WEBSTER'S
NEW WRLD®
ITALIAN
DICTIONARY
SECOND EDITION

ITALIAN-ENGLISH
ENGLISH-ITALIAN

D0905902

HOUGHTON MIFFLIN HARCOURT
BOSTON   NEW YORK

ISBN: 978-0-544-74553-7

Visit our website: hmhco.com

Library of Congress Cataloging-in-Publication Data

Title: Webster's new world Italian dictionary.
Description: Second edition / edited by Gabriella Bacchelli, Susie Beattie, Andrea Cavatorti, Ariella Germinario, Helen Hyde, et al. | Boston : Houghton Mifflin Harcourt Publishing Company, [2017] | This publication includes English and Italian words. | "Italiano-Inglese /Inglese-Italiano = Italian-English/English-Italian Dictionary."
Identifiers: LCCN 2017005129 | ISBN 9780544745537
Subjects: LCSH: Italian language—Dictionaries—English. | English language—Dictionaries—Italian.
Classification: LCC PC1640 .W24 2017 | DDC 453/.21—dc23
LC record available at https://lccn.loc.gov/2017005129

Printed in the United States of America

2 3 4 5 6 7 8 9 10 – DOC – 23 22 21 20 19 18

4500701708

DIZIONARIO
ITALIANO-INGLESE
INGLESE-ITALIANO

ITALIAN-ENGLISH
ENGLISH-ITALIAN
DICTIONARY

editors, HarperCollins

Gabriella Bacchelli
Susie Beattie
Andrea Cavatorti
Ariella Germinario
Helen Hyde
Joyce Littlejohn
Persephone Lock
Francesca Logi
Stefano Longo
Gabriella Martinez
Debora Mazza Magne
Stefano Ondelli
Liz Potter
Loredana Riu
Annamaria Rubino
Maggie Seaton

editors, Houghton Mifflin Harcourt

Peter Chipman
Steve Kleinedler
Emily Snyder
Vali Tamm

production, Houghton Mifflin Harcourt

Christopher J. Granniss
Donna Baxter McCarthy
Margaret Anne Miles
Diane Varone

computing support

Thomas Callan
Agnieszka Urbanowicz
Thomas Widmann

for HarperCollins

Gerry Breslin
Lucy Cooper
Kerry Ferguson
Elaine Higgleton

contributors to previous editions

Mirella Alessio, Anne-Marie Banks, Carmela Celino,
Anne Convery, Daphne Day, Prof. John M. Dodds,
Sandra Harper, Angela Jack, David Katan, Val
McNulty, Cindy Mitchell, Judy Moss, Gail Norfolk,
Carol Peters, Eugenio Picchi, Martin de Sa'Pinto,
Timothy Shaw, Katherine Snell, Jill Williams

INDICE

CONTENTS

INTRODUZIONE

Nato da una moderna concezione lessicografica che privilegia la lingua attuale, i modi di dire colloquiali, il linguaggio dei mass media, senza tuttavia trascurare le espressioni di carattere più formale, il *Webster's New World Italian Dictionary* è un'opera di consultazione completa, moderna ed affidabile. L'opera include i neologismi entrati a far parte della lingua inglese e di quella italiana in questi ultimi anni e molti termini tratti da linguaggi settoriali come quello informatico, commerciale e scientifico, oggi sempre più diffusi. La scelta di lemmi, significati e locuzioni di quest'opera, basata su criteri di frequenza d'uso, è stata dettata dalla volontà di presentare all'utente l'inglese e l'italiano attuali. Per la scelta e la verifica di lemmi, locuzioni e traduzioni i lessicografi hanno potuto consultare il Collins Corpus, un database costituito da migliaia e migliaia di libri, giornali, riviste, opuscoli, conversazioni e trasmissioni radiotelevisive. Con oltre 4,5 miliardi di parole, esso rappresenta attualmente la fonte linguistica più esauriente utilizzata per un dizionario bilingue di queste dimensioni. La modernità dei contenuti, l'affidabilità delle traduzioni e la ricchezza di esempi ed espressioni idiomatiche fanno di quest'opera uno strumento indispensabile per esprimersi in un inglese corretto e idiomatico.

INTRODUCTION

The *Webster's New World Italian Dictionary* is comprehensive, up-to-date, and reliable. It is based on modern principles, with its main focus on present-day language, including colloquial expressions, slang, and the language of the mass media. More formal language, however, is by no means neglected. The dictionary includes many recent additions to the English and Italian languages, and widely-used terms from key fields such as computing, business, and science. The criteria governing the selection of material for inclusion in the dictionary were frequency of use, typicality, and naturalness. To this end, the Collins corpus was an invaluable resource available to compilers and translators. This database consists of many thousands of texts: books, newspapers, magazines, leaflets, conversations, and radio and television broadcasts. With its body of 4.5 billion words, it provides an authoritative basis to judge whether particular words or structures merit inclusion because of the frequency of their occurrence, and to establish how they are typically used. Whether you wish to read, speak, or write Italian, you will find this dictionary an indispensable tool, thanks to the range of words treated, the accuracy and clarity of translations, and the wealth of examples and illustrative phrases.

COME USARE IL DIZIONARIO

Il dizionario contiene moltissime informazioni, rappresentate in modo sintetico. Alcune parole sono complesse in quanto hanno molti significati e diverse traduzioni, altre possono avere più di una funzione grammaticale, cioè possono essere sia sostantivo sia aggettivo oppure verbo, avverbio e così via, a seconda del contesto. È importante sviluppare una strategia di consultazione per evitare inutili frustrazioni e perdite di tempo nella consultazione, ed è per questo che occorre conoscere le convenzioni usate se si vuole accedere in modo ottimale alle informazioni di cui si ha bisogno. Nel dizionario sono stati usati numeri, simboli e caratteri tipografici diversi (neretto, corsivo, tondo ecc.); è necessario capire come sono stati usati e farvi attenzione.

piccoli rombi neri

Quando una parola ha più di una funzione grammaticale, il passaggio da una parte del discorso a un'altra è segnalato da un piccolo rombo nero ♦. Se per esempio volete tradurre la parola **fondere** in frasi come "il metallo fonde a temperature elevate", stabilirete innanzitutto quale sia la funzione grammaticale del verbo nel vostro contesto. In questo caso il verbo **fondere** è usato intransitivamente e quindi la traduzione va cercata nella categoria ♦ VI. L'elenco delle abbreviazioni usate per indicare le diverse parti del discorso si trova a pagina xx.

fondere ['fondere] (irreg) / 25/ vt 1 (gen) to melt; (metallo) to fuse, melt; (fig: colori) to blend, merge; (: enti, classi: Inform) to merge 2 (statua, campana) to cast ♦ vi aus avere to melt; **mi fonde il cervello** (fig) I can't think straight any more, my brain has seized up; **fondersi** vr (uso reciproco: unirsi: correnti, enti) to merge, unite; **fondersi** vip (sciogliersi) to melt

numeri

I numeri sono stati usati in due modi:

Numeri in posizione esponenziale

I numeri in posizione esponenziale rispetto al lemma sono stati usati per distinguere gli omografi, ossia parole che presentano la stessa grafia ma che sono completamente diverse dal punto di vista del significato, come in italiano **diritto**[1] (retto) e **diritto**[2] (prerogativa) e in inglese **fine**[1] (bello) e **fine**[2] (multa). Se quello che trovate nella prima voce non è quello di cui avete bisogno, consultate la seconda o eventualmente la terza.

Numeri all'interno della voce

I numeri all'interno della voce differenziano i diversi significati di una parola. Possono farvi risparmiare tempo, specialmente se avete a che fare con una paro-

HOW TO USE THE DICTIONARY

The dictionary contains a great deal of information, in a condensed form. Some words are complicated — they have a large number of senses, or they have several different meanings. They may also be categorized as members of more than one part of speech — they may serve as a verb, a noun, an adjective, an adverb, etc. To avoid time-wasting and frustration, you should develop a strategy for approaching entries, and to do this you need to be aware of the pointers that are provided to guide you to the particular information you want. These pointers are black diamonds, numbers, and typefaces: it is important to understand how they are used and to pay attention to them.

black diamonds

When a word is not just a noun, or just a verb, (i.e. if it can be more than one part of speech), a black diamond ♦ is used along with the part of speech to indicate each additional function it can perform. Thus, if you want to translate "he cleaned his apartment," and you need to look up **clean**, decide first of all what function the word has. Having decided that it is a verb with an object (i.e. a transitive verb) you can then run your eye down the numbered items in the entry until you get to ♦ VT (verb, transitive) — which is what you want. Abbreviations used to indicate parts of speech appear on page xx.

clean [kli:n] ADJ (comp -er, superl -est) (gen) pulito(-a); (sheet of paper) nuovo(-a); (smooth, clear: outline, movement, break) netto(-a); (fair: fight, game) leale, corretto(-a); **to wipe sth clean** pulire qc . . . ♦ ADV : **he clean forgot** si è completamente dimenticato; **he got clean away** se l'è svignata senza lasciare tracce. . . ♦ N pulita, ripulitura ♦ VT (gen) pulire; (blackboard) . . .

numbers

Numbers are used in two ways:

Numbers at the end of a headword

When words are spelled the same, but are actually separate entities — e.g. **fine** in English (which could mean good, or a financial penalty) or **piano** in Italian (which could mean flat, a plan, or a musical instrument) they are given as separate entries, with the headword followed by a superscript number. If what you find at the first entry is obviously not what you want, go on to look at the following one(s).

Numbers within an entry

These are used to distinguish different senses of a word. Paying attention to them can save a lot of time when you are dealing with a word such as **get** that has

la come **attaccare**, che ha svariati significati. Se per esempio volete tradurre la frase "mi ha attaccato l'influenza" e cercate **attaccare**, dovete innanzitutto individuare la funzione grammaticale della parola; dato che si tratta di un verbo transitivo, andrete a **VT**. Dovete quindi stabilire che significato ha la parola nel vostro contesto. **1** (far aderire) è la prima possibilità, ma non si adatta al contesto; nemmeno **2** (Mil, Sport, fig) e **3** (cominciare: discorso, lite) coprono il significato del verbo nella vostra frase; passate quindi a **4** (contagiare, anche fig), che vi darà la traduzione appropriata.

Quando cercate una parola inglese e trovate una serie di traduzioni diverse, scorrete velocemente le sezioni precedute dai numeri per trovare quella che si adatta al vostro contesto.

attaccare [attak'kare] / 20/ vt **1** (*far aderire*) to attach; (*incollare*: *manifesto*) to stick up; (: *francobollo*) to stick (on); (*cucire*) to sew (on); (*legare*) to tie (up); (*appendere*: *quadro*) to hang (up); **devo attaccare due bottoni** I've got to sew two buttons on; **non so dove attaccare questo poster** I don't know where to stick this poster **2** (*Mil, Sport, o fig*) to attack **3** (*cominciare*: *discorso, lite*) to start, begin; **attaccare discorso con qn** to start a conversation with sb **4** (*contagiare, anche fig*) to affect

indicazioni in corsivo

Il testo in corsivo aiuta a individuare i significati di una parola: può trattarsi di un sinonimo, un aggettivo o un sostantivo che compaiono spesso assieme alla parola, quando essa ha un certo significato. Per esempio, quando **dare** significa **organizzare**, tra le cose che si possono organizzare ci sono una festa, un banchetto, oppure uno spettacolo: queste parole compaiono in corsivo. Quando si cerca di individuare la traduzione giusta va tenuto conto di queste indicazioni in corsivo, che si differenziano sia dal testo nella lingua di partenza, che appare in grassetto, sia dalle traduzioni, che appaiono in tondo.

dove cercare i lemmi

I lemmi sono elencati in ordine alfabetico. Si noti che vanno ignorati nell'ordinamento alfabetico i trattini all'interno di parola. Il carattere &, usato in parole come **B & B, R & R** ecc. viene trattato come "and": l'ordine sarà pertanto come appare nel seguente esempio: **candour, C & W, candy**.

dove cercare i lemmi composti

In inglese sono stati considerati come lemmi a sé stanti anche alcuni composti formati da due o più parole aventi grafia separata, come **fast food** e **state of the art**, che sono elencati quindi in ordine alfabetico. Dovendo tradurre espressioni come **back page** e **back number**, potreste essere incerti su dove cercarle

all sorts of meanings: if, for example, you wanted to translate "I was starting to get tired" and were looking up **get**, you would first decide on the word's grammatical function (it's a verb without an object, i.e. an intransitive verb) — that would take you to ♦ **VI**. Next you would need to decide what meaning the word has in your particular context. **1** (go) is the first possibility, but this doesn't fit — so you would look next at **2** (become, be) — which would take you to the right translation.

When you look up an Italian word and find a number of different translations, scan the numbered sections for the one that fits your context.

Looking first at the numbered categories means you waste no time looking at irrelevant sections.

material appearing in italics

Material appearing in italics helps you pinpoint the sense of a word. It may be another way of saying the same thing, or an adjective, noun etc. that often occurs with the word when it has a particular sense — e.g. when **get** means "receive," letters and presents are typical examples of things you can get, so these appear in italics. When you are trying to track down the right translation, make sure you take note of these italic pointers, which are distinguishable at a glance from the bold type used for the source language and from the normal type used for translations.

where to look for headwords

Headwords are listed in alphabetical order. However you should note that hyphens are ignored and the character & (which appears in forms like **B & B, R & R**, etc.) is treated as "and" when deciding alphabetical order. The order is therefore as follows: **candour, C & W, candy**.

where to look for combinations of words

When faced by such combinations as **back number** and **back page** you may be uncertain where to look. Is **back** an adjective, in which case you should look in the appropriate section under **back**, or is it the first element in a compound word, which you should look for in its alphabetical place?

e chiedervi se **back** vada considerato un aggettivo, nel qual caso bisognerebbe guardare nella relativa sezione sotto **back**, oppure sia il primo elemento di una parola composta, che andrebbe cercata al suo posto nell'ordine alfabetico.

Sarà utile ricordare che se la combinazione non compare come lemma a sé stante, bisognerà cercarla sotto il primo elemento che la compone – cioè sotto **back** e non sotto **page** o **number**.

In italiano invece nomi composti come **pesce rosso** o **acqua di rose** non compaiono come parole a sé stanti ma vanno in genere ricercati sotto il primo elemento che li compone.

dove cercare i verbi + avverbio/preposizione

Nelle frasi "she came into the room" e "she came into a large fortune" compaiono lo stesso verbo e la stessa preposizione ("come" e "into") ma solo nel secondo caso si tratta di un phrasal verb, cioè di una combinazione fissa con un significato particolare (**ereditare**), che compare come voce a sé stante, contrassegnata dal simbolo ▸.

Per tradurre il primo esempio, invece, bisogna guardare sotto il verbo **come**. In caso di dubbio, verificate innanzitutto se si tratta di un phrasal verb. Se la ricerca non vi fornirà le indicazioni di cui avete bisogno, cercate sotto il verbo in questione.

dove cercare le locuzioni

In genere locuzioni ed espressioni idiomatiche si trovano sotto il primo elemento fondamentale della locuzione. Per esempio "filare diritto" si trova sotto **filare** e "to burn one's boats", sotto **burn**. Tuttavia, nel caso di verbi con molti significati, come **fare, mettere, prendere** o **set, do** e **get**, le locuzioni compaiono generalmente sotto un'altra parola che compone l'espressione. Per esempio "to set a trap" è stata posta sotto **trap** per facilitare l'utente, che troverà più rapidamente l'espressione alla voce breve **trap** piuttosto che alla voce **set**, molto più complessa.

LEMMARIO E STRUTTURA DELLE VOCI

L'intento di questa sezione è di fornire un elenco completo degli elementi che costituiscono il dizionario e delle informazioni che è possibile ricavarne. Una conoscenza approfondita di questi elementi insieme a una corretta strategia di consultazione consentiranno all'utente di sfruttare al meglio il dizionario.

The important things to remember are:

1 You should look for such items under their first element — e.g. under **back**, not under **number** or **page**.

2 You should bear in mind that the combination may appear as a separate entry, as does **back number**, or under the first element, as does **back page**. If you don't find it at the first option, try the second.

Italian combinations of two words or more such as **pesce rosso** and **acqua di rose** are not treated as separate entries but generally appear under their first element.

where to find verb + adverb/preposition combinations

"She came into the room" and "she came into a large fortune" include the same verb + preposition, (**come + into**), but the second combination is a phrasal verb, with a special sense (**inherit**), and is treated in a separate entry, which is marked by the symbol ▸.

To find how to translate the first example you should look under **come**. If you are in doubt in such cases, the quickest thing is to look first for a phrasal verb entry. If that doesn't provide the information you need, look then at the entry for the verb on its own.

where to look for phrases

Idioms and set phrases generally appear under their first important element, thus "filare diritto" appears under **filare** and "to burn one's boats" appears under **burn**. However, in the case of verbs that have a great many meanings, such as **prendere, fare, mettere**, or **set, do**, and **get**, phrases appear under another key word in the expression. For exmple, "to set a trap" comes under **trap**. This is to make things easier for the user, who will find the phrase more quickly in the short entry **trap** than in the long and complicated entry **set**.

THE DESIGN OF THE DICTIONARY

The previous section is intended to help solve problems that may be encountered in using the dictionary. However, to fully exploit the information this dictionary offers, users will find it worthwhile to familiarize themselves in more detail with the way the dictionary is organized and the way entries are structured.

lemmario: I lemmi sono elencati naturalmente in ordine alfabetico e sono stampati in neretto. Nel margine superiore di ogni pagina compare una testatina che riporta il primo e l'ultimo lemma di quella pagina: ciò renderà più rapida la consultazione del dizionario.

derivati: Per maggiore facilità di consultazione i derivati, ad esempio **fortunately, delivery, deliverance** e **installazione, utilità, utilmente**, compaiono tutti come lemmi principali (in alcuni dizionari essi compaiono sotto la parola da cui derivano).

nomi composti: nailbrush, backache, accendisigari e **capostazione** sono nomi composti e sono inseriti in ordine alfabetico. Nella parte inglese-italiano anche molti nomi composti formati da due o più parole (es. **news agency**), o ancora da due o più parole unite da un trattino (es. **do-it-yourself**), compaiono come lemmi principali in ordine alfabetico.

Nella parte italiano-inglese, questi compaiono all'interno della voce corrispondente alla prima parola, preceduti dal simbolo ♦.

phrasal verbs: I phrasal verbs come **make up** o **put up with** compaiono in forma di sottolemmi in ordine alfabetico, in neretto, dopo il lemma principale. ► è il simbolo che precede i phrasal verbs nella parte inglese-italiano.

sigle e abbreviazioni: Per maggior facilità di consultazione le abbreviazioni e le sigle come **IVA, UNESCO,** e **ab.** sono state inserite nel testo.

LA STRUTTURA DELLE VOCI

suddivisione in sillabe

Sulla parte inglese-italiano è stata data indicazione, mediante l'introduzione di puntini, di come possono essere suddivise le parole inglesi, come per esempio **pae·di·at·ric**.

trascrizione fonetica

Tutti i lemmi sono seguiti dalla pronuncia, che si trova tra parentesi quadre. Come in tutti i principali dizionari moderni è stato adottato il sistema noto come "alfabeto fonetico internazionale". A pagina xix troverete un elenco completo dei caratteri utilizzati in questo sistema.

Nella parte inglese-italiano, per la pronuncia di nomi composti formati da due o più parole non unite dal trattino, si dovrà cercare la trascrizione di ciascuna parola alla rispettiva posizione alfabetica.

Headwords are listed in alphabetical order and printed in bold. The running heads at the top of each page show you the first and last headword on each page in order to make it quicker to find the word you are looking for.

Derived words such as **fortunately, delivery, deliverance,** and **installazione, utilità, utilmente** appear as headwords. (In some dictionaries such words are treated under the word they derive from.)

Compound words in English may consist of one word (e.g. **housewife**), two or more words (e.g. **news agency, state of the art**), or two or more words joined by a hyphen (e.g. **do-it-yourself**). All types can appear as headwords. Compounds consisting of two or more words are set as headwords.

In Italian, compounds proper consist of a single word, e.g. **accendisigari, capostazione,** and these appear as headwords. Combinations of two words or more, such as **strisce pedonali** or **acqua minerale** are to be found under their first element (i.e. **striscia** or **acqua**). If the compound shows a new sense of the headword, it is preceded by the symbol ♦.

Phrasal verbs, for example **make up** or **put up with**, appear in bold type, under the main verb. They are marked by the symbol ►.

Acronyms and abbreviations, for example **VAT, UNESCO,** and **ad,** appear in the main body of the dictionary.

THE ORGANIZATION OF ENTRIES

syllable points

On the English-Italian side of the dictionary, syllable points appear in headwords, to show how they may be hyphenated: **pae·di·at·ric**.

phonetic transcription

Headwords are followed by their pronunciation in square brackets, in the International Phonetic Alphabet. You will find a full list of the symbols used in this system on page xix.

categorie grammaticali

Quando il lemma ha una sola funzione grammaticale la categoria grammaticale di appartenenza compare in maiuscoletto subito dopo la trascrizione fonetica.

lemma	pronuncia	categoria grammaticale	traduzione
rissa	[ˈrissa]	SF	fight, brawl

Se invece ha più di una funzione, ogni categoria grammaticale dopo la prima viene contrassegnata dal simbolo ♦.

col·lar [ˈkɒləʳ] N (*of shirt, blouse, coat*) colletto, collo; (*for dog*) collare *m*; (*Tech*) anello, fascetta; **to grab sb by the collar** afferrare qn per il bavero ♦ VT (*fam: person, object*) beccare

parts of speech

If the headword functions only as a noun, verb, etc., the relevant part of speech appears in small capitals after the phonetics.

headword	pronunciation	part of speech category	translations
collar	[ˈkɒləʳ]	N	colletto, collo

If it has more than one function, each part of speech after the first is indicated with a ♦.

col·lar [ˈkɒləʳ] N (*of shirt, blouse, coat*) colletto, collo; (*for dog*) collare *m*; (*Tech*) anello, fascetta; **to grab sb by the collar** afferrare qn per il bavero ♦ VT (*fam: person, object*) beccare

categorie di significato

Quando un lemma ha più di un significato la voce viene suddivisa in categorie di significato, ognuna preceduta da un numero: **1, 2, 3**, ecc.

Ciascuna categoria di significato può riportare una o più accezioni seguite da una serie di frasi illustrative in grassetto, seguite dalle relative traduzioni in tondo.

al·to·geth·er [ˌɔːltəˈgeðəʳ] ADV **1** (*in all*) in tutto, complessivamente; (*on the whole*) tutto considerato, tutto sommato, nel complesso, nell'insieme; **you owe me twenty pounds altogether** in tutto mi devi venti sterline; **altogether it was rather unpleasant** tutto sommato *or* in complesso è stato piuttosto spiacevole; **how much is that altogether?** quant'è in tutto? **2** (*entirely*) del tutto, completamente; **I'm not altogether sure** non sono del tutto *or* proprio sicuro

meaning categories

When a headword has more than one sense, the entry is divided into sections marked by a number: **1, 2, 3**, etc.

Each meaning category can include a number of related senses. At the end of each category there may be phrases, in bold type, with translations in roman.

al·to·geth·er [ˌɔːltəˈgeðəʳ] ADV **1** (*in all*) in tutto, complessivamente; (*on the whole*) tutto considerato, tutto sommato, nel complesso, nell'insieme; **you owe me twenty pounds altogether** in tutto mi devi venti sterline; **altogether it was rather unpleasant** tutto sommato *or* in complesso è stato piuttosto spiacevole; **how much is that altogether?** quant'è in tutto? **2** (*entirely*) del tutto, completamente; **I'm not altogether sure** non sono del tutto *or* proprio sicuro

indicatori

Si chiamano "indicatori" le informazioni in corsivo tra parentesi che introducono le diverse accezioni di un lemma. Come già accennato al paragrafo **indicazioni in corsivo**, la funzione degli indicatori è di guidare l'utente nella scelta della traduzione più adatta ad un contesto specifico. A volte gli indicatori appaiono dopo una traduzione per segnalarne il registro o l'ambito d'uso.

Moltissime parole hanno più di un significato o diverse sfumature di significato; altre, pur mantenendo un significato relativamente unitario, si traducono in modo diverso a seconda del contesto in cui si trovano o dei loro collocatori, cioè delle parole assieme alle quali vengono usate più di frequente. Nel dizionario sono stati usati diversi tipi di indicatori:

1 indicatori che sostituiscono il lemma
2 indicatori contestuali
3 indicatori di campo semantico
4 indicatori di stile o registro

indicators

The section on page viii on **material appearing in italics** gives a partial explanation of the pointers, or indicators, which are provided to help the user choose the most suitable translation for a particular context.

Clear and effective indicators are of great importance since many words have several meanings or shades of meaning, while others, which seem to have only one meaning in one language, call for different translations, depending on context or the other words (collocates) used with them. The full range of indicators used in the dictionary can be listed as follows:

1 substitutes for the headword
2 contextual indicators
3 subject field indicators
4 style and register labels
5 chronological labels
6 literal/figurative labels
7 regional labels

Questi indicatori si riferiscono alla lingua di partenza, e sono in italiano nella parte italiano-inglese e in inglese nella parte inglese-italiano; compaiono tra parentesi tonde e in corsivo subito prima della traduzione.

Indicatori che sostituiscono il lemma

Uno degli indicatori che troverete più di frequente consiste in un sinonimo o in una parziale definizione del lemma.

malizia [ma'littsja] SF (*cattiveria*) malice, spite; (*furbizia*) mischievousness; (*astuzia*) clever trick; **con malizia** maliciously, spitefully; mischievously; cleverly

Indicatori contestuali

Gli indicatori contestuali forniscono i contesti tipici in cui è possibile trovare il lemma. Possono essere di vario tipo: qui di seguito troverete gli indicatori contestuali più comuni.

8 soggetto tipico di un verbo intransitivo: **fiorire** ... (*albero*) ...(*fig*: *sentimento*) ... (: *commercio, arte*) ...
9 oggetto tipico di un verbo transitivo: **dissotterrare** ... (*cadavere*) ... (*tesori, rovine*) ... (*fig*: *sentimento*) ...
10 sostantivo che viene usato spesso in combinazione con l'aggettivo in questione: **collerico** ...(*persona*) ...(*parole*) ...(*temperamento*) ...
11 sostantivo che viene usato spesso in combinazione con il sostantivo in questione: **groviglio** ...(*di fili, lana*) ... (*fig*: *di idee*) ...
12 aggettivo che viene usato spesso in combinazione con l'avverbio in questione: **tenuamente** ... (*colorato*) ...(*illuminato*) ...
13 verbo che viene usato spesso in combinazione con l'avverbio in questione: **involontariamente** ...(*sorridere*) ...(*spingere*) ...

Indicatori di campo semantico

Gli indicatori di campo semantico (cioè *Med, Pol, Bot* ecc.) vengono usati per differenziare i vari significati del lemma secondo una specifica suddivisione in campi semantici. Questi indicatori, sempre tra parentesi e in corsivo, hanno l'iniziale maiuscola e sono spesso abbreviazioni (per l'elenco completo delle abbreviazioni vedere pagina xx).

nervatura [nerva'tura] SF (*Anat*) nerves *pl*, nervous system; (*Bot*) veining; (*Archit, Tecn*) rib

Questi indicatori vengono anche usati quando il significato di una parola è chiaro nella lingua d'origine ma può essere ambiguo nella lingua d'arrivo. Per esempio

These labels relate to the source language and are in English on the English-Italian side of the dictionary, and in Italian on the Italian-English side.

They appear in italics, within round brackets, and immediately precede the translation.

Substitutes for the headword

Synonyms or partial definitions of the headword often appear as indicators.

dis·trac·tion [dɪs'træk ʃən] N **1** (*interruption*) distrazione *f*; (*entertainment*) distrazione, diversivo; **a distraction from our concerns** una distrazione dalle nostre preoccupazioni **2** (*distress, madness*): **to drive sb to distraction** far impazzire qn

Contextual indicators

These provide typical contexts in which the user may find or wish to use the headword. They are of various types: some of the commonest are listed below:

8 typical noun subjects of an intransitive verb: **fluc·tu·ate** ...(*cost*) ...(*person*) ...
9 typical noun objects of a transitive verb: **ful·fil** ... (*duty*) ...(*promise*) ...
10 typical noun complements of an adjective: **full-length** ...(*portrait*) ...(*dress*) ...
11 typical noun complements of another noun: **full·ness** ...(*of detail*) ...
12 typical adjective complements of an adverb: **in·tense·ly** ...(*moved*) ...
13 typical verb complements of an adverb: **un·fair·ly** ...(*treat, criticize*) ...

Subject field indicators

Subject field indicators (for example, *Med, Pol, Bot*) are used to distinguish meanings of the headword according to specific fields of application. They begin with capital letters and are often abbreviated. For the full list, and explanations of what the abbreviations stand for, see page xx.

at·tack [ə'tæk] N **1** (*Mil, also fig*) attacco; (*on individual*) aggressione *f*; **a savage attack** una feroce aggressione; **surprise attack** attacco a sorpresa; **attack on sb's life** attentato alla vita di qn; **to be under attack (from)** essere attaccato(-a) (da); **to launch an attack (on)** (*Mil, Sport: fig*) ...

They are also used when the meaning in the source

il sostantivo **oratorio** in inglese ha solo il significato musicale, mentre in italiano può indicare anche l'edificio annesso alla chiesa in cui si svolgono attività ricreative e spirituali per ragazzi.

Indicatori di stile e di registro

Gli indicatori di stile o registro sono stati usati per tutti i vocaboli che esulano dal linguaggio standard. Alcuni indicatori compaiono sia nella sezione inglese-italiano che in quella italiano-inglese; si tratta di (*frm*) per l'uso formale, (*fam*) per l'uso informale o colloquiale e (*iro*) per l'uso ironico. L'uso letterario è contrassegnato da (*liter*) nella parte inglese e da (*letter*) in quella italiana.

Per quello scherzoso sono stati usati rispettivamente (*hum*) e (*scherz*), mentre (*euph*) ed (*euf*) evidenziano le espressioni eufemistiche e (*pej*) e (*pegg*) l'uso peggiorativo.

Le espressioni informali e volgari, pur essendo largamente diffuse, sono a nostro parere da usare con estrema cautela. Per aiutare il lettore ad identificarle è stato usato l'indicatore (*fam!*).

Da evitare anche quelle parole contrassegnate dagli indicatori (*offensive*) ed (*offensivo*).

Indicatori cronologici

Quando l'uso di una parola o di un'espressione è da considerarsi ormai sorpassato, compare l'indicatore (*old*) in inglese e (*ant*) in italiano.

Indicatori di uso letterale e figurato

Sono (*lit*) per l'uso letterale e (*fig*) per quello figurato.

Indicatori di uso regionale

Tra gli indicatori di uso regionale ricordiamo (*Scot*) per le parole o espressioni scozzesi, (*Ir*) per quelle irlandesi e (*dial*) per segnalare che una parola o espressione è di uso prevalentemente dialettale.

Americanismi

L'abbreviazione (*USA*) segnala le grafie e le pronunce americane e le parole ed espressioni che, sebbene generalmente conosciute sia dai parlanti americani che da quelli inglesi, sono usate con maggiore frequenza negli Stati Uniti.

Quando una parola o un'espressione viene usata prevalentemente nell'inglese britannico, ciò è segnalato dall'indicatore (*Brit*).

Uso della punteggiatura negli indicatori

Prima di una traduzione troverete spesso due o più indicatori, in corsivo e nella stessa parentesi. Nella

language is clear, but possibly ambiguous in the target language. This is true in the case of **oratorio**, which in English has only a musical sense, but in Italian can also be an oratory.

Style and register labels

These have been given to words that are not neutral language. On both sides of the dictionary you will find the labels (*frm*) = formal, (*fam*) = informal or colloquial and (*iro*) = ironic. Literary use is marked as (*liter*) on the English side and (*letter*) on the Italian. Humorous use is labelled (*hum*) on the English side, and (*scherz*) on the Italian side. (*euph*) or (*euf*) indicates euphemistic use and (*pej*) or (*pegg*) pejorative language. The labels (*offensive*) or (*offensivo*) speak for themselves.

In all languages there are colloquial and vulgar expressions which are widely used, but which non-native speakers need to approach with caution. Such words are marked (*fam!*).

Chronological labels

When a word or expression would generally be regarded as old fashioned, we have the label (*old*), or (*ant*) on the Italian side.

Literal/figurative labels

(*lit*) and (*fig*) indicate literal and figurative senses.

Regional labels

These include (*Scot*) = Scottish, (*Ir*) = Irish and (*dial*) = dialect.

American English

(*USA*) is used to mark American spellings and pronunciations, and words and expressions that are more current in the United States than in Britain—though they may be familiar to many speakers of British English. (*Brit*) labels words and phrases used mainly in Britain.

The use of punctuation in indicators

You will often find two or more words in italics (indicators) preceding a translation. In the entry for **passen-**

voce **marino**, riportata qui di seguito, il fatto che *aria* e *fondali* siano separati tra loro da una virgola indica che la traduzione **sea** funziona sia dovendo tradurre "aria marina" che "fondale marino". Analogamente **seaside** può essere usata sia per tradurre "città marina" che "colonia marina".

marino,-a [maˈrino] AGG (*aria, fondali*) sea *attr*; (*fauna*) marine; (*città, colonia*) seaside *attr*

Se invece gli indicatori sono separati da due punti, come ad esempio in **refresh** riportato qui sotto, ciò indica che essi si riferiscono insieme alla traduzione. Se il soggetto di **refresh** è **drink**, la traduzione adatta è **rinfrescare**, mentre se il soggetto del verbo è **sleep** oppure **bath**, la traduzione è **ristorare**. L'indicatore "subj" non viene ripetuto la seconda volta, ma viene richiamato dai due punti. Ogni volta che i due punti compaiono come primo elemento dell'indicatore ci si dovrà riferire all'indicatore precedente.

re·fresh [rɪˈfrɛʃ] VT (*subj: drink*) rinfrescare; (: *food, sleep, bath*) ristorare; (*fig: memory*) rinfrescare; **this will refresh your memory** questo ti rinfrescherà la memoria

ger (see below), the fact that there are commas between *boat, plane,* and *car* shows that the translation "passeggero" works in relation to all three words. Similarly, when used as an adjective with "aircraft" or "liner" the word can be translated "di linea" or "passeggeri."

pas·sen·ger [ˈpæsɪndʒəʳ] N (*in boat, plane, car*) passeggero(-a); (*on train*) viaggiatore(-trice), passeggero(-a) ♦ ADJ (*aircraft, liner*) di linea, passeggeri *inv*; (*train*) viaggiatori *inv*

If, however, there is a colon between words in italics, as in the entry **refresh** (see below), a different reading is called for. In the case of **refresh**, if the subject of the verb is a drink, the appropriate translation is "rinfrescare," while if the subject is "sleep," or a "bath," it is "ristorare." (*Subj*) is not repeated a second time—the colon which appears at the beginning of the second set of brackets stands for it. Whenever a colon is the first element inside brackets it refers back to a word that has already appeared as an indicator.

re·fresh [rɪˈfrɛʃ] VT (*subj: drink*) rinfrescare; (: *food, sleep, bath*) ristorare; (*fig: memory*) rinfrescare; **this will refresh your memory** questo ti rinfrescherà la memoria

use of "tu" and "lei"

Partly as a consequence of the dictionary's emphasis on colloquial language, and also to avoid confusion between the 2nd and 3rd person use of "lei," the familiar form "tu" (you) occurs in examples somewhat more often that the formal "lei."

traduzioni

Tutte le traduzioni nel dizionario corrispondono il più possibile ai loro equivalenti nella lingua di partenza, sia a livello semantico che a livello sintattico e di registro linguistico. Particolare attenzione è stata fatta alle costruzioni tipiche e ai loro equivalenti nella lingua di arrivo.

Spesso, dopo uno stesso indicatore, compaiono più traduzioni separate tra di loro da una virgola, come ad esempio in **ammonimento**.

ammonimento [ammoniˈmento] SM (*rimprovero*) reprimand, admonishment; (*lezione*) lesson, warning

Va sottolineato che queste traduzioni sono sempre intercambiabili con riferimento al significato riportato dall'indicatore. Ogni volta che un contesto diverso ha richiesto una traduzione diversa, questo è stato segnalato inserendo un nuovo indicatore.

translations

It will often be found that a particular indicator is followed by two or more translations, separated by commas. These translations are interchangeable, each of them serving equally well to translate the sense in question.

When a different sense calls for a different translation a further indicator appears.

Sometimes part of a translation is optional, and therefore appears in brackets, thus at **neo** (mole) the translation for the figurative use is "(slight) flaw."

neo [ˈnɛo] SM (*gen*) mole; (*sul viso*) beauty spot; (*fig: imperfezione*) (slight) flaw; (: *di persona*) slight defect

A volte parte della traduzione è opzionale, e quindi compare tra parentesi. Per esempio alla voce **neo** la traduzione per il senso figurato è (slight) flaw.

neo ['nɛo] SM (gen) mole; (sul viso) beauty spot; (fig: imperfezione) (slight) flaw; (: di persona) slight defect

glosse esplicative ed equivalenti culturali

Non sempre è possibile fornire una traduzione corrispondente al lemma di partenza. A volte è stato quindi necessario usare una glossa esplicativa, che compare in corsivo (vedere ad esempio le voci **angel dust** o **ginnasio**); altre volte è stato dato un equivalente approssimativo nell'altra lingua (vedere ad esempio **ACI** o **Speaker** (Brit Parliament). ≈ è il simbolo che precede gli equivalenti culturali.

explanatory glosses and cultural equivalents

It is not always possible to give a direct translation of words or phrases. Sometimes it is necessary to offer instead an explanatory gloss, which appears in italics—see for example **angel dust** or **ginnasio**. In other cases an approximate equivalent is given—see for example **ACI** or **Speaker**. Such equivalents are preceded by the symbol ≈ .

INFORMAZIONI GRAMMATICALI

genere

Sia nel lato italiano-inglese sia in quello inglese-italiano sono state indicate le desinenze femminili degli aggettivi italiani e dei sostantivi riferiti a persona.

GRAMMATICAL INFORMATION

gender

Both sides of the dictionary give the feminine endings for Italian adjectives and, where appropriate, the feminine form of nouns.

plurali

I plurali irregolari e quelli la cui formazione può creare delle difficoltà compaiono dopo il lemma in entrambe le lingue. Plurali irregolari quali **mice** (topi) e **buoi** compaiono in ordine alfabetico con un rimando alla voce principale.

plurals

Irregular plurals and those presenting any sort of difficulty appear after the headword. Irregular plurals of nouns, such as **mice** and **buoi** (oxen), also appear alphabetically in the word list, with a cross reference to the singular.

verbi irregolari

Allo stesso modo, e per rendere più agevole la ricerca, abbiamo inserito in ordine alfabetico anche le principali forme irregolari di verbi e sostantivi, quali l'inglese **gone** o l'italiano **corso**, con un rimando alla voce in cui il lemma viene trattato per esteso.

È stata data indicazione dell'irregolarità dei verbi italiani subito dopo la categoria grammaticale; per i verbi irregolari inglesi sono state introdotte, subito dopo il lemma, le forme irregolari del passato e del participio passato.

irregular verbs

Similarly, irregular verb forms such as **went, gone**, **abbia**, and **corso** are listed, and cross-referred to their infinitives.

The fact that an Italian verb is irregular is noted immediately after the part of speech number. English irregular verbs are followed immediately by their past tenses and past participles.

verbi ausiliari

È stato indicato l'ausiliare **essere** o **avere** per tutti i verbi intransitivi italiani; per i verbi transitivi non compare alcuna indicazione in quanto i tempi composti di tali verbi si formano sempre con l'ausiliare **avere**.

auxiliary verbs

Information is given on whether Italian intransitive verbs take the auxiliary **essere** or **avere**. No such information is given for transitive verbs, since they always form compound tenses with **avere**.

verbi riflessivi e intransitivi pronominali

I verbi riflessivi come **radersi** e **vestirsi** sono stati distinti dai verbi intransitivi pronominali come **sbagliarsi** e **ricordarsi** mediante la distinzione tra le categorie grammaticali VR (verbo riflessivo) e VIP (verbo intransitivo pronominale). Le forme riflessive reciproche (come "si amano") e le forme riflessive indirette (come "lavarsi le mani") sono state differenziate all'interno della voce principale. Le forme riflessive reciproche compaiono nella categoria grammaticale VR, precedute dall'indicatore (*uso reciproco*), mentre quelle riflessive indirette sono state inserite come esempi sotto la categoria del transitivo, dato che si tratta di forme pronominali transitive in quanto prendono l'oggetto diretto. In inglese non esiste la forma pronominale del verbo, e quando un verbo viene usato insieme a **oneself** traduce in generale una forma riflessiva vera e propria. Si confrontino, ad esempio, le traduzioni di **ammazzarsi** nel senso di **suicidarsi** e quindi realmente riflessivo (**to kill o.s.**) e **ammazzarsi** nel senso di trovare la morte (**to die, be killed**).

phrasal verbs

Verbi come **get off** e **make up**, i cosiddetti phrasal verbs, costituiscono spesso un problema per gli studenti stranieri che incontrano difficoltà nel distinguerli dalle normali costruzioni con avverbi o preposizioni (ad esempio "he came into the room", normale costruzione con preposizione, e il phrasal verb "he came into money"). I phrasal verbs sono suddivisi in base alla funzione grammaticale degli elementi che li costituiscono. Alla voce **get off**, come vediamo qui di seguito, le qualifiche grammaticali sono VT + ADV, VI + PREP e VI + ADV. Alcuni phrasal verbs sono composti da tre elementi, come per esempio **get off with**.

> ▸ **get off** VT + ADV 1 (*remove: clothes, stain*) levare, togliere 2 (*send off*) spedire 3 (*save from punishment*) far assolvere, tirar fuori 4 (*have as holiday: day, time*) prendersi; **we got 2 days off** abbiamo avuto 2 giorni liberi ♦ VI + PREP (*bus, train, plane, bike*) scendere da; (*fam: escape: chore, lessons*) evitare, sfuggire a
>
> ...
>
> ▸ **get off with** VI + ADV + PREP (*fam: start relationship with*) mettersi con

Italian reflexive and pronominal verbs

Reflexive verbs such as **radersi** and **vestirsi** are distinguished from intransitive pronominal verbs such as **sbagliarsi** and **ricordarsi**. Reflexives are to be found under the part of speech headed VR (*verbo riflessivo*), pronominal verbs under VIP (*verbo intransitivo pronominale*). Some verbs can be used both ways: **ammazzarsi**, for example, used reflexively, means "to kill oneself," while used as a pronominal intransitive means "to die."

ammazzare [ammat'tsare] / **72**/ VT (*uccidere*) to kill; (*fig*: *affaticare*) to exhaust, wear out; **ammazzare il tempo** to kill time; **ammazzarsi** VR (*uso reciproco*) to kill each other; (*suicidarsi*) to kill o.s, commit suicide; **ammazzarsi di lavoro** to kill o.s. with work, work o.s. to death; **ammazzarsi** VIP (*rimanere ucciso*) to die, be killed

Reciprocal reflexives are treated under the VR heading: **ammazzarsi** can also translate as "to kill each other."

Indirect reflexives, such as **lavarsi le mani**, which take a direct object, are to be found as examples under the transitive verb category.

parole chiave

Alle parole che in qualche modo costituiscono i cardini della lingua, come i verbi ausiliari, le principali preposizioni, congiunzioni e così via, è stato riservato un trattamento particolare, sia dal punto di vista grafico sia da quello linguistico, con una strutturazione più chiara e articolata e una fraseologia molto ricca. Tali voci sono contrassegnate dal titoletto **PAROLA CHIAVE** sul lato italiano-inglese e dal titoletto **KEYWORD** sul lato inglese-italiano

---
PAROLA CHIAVE

a [a] PREP *a+il*=al, *a+lo*=allo, *a+l'*=all', *a+la*=alla, *a+i*=ai, *a+gli*=agli, *a+le*=alle

1 (*complemento di termine*) to (*spesso omesso*); **dare qc a qn** to give sth to sb, give sb sth; **ho dato un giocattolo a Sandro** I gave Sandro a toy, I gave a toy to Sandro

keywords

Words that are the nuts and bolts of the language, such as auxiliary and modal verbs, and the main prepositions and conjunctions, are given specially clear and detailed treatment, with a large number of examples. These entries are identified by the term **KEYWORD** on the English-Italian side and **PAROLA CHIAVE** on the Italian-English side:

KEYWORD

a [eɪ, ə] INDEF ART (*before vowel and silent h* an [æn, ən, n])

1 un *m*, uno (+ *s impure, gn, pn, ps, x, z*), una *f*, un' (*plus vowel*); **he's a friend** è un amico; **a herring** un'aringa; **an apple** una mela; **I haven't got a car** non ho la macchina; ...

"falsi amici"

Esistono parole molto simili, o addirittura identiche, in italiano e in inglese, che però hanno un significato del tutto diverso. Per aiutare il lettore ad evitare potenziali errori nella traduzione, al termine della voce in questione è stata introdotta una nota col segno ❑:

   ❑ **fondo** non si traduce mai con la parola inglese *fond*

false friends

Words which are similar or identical in both languages can be easily confused. In order to help users to avoid these potential translation pitfalls, a note has been given at the end of the dictionary entry where such confusion could occur. These notes are identified with the symbol ❑:

   ❑ **gentle** is not translated by the Italian word *gentile*

TRASCRIZIONE FONETICA

Consonanti

p, b, t, d, k, g in inglese sono seguiti dall'aspirazione.

PHONETIC TRANSCRIPTION

Consonants

p, b, t, d, k, g are not aspirated in Italian.

Italiano	Simbolo	English
*p*adre	p	*pupp*y
*b*am*b*ino	b	*b*a*b*y
*tut*to	t	*ten*t
*d*a*d*o	d	*d*a*dd*y
*c*ane *ch*e	k	*c*ork *k*iss *ch*ord
*g*ola *gh*iro	g	*g*a*g g*uess
*s*ano	s	*s*o ri*c*e ki*ss*
*s*vago e*s*ame	z	cou*s*in bu*zz*
*sc*ena	ʃ	*sh*eep *s*ugar
	ʒ	plea*s*ure bei*g*e
pe*c*e lan*ci*are	tʃ	*ch*urch
*g*iro *g*ioco	dʒ	*j*u*dg*e *g*eneral
a*f*a *f*aro	f	*f*arm ra*ff*le
*v*ero bra*v*o	v	*v*ery re*v*
	θ	*th*in pa*th*
	ð	*th*at o*th*er
*l*etto a*l*a	l	*l*itt*l*e ba*ll*
*gl*i	ʎ	
*r*ete a*r*co	r	*r*at b*r*at
ra*m*o *m*adre	m	*m*u*mm*y co*m*b
*n*o fuma*n*te	n	*n*o ra*n*
*gn*omo	ɲ	
	ŋ	si*ng*ing ba*n*k
	h	*h*at re*h*eat
bu*i*o p*i*acere	j	*y*et
*u*omo *gu*aio	w	*w*all be*w*ail
	x	lo*ch*

Vocali

La messa in equivalenza di certi suoni indica solo una rassomiglianza approssimativa.

Vowels

The pairing of of some vowel sounds only indicates approximate equivalence.

vino idea	iː i	heel bead
	ɪ	hit pity
stella edera	e	set tent
epoca eccetto	ɛ	
mamma amore	æ a	apple bat
	ɑː	car calm
	ʌ	fun cousin
	ə	over above
	ɛː	urn fern work
rosa occhio	ɒ ɔ	wash pot
	ɔː	born cork
ponte ognuno	o	
utile zucca	u	full soot
	uː	boon lewd

Dittonghi / Diphthongs

ɪə	beer tier
ɛə	bear fair there
eɪ	date place day
aɪ	life buy cry
aʊ	owl foul now
əʊ	low no
ɔɪ	boil boy oily
ʊə	poor tour

Varie / Miscellaneous

ʳ per l'inglese: la 'r' finale viene pronunciata se seguita da una vocale

ˈ primary or strong

ˌ stress secondary or weak stress

ABBREVIAZIONI

abbreviazione	*abbr*	abbreviation
aggettivo	*adj*	adjective
amministrazione	*Admin*	administration
avverbio	*adv*	adverb
aeronautica, trasporti aerei	*Aer*	aviation, aeronautics
aggettivo	*agg*	adjective
agricoltura	*Agr*	agriculture
amministrazione	*Amm*	administration
anatomia	*Anat*	anatomy
antico	*ant*	old
archeologia	*Archeol*	archaeology
architettura	*Archit*	architecture
articolo	*art*	article
astrologia	*Astrol*	astrology
astronomia	*Astron*	astronomy
attributivo	*attr*	attributive
ausiliare	*aus*	auxiliary
automobile, automobilismo	*Aut*	cars and motoring
ausiliare	*aux*	auxiliary
avverbio	*avv*	adverb
biologia	*Bio*	biology
botanica	*Bot*	botany
britannico, Gran Bretagna	*Brit*	British, Great Britain
chimica	*Chem, Chim*	chemistry
cinema	*Cine*	cinema
commercio	*Comm*	commerce
comparativo	*comp*	comparative
informatica, computer	*Comput*	computing
condizionale	*cond*	conditional
congiunzione	*cong*	conjunction
congiuntivo	*congiunt*	subjunctive
congiunzione	*conj*	conjunction
edilizia	*Constr*	building trade
culinaria, cucina	*Culin*	cooking
davanti a	*dav a*	before
determinativo	*def*	definite
dimostrativo	*dem*	demonstrative
determinativo	*det*	definite
dialetto	*dial*	dialect
difettivo	*dif*	defective
dimostrativo	*dimostr*	demonstrative
diritto	*Dir*	law

ABBREVIATIONS

ABBREVIAZIONI		ABBREVIATIONS
eccetera	*ecc*	et cetera
economia	*Econ*	economics
edilizia	*Edil*	building trade
elettricità, elettronica	*Elec, Elettr*	electricity, electronics
esclamazione	*escl*	exclamation
specialmente	*esp*	especially
eccetera	*etc*	et cetera
eufemismo	*euf, euph*	euphemistic
esclamazione	*excl*	exclamation
femminile	*f*	feminine
familiare, colloquiale	*fam*	informal, colloquial, familiar
volgare, tabù	*fam!*	vulgar, taboo
ferrovia	*Ferr*	railways
figurato	*fig*	figurative
finanza	*Fin*	finance
fisica	*Fis*	physics
fotografia	*Fot*	photography
formale	*frm*	formal
calcio	*Ftbl*	football
generale, nella maggior parte dei casi	*gen*	generally, in most senses
geografia	*Geog*	geography
geologia	*Geol*	geology
geometria	*Geom*	geometry
grammatica	*Gram, Gramm*	grammar
scherzoso	*hum*	humorous
impersonale	*impers*	impersonal
indefinito	*indef*	indefinite
indeterminativo	*indet*	indefinite
indicativo	*indic*	indicative
indiretto	*indir*	indirect
infinito	*infin*	infinitive
informatica, computer	*Inform*	computing
interrogativo	*interrog*	interrogative
invariabile	*inv*	invariable
irlandese	*Ir*	Irish
ironico	*iro*	ironic
irregolare	*irreg*	irregular
linguistica	*Ling*	linguistics
letterale	*lit*	literal
letterario	*liter*	literary
maschile	*m*	masculine

ABBREVIAZIONI		ABBREVIATIONS
matematica	*Mat, Math*	mathematics
medicina	*Med*	medicine
meteorologia	*Met, Meteor*	meteorology, weather
maschile o femminile,	*m/f*	either masculine or feminine
secondo il sesso		depending on sex
militare	*Mil*	military
mitologia	*Mitol*	mythology
musica	*Mus*	music
mitologia	*Myth*	mythology
sostantivo	*n*	noun
nautica	*Naut*	nautical, naval
negativo	*neg*	negative
non ha plurale	*no pl*	no plural
sostantivo sempre plurale	*npl*	plural noun
sostantivo sempre singolare	*nsg*	singular noun
oggetto	*ogg, obj*	object
	o.s.	oneself
passivo	*pass*	passive
passato remoto	*pass rem*	past historic
peggiorativo	*pegg, pej*	pejorative
persona, personale	*pers*	person, personal
fotografia	*Phot*	photography
fisica	*Phys*	physics
plurale	*pl*	plural
poetico, letterario	*poet*	poetic, literary
politica	*Pol*	politics
possessivo	*poss*	possessive
participio passato	*pp*	past participle
predicativo	*pred*	predicative
prefisso	*pref*	prefix
preposizione	*prep*	preposition
presente	*pres*	present
pronome	*pron*	pronoun
participio presente	*prp*	present participle
psicologia	*Psic, Psych*	psychology
passato	*pt*	past tense
qualcosa	*qc*	something
qualcuno	*qn*	someone
ferrovia	*Rail*	railways
religione	*Rel*	religion
relativo	*rel*	relative
sostantivo	*s*	noun

ABBREVIAZIONI		ABBREVIATIONS
qualcuno	*sb*	somebody
scherzoso	*scherz*	humorous
scienza	*Sci*	science
sistema scolastico	*Scol*	school
scozzese	*Scot*	Scottish
singolare	*sg*	singular
sociologia	*Sociol*	sociology
soggetto	*sogg*	subject
specialmente	*spec*	especially
qualcosa	*sth*	something
congiuntivo	*sub*	subjunctive
soggetto	*subj*	subject
suffisso	*suff*	suffix
superlativo	*superl*	superlative
tecnica, tecnologia	*Tech, Tecn*	technology, technical
telecomunicazioni	*Telec*	telecommunications
tipografia	*Tip*	typography, printing
televisione	*TV*	television
tipografia	*Typ*	typography, printing
università	*Univ*	university
Stati Uniti	*USA*	United States
di solito	*usu*	usually
verbo	*vb*	verb
verbo intransitivo	*vi*	intransitive verb
verbo intransitivo pronominale	*vip*	intransitive pronominal verb
verbo riflessivo	*vr*	reflexive verb
verbo transitivo	*vt*	transitive verb
zoologia	*Zool*	zoology
marchio registrato	®	registered trademark
introduce un'equivalenza culturale	≈	introduces a cultural equivalent

ITALIAN VERBS

a Gerund **b** Past participle **c** Present **d** Imperfect **e** Past historic **f** Future **g** Conditional **h** Present subjunctive **i** Imperfect subjunctive **j** Imperative

1 **abbattere** e abbattei, abbattesti (*doesn't have alternative forms* -etti, -ette, -ettero)

2 **accendere** b acceso e accesi, accendesti

3 **accludere** b accluso e acclusi, accludesti

4 **accorgersi** b accorto e mi accorsi, ti accorgesti

5 **aggiungere** b aggiunto e aggiunsi, aggiungesti

6 **andare** c vado, vai, va, andiamo, andate, vanno f andrò *etc.* h vada j va'!, vada!, andate!, vadano!

7 **apparire** b apparso c appaio, appari *or* apparisci, appare *or* apparisce, appaiono *or* appariscono e apparvi *or* apparsi, apparisti, apparve *or* appari *or* apparse, apparvero *or* apparirono *or* apparsero h appaia *or* apparisca

8 **appendere** b appeso e appesi, appendesti

9 **aprire** b aperto c apro e aprii, apristi h apra

10 **ardere** b arso e arsi, ardesti

11 **assistere** b assistito e assistei *or* assistetti, assistesti

12 **assumere** b assunto e assunsi, assumesti

13 **AVERE** c ho, hai, ha, abbiamo, avete, hanno e ebbi, avesti, ebbe, avemmo, aveste, ebbero f avrò *etc.* h abbia *etc.* j abbi!, abbia!, abbiate!, abbiano!

14 **baciare** *when the ending begins with* -e*, the* i *is dropped* → bacerò (*not* bacierò)

15 **bagnare** c bagniamo, bagniate h bagniamo, bagniate (*not* bagnamo, bagnate)

16 **bere** a bevendo b bevuto c bevo *etc.* d bevevo *etc.* e bevvi *or* bevetti, bevesti f berrò *etc.* h beva *etc.* i bevessi *etc.*

17 **bollire** c bollo *or* bollisco, bolli *or* bollisci etc.

18 **cadere** e caddi, cadesti f cadrò *etc.*

19 **cambiare** *drops the* i *of the root if the ending starts with* i (cambi, cambino *not* cambii, cambiino (*cf.* inviare)

20 **caricare** *when* c *in the root is followed by* -i *or* -e *an* h *should be inserted* (for example carichi, carichiamo, caricherò)

21 **chiedere** b chiesto e chiesi, chiedesti

22 **chiudere** b chiuso e chiusi, chiudesti

23 **cogliere** b colto c colgo, colgono e colsi, cogliesti h colga

24 **compiere** b compiuto e compii, compisti

25 **confondere** b confuso e confusi, confondesti

26 **conoscere** b conosciuto e conobbi, conoscesti

27 **consigliare** *when the ending begins with* -i*, the* i *of the root is dropped* → consigli (*not* consiglii)

28 **correre** b corso e corsi, corresti

29 **CREDERE** a credendo b creduto c credo, credi, crede, crediamo, credete, credono d credevo, credevi, credeva, credevamo, credevate, credevano e credei *or* credetti, credesti, credé *or* credette, credemmo, credeste, crederono *or* credettero f crederò, crederai, crederà, crederemo, crederete, crederanno g crederei, crederesti, crederebbe, crederemmo, credereste, crederebbero h creda, creda, creda, crediamo, crediate, credano i credessi, credessi, credesse, credessimo, credeste, credessero j credi!, creda!, credete!, credano!

30 **crescere** b cresciuto e crebbi, crescesti

31 **cucire** *when* c *or* g *in the root is followed by* -o *or* -a *an* i *should be inserted* (ie cucio, cucia)

32 **cuocere** b cotto c cuocio, cociamo, cuociono e cossi, cocesti

33 **dare** b do, dai, dà, diamo, date, danno e diedi *or* detti, desti f darò *etc.* h dia *etc.* i dessi *etc.* j da'!, dai!, date!, diano!

34 **decidere** b deciso e decisi, decidesti

35 **deludere** b deluso e delusi, deludesti

36 **difendere** b difeso e difesi, difendesti

37 **dipingere** b dipinto e dipinsi, dipingesti

38 **dire** a dicendo b detto c dico, dici, dice, diciamo, dite, dicono d dicevo *etc.* e dissi, dicesti f dirò *etc.* h dica, diciamo, diciate, dicano i dicessi *etc.* j di'!, dica!, dite!, dicano!

39 **dirigere** b diretto e diressi, dirigesti

40 discutere b discusso e discussi, discutesti

41 disfare *like* fare *but* c disfo, disfi *etc.* f disferò, disferai *etc.* i disfi, disfi *etc.* (*regular forms*)

42 distinguere b distinto e distinsi, distinguesti

43 dividere b diviso e divisi, dividesti

44 dolere c dolgo, duoli, duole, dolgono e dolsi, dolesti f dorrò *etc.* h dolga

45 DORMIRE a dormendo b dormito c dormo, dormi, dorme, dormiamo, dormite, dormono d dormivo, dormivi, dormiva, dormivamo, dormivate, dormivano e dormii, dormisti, dormì, dormimmo, dormiste, dormirono f dormirò, dormirai, dormirà, dormiremo, dormirete, dormiranno g dormirei, dormiresti, dormirebbe, dormiremmo, dormireste, dormirebbero h dorma, dorma, dorma, dormiamo, dormiate, dormano i dormissi, dormissi, dormisse, dormissimo, dormiste, dormissero j dormi!, dorma!, dormite!, dormano!

46 dovere c devo *or* debbo, devi, deve, dobbiamo, dovete, devono *or* debbono f dovrò *etc.* h debba, dobbiamo, dobbiate, devano *or* debbano

47 esigere b esatto (*not common*) e esigei *or* esigetti, esigesti

48 espellere b espulso e espulsi, espellesti

49 esplodere b esploso e esplosi, esplodesti

50 esprimere b espresso e espressi, esprimesti

51 ESSERE b stato c sono, sei, è, siamo, siete, sono d ero, eri, era, eravamo, eravate, erano e fui, fosti, fu, fummo, foste, furono f sarò *etc.* h sia *etc.* i fossi, fossi, fosse, fossimo, foste, fossero j sii!, sia!, siate!, siano!

52 evadere b evaso e evasi, evadesti

53 fare a facendo b fatto c faccio, fai, fa, facciamo, fate, fanno d facevo *etc.* e feci, facesti f farò *etc.* h faccia *etc.* i facessi *etc.* j fa'!, faccia!, fate!, facciano!

54 fingere b finto e finsi, fingesti

55 FINIRE a finendo b finito c finisco, finisci, finisce, finiamo, finite, finiscono d finivo, finivi, finiva, finivamo, finivate, finivano e finii, finisti, finì, finimmo, finiste, finirono f finirò, fini-

rai, finirà, finiremo, finirete, finiranno g finirei, finiresti, finirebbe, finiremmo, finireste, finirebbero h finisca, finisca, finisca, finiamo, finiate, finiscano i finissi, finissi, finisse, finissimo, finiste, finissero j finisci!, finisca!, finite!, finiscano!

56 friggere b fritto e frissi, friggesti

57 giacere b giaciuto e giacqui, giacesti

58 godere f godrò, godrai *etc.* g godrei, godresti *etc.*

59 immergere b immerso e immersi, immergesti

60 inviare c (tu) invii f (essi) inviino

61 leggere b letto e lessi, leggesti

62 mangiare *when the ending begins with* -e, *the* i *is dropped* → mangerò (*not* mangierò)

63 mettere b messo e misi, mettesti

64 mordere b morso e morsi, mordesti

65 morire b morto c muoio, muori, muore, moriamo, morite, muoiono f morirò *or* morrò *etc.* h muoia

66 muovere b mosso e mossi, muovesti

67 nascere b nato e nacqui, nascesti

68 nascondere b nascosto e nascosi, nascondesti

69 nuocere b nuociuto c nuoccio, nuoci, nuoce, nociamo *or* nuociamo, nuocete, nuocciono d nuocevo *etc.* e nocqui, nuocesti f nuocerò *etc.* g nuoccia

70 offrire b offerto c offro e offersi *or* offrii, offristi h offra

71 parere b parso c paio, paiamo, paiono e parvi *or* parsi, paresti f parrò *etc.* h paia, paiamo, paiate, paiano

72 PARLARE a parlando b parlato c parlo, parli, parla, parliamo, parlate, parlano d parlavo, parlavi, parlava, parlavamo, parlavate, parlavano e parlai, parlasti, parlò, parlammo, parlaste, parlarono f parlerò, parlerai, parlerà, parleremo, parlerete, parleranno g parlerei, parleresti, parlerebbe, parleremmo, parlereste, parlerebbero h parli, parli, parli, parliamo, parliate, parlino i parlassi, parlassi, parlasse, parlassimo, parlaste, parlassero j parla!, parli!, parlate!, parlino!

73 **perdere** b perso *or* perduto e persi, perdesti

74 **piacere** b piaciuto c piaccio, piacciamo, piacciono e piacqui, piacesti h piaccia *etc.*

75 **piangere** b pianto e piansi, piangesti

76 **piovere** b piovuto e piovve

77 **porre** a ponendo b posto c pongo, poni, pone, poniamo, ponete, pongono d ponevo *etc.* e posi, ponesti f porrò *etc.* h ponga, poniamo, poniate, pongano i ponessi *etc.*

78 **potere** c posso, puoi, può, possiamo, potete, possono f potrò *etc.* h possa, possiamo, possiate, possano

79 **prefiggersi** b prefisso e mi prefissi, ti prefiggesti

80 **pregare** *when* g *in the root is followed by* -i *or* -e *an* h *should be inserted* (for example, preghi, preghiamo, pregherò)

81 **prendere** b preso e presi, prendesti

82 **prevedere** *like* vedere *but* f prevederò, prevederai *etc.* g prevederei *etc.*

83 **proteggere** b protetto e protessi, proteggesti

84 **pungere** b punto e punsi, pungesti

85 **radere** b raso e rasi, radesti

86 **redimere** b redento e redensi, redimesti

87 **reggere** b retto e ressi, reggesti

88 **rendere** b reso e resi, rendesti

89 **ridere** b riso e risi, ridesti

90 **ridurre** a riducendo b ridotto c riduco *etc.* d riducevo *etc.* e ridussi, riducesti f ridurrò *etc.* h riduca *etc.* i riducessi *etc.*

91 **riempire** a riempiendo c riempio, riempi, riempie, riempiono

92 **riflettere** b riflettuto *or* riflesso

93 **rimanere** b rimasto c rimango, rimangono e rimasi, rimanesti f rimarrò *etc.* h rimanga

94 **risolvere** b risolto e risolsi, risolvesti

95 **rispondere** b risposto e risposi, rispondesti

96 **rivolgere** b rivolto e rivolsi, rivolgesti

97 **rompere** b rotto e ruppi, rompesti

98 **salire** c salgo, sali, salgono h salga

99 **sapere** c so, sai, sa, sappiamo, sapete, sanno e seppi, sapesti f saprò *etc.* h sappia *etc.* j sappi!, sappia!, sappiate!, sappiano!

100 **scegliere** b scelto c scelgo, scegli, sceglie, scegliamo, scegliete, scelgono e scelsi, scegliesti h scelga, scegliamo, scegliate, scelgano j scegli!, scelga!, scegliamo!, scegliete!, scelgano!

101 **scendere** b sceso e scesi, scendesti

102 **scindere** b scisso e scissi, scindesti

103 **sciogliere** b sciolto c sciolgo, sciogli, scioglie, sciogliamo, sciogliete, sciolgono e sciolsi, sciogliesti h sciolga, sciogliamo, sciogliate, sciolgano j sciogli!, sciolga!, sciogliamo!, sciogliete!, sciolgano!

104 **sconfiggere** b sconfitto e sconfissi, sconfiggesti

105 **scrivere** b scritto e scrissi, scrivesti

106 **scuotere** b scosso e scossi, scuotesti

107 **sedere** c siedo, siedi, siede, siedono h sieda

108 **solere** b solito e soglio, suoli, suole, sogliamo, solete, sogliono h soglia (*regular imperfect, gerund, past participle; no other verb forms*)

109 **sorgere** b sorto e sorse, sorsero

110 **spandere** b spanto e spansi, spandesti

111 **spargere** b sparso e sparse, sparsero

112 **sparire** e sparii, sparisti

113 **spegnere** b spento c spengo, spengono e spensi, spegnesti h spenga

114 **spingere** b spinto e spinsi, spingesti

115 **sporgere** b sporto e sporsi, sporgesti

116 **stare** b stato c sto, stai, sta, stiamo, state, stanno e stetti, stesti f starò *etc.* h stia *etc.* i stessi *etc.* j sta'!, stia!, state!, stiano!

117 **stringere** b stretto e strinsi, stringesti

118 **succedere** b successo e successi, succedesti

119 **tacere** b taciuto c taccio, tacciono e tacqui, tacesti h taccia

120 **tendere** b teso e tesi, tendesti

121 **tenere** c tengo, tieni, tiene, tengono e tenni, tenesti f terrò *etc.* h tenga

122 **togliere** b tolto c tolgo, togli, toglie, togliamo, togliete, tolgono e tolsi, togliesti h tolga j togli!, tolga!, togliamo!, togliete!, tolgano!

123 **trarre** **a** traendo **b** tratto **c** traggo, trai, trae, traiamo, traete, traggono **d** traevo *etc.* **e** trassi, traesti **f** trarrò *etc.* **h** tragga **i** traessi *etc.*

124 **udire** **c** odo, odi, ode, odono **h** oda

125 **uscire** **c** esco, esci, esce, escono **h** esca

126 **valere** **b** valso **c** valgo, valgono **e** valsi, valesti **f** varrò *etc.* **h** valga

127 **vedere** **b** visto *or* veduto **e** vidi, vedesti **f** vedrò *etc.*

128 **venire** **b** venuto **c** vengo, vieni, viene, vengono **e** venni, venisti **f** verrò *etc.* **h** venga

129 **vincere** **b** vinto **e** vinsi, vincesti

130 **vivere** **b** vissuto **e** vissi, vivesti

131 **volere** **c** voglio, vuoi, vuole, vogliamo, volete, vogliono **e** volli, volesti **f** vorrò *etc.* **h** voglia *etc.* **j** *not common*

VERBI INGLESI

PRESENT	PT	PP
arise	arose	arisen
awake	awoke	awoken
be (am, is, are; being)	was, were	been
bear	bore	born(e)
beat	beat	beaten
become	became	become
befall	befell	befallen
begin	began	begun
behold	beheld	beheld
bend	bent	bent
beset	beset	beset
bet	bet, betted	bet, betted
bid (*at auction, cards*)	bid	bid
bid (*say*)	bade	bidden
bind	bound	bound
bite	bit	bitten
bleed	bled	bled
blow	blew	blown
break	broke	broken
breed	bred	bred
bring	brought	brought
build	built	built
burn	burnt, burned	burnt, burned
burst	burst	burst
buy	bought	bought
can	could	(been able)
cast	cast	cast
catch	caught	caught
choose	chose	chosen
cling	clung	clung
come	came	come
cost	cost	cost
cost (*work out price of*)	costed	costed
creep	crept	crept
cut	cut	cut
deal	dealt	dealt
dig	dug	dug
do (*3rd person:* he/ she/it **does**)	did	done
draw	drew	drawn
dream	dreamed, dreamt	dreamed, dreamt

PRESENT	PT	PP
drink	drank	drunk
drive	drove	driven
dwell	dwelt	dwelt
eat	ate	eaten
fall	fell	fallen
feed	fed	fed
feel	felt	felt
fight	fought	fought
find	found	found
flee	fled	fled
fling	flung	flung
fly	flew	flown
forbid	forbad(e)	forbidden
forecast	forecast	forecast
forget	forgot	forgotten
forgive	forgave	forgiven
forsake	forsook	forsaken
freeze	froze	frozen
get	got	got, (*USA*) gotten
give	gave	given
go (goes)	went	gone
grind	ground	ground
grow	grew	grown
hang	hung	hung
hang (*execute*)	hanged	hanged
have	had	had
hear	heard	heard
hide	hid	hidden
hit	hit	hit
hold	held	held
hurt	hurt	hurt
keep	kept	kept
kneel	knelt, kneeled	knelt, kneeled
know	knew	known
lay	laid	laid
lead	led	led
lean	leaned, leant	leaned, leant
leap	leaped, leapt	leaped, leapt
learn	learned, learnt	learned, learnt
leave	left	left
lend	lent	lent
let	let	let

PRESENT	PT	PP	PRESENT	PT	PP
lie (lying)	lay	lain	**smell**	smelt, smelled	smelt, smelled
light	lit, lighted	lit, lighted	**sow**	sowed	sown, sowed
lose	lost	lost	**speak**	spoke	spoken
make	made	made	**speed**	sped, speeded	sped, speeded
may	might	—	**spell**	spelled, spelt	spelled, spelt
mean	meant	meant	**spend**	spent	spent
meet	met	met	**spill**	spilled, spilt	spilled, spilt
mistake	mistook	mistaken	**spin**	spun	spun
mow	mowed	mown, mowed	**spit**	spat	spat
must	(had to)	(had to)	**spoil**	spoiled, spoilt	spoiled, spoilt
pay	paid	paid	**spread**	spread	spread
put	put	put	**spring**	sprang	sprung
quit	quit, quitted	quit, quitted	**stand**	stood	stood
read	read	read	**steal**	stole	stolen
ride	rode	ridden	**stick**	stuck	stuck
rid	rid	rid	**sting**	stung	stung
ring	rang	rung	**stink**	stank	stunk
rise	rose	risen	**stride**	strode	stridden
run	ran	run	**strike**	struck	struck
saw	sawed	sawed, sawn	**strive**	strove	striven
say	said	said	**swear**	swore	sworn
seek	sought	sought	**sweep**	swept	swept
see	saw	seen	**swell**	swelled	swollen, swelled
sell	sold	sold	**swim**	swam	swum
send	sent	sent	**swing**	swung	swung
set	set	set	**take**	took	taken
sew	sewed	sewn	**teach**	taught	taught
shake	shook	shaken	**tear**	tore	torn
shear	sheared	shorn, sheared	**tell**	told	told
shed	shed	shed	**think**	thought	thought
shine	shone	shone	**throw**	threw	thrown
shoot	shot	shot	**thrust**	thrust	thrust
show	showed	shown	**tread**	trod	trodden
shrink	shrank	shrunk	**wake**	woke, waked	woken, waked
shut	shut	shut	**wear**	wore	worn
sing	sang	sung	**weave**	wove	woven
sink	sank	sunk	**weave** (*wind*)	weaved	weaved
sit	sat	sat	**wed**	wedded, wed	wedded, wed
slay	slew	slain	**weep**	wept	wept
sleep	slept	slept	**wind**	wound	wound
slide	slid	slid	**win**	won	won
sling	slung	slung	**wring**	wrung	wrung
slit	slit	slit	**write**	wrote	written

Italiano — Inglese

Italian — English

Aa

A¹, a¹ [a] SF INV, SM INV (*lettera*) A, a; **A come Ancona** ≈ A for Andrew (*Brit*), ≈ A for Able (*USA*); **dalla a alla zeta** from A to Z

A² [a] ABBR **1** = **autostrada**; **sull'A1** ≈ on the M1 (*Brit*) **2** (= *altezza*) h **3** (= *area*) A

PAROLA CHIAVE

a [a] PREP *a+il=al*, *a+lo=allo*, *a+l'=all'*, *a+la=alla*, *a+i=ai*, *a+gli=agli*, *a+le=alle*

1 (*complemento di termine*) to (*spesso omesso*); **dare qc a qn** to give sth to sb, give sb sth; **ho dato un giocattolo a Sandro** I gave Sandro a toy, I gave a toy to Sandro

2 (*stato in luogo: posizione*) at; (: *in*) in; (: *su*) on; **abitare a Milano/al terzo piano** to live in Milan/on the third floor; **è a 10 chilometri da qui** it's 10 kilometres from here; **essere a scuola/a casa/al cinema** to be at school/at home/at the cinema; **lavora alle poste/alle ferrovie** he works at the Post Office/for the railway; **alla radio** on the radio; **alla televisione** on television

3 (*moto a luogo*) to; **andare a casa/a Roma/al mare** to go home/to Rome/to the seaside

4 (*tempo*) at; (*epoca, stagione*) in; (*fino a*) to, till, until; **alle 3** at 3 o'clock; **all'alba** at dawn; **a 18 anni si diventa maggiorenni** at 18 you come of age; **dalle 3 alle 5** from 3 to o till 5 (o'clock); **a domani!** see you tomorrow!; **tornerà a giorni** he'll be back in a few days; **a lunedì!** see you on Monday!; **a maggio** in May; **a mezzanotte** at midnight; **tornerà a minuti** he'll be back in a few minutes; **a Natale** on Christmas; **a primavera** in spring

5 (*mezzo, modo*): **andare a cavallo** to go on horseback; **bistecca ai ferri** grilled steak; **bistecca alla fiorentina** T-bone steak; **fatto a mano** made by hand, handmade; **scrivere qc a matita** to write sth in pencil o with a pencil; **alla milanese** Milanese-style, in the Milanese fashion; **una barca a motore** a motorboat; **andare a piedi** to go on foot; **gonna a pieghe** pleated skirt; **pasta al pomodoro** pasta with o in tomato sauce; **gonna a righe** striped skirt; **entrare a uno a uno** to come in one by one

6 (*rapporto*) by, per; (*con prezzi*) at; **essere pagato a giornata** to be paid by the day; **vendere qc a 6 euro il chilo** to sell sth at 6 euros a o per kilo; **prendo 2000 euro al mese** I get 2000 euros a o per month; **viaggiare a 100 km all'ora** to travel at 100 km an o per hour; **essere pagato a ore** to be paid by the hour

7 (*scopo, fine*) for, to; **restare a cena** to stay for o to dinner

AA SIGLA = **Alto Adige**

AAST [a'a'esse'ti] SIGLA F = **Azienda Autonoma di Soggiorno e Turismo**

AA.VV. ABBR = **autori vari**

ab. ABBR = **abitante**

abate [a'bate] SM abbot

abbacchiato, -a [abbak'kjato] AGG (*fam*) down, depressed; **ha un'aria abbacchiata** he's looking a bit down

abbacinare [abbatʃi'nare] /72/ VT to dazzle

abbagliante [abbaʎ'ʎante] AGG dazzling; **fare uso dei fari abbaglianti** to have one's headlights on full (*Brit*) o high (*USA*) beam ♦ SM (*gen pl: Aut*): **accendere gli abbaglianti** to put one's headlights on full (*Brit*) o high (*USA*) beam

abbagliare [abbaʎ'ʎare] /27/ VT (*anche fig*) to dazzle; (*illudere*) to delude; **non lasciarti abbagliare** don't let yourself be taken in

abbaglio, -gli [ab'baʎʎo] SM blunder; **prendere un abbaglio** to blunder, make a blunder

abbaiare [abba'jare] /19/ VI: **abbaiare (a)** to bark (at); (*fig: gridare rabbiosamente*) to bawl (at)

abbaino [abba'ino] SM (*finestra*) dormer window; (*soffitta*) attic room

abbandonare [abbando'nare] /72/ VT **1** (*gen*) to abandon; (*famiglia, paese*) to abandon, desert; **abbandonare qn a se stesso** to leave sb to his (o her) own devices; **i suoi genitori lo hanno abbandonato quando era piccolo** his parents abandoned him when he was little; **il coraggio lo abbandonò** his courage deserted him; **abbandonare la nave** (*anche fig*) to abandon ship; **abbandonare il campo** (*Mil, o fig*) to retreat **2** (*trascurare: casa, lavoro*) to neglect **3** (*rinunciare a*) to give up; (*studi, progetto, speranza*) to abandon, give up; **abbandonare la gara** to withdraw from the race; **hanno abbandonato tutte le speranze** they gave up all hope **4** (*lasciare andare: redini*) to slacken; **abbandonò la testa sul cuscino** he let his head fall back on the pillow; **abbandonarsi** VR to let o.s. go; **si abbandonò sul divano** he sank onto the couch; **abbandonarsi a qc** (*ricordi, passioni*) to give o.s. up to sth; **abbandonarsi a qn** (*affidarsi*) to put o.s. in sb's hands

abbandonato, -a [abbando'nato] AGG **1** (*casa*) deserted; (*miniera*) disused **2** (*trascurato: terreno, podere*) neglected **3** (*bambino*) abandoned

abbandono [abban'dono] SM **1** (*di famiglia, paese*) desertion, abandonment; **abbandono del tetto coniugale** (*Dir*) desertion **2** (*trascuratezza*) neglect; **in abbandono** (*edificio, giardino*) neglected; **lasciare qc in stato di abbandono** to neglect sth **3** (*rinuncia: di progetto*) abandonment, dropping, giving up **4** (*Sport*) withdrawal; **vincere per abbandono dell'avversario** to win by default **5** (*rilassamento, cedimento*) abandon; **momenti di abbandono** moments of abandon

abbarbicarsi [abbarbi'karsi] /61/ VIP: **abbarbicarsi (a)** (*anche fig*) to cling (to)

abbassamento [abbassa'mento] SM lowering; (*di pressione, livello dell'acqua*) fall; (*di prezzi*) reduction; **abbassamento di temperatura** drop in temperature

abbassare [abbas'sare] /72/ VT **1** to lower; (*leva*) to press down; (*finestrino della macchina*) to lower; (*finestrino del treno, tapparella*) to pull down; **abbassare le armi** (*Mil*) to lay down one's arms; **abbassò la testa per la vergogna** he hung his head in shame; **abbassare la guardia** (*Sport, o fig*) to drop one's guard **2** (*volume, radio, TV*) to turn down; (*voce*) to lower; **ti dispiace abbassare il volume?** would you mind turning down the volume? **3** (*diminuire: prezzi*) to reduce, bring down **4** (*luce*) to dim; (*fari*) to dip (*Brit*), dim (*USA*) **5** (*Geom: perpendicolare*) to drop; **abbassarsi** VR (*chinarsi*) to bend down, stoop; (*per evitare*) to duck; (*fig: umiliarsi*) to demean o.s.; **abbassarsi a fare qc** to lower o.s. to do sth; **abbassarsi** VIP **1** (*temperatura, prezzi*) to drop, fall; (*marea*) to go out, fall; (*livello*) to go down; (*sipario*) to fall **2** (*peggiorare: vista*) to deteriorate

abbasso [ab'basso] ESCL: **abbasso il re!** down with the king!

abbastanza [abbas'tantsa] AVV **1** (*a sufficienza*) enough; **non mangia abbastanza** he doesn't eat enough; **non avevo studiato abbastanza** I hadn't studied enough; **non ho abbastanza tempo/denaro** I don't have o haven't got enough o sufficient time/money; **hai trovato una casa abbastanza grande per la tua famiglia?** have you found a big enough house for your family?; **non ho abbastanza soldi per comprarlo** I don't have enough money to buy it; **averne abbastanza di qn/qc** to have had enough of sb/sth, be fed up with sb/sth **2** (*alquanto*) quite, rather, fairly; **un vino abbastanza dolce** quite a sweet wine, a fairly sweet wine; **è abbastanza alto** he's quite tall; **vanno abbastanza d'accordo** they get on O.K.; **l'esame era abbastanza difficile** the exam was quite difficult; **ti piace il film? — sì, abbastanza** are you enjoying the film? — yes, quite o it's o.k.

abbattere [ab'battere] /1/ VT **1** (*edificio, muro, ostacolo*) to knock down; (*albero*) to fell, cut down; (*sogg: vento*) to bring down; (*aereo*) to shoot down; (*porta*) to break down; (*fig: governo*) to overthrow; **hanno dovuto abbattere molti edifici**

pericolanti they had to knock down a lot of unsafe buildings **2** (*uccidere: persona, selvaggina*) to shoot; (: *bestie da macello*) to slaughter; (: *cane, cavallo*) to destroy, put down **3** (*prostrare: sogg: malattia, disgrazia*) to lay low; **non lasciarti abbattere** don't be disheartened, don't let it get you down; **abbattersi** VIP **1** (*cadere*): **abbattersi al suolo** to fall to the ground **2** (*colpire*): **abbattersi su** (*sogg: maltempo*) to beat down on; (: *disgrazia*) to hit, strike **3** (*avvilirsi*) to lose heart

abbattimento [abbatti'mento] SM **1** (*di albero*) felling; (*di muro*) knocking down; (*di casa*) demolition; (*di aereo*) downing down (*Brit*), downing (*USA*); (*di animali: a caccia*) shooting; (: *morale*) despondency

abbattuto, -a [abbat'tuto] AGG despondent, depressed; **mi è sembrato un po' abbattuto** he seemed a bit depressed

abbazia [abbat'tsia] SF abbey; **l'abbazia di Westminster** Westminster Abbey

abbecedario, -ri [abbetʃe'darjo] SM ABC book

abbellimento [abbelli'mento] SM **1** (*ornamento*) embellishment **2** (*Mus*) embellishment, grace note

abbellire [abbel'lire] /55/ VT to make (more) attractive; (*racconto*) to embellish; **abbellirsi** VIP to become more attractive

abbeverare [abbeve'rare] /72/ VT to water; **abbeverarsi** VR to drink

abbeveratoio, -oi [abbevera'tojo] SM drinking trough

abbi, abbia, abbiamo, abbiate, abbiano VB vedi avere

abbiccì [abbit'tʃi] SM INV (*alfabeto*) ABC, alphabet; (*fig*) ABC, rudiments pl; (*abbecedario, sillabario*) ABC book; **l'abbiccì del fai da te** the abc of do-it-yourself

abbiente [ab'bjɛnte] AGG well-to-do, well-off; **una famiglia abbiente** a well-off family ♦ **gli abbienti** SMPL the well-to-do; **gli abbienti e i non abbienti** the haves and the have-nots

abbietto ecc [ab'bjɛtto] AGG = **abietto**

abbiezione [abbjet'tsjone] SF = **abiezione**

abbigliamento [abbiλλa'mento] SM (*modo di vestire*) clothes pl; (*vestiario*) clothing; **abbigliamento maschile/femminile** menswear/ladieswear; **capo di abbigliamento** article of clothing; **industria dell'abbigliamento** clothing industry, fashion business; **spende molto per l'abbigliamento** he spends a lot on clothes

abbigliare [abbiλ'λare] /27/ VT (*aiutare a vestire*) to dress; (*agghindare*) to dress up; **abbigliarsi** VR to dress

abbinamento [abbina'mento] SM (*vedi vb*) combination; linking; matching

abbinare [abbi'nare] /72/ VT: **abbinare (con o a)** (*gen*) to combine (with); (*nomi*) to link (with); (*colori ecc*) to match (with), to go (with); **ha una camicia da abbinare a questi pantaloni?** have you got a shirt to go with these pants?

abbindolare [abbindo'lare] /72/ VT (*fig*) to trick, take in, cheat; **si è fatto abbindolare** he was done in

abboccamento [abbokka'mento] SM **1** (*colloquio*) preliminary meeting **2** (*Tecn: di tubi*) connection

abboccare [abbok'kare] /20/ VI (*aus avere*) (*pesce*) to bite; (*fig: farsi raggirare*) to swallow the bait; **abboccare all'amo** (*anche fig*) to rise to the bait ♦ VT (*Tecn: tubi, condutture*) to connect, join (up)

abboccato, -a [abbok'kato] AGG (*vino*) medium sweet

abbonamento [abbona'mento] SM **1** **abbonamento (a)** (*rivista*) subscription (to); (*teatro, trasporti*) season ticket (for); **l'abbonamento ad una rivista** a magazine subscription; **abbonamento settimanale/mensile** (*a teatro, trasporti*) weekly/monthly ticket; **fare l'abbonamento (a qc)** to take out a subscription (to sth), buy a season ticket (for sth); **in abbonamento** for subscribers only, for season ticket holders only **2** (*al telefono*) rental; **abbonamento alla televisione** television licence

abbonare¹ [abbo'nare] /72/ VT (*cifra*) to deduct; (*fig: perdonare*) to forgive

abbonare² [abbo'nare] /72/ VT: **abbonare qn (a qc)** (*rivista*) to take out a subscription for sb (to sth); (*teatro, trasporti*) to buy sb a season ticket (for sth); (*televisione ecc*) to get o buy a licence (for sth) for sb; **abbonarsi** VR: **abbonarsi (a)** (*rivista*) to subscribe (to); (*teatro, trasporti*) to buy a season ticket (for); **abbonarsi al telefono** to have a telephone installed o

put in; **abbonarsi alla televisione** to get o buy a television licence

abbonato, -a [abbo'nato] AGG **essere abbonato** (*a rivista*) to be a subscriber; (*a teatro, trasporti*) to be a season ticket holder; (*alla televisione ecc*) to be a licence holder: (*fig: abituato*): **viene a cena da noi ogni settimana: ormai c'è abbonato!** he comes to our house for dinner every week: it's part of his routine! ♦ SM, SF vedi **abbonare²** subscriber; season ticket holder; licence holder; **abbonato al telefono** telephone subscriber; **elenco abbonati** telephone directory

abbondante [abbon'dante] AGG **1** (*gen*) abundant, plentiful; (*misure*) generous; (*nevicata*) heavy; **un'abbondante colazione** a big breakfast; **in quel ristorante le porzioni sono più abbondanti** the portions are bigger in that restaurant **2** (*abito: troppo grande*) too big, on the large side; (: *ampio*) loose-fitting

abbondanza [abbon'dantsa] SF **1** (*gran quantità*) abundance; **in abbondanza** plenty; **ne ho in abbondanza** I've got plenty; **dovresti mangiare frutta e verdura in abbondanza** you should eat plenty of fruit and vegetables; **ci sono pere in abbondanza** there are plenty of pears, there is an abundance of pears **2** (*ricchezza*) plenty; **vivere nell'abbondanza** to live in plenty

abbondare [abbon'dare] /72/ VI **1** (*aus essere*) to abound, be plentiful **2** (*aus avere*) **abbondare di** to be full of, abound in; **abbondare in o di cortesie** to be extremely polite

abbordabile [abbor'dabile] AGG (*persona*) approachable; (*prezzo*) affordable

abbordare [abbor'dare] /72/ VT **1** (*Naut*) to go alongside; (*nave nemica*) to board **2** (*curva, salita*) to take **3** (*persona*) to accost; (*questione, argomento*) to tackle

abbottonare [abbotto'nare] /72/ VT to button (up), do up; **abbottonarsi il cappotto** to button (up) one's coat; **abbottonarsi** VR (*fig: fam: diventare riservato*) to clam up

abbottonato, -a [abbotto'nato] AGG (*camicia ecc*) buttoned (up); (*fig*) buttoned up

abbottonatura [abbottona'tura] SF buttons pl; **questo cappotto ha l'abbottonatura da uomo/da donna** this coat buttons on the man's/woman's side

abbozzare [abbot'tsare] /72/ VT **1** (*scultura*) to rough-hew; (*disegno*) to sketch, outline; (*romanzo*) to sketch out **2** (*fig: idea, progetto*) to outline; (: *contratto*) to draft; **abbozzare un sorriso** to give a faint smile o a hint of a smile; **abbozzare un saluto** (*con la mano*) to half wave; (*con un cenno del capo*) to half nod

abbozzo [ab'bottso] SM **1** (*di scultura, disegno*) sketch, outline; (*di libro*) rough outline **2** (*di progetto*) outline; (*di contratto*) draft; (*fig: accenno*) hint; **un abbozzo di sorriso** the ghost of a smile

abbracciare [abbrat'tʃare] /14/ VT **1** (*persona*) to embrace, hug; **ti abbraccio** (*in una lettera*) lots of love **2** (*professione*) to take up; (*fede*) to embrace **3** (*includere*) to include; **abbracciare qc con lo sguardo** to take sth in at a glance; **la sua opera abbraccia due secoli di storia** his work covers two hundred years of history; **abbracciarsi** VR (*uso reciproco*) to hug o embrace (one another)

abbraccio, -ci [ab'brattʃo] SM embrace, hug; **ci siamo salutati con un abbraccio** we hugged and said goodbye; **un abbraccio** (*in lettera, cartolina*) love; **un abbraccio, Francesca** (lots of) love, Francesca

abbreviare [abbre'vjare] /19/ VT (*gen*) to shorten; (*parola*) to abbreviate, shorten

abbreviazione [abbrevjat'tsjone] SF (*vedi vb*) shortening; abbreviation

abbronzante [abbron'dzante] AGG (*prodotto*) suntan attr, sun attr ♦ SM (*crema*) suntan cream; (*olio*) suntan oil

abbronzare [abbron'dzare] /72/ VT (*pelle*) to tan; (*metalli*) to bronze; **abbronzarsi** VIP to get a tan; **stare ad abbronzarsi** to sunbathe

abbronzato, -a [abbron'dzato] AGG (sun)tanned; **è abbronzatissima** she's very tanned

abbronzatura [abbrondza'tura] SF (sun)tan

abbrustolire [abbrusto'lire] /55/ VT (*pane*) to toast; (*semi, caffè*) to roast; **abbrustolirsi** VIP: **abbrustolirsi al sole** (*fig*) to soak up the sun

abbrutimento [abbruti'mento] SM degradation

abbrutire [abbru'tire] /55/ VT (*degradare*) to degrade; **essere abbrutito dall'alcol** to be ruined by drink; **la guerra abbrutisce l'uomo** war brutalizes people; **abbrutirsi** VIP to be degraded, be brutalized

abbuffarsi [abbuf'farsi] /72/ VR (*fam*): **abbuffarsi (di qc)** to stuff o.s. (with sth)

abbuffata [abbuf'fata] SF (*fam*) nosh-up, blow-out; (*fig*) binge; **farsi un'abbuffata** to stuff o.s.

abbuonare [abbwo'nare] /72/ VT = **abbonare¹**

abbuono [ab'bwono] SM **1** (*Comm*) discount **2** (*Ippica*) handicap

abdicare [abdi'kare] /20/ VI **1** (*al trono*): **abdicare (a)** to abdicate (from); (*rinunciare*): **abdicare a** to renounce, give up; **abdicare a una carica** to give up a position **2** (*venir meno a: responsabilità, dovere*) to abdicate

abdicazione [abdikat'tsjone] SF abdication

aberrazione [aberrat'tsjone] SF aberration

abetaia [abe'taja] SF fir wood

abete [a'bete] SM (*albero*) fir (tree); (*legno*) fir; **abete bianco** silver fir; **abete rosso** spruce

abietto, -a [a'bjetto] AGG (*spregevole: persona, azione*) despicable, vile; (*squallido: condizioni*) abject, appalling

abiezione [abjet'tsjone] SF (*vedi agg*) vileness; abjectness

abile ['abile] AGG **1** (*capace*) skilful, able; **essere abile in qc** to be good at sth; **è molto abile nel suo lavoro** he's very good at his job; **un abile chirurgo/artigiano** a skilful surgeon/craftsman **2** (*accorto*) clever; (*astuto*) shrewd; **un'abile mossa** a good o clever move; **un'abile donna d'affari** a shrewd businesswoman **3** (*idoneo*): **abile (a qc/a fare qc)** fit (for sth/to do sth); **abile al servizio militare** fit for military service

abilità [abili'ta] SF INV **1** (*capacità*) ability; (*destrezza*) skill; **questo lavoro richiede una grande abilità** this work requires great skill; **abilità nel fare qc** ability to do sth; **una grande abilità nella guida** great skill in driving **2** (*accortezza*) cleverness; (*astuzia*) shrewdness

abilitante [abili'tante] AGG qualifying; **corsi abilitanti** (*Scol*) ≈ teacher training *sg*

abilitare [abili'tare] /72/ VT: **abilitare qn a qc/a fare qc** to qualify sb for sth/to do sth; **è stato abilitato all'insegnamento** he has qualified as a teacher

abilitato, -a [abili'tato] AGG **1** (*qualificato*) qualified **2** (*Telec*) which has an outside line ♦ SM, SF qualified person; **solo gli abilitati possono partecipare** only those with the required qualifications may take part

abilitazione [abilitat'tsjone] SF qualification; **esame di abilitazione** qualifying exam; **conseguire l'abilitazione** to qualify

abissale [abis'sale] AGG abysmal; (*fig: senza limiti: ignoranza*) profound; **Mario è di un'ignoranza abissale!** Mario is a total ignoramus!

abissino, -a [abis'sino] AGG, SM, SF Abyssinian

abisso [a'bisso] SM (*anche fig*) abyss, gulf; **gli abissi marini** the depths of the sea; **tra noi c'è un abisso** we are poles apart; **essere sull'orlo dell'abisso** to be on the brink of ruin; **è un abisso di ignoranza** he is utterly ignorant

abitabilità [abitabili'ta] SF INV: **licenza o autorizzazione di abitabilità** *document stating that a property is fit for habitation*

abitacolo [abi'takolo] SM (*di aereo*) cockpit; (*di macchina*) inside; (*di camion*) (driver's) cab

abitante [abi'tante] SM, SF (*di città, paese*) inhabitant; (*di casa*) occupant

abitare [abi'tare] /72/ VI (*aus avere*) **abitare in, a** to live (in); **abitare in campagna/a Roma/all'estero** to live in the country/in Rome/abroad; **dove abiti?** where do you live?; **abito a Firenze** I live in Florence; **tra noi è un abisso** no idea; **abito qui da sei anni** I've been living here for six years; **abita al numero 10** she lives at number 10; **abitano al sesto piano** they live on the sixth floor ♦ VT (*casa*) to live in, dwell in; (*luogo*) to inhabit

abitato, -a [abi'tato] AGG (*casa, appartamento*) occupied, inhabited ♦ SM (*anche: centro abitato*) built-up area

abitazione [abitat'tsjone] SF (*casa*) house, residence (*frm*)

abito ['abito] SM **1** (*da donna*) dress; (*da uomo*) suit; **in abito da cerimonia** in formal dress; **"è gradito l'abito scuro"**

"dress formal"; **in abito da sera** in evening dress; **abito da sposa** wedding dress **2** (*vestiti*): **abiti** SMPL clothes, dress *no pl*; **abiti civili** civilian clothes *pl*, civvies *pl* (*fam*) **3** (*disposizione*): **abito mentale** way of thinking **4** (*Rel*) habit; **l'abito non fa il monaco** (*Proverbio*) you can't tell a book by its cover, you can't judge by appearances

abituale [abitu'ale] AGG usual; (*cliente, frequentatore*) regular

abitualmente [abitual'mente] AVV usually, normally

abituare [abitu'are] /72/ VT: **abituare qn (a qc/a fare qc)** to accustom sb to sth/to doing sth, get sb used to sth/to doing sth; **abituarsi** VR: **abituarsi a qc/a fare qc** to get used to o accustomed to sth/to doing sth, accustom o.s. to sth/to doing sth (*frm*); **adesso mi ci sono abituato** I'm used to it now

abitudinario, -ria, -ri, -rie [abitudi'narjo] AGG: **essere abitudinario** to be set in one's ways; **è un po' abitudinario** he's rather set in his ways ♦ SM, SF creature of habit

abitudine [abi'tudine] SF habit; **aver l'abitudine di fare qc** to be in the habit of doing sth; **prendere/perdere l'abitudine di fare qc** to get into/out of the habit of doing sth; **per abitudine** from o out of habit; **come d'abitudine** as usual; **d'abitudine** usually; **buona o bella/cattiva o brutta abitudine** good/bad habit; **ci ho fatto l'abitudine** I've got used to it

abiurare [abju'rare] /72/ VT (*Rel*) to abjure; (*principi*) to renounce

ablativo [abla'tivo] SM, AGG ablative

abnegazione [abnegat'tsjone] SF (self-)abnegation, self-denial; **con abnegazione** selflessly

abnorme [ab'norme] AGG (*enorme*) extraordinary; (*anormale*) abnormal

abolire [abo'lire] /55/ VT to abolish; (*Dir*) to repeal; **abbiamo abolito lo zucchero dalla nostra dieta** we have eliminated sugar from our diet; **abolire una legge/tassa** to abolish a law/tax

abolizione [abolit'tsjone] SF abolition

abominevole [abomi'nevole] AGG abominable

aborigeno, -a [abo'ridʒeno] AGG aboriginal ♦ SM, SF aboriginal, aborigine; **aborigeno australiano** Aborigine

aborrire [abor'rire] /17/ VT to abhor, loathe

abortire [abor'tire] /55/ VI **1** (*aus avere*) (*Med*) to abort; (*accidentalmente*) to have a miscarriage, miscarry; (*volontariamente*) to have an abortion **2** (*aus essere*) (*fig: progetto ecc*) to fail, come to nothing, miscarry (*frm*); (*Inform*) to abort

aborto [a'borto] SM **1** (*provocato*) abortion; (*spontaneo*) miscarriage; **aborto clandestino** backstreet abortion **2** (*feto*) aborted foetus; (*fig*) freak; **è un aborto di quadro** (*fig*) it's a ghastly painting

abrasione [abra'zjone] SF abrasion

abrasivo, -a [abra'zivo] AGG, SM abrasive

abrogare [abro'gare] /80/ VT (*legge*) to repeal, abrogate (*frm*)

abrogazione [abrogat'tsjone] SF repeal, abrogation (*frm*)

abruzzese [abrut'tsese] AGG of o from the Abruzzi ♦ SM, SF inhabitant o native of the Abruzzi

Abruzzo [a'bruttso] SM: **l'Abruzzo** the Abruzzi

ABS [abi'esse] SIGLA M (= *Anti-Blockier System*) ABS (= *anti-lock braking system*)

abside ['abside] SF apse

Abu Dhabi [abu'dabi] SF Abu Dhabi

abulico, -a, -ci, -che [a'buliko] AGG abulic; lethargic

abusare [abu'zare] /72/ VI (*aus avere*) **abusare di qc** (*fare uso eccessivo: di pazienza, cortesia*) to take advantage of; (: *di alcol, stupefacenti*) to abuse; (*fare uso indebito: di potere, autorità, fiducia*) to abuse; **abusare di qn** to abuse sb; **non vorrei abusare della tua gentilezza** I don't want to take advantage of your kindness

abusivismo [abuzi'vizmo] SM (*anche: abusivismo edilizio*) unlawful building, building without planning permission (*Brit*)

abusivo, -a [abu'zivo] AGG unauthorized; **edilizia abusiva** unauthorized building; **occupante abusivo** (*di una casa*) squatter; **taxi abusivo** unlicensed taxi

❑ **abusivo** non si traduce mai con la parola inglese *abusive*

abuso [a'buzo] SM **1** (*uso eccessivo*) excessive use; (*uso impro-*

prio) abuse, misuse; **fare abuso di** (*stupefacenti, medicine*) to abuse; **abuso di potere** abuse of power; **abuso di medicinali** drug abuse **2** (*violenza*) abuse; **abusi sessuali sui minori** child abuse

a.C. ABBR (= *avanti Cristo*) BC; **il primo secolo a.c.** the first century BC

acacia, -cie [aˈkatʃa] SF acacia

acca [ˈakka] SF letter H; **non capire un'acca** not to understand a thing; **non sai un'acca di latino** you don't know a thing about Latin

accadde ecc VB *vedi* accadere

accademia [akkaˈdɛmja] SF (*scuola: d'arte, militare*) academy; (*società*) learned society; **accademia d'arte drammatica** drama school; **accademia di Belle Arti** art school; **accademia militare** military academy; **Accademia della Crusca** *national academy for the study and preservation of the Italian language*

accademico, -a, -ci, -che [akkaˈdɛmiko] AGG academic; (*fig: pedante*) academic, pedantic; **anno accademico** academic year ♦ SM, SF academician

accadere [akkaˈdere] VB IRREG (*aus essere*) /18/ VI to happen, occur; **mi è accaduto di incontrarlo** I happened to meet him; **è accaduto l'anno scorso** it happened last year ♦ VB IMPERS to happen; **accadde che...** it happened that ...

accaduto [akkaˈduto] SM event; **raccontare l'accaduto** to describe what happened; **in seguito all'accaduto** following what happened

accalappiacani [akkalappjaˈkani] SM INV dog-catcher

accalappiare [akkalapˈpjare] /19/ VT (*animali*) to catch; (*fig: persona*) to trick, dupe

accalcare [akkalˈkare] /20/ VT , **accalcarsi** VIP to crowd, throng; **i tifosi accalcavano lo stadio, i tifosi si accalcavano nello stadio** the fans crowded *o* thronged the stadium

accaldarsi [akkalˈdarsi] /61/ VIP to get hot

accaldato, -a [akkalˈdato] AGG hot; **era tutto accaldato dopo la corsa** he was boiling hot after the race

accalorarsi [akkaloˈrarsi] /61/ VR (*infervorarsi*) to become worked up, get excited

accampamento [akkampaˈmento] SM (*Mil: di zingari ecc*) camp, encampment; **togliere/porre l'accampamento** to strike/pitch camp

accampare [akkamˈpare] /72/ VT **1** (*Mil*) to encamp **2** (*fig: diritti*) to assert; (: *pretese*) to advance; **accampare scuse** to make excuses; **accamparsi** VR (*Mil*) to pitch camp; (*fare campeggio*) to camp; (*sistemarsi alla meglio*) to bed down

accanimento [akkaniˈmento] SM (*odio, furia*) fury; (*tenacia*) tenacity, perseverance; **con accanimento** (*furiosamente*) furiously; (*tenacemente*) assiduously; **lavorare con accanimento** to work extremely hard; **accanimento terapeutico** *medical treatment that uselessly prolongs the life of a terminally ill patient*

accanirsi [akkaˈnirsi] /55/ VIP **1** (*infierire*): **accanirsi (contro)** to rage (against) **2** (*ostinarsi*): **accanirsi a** *o* **nel fare qc** to persist in doing sth; **accanirsi nello studio** to study very hard; **è inutile che ti accanisci a fare domande** there's no point going on and on asking questions

accanitamente [akkanitaˈmente] AVV (*vedi agg*) fiercely; assiduously

accanito, -a [akkaˈnito] AGG (*odio*) fierce; (*lavoratore*) assiduous; (*giocatore*) inveterate; (*tifoso, sostenitore*) keen; **fumatore accanito** chain smoker

accanto [akˈkanto] AVV nearby, near; **abito qui accanto** (*di fianco*) I live next door; (*vicino*) I live near here; **la casa accanto** the house next door ♦ **accanto a** PREP next to, beside; **accanto alla porta** by the door; **la tua camera è accanto alla mia** your room's next to mine; **siediti accanto a me** sit next to me

accantonare [akkantoˈnare] /72/ VT (*progetto, idea, problema*) to shelve; (*argomento*) to leave aside; (*denaro, viveri*) to put aside, set aside; **abbiamo deciso di accantonare il progetto per il momento** we decided to shelve the project for the moment; **sono riusciti ad accantonare una bella somma** they managed to set aside a considerable sum of money

accaparramento [akkaparraˈmento] SM (*Comm*) buying up

accaparrare [akkaparˈrare] /72/ VT **1** (*Comm*) to buy up **2**

(*assicurare con caparra*) to pay a deposit on, secure (by deposit) **3 accaparrarsi qc** (*simpatia, voti*) to secure sth (for o.s.); **accaparrarsi il mercato** to corner the market; **accaparrarsi il posto migliore** to grab the best seat

accapigliarsi [akkapiʎˈʎarsi] /27/ VR (*uso reciproco*) to come to blows; (*fig*) to squabble

accappatoio, -oi [akkappaˈtojo] SM (*da bagno*) bathrobe; (*da spiaggia*) beach robe

accapponare [akkappoˈnare] /72/ VI (*aus essere*), **accapponarsi** VIP: **mi si è accapponata la pelle** I came out in goosepimples *o* gooseflesh; **uno spettacolo da far accapponare la pelle** a sight to make your flesh creep

accarezzare [akkaretˈtsare] /72/ VT **1** to caress; (*in modo spinto*) to fondle; (*animali*) to stroke; **accarezzarsi il mento** to stroke one's chin; (*capelli*) to stroke; **stava accarezzando il gatto** he was petting the cat **2** (*fig: idea, progetto*) to toy with

accartocciare [akkartotˈtʃare] /14/ VT (*carta*) to roll up, screw up; **accartocciarsi** VIP (*foglie*) to curl up

accasarsi [akkaˈsarsi] /27/ VR (*sposarsi*) to get married; (*mettersi su casa*) to set up house

accasciarsi [akkaʃˈʃarsi] /14/ VIP to collapse; (*fig: deprimersi*) to lose heart; **accasciarsi su una sedia** to collapse into a chair; **si è accasciata al suolo all'improvviso** she suddenly collapsed onto the ground

accatastare [akkatasˈtare] /72/ VT to stack, pile

accattonaggio [akkattoˈnaddʒo] SM begging

accattone, -a [akkatˈtone] SM, SF beggar

accavallare [akkavalˈlare] /72/ VT: **accavallare le gambe** to cross one's legs; **accavallarsi** VIP (*sovrapporsi: muscolo, nervo*): **mi si è accavallato un tendine** I've pulled a tendon; (*fig: avvenimenti*) to overlap; (*addensarsi: pensieri, nubi*) to gather

accecare [attʃeˈkare] /20/ VT to blind; (*abbagliare*) to dazzle; **accecarsi** VIP to become *o* go blind

accedere [atˈtʃedere] /29/ VI IRREG; **accedere a 1** (*aus essere*) (*luogo*) to enter; (*scuola: essere ammesso*) to enter, be admitted to **2** (*avere accesso a: notizia, fonte*) to gain access to **3** (*acconsentire: richiesta*) to accede to

accelerare [attʃeleˈrare] /72/ VI (*aus avere*) to accelerate, speed up ♦ VT to speed up; **accelerare il passo** to quicken one's pace

accelerato, -a [attʃeleˈrato] AGG (*rapido*) quick, rapid; **tempo/ritmo accelerato** fast tempo/rhythm ♦ SM (*treno: ant*) local train, stopping train

acceleratore [attʃeleraˈtore] SM (*Aut*) accelerator

accelerazione [attʃeleratˈtsjone] SF acceleration

accendere [atˈtʃɛndere] VB IRREG /2/ VT **1** (*fiammifero, candela, sigaretta, fuoco*) to light; **accendere il camino** to light the fire; **abbiamo acceso le candeline** we lit the candles; **mi fa accendere?** do you have a light? **2** (*radio, TV, luce, lampada*) to switch *o* turn on; (*gas*) to light; (*Aut: motore*) to switch on; **accendi il computer/il telefonino** switch on the computer/ the phone **3** (*fig: speranza, desiderio*) to arouse **4** (*Fin: conto*) to open; (: *ipoteca*) to raise; **accendere un debito** to take out a loan; **accendersi** VIP **1** (*fuoco*) to start; (*legna secca*) to catch fire; (*riscaldamento, luce, TV*) to come on **2** (*fig: di sentimenti*): **accendersi di gioia** (*occhi, volto*) to light up with joy; **accendersi in volto** (*per la vergogna*) to turn red **3** (*fig: disputa*) to flare up

accendino [attʃenˈdino] SM (*cigarette*) lighter; **accendino a gas/elettronico** gas/electronic lighter

accennare [attʃenˈnare] /72/ VT **1** (*indicare*) to indicate, point out; **le accennai la porta** I showed her the door **2** (*abbozzare*): **accennare un saluto** (*con la mano*) to make as if to wave; (*col capo*) to half nod; **accennare un sorriso** to half smile **3** (*citare*) to mention; **mi ha accennato qualcosa a proposito del suo progetto** he mentioned something to me about his project **4** (*canzone, melodia: al piano*) to pick out; (: *canticchiando*) to hum ♦ VI (*aus avere*) **1** (*far cenno*): **mi accennò di star zitto** he signalled to me to keep quiet **2** (*far atto di*): **accennare a fare qc** to show signs of doing sth; **accennò ad alzarsi, ma poi si trattenne** he made as if to get up but then stopped; **accenna a piovere** it looks as if it's going to rain **3** (*fig*) **accennare a** (*menzionare*) to mention; (*alludere a*) to hint at; **ha accennato al fatto che vuole partire** he mentioned that he wants to leave

accenno [atˈtʃenno] SM (*menzione, allusione, abbozzo*) hint;

(*segno premonitore*) sign; **fare accenno a qc** to mention sth; **non ha fatto accenno all'accaduto** he made no mention of what had happened; **con un accenno di sorriso** with a hint of a smile

accensione [attʃenˈsjone] SF **1** (*Aut*) ignition **2** (*di fiammifero, candela, sigaretta, fuoco*) lighting **3** (*di radio, TV, luce, lampada*) switching o turning on; (*di gas*) lighting, turning on **4** (*Fin: di conto*) opening; (: *di ipoteca*) raising; (: *di debito*) contracting

accentare [attʃenˈtare] /72/ VT (*scrivendo*) to put an accent on; (*parlando*) to stress; **gli articoli non sono accentati** there is no (written) accent on articles

accentazione [attʃentatˈtsjone] SF (*vedi vb*) marking with an accent; stressing

accento [atˈtʃento] SM **1** (*pronuncia*) accent; **parla con un accento straniero** he speaks with a foreign accent **2** (*Fonetica*) accent, stress; (*fig*) stress, emphasis; **l'accento cade sulla penultima sillaba** the stress is on the penultimate syllable; **mettere l'accento su qc** (*fig*) to stress sth **3** (*segno grafico*) accent; **accento grave/acuto/circonflesso** grave/acute/circumflex accent; **si scrive con l'accento sulla "u"** it's spelled with an accent on the "u" **4** (*inflessione*) tone (of voice); **un breve accento di tristezza** a slight note of sadness

accentramento [attʃentraˈmento] SM (*Amm*) centralization

accentrare [attʃenˈtrare] /72/ VT (*potere ecc*) to centralize; (*fig: interesse, sguardi*) to attract, draw

accentratore, -trice [attʃentraˈtore] AGG (*persona*) unwilling to delegate; **politica accentratrice** policy of centralization; **governo accentratore** centralizing government

accentuare [attʃentuˈare] /72/ VT **1** (*mettere in rilievo*) to emphasize, accentuate **2** (*sillaba, parola*) to stress, emphasize; **accentuarsi** VIP (*tendenza*) to become more marked o pronounced o noticeable; (*crisi*) to become worse

accerchiare [attʃerˈkjare] /19/ VT to encircle, surround; **accerchiarono il castello** they surrounded the castle

accertamento [attʃertaˈmento] SM (*verifica*) check; (*Fisco*) assessment; (*Dir*) investigation; **essere in corso di accertamento** to be under investigation; **è stato ricoverato per ulteriori accertamenti** he's been admitted to (the) hospital for further tests; **accertamento d'imposta** tax assessment

accertare [attʃerˈtare] /72/ VT **1** (*verificare*) to verify, check **2** (*Fisco: reddito*) to assess; **accertarsi** VR: **accertarsi di qc/che** to make sure of sth/that, ascertain sth/that

acceso, -a [atˈtʃeso] PP *di* **accendere** ♦ AGG **1** (*fuoco, lampada*) lit; (*luce, televisore, gas*) on; (*Fin*) open; **c'era la luce accesa** the light was on; **aveva in mano una candela accesa** he was holding a lighted candle **2** (*intenso: colore*) bright, vivid; (*infervorato: discussione, parole*) heated; **acceso di** (*ira, entusiasmo ecc*) burning with

accessibile [attʃesˈsibile] AGG (*luogo*) accessible; (*persona*) approachable; (*prezzo*) affordable; **accessibile a tutti** (*prezzo, articolo*) within everyone's means, affordable; (*concetto, materia*) within the reach of everyone; **la zona è facilmente accessibile in macchina** the area is easily accessible by car

accesso [atˈtʃesso] SM **1** (*gen, Inform*) access; **vietato l'accesso** no entry, no admittance; **di facile accesso** (*luogo*) (easily) accessible; **avere accesso a** to have access to; **nessuno aveva accesso all'edificio** nobody had access to the building; **dare accesso a** (*sogg: porta, scala*) to lead to; (: *corso*) to lead to, open the door to; (: *qualifica*) to open the door to; **tempo di accesso** (*Inform*) access time; **accesso casuale** random access; **accesso sequenziale** sequential access; **accesso seriale** serial access **2** (*impulso violento: di rabbia, gelosia, Med: di tosse*) fit; (: *di febbre*) attack, bout

accessoriato, -a [attʃessoˈrjato] AGG (*Aut*) (fitted) with accessories

accessorio, -ria, -ri, -rie [attʃesˈsɔrjo] AGG secondary, of secondary importance ♦ SM (*Aut, Moda, etc*) accessory

accetta [atˈtʃetta] SF hatchet; **fatto con l'accetta** (*fig: lavoro ecc*) clumsily done; **tagliato con l'accetta** (*dal carattere grossolano*) uncouth; (*dai lineamenti marcati*) craggy

accettabile [attʃetˈtabile] AGG acceptable

accettare [attʃetˈtare] /72/ VT (*gen, Comm*) to accept; (*proposta*) to agree to, accept; **ha accettato l'invito** she accepted the invitation; **accettare di fare qc** to agree to do sth; **accettare qn come socio** to accept sb as a member

accettazione [attʃettatˈtsjone] SF **1** (*gen*) acceptance; **accettazione bancaria** bank acceptance **2** (*di albergo, ospedale ecc*) reception; **accettazione bagagli** (*Aer*) check-in (desk)

accetto, -a [atˈtʃetto] AGG: **bene/male accetto** welcome/unwelcome; **ben accetto a tutti** (*persona*) well-liked by everybody

accezione [attʃetˈtsjone] SF meaning, sense

acchiappare [akkjapˈpare] /72/ VT (*prendere, catturare*) to catch; (*afferrare*) to seize; **l'ho rincorso ma non sono riuscito ad acchiapparlo** I ran after him but couldn't catch him

acchito [akˈkito] SM: **di primo acchito** at first

acciaccato, -a [attʃakˈkato] AGG **1** (*persona*) full of aches and pains **2** (*abito, cappello*) crushed; (*macchina*) battered

acciacco, -chi [atˈtʃakko] SM ailment; **acciacchi** SMPL aches and pains

acciaieria [attʃajeˈria] SF steelworks *sg*

acciaio, -ai [atˈtʃajo] SM steel; **d'acciaio** (*trave*) steel *attr*, of steel; (*fig: uomo, nervi*) of steel; **acciaio al carbonio** carbon steel; **acciaio inossidabile** stainless steel

accidentale [attʃidenˈtale] AGG accidental; **in circostanze accidentali** accidentally

accidentalmente [attʃidentalˈmente] AVV (*per caso*) by chance; (*non deliberatamente*) accidentally, by accident

accidentato, -a [attʃidenˈtato] AGG (*terreno*) uneven, rough; (*strada*) bumpy, uneven

accidente [attʃiˈdente] SM **1** (*gen, Filosofia*) accident; (*disgrazia*) mishap **2** (*fam: colpo apoplettico*) stroke; (: *fig*) fit, shock; **quando l'ho visto il conto mi è venuto un accidente!** I had a fit when I saw the bill!; **mandare un accidente a qn** to curse sb **3** (*fig: niente*): **non vale un accidente** it's not worth a damn; **non capisco un accidente** it's as clear as mud to me

accidia [atˈtʃidja] SF sloth; (*Rel*) accidie

accigliato, -a [attʃiʎˈʎato] AGG frowning

accingersi [atˈtʃindʒersi] /54/ VR IRREG: **accingersi a fare** to be all set to do; **mi accingevo ad andare a letto** I was about to go to bed

acciottolato [attʃottoˈlato] SM cobblestones *pl*

acciuffare [attʃufˈfare] /72/ VT to seize, catch

acciuga, -ghe [atˈtʃuga] SF anchovy; **magro come un'acciuga** as thin as a rake; **stretti come acciughe** packed like sardines

acclamare [akklaˈmare] /72/ VT **1** (*applaudire*) to cheer, applaud **2** (*eleggere*) to acclaim ♦ VI (*aus avere*) acclamare a to cheer, applaud

acclamazione [akklamatˈtsjone] SF (*vedi vb*) applause; acclamation

acclimatare [akklimaˈtare] /72/ VT to acclimatize; **acclimatarsi** VR to become acclimatized

acclimatazione [akklimatatˈtsjone] SF acclimatization

accludere [akˈkludere] /35/ VT: **accludere (a)** to enclose (with); **accludo una copia di...** I enclose a copy of ...

accluso, -a [akˈkluzo] PP *di* **accludere** ♦ AGG enclosed; **qui accluso troverete...** please find enclosed ...

accoccolarsi [akkokkoˈlarsi] /72/ VR to crouch (down)

accodarsi [akkoˈdarsi] /72/ VR to follow, tag along (behind)

accogliente [akkoʎˈʎente] AGG (*atmosfera*) welcoming, friendly; (*stanza*) pleasant, cosy

accoglienza [akkoʎˈʎentsa] SF welcome, reception; **fare una buona accoglienza a** to welcome sb; **fare una cattiva accoglienza a qn** to give sb a cool reception

accogliere [akˈkɔʎʎere] /23/ VT IRREG **1** (*persona: ricevere*) to receive; (: *calorosamente*) to welcome; (*sogg: sala, stadio*) to accommodate, hold; **mi ha accolto a braccia aperte** she welcomed me with open arms; **questa sala può accogliere 600 persone** this hall can hold o accommodate 600 people **2** (*notizia*) to receive **3** (*richiesta*) to agree to, accept

accolgo *ecc* [akˈkɔlgo] VB *vedi* **accogliere**

accollare [akkolˈlare] /72/ VT: **accollare qc a qn** (*spesa, responsabilità, obbligo*) to force sth on sb; **accollarsi qc** to take sth upon o.s., shoulder sth

accollato, -a [akkolˈlato] AGG (*vestito*) high-necked; (*scarpa*) ankle-high

accolsi *ecc* [akˈkɔlsi] VB *vedi* **accogliere**

accoltellare [akkoltelˈlare] /72/ VT to knife, stab; **l'hanno accoltellato in una rissa** he was stabbed in a fight;

accoltellarsi VR (*uso reciproco*) to attack each other with knives

accolto, -a [ak'kɔlto] PP *di* **accogliere**

accomandita [akko'mandita] SF (*Dir*): (**società** in) **accomandita** limited partnership

accomiatare [akkomja'tare] /72/ VT to dismiss; **accomiatarsi** VR: **accomiatarsi (da)** to take one's leave (of), say goodbye (to)

accomodamento [akkomoda'mento] SM (*accordo*) arrangement, agreement; **trovare un accomodamento** to come to an agreement
❑ **accomodamento** non si traduce mai con la parola inglese *accommodation*

accomodante [akkomo'dante] AGG accommodating

accomodare [akkomo'dare] /72/ VT 1 (*riparare*) to fix, repair, mend 2 (*sistemare*) to arrange; (*fig: questione, lite*) to settle; **accomodarsi** VIP: **le cose col tempo si accomoderanno** things will get sorted out in time; **accomodarsi** VR 1 (*sedersi*) to sit down; **si accomodi!** (*venga avanti*) come in!; (*mi segua*) this way please!; (*si sieda*) please take a seat! 2 (*uso reciproco: accordarsi*): **accomodarsi (con qn su qc)** to come to an agreement (with sb on sth)
❑ **accomodare** non si traduce mai con la parola inglese *accommodate*

accompagnamento [akkompaɲɲa'mento] SM 1 (*Mus*) accompaniment; **senza accompagnamento** unaccompanied 2 (*Comm*): **lettera di accompagnamento** accompanying letter 3 (*Dir*): **indennità di accompagnamento** attendance allowance

accompagnare [akkompaɲ'ɲare] /15/ VT 1 (*gen*) to accompany, come *o* go with; (*Mus*) to accompany; **accompagnare qn a casa** to see sb home; **ti accompagno** I'll come with you; **ti accompagno io all'aeroporto** I'll take you to the airport; **mi ha accompagnato a casa in macchina** she took me home in her car; **accompagnare qn alla porta** to show sb out; **accompagnare qn con lo sguardo** to follow sb with one's eyes; **accompagnare la porta** to close the door gently; **accompagnare il colpo** (*Tennis*) to follow through; **accompagnarsi** VIP (*armonizzarsi*) to go well together; **accompagnarsi a** (*colori*) to go with, match; (*cibi*) to go with; **accompagnarsi** VR (*frequentare*): **accompagnarsi a qn** to associate with sb

accompagnatore, -trice [akkompaɲɲa'tore] SM, SF 1 companion, escort; **il suo accompagnatore** her escort 2 (*Mus*) accompanist 3 (*Sport*) team manager; **accompagnatore turistico** tour guide

accomunare [akkomu'nare] /72/ VT 1 (*persone*) to unite, join; **molti interessi ci accomunano** we have many interests in common; **non voglio che mi si accomuni a lui** I don't want to be associated with him 2 (*ricchezze, idee*) to pool, share

acconciatura [akkontʃa'tura] SF (*pettinatura*) hairstyle; (*ornamento*) headdress

accondiscendente [akkondiʃʃen'dɛnte] AGG affable

accondiscendere [akkondiʃ'ʃendere] /101/ VI IRREG (*aus avere*) **accondiscendere a** to agree to, consent to

accondisceso, -a [akkondiʃ'ʃeso] PP *di* **accondiscendere**

acconsentire [akkonsen'tire] /17/ VI (*aus avere*) **acconsentire (a)** to agree (to), consent (to); **ha acconsentito a darci le informazioni in suo possesso** he agreed to give us the information he had; **chi tace acconsente** (*Proverbio*) silence means consent

accontentare [akkonten'tare] /72/ VT to satisfy; **cercare di accontentare tutti** to try to please everybody; **è molto difficile da accontentare** she's very difficult to please; **accontentarsi** VIP: **accontentarsi (di)** to be content *o.s.* (with); **mi dovrò accontentare di vederlo in TV** I'll have to make do with seeing it on TV; (*essere soddisfatto*) to be content (with), be satisfied (with); **accontentarsi di poco** to be easily pleased; **chi si accontenta gode** (*Proverbio*) well pleased is well served

acconto [ak'konto] SM (*sullo stipendio*) advance; (*caparra*) deposit, down payment; **versare una somma in acconto** to pay a sum of money as a deposit; **ho versato un acconto**

per il viaggio I've paid a deposit for the trip; **acconto di dividendo** (*Fin*) interim dividend

accoppiamento [akkoppja'mento] SM (*vedi vb*) pairing off; mating; coupling, connecting (up)

accoppiare [akkop'pjare] /19/ VT 1 (*persone, cose*) to pair off; **essere ben accoppiati** to be well matched, go well together 2 (*animali*) to mate 3 (*Tecn*) to couple, connect (up); **accoppiarsi** VR (*animali*) to mate; (*persone: formare una coppia*) to pair off

accoppiatore [akkoppja'tore] SM (*Tecn*) coupler; **accoppiatore acustico** (*Inform*) acoustic coupler

accorato, -a [akko'rato] AGG heartfelt

accorciare [akkor'tʃare] /14/ VT to shorten; **far accorciare una gonna** to have a skirt shortened; **devo accorciare questi jeans** I need to shorten these jeans; **accorciarsi** VIP to grow *o* get shorter; **le giornate si stanno accorciando** the days are getting shorter

accordare [akkor'dare] /72/ VT 1 (*concedere*): **accordare qc a qn** to grant sb sth *o* sth to sb 2 (*Mus*) to tune 3 (*Gramm*): **accordare qc (con qc)** to make sth agree (with sth); **accordarsi** VR (*uso reciproco: mettersi d'accordo*): **accordarsi (con qn su per qc)** to agree (on sth with sth); **accordarsi** VIP (*intonarsi: sogg: colore*): **accordarsi (con qc)** to match (sth)

accordo [ak'kɔrdo] SM 1 (*gen, Gramm*) agreement; (*armonia*) harmony; **andare d'accordo (con qn)** to get along well (with sb); **vanno d'accordo** they get along well together; **non vado d'accordo con i miei** I don't get along well with my parents; **essere d'accordo** to agree, be in agreement; **su questo siamo tutti d'accordo** we all agree on this; **mettersi d'accordo (con qn)** to agree *o* come to an agreement (with sb); **mettersi d'accordo per fare qc** to arrange to do sth; **ci siamo messi d'accordo per andare al cinema** we arranged to go to the cinema; **rimanere d'accordo** to agree; **siamo rimasti d'accordo che sarebbe venuto a prendermi** we agreed that he'd come and pick me up; **d'accordo!** agreed!, all right!, O.K.! (*fam*); **sono d'accordissimo** I quite agree; **decidere di comune accordo di fare qc** to make a joint decision to do sth; **prendere accordi con** to reach an agreement with; **stringere un accordo** to reach an agreement 2 (*Mus*) chord; **conosci gli accordi di quella canzone?** can you play that song? ♦ **accordo commerciale** trade agreement; **accordo di esclusiva** exclusive agency agreement; **Accordo generale sulle tariffe doganali ed il commercio** General Agreement on Tariffs and Trade

accorgersi [ak'kɔrdʒersi] /4/ VIP IRREG: **accorgersi di** (*notare*) to notice; (*capire*) to realize; **accorgersi che** to notice (*o* realize) that; **non si sono accorti di niente** they didn't notice anything; **si è accorto del furto solo il giorno dopo** he only noticed it had been stolen the next day; **mi sono accorto subito che qualcosa non andava** I immediately realized something was wrong

accorgimento [akkordʒi'mento] SM 1 (*espediente*) trick, device 2 (*astuzia*) shrewdness *no pl*

accorrere [ak'korrere] /28/ VI IRREG (*aus essere*) **accorrere (a)** to rush up (to), hurry (to), run up (to); **la gente accorreva da tutte le direzioni** people came running from all directions; **accorrere in aiuto di qn** to rush to sb's aid

accorsi [ak'korsi] VB 1 *vedi* **accorgersi** 2 *vedi* **accorrere**

accorso, -a [ak'korso] PP *di* **accorrere**

accortezza [akkor'tettsa] SF (*avvedutezza*) good sense; (*astuzia*) shrewdness

accorto, -a [ak'kɔrto] PP *di* **accorgersi** ♦ AGG shrewd, alert; **stare accorto** to be on one's guard

accostamento [akkosta'mento] SM (*di colori ecc*) combination

accostare [akkos'tare] /72/ VT 1 **accostare qc a qc** (*mettere vicino: oggetto*) to move sth near sth; (*: colori, stili*) to match sth with; (*appoggiare: scala*) to lean sth against sth; **accosta la sedia al tavolo** move your chair nearer the table; **ha accostato la tazza alle labbra** he put the cup to his lips 2 (*avvicinare: persona*) to approach, come up to 3 (*socchiudere: persiane*) to half-close; (*: porta*) to push (*o* pull) to; **lasciare la porta accostata** to leave the door ajar; **ha accostato le imposte** he half-closed the shutters ♦ VI (*aus avere*) 1 **accostare (a)** (*Aut*) to draw up (at); (*Naut*) to come alongside; **accosti per favore!** pull in, please! 2 (*Naut: modificare la* *rotta*) to alter course; **accostarsi** VR **1** (*andare o venire vicino*): **accostarsi (a)** to approach, go (*o* come) nearer; **accostarsi a qc/qn** (*Aut*) to draw up at sth/next to sb; (*Naut*) to come alongside **2** (*fig: abbracciare: fede, religione*): **accostarsi (a)** to turn to (*idee politiche*) to come to agree with **3** (*somigliare*): **accostarsi (a)** to be like, resemble

accovacciarsi [akkovat'tʃarsi] /14/ VR to crouch (down)

accozzaglia [akkot'tsaʎʎa] SF (*pegg: di persone*) odd assortment; (: *di oggetti, colori, idee*) jumble, hotchpotch

accrebbi *ecc* [ak'krebbi] VB *vedi* **accrescere**

accreditare [akkredi'tare] /72/ VT **1** (*Comm, Fin*): **accreditare qc a** *o* **a favore di qn** to credit sb with sth; **accreditare su un conto** to credit to an account **2** (*convalidare*) to confirm; (*voce*) to substantiate; (*notizia*) to confirm the truth of **3** (*diplomatico*) to accredit; **accreditarsi** VIP (*teoria ecc*) to gain ground *o* credence

accredito [ak'kredito] SM (*Comm, Fin :atto*) crediting; (: *effetto*) credit

accrescere [ak'kreʃʃere] VB IRREG /30/ VT to increase; **accrescersi** VIP to grow, increase

accrescimento [akkreʃʃi'mento] SM increase, growth

accrescitivo, -a [akkreʃʃi'tivo] AGG, SM (*Gramm*) augmentative

accresciuto, -a [akkreʃ'ʃuto] PP *di* **accrescere**

accucciarsi [akkut'tʃarsi] /14/ VR (*cane*) to lie down; (*persona*) to crouch down

accudire [akku'dire] /55/ VI (*aus avere*) **accudire a** to attend to ♦ VT to look after

acculturazione [akkulturat'tsjone] SF (*Sociol*) acculturation, integration

accumulare [akkumu'lare] /72/ VT (*gen*) to accumulate; (*energia*) to store; **il treno ha accumulato un ritardo di 3 ore** the train is running 3 hours late; **accumulare degli arretrati** to have backpay due *o* owing; **accumularsi** VIP to accumulate; (*Fin*) to accrue

accumulatore [akkumula'tore] SM (*Elettr*) accumulator, (storage) battery

accumulazione [akkumulat'tsjone] SF (*vedi vb*) accumulation; storage

accumulo [ak'kumulo] SM accumulation

accuratamente [akkurata'mente] AVV carefully, thoroughly

accuratezza [akkura'tettsa] SF (*precisione*) accuracy; (*diligenza*) care, thoroughness

accurato, -a [akku'rato] AGG (*preciso*) accurate; (*diligente*) careful, thorough; **una descrizione accurata** a detailed description; **un lavoro accurato** a careful piece of work

accusa [ak'kuza] SF (*gen*) accusation; (*Dir*) charge; **fare** *o* **muovere un'accusa a qn** to make an accusation against sb; **l'accusa, la pubblica accusa** (*Dir*) the prosecution; **mettere qn sotto accusa** (*Dir*) to indict sb; **in stato di accusa** (*Dir*) committed for trial

accusare [akku'zare] /72/ VT **1** (*incolpare*): **accusare qn di** (*fare*) **qc** to accuse sb of (doing) sth; **mi ha accusato di avergli rotto lo stereo** he accused me of breaking his stereo; **accusare qn/qc di qc** (*biasimare*) to blame sb/sth for sth; **accusare qn di qc** (*Dir*) to charge sb with sth **2** (*sentire: dolore*) to feel; (*mostrare*): **accusare la fatica** to show signs of exhaustion; **ha accusato il colpo** (*fig*) you could see that he had felt the blow **3** (*Comm*): **accusare ricevuta (di)** to acknowledge receipt (of)

accusativo [akkuza'tivo] AGG, SM (*Gramm*) accusative

accusato, -a [akku'zato] SM, SF accused

accusatore, -trice [akkuza'tore] AGG accusing ♦ SM, SF accuser; (*Dir*) prosecutor

acerbo, -a [a'tʃerbo] AGG (*non maturo: frutto*) unripe; (: *fig: bellezza*) adolescent; (: *persona*) very young

acero [a'tʃero] SM maple; **acero campestre** field maple

acerrimo, -a [a'tʃerrimo] AGG bitter

acetato [atʃe'tato] SM acetate

aceto [a'tʃeto] SM vinegar; **sotto aceto** pickled; **mettere sotto aceto** to pickle; **aceto balsamico** balsamic vinegar

acetone [atʃe'tone] SM (*Chim*) acetone; (*per unghie*) nail polish remover

ACI [a'tʃi] SIGLA M (= *Automobile Club d'Italia*) ≈ AA (*Brit*), ≈ AAA (*USA*)

acidità [atʃidi'ta] SF INV (*vedi agg*) acidity, sourness, tartness; **acidità (di stomaco)** heartburn

acido, -a [a'tʃido] AGG (*anche fig*) acid, sour, tart; (*Chim*) acid; **latte acido** sour milk; **giallo/verde acido** acid yellow/green ♦ SM acid; **sapere di acido** to taste sour ♦ **acido acetico** acetic acid; **acido acetilsalicilico** acetylsalicylic acid; **acido cloridrico** hydrogen chloride; **acido lisergico** lysergic acid; **acido muriatico** hydrochloric acid; **acido solfidrico** hydrogen sulphide; **acido solforoso** sulphurous acid

acidulo, -a [a'tʃidulo] AGG slightly sour, slightly acid

acino [a'tʃino] SM: **acino (d'uva)** grape

acme ['akme] SF acme, peak; (*Med*) crisis

acne ['akne] SF (*anche:* **acne giovanile**) acne

ACNUR ['aknur] SIGLA M (= *Alto Commissariato delle Nazioni Unite per i Rifugiati*) UNHCR (= *United Nations High Commission for Refugees*)

acqua ['akkwa] SF **1** (*gen*) water; (*pioggia*) rain; **le acque** SFPL (*Med*) the waters; **mi dai un bicchiere d'acqua, per favore?** could I have a glass of water please?; **prendere l'acqua** to get caught in the rain, get wet; **far la cura delle acque** to go to a spa **2** (*fraseologia*): **acqua, acqua!** (*in giochi*) you're cold!; **acqua in bocca!** mum's the word!; **(all')acqua e sapone** (*faccia, ragazza: senza trucco*) without makeup; (: *semplice*) natural; **buttare acqua sul fuoco** to pour oil on troubled waters; **è sempre stata un'acqua cheta** she has always seemed a quiet one; **fare acqua (da tutte le parti)** (*situazione, posizione*) to be shaky; **la sua versione dei fatti fa acqua da tutte le parti** his version of what happened won't hold water; **essere con** *o* **avere l'acqua alla gola** to be snowed under; **tirare acqua al proprio mulino** to feather one's own nest; **è acqua passata** that's (ancient) history; **è passata molta acqua sotto i ponti** a lot of water has flowed under the bridge; **trovarsi** *o* **navigare in cattive acque** to be in deep water ♦ **acqua di calce** limewater; **acqua di colonia** eau de Cologne, cologne; **acqua corrente** running water; **acqua distillata** distilled water; **acqua dolce** fresh water; **acqua gassata** fizzy water; **acqua di mare** sea water; **acqua minerale** mineral water; **acqua ossigenata** hydrogen peroxide; **acqua pesante** (*Fis*) heavy water; **acqua piovana** rain water; **acqua potabile** drinking water; **acqua ragia** = **acquaragia**; **acqua di rose** rose water; **all'acqua di rose** mild; **acqua del rubinetto** tap water; **acqua salata** salt water; **acqua santa** = **acquasanta**; **acqua sorgiva** *o* **di sorgente** spring water; **acqua tonica** tonic water; **acque superficiali** (*Geog*) surface runoff *sg*; **acque territoriali** territorial waters *pl*

acquaforte [akkwa'fɔrte] SF (*pl* **acqueforti**) etching

acquaio, -ai [ak'kwajo] SM (kitchen) sink

acquaragia [akkwa'radʒa] SF turpentine

acquario, -ri [ak'kwarjo] SM **1** (*vasca per pesci, edificio*) aquarium **2** (*Astrol*): **Acquario** Aquarius; **essere dell'Acquario** to be Aquarius *o* (an) Aquarian

acquartierare [akkwartje'rare] /72/ VT, **acquartierarsi** VR (*Mil*) to quarter

acquasanta [akkwa'santa] SF holy water

acquascooter [akkwas'kuter] SM INV personal watercraft

acquatico, -a, -ci, -che [ak'kwatiko] AGG aquatic; (*sport, sci*) water *attr*; **sport acquatici** water sports; **uccello acquatico** waterfowl

acquattarsi [akkwat'tarsi] /72/ VR to crouch (down)

acquavite [akkwa'vite] SF (*pl* **acquaviti** *o* **acqueviti**) spirit

acquazzone [akkwat'tsone] SM downpour

acquedotto [akkwe'dotto] SM (*conduttura*) aqueduct; (*intero sistema*) water system; **un acquedotto romano** a Roman aqueduct

acqueo, -a ['akkweo] AGG: **vapore acqueo** water vapour (*Brit*) *o* vapor (*USA*); **umore acqueo** aqueous humour (*Brit*) *o* humor (*USA*)

acquerello [akkwe'rello] SM (*tecnica*) watercolours (*Brit*), watercolors (*USA*); (*opera*) watercolour (*Brit*), watercolor (*USA*)

acquerugiola [akkwe'rudʒola] SF drizzle

acquietare [akkwje'tare] /72/ VT (*dolore*) to ease; (*desiderio, fame*) to appease; **acquietarsi** VIP to calm down

acquirente [akkwi'rente] SM, SF buyer

acquisire [akkwi'zire] /55/ VT (*diritto, proprietà*) to acquire; (*qualità, cognizione*) to acquire, gain

acquisizione [akkwizit'tsjone] SF acquisition

acquistare [akkwis'tare] /72/ VT 1 (*casa, mobili*) to buy, purchase; (*beni, diritti*) to acquire; **acquistare a rate** to buy in installments; **acquistare in contanti** to buy for cash 2 (*fig: esperienza, pratica ecc*) to gain; **acquistare importanza** to become important; **acquistare terreno** to gain ground ♦ VI (*aus* avere) to improve; **acquistare in bellezza** to become more beautiful; **ha acquistato in salute** his health has improved

acquisto [ak'kwisto] SM purchase; **andare a fare acquisti** to go shopping; **fare molti acquisti** to buy a lot of things; **fare un buon/cattivo acquisto** (*anche fig*) to get a good/bad buy; **ecco il nostro ultimo acquisto** (*persona*) here is our latest recruit; **campagna acquisti** (*Sport*) transfer season; **potere d'acquisto** (*Econ*) buying power; **acquisto d'impulso** impulse buying; **acquisto rateale** instalment purchase, hire purchase (*Brit*)

acquitrino [akkwi'trino] SM bog, marsh

acquolina [akkwo'lina] SF: **far venire l'acquolina in bocca a qn** to make sb's mouth water; **solo a vederlo ti fa venire l'acquolina in bocca!** it makes your mouth water just to look at it!; **ho l'acquolina in bocca, mi viene l'acquolina in bocca** my mouth is watering

acquoso, -a [ak'kwoso] AGG watery; **soluzione acquosa** aqueous solution

acre ['akre] AGG (*sapore, odore*) acrid, pungent; (*fig: polemica*) bitter; (: *critica*) harsh, biting

acredine [a'kredine] SF (*fig*) bitterness

acrilico, -a, -ci, -che [a'kriliko] AGG, SM acrylic

acritico, -a, -ci, -che [a'kritiko] AGG uncritical

acrobata, -i, -e [a'krɔbata] SM, SF acrobat

acrobatico, -a, -ci, -che [akro'batiko] AGG (*ginnastica*) acrobatic; (*Aer*) aerobatic

acrobazia [akrobat'tsia] SF 1 (*ginnica*) acrobatic feat; **fare acrobazie** (*anche fig*) to perform acrobatics 2 (*aerea*) aerobatic feat; **acrobazie aeree** aerobatics

acronimo [a'krɔnimo] SM acronym

acropoli [a'krɔpoli] SF INV: **l'Acropoli** the Acropolis

acuire [aku'ire] /55/ VT to sharpen; (*desiderio*) to increase; **acuirsi** VIP (*gen*) to increase; (*crisi, dissidio*) to worsen

aculeo [a'kuleo] SM (*di riccio, istrice*) quill (*pianta*) prickle; (*di vespa, ape*) sting

acume [a'kume] SM perspicacity; **con grande acume** with great shrewdness; **non ci vuole tanto acume per capire che...** you don't need to be a genius to realize that ...

acuminato, -a [akumi'nato] AGG sharp

acustico, -a, -ci, -che [a'kustiko] AGG acoustic; **apparecchio acustico** hearing aid; **chitarra acustica** acoustic guitar; **cornetto acustico** ear trumpet

acutezza [aku'tettsa] SF (*vedi agg*) acuteness; keenness; intensity; sharpness; shrillness; (*Mus*) high pitch

acutizzare [akutid'dzare] /72/ VT to intensify; **acutizzarsi** VIP (*crisi, malattia*) to become worse, worsen

acuto, -a [a'kuto] AGG 1 (*Mat, Med, Gramm*) acute; (*vista, udito, senso dell'umorismo*) keen; (*desiderio, fastidio, sofferenza*) intense; (*mente, osservazione, dolore*) sharp, acute; **ho sentito un dolore acuto al braccio** I felt a sharp pain in my arm 2 (*suono, voce*) shrill, high-pitched, piercing; (*Mus*) high ♦ SM (*Mus*) high note

ad [ad] PREP (*davanti a vocale*) = **a**

adagiare [ada'dʒare] /62/ VT to lay *o* set down carefully; **adagiarsi** VR (*mettersi comodo*) to make *o.s.* comfortable; (*sdraiarsi*) to lie down, stretch out; **si è adagiato (nell'ozio)** (*fig*) he just sat back (in this situation)

adagio¹ [a'dadʒo] AVV (*lentamente*) slowly; (*con cura*) with care, gently; **vacci adagio con la birra!** go easy on the beer!; **adagio!** easy does it!; **adagio adagio** gradually

adagio², -gi [a'dadʒo] SM 1 (*Mus*) adagio 2 (*proverbio*) adage, saying

adamitico, -a, -ci, -che [ada'mitiko] AGG: **in costume adamitico** in one's birthday suit

adattabile [adat'tabile] AGG (*persona*) adaptable

adattabilità [adattabili'ta] SF adaptability

adattamento [adatta'mento] SM (*Bio, Med: di romanzo*) adaptation; (*di stanza, edificio*) conversion; **avere spirito di adattamento** to be adaptable

adattare [adat'tare] /72/ VT (*gen*): **adattare qc (a)** to adapt sth (to); (*camera*) to convert sth (into); **si era fatta adattare il cappotto della madre** she had her mother's coat altered to fit her; **adattarsi** VR 1 (*adeguarsi*): **adattarsi (a)** (*ambiente, situazione, tempi*) to adapt (to); **si adatta facilmente** she adapts easily, she's very adaptable; **si sta adattando alla situazione** she is adapting to the situation 2 (*accontentarsi*): **adattarsi a qc/a fare qc** to make the best of sth/of doing sth; **dobbiamo adattarci** we'll have to make the best of it; **adattarsi** VIP (*addirsi*): **adattarsi a** to be suitable for

adattatore [adatta'tore] SM (*Elettr*) adapter, adaptor

adatto, -a [a'datto] AGG: **adatto (a)** (*giusto*) right (for); (*appropriato*) suitable (for); **è la persona più adatta per** *o* **a fare questo lavoro** he is the most suitable person for this job *o* to do this job; **non è il momento adatto** it's not the right moment; **un vestito adatto all'occasione** a suitable dress for the occasion

addebitare [addebi'tare] /72/ VT: **addebitare qc a qn** to charge sth to sb; **mi hanno addebitato un'interurbana** they charged a long-distance call to me; (*fig: incolpare*) to blame sb for sth; **addebitare qc in conto a qn** (*Comm*) to debit sb's account with sth

addebito [ad'debito] SM 1 (*Comm*) debit 2 (*imputazione*) blame; **muovere (un) addebito di qc a qn** to accuse sb of sth

addensamento [addensa'mento] SM (*vedi vb*) thickening; gathering

addensare [adden'sare] /72/ VT to thicken; **addensarsi** VIP (*nebbia*) to get thicker; (*nuvole, folla*) to gather; (*salsa, sugo*) to thicken

addentare [adden'tare] /72/ VT to bite into; **ha addentato il panino** he bit into the roll

addentrarsi [adden'trarsi] /72/ VIP: **addentrarsi in** (*posto*) to penetrate, go into; (*fig: problema*) to go (deeply) into; **si sono addentrati nel bosco** they went deep into the woods

addentro [ad'dentro] AVV (*fig*): **essere (molto) addentro a** *o* **in qc** to be well up on sth, be well-versed in sth

addestramento [addestra'mento] SM (*gen*) training; (*Mil*) drill; (*Equitazione: specialità*) dressage; **il corso di addestramento dura un mese** the training course lasts a month; **addestramento professionale** vocational training

addestrare [addes'trare] /72/ VT: **addestrare qn/qc a** *o* **per qc** to train sb/sth for sth; **quel cane è stato addestrato alla guardia** that dog has been trained as a watchdog; **addestrarsi** VR: **addestrarsi (a** *o* **in qc)** to train (in sth), practise (*Brit*) *o* practice (*USA*) sth

addetto, -a [ad'detto] PP *di* **addirsi** ♦ AGG: **addetto a** (*persona*) employed on, in charge of; (*oggetto*) intended for ♦ SM, SF **l'addetto alla manutenzione** the maintenance man; **gli addetti ai lavori** authorized personnel *sg*; (*fig*) those in the know; **"vietato l'ingresso ai non addetti ai lavori"** "authorized personnel only"; **addetti alle pulizie** cleaning staff; **addetto stampa** press officer; **addetto al telex** telex operator 2 (*Diplomazia*) attaché; **addetto commerciale** commercial attaché; **addetto militare** military attaché ❑ **addetto** non si traduce mai con la parola inglese *addict*

addì [ad'di] AVV (*Amm*): **addì 31 luglio 2004** on (the) 31st (of) July 2004, on July 31st 2004

addiaccio [ad'djatt∫o] SM: **all'addiaccio** (*Mil*) without shelter; **dormire all'addiaccio** to sleep in the open

addietro [ad'djetro] AVV (*letter: nel passato, prima*) before, ago; **l'aveva conosciuto anni addietro** she'd met him years before

addio [ad'dio] ESCL goodbye, farewell; **dire addio a qn** *o* **qc** (*anche fig*) to say goodbye to sb/sth; **se arrivano i bambini, addio pace!** if the children turn up, that'll be the end of our peace and quiet! ♦ SM goodbye, farewell; **serata d'addio** (*Teatro*) farewell performance

addirittura [addirit'tura] AVV (*perfino*) even; **gli hanno addirittura proibito di uscire di casa** they've even forbidden him to leave the house; **il suo comportamento è addirittura**

ridicolo his behaviour is downright ridiculous; **addirittura?!** really!; **gli hanno proibito di uscire di casa - addirittura?!** they've forbidden him to leave the house - really?!

addirsi [ad'dirsi] /38/ VIP IRREG E DIF: **addirsi a** to suit, be suitable for

Addis Abeba [ad'dis a'beba] SF Addis Ababa

additare [addi'tare] /72/ VT to point out; (fig) to expose

additivo, -a [addi'tivo] AGG, SM additive

addizionale [addittsjo'nale] AGG additional ♦ SF (anche: imposta addizionale) surtax

addizionare [addittsjo'nare] /72/ VT (Mat) to add (up); **addizionare qc a qc** to add sth to sth

addizione [addit'tsjone] SF (Mat, Chim) addition; **fare un'addizione** to do a sum

❑ addizione non si traduce mai con la parola inglese addiction

addobbare [addob'bare] /72/ VT 1 (chiesa, sala, vetrina) to decorate; **addobbare a festa** to deck out 2 (scherz: persona) to put on one's glad rags; **addobbarsi** VR (scherz) to dress up

addobbo [ad'dobbo] SM decoration; **addobbi natalizi** Christmas decorations

addolcire [addol't∫ire] /55/ VT 1 (caffè, bevanda) to sweeten 2 (fig: mitigare: brutta notizia, carattere) to soften; (: calmare) to soothe, calm 3 (Tecn: acqua) to soften; (: acciaio) to temper; **addolcirsi** VIP (fig: carattere, persona) to mellow, soften

addolorare [addolo'rare] /72/ VT to grieve, sadden; **la notizia mi ha addolorato molto** I was very sad to hear the news; **mi ha addolorato molto sapere che...** I was very sad to hear that ...; **addolorarsi** VIP: **addolorarsi (per)** to be saddened (by)

addolorato, -a [addolo'rato] AGG upset, distressed

addome [ad'dome] SM abdomen

addomesticare [addomesti'kare] /20/ VT (anche fig) to tame; **è riuscita ad addomesticare quel terreno selvaggio** she's managed to tame that wild field

addominale [addomi'nale] AGG abdominal; **un dolore addominale** an abdominal pain; **addominali** SMPL (muscoli) stomach muscles; (esercizi) sit-ups; **fare un po' di addominali** to do sit-ups

addormentare [addormen'tare] /72/ VT (anche fig): (far) addormentare to send to sleep; **addormentarsi** VIP to go to sleep, fall asleep; **non voleva addormentarsi** he didn't want to go to sleep; **mi sono addormentato davanti alla TV** I fell asleep in front of the TV; **mi si è addormentato un piede** my foot has gone to sleep

addormentato, -a [addormen'tato] AGG sleeping, asleep; (fig: tardo) stupid, dopey; **un bambino addormentato** a sleeping baby; **ero ancora mezzo addormentato** I was still half asleep

addossare [addos'sare] /72/ VT 1 (appoggiare): **addossare qc a qc** to lean sth against sth 2 (attribuire): **addossare la colpa/la responsabilità** to lay the blame/the responsibility for sth on sb; **si addossò la colpa** he took the blame; **addossarsi** VR (appoggiarsi): **addossarsi a** to stand against; **stava addossato al muro** he was leaning against the wall; **si sono addossati gli uni agli altri** they crowded together

addosso [ad'dosso] AVV (sulla persona) on; **avere addosso** to wear; **aveva addosso un vecchio impermeabile** she was wearing an old raincoat; **mettersi addosso il cappotto** to put one's coat on; **addosso non ho molti soldi** I don't have much money on me; **ho una tale sfortuna addosso** I've had such a run of bad luck; **farsela addosso** to wet o.s. ♦ **addosso a** PREP (sopra) on; (molto vicino) right next to; **uno addosso all'altro** on top of each other; **gli ombrelloni sono praticamente uno addosso all'altro** the beach umbrellas are practically on top of each other; **andare (o venire) addosso a** (Aut: altra macchina) to run into; (: pedone) to run over; **cadere addosso a qn** to fall on top of sb; **mettere gli occhi addosso a qn/qc** to set one's eyes on sb/sth; **mettere le mani addosso a qn** (picchiare) to hit sb, lay hands on sb; (catturare) to seize sb; (molestare) to touch sb up; **dare addosso a qn** (fig) to attack sb; **il mio capo mi sta addosso** my boss is breathing down my neck

addotto, -a [ad'dotto] PP di **addurre**

adduco ecc [ad'duko] VB vedi **addurre**

addurre [ad'durre] /90/ VT IRREG 1 (Dir: fatti, prove, ragioni) to produce 2 (citare: esempi, scuse, argomenti, fatti) to advance, put forward

addussi ecc [ad'dussi] VB vedi **addurre**

adeguare [ade'gware] /72/ VT: **adeguare qc (a)** (stipendio) to adjust sth (to); (produzione, struttura) to bring into line (with); **adeguarsi** VR (conformarsi): **adeguarsi (a)** to adapt (to)

adeguatezza [adegwa'tettsa] SF (vedi agg) adequacy; suitability; fairness

adeguato, -a [ade'gwato] AGG: **adeguato (a)** (proporzionato) adequate (to); (adatto) suitable (for); (equo) fair; **una preparazione adeguata** proper preparation; **un compenso adeguato** fair payment; **uno stipendio adeguato al mio titolo di studio** a salary adequate for my qualifications

adempiere [a'dempjere] /24/ VT, VI (aus avere) **adempiere (a)** (promessa) to carry out, fulfil (Brit), fulfill (USA); (ordine) to carry out; **adempiere al proprio dovere** to do one's duty

adempimento [adempi'mento] SM (di dovere, ordine) carrying out; (di promessa) fulfilment (Brit), fulfillment (USA); **nell'adempimento del proprio dovere** in the performance of one's duty

adempire [adem'pire] /17/ VT = adempiere

Aden ['aden] SF Aden; **il golfo di Aden** the Gulf of Aden

adenoidi [ade'nɔidi] SFPL adenoids

adepto, -a [a'dɛpto] SM, SF disciple, follower

aderente [ade'rɛnte] AGG 1 (abiti) tight-fitting 2 (fig: fedele): **una traduzione aderente al testo originale** a translation faithful to the original ♦ SM, SF: **aderente (a)** follower (of), supporter (of)

aderenza [ade'rɛntsa] SF 1 (gen, Med) adhesion; (Aut: di ruota) grip 2 (fig: conoscenze) **aderenze** SFPL connections, contacts

aderire [ade'rire] /55/ VI (aus avere) **aderire (a)** 1 (stare attaccato) to adhere (to), stick (to); **aderire alla strada** (Aut) to grip the road 2 (partito) to join; (idea) to support 3 (richiesta) to agree to

adescare [ades'kare] /20/ VT 1 (Dir) to solicit; (attirare) to lure, entice 2 (Tecn: pompa) to prime

adesione [ade'zjone] SF 1 (iscrizione: a partito) joining; (assenso) agreement, acceptance; (appoggio) support; **dare/rifiutare la propria adesione ad un'iniziativa** to give one's support to/to refuse to support a proposal 2 (Fis) adhesion

adesivo, -a [ade'zivo] AGG adhesive; **nastro adesivo** sticky tape ♦ SM 1 (sostanza) adhesive 2 (anche: autoadesivo) sticker; **faccio collezione di adesivi** I collect stickers

adesso [a'dɛsso] AVV (ora) now; (poco fa) just now; (fra poco) any moment now; **adesso non posso, sto studiando** I can't do it now, I'm studying; **e me lo dici adesso?** now you tell me!; **da adesso in poi** from now on; **per adesso** for the moment, for now

adiacente [adja't∫ɛnte] AGG adjacent, adjoining; **adiacente a** adjacent to

adibire [adi'bire] /55/ VT: **adibire qc a** to use sth as; **questo edificio è adibito a deposito merci** this building is used as a goods depot; **la stanza era stata adibita a studio** the room had been used as a study

Adige ['adidʒe] SM: **l'Adige** the Adige

adipe ['adipe] SM (adipose) fat

adiposo, -a [adi'poso] AGG (Anat) adipose

adirarsi [adi'rarsi] /72/ VIP: **adirarsi (con qn per qc)** to get angry (with sb over sth); **si è adirato moltissimo** he got very angry

adirato, -a [adi'rato] AGG angry

adire [a'dire] /55/ VT (Dir): **adire le vie legali** to institute o commence legal proceedings; **adire un'eredità** to take legal possession of an inheritance

adito [a'dito] SM: **dare adito a** (sospetti) to give rise to

adocchiare [adok'kjare] /19/ VT (scorgere) to catch sight of; (desiderare) to have one's eye on

adolescente [adole∫'∫ente] AGG adolescent ♦ SM, SF adolescent, teenager

adolescenza [adole∫'∫entsa] SF adolescence

adolescenziale [adoleʃʃen'tsjale] AGG of adolescence
adombrare [adom'brare] /72/ VT (fig: celare) to veil, conceal; **adombrarsi** VIP (cavallo) to shy; (persona: offendersi) to be offended; (: insospettirsi) to grow suspicious
adoperare [adope'rare] /72/ VT to use; **adoperarsi** VR: **adoperarsi (per** o **per fare qc)** to make every effort (to do sth), strive (to do sth); **adoperarsi in favore di qn** to do one's best for sb
adorabile [ado'rabile] AGG adorable
adorare [ado'rare] /72/ VT (gen) to adore; (Rel) to adore, worship; **adoro le ciliegie!** I love cherries!
adorazione [adorat'tsjone] SF (gen) adoration; (Rel) worship, adoration
adornare [ador'nare] /72/ VT (anche fig): **adornare (di** o **con)** to adorn (with); **adornarsi** VR: **adornarsi (di** o **con)** to adorn o.s. (with)
adorno, -a [a'dorno] AGG: **adorno (di)** adorned (with)
adottare [adot'tare] /72/ VT (gen) to adopt; (libro di testo) to choose, select; (decisione, provvedimenti) to pass; **è stato adottato** he was adopted; **dovremo adottare una soluzione diversa** we'll have to find another solution
adottivo, -a [adot'tivo] AGG (genitori) adoptive; (figlio, patria) adopted
adozione [adot'tsjone] SF (vedi vb) adoption; selection; **si rende necessaria l'adozione di misure di sicurezza** security measures will have to be adopted; **adozione a distanza** child sponsorship
adrenalinico, -a, -ci, -che [adrena'liniko] AGG (fig: vivace, eccitato) charged-up
adriatico, -a, -ci, -che [adri'atiko] AGG Adriatic ♦ SM: **l'Adriatico** the Adriatic
ADSL [adiesse'elle] SIGLA M (Inform) ADSL (= Asymmetric Digital Subscriber Line)
adulare [adu'lare] /72/ VT to flatter
adulatore,-trice [adula'tore] SM, SF flatterer
adulatorio,-ria,-ri,-rie [adula'tɔrjo] AGG flattering
adulazione [adulat'tsjone] SF flattery
adulterare [adulte'rare] /72/ VT to adulterate; (fig: informazione) to distort
adulterio,-ri [adul'tɛrjo] SM adultery
adultero,-a [a'dultero] AGG adulterous ♦ SM, SF adulterer
adulto, -a [a'dulto] AGG adult; (fig) mature ♦ SM, SF adult, grown-up
adunanza [adu'nantsa] SF meeting, assembly
adunare [adu'nare] /72/ VT, **adunarsi** VIP to assemble, gather
adunata [adu'nata] SF (Mil) muster, parade
adunco,-a,-chi,-che [a'dunko] AGG hooked
aerazione [aerat'tsjone] SF 1 ventilation 2 (Tecn) aeration
aereo,-a [a'ɛreo] AGG 1 (gen, Aer, Posta) air attr; (navigazione, fotografia) aerial; (linea elettrica) overhead attr; **traffico aereo** air traffic; **per via aerea** by airmail 2 (Bot: radice) aerial ♦ SM (anche: **aeroplano**) plane; **l'aereo era in ritardo** the plane was late; **viaggiare in aereo** to fly; **mi piace viaggiare in aereo** I like flying; **aereo da caccia** fighter (plane); **aereo da guerra** warplane; **aereo di linea** airliner; **aereo a reazione** jet (plane); **aereo da trasporto merci** cargo plane; **aereo da turismo** light aircraft inv
aerobica [ae'rɔbika] SF aerobics sg; **faccio aerobica due volte alla settimana** I do aerobics twice a week
aerodinamico, -a, -ci, -che [aerodi'namiko] AGG (Fis) aerodynamic; (affusolato) streamlined
aeromodello [aeromo'dɛllo] SM model aircraft
aeronautica [aero'nautika] SF (scienza) aeronautics sg; **aeronautica civile** civil aviation; **aeronautica militare** air force
aeronavale [aerona'vale] AGG (forze, manovre) air and sea attr
aeroplano [aero'plano] SM (aero)plane (Brit), (air)plane (USA)
aeroporto [aero'pɔrto] SM airport; **ci vediamo in aeroporto** I'll meet you at the airport; **l'aeroporto di Heathrow** Heathrow Airport
aeroportuale [aeroportu'ale] AGG airport attr
aeroscalo [aeros'kalo] SM airstrip
aerosol [aero'sɔl] SM INV aerosol
aerospaziale [aerospat'tsjale] AGG aerospace

aerostatico, -a, -ci, -che [aeros'tatiko] AGG aerostatic; **pallone aerostatico** air balloon
aerostato [ae'rɔstato] SM aerostat
AF SIGLA (= alta frequenza) HF ♦ ABBR (Amm) = assegni familiari
afa ['afa] SF closeness; **c'è un'afa terribile** it's terribly close
affabile [af'fabile] AGG friendly
affabilità [affabili'ta] SF affability
affaccendarsi [affattʃen'darsi] /72/ VR: **affaccendarsi a fare qc** to be busy doing sth, bustle about doing sth
affaccendato, -a [affattʃen'dato] AGG busy; **sono molto affaccendato** I'm very busy
affacciarsi [affat'tʃarsi] /14/ VR (sporgersi): **affacciarsi (a)** to appear (at); **affacciarsi alla finestra** to appear at the window; **affacciarsi alla vita** (bambino) to come into the world; **un dubbio gli si affacciò alla mente** a sudden doubt came into his mind ♦ VIP (guardare): **affacciarsi su, il balcone si affaccia sulla piazza** the balcony looks (out) onto the square
affamato, -a [affa'mato] AGG starving, hungry; **affamato d'affetto** starved for affection
affannare [affan'nare] /72/ VT to leave breathless; **affannarsi** VR (preoccuparsi): **affannarsi (per)** to worry (about), get worked up (about); **affannarsi a fare qc** to do one's utmost to do sth, hurry o race to do sth; **è inutile che ti affanni a trovar scuse** don't waste your breath looking for excuses
affanno [af'fanno] SM 1 breathlessness; **ho fatto le scale a piedi e mi è venuto l'affanno** I got out of breath going up the stairs, I was panting after walking up the stairs 2 (preoccupazione) worry
affannosamente [affannosa'mente] AVV (respirare) with difficulty; (freneticamente) anxiously
affannoso, -a [affan'noso] AGG (respiro) laboured; (fig: ricerca: di oggetto, regalo) frantic; (: della verità) painstaking
affare [af'fare] SM 1 (faccenda) matter, affair; (Dir) case; **è stato un brutto affare** it was a nasty business; **questo non è affar tuo** this is none of your business; **sono affari miei** that's my business; **fatti gli affari tuoi!** mind your own business!; **affare di cuore** love affair; **affare di Stato** (Pol, anche fig) affair of state 2 (Comm: transazione) piece of business, (business) deal; (occasione) bargain; **affare fatto!** done!, it's a deal!; **concludere un affare** to conclude a (business) deal; **hai fatto un (buon) affare** you got a bargain; **a quel prezzo è proprio un affare** it's a real bargain at that price 3 (fam: coso) thing; **come funziona quest'affare?** how does this thing work? 4 **affari** SMPL (gen, Pol) affairs; (commercio) business sg; **come vanno gli affari?** how's business?; **un viaggio d'affari** a business trip; **è qui per affari** she's here on business; **uomo d'affari** businessman; **ministro degli Affari Esteri** Foreign Secretary (Brit), Secretary of State (USA); **affari esteri** (Pol) external affairs
affarista, -i, -e [affa'rista] SM, SF shrewd businessperson; (pegg) profiteer, unscrupulous businessperson
affascinante [affaʃʃi'nante] AGG (uomo, donna) attractive; (argomento, libro) fascinating
affascinare [affaʃʃi'nare] /72/ VT (ammaliare) to bewitch, enchant; (sedurre) to charm, fascinate; **il racconto mi ha affascinato** I was charmed by the story
affaticamento [affatika'mento] SM tiredness
affaticare [affati'kare] /20/ VT: **la salita mi ha affaticato molto** the climb tired me out; **affaticarsi** VR (stancarsi) to get tired; **non voglio affaticarmi troppo** I don't want to get too tired; **affaticarsi a fare qc** to tire o.s. out doing sth
affaticato, -a [affati'kato] AGG tired
affatto [af'fatto] AVV (interamente) completely; **non...affatto** not ...at all; **non mi piace affatto** I don't like it at all; **non sei affatto divertente** you're not at all funny; **niente affatto!** not at all!
affermare [affer'mare] /72/ VT (dichiarare) to declare; (diritti) to assert; **afferma di essere innocente** he maintains that he is innocent; **ha affermato di averlo visto** she said she'd seen him; **affermò col capo** he nodded in agreement; **affermarsi** VR (imporsi) to make o.s. o one's name known; **si è affermato come avvocato** he made his name as a lawyer
affermativamente [affermativa'mente] AVV in the affirmative, affirmatively

affermativo, -a [afferma'tivo] AGG affirmative; **dare una risposta affermativa** to say yes

affermato, -a [affer'mato] AGG established, well-known

affermazione [affermat'tsjone] SF 1 (*dichiarazione*) statement; (*di diritti, verità*) assertion 2 (*successo*) achievement; **una grande affermazione degli azzurri** a great triumph for the Italian team

afferrare [affer'rare] /72/ VT (*prendere*) to seize, grasp; (*fig: idea*) to grasp, get; **l'hanno afferrato per un braccio** they grabbed him by the arm; **afferrare un'occasione** to seize an opportunity; **afferrare un concetto** to get an idea; **afferri il concetto?** do you get the idea?; **non ho afferrato quello che hai detto** (*sentito*) I didn't get *o* catch what you said; (*capito*) I didn't understand what you said; **scusa, non ho afferrato il tuo nome** sorry, I didn't catch your name; **afferrarsi** VR: **afferrarsi a** to cling to

Aff. Est. ABBR = **Affari Esteri**

affettare¹ [affet'tare] /72/ VT (*tagliare a fette*) to slice

affettare² [affet'tare] /72/ VT (*ostentare*) to affect

affettato¹, -a [affet'tato] AGG sliced ♦ SM (sliced) cold meat (*ham ecc*)

affettato², -a [affet'tato] AGG (*lezioso*) affected

affettatrice [affetta'tritʃe] SF meat slicer

affettazione [affettat'tsjone] SF affectation

affettivo, -a [affet'tivo] AGG (*vita*) emotional; **la sfera affettiva** the area of feelings and emotions; **la vita affettiva** personal relationships; **avere un valore affettivo** to have sentimental value; **una collanina con un valore puramente affettivo** a little necklace with only sentimental value

affetto¹ [af'fetto] SM 1 (*sentimento*) affection; **trova difficile dimostrare il suo affetto** he finds it difficult to show affection; **con affetto** (*nelle lettere*) with love, affectionately yours 2 (*persona, cosa*) object of affection; **gli affetti familiari** one's nearest and dearest

affetto², -a [af'fetto] AGG: **essere affetto da** to suffer from

affettuosamente [affettuosa'mente] AVV affectionately; **(ti saluto) affettuosamente, Roberta** (*nelle lettere*) love Roberta

affettuosità [affettuosi'ta] SF INV 1 affection 2 affettuosità SFPL: *manifestazioni* demonstrations of affection

affettuoso, -a [affettu'oso] AGG affectionate; **il mio gatto è molto affettuoso** my cat's very affectionate; **un saluto** *o* **un abbraccio affettuoso, Roberta** (*nelle lettere*) love Roberta

affezionarsi [affettsjo'narsi] /72/ VIP: **affezionarsi a** to become *o* grow fond of; **mi sono molto affezionata a lei** I became very fond of her

affezionato, -a [affettsjo'nato] AGG 1 **affezionato a** fond of; (*attaccato*) attached to; **sono molto affezionato a mia zia** I'm very fond of my aunt 2 (*abituale: cliente*) regular

affezione [affet'tsjone] SF 1 (*Med*) ailment, disorder 2 (*affetto*) affection

affiancare [affjan'kare] /20/ VT 1 (*mettere a fianco: due oggetti*) to place side by side; **affiancare qc a qc** (*un oggetto a un altro*) to put sth beside *o* next to sth 2 (*Mil*) to flank 3 (*fig: sostenere*) to support; **affiancarsi** VR: **affiancarsi a qn** to stand beside sb

affiatamento [affjata'mento] SM team spirit; **c'è molto affiatamento fra di loro** (*giocatori, colleghi*) they make a good team

affiatato, -a [affja'tato] AGG: **essere affiatati** to get on; **formano una squadra affiatata** they make a good team; **una coppia molto affiatata** a very close couple

affibbiare [affib'bjare] /19/ VT 1 (*appioppare*): **affibbiare qc a qn** (*soprannome, colpa*) to pin sth on sb; (*compito sgradevole*) to saddle sb with sth; **affibbiare uno schiaffo a qn** to slap sb in the face 2 (*allacciare*) to buckle, do up

affidabile [affi'dabile] AGG (*persona, fonte d'informazioni*) reliable; **una macchina affidabile** a reliable car

affidabilità [affidabili'ta] SF reliability

affidamento [affida'mento] SM 1 (*fiducia*) trust, confidence; (*garanzia*) assurance; **dare affidamento** to seem reliable; **fare affidamento su qn/qc** to rely *o* count on sb/sth; **sai che puoi fare affidamento su di me** you know you can rely on me; **non si può fare affidamento sui mezzi pubblici!** you can't rely on public transport!; **quel tipo non mi dà**

nessun affidamento I don't trust that chap at all 2 (*Dir: di bambino*) fostering; **avere/dare in affidamento** to foster; **bambini in affidamento** foster children

affidare [affi'dare] /72/ VT: **affidare qn/qc a qn** to entrust sb/sth to sb; **affidare un incarico a qn** to entrust sb with a task; **affidarsi** VR: **affidarsi a** to place one's trust in; **mi affido alla tua discrezione** I rely on your discretion

affievolire [affjevo'lire] /55/ VT (*forze*) to weaken; (*suoni*) to make faint; **affievolirsi** VIP (*suoni*) to grow faint; (*passione, affetto*) to fade, grow less

affiggere [af'fiddʒere] /104/ VT IRREG to stick up

affilare [affi'lare] /72/ VT to sharpen; **affilarsi** VIP (*viso, naso*) to get thinner

affilato, -a [affi'lato] AGG (*gen*) sharp; (*volto, naso*) thin; **attento, quel coltello è molto affilato** be careful, that knife's very sharp!

affiliare [affi'ljare] /19/ VT (*aggregare*) to affiliate; **affiliarsi** VR: **affiliarsi a qc** to join (sth), become a member (of sth)

affinare [affi'nare] /72/ VT (*Tecn, o fig: gusto*) to refine; (: *ingegno*) to sharpen

affinché [affin'ke] CONG (+ *congiunt*) in order that, so that

affine [af'fine] AGG similar ♦ SM, SF 1 (*di coniuge*) in-law 2 (*prodotto dello stesso tipo*) similar product; **sapone e affini** soap and allied products

affinità [affini'ta] SF INV affinity

affiorare [affjo'rare] /72/ VI (*aus essere*) 1 (*venire in superficie*) to appear on the surface; **affiorare alla** *o* **in superficie** to come to the surface; **affiorare da** to emerge from 2 (*fig: indizi*) to come to light

affissi ecc [af'fissi] VB *vedi* **affiggere**

affissione [affis'sjone] SF billposting; **"divieto di affissione"** "post no bills"

affisso, -a [af'fisso] PP *di* **affiggere** ♦ SM 1 (*avviso*) notice; (*manifesto*) poster, bill 2 (*Gramm*) affix

affittacamere [affitta'kamere] SM INV, SF INV landlord (landlady); **fare l'affittacamere** to take in lodgers

affittare [affit'tare] /72/ VT 1 (*dare in affitto: casa*) to rent (out), let; (: *macchina*) to hire (out) (*Brit*), rent (out); **"affittasi"** "to let"; **hanno affittato la casa a degli studenti** they've rented the house to students 2 (*prendere in affitto: casa*) to rent; (: *macchina*) to hire (*Brit*), rent; **ho affittato una casa al mare** I rented a house at the seaside

affitto [af'fitto] SM 1 (*vedi vb*) renting; hiring; **dare in affitto** to rent (out), let; to hire (out); **prendere in affitto** to rent; to hire; **contratto d'affitto** lease 2 (*prezzo*) rent; **quant'è l'affitto?** how much is the rent?

affittuario, -ri [affittu'arjo] SM tenant

affliggere [af'fliddʒere] VB IRREG /104/ VT (*sogg: malattia*) to trouble; (: *notizia*) to grieve, distress; (: *persona: con lamentele*) to torment; **i dolori reumatici la affliggono da tempo** she has been troubled with rheumatism for years; **la malattia che lo affligge** the illness he suffers from; **continua ad affliggermi con quella vecchia storia** he's for ever boring me to death with that old story; **affliggersi** VIP: **affliggersi** (*per*) (*preoccuparsi*) to worry; **non affliggerti per simili sciocchezze** don't worry over such silly things

afflissi ecc [af'flissi] VB *vedi* **affliggere**

afflitto, -a [af'flitto] PP *di* **affliggere** ♦ AGG: **aver l'aria afflitta** to look miserable ♦ SM, SF: **gli afflitti** SMPL the afflicted

afflizione [afflit'tsjone] SF distress, torment

afflosciarsi [afflo∫'ʃarsi] /14/ VIP 1 (*perdere tensione: vela, tenda*) to become limp; (: *pelle*) to become flabby, sag; (*sgonfiarsi: palloncino*) to go down 2 (*accasciarsi: persona*) to collapse, go limp

affluente [afflu'ɛnte] SM (*Geog*) tributary

affluenza [afflu'ɛntsa] SF (*di persone, merci*) influx; (*di liquidi*) flow; (*degli elettori*) turnout

❑ **affluenza** non si traduce mai con la parola inglese *affluence*

affluire [afflu'ire] /55/ VI (*aus essere*) 1 (*liquidi*) to flow 2 (*persone, merci*) to pour in; **affluire in** to pour into

afflusso [af'flusso] SM (*di gente, prodotti*) influx; (*di liquidi*) flow

affogare [affo'gare] /80/ VI (*aus essere*) (*anche fig*) to drown; **per poco non affogai** I nearly drowned; **affogare in un bicchier d'acqua** to be unable to cope with the slightest difficulty ♦ VT (gen, o fig) to drown; **affogare i dispiaceri nell'alcol** to drown one's sorrows in drink; **affogarsi** VR to drown o.s.

affogato, -a [affoˈgato] AGG **1** drowned; **è morta affogata** she drowned **2** (Culin: uova) poached ♦ SM: **un affogato al caffè** coffee with ice cream

affollamento [affollaˈmento] SM **1** crowding **2** (folla) crowd

affollare [affolˈlare] /72/ VT (gen, o fig) to crowd; **affollarsi** VIP (gen, anche fig) to crowd; **affollarsi intorno a qn/qc** to crowd around sb/sth

affollato, -a [affolˈlato] AGG: **affollato (di)** crowded (with); **la spiaggia era affollatissima** the beach was very crowded

affondamento [affondaˈmento] SM (di nave) sinking; (di àncora) dropping

affondare [affonˈdare] /72/ VT **1** (mandare a fondo: nave) to sink; (: àncora) to drop **2** (immergere): **affondare in qc** to sink into sth; **affondare le mani in tasca** to plunge one's hands into one's pockets ♦ VI (aus essere) **1** (andare a fondo) to sink; **la nave è affondata rapidamente** the ship sank quickly **2** (penetrare): **affondare in qc** to sink into sth; **sono affondato nella neve fino al ginocchio** I sank up to my knees in the snow

affrancare [affranˈkare] /20/ VT **1** (con francobolli) to stamp; **ricorda di affrancare la lettera prima di imbucarla** remember to put a stamp on the letter before you post it; **affrancare (a macchina)** to frank (Brit), meter (USA) **2** (liberare: schiavo, popolo) to liberate, free; (beni, proprietà) to redeem; **affrancarsi** VR (da schiavitù, passione, debiti) to free o.s.

affrancatrice [affrankaˈtritʃe] SF franking machine (Brit), postage meter (USA)

affrancatura [affrankaˈtura] SF (valore) postage; (operazione) stamping, franking (Brit), metering (USA); **affrancatura a carico del destinatario** postage paid (Brit), post-paid (USA)

affranto, -a [afˈfranto] AGG (dallo sconforto, dal dolore): **affranto (da)** overcome (with)

affresco, -schi [afˈfresko] SM fresco

affrettare [affretˈtare] /72/ VT (lavoro, operazione) to speed up; (partenza) to bring forward, **affrettare il passo** to quicken one's pace; **affrettarsi** VR (sbrigarsi) to hurry up; **affrettati o perderai il treno** hurry up, or you'll miss the train; **affrettarsi a fare qc** to hurry o hasten to do sth

affrettato, -a [affretˈtato] AGG **1** (veloce: passo, ritmo) quick, fast **2** (frettoloso: decisione) hurried, hasty; (: lavoro) rushed

affrontare [affronˈtare] /72/ VT (nemico, pericolo) to face, confront; (situazione) to face up to; (questione) to deal with, tackle; (Equitazione: ostacolo) to negotiate; **affrontare una spesa** to meet an expense; **prima o poi dovrai affrontare il problema** sooner or later you'll have to face up to the problem; **è un argomento difficile da affrontare** it's a difficult thing to talk about; **affrontano domani la prova decisiva per il campionato** tomorrow they face the decider for the championship; **affrontarsi** VR (uso reciproco: scontrarsi) to confront each other

affronto [afˈfronto] SM affront; **fare un affronto a qn** to insult sb

affumicare [affumiˈkare] /20/ VT **1** (riempire di fumo) to fill with smoke **2** (annerire) to blacken with smoke **3** (alimenti) to smoke

affumicato, -a [affumiˈkato] AGG (salmone, prosciutto) smoked; (lenti) tinted

affusolato, -a [affusoˈlato] AGG tapering

afgano, -a, afghano, -a [afˈgano] AGG, SM, SF Afghan

Afghanistan [afˈganistan] SM Afghanistan

aforisma, -i [afoˈrizma] SM aphorism

afoso, -a [aˈfoso] AGG close; **oggi è una giornata afosa** it's muggy today

Africa [ˈafrika] SF Africa; **vengono dall'Africa** they come from Africa

africano, -a [afriˈkano] AGG, SM, SF African

afroasiatico, -a, -ci, -che [afroaˈzjatiko] AGG Afro-Asian

afrodisiaco, -a, -ci, -che [afrodiˈziako] AGG, SM aphrodisiac

AG SIGLA = Agrigento

agenda [aˈdʒenda] SF **1** (taccuino) diary; **l'ho segnato sull'agenda** I noted it in my diary; **agenda elettronica** personal organizer; **agenda tascabile** pocket diary; **agenda da tavolo** desk diary **2** (in una riunione) agenda

agente [aˈdʒɛnte] SM **1** (Polizia) policeman, police officer **2** (incaricato) agent, representative **3** (Chim, Med, Meteor) agent; **resistente agli agenti atmosferici** weather-resistant ♦ **agente assicurativo** insurance agent; **agente di cambio** stockbroker; **agente di custodia** prison officer; **agente immobiliare** estate agent (Brit), realtor (USA); **agente marittimo** shipping agent; **agente di polizia** o **di Pubblica Sicurezza** police officer; **agente provocatore** agent provocateur; **agente segreto** secret agent; **agente teatrale** theatrical agent; **agente di vendita** sales agent

agenzia [adʒenˈtsia] SF **1** (impresa) agency **2** (succursale) branch office ♦ **agenzia di collocamento** employment agency; **agenzia immobiliare** estate agent's (office) (Brit), real estate office (USA); **agenzia d'informazioni** news agency; **agenzia matrimoniale** marriage bureau; **agenzia pubblicitaria** advertising agency; **agenzia di stampa** press agency; **agenzia di viaggi** travel agency

agevolare [adʒevoˈlare] /72/ VT **1** (facilitare: compito, operazione): **agevolare qc (a qn)** to make sth easier (for sb), facilitate sth (for sb) **2** (aiutare): **agevolare qn (in qc)** to help sb (with sth); **ho cercato di agevolarlo in ogni modo** I tried to help him in every way possible

agevolazione [adʒevolatˈtsjone] SF (facilitazione economica): **concedere delle agevolazioni** to give special terms; **agevolazione di pagamento** payment on easy terms; **agevolazioni creditizie** credit facilities; **agevolazioni fiscali** tax relief

agevole [aˈdʒevole] AGG (salita, compito) easy; (strada) smooth; **gli ha reso più agevole il compito** it made things easier for him

agganciare [aggganˈtʃare] /14/ VT (unire con un gancio) to hook; (ricevitore del telefono) to hang up; (Ferr: vagone, vettura) to couple; (fig) to pick up, to hook up

aggancio, -ci [agˈgantʃo] SM **1** (Tecn) coupling **2** (fig: conoscenza) contact

aggeggio, -gi [adˈdʒeddʒo] SM (fam) thingy; **a cosa serve quest'aggeggio?** what's this thing for?

aggettivo [addʒetˈtivo] SM adjective

agghiacciante [agggjatˈtʃante] AGG chilling

agghiacciare [agggjatˈtʃare] /14/ VT: **agghiacciare qn, agghiacciare il sangue a qn** to make sb's blood run cold; **agghiacciarsi** VIP: **mi si è agghiacciato il sangue** my blood ran cold

agghindarsi [aggginˈdarsi] /61/ VR to dress o.s. up

aggiornamento [addʒornaˈmento] SM (vedi vb) updating; revision; postponement, adjournment; **corso di aggiornamento** refresher course

aggiornare [addʒorˈnare] /72/ VT **1** (testo) to update; (rivedere) to revise; (persona) to bring up-to-date; **mi piace tenermi aggiornato (su ciò che succede)** I like to keep up to date with what's happening; **tienimi aggiornato! keep me posted!**; **"Aggiorna"** (Inform) "Refresh" **2** (rimandare): **aggiornare (a)** to postpone (till), put off (till) (Dir) to adjourn (till); **la seduta è stata aggiornata a lunedì** the session has been postponed until Monday; **aggiornarsi** VR: **aggiornarsi (su qc)** to bring (o keep) o.s. up to date (about sth)

aggiornato, -a [addʒorˈnato] AGG up-to-date; **un orario aggiornato** an up-to-date timetable; **tenersi aggiornato su qc** to keep up to date with sth; **mi tengo aggiornato sulle novità nel mondo della musica** I keep up to date with the new releases

aggiotaggio, -gi [addʒoˈtaddʒo] SM (Econ) rigging the market

aggirare [addʒiˈrare] /72/ VT (andare intorno a) to go round; **aggirare un ostacolo/problema** (fig) to get round an obstacle/problem; **aggirarsi** VIP **1 aggirarsi in** o **per** (girare qua o là) to go about, wander about (tipo sospetto) to hang about; **l'ho visto che si aggirava da queste parti** I've seen him wandering about this area **2** (approssimarsi) to be around; **il prezzo s'aggira sul milione** the price is around the million mark

aggiudicare [addʒudiˈkare] /20/ VT (premio, merito): **aggiudicare qc a qn** to award sb sth, award sth to sb; (all'asta) to knock sth down to sb; **aggiudicato!** (*all'asta*) gone!; **si è aggiudicato il primo posto** he won first place

aggiungere [ad'dʒundʒere] VB IRREG /5/ VT to add; **aggiungi ancora un po' di latte** add a bit more milk; **aggiungersi** VIP: **aggiungersi a** to add to

aggiunsi *ecc* [ad'dʒunsi] VB *vedi* **aggiungere**

aggiunto, -a [ad'dʒunto] PP *di* **aggiungere** ♦ AGG (*Amm: aiuto*) assistant *attr*; (: *sostituto*) stand-in; **sindaco aggiunto** deputy mayor ♦ SM (*Amm*) assistant

aggiustare [addʒus'tare] /72/ VT 1 (*riparare*) to repair, mend; **mi ha aggiustato la bicicletta** he repaired my bike for me 2 (*adattare: vestito*) to alter; (*regolare: tiro, mira*) to adjust; **si è aggiustato la cravatta** he straightened his tie; **gli aggiustò un manrovescio** he gave him a backhander · 3 (*fig: sistemare: lite, conti*) to settle; **ti aggiusto io!** I'll fix you!; **aggiustarsi** VR 1 (*uso reciproco: accordarsi*) to come to an agreement; (*per soldi*) to settle (up) 2 (*arrangiarsi*): **mi aggiusterò sul divano** the sofa will be fine

agglomerato [agglome'rato] SM 1 (*di rocce*) agglomerate, conglomerate; **agglomerato urbano** built-up area 2 (*Tecn*) agglomeration; **agglomerato di legno** chipboard

aggrapparsi [aggrap'parsi] /72/ VR (*anche fig*): **aggrapparsi (a)** to hold (onto); **si è aggrappato alla ringhiera** he held onto the banister; **aggrappati a me!** hold onto me!

aggravamento [aggrava'mento] SM worsening; **c'è stato un aggravamento** there has been a turn for the worse

aggravante [aggra'vante](*Dir*) AGG aggravating ♦ SF aggravating circumstance

aggravare [aggra'vare] /72/ VT (*peggiorare*) to worsen; (*accrescere*) to increase; **la pioggia ha aggravato ulteriormente la situazione** the rain has made the situation even worse; **aggravarsi** VIP (*situazione, malato*) to get worse

aggravio, -vi [ag'gravjo] SM: **aggravio fiscale** tax increase

aggraziato, -a [aggrat'tsjato] AGG (*movimenti*) graceful; (*lineamenti*) pretty; (*modi*) gracious

aggredire [aggre'dire] /55/ VT to attack; **è stato aggredito mentre tornava in albergo** he was attacked as he was going back to his hotel

aggregare [aggre'gare] /80/ VT: **aggregare qn a qc** to include sb in sth; (*a un club*) to admit sb to sth; **aggregarsi** VR: **aggregarsi (a)** to join; (*a un club*) to become a member of; **aggregarsi** VIP (*Geol,Bio*) to aggregate

aggregato, -a [aggre'gato] AGG (*associato*) associated; **socio aggregato** associate member; **aggregato a un reparto** attached to a section ♦ SM (*gen, Bot, Geol*) aggregate; **aggregato urbano** built-up area

aggressione [aggres'sjone] SF 1 (*contro una persona*) attack, assault; **subire un'aggressione** to be attacked; **aggressione a mano armata** armed assault 2 (*Mil, Pol: contro un paese*) aggression; **patto di non aggressione** non-aggression pact 3 (*fig: a volto, capelli, monumento*) attack

aggressività [aggressivi'ta] SF aggressiveness

aggressivo,-a [aggres'sivo] AGG (*anche fig*) aggressive

aggressore [aggres'sore] SM (*persona*) attacker; (*Pol*) aggressor ♦ AGG (*stato, esercito*) aggressor *attr*

aggrottare [aggrot'tare] /72/ VT: **aggrottare le sopracciglia/la fronte** to frown

aggrovigliare [aggroviʎ'ʎare] /27/ VT (*fili, matassa*) to (en)tangle; **aggrovigliare la matassa** (*fig*) to complicate things; **aggrovigliarsi** VIP to become tangled; (*fig*) to become complicated

agguantare [aggwan'tare] /72/ VT to catch (hold of), seize

agguato [ag'gwato] SM 1 (*insidia*) trap; **tendere un agguato a qn** to set a trap for sb; (*cadere in un agguato* to fall into a trap 2 (*appostamento*) ambush; **stare** *o* **essere in agguato** to lie in ambush

agguerrito, -a [aggwer'rito] AGG (*sostenitore, nemico*) fierce

agiatezza [adʒa'tettsa] SF prosperity; **vivere nell'agiatezza** to live in comfort

agiato, -a [a'dʒato] AGG (*vita, condizione*) comfortable, easy; (*persona, famiglia*) well-off, well-to-do

agile ['adʒile] AGG agile, nimble

agilità [adʒili'ta] SF agility, nimbleness

agio, -gi ['adʒo] SM 1 ease, comfort; **sentirsi/trovarsi a proprio agio** to feel/be at ease; **mi sono sentito subito a mio**

agio I immediately felt at ease; **mettere qn a proprio agio** to put sb at their ease; **ha fatto del suo meglio per mettermi a mio agio** he did his best to put me at my ease; **mettersi a proprio agio** to make o.s. at home *o* comfortable 2 (*opportunità*): **dare agio a qn di fare qc** to give sb the chance of doing sth 3 *agi* SMPL comforts; **vivere negli agi** to live in comfort

agire [a'dʒire] /55/ VI 1 (*gen*) to act; (*comportarsi*) to behave; **bisogna agire** we must act *o* take action at once; **agisce senza riflettere** he acts without thinking; **ha agito male verso i colleghi** he behaved badly towards his colleagues; **non mi piace il suo modo di agire** I don't like the way he goes about things; **agire su qn/qc** to act on sb/sth 2 (*esercitare un'azione*) to work, function; **la leva agisce sul cambio** the lever operates the gear; **una medicina che agisce rapidamente** a medicine which acts *o* takes effect quickly 3 (*Dir*): **agire contro qn** to take (legal) action against sb, start proceedings against sb

agitare [adʒi'tare] /72/ VT 1 (*liquido, bottiglia*) to shake; (*mano, fazzoletto*) to wave; **"agitare prima dell'uso"** "shake well before use"; **il vento agitava i rami** the wind was shaking the branches 2 (*fig: incitare*) to incite; (: *turbare*) to trouble, disturb; **agitarsi** VIP (*rami*) to sway; (*bambino*) to fidget; (*mare*) to get rough; (*dubbio, pensiero*) to stir; (*folla*) to become restless; **agitarsi nel sonno** to toss and turn in one's sleep 2 (*turbarsi*) to get worked up, get upset; (*eccitarsi*) to get excited; **non è il caso di agitarsi tanto** there's no need to get so worked up 3 (*Pol*) to agitate

agitato, -a [adʒi'tato] AGG 1 (*malato*) restless; (*bambino*) fidgety; (*mare*) rough 2 (*persona: turbato*) worried, upset; (: *eccitato*) excited

agitatore,-trice [adʒita'tore] SM, SF (*Pol*) agitator

agitazione [adʒitat'sjone] SF 1 (*inquietudine*) agitation; **essere in uno stato di agitazione** to be worked up; **mettersi in agitazione** to get worked up; **mettere in agitazione qn** to upset *o* distress sb 2 (*Pol*) agitation, unrest; **entrare in agitazione** to take industrial action

agli ['aʎʎi] PREP + ART *vedi* **a**

aglio, -gli ['aʎʎo] SM garlic; **uno spicchio d'aglio** a clove of garlic

agnello [aɲ'ɲello] SM lamb; **agnello arrosto** roast lamb; **Agnello di Dio** (*Rel*) Lamb of God

agnostico,-a, -ci,-che [aɲ'ɲɔstiko] AGG, SM, SF agnostic

ago, aghi ['ago] SM (*gen*) needle; (*della bilancia*) pointer; **lavoro ad ago** needlework; **è come cercare un ago in un pagliaio** it's like looking for a needle in a haystack; **ago da calza** knitting needle; **ago magnetico** magnetic needle

ago. ABBR (= *agosto*) Aug.

agonia [ago'nia] SF 1 (*Med*) death throes *pl*; **entrare in agonia** to be close to death; **è stata una lunga agonia** it was a slow death 2 (*fig*) agony

agonistico, -a, -ci,-che [ago'nistiko] AGG (*Sport, o fig*) competitive

agonizzante [agonid'dzante] AGG dying

agonizzare [agonid'dzare] /72/ VI (*aus avere*) (*malato*) to be dying; (*fig: civiltà*) to decline

agopuntura [agopun'tura] SF acupuncture

agorafobia [agorafo'bia] SF agoraphobia

agosto [a'gosto] SM August; *vedi* **luglio**

agrario, -ria, -ri, -rie [a'grarjo] AGG (*scuola, scienza*) agricultural; (*leggi*) agrarian; **scienze agrarie** agricultural science; **riforma agraria** land reform ♦ SM landowner

agricolo, -a [a'grikolo] AGG (*gen*) agricultural; (*lavoratori, prodotti, macchine*) farm *attr*; (*popolazione*) farming; **terreno agricolo** agricultural land

agricoltore [agrikol'tore] SM farmer; **fa l'agricoltore** he's a farmer

agricoltura [agrikol'tura] SF agriculture; **agricoltura biologica** organic farming; **agricoltura intensiva** intensive farming

agrifoglio,-gli [agri'fɔʎʎo] SM holly

agrimensore [agrimen'sore] SM land surveyor

agriturismo [agritu'rizmo] SM farm holidays *pl*

agrituristico, -a, -ci,-che [agritu'ristiko] AGG farm holiday *attr*

agro,-a ['agro] AGG bitter, sharp

agrodolce [agro'doltʃe] AGG (*sapore*) bittersweet; (*salsa*) sweet and sour ♦ SM (*Culin*) sweet-and-sour sauce; **in agrodolce** sweet and sour; **maiale in agrodolce** sweet and sour pork
agronomia [agrono'mia] SF agronomy
agronomo, -a [a'grɔnomo] SM, SF agronomist
agrume [a'grume] SM (*spesso al pl: pianta*) citrus; (: *frutto*) citrus fruit
agrumeto [agru'meto] SM citrus grove
aguzzare [agut'tsare] /72/ VT to sharpen; **aguzzare la vista** *o* **gli occhi** to strain to see; **aguzzare le orecchie** to prick up one's ears; **aguzzare l'ingegno** to sharpen one's wits; **il bisogno aguzza l'ingegno** (*Proverbio*) necessity is the mother of invention
aguzzino, -a [agud'dzino] SM, SF jailer; (*fig*) tyrant
aguzzo, -a [a'guttso] AGG sharp
ahi [ˈai] ESCL (*dolore*) ouch!
ahimè [ai'mε] ESCL (*spec letter*) alas!
ai [ˈai] PREP + ART *vedi* **a**
Aia [ˈaja] SF: **L'Aia** The Hague
aia [ˈaja] SF (*cortile*) farmyard; (*per battere il grano*) threshing floor
AIDS [ˈaidz, aidiˈesse] SIGLA M, SIGLA F AIDS
AIEA [a'jea] SIGLA F (= *Agenzia Internazionale per l'Energia Atomica*) IAEA
aiola [a'jɔla] SF = **aiuola**
airbag [ˈɛəbæg] SM INV airbag; **airbag laterali** side airbags; **airbag lato guida/passeggero** driver/passenger airbag
airone [ai'rone] SM heron; **airone bianco** great white egret
aitante [ai'tante] AGG robust
aiuola [a'jwɔla] SF flower bed; **"non calpestare le aiuole"** "keep off the flower beds"; **aiuola spartitraffico** (*Aut*) traffic island
aiutante [aju'tante] SM, SF 1 (*nel lavoro*) assistant; **fare da aiutante a qn** to be sb's assistant 2 (*Mil*) adjutant; **aiutante di campo** aide-de-camp 3 (*Naut*) master-at-arms; **aiutante di bandiera** flag lieutenant
aiutare [aju'tare] /72/ VT to help; (*assistere*) to assist; **ha detto che ci avrebbe aiutati** he said he would help us; **aiutare qn (a fare qc)** to help sb (to do sth); **mi puoi aiutare a compilare questo modulo?** can you help me to fill in this form?; **aiutare la digestione** to aid (the) digestion; **aiutarsi** VR 1 to help o.s.; **aiutati, che Dio ti aiuta** God helps those who help themselves 2 (*uso reciproco*) to help one another
aiuto [a'juto] SM 1 (*soccorso*) help, assistance, aid; **mi serve il tuo aiuto** I need your help; **prestare** *o* **dare aiuto a qn** to help sb; **venire in aiuto di qn** to help sb, come to sb's assistance *o* aid; **essere di aiuto (a qn)** (*persona*) to be a help (to sb); (*cosa*) to be useful (to sb); **se questo esserti d'aiuto...** if I can be of help to you ...; **mi è stata di grande aiuto** she has been a great help to me; **grazie per la guida, mi è stata di grande aiuto** thanks for the guidebook, it was very useful; **chiedere aiuto a qn** to ask sb for help; **correre in aiuto di qn** to rush to sb's assistance; **gridare aiuto** to shout for help; **c'è qualcuno che grida aiuto** there's somebody shouting for help; **aiuti** SMPL (*viveri, finanziamenti ecc.*) aid *sg*; **aiuti umanitari** humanitarian aid 2 (*aiutante, assistente*) assistant; **aiuto contabile** junior accountant; **aiuto giardiniere** under gardener; **aiuto regista** assistant director ♦ ESCL help!
aizzare [ait'tsare] /72/ VT 1 (*cani*): **aizzare contro qn** to set on sb 2 (*folla*) to incite; (*contendenti*) to urge on
al [al] PREP + ART *vedi* **a**
a.l. ABBR = **anno luce**
ala [ˈala] SF (*pl* **ali**) (*gen*) wing; (*di cappello*) brim; (*di mulino*) sail; **ala destra/sinistra** (*Sport*) right/left wing(er); **fare ala** to make way; **avere le ali ai piedi** to have wings; **prendere qn sotto la propria ala protettrice** to take sb under one's wing; **spiegare le ali** (*fig*) to spread one's wings; **tarpare le ali a qn** to clip sb's wings
alabastro [ala'bastro] SM alabaster; **una lampada di alabastro** an alabaster lamp
alacre [ˈalakre] AGG (*persona*) eager; (*mente, fantasia*) lively
alacrità [alakri'ta] SF promptness, speed
alambicco, -chi [alam'bikko] SM still (*Chim*)
alano [a'lano] SM Great Dane

alare¹ [a'lare] AGG wing *attr*
alare² [a'lare] SM (*di camino*) firedog, andiron
Alaska [a'laska] SF Alaska
alato, -a [a'lato] AGG winged
alba [ˈalba] SF dawn; **all'alba** at dawn, at daybreak; **alzarsi all'alba** to get up at dawn; **spunta l'alba** dawn is breaking
albanese [alba'nese] AGG, SM, SF Albanian
Albania [alba'nia] SF Albania; **viene dall'Albania** he comes from Albania
albatro [ˈalbatro] SM , **albatros** [ˈalbatros] SM INV albatross
albeggiare [albed'dʒare] /62/ VB IMPERS (*aus essere*) to dawn; **comincia ad albeggiare** day is dawning; **albeggiava quando arrivò a casa** day was breaking when he arrived home
alberato, -a [albe'rato] AGG (*viale, piazza*) lined with trees, tree-lined
alberatura [albera'tura] SF (*Naut*) masts *pl*
albergare [alber'gare] /80/ VT (*letter: sentimenti*) to harbour ♦ VI (*aus avere*) (*letter*) to dwell
albergatore, -trice [alberga'tore] SM, SF (*proprietario*) hotel owner, hotelier; (*gestore*) hotel manager (manageress)
alberghiero, -a [alber'gjɛro] AGG (*settore, industria*) hotel *attr*; **scuola alberghiera** catering college; **faccio la scuola alberghiera** I'm at catering college (*Brit*), I go to Hotel Administration School (*USA*)
albergo, -ghi [al'bεrgo] SM hotel; **ho dormito in albergo** I spent the night in a hotel; **albergo diurno** public toilets with washing and shaving facilities *ecc*
albero [ˈalbero] SM 1 (*pianta*) tree; **albero da frutto** fruit tree; **albero genealogico** family tree; **albero di mele** apple tree; **albero di Natale** Christmas tree 2 (*Naut*) mast; **albero maestro** mainmast 3 (*Tecn*) shaft; **albero a camme** *o* **della distribuzione** camshaft; **albero motore** *o* **a gomiti** crankshaft; **albero di trasmissione** transmission shaft
albicocca, -che [albi'kɔkka] SF apricot; **marmellata di albicocche** apricot jam
albicocco, -chi [albi'kokko] SM apricot tree
albino, -a [al'bino] AGG, SM, SF (*Bio*) albino
albo [ˈalbo] SM (*registro professionale*) register; (*fascicolo illustrato*) album; **radiare dall'albo** to strike off
album [ˈalbum] SM INV (*libro, disco*) album; **hai sentito il suo ultimo album?** have you heard her latest album?; **album per francobolli/fotografie** stamp/photo album; **album da disegno** sketch book
albume [al'bume] SM egg white, albumen (*termine tecn*)
albumina [albu'mina] SF albumin
alce [ˈaltʃe] SM elk, moose
alchimia [alki'mia] SF alchemy
alchimista, -i, -e [alki'mista] SM, SF alchemist
alcol [ˈalkol] SM INV (*gen, Chim*) alcohol; **alcol denaturato** methylated spirits *pl* (*Brit*), wood alcohol (*USA*); **alcol etilico** ethyl alcohol, ethanol; **alcol metilico** methyl alcohol
alcolicità [alkoliʧi'ta] SF alcoholic strength
alcolico, -a, -ci, -che [al'kɔliko] AGG alcoholic; **è alcolico?** is it alcoholic? ♦ SM alcohol; **non bevo alcolici** I don't drink; **non vendono alcolici** they don't sell alcoholic drinks
alcolismo [alko'lizmo] SM alcoholism
alcolista, -i, -e [alko'lista] SM, SF alcoholic
alcolizzato, -a [alkolid'dzato] AGG, SM, SF alcoholic
alcoltest [alkol'test] SM INV Breathalyzer (*Marchio registrato*)
alcool *ecc* [ˈalkool] SM INV = **alcol**
alcova [al'kɔva] SF alcove
alcuno, -a [al'kuno] AGG *dav sm*: **alcun** + *consonante, vocale*, alcuno + *s impura, gn, pn, ps, x, z*; *dav sf*: **alcuna** + *consonante*, **alcun'** + *vocale* 1 (*nessuno*): **non... alcuno** no, not any; **non c'è alcuna fretta** there's no hurry, there isn't any hurry; **senza alcun riguardo** without any consideration 2 **alcuni(e)** some, a few; **sono uscito con alcuni amici** I went out with some friends ♦ **alcuni(e)** PRON PL some, a few; **ne ho prese alcune** I took some
aldilà [aldi'la] SM: **l'aldilà** the next life, the after-life
aleatorio, -ria, -ri, -rie [alea'tɔrjo] AGG (*incerto*) uncertain
aleggiare [aled'dʒare] /62/ VI (*aus avere*) (*fig: profumo, sospetto*) to be in the air

Alessandria [ales'sandria] SF Alessandria; **Alessandria d'Egitto** Alexandria

aletta [a'letta] SF (*Tecn, Zool*) fin; (*Aer*) tab

alettone [alet'tone] SM (*Aer*) aileron; (*Aut*) spoiler

Aleutine [aleu'tine] SFPL: **le isole Aleutine** the Aleutian Islands

alfabetico, -a, -ci, -che [alfa'betiko] AGG alphabetical; **in ordine alfabetico** in alphabetical order

alfabeto [alfa'beto] SM alphabet; **alfabeto fonetico** phonetic alphabet; **alfabeto Morse** Morse code

alfanumerico, -a, -ci, -che [alfanu'meriko] AGG alphanumeric

alfiere [al'fjere] SM (*Mil*) standard-bearer; (*Scacchi*) bishop

alfine [al'fine] AVV finally, in the end

alga, -ghe ['alga] SF strand of seaweed, alga (*Bot*); **alghe** SFPL seaweed *sg*, algae (*Bot*)

algebra ['alʒebra] SF algebra; **questo per me è algebra** (*fig*) this is Greek to me

Algeri [al'dʒeri] SF Algiers

Algeria [aldʒe'ria] SF Algeria; **viene dall'Algeria** he comes from Algeria

algerino, -a [aldʒe'rino] AGG, SM, SF Algerian; **è algerina** she's Algerian

algoritmo [algo'ritmo] SM algorithm

aliante [ali'ante] SM (*Aer*) glider

alibi ['alibi] SM INV alibi; **aveva un alibi di ferro** he had a cast-iron alibi

alice [a'litʃe] SF anchovy

alienare [alje'nare] /72/ VT (*gen*) to alienate; (*Dir: trasferire*) to transfer; **alienarsi un amico** to alienate a friend; **alienarsi** VR: **alienarsi (da)** to cut o.s. off (from)

alienato, -a [alje'nato] AGG (*gen*) alienated; (*Dir*) transferred; (*pazzo*) insane ♦ SM, SF lunatic, insane person

alienazione [aljenat'tsjone] SF (*gen*) alienation; (*Dir*) transfer; **alienazione mentale** (*Psic*) insanity

alieno, -a [a'ljeno] AGG: **alieno (da)** opposed (to), averse (to) ♦ SM, SF alien

alimentare¹ [alimen'tare] /72/ AGG food *attr*; **generi alimentari** foodstuffs; **regime alimentare** diet

alimentare² [alimen'tare] /72/ VT 1 (*Tecn*) to feed, supply; (*stufa*) to add fuel to; (*caldaia*) to stoke; (*fuoco*) to stoke up 2 (*fig: tener vivo*) to keep alive 3 (*nutrire*) to nourish, feed; **alimentarsi** VR: **alimentarsi di** to live o feed on

alimentari [alimen'tari] SMPL foodstuffs ♦ SM (*anche: negozio di alimentari*) grocer's shop; **c'è un (negozio di) alimentari qui vicino?** is there a grocer's near here?

alimentatore [alimenta'tore] SM 1 (*Tecn, Elettr*) feeder 2 (*operaio*) stoker

alimentazione [alimentat'tsjone] SF 1 (*nutrizione*) nutrition; (*cibi*) diet; **alimentazione equilibrata/priva di grassi** balanced/low-fat diet 2 (*Tecn*) feeding; (*di caldaia*) stoking 3 (*Inform: di carta*) feed; **alimentazione a fogli singoli** sheet feed; **alimentazione a modulo continuo** stream feed

alimento [ali'mento] SM 1 (*cibo*) food; **contenitore per alimenti** food container 2 (*Dir*); **alimenti** SMPL alimony; **pagare gli alimenti** to pay alimony
❑ **alimento** non si traduce mai con la parola inglese *ailment*

aliquota [a'likwota] SF 1 (*Mat*) aliquot 2 (*Fin*) rate; **aliquota d'imposta** (*Fisco*) tax rate; **aliquota minima** (*Fisco*) basic rate

aliscafo [alis'kafo] SM hydrofoil

alito ['alito] SM (*anche fig*) breath; **avere l'alito cattivo** to have bad breath; **non c'è un alito di vento** there isn't a breath of wind

all. ABBR (= *allegato*) enc.

alla ['alla] PREP + ART *vedi* a

allacciamento [allattʃa'mento] SM (*Tecn*) connection; **allacciamento all'elettricità** connection to the power supply; **far fare l'allacciamento dell'acqua/del gas** to have the water/gas connected

allacciare [allat'tʃare] /14/ VT 1 (*cintura, mantello, cerniera*) to fasten, do up; (*scarpe*) to lace (up), tie; **allacciare o allacciarsi la cintura di sicurezza** to fasten one's seat belt;

allacciarsi il cappotto to fasten one's coat; **allacciare due funi** to join two ropes together; **allacciati le scarpe** lace up your shoes 2 (*Tecn: luce, gas, telefono*) to connect; (*due località*) to link; **il telefono non è ancora allacciato** the phone hasn't been connected yet 3 (*fig: rapporti*) to start

allacciatura [allattʃa'tura] SF fastening

allagamento [allaga'mento] SM (*atto*) flooding *no pl*; (*effetto*) flood

allagare [alla'gare] /80/ VT to flood; **la pioggia aveva allagato le strade** the rain had flooded the roads; **allagarsi** VIP to flood, be flooded; **si è allagato lo scantinato** the basement is flooded

allampanato, -a [allampa'nato] AGG lanky

allargare [allar'gare] /80/ VT 1 (*passaggio*) to widen; (*buco*) to enlarge; (*vestito*) to let out; (*scarpe nuove*) to break in; (*fig: orizzonti*) to widen, broaden; **stanno allargando la strada** they're widening the road 2 (*aprire: braccia*) to open ♦ VI (*aus avere*) (*Aut*): **allargare in curva** to take a bend wide; **allargarsi** VIP (*gen*) to widen; (*scarpe, pantaloni*) to lose its shape; (*espandersi: problema, fenomeno*) to spread; **si sentì allargare il cuore** he felt his heart swell

allarmare [allar'mare] /72/ VT to alarm; **non volevo allarmarti** I didn't want to alarm you; **allarmarsi** VIP to become alarmed

allarme [al'larme] SM (*gen*) alarm; **dare l'allarme** to give o sound the alarm; **essere in allarme per qc** to be alarmed about sth; **mettere qn in allarme** to alarm sb; **i ladri hanno fatto scattare l'allarme** the burglars set off the alarm; **era solo un falso allarme** it was just a false alarm; **allarme aereo** air-raid warning; **allarme rosso** red alert

allarmismo [allar'mizmo] SM scaremongering

allarmista, -i, -e [allar'mista] SM, SF alarmist, scaremonger

allattare [allat'tare] /72/ VT (*sogg: donna*) to (breast-)feed; (*: animale*) to suckle; **allattare artificialmente** to bottle-feed

alle ['alle] PREP + ART *vedi* a

alleanza [alle'antsa] SF alliance; **Alleanza Democratica** (*Pol*) moderate centre-left party; **Alleanza Nazionale** (*Pol*) party on the far right

alleare [alle'are] /72/ VT to unite; **allearsi** VR to form an alliance; **allearsi a o con qn/qc** to become allied with sb/sth; **l'Italia e la Germania si allearono contro la Francia** Italy and Germany joined forces against France

alleato, -a [alle'ato] AGG allied ♦ SM, SF ally; **gli Alleati** SMPL the Allies

alleg. ABBR (= *allegato*) encl.

allegare [alle'gare] /80/ VT 1 (*in lettera*): **allegare (a)** to enclose (with); **alleghiamo alla presente una fotocopia** we enclose herewith a photocopy; **allego una copia di...** I enclose a copy of ... 2 (*in e-mail*) to attach; **hai dimenticato di allegare il file!** you forgot to attach the file! 3 (*gen, anche Dir: addurre*) to adduce, put forward 4 (*denti*) to set on edge

allegato, -a [alle'gato] AGG enclosed ♦ SM (*in e-mail*) attachment; (*in lettera*) enclosure; **l'allegato può contenere un virus** the attachment may contain a virus; **in allegato Vi inviamo...** (*in e-mail*) please find attached ...; (*in lettera*) please find enclosed ...

alleggerire [alleddʒe'rire] /55/ VT 1 (*rendere più leggero*) to lighten, make lighter; (*fig: responsabilità*) to lighten; (*: sofferenza*) to relieve, lessen, alleviate; (*: lavoro, tasse*) to reduce; (*: coscienza*) to ease; **hanno alleggerito del portafoglio** (*scherz*) he's had his wallet pinched 2 (*Sci*) to unweight

allegoria [allego'ria] SF allegory

allegorico, -a, -ci, -che [alle'gɔriko] AGG allegorical

allegria [alle'gria] SF cheerfulness, gaiety; **mettere allegria a qn** to cheer sb up; **su, un po' di allegria!** come on, cheer up!; **tutte queste luci colorate fanno allegria** all these coloured lights make things more cheerful o brighten the place up

allegro, -a [al'legro] AGG 1 (*persona*) cheerful; (*colore*) bright; (*musica*) lively; **è sempre allegro** he's always cheerful; **c'è poco da stare allegri** things are pretty grim, there's not much to be cheerful about 2 (*un po' brillo*) merry, tipsy ♦ SM (*Mus*) allegro

allenamento [allena'mento] SM training; **si è fatto male al braccio durante l'allenamento** he hurt his arm during training; **essere fuori allenamento** (*anche fig*) to be out of practice

allenare [alle'nare] /72/ vt to train; **ha allenato la squadra per due anni** he trained the team for two years; **allenarsi** vr to train; **ci alleniamo ogni giovedì** we train every Thursday

allenatore, -trice [allena'tore] sm, sf trainer, coach; **l'allenatore della nazionale italiana** the Italian national coach

allentare [allen'tare] /72/ vt 1 (*nodo, cintura, vite*) to loosen; **allentare le redini** (*anche fig*) to slacken the reins; **allentare il passo** to slacken one's pace 2 (*diminuire: disciplina*) to relax; **allentarsi** vip (*nodo, stringhe*) to loosen, become loose; (*ingranaggio, vite*) to loosen, work loose

allergia, -gie [aller'dʒia] sf allergy

allergico, -a, -ci, -che [al'lɛrdʒiko] agg: **allergico (a)** allergic (to); **sono allergico alle fragole** I'm allergic to strawberries

allestimento [allesti'mento] sm preparation, setting up; **in allestimento** in preparation

allestire [alles'tire] /55/ vt 1 (*spettacolo, mostra, fiera*) to organize, stage; (*vetrina*) to dress; (*cena*) to prepare; **hanno allestito la mostra in fretta e furia** they organized the exhibition in a mad rush 2 (*esercito, nave*) to equip

allettante [allet'tante] agg attractive; **una prospettiva allettante** an attractive prospect

allettare [allet'tare] /72/ vt to attract, entice; **l'idea non mi alletta** the idea doesn't appeal to me

allevamento [alleva'mento] sm 1 (*di animali*) breeding, rearing; **pollo d'allevamento** battery hen 2 (*luogo*) (stock) farm; (*per cavalli*) stud farm; (*per cani*) kennels *pl*

allevare [alle'vare] /72/ vt (*animali*) to breed, rear; (*bambini*) to bring up; **allevato male** (*bambino*) badly brought up

allevatore, -trice [alleva'tore] sm, sf breeder

alleviare [alle'vjare] /19/ vt (*pene, stanchezza*) to alleviate, relieve

allibire [alli'bire] /55/ vi (*aus essere*) (*dallo stupore*) to be appalled; (*dalla paura*) to go white

allibito, -a [alli'bito] agg (*vedi vi*) appalled; white; **rimanere allibito** to be appalled

allibratore [allibra'tore] sm bookmaker

allietare [allje'tare] /72/ vt to delight, gladden; **allietarsi** vip to be delighted, rejoice

allievo, -a [al'ljevo] sm, sf pupil, student; **è uno dei miei migliori allievi** he's one of my best pupils; **allievo ufficiale** (*Mil*) cadet

alligatore [alliga'tore] sm alligator

allineamento [allinea'mento] sm alignment

allineare [alline'are] /72/ vt (*persone, cose*) to line up; (*Tip*) to align; (*Mil*) to draw up in lines; (*fig: economia, salari*) to adjust; **ci ha allineati in fondo alla palestra** he lined us up at the back of the gym; **allinearsi** vr (*anche Mil*) to line up; **allinearsi a** o **con** (*conformarsi*) to go along with

allineato, -a [alline'ato] agg aligned, in line; **testo allineato/ non allineato** justified/unjustified text; **paesi non allineati** (*Pol*) non-aligned countries

allo ['allo] prep + art *vedi* **a**

allocare [allo'kare] /20/ vt to allocate

allocco, -a, -chi, -che [al'lɔkko] sm (*Zool*) tawny owl ♦ sm, sf fool

allocuzione [allokut'tsjone] sf address

allodola [al'lɔdola] sf (sky)lark

alloggiare [allod'dʒare] /62/ vi (*aus avere*) **alloggiare (in)** to stay (at); **alloggia al Ritz** he's staying at the Ritz; **ho alloggiato presso una famiglia scozzese** I stayed with a Scottish family ♦ vt to accommodate, put up

alloggio, -gi [al'lɔddʒo] sm 1 (*abitazione provvisoria*) accommodation (*Brit*), accommodations (*USA*); **l'alloggio è compreso nel prezzo** accommodation is included in the price; **vitto e alloggio** board and lodging 2 (*appartamento*) flat (*Brit*), apartment (*USA*); **la crisi degli alloggi** the housing problem; **cercare alloggio** to look for somewhere to live

allontanamento [allontana'mento] sm (*gen*) separation; (*affettivo*) estrangement; (*di funzionario*) removal; (*di studente*) exclusion, expulsion; **c'è stato un graduale allontanamento fra i due paesi** relations between the two countries have grown cooler

allontanare [allonta'nare] /72/ vt 1 (*persona*) to take away; (*oggetto*) to move away, take away; (*fig: affetti, amici*) to alienate; **allontanare una poltrona dal fuoco** to move an armchair away from the fire; **la polizia fece allontanare i passanti** the police moved on the bystanders; **la maestra ha allontanato Maria da Roberto** the teacher has separated Maria and Roberto 2 (*mandare via*) to send away, send off; (*licenziare*) to dismiss 3 (*fig: pericolo*) to avert; (: *sospetti*) to divert; **allontanarsi** vr: **allontanarsi (da)** to go away (from), to move away (from); (*fig: possibilità*) to grow more remote; **c'eravamo allontanati troppo** we had wandered too far; **allontanati dall'orlo, è pericoloso** move away from the edge, it's dangerous; **allontanarsi da qn** to wander away from sb; (*fig*) to grow away from sb

allora [al'lora] avv 1 (*in quel momento*) then, at that moment; (*a quel tempo*) then, in those days, at that time; **proprio allora ha squillato il telefono** just at that moment the phone rang; **è stato allora che ho capito che tipo era** it was then that I realized what kind of person he was; **allora non lo sapevo** I didn't know about it then; **da allora non l'ho più visto** I haven't seen him since then; **da allora in poi** since then, from then on; **allora aveva ancora i capelli lunghi** at that time she still had long hair; **la gente di allora** people then o in those days 2 (*in questo caso*) then, in that case, so; (*dunque*) well then, so; **hai paura? — allora dillo!** are you frightened? — (well) then, say so!; **allora, che facciamo stasera?** so, what are we going to do this evening?; **allora? Com'è andata?** so, how did it go?; **allora vieni?** well (then), are you coming?; **e allora?** (*che fare?*) what now?; (*e con ciò?*) so what?

allorché [allor'ke] cong (*letter*) when, as soon as

alloro [al'lɔro] sm laurel; **una foglia d'alloro** a bay leaf; **riposare** o **dormire sugli allori** to rest on one's laurels

alluce [al'lutʃe] sm big toe

allucinante [allutʃi'nante] agg (*scena, spettacolo*) awful, terrifying; (*fam: incredibile*) amazing

allucinato, -a [allutʃi'nato] agg (*persona*) suffering from hallucinations; (*fig*) shocked; (*sguardo*) staring ♦ sm, sf: **sguardo da allucinato** staring eyes

allucinazione [allutʃinat'tsjone] sf hallucination; **avere le allucinazioni** (*anche fig*) to hallucinate

alludere [al'ludere] /35/ vi irreg (*aus avere*) **alludere a** to allude to, hint at; **a cosa alludevi?** what were you referring to?

alluminio [allu'minjo] sm aluminium (*Brit*), aluminum (*USA*)

allunaggio, -gi [allu'naddʒo] sm moon landing

allunare [allu'nare] /72/ vi (*aus essere*) to land on the moon

allungare [allun'gare] /80/ vt 1 (*rendere più lungo*) to lengthen; **basterebbe allungare un po' la gonna** the skirt just needs lengthening a bit; **allungare il passo** to hurry up; **allungare la strada** to take the long way round 2 (*tendere*) to stretch out; **allungare le gambe** to stretch one's legs; **non c'era posto per allungare le gambe** there was no room to stretch your legs; **allungare le orecchie/il collo** to strain one's ears/crane one's neck; **allungare le mani** (*rubare*) to pick pockets; (*picchiare*) to become violent 3 (*fam: dare*) to pass, hand; **mi allunghi il sale per favore?** could you pass me the salt please?; **gli allungò uno schiaffo** he gave him a slap 4 (*diluire*) to dilute, water down; **allungarsi** vip (*diventare più lungo*) to grow o get longer; (*ombre*) to lengthen; (*pianta*) to grow taller; (*vestito, maglione*) to stretch; **le giornate si stanno allungando** the days are getting longer; **allungarsi** vr (*stendersi*) to stretch out

allusi ecc [al'luzi] vb *vedi* **alludere**

allusione [allu'zjone] sf: **allusione (a)** allusion (to), hint (at); **un'allusione velata** a veiled hint

alluso, -a [al'luzo] pp *di* **alludere**

alluvione [allu'vjone] sf flood; **l'alluvione ha causato molti danni** the flood caused a lot of damage

almanacco, -chi [alma'nakko] sm almanac

almeno [al'meno] avv at least; **potevi almeno telefonare, no?** you could at least have phoned, couldn't you?; **dammene almeno uno!** at least give me one!; **ci saranno state almeno tremila persone** there must have been at least three thousand people ♦ cong: **(se) almeno** if only; **(se) almeno piovesse!** if only it would rain!; **se almeno sapessi dov'è!** if only I knew where it was!

alogeno, -a [a'lɔdʒeno] AGG (luce, lampada) halogen attr ♦ SF (lampada) halogen lamp ♦ SM (Chim) halogen

alone [a'lone] SM (di sole, luna) halo; (di fiamma, lampada) glow; (di macchia) ring; **un alone di mistero** an aura o air of mystery

alpestre [al'pestre] AGG (delle Alpi) alpine; (montuoso) mountainous

Alpi ['alpi] SFPL: **le Alpi** the Alps

alpinismo [alpi'nizmo] SM mountaineering, climbing

alpinista, -i, -e [alpi'nista] SM, SF mountaineer, climber

alpino, -a [al'pino] AGG (montano) alpine, mountain attr; (delle Alpi) Alpine; **il paesaggio alpino** the Alpine scenery ♦ SM (Mil): **gli alpini** Italian Alpine troops

alquanto, -a [al'kwanto] AGG INDEF a certain amount of, some; **alquanti(e)** quite a few, several ♦ PRON INDEF PL: **alquanti(e)** quite a few, several ♦ AVV rather, somewhat

Alsazia [al'sattsja] SF Alsace

alt [alt] ESCL halt!, stop! ♦ SM: **dare l'alt** to call a halt

altalena [alta'lena] SF (a funi) swing; (a bilico, anche fig) seesaw; **un'altalena di fortuna e disgrazie** a series of ups and downs

altamente [alta'mente] AVV (specializzato, qualificato) highly; (seccato, scocciato) extremely; **me ne frego altamente** I don't give a damn

altare [al'tare] SM altar; **altare maggiore** high altar

alterare [alte'rare] /72/ VT 1 (fatti, verità) to distort; (registro) to falsify; (qualità, colore) to affect, impair; (alimenti) to adulterate 2 (piani) to alter, change; (persona) to irritate; **alterarsi** VIP 1 (alimenti) to go bad o off; (vino) to spoil 2 (irritarsi) to get angry, lose one's temper

alterazione [alterat'tsjone] SF (vedi vt) distortion; falsification; impairment; adulteration; alteration, change; **alterazione del polso** change in the pulse rate

alterco, -chi [al'terko] SM row, altercation

alternanza [alter'nantsa] SF alternation; (Agr) rotation

alternare [alter'nare] /72/ VT (avvicendare): **alternare qc a o con qc** to alternate sth with sth; (Agr) to rotate; **alternarsi** VR: **alternarsi (a o con)** to alternate (with)

alternativo, -a [alterna'tivo] AGG (energia, medicina ecc) alternative

alternato, -a [alter'nato] AGG alternate; (Elettr) alternating; **passo alternato** (Sci) classic striding

alternatore [alterna'tore] SM alternator

alterno, -a [al'terno] AGG (gen) alternate; (mutevole: fortuna, vicenda) changing; **a giorni alterni** every other day, on alternate days; **circolazione a targhe alterne** (Aut) vedi **circolazione**

altero, -a [al'tero] AGG proud

altezza [al'tettsa] SF 1 (di edificio, persona) height; (quota) height, altitude; (di suono) pitch; (di acqua, pozzo) depth; (di tessuto) width; (fig: d'animo) greatness; **è di altezza media** she's of medium height; **avere un'altezza di...** to be ... high; **ha un'altezza di cinque centimetri** it's five centimetres high; **altezza sul mare** height above sea level; **da un'altezza di 2000 metri** from a height of 2000 metres; **essere all'altezza di una situazione** (fig) to be equal to a situation; **non sono all'altezza** (fig) I'm not up to it 2 (Geom) perpendicular height; (linea) perpendicular; (Astron) elevation, altitude 3 (prossimità): **all'altezza di** near; **l'albergo è all'altezza di piazza Verdi** the hotel is near piazza Verdi; **all'altezza di Capo Horn** off Cape Horn 4 (titolo) highness; **Sua Altezza** Your Highness

altezzoso, -a [altet'tsoso] AGG haughty, arrogant

alticcio, -cia, -ci, -ce [al'tittʃo] AGG tipsy

altipiano [alti'pjano] SM = altopiano

altisonante [altiso'nante] AGG high-sounding, pompous

altitudine [alti'tudine] SF altitude

alto, -a ['alto] AGG 1 (gen) high, tall; **un edificio alto** a tall building; **un muro alto 10 metri** a wall 10 metres high; **quanto sei alto?** how tall are you?; **è alto 1 metro e 80** ≈ he's 6 foot (tall); **Marisa è più alta di me** Marisa's taller than me; **Matteo è il più alto della famiglia** Matteo is the tallest in the family; **andare a testa alta** (fig) to carry one's head high; **aveva la febbre alta** she had a high temperature; **salto in alto** high jump 2 (suono: elevato) high(-pitched); (: forte)

loud; **ad alta voce** out loud, aloud; **l'ha detto a voce alta perché sentissero tutti** she said it in a loud voice so that everybody would hear; **abbassa un po', è troppo alto** turn it down a bit, it's too loud; **ad alto rischio** high-risk 3 (fig: elevato: carica, dignitario) high; (: sentimenti, pensieri) lofty, noble; **avere un'alta opinione di sé** to have a high opinion of o.s. 4 (profondo: acqua) deep; **in quel punto l'acqua è molto alta** the water's very deep there; **essere ancora in alto mare** (fig) to still have a long way to go; **a notte alta** in the dead of night 5 (Geog): **l'alta Italia** Northern Italy; **l'alto Po** the upper reaches of the Po 6 (largo: tessuto) wide ♦ SM (parte superiore) top (part); **in alto** up; **mani in alto!** hands up!; **guardare in alto** to look up; **là in alto up** there; **dall'alto** (fig) from on high; **dall'alto di** from the top of; **dall'alto della torre si vede tutta la città** from the top of the tower you can see the whole city; **dall'alto in** o **al basso** up and down; **guardare dall'alto in basso qn** (fig) to look down on sb; **alti e bassi** ups and downs; **la sua carriera ha avuto alti e bassi** his career has had its ups and downs ♦ AVV (volare) high; **"alto"** (su casse di imballaggio) "this side up" ♦ **alta definizione** high definition; **alta fedeltà** high fidelity, hi-fi; **alta moda** haute couture; **alta pressione** (Meteor) high pressure; **alta società** high society; **alta stagione** high o peak season; **alta velocità** (Ferr) high speed rail system; **alto comando** (Mil) high command; **alto commissario** high commissioner; **l'Alto Medioevo** the Early Middle Ages

altoatesino, -a [altoate'zino] AGG of o from the Alto Adige ♦ SM, SF inhabitant o native of the Alto Adige

altoforno [alto'forno] SM blast furnace

altolocato, -a [altolo'kato] AGG of high rank, highly placed; **amicizie altolocate** friends in high places

altoparlante [altopar'lante] SM (loud)speaker

altopiano [alto'pjano] SM (pl **altipiani**) upland plain, plateau; **altopiano basaltico** lava plateau

altrettanto, -a [altret'tanto] AGG as much; **altrettanti(e)** as many; **ho altrettanta fiducia in te** I have as much o the same confidence in you ♦ PRON as much; **altrettanti(e)** as many; **domani dovrò comprarne altrettanto** I'll have to buy as much o the same tomorrow; **sono 2 mesi che cerco lavoro, e temo che ne passeranno altrettanti prima di trovarlo** I have been looking for work for 2 months now, and I'm afraid it'll be as long again before I find any; **se n'è andato ed io ho fatto altrettanto** he left and so did I o and I followed suit; **tanti auguri! — grazie, altrettanto** all the best! — thank you, the same to you ♦ AVV equally; **lui è altrettanto bravo** he is equally clever, he is just as clever

altri ['altri] PRON PERS SG (qualcun altro) someone else; (in frasi negative) anyone else; **né tu né altri potrete convincermi** neither you nor anyone else is going to persuade me; **non si tocca la roba d'altri** you shouldn't touch other people's things

altrimenti [altri'menti] AVV 1 (in caso contrario) otherwise, or else; **sbrigati, altrimenti arriveremo in ritardo** hurry up or we'll be late 2 (in modo diverso) differently; **non posso fare altrimenti** I can't do otherwise

altro, -a ['altro] AGG INDEF

1 (diverso) other, different; **questa è un'altra cosa** that's another o a different thing; **erano altri tempi** things were different then

2 (supplementare) other; **prendi un altro cioccolatino** have another chocolate; **gli altri allievi usciranno più tardi** the other pupils o the rest of the pupils will come out later

3 (opposto) other; **dall'altra parte della strada** on the other o opposite side of the street; **d'altra parte** on the other hand

4 (nel tempo): **domani l'altro** the day after tomorrow; **l'altro giorno** the other day; **l'altro ieri** the day before yesterday; **quest'altro mese** next month

5 **chi/dove/chiunque altro** who/where/anybody else; **noi altri = noialtri; voi altri = voialtri**

♦ PRON INDEF

1 (persona, cosa diversa o supplementare): **un altro/un'altra** another (one); **altri(e)** others; (altre persone) other people; **prendine un altro** take another one; **se non lo fai tu lo farà un altro** if you don't do it someone else will; **da un giorno**

all'altro (*improvvisamente*) from one day to the next; (*presto*) any day now; **aiutarsi l'un l'altro** to help one another *o* each other
2 (*opposizione*): **l'altro(a)** the other (one); **gli altri/ le altre** the others; **l'uno e l'altro** both (of them); **o l'uno o l'altro** either (of them); **né l'uno né l'altro** neither (of them); **non questo, l'altro** not this one, the other one
3 (*sostantivato: solo maschile*) something else; (*in espressioni interrogative*) anything else; **non faccio altro che studiare** I do nothing but study, all I do is study; **non ho altro da dire** I have nothing else to say, I don't have anything else to say; **desidera altro?** (would you like) anything else?; **gli dirò questo ed altro!** I'll tell him this and more besides!; **ci mancherebbe altro!** that's all we need!; **più che altro** above all; **se non altro** at least; **tra l'altro** among other things; **sei contento? — tutt' altro!** are you pleased? — far from it! *o* anything but!; **ci vuole altro per spaventarmi!** it takes a lot more (than this) to frighten me!
altroché [altro'ke] ESCL certainly!, and how!
altronde [al'tronde] AVV: **d'altronde** on the other hand
altrove [al'trove] AVV elsewhere, somewhere else
altrui [al'trui] AGG INV other people's, others'; **la roba altrui** other people's things *pl*
altruismo [altru'izmo] SM altruism
altruista, -i, -e [altru'ista] AGG altruistic ♦ SM, SF altruist
altura [al'tura] SF **1** (*rialto*) height, high ground **2** (*Naut*): **d'altura** deep-sea
alunno, -a [a'lunno] SM, SF pupil
alveare [alve'are] SM (bee)hive
alveo [alveo] SM riverbed
alzabandiera [altsaban'djɛra] SM INV (*Mil*): **l'alzabandiera** the raising of the flag
alzare [al'tsare] /72/ VT **1** (*gen*) to raise; (*peso*) to lift; **è troppo pesante, non riesco nemmeno ad alzarla** it's too heavy, I can't even lift it; **alzare gli occhi** *o* **lo sguardo** to raise one's eyes; **lo sciopero fece alzare i prezzi** the strike caused an increase in prices **2** (*issare: bandiera, vela*) to hoist **3** (*costruire*) to build, erect **4** (*fraseologia*): **alzare le carte** to cut the cards; **non ha alzato un dito per aiutarmi** he didn't lift a finger to help me; **alzare il gomito** to drink too much; **alzare le mani su qn** to lay hands on sb; **alzare le spalle** to shrug one's shoulders; **alzare i tacchi** to take to one's heels; **alzare la voce** (*per farsi sentire*) to speak up; (*per intimidire, in collera*) to raise one's voice; **alzarsi** VR (*persona*) to rise, get up; **a che ora ti alzi la mattina?** what time do you get up in the morning?; **si è alzato e se n'è andato** he got up and went away; **alzarsi (in piedi)** to stand up, get to one's feet; **alzarsi da tavola** to get up from the table; **alzarsi col piede sbagliato** to get out of bed on the wrong side; **alzarsi** VIP **1** (*sorgere: sole, luna*) to rise; (: *vento*) to rise, get up **2** (*aumentare: temperatura*) to rise; (*fiamma*) to leap up
alzata [al'tsata] SF **1** (*vedi vb*) raising; lifting; **un'alzata di spalle** a shrug; **un'alzata d'ingegno** a flash of genius; **votare per alzata di mano** to vote by show of hands **2** (*di mobile*) upper part, top **3** (*per dolci*) cakestand
amabile [a'mabile] AGG **1** (*persona, conversazione*) pleasant, amiable **2** (*vino*) sweet
amaca, -che [a'maka] SF hammock
amalgamare [amalga'mare] /72/ VT to amalgamate, combine; (*impastare*) to mix; **amalgamarsi** VIP (*sostanze*) to amalgamate, combine; (*Culin*) to mix; (*fig: gruppo, squadra*) to become unified
amante [a'mante] AGG (*appassionato*): **amante di** fond of, keen on; **è amante del jazz** he's keen on jazz ♦ SM, SF lover; (*extraconiugale: uomo*) lover; (: *donna*) lover, mistress; **sono amanti da anni** they've been lovers for years
amaramente [amara'mente] AVV bitterly
amaranto [ama'ranto] SM (*Bot*) love-lies-bleeding ♦ AGG INV: **color amaranto** reddish purple
amare [a'mare] /72/ VT (*provare affetto*) to love; (*amante, marito, moglie*) to love, be in love with; (*amico, musica, sport*) to be fond of, love; **ti amo** I love you; **mi ami?** do you love me?; **noi amiamo la musica classica** we love *o* enjoy *o* are fond of classical music; **amare fare qc** to like *o* love doing sth to do; **farsi amare da qn** to win sb's love; **amarsi** VR (*uso reciproco*) to be in love, love each other; **si amano** they love each other

amareggiare [amared'dʒare] /62/ VT to embitter; **amareggiarsi la vita** to make one's life a misery; **amareggiarsi** VR to get upset
amareggiato, -a [amared'dʒato] AGG embittered
amarena [ama'rena] SF (sour) black cherry
amaretto [ama'retto] SM (*biscotto*) amaretto biscuit; (*liquore*) amaretto liqueur
amarezza [ama'rettsa] SF bitterness; **le amarezze della vita** life's disappointments
amaro, -a [a'maro] AGG (*sapore, anche fig*) bitter; (*caffè*) without sugar; (*spiacevole*) unpleasant, bitter; (*triste*) unhappy; (*doloroso*) painful; **avere la bocca amara** to have a bitter taste in one's mouth ♦ SM **1** (*liquore*) bitters *pl* **2** (*gusto*) bitter taste; (*fig: tristezza, dolore*) bitterness; **mi ha lasciato l'amaro in bocca** it left a bitter taste in my mouth
amarognolo, -a [amaro'ɲɲolo] AGG slightly bitter
amato, -a [a'mato] AGG beloved, loved, dear ♦ SM, SF loved one
amatore, -trice [ama'tore] SM, SF **1** (*amante*) lover **2** (*appassionato*) lover; (*intenditore: di vini ecc*) connoisseur; **pezzo da amatore** collector's item **3** (*dilettante*) amateur
amazzone [a'maddzone] SF **1** (*Mitol*) Amazon; **il Rio delle Amazzoni** (*Geog*) the (river) Amazon **2** (*cavallerizza*) horsewoman; (*abito*) riding habit; **cavalcare all'amazzone** to ride sidesaddle
Amazzonia [amad'dzɔnja] SF Amazonia
amazzonico, -a, -ci, -che [amad'dzɔniko] AGG (*gen*) Amazonian; (*giungla, bacino*) Amazon *attr*
ambasceria [ambaʃʃe'ria] SF embassy
ambasciata [ambaʃʃata] SF embassy; (*messaggio*) message; **l'ambasciata britannica** the British Embassy
ambasciatore, -trice [ambaʃʃa'tore] SM, SF ambassador; **ambasciator non porta pena!** don't take it out on me (*o* him *ecc*)!
ambedue [ambe'due] AGG INV both; **ambedue i ragazzi** both boys ♦ PRON INV both
ambidestro, -a [ambi'destro] AGG ambidextrous
ambientale [ambjen'tale] AGG (*temperatura*) ambient *attr*; (*problemi, tutela*) environmental
ambientalismo [ambjenta'lizmo] SM environmentalism
ambientalista, -i, -e [ambjenta'lista] AGG environmental ♦ SM, SF environmentalist
ambientare [ambjen'tare] /72/ VT (*film, racconto*) to set; **il film è ambientato nella Chicago degli anni venti** the film is set in Chicago in the twenties; **ambientarsi** VR to get used to one's surroundings, settle down; **ti stai ambientando nella nuova scuola?** are you settling into your new school?
ambientazione [ambjentat'tsjone] SF (*di film, racconto*) setting
ambiente [am'bjɛnte] SM **1** environment; **la difesa dell'ambiente** the protection of the environment; **negli ambienti politici** in political circles **2** (*stanza*) room ♦ AGG INV: **temperatura ambiente** room temperature
ambiguità [ambigui'ta] SF INV ambiguity
ambiguo, -a [am'biguo] AGG ambiguous; (*persona*) shady; **una risposta ambigua** an ambiguous answer
ambire [am'bire] /55/ VT, VI (*aus avere*) **ambire a** to aspire to; **un premio molto ambito** a much sought-after prize
ambito [am'bito] SM area; (*tecnico, specialistico*) field; (*fig: cerchia*) sphere, circle
ambivalente [ambiva'lɛnte] AGG (*termini*) with two possible interpretations
ambizione [ambit'tsjone] SF ambition; **la mia ambizione è fare il giornalista** my ambition is to be a journalist
ambizioso, -a [ambit'tsjoso] AGG ambitious
ambo ['ambo] AGG (*pl m* **ambo** *o* **ambi** *pl f* **ambo** *o* **ambe**) both; **da ambo** *o* **ambe le parti** from *o* on both sides ♦ SM (*al gioco*) double
ambra ['ambra] SF amber; **ambra grigia** ambergris
ambulante [ambu'lante] AGG travelling, itinerant; (*biblioteca*) mobile; **un venditore ambulante** a travelling salesperson; **sei un'enciclopedia ambulante!** you're a walking encyclopaedia! ♦ SM pedlar
ambulanza [ambu'lantsa] SF (*veicolo*) ambulance; (*Mil*) field hospital; **devo chiamare l'ambulanza?** shall I call an ambulance?

ambulatoriale [ambulato'rjale] AGG (*Med*) outpatients *attr*; **intervento ambulatoriale** operation in a doctor's surgery; **visita ambulatoriale** visit to the doctor's surgery (*Brit*) *o* office (*USA*)

ambulatorio, -ri [ambula'torjo] SM (*di medico*) surgery (*Brit*), doctor's office (*USA*); (*di ospedale*) outpatients' department; **a che ora apre l'ambulatorio?** what time does the surgery open?

ameba [a'mɛba] SF amoeba (*Brit*), ameba (*USA*)

amenità [ameni'ta] SF INV 1 (*di luogo, pensieri*) pleasantness *no pl* 2 (*facezia*) pleasantry

ameno, -a [a'mɛno] AGG 1 (*luogo, lettura, pensieri*) pleasant, agreeable 2 (*faceto: tipo, discorso*) droll, amusing

America [a'mɛrika] SF America; **l'America latina** Latin America; **l'America meridionale** South America; **l'America settentrionale** North America; **vengono dall'America** they come from America

americanata [amerika'nata] SF (*pegg*): **le Olimpiadi sono state una vera americanata** the Olympics were a typical American extravaganza; **gli piacciono le americanate** he likes everything that's typically American

americanismo [amerika'nizmo] SM (*espressione*) Americanism; (*ammirazione*) love of America

americano, -a [ameri'kano] AGG American; **confronto all'americana** identity parade; **servizio all'americana** table mats ♦ SM, SF American

ametista [ame'tista] SF amethyst

amianto [a'mjanto] SM asbestos

amichevole [ami'kevole] AGG (*anche Sport*) friendly; **potresti avere un atteggiamento un po' più amichevole** you could be a bit friendlier; **in via amichevole** amicably ♦ SF (*Sport*) friendly match

amicizia [ami'tʃittsja] SF 1 (*rapporto*) friendship; **ci tengo molto alla sua amicizia** her friendship is very important to me; **fare amicizia con qn** to make friends with sb; **abbiamo fatto subito amicizia** we immediately became friends; **un'affettuosa amicizia** (*euf: relazione sentimentale*) a close friendship 2 **amicizie** (*amici*) friends; **ha molte amicizie influenti** she has a lot of influential friends *o* friends in high places

amico, -a, -ci, -che [a'miko] AGG friendly ♦ SM, SF 1 friend; **la mia migliore amica** my best friend; **ha molti amici** she's got a lot of friends; **amico del cuore** best friend; **amico d'infanzia** childhood friend; **amico intimo** close friend; **Michela e le sue amiche** Michela and her (girl)friends; **siamo molto amici** we're good friends; **sono amici per la pelle** they're great pals; **è un mio amico** he's a friend of mine; **un mio amico avvocato** a lawyer friend of mine; **farsi qn amico** to make friends with sb; **senza amici** friendless; **aggiungere qn agli amici** (*Inform*) to friend sb; **rimuovere qn dagli amici** (*Inform*) to unfriend sb 2 (*euf: amante*) friend, man friend/lady friend 3 (*appassionato*) lover, enthusiast; **amico degli animali** animal lover; **club degli amici della musica** music club

amido ['amido] SM starch

ammaccare [ammak'kare] /20/ VT (*auto, pentola, cappello*) to dent; (*frutta, parte del corpo*) to bruise; **ammaccarsi** VIP (*vedi vt*) to get dented; bruise

ammaccatura [ammakka'tura] SF (*segno: su auto ecc*) dent; (*: su parte del corpo*) bruise; **c'è un'ammaccatura sullo sportello** there's a dent in the door

ammaestrare [ammaes'trare] /72/ VT (*addestrare*) to teach; (*animali*) to train; (*scherz, o fig: persona*) tame; **orso/cavallo ammaestrato** performing bear/horse

ammainare [ammai'nare] /72/ VT (*vela, bandiera*) to lower, haul down

ammalarsi [amma'larsi] /72/ VIP to fall *o* become ill; **mi sono ammalato e non sono potuto partire** I got ill and couldn't go

ammalato, -a [amma'lato] AGG ill, unwell, sick; **metà della classe era ammalata** half the class was ill ♦ SM, SF sick person; (*paziente*) patient

ammaliare [amma'ljare] /19/ VT (*con sortilegio*) to bewitch; (*fig*) to bewitch, enchant, charm

ammaliatore, -trice [ammalja'tore] SM, SF (*uomo*) charmer; (*donna*) enchantress ♦ AGG bewitching, charming

ammanco, -chi [am'manko] SM (*Amm, Econ*) deficit; **c'è stato un ammanco di cassa di 300 euro** the till was 300 euros short

ammanettare [ammanet'tare] /72/ VT to handcuff

ammanicato, -a [ammani'kato], **ammanigliato, -a** [ammaniʎ'ʎato] AGG (*fam*) well-connected, with friends in high places

ammansire [amman'sire] /55/ VT (*animale*) to tame; (*fig: persona*) to calm (down)

ammantarsi [amman'tarsi] /72/ VR (*persona*) to wrap o.s.; (*fig*): **ammantarsi di virtù** to pretend virtue ♦ VIP: **ammantarsi di** (*prato: di fiori*) to be carpeted with; (*cielo: di stelle*) to be studded with

ammaraggio, -gi [amma'raddʒo] SM (*vedi vb*) (sea) landing; splashdown

ammarare [amma'rare] /72/ VI (*aus essere*) (*aereo*) to make a sea landing; (*astronave*) to splash down

ammassare [ammas'sare] /72/ VT (*cose: o fig: ricchezze*) to pile up, accumulate, amass; (*persone*) to pack; **ammassarsi** VIP (*cose*) to pile up, accumulate; (*persone*) to crowd; **la gente si era ammassata sull'autobus** people were crammed together on the bus

ammasso [am'masso] SM (*cumulo*) pile, heap; (*Econ*) stockpile; **portare all'ammasso** (*grano, olio*) to stockpile

ammattire [ammat'tire] /55/ VI (*aus essere*) (*anche fig*) to go mad, be driven mad

ammazzare [ammat'tsare] /72/ VT (*uccidere*) to kill; (*fig: affaticare*) to exhaust, wear out; **ammazzare il tempo** to kill time; **ammazzarsi** VR (*uso reciproco*) to kill each other; (*suicidarsi*) to kill o.s., commit suicide; **ammazzarsi di lavoro** to kill o.s. with work, work o.s. to death; **ammazzarsi** VIP (*rimanere ucciso*) to die, be killed

ammenda [am'menda] SF 1 (*Dir, Sport*) fine 2 (*riparazione*): **fare ammenda di qc** to make amends for sth

ammesso, -a [am'messo] PP *di* ammettere

ammettere [am'mettere] /63/ VT IRREG 1 (*far entrare: visitatore*) to admit, let in, allow in; (*accettare: nuovo socio, studente*) to admit; **ammettere qn ad un club** to admit sb to a club; **essere ammesso agli esami orali** to be admitted to *o* to be allowed to do the oral exams 2 (*riconoscere: colpa, errore, fatto*) to admit, acknowledge; **ha ammesso di avere torto** she admitted she was wrong 3 (*supporre*) to suppose, assume; **ammettiamo che sia vero** let us suppose *o* assume that it's true; **ammettiamo che venga...** suppose he comes ...; **ammesso (e non concesso) che...** (just) assuming that ... 4 (*tollerare: scuse, comportamento*) to accept; (*permettere*) to allow; **non ammetto che mi si bestemmi** I will not tolerate swearing; **non ammetto scuse** I won't accept any excuses

ammezzato [ammed'dzato] SM (*anche*: **piano ammezzato**) mezzanine, entresol

ammiccare [ammik'kare] /20/ VI (*aus avere*) **ammiccare (a)** to wink (at)

amministrare [amminis'trare] /72/ VT 1 (*ditta*) to manage, run; (*patrimonio*) to administer; (*stato*) to run, govern 2 (*Rel, Dir*) to administer

amministrativo, -a [amministra'tivo] AGG administrative

amministratore [amministra'tore] SM (*Amm*) administrator; (*di stabile*) manager of flats; **amministratore aggiunto** associate director; **amministratore di condominio** house manager; **amministratore delegato** managing director, chief executive; **amministratore fiduciario** trustee; **amministratore unico** sole director

amministrazione [amministrat'tsjone] SF (*vedi vb*) management, running; administration; government; **consiglio d'amministrazione** board of directors; **amministrazione controllata** temporary receivership; **amministrazione fiduciaria** trusteeship; **amministrazione locale** local government; **amministrazione pubblica** public administration, ≈ civil service; **amministrazione straordinaria** *control by a government-appointed administrator*

ammiraglia [ammi'raʎʎa] SF (*nave*) flagship

ammiragliato [ammiraʎ'ʎato] SM (*ufficio*) admiralship; (*consesso, sede*) admiralty

ammiraglio, -gli [ammi'raʎʎo] SM admiral

ammirare [ammi'rare] /72/ VT to admire; **ci siamo fermati**

ad ammirare il paesaggio we stopped to admire the view; **lo ammiro** I admire him

ammiratore, -trice [ammira'tore] SM, SF admirer

ammirazione [ammirat'tsjone] SF admiration

ammisi ecc [am'mizi] VB vedi **ammettere**

ammissibile [ammis'sibile] AGG (comportamento) acceptable; (Dir: testimonianza) admissible

ammissione [ammis'sjone] SF 1 (a club) admission, entry; (a scuola) entrance, acceptance; **esame d'ammissione** entrance exam 2 (di colpa, errore) admission

Amm.ne ABBR = **amministrazione**

ammobiliare [ammobi'ljare] /19/ VT to furnish

ammobiliato, -a [ammobi'ljato] AGG (camera, appartamento) furnished

ammodernare [ammoder'nare] /72/ VT to modernize

ammodo, a modo [am'mɔdo] AVV (per bene) well, properly ♦ AGG INV respectable, nice

ammogliare [ammoʎ'ʎare] /27/ VT to find a wife for; **ammogliarsi** VR to marry, take a wife (ant)

ammollo [am'mɔllo] SM soaking; **mettere/lasciare i panni in ammollo** to leave the clothes to soak

ammoniaca [ammo'niaka] SF ammonia

ammonimento [ammoni'mento] SM (rimprovero) reprimand, admonishment; (lezione) lesson, warning

ammonire [ammo'nire] /55/ VT 1 (rimproverare) to admonish, reprimand; (avvertire) to warn; **è stato ammonito dall'insegnante** he was reprimanded by the teacher 2 (Dir) to caution; (Calcio) to book; **è stato ammonito dall'arbitro** he was booked by the referee

ammonizione [ammonit'tsjone] SF 1 (monito) warning; (rimprovero) reprimand 2 (Dir) caution; (Calcio) booking

ammontare [ammon'tare] /72/ VI (aus essere) **ammontare a** to amount to, add up to; **a quanto ammonta il totale?** what does the total come to? ♦ SM (somma) (total) amount

ammonticchiare [ammontik'kjare] /19/ VT to pile up, heap up

ammorbare [ammor'bare] /72/ VT 1 (diffondere malattia) to infect 2 (sogg. odore) to foul, **un tanfo tremendo ammorbava l'aria** a terrible stench poisoned the air

ammorbidente [ammorbi'dente] SM fabric softener

ammorbidire [ammorbi'dire] /55/ VT to soften; **ammorbidirsi** VIP to soften; **ammorbidirsi con l'età** (fig) to mellow with age

ammortamento [ammorta'mento] SM (Fin: estinzione di debito) redemption, amortization; (: in bilancio) depreciation; **ammortamento fiscale** capital allowance

ammortare [ammor'tare] /72/ VT (Fin: debito) to pay off, redeem; (: spese d'impianto) to write off

ammortizzare [ammortid'dzare] /72/ VT 1 (Fin: debito) to pay off, redeem; (: spese d'impianto) to write off 2 (Aut, Tecn: attutire) to cushion, absorb

ammortizzatore [ammortiddza'tore] SM (Aut, Tecn) shock absorber; **ammortizzatori sociali** measures to cushion the effects of unemployment

ammucchiare [ammuk'kjare] /19/ VT (disporre in mucchio) to heap, pile up; (denaro) to pile up, accumulate; **ha ammucchiato le sue cose in un angolo** she piled up her things in a corner; **ammucchiarsi** VIP (cose) to pile up, accumulate; (persone) to crowd

ammuffire [ammuf'fire] /55/ VI (aus essere) to go o grow mouldy (Brit) o moldy (USA); (fig: persona) to moulder, languish; **il pane è ammuffito** the bread's gone mouldy

ammutinamento [ammutina'mento] SM mutiny

ammutinarsi [ammuti'narsi] /72/ VIP to mutiny

ammutinato, -a [ammuti'nato] AGG mutinous ♦ SM mutineer

ammutolire [ammuto'lire] /55/ VI (aus essere) to be struck dumb

amnesia [amne'zia] SF amnesia

amnistia [amnis'tia] SF amnesty

amo ['amo] SM (Pesca) (fish) hook; (fig) bait; **l'abbiamo preso all'amo** (fig) he's swallowed the bait; **gettare l'amo** to cast one's line; (fig) to lay bait

amorale [amo'rale] AGG amoral

amore [a'more] SM 1 (affetto) love, affection; (sessuale) love; **una canzone d'amore** a love song; **il suo amore per lui/ per le piante** her love for him/of plants; **fare qc con amore** to do sth with loving care; **fare l'amore** o **all'amore** (con qn)** to make love (with sb); **mi ha raccontato tutto dei suoi amori** he told me all about his love affairs 2 (persona) love; **vieni, amore** come here, darling o love; **il tuo bambino è un amore** your baby is a darling 3 (fraseologia): **per amore di** for the sake of; **per l'amor del cielo!** for heaven's sake!; **per l'amor di Dio!** for God's sake!; **per amore o per forza** willy-nilly; **andare d'amore e d'accordo con qn** to get on like a house on fire with sb; **che amore di vestito!** what a lovely dress!; **amore libero** free love; **amore di sé** egoism, selfishness; **amor proprio** self-esteem, pride

amoreggiare [amored'dʒare] /62/ VI (aus avere) to flirt

amorevole [amo'revole] AGG loving, affectionate

amorfo, -a [a'morfo] AGG amorphous; (fig: persona) colourless; **ma come sei amorfo!** how apathetic you are!

amorino [amo'rino] SM cupid

amoroso, -a [amo'roso] AGG (affettuoso) loving, affectionate; (d'amore: sguardo) amorous; (: poesia, lettera) love attr; **uno sguardo amoroso** an amorous look; **una relazione amorosa** an affair ♦ SM, SF (fam) sweetheart

ampere [ã'per] SM INV (Elettr) amp(ère)

ampiezza [am'pjettsa] SF 1 (di sala) (large) size; (di gonna) fullness; (fig: di fenomeno) scale; **ampiezza di vedute** broad-mindedness 2 (Fis) amplitude, range; (Geom) size; (Mus) range

ampio, -pia, -pi, -pie ['ampjo] AGG 1 (vasto: spazio, sala) spacious; (: strada, corridoio) wide, broad; **di ampio respiro** (fig: ricerca, articolo) wide-ranging; **di ampie vedute** broad-minded 2 (largo: vestito) loose; **una gonna ampia** a full skirt 3 (abbondante: garanzie) ample

amplesso [am'plesso] SM (sessuale) intercourse

ampliamento [amplia'mento] SM (di strada) widening; (di aeroporto) expansion; (fig) broadening

ampliare [ampli'are] /19/ VT (allargare) to widen; (fig: discorso) to enlarge (up)on; (: raggio di azione) to widen; **ampliare le proprie conoscenze** to broaden one's knowledge; **vorrei ampliare la cucina** I'd like to make the kitchen bigger; **ampliarsi** VIP to grow, increase

amplificare [amplifi'kare] /20/ VT (suono) to amplify; (fig: sensazione) to increase; (: pregi) to extol

amplificatore [amplifika'tore] SM (Tecn, Mus) amplifier

amplificazione [amplifikat'tsjone] SF amplification

ampolla [am'polla] SF 1 (per olio, aceto) cruet 2 (Chim) round-bottom flask

ampolloso, -a [ampol'loso] AGG bombastic

amputare [ampu'tare] /72/ VT (Med) to amputate; (fig: testo, scritto) to cut

amputazione [amputat'tsjone] SF amputation

Amsterdam [amster'dam] SF Amsterdam

amuleto [amu'leto] SM lucky charm

AN [a'enne] SIGLA = **Ancona** ♦ SIGLA F (Pol: = Alleanza Nazionale) National Alliance, Italian right-wing party

anabbagliante [anabbaʎ'ʎante] (Aut) AGG dipped (Brit), dimmed (USA) ♦ SM dipped (Brit) o dimmed (USA) headlight

anabolizzante [anabolid'dzante] SM anabolic steroid ♦ AGG (sostanza) anabolic

anacronismo [anakro'nizmo] SM anachronism

anagrafe [a'nagrafe] SF (Amm: registro) register of births, marriages and deaths; (: ufficio) registry o register office (Brit), office of vital statistics (USA); **anagrafe tributaria** central tax records

anagrafico, -a, -ci, -che [ana'grafiko] AGG (Amm): **dati anagrafici** personal data o records; **luogo di residenza anagrafica** place of residence

anagramma, -i [ana'gramma] SM anagram

analcolico, -a, -ci, -che [anal'kɔliko] AGG non-alcoholic; **bevanda analcolica** non-alcoholic drink; **bibita analcolica** soft drink; **birra analcolica** alcohol-free beer ♦ SM non-alcoholic aperitif

anale [a'nale] AGG anal

analfabeta, -i, -e [analfa'beta] AGG, SM, SF illiterate

analfabetismo [analfabe'tizmo] SM illiteracy

analgesico [anal'dʒeziko] SM painkiller, analgesic

analisi [a'nalizi] SF INV **1** (*gen*) analysis; (*di orina, sangue*) test; **analisi del sangue** blood test; **all'analisi dei fatti** on examining the facts; **in ultima analisi** all in all, in the final analysis; **sono in analisi da 5 anni** (*Psic*) I've been in analysis for the past 5 years; **analisi dei costi** cost analysis; **analisi di mercato** market analysis; **analisi dei sistemi** systems analysis; **analisi delle vendite** sales analysis **2** (*Gramm*): **analisi grammaticale** parsing; **analisi logica** sentence analysis

analista, -i, -e [ana'lista] SM, SF (*Chim, Med, Inform*) analyst; (*Psic*) (psycho)analyst; **analista finanziario** financial analyst; **analista di sistemi** systems analyst

analitico, -a, -ci, -che [ana'litiko] AGG analytic(al); **indice analitico** index

analizzare [analid'dzare] /72/ VT (*gen*) to analyse (*Brit*), analyze (*USA*); (*sangue, orina*) to test, analyse; (*Gramm: frase*) to parse; (*poesia, testo*) to give a commentary on

analogia, -gie [analo'dʒia] SF analogy; **per analogia (con)** by analogy (with)

analogico, -a, -ci, -che [ana'lɔdʒiko] AGG analogical; (*calcolatore, orologio*) analog(ue)

analogo, -a, -ghi, -ghe [a'nalogo] AGG: **analogo (a)** analogous (to), similar (to)

ananas ['ananas] SM INV pineapple

anarchia [anar'kia] SF anarchy

anarchico, -a, -ci, -che [a'narkiko] AGG anarchistic; (*disordinato*) anarchic(al); **un poeta anarchico** an anarchist poet ♦ SM, SF anarchist; **gli anarchici** the anarchists

anarco-insurrezionalista, -i, -e [a'narko insurrettsjona'lista], **anarchico-insurrezionalista, -i, -e** AGG anarcho-insurrectionalist

anatema, -i [ana'tɛma] SM (*Rel*) anathema; **scagliare** *o* **gettare l'anatema contro** *o* anathematize

anatomia [anato'mia] SF (*gen*) anatomy; (*analisi*) analysis

anatomico, -a, -ci, -che [ana'tɔmiko] AGG anatomical; **sedile anatomico** contoured *o* anatomical seat

anatra ['anatra] SF duck; **anatra all'arancia** duck with orange sauce; **anatra selvatica** mallard

anatroccolo [ana'trɔkkolo] SM duckling

anca, -che ['anka] SF (*di persona*) hip; (*di animale*) haunch

anche ['anke] CONG **1** (*pure*) also, too; **e va anche a Roma** and he's going to Rome too, and he's also going to Rome; **parla inglese e anche italiano** he speaks English and Italian too *o* as well; **vengo anch'io!** I'm coming too!; **sono stanchissimo! - anch'io!** I'm really tired! - me too!; **gli ho parlato ieri — anch'io** I spoke to him yesterday — so did I; **anche oggi non potrò venire** I won't be able to come today either; **potrebbe anche cambiare idea, ma...** he may change his mind, but ...; **avresti anche potuto avvertirmi** you could have let me know **2** (*perfino*) even; **lo saprebbe fare anche un bambino** even a child could do it; **anche se** (*ipotesi*) even if; (*nonostante*) although; **anche se dovesse piovere** even if it rained; **me lo ricordo anche se avevo solo sei anni** I remember it, although I was only six; **anche volendo, non finiremmo in tempo** however much we wanted to, we wouldn't finish in time

ancheggiare [anked'dʒare] /62/ VI (*aus* avere) to wiggle (one's hips)

anchilosato, -a [ankilo'zato] AGG stiff

anconetano, -a [ankone'tano] AGG of *o* from Ancona ♦ SM, SF inhabitant *o* native of Ancona

ancora¹ ['ankora] SF (*Naut* o *fig*) anchor; **gettare/levare l'ancora** to cast/weigh anchor; **ancora galleggiante** sea anchor; **ancora di salvezza** (*fig*) last hope

ancora² ['ankora] AVV **1** (*tuttora*) still; **è ancora arrabbiato con me** he's still angry with me; **ancora oggi** still today; **stava ancora dormendo** he was still asleep **2** (*di nuovo*) again; **ancora tu!** (not) you again!; **sei andato ancora a Parigi da allora?** have you been back to Paris since then? **3 non ancora** not yet; **è pronto? — no, non ancora** is it ready? — no, not yet; **il direttore non è ancora qui** the manager isn't here yet **4** (*più*) (some) more; **ancora un po'** a little more; **vuoi ancora zucchero?** would you like some more sugar?; **mi dai ancora un po' di gelato?** could I have a bit more

ice-cream?; **vorrei ancora latte** I'd like more milk; **ne vorrei ancora** I'd like some more; **prendi ancora un biscotto** have another biscuit; **ci sono ancora caramelle?** are there any sweets left?; **cosa vuoi ancora?** what else do you want?; **ancora per una settimana** for another week, for one week more; **ancora una volta** once more, once again; **ancora un po' e finivamo in acqua** we almost ended up in the water ♦ CONG (*nei comparativi*) even, still; **ancora di più/meno** even more/less; **ancora meglio/peggio** even *o* still better/worse; **ancora altrettanto** as much again; **oggi fa ancora più freddo** it's even colder today

ancoraggio, -gi [anko'raddʒo] SM anchorage; **tassa d'ancoraggio** anchorage dues *pl*

ancorare [anko'rare] /72/ VT , **ancorarsi** VR (*anche fig*) to anchor

ANCR [ankr] SIGLA F (= *Associazione Nazionale Combattenti e Reduci*) servicemen's and ex-servicemen's association

Andalusia [andalu'zia] SF Andalusia

andaluso, -a [anda'luzo] AGG, SM, SF Andalusian

andamento [anda'mento] SM (*di malattia*) course; (*della Borsa, del mercato*) trend; (*del lavoro*) progress

andante [an'dante] SM (*Mus*) andante ♦ AGG (*corrente*) current; (*di poco pregio*) cheap, second-rate

---

PAROLA CHIAVE

andare [an'dare] /6/ VI IRREG (*aus* essere)

1 (*gen*) to go; **andare in bicicletta** to cycle; **andare a casa** to go home; **andare a cavallo** to ride; **dove va (messa) questa vite?** where does this screw go?; **andare a letto** to go to bed; **andare lontano** (*anche fig*) to go far; **andare in macchina** to drive; **andare a male** to go bad; **andare per i 50** (*età*) to be getting on for 50; **andare in città a piedi** to walk to town; **andare a Roma** to go to Rome; **andrò all'università l'anno prossimo** I'm going to university next year; **vado e vengo** I'll be back in a minute; **andare e venire** to come and go

2 (*essere*): **se non vado errato** if I'm not mistaken; **va fatto entro oggi** it's got to be done today; **andare fiero di qc/qn** to be proud of sth/sb; **ne va della nostra vita** our lives are at stake; **vado pazzo per la pizza** I'm crazy about pizza, I adore pizza; **la situazione va peggiorando** the situation is getting worse; **andare perduto** to go missing; **non va trascurato il fatto che...** we shouldn't forget *o* overlook the fact that ...; **va sempre vestita di rosso** she always wears red

3 (*salute, situazione*): **come va? — bene grazie** how are you? — fine thanks; **va bene** (*d'accordo*) all right, O.K (*fam*); **ti è andata bene** you got away with it; **andare di bene in meglio** to get better and better; **come è andata?** how did it go?; **come va (la salute)? — va bene** how are you? — I'm fine; **come va la scuola?** how's school?; **come vai a scuola?** how are you getting on at school?

4 (*funzionare*) to work; **la macchina va a benzina** the car runs on petrol; **non riesco a far andare la macchina** I can't start the car; **la lavatrice non va** the washing machine won't work

5 andare a qn (*calzare: scarpe, vestito*) to fit sb: (*essere gradito*): **quest'idea non mi va** I don't like this idea; **questi jeans non mi vanno più** these jeans don't fit me any more; **ti va il cioccolato?** do you like chocolate?; **ti va di andare al cinema?** do you like the idea of going to the cinema?; **ti va (bene) se ci vediamo alle 5?** is it ok if we meet at 5?

6 (*essere venduto*) to sell; (*essere di moda*) to be fashionable; **un modello che va molto** a style that sells well

7 (+ *infinito*): **andare a pescare** to go fishing; **andare a prendere qc/qn** to go and get sth/sb; **andare a sciare** to go skiing; **andare a vestirsi** to go and get dressed

8 (*fraseologia*): **va là che ti conosco bene** come off it, I know you too well; **vai a quel paese!** (*fam*) get lost!; **vada per una birra** ok, I'll have a beer; **chi va piano va sano e va lontano** (*Proverbio*) more haste less speed; **va da sé** (*è naturale*) it goes without saying; **per questa volta vada** let's say no more about it this time; **andiamo!** let's go!; (*coraggio!*) come on!

9 andarsene to go away; **me ne vado** I'm off, I'm going; **se ne sono andati** they've gone

10 (+ *avverbio, preposizione*) *vedi* **fuori via²**

♦ SM: **a lungo andare** in time, in the long run; **con l'andar**

del tempo with the passing of time; **racconta storie a tutto andare** he's forever talking rubbish; **andare e venire** coming and going

andata [anˈdata] SF (*viaggio*) outward journey; **all'andata c'era brutto tempo** on the outward journey there was bad weather; **all'andata ci ho messo due ore** it took me two hours to get there; **biglietto di sola andata** single (*Brit*) o one-way ticket; **biglietto di andata e ritorno** return (*Brit*) o round-trip (*USA*) ticket; **partita/girone di andata** (*Sport*) first leg/first half of the season

andatura [andaˈtura] SF **1** (*modo di camminare*) gait, walk **2** (*Sport*) pace; **imporre l'andatura** to set the pace **3** (*Naut*) tack

andazzo [anˈdattso] SM (*pegg*): **con** o **di questo andazzo, finiremo male** the way things are going, we'll end up in a mess; **le cose hanno preso un brutto andazzo** things have taken a turn for the worse

Ande [ˈande] SFPL: **le Ande** the Andes

andino, -a [anˈdino] AGG Andean

andirivieni [andiriˈvjɛni] SM INV coming and going

Andorra [anˈdɔrra] SF Andorra

andrò ecc [anˈdrɔ] VB *vedi* **andare**

androne [anˈdrone] SM entrance hall

aneddoto [aˈneddoto] SM anecdote

anelare [aneˈlare] /72/ VI (*aus* avere) **anelare a qc/a fare qc** to long o yearn for sth/to do sth

anelito [aˈnɛlito] SM (*letter*): **anelito (di)** longing (for), yearning (for)

anello [aˈnello] SM (*gen*, o *fig*) ring; (*di catena*) link; **un anello d'oro** a gold ring; **ad anello** ring-shaped; **anello di fidanzamento/nuziale** engagement/wedding ring; **anello di congiunzione/mancante** (*fig*) connecting/missing link

anemia [aneˈmia] SF anaemia (*Brit*), anemia (*USA*); **anemia falciforme** sickle-cell anaemia

anemico, -a, -ci, -che [aˈnɛmiko] AGG anaemic (*Brit*), anemic (*USA*) ♦ SM, SF an(a)emic person

anemone [aˈnɛmone] SM anemone; **anemone di bosco** wood anemone; **anemone di mare** sea anemone

anestesia [anesteˈzia] SF anaesthesia (*Brit*), anesthesia (*USA*); **fare l'anestesia a qn** to give sb an anaesthetic; **sotto anestesia** under anaesthetic, under anaesthesia; **anestesia locale** local anaesthetic; **anestesia totale** general anaesthetic

anestesista, -i, -e [anesteˈzista] SM, SF anaesthetist (*Brit*), anesthetist (*USA*)

anestetico, -a, -ci, -che [anesˈtɛtiko] AGG, SM anaesthetic (*Brit*), anesthetic (*USA*)

anestetizzare [anestetidˈdzare] /72/ VT to anaesthetize (*Brit*), anesthetize (*USA*)

anfetamina [anfetaˈmina] SF amphetamine

anfetaminico, -a, -ci, -che [anfetaˈminiko] AGG (*fig*) hyper (*fam*)

anfibio, -bia, -bi, -bie [anˈfibjo] AGG amphibious ♦ SM **1** (*Zool*) amphibian; (*veicolo*) amphibious **2** **anfibi** SMPL (*scarpe*) heavy-duty boots

anfiteatro [anfiteˈatro] SM amphitheatre (*Brit*), amphitheater (*USA*)

anfitrione [anfitriˈone] SM (*letter*) host

anfora [ˈanfora] SF amphora

anfratto [anˈfratto] SM cleft

angelico, -a, -ci, -che [anˈdʒeliko] AGG angelic(al)

angelo [ˈandʒelo] SM angel; **fabbricante d'angeli** (*euf*) back-street abortionist; **angelo custode** guardian angel

angheria [angeˈria] SF vexation

angina [anˈdʒina] SF (*tonsillite*) tonsillitis; **angina pectoris** angina (pectoris)

anglicano, -a [angliˈkano] AGG, SM, SF Anglican

anglicismo [angliˈtʃizmo] SM anglicism

anglofilo, -a [anˈglɔfilo] AGG anglophilic, anglophile ♦ SM, SF anglophile

anglosassone [angloˈsassone] AGG, SM, SF Anglo-Saxon

Angola [ˈangola] SF Angola

angolano, -a [angoˈlano] AGG, SM, SF Angolan

angolare [angoˈlare] AGG (*gen*, *Geom*) angular; **mobile**

angolare corner unit; **pietra angolare** (*Archit*, *anche fig*) cornerstone

angolazione [angolatˈtsjone] SF (*Fot*, *Cine*, *TV*, o *fig*) angle; **visto da questa angolazione** seen from this angle

angolo [ˈangolo] SM **1** (*di stanza*, *tavolo*, *strada*, *bocca*) corner; **fare angolo con** (*strada*) to run into; **sull'** o **all'angolo della strada** on o at the corner of the street; **è la casa all'angolo con via Garibaldi** it's the house on the corner of Via Garibaldi; **faccio un salto al negozio all'angolo** I'm just popping out to the corner shop; **dietro l'angolo** (*anche fig*) round the corner; **il cinema è proprio dietro l'angolo** the cinema's just round the corner; **abito in via Cairoli angolo via Bersaglio** I live on the corner of via Cairoli and via Bersaglio; **ho scoperto degli angoli di Londra che non conoscevo** I've discovered some out-of-the-way bits of London I never knew before; **starsene in un angolo** to stay all by one's self; **non startene sempre in un angolo, vieni con noi** don't stay on your own all the time, come with us; **angolo cottura** (*di appartamento*) kitchen area **2** (*Geom*) angle; **angolo retto/acuto/ottuso** right/acute/obtuse angle

angoloso, -a [angoˈloso] AGG (*oggetto*) angular; (*volto*, *corpo*) angular, bony

angora [ˈangora] SF: **lana d'angora** angora

angoscia [anˈgɔʃʃa] SF (*gen*, *Psic*) anguish *no pl*

angosciare [angoʃˈʃare] /14/ VT to cause anguish to; **la scena mi ha angosciato** I was very upset by what I saw; **il pensiero della morte mi angoscia** the thought of dying terrifies me; **angosciarsi** VIP: **angosciarsi (per)** (*preoccuparsi*) to become anxious (about); (*provare angoscia*) to get upset (about o over)

angoscioso, -a [angoʃˈʃoso] AGG (*scena*, *situazione*) distressing, harrowing; (*attesa*) agonizing

anguilla [anˈgwilla] SF eel

anguria [anˈgurja] SF watermelon

angustia [anˈgustja] SF **1** (*di spazio*) lack of space **2** (*povertà*) poverty, want; **vive in angustia** he lives in straitened circumstances **3** (*ansia*) anguish, distress

angustiare [angusˈtjare] /19/ VT to torment, distress; **angustiarsi** VIP: **angustiarsi (per)** to become distressed (about)

angusto, -a [anˈgusto] AGG (*stanza*, *letto*) narrow; (*fig*: *pensiero*) mean, petty; (: *mente*) narrow

anice [ˈanitʃe] SM **1** (*Bot*: *pianta*) anise; (: *frutto*) aniseed; **una caramella all'anice** an aniseed sweet **2** (*liquore*) anisette

anidride [aniˈdride] SF (*Chim*): **anidride carbonica** carbon dioxide; **anidride solforosa** sulphur dioxide

anima [ˈanima] SF **1** (*gen*) soul; **volere un bene dell'anima a qn** to be extremely fond of sb; **con tutta l'anima** with all one's heart; **mettere l'anima in qc/nel fare qc** to put one's heart and soul into sth/into doing sth; **vendere l'anima (al diavolo)** to sell one's soul (to the devil); **anima e corpo** body and soul, wholeheartedly; **rompere l'anima a qn** to drive sb mad; **mi hai rotto l'anima** I've had enough of you; **il nonno buon'anima...** Grandfather, God rest his soul ...; **la buon'anima di Mario** (*defunto*) the dear departed Mario **2** (*persona*) soul; (*abitante*) inhabitant; **il paese conta 1.000 anime** the town has 1,000 inhabitants; **un'anima in pena** (*anche fig*) a tormented soul; **anima gemella** soul mate; **l'anima della festa** the life and soul of the party; **non c'era neanche un'anima** there wasn't a soul; **non c'era anima viva** there wasn't a living soul

animale [aniˈmale] SM (*gen*, o *fig*) animal ♦ AGG animal; **grasso animale** animal fat

animalesco, -a, -schi, -sche [animaˈlesko] AGG (*gesto*, *atteggiamento*) animal-like

animalista, -i, -e [animaˈlista] AGG animal rights *attr*; **il movimento animalista** the animal rights movement ♦ SM, SF animal rights activist

animare [aniˈmare] /72/ VT **1** (*dare vita a*) to animate; (*serata*, *conversazione*) to liven up, enliven; **la gioia le animava il volto** her face shone with joy **2** (*sogg*: *sentimento*) to drive, impel; **era animato dal desiderio di libertà** he was driven by the desire for freedom **3** (*incoraggiare*: *persona*, *commercio*) to encourage; **animarsi** VIP (*persona*, *oggetto*, *strada*) to come to life; (*festa*) to liven up, become animated; (*scaldarsi*: *conversazione*, *persona*) to become animated

animato, -a [ani'mato] AGG **1** (*vivace: strada*) lively, busy; (: *conversazione*) lively, animated **2** (*vivo*) animate

animatore, -trice [anima'tore] AGG (*principio*) guiding; (*forza*) driving ♦ SM, SF (*turistico, di festa, gruppo*) organizer; (*di spettacolo*) compère; (*Cine*) animator; **è sempre lui l'animatore della festa** he's always the life and soul of the party

animazione [animat'tsjone] SF (*eccitazione*) excitement; (*vivacità*) liveliness; (*di città, strada*) bustle; (*Cine*) animation; **animazione teatrale** amateur dramatics

animo ['animo] SM **1** (*mente*) mind; (*disposizione*) character, disposition; **stato d'animo** state of mind; **avere in animo di fare qc** to have a mind to do sth, intend to do sth; **mettersi l'animo in pace** to set one's mind at rest; **fare qc di buon/ mal animo** to do sth willingly/unwillingly **2** (*coraggio*) courage; **perdersi d'animo** to lose heart; **fare animo a qn** to cheer sb up; **farsi animo** to pluck up courage; **fatti animo!, animo!** cheer up!

animosità [animosi'ta] SF animosity

anitra ['anitra] SF = **anatra**

Ankara ['ankara] SF Ankara

annacquare [annak'kware] /72/ VT to dilute; (*vino*) to water down

annaffiare [annaf'fjare] /19/ VT (*fiori, piante*) to water

annaffiatoio, -oi [annaffja'tojo] SM watering can

annali [an'nali] SMPL annals

annaspare [annas'pare] /72/ VI (*aus avere*) (*nell'acqua*) to flounder; (*fig: nel buio, nell'incertezza*) to grope

annata [an'nata] SF (*gen*) year; (*di vino*) vintage, year; (*importo annuo*) annual amount; **è stata una buona annata** it was a good year; **vino di annata** vintage wine

annebbiare [anneb'bjare] /19/ VT (*gen, o fig*) to cloud; **annebbiarsi** VIP to become foggy; (*vista*) to become blurred

annegamento [annega'mento] SM drowning; **è morto per annegamento** he drowned

annegare [anne'gare] /80/ VI (*aus essere*) to drown; **non sapeva nuotare ed è annegato** he couldn't swim and drowned ♦ VT to drown; **annegare i dispiaceri nel vino** to drown one's sorrows; **annegarsi** VR to drown o.s.

annerire [anne'rire] /55/ VT to blacken VI (*aus essere*), **annerirsi** VIP to go o become black

annessione [annes'sjone] SF (*Pol*) annexation

annesso, -a [an'nesso] PP *di* **annettere** ♦ AGG (*attaccato: gen*) attached; (: *Pol*) annexed ♦ SMPL: **fra annessi e connessi...** what with one thing and another ...; **...e tutti gli annessi e connessi** ... and so on and so forth; **mi occupo del nuovo progetto con tutti gli annessi e connessi** I'm working on the new project and everything relating to it

annettere [an'nettere] /63/ VT IRREG (*Pol*) to annexe (*Brit*), annex (*USA*); (*accludere*) to attach

annichilire [anniki'lire] /55/, **annichilare** [anniki'lare] VT to annihilate; (*fig*) to devastate

annidarsi [anni'darsi] /72/ VR (*uccello*) to nest; (*fig: persona*) to hide ♦ VIP (*paura, dubbio, invidia*) to take root

annientamento [annjenta'mento] SM annihilation, destruction

annientare [annjen'tare] /72/ VT to annihilate, destroy

anniversario, -ri [anniver'sarjo] SM anniversary; **è il loro anniversario di matrimonio** it's their wedding anniversary

anno ['anno] SM **1** year; **l'anno scorso** last year; **l'anno prossimo** next year; **anno per o dopo anno** year after year; **è aperto tutto l'anno** it's open all year round; **uno studente del primo anno** a first year student; **gli anni venti** the twenties; **gli anni novanta** the nineties; **un anno di affitto** a year's rent; **sono anni che non ti vedo** it's been ages since I last saw you, I haven't seen you for ages o years; **correva l'anno di grazia ...** it was in the year of grace ...; **Buon Anno!** Happy New Year!; **gli anni di piombo** *the Seventies in Italy, a time of terrorist outrages* **2** (*età*): **quanti anni hai? — ho 40 anni** how old are you? — I'm 40; **quando compi gli anni?** when is your birthday?; **una ragazza di vent'anni** a girl of twenty; **un bambino di 6 anni** a 6-year-old child; **porta bene gli anni** he doesn't look his age; **porta male gli anni** he looks older than he is ♦ **anno accademico** academic year; **anno bisestile** leap year; **anno commerciale** business year; **anno finanziario** financial year; **anno giudiziario** legal

year; **anno luce** (*Astron*) light year; **anno sabbatico** sabbatical year; **anno santo** (*Rel*) holy year

annodare [anno'dare] /72/ VT (*lacci*) to tie; (*cravatta*) to knot, tie; (*fune, corda*) to knot; (*due corde*) to knot o tie together; **annodarsi la cravatta** to tie o knot one's tie; **annodarsi** VIP to become o get knotted o tangled

annoiare [anno'jare] /19/ VT (*tediare*) to bore; **scusa, ti sto annoiando?** sorry, am I boring you?; **annoiarsi** VIP to get bored; **a stare a casa mi annoio** I get bored staying at home; **annoiarsi di qc/di fare qc** to be bored with sth/with doing sth
❏ **annoiare** non si traduce mai con la parola inglese *annoy*

annoso, -a [an'noso] AGG (*questione, problema*) age-old

annotare [anno'tare] /72/ VT (*scrivere*) to note, note down (*Brit*), take down **2** (*commentare: testo*) to annotate

annotazione [annotat'tsjone] SF **1** (*appunto*) note **2** (*di testo*) annotation

annoverare [annove'rare] /72/ VT to number

annuale [annu'ale] AGG (*gen*) annual, yearly; (*pianta*) annual

annualmente [annual'mente] AVV annually, yearly

annuario, -ri [annu'arjo] SM (*gen*) annual publication; (*di scuola ecc*) yearbook

annuire [annu'ire] /55/ VI (*aus avere*) (*assentire: anche: annuire col capo*) to nod

annullamento [annulla'mento] SM (*vedi vb*) cancellation; annulment; quashing; destruction

annullare [annul'lare] /72/ VT **1** (*francobollo, ordine, contratto*) to cancel; (*Dir: testamento, matrimonio*) to annul; (: *sentenza*) to quash; (: *partita, risultati*) to declare void; **hanno annullato il viaggio** they cancelled the trip **2** (*distruggere*) to destroy; **annullarsi** VR: **annullarsi (a vicenda)** to cancel each other out

annunciare [annun't∫are] /14/ VT (*gen*) to announce; (*predire*) to foretell; (*essere segno di*) to be a sign of; **annunciare una brutta notizia a qn** to break bad news to sb; **il barometro annuncia pioggia** the barometer is indicating rain; **entrò senza farsi annunciare** he came in unannounced

annunciatore, -trice [annunt∫a'tore] SM, SF (*Radio, TV*) announcer

Annunciazione [annunt∫at'tsjone] SF (*Rel*): **l'Annunciazione** the Annunciation

annuncio, -ci [an'nunt∫o] SM (*gen*) announcement; (*presagio*) sign; **hanno dato l'annuncio ieri** they made the announcement yesterday; **mettere un annuncio sul giornale** to place o put an advert(isement) in the newspaper; **annunci economici** classified ad(vertisement)s, small ads; **annunci mortuari** (*colonna*) death announcements; **annuncio pubblicitario** advertisement

annuo, -a ['annuo] AGG annual, yearly

annusare [annu'sare] /72/ VT (*anche fig*) to smell; (*cane*) to smell, sniff; **il cane mi ha annusato le mani** the dog sniffed my hands; **annusare tabacco** to take snuff

annuvolamento [annuvola'mento] SM clouding (over)

annuvolare [annuvo'lare] /72/ VT to cloud; **annuvolarsi** VIP to become cloudy, cloud over

ano ['ano] SM anus

anodo ['anodo] SM anode

anomalia [anoma'lia] SF (*gen*) anomaly; (*Med*) abnormality; **anomalia di funzionamento** (*Tecn*) technical fault

anomalo, -a [a'nomalo] AGG anomalous

anonimato [anoni'mato] SM anonymity; **conservare l'anonimato** to remain anonymous

anonimo, -a [a'nonimo] AGG anonymous; **una telefonata anonima** an anonymous phone call; **un tipo anonimo** (*banale*) a colourless (*Brit*) o colorless (*USA*) character ♦ SM, SF (*persona*) unknown person; (*pittore, autore ecc*) anonymous painter (*o writer ecc*)

anoressia [anores'sia] SF anorexia; **anoressia nervosa** anorexia nervosa

anoressico, -a, -ci, -che [ano'ressiko] AGG anorexic

anormale [anor'male] AGG abnormal ♦ SM, SF person who is abnormal

anormalità [anormali'ta] SF INV abnormality

ANSA ['ansa] SIGLA F (= *Agenzia Nazionale Stampa Associata*) *national press agency*

ansa ['ansa] SF (*curva*) loop, bend; (*di vaso*) handle; (*Anat*) loop

ansante [an'sante] AGG out of breath, panting

ansia ['ansja] SF anxiety; **stare** *o* **essere in ansia (per qn/qc)** to be anxious (about sb/sth); **con ansia** anxiously

ansietà [ansje'ta] SF INV anxiety

ansimare [ansi'mare] /72/ VI (*aus* **avere**) to pant, gasp for breath; (*respirare pesantemente*) to breathe heavily

ansioso, -a [an'sjoso] AGG (*agitato*) anxious; (*desideroso*): **ansioso di fare qc** anxious *o* eager to do sth

anta ['anta] SF (*di armadio*) door; (*di finestra*) shutter

antagonismo [antago'nizmo] SM antagonism

antagonista, -i, -e [antago'nista] SM, SF antagonist ♦ AGG antagonistic

antartico, -a, -ci, -che [an'tartiko] AGG Antarctic ♦ SM: **l'Antartico** the Antarctic

Antartide [an'tartide] SF Antarctica

antebellico, -a, -ci, -che [ante'belliko] AGG prewar *attr*

antecedente [antetʃe'dɛnte] AGG previous, preceding ♦ SM **1** (*Gramm, Filosofia*) antecedent **2** (*antefatto*): **gli antecedenti** previous history *sg*

antefatto [ante'fatto] SM prior event; **gli antefatti dell'incidente** the events leading up to the accident, what happened before the accident

anteguerra [ante'gwɛrra] SM prewar period; **dell'anteguerra** prewar ♦ AGG INV prewar; (*scherz*) ancient

antenato [ante'nato] SM ancestor, forefather

antenna [an'tenna] SF (*Zool*) antenna, feeler; (*Radio, TV*) aerial; **bisogna regolare l'antenna** the aerial needs adjusting; **(d)rizzare le antenne** (*fig*) to prick up one's ears; **antenna parabolica** (satellite) dish

anteporre [ante'porre] /77/ VT IRREG: **anteporre qc a qc** to place *o* put sth before sth

anteposto, -a [ante'posto] PP *di* anteporre

anteprima [ante'prima] SF (*Teatro, Cine*) preview; **presentare qc in anteprima** to preview sth; **comunichiamo in anteprima la notizia di...** we are bringing you advance news of ...; **anteprima di stampa** (*Inform*) print preview

anteriore [ante'rjore] AGG **1** (*tempo*) previous, preceding **2** (*spazio*) front *attr*; **lo sportello anteriore** the front door; **zampe anteriori** forelegs

antesignano [antesiɲ'ɲano] SM forerunner; (*Storia*) standard-bearer

antiaderente [antiade'rɛnte] AGG non-stick

antiaereo, -a [antia'ɛreo] AGG anti-aircraft *attr*

antiallergico, -a, -ci, -che [antial'lɛrdʒiko] AGG, SM hypoallergenic

antiatomico, -a, -ci, -che [antia'tɔmiko] AGG anti-nuclear; **rifugio antiatomico** fallout shelter

antibiotico, -a, -ci, -che [antibi'ɔtiko] AGG, SM antibiotic

anticaglia [anti'kaʎʎa] SF piece of old junk; **anticaglie** SFPL old junk; **negozio di anticaglie** junk shop

anticalcare [antikal'kare] AGG (*prodotto, detersivo*) anti-limescale ♦ SM limescale remover

anticamera [anti'kamera] SF (*ingresso*) hall; (*sala d'attesa*) antechamber, anteroom; **fare anticamera** to be kept waiting; **non mi passerebbe neanche per l'anticamera del cervello** it wouldn't even cross my mind

anticarie [anti'karje] AGG INV which fights tooth decay

antichità [antiki'ta] SF INV **1** antiquity; **nell'antichità** in ancient times **2** antichità SFPL antiques; **negozio di antichità** antique shop

anticiclone [antitʃi'klone] SM anticyclone

anticipare [antitʃi'pare] /72/ VT **1** (*spostare prima nel tempo*) to bring forward; **anticipare un incontro di 3 giorni** to bring a meeting forward 3 days; **anticipare i tempi** (*accelerare*) to speed things up; (*precorrere*) to be ahead of one's time **2** (*precedere: reazione, risposta*) to anticipate; **anticipare qn nel fare qc** to do sth before sb; **mi ha anticipato** he did it before me; **anticipare la palla/l'avversario** (*Sport*) to keep ahead of the ball/one's opponent **3** (*sorpresa, notizia*) to reveal **4** (*pagare*) to pay in advance; (*prestare*) to lend; **puoi anticiparmi un po' di soldi?** can you lend me some money? ♦ VI (*aus* avere) to come early, arrive early; **anticipare di un'ora** to come *o* arrive an hour earlier

anticipato, -a [antitʃi'pato] AGG (*prima del previsto*) early; **pagamento anticipato** payment in advance; **pensionamento anticipato** early retirement

anticipazione [antitʃipat'tsjone] SF **1** (*spostamento*) bringing forward **2** (*di notizia*) anticipation; (*pronostico*) forecast; **vi diamo delle anticipazioni sui risultati** we have advance news for you on the results; **è difficile fare delle anticipazioni sull'esito della partita** it's difficult to predict the result of the match **3** (*di denaro*) advance; **anticipazione bancaria** bank loan

anticipo [an'titʃipo] SM (*gen, Fin*) advance; **con due giorni di anticipo** two days in advance; **con mezz'ora di anticipo** half an hour early; **in anticipo** early; **sei in anticipo** you're early; **arrivare in anticipo** to arrive early *o* ahead of time; **avvertire qn in anticipo** to warn sb in advance *o* beforehand; **pagare in anticipo** to pay in advance; **gli ho dato un anticipo sullo stipendio** I gave him an advance on his salary; **con un sensibile anticipo** well in advance

anticlan [anti'klan] AGG INV (*magistrato, processo*) anti-mafia

antico, -a, -chi, -che [an'tiko] AGG **1** (*vecchio: mobile, quadro*) antique; (: *manoscritto*) ancient; **abitano in un'antica villa di campagna** they live in an old house in the country; **un mobile antico** an antique; **all'antica** old-fashioned; **un uomo all'antica** an old-fashioned man **2** (*dell'antichità*) ancient; **gli antichi Romani** the ancient Romans; **nei tempi antichi** in ancient times ♦ **gli antichi** SMPL the ancients

anticoncezionale [antikontʃettsjo'nale] AGG, SM contraceptive

anticonformista, -i, -e [antikonfor'mista] AGG unconventional ♦ SM, SF unconventional person

anticongelante [antikondʒe'lante] AGG, SM antifreeze

anticongiunturale [antikondʒuntu'rale] AGG (*Econ*): **misure anticongiunturali** measures to remedy the economic situation; **soluzione anticongiunturale** solution to the (unfavourable) economic situation

anticorpo [anti'kɔrpo] SM antibody

anticostituzionale [antikostituttsjo'nale] AGG unconstitutional

antidepressivo, -a [antidepres'sivo] AGG, SM antidepressant

antidiluviano, -a [antidilu'vjano] AGG (*fig: antiquato*) ancient, antediluvian

antidolorifico, -ci [antidolo'rifiko] SM painkiller

antidoping [anti'dɔpin(g)] AGG INV drug testing; **legge antidoping** drug testing regulations; **test antidoping** drug *o* drugs (*Brit*) test ♦ SM INV drug *o* drugs (*Brit*) test; **risultare positivo all'antidoping** to fail a drug test

antidoto [an'tidoto] SM antidote

antidroga [anti'drɔga] AGG INV anti-drugs *attr*

antiestetico, -a, -ci, -che [anties'tɛtiko] AGG unsightly

antifona [an'tifona] SF (*Mus, Rel*) antiphon; **capire l'antifona** (*fig*) to take the hint; **ha capito l'antifona e se n'è andato** he took the hint and left

antiforfora [anti'forfora] AGG INV anti-dandruff

antifurto [anti'furto] AGG INV, SM INV alarm

antigelo [anti'dʒelo] AGG INV antifreeze *attr* ♦ SM INV (*per motore*) antifreeze; (*per cristalli*) de-icer

antigene [an'tidʒene] SM (*Bio*) antigen

antigienico, -a, -ci, -che [anti'dʒeniko] AGG unhygienic

antiglobalizzazione [antiglobaliddzat'tsjone] AGG INV (*movimento*) anti-globalization *attr*

Antille [an'tille] SFPL: **le Antille** the Antilles

antilope [an'tilope] SF antelope

antimafia [anti'mafja] AGG INV anti-Mafia *attr*

antincendio [antin'tʃendjo] AGG INV fire *attr*; **scala antincendio** fire escape

antinebbia [anti'nebbja] SM INV (*Aut: anche: faro antinebbia*) fog light

antinevralgico, -a, -ci, -che [antine'vraldʒiko] AGG painkilling ♦ SM painkiller

antinfiammatorio, -a [antinfjamma'tɔrjo] AGG, SM anti-inflammatory

antiorario, -ria, -ri, -rie [antio'rarjo] AGG anticlockwise (*Brit*), counterclockwise (*USA*); **in senso antiorario** in an anticlockwise *o* counterclockwise direction

antipasto [anti'pasto] SM hors d'oeuvre, starter

antipatia [antipa'tia] SF antipathy, dislike; **avere antipatia per** not to like; **ho una certa antipatia per i viaggi in pullman** I don't really like travelling by coach; **prendere in antipatia** to take a dislike to; **l'ha preso subito in antipatia** she took an instant dislike to him

antipatico, -a, -ci, -che [anti'patiko] AGG unpleasant, disagreeable; **un tipo antipatico** an unpleasant person ♦ SM, SF unpleasant person; (*rompiscatole*) nuisance

antiplacca [anti'plakka] AGG INV (*dentifricio*) anti-plaque

antipodi [an'tipodi] SMPL: **gli antipodi** the antipodes; **essere agli antipodi** (*fig*) to be poles apart

antiproiettile [antipro'jettile] AGG INV bulletproof

antiquariato [antikwa'rjato] SM (*cose antiche*) antiques *pl*; (*Comm*) antique trade; **negozio di antiquariato** antique shop; **un pezzo d'antiquariato** an antique

antiquario, -ri [anti'kwarjo] SM antique dealer; **fa l'antiquario** he's an antique dealer; **negozio di antiquario** antique shop

antiquato, -a [anti'kwato] AGG antiquated, old-fashioned

antiriciclaggio [antirit∫i'kladdʒo] AGG INV (*attività, legge*) anti-laundering

antiriflesso [antiri'flesso] AGG INV (*schermo, lenti*) non-glare *attr*

antiruggine [anti'ruddʒine] AGG INV anti-rust *attr* ♦ SM INV rust preventer

antirughe [anti'ruge] AGG INV (*crema, prodotto*) anti-wrinkle ♦ SM INV anti-wrinkle cream

antisemita, -i, -e [antise'mita] AGG anti-semitic ♦ SM, SF anti-semite

antisemitismo [antisemi'tizmo] SM anti-semitism

antisettico, -a, -ci, -che [anti'settiko] AGG, SM antiseptic

antistaminico, -a, -ci, -che [antista'miniko] AGG, SM antihistamine

antistante [antis'tante] AGG opposite

antitartaro [anti'tartaro] AGG INV anti-tartar

antiterrorismo [antiterro'rizmo] SM antiterrorism, anti-terrorist measures *pl* ♦ SM AGG INV antiterrorist *attr*

antitesi [an'titezi] SF INV antithesis

antitraspirante [antitraspi'rante] AGG (*deodorante*) antiperspirant

antivipera [anti'vipera] AGG INV: **siero antivipera** remedy for snake bites

antivirale AGG antiviral

antivirus [anti'virus] SM INV (*Inform*) antivirus software *no pl*

antologia, -gie [antolo'dʒia] SF anthology

antonomasia [antono'mazja] SF antonomasia; **per antonomasia** par excellence

antracite [antra't∫ite] SF anthracite

antro ['antro] SM cave, cavern

antropofago, -a, -gi, -ghe [antro'pɔfago] AGG cannibal *attr* ♦ SM cannibal

antropologia [antropolo'dʒia] SF anthropology; **antropologia criminale** criminology

antropologico, -a, -ci, -che [antropo'lɔdʒiko] AGG anthropological

antropologo, -a, -gi, -ghe [antro'pɔlogo] SM, SF anthropologist

anulare [anu'lare] AGG ring *attr*; **raccordo anulare** (*Aut*) ring road ♦ SM (*Anat*) ring finger

Anversa [an'versa] SF Antwerp

anzi ['antsi] AVV 1 (*avversativo*) on the contrary; **non mi dispiace, anzi sono contento** I don't mind, in fact I'm glad 2 (*rafforzativo*) or rather, or better still

anzianità [antsjani'ta] SF INV (*età avanzata*) old age; (*Amm*) seniority; **anzianità di servizio** length of service

anziano, -a [an'tsjano] AGG (*vecchio*) elderly, old; (*socio*) senior; **è tuo nonno quel signore anziano?** is that old gentleman your grandfather? ♦ SM, SF senior citizen (*euf*), old person; (*di associazione*) senior member; **un anziano** an old man; **un'anziana** an old woman; **gli anziani** the elderly
  ❑ **anziano** non si traduce mai con la parola inglese *ancient*

anziché [antsi'ke] CONG rather than; **preferisco telefonare anziché scrivere** I prefer to phone rather than write; **ho**

comprato quello giallo anziché quello rosso I bought the yellow one rather than the red one; **quest'anno andiamo al mare anziché in montagna** this year we're going to the seaside instead of to the mountains

anzitempo [antsi'tempo] AVV (*in anticipo*) early; **morire anzitempo** to die before one's time

anzitutto [antsi'tutto] AVV first of all

AO SIGLA = Aosta

aorta [a'ɔrta] SF aorta

aostano, -a [aos'tano] AGG of *o* from Aosta ♦ SM, SF inhabitant *o* native of Aosta

AP SIGLA = Ascoli Piceno

apartitico, -a, -ci, -che [apar'titiko] AGG (*Pol*) non-party *attr*

apatia [apa'tia] SF apathy

apatico, -a, -ci, -che [a'patiko] AGG apathetic

a.p.c. ABBR (= *a pronta cassa*) *vedi* **pronto**

ape ['ape] SF bee; **ape regina** queen bee
  ❑ **ape** non si traduce mai con la parola inglese *ape*

aperitivo [aperi'tivo] SM aperitif; **prendiamo un aperitivo?** shall we have an aperitif?

apertamente [aperta'mente] AVV openly; **ne abbiamo parlato apertamente** we talked about it frankly

aperto, -a [a'pɛrto] PP *di* **aprire** ♦ AGG (*gen, o fig*) open; (*rubinetto*) on, running; (*gas*) on; **hai lasciato la porta aperta** you've left the door open; **lasciare la macchina aperta** to leave the car unlocked; **di mentalità aperta** open-minded; **i miei sono molto aperti** my parents are very open-minded; **a cuore aperto** (*intervento*) open heart *attr*; (*fig*) frankly, sincerely; **a bocca aperta** open-mouthed; **rimanere a bocca aperta** (*fig*) to be taken aback; **sognare ad occhi aperti** to daydream; **all'aria aperta** in the open air ♦ SM: **all'aperto** outdoors; (*cinema, piscina*) open-air *attr*; (*giochi, vacanze*) outdoor *attr*; **abbiamo dormito all'aperto** we slept outdoors

apertura [aper'tura] SF 1 (*gen, Carte*) opening; (*Pol*) opening up; (*Fot*) aperture; **orario di apertura** opening times; **in apertura di** at the beginning of; **movimento di apertura** (*Tennis*) backswing; **apertura di credito** (*Comm*) granting of credit 2 (*ampiezza*) width, spread; **apertura alare** wing span; **apertura mentale** open-mindedness

apice ['apit∫e] SM peak, summit; (*fig*) height, peak; **essere all'apice del successo** to be at the height *o* peak of one's success

apicoltore, -trice [apikol'tore] SM, SF beekeeper

apicoltura [apikol'tura] SF beekeeping

apnea [ap'nea] SF: **immergersi in apnea** to dive without breathing apparatus

apocalisse [apoka'lisse] SF (*Rel*): **l'Apocalisse** (the book of) Revelation, the Apocalypse; (*fig*) apocalypse

apocalittico ...

apogeo [apo'dʒɛo] SM (*Astron*) apogee; (*fig: culmine*) zenith, apogee

apolide [a'pɔlide](*Pol*) AGG stateless ♦ SM, SF stateless person

apolitico, -a, -ci, -che [apo'litiko] AGG (*neutrale*) non-political; (*indifferente*) apolitical

apologia, -gie [apolo'dʒia] SF (*frm*) apologia; **fare l'apologia di** to extol the virtues of; **accusare qn di apologia di reato** (*Dir*) to accuse sb of attempting to defend criminal acts

apoplessia [apoples'sia] SF (*Med*) apoplexy

apoplettico, -a, -ci, -che [apo'plettiko] AGG apoplectic; **colpo apoplettico** apoplectic fit

apostolo [a'pɔstolo] SM apostle

apostrofare¹ [apostro'fare] /72/ VT (*parola*) to write with an apostrophe

apostrofare² [apostro'fare] /72/ VT (*persona*) to address indignantly

apostrofo [a'pɔstrofo] SM (*segno*) apostrophe

app. ABBR (= *appendice*) app.

appagamento [appaga'mento] SM (*vedi vb*) satisfaction; fulfilment

appagare [appa'gare] /80/ VT (*gen*) to satisfy; (*desiderio*) to fulfil; (*fame*) to satisfy; (*sete*) to quench; **appagarsi** VR: **appagarsi di** to be satisfied with

appagato, -a [appa'gato] AGG satisfied

appaiare [appa'jare] /19/ VT (*oggetti*) to pair; (*animali*) to match, couple

appaio *ecc* [ap'pajo] VB *vedi* **apparire**

appallottolare [appallotto'lare] /72/ VT (*carta, foglio*) to screw into a ball; **appallottolarsi** VR (*gatto*) to roll up into a ball

appaltatore, -trice [appalta'tore] SM contractor ♦ AGG contracting

appalto [ap'palto] SM contract; **dare in appalto** to put out to contract; **prendere in appalto** to take on a contract for; **gara di appalto** invitation to tender

appannaggio, -gi [appan'naddʒo] SM (*Pol: compenso*) annuity; (*fig*) prerogative

appannare [appan'nare] /72/ VT (*vetro*) to steam up, mist up; (*metallo*) to tarnish; (*vista*) to blur; **appannarsi** VIP (*vedi vt*) to steam up, mist up; to tarnish; (*vista: offuscarsi*) to blur; (: *affievolirsi*) to grow dim

apparato [appa'rato] SM 1 (*impianto*) equipment, machinery; **apparato burocratico** bureaucratic machinery; **apparato scenico** (*Teatro*) set 2 (*Anat, Bio*) apparatus; **apparato circolatorio** circulatory system 3 (*sfoggio*) display, pomp

apparecchiatura [apparek'kjare] /19/ VT: **apparecchiare (la tavola)** to set o lay the table; **ti aiuto ad apparecchiare?** shall I help you to set the table?

apparecchiatura [apparekkja'tura] SF (*Tecn: impianto*) equipment *no pl*; (: *macchina*) machine, device

apparecchio, -chi [appa'rekkjo] SM 1 (*gen*) instrument, device, piece of equipment; **un complicato apparecchio elettronico** a complex electronic device; **apparecchio acustico** hearing aid; **apparecchio telefonico** telephone 2 (*per denti*) brace; **porta l'apparecchio** he wears a brace 3 (*Radio, TV*) set 4 (*Aer*) aircraft *inv*

apparente [appa'rente] AGG apparent

apparentemente [apparente'mente] AVV apparently

apparenza [appa'rentsa] SF 1 (*aspetto*) appearance; **l'apparenza inganna** appearances can be deceptive; **in** o **all'apparenza** to all appearances, seemingly 2 **apparenze** SFPL (*convenienze sociali*) appearances; **badare alle apparenze** to care about appearances; **salvare le apparenze** to keep up appearances; **giudicare dalle apparenze** to judge by appearances

apparire [appa'rire] /7/ VI IRREG (*aus* essere) 1 (*mostrarsi*) to appear; **apparire in sogno** to appear in a dream; **l'uomo gli apparve davanti all'improvviso** the man suddenly appeared in front of o before him 2 (*essere evidente*): **apparire (chiaro)** to seem clear; **dalle indagini è apparso chiaro il suo coinvolgimento** the enquiries clearly demonstrate his involvement 3 (*sembrare*) to seem, appear; **appare che...** it appears o turns out that ...; **apparve sorpreso di vedermi** he seemed surprised to see me

appariscente [apparif'ʃente] AGG (*vestito*) showy; (*colore*) gaudy, garish; (*bellezza*) striking

apparizione [apparit'tsjone] SF (*comparsa*) appearance; (*fantasma*) apparition

apparso, -a [ap'parso] PP *di* **apparire**

appartamento [apparta'mento] SM flat (*Brit*), apartment (*USA*); **un appartamento ammobiliato** a furnished flat

appartarsi [appar'tarsi] /72/ VR to withdraw, to stand aloof

appartato, -a [appar'tato] AGG (*luogo*) secluded

appartenenza [apparte'nentsa] SF: **appartenenza (a)** (*gen*) belonging (to); (*a un partito, club*) membership (of)

appartenere [apparte'nere] /121/ VI IRREG (*aus* avere o essere) **appartenere a** 1 (*chiesa, fede*) to belong to; (*club, partito*) to be a member of 2 (*essere di proprietà*) to belong to; **mi appartiene di diritto** it belongs to me by right; **questa collana apparteneva a mia nonna** this necklace belonged to my grandma; **a chi appartiene questo libro?** who does this book belong to?

apparvi *ecc* [ap'parvi] VB *vedi* **apparire**

appassionante [appassjo'nante] AGG thrilling, exciting

appassionare [appassjo'nare] /72/ VT to grip, fascinate; **il romanzo mi ha appassionato molto** the novel really gripped me; **appassionarsi** VIP: **appassionarsi a qc** to develop a passion for sth, get very interested in sth

appassionato, -a [appassjo'nato] AGG 1 (*entusiasta*): **essere appassionato di qc** to love sth; **è appassionato di musica jazz** he loves jazz 2 (*passionale*) passionate ♦ SM, SF enthusiast

appassire [appas'sire] /55/ VI (*aus* essere) (*pianta*) to wither; (*fig: bellezza, speranze*) to fade

appassito, -a, appassita AGG dead

appellare [appel'lare] /72/ VI (*aus* avere) (*Dir*): **appellare (contro)** to appeal (against); **appellarsi** VIP 1 **appellarsi a** (*rivolgersi*) to appeal to; **mi appello alla vostra generosità** I appeal to your generosity 2 (*Dir*): **appellarsi contro** to appeal against; **si è appellato contro la sentenza** he appealed against the sentence

appello [ap'pello] SM 1 (*chiamata per nome*) roll-call; **fare l'appello** (*Scol*) to call the register; (*Mil*) to call the roll 2 (*Univ: sessione d'esame*) exam session 3 (*Dir*) appeal; **corte d'appello** court of appeal 4 (*invocazione*) appeal; **fare appello a** (*anche fig*) to call upon, appeal to

appena [ap'pena] AVV (*a stento*) hardly, scarcely; (*solamente, da poco*) just; **ci si vede appena** you can hardly see; **se n'è appena andato** he's just left; **sono appena le 9** it's only just 9 o'clock; **l'indirizzo era appena leggibile** the address was only just legible; **sarà alto appena un metro e 80** he is certainly no more than 6 foot tall; **un po' di latte? — grazie, appena un goccio** milk? — yes please, just a drop; **appena in tempo** just in time ♦ CONG as soon as; **l'ho riconosciuto appena l'ho visto** I recognized him as soon as I saw him; **ha detto che sarebbe venuto appena possibile** he said he'd come as soon as possible; **(non) appena (furono) arrivati...** as soon as they had arrived ...; **appena...che** o **quando** no sooner ..than; **era appena tornato quando è dovuto ripartire** no sooner o scarcely had he returned than he had to leave again; **non appena ho finito, vado** I'll leave the moment I've finished

appendere [ap'pendere] VB IRREG /8/ VT: **appendere (a)** to hang (on o up); **dove posso appendere il cappotto?** where can I hang my coat?; **appendersi** VR: **appendersi a qc** to hang on to sth

appendiabiti [appendi'abiti] SM INV hook, peg; (*mobile*) hall stand (*Brit*), hall tree (*USA*)

appendice [appen'ditʃe] SF (*Anat: di libro*) appendix; **romanzo d'appendice** popular serial (*formerly appearing in newspapers*)

appendicite [appendi't ʃite] SF appendicitis; **ha un'appendicite acuta** he's got acute appendicitis

appendino [appen'dino] SM (*coat*) hook

Appennini [appen'nini] SMPL: **gli Appennini** the Apennines

appesantire [appesan'tire] /55/ VT (*anche fig*) to weigh down; (*atmosfera*) to make strained; **i soldati erano appesantiti dall'armatura** the soldiers were weighed down by the armour; **quella torta mi ha appesantito lo stomaco** that cake is sitting on my stomach; **appesantirsi** VIP (*gen*) to grow heavier; (*ingrassare*) to put on weight; (*fig: atmosfera, situazione*) to become strained

appeso, -a [ap'peso] PP *di* **appendere**

appetito [appe'tito] SM 1 (*gen*) appetite; **la camminata mi ha messo appetito** the walk has given me an appetite; **avere appetito** to have an appetite; **non ho appetito** I'm not hungry; **perdere l'appetito** to lose one's appetite; **buon appetito!** enjoy your meal! (*said by waiter*), bon appétit! (*said by fellow diner*); **stuzzicare l'appetito** (*anche fig*) to whet one's appetite 2 (*istinti*): **appetiti** SMPL instincts; **soddisfare/frenare i propri appetiti** satisfy/curb one's instincts o appetite

appetitoso, -a [appeti'toso] AGG (*cibo*) appetizing; (*fig*) attractive, desirable

appezzamento [appettsa'mento] SM (*anche:* **appezzamento di terreno**) plot, piece of ground

appianare [appja'nare] /72/ VT (*terreno*) to flatten, level; (*fig: contesa, lite*) to settle; (*difficoltà*) to iron out, smooth away; **appianarsi** VIP (*divergenze*) to be ironed out

appiattire [appjat'tire] /55/ VT to flatten; (*fig: rendere monotono*) to make dull, make boring; **appiattirsi** VR (*farsi piatto: persona, animale*) to flatten o.s.; **si appiatti al** o **contro il muro** he flattened himself against the wall; **appiattirsi al suolo** to lie flat on the ground; **appiattirsi** VIP (*diventare piatto: oggetto*) to become flatter; (*fig*) to become dull

appiccare [appik'kare] /20/ VT (*dare inizio*) to start; **appiccare il fuoco a qc** to set fire to sth, set sth on fire

appiccicare [appittʃi'kare] /20/ VT: **appiccicare (a** o **su)** to stick (on); **appiccicare un soprannome a qn** (*fig: appioppare*) to pin a nickname on sb; **questa colla non appiccica bene** this glue doesn't stick very well; **appicicarsi** VR: **appicicarsi (a)** to stick (to); (*fig: persona*) to cling (to)

appiccicaticcio, -cia, -ci, -ce [apittʃikaˈtittʃo] AGG sticky

appiedato, -a [appjeˈdato] AGG: **rimanere appiedato** to be left without means of transport

appieno [apˈpjɛno] AVV fully

appigliarsi [appiʎˈʎarsi] /27/ VR: **appigliarsi a** to grasp, seize (hold of), take hold of; (*fig: scusa, pretesto*) to cling to; **non appigliarti a quella scusa** don't try that as an excuse

appiglio, -gli [apˈpiʎʎo] SM (hand)hold; (*fig: pretesto*) pretext, excuse

appioppare [appjopˈpare] /72/ VT: **appioppare qc a qn** (*nomignolo*) to pin sth on sb; (*compito difficile*) to saddle sb with sth; **gli ha appioppato un pugno sul muso** he punched him in the face

appisolarsi [appizoˈlarsi] /72/ VIP to doze off; **mi ero appisolato un attimo** I dozed off for a moment

applaudire [applauˈdire] /45/ VI (*aus avere*) **applaudire (a)** to applaud, clap; (*fig*) to applaud; **applaudivano tutti** everybody was clapping ♦ VT (*anche fig*) to applaud

applauso [apˈplauzo] SM applause *no pl*; **hanno ricevuto molti applausi** they got a lot of applause; **un applauso** a round of applause

applicabile [appliˈkabile] AGG: **applicabile (a)** applicable (to)

applicare [appliˈkare] /20/ VT (*gen*) to apply; (*cucire*) to sew on; **applicare la mente a qc** to apply one's mind to sth; (*fare*) **applicare una legge/un regolamento** to enforce a law/a regulation; **applicare una tassa** to impose a tax; **applicarsi** VR: **applicarsi (a o in)** to apply o.s. (to)

applicato, -a [appliˈkato] AGG (*arte, scienze*) applied ♦ SM, SF (*Amm*) clerk

applicatore [applikaˈtore] SM applicator

applicazione [applikatˈtsjone] SF 1 (*gen*) application; (*di legge, norma*) enforcement 2 (*su stoffa*) appliqué 3 (*Inform: programma*) application

appoggiare [appodˈdʒare] /62/ VT 1 (*posare*): **appoggiare qc su qc** to put sth (down) on sth, lay sth (down) on sth; **puoi appoggiare il pacco sul tavolo** you can put the parcel on the table 2 (*mettere contro*): **appoggiare qc a qc** to lean o rest sth against sth; **appoggia la scala al muro** lean the ladder against the wall 3 (*sostenere: idea, candidato*) to support, back ♦ VI (*aus avere*) **appoggiare su** to rest on; **appoggiarsi** VR: **appoggiarsi a o su** (*reggersi*) to lean against; (*fig*) to rely on o upon; **si è dovuto appoggiare al muro per sostenersi** he had to lean against the wall for support

appoggio, -gi [apˈpoddʒo] SM (*gen, fig*) support; (*Alpinismo*) press hold; **ho bisogno di tutto il vostro appoggio** I need all your support; **appoggio morale** moral support; **ho un appoggio importante al ministero** I have an important contact in the ministry

appollaiarsi [appollaˈjarsi] /72/ VR (*anche fig*) to perch; **se ne stava appollaiato sullo sgabello** he was perched on the stool

appongo *ecc* [apˈpongo] VB *vedi* **apporre**

apporre [apˈporre] /77/ VT IRREG (*firma*) to append; (*sigillo, nome*) to affix

apportare [apporˈtare] /72/ VT (*novità, cambiamento*) to bring (about); **apportare (delle) modifiche a** to modify

apporto [apˈporto] SM (*gen, Fin*) contribution; **dare il proprio apporto a qc** to make one's contribution to sth

apposi *ecc* [apˈposi] VB *vedi* **apporre**

appositamente [appozitaˈmente] AVV (*apposta*) on purpose; (*specialmente*) specially

apposito, -a [apˈpozito] AGG (*adatto*) appropriate, proper; (*fatto appositamente*) specially made; **i rifiuti vanno gettati negli appositi cestini** rubbish should be put in the bins provided

apposta [apˈposta] AVV (*intenzionalmente*) on purpose, intentionally, deliberately; (*proprio*) specially; **scusa, non l'ho fatto apposta** I'm sorry, I didn't do it on purpose; **neanche a farlo apposta,...** by sheer coincidence, ...; **sono venuto apposta per (vedere) te** I came here specially for you/to see you

appostare [apposˈtare] /72/ VT (*Mil*) to post, station; **appostarsi** VR to lie in wait

apposto, -a [apˈposto] PP *di* **apporre**

apprendere [apˈprɛndere] /81/ VT IRREG (*imparare*) to learn; (*venire a sapere*) to learn, find out; **hai appreso la notizia?** have you heard the news?

❑ **apprendere** non si traduce mai con la parola inglese *apprehend*

apprendimento [apprendiˈmento] SM learning

apprendista, -i, -e [apprenˈdista] SM, SF apprentice

apprendistato [apprendisˈtato] SM apprenticeship; **fare l'apprendistato** to serve one's apprenticeship

apprensione [apprenˈsjone] SF apprehension; **essere in uno stato di apprensione** to be anxious; **non stare in apprensione** don't worry

apprensivo, -a [apprenˈsivo] AGG apprehensive, anxious

appreso, -a [apˈpreso] PP *di* **apprendere**

appresso [apˈpresso] AVV (*vicino*) nearby, close up; (*con sé*) with me (*o* you ecc); (*dietro*) behind me (*o* you ecc); **me lo porto sempre appresso** I always carry it with me; **stammi appresso** stay *o* keep close to me ♦ PREP: **appresso a** near, close to; **andare appresso a qn** to go after sb, follow sb ♦ AGG INV (*dopo*): **il giorno appresso** the next day, the day after

apprestare [appresˈtare] /72/ VT to prepare, get ready; **apprestarsi** VR: **apprestarsi a fare qc** to prepare *o* get ready to do sth

appretto [apˈpretto] SM starch

apprezzabile [apprɛtˈtsabile] AGG (*notevole*) noteworthy, significant; (*percepibile*) appreciable; **è un'opera apprezzabile da tutti** it is a work which everybody can enjoy

apprezzamento [apprɛttsaˈmento] SM 1 appreciation 2 (*commento*) comment; **fare apprezzamenti su** to make comments about, pass comment on

apprezzare [apprɛtˈtsare] /72/ VT to appreciate

approccio, -ci [apˈprɔttʃo] SM approach

approdare [approˈdare] /72/ VI (*aus avere o essere*) (*Naut*) to land; **approdare a** (*fig*) to arrive at; **non approderà a nulla** (*piano, progetto*) it won't come to anything; (*persona*) he won't achieve anything

approdo [apˈprɔdo] SM (*Naut: l'approdare*) landing; (*luogo*) landing place

approfittare [approfitˈtare] /72/ VI (*aus avere*) **approfittare di** (*persona, situazione ecc*) to take advantage of, make the most of; (*occasione*) **dovresti approfittare dell'occasione** you should make the most of the opportunity; **approfittiamo della bella giornata e andiamo al parco!** let's make the most of the weather and go to the park!; **approfittane!** make the most of it!; **approfittarsi di qn** to take advantage of sb

❑ **approfittare** non si traduce mai con la parola inglese *profit*

approfondire [approfonˈdire] /55/ VT (*fossa*) to deepen, make deeper; (*fig: conoscenza*) to deepen, increase; (*argomento*) to go into, study in depth; **approfondire un problema** to go into a problem in more depth; **vorrei approfondire la materia** I'd like to study the subject in depth; **approfondirsi** VIP (*gen, o fig*) to deepen

approntare [approŋˈtare] /72/ VT to prepare, get ready

appropriarsi [approˈprjarsi] /19/ VIP: **appropriarsi di qc** to appropriate sth; **si è appropriato del mio motorino** he took my moped; **appropriarsi indebitamente di** to embezzle

appropriato, -a [approˈprjato] AGG appropriate, suitable

appropriazione [approprjatˈtsjone] SF appropriation; **appropriazione indebita** (*Dir*) embezzlement, misappropriation

approssimare [approssiˈmare] /72/ VT (*cifra*): **approssimare per eccesso/per difetto** to round up/down; **approssimarsi** VR (*frm*) to approach, draw near

approssimativo, -a [approssimaˈtivo] AGG (*calcolo*) rough, approximate; (*numero*) approximate; **è solo un calcolo approssimativo** it's only a rough estimate; **è stato molto approssimativo nel darmi informazioni** the information he gave me was very vague

approssimazione [approssimatˈtsjone] SF approximation; **per approssimazione** approximately, roughly

approvare [appro'vare] /72/ VT 1 (*comportamento, decisione, azione*) to approve of; **non approvo ciò che hai fatto** I don't approve of what you've done 2 (*candidato, legge*) to pass; (*mozione*) to approve; **hanno approvato il progetto** they approved the project

approvazione [approvat'tsjone] SF (*vedi vb*) approval; passing

approvvigionamento [approvvidʒona'mento] SM 1 (*atto*) supplying 2 (*provviste*): **approvvigionamenti** SMPL supplies

approvvigionare [approvvidʒo'nare] /72/ VT: **approvvigionare (di)** to supply (with); **approvvigionarsi** VR (*fare provviste*): **approvvigionarsi (di)** to stock up (with)

appuntamento [appunta'mento] SM (*d'affari, dal medico*) appointment; (*amoroso*) date; **darsi appuntamento** to arrange to meet (one another); **ci siamo dati appuntamento alle otto davanti al cinema** we arranged to meet at eight in front of the cinema; **il medico mi ha dato un appuntamento per mercoledì** the doctor gave me an appointment for Wednesday; **venerdì ho un appuntamento dal dentista** I've got a dental appointment on Friday; **stasera ho appuntamento con il mio ragazzo** I've got a date with my boyfriend tonight; **appuntamento al buio** blind date

appuntare¹ [appun'tare] /72/ VT 1 (*fissare: con spillo: foglio ecc*) to pin (on); (: *due cose tra loro*) to pin (together); (: *piega dei pantaloni ecc*) to pin 2 (*puntare: dito*) to point; (: *sguardo*) to fix, rivet; **appuntarsi** VIP (*interesse, attenzione*): **appuntarsi su** to be focussed on

❏ **appuntare** non si traduce mai con la parola inglese **appoint**

appuntare² [appun'tare] /72/ VT (*annotare*) to note down, take note of

appuntato [appun'tato] SM (*Polizia*) corporal

appuntino [appun'tino] AVV (*anche:* **a puntino**) perfectly; **cotto appuntino** cooked to perfection

appuntire [appun'tire] /55/ VT to sharpen

appunto¹ [ap'punto] SM 1 (*nota*) note; **prendere appunti** to take notes; **non avevo preso appunti** I hadn't taken notes 2 (*rimprovero*) reproach; **fare/muovere un appunto a qn** to find fault with sb

appunto² [ap'punto] AVV (*precisamente, proprio*) exactly, just; **dicevo appunto ieri** I was just saying yesterday; **si parlava (per l')appunto di questo** we were talking about that very thing; **stavo appunto per chiederti di venire** I was (actually) just going to ask you to come; **per l'appunto!, appunto!** exactly!

appurare [appu'rare] /72/ VT (*verificare*) to check, verify; (*verità*) to ascertain; **appurarsi** VR: **appurarsi di qc/che** to make sure of sth/that, check sth/that

apr. ABBR (= *aprile*) Apr.

apribottiglie [apribot'tiʎʎe] SM INV bottle-opener

aprile [a'prile] SM April; **pesce d'aprile!** April Fool!; **aprile dolce dormire** (*Proverbio*) April slumbers; *vedi* **luglio**

aprire [a'prire] VB IRREG /9/ VT 1 (*gen*) to open; (*porta chiusa a chiave*) to unlock; (*camicia*) to undo, unfasten; (*ali, anche fig*) to spread; **va' ad aprire (la porta)** go and open o answer the door; **posso aprire la finestra?** can I open the window?; **dai, non apri i regali?** come on, aren't you going to open your presents?; **non ha aperto bocca** he didn't say a word, he didn't open his mouth; **tutto ciò mi ha aperto gli occhi** all that was an eye-opener to me; **apri bene gli orecchi** listen carefully; **aprirsi una varco tra la folla** to cut one's way through the crowd 2 (*acqua, rubinetto*) to turn on; (*gas*) to turn on, switch on; **non riesco ad aprire il rubinetto** I can't turn the tap on 3 (*istituire: negozio, club, conto*) to open; (*inchiesta*) to open, set up; (*strada*) to build; **aprire bottega** to open shop 4 (*dare inizio: anno, stagione*) to start, open; (*lista*) to head; (*processione*) to lead; **aprire (il gioco)** (*Carte*) to open play; **aprire il fuoco** to open fire; **aprire le ostilità** (*Mil*) to begin hostilities; **aprire una sessione** (*Inform*) to log on 5 (*Dir: testamento*) to read ♦ VI (*aus* **avere**) to open; **a che ora apre la banca?** what time does the bank open?; **la banca apre alle otto** the bank opens at eight; **aprirsi** VIP (*gen*) to open; (*fiore*) to open (up); **la finestra si apre sulla piazza** the window looks onto the square; **la porta dev'essersi aperta** the door must have come open; **quest'abito si apre sul davanti** this dress opens at the front; **la vita che le**

si apre davanti the life which is opening in front of o before her; **mi si aprì davanti la vista del mare** the sea appeared before her; **davanti a quella scena le si è aperto il cuore** (*commuoversi*) she was moved by the scene before her; (*rallegrarsi*) the scene gladdened her heart; **apriti cielo!** heaven forbid!; (*cominciare*) to start, open; **aprirsi** VR (*confidarsi*): **aprirsi (con qn)** to open one's heart (to sb), confide (in sb)

apriscatole [apris'katole] SM INV tin (*Brit*) o can opener

APT [api'ti] SIGLA F (= *Azienda di Promozione Turistica*) tourist board

AQ SIGLA = **L'Aquila**

aquagym [akkwa'dʒim] SF aquarobics

aquario, -ri [a'kwarjo] SM = **acquario**

aquila ['akwila] SF eagle; **sei un'aquila!** (*anche iro*) you're a genius!; **aquila reale** golden eagle

aquilino, -a [akwi'lino] AGG aquiline; **naso aquilino** aquiline nose

aquilone [akwi'lone] SM 1 (*giocattolo*) kite; **facciamo volare l'aquilone!** let's fly the kite! 2 (*vento*) north wind

AR SIGLA = **Arezzo**

A/R ABBR (= *andata e ritorno*) return (*Brit*), round trip (*USA*)

arabesco, -schi [ara'besko] SM arabesque

Arabia Saudita [a'rabja sau'dita] SF Saudi Arabia; **vengono dall'Arabia Saudita** they come from Saudi Arabia

arabico, -a, -ci, -che [a'rabiko] AGG Arabic; **il deserto arabico** the Arabian desert; **la penisola arabica** the Arabian peninsula

arabile [a'rabile] AGG arable

arabo, -a ['arabo] AGG (*popolo, paesi*) Arab; (*lingua, arte*) Arabic, Arab; **numeri arabi** Arabic numerals ♦ SM, SF (*persona*) Arab ♦ SM (*lingua*) Arabic; **parlano l'arabo** they speak Arabic; **questo per me è arabo** (*fig*) it's all Greek to me; **ma parlo arabo?** (*fig*) don't you understand English?

arachide [a'rakide] SF peanut, groundnut; **olio di semi di arachide** peanut oil

aragosta [ara'gosta] SF lobster ♦ AGG INV: **color aragosta** bright orange

araldica [a'raldika] SF heraldry

araldo [a'raldo] SM herald

aranceto [aran't∫eto] SM orange grove

arancia, -ce [a'rant∫a] SF orange; **arancia amara** Seville orange; **succo d'arancia** orange juice

aranciata [aran't∫ata] SF orangeade; **aranciata amara** bitter orange (drink)

arancio, -ci [a'rant∫o] SM orange tree; (*colore*) orange; **fiori di arancio** orange blossom *sg* ♦ AGG INV (*colore*) orange

arancione [aran't∫one] AGG INV, SM bright orange; **una maglietta arancione** an orange T-shirt ♦ SM, SF (*fam*): **gli arancioni** the Hare Krishna people

arare [a'rare] /72/ VT to plough (*Brit*), plow (*USA*) ♦ VI (*aus* **avere**); (*Naut: ancora*) to drag

aratore [ara'tore] SM ploughman (*Brit*), plowman (*USA*)

aratro [a'ratro] SM plough (*Brit*), plow (*USA*)

aratura [ara'tura] SF ploughing (*Brit*), plowing (*USA*)

arazzo [a'rattso] SM tapestry

arbitraggio, -gi [arbi'traddʒo] SM 1 (*Sport*) refereeing; (*Tennis, Cricket*) umpiring 2 (*Dir*) arbitration 3 (*Fin*) arbitrage

arbitrare [arbi'trare] /72/ VT (*Sport*) to referee; (*Tennis, Cricket*) to umpire; (*Dir*) to arbitrate

arbitrario, -ria, -rie [arbi'trarjo] AGG arbitrary

arbitrato [arbi'trato] SM (*Sport, Dir*) arbitration

arbitrio, -rii [ar'bitrjo] SM 1 (*capacità, potere*) will; (*atto*) arbitrary act; **libero arbitrio** free will; **prendersi l'arbitrio di fare qc** to take the liberty of doing sth 2 (*sopruso*): **commettere un arbitrio** to act unlawfully

arbitro ['arbitro] SM 1 (*Sport*) referee; (*Cricket, Tennis*) umpire 2 (*di contese*) arbitrator; (*fig*): **un arbitro di eleganza** an arbiter of fashion

arbusto [ar'busto] SM shrub

arca ['arka] SF ark; **l'Arca di Noè** Noah's Ark

arcaico, -a, -ci, -che [ar'kaiko] AGG archaic

arcaismo [arka'izmo] SM archaism

arcangelo [ar'kandʒelo] SM archangel

arcano, -a [ar'kano] AGG arcane ♦ SM mystery

arcata [ar'kata] SF (*Anat*) arch

archeologia [arkeolo'dʒia] SF arch(a)eology; **è laureata in archeologia** she's got a degree in archaeology

archeologico, -a, -ci, -che [arkeo'lɔdʒiko] AGG arch(a)eological

archeologo, -a, -gi, -ghe [arke'ɔlogo] SM, SF arch(a)eologist

archetipo [ar'ketipo] SM archetype

archetto [ar'ketto] SM (*Mus*) bow

architettare [arkitet'tare] /**72**/ VT (*ideare*) to devise; (*macchinare*) to plan, concoct

architetto [arki'tetto] SM architect; **sua madre fa l'architetto** his mother is an architect

architettonico, -a, -ci, -che [arkitet'tɔniko] AGG architectural

architettura [arkitet'tura] SF architecture; **studia architettura** he's studying architecture; **architettura del paesaggio** landscaping

archiviare [arki'vjare] /**19**/ VT (*documenti*) to file; (*Dir*) to dismiss; **archiviare un caso** to dismiss a case; **per questa volta archiviamo la faccenda** (*passiamoci sopra*) let's forget about it this time

archiviazione [arkivjat'tsjone] SF (*vedi vb*) filing; dismissal

archivio, -vi [ar'kivjo] SM (*insieme di documenti, luogo*) archives pl; (*mobile*) filing cabinet; (*Inform*) archive

archivista, -i, -e [arki'vista] SM, SF (*Amm*) archivist; (*in ufficio*) filing clerk

arciduca, -chi [artʃi'duka] SM archduke

arciere [ar'tʃere] SM archer

arcigno, -a [ar'tʃiɲɲo] AGG (*espressione*) frowning, grim; (*persona*) severe

arcipelago, -ghi [artʃi'pelago] SM archipelago

arcivescovo [artʃi'veskovo] SM archbishop

arco, -chi ['arko] SM **1** (*arma, Mus*) bow; **arco e frecce** bow and arrows; **strumento ad arco** string(ed) instrument; **archi** SMPL (*Mus*) strings **2** (*Geom*) arc; (*Archit: forma*) arch; **ad arco** arched; **arco costituzionale** *parties formulating Italy's post-war constitution*; **arco trionfale** triumphal arch **3** (*lasso di tempo*) space; **nell'arco di 3 settimane** within the space of 3 weeks; **la somma verrà pagata in un arco di 6 mesi** the sum will be paid over a period of 6 months

arcobaleno [arkoba'leno] SM rainbow

arcuato, -a [arku'ato] AGG (*gen*) curved, bent; (*sopracciglia*) arched; **dalle gambe arcuate** bow-legged

ardente [ar'dɛnte] AGG (*sole, fuoco*) blazing, burning; (*sguardo*) passionate; (*ammiratore*) ardent; (*passione*) ardent, burning; (*preghiera, desiderio*) fervent

ardere ['ardere] VB IRREG /**10**/ VT (*anche fig*) to burn; **legna da ardere** firewood ♦ VI (*aus essere*) to burn; **ardere di passione/dalla curiosità** to burn with passion/curiosity; **ardere d'amore** to burn with love

ardesia [ar'dezja] SF (*minerale*) slate; (*colore*) slate-grey

ardimento [ardi'mento] SM daring

ardire [ar'dire] /**55**/ VI *vb dif*: (*aus avere*) **ardire (di) fare qc** to dare (to) do sth ♦ SM (*audacia*) daring, boldness; (*impudenza*) impudence

ardito, -a [ar'dito] AGG (*coraggioso*) brave, daring; (*temerario*) daring; (*impertinente*) impertinent, bold; **impresa ardita** risky undertaking; **scollatura ardita** daring neckline

ardore [ar'dore] SM (*calore intenso*) (blazing) heat; (*fig: passione*) ardour; (: *fervore*) fervour, eagerness

arduo, -a [ar'duo] AGG (*impresa*) arduous, difficult; (*problema*) difficult; (*salita*) steep

area ['area] SF **1** (*gen, Geom*) area; **nell'area dei partiti di sinistra** among the parties of the left **2** (*Edil*) land, ground; **un'area di 25 chilometri quadrati** an area of 25 square kilometres; **area di attesa** (*Aer*) holding position; **area convocazione gruppi** (*Aer*) meeting point; **area edificabile** building land; **area di meta** (*Rugby*) in-goal area; **area della porta** (*Calcio*) goal area; **area di rigore** (*Calcio*) penalty area; **area di servizio** (*Aut*) service area

arena [a'rena] SF **1** (*gen, o fig*) arena; (*per corride*) bullring **2** (*letter: sabbia*) sand

arenaria [are'narja] SF sandstone

arenarsi [are'narsi] /**72**/ VIP (*Naut*) to run aground; (*fig:*

trattative) to come to a standstill; **la mia pratica si è arenata** my file is gathering dust

areoplano [areo'plano] SM = **aeroplano**

aretino, -a [are'tino] AGG of *o* from Arezzo ♦ SM, SF inhabitant *o* native of Arezzo

argano ['argano] SM winch; (*Naut*) capstan

argentato, -a [ardʒen'tato] AGG silver-plated; (*colore*) silver, silvery; (*capelli*) silver(-grey)

argenteo, -a [ar'dʒenteo] AGG silver, silvery

argenteria [ardʒente'ria] SF (*oggetti*) silverware, silver; (*fabbrica*) silverware factory

Argentina [ardʒen'tina] SF Argentina; **vengono dall'Argentina** they come from Argentina

argentino, -a, argentina [ardʒen'tino] AGG, SM, SF (*dell'Argentina*) Argentinian ♦ SF crewneck sweater

argento [ar'dʒento] SM **1** silver; **un anello d'argento** a silver ring; **piatto d'argento** silver dish; **capelli d'argento** silver(-grey) hair; **avere l'argento vivo addosso** (*fig*) to be fidgety; **argento dorato** silver gilt; **argento vivo** (*Chim*) quicksilver **2 argenti** SMPL (*argenteria*) silverware *sg*, silver *sg*

argilla [ar'dʒilla] SF clay; **un vaso d'argilla** a clay pot

argilloso, -a [ardʒil'loso] AGG (*contenente argilla*) clayey; (*simile ad argilla*) clay-like

arginare [ardʒi'nare] /**72**/ VT (*fiume, acque*) to embank; (*con diga*) to dyke up; (*fig: inflazione, corruzione*) to check; (: *spese*) to limit; **arginare la piena** to stem the flow of water; **arginare l'avanzata nemica** to check the enemy advance

argine [ar'dʒine] SM (*di fiume*) embankment, bank; **rompere gli argini** to break the banks; **porre un argine a** (*fig*) to check, hold back

argomentare [argomen'tare] /**72**/ VI (*aus avere*) **argomentare (su *o* di qc)** to argue (about sth)

argomento [argo'mento] SM **1** (*tema*) subject; **argomento di conversazione** topic of conversation; **qual è l'argomento del film/del libro?** what is the film/book about?; **cambiare argomento** to change the subject; **visto che siamo entrati in argomento...** since we're on the subject ...; **tornare sull'argomento** to bring the matter up again **2** (*argomentazione*) argument; **addurre/confutare un argomento** to put forward/refute an argument

arguire [argu'ire] /**55**/ VT to deduce, infer

arguto, -a [ar'guto] AGG (*battuta, conversazione*) witty; (*persona*) quick-witted; (*sguardo*) sharp, keen

arguzia [ar'guttsja] SF (*spirito*) wit; (*battuta*) witty remark

aria¹ ['arja] SF **1** (*gen*) air; **aria di mare/montagna** sea/mountain air; **all'aria** (*aperta*) in the open (air); **vivere all'aria aperta** to live an outdoor life; **mettere le lenzuola all'aria** to air the sheets; **cambiare l'aria in una stanza** to air a room; **è meglio cambiare aria** (*fig: fam: andarsene*) we'd better make ourselves scarce; **esco a prendere una boccata d'aria** I'm going out for a breath of (fresh) air; **manca l'aria** it's stuffy; **un po' d'aria fresca** a bit of fresh air; **che aria tira?** (*fig: atmosfera*) what's the atmosphere like?; **c'è aria di burrasca** (*anche fig*) there's a storm brewing; **vivere *o* campare d'aria** to live on thin air; **aria!** (*fam: vattene*) out of the way!, move!; **aria compressa** compressed air; **aria condizionata** air conditioning **2 andare all'aria** (*piano, progetto*) to come to nothing; **buttare *o* mandare all'aria** (*progetto, piano*) to ruin, upset; **buttare all'aria qc** (*mettere a soqquadro*) to turn sth upside-down; **discorsi a mezz'aria** vague remarks; **ha la testa per aria** he's got his head in the clouds; **lasciare tutto per aria** (*in disordine*) to leave everything in a mess; **sta sempre con la pancia all'aria** he's always lazing about

aria² ['arja] SF **1** (*espressione, aspetto*) look, air; (*modi*) manner, air; **avere l'aria allegra** to look happy; **avere l'aria stanca** to look tired; **hai l'aria così stanca oggi** you look so tired today; **quel ragazzo ha l'aria intelligente** that boy looks *o* seems intelligent; **ha l'aria della persona onesta** he looks (like) *o* seems (to be) an honest person; **ha l'aria di voler piovere** it looks like *o* as if it's going to rain; **ha un'aria di famiglia** there is a family likeness; **cos'è quell'aria funerale?** what are you looking so gloomy about? **2 arie** SFPL airs (and graces); **darsi delle arie** to put on airs; **si dà un sacco di arie** he thinks he's so important!

aria³ ['arja] SF (*Mus: di opera*) aria; (: *di canzonetta*) tune

aridità [aridi'ta] SF aridity, dryness; (*fig*) lack of feeling

arido, -a [ˈarido] AGG (*suolo, regione*) arid; (*clima*) dry; (*fig: persona*) insensitive; **cuore arido** heart of stone

arieggiare [arjedˈdʒare] /62/ VT **1** (*stanza, abiti*) to air **2** (*imitare*) to imitate

ariete [aˈrjɛte] SM **1** (*Zool*) ram **2** (*Astrol*): **Ariete** Aries; **essere dell'Ariete** to be Aries **3** (*Storia, Mil*) battering ram

aringa, -ghe [aˈringa] SF herring; **aringa affumicata** smoked herring, kipper; **aringa marinata** pickled herring

arioso, -a [aˈrjoso] AGG (*ambiente, stanza*) airy; (*Mus*) ariose

arista [ˈarista] SF (*Culin*) chine of pork for roasting

aristocratico, -a, -ci, -che [aristoˈkratiko] AGG (*gen, o fig*) aristocratic ♦ SM, SF aristocrat

aristocrazia [aristokratˈtsia] SF aristocracy

aritmetica [aritˈmetika] SF arithmetic

aritmetico, -a, -ci, -che [aritˈmetiko] AGG arithmetical

arlecchino [arlekˈkino] SM (*Teatro*) harlequin

arma, -i [ˈarma] SF **1** (*anche fig*) weapon; **un'arma pericolosa** a dangerous weapon; **battersi all'arma bianca** to fight with blades; **all'armi!** to arms!; **passare qn per le armi** to execute sb; **arma a doppio taglio** (*fig*) double-edged weapon; **combattere ad armi pari** (*anche fig*) to fight on equal terms; **deporre le armi** (*anche fig*) to lay down one's arms; **essere alle prime armi** (*fig*) to be a novice, have just started; **come batterista sono ancora alle prime armi** I've just started playing the drums; **prendere armi e bagagli e partire** (*fig*) to pack up and go; **traffico d'armi** arms trafficking; **arma da fuoco** firearm; **armi atomiche** atomic weapons; **armi biologiche** biological weapons; **armi convenzionali/non convenzionali** conventional/unconventional weapons; **armi di distruzione di massa** weapons of mass destruction **2** (*corpo dell'esercito*) arm, force; (*dei carabinieri*) force **3** (*servizio militare*): **essere sotto le armi** to be in the army *o* in the forces; **andare sotto le armi** to join the army *o* forces; **chiamare alle armi** to call up (*Brit*), draft (*USA*)

armadietto [armaˈdjetto] SM (*dei medicinali*) medicine cabinet *o* cupboard; (*in cucina*) (kitchen) cupboard; (*per abiti*) locker

armadio, -di [arˈmadjo] SM (*gen*) cupboard, closet (*USA*); (*per abiti*) wardrobe; **armadio a muro** built-in cupboard

armamentario, -ri [armamenˈtarjo] SM (*attrezzatura*) equipment, tools *pl*; (*scherz*) paraphernalia

armamento [armaˈmento] SM **1** (*armi: di soldato*) arms *pl*, weapons *pl*; **armamenti** SMPL arms, armaments; **la corsa agli armamenti** the arms race; **società di armamenti** shipowning company **2** (*azione: di nazione*) armament; (: *Naut*) fitting out, equipping; (: *provvedere di uomini*) manning

armare [arˈmare] /72/ VT **1** (*persona, nazione, fortezza*) to arm; (*arma da fuoco*) to cock **2** (*Naut*) to equip, fit out; (*di uomini*) to man **3** (*Edil*) to prop up, shore up; **armarsi** VR (*Mil*) to take up arms; **armarsi di** (*anche fig*) to arm o.s. (with)

armato, -a [arˈmato] AGG **1 armato (di)** (*anche fig*) armed (with); **era armato di coltello** he was armed with a knife; **armato fino ai denti** armed to the teeth; **sono partiti armati di tutto punto** they set off equipped for anything; **rapina a mano armata** armed robbery **2** (*Tecn: cemento, volta*) reinforced ♦ SM (*soldato*) soldier

armatore, -trice [armaˈtore] AGG shipping *attr* ♦ SM shipowner

armatura [armaˈtura] SF **1** (*corazza*) (suit of) armour *no pl* (*Brit*), armor *no pl* (*USA*) **2** (*struttura di sostegno*) framework; (*impalcatura*) scaffolding **3** (*Elettr: di cavo*) sheath; (: *di condensatore*) plate

armeggiare [armedˈdʒare] /62/ VI (*aus avere*) (*affaccendarsi*): **armeggiare (intorno a qc)** to mess about (with sth)

armeno, -a [arˈmɛno] AGG, SM, SF Armenian

armeria [armeˈria] SF (*deposito*) armoury (*Brit*), armory (*USA*); (*negozio*) gun shop; (*collezione*) collection of arms

armistizio, -zi [armisˈtittsjo] SM armistice

armonia [armoˈnia] SF (*concordia, Mus*) harmony; (*conformità*) agreement; **vivere in armonia con qn** to live in harmony with sb, get on very well with sb

armonico, -a, -ci, -che [arˈmɔniko] AGG **1** (*Mus*) harmonic; **cassa armonica** sound box **2** (*ben proporzionato*) harmonious

armonioso, -a [armoˈnjoso] AGG (*voce*) melodious; (*suono*) harmonious; (*lingua*) musical; (*movimenti*) graceful; (*corpo*) well-proportioned

armonizzare [armonidˈdzare] /72/ VT (*Mus: leggi*) to harmonize; (*fig: colori*) to match ♦ VI (*aus avere*) **armonizzare (con)** to harmonize (with); to match

arnese [arˈnese] SM **1** (*strumento, utensile*) tool, implement; **arnesi da giardino/falegname** gardening/carpenter's tools **2** (*oggetto qualsiasi*) gadget, thing **3 essere male in arnese** (*vestito male*) to be poorly *o* badly dressed; (*di salute malferma*) to be in poor health; (*di condizioni economiche*) to be hard up

arnia [ˈarnja] SF (bee)hive

aroma, -i [aˈroma] SM **1** (*odore*) aroma **2** (*erbe*): **aromi** SMPL herbs (and spices); **aromi naturali/artificiali** natural/artificial flavouring *sg* (*Brit*) *o* flavoring *sg* (*USA*)

aromaterapia [aromateraˈpia] SF aromatherapy

aromatico, -a, -ci, -che [aroˈmatiko] AGG aromatic; (*cibo*) spicy; **erbe aromatiche** herbs

aromatizzare [aromatidˈdzare] /72/ VT flavour (*Brit*), flavor (*USA*)

arpa [ˈarpa] SF harp

arpeggio, -gi [arˈpeddʒo] SM arpeggio

arpia [arˈpia] SF (*Mitol*) Harpy; (*fig*) harpy

arpione [arˈpjone] SM (*Pesca*) harpoon; (*uncino, Alpinismo*) hook; (*cardine*) hinge

arrabattarsi [arrabatˈtarsi] /72/ VIP: **arrabattarsi per fare qc** to do all one can to do sth, strive to do sth

arrabbiare [arrabˈbjare] /19/ VI (*aus essere*) **1** (*cane*) to be affected with rabies **2** (*persona*): **far arrabbiare qn** to make sb angry; **mi ha fatto veramente arrabbiare** he really made me angry; **arrabbiarsi** VIP to get angry, fly into a rage; **non ti arrabbiare!** don't get angry!; **arrabbiarsi per qc** to get angry about sth

arrabbiato, -a [arrabˈbjato] AGG **1** (*cane*) rabid, with rabies **2** (*persona*) angry; **era molto arrabbiato** he was very angry; **è più arrabbiato di lei** he's angrier than she is; **Gianni era il più arrabbiato di tutti** Gianni was the angriest of all; **un giocatore arrabbiato** (*fig: entusiasta*) a keen player

arrabbiatura [arrabbjaˈtura] SF: **prendersi un'arrabbiatura (per qc)** to become furious (over sth)

arraffare [arrafˈfare] /72/ VT to snatch, seize; (*rubare*) to pinch

arrampicarsi [arrampiˈkarsi] /20/ VIP to climb (up); **arrampicarsi sul tetto** to climb (up) onto the roof; **arrampicarsi sugli specchi** *o* **sui vetri** (*fig*) to clutch at straws

arrampicata [arrampiˈkata] SF climb; **arrampicata libera** free climbing

arrampicatore, -trice [arrampikaˈtore] SM, SF (*gen, Sport*) climber; **arrampicatore sociale** (*fig*) social climber

arrancare [arranˈkare] /20/ VI (*aus avere*) to limp, hobble; (*fig*) to struggle along

arrangiamento [arrandʒaˈmento] SM (*Mus*) arrangement

arrangiare [arranˈdʒare] /62/ VT (*gen, Mus*) to arrange; **abbiamo arrangiato un pranzo alla bell'e meglio** we've rustled up some lunch; **ti arrangio io!** (*fam*) I'll fix you!, I'll sort you out!; **arrangiarsi** VIP (*cavarsela*) to get by *o* along, manage; **con l'arte di arrangiarsi si risolve tutto** with a bit of ingenuity you can sort anything out; **arrangiati un po' tu!** (*fam*) sort it out for yourself!

arrecare [arreˈkare] /20/ VT (*causare*) to cause; **arrecare danni/disturbo** to do damage/cause trouble

arredamento [arredaˈmento] SM **1** (*azione*) furnishing; (*mobilia*) furniture **2** (*arte*) interior design

arredare [arreˈdare] /72/ VT to furnish

arredatore, -trice [arredaˈtore] SM, SF interior designer

arredo [arˈredo] SM furnishings *pl*; **per l'arredo della vostra casa...** to furnish your home ...; **arredi sacri** religious ornaments; **arredo urbano** street furniture

arrembaggio, -gi [arremˈbaddʒo] SM (*Naut*) boarding; **si buttarono all'arrembaggio dei posti migliori** (*fig*) there was a mad scramble for the best seats

arrendersi [arˈrendersi] /88/ VIP IRREG (*persona*): **arrendersi (a)** (*polizia, nemico*) to give o.s. up (to), surrender (to); **si sono arresi alla polizia** they surrendered to the police;

arrendersi all'evidenza (dei fatti) to accept *o* yield to the evidence; **non ce la faccio, mi arrendo** I can't do it, I give up

arrendevole [arren'devole] AGG (*persona*) yielding, compliant

arrendevolezza [arrendevo'lettsa] SF compliancy

arreso, -a [ar'reso] PP *di* **arrendersi**

arrestare [arres'tare] /72/ (*Dir*) to arrest; (*fermare*) to stop, halt; **i rapinatori sono stati arrestati ieri** the robbers were arrested yesterday; **arrestarsi** VR to stop

arrestato, -a [arres'tato] SM, SF person under arrest

arresto [ar'resto] SM 1 (*Dir*) arrest; **mandato d'arresto** warrant of arrest *o* arrest warrant; **essere in stato di arresto** to be under arrest; **la dichiaro in arresto** I'm putting you under arrest; **essere/mettere agli arresti** (*Mil*) to be/place under arrest; **arresti domiciliari** house arrest 2 (*azione*) stopping; (*sosta, pausa*) interruption; (*Comm: nella produzione*) stoppage; **aspettate l'arresto del treno** wait until the train stops *o* comes to a stop; **segnale d'arresto** stop sign; **il gioco ha avuto una battuta d'arresto** the game was interrupted; **le discussioni fra i due partiti subirono un arresto** discussions between the two parties came to a standstill; **arresto cardiaco** (*Med*) cardiac arrest

arretrare [arre'trare] /72/ VI (*aus* **essere**) to move back, withdraw; **arretrare davanti** *o* **di fronte a qc** (*fig*) to shrink from sth ♦ VT to move back

arretrato, -a [arre'trato] AGG 1 (*paese, zona*) backward; **un paese arretrato** a backward country 2 (*numero di giornale, pagamento, interesse*) back *attr*; **numero arretrato** back number; **ho un sacco di lavoro arretrato da finire** I've got a huge backlog of work to finish ♦ SM 1 **essere in arretrato con qc** to be behind with sth 2 **arretrati** SMPL arrears; **gli arretrati dello stipendio** back pay *sg*

arricchimento [arrikki'mento] SM (*anche fig*) enrichment

arricchire [arrik'kire] /55/ VT to make rich; **arricchire qc di** *o* **con qc** (*fig*) to enrich sth with sth; **arricchirsi** VIP (*persona*) to grow *o* become *o* get rich; (*collezione*): **arricchirsi di** to be enriched with

arricchito, -a [arrik'kito] SM, SF nouveau riche

arricciare [arrit'tʃare] /14/ VT (*capelli, baffi*) to curl; **arricciare il naso** to turn up one's nose; **arricciarsi** VIP to become curly

arridere [ar'ridere] /89/ VI IRREG (*aus* **avere**) (*fortuna, successo*): **arridere a qn** to smile on sb

arringa [ar'ringa] SF (*gen*) (formal) address; (*Dir*) address by counsel

arrischiare [arris'kjare] /19/ VT (*parola, giudizio*) to venture, hazard; **arrischiarsi** VR: **arrischiarsi (a fare qc)** to venture (to do sth), dare (to do sth)

arrischiato, -a [arris'kjato] AGG (*pericoloso: impresa, speculazione*) risky; (*avventato: giudizio, ipotesi*) rash

arriso, -a [ar'riso] PP *di* **arridere**

arrivare [arri'vare] /72/ VI (*aus* **essere**) 1 (*essere a destinazione*) to arrive; (*avvicinarsi*) to come; (*raggiungere*): **arrivare a** to reach, arrive at, get to; **arrivare in orario** to arrive on time; **arrivare in ritardo** to arrive late; **arrivare a casa** to arrive *o* get *o* reach home; **arrivare a Roma/in Italia** to arrive in Rome/in Italy; **arrivare a Londra alle sette** I arrived in London at seven; **a che ora arrivi a scuola?** what time do you arrive at school?; **mi è arrivato un pacco dall'Italia** a parcel has arrived for me from Italy, I've had a parcel from Italy; **come si arriva al castello?** how do you get to the castle?; **arrivare a destinazione** to arrive at *o* reach one's destination; **arrivare a una conclusione** to reach a conclusion; **arrivare allo scopo** to reach one's goal; **arrivare al potere** to come to power; **arrivare primo** (*in un luogo*) to be the first to arrive; (*in classifica*) to come (in) first; **non credevo arrivasse a tanto** *o* **a quel punto** I didn't think he'd go that far; **arrivo!** (I'm) coming!; **siamo arrivati** we're here; **per fare arrivare la corrente alla macchina** in order to connect the machine up to the electricity supply; **l'acqua mi arrivava alle ginocchia** the water came up to my knees; **la notizia è arrivata fino a lui** the news (even) reached him; **non ci arrivo** (*a prendere qc*) I can't reach it; (*a capire qc*) I can't understand it, I don't get it; **è arrivato il momento di...** the time has come to ...; **a questo siamo arrivati!** so this is what we've come to!; **il suo stipendio non arriva a 1.000 euro** his salary is less than

1,000 euros; **dove ti arriva la gonna?** how long is the skirt on you?; **chi tardi arriva male alloggia** (*Proverbio*) the early bird catches the worm 2 (*riuscire*): **arrivare a fare qc** to manage to do sth, succeed in doing sth; **non arriverò mai a capirlo** I'll never understand him; **non arriverà a niente** he'll never get anywhere, he'll never achieve anything; **non ci arrivo da solo** I can't do it on my own

arrivato, -a [arri'vato] AGG 1 (*persona di successo*) successful 2 **ben arrivato!** welcome! ♦ SM, SF 1 (*persona di successo*): **essere un arrivato** to have made it 2 **nuovo arrivato** newcomer; **l'ultimo arrivato** the last to arrive

arrivederci [arrive'dertʃi] ESCL goodbye!; **arrivederci, signora Cooper!** goodbye, Mrs Cooper!; **arrivederci a domani!** see you tomorrow!

arrivederla [arrive'derla] ESCL goodbye!

arrivismo [arri'vizmo] SM social climbing

arrivista, -i, -e [arri'vista] SM, SF social climber

arrivo [ar'rivo] SM 1 arrival; **al mio arrivo** on my arrival; **telefonami al tuo arrivo in Italia** phone me when you arrive in *o* get to Italy; **essere in arrivo** to be arriving; **il treno proveniente da Roma è in arrivo sul binario 1** the train from Rome is arriving *o* coming in at platform 1; **arrivi e partenze** arrivals and departures 2 (*Sport*) finish, finishing line 3 (*Comm*): **questi sono gli ultimi arrivi** these have just come in; **ci sono nuovi arrivi?** has anything new come in?

arrogante [arro'gante] AGG arrogant

arroganza [arro'gantsa] SF arrogance

arrogare [arro'gare] /80/ VT: **arrogarsi il diritto di fare qc** to assume the right to do sth; **arrogarsi il merito di qc** to claim credit for sth

arrossamento [arrossa'mento] SM reddening

arrossare [arros'sare] /72/ VT (*occhi, pelle*) to redden, make red; **arrossarsi** VIP to go *o* turn red

arrossire [arros'sire] /55/ VI (*aus* **essere**) **arrossire (di, per)** (*vergogna, imbarazzo*) to blush (with); (*piacere*) to flush (with); **è arrossito per l'imbarazzo** he went red with embarrassment; **arrossire fino alle orecchie** to go *o* turn bright red, blush to the roots of one's hair

arrostire [arros'tire] /55/ VT (*al forno*) to roast; (*ai ferri, alla griglia*) to grill; **sotto un sole che arrostiva** under a blazing sun; **arrostirsi** VIP: **arrostirsi al sole** to soak up *o* roast in the sun

arrosto [ar'rosto] AGG INV (*vedi vb*) roast; grilled; **pollo arrosto** roast chicken ♦ SM roast; **arrosto arrotolato** stuffed rolled veal; **arrosto di manzo** roast beef ♦ AVV: **fare** *o* **cuocere arrosto** (*vedi vb*); to roast; to grill; **pollo da fare arrosto** roasting chicken

arrotare [arro'tare] /72/ VT 1 (*lame, coltelli*) to sharpen; (*denti*) to grind 2 **arrotare la erre** to roll one's r's 3 (*investire con un veicolo*) to run over

arrotino [arro'tino] SM knife-grinder

arrotolare [arroto'lare] /72/ VT (*stoffa, sigaretta*) to roll; (*carta*) to roll up

arrotondare [arroton'dare] /72/ VT (*cifra*) to round up; (*per difetto*) to round down; (*forma, oggetto*) to (make) round; (*fig: stipendio*) to supplement; **fa dei lavoretti extra per arrotondare lo stipendio** he does part-time jobs to supplement his salary

arrovellare [arrovel'lare] /72/ VT: **arrovellarsi il cervello** to rack one's brains; **arrovellarsi** VR: **arrovellarsi (per qc)** to rack one's brains (about sth)

arroventato, -a [arroven'tato] AGG red-hot

arruffare [arruf'fare] /72/ VT to ruffle; (*fili*) to tangle; **arruffarsi** VIP to become tousled

arrugginire [aruddʒi'nire] /55/ VI (*aus* **essere**) to rust, get rusty ♦ VT to rust; **arrugginirsi** VIP (*metallo*) to rust, get rusty; (*fig: atleta, memoria*) to become rusty

arrugginito, -a [aruddʒi'nito] AGG (*anche fig*) rusty; **un lucchetto arrugginito** a rusty padlock

arruolamento [arrwola'mento] SM enlistment

arruolare [arrwo'lare] /72/ VT to enlist; **arruolarsi** VR to enlist; **arruolarsi volontario** to join up, enlist

arsenale [arse'nale] SM (*cantiere navale*) dockyard; (*di armi*) arsenal; **si è portato dietro un arsenale** he brought everything but the kitchen sink

arsenico [ar'sɛniko] SM arsenic
arsi ecc ['arsi] VB vedi **ardere**
arso, -a ['arso] PP di **ardere** ♦ AGG (bruciato) burnt; (arido) dry
arsura [ar'sura] SF **1** (siccità) drought; (sete) thirst **2** (calore: del sole) burning heat; (: di febbre) burning
art. ABBR (= articolo) art.
arte ['arte] SF **1** (gen) art; (abilità) skill; (mestiere, attività) craft; **galleria d'arte** art gallery; **opera d'arte** work of art; **con arte** skilfully; **a regola d'arte** (fig) perfectly; **avere l'arte di fare qc** to have the knack of doing sth; **senz'arte né parte** penniless and jobless; **arti figurative** visual arts **2** (Storia) guild; **l'arte della lana** the woollen guild; **arti e mestieri** arts and crafts; **arti marziali** martial art
artefatto, -a [arte'fatto] AGG (stile, modi) artificial
artefice [ar'tefitʃe] SM, SF (autore) author; **il sommo artefice** (Dio) the supreme Architect
arteria [ar'tɛrja] SF (Anat, o fig) artery
arteriosclerosi [arterjoskle'rɔzi] SF arteriosclerosis (Med), hardening of the arteries
arterioso, -a [arte'rjoso] AGG (Anat) arterial
artico, -a, -ci, -che ['artiko] AGG Arctic; **il Circolo polare artico** the Arctic Circle; **l'Oceano artico** the Arctic Ocean ♦ SM: **l'Artico** the Arctic
articolare[1] [artiko'lare] /72/ AGG (Anat) articular, of the joints
articolare[2] [artiko'lare] /72/ VT **1** (muovere: giunture) to move **2** (pronunciare: parole) to articulate **3** (suddividere: discorso, periodo) to split (up), divide; **ha articolato bene la sua relazione** his presentation was well organized; **articolarsi** VIP (discorso, progetto): **articolarsi in** to be divided into
articolato, -a [artiko'lato] AGG **1** (snodato) articulated **2** (linguaggio) articulate; **un ragionamento ben articolato** a clear and well developed argument **3** (Gramm): **preposizione articolata** preposition combined with the definite article
articolazione [artikolat'tsjone] SF **1** (Anat, Tecn) joint; **ha dolori alle articolazioni** her joints ache **2** (di voce, concetto) articulation
articolo [ar'tikolo] SM **1** (Gramm) article; **articolo determinativo/indeterminativo** definite/indefinite article **2** (di giornale, legge, regolamento) article; **abbiamo letto un articolo sull'effetto serra** we read an article about the greenhouse effect; **articolo di fede** (Rel) article of faith; **articolo di fondo** (Stampa) editorial, leader, leading article **3** (Comm) item, article; **quel suo amico è un bell'articolo** (fig) that friend of his is a real character; **negozio di articoli sportivi** sports shop; **articoli di cancelleria** stationery; **articoli casalinghi** kitchenware; **articoli di lusso** luxury goods; **articoli di marca** branded o brand-name goods; **articoli da regalo** gifts; **articolo civetta** loss leader
Artide ['artide] SM: **l'Artide** the Arctic
artificiale [artifi'tʃale] AGG (gen) artificial; (allegria) forced, unnatural
artificiere [artifi'tʃere] SM (Mil) artificer; (per disinnescare bombe) bomb disposal expert
artificio, -ci [arti'fitʃo] SM (espediente) trick; (ricerca di effetto) artificiality; **fuochi d'artificio** fireworks
artificioso, -a [artifi'tʃoso] AGG (comportamento) unnatural; (argomento) forced
artigianale [artidʒa'nale] AGG craft attr; **laboratorio artigianale** workshop; **lavoro artigianale** craftsmanship; **è un pezzo artigianale** it was made by a craftsman; **produzione artigianale** production by craftsmen
artigianato [artidʒa'nato] SM **1** (arte) craft; **corso di artigianato arts and crafts course; **fiera dell'artigianato** craft fair **2** (prodotti) arts and crafts pl; **un negozio di artigianato locale** a shop selling local crafts **3** (categoria) artisans pl, craftsmen pl
artigiano, -a [arti'dʒano] AGG craft attr ♦ SM, SF artisan; (idraulico, elettricista) engineer
artigliere [artiʎ'ʎɛre] SM artilleryman
artiglieria [artiʎʎe'ria] SF artillery; **tiro di artiglieria** artillery fire
artiglio [ar'tiʎʎo] SM (di felini) claw; (di rapaci) talon; **sfoderare gli artigli** (fig) to show one's claws; **cadere negli artigli di qn** (fig) to fall into sb's clutches

artista, -i, -e [ar'tista] SM, SF (pittore, scultore ecc) artist; (di spettacolo, circo) artiste; **è un artista** he's an artist; **un lavoro da artista** (fig) a professional piece of work; **artista di varietà** variety artist
artistico, -a, -ci, -che [ar'tistiko] AGG artistic; **non ho nessuna inclinazione artistica** I'm not at all artistic; **liceo artistico** secondary school specializing in art
arto ['arto] SM limb
artrite [ar'trite] SF arthritis
artrosi [ar'trɔzi] SF INV osteoarthritis
arzigogolato, -a [ardzigogo'lato] AGG tortuous
arzillo, -a [ar'dzillo] AGG lively, sprightly
ascella [aʃ'ʃella] SF armpit
ascendente [aʃʃen'dɛnte] AGG (moto, piano) ascending, upward; (Mus: scala) ascending ♦ SM **1** (influenza): **ascendente (su)** ascendancy (over) **2** (Astrol) ascendant **3** (antenato) ancestor
ascendere [aʃ'ʃendere] /101/ VI IRREG (aus essere) (frm): **ascendere al trono** to ascend the throne; **ascendere a grandi onori** to rise to great honours
ascensione [aʃʃen'sjone] SF **1** (Alpinismo) ascent, climb; (Aer) ascent **2** (Rel): **l'Ascensione** the Ascension **3** (isola dell') **Ascensione** Ascension Island
ascensore [aʃʃen'sore] SM lift (Brit), elevator (USA); **l'ascensore è guasto** the lift's out of order
ascesa [aʃ'ʃesa] SF (gen) ascent, climb; (fig: al trono) accession; (: al potere, successo) rise
ascesi [aʃ'ʃezi] SF asceticism
asceso, -a [aʃ'ʃeso] PP di **ascendere**
ascesso [aʃ'ʃesso] SM abscess
asceta, -i [aʃ'ʃeta] SM, SF ascetic
ascia, -sce [aʃʃa] SF axe; (più piccola) hatchet
asciugacapelli [aʃʃugaka'pelli] SM INV hair dryer
asciugamano [aʃʃuga'mano] SM towel; **asciugamano da bagno** bath towel
asciugare [aʃʃu'gare] /80/ VT (gen) to dry; (sudore) to wipe; **asciugare i piatti** to wipe o dry the dishes; **asciugarsi le mani/le lacrime** to dry one's hands/one's tears; **asciugarti i capelli** dry your hair; **asciugarsi** VIP (panni) to dry; **la maglietta si è asciugata in fretta** the T-shirt soon got dry; **asciugarsi al sole** to dry in the sun; **asciugarsi** VR (persona) to dry o.s.; **asciugarsi al sole** to dry off in the sun
asciugatrice [aʃʃuga'tritʃe] SF spin-dryer; **asciugatrice a centrifuga** tumble dryer
asciuttezza [aʃʃut'tettsa] SF (vedi agg) dryness; leanness; curtness
asciutto, -a [aʃ'ʃutto] AGG (gen, o fig) dry; (magro: viso, corpo ecc) lean; (brusco: risposta) curt; **è asciutta la maglietta?** is the T-shirt dry?; **rimanere o restare a bocca asciutta** (fig) to be disappointed ♦ SM: **tenere all'asciutto** to keep in a dry place; **rimanere o restare all'asciutto** (fig) to be broke; **sono rimasto all'asciutto, puoi prestarmi 50 euro?** I'm broke, can you lend me 50 euros?
ascolano, -a [asko'lano] AGG of o from Ascoli ♦ SM, SF inhabitant o native of Ascoli
ascoltare [askol'tare] /72/ VT (persona, musica, radio, discorso ecc) to listen to; **mi stai ascoltando?** are you listening to me?; **ascoltare qn parlare/cantare** to listen to sb talk/sing; **ascoltare qn con un orecchio solo** to half listen to sb; **ascoltare il consiglio di qn** to listen to o heed sb's advice; **ascoltare la messa/una lezione** to attend Mass/a class; **ascoltare un testimone** (Dir) to hear a witness
ascoltatore, -trice [askolta'tore] SM, SF listener
ascolto [as'kolto] SM **1** (Radio) reception; (gen, programma): **essere o stare in ascolto (di qc)** to be listening (to sth); **mettersi in ascolto (di qc)** to listen (to sth); **indice di ascolto** (TV, Radio) audience rating **2** (attenzione): **dare o prestare ascolto a qn/ai consigli di qn** to listen to o heed sb/sb's advice; **non presterai ascolto a queste chiacchiere** you won't take any notice of o you won't listen to these rumours, will you?
ascritto, -a [as'kritto] PP di **ascrivere**
ascrivere [as'krivere] /105/ VT IRREG **1** (attribuire): **ascrivere qc a qn** to attribute sth to sb; **ascrivere qc a merito di qn** to give sb credit for sth **2** (annoverare): **ascrivere (tra)** to number (among)

asettico, -a, -ci, -che [aˈsettiko] AGG aseptic
asfaltare [asfalˈtare] /72/ VT to asphalt
asfalto [asˈfalto] SM asphalt
asfissia [asfisˈsia] SF asphyxia, asphyxiation
asfissiante [asfisˈsjante] AGG (gas) asphyxiant, asphyxiating; (fig: calore, ambiente) stifling, suffocating; (: persona) tiresome
asfissiare [asfisˈsjare] /19/ VT to asphyxiate, suffocate; (fig: opprimere) to stifle; (fig: infastidire) to get on sb's nerves; **asfissiare (con il gas)** to gas; **è morto asfissiato** he died of suffocation; **le sta asfissiando con la sua gelosia** she's stifling her with her jealousy ♦ VI (aus essere) to suffocate, asphyxiate; **asfissiarsi** VR to suffocate o.s.; **asfissiarsi col gas** to gas to o.s.
Asia [ˈazja] SF Asia; **vengono dall'Asia** they come from Asia
asiatico, -a, -ci, -che [aˈzjatiko] AGG Asian, Asiatic ♦ SM, SF Asian, Asiatic ♦ SF (Med) Asian flu
asilo [aˈzilo] SM 1 **asilo (infantile)** nursery (school); **Paolo va all'asilo** Paolo goes to nursery school; **asilo nido** day nursery (for children aged 0 to 3), crèche 2 (rifugio) shelter, refuge; (Pol) asylum; **diritto di asilo** right of asylum; **dare/chiedere asilo** to grant/seek political asylum
asimmetrico, -a, -ci, -che [asimˈmetriko] AGG asymmetric(al)
asino [ˈazino] SM (Zool) donkey, ass; (fig) fool, ass; (scolaro) dunce; **a dorso d'asino** on the back of a donkey; **qui casca l'asino!** there's the rub!
ASL [azl] SIGLA F (= Azienda Sanitaria Locale) local health centre
asma [ˈazma] SF asthma
asmatico, -a, -ci, -che [azˈmatiko] AGG, SM, SF asthmatic
asociale [asoˈtʃale] AGG antisocial; (chiuso) unsociable ♦ SM, SF unsociable person
asola [ˈazola] SF buttonhole
asparago, -gi [asˈparago] SM asparagus no pl; **gli asparagi sono buoni** asparagus is good; **un mazzo di asparagi** a bunch of asparagus
aspergere [asˈperdʒere] /59/ VT IRREG: **aspergere (di o con)** to sprinkle (with)
asperità [asperiˈta] SF INV (di terreno, roccia) roughness no pl, ruggedness no pl; (fig) harshness no pl; **le asperità della vita** the trials of life
aspersi ecc [asˈpersi] VB vedi aspergere
asperso, -a [asˈperso] PP di aspergere
aspettare [aspetˈtare] /72/ VT 1 (attendere) to wait for, await (frm); **è un'ora che aspetto** I've been waiting for an hour; **aspettiamo che arrivi** let's wait for him to come; **aspetta un po'** wait a second o moment, hold on; **aspetta un attimo!** wait a minute!; **aspetta a giudicare** wait and see!; **aspettare la fine** (di film ecc) to wait until the end; **aspettare conferma** (Comm) to await confirmation; **sto aspettando una telefonata importante** I'm expecting an important phone call; **aspettare un bambino** (essere incinta) to be expecting (a baby); **mia sorella aspetta un bambino** my sister's expecting a baby; **aspettare qn** to wait for sb; **è mezz'ora che ti aspetto** I've been waiting for you for half an hour; **sto aspettando un'amica** I'm waiting for a friend; **aspettami, vengo anch'io!** wait for me, I'm coming too!; **fare aspettare qn** to keep sb waiting; **mi ha fatto aspettare un'ora** he kept me waiting for an hour; **farsi aspettare** to keep people waiting; **aspetta e spera!** that'll be the day!; **chi la fa, l'aspetti!** (Proverbio) it'll all come home to roost 2 (essere in serbo: notizia, evento ecc) to be in store for, lie ahead of; **non sapeva che cosa lo aspettasse** he didn't know what was in store for him o lay ahead of him 3 **aspettarsi qc** to expect sth; **non mi aspettavo che partisse** I didn't expect him to leave; **era meglio di quanto mi aspettassi** it was better than I expected; **quando meno te l'aspetti** when you least expect it; **me l'aspettavo!** I thought as much!
aspettativa [aspettaˈtiva] SF 1 (previsione, speranza) expectation; **contro ogni mia aspettativa** against all my expectations; **inferiore/superiore all'aspettativa** worse/better than expected; **corrispondere alle/deludere le aspettative di qn** to come up to/fall short of sb's expectations; **superare ogni aspettativa** to exceed o go beyond all expectations;

aspettativa di vita life expectancy 2 (Amm): **chiedere l'aspettativa** to ask for o put in for leave; **essere/mettersi in aspettativa** to be on/take leave (of absence)
aspetto [asˈpetto] SM 1 (apparenza) appearance, look; **cura molto il suo aspetto** he takes great care of his appearance; **un uomo di bell'aspetto** a good-looking man; **all'aspetto o a giudicare dall'aspetto, pare una persona onesta** as far as we can tell, he seems an honest person; **avere l'aspetto di** to look like 2 (di questione ecc) aspect, side; **un aspetto positivo** a positive aspect; **sotto un certo aspetto** in some ways
aspirante [aspiˈrante] AGG 1 (Tecn) suction attr 2 (artista) aspiring; **un aspirante attore** an aspiring actor ♦ SM, SF (a un titolo) aspirant; (candidato) candidate
aspirapolvere [aspiraˈpolvere] SM INV vacuum cleaner; **passare l'aspirapolvere** to vacuum
aspirare [aspiˈrare] /72/ VT 1 (fumo) to inhale; (aria, profumo) to breathe in 2 (Tecn) to suck (up) 3 (Fonetica) to aspirate ♦ VI (aus avere) (anelare): **aspirare a qc/a fare qc** to aspire to sth/to do sth
aspiratore [aspiraˈtore] SM (di aria, gas) extractor fan; (di liquidi) aspirator, extractor
aspirazione [aspiratˈtsjone] SF 1 (Tecn) suction 2 (anelito) aspiration; (ambizione) ambition 3 (Fonetica) aspiration
aspirina [aspiˈrina] SF (Marchio registrato) aspirin; **prendi due aspirine** take two aspirins
asportare [asporˈtare] /72/ VT to take away; (Med) to remove
asprezza [asˈprettsa] SF INV (vedi agg) sourness; sharpness; pungency; rugged nature; severity; harshness, roughness; strictness
aspro, -a [ˈaspro] AGG 1 (agrumi) sour; (vino) sharp; (odore) pungent, acrid; (paesaggio) rugged; (clima) severe, harsh; **questo pompelmo è molto aspro** this grapefruit is very sour 2 (fig: voce, giudizio) harsh, rough; (: disciplina, regime) strict 3 (Fonetica): **"s" aspra** unvoiced "s"
Ass. ABBR 1 = assicurazione 2 = assicurata 3 = assegno
assaggiare [assadˈdʒare] /62/ VT (pietanza, bevanda) to taste, try; **vuoi assaggiare?** would you like to taste it?; **fammi assaggiare** let me have a taste
assaggini [assadˈdʒini] SMPL (Culin) selection of first courses
assaggio, -gi [asˈsaddʒo] SM (prova, degustazione) tasting, sampling; (piccola quantità) taste; (campione) sample
assai [asˈsai] AVV (molto) a lot, much; (con agg) very; **è assai più giovane di me** she is very much o a lot younger than me; **sono assai contento del risultato** I'm very pleased with the result; **m'importa assai di lui!** what do I care about him!
assalgo ecc [asˈsalgo] VB vedi assalire
assalire [assaˈlire] /98/ VT IRREG to attack, assail; (fig) to assail; **fu assalito dai malviventi** he was attacked by thugs; **assalire a parole** to attack verbally
assalitore, -trice [assaliˈtore] SM, SF attacker, assailant
assaltare [assalˈtare] /72/ VT (Mil) to storm; (banca) to raid; (treno, diligenza) to hold up
assalto [asˈsalto] SM 1 (Mil) attack, assault; **truppe d'assalto** assault troops; (fig: editoria, giornalista ecc) aggressive 2 (rapina) raid; **prendere d'assalto** (fig: negozio, treno) to storm; (: personalità) to besiege
assaporare [assapoˈrare] /72/ VT (anche fig) to savour (Brit), savor (USA)
assassinare [assassiˈnare] /72/ VT (gen) to murder; (Pol) to assassinate
assassinio, -nii [assasˈsinjo] SM murder; (politico) assassination
assassino, -a [assasˈsino] SM, SF murderer; (Pol) assassin ♦ AGG (mania, tendenza) murderous; (seducente: sguardo, occhiata) seductive
asse¹ [ˈasse] SF (di legno) board; **asse di equilibrio** (Ginnastica) beam; **asse del gabinetto** lavatory seat; **asse da stiro** ironing board
asse² [ˈasse] SM (Geom) axis; (Tecn) axle; **l'asse terrestre** the earth's axis; **l'asse Roma-Berlino** (alleanza) the Rome-Berlin axis
assecondare [assekonˈdare] /72/ VT: **assecondare qn (in qc)** to go along with sb (in sth); **assecondare i desideri di qn** to go along with sb's wishes; **assecondare i capricci di qn** to give in to sb's whims

assediare [asse'djare] /19/ vt (anche fig) to besiege

assedio, -di [as'sedjo] sm (anche fig) siege; **porre in stato di assedio** to lay siege to; **cingere d'assedio** to besiege

assegnare [assep'pare] /15/ vt: **assegnare (a)** (gen) to assign (to); (premio, borsa di studio) to award (to); (somma) to allocate (to), allot (to)

assegnatario, -ria, -ri, -rie [assepppa'tarjo] sm, sf (Dir) assignee; **l'assegnatario del premio** the person awarded the prize

assegnazione [assepppat'tsjone] sf (di casa, somma) allocation; (di carica) assignment; (di premio, borsa di studio) awarding

assegno [as'seppo] sm 1 (Comm): **contro assegno** cash on delivery 2 (somma integrativa): **assegni familiari** ≈ child benefit sg; **assegno di studio** ≈ study grant 3 (Fin): **assegno (bancario)** cheque (Brit), check (USA); **un assegno per o di 500 euro** a cheque for 500 euros; **ha pagato con un assegno** he paid by cheque; **assegno in bianco** blank cheque; **assegno circolare** bank draft; **"assegno non trasferibile" "account payee only"**; **assegno post-datato** post-dated cheque; **assegno sbarrato** crossed cheque; **assegno a vuoto** dud cheque

assemblaggio, -gi [assem'bladdʒo] sm (Industria) assembly; (Inform) assembling

assemblare [assem'blare] /72/ vt (Industria, Inform, anche fig) to assemble

assemblea [assem'blea] sf (gen) assembly; (raduno, adunanza) meeting; **assemblea generale** general meeting

assembramento [assembra'mento] sm (public) gathering; **divieto di assembramento** ban on public meetings

assennato, -a [assen'nato] agg sensible, wise

assenso [as'senso] sm approval, assent; (Dir) consent; **dare/negare il proprio assenso** give/not give o withhold one's consent

assentarsi [assen'tarsi] /72/ vip (gen) to go out; **il direttore dovrà assentarsi per un paio di giorni** the manager will be away for a couple of days; **si assenta spesso dal lavoro** he is frequently absent from work

assente [as'sente] agg 1 **assente (da)** (gen) away (from); (malato, studente) absent (from); **il direttore è momentaneamente assente** the manager is out at the moment; **oggi sono assenti due scolari** two pupils are absent today 2 (espressione, sguardo) vacant, faraway; **avere lo sguardo assente** to look miles away ♦ sm, sf absentee; **quanti assenti ci sono oggi?** how many people are absent today?; **non sparlare degli assenti** you shouldn't talk behind people's backs; **il grande assente alla riunione** the most notable absentee at the meeting

assenteismo [assente'izmo] sm absenteeism

assenteista, -i, -e [assente'ista] sm, sf (dal lavoro) absentee; **è un assenteista** he is often absent

assentire [assen'tire] /45/ vi (aus avere) **assentire (a)** to agree (to), assent (to)

assenza [as'sentsa] sf absence; **in assenza di** in the absence of; **in mia assenza** in my absence; **non ho fatto nessuna assenza a scuola/in ufficio** I haven't missed a day at school/at the office; **quanto durerà la sua assenza?** how long will he be away for?

asserire [asse'rire] /55/ vt to maintain, assert; **ha asserito di avere ragione** he maintained (that) he was right

asserragliarsi [asserraʎ'ʎarsi] /27/ vr: **asserragliarsi (in)** to barricade o.s. (in)

asservire [asser'vire] /55/ vt to enslave; (fig: animo, passioni) to subdue; **asservirsi** vr: **asservirsi (a)** to submit (to)

asserzione [asser'tsjone] sf assertion

assessorato [assesso'rato] sm (carica) councillorship; **assessorato alla cultura** local authority arts and entertainment department

assessore [asses'sore] sm councillor

assestamento [assesta'mento] sm (gen, Geol, Edil) settlement; **essere in via di assestamento** (terreno) to be settling; **la situazione è in via di assestamento** things are settling down

assestare [asses'tare] /72/ vt (gen, Geol) to settle; **assestare un colpo a qn** to deal sb a blow; **assestare la mira** to adjust

one's aim; **assestarsi** vip (situazione ecc) to settle down; (terreno) to settle

assetato, -a [asse'tato] agg thirsty; **assetato di** (fig) thirsting for; **assetato di potere** greedy for power; **assetato di sangue** bloodthirsty

assetto [as'setto] sm 1 (ordine) order, arrangement; **dare un assetto nuovo a qc** to (re)arrange sth; **in assetto di guerra** ready for war; **in assetto antisommossa** in riot gear 2 (Aer, Naut) trim; (Aut) balance; (Equitazione) seat; **assetto delle ruote** (Aut) (wheel) alignment; **assetto territoriale** country planning

assicurare [assiku'rare] /72/ vt 1 (Assicurazione: vita, casa) to insure; (lettera, pacco) to register; **la macchina non era assicurata contro il furto** the car wasn't insured against theft 2 (garantire) assure; **assicurare l'avvenire ai figli** to secure the children's future; **assicurarsi qc** to secure o ensure sth for o.s.; **assicurarsi un posto** to get a job for o.s.; **assicurare qn alla giustizia** (arrestare) to arrest sb 3 (per tranquillizzare): **assicurare qn che** to assure sb that; **mi ha assicurato che sarebbe venuto** he assured me that he'd come; **te l'assicuro!** I assure you! 4 (fermare, legare): **assicurare (a)** to secure (to); (Alpinismo) to belay; **assicurarsi** vr 1 (Assicurazione): **assicurarsi (contro qc)** to insure o.s. (against sth) 2 (accertarsi): **assicurarsi di/che** to make sure of/that; **assicurati che la porta sia ben chiusa** make sure the door's closed properly 3 (legarsi): **assicurarsi (a)** to fasten o.s. (to), tie o.s. (to)

assicurato, -a [assiku'rato] agg insured ♦ sm, sf policy holder

assicuratore, -trice [assikura'tore] agg insurance attr; **società assicuratrice** insurance company ♦ sm, sf insurance agent

assicurazione [assikurat'tsjone] sf 1 (conferma, garanzia) assurance 2 (contratto) insurance (policy); **fare un'assicurazione** to take out insurance; **assicurazione contro furti** theft insurance; **assicurazione contro incendi** fire insurance; **assicurazione contro terzi** third party insurance; **assicurazione multi-rischio** comprehensive insurance; **assicurazione sulla vita** life insurance 3 (Alpinismo) belaying

assideramento [assidera'mento] sm (Med) exposure

assiderare [asside'rare] /72/ vt to freeze; **questo freddo mi sta assiderando** (fig) I'm chilled to the bone; **assiderarsi** vip to freeze

assiduo, -a [as'siduo] agg (cure, studio, applicazione) assiduous; (visitatore, lettore) regular

assieme [as'sjeme] avv (insieme) together ♦ prep: **assieme a** (together) with

assillante [assil'lante] agg (dubbio, pensiero) nagging; (creditore) pestering

assillare [assil'lare] /72/ vt (sogg: dubbio, pensiero, persona) to nag at; (: creditore) to hound; **continua ad assillarmi con i suoi problemi** he keeps pestering me with his problems

assillo [as'sillo] sm 1 (pensiero tormentoso) nagging worry, worrying thought; **aver l'assillo di qc** to be constantly worrying about sth 2 (Zool) horsefly, gadfly

assimilare [assimi'lare] /72/ vt (anche fig) to assimilate

assimilazione [assimilat'tsjone] sf assimilation

assioma [as'sjoma] sm axiom

assiomatico, -a, -ci, -che [assjo'matiko] agg axiomatic

assise [as'size] sfpl (Dir): **la Corte d'Assise** ≈ the crown court (Brit)

assistente [assis'tente] sm, sf (gen) assistant; **la direttrice ha chiamato una sua assistente** the manager called one of her assistants; **assistente ai lavori** supervisor; **assistente dell'arbitro** (Calcio) assistant referee; **assistente di polizia** inspector; **assistente sanitario** health worker; **assistente sociale** social worker; **assistente universitario** ≈ (assistant) lecturer; **assistente di volo** (Aer) flight attendant

assistenza [assis'tentsa] sf (aiuto) assistance; **dare o prestare assistenza a qn** to assist sb, give assistance to sb; **fare opera di assistenza** to help out; **assistenza all'infanzia** childcare; **assistenza legale** legal aid; **assistenza ospedaliera** free hospital treatment; **assistenza sanitaria** health service; **assistenza sociale** social security; **assistenza tecnica** after-sales service; **assistenza a terra** (Aer) ground handling

assistenziale [assisten'tsjale] agg (ente, organizzazione) welfare attr; (opera) charitable

assistenzialismo [assistentsja'lizmo] SM (*pegg*) excessive state aid

assistere [as'sistere] VB IRREG /11/ VI (*aus* avere) assistere a (*essere presente*) to be present at, attend; (*incidente, scena*) to witness; (*spettacolo*) to watch; (*sorvegliare: lavori, esami*) to supervise ♦ VT (*aiutare*) to assist; (*malato*) to look after; (*curare*) to treat; **assiste la madre ammalata** she's looking after her sick mother

assistito, -a [assis'tito] PP *di* assistere ♦ SM, SF (*di medico*) patient; (*di avvocato, ente assistenziale*) client ♦ AGG assisted; **fecondazione assistita** assisted conception; **traduzione assistita** assisted translation

asso ['asso] SM 1 (*carta, dado*) ace; **asso di picche/cuori** *ecc* ace of spades/hearts *ecc*; **avere un** *o* **l'asso nella manica** (*fig*) to have an ace up one's sleeve; **piantare qn in asso** to leave sb in the lurch 2 (*campione*) ace; **asso del volante** ace driver

associare [asso'tʃare] /14/ VT 1 (*idee, parole, fatti*): associare (a) to associate (with); **il suo nome è stato associato alla Mafia** his name has been linked with the Mafia 2 associare **qn a** (*un circolo*) to make sb a member of; (*ad una ditta*) to take sb into partnership in; **associare qn alle carceri** to take sb to prison; **associarsi** VR 1 associarsi con qn (*in una ditta*) to enter into partnership with sb 2 associarsi a (*circolo*) to join, become a member of; (*dolori, gioie, lutto*) to share in

associazione [assotʃat'tsjone] SF 1 (*gen, Pol, Sport ecc*) association; **associazione a** *o* **per delinquere** (*Dir*) criminal association; **associazione di categoria** trade association; **Associazione Europea di Libero Scambio** European Free Trade Association; **associazione in partecipazione** (*Comm*) joint venture 2 (*di idee*) association; **per associazione di idee** by association of ideas

assodare [asso'dare] /72/ VT 1 (*accertare: fatti, verità*) to ascertain 2 (*muro, posizione*) to strengthen; **assodarsi** VIP (*sostanza*) to harden

assodato, -a [asso'dato] AGG well-founded

assoggettare [assoddʒet'tare] /72/ VT (*persone*) to subjugate; (*fig: passioni, istinti*) to curb; **assoggettarsi** VR: assoggettarsi **a** to submit to; (*adattarsi*) to adapt to

assolato, -a [asso'lato] AGG sunny

assoldare [assol'dare] /72/ VT (*sicario*) to hire; (*spia*) to recruit

assolsi *ecc* [as'solsi] VB *vedi* assolvere

assolto, -a [as'sɔlto] PP *di* assolvere

assolutamente [assoluta'mente] AVV absolutely; **è assolutamente incredibile** it's absolutely incredible; **devo assolutamente andare** I've simply got to go; **assolutamente no** certainly not

assoluto, -a [asso'luto] AGG (*gen, Pol, Gramm*) absolute; **in caso di assoluta necessità** if absolutely essential; **è in assoluto il più bravo** he is without doubt *o* altogether the best ♦ SM (*Filosofia*): **l'assoluto** the absolute

assoluzione [assolut'tsjone] SF (*Rel*) absolution; (*Dir*) acquittal; **dare l'assoluzione a qn** to give sb absolution; **concedere l'assoluzione a qn** to acquit sb

assolvere [as'sɔlvere] /94/ VT IRREG 1 assolvere qn (da) (*Rel*) to absolve sb (from); (*Dir*) to acquit sb (of); **è stato assolto dall'accusa di omicidio** he was acquitted of murder 2 (*adempiere: mansioni, compiti*) to carry out, perform; **assolvere il proprio dovere** to perform one's duty

assomigliare [assomiʎ'ʎare] /27/ VI (*aus* avere *o* essere) assomigliare a (*nell'aspetto*) to resemble, look like; (*nel carattere*) to be like; **assomigliarsi** VR (*uso reciproco*) to be alike, resemble each other; **si assomigliano come due gocce d'acqua** they are as like as two peas (in a pod)

assonnato, -a [asson'nato] AGG sleepy; **hai l'aria assonnata** you look sleepy

assopire [asso'pire] /55/ VT 1 far assopire to make drowsy 2 (*dolore*) to soothe; **assopirsi** VIP to doze off

assorbente [assor'bɛnte] AGG absorbent; **carta assorbente** blotting paper ♦ SM: **assorbente (igienico)** sanitary towel; **assorbente interno** tampon

   ❑ assorbente non si traduce mai con la parola inglese *absorbing*

assorbire [assor'bire] /17/ VT (*liquidi*) to absorb, soak up; (*suono*) to absorb; (*tempo, attenzione*) to take up, occupy; (*cultura, influenza*) to assimilate, absorb

assordante [assor'dante] AGG (*rumore, musica*) deafening

assordare [assor'dare] /72/ VT to deafen; **abbassa il volume, mi stai assordando!** turn down the volume, you're deafening me!

assortimento [assorti'mento] SM assortment, variety

assortire [assor'tire] /55/ VT (*combinare*) to combine; (*colori*) to match; (*disporre*) to arrange

assortito, -a [assor'tito] AGG 1 (*combinato: persone, cose, colori*): bene/male assortito well/badly matched 2 (*caramelle, cioccolatini*) assorted; **una scatola di cioccolatini assortiti** a box of assorted chocolates

assorto, -a [as'sɔrto] AGG: essere assorto in qc to be engrossed in sth

assottigliare [assotti'ʎʎare] /27/ VT 1 (*affilare*) to sharpen 2 (*ridurre: spessore*) to make thinner, thin (down); (: *proviste*) to reduce; (: *caviglie*) to slim; (: *girovita*) to reduce, slim down; **assottigliarsi** VIP (*proviste*) to dwindle; (*caviglie, girovita*) to slim down

assuefare [assue'fare] VB IRREG /41/ VT: assuefare a to get used to, accustom to; **assuefarsi** VR: assuefarsi a to become *o* get accustomed *o* used to; (*droga*) to become addicted to

assuefatto, -a [assue'fatto] PP *di* assuefare

assuefazione [assuefat'tsjone] SF (*Med*) addiction; **questo medicinale non dà assuefazione** this drug is not habit-forming

assumere [as'sumere] /12/ VT IRREG 1 (*impiegato*) to take on, engage, employ; **l'azienda assumerà due operai** the company is going to take on two workers; **essere assunto** to get a job; **è stata assunta come programmatrice** she's got a job as a programmer 2 (*atteggiamento, espressione*) to assume, put on; (*comando, potere*) to assume, take over; (*incarico*) to take up; **assumersi il compito di fare qc** to take on the job of doing sth; **si è assunto ogni responsabilità** he's taken responsibility for everything; **assumere informazioni su qn/ qc** to make enquiries about sb/sth 3 (*supporre*) to assume; **assumendo (come ipotesi) che...** assuming that ... 4 (*droga*) to take 5 (*innalzare a dignità*) to raise

assunsi *ecc* [as'sunsi] VB *vedi* assumere

assunto, -a [as'sunto] PP *di* assumere ♦ SM (*Filosofia*) proposition

assunzione [assun'tsjone] SF 1 (*di impiegati*) employment, engagement; **ci sono state poche assunzioni** few people have been taken on; **il problema delle assunzioni** the employment problem 2 (*Rel*): **l'Assunzione** the Assumption

assurdità [assurdi'ta] SF INV absurdity; **l'assurdità della situazione** the absurdity of the situation; **che assurdità!** how absurd!; **dire delle assurdità** to talk nonsense

assurdo, -a [as'surdo] AGG absurd; **che idea assurda!** what a ridiculous idea!; **è assurdo!** it's ridiculous!

asta ['asta] SF 1 (*palo*) pole; salto con l'asta pole vault; **bandiera a mezz'asta** flag at half-mast 2 (*di occhiali*) arm (*Brit*), stem (*USA*); (*di compasso, bilancia*) arm; (*Sci: di skilift*) bar 3 (*Comm*) auction; **mettere all'asta** to put up for auction; **vendere all'asta** to auction off; **vendita all'asta** auction sale; **asta fallimentare** bankruptcy sale 4 (*nella scrittura*) stroke

astante [as'tante] SM, SF bystander

astanteria [astante'ria] SF casualty department

astemio, -mia, -mi, -mie [as'tɛmjo] AGG teetotal ♦ SM, SF teetotaller

   ❑ astemio non si traduce mai con la parola inglese *abstemious*

astenersi [aste'nersi] /121/ VR IRREG: astenersi (dal fare qc/ da qc) to abstain *o* refrain (from doing sth/from sth); **astenersi dal dire** to refrain from saying; **astenersi dal bere/ dal fumo** to keep off drink/cigarettes; **astenersi (dal voto)** (*Pol*) to abstain

astensione [asten'sjone] SF abstention

astensionista, -i, -e [astensjo'nista] SM, SF (*Pol*) abstentionist

asterisco, -schi [aste'risko] SM asterisk; (*di telefono, computer*) star key

asteroide [aste'rɔide] SM asteroid

astice ['astitʃe] SM lobster

astigiano, -a [asti'dʒano] AGG of *o* from Asti ♦ SM, SF inhabitant *o* native of Asti

astigmatico, -a, -ci, -che [astig'matiko] AGG astigmatic ♦ SM, SF person suffering from astigmatism

astinenza [asti'nɛntsa] SF abstinence; **fare astinenza (da)** (*Rel*) to abstain (from); **essere in crisi di astinenza** (*di droga*) to suffer from withdrawal symptoms

astio ['astjo] SM: **astio (contro)** rancour (against), resentment (towards); **portare astio a qn** to bear sb a grudge

astioso, -a [as'tjoso] AGG resentful

astrattismo [astrat'tizmo] SM (*Arte*) abstract art

astratto, -a [as'tratto] PP *di* **astrarre** ♦ AGG, SM abstract; **in astratto** in the abstract

astringente [astrin'dʒɛnte] AGG, SM astringent

astro ['astro] SM (*Astron, o fig*) star; (*Bot*) aster; **un astro nascente del cinema italiano** a rising star of Italian cinema

astrologia [astrolo'dʒia] SF astrology

astrologico, -a, -ci, -che [astro'lɔdʒiko] AGG astrological

astrologo, -a, -gi, -ghe [as'trɔlogo] SM, SF astrologer

astronauta, -i, -e [astro'nauta] SM, SF astronaut

astronautica [astro'nautika] SF astronautics *sg*

astronave [astro'nave] SF spaceship

astronomia [astrono'mia] SF astronomy

astronomico, -a, -ci, -che [astro'nɔmiko] AGG (*anche fig*) astronomic(al); **prezzi astronomici** astronomical prices

astronomo, -a [as'trɔnomo] SM, SF astronomer

astruso, -a [as'truzo] AGG (*discorso, ragionamento*) abstruse

astuccio, -ci [as'tuttʃo] SM (*per gioielli*) box, case; (*per compasso, matite*) case; **un astuccio portapenne** a pencil case

astuto, -a [as'tuto] AGG astute, shrewd, cunning; **un'astuta donna d'affari** a shrewd businesswoman; **astuto come una volpe** cunning as a fox

astuzia [as'tuttsja] SF (*qualità*) astuteness, shrewdness, cunning; (*azione*) trick

AT SIGLA = **Asti** ♦ ABBR (= *alta tensione*) HT

atavico, -a, -ci, -che [a'taviko] AGG primitive, atavistic (*frm*)

ateismo [ate'izmo] SM atheism

atelier [ata'lje] SM INV (*sartoria*) fashion house; (*studio*) studio; (*laboratorio*) workshop

Atene [a'tene] SF Athens; **quest'estate andremo ad Atene** we're going to Athens this summer; **abita ad Atene** she lives in Athens

ateneo [ate'neo] SM university

ateniese [ate'njese] AGG, SM, SF Athenian

ateo, -a ['ateo] AGG atheistic; **essere ateo** to be an atheist ♦ SM, SF atheist

atipico, -a, -ci, -che [a'tipiko] AGG atypical; (*lavoro, lavoratore*) not permanent

atlante [a'tlante] SM (*libro, Anat*) atlas

atlantico, -a, -ci, -che [a'tlantiko] AGG Atlantic ♦ SM: **l'(Oceano) Atlantico** the Atlantic (Ocean)

atleta, -i, -e [a'tleta] SM, SF athlete

atletica [a'tletika] SF athletics *sg*; **guardo sempre l'atletica in TV** I always watch the athletics on TV; **atletica leggera** track and field events *pl*; **atletica pesante** weightlifting and wrestling

atmosfera [atmos'fera] SF (*anche fig*) atmosphere; **c'era una bella atmosfera** there was a nice atmosphere; **atmosfera controllata** protective atmosphere

atmosferico, -a, -ci, -che [atmos'feriko] AGG atmospheric

atollo [a'tɔllo] SM atoll

atomico, -a, -ci, -che [a'tɔmiko] AGG atomic; (*nucleare*) nuclear; **numero atomico** atomic number; **bomba atomica** atom bomb; **guerra atomica** nuclear war

atomizzatore [atomiddza'tore] SM (*di acqua, lacca*) spray; (*di profumo*) atomizer

atomo ['atomo] SM atom

atono, -a ['atono] AGG (*Fonetica*) unstressed

atrio, -ri ['atrjo] SM (*di albergo*) entrance hall, lobby; (*di stazione, aeroporto*) concourse; (*Storia, Anat*) atrium

atroce [a'trotʃe] AGG (*delitto*) atrocious; (*sofferenza, destino*) terrible, dreadful; (*dolore*) excruciating; (*tempo*) ghastly, dreadful; **un mal di testa atroce** a terrible headache; **fa un freddo atroce** it's dreadfully cold; **in modo atroce** dreadfully; **ho l'atroce dubbio che...** I have the horrible feeling that ...

atrocità [atrotʃi'ta] SF INV (*caratteristica*) atrocity, atrociousness; (*azione*) atrocity

atrofia [atro'fia] SF atrophy

attaccabrighe [attakka'brige] SM INV, SF INV quarrelsome person

attaccamento [attakka'mento] SM (*a tradizioni ecc*) attachment; (*a persona, famiglia*) affection; **il suo attaccamento alla madre** his affection for his mother

attaccante [attak'kante] SM, SF (*Calcio*) forward; **gioca da attaccante** he's a forward

attaccapanni [attakka'panni] SM INV (*su parete*) hook, peg; (*mobile*) hall stand

attaccare [attak'kare] /20/ VT 1 (*far aderire*) to attach; (*incollare: manifesto*) to stick up; (: *francobollo*) to stick (on); (: *cucire*) to sew (on); (: *legare*) to tie (up); (: *appendere: quadro*) to hang (up); **devo attaccare due bottoni** I've got to sew two buttons on; **non so dove attaccare questo poster** I don't know where to stick this poster 2 (*Mil, Sport, o fig*) to attack 3 (*cominciare: discorso, lite*) to start, begin; **attaccare discorso con qn** to start a conversation with sb 4 (*contagiare, anche fig*) to affect; **ha attaccato il morbillo a sua cugina** he's given his cousin the measles; **non vorrei attaccarti il raffreddore** I wouldn't want to give you my cold ♦ VI (*incollare*) 1 to stick 2 (*aver successo*): **la nuova moda non attacca** the new fashion isn't catching on; **con me non attacca!** it doesn't work with me!, that won't work with me! 3 (*cominciare*) to start, begin; **attaccare a suonare** to strike up; **quando attacca a cantare non la smette più** once she starts singing she never stops; **ha attaccato con una delle sue lamentele** *o* **a lamentarsi** he started whining; **attaccarsi** VIP 1 **attaccarsi (a)** (*appiccicarsi*) to stick (to); (*aggrapparsi, anche fig*) to cling (to); **le pagine si sono attaccate** the pages have stuck together; **attaccati alla corda!** hold on tight to the rope!; **è inutile che ti attacchi a dei pretesti** there's no point (in) making excuses; **attaccarsi alla bottiglia** (*fig*) to take to the bottle; **il sugo si è attaccato** the sauce has stuck 2 (*affezionarsi*): **attaccarsi a** to become attached to 3 (*trasmettersi per contagio*) to be contagious

attaccaticcio, -cia, -ci, -ce [attakka'tittʃo] SM: **sapere d'attaccaticcio** to taste burnt ♦ AGG sticky; **è una persona attaccaticcia** (*fig*) he (*o* she) is a very clingy person

attaccatura [attakka'tura] SF (*di manica*) join; **attaccatura dei capelli** hairline

attacco, -chi [at'takko] SM 1 (*Mil, Sport, anche fig*) attack; (*giocatori*) forward line, forwards *pl*; (*Alpinismo*) start; **giocare in attacco** to play an attacking game 2 (*Med*) fit; **un attacco di tosse** a coughing fit; **un attacco epilettico** an epileptic fit; **un attacco d'asma** an asthma attack 3 (*Sci*) binding; **attacchi di sicurezza** safety bindings 4 (*Tecn*) connection; (*Elettr*) socket

attanagliare [attanaʎ'ʎare] /27/ VT (*anche fig*) to grip; **attanagliato dalla paura** gripped by fear

attardarsi [attar'darsi] /72/ VIP to linger; **attardarsi a fare qc** (*fermarsi*) to stop to do sth; (*stare più a lungo*) to stay behind to do sth; **dev'essersi attardato in ufficio** he must have stayed on *o* behind at the office

attecchire [attek'kire] /55/ VI (*aus avere*) (*pianta*) to take root; (*fig*) to catch on

atteggiamento [attedʒa'mento] SM (*disposizione mentale*) attitude; (*aria*) air; (*del corpo*) pose; **non mi piace il suo atteggiamento** I don't like his attitude; **atteggiamento dimesso** unassuming attitude; **perché hai avuto quell'atteggiamento strano quando l'abbiamo incontrato?** why did you act so strangely when we met him?; **è tutto un atteggiamento il suo** it's all an act with him

atteggiare [atted'dʒare] /62/ VT: **atteggiare il viso a compassione** to assume a sympathetic expression; **atteggiarsi** VR: **atteggiarsi ad artista** to play *o* act the artist

attempato, -a [attem'pato] AGG elderly

attendente [atten'dente] SM (*Mil*) orderly, batman

attendere [at'tendere] VB IRREG /120/ VT (*aspettare*) to wait for, await (*frm*); **cosa sta attendendo?** what are you waiting for?; **attendo l'arrivo di mio fratello** I'm waiting for my brother to arrive; **attenda in linea** hold the line, please ♦ VI (*aus avere*) **attendere a** (*dedicarsi*) to attend to

attendibile [atten'dibile] AGG (*scusa, storia*) credible; (*fonte, testimone, notizia*) reliable; (*persona*) trustworthy

attenersi [atte'nersi] /121/ VR IRREG: **attenersi a** (*istruzioni, regolamento*) to keep to, stick to

attentare [atten'tare] /72/ VI (*aus* avere) **attentare a** (*libertà, diritti*) to attack; **attentare alla vita di qn** to make an attempt on sb's life

attentato [atten'tato] SM (*a libertà, onore*) attack; (*contro persona*) assassination attempt; **un attentato terroristico** a terrorist attack; **un attentato suicida** suicide bombing, a suicide attack; **commettere un attentato contro qn** *o* **alla vita di qn** to make an attempt on sb's life

attentatore, -trice [attenta'tore] SM, SF attacker

attento, -a [at'tɛnto] AGG **1** (*che presta attenzione*) attentive; **avere lo sguardo attento** to watch attentively **2** (*avviso di pericolo*): **attento!** (be) careful!, look *o* watch out!; **attenti al cane** beware of the dog; **attento alle dita!** mind your fingers!; **stai attento!** (*non distrarti*) pay attention!; (*stai in guardia*) be careful!; **stai attento quando attraversi la strada** be careful when you cross the road **3** (*accurato: esame, ricerca*) careful, thorough

attenuante [attenu'ante](*Dir*) AGG: **circostanze attenuanti** extenuating circumstances ♦ SF extenuating *o* mitigating circumstance; **concedere le attenuanti** (*generiche/specifiche*) to make allowances for the (general/particular) extenuating circumstances

attenuare [attenu'are] /72/ VT (*dolore*) to ease, alleviate; (*rumore*) to reduce, deaden; (*colpo*) to soften; (*Dir: colpa*) to mitigate; **attenuarsi** VIP to ease, abate

attenuazione [attenuat'tsjone] SF (*vedi vb*) easing, alleviation; reduction; softening; mitigation

attenzione [atten'tsjone] ESCL watch out!, (be) careful! ♦ SF **1** (*gen*) attention; (*cura*) care; **gli piace essere al centro dell'attenzione** he likes to be the centre of attention; **cerca di richiamare l'attenzione del cameriere** try and attract the waiter's attention; **con attenzione** (*ascoltare*) carefully, attentively; (*esaminare*) carefully, closely; **attenzione al gradino** mind the step; **prestare attenzione** (*stare in guardia*) to be careful; (*ascoltare, guardare*) to pay attention; **alla cortese attenzione di** (*Comm*) for the attention of **2** **attenzioni** SFPL (*gentilezze*) attentions; **avere mille attenzioni per qn, coprire qn di attenzioni** to lavish attentions on sb

atterraggio, -gi [atter'raddʒo] SM landing; **all'atterraggio** on landing; **essere in fase di atterraggio** to be coming in to land; **atterraggio di fortuna** emergency landing

atterrare [atter'rare] /72/ VI (*aus* avere *o* essere) (*aereo, persona*) to land; **l'aereo ha appena atterrato** the plane has just landed ♦ VT (*avversario*) to floor, bring down

atterrire [atter'rire] *vb dif* /55/ VT to terrify; **atterrirsi** VIP to become terrified

attesa [at'tesa] SF wait; **dopo una lunga attesa** after a long wait; **lista d'attesa** waiting list; **sala d'attesa** waiting room; **l'attesa durò a lungo** it was a long wait; **essere in attesa di qc** to be waiting for sth; **è in attesa del terzo figlio** she is expecting her third baby; **in attesa di una vostra risposta** (*Comm*) awaiting your reply; **restiamo in attesa di Vostre ulteriori notizie** (*Comm*) we look forward to hearing (further) from you

attesi *ecc* [at'tesi] VB *vedi* **attendere**

atteso, -a [at'teso] PP *di* **attendere** ♦ AGG long-awaited

attestare [attes'tare] /72/ VT: **attestare qc/che** to testify *o* sth/(to the fact) that

attestato [attes'tato] SM (*certificato*) certificate; **quest'attestato certifica che** this document testifies to the fact that

attestazione [attestat'tsjone] SF (*certificato*) certificate; (*dichiarazione*) statement

attico, -ci [at'tiko] SM (*soffitta*) attic; (*di lusso*) penthouse

attiguo, -a [at'tiguo] AGG (*contiguo*) adjoining; (*adiacente*) adjacent; **il suo appartamento è attiguo al nostro** his apartment is next to ours

attillato, -a [attil'lato] AGG (*vestito*) skin-tight, close-fitting

attimo ['attimo] SM moment; **aspetta un attimo** wait a minute; **un attimo, per favore** just a moment, please; **un attimo di pazienza!** wait a moment!; **fra un attimo** in a minute *o*

moment; **un attimo fa** a moment ago; **ci metto un attimo** I'll just be a minute; **torno tra un attimo** I'll be back in a minute; **in un attimo** in a moment; **attimo per attimo** moment by moment

attinente [atti'nɛnte] AGG: **attinente a** relating to, concerning

attinenza [atti'nɛntsa] SF connection

attingere [at'tindʒere] /37/ VT IRREG: **attingere** *o* **da** (*acqua*) to draw from; (*denaro, risorse*) to draw on, obtain from; **attingere informazioni a una fonte sicura** to obtain information from a reliable source

attinto, -a [at'tinto] PP *di* **attingere**

attirare [atti'rare] /72/ VT (*attenzione, persona*) to attract; **l'idea mi attira** the idea appeals to me; **attirarsi delle critiche** to incur criticism

❏ **attirare** non si traduce mai con la parola inglese *attire*

attitudine [atti'tudine] SF (*disposizione*) aptitude; **avere attitudine per qc** to have a flair for sth

❏ **attitudine** non si traduce mai con la parola inglese *attitude*

attivare [atti'vare] /72/ VT (*motore, azienda*) to start; (*dispositivo, mina*) to activate; **attivare la circolazione** (*Med*) to stimulate the circulation

attivista, -i, -e [atti'vista] SM, SF activist

attività [attivi'ta] SF INV **1** (*gen*) activity; **mi piacciono le attività all'aria aperta** I like outdoor activities; **essere/entrare in attività** to be/become active **2** (*Comm: azienda*) business; **le attività e passività di un'azienda** the assets and liabilities of a business; **attività liquide** liquid assets

attivo, -a [at'tivo] AGG (*gen, Gramm*) active; (*Comm*) profit-making; **bilancio attivo** credit balance; **un'azienda attiva** a going concern; **popolazione attiva** working population ♦ SM (*Comm*) assets *pl*; **in attivo** in credit; **chiudere in attivo** to show a profit; **avere qc al proprio attivo** (*fig*) to have sth to one's credit

attizzare [attit'tsare] /72/ VT (*fuoco*) to poke (up); (*fig: passioni, odi*) to stir up

attizzatoio, -oi [attittsa'tojo] SM poker

atto[1] ['atto] SM **1** (*azione, gesto*) action, deed, act; **atti di sabotaggio** acts of sabotage; **atto eroico** heroic feat; **essere in atto** to be under way; **cogliere** *o* **sorprendere qn nell'atto di fare qc** to catch sb in the act of doing sth; **all'atto pratico** in practice; **mettere in atto qc** to put into action *o* practice; **fare (l')atto di fare qc** to make as if to do sth; **atti osceni (in luogo pubblico)** (*Dir*) indecent exposure *o* (*obscene behaviour*) **2** (*dimostrazione*): **atto di fede/affetto** *ecc* act of faith/friendship *ecc*; **dare atto a qn di qc** to give sb credit for sth; **prendere atto di qc** to take note of sth **3** (*Dir: documento*) document; (*del parlamento*) act; (*notarile*) deed; **atti** SMPL (*di congresso ecc*) proceedings; (*di processo*) records; **mettere agli atti** to put on record; **atto di morte** death certificate; **atto di nascita** birth certificate; **atto di proprietà** title deed; **atto pubblico** official document; **atto di vendita** bill of sale **4** (*Teatro*) act; **durante il secondo atto** during the second act; **una commedia in 3 atti** a three-act play; **atto unico** one-act play

atto[2], **-a** ['atto] AGG: **atto a** fit for, capable of; **atto alle armi** fit for military service; **atto a proseguire gli studi** capable of going on with one's studies

attonito, -a [at'tɔnito] AGG astonished, amazed, dumbfounded

attorcigliare [attortʃiʎ'ʎare] /27/ VT to twist; **attorcigliarsi** VIP to twist; **le funi si sono attorcigliate** the cords have got twisted; **attorcigliarsi** VR (*serpente*) to coil

attore, -trice [at'tore] SM, SF actor (actress); (*Dir*) plaintiff; **un attore famoso** a famous actor

attorniare [attor'njare] /19/ VT (*circondare*) to surround; **attorniarsi** VR: **attorniarsi di** to surround o.s. with

attorno [at'torno] AVV around; **è entrato ed è guardato attorno** he came in and looked around *o* about him; **tutt'attorno** all around; **d'attorno = di torno** ♦ PREP: **attorno a** around, round; **stare attorno a qn** to hang round sb; **attorno al fuoco** around *o* round the fire; **seduti attorno al fuoco abbiamo cantato fino all'alba** we sat round the fire and sang until dawn

attraccare [attrak'kare] /20/ VT, VI (*aus* avere *o* essere) (*Naut*) to dock, berth

attracco, -chi [at'trakko] SM (*Naut: manovra*) docking, berthing; (: *luogo*) berth

attrae *ecc* [at'trae] VB *vedi* **attrarre**

attraente [attra'ente] AGG (*gen*) attractive; **dai modi attraenti** charming; **una prospettiva ben poco attraente** not a particularly attractive *o* exciting prospect

attraggo *ecc* [at'traggo] VB *vedi* **attrarre**

attrarre [at'trarre] /123/ VT IRREG (*anche fig*) to attract; **l'idea non mi attrae per niente** the idea doesn't appeal to me at all; **l'attrasse a sé** he drew her into his arms

attrassi *ecc* [at'trassi] VB *vedi* **attrarre**

attrattiva [attrat'tiva] SF 1 (*fascino*) attraction, charm; **esercitare una grande *o* forte attrattiva su qn** to hold a great attraction for sb; **dotato di grande attrattiva** charming 2 (*cosa attraente*): **attrattive** SFPL attractions; **una località che offre molte attrattive per i giovani** a town with a lot to offer to young people

attratto, -a [at'tratto] PP *di* **attrarre**

attraversamento [attraversa'mento] SM crossing; **attraversamento pedonale** pedestrian crossing

attraversare [attraver'sare] /72/ VT (*strada, fiume, ponte*) to cross; (*bosco, città, periodo*) to go through; (*sogg: fiume*) to run through; **attraversare la strada di corsa** to rush across the road; **stai attento quando attraversi la strada** be careful when you cross the road; **attraversare il fiume a nuoto** to swim across the river; **attraversare il ponte correndo** to run across the bridge; **il fiume attraversava la città** the river passes through the town; **la pallottola gli ha attraversato il braccio** the bullet went straight through his arm; **attraversare un brutto periodo** to go through a bad patch; **sta attraversando un periodo difficile** she's going through a difficult time

attraverso [attra'verso] PREP 1 (*gen*) through; **abbiamo camminato attraverso i campi** we walked through the fields; **sono entrati attraverso la finestra** they got in through the window; **ha ottenuto il lavoro attraverso suo zio** he got the job through his uncle 2 (*da una parte all'altra*) across; **ha nuotato attraverso il fiume** he swam across the river 3 (*di tempo*) over, through; **attraverso i secoli** over *o* through the centuries

attrazione [attrat'tsjone] SF 1 (*gen, Fis*) attraction; **esercitare una grande attrazione su qc** to hold a great attraction for sb; **provare attrazione per qn** to feel attracted to sb; **uno spettacolo di grande attrazione** a very entertaining show 2 (*di circo, luna park*) attraction

attrezzare [attret'tsare] /72/ VT (*gen*) to equip; (*nave*) to rig

attrezzatura [attrettsa'tura] SF equipment *no pl*; (*di nave*) rigging; **attrezzature sportive** sports facilities; **attrezzature per uffici** office equipment

attrezzo [at'trettso] SM tool, implement; **attrezzi da giardinaggio** gardening tools; **carro attrezzi** breakdown truck; **gli attrezzi** SMPL: *Atletica*: the apparatus *sg*

attribuire [attribu'ire] /55/ VT: **attribuire qc a qn** (*gen*) to attribute sth to sb; (*premio*) to give *o* award sth to sb; **non attribuirmi colpe che non ho** don't blame me for things I didn't do; **va attribuito a lui il merito di tale successo** he should be given the credit for this success; **attribuirsi il merito di qc** to take the credit for sth; **il dipinto è stato attribuito a Picasso** the painting has been attributed to Picasso

attributo [attri'buto] SM (*anche Gramm*) attribute

attrice [at'tritʃe] SF actress; **un'attrice famosa** a famous actress

attrito [at'trito] SM (*anche fig*) friction

attuabile [attu'abile] AGG feasible

attuabilità [attuabili'ta] SF feasibility

attuale [attu'ale] AGG (*presente*) present; (*di attualità*) topical; (*che è in atto*) current; **al momento attuale** at the present moment; **l'attuale proprietario** the present owner; **lo stato attuale dell'economia** the present state of the economy; **l'attuale situazione politica** the current political situation; **le leggi attuali** the current legislation; **un problema attuale** a current problem; **il suo attuale lavoro** her current job; **è un filosofo ancora attuale** his philosophy is still

relevant today; **il marrone è molto attuale** (*di moda*) brown is very fashionable

❏ **attuale** non si traduce mai con la parola inglese *actual*

attualità [attuali'ta] SF INV 1 (*di argomento*) topicality; **un problema di grande attualità** a very topical question; **argomento d'attualità** topical subject 2 (*avvenimenti*) current affairs *pl*; **un programma di attualità** a current affairs programme; **notizie d'attualità** the news *sg*; **settimanale d'attualità** (weekly) news magazine

❏ **attualità** non si traduce mai con la parola inglese *actuality*

attualizzare [attualid'dzare] /72/ VT to focus attention on

attualmente [attual'mente] AVV at the moment, at present; **attualmente sono in tournée in America** they're on tour in America at the moment

❏ **attualmente** non si traduce mai con la parola inglese *actually*

attuare [attu'are] /72/ VT to carry out; **attuarsi** VIP to be realized

attuazione [attuat'tsjone] SF carrying out; **di facile/difficile attuazione** easy/difficult to carry out; **l'attuazione del progetto sembra impossibile** it seems an impossible plan to carry out

attutire [attu'tire] /55/ VT (*colpo, caduta*) to cushion; (*suono*) to deaden; (*dolore*) to ease, reduce; **attutirsi** VIP (*suono*) to die down; (*dolore*) to ease

AU ABBR = **allievo ufficiale**

audace [au'datʃe] AGG 1 (*coraggioso: persona*) daring, audacious; (: *impresa*) daring, bold 2 (*ipotesi*) daring; (*proposta*) suggestive; (*provocante: scollatura*) daring; (*sfacciato*) impudent, bold

audacia [au'datʃa] SF (*vedi agg*) daring, audacity; boldness; impudence; **tutti hanno notato l'audacia del suo stile** everyone noticed his daring design

audio ['audjo] SM INV (*TV, Radio, Cine*) sound; **il video funziona ma l'audio no** there's a picture but no sound

audiocassetta [audjokas'setta] SF (audio) cassette

audioleso, -a [audjo'lezo] SM, SF person who is hard of hearing

audiovisivo, -a [audjovi'zivo] AGG audiovisual; **sussidi audiovisivi** audiovisual aids

auditorio, -ri [audi'tɔrjo], **auditorium** [audi'tɔrjum] SM auditorium

audizione [audit'tsjone] SF hearing; (*Mus*) audition

auge ['audʒe] SF: **essere in auge** to be at the top

augurale [augu'rale] AGG: **messaggio augurale** greeting

augurare [augu'rare] /72/ VT (*buon viaggio, buonanotte ecc*) to wish; **ti auguro Buon Natale** I wish you a Merry Christmas; **gli augurò di guarire presto** he wished him a speedy recovery; **augurarsi qc/che succeda qc** to hope for sth/that sth will happen; **me lo auguro** I hope so; **mi auguro di no/sì** I hope not/so; **mi auguro che tu guarisca presto** I hope you get well soon

augurio, -ri [au'gurjo] SM 1 greeting; **auguri di Natale/Pasqua** Christmas/Easter greetings; **biglietto di auguri** greeting card; **fare gli auguri a qn** to give sb one's best wishes, wish sb all the best; **tanti auguri!** best wishes!, all the best!; (*di compleanno*) happy birthday!; (*buona fortuna*) good luck!; **auguri di pronta guarigione!** get well soon! 2 (*presagio*): **essere di cattivo/di buon augurio** to be ominous/a good omen

aula ['aula] SF (*di scuola*) classroom; (*di università*) lecture room *o* theatre; (*di tribunale*) courtroom; (*di Parlamento ecc*) chamber; **silenzio in aula!** silence in court!; **aula bunker** *high security court for Mafia trials*; **aula magna** main hall

aumentare [aumen'tare] /72/ VT (*prezzo*) to increase, put up; (*stipendio*) to increase, raise; **gli hanno aumentato l'affitto** his rent's gone up ♦ VI (*aus* essere) (*gen*) to increase; (*prezzi*) to go up, rise, increase; (*livello*) to rise; (*qualità*) to improve; **il prezzo della benzina è aumentato** the price of petrol has gone up; **aumentare di peso** (*persona*) to put on weight; **la produzione è aumentata del 50%** production has increased by 50%; **la disoccupazione è aumentata del 10%** unemployment's gone up by 10%

aumento [au'mento] SM: **aumento (di)** increase (in), rise (in); **un imprevisto aumento delle nascite** an unexpected rise in the birth rate; **c'è stato un aumento del 5% sul prezzo** there's been a 5% increase in the price; **aumento di stipendio** pay rise; **ottenere un aumento (di stipendio)** to get a (pay) rise; **essere in aumento** (*gen*) to be rising, be going up; (*qualità*) to be improving; **i prezzi sono in aumento** prices are rising

aureo, -a ['aureo] AGG (*di oro*) gold *attr*; (*fig: colore, periodo*) golden

aureola [au'reola] SF (*Rel, Astron*) halo

aurora [au'rɔra] SF (*anche fig*) dawn

ausiliare [auzi'ljare] AGG, SM (*gen, Gramm*) auxiliary

ausilio [au'ziljo] SM aid; **con l'ausilio di** with the aid of

auspicabile [auspi'kabile] AGG desirable; **è auspicabile che** it is to be hoped that

auspicare [auspi'kare] /20/ VT to hope for; **ci si auspica che** it is hoped that

auspicio, -ci [aus'pitʃo] SM 1 (*presagio*) omen; **essere di buon auspicio** to be a good omen, augur well 2 (*aiuto, protezione*) auspices *pl*; **sotto gli auspici di** under the auspices of

austerità [austeri'ta] SF (*gen, Econ*) austerity

austero, -a [aus'tero] AGG (*persona, vita*) austere; (*disciplina*) strict

australe [aus'trale] AGG southern

Australia [aus'tralja] SF Australia; **ti è piaciuta l'Australia?** did you like Australia?; **quest'estate andremo in Australia** we're going to Australia this summer

australiano, -a [austra'ljano] AGG, SM, SF Australian

Austria ['austria] SF Austria; **ti è piaciuta l'Austria?** did you like Austria?; **quest'estate andremo in Austria** we're going to Austria this summer

austriaco, -a, -ci, -che [aus'triako] AGG, SM, SF Austrian

autarchico, -a, -ci, -che [au'tarkiko] AGG (*sistema*) self-sufficient, autarkic; (*prodotto*) home *attr*, home-produced

aut aut ['aut 'aut] SM INV ultimatum; **dare un aut aut** to give *o* issue *o* deliver an ultimatum

autenticare [autenti'kare] /20/ VT to authenticate

autenticità [autentit ʃi'ta] SF authenticity

autentico, -a, -ci, -che [au'tentiko] AGG (*quadro, firma*) authentic, genuine; (*notizia, sentimento, fatto*) true; **la firma è autentica** the signature is genuine; **è un autentico cretino** he's an absolute fool

autista, -i, -e [au'tista] SM, SF driver; (*personale*) chauffeur; **fa l'autista di autobus** he's a bus driver; **auto con autista** chauffeur-driven car

auto ['auto] SF INV (*motor*) car, automobile (*USA*); **verremo in auto** we'll come by car; **auto blu** official car; **auto da corsa** racing car (*Brit*), race car (*USA*)

autoabbronzante [autoabbron'dzante] AGG self-tanning ♦ SM self-tanning cream

autoadesivo, -a [autoade'zivo] AGG self-adhesive ♦ SM sticker

autoarticolato [autoartiko'lato] SM articulated lorry (*Brit*), semi (trailer) (*USA*)

autobiografia [autobiogra'fia] SF autobiography

autobiografico, -a, -ci, -che [autobio'grafiko] AGG autobiographic(al); **un romanzo autobiografico** an autobiographical novel

autoblinda [auto'blinda] SF INV armoured (*Brit*) *o* armored (*USA*) car

autobomba [auto'bomba] SF INV car carrying a bomb; **l'autobomba si trovava a pochi metri** the car bomb was a few metres away

autobotte [auto'botte] SF tanker

autobus ['autobus] SM INV bus; **vado a scuola in autobus** I go to school by bus; **autobus a due piani** double-decker bus

autocarro [auto'karro] SM lorry (*Brit*), truck

autocertificazione [autot ʃertifikat'tsjone] SF self-declaration

autocisterna [autot ʃis'terna] SF tanker

autocolonna [autoko'lonna] SF convoy

autocontrollo [autokon'trɔllo] SM self-control

autocorriera SF coach, bus

autocratico, -a, -ci, -che [auto'kratiko] AGG autocratic

autocritica, -che [auto'kritika] SF self-criticism

autoctono, -a [au'tɔktono] AGG, SM, SF native

autodemolizione [autodemolit'tsjone] SF breaker's yard (*Brit*), junk yard (*USA*)

autodidatta, -i, -e [autodi'datta] SM, SF self-taught person, autodidact (*frm*); **è un autodidatta** he is self-taught

autodifesa [autodi'fesa] SF self-defence

autodistruttivo, -a [autodistrut'tivo] AGG (*persona, comportamento*) self-destructive

autoferrotranviario, -ria, -ri, -rie [autoferrotran'vjarjo] AGG public transport *attr*

autogestione [autodʒes'tjone] SF worker management

autogestito, -a [autodʒes'tito] AGG (*fabbrica*) under worker management

autogol [auto'gɔl] SM INV (*Calcio, anche fig*) own goal; **ha fatto autogol** he scored an own goal

autografo, -a [au'tɔgrafo] AGG, SM autograph; **mi ha fatto l'autografo!** he gave me his autograph!

autogrill [auto'gril] SM INV motorway café (*Brit*), roadside restaurant (*USA*)

autoimmune [autoim'mune] AGG autoimmune

autolesionismo [autolezjo'nizmo] SM self-destruction; (*fisicamente*) self-mutilation

autolinea [auto'linea] SF bus service

automa, -i [au'tɔma] SM (*anche fig*) automaton

automatico, -a, -ci, -che [auto'matiko] AGG automatic; **porte a chiusura automatica** automatic doors; **selezione automatica** (*Telec*) direct dialling, subscriber trunk dialling ♦ SM (*bottone*) press stud, snap fastener ♦ SF: (*pistola*) **automatica** automatic (pistol)

automazione [automat'tsjone] SF automation; **automazione delle procedure d'ufficio** office automation

automedicazione [automedikat'tsjone] SF: **medicinale di automedicazione** self-medication

automezzo [auto'mɛddzo] SM motor vehicle

automobile [auto'mɔbile] SF (motor) car, automobile (*USA*); **viaggiare in automobile** to travel by car

automobilismo [automobi'lizmo] SM (*gen*) motoring; (*Sport*) motor racing

automobilista, -i, -e [automobi'lista] SM, SF motorist

automobilistico, -a, -ci, -che [automobi'listiko] AGG (*industria, assicurazione, incidente*) car *attr*, automobile *attr* (*USA*); (*sport*) motor *attr*

autonoleggio, -gi [autono'leddʒo] SM car hire (*Brit*), car rental; **c'è un autonoleggio da queste parti?** is there a car rental agency near here?

autonomia [autono'mia] SF (*Pol*) autonomy; (*fig: di idee, comportamento*) independence; (*Tecn: di macchine, motori*) range; **autonomia di volo** (*Aer*) flight range

autonomo, -a [au'tɔnomo] AGG (*Pol*) autonomous; (*sindacato, pensiero*) independent; **lavoro autonomo** self-employment ♦ **autonomi** SMPL *independent trade union members*

autoparco, -chi [auto'parko] SM (*insieme di automezzi*) transport fleet; (*parcheggio*) car park (*Brit*), parking lot (*USA*)

autopompa [auto'pompa] SF fire engine

autopsia [autop'sia] SF autopsy, post-mortem (examination)

autoradio [auto'radjo] SF INV (*apparecchio*) car radio; (*autoveicolo*) radio car; **gli hanno rotto il finestrino per rubare l'autoradio** they broke the window to steal his car radio

autore, -trice [au'tore] SM (*gen, scrittore*) author; (*di pittura*) painter; (*di scultura*) sculptor; (*di musica*) composer; **l'autore del delitto/del furto** the person who committed the crime/the robbery; **quadro d'autore** painting by a famous artist; **diritti d'autore** copyright *sg*; (*compenso*) royalties

autoreggente [autored'dʒɛnte] AGG: **calze autoreggenti** hold-up stockings, hold-ups

autoregolamentazione [autoregolamentat'tsjone] SF self-regulation

autorevole [auto'revole] AGG (*giudizio*) authoritative; (*fonte*) reliable; (*influente: persona*) influential

autoricaricabile [autorikari'kabile] AGG: **scheda autoricaricabile** top-up card

autorimessa [autori'messa] SF garage

autorità [autori'ta] SF INV 1 (*potere*) authority; **agire d'autorità** to act with authority, have the authority to act; **esercitare la propria autorità su qn** to exercise one's authority over sb 2 (*Amm: governo, ente*): **l'autorità, le autorità** the authorities *pl*; **le autorità competenti** the relevant authorities; **erano presenti tutte le autorità** all the public services were represented 3 (*esperto*) authority, expert; **è una vera autorità in questo campo** he's a real expert in this field 4 (*prestigio*) repute

autoritratto [autori'tratto] SM self-portrait

autorizzare [autorid'dzare] /72/ VT to give permission for, authorize; **autorizzare qn a fare qc** to give sb permission to do sth; **mi hanno autorizzato ad aprire la corrispondenza** I was given permission to open correspondence; **"vietato l'accesso al personale non autorizzato"** "authorized personnel only"

autorizzazione [autoriddzat'tsjone] SF (*permesso*) authorization, permission; (*documento*) permit; **autorizzazione a procedere** (*Dir*) authorization to proceed

autoscatto [autos'katto] SM (*Fot*) self-timer

autoscontro [autos'kontro] SM dodgem car (*Brit*), bumper car (*USA*)

autoscuola [autos'kwɔla] SF driving school

autosnodato [autozno'dato] SM articulated vehicle

autostima [autos'tima] SF self-esteem

autostop [autos'tɔp] SM hitchhiking; **fare l'autostop** to hitchhike; **è andato a Parigi in** *o* **con l'autostop** he hitchhiked to Paris

autostoppista, -i, -e [autostop'pista] SM, SF hitchhiker; **abbiamo dato un passaggio ad un autostoppista** we gave a hitchhiker a lift

autostrada [autos'trada] SF motorway (*Brit*), highway (*USA*); **autostrada informatica** information (super)highway

autosufficiente [autosuffi'tʃɛnte] AGG self-sufficient

autosufficienza [autosuffi'tʃɛntsa] SF self-sufficiency

autotreno [auto'treno] SM lorry with trailer (*Brit*), trailer truck (*USA*)

autoveicolo [autove'ikolo] SM motor vehicle

autovettura [autovet'tura] SF (motor) car

autunnale [autun'nale] AGG (*di autunno*) autumn *attr*, fall *attr* (*USA*); (*da autunno*) autumnal

autunno [au'tunno] SM autumn, fall (*USA*); **in autunno** in autumn; **l'autunno della vita** the autumn of life *o* one's years

AV SIGLA = Avellino

avallare [aval'lare] /72/ VT (*Fin*) to guarantee; (*sostenere*) to back; (*confermare*) to confirm

avallo [a'vallo] SM (*Fin*) guarantee

avambraccio, -ci [avam'brattʃo] SM forearm

avamposto [avam'posto] SM (*Mil*) outpost

Avana [a'vana] SF Havana

avana [a'vana] SM INV (*sigaro*) Havana (cigar); (*colore*) tobacco brown ♦ AGG (*colore*) tobacco-brown, tobacco-coloured

avanguardia [avan'gwardja] SF 1 (*Mil, o fig*) vanguard; **essere all'avanguardia** to be in the vanguard 2 (*Arte*) avant-garde; **d'avanguardia** avant-garde *attr*

avanscoperta [avansko'perta] SF (*Mil*) reconnaissance; **andare in avanscoperta** to reconnoitre

avanti [a'vanti] AVV 1 (*moto: andare, venire*) forward; **fare un passo avanti** to take a step forward; **ho fatto un passo avanti** I took a step forward; **farsi avanti** to come forward; **avanti e indietro** backwards and forwards, to and fro; **essere avanti negli studi** (*a scuola*) to be well ahead in one's studies; **essere avanti di 5 punti** (*Sport, etc*) to be ahead *o* be leading by 5 points; **tirare avanti** (*fig*) to get by, survive; **in avanti** forward; **spostalo un po' in avanti** move it forward a bit; **piegarsi in avanti** to bend forward; **più avanti** further on 2 (*tempo: prima*) before; **l'anno avanti** the year before 3 (*tempo: posteriore a*): **d'ora in avanti** from now on; **più avanti** later; **essere avanti con gli** *o* **negli anni** to be well on in years; **il mio orologio è** *o* **va avanti** my watch is fast; **mettere avanti l'orologio** to put the clock forward; **bisogna mettere l'orologio avanti di un'ora** you have to put the clock forward an hour; **guardare avanti** to look ahead 4 **andare avanti** to go forward; (*continuare*) to go on, carry on; (*fig: fare progressi*) to get on; (*: sopravvivere*) to get by; **non aspettatemi, andate avanti!** don't wait for me, go on (ahead)!; **non possiamo andare avanti così** we can't carry *o* go on like this; **la mia tesi sta andando avanti** my thesis is coming on 5 **mandare avanti la famiglia** to provide for one's family; **mandare avanti un'azienda** to run a business 6 **avanti!** (*entra*) come in!; (*non fare così*) come on!; **avanti! si accomodi!** come (*o* go) in and sit down!; **avanti il prossimo!** next please!; **avanti, assaggialo!** go on, taste it!; **avanti, march!** forward, march!; **avanti tutta!** (*Naut*) full speed ahead! ♦ PREP: **avanti a** (*luogo*) before, in front of; (*tempo*) before; **avanti Cristo** before Christ; **nel 55 avanti Cristo** in 55 BC ♦ SM INV (*Sport*) forward

avantreno [avan'treno] SM (*Aut*) front chassis

avanzamento [avantsa'mento] SM (*gen*) advance; (*progresso*) progress; (*promozione di grado*) promotion

avanzare¹ [avan'tsare] /72/ VT (*proposta ecc*) to put forward; (*spostare in avanti: oggetto*) to move forward; **avanzare di grado** to promote sb ♦ VI (*aus avere o essere*) (*procedere*) to advance, move forward; (*stagioni*) approach; (*fig: nello studio ecc*) to make progress; **avanzare negli anni** to grow older, get on; **con l'avanzare degli anni** with the passing of time; **avanzare di grado** to be promoted

avanzare² [avan'tsare] /72/ VI (*aus essere*) 1 (*essere d'avanzo*) to be left over, remain; **è avanzato del pane da ieri** there is some bread left over from yesterday; **non m'avanza molto tempo** I haven't (got) much time left; **basta e avanza** that's more than enough 2 (*Mat*): **sette diviso tre fa due e avanza uno** seven divided by three is two remainder one ♦ VT: **avanzare qc (da qn)** (*essere creditore*) to be owed sth by sb; **avanzo dieci euro da te** you owe me ten euros

avanzato, -a [avan'tsato] AGG (*teoria, tecnica*) advanced; **essere in età avanzata** to be of an advanced age; **a primavera avanzata** late in *o* in late spring; **a un'ora avanzata della notte** late at night

avanzo [a'vantso] SM 1 (*gen, Mat*) remainder; (*di stoffa*) remnant; (*di carta*) scrap; **avanzo di galera** (*fig*) jailbird; **avanzi** SMPL (*di cibo*) leftovers 2 (*sovrappiù*): **averne d'avanzo (di qc)** to have more than enough (of sth); **ce n'è d'avanzo** there is more than enough 3 (*Comm*) surplus; (*eccedenza di bilancio*) profit carried forward

❑ **avanzo** non si traduce mai con la parola inglese *advance*.

avaria [ava'ria] SF (*guasto meccanico*) breakdown, failure; (*danneggiamento*) damage; **motore in avaria** engine out of action; **subire un'avaria all'elica** to suffer *o* have a damaged propeller

avariato, -a [ava'rjato] AGG (*cibo*) off; (*merce*) damaged

avarizia [ava'rittsja] SF (*peccato*) avarice; (*tirchieria*) meanness, stinginess; **crepi l'avarizia!** hang the expense!

avaro, -a [a'varo] AGG (*tirchio*) mean, stingy, tight-fisted; **è più avara di lui** she's stingier than him 2 **avaro di** (*complimenti, parole*) sparing (with) ♦ SM, SF miser

avena [a'vena] SF oats *pl*

PAROLA CHIAVE

avere [a'vere] VB IRREG /13/ VT

1 (*gen*) to have; (*ricevere, ottenere*) to get; (*indossare*) to wear, have on; **avere da bere** to have something to drink; **avere da mangiare** to have something to eat; **non ha soldi** he has no money, he doesn't have any money, he hasn't got any money; **ho le mani sporche** my hands are dirty; **aveva le mani che gli tremavano** his hands were shaking

2 (*età, forma, colore*) to be; **quanti anni hai?** how old are you?; **ho vent'anni** I am twenty (years old); **ha 2 anni più di me** he's two years older than me; **aveva la mia stessa età** he was the same age as me; **avere fame** to be hungry; **avere paura** to be afraid

3 (*tempo*): **ne hai ancora per molto?** have you got much longer to go?; **ne avremo ancora per due giorni prima di arrivare a Londra** we've got another two days to go before we get to London; **quanti ne abbiamo oggi?** what's the date today?

4 (*fraseologia*): **averne fin sopra i capelli** (*fam*) to be fed up to

the teeth; **ce l'hai con me?** are you angry with me?; **cos'hai?** what's wrong o what's the matter (with you)?; **avere qc da fare** to have sth to do; **ho ancora due lettere da scrivere** I have to o must write another two letters, I've still got two letters to write; **non hai che da dirglielo** you only have to tell him; **non hai da preoccuparti per me** you don't have to o needn't worry about me; **ma cos'hai da lamentarti?** what have you got to complain about?

♦ VB AUS (*con participio passato*): **lo hai/avevi sentito?** have/ had you heard from him?; **l'ho incontrata ieri** I met her yesterday; **quando l'avrò visto, ti dirò** when I've seen him, I'll let you know

♦ VB IMPERS: **si è avuto un risultato imprevisto** there was a surprising result; **ieri si è avuto un abbassamento di temperatura** there was a drop in temperature yesterday

♦ SM

1 il dare e l'avere (*Fin*) debits and credits *pl*
2 (*richezze*): **gli averi** SMPL wealth *sg*, fortune *sg*

aviario, -a AGG bird *attr*; **influenza aviaria** bird flu

aviatore, -trice [avja'tore] SM, SF pilot, aviator

aviazione [avjat'tsjone] SF aviation; **aviazione civile** civil aviation; **aviazione militare** air force

avicoltura [avikol'tura] SF (*di pollame*) poultry farming; (*di uccelli*) bird breeding

avidità [avidi'ta] SF: **avidità (di)** (*denaro ecc*) greed (for); (*gloria*) thirst (for)

avido, -a ['avido] AGG: **avido (di)** (*pegg*) greedy (for); (*fig: di conoscenza*) eager (for)

aviere [a'vjere] SM (*Mil*) airman

avitaminosi [avitami'nɔzi] SF vitamin deficiency

avo ['avo] SM (*antenato*) ancestor; (*letter: nonno*) grandfather; **i miei avi** my forebears; **i nostri avi** our ancestors

avocado [avo'kado] SM INV (*albero*) avocado; (*frutto*) avocado (pear)

avorio, -ri [a'vɔrjo] SM ivory; **torre d'avorio** (*fig*) ivory tower

avulso, -a [a'vulso] AGG: **parole avulse dal contesto** words taken out of context; **avulso dalla società** (*fig*) cut off from society

Avv. ABBR = **Avvocato**

avvalersi [avva'lersi] /126/ VIP: **avvalersi di** to avail o.s. of

avvallamento [avvalla'mento] SM (*Geol*) depression, sinking *no pl*; (*di strada ecc*) subsidence

avvalorare [avvalo'rare] /72/ VT (*comprovare*) to confirm; **avvalorare una tesi** to confirm a theory

avvantaggiare [avvantad'dʒare] /62/ VT (*favorire*) to favour (*Brit*), favor (*USA*); **avvantaggiarsi** VR **1** (*acquistare vantaggio*) to gain an advantage o get ahead; **avvantaggiarsi negli affari** to get ahead in business; **avvantaggiarsi nella carriera/nello studio** to get ahead in one's career/in one's studies; **avvantaggiarsi di qualche metro/minuto** to gain a few metres/minutes; **avvantaggiarsi su qn** to get ahead of sb **2** (*avvalersi*): **avvantaggiarsi di** to take advantage of

avvedersi [avve'dersi] /127/ VIP IRREG: **avvedersi di qn/qc** to notice sb/sth

avveduto, -a [avve'duto] AGG (*accorto*) prudent; (*scaltro*) astute

avvelenamento [avvelena'mento] SM poisoning

avvelenare [avvele'nare] /72/ VT to poison; **avvelenare l'esistenza a qn** to make sb's life a misery; **è inutile avvelenarsi il sangue per così poco** there's no point in making yourself miserable over nothing; **avvelenarsi** VR to poison o.s.

avvenente [avve'nente] AGG attractive

avvenenza [avve'nentsa] SF attractiveness

avvengo *ecc* [av'vengo] VB *vedi* **avvenire**

avvenimento [avveni'mento] SM event; **i principali avvenimenti sportivi** the main sporting events

avvenire [avve'nire] /128/ VI IRREG (*aus essere*) to happen, occur ♦ AGG INV future *attr* ♦ SM (*gen*) future; (*carriera*) future, prospects *pl*; **fa progetti per l'avvenire** she's making plans for the future; **in avvenire** in the future

avvenni *ecc* [av'venni] VB *vedi* **avvenire**

avventare [avven'tare] /72/ VT (*scagliare*): **gli avventò contro il cane** he set the dog on him; **avventarsi** VR (*scagliarsi*): **avventarsi su** o **contro qn/qc** to hurl o.s. at sb/sth

avventato, -a [avven'tato] AGG (*giudizio*) rash; **è stata una decisione avventata** it was a rash decision

avventizio, -zia, -zi, -zie [avven'tittsjo] AGG (*impiegato*) temporary; (*guadagno*) casual ♦ SM temporary clerk

avvento [av'vento] SM **1** (*venuta*) coming, advent; **avvento al trono** accession to the throne **2** (*Rel*): **l'Avvento** Advent

avventore [avven'tore] SM customer

avventura [avven'tura] SF (*gen*) adventure; (*vicenda amorosa*) (love) affair; **è la vacanza ideale per chi ama l'avventura** it's an ideal holiday for anyone who likes adventure; **ha avuto un'avventura con una sposata** he had an affair with a married woman

avventurarsi [avventu'rarsi] /72/ VR: **avventurarsi (in qc)** to venture (into sth)

avventuriero, -a [avventu'rjero] SM, SF adventurer

avventuroso, -a [avventu'roso] AGG adventurous

avvenuto, -a [avve'nuto] PP *di* **avvenire**

avverarsi [avve'rarsi] /72/ VIP to come true; **il suo sogno si è avverato** her dream came true

avverbio, -bi [av'verbjo] SM adverb

avversare [avver'sare] /72/ VT to oppose

avversario, -ria, -ri, -rie [avver'sarjo] AGG opposing; **la squadra avversaria** the opposing team ♦ SM, SF (*Sport*) opponent; (*Pol*) adversary, opponent; **ha battuto l'avversario** he beat his opponent

avversione [avver'sjone] SF: **avversione (per)** loathing (for), aversion (to); **nutrire un'avversione per** to harbour a dislike for

avversità [avversi'ta] SF INV adversity; **le avversità della vita** life's tribulations

avverso, -a [av'verso] AGG (*forze, sorte*) adverse, hostile; (*tempo*) unfavourable (*Brit*), unfavorable (*USA*), adverse; (*persona: contrario*): **avverso a** against

avvertenza [avver'tentsa] SF **1** (*avviso*) warning; **avvertenza ai lettori** (*prefazione*) foreword **2** (*cautela*) care *no pl* **3** (*per l'uso*) **avvertenze** SFPL instructions

avvertimento [avverti'mento] SM warning
❑ **avvertimento** non si traduce mai con la parola inglese *advertisement*

avvertire [avver'tire] /45/ VT **1** (*informare*): **avvertire (di)** to inform (of), let know (of); **avvertimi prima di partire** let me know when you're leaving; **avresti anche potuto avvertirmi** you could have told me **2** (*ammonire*) to warn; **ti avevo avvertito!** I warned you! **3** (*percepire: suono*) to perceive, hear; (*sentire: dolore*) to feel

avvezzo, -a [av'vettso] AGG: **avvezzo a** accustomed to, used to

avviamento [avvia'mento] SM **1** (*gen, atto*) starting; (*effetto*) start **2** (*insegnamento preparatorio: ad una carriera*) training; (: *ad uno studio*) introduction **3** (*Meccanica: messa in moto*) starting; **avviamento a freddo** cold start; **motorino d'avviamento** starter (motor) **4** (*Comm*) goodwill

avviare [avvi'are] /60/ VT **1** (*indirizzare: a studi, mestiere*) to lead, direct **2** (*mettere in moto*) to start (up); **avviare con la manovella** (*Aut*) to crank, give a crank start to **3** (*iniziare: attività, impresa*) to start up, set up; (: *trattative*) to set in motion; (: *discussione*) to get going; (: *lavoro a maglia*) to cast on; **avviarsi** VIP (*incamminarsi*): **avviarsi (a** o **verso qc)** to set out o off (for sth); **avviarsi a fare qc** to be about to do sth, be on the point of doing sth; **avviati, poi ti raggiungo** you go on ahead and I'll catch up with you; **l'estate si avvia alla fine** summer is drawing to an end

avvicendamento [avvitʃenda'mento] SM (*gen*) alternation; (*Agr: delle colture*) rotation; **c'è molto avvicendamento di personale** there is a high turnover of staff

avvicendare [avvitʃen'dare] /72/ VT to alternate; **avvicendarsi** VR (*uso reciproco*) to alternate

avvicinamento [avvitʃina'mento] SM (*Mil, Aer*) approach; **ha ottenuto un avvicinamento** (*soldato*) he has been posted nearer home; (*in un lavoro*) he has been given a transfer nearer home

avvicinare [avvitʃi'nare] /72/ VT **1** (*mettere vicino*): **avvicinare (a)** to bring near (to); **avvicina la sedia al tavolo** bring the chair nearer to the table, draw the chair up to the table; **dovrò avvicinare il tavolo alla finestra** I'll have to move the table closer to the window; **il dolore li ha avvicinati** (*fig*) their sorrow has brought them closer together **2** (*farsi vicino a: persona*) to approach; **lo avvicinò per strada e si**

presentò she came up to him in the street and introduced herself; **avvicinarsi** VIP 1 (*andare vicino*): **avvicinarsi (a)** to approach, go (*o* come) up to; **il treno si avvicinava alla stazione** the train was approaching the station; **avvicinati! come here!, come closer!; mi ha fatto cenno di avvicinarmi** he beckoned to me to come closer 2 (*essere imminente: stagione, periodo*) to draw near 3 (*somigliare*): **avvicinarsi (a)** be similar (to), be close (to)

avvilente [avvi'lɛnte] AGG (*umiliante*) humiliating; (*scoraggiante*) discouraging, disheartening

avvilimento [avvili'mento] SM (*vedi vb*) humiliation; discouragement

avvilire [avvi'lire] /55/ VT (*mortificare*) to humiliate; (*scoraggiare*) to dishearten, discourage; (*degradare*) to degrade; **avvilirsi** VIP to lose heart, become discouraged

avvilito, -a [avvi'lito] AGG (*scoraggiato*) disheartened, discouraged; (*depresso*) depressed

avviluppare [avvilup'pare] /72/ VT 1 (*avvolgere*): **avviluppare (in)** to wrap up (in); (*sogg: nebbia*) to envelop (*ingarbugliare*) to entangle; **avvilupparsi** VR (*avvolgersi*): **avvilupparsi in qc** to wrap o.s. up in sth; **avvilupparsi** VIP (*aggrovigliarsi*) to get entangled *o* tangled up

avvinazzato, -a [avvinat'tsato] AGG drunken ♦ SM, SF drunkard

avvincente [avvin't ʃɛnte] AGG (*spettacolo, lettura*) enthralling

avvincere [av'vint ʃere] /129/ VT IRREG (*sogg: spettacolo, lettura*) to enthral, fascinate

avvinghiare [avvin'gjare] /19/ VT to clutch, clasp; **avvinghiarsi** VR: **avvinghiarsi a** to cling to; **la bambina gli si avvinghiò al collo** the girl threw her arms round his neck

avvinsi ecc [av'vinsi] VB *vedi* **avvincere**

avvinto, -a [av'vinto] PP *di* **avvincere**

avvio, -vii [av'vio] SM start, beginning; **dare l'avvio a qc** to start sth off; **prendere l'avvio** to get going, get under way

avvisaglia [avvi'zaʎʎa] SF: **le prime avvisaglie** (*sintomo: di temporale ecc*) the first signs; (: *di malattia*) the first signs, the first symptoms

avvisare [avvi'zare] /72/ VT 1 (*informare*) to inform, notify 2 (*mettere in guardia*) to warn; **uomo avvisato, mezzo salvato** (*Proverbio*) forewarned is forearmed

avvisatore [avviza'tore] SM (*apparecchio d'allarme*) alarm; **avvisatore acustico** horn; **avvisatore d'incendio** fire alarm

avviso [av'vizo] SM 1 (*comunicazione: al pubblico*) notice; **hai letto l'avviso in bacheca?** have you read the notice on the board?; **dare l'avviso a qn di qc** to give sb notice of sth; **fino a nuovo avviso** until further notice; **avviso di chiamata** (*servizio*) call waiting; (*segnale*) call waiting signal 2 (*documento di notificazione*) notice; **avviso di garanzia** notification (*of impending investigation and of the right to name a defence lawyer*); **avviso di sfratto** eviction order 3 (*Comm*): **avviso di consegna** consignment note; **avviso di pagamento** payment advice; **avviso di spedizione** delivery note 4 (*consiglio, avvertimento*) warning; **dare un avviso a qn** to warn sb; **mettere qn sull'avviso** to put sb on their guard 5 (*opinione*) opinion; **a mio avviso** in my opinion 6 (*inserzione pubblicitaria*) advertisement, ad

❑ **avviso** non si traduce mai con la parola inglese *advice*

avvistamento [avvista'mento] SM sighting

avvistare [avvis'tare] /72/ VT to sight

avvitare [avvi'tare] /72/ VT (*vite*) to screw in (*o* down); (*fissare con viti*) to screw; (*lampadina*) to screw in; **avvitarsi** VR (*vite, lampadina*) to screw in; (*Aer*) to spin, go into a spin

avvizzire [avvit'tsire] /55/ VI (*aus essere*) to wither; **avvizzirsi** VIP to wither, shrivel

avvocato [avvo'kato] SM 1 (*gen*) lawyer; (*in corti inferiori*) solicitor; (*in corti superiori*) barrister (*Brit*), attorney(-at-law) (*USA*); **suo padre fa l'avvocato** his father's a lawyer; **consultare il proprio avvocato** to consult one's lawyer; **avvocato di parte civile/difensore** counsel for the plaintiff/the defence 2 (*fig*) advocate, defender; **avvocato delle cause perse** defender of lost causes; **avvocato del diavolo** devil's advocate; **fare l'avvocato del diavolo** to play devil's advocate

avvolgere [av'vɔldʒere] VB IRREG /96/ VT 1 (*bambino, oggetto*) to wrap (up); (*arrotolare: tappeto*) to roll up; (: *bobina*) to

wind up; **puoi avvolgere la scatola con questa carta** you can wrap the box in this paper; **avvolto dalla nebbia** enveloped in fog; **avvolto dal mistero/silenzio** shrouded in mystery/silence 2 **avvolgere qc intorno a qc** to wind sth round sth; **avvolgersi** VR to wrap o.s. up; **si è avvolto nella coperta** he wrapped himself up in the blanket

avvolgibile [avvol'dʒibile] AGG roll-up *attr*, roller *attr* ♦ SM (*roller*) blind (*Brit*), window shade (*USA*)

avvolgimento [avvoldʒi'mento] SM (*Elettr*) winding

avvolsi ecc [av'vɔlsi] VB *vedi* **avvolgere**

avvolto, -a [av'vɔlto] PP *di* **avvolgere**

avvoltoio, -oi [avvol'tojo] SM (*gen, o fig*) vulture

azalea [addza'lɛa] SF azalea

Azerbaigian [addzerbai'dʒan] SM Azerbaijan

azerbaigiano, -a [addzerbai'dʒano] AGG Azerbaijani ♦ SM, SF Azerbaijani ♦ SM (*lingua*) Azerbaijani

azero [ad'dʒɛro] AGG, SM, SF Azeri

azienda [ad'dzjenda] SF (*gen*) company, business, firm, concern; **azienda agricola** commercial farm; **azienda (autonoma) di soggiorno e turismo** tourist board; **azienda avicola** poultry farm; **azienda a partecipazione statale** *company in which the state has a controlling interest*; **azienda pubblica** state (run) company

aziendale [addzjen'dale] AGG company *attr*; **la nostra politica aziendale** our company policy; **gestione aziendale** business management; **mensa aziendale** company canteen; **organizzazione aziendale** business administration

azionare [attsjo'nare] /72/ VT to activate

azionario, -ria, -ri, -rie [attsjo'narjo] AGG share *attr*; **mercato azionario** stock market; **capitale azionario** share capital

azione¹ [at'tsjone] SF 1 (*l'agire*) action; **entrare in azione** (*piano*) to come into operation; **passare all'azione** to take action; (*Mil*) to go into action 2 (*atto*) action, act; **bequ a/cattiva azione** good/bad deed 3 (*effetto*) action; **l'azione dei gas tossici** the action of toxic gases 4 (*Teatro, Sport*) action; (*trama*) plot; **film d'azione** action movie 5 (*Dir: processo*) (law)suit, action

azione² [at'tsjone] SF (*Fin: titolo*) share (*Brit*), stock (*USA*); **azioni ordinarie** ordinary shares; **azioni preferenziali** preference shares (*Brit*), preferred stock *sg* (*USA*)

azionista, -i, -e [attsjo'nista] SM, SF shareholder

azoto [ad'dzɔto] SM nitrogen

azteco, -a, -chi, -che [as'tɛko] AGG, SM, SF Aztec

azzannare [attsan'nare] /72/ VT to maul, bite

azzardare [addzar'dare] /72/ VT (*domanda, ipotesi*) to hazard, venture; (*uso assoluto*) to take a risk; **azzardarsi** VIP: **azzardarsi a fare qc** to dare (to) do sth

azzardato, -a [addzar'dato] AGG (*ipotesi, risposta*) rash; (*impresa*) risky; **non voglio dare un parere azzardato, ma...** I don't want to be hasty *o* rash, but ...

azzardo [ad'dzardo] SM risk; **gioco d'azzardo** gambling; **gli piace giocare d'azzardo** (*anche fig*) he likes gambling

azzeccare [attsek'kare] /20/ VT (*bersaglio*) to hit, strike; (*indovinare: risposta, pronostico*) to guess; **ha azzeccato il pronostico al totocalcio** he had a win on the pools; **non ne azzecca mai una** he never gets anything right; **che ci azzecca?** (*fam*) what's that got to do with it?

azzeramento [addzera'mento] SM (*Inform*) reset

azzerare [addze'rare] /72/ VT 1 (*Mat, Fis*) to make equal to zero, reduce to zero 2 (*Tecn: strumento*) to (re)set to zero; (*Inform*) to reset

azzimo, -a ['addzimo] AGG (*non lievitato: pane*) unleavened ♦ SM unleavened bread

azzoppare [attsop'pare] /72/ VT to lame, make lame; **azzopparsi** VIP to become lame

Azzorre [ad'dzɔrre] SFPL: **le Azzorre** the Azores

azzuffarsi [attsuf'farsi] /72/ VIP (*gen*) to come to blows; (*bambini*) to squabble

azzurro, -a [ad'dzurro] AGG 1 (*colore*) blue, azure; **occhi azzurri** blue eyes; **il principe azzurro** Prince Charming 2 (*Sport: della nazionale italiana*) of the Italian team 3 (*Pol*) *relating to the political party Forza Italia* ♦ SM 1 (*colore*) blue, azure 2 (*Sport: atleta*) member of the Italian team; **gli azzurri** SMPL the Italian team

azzurrognolo, -a [addzur'roɲɲolo] AGG bluish

Bb

B, b [bi] SF INV, SM INV (*lettera*) B, b; **B come Bologna** ≈ B for Benjamin (*Brit*), ≈ B for Baker (*USA*)

BA SIGLA = **Bari**

babau [baˈbau] SM INV ogre, bogey man

babbeo [babˈbɛo] SM fool, idiot

babbo [ˈbabbo] SM (*fam*) dad, daddy; **è un regalino per il mio babbo** it's a little present for my dad; **Babbo Natale** Father Christmas, Santa Claus

babbuccia, -ce [babˈbuttʃa] SF (Turkish) slipper; (*per neonati*) bootee

babbuino [babbuˈino] SM baboon

babilonese [babiloˈnese] AGG, SM, SF Babylonian

Babilonia [babiˈlɔnja] SF Babylon

babordo [baˈbordo] SM (*Naut*) port side; **a babordo** to port

babysitter [ˈbeɪbsɪtəʳ] SM INV, SF INV baby-sitter

bacato, -a [baˈkato] AGG (*frutto*) worm-eaten, maggoty; (*fig: mente*) diseased; (: *persona*) corrupt

bacca, -che [ˈbakka] SF berry

baccalà [bakkaˈla] SM INV (*pesce*) dried salted cod; (*fig: persona sciocca*) dummy; **secco come un baccalà** (*magro*) as thin as a rake

baccano [bakˈkano] SM row, din; **fare baccano** to make a row *o* din; **smettetela di fare baccano!** stop making this racket!

baccello [batˈtʃɛllo] SM pod

bacchetta [bakˈketta] SF (*bastoncino*) rod, stick; (*di tamburo*) drumstick; (*di direttore d'orchestra*) baton; (*per mangiare alla cinese*) chopstick; **comandare a bacchetta** to rule with a rod of iron; **bacchetta magica** magic wand

bacheca, -che [baˈkeka] SF 1 (*per affissione*) notice board (*Brit*), bulletin board (*USA*); **appendilo in bacheca** put it on the notice board; **bacheca elettronica** (*Inform*) bulletin board 2 (*mobile*) showcase, display case

baciamano [batʃaˈmano] SM: **fare il baciamano a qn** to kiss sb's hand

baciare [baˈtʃare] /14/ VT to kiss; **lo baciò sulla guancia** she kissed him on the cheek, she kissed his cheek; **le sponde baciate dal sole** the sun-kissed shores; **baciarsi** VR (*uso reciproco*) to kiss (each other *o* one another); **ci siamo baciati** we kissed

bacillo [baˈtʃillo] SM bacillus, germ

bacinella [batʃiˈnella] SF (*gen, recipiente*) bowl; (*per lavarsi*) basin; **una bacinella di plastica** a plastic bowl

bacino [baˈtʃino] SM 1 (*Anat*) pelvis; **sollevate il bacino** raise your pelvis 2 (*Geog*) basin 3 (*Geol*) field, bed; **bacino carbonifero** coalfield; **bacino petrolifero** oilfield 4 (*Naut*) dock; **bacino di carenaggio** dry dock; **bacino galleggiante** floating dock

bacio, -ci [ˈbatʃo] SM 1 kiss; **dare un bacio a qn** to give sb a kiss; **coprire qn di baci** to smother sb with kisses; **dare il bacio della buonanotte a qn** to kiss sb goodnight; **tanti baci** (*fine di lettera*) love and kisses, lots of love; **un bacio sulla guancia** a kiss on the cheek 2 (*gusto di gelato*) chocolate and hazelnut

baco, -chi [ˈbako] SM (*gen, verme*) worm, maggot; (*larva*) grub; (*Inform*) bug; **questa mela ha il suo baco** there's a worm in this apple; **baco da seta** silkworm

bada [ˈbada] SF: **tenere qn a bada** (*tener d'occhio*) to keep an eye on sb; (*tenere a distanza*) to hold sb at bay

badante [baˈdante] SM, SF care worker

badare [baˈdare] /72/ VI (*aus avere*) **badare a** 1 (*occuparsi di: negozio, casa*) to look after, mind; (: *bambino, malato*) to take care of, look after; (: *cliente*) to attend to; **bada agli affari tuoi!, bada ai fatti tuoi!** mind your own business! 2 (*fare attenzione*) to pay attention to, mind; **nessuno gli ha badato** nobody paid any attention to him; **bada (a te)!** watch out!; **bada a non cadere** mind *o* be careful you don't fall 3

(*preoccuparsi*) to care about; **non bada a ciò che dice la gente** he doesn't care what people say; **è un tipo che non bada a spese** he doesn't mind how much he spends

badia [baˈdia] SF abbey

badile [baˈdile] SM shovel

baffo [ˈbaffo] SM 1 **baffi** SMPL (*di persona*) moustache *sg*; (*di animale*) whiskers; **un pranzo da leccarsi i baffi** a mouth-watering meal; **ridere sotto i baffi** to laugh up one's sleeve; **di quello che mi ha detto me ne faccio un baffo** (*fam*) I don't give *o* care a damn about what he said 2 (*sgorbio, sbavatura*) smear, smudge

bagagliaio, -ai [bagaʎˈʎajo] SM 1 (*di auto*) boot (*Brit*), trunk (*USA*); (*di treno*) luggage van (*Brit*), baggage car (*USA*); (*di aereo*) hold; **puoi mettere la valigia nel bagagliaio** you can put your case in the boot 2 (*deposito bagagli*) left-luggage office

bagaglio, -gli [baˈgaʎʎo] SM luggage *no pl*, baggage *no pl*; **hai molti bagagli?** have you got a lot of luggage?; **ho lasciato i miei bagagli all'albergo** I left my luggage at the hotel; **dove si ritirano i bagagli?** where's the baggage reclaim?; **fare/disfare i bagagli** to pack/unpack; **hai già fatto i bagagli?** have you packed?; **ho preso armi e bagagli e me ne sono andato** I packed up and left; **un bagaglio culturale** a store of knowledge; **bagaglio appresso** accompanied luggage; **bagaglio consentito** free luggage allowance; **bagaglio in eccesso** excess luggage; **bagaglio a mano** hand luggage

bagattella [bagatˈtɛlla] SF 1 (*inezia*) trifle, trifling matter 2 (*Mus*) bagatelle

baggianata [baddʒaˈnata] SF foolish action; **dire baggianate** to talk nonsense

Baghdad [baˈdʒdad] Baghdad

bagliore [baʎˈʎore] SM (*di fuoco*) glow; (*di fari*) glare; (*di lampi*) flash; **un bagliore di speranza** a gleam *o* ray of hope

bagnante [baɲˈɲante] SM, SF bather

bagnare [baɲˈɲare] /15/ VT 1 (*gen*) to wet; (*inzuppare*) to soak; (*labbra*) to moisten; (*annaffiare*) to water; **bagnarsi le labbra** to moisten one's lips; **le lacrime bagnavano il suo viso** her face was bathed in tears; **hai bagnato le piante?** did you water the plants?; **non voglio bagnarmi le scarpe** I don't want to get my shoes wet 2 (*sogg: fiume*) to flow through; (: *mare*) to wash, bathe; **il Mediterraneo bagna Genova** Genoa stands on the Mediterranean coast 3 (*fam: festeggiare bevendo*) to drink to, toast; **abbiamo bagnato la sua promozione** we celebrated his promotion; **bagnarsi** VR (*fare il bagno*) to bathe; **il bambino si è bagnato** the baby has wet himself; **bagnarsi** VIP (*prendere acqua*) to get wet; (*inzupparsi*) to get soaked, get drenched; **ci siamo bagnati anche se avevamo l'ombrello** we got soaked even though we had an umbrella

bagnato, -a [baɲˈɲato] AGG wet; **ho i capelli bagnati** my hair's wet; **bagnato di lacrime** bathed in tears; **bagnato di sudore** (*viso, fronte*) bathed in sweat; (*camicia*) soaked with sweat; **bagnato fino alle ossa** soaked to the skin; **bagnato fradicio** wet through, drenched; **sei bagnato fradicio!** you're soaking wet!; **essere bagnato come un pulcino** to be like a drowned rat, be sopping wet; **sembrare un pulcino bagnato** to look a pathetic sight ♦ SM wet surface; **piove sempre sul bagnato** (*fig*) it never rains but it pours

bagnino, -a [baɲˈɲino] SM, SF lifeguard; (*in piscina*) swimming pool attendant; **fa il bagnino** he's a lifeguard

bagno [ˈbaɲɲo] SM 1 (*gen, Chim, Fot*) bath; (*in piscina*) swim; (*al mare*) swim, bathe; **fare il bagno** (*nella vasca*) to have a bath; (*in piscina*) to go swimming; (*al mare*) to go swimming *o* bathing; **preferisci il bagno o la doccia?** which do you prefer, a bath or a shower?; **fare il bagno a qn** to give sb a bath; **mettere qc a bagno** to leave sth to soak; **vasca**

da bagno bath, bathtub **2** (*locale: anche:* **stanza da bagno**) bathroom; **qui c'è il bagno e lì la camera da letto** the bathroom's here, and the bedroom's there; **scusi, dov'è il bagno?** where's the toilet *o* loo, please? (*Brit*), where's the bathroom, please? (*USA*) **3** (*stabilimento balneare*) private beach ♦ **bagni di mare** sea bathing *sg*; **bagni pubblici** public baths; **bagno di fango** mud bath; **bagno di folla** (*fig*) adulation of the crowd; **bagno di sabbia** sand bath; **bagno di sangue** (*fig*) blood bath; **bagno turco** Turkish bath

bagnomaria [baɲɲoma'ria] SM INV: **cuocere a bagnomaria** to cook in a bain marie (*Brit*), to cook in a double boiler (*USA*)

bagnoschiuma [baɲɲo'skjuma] SM INV bubble bath

Bahama [ba'hama] SFPL: **le Bahama** the Bahamas

Bahrein [ba'rein] SM Bahrain *o* Bahrein

baia ['baja] SF (*Geog*) bay

baionetta [bajo'netta] SF bayonet; **innesto a baionetta** bayonet fitting

baita ['baita] SF mountain hut

balaustra [bala'ustra], **balaustrata** [balaus'trata] SF balustrade

balbettare [balbet'tare] /72/ VT (*gen*) to stammer (out); (*sogg: bambino*) to babble; **balbettare delle scuse** to mumble an excuse ♦ VI (*vedi vt*) to stammer; to babble

balbuzie [bal'buttsje] SF INV stammer; **essere affetto da balbuzie** to have a stammer

balbuziente [balbut'tsjente] AGG stammering; **essere balbuziente** to stammer ♦ SM, SF stammerer

Balcani [bal'kani] SMPL: **i Balcani** the Balkans

balcanico, -a, -ci, -che [bal'kaniko] AGG Balkan

balcone [bal'kone] SM balcony; **il balcone dà sul giardino** the balcony looks onto the garden

baldacchino [baldak'kino] SM canopy; **letto a baldacchino** four-poster (bed)

baldanza [bal'dantsa] SF (*sicurezza*) self-confidence; (*spavalderia*) audacity, boldness

baldo, -a ['baldo] AGG bold

baldoria [bal'dɔrja] SF merrymaking, revelry; **fare baldoria** to have a good time

Baleari [bale'ari] SFPL: **le (isole) Baleari** the Balearic Islands

balena [ba'lena] SF (*Zool*) whale; (*fig: pegg*) barrel of lard; **caccia alla balena** whaling; **olio di balena** whale oil

balenare [bale'nare] /72/ VI (*aus essere*) (*gen*) to flash; **mi è balenata un'idea** an idea flashed into *o* through my mind; **l'ira balenò nel suo sguardo** his eyes flashed with rage

baleniera [bale'njera] SF (*per la caccia*) whaler, whaling ship

baleno [ba'leno] SM flash of lightning; **in un baleno** in a flash

balera [ba'lera] SF (*locale*) dance hall; (*pista*) dance floor

balestra [ba'lɛstra] SF **1** (*arma*) crossbow **2** (*Tecn*) leaf spring

balia¹ ['balja] SF (*anche fig*) wet-nurse; **balia asciutta** nanny

balia² [ba'lia] SF (*potere assoluto*): **essere in balia di** to be at the mercy of; **la nave era in balia delle onde** the ship was at the mercy of the waves; **essere lasciato in balia di se stesso** to be left to one's own devices

balilla [ba'lilla] SM INV (*Storia*) member of Fascist youth group

balistico, -a, -ci, -che [ba'listiko] AGG ballistic; **perito balistico** ballistics expert

balla ['balla] SF **1** (*quantità*) bale **2** (*fam: fandonia*) rubbish *no pl*; **raccontare una balla a qn** to tell sb a lie; **un sacco di balle** a pack of lies, a load of rubbish

ballabile [bal'labile] SM (*Mus*) dance number, dance tune

ballare [bal'lare] /72/ VI (*aus avere*) **1** to dance; **abbiamo ballato tutta la sera** we danced all night; **andare a ballare** to go dancing; **andiamo a ballare?** shall we go dancing?; **ballare come un orso** to dance like an elephant **2** (*traballare: mobile*) to wobble; **le onde facevano ballare la nave** the waves tossed the ship about; **abbiamo ballato in volo** we had a bumpy flight; **quella giacca gli balla addosso** he's lost in that jacket ♦ VT to dance; **ballare il valzer** to (dance the) waltz

ballata [bal'lata] SF ballad

ballatoio, -oi [balla'tojo] SM (*balcone*) gallery, walkway

ballerina [balle'rina] SF **1** (*female*) dancer; **prima ballerina** prima ballerina; **ballerina classica** ballerina, ballet dancer;

voleva fare la ballerina she wanted to be a dancer; **ballerina di rivista** chorus girl **2** (*scarpa*) pump **3** (*uccello*) wagtail; **ballerina gialla** grey wagtail

ballerino [balle'rino] SM (*male*) dancer; (*classico*) ballet dancer; **un ottimo ballerino** a very good dancer

balletto [bal'letto] SM **1** (*spettacolo*) ballet; (*Mus*) ballet music **2** (*corpo di ballo*) dance troupe; (*classico*) corps de ballet

ballo ['ballo] SM (*danza, festa*) dance, ball; (*giro di danza*) dance; **un ballo sudamericano** a Latin American dance; **fare un ballo** to have a dance; **essere in ballo** (*fig*) to be at stake; **tirare in ballo qn** (*fig*) to involve sb; **tirare in ballo qc** to bring sth up, raise sth; **entrare in ballo** (*fig: persona*) to become *o* get involved; (: *cosa*) to come into the picture, become a factor; **ballo liscio** ballroom dancing; **ballo in maschera** *o* **mascherato** fancy-dress ball

ballottaggio, -gi [ballot'taddʒo] SM (*Pol*) second ballot

balneare [balne'are] AGG bathing *attr*; **località balneare** seaside town; **la stagione balneare** the summer season; **governo balneare** (*Pol*) caretaker government

balocco, -chi [ba'lɔkko] SM toy, plaything

balordo, -a [ba'lordo] AGG (*sciocco*) stupid, silly, foolish; (*di poco affidamento*) unreliable; (*strampalato*) odd, peculiar ♦ SM, SF (*sciocco*) fool, stupid person; (*tipo strampalato*) odd sort

balsamico, -a, -ci, -che [bal'samiko] AGG (*aria, brezza*) balmy; **pomata balsamica** balsam

balsamo ['balsamo] SM (*lenimento*) balsam, balm; (*fig*) balm; **balsamo (per capelli)** (hair) conditioner

baltico, -a, -ci, -che ['baltiko] AGG Baltic ♦ SM: **il (mar) Baltico** the Baltic (Sea)

baluardo [balu'ardo] SM (*bastione*) bulwark, rampart; (*fig*) bulwark

balza ['baltsa] SF **1** (*di stoffa*) frill **2** (*rupe*) crag **3** (*di cavallo*) white sock

balzano, -a [bal'tsano] AGG (*persona, idea*) queer, odd; **è un cervello balzano** he's a queer fish

balzare [bal'tsare] /72/ VI (*aus essere*) to leap, jump; **balzare in piedi** to leap *o* jump to one's feet; **balzare giù dal letto/dalla sedia** to leap *o* jump out of bed/up from one's chair; **balzare in macchina/a cavallo** to jump into a car/onto a horse; **il cuore le balzò in gola per la gioia/paura** her heart leapt with joy/fear; **la verità balza agli occhi** the truth is obvious; **gli balzò in mente che...** it came to him that ...

balzo¹ ['baltso] SM (*salto*) leap, jump; (*di palla*) bounce; **fare un balzo** to jump; **fare un balzo in avanti** to leap forward; **un balzo in avanti** (*fig*) a great leap forward; **prendere la palla al balzo** (*fig*) to seize one's opportunity

balzo² ['baltso] SM (*di rupe*) crag, cliff

bambagia, -gie [bam'badʒa] SF (*ovatta*) cottonwool (*Brit*), absorbent cotton (*USA*); (*cascame*) cotton waste; **tenere qn nella bambagia** (*fig*) to mollycoddle sb

bambinaia [bambi'naja] SF nursemaid

bambino, -a [bam'bino] SM, SF (*gen*) child, (little) boy/girl; (*neonato*) baby; **quando ero bambino** when I was a child; **chi è quel bambino?** who's that little boy?; **aspetta un bambino** she's expecting a baby; **c'erano dei bambini che giocavano nel parco** there were some children playing in the park; **lo saprebbe fare anche un bambino!** a child could do it!; **fare il bambino** to behave childishly; **è un bambino!** he's really childish! ♦ AGG: **una scienza ancora bambina** a science still in its infancy

bamboccio, -ci [bam'bɔttʃo] SM (*bambino*) bouncing child; (*pupazzo*) rag doll; (*fig*) big baby

bambola ['bambola] SF (*giocattolo*) doll, dolly; (*fig: donna*) doll

bambolotto [bambo'lɔtto] SM male doll

bambù [bam'bu] SM bamboo; **di bambù** bamboo

banale [ba'nale] AGG (*gen*) banal, commonplace; (*idea, scusa*) trite; (*incidente*) trivial, minor; (*persona*) ordinary; (*vita*) humdrum, dull; **è solo un banale raffreddore** it's just a common *o* garden cold; it's just an ordinary cold; **si è trattato di un banale incidente** it was a minor accident; **la trama del libro era un po' banale** the plot of the book was rather banal

banalità [banali'ta] SF INV **1** (*vedi agg*) banality; triteness; triviality; ordinariness; dullness **2** (*parole*) truism, trite remark; **dire una banalità** to make a trite remark

banana [ba'nana] SF banana; **banana split** banana split

banano [ba'nano] SM banana tree

banca, -che ['banka] SF (*istituto, edificio*) bank; **in banca** in the bank; **andare in banca** to go to the bank; **devo andare in banca** I need to go to the bank; **avere un conto in banca** to have a bank account; **banca dati** (*Inform*) data bank; **banca del sangue** blood bank; **banca del tempo** local exchange and trading system, LETS

bancarella [banka'rɛlla] SF stall; **l'ho comprato in una bancarella al mercato** I bought it from a stall in the market

bancario, -ria, -ri, -rie [ban'karjo] AGG banking; **il settore bancario** the banking sector; **prestito bancario** bank loan; **assegno bancario** (bank) cheque ♦ SM, SF bank employee

bancarotta [banka'rotta] SF (*Fin*) bankruptcy; (*fig*) failure; **andare in bancarotta, fare bancarotta** to go bankrupt

bancarottiere, -a [bankarot'tjɛre] SM, SF bankrupt

banchetto [ban'ketto] SM banquet; **fare un banchetto (a base di qc)** to feast (on sth)

banchiere [ban'kjɛre] SM (*Fin: nei giochi*) banker

banchina [ban'kina] SF **1** (*di porto*) quay, wharf **2** (*di stazione*) platform **3** (*per pedoni*) footway; (*per ciclisti*) cycle path; **banchina cedevole** (*Aut*) soft verge (*Brit*) o shoulder (*USA*); **banchina spartitraffico** (*Aut*) central reservation (*Brit*), median (strip) (*USA*)

banchisa [ban'kiza] SF pack ice

banco, -chi ['banko] SM **1** (*sedile*) seat, bench; (*in Parlamento*) bench; **banco di chiesa** pew; **banco degli imputati** (*Dir*) dock; **banco di scuola** desk; **banco dei testimoni** witness box (*Brit*) o stand (*USA*) **2** (*di negozio*) counter; (*di mercato*) stall; **medicinali da banco** over-the-counter medicines; **sotto banco** (*fig*) under the counter; **banco del Lotto** lottery-ticket office **3** (*di officina*) (work)bench; **banco di prova** test bed; (*fig*) testing ground **4** (*Fin*) bank; **tenere il banco** (*nei giochi*) to be (the) banker; **tener banco** (*fig*) to monopolize the conversation **5** (*Meteor*) bank, patch; **banco di nebbia** fog bank **6** (*Geol: strato*) layer; (: *di coralli*) reef; **banco di ghiaccio** ice floe; **banco di sabbia** sandbank **7** (*di pesci*) shoal

bancogiro [banko'dʒiro] SM credit transfer

banconota [banko'nɔta] SF banknote; **una banconota da cento euro** a hundred euro note

banda¹ ['banda] SF (*di suonatori*) band; (*di ladri, guerriglieri*) band, gang; (*di amici*) gang, group; **suona nella banda del paese** she plays in the village band; **una banda di rapinatori** a gang of robbers

banda² ['banda] SF **1** (*di stoffa*) band, strip; (*di metallo*) band, strip (*di carta*) strip; (*di calcolatore*) tape; **banda larga** (*Inform*) broadband; **banda perforata** (*Inform*) punch tape; **banda stretta** (*Inform*) narrowband **2** (*Fis, Radio*) band

banderuola [bande'rwɔla] SF (*Meteor*) weathercock, weathervane; **essere una banderuola** (*fig*) to be fickle

bandiera [ban'djera] SF flag; **alzare bandiera bianca** to show the white flag; **la bandiera italiana** the Italian flag; **battere bandiera italiana** (*nave*) to fly the Italian flag; **cambiare bandiera** (*fig*) to change sides; **bandiera ombra** o **di comodo** flag of convenience

bandire [ban'dire] /55/ VT **1** (*annunciare*) to announce, proclaim; **bandire un concorso** to announce a competition (*for posts in large organizations*) **2** (*porre al bando: prodotto*) to ban; (: *sentimenti*) to banish; (: *complimenti, ciance*) to dispense with; (: *persona*) to exile; **l'hanno bandito dall'ordine degli avvocati** he has been struck off

bandito [ban'dito] SM bandit, outlaw; (*fig: persona senza scrupoli*) rogue

banditore [bandi'tore] SM **1** (*Storia*) town crier **2** (*di aste*) auctioneer

bando ['bando] SM **1** (*annuncio*) (public) announcement, (public) notice; **bando di concorso** announcement of a public examination **2** (*esilio*) exile; **mettere al bando qn** to exile sb; (*fig*) to freeze sb out; **bando alle ciance!** that's enough talk!

bandolo ['bandolo] SM (*di matassa*) end; **trovare il bandolo della matassa** (*fig*) to find the key to the problem

Bangkok [ban'kɔk] SF Bangkok

Bangladesh [bangla'deʃ] SM Bangladesh

bar [bar] SM INV (*locale*) bar (*serving coffee, alcoholic drinks, snacks ecc*); (*mobile*) cocktail cabinet

bara ['bara] SF coffin

baracca, -che [ba'rakka] SF hut; (*pegg*) hovel; (*fam, pegg: oggetto*) piece of junk; **mandare avanti la baracca** to keep things going; **come va la baracca?** how are you managing?; **piantare baracca e burattini** to throw everything up

baraccato, -a [barak'kato] SM, SF *person living in temporary camp or shanty town*

baracchino [barak'kino] SM **1** (*chiosco*) stall **2** (*apparecchio*) CB radio

baraccone [barak'kone] SM booth, stall; **baracconi** SMPL (*parco dei divertimenti*) funfair sg

baraccopoli [barak'kɔpoli] SF INV shanty town

baraonda [bara'onda] SF (*confusione*) chaos; (*movimento di gente*) hubbub, bustle

barare [ba'rare] /72/ VI (*aus avere*) to cheat; **hai barato!** you cheated!

baratro ['baratro] SM (*anche fig*) abyss

barattare [barat'tare] /72/ VT: **barattare qc con qc** (*merce*) to barter sth for sth; (*francobolli*) to swap sth for sth (*Brit*), to trade sth for sth (*USA*)

baratto [ba'ratto] SM (*Comm*) barter; (*scambio*) exchange; **fare un baratto con qn** to swap with sb (*Brit*), to trade with sb (*USA*)

barattolo [ba'rattolo] SM (*di vetro*) jar; (*di latta*) tin, can; (*di plastica*) pot

barba ['barba] SF **1** beard; **ha la barba** he's got a beard; **farsi la barba** to shave; **una barba di 3 giorni** 3 days' growth; **farsi crescere la barba** to grow a beard; **farla in barba a qn** (*fig*) to fool sb; **servire qn di barba e capelli** (*fig*) to teach sb a lesson; **che barba!** (*persona, libro*) what a bore! **2** (*Bot*) (*fine*) root

barbabietola [barba'bjetola] SF beetroot (*Brit*), beet (*USA*); **barbabietola da zucchero** sugar beet

Barbados [bar'bados] SF Barbados sg

barbarico, -a, -ci, -che [bar'bariko] AGG (*invasione*) barbarian; (*usanze, metodi*) barbaric

barbarie [bar'barje] SF INV (*condizione*) barbarism; (*crudeltà*) barbarity

barbaro, -a ['barbaro] AGG (*popolo*) barbarian; (*comportamento, crimine*) barbaric, barbarous; (*stile, gusto*) appalling ♦ SM barbarian; **i Barbari** SMPL the Barbarians

barbecue [bar'bikju:] SM INV barbecue

barbiere [bar'bjere] SM barber; **fa il barbiere** he's a barber; **devo andare dal barbiere** I need a haircut

barbiturico, -a, -ci, -che [barbi'turiko] AGG barbituric ♦ SM barbiturate

barbone¹ [bar'bone] SM (*anche: cane barbone*) (French) poodle

barbone², -a SM, SF (*vagabondo*) tramp, vagrant

barbuto, -a [bar'buto] AGG bearded

barca¹, -che ['barka] SF boat; **andare in barca** (*a vela*) to go sailing; (*a remi*) to go boating; **si è comprato una barca** he's bought himself a boat; **barca a motore** motorboat; **barca a remi** rowing boat (*Brit*), rowboat (*USA*); **barca a vela** sailing boat (*Brit*), sailboat (*USA*)

barca² ['barka] SF (*fig: quantità*): **una barca di** heaps of, tons of; **ha una barca di soldi** she's got loads of money

barcaiolo [barka'jolo] SM boatman

barcamenarsi [barkame'narsi] /72/ VIP (*nel lavoro*) to get by

Barcellona [bartʃel'lona] SF Barcelona

barcollare [barkol'lare] /72/ VI (*aus avere*) to stagger; **ha barcollato ed è caduto** he staggered and fell

barcone [bar'kone] SM (*quadrangolare*) scow; (*per costruzione di ponti*) pontoon

barella [ba'rɛlla] SF (*per malati*) stretcher; **l'hanno portato via in barella** he was carried away on a stretcher

Barents ['barents] SM: **il mare di Barents** the Barents Sea

barese [ba'rese] AGG of o from Bari ♦ SM, SF inhabitant o native of Bari

baricentro [barit'ʃentro] SM centre (*Brit*) o center (*USA*) of gravity

barile [ba'rile] SM (*gen*) barrel; (*di vino*) cask, barrel

barista, -i, -e [ba'rista] SM, SF (*cameriere*) barman (barmaid); (*proprietario*) bar owner; **fa la barista** she works in a bar
- ❏ **barista** non si traduce mai con la parola inglese *barrister*

baritono [ba'ritono] SM baritone

barlume [bar'lume] SM (faint) light; (*fig: di speranza, idea*) glimmer

baro ['baro] SM (*Carte*) cardsharp

barocco, -a, -chi, -che [ba'rɔkko] AGG, SM baroque

barometro [ba'rɔmetro] SM barometer

barone [ba'rone] SM baron; **i baroni della medicina** (*fig: pegg*) the big shots in the medical profession

baronessa [baro'nessa] SF baroness

barra ['barra] SF **1** (*gen*) bar; (*di legno, metallo*) rod, bar; **barra delle applicazioni** (*Inform*) taskbar; **barra di rimorchio** (*Aut*) tow bar; **barra di scorrimento** (*Inform*) scroll bar; **barra spaziatrice** space-bar; **barra stabilizzatrice** (*Aut*) anti-roll bar; **barra degli strumenti** (*Inform*) toolbar; **barre laterali** *o* **antintrusione** (*Aut*) side impact bars **2** (*Naut*) helm; (*piccola*) tiller **3** (*segno tipografico*) slash; **barra inversa** backslash

barrare [bar'rare] /72/ VT to bar; **barrate la risposta esatta** tick the right answer

barricare [barri'kare] /20/ VT to barricade; **barricarsi** VR: **barricarsi in/dietro** to barricade o.s. in/behind; **barricarsi in camera** to shut o.s. up in one's room

barricata [barri'kata] SF barricade; **essere dall'altra parte della barricata** (*fig*) to be on the other side of the fence

barriera [bar'rjera] SF (*gen, anche fig, o Fis*) barrier; (*corallina*) reef; (*Calcio*) wall; (*Equitazione: ostacolo*) pole; **la Grande Barriera Corallina** the Great Barrier Reef; **barriera doganale** trade *o* tariff barrier; **la barriera del suono** the sound barrier; **le barriere architettoniche** physical obstacles (*preventing access to buildings by the disabled*)

barroccio, -ci [bar'rɔttʃo] SM cart

baruffa [ba'ruffa] SF quarrel, row; **fare baruffa** to quarrel, have a row

barzelletta [bardzel'letta] SF joke, funny story; **raccontare una barzelletta** to tell a joke; **mi ha raccontato una barzelletta molto divertente** he told me a very funny joke

basamento [baza'mento] SM (*parte inferiore, piedistallo*) base; (*Tecn*) bed, base plate
- ❏ **basamento** non si traduce mai con la parola inglese *basement*

basare [ba'zare] /72/ VT: **basare (su)** (*argomento*) to base (on), found (on); (*edificio*) to build on; **il film è basato su un fatto realmente accaduto** the film is based on a true story; **basarsi** VR: **basarsi su** (*sogg: argomento, fatti, prove*) to be based on, be founded on; (: *persona*) to base o.s. on, base one's arguments on; (: *edificio*) to be built on; **mi baso sulle esperienze precedenti** I'm going on past experience

basco, -a, -schi, -sche ['basko] AGG Basque ♦ SM, SF Basque ♦ SM (*lingua*) Basque ♦ SF (*berretto*) beret

bascula [baskula], **basculla** [bas'kulla] SF weighing machine, weighbridge

base ['baze] SF **1** (*gen, Mil, Chim, Mat*) base; **la base della lampada** the lamp base; **la base del partito** (*Pol*) the rank and file of the party **2** (*fig: fondamento*) basis; (: *di problema, idea*) origin, root; **base di partenza** starting point **3** base SFPL (*fondamento*) basis *sg*, foundation *sg*; **gettare le basi per qc** to lay the basis *o* foundations for sth; **avere buone basi** (*Scol*) to have a sound educational background **4** (*fraseologia*): **prodotto a base di carne** meat-based product; **liquore a base di caffè** coffee liqueur; **essere alla base di qc** to be at the basis of; (*di problema*) to be at the root of; **la fiducia stava alla base della nostra amicizia** trust was the basis of our friendship; **servire da o come base a** (*punto di partenza*) to act as the basis for; **di base** basic; **il suo stipendio di base è piuttosto basso** her base salary is quite low; **regole di base** basic rules; **in base a** (*notizie, informazioni*) according to; **in base a ciò...** on that basis ...; **in base a questo depliant ci sono tre alberghi** according to this brochure there are three hotels; **sulla base di** on the basis of ♦ AGG INV (*prezzo, problema, stipendio*) basic

baseball ['bezbol] SM INV baseball

basetta [ba'zetta] SF side whisker, sideburn

basilare [bazi'lare] AGG basic, fundamental

Basilea [basi'lea] SF Basle

basilica, -che [ba'zilika] SF basilica

basilico [ba'ziliko] SM (*Bot*) (sweet) basil

basket ['basket] SM INV (*sport*) basketball; **gioco a basket** I play basketball

bassezza [bas'settsa] SF (*d'animo, di sentimenti*) baseness; (*azione*) base action

bassista, -i, -e [bas'sista] SM, SF bass player

basso, -a ['basso] AGG **1** (*gen*) low; (*persona*) short; (*suono*) soft, low; (*profondo*) deep; **il volume è troppo basso** the sound's too low; **parlare a voce bassa** to speak in a low voice; **è basso** he's short; **Simona è più bassa di me** Simona is shorter than me; **i rami bassi** the lower *o* bottom branches; **a occhi bassi** with lowered eyes; **l'ho avuto a basso prezzo** I got it cheap; **c'è bassa marea** it's low tide, the tide is out; **in quel punto l'acqua è bassa** the water's shallow there; **in bassa stagione** in the low season **2** (*inferiore: qualità*) poor, inferior; (*abietto: azione, istinto*) base, mean **3** (*Geog*): **il basso Po** the lower Po; **i Paesi Bassi** the Netherlands **4** (*Storia: tardo*) late; **il basso Medioevo** the late Middle Ages; **basso latino** low Latin ♦ AVV (*volare, mirare*) low; (*parlare*) softly, in a low voice ♦ SM **1** (*parte inferiore*) bottom, lower part; (*di pagina*) foot, bottom; in basso at the bottom; **io sono quella in basso a destra nella foto** I'm the one in the bottom right of the photo; **è là in basso** it's down there; **più in basso** lower down; **mettilo un po' più in basso** put it a bit lower down; **scendere da basso** to go downstairs; **cadere in basso** (*fig*) to come down in the world **2** (*Mus*) bass; **suonare il basso** to play bass (guitar)

bassofondo [basso'fondo] SM (*pl* **bassifondi**) shallows *pl*; **i bassifondi (della città)** (*quartieri emarginati*) the seediest parts of the town

bassorilievo [bassori'ljevo] SM (*pl* **bassorilievi**) bas-relief

bassotto, -a [bas'sɔtto] AGG squat ♦ SM (*cane*) dachshund

'basta ESCL (that's) enough!, that will do!

bastardo, -a [bas'tardo] AGG bastard *attr*; (*animale*) cross-bred; (*pianta*) hybrid; **cane bastardo** mongrel ♦ SM, SF (*figlio, anche insulto*) bastard; **bastardo!** (*fam*) (you) bastard! ♦ SM (*cane*) mongrel

bastare [bas'tare] /72/ VI (*aus essere*) **1** to be enough, be sufficient; **questa pasta non basta per cinque persone** this pasta isn't enough for five people; **bastare a qn** to be enough for sb; **mi bastano 10 euro per oggi** 10 euro will do me *o* will be sufficient (for me) for today; **75 euro ti bastano per 2 giorni** 75 euro will last you 2 days; **fatti bastare questi soldi!** mind you make this money last!; **bastare a se stesso** to be self-sufficient **2** (*fraseologia*): **basta!** that's enough!, stop it!, that will do!; **punto e basta!** and that's that!; **basta con queste scuse** enough of these excuses; **dimmi basta** (*versando da bere*) say when!; **basta così?** (*al bar ecc*) will that be all?; **basta così, grazie** that's enough, thank you; (*nei negozi*) that's all, thank you; **basta e avanza** that's more than enough ♦ VB IMPERS: **basta chiedere** *o* **che chieda a un vigile** you have only to *o* need only ask a policeman; **basta rivolgersi all'ufficio competente** you just have to contact the relevant department; **non basta volerlo, bisogna sapere come fare** it's not enough to want to, you have to know how to; **e come se non bastasse...** and as if that wasn't enough ...; **basti dire che...** suffice it to say that ...; **basta un niente per farla arrabbiare** the slightest thing will get her annoyed, it only takes the slightest thing to annoy her; **quanto basta** as much as is necessary; **basta che** (*purché*) provided (that); **basta che tu lo chieda** you only have to ask

bastian [bas'tjan] SM: **bastian contrario** awkward customer

bastimento [basti'mento] SM ship, vessel

bastione [bas'tjone] SM bastion

bastonare [basto'nare] /72/ VT to beat, thrash; **avere l'aria di un cane bastonato** to look crestfallen

bastonata [basto'nata] SF blow (*with a stick*); **prendere qn a bastonate** to give sb a beating; **l'hanno ucciso a bastonate** they beat him to death

bastoncino [baston'tʃino] SM (*piccolo bastone*) small stick;

(*Tecn*) rod; (*Sci*) ski pole; **bastoncini di pesce** (*Culin*) fish fingers (*Brit*), fish sticks (*USA*)

bastone [bas'tone] SM **1** (*gen*) stick; (*Rel*) staff; **l'ha picchiato con un bastone** he hit him with a stick; **mettere i bastoni fra le ruote a qn** (*fig*) to put a spoke in sb's wheel; **bastone da passeggio** walking stick **2 bastoni** SMPL (*Carte*) *suit in Neapolitan pack of cards*

battage [ba'taʒ] SM INV: **battage promozionale** *o* **pubblicitario** hype

battaglia [bat'taʎʎa] SF (*Mil*) battle; (*fig*) fight

battaglio, -gli [bat'taʎʎo] SM (*di campana*) clapper; (*di porta*) (door-)knocker

battaglione [battaʎ'ʎone] SM battalion

battello [bat'tɛllo] SM (*gen*) boat; (*canotto*) dinghy; **battello pneumatico** rubber dinghy; **battello di salvataggio** lifeboat

battente [bat'tɛnte] SM **1** (*di finestra*) shutter; (*di porta*) one *side of a double door*; **porta a due battenti** double door; **chiudere i battenti** (*fig*) to shut up shop **2** (*per bussare*) (door-)knocker **3** (*di orologio*) hammer

battere ['battere] /1/ VT **1** (*percuotere: persona*) to beat, strike, hit; (: *panni, tappeti*) to beat; (: *ferro*) to hammer; (: *grano*) to thresh; **battere il ferro finché è caldo** (*fig*) to strike while the iron is hot; **batté un pugno sul tavolo** he beat his fist on the table; **battersi il petto** to beat one's breast; (*fig*) to repent; **battere (a macchina)** to type; **battere il tempo**, **battere il ritmo** (*Mus*) to beat time **2** (*avversario*) to beat, defeat; (*concorrenza, record*) to beat; **in matematica nessuno lo batte** there's no one to beat him at math(s); **li abbiamo battuti due a zero** we beat them two nil; **ha battuto il record mondiale** she's beaten the world record **3** (*urtare: parte del corpo*) to hit; **ha battuto il mento sul gradino** he hit his chin on the step; **batteva i denti per il freddo** his teeth were chattering with the cold; **battere i piedi** to stamp one's feet; **battere i tacchi** to click one's heels; **battere le mani** to clap one's hands **4** (*sbattere: ali*) to beat; **senza battere ciglio** without batting an eyelid; **in un batter d'occhio** in the twinkling of an eye **5** (*rintoccare: le ore*) to strike; **il pendolo batteva le 8** the grandfather clock was striking 8 o'clock **6** (*Culin*) to beat **7** (*Sport: palla*) to hit; **battere un rigore** (*Calcio*) to take a penalty **8** (*percorrere: campagna, paese*) to scour, comb; (*Caccia*) to beat **9 battersela** to run off **10** (*Fin*): **battere moneta** to mint coin ♦ VI (*aus avere*) **1** (*cuore, polso*) to beat; (*pioggia, sole*): **gli batteva forte il cuore** his heart was beating fast; **battere (su)** to beat down (on); **la pioggia batteva sui vetri** the rain beat *o* lashed against the window panes; **battere in testa** (*Aut*) to knock **2** (*insistere*): **battere su** to insist on; **battere su un argomento** to harp on a topic **3** (*bussare*): **battere (a)** to knock (at) **4 battere in ritirata** to beat a retreat, fall back; **battersi** VIP (*lottare*) to fight; (*fig*) to fight, battle; **battersi all'ultimo sangue** to fight to the last

batteria [batte'ria] SF **1** (*Elettr, Mil, Agr*) battery; **la batteria è scarica** the battery's flat; **batteria da cucina** pots and pans *pl* **2** (*Sport*) heat **3** (*Mus*): **la batteria** the drums *pl*; **suona la batteria** he plays the drums

batterio, -ri [bat'tɛrjo] SM bacterium; **batteri patogeni** bacteria which cause disease

batteriologia [batterjolo'dʒia] SF bacteriology

batterista, -i, -e [batte'rista] SM, SF drummer

battesimo [bat'tezimo] SM **1** (*sacramento*) baptism; (*rito*) christening, baptism; **nome di battesimo** Christian name; **tenere qn a battesimo** to be godfather *o* godmother) to sb **2** (*cerimonia inaugurale: di nave*) christening; **battesimo dell'aria** first flight; **battesimo del fuoco** baptism of fire

battezzare [batted'dzare] /72/ VT **1** (*Rel*) to baptize, christen; (*nave*) to christen **2** (*chiamare*) to call, name, christen; (*fig: dare un soprannome*) to nickname

battibaleno [battiba'leno] SM: **in un battibaleno** in a flash

battibecco, -chi [batti'bekko] SM squabble

batticuore [batti'kwɔre] SM palpitations *pl*; **avevo il batticuore** (*fig*) my heart was thumping

battigia, -gie [bat'tidʒa] SF water's edge

battimano [batti'mano] SM applause *no pl*, clapping *no pl*

battipanni [batti'panni] SM INV carpet beater

battistero [battis'tɛro] SM baptist(e)ry

battistrada [battis'trada] SM INV **1** (*di pneumatico*) tread **2** (*Sport*) pacemaker; **fare da battistrada** (*in una gara*) to set the pace, make the running; **fare da battistrada a qn** (*fig*) to prepare the way for sb

battitappeto [battitap'peto] SM INV upright vacuum cleaner; **passare il battitappeto** to vacuum, hoover

battito ['battito] SM (*pulsazione*) beat, throb; **battito della pioggia/dell'orologio** drumming of the rain/ticking of the clock; **battito cardiaco** heartbeat

battitore [batti'tore] SM **1** (*Cricket*) batsman; (*Baseball*) batter **2** (*Caccia*) beater

battitura [batti'tura] SF **1** (*anche:* **battitura a macchina**) typing **2** (*del grano*) threshing

battuta [bat'tuta] SF **1** (*Teatro*) cue; (*osservazione*) remark; (*spiritosaggine*) witty remark; **fare una battuta** to crack a joke, make a witty remark; **aver la battuta pronta** (*fig*) to have a ready answer; **ma dai, era solo una battuta** come on, it was only a joke; **non ho perso una battuta della loro conversazione** I didn't miss a word of what they were saying; **è ancora alle prime battute** (*progetto, commedia*) it's just started **2** (*di caccia*) beat, beating; (*di polizia*): **fare una battuta in una zona** to scour *o* comb an area **3** (*Tennis*) service; **alla battuta Federer** Federer is now serving **4** (*Mus*) bar; **battuta d'arresto** *o* **d'aspetto** bar rest; **gli affari hanno subito una battuta d'arresto** it's a slack period for business **5** (*di macchina da scrivere*) key stroke

batuffolo [ba'tuffolo] SM wad; **un batuffolo di cotone** a wad of cotton wool

baule [ba'ule] SM (*valigia*) trunk; (*Aut*) boot (*Brit*), trunk (*USA*)

bauxite [bauk'site] SF bauxite

bava ['bava] SF (*di persona, bambino*) dribble; (*di animale*) slaver, slobber; (*di cane idrofobo*) foam; (*di lumaca*) slime; (*di baco da seta*) silk filament; **aver la bava alla bocca** (*anche fig*) to be foaming at the mouth; **non c'era nemmeno una bava di vento** there wasn't a breath of wind

bavaglino [bavaʎ'ʎino] SM bib

bavaglio, -gli [ba'vaʎʎo] SM gag; **mettere il bavaglio a qn/qc** (*anche fig*) to gag sb/sth; **si è liberato del bavaglio** he got the gag off

bavarese [bava'rese] AGG, SM, SF Bavarian ♦ SF (*Culin*) bavarois

bavero ['bavero] SM collar

Baviera [ba'vjera] SF Bavaria

bazar [bad'dzar] SM INV bazaar

bazzecola [bad'dzekola] SF (*mere*) trifle

bazzicare [battsi'kare] /20/ VT (*persona*) to hang about with; (*posto*) to hang about *o* around ♦ VI (*aus avere*) **bazzicare con qn** to hang about *o* around with sb; **bazzicare in un posto** to hang about *o* around a place

BCE [bit ʃi'e] SIGLA F (= *Banca Centrale Europea*) ECB (= *European Central Bank*)

bearsi [be'arsi] /72/ VIP: **bearsi di qc/fare qc** to delight in sth/in doing sth; **bearsi alla vista di** to feast one's eyes on

beatitudine [beati'tudine] SF (*Rel*) beatitude; (*felicità*) bliss

beato, -a [be'ato] AGG (*Rel*) blessed; (*felice*) blissfully happy; **una vita beata** a life of bliss; **beata ignoranza** blissful ignorance; **beato lui!** lucky him!, how lucky he is!; **beato chi ti vede!** (*fam*) long time no see!

bebè [be'bɛ] SM INV baby

beccaccia, -ce [bek'kattʃa] SF woodcock; **beccaccia di mare** oystercatcher

beccare [bek'kare] /20/ VT **1** (*sogg: uccello*) to peck (at) **2** (*fam: cogliere sul fatto*) to nab, catch; **l'hanno beccato a rubare in un negozio** they caught him shoplifting; **non mi becchi più!** you won't catch me out like that again! **3** (*fam: anche: beccarsi*) to get; **beccarsi un raffreddore** to catch a cold; **beccarsi** VR (*uso reciproco: uccelli*) to peck (at) one another; (: *fig: litigare*) to squabble

beccata [bek'kata] SF peck

beccheggiare [bekked'dʒare] /62/ VI (*aus avere*) (*Aer, Naut*) to pitch

beccherò ecc [bekke'rɔ] VB *vedi* **beccare**

becchime [bek'kime] SM birdseed

becchino [bek'kino] SM gravedigger

becco¹, -chi ['bekko] SM 1 (*di uccello*) beak, bill; **non ho il becco di un quattrino** (*fam*) I'm broke 2 (*fam: bocca*) mouth; **chiudi il becco!** shut your mouth!; **mettere il becco in qc** to poke one's nose into sth; **tu non mettere becco!** you keep out of this! 3 (*bruciatore*) burner; **becco Bunsen** Bunsen burner 4 (*di caffettiera*) spout

becco², -chi ['bekko] SM (*Zool*) billy-goat; (*fig: fam*) cuckold

Befana [be'fana] SF 1 (*festività*) national holiday (*Jan 6, feast of the Epiphany*) 2 (*personaggio*) kind old woman who, according to legend, comes down the chimney 3 (*donna brutta*) old hag, old witch

beffa ['beffa] SF: **farsi beffa** o **beffe di qn** to make a fool of sb; **farsi beffa** o **beffe di qc** to make fun of sth; **ma questa è una beffa!** this is some kind of sick joke!

beffardo, -a [bef'fardo] AGG mocking

beffare [bef'fare] /72/ VT to make a fool of, mock; **beffarsi** VIP: **beffarsi di** to scoff at

bega, -ghe ['bɛga] SF (*litigio*) quarrel, dispute; (*problema*): **non voglio beghe** I don't want any trouble

begli ['beʎʎi] AGG *vedi* **bello**

beige [bɛʒ] AGG INV beige; **una gonna beige** a beige skirt

Beirut [bei'rut] SF Beirut

bel [bɛl] AGG *vedi* **bello**

belare [be'lare] /72/ VI (*aus avere*) (*Zool, o fig*) to bleat

belato [be'lato] SM bleating

belga, -gi, -ghe ['bɛlga] AGG, SM, SF Belgian

Belgio ['bɛldʒo] SM Belgium; **andremo in Belgio quest'estate** we're going to Belgium this summer; **mi è piaciuto molto il Belgio** I really liked Belgium

Belgrado [bel'grado] SF Belgrade

bella ['bɛlla] SF 1 beauty, belle; (*innamorata*) sweetheart; **la Bella addormentata nel bosco** Sleeping Beauty 2 (*anche: bella copia*) fair copy 3 (*Sport, Carte*) deciding match

bellezza [bel'lettsa] SF 1 (*qualità*) beauty; (*di donna*) beauty, loveliness; (*di uomo*) handsomeness; **una donna di eccezionale bellezza** an exceptionally beautiful woman; **un istituto di bellezza** a beauty salon; **chiudere** o **finire qc in bellezza** to finish sth with a flourish; **e per finire in bellezza...** (*iro*) and to round it all off perfectly ...; **che bellezza!** fantastic! 2 (*persona, cosa*) beauty; **ciao bellezza!** hello gorgeous!; **le bellezze di Roma** the beauties o sights of Rome; **questo vestito è una bellezza** this dress is really lovely 3 (*quantità*): **ho pagato la bellezza di trecento euro** I paid three hundred euros, no less; **ha impiegato la bellezza di 2 anni a finirlo** he took a good 2 years to finish it

bellicoso, -a [belli'koso] AGG (*popolo, nazione*) warlike; (*fig: persona*) quarrelsome

belligerante [bellidʒe'rante] AGG belligerent

bellimbusto [bellim'busto] SM dandy

PAROLA CHIAVE

bello, -a ['bɛllo] AGG *davanti sm* bel + *consonante*, bell' + *vocale*, bello + *s impura, gn, pn, ps, x, y, z, pl* bei + *consonante*, begli + *s impura ecc o vocale*

1 (*oggetto, donna, paesaggio*) beautiful, lovely; (*uomo*) handsome, good-looking; **le Belle Arti** fine arts; **che bello!** how lovely!; **belle maniere** elegant manners; **il bel mondo** high society; **una bella pettinatura** a nice hairstyle
2 (*tempo*) fine, beautiful, lovely; **fa bello** the weather's lovely o beautiful; **è una bella giornata** it's a lovely o beautiful day; **fa bel tempo** it's lovely weather
3 (*quantità*) considerable; **una bella cifra** a considerable sum of money; **ha avuto un bel coraggio** he was very brave; (*iro*) he had a nerve; **ce n'è rimasto un bel pezzo** there's still a good bit left
4 (*buono*) good, fine; **una bella azione** a good deed; **fare una bella dormita** to have a nice long sleep; **una bella idea** a good o nice idea; **un bel pensiero** a kind thought; **una bella tazza di tè** a nice cup of tea
5 (*rafforzativo*): **è una truffa bella e buona!** it's a real con!; **è bell'e fatto** it's done now; **sei un bel matto** you're absolutely crazy; **nel bel mezzo di** right in the middle of; **non mi ha dato un bel niente** he gave me absolutely nothing
6 (*fraseologia*): **dirne delle belle** to tell some whoppers; **farne delle belle** to get up to mischief; **farsi (più) bello** to get better looking; **farsi bello di qc** (*vantarsi*) to show off

about sth; **alla bell'e meglio** somehow or other; **oh bella!, questa è bella!** (*iro*) that's nice!

♦ SM

1 **il bello** the beautiful, beauty; **amare il bello** to love beauty o beautiful things; **il bello è che...** the best bit about it is that ...; **adesso viene il bello** (*iro*) now comes the best bit; **che fai di bello stasera?** what are you doing this evening?; **proprio sul più bello** at that very moment
2 (*tempo*): **si sta mettendo al bello** the weather is clearing up

♦ SM, SF (*fidanzato*) sweetheart

bellunese [bellu'nese] AGG *o* from Belluno ♦ SM, SF inhabitant *o* native of Belluno

belva ['belva] SF wild beast *o* animal; **essere una belva** (*fig*) to be an animal

belvedere [belve'dere] SM INV panoramic viewpoint

benché [ben'ke] CONG although, though

benda ['benda] SF (*Med*) bandage; (*per gli occhi*) blindfold; **avere gli occhi coperti da una benda** to be blindfolded; **avere la benda agli occhi** (*fig*) to be blind

bendaggio, -gi [ben'daddʒo] SM (*atto*) bandaging; (*effetto*) bandage; **bendaggio gastrico** (*anello*) gastric band; (*operazione*) gastric band surgery

bendare [ben'dare] /72/ VT (*ferita*) to bandage; (*occhi*) to blindfold; **mi ha bendato la mano** he bandaged my hand; **l'hanno bendato e imbavagliato** he was blindfolded and gagged

bendisposto, -a [bendis'posto] AGG: **essere bendisposto verso qn/qc** to be well-disposed towards sb/sth

PAROLA CHIAVE

bene ['bɛne] AVV

1 (*gen*) well; (*funzionare*) well; **faresti bene a studiare** you'd do well o you'd be well advised to study; **hai fatto bene** you did the right thing; **ben fatto!** well done!; **guida bene** he drives well, he's a good driver; **parla bene l'italiano** he speaks Italian well, he speaks good Italian; **parlare bene di qn** to speak well of sb; **gente per bene** respectable people; **sto poco bene** I'm not very well; **ha preso bene la notizia** he took the news well; **se ben ricordo, se ricordo bene** if I remember correctly; **sto bene** I'm fine; **va bene** all right, okay
2 (*con attenzione, completamente*): **ascoltami bene** listen to me carefully; **ben bene** thoroughly; **ho legato il pacco ben bene** I've tied the parcel securely; **hai capito bene?** do you understand?; **chiudi bene la porta** close the door properly; **per bene** thoroughly
3 (*molto: + aggettivo*) very; (: + *comparativo, avverbio*) (very) much; **ben contento** very pleased; **è ben difficile** it's very difficult; **ben più caro** much more expensive; **ben più lungo** much longer
4 (*rafforzativo: appunto*): **lo credo bene** I'm not surprised; **te l'avevo ben detto io che...** I DID tell you that ..., I certainly did tell you that ...; **sai bene che non dovresti uscire** you know perfectly well you shouldn't go out; **come tu sen sai** as you well know; **lo so ben io, lo so fin troppo bene** I know only too well; **lo spero bene** I certainly hope so
5 (*addirittura, non meno di*) at least; **hai fatto ben 7 errori** you've made at least 7 mistakes; **sono ben 3 giorni che non la vedo** I haven't seen her for at least 3 days
6 (*in esclamazioni*): **ho finito — bene!** I've finished — good!; **bene, allora possiamo partire** right then, we can go; **bene, puoi continuare da solo** all right, you can continue on your own; **bene bene!** good (good)!
7 (*fraseologia*): **né bene né male** so-so; **di bene in meglio** better and better; **tutto è bene quel che finisce bene** all's well that ends well

♦ AGG INV: **la gente bene** (*ricca, snob*) well-to-do people; **la Roma bene** the Roman bourgeois

♦ SM

1 good; **far del bene** to do good; **fare del bene a qn** to do sb a good turn; **fare bene a** (*salute*) to be good for; **quella vacanza ti ha fatto bene** that holiday has done you good; **a fin di bene** for a good reason; **sul tavolo c'era ogni ben di Dio** there were all sorts of good things on the table; **l'ho fatto per il suo bene** I did it for his own good; **è stato un bene**

it was a good thing; **volere un bene dell'anima a qn** to love sb very much; **vuole molto bene a suo padre** he loves his father very much, he's very fond of his father
2 beni SMPL (*proprietà, anche Dir*) possessions, propèrty *sg*; (*Econ*) goods; **beni ambientali** the environment *sg*; **beni di consumo** consumer goods; **beni culturali** cultural heritage *sg*; **beni (di) rifugio** *safe assets bought during periods of inflation*; **beni immobili** property *sg* (*Brit*), real estate *sg* (*USA*); **beni mobili** personal *o* movable property *sg*; **beni patrimoniali** fixed assets; **beni privati** private property *sg*; **beni pubblici** public property *sg*

benedetto, -a [bene'detto] PP *di* **benedire** ♦ AGG blessed; (*santo*) holy; **acqua benedetta** holy water; **Dio benedetto!** Good Lord!

benedire [bene'dire] /38/ VT IRREG (*persona*) to bless; (*chiesa*) to consecrate; **che Dio ti benedica!** God bless you!; **l'ho mandato a farsi benedire** (*fig*) I told him to go to hell

benedizione [benedit'tsjone] SF (*atto*) blessing; (*funzione*) benediction; **dare la propria benedizione a qn** to bless sb

beneducato, -a [benedu'kato] AGG well-mannered, polite

benefattore, -trice [benefat'tore] SM, SF benefactor

beneficenza [benefi'tʃentsa] SF charity; **fare opera di beneficenza** to do charity work; **istituto di beneficenza** charitable organization; **festa di beneficenza** charity event; **concerto di beneficenza** charity concert

beneficiare [benefi'tʃare] /14/ VI (*aus* avere) **beneficiare di** to benefit by, benefit from; **beneficiare di una borsa di studio** to be awarded a scholarship

beneficiario, -ria, -ri, -rie [benefi'tʃarjo] AGG, SM, SF (*Dir*) beneficiary

beneficio, -ci [bene'fitʃo] SM benefit; **trarre beneficio da** to benefit from *o* by; **il beneficio del dubbio** the benefit of the doubt; **con beneficio d'inventario** (*fig*) with reservations; **trarre beneficio da** to benefit from

benefico, -a, -ci, -che [be'nefiko] AGG (*gen*) beneficial; (*persona*) charitable; **un effetto benefico** a beneficial effect; **un'associazione benefica** a charitable organization

Benelux [ˈbeneluks] SM: **il Benelux** the Benelux countries, Benelux

benemerenza [beneme'rentsa] SF merit; **attestato di benemerenza** certificate of merit

benemerito, -a [bene'merito] AGG meritorious

beneplacito [bene'platʃito] SM (*approvazione*) approval; (*permesso*) permission

benessere [be'nessere] SM *no pl* (*salute*) well-being; (*agiatezza*) comfort

benestante [benes'tante] AGG well-to-do, well-off; **una famiglia benestante** a well-off family; **viene da una famiglia più benestante della mia** his family is better off than mine ♦ SM, SF: **essere un benestante** to be well-off; **i benestanti** SMPL the well-off

benestare [benes'tare] SM INV approval

benevolenza [benevo'lentsa] SF benevolence; **trattare qn con benevolenza** to treat sb kindly

benevolo, -a [be'nevolo] AGG benevolent

bengodi [ben'godi] SM land of plenty

beniamino, -a [benja'mino] SM, SF favourite (*Brit*), favorite (*USA*); **Marco è il beniamino della maestra** Marco is the teacher's pet

benigno, -a [be'niɲɲo] AGG (*gen, Med*) benign; (*sguardo, sorriso*) kindly, kind; (*critica*) favourable (*Brit*), favorable (*USA*); **tumore benigno** benign tumour

benintenzionato, -a [benintentsjo'nato] AGG well-meaning; **in fondo era benintenzionato** after all he meant well

beninteso [benin'teso] AVV (*certamente*) of course, certainly ♦ **beninteso che** CONG provided that

benpensante [benpen'sante] SM, SF conformist

benservito [benser'vito] SM reference; **dare il benservito a qn** (*sul lavoro*) to give sb the sack, fire sb; (*fig*) to send sb packing

bensì [ben'si] CONG (*ma*) but (rather); (*anzi*) on the contrary

benvenuto, -a [benve'nuto] AGG welcome; **benvenuti a Roma!** welcome to Rome! ♦ SM, SF: **essere il(la) benvenuto(a)** to be welcome ♦ SM welcome; **dare il benvenuto a qn** to welcome sb

benvisto, -a [ben'visto] AGG: **essere benvisto (da)** to be well thought of (by)

benvolere [benvo'lere] /131/ VT *vb dif*: **farsi benvolere da tutti** to win everybody's affection; **prendere a benvolere qn/qc** to take a liking to sb/sth

benzina [ben'dzina] SF petrol (*Brit*), gas(oline) (*USA*); **rimanere senza benzina** to run out of petrol *o* gas; **siamo rimasti senza benzina** we ran out of petrol; **fare benzina** to get petrol *o* gas; **benzina verde** *o* **senza piombo** unleaded petrol *o* gas, lead-free petrol *o* gas

benzinaio, -aia, -ai, -aie [bendzi'najo] SM, SF (*persona*) petrol (*Brit*) *o* gas (*USA*) pump attendant ♦ SM (*posto*) petrol station

beone, -a [be'one] SM heavy drinker

bere [ˈbere] /16/ VT IRREG (*gen*) to drink; (*fig: assorbire*) to soak up; **vuoi bere qc?** would you like sth to drink?; **bere un bicchiere di vino/un caffè** to have a glass of wine/a (cup of) coffee; **chi porta da bere?** who's going to bring the drinks?; **ti offro *o* ti pago da bere** I'll buy you a drink; **bere qc tutto d'un fiato** to down sth in one gulp; **bevi un po' d'acqua** have a drink of water; **sono le preoccupazioni a farlo bere** his problems have made him turn to drink; **bere come una spugna** to drink like a fish; **bere per dimenticare** to drown one's sorrows (in drink); **bere alla salute di qn** to drink to sb's health; **il motore beve la benzina** the engine is heavy on petrol; **bere le parole di qn** to drink in sb's words; **questa volta non me la dai a bere!** I won't be taken in this time!; **questa non la bevo** I'm not buying that ♦ SM drink; **si è dato al bere** he has turned to drink

bergamasco, -a, -schi, -sche [berga'masko] AGG of *o* from Bergamo ♦ SM, SF inhabitant *o* native of Bergamo

Bering [ˈberiŋ] SM: **il mar di Bering** the Bering Sea

berlina[1] [ber'lina] SF: **mettere alla berlina** (*fig*) to hold up to ridicule

berlina[2] [ber'lina] SF (*Aut*) saloon (car) (*Brit*), sedan (*USA*)

Berlino [ber'lino] SF Berlin; **nella vecchia Berlino est...** in former East Berlin...

Bermuda [ber'muda] SFPL: **le Bermuda** Bermuda *sg*

bermuda [ber'muda] SMPL (*calzoni*) Bermuda shorts; **un paio di bermuda** a pair of Bermuda shorts

Berna [ˈberna] SF Bern

bernoccolo [ber'nɔkkolo] SM bump; **ho un bernoccolo in fronte** I've got a bump on my forehead; **avere il bernoccolo di qc** (*fig: disposizione*) to have a bent *o* flair for sth

berretto [ber'retto] SM cap; **berretto da baseball** baseball cap; **berretto con visiera** peaked cap

berrò ecc [ber'rɔ] VB *vedi* **bere**

bersagliare [bersaʎ'ʎare] /27/ VT (*colpire ripetutamente*) to bombard; **bersagliare di pugni** to rain blows on; **bersagliare di domande** to bombard with questions; **è bersagliato dalla sfortuna** he's dogged by ill fortune

bersagliere [bersaʎ'ʎere] SM *member of rifle regiment in Italian army*

bersaglio, -gli [ber'saʎʎo] SM target; (*fig*) target, butt; **colpire il bersaglio** to hit the target; (*fig*) to reach one's target; **ha mancato il bersaglio** he missed the target; **era il bersaglio di tutti i loro scherzi** he was the butt of all their jokes

besciamella [beʃʃa'mella] SF béchamel sauce

bestemmia [bes'temmja] SF (*gen*) curse; (*Rel*) blasphemy; **dire una bestemmia** to swear; (*Rel*) to blaspheme

bestemmiare [bestem'mjare] /19/ VT (*gen*) to curse, swear; (*Rel*) to blaspheme; **non l'ho mai sentito bestemmiare** I've never heard him swear; **bestemmiare come un turco** to swear like a trooper

bestia [ˈbestja] SF (*anche fig*) beast, animal; **non voglio bestie in casa!** I don't want animals in the house!; **andare in bestia** to fly into a rage; **lavorare come una bestia** to work like a dog; **mi guardavano come se fossi una bestia rara** they looked at me as if I came from another planet; **bestia!** (*sciocco*) you stupid fool!; **bestia feroce** wild beast *o* animal; **bestia da macello** animal for slaughter; **bestia da soma** beast of burden; **bestia da tiro** draught animal

bestiale [bes'tjale] AGG (*gen*) brutal; (*passione, istinto*) animal *attr*; (*fam: terribile*) beastly, terrible; **ha fatto un freddo bestiale** it's been terribly cold; **fa un caldo bestiale** it's absolutely boiling, it's terribly hot; **ho una fame bestiale** I could eat a horse

bestialità [bestjali'ta] SF INV 1 (*qualità*) brutality; (*perversione sessuale*) bestiality 2 **dire/fare una bestialità dopo l'altra** to say/do one idiotic thing after another

bestiame [bes'tjame] SM livestock; (*bovino*) cattle *pl*

Betlemme [bet'lɛmme] SF Bethlehem

betoniera [beto'njɛra] SF cement mixer

bettola ['bettola] SF tavern; (*pegg*) dive; **contegno da bettola** coarse behaviour

betulla [be'tulla] SF birch; **betulla argentata** *o* **bianca** silver birch

bevanda [be'vanda] SF drink, beverage (*frm*); **bevanda alcolica/non alcolica** alcoholic/soft drink

bevitore, -trice [bevi'tore] SM, SF drinker; **un gran bevitore** a heavy drinker

bevo *ecc* ['bevo] VB *vedi* **bere**

bevuto, -a [be'vuto] PP *di* **bere**

bevvi *ecc* ['bevvi] VB *vedi* **bere**

BG SIGLA = Bergamo

BI [bi] SIGLA F = Banca d'Italia ♦ SIGLA = Biella

biada ['bjada] SF fodder

biancheria [bjanke'ria] SF (*per casa*) linen; **biancheria da donna** ladies' underwear, lingerie; **biancheria intima** underwear

bianco, -a, -chi, -che ['bjanko] AGG 1 (*gen*) white; **essere bianco come un cencio** to be as white as a sheet; **avere i capelli bianchi** to have white hair, be white-haired; **ha i capelli bianchi** she's got white hair; **far venire i capelli bianchi a qn** (*fig*) to make sb's hair turn white; **notte bianca** *o* **in bianco** sleepless night 2 (*pagina*) blank; **votare scheda bianca** to return a blank voting slip 3 (*Mus*): **voce bianca** treble (voice) ♦ SM 1 (*colore*) white; (*intonaco*) whitewash; (*vino*) white wine; **vestire di bianco** to dress in white; **in bianco e nero** (*TV, Fot*) black and white; **passare una notte in bianco** to have a sleepless night; **andare in bianco** (*non riuscire*) to fail; (*fam: in amore*) to fail to score 2 (*non scritto*): **un assegno in bianco** a blank cheque; **lasciare in bianco** to leave blank 3 (*Culin*): **bianco d'uovo** egg-white; **pesce/carne in bianco** boiled fish/meat; **mangiare in bianco** to be on a light *o* bland diet ♦ SM, SF (*persona*) white person

biancosegno [bjanko'seɲɲo] SM (*Dir*) signature to a blank document

biancospino [bjankos'pino] SM hawthorn

biascicare [bjaʃʃi'kare] /20/ VT to mumble

biasimare [bjazi'mare] /72/ VT (*persona*) to blame; (*condotta, azione*) to disapprove of, censure; **non posso biasimarti** I don't blame you

biasimo ['bjazimo] SM (*vedi vt*) blame; disapproval, censure; **degno di biasimo** blameworthy

Bibbia ['bibbja] SF Bible

biberon [bibɔ'rɔn] SM INV (baby's) bottle, feeding bottle

bibita ['bibita] SF drink; **vendono gelati e bibite** they sell ice cream and drinks; **bibita analcolica** soft drink

bibliografia [bibljogra'fia] SF bibliography

biblioteca, -che [bibljo'tɛka] SF (*edificio*) library; (*mobile*) bookcase

bibliotecario, -ria, -ri, -rie [bibljote'karjo] SM, SF librarian

bicamerale [bikame'rale] AGG (*sistema*) bicameral *attr* ♦ SF (*anche*: **commissione bicamerale**) *parliamentary commission consisting of members of both houses*

bicarbonato [bikarbo'nato] SM: **bicarbonato (di sodio)** bicarbonate (of soda)

bicchiere [bik'kjɛre] SM glass; **bicchiere di vino** glass of wine; **bere un bicchiere** to have a drink; **è (facile) come bere un bicchier d'acqua** it's as easy as pie; **bicchiere a calice** goblet; **bicchiere di carta** paper cup; **bicchiere graduato** measuring cup; **bicchiere da vino** wine glass

bicicletta [bitʃi'kletta] SF bicycle, bike; **andare in bicicletta** to cycle, to ride a bike; **sai andare in bicicletta?** can you ride a bike?; **ci andai in bicicletta** I went there on my bike; **bicicletta da corsa** racing cycle

bicipite [bi'tʃipite] AGG 1 (*Anat*): (*muscolo*) **bicipite** biceps *sg o pl* 2 (*che ha due teste*) two-headed ♦ SM biceps *sg o pl*

bidè, bidet [bi'dɛ] SM INV bidet

bidello, -a [bi'dɛllo] SM, SF (*di scuola*) janitor; (*di università*) porter

bidirezionale [bidirettsjo'nale] AGG bidirectional

bidonare [bido'nare] /72/ VT (*fam: imbrogliare*) to cheat, swindle; (: *piantare in asso*) to let down

bidonata [bido'nata] SF (*fam: imbroglio*) swindle; (: *delusione*) let-down; **fare** *o* **tirare una bidonata a qn** (*imbrogliare*) to cheat *o* do sb; (*deludere*) to let sb down

bidone [bi'done] SM 1 (*recipiente*) drum; (*più piccolo*) can; **bidone da latte** churn; **bidone per la spazzatura** *o* **dei rifiuti** *o* **dell'immondizia** dustbin 2 = **bidonata**

bidonville [bidɔ̃'vil] SF INV shanty town

bieco, -a, -chi, -che ['bjɛko] AGG sinister

biella ['bjɛlla] SF (*Tecn*) connecting rod

Bielorussia [bjelo'russja] SF Belarus, Belorussia

bielorusso, -a SM, SF Belarussian, Belorussian

biennale [bien'nale] AGG (*che dura 2 anni*) two-year *attr*; (*che avviene ogni 2 anni*) two-yearly, biennial; **la mostra è biennale** the exhibition is held every two years ♦ SF: **la Biennale di Venezia** *the Venice Arts Festival*

biennio, -ni [bi'ennjo] SM 1 period of two years; **nel prossimo biennio** over the next two years 2 (*Univ*) two-year foundation course

bierre [bi'erre] SM, SF *member of the Red Brigades*

bietola [bjɛtola] SF (*Bot*) chard; (*fam: barbabietola*) beet

bifamiliare [bifami'ljare] AGG (*villa, casetta*) semi-detached ♦ SF semi-detached house

bifocale [bifo'kale] AGG bifocal

bifolco, -a, -chi, -che [bi'folko] SM, SF (*pegg*) bumpkin, yokel

bifora ['bifora] SF (*Archit*) mullioned window

biforcarsi [bifor'karsi] /20/ VIP (*fiume, strada*) to divide, fork; (*Ferr*) to branch

biforcazione [biforkat'tsjone] SF (*di fiume, strada*) fork; (*Ferr*) junction

biforcuto, -a [bifor'kuto] AGG (*anche fig*) forked; **lingua biforcuta** forked tongue

bigamia [biga'mia] SF bigamy

bigamo, -a ['bigamo] AGG bigamous ♦ SM, SF bigamist

bighellonare [bigello'nare] /72/ VI (*aus avere*) to loaf about

bighellone, -a [bigel'lone] SM, SF loafer

bigiotteria [bidʒotte'ria] SF (*gioielli*) costume jewellery (*Brit*) *o* jewelry (*USA*); (*negozio*) shop selling costume jewel(le)ry

bigliardo [biʎ'ʎardo] SM = **biliardo**

bigliettaio, -aia, -ai, -aie [biʎʎet'tajo] SM, SF (*in treno*) ticket inspector; (*in autobus*) conductor; (*in cinema, teatro*) box-office attendant

biglietteria [biʎʎette'ria] SF (*gen*) ticket office; (*di teatro*) box office; (*per prenotazioni*) booking office

biglietto [biʎ'ʎetto] SM 1 (*per viaggio, entrata*) ticket; **fare/comprare il biglietto** to get/buy one's ticket; **hai fatto il biglietto?** have you got a ticket?; **biglietto di andata e ritorno** return (ticket) (*Brit*), round-trip ticket (*USA*); **biglietto aperto** (*Aer*) open ticket; **biglietto chiuso** (*Aer*) closed ticket; **biglietto omaggio** complimentary ticket; **biglietto di (sola) andata** single (ticket) (*Brit*), one-way ticket (*USA*) 2 (*banconota*): **biglietto (di banca)** banknote, note, bill (*USA*); **un biglietto da 10 euro** a 10 euro note 3 (*nota*) note; (*cartoncino*) card; **mi ha mandato un biglietto per il compleanno** he sent me a card for my birthday; **biglietto d'auguri** greetings card; **biglietto da visita** visiting card

bignè [biɲ'ɲɛ] SM INV cream puff

bigodino [bigo'dino] SM roller

bigotto, -a [bi'gɔtto] AGG pharisaic ♦ SM, SF pharisee

bikini [bi'kini] SM INV bikini

bilancia, -ce [bi'lantʃa] SF 1 (*gen*) scales *pl*; (*a due piatti*) pair of scales; (*di precisione*) balance; (*bascula*) weighing machine; **mettere qc sulla bilancia** to weigh sth; (*fig*) to weigh sth up; **hai una bilancia?** have you got any scales? 2 (*Astrol: anche*: **Bilancia**) Libra; **essere della Bilancia** to be Libra 3 (*Econ*): **bilancia commerciale/dei pagamenti** balance of trade/payments 4 (*Pesca*) drop-net

bilanciare [bilan'tʃare] /14/ VT 1 (*tenere in equilibrio*) to balance; **bilanciare il carico** to spread the load evenly 2 (*Comm*) to balance; **bilanciare le uscite e le entrate** to balance expenditure and revenue; **le uscite bilanciano le entrate** expenditure and revenue balance out **3** (*fig: valutare*) to weigh up; **bilanciarsi** VR **1** (*uso reciproco: equipararsi*) to be equal **2** (*stare in equilibrio*) to balance (o.s.)

bilancio, -ci [bi'lantʃo] SM (*Comm: cifre*) balance; (: *documento*) balance sheet; **fare il bilancio, chiudere il bilancio** to draw up the balance sheet; **far quadrare il bilancio** to balance the books; **chiudere il bilancio in attivo/passivo** to make a profit/loss; **fare il bilancio della situazione** (*fig*) to assess the situation; **bilancio consolidato** consolidated balance; **bilancio consuntivo** final balance; **bilancio preventivo** budget; **bilancio mensile/settimanale** monthly/weekly balance; **bilancio dello stato** budget; **bilancio di verifica** trial balance

bilaterale [bilate'rale] AGG bilateral

bile ['bile] SF (*Med*) bile; (*fig: rabbia*) anger, rage; **era verde dalla bile** he was white with rage

biliardino [biljar'dino] SM (small) billiard table; (*elettrico*) pinball

biliardo [bi'ljardo] SM pool; (*tavolo*) pool table; **giocare a biliardo** to play pool; **sai giocare a biliardo?** can you play pool?; **sala da biliardo** poolroom

bilico ['biliko] SM: **essere** *o* **stare in bilico** to be balanced; (*fig*) to be undecided; **essere in bilico tra la vita e la morte** to be suspended between life and death; **tenere qn in bilico** to keep sb in suspense

bilingue [bi'lingwe] AGG bilingual

bilione [bi'ljone] SM (*mille milioni*) thousand million, billion (*USA*); (*milione di milioni*) billion (*Brit*), trillion (*USA*)

bilocale [bilo'kale] SM two-room flat (*Brit*) *o* apartment (*USA*)

bimbo, -a ['bimbo] SM, SF (*bambino*) child, little boy (girl); (*bebè*) baby

bimensile [bimen'sile] AGG twice-monthly, fortnightly (*Brit*)

bimestrale [bimes'trale] AGG (*che dura 2 mesi*) two-month attr; (*che avviene ogni 2 mesi*) two-monthly, bimonthly; **pagamento bimestrale** payment every 2 months; **rivista bimestrale** bimonthly magazine

bimestre [bi'mestre] SM two-month period; **ogni bimestre** every two months

binario¹, -ria, -ri, -rie [bi'narjo] AGG (*Astron, Chim, Mat, Mus*) binary

binario², -ri [bi'narjo] SM (*rotaie*) (railway) track *o* line; (*piattaforma*) platform; **uscire dai binari** to come off the rails; (*fig*) to go off the rails; **camminare lungo il binario** he was walking along the track; **da quale binario parte il treno per Cambridge?** which platform does the Cambridge train go from?; **binario morto** dead-end track; **siamo su un binario morto** (*fig*) we're not going to get anywhere; **binario unico/doppio** single/double track

binocolo [bi'nɔkolo] SM (*gen*) binoculars *pl*; (*da teatro*) opera glasses *pl*; **guardava gli uccelli con il binocolo** she was looking at the birds through binoculars; **binocolo prismatico** prism binoculars

bio- ['bio] PREF bio-

biocarbu'rante SM biofuel

biochimica [bio'kimika] SF biochemistry

biodegradabile [biodegra'dabile] AGG biodegradable

bio'diesel [bio'dizel] SM INV biodiesel

biodinamico, -a, -ci, -che [biodi'namiko] AGG biodynamic

biodiversità [biodiversi'ta] SF INV biodiversity

bioetica [bio'etika] SF bioethics *sg*

bioetico, -a, -ci, -che [bio'etiko] AGG bioethical

biofabbrica [bio'fabbrika] SF factory producing biological control agents

biofisica [bio'fizika] SF biophysics *sg*

biografia [biogra'fia] SF biography

biografico, -a, -ci, -che [bio'grafiko] AGG biographical

biografo, -a [bi'ɔgrafo] SM, SF biographer

biologia [biolo'dʒia] SF biology

biologico, -a, -ci, -che [bio'lɔdʒiko] AGG (*scienze, fenomeni ecc*) biological; (*agricoltura, prodotti*) organic; **guerra biologica** biological warfare

biologo, -a, -gi, -ghe [bi'ɔlogo] SM, SF biologist; **è biologa** she's a biologist

biondo, -a ['bjondo] AGG (*capelli*) fair, blond; (*persona*) fair, fair-haired; **biondo cenere/platino** ash/platinum blond ♦ SM (*colore*) blond; (*uomo*) fair-haired man ♦ SF (*donna*) blonde

bionico, -a, -ci, -che [bi'ɔniko] AGG bionic

biopsia [biop'sia] SF biopsy

bioritmo [bio'ritmo] SM biorhythm

biosfera [bios'fɛra] SF biosphere

biotecnologia [bioteknolo'dʒia] SF biotechnology

bipartito, -a [bipar'tito](*Pol*) AGG two-party attr ♦ SM two-party alliance

birba ['birba] SF rascal, rogue

birbante [bir'bante] SM rascal, rogue

birbonata [birbo'nata] SF naughty trick

birbone, -a [bir'bone] AGG (*bambino*) naughty; **fare un tiro birbone a qn** to play a naughty trick on sb ♦ SM, SF (*bambino*) little rascal

birichino, -a [biri'kino] AGG (*bambino*) mischievous, impish; (*adulto*) sly; **sguardo birichino** sly look ♦ SM, SF (*bambino*) little rascal, scamp

birillo [bi'rillo] SM skittle (*Brit*), pin (*USA*); **birilli** SMPL (*gioco*) skittles *sg*

Birmania [bir'manja] SF Burma

birmano, -a [bir'mano] AGG, SM, SF Burmese ♦ SM (*lingua*) Burmese

birra ['birra] SF (*gen*) beer, ale; **fabbrica di birra** brewery; **a tutta birra** (*fig: veloce*) at top speed, flat out; **birra in bottiglia** bottled beer; **birra chiara** lager; **birra scura** stout; **birra alla spina** draught beer

birreria [birre'ria] SF (*locale*) ≈ bierkeller; (*fabbrica*) brewery

bis [bis] ESCL encore! ♦ SM INV encore; **chiedere il bis** (*Teatro*) to call for an encore; (*fig: a tavola*) to ask for a second helping; **fare il bis di** to have some more; **facciamo il bis di gelato?** shall we have some more ice cream? ♦ AGG INV (*treno, autobus*) relief attr (*Brit*), additional; (*numero*): **12 bis** 12a

bisaccia, -ce [bi'zattʃa] SF knapsack

Bisanzio [bi'zantsjo] SF Byzantium

bisbetico, -a, -ci, -che [biz'bɛtiko] AGG ill-tempered, crabby

bisbigliare [bizbiʎ'ʎare] /27/ VT, VI (*aus avere*) (*anche fig*) to whisper; **mi ha bisbigliato qc all'orecchio** he whispered sth in my ear

bisbiglio¹, -glii [bizbiʎ'ʎio] SM (*anche fig*) whisper

bisbiglio², -gli [biz'biʎʎio] SM (*anche fig*) whispering

bisboccia, -ce [biz'bɔttʃa] SF binge, spree; **fare bisboccia** to go on a binge

bisca, -sche ['biska] SF gambling den

Biscaglia [bis'kaʎʎa] SF: **il golfo di Biscaglia** the Bay of Biscay

bischero ['biskero] SM **1** (*fam: toscano*) fool, idiot **2** (*Mus*) peg

biscia, -sce ['biʃʃa] SF grass snake; **biscia d'acqua** water snake

biscottato, -a [biskot'tato] AGG crisp; **fette biscottate** rusks

biscotto [bis'kɔtto] SM biscuit

bisessuale [bisessu'ale] AGG, SM, SF bisexual

bisestile [bizes'tile] AGG: **anno bisestile** leap year

bisezione [biset'tsjone] SF (*Geom*) bisection

bislacco, -a, -chi, -che [biz'lakko] AGG odd, weird; **è una testa bislacca** he's an odd fellow

bislungo, -a, -ghi, -ghe [biz'lungo] AGG oblong

bisnonno, -a [biz'nɔnno] SM, SF great-grandfather (grandmother); **i miei bisnonni** my great-grandparents

bisognare [bizoɲ'ɲare] /15/ VB IMPERS: **bisogna partire** we must leave, we've got to go, we'll have to leave; **bisogna parlargli** we (*o* I'll) have to talk to him; **bisogna arrivare un'ora prima per il check-in** you have to get there an hour earlier to check in; **bisogna prenotare?** is it necessary to book?; **bisogna che arriviate in tempo** you must *o* you'll have to arrive on time; **bisognerebbe che si decidesse** he should make up his mind; **bisognerebbe telefonargli** we should phone him; **non bisogna lamentarsi sempre** one *o* you shouldn't complain all the time; **bisogna vedere!** (*dipende*) I'll (*o* you'll *ecc*) have to see how things go!; **bisogna proprio dire che...** it has to be said that ... ♦ VI (*aus* essere) (*aver bisogno*) to need, want; **cosa le bisogna?** (*ant: in negozio*) can I help you?

bisogno [bi'zoɲɲo] SM **1** (*necessità*) need, necessity; **aver bisogno di** to need, be in need of; **hai bisogno di qc?** do you need anything?; **aver bisogno di fare qc** to need to do sth; **ho bisogno di cambiare dei soldi** I need to change some money; **sentire il bisogno di qc/di fare qc** to feel the need for sth/to do sth; **c'è bisogno di te qui** we need you here; **non c'è bisogno che venga anche tu** there's no need for you to come too; **non c'è bisogno di gridare** there's no need to shout; **in caso di bisogno** if need be, if necessary; **nel momento del bisogno** in one's hour of need **2** (*povertà*) poverty, need; **trovarsi nel bisogno** to be in want **3** (*euf: necessità corporali*): **fare i bisogni** (*persona*) to go to the toilet; (*animale*) to do its business

bisognoso, -a [bizoɲ'ɲoso] AGG **1** (*che ha bisogno*): **bisognoso di** in need of, needing; **essere bisognoso di qc** to need sth **2** (*povero*) poor, needy; **le famiglie più bisognose** the poorest families

bisonte [bi'zonte] SM (*Zool*) bison

bistecca, -che [bis'tekka] SF steak; **bistecca al sangue/ai ferri** rare/grilled steak

bisticciare [bistit'tʃare] /14/ VI (*aus* avere), **bisticciarsi** VR (*uso reciproco*) to bicker, squabble, quarrel; **bisticciano sempre** they're always quarrelling

bisticcio, -ci [bis'tittʃo] SM **1** (*litigio*) quarrel, squabble **2** (*gioco di parole*) pun, play on words

bistrattare [bistrat'tare] /72/ VT to maltreat

bisturi ['bisturi] SM INV (*Med*) scalpel

bisunto, -a [bi'zunto] AGG (*unto*) very greasy; **un cappotto unto e bisunto** a filthy, greasy coat

bitorzolo [bi'tortsolo] SM (*sulla testa*) bump; (*sul corpo*) lump

bitter ['bitter] SM INV bitters *pl*

bitume [bi'tume] SM bitumen

bivaccare [bivak'kare] /20/ VI (*aus* avere) (*Mil*) to bivouac; (*fig*) to bed down

bivacco, -chi [bi'vakko] SM bivouac

bivio, -vi ['bivjo] SM (*di una strada*) fork, junction; **al bivio prendi la strada che va a destra** go right at the junction; **trovarsi davanti a un bivio** (*fig*) to be at a crossroads

bizantino, -a [biddzan'tino] AGG Byzantine; (*fig: pedante*) pedantic; **questioni bizantine** convoluted questions

bizza ['biddza] SF tantrum; **fare le bizze** to throw a tantrum; **la macchina fa le bizze oggi** the car is acting up today

bizzarro, -a [bid'dzarro] AGG **1** (*strano, eccentrico*) odd, queer, eccentric **2** (*focoso: cavallo*) frisky

bizzeffe [bid'dzeffe] AVV: **a bizzeffe** in abundance, in plenty, galore; **avere soldi a bizzeffe** to be rolling in money

BL SIGLA = Belluno

blandire [blan'dire] /55/ VT (*alleviare*) to soothe; (*lusingare*) to flatter

blando, -a ['blando] AGG (*medicina, rimedio*) mild, gentle; (*liquore*) weak; (*sapore, cibo*) bland; (*punizione*) light, mild

blasfemo, -a [blas'femo] AGG blasphemous ♦ SM, SF blasphemer

blasone [bla'zone] SM coat of arms, escutcheon

blaterare [blate'rare] /72/ VI (*aus* avere) to blether ♦ VT to blether about; **ma cosa vai blaterando?** what are you blethering about?

blatta ['blatta] SF cockroach

blindare [blin'dare] /72/ VT (*veicolo*) to armour; (*porta*) to reinforce

blindata [blin'data] SF (*macchina*) armoured car *o* limousine

blindato, -a [blin'dato] AGG armoured (*Brit*), armored (*USA*); **camera blindata** strongroom; **mezzo blindato** armoured vehicle; **porta blindata** reinforced door; **vetro blindato** bulletproof glass; **condurre una vita blindata** (*fig*) to live surrounded by maximum security

bloccare [blok'kare] /20/ VT **1** (*ostruire: strada*) to block (up); (*fermare: assegno, pallone, persona*) to stop; (*: comandi, meccanismo*) to jam; (*: merci*) to stop, hold up; (*: negoziati*) to block, hold up; (*: prezzi, affitti*) to freeze; **la strada è bloccata da una frana** the road is blocked by a landslide; **la neve ha bloccato molti paesi** the snow has cut off many villages, many villages are snow-bound; **la polizia ha bloccato le vie** d'accesso alla città the police have blocked off the roads leading to the city; **ha bloccato la macchina** he braked suddenly, he slammed on the brakes; **blocca la sicura** put on the safety catch; **rimanere bloccato** to be stuck; **sono rimasto bloccato in un ingorgo/nell'ascensore** I was stuck in a traffic jam/in the lift **2** (*Mil*) to blockade **3** (*Inform*) to block; **bloccarsi** VIP (*motore*) to stall; (*freni, porta*) to jam, stick; (*ascensore*) to get stuck, stop; **si è bloccato nel bel mezzo del discorso** he suddenly stopped in the middle of what he was saying; **ho frenato ma la macchina non si è bloccata** I braked, but the car didn't stop

bloccasterzo [blokkas'tertso] SM (*Aut*) steering lock

bloccherò ecc [blokke'rɔ] VB *vedi* bloccare

blocchetto [blok'ketto] SM notebook; (*di biglietti*) book; **un blocchetto di biglietti per l'autobus** a book of tickets for the bus; **blocchetto delle ricevute** receipt book

blocco¹, -chi ['blɔkko] SM **1** (*gen*) block; **in blocco** (*Comm*) in bulk; **considerare/condannare qc in blocco** (*fig*) to take/condemn sth as a whole; **blocchi di partenza** (*Sport*) starting blocks **2** (*per appunti*) notebook; (*di carta da lettere*) (*writing*) pad **3** (*Pol*) bloc, coalition; **l'ex blocco orientale** the former Eastern bloc **4** (*Aut*): **blocco cilindri** cylinder block; **blocco motore** engine block

blocco², -chi ['blɔkko] SM **1** (*Mil*) blockade; **posto di blocco** (*sul confine*) frontier post; (*di polizia: anche: blocco stradale*) road block **2** (*Comm*) freeze; **blocco degli affitti** rent freeze; **blocco dei salari** wage freeze **3** (*Med*): **blocco cardiaco** cardiac arrest; **blocco mentale** mental block; **blocco renale** kidney failure

bloc-notes [blɔk'nɔt] SM INV notebook, notepad

blog [blog] SM INV blog

'bloggare /80/ VI to blog

blogos'fera [blogos'fera] SF blogosphere

blu [blu] AGG INV, SM INV dark blue; **blu scuro** navy (blue); **blu elettrico** electric blue

bluff [blʌf] SM INV (*anche fig*) bluff; **un bluff pubblicitario** a publicity stunt

bluffare [bluf'fare] /72/ VI (*aus* avere) (*anche fig*) to bluff

blusa ['bluza] SF (*camicetta*) blouse; (*per pittore*) smock; (*per operaio*) overall

BN SIGLA = Benevento

BO SIGLA = Bologna

boa¹ ['bɔa] SM INV **1** (*serpente*) boa (constrictor) **2** (*sciarpa*) feather boa

boa² ['bɔa] SF (*Naut*) buoy

boato [bo'ato] SM (*di esplosione*) noise; (*di folla*) roar; (*di tuono*) rumble; **boato sonico** sonic boom

bob [bɔb] SM INV bobsleigh

bobina [bo'bina] SF **1** (*Elettr*) coil; **bobina d'accensione** (*Aut*) ignition coil **2** (*di film*) reel; (*di pellicola*) spool **3** (*di cotone*) reel, bobbin, spool

bocca, -che ['bokka] SF **1** (*gen*) mouth; **per bocca** orally; **rimanere a bocca asciutta** to have nothing to eat; (*fig*) to be disappointed; **rimanere a bocca aperta** (*fig*) to be taken aback; **non ha aperto bocca** (*parlare*) he didn't open his mouth; **vuoi chiudere la bocca?** (*star zitto*) will you shut up?; **essere sulla bocca di tutti** (*persona, notizia*) to be the talk of the town; **essere di bocca buona** to eat anything; (*fig*) to be easily satisfied; **fare la bocca a qc** to acquire a taste for sth; **non voglio metter bocca in questa storia** I don't want to interfere; **mi hai tolto la parola di bocca** you took the words out of my mouth; **in bocca al lupo!** good luck!; **respirazione bocca a bocca** mouth-to-mouth resuscitation, kiss of life (*fam*) **2** (*di fiume, recipiente*) mouth; **bocca d'acqua** hydrant **3** (*Bot*): **bocca di leone** snapdragon

boccaccia, -ce [bok'kattʃa] SF **1** (*smorfia*): **fare le boccacce** to pull faces **2** (*persona maldicente*) foul-mouthed person

boccaglio, -gli [bok'kaʎʎo] SM (*Tecn*) nozzle; (*di respiratore*) mouthpiece

boccale [bok'kale] SM (*recipiente*) jug; (*per bere*) mug; **boccale da birra** beer mug, tankard

boccascena [bokkaʃ'ʃena] SM INV proscenium

boccata [bok'kata] SF mouthful; (*di fumo*) puff; **prendere una boccata d'aria** to go out for a breath of (fresh) air

boccetta [bot'tʃetta] SF phial, small bottle

boccheggiare [bokked'dʒare] /62/ VI (aus avere) to gasp

bocchino [bok'kino] SM (di pipa, strumento musicale) mouthpiece; (per sigarette) cigarette holder

boccia, -ce ['bɔttʃa] SF 1 (palla di legno, metallo) bowl; il gioco delle bocce bowls sg; giocare a bocce to play bowls 2 (bottiglia) bottle; (da vino) carafe

bocciare [bot'tʃare] /14/ VT 1 (respingere) to reject; (agli esami) to fail; essere bocciato agli esami to fail one's exams; andava male in tutte le materie ed è stato bocciato he did badly in all subjects and was kept back 2 (alle bocce) to hit

bocciatura [bottʃa'tura] SF (agli esami) failure

bocciolo [bot'tʃɔlo] SM bud; bocciolo di rosa rosebud

boccolo ['bokkolo] SM curl

bocconcino [bokkon'tʃino] SM (pietanza deliziosa) delicacy

boccone [bok'kone] SM (quantità di cibo) mouthful; un boccone di pane a mouthful of bread; mangiare un boccone to have a bite to eat; finire tutto in un boccone to gulp everything down at once; inghiottire un boccone amaro (fig) to swallow a bitter pill; boccone del prete (Culin) parson's nose

bocconi [bok'koni] AVV face downwards; cadere bocconi to fall flat on one's face

Boemia [bo'ɛmja] SF Bohemia

boemo, -a [bo'ɛmo] AGG, SM, SF Bohemian

bofonchiare [bofon'kjare] /19/ VI (aus avere) to grumble

Bogotà [bogo'ta] SF Bogotá

boia ['bɔja] SM INV 1 (carnefice) executioner; (in impiccagione) hangman; (fig: mascalzone) rogue, scoundrel 2 (in escl: fam): boia d'una miseria!, boia d'un mondo ladro! damn!, blast! ♦ AGG INV (fam): fa un freddo boia it's cold as hell

boiata [bo'jata] SF (fam: robaccia) rubbish; quel film era una boiata that film was (a load of) rubbish; non dire boiate! (sciocchezze) don't talk rubbish!

boicottaggio, -gi [boikot'taddʒo] SM boycott; (fig) sabotage

boicottare [boikot'tare] /72/ VT (Econ, o fig: persona) to boycott; (: piani) to sabotage

bolgia, -ge ['bɔldʒa] SF (fig): c'era una tale bolgia al cinema the cinema was absolutely mobbed

bolide ['bɔlide] SM 1 (Astron) meteor; come un bolide like a flash, at top speed; entrare/uscire come un bolide to charge in/out 2 (auto da corsa) racing car (Brit), race car (USA)

Bolivia [bo'livja] SF Bolivia

boliviano, -a [boli'vjano] AGG, SM, SF Bolivian

bolla[1] ['bɔlla] SF bubble; (Med) blister; fare le bolle di sapone to blow bubbles; finire in una bolla di sapone (fig) to come to nothing; bolla speculativa speculative bubble

bolla[2] ['bɔlla] SF 1 (Comm) bill, receipt; bolla di accompagnamento waybill; bolla di consegna delivery note 2 (Rel): bolla papale papal bull

bollare [bol'lare] /72/ VT (timbrare) to stamp; (sigillare) to seal; (fig) to brand; bollato a vita (fig) branded for life; carta bollata official stamped paper

bollente [bol'lente] AGG (che bolle) boiling; (caldissimo) boiling (hot); cuocere in acqua bollente cook in boiling water; la minestra è bollente! the soup is boiling hot!; calmare i bollenti spiriti to calm down

bolletta [bol'letta] SF 1 (conto: del gas, telefono) bill; bolletta della luce electricity bill 2 (ricevuta) receipt; bolletta di carico bill of lading; bolletta di consegna delivery note; bolletta doganale clearance certificate; bolletta di trasporto aereo air waybill 3 (fam: senza soldi): essere in bolletta to be broke, be hard up

bollettino [bollet'tino] SM 1 (comunicato, periodico) bulletin; bollettino meteorologico weather report 2 (Comm: dei prezzi, cambi) list; (: modulo) form; bollettino di ordinazione order form; bollettino di spedizione consignment note

bollicina [bolli'tʃina] SF bubble; acqua con le bollicine fizzy water

bollire [bol'lire] /17/ VT to boil; fare bollire (acqua) to boil, bring to the boil; (biberon) to sterilize; (panni) to boil ♦ VI (aus avere) to boil, be boiling; l'acqua bolle the water's boiling; qui dentro si bolle (dal caldo) it's boiling (hot) in here; qualcosa bolle in pentola (fig) there's something brewing

bollito, -a [bol'lito] AGG boiled ♦ SM (Culin) ≈ boiled beef

bollitore [bolli'tore] SM 1 (per acqua) kettle; (per latte) milk pan 2 (Tecn) boiler

bollitura [bolli'tura] SF 1 (azione) boiling 2 (acqua) cooking liquid

bollo ['bollo] SM (timbro) stamp; (sigillo) seal; (su bestiame) brand; carta da bollo official stamped paper; marca da bollo revenue stamp; tassa di bollo stamp duty; bollo di circolazione (Aut) road tax; bollo per patente driving licence tax; bollo postale postmark

bollore [bol'lore] SM: dare un bollore a qc to bring sth to the boil (Brit) o a boil (USA); i bollori della gioventù (fig) youthful enthusiasm sg; ti sono passati i bollori? have you calmed down?

Bologna [bo'loɲɲa] SF Bologna

bolognese [boloɲ'ɲese] AGG Bolognese, of o from Bologna; spaghetti alla bolognese spaghetti bolognese ♦ SM, SF inhabitant o native of Bologna

bomba ['bomba] SF bomb; (Calcio: tiro violento) drive; è scoppiata una bomba alla stazione a bomb went off at the station; la notizia fu una bomba the news came as a bombshell; sei stato una bomba! you were tremendous!; guarda che bomba! (persona, macchina) what a beauty!; tornare a bomba (al punto) to get back to the point; bomba atomica atom bomb; bomba chimica chemical weapon; bomba a mano hand grenade; bomba N Neutron bomb; bomba ad orologeria time bomb; bomba umana suicide bomber

bombardamento [bombarda'mento] SM (vedi vb) bombardment; bombing; shelling; un bombardamento aereo an air raid; è rimasto ucciso durante il bombardamento aereo he was killed in the bombing; bombardamento a tappeto saturation bombing

bombardare [bombar'dare] /72/ VT (gen, Fis) to bombard; (con bombe) to bomb; (con cannone) to shell; bombardare di domande/lettere to bombard with questions/letters

bombardiere [bombar'djere] SM (aereo) bomber; (persona) bombardier

bombetta [bom'betta] SF bowler (hat) (Brit), derby (USA); la classica bombetta inglese the famous English bowler hat

bombola ['bombola] SF cylinder; bombola del gas gas cylinder; bombola d'insetticida fly spray; bombola di ossigeno oxygen cylinder

bomboletta [bombo'letta] SF spray can

bomboniera [bombo'njera] SF box of sweets (as souvenir at weddings, first communions)

bonaccia [bo'nattʃa] SF (Naut) dead calm; (fig) lull; il mare è in bonaccia the sea is dead calm

bonaccione, -a [bonat'tʃone] AGG good-natured, easy-going ♦ SM, SF good-natured sort

bonario, -ria, -ri, -rie [bo'narjo] AGG (persona) good-natured, affable; (modi, aspetto) kindly

bonifica, -che [bo'nifika], **bonificazione** [bonifikat'tsjone] SF (operazione) reclamation; (terreno) reclaimed land; opere di bonifica land reclamation works

bonifico, -ci [bo'nifiko] SM (Comm: riduzione, abbuono) discount; (Banca) credit transfer

Bonn [bɔn] SF Bonn

bontà [bon'ta] SF (gen) goodness, kindness; (di prodotti) quality; bontà d'animo o di cuore goodness of heart; bontà sua! (iro) how kind of him!; abbia la bontà di ascoltarmi! will you please listen to me?

borbonico, -a, -ci, -che [bor'boniko] AGG Bourbon; (pegg) backward, out of date ♦ SM, SF Bourbon

borbottare [borbot'tare] /72/ VT (pronunciare confusamente) to mutter ♦ VI (aus avere) to mutter; (lamentarsi) to moan, grumble; (tuono, stomaco) to rumble

borbottio, -tii [borbot'tio] SM (vedi vb) muttering, moaning, grumbling; rumbling

borchia ['borkja] SF (di abiti, cinture, borse) stud; (Tecn) boss; (da tappezziere) upholsterer's nail

bordatura [borda'tura] SF (di abiti, tende) border, edge

bordeaux [bor'do] SM INV (colore) burgundy, maroon; (vino) Bordeaux

bordello [bor'dello] SM brothel; fare bordello (fam!) to kick up a hell of a row

bordo ['bordo] SM 1 (*orlo*) edge; (*guarnizione*) border; (*di cratere, ruota*) rim; **il bordo del tavolo/letto** the edge of the table/bed; **sul bordo della strada** at the roadside; **eravamo seduti sul bordo della piscina** we were sitting on the edge of the pool; **è nero, con un bordo rosso** it's black, with a red border; **a bordo campo** (*Calcio*) on the touchline 2 (*Naut: fiancata di nave*) ship's side; **virare di bordo** (*anche fig*) to change course; **fuori bordo** overboard; **a bordo di** (*nave, aereo*) aboard, on board; **era a bordo di una macchina rossa** he was in a red car; **c'erano cento passeggeri a bordo dell'aereo** there were a hundred passengers on board the plane; **salire a bordo (di qc)** (*aereo, nave*) to go on board (sth), board (sth); (*macchina*) to get in(to sth); **siamo saliti a bordo dell'aereo** we got on the plane; **persona d'alto bordo** (*fig*) VIP

bordura [bor'dura] SF (*di abiti, aiuole*) border; (*di pietanze*) garnish

borgata [bor'gata] SF (*in campagna*) hamlet; (*a Roma*) working-class suburb

borghese [bor'gese] AGG 1 (*gen*) middle-class; (*pegg*) bourgeois; **una famiglia borghese** a middle-class family 2 **essere in (abito) borghese** to be in civilian clothes *o* in civvies; **poliziotto in borghese** plainclothes policeman ♦ SM, SF (*vedi agg*) middle-class person; bourgeois; **piccolo borghese** (*pegg*) petty bourgeois

borghesia [borge'zia] SF bourgeoisie, middle classes *pl*; **alta/ piccola borghesia** upper/lower middle classes *pl*

borgo, -ghi ['borgo] SM (*paese*) village; (*quartiere cittadino*) district; (*sobborgo*) suburb

boria ['borja] SF conceit, arrogance

borioso, -a [bo'rjoso] AGG conceited, arrogant

borlotto [bor'lotto] SM kidney bean

Borneo ['borneo] SM Borneo

borraccia, -ce [bor'rattʃa] SF (*per soldati, cowboy*) water-bottle, flask

borsa ['borsa] SF (*gen*) bag; (*borsetta*) handbag (*Brit*), purse (*USA*); (*Ciclismo*) pannier; **ho una valigia e una borsa** I've got one case and one bag; **o la borsa o la vita!** your money or your life!; **aver le borse sotto gli occhi** to have bags under one's eyes ♦ **borsa dell'acqua calda** hot water bottle; **borsa del ghiaccio** ice bag; **borsa portalavoro** knitting bag; **borsa del postino** mailbag; **borsa della spesa** shopping bag; **borsa di studio** (*per studente bisognoso*) (student's) grant; (*per studente meritevole e bisognoso*) scholarship; **borsa del tabacco** tobacco pouch; **borsa degli utensili** toolbag; **borsa da viaggio** travelling bag

borsaiolo, -a [borsa'jolo] SM, SF pickpocket

borseggio, -gi [bor'seddʒo] SM pickpocketing

borsellino [borsel'lino] SM purse

borsello [bor'sello], **borsetto** [bor'setto] SM handbag (*for man*)

borsetta [bor'setta] SF handbag; **borsetta da sera** evening bag

borsista, -i, -e [bor'sista] SM, SF 1 (*di borsa di studio*) grant holder 2 (*Borsa*) speculator

boscaglia [bos'kaʎʎa] SF brush

boscaiolo [boska'jolo], **boscaiuolo** [boska'jwɔlo] SM (*legnaiuolo*) woodcutter, lumberjack (*USA*); (*guardiano*) forester

boschetto [bos'ketto] SM copse, grove

bosco, -schi ['bɔsko] SM wood; **un bosco di querce** an oak wood; **una passeggiata nel bosco** a walk in the woods

boscoso, -a [bos'koso] AGG wooded

bosniaco, -a, -ci, -che [boz'niako] AGG, SM, SF Bosnian

Bosnia-Erzegovina ['bɔznja erdze'govina] SF Bosnia-Herzegovina

bossolo ['bɔssolo] SM cartridge case

Bot, bot [bɔt] SIGLA M INV = **buono ordinario del Tesoro**

botanico, -a, -ci, -che [bo'taniko] AGG botanic(al); **orto** *o* **giardino botanico** botanical gardens *pl* ♦ SM, SF botanist

botola ['bɔtola] SF trap door

Botswana [bots'wana] SM Botswana

botta ['bɔtta] SF 1 (*percossa*) blow; (*fig: colpo, danno*) blow, shock; **gli menò una botta in testa** he struck him a blow on the head; **dare (un sacco di) botte a qn** to give sb a good thrashing; **prendere una botta** to be hit; **ha preso una botta sulla testa** he was hit on the head; **fare a botte** to fight 2 (*Scherma*) thrust; **botta e risposta** (*fig*) cut and thrust

botte ['botte] SF barrel, cask; **volta a botte** (*Archit*) barrel vault; **volere la botte piena e la moglie ubriaca** (*Proverbio*) to want to have one's cake and eat it; **essere in una botte di ferro** (*fig*) to be (as) safe as houses

bottega, -ghe [bot'tega] SF (*negozio*) shop; (*laboratorio*) workshop; **aprire/mettere su bottega** to open/set up shop; **chiudere bottega** to shut up shop; (*fig*) to give up; **stare a bottega (da qn)** to serve one's apprenticeship (with sb); **avere la bottega aperta** (*fam*) to have one's flies undone

bottegaio, -aia, -ai, -aie [botte'gajo] SM, SF shopkeeper

botteghino [botte'gino] SM (*Teatro, Cine*) box office; (*del lotto*) lottery office

bottiglia [bot'tiʎʎa] SF bottle; **bottiglia di vino** bottle of wine; **una bottiglia da 1 litro** a litre bottle; **in bottiglia** bottled; **birra in bottiglia** bottled beer; **vino in bottiglia** bottled wine; **bottiglia Molotov** Molotov cocktail; **bottiglia da vino** wine bottle ♦ AGG INV: **verde bottiglia** bottle green

bottiglieria [bottiʎʎe'ria] SF (*negozio*) wine shop; (*deposito*) wine cellar

bottino [bot'tino] SM (*di guerra*) booty; (*di rapina, furto*) loot; **fare bottino di qc** to make off with sth

botto ['bɔtto] SM (*di mortaretti*) thud; (*spari*) rattle; **abbiamo sentito un gran botto** we heard a loud bang; **di botto** (*fam*) suddenly; **si è fermato di botto** he stopped suddenly; **in un botto** (*fam*) in a flash

bottone [bot'tone] SM 1 (*di giacca, radio*) button; **premere** *o* **spingere un bottone** to press a button; **stanza dei bottoni** control room; (*fig*) nerve centre; **attaccare un bottone** (*alla camicia*) to sew on a button; **attaccare un bottone a qn** (*fig: trattenere*) to buttonhole sb; **attaccare bottone con qn** (*fig: conversare*) to strike up a conversation with sb; **bottone automatico** press stud 2 (*Bot*) bud; **bottone d'oro** buttercup

bovino, -a [bo'vino] AGG bovine; (*allevamento*) cattle *attr*; **carne bovina** beef; **occhi bovini** (*fig*) protruding eyes ♦ **bovini** SMPL cattle

box [bɔks] SM INV (*per cavalli*) horsebox; (*per macchina*) lockup, garage; (*per macchina da corsa*) pit; (*per bambini*) playpen; **metti la macchina nel box** put the car in the garage; **tuo fratello è nel box** your brother is in his playpen; **box doccia** shower cubicle

❏ **box** non si traduce mai con la parola inglese *box*

boxe [bɔks] SF INV boxing; **un incontro di boxe** a boxing match

boxer ['bɔkser] SM INV (*cane*) boxer ♦ SMPL (*mutande*): **un paio di boxer** a pair of boxer shorts

bozza ['bɔttsa] SF (*di lettera, contratto, romanzo*) draft; (*Tip: di stampa*) proof; **rivedere** *o* **correggere le bozze** to proofread; **prima/seconda/terza bozza** first/revised proof; **bozza in colonna** galley proof; **bozza impaginata** page proof

bozzetto [bot'tsetto] SM (*disegno*) sketch; (*modello*) scale model

bozzolo ['bɔttsolo] SM cocoon; **uscire dal bozzolo** (*fig*) to come out of one's shell; **chiudersi nel proprio bozzolo** (*fig*) to withdraw into one's shell

BR [bi'erre] SIGLA FPL = **Brigate Rosse** ♦ SIGLA = **Brindisi**

braca, -che ['braka] SF 1 **brache** *pl* (*fam: pantaloni*) trousers, pants (*USA*); (: *mutandoni*) drawers; **calare** *o* **calarsi le brache** (*fig: fam*) to chicken out 2 (*allacciatura: per operai*) (safety) harness

braccare [brak'kare] /20/ VT (*anche fig*) to hunt

braccetto [brat'tʃetto] AVV: **a braccetto** arm in arm; **prendere qn a braccetto** to take sb by the arm; **tenersi a braccetto** to be arm in arm; **si tenevano a braccetto** they were walking arm in arm

braccherò ecc [brakke'rɔ] VB *vedi* **braccare**

bracciale [brat'tʃale] SM (*ornamento*) bracelet; (*distintivo*) armband; **bracciali** (*per nuotare*) armbands

braccialetto [brattʃa'letto] SM bracelet, bangle; **un braccialetto d'argento** a silver bracelet; **braccialetto elettronico** electronic tag

bracciante [brat'tʃante] SM, SF (day) labourer

bracciata [bratˈtʃata] SF 1 (*quantità*) armful; **a bracciate** by the armful 2 (*nel nuoto*) stroke

braccio [ˈbrattʃo] SM 1 (*pl f* **braccia**): *Anat*: arm; **mi fa male il braccio** my arm hurts; **tenere/prendere in braccio** to hold/ take in one's arms; **dare** o **offrire il braccio a qn** to give sb one's arm; **camminare sotto braccio** to walk arm in arm; **è il suo braccio destro** (*fig*) he's his right-hand man; **braccio di ferro** (*anche fig*) trial of strength; **alzare le braccia al cielo** to throw up one's arms; **a braccia** (*sollevare, portare*) with one's own hands; **a braccia aperte** with open arms; **incrociare le braccia** to fold one's arms; (*fig*) to down tools; **gettare le braccia al collo a qn** to throw one's arms round sb's neck; **mi sono cascate le braccia** (*fig*) I could have wept; **avere buone braccia** to be big and strong 2 (*pl f* **braccia**): (*Naut*: *unità di misura*) fathom 3 (*pl m* **bracci**) (*di croce, gru, fiume, grammofono*) arm; (*di edificio*) wing; **braccio di mare** sound; **braccio della morte** death row

bracciolo [bratˈtʃɔlo] SM arm

bracco, -chi [ˈbrakko] SM hound

bracconiere [brakkoˈnjɛre] SM poacher

brace [ˈbratʃe] SF embers *pl*; **alla brace** barbecued; **pollo alla brace** barbecued chicken

❑ **brace** non si traduce mai con la parola inglese *brace*

braciere [braˈtʃɛre] SM brazier

braciola [braˈtʃɔla] SF (*con osso*) chop; (*senza osso*) steak; **una braciola di maiale** a pork chop

bradipo [ˈbradipo] SM (*Zool*) sloth

brado, -a [ˈbrado] AGG (*animale*) wild; **allo stato brado** in the wild o natural state

brama [ˈbrama] SF: **brama (di/di fare)** longing (for/to do), yearning (for/to do)

bramare [braˈmare] /72/ VT: **bramare (qc/di fare qc)** to long (for sth/to do sth), yearn (for sth/to do sth)

bramosia [bramoˈsia] SF: **bramosia (di)** longing (for), yearning (for)

branca, -che [ˈbranka] SF 1 (*settore, ramo*) branch; **una branca della medicina** a branch of medicine 2 (*fig*: *artigli*) branche SFPL (*di vizio*) grip; (*di usuraio*) clutches

branchia [ˈbrankja] SF (*Zool*) gill

branco, -chi [ˈbranko] SM (*di uccelli, pecore*) flock; (*di cani, lupi*) pack; (*di balene, delfini*) school; (*fig*: *pegg*: *di persone*) gang, pack; **entrare nel branco** (*fig*) to go with the crowd

brancolare [brankoˈlare] /72/ VI (*aus avere*) to grope, feel one's way; **brancolare nel buio** (*fig*) to grope in the dark

branda [ˈbranda] SF (*da campo, per militari*) camp bed, folding bed; (*per marinai*) hammock; **giù dalle brande!** everybody up!

brandello [branˈdɛllo] SM scrap, shred; **a brandelli** in tatters, in rags; **fare a brandelli** to tear to shreds

brandina [branˈdina] SF camp bed (*Brit*), cot (*USA*)

brandire [branˈdire] /55/ VT to brandish

brano [ˈbrano] SM (*gen*) piece; (*di libro*) passage; **un brano di musica classica** a piece of classical music; **abbiamo letto un brano da "I Promessi Sposi"** we read a passage from "I Promessi Sposi"; **fare a brani** (*fig*) to tear to pieces

brasare [braˈzare] /72/ VT 1 (*Culin*) to braise 2 (*Tecn*) to braze

brasato, -a [braˈzato] AGG (*Culin*) braised ♦ SM braised beef

Brasile [braˈzile] SM Brazil; **andremo in Brasile quest'estate** we're going to Brazil this summer; **mi è piaciuto molto il Brasile** I really liked Brazil

Brasilia [braˈzilja] SF Brasilia

brasiliano, -a [braziˈljano] AGG, SM, SF Brazilian

bravata [braˈvata] SF (*azione spavalda*) act of bravado; **bravate** SFPL bravado *sg*

bravo, -a [ˈbravo] AGG 1 (*abile*) good, clever, skilful, capable; **essere bravo in qc/a fare qc** to be good at sth/at doing sth; **sono abbastanza bravo in inglese** I'm quite good at English; **un bravo insegnante/medico** a good teacher/doctor; **essere bravo a scuola** to do well at school; **il più bravo** the best; **è il più bravo della classe** he's the best in the class; **bravo!** well done!; **bravi!** (*in chiusura di spettacolo*) bravo! 2 (*buono*) good; (*onesto*) honest; **è un brav'uomo** he's a decent chap; **sono brave persone** they're good people; **fai il bravo**

be good; **su da bravo!** (*fam*) there's a good boy! 3 (*coraggioso*) brave 4 (*rafforzativo*): **mi sono fatto le mie brave 8 ore di lavoro** I put in a full 8 hours' work

bravura [braˈvura] SF cleverness, skill; **pezzo di bravura** (*Mus*) bravura piece

breccia, -ce [ˈbrettʃa] SF breach; (*Geol*) breccia; **essere sulla breccia** (*fig*) to be going strong; **fare breccia nell'animo** o **nel cuore di qn** to find the way to sb's heart

Brema [ˈbrɛma] SF Bremen

bresaola [breˈzaola] SF (*Culin*) *kind of dried salted beef*

bresciano, -a [breʃˈʃano] AGG o from Brescia ♦ SM, SF inhabitant o native of Brescia

Bretagna [breˈtaɲɲa] SF Brittany; **Gran Bretagna** Great Britain

bretella [breˈtella] SF 1 (*di sottoveste, reggiseno*) strap; **bretelle** (*di calzoni*) braces 2 (*raccordo stradale*) motorway link road; (*Aer*) exit runway

bretone [ˈbretone] AGG, SM, SF Breton

breve [ˈbrɛve] AGG (*gen*) brief, short; (*vita, strada*) short; **una breve visita** a short visit; **tra breve** shortly; **a breve distanza** near, not far; **sarò breve** I'll be brief; **per farla breve** to cut a long story short; **in breve** in short; **a breve** (*Comm*) short-term ♦ SF 1 (*Mus*) breve 2 (*vocale*) short vowel; (*sillaba*) short syllable

brevettare [brevetˈtare] /72/ VT to patent

brevetto [breˈvetto] SM 1 (*d'invenzione*) patent; **Ufficio Brevetti** Patent Office 2 (*patente*): **brevetto di pilota** pilot's licence (*Brit*) o license (*USA*)

brevità [breviˈta] SF brevity

brezza [ˈbreddza] SF breeze; **brezza di terra/mare** land/sea breeze

bricco, -chi [ˈbrikko] SM jug; **bricco del caffè** coffeepot; **bricco del latte** milk jug

bricconata [brikkoˈnata] SF mischievous trick

briccone [brikˈkone] SM, SF rascal, rogue

briciola [ˈbritʃola] SF (*di pane*) crumb; (*frammento*) scrap; **non ha lasciato che le briciole** (*anche fig*) he only left the scraps; **ridurre in briciole** (*biscotto*) to crumble up; (*fig*: *persona*) to take to pieces

briciolo [ˈbritʃolo] SM bit; (*fig*: *di buon senso, verità*) grain; **non ha un briciolo di cervello** she hasn't got a bit of sense

bridge [bridʒ] SM INV bridge

briga, -ghe [ˈbriga] SF 1 (*cura, fastidio*) bother, trouble; **darsi** o **prendersi la briga di fare qc** to take the trouble to do sth; **si è preso la briga di telefonare a tutti** he took the trouble to phone everybody 2 (*lite*): **attaccar briga** to start a quarrel

brigadiere [brigaˈdjɛre] SM (*dei Carabinieri, Finanza*) ≈ sergeant

brigante [briˈgante] SM brigand, bandit; (*fig*: *bambino*) rascal

brigata [briˈgata] SF 1 (*gruppo*) group; (*comitiva*) party; **un'allegra brigata di amici** a lively bunch of friends 2 (*Mil*) brigade; **generale di brigata** brigadier (*Brit*), brigadier general (*USA*); **le Brigate Rosse** (*Pol*) the Red Brigades

brigatismo [brigaˈtizmo] SM *phenomenon of the Red Brigades*

brigatista, -i, -e [brigaˈtista] SM, SF (*Pol*) *member of the Red Brigades*

briglia [ˈbriʎʎa] SF (*di cavallo*) rein, bridle; (*per bambino*) rein; **a briglia sciolta** at full gallop; (*fig*) at full speed; **allentare/tirare la briglia** (*anche fig*) to slacken/tighten the reins

brillante [brilˈlante] AGG 1 (*luce, raggi, colori*) bright; (*più intenso*) brilliant; (*che luccica*) shining; (*occhi*) sparkling; **una camicia verde brillante** a bright green shirt 2 (*successo, carriera, studioso*) brilliant; (*conversazione*) brilliant, sparkling; **è una persona brillante** he has a sparkling wit ♦ SM (*diamante*) diamond; (*anello*) diamond ring; **un anello con brillante** a diamond ring

brillantina [brillanˈtina] SF brilliantine

brillare [brilˈlare] VI (*aus avere*) 1 (*sole*) to shine; (*stelle*) to shine, twinkle; (*occhi*) to shine, sparkle; (*diamante*) to sparkle; **le stelle brillano in cielo** the stars are shining in the sky; **gli occhi le brillavano di gioia** her eyes sparkled o shone with joy; **brilla per la sua bellezza/intelligenza** she is outstandingly beautiful/intelligent; **brillare per la propria**

assenza to be conspicuous by one's absence 2 (*mina*) to go off, explode ♦ VT (*mina*) to set off

brillo, -a ['brillo] AGG (*fam*) tipsy, merry; **era un po' brillo** he was a bit tipsy

brina ['brina] SF (hoar)frost; **c'è ancora la brina sui campi** there's still frost on the fields

brindare [brin'dare] /72/ VI (*aus* avere) to make a toast; **brindare a qn/qc** to drink to o toast sb/sth; **brindare alla salute di qn** to drink sb's health; **brindiamo alla macchina nuova!** let's drink to the new car!

brindisi ['brindizi] SM INV toast; **fare un brindisi (a qn/qc)** to drink a toast (to sb/sth); **facciamo un brindisi!** let's drink a toast!

brio ['brio] SM (*brio*) liveliness; **essere pieno di brio** to be very lively o full of life

brioche [bri'ɔʃ] SF INV brioche

brioso, -a [bri'oso] AGG lively

briscola ['briskola] SF (*gioco di carte*) type of card game; (*seme vincente*) trump(s); (*carta*) trump card

britannico, -a, -ci, -che [bri'tanniko] AGG British; **le isole britanniche** the British Isles ♦ SM, SF British person, Briton; **i britannici** SMPL the British

brivido ['brivido] SM (*di freddo*) shiver; (*di ribrezzo*) shudder; (*di piacere*) thrill; **avere i brividi** (*anche fig*) to have the shivers; **ho i brividi** I've got the shivers; **far venire i brividi a qn** (*fig*) to give sb the shivers; **racconti del brivido** suspense stories

brizzolato, -a [brittso'lato] AGG greying; (*persona*) greyhaired; **capelli brizzolati** greying hair

brocca, -che ['brɔkka] SF jug

broccato [brok'kato] SM brocade

broccolo ['brɔkkolo] SM (*Bot, Culin*) broccoli *no pl*

brodaglia [bro'daʎʎa] SF (*pegg*) dishwater

brodo ['brɔdo] SM broth; (*per cucinare*) stock; **riso/pasta in brodo** rice/noodle soup; **dadi da brodo** stock cubes; **tutto fa brodo** (*fig*) every little helps; **lasciare (cuocere) qn nel suo brodo** (*fig*) to let sb stew (in his own juice); **brodo di manzo** beef tea; **brodo di pollo** chicken soup; **brodo ristretto** consommé

broglio, -gli ['brɔʎʎo] SM: **broglio elettorale** gerrymandering

bromo ['brɔmo] SM (*Chim*) bromine

bronchite [bron'kite] SF bronchitis

broncio, -ci ['brontʃo] SM sulky expression; (*malumore*) sulkiness; **avere** o **tenere il broncio** to sulk; **gli tiene il broncio** he's not speaking to him

bronco, -chi ['bronko] SM bronchial tube

brontolare [bronto'lare] /72/ VT to mutter, mumble ♦ VI (*aus* avere) (*mormorare*) to mutter, mumble; (*protestare*) to grumble; **non fa altro che brontolare** he's always grumbling; **mi brontola lo stomaco** my stomach is rumbling

brontolio, -lii [bronto'lio] SM (*vedi vb*) muttering, mumbling; grumbling; rumbling

brontolone, -a [bronto'lone] AGG grumbling ♦ SM, SF grumbler

bronzina [bron'dzina] SF (*Tecn*) bush

bronzo ['brondzo] SM (*metallo, oggetto*) bronze; **ha vinto la medaglia di bronzo** she won the bronze medal; **che faccia di bronzo!** what (brazen) insolence!

bross. ABBR = **in brossura**; *vedi* **brossura**

brossura [bros'sura] SF: **in brossura** (*libro*) paperback

browser ['brauzer] SM INV (*Inform*) browser

brucare [bru'kare] /20/ VT to browse on, nibble at

brucherà *ecc* [bruke'ra] VB *vedi* **brucare**

bruciacchiare [brutʃak'kjare] /19/ VT to singe, scorch; **bruciacchiarsi** VIP to get singed o scorched

bruciapelo [brutʃa'pelo] AVV: **a bruciapelo** point-blank; **sparare a bruciapelo** to fire at point-blank range

bruciare [bru'tʃare] /14/ VT 1 (*gen*) to burn; (*edificio*) to burn down; (*stoffa: stirando*) to scorch; (*Med: verruca*) to cauterize; **oh no, ho bruciato la torta!** oh no, I've burnt the cake!; **mi sono bruciata un dito** I've burnt my finger; **bruciato dal sole** (*terreno*) sun-scorched; (*volto*) sunburnt (*ustionato*) burnt by the sun 2 (*fraseologia*): **bruciare gli avversari** (*Sport, anche fig*) to leave the rest of the field behind; **bruciare**

le cervella a qn to blow sb's brains out; **bruciare le tappe** o **i tempi** (*Sport, anche fig*) to shoot ahead; **bruciarsi le ali** (*fig*) to burn one's fingers; **bruciarsi la carriera** to ruin one's career ♦ VI (*aus* essere) 1 (*gen*) to burn; (*edificio, bosco*) to be on fire 2 (*essere molto caldo*) to be burning (hot); (*sole*) to be scorching, be burning; **bruciare di febbre** to run a high temperature 3 (*produrre bruciore*): **gli occhi mi bruciano** my eyes are smarting o stinging; **il viso mi brucia** my face is burning; **mi brucia molto questa offesa** that insult really rankles; **bruciarsi** VR, VIP (*persona*) to burn o.s.; **mi sono bruciata!** I've burnt myself!; **si è bruciato l'arrosto** the joint is burnt; **si è bruciata una lampadina** a bulb has blown

bruciatore [brutʃa'tore] SM (*Tecn*) burner

bruciatura [brutʃa'tura] SF 1 (*atto*) burning *no pl* 2 (*parte bruciata*) burn; (*scottatura*) scald; **una bruciatura di primo grado** a first-degree burn

bruciore [bru'tʃore] SM burning o smarting sensation; **provocare bruciore** to sting

bruco, -chi ['bruko] SM (*Zool*) grub; (*di farfalla*) caterpillar

brufolo ['brufolo] SM pimple, spot

brughiera [bru'gjera] SF moor, heath

brulicare [bruli'kare] /20/ VI (*aus* avere) to swarm; **il mercato brulicava di gente** the market was heaving with people

brulichio, -chii [bruli'kio] SM swarming

brullo, -a ['brullo] AGG bare

bruma ['bruma] SF mist, haze

bruno, -a ['bruno] AGG (*capelli*) brown, dark; (*carnagione*) dark; (*persona*) dark(-haired); **è bruno** he's got dark hair ♦ SM, SF dark-haired person

bruscamente [bruska'mente] AVV (*frenare, fermarsi*) suddenly; (*rispondere, reagire*) sharply

brusco, -a, -schi, -sche ['brusko] AGG (*movimento*) abrupt, sudden; (*modi, persona*) abrupt, brusque; **ha fatto una brusca frenata** he braked suddenly; **è stato un po' brusco con me** he was a bit abrupt with me

brusio, -sii [bru'zio] SM hubbub, buzz; **il brusio degli insetti** the buzzing of the insects

brutale [bru'tale] AGG rough, brutal; **per dirla in modo brutale** to put it bluntly

brutalità [brutali'ta] SF INV brutality

bruto, -a ['bruto] AGG brute; **forza bruta** brute force o strength ♦ SM (*uomo violento*) brute

brutta ['brutta] SF rough copy, first draft

bruttezza [brut'tettsa] SF ugliness

brutto, -a ['brutto] AGG 1 (*persona, vestito, casa*) ugly; **è proprio brutto!** he's really ugly!; **è il posto più brutto che abbia mai visto** it's the ugliest place I've ever seen; **brutto come la fame** as ugly as sin 2 (*cattivo: gen*) bad; (: *ferita, malattia, strada, affare*) nasty; (: *carattere*) unpleasant, nasty; **ho un brutto raffreddore** I've got a bad cold; **ho fatto un brutto sogno** I had a bad dream; **ho preso un brutto voto in matematica** I got a bad mark in mathematics; **ha fatto brutto (tempo) ieri** yesterday the weather was bad; **che brutta giornata!** what a horrible day!; **brutto stupido!** you stupid clown!; **avere un brutto male** (*euf*) to have cancer; **passare un brutto momento** to go through a difficult period; **passare un brutto quarto d'ora** to have a nasty time of it; **vedersela brutta** (*per un attimo*) to have a nasty moment; (*per un periodo*) to have a bad time of it; **brutta copia** rough copy ♦ SM: **il brutto** the ugly; **è il brutto della famiglia** he's the ugly member of the family; **il brutto è che...** the problem o unfortunate thing is that ...; **stiamo andando verso il brutto** (*Meteor*) the weather is taking a turn for the worse ♦ AVV: **guardare qn di brutto** to give sb a nasty look; **picchiare qn di brutto** to give sb a bad o nasty beating; **sta lavorando di brutto** he's working furiously

bruttura [brut'tura] SF (*oggetto*) ugly thing

Bruxelles [bry'sɛl] SF Brussels; **vivo a Bruxelles** I live in Brussels

BS SIGLA = Brescia

BSE [bi'esse'e] SIGLA F BSE (= *Bovine Spongiform Encephalopathy*)

BT [bi'ti] ABBR (= *bassa tensione*) LT ♦ SIGLA M = **buono del Tesoro**

btg ABBR = **battaglione**

BTP [bitiˈpi] SIGLA M INV = **buono del Tesoro poliennale**

bubbone [bubˈbone] SM swelling

buca, -che [ˈbuka] SF (gen, Golf) hole; (più profondo) pit; (di biliardo) pocket; (avvallamento) hollow; **la strada è piena di buche** the road is full of holes; **mi ha dato buca** (fam) she didn't turn up; **buca delle lettere** (per imbucare) post box; (in portone) letterbox; **buca del suggeritore** (Teatro) prompter's box

bucaneve [bukaˈneve] SM INV snowdrop

bucare [buˈkare] /20/ VT (forare) to make a hole (o holes) in; (biglietto) to punch; (gomma) to puncture; (pungere) to pierce; **ho bucato (una gomma)** I've got a puncture; **abbiamo bucato e siamo arrivati in ritardo** we had a puncture and arrived late; **avere le mani bucate** (fig) to be a spendthrift; **bucarsi** VR (pungersi) to prick o.s.; **bucarsi** VIP (forarsi: gomma, palla) to puncture; (fam: drogarsi) to mainline; **si è bucata una gomma** I've got a puncture

Bucarest [ˈbukarest] SF Bucharest

bucato [buˈkato] SM washing; **fare il bucato** to do the washing; **stirare il bucato** to do the ironing; **lenzuola di bucato** freshly-laundered sheets

buccia, -ce [ˈbuttʃa] SF 1 (di verdura, frutta: gen) skin; (: di agrumi, patate) skin, peel; (: di piselli) pod; **una buccia di banana** a banana skin; **aggiungi un po' di buccia di limone grattugiata** add some grated lemon rind 2 (di salumi) skin; (di formaggio) rind 3 (corteccia) bark

bucherellare [bukerelˈlare] /72/ VT to riddle with holes

bucherò ecc [bukeˈrɔ] VB vedi **bucare**

buco, -chi [ˈbuko] SM (gen) hole; (omissione) gap; (orifizio, apertura) aperture; **c'è un buco nella tasca** there's a hole in the pocket; **il buco della serratura** keyhole; **fare un buco nell'acqua** to fail, draw a blank; **farsi un buco** (fam: drogarsi) to have a fix; **buco nero** (anche fig) black hole

Budapest [ˈbudapest] SF Budapest

Budda [ˈbudda] SM INV Buddha

buddismo [budˈdizmo] SM Buddhism

budello [buˈdɛllo] SM 1 (pl f budella): intestino: bowel, intestine, gut 2 (materiale) gut 3 (vicolo) alley

budino [buˈdino] SM pudding; **budino al cioccolato** chocolate pudding

bue [ˈbue] SM (pl buoi) 1 (Zool) ox; **bue marino** dugong; **bue muschiato** musk ox; **bue selvatico** bison 2 (Culin) beef; **carne di bue** beef

Buenos Aires [bwenosˈaires] SF Buenos Aires

bufalo, -a [ˈbufalo] SM buffalo; **bufalo indiano** water buffalo

bufera [buˈfɛra] SF (anche fig) storm

buffetto [bufˈfetto] SM flick

buffo, -a [ˈbuffo] AGG (ridicolo) funny, comical; (divertente) funny, amusing; (strano) funny, odd; (Teatro) comic; **pensa a qc di più buffo** think of sth funnier; **è la cosa più buffa che abbia mai sentito** it's the funniest thing I've ever heard

buffonata [buffoˈnata] SF (azione) prank, jest; (parola) jest; **fare buffonate** (anche fig) to clown about; **dire buffonate** to joke; (fig) to talk rubbish

buffone [bufˈfone] SM (anche fig) clown, buffoon; (pegg) joker; **fare il buffone** (fig) to play the fool, clown about; **buffone di corte** court jester

buggerare [buddʒeˈrare] /72/ VT (fam) to swindle, cheat

bugia¹, -gie [buˈdʒia] SF (menzogna) lie; **dire o raccontare bugie** to tell lies; **non dirci mai le bugie** I never tell lies; **bugia pietosa** white lie; **le bugie hanno le gambe corte** (Proverbio) truth will out

bugia², -gie [buˈdʒia] SF (candeliere) candleholder

bugiardo, -a [buˈdʒardo] AGG lying, deceitful; **essere bugiardo** to be a liar ♦ SM, SF liar; **mi ha dato del bugiardo** he called me a liar; **bugiardo patologico** compulsive liar

bugigattolo [budʒiˈgattolo] SM (ripostiglio) boxroom; (pegg) poky little room

buio, -a, -i o, -ii, -e [ˈbujo] AGG (oscuro) dark; (tetro, triste) gloomy, dismal; **un vicolo buio** a dark alley ♦ SM dark, darkness; **al buio** in the dark; **si sta facendo buio** (imbrunisce) it is growing o getting dark; **ha paura del buio** she's afraid of the dark; **buio pesto** pitch-dark, pitch-black

bulbo [ˈbulbo] SM 1 (gen, Bot) bulb 2 **bulbo oculare** eyeball 3 (Naut) ballast

Bulgaria [bulgaˈria] SF Bulgaria

bulgaro, -a [ˈbulgaro] AGG, SM, SF Bulgarian; **i Bulgari** Bulgarians ♦ SM (lingua) Bulgarian

bulimia [buliˈmia] SF bulimia

bulimico, -a, -ci, -che [buˈlimiko] AGG, SM, SF bulimic

bullismo [bulˈlizmo] SM bullying

bullo [ˈbullo] SM (persona) tough; **fare il bullo** to act tough
　❏ **bullo** non si traduce mai con la parola inglese bull

bullone [bulˈlone] SM bolt

buoi [ˈbwɔji] SMPL di **bue**

buonafede [bwonaˈfede] SF good faith; **in buonafede** in good faith

buonanima [bwoˈnanima] SF: **mio nonno buonanima, la buonanima di mio nonno** my grandfather, God rest his soul

buonanotte [bwonaˈnotte] ESCL good night! ♦ SF: **dare la buonanotte a qn** to say good night to sb

buonasera [bwonaˈsera] ESCL (anche: buona sera) good evening! ♦ SF: **dare la buonasera a qn** to wish sb good evening; **signorina buonasera** (TV) female TV announcer

buoncostume [bwonkosˈtume] SM public morality ♦ SF: **la (squadra del) buoncostume** (Polizia) the vice squad

buondì [bwonˈdi] ESCL hello!

buongiorno [bwonˈdʒorno] ESCL good morning (o afternoon)! ♦ SM: **dare il buongiorno a qn** to wish sb good morning

buongrado [bwonˈgrado] AVV: **di buongrado** willingly

buongustaio, -aia, -ai, -aie [bwongusˈtajo] SM, SF gourmet

buongusto [bwonˈgusto] SM (good) taste; **abbi il buongusto di non farti più vedere** I hope you'll have the decency not to show your face again

---
PAROLA CHIAVE
---

buono¹, -a [ˈbwɔno] AGG (comp migliore, superl ottimo)

1 davanti sm: buon + consonante, vocale, buono + s impura, gn, pn, ps, x, z; davanti sf: buona + consonante, buon' + vocale (gen) good; (prodotto) good (quality); (odore, ambiente, atmosfera) good, nice, pleasant; (posizione, ditta, impresa) sound; **essere in buona compagnia** to be in good company; **essere di buona famiglia** to come from a good family; **avere un buon odore** to smell good o nice; **più buono** better; **avere un buon sapore** to taste good o nice; **buon senso** = **buonsenso**; **buona società** polite society; **stai buono!** behave!; **tenere buono qn** (bambino) to keep sb quiet; (fig: persona influente) to keep sb sweet

2 (generoso: persona, azione) good, kind, kindly; **una persona di buon cuore** a good-hearted person; **essere buono come il pane** to have a heart of gold

3 (abile, idoneo) good o buono a nulla o to use at anything; **quest'acqua non è buona da bersi** this water isn't safe to drink; **buono da buttar via** fit for the dustbin; **mi sembra buono per questo lavoro** he seems suitable for the job

4 (utile, vantaggioso): **a buon mercato** cheap; **buono a sapersi** that's good to know; **è stata una buona scelta** it was a good choice

5 (giusto, valido) correct, right; (motivo) valid; **ad ogni buon conto** in any case; **a buon diritto** rightfully; **al momento buono** at the right moment

6 (utilizzabile) usable; (biglietto, passaporto) valid; **è ancora buona questa vernice?** is this paint still okay o usable?; **non è più buono** (latte) it's off; (pane) it's stale

7 (con valore intensivo) good; **peserà dieci chili buoni** it must weigh a good ten kilos; **di buon mattino** early in the morning; **ci vuole un mesetto buono** it takes a good month o a month at least; **un buon numero** a good o large number; **deciditi una buona volta!** make up your mind once and for all!

8 (auguri): **buon appetito!** enjoy your meal!; **buon compleanno!** happy birthday!; **tante buone cose!** all the best!; **buon divertimento!** have a nice time!; **buona fortuna!** good luck!; **buon giorno!** (in mattinata) good morning!; (di pomeriggio) good afternoon!; **buon Natale!** Merry Christmas!; **buona notte!** good night!; **buona permanenza!** enjoy your stay!; **buon riposo!** sleep well!; **buona sera!** good evening!; **buon viaggio!** have a good trip!

9 (*fraseologia*): **fare qc alla buona** to do sth simply *o* in a simple way; **stasera mi vesto alla buona** I'm not getting dressed up this evening; **è un tipo alla buona** he's an easy-going sort; **accetterà con le buone o con le cattive** he'll have to agree whether he wants to or not; **l'ho fatto di buon grado** I did it willingly; **che Dio ce la mandi buona!** here's hoping!; **essere in buone mani** to be in good hands; **con le buone maniere** in a kind *o* friendly way; **mettere una buona parola per qn** to put in a good word for sb; **essere a buon punto** to be well advanced; **siamo a buon punto con il pranzo** dinner's nearly ready; **questa sì che è buona!** that's a good one!; **mi dica, buon uomo** tell me, my good man; **fare buon viso a cattivo gioco** to put a brave face on things

♦ SM, SF (*persona*) good *o* upright person; **i buoni e i cattivi** (*in film*) the good guys and the bad guys; **un buono a nulla** a good-for-nothing

♦ SM (*non ha plurale*) (*bontà*) goodness, good; **di buono c'è che...** the good thing about it is that ...; **essere un poco di buono** to be a nasty piece of work

buono² [ˈbwɔno] SM **1** (*Comm*) coupon, voucher **2** (*Fin*) bill, bond; **buono d'acquisto** credit note, credit slip; **buono benzina** petrol coupon; **buono di cassa** cash voucher; **buono di consegna** delivery note; **buono fruttifero** interest-bearing bond; **buono d'imbarco** shipping note; **buono d'imposta** special credit instrument for tax-relief purposes; **buono mensa** canteen voucher; **buono pasto** meal ticket; **buono (ordinario) del Tesoro** short-term treasury bond, treasury bill; **buono postale fruttifero** interest-bearing bond (*issued by Italian Post Office*); **buono sconto** coupon; **buono del Tesoro poliennale** (*Econ*) long-term treasury bond

buonsenso [bwonˈsɛnso] SM *no pl* common sense

buontempone, -a [bwontemˈpone] SM, SF jovial person

buonuscita [bwonuʃˈʃita] SF **1** (*Industria*) golden handshake **2** (*di affitti*) sum paid for the relinquishing of tenancy rights

burattinaio, -ai [burattiˈnajo] SM puppeteer, puppet master

burattino [buratˈtino] SM (*anche fig*) puppet

burbero, -a [ˈburbero] AGG surly, gruff ♦ SM, SF surly person, gruff person; **un burbero benefico** a rough diamond

burla [ˈburla] SF prank, trick; **per burla** for fun, for a joke

burlare [burˈlare] /72/ VT to make fun of; **burlarsi di** = **burlare** VT

burlarsi di = **burlare** VT

burocrate [buˈrɔkrate] SM (*anche pegg*) bureaucrat

burocratico, -a, -ci, -che [buroˈkratiko] AGG bureaucratic; **lungaggini burocratiche** red tape

burocrazia [burokratˈtsia] SF bureaucracy

burrasca, -sche [burˈraska] SF (*anche fig*) storm; **c'è o tira aria di burrasca** (*anche fig*) there's a storm brewing *o* in the air; **mare in burrasca** stormy sea; **c'è burrasca in famiglia** there's trouble at home

burrascoso, -a [burrasˈkoso] AGG (*anche fig*) stormy

burro [ˈburro] SM butter; **pane e burro** bread and butter; **pasta/riso al burro** buttered pasta/rice; **uovo al burro** egg fried in butter; **questa bistecca è un burro** (*tenero*) this steak melts in your mouth; **avere le mani di burro** (*fig*) to be butter-fingered; **burro di cacao** cocoa butter; (*per labbra*) lip salve

burrone [burˈrone] SM ravine, gorge

buscare [busˈkare] /20/ VT (*anche:* **buscarsi**: *raffreddore, schiaffo*) to get; **buscarle** to catch it, get a good hiding; (*essere battuto*) to get a drubbing

buscherò ecc [buskeˈrɔ] VB *vedi* **buscare**

bussare [busˈsare] /72/ VI (*aus* avere) **1** to knock; **bussare alla porta** to knock at the door; **ho bussato alla porta** I knocked at the door; **stanno bussando** there's somebody at the door **2** (*Carte*) to knock on the table to induce partner to play his highest card

bussola [ˈbussola] SF **1** (*strumento nautico*) compass; **bussola giroscopica/magnetica** gyro/magnetic compass; **perdere la bussola** (*fig*) to lose one's head, lose one's bearings **2** (*porta*) revolving door **3** (*cassetta sigillata*) collection box

busta [ˈbusta] SF **1** (*da lettera*) envelope; **in busta aperta/chiusa** in an unsealed/sealed envelope; **busta a finestra** window envelope; **busta paga** pay packet; (*listino*) pay slip **2** (*astuccio: di occhiali*) case; **busta portatrucco** make-up bag

bustarella [bustaˈrella] SF bribe, backhander; **dare una bustarella a qn** to slip sb a backhander; **lo scandalo delle bustarelle** the bribes scandal

bustina [busˈtina] SF **1** (*piccola busta*) envelope **2** (*di cibi, farmaci*) sachet; **una bustina di zucchero** a sachet of sugar; **bustina di tè** tea bag **3** (*Mil*) forage cap

busto [ˈbusto] SM **1** (*Anat, Scultura*) bust; **a mezzo busto** (*fotografia, ritratto*) half-length; **stare a busto eretto** to stand up straight; **piegate il busto in avanti** bend your trunk forward **2** (*indumento*) corset

butano [buˈtano] SM butane

buttare [butˈtare] /72/ VT **1** (*gettare*) to throw; **ha buttato il cappotto sul letto** he threw his coat onto the bed; **buttare fuori qn** to throw sb out; **buttare qc addosso a qn** to throw sth at sb; **buttare qc a qn** to throw sth to sb; **buttare qc per terra** to throw sth on the ground; **buttare la pasta/il riso** (*Culin*) to put pasta/rice into boiling water; **hai già buttato la pasta?** have you put the pasta in?; **buttarsi il cappotto sulle spalle** to throw one's coat round one's shoulders; **buttarsi qc dietro le spalle** to throw sth over one's shoulder; (*fig: passato*) to put sth behind one **2** (*anche:* **buttare via**: *nella spazzatura*) to throw away, discard; (*sprecare: soldi, tempo*) to waste; **era rotto e l'ho buttato via** it was broken and I threw it away; **non è una macchina da buttar via** it's not a bad looking car **3** **buttare giù** (*scritto*) to jot down, scribble down; (*cibo, boccone*) to gulp down; (*edificio*) to pull down, knock down; (*governo*) to bring down; **buttare giù un muro** to knock down a wall; **buttare giù due righe** to scribble a couple of lines; **buttare giù qn** (*deprimere*) to get sb down **4** (*fraseologia*): **buttare la colpa addosso a qn** to lay the blame on sb; **buttare a mare** (*fig: soldi, occasione*) to throw away; **buttare i soldi dalla finestra** to throw money down the drain; **ho buttato là una frase** I mentioned it in passing; **gli ha buttato in faccia tutto il suo disprezzo** she told him to his face how much she despised him; **mi ha buttato in faccia tutta la verità** he flung the truth at me ♦ VI (*aus* avere) (*fam: apparire*): **la faccenda butta male** things are looking bad; **buttarsi** VR (*saltare*) to jump; **buttiamoci!** (*saltiamo*) let's jump!; (*rischiamo*) let's have a go!; **buttarsi in acqua** to jump into the water; **buttarsi dalla finestra** to jump out of the window; **buttarsi su** *o* **addosso a qn** to launch o.s. at sb; **buttarsi nelle braccia di qn** to throw o.s. into sb's arms; **buttarsi in ginocchio** to throw o.s. down on one's knees; **buttarsi (anima e corpo) in qc** to throw o.s. (wholeheartedly) into sth; **buttarsi giù** (*stendersi*) to lie down; (*stimarsi poco*) to have a low opinion of o.s.; (*scoraggiarsi*) to get depressed *o* miserable; **buttarsi nella mischia** (*anche fig*) to throw o.s. into the fray; **buttarsi sulla preda** (*anche fig*) to pounce on one's prey

buzzo [ˈbuddzo] SM: **di buzzo buono** (*con impegno*) with a will

byte [ˈbait] SM INV (*Inform*) byte

Cc

C¹, c¹ [tʃi] SF INV, SM INV (*lettera*) C, c; **C come Como** ≈ C for Charlie

C² [tʃi] ABBR **1** (*Geog*) = **capo 2** (= *Celsius, centigrado*) C **3** (= *conto*) a/c ♦ SIGLA M (*Inform*) C

CA SIGLA = Cagliari

c.a. ABBR **1** (*Elettr*: = *corrente alternata*) AC **2** (*Comm*: = **corrente anno**)

cabaret [kabaˈrɛ] SM INV cabaret

cabina [kaˈbina] SF (*di nave*) cabin; (*di ascensore*) cage; (*di funivia*) car; (*in spiaggia*) beach hut; (*in piscina*) cubicle; **una cabina di seconda classe** a second-class cabin ♦ **cabina di blocco** *o* **di manovra** (*Ferr*) signal box; **cabina elettorale** polling booth; **cabina elettrica** substation; **cabina di guida** driver's cab; **cabina passeggeri** (*Aer*) passenger cabin *o* compartment; **cabina di pilotaggio** (*Aer: gen*) cockpit; (: *in aereo di linea*) flight deck; **cabina di proiezione** (*Cine*) projection booth; **cabina di prova** changing room (*in shop*); **cabina di regia** control room (*Radio, TV*); **cabina telefonica** telephone booth *o* box, callbox

cabinato, -a [kabiˈnato] AGG (*Naut*) with a cabin ♦ SM cabin cruiser

cablaggio, -gi [kaˈbladdʒo] SM wiring

cablogramma, -i [kabloˈgramma] SM cable(gram)

cacao [kaˈkao] SM INV (*albero*) cacao; (*polvere*) cocoa

cacca [ˈkakka] SF (*fam, anche fig*) shit (*fam!*); **fare la cacca** (*linguaggio infantile*) to go poop; **dover fare la cacca** to have to go poop

caccia¹ [ˈkattʃa] SF **1** hunting; (*con fucile*) shooting, hunting; **sono contro la caccia** I'm against hunting; **andare a caccia** to go hunting; **la domenica vanno a caccia** they go hunting on Sundays; **andare a caccia di leoni** to go lion-hunting; **battuta di caccia** hunting party **2** (*anche: stagione di caccia*) hunting (*o* shooting) season **3** (*cacciagione*) game **4** (*fig: inseguimento, ricerca*) chase; **dare la caccia a qn** to give chase to sb; **la polizia gli dava la caccia** the police was going after him; **essere a caccia di notizie/libri** to be on the lookout for news/books; **essere a caccia di un impiego/una casa** to be job-hunting *o* house-hunting; **essere a caccia di uomini/soldi** to be after men/money; **andare a caccia di guai** to go looking for trouble ♦ **caccia al cervo** deer hunting, deerstalking; **caccia grossa** big game hunting; **caccia alle streghe** witch-hunt; **caccia subacquea** harpoon fishing; **caccia al tesoro** treasure hunt; **caccia all'uomo** manhunt

caccia² [ˈkattʃa] SM INV (*aereo*) fighter; (*nave*) destroyer

cacciabombardiere [kattʃabombarˈdjere] SM fighter-bomber

cacciagione [kattʃaˈdʒone] SF game

cacciare [katˈtʃare] /14/ VT **1** (*Sport*) to hunt; (*con fucile*) to shoot, hunt; **ha imparato a cacciare e a pescare da bambino** he learned to hunt and fish as a child **2** (*mandar via: persona*): **cacciare qn da casa/dal paese/dalla scuola** to throw sb out of the house/the country/school (*nemico*) to drive away; (*tristezza, malinconia, dubbio*) to chase away; **se continua così, lo cacceranno dalla squadra** if he goes on like this, they'll throw him out of the team **3** (*fam: mettere*): **cacciare qn in prigione** to throw sb into prison; **cacciarsi qc in testa** (*cappello*) to pull sth on; (*idea*) to get sth into one's head; **dove hai cacciato quel libro?** where have you put that book? **4** (*fam: emettere*): **cacciare un grido** to let out a cry *o* yell **5** (*fam: estrarre*): **cacciare fuori** to pull out; **cacciare fuori un coltello** to pull out a knife; **cacciare fuori la lingua** to stick out one's tongue; **cacciare fuori i soldi!** pay up!, cough up!; **cacciarsi** VR **1** (*fam: nascondersi*) to hide o.s.; **ma dove si sarà cacciato?** where can he (*o* it) have got to? **2** (*fam: mettersi*): **cacciarsi nei guai** *o* **in un bel pasticcio** to get into a lot of trouble

cacciatora [kattʃaˈtora] SF **1** (*giacca*) hunting jacket **2** (*Culin*): **pollo** *ecc* **alla cacciatora** chicken *ecc* chasseur

cacciatore [kattʃaˈtore] SM hunter; **cacciatore di dote** fortune-hunter; **cacciatore di frodo** poacher; **cacciatore di teste** (*anche fig*) headhunter

cacciatorpediniere [kattʃatorpediˈnjere] SM destroyer

cacciavite [kattʃaˈvite] SM INV screwdriver; **cacciavite cercafase** mains tester; **cacciavite a croce** *o* **a stella** Philips screwdriver

cachemire [kaʃˈmir] SM INV cashmere

cachet [kaˈʃɛ] SM INV **1** (*Med*: *compressa*) tablet; (: *capsula*) capsule **2** (*compenso*) fee **3** (*colorante per capelli*) rinse

cachi¹ [ˈkaki] SM INV (*albero, frutto*) persimmon

cachi² [ˈkaki] AGG INV, SM khaki

cacio, -ci [ˈkatʃo] SM cheese; **venire** *o* **cadere come il cacio sui maccheroni** (*fig*) to turn up at the right moment

cactus [ˈkaktus] SM INV cactus

cadavere [kaˈdavere] SM corpse, (dead) body; **sembrare un cadavere ambulante** to look like death warmed up

cadaverico, -a, -ci, -che [kadaˈveriko] (*fig*) deathly pale; **rigidità cadaverica** rigor mortis

caddi *ecc* [ˈkaddi] VB *vedi* **cadere**

cadente [kaˈdɛnte] AGG falling; (*fig: edificio*) tumbledown; (: *persona*) decrepit; **stella cadente** falling *o* shooting star

cadenza [kaˈdɛntsa] SF **1** (*gen*) cadence; (*ritmo*) rhythm; (*inflessione*) intonation; (*Mus*) cadenza; **a cadenza regolare** at regular intervals

cadere [kaˈdere] /18/ VI IRREG (*aus essere*) **1** (*persona, oggetto*) to fall; (*tetto*) to fall in; (*aereo*) to crash; **ho inciampato e sono caduta** I tripped and fell; **cadere dalla bicicletta/da un albero/dalle scale** to fall off one's bicycle/ from a tree/down the stairs; **è caduto dalla bicicletta** he fell off his bike; **sono caduto dal letto** I fell out of bed; **cadere bocconi** to fall flat on one's face; **cadere in ginocchio** to fall on(to) one's knees; **cadere lungo disteso** to fall flat on one's back; **cadere in piedi** (*anche fig*) to land on one's feet; **cadere ai piedi di qn** to fall at sb's feet; **cadere dal sonno** to be falling asleep on one's feet; **cadere a terra** to fall down, fall to the ground; **far cadere** (*urtando*) to knock over *o* down; (*dall'alto*) to drop; **cadere dalle nuvole** (*fig*) to be taken aback; **quando gliel'ho detto è caduto dalle nuvole** when I told him about it he was very surprised; **la conversazione cadde su Garibaldi** the conversation came round to Garibaldi; **mi è caduto lo sguardo su una vecchia foto** my eye fell upon an old photo; **ti è caduta la sciarpa** you've dropped your scarf; **questi pantaloni cadono bene** these trousers hang well **2** (*staccarsi: denti, capelli*) to fall out; (: *foglie*) to fall **3** (*scendere: pioggia, neve*) to fall, come down; (: *notte, stella*) to fall **4** (*cessare: vento*) to drop; **è caduta la linea** I (*o* you *ecc*) have been cut off **5** (*data*) to fall; **quest'anno il mio compleanno cade di martedì** my birthday falls on a Tuesday this year **6** (*venire a trovarsi*): **cadere ammalato** to fall ill; **cadere in disgrazia** to fall into disgrace; **cadere in errore** to make a mistake; **cadere in trappola** fall into a trap; **cadere in miseria/oblio** to sink into poverty/ oblivion **7** (*soldato, fortezza, governo*) to fall; **far cadere il governo** to bring down the government **8** **lasciar cadere** (*oggetto, anche fig: discorso, proposta*) to drop; (*frase, parola*) to slip in; **si lasciò cadere sulla poltrona** he dropped *o* fell into the armchair

cadetto, -a [kaˈdetto] AGG **1** younger; **ramo cadetto** cadet branch **2** (*Sport*) junior *attr* ♦ SM (*gen, Mil*) cadet; (*Sport*) junior

cadrò *ecc* [kaˈdrɔ] VB *vedi* **cadere**

caduta [kaˈduta] SF (*gen, Rel*) fall; **ha fatto una brutta caduta** he had a nasty fall; **la caduta dei capelli** hair loss ♦

caduta libera (*Fis*) free fall; **caduta massi** falling rocks; **caduta del sistema** (*Inform*) system failure; **caduta di tensione** (*Elettr*) voltage drop

caduto, -a [ka'duto] PP *di* cadere ♦ AGG (*morto*) dead ♦ SM dead soldier; **monumento ai caduti** war memorial

caffè [kaf'fɛ] SM INV (*bevanda*) coffee; (*bar*) cafè; **si sono incontrati in un caffè** they met in a café; **un gelato al caffè** a coffee ice cream; **caffè corretto** coffee with a shot of spirits; **caffè decaffeinato** decaffeinated coffee; **caffè espresso** espresso coffee; **caffè in grani** coffee beans; **caffè lungo** weak black coffee; **caffè macchiato** coffee with a dash of milk; **caffè macinato** ground coffee; **caffè d'orzo** barley coffee; **caffè ristretto** strong black coffee; **caffè solubile** instant coffee

caffeina [kaffe'ina] SF caffeine

caffellatte [kaffel'latte] SM INV white coffee

caffetteria [kaffette'ria] SF coffee shop, coffee bar

caffettiera [kaffet'tjera] SF (*per fare il caffè*) coffee-maker; (*per servire il caffè*) coffeepot

cafone, -a [ka'fone] SM, SF (*persona*) boor, ill-mannered person; **comportarsi da cafone** to be ill-mannered ♦ AGG (*persona, comportamento, risposta*) boorish, ill-mannered

cagionare [kadʒo'nare] /72/ VT to cause, be the cause of

cagionevole [kadʒo'nevole] AGG delicate, weak

cagliare [kaʎ'ʎare] /27/ VI (*aus* essere), VT to curdle

cagliaritano, -a [kaʎʎari'tano] AGG of o from Cagliari ♦ SM, SF inhabitant o native of Cagliari

cagna ['kaɲɲa] SF (*Zool*) bitch

cagnara [kaɲ'nara] SF uproar; **far cagnara** to make a din

cagnesco [kaɲ'ɲesko] AGG: **guardare qn in cagnesco** to scowl at sb

Cairo ['kairo] SF Cairo

calabrese [kala'brese] AGG, SM, SF Calabrian

calabrone [kala'brone] SM hornet

calamaio, -ai [kala'majo] SM inkpot, inkwell

calamaro [kala'maro] SM squid; **calamari alla griglia** grilled squid

calamita [kala'mita] SF (*anche fig*) magnet

calamità [kalami'ta] SF INV disaster, calamity; **è una calamità naturale** (*fig*) he's a walking disaster; **calamità naturale** natural disaster

calare [ka'lare] /72/ VT (*gen*) to lower; (*Maglia*) to decrease; (*ancora*) to drop, lower; (*perpendicolare*) to drop; (*fam: ecstasy*) to drop; **calare il sipario** to lower the curtain ♦ VI (*aus* essere) 1 (*gen*) to come down, fall; (*sole*) to set, go down; (*notte, silenzio*) to fall 2 (*diminuire: vento, febbre*) to drop; (: *temperatura, prezzo*) to drop, fall; (: *suono*) to die away; **la popolazione è calata del dieci per cento** the population has decreased by ten percent; **il prezzo della benzina è calato** the price of petrol has fallen; **la temperatura è calata improvvisamente** the temperature suddenly dropped; **calare di peso** to lose weight; **sono calato (di) 3 chili** I've lost 3 kilos; **cala!** (*non esagerare*) come off it! 3 (*invadere*): **calare (su)** to descend (on); **calarsi** VR 1 (*discendere*) to lower o.s.; **calarsi da una finestra/in un crepaccio** to lower o.s. from a window/into a crevasse 2 **calarsi nella parte** (*Teatro*): **si è calato nella parte** he has really got into the part ♦ SM: **al calar del sole** at sunset; **al calar della luna** when the moon goes down

calata [ka'lata] SF (*invasione*) invasion

calca ['kalka] SF throng, press

calcagno [kal'kaɲɲo] SM (*pl* calcagna) (*negli usi figurati: Anat: di scarpa*) heel; **aveva la polizia alle calcagna** the police were hot on his heels; **il mio capo mi sta sempre alle calcagna** my boss is never off my back

calcare¹ [kal'kare] /20/ VT 1 (*premere*) to press down; (*coi piedi*) to tread, press down; **calcarsi il cappello sugli occhi** to pull one's hat down over one's eyes; **le scene** (*fig*) to be on the stage; **calcare le orme di qn** (*fig*) to follow in sb's footsteps; **calcare la mano** (*fig*) to overdo it, exaggerate 2 (*mettere in rilievo*) to stress; **calcare le parole** to accentuate each syllable

calcare² [kal'kare] /20/ SM limestone; (*incrostazione*) (lime) scale

calce¹ ['kaltʃe] SF lime; **calce spenta** slaked lime; **calce viva** quicklime

calce² ['kaltʃe] SM (*Amm*): **in calce** at the foot of; **"firma in calce"** "please sign below"

calcestruzzo [kaltʃes'truttso] SM concrete

calcetto [kal'tʃetto] SM (*calcio-balilla*) table football; (*calcio a cinque*) five-a-side (football)

calcherò ecc [kalke'rɔ] VB *vedi* calcare¹

calciare [kal'tʃare] /14/ VI (*aus* avere), VT to kick

calciatore [kaltʃa'tore] SM (*Calcio*) (football) player, footballer; (*Rugby*) kicker

calcina [kal'tʃina] SF (lime) mortar

calcinaccio, -ci [kaltʃi'nattʃo] SM flake of plaster; **un mucchio di calcinacci** a pile of rubble

calcio¹, -ci ['kaltʃo] SM 1 (*pedata, anche Sport*) kick; **dare un calcio a qn** to give sb a kick, kick sb; **mi ha dato un calcio** he gave me a kick 2 (*sport*) football; **giochi a calcio?** do you play football?; **una partita di calcio** a football match; **squadra di calcio** football team 3 (*di pistola, fucile*) butt ♦ **calcio d'angolo** corner (kick); **calcio d'inizio** kick-off; **calcio di prima** (*Calcio*) direct free kick; **calcio di punizione** free kick; **calcio di rigore** penalty kick; **calcio di rimessa** (*Calcio*) goal kick; **calcio di rinvio** (*Rugby*) drop-out; **calcio di seconda** (*Calcio*) indirect free kick

calcio² ['kaltʃo] SM (*Chim*) calcium

calco, -chi ['kalko] SM (*Scultura*) cast, mould (*Brit*), mold (*USA*), casting, moulding (*Brit*), molding (*USA*); (*di disegno*) tracing; (*Ling*) calque, loan translation

calcolare [kalko'lare] /72/ VT (*fare il conto di*) to calculate, work out; (*considerare*) to reckon on, take into account; (*ponderare*) to weigh (up); **hai calcolato quanto viene a testa?** have you worked out how much it comes to each?; **calcolo che sarò di ritorno fra 5 giorni** I reckon I'll be back in 5 days' time; **calcolare i pro e i contro** to weigh up the pros and cons

calcolatore, -trice [kalkola'tore] AGG (*fig*) calculating ♦ SM computer ♦ SF (*anche*: **macchina calcolatrice**) calculator ♦ SM, SF (*persona*) calculating person

calcolo ['kalkolo] SM 1 (*anche Mat*) calculation; **fare il calcolo di qc** to work sth out; **ho fatto il calcolo di quanto gli dovevo** I worked out how much I owed him; **ho fatto un rapido calcolo** I did a quick calculation; **fare i propri calcoli** (*fig*) to weigh up the pros and cons; **per calcolo** out of self-interest; **a un calcolo approssimativo** at a rough estimate; **calcolo differenziale** differential calculus; **calcolo infinitesimale** infinitesimal calculus; **calcolo integrale** integral calculus 2 (*Med*) stone, calculus (*termine tecn*); **calcolo renale** (*Med*) stone in the kidneys

caldaia [kal'daja] SF boiler

caldarrosta [kaldar'rɔsta] SF roast chestnut

caldeggiare [kalded'dʒare] /62/ VT to support

caldo, -a ['kaldo] AGG (*gen, anche fig*) warm; (*molto caldo*) hot; (*appassionato*) keen; (*cordiale: persona, accoglienza*) warm, friendly, cordial; **l'acqua calda** hot water; **la minestra è troppo calda** the soup's too hot; **il tuo cappotto è più caldo del mio** your coat is warmer than mine; **è il mese più caldo** it's the hottest month; **una bella coperta calda** a nice warm blanket; **batti il ferro finché è caldo** strike while the iron is hot; **piangere a calde lacrime** to weep bitterly; **essere una testa calda** to be hot-headed ♦ SM heat; **non sopporto il caldo** I can't stand the heat; **fa caldo** it's warm; (*molto caldo*) it's hot; **fa caldo qui, non trovi?** it's hot here, isn't it?; **col caldo che fa...** in this heat ...; **ho caldo** I'm warm; (*molto caldo*) I'm hot; **ti tengo in caldo la minestra** I'm keeping your soup hot for you; **non mi fa né caldo né freddo** I couldn't care less; **quel ragazzo non mi fa né caldo né freddo** I'm indifferent to that boy; **a caldo** (*fig*) in the heat of the moment

❑ **caldo** non si traduce mai con *cold*

caleidoscopio, -pi [kaleidos'kɔpjo] SM kaleidoscope

calendario, -ri [kalen'darjo] SM calendar; **calendario degli incontri** (*Calcio*) fixtures list

calende [ka'lɛnde] SFPL calends; **rimandare qc alle calende greche** to put sth off indefinitely

calesse [ka'lesse] SM (*carrozza*) gig

calibro ['kalibro] SM (*di arma*) calibre, bore; (*strumento*) callipers *pl*; (*fig*) calibre; **di grosso calibro** (*fig*) prominent; **un personaggio di grosso calibro** a prominent figure

calice ['kalitʃe] SM (*coppa*) goblet; (*bicchiere*) stem glass; (*Rel*) chalice

California [kali'fɔrnja] SF California; **vengono dalla California** they come from California

californiano, -a [kalifor'njano] AGG, SM, SF Californian

caligine [ka'lidʒine] SF (*nebbia*) fog; (*mista a fumo*) smog

calligrafia [kalligra'fia] SF (*scrittura*) handwriting; (*arte*) calligraphy; **non capisco la sua calligrafia** I can't read her writing

callo ['kallo] SM callus; (*sui piedi*) corn; **pestare i calli a qn** (*fig*) to tread on sb's toes; **fare il callo a qc** to get used to sth; **callo osseo** callus

calma ['kalma] SF (*vedi agg*) quietness, peacefulness; stillness; calm; (*tranquillità*) peace (and quiet), quietness; **finalmente un po' di calma** a bit of peace at last; **con calma** (*senza fretta*) slowly; **fai con calma** take your time; **mare in calma** calm sea; **calma!** steady on!; **calma, non spingete!** steady on, don't push!; **calma e sangue freddo!** keep cool o calm!; **è un giorno di calma nel negozio** it's a quiet day in the shop

calmante [kal'mante] AGG relaxing ♦ SM (*Med: analgesico*) painkiller; (: *sedativo*) tranquillizer, sedative

calmare [kal'mare] /72/ VT (*gen*) to calm; (*persona*) to calm (down); (*dolore*) to soothe; **ho cercato di calmarlo** I tried to calm him down; **non riusciva a calmare i dolori** he couldn't relieve the pain; **calmarsi** VIP (*mare, persona*) to calm down, grow calm; (*dolore*) to ease; (*febbre, rabbia*) to subside; (*vento*) to abate; **calmati e dimmi tutto** calm down and tell me everything

calmiere [kal'mjɛre] SM (*Comm*): **calmiere dei prezzi** price control(s)

calmo, -a ['kalmo] AGG (*atmosfera*) quiet, peaceful; (*aria, cielo*) still; (*persona, mare*) calm; **il mare è calmo, oggi** the sea's calm today; **stare calmo** to keep calm; **state calmi, non c'è pericolo** keep calm, there's no danger

calo ['kalo] SM: **calo (di)** (*gen*) fall (in), drop (in); (*di prezzi*) fall (in); (*di peso*) loss (of); (*di volume*) shrinkage; **un forte calo delle vendite** a big drop in sales; **un calo di prezzi** a fall in prices; **calo di peso** weight loss; **la sua popolarità ha subito un grosso calo** his popularity has fallen sharply

calore [ka'lore] SM (*gen*) warmth; (*intenso: Fis*) heat; (*fig: entusiasmo*) fervour; **accogliere qn con calore** to welcome sb warmly; **essere in calore** (*animale*) to be on heat

caloria [kalo'ria] SF calorie

calorifero [kalo'rifero] SM radiator

caloroso, -a [kalo'roso] AGG (*persona, accoglienza*) warm; (*applauso*) hearty, enthusiastic; **un'accoglienza calorosa** a warm welcome; **è un tipo caloroso** he doesn't feel the cold

calpestare [kalpes'tare] /72/ VT to tread on, trample on; "**vietato calpestare l'erba**" "keep off the grass"; **calpestare i diritti di qn** to encroach on sb's rights; **non farti calpestare** (*fig*) don't let people walk all over you

calunnia [ka'lunnja] SF slander; **spargere calunnie sul conto di qn** to spread slander about sb

calunniare [kalun'njare] /19/ VT to slander

Calvario [kal'varjo] SM (*Rel*) Calvary; (*fig*) ordeal, trial; **da allora la sua vita è stata un calvario** her life since then has been one of suffering

calvizie [kal'vittsje] SF baldness

calvo, -a ['kalvo] AGG bald ♦ SM bald man

calza ['kaltsa] SF (*da uomo*) sock; (*da donna: con reggicalze*) stocking; **una calza bucata** a sock with a hole in it; **fare la calza** to knit; **calze** (*calzini, calzettoni*) socks; (*collant*) tights; (*con reggicalze*) stockings; **calze elastiche** support stockings (o tights); **calze di nailon** nylons, (nylon) stockings (o tights)

calzamaglia [kaltsa'maʎʎa] SF tights pl; (*per danza, ginnastica*) leotard; **una calzamaglia** a pair of tights; **una calzamaglia di lana** a pair of woollen tights

calzare [kal'tsare] /72/ VT (*scarpe, guanti: portare*) to wear; (: *mettere*) to put on ♦ VI (*aus avere, nel senso fig essere*) to fit; **calzare a pennello** to fit like a glove; **questa descrizione gli calza a pennello** that describes him to a T

calzatura [kaltsa'tura] SF footwear; **negozio di calzature** shoeshop

calzaturificio, -ci [kaltsaturi'fitʃo] SM shoe factory

calzetta [kal'tsetta] SF ankle sock; **una mezza calzetta** (*fig*) a nobody

calzettone [kaltset'tone] SM knee-length sock; **un paio di calzettoni** a pair of knee socks

calzino [kal'tsino] SM (short) sock; **un paio di calzini** a pair of socks

calzolaio, -ai [kaltso'lajo] SM (*che ripara*) cobbler; (*che fabbrica*) shoemaker; **mio padre fa il calzolaio** my father's a cobbler

calzoleria [kaltsole'ria] SF (*negozio*) shoe shop; (*arte*) shoe-making

calzoncini [kaltson'tʃini] SMPL shorts; **calzoncini da bagno** (swimming) trunks

calzone [kal'tsone] SM **1** **calzone destro/sinistro** right/left trouser leg **2 calzoni** SMPL trousers (*Brit*), pants (*USA*); **portare i calzoni** (*anche fig*) to wear the trousers; **calzoni alla cavallerizza** jodhpurs; **calzoni corti** shorts; **calzoni alla zuava** knickerbockers **3** (*Culin*) calzone (*savoury turnover made with pizza dough*)

camaleonte [kamale'onte] SM (*Zool, anche fig*) chameleon

cambiale [kam'bjale] SF (*Comm*) bill (of exchange); (*pagherò cambiario*) promissory note; **firmare cambiali per qc** to pay sth up in instalments; **cambiale di comodo** o **favore** accommodation bill

cambiamento [kambja'mento] SM change; **un cambiamento di orario** a change in the timetable

cambiare [kam'bjare] /19/ VT **1** (*gen*) to change; (*modificare*) to alter; **cambiare (l')aria in una stanza** to air a room; **vado in montagna per cambiare aria** I'm going to the mountains for a change of air; **è ora di cambiare aria** (*andarsene*) it's time to move on; **cambiare casa** to move (house); **ha cambiato casa il mese scorso** she moved house last month; **cambiare indirizzo** to change address; **cambiare treno** to change trains; **cambiare marcia** (*Aut*) to change gear; **cambiamo argomento** let's change the subject; **cambiare idea** to change one's mind; **scusi, ho cambiato idea, prendo quell'altro** sorry, I've changed my mind, I'll have that one; **cambiare le carte in tavola** (*fig*) to change one's tune **2** (*barattare*): **cambiare (qc con qn/qc per qc)** to exchange (sth with sb/sth for sth); **ho cambiato la mia macchina con quella del mio amico** I exchanged cars with my friend; **se non va bene me lo cambia?** if it's not right will you change it? **3** (*valuta*) to change; **mi puoi cambiare 100 euro?** can you change 100 euros for me?; **vorrei cambiare questi euro in sterline** I'd like to change these euros into pounds ♦ VI (*aus essere*) (*variare*) to change, alter; **ultimamente è molto cambiato** he's changed a lot recently; **cambiarsi** VIP (*modificarsi*) to change; **cambiarsi** VR: **cambiarsi (d'abito)** to get changed, change (one's clothes); **devo andare a casa a cambiarmi** I've got to go home and get changed

cambiavalute [kambjava'lute] SM INV exchange office

cambio, -bi ['kambjo] SM **1** (*gen*) change; (*modifica*) alteration, change; **dare il cambio a qn** to take over from sb, relieve sb; **se sei stanco ti do il cambio** if you're tired I'll take over from you; **fare il** o **un cambio** to change (over); **facciamo a cambio** let's change over o swap; **effettuare il cambio di campo** (*Sport*) to change ends; **in cambio di** in exchange for; **mi ha dato un CD in cambio del pallone** he gave me a CD in exchange for the football; **ho portato solo un cambio d'abito** I've only brought one change of clothes; **il cambio della guardia** the changing of the guard **2** (*Fin*) exchange; (*anche:* **tasso di cambio**) rate of exchange; **agenzia di cambio** bureau de change; **cambio a termine** forward exchange **3** (*Aut, Ciclismo*) gears pl; **cambio di marcia** gear change; **macchina con il cambio automatico** automatic (car)

Cambital ['kambital] SIGLA M = **Ufficio italiano dei cambi**

Cambogia [kam'bodʒa] SF Cambodia

cambogiano, -a [kambo'dʒano] AGG, SM, SF Cambodian

cambusa [kam'buza] SF pantry (*on ship*)

camera ['kamera] SF **1** (*gen*) room; (*anche:* **camera da letto**) bedroom; (*mobili*) bedroom suite; **una camera grande** a large room; **è rimasto in camera sua tutto il pomeriggio** he stayed in his bedroom the whole afternoon **2** (*Pol*) Chamber, House; **le Camere** ≈ (the Houses of) Parliament (*Brit*),

Congress (*USA*) ♦ **camera ardente** chapel of rest; **camera d'aria** (*di pneumatico*) inner tube; (*di pallone*) bladder; **camera blindata** strongroom; **camera a bolle** (*Fis*) bubble chamber; **camera di combustione** combustion chamber; **Camera di commercio** Chamber of Commerce; **camera di decompressione** decompression chamber; **Camera dei Deputati** Chamber of Deputies, ≈ House of Commons (*Brit*), ≈ House of Representatives (*USA*); **camera a due letti** twin-bedded room; **camera a gas** gas chamber; **camera del lavoro** trades union centre (*Brit*), labor union centre (*USA*); **camera matrimoniale** double room; **camera a nube** (*Fis*) cloud chamber; **camera oscura** (*Fot*) darkroom; **camera da pranzo** dining room; **camera singola** single room
❑ **camera** non si traduce mai con la parola inglese *camera*

camerata¹ [kameˈrata] SF (*dormitorio*) dormitory

camerata² [kameˈrata] SM, SF comrade (*of right-wing group*)

cameratismo [kameraˈtizmo] SM comradeship

cameriera [kameˈrjɛra] SF (*domestica*) maid; (*che serve a tavola*) waitress; (*che fa le camere*) chambermaid

cameriere [kameˈrjɛre] SM (*domestico*) (man)servant; (*di ristorante*) waiter; **fa il cameriere** he's a waiter; **scusi, cameriere!** excuse me!

camerino [kameˈrino] SM (*Teatro*) dressing room

Camerun [ˈkamerun] SM Cameroon

camice [ˈkamitʃe] SM (*di medico, tecnico*) white coat; (*di chirurgo*) gown; (*di sacerdote*) alb

camicetta [kamiˈtʃetta] SF blouse

camicia, -cie [kaˈmitʃa] SF 1 (*da uomo*) shirt; (*da donna*) blouse; **nascere con la camicia** (*fig*) to be born with a silver spoon in one's mouth; **sudare sette camicie** (*fig*) to have a hell of a time 2 (*Tecn: involucro*) jacket ♦ **camicia di forza** straitjacket; **camicia nera** (*fascista*) Blackshirt; **camicia da notte** (*da donna*) nightdress; (*da uomo*) nightshirt; **camicia verde** *supporter of Lega Nord*

camiciaio, -aia, -ai, -aie [kamiˈtʃajo] SM, SF (*sarto*) shirtmaker; (*che vende camicie*) shirtseller

camiciola [kamiˈtʃɔla] SF vest

camiciotto [kamiˈtʃɔtto] SM (*camicia sportiva*) casual shirt; (*per operai*) smock

caminetto [kamiˈnetto] SM hearth, fireplace

camino [kaˈmino] SM 1 (*focolare*) fireplace, hearth; **accendere il camino** to light the fire 2 (*comignolo, ciminiera, di vulcano*) chimney

camion [ˈkamjon] SM INV lorry (*Brit*), truck (*USA*)

camioncino [kamjonˈtʃino] SM van

camionetta [kamjoˈnetta] SF jeep

camionista, -i [kamjoˈnista] SM, SF lorry driver (*Brit*), truck driver (*USA*); **mio padre fa il camionista** my father's a lorry (truck) driver

camma [ˈkamma] SF cam; **albero a camme** camshaft

cammello [kamˈmello] SM (*Zool: colore*) camel; (*stoffa*) camel hair

cammeo [kamˈmɛo] SM cameo

camminare [kammiˈnare] /72/ VI (*aus avere*) 1 (*gen*) to walk; **non sono abituato a camminare tanto** I'm not used to walking so much; **camminare a carponi** *o* **a quattro zampe** to go on all fours, crawl; **camminare a grandi passi** to stride (along); **camminare a testa alta** (*fig*) to walk with one's head held high; **cammina cammina, siamo arrivati** after a long walk, we arrived; **cammina!** (*spicciati*) come on!; (*levati di torno*) go away! 2 (*funzionare*) to work, go; **il mio orologio non cammina più** my watch has stopped

camminata [kammiˈnata] SF walk; **fare una camminata** to go for a walk

cammino [kamˈmino] SM (*viaggio*) walk; (*sentiero*) path; (*itinerario, direzione, tragitto*) way; **un'ora di cammino** an hour's walk; **lungo il cammino** along the way; **mettersi in cammino** to set *o* start off; **riprendere il cammino** to continue on one's way; **cammin facendo** on the way; **il cammino della virtù** (*fig*) the path of virtue

camomilla [kamoˈmilla] SF (*Bot*) camomile; (*infuso*) camomile tea

camorra [kaˈmorra] SF Camorra; (*fig*) racket

camorrista, -i, -e [kamorˈrista] SM, SF member of the Camorra; (*fig*) racketeer

camoscio, -sci [kaˈmoʃʃo] SM (*Zool: pelle*) chamois; **scarpe di camoscio** suede shoes

campagna [kamˈpaɲɲa] SF 1 (*gen*) country, countryside; (*paesaggio*) countryside; **vivere/abitare in campagna** to live in the country; **andare in campagna** to go to the country; **siamo andati in campagna a passeggiare** we went for a walk in the country; **la campagna inglese è proprio bella** the English countryside is really beautiful 2 (*terra coltivata*) land 3 (*Pol, Comm, Mil*) campaign; **fare una campagna** to campaign; **campagna acquisti** (*Calcio*) *negotiations between football clubs to buy and sell players*; **campagna promozionale vendite** sales campaign; **campagna pubblicitaria** publicity campaign

campagnolo, -a [kampaɲˈɲɔlo] AGG country *attr* ♦ SM, SF countryman *o* countrywoman ♦ SF (*Aut*) cross-country vehicle

campale [kamˈpale] AGG (*Mil*) field *attr*; **una giornata campale** (*fig*) a hectic *o* hard day

campana [kamˈpana] SF bell; **suonare le campane a martello/a morte** to sound the alarm bell/death knell; **sordo come una campana** as deaf as a doorpost; **sentire l'altra campana** (*fig*) to hear the other side of the story; **campana (per la raccolta del vetro)** bottle bank; **campana pneumatica** diving bell; **campana di vetro** bell jar; **tenere qn sotto una campana di vetro** (*fig*) to wrap sb up in cotton wool

campanella [kampaˈnella] SF 1 (*a scuola*) (school) bell 2 (*di tenda*) curtain ring 3 (*Bot*) campanula; **campanella scozzese** harebell

campanello [kampaˈnello] SM (*di porta, bicicletta, da tavola*) bell; **hai suonato il campanello?** have you rung the bell?; **campanello d'allarme** (*anche fig*) alarm bell

campanile [kampaˈnile] SM bell tower, belfry

campanilismo [kampaniˈlizmo] SM parochialism

campano, -a [kamˈpano] AGG of *o* from Campania

campare [kamˈpare] /72/ VI (*aus essere*) (*vivere*) to live; (*tirare avanti*) to get by, manage; **campare d'aria** (*fig*) to live on air; **campare alla giornata, tirare a campare** to live from day to day

campato, -a [kamˈpato] AGG: **campato in aria** (*ragionamento ecc*) unsound, unfounded

campeggiare [kampedˈdʒare] /62/ VI (*aus avere*) 1 (*gen, anche Mil*) to camp 2 (*risaltare*) to stand out

campeggiatore, -trice [kampeddʒaˈtore] SM, SF camper

campeggio, -gi [kamˈpeddʒo] SM (*luogo*) camp site; (*attività*) camping; **c'è un campeggio qui vicino?** is there a camp site near here?; **nel campeggio** on the camp site; **andare in campeggio** to go camping; **quest'estate andremo in campeggio** we're going camping this summer; **"vietato il campeggio"** "no camping"

camper [ˈkæmpə'] SM INV motor caravan (*Brit*), motor home (*USA*)

campestre [kamˈpɛstre] AGG country *attr*, rural; **corsa campestre** cross-country race

Campidoglio [kampiˈdɔʎʎo] SM: **il Campidoglio** the Capitol, one of the Seven Hills of Rome

camping [ˈkæmpiŋ] SM INV camp site
❑ **camping** non si traduce mai con la parola inglese *camping*

campionamento [kampjonaˈmento] SM sampling

campionario, -ria, -ri, -rie [kampjoˈnarjo] SM (*Comm*) collection of samples ♦ AGG: **fiera campionaria** trade fair

campionato [kampjoˈnato] SM championship; **il campionato di calcio** the Premiership, the Premier League (*Brit*); **il campionato di serie A** (*di calcio*) the Italian Premier League

campionatura [kampjonaˈtura] SF (*Statistica: azione*) sampling; (: *campioni*) range of samples, collection of samples; (*Mus*) sampling

campione¹, -essa [kamˈpjone] SM, SF (*Sport*) champion; **campione di tennis/del mondo** tennis/world champion; **il campione del mondo di sci** the world skiing champion; **sei un campione in matematica** (*fig*) you're brilliant at mathematics

campione² [kam'pjone] AGG INV 1 (*Sport: squadra, pugile*) champion *attr* 2 (*Statistica: test, analisi, indagine*) sample *attr* ♦ SM (*Comm, Statistica*) sample; **vendita su campione** sale on sample ♦ **campione casuale** (*Statistica*) random sample; **campione gratuito** free sample; **campione di misura** (*Fis*) standard measure; **campione senza valore** sample only

campo ['kampo] SM 1 (*gen, anche Agr, Fis*) field; **campo di grano** cornfield; **la vita dei campi** life in the country, country life; **fiori di campo** wild flowers; **nel suo campo è uno dei migliori** he's one of the best in his field; **a tutto campo** (*Sport*) attacking and defending; (*fig: colloqui, inchiesta*) open-ended 2 (*di calcio*) field, pitch; (*da golf*) course; (*da tennis*) court; (*da cricket*) pitch; **campo ostacoli** (*Equitazione*) jumping arena; **campo in terra battuta** (*Tennis*) clay court 3 (*Mil*) field, battlefield; (*accampamento*) camp; **abbandonare il campo** (*anche fig*) to leave the field; **scendere in campo** (*anche fig*) to enter the field, join the fray 4 (*pittura*) background; (*Araldica*) field ♦ **campo da aviazione** airfield; **campo base** (*Alpinismo*) base camp; **campo di battaglia** battlefield; **campo carbonifero** coalfield; **campo di concentramento** concentration camp; **campo di forze** (*Fis*) force field; **campo giochi** play area; **campo lungo** (*Cine, TV, Fot*) long shot; **campo nomadi** travellers' camp; **campo petrolifero** oilfield; **campo profughi** refugee camp; **campo sportivo** sports ground; **campo di visibilità** range of visibility; **campo visivo** field of vision

campobassano, -a [kampobas'sano] AGG of *o* from Campobasso ♦ SM/F inhabitant *o* native of Campobasso

camposanto [kampo'santo] SM (*pl* campisanti) cemetery

camuffare [kamuf'fare] /72/ VT: **camuffare (da)** to disguise (as); **camuffarsi** VR: **camuffarsi (da)** to disguise o.s. (as)

Can. ABBR = canale

Canada [kana'da] SM: **il Canada** Canada; **andremo in Canada quest'estate** we're going to Canada this summer; **mi è piaciuto molto il Canada** I really liked Canada

canadese [kana'dese] AGG, SM, SF Canadian ♦ SF (*anche:* **tenda canadese**) ridge tent

canaglia [ka'naʎʎa] SF (*persona*) scoundrel, rogue; **stato canaglia** rogue state

canale [ka'nale] SM (*gen, anche Elettr, TV: fig*) channel; (*artificiale*) canal; (*condotto*) conduit; (*Anat*) duct, canal; (*Alpinismo*) gully; **su che canale è il film?** which channel is the film on?; **canale di bonifica** *o* **di drenaggio** drainage canal; **i canali di Venezia** the canals of Venice; **il canale di Panama** the Panama Canal; **il Canal Grande** the Grand Canal; **il canale della Manica** the English Channel

canapa ['kanapa] SF (*Bot: tessuto*) hemp; **canapa indiana** (*Bot*) Indian hemp; (*droga*) cannabis

Canarie [ka'narje] SFPL: **le (isole) Canarie** the Canary Islands, the Canaries

canarino [kana'rino] SM canary

Canberra [kan'berra] SF Canberra

cancellare [kantʃel'lare] /72/ VT 1 (*con gomma*) to erase, rub out; (*con penna*) to cross out, score out 2 (*fig: ricordo*) erase; (*volo, treno, appuntamento*) to cancel; **cancellare la lavagna** to clean the blackboard; **cancellare qn dalla faccia della terra** to wipe sb off the face of the earth; **cancellarsi** VIP (*ricordo*) to fade

cancellata [kantʃel'lata] SF railing(s *pl*)

cancelleria [kantʃelle'ria] SF 1 (*materiale per scrivere*) stationery 2 (*Dir, Amm*) chancery

cancelliere [kantʃel'ljere] SM 1 (*di tribunale*) clerk of the court 2 (*Pol*) chancellor; **Cancelliere dello Scacchiere** Chancellor of the Exchequer (*Brit*)

cancello [kan'tʃello] SM gate

cancerogeno, -a [kantʃe'rɔdʒeno] AGG carcinogenic ♦ SM carcinogen

canceroso, -a [kantʃe'roso] AGG (*Med*) cancerous ♦ SM, SF cancer patient

cancrena [kan'krena] SF (*Med*) gangrene; (*fig: corruzione*) corruption; **andare in cancrena** to become gangrenous

cancro ['kankro] SM 1 (*Med, anche fig*) cancer; (*Bot*) canker; **cancro ai polmoni** lung cancer 2 (*Astron, Astrol*): **Cancro** Cancer; **essere del Cancro** to be Cancer

candeggiare [kanded'dʒare] /62/ VT to bleach

candeggina [kanded'dʒina] SF bleach

candeggio, -gi [kan'deddʒo] SM bleaching; **fare il candeggio (di qc)** to bleach (sth)

candela [kan'dela] SF 1 candle; **a lume di candela** by candlelight; **tenere la candela** (*fig*) to play gooseberry (*Brit*), be a third wheel (*USA*) 2 (*Aut*) spark(ing) plug 3 (*Elettr*): **una lampadina da 100 candele** a 100-watt bulb

candelabro [kande'labro] SM candelabra *inv*

candeliere [kande'ljere] SM 1 candlestick 2 (*Naut*) stanchion

❏ **candeliere** non si traduce mai con *chandelier*

candelotto [kande'lɔtto] SM candle; **candelotto di dinamite** stick of dynamite; **candelotto fumogeno** smoke-bomb; **candelotto lacrimogeno** tear gas grenade

candidare [kandi'dare] /72/ VT to present as candidate; **candidarsi** VR: **candidarsi (per *o* a)** (*Pol*) to stand (*Brit*) *o* run (*USA*) as candidate (for)

candidato, -a [kandi'dato] SM, SF: **candidato (a)** (*a una carica*) candidate (for); (*a un lavoro*) applicant (for)

candidatura [kandida'tura] SF (*a una carica*) candidature; (*a un lavoro*) application; **presentare la propria candidatura alle elezioni** to stand (*Brit*) *o* run (*USA*) for election

candido, -a ['kandido] AGG 1 (*bianco*) (pure) white; **bianco candido** pure white; **candido come la neve** (as) white as snow 2 (*fig: ingenuo*) ingenuous, naïve; (: *sincero*) candid, frank; (: *innocente*) pure, innocent

candito, -a [kan'dito] AGG candied ♦ **canditi** SMPL candied fruit *sg*

candore [kan'dore] SM (*vedi agg*) brilliant white; ingenuousness, naïvety; candour (*Brit*), candor (*USA*), frankness; purity, innocence

cane ['kane] SM (*Zool*) dog; (*di pistola*) cock, hammer; **qui si mangia da cani** the food is rotten here; **che vita da cani!** it's a dog's life!; **questo lavoro è fatto da cani** this job is a real botch-up; **quell'attore è un cane** he's a rotten actor; **fa un freddo cane** it's bitterly cold; **non c'era un cane** there wasn't a soul; **essere solo come un cane** to be all on one's own; **essere come cane e gatto** to fight like cat and dog ♦ **cane barbone** (French) poodle; **cane da caccia** hunting dog; **cane per ciechi** guide dog (*Brit*), seeing eye dog (*USA*); **cane da guardia** watchdog, guard dog; **cane lupo** alsatian (dog) (*Brit*), German shepherd (dog) (*USA*); **cane delle praterie** prairie dog; **cane da punta** pointer; **cane randagio** stray dog; **cane di razza** pedigree dog; **cane da salotto** lap dog; **cane da slitta** husky

❏ **cane** non si traduce mai con la parola inglese *cane*

canestro [ka'nestro] SM (*gen, anche Sport*) basket; **centrare il canestro** *o* **fare (un) canestro** (*Sport*) to shoot a basket

canfora ['kanfora] SF camphor

cangiante [kan'dʒante] AGG iridescent; **seta cangiante** shot silk

canguro [kan'guro] SM kangaroo

canicola [ka'nikola] SF scorching heat

canile [ka'nile] SM kennel; (*di allevamento*) kennels *pl*; **canile municipale** dog pound

canino, -a [ka'nino] AGG 1 (*razza*) canine; (*mostra*) dog *attr*; **tosse canina** whooping cough; **rosa canina** dog rose 2 (*dente*) canine ♦ SM (*dente*) canine, eyetooth

canna ['kanna] SF 1 (*Bot*) reed; **canna da zucchero** sugar cane 2 (*bastone*) stick, cane; **canna da pesca** (fishing) rod 3 (*di fucile*) barrel; (*di organo*) pipe; (*di bicicletta*) crossbar; **canna fumaria** chimney flue 4 (*Droga: gergo*) joint

cannella¹ [kan'nella] SF (*di conduttura, botte*) tap

cannella² [kan'nella] SF (*Bot, Culin*) cinnamon

cannelloni [kannel'loni] SMPL (*Culin*) cannelloni *sg*; **i cannelloni sono buoni** the cannelloni is good

canneto [kan'neto] SM bed of reeds

cannibale [kan'nibale] SM, SF cannibal

cannocchiale [kannok'kjale] SM telescope

cannonata [kanno'nata] SF cannon shot; **cannonata a salve** gun salute; **è una vera cannonata!** (*fig*) it's (*o* he's *ecc*) fantastic

cannone [kan'none] SM 1 (*arma*) gun; (*Storia*) cannon; (*fig*: *chi eccelle*) ace; **donna cannone** (*in circo*) fat lady 2 (*tubo*) pipe, tube 3 (*di abito*) box pleat 4 (*Sci*): **cannone per innevamento artificiale** snow cannon

cannoniere [kanno'njere] SM 1 (*Naut*) gunner 2 (*Calcio*) goal scorer

cannuccia, -ce [kan'nuttʃa] SF (drinking) straw

canoa [ka'nɔa] SF canoe; **andare in canoa** to go canoeing

canone ['kanone] SM 1 **canoni** SMPL (*criteri*) canons, rules; (*di comportamento*) norm 2 (*pagamento periodico*) rent, fee; **legge dell'equo canone** fair rent act; **canone d'abbonamento alla TV** TV licence fee (*Brit*); **canone d'affitto** rent; **canone agricolo** land rent 3 (*Rel, Mus*) canon

canonica [ka'nɔnika] SF presbytery

canonico, -a, -ci, -che [ka'nɔniko](*Rel*) AGG canonical; **diritto canonico** canon law ♦ SM canon

canonizzare [kanonid'dzare] /72/ VT to canonize

canoro, -a [ka'nɔro] AGG: **uccello canoro** songbird

canotta [ka'nɔtta] SF = canottiera

canottaggio, -gi [kanot'taddʒo] SM rowing; **circolo di canottaggio** rowing club; **gara di canottaggio** boat race

canottiera [kanot'tjera] SF vest (*Brit*), undershirt (*USA*)

canotto [ka'nɔtto] SM dinghy; **canotto pneumatico** rubber dinghy; **canotto di salvataggio** lifeboat

canovaccio, -ci [kano'vattʃo] SM 1 (*tela*) canvas; (*per lavare i piatti*) dishcloth; (*per asciugare i piatti*) tea towel (*Brit*), dish towel (*USA*); (*per pulire*) duster 2 (*Teatro*: *trama*) plot

cantante [kan'tante] SM, SF singer; **fare il cantante** to be a singer; **cantante lirico** o **d'opera** opera singer

cantare [kan'tare] /72/ VI (*aus avere*) (*gen, uccelli*) to sing; (*gallo*) to crow; **ha cantato per tutta la sera** he sang all evening; **cantare da tenore/da soprano** to be a tenor/soprano; **fare cantare qn** (*fig*) to make sb talk; **i complici hanno cantato** (*fam*) his accomplices talked ♦ VT (*Mus*) to sing; (*Poesia*: *anche*: **cantare in versi**) to sing of; **cantare messa** to sing mass; **cantare vittoria** to crow

cantastorie [kantas'tɔrje] SM INV, SF INV story-teller

cantautore, -trice [kantau'tore] SM, SF singer-songwriter

canterellare [kanterel'lare] /72/ VT, VI (*aus avere*) to sing to o.s.; (*a bocca chiusa*) to hum

canticchiare [kantik'kjare] /19/ VT, VI (*aus avere*) sing to o.s.; (*a bocca chiusa*) to hum

cantiere [kan'tjere] SM 1 (*anche*: **cantiere navale**) shipyard 2 (*anche*: **cantiere edile**) building site

cantilena [kanti'lena] SF (*filastrocca*) lullaby; (*intonazione*) singsong; (*fig*: *lamentela*) whining

cantina [kan'tina] SF (*locale*) cellar; **è in cantina** it's in the cellar; **cantina sociale** cooperative winegrowers' association
☐ **cantina** non si traduce mai con **canteen**

canto[1] ['kanto] SM (*il cantare*: *arte*) singing; (*canzone*) song; (*Poesia*) lyric poem; (*capitolo*) canto; **lezioni di canto** singing lessons; **il canto dell'usignolo** (*il cantare*) the singing of the nightingale; (*melodia*) the song of the nightingale; **al canto del gallo** at cockcrow; **il canto del cigno** (*fig*) swan song; **canto gregoriano** Gregorian chant; **canto di Natale** (Christmas) carol

canto[2] ['kanto] SM: **da un canto... d'altro canto** on the one hand ... on the other hand; **da un canto ti capisco** in a way I understand you; **dal canto mio** (*per ciò che mi riguarda*) for my part, as for me, as far as I'm concerned

cantonata [kanto'nata] SF (*di edificio*) corner; **prendere una cantonata** (*fig*) to blunder

cantone [kan'tone] SM (*Amm*) canton

cantoniera [kanto'njera] AGG: (*casa*) **cantoniera** road inspector's house

cantuccio, -ci [kan'tuttʃo] SM corner, nook

canuto, -a [ka'nuto] AGG (*persona*) white-haired; (*barba, capelli*) white

canzonare [kantso'nare] /72/ VT to tease, make fun of

canzonatura [kantsona'tura] SF teasing; (*beffa*) joke

canzone [kan'tsone] SF (*Mus*) song; (*poesia*) canzone; **è sempre la stessa canzone** (*fig*) it's always the same old story; **canzone di gesta** (*poema epico*) chanson de geste

canzoniere [kantso'njere] SM (*Mus*) song book; (*Letteratura*) collection of poems

caos ['kaos] SM INV (*anche fig*) chaos

caotico, -a, -ci, -che [ka'ɔtiko] AGG chaotic

CAP [kap] SIGLA M = **codice di avviamento postale**

cap. ABBR (= *capitolo*) ch.

capace [ka'patʃe] AGG 1 (*capiente*) large, capacious; **una stanza capace** a large room; **questa borsa è poco capace** this bag doesn't hold much 2 (*in grado, dotato*) able, capable; **un insegnante molto capace** a very able teacher; **capace di fare qc** able to do sth, capable of doing sth; **sei capace di farlo da solo?** can you o are you able to do it on your own?; **sei capace di nuotare?** can you swim?; **non è stata capace di farlo** she couldn't do it; **è capace di tutto** he's capable of anything; **capace d'intendere e di volere** (*Dir*) in full possession of one's faculties; **è capace di venire nonostante tutto** he's quite likely to come in spite of everything

capacità [kapat'ʃita] SF INV 1 (*capienza*) capacity; **misure di capacità** measures of capacity 2 (*abilità*) ability, capability; **ha la capacità di trarre il meglio dagli altri** he has the ability to bring out the best in others; **è un compito superiore alle sue capacità** it's a task beyond his capabilities 3 (*Dir, Fis*) capacity; **capacità giuridica** legal capacity 4 **capacità produttiva** (*di impresa*) production capacity

capacitarsi [kapatʃi'tarsi] /72/ VIP: **capacitarsi (di qc)** to comprehend

capanna [ka'panna] SF hut

capannello [kapan'nello] SM knot (of people)

capanno [ka'panno] SM (*di cacciatori*) hide; (*da spiaggia*) bathing hut; (*degli attrezzi*) tool shed

capannone [kapan'none] SM (*gen*) shed; (*Agr*) barn; (*Aer*) hangar

caparbietà [kaparbje'ta] SF stubbornness, obstinacy

caparbio, -bia, -bi, -bie [ka'parbjo] AGG stubborn, obstinate

caparra [ka'parra] SF deposit, down payment

capatina [kapa'tina] SF: **fare una capatina da qn/in centro** to pop in on sb/into town

capeggiare [kaped'dʒare] /62/ VT (*rivolta*) to head, lead

capello [ka'pello] SM (*uno*) hair; **capelli** SMPL hair sg; **c'è un capello nella minestra** there's a hair in the soup; **mi lavo i capelli ogni giorno** I wash my hair every day; **ho i capelli ancora bagnati** my hair is still wet; **ha i capelli ricci** she's got curly hair; **avere i capelli bianchi** to have white hair; **dai capelli scuri** dark-haired; **capelli d'angelo** (*Culin*) long thin pasta; **avere un diavolo per capello** to be in a foul temper; **averne fin sopra i capelli di qc/qn** to be fed up to the (back) teeth with sth/sb; **mettersi le mani nei capelli** (*fig*) to be in despair; **prendersi per i capelli** (*fig*) to tear one's hair out; **mi ci hanno tirato per i capelli** (*fig*) they dragged me into it; **tirato per i capelli** (*spiegazione*) far-fetched

capellone, -a [kapel'lone] SM, SF hippie

capelluto, -a [kapel'luto] AGG: **il cuoio capelluto** the scalp

capezzale [kapet'tsale] SM bolster; (*fig*) bedside; **accorrere al capezzale di qn** to rush to sb's bedside

capezzolo [ka'pettsolo] SM nipple

capiente [ka'pjente] AGG capacious

capienza [ka'pjentsa] SF capacity

capigliatura [kapiλλa'tura] SF hair, head of hair

capillare [kapil'lare] AGG (*Anat, Fis*) capillary; (*fig*: *analisi, ricerca*) detailed ♦ SM (*Anat*: *anche*: **vaso capillare**) capillary

capire [ka'pire] /55/ VT to understand; **si capisce che...** it is clear that ...; **si capisce!** (*certamente!*) of course!, certainly!; **capisco I see, I understand; va bene, capisco** ok, I understand; **fammi capire...** let's get this straight ...; **capisci, è un problema di soldi** you see, it's a problem of money; **non ho capito una parola** I didn't understand a word; **non capito, puoi ripetere?** I don't understand, could you say it again?; **bisogna capirla, poverina** you've got to try and understand her, poor thing; **capire al volo** to catch on straight away; **capire male** to misunderstand; **farsi capire** to make o.s. understood; **capirai!** (*sai che sforzo!*) big deal!; **capirsi** VR (*uso reciproco*) to understand each other o one another

capitale [kapi'tale] AGG 1 (*mortale*): **pena capitale** capital punishment; **sentenza capitale** death sentence; **i sette**

peccati capitali the seven deadly sins **2** (*fondamentale*) main *attr*, chief *attr*; **d'importanza capitale** of capital *o* the utmost importance ♦ SF (*Amm*) capital (city); (*fig: centro*) centre ♦ SM (*Fin, Econ*) capital; **ho speso un capitale per quella macchina** (*fig*) I've spent a fortune on that car; **capitale azionario** equity capital, share capital; **capitale d'esercizio** working capital; **capitale fisso** capital assets *pl*, fixed capital; **capitale immobile** real estate; **capitale liquido** cash assets *pl*; **capitale mobile** movables *pl*; **capitale nominale** authorized capital; **capitale di rischio** risk capital; **capitale sociale** (*di società*) authorized capital; (*di club*) funds *pl*; **capitale di ventura** venture capital, risk capital

capitalismo [kapita'lizmo] SM capitalism

capitalista, -i, -e [kapita'lista] AGG, SM, SF capitalist

capitalizzare [kapitalid'dzare] /72/ VT to capitalize

capitalizzazione [kapitaliddzat'tsjone] SF capitalization

capitanare [kapita'nare] /72/ VT to lead; (*Calcio*) to captain

capitaneria [kapitane'ria] SF: **capitaneria (di porto)** port authorities *pl*

capitano [kapi'tano] SM (*Mil, Naut, Sport*) captain; (*Aer: di squadriglia*) flight lieutenant (*Brit*), captain (*USA*); **capitano di industria** captain of industry; **capitano di lungo corso** master mariner; **capitano di ventura** (*Storia*) mercenary leader

capitare [kapi'tare] /72/ VI (*aus essere*) **1** (*giungere casualmente*) to arrive, find o.s.; (*presentarsi: cosa*) to turn up, present itself; **capitare a proposito/bene/male** to turn up at the right moment/at a good time/at a bad time; **siamo capitati nella zona più pericolosa della città** we found ourselves in the most dangerous area of the city **2** (*accadere*) to happen; **se ti capita di vederlo** if you happen to see him; **mi è capitato un guaio** I had a spot of trouble; **non mi è mai capitato** it's never happened to me; **sono cose che capitano** these things happen ♦ VB IMPERS (*aus essere*) to happen; **capita spesso di incontrarci** *o* **che ci incontriamo** we often bump into one another

capitello [kapi'tɛllo] SM (*Archit*) capital

capitolare [kapito'lare] /72/ VI (*aus avere*) (*Mil*) to capitulate, surrender; (*fig*) to give in

capitolazione [kapitolat'tsjone] SF (*Mil, anche fig*) capitulation

capitolo [ka'pitolo] SM **1** (*di testo, anche Rel*) chapter; **non ho voce in capitolo** (*fig*) I have no say in the matter **2** (*di bilancio*) item

capitombolo [kapi'tombolo] SM tumble, headlong fall; **fare un capitombolo** to take a tumble

capo ['kapo] SM **1** (*Anat*) head; **a capo chino/alto** with one's head bowed/held high; **da capo a piedi** from head to foot; **era coperto di fango da capo a piedi** he was covered in mud from head to foot; **mal di capo** headache; **rompersi il capo** (*fig*) to rack one's brains; **fra capo e collo** (*all'improvviso*) out of the blue **2** (*di fabbrica, ufficio*) head, boss; (*di tribù*) chief; **il mio capo è molto esigente** my boss is very demanding; (*di partito, movimento*) leader; **essere a capo di qc** to head sth, be at the head of sth; **capo del personale** personnel manager; **capo di stato** head of state **3** (*oggetto*) item, article; **un capo di biancheria (intima)/vestiario** an item of underwear/clothing; **capo di bestiame** head *inv* of cattle **4** (*estremità: di tavolo, scale*) head, top; (: *di filo*) end; **era seduto all'altro capo del tavolo** he was sitting at the other end of the table; **da un capo all'altro** from one end to the other; **in capo a** (*tempo*) within; (*luogo*) at the top of; **andare in capo al mondo per qn** (*fig*) to go to the ends of the earth for sb; **da capo** all over again; **ricominciare da capo** to start all over again; **ha sbagliato e ha dovuto ricominciare da capo** he made a mistake and had to start all over again; **a capo** new paragraph; **andare a capo** to start a new paragraph; **"punto a capo"** "full stop - new paragraph"; **fare un discorso senza né capo né coda** to talk nonsense; **un discorso senza né capo né coda** a senseless *o* meaningless speech **5** (*di corda, lana*) ply; **lana a 3 capi** 3-ply wool **6** (*Geog*) cape; **Capo di Buona Speranza** Cape of Good Hope; **Capo Horn** Cape Horn **7** (*Dir*): **capo d'accusa** charge ♦ AGG INV (*giardiniere, sorvegliante*) head *attr*; **redattore capo** chief editor

capobanda [kapo'banda] SM (*pl* **capibanda**) (*Mus*) bandmaster; (*di malviventi: fig*) gang leader

capoccia [ka'pɔttʃa] SM INV (*di lavoranti*) overseer; (*pegg: capobanda*) boss

capoclasse [kapo'klasse] SM, SF (*pl m* **capiclasse**, *pl f* **capoclasse**) (*Scol*) ≈ form captain (*Brit*), ≈ class president (*USA*)

capocuoco, -a [kapo'kwɔko] SM, SF (*pl m* **capocuochi** *o* **capicuochi** *pl f* **capocuoche**) head cook *o* chef

Capodanno [kapo'danno] SM New Year; **il veglione di Capodanno** New Year's Eve party

capofamiglia [kapofa'miʎʎa] SM, SF (*pl m* **capifamiglia**, *pl f* **capofamiglia**) head of the family

capofitto [kapo'fitto] **a capofitto** AVV headlong, headfirst; **gettarsi a capofitto in qc** (*fig*) to rush headlong into sth

capogiro [kapo'dʒiro] SM dizziness *o* dizzy spell; **ho avuto un capogiro** I felt dizzy; **far venire il capogiro a qn** to make sb dizzy; **da capogiro** (*fig*) astonishing, staggering

capogruppo [kapo'gruppo] SM, SF (*pl m* **capigruppo**, *pl f* **capogruppo**) group leader

capolavoro [kapola'voro] SM (*anche fig*) masterpiece

capolinea [kapo'linea] SM (*pl* **capilinea**) terminus; (*fig*) the end of the line

capolino [kapo'lino] SM: **far capolino** to peep out (*o* in *ecc*)

capolista [kapo'lista] SM, SF (*pl m* **capilista**, *pl f* **capolista**) (*Pol*) top candidate on electoral list ♦ SF (*Sport*) top team

capoluogo [kapo'lwɔgo] SM (*pl* **capoluoghi** *o* **capiluoghi**): **capoluogo (di provincia)** ≈ county town (*Brit*), county seat (*USA*), administrative centre (*Brit*) *o* center (*USA*)

capomastro [kapo'mastro] SM (*pl* **capomastri** *o* **capimastri**) master builder

caporale [kapo'rale] SM (*Mil*) lance corporal (*Brit*), private first class (*USA*)

caporeparto [kapore'parto] SM, SF (*pl m* **capireparto**, *pl f* **caporeparto**) (*di operai*) foreman; (*di ufficio*) head of department; (*di negozio*) floor-manager

caposala [kapo'sala] SM, SF (*pl m* **capisala**, *pl f* **caposala**) (*in ospedale*) head nurse; (*donna*) ward sister

caposaldo [kapo'saldo] SM (*pl* **capisaldi**) (*Mil*) stronghold; (*Topografia*) datum point; (*fig: fondamento*) cornerstone, basis

caposquadra [kapos'kwadra] SM, SF (*pl m* **capisquadra**, *pl f* **caposquadra**) (*di operai*) foreman, ganger; (*Mil*) squad leader; (*Sport*) team captain

capostazione [kapostat'tsjone] SM, SF (*pl m* **capistazione**, *pl f* **capostazione**) (*Ferr*) station master

capostipite [kapos'tipite] SM, SF (*pl* **capostipiti**) progenitor; (*fig*) earliest example

capotavola [kapo'tavola] SM, SF (*pl m* **capitavola**, *pl f* **capotavola**) (*persona*) head of the table; **sedere a capotavola** to sit at the head of the table

capote [ka'pɔt] SF INV (*Aut*) hood (*Brit*), top

capotreno [kapo'treno] SM, SF (*pl m* **capitreno** *o* **capotreni** *pl f* **capotreno**) (*Ferr*) guard (*Brit*), conductor (*USA*)

capoufficio [kapouf'fitʃo] SM, SF (*pl m* **capiufficio**, *pl f* **capoufficio**) head clerk

Capo Verde ['kapo 'verde] SM: **il Capo Verde** Cape Verde

capoverso [kapo'verso] SM **1** (*di verso, periodo*) first line; (*Tip*) indent; (*paragrafo*) paragraph **2** (*Dir: comma*) section

capovolgere [kapo'vɔldʒere] VB IRREG /96/ VT (*gen*) to turn upside down; (*barca*) to capsize, overturn; (*macchina*) to overturn; (*fig: situazione, posizione*) to reverse, change completely; **capovolgersi** VIP (*gen*) to overturn; (*barca*) to capsize; (*fig*) to be reversed

capovolgimento [kapovold'ʒimento] SM (*fig*) reversal, complete change

capovolto, -a [kapo'vɔlto] PP *di* **capovolgere** ♦ AGG upside down; (*barca*) capsized

cappa ['kappa] SF **1** (*mantello*) cloak, cape; **film/romanzo di cappa e spada** swashbuckler; **sentirsi sotto una cappa di piombo** to feel oppressed **2** (*del camino*) hood; (*Industria*) chimney; **cappa aspirante** (*per cucina*) extractor hood **3** (*Naut*): **mettersi in cappa** to heave to

cappella [kap'pella] SF (*Rel*) chapel; (*cantori*) choir

cappellano [kappel'lano] SM chaplain; **cappellano militare** army chaplain

cappello [kap'pello] SM hat; (*di fungo*) cap; **cappello di paglia** straw hat; **levarsi/togliersi il cappello** to raise/take off one's hat; **ti faccio tanto di cappello!** (*fig*) I take my hat off to you!; **cappello a bombetta** bowler (hat) (*Brit*), derby (*USA*); **cappello a cilindro** top hat

cappero ['kappero] SM (*Bot, Culin*) caper; **capperi!** (*fam*) gosh!

cappone [kap'pone] SM capon

cappottare [kappot'tare] /**72**/ VI (*aus avere*) (*Aut*) to overturn; **la macchina ha cappottato in curva** the car overturned on the bend

cappotto [kap'potto] SM (over)coat; **m'infilo il cappotto e sono pronta** I'll put my coat on and I'll be ready

cappuccino[1] [kapput'tʃino] AGG, SM (*Rel*) Capuchin

cappuccino[2] [kapput'tʃino] SM (*caffè*) cappuccino

cappuccio, -ci [kap'puttʃo] SM **1** (*copricapo*) hood; (*di frate*) cowl; (*di biro*) cap; **una felpa col cappuccio** a sweatshirt with a hood **2** (*fam*) = **cappuccino[2]**

capra ['kapra] SF **1** (*Zool*) (she-)goat, nanny-goat (*fam*); **formaggio di capra** goat cheese **2** (*Tecn*) trestle

caprese [ka'prese] AGG from *o* of Capri ♦ SM, SF inhabitant *o* native of Capri

capretto [ka'pretto] SM kid

capriccio, -ci [ka'prittʃo] SM **1** (*gen*) whim, caprice; (*di bambino*) tantrum; **è solo un capriccio** it's just a whim; **levarsi** *o* **togliersi il capriccio** to indulge one's whim; **fare i capricci** to be awkward, be naughty; **fare un capriccio** to throw a tantrum; **capricci della moda** whims of fashion; **capriccio della natura** freak of nature; **capriccio della sorte** quirk of fate **2** (*Mus*) capriccio

capriccioso, -a [kaprit'tʃoso] AGG (*persona*) capricious; (*bambino*) naughty; (*tempo*) changeable; **un bambino capriccioso** a naughty boy; **insalata capricciosa** (*Culin*) mixed salad *with mayonnaise*

Capricorno [kapri'kɔrno] SM Capricorn; **essere del Capricorno** (*Astrol*) to be Capricorn; **sono del Capricorno** I'm Capricorn

caprifoglio, -gli [kapri'fɔʎʎo] SM honeysuckle

capriola [kapri'ɔla] SF (*salto*) somersault; (*Danza*) cabriole; (*Equitazione*) caper; **fare una capriola** to turn a somersault; **sai fare le capriole?** can you do somersaults?; **fare le capriole per la gioia** to be jumping for joy

capriolo [kapri'ɔlo] SM roe deer; (*maschio*) roebuck

capro ['kapro] SM (he-)goat, billy-goat (*fam*); **capro espiatorio** (*fig*) scapegoat

caprone [ka'prone] SM (he-)goat, billy-goat (*fam*)

capsula ['kapsula] SF (*di medicinali, spaziale, anche Anat*) capsule; (*di dente*) crown; (*di arma, bottiglia*) cap

captare [kap'tare] /**72**/ VT (*segnale radio*) to pick up; (*pensiero*) to read; **captare lo sguardo di qn** to catch sb's eye

CAR [kar] SIGLA M = Centro Addestramento Reclute

carabina [kara'bina] SF rifle

carabiniere [karabi'njere] SM carabiniere

Caracas [ka'rakas] SF Caracas

caraffa [ka'raffa] SF carafe

Caraibi [ka'raibi] SMPL: **i Caraibi** the Caribbean *sg*; **andrò ai Caraibi quest'estate** I'm going to the Caribbean this summer; **il mar dei Caraibi** the Caribbean (Sea)

caraibico, -a, -ci, -che [kara'ibiko] AGG Caribbean

caramella [kara'mella] SF (*dolciume*) sweet; (*monocolo*) monocle; **vuoi una caramella?** would you like a sweet?; **una caramella alla menta** a mint

caramello [kara'mello] SM caramel

carato [ka'rato] SM **1** (*di oro, diamante*) carat **2** (*Naut*) twenty-fourth part of the ownership of a ship

carattere [ka'rattere] SM **1** (*gen*) character, nature; **avere un buon/brutto carattere** to be good-/ill-natured, be good-/bad-tempered; **aver carattere** to have character; **mancare di/avere poco carattere** to lack character, have no backbone; **informazione di carattere tecnico/confidenziale** information of a technical/confidential nature; **essere in carattere con qc** (*intonarsi*) to be in harmony with sth; **incompatibilità di carattere** personality clash **2** (*spesso pl*: *caratteristica*) characteristic, feature, trait; **caratteri sessuali** sexual characteristics **3** (*Tip*) character, letter; **in carattere corsivo/neretto** *o* **grassetto** in italic/bold type; **carattere jolly** (*Inform*) wild card

caratterino [karatte'rino] SM difficult nature *o* character

caratteristico, -a, -ci, -che [karatte'ristiko] AGG (*tipico*) typical, characteristic; (*distintivo*) distinctive; **il sapore caratteristico del caviale** the distinctive taste of caviar; **un elemento caratteristico dell'architettura locale** a distinctive feature of the local architecture; **un ristorante caratteristico** a traditional restaurant; **segni caratteristici** (*su passaporto*) distinguishing marks

caratterizzare [karatterid'dzare] /**72**/ VT (*essere tipico*) to characterize, be typical *o* characteristic of; (*descrivere*) to distinguish

carboidrato [karboi'drato] SM carbohydrate

carbonaio, -ai [karbo'najo] SM (*chi fa carbone*) charcoal-burner; (*commerciante*) coalman, coal merchant

carbone [kar'bone] SM coal; (*anche:* **carbone dolce** *o* **di legna**) charcoal; (*di lampada ad arco*) carbon; **essere** *o* **stare sui carboni ardenti** to be like a cat on hot bricks (*Brit*) *o* on a hot tin roof (*USA*); **carbone bianco** hydroelectric power; **carbone fossile** (pit) coal

carbonio [kar'bɔnjo] SM (*Chim*) carbon

carbonizzare [karbonid'dzare] /**72**/ VT (*legna*) to carbonize; (*parzialmente*) to char; **morire carbonizzato** to be burned to death; **hanno trovato i resti carbonizzati della vittima** they found the charred remains of the victim

carburante [karbu'rante] AGG combustible ♦ SM (motor) fuel; **siamo rimasti senza carburante** we've run out of fuel

carburatore [karbura'tore] SM carburettor (*Brit*), carburetor (*USA*)

carcassa [kar'kassa] SF **1** (*di animale*) carcass; (*fig*: *pegg*: *macchina*) (old) wreck **2** (*struttura portante*) framework, frame; (*di nave*) hulk **3** (*Aut*: *pneumatico*) carcass; **pneumatico a carcassa radiale/diagonale** radial/cross-ply tyre (*Brit*) *o* tire (*USA*)

carcerato, -a [kartʃe'rato] SM, SF prisoner

carcere ['kartʃere] SM (*pl f carceri*) (*edificio*) prison, jail; (*pena*) imprisonment; **sono evasi dal carcere** they escaped from prison; **essere/mettere in carcere** to be in/send to prison *o* jail; **gli hanno dato dieci anni di carcere** he was sent to prison for ten years; **condannato a due anni di carcere** sentenced to two years' imprisonment; **carcere di massima sicurezza** top-security prison

carceriere, -a [kartʃe'rjere] SM, SF (*anche fig*) jailer

carciofo [kar'tʃɔfo] SM artichoke

cardellino [kardel'lino] SM goldfinch

cardiaco, -a, -ci, -che [kar'diako] AGG cardiac, heart *attr*; **attacco cardiaco** heart attack

cardinale [kardi'nale] AGG cardinal ♦ SM (*Rel*) cardinal

cardine ['kardine] SM (*di porta, finestra*) hinge; (*fig*: *fondamento*) cornerstone, foundation

cardiologia [kardjolo'dʒia] SF cardiology

cardiologo, -a, -gi [kar'djɔlogo] SM, SF heart specialist, cardiologist

cardo ['kardo] SM (*Bot*) thistle; (*commestibile*) cardoon

carente [ka'rente] AGG: **carente di** lacking in

carenza [ka'rentsa] SF shortage, lack, scarcity; (*Med*) deficiency; **carenza vitaminica** vitamin deficiency

carestia [kares'tia] SF famine; (*fig*: *penuria*) scarcity, lack, dearth; **migliaia di persone rischiano di morire a causa della carestia** thousands of people may die as a result of the famine

carezza [ka'rettsa] SF caress; **dare** *o* **fare una carezza a** (*persona*) to caress; (*animale*) to stroke, pat

carezzare [karet'tsare] /**20**/ VT = **accarezzare**

carezzevole [karet'tsevole] AGG sweet, endearing

cargo, -ghi ['kargo] SM (*nave*) cargo boat, freighter; (*aereo*) freighter

cariare [ka'rjare] /**20**/ VT to decay; **lo zucchero caria i denti** sugar decays teeth; **cariarsi** VIP (*denti*) to decay

carica, -che ['karika] SF (*ufficio, funzione*) position, office; **ricoprire** *o* **rivestire una carica** to hold a position; **in carica** in office; **il presidente in carica** the president in office; **rimanere in carica per...** to hold office for...; **il Presidente è rimasto in carica per cinque anni** the President held office for five years; **entrare/essere in carica** to come into/be in office; **uscire di carica** to leave office; **carica onorifica** honorary appointment **2** (*di orologio*) winding; **è finita la carica** it's wound down; **dare la carica all'orologio** to wind up the clock **3** (*di arma, missile*) charge **4** (*attacco: Mil: di animali*) charge; **tornare alla carica** (*fig*) to insist, persist; **entrare a passo di carica** to charge in **5** (*fig: energia*) drive; **dare la carica a qn** to give sb strength, encourage sb; **ha una forte carica di simpatia** he's very likeable

caricabatteria [karikabatte'ria] SM INV (*Aut*) battery charger; (*di telefonino*) charger

caricare [kari'kare] /20/ VT **1** (*gen*) to load; (*fig: esagerare*) to exaggerate; (*tinta*) to deepen **2 caricare su/in** (*merci ecc*) to load on/into; **caricare in macchina** (*passeggero*) to give a lift to; (*valigie*) to put into the car **3** (*sovraccaricare*): **caricare di** (*merci ecc*) to overload with; (*fig: di lavoro, responsabilità*) to overload with, to overburden with **4** (*orologio*) to wind up; (*batteria, accumulatore*) to charge; (*fucile, macchina fotografica*) to load; (*pipa, stufa*) to fill; (*caldaia, altoforno*) to stoke; **avevo dimenticato di caricare la sveglia** I'd forgotten to wind the alarm clock; **come si carica questa macchina fotografica?** how do you load the film in this camera?; **caricare un programma** (*Inform*) to load a program; **hai caricato il programma?** have you loaded the program? **5** (*attaccare: Mil*) to charge; (*: Sport*) to tackle; **la polizia ha caricato i dimostranti** the police charged the demonstrators; **caricarsi** VR **1 caricarsi di** to overburden o overload o.s. with; (*fig: di responsabilità, impegni*) to overburden o.s. with **2** (*concentrarsi*): **caricarsi per una gara** to gear o.s. up for a race

caricatura [karika'tura] SF caricature; **fare la caricatura di qn** to do a caricature of sb

carico, -a, -chi, -che ['kariko] AGG **1** (*veicolo*): **carico (di)** loaded o laden (with), full (of); (*persona*): **carico di** laden with; **è tornato carico di pacchi e pacchetti** he came back loaded with parcels; **un camion carico di mattoni** a truck with a load of bricks; **carico di debiti** up to one's ears in debt; **carico di lavoro** weighed down with work **2** (*forte: colore*) strong, deep; (*: caffè, tè*) strong **3** (*caricato: orologio*) wound up; (*: fucile, macchina fotografica*) loaded; (*: pipa*) full; (*: batteria*) charged; (*: bomba*) live; **il fucile era carico** the gun was loaded ♦ SM (*il caricare*) loading; **fare il carico** to load; **operazioni di carico** loading operations **2** (*materiale caricato*) load; (*su nave*) freight, cargo; (*Comm*) shipment; **trasportava un carico di arance** it was carrying a load of oranges; **a pieno carico** with a full load; **capacità di carico** cargo capacity; **carico utile** pay load **3** (*Elettr*) charge **4** (*Econ*): **essere a carico di qn** (*onere, spese ecc*) to be charged to sb, be payable by sb; (*persona*) to be dependent on sb, be supported by sb; **a carico del cliente** at the customer's expense; **ha dei familiari a carico?** do you have any dependents? **5** (*Dir*) charge; **ha carichi pendenti** do you have any charges pending?; **essere a carico di qn** (*accusa, prova*) to be against sb; **testimone a carico** witness for the prosecution **6** (*fig: peso*) burden, weight; **farsi carico di** (*problema, responsabilità*) to take on; **carico di lavoro** (*di ditta, reparto*) workload; **carico fiscale** tax burden

carie ['karje] SF (*Med*) decay; (*Bot*) rot; **ho una carie** I've got a cavity in one of my teeth

carino, -a [ka'rino] AGG (*gen*) nice; (*ragazza, bambino*) pretty, lovely; (*ragazzo*) good-looking; **carina questa maglietta!** that's a nice T-shirt!; **ha una casa molto carina** she's got a very nice house; **è stato tuo fratello** your brother's nice-looking; **essere carino con qn** to be nice to sb; **sono stati molto carini con me** they were very nice to me; **è stato molto carino da parte tua** that was really o kind of you

carisma [ka'rizma] SM charisma

carismatico, -a, -ci, -che [kariz'matiko] AGG charismatic

carità [kari'ta] SF INV (*gen, anche Rel*) charity; **chiedere la carità (a qn)** to beg for charity (from sb); (*fig*) to come begging (to sb); **c'era uno che chiedeva la carità fuori dalla chiesa** there was a man begging outside the church; **fare la carità a** to give (something) to; **vivere di carità** to live on charity; **per carità!** (*figurarsi*) you've got to be joking!; (*per favore*) please!; (*non ti disturbare!*) please don't bother!; (*non è un disturbo*) not at all!, it's no trouble at all!; (*neanche per*

sogno) good heavens, no!; **uscire con lui? Per carità!** go out with him? You're joking!; **fammi la carità di star zitto** please be so kind as to keep quiet

caritatevole [karita'tevole] AGG charitable

carnagione [karna'dʒone] SF complexion; **ha la carnagione chiara** she's got a fair complexion

carnale [kar'nale] AGG **1** (*sessuale: desiderio, conoscenza*) carnal; **violenza carnale** rape **2** (*consanguineo: fratello, sorella*) full *attr*, blood *attr*

carne ['karne] SF **1** (*gen, anche fig*) flesh; **in carne e ossa** in the flesh, in person; **era proprio lui, in carne e ossa!** it was really him, in the flesh!; **carne da macello** (*fig*) cannon fodder; **color carne** flesh coloured; **carne viva** raw flesh; **essere (bene) in carne** to be well padded, be plump; **è carne della mia carne** he's my own flesh and blood **2** (*Culin*) meat; **preferisci la carne o il pesce?** which do you prefer, meat or fish?; **non essere né carne né pesce** (*fig*) to be neither fish nor fowl; **mettere troppa carne al fuoco** (*fig*) to have too many irons in the fire; **carne arrosto/ai ferri** roast/grilled meat; **carne bianca** (*di pollo, agnello, coniglio*) white meat; **carne bovina** o **di manzo** beef; **carne di cavallo** o **equina** horseflesh, horse meat; **carne suina** o **di maiale** pork; **carne ovina** o **di pecora** mutton; **carne rossa** (*di manzo o maiale*) red meat; **carne in scatola** tinned (*Brit*) o canned (*USA*) meat; **carne tritata** mince (*Brit*), hamburger meat (*USA*), minced (*Brit*) o ground (*USA*) meat; **carne di vitello** veal

carnefice [kar'nefitʃe] SM (*boia*) executioner; (*nell'impiccagione*) hangman; (*fig*) torturer

carneficina [karnefi'tʃina] SF carnage; (*fig*) disaster; **fare una carneficina** to carry out a massacre

carnevale [karne'vale] SM carnival period; **il carnevale di Venezia** the Venice Carnival

carnivoro, -a [kar'nivoro] AGG carnivorous ♦ SM carnivore

carnoso, -a [kar'noso] AGG (*gen*) fleshy; (*pianta, frutto, radice*) pulpy; (*labbra*) full

caro, -a [ˈkaro] AGG **1** (*amato*): **caro (a)** dear (to) (*ricordo*) fond; **mi è tanto caro** it (o he) is very dear to me; **Caro Paolo** (*nelle lettere*) Dear Paul; **tanti cari saluti** best wishes; **cara signora!** my dear lady!; **se ti è cara la vita** if you value your life; **tener caro il ricordo di qn/qc** to cherish the memory of sb/sth **2** (*costoso*) dear, expensive; **a caro prezzo** at a high price; **vendere cara la pelle** to sell one's life dear ♦ SM, SF: **mio caro, mia cara** my dear; **i miei cari** my dear ones ♦ AVV (*costare, pagare*) a lot, a great deal; **questo insulto ti costerà caro** you'll pay dearly for that insult; **lo pagherai caro** you'll pay a lot for it

carogna [ka'roɲɲa] SF carrion *inv*; (*fam: persona vile*) swine *inv*; **sei una carogna!** you're a pig!

carosello [karo'zello] SM (*giostra*) merry-go-round, carousel (*USA*); (*movimento vorticoso: di automobili, idee*) whirl; **all'uscita dello stadio si sono formati dei caroselli** outside the stadium there was a whirl of cars

carota [ka'rɔta] SF **1** carrot **2** (*Mineralogia*) core

carovana [karo'vana] SF (*gen*) caravan; (*convoglio*) convoy

carovita [karo'vita] SM INV high cost of living; (*indennità*) cost of living allowance

carpa ['karpa] SF (*pesce*) carp

Carpazi [kar'pattsi] SMPL: **i Carpazi** the Carpathian Mountains, the Carpathians

carpenteria [karpente'ria] SF carpentry

carpentiere [karpen'tjere] SM carpenter

carpire [kar'pire] /55/ VT: **carpire qc a qn** (*denaro*) to get sth out of sb; **carpire un segreto/un'informazione a qn** to worm a secret/information out of sb

carponi [kar'poni] AVV on all fours, on one's hands and knees; **mettersi/stare a carponi** to get down/be on all fours

carrabile [kar'rabile] AGG suitable for vehicles; **"passo carrabile"** "keep clear"

carraio, -aia, -ai, -aie [kar'rajo] AGG carriage *attr*; **passo carraio** driveway

carré [kar're] SM INV **1** (*Culin: lombata*) loin **2** (*taglio di capelli*) bob ♦ AGG INV: **pan carré** toasting loaf

carreggiata [karred'dʒata] SF (*Aut*) carriageway (*Brit*), roadway; **strada a due carreggiate** dual carriageway (*Brit*), divided highway (*USA*); **tenersi in carreggiata** (*fig*) to keep to the right path; **rimettersi in carreggiata** (*fig: recuperare*) to catch up

carrellata [karrelˈlata] SF (*Cine, TV: tecnica*) tracking; (: *scena*) tracking shot; **carrellata di successi** medley of hits; **una carrellata su...** a brief look at ...

carrello [karˈrɛllo] SM (*gen, anche Ferr*) trolley; (*di teleferica*) car; (*Aer*) undercarriage; (*di macchina da scrivere*) carriage; (*Cine, TV*) dolly; **carrello elevatore** fork-lift truck; **carrello per la spesa** shopping trolley (*Brit*); shopping cart (*USA*); **carrello portaverdure** vegetable rack; **carrello portavivande** (food) trolley

carretta [karˈretta] SF (*piccolo carro*) cart; (*pegg: veicolo*) old wreck; **tirare la carretta** (*fig*) to plod along; **carretta del mare** old and unsafe boat, generally used to carry undocumented immigrants

carretto [karˈretto] SM handcart; **carretto a mano** wheelbarrow

carriera [karˈrjɛra] SF career; **fare carriera** to get on (in one's job), to have a successful career; **non è facile far carriera per una donna con figli** it's not easy for a woman with children to have a career; **farà sicuramente carriera** he'll get on; **una brillante carriera universitaria** a brilliant university career; **prospettive di carriera** career prospects; **ufficiale di carriera** (*Mil*) regular officer; **di** o **a gran carriera** (*fig*) at full speed

carriola [karriˈɔla] SF wheelbarrow

carro [ˈkarro] SM 1 cart, wagon; (*per carnevale*) float; **mettere il carro davanti ai buoi** (*fig*) to put the cart before the horse 2 (*Astron*): **il Gran/Piccolo Carro** the Great/Little Bear ♦ **carro armato** (*Mil*) tank; **carro attrezzi** (*Aut*) breakdown van (*Brit*), tow truck (*USA*); **carro bestiame** (*Ferr*) animal wagon; **carro funebre** hearse; **carro merci** (*Ferr*) goods wagon (*Brit*), freight car (*USA*)

carroccio [karˈrottʃo] SM (*Pol*) : **il Carroccio** symbol of Lega Nord

carrozza [karˈrɔttsa] SF (*gen, anche Ferr*) carriage, coach; (**signori**) **in carrozza!** all aboard!; **carrozza belvedere** observation car; **carrozza letto** sleeper (*Brit*), Pullman (*USA*); **carrozza ristorante** dining o restaurant car

carrozzella [karrotˈtsɛlla] SF (*per bambini*) pram (*Brit*), baby carriage (*USA*); (*per invalidi*) wheelchair

carrozzeria [karrottseˈria] SF 1 (*Aut: rivestimento*) bodywork, body, coachwork (*Brit*); **carrozzeria portante** chassis 2 (*Aut: officina*) body shop

carrozziere [karrotˈtsjere] SM (*Aut: progettista*) car designer; (: *meccanico*) panel beater (*Brit*), auto bodyworker (*USA*)

carrozzina [karrotˈtsina] SF pram (*Brit*), baby carriage (*USA*)

carrozzone [karrotˈtsone] SM (*di circo, zingari*) caravan (*Brit*), wagon (*USA*)

carrucola [karˈrukola] SF pulley

carta [ˈkarta] SF 1 (*gen*) paper; (*statuto*) charter; **un foglio di carta** a sheet of paper; **sulla carta** (*in teoria*) on paper 2 (*da gioco*) card; **dare le carte** to deal the cards; **giocare una carta** to play a card; **giocare l'ultima carta** (*anche fig*) to play one's last card; **a carte scoperte** (*anche fig*) cards on the table; **mettere le carte in tavola** to lay one's cards on the table; **cambiare le carte in tavola** (*fig*) to shift one's ground; **fare le carte a qn** (*Cartomanzia*) to tell sb's fortune using cards 3 (*documenti*): **carte** SFPL papers, documents; **devo fare tutte le carte per il passaporto** I've got to sort out all the documents and forms for the passport application; **fare carte false** (*fig*) to go to great lengths; **avrebbe fatto carte false pur di ottenere quel posto** he would have gone to any lengths to get that job 4 (*al ristorante*) menu; **alla carta** à la carte ♦ **carta di alluminio** aluminium (*Brit*) o aluminum (*USA*) foil; **carta assegni** bank card; **carta assorbente** blotting paper; **carta automobilistica** road map; **carta bianca** carte blanche; **dare carta bianca a qn** to give sb carte blanche; **carta da bollo** o **bollata** o **legale** (*Amm*) official stamped paper; **carta di credito** credit card; **carta di credito telefonica** phone card (*for calls that are charged to the phone bill*); **carta da cucina** kitchen roll o paper o towel (*Brit*), paper towel (*USA*); **carta da disegno** drawing paper; **carta geografica** map; **carta di giornale** newsprint; **carta d'identità** identity card; **carta igienica** toilet paper; **carta d'imbarco** boarding card; **carta intelligente** smart card; **carta da lettere** writing paper;

carta libera o **semplice** (*Amm*) unstamped paper; **carta lucida** tracing paper; **carta millimetrata** graph paper; **carta moschicida** fly-paper; **carta nautica** (nautical) chart; **carta oleata** waxed o wax paper (*spec USA*); **carta da pacchi** o **da imballaggio** wrapping paper, brown paper; **carta paraffinata** o **vegetale** (*Culin*) greaseproof paper (*Brit*); **carta da parati** wallpaper; **carta per prelievi automatici** cash card; **carta da regalo** (gift) wrapping paper; **carta stagnola** tinfoil (*Brit*); **carta stradale** o **automobilistica** road map; **carta velina** tissue paper; **carta verde** (*Aut*) green card (*Brit*); **carta vetrata** glasspaper, sandpaper; **carta dei vini** wine list; **carta da visita** visiting card; **(color) carta da zucchero** mid blue; **carte da gioco** playing cards

cartacarbone [kartakarˈbone] SF carbon paper

cartaccia, -ce [karˈtattʃa] SF waste paper

cartamodello [kartamoˈdello] SM (*Cucito*) paper pattern

cartamoneta [kartamoˈneta] SF paper money

cartapecora [kartaˈpekora] SF parchment, vellum

cartapesta [kartaˈpesta] SF papier-mâché; **di cartapesta** papier-mâché *attr*; (*fig*) weak; **eroe di cartapesta** tin god

cartastraccia, -ce [kartasˈtrattʃa] SF waste paper

carteggio, -gi [karˈteddʒo] SM correspondence

cartella [karˈtɛlla] SF 1 (*custodia: di cartoncino*) folder; (*borsa: di professionista*) briefcase; (: *di scolaro*) schoolbag, satchel; (*pratica, incartamento*) file, dossier; (*Inform*) folder; **cartella trasparente** transparent folder 2 (*Tip*) page 3 (*Lotto*) lottery ticket; (*Tombola*) tombola card 4 **cartella clinica** (*Med*) case sheet

cartellino [kartelˈlino] SM (*del prezzo*) price label, price tag; (*scheda*) card; **timbrare il cartellino** (*all'entrata*) to clock in o on; (*all'uscita*) to clock out o off; **cartellino giallo/rosso** (*Calcio*) yellow/red card; **cartellino di presenza** o **orario** clock card, timecard

cartello[1] [karˈtello] SM (*avviso*) notice, sign; (*stradale*) sign, signpost; (*di dimostranti, pubblicitario*) placard, poster; (*di negozio*) sign; **cosa indica quel cartello?** what does that sign say?; **sul cartello c'era scritto "tutto esaurito"** the sign said "sold out"

cartello[2] [karˈtello] SM (*Econ, Pol*) cartel

cartellone [kartelˈlone] SM (*pubblicitario*) placard, (advertising) poster; (*Teatro*) bill, playbill; (*Cine*) poster; (*di tombola*) scoring frame, board; **tenere il cartellone** (*Teatro*) to have a long run

cartiera [karˈtjɛra] SF paper mill

cartilagine [kartiˈladʒine] SF cartilage

cartina [karˈtina] SF 1 (*Geog*) map 2 (*di sigarette*) cigarette paper; (*piccolo involto*) packet

cartoccio, -ci [karˈtɔttʃo] SM 1 (*involucro*) cornet; **cuocere al cartoccio** (*Culin*) to bake in tinfoil o aluminium (*Brit*) o aluminum (*USA*); **patate al cartoccio** ≈ jacket potatoes (*Brit*) 2 (*Mil*) powder charge

cartografia [kartograˈfia] SF cartography

cartolaio, -aia, -ai, -aie [kartoˈlajo] SM, SF stationer

cartolarizzazione [kartolariddzatˈtsjone] SF *the conversion of credits of banks, companies and public bodies into shares that can be bought and sold*

cartoleria [kartoleˈria] SF stationer's (shop); **lo trovi in cartoleria** you'll get it at a stationer's

cartolina [kartoˈlina] SF postcard; **mandami una cartolina** send me a postcard; **cartolina di auguri** greetings card; **cartolina illustrata** picture postcard; **cartolina postale** stamped postcard; **cartolina precetto** o **rosa** (*Mil*) call-up papers *pl* (*Brit*), draft card (*USA*)

cartomante [kartoˈmante] SM, SF fortune-teller (*using cards*)

cartoncino [kartonˈtʃino] SM (*materiale*) thin cardboard; (*biglietto*) card

cartone [karˈtone] SM 1 (*materiale*) cardboard; **una scatola di cartone** a cardboard box 2 (*Arte*) cartoon; **cartone animato** (*Cine*) cartoon; **i cartoni animati di Tom e Jerry** Tom and Jerry cartoons 3 (*imballaggio*) large cardboard box; (*scatola: del latte, dell'aranciata*) carton; **un cartone di latte** a carton of milk

cartuccia, -ce [karˈtuttʃa] SF (*di arma*) cartridge; (*di penna*) refill, cartridge; **mezza cartuccia** (*fig: persona da poco*) good-for-nothing; **cartuccia a salve** blank (cartridge)

casa [ˈkasa] SF **1** (*edificio*) house; **una bella casa grande** a nice big house; **casa a quattro piani** four-storey(ed) (*Brit*) o four-storied (*USA*) house; **casa di campagna** (*grande*) house in the country; (*piccola*) country cottage; **casa di mattoni** brick house; **case a schiera** terraced (*Brit*) o row (*USA*) houses; **hanno una bella casa** they have a nice apartment; **la Casa Bianca** (*Pol*) the White House **2** (*abitazione*) home; **essere/stare a** o **in casa** to be/stay at home; **sono stato in casa tutta la sera** I was at home all evening; **eravamo a casa mia** we were at my house; **non è a casa** she isn't at home; **sarò a casa tra un'ora** I'll be home in an hour; **tornare a casa** to come/go back home; **è tornato a casa tardi** he got home late; **andare a casa** to go home; **vado a casa mia/tua** I'm going home/to your house; **c'è nessuno in casa?** is anybody in?; **vieni a casa nostra?** are you coming to our house o place?; **uscire di casa** to leave home; **dove sta di casa?** where does he live?; **non sa dove stia di casa la cortesia** he doesn't know the meaning of courtesy; **essere di casa** to be like one of the family; **fatto in casa** home-made; **pane fatto in casa** home-made bread; **fai come se fossi a casa tua** make yourself at home; **abitare a casa del diavolo** to live in the back of beyond; **"tanti saluti a casa"** "best wishes to all the family" **3** (*casato, stirpe*) house, family; **casa d'Asburgo** House of Hapsburg **4** (*ditta*) firm, company ♦ **casa di correzione** ≈ community home (*Brit*), ≈ reform school (*USA*), reformatory (*USA*); **casa di cura** nursing home; **casa discografica** record company; **casa editrice** publishing house; **casa famiglia** (*per bambini, anziani*) (care) home; (*per malati di mente, ex-tossicodipendenti*) halfway house; **casa madre** head office; **casa di moda** fashion house; **casa popolare** ≈ council house o flat (*Brit*), ≈ public housing unit (*USA*); **casa di riposo** (old people's) home, care home; **casa dello studente** hall of residence (*Brit*), dormitory (*USA*); **casa di tolleranza** o **d'appuntamenti** brothel

casacca, -che [kaˈzakka] SF (*Mil*) coat; (*giacca*) jacket; (*di fantino*) blouse

casale [kaˈsale] SM (*gruppo di case*) hamlet; (*casolare*) farmhouse

casalingo, -a, -ghi, -ghe [kasaˈlingo] AGG **1** (*occupazione, lavoro*) domestic, household **2** (*fatto in casa*) home-made; (*semplice*) homely; (*amante della casa*) home-loving; **cucina casalinga** (plain) home cooking ♦ **casalinghi** SMPL (*oggetti*) household articles

casata [kaˈsata] SF family, (family) lineage

casato [kaˈsato] SM family name; **è di nobile casato** he's of noble birth

cascamorto [kaskaˈmɔrto] SM love-sick Romeo; **fare il cascamorto** to play the love-sick Romeo; **non fare il cascamorto con me** there's no point in chasing after me

cascare [kasˈkare] /20/ VI (*aus* essere) to fall; **far cascare qc** to drop sth; **cascare per terra** to fall to the ground, fall down; **è cascato dal letto** he fell out of bed; **cascare dalla fame** to be faint with hunger; **cascare dal sonno** to be falling asleep on one's feet; **cascare bene/male** (*fig*) to land lucky/unlucky; **cascare bene/male** (*fig*) to land lucky/unlucky; **cascarci** to fall for it; **gli ho detto che tu eri partito e lui c'è cascato** I told him you had left and he fell for it; **casca il mondo** no matter what; **non cascherà il mondo se...** it won't be the end of the world if ...

cascata [kasˈkata] SF (*di acqua*) waterfall, cascade; (*fig: di capelli*) cascade; **sono le cascate più alte del mondo** they're the biggest waterfalls in the world; **cascata di ghiaccio** icefall; **le cascate del Niagara** the Niagara Falls; **le cascate Vittoria** the Victoria Falls

cascherò ecc [kaskeˈrɔ] VB vedi cascare

cascina [kaʃˈʃina] SF farmstead

cascinale [kaʃʃiˈnale] SM (*casolare*) farmhouse; (*cascina*) farmstead

casco, -schi [ˈkasko] SM **1** (*Mil, Sport*) helmet; (*da motociclista*) crash helmet; (*da parrucchiere*) (hair-)dryer; **i caschi blu** UN troops, the Blue Helmets **2** (*di banane*) bunch

caseggiato [kasedˈdʒato] SM (*edificio*) large block of flats (*Brit*), large apartment building (*USA*) o house; (*gruppo di case*) group of houses

caseificio, -ci [kazeiˈfitʃo] SM creamery

casella [kaˈsɛlla] SF (*quadretto*) box; (*di scacchiera*) square; (*di mobile, schedario*) pigeonhole; **casella postale** post office box; **casella di posta elettronica** mailbox; **casella di ricezione** (*Inform*) stacker

casellario, -ri [kaselˈlarjo] SM (*mobile*) filing cabinet; (*raccolta di pratiche*) files pl; **casellario giudiziale** o **giudiziario** court records pl; **casellario penale** police files pl

casello [kaˈsɛllo] SM (*Ferr*) signal box (*Brit*), signal tower (*USA*); (*di autostrada*) tollgate

casereccio, -cia, -ci, -ce [kaseˈrettʃo] AGG home-made

caserma [kaˈzɛrma] SF barracks pl; **caserma dei vigili del fuoco** fire station

casertano, -a [kazerˈtano] AGG of o from Caserta ♦ SM, SF inhabitant o native of Caserta

casino [kaˈsino] SM **1** (*fam: bordello*) brothel **2** (*fig: fam: rumore*) row, racket; (: *disordine*) mess; (: *guaio*) trouble; **ha fatto un casino** he made an awful row; he messed everything up; **cos'è questo casino?** what's this bloody racket?; **in camera mia c'è un gran casino** my bedroom is in a hell of a mess; **in questo periodo ho tanti casini** I've got loads of problems at the moment; **mettere qn nei casini** put sb in a hell of a mess **3** (*fam: grande quantità*) loads; **mi piace un casino** I really like it; **un casino di** loads of; **c'era un casino di gente** there were loads of people; **c'era un casino di macchine** there was a hell of a lot of traffic **4** **casino di caccia** hunting lodge

casinò [kaziˈnɔ] SM INV casino

casistica [kaˈzistika] SF record of cases; **secondo la casistica degli incidenti stradali** according to road accident data

caso [ˈkazo] SM **1** (*fatalità, destino*) chance; **è un puro caso** it's sheer chance; **il caso ha voluto che...** by chance ...; **non è un caso** it's no coincidence; **si dà il caso che...** it so happens that ...; **guarda caso** strangely enough; **a caso** at random; **ho aperto il libro a caso** I opened the book at random **2** (*fatto, anche Gramm, Med, Dir*) case; **per lui è un caso di coscienza** to him it is a moral dilemma; **questi sono i casi della vita!** that's life!; **caso limite** borderline case **3** (*bisogno*): **fare al caso di qn** to be just what sb needs; **fa al caso mio** it's just what I need; **non è il caso che tu te la prenda** there's no need for you to be upset; **non è il caso di arrabbiarsi!** there's no point getting angry!; **non mi sembra il caso di insistere** I wouldn't insist on that; **è il caso che ce ne andiamo** we'd better go; **forse sarebbe il caso di andarcene** perhaps we'd better go **4** (*possibilità, evenienza*) possibility, event; **i casi sono due** there are two possibilities; **in ogni caso** in any case; **in ogni caso non ci perdi niente** in any case you've got nothing to lose; **in caso contrario** otherwise; **in tal caso, in quel caso** in that case; **be', in tal caso dovremo rimandare la partenza** well, in that case we'll have to put off our departure; **in caso di necessità** o **bisogno** in case of need; **al caso** if need be, should the opportunity arise; **per caso** by chance, by accident; **l'ho incontrato per caso** I met him by chance; **nel caso che...** in case ...; **ti do il mio numero di telefono, nel caso che tu venga a Roma** I'll give you my phone number, in case you come to Rome; **caso mai** if by chance; **caso mai non dovessi venire...** if (by chance) you can't come ...; **dovrei essere lì alle 5, caso mai aspetta** I should be there for 5; if (by any chance) I'm not, wait; **fare** o **porre** o **mettere il caso che...** to suppose that ...; **mettiamo il caso che** supposing; **mettiamo il caso che ti inviti: accetteresti?** supposing he invited you, would you go?; **a seconda dei casi** depending on the circumstances; **nel migliore dei casi** at best; **nel peggiore dei casi** at worst **5** (*attenzione*): **far caso a qn/qc** to pay attention to sb/sth; **hai fatto caso al suo cappello?** did you notice his hat?; **non ci ho fatto caso** I didn't notice; **non farci caso** don't pay any attention

casolare [kasoˈlare] SM cottage

Caspio [ˈkaspjo] SM: **il mar Caspio** the Caspian Sea

caspita [ˈkaspita] ESCL (*di sorpresa*) good heavens!; (*di impazienza*) goodness' sake!

cassa [ˈkassa] SF **1** (*gen, anche Tip: di orologio*) case; (*gabbia*) crate; (*mobile*) chest; (*scatola*) box; **ho comprato una cassa di birra** I bought a case of beer **2** (*Comm: macchina*) cash register; (: *sportello*) cash desk; (: *in supermercato*) checkout (counter); **"si prega di pagare alla cassa"** "please pay at the desk"; **"cassa"** "pay here"; **registratore di cassa** till; **piccola**

cassa petty cash; **battere cassa** (*fig*) to come looking for money **3** (*ente finanziario*) fund **4** (*istituto bancario*) bank ♦ **cassa acustica** (*Mus*) speaker; **cassa d'aria** (*Naut*) airlock; **cassa armonica** (*Mus*) soundbox; **cassa automatica prelievi** cashpoint (*USA*), cash dispenser (*Brit*), automatic telling machine (*Brit*); **cassa comune** kitty; **cassa continua** night safe (*Brit*), night depository (*USA*); **cassa del fucile** rifle stock; **cassa da imballaggio** packing case; **cassa integrazione** *system whereby the state pays part of the salaries of employees of a company that is in difficulty for a certain period of time*; **mettere in cassa integrazione** ≈ to lay off; **cassa da morto** coffin; **cassa mutua** *o* **malattia** health insurance scheme; **cassa di risonanza** (*Fis*) resonance chamber; (*fig*) platform; **cassa di risparmio** savings bank; **cassa rurale e artigiana** credit institution (*for farmers and artisans*); **cassa toracica** (*Anat*) chest

cassaforte [kassaˈfɔrte] SF (*pl* **casseforti**) safe; **hanno forzato la cassaforte** they forced open the safe

cassapanca, -che [kassaˈpanka] SF settle

casseruola [kasseˈrwɔla] SF saucepan; **pollo in casseruola** chicken casserole

cassetta [kasˈsetta] SF **1** (*gen*) box; (*musicassetta*) cassette; **una cassetta di mele** a box of apples; **ce l'ho sia su CD che su cassetta** I've got it on CD and on cassette; **pane a** *o* **in cassetta** toasting loaf; **cassetta degli arnesi** toolbox; **cassetta delle lettere** letterbox; **cassetta di sicurezza** strongbox **2** (*Cine, Teatro: incasso*) box-office takings *pl*; **far cassetta** to be a box-office success; **film di cassetta** (*commerciale*) box-office draw

cassetto [kasˈsetto] SM drawer; **è nel primo cassetto** it's in the top drawer

cassettone [kassetˈtone] SM (*mobile*) chest of drawers; **soffitto a cassettoni** (*Archit*) panelled ceiling

cassiere, -a [kasˈsjɛre] SM, SF cashier; (*in supermercato*) check-out assistant (*Brit*), check-out clerk (*USA*); **cassiere di banca** bank teller

cassintegrato, -a [kassinteˈɡrato] SM, SF *worker who has been laid off and receives money from the state*

cassone [kasˈsone] SM (*cassa*) large case, large chest

cassonetto [kassoˈnetto] SM (*per rifiuti*) wheelie-bin

casta [ˈkasta] SF caste

castagna [kasˈtaɲɲa] SF chestnut; **prendere qn in castagna** (*fig*) to catch sb in the act; **castagna d'acqua** water chestnut

castagno [kasˈtaɲɲo] SM (*albero*) chestnut (tree); (*legno*) chestnut; **castagno comune** *o* **dolce** sweet chestnut

castano, -a [kasˈtano] AGG (*capelli*) chestnut (brown); (*occhi*) brown; (*persona*) brown-haired; **ha gli occhi e i capelli castani** she's got brown eyes and brown hair

castello [kasˈtello] SM **1** castle; **castello di carte** house of cards; **castello di sabbia** sand castle; **fare castelli in aria** to build castles in the air; **letti a castello** bunk-beds **2** (*Naut*): **castello di poppa** quarter-deck; **castello di prua** foˈcˈsle **3** (*Tecn*) scaffolding

castigare [kastiˈɡare] /80/ VT to punish, chastise

castigato, -a [kastiˈɡato] AGG (*casto, modesto*) pure, chaste; (*abbigliamento*) demure; (*emendato: prosa, versione*) expurgated, amended

castigo, -ghi [kasˈtiɡo] SM punishment; **per castigo** as a punishment; **mettere/essere in castigo** to punish/be punished; **sono in castigo e non posso uscire** I'm being punished and I'm not allowed to go out; **castigo di Dio** (*fig*) scourge

castità [kastiˈta] SF chastity

casto, -a [ˈkasto] AGG chaste, pure

castoro [kasˈtɔro] SM beaver

castrante [kasˈtrante] AGG frustrating

castrare [kasˈtrare] /72/ VT (*gen*) to castrate; (*cavallo*) to geld; (*gatto*) to neuter, doctor (*Brit*), fix (*USA*); (*fig: iniziativa*) to frustrate

castroneria [kastroneˈria] SF (*fam*): **dire castronerie** to talk rubbish

casuale [kazuˈale] AGG chance *attr*, fortuitous

casupola [kaˈsupola] SF simple little cottage

cataclisma, -i [kataˈklizma] SM cataclysm; (*fig*) catastrophe; **sembra che ci sia stato un cataclisma qui** this place looks as though a bomb has hit it

catacomba [kataˈkomba] SF catacomb

catafascio [kataˈfaʃʃo] SM: **mandare a catafascio** to wreck; **andare a catafascio** to go to rack and ruin

catalitico, -a, -ci, -che [kataˈlitiko] AGG: **marmitta catalitica** catalytic converter

catalizzare [katalidˈdzare] /72/ VT (*anche fig*) to act as a catalyst (up)on

catalizzato, -a [katalidˈdzato] AGG (*Aut*) fitted with a catalytic converter

catalizzatore [kataliddzaˈtore] SM (*Aut*) catalytic converter; (*Chim, fig*) catalyst

Catalogna [kataˈloɲɲa] SF Catalonia

catalogo [kaˈtaloɡo] SM catalogue

catanese [kataˈnese] AGG of *o* from Catania ♦ SM, SF inhabitant *o* native of Catania

catanzarese [katandzaˈrese] AGG of *o* from Catanzaro ♦ SM, SF inhabitant *o* native of Catanzaro

catapecchia [kataˈpekkja] SF hovel

catapulta [kataˈpulta] SF catapult

catarifrangente [katarifranˈdʒɛnte] AGG reflecting ♦ SM reflector

catarro [kaˈtarro] SM catarrh

catarsi [kaˈtarsi] SF INV catharsis

catasta [kaˈtasta] SF pile, stack

catasto [kaˈtasto] SM (*Amm: inventario*) land register, cadaster; (*anche: ufficio del catasto*) land registry (office)

catastrofe [kaˈtastrofe] SF catastrophe, disaster

catastrofico, -a, -ci, -che [katasˈtrɔfiko] AGG (*evento*) catastrophic, disastrous; (*persona, previsione*) pessimistic

catastrofista, -i, catastrofisti, -e, catastrofiste AGG, SM, SF doom-monger; **non fare il catastrofista** don't be so pessimistic

catechismo [kateˈkizmo] SM catechism

categoria [kateɡoˈria] SF (*gen*) category; (*di albergo*) class; **di terza categoria** (*albergo, locale, anche pegg*) third-class

categorico, -a, -ci, -che [kateˈɡɔriko] AGG (*gen*) categorical; (*rifiuto*) categorical, flat

catena [kaˈtena] SF (*gen, di negozi*) chain; (*di montagne*) range, chain; (*fig: legame*) bond, chain; **reazione a catena** (*anche fig*) chain reaction; **susseguirsi a catena** to happen in quick succession; **tenere un cane alla catena** to keep a dog on a chain; **catena alimentare** food chain; **catena di montaggio** (*Tecn*) assembly line; **catena di Sant'Antonio** chain letter; **catena umana** human chain; **catene da neve** (*Aut*) snow chains

catenaccio, -ci [kateˈnattʃo] SM bolt; **chiudere con il catenaccio** to bolt; **fare catenaccio** (*Calcio*) to play defensively

catenella [kateˈnella] SF (*ornamento*) chain; (*di orologio*) watch chain; (*di porta*) door chain; **punto catenella** (*in ricamo, maglia*) chain stitch

cate'nina SF (*gioiello*) (thin) chain

cateratta [kateˈratta] SF **1** (*Med, Geog*) cataract **2** (*saracinesca*) sluice(gate)

caterva [kaˈtɛrva] SF (*di cose*) loads *pl*, heaps *pl*; (*di persone*) horde

catetere [kateˈtɛre] SM (*Med*) catheter

catinella [katiˈnella] SF basin; **piovere a catinelle** to rain cats and dogs

catino [kaˈtino] SM basin

catodico, -a, -ci, -che [kaˈtɔdiko] AGG cathode *attr*; **tubo a raggi catodici** cathode-ray tube

catorcio, -ci [kaˈtɔrtʃo] SM (*pegg*) old wreck

catrame [kaˈtrame] SM tar

cattedra [ˈkattedra] SF **1** (*mobile*) (teacher's) desk; **cattedra episcopale** bishop's throne; **salire** *o* **montare in cattedra** (*fig*) to pontificate **2** (*incarico: Scol*) teaching post; (: *Univ*) chair, professorship

cattedrale [katteˈdrale] SF cathedral

cattedratico, -a, -ci, -che [katteˈdratiko] AGG (*insegnamento*) university *attr*; (*pegg*) pedantic ♦ SM professor

cattiveria [kattiˈverja] SF **1** (*qualità*) wickedness, nastiness; (*di bambino*) naughtiness; **lo ha fatto per pura cattiveria** he did it out of sheer spite **2** (*azione*) nasty *o* wicked action; **fare una cattiveria** to do something nasty *o* wicked;

(*bambino*) to be naughty **3** (*discorso*): **dire una cattiveria to say sth spiteful**

cattività [katti'ta] SF (*di animali*) captivity

cattivo, -a [kat'tivo] AGG **1** (*persona, azione*) bad, wicked; (*bambino: birichino*) naughty, bad; **un bambino cattivo** a naughty boy; **brutto cattivo!** you naughty boy!; **quel ragazzo è un cattivo soggetto** that boy's a bit of a rascal; **farsi cattivo sangue** to worry, get in a state; **farsi un cattivo nome** to earn a bad reputation for o.s., **earn o.s.** a bad reputation **2** (*di qualità: gen*) bad; (*odore, sapore*) bad, nasty; (*cibo guasto*) off; (*insegnante, salute*) bad, poor; (*mare*) rough; **è sempre di cattivo umore** he's always in a bad mood; **ha un cattivo odore** it's got a nasty smell; **con le buone o con le cattive (maniere)** by hook or by crook ♦ SM, SF bad *o* wicked person; (*nei film*) villain; **fa sempre la parte del cattivo** he always plays the villain; **fare il cattivo** (*bambino*) to be naughty; **i cattivi** (*nei film*) the baddies (*Brit*), the bad guys (*USA*)

cattocomunista, -i, -e AGG combining Catholic and Communist ideas ♦ SM, SF Catholic-communist

cattolicesimo [kattoli't'ʃezimo] SM Catholicism

cattolico, -a, -ci, -che [kat'tɔliko] AGG, SM, SF (Roman) Catholic

cattura [kat'tura] SF capture; **ordine di cattura** (*Dir*) warrant of *o* for arrest

catturare [kattu'rare] /72/ VT (*gen, anche fig: attenzione*) to capture, catch

caucasico, -a, -ci, -che [kau'kaziko] AGG, SM, SF Caucasian

Caucaso [kaukazo] SM: **il Caucaso** the Caucasus

caucciù [kaut'tʃu] SM INV India rubber

causa ['kauza] SF **1** (*motivo, ragione*) cause, reason; (*ideale*) cause; **quella è stata la causa principale** that was the main cause; **essere causa di qc** to be the cause of sth, be the reason for sth; **l'aeroporto è chiuso a causa della nebbia** the airport is closed because of the fog; **per causa sua** because of him; **causa persa** (*anche fig*) lost cause; **far causa comune** to make common cause; **giusta causa** true and just cause **2** (*Dir*) case, lawsuit, action; **intentare** *o* **fare** *o* **muovere causa a qn** to sue sb; **mi ha fatto causa** he sued me; **perorare una causa** to plead a case; **parte in causa** litigant; **tu non sei parte in causa in tutto ciò** all this doesn't concern you; **rimettere qc in causa** (*fig*) to bring sth up again **3** (*Gramm*): **complemento di causa** complement of cause

causale [kau'zale] AGG (*rapporto, nesso, anche Gramm*) causal ♦ SF cause, reason; **causale di versamento** (*Amm*) description of payment

causare [kau'zare] /72/ VT to cause; **potrebbe causare dei problemi** it might cause problems

caustico, -a, -ci, -che ['kaustiko] AGG (*Chim, anche fig*) caustic

cautela [kau'tela] SF **1** (*prudenza*) caution, prudence; **"maneggiare con cautela"** "handle with care" **2** (*precauzione*) precaution

cautelare [kaute'lare] /72/ VT to protect; **cautelarsi** VR: **cautelarsi (da** *o* **contro)** to take precautions (against)

cauto, -a ['kauto] AGG prudent, cautious; **andare cauto** (*fig*) to tread carefully

cauzionare [kauttsjo'nare] /72/ VT to guarantee

cauzione [kaut'tsjone] SF **1** (*Dir: deposito*) security, guarantee; (: *per libertà provvisoria*) bail; **rilasciare dietro cauzione** to release on bail **2** (*somma*) caution money

cav. ABBR = **cavaliere**

cava ['kava] SF quarry (*Geol*)

❑ **cava** non si traduce mai con *cave*

cavalcare [kaval'kare] /20/ VT (*sogg: persona: cavallo*) to ride; (: *muro*) to sit astride; (*sogg: ponte*) to span ♦ VI (*aus avere*) (*andare a cavallo*) to ride; **sai cavalcare?** can you ride?; **andare a cavalcare** to go riding

cavalcata [kaval'kata] SF ride; **fare una cavalcata** to go for a ride; **abbiamo fatto una cavalcata nel bosco** we went for a ride in the woods

cavalcavia [kavalka'via] SM INV flyover (*Brit*), overpass (*USA*); (*sopra ferrovia*) railway bridge

cavalcioni [kaval'tʃoni] **a cavalcioni (di)** AVV astride; **era seduto a cavalcioni del muretto** he was sitting astride the wall

cavaliere [kava'ljere] SM **1** rider, horseman; (*Mil*) cavalryman, trooper **2** (*accompagnatore*) escort; (*nel ballo*) partner; (*gentiluomo*) gentleman **3** (*titolo, anche Storia*) knight; **l'hanno fatto cavaliere del lavoro** he has been knighted for services to industry

cavalleggero [kavalled'dʒero] SM light cavalryman

cavalleresco, -a, -schi, -sche [kavalle'resko] AGG knightly; (*fig: comportamento*) chivalrous, noble; **poema cavalleresco** poem of chivalry

cavalleria [kavalle'ria] SF **1** (*Mil*) cavalry **2** (*Storia, anche fig*: *lealtà, cortesia*) chivalry

cavallerizzo, -a [kavalle'rittso] SM, SF (*nel circo*) circus rider; (*maestro di equitazione*) riding instructor

cavalletta [kaval'letta] SF (*Zool*) grasshopper; (*dannosa*) locust

cavalletto [kaval'letto] SM (*supporto*) trestle; (*da pittore*) easel; (*Fot*) tripod

cavallina [kaval'lina] SF **1** (*Zool*) filly **2** (*gioco*) leapfrog **3** (*attrezzo ginnico*) (vaulting) horse; **correre la cavallina** (*fig*) to sow one's wild oats

cavallo [ka'vallo] SM **1** horse; **ti piacciono i cavalli?** do you like horses?; **a cavallo** on horseback; **a cavallo di** (*sedia, moto, bici*) astride, straddling; **andare a cavallo** to go on horseback, ride; **sai andare a cavallo?** can you ride?; **essere a cavallo** (*fig*) we've made it; **montare a/scendere da cavallo** to mount/dismount; **denti da cavallo** horsy teeth; **da cavallo** (*fig: dose*) drastic; (: *febbre*) raging; **a cavallo tra** halfway between; **vivere a cavallo tra due periodi** to straddle two periods; **a caval donato non si guarda in bocca** (*Proverbio*) don't look a gift horse in the mouth **2** (*dei pantaloni*) crotch; (*Scacchi*) knight; (*attrezzo ginnico*) (vaulting) horse **3** (*anche: cavallo vapore*) horsepower ♦ **cavallo di battaglia** (*Teatro*) tour de force; (*fig*) hobby-horse; **cavallo da corsa** racehorse; **cavallo a dondolo** rocking horse; **cavallo di Frisia** (*Mil*) cheval-de-frise; **cavallo purosangue** *o* **di razza** thoroughbred; **cavallo di sella** saddle horse; **cavallo da soma** packhorse; **cavallo vincente** (*lett*) winning horse; (*fig: persona*) (surefire) winner

cavare [ka'vare] /72/ VT **1** (*gen*) to take out, draw out; (*marmo*) to extract; (*dente*) to pull, extract; (*informazioni, soldi*) to obtain, get; **cavare gli occhi a qn** (*anche fig*) to scratch sb's eyes out; **me l'hai cavato di bocca** you took the words out of my mouth; **non gli ho cavato una parola (di bocca)** I couldn't get a word out of him **2** **cavarsi** (*capriccio, voglia*) to satisfy; (*fame*) to satisfy, appease; (*sete*) to quench, slake; (*giacca, scarpe*) to take off; **cavarsi il pane di bocca** (*fig*) to make sacrifices **3** **cavarsela** (*farcela*) to manage, get on all right; (*da impiccio*) to find a way out; **come te la cavi?** how are things?; **cavarsela (a buon mercato)** to come off lightly, get away with it; **se l'è cavata bene** (*in un processo*) he got off lightly; (*in un esame*) he did quite well; **se l'è cavata con qualche graffio** she came out of it with only a few scratches

cavatappi [kava'tappi], **cavaturaccioli** [kavatu'ratt'ʃoli] SM INV corkscrew

caverna [ka'verna] SF cave, cavern; **uomo delle caverne** caveman

cavernoso, -a [kaver'noso] AGG (*voce*) deep

cavezza [ka'vettsa] SF halter

cavia ['kavja] SF (*anche fig*) guinea pig; **fare da cavia** to act as a guinea pig

caviale [ka'vjale] SM caviar

caviglia [ka'viʎʎa] SF (*Anat*) ankle; (*cavicchio*) pin, peg

cavillare [kavil'lare] /72/ VI (*aus avere*) to quibble, split hairs

cavillo [ka'villo] SM quibble

cavilloso, -a [kavil'loso] AGG quibbling, hairsplitting

cavità [kavi'ta] SF INV hollow; (*Anat*) cavity; **cavità sotterranea** underground cave

cavo¹, -a ['kavo] AGG hollow ♦ SM (*Anat*) cavity

cavo² ['kavo] SM (*gen, anche Tecn, Telec*) cable; (*Naut*) rope; **televisione via cavo** cable television; **cavo di traino** (*Aut*) tow rope

cavolata [kavo'lata] SF (*fam*) stupid thing, foolish thing; **dire cavolate** to talk rubbish *o* nonsense; **fare cavolate** to do stupid things

cavolfiore [kavol'fjore] SM cauliflower

cavolo [ˈkavolo] SM 1 (*Bot*) cabbage; **una minestra di cavolo** cabbage soup; **cavolo cappuccio** spring cabbage; **cavolo da foraggio** kale; **questo c'entra come il cavolo a merenda** that's completely beside the point 2 (*fam, euf: per cazzo*): **non fa un cavolo dalla mattina alla sera** he doesn't do a damn thing from morning till night; **non m'importa un cavolo** I don't give a damn; **che cavolo vuoi?** what the heck do you want?; **cavolo!** (*imprecazione*) damn!; (*di ammirazione*) wow!; **ci presterà la macchina? — sì, col cavolo!** will she lend us the car? — fat chance!

cazzata [katˈtsata] SF (*fam!: stupidaggine*) stupid thing, something stupid; **dire cazzate** to talk crap (*fam!*); **ha fatto un'altra delle sue cazzate!** he's boobed again!, he's ballsed things up again; **quel film è una vera cazzata** that film is a load of crap (*fam!*)

cazzo [ˈkattso] SM 1 (*fam!: pene*) prick (*fam!*) 2 (*fig: fam!*): **non gliene importa un cazzo** he doesn't give a shit (*fam!*) o fuck (*fam!*) about it; **che cazzo vuoi?** what the fuck (*fam!*) do you want?; **cazzo!** fuck! (*fam!*); **testa di cazzo** dickhead (*fam!*), prick (*fam!*); **che film del cazzo** what a crap (*fam!*) film!; **grazie al cazzo!** thanks for nothing!; **stare sul cazzo a qn** to get up sb's nose

cazzotto [katˈtsɔtto] SM punch; **tirare un cazzotto** to throw a punch; **fare a cazzotti** to have a punch-up (*Brit*), to have a fist fight (*USA*)

cazzuola [katˈtswɔla], **cazzola** [katˈtsɔla] SF trowel

CB SIGLA = Campobasso ♦ SIGLA M INV (= *Citizens' Band*) CB radio

CC ABBR = Carabinieri

cc ABBR (= *centimetro cubo*) cc

C.C. ABBR = codice civile

c.c. ABBR 1 (= *conto corrente*) c/a, a/c 2 (*Elettr*: = *corrente continua*) DC

CCD [tʃitʃiˈdi] SIGLA M (*Pol*: = *Centro Cristiano Democratico*) Christian Democratic Centre (*Italian political party of the centre*)

CD [tʃiˈdi] SM INV (= *compact disc*) CD; (*lettore*) CD player ♦ ABBR (= *Corpo Diplomatico*) CD

cd. ABBR = cosiddetto

C.d.A. [tʃidiˈa] SIGLA M = consiglio d'amministrazione; *vedi* consiglio

c.d.d. ABBR (= *come dovevasi dimostrare*) QED (= *quod erat demonstrandum*)

CD-ROM [tʃidiˈrɔm] SM INV (= *Compact Disc Read Only Memory*) CD-Rom

C.D.U. [tʃidiˈu] SIGLA M (= *Cristiano Democratici Uniti*) United Christian Democrats (*Italian centre-right political party*)

CE SIGLA = Caserta ♦ [tʃiˈe] SIGLA F 1 = Consiglio d'Europa 2 = Comunità Europea

ce [tʃe] PRON, AVV *vedi* ci

cecchino [tʃekˈkino] SM sniper; (*Pol*) *member of parliament who votes against his own party*

cece [ˈtʃetʃe] SM chickpea, garbanzo (*USA*)

Cecenia [tʃeˈtʃɛnja] SF Chechnya

ceceno, -a [tʃeˈtʃɛno] AGG, SM, SF Chechen

cecità [tʃetʃiˈta] SF blindness; **cecità da neve** snow blindness

ceco, -a, -chi, -che [ˈtʃɛko] AGG, SM, SF Czech; **la Repubblica ceca** the Czech Republic ♦ SM (*lingua*) Czech

Cecoslovacchia [tʃekozloˈvakkja] SF Czechoslovakia

cecoslovacco, -a, -chi, -che [tʃekozloˈvakko] AGG, SM, SF Czechoslovakian

CED [tʃed] SIGLA M = centro elaborazione dati

cedere [ˈtʃɛdere] /29/ VT 1 (*concedere*): **cedere qc (a qn)** to give sth up (to sb); (*eredità, diritto*) to transfer sth (to sb), make sth over (to sb); **cedere il posto a qn** (*in autobus*) to give sb one's seat; **le ho ceduto il posto** I gave her my seat; **cedere il passo (a qn)** to let (sb) pass in front; **cedere il passo a qc** (*fig*) to give way to sth; **cedere la parola (a qn)** to hand over (to sb) 2 (*Comm: vendere*) to sell; **"cedo", "cedesi" "for sale"** ♦ VI 1 (*crollare: persona*) to give in; (*: terreno*) to give way, subside; (*: muro*) to collapse, fall down; **la sedia a sdraio ha ceduto sotto il suo peso** the deckchair collapsed under his weight; **il suo cuore ha ceduto** his heart couldn't take the strain; **ha insistito tanto che alla fine ho**

ceduto she was so insistent that in the end I gave in 2 (*soccombere*): **cedere a** to give way to, to surrender to, yield to, give in to 3 (*deformarsi: tessuto, scarpe*) to give

cedevole [tʃeˈdevole] AGG (*materiale*) supple, pliable, yielding; (*terreno*) soft

cedola [ˈtʃɛdola] SF (*Comm, Fin*) coupon, voucher; (*di assegno*) counterfoil

cedrata [tʃeˈdrata] SF citron juice

cedro¹ [ˈtʃɛdro] SM (*frutto, albero*) citron

cedro² [ˈtʃɛdro] SM (*legno, albero*) cedar; **cedro bianco** Lawson's cypress; **cedro del Libano** cedar of Lebanon

CEE [ˈtʃee] SIGLA F (= *Comunità Economica Europea*) EEC (= *European Economic Community*)

ceffo [ˈtʃeffo] SM (*pegg*) ugly mug

ceffone [tʃefˈfone] SM slap, smack; **dare un ceffone a qn** slap sb

ceko, -a [ˈtʃeko] AGG, SM, SF = ceco

celare [tʃeˈlare] /72/ VT to conceal; **celare qc alla vista di qn** to conceal sth from sb; **celarsi** VR (*nascondersi*) to hide, conceal o.s.; (*stare nascosto*) to be hidden, be concealed

celebrare [tʃeleˈbrare] /72/ VT (*messa, matrimonio, festa*) to celebrate; (*cerimonia*) to hold; **celebrare le lodi di qn/qc** to sing the praises of sb/sth

celebrazione [tʃelebratˈtsjone] SF celebration

celebre [ˈtʃɛlebre] AGG famous, celebrated

celebrità [tʃelebriˈta] SF INV (*fama, notorietà*) fame; (*persona*) celebrity; **arrivare alla celebrità** to become famous; **raggiungere la celebrità** to rise to fame

celere [ˈtʃɛlere] AGG quick, fast, swift; (*Scol, Univ: corso*) crash *attr* ♦ SF (*Polizia*) riot police

celeste [tʃeˈlɛste] AGG 1 (*colore*) pale blue, sky-blue; **una gonna celeste** a pale blue skirt; **ha gli occhi celesti** she's got blue eyes 2 (*di cielo*) celestial; (*divino*) heavenly, celestial; **la volta celeste** the vault o canopy of heaven ♦ SM (*colore*) pale blue, sky blue

celia [ˈtʃɛlja] SF joke; **per celia** as a joke, in jest

celibato [tʃeliˈbato] SM celibacy

celibe [ˈtʃɛlibe] AGG single, unmarried; (*prete*) celibate ♦ SM single o unmarried man, bachelor

cella [ˈtʃɛlla] SF cell; **cella a combustione** (*Fis*) fuel cell; **cella frigorifera** cold store; **cella di isolamento**; **essere in cella di isolamento** to be in solitary confinement; **cella di rigore** punishment cell; **cella a secco** (*Chim*) dry cell

cellula [ˈtʃɛllula] SF (*in ogni senso*) cell; **cellula nervosa** neuron, nerve cell; **cellula uovo** ovum

cellulare [tʃelluˈlare] AGG cellular; **differenziazione/divisione cellulare** (*Bio*) cell differentiation/division; **segregazione cellulare** (*Dir*) solitary confinement ♦ SM (*furgone*) police van; (*telefono*) cellphone

cellulite [tʃelluˈlite] SF cellulitis; **una crema contro la cellulite** an anti-cellulite cream

celta [ˈtʃɛlta] SM, SF Celt

celtico, -a, -ci, -che [ˈtʃɛltiko] AGG, SM Celtic

cembalo [ˈtʃembalo] SM (*Mus*) harpsichord

cementare [tʃemenˈtare] /72/ VT (*anche fig*) to cement

cemento [tʃeˈmento] SM cement; **cemento armato** reinforced concrete

cena [ˈtʃena] SF dinner; (*leggera*) supper; **invitare qn a cena** to invite sb to dinner; **mi hanno invitato a cena** they've invited me to dinner; **vieni a cena da noi?** would you like to come and have dinner with us?; **andare fuori a cena** to go out for dinner; **ti telefono all'ora di cena** I'll phone you at dinner time; **l'Ultima Cena** (*Rel*) the Last Supper

cenacolo [tʃeˈnakolo] SM (*circolo*) coterie, circle; (*Rel: dipinto*) (the) Last Supper

cenare [tʃeˈnare] /72/ VI (*aus avere*) to have dinner, dine; **hai cenato?** have you had dinner?

cencio, -ci [ˈtʃentʃo] SM (*straccio*) rag; (*per pulire*) cloth; (*per spolverare*) duster; **vestito di cenci** dressed in rags; **essere ridotto a un cencio** to feel washed out; **essere bianco come un cencio** to be as white as a sheet

cenere [ˈtʃenere] SF ash, ashes *pl*; (*di carbone, legno*) cinders *pl*; **ceneri** SFPL ashes; **biondo cenere** ash blonde

Cenerentola [tʃeneˈrentola] SF (*anche fig*) Cinderella

cenno [ˈtʃenno] SM 1 (*segno*) sign, signal; (*con la testa*) nod;

(*con gli occhi*) wink; (*con la mano*) gesture; (*di saluto*) wave; **capirsi/parlare a cenni** to understand each other/speak with gestures; **cenno d'intesa** sign of agreement; **fare cenno di sì/no** to nod (one's head)/shake one's head; **mi fece un cenno di saluto con la mano/con la testa** he waved/nodded to me; **far cenno di no** (*con il dito*) to wag one's finger; **far cenno a qn** to gesture to sb; **mi ha fatto cenno di avvicinarmi** he beckoned to me to come forward **2** (*breve esposizione*) mention, short account; (*allusione*) hint; **fare cenno a qn/qc** to mention sb/sth; **cenni di storia dell'arte** an outline of the history of art **3** (*indizio*) sign; **al primo cenno di pioggia** at the first sign of rain

censimento [tʃensi'mento] SM census; **fare il censimento** to take a census

censire [tʃen'sire] /55/ VT: **censire qc** to take a census of sth

censore [tʃen'sore] SM (*anche Storia*) censor; (*fig: critico*) critic

censura [tʃen'sura] SF (*Psic, Cine, Stampa: controllo*) censors; (*ufficio*) board of censors, censor's office; (*fig, o Pol, Rel*) censure

censurare [tʃensu'rare] /72/ VT (*Psic, Cine, Stampa*) to censor; (*fig, o Pol, Rel*) to censure

cent. ABBR = centesimo

centellinare [tʃentelli'nare] /72/ VT to sip; (*fig*) to savour (*Brit*), savor (*USA*)

centenario, -ria, -ri, -rie [tʃente'narjo] AGG **1** (*che ha cento anni*) hundred-year-old; **un edificio centenario** a (one) hundred-year-old building **2** (*che ricorre ogni cento anni*) centennial *attr*, centenary *attr* ♦ SM, SF (*persona*) centenarian ♦ SM (*anniversario*) centenary, centennial (*USA*)

centesimo, -a [tʃen'tezimo] AGG hundredth ♦ SM (*centesima parte*) hundredth; (*moneta: di dollaro, euro*) cent; **costa ottanta centesimi** it costs eighty cents; **non vale un centesimo** it's not worth a penny (*Brit*) o one red cent (*USA*); **essere senza un centesimo** to be penniless; **pochi centesimi di secondo** a few hundredths of a second

centigrado, -a [tʃen'tigrado] AGG centigrade; **20 gradi centigradi** 20 degrees centigrade

centilitro [tʃen'tilitro] SM centilitre (*Brit*), centiliter (*USA*)

centimetro [tʃen'timetro] SM **1** (*misura*) centimetre (*Brit*), centimeter (*USA*); **lungo venti centimetri** twenty centimetres long **2** (*nastro*) measuring tape (*in centimetres*)

centinaio [tʃenti'najo] SM (*pl f* **centinaia**) hundred; **un centinaio di** about a hundred; **un centinaio di persone** about a hundred people, a hundred or so people; **centinaia hundreds**; **ci sono stato centinaia di volte** I've been there hundreds of times; **diverse centinaia di sterline** several hundred pounds; **a centinaia** (*merce: vendere*) by the hundred; (*persone: venire*) in (their) hundreds

cento ['tʃento] AGG INV a hundred, one hundred; **centouno** one o a hundred and one; **seicento** six hundred; **cento di questi giorni!** many happy returns (of the day)! ♦ SM INV a hundred, one hundred; **per cento** per cent; **cinque per cento** five per cent; **al cento per cento** a hundred per cent; **ne sono sicuro al cento per cento** I'm a hundred per cent sure; **cento di questi giorni!** many happy returns!; *vedi* **cinque**

centodieci [tʃento'djetʃi] AGG, SM INV one hundred and ten; **laurearsi con centodieci e lode** (*Univ*) ≈ to graduate with first-class honours (*Brit*), ≈ to graduate summa cum laude (*USA*)

centomila [tʃento'mila] AGG INV a o one hundred thousand; **te l'ho detto centomila volte** (*fig*) I've told you a thousand times

centrale [tʃen'trale] AGG (*gen*) central; (*stazione, ufficio*) main; **dov'è la stazione centrale?** where's the main station?; **l'albergo è molto centrale** the hotel is very central; **sede centrale** head office; **la sede centrale è a Roma** the head office is in Rome ♦ SF (*sede principale*) head office; **centrale elettrica** power station o plant (*USA*); **centrale del latte** dairy; **centrale nucleare** nuclear power station o plant (*USA*); **centrale di polizia** police headquarters *pl*; **centrale telefonica** (telephone) exchange; **centrale termoelettrica** thermal power station o plant (*USA*)

centralinista, -i, -e [tʃentrali'nista] SM, SF (*Telec*) operator; (*in ditta, albergo*) switchboard operator

centralino [tʃentra'lino] SM (*Telec*) (telephone) exchange; (*di ditta, albergo*) switchboard

centralizzare [tʃentralid'dzare] /72/ VT to centralize

centraliz'zato, -a, centralizzata [tʃentralid'dzato] AGG central

centrare [tʃen'trare] /72/ VT (*gen*) to hit the centre (*Brit*) o center (*USA*) of; (*Sport, Tecn*) to centre; (*bersaglio*) to hit in the centre; **centrare (in pieno)** (*freccette*) to score a bull's eye; **centrare una risposta** to get the right answer; **hai centrato il problema** you've hit the nail on the head

centra'vanti [tʃentra'vanti] SM INV centre forward

centrifuga, -ghe [tʃen'trifuga] SF (*Tecn*) centrifuge; (*di lavatrice*) spin-dryer; **centrifuga lunga/corta** long/short spin; **centrifuga elettrica** juice extractor; **centrifuga scolaverdure** (*Culin*) salad spinner

centrifugare [tʃentrifu'gare] /80/ VT (*Tecn*) to centrifuge; (*biancheria*) to spin-dry; (*Culin: verdura, frutta*) to extract the juice from

centro ['tʃentro] SM (*gen*) centre (*Brit*), center (*USA*); (*di città*) (town o city) centre; (*di bersaglio*) bull's eye; **al centro della piazza c'è una fontana** there's a fountain in the centre of the square; **siamo andati in centro a fare spese** we went into the town centre to do some shopping; **abiti in centro o in periferia?** do you live in the town centre or in the suburbs?; **fare centro** to hit the bull's eye; (*Calcio*) to score; (*fig*) to hit the nail on the head ♦ **centri vitali** (*anche fig*) vital organs; **centro di accoglienza** reception centre; **centro balneare** seaside resort; **centro benessere** wellness centre; **centro commerciale** shopping centre o mall (*USA*); (*città*) commercial centre; **centro di costo** cost centre; **centro elaborazione dati** data-processing unit; **centro nervoso** (*Anat*) nerve centre; **centro ospedaliero** hospital complex; **centro di ricerche** research centre; **centro sociale** community centre; **centro sportivo** sports centre; **centro storico** old town

centrodestra [tʃentro'destra] SM (*Pol*) centre right

centromediano [tʃentrome'djano] SM (*Calcio*) centre half

centrosinistra [tʃentrosi'nistra] SM (*Pol*) centre left

ceppo ['tʃeppo] SM **1** (*di albero*) (tree) stump; (*fig: genealogico*) stock **2** (*ciocco*) log; (*per decapitazione*) (chopping) block **3** (*di aratro, ancora*) stock; (*Tecn*) brake shoe **4 ceppi** SMPL (*di prigioniero*) shackles, fetters

cera ['tʃera] SF **1** (*sostanza*) wax; **cera per pavimenti** floor polish; **dare la cera (a qc)** to polish (sth); **museo delle cere** waxworks *sg*; **cera d'api** beeswax **2** (*fig: aspetto*): **avere una bella/brutta cera** to look well/ill

ceralacca [tʃera'lakka] SF sealing wax

ceramica [tʃe'ramika] SF **1** (*materiale*) baked clay, ceramic; (*Arte*) ceramics *sg*; **una tazza di ceramica** a china cup **2 ceramiche** SFPL pottery

cerbiatto [tʃer'bjatto] SM (*animale*) fawn

cerca ['tʃerka] SF: **andare/essere in cerca di** to go/be looking for, go/be in search of

cercapersone [tʃerkaper'sone] SM INV pager, bleeper (*Brit*), beeper (*USA*)

cercare [tʃer'kare] /20/ VT (*gen*) to look for, search for; (*fama, gloria*) to seek; **le ho cercate dappertutto** I've looked for them everywhere; **l'hai cercato sul dizionario?** have you looked it up in the dictionary?; **cercare lavoro/casa** to look for work/a house; **stai cercando lavoro?** are you looking for a job?; **cercare moglie/marito** to be looking for a wife/husband; **cercare qn con gli occhi** to look round for sb; **cercare le parole** to search for words; **cercare guai** to be looking for trouble; **cercare fortuna** to seek one's fortune ♦ VI (*aus avere*) **cercare di fare qc** to try to do sth; **cerca di non far tardi** try not to be late; **ho cercato di spiegargli il motivo** I tried to explain the reason to him

cercherò *ecc* [tʃerke'rɔ] VB *vedi* **cercare**

cerchia ['tʃerkja] SF (*anche fig*) circle; **cerchia di mura** city walls

cerchiato, -a [tʃer'kjato] AGG: **occhiali cerchiati d'osso** horn-rimmed spectacles; **hai gli occhi cerchiati** you've got dark rings under your eyes

cerchietto [tʃer'kjetto] SM **1** (*per capelli*) hairband; **cerchietto d'oro** (*anello*) gold band **2** (*gioco*): **cerchietti** SMPL game *between 2 players in which each tries to throw a hoop over the other's stick*

cerchio, -chi [tʃerkjo] SM (*gen, anche Geom: di persone*) circle; (*di ruota*) rim; (*giocattolo, di botte*) hoop; **mettersi in cerchio** to stand in a circle; **eravamo seduti in cerchio** we were sitting in a circle; **dare un colpo al cerchio e uno alla botte** (*fig*) to keep two things going at the same time; **avere un cerchio alla testa** (*fig: mal di testa*) to have a headache; **cerchi in lega leggera** (*Aut*) light-alloy wheels

cerchione [tʃerkjone] SM (*wheel*)rim

cereale [tʃereale] AGG, SM cereal

cerebrale [tʃerebrale] AGG cerebral

cerimonia [tʃerimɔnja] SF 1 ceremony; (*Rel*) service 2 **cerimonie** SFPL ceremony *sg*; **fare cerimonie** to stand on ceremony; **senza tante cerimonie** (*senza formalità*) informally; (*bruscamente*) unceremoniously, without so much as a by-your-leave

cerimoniale [tʃerimonjale] SM (*regole*) ritual, custom, etiquette; (*libro*) book of etiquette, ceremonial; **cerimoniale di corte** court etiquette

cerimoniere [tʃerimonjɛre] SM master of ceremonies

cerimonioso, -a [tʃerimonjoso] AGG ceremonious, formal

cerino [tʃerino] SM (*fiammifero*) wax match; (*stoppino*) taper; **una scatola di cerini** a box of wax matches

CERN [tʃɛrn] SIGLA M (= *Consiglio Europeo per la Ricerca Nucleare*) CERN

cernia [tʃɛrnja] SF (*anche:* **cernia gigante**) groper; (*anche:* **cernia di fondo**) stone bass

cerniera [tʃernjɛra] SF (*di porte, finestre*) hinge; (*di abito: anche:* **cerniera lampo**) zip (fastener) (*Brit*), zipper (*USA*); (*di bracciale*) clasp

cernita [tʃernita] SF selection; **fare una cernita di** to select

cero [tʃero] SM (*church*) candle

cerone [tʃerone] SM (*trucco*) greasepaint

cerotto [tʃerɔtto] SM (*Med*) (sticking) plaster (*Brit*), adhesive bandage (*USA*)

certamente [tʃertamente] AVV certainly, surely

certezza [tʃertettsa] SF certainty; **avere la certezza che...** to be certain *o* sure that ...; **sapere con certezza che...** to know for sure that ...

certificare [tʃertifikare] /20/ VT to certify

certificato [tʃertifikato] SM certificate; **certificato azionario** share certificate; **certificato di credito del Tesoro** government bond, treasury bill (*USA*); **certificato di matrimonio** marriage certificate; **certificato medico** doctor's certificate, medical certificate; **certificato di nascita** birth certificate

certificazione [tʃertifikatstsjone] SF 1 (*di documento*) certification 2 **certificazione di bilancio** (*Econ*) external audit

certo, -a [tʃerto] AGG 1 (*dopo sostantivo: sicuro: gen*) certain; (: *prova*) positive, definite; **è cosa certa** it's quite certain, there's no doubt about it; **è un sintomo certo di malattia** it's a sure sign of illness 2 (*sicuro*) certain, sure; **essere certo di qc/di fare qc** to be sure *o* certain of sth/of doing sth; **sono certo che verrà** I'm sure she'll come; **ne sono più che certo** I'm absolutely sure of it; **non sono certo di poter venire** I'm not sure I can come ♦ AGG INDEF (*prima del sostantivo*) 1 certain; **devo sbrigare una certa faccenda** there is a certain matter I must attend to; **un certo signor Bonanno** a (certain) Mr Bonanno; **c'è un certo Stefano che ti cerca** someone called Stefano is looking for you; **in un certo senso** in a way, in a certain sense; **in certi casi** in some *o* certain cases; **un certo non so che** an indefinable something; **fino ad un certo punto** up to a point 2 (*con valore intensivo*) some; **certe volte** sometimes; **certe volte non ti capisco proprio!** sometimes I just don't understand you!; **avere una certa età** to be getting on; **di una certa età** past one's prime, not so young; **un fatto di una certa importanza** a fact of some importance; **certi giorni l'ufficio apre più tardi** some days the office opens later; **certa gente non è mai contenta** some people are never satisfied; **non vado a vedere certi film** I don't watch such bad films; **in quel locale c'erano certe facce!** there were some really unpleasant faces in that place! ♦ PRON INDEF PL: **certi/e** (*persone*) some (people); (*cose*) some ♦ AVV (*senz'altro*) of course; **certo che sì/no** certainly/certainly not; **posso portare un amico? — ma certo!** may I bring a friend? — yes, of course!; **certo**

che puoi! of course you can!; **sì certo** yes indeed; **no certo** certainly not ♦ SM: **di certo** certainly

certosino [tʃertozino] SM Carthusian monk; (*liquore*) chartreuse; **è un lavoro da certosino** it's a pernickety job

certuni [tʃertuni] PRON INDEF PL some (people)

cerume [tʃerume] SM (ear) wax

cerva [tʃerva] SF female (deer), doe

cervello [tʃervɛllo] SM 1 ((*Anat*) *pl f* **cervella**) brain, brains; **far saltare le cervella a qn** to blow sb's brains out 2 (*fig: intelligenza*): **avere molto cervello** to be very clever; **ha poco cervello** he's not very bright; **avere il cervello fino** to be sharp-witted; **avere il cervello di una gallina** to be brainless *o* peabrained; **dovevi avere abbastanza cervello da evitarlo** you should have had enough sense to avoid it; **gli ha dato di volta il cervello** he's gone off his head; **cervello elettronico** computer 3 (*persona*) mind; **è lui il cervello della banda?** is he the brains behind the operation?; **fuga dei cervelli** brain drain

cervicale [tʃervikale] AGG cervical

cervo [tʃervo] SM 1 (*mammifero*) deer; (*maschio*) stag; (*femmina*) doe; **carne di cervo** venison 2 (*insetto*): **cervo volante** stag beetle

cesellare [tʃezellare] /72/ VT to chisel; (*incidere*) to engrave

cesello [tʃezɛllo] SM (*strumento*) chisel; (*Arte*) engraving

cesoie [tʃezoje] SFPL shears

cespuglio, -gli [tʃespuʎʎo] SM bush

cessare [tʃessare] /72/ VI 1 (*aus essere*) (*aver termine: pioggia, vento, rumore*) to stop 2 (*aus essere*) (*smettere*): **cessare di fare qc** to stop doing sth; **non ha ancora cessato di piovere** it hasn't stopped raining yet ♦ VT to stop, put an end to; (*produzione*) to discontinue; **cessare il fuoco** (*Mil*) to cease fire; **"cessato allarme" "all clear"**

cessate il fuoco [tʃessateilfwoko] SM INV ceasefire

cessazione [tʃessatstsjone] SF cessation; (*interruzione*) suspension

cessione [tʃessjone] SF transfer

cesso [tʃesso] SM (*fam: gabinetto*) bog (*Brit*), john (*USA*); (: *pegg: luogo*) dive; **quel film era proprio un cesso** that film was a load of shit (*fam!*)

cesta [tʃesta] SF (*large*) basket

cestello [tʃestɛllo] SM (*per bottiglie*) crate; (*di lavatrice*) drum

cestinare [tʃestinare] /72/ VT to throw away; (*fig: proposta*) to turn down; (: *romanzo*) to reject

cestino [tʃestino] SM basket; (*per la carta straccia*) wastepaper basket; **un cestino di fragole** a container of strawberries; **cestino da lavoro** (*Cucito*) work basket, sewing basket; **cestino dei rifiuti** litter bin (*Brit*), trashcan (*USA*); **cestino da viaggio** packed lunch *o* dinner (*for train travellers*); **cestino di vimini** wicker basket

cesto [tʃesto] SM (*gen, anche Sport*) basket

cesura [tʃezura] SF caesura

cetaceo [tʃetatʃeo] SM sea mammal

ceto [tʃeto] SM (social) class

cetra [tʃetra] SF zither

cetriolino [tʃetriolino] SM gherkin

cetriolo [tʃetriɔlo] SM cucumber

CFC [tʃiɛffetʃi] SIGLA MPL (= *clorofluorocarburi*) CFC

cfr., cf. ABBR (= *confronta*) cf.

cg ABBR (= *centigrammo*) cg

CGIL [tʃidʒiɛlle] SIGLA F (= *Confederazione Generale Italiana del Lavoro*) trades union organization

CH SIGLA = **Chieti**

chalet [ʃaˈlɛ] SM INV chalet

champagne [ʃãˈpaɲ] SM INV champagne

chance [ʃãs] SF INV chance

charme [ʃarm] SM charm

charter [tʃaːtə] AGG INV (*volo*) charter *attr*; (*aereo*) chartered ♦ SM INV (*aereo*) chartered plane

chat line [tʃatˈlaen] SF INV (*sito*) chat room

chattare [tʃattare] /72/ VI (*aus avere*) to chat (online)

chat'tata [tʃatˈtata] SF chat

che [ke] PRON

1 (*relativo: persona: soggetto*) who; (: *oggetto*) whom, that;

(: *cosa, animale*) which, that (*spesso omesso*); **l'uomo che sta parlando** the man who is speaking; **la ragazza che hai visto** the girl whom you saw; **i bambini che vedi nel cortile** the children whom *o* that you see in the yard; **il giorno che... the day (that) ...; la sera che ti ho visto** the evening I saw you; **il libro che è sul tavolo** the book which *o* that is on the table **2** (*la qual cosa*) which; **dovrei ottenere il massimo dei voti, il che è improbabile** I would have to get top marks, which is unlikely **3** (*indefinito*): **quell'uomo ha un che di losco** there's something suspicious about that man; **un certo non so che** an indefinable something; **quel film non era un gran che** that film was nothing special; **quella donna ha un non so che di affascinante** there's something fascinating about that woman **4** (*interrogativo*) what; **che (cosa) fai?** what are you doing?; **di che (cosa) hai bisogno?** what do you need?; **non so che dire** I don't know what to say; **ma che dite!** what are you saying!

♦ AGG

1 (*interrogativo*) what; (*di numero limitato*) which; **che giorno è oggi?** what day is it today?; **che vestito ti vuoi mettere?** what (*o* which) dress do you want to put on?; **di che attore stai parlando?** which actor are you talking about?

2 (*esclamativo*) what; **che bel vestito!** what a lovely dress!; **che buono!** how delicious!; **guarda in che stato sei ridotto!** look at the mess you're in!

♦ CONG

1 (*con proposizioni subordinate*) that (*talvolta omesso*); **ero così felice che corsi a dirlo a tutti** I was so happy (that) I ran off to tell everyone; **nasconditi qui che non ti veda nessuno** hide here, so nobody can see you; **so che tu c'eri** I know (that) you were there; **voglio che ti venga** I want you to come **2** (*temporale*): **mi sono svegliato che era ancora buio** it was still dark when I woke up; **sono anni che non lo vedo** I haven't seen him for *o* in years, it's years since I saw him; **era appena uscita di casa che suonò il telefono** she had no sooner gone out than *o* she had hardly gone out when the telephone rang; **arrivai che eri già partito** you had already left when I arrived **3** (*in frasi imperative, in concessive*): **che venga pure!** let him come by all means!; **che sia benedetto!** may God bless him! **4** **non che sia stupido** not that he's stupid; **non è che non mi interessi la commedia, è che sono stanco e vorrei andare a letto** it's not that the play doesn't interest me, it's just that I'm tired and I'd like to go to bed; **che tu venga o no, noi partiamo lo stesso** we're leaving whether you come or not **5** (*comparativo*: con *più, meno*) than; **è più furbo che intelligente** he's more cunning than intelligent; *vedi* **non più, meno così**

chef [ʃef] SM INV chef
chemioterapia [kemjoteraˈpia] SF chemotherapy
cherosene [keroˈzene] SM paraffin (*Brit*), kerosene (*USA*)
cherubino [keruˈbino] SM (*anche fig*) cherub
chetare [keˈtare] /72/ VT to hush, silence; **chetarsi** VIP to quieten down, fall silent
chetichella [ketiˈkɛlla] AVV: **alla chetichella** unobtrusively, stealthily; **andarsene alla chetichella** to slip away
cheto, -a [ˈketo] AGG quiet, silent

PAROLA CHIAVE

chi [ki] PRON

1 (*interrogativo*: *soggetto*) who; (: *oggetto*) who, whom; **non sapevo a chi rivolgermi** I didn't know who to ask; **con chi desidera parlare?** who do you wish to speak to (*Brit*) or with (*USA*)?; **con chi parli?** who are you talking to?, to whom are you talking?; **di chi è questo libro?** whose book is this?, whose is this book?; **di chi stai parlando?** who are you talking about?; **dimmi chi ti piace di più tra loro** tell me which of them you like best; **ha telefonato non so chi per te** somebody or other phoned up for you; **chi l'ha visto?** who saw him?; **chi viene di voi?** which of you is coming?; **chi hai visto?** who *o* whom did you see?

2 (*relativo*) whoever, anyone who; **lo racconterò a chi so io**

I know who I'll tell about it; **lo riferirò a chi di dovere** I'll pass it on to the relevant person; **esco con chi mi pare** I'll go out with whoever I like; **so io di chi o di chi parlo** I'm naming no names; **invita chi vuoi** invite whoever *o* anyone you like; **chi arriva prima vince** whoever gets there first wins **3** (*indefinito*): **chi... chi...** some ... some ..., some ... others ...; **i bambini hanno avuto i regali: chi dolci, chi giocattoli e così via** the children have had their presents: some got sweets, others toys and so on; **chi dice una cosa, chi un'altra** some say one thing, some another **4** (*fraseologia*): **ride bene chi ride ultimo** (*Proverbio*) he who laughs last laughs longest (*Brit*) *o* best (*USA*); **si salvi chi può** every man for himself; **chi si somiglia si piglia** (*Proverbio*) birds of a feather flock together; **chi va piano va sano e va lontano** (*Proverbio*) more haste less speed

chiacchiera [ˈkjakkjera] SF **1** **chiacchiere** SFPL (*conversazione*) chatter SG; (*pettegolezzi*) gossip SG, talk SG; **fare due** *o* **quattro chiacchiere** to have a chat; **perdersi in chiacchiere** to waste time talking **2** (*loquacità*) talkativeness; **con la sua chiacchiera convincerebbe chiunque** with his gift of the gab he could persuade anyone
chiacchierare [kjakkjeˈrare] /72/ VI (*aus avere*) to chat; (*discorrere futilmente*) to chatter; (*spettegolare*) to gossip; **ci siamo fermati a chiacchierare sotto casa sua** we stopped to chat outside her house; **una relazione molto chiacchierata** a much talked about relationship
chiacchierata [kjakkjeˈrata] SF chat; **farsi una chiacchierata** to have a chat
chiacchierone, -a [kjakkjeˈrone] SM, SF chatterbox; (*pegg*) gossip ♦ AGG talkative, chatty; (*pegg*) gossipy
chiamare [kjaˈmare] /72/ VT **1** (*persona*) to call; (*nome*) to call out; (*per telefono*) to call, phone; **chiamare qn per nome** to call *o* address sb by his (*o* her) name; **chiamare qn a gran voce** to call out loudly to sb; **chiamare qn da parte** to take sb aside; **chiamare (qn in) aiuto** to call (sb) for help; **mandare a chiamare qn** to send for sb, call sb in; **mi sono fatto chiamare presto stamattina** (*svegliare*) I asked to be called early this morning; **hanno chiamato la polizia** they called the police; **l'ho chiamato ma non mi ha sentito** I called to him but he didn't hear me; **ha chiamato Loredana** Loredana phoned; **chiamare il 113** to call the police; **chiamare il 118** to call an ambulance **2** (*dare un nome*) to call, name; (*soprannominare*) to (nick)name, call; **e chiamala sfortuna!** and you call that bad luck! **3** (*Mil*): **chiamare alle armi** to call up **4** (*Dir*): **chiamare qn in giudizio** *o* **in causa** to summons sb; **non mi chiamare in causa!** (*fig*) don't bring me into it!; **chiamarsi** VIP: **come ti chiami?** — **mi chiamo Michela** what's your name? *o* what are you called? — my name is Michela *o* I'm called Michela; **questo è quello che si chiama un buon affare** that's what you call a bargain; **questa si chiama fortuna!** that's what I call luck!
chiamata [kjaˈmata] SF (*gen*) call; (*Dir*) summons; **fare una chiamata** (*Telec*) to make a (phone) call; **chiamata alle armi** (*Mil*) call-up (*Brit*), draft (*USA*); **chiamata urbana** local call; **chiamata alle urne** (*Pol*) election
chiappa [ˈkjappa] SF (*fam*: *natica*) cheek; **chiappe** SFPL backside SG; **alza le chiappe!** get up off your backside!
chiara [ˈkjara] SF (*fam*) egg white
chiarezza [kjaˈrettsa] SF (*anche fig*) clearness, clarity
chiarificare [kjarifiˈkare] /20/ VT (*anche fig*) to clarify, make clear
chiarificazione [kjarifikatˈtsjone] SF clarification *no pl*, explanation
chiarimento [kjariˈmento] SM clarification *no pl*, explanation
chiarire [kjaˈrire] /55/ VT **1** (*gen*) to clarify, make clear, explain; (*mistero, dubbio*) to clear up; **vorrei chiarire alcuni punti** I'd like to get some points clear; **alla fine il mistero è stato chiarito** in the end the mystery was solved; **chiarire le idee a qn** to clarify things for sb; **ti chiarisco io le idee!** I'll sort you out!
chiaro, -a [ˈkjaro] AGG **1** (*di colore*: *mobili, vestiti*) light-coloured; (*colore*) light; (*capelli, carnagione*) fair; **pantaloni verde chiaro** light green trousers; **ha i capelli chiari** she's got fair hair (*limpido, anche fig*) clear; (*luminoso*) bright; **si sta facendo chiaro** it's getting light, the day is dawning; **un no chiaro e tondo** a very definite no; **sarò chiaro** I'll come

to the point; **sia chiara una cosa** let's get one thing straight **3** (*evidente, ovvio*) obvious, clear; **è chiaro!** it's blatantly obvious; **non voglio averci niente a che fare, è chiaro?** I want nothing to do with it, is that clear?; **era chiaro che non se l'aspettava** he clearly wasn't expecting it ♦ SM **1** (*colore*): **vestirsi di chiaro** to wear light colours *o* light-coloured clothes **2** (*luce, luminosità*) day, daylight; **fare chiaro** to get light; **fa chiaro alle 7** it gets light at 7 o'clock; **chiaro di luna** moonlight; **mettere in chiaro qc** (*fig*) to clear sth up; **trasmissione in chiaro** (*TV*) uncoded broadcast ♦ AVV (*parlare, vedere*) clearly; **parliamoci chiaro** let's be frank

chiarore [kja'rore] SM (*diffuse*) light; **col chiarore della luna** in the moonlight

chiaroveggente [kjaroved'dʒɛnte] AGG, SM, SF clairvoyant

chiasso ['kjasso] SM din, uproar; **cos'è tutto questo chiasso?** what's all this noise?; **far chiasso** to make a din; (*fig*) to make a fuss; (*scalpore*) to cause a stir; **smettetela di fare chiasso!** be quiet!

chiassoso, -a [kjas'soso] AGG (*rumoroso*) noisy, rowdy; (*vistoso: colori*) showy, gaudy

chiatta ['kjatta] SF barge

chiave ['kjave] SF **1** (*gen, anche fig*) key; **ho perso le chiavi di casa** I've lost my house keys; **chiudere a chiave** to lock; **mi raccomando, chiudi a chiave la porta** make sure you lock the door; **tenere sotto chiave** (*anche fig*) to keep under lock and key; **prezzo chiavi in mano** (*di macchina*) on-the-road price (*Brit*), sticker price (*USA*); (*di casa*) price with immediate entry *o* possession; **in chiave politica** in political terms; **rifare qc in chiave moderna** to produce a modern version of sth; **la chiave di lettura di questo brano...** the key to an understanding of this passage ...; **chiave di basso/di violino** (*Mus*) bass/treble clef; **chiave d'accensione** (*Aut*) ignition key **2** (*Tecn*) spanner (*Brit*), wrench (*USA*); **chiave a brugola** Allen key *o* Allen wrench (*USA*); **chiave a bussola** socket wrench; **chiave a croce** spider; **chiave fissa** spanner (*Brit*), wrench (*USA*); **chiave a forcella** fork spanner (*Brit*) *o* wrench (*USA*); **chiave inglese** monkey wrench; **chiave a rullino** adjustable spanner (*Brit*) *o* wrench (*USA*); **chiave torsiometrica** *o* **tarata** torque wrench **3** (*Archit*): **chiave di volta** (*anche fig*) keystone ♦ AGG INV key *attr*

chiavistello [kjavis'tɛllo] SM bolt

chiazza ['kjattsa] SF stain, splash; **una chiazza verde sul vestito** a green mark on her dress; **chiazza di petrolio** oil slick

chiazzare [kjat'tsare] /72/ VT to stain, splash

chic [ʃik] AGG INV chic, elegant

chicchessia [kikkes'sia] PRON INDEF anyone, anybody

chicco, -chi ['kikko] SM (*di cereale, riso*) grain; (*di caffè*) bean; (*d'uva*) grape; (*di rosario*) bead; (*di grandine*) hailstone

chiedere ['kjedere] VB IRREG /21/ VT **1** (*per sapere*) to ask; (*per avere*) to ask for; (*intervista*) to ask for, request; (*intervento, volontari*) to call for; **chiedere qc a qn** to ask sb for sth, ask sb sth; **chiedi a Lidia come si chiama il suo cane** ask Lidia what her dog's called; **mi ha chiesto l'ora** he asked me the time; **ho chiesto il conto al cameriere** I asked the waiter for the bill; **mi ha chiesto degli spiccioli** he asked me for some change; **chiedersi (se)** to wonder (whether); **mi chiedo cosa stia facendo** I wonder what she's doing; **chiedere scusa a qn** to apologize to sb; **ho chiesto scusa a Marco** I apologized to Marco; **chiedo scusa!** I'm sorry!; **chiedere a qn di fare qc** *o* **che faccia qc** to ask sb to do sth; **chiedi a Giulia di spostarsi un po'** ask Giulia to move over a bit; **chiedere il permesso di fare qc** to ask permission to do sth; **chiedere notizie di qn** to inquire *o* ask after sb; **mi ha chiesto del mio viaggio** he asked me about my trip; **ci chiede di partire** he wants us *o* is asking us to go **2** (*fraseologia*): **chiedere il divorzio** to ask for a divorce; **chiedere l'elemosina** to beg; **chiedere giustizia** to demand justice; **chiedere l'impossibile** to ask (for) the impossible; **chiedere la mano di qn** to ask for sb's hand in marriage; **chiedere la pace** to sue for peace; **non chiedo altro** that's all I want; **non chiedo altro che partire con te** all I want is to leave with you ♦ VI (*aus avere*) **chiedere di qn** (*salute*) to ask about *o* after sb; (*al telefono*) to ask for sb, want sb; (*per vederlo*) to ask for sb; **tutti i miei amici chiedono di te** all my friends are asking after you; **c'è un certo Andrea che chiede di te** someone called

Andrea is looking for you; **il padrone chiede di te** the boss wants to see you

chierichetto [kjeri'ketto] SM altar boy

chierico, -ci ['kjeriko] SM (*Rel*) cleric; (*seminarista*) seminarist

chiesa ['kjɛza] SF church; **va in chiesa ogni domenica** he goes to church every Sunday; **Chiesa anglicana** Church of England; **Chiesa cattolica** (Roman) Catholic Church; **essere di chiesa** to be a churchgoer

chiesi *ecc* ['kjɛzi] VB *vedi* chiedere

chiesto, -a ['kjɛsto] PP *di* chiedere

Chigi ['kidʒi] SM: **palazzo Chigi** (*Pol*) *offices of the Italian Prime Minister*

chiglia ['kiʎʎa] SF keel

chilo ['kilo] SM kilo; **quarantacinque chili** forty five kilos; **mezzo chilo di ciliegie** half a kilo of cherries ♦ PREF: **chilo-** kilo-

chilogrammo [kilo'grammo] SM kilogram(me)

chilometraggio, -gi [kilome'traddʒo] SM (*Aut*) ≈ mileage

chilometrico, -a, -ci, -che [kilo'metriko] AGG kilometric; (*fig*) endless

chilometro [ki'lɔmetro] SM kilometre (*Brit*), kilometer (*USA*); **cinquanta chilometri all'ora** ≈ thirty miles per hour; **abbiamo camminato per dei chilometri** ≈ we walked for miles

chimico, -a, -ci, -che ['kimiko] AGG chemical; **sostanza chimica** chemical ♦ SM, SF chemist; **fa il chimico** he's a chemist

chimono [ki'mɔno] SM INV kimono

china¹ ['kina] SF (*pendio*) slope, descent; (*salita*) incline; **risalire la china** (*fig*) to be on the road to recovery

china² ['kina] SF (*inchiostro*) Indian ink

chinare [ki'nare] /72/ VT to lower, bend; **chinare il capo** (*anche fig*) to bow one's head; **chinarsi** VR to stoop, bend (over)

chincaglieria [kinkaʎʎe'ria] SF **1** (*negozio*) fancy-goods shop **2 chincaglierie** SFPL (*cianfrusaglie*) fancy goods, knick-knacks

chinino [ki'nino] SM quinine

chino, -a ['kino] AGG: **a capo chino, a testa china** head bent *o* bowed

chioccia, -ce ['kjɔttʃa] SF broody hen

chioccio, -cia, -ci, -ce ['kjɔttʃo] AGG (*voce*) clucking

chiocciola ['kjɔttʃola] SF **1** (*Zool*) snail; (*di indirizzo e-mail*) at; **scala a chiocciola** spiral staircase

chiodo ['kjɔdo] SM **1** (*Tecn*) nail; (*per lamiere*) rivet; (*da scarpone*) hobnail; (*Alpinismo*) piton; (*di scarpe da calcio*) stud; (*di scarpe da atleta, pneumatico*) spike; **chiodo a espansione** expansion bolt; **chiodo da ghiaccio** (*Alpinismo*) ice piton **2** (*Culin*): **chiodo di garofano** clove **3** (*fraseologia*): **roba da chiodi!** it's unbelievable!; **chiodo scaccia chiodo** (*Proverbio*) one problem drives away another; **chiodo fisso** fixation; **per lui è diventato un chiodo fisso** it's become a fixation with him

chioma ['kjɔma] SF (*capelli*) head of hair; (*di cavallo*) mane; (*di albero*) foliage; (*di cometa*) tail

chiosco, -schi ['kjɔsko] SM kiosk, stall

chiostro ['kjɔstro] SM cloister

chiromante [kiro'mante] SM, SF palmist; (*indovino*) fortune-teller

chirurgia [kirur'dʒia] SF surgery; **chirurgia estetica** *o* **plastica** plastic surgery; **specialista in chirurgia plastica** plastic surgeon

chirurgico, -a, -ci, -che [ki'rurdʒiko] AGG (*Med, anche fig*) surgical

chirurgo, -ghi *o* **, -gi** [ki'rurgo] SM surgeon; **fa il chirurgo** he's a surgeon

chissà [kis'sa] AVV (*chissà!* who knows!, I wonder!; **chissà chi/come** goodness knows who/how; **chissà che non riesca** you never know, he might succeed; **chissà se verrà alla festa** I wonder if he'll come to the party; **chissà chi gliel'ha detto** I wonder who told him

chitarra [ki'tarra] SF guitar; **suona la chitarra** he plays the guitar; **una chitarra elettrica** an electric guitar

chitarrista, -i, -e [kitar'rista] SM, SF guitarist, guitar player

chiudere ['kjudere] VB IRREG /22/ VT **1** to close, shut; (*pugno, lista, caso*) to close; (*busta, lettera*) to seal; (*giacca, camicia*) to do up, fasten; (*gas, rubinetto*) to turn off; **chiudere a chiave** to lock; **sei sicuro di aver chiuso a chiave?** are you sure you locked it?; **chiudere col catenaccio** to bolt; **sta sempre chiusa in casa** she never goes out; **chiudere la porta in faccia a qn** (*anche fig*) to slam the door in sb's face; **chiudere un occhio su** to turn a blind eye to; **chiudere gli occhi davanti a** (*fig*) to close one's eyes to; **chiudersi le dita nella porta** to catch one's fingers in the door; **non ho chiuso occhio tutta la notte** I didn't sleep a wink all night; **chiudi la bocca!** *o* **il becco!** (*fam*) shut up!; **chiudi la finestra, per favore** close the window please; **ricordati di chiudere il gas** remember to turn off the gas; **chiudi bene il rubinetto** turn the tap off properly; **chiuditi la camicia** do up your shirt **2** (*strada*) to block off; (*frontiera*) to close; (*aeroporto, negozio, scuola*) to close (down), shut (down); (*definitivamente: fabbrica*) to close down, shut down; **il centro è stato chiuso al traffico** the town centre was closed to traffic **3** (*recingere*) to enclose **4** (*terminare*) to end; **con lui ho chiuso** I've finished with him ♦ *vi* (*aus avere*) (*scuola, negozio*) to close, shut; (*definitivamente*) to close down, shut down; **a che ora chiude il negozio?** what time does the shop close?; **la fabbrica ha chiuso due anni fa** the factory closed two years ago; **chiudersi** *vip* (*porta, ombrello*) to close, shut; (*fiore, ferita*) to close up; (*periodo lungo, vacanze*) to finish; **la porta si è chiusa** the door closed; **chiudersi** *vr*: **chiudersi in casa** to shut o.s. up in the house; **chiudersi in se stesso** to withdraw into o.s.

chiunque [ki'unkwe] *pron rel* whoever, anyone who; **chiunque sia** whoever it is; **chiunque chiami, di' che non ci sono** if anyone phones, tell them I'm not in; **chiunque sia, fallo entrare** whoever that is, let them in; **di chiunque sia la colpa, nessuno la passerà liscia** I don't care who is to blame, nobody's going to get away with it; **chiunque lo abbia fatto...** whoever did it ... ♦ *pron indef* anyone, anybody; **chiunque ti direbbe che hai torto** anybody'd tell you you're wrong; **potrebbe farlo chiunque** anyone could do it; **puoi chiederlo a chiunque** you can ask anybody; **attacca discorso con chiunque** she'll talk to anyone; **chiunque altro** anyone else, anybody else; **posso farlo meglio di chiunque altro** I can do it better than anyone else

chiusi *ecc* ['kjusi] *vb vedi* **chiudere**

chiuso, -a ['kjuso] *pp di* **chiudere** ♦ *agg* **1** (*porta*) shut, closed; (*a chiave*) locked; (*senza uscita: strada, corridoio*) blocked off; (*rubinetto*) off; **"chiuso"** (*negozio ecc*) "closed"; **"chiuso al pubblico"** "no admittance to the public"; **una finestra chiusa** a closed window; **la porta era chiusa** the door was shut; **la banca è chiusa per sciopero** the bank is closed because of a strike; **a occhi chiusi** with one's eyes closed; **lo saprei fare ad occhi chiusi** I could do it with my eyes closed; **sono rimasto chiuso fuori** I was locked out; **chiuso a chiave** locked; **ho il naso chiuso** my nose is stuffed up **2** (*persona*) uncommunicative, introverted; (*mente*) narrow; (*ambiente, club*) exclusive; **un ragazzo molto chiuso** a very introverted boy **3** (*concluso: discussione, seduta*) finished; (: *iscrizione, lista*) closed ♦ *sm*: **stare al chiuso** (*fig*) to be shut up; **odore di chiuso** musty smell

chiusura [kju'sura] *sf* **1** (*fine*) end; (*Comm: definitiva*) closing down; **chiusura anticipata** early closing; **orario di chiusura** closing time; **termine di chiusura** closing date; **discorso di chiusura** closing speech **2** (*di porta, cassaforte*) lock; (*di vestito*) fastening, fastener; **chiusura centralizzata (delle porte)** (*Aut*) central locking (device); **chiusura ermetica** hermetic seal; **a chiusura ermetica** airtight; **un recipiente a chiusura ermetica** an airtight container; **chiusura lampo** zip (fastener) (*Brit*), zipper (*USA*); **chiusura di sicurezza** safety lock; **chiusura sicurezza bambini** (*Aut*) child-proof lock **3** (*Pol*): **chiusura verso la destra/sinistra** refusal to collaborate with the right/left

ci [tʃi] *dav lo la, li, le, ne diventa* ce *pron pers* **1** (*ogg diretto*) us; (*a noi*) to us; **ci hanno visto** they saw us; **ascoltaci** listen to us; **ci chiamava** he was calling to us **2** (*complemento di termine*) (to) us; **ci dai da mangiare?** will you give us something to eat?; **ce l'hanno dato** they gave it to us; **ci dissero di tornare più tardi** they told us to come back later; **ci sembrava una buona idea** it seemed a good idea to us; **ci ha sorriso** he smiled at us **3** (*con verbi riflessivi, pronominali, reciproci*): **ci siamo divertiti** we enjoyed ourselves; **ci siamo annoiati** we got bored; **ci vediamo più tardi!** see you later!; **ci amiamo** we love each other; **ci siamo preparati** we prepared ourselves; **ci siamo stancati** we got tired; **ci siamo lavati i denti** we brushed our teeth ♦ *pron dimostr* (*di ciò, su ciò, in ciò ecc*) about (*o on o of*) it; **non so che farci** I don't know what to do about it; **che c'entro io?** what have I got to do with it?; **cosa c'entra?** what's that got to do with it?; **ci puoi giurare, ci puoi scommettere** you can bet on it; **ci puoi contare** you can depend on it; **ci penserò** I'll think about it; **non ci credo** ♦ *avv* **1** (*qui*) here; (*lì*) there; **qui non ci ritorno più** I'm not coming back here again; **son qui e ci resto** here I am and here I stay; **ci andiamo?** shall we go there?; **ci andrò domani** I'll go tomorrow; **ci sei mai stato?** have you ever been there?; **ci sei?** (*sei pronto*) are you ready?; (*hai capito*) do you follow?; **non ci si sta tutti, non ci stiamo tutti** we won't all fit in **2** c'è there is; ci sono there are; **non c'era nessuno** there was nobody there; **c'è nessuno in casa?** is (there) anybody in?; **c'era una volta...** once upon a time ... **3** (*con verbi di moto*): **ci passa sopra un ponte** a bridge passes over it; **non ci passa più nessuno per di qua** nobody comes this way anymore; *vedi* **mancare**, **stare**, **volere**

C.I. *abbr* = **carta d'identità**; *vedi* **carta**

CIA ['tʃia] *sigla f* (= *Central Intelligence Agency*) CIA

C.ia *abbr* = **compagnia**) Co.

ciabatta [tʃa'batta] *sf* slipper; **trattare qn come una ciabatta** to treat sb like dirt

ciabattino [tʃabat'tino] *sm* cobbler

ciac [tʃak] *escl* (*camminando sul fango ecc*) squelch!; **ciac, si gira!** action! ♦ *sm* (*Cine*) clapper board

Ciad [tʃad] *sm* Chad

cialda ['tʃalda] *sf* wafer

cialtrone, -a [tʃal'trone] *sm, sf* rascal, scoundrel

ciambella [tʃam'bella] *sf* **1** (*Culin*) ring-shaped cake; **non tutte le ciambelle riescono col buco** (*Proverbio*) things can't be expected to turn out right every time **2** (*oggetto: gen*) ring; (: *cuscino*) round cushion; (: *salvagente*) rubber ring; **a ciambella** ring-shaped

ciancia, -ce ['tʃantʃa] *sf* gossip *no pl*, tittle-tattle *no pl*

cianfrusaglia [tʃanfru'zaʎʎa] *sf* knick-knack; **cianfrusaglie** *sfpl* bits and pieces

cianuro [tʃa'nuro] *sm* cyanide

ciao [tʃao] *escl* (*all'arrivo*) hello!, hi!; (*alla partenza*) bye!, bye-bye!

ciarlare [tʃar'lare] /72/ *vi* (*aus avere*) to chatter; (*pegg*) to gossip

ciarlatano [tʃarla'tano] *sm* (*pegg: gen*) charlatan; (: *medico*) quack

ciascuno, -a [tʃas'kuno] *agg dav sm*: ciascun + *consonante, vocale*, ciascuno + *s impura, gn, pn, ps, x, z*; *dav sf*: ciascuna + *consonante*, ciascun' + *vocale* (*con valore distributivo*) every, each; (*ogni*) every; **ciascun ragazzo** every *o* each boy; **ciascun uomo nasce libero** every man is born free; **ciascun candidato deve presentare un tema** each candidate has to submit an essay ♦ *pron indef* (*con valore distributivo*) each (one); ciascuno di each (one) *o* every one of; **ciascuno di noi avrà la sua parte** each of us will have his share; **ci ha dato 20 euro (per) ciascuno** he gave each of us 20 euros; **ne avevamo uno per ciascuno** we had one each; **costano cinquanta euro ciascuno** they cost fifty euros each

cibare [tʃi'bare] /72/ *vt* to feed; **cibarsi** *vr*: **cibarsi di** (*anche fig*) to live on

cibarie [tʃi'barje] *sfpl* foodstuffs, provisions

cibernauta, -i, -e [tʃiber'nauta] *sm, sf* = **cybernauta**

cibernetica [tʃiber'netika] *sf* cybernetics *sg*

ciberspazio [tʃiber'spattsjo] *sm* = **cyberspazio**

cibo ['tʃibo] *sm* food; **cibi precotti** ready-cooked food; **son 2 giorni che non tocca cibo** he hasn't eaten for 2 days

cicala [tʃi'kala] *sf* (*Zool*) cicada; **cicala di mare** squilla

cicatrice [tʃika'tritʃe] *sf* (*anche fig*) scar

cicatrizzare [tʃikatrid'dzare] /72/ *vt, vi* (*aus avere*) to heal; **cicatrizzarsi** *vip* to form a scar, heal (up)

cicca, -che ['tʃikka] *sf* **1** (*mozzicone: di sigaretta*) cigarette end, stub; (: *di sigaro*) cigar butt; **non vale una cicca** (*fig*) it's not worth tuppence (*Brit*) *o* one red cent (*USA*), it's worthless **2** (*fam: sigaretta*) cigarette

ciccia [ˈtʃittʃa] SF (*fam: grasso umano*) fat, flab; (: *carne*) meat; **avere troppa ciccia** to be on the plump side

ciccione, -a [tʃitˈtʃone] SM, SF (*fam*) fatty

cicerone [tʃitʃeˈrone] SM (*guida turistica*) guide; **fare da cicerone a qn** to show sb around

ciclamino [tʃiklaˈmino] SM cyclamen

ciclismo [tʃiˈklizmo] SM cycling; **un campione di ciclismo** a cycling champion

ciclista, -i, -e [tʃiˈklista] SM, SF cyclist; **un ciclista professionista** a professional cyclist

ciclo [ˈtʃiklo] SM (*gen, anche Chim, Fis*) cycle; (*di lezioni, conferenze*) series, course; **la malattia deve fare il suo ciclo** the illness must run its course; **un ciclo di film di fantascienza** a series of sci-fi films; **ciclo dell'azoto** nitrogen cycle; **ciclo biologico** life history; **ciclo del carbonio** carbon cycle

ciclomotore [tʃiklomoˈtore] SM moped

ciclone [tʃiˈklone] SM cyclone; (*fig*) whirlwind

ciclostile [tʃiklosˈtile] SM 1 (*macchina*) cyclostyle (*Brit*), duplicator 2 (*foglio*) duplicate copy

cicogna [tʃiˈkoɲɲa] SF 1 (*uccello*) stork 2 (*autotreno*) trailer lorry *o* truck

cicoria [tʃiˈkɔrja] SF chicory

cieco, -a, -chi, -che [ˈtʃeko] AGG (*anche fig*) blind; **essere cieco da un occhio** to be blind in one eye; **il mio cane è cieco da un occhio** my dog's blind in one eye; **alla cieca** (*anche fig*) blindly; **andare alla cieca** to grope along; **cieco come una talpa** as blind as a bat; **essere cieco d'amore** to be blinded by love; **vicolo cieco** (*anche fig*) blind alley ♦ SM, SF blind person; **i ciechi** the blind

ciellino, -a [tʃielˈlino] SM, SF (*Pol*) member of CL movement

cielo [ˈtʃelo] SM 1 sky; (*letter*) heavens *pl*; **un cielo azzurro** a blue sky; **miniera a cielo aperto** opencast mine; **toccare il cielo con un dito** to walk on air; **essere al settimo cielo** to be in seventh heaven; **volare nel cielo italiano** (*Aer*) to fly in Italian airspace 2 (*Rel*) heaven; **il regno dei cieli** the kingdom of heaven; **santo cielo!** good heavens!; **per amor del cielo!** for heaven's sake!; **voglia il cielo che torni presto** I hope to heaven (that) he comes back soon

cifra [ˈtʃifra] SF 1 (*numero*) figure, numeral; **un numero di 5 cifre** a five-figure number; **scrivere un numero in cifre** to write a number in figures; **fare cifra tonda** to make a round figure; **una cifra** (*fam: molto*) loads; **di questi ne abbiamo venduti una cifra** we've sold loads of these; **ci siamo divertiti una cifra** we had a brilliant time 2 (*somma di denaro*) figure, sum; **è una cifra astronomica** it's an astronomical figure; **mi è costato una cifra** (*fam*) it cost me a fortune; **l'ha pagato una bella cifra** he paid a lot for it 3 **cifre** SFPL (*monogramma*) initials, monogram *sg* 4 (*codice*) code, cipher

cifrare [tʃiˈfrare] /72/ VT 1 (*messaggio*) to (put into) code, encode, cipher 2 (*lenzuola, camicie*) to embroider initials *o* a monogram on

ciglio, -gli [ˈtʃiʎʎo] SM 1 (*pl f* **ciglia**) (eye)lash; **ciglia finte** false eyelashes; **non ha battuto ciglio** (*fig*) he didn't bat an eyelid 2 (*di strada, fossato*) edge, side; **sul ciglio della strada** at the edge of the road

cigno [ˈtʃiɲɲo] SM swan

cigolante [tʃigoˈlante] AGG (*vedi vb*) squeaking, creaking

cigolare [tʃigoˈlare] /72/ VI (*aus avere*) (*porta*) to squeak, creak; (*ruota*) to squeak; (*parquet*) to creak

Cile [ˈtʃile] SM Chile; **viene dal Cile** he comes from Chile

cilecca [tʃiˈlekka] SF: **far cilecca** (*fucile*) to misfire; (*fig*) to fail; **le ginocchia mi hanno fatto cilecca** my knees gave way

cileno, -a [tʃiˈleno] AGG, SM, SF Chilean

ciliegia, -gie *o* **-ge** [tʃiˈljɛdʒa] SF cherry; **marmellata di ciliegie** cherry jam

ciliegina [tʃiljeˈdʒina] SF glacé cherry; **la ciliegina sulla torta** (*fig*) the icing *o* cherry on the cake

ciliegio, -gi [tʃiˈljɛdʒo] SM (*albero*) cherry (tree); (*legno*) cherry (wood); **ciliegio dolce** wild cherry

cilindrata [tʃilinˈdrata] SF (*Aut*) (cubic) capacity; **macchina di grossa/piccola cilindrata** a big-engined/small-engined car; **qual è la cilindrata della tua auto?** what's the engine capacity of your car?

cilindro [tʃiˈlindro] SM (*gen, anche Tecn, Geom*) cylinder; (*di macchina da scrivere*) roller; (*cappello*) top hat

CIM [tʃim] SIGLA M (= *Centro d'Igiene Mentale*) mental health centre

cima [ˈtʃima] SF 1 (*gen*) top; (*estremità*) end; (*di montagna*) top, summit, peak; **sulla cima del monte** on the top of the mountain; **si è posato sulla cima dell'albero** it landed on the top of the tree; **conquistare una cima** (*Alpinismo*) to conquer a peak; **in cima a** (*lista, classifica*) at the top of; (*montagna*) at the top of, on the summit of; **sono in cima alla classifica** they're at the top of the league; **da cima a fondo** from top to bottom; **leggere qc da cima a fondo** to read sth from beginning to end; **hanno perquisito la casa da cima a fondo** they searched the house from top to bottom 2 (*persona*) genius; **essere una cima** to be a genius; **non è una cima, ma se la cava** he's not a genius, but he does OK 3 (*Naut*) rope, cable 4 (*Bot*) top, head

cimelio, -li [tʃiˈmɛljo] SM relic

cimentare [tʃimenˈtare] /72/ VT (*pazienza, persona*) to try, to put to the test; **cimentarsi** VR: **cimentarsi in qc** to undertake (the challenge of) sth; (*atleta, concorrente*) to try one's hand at sth; **cimentarsi con qn** to compete with sb

cimice [ˈtʃimitʃe] SF 1 (*Zool*) (bed)bug 2 (*radiotrasmittente*) bug

ciminiera [tʃimiˈnjɛra] SF (*di fabbrica*) chimney (stack); (*di nave*) funnel

cimitero [tʃimiˈtero] SM cemetery, graveyard; **cimitero di automobili** scrapyard; **questo posto è un cimitero!** (*fig*) this place is like a morgue!

cimurro [tʃiˈmurro] SM distemper

Cina [ˈtʃina] SF China; **andremo in Cina a Pasqua** we're going to China at Easter; **mi è piaciuta molto la Cina** I really liked China

cincin, cin cin [tʃinˈtʃin] ESCL cheers!

cincischiare [tʃintʃisˈkjare] /19/ VI (*aus avere*) (*perder tempo*) to mess about, fiddle about

cine [ˈtʃine] SM INV (*fam*) cinema; **andare al cine** to go to the cinema

cineasta, -i, -e [tʃineˈasta] SM, SF 1 person in the film (*Brit*) *o* movie (*USA*) industry; **è un cineasta** he's in films 2 film-maker (*Brit*), moviemaker (*USA*)

cinegiornale [tʃinedʒorˈnale] SM newsreel

cinema [ˈtʃinema] SM INV cinema; **andare al cinema** to go to the cinema *o* movies (*USA*); **andiamo al cinema?** shall we go to the cinema?; **cosa danno al cinema stasera?** what's on at the cinema tonight?; **fare del cinema** to be in the film business; **industria/divo del cinema** film industry/star; **cinema muto** silent films

cinematografico, -a, -ci, -che [tʃinematoˈgrafiko] AGG 1 (*attore, critica: festival*) film (*Brit: attr, movie* (*USA: attr*; **casa cinematografica** film studio, film company; **festival cinematografico** film festival; **regista cinematografico** film director; **sala cinematografica** cinema; **successo cinematografico** box-office success 2 (*fig: stile*) cinematographic

cinematografo [tʃinemaˈtografo] SM (*locale*) cinema (*Brit*), movie theatre (*USA*); (*arte*) cinema, films *pl* (*Brit*), movies *pl* (*USA*)

cinepresa [tʃineˈpresa] SF cine camera

cinese [tʃiˈnese] AGG Chinese ♦ SM, SF Chinese person; **i Cinesi** the Chinese ♦ SM (*lingua*) Chinese; **parla cinese** she speaks Chinese

cineteca, -che [tʃineˈteka] SF (*collezione*) film collection, film library; (*locale*) film library

cinetico, -a, -ci, -che [tʃiˈnetiko] AGG kinetic

cingere [ˈtʃindʒere] /54/ VT IRREG 1 (*circondare*) to surround, encircle; **cingere una città di mura** to surround a city with walls; **cingere d'assedio** to besiege, lay siege to 2 (*avvolgere*): **le cinse la vita con le braccia** he put his arms round her waist; **cingersi la vita con una corda** to tie a rope round one's waist; **cingersi la testa con fiori** to wreath one's head with flowers

cinghia [ˈtʃingja] SF (*cintura*) belt, strap; (*di portabagagli, zaino*) strap; (*Tecn*) belt; (*Equitazione*) girth; **tirare la cinghia** (*fig*) to tighten one's belt; **cinghia di trasmissione** drive belt; **cinghia del ventilatore** fan belt

cinghiale [tʃinˈgjale] SM (*animale*) wild boar; (*pelle*) pigskin

cinguettare [tʃingwetˈtare] /72/ vi (aus avere) (uccelli) to twitter; (bambini) to chatter

cinico, -a, -ci, -che [ˈtʃiniko] AGG cynical ♦ SM, SF cynic

cinismo [tʃiˈnizmo] SM cynicism

cinquanta [tʃinˈkwanta] AGG INV, SM INV fifty; **ha cinquant'anni** he is fifty; **gli anni cinquanta** the Fifties, the 50s; **cinquantuno** fifty-one

cinquantenario, -ri [tʃinkwanteˈnarjo] SM fiftieth anniversary

cinquantenne [tʃinkwanˈtenne] AGG fifty-year-old; **un signore cinquantenne** a man of fifty, a fifty-year-old man ♦ SM, SF fifty-year-old person; (sulla cinquantina) man (woman) in his (her) fifties

cinquantesimo, -a [tʃinkwanˈtezimo] AGG, SM, SF fiftieth

cinquantina [tʃinkwanˈtina] SF **1** **una cinquantina (di)** about fifty, fifty or so; **eravamo una cinquantina** there were about fifty of us **2** (età): **avere una cinquantina d'anni, essere sulla cinquantina** (persona) to be about fifty, be in one's fifties; **avere una cinquantina d'anni** (mobile, casa) to be about fifty years old

cinque [ˈtʃinkwe] AGG INV five; **paragrafo/pagina/capitolo cinque** paragraph/page/chapter five; **i cinque settimi della cifra** five-sevenths of the amount; **abito in Via Cavour, numero cinque** I live at number five Via Cavour; **un bambino di cinque anni** a child of five; **ha cinque anni** he is five; **un biglietto da cinque sterline** a five-pound note; **siamo in cinque** there are five of us; **sono le due meno cinque** it's five to two; **sono arrivati alle cinque** they arrived at five o'clock; **le cinque di sera** five o'clock in the evening; **cinque volte su dieci** five times out of ten; **mettersi in fila per cinque** to form rows of five ♦ SM INV five; **due più tre fa cinque** two plus three make five; **il cinque nel dieci ci sta due volte** five goes into ten twice; **uno sconto del cinque per cento** a five percent discount; **abito in Via Cavour cinque** I live at 5 Via Cavour; **il cinque dicembre 1988** the fifth of December 1988; **arrivare il cinque ottobre** to arrive on October 5th; **prendere un cinque** (Scol) to get five out of ten; **il cinque di fiori** (Carte) the five of clubs

cinquecentesco, -a, -schi, -sche [tʃinkwetʃenˈtesko] AGG sixteenth-century

cinquecento [tʃinkweˈtʃento] AGG INV five hundred; **cinquecento sterline** five hundred pounds ♦ SM INV five hundred; **il Cinquecento** (secolo) the sixteenth century ♦ SF INV (Aut) Fiat 500

cinquemila [tʃinkweˈmila] AGG INV, SM INV five thousand

cinsi ecc [ˈtʃinsi] VB vedi cingere

cinta [ˈtʃinta] SF (anche: **cinta muraria**) city walls pl; **muro di cinta** (di giardino) surrounding wall

cintare [tʃinˈtare] /72/ VT to enclose

cinto, -a [ˈtʃinto] PP di cingere ♦ SM: **cinto erniario** truss

cintola [ˈtʃintola] SF (cintura) belt; (vita) waist

cintura [tʃinˈtura] SF **1** belt; **una cintura di pelle** a leather belt; **cintura dei pesi** (di subacqueo) weight belt; **cintura di salvataggio** lifebelt (Brit), life preserver (USA); **cintura di sicurezza** (Aut, Aer) safety o seat belt; **allacciare la cintura (di sicurezza)** to fasten one's safety o seat belt **2** (vita) waist **3** (Urbanistica): **cintura industriale** industrial belt; **cintura verde** green belt

cinturino [tʃintuˈrino] SM strap; **cinturino dell'orologio** watch strap

CIO [ˈtʃio] SIGLA M (= Comitato olimpico internazionale) IOC (= International Olympic Committee)

ciò [tʃɔ] PRON DIMOSTR **1** (questa cosa) this; (quella cosa) that; **ciò è vero** this (o that) is true; **ciò significa che...** this means that ...; **di ciò parleremo più tardi** we'll talk about this (o that) later; **con tutto ciò** for all that, in spite of everything; **da ciò deduco che...** from this I deduce that ...; **e con ciò me ne vado!** and now I'm off!; **e con ciò ha concluso il suo discorso** and with that he finished his speech; **e con ciò?** so what?; **oltre a ciò** besides that, furthermore; **nonostante ciò, ciò nonostante** nevertheless, in spite of that; **aveva la febbre e ciò nonostante è uscito** he had a temperature, but went out anyway; **detto ciò...** having said that ... **2** **ciò che** what; **ciò che voglio dirti è importante** what I want to tell you is important; **gli sarò sempre grato per ciò che ha fatto** I'll always be grateful for what he's done;

l'hanno sgridato per ciò che ha fatto he got told off for what he did; **è questo tutto ciò che hai fatto?** is this all (that) you've done?

ciocca, -che [ˈtʃɔkka] SF (di capelli) lock; **perde i capelli a ciocche** her hair is coming out in handfuls

cioccolata [tʃokkoˈlata] SF chocolate; **una tavoletta di cioccolata** a bar of chocolate; **una (tazza di) cioccolata calda** a (cup of) hot chocolate

cioccolatino [tʃokkolaˈtino] SM chocolate; **una scatola di cioccolatini** a box of chocolates

cioccolato [tʃokkoˈlato] SM chocolate; **cioccolato al latte/fondente** milk/plain chocolate

cioè [tʃoˈɛ] AVV that is (to say); **vengo tra poco — cioè** I'll come soon — what do you mean by soon?; **partirò il tredici, cioè domenica prossima** I'm leaving on the thirteenth, that's next Sunday; **questo è il mio, cioè no, il tuo!** this is mine, or rather, I mean yours!

ciondolare [tʃondoˈlare] /72/ vi (aus avere) to dangle; (fig: bighellonare) to hang around, loaf (about); **l'ubriaco camminava ciondolando** the drunk swayed from side to side as he walked ♦ VT (far dondolare) to dangle, swing

ciondolo [ˈtʃondolo] SM pendant; **ciondolo portafortuna** good-luck charm

ciondoloni [tʃondoˈloni] AVV: **con le braccia/gambe ciondoloni** with arms/legs dangling

ciononostante [tʃononosˈtante] AVV nonetheless, nevertheless

ciotola [ˈtʃɔtola] SF bowl

ciottolo [ˈtʃɔttolo] SM (di fiume) pebble; (di strada) cobble, cobblestone

cipiglio [tʃiˈpiʎʎo] SM frown

cipolla [tʃiˈpolla] SF **1** onion; (di tulipano) bulb; **mangiare pane e cipolla** (fig) to live on bread and dripping **2** (Med) bunion **3** (scherz: orologio) timepiece

cipollina [tʃipolˈlina] SF (baby) onion; **cipolline sottaceto** pickled onions; **cipolline sottolio** baby onions in oil

cipresso [tʃiˈpresso] SM cypress

cipria [ˈtʃiprja] SF (face) powder; **cipria compatta/in polvere** solid/loose powder

cipriota, -i, -e [tʃipriˈɔta] AGG Cypriot; **la questione cipriota** the Cyprus question ♦ SM, SF Cypriot

Cipro [ˈtʃipro] SM Cyprus

circa [ˈtʃirka] PREP: **circa (a)** regarding, concerning, about; **circa gli accordi presi in precedenza** with reference to previous agreements; **non mi ha detto niente circa i suoi progetti** he didn't tell me anything about his plans ♦ AVV (quasi) about, approximately, roughly; **costerà circa venti sterline** it'll cost about twenty pounds; **erano circa le 3 quando è partita, è partita alle 3 circa** she left at about 3; **mancano 20 minuti circa all'arrivo del treno** the train is due in about 20 minutes; **a mezzogiorno circa** (at) about midday

circo, -chi [ˈtʃirko] SM **1** (Storia romana) circus; **circo (equestre)** (spettacolo) circus; **il circo bianco** world cup skiers and their entourages **2** (Geog) cirque, corrie

circolare¹ [tʃirkoˈlare] /72/ vi (aus avere o essere) (gen, anche Anat, Econ) to circulate; (persone) to go about; (notizie, idee) to circulate, go about; **circolare!** move along!; **circolare in città diventa sempre più difficile** (Aut) driving in town is getting more and more difficult; **i camion non possono circolare di domenica** trucks are not allowed on the roads on Sundays; **circola voce che...** there is a rumour going about that ...; **far circolare qc** to pass sth round; **Luca ne ha fatto circolare una copia in classe** Luca passed a copy round the class

circolare² [tʃirkoˈlare] /72/ AGG circular; **assegno circolare** banker's draft; **un movimento circolare** a circular movement ♦ SF **1** (Amm) circular (letter); **ha inviato una circolare** he's sent out a circular **2** (linea di autobus) circle line

circolazione [tʃirkolatˈtsjone] SF (di sangue, aria, moneta) circulation; (di merci, veicoli) movement; **mettere in circolazione** (moneta) to put into circulation; (fig: voce, notizia) to spread, put about; **togliere dalla circolazione** (moneta) to withdraw from circulation; (fig: persona) to remove; **tassa di circolazione** (Aut) road tax; **libretto di circolazione** (Aut) registration document (Brit), registration (USA);

circolazione monetaria money in circulation; **circolazione stradale** (*Aut*) traffic; **circolazione a targhe alterne** *anti-pollution measure*

circolo [tʃirkolo] SM **1** (*gen, anche Geog, Mat*) circle; **entrare in circolo** (*Med*) to enter the bloodstream; **circolo vizioso** vicious circle **2** (*club*) club; **circolo giovanile** youth club; **circolo letterario** literary circle *o* society; **circolo ufficiali** officers' club

circoncisione [tʃirkontʃiˈzjone] SF circumcision

circondare [tʃirkonˈdare] /72/ VT (*gen*) to surround; (*racchiudere*) to encircle; (*con uno steccato*) to enclose; **la polizia aveva circondato il palazzo** the police had surrounded the building; **circondare qn di cure** to give sb the best of attention; **circondare qn di attenzioni** to be very attentive towards sb; **è sempre stato circondato d'affetto** he has always been surrounded by affection; **circondarsi** VR: **circondarsi di** to surround o.s. with

circondariale [tʃirkondaˈrjale] AGG: **casa circondariale di pena** district prison

circondario, -ri [tʃirkonˈdarjo] SM **1** (*Dir*) administrative district **2** (*zona circostante*) neighbourhood (*Brit*), neighborhood (*USA*)

circonferenza [tʃirkonfeˈrentsa] SF circumference; **circonferenza fianchi/vita** hip/waist measurement

circonvallazione [tʃirkonvallatˈtsjone] SF ring road (*Brit*), beltway (*USA*); (*per evitare una città*) by-pass

circoscritto, -a [tʃirkosˈkritto] PP *di* **circoscrivere** ♦ AGG (*zona*) limited; (*fenomeno, contagio*) localized

circoscrivere [tʃirkosˈkrivere] /105/ VT IRREG (*Geom*) to circumscribe; (*zona*) to mark out; (*incendio, contagio*) to contain, confine; (*fig: problema, concetto*) to define, describe

circoscrizione [tʃirkoskritˈtsjone] SF (*Amm*) district, area; **circoscrizione elettorale** constituency

circospetto, -a [tʃirkosˈpetto] AGG circumspect, cautious; **un'occhiata circospetta** a cautious look; **con fare circospetto** with a suspicious air

circostante [tʃirkosˈtante] AGG (*territorio*) surrounding, neighbouring (*Brit*), neighboring (*USA*); (*persone*) in the vicinity

circostanza [tʃirkosˈtantsa] SF (*occasione*) occasion; **circostanze** SFPL circumstances; **in questa circostanza** on this occasion; **date le circostanze** in view of *o* under the circumstances; **date le circostanze, è stato un buon risultato** in the circumstances, it was a good result; **circostanze aggravanti/attenuanti** (*Dir*) aggravating/mitigating circumstances; **parole di circostanza** words suited to the occasion

circuire [tʃirkuˈire] /55/ VT (*fig*) to fool, take in

circuito [tʃirˈkuito] SM **1** (*Elettr*) circuit; **andare in** *o* **fare corto circuito** to short-circuit; **circuito chiuso/integrato** closed/integrated circuit; **televisione a circuito chiuso** closed-circuit television **2** (*Aut*) track, circuit; **circuito di attesa** (*Aer*) holding pattern; **circuito di gara** racing track; **circuito di prova** test circuit **3** (*sale cinematografiche*) circuit

cirillico, -a, -ci, -che [tʃirˈrilliko] AGG Cyrillic

cirrosi [tʃirˈrɔzi] SF (*Med*) cirrhosis; **cirrosi epatica** cirrhosis (of the liver)

ciste [ˈtʃiste] SF = **cisti**

cisterna [tʃisˈterna] SF tank, cistern ♦ AGG INV: **nave cisterna** (*per petrolio*) tanker; (*per acqua*) water-supply ship; **camion cisterna** tanker (truck)

cisti [ˈtʃisti] SF INV cyst

cistite [tʃisˈtite] SF cystitis

CIT [tʃit] SIGLA F = **Compagnia Italiana Turismo**

cit. ABBR (= *citato, citata*) cit.

citare [tʃiˈtare] /72/ VT **1** (*Dir*) to summon; (*testimone*) to subpoena; **citare qn per danni** to sue sb for damages **2** (*passo, testo, autore*) to cite; **citare qn/qc a modello** *o* **ad esempio** to cite sb/sth as an example

citazione [tʃitatˈtsjone] SF **1** (*Dir: vedi vb*) summons *sg*; subpoena **2** (*di testo*) quotation, citation **3** (*menzione*) citation; **citazione all'ordine del giorno** (*Mil*) mention in dispatches

citofono [tʃiˈtɔfono] SM (*di appartamento*) entry phone; (*in uffici*) intercom

citologico, -a, -ci, -che [tʃitoˈlɔdʒiko] AGG: **esame citologico** *test for detection of cancerous cells*

citrico, -a, -ci, -che [ˈtʃitriko] AGG citric

città [tʃitˈta] SF INV (*gen*) town; (*grande*) city; **la mia città** my home town; **Firenze è una bella città** Florence is a beautiful city; **ti faccio visitare la città** I'll show you round the town; **abitare in città** to live in town *o* in the city; **abiti in città o in campagna?** do you live in town or in the country?; **andare in città** to go to *o* into town; **vita di città** town *o* city life; **la città vecchia/nuova** the old/new (part of) town; **Città del Capo** Cape Town; **città di mare/di provincia** seaside/provincial town; **la Città Santa** (*Gerusalemme*) the Holy City; **città dormitorio** dormitory town; **città giardino** garden city; **città mercato** shopping centre *o* mall (*USA*); **città satellite** satellite town; **città degli studi** *o* **universitaria** university campus

cittadella [tʃittaˈdella] SF citadel, stronghold

cittadinanza [tʃittadiˈnantsa] SF **1** (*città, popolazione*) town, citizens *pl*, inhabitants *pl* of a town *o* city; **tutta la città** the whole town **2** (*Dir*) citizenship; **avere/prendere la cittadinanza britannica** to have/take British citizenship; **ha la cittadinanza britannica** he has British citizenship

cittadino, -a [tʃittaˈdino] AGG (*vie, popolazione, vita*) town *attr*, city *attr* ♦ SM, SF (*abitante di città*) city *o* town dweller; (*di uno Stato*) citizen; **privato cittadino** private citizen; **cittadino britannico** British subject *o* citizen

ciuccio, -ci [ˈtʃiuttʃo] SM (*fam*) comforter, dummy (*Brit*), pacifier (*USA*)

ciuco, -chi [ˈtʃuko] SM, SF ass; (*fig: persona*) ass, fool

ciuffo [ˈtʃuffo] SM (*gen*) tuft; (*di prezzemolo*) bunch; (*di capelli*): **porta il ciuffo di lato** she wears her fringe to the side

ciurma [ˈtʃurma] SF (*di nave*) crew

civetta [tʃiˈvetta] SF **1** owl; **civetta notturna** little owl **2** (*fig: donna*) flirt, coquette; **fare la civetta con qn** to flirt with sb ♦ AGG INV: **auto/nave civetta** decoy car/ship

civettare [tʃivetˈtare] /72/ VI (*aus avere*) **civettare (con qn)** to flirt (with sb)

civetteria [tʃivetteˈria] SF flirtatiousness, coquetry

civettuolo, -a [tʃivetˈtwolo] AGG flirtatious, coquettish; **un cappellino civettuolo** a pert little hat

civico, -a, -ci, -che [ˈtʃiviko] AGG **1** (*museo*) town *attr*, municipal; **centro civico** civic centre; **guardia civica** (*town*) policeman; **museo civico** town museum **2** (*dovere*) civic; **senso civico** public spirit; **educazione civica** civics *sg*

civile [tʃiˈvile] AGG **1** civil; **Diritto Civile** Civil Law; **diritti civili** civil rights; **convivenza civile** life in society; **società civile** civil society; **stato civile** marital status **2** (*non militare*) civilian; **abiti civili** civilian clothes **3** (*civilizzato*) civilized; (*educato*) polite, civil; **un paese civile** a civilized country ♦ SM private citizen, civilian

civilista, -i, -e [tʃiviˈlista] SM, SF (*avvocato*) civil lawyer; (*studioso*) expert in civil law

civilizzare [tʃiviliddzare] /72/ VT (*paese, popolo*) to civilize; **civilizzarsi** VR (*fig*) to become civilized, become more refined

civilizzazione [tʃiviliddzatˈtsjone] SF civilization

civiltà [tʃivilˈta] SF INV **1** (*civilizzazione*) civilization; **una società con un alto grado di civiltà** a highly civilized society **2** (*gentilezza, educazione*) courtesy, civility; **con civiltà** in a civilized manner

civismo [tʃiˈvizmo] SM civic-mindedness, public spirit

CL [tʃiˈelle] SIGLA F (*Pol: = Comunione e Liberazione*) *Catholic youth movement* ♦ SIGLA = **Caltanissetta**

cl ABBR (= *centilitro*) cl

clacson [ˈklakson] SM INV (*Aut*) horn, hooter (*Brit*); **suonare il clacson** to sound the horn

clamore [klaˈmore] SM (*frastuono*) din, uproar, clamour (*Brit*), clamor (*USA*); (*fig: scalpore*) outcry; **suscitare** *o* **destare clamore** to cause a sensation

clamoroso, -a [klamoˈroso] AGG (*sconfitta*) resounding; (*applausi*) noisy; (*fig: notizia, processo*) sensational
❑ **clamoroso** non si traduce mai con *clamorous*

clan [klan] SM INV clan; (*fig: gruppo*) team; (*: mafioso*) gang, clan

clandestinità [klandestiniˈta] SF INV (*di attività*) secret nature; **vivere nella clandestinità** to live in hiding; (*ricercato politico*) to live underground

clandestino, -a [klandesˈtino] AGG (*illecito*) illicit; (*segreto:*

matrimonio, incontro) clandestine, secret; (: *movimento, radio*) underground *attr* ♦ SM, SF (*anche*: **immigrato clandestino**) undocumented immigrant; (*anche*: **passeggero clandestino**) stowaway

clarinetto [klari'netto] SM clarinet

classe ['klasse] SF **1** (*gen, anche fig*) class; **lotta di classe** class struggle; **classe di leva 1958** (*Mil*) class of 1958; **viaggiare in prima/seconda classe** to travel first/second class; **un albergo di prima classe** a first-class hotel; **classe turistica** (*Aer*) economy class; **una persona di (gran) classe** a person with class **2** (*Scol*) class; (*aula*) classroom; **compagno di classe** schoolmate; **un mio compagno di classe** a boy in my class; **che classe fai quest'anno?** what class are you in this year?; **siamo rimasti in classe durante l'intervallo** we stayed in the classroom during the break

classicismo [klassi't∫izmo] SM classicism

classico, -a, -ci, -che ['klassiko] AGG **1** (*arte, letteratura, civiltà*) classical; **studi classici** classical studies; **musica classica** classical music; **non mi piace la musica classica** I don't like classical music **2** (*moda, esempio*) classic; un **film classico** a classic film; **classico! that's typical!** ♦ SM **1** (*autore antico*) classical author; (*opera famosa*) classic; **un classico del cinema francese** a classic of the French cinema **2** (*anche*: **liceo classico**) *secondary school with emphasis on the humanities*

classifica, -che [klas'sifika] SF (*di gara sportiva*) placings *pl*; (*di concorso, esame*) list; (*di dischi*) charts *pl*; **essere primo in classifica** to be placed first, come first; (*disco*) to be number one (in the charts); (*squadra*) to be top of the league; **classifica finale** final results *pl*; **classifica generale** overall placings *pl*; **classifica del campionato** (*Calcio*) league table

classificare [klassifi'kare] /20/ VT (*catalogare*) to classify; (*candidato, compito*) to grade; **classificarsi** VIP (*Sport*) to be placed; **classificarsi primo/secondo** to be placed first/second; **si è classificata prima** she was placed first

classificatore [klassifika'tore] SM (*cartella*) loose-leaf file; (*mobile*) filing cabinet

classificazione [klassifikat'tsjone] SF (*vedi vt*) classification; grading

classista, -i, -e [klas'sista] AGG   class-conscious ♦ SM, SF class-conscious person

claudicante [klaudi'kante] AGG (*zoppo*) lame; (*fig: prosa*) halting

clausola ['klauzola] SF clause

claustrofobico, -a, -ci, -che [klaustrofo'biko] AGG claustrophobic

clausura [klau'zura] SF (*Rel*): **monaca di clausura** nun belonging to an enclosed order; **fare una vita di clausura** (*fig*) to lead a cloistered life

clava ['klava] SF (*arma primitiva*) club; (*attrezzo da ginnastica*) Indian club

clavicembalo [klavi't∫embalo] SM harpsichord

clavicola [kla'vikola] SF collarbone, clavicle (*termine tecn*); **si è fratturato la clavicola** he broke his collarbone

clemente [kle'mente] AGG (*persona*) merciful; (*tempo, stagione*) mild

clemenza [kle'mentsa] SF (*di persona*) mercy, clemency; (*di tempo, stagione*) mildness

cleptomane [klep'tomane] SM, SF kleptomaniac

clericale [kleri'kale] AGG clerical; **potere clericale** power of the clergy ♦ SM, SF clericalist, supporter of the power of the clergy

clero ['klɛro] SM clergy

clessidra [kles'sidra] SF (*a sabbia*) hourglass; (*ad acqua*) water clock

cliccare [klik'kare] /20/ VI (*aus avere*) (*Inform*): **cliccare su** to click on

cliché [kli'∫e] SM INV (*Tip*) plate; (*fig*) cliché

cliente [kli'ɛnte] SM, SF (*gen*) customer; (*di albergo*) guest; (*di professionista*) client; **il negozio era pieno di clienti** the shop was full of customers; **cliente abituale/occasionale** regular/occasional customer; **sono un cliente fisso di quel bar** I'm a regular at that bar

clientela [klien'tela] SF (*di negozio*) customers *pl*; (*di professionista*) clients *pl*; (*di sartoria*) clientele

clientelismo [kliente'lizmo] SM: **clientelismo politico** political nepotism

clima, -i ['klima] SM climate; (*fig*) atmosphere; **c'è un clima piuttosto teso** there's a rather tense atmosphere ♦ ABBR (*Aut: climatizzatore*) air con

climatico, -a, -ci, -che [kli'matiko] AGG climatic; **stazione climatica** health resort

climatizzatore [klimatiddza'tore] SM (*Aut*) air conditioner; **una macchina con il climatizzatore** a car with air conditioning

climatizzazione [klimatiddzat'tsjone] SF air conditioning

clinico, -a, -ci, -che ['kliniko] AGG (*medico, esame*) clinical; **quadro clinico** case history; **avere l'occhio clinico** (*fig*) to have an expert eye ♦ SM (*medico*) clinician; (*docente*) professor of clinical medicine

clistere [klis'tere] SM (*Med*) enema; (*apparecchio*) enema (syringe)

cloaca, -che [klo'aka] SF **1** (*fogna*) sewer; (*pozzo nero*) cesspool, cesspit **2** (*Anat*) cloaca

cloche [klɔ∫] SF INV (*Aer*) control stick, joystick; **cambio a cloche** (*Aut*) (floor-mounted) gear lever (*Brit*) o stick (*Brit*) o shaft (*USA*); **cappello a cloche** cloche hat

clonare [klo'nare] /72/ VT (*Bio, anche fig*) to clone

clonazione [klonat'tsjone] SF (*Bio, anche fig*) cloning

cloro ['klɔro] SM chlorine

clorofilla [kloro'filla] SF chlorophyll (*Brit*), chlorophyl (*USA*)

cloroformio [kloro'fɔrmjo] SM chloroform

cloud computing [klaud kom'pjutin] SM INV cloud computing

club [klub] SM INV club

cm ABBR (= *centimetro*) cm

c.m. ABBR (= *corrente mese*) inst

CN SIGLA = Cuneo

CNEN [knen] SIGLA M (= *Comitato Nazionale per l'Energia Nucleare*) ≈ AEA (*Brit*), AEC (*USA*)

CNR [t∫i'enne'ɛrre] SIGLA M (= *Consiglio Nazionale delle Ricerche*) science research council

CNRN SIGLA M = Comitato Nazionale Ricerche Nucleari

CO SIGLA = Como

Co. ABBR (= *compagnia*) Co.

c/o ABBR (= *care of*) c/o

coabitare [koabi'tare] /72/ VI (*aus avere*) to live in the same flat (*Brit*) o apartment (*USA*) o house

coagulare [koagu'lare] /72/ VT , **coagularsi** VIP (*sangue*) to coagulate, clot; (*latte*) to curdle

coalizione [koalit'tsjone] SF coalition; **governo di coalizione** coalition government

coatto, -a [ko'atto] AGG (*Dir*) compulsory, forced; **condannare al domicilio coatto** to place under house arrest

COBAS ['kɔbas] SIGLA MPL (= *Comitati di base*) *independent trades unions*

cobra ['kɔbra] SM INV cobra

coca ['kɔka] SF **1** (*bevanda*) cola **2** (*fam: cocaina*) coke

cocaina [koka'ina] SF cocaine

coccarda [kok'karda] SF cockade

cocchiere [kok'kjere] SM coachman

cocchio, -chi ['kɔkkjo] SM (*carrozza*) coach; (*biga*) chariot

coccinella [kott∫i'nella] SF ladybird (*Brit*), ladybug (*USA*)

coccio, -ci ['kɔtt∫o] SM **1** earthenware; **un vaso di coccio** an earthenware pot **2** (*frammento*) fragment (of pottery), potsherd; **chi rompe paga e i cocci sono suoi** (*Proverbio*) any damage must be paid for

cocciutaggine [kott∫u'taddʒine] SF stubbornness, pigheadedness

cocciuto, -a [kot't∫uto] AGG stubborn, pig-headed

cocco[1], -chi ['kɔkko] SM coconut palm; **noce di cocco** coconut; **latte di cocco** coconut milk; **gelato al cocco** coconut ice cream

cocco[2], -a, -chi, -che ['kɔkko] SM, SF (*fam*) love, darling; **è il cocco della mamma** he's mummy's darling

coccodrillo [kokko'drillo] SM crocodile; **lacrime di coccodrillo** (*fig*) crocodile tears

coccolare [kokko'lare] /72/ VT to cuddle; **coccolarsi** VR (*uso reciproco*) to cuddle

cocente [ko'tʃɛnte] AGG (*sole*) burning, scorching; (*fig: dolore*) burning; (: *rimorso*) bitter

cocomero [ko'kɔmero] SM watermelon

cocuzzolo [ko'kuttsolo] SM (*di montagna*) summit, top; (*della testa*) crown, top (of the head)

cod. ABBR = **codice**

coda ['koda] SF **1** tail; (*di abiti*) train; **coda di cavallo** (*acconciatura*) ponytail; **ha la coda di cavallo** she's got a ponytail; **vettura/fanale di coda** rear coach/light; **in coda a** (*veicolo, treno*) at the rear of; (*processione*) at the rear end of; **con la coda fra le gambe** (*fig*) with one's tail between one's legs; **avere la coda di paglia** (*fig*) to have a guilty conscience; **guardare con la coda dell'occhio** to look out of the corner of one's eye; **incastro a coda di rondine** dovetail joint **2** (*fila*) queue (*Brit*), line (*USA*); **fare la coda, mettersi in coda** to join the queue, queue (up) (*Brit*), line up (*USA*); **prendi il vassoio e mettiti in coda** take a tray and join the queue; **la coda si fa da questa parte** queue this side **3** (*Culin*): **coda di rospo** frogfish tail

codardia [kodar'dia] SF cowardice

codardo, -a [ko'dardo] AGG cowardly ♦ SM, SF coward

codesto, -a [ko'desto] AGG, PRON DIMOSTR (*letter, o toscano*) this, that

codice ['kɔditʃe] SM **1** code; **messaggio in codice** message in code, coded message **2** (*manoscritto antico*) codex ♦ **codice di avviamento postale** postcode (*Brit*), zip code (*USA*); **codice a barre** bar code; **codice di carattere** (*Inform*) character code; **codice civile** civil code; **codice fiscale** tax code; **codice genetico** genetic code; **codice macchina** (*Inform*) machine code; **codice penale** penal code; **codice postale** postcode; **codice professionale** code of practice; **codice segreto** (*di tessera magnetica*) PIN (number)

codifica [ko'difika] SF codification; (*Inform: di programma*) coding

codificare [kodifi'kare] /20/ VT (*Dir*) to codify; (*informazioni, segreti, dati*) to encode

codificazione [kodifikat'tsjone] SF (*vedi vb*) codification; encoding

coercizione [koertʃit'tsjone] SF coercion

coerente [koe'rɛnte] AGG (*Geol*) coherent; (*fig: pensiero, azione*) consistent, coherent

coerenza [koe'rɛntsa] SF (*vedi agg*) coherence; consistency

coesione [koe'zjone] SF cohesion

coesistere [koe'zistere] /11/ VI IRREG (*aus* essere) to coexist

coetaneo, -a [koe'taneo] AGG (of) the same age; **essere coetaneo di qn** to be the same age as sb; **ma allora siamo coetanei!** so we're the same age! ♦ SM, SF contemporary; **preferisco la compagnia dei miei coetanei** I prefer the company of people my own age

cofanetto [kofa'netto] SM casket; **cofanetto dei gioielli** jewel case; **cofanetto da lavoro** workbox; **cofanetto regalo** gift box

cofano ['kɔfano] SM **1** coffer **2** (*Aut*) bonnet (*Brit*), hood (*USA*)

coffa ['kɔffa] SF (*Naut*) top

cogli [ko'ʎʎi] PREP + ART *vedi* con

cogliere ['kɔʎʎere] /23/ VT IRREG **1** (*fiori, frutta*) to pick, gather; **ho colto una mela dall'albero** I picked an apple off the tree **2** (*fig: afferrare*) to grasp, seize, take; **cogliere il significato di qc** to grasp the meaning of sth; **cogliere l'occasione** o **l'opportunità (per fare)** to take the opportunity (to do); **ha colto l'occasione buona** he chose the right moment; **cogliere nel segno** (*fig*) to hit the nail on the head **3** (*sorprendere*) to catch, surprise; **cogliere sul fatto** o **in flagrante/alla sprovvista** to catch red-handed/unprepared; **l'ho colto sul fatto** I caught him red-handed; **cogliere qn in fallo** to catch sb out

coglione, -a [koʎ'ʎone] SM: **coglioni** SMPL balls (*fam!*); **rompere i coglioni a qn** to get on sb's tits (*Brit fam!*) ♦ SM, SF (*fam!: persona sciocca*) dickhead (*fam!*)

cognac [kɔ'ɲak] SM INV cognac

cognato, -a [koɲ'ɲato] SM, SF brother-(sister)-in-law

cognitivo, -a [koɲɲi'tivo] AGG cognitive

cognizione [koɲɲit'tsjone] SF (*conoscenza*) knowledge; (*Dir*) cognizance; (*Filosofia*) cognition; **con cognizione di causa** with full knowledge of the facts

cognome [koɲ'ɲome] SM surname; **come ti chiami di cognome?** what's your surname?

coi ['koi] PREP + ART *vedi* con

coibente [koi'bɛnte] AGG insulating

coincidenza [kointʃi'dɛntsa] SF **1** coincidence; **che coincidenza, vado anch'io a Bologna** what a coincidence, I'm going to Bologna too **2** (*Ferr, Aer: di autobus*) connection; **ho perso la coincidenza** I missed my connection

coincidere [koin'tʃidere] /34/ VI IRREG (*aus* avere) to coincide

coinciso, -a [koin'tʃizo] PP *di* **coincidere**

coinquilino [koinkwi'lino] SM (*in condominio*) fellow tenant; (*in appartamento*) flatmate (*Brit*), roommate (*USA*)

cointeressenza [kointeres'sentsa] SF (*Comm*): **avere una cointeressenza in qc** to own shares in sth; **cointeressenza dei lavoratori** profit-sharing

coinvolgere [koin'vɔldʒere] /96/ VT IRREG to involve, implicate; **coinvolgere qn in qc** to involve sb in sth; **non mi coinvolgere in questa storia** don't involve me in this business

coinvolgimento [koinvoldʒi'mento] SM involvement

coinvolto, -a [koin'vɔlto] PP *di* **coinvolgere**

col [kol] PREP + ART *vedi* con

Col. ABBR (= *colonnello*) Col.

colà [ko'la] AVV there

colabrodo [kola'brɔdo] SM INV colander, strainer

colapasta [kola'pasta] SM INV colander

colare [ko'lare] /72/ VT **1** (*liquido*) to strain; (*pasta*) drain; **hai colato la pasta?** have you drained the pasta? **2** (*metalli*) to cast; (*oro fuso*) to pour ♦ VI (*aus* essere) **1** (*cadere a gocce*) to drip; (*cera, formaggio*) to run; **il sudore gli colava dalla fronte** sweat dripped from his brow; **mi cola il naso** my nose is running; **mi cola il sangue dal naso** my nose is bleeding **2** (*perdere: botte*) to leak **3** (*nave*): **colare a picco** to sink straight to the bottom

colata [ko'lata] SF (*di metallo fuso*) casting; (*di lava*) flow

colazione [kolat'tsjone] SF (*anche*: **prima colazione**) breakfast; (*anche*: **seconda colazione**) lunch; **cosa mangi a colazione?** what do you have for breakfast?; **fare colazione** to have breakfast o lunch; **colazione all'inglese** English o full breakfast; **colazione di lavoro** working lunch

Coldiretti [koldi'retti] SIGLA F (= *Confederazione nazionale coltivatori diretti*) federation of Italian farmers

colei [ko'lei] PRON DIMOSTR (*sogg*) she; (*complemento*) her; **colei che** the woman who, the one who

colera [ko'lera] SM INV cholera

colesterolo [koleste'rɔlo] SM cholesterol

colf [kɔlf] SF INV home help

colgo ecc ['kɔlgo] VB *vedi* **cogliere**

colibrì [koli'bri] SM INV hummingbird

colica ['kɔlika] SF (*Med*) colic

colino [ko'lino] SM strainer; **colino per il tè** tea strainer

colla¹ ['kɔlla] SF glue; **un tubetto di colla** a tube of glue; **colla di farina** paste; **colla di pesce** fish glue, isinglass

colla² ['kolla] PREP + ART *vedi* con

collaborare [kollabo'rare] /72/ VI (*aus* avere) (*lavorare insieme*) to cooperate; (*Pol*) to collaborate; **collaborare a** (*progetto*) to contribute to, collaborate on; **ho collaborato ad un progetto molto interessante** I worked on a very interesting project; **collaborare a un giornale** to contribute to a newspaper; **collaborare con la polizia** to help the police with their enquiries; **tu e Luca dovete cercare di collaborare** you and Luca must try to work together

collaboratore, -trice [kollabora'tore] SM, SF (*vedi vb*) contributor; collaborator; **tutti i nostri collaboratori** all the members of our team; **è uno dei nostri collaboratori più validi** he's one of our best people; **stiamo cercando due collaboratori per questo progetto** we're looking for two people to work on this project; **collaboratore di un giornale** contributor to a newspaper; **collaboratrice domestica/familiare** home help; **collaboratore esterno** freelance, freelancer; **collaboratore di giustizia** = **pentito**

collaborazione [kollaborat'tsjone] SF (*vedi vb*) cooperation; collaboration; contribution; **in collaborazione con** in collaboration with

collana [kol'lana] SF **1** necklace; **collana di fiori** garland of flowers **2** (*raccolta di libri, scritti*) collection, series *sg*

collant [kɔˈlã] SM INV tights pl; **un paio di collant** a pair of tights

collare [kolˈlare] SM collar

collasso [kolˈlasso] SM (Med) collapse; **avere un collasso** to collapse; **ha avuto un collasso mentre giocava a pallone** he collapsed while playing football; **un collasso cardiaco** heart failure

collaterale [kollateˈrale] AGG collateral; **effetti collaterali** side effects

collaudare [kollauˈdare] /72/ VT to test, try out

collaudo [kolˈlaudo] SM (azione) testing no pl; (prova) test; **fare il collaudo di qc** to test sth; **volo/giro di collaudo** test flight/run

colle¹ [ˈkɔlle] SM (collina) hill; (valico) pass

colle² [ˈkɔlle] PREP + ART vedi **con**

collega, -ghi, -ghe [kolˈlega] SM, SF colleague; **un suo collega** a colleague of hers

collegamento [kollegaˈmento] SM 1 (gen, anche fig: legame) connection 2 (Mil) liaison; **ufficiale di collegamento** liaison officer 3 (Radio) link(-up); **siamo ora in collegamento con...** we are now linked to ... 4 (Inform) link; **collegamento ipertestuale** hyperlink

collegare [kolleˈgare] /80/ VT to connect, join, link; (città, zone) to join, link; (Elettr) to connect (up); **devi collegare la stampante al computer** you have to connect the printer to the computer; **l'autostrada collega Bologna a Firenze** the motorway links Bologna and Florence; **collegarsi** VIP to join, meet; (Radio, TV) to link up; **collegarsi a** to connect to; **collegarsi con** (Telec) to get through to

collegiale [kolleˈdʒale] AGG (riunione, decisione) collective; (Scol) boarding school attr ♦ SM, SF boarder; (fig: persona timida e inesperta) schoolboy (schoolgirl)

collegio, -gi [kolˈledʒo] SM 1 (ordine di professionisti, anche Rel) college 2 (convitto) boarding school; **collegio militare** military college 3 (Amm): **collegio** constituency

collera [ˈkɔllera] SF anger; **andare in collera** to get angry; **essere in collera con qn** to be angry with sb

collerico, -a, -ci, -che [kolˈleriko] AGG (persona) quick-tempered, irascible; (parole) angry; (temperamento) choleric

colletta [kolˈletta] SF collection; **abbiamo fatto una colletta per comprarle un regalo** we had a collection to buy her a present

collettività [kollettiviˈta] SF community

collettivo, -a [kolletˈtivo] AGG (benessere, bisogno, interesse) common, general; (responsabilità) collective; (impresa) group attr; **fenomeno collettivo** popular phenomenon; **nome collettivo** (Gramm) collective noun; **società in nome collettivo** (Comm) partnership ♦ SM (Pol) collective

colletto [kolˈletto] SM (di vestito: anche Bot: di albero) collar; (di dente) neck; **colletti bianchi** (fig) white-collar workers

collezionare [kollettsjoˈnare] /72/ VT to collect; **colleziono cartoline da tutto il mondo** I collect postcards from all over the world

collezione [kolletˈtsjone] SF (gen) collection; **una collezione di francobolli** a stamp collection; **fare collezione di** (francobolli) to collect

collezionista, -i, -e [kollettsjoˈnista] SM, SF collector; **un collezionista di francobolli** a stamp collector

collimare [kolliˈmare] /72/ VI (aus avere) **collimare (con)** (idee) to coincide (with), agree (with)

collina [kolˈlina] SF hill; (zona) hills; **una città di collina** a town in the hills, a hill town

collinare [kolliˈnare] AGG hill attr

collirio, -ri [kolˈlirjo] SM eyedrops pl; **vorrei un collirio** I'd like some eyedrops

collisione [kolliˈzjone] SF (di veicoli) collision; (fig) clash, conflict; **entrare in collisione con qc** to collide with sth

collo¹ [ˈkɔllo] SM neck; (di abito) neck, collar; **a collo alto** (maglione) high-necked; **portare qc al collo** to wear sth round one's neck; **buttare le braccia al collo di qn** to throw one's arms round sb; **portava un foulard al collo** she had a scarf round her neck; **fino al collo** (anche fig) up to one's neck; **essere nei guai fino al collo** to be in deep trouble; **è nei guai fino al collo** he's up to his neck in it; **collo del piede** instep

collo² [ˈkɔllo] SM (pacco) parcel, package; (bagaglio) piece of luggage

collo³ [ˈkɔllo] PREP + ART vedi **con**

collocamento [kollokaˈmento] SM (impiego) employment; (disposizione) placing, arrangement; **agenzia di collocamento** employment agency; **ufficio di collocamento** ≈ Jobcentre (Brit), state o federal employment agency (USA); **collocamento a riposo** retirement

collocare [kolloˈkare] /20/ VT 1 (porre: libri, mobili) to place, position; (: cavi) to lay; **questo libro va collocato fra le sue opere migliori** this book ranks among his best works 2 (trovare un impiego a qn) to place, find a job for; **collocare qn a riposo** to pension sb off, retire sb 3 (Comm: merce) to place, find a market for

collocazione [kollokatˈtsjone] SF 1 (gen) placing, positioning; **l'opera va considerata nella sua collocazione storica** the work has to be considered within its historical setting 2 (in biblioteca) classification

colloquiale [kollokˈkwjale] AGG (gen) colloquial; (tono) informal

colloquio, -qui [kolˈlɔkwjo] SM 1 (conversazione) talk, conversation; (ufficiale, per un lavoro) interview; **domani ha un colloquio di lavoro** she's got a job interview tomorrow; **concedere un colloquio a qn** to grant sb an interview; **avviare un colloquio con qn** (Pol) to start talks with sb 2 (Univ) preliminary oral exam

colloso, -a [kolˈloso] AGG sticky

collottola [kolˈlɔttola] SF nape of the neck; **afferrare qn per la collottola** to grab sb by the scruff of the neck

collusione [kolluˈzjone] SF (Dir) collusion

colluttazione [kolluttatˈtsjone] SF scuffle

colmare [kolˈmare] /72/ VT: **colmare (di)** (riempire) to fill (to the brim) (with); (fig) to fill (with); (spazio) **colmare una lacuna** (fig) to fill a gap; **colmare un divario** (fig) to bridge a gap; **colmare qn di** to shower sb with; **colmare qn di gentilezze** to overwhelm sb with kindness

colmo¹, -a [ˈkolmo] AGG: **colmo (di)** full (of)

colmo² [ˈkolmo] SM (punto più alto) summit, top; (fig): **il colmo della maleducazione** the height of bad manners; **essere al colmo della disperazione** to be in the depths of despair; **essere al colmo dell'ira** to be in a towering rage; **e per colmo di sfortuna... and to cap it all ...; il colmo!** that beats everything!; **questo è il colmo!** this is ridiculous!

colomba [koˈlomba] SF dove; **colomba dal collare** collared dove; **colomba pasquale** (Culin) dove-shaped Easter cake

Colombia [koˈlombja] SF Colombia

colombiano, -a [kolomˈbjano] AGG, SM, SF Colombian

colombo [koˈlombo] SM (Zool) pigeon; **colombi** SMPL love-birds

Colonia [koˈlɔnja] SF Cologne

colonia¹ [koˈlɔnja] SF (gen) colony; (per bambini) holiday camp; **era una colonia britannica** it was a British colony; **colonia marina** seaside holiday camp

colonia² [koˈlɔnja] SF (anche: **acqua di colonia**) (eau de) cologne

coloniale [koloˈnjale] AGG colonial ♦ SM, SF colonist, settler

colonico, -a, -ci, -che [koˈlɔniko] AGG: **casa colonica** farmhouse

colonizzare [kolonidˈdzare] /72/ VT to colonize

colonna [koˈlonna] SF (gen) column; **le colonne di un tempio** the columns of a temple; **le colonne di Ercole** (Geog) the Pillars of Hercules; **in colonna** in a column; **stare in colonna** (Aut) to be caught in a tailback (Brit) o backup (USA); **una colonna di 10 chilometri** (Aut) a 10-kilometre tailback; **colonna sonora** (Cine) sound track; **colonna vertebrale** spine, spinal column

colonnello [kolonˈnello] SM colonel

colono [koˈlɔno] SM 1 (contadino) (tenant) farmer 2 (abitante di una colonia) colonist, settler

colorante [koloˈrante] AGG colouring (Brit), coloring (USA) ♦ SM colorant; (alimentare) colo(u)ring

colorare [koloˈrare] /72/ VT to colour (Brit), to color (USA); (disegno) to colo(u)r in; **colorarsi** VIP: **il cielo si colorava di rosso** the sky was turning red

colore [koˈlore] SM 1 (gen, anche fig) colour (Brit), color

(*USA*); (*pittura*) paint; (*Carte*) suit; **di che colore è?** what colo(u)r is it?; **di (un) colore chiaro/scuro** light-/dark-colo(u)red; **un cappotto color ruggine** a rust-coloured coat; **color fragola** strawberry-colo(u)red; **senza** *o* **privo di colore** (*fig*) colo(u)rless; **di colore** colo(u)red; **gente di colore** black people, people of colo(u)r; **cambiare colore** (*anche fig*) to change colo(u)r; **a colori** (*film: anche TV: foto*) colo(u)r *attr*, in colo(u)r; **TV a colori** colour TV; **colori a olio/a tempera** oil/tempera paints **2** (*fraseologia*): **riprendere colore** (*fig*) to get one's colo(u)r back; **diventare di tutti i colori** to turn scarlet; **è diventato di tutti i colori per l'imbarazzo** he went red with embarrassment; **dirne di tutti i colori a qn** to hurl insults at sb; **farne di tutti i colori** to get up to all sorts of tricks *o* mischief; **in gita ne abbiamo fatte di tutti i colori** on the trip we got up to all sorts of things; **passarne di tutti i colori** to go through all sorts of problems

colorito, -a [kolo'rito] AGG (*guance, viso*) rosy, pink; (*racconto, linguaggio*) colourful (*Brit*), colorful (*USA*); **sei più colorito oggi** you've got more colo(u)r in your cheeks today
♦ SM (*carnagione*) complexion

coloro [ko'loro] PRON DIMOSTR PL (*sogg*) they; (*complemento*) them; **coloro che** those who; *vedi anche* **colui**

colossale [kolos'sale] AGG colossal, huge, enormous

colosso [ko'lɔsso] SM (*statua*) colossus; (*fig*) giant, colossus; **è un colosso!** (*fisicamente*) he's enormous!

colpa ['kolpa] SF (*responsabilità*) fault; (*colpevolezza*) guilt; (*biasimo*) blame; (*morale*) sin; **di chi è la colpa?** whose fault is it?; **è colpa mia** it's my fault; **per colpa di** because of, thanks to; **per colpa sua** because of him, thanks to him; **l'incidente è successo per colpa sua** the accident was his fault; **per colpa sua non possiamo uscire** it's his fault we can't go out; **essere in colpa** to be at fault; **sentirsi in colpa** to feel guilty; **se non ci vado mi sento in colpa** if I don't go I feel guilty; **senso di colpa** sense of guilt; **confessare le proprie colpe** to admit one's faults; **dare la colpa di qc a qn** to blame sb for sth; **non dare la colpa a me!** don't blame me!; **addossarsi la colpa di qc** to take the blame for sth; **si è addossato lui la colpa** he took the blame

colpevole [kol'pevole] AGG guilty; **dichiarare qn colpevole (di qc)** to find sb guilty (of sth); **dichiararsi colpevole** to plead guilty; **colpevole di omicidio** guilty of murder ♦ SM, SF culprit; **non hanno trovato il colpevole** they haven't found the culprit

colpevolizzare [kolpevolid'dzare] /72/ VT: **colpevolizzare qn** to make sb feel guilty

colpire [kol'pire] /55/ VT (*anche fig*) to hit, strike; (*toccare*) to affect; **è stata colpita alla testa** she was hit *o* struck on the head; **colpire qn con un pugno** to punch sb; **lo ha colpito con un pugno** he punched him; **colpire qn a morte** to strike sb dead; **il nuovo provvedimento colpirà gli spacciatori** the new measure will hit drug pushers; **colpire nel segno** (*fig*) to hit the nail on the head, be spot on (*Brit*); **rimanere colpito da qc** to be amazed *o* struck by sth; **sono rimasto colpito dalla sua reazione** I was shocked by his reaction; **la sua bellezza mi ha colpito** I was struck by her beauty; **qual è la cosa che ti ha colpito di più?** what's the thing that struck you most?; **colpire l'immaginazione** to catch the imagination; **un'epidemia che colpisce le persone anziane** an epidemic which affects old people; **le regioni colpite dal maltempo** the regions affected by the bad weather; **colpito dalla paralisi/dalla sfortuna** stricken with paralysis/by misfortune; **è stato colpito da ordine di cattura** there is a warrant out for his arrest

colpo ['kolpo] SM **1** (*aggressivo*) blow; (*urto*) knock; (*fig: affettivo*) blow, shock; **colpo basso** below the belt; **colpo mortale** mortal blow; **colpo di spada** sword blow; **colpo di remo** oar stroke; **dare un colpo a qn** to hit sb; **un colpo in testa** a blow on the head; **dare un colpo in testa a qn** to hit sb over the head; **gli ha dato un colpo in testa** he hit him on the head; **prendere un colpo** *o* **alla testa** to bump one's head; **prendere qn a colpi di bastone** to set about sb with a stick; **darsi un colpo di pettine** to run a comb through one's hair; **è stato un brutto colpo per lui** it came as a hard blow to him; **un colpo di coda** (*di cavallo*) a flick of the tail; **con un colpo d'ala l'uccello si è librato in volo** with a flap of its wings bird took flight **2** (*di arma da fuoco*) shot; **hanno**

sparato 10 colpi di cannone they fired 10 cannon shots; **mi restano solo 2 colpi** I've only got 2 rounds left; **abbiamo sentito dei colpi** we heard shots; **sparare un colpo in aria; ha sparato dei colpi in aria** he fired into the air **3** (*Med*) stroke; **colpo (apoplettico)** (apoplectic) fit; **ti venisse un colpo!** (*fam*) drop dead!; **mi hai fatto venire un colpo!** what a fright you gave me!; **colpo d'aria** chill; **ho preso un colpo d'aria** I've caught a chill; **colpo di calore** heat stroke; **colpo di frusta** *o* **della strega** whiplash; **colpo di sole** sunstroke; **colpo di tosse** fit of coughing **4** (*Pugilato*) punch; (*Scherma*) hit; **colpo basso** (*Pugilato, anche fig*) blow *o* punch below the belt **5** (*furto*) raid; **fare un colpo** to carry out a raid; **hanno preso gli autori di quel colpo in banca** they caught those responsible for the bank job *o* raid; **tentare il colpo** (*fig*) to have a go; **ho fatto un buon colpo** I pulled it off **6** (*fraseologia*): **al primo colpo** at the first attempt; **di colpo, tutto d'un colpo** suddenly; **si è fermato di colpo** he stopped suddenly; **far colpo** to cause a sensation; **hai fatto colpo sulla mia amica!** you were a hit with my friend!; **sul colpo** instantly; **è morto sul colpo** he died instantly; **sono andato in quel negozio a colpo sicuro** I went into that shop knowing I would find what I wanted; **il motore perde colpi** (*Aut*) the engine is misfiring ♦ **colpi di sole** (*nei capelli*) highlights; **colpo d'approccio** (*Tennis*) approach shot; **colpo di fortuna** stroke of (good) luck; **colpo di fulmine** love at first sight; **è stato un colpo di fulmine** it was love at first sight; **colpo giornalistico** newspaper coup; **colpo gobbo** smart move; (*al gioco*) lucky strike; **colpo di grazia** (*fig*) coup de grâce; **colpo di mano** (*Mil*) surprise attack; (*fig*) surprise action; **colpo d'occhio; a colpo d'occhio** at a glance; **avere colpo d'occhio** to have a good eye; **colpo di rimbalzo** (*Tennis*) ground stroke; **colpo di scena** (*Teatro*) coup de théâtre; (*fig*) dramatic turn of events; **colpo di Stato** coup (d'état); **colpo di telefono** phone call; **dare un colpo di telefono a qn** to give sb a ring; **ti do un colpo di telefono domani sera** I'll give you a ring tomorrow evening; **colpo di testa** (*Calcio*) header (*Brit*); (*fig*) (sudden) impulse *o* whim; **colpo di vento** gust (of wind)

colposo, -a [kol'poso] AGG: **omicidio colposo** manslaughter

colsi *ecc* ['kɔlsi] VB *vedi* **cogliere**

coltellata [koltel'lata] SF (*colpo*) stab; (*ferita*) knife *o* stab wound; **dare una coltellata a qn** to stab sb

coltello [kol'tɛllo] SM knife; **avere il coltello dalla parte del manico** to have the whip hand; **c'era una nebbia che si tagliava con il coltello** the fog was so thick you could have cut it with a knife; **coltello da cucina** kitchen knife; **coltello a serramanico** flick knife, clasp knife

coltivare [kolti'vare] /72/ VT (*terreno, anche fig: amicizia*) to cultivate; (*piante*) to grow, cultivate; **coltivavano pomodori** they grew tomatoes; **coltivare un campo a grano** to plant a field with corn; **coltivare la mente** to cultivate one's mind

coltivatore, -trice [koltiva'tore] SM grower, farmer; **coltivatore diretto** small independent farmer

coltivazione [koltivat'tsjone] SF growing, cultivation; **la coltivazione del mais** maize growing; **coltivazione intensiva** intensive farming

colto¹, -a ['kolto] AGG (*istruito*) cultured, well-educated; **una persona molto colta** a very well-educated person

colto², -a ['kolto] PP *di* **cogliere**

coltre ['koltre] SF (*anche fig*) blanket

coltura [kol'tura] SF **1** cultivation; **coltura alternata** crop rotation **2** (*Bio*) culture; **coltura batterica** bacterial culture

colui [ko'lui] PRON DIMOSTR (*sogg*) he; (*complemento*) him; **colui che** the man who, the one who; **colui che parla** the one *o* the man *o* the person who is speaking

com. ABBR = **comunale commissione**

coma ['koma] SM INV coma; **essere in coma** to be in a coma; (*fig*) to be dead tired; **oggi sono in coma!** I'm half dead today!; **entrare in coma** to go into a coma; **è entrato in coma** he's gone into a coma

comandamento [komanda'mento] SM commandment

comandante [koman'dante] SM (*Mil*) commander, commandant; (*di reggimento*) commanding officer; (*Aer, Naut*) captain; **comandante del porto** harbour master; **comandante in seconda** second-in-command

comandare [koman'dare] /72/ VT **1** (*ordinare*) to order, command; (*essere al comando di*) to command, be in charge of; **comandare a qn di fare qc** to order sb to do sth; **comandare a bacchetta** to rule with a rod of iron 2 (*azionare*) to operate, control; **comandare a distanza** to operate by remote control ♦ vi (*aus* avere) to be in charge, be in command; **qui comando io!** I'm in charge here!; **è lei che comanda in casa** she's the boss in the house

comando [ko'mando] SM 1 (*ordine*) command, order; (*Inform*) command; **ubbidire a un comando** to obey an order 2 (*autorità, sede*) command; **essere al comando (di)** to be in command *o* in charge (of); (*Sport: di classifica*) to be at the top (of); (: *di gara*) to be in the lead (in); **assumere il comando di** to assume command of; (*Sport*) to take the lead in; **comando generale** general headquarters *pl* 3 (*Tecn*) control; **doppi comandi** dual controls; **comandi manuali** hand controls; **comando a distanza** remote control

comare [ko'mare] SF (*madrina*) godmother; (*donna pettegola*) gossip; **le allegre comari di Windsor** the Merry Wives of Windsor

comasco, -a, -schi, -sche [ko'masko] AGG *of o* from Como ♦ SM, SF inhabitant *o* native of Como

combaciare [komba't∫are] /14/ vi (*aus* avere) to fit together; (*fig: coincidere*) to agree, coincide, correspond; **i due pezzi combaciano perfettamente** the two pieces fit together perfectly; **le tue idee non combaciano con le mie** your ideas are different from mine

combattente [kombat'tente] AGG fighting, combatant ♦ SM fighter, combatant; **ex-combattente** ex-serviceman

combattere [kom'battere] /1/ vt to fight; (*fig: teoria, malattia*) to combat, fight (against); **hanno sempre combattuto contro l'ingiustizia** they've always fought against injustice ♦ vi (*aus* avere) to fight

combattimento [kombatti'mento] SM (*Mil*) battle, fight, fighting *no pl*; (*Pugilato*) match; **mettere fuori combattimento** to knock out; **combattimento (a) corpo a corpo** hand-to-hand combat; **combattimento di galli** cockfighting

combattivo, -a [kombat'tivo] AGG pugnacious

combattuto, -a [kombat'tuto] AGG 1 (*incerto: persona*) uncertain, undecided; **combattuto tra due possibilità** torn between two possibilities 2 (*gara, partita*) hard-fought

combinare [kombi'nare] /72/ vt 1 (*mettere insieme*) to combine 2 (*organizzare: incontro*) to arrange; (*concludere: affare*) to conclude; **che cosa stai combinando?** what are you up to?; **che cosa hai combinato?** what have you gone and done?; **ci hai combinato un bel guaio!** you've got us into a nice mess!; **oggi non ho combinato nulla** I haven't got anything done today ♦ vi (*aus* avere) (*corrispondere*): **combinare (con)** to correspond (with); **combinarsi** vr (*fam: conciarsi*): **ma come ti sei combinato?** what on earth have you got on?, what on earth have you done to yourself?; **combinarsi** vip (*Chim*) to combine

combinazione [kombinat'tsjone] SF 1 (*accostamento, unione*) combination 2 (*caso fortuito*) chance, coincidence; **per combinazione** by chance; **per combinazione era lì anche lui** by chance he was there too; (*guarda*) **che combinazione!** what a coincidence! 3 (*di cassaforte*) combination

combriccola [kom'brikkola] SF (*gruppo di amici*) party; (*banda*) gang

combustibile [kombus'tibile] AGG combustible ♦ SM fuel

combustione [kombus'tjone] SF combustion; **a lenta combustione** slow-burning

combutta [kom'butta] SF: **essere in combutta** to be in league *o* in cahoots; **fare combutta con qn** to be in league *o* in cahoots with sb

PAROLA CHIAVE

come ['kome] AVV

1 (*alla maniera di, nel modo che*) as, like (*davanti a sostantivo, pronome*); **com'è vero Dio** as God is my witness; **bianco come la neve** (as) white as snow; **veste come suo padre** he dresses like his father; **a scuola come a casa** both at school and at home, at school as well as at home; **ci vuole uno come lui** we need somebody like him; **è come parlare al muro** it's like talking to the wall

2 (*in quale modo: interrogativo, esclamativo*) how; **come mai?**

how come?; **come mai non sei partito?** why didn't you leave?; **non hanno accettato il mio assegno — come mai?** they didn't accept my cheque — why not?; **vieni? — come no!** are you coming? — of course!; **come stai?** how are you?; **come glielo dico?** how will I tell him?; **non so come dirglielo** I don't know how to tell him; **come?, come dici?** pardon? (*Brit*), sorry?, excuse me? (*USA*), what did you say?; **com'è il tuo amico?** what's your friend like?; **com'è che non hai telefonato?** how come you didn't phone?

3 (*il modo in cui*): **mi piace come scrive** I like the way he writes, I like his style of writing; **ecco come è successo** this is how it happened; **attento a come parli!** mind your tongue!

4 (*in qualità di*) as; **ti parlo come amico** I'm speaking to you as a friend; **come presidente, dirò che...** speaking as your president I must say that ...; **lo hanno scelto come rappresentante** they've chosen him as their representative

5 (*quanto*): **come è brutto!** how ugly he (*o* it) is!; **come mi dispiace!** I'm terribly sorry!

6 A **come** Ancona ≈ A for Andrew; **come non detto** let's forget it; **oggi come oggi** at the present time; **ora come ora** right now; *vedi anche* **così tanto**

♦ CONG

1 (*in quale modo*): **mi scrisse come si era rotto un braccio** he wrote to tell me about how he had broken an arm; **mi ha spiegato come l'ha conosciuto** he told me how he met him

2 (*quanto*) how; **sai come sia sensibile** you know how sensitive he is

3 (*correlativo*) as; (*con comparativi di maggioranza*) than; **si comporta come ha sempre fatto** he behaves as he has always done; **è meglio/peggio di come mi aspettavo** it is better/worse than I expected

4 (*appena che, quando*) as soon as; **come arrivò si mise a lavorare** as soon as he arrived he set to work, no sooner had he arrived than he set to work; **come se n'è andato, tutti sono scoppiati a ridere** as soon as he left, everyone burst out laughing

5 **come (se)** as if, as though; **tratta la sua Panda come (se) fosse una Ferrari** he treats his Panda as if it were a Ferrari

6 (*in proposizioni incidentali*) as; **come puoi constatare** as you can see; **come sai** as you know

♦ SM INV: **il come e il perché** the whys and the wherefores; **non so dirti il come e il quando di tutta questa faccenda** I couldn't tell you how and when all this happened

comedone [kome'done] SM blackhead

cometa [ko'meta] SF comet

comico, -a, -ci, -che ['komiko] AGG (*gen, buffo*) comic(al); (*Teatro*) comic; **una scena comica** a funny scene ♦ SM 1 (*comicità*) comic spirit, comedy; **il comico è che...** the funny thing is that ... 2 (*attore*) comedian, comic actor; **è un comico famoso** he's a well-known comedian

comignolo [ko'miɲɲolo] SM chimney (top)

cominciare [komin't∫are] /14/ vt *o* to start, begin; **hai cominciato il libro che ti ho prestato?** have you started the book I lent you?; **cominciare a fare/col fare** to begin to do/by doing; **ha cominciato a ridere** she started to laugh; **ha cominciato a piangere** she started crying ♦ vi (*aus* essere) to start, begin; **una parola che comincia per J** a word beginning with J; **il film comincia con un'esplosione** the film starts with an explosion; **tanto per cominciare** to start with; **tanto per cominciare non sappiamo se funzionerà** in the first place we don't know if it'll work; **a cominciare da domani** starting (from) tomorrow; **cominciamo bene!** (*iro*) we're off to a fine start!

comitato [komi'tato] SM committee, board; **far parte di un comitato** to be on a committee; **comitato direttivo** steering committee; **comitato di gestione** works council; **Comitato Interministeriale per la Programmazione Economica** interdepartmental committee for economic planning; **Comitato Interministeriale di coordinamento per la Politica Industriale** interdepartmental committee for industrial development; **Comitato Interministeriale dei Prezzi** interdepartmental committee on prices; **comitato di redazione** committee of journalists (*meeting to decide on something, for example whether to strike*)

comitiva [komi'tiva] SF group, party; **viaggiare in comitiva**

to travel in *o* as a group; **una comitiva di turisti** a group of tourists; **sconto per comitive** group discount

comizio, -zi [ko'mittsjo] SM rally; **comizio elettorale** election rally

comma, -i ['kɔmma] SM (*Dir*) subsection

commando [kom'mando] SM INV commando unit

commedia [kom'mɛdja] SF **1** (*Teatro*) play; (*comica*) comedy; **commedia musicale** musical; **la Divina Commedia** the Divine Comedy **2** (*finzione*) sham, play-acting *no pl*; **è tutta una commedia** it's just play-acting; **fare la commedia** to play-act; **commedia dell'arte** commedia dell'arte; **commedia all'italiana** *Italian satirical film comedies made in the 1950s and 1960s*

commediante [komme'djante] SM, SF comedian (comedienne); (*pegg*) third-rate actor (actress); (*fig*: *ipocrita*) sham

commediografo, -a [komme'djɔgrafo] SM, SF (*autore*) comedy writer

commemorare [kommemo'rare] /72/ VT to commemorate

commemorazione [kommemorat'tsjone] SF commemoration

commendatore [kommenda'tore] SM *official title awarded for services to one's country*

commensale [kommen'sale] SM, SF table companion

commentare [kommen'tare] /72/ VT (*dare un giudizio su: fatto, avvenimento*) to comment on; (*Radio, TV*) to give a commentary on; (*annotare*) to annotate; **qualcuno vuole commentare quello che ho detto?** does anyone want to comment on what I've been saying?

commentatore, -trice [kommenta'tore] SM, SF (*Radio, TV*) commentator; (*di testo*) annotator

commento [kom'mento] SM (*osservazione*) comment; (*letterario: Radio, TV*) commentary; **fare un commento su qn/qc** to comment on sb/sth; **fare il commento di una partita** to give the commentary on a match; **senza fare commenti** without passing comment; **è meglio che io non faccia commenti** it is better if I don't say anything; **commento musicale** (*Cine*) background music

commerciale [kommer'tʃale] AGG (*gen*) commercial; (*corrispondenza*) business *attr*, commercial; (*fiera, bilancio*) trade *attr*; (*pegg: film*) commercial; **le attività industriali e commerciali** industrial and commercial activities; **un'attività commerciale** a business; **avere rapporti commerciali con** to trade with; **interrompere i rapporti commerciali con** to interrupt trade with

commercialista, -i, -e [kommertʃa'lista] SM, SF (*laureato*) graduate in economics and commerce; (*consulente*) business consultant; (*fiscale, per contabilità*) accountant

commercializzare [kommertʃalid'dzare] /72/ VT (*prodotto*) to market; (*pegg: arte*) to commercialize

commercializzazione [kommertʃaliddzat'tsjone] SF marketing

commerciante [kommer'tʃante] SM, SF trader, dealer; (*negoziante*) shopkeeper, tradesman; **i commercianti del centro** the shopkeepers in the town centre; **commerciante di legname** timber merchant; **commerciante all'ingrosso** wholesaler; **commerciante in proprio** sole trader

commerciare [kommer'tʃare] /14/ VI (*aus* avere) commerciare in to deal *o* trade in; **commerciare con qn** to do business with sb ♦ VT to deal *o* trade in

commercio, -ci [kom'mertʃo] SM (*vendita, affari*) trade, commerce; **il commercio della lana** the wool trade; **essere in commercio** (*prodotto*) to be in the shops, be on the market *o* on sale; **mettere in commercio** to put on the market; **essere nel commercio** (*persona*) to be in business; **economia e commercio** economics and business studies; **commercio elettronico** e-commerce, e-business; **commercio equo e solidale** fair trade; **commercio all'ingrosso** wholesale trade; **commercio al minuto** retail trade

commesso, -a [kom'messo] PP *di* **commettere** ♦ SM, SF (*addetto alla vendita*) shop assistant (*Brit*), sales clerk (*USA*); **fa la commessa** she's a shop assistant; **commesso viaggiatore** travelling salesman ♦ SM (*impiegato*) clerk; **commesso di banca** bank clerk

commestibile [kommes'tibile] AGG edible ♦ **commestibili** SMPL foodstuffs

commettere [kom'mettere] /63/ VT IRREG **1** (*errore*) to make; (*delitto, peccato*) to commit **2** (*ordinare*) to commission, order

commiato [kom'mjato] SM leave-taking; **prendere commiato da qn** to take one's leave of sb

comminare [kommi'nare] /72/ VT (*Dir*) to make provision for

commiserare [kommize'rare] /72/ VT to commiserate with, sympathize with

commiserazione [kommizerat'tsjone] SF commiseration; **sorriso di commiserazione** (*anche pegg*) pitying smile

commisi ecc [kom'mizi] VB *vedi* **commettere**

commissariamento [kommissarja'mento] SM temporary receivership

commissariare [kommissa'rjare] /19/ VT to put under temporary receivership

commissariato [kommissa'rjato] SM **1** (*di polizia*) police station **2** (*carica*) commissionership; (*sede*) commissioner's office

commissario, -ri [kommis'sarjo] SM **1** (*funzionario*): **commissario (di Pubblica Sicurezza)** ≈ (police) superintendent (*Brit*), (police) captain (*USA*); **alto commissario** high commissioner; **commissario di bordo** (*Naut*) purser; (*Aer*) chief steward, purser; **commissario d'esame** member of an examining board (*Sport*) steward; **commissario di gara** race official; **commissario tecnico (della Nazionale)** national team manager

commissionare [kommissjo'nare] /72/ VT to order, place an order for

commissionario, -ri [kommissjo'narjo] SM (*Comm, Fin*) agent, broker

commissione [kommis'sjone] SF **1** (*incarico*) errand; **fare una commissione** to go on an errand; **devo fare delle commissioni** I have some shopping to do **2** (*Comm: ordinazione*) order; (: *percentuale*) commission; **fatto su commissione** made to order; **vendere su commissione** to sell on commission; **ha una commissione sulle vendite** he gets commission on sales; **commissioni bancarie** bank charges **3** (*comitato*) committee, board; **commissione d'esame** examining board; **Commissione Europea** European Commission; **commissione d'inchiesta** committee of enquiry; **commissione parlamentare** parliamentary (*Brit*) *o* Congressional (*USA*) commission; **commissione permanente** standing committee

committente [kommit'tente] SM, SF (*Comm*) purchaser, customer

commosso, -a [kom'mɔsso] PP *di* **commuovere** ♦ AGG moved, touched; **essere commosso fino alle lacrime** to be moved to tears

commovente [kommo'vente] AGG moving, touching; **una storia commovente** a moving story

commozione [kommot'tsjone] SF **1** (*emozione*) emotion, deep feeling; **non riusciva a nascondere la commozione** he couldn't hide his emotion; **si è messa a piangere per la commozione** she got emotional and started to cry **2** (*Med*): **commozione cerebrale** concussion

commuovere [kom'mwɔvere] VB IRREG /66/ VT to move, touch, affect; **mi hai commosso** I'm touched *o* moved; **commuoversi** VIP to be moved, get emotional; **si è commosso** he got emotional

commutare [kommu'tare] /72/ VT **1** (*Dir: pena*) to commute **2** (*Elettr*) to switch *o* change over, commutate (*termine tecn*)

commutazione [kommutat'tsjone] SF (*Dir, Elettr*) commutation; **commutazione di pacchetto** (*Inform*) packet switching

comò [ko'mɔ] SM INV chest of drawers, bureau (*USA*)

comodino [komo'dino] SM bedside table

comodità [komodi'ta] SF INV **1** (*vedi agg*) convenience; handiness; comfort; **la comodità di abitare in centro** the convenience of living in the town centre; **ho la comodità di avere la fermata sotto casa** conveniently for me, the stop is outside my house **2 le comodità della vita moderna** modern conveniences

❑ **comodità** non si traduce mai con *commodity*

comodo, -a ['kɔmodo] AGG (*conveniente*) convenient; (*prati-*

co) handy; (*utile*) useful; (*confortevole*) comfortable; (*facile*) easy; **una poltrona comoda** a comfortable chair; **gli piace la vita comoda** he likes an easy life; **stia comodo! don't bother to get up!; stai comodo lì?** are you comfortable there?; **è comodo dare la colpa agli altri** it's easy to blame other people; **sarebbe più comodo incontrarci in centro** it would be more convenient to meet in the town centre ♦ SM: **con comodo** at one's convenience *o* leisure; **fai con comodo** take your time; **fare il proprio comodo** to please o.s., do as one pleases; **amare il proprio comodo** to like one's comforts; **far comodo** to be a help; **quei soldi mi hanno fatto comodo** that money came in handy; **una macchina mi farebbe comodo** a car would do me nicely, a car would be very handy; **una soluzione di comodo** a convenient arrangement

compact disc ['kɔmpakt 'disk] SM INV compact disc

compaesano, -a [kompae'zano] SM, SF (*dello stesso paese*) fellow countryman (woman); (*della stessa città*) person from the same town; **è un mio compaesano** he comes from the same town *o* country as I do

compagine [kom'padʒine] SF 1 (*Pol*) : **la compagine del partito** the party en bloc; **la compagine dello Stato** the government as a whole 2 (*squadra*) team

compagnia [kompa'ɲia] SF 1 company; **fare compagnia a qn** to keep sb company; **quand'era malato andavo a fargli compagnia** when he was ill I used to go and keep him company; **essere di compagnia** to be sociable; **è un tipo di compagnia** he's a sociable kind of person; **dama di compagnia** lady-in-waiting 2 (*gruppo di persone*) group, party; (*Mil, Comm, Teatro*) company; **compagnia aerea** airline; **compagnia di bandiera** (*aerea*) national airline; **lavora in una compagnia di assicurazioni** he works for an insurance company; **frequentare cattive compagnie** to keep bad company; **...e compagnia bella** (*e gli altri*) ...and co.; (*eccetera, eccetera*) ...and so on

compagno, -a [kom'paɲɲo] SM, SF (*gen*) companion; (*nel gioco*) partner; (*della vita*) life companion; (*Pol*) comrade; **compagno di classe** classmates; **i miei compagni di classe** my classmates; **un mio compagno di classe** a boy in my class; **compagno di giochi** playmate; **compagno di lavoro** workmate; **compagno di scuola** schoolfriend; **è una mia compagna di scuola** she's one of my schoolfriends; **compagno di squadra** team-mate; **compagno di sventura** companion in misfortune; **compagno di viaggio** fellow traveller

compaio ecc [kom'pajo] VB *vedi* **comparire**

comparare [kompa'rare] /72/ VT to compare

comparativo, -a [kompara'tivo] AGG, SM comparative

comparazione [komparat'tsjone] SF comparison

compare [kom'pare] SM (*padrino*) godfather; (*complice*) accomplice; (*fam: amico*) old pal, old mate

comparire [kompa'rire] /7/ VI IRREG (*aus* **essere**) (*presentarsi*) to appear; (*uscire: libro, giornale*) to come out; **comparire in giudizio** (*Dir*) to appear before the court

comparizione [komparit'tsjone] SF (*Dir*) appearance; **mandato di comparizione** summons *sg*

comparso, -a [kom'parso] PP *di* **comparire**

compartecipare [kompartetʃi'pare] /72/ VI (*aus* **avere**) (*Comm*): **compartecipare a** to have a share in; **compartecipare agli utili** to share in the profits

compartecipazione [kompartetʃipat'tsjone] SF (*divisione con altri*) sharing; (*quota*) share; **compartecipazione agli utili** profit-sharing; **in compartecipazione** jointly

compartimento [komparti'mento] SM 1 (*Amm: circoscrizione*) district 2 (*Naut*): **compartimento stagno** watertight compartment

comparvi ecc [kom'parvi] VB *vedi* **comparire**

compassato, -a [kompas'sato] AGG (*persona*) composed; **freddo e compassato** cool and collected

compassione [kompas'sjone] SF compassion, pity; **provare** *o* **sentire compassione per qn, avere compassione di qn** to pity sb, feel sorry for sb; **fare compassione** to arouse pity; **mi ha fatto compassione vederli ridotti così** I was sorry to see them in such a state; **ha perso tutti gli amici e mi fa proprio compassione** he's lost all his friends, and I feel really sorry for him

compassionevole [kompassjo'nevole] AGG (*che sente compassione*) compassionate; (*che suscita compassione*) pitiful, pathetic

compasso [kom'passo] SM (pair of) compasses *pl*; **compasso per spessori** callipers *pl*

compatibile [kompa'tibile] AGG 1 (*conciliabile, anche Inform*) compatible 2 (*scusabile*) understandable, excusable

compatimento [kompati'mento] SM: **con aria di compatimento** with a condescending air

compatire [kompa'tire] /55/ VT (*aver compassione di*) to feel sorry for, sympathize with; (*scusare*) to make allowances for; **bisogna compatirlo, poveretto** (*iro*) you've got to make allowances for him, poor thing

compatriota, -i, -e [kompatri'ɔta] SM, SF fellow countryman *o* countrywoman, compatriot

compattezza [kompat'tettsa] SF (*solidità*) compactness; (*fig: unità*) solidarity

compatto, -a [kom'patto] AGG (*roccia*) solid; (*folla*) dense; (*partito*) united; (*gruppo*) close-knit

compendio, -di [kom'pɛndjo] SM compendium, outline

compensare [kompen'sare] /72/ VT 1 (*lavoro*) to pay for; (*danno*) to give compensation for; **è stato compensato per il danno ricevuto** he has received compensation for the damage 2 (*bilanciare*) to compensate for, make up for; **le perdite dell'anno scorso saranno compensate dagli utili di quest'anno** this year's profits will compensate for last year's losses; **compensarsi** VR (*uso reciproco*) to balance each other out

compensato [kompen'sato] SM (*anche:* **legno compensato**) plywood

compenso [kom'penso] SM (*retribuzione*) remuneration, payment; (*onorario*) fee; (*ricompensa*) reward, compensation; **in compenso** (*d'altra parte*) on the other hand; **è caro, ma in compenso è molto utile** it's expensive, but it's very useful; **ha un lavoro noiosissimo, in compenso è pagato molto bene** his job is very boring, the plus side is that it's very well paid

compera ['kompera] SF: **fare le compere** to do the shopping

comperare [kompe'rare] /72/ VT = **comprare**

competente [kompe'tente] AGG (*gen, anche Dir*) competent; (*capace*) capable; **è lui il competente in materia** he's the expert; **rivolgersi all'ufficio competente** to apply to the office concerned

competenza [kompe'tentsa] SF 1 (*capacità*) competence, expertise; (*Dir: autorità*) jurisdiction; **non ho competenza in materia** I'm not an expert on that; **è di competenza del tribunale di Milano** it comes under the jurisdiction of the Milan courts; **l'argomento non è di mia competenza** I am not qualified to speak on that subject; **questo lavoro non è di mia competenza** that's not my job; **definire le competenze** to establish responsibilities 2 (*onorario*): **competenze** SFPL fees

competere [kom'petere] /45/ VI *vb dif* 1 (*gareggiare*) to compete, vie 2 (*Dir*): **competere a** to lie with, come under the jurisdiction of, lie within the competence of; (*spettare: compito*) to lie with; (: *denaro*) to be due to; **non mi compete** it's not my responsibility; **avrai ciò che ti compete** you'll have what is due to you

competitività [kompetitivi'ta] SF competitiveness

competitivo, -a [kompeti'tivo] AGG competitive

competitore, -trice [kompeti'tore] SM, SF competitor

competizione [kompetit'tsjone] SF competition, contest; **spirito di competizione** competitive spirit; **auto da competizione** racing car

compiacente [kompja'tʃente] AGG obliging, courteous; (*pegg*) accommodating

compiacenza [kompja'tʃentsa] SF courtesy; **abbia la compiacenza di aspettarmi** please be so good as to wait for me

compiacere [kompja'tʃere] VB IRREG /74/ VI (*aus* **avere**) **compiacere a** to gratify, please ♦ VT to please, make happy; **compiacersi** VIP (*provare soddisfazione*): **compiacersi di** *o* **per qc** to be delighted at sth, be pleased with sth; (*rallegrarsi*): **compiacersi con qn per qc** to congratulate sb for *o* on sth

compiacimento [kompjatʃi'mento] SM satisfaction

compiaciuto, -a [kompja'tʃuto] PP *di* **compiacere**

compiangere [kom'pjandʒere] /75/ VT IRREG to feel sorry for, sympathize with

compianto, -a [kom'pjanto] PP *di* **compiangere** ♦ AGG: **il compianto presidente** the late lamented president ♦ SM mourning, grief

compiere ['kompjere] /24/ VT (*adempiere*) to carry out, fulfil (*Brit*), fulfill (*USA*); (*finire*) to finish, complete; **compiere gli anni** to have one's birthday; **quando compi gli anni?** when is your birthday?; **quanti anni compi?** how old will you be?; **ha compiuto 18 anni il mese scorso** he turned 18 last month; **compiere il proprio dovere** to carry out one's duty; **compiere una buona azione** to do a good deed; **compiersi** VIP **1** (*giungere a termine*) to end **2** (*avverarsi: speranze*) to be fulfilled; (*: profezie*) to come true

compilare [kompi'lare] /72/ VT (*gen*) to compile; (*modulo*) to complete, fill in, fill out (*USA*); **compilare il modulo in stampatello** fill in the form in block letters

compilatore, -trice [kompila'tore] SM, SF compiler

compilazione [kompilat'tsjone] SF (*vedi vb*) compilation; completion

compimento [kompi'mento] SM (*termine, conclusione*) completion, fulfilment (*Brit*), fulfillment (*USA*); **portare a compimento qc** to conclude sth, bring sth to a conclusion

compire *ecc* /92/ VB = **compiere**

compito¹, -a [kom'pito] AGG well-mannered, polite

compito² ['kompito] SM **1** (*incarico*) job, task, duty; (*dovere*) duty; **a me è toccato il compito di portare le bibite** it was my job to bring the drinks **2** (*Scol: a casa*) piece of homework; (*: in classe*) class test; **domani c'è il compito in classe di matematica** we've got a math(s) test tomorrow; **fare i compiti** to do one's homework; **non posso, devo fare i compiti** I can't, I've got to do my homework

compiutezza [kompju'tettsa] SF (*completezza*) completeness; (*perfezione*) perfection

compiuto, -a [kom'pjuto] AGG: **a 20 anni compiuti** at 20 years of age, at age 20; **ho dieci anni compiuti** I'm ten; **un fatto compiuto** a fait accompli

compleanno [komple'anno] SM birthday; **buon compleanno!** happy birthday!

complementare [komplemen'tare] AGG (*gen, anche Geom*) complementary; (*materia di studio, esame*) subsidiary

complemento [komple'mento] SM **1** (*Gramm*) complement; **complemento oggetto** *o* **diretto/indiretto** direct/indirect object **2** (*Mil*) reserve (troops *pl*); **di complemento** reserve *attr*

complessato, -a [komples'sato] AGG, SM, SF: **essere (un) complessato** to be full of complexes

complessità [komplessi'ta] SF complexity

complessivamente [komplessiva'mente] AVV (*nell'insieme*) on the whole, in all; (*in tutto*) altogether

complessivo, -a [komples'sivo] AGG (*ammontare, prezzo, spesa*) total; (*voti*) overall; **visione complessiva** overview

complesso, -a [kom'plesso] AGG complex, complicated; **un problema complesso** a complex problem; **numeri complessi** complex numbers; **proposizione complessa** compound sentence ♦ SM **1** (*insieme*) whole; (*di leggi*) body; (*organizzazione, posto*) complex; **nel** *o* **in complesso** by and large, generally speaking, on the whole; **nel complesso mi è piaciuto abbastanza** on the whole I quite liked it; **è stato un complesso di cose a farmi cambiare idea** it was a combination of things that made me change my mind; **il complesso delle manifestazioni culturali avverrà in luglio** the vast majority of cultural events will take place in July; **complesso industriale** industrial complex; **complesso vitaminico** multi-vitamin **2** (*Psic*) complex; **complesso d'inferiorità** inferiority complex **3** (*Mus*) band, ensemble; (*di musica leggera*) group; **suona in un complesso** he plays in a band

completamente [kompleta'mente] AVV completely

completamento [kompleta'mento] SM completion

completare [komple'tare] /72/ VT to complete, finish

completo, -a [kom'pleto] AGG (*gen*) complete; (*resoconto, elenco*) full, complete; (*fiasco, fallimento*) complete, utter; **è stato un disastro completo!** it was a complete disaster!; **computer completo di stampante** computer complete

with printer ♦ SM (*abito*) suit; (*di lenzuola*) set; **completo di lenzuola singole/matrimoniali** set of sheets for a single/double bed; **portava un completo grigio** he was wearing a grey suit; **completo da sci** ski suit; **essere al completo** (*albergo*) to be full; (*teatro*) to be sold out

complicare [kompli'kare] /20/ VT to complicate; **non per complicarti la vita, ma...** not that I want to make life difficult for you, but ...; **complicarsi** VIP to become complicated

complicazione [komplikat'tsjone] SF complication; **salvo complicazioni** unless any difficulties arise; (*Med*) unless there are any complications

complice ['komplitʃe] SM, SF accomplice

complicità [komplitʃi'ta] SF INV complicity; **un sorriso/uno sguardo di complicità** a knowing smile/look

complimentarsi [komplimen'tarsi] /72/ VIP: **complimentarsi con qn per qc** to congratulate sb on sth

complimento [kompli'mento] SM **1** (*lode*) compliment; **fare un complimento a qn** to compliment sb, pay sb a compliment **2 complimenti** SMPL (*congratulazioni*) congratulations; **le faccio i miei complimenti per...** may I congratulate you on ...; **complimenti!** congratulations!; **complimenti per la promozione!** congratulations on your promotion!; **complimenti, parli molto bene l'italiano!** you speak very good Italian!; **complimenti, che bella casa!** your house is lovely! **3 complimenti** SMPL (*cerimonie*) ceremony *sg*; **fa sempre tanti complimenti** he always stands on ceremony; **senza complimenti!** (*offrendo qualcosa*) help yourself!; **non fare complimenti** *o* **senza complimenti, se ti fa piacere resta con noi** feel free to stay with us if you'd like to; **senza tanti complimenti ha preso la mia macchina e se n'è andato** without so much as a by your leave he took my car and off he went

complottare [komplot'tare] /72/ VI (*aus avere*) to plot, conspire

complotto [kom'plotto] SM plot, conspiracy

compone *ecc* [kom'pone] VB *vedi* **comporre**

componente [kompo'nente] AGG component ♦ SM, SF (*persona*) member ♦ SM (*Elettr*) component, part; (*Chim*) component ♦ SF (*fig: elemento*) element; **c'era in lui una componente di sadismo** there was an element of sadism in his character

compongo *ecc* [kom'pongo] VB *vedi* **comporre**

componibile [kompo'nibile] AGG (*mobili, cucina*) fitted

componimento [komponi'mento] SM **1** (*gen, anche Mus*) composition; (*Letteratura*) work, writing **2** (*Dir*) settlement

comporre [kom'porre] VB IRREG /77/ VT **1** (*creare: musica, poesia*) to compose; **ha composto la colonna sonora** he composed the soundtrack; **essere composto da** to be composed of, consist of; **la casa è composta da tre stanze** the house consists of three rooms **2** (*mettere in ordine*) to arrange **3** (*Telec*) to dial; **alzare il ricevitore e comporre il numero** to lift the receiver and dial the number **4** (*Tip*) to set **5** (*Dir: vertenza*) to settle; **comporsi** VIP: **comporsi di** to consist of, be composed of

comportamentale [komportamen'tale] AGG behavioural (*Brit*), behavioral (*USA*)

comportamento [komporta'mento] SM (*umano, animale*) behaviour (*Brit*), behavior (*USA*); (*di prodotto*) performance; **non capisco il suo comportamento** I don't understand her behaviour

comportare [kompor'tare] /72/ VT (*richiedere*) to call for, require; (*implicare*) to imply, involve, entail; **ciò comporta una spesa ingente** it involves a huge financial outlay; **comportarsi** VIP to behave; **comportati bene!** behave!; **non ci si comporta così** that's no way to behave; **comportarsi da vigliacco** to behave like a coward

composi *ecc* [kom'pozi] VB *vedi* **comporre**

compositore, -trice [kompozi'tore] SM, SF (*Mus*) composer ♦ SM (*Tip*) compositor, typesetter ♦ SF (*Tip*) typesetting machine

composizione [kompozit'tsjone] SF **1** (*gen, anche Chim, Mus*) composition **2** (*Tip*) typesetting, composition **3** (*Dir*) settlement

composta [kom'posta] SF (*Culin*) stewed fruit, compote

compostezza [kompos'tettsa] SF (*vedi agg*) composure; decorum

composto, -a [kom'posto] PP di **comporre** ♦ AGG **1** (*Gramm*) compound *attr*; (*Mat*) composite; (*formato da più elementi*) compound *attr* **2** (*atteggiamento*) composed; (*persona: decoroso*) dignified; **stai seduto composto** sit properly ♦ SM (*Chim*) compound; (*Culin*) mixture; (*Agr*) compost

comprare [kom'prare] /72/ VT **1** to buy; **cosa hai comprato?** what did you buy?; **comprare qc a qn** to buy sth for sb, buy sb sth; **ho comprato un regalino per mia sorella** I bought a little present for my sister; **comprare qc a occhi chiusi** *o* **a scatola chiusa** to buy sth with complete confidence **2** (*corrompere*: *giudice*, *testimone*) to bribe; (*voti*) to buy; **comprare il silenzio di qn** to bribe sb to keep quiet, buy sb's silence

compratore, -trice [kompra'tore] SM, SF buyer, purchaser

compravendita [kompra'vendita] SF (*Comm*) (contract of) sale; **un atto di compravendita** a deed of sale

comprendere [kom'prendere] /81/ VT IRREG **1** (*includere*) to include; (*contenere*) to comprise, consist of **2** (*capire*) to understand

comprendonio [kompren'dɔnjo] SM: **essere duro di comprendonio** to be slow on the uptake

comprensibile [kompren'sibile] AGG understandable

comprensione [kompren'sjone] SF understanding

comprensivo, -a [kompren'sivo] AGG **1** (*Comm*): **comprensivo (di)** (*prezzo*) inclusive (of) **2** (*tollerante*) understanding; **è molto comprensivo** he's very understanding ❏ **comprensivo** non si traduce mai con *comprehensive*

comprensorio, -ri [kompren'sɔrjo] SM (*Amm*: *territorio*) district

compreso, -a [kom'preso] PP di **comprendere** ♦ AGG (*incluso*) inclusive, included; **tutto compreso** all inclusive, all-in (*Brit*); **la vacanza, tutto compreso, costa mille euro** the holiday costs one thousand euros, all-inclusive; **dall'8 al 22 compreso** from the 8th to the 22nd inclusive; **aperto tutta la settimana domenica compresa** open all week including Sunday

compressa [kom'pressa] SF (*Med*: *pastiglia*) tablet; (: *garza*) compress

compressione [kompres'sjone] SF compression

compresso, -a [kom'presso] PP di **comprimere** ♦ AGG compressed, pressed

compressore [kompres'sore] SM **1** compressor **2** (*anche*: **rullo compressore**) steamroller

comprimario, -ria, -ri, -rie [kompri'marjo] SM, SF (*Teatro*) supporting actor (actress)

comprimere [kom'primere] /50/ VT IRREG to compress, press; (*file*) to compress

compromesso, -a [kompro'messo] PP di **compromettere** ♦ SM (*accordo*) compromise; (*Dir*) arbitration agreement; **arrivare a un compromesso** to reach a compromise; **soluzione di compromesso** compromise solution; **vive di compromessi** his life is a series of compromises

compromettere [kompro'mettere] VB IRREG /63/ VT (*reputazione*) to compromise, jeopardize; (*libertà*, *avvenire*, *risultato*) to jeopardize; **compromettersi la reputazione** to compromise *o* jeopardize one's reputation; **compromettersi** VR to compromise o.s.

comproprietà [komproprje'ta] SF (*Dir*) joint ownership

comprovare [kompro'vare] /72/ VT to prove, confirm

compunto, -a [kom'punto] AGG (*contrito*) contrite; **con fare compunto** (*iro*) with a solemn air

compunzione [kompun'tsjone] SF (*vedi agg*) contrition; solemnity

computare [kompu'tare] /72/ VT to calculate, estimate

computer [kəm'pjuːtər] SM INV computer; **lavora molto col computer** he works a lot on the computer; **computer di bordo** (*Aut*) trip computer

computerizzato, -a [kompjuterid'dzato] AGG computerized

computerizzazione [kompjuteriddzat'tsjone] SF computerization

computisteria [komputiste'ria] SF (*Comm*) book-keeping, accounting

computo ['kɔmputo] SM (*calcolo*) counting, calculation; **fare il computo di** to count

comunale [komu'nale] AGG (*del comune*) town *attr*, municipal; **è un impiegato comunale** he works for the local council; **consiglio/palazzo comunale** town council/hall

comune¹ [ko'mune] AGG **1** (*gen*, *anche Gramm*) common; (*diffuso*) common, widespread; (*consueto*) everyday; **è un problema molto comune** it's a very common *o* widespread problem; **di intelligenza non comune** of exceptional intelligence; **un nostro comune amico** a mutual friend of ours; **il bene comune** the common good; **di comune accordo** by common consent; **di uso comune** in common use; **un luogo comune** a commonplace; **cassa comune** kitty; **fare cassa comune** to pool one's money; **mal comune, mezzo gaudio** a trouble shared is a trouble halved **2** (*ordinario*) ordinary; (*di livello medio*) average; **la gente comune** ordinary folk ♦ SM **1** (*di più persone*): **avere qc in comune** to have sth in common, share sth; **non abbiamo niente in comune** we haven't got anything in common; **abbiamo un amico in comune** we've got a mutual friend; **avere il bagno in comune** to share a bathroom, have a communal bathroom; **mettere le provviste in comune** to pool *o* share one's provisions **2** fuori del comune out of the ordinary

comune² [ko'mune] SM (*Amm*: *sede*) town hall; (: *autorità*) town council; **lavora per il comune** she works for the council; **l'età dei Comuni** (*Storia*) the age of the city states; **la Camera dei Comuni, i Comuni** (*in Gran Bretagna: Pol*) the House of Commons, the Commons

comune³ [ko'mune] SF (*comunità*, *anche Storia*) commune

comunicare [komuni'kare] /20/ VT **1** (*trasmettere*) to communicate; **comunicare una notizia a qn** to give sb a piece of news; **comunicare qc a qn** to inform sb of sth **2** (*Rel*) to administer communion to ♦ VI (*aus avere*) (*stanze*, *percorsi*) to communicate; **questa porta comunica con l'esterno** this door leads outside; **comunicarsi** VIP **1** (*propagarsi*) to spread **2** (*Rel*) to receive communion

comunicativo, -a [komunika'tivo] AGG communicative

comunicato [komuni'kato] SM communiqué; **comunicato stampa** press release

comunicazione [komunikat'tsjone] SF **1** (*collegamento*) communication; **porta di comunicazione** communicating door; **essere in comunicazione (con)** (*Anat*, *Tecn*) to be connected (with); **mettersi in comunicazione con qn** to contact sb; **vie di comunicazione** means of communication; **le comunicazioni ferroviarie/stradali/telefoniche sono interrotte** rail/road/telephone communications have broken down; **non c'è più comunicazione tra loro** there's no longer any communication between them **2** (*Telec*) call; **passare la comunicazione a qn** to put sb through; **le passo la comunicazione** I'll put the call through to you; **ottenere la comunicazione** to get through; **non riesco ad avere la comunicazione** I can't get through; **si è interrotta la comunicazione** we've been cut off **3** (*messaggio*) message, communication; (*annuncio*) announcement; **ho una comunicazione urgente per lei** I have an urgent message for you; **salvo comunicazioni contrarie da parte Vostra** unless we hear from you to the contrary

comunione [komu'njone] SF (*Rel*, *anche fig*) communion; **fare la comunione** to receive communion; **prima comunione** first communion; **fare la prima comunione** to make one's first communion; **comunione dei beni** (*Dir*: *tra coniugi*) joint ownership of property

comunismo [komu'nizmo] SM communism

comunista, -i, -e [komu'nista] AGG, SM, SF communist

comunità [komuni'ta] SF INV community; **c'è una grossa comunità britannica in Toscana** there's a big British community in Tuscany; **Comunità (Economica) Europea** European (Economic) Community; **comunità terapeutica** therapeutic community (*rehabilitation centre run by voluntary organization for people with drug, alcohol etc dependency*)

comunitario, -ria, -ri, -rie [komuni'tarjo] AGG community *attr*

comunque [ko'munkwe] AVV (*in ogni modo*) anyhow, anyway, in any case; **devi farlo comunque** you'll have to do it anyway; **accetterà comunque** he'll accept in any case; **i miei non vogliono, ma ci vado comunque** my parents don't want me to, but I'm going anyway; **e comunque al biglietto ci penso io** and as for the ticket I'll see to that ♦ CONG **1** (*in* *qualunque modo*) however, no matter how; **comunque vada** whatever happens; **comunque vada, sono contento che sia finita** however it turns out, I'm glad it's over; **comunque sia** however that may be **2** (*tuttavia*) however, nevertheless; **comunque potevi avvertirmi** however *o* nevertheless you could have let me know, you could have let me know though

con [kon] PREP *può fondersi con l'articolo determinativo:* con + il = col, con + lo = collo, con + l' = coll', con + la = colla, con + i = coi, con + gli = cogli, con + le = colle **1** (*gen*) with; **ci andrò con lei** I'll go with her; **con chi sei stato?** who were you with?; **con chi era il film?** who was in the film?; **riso col burro** rice with butter; **un ragazzo con gli occhi azzurri** a boy with blue eyes, a blue-eyed boy; **è a letto con la febbre** he's in bed with a temperature **2** (*complemento di relazione*) with; (*nei confronti di*) with, towards; **sono in contatto con loro** I am in touch with them; **è sposata con uno scozzese** she's married to a Scot; **si è sposata con uno scozzese** she married a Scot, she got married to a Scot; **hai parlato con lui?** have you spoken to him?; **essere gentile con** to be kind to sb; **è gentile con tutti** she's nice to everybody; **è brava con i bambini** she's good with children; **confrontare qc con qc** to compare sth with *o* to sth; **sono tutti con lui** (*dalla sua parte*) they are all on his side, they are all behind him **3** (*per mezzo di*) with; (*aereo, macchina*) by; **scrivere con la penna** to write with a pen; **prendilo con le mani** pick it up with your hands; **condisci l'insalata con l'olio** dress the salad with oil; **arrivare col treno/l'aereo/con la macchina** to arrive by train/plane/by car; **lo hanno fatto venire con una scusa** they used a pretext to get him to come, they got him to come by means of a pretext **4** (*complemento di modo o maniera*) with; **con pazienza** with patience, patiently; **con la forza** by force; **con molta attenzione** with great attention, very attentively; **con mia grande sorpresa/mio grande stupore** to my great surprise/astonishment **5** (*complemento di causa*): **con questo freddo non potremo partire** we can't leave in this cold weather; **con i debiti che ha...** with all his debts ..., given all his debts ...; **con il 1° di ottobre** as of October 1st; **con l'autunno cadono le foglie** with the coming of autumn the leaves fall from the trees **6** (*nonostante*): **con tutti i suoi difetti...** in spite of all his faults ...; **con tutto ciò** in spite of that, for all that; **con tutto che era arrabbiato** even though he was angry, in spite of the fact that he was angry **7** (*con l'infinito*): **finì col dirgli che aveva ragione lei** he ended up saying she was right; **con l'insistere tanto l'hai fatto arrabbiare** you've annoyed him with your pestering; **col passar del tempo** with the passing of time, in the course of time; **col sorgere del sole** with the dawn **8** **e con ciò se n'è andato** and with that he left; **e con questo?** so what?; **come va con la tua gamba?** how's your leg?; **come va con Alberto?** how are you getting on with Alberto?

conato [ko'nato] SM **conato di vomito** retching; **avere un conato di vomito** to retch

conca,-che ['konka] SF (*Geog*) valley, basin

concatenare [konkate'nare] /72/ VT to link up, connect; **concatenarsi** VR (*uso reciproco*) to be connected

concavo,-a ['kɔnkavo] AGG concave

concedere [kon't∫edere] /29/ VT IRREG **1** (*permettere*): **concedere a qn di fare qc** to allow sb to do sth; (*dare*): **concedere qc a qn** to grant sb sth; **gli concesse di uscire** he gave him permission to go out; **concedere un prestito** to grant a loan; **mi hanno concesso un prestito** they gave me a loan; **mi concedi un minuto d'attenzione** may I have your attention? **2** (*ammettere*): **concedere (che)** to concede (that) **3** **concedersi qc/di fare qc** (*permettersi*) to allow o.s. sth/to do sth, to treat o.s. to sth; **concedersi il lusso di andare in vacanza** to allow o.s. the luxury of a holiday; **si è concesso una bella macchina** he treated himself to a nice car; **concedersi un'intervista** to grant, allow; **si é concessa as una intervista** she granted him an interview

concentramento [kont∫entra'mento] SM concentration

concentrare [kont∫en'trare] /72/ VT to concentrate; **concentrare l'attenzione su qc** to focus one's attention on sth; **concentrarsi** VR: **concentrarsi (in)** (*raccogliere l'attenzione*) to concentrate (on); (*adunarsi*) to assemble (in)

concentrato,-a [kont∫en'trato] SM concentrate; **concentrato di pomodoro** tomato purée

concentrazione [kont∫entrat'tsjone] SF (*gen*) concentration; **concentrazione orizzontale/verticale** (*Econ*) horizontal/vertical integration

concentrico,-a,-ci,-che [kon't∫entriko] AGG (*Geom*) concentric

concepibile [kont∫e'pibile] AGG conceivable

concepimento [kont∫epi'mento] SM conception

concepire [kont∫e'pire] /55/ VT **1** (*bambino*) to conceive **2** (*idea*) to conceive; (*progetto*) to devise, conceive; (*metodo, piano*) to devise; **un elettrodomestico concepito per vari usi** an electrical appliance devised for various purposes **3** (*immaginare*) to imagine, understand, conceive (of); **non riesco a concepire una cosa simile** I just can't imagine such a thing

concernere [kon't∫ernere] /45/ VT *vb dif* to concern, regard; **per quanto mi concerne** as far as I'm concerned

concertare [kont∫er'tare] /72/ VT (*ordire: piano*) to devise, plan; (*Mus: spartito*) to harmonize; (: *sinfonia*) to rehearse

concertista,-i,-e [kont∫er'tista] SM, SF concert performer

concerto [kon't∫erto] SM (*Mus*) concert; (*componimento*) concerto; **sala per concerti** concert hall

concessi *ecc* [kon't∫essi] VB *vedi* **concedere**

concessionario,-a,-ria,-ri,-rie [kont∫essjo'narjo] AGG concessionary ◆ SM (*Comm*) agent, dealer; **concessionario esclusivo (di)** sole agent (for)

concessione [kont∫es'sjone] SF concession

concesso,-a [kon't∫esso] PP *di* **concedere**

concetto [kon't∫etto] SM (*nozione*) concept; (*opinione*) opinion; **non ho afferrato bene il concetto** I haven't quite got the idea; **farsi un concetto di** to form an opinion of; **è un impiegato di concetto** ≈ he's a white-collar worker; **lascialo in pace, sta facendo un lavoro di concetto** (*iro*) leave him alone, he's concentrating

concezione [kont∫et'tsjone] SF **1** (*idea*) view, idea; **che concezione hai della vita?** how do you see life?, what is your view of life? **2** (*ideazione*) conception

conchiglia [kon'kiʎʎa] SF (*Zool*) shell; (*Culin*) pasta shell

concia ['kont∫a] SF (*vedi vt a*) tanning; curing

conciare [kon't∫are] /14/ VT **1** (*pelli*) to tan; (*tabacco*) to cure **2** (*maltrattare: scarpe, libri*) to treat badly; (: *persona*) to ill-treat; **guarda come hai conciato quei libri** look at the mess you've made of those books; **ti hanno conciato male** *o* **per le feste!** they've really beaten you up!; **conciarsi** VR (*ridursi male*) to get into a mess; (*vestirsi male*): **ma guarda come si è conciata!** what on earth has she got on?

conciliabile [kont∫i'ljabile] AGG compatible

conciliabolo [kont∫i'ljabolo] SM secret meeting

conciliante [kont∫i'ljante] AGG conciliatory

conciliare [kont∫i'ljare] /19/ VT **1** (*mettere d'accordo*) to reconcile; **conciliare una contravvenzione** to settle a fine on the spot **2** (*favorire: sonno*) to be conducive to, induce; **conciliil il sonno** it helps you sleep **3** **conciliarsi qc** (*stima, simpatia*) to gain *o* win sth (for o.s.); **conciliarsi qc** VIP: **lo studio non si concilia con il mio lavoro** I can't combine studying with my job

conciliazione [kont∫iljat'tsjone] SF (*accordo*) reconciliation; (*Dir*) settlement; **la Conciliazione** (*Storia*) the Lateran Pact

concilio,-lii [kon't∫iljo] SM **1** (*Rel*) council **2** (*riunione*) conference, meeting

concimare [kont∫i'mare] /72/ VT to fertilize; (*con letame*) to manure

concime [kon't∫ime] SM (*chimico*) fertilizer; (*letame*) manure

concisione [kont∫i'zjone] SF concision, conciseness

conciso,-a [kon't∫izo] AGG concise, succinct

concitato,-a [kont∫i'tato] AGG excited, agitated

concittadino,-a [kont∫itta'dino] SM, SF fellow citizen

conclave [kon'klave] SM (*Rel*) conclave

concludere [kon'kludere] VB IRREG /93/ VT **1** (*affare, trattato*) to conclude; (*discorso*) to finish, end, conclude, bring to an end; (*operare positivamente*) to achieve; **non ho concluso nulla oggi** I haven't achieved anything today; **per concludere...** to conclude ...; **cerchiamo di concludere** let's try to come to a conclusion **2** (*dedurre*) **concludere che** to conclude that, come to the conclusion that; **cosa possiamo concludere dalla discussione?** what can we conclude from the debate?; **concludersi** VIP (*finire*) to end, conclude, come to an end

conclusione [konklu'zjone] SF (*gen*) conclusion; (*di discorso*) close, end; (*risultato*) result; **trarre una conclusione** to draw a conclusion; (*Calcio*) shot on goal; **in conclusione** in conclusion

conclusivo, -a [konklu'zivo] AGG (*finale*) final, closing, conclusive

concluso, -a [kon'kluzo] PP *di* **concludere**

concomitanza [konkomi'tantsa] SF (*di circostanze, fatti*) combination

concordanza [konkor'dantsa] SF (*anche Gramm*) agreement; **concordanze** SFPL concordances

concordare [konkor'dare] /72/ VT (*fissare: prezzo*) to agree on; (*Gramm*) to make agree; **concordare una tregua** to agree to a truce ♦ VI (*aus avere*) (*essere d'accordo*) to agree, coincide; (*testimonianze*) to agree, tally

concordato [konkor'dato] SM (*patto*) agreement; (*Rel*) concordat

concorde [kon'kɔrde] AGG (*d'accordo*) in agreement; (*simultaneo*) simultaneous; **concordi nel condannarlo** unanimous in their condemnation of him

concordia [kon'kɔrdja] SF concord, harmony

concorrente [konkor'rente] AGG 1 (*Geom*) concurrent 2 (*Comm*) competing *attr* ♦ SM, SF (*Comm, Sport*) competitor; (*a un concorso di bellezza*) contestant

concorrenza [konkor'rentsa] SF competition; **le due ditte si fanno una concorrenza spietata** the two firms are in fierce competition with each other, there is fierce competition between the two firms; **non temono la concorrenza** they are unbeatable; **a prezzi di concorrenza** at competitive prices; **concorrenza sleale** unfair competition

concorrenziale [konkorren'tsjale] AGG competitive

concorrere [kon'korrere] /28/ VI IRREG (*aus avere*) 1 **concorrere a** (*contribuire: a guarigione, spesa*) to contribute (to); (*partecipare: a un'impresa*) to take part (in); **concorri alla gara di domani?** are you taking part in the competition tomorrow? 2 (*competere*) **concorrere a** to compete (for); (*a una cattedra*) to apply (for) 3 **concorrere (in)** (*Mat*) to converge *o* meet (in)

concorso, -a [kon'korso] PP *di* **concorrere** ♦ SM 1 (*gen*) competition; (*esame*) competitive examination; **partecipanti fuori concorso** non-competitors; **concorso di bellezza** beauty contest; **concorso ippico** showjumping event; **concorso a premi** competition; **ha partecipato ad un concorso a premi e ha vinto** she went in for a competition and won; **concorso per titoli** competitive examination for qualified candidates 2 (*partecipazione*): **concorso (a)** contribution (to); **concorso di colpa** (*Dir*) contributory negligence; **concorso in reato** (*Dir*) complicity in a crime 3 (*affluenza*) gathering; **concorso di circostanze** combination of circumstances

concreto, -a [kon'krɛto] AGG (*gen*) concrete; (*vantaggi*) positive; **una prova concreta** concrete evidence ♦ SM: **in concreto** in reality; **ma cosa fa in concreto?** what's he actually doing?; **fare qualcosa di concreto** to get something concrete done

concubina [konku'bina] SF concubine

concussione [konkus'sjone] SF (*Dir*) extortion

❏ **concussione** non si traduce mai con *concussion*

condanna [kon'danna] SF 1 (*Dir: sentenza*) sentence; **scontare una condanna** to serve a sentence; **ha già avuto due condanne per furto** he has two previous convictions for theft; **condanna a morte** death sentence 2 (*disapprovazione*) condemnation

condannare [kondan'nare] /72/ VT 1 (*Dir*): **condannare (a)** to sentence (to); **condannare qn a 5 anni di prigione** to sentence sb to 5 years' imprisonment; **l'hanno condannato a cinque anni di prigione** he's been sentenced to five years in prison; **condannare qn per** to convict sb of; **condannare qn per rapina a mano armata** to convict sb *o* find sb guilty of armed robbery; **li hanno condannati per rapina a mano armata** they were convicted of armed robbery; **è condannato al letto** he is confined to bed 2 (*disapprovare*) to condemn, censure; **non me la sento di condannarlo** I don't condemn him

condannato, -a [kondan'nato] SM, SF prisoner, convict

condensa [kon'densa] SF condensation

condensare [konden'sare] /72/ VT, **condensarsi** VIP to condense

condensatore [kondensa'tore] SM condenser, capacitor

condensazione [kondensat'tsjone] SF condensation

condimento [kondi'mento] SM (*di insalata*) dressing; (*di carne*) seasoning; (*salsa*) sauce

condire [kon'dire] /55/ VT (*cibo*) to season, flavour; (*insalata*) to dress; (*fig*) to spice, season; **una salsa per condire la pasta** a sauce for pasta; **hai condito la pasta?** have you mixed the sauce with the pasta?

condiscendente [kondiʃʃen'dente] AGG (*indulgente*) obliging; (*arrendevole*) compliant

condiscendenza [kondiʃʃen'dentsa] SF (*disponibilità*) obligingness; (*arrendevolezza*) compliance

condiscendere [kondiʃ'ʃendere] /101/ VI IRREG (*aus avere*) **condiscendere a** to agree to

condisceso, -a [kondiʃ'ʃeso] PP *di* **condiscendere**

condividere [kondi'videre] /43/ VT IRREG to share; **condivide l'appartamento con il fratello** he shares the apartment with his brother; **condividere l'opinione di qn** to agree with sb; **non condivido le tue opinioni** I don't agree with you

condiviso, -a [kondi'vizo] PP *di* **condividere**

condizionale [kondittsjo'nale] AGG (*Gramm*) conditional ♦ SM (*Gramm*) conditional (mood) ♦ SF 1 (*Gramm*) conditional clause 2 (*Dir*) suspended sentence

condizionamento [kondittsjona'mento] SM conditioning; **condizionamento d'aria** air conditioning

condizionare [kondittsjo'nare] /72/ VT (*gen, anche Psic*) to condition

condizionatore [kondittsjona'tore] SM: **condizionatore (d'aria)** air conditioner

condizione [kondit'tsjone] SF 1 (*stato*) condition; **in buone condizioni** in good condition; **la macchina è ancora in buone condizioni** the car is still in good condition; **in condizioni pessime** in a very bad state, in poor condition; **condizioni di salute** state of health; **migliorare le proprie condizioni finanziarie** to improve one's financial position; **non sei in condizione di guidare** you're not in a fit state to drive; **condizioni di lavoro** working conditions 2 (*situazione*) situation; **essere** *o* **trovarsi in condizione di fare qc** to be in a position to do sth; **mettere qn in condizione di fare qc** to make it possible for sb to do sth; **mi trovo in una condizione assurda** I'm in an absurd situation 3 (*di patto*) condition; (*di contratto*) condition, term; (*di pagamento*) term, condition; **porre una condizione** to lay down *o* make a condition; **ad un'unica condizione** on one condition; **non lo farò a nessuna condizione** on no account will I do it; **a condizione che** on condition that, provided that; **condizioni a convenirsi** terms to be arranged; **condizioni di vendita** sales terms

condoglianze [kondoʎ'ʎantse] SFPL condolences; **fare le proprie condoglianze a qn** to offer one's sympathy *o* condolences to sb

condominiale [kondomi'njale] AGG: **riunione condominiale** residents' meeting; **spese condominiali** common charges

condominio, -nii [kondo'minjo] SM (*Dir*) condominium, joint ownership; (*edificio*) jointly-owned block of flats (*Brit*), condominium (*USA*)

❏ **condominio** non si traduce mai con la parola inglese *condom*

condomino [kon'domino] SM joint owner

condonare [kondo'nare] /72/ VT (*Dir*) to remit

condono [kon'dono] SM (*Dir*) remission; **condono edilizio** *conditional amnesty for work done without planning permission*; **condono fiscale** *conditional amnesty for people evading tax*; **condono tombale** tax amnesty (*for all past offences*)

condotta [kon'dotta] SF 1 (*comportamento*) conduct, behaviour (*Brit*), behavior (*USA*); (*di un affare ecc*) handling; **tenere una buona/cattiva condotta** to behave well/badly 2 (*Amm: di medico*) *country medical practice controlled by a local authority* 3 (*Tecn: tubature*) piping

condotto, -a [kon'dotto] PP *di* **condurre** ♦ AGG: **medico condotto** local authority doctor (*in a country district*) ♦ SM 1 (*Anat*) duct;

condotto uditivo auditory canal **2** (*Tecn*: *di liquido*) pipe, conduit; (: *di aria*) duct
conducente [kondu't∫ɛnte] SM, SF driver; **il conducente dell'autobus** the bus driver
conduco *ecc* [kon'duko] VB *vedi* **condurre**
condurre [kon'durre] VB IRREG /**90**/ VT **1** (*persona: accompagnare*) to take; (: *guidare*) to lead; **condurre qn a casa** (*a piedi*) to walk sb home; (*in macchina*) to drive *o* take sb home; **mi ha condotto a casa** he took me home; **condurre qn per mano** to take sb by the hand; **condurre alla vittoria** to lead to victory; **condurre in salvo qn** to lead sb to safety; **condurre qn alla follia** to drive sb mad; **questo ci conduce a pensare che...** this leads us to think that ... **2** (*azienda, affari*) to run, manage; (*trattative*) to hold, conduct; (*orchestra*) to conduct; **condurre (la gara)** (*Sport*) to lead, be in the lead; **condurre a termine** to conclude **3** (*automobile*) to drive; (*aereo*) to pilot; (*barca*) to steer **4** (*trasportare: acqua, gas*) to convey **5** (*Fis*) to conduct; **condursi** VR to behave, conduct o.s.
condussi *ecc* [kon'dussi] VB *vedi* **condurre**
conduttore, -trice [kondut'tore] AGG: **filo conduttore** (*fig*) thread; **motivo conduttore** leitmotiv ♦ SM **1** (*Fis*) conductor **2** (*di mezzi pubblici*) driver
conduttura [kondut'tura] SF (*gen*) pipe; (*di acqua, gas*) main
conduzione [kondut'tsjone] SF **1** (*di affari, ditta*) management; **a conduzione familiare** (*ditta*) family-run **2** (*Dir: locazione*) lease **3** (*Fis*) conduction
confabulare [konfabu'lare] /**72**/ VI (*aus* avere) to confab
confacente [konfa't∫ɛnte] AGG: **confacente a qn/qc** suitable for sb/sth; **clima confacente alla salute** healthy climate
confarsi [kon'farsi] /**53**/ VIP (*essere adatto*): **confarsi a qn/ qc** to be suitable for sb/sth, suit sb/sth; **questo modo di parlare non ti si confà** it doesn't become you to speak like that; **questo clima non mi si confà** this climate isn't good for me; **il lavoro non gli si confà** (*scherz*) work doesn't agree with him!
confederazione [konfederat'tsjone] SF confederacy, confederation; **confederazione imprenditoriale** employers' association
conferenza [konfe'rentsa] SF **1** (*discorso*) lecture; **fare** *o* **tenere una conferenza su qc** to give a lecture on sth, lecture on sth; **terrà una conferenza nell'aula magna** he's going to give a lecture in the main hall; **sala conferenze** lecture theatre **2** (*Pol, Amm: riunione*) conference; **una conferenza sull'inquinamento atmosferico** a conference on air pollution; **conferenza stampa** press conference; **conferenza al vertice** summit conference
conferenziere, -a [konferen'tsjere] SM, SF lecturer, speaker
conferimento [konferi'mento] SM conferring, awarding
conferire [konfe'rire] /**55**/ VT: **conferire (a)** (*premio, titolo, incarico*) to confer (on); (*tono, aria*) to give (to) ♦ VI (*aus* avere) **1** (*avere un colloquio*) to confer **2** (*contribuire, giovare*): **conferire a qn/qc** to be good for sb/sth
conferma [kon'ferma] SF confirmation; **dare conferma** to confirm; **a conferma di** in confirmation of
confermare [konfer'mare] /**72**/ VT to confirm; **l'eccezione conferma la regola** the exception proves the rule; **devo confermare la prenotazione** I've got to confirm the booking; **ha confermato che verrà** he's confirmed that he's coming; **si è confermato campione** he has confirmed his position as champion
confessare [konfes'sare] /**72**/ VT (*gen*) to confess, admit; (*Rel*) to confess; **ti confesso che...** I must confess that....; **confesso di essere stupito** I must admit I'm amazed; **l'omicida ha confessato** the murderer confessed; **confessarsi** VR to confess; **(andare a) confessarsi** to go to confession **2 confessarsi colpevole** to admit one's guilt
confessionale [konfessjo'nale] AGG confessional ♦ SM (*Rel*) confessional (box)
confessione [konfes'sjone] SF **1** (*gen, anche Rel*) confession **2** (*fede*) denomination
confesso, -a [kon'fesso] AGG: **essere reo confesso** to have pleaded guilty
confessore [konfes'sore] SM (*Rel*) confessor
confetto [kon'fetto] SM **1** (*dolciume*) sugared almond; **a**

quando i confetti? when are we going to be hearing wedding bells? **2** (*pillola*) pill
confettura [konfet'tura] SF (*gen*) jam; (*di arance*) marmalade
confezionare [konfettsjo'nare] /**72**/ VT **1** (*pacco, merce: involgere*) to wrap up; (: *per vendita*) to package **2** (*articoli di abbigliamento*) to make (up)
confezione [konfet'tsjone] SF **1** (*gen*) making, preparation; (*di abiti da uomo*) tailoring; (*di abiti da donna*) dressmaking **2** (*imballaggio*) packaging; **una confezione di caramelle** a packet of sweets; **confezione natalizia** Christmas pack; **confezione regalo** gift pack; **fare una confezione regalo** to giftwrap; **mi può fare una confezione regalo?** can you giftwrap it for me?; **confezione risparmio** economy size; **confezione da viaggio** travel pack; **confezioni per signora** ladies' wear *no pl*; **confezioni da uomo** menswear *no pl*
conficcare [konfik'kare] /**20**/ VT: **conficcare in** (*chiodo, punta*) to hammer into, drive into, stick into; (*unghie*) to stick into, dig into; **mi si è conficcata una spina nel dito** a thorn got stuck in my finger; **conficcarsi** VIP to stick
confidare [konfi'dare] /**72**/ VT: **confidare qc a qn** to confide sth to sb; **ti voglio confidare un segreto** I want to tell you a secret ♦ VI (*aus* avere) **confidare in** (*persona, capacità ecc*) to have confidence in; **confido nella tua discrezione** I am relying on your discretion; **confido in una buona riuscita** I am confident of a successful outcome; **confidarsi** VR: **confidarsi con qn** to confide in sb; **aveva bisogno di confidarsi con qualcuno** she needed to confide in somebody
confidente [konfi'dɛnte] AGG confiding, trusting ♦ SM, SF (*persona amica*) confidant (confidante); (*informatore*) informer; **è un confidente della polizia** he is a police informer
confidenza [konfi'dentsa] SF **1** (*familiarità*) intimacy, familiarity; **essere in confidenza** *o* **avere confidenza con qn** to be on friendly terms with sb; **prendersi (troppe) confidenze** to take liberties **2** (*rivelazione*) confidence; **fare una confidenza a qn** to confide something to sb; **dire qc in confidenza a qn** to tell sb sth in confidence **3** (*dimestichezza*): **prendere confidenza col proprio lavoro** to become more confident about one's work
confidenziale [konfiden'tsjale] AGG (*lettera, informazione*) confidential; (*maniere, parole*) familiar; **in via confidenziale** confidentially
configurare [konfigu'rare] /**72**/ VT (*Inform*) to set; **configurarsi** VIP (*fig*) to take shape
configurazione [konfigurat'tsjone] SF (*gen*) shape, configuration; (*Astron, Geog*) configuration; (*Inform*) setting
confinante [konfi'nante] AGG neighbouring (*Brit*), neighboring (*USA*)
confinare [konfi'nare] /**72**/ VI (*aus* avere) **confinare con** (*anche fig*) to border on; **l'Italia confina ad ovest con la Francia** Italy has a border with France to the west ♦ VT **1** (*relegare*) to confine; **confinare qn in** to confine sb to; **la malattia l'ha confinata in casa** her illness confined her to the house **2** (*Pol*) to intern; **confinarsi** VR (*isolarsi*): **confinarsi in** to shut o.s. up in
confinato, -a [konfi'nato] AGG interned ♦ SM, SF internee
confine [kon'fine] SM (*di territorio, nazione*) border, frontier; (*di proprietà*) boundary; **abbiamo passato il confine** we crossed the border; **territorio di confine** border zone; **senza confine** (*fig*) boundless; **i confini della scienza** the frontiers of science
confino [kon'fino] SM (*Pol*) internment; **mandare al confino qn** to send sb into internal exile
confisca [kon'fiska] SF confiscation
confiscare [konfis'kare] /**20**/ VT to confiscate
conflagrazione [konflagrat'tsjone] SF (*incendio*) conflagration; (*fig: guerra*) sudden outbreak of hostilities
conflitto [kon'flitto] SM (*gen, anche Mil*) conflict; (*fig: contrasto*) clash, conflict; **essere in conflitto con qc** to clash with sth; **essere in conflitto con qn** to be at loggerheads with sb; **conflitto d'interessi** conflict of interests
conflittuale [konflittu'ale] AGG: **rapporto conflittuale** relationship based on conflict
conflittualità [konflittuali'ta] SF INV conflicts *pl*
confluenza [konflu'entsa] SF (*di fiumi, anche fig*) confluence; (*di strade*) junction

confluire [konfluˈire] /55/ VI (aus avere o essere) (fiumi) to meet, flow into each other; (strade) to meet; (fig: idee, persone) to meet, come together

confondere [konˈfondere] VB IRREG /25/ VT **1** (mischiare) to mix up, confuse; **confondere le idee a qn** to mix sb up, confuse sb; **tutti questi discorsi mi confondono le idee** all this talk is getting me confused; **confondere le carte in tavola** (fig) to confuse the issue **2** (scambiare): **confondere qc con qc** to confuse sth with sth; **confondo sempre i due fratelli** I always get the two brothers mixed up; **non starai confondendo i nomi?** you're not mixing up the names, are you?; **ho confuso le date** I mixed up the dates **3** (turbare) to confuse; (imbarazzare) to embarrass; (disorientare: nemico, avversario) to trick; **confondersi** VIP **1** (colori, sagoma) to merge; (ricordi) to become confused; (persona): **confondersi tra la folla** to mingle with the crowd **2** (sbagliarsi) to be mistaken, get mixed up; **no, scusa, mi sono confuso: era ieri** no, sorry, I've got mixed up: it was yesterday **3** (turbarsi) to become confused

conformare [konforˈmare] /72/ VT: **conformare (a)** (adeguare) to adapt (to); **conformarsi** VR: **conformarsi (a)** to conform (to)

conforme [konˈforme] AGG: **conforme a** (simile) similar to; (corrispondente) in keeping with

conformemente [konformeˈmente] AVV accordingly; **conformemente a** in accordance with, according to

conformismo [konforˈmizmo] SM conformity

conformista [konforˈmista] SM, SF (gen) conformist

conformità [konformiˈta] SF conformity; **in conformità a** in conformity with

confortare [konforˈtare] /72/ VT **1** (consolare) to comfort, console; **mi conforta sapere...** I'm glad to know ... **2** (tesi, accusa) to strengthen, support

confortevole [konforˈtevole] AGG (comodo) comfortable; (confortante) comforting

conforto [konˈforto] SM **1** (consolazione, sollievo) comfort, consolation; **i conforti (religiosi)** the last sacraments **2** (conferma) support; **a conforto di qc** in support of sth

confraternita [konfraˈternita] SF brotherhood

confrontare [konfronˈtare] /72/ VT (paragonare) to compare; **abbiamo confrontato le nostre scuole** we compared our schools; **confrontarsi** VR (scontrarsi) to have a confrontation
❑ confrontare non si traduce mai con confront

confronto [konˈfronto] SM **1** (paragone) comparison; (Dir, Mil, Pol) confrontation; **a confronto di** o in comparison a compared with o to, in comparison with o to; **mettere a confronto** to compare; (Dir) to confront; **fare un confronto fra due cose** to compare two things; **non c'è confronto!** there's no comparison!; **senza confronti** beyond comparison; **reggere al confronto con** to stand comparison with; **confronto all'americana** (Dir) identity parade **2** (di testi) collation **3 nei miei** (o tuoi ecc) **confronti** towards me (o you ecc); **non ho risentimento nei suoi confronti** I don't feel any resentment towards him

confusi ecc [konˈfuzi] VB vedi **confondere**

confusione [konfuˈzjone] SF (disordine, errore) confusion; (chiasso) racket, noise; (imbarazzo) embarrassment; **c'è stata confusione tra i due nomi** there's been a mix-up over the two names, the two names have been confused; **ha approfittato della confusione per scappare** he took advantage of the confusion to escape; **che confusione!** what a mess!; **far confusione** (disordine) to make a mess; (chiasso) to make a racket; (confondere) to confuse things; **essere in uno stato di confusione mentale** to be confused in one's mind

confuso, -a [konˈfuzo] PP di **confondere** ♦ AGG (gen) confused; (discorso, stile) muddled; (persona: turbato) embarrassed; (immagine, ricordo) hazy; **sono un po' confuso** I'm a bit confused; **la situazione è ancora confusa** the situation is still confused

confutare [konfuˈtare] /72/ VT to confute, refute

congedare [kondʒeˈdare] /72/ VT (gen) to dismiss; (Mil: soldati) to demobilize; (licenziare) to sack; **congedare per invalidità** to invalid out; **congedarsi** VR: **congedarsi (da)** to take one's leave (of); (soldato) to be demobilized (from)

congedo [konˈdʒedo] SM **1** (permesso, anche Mil) leave; **andare in congedo** to go on leave; **chiedere un congedo per motivi di salute** to apply for sick leave; **congedo assoluto** (Mil) discharge; **congedo parentale** parental leave **2** (commiato): **prendere congedo da qn** to take one's leave of sb **3** (Teatro: finale) finale; (Poesia: coda) envoy

congegnare [kondʒeɲˈɲare] /15/ VT (motore) to construct, put together; (fig: trama, scherzo) to devise

congegno [konˈdʒeɲɲo] SM (dispositivo) device; (meccanismo) mechanism

congelamento [kondʒelaˈmento] SM (gen) freezing; (Med) frostbite; **congelamento dei prezzi** (Econ) price freeze; **congelamento salariale** wage freeze

congelare [kondʒeˈlare] /72/ VT (gen, anche Econ) to freeze; **congelarsi** VIP to freeze
❑ congelare non si traduce mai con congeal

congelatore [kondʒelaˈtore] AGG freezer attr ♦ SM (macchina) deepfreeze, freezer

congenito, -a [konˈdʒenito] AGG congenital

congerie [konˈdʒɛrje] SF INV (di oggetti) heap; (di idee) muddle, jumble

congestionare [kondʒestjoˈnare] /72/ VT (Med: strada) to congest; **essere congestionato** (persona, viso) to be flushed; (zona: per traffico) to be congested

congestione [kondʒesˈtjone] SF congestion

congettura [kondʒetˈtura] SF conjecture, supposition; **fare mille congetture** to let one's imagination run riot

congiungere [konˈdʒundʒere] VB IRREG /5/ VT (gen) to join (together); (punti) to join, connect; (luoghi) to link, connect; **il ponte congiunge l'isoletta alla terraferma** the bridge links the island to the mainland; **congiungersi** VIP (gen) to join (together); (Mil) to join forces; **congiungersi in matrimonio** to be joined in matrimony

congiuntivite [kondʒuntiˈvite] SF (Med) conjunctivitis; **ha la congiuntivite** she's got conjunctivitis

congiuntivo, -a [kondʒunˈtivo] AGG, SM (Gramm) subjunctive

congiunto, -a [konˈdʒunto] PP di **congiungere** ♦ AGG (mani) clasped, joined; (azione, sforzo) joint ♦ SM, SF (parente) relative

congiuntura [kondʒunˈtura] SF **1** (punto di contatto) join, junction; (Anat) joint **2** (circostanza) juncture, circumstance; (opportunità) occasion; **in questa congiuntura** at this juncture **3** (Econ) economic situation; **superare la (bassa) congiuntura** to overcome the economic crisis

congiunturale [kondʒuntuˈrale] AGG of the economic situation; **crisi congiunturale** economic crisis

congiunzione [kondʒunˈtsjone] SF (gen) join; (Anat) joint; (di due linee ferroviarie) junction; (Astron, Gramm) conjunction

congiura [konˈdʒura] SF (anche fig) conspiracy, plot

congiurare [kondʒuˈrare] /72/ VI (aus avere) **congiurare (ai danni di** o **contro qn)** to conspire (against sb), plot (against sb); **tutto sembra congiurare contro di me** everything seems to be conspiring against me
❑ congiurare non si traduce mai con conjure

conglomerato [konglomeˈrato] SM (gen) conglomeration; (Geol) conglomerate; (Edil) concrete

Congo [ˈkɔngo] SM (paese, fiume) the Congo

congolese [kongoˈlese] AGG, SM, SF Congolese inv

congratularsi [kongratuˈlarsi] /72/ VIP: **congratularsi con qn (per qc)** to congratulate sb (on sth)

congratulazioni [kongratulatˈtsjoni] SFPL congratulations; **congratulazioni per la promozione!** congratulations on your promotion!; **fare le (proprie) congratulazioni a qn per qc** to congratulate sb on sth

congrega, -ghe [konˈgrega] SF gang, band, bunch

congregazione [kongregatˈtsjone] SF congregation

congressista, -i, -e [kongresˈsista] SM, SF participant at a congress

congresso [konˈgresso] SM congress; **sala (dei) congressi** conference hall; **il congresso del partito socialista** the Socialist Party conference

congruo, -a [ˈkongruo] AGG (prezzo, compenso) adequate, fair; (ragionamento) coherent, consistent

conguagliare [kongwaʎ'ʎare] /27/ VT (*Comm*) to balance; (*stipendio*) to adjust

conguaglio, -gli [kon'gwaʎʎo] SM 1 (*vedi vb*) balancing; adjusting 2 (*somma di denaro*) balance

CONI ['koni] SIGLA M = Comitato Olimpico Nazionale Italiano

coniare [ko'njare] /19/ VT (*monete*) to mint; (*medaglie*) to strike; (*fig: parole nuove*) to coin

coniazione [konjat'tsjone] SF (*vedi vb*) minting; striking; coining

conico, -a, -ci, -che ['koniko] AGG conic(al), cone-shaped

conifera [ko'nifera] SF conifer

conigliera [koniʎ'ʎera] SF (*gabbia*) rabbit hutch; (*più grande*) rabbit run

coniglietto [koniʎ'ʎetto] SM bunny

coniglio, -gli [ko'niʎʎo] SM (*Zool*) rabbit; (*maschio*) buck; **pelliccia di coniglio** rabbit fur; **sei un coniglio!** (*fig*) you're chicken!

coniugale [konju'gale] AGG (*amore, diritti*) conjugal; (*vita*) married, conjugal

coniugare [konju'gare] /80/ VT 1 (*Gramm*) to conjugate 2 (*far coesistere*) to combine; **coniugare lo sviluppo industriale con il rispetto dell'ambiente** to combine industrial development with respect for the environment

coniugato, -a [konju'gato] AGG (*Amm*) married

coniugazione [konjugat'tsjone] SF (*Gramm*) conjugation

coniuge ['kɔnjudʒe] SM, SF spouse; **i coniugi** the couple, the husband and wife; **una coppia di coniugi** a married couple; **i coniugi Bianchi** Mr and Mrs Bianchi

connaturato, -a [konnatu'rato] AGG inborn

connazionale [konnattsjo'nale] AGG of the same country ♦ SM, SF compatriot, fellow-countryman (woman)

connessione [konnes'sjone] SF connection; (*Inform: a internet*) connection; **connessione di idee** association of ideas; **connessione remota** (*Inform*) remote connection

connesso, -a [kon'nɛsso] PP *di* connettere ♦ AGG connected

connettere [kon'nettere] /63/ VT IRREG 1 (*uso assoluto: ragionare*) to think straight; **la mattina non riesco a connettere** I can't think straight in the morning 2 **connettere (a)**; (*gen, anche fig*) to connect (with), link (to); (*Elettr*) to connect (with); **non avevo connesso i due fatti** I hadn't connected the two facts

connettore [konnet'tore] SM (*Elettr*) connector

connivente [konni'vɛnte] AGG: **essere connivente (in qc con qn)** to connive (at sth with sb)

connotati [konno'tati] SMPL distinguishing marks; **dare i connotati di qn** to give a description of sb; **rispondere ai connotati** to fit the description; **cambiare i connotati a qn** (*fam*) to beat sb up

connubio, -bi [kon'nubjo] SM (*matrimonio*) marriage; (*fig*) union

cono ['kɔno] SM (*in tutti i sensi*) cone; **un cono al cioccolato** a chocolate cone; **cono gelato** ice-cream cone

conobbi *ecc* [ko'nobbi] VB *vedi* **conoscere**

conoscente [konoʃ'ʃɛnte] SM, SF acquaintance; **una mia conoscente** an acquaintance of mine

conoscenza [konoʃ'ʃentsa] SF 1 (*sapere, nozione*) knowledge *no pl*; (*Filosofia*) cognition; **essere a conoscenza di qc** to know sth; **venire a conoscenza di qc** to get to know sth, learn of sth; **portare qn a conoscenza di qc** to inform sb of sth; **la polizia è venuta a conoscenza del fatto che...** it has come to the knowledge of the police that ...; **le mie conoscenze in questo campo** my knowledge in this field; **per vostra conoscenza** for your information; **prendere conoscenza di qc** (*Dir, Amm*) to take cognizance of sth; **conoscenza tecnica** know-how 2 (*amicizia, persona*) acquaintance; **fare la conoscenza di qn** to make sb's acquaintance; **lieto di fare la sua conoscenza** pleased to meet you; **ha ottenuto il lavoro grazie alle sue conoscenze** she got the job because of her contacts 3 (*sensi, coscienza*) consciousness; **perdere/riprendere conoscenza** to lose/regain consciousness

conoscere [ko'noʃʃere] VB IRREG /26/ VT 1 (*gen*) to know; (*persona, avvenimento*) to be acquainted with, know; (*testo, abitudine*) to be familiar with, know; (*posto, ristorante*) to know of; **conoscere qn di vista** to know sb by sight; **lo conosco solo di vista** I only know him by sight; **l'ha conosciuto**

all'università she met him at university; **conosci i motori?** do you know anything about engines?; **non conosco bene la città** I don't know the town well; **conosco la canzone** (*fig*) I've heard it all before; **conosce il fatto suo** he knows what he's talking about; **non conosce il mondo** he isn't very worldly-wise 2 (*successo*) to enjoy, have; (*privazioni*) to know, experience; **conoscere tempi difficili** to go through hard times 3 **far conoscere qn/qc** to make sb/sth known; **ti farò conoscere mio marito** I'll introduce you to my husband; **mi ha fatto conoscere la musica classica** he introduced me to classical music; **farsi conoscere** (*fig*) to make a name for o.s. 4 (*riconoscere*): **conoscere qn dalla voce** to recognize sb by his voice; **conoscersi** VR 1 (*se stessi*) to know o.s. 2 (*uso reciproco*) to know each other; (*incontrarsi*) to meet; **si sono conosciuti un anno fa** they (first) met a year ago; **ci siamo conosciuti in vacanza** we met on holiday; **da quanto vi conoscete?** how long have you known one another?; **ci conosciamo da poco tempo** we haven't known each other long

conoscitore, -trice [konoʃʃi'tore] SM, SF connoisseur

conosciuto, -a [konoʃ'ʃuto] PP *di* **conoscere** ♦ AGG (*universo*) known; (*attore, autore, artista*) well-known; **un attore conosciuto** a well-known actor; **conosciuto in tutto il mondo** well-known throughout the world, world-famous

conquista [kon'kwista] SF (*anche fig*) conquest; **partire alla conquista di qc** to set out to conquer sth; **le conquiste della scienza** the achievements of science

conquistare [konkwis'tare] /72/ VT (*territorio, fortezza*) to conquer; (*felicità, successo, ricchezza*) to gain; (*simpatia, fiducia*) to win, gain; (*cuore*) to win over; **si è conquistato la simpatia di tutti** he's made himself popular with everybody

conquistatore, -trice [konkwista'tore] AGG (*esercito, truppe*) conquering ♦ SM (*in guerra*) conqueror; (*seduttore*) lady-killer

cons. ABBR = consiglio

consacrare [konsa'krare] /72/ VT 1 (*Rel*) to consecrate; (*sacerdote*) to ordain; (*re*) to anoint; (*abitudine, tradizione, uso*) to establish 2 (*vita, tempo, sforzi*): **consacrare qc a** to dedicate (to), devote (to); **consacrarsi** VR (*dedicarsi*): **consacrarsi a qn/qc** to dedicate o.s. to sb/sth

consanguineo, -a [konsan'gwineo] AGG related by blood ♦ SM, SF blood relation

consapevole [konsa'pevole] AGG: **consapevole di qc** aware of, conscious of sth; **rendere qn consapevole di qc** to make sb aware of sth

consapevolezza [konsapevo'lettsa] SF awareness, consciousness; **acquistare consapevolezza di qc** to become aware o conscious of sth

consciamente [konʃa'mente] AVV consciously; **non l'ha fatto consciamente** he didn't know what he was doing

conscio, -a, -sci, -sce ['kɔnʃo] AGG: **conscio (di)** aware (of), conscious (of); **è conscio dei suoi limiti** he is aware of o knows his limitations ♦ SM (*Psic*): **il conscio** the conscious

consecutivo, -a [konseku'tivo] AGG (*Gramm: senza interruzione*) consecutive; (*successivo: giorno*) following, next; **per tre giorni consecutivi** for three consecutive days; **consecutivo a** following upon

consegna [kon'seɲɲa] SF 1 (*Comm: il consegnare*) delivery; (*: merce consegnata*) consignment; **la consegna è garantita in giornata** same-day delivery is guaranteed; **alla consegna** on delivery; **si può pagare alla consegna** you can pay on delivery; **pagamento alla consegna** cash on delivery; **consegna in contrassegno** cash on delivery; **consegna a domicilio** home delivery; **consegna sollecita** prompt delivery 2 (*custodia*) care; **prendere in consegna qn** (*bambino*) to take sb into one's care; (*prigioniero*) to take custody of sb; **prendere qc in consegna** to take sth into safekeeping; **dare qc in consegna a qn** to give sth to sb for safekeeping, entrust sth to sb 3 (*Mil: ordine*) orders *pl*; (*: punizione*) confinement to barracks; **un soldato fedele alla consegna** a soldier who obeys orders; **passare le consegne a qn** to hand over to sb

consegnare [konse'ɲɲare] /15/ VT 1 **consegnare qc (a qn)** (*lettera, pacco, merce*) to deliver sth (to sb); (*lavoro finito*) to hand sth in (to sb), submit sth (to sb); **mi hanno consegnato il pacco stamattina** the parcel was delivered to me this morning; **il meccanico non mi ha ancora consegnato la**

macchina I haven't had the car back from the mechanic yet; **consegnare qn alla polizia** to hand sb over to the police **2** (*Mil: soldato*) to confine to barracks

consegnatario, -ria, -ri, -rie [konseɲɲaˈtarjo] SM, SF consignee

conseguente [konseˈgwɛnte] AGG consequent

conseguentemente [konsegwɛnteˈmente] AVV (*come conseguenza*) consequently; (*comportarsi*) consistently

conseguenza [konseˈgwɛntsa] SF consequence; **di** o **per conseguenza** consequently; **senza lasciare conseguenze** without having any effect; **pagare le conseguenze** to pay the consequences

conseguimento [konsegwiˈmento] SM (*di scopo, risultato*) achievement, attainment; **al conseguimento della laurea** on graduation

conseguire [konseˈgwire] /17/ VT (*scopo*) to achieve, attain; (*vittoria*) to gain; **conseguire la laurea** to graduate, obtain one's degree ♦ VI (*aus essere*) (*derivare*): **ne consegue che...** it follows that ...

consenso [konˈsɛnso] SM (*permesso*) consent; (*approvazione*) approval; **dare/negare il proprio consenso a qc** to give/refuse one's consent to sth; **per consenso unanime** unanimously; **consenso informato** informed consent

consensuale [konsensuˈale] AGG (*Dir*) by mutual consent

consentire [konsenˈtire] /45/ VI (*aus avere*) **consentire a qc/a fare qc** to agree o consent to sth/to do sth ♦ VT: **consentire a qn qc/di fare qc** to allow o permit sb sth/to do sth; **è un lavoro che non consente distrazioni** you can't afford to be distracted in this kind of job; **mi si consenta di ringraziare...** I would like to thank ...

consenziente [konsenˈtsjɛnte] AGG (*gen, anche Dir*) consenting

conserto, -a [konˈsɛrto] AGG: **a braccia conserte** with one's arms folded

conserva [konˈsɛrva] SF: **mettere cibi in conserva** to preserve food; **conserva di frutta** jam, preserve; **conserva di pomodoro** tomato purée; **conserve alimentari** tinned (*Brit*) o canned (*USA*) o bottled foods

conservante [konserˈvante] SM (*per alimenti*) preservative

conservare [konserˈvare] /72/ VT **1** (*gen*) to keep; (*andatura, velocità*) to maintain; **lo conservo in una scatola** I keep it in a box; **conservare la calma** to keep calm; **conservare il proprio sangue freddo** (*fig*) to keep one's head; **conservo sempre un buon ricordo di lui** I still have fond memories of him **2** (*monumenti*) to preserve **3** (*Culin*) to preserve; (*in frigo*) to keep; **conservare le cipolline sott'aceto** to pickle onions; **conservare i pomodori in bottiglia** to bottle tomatoes; **conservarsi** VIP (*cibo*) to keep; **si conserva bene per alcune settimane** it keeps well for several weeks; **conservarsi in buona salute** to keep healthy; **si conserva bene** (*persona*) he (o she) is well-preserved

conservatore, -trice [konservaˈtore] AGG (*gen, anche Pol*) conservative; **il partito Conservatore** the Conservative Party ♦ SM, SF **1** (*di museo*) curator; (*di biblioteca*) librarian; (*di archivio*) keeper **2** (*Pol*) Conservative

conservatorio, -ri [konservaˈtɔrjo] SM (*di musica*) conservatory; **studio al conservatorio** I'm at music school

conservatorismo [konservatoˈrizmo] SM (*Pol*) conservatism

conservazione [konservatˈtsjone] SF **1** (*di cibi, monumenti*) preservation; **in buono stato di conservazione** well-preserved; **istinto di conservazione** instinct of self-preservation; **a lunga conservazione** (*latte, panna*) long-life attr **2** (*di energia, dell'ambiente naturale*) conservation

consesso [konˈsɛsso] SM (*assemblea*) assembly; (*riunione*) meeting

considerabile [konsideˈrabile] AGG worthy of consideration

considerare [konsideˈrare] /72/ VT **1** (*gen*) to consider, regard; **considerato che...** considering that ...; **giochi bene, considerato che hai cominciato da poco** you play well, considering that you only started recently; **tutto considerato** all things considered; **tutto considerato non è male** it's not bad, all things considered; **ti considero un amico** I think of you as o consider you a friend; **bisogna considerare i pro e i contro** you have to consider the pros and cons; **considerare un onore fare qc** to consider it an honour to

do sth **2** (*stimare*): **considerare molto qn** to think highly of sb **3** (*Dir: contemplare*): **la legge non considera questo caso** the law does not provide for this case; **considerarsi** VR: **considerarsi un genio** to consider o.s. a genius; **si considerano amici** they consider themselves friends; **puoi considerarti fortunato!** you can think yourself lucky!; **si considera il migliore** he thinks he's the best

considerato, -a [konsideˈrato] AGG **1** (*stimato*) highly thought of, esteemed **2** (*prudente*) cautious, careful

considerazione [konsideratˈtsjone] SF **1** (*esame, riflessione*) consideration; **agire senza considerazione** to act rashly; **voglio che tu agisca con considerazione** I'd like you to think carefully about what you're doing; **meritare considerazione** to be worthy of consideration; **prendere qn/qc in considerazione** to take sb/sth into consideration **2** (*stima*) esteem, regard; **godere di molta considerazione** to be very highly thought of; **avere (una grande) considerazione per qn** to think highly of sb **3** (*pensiero, osservazione*) observation

considerevole [konsideˈrevole] AGG considerable

consigliabile [konsiʎˈʎabile] AGG advisable

consigliare [konsiʎˈʎare] /27/ VT **1** (*raccomandare: ristorante, film, prudenza*): **consigliare (a qn)** to recommend (to sb); **che cosa mi consigli?** what do you recommend?; **ti consiglio la pizza** I'd recommend the pizza **2** (*suggerire*): **consigliare a qn di fare qc** to advise sb to do sth; **si consiglia ai passeggeri di...** passengers are advised to ...; **gli ha consigliato di andarsene prima possibile** she advised him to leave as soon as possible; **ti consiglierei di sbrigarti** I'd advise you to get a move on; **ti consiglio di non accettare l'invito** I advise you not to accept the invitation; **consigliarsi** VIP: **consigliarsi con qn** to ask sb's advice, ask sb for advice; **consigliarsi col proprio avvocato** to consult one's lawyer

consigliere, -a [konsiʎˈʎɛre] SM, SF (*gen*) adviser; (*Pol, Amm*) councillor, councilman; **consigliere d'amministrazione** (*Comm*) board member; **consigliere comunale** town councillor; **consigliere delegato** (*Comm*) managing director

consiglio, -gli [konˈsiʎʎo] SM **1** advice *no pl*; **un consiglio** some advice, a piece of advice; **mi ha chiesto un consiglio** she asked me for advice; **ti do due consigli...** I'll give you two bits of advice...; **un consiglio da amico** a friendly piece of advice; **seguire il consiglio** o **i consigli di qn** to take sb's advice; **ho seguito i tuoi consigli** I followed your advice **2** (*assemblea*) council; **hanno fatto un consiglio di famiglia** they held a family conference; **consiglio d'amministrazione** board of directors, board; **consiglio comunale** town council (*headed by the sindaco (mayor): it elects the giunta comunale, which is responsible for running a comune*); **Consiglio d'Europa** European Council; **consiglio di fabbrica** works council; **Consiglio dei Ministri; il Consiglio dei Ministri** the *Italian Cabinet*; **Consiglio di Sicurezza** Security Council; **Consiglio di stato** *advisory body to the Italian government on administrative matters and their legal implications*; **Consiglio superiore della magistratura** *magistrates' governing body*

consimile [konˈsimile] AGG similar

consistente [konsisˈtɛnte] AGG (*tessuto*) solid; (*fig: prova, testimonianza*) sound; (*somma*) sizeable

❏ **consistente** non si traduce mai con *consistent*

consistenza [konsisˈtɛntsa] SF **1** (*di impasto*) consistency; (*di stoffa*) texture **2** (*di sospetti, voci, ragionamenti*): **senza consistenza** ill-founded, groundless; **acquistare consistenza** to gain substance **3** (*Comm*): **consistenza di cassa** cash in hand; **consistenza di magazzino** stock in hand; **consistenza patrimoniale** financial solidity

consistere [konˈsistere] VI IRREG (*aus essere*) (*essere composto di*): **consistere di qc** to consist of sth, be made up of sth; (*fondarsi, risiedere in*): **consistere in qc/nel fare qc** to consist in sth/in doing sth; **in che consiste il tuo lavoro?** what does your job entail?

consistito, -a [konsisˈtito] PP *di* consistere

CONSOB [ˈkonsɔb] SIGLA F (= *Commissione nazionale per le società e la borsa*) *regulatory body for the Italian Stock Exchange*

consociarsi [konsoˈtʃarsi] /14/ VR to go into partnership

consociativismo [konsotʃatiˈvizmo] SM (*Pol*) pact-building

consociativo, -a [konsotʃaˈtivo] AGG (*Pol: democrazia*) based on pacts

consociato, -a [konso't∫ato] AGG associated ♦ SM, SF associate ♦ SF associated company

consolante [konso'lante] AGG consoling, comforting

consolare [konso'lare] /72/ VT (confortare) to console, comfort; (rallegrare) to cheer up; **ho cercato di consolarla un po'** I tried to cheer her up a bit; **se ti può consolare...** if it is of any consolation o comfort to you ...; **consolarsi** VIP (trovare conforto) to console o.s., be comforted; (rallegrarsi) to cheer up; **si è consolato presto dopo la morte del cane** he got over the death of his dog quickly; **il bambino si è consolato vedendo le caramelle** the child cheered up when he saw the sweets

consolato [konso'lato] SM (officio) consulate; (carica) consulship; **il consolato italiano** the Italian consulate

consolazione [konsolat'tsjone] SF **1** comfort, consolation; **l'unica consolazione è che...** the only consolation is that ...; **sei la mia unica consolazione** you're my one consolation; **premio di consolazione** consolation prize **2** (piacere): **è una consolazione vederlo di nuovo in salute** it's a pleasure o joy to see him well again

console ['konsole] SM consul

consolidamento [konsolida'mento] SM consolidation, strengthening; (Econ) funding operations pl

consolidare [konsoli'dare] /72/ VT (anche fig) to consolidate, strengthen, reinforce; **consolidare le proprie posizioni** (Mil) to consolidate one's position; **consolidarsi** VIP (Geol) to consolidate; (fig: patrimonio, posizione) to become more stable; **la società si è consolidata** the company has consolidated its position

consolidazione [konsolidat'tsjone] SF consolidation, strengthening

consommé [kɔsɔ'me] SM INV consommé

consonante [konso'nante] SF consonant

consonanza [konso'nantsa] SF consonance

consono, -a ['kɔnsono] AGG: **consono a** consistent with, consonant with

consorte [kon'sɔrte] SM, SF (coniuge) consort ♦ AGG: **principe consorte** prince consort

consorzio, -zi [kon'sɔrtsjo] SM consortium; **consorzio agrario** farmers' cooperative; **consorzio di garanzia** (Comm) underwriting syndicate

constare [kon'stare] /72/ VI (aus essere) (essere composto): **constare di** to consist of, be composed of, be made up of ♦ VB IMPERS (essere noto): **mi consta che...** I know that ...; **a quanto mi consta** as far as I know

constatare [konsta'tare] /72/ VT vb dif **1** (notare) to notice, note, observe; **come può constatare** as you can see; **non faccio che constatare** I'm merely making an observation **2** (verificare) to establish, verify; (decesso) to certify

constatazione [konstatat'tsjone] SF observation; **fare una constatazione** to make an observation; **constatazione amichevole** (in incidenti stradali) jointly-agreed statement for insurance purposes

consueto, -a [konsu'eto] AGG usual, habitual; **il suo consueto buonumore** his usual good humour ♦ SM: **come di consueto** as usual; **più/meno del consueto** more/less than usual

consuetudinario, -ria, -ri, -rie [konsuetudi'narjo] AGG (abituale) usual, habitual; **diritto consuetudinario** (Dir) common law ♦ SM, SF (persona: abitudinario) creature of habit, lover of routine

consuetudine [konsue'tudine] SF **1** (abitudine) habit; (tradizione) custom; **è consuetudine alzarsi prestissimo** he usually gets up very early, he is in the habit of getting up very early; **secondo la consuetudine** according to custom **2** (Dir) common law

consulente [konsu'lente] AGG consulting ♦ SM, SF (tecnico, amministrativo) consultant; **consulente aziendale** management consultant; **consulente legale** legal adviser

consulenza [konsu'lentsa] SF (prestazione professionale) consultancy; (consigli) advice; **chiedere una consulenza** to ask for professional advice; **contratto di consulenza** consultancy agreement; **ufficio di consulenza fiscale** tax consultancy office; **consulenza legale** legal advice; **consulenza medica** medical advice; **consulenza tecnica** technical consultancy o advice

consultare [konsul'tare] /72/ VT (medico, esperto) to consult, seek the advice of; (dizionario) to look up, consult; **consultarsi** VR (scambiarsi pareri: uso reciproco) to confer, consult each other; **consultarsi** VIP (chiedere consiglio): **consultarsi con qn** to consult (with) sb, seek the advice of sb

consultazione [konsultat'tsjone] SF consultation; (Pol): **consultazioni** SFPL talks, consultations; **dopo lunga consultazione** after much consultation; **libro di consultazione** reference book; **consultazione popolare** referendum

consultivo, -a [konsul'tivo] AGG consultative

consultorio, -ri [konsul'tɔrjo] SM: **consultorio familiare** family planning clinic; **consultorio pediatrico** children's clinic

consumare [konsu'mare] /72/ VT **1** (logorare: scarpe, vestiti) to wear out; **ho consumato la suola delle scarpe** I've worn the soles of my shoes out **2** (cibo) to consume; (sogg: malattia, passione) to consume, devour; **desidera consumare i pasti in camera?** (in albergo) would you like to have your meals brought up to your room? **3** (usare: acqua, luce, benzina) to use; (finire) to use up; **quanto consuma questa macchina?** what sort of mileage does this car get?; **la mia moto consuma molto** my motorbike uses a lot of petrol (Brit) o gas (USA) **4** (Dir: matrimonio) to consummate; **consumarsi** VIP (vestiario) to wear (out); (candela) to burn down; (penna, pennarello) to run dry; (persona: per malattia) to waste away; **consumarsi (di)** to be consumed (with)

consumato, -a [konsu'mato] AGG **1** (vestiti, scarpe, tappeto) worn **2** (persona: esperto) accomplished

consumatore, -trice [konsuma'tore] SM, SF (Comm) consumer

consumazione [konsumat'tsjone] SF **1** (al bar: bibita) drink; (: spuntino) snack **2** (Dir: del matrimonio) consummation

consumismo [konsu'mizmo] SM consumerism

consumo [kon'sumo] SM **1** (gen) consumption, use; **consumo di benzina** petrol (Brit) o gas (USA) consumption; **fare largo consumo di qc** to use sth heavily; **per mio uso e consumo** for my personal use **2** (Econ): **generi o beni di consumo** consumer goods; **beni di largo consumo** basic commodities; **imposta di consumo** tax on consumer goods; **la società dei consumi** the consumer society

consuntivo, -a [konsun'tivo] AGG (Econ: bilancio) final ♦ SM (Econ) final balance; **fare un consuntivo (della situazione)** (fig) to take stock (of the situation)

consunto, -a [kon'sunto] AGG (abiti) worn out, shabby; (volto) wasted

conta ['konta] SF (nei giochi): **fare la conta** to see who is going to be 'it'

contabile [kon'tabile] AGG (Comm) book-keeping attr, accounts attr, accounting attr; **la situazione contabile** the accounting situation; **i libri contabili** the accounts ♦ SM, SF book-keeper, accountant

contabilità [kontabili'ta] SF (attività, tecnica) accounting, accountancy; (insieme dei libri) books pl, accounts pl; **tenere la contabilità** to keep the accounts; (ufficio) **contabilità** accounts department; **contabilità finanziaria** financial accounting; **contabilità di gestione** management accounting

contachilometri [kontaki'lɔmetri] SM INV ≈ mileometer (Brit), odometer (USA)

contadino, -a [konta'dino] AGG (di campagna) country attr; (rurale) peasant attr; **la rivolta contadina** the peasant revolt ♦ SM, SF **1** countryman (woman); (bracciante) farm worker; **mio zio è contadino** my uncle works on the land **2** (Storia, anche pegg) peasant ♦ SM (fattore) tenant farmer

contagiare [konta'dʒare] /62/ VT (anche fig) to infect

contagio, -gi [kon'tadʒo] SM **1** infection; (per contatto diretto) contagion; **il vaiolo si prende per contagio** smallpox is contracted by touch **2** (malattia) disease; (epidemia) epidemic

contagioso, -a [konta'dʒoso] AGG (gen) infectious; (per contatto) contagious; (fig: riso, allegria) infectious, contagious; **una malattia contagiosa** an infectious disease; **non preoccuparti, non è contagioso** don't worry, it's not contagious

contagiri [konta'dʒiri] SM INV (Aut) rev counter

contagocce [konta'gottʃe] SM INV dropper; **mi dà i soldi con il contagocce** he counts every penny he gives me

contaminare [kontami'nare] /72/ VT (gen) to contaminate; (buon nome) to tarnish; (testo) to corrupt

contaminazione [kontaminat'tsjone] SF contamination

contante [kon'tante] AGG: **denaro contante** cash ♦ **contanti** SMPL cash sg; **pagare in contanti** to pay cash

contare [kon'tare] /72/ VT 1 (calcolare, enumerare) to count; **li ho contati, sono quindici** I've counted them, there are fifteen; **le telefonate non si contavano più** I (o you ecc) couldn't keep count of the telephone calls; **ha sempre i minuti contati** he never has a spare moment; **ha i giorni contati, ha le ore contate** his days are numbered; **ho i soldi contati** I haven't a penny to spare; **amici così si contano sulla punta delle dita** you can count the number of friends like that on the fingers of one hand 2 (considerare) to include, count (in), consider; **senza contare** (senza includere) not counting; (senza parlare di) not to mention; **eravamo in dieci, senza contare i professori** there were ten of us, not counting the teachers; **contare di fare qc** to intend to do sth, to think of; **contavamo di partire nel pomeriggio** we were thinking of leaving in the afternoon; **conto di essere lì per mezzogiorno** I think I'll be there by midday 3 (fam: raccontare) to tell; **contarle grosse** to tell tall stories ♦ VI (aus avere) 1 (calcolare) to count; **contare fino a 100** to count to 100; **conta fino a cinquanta e poi vieni a cercarci** count to fifty and then come and look for us 2 (fare assegnamento): **contare su qn/qc** to count on sb/sth, rely on sb/sth; **sai che puoi contare su di me** you know you can count on me; **puoi contarci** you can count on it 3 (avere importanza) to count, matter, be of importance; **la gente che conta** the people who matter; **alla sua festa c'era tutta la Milano che conta** everybody who is anybody in Milan was at her party

contascatti [kontas'katti] SM INV telephone meter

contatore [konta'tore] SM counter; (della luce) meter; **contatore del gas** gas meter

contattare [kontat'tare] /72/ VT to contact

contatto [kon'tatto] SM 1 (gen) contact; **essere/venire a contatto con qc** to be in/come into contact with sth; **a contatto con l'aria** in contact with (the) air; **non sopporto la lana a contatto con la pelle** I can't wear wool next to my skin; **mettere qc a contatto con qc** to put sth against sth; **essere in contatto con qn** to be in touch with sb; **prendere contatto con qn** to get in touch o contact with sb; **mantenere i contatti (con qn)** to maintain contact (with sb), keep in touch (with sb); **mettersi in contatto con qn** to contact sb; **devo mettermi in contatto con John** I must contact John; **mantenersi in contatto** to keep in touch; **ci siamo mantenuti in contatto** we've kept in touch; **il loro contatto negli Stati Uniti era Chris** their contact in the United States was Chris 2 (Elettr, Radio) contact; **aprire/chiudere il contatto** (Elettr) to make/break contact; **fare contatto** (Elettr: fili) to touch; **stabilire il contatto** (Radio) to make contact

conte ['konte] SM (in Europa) count; (in Gran Bretagna) earl

contea [kon'tea] SF 1 (Storia: in Europa) domain of a count; (: in Gran Bretagna) earldom 2 (Amm: nei paesi anglosassoni) county

conteggiare [konted'dʒare] /62/ VT (fare il conto di) to work out; (addebitare) to charge (for), put on the bill

conteggio, -gi [kon'teddʒo] SM 1 (gen) reckoning, calculation; **fare il conteggio di** to calculate 2 **conteggio alla rovescia** countdown 3 (Pugilato) count

contegno [kon'teɲ ɲo] SM (comportamento) behaviour (Brit), behavior (USA); (atteggiamento) attitude; **avere o tenere un contegno esemplare** to behave perfectly; **ha assunto un contegno poco simpatico nei nostri confronti** he assumed a rather unpleasant attitude towards us; **darsi un contegno** (ostentare disinvoltura) to act nonchalant; (ricomporsi) to pull o.s. together

contegnoso, -a [konteɲ'ɲoso] AGG (dignitoso) dignified; (riservato) reserved

contemplare [kontem'plare] /72/ VT (paesaggio) to gaze at; (possibilità) to contemplate; (Dir: considerare) to provide for, make provision for

contemplativo, -a [kontempla'tivo] AGG contemplative

contemplazione [kontemplat'tsjone] SF contemplation

contempo [kon'tempo] SM: **nel contempo** meanwhile, in the meantime

contemporaneamente [kontemporanea'mente] AVV at the same time, simultaneously, contemporaneously; **sono arrivati contemporaneamente** they arrived at the same time; **contemporaneamente a** at the same time as

contemporaneo, -a [kontempo'raneo] AGG: **contemporaneo (di o a)** contemporary (with); **la sua partenza fu contemporanea al mio arrivo** his departure coincided with my arrival; **l'arte contemporanea** contemporary o modern art ♦ SM, SF contemporary

contendente [konten'dente] AGG contending ♦ SM, SF (avversario) opponent, adversary; (per un titolo) contestant

contendere [kon'tendere] VB IRREG /120/ VT (contestare): **contendere qc a qn** to contend with o be in competition with sb for sth; **si contendono il titolo** they are competing for the title; **si contendevano l'affetto della madre** they were vying with each other for their mother's affection ♦ VI (aus avere) (disputare, litigare) to quarrel; (competere) to compete; **contendere per qc** to quarrel over o about sth

contenere [konte'nere] VB IRREG /121/ VT 1 (racchiudere) to contain; (sogg: recipienti, locali pubblici) to hold; (cinema, veicoli) to hold, seat; **questo succo non contiene zucchero** this juice does not contain sugar; **lo stadio può contenere centomila spettatori** the stadium can hold a hundred thousand spectators 2 (frenare: entusiasmo, sentimenti, epidemia) to contain; (: truppe, avanzata nemica) to hold in check; **contenersi** VR to contain o.s

contenitore [konteni'tore] SM container; **un contenitore di plastica** a plastic container

contentabile [konten'tabile] AGG: **essere difficilmente contentabile** to be hard o difficult to please

contentare [konten'tare] /72/ VT to please; (soddisfare) to satisfy; **contentarsi** VIP: **contentarsi (di)** to content o.s. (with); **si contenta di poco** he is easily satisfied; **chi si contenta gode** (Proverbio) a contented mind is a perpetual feast

contentezza [konten'tettsa] SF (felicità) happiness; (soddisfazione) contentment

contentino [konten'tino] SM sop

contento, -a [kon'tento] AGG (lieto) happy, glad; (soddisfatto) satisfied, pleased; **contento di** (auto, persona) pleased with; (promozione, cambiamento) happy o pleased about; **sono contento di vederti** I'm glad to see you; **sono contento di averti ritrovato** I'm happy to have met up with you again; **e non contento di ciò...** and not content with that ...; **far contento qn** to make sb happy; **sono andato per far contenta la mamma** I went to make my mum happy; **sono contento così** (mi basta) I've got enough; **sei contento adesso?** are you happy now?; **sono contenta che ti piaccia** I'm glad you like it; **oggi sono più contento** I'm happier today

contenuto, -a [konte'nuto] AGG (ira, entusiasmo) restrained, suppressed; (forza) contained ♦ SM (di cassa, valigia) contents pl; (di libro, film, discorso) content; **ha rovesciato sul tavolo il contenuto della borsa** he tipped the contents of the bag out onto the table

contenzioso, -a [konten'tsjoso] AGG (Dir) contentious ♦ SM (Amm: ufficio) legal department

conteso, -a [kon'teso] PP di **contendere** ♦ AGG (premio, carica) sought after

contessa [kon'tessa] SF countess

contestare [kontes'tare] /72/ VT 1 (criticare) to question, protest against; **contestare il sistema** to protest against the system 2 (disputare) to dispute, contest; **contestare a qn il diritto di fare qc** to contest sb's right to do sth 3 (Dir: notificare) to notify; **contestare un reato a qn** to charge sb with a crime; **contestare una contravvenzione a qn** to issue sb with a fine

contestatore, -trice [kontesta'tore] AGG anti-establishment ♦ SM, SF protester

contestazione [kontestat'tsjone] SF 1 (Pol) anti-establishment activity; **la contestazione studentesca del '68** the student protests of '68 2 (Dir: disputa) dispute; **in caso di contestazione** if there are any objections 3 (Dir: notifica) notification; **si proceda alla contestazione delle accuse** please read out the charges

contesto [kon'testo] SM context; **visto nel contesto** seen in context

❏ **contesto** non si traduce mai con **contest**

contiguo, -a [kon'tiguo] AGG (*camere, case*) adjoining, adjacent; **essere contiguo a** to be adjacent o next to
continentale [kontinen'tale] AGG continental; **l'Europa continentale** (*Geog*) continental Europe; (*per gli inglesi*) the Continent
continente [konti'nɛnte] SM (*gen*) continent; (*terraferma*) mainland
continenza [konti'nɛntsa] SF continence
contingente [kontin'dʒɛnte] AGG contingent ♦ SM 1 (*gen, anche Mil, Filosofia*) contingent; **contingente di leva** draft (*USA*), group *of soldiers called up for military service* 2 (*Comm*) quota
contingenza [kontin'dʒɛntsa] SF 1 (*gen*) contingency; (*circostanza*) circumstance 2 (*anche:* **indennità di contingenza**) cost-of-living allowance
continuamente [kontinua'mente] AVV (*senza interruzione*) continuously, nonstop; (*ripetutamente*) continually; **perché vieni continuamente a disturbarmi?** why do you keep coming and bothering me?; **è piovuto continuamente** it rained nonstop; **cambia idea continuamente** she keeps changing her mind
continuare [kontinu'are] /72/ VT (*studi, progetto*) to continue (with), carry on with, go on with; (*viaggio*) to continue; (*tradizione*) to continue, carry on; **continuò la lettura** he went on reading ♦ VI (*riferito a persona: aus* avere *riferito a cosa: aus* avere o essere) to continue, go on; **continui pure** do go on; **per oggi basta, continueremo domani** that's enough for today, we'll carry on tomorrow; **continuano le trattative** negotiations are continuing; **continuare a fare qc** to go on o keep on o continue doing sth; **ha continuato a dormire nonostante il chiasso** she went on sleeping despite the noise; **continuava a credere in lei** she continued to believe in her; **continuò per la sua strada** he continued on his way; **la strada continua fino al bosco** the road carries on o continues as far as the wood; **se continua così...** if it (*o* he *o* she) goes on like this ...; **se i dolori continuano...** if the pain persists ...; **"continua"** (*di romanzi a puntate*) "to be continued"; **"continua a pagina 9"** "continued on page 9" ♦ VB IMPERS (*aus* avere o essere) **continua a nevicare/a fare freddo** it's still snowing/cold
continuativo, -a [kontinua'tivo] AGG (*occupazione*) permanent; (*periodo*) consecutive
continuazione [kontinuat'tsjone] SF continuation; **la continuazione di un romanzo** the sequel to a novel; **in continuazione** continuously
continuità [kontinui'ta] SF continuity
continuo, -a [kon'tinuo] AGG (*ininterrotto*) continuous; (*che si ripete*) continual; (*Elettr: corrente*) direct; **sono stufa delle sue lamentele continue** I'm fed up with her constant complaints; **c'è un continuo viavai di gente** there are people constantly coming and going; **di continuo** continually; **piove di continuo da tre giorni** it's been raining nonstop for three days
conto [konto] SM 1 (*calcolo*) calculation; **fare di conto** to count; **ho fatto un rapido conto** I did a quick calculation 2 (*Banca, Comm*) account; (*fattura: di ristorante, albergo*) bill; (: *di prestazione*) account, bill; **il conto, per favore** could I have the bill, please?; **pagare** o **saldare il conto** to pay the bill; **fare i conti** to do the accounts; **dobbiamo fare il conto delle spese** we must work out the expenses; **far bene/male i propri conti** (*anche fig*) to get one's sums right/wrong; **non aveva fatto i conti con possibili imprevisti** he hadn't allowed for anything unexpected happening; **fare i conti senza l'oste** to forget the most important thing; **fare i conti con qn** to settle one's account with sb; **farò i conti con te più tardi!** I'll sort you out later!; **avere un conto in sospeso (con qn)** to have an outstanding account (with sb); (*fig*) to have a score to settle (with sb); **fare i conti in tasca a qn** to pry into sb's financial affairs ♦ (*stima, considerazione*): **di poco/nessun conto** of little/no importance; **tener conto di qn/qc** to take sb/sth into consideration o account; **non avevo tenuto conto del fuso orario** I hadn't allowed for the time difference; **tenere qc da conto** to take great care of sth ♦ (*fraseologia*): **a conti fatti, in fin dei conti** all things considered, when all is said and done; **be', in fin dei conti non ha tutti i torti** well, after all, he's quite right; **ad ogni**

buon conto in any case; **per conto mio** (*a mio avviso*) in my opinion, as far as I'm concerned; (*a nome mio*) on my behalf; (*da solo*) on my own; **per conto mio la faccenda è un po' strana** in my opinion it's all rather strange; **voglio starmene per conto mio** I want to be on my own; **ci vado per conto mio** I'm going on my own; **per conto di** on behalf of; **telefono per conto di Sara** I'm phoning on behalf of Sara; **sul conto di** about; **girano strane voci sul conto di Luca** I've heard some strange things about Luca; **mi hanno detto strane cose sul suo conto** I've heard some strange things about him; **fare conto che...** (*supporre*) to suppose that ...; **fare conto su qn/qc** to rely o depend o count on sb/sth; **chiedere conto di qc a qn** to ask sb to give an account o explanation of sth; **rendere conto a qn di qc** to be accountable to sb for sth; **rendersi conto di qc/che...** to realize sth/that; **non si era reso conto che c'ero anch'io** he hadn't realized I was there too; **non ti rendi conto delle conseguenze!** you don't realize what will happen!; **essere alla resa dei conti ...** to come to the day of reckoning ♦ **conto in banca** o **bancario** bank account; **conto capitale** capital account; **conto cassa** cash account; **conto cifrato** numbered account; **conto corrente** current account (*Brit*), checking account (*USA*); **conto corrente postale** ≈ National Girobank payment, post office account; **conto in partecipazione** joint account; **conto passivo** account payable; **conto profitti e perdite** profit and loss account; **conto alla rovescia** countdown; **conto scoperto** overdrawn account; **avere il conto scoperto** to be overdrawn; **conto valutario** foreign currency account
contorcere [kon'tortʃere] VB IRREG /106/ VT to twist; (*viso*) to contort; **contorcersi** VR: **contorcersi dal dolore** to writhe with pain; **contorcersi dalle risa** to double up with laughter
contornare [kontor'nare] /72/ VT (*gen, anche fig*) to surround; (*ornare*) to decorate, trim; **contornarsi** VR: **contornarsi di** to surround o.s. with
contorno [kon'torno] SM 1 (*linea esterna*) outline, contour; (*ornamento*) border; **fare da contorno a** to surround 2 (*Culin*) vegetables *pl*; **non prendo il contorno** I don't want any vegetables; **cosa prendi come contorno?** what would you like to go with it?; **arrosto con contorno di piselli** roast meat served with peas
contorsione [kontor'sjone] SF contortion
contorto, -a [kon'tɔrto] PP *di* contorcere ♦ AGG twisted; (*fig: ragionamento, stile*) tortuous
contrabbandare [kontrabban'dare] /72/ VT to smuggle
contrabbandiere, -a [kontrabban'djere] SM, SF smuggler
contrabbando [kontrab'bando] SM smuggling, contraband; **fare il contrabbando** to smuggle; **di contrabbando** contraband, smuggled; **sigarette di contrabbando** contraband cigarettes; **merce di contrabbando** contraband *no pl*, smuggled goods *pl*; **contrabbando di droga** drug smuggling
contrabbasso [kontrab'basso] SM (*Mus*) (double) bass
contraccambiare [kontrakkam'bjare] /19/ VT (*favore, auguri*) to return; (*gentilezza*) to repay; **vorrei contraccambiare** I'd like to show my appreciation
contraccettivo, -a [kontrattʃet'tivo] AGG, SM contraceptive
contraccolpo [kontrak'kolpo] SM (*gen*) rebound; (*di arma da fuoco*) recoil; (*fig*) repercussion
contrada [kon'trada] SF (*letter: paese*) land; (*quartiere*) quarter, district; (*via*) street
contraddetto, -a [kontrad'detto] PP *di* contraddire
contraddire [kontrad'dire] VB IRREG /38/ VT to contradict; **mi contraddice sempre** he's always contradicting me; **contraddirsi** VR to contradict o.s.; (*uso reciproco: persone*) to contradict each other; (: *testimonianze*) to be contradictory
contraddistinguere [kontraddis'tingwere] VB IRREG /42/ VT (*merce*) to mark; (*fig: atteggiamento, persona*) to distinguish; **contraddistinguersi** VIP: **l'opera si contraddistingue per rigore scientifico** the work stands out because of its scientific accuracy
contraddistinto, -a [kontraddis'tinto] PP *di* contraddistinguere
contraddittorio, -ria, -ri, -rie [kontraddit'tɔrjo] AGG (*affermazione, testimonianza, personaggio*) contradictory; (*comportamento*) inconsistent; (*sentimenti*) conflicting ♦ SM (*Dir: di testimoni*) cross-examination; (*Pol: dibattito*) debate

contraddizione [kontraddit'tsjone] SF contradiction; cadere in contraddizione to contradict o.s.; essere in contraddizione (tesi, affermazioni) to contradict one another; essere in contraddizione con to contradict; spirito di contraddizione argumentativeness

contrae ecc [kon'trae] VB vedi contrarre

contraente [kontra'ente] AGG (Dir: parte) contracting ♦ SM, SF contracting party, contractor

contraerea [kontra'erea] SF (Mil) anti-aircraft artillery

contraereo, -a [kontra'ereo] AGG (Mil) anti-aircraft attr

contraffare [kontraf'fare] /41/ VT IRREG (firma) to forge; (banconota) to forge, counterfeit; (voce) to disguise; (cibo, vino) to adulterate

contraffatto, -a [kontraf'fatto] PP di contraffare ♦ AGG (firma) forged; (banconota) forged, counterfeit; (voce) disguised; (cibo, vino) adulterated

contraffazione [kontraffat'tsjone] SF 1 (vedi vb) forging no pl, forgery; counterfeiting; disguising no pl; adulteration 2 (esemplare contraffatto) forgery

contrafforte [kontraf'forte] SM 1 (Archit) buttress 2 (Geog) spur

contraggo [kon'traggo] VB vedi contrarre

contralto [kon'tralto] SM (Mus) contralto; (voce maschile) alto

contrappello [kontrap'pello] SM (Mil) second roll call

contrappesare [kontrappe'sare] /72/ VT to counterbalance; (fig: decisione) to weigh up; contrapparsi VR (uso reciproco) to counterbalance each other

contrappeso [kontrap'peso] SM counterbalance, counterweight

contrapporre [kontrap'porre] VB IRREG /77/ VT 1 (opporre): contrapporre qc a qc to counter sth with sth; contrapporre un rifiuto ad una richiesta to counter a request with a refusal; contrapporre un ostacolo a qc to set an obstacle in the way of sth 2 (paragonare): contrapporre qc (a qc) to compare sth (with sth); contrapporsi VR: contrapporsi a qc to contrast with sth, be opposed to sth; i loro punti di vista si contrappongono they hold opposing points of view

contrapposto, -a [kontrap'posto] PP di contrapporre ♦ AGG (argomenti, concetti) contrasting; (posizioni) opposing

contrariamente [kontrarja'mente] AVV: contrariamente a contrary to; contrariamente al solito just for once; contrariamente al solito non ha ottenuto un buon risultato unusually for him he wasn't successful

contrariare [kontra'rjare] /19/ VT (ostacolare: persona) to oppose; (: piani) to thwart; (: irritare) to annoy

contrariato, -a [kontra'rjato] AGG annoyed

contrarietà [kontrarje'ta] SF INV (avversità) adversity, misfortune; (fastidio) trouble; (avversione) aversion

contrario, -ria, -ri, -rie [kon'trarjo] AGG (gen) opposite; (sfavorevole) unfavourable (Brit), unfavorable (USA); (avverso: sorte) adverse; (: venti) contrary; essere contrario a qc (persona) to be against sth; sono contrario alla vivisezione I'm against vivisection; sono contrario a questo tuo modo di comportarti I disapprove of the way you're behaving; è contrario ai miei principi it's against my principles; in caso contrario otherwise; in direzione contraria in the opposite direction ♦ SM opposite; al contrario on the contrary; al contrario di contrary to; al contrario di quanto si crede, è piuttosto grande contrary to what people think, it's quite big; avere qualcosa in contrario to have some objection; io avrei qualcosa in contrario I have an objection; non ho niente in contrario I've no objection; è esattamente il contrario it's quite the opposite o reverse; fa tutto il contrario di quello che dice he does the complete opposite of what he says

contrarre [kon'trarre] VB IRREG /123/ VT 1 (muscoli, volto) to tense; contrarre un muscolo to contract a muscle 2 (malattia, debito, prestito) to contract; (abitudine, vizio) to pick up; (accordo, patto) to enter into; contrarre una malattia to contract an illness; contrarre matrimonio to marry; contrarsi VIP (gen, anche Gramm) to contract

contrassegnare [kontrasse p'nare] /15/ VT to mark

contrassegno [kontras'se p no] SM (distinguishing) mark ♦ AVV (Comm): spedire in contrassegno to send COD

contrassi ecc [kon'trassi] VB vedi contrarre

contrastante [kontras'tante] AGG contrasting

contrastare [kontras'tare] /72/ VT (avanzata, piano) to hinder; (desiderio, diritto) to dispute, contest; una vittoria contrastata a hard-fought victory ♦ VI (aus avere) (discordare): contrastare (con) to clash (with), contrast (with); questi colori contrastano fra di loro these colours clash

contrasto [kon'trasto] SM 1 (gen, anche TV, Fot) contrast; per contrasto in contrast 2 (conflitto) conflict; (disputa, litigio) quarrel, dispute; un contrasto di opinioni a difference of opinion; essere in/venire a contrasto con qn to be in/get into a disagreement with sb

contrattacco [kontrat'takko] SM counterattack; passare al contrattacco (fig) to fight back

contrattare [kontrat'tare] /72/ VT (uso assoluto: trattare) to negotiate; (: mercanteggiare) to bargain; (: terreno, merce) to bargain over, negotiate the price of; contrattare il prezzo to negotiate the price

contrattempo [kontrat'tempo] SM hitch; per una serie di contrattempi because of a series of difficulties; sono arrivato in ritardo per un contrattempo there was a problem, and I arrived late

contratto, -a [kon'tratto] PP di contrarre ♦ AGG (volto, mani) tense; (muscoli) tense, contracted; (Gramm) contracted ♦ SM contract; il contratto sarà firmato domani the contract will be signed tomorrow; contratto di acquisto purchase agreement; contratto di affitto lease; contratto collettivo di lavoro collective agreement; contratto di lavoro contract of employment; contratto di locazione lease; contratto a termine forward contract

contrattuale [kontrattu'ale] AGG contractual; forza contrattuale (di sindacato) bargaining power

contravvenire [kontravve'nire] /128/ VI IRREG (aus avere) contravvenire a (legge, regolamento) to contravene; (obbligo) to fail to meet

contravventore, -trice [kontravven'tore] SM, SF offender

contravvenuto, -a [kontravve'nuto] PP di contravvenire

contravvenzione [kontravven'tsjone] SF 1 (Aut: multa) fine; elevare una contravvenzione a qn to fine sb 2 (trasgressione): contravvenzione (a) contravention (of)

contrazione [kontrat'tsjone] SF (gen, anche Med, Gramm) contraction; contrazione (di) (di prezzi, vendite) decrease (in), fall (in)

contribuente [kontribu'ente] SM, SF (Fisco) taxpayer

contribuire [kontribu'ire] /55/ VI (aus avere) contribuire a qc to contribute to sth; abbiamo contribuito tutti alla spesa we all contributed to the cost; contribuire a fare qc to help do sth; tutto ciò ha contribuito a peggiorare la situazione all this has made things worse

contributivo, -a [kontribu'tivo] AGG contributory

contributo [kontri'buto] SM 1 (gen) contribution; dare il proprio contributo a qc to make one's contribution to sth 2 contributi SMPL (tasse) charges, tax; (sovvenzioni) subsidy, contribution; contributi previdenziali ≈ national insurance (Brit) o welfare (USA) contributions; contributi sindacali trade (Brit) o labor (USA) union dues

contrito, -a [kon'trito] AGG contrite, penitent; con aria contrita penitently

contro [kontro] PREP 1 (gen) against; non ho niente contro di lui I've nothing against him; sono tutti contro di me they are all against me; lottare contro qn/qc to fight against sb/sth; la lotta contro la droga the fight against drugs; è contro il divorzio he's against o opposed to divorce; il Milan contro la Juventus Milan versus o against Juventus; pastiglie contro la tosse throat lozenges; un ottimo rimedio contro l'influenza an excellent treatment for flu 2 (contatto, direzione) against; si appoggiò contro la porta he leaned against the door; ho sbattuto contro la porta I bumped into the door; si è schiantato contro un albero it crashed into a tree; puntò la pistola contro di me he pointed his gun at me; spararono contro la polizia they shot at the police 3 (Comm: in cambio di): contro pagamento/ricevuta on payment/receipt 4 (contrariamente a): contro ogni mia aspettativa contrary to my expectations 5 contro corrente, contro luce, contro vista ecc vedi controcorrente, controluce, controvoglia ♦ AVV against; votare contro to vote against; hanno votato contro they voted against it;

dar contro a qn to contradict sb; per contro on the oth-er hand ♦ SM INV con; il pro e il contro the pros and cons ♦ PREF counter-

controbattere [kontro'battere] /1/ VT (ribattere) to answer back; (confutare) to refute

controbilanciare [kontrobilan't∫are] /14/ VT (gen, anche fig) to counterbalance

controcorrente [kontrokor'rente] AVV: nuotare controcor-rente (in un fiume) to swim upstream; (nel mare) to swim against the tide; andare controcorrente (fig) to swim against the tide

controcultura [kontrokul'tura] SF counterculture

contro'esodo SM return from holiday

controfax [kontro'faks] SM INV reply to a fax

controffensiva [kontroffen'siva] SF (Mil, anche fig) counter-offensive

controfigura [kontrofi'gura] SF (Cine) stuntman (woman), double; essere la controfigura di qn to play sb's double

controfirmare [kontrofir'mare] /72/ VT to countersign

controllare [kontrol'lare] /72/ VT 1 (verificare: gen) to check; (: biglietto) to inspect, check; controlla che la porta sia ben chiusa check that the door is shut properly; mi hanno con-trollato il passaporto my passport was checked 2 (sorve-gliare) to watch, keep a close watch on; (ufficio, impiegato) to supervise 3 (tenere a freno, dominare, anche Mil, Calcio) to control; controllarsi VR to control o.s.; non riuscivo a con-trollarmi I couldn't control myself

controllato, -a [kontrol'lato] AGG (persona: non impulsivo) self-controlled, self-possessed; (reazioni) controlled

controllo [kon'trollo] SM 1 (verifica: gen) check; (: di biglietti) inspection; fare un controllo di to check sth, to inspect sth; visita di controllo (Med) checkup 2 (sorveglianza) super-vision; telefono sotto controllo tapped telephone; base di controllo (Aer) ground control 3 (padronanza, regolamenta-zione) control; sotto controllo under control; la situazione è sotto controllo the situation is under control; esercitare il controllo su qc to have control over sth; perdere il control-lo (di qc) (di macchina, situazione) to lose control (of sth); ha perso il controllo della macchina he lost control of the car; ha perso il controllo (di sé) he lost control (of himself), he lost his self-control ♦ controllo bagagli baggage o luggage check; controllo dei costi cost control; controllo dogana-le customs inspection; controllo di gestione management control; controllo delle nascite birth control; controllo passaporti passport control; controllo dei prezzi price control; controllo qualità quality control; controllo di si-curezza (in aeroporto) security check; controllo del traffico aereo air-traffic control

controllore [kontrol'lore] SM (di autobus, treno) (ticket) in-spector; (doganale) customs officer; controllore di volo air-traffic controller

controluce [kontro'lut∫e] SF INV (Fot) backlit shot ♦ AVV: (in) controluce against the light; (fotografare) into the light; guardala controluce look at it against the light

contromano [kontro'mano] AVV: guidare contromano to drive on the wrong side of the road; (in un senso unico) to drive the wrong way up a one-way street

contropartita [kontropar'tita] SF (fig: compenso): come con-tropartita in return

contropiede [kontro'pjɛde] SM (Sport): azione di contropie-de sudden counter-attack; prendere qn in contropiede to wrong-foot sb; (fig) to catch sb off his (o her) guard

controproducente [kontroprodu't∫ɛnte] AGG counter-productive

contrordine [kon'trordine] SM counter-order; salvo contror-dine unless I (o you ecc) hear to the contrary

controsenso [kontro'sɛnso] SM (contraddizione) contradic-tion in terms; (assurdità) nonsense

controspionaggio, -gi [kontrospio'nadd3o] SM counteres-pionage

controvalore [kontrova'lore] SM equivalent (value)

controvento [kontro'vɛnto] AVV against the wind; navigare controvento to sail to windward

controversia [kontro'vɛrsja] SF (gen) controversy; (Dir) dis-pute; ha suscitato molte controversie it provoked a great

deal of controversy; controversia sindacale industrial dis-pute

controverso, -a [kontro'vɛrso] AGG controversial

controvoglia [kontro'vɔʎʎa] AVV: (di) controvoglia reluc-tantly, unwillingly; l'ho mangiato controvoglia I ate it, though I didn't want to

contumace [kontu'mat∫e] AGG (Dir): rendersi contumace to default, fail to appear in court ♦ SM, SF (Dir) defaulter

contumacia [kontu'mat∫a] SF (Dir) default; processare qn in contumacia to try sb in his (o her) absence; giudizio in contumacia judgment by default

contundente [kontun'dente] AGG: corpo contundente blunt instrument

conturbante [kontur'bante] AGG (sguardo, bellezza) perturb-ing, thrilling

conturbare [kontur'bare] /72/ VT to perturb, thrill

contusione [kontu'zjone] SF (Med) bruise

convalescente [konvale∫'∫ɛnte] AGG, SM, SF convalescent

convalescenza [konvale∫'∫ɛntsa] SF convalescence; essere in convalescenza to be convalescing; ha fatto una conva-lescenza di 3 mesi he spent 3 months convalescing

convalida [kon'valida] SF (vedi vb) validation; stamping; con-firmation

convalidare [konvali'dare] /72/ VT (Amm) to validate; (biglietto) to stamp; (Dir, fig: dubbi, sospetti) to confirm

convegno [kon've ɲɲo] SM (incontro) meeting; (riunione uf-ficiale) convention, conference, congress; darsi convegno (appuntamento) to arrange to meet

convenevoli [konve'nevoli] SMPL courtesies, civilities; scam-biarsi i convenevoli to exchange the usual courtesies

conveniente [konve'njɛnte] AGG 1 (adatto, opportuno): con-veniente (a) suitable (for), fitting (for) 2 (vantaggioso: prez-zo) cheap; (: affare) profitable

convenienza [konve'njɛntsa] SF 1 (l'essere vantaggioso di: prezzo) cheapness; (: affare) advantage, profit; non vedo la convenienza di trovarci a Milano I don't think Milan is the most convenient place to meet; fare qc per convenienza to do sth out of self-interest; non c'è convenienza a vendere adesso there's no advantage in selling at the moment; la convenienza di abitare in centro the advantage of living in the centre; matrimonio di convenienza marriage of convenience 2 (decoro) propriety; andare oltre i limiti del-la convenienza to go beyond the pale 3 (norme sociali): le convenienze SFPL the proprieties, social conventions

convenire [konve'nire] VB IRREG /128/ VT to agree upon; come convenuto as agreed; resta convenuto che... it is agreed that ...; in data da convenire a date to be agreed ♦ VI (aus essere; nel senso 1 avere) 1 (aus avere) (essere d'ac-cordo): convenire (su qc/che...) to agree (upon sth/that ...); devi convenire che hai torto you must admit you are in the wrong; non convengo I agree 2 (essere meno caro) to be cheap 3 (riunirsi) to gather, assemble 4 convenire a qn (es-sere vantaggioso) to be worthwhile for sb; (essere consigliabile) to be advisable for sb; questo affare non mi conviene this transaction isn't worth my while; ti conviene accettare you would be well advised to accept; non gli conviene fare il furbo he'd better not try to get clever; se vuoi evitare il traf-fico ti conviene partire presto if you want to avoid the traf-fic you'd better leave early ♦ VB IMPERS (aus essere) conviene fare così it is advisable to do this; conviene andarsene we'd better go, we should go; comprare al supermercato convi-ene sempre it's always cheaper to shop at the supermarket; converrebbe rimandare la gita we'd better put off the trip; convenirsi VIP: convenirsi a to suit, befit; come si conviene a persone civili as befits civilized people

conventicola [konven'tikola] SF (cricca) clique

convento [kon'vɛnto] SM (di suore) convent; (di frati) mon-astery; entrare in convento (suora) to enter a convent; ac-contentiamoci di quel che passa il convento let's make the best of things

convenuto, -a [konve'nuto] PP di convenire ♦ AGG (ora, luo-go, prezzo) agreed ♦ SM 1 (cosa pattuita) agreement; secon-do il convenuto as agreed 2 (Dir) defendant 3 (i presente) i convenuti SMPL those present

convenzionale [konventsjo'nale] AGG (gen) conventional

convenzionato, -a [konventsjo'nato] AGG (ospedale, clinica) providing free health care, ≈ National Health Service *attr* (*Brit*)

convenzione [konven'tsjone] sf 1 (*Dir, Pol*) agreement 2 (*assunto generale, tradizione*) convention; (*tacito accordo*) understanding; **le convenzioni (sociali)** social conventions 3 (*Pol, Dir: convegno*) convention

convergente [konver'dʒɛnte] AGG convergent

convergenza [konver'dʒɛntsa] sf convergence; (*Aut*) toe-in

convergere [kon'vɛrdʒere] /59/ VI IRREGvb *dif*: (*aus essere*) **convergere (su);** (*gen, anche Mat*) to converge (on); (*interesse*) to centre (on)

conversa [kon'vɛrsa] sf (*Rel*) lay sister

conversare [konver'sare] /72/ VI (*aus avere*) to talk, to have a conversation

conversazione [konversat'tsjone] sf conversation; **fare conversazione** (*chiacchierare*) to chat, have a chat

conversione [konver'sjone] sf (*gen*) conversion (a/in) conversion (to/into); **conversione a U** (*Aut*) U-turn

converso, -a [kon'vɛrso] PP di convergere ♦ **per converso** AVV conversely

convertire [konver'tire] /45/ VT (*gen, anche Inform*) to convert; (*persuadere*): **convertire qn (a qc)** to convert sb (to sth); **convertire qc in qc** to convert sth into sth; **convertirsi** VR: **convertirsi (a qc)** to be converted (to sth); **si è convertito al buddismo** he has become a Buddhist; **convertirsi** VIP: **l'amore si convertì in odio** love turned to hate

convertito, -a [konver'tito] AGG converted ♦ SM, SF convert

convertitore [konverti'tore] SM (*Elettr*) converter; **convertitore di coppia** (*Aut*) torque converter

convesso, -a [kon'vɛsso] AGG convex

convincente [konvin't∫ɛnte] AGG convincing; **una spiegazione convincente** a convincing explanation

convincere [kon'vint∫ere] VB IRREG /129/ VT to convince; **va bene, mi hai convinto** ok, you've convinced me; **convincere qn di qc** to convince sb of sth; **convincere qn a fare qc** to persuade sb to do sth, talk sb into doing sth; **mi ha convinto a comprarlo** she persuaded me to buy it; **convincersi** VR: **convincersi di qc/che...** to convince o.s. of sth/that ...

convinto, -a [kon'vinto] PP di convincere ♦ AGG convinced; **in tono convinto** with conviction

convinzione [konvin'tsjone] sf conviction, firm belief; **fare opera di convinzione su qn** to try to convince sb

convissuto [konvis'suto] PP di convivere

convitato, -a [konvi'tato] SM, SF guest

convitto [kon'vitto] SM boarding school

convivente [konvi'vɛnte] SM, SF (*partner*) partner; (*compagno di appartamento*) flatmate (*Brit*), roommate (*USA*)

convivenza [konvi'vɛntsa] sf living together; (*Dir*) cohabitation; **la convivenza è sempre più comune** living together is becoming more common

convivere [kon'vivere] /130/ VI IRREG (*aus essere*) to live together; (*Dir*) to cohabit; **convivere con qn** to live with sb

conviviale [konvi'vjale] AGG convivial

convocare [konvo'kare] /20/ VT (*riunione*) to convene, call; (*parlamento*) to convene; (*persona subordinata*) to summon, send for; **convocare una riunione** to call a meeting; **tutti i genitori sono stati convocati** all parents have been asked to attend; **il giocatore è stato convocato in nazionale** the player has been chosen to play for the national team

convocazione [konvokat'tsjone] sf 1 (*atto: vedi vb*) convening; summoning; **lettera di convocazione** (letter of) notification to appear o attend 2 (*riunione*) meeting, summons sg

convogliare [konvoʎ'ʎare] /27/ VT 1 (*dirigere*) to direct, send; (*acque*) to channel; (*fig: energie*): **convogliare su** to channel into 2 (*trasportare*) to carry, transport, convey

convoglio, -gli [kon'vɔʎʎo] SM 1 (*Naut, Mil*) convoy; **convoglio (ferroviario)** train 2 (*corteo funebre*) funeral procession

convolare [konvo'lare] /72/ VI (*aus essere*) **convolare a (giuste) nozze** (*scherz*) to tie the knot

convulsione [konvul'sjone] sf (*Med*) convulsion; (*di riso*) fit

convulso, -a [kon'vulso] AGG (*gen*) convulsive; (*pianto*) uncontrollable, violent; (*fig: stile, parlare*) jerky; (: *attività, ritmo*) feverish

Coop. [ko'ɔp] ABBR F = **cooperativa**

cooperare [koope'rare] /72/ VI (*aus avere*) **cooperare (a qc/a fare qc)** to cooperate (in sth/to do sth); **le autorità francesi e britanniche stanno cooperando** the French and British authorities are working together; **cooperare ad un progetto** to work together on a project

cooperativa [koopera'tiva] sf cooperative; **cooperativa edilizia** building cooperative (*selling houses to its members*)

cooperazione [kooperat'tsjone] sf cooperation

coordinamento [koordina'mento] SM coordination

coordinare [koordi'nare] /72/ VT to coordinate

coordinato, -a [koordi'nato] AGG (*Mat, Ling*) coordinate; (*movimenti*) coordinated ♦ **coordinati** SMPL (*abbigliamento, arredamento*) coordinates

coordinazione [koordinat'tsjone] sf coordination

coperchio, -chi [ko'pɛrkjo] SM cover; (*di pentola*) lid

coperta [ko'pɛrta] sf 1 (*di lana*) blanket; (*da viaggio*) rug; **una bella coperta calda** a nice warm blanket; **stare sotto le coperte** to be in bed; **coperta elettrica** electric blanket 2 (*Naut*) deck; **tutti in coperta!** all hands on deck!

copertina [koper'tina] sf (*di libro, rivista*) cover; (*sovraccoperta*) jacket; **la sua faccia è sulla copertina di questa settimana** her picture is on this week's cover; **in copertina** on the cover; **ragazza copertina** cover girl

coperto, -a [ko'pɛrto] PP di coprire ♦ AGG (*gen, anche Assicurazione*) covered; (*luogo: riparato*) sheltered; (*piscina, campo da tennis*) indoor *attr*; (*cielo*) overcast; **essere ben coperto** to be wearing warm clothes; **sei ben coperto?** are you wearing warm clothes?; **tieni il bambino ben coperto** keep the child well wrapped up; **coperto di** covered with; **libri coperti di polvere** books covered with dust; **una parete coperta di poster** a wall covered with posters; **una piscina coperta** an indoor pool; **il cielo è coperto** the sky is overcast ♦ SM 1 al coperto cover, indoors; **in caso di pioggia la festa si svolgerà al coperto** if it rains, the party will be held indoors; **mettersi al coperto** to take shelter; **essere al coperto** (*fig*) to be safe 2 (*posto a tavola*) place; **ho messo 12 coperti** I've set the table for 12; **(prezzo del) coperto** (*al ristorante*) cover charge; **il coperto è compreso nel conto** the cover charge is included in the bill

copertone [koper'tone] SM 1 (*Aut*) tyre (*Brit*), tire (*USA*) (*telone impermeabile*) tarpaulin

copertura [koper'tura] sf 1 (*gen, atto*) covering; (*Edil*) roofing; **attività di copertura** cover-up; **materiali da copertura** roofing (materials) 2 (*Econ, Comm, Assicurazione*) cover; **copertura assicurativa** insurance cover 3 (*Sport*): **fare un gioco di copertura** to play a defensive game 4 (*Mil*) cover

copia ['kɔpja] sf (*gen*) copy; (*Fot*) print; **non è l'originale, è una copia** it's not the original, it's a copy; **brutta/bella copia** rough/final copy; **essere l'esatta copia di qn/qc** to be the spitting image of sb/sth; **hanno venduto un milione di copie dell'album** a million copies of the album have been sold; **vorrei due copie di ciascuna foto** I'd like two prints of each photo; **copia carbone** carbon copy; **copia conforme** (*Dir*) certified copy; **copia omaggio** presentation copy

copiare [ko'pjare] /19/ VT to copy; (*Inform*) to back up, copy; **copiare (qc da qn)** (*in compito a scuola*) to copy (sth from sb); **non dovete copiare** you mustn't copy

copiatrice [kopja'trit∫e] sf copier, copying machine

copincol·lare /72/ VT to copy and paste

copin'collo [ko'pjone] SM copy and paste

copione [ko'pjone] SM (*Cine, Teatro*) script; **come da o secondo copione** according to plan, as planned

coppa ['kɔppa] sf 1 (*gen*) cup; (*Sport*) trophy, cup; (*per gelato, frutta*) bowl; (*per spumante*) champagne glass; (*Rel*) chalice; **coppa di gelato** (*in confezione*) tub of ice cream; **prendi un cono o una coppa?** are you going to have a cone or a tub?; **una coppa di champagne** a glass of champagne; **la nostra squadra ha vinto la coppa** our team won the cup; **coppa dell'olio** (*Aut*) oil sump (*Brit*) o pan (*USA*); **coppa della ruota** (*Aut*) hubcap 2 (*Carte*): **coppe** SFPL suit in Neapolitan pack of cards

coppia ['kɔppja] sf (*di persone*) couple; (*di animali; Sport*) pair; **sono una bella coppia** they're a nice-looking couple; **fare una bella coppia** to make a nice couple; **una coppia di sposi** a married couple; **una coppia di canarini** a pair of

canaries; **a coppie, in coppia** in pairs; **gara a coppie** competition for pairs; **coppia di forze** (Fis) torque
coprente [ko'prɛnte] AGG (colore, cosmetico) covering; (calze) opaque
copricapo [kopri'kapo] SM headgear no pl; (cappello) hat
coprifuoco, -chi [kopri'fwɔko] SM curfew
copriletto [kopri'letto] SM INV bedspread
copripiumino [kopripju'mino] SM INV duvet cover
coprire [ko'prire] VB IRREG /9/ VT (gen) to cover; (occupare: carica, posto) to hold; (persona: proteggere, anche fig) to cover, shield; (fig: suono) to drown; (: segreto, sentimenti) to conceal; **copri bene il bambino** wrap the child up well; **coprire di o con** (gen) to cover with; **era coperto di lividi** he was bruised all over o covered in bruises; **ho coperto la bici con un telo di plastica** I covered the bike with a plastic sheet; **coprire qn di insulti/di doni** to shower insults/gifts on sb; **coprire qn di ridicolo** to cover sb with ridicule; **coprire qn di baci** to smother sb with kisses; **coprire (le spalle a) qn** (in una sparatoria) to cover sb; **coprire un rischio** (Econ, Assicurazione) to cover a risk; **coprire le spese** to break even; **coprire un percorso in un'ora** to cover a distance in one hour; **coprirsi** VR (persona) to wrap (o.s.) up; (Assicurazione): **coprirsi contro** to insure o.s. against; **coprirsi di gloria/di ridicolo** to cover o.s. with glory/with ridicule; **coprirsi** VIP (cielo) to cloud over; (rivestirsi): **coprirsi di** (muffa, macchie) to be covered in
coque [kɔk] SF INV: **uovo alla coque** (soft-)boiled egg
coraggio [ko'raddʒo] SM 1 courage, bravery; **aver coraggio** to be courageous, be brave; **avere il coraggio di fare qc** to be brave enough to do sth; **ha avuto il coraggio di dire la verità** he was brave enough to tell the truth; **non ho avuto il coraggio di chiederglielo** I hadn't the nerve to ask him; **avere il coraggio delle proprie azioni** to have the courage of one's convictions; **ha dimostrato molto coraggio** she showed great courage; **dimostrare coraggio in battaglia** to show courage o bravery in battle; **aver un coraggio da leone** to be as brave as a lion; **farsi coraggio** to pluck up courage; **si è fatto coraggio e le ha chiesto di uscire con lui** he plucked up courage and asked her to go out with him; **fare coraggio a qn** to cheer sb up; **coraggio!** (forza!) come on!; (animo!) cheer up!; **coraggio, siamo quasi arrivati!** come on, we're nearly there! 2 (sfacciataggine) nerve; **hai un bel coraggio!** you've got a nerve!
coraggioso, -a [korad'dʒoso] AGG brave, courageous
corale [ko'rale] AGG (Mus) choral; (adesione, consenso) unanimous
corallo [ko'rallo] SM coral; **il mar dei Coralli** the Coral Sea
Corano [ko'rano] SM: **il Corano** the Koran
corazza [ko'rattsa] SF (Storia) cuirass; (Mil) armo(u)r(-plate); (Sport) protective clothing; (di animali) carapace, shell; **corazza di indifferenza** hard shell of indifference
corazzato, -a [korat'tsato] AGG (Mil) armo(u)red; **essere corazzato contro le avversità** to be hardened o proof against adversities
corazziere [korat'tsjere] SM (Storia) cuirassier; (guardia presidenziale) carabiniere of the President's guard
corbelleria [korbelle'ria] SF (parola) stupid remark; (azione) foolish action; **non dire corbellerie!** don't talk nonsense!, don't be so silly!
corda [ˈkɔrda] SF 1 (fune) rope; (Pugilato): **le corde** the ropes; **una corda per saltare** a skipping rope; **saltare la corda** to skip (Brit), jump rope (USA); **di corda** (suole) rope attr; **scarpe di corda** espadrilles 2 (di violino, arco, racchetta) string; **strumenti a corda** stringed instruments 3 (Anat): **corda vocali** vocal cords; **corda dorsale** (Zool) spinal chord 4 (Geom) chord 5 (fraseologia): **dare corda a qn** to let sb have his (o her) way; **dare la corda a un orologio** to wind a clock; **mettersi la corda al collo** (fig) to put one's head in the noose; **tenere sulla corda qn** to keep sb on tenterhooks; **essere giù di corda** to feel down; **oggi sono un po' giù di corda** I'm feeling a bit down today; **tagliare la corda** to sneak off, slip away; **tendere o tirare troppo la corda** (fig) to push one's luck
cordata [kor'data] SF (Alpinismo) roped party; (fig: Pol) network, alliance system in financial and business world; **in cordata** roped together

cordiale [kor'djale] AGG (accoglienza) warm, cordial; (persona) warm; **una persona molto cordiale** a very friendly person; **è la ragazza più cordiale che abbia mai conosciuto** she's the friendliest girl I've ever met; **cordiali saluti** (in lettere) best regards; **c'è una cordiale antipatia tra noi** we cordially dislike one another ♦ SM (bevanda) cordial
cordialità [kordjali'ta] SF 1 warmth, cordiality 2 (saluti): **cordialità** SFPL best wishes
cordless [ˈkordles] SM INV, AGG INV (anche: telefono cordless) cordless phone
cordoglio [kor'dɔʎʎo] SM grief, sorrow; (lutto) mourning; **esprimere il proprio cordoglio a qn** to offer sb one's sympathy o condolences
cordone [kor'done] SM (gen) cord; (di telefono) cord, flex; (di borsa) string; (linea: di poliziotti, soldati) cordon; **cordone litoraneo** (Geog) offshore bar; **cordone ombelicale** (Anat) umbilical cord; **cordone sanitario** quarantine line, cordon sanitaire
Corea [ko'rea] SF Korea; **la Corea del Nord/Sud** North/South Korea
coreano, -a [kore'ano] AGG, SM, SF Korean
coreografia [koreogra'fia] SF choreography
coreografo, -a [kore'ografo] SM, SF choreographer
coriaceo, -a [ko'rjat'feo] AGG (Bot, Zool) coriaceous; (fig) tough
coriandolo [ko'rjandolo] SM 1 (per carnevale): **coriandoli** SMPL confetti sg 2 (Bot) coriander
coricare [kori'kare] /20/ VT (persona: a letto) to put to bed; (: a terra, su divano) to lay down, lay down; (: bottiglia) to rest, lay; **coricarsi** VR (andare a letto) to go to bed; (riposarsi) to lie down
coricherò ecc VB vedi **coricare**
Corinto [ko'rinto] SF Corinth
corista, -i, -e [ko'rista] SM, SF (Rel) choir member, chorister; (Teatro) member of the chorus; **i coristi** (Teatro) the chorus ♦ SM tuning fork
corna [ˈkɔrna] SFPL vedi **corno**
cornacchia [kor'nakkja] SF crow; **cornacchia grigia** hooded crow; **cornacchia nera** carrion crow
cornamusa [korna'muza] SF bagpipes pl
cornea [ˈkɔrnea] SF (Anat) cornea
corner [ˈkorner] SM INV (Calcio) corner (kick); **salvarsi in corner** (fig: in gara, esame) to get through by the skin of one's teeth; **mi son salvato in corner** (in situazione imbarazzante) I just managed to wriggle out of it
cornetta [kor'netta] SF (Mus) cornet; (di telefono) receiver; **sollevare la cornetta e comporre il numero** lift the receiver and dial the number; **riattaccare la cornetta** to hang up
cornetto [kor'netto] SM 1 (Culin: brioche) croissant; (: gelato) cone, cornet (Brit); (: fagiolino) runner bean (Brit), string bean (USA) 2 (amuleto) horn-shaped talisman 3 **cornetto acustico** ear trumpet
cornice [kor'nitfe] SF (gen) frame; (Archit, Sci) cornice; (Geog) ledge; (fig) background, setting; **una cornice d'argento** a silver frame; **fare da cornice a** (fig) to frame
cornicione [korni'tfone] SM (di edificio) ledge; (Archit) cornice
corno [ˈkɔrno] SM (pl m corni) (Mus) horn; **corno da caccia** hunting horn; **corno inglese** (Mus) English horn, cor anglais ♦ SM no pl 1 (materiale) horn; **di corno** (bottone, manico) horn attr 2 (fam): **un corno!** not on your life!; **felice? — un corno!** — anything but!; **non me ne importa un corno!** I don't give a damn!; **non è vero un corno!** that's rubbish! 3 (Geog): **il Corno d'Africa** Horn of Africa; **i paesi del Corno d'Africa** Somaliland ♦ SM (pl f corna) 1 (Zool: di toro, lumaca) horn; (: di cervo) antler 2 (fam): **fare le corna** (per scaramanzia) to keep one's fingers crossed; **fare le corna a qn** (a marito, moglie) to cheat on sb; **dire peste e corna di qn** to call sb every name under the sun; **rompersi le corna** to burn one's fingers
❏ **corno** non si traduce mai con **corn**
Cornovaglia [korno'vaʎʎa] SF Cornwall; **andremo in Cornovaglia a Pasqua** we're going to Cornwall at Easter; **mi è piaciuta molto la Cornovaglia** I really liked Cornwall
cornuto, -a [kor'nuto] AGG 1 (con corna) horned 2 (fam:

tradito) cheated on; **arbitro cornuto!** bloody ref! ♦ SM, SF (*fam*) cheated-on husband (wife); **cornuto!** (*fam.!*) bastard! (*fam.!*)

coro [ˈkɔro] SM (*gen, anche fig*) chorus; (*Rel: cantori, luogo*) choir; **canta in un coro** he sings in a choir; **un coro di proteste** a chorus of protests; **in coro** in chorus; **tutti in coro** all together

corollario, -ri [korolˈlarjo] SM corollary

corona [koˈrona] SF **1** (*di re*) crown; (*di nobile*) coronet; **cingere la corona** to assume the crown; **fare corona intorno a qn** (*fig*) to form a circle round sb **2** (*di fiori*) wreath; **corona d'alloro** laurel wreath; **corona funebre** *o* **mortuaria** funeral wreath; **corona del rosario** rosary, rosary beads *pl*; **corona di spine** crown of thorns **3** (*di dente*) crown **4** (*Geom*): **corona circolare** outer circle

coronamento [koronaˈmento] SM **1** (*di impresa*) completion; (*di carriera*) crowning achievement; **il coronamento dei propri sogni** the fulfilment of one's dreams **2** (*Edil*) crown; (*Naut*) taffrail

coronare [koroˈnare] /72/ VT **1** (*cingere*): **coronare (di)** (*anche fig*) to crown (with) **2** (*realizzare: impresa*) to bring to a successful conclusion; **coronare i propri sogni** to fulfil one's dreams; **uno sforzo coronato dal successo** an effort crowned with success

coronaria [koroˈnarja] SF coronary artery

corpo [ˈkɔrpo] SM (*gen, anche Chim, fig*) body; (*cadavere*) corpse, (dead) body; (*di opere*) corpus; **corpo liquido/gassoso** liquid/gaseous substance; **non ho niente in corpo da stamattina** I haven't eaten anything since this morning; **darsi anima e corpo a** to give o.s. heart and soul to; (a) **corpo a corpo** agg hand-to-hand; **andare di corpo** to empty one's bowels; **dare corpo a qc** to give substance to sth; **prendere corpo** (*idea, progetto*) to take shape; **a corpo morto** (*fig*) like a dead weight, heavily; **lo colpì con tutta la forza che aveva in corpo** she hit him with all her strength; **l'incendio ha divorato l'intero corpo dell'edificio** the fire destroyed the entire building; **l'intero corpo delle opere di Leopardi** the entire works of Leopardi; **esercizi a corpo libero** floor exercises ♦ **corpo d'armata** army corps *sg*; **corpo di ballo** corps de ballet; **corpo dei carabinieri** ≈ police force; **corpo celeste** heavenly body; **corpo a corpo** (*lotta*) hand-to-hand fight; **corpo diplomatico** diplomatic corps *sg*; **corpo elettorale** electorate; **corpo estraneo** foreign body; **corpo di guardia** (*soldati*) guard; (*locale*) guardroom; **corpo insegnante** teachers *pl*, teaching staff; **corpo dei pompieri** fire brigade; **corpo del reato** material evidence; **corpo di spedizione** (*Mil*) task force

corporale [korpoˈrale] AGG (*bisogni*) bodily; (*punizione*) corporal ♦ SM (*Rel*) corporal

corporatura [korporaˈtura] SF build, physique; **di corporatura media** of medium build

corporazione [korporatˈtsjone] SF professional body, corporation; (*Storia*) guild

corporeo, -a [korˈpɔreo] AGG bodily, physical

corposo, -a [korˈposo] AGG (*vino*) full-bodied

corpulento, -a [korpuˈlento] AGG stout, corpulent

corpulenza [korpuˈlentsa] SF stoutness, corpulence

corpuscolo [korˈpuskolo] SM corpuscle

corredare [korreˈdare] /72/ VT: **corredare di** (*apparecchio, laboratorio*) to provide *o* furnish *o* equip with; **un elettrodomestico corredato di vari accessori** an electrical appliance complete with various accessories; **domanda corredata dai seguenti documenti** application accompanied by the following documents; **corredarsi** VR: **corredarsi di** to equip o.s. with

corredo [korˈredo] SM (*di attrezzi*) kit; (*da sposa*) trousseau

correggere [korˈreddʒere] VB IRREG /87/ VT (*gen*) to correct; (*compiti*) to correct, mark (*Brit*), grade (*USA*); (*Tip*) to proofread; (*fig: abuso*) to remedy; **deve ancora correggere i compiti di ieri** she hasn't marked yesterday's homework yet; ... **correggimi se sbaglio** ... if I'm not mistaken; **correggere il caffè con la grappa** to lace one's coffee with grappa; **correggersi** VR to correct o.s.

corrente [korˈrɛnte] AGG **1** (*acqua del rubinetto*) running; **acqua corrente** running water **2** (*uso, anno*) current; (*moneta*) valid; **è opinione corrente che...** it is commonly

believed that ...; **la vostra lettera del 5 corrente mese** (*in lettere commerciali*) in your letter of the 5th of this month, in your letter of the 5th inst. (*Brit: frm*) **3** (*ordinario: merce*) ordinary; **articoli di qualità corrente** average-quality products **4** (*quotidiano: spese, affari*) everyday ♦ SM: **essere al corrente di** (*notizia*) to know about; (*scoperte scientifiche*) to be well-informed about; **tenere qn al corrente** to keep sb informed; **mettere qn al corrente (di)** to inform sb (of); **mi ha messo al corrente degli ultimi sviluppi** she told me about the latest developments ♦ SF (*Elettr: di acque*) current; (*di aria*) airstream, current of air; (*spiffero*) draught (*Brit*), draft (*USA*); (*di opinioni*) trend; **c'è corrente qui dentro** there's a draught in here; **tagliare la corrente** (*Elettr*) to cut off the power; **è andata via la corrente** (*Elettr*) the electricity's gone off; **presa di corrente** socket; **una corrente di simpatia** a wave of sympathy; **la corrente l'ha trascinato al largo** the current carried him out to sea; **andare contro corrente** (*anche fig*) to swim against the stream; **seguire la corrente** (*fig*) to follow the trend; **corrente alternata** alternating current; **corrente continua** direct current; **la Corrente del Golfo** the Gulf Stream; **corrente di risacca** (*Geog*) undertow

correntemente [korrenteˈmente] AVV (*comunemente*) commonly; **parlare una lingua correntemente** to speak a language fluently; **parla correntemente il francese** she speaks French fluently

correntista, -i, -e [korrenˈtista] SM, SF (*Fin*) (current (*Brit*) *o* checking (*USA*)) account holder

correo, -a [korˈreo] SM, SF (*Dir*) accomplice

correre [ˈkorrere] VB IRREG /28/ VI (*quando si esprime o sottintende una meta*) (*aus* **essere**) (*senza una meta e nel senso Sport*) (*aus* **avere**) (*gen*) to run; (*affrettarsi*) to hurry; (*precipitarsi*) to rush; (*Sport*) to race, run; (*diffondersi: notizie*) to go round; **abbiamo corso come pazzi per non perdere il treno** we ran like mad to catch the train; **sono corso subito fuori** I immediately rushed outside; **oggi ho corso un'ora** I went running for an hour today; **corre troppo in macchina** he drives too fast; **non correre!** (*anche fig*) not so fast!; **correre dietro a qn** (*anche fig*) to run after sb; **ci corre!** (*c'è una differenza*) there's a big difference!; **correva l'anno 1265** it was the year 1265; **corre voce che...** it is rumoured that ...; **il tempo corre** time is getting on ♦ VT (*gen*) to run; (*pericolo*) to face; (*Sport*) to run; (*gara*) to compete in; **correre i 100 metri** to run in the 100 metres; **correre i 100 metri a tempo di record** to run the 100 metres in record time; **correre un rischio** to run a risk; **non voglio correre il rischio di non trovare posto** I don't want to risk not getting a seat

corresponsabilità [korresponsabiliˈta] SF (*vedi agg*) joint responsibility; joint liability

corresponsione [korresponˈsjone] SF payment

corressi ecc [korˈressi] VB vedi **correggere**

correttezza [korretˈtettsa] SF (*di comportamento*) correctness; (*Sport*) fair play; **è questione di correttezza** it's a question of propriety *o* good manners

corretto, -a [korˈretto] PP *di* **correggere** ♦ AGG (*gen*) correct; (*comportamento*) proper, correct; **caffè corretto al cognac** coffee with a shot of cognac; **la risposta corretta** the correct answer

correttore, -trice [korretˈtore] SM, SF: **correttore di bozze** proofreader ♦ SM **1** (*liquido*) **correttore** correction *o* correcting fluid **2** (*cosmetico*) blemish cover; **correttore ortografico** (*Inform*) spellchecker

correzione [korretˈtsjone] SF **1** (*gen*) correction; (*di compiti*) marking (*Brit*), grading (*USA*); (*miglioramento*) improvement; **correzione di bozze** proofreading; **correzione ortografica** (*Inform: atto*) spelling check; (: *processo*) spellchecking **2** (*castigo*): **casa di correzione** ≈ community home (*Brit*), ≈ reform school (*USA*), reformatory (*USA*)

corrida [korˈrida] SF bullfight

corridoio, -oi [korriˈdojo] SM (*gen*) corridor, passage; (*laterale: di aereo, treno*) (*centrale: di aereo, pullman*) aisle; (*Tennis*) alley; **manovre di corridoio** (*Pol*) lobbying *sg*; **corridoio aereo** air corridor

corridore [korriˈdore] SM (*Sport*) runner; (*su veicolo*) racer

corriera [korˈrjera] SF bus, coach (*Brit*)

corriere [korˈrjere] SM **1** (*gen*) messenger; (*Mil: diplomatico*) courier; (*spedizioniere*) carrier **2** (*Zool*): **corriere grosso ringed plover**

corrimano [korri'mano] SM handrail

corrispettivo [korrispet'tivo] SM amount due; **versare a qn il corrispettivo di una prestazione** to pay sb the amount due for his (*o* her) services

corrispondente [korrispon'dɛnte] AGG corresponding ♦ SM, SF (*gen, anche Stampa, TV*) correspondent

corrispondenza [korrispon'dɛntsa] SF **1** (*conformità*) correspondence; (*fig*) connection, relation; **non c'è corrispondenza tra le due versioni** the two versions do not correspond **2** (*posta*: *atto di scrivere*) correspondence; (*insieme di lettere*) mail; **evadere la corrispondenza** to deal with one's correspondence; **corrispondenza in arrivo/partenza** incoming/outgoing mail; **corso per corrispondenza** correspondence course; **vendita per corrispondenza** mail-order shopping **3** (*Mat*) relation

corrispondere [korris'pondere] VB IRREG /95/ VT **1** (*pagare*) to pay **2** (*ricambiare*: *amore*) to return ♦ VI (*aus* avere) **1** (*equivalere*): **corrispondere (a)** to correspond (to); **quello che ha detto non corrisponde a verità** what he said doesn't fit the facts; **a ciascun numero corrisponde una lettera** each number corresponds to a letter **2** (*per lettera*): **corrispondere con** to correspond with

corrisposto, -a [korris'posto] PP *di* corrispondere ♦ AGG (*affetto, sentimento*) reciprocated

corroborare [korrobo'rare] /72/ VT (*rinvigorire*) to invigorate, strengthen, fortify; (*fig*: *ipotesi*) to corroborate, bear out

corrodere [kor'rodere] VB IRREG /49/ VT (*metalli, anche fig*) to corrode; (*legno*) to eat into; **la carie corrode i denti** teeth are eaten away by decay; **corrodersi** VIP to corrode; (*roccia*) to erode, wear away

corrompere [kor'rompere] VB IRREG /97/ VT (*gen, anche fig*) to corrupt; (*testimone, giudice*) to bribe, corrupt; (*linguaggio*) to debase; **corrompersi** VIP (*costumi*) to become corrupt

corrosione [korro'zjone] SF corrosion

corrosivo, -a [korro'sivo] AGG, SM corrosive

corroso, -a [kor'roso] PP *di* corrodere

corrottamente [korrotta'mente] AVV corruptly

corrotto, -a [kor'rotto] PP *di* corrompere ♦ AGG corrupt

corrucciarsi [korrut't∫arsi] /14/ VIP to become upset; **si corrucciò in viso** his face took on a worried expression

corrugare [korru'gare] /80/ VT: **corrugare la fronte** *o* **le sopracciglia** to frown, knit one's brows

corruppi ecc [kor'ruppi] VB *vedi* corrompere

corruttela [korrut'tela] SF (*letter*) corruption, depravity

corruzione [korrut'tsjone] SF corruption; (*con denaro*) bribery; **corruzione di minorenne** (*Dir*) corruption of a minor

corsa [korsa] SF **1** (*azione*) running *no pl*; **andare** *o* **essere di corsa** to be in a hurry; **andarsene/arrivare di corsa** to rush off/in; **fare qc di corsa** to do sth quickly; **ho fatto i compiti di corsa e sono uscito** I did my homework quickly and went out; **ho mangiato di corsa un panino e sono uscito** I had a quick sandwich and went out; **ho dovuto fare una corsa** I had to dash; **"vietato scendere dal treno in corsa"** "do not alight from the train while it is in motion"; **abbiamo preso i cappotti e via di corsa** we grabbed our coats and off we went; **faccio una corsa e torno!** I'll be straight back!; **è una corsa contro il tempo** it's a race against time; **corsa all'oro** gold rush **2** (*Sport*: *gara*) race; (*: disciplina*) racing *no pl*; (*: atletica*) running *no pl*; **da corsa** (*auto, moto*) racing; **auto da corsa** racing car; **cavallo da corsa** racehorse; **fare una corsa** to run a race; **va spesso alle corse** he often goes to the races; **corsa automobilistica/ciclistica** motor/cycle racing; **corsa con i sacchi** sack race; **corsa campestre** cross-country race; **corsa ad ostacoli** (*Ippica*) steeplechase; (*Atletica*) hurdles *sg*; **corsa piana** *o* **in piano** (*Ippica*) flat race; **corsa a siepi** (*Ippica*) hurdle race **3** (*di autobus, taxi*) trip, journey; **a che ora c'è l'ultima corsa?** when is the last bus?; **quanto costa la corsa?** what's the fare? **4** (*Fis*: *di pendolo*) movement; (*: di pistone*) stroke **5** (*Naut, Mil*): **guerra di corsa** privateering

corsaro, -a [kor'saro] AGG: **nave corsara** privateer ♦ SM privateer, corsair

corsi ecc [korsi] VB *vedi* correre

corsia [kor'sia] SF **1** (*gen*) gangway, passage; (*Aut, Sport*) lane; **autostrada a 4 corsie** 4-lane motorway (*Brit*) *o* freeway (*USA*); **corsia di accelerazione** (*Aut*) acceleration lane; **corsia di decelerazione** (*Aut*) deceleration lane; **corsia di emergenza** (*Aut*) hard shoulder (*Brit*), shoulder (*USA*); **corsia preferenziale** ≈ bus lane; (*fig*) fast track; **corsia di sorpasso** (*Aut*) overtaking lane, fast lane **2** (*in ospedale*) ward; **è ricoverato in corsia** he's a patient in the ward

Corsica [korsika] SF Corsica

corsivo, -a [kor'sivo] AGG (*scrittura*) cursive; (*Tip*) italic ♦ SM **1** cursive (writing); (*Tip*) italics *pl* **2** (*Stampa*) brief article of comment (*in italics*)

corso¹, -a [korso] PP *di* correre

corso², -a [korso] SM Corsican

corso³ [korso] SM **1** (*fluire*: *di acqua, tempo*) course; **corso d'acqua** (*naturale*) river, stream; (*artificiale*) waterway; **discendere il corso del Nilo** to go down the Nile; **dare corso a** to start; **dar libero corso a** to give free expression to; **in corso** (*lavori*) in progress, under way; (*anno, mese*) current; **in corso di riparazione** in the process of being repaired; **nel corso di** during; **nel corso del tempo** in the course of time; **il nuovo corso del partito laburista** the new direction of the Labour Party **2** (*Scol, Univ*) course; **un corso d'inglese** an English course; **seguire un corso serale** to go to an evening class; **tenere un corso su** to give a course on; **primo anno di corso** first year; **studente fuori corso** undergraduate who *has not completed course in due time*; **corso di aggiornamento** refresher course **3** (*strada cittadina*) main street; (*nei nomi di strada*) avenue; **ha un negozio sul corso** she's got a shop in the main street **4** (*Fin*: *di moneta*) circulation; (*: di titoli, valori*) rate, price; **aver corso legale** to be legal tender; **una banconota fuori corso** a banknote no longer legal tender

corte [korte] SF **1** (*seguito del re*) court **2** (*attenzioni, gentilezze*): **fare la corte a qn** (*per amore*) to court sb; (*per interesse*) to butter sb up **3** (*Dir*) court; **Corte d'Appello** court of appeal; **Corte d'Assise** (*in Inghilterra e Galles*) ≈ crown court; (*in Scozia*) ≈ high court; **Corte di Cassazione** court of cassation, *the highest judicial authority*; **Corte dei Conti** audit court; **Corte Costituzionale** *special court dealing with constitutional and ministerial matters*; **corte marziale** court-martial **4** (*cortile*) (court)yard

corteccia, -ce [kor'tett∫a] SF (*di albero*) bark; (*Anat*) cortex

corteggiamento [korteddʒa'mento] SM courtship

corteggiare [korted'dʒare] /62/ VT to court, woo

corteggiatore [korteddʒa'tore] SM suitor

corteo [kor'tɛo] SM procession; **i dimostranti hanno sfilato in corteo** the demonstrators marched past; **corteo funebre** funeral cortège

cortese [kor'teze] AGG courteous; (*Letteratura*) courtly

cortesia [korte'zia] SF (*qualità*) courtesy; (*atto*) favour; **fare una cortesia a qn** to do sb a favour; **mi faresti una cortesia?** would you do me a favour?; **fammi la cortesia di star zitto!** do me a favour and shut up!; **fammi una cortesia, spegni quella radio** would you please turn off that radio; **per cortesia, dov'è...?** excuse me, please, where is ...?; **per cortesia, dov'è il bagno?** excuse me, where's the toilet?

cortigiano, -a [korti'dʒano] SM, SF courtier ♦ SF (*euf*: *prostituta*) courtesan

cortile [kor'tile] SM (*di edificio*: *all'interno*) (court)yard; (*: davanti*) forecourt; (*: all'esterno, dietro*) yard; (*: di cascina*) farmyard

cortina [kor'tina] SF curtain, drape (*USA*); (*anche fig*) screen; **una cortina di fumo/nebbia** a wall of smoke/mist; **la cortina di ferro** the Iron Curtain; **una cortina di silenzio** a wall of silence

cortisone [korti'zone] SM cortisone

corto, -a [korto] AGG (*tutti i sensi*) short; **maniche corte** short sleeves; **questi pantaloni sono troppo corti** these trousers are too short; **la settimana corta** the 5-day week; **la strada più corta** (*anche fig*) the quickest way; **avere la vista corta** (*anche fig*) to be short-sighted; **essere** *o* **rimanere a corto di qc** to be short of sth; **sono a corto di soldi** I'm short of money; **essere a corto di parole** to be at a loss for words ♦ AVV: **tagliare corto** to come straight to the point ♦ SM (*Cine*) short

❏ **corto** non si traduce mai con *curt*

cortocircuito [kortotʃirˈkuito] SM short-circuit

cortometraggio, -gi [kortomeˈtraddʒo] SM (*Cine*) short (feature film)

corvino, -a [korˈvino] AGG: **capelli corvini** jet-black hair

corvo [ˈkɔrvo] SM (*anche:* **corvo imperiale**) raven; **corvo comune** *o* **nero** rook

cosa [ˈkɔsa] SF 1 (*gen*) thing; **ogni cosa, tutte le cose** everything; **il terremoto ha distrutto ogni cosa** the earthquake destroyed everything; **qualche cosa** something; **c'è qualche altra cosa da discutere** there's something else to discuss; **vuole qualche cosa da mangiare?** would you like something to eat?; **nessuna cosa** nothing; **è una cosa da poco** it's nothing; **devo dirti una cosa** I've got something to tell you; **come prima cosa** first of all; **facciamo le cose per bene** let's do things properly; **la cosa migliore sarebbe partire di mattina** the best thing would be to leave in the morning; **tante belle cose!** all the best! 2 (*situazione, fatto*) it, things *pl*; **la cosa non è chiara** it isn't clear, things aren't clear; **ti voglio spiegare la cosa** let me explain things to you; **è successa una cosa strana** something strange has happened; **sono cose da ragazzi** that's kids for you; **ormai è cosa fatta!** (*positivo*) it's in the bag!; (*negativo*) it's done now!; **a cose fatte** when all is said and done, when it's all over; **le cose stanno così** this is how things stand; **sono cose che capitano!** these things happen! 3 (*preoccupazione, problema*) matter, affair, business *no pl*; **brutta cosa!** it's a nasty business *o* matter!; **la cosa non mi riguarda** the matter doesn't concern me; **è tutt'altra cosa** that's quite another matter; **eh no, non è la stessa cosa!** excuse me, but that's not the same thing! ♦ PRON INTERROG: **(che) cosa?** what?; **(che) cos'è?** what is it?; **a cosa pensi?** what are you thinking about?; **cosa stai facendo?** what are you doing?; **che cosa ha detto?** what did he say?; **cosa?!** what?!; *vedi anche* **che**

Cosa Nostra [koza ˈnɔstra] SF Cosa Nostra

cosca, -sche [ˈkɔska] SF (*di mafiosi*) clan

coscia, -sce [ˈkɔʃʃa] SF (*Anat*) thigh; (*Culin: di pollo*) leg; **una coscia di pollo** a chicken leg; **una coscia d'agnello** a leg of lamb

cosciente [koʃˈʃɛnte] AGG (*gen, anche Med*) conscious; (*consapevole*): **cosciente di** conscious *o* aware of

coscienza [koʃˈʃɛntsa] SF 1 (*morale*) conscience; **aver qc sulla coscienza** to have sth on one's conscience; **avere la coscienza a posto/sporca** to have a good *o* clear/bad *o* guilty conscience; **in (tutta) coscienza** in all conscience *o* honesty 2 (*sensi*) consciousness; **perdere/riacquistare coscienza** to lose/regain consciousness 3 (*psicologica*) awareness; **avere coscienza di/che...** to be aware *o* conscious of/that ...; **prendere coscienza di qc** to become aware of sth, realize sth; **coscienza politica** political awareness 4 (*serietà*) conscientiousness; **coscienza professionale** conscientiousness; **persona di coscienza** honest *o* conscientious person

coscienzioso, -a [koʃʃenˈtsjoso] AGG conscientious

cosciotto [koʃˈʃɔtto] SM (*Culin*) leg

coscritto [kosˈkritto] SM (*Mil*) conscript

coscrizione [koskritˈtsjone] SF (*Mil*) conscription

così [koˈsi] AVV 1 (*in tal modo*) so; (*in questo modo*) (in) this way, like this, like that; **devi ripiegarlo così** you have to fold it like this; **se lo tiri così lo rompi** if you pull it like that you'll break it; **ho detto così** that's what I said; **ha detto così:"sei bugiardo"** this is what he said:"you're a liar"; **non ho detto così** I didn't say that; **se fosse così** if this were the case; **le cose stanno così** this is how things stand; **vorrei una scatola larga così e lunga così** (*accompagnato da gesti*) I'd like a box this *o* so wide and this *o* so long; **non scriverlo così, ma così!** don't write it like that, write it like this!; **e così feci anch'io** and I did likewise; **basta così!** that's enough! 2 (*talmente*) so; **fa così bello oggi** it's such a lovely day, the weather's so lovely today; **una persona così gentile** such a kind person; **è così simpatica!** she's so nice!; **è così lontano** it's so far away; **non sono così stupido!** I'm not that stupid!; **così... che...** so ... that ...; **era così stanco che è andato subito a letto** he was so tired that he went to bed immediately 3 **così... come** as ... as; **non è così onesto come credi** he's not as *o* so honest as you think; **se si comporta così come ha sempre fatto...** if he goes on behaving like this ...; **me lo dia così com'è** give it to me as it is 4 **per così dire** so to

speak, so to say; **e così via** and so on; **è così o non è così?** isn't that so?; **così così** so so; **com'era il concerto? — così così** what was the concert like? — so-so; **e così?** well? ♦ AGG INV (*tale*): **non ho mai visto un film così** I've never seen such a film; **non ho mai conosciuto una persona così** I've never met such a person, I've never met a person like that; **i tipi così mi danno ai nervi** people like that get on my nerves ♦ CONG (*perciò*) so, therefore; **pioveva, così sono rimasto a casa** it was raining so I stayed at home

cosicché [kosikˈke] CONG so (that)

cosiddetto, -a [kosidˈdetto] AGG so-called

cosmesi [kozˈmɛzi] SF INV (*scienza*) cosmetics sg; (*prodotti*) cosmetics pl; (*trattamento*) beauty treatment

cosmetico, -a, -ci, -che [kozˈmɛtiko] AGG, SM cosmetic

cosmico, -a, -ci, -che [ˈkɔzmiko] AGG cosmic

cosmo [ˈkɔzmo] SM (*universo*) cosmos; (*spazio*) outer space

cosmonauta, -i, -e [kozmoˈnauta] SM, SF cosmonaut

cosmopolita, -i, -e [kozmopoˈlita] AGG, SM, SF (*anche fig*) cosmopolitan

coso [ˈkɔso] SM (*fam: oggetto*) thing, thingummy (*Brit*), thingumajig (*USA*); (: *aggeggio*) contraption; (: *persona*) what's his name, thingummy

cospargere [kosˈpardʒere] /111/ VT IRREG: **cospargere di** to sprinkle with

cosparso, -a [kosˈparzo] PP di **cospargere**

cospetto [kosˈpetto] SM (*presenza*): **in** *o* **al cospetto di** in the presence of, in front of; **giurare al cospetto di Dio** to swear before God

cospicuità [kospikuiˈta] SF vast quantity; **la cospicuità delle sue risorse** his considerable resources

cospicuo, -a [kosˈpikuo] AGG considerable, large

cospirare [kospiˈrare] /72/ VI (*aus avere*) (*gen*) to conspire, plot; (*fig: circostanze*) to conspire

cospiratore, -trice [kospiraˈtore] SM, SF plotter, conspirator; **con fare da cospiratore** with a conspiratorial air

cospirazione [kospiratˈtsjone] SF (*anche fig*) plot, conspiracy

cossi ecc [ˈkɔssi] VB *vedi* **cuocere**

Cost. ABBR = **costituzione**

costa [ˈkɔsta] SF 1 (*litorale*) coast; (*spiaggia*) shore; (*tra terra e mare*) coastline; **una città sulla costa** a town on the coast; **navigare sotto costa** to hug the coast; **la Costa d'Avorio** the Ivory Coast; **la Costa Azzurra** the French Riviera 2 (*di montagna*) slope; **a mezza costa** halfway up (*o* down) the slope 3 (*nervatura: di nave, Bot*) rib; (: *di tessuto*) ribbing *no pl*; (*dorso: di libro*) spine; **punto a coste** (*Maglia*) rib (stitch); **velluto a coste** corduroy

costà [kosˈta] AVV (*letter*) there

costante [kosˈtante] AGG (*gen, anche Mat*) constant; (*persona*) steadfast ♦ SF (*Mat*) constant; **è una costante della letteratura del '900** it is a standard feature of 20th century literature

costanza [kosˈtantsa] SF (*gen*) constancy; (*fig: fermezza*) constancy, steadfastness; **il Lago di Costanza** Lake Constance

costare [kosˈtare] /72/ VI (*aus essere*) (*anche fig*) to cost; **quanto costa quell'anello?** how much does that ring cost?; **quanto t'è costato?** how much did it cost you?; **è costato trenta euro** it cost thirty euros; **costare caro** to be expensive, cost a lot; **mangiare fuori tutte le sere costa caro** eating out every evening is expensive; **costare poco** to be cheap; **cosa vuoi che ti costi** I am not asking much of you; **costare un occhio della testa** to cost a fortune; **costi quel che costi** no matter what; **gli è costato la vita** it cost him his life

Costa Rica [ˈkɔsta ˈrika] SF Costa Rica

costata [kosˈtata] SF (*Culin: di manzo*) large chop

costato [kosˈtato] SM (*Anat*) ribs pl

costeggiare [kostedˈdʒare] /62/ VT (*Naut*) to hug, skirt; (*sogg: persona*) to walk (*o* drive *ecc*) alongside; (: *strada*) to run alongside

costei [kosˈtei] PRON DIMOSTR (*sogg*) she; (*complemento*) her; (*pegg*) this woman

costellazione [kostellatˈtsjone] SF constellation

costernare [kosterˈnare] /72/ VT to dismay, fill with consternation

costernato, -a [kosterˈnato] AGG dismayed

costernazione [kosternat'tsjone] SF dismay, consternation

costiero, -a [kos'tjɛro] AGG coastal, coast *attr*; **nave costiera** coaster

costipato, -a [kosti'pato] AGG (*stitico*) constipated; (*raffreddato*): **essere costipato** to have a bad cold

costituire [kostitu'ire] /55/ VT 1 (*fondare: società, comitato, governo*) to set up, form; (*accumulare: patrimonio, raccolta*) to build up, put together; **hanno costituito un nuovo gruppo** they've formed a new group 2 (*formare: sogg: elementi, parti*) to constitute, make up 3 (*essere, rappresentare*) to be, constitute; **costituisce un vero problema!** it's a real problem!; **il fatto non costituisce reato** (*Dir*) this is not a crime 4 (*Dir: nominare*) to appoint; (*Dir*) to appoint sb chairman/one's heir; **costituirsi** VR 1 (*organizzarsi*): **costituirsi in società** to form a company; **costituirsi in regione autonoma** to become an independent region 2 (*ricercato*): **costituirsi (alla polizia)** to give o.s. up (to the police) 3 (*Dir*): **costituirsi parte civile** *to associate in an action with the public prosecutor for damages*

costitutivo, -a [kostitu'tivo] AGG constituent, component; **atto costitutivo** (*Dir: di società*) memorandum of association

costituzionale [kostituttsjo'nale] AGG constitutional

costituzione [kostitut'tsjone] SF 1 (*formazione*) setting-up, establishment; (*struttura*) composition, make-up; (*Med*) constitution; **certificato di sana e robusta costituzione** certificate of good health 2 (*Dir*) constitution

costo ['kɔsto] SM (*anche fig*) cost; **il costo della vacanza** the cost of the holiday; **determinazione dei costi** costing; **sotto costo** for less than cost price; **a ogni o qualunque costo, a tutti i costi** at all costs; **dev'essere evitato a tutti i costi** it must be avoided at all costs; **l'ha voluto portare a tutti i costi** he was determined to bring it, no matter what; **non vuol cedere a nessun costo** there's no way he'll give in, he won't give in no matter what ♦ **costi di esercizio** running costs; **costi fissi** fixed costs; **costi di gestione** operating costs; **costi d'impianto** set-up costs; **costi indiretti** indirect costs; **costi di produzione** production costs; **costo, assicurazione e nolo** cost, insurance and freight; **costo del denaro** cost of money; **costo del lavoro** cost of labour; **costo e nolo** cost and freight; **costo della vita** cost of living

costola ['kɔstola] SF (*Anat, Bot, Archit*) rib; **mi sono rotto una costola** I broke a rib; **è magrissimo, gli si contano le costole** he's so thin you can see his ribs; **ha la polizia alle costole** the police are hard on his heels

costoletta [kosto'letta] SF (*Culin*) cutlet

costoro [kos'toro] PRON DIMOSTR PL (*sogg*) they; (*complemento*) them; (*pegg*) these people

costoso, -a [kos'toso] AGG costly, expensive; **un albergo costoso** an expensive hotel

costretto, -a [kos'tretto] PP *di* **costringere**

costringere [kos'trindʒere] /117/ VT IRREG: **costringere qn (a fare qc)** to force o compel sb (to do sth); **mi ci hanno costretto con la forza** they forced me to do it; **mi ha costretto a dire la verità** she made me tell the truth; **la paralisi lo costringe a una sedia a rotelle** the paralysis confines him to a wheelchair; **è stato costretto a ritirarsi dalla gara** he had to withdraw from the competition; **vedersi costretto a fare qc** to find o.s. forced o compelled to do sth

costrittivo, -a [kostrit'tivo] AGG coercive

costrizione [kostrit'tsjone] SF 1 (*obbligo*) compulsion; **è legato da costrizione morale** he is morally obliged 2 (*violenza*) coercion, duress

costruire [kostru'ire] /55/ VT IRREG (*gen*) to build, construct; (*fig: teoria, frasi, fortuna*) to construct, build up; **qui costruiranno il nuovo stadio** they're going to build the new stadium here; **in questa città non si costruisce più da anni** there's been no building work done in this town for years; **questo verbo si costruisce con il congiuntivo** this verb takes the subjunctive; **costruire sulla sabbia** (*fig*) to build on sand

❏ **costruire** non si traduce mai con *construe*

costruttivo, -a [kostrut'tivo] AGG (*Edil*) building *attr*; (*fig*) constructive; **schema costruttivo** (*Tecn*) design, plan; **tecnica costruttiva** (*Edil*) building techniques *pl*; (*Ingegneria*) assembly techniques *pl*

costruzione [kostrut'tsjone] SF 1 (*fabbricazione*) building, construction; (*struttura, anche Tecn, Gramm*) construction; **la costruzione del ponte è durata sette anni** it took seven years to build the bridge; **di recente costruzione** recently built; **in (via di) costruzione** under construction; **essere in costruzione** to be under construction; **l'autostrada è in costruzione** the motorway is under construction; **materiali/legno da costruzione** building materials/timber; **scienza delle costruzioni** construction theory; **le costruzioni** (*gioco*) building blocks 2 (*edificio*) building; **una costruzione in vetro e acciaio** a building made of glass and steel

costui [kos'tui] PRON DIMOSTR (*sogg*) he; (*complemento*) him; (*pegg*) this fellow, this man; **si può sapere chi è costui?** (*pegg*) just who is that fellow?

costume [kos'tume] SM 1 (*gen*) custom; (*abitudine*) habit; **usi e costumi di una popolazione** habits and customs of a people; **di facili costumi** of loose morals, of easy virtue; **il buon costume** public morality 2 (*indumento*) costume; **costume nazionale** national costume *o* dress; **costume da bagno** (*da donna*) bathing *o* swimming costume (*Brit*), swimsuit; (*da uomo*) bathing *o* swimming trunks *pl*

costumista, -i, -e [kostu'mista] SM, SF (*Cine, Teatro, TV*) costume maker, costume designer

cotenna [ko'tenna] SF bacon rind

cotogna [ko'toɲɲa] SF (*anche*: **mela cotogna**) quince

cotoletta [koto'letta] SF (*di maiale, montone*) chop; (*di vitello, agnello*) cutlet

cotonare [koto'nare] /72/ VT (*capelli*) to backcomb

cotone [ko'tone] SM 1 (*gen*) cotton; **di cotone** cotton *attr*; **una maglietta di cotone** a cotton T-shirt; **cotone mercerizzato** mercerised cotton; **cotone pettinato** brushed cotton; **cotone da rammendo** darning thread 2 (*anche*: **cotone idrofilo**) cotton wool (*Brit*), cotton (*USA*); **batuffolo di cotone** wad of cotton wool (*Brit*) *o* cotton (*USA*)

cotonificio, -ci [kotoni'fitʃo] SM cotton mill

cotta¹ ['kɔtta] SF (*fam*): **prendersi una cotta (per qn)** to get a crush (on sb)

cotta² ['kɔtta] SF 1 (*Rel*) surplice 2 (*Storia*): **cotta d'arme** surcoat; **cotta di maglia** chain mail

cottimo ['kɔttimo] SM (*anche*: **lavoro a cottimo**) piecework; **lavorare a cottimo** to do piecework

cotto, -a ['kɔtto] PP *di* **cuocere** ♦ AGG (*Culin*) cooked; **cotta o cruda?** cooked or raw?; **sono cotti gli spaghetti?** is the spaghetti done?; **mele cotte** stewed apples; **ben cotto** well cooked; (*carne*) well done; **poco cotto** underdone; **troppo cotto** overdone; **cotto a puntino** cooked to perfection; **essere cotto (di qn)** (*fig: fam*) to have a crush (on sb); **è proprio cotto!** he's smitten!, he's head-over-heels in love; **essere cotto (di sonno/stanchezza)** (*fam*) to be dead tired; **dirne di cotte e di crude a qn** to call sb every name under the sun; **farne di cotte e di crude** to get up to all kinds of mischief ♦ SM brickwork; **mattone di cotto** fired brick; **pavimento in cotto** tile floor

cottura [kot'tura] SF (*Culin: gen*) cooking; (*in forno*) baking; (*di arrosto*) roasting; (*in umido*) stewing; **cottura a fuoco lento** simmering

covare [ko'vare] /72/ VI (*aus* avere) (*fuoco, anche fig: odio, rancore*) to smoulder (*Brit*), smolder (*USA*); **qui gatta ci cova** there's something fishy about this ♦ VT 1 (*sogg: uccello: uova*) to sit on; (*uso assoluto*) to sit on its eggs 2 (*fig: malattia*) to be sickening for; (: *odio, rancore*) to nurse; **covare un raffreddore** he is sickening for a cold; **covare odio verso qn** to nurse hatred for sb

covata [ko'vata] SF (*anche fig*) brood

covo ['kɔvo] SM den, lair; **un covo di terroristi** a terrorist base

covone [ko'vone] SM sheaf

cozza ['kɔttsa] SF mussel; **spaghetti con le cozze** spaghetti with mussels

cozzare [kot'tsare] /72/ VI (*aus* avere) (*animali: con le corna*) to butt; (*veicoli*) to collide; (*fig: caratteri, idee*) to clash; **cozzare contro o contro a** to collide with; **cozzare contro un muro** to crash into a wall ♦ VT (*fig*): **cozzare il capo contro il muro** to bang one's head against a brick wall

cozzo ['kɔttso] SM (*di corna*) butt; (*di veicoli*) crash, collision; (*fig: di idee*) clash

C.P. ABBR **1** (= *cartolina postale*) pc **2** (= *casella postale*) P.O. box **3** (*Naut*) = capitaneria (di porto) **4** (*Dir*) = **codice penale**

craccare [krak'kare] /20/ VT (*Inform*) to crack

crack [krak] SM INV (*droga*) crack

Cracovia [kra'kɔvja] SF Cracow

crampo ['krampo] SM cramp; **avere un crampo alla gamba** to have a cramp in one's leg; **ho un crampo alla gamba** I've got a cramp in my leg; **avere i crampi allo stomaco** to have stomach cramps; **ho i crampi allo stomaco dalla fame** I've got hunger pangs

cranio, -ni ['kranjo] SM **1** skull; (*Anat*) cranium; **avere il cranio duro** (*fig*) to be pig-headed; **fa trenta euro a cranio** (*fam*) it's thirty euro a head **2** (*genio*): **essere un cranio (in qc)** to be a genius (at sth)

cratere [kra'tɛre] SM crater

cravatta [kra'vatta] SF tie; **fare il nodo alla cravatta** to tie one's tie; **cravatta a farfalla** bow tie

cravattino [kravat'tino] SM bow tie

creanza [kre'antsa] SF (good) manners *pl*; **per buona creanza** out of politeness

creare [kre'are] /72/ VT (*gen*) to create; (*eleggere*) to make, appoint; (*fondare*) to set up; **creare un precedente** to create a precedent; **creare un problema a qn** to create a problem for sb; **mi ha creato un sacco di problemi** it's caused me a lot of problems; **crearsi una clientela** to build up a clientele; **ha creato un personaggio molto divertente** he created a very funny character; **la notizia ha creato il panico** the news caused panic

creatività [kreati'vita] SF INV creativity

creato [kre'ato] SM: **il creato** the Creation

creatore, -trice [krea'tore] AGG creative ♦ SM, SF creator; (*fondatore*) founder; **un creatore di alta moda** fashion designer; **il Creatore** (*Dio*) the Creator; **andare al Creatore** to go to meet one's maker

creatura [krea'tura] SF creature; (*bimbo*) baby, infant; **povera creatura!** poor thing!; **le mie creature** my babies

creazione [kreat'tsjone] SF (*gen*) creation; (*fondazione*) foundation, establishment

crebbi ecc VB vedi **crescere**

credente [kre'dɛnte] SM, SF (*Rel*) believer

credenza¹ [kre'dɛntsa] SF (*fede, opinione*) belief

credenza² [kre'dɛntsa] SF (*armadio*) sideboard

credenziale [kreden'tsjale] AGG: **lettere credenziali** credentials ♦ **credenziali** SFPL (*anche fig*) credentials

credere ['kredere] /29/ VT **1** to believe; **lo** o **ci credo** I believe it; **come puoi credere una cosa simile?** how can you believe such a thing?; **lo credo bene!** I should think so too! **2** (*pensare*) to believe, think; **ti credevo meno ingenuo** I didn't think you were so naive; **lo credo onesto** I believe him to be honest; **ti credevo morto** I thought you were dead; **credo che sia stato lui** (*a farlo*) I think it was him, I think he did it; **credo che arrivi domani** I think he's arriving tomorrow; **credeva di aver perso le chiavi** she thought she had lost her keys; **credo di sì/no** I think/don't think so; **voleva farmi credere che...** he wanted me to think that ...; **voleva darmi a credere che non la conosceva** he tried to convince me that he didn't know her **3** (*ritenere opportuno*): **fai quello che credi** o **come credi** do as you please; **ha creduto bene di mollare tutto** he thought it best to let everything go ♦ VI (*aus avere*) to believe; **credere a qn/qc** to believe sb/sth; **non ti credo** I don't believe you; **non dirmi che credi ai fantasmi!** don't tell me you believe in ghosts!; **come puoi credere a una cosa simile?** how can you believe such a thing?; **non posso crederci!** I can't believe it!; **credere in qn/qc** to believe in sb/sth; **credere in Dio** to believe in God; **ti credo sulla parola** I'll take your word for it; **gli credo poco** I have little faith in him; **non credeva ai suoi occhi/alle sue orecchie** he could not believe his eyes/ears; **credevo a uno scherzo** I thought it was a joke; **si è creduto ad una truffa** it looked like a swindle; **credersi** VR: **si crede furbo** he thinks he's smart; **chi ti credi di essere!** who do you think you are!

credibile [kre'dibile] AGG credible, believable

credibilità [kredibili'ta] SF credibility

creditizio, -zia, -zi, -zie [kredi'tittsjo] AGG credit *attr*

credito ['kredito] SM **1** (*Fin*) credit; **comprare/vendere a credito** to buy/sell on credit o easy terms; **"non si fa credito"** "no credit", "cash terms only"; **essere in credito** to be owed money; (*Banca*) to be in credit; **credito agevolato** easy credit terms; **credito formativo** (*Scol*) *a system that gives students credit for extra work done*; *vedi anche* **debito²** formativo; **credito d'imposta** tax credit **2** (*credibilità*) credit; **acquistare credito** (*teoria, partito*) to gain acceptance; **dare credito a qc** to give credit to sth; **non puoi dar credito alla sua parola** you can't trust him; **trovare credito presso qn** to win sb's trust

creditore, -trice [kredi'tore] AGG, SM, SF creditor

credo ['krɛdo] SM INV (*Rel, anche fig*) creed; **credo politico** political credo

credulo, -a [kre'dulo] AGG credulous

credulone, -a [kredu'lone] SM, SF gullible person

crema ['krɛma] SF (*Culin*) cream; (*con uova, zucchero ecc*) custard; (*cosmetico, fig*) cream; **un gelato alla crema** a vanilla ice; **una pasta con la crema** a cake with a custard filling ♦ **crema da barba** shaving cream; **crema di bellezza** beauty cream; **crema di cacao** (*liquore*) crème de cacao; **crema al cioccolato** chocolate custard; **crema idratante** moisturizing cream; **crema pasticciera** confectioner's custard; **crema di riso** rice custard; **crema solare** sun cream

cremare [kre'mare] /72/ VT to cremate

crematorio, -ria, -ri, -rie [krema'tɔrjo] AGG crematory ♦ SM crematorium

cremazione [kremat'tsjone] SF cremation

cremisi ['kremizi] AGG INV, SM INV crimson

Cremlino [krem'lino] SM: **il Cremlino** the Kremlin

cremonese [kremo'nese] AGG of o from Cremona ♦ SM, SF inhabitant o native of Cremona

cremoso, -a [kre'moso] AGG creamy

crepa ['krɛpa] SF crack

crepaccio, -ci [kre'pattʃo] SM (*nella roccia*) large crack, fissure; (*nel ghiaccio*) crevasse

crepacuore [krepa'kwɔre] SM: **morire di crepacuore** to die of a broken heart

crepapelle [krepa'pɛlle] AVV: **ridere a crepapelle** to split one's sides laughing; **mangiare a crepapelle** to eat till one bursts

crepare [kre'pare] /72/ VI (*aus essere*) (*fam: morire*) to kick the bucket, snuff it (*Brit*); **crepare dal ridere** o **dalle risa** to kill o.s. laughing, split one's sides laughing; **crepare dall'invidia** to be green with envy; **creparsi** VIP (*spaccarsi*) to crack

crêpe [krɛp] SF INV (*Culin*) pancake; **una crêpe al cioccolato** a chocolate pancake

crepitare [krepi'tare] /72/ VI (*aus avere*) (*fuoco*) to crackle; (*pioggia*) to patter; (*foglie*) to rustle

crepitio, -tii [krepi'tio] SM (*vedi vb*) crackling; pattering; rustling

crepuscolo [kre'puskolo] SM (*anche fig*) twilight, dusk; **al crepuscolo** at twilight

crescendo [kreʃ'ʃɛndo] SM (*Mus, anche fig*) crescendo; **suonare in crescendo** to play a crescendo; **la sua carriera è stata un crescendo di successi** his career has gone from strength to strength

crescente [kreʃ'ʃɛnte] AGG (*gen*) growing, increasing; (*luna*) waxing; **luna crescente** waxing moon

crescere ['kreʃʃere] VB IRREG /30/ VI (*aus essere*) **1** (*gen*) to grow; (*persona: diventare adulto*) to grow up; (: *diventare più alto*) to grow tall; **il bambino/l'albero è cresciuto** the child/tree has grown; **com'è cresciuto tuo fratello!** how your brother has grown!; **i suoi capelli non crescono molto** her hair doesn't grow very fast; **sono cresciuto in Sardegna** I grew up in Sardinia; **farsi crescere la barba/i capelli** to grow a beard/one's hair; **si sta facendo crescere i capelli** she's growing her hair **2** (*aumentare: rumore, prezzo, numero*) to increase; (: *città, quartiere*) to expand; (: *luna*) to wax; **la popolazione mondiale cresce velocemente** the world's population is increasing rapidly; **i prezzi crescono ogni giorno** prices are going up daily; **la città è cresciuta a vista d'occhio** the city has grown before our very eyes ♦ VT (*fam coltivare*) to grow; (: *allevare: figli*) to bring up

crescione [kreʃ'ʃone] SM watercress; **crescione inglese** o **degli orti** garden cress

crescita ['kreʃʃita] SF: **crescita (di)** growth (in); **crescita zero** zero growth

cresciuto,-a [kreʃ'ʃuto] PP *di* crescere

cresima ['krɛzima] SF (*Rel*) confirmation; **fare la cresima** to be confirmed

cresimare [krezi'mare](*Rel*) /72/ VT to confirm; **cresimarsi** VIP to be confirmed

crespo,-a ['krɛspo] AGG (*capelli*) frizzy; (*tessuto*) puckered; **ha i capelli crespi** she's got frizzy hair ♦ SM (*tessuto*) crêpe

cresta ['krɛsta] SF (*gen*) crest; (*di uccello*) crest; (*di pollo*) comb; (*di montagna*) ridge; **alzare la cresta** (*fig*) to become cocky; **abbassare la cresta** (*fig*) to climb down; **far abbassare la cresta a qn** to take sb down a peg or two; **far la cresta sulla spesa** to keep some of the shopping money for o.s.; **essere sulla cresta dell'onda** to be riding high; **cresta di gallo** (*Bot*) cockscomb; (*Med: fam*) condyloma

Creta ['krɛta] SF Crete

creta ['krɛta] SF (*argilla*) clay

cretese [kre'tese] AGG, SM, SF Cretan

cretinata [kreti'nata] SF (*fam*): **dire/fare una cretinata** to say/do something stupid; **non dire cretinate!** don't talk rubbish!

cretino,-a [kre'tino] AGG (*Med*) cretinous; (*pegg*) cretinous, moronic; **ma come sei cretina!** you're so stupid! ♦ SM, SF (*vedi agg*) cretin; cretin, moron; **quel cretino mi ha quasi investito** that idiot nearly ran me over

CRI [kri] SIGLA F = **Croce Rossa Italiana**

cric [krik] SM INV (*martinetto*) jack

cricca,-che ['krikka] SF clique

criceto [kri'tʃeto] SM hamster

criminale [krimi'nale] AGG criminal ♦ SM, SF criminal; **criminale di guerra** war criminal

criminalità [kriminali'ta] SF 1 criminal nature 2 (*delinquenza*) crime; **la criminalità organizzata** organized crime

Criminalpol [kriminal'pɔl] SIGLA F = **polizia criminale**

crimine ['krimine] SM (*anche fig*) crime; **crimini di guerra** war crimes

criminologia [kriminolo'dʒia] SF criminology

criminoso,-a [krimi'noso] AGG criminal

crinale [kri'nale] SM ridge, crest

crine ['krine] SM horsehair; **di crine** horsehair *attr*; **crine vegetale** vegetable fibre

criniera [kri'njera] SF (*di animale*) mane

cripta ['kripta] SF crypt

criptare [krip'tare] /72/ VT (*TV*) to encrypt

criptato,-a [krip'tato] AGG (*programma, messaggio*) encrypted

crisantemo [krizan'temo] SM chrysanthemum

crisi ['krizi] SF INV 1 (*gen, anche Pol, Econ*) crisis; **il paese sta uscendo dalla crisi (economica)** the country is emerging from the (economic) crisis; **essere in crisi** (*partito, impresa*) to be in a state of crisis; (*persona*) to be upset; **in questo periodo sono in crisi** I've got a lot of problems at the moment; **mettere qn in crisi** to put sb in a difficult position; **la crisi degli alloggi** the housing crisis; **crisi energetica** energy crisis 2 (*Med*) attack; (*di epilessia*) fit; **crisi da astinenza** withdrawal symptoms *pl*; **crisi di nervi** fit of hysterics, attack of nerves; **crisi di pianto** fit of tears

cristalleria [kristalle'ria] SF (*fabbrica*) crystal glassworks *sg*; (*oggetti*) crystalware

cristallino,-a [kristal'lino] AGG (*Mineralogia*) crystalline; (*fig: suono, acque*) crystal clear ♦ SM (*Anat*) crystalline lens

cristallizzare [kristalliddzare] /72/ VI (*aus* essere), **cristallizzarsi** VIP to crystallize; (*fig*) to become fossilized ♦ VT (*gen*) to crystallize, turn into crystals; **zucchero cristallizzato** granulated sugar

cristallo [kris'tallo] SM crystal; (*di finestra*) pane (of glass); **un bicchiere di cristallo** a crystal glass; **a cristalli liquidi** (*schermo, display*) liquid crystal; **cristallo liquido** liquid crystal; **cristallo di rocca** rock crystal

cristianesimo [kristja'nezimo] SM Christianity

cristianità [kristjani'ta] SF (*condizione*) Christianity; (*popoli, territorio*) Christendom

cristiano,-a [kris'tjano] AGG Christian ♦ SM, SF (*anche fig*) Christian; **un povero cristiano** (*fig*) a poor soul *o* beggar;

non c'era un cristiano per le strade there wasn't a soul in the streets; **comportarsi da cristiano** (*fig*) to behave in a civilized manner

cristo ['kristo] SM 1 Cristo Christ; **nell'anno 54 avanti/dopo Cristo** in 54 B.C./A.D; (*un*) **povero cristo** (a) poor beggar 2 (*immagine, oggetto*) figure of Christ

criterio,-ri [kri'terjo] SM 1 (*norma*) criterion, rule; **con criterio approssimativo** approximately 2 (*buon senso*) (common) sense; **dovresti avere più criterio** you should have more sense; **è una persona di poco criterio** he doesn't have much common sense

critica ['kritika] SF 1 (*biasimo*) criticism; **una critica costruttiva** constructive criticism 2 **la critica** (*attività*) criticism; (*i critici*) critics *pl*; (*opera, studio*) appreciation, critique; (*recensione*) review; **fare la critica di** (*libro, film*) to review; **una critica sul film** a review of the film

criticare [kriti'kare] /20/ VT (*biasimare*) to criticize, find fault with; (*giudicare: opera*) to give a critique of

critico,-a,-ci,-che ['kritiko] AGG critical; **aver spirito critico** to have a critical mind; **al momento critico** at the critical moment; **età critica** (*gen*) difficult age; (*menopausa*) change of life ♦ SM (*gen*) critic; (*recensore*) reviewer; **critico cinematografico** film critic; **critico letterario** literary critic

criticone,-a [kriti'kone] SM, SF faultfinder; **sei il solito criticone!** you're always finding fault!

crivellare [krivel'lare] /72/ VT: **crivellare (di)** to riddle (with)

crivello [kri'vello] SM riddle

croato,-a [kro'ato] AGG, SM, SF Croatian, Croat

Croazia [kro'attsja] SF: **la Croazia** Croatia; **ti è piaciuta la Croazia?** did you like Croatia?; **andrò in Croazia quest'estate** I'm going to Croatia this summer

croccante [krok'kante] AGG crisp, crunchy; **un biscotto croccante** a crispy biscuit; **un panino croccante** a crusty roll ♦ SM (*Culin*) almond crunch

crocchia ['krɔkkja] SF chignon, bun

crocchio,-chi ['krɔkkjo] SM (*di persone*) small group, cluster

croce ['krotʃe] SF (*gen*) cross; **farsi il segno della croce** to make the sign of the cross, cross o.s.; **Cristo in croce** *o* **sulla croce** Christ on the cross; **in croce** (*di traverso*) crosswise; (*fig*) on tenterhooks; **mettere in croce** (*anche fig: criticare*) to crucify; (*tormentare*) to nag to death; **facciamoci una croce sopra** let's forget about it; **quella malattia è la sua croce** that illness is her cross in life; **ognuno ha la sua croce da portare** we each have our cross to bear; **punto croce** (*Maglia*) cross stitch; **croce greca** Greek cross; **croce latina** Latin cross; **Croce di Malta** Maltese cross; **croce uncinata** swastika; **la Croce Rossa** the Red Cross; **chiama la Croce Rossa!** (*uso improprio*) call an ambulance!

crocefiggere ecc = **crocifiggere**

crocerossina [krotʃeros'sina] SF Red Cross nurse

crocevia [krotʃe'via] SM INV crossroads *sg*

crociato,-a [kro'tʃato] AGG cross-shaped; **parole crociate** crossword puzzle *sg* ♦ SM (*anche fig*) crusader

crocicchio,-chi [kro'tʃikkjo] SM crossroads *sg*

crociera [kro'tʃera] SF 1 (*viaggio*) cruise; **velocità di crociera** (*Aut, Aer, Naut*) cruising speed; **altezza di crociera** (*Aer*) cruising height; **andare in crociera, fare una crociera** to go on a cruise; **sono andati in crociera nel Mediterraneo** they went on a Mediterranean cruise 2 (*Archit*) transept; **volta a crociera** cross vault

crocifiggere [krotʃi'fiddʒere] /104/ VT IRREG (*anche fig*) to crucify

crocifissione [krotʃifis'sjone] SF (*anche fig*) crucifixion

crocifisso,-a [krotʃi'fisso] PP *di* crocifiggere ♦ SM crucifix

crogiolarsi [krodʒo'larsi] /72/ VIP 1 (*scaldarsi*): **crogiolarsi al sole** to bask in the sun 2 (*bearsi*): **crogiolarsi nelle illusioni** to harbour (*Brit*) *o* harbor (*USA*) illusions

crogiolo [kro'dʒɔlo], **crogiuolo** [kro'dʒwɔlo] SM (*Chim, Metallurgia*) crucible; (*Vetreria*) pot; (*fig: di popoli*) melting pot

crollare [krol'lare] /72/ VI (*aus* essere) (*gen, anche fig*) to collapse; (*tetto*) to cave in; (*prezzi, titoli*) to slump; **il ponte è crollato** the bridge collapsed; **si lasciò crollare sul letto** he collapsed onto the bed; **dopo 2 giorni di interrogatorio è crollato** he broke down after 2 days of interrogation

crollo [ˈkrɔllo] SM (*anche fig*) collapse; (*Fin*) slump, sudden fall; **avere un crollo** (*fisico*) to collapse; (*psichico*) to have a breakdown; **crollo in Borsa** slump in prices on the Stock Exchange; **il crollo del '29** the Wall Street Crash

croma [ˈkrɔma] SF (*Mus*) quaver (*Brit*), eighth note (*USA*)

cromato, -a [kroˈmato] AGG chromium-plated

cromo [ˈkrɔmo] SM (*Chim*) chromium ♦ AGG INV: **giallo cromo** chrome yellow

cromosoma, -i [kromoˈsɔma] SM chromosome

cronaca, -che [ˈkrɔnaka] SF 1 (*Storia*) chronicle 2 (*di giornale*) news *sg*; (*resoconto: sportivo*) commentary; (: *di viaggio*) coverage; **fatto** *o* **episodio di cronaca** news item; **cronaca mondana** *o* **rosa** gossip column; **cronaca nera** crime news *sg*; (*rubrica*) crime column

cronico, -a, -ci, -che [ˈkrɔniko] AGG (*anche fig*) chronic ♦ SM (*Med*) chronic invalid

cronista, -i, -e [kroˈnista] SM, SF (*Stampa*) columnist; (*Radio, TV*) commentator; (*storico*) chronicler

cronistoria [kronisˈtɔrja] SF chronicle; (*fig*) blow-by-blow account

cronografo [kroˈnografo] SM chronograph

cronologia [kronoloˈdʒia] SF chronology; "**Cronologia**" (*Inform*) "History"

cronometrare [kronomeˈtrare] /72/ VT to time

cronometro [kroˈnɔmetro] SM chronometer; (*a scatto*) stopwatch

crosta [ˈkrɔsta] SF (*di formaggio, pane*) crust; (*Med*) scab; (*Zool*) shell; (*di ghiaccio*) layer; (*fig: pegg: quadro*) daub; **crosta lattea** (*Anat*) cradle cap; **crosta terrestre** the earth's crust

crostaceo [krosˈtatʃeo] SM (*Zool*) shellfish *no pl*

crostata [krosˈtata] SF (*Culin*) tart; **una crostata di albicocche** an apricot tart

crostino [krosˈtino] SM (*da brodo*) croûton; (*da antipasto*) canapé

crucciare [krutˈtʃare] /14/ VT to torment, worry; **crucciarsi** VIP: **crucciarsi per** to torment o.s. over

cruccio, -ci [ˈkruttʃo] SM torment, worry

cruciale [kruˈtʃale] AGG crucial

cruciverba [krutʃiˈverba] SM INV crossword (puzzle)

crudele [kruˈdele] AGG (*anche fig*) cruel; **non essere così crudele!** don't be so cruel!

crudeltà [krudelˈta] SF INV (*anche fig*) cruelty

crudo, -a [ˈkrudo] AGG 1 (*Culin, Tecn*) raw; **mangia carne cruda** he eats raw meat; **la bistecca è un po' cruda** the steak is underdone 2 (*fig: descrizione, linguaggio*) blunt; **cruda realtà** harsh reality
❑ **crudo** non si traduce mai con *crude*

cruento, -a [kruˈento] AGG bloody

crumiro, -a [kruˈmiro] SM, SF (*pegg*) scab, blackleg (*Brit*)

cruna [ˈkruna] SF eye (of a needle)

crusca [ˈkruska] SF bran

cruscotto [krusˈkɔtto] SM (*Aut*) dashboard

CS SIGLA 1 = Cosenza ♦ ABBR 1 (*Mil*: = comando supremo) 2 (*Aut*: = codice della strada)

CSM, Csm [tʃiˈɛsseˈɛmme] SIGLA M (= Consiglio Superiore della Magistratura) magistrates' internal board of supervisors

CT SIGLA = Catania ♦ ABBR = commissario tecnico

Cuba [ˈkuba] SF Cuba

cubano, -a [kuˈbano] AGG, SM, SF Cuban

cubetto [kuˈbetto] SM (small) cube; **cubetto di ghiaccio** ice cube

cubico, -a, -ci, -che [ˈkubiko] AGG (*gen*) cubic; **radice cubica** cube root

cubista, -i, -e [kuˈbista] AGG (*pittore, quadro etc*) Cubist ♦ SM, SF (*in discoteca*) platform dancer, *dancer who performs on raised platform in a club*

cubo [ˈkubo] AGG cubic ♦ SM 1 (*gen*) cube; **elevare al cubo** (*Mat*) to cube 2 (*in discoteca*) platform

cuccagna [kukˈkaɲa] SF abundance, plenty; **paese della cuccagna** land of plenty; **è finita la cuccagna!** the party's over!; **albero della cuccagna** greasy pole (*fig*)

cuccetta [kutˈtʃetta] SF (*di treno*) couchette; (*di nave*) berth

cucchiaiata [kukkjaˈjata] SF spoonful, tablespoonful

cucchiaino [kukkjaˈino] SM coffee spoon, ≈ teaspoon;

(*contenuto*) ≈ teaspoonful; (*Pesca*) spinner; **due cucchiaini di zucchero** two teaspoons of sugar

cucchiaio, -ai [kukˈkjajo] SM (*gen*) spoon; (*da tavola*) tablespoon; (*cucchiaiata*) spoonful; tablespoonful; **forchetta, coltello e cucchiaio** fork, knife and spoon; **aggiungere un cucchiaio di farina** add a spoonful of flour; **ha mangiato qualche cucchiaio di minestra** she ate a few spoonfuls of soup; **cucchiaio da portata** serving spoon

cuccia, -ce [ˈkuttʃa] SF (*di cane: letto*) dog's basket; (: *canile*) kennel; **a cuccia!, fai la cuccia!** down (boy)!

cucciolata [kuttʃoˈlata] SF litter; **era il più piccolo della cucciolata** it was the smallest of the litter

cucciolo [ˈkuttʃolo] SM (*gen*) cub; (*di cane*) pup, puppy; (*fig: persona*): **vieni qua, cucciolo!** come here, pet!

cucina [kuˈtʃina] SF (*locale*) kitchen; (*arte culinaria*) cooking, cookery; (*cibo*) cooking, food; (*elettrodomestico*) cooker; **una cucina spaziosa** a big kitchen; **mi piace la cucina greca** I like Greek cooking; **è molto bravo in cucina** he's very good at cooking; **da cucina** (*utensile*) kitchen *attr*; **di cucina** (*libro, lezione*) cookery *attr*; **cucina da campo** primus stove; **cucina componibile** fitted kitchen; **cucina economica** kitchen range; **cucina a gas** gas cooker (*Brit*), gas stove (*USA*)

cucinare [kutʃiˈnare] /72/ VT to cook; **oggi cucino io!** I'll cook today!; **chi ha cucinato?** who did the cooking?

cucinino [kutʃiˈnino] SM kitchenette

cucire [kuˈtʃire] /31/ VT (*gen*) to sew; (*vestito: Med: ferita*) to sew up; (*libro, cuoio*) to stitch; **non so cucire** I can't sew; **cucire a macchina** to machine-sew; **macchina da cucire** sewing machine; **cucire la bocca a qn** (*fig*) to shut sb up

cucito, -a [kuˈtʃito] AGG (*vedi vb*) sewn; stitched; **cucito a mano** hand-sewn; **stare cucito addosso a qn** (*fig: persona*) to cling to sb ♦ SM sewing

cucitrice [kutʃiˈtritʃe] SF (*per fogli*) stapler; (*Tip: per libri*) stitching machine

cucitura [kutʃiˈtura] SF (*di stoffa, cuoio, libro*) stitching; (*costura*) seam

cucù [kuˈku] PRON REL 1 (*Zool: anche: cuculo*) cuckoo 2 (*verso del cuculo*): **far cucù** to go boo; **cucù, eccomi qua!** peek-a-boo!; **orologio a cucù** cuckoo clock

cuffia [ˈkuffja] SF bonnet, cap; (*da infermiera*) cap; (*per ascoltare*) headphones *pl*, headset; (*Tecn*) casing; (*Bot*) root cap; **cuffia da bagno** (*da piscina*) bathing cap; (*da doccia*) shower cap

cugino, -a [kuˈdʒino] SM, SF cousin

cui [ˈkui] PRON REL 1 (*nei complementi indiretti: riferito a persona*) whom; (: *riferito a oggetto, animale*) which; **la persona (a) cui si riferiva** the person he referred to *o* to whom he referred; **le donne di cui ti ho parlato** the women I spoke to you about *o* about whom I spoke to you; **il libro di cui parlavo** the book I was talking about *o* about which I was talking; **il motivo per cui non insisto** the reason I'm not insisting; **il motivo per cui non sono venuto** the reason why I didn't come; **il quartiere in cui abito** the area *o* district where I live; **l'anno in cui prese la laurea** the year he took his degree, the year when *o* in which he took his degree; **il ponte su cui camminavamo** the bridge we were walking on 2 (*come genitivo possessivo: riferito a persona*) whose; (: *riferito a oggetto, animale*) of which, whose; **il signore la cui figlia ho incontrato ieri** the gentleman whose daughter I met yesterday; **la persona di cui le ho dato il numero di telefono ieri** the person whose telephone number I gave you yesterday; **un'attrice il cui nome mi sfugge** an actress whose name I can't remember 3 **per cui** (*perciò*) therefore, so; **io non c'ero, per cui non chiedere a me** I wasn't there, so don't ask me

culinaria [kuliˈnarja] SF cuisine, cookery

culinario, -ria, -ri, -rie [kuliˈnarjo] AGG culinary

culla [ˈkulla] SF (*anche fig*) cradle; **fin dalla culla** from the cradle, since I was (*o* you were *ecc*) a baby

cullare [kulˈlare] /72/ VT (*bambino*) to rock; (*fig: idea, speranza*) to cherish; **cullarsi** VIP (*persona*) to sway; **cullarsi in vane speranze** to cherish fond hopes; **cullarsi nel dolce far niente** to sit back and relax

culminante [kulmiˈnante] AGG: **posizione culminante** (*Astron*) highest point; **punto** *o* **momento culminante** (*fig*) climax

culminare [kulmi'nare] /72/ VI (aus essere) culminare (in) (Astron) to reach its highest point (at); culminare in o con (fig) to culminate in

culmine ['kulmine] SM (di torre, monte) summit, top; (fig): ero al culmine della felicità my happiness knew no bounds; essere al culmine del successo to be at the peak of one's success; era al culmine del successo he was at the peak of his success

culo ['kulo] SM (fam!) 1 (sedere) arse (Brit fam!), ass (USA: fam!); alza il culo! get off your arse!; prendere qn per il culo to take the piss out of sb (Brit fam!), to fool sb 2 (fortuna): aver culo to be lucky; che culo! lucky bastard! (fam!)

culto ['kulto] SM (religione) religion; (adorazione) worship, adoration; (venerazione, anche fig) cult; culto della personalità personality cult; culto degli eroi hero worship; avere il culto della propria persona to be vain about one's personal appearance

cultura [kul'tura] SF (gen) culture; (conoscenza) learning, knowledge, education; di cultura (persona) cultured; (istituto) cultural, of culture; la cultura occidentale western culture; avere una certa cultura to be educated; una persona di grande cultura a well-educated person; una persona di scarsa cultura a person without much education; cultura generale general knowledge; una domanda di cultura generale a general knowledge question; cultura di massa mass culture

culturale [kultu'rale] AGG cultural; una serie di manifestazioni culturali a series of cultural events; scambi culturali cultural exchanges

culturismo [kultu'rizmo] SM body-building

cumulare [kumu'lare] /72/ VT (gen) to accumulate, amass; (Amm: impieghi) to hold concurrently

cumulativo, -a [kumula'tivo] AGG (gen) cumulative; (prezzo) (all-)inclusive; (biglietto) group attr; un biglietto cumulativo a group ticket

cumulo ['kumulo] SM 1 (mucchio) heap, pile; cumulo delle pene (Dir) consecutive sentences; cumulo dei redditi (Fisco) combined incomes 2 (Meteor) cumulus

cuneo ['kuneo] SM wedge

cunetta [ku'netta] SF 1 (di strada) dip; pieno di cunette bumpy 2 (scolo: nelle strade di città) gutter; (: di campagna) ditch

cunicolo [ku'nikolo] SM (galleria) tunnel; (di miniera) pit, shaft; (di talpa) hole

cuocere ['kwɔtʃere] VB IRREG /32/ VT 1 (gen): (far) cuocere to cook; cuocere al forno (pane) to bake; (arrosto) to roast; cuocere in umido/a vapore/in padella to stew/steam/fry; da cuocere (frutta) cooking attr 2 (mattoni) to fire ♦ VI (aus essere) to cook; cuocersi VIP (cibo) to cook

cuoco, -a, -chi, -che ['kwɔko] SM, SF cook; (di ristorante) chef

cuoiame [kwo'jame] SM leather goods pl

cuoio, -oi [kwɔjo] SM 1 (pelle di animale) leather; (prima della concia) hide; in o di cuoio leather attr; scarpe di cuoio leather shoes 2 (Anat): il cuoio capelluto the scalp 3 cuoia SFPL: tirare le cuoia (fam) to kick the bucket

cuore ['kwɔre] SM 1 (Anat, anche fig: cosa centrale) heart; la ginnastica fa bene al cuore exercise is good for your heart; un'operazione al cuore a heart operation; a cuore heart-shaped; una scatola a forma di cuore a heart-shaped box; nel cuore della città/della notte/della mischia in the heart of the city/middle of the night/midst of the fight; intervento a cuore aperto open-heart operation 2 (fig: animo): aver buon cuore to be kind-hearted; una persona di buon cuore a kind-hearted soul; parlare col cuore in mano to speak frankly; col cuore in gola with one's heart in one's mouth; senza cuore heartless; aprire il proprio cuore a qn to open one's heart to sb; non ho il cuore di dirglielo I haven't the heart to tell him; il cuore mi dice che... I feel in my heart that ...; avere un cuore da leone to be brave-hearted; mettiti il cuore in pace, non tornerà mai più you'll have to accept that he'll never come back; avere la morte nel cuore to be sick at heart; nel profondo del cuore in one's heart of hearts; ringraziare di cuore to thank sincerely; un grazie di cuore heartfelt thanks; ho a cuore il successo del progetto the success of the project matters to me; mi sta molto a cuore it's very important to me; mi si stringeva il cuore,

mi piangeva il cuore my heart ached; mi piange il cuore a vedere questo spreco I hate to see such waste; toccare il cuore a qn to move sb; club dei cuori solitari lonely hearts club 3 (Carte); cuori SMPL hearts

cupidigia [kupi'didʒa] SF greed, covetousness

cupo, -a ['kupo] AGG (caverna, notte) pitch-black; (voce, abisso) deep; (colore, cielo) dark; (suono) dull; (fig: carattere) sullen, morose

cupola ['kupola] SF (di chiesa, osservatorio) dome; (più piccola) cupola; (fig: della Mafia) Mafia high command; a cupola dome-shaped

cura ['kura] SF 1 care; avere o prendersi cura di qn/qc to look after sb/sth; abbi cura che come ti ho detto be sure to do exactly as I've told you, take care to do exactly as I've told you; abbi cura di te take care of yourself, look after yourself; si dedica completamente alla cura dell'azienda he devotes all his time to running the company; questa pianta ha bisogno di molte cure this plant needs a lot of attention; a cura di (Stampa) edited by; trasmissione a cura di (TV, Radio) programme produced by 2 (accuratezza) care, accuracy; con cura carefully; "maneggiare con cura" "handle with care"; senza cura carelessly; se lo facessi con un po' più di cura... if you took a bit more care over it ... 3 (Med: trattamento) (course of) treatment; fare una cura to follow a course of treatment; sto facendo una cura contro l'acne I'm having treatment for my acne; è in cura presso il dott. Bianchi he's one of Dr. Bianchi's patients; è stato in cura presso i migliori medici he has received treatment from the best doctors; non hanno ancora trovato una cura they haven't found a cure yet; cura dimagrante diet; cura del sonno sleep therapy

curabile [ku'rabile] AGG curable

curante [ku'rante] AGG: medico curante doctor (in charge of a patient)

curare [ku'rare] /72/ VT 1 (Med) to treat; (guarire) to cure; gli curarono la pertosse they treated him for whooping cough; farsi curare da qn per qc to be treated by sb for sth; devi curare o curarti questo raffreddore you must see about that cold 2 (occuparsi di) to look after; (azienda) to run, look after; (libro) to edit; curare l'edizione di un'antologia to be the editor of an anthology; curarsi VR 1 (gen) to take care of o.s., look after o.s.; (Med) to follow a course of treatment; si sta curando con le vitamine he's taking vitamins 2 (esteticamente) to take trouble over one's appearance; curarsi di VIP (occuparsi di) to look after; (preoccuparsi di) to bother about

curato [ku'rato] SM (Rel) parish priest; (protestante) vicar, minister

curatore, -trice [kura'tore] SM, SF 1 (Dir) guardian; (di testamento) administrator; curatore fallimentare (official) receiver 2 (di antologia) editor

curdo, -a ['kurdo] AGG, SM (lingua) Kurdish ♦ SM, SF Kurd

curia ['kurja] SF 1 (Rel): la Curia (Romana) the (Roman) Curia; curia vescovile diocesan administration 2 (Dir) local lawyers' association; curia notarile notaries' association o guild

curiosaggine [kurjo'saddʒine] SF nosiness

curiosare [kurjo'sare] /72/ VI (aus avere) (aggirarsi) to look round, wander round; curiosare nei negozi to look round o wander around the shops; curiosare tra vecchi giornali to browse through old newspapers; curiosare nelle faccende altrui to poke one's nose into other people's affairs

curiosità [kurjosi'ta] SF INV 1 (gen) curiosity; (pegg) curiosity, inquisitiveness; provare curiosità per to be curious about; siamo andati per curiosità we went out of curiosity; per curiosità, quanto l'hai pagato? as a matter of interest, how much did you pay for it? 2 (cosa rara) curio, curiosity

curioso, -a [ku'rjoso] AGG (gen) curious; (che vuol sapere) inquiring; (pegg) curious, inquisitive; (strano) odd, strange, curious; un fatto/tipo curioso an odd thing/person; essere curioso di qc/di sapere qc to be curious about sth/to know sth ♦ SM, SF busybody, nosy parker (Brit fam); una folla di curiosi a crowd of onlookers ♦ SM: il curioso è che... the funny o curious thing is that ...

curriculum [kur'rikulum] SM INV: curriculum (vitae) curriculum vitae, CV

cursore [kur'sore] SM (*su strumento di misura, videoterminale*) cursor; (*su radio*) slider

curva ['kurva] SF 1 (*gen, anche Mat, Tecn*) curve; (*traiettoria*) trajectory; **un fisico tutte curve** (*fam*) a curvaceous *o* voluptuous physique 2 (*di strada, fiume*) bend; **prendere una curva** (*Aut*) to take a bend; **sorpassare in curva** to overtake on a bend; **curva a gomito** hairpin bend; **curva stretta** sharp bend 3 (*Geog*) contour; **curva di livello** contour line 4 (*Sci*) turn; **curva a sci uniti** parallel turn; **curva a spazzaneve** snow-plough turn, basic turn 5 (*Calcio*) *curved area behind the goal where the hard-core fans go*

curvare [kur'vare] /72/ VT to bend ♦ VI (*aus avere*) 1 (*strada*) to bend; **curvare a sinistra/destra** to bend to the left/right 2 (*veicolo*) to take a bend; **curvare a sinistra/destra** to follow the road to the left/right; **curvarsi** VR (*chinarsi*) to bend down; **curvarsi** VIP (*legno*) to warp; (*persona*): **curvarsi con la vecchiaia** to become bent with age

curvo, -a ['kurvo] AGG (*gen*) curved; (*piegato*) bent; **camminare curvo** to walk with a stoop; **stare curvo** to slouch; **non stare curvo!** don't slouch!; **una linea curva** a curved line

cuscinetto [kuʃʃi'netto] SM 1 (*per timbri*) pad; (*puntaspilli*) pincushion; (*Tecn*) bearing; **cuscinetto a sfere** ball bearing 2 (*fam: deposito adiposo*) spare tyre (*Brit*) *o* tire (*USA*) ♦ AGG INV: **stato cuscinetto** (*fig*) buffer state

cuscino [kuʃ'ʃino] SM (*gen*) cushion; (*guanciale*) pillow; **cuscino di fiori** wreath

cuspide ['kuspide] SF (*Mat, Astron, Astrol*) cusp; (*Archit*) spire

custode [kus'tode] SM, SF (*di museo*) keeper, custodian; (*di parco*) warden; (*di casa*) concierge; (*di fabbrica, carcere*) guard

custodia [kus'tɔdja] SF 1 care; **avere qc in custodia** to look after sth; **dare qc in custodia a qn** to entrust sth to sb's care 2 (*Dir*) custody; **affidare a qn la custodia di** to give sb custody of; **agente di custodia** prison warder; **custodia delle carceri** prison security; **custodia cautelare** remand (*Brit*) 3 (*astuccio*) case, holder

custodire [kusto'dire] /55/ VT (*conservare*) to keep; (*fare la guardia: casa, carcere*) to guard; **i gioielli sono custoditi in cassaforte** the jewels are kept in a safe

cute ['kute] SF (*Anat*) skin

cuticola [ku'tikola] SF cuticle

CV ABBR (= *cavallo vapore*) h.p.

c.v.d. ABBR (= *come volevasi dimostrare*) QED (= *quod erat demonstrandum*)

c.vo ABBR = **corsivo**

cybercaffè [tʃiberkaf'fɔ] SM INV cybercafe

cybernauta, -i, -e [tʃiber'nauta] SM, SF cybernaut

cyberspazio [tʃiber'spattsjo] SM cyberspace

Dd

D¹, d¹ [di] SF INV, SM INV (*lettera*) D, d; **D come Domodossola** ≈ D for David (*Brit*), ≈ D for Dog (*USA*)

D² [di] ABBR **1** (= *destra*) R **2** (*Ferr*) = diretto

PAROLA CHIAVE

da [da] PREP *a + il*= dal, *da + lo*= dallo, *da + l'*= dall', *da + la*= dalla, *da + i*= dai, *da + gli*= dagli, *da + le*= dalle

1 (*agente, mezzo*) by; **fare qc da sé** to do sth (for) o.s.; **dipinto da un grande artista** painted by a great artist; **riconoscere qn dal passo** to recognize sb by his (*o* her) step

2 (*causa*): **tremare dal freddo** to shiver with cold; **morire dallo spavento** to die of fright

3 (*provenienza, distanza, separazione*) from; (*fuori di*) out of; (*giù da*) off; **a 3 km da Roma** 3 km(s)from Rome; **arrivare da Milano** to arrive from Milan; **da dove vieni?** where do you come from?; **l'aereo parte da Gatwick** the plane departs from Gatwick; **scendere dal treno** to get off the train; **staccarsi da qn** to leave *o* part from sb; **toglitelo dalla testa** get it out of your head; **uscire dalla scuola** to come out of school

4 (*stato in luogo*) at; (*presso*) at, with; **abita da quelle parti** he lives somewhere round there, he lives in that area; **ti aspetto dal macellaio** I'll wait for you at the butcher's; **sono da Pietro** I'm at Pietro's (house); **vive da un amico** he's living at a friend's *o* with a friend

5 (*moto a luogo*) to; (*moto per luogo*) through; **questo treno passa da Genova** this train goes through Genoa; **è uscito dalla finestra** he went out through *o* by (way of) the window; **vado da Pietro/dal giornalaio** I'm going to Pietro's (house)/to the newsagent's

6 (*tempo: durata*) for; (: *a partire da:* nel passato) since; (: *nel futuro*) from; **da allora** since then; **vivo qui da un anno** I've been living here for a year; **è a Londra da martedì** he has been in London since Tuesday; **da oggi in poi** from today onwards; **d'ora in poi** *o* **in avanti** from now on; **da quando sei qui** since you have been here; **sono qui dalle sei** I've been here since six o'clock

7 (*qualità, caratteristica*): **una ragazza dai capelli biondi** a fair-haired girl, a girl with fair hair; **un vestito da 300 euro** a 300-euro dress; **un ragazzo dagli occhi azzurri** a blue-eyed boy, a boy with blue eyes; **sordo da un orecchio** deaf in one ear; **è una cosa da poco** it's nothing special

8 (*modo*) like; **trattare qn da amico** to treat sb like *o* as a friend; **non è da lui** it's not like him; **comportarsi da uomo** to behave like a man

9 (*predicativo*) as; **da bambino piangevo molto** I cried a lot as a child *o* when I was a child; **da giovane** as a young man *o* woman; **fare da guida** to act as a guide; **fare da maestro** to act as a teacher; **fare da padre a** to be a father to; **da studente** as a student

10 (*fine, scopo*): **cavallo da corsa** racehorse; **macchina da corsa** racing car; **vino da pasto** table wine; **abito da sera** evening dress

11 (*seguito da infinito: consecutivo*) that (*spesso omesso*); (: *finale*) to; **casa da affittare** house to let; **qualcosa da bere** something to drink; **qualcosa da mangiare** something to eat; **ero così stanco da non stare più in piedi** I was so tired (that) I couldn't stand; **casa da vendere** house for sale

12 da... a... from ... to ...; **contare da 1 a 10** to count from 1 to 10; **dalle 3 alle 5** from 3 to *o* till 5 (o'clock); **c'erano dalle 30 alle 40 persone** there were between 30 and 40 people there; **è cambiato dall'oggi al domani** he changed overnight

dà [da] VB *vedi* dare

dabbene [dab'bɛne] AGG INV honest, decent

Dacca ['dakka] SF Dacca

daccapo [dak'kapo] AVV = **da capo**; *vedi* capo; **ricominciare daccapo** to start all over again

dacché [dak'ke] CONG (*letter*) since

dado ['dado] SM (*nel gioco*) dice *pl inv*; (*Culin*) stock cube (*Brit*), bouillon cube (*USA*); (*Tecn*) (screw) nut; (*Archit*) dado; **giocare a dadi** to play dice; **tagliare a dadi** (*Culin*) to dice; **il dado è tratto** (*fig*) the die is cast

daffare [daf'fare] SM INV work; **avere un gran daffare** to be very busy; **darsi daffare perché si faccia qc** to work hard to get sth done

dagli ['daʎʎi], **dai** [dai] PREP + ART *vedi* da

daino ['daino] SM (*maschio*) (fallow) deer *pl inv*; (*femmina*) female fallow deer *pl inv*, doe; **pelle di daino** buckskin, chamois leather

Dakar [da'kar] SF Dakar

dal¹ [dal] PREP + ART *vedi* da

dal² ABBR (= *decalitro*) dal

dall' [dall], **dalla** ['dalla], **dalle** ['dalle], **dallo** ['dallo] PREP + ART *vedi* da

daltonico, -a, -ci, -che [dal'tɔniko] AGG colour-blind (*Brit*), colorblind (*USA*) ♦ SM, SF colo(u)r-blind person

dam ABBR (= *decametro*) dam

dama ['dama] SF **1** lady; (*nei balli*) partner; **dama di compagnia** lady's companion; **dama di corte** lady-in-waiting **2** (*gioco*) draughts *sg* (*Brit*), checkers *sg* (*USA*); **giocare a dama** to play draughts/checkers; **far dama** to crown a king (*USA*), to crown a draughtsman (*Brit*), to crown a king (*USA*)

Damasco [da'masko] SF Damascus

damigella [dami'dʒɛlla] SF (*Storia*) damsel; **damigella d'onore** (*di sposa*) bridesmaid

damigiana [dami'dʒana] SF demijohn

dammeno [dam'meno] AGG INV: **per non essere dammeno di qn** so as not to be outdone by sb; **è un grande imbroglione e sua moglie non è dammeno** he's an out-and-out crook and so is his wife

danaro [da'naro] SM = denaro

danaroso, -a [dana'roso] AGG wealthy

danese [da'nese] AGG Danish ♦ SM, SF Dane; **i danesi** the Danes ♦ SM **1** (*lingua*) Danish; **parli danese?** do you speak Danish? **2** (*cane*) Great Dane

Danimarca [dani'marka] SF Denmark; **ti è piaciuta la Danimarca?** did you like Denmark?; **andrò in Danimarca quest'estate** I'm going to Denmark this summer

dannare [dan'nare] /72/ VT (*Rel*) to damn; **far dannare qn** (*fig*) to drive sb mad; **dannarsi l'anima per qc** (*affannarsi*) to work o.s. to death for sth; **dannarsi** VR (*affannarsi*): **dannarsi per fare qc** to wear o.s. out doing sth

dannato, -a [dan'nato] AGG damned; **quella dannata macchina!** (*fam*) that damned car! ♦ **i dannati** SMPL the damned

dannazione [dannat'tsjone] SF damnation ♦ ESCL: **dannazione!** damn!

danneggiare [danned'dʒare] /62/ VT (*gen*) to damage; (*rovinare*) to spoil; (*fig: persona*) to harm; **la parte danneggiata** (*Dir*) the injured party

danno¹ ['danno] SM (*gen*) damage; (*a persona*) harm, injury; **arrecare danno a qc** to damage sth; **arrecare danno a qn** to harm sb, do sb harm; **il maltempo ha provocato ingenti danni** the bad weather caused serious damage; **ho provocato un piccolo danno alla macchina** I damaged the car slightly; **fare danni** to do damage; **la grandine ha fatto molti danni** the hail did a lot of damage; **senza fare danni** without doing any damage; **il danno ormai è fatto** the damage has been done; **a danno di qn** to sb's detriment; **non c'è stato nessun danno alle persone** nobody was hurt; **in caso di perdita o danno** in case of loss or damage; **chiedere/risarcire i danni** to sue for/pay damages; **due milioni di risarcimento danni** two million in damages

danno² ['danno] VB *vedi* dare

dannoso, -a [dan'noso] AGG: **dannoso (a** *o* **per)** harmful (to), bad (for); **una sostanza dannosa** a harmful substance; **il fumo è dannoso alla salute** smoking damages your health

dantesco, -a, -schi, -sche [dan'tesko] AGG Dantesque; **l'opera dantesca** Dante's work

Danubio [da'nubjo] SM: **il Danubio** the Danube

danza ['dantsa] SF: **la danza** dancing; **una danza** a dance; **fare danza** to study dancing; **scuola/maestro di danza** dancing school/master; **danza classica** ballet dancing; **danza di guerra** war dance

danzante [dan'tsante] AGG dancing; **serata danzante** dance

danzare [dan'tsare] /72/ VT, VI (*aus* avere) to dance

danzatore, -trice [dantsa'tore] SM, SF dancer

dappertutto [dapper'tutto] AVV everywhere

dappoco [dap'pɔko] AGG INV (*anche:* **da poco:** *inetto*) inept; (*insignificante*) insignificant, negligible

dapprima [dap'prima] AVV at first

Dardanelli [darda'nɛlli] SMPL: **i Dardanelli** the Dardanelles

dardo ['dardo] SM dart, arrow

dare ['dare] VB IRREG /33/ VT 1 (*gen*) to give; (*premio, borsa di studio*) to give, award; **dare qc a qn** to give sb sth, give sth to sb; **gli ho dato un libro** I gave him a book; **gli ho dato la cartina** I gave the map to him; **dammelo** give it to me; **dare qc da fare a qn** to give sb sth to do; **dare da mangiare/bere a qn** to give sb sth to eat/drink; **dare uno schiaffo/un calcio a qn** to give sb a slap/kick, to slap/kick sb; **mi dai la macchina?** can I have the car?; **dare a qn il permesso di fare qc** to give sb permission to do sth; **gli hanno dato ordine di sparare** they gave him the order to fire; **questo trucco ti dà un'aria volgare** that make-up makes you look common; **ha dato sedicimila euro per la macchina** he paid sixteen thousand euros for the car; **gli hanno dato 5 anni** (*di prigione*) they gave him 5 years; **quanti anni mi dai?** how old do you think I am?; **queste scene mi danno il voltastomaco** these scenes make me feel sick; **dare del cretino a qn** to call sb a fool; **dare la vita per qc** to give (up) one's life for sth; **dare tutto se stesso a qn/qc** to give one's all to sb/sth; **darsi una pettinata** to give one's hair a comb 2 (*organizzare: festa, banchetto*) to hold, give; (: *spettacolo*) to perform, put on; (: *film*) to show; **danno ancora quel film?** is that film still showing? 3 (*produrre: frutti, soldi*) to yield, produce; (: *calore*) to give off; (: *suono*) to make; **gli investimenti hanno dato il 10% di interesse** the investments yielded 10% interest; **gli ha dato un figlio** she bore him a son 4 **dare qc per certo** to be sure of sth; **dare qn per disperso** to report sb missing; **dare qn per morto** to give sb up for dead; **dare qc/qn per perso** to give sth/sb up for lost; **dare qc per scontato** to take sth for granted; **dare ad intendere a qn che...** to lead sb to believe that ...; **ciò mi dà da pensare** (*insospettire*) that gives me food for thought; (*preoccupare*) that worries me; **non è dato a tutti di essere intelligenti** not everyone is blessed with intelligence; **dar via** to give away ♦ VI (*aus* avere) 1 (*finestra, casa: guardare*): **dare su** to overlook, give onto, look (out) onto; **la mia finestra dà sul giardino** my window looks onto the garden; **il giardino dà sulla strada** the garden faces onto the road 2 (*colore: tendere*): **dare su** to tend towards; **un colore che dà sul verde** a greenish colour; **darsi** VR: **darsi a** (*musica, politica*) to devote o.s. to; **darsi al bere/al gioco** to take to drink/to gambling; **darsi alla bella vita** to have a good time; **darsi ammalato** to report sick; **darsi prigioniero** to surrender; **darsi per vinto** to give in; **darsi da fare per fare qc** to go to a lot of bother to do sth; **devi darti da fare** you'll have to get busy; **coraggio, diamoci da fare!** come on, let's get on with it!; **darsi** VIP 1 **può darsi** maybe, perhaps; **può darsi che venga** he may come, perhaps he will come; **si dà il caso che...** it so happens that ... 2 **darsela a gambe** to take to one's heels ♦ SM (*Fin*): **il dare e l'avere** debits and credits *pl*

❏ **dare** non si traduce mai con la parola inglese *dare*

Dar-es-Salaam [daresa'lam] SF Dar-es-Salaam

darsena ['darsena] SF (*Naut*) dock

data ['data] SF date; **che data è oggi?** what's today's date?; **in data da destinarsi** on a date still to be announced; **lettera in data 4 febbraio** letter dated the 4th February; **in data odierna** as of today; **senza data** undated; **amicizia di lunga** *o* **vecchia data** long-standing friendship; **data di emissione**

date of issue; **data di nascita** date of birth; **data di scadenza** expiry date

datare [da'tare] /72/ VT to date; **non datato** undated ♦ VI: **datare da** to date back to, date from; **a datare da oggi** dating from today

datato, -a [da'tato] AGG (*film, romanzo*) dated

dativo [da'tivo] SM (*Gramm*) dative

dato, -a ['dato] AGG 1 (*certo*): **in quel dato giorno** on that particular day; **in dati casi** in certain cases 2 (*stabilito*): **entro quel dato giorno** by that particular day; **in un dato periodo** at a given time 3 (*considerato*): **data la situazione** given *o* considering *o* in view of the situation; **dato che...** given that ... ♦ SM (*Mat, Sci*) datum; **dati** SMPL data *pl inv*; **è un dato di fatto** it's a fact; **dati sensibili** sense data

datore, -trice [da'tore] SM, SF: **datore di lavoro** employer

dattero ['dattero] SM (*Bot: albero*) date palm; (: *frutto*) date 2 (*Zool*): **dattero di mare** date mussel

dattilografare [dattilogra'fare] /72/ VT to type

dattilografia [dattilogra'fia] SF typing

dattilografo, -a [datti'lɔgrafo] SM, SF typist; **fa il dattilografo** he's a typist

dattiloscritto, -a [dattilos'kritto] AGG typewritten ♦ SM typescript

davanti [da'vanti] AVV in front; (*all'inizio di: gruppo*) at the front; (*dirimpetto*) opposite; **posso andare davanti?** (*in macchina*) can I go *o* sit in front?; **davanti c'era un bel giardino** at the front there was a nice garden ♦ **davanti a** PREP 1 (*posizione: gen*) in front of; (: *dirimpetto a*) opposite; (: *distanza*) ahead of; **ogni mattina passo davanti a casa tua** every morning I go past your house; **camminava davanti a me** he was walking ahead of *o* in front of me; **era seduto davanti a me** (*più in là*) he was sitting in front of me; (*faccia a faccia*) he was sitting opposite *o* facing me; **era seduto davanti a me al cinema** he was sitting in front of me at the cinema; **la casa davanti alla mia** the house opposite mine; **la mia casa è davanti al municipio** my house is opposite *o* faces the town hall 2 (*al cospetto di*) before, in front of; **comparire davanti al giudice** to appear before the judge; **davanti al pericolo** in the face of danger ♦ AGG INV front *attr*; **le file davanti sono occupate** the front rows are taken; **le zampe davanti** the front *o* fore paws ♦ SM INV front

davanzale [davan'tsale] SM (window)sill

davanzo [da'vantso] AVV (= *d'avanzo*) *vedi* avanzo

davvero [dav'vero] AVV really; **è successo davvero** it really happened; **dico davvero** I mean it

daziario, -ria, -ri, -rie [dat'tsjarjo] AGG excise *attr*

dazio, -zi ['dattsjo] SM (*somma*) duty, tax; (*luogo*) customs *pl*; **dazio doganale** customs duty; **dazio d'importazione** import duty

dB ABBR (= *decibel*) dB, db

d.C. ABBR (= *dopo Cristo*) A.D.

DDT [didi'ti] SIGLA M (= *dicloro-difenil-tricloroetano*) D.D.T.

dea ['dɛa] SF (*anche fig*) goddess

debbo *ecc* ['dɛbbo] VB *vedi* dovere

debellare [debel'lare] /72/ VT to overcome

debilitare [debili'tare] /72/ VT to debilitate; **debilitarsi** VIP to become debilitated

debitamente [debita'mente] AVV (*vedi agg*) duly; properly

debito[1], -a ['debito] AGG (*dovuto*) due; (*appropriato*) proper; **a tempo debito** at the right *o* appropriate time; **ogni cosa a tempo debito** I'll (*o* we'll) think about it when the time comes, everything in due time

debito[2] ['debito] SM 1 (*anche fig*) debt; **ha molti debiti** he's got a lot of debts; **far debiti** to get into debt; **essere/sentirsi in debito verso qn** to be/feel indebted to sb; **debito formativo** (*Scol*) a system that allows a student who has not reached a significant standard in a subject to move up to the next year, and make up the insufficiency at a later date; vedi anche **credito formativo** 2 (*Comm*) debit; **debito consolidato** consolidated debt; **debito formativo** failure to achieve the required standard; **debito d'imposta** tax liability; **debito pubblico** national debt

debitore, -trice [debi'tore] SM, SF debtor; **ti sono debitore** (*anche fig*) I'm in your debt; **ti sono debitore di un favore** I owe you a favour

debole [ˈdebole] AGG (gen) weak, feeble; (luce) dim, faint; (speranza, lamento, suono) faint; (polso) faint, weak; (argomentazioni) weak, poor; **mi sento debole** I feel weak; **essere debole di vista** to have weak o poor eyesight; **essere debole di stomaco** to have a delicate stomach; **essere debole in matematica** to be bad at mathematics; **un debole suono** a faint sound; **una luce debole** a dim light ♦ SM, SF (persona) weakling; **i deboli** the weak ♦ SM weakness; **ha un debole per la cioccolata** he's got a weakness for chocolate; **ha un debole per me** she's got a soft spot for me

debolezza [deboˈlettsa] SF (anche fig) weakness

debuttante [debutˈtante] SM, SF (gen) beginner, novice; (Teatro) actor o actress at the beginning of his (o her) career; **ballo delle debuttanti** debutantes' ball

debuttare [debutˈtare] /72/ VI (aus avere) to make one's debut

debutto [deˈbutto] SM (anche fig) debut; **fare il proprio debutto** (anche fig) to make one's debut

decade [ˈdɛkade] SF period of ten days

decadente [dekaˈdente] AGG, SM, SF (gen, anche Arte) decadent

decadenza [dekaˈdentsa] SF 1 (processo) decline; (stato) decadence; **una civiltà in decadenza** a civilisation in decline 2 (Dir) loss, forfeiture

decadere [dekaˈdere] /18/ VI IRREG (aus essere) 1 (costumi) to fall into decline 2 (scadere) to lapse

decaduto, -a [dekaˈduto] AGG (nobile) impoverished; (norma) no longer in force

decaffeinato, -a [dekaffeiˈnato] AGG decaffeinated; **caffè decaffeinato** decaffeinated coffee ♦ SM decaffeinated coffee, decaf (fam); **un decaffeinato** a decaf

decalogo, -ghi [deˈkalogo] SM (Rel) Decalogue; (fig) rulebook

decano [deˈkano] SM (Rel) dean; (fig) doyen

decantare [dekanˈtare] /72/ VT (virtù, bravura) to hymn; (persona) to sing the praises of

decapitare [dekapiˈtare] /72/ VT (gen) to decapitate; (per pena capitale) to behead

decappottabile [dekappotˈtabile] AGG, SF (Aut) convertible; **una macchina decappottabile** a convertible

deceduto, -a [detʃeˈduto] AGG deceased

decelerare [detʃeleˈrare] /72/ VT, VI (aus avere) to decelerate, slow down

decennale [detʃenˈnale] AGG (che dura 10 anni) ten-year attr; (che ricorre ogni 10 anni) ten-yearly, every ten years ♦ SM (ricorrenza) tenth anniversary

decenne [deˈtʃenne] AGG: **un bambino decenne** a ten-year-old child, a child of ten

decennio, -ni [deˈtʃɛnnjo] SM decade

decente [deˈtʃɛnte] AGG (decoroso: abiti) decent, respectable; (contegno) proper; (accettabile) satisfactory, decent

decentramento [detʃentraˈmento] SM , **decentralizzazione** [detʃentraliddzatˈtsjone] SF decentralization

decentrare [detʃenˈtrare] /72/, **decentralizzare** [detʃentralidˈdzare] VT to decentralize

decenza [deˈtʃentsa] SF decency, propriety

decesso [deˈtʃɛsso] SM (frm) death; **atto di decesso** death certificate

decidere [deˈtʃidere] VB IRREG /34/ VT 1 (stabilire): **decidere qc** to decide on sth; **decidere una data/un'ora** to agree on a date/time, fix a date/time; **decidere che** to decide that; **decidere di fare qc/di non fare qc** to decide to do sth/ against doing sth; **ho deciso di non andarci** I decided not to go; **sta a lui decidere** it's up to him to decide; **ha deciso il nostro futuro** it determined our future 2 (risolvere: disputa) to settle, resolve; **decidere una lite** (Dir) to settle a dispute ♦ VI (aus avere) (persona) to decide, make up one's mind; **hai deciso?** have you decided?; **è venuto il momento di decidere** it's time to decide o make a decision; **non so decidere tra questi modelli** I can't decide which of these models to choose; **hai quel fatto a decidere del mio futuro** that was what decided o determined my future; **decidersi** VIP (persona) to come to o make a decision; **non so decidermi** I can't decide; **decidersi a fare** to make up one's mind to do; **finalmente si è deciso a parlare** he finally made up his mind to talk

decifrare [detʃiˈfrare] /72/ VT (codice) to decode, decipher; (calligrafia) to decipher, make out; (enigma) to find the key to; (fig: intenzioni, atteggiamento) to work out

decilitro [deˈtʃilitro] SM decilitre (Brit), deciliter (USA)

decimale [detʃiˈmale] AGG, SM decimal

decimare [detʃiˈmare] /72/ VT (anche fig) to decimate

decimetro [deˈtʃimetro] SM decimetre (Brit), decimeter (USA)

decimo, -a [ˈdɛtʃimo] AGG tenth ♦ SM 1 (Mat) tenth 2 (Med): **avere dieci decimi di vista** to have twenty-twenty vision ♦ SM, SF (in ordine, graduatoria): **il decimo da sinistra** the tenth from the left

decina [deˈtʃina] SF 1 (Mat): **la colonna delle decine** the tens column 2 (circa 10) about ten, ≈ about a dozen; **una decina di macchine** ≈ about a dozen cars; **decine di lettere** ≈ dozens of letters, ≈ letters by the dozen

decisi ecc [deˈtʃizi] VB vedi **decidere**

decisionale [detʃizjoˈnale] AGG decision-making attr

decisione [detʃiˈzjone] SF 1 (scelta, anche Dir) decision; **prendere una decisione** to take o make a decision; **ho preso una decisione** I've made a decision 2 (risolutezza) decisiveness; **con decisione** decisively, resolutely; **agire con decisione** to act decisively

decisivo, -a [detʃiˈzivo] AGG (gen) decisive; (fattore) deciding; **il suo voto è stato decisivo** his vote was decisive

deciso, -a [deˈtʃizo] PP di **decidere** ♦ AGG 1 (persona, carattere) determined; (tono) firm, resolute; **essere deciso a fare qc** to be determined to do sth; **essere deciso a tutto** to be ready to do anything; **sei proprio deciso?** are you quite sure?; **entrò con passo deciso** he marched in resolutely 2 (netto: colpo) clean 3 (definitivo): **non c'è ancora niente di deciso** nothing has been decided yet

declassare [deklasˈsare] /72/ VT to downgrade; **1ª declassata** (Ferr) first-class carriage which may be used by second-class passengers

declinare [dekliˈnare] /72/ VI (aus avere) (pendio) to slope down; (fig: popolarità) to decline ♦ VT 1 (Gramm) to decline 2 (rifiutare: invito, offerta) to decline, turn down; **ho declinato l'offerta** I turned down the offer; **declinare ogni responsabilità** to disclaim all responsibility 3 **declinare le proprie generalità** (frm) to give one's particulars

declinazione [deklinatˈtsjone] SF 1 (Gramm) declension 2 (Fis, Astron) declination

declino [deˈklino] SM decline; **in declino** declining, on the decline

declivio, -vi [deˈklivjo] SM (downward) slope

decodificare [dekodifiˈkare] /20/ VT to decode

decodificatore [dekodifikaˈtore] SM decoder

decollare [dekolˈlare] /72/ VI (aus avere) (anche fig) to take off; **l'aereo è decollato alle otto** the plane took off at eight o'clock

décolleté [dekolaˈte] AGG INV (abito) low-necked, low-cut; **scarpa décolleté** court shoe ♦ SM INV (di abito) low neckline; (di donna) cleavage

decollo [deˈkɔllo] SM (Aer, anche fig) take-off; **al decollo** on take-off; **in fase di decollo** during take-off; **decollo verticale** vertical take-off

decolorare [dekoloˈrare] /72/ VT (vedi agg) to decolorize o decolour; to bleach

decomporre [dekomˈporre] VB IRREG /77/ VT , **decomporsi** VIP to decompose

decomposizione [dekompozitˈtsjone] SF decomposition; **un cadavere in decomposizione** a decomposing corpse

decomposto, -a [dekomˈposto] PP di **decomporre**

decompressione [dekompresˈsjone] SF decompression; **fare la decompressione** to decompress

decongelare [dekondʒeˈlare] /72/ VT to defrost

decongestionare [dekondʒestjoˈnare] /72/ VT (Med: traffico) to relieve congestion in

decorare [dekoˈrare] /72/ VT (ornare, anche Mil) to decorate; **decorare qn al valor militare** to decorate somebody for bravery

decorativo, -a [dekoraˈtivo] AGG decorative

decoratore, -trice [dekoraˈtore] SM, SF 1 (interior) decorator 2 (Teatro) set designer

decorazione [dekorat'tsjone] SF (*ornamento, medaglia*) decoration

decoro [de'kɔro] SM (*decenza*) decorum; (*dignità*) dignity; **vestirsi con decoro** to be properly dressed

decoroso, -a [deko'roso] AGG (*contegno, abito*) dignified, decorous; (*fig: stipendio*) decent

decorrenza [dekor'rɛntsa] SF: **con decorrenza da** (as) from

decorrere [de'korrere] /28/ VI IRREG (*aus* **essere**) **1** decorrere da to have effect from, run from; **a decorrere da** (as) from, starting from **2** (*trascorrere*) to pass, elapse (*frm*); **è decorso un anno dalla sua morte** a year has passed *o* elapsed since he died

decorso, -a [de'korso] PP *di* **decorrere** ♦ SM (*di malattia*) course

decrebbi *ecc* [de'krebbi] VB *vedi* **decrescere**

decrepito, -a [de'krɛpito] AGG (*vecchio*) decrepit; (*fig*) obsolete

decrescere [de'kreʃʃere] /30/ VI IRREG (*aus* **essere**) (*gen*) to decrease, diminish; (*prezzi, febbre*) to go down; (*piena*) to subside; (*luna*) to wane; (*marea*) to ebb

decresciuto, -a [dekreʃʃuto] PP *di* **decrescere**

decretare [dekre'tare] /72/ VT (*Dir*) to decree; (*stabilire*) to order; **decretare lo stato d'emergenza** to declare a state of emergency; **decretare la nomina di qn** to nominate sb for appointment

decreto [de'kreto] SM decree; **decreto legge** ≈ decree with the force of law; **decreto di sfratto** eviction order

decurtare [dekur'tare] /72/ VT (*debito, somma*) to reduce

decurtazione [dekurtat'tsjone] SF reduction

dedalo ['dɛdalo] SM maze, labyrinth

dedica, -che ['dɛdika] SF dedication

dedicare [dedi'kare] /20/ VT (*gen, anche Rel*) to dedicate; (*energie, sforzi*) to devote; **le ha dedicato una canzone** he dedicated a song to her; **ha dedicato la sua vita alla scienza** he devoted his life to science; **dedicarsi** VR: **dedicarsi a** (*votarsi*) to devote o.s. to; **mi dedicherò alla musica** I'm going to devote myself to music; **dedicarsi alla casa** (*occuparsene*) to look after the house; **dedicarsi anima e corpo a** to give o.s. up body and soul to

dedicherò *ecc* [dedike'rɔ] VB *vedi* **dedicare**

dedito, -a ['dɛdito] AGG: **dedito a** (*studio*) dedicated *o* devoted to; (*vizio*) addicted to; **essere dedito allo studio** to be a very keen student; **essere dedito al bere** to be a heavy drinker; **essere dedito al gioco** to be a gambler

dedotto, -a [de'dotto] PP *di* **dedurre**

deduco *ecc* [de'duco] VB *vedi* **dedurre**

dedurre [de'durre] /90/ VT IRREG **1** (*capire, concludere*) to deduce, infer; **ne deduco che...** I deduce from this that...; **dal suo comportamento ho dedotto che era stanco** I realized from the way he was behaving that he was tired **2** (*togliere*): **dedurre (da)** to deduct (from); **l'IVA va dedotta alla fine** VAT is deducted at the end

dedussi *ecc* [de'dussi] VB *vedi* **dedurre**

deduzione [dedut'tsjone] SF (*in tutti i sensi*) deduction

defalcare [defal'kare] /20/ VT to deduct

defenestrare [defenes'trare] /72/ VT (*fig*) to remove from office; (*in senso proprio*) to throw out of the window

deferente [defe'rɛnte] AGG **1** (*persona*) deferential **2** (*Anat: dotto, canale*) deferent

deferire [defe'rire] /55/ VT: **deferire qc a** (*Dir*) to refer sth to

defezione [defet'tsjone] SF (*vedi vb*) defection; desertion

deficiente [defi'tʃɛnte] AGG **1** (*fam, peg: sciocco*) half-witted, half-wit **2** (*mancante*): **deficiente di** deficient in ♦ SM, SF (*fam, peg: sciocco*) idiot, fool

deficienza [defi'tʃɛntsa] SF (*gen*) deficiency; (*carenza*) shortage; (*fig: lacuna*) weakness

deficit ['dɛfitʃit] SM INV deficit

definire [defi'nire] /55/ VT **1** (*descrivere*) to define; **il suo comportamento si può definire irresponsabile** his behaviour can be described as irresponsible **2** (*risolvere: vertenza*) to settle; **dobbiamo definire la questione al più presto** we must settle this matter as soon as possible **3** (*determinare*) to define

definitivo, -a [defini'tivo] AGG (*gen*) final, definitive; (*chiusura, vittoria, edizione*) definitive

definito, -a [defi'nito] AGG (*gen*) definite; **ben definito** clear, clear cut

definizione [definit'tsjone] SF (*gen*) definition; (*di disputa, vertenza*) settlement; (*di tempi, obiettivi*) establishment; **ad alta definizione** (*Fot, TV*) high definition

deflagrazione [deflagrat'tsjone] SF explosion

deflazione [deflat'tsjone] SF (*Econ*) deflation

deflettore [deflet'tore] SM (*Aut*) quarterlight (*Brit*), deflector (*USA*)

defluire [deflu'ire] /55/ VI (*aus* **essere**) **defluire da** (*liquido*) to flow away from; (*folla*) to stream

deflusso [de'flusso] SM (*anche fig*) flow; (*di marea*) ebb

deformare [defor'mare] /72/ VT (*oggetto*) to put out of shape; (*legno*) to warp; (*corpo*) to deform; (*fig: immagine, visione, verità, fatto*) to distort; **deformarsi** VIP (*vedi vt*) to lose its shape; to warp; to become deformed; (*fig: immagine*) to become distorted

deformazione [deformat'tsjone] SF (*Med*) deformation; **questa è deformazione professionale!** that's how you get when you do this job!

deforme [de'forme] AGG (*mani, piedi, corpo*) misshapen; (*volto*) disfigured; (*fig: brutto, sgradevole*) hideous

deformità [deformi'ta] SF INV (*Med*) deformity

defraudare [defrau'dare] /72/ VT: **defraudare qn di qc** to cheat *o* swindle sb out of sth, defraud sb of sth

defunto, -a [de'funto] AGG dead, late *attr*; **il defunto presidente** the late president ♦ SM, SF deceased person; **il defunto** the deceased; **i defunti** the dead; **commemorazione dei defunti** (*ricorrenza*) All Souls' Day

degenerare [dedʒene'rare] /72/ VI (*aus* **avere**) **degenerare (in)** to degenerate (into)

degenerazione [dedʒenerat'tsjone] SF degeneration, degeneracy

degenere [de'dʒenere] AGG degenerate

degente [de'dʒɛnte] SM, SF (*di ospedale*) in-patient

degenza [de'dʒɛntsa] SF confinement in *o* to bed; **degenza ospedaliera** period in hospital

degli ['deʎʎi] PREP + ART *vedi* **di**

deglutire [deglu'tire] /55/ VT to swallow

degnare [deɲ'ɲare] /15/ VT: **non mi ha degnato di uno sguardo** he didn't so much as look at me; **non mi ha degnato di una risposta** he didn't deign to answer me; **degnarsi** VIP: **degnarsi di fare qc** to deign *o* condescend to do sth; **vedo che ti sei degnato!** (*iro*) how gracious of you!

degno, -a ['deɲɲo] AGG (*gen*) worthy; (*dignitoso*) dignified; **degno di** worthy of; **degno di fiducia** trustworthy; **degno di fede** (*persona, testimonianza*) reliable; **degno di lode** praiseworthy; **non è degno di te** (*persona*) he is not worthy of you; **fare una cosa del genere non è degno di te** it's unworthy of you to do a thing like that; **non è degno di essere chiamato padre** he is not fit to be called a father; **il suo degno figlio** (*anche iro*) his good *o* worthy son

degradare [degra'dare] /72/ VT (*Mil*) to demote; (*fig: persona*) to degrade; **degradarsi** VR to degrade o.s., demean o.s.

degrado [de'grado] SM: **degrado urbano** urban decay

degustare [degus'tare] /72/ VT to sample, taste

degustazione [degustat'tsjone] SF **1** (*azione*) tasting, sampling **2** (*negozio*): **degustazione di vini** specialist wine bar; **degustazione di caffè** specialist wine shop

dei ['dei] PREP + ART *vedi* **di**

del [del] PREP + ART *vedi* **di**

delatore, -trice [dela'tore] SM, SF (*police*) informer

delazione [delat'tsjone] SF informing

delega, -ghe ['dɛlega] SF **1** (*di autorità, poteri*) delegation **2** (*procura*) proxy; **per delega** by proxy; **per delega notarile** ≈ through a solicitor (*Brit*) *o* lawyer

delegare [dele'gare] /80/ VT to delegate; **delegare qn a fare qc** to delegate sb to do sth; (*Dir*) to empower *o* authorise sb to do sth

delegato, -a [dele'gato] AGG: **amministratore delegato, consigliere delegato** managing director ♦ SM, SF delegate

delegazione [delegat'tsjone] SF delegation

delegherò *ecc* [delege'rɔ] VB *vedi* **delegare**

deleterio, -ria, -ri, -rie [dele'tɛrjo] AGG (*effetto*) deleterious; (*sostanza*) noxious

delfino¹ [del'fino] SM (*Zool*) dolphin; **nuotare a delfino** (*Sport*) ≈ to do the butterfly (stroke)

delfino² [del'fino] SM (*Storia*) dauphin; (*fig: successore*) probable successor

Delhi ['deli] SF Delhi

delibera [de'libera] SF decision; (*del Parlamento*) resolution

deliberare [delibe'rare] /72/ VT: **deliberare qc** to come to a decision on sth; **deliberare di fare qc** to decide to do sth ♦ VI (*aus avere*) (*Dir*): **deliberare su qc** to rule on sth

delicatezza [delika'tettsa] SF (*vedi agg*) delicacy; softness, paleness; lightness; gentleness; frailty; fragility; thoughtfulness, considerateness, tactfulness

delicato, -a [deli'kato] AGG **1** (*gen*) delicate; (*tessuto*) delicate, fine; (*colore*) delicate, soft, pale; (*profumo*) delicate, light; (*carezza*) gentle, soft; (*salute*) delicate, frail; (*meccanismo*) delicate, fragile; **è delicato di stomaco** he has a delicate stomach **2** (*che richiede tatto*) delicate; (*che dimostra tatto*) thoughtful, considerate, tactful

delimitare [delimi'tare] /72/ VT (*anche fig*) to delimit (*frm*)

delineare [deline'are] /72/ VT (*anche fig*) to outline; **delinearsi** VIP to be outlined; (*fig: situazione*) to take shape; **si sta delineando un periodo difficile** there are hard times ahead

delinquente [delin'kwɛnte] SM, SF delinquent, criminal; (*fig: mascalzone*) scoundrel, wretch; **la polizia ha arrestato il delinquente** the police arrested the criminal; **delinquente abituale** (*Dir*) persistent offender

delinquenza [delin'kwɛntsa] SF delinquency, criminality; **un aumento della delinquenza** an increase in crime; **delinquenza minorile** juvenile delinquency; **delinquenza organizzata** organized crime

deliquio, -qui [de'likwjo] SM (*frm*) swoon; **cadere in deliquio** to swoon

delirante [deli'rante] AGG (*Med*) delirious; (*fig: folla*) frenzied; (: *discorso, mente*) insane

delirare [deli'rare] /72/ VI (*aus avere*) (*Med*) to be delirious; (*fig*) to rave

delirio, -ri [de'lirjo] SM (*Med*) delirium; **in delirio** (*Med*) delirious; **andare in delirio per qc** to go wild about sth; **mandare in delirio** to send into a frenzy; **la folla in delirio** the frenzied crowd

delitto [de'litto] SM (*misfatto, anche fig*) crime, offence

delittuoso, -a [delittu'oso] AGG criminal

delizia [de'littsja] SF delight; **con mia grande delizia** to my great delight; **che delizia!** how delightful!

deliziare [delit'tsjare] /19/ VT to delight; **deliziarsi** VIP: **deliziarsi di qc/a fare qc** to take delight in sth/in doing sth

delizioso, -a [delit'tsjoso] AGG (*gen*) delightful; (*sapore, odore, cibo*) delicious

della [*della*], **delle** ['delle], **dello** ['dello] PREP + ART *vedi* **di**

delta ['dɛlta] SM INV (*Geog*) delta ♦ SM INV, SF INV **1** (*in alfabeto greco*) delta **2** (*Aer*): **ala a delta** delta wing

deltaplano [delta'plano] SM hang-glider; **volo col deltaplano** hang-gliding; **andare in deltaplano** to hang-glide

delucidazione [delutʃidat'tsjone] SF clarification *no pl*; **vorrei delle delucidazioni in merito** I would like some more details on that

deludente [delu'dɛnte] AGG disappointing; **un film un po' deludente** a rather disappointing film

deludere [de'ludere] /35/ VT IRREG to disappoint; **mi hai molto deluso** you've really disappointed me; **il suo ultimo film mi ha deluso** his last film was disappointing
  ❏ **deludere** non si traduce mai con la parola inglese *delude*

delusione [delu'zjone] SF disappointment; **è stata una delusione** it was a disappointment; **che delusione!** what a disappointment!; **dare una delusione a qn** to disappoint sb; **avere una delusione amorosa** to be disappointed in love
  ❏ **delusione** non si traduce mai con la parola inglese *delusion*

deluso, -a [de'luzo] PP *di* **deludere** ♦ AGG disappointed; **sono deluso del voto che ho preso** I'm disappointed with the mark I got

demagogico, -a, -ci, -che [dema'gɔdʒiko] AGG (*politica, iniziativa*) popularity-seeking

demagogo, -ghi [dema'gɔgo] SM demagogue

demanio [de'manjo] SM (*Amm*) state property; (*ufficio*) state property office

demente [de'mɛnte] SM, SF (*anche fig*) lunatic ♦ AGG (*Med*) demented, mentally deranged; (*fam*) crazy, mad

demenza [de'mɛntsa] SF (*anche fig*) madness, insanity; **demenza senile** (*Med*) senile dementia

demenziale [demen'tsjale] AGG insane; (*comicità*) surreal, off-the-wall

demmo ['demmo] VB *vedi* **dare**

democratico, -a, -ci, -che [demo'kratiko] AGG democratic ♦ SM, SF democrat; **Democratici di sinistra** (*Pol*) Democrats of the Left (*Italian left-wing party*)

democrazia [demokrat'tsia] SF democracy; **le democrazie occidentali** the western democracies; **la Democrazia Cristiana** the Christian Democrat Party

democristiano, -a [demokris'tjano] AGG, SM, SF Christian Democrat

demografia [demogra'fia] SF demography

demografico, -a, -ci, -che [demo'grafiko] AGG demographic; **incremento demografico** increase in population

demolire [demo'lire] /55/ VT (*casa, oggetto, teoria*) to demolish; (*persona: criticare*) to tear to pieces

demolizione [demolit'tsjone] SF (*anche fig*) demolition

demone ['demone] SM demon

demonio, -ni [de'mɔnjo] SM demon, devil; (*fig: genio*) genius; **il Demonio** the Devil; **quel ragazzino è un demonio** that child is a little devil

demonizzare [demonid'dzare] /72/ VT to make a monster of

demonizzazione [demoniddzat'tsjone] SF demonizing, demonization

demoralizzare [demoralid'dzare] /72/ VT to demoralize; **demoralizzarsi** VIP to become demoralized; **non demoralizzarti** don't let it get you down

demordere [de'mɔrdere] /64/ VI IRREG (*aus avere*) to give up; **non demordere (da)** to refuse to give up

demotivare [demoti'vare] /72/ VT: **demotivare qn** to take away sb's motivation

demotivato, -a [demoti'vato] AGG demotivated, lacking motivation

denaro [de'naro] SM **1** money; **denaro contante** *o* **liquido** cash; **non ho molto denaro con me** I haven't got much money with me **2** (*misura di fibre tessili*) denier **3 denari** SMPL (*Carte*) suit in Neapolitan pack of cards

denaturato, -a [denatu'rato] AGG: **alcol denaturato** methylated spirits, denatured alcohol (*USA*)

denigrare [deni'grare] /72/ VT to denigrate, run down

denominare [denomi'nare] /72/ VT to name

denominatore [denomina'tore] SM (*Mat*) denominator; **denominatore comune** (*anche fig*) common denominator

denominazione [denominat'tsjone] SF (*gen*) name, designation (*frm*); (*classificazione*) denomination; **denominazione di origine controllata** mark guaranteeing the quality and origin of a wine

denotare [deno'tare] /72/ VT to indicate, denote

densità [densi'ta] SF (*gen, anche Fis*) density; (*di nebbia*) thickness, denseness; (*di vernice*) thickness; (*di folla*) denseness; **ad alta/bassa densità di popolazione** densely/sparsely populated; **ad alta densità di manodopera** labour-intensive; **a doppia/alta densità** (*Inform*) double-/high-density

denso, -a ['dɛnso] AGG (*gen*) dense, thick; (*vernice, fumo, minestra*) thick; **una minestra densa** a thick soup; **una frase densa di significato** a phrase charged with meaning

dentale [den'tale] AGG dental

dentario, -ria, -ri, -rie [den'tarjo] AGG dental

dentatura [denta'tura] SF **1** set of teeth, teeth *pl* **2** (*Tecn: di ruota*) serration

dente ['dɛnte] SM **1** (*Anat*) tooth; **denti sporgenti** buck teeth; **mettere i denti** to teethe; **mal di denti** toothache; **avere mal di denti** to have a toothache; **lavarsi i denti** to clean *o* brush one's teeth; **mi lavo i denti dopo ogni pasto** I clean my teeth after every meal; **dente del giudizio** wisdom tooth; **dente da latte** milk tooth **2** (*di sega, pettine*) tooth; (*di*

ingranaggio) cog; (di forchetta, tridente) prong **3** (Geog) jagged peak **4** (Bot): **dente di leone** dandelion **5** (fraseologia): **al dente** (Culin) al dente; **avere il dente avvelenato contro** o **con qn** to bear sb a grudge; **via il dente, via il dolore** once it's over I'll (o you'll ecc) feel better; **mettere qc sotto i denti** to have a bite to eat; **mostrare i denti** to show one's teeth; **parlare a denti stretti** to speak unwillingly; **stringere i denti** to grit one's teeth
❏ **dente** non si traduce mai con la parola inglese **dent**

dentice ['dɛntitʃe] SM (Zool) sea bream

dentiera [den'tjɛra] SF **1** (Med) dentures pl, (set of) false teeth pl (fam); **porta la dentiera** she's got false teeth **2** (Tecn) rack

dentifricio, -cia, -ci, -cie [denti'fritʃo] SM toothpaste; **dentifricio al fluoro** fluoride toothpaste ♦ AGG: **pasta dentifricia** toothpaste

dentista, -i, -e [den'tista] SM, SF dentist; **fa la dentista** she's a dentist

dentro ['dentro] AVV **1** (all'interno) inside; (in casa) indoors; **qui/là dentro** in here/there; **andare dentro** to go inside (o indoors); **vai dentro** go inside; **non va dentro** it won't go in (here); **vieni dentro** come inside o in; **col freddo che c'era, dentro si stava bene** with the cold weather we were better off indoors; **hai visto dentro?** have you seen inside?; **cioccolatini con dentro le nocciole** chocolates with hazelnut centres; **piegato in dentro** folded over; o **dentro o fuori!** either come in or go out!; **darci dentro** (fig: fam) to slog away, work hard **2** (fam: in carcere) inside; **l'hanno messo dentro** they've put him away o inside; **non va dentro** it won't go; **è dentro da un anno** he's been inside for a year **3** (fig: nell'intimo) inwardly; **sentire qc dentro** to feel sth deep down inside o.s.; **tenere tutto dentro** to keep everything bottled up (inside o.s.) ♦ PREP: **dentro (a)** in; **dentro l'armadio** in the cupboard; **dentro le mura/i confini** within the walls/frontiers; **è dentro a quel cassetto** it's in that drawer; **è dentro alla politica/agli affari** he's involved in politics/business; **dentro di me pensai...** I thought to myself ...; **ci sono dentro fino al collo** (fig) I'm in it up to my neck ♦ SM inside

denuclearizzato, -a [denuklearid'dzato] AGG (comune, zona) denuclearized, nuclear-free

denudare [denu'dare] /72/ VT (persona) to strip; (parte del corpo) to bare; **denudarsi** VR to strip

denuncia, -ce o **, -cie** [de'nuntʃa], **denunzia** [de'nuntsja] SF **1** (Dir): **sporgere denuncia contro qn** to report sb to the police **2** (dichiarazione) notification; **denuncia delle nascite** registration of births; **denuncia dei redditi** income tax return

denunciare [denun'tʃare] /19/, **denunziare** [denun'tsjare] VT **1** (Dir): **denunciare qn/qc (alla polizia)** to report sb/sth (to the police); **lo ha denunciato alla polizia** he reported him to the police **2** (dichiarare: nascite, redditi) to declare; (accusare pubblicamente) to denounce; (rivelare) to expose; **ha denunciato la corruzione all'interno del partito** he exposed the corruption within the party

denutrito, -a [denu'trito] AGG undernourished

denutrizione [denutri'tsjone] SF malnutrition

deodorante [deodo'rante] AGG, SM deodorant

deontologia [deontolo'dʒia] SF: **deontologia professionale** professional code of conduct

depenalizzazione [depenaliddzat'tsjone] SF decriminalization

dépendance [depã'dãs] SF INV outbuilding

deperibile [depe'ribile] AGG perishable; **merce deperibile** perishables pl, perishable goods pl

deperimento [deperi'mento] SM (di persona) wasting away; (di merci) deterioration; **il loro deperimento è dovuto a denutrizione** they are in a serious state because of malnutrition

deperire [depe'rire] /55/ VI (aus essere) (persona) to waste away; (pianta) to wilt; **ti trovo un po' deperito** you look rather run-down to me

depilare [depi'lare] /72/ VT to depilate; **depilarsi le sopracciglia** to pluck one's eyebrows; **depilarsi le gambe** (con rasoio) to shave one's legs; (con ceretta) to wax one's legs

depilatorio, -ria, -ri, -rie [depila'tɔrjo] AGG hair-removing attr, depilatory; **crema depilatoria** hair-removing cream ♦ SM (sostanza) hair-remover, depilatory

depilazione [depilat'tsjone] SF depilation, hair-removal

depistaggio, -gi [depis'taddʒo] SM: **un tentativo di depistaggio delle indagini** an attempt to throw the inquiry off the track

depistare [depis'tare] /72/ VT (polizia, autorità) to set on the wrong track

dépliant [depli'ã] SM INV leaflet; (opuscolo) brochure

deplorare [deplo'rare] /72/ VT (biasimare) to deplore; (perdita) to lament

deplorevole [deplo'revole], **deplorabile** [deplo'rabile] AGG deplorable

depone ecc [de'pone] VB vedi **deporre**

deporre [de'porre] VB IRREG /77/ VT **1** (gen, valigia) to put down; (fig: abbandonare: orgoglio, vecchio rancore) to put aside, forget; **deporre le armi** (Mil) to lay down arms **2** (rimuovere: persona) to remove; (: re) to depose; **lo deposero dalla carica** they removed him from office **3** (sogg: uccello): **deporre le uova** to lay eggs **4** (Dir): **deporre il vero** to tell the truth; **deporre il falso** to give false evidence ♦ VI (aus avere) (Dir) to testify

deportare [depor'tare] /72/ VT to deport

deportato, -a [depor'tato] SM, SF deportee

deportazione [deportat'tsjone] SF deportation

deposi ecc [de'posi] VB vedi **deporre**

depositante [depozi'tante] SM, SF (Comm) depositor

depositare [depozi'tare] /72/ VT **1** (gen, oggetto) to put down, lay down; (merci) to store; **depositare qc per terra** to put sth down; **ha depositato qui tutti i libri e se n'è andato** he dumped all his books here and left **2** (Banca) to deposit; **depositare una somma in banca** to pay a sum of money into the bank **3** (sogg: fiume, vino) to deposit ♦ VI (aus avere) (liquido) to leave some sediment; **depositarsi** VIP (sabbia, polvere) to settle

depositario, -ria, -ri, -rie [depozi'tarjo] SM, SF (gen) depository; (fig: confidente) repository; (: custode: di verità, tradizioni) custodian

deposito [de'pɔzito] SM **1** (atto): **il deposito della merce ci è costato molto** storing the goods cost us a lot; **il deposito dei bagagli è gratuito** there is no charge for left luggage **2** (di liquidi) sediment, deposit; (di acqua calcarea) fur, (lime) scale; **deposito alluvionale** drift **3** (Fin) deposit; **fare o eseguire un deposito** to put down o pay a deposit; **denaro in deposito** money on deposit; **deposito bancario** bank deposit; **deposito cauzionale** deposit **4** (magazzino) warehouse; (Mil: di autobus) depot; **lasciare in deposito** (merce) to store; **deposito bagagli** left-luggage office; **deposito di munizioni** ammunition dump

deposizione [depozit'tsjone] SF **1** (gen, anche Dir) deposition; (da una carica) removal; **fare una falsa deposizione** to perjure o.s. **2** (Arte, Rel): **la Deposizione** the Deposition

deposto, -a [de'posto] PP di **deporre**

depravare [depra'vare] /72/ VT to corrupt, pervert

depravato, -a [depra'vato] AGG depraved ♦ SM, SF degenerate

deprecare [depre'kare] /20/ VT to deplore, deprecate

depredare [depre'dare] /72/ VT to plunder, loot; **depredare qn di qc** to rob sb of sth

depressione [depres'sjone] SF **1** (in tutti i sensi) depression; **area** o **zona di depressione** (Meteor) area of low pressure; **essere in uno stato di depressione** (Med) to be depressed, be in a state of depression

depresso, -a [de'presso] PP di **deprimere** ♦ AGG depressed; **zona depressa** (Econ) depressed area

deprezzamento [deprettsa'mento] SM: **deprezzamento (di)** depreciation (of)

deprezzare [depret'tsare] /72/ VT to bring down the value of; **deprezzarsi** VIP to depreciate

deprimente [depri'mente] AGG depressing

deprimere [de'primere] VB IRREG /50/ VT to depress; **deprimersi** VIP to become depressed

depurare [depu'rare] /72/ VT (liquido) to purify; (sangue) to cleanse; **depurarsi** VIP (liquido) to be purified; (corpo) to be cleansed

depuratore, -trice [depura'tore] AGG purifying ♦ SM: **depuratore d'acqua** water purifier; **depuratore di gas** scrubber

deputato, -a [depu'tato] SM, SF **1** (*Pol*) deputy, ≈ member of Parliament (*Brit*), ≈ representative (*USA*), ≈ Congressman *o* Congresswoman (*USA*) **2** (*Amm*) delegate, representative

deputazione [deputat'tsjone] SF (*gruppo*) deputation, delegation

deragliamento [deraʎʎa'mento] SM derailment

deragliare [deraʎ'ʎare] /**27**/ VI (*aus* avere) to be derailed, go off the rails; **far deragliare un treno** to derail a train

derapare [dera'pare] /**72**/ VI (*aus* avere) (*veicolo, anche Aer*) to skid; (*Sci*) to sideslip

derattizzazione [derattiddzat'tsjone] SF rodent control

deregolamentare [deregolamen'tare] /**72**/ VT to deregulate

deregolamentazione [deregolamentat'tsjone] SF deregulation

derelitto, -a [dere'litto] AGG abandoned; (*casa*) derelict, abandoned ♦ SM, SF destitute person; **i derelitti** the destitute

deretano [dere'tano] SM (*fam*) backside

deridere [de'ridere] /**89**/ VT IRREG to mock, deride

derisi *ecc* [de'risi] VB *vedi* **deridere**

derisione [deri'zjone] SF mockery, derision

deriso, -a [de'rizo] PP *di* **deridere**

derisorio, -ria, -ri, -rie [deri'zɔrjo] AGG (*gesto, tono*) mocking

deriva [de'riva] SF **1** (*Aer, Naut*) drift; **andare alla deriva** (*anche fig*) to drift; **la deriva dei continenti** (*Geol*) continental drift **2** (*dispositivo: Aer*) fin; (: *Naut*) centreboard (*Brit*), centerboard (*USA*) **3** (*Naut: barca*) dinghy

derivare [deri'vare] /**72**/ VI (*aus* essere) **derivare da** to derive from; (*corso d'acqua*) to spring from; **questa parola deriva dal francese** this word is of French derivation; **da quella decisione non sono derivati altro che guai** nothing but trouble has come out of that decision ♦ VT **1** (*Chim, Gramm, Mat*) to derive; **"gas" deriva dalla parola greca "chaos"** "gas" derives from the Greek word "chaos"; **da ciò ha derivato che...** hence he concluded that ... **2** (*corso d'acqua*) to divert

derivato, -a [deri'vato] AGG derived ♦ SM (*Chim, Gramm*) derivative; (*prodotto*) by-product

derivazione [derivat'tsjone] SF (*gen*) derivation; (*di acque*) diversion; (*Elettr*) shunt; (*Telec*) extension (*in house*)

dermatite [derma'tite] SF dermatitis

dermatologia [dermatolo'dʒia] SF dermatology

dermatologo, -a, -gi, -ghe [derma'tɔlogo] SM, SF dermatologist

dermoprotettivo, -a [dermoprotet'tivo] AGG (*crema, trattamento*) protecting the skin

deroga, -ghe ['dɛroga] SF (*special*) dispensation; **in deroga a** as a (special) dispensation to; **è una norma che non ammette deroghe** there can be no exceptions to this rule

derogare [dero'gare] /**80**/ VI (*aus* avere) (*Dir*): **derogare a** to repeal in part

derrate [der'rate] SFPL: **derrate alimentari** foodstuffs

derubare [deru'bare] /**72**/ VT: **derubare qn di qc** to rob sb of sth; **lo hanno picchiato e derubato** he was attacked and robbed; **mi hanno derubato del portafoglio** I had my wallet stolen

descritto, -a [des'kritto] PP *di* **descrivere**

descrivere [des'krivere] /**105**/ VT IRREG (*in tutti i sensi*) to describe; **descrivere qc a qn** to describe sth to sb; **mi ha descritto ciò che aveva trovato** he described to me what he had found

descrizione [deskrit'tsjone] SF description; **fare una descrizione** to give a description

deserto, -a [de'zɛrto] AGG deserted; **le strade erano deserte** the streets were deserted; **isola deserta** desert island ♦ SM desert

desiderabile [deside'rabile] AGG desirable

desiderare [deside'rare] /**72**/ VT **1** (*volere*) to want, wish for; **desiderare (di) fare qc** to want *o* wish to do sth; **desidererei andarmene** I would like to leave; **desidero che lei venga domani** I'd like you to come tomorrow; **desiderava migliorare il suo inglese** he wanted to improve his English; **desidero parlarvi subito** I'd like to speak to you immediately;

desidera? (*in bar*) what would you like?; (*in negozio, ufficio*) can I help you?; **sei desiderato al telefono** you're wanted on the phone; **farsi desiderare** (*fare il prezioso*) to play hard to get; (*farsi aspettare*) to take one's time; **lascia molto a desiderare** it leaves a lot to be desired; **la casa lascia un po' a desiderare** the house is not ideal **2** (*sessualmente*) to desire

desiderio, -ri [desi'dɛrjo] SM (*gen*) wish; (*più intenso, carnale*) desire; **sentì il desiderio di andarsene** he felt a desire to leave; **esprimi un desiderio!** make a wish!

desideroso, -a [deside'roso] AGG: **desideroso di** longing *o* eager for

designare [desiɲ'pare] /**15**/ VT (*persona*) to designate, appoint; (*data, ora*) to fix; **la vittima designata** the intended victim

designazione [desiɲɲat'tsjone] SF designation, appointment

desinare [dezi'nare] (*toscano*) /**72**/ VI (*aus* avere) to dine, have dinner ♦ SM dinner

desinenza [dezi'nɛntsa] SF (*Gramm*) ending, inflexion

desistere [de'sistere] /**11**/ VI IRREG (*aus* avere) **desistere (da qc/dal fare qc)** to give up (sth/doing sth), desist from (doing sth) (*frm*)

desistito, -a [desis'tito] PP *di* **desistere**

desolante [dezo'lante] AGG distressing

desolato, -a [dezo'lato] AGG (*paesaggio*) desolate; (*persona: sconsolato*) distressed; **essere desolato (per qc)** (*spiacente*) to be terribly sorry (about sth); **sono desolato!** I'm terribly sorry!

desolazione [dezolat'tsjone] SF desolation

despota, -i ['dɛspota] SM despot

dessi *ecc* ['dessi] VB *vedi* **dare**

destabilizzare [destabilid'dzare] /**72**/ VT to destabilize

destare [des'tare] /**72**/ VT (*svegliare*) to wake (up); (*fig: dubbio, sospetti, pietà*) to arouse; (: *curiosità, invidia*) to arouse, to awaken; **destare la preoccupazione/la sorpresa di qn** to cause sb concern/surprise; **non destare il can che dorme** (*Proverbio*) let sleeping dogs lie; **destarsi** VIP to wake up

deste *ecc* ['deste] VB *vedi* **dare**

destinare [desti'nare] /**72**/ VT **1** (*designare*): **destinare qc a qn** to intend *o* mean sth for sb; **era destinato a morir giovane** he was destined *o* fated to die young; **la sorte che gli è stata destinata** the fate that was in store for him; **libri destinati ai bambini** books (written) for children **2** (*devolvere*): **destinare una somma all'acquisto di qc** to intend *o* use *o* earmark a sum to buy sth; **i fondi saranno destinati alla ricerca** the money will be used for research **3** (*assegnare*) to appoint, assign; **è destinato alla nuova filiale** he's been appointed to the new branch **4** (*indirizzare*) to address; **sai dov'è destinata la lettera?** do you know where the letter is going? **5** (*decidere*): **destinare un giorno a qc/a fare qc** to set aside a day for sth/to do sth; **in data da destinarsi** at some future date, at a date to be decided **6** (*Fin*) to ring-fence

destinatario, -ria, -ri, -rie [destina'tarjo] SM, SF (*di lettera*) addressee; (*di merce*) consignee; (*di mandato*) payee

destinazione [destinat'tsjone] SF destination; (*scopo*) purpose; **giungere a destinazione** to reach one's destination; **sono giunti a destinazione** they reached their destination

destino [des'tino] SM (*sorte*) fate, destiny; (*futuro*) destiny; **il mio destino** my destiny; **era destino che accadesse** it was fated *o* destined to happen

destituire [destitu'ire] /**55**/ VT (*funzionario*) to dismiss, remove

destituzione [destitut'tsjone] SF dismissal, removal

❑ **destituzione** non si traduce mai con la parola inglese *destitution*

desto, -a ['desto] AGG (*wide*) awake; **tener desto l'interesse del pubblico** to hold the public's attention; **sogno o son desto?** am I dreaming?

destra ['dɛstra] SF **1** (*mano*) right hand; **scrivo con la destra** I write with my right hand **2** (*parte*) right, right-hand side; **a destra** (*stato in luogo*) on the right; (*moto a luogo*) to the right; **a destra di** to the right of; **alla destra, nella foto...** on the right of the photograph ...; **corsia di destra** right-hand lane; **guida a destra** right-hand drive; **tenere la destra** to keep to the right; **voltare a destra** to turn right; **spostarsi verso destra** to move to the right **3** (*Pol*): **la destra** the right; **di destra** right-wing; **un partito di destra** a rightwing party

destreggiarsi [destred'dʒarsi] /**62**/ VIP to manoeuvre (*Brit*), maneuver (*USA*)

destrezza [des'trettsa] SF skill, dexterity

destro, -a ['dɛstro] AGG **1** (*mano, braccio*) right; (*lato*) righthand **2** (*persona: abile*) adroit, skilful (*Brit*), skillful (*USA*) ♦ SM (*Boxe*) right

desumere [de'sumere] /**12**/ VT IRREG (*dedurre*) to infer, deduce; (*trarre: informazioni*) to obtain; **desumo da ciò che te ne vuoi andare** I gather from this that you want to leave

desunto, -a [de'sunto] PP *di* **desumere**

detassare [detas'sare] /**72**/ VT to remove the duty (*o* tax) from

detenere [dete'nere] /**121**/ VT IRREG (*incarico, primato*) to hold; (*proprietà*) to have, possess; (*prigioniero*) to detain, hold

detengo *ecc* [de'tɛngo] VB *vedi* **detenere**

detentivo, -a [deten'tivo] AGG: **pena detentiva** prison sentence

detentore, -trice [deten'tore] SM, SF (*di titolo, primato*) holder

detenuto, -a [dete'nuto] SM, SF prisoner

detenzione [deten'tsjone] SF **1** (*di titolo, primato*) holding; (*di armi, stupefacenti*) possession **2** (*Dir*) detention

detergente [deter'dʒɛnte] AGG (*gen*) detergent; (*crema, latte*) cleansing *attr*; **latte detergente** cleansing milk ♦ SM (*detersivo*) detergent; (*cosmetico*) cleanser

detergere [de'tɛrdʒere] /**111**/ VT IRREG (*gen*) to clean; (*pelle, viso*) to cleanse; (*sudore*) to wipe (away)

deterioramento [deterjora'mento] SM: **deterioramento (di)** deterioration (in)

deteriorare [deterjo'rare] /**72**/ VT (*macchinari, merce*) to damage, cause to deteriorate; (*alimenti*) to spoil, cause to go bad; **deteriorarsi** VIP (*vedi vt*) to deteriorate; to go bad

deteriore [dete'rjore] AGG (*merce*) second-rate; (*significato*) pejorative

determinante [determi'nante] AGG decisive, determining

determinare [determi'nare] /**72**/ VT (*gen*) to determine; (*causare*) to bring about, cause

determinativo, -a [determina'tivo] AGG determining; **articolo determinativo** (*Gramm*) definite article

determinato, -a [determi'nato] AGG **1** (*gen*) certain; (*particolare*) specific; **in determinate circostanze** in certain circumstances **2** (*risoluto*) determined, resolute; **è molto determinato** he's very determined

determinazione [determinat'tsjone] SF (*atto*) determining; (*decisione*) decision; (*risolutezza*) determination; **determinazione dei costi** (*Econ*) costing

deterrente [deter'rente] AGG, SM deterrent

deterrò *ecc* [deter'rɔ] VB *vedi* **detenere**

detersivo [deter'sivo] SM (*gen*) detergent; (*per bucato*) washing powder (*Brit*), soap powder; **un detersivo neutro** a mild detergent; **detersivo per bucato a mano** hand-washing powder/liquid; **detersivo per lavatrice** detergent for use in washing machines; **detersivo per i pavimenti** floor cleaner; **detersivo per i piatti** washing-up liquid

deterso, -a [de'tɛrso] PP *di* **detergere**

detestare [detes'tare] /**72**/ VT to detest, hate, loathe; **lo detesto!** I detest him!; **detesto mentire** I hate lying

detiene *ecc* [de'tjɛne] VB *vedi* **detenere**

detonare [deto'nare] /**72**/ VI (*aus avere*) to detonate, explode

detonatore [detona'tore] SM detonator

detonazione [detonat'tsjone] SF (*di esplosivo*) detonation, explosion; (*di arma*) bang; (*di motore*) knocking, pinking (*Brit*)

detrae *ecc* [de'trae] VB *vedi* **detrarre**

detrarre [de'trarre] /**123**/ VT IRREG: **detrarre (da)** to deduct (from), take away (from)

detrassi *ecc* [de'trassi] VB *vedi* **detrarre**

detratto, -a [de'tratto] PP *di* **detrarre**

detrazione [detrat'tsjone] SF deduction; **detrazione d'imposta** tax allowance

detrimento [detri'mento] SM: **a detrimento di** to the detriment of

detrito [de'trito] SM (*Geol*) detritus; (*fluviale*) silt, alluvium

detronizzare [detronid'dzare] /**72**/ VT (*anche fig*) to dethrone

detta ['detta] SF: **a detta di** according to; **a detta sua** according to him (*o* her)

dettagliante [dettaʎ'ʎante] SM, SF (*Comm*) retailer, retail dealer

dettagliare [dettaʎ'ʎare] /**27**/ VT (*racconto, descrizione*) to detail, give full details of

dettagliatamente [dettaʎʎata'mente] AVV in detail

dettaglio, -gli [det'taʎʎo] SM **1** detail; **in dettaglio** in detail; **entrare o scendere nei dettagli** to go into details *o* particulars **2** (*Comm*): **al dettaglio** (*prezzo, vendita*) retail; **prezzo al dettaglio** retail price; **vendere al dettaglio** to (sell) retail

dettame [det'tame] SM dictate

dettare [det'tare] /**72**/ VT (*lettera, condizioni*) to dictate; **dettare legge** (*fig*) to lay down the law; **fa' come ti detta il cuore** follow your heart

dettato [det'tato] SM dictation

dettatura [detta'tura] SF dictation; **scrivere qc sotto dettatura** to take sth down from dictation; **l'ha scritto sotto dettatura** it was dictated to him

detto, -a ['detto] PP *di* **dire** ♦ AGG **1** (*Amm, Comm*: *suddetto*) above-mentioned, aforementioned; **detti prodotti vi saranno consegnati in settimana** the above-mentioned products will be delivered to you by the end of the week; **nel detto giorno** on that day **2** (*soprannominato*) called, known as **3** (*fraseologia*): **detto fatto** no sooner said than done; **è presto detto!** it's easier said than done!; **come non detto** let's forget it ♦ SM (*motto*) saying; **un detto cinese** a Chinese saying

deturpare [detur'pare] /**72**/ VT (*anche fig*) to disfigure; (*moralmente*) to sully

devastante [devas'tante] AGG (*anche fig*) devastating

devastare [devas'tare] /**72**/ VT to devastate; (*fig: sogg: malattia*) to ravage

devastazione [devastat'tsjone] SF devastation, destruction

deviare [devi'are] /**19**/ VI (*aus avere*) (*veicolo*): **deviare (da)** to turn off (from); (*pallone*) to deflect; **il viale devia dal corso principale** the avenue leads off the main road; **deviare dalla retta via** to go astray ♦ VT (*traffico, fiume, conversazione*) to divert; (*proiettile, colpo, pallone*) to deflect; **il traffico è stato deviato** the traffic has been diverted; **deviare qn dalla retta via** to lead sb astray

deviato, -a [devi'ato] AGG (*fig: organizzazione*) corrupt, bent (*fam*)

deviazione [deviat'tsjone] SF (*gen*) deviation; (*Aut*) diversion; **fare una deviazione** to make a detour; **deviazione della colonna vertebrale** curvature of the spine

devo *ecc* ['devo] VB *vedi* **dovere**

devoluto, -a [devo'luto] PP *di* **devolvere**

devoluzione [devolut'tsjone] SF **1** (*di beni*) transfer **2** (*Pol*) devolution

devolvere [de'volvere] /**94**/ VT IRREG (*somma*) to transfer; **devolvere qc in beneficenza** to give sth to charity

devoto, -a [de'vɔto] AGG (*Rel*) devout, pious; (*affezionato*) devoted ♦ SM, SF devout person; **i devoti** (*i fedeli*) the faithful

devozione [devot'tsjone] SF (*Rel*) devoutness; (*affetto, dedizione*) devotion; **avere una devozione per qn** to worship sb; **dire/fare le devozioni** (*Rel: preghiere*) to say/make one's devotions

dezip'pare [dedzip'pare] /**72**/ VT (*Inform*) to unzip

dg ABBR (= *decigrammo*) dg

PAROLA CHIAVE

di [di] *di + il* = **del**, *di + lo* = **dello**, *di + l'* = **dell'**, *di + la* = **della**, *di + i* = **dei**, *di + gli* = **degli**, *di + le* = **delle** PREP

1 (*possesso*) of; (*composto da, scritto da*) by; **la macchina del mio amico/dei miei amici** my friend's/friends' car; **la figlia dell'amica di mia madre** the daughter of my mother's friend, my mother's friend's daughter; **una commedia di Goldoni** a play by Goldoni; **l'ultimo libro di Umberto Eco** Umberto Eco's latest book, the latest book by Umberto Eco

2 (*specificazione, denominazione*) of; **il sindaco di Milano** the mayor of Milan; **il mese di marzo** the month of March; **la vita di campagna** country life; **tavolo di cucina** kitchen table; **sala di lettura** reading-room; **il direttore dell'azienda** the manager of the company; **il professore d'inglese** the English teacher, the teacher of English; **il nome di Maria** the name Mary

3 (*materiale*): **fatto di legno** made of wood; **una casa di mattoni** a brick house, a house made of brick(s); **un'orologio d'oro** a gold watch; **un sacchetto di plastica** a plastic bag **4** (*provenienza*) from, out of; (*posizione*) in, on; **uscire di casa** to come out of *o* leave the house; **i negozi di Milano** the Milan shops, the shops in Milan; **i vicini del piano di sopra** the upstairs neighbours, the people who live on the floor above us; **sono di Roma** I am *o* come from Rome

5 (*tempo*): **di domenica** on Sundays; **d'estate** in (the) summer; **di giorno** by day, during the day; **di mattina** in the morning; **di notte** by night; at night; in the night; **di sera** in the evening

6 (*misura*): **un bimbo di 2 anni** a 2-year-old child, a child of two; **un viaggio di 100 chilometri** a 100-kilometre journey; **un chilo di farina** a kilo of flour; **un viaggio di 2 giorni** a 2-day journey; **un milione di euro** a million euro; **una stanza di 2 metri per 3** a room measuring 2 metres by 3; **un gioiello di valore** a valuable piece of jewellery; **un bicchiere di vino** a glass of wine

7 (*mezzo, modo, causa*): **vestirsi di bianco** to dress in white; **fermarsi di botto** to stop dead *o* suddenly; **rispondere di brutto** to answer brusquely; **è debole di cuore** he has a weak heart; **urlare di dolore** to scream with pain; **ridere di gusto** to laugh heartily; **morire di cancro** to die of cancer; **spalmare di burro** to spread with butter; **sporcare qc di sugo** to get sauce on sth

8 (*argomento*) about, of; **discutere del tempo** to talk about the weather; **trattato di medicina** medical treatise; **parlare di qc** to talk about sth; **libro di storia** history book

9 (*abbondanza, privazione*): **pieno di** full of; **povero di carbone** poor in coal; **privo di** lacking in; **ricco di risorse naturali** rich in natural resources

10 (*paragone nei comparativi*) than; (*paragone nei superlativi*) of; **il migliore della classe** the best in the class; **è meglio di me** he's better than me; **è il migliore di tutti** he is the best of all; **il migliore dei suoi libri** his best book, the best of his books; **il migliore della città** the best in the city

11 (*seguito da infinito*): **sa di aver sbagliato** he knows (that) he did the wrong thing; **credo di capire** I think (that) I understand; **ti chiedo di dirmi la verità** I beg you to tell me the truth; **è degno di esser ricordato** it's worth remembering; **tentò di scappare** he tried to escape

♦ ART PARTITIVO (*affermativo*) some; (*negativo*) any; (*interrogativo*) any, some; **vuoi dei biscotti?** would you like some biscuits?, do you want any biscuits?; **non ho dei libri** I haven't any books, I have no books; **non vedo niente di meglio** I can't see anything better; **c'erano delle persone che non conoscevo** there were some people I didn't know; **ho dei soldi** I've got some money; **non c'è nulla di strano** there's nothing odd about it; **c'è del vero in quello che dici** there's some truth in what you say; **vuoi del vino?** would you like some wine?, do you want any wine?

dì [di] SM (*letter*) day; **buon dì!** good day (to you)!; **a dì = addì**

DIA [ˈdia] SIGLA F = **Direzione Investigativa Antimafia**

diabete [diaˈbɛte] SM diabetes *sg*

diabetico, -a, -ci, -che [diaˈbɛtiko] AGG, SM, SF diabetic

diabolico, -a, -ci, -che [djaˈbɔliko] AGG (*anche fig*) diabolical

diacono [diˈakono] SM (*Rel*) deacon

diadema, -i [diaˈdɛma] SM (*di sovrano*) diadem; (*di donna*) tiara

diafano, -a [diˈafano] AGG diaphanous; (*fig: mani, volto*) transparent

diaframma, -i [diaˈframma] SM (*Anat, Fot*) diaphragm; (*contraccettivo*) diaphragm, Dutch cap; (*schermo*) screen

diagnosi [diˈaɲɲozi] SF INV (*anche fig*) diagnosis *sg*; **diagnosi prenatale** prenatal diagnosis

diagnosticare [diaɲɲostiˈkare] /20/ VT (*anche fig*) to diagnose

diagnostico, -a, -ci, -che [djaɲˈɲɔstiko] AGG diagnostic; **aiuti diagnostici** (*Inform*) debugging aids ♦ SM diagnostician

diagonale [diagoˈnale] AGG (*motivo, disegno*) diagonal; **in linea diagonale** diagonally; **tessuto diagonale** twill; **tiro diagonale** (*Calcio*) cross ♦ SF diagonal; **in diagonale** diagonally ♦ SM **1** (*Calcio*) cross; (*Tennis*) crosscourt shot; **diagonale incrociato** (*Tennis*) return crosscourt shot

diagramma, -i [diaˈgramma] SM (*gen, anche Mat*) diagram; (*grafico*) chart, graph; **diagramma a barre** bar chart; **diagramma di flusso** flow chart; **diagramma a torta** pie chart

dialettale [dialetˈtale] AGG dialectal; **poesia dialettale** poetry in dialect

dialetto [diaˈletto] SM dialect

dialisi [diˈalizi] SF INV (*Chim, Med*) dialysis *sg*

dialogante [dialoˈgante] AGG: **unità dialogante** (*Inform*) interactive terminal

dialogare [dialoˈgare] /80/ VI (*aus avere*) **dialogare (con)** to have a dialogue (*Brit*) *o* dialog (*USA*) (with); (*conversare*) to converse (with) ♦ VT (*scena*) to write the dialogue (*Brit*) *o* dialog (*USA*) for

dialogo, -ghi [diˈalogo] SM dialogue (*Brit*), dialog (*USA*); **tra noi non c'è più dialogo** we don't talk anymore

diamante [diaˈmante] SM **1** (*gen*) diamond; (*di diamante*) diamond *attr*; **un anello con diamante** a diamond ring; **nozze di diamante** diamond wedding anniversary **2** (*Naut: di ancora*) crown

diametro [diˈametro] SM diameter

diamine [ˈdjamine] ESCL: **che diamine?** what on earth?

diapositiva [diapoziˈtiva] SF slide, transparency

diaria [diˈarja] SF daily (expense) allowance

diario, -ri [diˈarjo] SM (*gen*) diary, journal; **tenere un diario** to keep a diary; **diario di bordo** (*Naut*) log(book); **diario di classe** (*Scol*) class register; **diario degli esami** (*Scol*) exam timetable; **diario scolastico** homework diary

diarrea [diarˈrea] SF diarrhoea (*Brit*), diarrhea (*USA*)

diatriba [diˈatriba] SF diatribe

diavoleria [djavoleˈria] SF **1** (*azione*) act *o* piece of mischief **2** (*aggeggio*) weird contraption

diavolo [ˈdjavolo] SM **1** devil; **povero diavolo!** poor devil!; **è un buon diavolo** he's a good sort; **avere un diavolo per capello** to be in a foul temper; **avere il diavolo in corpo** (*bambino*) to have the devil in one; (*adulto*) to be fidgety; **avere una fame/un freddo del diavolo** to be ravenously hungry/frozen stiff; **mandare qn al diavolo** (*fam*) to tell sb to go to hell; **l'ho mandato al diavolo** I told him to go to hell; **va al diavolo!** (*fam*) go to hell!; **fare il diavolo a quattro** to kick up a fuss **2 diavolo!** for goodness' sake!; **che diavolo vuoi?** what the hell do you want?; **dove diavolo è finito?** where the hell has it (*o* he) got to? **3** (*Zool*): **diavolo orsino** Tasmanian devil

dibattere [diˈbattere] /1/ VT (*argomento*) to debate, discuss; **dibattersi** VR (*anche fig*) to struggle, wrestle; **dibattersi tra mille difficoltà** to have to contend with a host of difficulties; **dibattersi nel dubbio** to be racked by indecision

dibattimento [dibattiˈmento] SM (*dibattito*) debate, discussion; (*Dir*) hearing

dibattito [diˈbattito] SM (*gen*) debate, discussion; (*in parlamento*) debate

dic. ABBR (= *dicembre*) Dec

dicastero [dikasˈtero] SM ministry

dice ecc VB *vedi* **dire**

dicembre [diˈtʃembre] SM December; *vedi* **luglio**

diceria [ditʃeˈria] SF rumour (*Brit*), rumor (*USA*), piece of gossip; **sono solo dicerie** it's just gossip

dichiarare [dikjaˈrare] /72/ VT (*gen*) to declare; (*annunciare*) to announce; **dichiarare guerra (a)** to declare war (on); **dichiarare qn colpevole** to declare sb guilty; **si dichiara che...** it is hereby declared that ...; **il portavoce ha dichiarato che...** the spokesman said that ...; **vi dichiaro marito e moglie** I pronounce you man and wife; **articoli da dichiarare** (*Dogana*) goods to declare; **nulla da dichiarare** (*Dogana*) nothing to declare; **dichiararsi** VR **1** to declare o.s.; **dichiararsi soddisfatto** to declare o.s. satisfied; **dichiararsi a favore di/contro** to declare o.s. *o* come out in favour of/against; **dichiararsi colpevole/non colpevole** to plead guilty/not guilty; **dichiararsi vinto** to

acknowledge defeat **2** (*innamorato*) to declare one's love
dichiarato, -a [dikja'rato] AGG (*nemico, ateo*) avowed; (*cocainomane, anarchico*) self-confessed
dichiarazione [dikjarat'tsjone] SF (*proclamazione*) declaration; (*discorso, commento*) statement; **ha rilasciato una dichiarazione alla polizia** he made a statement to the police; **dichiarazione (d'amore)** declaration of love; **le ha fatto una dichiarazione d'amore** he told her he loved her; **dichiarazione doganale** customs declaration; **dichiarazione di guerra** declaration of war; **dichiarazione d'indipendenza** declaration of independence; **dichiarazione dei redditi** statement of income; (*modulo*) tax return
diciannove [dit∫an'nɔve] AGG INV, SM INV nineteen
diciannovenne [dit∫anno'venne] AGG, SM, SF nineteen-year-old
diciassette [dit∫as'sette] AGG INV, SM INV seventeen
diciassettenne [dit∫asset'tɛnne] AGG, SM, SF seventeen-year-old
diciottenne [dit∫ot'tenne] AGG, SM, SF eighteen-year-old
diciotto [di't∫ɔtto] AGG INV eighteen ♦ SM INV eighteen; (*Univ*) *minimum (pass) mark awarded in Italian universities for any individual exam*
dicitura [dit∫i'tura] SF wording, words *pl*
dico *ecc* ['diko] VB *vedi* **dire**
didascalia [didaska'lia] SF (*di illustrazione*) caption; (*Teatro*) stage directions *pl*; (*Cine*) subtitle; (*in film muto*) title
didattico, -a, -ci, -che [di'dattiko] AGG (*gen*) didactic; (*programma, metodo*) teaching; (*centro, libro*) educational
didentro [di'dentro] SM INV (*gen*) inside; (*di casa, auto*) interior; **dal didentro** from inside
didietro [di'djetro] SM INV (*di casa*) rear, back; (*euf*) bottom; **dal didietro** from behind
dieci ['djet∫i] AGG INV ten ♦ SM INV ten; **dare un dieci a qn** (*voto*) to give sb ten out of ten
diecimila [djet∫i'mila] AGG INV, SM INV ten thousand
diecina [dje't∫ina] SF = **decina**
diedi *ecc* ['djedi] VB *vedi* **dare**
dieresi [di'erezi] SF INV dieresis *sg*
diesel ['dizzəl] AGG INV, SM INV (*motore, automobile*) diesel; **motore diesel** diesel engine; **macchina diesel** diesel car
diessino, -a [dies'sino](*Pol*) AGG of (*o* belonging to) the Democrats of the Left (*Italian left-wing party*) ♦ SM, SF *member (o supporter) of Democrats of the Left*
dieta ['djeta] SF **1** diet; **essere *o* stare a dieta** to be on a diet; **mettersi a dieta** to diet, go on a diet; **rompere la dieta** to break one's diet **2** (*Storia*) diet, Diet
dietetica [die'tetika] SF dietetics *sg*
dietologo, -a, -gi, -ghe [dje'tɔlogo] SM, SF dietician
dietro ['djetro] AVV behind; (*in fondo: di gruppo, stanza*) at the back; **qua/là dietro** behind here/there; **dev'essere qua dietro** it must be behind here; **abita qua dietro** he lives round the corner; **2 file dietro** 2 rows (further) back; **vestito che si abbottona dietro** dress which buttons at the back; **non guardar dietro** don't look back; **guarda se arriva qualcuno (da) dietro** look and see if anyone is coming up behind us; **ti metti tu dietro?** (*in macchina*) are you going to go in the back?; **essere seduto dietro** (*in macchina*) to be sitting in the back; (*in autobus*) to be sitting at the back; **la firma è dietro** the signature is on the back; **attacca il foglio dietro** attach the sheet to the back; **passa dietro!** go round the back!; **di dietro** (*gen*) back; (*entrare, stare*) at the back; **la porta di dietro** the back door; **zampe di dietro** hind legs; **il sedile di dietro** the back seat; **da dietro** (*assalire*) from behind, from the rear; **da dietro non ti ho riconosciuto** I didn't recognize you from the back ♦ PREP **1** (*anche:* **dietro a: posizione**) behind; **era dietro alla scrivania** he was behind his desk; **dietro la casa/il banco** behind the house/the counter; **dietro la porta** behind the door; **dietro l'angolo** round the corner; **dietro di *o* a lui/lei** behind him/her; **sono seduti dietro di me** they're sitting behind me; **guarda cosa c'è scritto dietro il foglio** look what is written on the other side of the page; **camminare uno dietro l'altro** to walk one behind the other *o* in single file; **andare dietro a** (*anche fig*) to follow; **stare dietro a qn** (*sorvegliare*) to keep an eye on sb; (*corteggiare*) to hang around sb; **portarsi dietro qn/qc** to

bring sb/sth with one, bring sb/sth along; **gli hanno riso/parlato dietro** they laughed at/talked about him behind his back **2** (*anche: dietro a: dopo*) after; **uno dietro l'altro** (*dopo*) one after the other; (*in fila*) one behind the other; **sono arrivati uno dietro l'altro** they arrived one after the other **3** (*Amm, Comm*): **dietro pagamento/consegna** on payment/delivery; **dietro ricevuta di pagamento** on receipt of payment; **dietro richiesta** (*orale*) on demand, upon request; (*scritta*) on application ♦ SM INV (*di foglio, quadro, giacca*) back; (*di casa*) back, rear; (*di pantaloni*) seat ♦ AGG INV (*vedi sm*): **la parte dietro** the back; the rear; the seat; **le file dietro** the back rows
dietro front ['djetro 'front] ESCL about turn! (*Brit*), about face! (*USA*) ♦ SM INV (*Mil*) about-turn, about-face; (*fig*) volte-face, about-turn, about-face; **fare dietro front**; (*Mil*, *anche fig*) to about-turn, about-face; (*tornare indietro*) to turn (a)round; **dietro front da fermo** (*Sci*) kick turn
difatti [di'fatti] CONG in fact, as a matter of fact
difendere [di'fɛndere] VB IRREG **/36/** VT (*gen, anche Dir: proteggere*) to defend; (: *opinioni*) to defend, stand up for, uphold; (: *dal freddo*) to protect; **difendere gli interessi di qn** to look after sb's interests; **sapersi difendere** to know how to look after o.s.; **difendersi** VR **1** (*proteggersi*): **difendersi (da/contro)** to defend o.s. (from/against); **difendersi dal freddo** to protect o.s. from the cold **2** (*cavarsela*) to get by; **in matematica mi difendo** I get by in mathematics
difensivo, -a [difen'sivo] AGG defensive
difensore [difen'sore] SM, SF (*gen*) defender; (*di moralità*) upholder; (*Dir*) counsel for the defence ♦ AGG: **avvocato difensore** defence counsel, defense lawyer (*USA*), counsel for the defence (*Brit*) *o* defense (*USA*)
difesa [di'fesa] SF (*gen, anche Mil, Dir, Sport*) defence (*Brit*), defense (*USA*); **senza difese** defenceless; **per legittima difesa** in self-defence; **prendere le difese di qn** to defend sb, take sb's part; **la parola alla difesa** (*Dir*) the defence may speak; **giocare in difesa** (*Sport*) to play in defence; **Ministro/Ministero della Difesa** Minister/Ministry of Defence; **la difesa dell'ambiente** protection of the environment
difesi *ecc* [di'fesi] VB *vedi* **difendere**
difeso, -a [di'feso] PP *di* **difendere**
difettare [difet'tare] **/72/** VI (*aus avere*) **1** (*essere difettoso*) to be defective **2** (*mancare*): **difettare di** to be lacking in, lack
difettivo, -a [difet'tivo] AGG (*Gramm*) defective
difetto [di'fɛtto] SM **1** (*imperfezione: di fabbricazione*) fault, flaw, defect; (: *morale*) fault, failing, defect; (: *fisico*) defect; **ha molti difetti** he has many faults; **è senza difetti** (*persona*) he has no faults; **l'arroganza è il suo difetto** pride is his failing; **difetto di pronuncia** speech defect **2** (*mancanza*): **difetto di luce** lack of; **se la memoria non mi fa difetto** if my memory serves me well
difettoso, -a [difet'toso] AGG defective, faulty, imperfect
diffamare [diffa'mare] **/72/** VT (*a parole*) to slander; (*per iscritto*) to libel
diffamatorio, -ria, -ri, -rie [diffama'tɔrjo] AGG (*vedi vb*) slanderous; libellous (*Brit*), libelous (*USA*)
diffamazione [diffamat'tsjone] SF (*vedi vb*) slander; libel
differente [diffe'rɛnte] AGG: **differente (da)** different (from)
differenza [diffe'rɛntsa] SF **1** (*diversità*): **non c'è alcuna differenza** there's no difference; **differenza (di)** difference (in); **differenza di età** age difference, difference in age; **una differenza di prezzo** a difference in price; **non fare differenza (tra)** to make no distinction (between); **a differenza di** unlike; **a differenza del calcio qui il rugby non è molto diffuso** unlike football, rugby isn't very popular here; **con la differenza che...** with the difference that ...; **non fa differenza che venga o meno** it makes no difference whether he comes or not **2** (*Mat*) difference; **differenza di potenziale** (*Mat, Fis*) potential difference
differenziale [differen'tsjale] AGG differential ♦ SM (*Aut, Mat*) differential
differenziare [differen'tsjare] **/19/** VT to differentiate; **differenziarsi** VIP (*essere differente*) to be different, differ; (*diventare differente*) to become different
differire [diffe'rire] **/55/** VT (*gen*) to defer, postpone, put off; **differire qc di un mese** to postpone *o* defer sth for a month ♦ VI (*aus essere*) (*essere differente*): **differire (da/in)** to differ

(from/in), be different (from/in); **differire per grandezza** to differ *o* be different in size

differita [diffeˈrita] SF: **in differita** (*trasmettere*) prerecorded

difficile [difˈfitʃile] AGG **1** (*problema, lavoro, periodo*) difficult; (*situazione*) difficult, awkward; **un esercizio difficile** a difficult exercise; **difficile da fare** difficult *o* hard to do; **sta attraversando momenti difficili** he's going through a difficult period; **non farla tanto difficile** don't make it more difficult than it is **2** (*persona: intrattabile*) difficult, awkward; (: *nei gusti*) fussy; **un carattere difficile** an awkward character; **difficile da accontentare** hard to please; **essere difficile nel mangiare** to be fussy about one's food **3** (*improbabile*) unlikely; **è difficile che venga** he's unlikely to come ♦ SM, SF: **fare il (la) difficile** to be difficult, be awkward ♦ SM difficulty, difficult part; **il difficile è finire in tempo** the difficulty lies in finishing in time, the problem is getting finished in time; **ora che il difficile è fatto...** now that the difficult part has been done ...

difficilmente [diffitʃilˈmente] AVV **1** (*con difficoltà*) with difficulty **2** (*con scarsa. probabilità*): **difficilmente verrà** he's unlikely to come; **verrai? — difficilmente** will you come? — probably not

difficoltà [diffikolˈta] SF INV difficulty; **non arrenderti alla prima difficoltà** don't give up at the first difficulty; **difficoltà finanziarie** financial difficulties; **trovare difficoltà a fare qc** to find it difficult to do sth; **fare delle difficoltà** to make difficulties, raise objections; **trovarsi in difficoltà** to have problems

difficoltoso, -a [diffikolˈtoso] AGG (*compito*) difficult, hard; (*persona*) difficult, hard to please; **digestione difficoltosa** poor digestion

diffida [difˈfida] SF (*Dir*) notice, warning

diffidare [diffiˈdare] /72/ VI (*aus* **avere**) (*sospettare*): **diffidare di** to distrust, be suspicious *o* distrustful of; **diffido di lui** don't trust him ♦ VT (*Dir*): **diffidare qn dal fare qc** to warn sb not to do sth, caution sb against doing sth

diffidente [diffiˈdente] AGG: **diffidente (nei confronti di)** distrustful (of), suspicious (of); **è diffidente nei miei confronti** he's suspicious of me

❏ **diffidente** non si traduce mai con la parola inglese *diffident*

diffidenza [diffiˈdentsa] SF distrust, suspicion; **con diffidenza** suspiciously

❏ **diffidenza** non si traduce mai con la parola inglese *diffidence*

diffondere [difˈfondere] VB IRREG /25/ VT (*luce, calore*) to give out, spread, diffuse (*frm*); (*malattia, idea, notizie, scritto*) to spread, circulate; **la notizia è stata diffusa per radio** the news was broadcast *o* given out on the radio; **diffondersi** VIP (*anche fig*) to spread

diffusi *ecc* [difˈfuzi] VB *vedi* **diffondere**

diffusione [diffuˈzjone] SF (*gen*) diffusion; (*di giornale*) circulation; (*di cultura, religione, malattia*) spread; (*Fis*) scattering

diffuso, -a [difˈfuzo] PP *di* **diffondere** ♦ AGG **1** (*notizia, malattia*) widespread; **un'usanza diffusa** a common custom; **è opinione diffusa che...** it's widely held that ... **2** (*Fis*) diffuse; **luce diffusa** diffused light

difilato [difiˈlato] AVV (*subito*) straightaway, straight away; (*direttamente*) straight, directly; **ho lavorato per 8 ore difilato** I worked 8 hours without a break

difterite [difteˈrite] SF (*Med*) diphtheria

diga, -ghe [ˈdiga] SF (*sbarramento*) dam, dyke (*against flooding*); (*portuale*) breakwater

digerente [didʒeˈrente] AGG digestive

digerire [didʒeˈrire] /55/ VT (*cibo, anche fig: nozioni*) to digest; (: *insulto*) to stomach, put up with; **ci vogliono otto ore per digerire** it takes eight hours to digest; **non ho digerito bene** I've got indigestion

digestione [didʒesˈtjone] SF digestion

digestivo, -a [didʒesˈtivo] AGG digestive ♦ SM (after-dinner) liqueur

Digione [diˈdʒone] SF Dijon

digitale [didʒiˈtale] AGG (*Anat, Tecn*) digital; **impronta digitale** fingerprint; **orologio digitale** digital watch; **radio/TV digitale** digital radio/TV ♦ SF (*Bot*) foxglove ♦ SM (*settore*)

digital sector; **digitale terrestre** digital terrestrial

digitare [ˈdidʒiˈtare] /72/ VT (*dati*) to key (in)

digiunare [didʒuˈnare] /72/ VI (*aus* **avere**) (*gen, anche Rel*) to fast; **digiunare per protesta** to go on hunger strike

digiuno, -a [diˈdʒuno] SM fast, fasting; **alcune diete prevedono il digiuno** some diets involve fasting; **a digiuno** on an empty stomach; **sono a digiuno** I haven't eaten; **stare a digiuno** to fast; **è una medicina da prendersi a digiuno** this medicine should be taken before meals ♦ AGG: **digiuno di** (*fig: cognizioni*) ignorant of; **sono completamente digiuno di informatica** I haven't a clue about computers, I don't know anything about computers

dignità [diɲɲiˈta] SF dignity

dignitario, -ri [diɲɲiˈtarjo] SM dignitary

dignitoso, -a [diɲɲiˈtoso] AGG (*contegno, abito*) dignified; (*fig: stipendio*) decent

DIGOS [ˈdigos] SIGLA F (= *Divisione Investigazioni Generali e Operazioni Speciali*) police department dealing with political security, ≈ Special Branch

digressione [digresˈsjone] SF digression

digrignare [digriɲˈɲare] /15/ VT: **digrignare i denti** (*animale*) to bare its teeth; (*persona*) to grind one's teeth

dilagare [dilaˈgare] /80/ VI (*aus* **essere**) to overflow, flood; (*fig: corruzione*) to spread, be rampant; (: *malattia*) to spread

dilaniare [dilaˈnjare] /19/ VT to tear to pieces; **era dilaniato dal rimorso** (*fig*) he was overwhelmed by remorse

dilapidare [dilapiˈdare] /72/ VT to squander

dilatare [dilaˈtare] VT (*pupille*) to dilate; (*stomaco*) to dilate, cause to expand; (*gas, metallo*) to cause to expand; (*tubo, buco*) to enlarge; (*passaggio, cavità*) to open (up); **dilatarsi** VIP (*vedi vt*) to dilate; to expand; to become enlarged; to open up

dilatazione [dilataˈtsjone] SF (*Anat*) dilation; (*di gas, metallo*) expansion

dilazionare [dilattsjoˈnare] /72/ VT to defer, delay

dilazione [dilatˈtsjone] SF deferment

dileggiare [diledˈdʒare] /62/ VT to mock, scoff at, deride

dileguare [dileˈgware] /72/ VT to dispel, disperse; **il vento ha dileguato le nubi** the wind has dispersed the clouds; **dileguarsi** VIP (*nebbia*) to disperse; (*fig: dubbio, persona*) to vanish, disappear

dilemma, -i [diˈlemma] SM dilemma

dilettante [diletˈtante] AGG amateur *attr*; (*pegg*) amateur *attr*, dilettante *attr*; **un fotografo dilettante** an amateur photographer ♦ SM, SF (*vedi agg*) amateur; dilettante

dilettare [diletˈtare] /72/ VT **1** (*dar piacere*) to delight, please, give pleasure to; **mi dilettava l'idea di partire** the thought of going away was a delight **2** (*intrattenere*) to amuse, entertain; **dilettarsi** VIP: **dilettarsi a fare qc** to delight *o* take pleasure in doing sth, enjoy doing sth; **dilettarsi di qc** to have sth as a hobby; **si diletta di pittura** painting is a hobby of his

dilettevole [diletˈtevole] AGG delightful

diletto¹, -a [diˈletto] AGG beloved ♦ SM, SF beloved, loved one

diletto² [diˈletto] SM delight, pleasure; **trarre diletto da** to take pleasure *o* delight in; **per diletto** for pleasure

diligente [diliˈdʒente] AGG (*scrupoloso*) diligent, hard-working, assiduous; (*accurato*) careful, accurate; **un alunno diligente** a hard-working student

diligenza¹ [diliˈdʒentsa] SF (*qualità*) diligence

diligenza² [diliˈdʒentsa] SF (*carrozza*) stagecoach

diluire [diluˈire] /55/ VT (*gen, liquidi*) to dilute; (*vernice*) to thin (down); (*polverina, medicina*) to dissolve

dilungarsi [dilunˈgarsi] /80/ VIP to talk at length; **dilungarsi in una descrizione** to go into a detailed description

diluviare [diluˈvjare] /19/ VB IMPERS (*aus* **avere** *o* **essere**) to pour (down), rain hard; **sta diluviando** it's pouring

diluvio, -vi [diˈluvjo] SM (*pioggia*) downpour, deluge; (*fig: di insulti*) torrent; **ieri c'è stato un diluvio** there was torrential rain yesterday; **il diluvio universale** the Flood

dimagrante [dimaˈgrante] AGG slimming *attr*; **fare una cura dimagrante** to go on a diet

dimagrire [dimaˈgrire] /55/ VI (*aus* **essere**) to become thin, lose weight, get thinner; **è dimagrita** she's lost weight; **è dimagrito di 5 kg** he has lost 5 kg

dimenare [dimeˈnare] /72/ VT (*braccia*) to wave (about);

(*coda*) to wag; (*corpo, testa*) to shake; (*sedere*) to wiggle; **dimenarsi** VR (*agitarsi: nel letto*) to toss (about), toss and turn; (: *per liberarsi, ballando*) to fling o.s. about; (: *gesticolare*) to gesticulate wildly

dimensione [dimen'sjone] SF **1** (*Mat, Filosofia, Fis*) dimension, size; **a 3 dimensioni** 3-dimensional **2** (*misura*): **dimensioni** SFPL dimensions, measurements, size *sg*; **di quali dimensioni è la stanza?** what are the dimensions o measurements of the room?, what size is the room?, what does the room measure?; **di piccole dimensioni** small; **di grandi dimensioni** large **3** (*fig*): **ricondurre qc alle giuste dimensioni** to get sth back in perspective; **considerare un discorso nella sua dimensione politica** to look at a speech in terms of its political significance; **di dimensioni allarmanti** of alarming proportions

dimenticanza [dimenti'kantsa] SF (*svista*) oversight; **è stata una dimenticanza** it was an oversight

dimenticare [dimenti'kare] /20/ VT (*gen*) to forget; (*preoccupazioni*) to forget (about); (*omettere*) to leave out; **dimenticare di fare qc** to forget to do sth; **dimenticare o dimenticarsi qc** to forget sth; **ho dimenticato il tuo numero di telefono** I've forgotten your phone number; **ho dimenticato l'ombrello in ufficio** I left my umbrella at the office; **dimenticarsi** VIP: **dimenticarsi di qc/di fare qc** to forget (about) sth/to do sth; **non me ne dimenticherò** I won't forget

dimenticatoio [dimentika'tojo] SM (*scherz*): **cadere/mettere nel dimenticatoio** to sink into/consign to oblivion

dimentico, -a, -chi, -che [di'mentiko] AGG: **dimentico di** (*che non ricorda*) forgetful of; (*incurante*) oblivious of, unmindful of

dimesso, -a [di'messo] PP *di* **dimettere** ◆ AGG modest, unassuming, humble; **in abiti dimessi** simply dressed; **con voce dimessa** humbly

dimestichezza [dimesti'kettsa] SF (*familiarità*) familiarity; **avere dimestichezza con qc** to be familiar with sth

dimettere [di'mettere] VB IRREG /*72*/ (*da ospedale*) to discharge; (*da carcere*) to release; (*da carica*) to dismiss; **far dimettere qn** to have sb dismissed; **dimettersi** VR: **dimettersi (da)** to resign, hand o give in one's notice; **si è dimesso ieri** he resigned yesterday

dimezzare [dimed'dzare] /*72*/ VT to cut in half, halve

diminuire [diminu'ire] /*55*/ VT (*gen*) to reduce, decrease, diminish; (*prezzi*) to bring down, reduce; **la ditta ha deciso di diminuire i prezzi** the company has decided to cut its prices; **dobbiamo diminuire le spese del venti per cento** we must cut spending by twenty percent ◆ VI (*aus essere*) (*gen*) to diminish, to decrease; (*vento, rumore*) to die down, die away; (*prezzo, valore, pressione*) to go down, fall, decrease; **la popolazione è diminuita del dieci per cento** the population has decreased by ten percent; **il prezzo della carne è diminuito** the price of meat has fallen; **diminuire d'intensità** to decrease in intensity, subside; **diminuire di volume** (*massa*) to be reduced in volume; **diminuire di peso** (*persona*) to lose weight; (*Fis*) to be reduced in weight

diminutivo, -a [diminu'tivo] AGG, SM diminutive

diminuzione [diminut'tsjone] SF reduction; (*calo*) decrease; (*di temperatura, pressione*) fall; **in diminuzione** on the decrease; **temperature in diminuzione** drop in temperatures; **essere in diminuzione** to be dropping; **la temperatura è in diminuzione** the temperature is dropping; **diminuzione della produttività** fall in productivity; **diminuzione di peso** loss of weight

dimisi ecc [di'mizi] VB *vedi* **dimettere**

dimissionario, -ria, -ri, -rie [dimissjo'narjo] AGG outgoing

dimissioni [dimis'sjoni] SFPL resignation *sg*; **dare o rassegnare le dimissioni** to give/hand in o tender one's resignation, resign; **ha dato le dimissioni** he handed in his resignation

dimora [di'mɔra] SF (*abitazione*) residence; **senza fissa dimora** of no fixed address o abode; **estrema dimora** (*euf*) last resting place

dimorare [dimo'rare] /*72*/ VI (*aus avere*) (*anche fig: sentimenti*) to dwell

dimostrante [dimos'trante] SM, SF (*Pol*) demonstrator

dimostrare [dimos'trare] /*72*/ VT **1** (*verità, funzionamento*) to demonstrate, show; (*colpevolezza, teorema, tesi*) to prove,

demonstrate; **ciò dimostra che hai ragione** this proves o shows you are right **2** (*simpatia, affetto, interesse*) to show, display; **non dimostra la sua età** he doesn't look his age **3** (*Pol*) to demonstrate; **dimostrarsi** VR **1** (*rivelarsi*) to prove to be; **si è dimostrato coraggioso** he showed courage; **si è dimostrato esatto** it turned out to be correct **2** (*apparire*): **dimostrarsi entusiasta/interessato** to show one's enthusiasm/interest

dimostrativo, -a [dimostra'tivo] AGG (*gen, anche Gramm*) demonstrative; **azione dimostrativa** (*Mil*) demonstration

dimostrazione [dimostrat'tsjone] SF **1** demonstration, proof; **una dimostrazione d'affetto** a show of affection; **una chiara dimostrazione di inefficienza** (*prova*) clear proof of inefficiency **2** (*manifestazione, anche Mat*) demonstration; **una dimostrazione studentesca** a student demonstration

dinamico, -a, -ci, -che [di'namiko] AGG (*fig: persona, vita*) dynamic, dynamical; (*Fis, Mus*) dynamic

dinamismo [dina'mizmo] SM dynamism

dinamitardo, -a [dinami'tardo] AGG: **attentato dinamitardo** dynamite attack ◆ SM, SF dynamiter

dinamite [dina'mite] SF dynamite

dinamo ['dinamo] SF INV dynamo

dinanzi [di'nantsi] AVV ahead ◆ **dinanzi a** PREP (*di fronte*) in front of; (*al cospetto*) in the presence of, before; **si presentò dinanzi a me** he appeared before me; **dinanzi ad una tale situazione...** faced with such a situation ...

dinastia [dinas'tia] SF dynasty

diniego, -ghi [di'njego] SM (*rifiuto*) refusal; (*negazione*) denial; **ha opposto un netto diniego** he refused point-blank; **scuotere la testa in segno di diniego** to shake one's head

dinoccolato, -a [dinokko'lato] AGG lanky; **andatura dinoccolata** slouching walk

dinosauro [dino'sauro] SM dinosaur

dintorno [din'torno] AVV (a)round, (round)about

dio, dei ['dio] SM **1** (*Mitol, anche fig*) god; **gli dei** the gods; **si crede un dio** he thinks he's wonderful; **canta come un dio** he sings divinely **2** (*Rel*): **Dio** God; **credi in Dio?** do you believe in God?; **Dio padre** God the Father; **un senza Dio** a godless person; **il buon Dio** the good Lord **3** (*fraseologia*): **Dio mio!** my goodness!, my God!; **Dio buono** o **santo!** for God's sake!; **per Dio!** by God!; **grazie a Dio!** o **Dio sia lodato** o **ringraziato!** thank God!; **com'è vero Dio** as God is my witness; **Dio sa quando finirà** God knows when it's going to come to an end; **viene giù che Dio la manda** it's raining cats and dogs, it's pouring with rain; **Dio volle arrivammo** somehow or other we got there; **se Dio vuole...** God willing ...; (*che*) **Dio ce la mandi buona** let's hope for the best; **Dio ce ne scampi e liberi** God forbid

diocesi [di'ɔt∫ezi] SF INV diocese

diossina [dios'sina] SF dioxin

dipanare [dipa'nare] /*72*/ VT (*matassa*) to wind (up o into a ball); (*fig: questione*) to sort out, disentangle

dipartimento [diparti'mento] SM (*gen, anche Univ*) department

dipendente [dipen'dente] AGG **1** **personale dipendente** employees *pl* **2** (*gen*): **dipendente da** (*alcol, droga*) addicted to; **è completamente dipendente da sua madre** he's completely dependent on his mother ◆ SM, SF employee; **dipendenti** SMPL, SFPL employees, staff *sg* o *pl*, personnel *pl*; **un dipendente della ditta** an employee of the firm ◆ SF (*Gramm: anche*: **proposizione dipendente**) subordinate o dependent clause

dipendenza [dipen'dentsa] SF **1** dependency; (*economica*) dependence; (*da droga*) addiction; **un farmaco che provoca dipendenza** an addictive drug **2** **alle dipendenze di** employed by; **ha 10 persone alle sue dipendenze** (*datore di lavoro*) he employs 10 people; (*caporeparto*) he has 10 people under him

dipendere [di'pendere] /*8*/ VI IRREG (*aus essere*) **dipendere da 1** (*gen*) to depend on; **dipende!** it depends!; **dipende solo da te** it depends entirely on you, it's entirely up to you; **andiamo? — Non lo so. Dipende da Mario** are we going? — I don't know. It depends on Mario; **non voglio più dipendere dai miei genitori** I don't want to be dependent on my parents any longer; **la sua risposta è dipesa dal fatto**

che era nervosa she answered that way because she was irritated 2 (*impiegato, filiale*) to be answerable to; **la ditta dipendeva da una compagnia americana** the firm was controlled by an American company 3 (*essere mantenuto, soggetto*) to depend (up)on, be dependent on 4 (*Gramm*) to be subordinate (to)

dipesi *ecc* [di'pesi] VB *vedi* **dipendere**

dipeso, -a [di'peso] PP *di* **dipendere**

dipingere [di'pindʒere] VB IRREG /37/ VT (*gen, anche Arte*) to paint; (*fig*) to describe, depict; **dipingersi** VIP (*tingersi*): **il cielo si dipinse di rosso** the sky turned red; **gli si dipinse sul viso la delusione** (*fig*) his face expressed *o* clearly showed his disappointment

dipinsi *ecc* [di'pinsi] VB *vedi* **dipingere**

dipinto, -a [di'pinto] PP *di* **dipingere** ♦ SM (*quadro*) painting

diploma, -i [di'plɔma] SM diploma, certificate; **diploma di laurea** degree (certificate); **diploma di maturità** A level certificate (*Brit*), (high-school) graduation diploma (*USA*)

diplomare [diplo'mare] /72/ VT to award a diploma to, graduate (*USA*); **diplomarsi** VIP to obtain a diploma, graduate (*USA*)

diplomatico, -a, -ci, -che [diplo'matiko] AGG diplomatic; **cerca di essere diplomatico** try to be diplomatic; **rompere le relazioni diplomatiche** to break off diplomatic relations ♦ SM (*anche fig*) diplomat

diplomato, -a [diplo'mato] AGG qualified ♦ SM, SF qualified person, holder of a diploma, graduate (*USA*)

diplomazia [diplomat'tsia] SF (*anche fig*) diplomacy; (*corpo diplomatico*) diplomatic corps *sg*; **entrare in diplomazia** to enter *o* join the diplomatic service

diporto [di'pɔrto] SM: **imbarcazione da diporto** pleasure craft *inv*

diradare [dira'dare] /72/ VT (*vegetazione*) to thin (out); (*nebbia, gas*) to clear, dissipate; **diradare le visite** to call less frequently VI (*aus essere*), **diradarsi** VIP (*vegetazione*) to thin out; (*folla*) to disperse; (*nebbia*) to clear (up); (*visite*) to become less frequent

diramare [dira'mare] /72/ VT (*comunicato, ordine*) to issue; (*notizia*) to circulate; **diramare gli inviti** (*spedire*) to send out invitations; **diramarsi** VIP 1 (*sentiero, strada*) to branch off; (*vene*) to spread; (*fusti*) to branch 2 (*diffondersi*): **la notizia si è diramata** the news spread

<hr>

PAROLA CHIAVE

dire ['dire] /38/ VT IRREG

1 (*gen*) to say; **dire qc a qn** to say sth to sb, tell sb sth; **disse che accettava** he said he would accept; **dicono** *o* **si dice che...** (*impersonale*) they say that ..., it is said that ...; **dicono** *o* **si dice che siano ricchissimi** they are said to be very rich, people say they are very rich; **come dicono gli inglesi** as the English say; **come si dice in inglese?** how do you say it in English?; **come si dice 'penna' in inglese?** what is the English for 'penna'?; **lascialo dire** (*esprimersi*) let him have his say; (*ignoralo*) just ignore him, don't take any notice of him; **non disse una parola** he didn't say *o* utter a word; **dice sempre quello che pensa** he always says what he thinks; **di' liberamente ciò che pensi** feel free to say what you think; **dicano pure quello che vogliono** let them say what they like!; **sa quello che dice** he knows what he's talking about; **Roberta ... — sì, dimmi Roberta ...** — yes, what is it?; **dire di sì/no** to say yes/no; **"non ci vado", disse** "I'm not going," he said; **dica?** (*in negozio*) what can I do for you?

2 (*raccontare, riferire, indicare*) to tell; **dire a qn qc** to tell sb sth; **dire a qn di fare qc** to tell sb to do sth; **mi si dice che...** I am told that ...; **può dirmi da che parte devo andare?** can you tell me which way to go?; **mi ha detto tutto** he told me everything

3 (*significare*) to mean; **ti dice niente questo nome?** does this name mean anything to you?, does this name ring a bell?; **quel libro non mi ha detto niente** that book didn't appeal to me; **come sarebbe a dire?** what do you mean?

4 (*recitare*) to say, recite; **dire a memoria** to recite by heart; **dire (la) Messa** to say Mass; **dire le preghiere** to say one's prayers

5 (*pensare*) to think; **chi l'avrebbe mai detto!** who would have thought it!; **cosa** *o* **che ne dici di questa musica?** what

do you think of this music?; **che ne diresti di andarcene?** let's make a move, shall we?; **si direbbe che non menta** (*impersonale*) you would think he was telling the truth

6 (*ammettere*) to say, admit; **devi dire che ha ragione** you must admit that he's right

7 **far dire qc a qn** to make sb say sth; **non me lo farò dire due volte** I won't need to be asked twice; **gliel' ho fatto dire dalla segretaria** I had her secretary tell her about it, I got her secretary to tell her about it; **mandare a dire qc a qn** (*riferire*) to let sb know sth

8 **dirsi** to say to o.s.; (*definirsi*) to call o.s., claim to be; (*uso reciproco*) to say to each other; **"coraggio" - si disse** "come on" - he said to himself; **si dicono esperti** they claim to be experts; **si son detti addio** they said goodbye (to each other); **si son detti qualcosa all'orecchio** they whispered something to one another

9 (*fraseologia*): **per così dire** so to speak; **sono stanco — e a me lo dici?!** I'm tired — me too!; **non c'è che dire** there's no doubt about it; **avere** *o* **a che dire con qn** to have words with sb; **e chi mi dice che è vero?** and who's to say that's true?; **dimmi con chi vai e ti dirò chi sei** (*Proverbio*) you can tell what somebody is like by the company they keep; **trovare da dire su qc/qn** to find fault with sth/sb; **l'idea mi stuzzica, non dico di no** the idea is tempting, I don't deny it; **non ti dico la scena!** you can't imagine the scene!; **per così dire** so to speak; **lo conosco per sentito dire** I've heard about him; **a dir poco** to say the least; **dico sul serio** I'm serious; **il che è tutto dire** need I say more?; **a dire il vero...** to tell the truth ...

♦ SM: **tra il dire e il fare c'è di mezzo il mare** (*Proverbio*) it's easier said than done; **è un bel dire il suo** what he says is all very well

diressi *ecc* [di'ressi] VB *vedi* **dirigere**

diretta [di'retta] SF: **in diretta** (*trasmettere*) live; **un incontro di calcio in diretta** a live football match

direttamente [diretta'mente] AVV (*immediatamente*) directly, straight; (*personalmente*) directly; (*senza intermediari*) direct, straight; **andiamo direttamente a casa** let's go straight home; **non mi riguarda direttamente** it doesn't directly concern me; **parla direttamente col preside** speak directly to the headmaster

direttissima [diret'tissima] SF (*Dir*): **processo per direttissima** summary trial

direttissimo [diret'tissimo] SM (*Ferr*) fast (through) train

direttivo, -a [diret'tivo] AGG (*Pol, Amm*) executive; (*Comm*) managerial, executive ♦ SM leadership, leaders *pl*

diretto, -a [di'retto] PP *di* **dirigere** ♦ AGG (*gen, anche Gramm*) direct; **la strada più diretta** the most direct route; **è il suo diretto superiore** he's his immediate superior; **c'è una diretta dipendenza tra i due fatti** these two events are directly connected ♦ SM 1 (*Ferr: anche: treno diretto*) through train 2 (*Boxe*) jab

direttore [diret'tore] SM (*gen*) director; (*responsabile: di banca, fabbrica*) manager; **direttore artistico** (*Teatro, Mus*) artistic director; **direttore di carcere** prison governor (*Brit*) *o* warden (*USA*); **direttore didattico** (*primary school*) headmaster (*Brit*), (*elementary school*) principal (*USA*); **direttore di macchina** (*Naut*) chief engineer; **direttore d'orchestra** conductor; **direttore del personale** personnel manager; **direttore di produzione** (*Cine*) producer; (*Industria*) production manager; **direttore responsabile** (*Stampa*) editor (in chief); **direttore sportivo** team manager; **direttore tecnico** (*Sport*) trainer, coach

direzione [diret'tsjone] SF 1 (*senso, anche fig*) direction; **è nella direzione opposta** it's in the opposite direction; **in direzione di** towards, in the direction of; **in che direzione vai?** which way are you going?; **prendere la direzione giusta/sbagliata** to go the right/wrong way; **sbagliare direzione** to go the wrong way 2 (*conduzione: gen*) running; (: *di società*) management; (: *di giornale*) editorship; (: *di partito*) leadership; **assumere la direzione delle operazioni** to take charge of operations 3 **la direzione** (*direttori*) the management; (*ufficio*) director's (*o* manager's *o* editor's *o* headmaster's *ecc*) office

dirigente [diri'dʒente] AGG managerial; **classe dirigente** ruling class ♦ SM, SF executive

dirigenza [diri'dʒɛntsa] SF (di ditta) management; (di partito) leadership

dirigenziale [diridʒen'tsjale] AGG managerial

dirigere [di'ridʒere] VB IRREG /39/ VT 1 (condurre) to run; (ditta) to manage; (giornale) to edit; (partito, inchiesta) to lead; (operazioni, traffico) to direct; (orchestra) to conduct; **dirigere il traffico** to direct the traffic; **dirigere i lavori** to be in charge of the work 2 (arma): **dirigere verso o contro** to point at; **dirigere contro** (critiche) to direct at, aim at; **dirigere l'attenzione su qc/qn** to turn one's attention to sth/sb; **dirigere i propri passi verso** to make one's way towards; **dirigere lo sguardo verso** to look towards; **a chi era diretta quell'osservazione?** who was that remark intended for?; **era diretto verso casa** he was heading home; **dove sei diretto?** where are you heading?; **il treno era diretto a Pavia** the train was en route for Pavia; **eravamo diretti a nord** we were heading north; **mi hanno diretto qui** they sent me here 3 (pacco, lettera) to address; **dirigersi** VR (prendere una direzione): **dirigersi a o verso** (luogo) to make one's way towards, make o head for; **si è diretto verso la porta** he made for the door; **dirigersi verso** (persona) to come/go towards; **l'aereo si dirigeva a nord** the plane was on its way o flying north; **si diresse a o verso casa** he headed home, he set off home; **dove si è diretto?** which way did he go?

dirigibile [diri'dʒibile] SM airship

dirimpetto [dirim'petto] AVV opposite; **vivono qui dirimpetto** they live opposite ♦ **dirimpetto a** PREP opposite; **Roberto era seduto dirimpetto a me** Roberto was sitting opposite me; **la tua casa è dirimpetto alla mia** your house is opposite mine ♦ AGG INV opposite; **la casa dirimpetto** the house opposite

diritto¹, -a [di'ritto] AGG 1 (strada, palo, linea) straight; (persona: eretto) erect, upright; (fig: onesto) upright, honest, straight; **stare su diritto** to stand up straight; **una strada diritta** a straight road 2 (Maglia): **punto diritto** plain (stitch) ♦ AVV straight, directly; **verrò diritto al punto** I'll come straight to the point; **vai sempre diritto fino al semaforo** keep straight on till you get to the traffic lights; **è andato diritto dal direttore** he went straight to the manager ♦ SM 1 (di vestito) right side 2 (Tennis) forehand 3 (Maglia) plain stitch, knit stitch

diritto² [di'ritto] SM 1 (prerogativa) right; **ti spetta di diritto** it is yours by right; **a buon diritto** quite rightly; **avere il diritto di fare qc** to have the right to do sth; **aver diritto a qc** to be entitled to sth; **ho il diritto di sapere** I have a right to know; **diritto d'asilo** right of asylum; **diritto di voto** (elettore) right to vote; (azionista) voting right 2 (Dir): **il diritto** (the) law; **studia diritto** he's studying law 3 **diritti** SMPL (tasse) fees, dues; "**tutti i diritti sono riservati**" "all rights reserved"; **diritti d'autore** (compenso) royalties, copyright sg; **diritti di magazzinaggio** demurrage sg; **diritti di segreteria** administrative charges

dirittura [dirit'tura] SF 1 (Sport): **dirittura (d'arrivo)** (home o final) straight 2 (fig: rettitudine) rectitude

diroccato, -a [dirok'kato] AGG (semidistrutto) in ruins; (cadente) dilapidated, tumbledown

dirompente [dirom'pɛnte] AGG (anche fig) explosive; **bomba dirompente** fragmentation bomb

dirottamento [dirotta'mento] SM: **dirottamento (aereo)** hijacking, hijack

dirottare [dirot'tare] /72/ VT (aereo: sotto minaccia) to hijack; (traffico) to divert; (nave, aereo) to change the course of ♦ VI (aus avere) (Naut) to change course

dirottatore, -trice [dirotta'tore] SM, SF hijacker

dirotto, -a [di'rotto] AGG: **scoppiare in un pianto dirotto** to burst into tears; **piove a dirotto** it's pouring (with rain), it's raining cats and dogs

dirupo [di'rupo] SM precipice, crag

disabile [di'zabile] SM, SF disabled person ♦ AGG disabled

disabitato, -a [dizabi'tato] AGG uninhabited

disabituare [dizabitu'are] /72/ VT: **disabituare qn a qc/a fare qc** to break sb of a habit/the habit of doing sth; **disabituarsi** VIP: **disabituarsi a qc/a fare qc** to get out of the habit of sth/of doing sth

disaccordo [dizak'kɔrdo] SM 1 disagreement; **essere in disaccordo** to disagree 2 (Mus) discord

disadattato, -a [dizadat'tato] AGG maladjusted ♦ SM, SF maladjusted person, misfit

disadorno, -a [diza'dorno] AGG plain, unadorned

disaffezione [dizaffet'tsjone] SF disaffection

disagevole [diza'dʒevole] AGG (scomodo) uncomfortable; (difficile) difficult

disagiato, -a [diza'dʒato] AGG (povero) poor, needy; **vivere in condizioni disagiate** to live in poverty

disagio, -gi [di'zadʒo] SM 1 (scomodità) discomfort; (difficoltà) difficulty 2 (imbarazzo) awkwardness; **essere o trovarsi a disagio** to be ill-at-ease o uncomfortable; **mettere qn a disagio** to make sb feel ill-at-ease o uncomfortable; **sentirsi a disagio** to feel ill at ease

disamina [di'zamina] SF close examination; **sottoporre a disamina** to put under close scrutiny

disapprovare [dizappro'vare] /72/ VT: **disapprovare (qc)** to disapprove (of sth); **disapprovano il mio comportamento** they disapprove of my behaviour

disapprovazione [dizapprovat'tsjone] SF disapproval; **un'occhiata di disapprovazione** a disapproving glance; **con aria di disapprovazione** disapprovingly

disappunto [dizap'punto] SM (delusione) disappointment; (fastidio) annoyance; **con mio disappunto** to my disappointment (o annoyance)

disarcionare [dizartʃo'nare] /72/ VT to unseat

disarmante [dizar'mante] AGG (sorriso) disarming; (calma) soothing; **con fare disarmante** disarmingly

disarmare [dizar'mare] /72/ VT (Mil, anche fig) to disarm; (Naut) **to lay up** ♦ VI (aus avere) (Mil) to disarm; (fig) to surrender, give in

disarmo [di'zarmo] SM (Mil) disarmament; (di nave) laying up

disastro [di'zastro] SM (anche fig) disaster; **è il più grande disastro aereo mai avvenuto** it's the worst air disaster ever; **i disastri dovuti alla grandine** the damage caused by the hailstorm; **quel cameriere è un disastro!** that waiter is awful!

disastroso, -a [dizas'troso] AGG (gen) disastrous; **effetti disastrosi** disastrous effects; **in condizioni disastrose** in a terrible o appalling state

disattento, -a [dizat'tɛnto] AGG careless, inattentive

disattenzione [dizatten'tsjone] SF carelessness, lack of attention; **un errore di disattenzione** a careless mistake

disattivare [dizatti'vare] /72/ VT (bomba) to de-activate, defuse; (Inform) to deactivate

disavanzo [diza'vantso] SM (Econ) deficit

disavventura [dizavven'tura] SF misadventure, mishap

disbrigo, -ghi [diz'brigo] SM: **disbrigo (di)** (corrispondenza, pratiche) dealing (with)

discapito [dis'kapito] SM: **a discapito di** to the detriment of; **lo fai a tuo discapito** if you do this it will be to your disadvantage

discarica, -che [dis'karika] SF (di rifiuti) rubbish tip o dump

discendente [diʃʃen'dɛnte] AGG descending ♦ SM, SF descendant

discendere [diʃ'ʃɛndere] VB IRREG /101/ VI (aus essere) 1 (scendere) to come (o go) down, descend; **discendere da** (treno) to get off; (macchina) to get out of; (tetto) to get down from; **discendere da cavallo** to dismount, get off one's horse; **le tenebre discesero sulla città** darkness descended on the town 2 (provenire): **discendere da** to be descended from, come from ♦ VT (scale) to come (o go) down, descend

discepolo, -a [diʃ'ʃɛpolo] SM, SF (Rel) disciple; (seguace) follower, disciple; (scolaro) pupil

discernere [diʃ'ʃɛrnere] /29/ VT vb dif (distinguere, anche fig) to discern; **discernere il bene dal male** to distinguish good from evil

discernimento [diʃʃerni'mento] SM discernment

discesa [diʃ'ʃesa] SF 1 (atto) descent; **la discesa dei barbari** the barbarian invasion; **fare una discesa in corda doppia** (Alpinismo) to abseil; **discesa libera** (Sci) downhill (race) 2 (pendio) slope, downhill stretch; **una discesa ripida** a steep slope; **in discesa** downhill attr; **da casa nostra al paese la strada è in discesa** it's downhill from our house to the village

discesista, -i, -e [diʃʃeˈsista] SM, SF (Sci) downhill skier

disceso, -a [diʃˈʃeso] PP di **discendere**

dischiudere [disˈkjudere] /22/ VT IRREG (aprire) to open; (fig: rivelare) to disclose, reveal

dischiusi ecc [disˈkjusi] VB vedi **dischiudere**

dischiuso, -a [disˈkjuso] PP di **dischiudere**

discinto, -a [diʃˈʃinto] AGG half-undressed

disciogliere [diʃˈʃɔʎʎere] VB IRREG /103/ VT (sciogliere: medicina) to dissolve; (liquefare) to melt; **disciogliersi** VIP (vedi vt) to dissolve; to melt

disciplina [diʃʃiˈplina] SF (regola) discipline; (materia) discipline, subject

disciplinare¹ [diʃʃipliˈnare] /72/ VT to discipline

disciplinare² [diʃʃipliˈnare] /72/ AGG (provvedimento) disciplinary

disco, -schi [ˈdisko] SM 1 (gen, anche Anat) disc (Brit), disk (USA); (Inform) disk; (Sport) discus; **il lancio del disco** the discus; **chi ha vinto il lancio del disco?** who won the discus? 2 (Mus) record, disc; **uno dei miei dischi preferiti** one of my favourite records; **cambia disco!** (fam) change the subject!; **disco magnetico** (Inform) magnetic disk; **disco orario** (Aut) parking disc; **disco rigido** o **fisso** (Inform) hard disk o drive; **disco volante** flying saucer

discografia [diskograˈfia] SF 1 (tecnica) recording, record-making 2 (industria) record industry 3 (elenco) discography

discografico, -a, -ci, -che [diskoˈɡrafiko] AGG record attr, recording attr; **casa discografica** record(ing) company ♦ SM record producer

discolo, -a [ˈdiskolo] AGG (bambino) undisciplined, unruly ♦ SM, SF rascal

discolpare [diskolˈpare] /72/ VT: **discolpare qn** to prove sb's innocence, clear sb (of blame); **discolparsi** VR to clear o.s., prove one's innocence; (giustificarsi) to excuse o.s.

disconoscere [diskoˈnoʃʃere] /26/ VT IRREG (meriti) to ignore, disregard; **disconoscere la paternità di un figlio** (Dir) to deny paternity

disconosciuto, -a [diskonoʃˈʃuto] PP di **disconoscere**

discontinuo, -a [diskonˈtinuo] AGG (linea) discontinuous, broken; (rendimento, stile) irregular, erratic; (interesse): **essere discontinuo nel lavoro** to lack application

discorde [disˈkɔrde] AGG conflicting; **essere di parere discorde** to be of a different opinion

discordia [disˈkɔrdja] SF discord, dissension; **essere in discordia con** to be at variance with

discorrere [disˈkorrere] /28/ VI IRREG (aus avere) **discorrere (di)** to talk (about), chat (about)

discorso [disˈkorso] PP di **discorrere** ♦ SM 1 (gen) speech; **fare un discorso** (in pubblico) to make a speech; **gli ho fatto un bel discorso ieri** (iro) I gave him a piece of my mind yesterday; **cambiare discorso** to change the subject; **è un altro discorso** that's another matter; **non son discorsi da fare!** what sort of attitude is that? 2 (Ling): **analisi del discorso** discourse analysis; **discorso diretto/indiretto** direct/indirect o reported speech

discosto, -a [disˈkɔsto] AGG (letter): **discosto da** remote from; **tenersi discosto da** to stay away from ♦ AVV at a distance, at some distance, far away

discoteca, -che [diskoˈtɛka] SF 1 (sala da ballo) disco, club; **una discoteca alla moda** a popular club; **vado in discoteca di sabato** I go clubbing on Saturdays 2 (raccolta) record library 3 (negozio) record shop

discount [disˈkaunt] SM INV (supermercato) cut-price supermarket

discrepanza [diskreˈpantsa] SF discrepancy

discreto, -a [disˈkreto] AGG 1 (abbastanza buono) reasonable, fair; **un voto discreto** a reasonable mark 2 (non forte: tinta, trucco) subtle 3 (persona: riservato) discreet; **è una persona molto discreta** he's very discreet; **fu discreto da parte sua andarsene** it was tactful of him to leave

discrezione [diskretˈtsjone] SF 1 (riservatezza) discretion; **ti prego la massima discrezione** I'm relying on your absolute discretion 2 (arbitrio): **a propria discrezione** at one's own discretion 3 (discernimento): **l'età della discrezione** the age of discretion

discriminante [diskrimiˈnante] AGG (fattore, elemento) decisive ♦ SF (Dir) extenuating circumstance ♦ SM (Mat) discriminant

discriminare [diskrimiˈnare] /72/ VT to discriminate

discriminazione [diskriminatˈtsjone] SF discrimination; **la discriminazione razziale** racial discrimination

discussi ecc [disˈkussi] VB vedi **discutere**

discussione [diskusˈsjone] SF (gen) discussion; (lite) argument; **fare una discussione** to have a discussion; **avere una discussione** to have an argument; **abbiamo avuto una discussione col capo** (lite) I had words with my boss; **mettere in discussione** to bring into question; **questo è fuori discussione** this is out of the question; **fila a letto, senza discussioni!** go to bed and don't argue!

discusso, -a [disˈkusso] PP di **discutere** ♦ AGG controversial

discutere [disˈkutere] VB IRREG /40/ VT (dibattere) to discuss, debate; (contestare) to question, dispute; **è da discutere** (se ne parlerà ancora) it remains to be discussed; (è in dubbio) it's questionable; **discutere una proposta di legge** to debate a (parliamentary) bill; **discutere la tesi (di laurea)** to present o submit one's (degree) thesis ♦ VI (aus avere) 1 (conversare): **discutere (di)** to talk (about), to discuss; **discutono spesso di politica** they often discuss politics 2 (litigare) to argue; **non voglio mettermi a discutere con te** I don't want to argue with you; **mi ha ubbidito senza discutere** he obeyed me without question

discutibile [diskuˈtibile] AGG questionable

disdegnare [dizdeɲˈɲare] /15/ VT to disdain, to scorn

disdegno [dizˈdeɲɲo] SM disdain, contempt, scorn

disdegnoso, -a [dizdeɲˈɲoso] AGG (letter) disdainful, scornful, contemptuous

disdetto, -a [dizˈdetto] PP di **disdire**

disdicevole [dizdiˈtʃevole] AGG improper, unseemly

disdire [dizˈdire] /38/ VT IRREG (prenotazione, appuntamento) to cancel; **disdire un contratto d'affitto** (locatario) to give notice; (locatore) to give notice (to quit)

disegnare [diseɲˈɲare] /15/ VT 1 (gen) to draw; (a contorno) to outline; (fig: descrivere) to describe, portray; **mio fratello sta disegnando** my brother is drawing 2 (progettare: mobile, casa) to design; **disegna mobili** he designs furniture

disegnatore, -trice [diseɲɲaˈtore] SM, SF (tecnico) draughtsman o draughtswoman; (progettista) designer

disegno [diˈseɲɲo] SM 1 drawing; (schizzo) sketch; **un bel disegno** a beautiful drawing; **disegno a matita** pencil drawing; **disegno dal vero** from life drawing 2 (su carta, stoffa) design, pattern; **un disegno a fiori** a floral design 3 (fig: schema) outline, plan; (: progetto) plan, project; **disegno di legge** (Dir) bill

diserbante [dizerˈbante] AGG herbicidal ♦ SM herbicide, weed-killer

diseredare [dizereˈdare] /72/ VT to disinherit

disertare [dizerˈtare] /72/ VT to desert, abandon, leave; **ieri ho disertato la riunione** yesterday I gave the meeting a miss ♦ VI (aus avere) (Mil, anche fig): **disertare (da qc)** to desert (sth)

disertore [dizerˈtore] SM (Mil, anche fig) deserter

diserzione [dizerˈtsjone] SF (Mil, anche fig) desertion

disfacimento [disfatʃiˈmento] SM (di cadavere) decay; (fig: di istituzione, impero, società) decline, decay; **in disfacimento** in decay

disfare [disˈfare] VB IRREG /41/ VT 1 (gen) to undo; (nodo) to untie, undo; (sciogliere) to melt; (meccanismo) to take to pieces; **disfare il letto** to strip the bed; **disfare le valigie** to unpack (one's cases); **ha disfatto la valigia** he's unpacked; **ha disfatto il pacco** he undid the parcel 2 (distruggere) to destroy; **disfarsi** VR: **disfarsi di (liberarsi)** to get rid of; **ce ne siamo disfatti** we got rid of it; **disfarsi** VIP 1 (nodo, pacco) to come undone; (neve) to melt 2 (andare a pezzi) to fall to pieces

disfatta [disˈfatta] SF (anche fig) (utter) defeat

disfattista, -i, -e [disfatˈtista] SM, SF defeatist

disfatto, -a [disˈfatto] PP di **disfare** ♦ AGG (gen) undone, untied; (letto) unmade

disfunzione [disfunˈtsjone] SF (Med) dysfunction; **disfunzione cardiaca** heart trouble

disgelare [dizdʒeˈlare] /72/ VT, VI (*aus* essere), VB IMPERS, **disgelarsi** VIP to thaw

disgelo [dizˈdʒɛlo] SM thaw

disgrazia [dizˈgrattsja] SF 1 (*sventura*) bad luck, misfortune; **per disgrazia** unfortunately 2 (*incidente*) accident; (*calamità*) disaster; **è successa una disgrazia** something terrible has happened 3 (*sfavore*) disgrace; **cadere in disgrazia** to fall into disgrace

disgraziato, -a [dizgratˈtsjato] AGG (*persona: povero*) poor, wretched; (: *sfortunato*) unfortunate, unlucky; (: *pegg: sciagurato*) good-for-nothing; (*periodo, attività, impresa*) ill-fated ♦ SM, SF (*povero*) poor wretch; (*sciagurato*) rascal, rogue, scoundrel

disgregare [dizgreˈgare] /80/ VT to cause to disintegrate, break up; (*fig: partito, famiglia*) to break up; **disgregarsi** VIP to disintegrate, break up; (*fig*) to break up

disguido [dizˈgwido] SM hitch; **disguido postale** error in postal delivery

disgustare [dizgusˈtare] /72/ VT to disgust, sicken, make sick; **disgustarsi** VIP: **disgustarsi di** to be disgusted by, be sickened by

disgusto [dizˈgusto] SM (*anche fig*) disgust

disgustoso, -a [dizgusˈtoso] AGG disgusting

disidratare [dizidraˈtare] /72/ VT to dehydrate

disidratato, -a [dizidraˈtato] AGG dehydrated

disilludere [dizilˈludere] VB IRREG /72/ VT to disillusion, disenchant; **disilludersi** VIP to be disillusioned, be disenchanted

disillusione [dizilluˈzjone] SF disillusion, disenchantment

disimparare [dizimpaˈrare] /72/ VT to forget; **ho disimparato il francese** I've forgotten my French

disimpegnare [dizimpeɲˈɲare] /15/ VT 1 (*persona: da obblighi*): **disimpegnare da** to release (from); (*àncora*) to clear 2 (*oggetto in pegno*) to redeem, get out of pawn; **disimpegnarsi** VR: **disimpegnarsi da** (*obblighi*) to release o.s. from, free o.s. from

disincagliare [dizinkaʎˈʎare] /27/ VT (*barca*) to refloat; **disincagliarsi** VIP to get afloat again

disincantato, -a [dizinkanˈtato] AGG disenchanted, disillusioned

disincentivare [dizintʃentiˈvare] /72/ VT to discourage

disinfestare [dizinfesˈtare] /72/ VT to disinfest

disinfestazione [dizinfestatˈtsjone] SF disinfestation

disinfettante [dizinfetˈtante] AGG, SM disinfectant

disinfettare [dizinfetˈtare] /72/ VT to disinfect

disinfezione [dizinfetˈtsjone] SF disinfection

disingannare [dizingan'nare] /72/ VT to disillusion

disinganno [dizinˈganno] SM disillusion

disinibito, -a [diziniˈbito] AGG uninhibited

disinnescare [dizinnesˈkare] /20/ VT to defuse

disinnestare [dizinnesˈtare] /72/ VT (*marcia*) to disengage

disinquinare [dizinkwiˈnare] /72/ VT to free from pollution

disinstallare [dizinstalˈlare] /72/ VT (*programma*) to uninstall, to remove

disintegrare [dizinteˈgrare] /72/ VT (*gen*) to cause to disintegrate; (*edificio*) to shatter; (*fig: opposizione, avversari*) to annihilate; **disintegrarsi** VIP (*anche fig*) to disintegrate

disinteressare [dizinteresˈsare] /72/ VT: **disinteressare qn a qc** to cause sb to lose interest in sth; **disinteressarsi** VIP: **disinteressarsi di** to take no interest in

disinteresse [dizinteˈresse] SM 1 (*indifferenza*) disinterest, indifference 2 (*generosità*) disinterestedness, unselfishness

disintossicare [dizintossiˈkare] /20/ VT to detoxify; (*alcolizzato, drogato*) to treat for alcoholism (*o* drug addiction); **disintossicare l'organismo** to clear out one's system; **disintossicarsi** VR to clear out one's system; (*alcolizzato, drogato*) to be treated for alcoholism (*o* drug addiction)

disintossicazione [dizintossikatˈtsjone] SF (*vedi vb*) detoxification; treatment for alcoholism (*o* drug addiction)

disinvolto, -a [dizinˈvolto] AGG (*sicuro*) confident; (*spigliato*) casual, nonchalant, free and easy; **con fare disinvolto** nonchalantly

disinvoltura [dizinvolˈtura] SF (*vedi agg*) confidence; casualness, nonchalance, ease; **con disinvoltura** with ease, easily

dislessia [dizlesˈsia] SF dyslexia

dislivello [dizliˈvello] SM difference in height; (*fig*) gap

dislocare [dizloˈkare] /20/ VT 1 (*Mil, Amm*) to post 2 (*Naut*) to displace

dismisura [dizmiˈsura] SF: **a dismisura** excessively

disobbedire ecc [dizobbeˈdire] = **disubbidire**

disoccupato, -a [dizokkuˈpato] AGG unemployed, out of work; **è ancora disoccupato** he's still unemployed ♦ SM, SF unemployed person; **i disoccupati** the unemployed, people out of work

disoccupazione [dizokkupatˈtsjone] SF unemployment; **la disoccupazione è in aumento** unemployment is rising

disonestà [dizonesˈta] SF INV dishonesty; **è una disonestà** it's dishonest

disonesto, -a [dizoˈnesto] AGG dishonest ♦ SM, SF dishonest person

disonorare [dizonoˈrare] /45/ VT (*nome, famiglia*) to disgrace, bring disgrace upon, to dishonour (*Brit*), dishonor (*USA*); **disonorarsi** VR to bring disgrace on o.s., bring dishono(u)r on o.s.

disonore [dizoˈnore] SM disgrace, dishonour (*Brit*), dishonor (*USA*); **essere il disonore della propria famiglia** to be a disgrace to one's family

disopra [diˈsopra] AVV (= *di sopra*) *vedi* **sopra** ♦ SM INV top, upper part

disordinare [dizordiˈnare] /72/ VT to mess up, disarrange; (*Mil*) to throw into disorder

disordinato, -a [dizordiˈnato] AGG (*persona*) untidy, disorderly; (*compito*) untidy; (*fuga, vita*) disorderly; **un ragazzo disordinato** an untidy boy; **disordinato nel lavoro** disorganized in one's work

disordine [diˈzordine] SM 1 (*confusione*) untidiness, disorder; **non sopporto il disordine** I can't stand a mess; **che disordine!** what a mess!; **essere/mettere in disordine** to be/make untidy; **ho i capelli in disordine** my hair is in a mess; **disordine mentale** mental confusion 2 **disordini** SMPL (*Pol*) disorder *sg*; (*tumulti*) disturbances, riots; **i disordini della settimana scorsa** the disturbances of last week

disorganico, -a, -ci, -che [dizorˈganiko] AGG incoherent, disorganized

disorganizzato, -a [dizorganidˈdzato] AGG disorganized

disorientamento [dizorjentaˈmento] SM (*fig*) disorientation

disorientare [dizorjenˈtare] /72/ VT (*anche fig*) to disorientate, disorient; **disorientarsi** VIP (*anche fig*) to lose one's bearings, become disorientated

disorientato, -a [dizorjenˈtato] AGG disorientated, disoriented

disossare [dizosˈsare] /72/ VT (*Culin*) to bone

disotto [diˈsotto] AVV (= *di sotto*) *vedi* **sotto** ♦ SM INV bottom, underside

dispaccio, -ci [disˈpattʃo] SM dispatch, despatch

disparato, -a [dispaˈrato] AGG disparate; **le cose più disparate** the most oddly assorted things

dispari [ˈdispari] AGG INV (*numero*) odd, uneven; (*Mil: forze*) unequal; **numeri dispari** odd numbers

disparità [dispariˈta] SF INV: **disparità (di)** (*disuguaglianza*) disparity (in); (*divergenza*) difference (in)

disparte [disˈparte] **in disparte** AVV (*da lato*) aside, apart; **mettere qc in disparte** to put *o* set sth aside; **stare** *o* **starsene** *o* **tenersi in disparte** to stand apart; (*fig*) to keep to o.s., hold *o* keep o.s. aloof; **se ne stava in disparte** he was by himself

dispendio, -di [disˈpendjo] SM (*di denaro, energie*) expenditure; (*spreco*) waste

dispendioso, -a [dispenˈdjoso] AGG (*tenore di vita*) extravagant; (*impresa, viaggio*) expensive

dispensa [disˈpensa] SF 1 (*fascicolo*) instalment; (*Univ*) duplicated lecture notes *pl*, handout 2 (*esenzione*): **dispensa (da)** exemption (from); (*Rel*) dispensation (from) 3 (*locale*) larder, pantry; (*mobile*) sideboard

dispensare [dispenˈsare] /72/ VT 1 (*esonerare*): **dispensare qn da/dal fare qc** to exempt sb from/from doing sth 2 (*elemosine, favori*) to distribute, hand out; **dispensarsi** VR: **dispensarsi dal fare qc** to get out of *o* avoid doing sth

disperare [dispeˈrare] /72/ VI (*aus* avere) **disperare (di)** to despair (of); **disperare di fare qc** to despair of doing sth;

disperarsi VIP to despair; **non disperarti in quel modo!** don't get so upset!; **far disperare qn** to drive sb mad
disperato, -a [dispe'rato] AGG (*persona*) in despair; (*caso*) hopeless; (*tentativo, gesto*) desperate; **grido disperato** cry of despair; **è un caso disperato** he is a hopeless case; **un gesto disperato** a desperate gesture; **ho un disperato bisogno di soldi** I desperately need money ♦ SM, SF **1** (*fam: spiantato*): **è un povero disperato** he's a no-hoper **2 lavorare come un disperato** to work furiously *o* like mad
disperazione [disperat'tsjone] SF despair; **per disperazione in desperation; in preda alla disperazione** overcome by despair; **quel bambino è la mia disperazione** that child drives me mad
disperdere [dis'perdere] VB IRREG /73/ VT (*folla*) to disperse; (*nemico*) to scatter; (*fig: energia, sostanze*) to waste, squander; **la polizia ha disperso la folla** the police dispersed the crowd; **"non disperdere nell'ambiente"** (*vetro, lattine*) ≈ "please recycle"; (*pile, batterie*) ≈ "please dispose of carefully"; **disperdersi** VIP (*folla*) to disperse; (*nemico*) to scatter; (*energia, sostanze*) to be wasted; (*calore*) to be lost
dispersione [disper'sjone] SF (*vedi vb*) scattering, dispersal; waste; (*Chim, Fis*) dispersion; **dispersione di calore** heat loss
dispersivo, -a [disper'sivo] AGG (*lavoro*) disorganized
disperso, -a [dis'perso] PP *di* **disperdere** ♦ AGG (*sparpagliato*) scattered, dispersed; (*smarrito: persona*) missing ♦ SM, SF missing person; (*Mil*) missing soldier
dispetto [dis'petto] SM **1** (*molestia*) piece of spite; **fare un dispetto a qn** to play a nasty *o* spiteful trick on sb, to tease sb; **smettila di fargli dispetti** stop teasing him; **a dispetto di** in spite of, despite; **per dispetto** out of spite **2** (*stizza*) vexation; **con suo grande dispetto** much to his annoyance
dispettoso, -a [dispet'toso] AGG spiteful
dispiacere [dispja't∫ere] /74/ SM **1** (*rammarico*) regret, sorrow; (*dolore*) grief; **con mio grande dispiacere** much to my regret; **con grande dispiacere vi annuncio...** I regret to announce ...; **impazzire dal dispiacere** to go mad with grief **2** (*disappunto*) disappointment; **non puoi dare questo dispiacere a tua madre** you can't upset your mother in this way **3 dispiaceri** SMPL (*preoccupazioni*) worries, troubles; **il figlio le ha dato molti dispiaceri** her son has given her a lot of trouble ♦ VI IRREG (*aus* **essere**) **dispiacere a 1** (*causare dolore*) to upset; (*causare disagio, noia*) to displease; **ciò che hai fatto è dispiaciuto ai tuoi** your parents are upset (*o* displeased) at your behaviour, you have upset your parents by what you have done; **mi dispiace** I'm sorry; **non posso venire, mi dispiace** I'm sorry I can't come **2** (*risultare sgradito*): **ti dispiace se fumo?** do you mind if I smoke?; **se non le dispiace...** if you don't mind ...; **ti dispiace prestarmelo?** would you mind lending it to me?; **l'idea non mi dispiace** I don't dislike the idea; **dispiacersi** VIP: **dispiacersi (per** *o* **di qc)** to regret (sth)
dispiaciuto, -a [dispja't∫uto] PP *di* **dispiacere** ♦ AGG sorry
dispone *ecc* [dis'pone] VB *vedi* **disporre**
disponibile [dispo'nibile] AGG (*posto, merce*) available; (*persona: solerte, gentile*) helpful; **è disponibile in molti colori** it's available in many colours; **sei disponibile stasera?** are you free this evening?; **è sempre molto disponibile** he's always willing to help
disponibilità [disponibili'ta] SF INV **1** (*gen*) availability; (*solerzia, gentilezza*) helpfulness **2** (*Fin*); **disponibilità** SFPL available funds, resources
disporre [dis'porre] VB IRREG /77/ VT **1** (*mettere*) to place, put; (*sistemare*) to arrange; (*preparare*) to prepare, make ready **2** (*ordinare*) to order; **la legge dispone che...** the law lays down that ...; **ha disposto che nessuno se ne andasse** he gave orders that no-one should leave ♦ VI (*aus* **avere**) **1** (*decidere*) to decide; **abbiamo disposto diversamente** we have decided otherwise, we have made other arrangements **2 disporre di** to have, have at one's disposal; **lo stadio dispone di 50.000 posti** the stadium holds 50,000 people; **disporsi** VR **1** (*posizione*) to put o.s., place o.s., arrange o.s.; **disporsi in fila** to line up; **disporsi in cerchio** to form a circle **2** (*prepararsi*): **disporsi a fare qc** to prepare o.s. *o* get ready to do sth; **disporsi all'attacco** to prepare for an attack
disposi *ecc* [dis'posi] VB *vedi* **disporre**
dispositivo [dispozi'tivo] SM **1** (*meccanismo*) device; **dispo-**

-sitivo di controllo *o* **di comando** control device; **dispositivo di sicurezza** (*gen*) safety device; (*di arma da fuoco*) safety catch **2** (*Mil: posizione*) order; **dispositivo di marcia** marching order **3** (*Dir*) pronouncement
disposizione [disposit'tsjone] SF **1** (*sistemazione: di mobili*) arrangement; (*: di locali*) layout; (*Sport: di squadra*) positioning; **la disposizione dei mobili** the arrangement of the furniture; **ha cambiato la disposizione dei mobili** he rearranged the furniture **2** (*ordine*) order; (*Dir*) provision; **disposizioni** (*preparativi, misure*) measures; **dare disposizioni a qn affinché faccia qc** to give orders to sb to do sth; **ho dato disposizioni precise** I gave precise orders; **per disposizione di legge** by law; **le sue ultime disposizioni furono...** his last instructions were ...; **disposizione testamentaria** provisions of a will; **disposizioni di sicurezza** safety measures **3 a disposizione** at one's disposal; **avere a disposizione** to have available *o* at one's disposal; **abbiamo a disposizione cinque computer nuovi** we've got five new computers at our disposal; **sono a tua disposizione** I am at your disposal; **resti a disposizione della polizia** be prepared to assist the police with their enquiries **4 disposizione d'animo** mood, frame of mind **5** (*tendenza*) bent
disposto, -a [dis'posto] PP *di* **disporre** ♦ AGG (*incline*): **disposto a fare** disposed *o* prepared to do; **non sono disposta ad aiutarti se non mi paghi** I'm not prepared to help you if you don't pay me; **essere ben/mal disposto verso qn** to be well-/ill-disposed towards sb ♦ SM (*Dir*) provision
dispotico, -a, -ci, -che [dis'potiko] AGG despotic; (*fig*) tyrannical, overbearing
dispotismo [dispo'tizmo] SM despotism; (*fig*) tyranny
disprezzare [dispret'tsare] /72/ VT (*gen*) to scorn, to despise; (*persona*) to look down on
disprezzo [dis'prettso] SM scorn, contempt; **mi ha guardato con disprezzo** he looked at me with contempt; **ha agito con disprezzo del pericolo** he acted with a total disregard for the danger involved
disputa ['disputa] SF **1** (*dibattito*) discussion **2** (*lite*) argument, dispute
disputare [dispu'tare] /72/ VI (*aus* **avere**) **disputare di** (*dibattere*) to discuss ♦ VT **1** (*gara*) to take part in; (*partita*) to play; **quando si disputerà la gara?** when will the competition take place? **2** (*contrastare*) to contest, dispute; **gli hanno disputato il diritto di farlo** they disputed his right to do it **3 disputarsi qc** to compete for sth, fight for sth; **disputarsi il pallone** to fight for the ball
disquisire [diskwi'zire] /55/ VI to discourse on
disquisizione [diskwizit'tsjone] SF detailed analysis; **è inutile stare a fare disquisizioni sul perché** there's no point in discussing all the ins and outs of it
dissacrare [dissa'krare] /72/ VT to debunk
dissanguamento [dissangwa'mento] SM (*Med*) loss of blood
dissanguare [dissan'gware] /72/ VT (*fig: persona*) to bleed white *o* dry; **morire dissanguato** to bleed to death; **dissanguarsi** VIP (*Med*) to lose blood; (*fig*) to ruin o.s.
dissapore [dissa'pore] SM slight disagreement
disse *ecc* VB *vedi* **dire**
dissecare [disse'kare] /20/ VT to dissect
disseccare [dissek'kare] /20/ VT, **disseccarsi** VIP to dry up
disseminare [dissemi'nare] /72/ VT to scatter, spread; (*fig: malcontento*) to breed
dissennatezza [dissenna'tettsa] SF foolishness
dissenso [dis'sɛnso] SM (*protesta*) dissent; (*disapprovazione*) disapproval; **scrittori del dissenso** dissident writers
dissenteria [dissente'ria] SF dysentery
dissentire [dissen'tire] /45/ VI (*aus* **avere**) to dissent; **dissentire da qn su qc** to disagree with sb on sth
disseppellire [disseppel'lire] /55/ VT (*esumare: cadavere*) to disinter, exhume; (*dissotterrare, anche fig*) to dig up, unearth
dissertazione [dissertat'tsjone] SF dissertation
disservizio, -zi [disser'vittsjo] SM inefficiency; **i disservizi delle ferrovie** the inefficiency of the railways
dissestare [disses'tare] /72/ VT (*anche fig*) to upset, disturb; **dissestare il bilancio** to unbalance the budget

dissestato, -a [disses'tato] AGG (*fondo stradale*) uneven; (*economia, finanze*) shaky; **"strada dissestata"** (*per lavori in corso*) "road up" (*Brit*), "road out" (*USA*)

dissesto [dis'sesto] SM (*Fin, Econ*) disorder; **dissesto finanziario** serious financial difficulties; **in dissesto** in disorder; **dissesto idrogeologico** hydrogeological disturbance (*which could lead to natural disasters*)

dissetante [disse'tante] AGG refreshing, thirst-quenching; **una bevanda dissetante** a refreshing drink

dissetare [disse'tare] /72/ VT (*persona*) to quench the thirst of; (*animale*) to water, give water to; **dissetarsi** VR to quench one's thirst

dissezione [disset'tsjone] SF dissection

dissi *ecc* VB *vedi* dire

dissidente [dissi'dente] AGG, SM, SF dissident

dissidio, -di [dis'sidjo] SM disagreement; **dissidio di opinioni** difference of opinion

dissimile [dis'simile] AGG: **dissimile (da)** different (from), dissimilar (to)

dissimulare [dissimu'lare] /72/ VT (*nascondere*) to hide, conceal; (*mentire*) to dissemble (*frm*); **non sa dissimulare** he's not good at pretending

dissimulatore, -trice [dissimula'tore] SM, SF dissembler

dissimulazione [dissimulat'tsjone] SF (*vedi vb*) concealment; dissembling

dissipare [dissi'pare] /72/ VT 1 (*disperdere: nubi, nebbia*) to disperse; (*fig: dubbi, timori*) to dispel 2 (*sprecare*) to squander; **dissiparsi** VIP (*nubi*) to disperse; (*nebbia*) to clear, lift; (*dubbi, timori*) to vanish, disappear

dissipatezza [dissipa'tettsa] SF dissipation

dissipato, -a [dissi'pato] AGG dissolute, dissipated

dissipazione [dissipat'tsjone] SF 1 (*sperpero*) squandering, waste 2 (*dissipatezza*) dissipation

dissociare [disso't∫are] /14/ VT to dissociate; **dissociarsi** VR: **dissociarsi da** to dissociate o.s. from

dissolto, -a [dis'sɔlto] PP di **dissolvere**

disso'lubile AGG soluble

dissolutezza [dissolu'tettsa] SF dissoluteness; **vivere nella dissolutezza** to lead a dissolute life

dissolutivo, -a [dissolu'tivo] AGG (*forza*) divisive; **processo dissolutivo** (*anche fig*) process of dissolution

dissoluto, -a [disso'luto] AGG dissolute, licentious ♦ SM, SF dissolute person

dissolvenza [dissol'ventsa] SF (*Cine*) fade-out

dissolvere [dis'sɔlvere] VB IRREG /94/ VT (*sostanza*) to dissolve; (*nebbia*) to disperse, dispel, clear (away); (*neve*) to melt; (*fig: dubbio*) to dispel; **dissolversi** VIP (*vedi vt*) to dissolve; to disperse, dispel, clear (away); to melt; to be dispelled

dissonante [disso'nante] AGG (*suono*) dissonant, discordant

dissonanza [disso'nantsa] SF (*di suoni*) dissonance, discord; (*fig: di opinioni*) clash

dissotterrare [dissotter'rare] /72/ VT (*cadavere*) to disinter, exhume; (*tesori, rovine*) to dig up, unearth; (*fig: sentimenti, odio*) to bring up again, resurrect

dissuadere [dissua'dere] /88/ VT IRREG to dissuade; **dissuadere qn da qc/da fare qc** to dissuade sb from sth/from doing sth

dissuasione [dissua'zjone] SF dissuasion

dissuaso, -a [dissu'azo] PP di **dissuadere**

dissua'sore SM: **dissuasore di velocità** (*Aut*) speed bump

distaccamento [distakka'mento] SM (*Mil*) detachment

distaccare [distak'kare] /20/ VT 1 **distaccare (da)** (*persona*) to separate (from), take away (from); (*etichetta, francobollo*) to remove, take off; (*vagone, ricevuta*) to detach (from); **distaccare lo sguardo da qn** to look away from sb 2 (*Amm: dipendente*) to transfer; (*Mil: reparto*) to detach 3 (*Sport*) to outdistance, leave behind; **li distaccò di 20 metri** he outdistanced them by 20 metres; **distaccarsi** VIP 1 (*bottone, etichetta*): **distaccarsi (da qc)** to come off (sth) 2 **distaccarsi (da)** (*persona, famiglia: gradualmente*) to grow away (from); (: *nettamente*) to leave; (: *mondo*) to become detached (from) 3 (*distinguersi*) to stand out (from)

distacco, -chi [dis'takko] SM 1 (*separazione*) detachment; (*fig*) parting; **il distacco fu molto doloroso** it was very painful to part; **il distacco dalla famiglia è spesso difficile** leaving home is often difficult 2 (*indifferenza*) coldness; **con distacco** coldly; **mi guardava con distacco** he looked at me coldly 3 (*Sport*): **vincere con un distacco di 100 m** to win by a 100 m

distante [dis'tante] AGG 1 (*luogo*): **essere distante (da)** to be a long way (from); **la casa è molto distante dal centro** the house is a long way (away) from the (town) centre; **è distante da qui?** is it far from here?, is it a long way from here?; **non è distante** it's not far 2 (*tempo*): **essere distante nel tempo** to be in the distant past; **sono distanti gli anni in cui...** it's a long time since ... 3 (*fig: persona, atteggiamento*) distant ♦ AVV far away, a long way away; **non si vede da così distante** you can't see it from this distance *o* from so far away; **non abitano distante** they don't live far away

distanza [dis'tantsa] SF 1 (*gen*): **a tale distanza** at a certain distanza **distanza dal centro** I live a fair distance *o* quite a distance from the (town) centre; **qual è la distanza tra Glasgow ed Edimburgo?** how far is it from Glasgow to Edinburgh?, how far is Glasgow from Edinburgh?; **le 2 barche erano a 3 metri di distanza** the 2 boats were 3 metres apart; **era a 2 metri di distanza** she was 2 metres away; **a poca distanza da qui** not far from here; **comando a distanza** remote control; **distanza focale** focal length; **distanza di sicurezza** (*Aut*) braking distance; **distanza di tiro** (*Mil*) range; **distanza di visibilità** (*Aer, Naut*) visibility 2 (*tempo*): **a distanza di 2 giorni** 2 days later; **sono nati a qualche anno di distanza** they were born within a few years of one another 3 (*Sport*) distance; **gara su media/lunga distanza** middle-/long-distance race 4 (*fraseologia*): **prendere le distanze da qc/qn** to dissociate o.s. from sth/sb; **tenere** *o* **mantenere le distanze** to keep one's distance; **tenere qn a distanza** to keep sb at arm's length

distanziare [distan'tsjare] /19/ VT 1 (*oggetti*) to place at intervals; (*piante*) to space out 2 **distanziare qn** (*Sport*) to leave sb behind, outdistance sb; (*superare*) to outstrip, surpass

distare [dis'tare] /72/ VI *vb dif*: **distare (da)** to be a long way (from); **dista molto da qui?** is it far (away) from here?; **non dista molto** it's not far (away); **quanto dista?** how far is it?; **distiamo pochi chilometri da Roma** we are only a few kilometres (away) from Rome

distendere [dis'tendere] VB IRREG /120/ VT (*braccia, gambe*) to stretch (out); (*muscoli*) to relax; (*tovaglia*) to spread; (*bucato*) to hang out; **non c'era posto per distendere le gambe** there was no room to stretch your legs; **fecero distendere il ferito sul letto** they laid the injured man on the bed; **distendere i nervi** to relax; **è ottimo per distendere i nervi** it's just the thing to help you relax; **distendersi** VR (*persona*) to lie down, stretch out; (*fig: rilassarsi*) to relax; **distendersi** VIP (*estendersi*): **i prati si stendevano a perdita d'occhio** the fields stretched out as far as the eye could see

distensione [disten'sjone] SF (*Pol*) détente; (*rilassamento*) relaxation; (*estensione*) stretching

distensivo, -a [disten'sivo] AGG (*gen*) relaxing, restful; (*Pol*) conciliatory

disteso, -a [dis'teso] PP di **distendere** ♦ AGG (*allungato: persona, gamba*) stretched out; (*rilassato: persona, atmosfera*) relaxed; **essere disteso** to be lying; **era distesa sul letto** she was lying on the bed; **se ne stava distesa sul letto** he was stretched out on the bed; **cadere lungo disteso** to fall flat on one's face; **avere un volto disteso** to look relaxed

distillare [distil'lare] /72/ VT to distil; **acqua distillata** distilled water

distillato [distil'lato] SM distillate

distillazione [distillat'tsjone] SF distillation

distilleria [distille'ria] SF distillery

distinguere [dis'tingwere] VB IRREG /42/ VT 1 (*differenziare*) to distinguish, single out; **distinguere tra** to tell the difference between; **non li distinguo tra loro** I can't tell the difference between them; **distinguere il vero dal falso** to tell truth from falsehood; **la sua energia lo distingue dagli altri** his energy distinguishes him *o* sets him apart from the others 2 (*percepire*) to distinguish, discern; **era troppo buio per distinguere la sua faccia** it was too dark to see *o* make out his (*o* her) face; **non riesco a distinguere il numero dell'autobus** I can't see the number of the bus 3 (*contrassegnare*:

con etichetta) to mark, indicate **4** (*frm: dividere*) to divide, separate; **distinguersi** VIP **1** (*essere riconoscibile*) to be distinguished **2** (*emergere*) to stand out, be conspicuous, distinguish o.s.; **un whisky che si distingue per il suo aroma** a whisky with a distinctive bouquet; **si è sempre distinta per la sua eleganza** her elegance always makes her stand out from the crowd

distinguo [dis'tingwo] SM INV distinction

distinta [dis'tinta] SF (*Comm*) note; (*elenco*) list; **distinta di pagamento** receipt; **distinta di versamento** paying-in slip

distintivo, -a [distin'tivo] SM badge ♦ AGG distinguishing

distinto, -a [dis'tinto] PP *di* **distinguere** ♦ AGG **1** (*differente*) different, distinct; **due materie distinte** two distinct subjects **2** (*chiaro*) distinct, clear **3** (*elegante, dignitoso: signore*) distinguished; (: *modi*) refined; **un signore dall'aspetto distinto** a distinguished-looking man; **modi distinti** excellent manners; **distinti saluti** (*in lettera*) yours faithfully *o* truly

distinzione [distin'tsjone] SF **1** (*gen*) distinction; **non faccio distinzioni** (*tra persone*) I don't discriminate; (*tra cose*) it's all one *o* the same to me; **senza distinzione di razza/religione...** without distinction of race/religion ... **2** (*signorilità*) distinction, refinement **3** (*onore*) honour, distinction

distogliere [dis'tɔʎʎere] /122/ VT IRREG **1** (*allontanare*) to remove, take away; **distogliere lo sguardo** to look away **2** (*distrarre*) to distract; **cerca di distoglierla mentre portiamo via la torta** try and distract her while we take the cake away **3** (*fig: dissuadere*) to dissuade, deter; **distogliere qn da qc** to dissuade sb from sth

distolto, -a [dis'tɔlto] PP *di* **distogliere**

distorcere [dis'tɔrtʃere] /106/ VT IRREG **1** (*contorcere*) to twist; (*fig: verità, versione dei fatti*) to twist, distort; **distorcersi una caviglia** to sprain one's ankle **2** (*Fis, Ottica*) to distort; **distorcersi** VR (*contorcersi*) to twist

distorsione [distor'sjone] SF **1** (*Med*) sprain **2** (*Fis, Ottica*) distortion

distorto, -a [dis'tɔrto] PP *di* **distorcere** ♦ AGG (*Fis, Ottica, fig*) distorted

distrarre [dis'trarre] VB IRREG /123/ VT (*distogliere*) to distract, divert; (*divertire*) to amuse, entertain; **non distrarlo dal lavoro** don't distract him from his work; **distrarre lo sguardo** to look away; **distrarsi** VR (*non fare attenzione*) to let one's mind wander; (*svagarsi*) to take one's mind off things; **ho bisogno di distrarmi un po'** I need to take my mind off things; **si distrae spesso durante le lezioni** his mind often wanders during lessons; **non distrarti!** pay attention!

distrattamente [distratta'mente] AVV absent-mindedly, without thinking

distratto, -a [dis'tratto] PP *di* **distrarre** ♦ AGG (*persona*) absent-minded; (*pegg*) inattentive; **è molto distratto** he's very absent-minded; **scusa, ero distratta** I'm sorry, I wasn't paying attention

distrazione [distrat'tsjone] SF **1** (*caratteristica*) absent-mindedness; (*disattenzione*) carelessness; **errori di distrazione** slips of the pen, careless mistakes; **mi scusi, è stato un attimo di distrazione** I'm sorry, I wasn't thinking **2** (*divertimento*) distraction, amusement, entertainment

distretto [dis'tretto] SM (*circoscrizione*) district; **distretto militare** recruiting office

distribuire [distribu'ire] /55/ VT **1** (*dare: gen*) to distribute; (*posta*) to deliver; (*lavoro, mansioni: assegnare*) to allocate, assign; (: *ripartire*) to share out; (: *carte*) to deal (out); **distribuisci i quaderni** hand out the exercise books **2** (*disporre*) to arrange; (*Mil*) to deploy

distributore, -trice [distribu'tore] SM (*apparecchio*) dispenser; (*Aut, Elettr*) distributor; (*di sigarette, bibite*) vending machine, slot machine; (*di biglietti*) ticket machine; **distributore (di benzina)** (*pompa*) petrol (*Brit*) *o* gas (*USA*) pump; (*stazione*) petrol (*Brit*) *o* gas (*USA*) station ♦ SM, SF distributor

distribuzione [distribut'tsjone] SF **1** (*vedi vb*) distribution; delivery; allocation; assignment; sharing out, dealing; arrangement; deployment **2** (*Tecn*) distribution; **regolare la distribuzione** (*Aut*) to set the timing

districare [distri'kare] /20/ VT (*sbrogliare*) to unravel, to disentangle; (*fig: chiarire*) to unravel, sort out; **districarsi** VR **1** (*tirarsi fuori*) to extricate o.s. from **2** (*fig: cavarsela*) to manage, get by

distruggere [dis'truddʒere] /83/ VT IRREG (*gen*) to destroy; (*popolazione*) to wipe out; (*fig: speranze*) to ruin, destroy; (: *persona*) to shatter

distruttivo, -a [distrut'tivo] AGG destructive

distrutto, -a [dis'trutto] PP *di* **distruggere** ♦ AGG (*fig*): **sono distrutto!** (*stanco*) I'm exhausted *o* knackered (*fam*)!; (*dal dolore*) I'm devastated!

distruzione [distrut'tsjone] SF destruction

disturbare [distur'bare] /72/ VT (*importunare*) to disturb, trouble, bother; (*portar scompiglio*) to disturb, interrupt; **disturbo? am I disturbing you?; non vorrei disturbare** I don't want to be a nuisance; **"non disturbare"** "do not disturb"; **la disturba se fumo?** — **non mi disturba affatto** do you mind if I smoke? — no, I don't mind at all; **disturbarsi** VR to bother, to put o.s. out; **stia comodo, non si disturbi** please don't get up; **non doveva disturbarsi!** you shouldn't have gone to all that trouble!; **grazie del regalo, ma non dovevi disturbarti!** thank you for the present, but you shouldn't have!

disturbo [dis'turbo] SM **1** (*incomodo*) trouble, bother, inconvenience; **non è affatto un disturbo** it's no trouble at all; **ci scusiamo per il disturbo** we apologize for any inconvenience; **prendersi il disturbo di fare qc** to take the trouble to do sth; **disturbo della quiete pubblica** (*Dir*) breach of the peace **2** (*Med*) (slight) problem, ailment; **disturbi di stomaco** stomach trouble *sg* **3** (*Radio, TV*); **disturbi** SMPL noise *sg*, interference *sg*, static *sg*

disubbidiente [dizubbi'djɛnte] AGG disobedient

disubbidienza [dizubbi'djɛntsa] SF disobedience; **disubbidienza civile** civil disobedience

disubbidire [dizubbi'dire] /55/ VI (*aus avere*) disubbidire (a qn) to disobey (sb); **mi ha disubbidito** he disobeyed me; **disubbidire alla legge** to break the law

disuguaglianza [dizugwaʎ'ʎantsa] SF inequality

disuguale [dizu'gwale] AGG **1** (*gen, differente*) different; (*grandezze, altezze*) unequal **2** (*non uniforme: superficie*) uneven, irregular

disumanità [dizumani'ta] SF INV inhumanity

disumano, -a [dizu'mano] AGG inhuman; **un grido disumano** a terrible cry

disunione [dizu'njone] SF (*separazione*) disunity

disunire [dizu'nire] /55/ VT (*separare*) to take apart, separate; (*fig: disgregare*) to divide, disunite; **disunirsi** VIP (*oggetti*) to come apart; (*elementi*) separate

disuso [di'zuzo] SM disuse; **cadere in disuso** to fall into disuse

dita ['dita] SFPL *di* **dito**

ditale [di'tale] SM (*per cucire*) thimble; (*per ferita*) fingerstall

ditata [di'tata] SF (*colpo*) jab (with one's finger), poke; (*segno*) fingermark

dito ['dito] (*nell'insieme: pl f*) **dita**, (*singolarmente: pl m*) **diti** SM **1** (*di mano, guanto*) finger; **dito del piede** toe; **mettersi le dita nel naso** to pick one's nose **2** (*misura*): **per me solo un dito di vino** just a drop of wine for me; **accorciare una gonna di un dito** to shorten a skirt by an inch **3** (*fraseologia*): **avere sulla punta delle dita** (*materia*) to have at one's fingertips; **si possono contare sulle dita di una mano** you can count them on the fingers of one hand; **un pranzetto da leccarsi le dita** a scrumptious meal; **mettere il dito sulla piaga** (*fig*) to touch a sore spot; **non ha mosso un dito (per aiutarmi)** he didn't lift a finger (to help me); **ormai è segnato a dito** everyone knows about him now

ditta ['ditta] SF firm, business; **Spett. Ditta F.lli Gobi** (*su busta*) Messrs Gobi; (*su lettera*) Dear Sirs; **usa la macchina della ditta** he has the use of a company car; **son due giorni che non viene in ditta** he hasn't been into the office for the past two days

dittatore [ditta'tore] SM dictator; **fare il dittatore** to be bossy, act bossy

dittatura [ditta'tura] SF dictatorship

dittongo, -ghi [dit'tongo] SM diphthong

diurno, -a [di'urno] AGG day *attr*, daytime *attr*; **ore diurne** daytime *sg*; **spettacolo diurno** matinée; **albergo diurno** *public toilets with washing and shaving facilities*

diva ['diva] SF *vedi* **divo**

divagare [diva'gare] /80/ vi (*aus* avere) to digress; **divagare dal tema** to stray *o* wander from the point

divagazione [divagat'tsjone] sf digression

divampare [divam'pare] /72/ vi (*aus* essere) (*incendio*) to flare up, break out, blaze up; (*fig: rivolta*) to break out; (: *passione*) to blaze

divano [di'vano] sm sofa, settee; (*senza schienale*) divan; **sul divano** on the sofa; **divano letto** bed settee, sofa bed

divaricare [divari'kare] /20/ vt to open (wide); **a gambe divaricate** with his (*o* her) legs wide apart

divario, -ri [di'varjo] sm (*differenza*) difference; **divario tecnologico** technological gap

divengo *ecc* [di'vɛngo] vb *vedi* **divenire**

divenire [dive'nire] /128/ vi IRREG (*aus* essere) to become ♦ sm (*Filosofia*) becoming

divenni *ecc* [di'vɛnni] vb *vedi* **divenire**

diventare [diven'tare] /72/ vi (*aus* essere) (*gen*) to become; **diventare famoso/medico** to become famous/a doctor; **è diventato famoso** he became famous; **diventare vecchio** to grow old; **la situazione è diventata pericolosa** the situation has become dangerous; **le foglie sono diventate gialle** the leaves have turned yellow; **il latte è diventato acido** the milk has gone sour; **la maglietta è diventata rosa dopo il lavaggio** the T-shirt went pink in the wash; **è diventato rosso in faccia** he turned *o* grew red in the face; **come sei diventato grande!** how tall you've got!; **ora che sei diventato grande** now that you're grown up; **mangia la minestra, non farla diventare fredda** eat your soup, don't let it go *o* get cold; **c'è da diventare matti** it's enough to drive you mad

divenuto, -a [dive'nuto] pp *di* **divenire**

diverbio, -bi [di'vɛrbjo] sm dispute, quarrel, altercation (*frm*)

divergente [diver'dʒɛnte] agg divergent

divergenza [diver'dʒɛntsa] sf divergence; **divergenza d'opinioni** difference of opinion

divergere [di'vɛrdʒere] /59/ vi *vb dif* (*Mat*) to diverge, be divergent; (*fig: opinioni*) to differ, diverge

diverrò *ecc* [diver'rɔ] vb *vedi* **divenire**

diversamente [diversa'mente] avv 1 (*in modo differente*) differently; **diversamente da quanto stabilito** contrary to what had been decided 2 (*altrimenti*) otherwise

diversificare [diversifi'kare] /20/ vt (*gen*) to vary; (*Comm: prodotti*) to diversify; **diversificarsi** vip: **diversificarsi (per)** to differ (in)

diversificazione [diversifikat'tsjone] sf (*il diversificare*) diversification 2 (*diversità*) difference

diversione [diver'sjone] sf (*anche Mil*) diversion

diversità [diversi'ta] sf INV (*differenza*) difference; (*varietà*) variety, diversity

diversivo, -a [diver'sivo] agg diversionary; **fare un'azione diversiva** to create a diversion ♦ sm (*divertimento*) diversion, distraction

diverso, -a [di'vɛrso] agg (*differente*): **diverso (da)** different (from); **è diverso da me** he's different from me; **secondo me è diverso** I don't see it like that ♦ *agg indef*: **diversi(e)** *pl*: (*alcuni, parecchi*) several; **diversi amici** several friends; **diversi mesi fa** some *o* several months ago; **gliel'ho detto diverse volte** I told him several times; **c'era diversa gente** there were quite a few people; **diverse persone me l'hanno detto** several *o* various people told me that ♦ PRON INDEF: **diversi(e)** *pl* several; (*persone*) several (people); **diversi dicono che...** various people say that ...; **ne ho presi diversi** (*libri, bicchieri*) I took several (of them)

divertente [diver'tɛnte] agg (*piacevole*) amusing, entertaining; (*comico*) funny, amusing; **una barzelletta divertente** a funny joke; **Mario è molto divertente** Mario is very funny; **era molto divertente** it was great *o* good fun

divertimento [diverti'mento] sm 1 (*passatempo*) pastime; (*piacere*) amusement, pleasure, entertainment; **per divertimento** for fun; **fare qc per divertimento** to do sth for fun; **buon divertimento!** enjoy yourself!, have a good time!; **bel divertimento!** (*iro*) that sounds like fun! 2 (*Mus*) divertimento, divertissement

divertire [diver'tire] /45/ vt to amuse, entertain; **mi ha divertito molto la sua storia** I was very amused by her story; **far**

divertire qn to amuse sb; **divertirsi** vr to enjoy o.s., amuse o.s., have fun; **divertiti!** have a good time!; **ti sei divertito alla festa?** did you have a good time at the party?; **divertirsi a fare qc** to enjoy doing sth; **divertirsi alle spalle di qn** to have a laugh at sb's expense

divertito, -a [diver'tito] agg amused

dividendo [divi'dɛndo] sm (*Fin, Mat*) dividend

dividere [di'videre] vb IRREG /43/ vt 1 (*gen, anche Mat*) to divide; (*compito, risorse*) to share out; (*dolce*) to divide (up); **dividere in 5 parti/per 5** to divide *o* split into 5 parts/in 5; **dividere 100 per 2** to divide 100 by 2; **su questo argomento gli studiosi sono divisi** scholars are divided on this matter; **si stavano picchiando e hanno dovuto dividerli** they were fighting and had to be separated; **niente potrà dividerci** nothing can come between us; **si sono divisi il bottino** they split *o* divided the loot between them; **abbiamo diviso i soldi** we shared out the money; **è diviso dalla moglie** he's separated from his wife 2 (*condividere*) to share; **non ho niente da dividere con te** I have nothing in common with you; **dividersi** vr 1 **si divide tra casa e lavoro** he divides his time between home and work 2 (*uso reciproco: persone*) to separate, part; (: *coppia*) to separate; **dividersi** vip (*scindersi*): **dividersi (in)** to divide (into), split up (into); (*ramificarsi*) to fork; **il libro si divide in 5 capitoli** the book is divided into 5 chapters; **a questo punto le nostre strade si dividono** we must now go our separate ways

divieto [di'vjɛto] sm prohibition; "**divieto di accesso**" "no entry"; "**divieto di caccia**" "no hunting"; "**divieto di parcheggio**" "no parking"; "**divieto di sosta**" "no waiting"; "**divieto di transito**" "no thoroughfare"

divincolarsi [divinko'larsi] /72/ vr to wriggle (free), struggle (free); **cercava di divincolarsi** he was struggling to free himself

divinità [divini'ta] sf INV divinity

divino, -a [di'vino] agg (*gen*) divine; (*fig: fam*) divine, heavenly

divisa¹ [di'viza] sf (*uniforme*) uniform; **un ufficiale in divisa** a uniformed officer

divisa² [di'viza] sf (*Fin*) (foreign) currency

divisi *ecc* [di'vizi] vb *vedi* **dividere**

divisione [divi'zjone] sf (*gen*) division; **divisione del lavoro** division of labour; **divisione in sillabe** syllable division; (*a fine riga*) hyphenation

divismo [di'vizmo] sm (*esibizionismo*) prima donna behaviour; (*fanatismo di massa*) hero worship

diviso, -a [di'vizo] pp *di* **dividere**

divisorio, -ria, -ri, -rie [divi'zɔrjo] agg (*siepe, muro esterno*) dividing; (*muro interno*) dividing, partition *attr* ♦ sm (*in una stanza*) partition

divo, -a [di'vo] sm, sf star; **un divo del cinema** a film star; **come una diva** like a prima donna

divorare [divo'rare] /72/ vt (*fig: cibo, libro*) to devour; (: *patrimonio*) to squander; (*sogg: passione, malattia, fuoco*) to consume, devour; **divorare qn con gli occhi** to devour sb with one's eyes; **divorare qn con gli occhi** to eat sb up greedily; **questa macchina divora i chilometri** ≈ this car eats up the miles; **divorarsi** vip: **divorarsi da** (*rabbia, odio*) to be consumed *o* eaten up with

divorziare [divor'tsjare] /19/ vi (*aus* avere) to get divorced; **hanno divorziato** they got divorced; **divorziare dalla moglie/dal marito** to divorce one's wife/husband

divorziato, -a [divor'tsjato] agg divorced ♦ sm, sf divorcé(e)

divorzio, -zi [di'vortsjo] sm divorce

divulgare [divul'gare] /80/ vt 1 (*segreto*) to divulge, disclose 2 (*rendere accessibile: teoria, scienza*) to popularize; **divulgarsi** vip (*notizia, dottrina*) to spread

divulgazione [divulgat'tsjone] sf (*vedi vb*) disclosure; popularization; spread

dizionario, -ri [dittsjo'narjo] sm dictionary; **un dizionario di inglese** an English dictionary

dizione [dit'tsjone] sf 1 (*modo di parlare*) diction, delivery; (*recitazione*) recitation; (*pronuncia*) pronunciation; **corso di dizione** elocution classes *pl* 2 (*locuzione*) idiom, expression

DJ [di'dʒei] SIGLA M, SIGLA F DJ (= *disc jockey*)

Djakarta [dʒa'karta] sf Djakarta

dl ABBR (= *decilitro*) dl

dm ABBR (= *decimetro*) dm

DNA [di'ɛnne'a] SIGLA M (= *acido deossiribonucleico*) DNA ♦ SIGLA F = **Direzione Nazionale Antimafia**

do [dɔ] SM INV (*Mus*) C; (*solfeggiando la scala*) do(h)

dobbiamo [dob'bjamo] VB *vedi* **dovere**

DOC, doc [dɔk] ABBR = **denominazione di origine controllata** ♦ AGG INV: **vini doc** quality wines; **un fiorentino doc** a Florentine born and bred

doc. ABBR = **documento**

doccia, -ce ['dottʃa] SF 1 (*impianto*) shower; **fare la doccia** to have a shower; **doccia fredda** (*fig*) slap in the face 2 (*grondaia*) gutter

docciaschiuma [dottʃas'kjuma] SM INV shower gel

docente [do'tʃɛnte] AGG teaching; **personale non docente** non-teaching staff ♦ SM, SF (*di università*) lecturer (*Brit*), professor (*USA*)

docenza [do'tʃɛntsa] SF (*Univ*): **ottenere la libera docenza** to become a lecturer

DOCG [dotʃi'dʒi] ABBR (= *denominazione di origine controllata e garantita*) *label guaranteeing the quality and origin of a wine*

docile ['dɔtʃile] AGG (*persona*) docile, meek; (*cavallo*) docile, well-behaved; **capelli docili al pettine** manageable hair

docilità [dotʃili'ta] SF (*vedi agg*) docility; meekness

documentare [dokumen'tare] /72/ VT to document; **documentarsi** VR: **documentarsi (su)** to gather information *o* material (about)

documentario, -ria, -ri, -rie [dokumen'tarjo] AGG documentary ♦ SM documentary (film)

documentazione [dokumentat'tsjone] SF documentation

documento [doku'mento] SM 1 (*gen*) document; **documento di identità** proof of identity; **ha un documento (d'identità)?** do you have any identification?; **documenti** papers; **documenti prego!** may I see your papers, please?; **è andato a ritirare i documenti** he went to pick up the papers 2 (*storico*) historical document; **i dolmen sono un importante documento della preistoria** dolmen provide important evidence on the prehistoric period

Dodecanneso [dodekan'nezo] SM: **le isole del Dodecanneso** the Dodecanese Islands

dodicenne [dodi'tʃɛnne] AGG, SM, SF twelve-year-old

dodicesimo, -a [dodi'tʃɛzimo] AGG, SM, SF twelfth

dodici ['doditʃi] AGG INV, SM INV twelve

dogana [do'gana] SF customs *pl*; (*tassa*) (customs) duty; **passare la dogana** to go through customs; **pagare la dogana su qc** to pay duty on sth

doganale [doga'nale] AGG customs *attr*

doganiere [doga'njɛre] SM customs officer

doglie ['dɔʎʎe] SFPL (*Med*) labour *sg* (*Brit*), labor *sg* (*USA*); **avere le doglie** to be in labour

dogma, -i ['dɔgma] SM dogma

dogmatico, -a, -ci, -che [dog'matiko] AGG dogmatic ♦ SM, SF dogmatic person

dolce ['doltʃe] AGG 1 (*zuccherato, piacevole*) sweet; (*formaggio, clima*) mild; (*modi, carattere*) gentle, mild; (*suono, voce, colore*) soft; (*ricordo*) pleasant; (*pendio*) gentle; (*decollo*) smooth; (*legno, carbone*) soft; **un formaggio dolce** a mild cheese; **è molto dolce con me** he's very sweet to me; **cerca di essere più dolce con tua madre** try to be nicer to your mother; **il caffè mi piace dolce** I like my coffee sweet; **il dolce far niente** sweet idleness; **la dolce vita** the good life; **la dolce morte** euthanasia ♦ SM 1 **preferire il dolce al salato** to prefer sweet things to savoury foods 2 (*Culin: portata*) sweet, dessert; (: *torta*) cake; **hai ordinato il dolce?** have you ordered dessert?; **mi piacciono i dolci** I like sweet things

dolcemente [doltʃe'mente] AVV (*sorridere, cantare*) sweetly; (*parlare*) softly; (*baciare, trattare*) gently; **il pendio digradava dolcemente verso il mare** the land sloped gently down towards the sea

dolcezza [dol'tʃettsa] SF (*vedi agg a*) sweetness; mildness; gentleness; softness; pleasantness; smoothness; **parlare con dolcezza** to speak gently

dolciario, -ria, -ri, -rie [dol'tʃarjo] AGG confectionery *attr*

dolciastro, -a [dol'tʃastro] AGG (*sapore*) sweetish; (*stucchevole*) sickly sweet; (*fig: tono*) ingratiating

dolcificante [doltʃifi'kante] AGG sweetening ♦ SM sweetener

dolciumi [dol'tʃumi] SMPL sweets, confectionery *sg*

dolente [do'lɛnte] AGG 1 (*addolorato: espressione*) sorrowful, doleful, sad; **essere dolente per qc** to be very sorry about sth, regret sth profoundly 2 (*dolorante: braccio, gamba*) sore, painful; (: *dente, testa*) aching

dolere [do'lere] VB IRREG /44/ VI (*aus essere*) (*dente*) to ache; (*gamba, schiena*) to hurt, ache; **mi duole la testa** my head is aching, I've got a headache; **dolersi** VIP 1 **dolersi di** (*errore, cattiva azione*) to regret; (*peccato*) to repent of 2 (*protestare*) to complain

dolgo ecc ['dɔlgo] VB *vedi* **dolere**

dollaro ['dɔllaro] SM dollar

dolo ['dɔlo] SM 1 (*Dir*) malice 2 (*letter: frode*) fraud, deceit

Dolomiti [dolo'miti] SFPL: **le Dolomiti** the Dolomites

dolorante [dolo'rante] AGG aching, sore; **sono ancora dolorante** I'm still aching

dolore [do'lore] SM (*fisico*) pain; (*morale*) distress, sorrow, grief; **un dolore acuto** a sharp pain; **avere un dolore a** (*braccio, dito*) to have a pain in; **ho un dolore al braccio** I've got a pain in my arm; **ha dei dolori di testa** he gets headaches; **morire di dolore** to die of grief; **se lo scoprono sono dolori!** if they find out there'll be trouble!; **è con grande dolore che annunciamo la scomparsa di...** with great sorrow we announce the death of ...

doloroso, -a [dolo'roso] AGG (*operazione*) painful; (*situazione*) distressing; (*notizia*) sad; **è un'operazione dolorosa** it's a painful operation; **una notizia dolorosa** a sad piece of news

doloso, -a [do'loso] AGG (*Dir*) malicious; **incendio doloso** arson

dolsi ecc ['dɔlsi] VB *vedi* **dolere**

dom. ABBR (= *domenica*) Sun.

domanda [do'manda] SF 1 (*interrogazione*) question; **fare una domanda a qn** to ask sb a question; **ti ha fatto molte domande?** did he ask you a lot of questions? 2 **domanda (di)** (*richiesta*) request (for) (*d'impiego, iscrizione*) application (for); **hai spedito la domanda?** have you sent off your application?; **fare domanda d'impiego** to apply for a job; **presentare una domanda** to send in an application; **fare domanda all'autorità giudiziaria** to apply to the courts; **far regolare domanda (di qc)** to apply through the proper channels (for sth) 3 (*Econ*): **la domanda** demand; **la domanda e l'offerta** supply and demand

domandare [doman'dare] /72/ VT 1 (*per sapere: ora, nome, indirizzo*) to ask; **domandare qc a qn** to ask sb sth; **mi ha domandato l'ora** he asked me the time; **mi ha domandato se volevo andare alla festa** he asked me if I wanted to go to the party 2 (*per ottenere: informazione, consiglio, aiuto*) to ask for; **domandare qc a qn** to ask sb for sth; **domandare il permesso di** *o* **per fare qc** to ask permission to do sth; **domandare scusa a qn** to beg sb's pardon, say sorry to sb; **domandare un favore a qn** to ask sb a favour, ask a favour of sb; **domandare la parola** to ask leave *o* permission to speak 3 **domandarsi** to wonder, ask o.s.; **mi domando dove possa essere** I wonder where it can be; **mi domando e dico perché devo rimanere qua?** why on earth have I got to stay here? ♦ VI (*aus avere*) **domandare di qn** (*chiedere come sta*) to ask after sb; **mi ha domandato di te** she asked after you; (*voler vedere o parlare a*) to ask for sb; **c'è un signore che domanda di te** (*al telefono*) there's a gentleman asking to speak to you; (*voler vedere*) there's a gentleman asking to speak to *o* see you

❑ **domandare** non si traduce mai con la parola inglese *demand*

domani [do'mani] AVV tomorrow; **domani mattina** tomorrow morning; **domani stesso** tomorrow; **domani l'altro** the day after tomorrow; **domani a mezzogiorno** at midday tomorrow; **domani (a) otto** tomorrow week, a week tomorrow; **domani è sabato** tomorrow's Saturday; **a domani!** see you tomorrow!; **credi che ci presterà la macchina? — sì, domani!** (*fam, iro*) do you think he'll lend us the car? — fat chance! ♦ SM INV 1 (*il giorno dopo*) next day, the next *o* following day 2 **il domani** (*il futuro*) the future; **un domani** some day; **chi sa cosa ci riserva il domani** who knows what the future holds

domare [do'mare] /72/ VT (*belva*) to tame; (*cavallo*) to break in; (*fig: popolo, rivolta*) to subdue; (: *incendio*) to bring under control; (: *passione*) to master, control

domatore, -trice [doma'tore] SM, SF (*gen*) tamer; **domatore di cavalli** horsebreaker; **domatore di leoni** lion tamer

domattina [domat'tina] AVV tomorrow morning

domenica, -che [do'menika] SF Sunday; **ha messo il vestito della domenica** he is dressed in his Sunday best; **domenica delle Palme** Palm Sunday; **domenica di Pasqua** Easter Sunday; *vedi* **martedì**

domenicale [domeni'kale] AGG Sunday *attr*

domenicano, -a [domeni'kano] AGG, SM, SF (*Rel*) Dominican

domestico, -a, -ci, -che [do'mestiko] AGG (*lavori*) domestic, household *attr*; (*vita*) domestic, family *attr*; (*animale: addomesticato*) domestic, domesticated; **lavori domestici** housework; **animale domestico** (*di compagnia*) pet; **le pareti domestiche** one's own four walls ♦ SM, SF (*domestic*) servant; **domestica a ore** cleaning woman

domiciliare [domitʃi'ljare] /19/ AGG domiciliary; **essere agli arresti domiciliari** to be under house arrest; **fare una perquisizione domiciliare** to carry out a house search; **visita domiciliare** (*di medico*) home visit ♦ VT: **domiciliare una bolletta** to set up a direct debit; **domiciliarsi** VR to take up residence

domicilio, -li [domi'tʃiljo] SM (*gen*) residence; (*Dir*) domicile; (*indirizzo*) address, place of residence (*frm*); **qual è il suo domicilio?** where is your place of residence?; **cambiare domicilio** to change one's address; **visita a domicilio** (*di medico*) house call; **"recapito a domicilio"** "deliveries"; **violazione di domicilio** (*Dir*) breaking and entering

dominante [domi'nante] AGG (*colore, nota, anche Bio*) dominant; (*opinione*) prevailing; (*idea*) main *attr*, chief *attr*; (*posizione*) dominating *attr*; (*classe, partito*) ruling *attr* ♦ SF (*Mus*) dominant

dominare [domi'nare] /72/ VT (*gen*) to dominate; (*governare*) to rule; (*situazione*) to control; (*passioni, sentimenti*) to master; **la fortezza domina la pianura** the fortress has a commanding position overlooking the plain; **dominare i mari** to rule the seas *o* waves; **è dominato dal padre** he is dominated by his father; **da lassù si domina uno stupendo panorama** there is a wonderful view from up there ♦ VI (*aus avere*) 1 (*regnare*): **dominare (su)** to reign (over) 2 (*primeggiare*): **dominare su tutti per intelligenza** to excel everyone in intelligence; **dominarsi** VR (*controllarsi*) to control o.s.

dominatore, -trice [domina'tore] AGG ruling *attr* ♦ SM, SF ruler

dominazione [dominat'tsjone] SF domination

dominicano, -a [domini'kano] AGG, SM, SF Dominican; **la Repubblica Dominicana** the Dominican Republic

dominio, -ni [do'minjo] SM 1 (*Pol: supremazia*) dominion; (: *potere*) power; **esercitare il dominio su** to exercise power over; **domini coloniali** colonies; **il dominio indiscusso di un artista** an artist's undisputed pre-eminence; **essere di dominio pubblico** (*notizia*) to be common knowledge 2 (*controllo: gen*) control; (: *delle passioni, di una materia*) mastery; **dominio di sé** self-control

don [dɔn] SM (*sacerdote*) Father; (*titolo spagnolo o meridionale*) Don

donare [do'nare] /72/ VT (*gen*) to give; (*organo*) to donate; **mi ha donato un libro** he gave me a book; **donare il sangue** to give blood; **donare qc a qn** to give sb sth; **donare tutto se stesso a qn** to devote o.s. entirely to sb; **donare la vita per** to give one's life for ♦ VI (*aus avere*) (*abito, colore*): **donare a** to suit, become; **quel vestito ti dona** that dress suits you

donatore, -trice [dona'tore] SM, SF (*gen*) giver; (*Med*) donor; **donatore di organi** organ donor; **donatore di sangue** blood donor

donazione [donat'tsjone] SF donation; **atto di donazione** (*Dir*) deed of gift

donde [donde] AVV (*letter*) whence

dondolare [dondo'lare] /72/ VT (*sedia*) to rock; (*ciondolare: corda, gambe*) to dangle ♦ VI (*aus avere*) (*barca*) to rock, sway; (*altalena*) to sway; (*corda, lampadario*) to swing (to and fro); **dondolarsi** VR (*su sedia*) to rock (backwards and forwards); (*su altalena*) to swing (backwards and forwards)

dondolo [dondolo] SM: **cavallo/sedia a dondolo** rocking horse/chair

dongiovanni [dondʒo'vanni] SM INV Don Juan

donna [dɔnna] SF 1 woman; **ho visto due donne giovani** I saw two young women; **da donna** (*abito*) woman's, lady's; **donna di casa** housewife; **donna a ore** daily (help); **donna delle pulizie** cleaning lady, cleaner; **donna di servizio** maid; **donna di strada** prostitute, streetwalker; **figlio di buona donna!** (*fam*) son of a bitch! 2 (*titolo*) Donna 3 (*Carte*) queen

donnaiolo [donna'jɔlo] SM womanizer

donnola [dɔnnola] SF weasel

dono [dɔno] SM 1 (*regalo*) gift, present; (*donazione*) donation; **fare un dono a qn** to give sb a present; **portare qc in dono a qn** to bring sth as a gift *o* present for sb 2 (*dote*) gift, talent; **un dono di natura** a natural gift *o* talent; **il dono della parola** the gift of speech

doping [dɔpin(g)] SM doping

dopo [dopo] AVV 1 (*in seguito*) afterwards, after; (*poi*) then; (*più tardi*) later; **il giorno dopo** the next *o* following day; **un anno dopo** a year later; **è successo un anno dopo** it happened a year later; **parecchio/poco (tempo) dopo** long/not long after(wards); **prima studia, dopo usciremo** get your (school) work done first then we'll go out; **prima pensa e dopo parla** think before you speak; **è accaduto 2 mesi dopo** it happened 2 months later; **ci vediamo dopo** see you later; **ho rimandato tutto a dopo** I've postponed everything till later 2 (*oltre*) after, next; **ecco la chiesa - la mia casa è subito dopo** there's the church - my house is just past it; **non questa strada, quella dopo** not this street but the next one ♦ PREP (*gen*) after; **dopo un anno** after a year, a year later; **dopo le vacanze** after the holidays; **rimandare qc a dopo Natale** to postpone sth till after Christmas; **è arrivato dopo cena/di me** he arrived after supper/me; **non l'ho più sentito dopo la sua partenza** I haven't heard from him since he left; **uno dopo l'altro** one after the other; **è subito dopo la chiesa** it's just past the church; **la Cina del dopo Mao** post-Mao China; **dopo tutto = dopotutto** ♦ CONG (*temporale*): **dopo mangiato va a dormire** after eating *o* after a meal he has a sleep; **dopo aver mangiato è uscito** after having something to eat *o* after eating he went out; **dopo che è partito after he left; dopo tutto ciò che gli ho detto** after all I said to him; **dopo che = dopoché**

dopobarba [dopo'barba] SM INV after-shave

dopoché [dopo'ke] CONG after, when

dopodiché [dopodi'ke] AVV after which

dopodomani [dopodo'mani] AVV, SM the day after tomorrow; **ci vediamo dopodomani** see you the day after tomorrow

dopoguerra [dopo'gwɛrra] SM INV post-war period, postwar years *pl*

dopolavoro [dopola'voro] SM recreational club

dopopranzo [dopo'prandzo] SM INV afternoon ♦ AVV: **studierò dopopranzo** I'm going to study after lunch *o* this afternoon

doposcì [dopoʃ'ʃi] SM INV après-ski outfit

doposcuola [dopos'kwɔla] SM INV *supervised study and recreation after school hours*

doposole [dopo'sole] SM INV, AGG aftersun

dopotutto [dopo'tutto] AVV after all

doppiaggio, -gi [dop'pjaddʒo] SM (*Cine*) dubbing

doppiare¹ [dop'pjare] /19/ VT (*Cine*) to dub

doppiare² [dop'pjare] /19/ VT 1 (*Naut*) to round 2 (*Sport*) to lap

doppiatore, -trice [doppja'tore] SM, SF dubber

doppietta [dop'pjetta] SF 1 (*fucile*) double-barrelled (*Brit*) *o* double-barreled (*USA*) shotgun; (*sparo*) shot from both barrels 2 (*Calcio*) double; (*Boxe*) one-two 3 (*Aut*) double-declutch (*Brit*), double-clutch (*USA*)

doppiezza [dop'pjettsa] SF (*fig: di persona*) duplicity

doppio, -pia, -pi, -pie [doppjo] AGG (*gen*) double; (*vantaggio*) double, twofold; (*fig: persona*) deceitful; **battere una lettera in doppia copia** to type a letter with a carbon copy; **chiudere a doppia mandata** to double-lock; **un utensile a doppio uso** a dual-purpose utensil; **fare il doppio gioco** (*fig*) to play a double game; **doppio senso** double entendre; **frase a doppio senso** sentence with a double meaning; **strada a doppio senso di circolazione** two-way street; **un**

doppio whisky a double whisky; **doppi vetri** double-glazing; **fare doppio clic su** (*Inform*) to double-click on; **doppio fallo** (*Tennis*) double fault ♦ SM **1 pagare il doppio** to pay twice as much *o* double the amount; **10 è il doppio di 5** 10 is twice *o* two times 5 **2** (*Tennis*) doubles (match); **facciamo un doppio** let's have a game of doubles; **doppio misto** mixed doubles **3** (*attore*) understudy ♦ AVV double; **vedere** *o* **vederci doppio** to see double

doppiofondo [doppjoˈfondo] SM (*di valigia*) false bottom; (*Naut*) double hull

doppione [dopˈpjone] SM duplicate (copy)

doppiopetto [doppjoˈpɛtto] SM INV double-breasted jacket

doppista, -i, -e [dopˈpista] SM, SF (*Tennis*) doubles player

dorare [doˈrare] /72/ VT (*oggetto*) to gild; (*metallo*) to gold-plate; (*Culin: arrosto*) to brown; **dorare la pillola** (*fig*) to sugar the pill

dorato, -a [doˈrato] AGG (*oggetto*) gilt, gilded; (*abbronzatura, giallo*) golden

doratura [doraˈtura] SF **1** (*vedi vb*) gilding; gold-plating; browning **2** (*ornamento*) gilt, decoration

dormicchiare [dormikˈkjare] /19/ VI (*aus avere*) to doze

dormiente [dorˈmjente] AGG sleeping; **cellula dormiente** sleeper cell ♦ SM, SF sleeper

dormiglione, -a [dormiˈʎʎone] SM, SF sleepyhead; **sveglia, dormiglione!** wake up, sleepyhead!

dormire [dorˈmire] /45/ VI (*aus avere*) **1** to sleep; (*essere addormentato*) to be asleep, be sleeping; **sta dormendo** she's sleeping; **andare a dormire** to go to bed; **vado a dormire** I'm going to bed; **abbiamo dormito a Bologna** we spent the night in Bologna; **il caffè non mi fa dormire** coffee keeps me awake; **sono pensieri che non mi fanno dormire** I'm losing sleep thinking about all this; **i campi dormono sotto la neve** (*fig*) the fields slumber under the snow **2** (*fraseologia*): **dormire come un ghiro** to sleep like a log; **dormire della grossa** to sleep soundly, be dead to the world; **dormire con gli occhi aperti** to sleep with one eye open; **dormire in piedi** (*essere stanco*) to be asleep on one's feet; (*essere imbambolato*) to be half asleep; **dormire tranquillo** *o* **tra due guanciali** (*senza preoccupazioni*) to rest easy; **è meglio dormirci sopra** you'd (*o* we'd *ecc*) better sleep on it ♦ VT: **dormire sonni tranquilli/agitati** to have a good/bad night's sleep, sleep well/badly; **dormire il sonno del giusto** to sleep the sleep of the just; **dormire il sonno eterno** to sleep the sleep of the dead

dormita [dorˈmita] SF sleep; **fare una bella dormita** to have a good sleep

dormitorio, -ri [dormiˈtɔrjo] SM (*gen*) dormitory; **dormitorio pubblico** night shelter (*run by local authority*) ♦ AGG INV: **città dormitorio** dormitory town, commuter town

dormiveglia [dormiˈveʎʎa] SM INV: **essere nel dormiveglia** to be half-asleep, be drowsy; **nel dormiveglia ha sentito un rumore** he was half-asleep when he heard a noise

dorrò *ecc* [dorˈrɔ] VB *vedi* **dolere**

dorsale [dorˈsale] AGG **1** (*Anat*) dorsal, back *attr*; **spina dorsale** backbone, spine **2** (*Sport*): **nuoto dorsale** backstroke; **salto dorsale** Fosbury flop ♦ SF (*catena montuosa*) ridge ♦ SM (*di sedia*) back

dorso [ˈdorso] SM **1** (*gen*) back; (*di libro*) spine; (*di monte*) ridge, crest; **a dorso di cavallo** on horseback; **sdraiati sul dorso** lie on your back **2** (*Nuoto*) backstroke; **nuotare a dorso** to do the backstroke

dosaggio, -gi [doˈzaddʒo] SM (*atto*) measuring out; (*dose*) dosage (*frm*); **sbagliare il dosaggio** to get the amount wrong

dosare [doˈzare] /72/ VT (*ingredienti*) to measure out; (*Med*) to dose; (*fig: forze, risorse*) to husband; **saper dosare le proprie forze** to know how much effort to make

dose [ˈdɔze] SF (*Med*) dose; (*di farina, zucchero*) amount, quantity; (*di whisky, vodka*) measure; **ha avuto la sua dose di preoccupazioni** he's had his fair share of worries; **ci vuole una buona dose di coraggio** it takes a lot of courage

dossier [doˈsje] SM INV dossier, file

dosso [ˈdɔsso] SM **1** (*rilievo*) rise; (*di strada*) bump **2 levarsi i vestiti di dosso** to take one's clothes off; **levarsi un peso di dosso** (*fig*) to take a weight off one's mind

dotare [doˈtare] /72/ VT: **dotare di** (*attrezzature*) to equip with, provide *o* supply with; (*fig: qualità*) to endow with

dotato, -a [doˈtato] AGG **1** (*ricco di doti*) gifted, talented; **un bambino molto dotato** a highly gifted *o* talented child **2 dotato di** (*attrezzature*) equipped with; (*bellezza, intelligenza*) endowed with; **le vetture sono dotate di sofisticati strumenti di sicurezza** the cars are equipped with sophisticated safety devices

dotazione [dotatˈtsjone] SF **1** (*gen, anche Mil, Naut*) equipment; **dare qc in dotazione a qn** to issue sb with sth, issue sth to sb; **avere in dotazione una somma** to have a sum at one's disposal; **i macchinari in dotazione alla fabbrica** the machinery in use in the factory **2** (*rendita*) endowment

dote [ˈdɔte] SF (*di sposa*) dowry; (*Fin*) endowment; (*fig*) gift, talent; **portare qc in dote** to bring a dowry of sth; **avere doti naturali per** to have a natural talent for

Dott. ABBR (= *dottore*) Dr

dotto[1], -a [ˈdotto] AGG (*persona*) erudite, learned; (*citazione*) learned; **lingue dotte** classical languages ♦ SM, SF scholar

dotto[2] [ˈdotto] SM (*Anat*) duct

dottorato [dottoˈrato] SM ≈ PhD; **dottorato di ricerca** doctorate

dottore, -essa [dotˈtore] SM, SF **1** (*medico*) doctor; **andare dal dottore** to go to the doctor **2** (*laureato*) graduate; **dottore in lettere** ≈ Bachelor of Arts **3** (*studioso*) scholar

dottrina [dotˈtrina] SF (*Filosofia, Rel*) doctrine; (*cultura*) learning, erudition

Dott.ssa ABBR (= *dottoressa*) Dr.

double face [dublˈfas] AGG INV reversible

dove [ˈdove] AVV (*gen*) where; (*in cui*) where, in which; (*dovunque*) wherever; **dove vivi?** where do you live?; **di dove sei?** where are you from?, where do you come from?; **non so da dove iniziare** I don't know where to begin; **da dove è entrato?** where did he get in?; **la città dove abito** the city where *o* in which I live; **da dove abito vedo...** from where I live I can see ...; **per** *o* **da dove sei passato?** which way did you go?; **siediti dove vuoi** sit wherever you like; **ti do una mano fin dove posso** I'll help you as much as I can; **(fin) dove è arrivato con il programma?** (*insegnante*) how far has he got with the syllabus? ♦ CONG (*letter: allorquando*): **e dove non vi piacesse fate come volete** and if you are not happy about it do what you like ♦ SM where; **gente arrivava da ogni dove** people were arriving from all over; **per ogni dove** everywhere

dovere [doˈvere] /46/ VT IRREG (*soldi, riconoscenza*) to owe; **gli devo il mio successo** I owe my success to him, I have him to thank for my success; **devo tutto ai miei genitori** I owe everything to my parents; **crede che tutto gli sia dovuto** he thinks he has a god-given right to everything

♦ VB AUS (*nei tempi composti prende l'ausiliare del verbo che accompagna*)

1 (*obbligo*) to have to; **come si deve** (*bene*) properly; (*meritatamente*) properly, as he (*o* she *ecc*) deserves; **è una persona come si deve** he is a very decent person; **non avrebbe dovuto esserne informata che il giorno dopo** she was not supposed to hear about it until the following day; **non devi fare rumore** you mustn't *o* you're not to make a noise; **avrebbe dovuto farlo** he should have *o* ought to have done it; **lui deve farlo** he has (got) to do it, he must do it; **devo farlo subito?** do I have to *o* have I got to do it immediately?; **ha dovuto pagare** he had to pay; **è dovuto partire** he had to leave; **devo partire domani** I'm leaving tomorrow; (*purtroppo*) I've got to leave tomorrow; **non devi zuccherarlo** (*non è necessario*) there's no need to add sugar

2 (*fatalità*): **doveva accadere** it was bound to happen; **lo farò, dovessi morire** I'll do it if it kills me; **tutti dobbiamo morire** we all have to die

3 (*previsione*): **deve arrivare alle 10** he should *o* is due to arrive at 10; **sembra che le cose si debbano sistemare** things seem to be sorting themselves out

4 (*probabilità*): **deve essere difficile farlo** it must be difficult to do; **non deve essere uno stupido** he can't be stupid; **dev'essere tardi** it must be late; **devono essere le 4** it must be 4 o'clock; **devo averlo fatto** I must have done it

♦ SM (*obbligo*) duty; **a dovere** (*bene*) properly; (*debitamente*) as he (*o* she *ecc*) deserves; **rivolgersi a chi di dovere** to apply to the appropriate authority *o* person; **fare il proprio dovere di elettore** to do one's duty as a voter; **farsi un dovere di qc** to make sth one's duty; **avere il senso del dovere** to have a sense of duty

doveroso, -a [dove'roso] AGG (*ubbidienza*) dutiful; (*rispetto*) (right and) proper, due; **è doveroso avvertirlo** we (*o* you *ecc*) ought to warn him; **mi sembrava doveroso aiutarlo** I thought I ought to help him

dovizia [do'vittsja] SF abundance; **descrivere qc con dovizia di particolari** to give a very detailed description of sth

dovrò *ecc* [do'vrɔ] VB *vedi* **dovere**

dovunque [do'vunkwe] AVV **1** (*in qualsiasi luogo*) wherever; **dovunque vada** wherever I go; **dovunque tu sia** wherever you are; **ti troverò dovunque tu vada** I'll find you wherever you go **2** (*dappertutto*) everywhere; **si trovano dovunque** they can be found everywhere; **l'ho cercato dovunque** I've looked for it everywhere; **c'erano libri un po' dovunque** there were books all over the place

dovutamente [dovuta'mente] AVV (*debitamente*: *redigere, compilare*) correctly; (: *rimproverare*) as he (*o* she *ecc*) deserves

dovuto, -a [do'vuto] AGG (*denaro*) owing, owed; (*rispetto*) due; **essere dovuto a** to be due to; **il ritardo è dovuto al maltempo** the delay is due to the bad weather; **è dovuto al temporale** it's due to the storm, it's because of the storm; **nel modo dovuto** in the proper way, properly ♦ SM due; **mi hanno pagato più del dovuto** they paid me more than what I was owed; **ho lavorato più del dovuto** I worked more than I actually had to

dozzina [dod'dzina] SF dozen; **c'erano persone/libri a dozzine** there were dozens of people/books; **una dozzina di uova** a dozen eggs; **di** *o* **da dozzina** (*scrittore, spettacolo*) second-rate

dozzinale [doddzi'nale] AGG (*prodotto*) cheap, shoddy; (*persona*) second-rate

draga, -ghe ['draga] SF dredger

dragare [dra'gare] /80/ VT to dredge; **dragare il mare** (*per mine*) to sweep the sea (*for mines*)

dragherò *ecc* [drage'rɔ] VB *vedi* **dragare**

drago, -ghi ['drago] SM dragon; **in inglese è un drago** (*fig: fam*) he's a genius at English

dramma, -i ['dramma] SM **1** (*Teatro*) drama **2** (*fig: vicenda tragica*) drama, tragedy; **fare un dramma di qc** to make a drama out of sth

drammatico, -a, -ci, -che [dram'matiko] AGG **1** (*Teatro*): **arte drammatica** drama; **scuola d'arte drammatica** drama school; **autore drammatico** dramatist **2** (*situazione*) terrible **3** (*emotivo*) dramatic

drammatizzare [drammatid'dzare] /72/ VT to dramatize

drammaturgo, -a, -ghi, -ghe [dramma'turgo] SM, SF dramatist, playwright

drappeggiare [drapped'dʒare] /62/ VT to drape; **drappeggiarsi** VR to drape o.s.

drappeggio, -gi [drap'peddʒo] SM (*tessuto*) drapery; (*di abito*) folds

drappello [drap'pɛllo] SM (*Mil*) squad, platoon; (*gruppo*) group

drappo ['drappo] SM cloth

drastico, -a, -ci, -che ['drastiko] AGG drastic

drenaggio, -gi [dre'naddʒo] SM drainage

drenare [dre'nare] /72/ VT to drain

Dresda ['dresda] SF Dresden

dribblare [drib'blare] (*Calcio*) /72/ VI (*aus avere*) to dribble (the ball) ♦ VT (*avversario*) to avoid, dodge

dritto, -a ['dritto] AGG **1** = **diritto¹ 2** (*fam: scaltro*) sharp, crafty ♦ SM = **diritto¹** ♦ SM, SF (*fam: furbo*): **è un dritto** he's a crafty *o* sly one ♦ AVV = **diritto¹**

drizzare [drit'tsare] /72/ VT (*palo, quadro*) to straighten; (*innalzare: antenna, muro*) to erect; (*volgere: sguardo, occhi*) to turn, direct; **drizzare le orecchie** to prick up one's ears; **drizzarsi** VR: **drizzarsi in piedi** to rise to one's feet, stand up; **drizzarsi a sedere** to sit up

droga, -ghe ['drɔga] SF **1** (*stupefacente*) drug; **la droga**

drugs *pl*; **spacciare droga** to peddle drugs; **fare uso di droga** to take *o* be on drugs; **droghe leggere** soft drugs; **droghe pesanti** hard drugs **2** (*spezia*) spice

drogare [dro'gare] /80/ VT **1** (*persona, animale*) to drug, dope; **questa bevanda è drogata** this drink has been doped **2** (*Culin*) to season, spice; **drogarsi** VR to take drugs, be on drugs

drogato, -a [dro'gato] SM, SF drug addict

drogheria [droge'ria] SF ≈ grocer's (shop) (*Brit*), ≈ grocery (store) (*USA*)

drogherò *ecc* [droge'rɔ] VB *vedi* **drogare**

droghiere, -a [dro'gjere] SM, SF ≈ grocer

dromedario, -ri [drome'darjo] SM dromedary

DS [di'esse] SIGLA MPL (= *Democratici di Sinistra*) Democrats of the Left (*Italian left-wing party*)

dubbio, -bia, -bi, -bie ['dubbjo] SM (*incertezza*) doubt; **mettere in dubbio** (*affermazione, buona fede*) to doubt, question; (*esito, successo*) to put in doubt; **ha messo in dubbio la mia onestà** he questioned my honesty; **avere il dubbio che** to suspect (that), be afraid that; **ho il dubbio che sia stato lui** I suspect that it was him; **ho i miei dubbi in proposito** I have my doubts about it; **essere in dubbio** (*risultato*) to be doubtful *o* uncertain; **sono in dubbio se partire o no** I don't know whether to go or not; **essere in dubbio fra** to hesitate between; **nutrire seri dubbi su qc** to have grave doubts about sth; **senza dubbio** doubtless, no doubt, undoubtedly; **è senza dubbio uno dei suoi quadri più belli** it's undoubtedly one of his finest paintings; **senza alcun dubbio** without a doubt; **esprimere un dubbio su** to express (one's) doubts about ♦ AGG **1** (*incerto: gen*) doubtful; (: *avvenire*) uncertain **2** (*equivoco, discutibile: qualità, gusto*) dubious, questionable; **uno scherzo di dubbio gusto** a joke in poor taste; **di dubbia provenienza** of dubious origin

dubbioso, -a [dub'bjoso] AGG **1** (*esitante*) hesitant, uncertain; (*perplesso: persona*) uncertain; (: *sguardo, aria*) puzzled; **essere dubbioso su qc** to be uncertain about sth, question the truth of sth **2** (*incerto: esito*) uncertain, doubtful

dubitare [dubi'tare] /72/ VI (*aus avere*) **1** **dubitare di** (*onestà*) to doubt, have (one's) doubts as to; (*autenticità*) to question; (*riuscita*) to be doubtful of; **nessuno dubita della tua onestà** nobody doubts your honesty **2** (*ritenere improbabile*): **dubito che venga** I doubt if *o* whether he'll come; **pensi che telefonerà?** — **dubito** do you think he'll phone? — I doubt it; **non dubito che verrà** I have no doubt that he'll come, I'm sure he'll come **3** (*diffidare*): **dubitare di sé** to be unsure of o.s.; **dubitare di qn** to mistrust sb

Dublino [du'blino] SF Dublin; **vive a Dublino** he lives in Dublin

duca, -chi ['duka] SM duke

duce ['dutʃe] SM (*Storia*) (Roman) commander; (*del fascismo*) Duce

duchessa [du'kessa] SF duchess

due ['due] AGG INV **1** two; **due bambini** two children; **due volte** twice; **l'ho fatto due volte** I did it twice; **a due a due** two at a time, two by two **2** (*fig: pochi*) a couple, a few; **dire due parole** to say a few words; **vorrei dire due parole** I'd like to say a few words; **starò via due o tre giorni** I'll be away for two or three days; **ci metto due minuti** it'll only take me a couple of minutes ♦ SM INV two; *vedi* **cinque**

duecentesco, -a, -schi, -sche [duetʃen'tesko] AGG thirteenth-century

duecento [due'tʃento] AGG INV two hundred ♦ SM INV two hundred; **il Duecento** (*secolo*) the thirteenth century

duellare [duel'lare] /72/ VI (*aus avere*) to fight a duel

duello [du'ɛllo] SM duel; **sfidare a duello** to challenge to a duel

duemila [due'mila] AGG INV two thousand ♦ SM INV two thousand; **il duemila** the year two thousand

duepezzi, due pezzi [due'pɛttsi] SM INV (*da bagno*) bikini, two-piece swimsuit; (*abito*) two-piece (suit)

duetto [du'etto] SM (*Mus*) duet

dulcis in fundo [dultʃis in'fundo] AVV to cap it all

duna ['duna] SF dune

dunque ['dunkwe] CONG (*perciò*) therefore, so; (*allora*) well (now), well (then); **fallo dunque!** do it then!; **ho sbagliato,**

dunque è giusto che paghi I made a mistake, so it's fair I should pay; **dunque, come dicevo...** well, as I was saying...
♦ SM INV: **venire al dunque** to come to the point

duo [ˈduo] SM INV (*Mus*) duet; (*Teatro, Cine, fig*) duo; **formano un duo ben assortito** they're a well-matched pair o couple

duole *ecc* [ˈdwɔle] VB *vedi* **dolere**

duomo [ˈdwɔmo] SM cathedral

duplex [ˈdupleks] SM INV (*Telec*) party line

duplicato [dupliˈkato] SM duplicate

duplice [ˈduplitʃe] AGG (*gen*) double, twofold; (*incarico, scopo*) dual; **in duplice copia** in duplicate; **il problema ha un duplice aspetto** the problem is twofold

duplicità [duplitʃiˈta] SF (*fig*) duplicity

durante [duˈrante] PREP (*nel corso di*) during, in the course of; (*per tutta la durata di*) throughout, for; **durante la notte** during the night; **durante l'intera giornata** throughout the day, for the entire day; **vita natural durante** for life

durare [duˈrare] /72/ VI (*aus* avere o essere) (*gen*) to last; **la festa durò tutta la notte** the party went on all night; **lo stipendio ti deve durare tutto il mese** your salary will have to last you the month; **così non può durare!** this can't go on any longer!; **questa storia dura da un pezzo** this business has been going on for some time; **le batterie non sono durate a lungo** the batteries didn't last long; **durare in carica** to remain in office ♦ VT: **durare fatica a fare qc** to have a hard job doing sth, have difficulty in doing sth

durata [duˈrata] SF (*gen*) duration, length; (*di prodotto, pianta*) life; **per tutta la durata di** throughout; **di breve durata** (*vacanza*) short; (*felicità*) short-lived; **di lunga durata**

long-lasting; **durata della vita** life span; **durata media della vita** (*Statistica*) life expectancy

duraturo, -a [duraˈturo] AGG (*ricordo, fama*) enduring; (*pace*) lasting

durezza [duˈrettsa] SF (*gen, di acque*) hardness; (*di metallo*) strength; (*di spazzola*) stiffness; (*di voce*) harshness; (*fig: severità*) severity; (: *rigidità*) rigidity, severity; (: *ostinazione*) stubbornness

duro, -a [ˈduro] AGG **1** (*resistente: gen*) hard; (: *serratura*) stiff; (: *carne*) tough; **duro d'orecchi** (*sordo*) hard of hearing; **duro di comprendonio** o **di testa** slow-witted; **avere la pelle dura** (*fig: persona*) to be tough; **pane duro** stale bread; **il materasso è troppo duro per me** the mattress is too hard for me; **l'insegnamento è un lavoro duro** teaching is hard work **2** (*fig: severo: persona*) harsh, hard; (: *disciplina*) harsh, strict; (: *atteggiamento*) harsh, unbending; (: *inverno*) hard; **duro di cuore** hard-hearted; **non essere troppo duro con lui** don't be too hard on him **3** (*ostinato*) stubborn, obstinate **4** (*faticoso*) hard; **l'insegnamento è un lavoro duro** teaching is hard work ♦ SM **1** (*durezza*) hardness; (*parte dura*) hard part; **dormire sul duro** to sleep on a hard bed **2** (*fig: difficoltà*) hard part; **il duro deve ancora venire** the hard part is still to come ♦ SM, SF (*persona*) tough one; **fare il duro** to act tough ♦ AVV: **tener duro** (*resistere*) to stand firm, hold out

durone [duˈrone] SM (*callo*) hard skin

duttile [ˈduttile] AGG (*sostanza*) malleable; (*fig: carattere*) flexible; (: *stile*) adaptable

DVD [divuˈdi] SM INV (*disco*) DVD; (*lettore*) DVD player

Ee

E¹, e¹ [e] SF INV, SM INV (*lettera*) E, e; **E come Empoli** ≈ E for Edward (*Brit*), ≈ E for Easy (*USA*)

E² ABBR (= *Est*) E

'e [e] CONG *spesso ed dav a vocale* **1** and; **io e te** me and you; **Davide ed un suo amico** David and a friend of his; **un metro e novanta** one metre ninety; **ho speso 3 euro e settanta centesimi** I spent 3 euros seventy cents; **ho pagato quattro sterline e cinquanta** I paid four pounds fifty; **tutt'e tre** all three of them; **tutt'e due** both (of them); **è bell'e fatto** it's well and truly finished; **mi piace molto, e a te?** I like it a lot, what about you?; **io non ci vado, e tu?** I'm not going, how about you? **2** (*avversativo*) but; (*eppure*) and yet; **lo credevo onesto e non lo è** I thought he was honest but he isn't; **sapeva di sbagliare e l'ha fatto ugualmente** he knew it was a mistake but he did it all the same **3** (*ebbene*) well, well then; **e deciditi dunque!** well make up your mind then!; **e smettila!** stop it!

è [ε] VB *vedi* **essere**

EAD ABBR (= *elaborazione automatica dei dati*) A.D.P.

ebanisteria [ebaniste'ria] SF cabinet-making

ebano ['εbano] SM ebony

ebbene [eb'bene] CONG well (then)

ebbi *ecc* ['εbbi] VB *vedi* **avere**

ebbrezza [eb'brettsa] SF intoxication, inebriation; **in stato di ebbrezza** inebriated; (*ubriaco*) intoxicated; (*autista*) under the influence of drink; **l'ebbrezza del successo** the exhilaration of success

ebbro, -a ['εbbro] AGG intoxicated, inebriated; **ebbro di gioia** drunk with joy

ebete ['εbete] AGG slow-witted, moronic (*fam*) ♦ SM, SF half-wit, moron (*fam*)

ebetismo [ebe'tizmo] SM feeble mindedness

ebollizione [ebollit'tsjone] SF boiling; **in ebollizione** boiling; **portare ad ebollizione** to bring to the boil; **punto di ebollizione** boiling point

ebraico, -a, -ci, -che [e'braiko] AGG Jewish; (*scritture*) Hebrew; (*tradizione*) Hebraic ♦ SM (*lingua*) Hebrew

ebreo, -a [e'brεo] AGG Jewish; **è ebreo** he's Jewish ♦ SM, SF Jewish person; (*Storia*) Jew; **gli ebrei** the Jews; **l'Ebreo errante** the Wandering Jew

Ebridi ['εbridi] SFPL: **le (isole) Ebridi** the Hebrides

eburneo, -a [e'burneo] AGG (*letter, di avorio, anche fig*) ivory *attr*

EC ABBR = **Eurocity**

E/C ABBR = **estratto conto**

ecatombe [eka'tombe] SF (*fig: strage*) slaughter, massacre

ecc. ABBR (= *eccetera*) etc.; **vendono libri, dischi, magliette, poster ecc** they sell books, records, T-shirts, posters etc

eccedente [ettʃe'dεnte] SM excess

eccedenza [ettʃe'dεntsa] SF excess; **un'eccedenza di peso** some excess weight; **bagaglio in eccedenza** excess baggage

eccedere [et'tʃεdere] /29/ VT (*competenza, aspettative*) to exceed; (*limiti*) to overstep ♦ VI (*aus avere*) to go too far; **eccedere nel mangiare** to eat too much; **eccedere nel bere** to drink to excess

eccellente [ettʃel'lεnte] AGG excellent; (*cadavere, arresto*) of a prominent person

eccellenza [ettʃel'lεntsa] SF **1** excellence; **per eccellenza** par excellence **2** (*titolo*): **Sua Eccellenza** His (*o* Her) Excellency; **Vostra Eccellenza** Your Excellency

eccellere [et'tʃεllere] /45/ VI IRREG (*aus avere o essere*) **eccellere (in)** to excel (at); **eccellere in tutto** to excel at everything; **eccellere su tutti** to surpass everyone

eccelso, -a [et'tʃεlso] PP *di* **eccellere** ♦ AGG (*cima*) lofty; (*fig*) towering, lofty ♦ SM: **l'Eccelso** (*Rel*) the Almighty

eccentrico, -a, -ci, -che [et'tʃεntriko] AGG (*persona, anche*

Mat) eccentric; **suo zio è un po' eccentrico** his uncle's a bit eccentric; **si veste in modo eccentrico** she wears unusual clothes ♦ SM (*Tecn*) cam

eccessivo, -a [ettʃes'sivo] AGG excessive; **proibirgli di uscire mi sembra un po' eccessivo** I think it's a bit excessive to forbid him to go out

eccesso [et'tʃεsso] SM excess; **gentile fino all'eccesso** kind to a fault; **arrotondare una cifra per eccesso** to round up a figure; **dare in eccesso** to fly off the handle, fly into a rage; **devo smaltire il peso in eccesso** I must lose some excess weight; **eccesso di velocità** (*Aut*) speeding; **ha preso una multa per eccesso di velocità** she was fined for speeding; **eccesso di zelo** excess of zeal; **peccare per eccesso di zelo** to be overzealous

eccetera [et'tʃεtera] AVV et cetera, and so on; **...eccetera eccetera ...** and so on and so forth

eccetto [et'tʃεtto] PREP except; **tutti eccetto lui** everybody except him ♦ CONG: **eccetto che** (*tranne che*) except; **eccetto che (non) piova...** unless it rains ...

eccettuare [ettʃettu'are] /72/ VT: **se si eccettua...** apart from ..., other than ...; **eccettuati i presenti** present company excepted

eccezionale [ettʃettsjo'nale] AGG exceptional; **in via dell tutto eccezionale** in this one instance, exceptionally; **è un film eccezionale** it's a really good film; **in circostanze eccezionali** in exceptional circumstances

eccezione [ettʃet'tsjone] SF **1** exception; **d'eccezione** (*provvedimento*) exceptional, special; (*ospite*) special; **a eccezione o con l'eccezione di** with the exception of, except for; **l'eccezione che conferma la regola** the exception which proves the rule; **fare un'eccezione alla regola** to make an exception to the rule; **mi dispiace, non posso fare eccezioni** I'm sorry, I can't make exceptions; **va bene, ma lui è un'eccezione** okay, but he's an exception **2** (*Dir: obiezione*) objection

ecchimosi [ek'kimozi] SF INV bruise

eccidio, -di [et'tʃidjo] SM massacre

eccitante [ettʃi'tante] AGG (*gen*) exciting; (*sostanza*) stimulating ♦ SM stimulant

eccitare [ettʃi'tare] /72/ VT **1** (*persona: sessualmente*) to arouse; (*curiosità, interesse*) to arouse, excite; (*sensi, fantasia*) to stir; (*folla*) to incite **2** (*agitare*) to excite; **il caffè eccita** coffee acts as a stimulant; **eccitarsi** VIP (*sessualmente*) to become aroused; (*entusiasmarsi*) to get excited; (*innervosirsi*) to get worked up

eccitazione [ettʃitat'tsjone] SF (*gen*) excitement; (*del sistema nervoso*) stimulation; (*Elettr*) excitation

ecclesiastico, -a, -ci, -che [ekkle'zjastiko] AGG (*ufficio*) ecclesiastical; (*gerarchia, beni*) ecclesiastical, church *attr*; (*abito*) clerical ♦ SM ecclesiastic

ecco ['εkko] AVV: **ecco qui/là** here/there it is; **ecco i nostri amici** here are our friends; **ecco il treno** here comes *o* here's the train; **ecco! (prendi)** here you are!; **eccomi** here I am; **eccone due** here are two (of them); **ecco perché** that's why; **ah, ecco perché non è venuto!** so that's why he didn't come!; **ed ecco che sul più bello...** and just at that moment ...; **ecco fatto** there, that's done, there we are

eccome [ek'kome] AVV rather; **ti piace? — eccome!** do you like it? — I certainly do!; **era difficile? — eccome!** was it difficult? — yes it was!; **ti sei divertito? — eccome!** did you enjoy yourself? — yes I did!; **lo so eccome!** don't I know it!

ECG SIGLA M (= *elettrocardiogramma*) ECG

echeggiare [eked'dʒare] /62/ VI (*aus avere o essere*) to echo; **echeggiare di** to echo o resound with

eclettico, -a, -ci, -che [e'klεttiko] AGG, SM, SF eclectic

eclettismo [eklet'tizmo] SM eclecticism

eclissare [eklis'sare] /72/ VT (*anche fig*) to eclipse; **eclissarsi** VIP (*persona: scherz*) to disappear

eclissi [e'klissi] SF INV eclipse

eco ['eko] SM, SF (pl m echi) echo; **fare eco a qc/qn** to echo sth/sb; **suscitò** o **ebbe una vasta eco** it caused a considerable stir

ecografia [ekogra'fia] SF (Med) ultrasound, echography; **ho fatto un'ecografia** I had a scan

ecologia [ekolo'dʒia] SF ecology; **i problemi dell'ecologia** environmental issues

ecologico, -a, -ci, -che [eko'lɔdʒiko] AGG ecological; (detersivo, vernice ecc) environmentally friendly, eco-friendly; **un detersivo ecologico** an environmentally friendly detergent; **una catastrofe ecologica** an ecological disaster; **pelliccia ecologica** fake fur

ecologista, -i, -e [ekolo'dʒista] SM, SF ecologist; (ambientalista) environmentalist ♦ AGG (movimento) ecology attr; (gruppo, attivista) environmental

ecologo, -a, -gi, -ghe [e'kɔlogo] SM, SF ecologist

eco'mafia SF mafia involved in crimes related to the environment, in particular the illegal disposal of waste

economato [ekono'mato] SM (Scol, Univ) bursar's office

economia [ekono'mia] SF 1 (scienza) economics sg; (di paese, nazione) economy; **l'economia è in crisi** the economy is in crisis; **studia economia** he's studying economics; **economia aziendale** business management; **economia domestica** home economics sg; **economia di mercato** market economy; **economia e commercio** (Univ) business studies; **economia pianificata** planned economy; **economia politica** (Univ) political economy; **economia di scala** economy of scale; **economia sommersa** black (Brit) o underground (USA) economy 2 (impiego razionale) economy; (risparmio) saving; **dobbiamo fare economia** we must economize o make economies; **vivere in economia** to live frugally; **lavori in economia** (nei cantieri edili) building work involving direct labour

economico, -a, -ci, -che [eko'nɔmiko] AGG (Econ) economic; (che costa poco) inexpensive; (che fa risparmiare) economical; **un albergo economico** an inexpensive hotel; **più economico** cheaper; **è più economico viaggiare in pullman** it's cheaper to travel by coach; **crisi economica** economic crisis; **viaggiare in classe economica** to travel economy class; **edizione economica** low price edition

economista, -i, -e [ekono'mista] SM, SF economist

economizzare [ekonomid'dzare] /72/ VT (soldi, forze) to save ♦ VI (aus avere) **economizzare (su)** to economize (on), cut down (on)

economo, -a [e'kɔnomo] AGG thrifty ♦ SM, SF (Amm) bursar

ecosistema, -i [ekosis'tema] SM ecosystem

ecotassa [eko'tassa] SF green tax

ecstasy [eks'tazi] SF INV Ecstasy

Ecuador [ekwa'dɔr] SM Ecuador

ecumenico, -a, -ci, -che [eku'meniko] AGG ecumenical

eczema, -i [ek'dzɛma] SM eczema

ed [ed] CONG vedi **e**

Ed. ABBR = **editore**

ed. ABBR = **edizione**

edera ['edera] SF ivy

edicola [e'dikola] SF newspaper kiosk o stand, newsstand (USA)

edicolante [ediko'lante] SM, SF newspaper-seller

edificante [edifi'kante] AGG edifying; **è uno spettacolo poco edificante** it isn't a very edifying spectacle

edificare [edifi'kare] /20/ VT 1 (casa) to build; (teoria) to construct; (azienda) to set up 2 (indurre al bene) to edify

edificio, -ci [edi'fitʃo] SM (costruzione) building; (struttura: sociale) structure; (: filosofico, critico) framework

edile [e'dile] AGG building attr, construction attr; **un cantiere edile** a building site; **un operaio edile** a construction worker ♦ SM, SF construction worker

edilizio, -zia, -zi, -zie [edi'littsjo] AGG building attr

Edimburgo [edim'burgo] SF Edinburgh; **abita ad Edimburgo** she lives in Edinburgh; **domani andremo a Edimburgo** we're going to Edinburgh tomorrow

edito, -a ['edito] AGG published

editore, -trice [edi'tore] AGG publishing attr ♦ SM, SF (imprenditore) publisher; (chi cura la pubblicazione) editor

editoria [edito'ria] SF publishing; **editoria elettronica** electronic publishing

editoriale [edito'rjale] AGG publishing attr; **l'industria editoriale** the publishing industry ♦ SM (articolo di fondo) leader, editorial

editto [e'ditto] SM edict

edizione [edit'tsjone] SF 1 (di libro, giornale) edition; **la seconda edizione del libro** the second edition of the book; **edizione economica** paperback; **si trova anche in edizione economica** it's also available in paperback; **edizione a tiratura limitata** limited edition 2 **la quarantesima edizione della Fiera di Milano** the fortieth Milan Trade Fair

edonismo [edo'nizmo] SM hedonism

edotto, -a [e'dɔtto] AGG informed; **rendere qn edotto su qc** to inform sb about sth

educanda [edu'kanda] SF boarder

educare [edu'kare] /20/ VT (gen, anche fig: gusto) to educate; (allevare) to bring up; **educare qn a rispettare qc** to bring sb up to respect sth

educativo, -a [eduka'tivo] AGG educational

educato, -a [edu'kato] AGG (gen) polite; (bambino) well-behaved, well-mannered; **è un ragazzo molto educato** he's a very polite boy; **non è educato fare così** it's not good manners o polite o nice to do that; **non è educato fissare la gente** it's rude to stare at people
- **educato** non si traduce mai con la parola inglese educated

educazione [edukat'tsjone] SF 1 (comportamento) (good) manners pl; **per educazione** out of politeness; **buona/cattiva educazione** good/bad manners; **questa è pura mancanza d'educazione!** this is sheer bad manners!; **ma che razza d'educazione!** how rude! 2 (formazione) education; (familiare) upbringing; **un'educazione umanistica** a classical education; **ha avuto un'educazione molto severa** he had a very strict upbringing; **educazione fisica** physical education o training

educherò [eduke'rɔ] VB vedi **educare**

EED [ee'di] SIGLA F (= elaborazione elettronica dei dati) EDP

EEG [eed'ʒi] SIGLA M (= elettroencefalogramma) EEG

efelide [e'fɛlide] SF freckle

effeminato, -a [effemi'nato] AGG effeminate

efferato, -a [effe'rato] AGG brutal, savage

effervescente [efferveʃ'ʃɛnte] AGG (gen) effervescent; (fig: persona, personalità) bubbly; **bibita effervescente** fizzy drink; **digestivo effervescente** liver salts

effettivamente [effettiva'mente] AVV (in effetti) in fact; (a dire il vero) really, actually
- **effettivamente** non si traduce mai con la parola inglese effectively

effettivo, -a [effet'tivo] AGG 1 (vero e proprio) real 2 (impiegato, professore) permanent; (Mil) regular ♦ SM 1 (Amm); **effettivi** SMPL permanent staff; (Mil) strength 2 (di patrimonio) sum total
- **effettivo** non si traduce mai con la parola inglese effective

effetto[1] [ef'fetto] SM 1 (risultato) effect; **avere o produrre un effetto (su)** to have o produce an effect (on); **l'effetto voluto** the desired effect; **far effetto** (medicina) to take effect, (start to) work; **la pastiglia farà effetto tra una mezz'ora** you'll feel the effect of the pill in about half an hour; **sotto l'effetto dell'alcool** under the influence of alcohol; **in effetti** in fact; **in effetti non ha tutti i torti** in fact she's quite right; **a questo o tale effetto** to this end; **la legge ha effetto retroattivo** the law is retroactive 2 (fig: impressione) effect, impression; **ebbe l'effetto di una bomba** it had a shattering effect; **fare effetto su qn** to make an impression on sb; **il sangue mi fa effetto** I can't take the sight of blood; **mi fa un effetto strano pensare che...** it gives me a strange feeling to think that ...; **che effetto fa?** what's it like?; **cercare l'effetto** to try to impress; **effetti speciali** (Cine) special effects; **un film ricco di effetti speciali** a film with lots of special effects; **effetto cocktail** (Med) cocktail effect; **effetto neve** (TV) snow; **effetto serra** (Meteor) greenhouse effect 3 (Sport: di palla) spin; **colpire d'effetto una palla** to put a spin on a ball 4 (Comm: cambiale) bill

effetto² [efˈfetto] SM, SPEC PL **effetti personali** personal effects, personal belongings

effettuare [effettuˈare] /72/ VT (gen) to make; (controllo, volontà altrui) to carry out; **effettuare una fermata** (treni, bus) to stop; **effettuarsi** VIP to take place

efficace [effiˈkatʃe] AGG (provvedimento, rimedio) effective; **un rimedio efficace contro il raffreddore** an effective remedy for colds

efficacia [effiˈkatʃa] SF effectiveness

efficiente [effiˈtʃɛnte] AGG (persona, macchina) efficient; (misura) effective; **un impiegato efficiente** an efficient worker

efficientismo [effitʃenˈtizmo] SM (show of) hyper-efficiency

efficienza [effiˈtʃɛntsa] SF efficiency

effigiare [effiˈdʒare] /62/ VT to represent, portray

effigie, -gi [efˈfidʒe] SF effigy; (ritratto) portrait

effimero, -a [efˈfimero] AGG (gen) ephemeral, fleeting; (speranza, gloria) short-lived

effluvio, -vi [efˈfluvjo] SM (anche iro) scent, perfume

effusione [effuˈzjone] SF 1 (gen) effusion; **effusione lavica** (Geol) lava flow 2 **con effusione** (salutare, abbracciare) warmly

e.g. ABBR (= exempli gratia) e.g.

egemonia [edʒemoˈnia] SF hegemony

Egeo [eˈdʒɛo] SM: **l'Egeo, il mar Egeo** the Aegean (Sea)

egida [ˈɛdʒida] SF: **sotto l'egida di** under the aegis of

Egitto [eˈdʒitto] SM Egypt; **andremo in Egitto questa primavera** we're going to Egypt this spring; **mi è piaciuto molto l'Egitto** I really liked Egypt

egiziano, -a [edʒitˈtsjano] AGG Egyptian ♦ SM, SF Egyptian ♦ SM (lingua) Ancient Egyptian

egizio, -zia, -zi, -zie [eˈdʒittsjo] AGG, SM, SF Ancient Egyptian

egli [ˈeʎʎi] PRON PERS (poco usato) he; **egli stesso** he himself

ego [ˈego] SM INV (Psic) ego

egocentrico, -a, -ci, -che [egoˈtʃɛntriko] AGG egocentric, self-centred (Brit), self-centered (USA) ♦ SM, SF self-centred (Brit) o self-centered (USA) person

egocentrismo [egotʃenˈtrizmo] SM egocentricity

egoismo [egoˈizmo] SM selfishness; (Psic) egoism

egoista, -i, -e [egoˈista] AGG selfish; (Psic) egoistic; **penso di essere stato molto egoista** I think I've been very selfish; **sei egoista!** you're selfish! ♦ SM, SF selfish person; (Psic) egoist; **è un grande egoista** he's a very selfish person

egoistico, -a, -ci, -che [egoˈistiko] AGG selfish; (Psic) egoistic

egotismo [egoˈtizmo] SM egotism

egotista, -i, -e [egoˈtista] AGG egotistic ♦ SM, SF egotist

Egr., egr. ABBR = Egregio

egregio, -gia, -gi, -gie [eˈgrɛdʒo] AGG distinguished; **Egregio Signore** (nelle lettere) Dear Sir

eguaglianza ecc [egwaʎˈʎantsa] = uguaglianza

egualitario, -ria, -ri, -rie [egwaliˈtarjo] AGG, SM, SF egalitarian

EI ABBR = Esercito Italiano

eiaculazione [ejakulatˈtsjone] SF (Fisiologia) ejaculation; **eiaculazione precoce** premature ejaculation

elaborare [elaboˈrare] /72/ VT (proposta) to elaborate, develop; (concetto, idea) to work out; (dati) to process

elaboratore [elaboraˈtore] SM (Inform): **elaboratore elettronico** computer

elaborazione [elaboratˈtsjone] SF (gen) elaboration; (di concetto, idea) working out ♦ (Inform): **elaborazione (automatica) dei dati** (automatic) data processing; **elaborazione a blocchi** batch processing; **elaborazione conversazionale** interactive computing; **elaborazione elettronica dei dati** electronic data processing; **elaborazione testi** word processing

elargire [elarˈdʒire] /55/ VT to give (generously)

elargizione [elardʒitˈtsjone] SF donation

elasticizzato, -a [elastitʃidˈdzato] AGG (tessuto) stretch attr; **tessuto elasticizzato** stretch material

elastico, -a, -ci, -che [eˈlastiko] AGG (materiale) elastic; (fig: andatura) springy; (: mente, vedute, misure) flexible; (: principi morali) lax ♦ SM (per cucito: nastro) elastic no pl; (di gomma) elastic band, rubber band

elefante [eleˈfante] SM elephant

elegante [eleˈgante] AGG elegant, smart; **una giacca elegante** a smart jacket; **è sempre elegante** she's always smart

eleganza [eleˈgantsa] SF elegance; (nel vestirsi) elegance, smartness

eleggere [eˈleddʒere] /61/ VT IRREG: **eleggere (a)** to elect (to); **hanno eletto il nuovo presidente** they've elected the new president

elementare [elemenˈtare] AGG (gen) elementary; (rozzo, rudimentale) rudimentary; (principi, nozioni) basic; (Chim) elemental; **alcune nozioni elementari di informatica** some basic knowledge of computing; **scuola elementare** primary (Brit) o grade (USA) school; **la prima elementare** the first year of primary (Brit) o grade (USA) school; **la seconda elementare** the second year at primary school (Brit) o grade (USA) school ♦ SFPL: **le elementari** primary (Brit) o grade (USA) school sg

elemento [eleˈmento] SM (gen, anche Chim) element; (di meccanismo) part, component; (di pila) cell; (di cucina componibile) unit; **un elemento chimico** a chemical element; **elementi di algebra** basic algebra; **la furia degli elementi** the fury of the elements; **non è stato scoperto nessun nuovo elemento** no new facts have come to light; **è il migliore elemento della squadra** he's the best player in the team; **essere nel proprio elemento** to be in one's element; **elementi in parallelo/in serie** (Fis) parallel/series elements

elemosina [eleˈmɔzina] SF charity, alms pl (ant); **chiedere l'elemosina** to beg; **per strada tanti chiedevano l'elemosina** there were a lot of people begging in the street; **dare qc in elemosina** to give sth to charity; **cassetta delle elemosine** (in chiesa) alms box; **non ho bisogno della tua elemosina** (fig) I don't need your charity

elemosinare [elemoziˈnare] /72/ VT to beg for ♦ VI (aus avere) to beg

elencare [elenˈkare] /20/ VT to list

elencherò ecc [elenkeˈrɔ] VB vedi **elencare**

elenco, -chi [eˈlenko] SM list; **fare un elenco di** (scritto) to make a list of, list; (orale) to list; **c'è un elenco di ostelli della gioventù** there's a list of youth hostels; **elenco telefonico** telephone directory o phone book; **l'ho cercato sull'elenco telefonico** I looked him up in the phone book

elessi ecc [eˈlessi] VB vedi **eleggere**

elettivo, -a [eletˈtivo] AGG (carica) elective

eletto, -a [eˈletto] PP di **eleggere** ♦ AGG (Pol) elected; (pubblico) select; **il popolo eletto** the chosen people ♦ SM 1 (Pol) elected member 2 (Rel); **gli eletti** SMPL the elect, the chosen

elettorale [elettoˈrale] AGG electoral, election attr; **campagna elettorale** election campaign; **sistema elettorale** electoral system

elettorato [elettoˈrato] SM: **elettorato (attivo)** electorate

elettore, -trice [eletˈtore] SM, SF voter

elettrauto [eletˈtrauto] SM INV (Aut: officina) workshop for electrical repairs; (: tecnico) electrician

elettricista, -i [elettriˈtʃista] SM electrician; **fa l'elettricista** he's an electrician

elettricità [elettritʃiˈta] SF electricity; **c'è elettricità nell'aria** (fig) the atmosphere is electric

elettrico, -a, -ci, -che [eˈlettriko] AGG (gen) electric; (impianto, corrente) electric(al); **un filo elettrico** an electric wire; **tariffe elettriche** electricity charges; **blu elettrico** electric blue ♦ SM (operaio) electrician, electricity worker, power worker

elettrificare [elettrifiˈkare] /20/ VT (linea ferroviaria) to electrify

elettrizzante [elettridˈdzante] AGG (fig) electrifying

elettrizzare [elettridˈdzare] /72/ VT to charge (with electricity); (fig: pubblico, atmosfera) to electrify; **elettrizzarsi** VIP to become charged with electricity; (fig: persona) to be electrified, be thrilled

elettro- [eˈlettro] PREF electro-

elettrocardiogramma, -i [elettrokardjoˈgramma] SM electrocardiogram

elettrodo [eˈlettrodo] SM electrode

elettrodomestico, -a, -ci, -che [elettrodoˈmestiko] AGG: **(apparecchio) elettrodomestico** domestic (electrical) appliance

elettroencefalogramma, -i [elettroentʃefaloˈgramma] SM electroencephalogram, EEG

elettrogeno, -a [eletˈtrɔdʒeno] AGG: **gruppo elettrogeno** generator

elettrolisi [eletˈtrɔlizi] SF electrolysis

elettromagnetico, -a, -ci, -che [elettromaɲˈɲɛtiko] AGG electromagnetic

elettromotrice [elettromoˈtritʃe] SF electric train

elettrone [eletˈtrone] SM electron

elettronico, -a, -ci, -che [eletˈtrɔniko] AGG (gen) electronic; (carica, microscopio) electron attr; **musica elettronica** electronic music; **posta elettronica** e-mail; **ingegneria elettronica** electronic engineering

elettroshock [elettroʃˈʃɔk] SM INV electroconvulsive therapy, (electro)shock treatment

elettrotecnico, -a, -ci, -che [elettroˈtɛkniko] AGG electrotechnical ♦ SM electrical engineer

elevare [eleˈvare] /72/ VT 1 (alzare: muro) to put up; (sguardo, occhi) to raise, lift; (tenore di vita) to raise; **elevare un edificio di un piano** to add a floor to a building; **elevare qn al rango di** to raise o elevate sb to the rank of; **elevare al trono** to raise to the throne 2 (Mat) to raise; **elevare un numero al quadrato** to square a number 3 (Amm): **elevare una contravvenzione a qn** to fine sb; **elevarsi** VIP, VR (gen) to rise; **elevarsi (con lo spirito)** (fig) to be uplifted

elevatezza [elevaˈtettsa] SF (altezza) elevation; (di animo, pensiero) loftiness

elevato, -a [eleˈvato] AGG (gen) high; (cime) high, lofty; (fig: stile, sentimenti) lofty; **poco elevato** not very high

elevazione [elevatˈtsjone] SF (gen, anche Mat) raising; (di terreno) elevation; (Sport) lift; **l'Elevazione** (Rel) the Elevation

elezione [eletˈtsjone] SF 1 (Pol, Amm) election; **indire le elezioni** to hold an election; **giorno delle elezioni** election day; **elezioni amministrative** ≈ local council election; **elezioni anticipate** early election (held before end of fixed term of legislature); **elezioni politiche** general election 2 (scelta) choice; **patria d'elezione** adopted country

elica, -che [ˈelika] SF (Aer, Naut) propeller, screw; (Mat) helix

elicottero [eliˈkɔttero] SM helicopter

elidere [eˈlidere] VB IRREG /89/ VT (Fonetica) to elide; **elidersi** VR (uso reciproco) to cancel each other out, neutralize each other

eliminare [elimiˈnare] /72/ VT (anche fig) to eliminate; **la nostra squadra è stata eliminata alle semifinali** our team was eliminated in the semi-final

eliminatorio, -ria, -ri, -rie [eliminaˈtɔrjo] AGG (prova, gara) eliminatory ♦ SF (Sport) heat, eliminating round

eliminazione [eliminatˈtsjone] SF elimination; **per eliminazione** by a process of elimination

elio [ˈɛljo] SM (Chim) helium

eliporto [eliˈpɔrto] SM heliport

elisabettiano, -a [elizabetˈtjano] AGG Elizabethan

elisir [eliˈzir] SM INV elixir; **elisir di lunga vita** elixir of life

eliso, -a [eˈlizo] PP di elidere

elisoccorso [elisokˈkorso] SM (servizio) air ambulance

elitario, -ria, -ri, -rie [eliˈtarjo] AGG elitist

élite [eˈlit] SF INV élite

ella [ˈella] PRON PERS (letter) she; **ella stessa** she herself

ellisse [elˈlisse] SF (Geom) ellipse

ellittico, -a, -ci, -che [elˈlittiko] AGG (Geom, Gramm) elliptic(al)

elmetto [elˈmetto] SM helmet

elmo [ˈelmo] SM helmet

elogiare [eloˈdʒare] /62/ VT to praise, laud (frm)

elogiativo, -a [elodʒaˈtivo] AGG laudatory

elogio, -gi [eˈlɔdʒo] SM 1 praise; **fare l'elogio di qn/qc** to praise sb/sth, speak highly of sb/sth 2 (ufficiale) eulogy; **elogio funebre** funeral oration

eloquente [eloˈkwɛnte] AGG eloquent; **un discorso eloquente** an eloquent speech; **questi dati sono eloquenti** these facts speak for themselves

eloquenza [eloˈkwɛntsa] SF eloquence

eloquio, -qui [eˈlɔkwjo] SM (letter) discourse

elucubrare [elukuˈbrare] /72/ VT (anche iro) to ponder (on o

over); **che cosa stai elucubrando?** what are you dreaming up now?

elucubrazioni [elukubratˈtsjoni] SFPL (anche iro) cogitations, ponderings

eludere [eˈludere] /35/ VT IRREG (gen) to evade, elude; (sorveglianza, nemico) to evade, dodge

elusi ecc [eˈluzi] VB vedi eludere

elusione [eluˈzjone] SF: **elusione fiscale** tax avoidance

elusivo, -a [eluˈzivo] AGG (risposta, parole) evasive

eluso, -a [eˈluzo] PP di eludere

elvetico, -a, -ci, -che [elˈvetiko] AGG Swiss

emaciato, -a [emaˈtʃato] AGG emaciated

e-mail, email [iˈmeil] SF INV (messaggio, sistema) email ♦ AGG INV (indirizzo) email

emanare [emaˈnare] /72/ VT 1 (odore, calore) to give off o out; (raggi) to emit; (fascino) to radiate 2 (emettere: legge) to promulgate; (: ordine, circolare) to issue ♦ VI (aus essere) **emanare da** to emanate from

emanazione [emanatˈtsjone] SF 1 (di raggi, calore) emission; (di odori) exhalation 2 (di legge) promulgation; (di ordine, circolare) issuing

emancipare [emantʃiˈpare] /72/ VT to emancipate; **emanciparsi** VR to become liberated o emancipated

emancipazione [emantʃipatˈtsjone] SF emancipation

emarginare [emardʒiˈnare] /72/ VT (socialmente) to marginalize

emarginato, -a [emardʒiˈnato] SM, SF marginalized person, disadvantaged person

emarginazione [emardʒinatˈtsjone] SF marginalization

ematologia [ematoloˈdʒia] SF (Med) haematology (Brit), hematology (USA)

ematoma, -i [emaˈtoma] SM bruise; (termine tecn) haematoma (Brit), hematoma (USA)

emblema, -i [emˈblɛma] SM emblem

emblematico, -a, -ci, -che [embleˈmatiko] AGG emblematic; (atteggiamento, parole) symbolic

embolia [emboˈlia] SF embolism

embrionale [embrioˈnale] AGG embryonic, embryo attr; **sacco embrionale** embryo sac; **allo stadio embrionale** (progetto, piano) at the embryo stage

embrione [embriˈone] SM embryo

emendamento [emendaˈmento] SM (Dir) amendment; (di scritto) emendation

emendare [emenˈdare] /72/ VT (legge) to amend; (testo) to emend

emergente [emerˈdʒɛnte] AGG emerging; **paesi emergenti** developing countries

emergenza [emerˈdʒɛntsa] SF emergency; **in caso di emergenza** in case of an emergency; **in caso di emergenza chiama questo numero** in case of emergency call this number; **stato di emergenza** state of emergency; **è un'emergenza** it's an emergency

  ❑ **emergenza** non si traduce mai con la parola inglese *emergence*

emergere [eˈmerdʒere] /59/ VI IRREG (aus essere) (sommergibile) to surface; (fig: verità, fatti) to emerge, to come out; (: persona: distinguersi) to stand out

emerito, -a [eˈmerito] AGG (insigne) distinguished; **professore emerito** professor emeritus; **è un emerito cretino!** he's a complete idiot!

emersi ecc [eˈmersi] VB vedi emergere

emerso, -a [eˈmerso] PP di emergere ♦ AGG (Geog): **le terre emerse** the world's land surface

emesso, -a [eˈmesso] PP di emettere

emettere [eˈmettere] /63/ VT IRREG 1 (Fis) to emit; (luce) to give out; (calore, odore) to give off; (suono, fischio) to give, let out; (Radio) to transmit; (Inform) to output; **emettere un grido di dolore** to give a cry of pain; **emettere un gemito** to groan, utter a groan 2 (Fin: titoli, assegno) to issue; (: moneta) to put into circulation, issue 3 (pronunciare: giudizio) to express, voice; (Dir: ordine, mandato di cattura) to issue; **emettere una sentenza** to pass sentence

emicrania [emiˈkranja] SF migraine; **aveva l'emicrania** he had a migraine

emigrante [emi'grante] AGG, SM, SF emigrant

emigrare [emi'grare] /72/ VI (aus essere) emigrare (in) (persona) to emigrate (to); (animale: migrare) to migrate (to); erano emigrati in Germania they had emigrated to Germany

emigrato, -a [emi'grato] AGG emigrant ♦ SM, SF emigrant; (Storia) émigré

emigrazione [emigrat'tsjone] SF (vedi vb) emigration; migration; emigrazione di capitali flight of capital

emiliano, -a [emi'ljano] AGG of o from Emilia ♦ SM, SF inhabitant o native of Emilia

eminente [emi'nente] AGG (posizione) high, lofty; (scienziato ecc) eminent, distinguished

eminenza [emi'nentsa] SF 1 (titolo: di cardinale): Eminenza Eminence; eminenza grigia (fig) éminence grise 2 (qualità) distinction, eminence

emirato [emi'rato] SM emirate; gli Emirati Arabi Uniti the United Arab Emirates

emiro [e'miro] SM emir

emisfero [emis'fero] SM (gen) hemisphere; emisfero australe/boreale southern/northern hemisphere

emisi ecc [e'mizi] VB vedi emettere

emissario, -ri [emis'sarjo] SM 1 (Geog) outflowing river 2 (inviato) emissary

emissione [emis'sjone] SF (di suoni, onde, calore, radiazioni) emission; (di energia) output; (di francobolli, titoli, assegni) issue

emittente [emit'tente] AGG (Radio, TV) transmitting, broadcasting; (banca) issuing ♦ SF (stazione) transmitting station, broadcasting station; emittente privata independent station; un'emittente radiofonica locale a local radio station

emofilia [emofi'lia] SF haemophilia (Brit), hemophilia (USA)

emofiliaco, -a, -ci, -che [emofi'liako] AGG, SM, SF haemophiliac (Brit), hemophiliac (USA)

emoglobina [emoglo'bina] SF haemoglobin (Brit), hemoglobin (USA)

emolliente [emol'ljente] AGG (crema, preparato) soothing

emorragia, -gie [emorra'dʒia] SF haemorrhage (Brit), hemorrhage (USA); emorragia interna internal bleeding

emorroidi [emor'rɔidi] SFPL haemorrhoids (Brit), hemorrhoids (USA), piles

emostatico, -a, -ci, -che [emos'tatiko] AGG haemostatic (Brit), hemostatic (USA); laccio emostatico tourniquet; matita emostatica styptic pencil

emotività [emotivi'ta] SF INV emotional nature

emotivo, -a [emo'tivo] AGG emotional; è molto emotiva she's very emotional

emozionante [emottsjo'nante] AGG (che appassiona) thrilling, exciting; (che commuove) moving; è stata un'avventura emozionante it was an exciting adventure

emozionare [emottsjo'nare] /72/ VT (appassionare) to thrill, excite; (commuovere) to move; emozionarsi VIP (vedi vt) to get excited; to be moved; emozionarsi facilmente to be excitable; to be easily moved

emozionato, -a [emotsjo'nato] AGG (commosso) moved; (agitato) nervous; scusami sono un po' emozionato sorry, I feel a bit overwhelmed; ero troppo emozionato per fare un discorso I was too emotional to make a speech; era molto emozionato all'esame he was very nervous during the exam

emozione [emot'tsjone] SF emotion; a caccia di emozioni in search of excitement; le tremava la voce per l'emozione her voice trembled with emotion

empio, -pia, -pi, -pie ['ɛmpjo] AGG (Rel) impious; (crudele) cruel

empirico, -a, -ci, -che [em'piriko] AGG empirical

emporio, -ri [em'pɔrjo] SM emporium, general store

emulare [emu'lare] /72/ VT to emulate

emulo, -a ['ɛmulo] SM, SF imitator

emulsione [emul'sjone] SF emulsion

EN SIGLA = Enna

enciclica, -che [en'tʃiklika] SF (Rel) encyclical

enciclopedia [entʃiklope'dia] SF encyclopaedia (Brit), encyclopedia (USA)

encomiabile [enko'mjabile] AGG commendable, praiseworthy

encomiare [enko'mjare] /19/ VT to commend, praise

encomio, -mi [en'kɔmjo] SM commendation; encomio solenne (Mil) mention in dispatches

endovenoso, -a [endove'noso] AGG (Med) intravenous; per via endovenosa intravenously ♦ SF intravenous injection

energetico, -a, -ci, -che [ener'dʒɛtiko] AGG (risorse, crisi) energy attr; (cibo, sostanza, alimento) energy-giving

energia, -gie [ener'dʒia] SF 1 (vigore) energy, strength, vigour (Brit), vigor (USA); avere molta energia to be very energetic; avere poca energia to lack energy, have little energy; dedicare tutte le proprie energie a qc to devote all one's energies to sth; come fai ad essere così pieno di energia? how do you manage to be so full of energy? 2 (Fis) energy; (Tecn) power; liberare energia to release energy; consumo di energia power consumption; energia alternativa; fonti di energia alternativa sources of alternative energy; energia nucleare nuclear energy; energia termica heat energy

energico, -a, -ci, -che [e'nɛrdʒiko] AGG (persona) energetic, vigorous; (resistenza, rifiuto) forceful, vigorous; (cura) potent, powerful; (provvedimenti) drastic

enfasi ['ɛnfazi] SF INV emphasis; (pegg) pomposity; con enfasi emphatically; (pegg) pompously; porre l'enfasi su to stress, place the emphasis on, emphasize

enfatico, -a, -ci, -che [en'fatiko] AGG (tono, discorso) emphatic; (pegg) pompous

enfatizzare [enfatid'dzare] /72/ VT to emphasize, stress

enfisema, -i [enfi'zɛma] SM (Med) emphysema; enfisema polmonare pulmonary emphysema

enigma, -i [e'nigma] SM (mistero) enigma, riddle; (gioco) puzzle, riddle; quell'uomo è un enigma that man is an enigma; il suo comportamento rimane un enigma his behaviour is inexplicable

enigmatico, -a, -ci, -che [enig'matiko] AGG enigmatic

ENIT ['enit] SIGLA M (= Ente Nazionale Italiano per il Turismo) Italian tourist board

ennesimo, -a [en'nɛzimo] AGG (Mat, anche fam) nth; all'ennesima potenza to the nth power o degree; per l'ennesima volta for the umpteenth time

enologia [enolo'dʒia] SF oenology (Brit), enology (USA)

enologo, -a, -gi [e'nɔlogo] SM, SF oenologist (Brit), enologist (USA), wine expert

enorme [e'nɔrme] AGG (gen) enormous, huge; (distesa, riserva) vast, enormous; (pazienza, forza) tremendous, enormous; è un negozio enorme it's a huge shop; ha avuto un enorme successo it was a huge success

enormità [enormi'ta] SF INV 1 (di peso, somma) hugeness; (di distesa) vastness; (di richiesta) enormity; (di prezzo) unreasonableness 2 (stupidaggine) blunder, howler; non dire enormità! don't talk nonsense!; l'ho pagato un'enormità I paid a fortune for it

enoteca, -che [eno'tɛka] SF (per vendita) wine shop, ≈ off-licence; (per degustazione) wine bar

ente ['ɛnte] SM 1 (Amm) body, corporation, board; ente autonomo ≈ local board; ente locale ≈ local authority (Brit), local government (USA); ente pubblico public body; ente di ricerca research organization 2 (Filosofia) being

enterite [ente'rite] SF (Med) enteritis

entità [enti'ta] SF INV 1 (di perdita, danni, investimenti) extent; (di popolazione) size; di scarsa/una certa entità (avvenimento, incidente) of slight/some importance 2 (Filosofia) entity

entrambi, -e [en'trambi] AGG, PRON both; entrambi i ragazzi both boys, both of the boys; entrambe le sorelle both sisters, both of the sisters; vennero entrambi they both came, both of them came; mi piacciono entrambi I like them both, I like both of them; si può parcheggiare su entrambi i lati della strada you can park on both sides of the street

entrante [en'trante] AGG (prossimo: mese, anno) next, coming

PAROLA CHIAVE

entrare [en'trare] /72/ VI (aus essere)

1 to go (o come) in, enter; (con la macchina) to drive in; entri pure! do come in!; "si prega di bussare prima di entrare" "knock before entering"; entrare dalla finestra to get in by the window; entrare in automobile to get into the car; non entrare in acqua subito dopo aver mangiato! don't go into

the water when you've just eaten!; **mi è entrato qualcosa nell'occhio** I've got something in my eye **2** (*soldi, prodotti*) to enter, come in; (*contenuto*) to go in; (*adattarsi*) to fit in; **il regalo non entra nella scatola** the present won't go o fit into the box; **queste scarpe non mi entrano** I can't get into these shoes; **entra acqua dal tetto** there's water coming in through the roof; **la matematica non mi entra proprio in testa** I just can't get the hang of mathematics **3 far entrare** (*visitatore, cliente*) to show in; (*animale*) to let in; (*oggetto*) to fit in; (*merce: d'importazione*) to bring in; (: *di contrabbando*) to smuggle in; **far entrare qn in banca** (*come impiegato*) to get sb a job in a bank; **far entrare qn in un club** (*ammettere*) to let sb into a club; **non riesco a fargli entrare in testa che ce la può fare** I can't get him to understand that he can do it; **gli hanno fatto entrare in testa la trigonometria** they've managed to teach him trigonometry **4 entrare in** (*club, partito*) to join, become a member of; (*professione*) to go into; **entrare in affari** to go into business; **entrare nei vent'anni di età** to turn twenty; **entrare in argomento** to get onto the subject; **entrare in ballo** to come into play; **entrare in carica** to take up office; **entrare in commercio con qn** to go into business with sb; **entrare in convalescenza** to begin one's convalescence; **entrare in convento** to enter a convent; **entrare in discussione con qn** to enter into discussions with sb; **entrare in gioco** to come into play; **entrare in guerra** (*all'inizio*) to go to war; (*a conflitto iniziato*) to come into the war; **entrare nella professione legale** to go into the law; **entrare al servizio di qn** to enter sb's service; **entrare in società con qn** to go into partnership with sb; **entrare nella storia** to go down in history; **entrare in vigore** (*legge*) to come into force o effect **5 entrarci** to have to do with; **quello che dici non c'entra** (*niente*) what you say has nothing to do with it; **tu non c'entri in questa faccenda** this is none of your business; **io non c'entro** it's got nothing to do with me

entrata [en'trata] SF **1** (*ingresso: di persona*) entry, entrance; (: *di merci, veicoli*) entry; **alla sua entrata** as he entered; **alla sua entrata in scena** (*Teatro*) on his entrance; (*fig*) when he came on to the scene; **all'entrata in guerra degli Stati Uniti** when the United States came into the war; **dopo la sua entrata in carica** after he took office; **con l'entrata in vigore dei nuovi provvedimenti...** once the new measures come into effect ... **2** (*accesso*) admission; "**entrata libera**" "admission free"; **biglietto di entrata** (entrance) ticket **3** (*porta*) entrance; (*vestibolo*) entrance (hall); **l'entrata principale è sulla via laterale** the main entrance is in the side street; **entrata degli artisti** (*Teatro*) stage door; **entrata di servizio** service o tradesmen's entrance **4 entrate** SFPL (*Econ*) income sg; (*Comm*) takings, receipts; **entrate e uscite** income and expenditure; **entrate tributarie** tax revenue sg

entro ['entro] PREP within; **entro un mese** within a month; **avremo i risultati entro un mese** we'll have the results within a month; **entro domani** by tomorrow; **entro febbraio** by the end of February; **entro quattro anni** within four years; **devo pagare entro il dodici febbraio** I've got to pay by the twelfth of February; **entro e non oltre il 25 aprile** no later than 25th April

entroterra [entro'terra] SM INV hinterland; **l'entroterra australiano** the (Australian) outback

entusiasmante [entuzjaz'mante] AGG exciting

entusiasmare [entuzjaz'mare] /72/ VT to fill with enthusiasm, excite; **entusiasmarsi** VIP: **entusiasmarsi per qc** to be enthusiastic about o over sth

entusiasmo [entu'zjazmo] SM enthusiasm; **all'inizio era pieno di entusiasmo** at the start he was full of enthusiasm

entusiasta, -i, -e [entu'zjasta] AGG: **entusiasta (di)** enthusiastic (about o over); **sono entusiasta dell'idea** I'm enthusiastic about the idea; **non sono entusiasta dei risultati** I'm not too happy about the results; **non era troppo entusiasta, ma ha accettato** he wasn't exactly delighted, but he agreed ♦ SM, SF enthusiast

entusiastico, -a, -ci, -che [entu'zjastiko] AGG enthusiastic

enucleare [enukle'are] /72/ VT (*frm: problema*) to clarify

enumerare [enume'rare] /72/ VT to enumerate, list

enunciare [enun'tʃare] /14/ VT (*pensiero*) to express; (*fatti*) to state; (*teorema, teoria*) to set out

enzima, -i [en'dzima] SM enzyme

eolico, -a, -ci, -che [e'ɔliko] AGG (*Geog*) aeolian

epatico, -a, -ci, -che [e'patiko] AGG hepatic; **cirrosi epatica** cirrhosis of the liver

epatite [epa'tite] SF hepatitis; **epatite virale** viral hepatitis

epico, -a, -ci, -che ['epiko] AGG (*anche fig*) epic

epidemia [epide'mia] SF epidemic; **un'epidemia di influenza** a flu epidemic

epidermico, -a, -ci, -che [epi'dɛrmiko] AGG (*Anat*) skin *attr*; (*fig: interesse, impressione*) superficial

epidermide [epi'dɛrmide] SF (*Anat*) skin, epidermis

Epifania [epifa'nia] SF Epiphany

epigono [e'pigono] SM imitator

epigrafe [e'pigrafe] SF epigraph; (*su libro*) dedication

epilessia [epiles'sia] SF epilepsy

epilettico, -a, -ci, -che [epi'lettiko] AGG, SM, SF epileptic; **una crisi epilettica** an epileptic fit

epilogo, -ghi [e'pilogo] SM epilogue; (*fig*) conclusion

episodico, -a, -ci, -che [epi'zɔdiko] AGG (*romanzo, narrazione*) episodic; (*fig: occasionale*) occasional

episodio, -di [epi'zɔdjo] SM episode; **sceneggiato a episodi** serial; **un episodio imbarazzante della sua vita** an embarrassing episode in her life; **un grave episodio di intolleranza razziale** a serious instance of racism

epistola [e'pistola] SF epistle

epistolare [episto'lare] AGG epistolary; **essere in rapporto o relazione epistolare con qn** to correspond o be in correspondence with sb

epiteto [e'piteto] SM (*Gramm*) attribute; (*fig*) epithet; **un epiteto irripetibile** an unrepeatable insult

epoca, -che ['ɛpoka] SF (*gen*) time; (*periodo storico*) age, era, epoch; (*Geol*) age; **all'epoca di** at the time of; **in epoca bizantina** in the Byzantine era; **viviamo in un'epoca difficile** we live in difficult times o in a difficult age; **a quell'epoca** at that time; **a quell'epoca mi trovavo a Londra** at that time I was in London; **mobili d'epoca** period furniture; **fare epoca** (*scandalo*) to cause a stir; (*cantante, moda*) to mark a new era; **lo sbarco sulla luna ha fatto epoca** the moon landing was an epoch-making event

epopea [epo'pea] SF (*anche fig*) epic

eppure [ep'pure] CONG and yet, nevertheless; **sembra impossibile, eppure è vero!** it seems impossible, and yet it's true!; **non è venuto all'appuntamento, eppure aveva promesso** he didn't come to the meeting, though he'd promised he would

epurare [epu'rare] /72/ VT (*Pol*) to purge

equanime [e'kwanime] AGG (*imparziale*) impartial

equatore [ekwa'tore] SM equator

equazione [ekwat'tsjone] SF equation

equestre [e'kwɛstre] AGG equestrian; **circo equestre** circus; **una statua equestre** an equestrian statue

equilatero [ekwi'latero] AGG equilateral

equilibrare [ekwili'brare] /72/ VT (*gen*) to balance; (*controbilanciare*) to counterbalance; **equilibrare qc con qc** to balance sth against sth (else); **equilibrarsi** VR (*uso reciproco: forze ecc*) to counterbalance each other

equilibrato, -a [ekwili'brato] AGG (*carico, giudizio, dieta, alimentazione*) balanced; (*persona*) well-balanced

equilibrio, -ri [ekwi'librjo] SM (*gen*) balance, equilibrium; (*armonia*) harmony; **perdere l'equilibrio** to lose one's balance; **ha perso l'equilibrio ed è caduto** he lost his balance and fell; **stare in equilibrio su** (*persona*) to balance on; (*oggetto*) to be balanced on; **equilibrio mentale** (mental) equilibrium o stability; **equilibrio economico** economic stability; **equilibrio politico** balance of power; **è una persona priva di equilibrio** he is not a well-balanced person, he is rather unstable

equilibrismo [ekwili'brizmo] SM tightrope walking; (*fig*) juggling; (*Pol*) balancing act

equino, -a [e'kwino] AGG horse *attr*, equine; **carne equina** horsemeat; **una razza equina** a breed of horses

equinozio, -zi [ekwi'nɔttsjo] SM equinox

equipaggiamento [ekwipadd3a'mento] SM **1** (*operazione: di nave*) equipping, fitting out; (: *di spedizione, esercito*) equipping, kitting out (*fam*) **2** (*attrezzatura*) equipment, gear; **equipaggiamento da sci/da sub** skiing/diving equipment

equipaggiare [ekwipad'd3are] /62/ VT (*nave, esercito, spedizione*) to equip; (*per uno sport*) to kit out; **equipaggiarsi** VR to equip o.s.

equipaggio, -gi [ekwi'padd3o] SM (*gen, anche Naut*) crew; (*Aer*) (air)crew; **l'equipaggio dell'aereo** the cabin crew

equiparare [ekwipa'rare] /72/ VT (*Amm: stipendi, gradi*) to make equal, level

équipe [e'kip] SF INV (*gen, anche Sport*) team; **lavorare in équipe** to work as a team; **lavoro d'équipe** teamwork

equità [ekwi'ta] SF INV equity, fairness

equitazione [ekwitat'tsjone] SF (horse-)riding; **c'è una scuola di equitazione qua vicino** there's a riding school near here

equivalente [ekwiva'lente] AGG: **equivalente (a)** equivalent (to) ♦ SM equivalent

equivalenza [ekwiva'lεntsa] SF equivalence

equivalere [ekwiva'lere] VB IRREG /126/ VI (*aus avere o essere*) **equivalere a** (*valore*) to be equivalent to; (*affermazione*) to be tantamount to; **equivale a dire che...** that is the same as saying that ...; **equivalersi** VR (*uso reciproco: forze*) to counterbalance each other; (: *soluzioni*) to amount to the same thing

equivalso, -a [ekwi'valso] PP di **equivalere**

equivocare [ekwivo'kare] /20/ VI (*aus avere*) (*capire male*): **equivocare (su qc)** to misunderstand (sth)

equivoco, -a, -ci, -che [e'kwivoko] AGG (*risposta, discorso*) equivocal, ambiguous; (*persona*) shady; (*locale*) disreputable ♦ SM (*malinteso*) misunderstanding; **dar luogo a un equivoco** to cause a misunderstanding; **cadere in un equivoco** to misunderstand; **è stato tutto un equivoco** it was all a misunderstanding; **ci dev'essere stato un equivoco** there must have been some misunderstanding; **a scanso di equivoci** (so as) to avoid any misunderstanding, so that it will be perfectly clear

equo, -a ['ekwo] AGG (*gen*) equitable, fair; **un equo compenso** a fair o adequate reward

era[1] ['era] SF (*gen*) era; (*Geol*) period; **l'era cristiana** the Christian era; **l'era glaciale** the ice age; **l'era spaziale** the space age

era[2] ['era] VB vedi **essere**

erariale [era'rjale] AGG: **ufficio erariale** ≈ tax office; **spese erariali** public expenditure *sg*; **imposte erariali** revenue taxes

erario, -ri [e'rarjo] SM: **l'erario** ≈ the Treasury

erba ['εrba] SF grass; (*Culin, Med*) herb; (*fam: marijuana*) grass, pot; **in erba** (*fig: pittore, scultore*) budding; **fare di ogni erba un fascio** (*fig*) to lump everything (o everybody) together; **eravamo sdraiati sull'erba** we were lying on the grass; **erba cipollina** chives *pl*; **erba medica** lucerne; **erbe aromatiche** herbs

erbaccia, -ce [er'battʃa] SF weed

erbivoro, -a [er'bivoro] AGG herbivorous ♦ SM, SF herbivore

erborista, -i, -e [erbo'rista] SM, SF herbalist

erboristeria [erboriste'ria] SF (*scienza*) herbalism; (*negozio*) herbalist's (shop)

erboso, -a [er'boso] AGG grassy; **tappeto erboso** lawn

erede [e'rede] SM, SF heir; (heiress); **erede di qc** heir to sth; **erede al trono** heir to the throne; **erede legittimo** heir-at-law; **nominare qn proprio erede** to make sb one's heir; **lei è l'unica erede** she's the only heir

eredità [eredi'ta] SF INV **1** (*Dir*) inheritance; (*fig*) heritage; **lasciare qc in eredità a qn** to leave o bequeath sth to sb; **suo padre gli ha lasciato in eredità una bella casa** his father left him a beautiful house; **ricevere qc in eredità** to inherit sth; **aveva paura di perdere l'eredità** he was afraid of losing his inheritance **2** (*Bio*) heredity

ereditare [eredi'tare] /72/ VT to inherit; **ereditare qc da qn** to inherit sth from sb; **ha ereditato la casa del nonno** she inherited her grandfather's house

ereditario, -ria, -ri, -rie [eredi'tarjo] AGG hereditary; **una malattia ereditaria** a hereditary disease

ereditiera [eredi'tjera] SF heiress

eremita, -i [ere'mita] SM hermit

eremitaggio, -gi [eremi'tadd3o] SM hermitage

eremo ['eremo] SM hermitage; (*fig*) retreat

eresia [ere'zia] SF (*Rel, anche fig*) heresy; **dire eresie** (*fig*) to talk nonsense

eressi *ecc* [e'ressi] VB vedi **erigere**

eretico, -a, -ci, -che [e'retiko] AGG heretical ♦ SM, SF heretic

eretto, -a [e'retto] PP di **erigere** ♦ AGG (*capo, busto*) erect, upright

erezione [eret'tsjone] SF **1** (*Fisiologia*) erection **2** (*costruzione: di monumento*) raising; (: *di palazzo, chiesa*) building

ergastolano, -a [ergasto'lano] SM, SF prisoner serving a life sentence, lifer (*fam*)

ergastolo [er'gastolo] SM (*pena*) life imprisonment; (*luogo di pena*) prison (*for those serving life sentence*); **condannato all'ergastolo** given a life sentence; **gli hanno dato tre ergastoli** he was given three life sentences

ergonomia [ergono'mia] SF ergonomics *sg*, biotechnology (*USA*)

ergonomico, -a, -ci, -che [ergo'nomiko] AGG ergonomic(al)

erica, -che ['εrika] SF heather

erigere [e'rid3ere] VB IRREG /39/ VT (*monumento*) to erect, raise; (*fig: fondare*) to found; **erigersi** VR (*fig: costituirsi*): **erigersi a giudice/difensore (di)** to set o.s. up as a judge/a defender (of)

eritema, -i [eri'tema] SM (*Med*) inflammation, erythema (*termine tecn*); **eritema solare** sunburn

Eritrea [eri'trea] SF Eritrea

ermellino [ermel'lino] SM (*animale: d'inverno*) ermine; (: *d'estate*) stoat; (: *pelliccia*) ermine

ermetico, -a, -ci, -che [er'metiko] AGG **1** (*contenitore*) airtight; (*fig: sguardo, volto*) inscrutable, impenetrable; **a chiusura ermetica** hermetically sealed **2** (*Letteratura*) hermetic

ernia ['εrnja] SF (*Med*) hernia; **ernia del disco** slipped disc

ero *ecc* ['εro] VB vedi **essere**

erodere [e'rodere] /49/ VT IRREG to erode

eroe [e'rɔe] SM hero

erogare [ero'gare] /80/ VT (*gas, luce*) to supply; (*somma*) to distribute

erogazione [erogat'tsjone] SF (*vedi vb*) supply; distribution

eroico, -a, -ci, -che [e'rɔiko] AGG heroic

eroina[1] [ero'ina] SF (*donna*) heroine; **l'eroina del romanzo** the heroine of the novel

eroina[2] [ero'ina] SF (*droga*) heroin; **l'eroina è una droga pesante** heroin is a hard drug

eroismo [ero'izmo] SM heroism

eros ['eros] SM INV Eros

erosione [ero'zjone] SF erosion; **erosione fiscale** tax avoidance

eroso, -a [e'roso] PP di **erodere**

erotico, -a, -ci, -che [e'rɔtiko] AGG erotic

erotismo [ero'tizmo] SM eroticism

erpete [er'pεte] SM (*Med*) herpes *sg*

erpice ['εrpitʃe] SM (*Agr*) harrow

errare [er'rare] /72/ VI (*aus avere*) **1** (*letter: vagare*): **errare (per)** to wander (about), roam (about); **errare con la fantasia** (*fig*) to let one's imagination wander **2** (*frm: sbagliare*) to be mistaken, make a mistake; **se non erro...** if I'm not mistaken ...

errato, -a [er'rato] AGG (*calcolo*) wrong, incorrect; (*idea, interpretazione*) mistaken, erroneous; **se non vado errato** if I am not mistaken

erroneo, -a [er'rɔneo] AGG erroneous, mistaken

errore [er'rore] SM mistake, error; **fare un errore** to make a mistake; **non ho fatto neanche un errore** I didn't make a single mistake; **per errore** by mistake; **salvo errori** (*scritto*) errors excepted; (*nel parlare*) if I am not mistaken; **salvo errori ed omissioni** errors and omissions excepted; **errore di calcolo** (*anche fig*) miscalculation; **errore giudiziario** miscarriage of justice; **errore di giudizio** o **di valutazione** error of judgment; **errore di ortografia** spelling mistake; **errore di stampa** printing error, misprint

erto, -a ['erto] AGG (*letter*) (very) steep

erudire [eru'dire] /55/ vt (frm, scherz) to teach, educate

erudito, -a [eru'dito] AGG (persona) learned, erudite; (opera) scholarly, learned ♦ SM, SF scholar

eruttare [erut'tare] /72/ vt (lava) to spew (out)

eruzione [erut'tsjone] SF (Geol) eruption; (Med) rash; **eruzione cutanea** rash

ES ABBR 1 (= elettroshock) ECT 2 = Eurostar

es. ABBR (= esempio) e.g.

ESA SIGLA M (= European Space Agency) ESA

esacerbare [ezat∫er'bare] /72/ vt to exacerbate

esagerare [ezadʒe'rare] /72/ vt (gen) to exaggerate; (eccedere) to go too far; **non esagerare!** don't exaggerate!; **esagerare con le pretese** to demand too much, expect too much; **esagerare con la prudenza** to be overcautious; **senza esagerare** without exaggeration; **non ti sembra di esagerare un po'?** don't you think that's a bit of an exaggeration?; **esagerare nel bere/nel mangiare** to drink/eat too much; **ha esagerato un po' nel bere** he had a bit too much to drink ♦ vt to exaggerate

esagerato, -a [ezadʒe'rato] AGG (notizia, proporzioni) exaggerated; (curiosità, pignoleria) excessive; (prezzo) exorbitant; **sarebbe esagerato dire che...** it would be an exaggeration to say that ... ♦ SM, SF: **sei il solito esagerato** you're exaggerating as usual

esagerazione [ezadʒerat'tsjone] SF exaggeration; **costare un'esagerazione** to cost the earth; **che esagerazione!** what nonsense!

esagonale [ezago'nale] AGG hexagonal

esagono [e'zagono] SM hexagon

esalare [eza'lare] /72/ vt (odori) to give off; **esalare l'ultimo respiro** to breathe one's last ♦ vi (aus essere) **esalare (da)** to emanate (from)

esalazione [ezalat'tsjone] SF (emissione) exhalation; (odore) fumes pl

esaltante [ezal'tante] AGG exciting

esaltare [ezal'tare] /72/ vt 1 (lodare: pregi, virtù) to extol 2 (eccitare: immaginazione) to fire; (: folla) to excite, stir; **esaltarsi** vr: **esaltarsi (per qc)** to grow excited (about sth)

esaltato, -a [ezal'tato] AGG (giovane, mente) overexcited ♦ SM, SF fanatic

esaltazione [ezaltat'tsjone] SF 1 (elogio) extolling 2 (mistica) exaltation

esame [e'zame] SM 1 (gen) examination, exam; **essere all'esame** to be under examination; **prendere in esame** to examine, consider; **fare un esame di coscienza** to examine one's conscience; **dopo un attento esame della situazione** after careful study o consideration of the situation 2 (Scol) exam, examination; **dare o sostenere un esame** to sit (Brit) o take an exam; **non ho passato l'esame** I didn't pass the exam; **quando saprai il risultato degli esami?** when will you get your exam results?; **esame di guida** driving test 3 (Med) examination, test; **farsi fare degli esami** to have some tests done o carried out; **gli faranno degli esami** he's having some tests done; **esame del sangue** blood test; **esame della vista** eye test

esaminare [ezami'nare] /72/ vt 1 (gen) to examine; (proposta, elementi) to consider, examine 2 (oggetto) to examine, study 3 (candidati) to interview; (Scol) to examine

esangue [e'zangwe] AGG (pallido) pale, wan; (privo di vigore) lifeless

esanime [e'zanime] AGG lifeless

esasperare [ezaspe'rare] /72/ vt (persona) to exasperate; (situazione) to exacerbate; **esasperarsi** vip to become exasperated

esasperazione [ezasperat'tsjone] SF exasperation

esattamente [ezatta'mente] AVV exactly; **è esattamente quello che intendevo** it's exactly what I meant

esattezza [ezat'tettsa] SF 1 (correttezza: di calcolo, affermazione) accuracy; **per l'esattezza** to be precise; **con esattezza** exactly; **rispondere con esattezza** (in modo corretto) to answer correctly, give a o the correct answer; (in modo preciso) to give a detailed answer 2 (accuratezza: di persona) precision

esatto, -a [e'zatto] PP di esigere ♦ AGG 1 (corretto: calcolo, risposta) correct, right; (ora) exact, right; (dimensioni, quantità) exact, precise; (prezzo, peso) exact; **sono le tre esatte** it's exactly three o'clock; **è l'esatto contrario** it's the exact opposite o it's just the opposite; **esatto!** exactly!; **allora, hai deciso di partire? — esatto!** so, you've decided to leave? — that's right!; **non mi ricordo le parole esatte** I can't remember the exact words; **ha dato la risposta esatta** he gave the correct answer 2 (accurato :resoconto, descrizione) accurate; (: impiegato) careful; **le scienze esatte** the exact sciences

esattore, -trice [ezat'tore] SM, SF: **esattore delle tasse** tax collector; **esattore del gas/della luce** gas/electricity man

esattoria [ezatto'ria] SF: **esattoria comunale** council tax office (Brit), assessor's office (USA)

esaudire [ezau'dire] /55/ vt (desiderio, richiesta) to grant, fulfil (Brit), fulfill (USA); (preghiera) to answer, grant

esauriente [ezau'rjente] AGG (gen) exhaustive; (risposta) complete

esaurimento [ezauri'mento] SM (gen) exhaustion; **svendita (fino) ad esaurimento della merce** clearance sale; **esaurimento nervoso** nervous breakdown

esaurire [ezau'rire] /55/ vt 1 (consumare: scorte, risorse) to exhaust, use up; (: pozzo, miniera) to exhaust; (: carburante) to use up; (: forze, energie) to expend, use up; **vorrei una borsa di paglia — mi spiace, le abbiamo esaurite** I'd like a straw bag — I'm sorry we've sold out of them; **l'aereo aveva esaurito il carburante** the plane had run out of fuel 2 (portare a termine: indagine) to conclude; (: argomento) to exhaust 3 (persona) to exhaust, wear out; **esaurirsi** vr (persona) to exhaust o.s., wear o.s. out; **esaurirsi** vip (provviste) to run out; (fondi) to run out, dry up; (ispirazione) to dry up

esaurito, -a [ezau'rito] AGG (gen) exhausted; (esausto: persona) run-down attr; (merci) sold out; (libro: non più stampato) out of print; **tutto esaurito** sold out; **i biglietti erano tutti esauriti** all the tickets were sold out; **registrare il tutto esaurito** (teatro) to have a full house; **essere esaurito** (persona) to be worn out; **sono un po' esaurito** I'm a bit run-down

esausto, -a [e'zausto] AGG (spossato) exhausted, worn out; **sono esausta!** I'm exhausted!

esautorare [ezauto'rare] /72/ vt (dirigente, funzionario) to deprive of authority; (parlamento, istituzione) to reduce the authority of

esazione [ezat'tsjone] SF collection (of taxes)

esca ['eska] SF (anche fig) bait; **mettere l'esca all'amo** to bait the hook

escamotage [eskamɔ'taʒ] SM INV subterfuge

escandescenza [eskandeʃ'ʃentsa] SF: **dare in escandescenze** to fly into a rage

esce ecc ['eʃʃe] VB vedi uscire

eschimese [eski'mese] AGG, SM, SF Eskimo

esci ecc ['eʃʃi] VB vedi uscire

escl. ABBR (= escluso) excl.

esclamare [eskla'mare] /72/ vi (aus avere) to exclaim, cry out

esclamativo, -a [esklama'tivo] AGG: **punto esclamativo** exclamation mark

esclamazione [esklamat'tsjone] SF exclamation

escludere [es'kludere] /3/ vt IRREG 1 (estromettere): **escludere qn (da)** to exclude sb (from); **fu escluso dall'elenco** his name was left off the list; **è stato escluso dalla gara** he was excluded from the competition 2 (ritenere o rendere impossibile) to rule out, exclude; **escludo che si tratti di omicidio** I think we can rule out murder; **la polizia ha escluso la tesi del suicidio** the police ruled out o excluded the possibility of suicide; **una teoria esclude l'altra** one theory excludes another; **vieni domani? — lo escludo!** o **è escluso!** are you coming tomorrow? — it's out of the question!

esclusi ecc [es'kluzi] VB vedi escludere

esclusione [esklu'zjone] SF exclusion; **a esclusione di** o **fatta esclusione per** except (for), apart from; **senza esclusione (alcuna)** without exception; **senza esclusione di colpi** (fig) with no holds barred; **procedere per esclusione** to follow a process of elimination; **esclusione sociale** social exclusion

esclusiva [esklu'ziva] SF 1 (Comm): **avere l'esclusiva di qc** to be the sole agent for sth; **avere l'esclusiva di vendita** to have the exclusive *o* sole selling rights **2** (*Stampa*) exclusive; **intervista in esclusiva** exclusive interview

esclusivamente [eskluziva'mente] AVV exclusively, solely; **non è una professione esclusivamente femminile** it's not an exclusively female profession; **la colpa è esclusivamente tua** the fault is entirely yours

esclusivo, -a [esklu'zivo] AGG exclusive; **un ristorante esclusivo** an exclusive restaurant

escluso, -a [es'kluzo] PP *di* **escludere** ♦ AGG: **nessuno escluso** without exception; **è escluso che venga** there is no question of his coming; **non è escluso che lo si faccia** the possibility can't be ruled out, we (*o* they) might do it; **tutti lo sapevano, escluso me** everybody knew about it, except me; **costa cinquecento sterline, escluso l'albergo** it costs five hundred pounds, not including the hotel; **IVA esclusa** excluding VAT, exclusive of VAT

esco *ecc* ['esko] VB *vedi* **uscire**

escogitare [eskodʒi'tare] /72/ VT to devise, think up

escono ['eskono] VB *vedi* **uscire**

escoriazione [eskorjat'tsjone] SF abrasion, graze

escrementi [eskre'menti] SMPL excrement *sg*, faeces *pl*

escursione [eskur'sjone] SF **1** (*gita*) excursion, trip; (*a piedi*) hike, walk; **escursione in montagna** hillwalking **2** (*Meteor*): **escursione termica** temperature range

escursionista, -i, -e [eskursjo'nista] SM, SF (*gitante*) (day) tripper; (: *a piedi*) hiker, walker

esecrare [eze'krare] /72/ VT to abhor, loathe; (*persona*) to loathe

esecutivo, -a [ezeku'tivo] AGG executive; **(potere) esecutivo** executive power ♦ SM (*comitato*) executive committee

esecutore, -trice [ezeku'tore] SM, SF **1** (*Dir*): **esecutore (testamentario)** executor (executrix); **l'esecutore del progetto** the person who realized the project **2** (*Mus*) performer

esecuzione [ezekut'tsjone] SF **1** (*di lavoro, ordini, piano*) execution, carrying out; (*Mus*) performance; **mettere in esecuzione** *o* **dare esecuzione a** (*progetto, ordine*) to carry out; **è responsabile dell'esecuzione dei lavori** he's responsible for carrying out the work **2** (*Dir*) execution; **esecuzione capitale** execution

esegeta, -i, -e [eze'dʒeta] SM, SF commentator

eseguire [eze'gwire] /45/ VT (*lavoro, ordini, piano*) to carry out, execute; (*Mus: sinfonia, pezzo*) to perform, execute; **ha fatto eseguire dei lavori** he had some work done; **eseguire un pagamento** to make a payment; **eseguire un programma** (*Inform*) to run a program; **"Esegui" "Run"**; **stava solo eseguendo gli ordini** he was only carrying out orders; **ha eseguito un valzer di Chopin** she performed a waltz by Chopin

esempio, -pi [e'zempjo] SM example; **ad** *o* **per esempio** for example *o* instance; **citare come** *o* **ad esempio** to quote as an example; **dare il buon/cattivo esempio** to set a good/bad example; **essere un esempio di virtù** to be a paragon of virtue; **fare un esempio** to give an example; **fammi un esempio** give me an example; **prendere (l')esempio da qn** to follow sb's example; **che ti serva d'esempio!** let that be a lesson to you!; **un esempio per tutti noi** an example to us all

esemplare¹ [ezem'plare] AGG (*vita, punizione*) exemplary; (*allievo*) model *attr*; **dare una punizione esemplare a qn** to make an example of sb

esemplare² [ezem'plare] SM (*Bot, Zool, Geol*) specimen; (*di francobollo, moneta*) example; (*di libro*) copy; **un esemplare rarissimo** a very rare specimen

esemplificare [ezemplifi'kare] /20/ VT to illustrate

esentare [ezen'tare] VT: **esentare qn/qc (da qc)** to exempt sb/sth (from sth)

esentasse [ezen'tasse] AGG INV tax-free

esente [e'zente] AGG: **esente da** (*dispensato da*) exempt from; **esente di dazio** duty-free; **esente di tasse** *o* **imposte** untaxed; **anche lui non è esente da difetti** even he has his failings

esenzione [ezen'tsjone] SF: **esenzione (da)** exemption (from); **esenzione fiscale** tax exemption

esequie [e'zekwje] SFPL funeral rites, obsequies

esercente [ezer'tʃɛnte] SM, SF (*gestore*) trader, owner of a business

esercitare [ezertʃi'tare] /72/ VT **1** (*professione*) to practise (*Brit*), practice (*USA*); (*diritto*) to exercise; **esercitare (su)** (*controllo, influenza*) to exert (over); (*pressione*) to exert (on); (*autorità, potere*) to exercise (over); **esercitare il proprio controllo su qn** to exert control over sb; **quel medico non esercita più** that doctor is no longer in practice **2** (*corpo, mente, voce*) to train, exercise; **esercitarsi** VR (*sportivo*) to train; (*musicista*) to practise; **esercitarsi nella guida** to practise one's driving; **esercitarsi a fare qc** to practise doing sth; **esercitarsi in palestra** to train in the gym

esercitazione [ezertʃitat'tsjone] SF **1** (*Univ: di materie scientifiche*) practical (class); (: *di lingue*) language class **2** (*Mil*): **esercitazione navale/militare** naval/military exercise; **esercitazioni di tiro** target practice *sg*

esercito [e'zɛrtʃito] SM (*Mil*) army; (*fig: di persone*) host

esercizio, -zi [ezer'tʃittsjo] SM **1** (*compito, movimento*) exercise; **abbiamo fatto un esercizio di matematica** we did a math(s) exercise; **essere fuori esercizio** to be out of practice; **fare (molto) esercizio** (*pratica*) to practise (*Brit*) *o* practice (*USA*) a lot; (*movimento*) to take a lot of exercise; **questi esercizi sviluppano gli addominali** these exercises develop the abdominal muscles **2** (*di professione, culto*) practice; (*di diritto*) exercising; (*di funzioni*) exercise; **nell'esercizio delle proprie funzioni** in the execution of one's duties **3** (*Comm, Amm: gestione*) running, management; (: *azienda gestita*) business, concern; **costi d'esercizio** overheads; **quella ditta è in esercizio da pochi mesi** that firm has only been in business for a few months; **aprire un esercizio** to set up a business, open a shop (*o* bar *o* restaurant *ecc*); **pubblico esercizio** commercial concern; **licenza d'esercizio** licence to trade **4** (*Fin: anche: esercizio finanziario*) financial year; **il bilancio dell'esercizio 2005** the budget for the 2005 financial year

esfoliante [esfo'ljante] SM exfoliator

esibire [ezi'bire] /55/ VT (*bravura, capacità*) to exhibit, display; (*documenti*) to produce, present; **esibirsi** VR (*attore, artista*) to perform; (*fig*) to show off

esibizione [ezibit'tsjone] SF **1** (*spettacolo*) performance, show **2** (*sfoggio*) exhibition, showing off **3** (*di documento*) presentation

esibizionista, -i, -e [ezibittsjo'nista] SM, SF exhibitionist; (*Psic*) exhibitionist, flasher (*Brit fam*)

esigente [ezi'dʒɛnte] AGG demanding; **un cliente molto esigente** a very demanding customer; **è esigente nel mangiare** he's particular about his food

esigenza [ezi'dʒɛntsa] SF requirement, need; **avere troppe esigenze** to be too demanding; **andare incontro alle esigenze del mercato** *o* **dei consumatori** to meet the demands of the market *o* of consumers; **sentire l'esigenza di qc/di fare qc** to feel the need for sth/to do sth

esigere [e'zidʒere] /47/ VT IRREG **1** (*pretendere*) to demand; (*comportare, richiedere*) to require, call for; **esigere qc da qn** to demand sth from *o* of sb; **il proprietario esige il pagamento immediato** the owner is demanding immediate payment; **esigere che qn faccia qc** to expect sb to do sth; **esige il rispetto di tutti** he demands everybody's respect; **è un lavoro che esige molta concentrazione** it's a job which demands a lot of concentration; **esigere troppo da se stessi** to expect too much of oneself **2** (*riscuotere: debito*) to collect

esigibile [ezi'dʒibile] AGG (*assegno, somma*) payable

esiguo, -a [e'ziguo] AGG (*numero, quantità*) small, tiny; (*patrimonio, compenso*) meagre; (*risorse*) scanty

esilarante [ezila'rante] AGG hilarious; **gas esilarante** laughing gas

esile [e'zile] AGG (*persona*) slender, slim; (*stelo*) thin; (*voce*) faint; **un esile filo di speranza** a faint ray of hope, a glimmer of hope

esiliare [ezi'ljare] /19/ VT (*Pol*) to exile; (*fig*) to banish; **esiliarsi** VR (*Pol*) to go into exile

esiliato, -a [ezi'ljato] AGG exiled ♦ SM, SF exile

esilio, -li [e'ziljo] SM exile; **vive in esilio da diversi anni** he's been living in exile for several years; **mandare in esilio** to exile

esimere [e'zimere] /29/ VT: **esimere qn da qc** to exempt sb from sth; **esimersi** VR: **esimersi da qc/dal fare qc** to get out of sth/doing sth

esistente [ezis'tɛnte] AGG (gen) existing; **tuttora esistente** (persona) still alive o living; (casa) which still stands

esistenza [ezis'tɛntsa] SF (gen) existence; (vita) life, existence

esistenzialismo [ezistentsja'lizmo] SM existentialism

esistere [e'zistere] /11/ VI IRREG (aus essere) (gen) to exist; **esistono ancora dubbi in merito** there are still some doubts about it; **questo modello esiste in due colori** this model comes o is available in two colours; **Babbo Natale non esiste** Santa Claus doesn't exist; **non esiste!** (fam) no way!

esistito, -a [ezis'tito] PP di **esistere**

esitante [ezi'tante] AGG hesitant, faltering

esitare [ezi'tare] /72/ VI (aus avere) to hesitate; **esitava a prendere una decisione** he was reluctant to take a decision; **esitava tra il sì e il no** he wasn't sure whether to say yes or no; **esitò a rispondere** he hesitated before answering; **senza esitare** without (any) hesitation

esitazione [ezitat'tsjone] SF hesitation; **dopo molte esitazioni** after much hesitation; **senza esitazioni** unhesitatingly, without (any) hesitation

esito ['ɛzito] SM result, outcome; **avere buon esito** to be successful; **le analisi hanno avuto esito negativo** the results of the tests were negative; **l'esito degli esami** the exam results

eskimo ['ɛskimo] SM (giaccone) parka

esodo ['ɛzodo] SM exodus; **l'esodo di Ferragosto** ≈ the August bank holiday exodus; **l'esodo dei capitali all'estero** the outflow of funds into overseas investments; **l'Esodo** (Bibbia) the Exodus

esofago, -gi [e'zofago] SM oesophagus (Brit), esophagus (USA)

esonerare [ezone'rare] /72/ VT: **esonerare da** (servizio militare) to exempt from; (lezioni) to excuse from

esorbitante [ezorbi'tante] AGG exorbitant, excessive

esorcismo [ezor't∫izmo] SM exorcism

esorcista, -i [ezor't∫ista] SM exorcist

esorcizzare [ezort∫id'dzare] /72/ VT (anche fig) to exorcize

esordiente [ezor'djɛnte] AGG: **un attore/calciatore esordiente** an actor/footballer making his professional debut ♦ SM, SF (attore, giocatore) newcomer

esordio, -di [e'zordjo] SM debut, first appearance; **un'attrice al suo esordio** come regista an actress making her directorial debut; **questo è il suo esordio in nazionale** this is his debut in the national team; **la sua carriera è ancora agli esordi** his career is just beginning

esordire [ezor'dire] /55/ VI (aus avere) (Cine, Teatro, Mus, Sport) to make one's debut; (fig) to start out, begin (one's career); **esordì giovanissima** she made her debut when she was very young; **esordì dicendo che...** he began by saying (that) ...

esortare [ezor'tare] /72/ VT to exhort, urge; **esortare qn a fare qc** to urge sb to do sth; **lo esortai a partire al più presto** I urged him to leave as soon as possible

esortazione [ezortat'tsjone] SF exhortation

esoso, -a [e'zozo] AGG 1 (prezzo) exorbitant 2 (persona: avido) grasping

esoterico, -a, -ci, -che [ezo'tɛriko] AGG esoteric

esotico, -a, -ci, -che [e'zɔtiko] AGG exotic; **frutta esotica** exotic fruit

espandere [es'pandere] /110/ VT IRREG (gen) to expand; (confini) to extend; (influenza) to extend, widen; **espandersi** VIP to expand; (influenza) to spread

espansione [espan'sjone] SF (estensione) expansion; **in espansione** (economia) booming; (universo) expanding; **a espansione** (Tecn: motori) expansion attr

espansività [espansivi'ta] SF INV expansiveness

espansivo, -a [espan'sivo] AGG (persona) expansive, communicative; **poco espansivo** reserved, not very forthcoming

espanso, -a [es'panso] PP di **espandere**

espatriare [espa'trjare] /19/ VI (aus essere) to leave the country

espatrio, -ri [es'patrjo] SM expatriation; **permesso di espatrio** authorization to leave the country

espediente [espe'djɛnte] SM expedient; **cercare un espediente per trarsi d'impaccio** to try and find a way out of a difficult situation; **vivere di espedienti** to live by o on one's wits

espellere [es'pɛllere] /48/ VT IRREG 1 **espellere (da)** (da partito, associazione, scuola) to expel (from); (da paese) to deport (from); **l'hanno espulso dalla scuola** he was expelled from the school; **espellere (dal campo)** (Sport) to send off (the field); **tutt'e due i calciatori sono stati espulsi** both players were sent off 2 (gas) to discharge; (cartucce usate) to eject

esperienza [espe'rjɛntsa] SF 1 experience; **senza esperienza** inexperienced; **avere molta esperienza di/in** to have a lot of experience of/in; **parlare/sapere per esperienza** to speak/know from experience; **fare o acquisire esperienza** to gain experience; **ha dieci anni di esperienza nell'insegnamento** he has ten years' teaching experience; **è stata un'esperienza molto utile** it was a very useful experience; **esperienza di lavoro** work experience 2 (scientifico) experiment

esperimento [esperi'mento] SM experiment; **a titolo di esperimento** by way of experiment; **sottoporre qc ad esperimento** to carry out an experiment on sth; **fare un esperimento** to carry out o do an experiment; **esperimenti nucleari** nuclear tests; **esperimenti sugli animali** animal experiments

esperto, -a [es'pɛrto] AGG 1 (competente) expert; (operaio) skilled 2 (che ha esperienza) experienced; **è abbastanza esperto nella guida** he is a fairly experienced driver ♦ SM, SF expert; **è un esperto di botanica** he is an expert on botany; **un esperto di computer** a computer expert

espianto [es'pjanto] SM (Med) removal

espiare [espi'are] /60/ VT to expiate, atone for

espiazione [espiat'tsjone] SF: **espiazione (di)** expiation (of), atonement (for)

espirare [espi'rare] /72/ VT, VI (aus avere) to breathe out, exhale

espletamento [espleta'mento] SM (Amm) carrying out; **l'espletamento delle pratiche richiede due mesi** the completion of all formalities will require two months

espletare [esple'tare] /72/ VT (Amm) to carry out

esplicare [espli'kare] /20/ VT (incarico, attività) to carry out, perform

esplicativo, -a [esplika'tivo] AGG explanatory

esplicito, -a [es'plit∫ito] AGG explicit; **proposizione esplicita** (Gramm) sentence (containing finite verb)

esplodere [es'plɔdere] /49/ VI IRREG (aus essere) (anche fig) to explode; (bomba) to explode, blow up; **far esplodere una bomba** to explode a bomb; **esplodere per la rabbia** to explode with anger; **esplodere in una risata** to burst out laughing; **è esplosa l'estate** summer has arrived with a bang; **l'ordigno è esploso uccidendo tre persone** the bomb exploded, killing three people ♦ VT: **esplodere un colpo contro qn** to fire a shot at sb

esplorare [esplo'rare] /72/ VT 1 (gen, anche fig) to explore; **appena arrivati siamo usciti ad esplorare la città** as soon as we arrived we went out to explore the town 2 (Mil) to reconnoitre

esploratore, -trice [esplora'tore] SM, SF explorer; **giovani esploratori** (boy) scouts ♦ SM (militare) scout; (nave) scout (ship)

esplorazione [esplorat'tsjone] SF exploration; (Mil) reconnaissance; **mandare qn in esplorazione** to send sb to scout ahead

esplosione [esplo'zjone] SF (gen, anche fig: di moda, crisi) explosion; (: di rabbia, gioia) outburst; **esplosione demografica** population explosion; **l'esplosione ha distrutto il palazzo** the explosion destroyed the building

esplosivo, -a [esplo'zivo] AGG, SM explosive; **una notizia esplosiva** a bombshell

esploso, -a [es'plɔzo] PP di **esplodere** ♦ AGG (disegno) exploded ♦ SM exploded view

esponente [espo'nɛnte] SM, SF (rappresentante) exponent, representative ♦ SM (Mat) exponent

esponenziale [esponen'tsjale] AGG (Mat) exponential

espongo [es'pongo], **esponi** ecc [es'poni] VB vedi **esporre**

esporre [es'porre] VB IRREG /77/ VT 1 (esibire: merce) to put on display, display; (: quadri) to exhibit, show; (: bandiera) to put out, raise; **esposto al pubblico** on display to the public; **ha esposto la merce in vetrina** he displayed the goods in the window; **espone i suoi quadri in una galleria d'arte** he's showing his paintings in an art gallery 2 (*spiegare*) to explain; (*argomento, teoria*) to put forward, expound; (*fatti, ragionamenti*) to set out; (*dubbi, riserve*) to express; **esporre a voce/per iscritto** to explain verbally/in writing; **ha esposto i fatti con grande chiarezza** she explained the facts very clearly 3 (*mettere in pericolo*): **esporre qn al pericolo** to expose sb to danger; **esporre il fianco a critiche** to lay o.s. open to criticism 4 (*alla luce, all'aria, anche Fot*) to expose ♦ **esporsi** vr: **esporsi a** (*sole, pericolo*) to expose o.s. to; (*critiche*) to lay o.s. open to; **stai attento a non esporti troppo** (*compromettersi*) be careful about sticking your neck out

esportare [espor'tare] /72/ vt to export

esportatore, -trice [esporta'tore] AGG exporting attr ♦ SM, SF exporter

esportazione [esportat'tsjone] SF (*azione*) exportation, export; (*di prodotti*) exports pl; **di esportazione** (*agenzia, permesso*) export attr; **prodotti per l'esportazione** export goods

espose ecc [es'pose] vb vedi **esporre**

esposimetro [espo'zimetro] SM (*Fot*) exposure meter, light meter

esposizione [espozit'tsjone] SF 1 (*di merce*) display; (*di fatti, ragioni: narrazione*) exposition; (: *spiegazione*) explanation 2 (*fiera, mostra*) exhibition, show 3 (*posizione di casa*) aspect; **casa con esposizione a nord** house facing north, north-facing house 4 (*Fot: al sole*) exposure; **tempo di esposizione** (*Fot*) shutter speed

esposto, -a [es'posto] PP di **esporre** ♦ AGG 1 (*edificio*): **esposto a nord** facing north, north-facing; **la casa è esposta a nord** the house faces north 2 (*Med: frattura*) compound attr 3 (*Alpinismo: passaggio, via*) exposed ♦ SM (*Amm*) statement, account; (*petizione*) petition; **fare un esposto a qn** to submit a report to sb, give sb a report

espressione [espres'sjone] SF (*gen, anche Mat*) expression; **libertà di espressione** freedom of expression; **ha usato un'espressione volgare** he used a coarse expression; **avere un'espressione stupita** to look surprised

espressivo, -a [espres'sivo] AGG expressive; **silenzio espressivo** eloquent silence

espresso¹, -a [es'presso] PP di **esprimere**

espresso², -a [es'presso] AGG (*desiderio, treno*) express; (*caffè*) espresso; **un caffè espresso** an espresso ♦ SM (*lettera*) express letter; (*treno*) express; (*caffè*) espresso (coffee); **un espresso e un cappuccino, per favore** an espresso and a cappuccino, please; **abbiamo preso l'espresso per Roma** we took the express train to Rome

esprimere [es'primere] VB IRREG /50/ vt to express; (*opinione*) to voice, express; **ognuno è libero di esprimere il proprio parere** everybody's free to express their own opinion; **esprimere un desiderio** to make a wish; **dai, esprimi un desiderio!** go on, make a wish!; **esprimersi** VIP to express o.s.; **trovo difficile esprimermi in inglese** I find it difficult to express myself in English; **esprimersi a gesti** to use sign language

espropriare [espro'prjare] /19/ vt (*terreni, edifici*) to place a compulsory purchase order on; **l'hanno espropriato dei suoi beni** they dispossessed him of his property, they expropriated his property

espropriazione [esproprjat'tsjone] SF, **esproprio** (pri) [es'prɔprjo] SM expropriation; **espropriazione per pubblica utilità** compulsory purchase (*Brit*), eminent domain (*USA*)

espugnare [espuɲ'ɲare] /15/ vt to take by force, storm

espulsi ecc [es'pulsi] vb vedi **espellere**

espulsione [espul'sjone] SF (*da partito, scuola ecc*) expulsion; (*da paese*) deportation; (*dal campo di gioco*) sending off

espulso, -a [es'pulso] PP di **espellere**

essa ['essa] PRON F (pl f esse) vedi **esso**

essenza [es'sɛntsa] SF 1 (*di argomento*) gist, essence; (*Filosofia*) essence 2 (*estratto: di piante*) (essential) oil, essence; (: *alimentare*) essence

essenziale [essen'tsjale] AGG: **essenziale (a)** essential (to o for); (*stile, linguaggio*) simple; **olio essenziale** essential oil; **requisiti essenziali** prerequisites ♦ SM: **l'essenziale** (*l'importante*) the main o most important thing; (*oggetti necessari*)

the (basic) essentials pl; (*punti principali*) the essentials pl; **riduciamo il discorso all'essenziale** let's restrict our discussion to the basic o essential points; **l'essenziale è che venga** the main o important thing is that he should come; **l'essenziale è che tu sia arrivato sano e salvo** the main thing is that you got here safe and sound

---

PAROLA CHIAVE

essere ['essere] (*aus* **essere**) /51/ VI

1 (*copulativo*) to be; **chi è quel tipo?** — **è Giovanni** who is that (guy)? — it's Giovanni; **è giovane/malato** he is young/ill; **siamo in dieci a volerci andare** there are ten of us wanting to go o who want to go; **è (un) professore** he is a teacher; **non è vero** that's not true

2 (*trovarsi*) to be; (*vivere*) to live; **essere in piedi** to be standing; **sono qui da tre ore** I've been here for three hours; **è a Roma dal 1990** he's been (living) in Rome since 1990; **è a tavola** he is eating

3 (*diventare*) to be; **quando sarai calmo** when you calm down; **quando sarai grande** when you grow up o are grown up; **quando sarai medico** when you are a doctor

4 (*esistere*) to be; **essere o non essere** to be or not to be; **sia la luce - e la luce fu** let there be light - and there was light; **è il miglior meccanico che ci sia** he is the best mechanic there is

5 (*provenire*): **è di Genova** he is o comes from Genoa

6 (*appartenere*): **di chi è questo libro?** — **è mio** whose book is this? — it's mine; **non potrò essere dei vostri quest'estate** I won't be able to join you this summer

7 (*data*): **è il 12 giugno** it is June 12th; **era il 1962** it was 1962; **erano gli anni Sessanta** it was the Sixties

8 (*ora*): **che ora è?** o **che ore sono?** — **sono le due** what's the time? o what time is it? — it's two o'clock; **saranno state le cinque** it must have been five o'clock

9 (+ *da* + *infinito*): **è da fare subito** it's to be done o needs to be done o is to be done immediately; **è da spedire stasera** it has (got) to be sent tonight

♦ **VB AUS**

1 (*tempi composti: attivo*): **è arrivato?** has he arrived?; **è arrivato ieri?** did he arrive yesterday?; **è andato in Inghilterra** he has gone to England; **è stato in Inghilterra** he has been to England; **sono cresciuto in Italia** I grew up in Italy

2 (*tempi composti: passivo*): **è stato fabbricato in India** it was made in India; **è stato investito da un'auto** he was run over by a car

3 (*tempi composti: riflessivo*): **si sono vestiti** they dressed, they got dressed (*reciproco*): **si sono baciati** they kissed; **non si sono visti** they didn't see each other

♦ **VB IMPERS**

1 **è che non mi piace** the fact is I don't like it; **che ne sarà della macchina?** what will happen to the car?; **sarà come dici tu** you may be right; **come sarebbe a dire?** what do you mean?; **come se niente fosse** as if nothing had happened; **è da tre ore che ti aspetto** I've been waiting for you for three hours; **non è da te** it's not like you; **sia detto fra noi** between you and me; **è Pasqua** it's Easter; **è possibile che venga** he may come; **può essere perhaps**; **sarà quel che sarà** what will be will be; **sia quel che sia, io me ne vado** whatever happens I'm off; **è tardi** it's late

2 (*costare*): **sono 200 euro** that's 200 euros, that comes to 200 euros; **quant'è?** how much is it?; **quant'è in tutto?** how much does that come to?

3 **esserci**: **c'è** there is; **ci sono** there are; **non c'è altro da dire** there's nothing else to be said o there's nothing more one can say; **che (cosa) c'è?** what's wrong o the matter?; **che c'è di nuovo?** what's new?; **ci sono 60 chilometri** it's 60 kilometres; **cosa c'è** what's wrong o the matter?; **c'è da strapparsi i capelli** it's enough to drive you up the wall; **ce n'è per tutti** there's enough for everybody; **quanti invitati ci saranno?** how many guests will there be?; **quanto c'è da qui a Verona?** how far is it from here to Verona?; **c'era una volta...** once upon a time there was ...; vedi anche **ci**

♦ SM being; **essere umano** human being; **gli esseri viventi** the living pl

essi ['essi] PRON MPL vedi **esso**

essiccare [essik'kare] /20/ vt (*gen*) to dry; (*legname*) to season;

(*bacino, palude*) to drain; **essiccarsi** VIP (*fiume, pozzo*) to dry up; (*vernice*) to dry (out)

esso, -a [ˈesso] PRON PERS (NEUTRO) it; (*riferito a persona: sogg*) he (she); (: *complemento*) him (her); **essi** *o* **esse** (*sogg*) they; (*complemento*) them; **...o chi per esso ...** or his delegate *o* representative

est [ɛst] SM **1** east; **a est (di)** east (of); **a est di Palermo** east of Palermo; **si trova a est della città** it's east of the city; **il sole sorge a est** the sun rises in the east; **verso est** eastward(s); **il vento dell'est** the east wind **2** (*Pol*) : **l'Est** the East; **l'Europa dell'Est** Eastern Europe; **i paesi dell'Est** the Eastern bloc *sg* ♦ AGG INV (*gen*) east; (*regione*) eastern; **è partito in direzione est** he set off eastwards *o* in an eastward direction

estasi [ˈɛstazi] SF INV (*Rel, anche fig*) ecstasy; **andare in estasi (per)** (*fig*) to go into ecstasies *o* raptures (over); **mandare in estasi** to send into ecstasies *o* raptures

estasiare [estaˈzjare] /19/ VT to send into raptures; **estasiarsi** VIP: **estasiarsi (a, davanti a)** to go into ecstasies *o* raptures (over)

estate [esˈtate] SF summer; **d'estate** *o* **in estate** in (the) summer; **un giorno d'estate** one summer's day, one day in summer; **passa l'estate al mare** she spends the summer by the sea

❏ estate non si traduce mai con la parola inglese *estate*

estatico, -a, -ci, -che [esˈtatiko] AGG ecstatic

estemporaneo, -a [estempoˈraneo] AGG (*discorso*) extempore, impromptu; (*brano musicale*) impromptu

estendere [esˈtɛndere] /120/ VT (*gen*) to extend; **estendersi** VIP **1** (*diffondersi: epidemia, rivolta*) to spread; (*allargarsi: città*) to spread, expand; (: *attività commerciale*) to increase, expand **2** (*foresta*) to stretch, extend; **la pianura si estendeva a perdita d'occhio** the plain stretched (away) as far as the eye could see

estensione [estenˈsjone] SF **1** (*ampliamento: di diritto, significato, contratto*) extension; (: *di commercio, dominio*) expansion; **per estensione** by extension, in a wider sense; **in tutta l'estensione del termine** in the widest sense of the word **2** (*ampiezza: di fenomeno, territorio*) extent; (*superficie*) expanse **3** (*Mus*) range, compass **4** (*Inform*) extension

estenuante [estenuˈante] AGG wearing, tiring

estenuare [estenuˈare] /72/ VT (*stancare*) to wear out, tire out

esteriore [esteˈrjore] AGG (*esterno: aspetto, segni, manifestazioni*) outward *attr*; **il mondo esteriore** the external world; **la sua sicurezza è solo esteriore** he seems confident, but he isn't really

esteriorità [esterjoriˈta] SF INV outward appearance

esteriorizzare [esterjoridˈdzare] /72/ VT (*gioia, sentimenti*) to show

esternare [esterˈnare] /72/ VT to express; **esternare un sospetto** to voice a suspicion

esterno, -a [esˈtɛrno] AGG **1** (*muro, superficie*) outer, exterior; (*scala, gabinetto*) outside *attr*; (*rivestimento*) exterior; aspetto esterno (*di persona*) outward appearance; **l'aspetto esterno della casa** the outside of the house; **il muro esterno** the outside wall; **per uso esterno** (*Med*) for external use only **2** (*fig: influenze, mondo*) external, outside *attr*; (: *interessi*) outside *attr*; (: *realtà*) external **3** (*Geom*): **angolo esterno** exterior angle **4** (*allievo*) day *attr*; (*candidato*) external; **commissione esterna** external examiners *pl* ♦ SM (*di edificio*) outside, exterior; (*di scatola*) outside; **all'esterno** on the outside; **dall'esterno** from outside; **l'esterno del palazzo** the outside of the building; **gli esterni sono stati girati a Boston** (*Cine*) the location shots were taken in Boston ♦ SM, SF (*allievo*) day pupil; (*candidato*) external candidate

estero, -a [ˈɛstero] AGG foreign; **vendono giornali esteri?** do they sell foreign newspapers? ♦ SM: **andare all'estero** *o* **partire per l'estero** to go abroad; **vivere all'estero** to live abroad *o* in a foreign country; **vorrei andare all'estero** I'd like to go abroad; **non è mai stato all'estero** he's never been abroad; **commercio con l'estero** foreign trade; **ministero degli Esteri** *o* **gli Esteri** Ministry for Foreign Affairs, ≈ Foreign Office (*Brit*), ≈ State Department (*USA*)

esterofilia [esterofiˈlia] SF passion for foreign things

esterrefatto, -a [esterreˈfatto] AGG (*costernato*) horrified; (*sbalordito*) astounded

estesi ecc [esˈtesi] VB *vedi* **estendere**

esteso, -a [esˈteso] PP *di* **estendere** ♦ AGG (*gen*) extensive, large; (*territorio*) vast; (*cultura, ricerca*) wide-ranging; **un'area molto estesa** a very large area; **(scrivere) per esteso** (to write) in full

esteticamente [estetikaˈmente] AVV aesthetically; **esteticamente non è il massimo, però funziona bene** it isn't much to look at, but it works fine

estetico, -a, -ci, -che [esˈtɛtiko] AGG aesthetic; **chirurgia estetica** plastic surgery, cosmetic surgery; **cura estetica** beauty treatment

estetista, -i, -e [esteˈtista] SM, SF beautician; **fa l'estetista** he's a beautician

estimo [ˈɛstimo] SM (*stima*) valuation; (*disciplina*) surveying

estinguere [esˈtingwere] /42/ VT **1** (*spegnere*) to put out, extinguish **2** (*Comm: debito*) to pay off; (: *conto in banca*) to close; **estinguersi** VIP (*fuoco*) to go out, die out; (*fama*) to fade away; (*stirpe*) to die out; (*specie*) to become extinct

estinsi ecc [esˈtinsi] VB *vedi* **estinguere**

estinto, -a [esˈtinto] PP *di* **estinguere** ♦ AGG **1** (*specie, stirpe*) extinct **2** (*Comm: debito*) paid off; (: *conto*) closed ♦ SM, SF: **il caro estinto** the dear departed

estintore [estinˈtore] SM (*fire*) extinguisher

estinzione [estinˈtsjone] SF (*gen, di specie*) extinction; (*di debito*) payment; (*di conto*) closing; (*di incendio*) putting out; **una specie in via di estinzione** a species on the verge of extinction

estirpare [estirˈpare] /72/ VT (*pianta*) to uproot, pull up; (*dente*) to extract; (*tumore*) to remove; (*fig: vizio*) to eradicate

estivo, -a [esˈtivo] AGG summer *attr*; **nei mesi estivi** in the summer months; **le vacanze estive** the summer holidays; **una giornata estiva** a summer's day

estone [ˈɛstone] AGG, SM, SF Estonian ♦ SM (*lingua*) Estonian

Estonia [esˈtɔnja] SF Estonia

estorcere [esˈtortʃere] /106/ VT IRREG: **estorcere qc (a qn)** to extort sth (from sb)

estorsione [estorˈsjone] SF extortion; **il denaro frutto delle estorsioni** money acquired by extortion

estorto, -a [esˈtɔrto] PP *di* **estorcere**

estradare [estraˈdare] /72/ VT (*Dir*) to extradite

estradizione [estradiˈtsjone] SF (*Dir*) extradition

estraggo [esˈtraggo], **estrai** ecc [esˈtrai] VB *vedi* **estrarre**

estraneo, -a [esˈtraneo] AGG (*gen*) extraneous; **corpo estraneo** foreign body; **estraneo a** (*tema, argomento*) unrelated to; **sentirsi estraneo a** (*famiglia, società*) to feel alienated from; **mantenersi** *o* **rimanere estraneo a** (*litigio, complotto*) to take no part in ♦ SM, SF stranger; **ingresso vietato agli estranei** no admittance to unauthorized personnel; **è difficile parlare di sé con un estraneo** it's difficult to talk about yourself to a stranger

estraniarsi [estraˈnjarsi] /19/ VR: **estraniarsi (da)** to cut o.s. off (from)

estrarre [esˈtrarre] /123/ VT IRREG **1** (*gen, anche Med, Mat*) to extract; (*carbone*) to mine; (*marmo*) to quarry **2** (*sorteggiare*) to draw; **estrarre a sorte** to draw lots

estrassi ecc [esˈtrassi] VB *vedi* **estrarre**

estratto, -a [esˈtratto] PP *di* **estrarre** ♦ SM **1** (*alimentare*) extract; (*per profumeria*) essence; **estratto di carne** meat extract **2** (*sommario: di discorso, documento*) resumé; (*brano: di libro*) extract, excerpt; **estratto conto** (*Banca*) (bank) statement; **estratto di nascita** (*Amm*) birth certificate

estrazione [estraˈtsjone] SF **1** (*vedi vb*) extraction; mining; quarrying; drawing **2** (*sorteggio*) draw **3** (*fig: origine*): **essere di estrazione borghese** to come from a middle-class family

estremamente [estremaˈmente] AVV extremely; **è stato estremamente gentile** he was extremely kind

estremismo [estreˈmizmo] SM extremism

estremista, -i, -e [estreˈmista] SM, SF extremist

estremità [estremiˈta] SF INV **1** (*gen*) end, extremity; (*di ago, matita*) point; (*di villaggio, lago, isola*) far end; **da un'estremità all'altra** from one end to the other; **c'è una scala alle due estremità del corridoio** there are stairs at both ends of the corridor **2** (*Anat*); **estremità** SFPL extremities

estremo, -a [es'trɛmo] AGG (gen) extreme; (ultimo: ora, tentativo) final, last; (misure) drastic, extreme; **estrema destra/sinistra** (Pol) extreme right/left; **l'Estrema Unzione** (Rel) Extreme Unction; **l'Estremo Oriente** the Far East; sport **estremo** extreme sport ♦ SM 1 (gen) extreme; (limite: di pazienza, forze) limit, end; **all'estremo della disperazione** in the depths of despair; **passare da un estremo all'altro** to go from one extreme to the other; **è pignolo (fino) all'estremo** he is extremely o exceedingly fussy; **spingere le cose agli estremi** to go too far 2 **estremi** SMPL (Amm: dati essenziali) details, particulars; (Dir) essential elements; **gli estremi del caso** the details of the case

estrinsecare [estrinse'kare] /20/ VT to express, show; **estrinsecarsi** VIP to express o.s.

estro [ˈɛstro] SM (ispirazione) inspiration; (talento) gift, bent; (capriccio) whim, fancy; **gli è venuto l'estro di scrivere** he has taken it into his head to become a writer

estromesso, -a [estro'messo] PP di **estromettere**

estromettere [estro'mettere] /63/ VT IRREG: **estromettere (da)** (partito, club) to expel (from); (discussione) to exclude (from)

estromissione [estromis'sjone] SF (vedi vb) expulsion; exclusion

estroso, -a [es'troso] AGG (capriccioso) fanciful; (creativo) talented, creative

estroverso, -a [estro'vɛrso] AGG extrovert(ed), outgoing; **Claudia è molto estroversa** Claudia's very outgoing ♦ SM, SF extrovert

estuario, -ri [estu'arjo] SM estuary

esuberante [ezube'rante] AGG exuberant

esuberanza [ezube'rantsa] SF (vitalità) exuberance; **esuberanza di personale** (eccedenza) surplus staff

esubero [e'zubero] SM: **esubero di personale** surplus staff; **in esubero** (personale) due to be laid off

esulare [ezu'lare] /72/ VI (aus avere) **esulare da** (competenza) to be beyond; (compiti) not to be part of; **esula dalle mie possibilità aiutarti** it is not within my power to help you

esule [ˈezule] SM, SF exile

esultanza [ezul'tantsa] SF exultation

esultare [ezul'tare] /72/ VI (aus avere) **esultare di gioia** to be full of joy; **esultare per la vittoria** to rejoice at one's victory

esumare [ezu'mare] /72/ VT (salma) to exhume, disinter; (fig) to unearth

età [e'ta] SF INV (gen) age; **all'età di 8 anni** at the age of 8, at 8 years of age, at (age) 8; **avere l'età per fare qc** to be old enough to do sth; **non ho più l'età per fare queste cose** I'm too old to do this sort of thing; **di mezza età** middle-aged; **con l'età è migliorato** he has improved with age; **in età avanzata** of advanced years; **gente della nostra età** people our age; **Sandra ha la mia età** Sandra's the same age as me; **raggiungere la maggior età** to come of age; **essere in età minore** to be under age; **è giunto ad una bella età** he has reached a good age; **limite di età** age limit; **l'età della ragione** the age of reason; **l'età della pietra** the Stone Age; **lei ha la mia età** she is the same age as me o as I am

etanolo [eta'nɔlo] SM ethanol

etc. ABBR etc.

etere [ˈɛtere] SM (Chim, anche letter) ether; **via etere** on the airwaves

etereo, -a [e'tɛreo] AGG ethereal

eternità [eterni'ta] SF INV (anche fig) eternity; **impiegare o mettere un'eternità a fare qc** to take ages to do sth; **ti aspetto da un'eternità** I've been waiting for you for ages; **è durato pochi minuti ma mi è sembrato un'eternità** it only lasted a few minutes but it seemed like an eternity

eterno, -a [e'tɛrno] AGG (Rel, Filosofia) eternal; (senza fine) eternal, everlasting; (duraturo) perpetual; (interminabile: lamenti, attesa) never-ending; **in eterno** for ever, eternally ♦ SM eternity; **l'Eterno** (Dio) the Eternal (being)

eterogeneo, -a [etero'dʒɛneo] AGG heterogeneous, mixed, varied

eterosessuale [eterosessu'ale] AGG, SM, SF heterosexual

etica [ˈɛtika] SF ethics sg; **etica professionale** professional ethics

etichetta [eti'ketta] SF label; **si è staccata l'etichetta** the label's come off; **l'etichetta** (cerimoniale) etiquette

etico, -a, -ci, -che [ˈɛtiko] AGG (anche banca, conto) ethical

etilometro [eti'lɔmetro] SM Breathalyzer (Marchio registrato, USA), drunkometer (Brit)

etimologia [etimolo'dʒia] SF etymology

etimologico, -a, -ci, -che [etimo'lɔdʒiko] AGG etymological

etiope [e'tiope] AGG, SM, SF Ethiopian

Etiopia [eti'ɔpja] SF Ethiopia

etiopico, -a, -ci, -che [eti'ɔpiko] AGG Ethiopian ♦ SM (lingua) Amharic

Etna [ˈɛtna] SM Etna

etnico, -a, -ci, -che [ˈɛtniko] AGG ethnic

etrusco, -a, -schi, -sche [e'trusko] AGG, SM, SF Etruscan

ettaro [ˈɛttaro] SM hectare (= 10,000 m^2)

etto [ˈɛtto] PREF: **etto... hecto...** ♦ ABBR SM di **ettogrammo**

ettogrammo [etto'grammo] SM hectogram(me) (= 100 grams)

ettolitro [et'tɔlitro] SM hectolitre (Brit), hectoliter (USA)

ettometro [et'tɔmetro] SM hectometre

EU ABBR (= Europa) E

eucalipto [euka'lipto] SM eucalyptus

eucaristia [eukaris'tia] SF: **l'eucaristia** the Eucharist

eufemismo [eufe'mizmo] SM euphemism

eufemistico, -a, -ci, -che [eufe'mistiko] AGG euphemistic

euforia [eufo'ria] SF euphoria

euforico, -a, -ci, -che [eu'fɔriko] AGG euphoric

Eurasia [eu'razja] SF Eurasia

eurasiatico, -a, -ci, -che [eura'zjatiko] AGG, SM, SF Eurasian

eu'ristico, -a, euristica, -ci, euristici, -che, euristiche AGG heuristic

euro [ˈeuro] SM INV euro; **cinque euro** five euros; **una banconota da 100 euro** a 100 euro note

eurocorpo [euro'kɔrpo] SM European force

eurodeputato, -a [eurodepu'tato] SM, SF Euro MP

eurodivisa [eurodi'viza] SF Eurocurrency

eurodollaro [euro'dɔllaro] SM Eurodollar

Eurolandia [euro'landja] SF Euroland

euromercato [euromer'kato] SM Euromarket

euromissile [euro'missile] SM Euro-missile

Europa [eu'rɔpa] SF Europe

europarlamentare [europarlamen'tare] SM, SF Member of the European Parliament, MEP

europeo, -a [euro'pɛo] AGG, SM, SF European; **l'Unione Europea** the European Union

euroscettico, -a, -ci, -che [euro'ʃʃettiko] SM, SF Euro-sceptic

eutanasia [eutana'zia] SF euthanasia

EV ABBR = Eccellenza Vostra

evacuare [evaku'are] /72/ VT, VI (aus avere) (gen, anche Med) to evacuate

evacuazione [evakuat'tsjone] SF evacuation

evadere [e'vadere] VB IRREG /52/ VT 1 (tasse, imposte) to evade; **evadere il fisco** to evade (income) tax 2 (Amm: pratica) to deal with, dispatch; (: corrispondenza) to deal with, clear; (: ordine) to deal with ♦ VI (aus essere) **evadere (da)** (prigione) to escape (from); **sono evasi dal carcere** they escaped from prison; **far evadere qn** to help sb to escape; **evadere dalla realtà quotidiana** to get away from the realities of daily life

evangelico, -a, -ci, -che [evan'dʒɛliko] AGG, SM, SF evangelical

evangelista, -i [evandʒe'lista] SM Evangelist

evaporare [evapo'rare] /72/ VT, VI (nel senso di 'trasformarsi in vapore': (aus essere) nel senso di 'ridursi per evaporazione': (aus avere) to evaporate

evaporazione [evaporat'tsjone] SF evaporation

evasi ecc [e'vazi] VB vedi **evadere**

evasione [eva'zjone] SF 1 (da prigione, anche fig) escape; **letteratura d'evasione** escapist literature 2 (Amm: disbrigo: di ordine) carrying out, fulfilment; **occuparsi dell'evasione della corrispondenza** to deal with the correspondence 3 (Fisco) evasion; **evasione fiscale** tax evasion

evasivo, -a [eva'zivo] AGG evasive

evaso, -a [e'vazo] PP di **evadere** ♦ SM, SF escaped prisoner

evasore [eva'zore] SM: **evasore (fiscale)** tax evader

evenienza [eve'njentsa] SF: **nell'evenienza che ciò succeda** should that happen; **essere pronto ad ogni evenienza** to be ready for any eventuality; **in ogni evenienza puoi metterti in contatto con me** you can get in touch with me should the need arise

evento [e'vento] SM (*anche Inform*) event

eventuale [eventu'ale] AGG: **contro eventuali danni** against any possible damage; **siamo assicurati contro eventuali danni** we're insured against any damage; **per scongiurare il pericolo di eventuali complicazioni** to avoid the risk of possible complications; **gli eventuali guadagni saranno devoluti in beneficenza** any profit will be given to charity; **per eventuali reclami rivolgersi a...** (any) claims should be addressed to ...; **per eventuali domande rivolgersi a...** if you have any queries contact.. ♦ SFPL: **varie ed eventuali** any other business

❑ **eventuale** non si traduce mai con la parola inglese *eventual*

eventualità [eventuali'ta] SF INV eventuality, possibility; **tenersi pronto a ogni eventualità** *o* **a tutte le eventualità** to be prepared for any eventuality *o* for all eventualities; **nell'eventualità di** in the event of; **nell'eventualità che non dovesse tornare...** should he not return ...

eventualmente [eventual'mente] AVV (*se necessario*) if need be, if necessary; **eventualmente ci fossero difficoltà...** should there be any problems ...; **se eventualmente cambiassi idea, sai dove trovarci** if by any chance you change your mind, you know where to find us; **eventualmente potremmo andare in treno** we could always go by train

❑ **eventualmente** non si traduce mai con la parola inglese *eventually*

Everest ['everest] SM: **l'Everest, il monte Everest** (Mount) Everest

eversione [ever'sjone] SF subversion

eversivo, -a [ever'sivo] AGG subversive

evidente [evi'dente] AGG obvious, evident; **è una prova evidente di...** it's clear proof of ...; **era evidente che non voleva venire** it was obvious he didn't want to come; **è evidente!** obviously!

evidentemente [evidente'mente] AVV (*palesemente*) obviously, clearly, evidently; **era evidentemente seccato** he was obviously annoyed; **evidentemente avevo capito male** I obviously misunderstood

evidenza [evi'dentsa] SF: **l'evidenza dei fatti è schiacciante** the facts are incontrovertible; **arrendersi (di fronte) all'evidenza** to yield to the evidence; **negare l'evidenza** to deny the facts *o* the obvious; **mettere in evidenza** (*problemi*) to highlight, bring to the fore

evidenziare [eviden'tsjare] /19/ VT (*sottolineare*) to emphasize, highlight; (*con evidenziatore*) to highlight

evidenziatore [evidentsja'tore] SM (*penna*) highlighter

evirare [evi'rare] /72/ VT to castrate

evitabile [evi'tabile] AGG avoidable

evitare [evi'tare] /72/ VT (*gen*) to avoid; (*colpo*) to dodge; (*sguardo*) to evade; **evitare di fare qc** to avoid doing sth; **evitare di uscire da solo la notte** avoid going out alone at night; **evita di fare rumore** try not to make any noise; **evitare che qc accada** to prevent sth (from) happening; **evitare qc a qn** to spare sb sth; **ciò gli ha evitato il fastidio di tornare indietro** that saved him the bother of going back; **passiamo di qui per evitare il traffico** we're going this way to avoid the traffic

evo ['evo] SM: **l'evo moderno/antico** modern/ancient times

evocare [evo'kare] /20/ VT (*gen*) to evoke; (*ricordo*) to recall, evoke

evocativo, -a [evoka'tivo] AGG evocative

evocherò ecc [evoke'rɔ] VB *vedi* evocare

evolutivo, -a [evolu'tivo] AGG (*gen, anche Bio*) evolutionary; (*Med*) progressive

evoluto, -a [evo'luto] PP *di* evolversi ♦ AGG (*popolo, civiltà*) (highly) developed, advanced; (*persona: emancipato*) independent; (: *senza pregiudizi*) broad-minded

evoluzione [evolut'tsjone] SF 1 (*gen*) evolution; (*progresso*) progress, development; **teoria dell'evoluzione** theory of evolution 2 (*movimento*) movement; (*Mil*) manoeuvre

evolversi [e'volversi] /94/ VIP IRREG to develop, evolve ♦ SM: **con l'evolversi della situazione** as the situation developed *o* develops

evviva [ev'viva] ESCL hurrah!; **evviva il re!** long live the King! ♦ SM INV applause *no pl*

ex [eks] PREF ex, ex-, former; **l'ex Primo ministro** the former Prime Minister ♦ SM INV, SF INV: **il mio ex** my ex

ex aequo [εg'z εkwo] AVV: **classificarsi primo ex aequo** to come joint first, come joint equal

extra ['εkstra] AGG INV, SM INV extra; **una spesa extra** an extra expense; **nel conto c'erano molti extra** there were a lot of extras on the bill

extracomunitario, -ria, -ri, -rie [ekstracomuni'tarjo] AGG non-EU; **i paesi extracomunitari** countries outside the European Union ♦ SM, SF non-EU national (*often referring to non-European immigrant*)

extraconiugale [ekstrakonju'gale] AGG extramarital

extraparlamentare [ekstraparlamen'tare] AGG, SM, SF extra-parliamentary

extrasensoriale [ekstrasenso'rjale] AGG extrasensory; **percezione extrasensoriale** extrasensory perception

extraterrestre [ekstrater'restre] AGG, SM, SF extraterrestrial

extraurbano, -a [ekstraur'bano] AGG suburban

Ff

F¹, f¹ [ˈɛffe] SF INV, SM INV (lettera) F, f; **F come Firenze** ≈ F for Frederick (Brit), ≈ F for Fox (USA)

F² ABBR (= Fahrenheit) F

F. ABBR (= fiume) R

fa¹ [fa] (3a pers sg del presente di **fare**) ♦ AVV: **10 anni fa** 10 years ago; **quanto tempo fa?** how long ago?; **l'ho incontrata due ore fa** I met her two hours ago

fa² [fa] SM INV (Mus) F; (solfeggiando) fa

fabbisogno [fabbiˈzoɲɲo] SM needs pl, requirements pl; **il fabbisogno nazionale di petrolio** the country's oil requirements; **il fabbisogno del settore pubblico** public sector borrowing requirement (Brit), government debt borrowing (USA)

fabbrica, -che [ˈfabbrika] SF factory; **fabbrica di mattoni** brickyard; **una fabbrica di automobili** a car factory

❏ **fabbrica** non si traduce mai con la parola inglese *fabric*

fabbricante [fabbriˈkante] SM, SF manufacturer, maker

fabbricare [fabbriˈkare] /20/ VT (produrre: gen) to make, manufacture; (: a livello industriale) to manufacture; (costruire: edificio) to build, put up; (fig: inventare: alibi, accuse) to fabricate; **è fabbricato in Cina** it's made in China

fabbricato [fabbriˈkato] SM building

fabbricazione [fabbrikatˈtsjone] SF (vedi vb) making; manufacture, manufacturing; building; fabrication; **di fabbricazione italiana** made in Italy, Italian made; **difetto di fabbricazione** manufacturing defect

fabbro [ˈfabbro] SM smith; **fabbro ferraio** (black)smith

faccenda [fatˈtʃɛnda] SF (affare) business, affair, matter; **una brutta faccenda** a nasty business; **è una faccenda complicata** it's a complicated matter; **devo sbrigare alcune faccende** I've got a few things to see to; **le faccende domestiche** the housework sg

faccendiere [fattʃenˈdjere] SM wheeler-dealer, (shady) operator

faccetta [fatˈtʃetta] SF (di pietra preziosa) facet

facchino [fakˈkino] SM (gen) porter; **lavoro da facchino** (fig) hard graft

faccia, -ce [ˈfattʃa] SF 1 (viso, espressione) face; **una faccia amica** a friendly face; **avere la faccia stanca** to look tired; **fare la faccia imbronciata** to sulk; **dovevi vedere la sua faccia quando...** you should have seen his face when ...; **avere il sole in faccia** to have the sun in one's eyes; **gliel'ho detto in faccia** I told him to his face; **ridere in faccia a qn** to laugh in sb's face; **leggere qc in faccia a qn** to see sth written all over sb's face; **cosa ti sei messa in faccia?** what have you got on your face?; **perdere/salvare la faccia** to lose/save (one's) face; **avere la faccia (tosta) di dire/fare qc** to have the cheek o nerve to say/do sth; **hai una bella faccia tosta!** you've got a real cheek! 2 (lato: gen) side; (: Geom) face, side; (: della terra) face; (: fig: di problema, questione) side, aspect; **vorrei cancellarlo dalla faccia della terra** I'd like to wipe him off the face of the earth 3 (fraseologia): **(a) faccia a faccia** face to face; **a faccia in su/giù** face up(wards)/down(wards); **fare qc alla faccia di qn** to do sth to spite sb; **di faccia** opposite, facing; **visto di faccia** seen from the front

facciata [fatˈtʃata] SF 1 (Archit) façade; (fig: apparenza esterna) appearances pl; **non giudicare dalla facciata** don't judge by appearances 2 (di pagina) side; **una lettera di 4 facciate** a 4-page letter; **scrivi su entrambe le facciate** write on both sides

fac'cina [fatˈtʃina] SF (Inform) emoticon

faccio ecc [ˈfattʃo] VB vedi **fare**

facente [faˈtʃɛnte] **facente funzione** SM, SF (Amm) deputy

facessi ecc [faˈtʃessi] VB vedi **fare**

faceto, -a [faˈtʃeto] AGG humorous

facevo ecc [faˈtʃevo] VB vedi **fare**

facezia [faˈtʃɛttsja] SF witticism, witty remark

fachiro [faˈkiro] SM fakir

facile [ˈfatʃile] AGG 1 (gen) easy; **è più facile a dirsi che a farsi** it's easier said than done; **è l'esercizio più facile del libro** it's the easiest exercise in the book; **è meno facile di quanto sembri** it's harder than it looks, it's not as easy as it looks; **non era facile come pensavo** it wasn't as easy as I thought; **far tutto facile** to make light o little of everything; **avere la pistola facile** to be trigger-happy; **avere la lacrima facile** to be easily moved to tears; **è facile all'ira/alla malinconia** he's apt to lose his temper/to get depressed; **avere un carattere facile** to be an easy-going person; **persona di facili costumi** person lacking restraint in sexual behavior 2 (probabile): **è facile che piova** it's probably going to rain; **è facile che venga** he may well come, he'll probably come

facilità [fatʃiliˈta] SF INV 1 (di lavoro, compito) easiness; (di vittoria) ease; **studia con facilità** he has no problem studying; **arrabbiarsi con facilità** to be apt to lose one's temper 2 (disposizione, dono) ability, aptitude; **ha facilità a fare amicizia** he makes friends easily

facilitare [fatʃiliˈtare] /72/ VT to facilitate (frm), make easier; **non faciliterà la situazione** it's not going to make matters any easier

facilitazione [fatʃilitatˈtsjone] SF: **facilitazioni di pagamento** easy terms, credit facilities

facilmente [fatʃilˈmente] AVV (gen) easily; (probabilmente) probably

facilone, -a [fatʃiˈlone] SM, SF (pegg) laid-back type

facinoroso, -a [fatʃinoˈroso] AGG violent ♦ SM, SF thug

facoltà [fakolˈta] SF INV 1 (capacità mentale) faculty; (Chim) property; **nel pieno possesso delle proprie facoltà mentali** in full possession of one's faculties 2 (autorità) power; **dare facoltà a qn di fare qc** to give sb the power o authority to do sth; **esula dalle mie facoltà** it's not within my power 3 (Univ) department, faculty; **è iscritta alla facoltà di legge** she's a student in the law department

facoltativo, -a [fakoltaˈtivo] AGG optional; **fermata facoltativa** request stop; **un corso facoltativo** an optional course

facoltoso, -a [fakolˈtoso] AGG wealthy

facsimile [fakˈsimile] SM INV facsimile; (fig: cosa simile) copy

faggio, -gi [ˈfaddʒo] SM (albero, legno) beech; **mobili di o in faggio** beech(wood) furniture

fagiano [faˈdʒano] SM pheasant; **fagiano di monte** black grouse

fagiolino [fadʒoˈlino] SM French (Brit) o string bean

fagiolo [faˈdʒɔlo] SM bean; **capitare a fagiolo** to come at the right time

fagocitare [fagotʃiˈtare] /72/ VT (Bio) to perform phagocytosis on; (fig: industria) to absorb, swallow up

fagotto¹ [faˈgotto] SM bundle; **fare fagotto** to pack up and go

fagotto² [faˈgotto] SM (Mus) bassoon

Fahrenheit [ˈfaːrənhait] SM INV Fahrenheit

fai [ˈfai] VB vedi **fare**

faida [ˈfaida] SF feud

fai da te [faidaˈte] SM INV DIY, do-it-yourself

faina [faˈina] SF (Zool) stone marten

falange [faˈlandʒe] SF (Anat, Mil) phalanx

falcata [falˈkata] SF stride

falce [ˈfaltʃe] SF scythe; **una falce di luna** a crescent moon; **falce e martello** (Pol) hammer and sickle

falcetto [falˈtʃetto] SM sickle

falciare [falˈtʃare] /14/ VT 1 (grano) to reap; (erba) to mow, cut; (con la falce) to scythe 2 (fig: uccidere): **furono falciati da una raffica di mitra** they were mown down by a hail of machine-gun fire; **migliaia di vite falciate dall'epidemia**

thousands of lives wiped out by the epidemic **3** (*Calcio*) to bring down

falciatrice [faltʃa'tritʃe] SF (*per grano*) reaping machine; (*per erba*) mowing machine

falco, -chi ['falko] SM (*Zool, o fig: Pol*) hawk; **occhio di falco!** you're sharp-eyed!; (*Zool*): **falco migratore** *o* **pellegrino** peregrine falcon; **falco di palude** marsh harrier; **falco pescatore** osprey

falcone [fal'kone] SM falcon

falda ['falda] SF (*Geol*) layer, stratum; (*di cappello*) brim; (*di cappotto*) tails *pl*; (*di monte*) lower slope; (*di tetto*) pitch; (*di neve*) flake

falegname [faleɲ'ɲame] SM carpenter, joiner (*Brit*); **mio padre fa il falegname** my father's a carpenter

falena [fa'lena] SF (*Zool*) moth

Falkland ['fɔːlklɔnd] SFPL: **le (isole) Falkland** the Falkland Islands

fallace [fal'latʃe] AGG deceptive

fallico, -a, -ci, -che ['falliko] AGG phallic

fallimentare [fallimen'tare] AGG (*Comm*) bankruptcy *attr*; **bilancio fallimentare** negative balance, deficit; **diritto fallimentare** bankruptcy law; **"tutto a prezzi fallimentari"** "everything at drastically reduced prices"; **il bilancio della sua vita era fallimentare** his life was a total failure; **fu un'esperienza fallimentare** it was a failure

fallimento [falli'mento] SM **1** (*fiasco*) failure, flop; **è stato un fallimento totale** it was a total failure **2** (*Comm, Dir*) bankruptcy; **molte aziende rischiavano il fallimento** many firms were facing bankruptcy; **essere/andare in fallimento** to be/go bankrupt

fallire [fal'lire] /55/ VT (*colpo, bersaglio*) to miss; **Federer ha fallito il colpo** Federer missed the ball ♦ VI (*aus essere*) **1** **fallire (in)** (*non riuscire*) to fail (in), be unsuccessful (in); **il nostro piano è destinato a fallire** our plan is bound to fail **2** (*Comm, Dir*) to go bankrupt; **la ditta è fallita** the firm has gone bankrupt

fallito, -a [fal'lito] AGG (*commerciante*) bankrupt; (*tentativo*) unsuccessful ♦ SM, SF (*Comm*) bankrupt; (*fig*) failure

fallo[1] ['fallo] SM **1** (*errore*) fault; **essere in fallo** to be at fault *o* in error; **mettere il piede in fallo** to slip; **ha messo il piede in fallo ed è caduto** he lost his footing and fell; **cogliere qn in fallo** to catch sb out; **mi ha colto in fallo** he caught me out; **senza fallo** without fail **2** (*difetto*) fault, defect, flaw **3** (*Sport*) fault, foul; (*Tennis*) fault; **fallo di piede** (*Tennis*) foot fault; **fare un fallo di mano** (*Calcio*) to handle the ball; **è stato espulso per un fallo sul portiere** he was sent off for a foul on the goalkeeper

fallo[2] ['fallo] SM (*Anat*) phallus; **fallo di mano** (*Calcio*) handball

fallocrate [fal'lɔkrate] SM (*pegg*) male chauvinist

falò [fa'lɔ] SM INV bonfire

falsare [fal'sare] /72/ VT (*notizia, realtà*) to distort

falsariga, -ghe [falsa'riga] SF lined page, ruled page; **sulla falsariga di...** (*fig*) along the lines of ...

falsario, -ri [fal'sarjo] SM (*di documenti, quadri*) forger; (*di monete*) counterfeiter

falsificare [falsifi'kare] /20/ VT (*firma, documento*) to forge; (*conti*) to falsify; (*monete*) to forge, counterfeit

falsità [falsi'ta] SF INV (*di persona, notizia*) falseness; (*bugia*) lie

falso, -a ['falso] AGG (*denaro, documenti*) forged, fake, counterfeit; (*oro, gioielli*) imitation *attr*; (*pudore, promessa*) false; **fare un passo falso** to stumble; (*fig*) to slip up; **sotto falsa luce** in a false light; **essere un falso magro** to be heavier than one looks; **un nome falso** a false name; **avere un passaporto falso** he had a forged passport; **un diamante falso** a fake diamond; **falsa partenza** (*anche fig*) false start; **falso allarme** false alarm ♦ SM **1** falsehood; **dire il falso** to lie, not to tell the truth; **giurare il falso** (*Dir*) to commit perjury **2** (*Dir*) forgery; **falso in atto pubblico** forgery (of a legal document) **3** (*opera d'arte*) fake; **il quadro era un falso** the painting was a fake **4 falso in bilancio** false accounting

fama ['fama] SF **1** (*celebrità*) fame, renown; **raggiungere la fama** to become famous; **di fama mondiale** world famous; **un attore di fama mondiale** a world-famous actor; **voglio fama e successo** I want fame and success **2** (*reputazione*)

reputation, name; **conoscere qn di** *o* **per fama** to know sb by reputation; **ha (la) fama di essere un dongiovanni** he has a reputation as a Don Juan; **ha una cattiva fama** he's got a bad reputation

fame ['fame] SF hunger; **aver fame** to be hungry; **hai fame?** are you hungry?; **ho una fame da lupo** I'm famished *o* starving, I could eat a horse; **aver fame di** (*fig: giustizia*) to hunger *o* long for; **fare la fame** (*fig*) to starve, scrape a living; **morire di fame** to be starving; **il problema della fame nel terzo mondo** the problem of hunger in the Third World

famelico, -a, -ci, -che [fa'meliko] AGG ravenous

famigerato, -a [famidʒe'rato] AGG notorious

famiglia [fa'miʎʎa] SF (*gen, anche Zool, Bot*) family; **essere di buona famiglia** to come from a good family; **metter su famiglia** to start a family; **amico/festa di famiglia** family friend/celebration; **in famiglia** (*matrimonio*) quiet; (*funerale*) private; **passare il Natale in famiglia** to spend Christmas with one's family; **è uno della famiglia** (*fig*) he's (quite) one of the family; **viene da una famiglia numerosa** he comes from a large family; **la Sacra Famiglia** the Holy Family

familiare [fami'ljare] AGG **1** (*di famiglia*) family *attr*; **vita familiare** family life; **un'azienda familiare** a family business; **cucina familiare** home cooking; **una FIAT familiare** a FIAT estate (*Brit*) *o* station wagon (*USA*) **2** (*noto*) familiar; **questo nome mi è familiare** I've heard this name before, I know the name; **un viso familiare** a familiar face **3** (*intimo: rapporti, atmosfera*) friendly; (*: tono*) informal; (*lessico: colloquiale*) informal, colloquial ♦ SM, SF relative, relation; **va in vacanza con dei familiari** he's going on holiday with relatives; **i miei familiari** my relations *o* family *sg*

familiarità [familjari'ta] SF (*dimestichezza*) familiarity; (*confidenza*) informality; **trattare qn con familiarità** to treat sb in a friendly way; **aver familiarità con qc** to be familiar with sth

familiarizzare [familjarid'dzare] /72/ VI (*aus avere*) **familiarizzare con qn** to get to know sb; **abbiamo familiarizzato subito** we got on well together from the start; **familiarizzare** *o* **familiarizzarsi con l'ambiente** to familiarize o.s. with one's surroundings

famoso, -a [fa'moso] AGG famous, well-known

fanale [fa'nale] SM (*Aut*) light; (*luce stradale*) lamp; (*Naut*) light; (*di faro*) beacon; **fanale di poppa** (*Naut*) stern light

fanatico, -a, -ci, -che [fa'natiko] AGG fanatical; **fanatico di** *o* **per** (*teatro, calcio*) wild *o* mad *o* crazy about; **essere fanatico di** to be mad about; **è fanatico di calcio** he's mad about football ♦ SM, SF fanatic; (*tifoso*) fan; **è un fanatico del golf/di Fellini** he is a golf/Fellini fanatic

fanatismo [fana'tizmo] SM fanaticism

fanciullezza [fantʃul'lettsa] SF childhood

fanciullo, -a [fan'tʃullo] SM, SF child

fandonia [fan'dɔnja] SF (tall) story, whopper; **fandonie!** nonsense! *sg*, rubbish! *sg*

fanfara [fan'fara] SF (*banda*) brass band; (*musica*) fanfare

fanfarone [fanfa'rone] SM braggart

fanghiglia [fan'giʎʎa] SF mire, mud

fango, -ghi ['fango] SM mud; **ero coperto di fango** I was covered with mud; **gettare fango addosso a qn** (*fig*) to sling mud at sb; **fare i fanghi** (*Med*) to take a course of mud baths

fangoso, -a [fan'goso] AGG muddy

fanno ['fanno] VB *vedi* **fare**

fannullone, -a [fannul'lone] SM, SF layabout

fantascienza [fantaʃ'ʃentsa] SF science fiction, sci-fi; **un film di fantascienza** a science fiction film

fantasia [fanta'zia] SF **1** (*facoltà*) imagination, fancy; **avere fantasia** to have imagination; **non ha fantasia** he hasn't got any imagination; **lavori troppo di fantasia** your imagination is running away with you; **sono fantasie le tue!** it's just your imagination!; **nel mondo della fantasia** in the realm(s) of fantasy *o* fancy **2** (*capriccio*) whim, caprice; **fantasia passeggera** passing fancy; **era solo una mia fantasia** it was just a fantasy of mine **3** (*decorazione*) pattern; **lo vuole tinta unita o fantasia?** would you like it plain or patterned?; **non mi piace questa fantasia** I don't like this pattern; **camicia fantasia** patterned shirt **4** (*Mus*) fantasia

fantasioso, -a [fanta'zjoso] AGG (*dotato di fantasia*) imaginative; (*bizzarro*) fanciful, strange

fantasma, -i [fan'tazma] SM (*spettro*) ghost, spectre (*letter*), phantom (*letter*) ♦ AGG: **governo fantasma** shadow cabinet; **città/scrittore fantasma** ghost town/writer

fantasticare [fantasti'kare] /20/ VI (*aus avere*) to daydream

fantasticheria [fantastike'ria] SF daydream

fantastico, -a, -ci, -che [fan'tastiko] AGG (*gen*) fantastic; (*potenza, ingegno*) imaginative; **un mondo fantastico** a world of fantasy, a fantasy world; **è una festa fantastica** it's a fantastic party; **fantastico!** fantastic!, terrific!

fante ['fante] SM **1** (*Mil*) infantryman **2** (*Carte*) jack

fanteria [fante'ria] SF (*Mil*) infantry

fantino [fan'tino] SM jockey

fantoccio, -ci [fan'tottʃo] SM (*manichino*) dummy; (*bambola*) doll; (*fig: persona*) puppet; **fantoccio di pezza** rag doll ♦ AGG INV: **governo fantoccio** puppet government

fantomatico, -a, -ci, -che [fanto'matiko] AGG (*personaggio*) mythical

farabutto [fara'butto] SM crook

faraona [fara'ona] SF (*anche: gallina faraona*) guinea fowl

faraone [fara'one] SM **1** (*Storia*) Pharaoh **2** (*Carte*) faro

faraonico, -a, -ci, -che [fara'ɔniko] AGG of the Pharaohs; (*fig*) enormous, huge

farcire [far'tʃire] /55/ VT (*carni, peperoni, pomodori*) to stuff; (*torte*) to fill; **farcito di errori** (*fig*) riddled with mistakes

fard [far] SM INV blusher

fardello [far'dello] SM bundle; (*fig*) burden

PAROLA CHIAVE

fare ['fare] VB IRREG /53/ VT

1 (*fabbricare: gen*) to make; (: *casa*) to build; (*quadro*) to paint; (*disegno*) to draw; (*pasto*) to cook; (*pane, dolci*) to bake; (*assegno*) to make out; **fanno la stessa classe** they are in the same year; **fare un corso** (*tenere*) to give a series of lessons, teach a course; (*seguire*) to do a course; **che cosa ne hai fatto di quei pantaloni?** what have you done with those trousers?; **fare un errore** to make a mistake; **ha fatto la mia felicità** he made me so happy; **fare una festa** to have *o* hold a party; **ha fatto un ciglio** she's had a baby; **quest'albero non fa frutti** this tree doesn't bear fruit; **hai fatto il letto?** have you made the bed?; **lo hanno fatto presidente** they made him president; **fare una promessa** to make a promise; **hai fatto la stanza?** have you cleaned the room?

2 (*attività: gen*) to do; (*vacanza, sogno*) to have; **a scuola facciamo chimica** at school we do chemistry; **fare i compiti** to do one's homework; **cosa fai?** (*adesso*) what are you doing?; (*nella vita*) what do you do?, what is your job?; **non posso farci nulla** I can't do anything about it; **fare la spesa** to do the shopping; **ho fatto una vacanza in Grecia** I went on holiday in Greece; **devi aver fatto un brutto sogno** you must have had a bad dream; **fare del tennis** to play tennis

3 (*funzione*) to be; (*Teatro*) to play, be, act; **fare l'avvocato** to be a lawyer; **fare finta di essere stanco** to pretend to be tired; **fare l'innocente** to act the innocent; **fare il malato** to pretend to be ill; **fare il medico** to be a doctor; **fare il morto** (*in acqua*) to float; **nel film fa il padre** in the film he plays the father

4 (*percorrere*) to do; **fare i 100 metri** (*competere*) to go in for *o* run in the 100 metres; **fa i 100 metri in 10,5** he does the 100 metres in 10.5; **abbiamo fatto 5 chilometri** we've done 5 kilometres; **fare una passeggiata** to go for *o* take a walk; **fare un viaggio** to go on a trip, make a journey

5 (*suscitare: sentimenti*): **fa niente** it doesn't matter; **mi fa orrore** it horrifies me; **fare paura a** to frighten; **mi fa rabbia** it makes me angry

6 (*considerare*): **ti facevo più intelligente** I thought you had more sense; **ti facevo al mare** I thought you were at the seaside; **lo facevo più vecchio** I thought he was older

7 (*ammontare*): **due più due fa quattro** two plus two make(s) *o* equal(s) four; **la città non fa più di 2 milioni di abitanti** the city hasn't more than 2 million inhabitants; **che differenza fa?** what difference does it make?; **fa 50 euro, signora** that'll be 50 euros, madam; **glielo faccio 100 euro** I'll give it to you *o* I'll let you have it for 100 euros; **che ora fa il tuo orologio?** what time is it by your watch?

8 (+ *infinito*): **le faremo avere la merce** we'll get the goods to you; **l'hanno fatto entrare in macchina** (*costringere*) they forced him into the car, they made him get into the car; (*lasciare*) they let him get into the car; **lo farò fare a lei** I'll get her to do it, I'll have her do it; **farsi fregare** to be taken for a ride; **far piangere qn** to make sb cry; **far riparare la macchina** to have one's car repaired; **far scongelare** to defrost, thaw out; **far soffrire qn** to make sb suffer; **mi son fatto tagliare i capelli** I've had my hair cut; **fammi vedere** let me see; **fare venire qn** to send for sb

9 farsi, farsi la barba to have a shave; **farsi la barca** to get a boat; **farsi una gonna** to make o.s. a skirt; **farsi la macchina** to get a car; **si fa da mangiare da solo** he does his own cooking; **farsi un nome** to make a name for o.s.

10 (*fraseologia*): **farla a qn** to get the better of sb; **me l'hanno fatta!** (*imbrogliare*) I've been done!; (*derubare*) I've been robbed!; (*lasciare nei guai*) I've been lumbered!; **farcela** to succeed, manage; **ne ha fatta una delle sue** he's done it again; **non ce la faccio più** (*a camminare*) I can't go on; (*a sopportare*) I can't take any more; **ce la facciamo?** do you think we'll make it?; **farla finita con qc** to have done with sth; **fare del proprio meglio** to do one's best; **non c'è niente da fare** it's no use; **ormai è stato deciso e non c'è niente da fare** it's been decided and there's nothing we can do about it; **ha fatto di sì con la testa** he nodded

♦ VI (*aus avere*)

1 (*agire*) to do; **fare presto** to be quick; **faccia pure!** go ahead!; **saperci fare con** (*situazioni, persone*) to know how to deal with; **ci sa fare coi bambini/le macchine** he's good with children/cars; **ci sa fare con le persone** he's a smooth operator; **ci sa fare** he's quite good; **fate come volete** do as you please

2 (*dire*): "**davvero?**" **fece** "really?" he said

3 questo non si fa it's not done, you (just) can't do that; **si fa così!** you do it like this, this is the way it's done; **non si fa così** (*rimprovero*) that's no way to behave!; **questa festa non si farà** this party won't take place!

4 (*fraseologia*): **fa proprio al caso nostro** it's just what we need; **avere a che fare con qn** to have sth to do with sb; **non so che farmene di lui** I don't know what to do with him; **fare da** (*funzioni*) to act as; **fare da padre a qn** to be like a father to sb; **la cucina fa anche da sala da pranzo** the kitchen also serves as *o* is also used as a dining room; **fai in modo che non ti vedano** make sure they don't see you; **fare per** (*essere adatto*) to be suitable for; (*essere sul punto di*) to be about to; **fece per uscire e poi si fermò** he made as if to go out and then stopped; **non fa per me** it isn't (suitable) for me; **fare a pugni** to come to blows; (*fig*) to clash; **fare in tempo a...** to be in time to ...; **il grigio fa vecchio** grey makes you *o* one look older

♦ VB IMPERS: **fa caldo** it's hot; **fa freddo** it's cold; **fa notte** it's getting dark; **farsi** VR

1 (*rendersi*): **farsi amico di qn** to make friends with sb; **farsi notare** to get *o.* noticed; **farsi prete** to become a priest

2 (*spostarsi*): **farsi avanti** to move forward; (*fig*) to come forward; **fatti più in là!** move along a bit!

3 (*gergo: drogarsi*) to do drugs; **farsi** VIP (*divenire*) to become; **farsi bello** to grow beautiful; **farsi grande** to grow tall; **si fa notte** it's getting dark; **farsi vecchio** to grow old

♦ SM: con fare distratto absent-mindedly; **ha un fare simpatico** he has a pleasant manner; **sul far del giorno/della notte** at daybreak/nightfall

faretra [fa'retra] SF (*per frecce*) quiver

farfalla [far'falla] SF **1** (*Zool*) butterfly **2** (*cravatta*) bow tie **3** (*Nuoto*) butterfly (stroke); **nuotare a farfalla** to do the butterfly (stroke); **i cento metri farfalla** the hundred metres butterfly **4** (*pasta*) bow **5** (*Aut*): **valvola a farfalla** butterfly valve **6** (*Naut*): **navigare a farfalla** to goosewing

farfugliare [farfuʎ'ʎare] /27/ VT, VI (*aus avere*) to mumble, mutter

farina [fa'rina] SF flour; **questa non è farina del tuo sacco** (*fig*) this isn't your own idea (*o* work); **farina di castagne** chestnut flour; **farina di grano saraceno** buckwheat; **farina di granoturco** *o* di mais *o* gialla maize (*Brit*) *o* corn (*USA*) flour; **farina integrale** wholemeal (*Brit*) *o* whole-wheat

(*USA*) flour; **farina di riso** ground rice; **farina di soia** soya flour; **farine animali** *animal feeds made from recycled livestock*

farinaceo, -a [fari'natʃeo] AGG farinaceous ♦ **farinacei** SMPL starches, starchy foods

faringe [fa'rindʒe] SF (*Anat*) pharynx

faringite [farin'dʒite] SF (*Med*) pharyngitis

farinoso, -a [fari'noso] AGG (*patate*) floury; (*mela*) woolly; (*neve*) powdery

farmaceutico, -a, -ci, -che [farma'tʃɛutiko] AGG pharmaceutical

farmacia, -cie [farma'tʃia] SF 1 (*negozio*) chemist's (shop) *o* chemist (*Brit*), pharmacy; **sto andando in farmacia** I'm going to the chemist's; **farmacia di turno** duty chemist 2 (*professione*) pharmacy

farmacista, -i, -e [farma'tʃista] SM, SF (dispensing) chemist (*Brit*), pharmacist

farmaco, -ci ['farmako] SM drug, medicine

farneticare [farneti'kare] /20/ VI (*aus* avere) (*anche fig*) to be delirious; **stai farneticando!** you're talking nonsense!

faro ['faro] SM 1 (*Naut*) lighthouse; (*Aer*) beacon; **faro d'atterraggio** landing light 2 (*Aut*) headlight, headlamp (*Brit*); **accendi i fari** switch on your headlights; **fari abbaglianti** headlights on full beam; **fari anabbaglianti** dipped headlights; **fari antinebbia** fog lights *o* lamps

farraginoso, -a [farradʒi'noso] AGG (*stile*) muddled, confused

farsa ['farsa] SF (*anche fig*) farce

farsesco, -a, -schi, -sche [far'sesko] AGG farcical

fasc. ABBR = **fascicolo**

fascia, -sce ['faʃʃa] SF 1 (*di tessuto, carta, anche fig*) strip, band; (*Med*) bandage; (*di sindaco, ufficiale*) sash; **fascia del cappello** hatband; **fascia elastica** elastic bandage; **essere in fasce** (*anche fig*) to be in one's infancy; **ti conosco da quando eri ancora in fasce** I've known you since you were a baby; **fascia di contribuenti** tax group *o* band; **fascia d'età** age group; **fascia blu** *city centre area wholly or partially closed to traffic*; **fascia oraria** (*Radio, TV*) slot; (*Telec*) time band 2 (*Geog*) strip, belt; **fascia equatoriale** equatorial belt 3 (*Tecn*): **fascia elastica** piston ring

fasciare [faʃ'ʃare] /14/ VT (*gen*) to bind; (*Med*) to bandage; **fasciare un bambino** to put on a baby's nappy (*Brit*) *o* diaper (*USA*); **fasciati il piede** bandage your foot; **gli hanno fasciato il ginocchio** they bandaged his knee; **quel vestito le fasciava i fianchi** the dress clung to her hips

fasciatura [faʃʃa'tura] SF (*azione*) bandaging; (*fascia*) bandage

fascicolo [faʃ'ʃikolo] SM (*opuscolo*) booklet, pamphlet; (*Amm*) file, dossier; (*di pubblicazione*) instalment; (*di rivista*) issue, number

fascino ['faʃʃino] SM charm, fascination; **avere fascino** (*persona*) to be fascinating; **subire il fascino di qn** to succumb to sb's charm

fascio, -sci ['faʃʃo] SM 1 (*di legna*) bundle; (*di fieno, frecce*) sheaf; (*di fiori*) bunch; (*di luce*) beam 2 (*Storia*) fasces *pl* 3 (*Pol*): **il Fascio** the Fascist Party

fascismo [faʃ'ʃizmo] SM fascism

fascista, -i, -e [faʃ'ʃista] AGG, SM, SF fascist; **è fascista** he's a fascist

fase ['faze] SF 1 (*gen, anche Chim, Astron*) phase; **in fase avanzata** at an advanced stage; **essere in fase di miglioramento** to be getting better, be improving; **in fase preliminare** in the preliminary stages; **in fase di espansione** in a period of expansion 2 (*Tecn*) stroke; **essere fuori fase** (*motore*) to be rough (*Brit*), run roughly; (*fig*) to feel rough (*Brit*) *o* rotten; **mettere il motore in fase** to tune the engine

fastidio, -di [fas'tidjo] SM (*disturbo*) trouble, bother; **che fastidio!** what a nuisance!; **dare fastidio a qn** to bother *o* annoy sb; **smettila! mi dai fastidio!** stop it! you're getting on my nerves!; **il rumore mi dava fastidio** the noise was annoying me; **mi dà fastidio il suo modo di fare** his whole attitude gets on my nerves; **le dà fastidio se fumo?** do you mind if I smoke?; **la caviglia mi dà ancora fastidio** my ankle is still bothering me; **sento un po' di fastidio** it hurts a bit; **ha avuto dei fastidi con la polizia** he has had some trouble *o* bother with the police

fastidioso, -a [fasti'djoso] AGG 1 (*gen*) annoying; (*persona*) tiresome, annoying; **un dolore fastidioso** a nagging pain; **è un bambino fastidioso** he's an annoying child 2 (*irritabile*) irritable

❑ **fastidioso** non si traduce mai con la parola inglese *fastidious*

fasto ['fasto] SM pomp, splendour (*Brit*), splendor (*USA*); **i fasti dell'antica Roma** the splendour(s) of ancient Rome

fastoso, -a [fas'toso] AGG sumptuous, lavish

fasullo, -a [fa'zullo] AGG (*gen*) fake; (*dichiarazione, persona*) false; (*pretesto*) bogus

fata ['fata] SF fairy; **fata morgana** (*miraggio*) Fata Morgana

fatale [fa'tale] AGG 1 (*inevitabile*) inevitable; **era fatale che succedesse** it was bound to happen 2 (*mortale: incidente, malattia*) fatal; (: *colpo*) fatal, mortal; **errore fatale** fatal error; **essere fatale a qn** to be *o* prove fatal to sb 3 (*irresistibile: sguardo*) irresistible; **donna fatale** femme fatale

fatalismo [fata'lizmo] SM fatalism

fatalità [fatali'ta] SF INV (*fato*) fate, destiny; (*inevitabilità*) inevitability; (*disgrazia*) misfortune

fatato, -a [fa'tato] AGG (*spada, chiave*) magic; (*castello*) enchanted

fatica, -che [fa'tika] SF 1 (*sforzo fisico*) hard work, toil; **animale da fatica** beast of burden; **divisa di fatica** (*Mil*) fatigues *pl*; **uomo di fatica** odd-job man; **fare fatica a fare qc** to have a job doing sth, find it difficult to do sth; **faccio fatica a crederlo** I find that hard to believe; **faccio fatica a capire la matematica** I find it difficult to understand math(s); **il paziente deve evitare ogni fatica** the patient must avoid any kind of physical exertion; **accusare *o* sentire fatica** to feel tired; **non si è preso nemmeno la fatica di dirmelo** he didn't even take the trouble to tell me; **risparmiarsi la fatica di fare qc** to save o.s. the bother *o* effort of doing sth; **ci vuole tempo e fatica** it takes time and effort; **che fatica!** it's hard work!; **le fatiche di Ercole** the labours of Hercules 2 (*difficoltà*): **a fatica** with difficulty; **respirare a fatica** to have difficulty (in) breathing; **riusciva a fatica a tenere la testa dritta** he could hardly keep his head up; **l'ho convinto a fatica** I had a hard job convincing him 3 (*di metalli*) fatigue

faticaccia, -ce [fati'kattʃa] SF (*fam*): **fu una faticaccia** it was a hell of a job

faticare [fati'kare] /20/ VI (*aus* avere) to work hard, toil; **faticare per fare qc** to struggle to do sth; **faticare a fare qc** to have difficulty in doing sth, have difficulty doing sth

faticata [fati'kata] SF hard work

fatichi ecc [fa'tiki] VB *vedi* **faticare**

faticoso, -a [fati'koso] AGG (*viaggio, camminata*) tiring, exhausting; (*lavoro*) laborious

fatidico, -a, -ci, -che [fa'tidiko] AGG fateful

fato ['fato] SM fate, destiny

fatt. ABBR (= *fattura*) inv

fattaccio, -ci [fat'tattʃo] SM foul deed

fattezze [fat'tettse] SFPL (*del viso*) features

fattibile [fat'tibile] AGG feasible, possible

fattispecie [fattis'petʃe] SF: **nella *o* in fattispecie** in this case *o* instance

fatto¹, -a ['fatto] PP *di* **fare** ♦ AGG 1 (*prodotto*) made; **fatto a macchina/a mano** machine-/hand-made; **fatto in casa** home-made; **abiti fatti** ready-made *o* off-the-peg clothes 2 (*fraseologia*): **sono fatto così** that's how I am, I'm like that; **essere fatto per qc** to be made *o* meant for sth; **è fatto per l'archeologia** he's got what it takes to be an archeologist; **è un uomo fatto** he's a grown man; **a giorno fatto** in broad daylight; **è fatta!** that's it!, I've (*o* you've *ecc*) done it!; **è completamente fatto** (*fam: drogato, ubriaco*) he's (completely) stoned

fatto² ['fatto] SM 1 (*accaduto*) fact; **i fatti parlano chiaro** the facts speak for themselves; **questo è un altro fatto** that's another matter; **di fatto in fatto**; **il fatto sta *o* è che** the fact remains *o* is that; **il fatto è che ha ragione lui** the fact is that he's right; **in fatto di macchine è un genio** when it comes to cars he's a genius 2 (*azione*) deed, act; **cogliere qn sul fatto** to catch sb red-handed *o* in the act; **li hanno colti sul fatto** they caught them red-handed; **porre qn di fronte al fatto compiuto** to present sb with a fait accompli; **c'è stato un nuovo fatto di sangue** there has been further bloodshed;

fatto d'arme (*frm*) feat of arms; **è uno che sa il fatto suo** he knows what he's about; **gli ho detto il fatto suo** I told him what I thought of him; **fare i fatti propri** to mind one's own business; **pensa ai fatti tuoi!** mind your own business!; **immischiarsi nei fatti altrui** to stick one's nose into other people's business **3** (*avvenimento*) event, occurrence; (*di romanzo, film*) action, story; **fatto di cronaca** news item; **fatto nuovo** new development; **è successo un fatto strano** a strange thing happened; **la mia versione dei fatti** my version of events

fattore [fat'tore] SM **1** (*elemento, anche Mat*) factor; **fattore di protezione** (*di crema solare*) (protection) factor; **fattore di protezione solare 6** (protection) factor 6 **2** (*Agr*) farm manager

fattoria [fatto'ria] SF (*gen*) farm; (*casa*) farmhouse
❏ **fattoria** non si traduce mai con la parola inglese *factory*

fattorino [fatto'rino] SM (*gen*) errand boy; (*di ufficio*) office junior, office boy; (*d'albergo*) porter

fattucchiera [fattuk'kjɛra] SF witch

fattura [fat'tura] SF **1** (*Comm*) invoice **2** (*confezione: di abito*) tailoring **3** (*stregoneria*) spell; **fare una fattura a qn** to cast a spell on sb

fatturare [fattu'rare] /72/ VT **1** (*Comm*) to invoice **2** (*adulterare*) to adulterate

fatturato [fattu'rato] SM (*Comm*) turnover

fatturazione [fatturat'tsjone] SF invoicing, billing

fatuo, -a ['fatuo] AGG fatuous, vain; **fuoco fatuo** (*anche fig*) will-o'-the-wisp

fauci ['fautʃi] SFPL (*di leone*) jaws; (*di vulcano*) mouth *sg*; **cadere nelle fauci di qn** (*fig*) to fall prey to sb

fauna ['fauna] SF (*Zool*) fauna

fausto, -a ['fausto] AGG (*frm*) happy, propitious; **un fausto evento** a happy event; **un fausto presagio** a good omen

fautore, -trice [fau'tore] SM, SF advocate, supporter

fava ['fava] SF broad bean

favella [fa'vɛlla] SF speech; **perdere il dono della favella** to be struck dumb

favilla [fa'villa] SF spark; (*fig: di speranza*) glimmer; **fare faville** (*fig: cantante*) to give a sparkling performance

favo ['favo] SM (*di api*) honeycomb

favola ['favola] SF (*fiaba*) fairy tale; (*d'intento morale*) fable; (*fig: fandonia*) tall tale, yarn; **essere la favola del paese** (*oggetto di chiacchiere*) to be the talk of the town; (*zimbello*) to be a laughing stock in the town; **la casa è una favola** the house is a dream

favoloso, -a [favo'loso] AGG (*gen*) fabulous; (*incredibile*) incredible; **prezzi favolosi** incredible prices; **un concerto favoloso** a fabulous concert

favore [fa'vore] SM favour (*Brit*), favor (*USA*); **chiedere/fare un favore a qn** to ask/do sb a favour; **posso chiederti un favore?** can I ask you a favour?; **mi faresti un favore?** would you do me a favour?; **per favore** please; **godere del favore del pubblico** to enjoy public favour; **prezzo/trattamento di favore** preferential price/treatment; **condizioni di favore** (*Comm*) favourable terms; **biglietto di favore** complimentary ticket; **a favore di** (*votare*) in favour of; (*testimoniare, raccogliere aiuti*) on behalf of; **essere a favore di** to be in favour of; **col favore delle tenebre** under cover of darkness

favoreggiamento [favoredd3a'mento] SM (*Dir*) aiding and abetting; **favoreggiamento bellico** collaboration (with the enemy)

favorevole [favo'revole] AGG: **favorevole (a)** (*situazione, vento*) favourable (*Brit*) o, favorable (*USA*) (to); (*persona*) in favour (of), favourable (to); **essere favorevole a** to be in favour of; **hanno avuto 70 voti favorevoli** they got 70 votes in favour; **aspettare il momento favorevole** to wait for the right moment

favorire [favo'rire] /55/ VT **1** (*gen*) to favour (*Brit*), favor (*USA*); (*commercio, industria, arti*) to promote, encourage; (*partito, opinione*) to support **2** (*in espressioni di cortesia*): **favorisca da questa parte** please come this way; **vuole favorire?** won't you help yourself?; **mi favorisca i documenti** please may I see your papers?; **favorisca alla cassa** please pay at the cash-desk

favoritismo [favori'tizmo] SM favouritism (*Brit*), favoritism (*USA*)

favorito, -a [favo'rito] AGG, SM, SF favourite (*Brit*), favorite (*USA*)

fax [faks] SM INV (*anche: telefax*) fax; **mandare qc via fax** to fax sth; **gli ho mandato un fax** I sent him a fax

faxare [fak'sare] /72/ VT to fax

fazione [fat'tsjone] SF faction

faziosità [fattsjosi'ta] SF INV bias

fazzoletto [fattso'letto] SM (*da naso*) handkerchief; (*di carta*) (paper) tissue; (*da collo*) neckerchief; **un fazzoletto di terra** a patch of land

FBI [efbi'ai] SIGLA F FBI (= *Federal Bureau of Investigation*)

FC ABBR *vedi* **fuoricorso**

f.co ABBR = **franco¹ 2**

FE SIGLA = **Ferrara**

febb. ABBR (= *febbraio*) Feb

febbraio [feb'brajo] SM February; *vedi* **luglio**

febbre ['febbre] SF **1** fever; **avere la febbre** to have a (high) temperature; **hai la febbre?** have you got a temperature?; **misurare la febbre a qn** to take sb's temperature; **misurarsi la febbre** to take one's temperature; **febbre da fieno** hay fever; **febbre gialla** yellow fever; **febbre reumatica** rheumatic fever **3** (*herpes*) cold sore **3** (*fig*): **la febbre dell'oro** gold fever

febbrile [feb'brile] AGG (*anche fig*) feverish

feccia, -ce ['fettʃa] SF (*anche fig*) dregs *pl*

feci¹ [fetʃi] SFPL faeces (*Brit*), feces (*USA*), excrement *sg*

feci² ['fetʃi] VB *vedi* **fare**

fecola ['fekola] SF starch; **fecola di patate** ≈ cornflour

fecondare [fekon'dare] /72/ VT to fertilize

fecondazione [fekondat'tsjone] SF fertilization; **fecondazione artificiale** artificial insemination; **fecondazione assistita** assisted conception

fecondità [fekondi'ta] SF INV (*Bio: di terreno, fig: ingegno*) fertility, productiveness; (*di scrittore*) prolificness

fecondo, -a [fe'kondo] AGG (*terreno, donna, anche fig: ingegno*) fertile; (*albero, fig: pensiero, lavoro*) fruitful; (: *scrittore*) prolific

fede ['fede] SF **1** (*credenza*) faith, belief; (*Rel*) faith **2** (*fiducia*) faith, trust; (*fedeltà*) loyalty; **aver fede in** to have faith in; **degno di fede** trustworthy, reliable; **tener fede a** (*ideale*) to remain loyal to; (*giuramento, promessa*) to keep; **in buona fede** in good faith; **ho agito in buona fede** I acted in good faith; **essere in buona/cattiva fede** to act in good/bad faith; **in fede mia!** on my word! **3** (*anello nuziale*) wedding ring **4** (*attestato*) certificate; **in fede di** in proof of o as evidence of; **far fede di** to be proof o evidence of; **"in fede"** (*Dir*) "in witness whereof"

fedele [fe'dele] AGG **1** (*leale*): **fedele (a)** faithful (to); **essere fedele a** to be faithful to; **gli è sempre stata fedele** she's always been faithful to him; **essere fedele alla parola data** to keep one's word; **un marito fedele** a faithful husband; **suddito fedele** loyal subject **2** (*veritiero*) true, accurate ♦ SM, SF (*Rel*) believer; (*seguace*) follower; **i fedeli** (*Rel*) the faithful *pl*

fedeltà [fedel'ta] SF INV **1** (*devozione*) loyalty, faithfulness; (*coniugale*) fidelity; **fedeltà verso o a** qn loyalty to **2** (*esattezza: di copia, traduzione*) accuracy **3** (*Radio, etc*): **alta fedeltà** high fidelity; **un impianto ad alta fedeltà** a hi-fi system

federa ['federa] SF pillowslip, pillowcase

federale [fede'rale] AGG federal

federalismo [federa'lizmo] SM federalism

federalista, -i, -e [federa'lista] AGG, SM, SF federalist

federazione [federat'tsjone] SF federation

fedifrago, -a, -ghi, -ghe [fe'difrago] AGG faithless, perfidious

fedina [fe'dina] SF (*Dir: anche: fedina penale*) record; **avere la fedina (penale) pulita** to have a clean record; **avere la fedina (penale) sporca** to have a police record

fegato ['fegato] SM **1** (*Anat, Culin*) liver; **fegato di vitello** calf's liver; **mangiarsi** o **rodersi il fegato** to be consumed with rage; **fegato ingrossato** (*Med*) enlarged liver; **non mi piace il fegato** I don't like liver **2** (*fig: coraggio*) guts *pl*, nerve; **ha fegato!** he's got guts!

felce [ˈfeltʃe] SF fern

felice [feˈlitʃe] AGG **1** (*contento*) happy; **sono felice di fare la sua conoscenza** pleased to meet you; **adesso sono più felice** I'm happier now; **è stato il giorno più felice della mia vita** it was the happiest day of my life; **felice come una pasqua** as happy as a sandboy **2** (*fortunato*) lucky; (*scelta*) fortunate, happy; (*vento*) favourable; **avere la mano felice** to have nimble fingers; **non ho scelto il momento più felice per venire** I don't seem to have chosen the best moment to come

felicità [feliˈtʃita] SF INV happiness

felicitarsi [felitʃiˈtarsi] /72/ VIP: **felicitarsi con qn (per qc)** (*congratularsi*) to congratulate sb (on sth)

felicitazioni [felitʃitatˈtsjoni] SFPL congratulations

felino, -a [feˈlino] AGG (*Zool*) feline; (*fig*) feline, catlike ♦ SM feline

felpa [ˈfelpa] SF (*maglia*) sweatshirt

felpato, -a [felˈpato] AGG (*tessuto*) brushed; (*passo*) stealthy; **con passo felpato** stealthily ♦ SM brushed cotton (*o* nylon *ecc*)

feltro [ˈfeltro] SM felt; **cappello di feltro** felt hat

femmina [ˈfemmina] SF (*Zool*, *Tecn*) female; **ho due figli, un maschio e una femmina** I've got two children, a boy and a girl; **una femmina di panda, un panda femmina** a female panda

femminile [femmiˈnile] AGG (*gen*, anche *Gramm*) feminine; (*sesso*) female; **moda femminile** women's fashion; **una rivista femminile** a women's magazine

femminilità [femminiliˈta] SF INV femininity; **un tocco di femminilità** a feminine touch

femminismo [femmiˈnizmo] SM feminism

femminista, -i, -e [femmiˈnista] SM, SF, AGG feminist; **è femminista** she's a feminist

femore [ˈfemore] SM (*Anat*) thighbone, femur

fendere [ˈfendere] /36/ VT IRREG (*fig*: *aria, flutti, onde*) to cut through, slice (through); **i fari fendevano la nebbia** the headlights pierced the fog; **fendere la folla** to push through the crowd

fendinebbia [fendiˈnebbja] SM INV (*Aut*) fog lamp

fenditura [fendiˈtura] SF (*gen*) crack; (*di roccia*) cleft, crack

fenomeno [feˈnɔmeno] SM (*gen*) phenomenon; (*persona*: *eccezionale*) character; (: *anormale*) freak; **un fenomeno inspiegabile** an inexplicable phenomenon

feretro [ˈferetro] SM coffin; **il feretro si avviava verso il cimitero** the funeral procession wound its way to the cemetery

feriale [feˈrjale] AGG: **giorno feriale** working day, weekday

ferie [ˈferje] SFPL holidays (*Brit*), vacation *sg* (*USA*); **ferie retribuite** paid holiday, holiday with pay; **andare in ferie** to go on holiday *o* vacation; **dove vai in ferie?** where are you going on holiday?; **ho fatto le ferie al mare** I spent my holidays at the seaside; **ho 2 settimane di ferie** I have 2 weeks' holidays; **un giorno di ferie** a day off; **prendere un giorno di ferie** to take a day off; **ho preso un giorno di ferie** I took a day off

ferimento [feriˈmento] SM wounding; **nella sparatoria si è avuto il ferimento di 3 persone** 3 people were hurt *o* wounded in the shooting

ferire [feˈrire] /55/ VT **1** (*gen*) to injure; (*Mil*) to wound; **fu ferito a morte** he was fatally wounded; **nell'incidente sono state ferite 4 persone** 4 people were injured in the accident; **la bomba ha ferito tre persone** the bomb injured three people; **il soldato è stato ferito ad una gamba** the soldier was wounded in the leg **2** (*fig*) to hurt, wound; **ferire qn nell'orgoglio** to hurt *o* wound *o* injure sb's pride; **le sue parole la ferirono** she was wounded *o* hurt by what he said; **ferirsi** VR to hurt o.s., injure o.s.; **ferirsi con un coltello** to cut o.s. with a knife; **mi sono ferito ad una mano** I've injured my hand

ferito, -a [feˈrito] SM, SF casualty; **hanno portato i feriti all'ospedale** the casualties were taken to the hospital; **nell'incidente ci sono stati due feriti** two people were injured in the accident; **un ferito grave** a seriously injured person

feritoia [feriˈtoja] SF slit

ferma [ˈferma] SF **1** (*Mil*) (period of) service **2** (*Caccia*): **cane da ferma** pointer

fermacarte [fermaˈkarte] SM INV paperweight

fermacravatta [fermakraˈvatta] SM INV tiepin (*Brit*), tie tack (*USA*)

fermaglio, -gli [ferˈmaʎʎo] SM (*gen*) clasp; (*per documenti*) clip

fermamente [fermaˈmente] AVV firmly

fermare [ferˈmare] /72/ VT **1** (*gen*) to stop, halt; **non cercare di fermarmi** don't try and stop me; **lo fermò con un gesto della mano** (*far cenno*) he gestured to him to stop; (*bloccare*) he put his hand out to stop him **2** (*fissare*: *bottone*) to make secure; (: *porta*) to stop **3** (*prenotare*: *stanza, albergo*) to book **4** (*Polizia*) to detain, hold ♦ VI (*aus avere*) to stop; **il treno ferma a...** the train calls at ...; **fermarsi** VIP (*gen*) to stop, halt; **fermarsi a guardare/fare** to stop to look/do; **non posso fermarmi di più** I can't stop *o* stay any longer; **mi sono fermato a salutarla** I stopped to say hello to her; **far segno di fermarsi a qn** to signal to sb to stop; (*ad automobilista*) to wave sb down; **fermati!** stop!; **la sua attenzione si fermò sul dipinto** his attention focused on the painting; **l'orologio si è fermato alle tre e cinque** the clock stopped at five past three

fermata [ferˈmata] SF stop; **scendo tra 2 fermate** I get off 2 stops from here; **la corriera fa una fermata a Montelupo** the coach stops *o* makes a stop at Montelupo; **fermata dell'autobus** bus stop; **fermata facoltativa** *o* **a richiesta** request stop

fermentare [fermenˈtare] /72/ VI (*aus avere*) to ferment ♦ VT (*fig*) to be in ferment

fermentazione [fermentatˈtsjone] SF fermentation

fermento [ferˈmento] SM **1** (*anche fig*) ferment; **in fermento** in a ferment **2** (*Culin*: *lievito*) yeast; **fermenti lattici** lactobacillus, probiotics

fermezza [ferˈmettsa] SF firmness, steadfastness; **fermezza di mente/d'animo** strength of mind/of character; **fermezza di propositi** steadiness of purpose; **rispondere con fermezza** to answer firmly, give a firm answer

fermo, -a [ˈfermo] AGG **1** (*immobile*: *persona*) still, motionless; (: *veicolo, traffico*) at a standstill, stationary; (*non in funzione*) not working; **era fermo in piedi** he was standing still; **stare fermo** to keep still; **non sta fermo un attimo** he can't keep still for a minute; **stai fermo!** keep still!; **stai fermo con le mani!** keep your hands still!; (*non toccarmi*) keep your hands to yourself!; **fermo!** don't move!, stay where you are!; **tenere fermo qn** to keep sb still; **c'era una macchina ferma al bordo della strada** there was a car stopped at the side of the road; **il treno era fermo in stazione** the train was standing in the station; **ero fermo al semaforo** I was waiting at the traffic lights; **gli affari sono fermi** business is at a standstill; **l'orologio è fermo** the clock has stopped **2** (*costante, risoluto*) firm; (*non tremante*: *voce, mano*) steady; **restare fermo sulle proprie posizioni** to stick to one's position; **resta fermo che...** it is settled that ...; **ferme restando che...** it being understood that ... ♦ SM **1** (*Dir*): **fermo di polizia** police custody (*before formal accusation of a crime*) **2** (*di porta*: *gancio*) catch **3 fermo immagine** pause (button)

fermo posta [ˈfermo ˈposta] AVV, SM, AGG poste restante (*Brit*), general delivery (*USA*)

feroce [feˈrotʃe] AGG (*animale*) ferocious, fierce; (*persona*) fierce, cruel; (*critica*) savage; (*fame, dolore*) raging; **le bestie feroci** wild animals

ferocia [feˈrotʃa] SF ferocity

Ferr. ABBR = **ferrovia**

ferraglia [ferˈraʎʎa] SF scrap iron; **rumore di ferraglia** clanking noise

ferragosto [ferraˈɡosto] SM (*festa*) feast of the Assumption; (*data*) August 15

ferramenta [ferraˈmenta] SFPL ironmongery *sg* (*Brit*), hardware *sg* ♦ SF (*anche*: **negozio di ferramenta**) ironmonger's (*Brit*), hardware shop *o* store (*USA*)

ferrare [ferˈrare] /72/ VT (*cavallo*) to shoe; (*botte*) to hoop

ferrato, -a [ferˈrato] AGG **1** (*Ferr*): **strada ferrata** railway line (*Brit*), railroad line (*USA*) **2** (*fig*): **essere ferrato in** (*materia*) to be well up in

ferravecchio, -chi [ferraˈvɛkkjo] SM = **ferrovecchio**

ferreo, -a [ˈferreo] AGG (*anche fig*) iron *attr*; **volontà ferrea** iron will; **salute ferrea** iron constitution

ferriera [fer'rjɛra] SF ironworks *sg o pl*

ferro ['fɛrro] SM **1** (*metallo*) iron; **ferro battuto** wrought iron; **l'età del ferro** the Iron Age; **di ferro** iron; **una sbarra di ferro** an iron bar; **minerali di ferro** iron ore; **ha una memoria di ferro** he has an excellent memory; **ha una salute di ferro** he has an iron constitution; **avere uno stomaco di ferro** to have a cast-iron stomach; **avere un alibi di ferro** to have a cast-iron alibi; **tocca ferro!** touch wood!; **battere il ferro finché è caldo** to strike while the iron is hot **2** (*strumento: gen*) tool; **i ferri del mestiere** the tools of the trade; **a ferro di cavallo** in the shape of a horseshoe; **i ferri del chirurgo** surgical instruments; **essere sotto i ferri** (*di chirurgo*) to be under the knife; **ai ferri** grilled; **una bistecca ai ferri** a grilled steak; **carne ai ferri** grilled meat; **cucinare** *o* **fare qc ai ferri** to grill sth; **ferri da calza** knitting needles; **ferro di cavallo** horseshoe; **ferro da stiro** iron **3** (*arma*) sword; **ferri** SMPL (*ceppi*) irons, chains; **incrociare i ferri** to cross swords; **mettere a ferro e fuoco** to put to the sword; **essere ai ferri corti** (*fig*) to be at daggers drawn

ferrotranviario, -ria, -ri, -rie [ferrotran'vjarjo] AGG public transport *attr*

Ferrotranvieri [ferrotran'vjeri] ABBR F (= *Federazione Nazionale Lavoratori Autoferrotranvieri e Internavigatori*) *transport workers' union*

ferrovecchio, -chi [ferro'vɛkkjo] SM (*commerciante: di oggetti di scarso valore*) junk dealer; (*: di ferro vecchio*) scrap merchant

ferrovia [ferro'via] SF railway (*Brit*), railroad (*USA*)

ferroviario, -ria, -rie, -ri [ferro'vjarjo] AGG railway *attr* (*Brit*), railroad *attr* (*USA*); **la stazione ferroviaria** the railway station

ferroviere [ferro'vjere] SM railwayman (*Brit*), railroad man (*USA*)

fertile ['fɛrtile] AGG (*anche fig*) fertile

fertilità [fertili'ta] SF INV fertility

fertilizzante [fertilid'dzante] AGG fertilizing ♦ SM fertilizer

fertilizzare [fertilid'dzare] /72/ VT to fertilize

fervente [fer'vente] AGG fervent, ardent

fervere ['fɛrvere] /29/ VI *vb dif*: **fervono i preparativi per l'arrivo del presidente** preparations for the president's arrival are in full swing

fervido, -a ['fɛrvido] AGG fervent, fervid, ardent; **fervide preghiere** impassioned pleas; **i miei più fervidi auguri** my very best wishes

fervore [fer'vore] SM fervour (*Brit*), fervor (*USA*), ardour (*Brit*), ardor (*USA*); **nel fervore di** (*discussione, lotta*) in the heat of

fesa ['feza] SF (*Culin*) rump of veal

fesseria [fesse'ria] SF stupidity; **quel film è una fesseria** that film is rubbish; **dire fesserie** to talk nonsense; **fare una fesseria** to do something stupid

fesso, -a ['fɛsso] PP *di* **fendere** ♦ SM, SF idiot, fool; **fare il fesso** to play the fool; **dare del fesso a qn** to call sb a fool ♦ AGG **1** (*fam*) stupid, daft **2** (*spaccato*) cracked; **con voce fessa** in a cracked voice

fessura [fes'sura] SF (*gen*) crack, split; (*per gettone, moneta*) slot; (*Alpinismo*) crack

festa ['fɛsta] SF **1** (*religiosa*) feast (day); (*civile*) holiday; **oggi è festa** today's a holiday; **giorno di festa** holiday; **il Natale è la festa dei bambini** Christmas is a time for children **2** (*vacanza*) holiday (*Brit*), vacation (*USA*); **cosa fai per le feste?** what are you doing over the holidays?; **la settimana scorsa ho avuto 3 giorni di festa** last week I was on holiday for 3 days, I had 3 days off (work) last week **3** (*ricorrenza: compleanno*) birthday; (*: onomastico*) name day; **quand'è la tua festa?** when is your birthday?; **la festa di San Giovanni** St John's Day, the feast of St John **4** (*sagra*) fair; **la festa del paese** the town festival; **festa della birra** beer festival **5** (*ricevimento*) party, celebration; **dare** *o* **fare una festa** to give *o* have a party; **ha dato una festa per il suo compleanno** he gave a party for his birthday **6** (*fraseologia*): **un'aria di festa** a festive air; **fare festa** (*non lavorare*) to have a holiday; (*far baldoria*) to live it up; **fare le feste a qn** to give sb a warm welcome; **tutta la città era in festa** the whole town was celebrating; **le campane suonavano a festa** the bells were pealing; **essere vestito a festa** to be dressed up to the nines

♦ **festa comandata** (*Rel*) holiday *o* holy day of obligation; **la festa della donna** International Women's Day; **la festa della mamma/del papà** Mother's/Father's Day; **festa del lavoro** May Day; **festa nazionale** national *o* public holiday; **la festa della repubblica** *national holiday*

festeggiamenti [festedddʒa'menti] SMPL celebrations

festeggiare [fested'dʒare] /62/ VT (*anniversario*) to celebrate; (*persona*) to have a celebration for, fête

festino [fes'tino] SM (*festa*) party; (*con balli*) ball

festivo, -a [fes'tivo] AGG (*atmosfera*) festive; **giorno festivo** holiday; **"sabato e festivi"** "Saturdays, Sundays and public holidays"

festoso, -a [fes'toso] AGG merry, joyful; **un'accoglienza festosa** a warm welcome

fetente [fe'tente] AGG (*puzzolente*) fetid; (*comportamento*) disgusting ♦ SM, SF (*fam*) stinker, rotter (*Brit*)

feticcio, -ci [fe'tittʃo] SM fetish

feto ['fɛto] SM foetus (*Brit*), fetus (*USA*)

fetore [fe'tore] SM stench, stink

fetta ['fetta] SF (*gen*) slice; (*di terra*) strip; (*fig: porzione*) share; **fare/tagliare a fette** (*pane, prosciutto*) to slice; (*fig: persona*) to make mincemeat of; **può tagliarmelo a fette?** can you slice it for me?; **una fetta di pane** a slice of bread; **una fetta del bottino** a share of the loot; **si vedeva solo una fetta di luna/cielo** you could just glimpse the moon/sky; **fette biscottate** crispbread *sg*

fettuccia, -ce [fet'tuttʃa] SF tape, ribbon

fettuccine [fettut'tʃine] SFPL (*Culin*) fettu(c)cine (*ribbon-shaped pasta*)

feudale [feu'dale] AGG feudal

feudo ['feudo] SM (*Storia*) fief; **un feudo democristiano** (*fig*) a Christian Democrat stronghold

ff ABBR **1** (*Amm*: = *facente funzioni*) **2** (= *fogli*) pp

FF.AA ABBR = *forze armate*

FF.SS. ABBR (= *Ferrovie dello Stato*) *Italian railways*

FG SIGLA = Foggia

FI SIGLA = Firenze ♦ ABBR = Forza Italia

fiaba ['fjaba] SF fairy tale; **paesaggio di fiaba** fairy-tale landscape

fiabesco, -a, -schi, -sche [fja'besko] AGG fairy-tale *attr*

fiacca ['fjakka] SF (*stanchezza*) weariness; (*svogliatezza*) listlessness; **avere la fiacca** to be listless; **battere la fiacca** to shirk

fiaccare [fjak'kare] /72/ VT to weaken; **l'artiglieria ha fiaccato le difese nemiche** the artillery wore down the enemy's defences (*Brit*) *o* defenses (*USA*)

fiaccherò ecc [fjakke'rɔ] VB *vedi* **fiaccare**

fiacco, -a, -chi, -che [fjakko] AGG (*stanco*) tired, weary; (*svogliato*) listless; (*debole*) weak; (*discorso*) weak, dull; (*fermo: mercato*) stagnant; **mi sento un po' più fiacco di ieri** I feel a bit wearier than I did yesterday

fiaccola ['fjakkola] SF torch (*with flame*)

fiaccolata [fjakko'lata] SF torchlight procession; (*Sci*) torchlit descent

fiala ['fjala] SF phial

fiamma ['fjamma] SF **1** flame; **andare in fiamme** to go up in flames; **la casa è andata in fiamme** the house went up in flames; **dare alle fiamme** to set on fire, burn; **essere in fiamme** to be ablaze; **morì tra le fiamme** he died in the blaze; **le fiamme dell'inferno** hellfire *sg*; **cucinare alla fiamma** (*Culin*) to flambé **2** (*fig: persona amata*) love, flame; **una vecchia fiamma** an old flame **3** (*Mil, Naut*) pennant

fiammante [fjam'mante] AGG (*colore*) flaming; **rosso fiammante** flame red, bright red; **nuovo fiammante** brand new

fiammata [fjam'mata] SF blaze

fiammeggiare [fjammed'dʒare] /62/ VI (*aus avere*) (*anche fig: cielo*) to blaze; (*: occhi*) to flash; (*: spada*) to gleam ♦ VT (*Culin: pollo*) to singe

fiammifero [fjam'mifero] SM match; **una scatola di fiammiferi** a box of matches

fiammingo, -a, -ghi, -ghe [fjam'mingo] AGG Flemish ♦ SM, SF Fleming; **i fiamminghi** the Flemish ♦ SM (*lingua*) Flemish

fiancata [fjan'kata] SF (*di nave, auto*) side

fiancheggiare [fjankedˈdʒare] /62/ vt (gen) to border; (Mil) to flank; (fig: sostenere) to support, back (up)

fianco, -chi [ˈfjanko] sm (gen) side; (di persona) hip; (di animale, esercito) flank; (di montagna) slope; **di fianco** from the side, sideways; **di fianco a** o **a fianco di qn/qc** beside o next to sb/sth; **si trova a fianco della chiesa** it's next to the church; **avere un dolore al fianco** to have a pain in one's side; **stare al fianco di qn** (anche fig) to stand by sb, stay by sb's side; **ho sempre avuto qualcuno al mio fianco** I have always had somebody by my side; **starò sempre al tuo fianco** I'll always stand by you; **fianco a fianco** side by side; **stare con le mani sui fianchi** to stand with one's hands on one's hips; **avere fianchi larghi/stretti** (persona) to have broad/narrow hips, be broad-/narrow-hipped; **fianchi larghi** wide hips; **dormo sempre su un fianco** I always sleep on my side; **una spina nel fianco** (fig) a thorn in one's side; **mostrare il fianco al nemico** (fig) to reveal one's weak spot o Achilles' heel to one's enemy; **offrire** o **prestare il fianco a critiche** to leave o.s. open to criticism; **fianco destr/sinistr!** (Mil) right/left turn!

Fiandre [ˈfjandre] sfpl Flanders sg

fiaschetteria [fjasketteˈria] sf wine shop

fiasco, -schi [ˈfjasko] sm bottle (in straw holder); (fig: fallimento) fiasco; **un fiasco di vino** a bottle of wine; **essere un fiasco** to be a fiasco; **la festa è stata un fiasco completo** the party was a complete fiasco; **fare fiasco** (persona) to come a cropper; (spettacolo) to be a flop, be a fiasco

fiatare [fjaˈtare] /72/ vi (aus avere) (fig: parlare): **senza fiatare** without saying a word; **non osarono fiatare** they didn't dare breathe; **non fiatate!** don't say a word!

fiato [ˈfjato] sm **1** breath; **fiato cattivo** bad breath; **avere il fiato grosso** to pant, be out of breath; **riprendere fiato** (anche fig) to get one's breath back, catch one's breath; **mi sono fermato a riprendere fiato** I stopped to get my breath back; **tirare il fiato** to draw breath; (fig) to have a breather; **essere senza fiato** to be out of breath; **sono senza fiato** I'm out of breath; **restare senza fiato** to be breathless; **rimanere senza fiato** to be speechless; **quando l'ho saputo sono rimasto senza fiato** I was speechless when I heard about it; **sono rimasto senza fiato** (fig) it took my breath away; **tutto d'un fiato** all in one go; **bere tutto d'un fiato** to drink all in one go o gulp; **me l'ha raccontato tutto d'un fiato** he told me the whole story without drawing breath; **è fiato sprecato** (fig) it's a waste of breath; **quella scena mi ha mozzato il fiato** that scene took my breath away **2** (capacità di resistenza) stamina, staying power; **non ho più molto fiato** I haven't got much stamina these days **3** (Mus): **i fiati** wind instruments, the winds; **strumento a fiato** wind instrument

fibbia [ˈfibbja] sf buckle

fibra [ˈfibra] sf **1** (gen) fibre (Brit), fiber (USA) **2** (costituzione) constitution; **persona di fibra forte** person with a strong constitution ♦ **fibra di vetro** fibreglass (Brit), fiberglass (USA); **fibre grezze** roughage sg, (dietary) fibre sg; **fibre ottiche** optic fibres; **fibre tessili** textile fibres

ficcanaso [fikkaˈnaso] sm, sf (pl m ficcanasi, pl f ficcanaso) busybody, nose(y) parker

ficcare [fikˈkare] /20/ vt **1** (infilare: in borsa, cassetto) to put; (: con forza) to thrust, push; (: palo, chiodo) to drive; **dove lo hai ficcato?** where did you put it?; **ha ficcato tutti i libri in borsa** she crammed all the books into her bag; **mi ha ficcato un dito nell'occhio** he poked his finger in my eye; **ficcalo da qualche parte** (fam) stick it somewhere; **ficcare il naso negli affari altrui** (fig) to poke o stick one's nose into other people's business; **non ficcare il naso nei miei affari** don't stick your nose into my business; **lo hanno ficcato dentro** (fam: in prigione) they put him away o inside **2 ficcarsi**, **ficcarsi le dita nel naso** to pick one's nose; **ficcarsi il cappello in testa** to put o thrust one's hat on one's head; **ficcarsi in testa qc** (fig) to get sth into one's head; **ficcarsi in testa di fare qc** (fig) to take it into one's head to do sth; **ficcarsi** vr (andare a finire) to get to; **dove si sarà ficcato?** where can he (o it ecc) have got to?; **ficcarsi nei pasticci** o **nei guai** to get into hot water o a fix; **perché ti devi sempre ficcare in mezzo?** why do you always have to stick your oar in?

ficcherò ecc [fikkeˈro] vb vedi ficcare

fiche [fiʃ] sf inv (nei giochi d'azzardo) chip

fico, -chi [ˈfiko] sm (Bot) fig; **fico d'India** prickly pear; **fico secco** dried fig; **non vale un fico secco** (fig) it's not worth a fig o a straw; **non ci capisco un fico secco** I don't understand a thing

fiction [ˈfikʃon] sf inv TV drama
❏ **fiction** non si traduce mai con la parola inglese fiction

fidanzamento [fidantsaˈmento] sm engagement; **anello/festa di fidanzamento** engagement ring/party

fidanzare [fidanˈtsare] /72/ vt: **fidanzare a** to betroth to; **fidanzarsi** vr (uso reciproco) to get engaged

fidanzato, -a [fidanˈtsato] agg engaged ♦ sm, sf fiancé (fiancée); **i fidanzati** the engaged couple

fidarsi [fiˈdarsi] vip: **fidarsi di** to trust; (fare affidamento) to rely on; **non mi fido di uscire con questo tempo** I daren't go out in this weather; **fidarsi è bene, non fidarsi è meglio** (Proverbio) better safe than sorry

fidato, -a [fiˈdato] agg (degno di fiducia) trustworthy, reliable; (leale) loyal, faithful

fideismo [fideˈizmo] sm unquestioning belief

fideistico, -a, -ci, -che [fideˈistiko] agg (atteggiamento, posizione) totally uncritical

fideiussore [fidejusˈsore] sm (Dir) guarantor

fidelizzare [fideliˈdzare] /72/ vt: **fidelizzare la clientela** to build customer loyalty; **fidelizzarsi** vr to stay loyal

fido¹, -a [ˈfido] agg faithful, loyal

fido² [ˈfido] sm (Comm) credit; **fido bancario** banker's credit

fiducia [fiˈdutʃa] sf **1** trust, confidence; **avere fiducia in qn** to have faith in sb, trust sb; **ho fiducia in lui** I trust him; **abbi fiducia in Dio** have faith in the Lord; **riporre la propria fiducia in qn/qc** to place one's trust in sb/sth; **fiducia in se stesso** self-confidence; **devi avere più fiducia in te stesso** you should have more confidence in yourself; **una persona di fiducia** a trustworthy o reliable person; **un prodotto di fiducia** a reliable product; **è il mio uomo di fiducia** he is my right-hand man; **ha un incarico di fiducia** he holds a responsible position; **ha tradito la nostra fiducia** he has betrayed our trust **2** (Pol): **voto di fiducia** vote of confidence; **fiducia del Parlamento al Governo** parliamentary vote of confidence; **porre la questione di fiducia** to ask for a vote of confidence

fiducioso, -a [fiduˈtʃoso] agg trusting

fiele [ˈfjɛle] sm (amarezza) bitterness, bile; (letter) **parole piene di fiele** (fig) bitter words

fienile [fjeˈnile] sm hayloft

fieno [ˈfjɛno] sm hay

fiera¹ [ˈfjɛra] sf (letter: animale) wild beast

fiera² [ˈfjɛra] sf fair; **fiera di beneficenza** charity bazaar, (garden) fête o fete; **fiera del bianco** linen sale; **fiera campionaria** trade fair

fierezza [fjeˈrettsa] sf pride

fiero, -a [ˈfjɛro] agg **1** (orgoglioso) proud; **essere** o **andare fiero di qn/qc** to be proud of sb/sth; **i suoi vanno molto fieri di lui** his parents are very proud of him **2** (valente) bold, intrepid

fievole [ˈfjevole] agg (luce) dim; (suono) faint

FIFA [ˈfifa] sigla f (= Fédération Internationale des Football Associations) FIFA

fifa [ˈfifa] sf (fam): **che fifa!** what a fright!; **avere fifa** to have the jitters, be afraid; **ho fifa** I've got the jitters

fifone, -a [fiˈfone] sm, sf (fam, scherz) chicken, scaredy cat (used by children)

fig. abbr (= figura) fig.

Figi [ˈfidʒi] sfpl: **le (isole) Figi** Fiji sg, the Fiji Islands

figlia [ˈfiʎʎa] sf **1** daughter; **è figlia unica** she's an only child; **figlia di papà** daddy's girl **2** (Comm) counterfoil (Brit), stub

figliare [fiʎˈʎare] /27/ vi (aus avere) (animali) to give birth

figliastro, -a [fiʎˈʎastro] sm, sf stepchild, stepson (stepdaughter)

figlio, -gli [ˈfiʎʎo] sm son; (senza distinzione di sesso) child; **hanno 2 figli** they have 2 children; **non vuole avere figli** she doesn't want to have children; **aspetta un figlio** she's expecting a baby; **aspetta il secondo figlio** she's expecting her second child; **suo figlio è all'estero** her son is abroad;

mio figlio ha sette anni my son is seven; **essere figlio d'arte** to come from a theatrical (*o* artistic *ecc*) family; **il Figlio di Dio/dell'uomo** (*Rel*) the Son of God/of Man; **figlio di papà** daddy's boy, spoilt and wealthy young man; **figlio di puttana** (*fam!*) son of a bitch (*fam!*); **figlio unico** only child; **è figlio unico** he's an only child

figlioccio, -cia, -ci, -ce [fiʎˈʎɔttʃo] SM, SF godchild, godson (goddaughter)

figliola [fiʎˈʎɔla] SF daughter

figliolo [fiʎˈʎɔlo] SM son

figura [fiˈgura] SF (*gen, anche Mat*) figure; (*illustrazione*) illustration, picture; (*Carte*) face card; **ritratto a mezza figura** half-length portrait; **fare bella/brutta figura** to create *o* make a good/bad impression; **ho fatto una brutta figura al colloquio** I made a bad impression at the interview; **far fare una brutta figura a qn** to show sb up, make sb look a fool; **fare la figura dello scemo** to look a fool; **che figura!** how embarrassing!; **fare figura** to look good *o* smart; **questo libro ha molte figure** this book has lots of pictures; **figura retorica** figure of speech

figuraccia, -ce [figuˈrattʃa] SF: **fare una figuraccia** to create a bad impression

figurare [figuˈrare] /72/ VT: **non riesco a figurarmelo** I can't picture it; **ti disturbo? — ma no, figurati!** am I disturbing you? — no, not at all!; **figurati che...** would you believe that ...?; **figurarsi se non accettava!** wouldn't you just know it — he accepted it! ♦ VI (*aus avere*) to appear, figure

figurativo, -a [figuraˈtivo] AGG figurative

figurina [figuˈrina] SF 1 (*statuetta*) figurine 2 (*da collezione*) picture card

figurinista, -i, -e [figuriˈnista] SM, SF dress designer

figurino [figuˈrino] SM fashion sketch; **sembra un figurino** she looks like a fashion plate

figuro [fiˈguro] SM: **un losco figuro** a suspicious character

figurona [figuˈrona] SF , **figurone** [figuˈrone] SM (*fam*): **fare una figurona** *o* **un figurone** (*persona, oggetto*) to look terrific; (*persona: con un discorso*) to make an excellent impression

fila [ˈfila] SF 1 (*gen*) line, row; (*coda*) queue; (*Mil*) rank; (*Teatro*) row; **una fila di alberi** a line of trees; **in fila** in a row *o* line; **in fila indiana** in single file; **mettetevi in fila per due** line up in twos; **ci hanno messo in fila per due** they lined us up in twos; **fare la fila** to queue; **c'era una lunga fila alla fermata dell'autobus** there was a long queue at the bus stop; **serrare/rompere le file** (*Mil*) to close/break ranks; **ero seduto in seconda fila** I was sitting in the second row 2 (*successione*): **di fila** in succession, one after the other; **è piovuto per due mesi di fila** it rained for two months on the trot *o* non-stop; **una fila di avvenimenti** a series of events; **fuoco di fila** (*di armi da fuoco, anche fig: di domande ecc*) volley

filamento [filaˈmento] SM filament

filanda [fiˈlanda] SF spinning mill

filante [fiˈlante] AGG: **stella filante** (*stella cadente*) shooting star; (*striscia di carta*) streamer

filantropia [filantroˈpia] SF philanthropy

filantropico, -a, -ci, -che [filanˈtrɔpiko] AGG philanthropic(al)

filantropo [fiˈlantropo] SM philanthropist

filare¹ [fiˈlare] /72/ VT 1 (*lana*) to spin; (*metallo*) to draw; **quando Berta filava** in the good old days 2 (*Naut: gomena*) to pay out; (: *remi*) to trail ♦ VI (*aus essere*) (*persona*) to dash off, run; **filare via, filarsela** to run away, make off, make o.s. scarce; **fila (via)!** clear off!; **fila a letto subito** off to bed with you; **far filare qn** (*fig*) to make sb behave; **filare dritto** to behave, toe the line 2 (*aus avere*) (*discorso, ragionamento*) to be coherent, hang together 3 (*aus avere*) (*amoreggiare*): **filare (con)** to go out (with), go steady (with) (*ant*) 4 (*aus avere*) (*liquido*) to trickle; (*candela*) to smoke; (*formaggio*) to go stringy

filare² [fiˈlare] /72/ SM (*di alberi*) row, line

filarmonico, -a, -ci, -che [filarˈmɔniko] AGG philharmonic

filastrocca, -che [filasˈtrɔkka] SF nursery rhyme

filatelia [filateˈlia] SF philately (*frm*), stamp collecting

filato¹, -a [fiˈlato] AGG 1 **zucchero filato** candy floss (*Brit*), cotton candy (*USA*) 2 (*di seguito*) without a break, straight off; **ha parlato per 4 ore filate** he spoke for 4 hours without stopping ♦ AVV: **vai dritto filato a casa** go straight home

filato² [fiˈlato] SM (*di lana*) yarn; (*di altri tessuti*) thread

filatura [filaˈtura] SF 1 (*operazione*) spinning 2 (*fabbrica*) spinning mill

filetto¹ [fiˈletto] SM 1 (*ornamento*) braid, trimming 2 (*Tecn*) thread 3 (*Equitazione*) snaffle (bit)

filetto² [fiˈletto] SM (*di carne, pesce*) fillet

filiale [fiˈljale] SF (*Comm*) branch; (*impresa dipendente*) subsidiary (company)

filibustiere [filibusˈtjɛre] SM pirate; (*fig*) adventurer

filigrana [filiˈgrana] SF (*di oro*) filigree; (*di banconota, francobollo*) watermark

filippica [fiˈlippika] SF invective

Filippine [filipˈpine] SFPL: **le Filippine** the Philippines

filippino, -a [filipˈpino] AGG, SM, SF Filipino

film [film] SM INV (*Fot*) film; (*Cine*) film, movie (*USA*)

filmare [filˈmare] /72/ VT (*persona*) to film; (*scena*) to film, shoot

filmato [filˈmato] SM short film

filmina [filˈmina] SF film strip

filo [ˈfilo] SM 1 (*di cotone*) thread; (*di lana*) yarn; (*di perle, burattini*) string; (*di telefono, lampada*) wire, flex; **maglietta di filo di Scozia** fine cotton T-shirt; **calzettoni di filo di Scozia** lisle socks; **i fili della luce/del telefono** the electricity/telephone wires; **il filo del traguardo** the finishing tape; **in fil di ruota** (*Naut*) on a dead run; **un filo d'erba** a blade of grass; **filo a piombo** plumb line; **un filo d'acqua** a trickle of water; **un filo d'aria** (*fig*) a breath of air; **un filo di luce** (*fig*) a ray of light; **un filo di speranza** (*fig*) a ray *o* glimmer of hope; **con un filo di voce** in a weak *o* feeble voice, in a whisper; **filo elettrico** electric wire; **filo di ferro/spinato** wire/barbed wire; **filo interdentale** dental floss 2 (*di lama, rasoio*) edge; **essere o camminare o trovarsi sul filo del rasoio** (*fig*) to be on the razor's edge 3 (*di legno*) grain 4 (*fraseologia*): **perdere il filo** (*di un discorso*) to lose the thread; **ripetere qc per filo e per segno** to repeat sth word for word; **dare del filo da torcere a qn** to create difficulties for sb, make life difficult for sb; **è appeso a un filo** it's hanging by a thread; **fare il filo a qn** (*corteggiare*) to be after sb, chase sb 5 **fila** SFPL: **fila di un complotto** the threads of a plot

filoamericano, -a [filoameriˈkano] AGG pro-American

filobus [ˈfilobus] SM INV trolley bus

filodiffusione [filodiffuˈzjone] SF rediffusion

filodrammatico, -a, -ci, -che [filodramˈmatiko] AGG: (**compagnia**) **filodrammatica** amateur dramatic society ♦ SM, SF amateur actor

filoncino [filonˈtʃino] SM ≈ French stick, baguette

filone [fiˈlone] SM 1 (*di minerale*) seam, vein; (*fig: culturale*) tradition; **un film che appartiene al filone western** a film in the Western genre 2 (*di pane*) ≈ Vienna loaf

filosofia [filozoˈfia] SF philosophy; **con filosofia** (*fig*) philosophically

filosofico, -a, -ci, -che [filoˈzɔfiko] AGG philosophical

filosofo, -a [fiˈlɔzofo] SM, SF philosopher

filosovietico, -a, -ci, -che [filosoˈvjetiko] AGG pro-Soviet

filovia [filoˈvia] SF (*linea*) trolley line; (*bus*) trolley bus

filtrare [filˈtrare] /72/ VT to filter; (*fig: selezionare*) to screen ♦ VI (*aus essere*) to filter; **la luce filtrava dalla finestra** the light filtered in through the window

filtro¹ [ˈfiltro] SM (*gen, anche Fot*) filter; **sigaretta con filtro** filter-tipped cigarette, filter tip; **filtro dell'aria** (*Aut*) air filter; **filtro dell'olio** (*Aut*) oil filter

filtro² [ˈfiltro] SM (*pozione*) potion

filza [ˈfiltsa] SF (*gen, anche fig*) string; **mi ha raccontato una filza di bugie** he told me a string of lies

finale [fiˈnale] AGG final; **il giudizio finale** (*Rel*) the Last Judgment; **proposizione finale** (*Gramm*) purpose clause ♦ SM (*di libro, film*) ending, end; (*Mus: di spettacolo*) finale; **finale a sorpresa** surprise ending; **non mi è piaciuto il finale** I didn't like the ending ♦ SF 1 (*Sport*) final; **entrare in finale** to reach the final; **sono entrati in finale** they reached the final; **la finale di Coppa** the Cup Final 2 (*Gramm*) last syllable (*o* letter)

finalista, -i, -e [finaˈlista] SM, SF finalist

finalità [finaliˈta] SF INV 1 (*scopo*) aim, purpose; **gioco a finalità educativa** educational game 2 (*Filosofia*) finality

finalizzare [finalid'dzare] /72/ vt: **finalizzare a** (*ricerca, iniziativa*) to direct towards, aim at; **l'iniziativa è finalizzata alla salvaguardia dell'ambiente** the aim of this project is to protect the environment

finalmente [final'mente] avv at (long) last, finally; **finalmente!** at (long) last!; **finalmente sei arrivato!** you're here at last!

finanza [fi'nantsa] sf **1** finance; **alta finanza** high finance; **finanza creativa** creative accounting **2 finanze** sfpl finances; **Ministro delle finanze** Minister of Finance, ≈ Chancellor of the Exchequer (*Brit*), ≈ Secretary of the Treasury (*USA*) **3** (*Amm*): **(Guardia di) finanza** (*di frontiera*) ≈ Customs and Excise (*Brit*), ≈ Customs Service (*USA*); **Intendenza di finanza** ≈ Inland Revenue (*Brit*), ≈ Internal Revenue Service (*USA*)

finanziamento [finantsja'mento] sm (*azione*) financing; (*denaro fornito*) funds pl; **la banca ha concesso un finanziamento alla ditta** the bank has agreed to finance o fund the company

finanziare [finan'tsjare] /19/ vt to finance, fund

finanziario, -ria, -ri, -rie [finan'tsjarjo] agg financial

finanziatore, -trice [finantsja'tore] agg: **ente finanziatore** financing body ♦ sm, sf backer

finanziere [finan'tsjere] sm **1** (*esperto di finanze*) financier **2** (*guardia*) ≈ customs officer

finché [fin'ke] cong (*fino a quando*) until; (*per tutto il tempo che*) as long as; **ti amerò finché vivrò** I'll love you as long as I live; **non uscirai finché non avrai finito il lavoro** you won't leave until you have finished your work; **finché vorrai** as long as you like; **rimani finché vuoi** stay as long as you like; **aspetta finché non sia uscito** wait until he goes (o comes) out; **aspetta finché non sarò tornato** wait until I come back

fine¹ ['fine] agg **1** (*sottile: lamina, fetta*) thin; (: *capelli, lineamenti, pioggia*) fine; (: *voce*) thin, frail; **penna a punta fine** fine-point pen **2** (*acuto: vista, udito*) sharp, keen; (: *odorato*) fine; (*fig: ingegno*) shrewd; (: *osservazione, ironia*) subtle **3** (*raffinato: persona*) refined, distinguished; **non è fine mangiare con le mani** it's not polite to eat with your fingers

fine² ['fine] sm **1** (*scopo*) aim, end, purpose; (*Filosofia*) end; **avere un secondo fine** to have an ulterior motive; **a fin di bene** with the best of intentions; **l'ho fatto a fin di bene** I did it with good intentions; **il fine giustifica i mezzi** the end justifies the means; **al fine di fare qc** (in order) to do sth **2** (*conclusione*) end; **condurre qc a buon fine** to bring sth to a successful conclusion

fine³ ['fine] sf (*gen*) end; (*di libro, film*) ending; **alla fine** in the end, finally; **senza fine** endlessly (*avv*), endless (*agg*); **porre fine a** to put an end to; **a fine anno/mese** at the end of the year/month; **alla fine** in the end; **alla fine della giornata** at the end of the day; **verso la fine di giugno** in late June; **fine settimana** weekend; **alla fin fine** at the end of the day, in the end; **in fin dei conti** when all is said and done; (*tutto sommato*) after all; **dall'inizio alla fine** from beginning to end; **a lieto fine** with a happy ending; **mi piacciono le storie a lieto fine** I like stories with a happy ending; **volgere alla fine** to draw to an end; **fare una brutta fine** to come to a bad end; **che fine ha fatto?** what became of him?; **essere in fin di vita** to be at death's door; **è la fine del mondo!** (*fig: stupendo*) it's out of this world!; (*pegg*) what's the world coming to?; **buona fine e buon principio!** (*augurio*) happy New Year!; **un quadro fine Ottocento** a late nineteenth-century painting; **articoli di fine serie** oddments; **svendita di fine stagione** end-of-season sale

fine settimana ['fine setti'mana] sm inv weekend

finestra [fi'nestra] sf (*gen, anche Inform*) window; **affacciarsi alla finestra** to appear at the window; **buttare il denaro dalla finestra** (*fig*) to throw money down the drain; **periodo finestra** symptom-free period; **finestra a battenti** casement window; **finestra a ghigliottina** sash window

finestrino [fines'trino] sm (*di treno, auto*) window

finezza [fi'nettsa] sf (*vedi fine*) thinness; fineness; sharpness, keenness; shrewdness; subtleness, subtlety; refinement

fingere ['findʒere] vb irreg **54** vt to feign (*letter*); **fingere di fare qc** to pretend to do sth; **fingiamo di dormire** let's pretend we're asleep; **ha finto di non conoscermi** he pretended

he didn't recognize me; **fingere un grande dolore** to pretend to be very upset ♦ vi (*aus avere*) to dissemble (*letter*); **sa fingere molto bene** he's very good at hiding his feelings; **fingersi** vr to pretend to be; **si è finto ubriaco** he pretended he was drunk; **fingersi medico** to pretend to be a doctor

finimenti [fini'menti] smpl (*di cavallo*) harness sg

finimondo [fini'mondo] sm pandemonium; **successe un finimondo** all hell broke loose

finire [fi'nire] /55/ vi (*aus essere*) **1** (*gen*) to finish, end; (*pioggia, neve*) to stop, cease; **il film finisce alle dieci** the film finishes at ten; **l'anno scolastico finisce a giugno** the school year ends in June; **un altro giorno è finito** another day is over o has come to an end; **tra noi è tutto finito** it's all over between us; **è finito di piovere/nevicare** it has stopped raining/snowing; **finire bene/male** (*film, libro*) to have a happy/an unhappy ending; **finire male** (*persona*) to come to a bad end; **per fortuna tutto è finito bene** luckily everything turned out well in the end; **finire per o col fare qc** to end up (by) doing sth; **finirà per crederle** he'll end up believing her; **finì col fare il lavoro lui** he ended up doing the job himself; **andare a finire** to end up; (*lavoro, corso*) to turn out; **dov'è andato a finire quel libro?, dov'è finito quel libro?** where has that book got to?; **dove vuoi andare a finire con questo discorso?** what are you driving o getting at?; **com'è andata a finire?** what happened in the end?; **è finita!** (*non c'è rimedio*) it's all over!; **com'è finita la partita?** how did the match end?; **finire in** to end with; **finire in galera** to end up o finish up in prison **2** (*esaurirsi*) to be finished; **l'olio è finito** we have run out of oil, there's no oil left ♦ vt **1** (*gen*) to finish, (*lavoro, corso*) to finish, complete; (*discorso*) to end; **finire di fare qc** to finish doing sth; **ho finito di leggere il libro** I've finished reading the book; **non ho ancora finito i compiti** I haven't finished my homework yet; **ha finito i propri giorni in prigione** he ended his days in prison; **finisci la minestra** finish o eat up your soup; **abbiamo finito il pane** we've run out of bread; **mi ha finito la crema** she's used up all my cream **2** (*smettere*) to stop; **finire di fare qc** to stop doing sth; **non finire più di fare qc** to keep on doing sth; **non finisco di meravigliarmi della sua pazienza** her patience never ceases to amaze me **3** (*dare il colpo di grazia*) to finish off **4** (*rifinire*) to finish off, put the finishing touches to **5** (*fam*): **finirla** to pack in; **è ora di finirla con queste storie!** it's time you stopped this nonsense!; **finiscila!** stop it!; **farla finita con qc** to have done with sth; **devi farla finita con questi capricci** you'll have to stop these tantrums; **l'ho fatta finita con la droga** I'm off drugs now; **ho deciso di farla finita con Maria** I've decided to finish with Maria; **farla finita (con la vita)** to put an end to one's life ♦ sm (*fine*) end; **sul finire della festa** towards the end of the party

finitura [fini'tura] sf finish; **le ultime finiture** the finishing touches

finlandese [finlan'dese] agg Finnish ♦ sm, sf Finn; **i finlandesi** the Finns ♦ sm (*lingua*) Finnish; **parli finlandese?** do you speak Finnish?

Finlandia [fin'landja] sf Finland; **ti è piaciuta la Finlandia?** did you like Finland?; **andrò in Finlandia quest'estate** I'm going to Finland this summer

fino¹, -a ['fino] agg **1** = **fine¹ 2** (*oro, argento*) pure; **cervello fino** quick brain; *vedi* **fine¹**

fino² ['fino] *spesso troncato, davanti a consonante, in* fin avv (*pure, anche*) even; **hai detto fin troppo** you have said too much o more than enough ♦ prep **1 fino a** (*tempo*) until, up to, till; (*luogo*) as far as; (+ *infin*) so that; **resto fino a venerdì/al 15 gennaio** I'm staying until Friday/until the 15th of January; **vengo con te fino al cinema** I'll come as far as the cinema with you; **ha lavorato fino ad ammalarsi** he worked so hard that he made himself ill; **fino a quando?, fin quando?** until when?; **fino a quando puoi rimanere?** how long can you stay?; **fino all'ultimo** until the end, to the end; **fino all'ultimo ha negato, poi ha ceduto** he denied it up till the last minute, then gave way; **arrivare fino a** (*livello*) to reach; **averne fin sopra i capelli** (*fig*) to be fed up to the back teeth, to have it up to here; **andare fino in fondo a qc** to get to the bottom of sth **2 fin da** since, from; **fin dalla nascita/dall'infanzia** from o since birth/infancy; **fin da quando sei arrivato** since you arrived, from the time you arrived; **fin d'ora** as of o from now; **fin dall'alba** since daybreak; **fin da domani** from tomorrow onwards; **fin da ieri** since yesterday

finocchio, -chi [fi'nɔkkjo] SM **1** (*Bot*) fennel **2** (*offensivo*) gay man

finora [fi'nora] AVV up till now, so far; **finora Marco non si è visto** Marco hasn't turned up yet; **finora abbiamo fatto solo il presente** so far we've only studied the present tense

finsi ecc ['finsi] VB *vedi* **fingere**

finto, -a ['finto] PP *di* **fingere** ♦ AGG (*capelli, denti*) false; (*fiori*) artificial; (*cuoio, pelle*) imitation *attr*; (*fig: simulato: pazzia*) feigned, pretended; **una giacca in finta pelle** an imitation leather jacket

finzione [fin'tsjone] SF (*simulazione*) pretence (*Brit*), pretense (*USA*), sham; **la finzione scenica** the stage illusion

fioccare [fjok'kare] /20/ VI (*aus* essere) (*neve*) to fall; (*fig: insulti*) to come thick and fast ♦ VB IMPERS to snow

fiocco¹, -chi ['fjɔkko] SM **1** (*di neve, cereali*) flake; **un fiocco di neve** a snowflake; **fiocchi di granturco** cornflakes **2** (*di lana*) flock **3** (*nastro*) bow; **coi fiocchi** (*fig*) first-rate; **un pranzo coi fiocchi** a slap-up meal

fiocco², -chi ['fjɔkko] SM (*Naut*) jib

fiocina [fjɔt'fina] SF (*Naut*) harpoon

fioco, -a, -chi, -che ['fjɔko] AGG (*luce*) dim, weak; (*suono, voce*) faint, weak; **la luce era sempre più fioca** the light was getting dimmer and dimmer

fionda ['fjonda] SF (*arma*) sling; (*giocattolo*) catapult

fioraio, -aia, -ai, -aie [fjo'rajo] SM, SF (*in negozio*) florist; (*ambulante*) flower seller; **sto andando dal fioraio** I'm going to the florist's

fiordaliso [fjorda'lizo] SM (*Bot*) cornflower; (*Araldica*) fleur-de-lis *o* -lys

fiordo ['fjɔrdo] SM fjord

fiore ['fjore] SM **1** (*gen, anche fig*) flower; (*di albero*) blossom; **fiori di campo** wild flowers; **essere in fiore** (*pianta, giardino*) to be in bloom; (*albero*) in blossom; (*fig*) to be in full bloom; **fiore d'arancio** orange blossom *sg*; **a fiori** with a flower pattern, flowered; **una gonna a fiori** a skirt with a flower pattern; **disegno a fiori** floral design; **nel fiore degli anni** in one's prime; **oggi sei un fiore** you're looking at your best today; **"non fiori ma opere di bene"** (*negli annunci mortuari*) "no flowers please, but donations to charity"; **fiori di Bach** Bach flower remedies **2** (*Carte*) **fiori** SMPL clubs **3 a fior di, a fior d'acqua** on (the surface of) the water; **a fior di labbra** in a whisper; **ho i nervi a fior di pelle** my nerves are all on edge **4** (*fraseologia*): **un fior di persona** a really lovely person; **è costato fior di quattrini** it cost a pretty penny; **aver fior di quattrini** to be rolling in money; **il fior fiore della società** the cream of society; **fiore all'occhiello** feather in the cap **5 fior di latte** cream

fiorente [fjo'rente] AGG (*industria, paese*) flourishing; (*salute*) blooming; (*petto*) ample; **fiorente di** (*boschi, vigneti*) rich in

fiorentino, -a [fjoren'tino] AGG *di o* from Florence, Florentine ♦ SM, SF inhabitant *o* native of Florence; **i fiorentini** the people of Florence

fioretto [fjo'retto] SM **1** (*Scherma*) foil **2** (*Tecn*) drilling bit

fiorino [fjo'rino] SM florin

fiorire [fjo'rire] /55/ VI (*aus* essere) (*fiore*) to flower, bloom; (*albero*) to blossom, flower; (*fig: sentimento*) to blossom; (: *commercio, arte*) to flourish

fiorista, -i, -e [fjo'rista] SM, SF florist

fioritura [fjori'tura] SF **1** (*di pianta*) flowering, blooming; (*di albero*) blossoming; (*fig: di commercio, arte*) flourishing **2** (*insieme dei fiori*) flowers *pl*; **il ciliegio ha avuto una fioritura abbondante quest'anno** the cherry tree produced a lot of flowers *o* blossom this year **3** (*Mus*) fioritura

fiotto ['fjɔtto] SM (*di lacrime*) flood; (*di sangue*) gush, spurt; **scorrere a fiotti** to gush out *o* fourth

Firenze [fi'rentse] SF Florence; **sto andando a Firenze** I'm going to Florence; **vive a Firenze** he lives in Florence

firma ['firma] SF signature; (*fig*) name; **apporre la propria firma** to put one's signature to; **la mia firma** my signature; **le grandi firme della moda** the big names in fashion

❏ **firma** non si traduce mai con la parola inglese *firm*

firmamento [firma'mento] SM firmament

firmare [fir'mare] /72/ VT to sign; **dove devo firmare?** where shall I sign?; **un maglione firmato da Missoni** a Missoni sweater, a sweater by Missoni

firmatario, -ria, -ri, -rie [firma'tarjo] SM, SF signatory

fisarmonica, -che [fizar'mɔnika] SF accordion

fiscale [fis'kale] AGG **1** fiscal, tax *attr*; **anno fiscale** tax year; **evasione fiscale** tax evasion; **scontrino fiscale** (shop) receipt; **ricevuta fiscale** official receipt (*for tax purposes*); **medico fiscale** doctor employed by Social Security to examine people on sick leave **2** (*fig: pegg: meticoloso*) nitpicking

fiscalista, -i, -e [fiska'lista] SM, SF tax consultant

fiscaliz'zare [fiskalid'dzare] /72/ VT to exempt from taxes

fischiare [fis'kjare] /19/ VT **1** (*canzone, motivo*) to whistle; **sai fischiare?** can you whistle?; **fischiare un rigore** to give a penalty; **l'arbitro ha fischiato un rigore** the referee blew his whistle for a penalty **2** (*in segno di disapprovazione*) to hiss, boo; **il pubblico lo ha fischiato** the audience booed him ♦ VI (*aus* avere) (*gen, o fig*) to whistle; (*serpente*) to hiss; (*uccello*) to sing; **mi fischiano le orecchie** I've got a ringing in my ears; (*fig: fam*) my ears are burning; **fischiare al cane** to whistle for one's dog

fischiettare [fiskjet'tare] /72/ VI (*aus* avere), VT to whistle

fischietto [fis'kjetto] SM (*strumento*) whistle

fischio, -chi ['fiskjo] SM (*suono*) whistle; **fare un fischio** to whistle, give a whistle; **prendere fischi per fiaschi** to get hold of the wrong end of the stick; **il fischio dell'arbitro** the referee's whistle

fisco ['fisko] SM tax authorities *pl*; (*Amm*) ≈ Inland Revenue (*Brit*), ≈ Internal Revenue (Service) (*USA*); (*fam*): **il fisco** the taxman

fisica ['fizika] SF physics *sg*

fisicamente [fizika'mente] AVV physically; **sono fisicamente impossibilitato a venire** it's physically impossible for me to come

fisico, -a, -ci, -che ['fiziko] AGG (*gen*) physical; **il contatto fisico** physical contact; **educazione fisica** PE; **aspetto fisico** appearance ♦ SM (*corpo*) physique; **avere un bel fisico** (*donna*) to have a good figure; (*uomo*) to have a good physique; **hai il fisico dell'atleta** you have an athletic physique *o* the physique of an athlete ♦ SM, SF (*studioso*) physicist; **un fisico nucleare** a nuclear physicist

fisima ['fizima] SF fixation

fisiologia [fizjolo'dʒia] SF physiology

fisionomia [fizjono'mia] SF physiognomy; **non ricordo bene la sua fisionomia** I don't remember his face very well

fisioterapia [fizjotera'pia] SF physiotherapy

fisioterapista, -i, -e [fizjotera'pista] SM, SF physiotherapist

fissaggio, -gi [fis'sadd'ʒo] SM (*Fot*) fixing; **bisogna aspettare 2 ore per il fissaggio di questa vernice** you must wait 2 hours for this paint to dry

fissante [fis'sante] AGG (*spray, lozione*) holding

fissare [fis'sare] /72/ VT **1** (*attaccare*): **fissare (a o su)** to fix (to), fasten (to); **fissare (su)** (*sguardo*) to fix (on), fasten (on); **fissare qn/qc** (*guardare*) to stare at sb/sth; **non fissarlo tutto il tempo** don't keep staring at him; **fissare qc in mente** to fix sth firmly in one's mind; **è fissato al muro** it's fixed to the wall **2** (*prezzo, data, condizioni*) to fix, set; (*regola*) to lay down; (*appuntamento*) to arrange, fix; **all'ora fissata** at the agreed time; **è tutto fissato** it's all fixed *o* arranged; **hai fissato la data?** have you fixed the date? **3** (*prenotare*) to book, reserve; **ho fissato una stanza per lunedì** I've booked a room for Monday **4** (*Fot, Chim*) to fix; **fissarsi** VIP **1 fissarsi di fare qc** (*mettersi in testa di*) to set one's heart on doing sth; (*ostinarsi*) to insist on doing sth; **si è fissato di partire con noi** he has set his heart on coming with us; **si è fissato che vuole vederlo subito** he insists on seeing him at once **2** (*concentrarsi*): **l'attenzione del pubblico si fissò su di lui** everybody was staring at him **3** (*uso reciproco*) to stare at each other

fissazione [fissat'tsjone] SF (*Psic*) obsession, fixation

fissione [fis'sjone] SF fission

fisso, -a ['fisso] AGG (*gen*) fixed; (*lavoro, lavoratore*) permanent; (*stipendio*) regular; (*presenza*) constant; (*immagine, elemento*) recurring; **senza fissa dimora** of no fixed abode; **prezzo fisso** fixed price; **un lavoro fisso** a permanent job; **uno**

stipendio fisso a regular income; **un ragazzo fisso** a steady boyfriend; **telefono fisso** landline ♦ sᴍ (*compenso*) fixed sum ♦ ᴀᴠᴠ: **guardar fisso (qn/qc)** to stare (at sb/sth)

fitotermalismo [fitotermaˈlizmo] sᴍ herbal hydrotherapy

fitta [ˈfitta] sꜰ sharp pain; **una fitta di dolore** a sharp twinge of pain; **a volte ho delle fitte al petto** I sometimes get sharp pains in my chest; **una fitta al cuore** (*fig*) a pang of grief

fittavolo [fitˈtavolo] sᴍ tenant

fittizio, -zia, -zi, -zie [fitˈtittsjo] ᴀɢɢ (*nome, personaggio*) fictitious, imaginary

fitto¹, -a [ˈfitto] ᴀɢɢ 1 (*bosco, pelo*) thick; (*nebbia*) thick, dense; (*tessuto*) closely-woven; (*pettine*) fine; (*mistero*) impenetrabile; **è buio fitto** it's pitch dark 2 (*intenso: fuoco d'artiglieria: pioggia*) heavy; **una giornata fitta di eventi** an eventful day ♦ ᴀᴠᴠ (*nevicare, piovere*) hard; **parlare fitto fitto** to be deep in conversation; **scrittto fitto fitto** closely written ♦ sᴍ: **nel fitto del bosco** in the heart *o* depths of the wood
❑ **fitto** non si traduce mai con la parola inglese *fit*

fitto² [ˈfitto] sᴍ (*affitto*) rent; **blocco dei fitti** rents freeze

fiumana [fjuˈmana] sꜰ (*fiume in piena*) torrent; (*fig: di gente*) flood, stream

fiume [ˈfjume] sᴍ river; (*fig: di gente, parole*) stream; **scorrere a fiumi** (*vino, sangue*) to flow in torrents; **sgorgare a fiumi (da)** (*acqua, sangue*) to pour out (from); **versare fiumi di inchiostro su qc** to write reams about sth ♦ ᴀɢɢ ɪɴᴠ: **romanzo fiume** roman-fleuve; **processo fiume** long-drawn-out *o* long-running trial

fiutare [fjuˈtare] /72/ ᴠᴛ 1 (*annusare*) to smell, sniff; (*sogg: cane da caccia*) to scent; **fiutare tabacco** to take snuff; **fiutare cocaina** to snort cocaine 2 (*intuire*): **fiutare un pericolo** to smell danger; **fiutare un buon affare** to sniff out a bargain; **fiutare qc di losco** to smell a rat

fiuto [ˈfjuto] sᴍ (*odorato*) sense of smell; (*fig: intuito*) nose; **avere fiuto per qc** to have a nose for sth; **avere fiuto nel fare qc** to have a flair for doing sth

flaccido, -a [ˈflattʃido] ᴀɢɢ flabby

flacone [flaˈkone] sᴍ (*di profumo ecc*) bottle

flagellare [fladʒelˈlare] /72/ ᴠᴛ to flog, scourge; (*sogg: onde*) to beat against; **flagellarsi** ᴠʀ to whip o.s.

flagello [flaˈdʒello] sᴍ 1 (*frusta, anche fig*) scourge 2 (*Bio*) flagellum

flagrante [flaˈɡrante] ᴀɢɢ: **cogliere qn in flagrante** to catch sb red-handed *o* in the act; **hanno colto il ladro in flagrante** they caught the burglar red-handed; **essere in flagrante contraddizione** (*evidente*) to be in blatant contradiction

flanella [flaˈnella] sꜰ flannel

flash [flæʃ] sᴍ ɪɴᴠ 1 (*Fot, Elettr*) flash 2 (*Radio, TV*) newsflash

flautista, -i, -e [flauˈtista] sᴍ, sꜰ flautist

flauto [ˈflauto] sᴍ: **flauto (traverso)** flute; **flauto dolce** recorder

flebile [ˈflɛbile] ᴀɢɢ feeble, faint

flebite [fleˈbite] sꜰ phlebitis

flemma [ˈflemma] sꜰ (*calma*) composure, coolness; **rispose con molta flemma** he answered very coolly

flemmatico, -a, -ci, -che [flemˈmatiko] ᴀɢɢ cool

flessibile [flesˈsibile] ᴀɢɢ (*materiale*) flexible, pliable; (*fig: carattere*) flexible, adaptable; **orario flessibile** flexitime ♦ sᴍ flex

flessibilità [flessibiliˈta] sꜰ ɪɴᴠ flexibility; **flessibilità (del lavoro)** flexibility

flessione [flesˈsjone] sꜰ 1 (*gen*) bending; (*Ginnastica: a terra*) sit-up; (*: in piedi*) forward bend; (*: sulle gambe*) knee-bend; (*: sulle braccia*) press-up; **fare una flessione** to bend 2 (*diminuzione*) slight drop *o* fall, blip; **una flessione economica** a downward trend in the economy 3 (*Ling*) inflection

flesso, -a [ˈflesso] ᴘᴘ *di* flettere

flessuoso, -a [flessuˈoso] ᴀɢɢ (*elastico*) supple, lithe; (*armonico: corpo*) graceful; (*: movimenti*) flowing, graceful

flettere [ˈflettere] ᴠʙ ɪʀʀᴇɢ /92/ ᴠᴛ 1 (*gen*) to bend; **flettere il busto in avanti** to bend forward from the waist 2 (*Ling*) to inflect; **flettersi** ᴠʀ to bend

flipper [ˈflipper] sᴍ ɪɴᴠ pinball machine; **giocare a flipper** to play pinball

flirt [flɜːt] sᴍ ɪɴᴠ brief romance, flirtation

flirtare [flirˈtare] /72/ ᴠɪ (*aus* avere) to flirt

F.lli ᴀʙʙʀ (= *Fratelli*) Bros

flora [ˈflɔra] sꜰ flora; **flora batterica intestinale** intestinal flora

florido, -a [ˈflɔrido] ᴀɢɢ (*industria*) flourishing, thriving, prosperous; (*aspetto*) healthy, glowing with health; (*salute*) excellent; **un'industria florida** a flourishing industry

floscio, -scia, -sci, -sce [ˈflɔʃʃo] ᴀɢɢ (*cappello, tessuto*) soft, floppy; (*muscoli, carni*) flabby

flotta [ˈflɔtta] sꜰ fleet; **flotta aerea** fleet of aircraft

flottante [flotˈtante] sᴍ (*Borsa*): **titoli a largo flottante** blue chips

fluido, -a [ˈfluido] ᴀɢɢ (*gen*) fluid ♦ sᴍ fluid; (*forza magica*) mysterious power

fluire [fluˈire] /55/ ᴠɪ (*aus* essere) to flow

fluorescente [fluoreʃˈʃɛnte] ᴀɢɢ fluorescent

fluoro [fluˈɔro] sᴍ fluorine; **un dentifricio al fluoro** a fluoride toothpaste

fluoruro [fluoˈruro] sᴍ fluoride

flusso [ˈflusso] sᴍ (*gen, anche fig*) flow; (*Fis, Elettr*) flux; **flusso e riflusso** ebb and flow; **flusso di cassa** (*Comm*) cash flow

flutto [ˈflutto] sᴍ (*letter: onda*) billow; **tra i flutti** among the waves

fluttuare [fluttuˈare] /72/ ᴠɪ (*aus* avere) 1 (*ondeggiare: mare*) to rise and fall; (*: barca*) to toss, rock; (*: bandiera*) to flutter 2 (*Econ: moneta*) to fluctuate

fluviale [fluˈvjale] ᴀɢɢ river *attr*; **pesca fluviale** freshwater fishing; **navigazione fluviale** river *o* inland navigation

FM ᴀʙʙʀ (= *modulazione di frequenza*) FM (= *frequency modulation*)

FMI [ˈeffeˈemmeˈi] sɪɢʟᴀ ᴍ (= *Fondo Monetario Internazionale*) IMF (= *International Monetary Fund*)

FO sɪɢʟᴀ = *Forlì*

fobia [foˈbia] sꜰ (*Med*) phobia; **ha la fobia dei ragni** he has a phobia about spiders

foca, -che [ˈfɔka] sꜰ (*Zool*) seal

focaccia, -ce [foˈkattʃa] sꜰ (*Culin*) kind of pizza; (*dolce*) bun; **rendere pan per focaccia** to get one's own back, give tit for tat

focale [foˈkale] ᴀɢɢ focal

focalizzare [fokalidˈdzare] /72/ ᴠᴛ (*Fot: immagine*) to get into focus; **focalizzare la situazione** to get the situation into perspective; **focalizzare l'attenzione su** to focus one's attention on

foce [ˈfotʃe] sꜰ (*Geog*) mouth; **la foce del Po** the mouth of the Po

focolaio, -ai [fokoˈlajo] sᴍ (*Med*) centre (*Brit*) *o* center (*USA*) of infection, focus; (*fig*) hotbed, breeding ground; **il focolaio della rivolta** the breeding ground of the rebellion

focolare [fokoˈlare] sᴍ hearth, fireside; (*Tecn*) furnace; **ritornare al focolare domestico** to return to hearth and home

focoso, -a [foˈkoso] ᴀɢɢ fiery; (*cavallo*) mettlesome, fiery

fodera [ˈfɔdera] sꜰ (*interna: di vestito*) lining; (*di libro*) dust jacket; (*di divano, poltrona*) cover

foderare [fodeˈrare] /72/ ᴠᴛ (*vestito*) to line; (*Culin*) to line (with pastry); (*libro*) to cover

fodero [ˈfɔdero] sᴍ (*di spada*) scabbard; (*di pugnale*) sheath; (*di pistola*) holster

foga [ˈfɔɡa] sꜰ enthusiasm, ardour (*Brit*), ardor (*USA*); **nella foga della passione/discussione** in the heat of passion/the discussion; **lavora con foga** he throws himself into his work (with great enthusiasm); **si precipitò con foga ad aprire** he rushed excitedly to the door

foggia, -ge [ˈfɔddʒa] sꜰ (*forma*) shape, form; (*moda*) style, fashion; **un abito di foggia strana** an odd looking suit/dress; **alla foggia degli anni venti** twenties style

foggiare [fodˈdʒare] /62/ ᴠᴛ to fashion; (*carattere*) to form

foglia [ˈfɔʎʎa] sꜰ (*Bot: di melo*) leaf; **gli alberi stanno mettendo le foglie** the trees are coming into leaf; **ha mangiato la foglia** (*fig*) he's caught on; **tremare come una foglia** (*fig*) to shake like a leaf; **foglia d'argento/oro** silver/gold leaf; **foglia di fico** fig leaf

fogliame [foʎˈʎame] sᴍ foliage, leaves *pl*

foglietto [foʎˈʎetto] SM 1 (*piccolo foglio*) slip *o* piece of paper; (*manifestino*) leaflet, handout 2 (*Anat*): **foglietto pleurico** pleural layer

foglio, -gli [ˈfɔʎʎo] SM 1 (*gen, di metallo*) sheet; (*di libro*) page, leaf; **foglio rigato** *o* **a righe** sheet of lined *o* ruled paper; **foglio a quadretti** sheet of squared paper; **foglio protocollo** foolscap; **foglio volante** leaflet 2 **foglio di calcolo** *o* **elettronico** spreadsheet; **foglio rosa** (*Aut: documento*) ≈ provisional driving licence; **foglio di via** (*Dir*) expulsion order 3 (*banconota*) (bank)note 4 (*Tip*): **in foglio** folio *attr*

fogna [ˈfoɲɲa] SF sewer; (*fig: luogo sporco*) pigsty; **topo di fogna** sewer rat; **sei una fogna!** (*fig: fam: ghiottone*) you're a greedy pig!

fognatura [foɲɲaˈtura] SF sewerage

föhn [føːn] SM INV hair-dryer

folata [foˈlata] SF gust; **il tuo arrivo ha portato una folata di novità** your arrival was like a breath of fresh air

folclore [folˈklore] SM folklore

folcloristico, -a, -ci, -che [folkloˈristiko] AGG (*spettacolo, canzone*) folk *attr*; (*scherz: bizzarro*) weird, freakish; **costume folcloristico** traditional dress

folgorare [folɡoˈrare] /72/ VT (*sogg: fulmine*) to strike (down); (: *alta tensione*) to electrocute; **mi folgorò con uno sguardo** (*fig*) he gave me a withering look ♦ VI (*aus avere*) (*rilucere*) to flash

folgorazione [folɡoratˈtsjone] SF electrocution; **ebbe una folgorazione** (*fig: idea*) he had a brainwave

folgore [ˈfolɡore] SF thunderbolt

folla [ˈfolla] SF (*di persone*) crowd, throng; (*pegg*) mob; **una folla di idee** a multitude *o* host of ideas

folle [ˈfolle] AGG 1 (*anche fig: idee, trovata*) mad, insane; **a ritmo** *o* **velocità folle** at breakneck speed 2 (*Tecn: ingranaggio*) idle ♦ SM, SF madman *o* madwoman ♦ SF (*Aut*): **in folle** in neutral; **assicurati che sia in folle** make sure it's in neutral

folleggiare [folledˈdʒare] /62/ VI (*aus avere*) (*divertirsi*) to paint the town red

folletto [folˈletto] SM elf

follia [folˈlia] SF (*pazzia*) madness; (*atto*) act of madness *o* folly; **in un momento di follia** in a moment of madness; **fare una follia** (*fig*) to do sth mad *o* crazy; **è una follia!** it's crazy!; **è stata una follia fare ciò che ha fatto** it was madness *o* folly to do what he did; **costare una follia** to cost the earth; **la sua macchina nuova dev'essere costata una follia** his new car must have cost the earth; **amare qn alla follia** to love sb to distraction; **lo amo alla follia** I'm madly in love with him; **che follia!** what folly!, what madness!

folto, -a [ˈfolto] AGG (*capelli, pelo, bosco*) thick; (*schiera*) dense ♦ SM: **nel folto della mischia** in the thick of the fray

fomentare [fomenˈtare] /72/ VT to stir up, foment (*frm*)

fon [fɔn] SM INV = **föhn**

fondale [fonˈdale] SM 1 (*del mare*) bottom; **il fondale marino** the sea bed 2 (*Teatro*) backdrop

fondamentale [fondamenˈtale] AGG fundamental, basic; **è fondamentale che...** it's of prime importance that ...

fondamentalista, -i, -e [fondamentaˈlista] AGG, SM, SF (*Rel*) fundamentalist

fondamento [fondaˈmento] SM 1 foundation, basis; **i fondamenti della matematica** the principles of mathematics 2 **fondamenta** SFPL (*Edil*) foundations; **gettare le fondamenta** (*anche fig*) to lay the foundations

fondare [fonˈdare] /72/ VT (*istituzione, città*) to found; (*fig: teoria, sospetti*) to base; **fondare qc su** to base sth on; **fondarsi** VIP: **fondarsi (su)** (*teorie*) to be based (on)

fondatezza [fondaˈtettsa] SF (*di ragioni*) soundness; (*di dubbio, sospetto*) basis in fact

fondato, -a [fonˈdato] AGG (*sospetto*) well-founded, valid; (*ragione*) valid, sound

fondazione [fondatˈtsjone] SF foundation

fondente [fonˈdɛnte] SM (*Metallurgia*) flux ♦ AGG: **cioccolato fondente** plain *o* dark chocolate

fondere [ˈfondere] VB IRREG /25/ VT 1 (*gen*) to melt; (*metallo*) to fuse, melt; (*fig: colori*) to blend, merge; (: *enti, classi: Inform*) to merge 2 (*statua, campana*) to cast ♦ VI (*aus avere*) to melt; **mi fonde il cervello** (*fig*) I can't think straight any more, my brain has seized up; **fondersi** VR (*uso reciproco*:

unirsi: *correnti, enti*) to merge, unite; **fondersi** VIP (*sciogliersi*) to melt

fonderia [fondeˈria] SF foundry

fondiario, -ria, -ri, -rie [fonˈdjarjo] AGG land *attr*; **possidente fondiario** landowner

fondina [fonˈdina] SF 1 (*portapistola*) holster 2 (*piatto fondo*) soup plate

fondo¹, -a [ˈfondo] AGG deep; **piatto fondo** soup plate; **a notte fonda** at dead of night; **una buca fonda 3 metri** a hole 3 metres deep; **qui l'acqua è fonda** the water is deep here ♦ SM 1 (*di recipiente, vallata, pozzo*) bottom; (*dei pantaloni*) seat; (*di mare, fiume*) bottom, bed; **fondo marino** sea floor; **fondo stradale** road surface; **doppio fondo** false bottom; **andare** *o* **colare a fondo** (*nave*) to go to the bottom, sink; **la nave è andata a fondo** the ship sank; **dar fondo (all'ancora)** (*Naut*) to drop anchor; **in fondo a** at the bottom of the sea; **in fondo alla sala** at the back of the room; **in fondo alla pagina** at the bottom of the page; **in fondo al vicolo** at the end of the alley; **laggiù in fondo** (*lontano*) over there; (*in profondità*) down there; **nel fondo del bosco** in the depths *o* heart of the wood; **nel fondo del suo cuore** deep down, in his (*o* her) heart of hearts; **il fondo del bicchiere** the bottom of the glass 2 **fondi** SMPL (*di vino, aceto*) dregs; (*di vino, birra*) lees; (*di caffè*) grounds; (*di tè*) leaves; **fondi di magazzino** old *o* unsold stock *sg* 3 (*sfondo*) background; (*Araldica*) ground; **bianco su fondo nero** white on a black background 4 (*Sport*): **di fondo** long-distance; **sci di fondo** cross-country *o* langlauf skiing; **linea di fondo** (*Tennis*) baseline; (*Calcio*) bye-line; **prova di fondo** (*Equitazione*) speed and endurance (test) 5 (*Giornalismo*): **articolo di fondo** editorial 6 (*fraseologia*): **conoscere a fondo** (*persona*) to know through and through; (*argomento, materia*) to have a thorough knowledge of, know inside out; **conosco a fondo la materia** I know this subject inside out; **studiare a fondo qc** to study sth thoroughly *o* in depth; **andare in fondo a/fino in fondo** (*fig*) to examine thoroughly; **dar fondo a qc** (*risorse*) to use up, consume; **abbiamo dato fondo alle provviste** we've used up all the food; **senza fondo** (*risorse*) infinite, inexhaustible; (*pozzo*) bottomless; **in fondo** after all, all things considered; **in fondo in fondo** actually; **in fondo in fondo avevi ragione** in fact you were right; **toccare il fondo** (*fig*) to plumb the depths

    ❏ **fondo** non si traduce mai con la parola inglese *fond*

fondo² [ˈfondo] SM 1 (*riserva*) fund; **a fondo perduto** unsecured, without security; **fondo (comune) d'investimento** investment trust; **fondo (di) cassa** cash in hand; (*per piccole spese*) petty cash; **Fondo Monetario Europeo** European Monetary Fund; **Fondo Monetario Internazionale** International Monetary Fund; **fondo pensione** pension fund; **fondo di previdenza** social insurance fund; **fondo di riserva** reserve fund 2 **fondi** SMPL (*capitale*): **fondi pubblici/segreti** public/secret funds; **fondi d'esercizio** working capital *sg* 3 (*bene immobile*) land, property, estate; **fondo rustico** country estate; **fondo urbano** town property

fondotinta [fondoˈtinta] SM INV (*cosmetico*) foundation

fonema [foˈnɛma] SM phoneme

fonetica [foˈnɛtika] SF phonetics *sg*

fonetico, -a, -ci, -che [foˈnɛtiko] AGG phonetic

fontana [fonˈtana] SF fountain; **piangere come una fontana** to weep (great) buckets of tears; **fare la fontana** (*Culin*) to make a well

fontanella [fontaˈnɛlla] SF 1 (*fontana*) drinking fountain 2 (*Anat*) fontanelle

fonte [ˈfonte] SF (*sorgente*) spring; (*fig: di calore, informazioni*) source; **risalire alle fonti** to go back to the origins *o* roots; **una fonte di informazioni** a source of information ♦ SM: **fonte battesimale** (*Rel*) font

fontina [fonˈtina] SF *full fat, hard, sweet cheese from Valle d'Aosta*

footing [ˈfutiŋ] SM jogging; **fare footing** to jog

foraggiare [foradˈdʒare] /62/ VT (*cavalli*) to fodder; (*fig: fam: sovvenzionare*) to bankroll; (: *illegalmente*) to bribe

foraggio, -gi [foˈraddʒo] SM fodder, forage

forare [fo'rare] /72/ VT (gen) to make a hole in, pierce; (biglietto) to punch; (pneumatico) to puncture; (pallone) to burst; **forare una gomma** to burst a tyre (Brit) o tire (USA) ♦ VI (aus avere) (Aut) to have a puncture; **abbiamo forato** we've got a puncture; **forarsi** VIP (gen) to develop a hole; (Aut: pallone, timpano) to burst

foratura [fora'tura] SF (vedi vb) piercing; punching; puncturing, puncture; bursting

forbice ['fɔrbitʃe] SF, SPEC PL scissors pl; (Statistica) range; **un paio di forbici** a pair of scissors; **dare un colpo di forbici a qc** to snip sth; **forbici da giardiniere** (gardening) shears; **forbici per potare** secateurs

forbicina [forbi'tʃina] SF (Zool) earwig

forbito, -a [for'bito] AGG (stile, modi) polished; **parla una lingua forbita** he has an elegant turn of phrase

forca ['forka] SF 1 (Agr) (pitch)fork 2 (per impiccagione) gallows sg o pl

forcella [for'tʃella] SF (gen, anche Tecn) fork; (per capelli) hairpin; (di volatile) wishbone; (di monte) pass

forchetta [for'ketta] SF fork; (Statistica) range; **essere una buona forchetta** to enjoy one's food, be a big eater

forcina [for'tʃina] SF hairpin

forcipe ['fɔrtʃipe] SM forceps pl

forcone [for'kone] SM pitchfork

forense [fo'rense] AGG (linguaggio) legal; **avvocato forense** barrister (Brit), lawyer

foresta [fo'resta] SF (anche fig) forest; **foresta pluviale** rain forest

forestale [fores'tale] AGG forest attr; **guardia forestale** forester, (forest) ranger

foresteria [foreste'ria] SF (di convento, palazzo) guest rooms pl, guest quarters pl

forestiero, -a [fores'tjero] SM, SF stranger; (dall'estero) foreigner ♦ AGG foreign

forfait [for'fε] SM INV 1 (prezzo a) forfait fixed o set price; **le diamo un forfait per il suo lavoro** we'll give you a lump sum for your work; **a forfait** on a lump-sum basis 2 **dichiarare forfait** (Sport) to withdraw; (fig) to give up

forfetario, -ria, -ri, -rie [forfe'tarjo], **forfettario, -ria, -ri, -rie** [forfet'tarjo] AGG: **prezzo forfetario** fixed o set price; **somma forfetaria** lump sum

forfora ['forfora] SF dandruff

'forgia, -ge, forge ['fɔrdʒa] SF forge

forgiare [for'dʒare] /62/ VT to forge; (fig: carattere) to mould, form

forma ['forma] SF 1 (gen, anche Gramm, Filosofia) form; (contorno) form, shape; **di forma quadrata** square; **a forma di cuore** heart-shaped; **di che forma è?** what shape is it?; **senza forma** (oggetto) shapeless; (pensiero) unformed; **prendere forma** (delinearsi) to take shape; **prendere una medicina in o sotto forma di compresse** to take a medicine in tablet form; **una forma rara di cancro** a rare form of cancer; **in forma ufficiale/privata** officially/privately; **forma mentale** o **mentis** way of thinking; **non c'è alcuna forma di vita sulla luna** there is no form of life on the moon; **forma attiva/passiva** (Gramm) active/passive voice 2 (stampo) mould (Brit), mold (USA); (per scarpe) last; **una forma di formaggio** a (whole) cheese 3 (modo di esprimersi) form; **errori di forma** stylistic errors 4 (anche: forma fisica) form; **essere/non essere in forma** (atleta, squadra) to be on/off form; (persona) to be in/out of shape; **in ottima forma e ha segnato tre gol** he was in great form and scored three goals; **la squadra non era in forma** the team was off form; **tenersi in forma** to keep fit o in shape; **mi tengo in forma nuotando tutti i giorni** I keep fit by swimming every day 5 (apparenze) appearances pl; **tenere alla forma** to care about appearances 6 **forme** SFPL (del corpo) figure, shape

formaggino [formad'dʒino] SM processed cheese; **un formaggino** a portion of processed cheese

formaggio, -gi [for'maddʒo] SM cheese; **un panino con il formaggio** a cheese sandwich

formale [for'male] AGG formal

formalità [formali'ta] SF INV formality; **senza tante formalità** (pasto) informal

formalizzare [formalid'dzare] /72/ VT to formalize; **forma-lizzarsi** VIP (farsi scrupoli sulla forma) to stand on ceremony; (scandalizzarsi) to be easily shocked

formare [for'mare] /72/ VT 1 (gen) to form, shape, make; (numero telefonico) to dial; **questi pezzi formano una croce** these pieces make o form a cross; **l'appartamento è formato da 3 stanze** the apartment comprises 3 rooms; **abbiamo formato un gruppo** we formed a group; **sollevate il ricevitore prima di formare il numero** lift the receiver before dialling the number; **formare una famiglia** to start a family 2 (educare: soldati, attori) to train; (carattere) to form, mould (Brit), mold (USA); **formarsi** VIP 1 to form, take shape; **il treno si forma a Milano** the train starts from Milan; **si è formata la fila allo sportello** a queue formed at the counter 2 (educarsi) to be educated; **Leopardi si formò sui classici greci** Leopardi had a classical Greek background

formato, -a [for'mato] AGG (maturo) fully-developed, fully-grown ♦ SM (dimensioni) size, format; (Inform) format; **foto formato tessera** passport-size photo; **formato famiglia** family size; **formato A4** A4 size; **una confezione formato gigante** a giant-size pack

formattare [format'tare] /72/ VT (Inform) to format

formattazione [formattat'tsjone] SF (Inform) formatting

formazione [format'tsjone] SF 1 (gen, anche Mil, Sport) formation; **la formazione del nuovo governo** the formation of the new government 2 (educazione) education; (addestramento) training; **formazione continua** continuing education; **formazione permanente** lifelong learning; **formazione professionale** vocational training; **un corso di formazione professionale** a vocational training course

formica, -che [for'mika] SF (Zool) ant

formicaio, -ai [formi'kajo] SM (sporgente) anthill; (sotterraneo) ants' nest; **quella spiaggia è un formicaio** (fig) that beach is always swarming with people

formicolare [formiko'lare] /72/ VI 1 (aus avere) (anche fig: brulicare): **formicolare di** to swarm with, be crawling o swarming with 2 (aus essere) **mi formicola un braccio** I've got pins and needles in my arm

formicolio, -lii [formiko'lio] SM (brulichio) swarming; (prurito) tingling; **avere un formicolio alla gamba** to have pins and needles in one's leg; **sento un formicolio al braccio** I've got pins and needles in my arm

formidabile [formi'dabile] AGG (temibile) formidable; (meraviglioso) amazing, tremendous, fantastic; (straordinario) remarkable; **ho una fame formidabile** I'm incredibly hungry

formoso, -a [for'moso] AGG shapely

formula ['formula] SF (gen, anche Chim, Mat) formula; **formula di struttura** (Chim) structural formula; **formula di cortesia** (nelle lettere) set phrase; **formula pubblicitaria** advertising slogan; **formula 1** (Sport) formula 1

formulare [formu'lare] /72/ VT (giudizio, pensiero) to formulate

fornace [for'natʃe] SF (Tecn) kiln

fornaio, -ai [for'najo] SM baker; **dal fornaio** at the baker's

fornello [for'nello] SM (cuocivivande: a spirito, petrolio) stove; (: elettrico) hotplate; (: a gas) ring; **fornello a gas** (di cucina) gas ring; (da campeggio) camping stove; **fornello elettrico** hotplate 2 (di pipa) bowl

fornire [for'nire] /55/ VT 1 (Comm): **fornire qc a qn** to supply sth to sb, supply sb with sth 2 (procurare: abiti, viveri): **fornire qc a qn, fornire qn di qc** to supply o provide sb with sth; **ci forniscono le materie prime** they supply us with raw materials; **fornire qn di informazioni** to supply o provide sb with information, supply o provide information to sb; **ci ha fornito tutte le informazioni necessarie** he gave us all the necessary information; **fornirsi** VR: **fornirsi (di procurarsi)** to provide o.s. with; **mi fornisco di pane da quel fornaio** I get my bread from that baker; **dobbiamo fornirci di legna per l'inverno** we'll have to stock up with wood for the winter

fornito, -a [for'nito] AGG: **ben fornito** (negozio) well-stocked

fornitore, -trice [forni'tore] AGG: **ditta fornitrice di...** company supplying ... ♦ SM supplier ♦ SM: **fornitore di accesso/servizi** (Inform) access/service provider

fornitura [forni'tura] SF supply; **forniture per ufficio** office supplies; **negozio** o **società di forniture navali** ship's chandler

❑ **fornitura** non si traduce mai con la parola inglese *furniture*

forno ['forno] SM (*gen*) oven; (*panetteria*) bakery; (*Industria*) furnace; (*per ceramica*) kiln; **cuocere al forno** (*dolci, patate*) to bake; (*carne, patate*) to roast; **pasta al forno** oven-baked pasta; **pollo al forno** roast chicken; **metti la torta nel forno** put the cake in the oven; **fare i forni** (*Med*) to have heat treatment; **questa stanza è un forno!** this room's like an oven!; **forno crematorio** cremator, cinerator (*USA*); **forno a microonde** microwave (oven)

foro¹ ['foro] SM (*buco*) hole

foro² ['foro] SM 1 (*Storia*) forum 2 (*Dir: tribunale*) (law) court; (: *autorità competente*): **del caso si occuperà il foro di Milano** the case will be dealt with by the Milan judiciary; **gli avvocati del foro** ≈ the Bar

forse ['forse] AVV 1 perhaps, maybe; **forse verrà più tardi** he may *o* might come later; **forse hai ragione** maybe you're right; **forse dovremmo andarcene** maybe we should leave; **verrà?** —**forse** will he come?—maybe 2 (*circa*) about; **ti devo forse 10 euro** I must owe you about 10 euros; **mancheranno forse 500 euro** we're about 500 euros short; **sei forse tu il mio padrone?** so you think you own me, do you? ♦ SM: **essere in forse** (*persona*) to be undecided; (*evento*) to be in doubt; **mettere in forse la propria vita** to put one's life in danger

forsennato, -a [forsen'nato] SM, SF madman *o* madwoman, lunatic ♦ AGG mad, crazy, insane

forte¹ ['forte] AGG 1 (*gen, anche fig*) strong; (*luce, tinta*) strong, bright; (*nevicata, pioggia*) heavy; (*voce, musica*) loud; (*ceffone, colpo*) hard; (*somma, aumento*) large, big; (*spesa*) considerable; **un vento forte** a strong wind; **è più forte di me** he's stronger than me; **ho un forte mal di testa/raffreddore** I have a bad headache/heavy cold; **questo curry è un po' forte** this curry is rather hot; **un forte fumatore** a heavy smoker; **un forte colpo in testa** a hard knock on the head; **un rumore forte** a loud noise; **taglie forti** (*Abbigliamento*) outsize; **usare le maniere forti** to use strong-arm methods *o* tactics; **piatto forte** (*Culin*) main dish; **pezzo forte** pièce de résistance; **dare man forte a qn** to back sb up, support sb; **essere forte in qc** to be good at sth; **è forte in matematica** he is good at math(s); **farsi forte di qc** to make use of sth, avail o.s. of sth; **non voglio piangere ma è più forte di me** I don't want to cry but I can't help it 2 (*fam: bello, bravo*) amazing, great; **che forte!** (*fam*) amazing!, fantastic!; **è proprio forte!** he's really good! ♦ AVV (*velocemente*) fast; (*a volume alto*) loud(ly); (*violentemente*) hard; **tenersi forte** to hold tight; **tieniti forte!** hold tight!; **giocare forte** to play for high stakes; **andare forte** (*fam: essere bravo*) to be amazing, be fantastic; (: *aver successo*) to be all the rage; **correva forte** he was running fast; **ha picchiato forte la testa** she hit her head hard; **non parlare così forte** don't speak so loud; **potresti parlare più forte?** could you speak louder? ♦ SM (*persona*): **il forte e il debole** the strong and the weak; (*punto forte*) strong point, forte

forte² ['forte] SM (*fortezza*) fort

fortezza [for'tettsa] SF (*luogo fortificato*) fortress; (*morale*) strength

fortificare [fortifi'kare] /20/ VT to strengthen, fortify

fortuito, -a [for'tuito] AGG chance, fortuitous, chance *attr*; **per un caso fortuito** by pure chance

fortuna [for'tuna] SF 1 (*destino*) fortune, destiny; (*favorevole*) luck; **predire la fortuna a qn** to tell sb's future; **la ruota della fortuna** the wheel of fortune; **è girata la fortuna** my (*o* your *ecc*) luck's changed; **tentare la fortuna** to try one's luck; **portare fortuna** to bring luck; **mi ha sempre portato fortuna** it's always brought me good luck; **colpo di fortuna** stroke of luck; **per fortuna** luckily, fortunately; **(per) fortuna che sei passato, è una fortuna che tu sia passato** it's lucky that you were passing; **per fortuna sei arrivato in tempo** luckily, you arrived in time; **aver fortuna** to be lucky; **avere la fortuna di fare qc** to be lucky enough to do sth; **è tutta fortuna la sua** he's just lucky; **che fortuna!** what luck!; **buona fortuna!** good luck! 2 (*successo, ricchezza*) fortune; **costa una fortuna** it costs a fortune; **fare fortuna** (*persona*) to make one's fortune; (*libro, film ecc*) to be successful; **cercare fortuna** to seek one's fortune 3 **di fortuna** (*riparazione*) makeshift, emergency *attr*; **atterraggio di fortuna** emergency landing; **albero/timone di fortuna** (*Naut*) jury mast

fortunale [fortu'nale] SM storm

fortunatamente [fortunata'mente] AVV luckily, fortunately

fortunato, -a [fortu'nato] AGG lucky, fortunate; (*felice*) happy; (*coronato da successo*) successful; **sei più fortunato di me** you're luckier than me; **è la persona più fortunata che conosca** she's the luckiest person I know; **numero fortunato** lucky number

fortunoso, -a [fortu'noso] AGG (*vita*) eventful; (*avvenimenti, vicende*) unlucky

foruncolo [fo'runkolo] SM boil

forviare [forvi'are] /19/ VI (*aus avere*) to go astray ♦ VT (*inseguitori, polizia*) to mislead; (*sospetti*) to allay; (*giovani: traviare*) to lead astray

forza ['fortsa] SF 1 (*vigore*) strength; **è per misurare la forza dei muscoli** it's to test the strength of the muscles; **perdere/riacquistare le forze** to lose/regain one's strength; **avere forza nelle braccia** to be strong in the arm; **ha riacquistato presto le forze** he quickly regained his strength; **ha molta forza** he's very strong; **senza forza** *o* **forze** weak; **bella forza!** (*iro*) how clever of you (*o* him *ecc*)!; **farsi forza** (*coraggio*) to pluck up one's courage; **fatti forza!** chin up!, come on!; **forza!** come on!; **con la forza della disperazione** with the strength born of desperation; **l'unione fa la forza** unity is strength; **forza d'animo** strength of mind; **forza di volontà** willpower 2 (*di vento, tempesta*) force; **vento forza 4** force 4 gale; **la forza del vento** the strength of the wind; **la forza dell'esplosione** the force of the explosion 3 (*violenza*) force; **ricorrere alla/adoperare la forza** to resort to/use violence; **a viva forza** by force; **forza bruta** brute force 4 (*Mil*): **le forze armate** the armed forces; **la forza pubblica** the police *pl*; **forza di pace** peacekeeping force 5 (*Dir*): **in forza in** force; **avere forza di legge** to have force of law 6 (*Fis, Tecn*) force; **forza di gravità** force of gravity; **forza motrice** motive power 7 **a forza, con la forza** by force; **mi ha costretto con la forza** he forced me to do it; **a forza di rimproveri/di lavorare** by dint of scolding/working; **perderai la voce a forza di gridare** you'll lose your voice if you shout so much; **con forza** (*violentemente*) violently; (*fermamente*) firmly; **per forza** (*ovviamente*) of course; (*contro la sua volontà*) against one's will; **lo devi fare per forza?** have you got to do it?; **l'ha fatto per forza** he had no choice but to do it, he was forced to do it; **per causa di forza maggiore** (*Dir*) by reason of force majeure; (*per estensione*) due to circumstances beyond one's control; **per forza di cose** through force of circumstances 8 **forza lavoro** (*Econ*) workforce 9 **Forza Italia** (*Pol*) centre-right party

forzare [for'tsare] /72/ VT 1 (*costringere*): **forzare qn (a fare qc)** to force sb (to do sth), compel sb (to do sth); **hanno forzato la mia volontà** they forced me to do it 2 (*cassaforte, porta*) to force (open); (*serratura*) to force; **la serratura è stata forzata** the lock has been forced 3 (*sforzare: voce*) to strain; **forzare l'andatura** to force the pace; **forzare il significato** (*di parola, testo*) to stretch the meaning; **non voglio forzare la situazione** I don't want to push things

forzato, -a [for'tsato] AGG forced; (*situazione*) artificial; **la mia è stata un'assenza forzata** my absence was due to circumstances beyond my control; **fare un sorriso forzato** to force a smile ♦ SM prisoner sentenced to hard labour (*Brit*) *o* labor (*USA*)

forziere [for'tsjere] SM strongbox; (*di pirati*) treasure chest

forzista, -i, -e [for'tsista] (*Pol*) AGG relating to supporters of the political party Forza Italia ♦ SM, SF member (*o* supporter) of Forza Italia

forzuto, -a [for'tsuto] AGG (*scherz*) big and strong

foschia [fos'kia] SF haze, mist; **oggi c'è molta foschia** it's very hazy *o* misty today

fosco, -a, -schi, -sche ['fosko] AGG (*colore*) dark; (*cielo*) dull, overcast; (*fig: futuro, pensiero*) dark, gloomy; **dipingere qc a tinte fosche** (*fig*) to paint a gloomy picture of sth

fosfato [fos'fato] SM (*Chim*) phosphate; **fosfato di sodio** sodium phosphate

fosforescente [fosfore∫'∫ente] AGG phosphorescent; (*insegna, lancetta dell'orologio*) luminous

fosforo ['fɔsforo] SM (*Chim*) phosphorus

fossa ['fɔssa] SF 1 pit, hole; (*Geol, Mil*) trench; **fossa biologica** cesspool, cesspit; **fossa tettonica** (*Geol*) rift valley 2 (*tomba*) grave; **essere con un piede nella fossa** to have one foot in the grave; **fossa comune** mass grave 3 (*Anat*) fossa

fossato [fos'sato] SM ditch; (*di castello*) moat

fossetta [fos'setta] SF dimple

fossi ecc ['fɔssi] VB *vedi* **essere**

fossile ['fɔssile] AGG, SM (*anche fig*) fossil *attr*

fosso ['fɔsso] SM ditch; (*di castello*) moat; **saltare il fosso** (*fig*) to take the plunge

foste ['foste] VB *vedi* **essere**

foto ['fɔto] SF INV, ABBR (*anche*: **fotografia**) photo, snap; **fare una foto** to take a photo *o* a snap; **ha fatto molte foto** he took a lot of photos; **una foto in bianco e nero** a black and white photo; **foto ricordo** souvenir photo; **foto tessera** passport (-type) photo

foto- ['fɔto] PREF photo-

fotocamera [foto'kamera] SF: **fotocamera digitale** digital camera; **telefonino con fotocamera integrata** camera phone

fotocompositore [fotokompozi'tore] SM filmsetter, photocomposer (*USA*)

fotocomposizione [fotokomposit'tsjone] SF filmsetting, (photo)typesetting, photocomposition (*USA*)

fotocopia [foto'kɔpja] SF photocopy

fotocopiare [fotoko'pjare] /19/ VT to photocopy

fotocopiatrice [fotokopja'tritʃe] SF photocopier, photocopying machine

fotocopisteria [fotokopiste'ria] SF photocopy shop

fotofo'nino SM camera phone

fotogenico, -a, -ci, -che [foto'dʒeniko] AGG photogenic

fotografare [fotogra'fare] /72/ VT to photograph

fotografia [fotogra'fia] SF (*arte*: *procedimento*) photography; (*immagine*) photograph; **un corso di fotografia** a photography course; **fotografia a colori/in bianco e nero** colour/black and white photograph; **fare una fotografia** to take a photograph; **farsi fare una fotografia** to have one's photograph taken

fotografico, -a, -ci, -che [foto'grafiko] AGG photographic; **macchina fotografica** camera; **servizio** *o* **reportage fotografico** photo feature; **studio fotografico** photographer's studio

fotografo, -a [fo'tɔgrafo] SM, SF photographer

fotogramma, -i [foto'gramma] SM (*Cine*) frame

fotomodello, -a [fotomo'dɛllo] SM, SF fashion *o* photographic model

fotomontaggio, -gi [fotomon'taddʒo] SM photomontage

fotoreporter [fotore'pɔrter] SM INV, SF INV newspaper (*o* magazine) photographer

fotoromanzo [fotoro'mandzo] SM photo love story

fotosintesi [foto'sintezi] SF (*Bot*) photosynthesis

fotovol'taico, -a, fotovoltaica, -ci, fotovoltaici, -che AGG photovoltaic; **pannelli fotovoltaici** solar panels

fottere ['fottere] /1/ VT (*fam!*) 1 (*avere rapporti sessuali*) to fuck (*fam!*), screw (*fam!*); **vai a farti fottere!** fuck off! (*fam!*) 2 (*rubare*) to pinch, swipe 3 (*fregare*): **mi hanno fottuto** they played a dirty trick on me, I've been screwed (*fam*)

fottuto, -a [fot'tuto] AGG (*fam!*) bloody, fucking (*attr: fam!*)

foulard [fu'lar] SM INV (head)scarf

FR SIGLA = Frosinone

fra¹ [fra] PREP = **tra**

fra² [fra] SM (*dav a nomi propri*) = **frate**

fracassare [frakas'sare] /72/ VT to smash, shatter; **fracassarsi** VIP to smash, break, shatter; (*veicolo*) to crash; (*fare a piccoli pezzi*) to smash to smithereens, shatter

fracasso [fra'kasso] SM (*baccano, confusione*) din; (*di piatti*) crash; **fare fracasso** to make a din

fradicio, -cia, -ci, -ce ['fraditʃo] AGG soaked, soaking (wet), drenched; **bagnato fradicio** soaking wet; **ubriaco fradicio** blind drunk; **ho la camicia fradicia** my shirt is soaked

fragile ['fradʒile] AGG (*gen, anche fig*) fragile; (*salute, nervi*) delicate; (*vetro*) brittle; **"fragile"** (*sui pacchi*) "fragile, (handle) with care"

fragilità [fradʒili'ta] SF INV (*vedi agg*) fragility; delicacy; brittleness

fragola ['fragola] SF strawberry

fragore [fra'gore] SM (*di cascate, carro armato*) roar; (*di tuono*) rumble

fragoroso, -a [frago'roso] AGG deafening, ear-splitting; **un fragoroso ceffone** a resounding slap; **una risata fragorosa** an uproarious burst of laughter; **scoppiare in una risata fragorosa** to roar with laughter

fragrante [fra'grante] AGG fragrant

fraintendere [frain'tendere] /120/ VT IRREG to misunderstand; **mi hai frainteso** you misunderstood me

fraintendimento [fraintendi'mento] SM misunderstanding

frainteso, -a [frain'teso] PP *di* **fraintendere**

frammento [fram'mento] SM (*di roccia*) fragment, bit; (*di testo*) passage, extract

frammisto, -a [fram'misto] AGG: **frammisto a** interspersed with, mixed with

frana ['frana] SF landslip, landslide; (*fig: persona*): **essere una frana in** to be useless *o* hopeless *o* rubbish at

franare [fra'nare] /72/ VI (*aus* **essere**) (*Geol*) to slip, slide down; (*roccia*) to fall; (*fig: resistenza*) to collapse

francamente [franka'mente] AVV frankly

francese [fran'tʃeze] AGG French ♦ SM, SF Frenchman *o* Frenchwoman; **i francesi** the French ♦ SM (*lingua*) French; **parli francese?** do you speak French?

franchezza [fran'kettsa] SF frankness, openness

franchigia, -gie [fran'kidʒa] SF 1 (*Amm*) exemption; **franchigia doganale** exemption from customs duty; **bagaglio in franchigia** (*Aer*) free baggage allowance 2 **franchigia assicurativa** insurance excess franchise 3 (*Naut*) shore leave

Francia ['frantʃa] SF France; **ti piace la Francia?** do you like France?; **andrò in Francia quest'estate** I'm going to France this summer

franco¹, -a, -chi, -che ['franko] AGG 1 (*persona, sguardo: sincero*) frank, candid, open, sincere; **rispondere in modo franco** to answer frankly 2 (*Comm*): **porto franco** free port; **franco bordo** free on board; **franco di dazio** *o* **dogana** duty-free; **franco fabbrica** ex factory, ex works; **prezzo franco fabbrica** ex-works price; **franco magazzino** ex warehouse; **franco di porto** carriage free; **franco vagone** free on rail 3 (*Mil*) **franco tiratore** irregular (soldier); (*cecchino*) sniper; (*Pol*) member of parliament who votes against his own party 4 **farla franca** to get away with it, get off scot-free ♦ AVV (*francamente*) frankly

franco², -chi ['franko] SM (*moneta*) franc

francobollo [franko'bollo] SM (postage) stamp

franco-canadese [frankokana'dese] AGG, SM, SF French Canadian

Francoforte [franko'fɔrte] SF Frankfurt

frangente [fran'dʒente] SM 1 (*onda*) breaker 2 (*scoglio affiorante*) reef 3 (*circostanza*) situation, circumstance

frangia, -ge ['frandʒa] SF (*gen*) fringe; **frangia costiera** coastal strip; **le frange estremiste del partito** (*fig*) the extremist fringe of the party

frangiflutti [frandʒi'flutti] SM INV breakwater

frangivento [frandʒi'vento] SM INV windbreak

frantoio, -oi [fran'tojo] SM (*Agr*) olive-press; (*Tecn*) crusher

frantumare [frantu'mare] /72/ VT to break (up), break into pieces, shatter; **frantumarsi** VIP to break, shatter, break into pieces

frantume [fran'tume] SM: **andare in frantumi, mandare in frantumi** to shatter, smash to pieces *o* smithereens

frappé [frap'pe] SM INV (*Culin*) milk shake

frasario, -ri [fra'zarjo] SM (*gergo*) language

frasca, -sche ['fraska] SF bough, (leafy) branch; **saltare di palo in frasca** to jump from one subject to another

frase ['fraze] SF 1 (*proposizione*) sentence; **la frase che ha detto non mi è piaciuta** I didn't like what he said; **traduci questa frase** translate this sentence; **frase fatta** stock *o* set phrase 2 (*Mus*) phrase

fraseologia [frazeolo'dʒia] SF phraseology

frassino ['frassino] SM ash (tree)

frastagliato, -a [frastaʎ'ʎato] AGG (*costa*) indented, jagged

frastornare [frastor'nare] /72/ VT (*intontire*) to daze; (*confondere*) to befuddle, bewilder

frastornato, -a [frastor'nato] AGG deafened; (*vedi vt*) dazed; bewildered

frastuono [fras'twɔno] SM noise, din

frate ['frate] SM (*Rel*) brother, friar, monk; **farsi frate** to become a monk

fratellanza [fratel'lantsa] SF (*sentimento*) brotherliness; (*associazione*) brotherhood, fraternity

fratellastro [fratel'lastro] SM stepbrother; (*con genitore in comune*) half brother

fratello [fra'tello] SM 1 (*gen*) brother; **questo è mio fratello** this is my brother; **hai fratelli?** have you any brothers or sisters?; **siamo fratelli, disse la donna** we are brother and sister, said the woman; **fratello d'armi** brother in arms; **fratello gemello** twin (brother) 2 (*Rel*) brother; **i fratelli cristiani** the Christian brethren

fraterno, -a [fra'terno] AGG fraternal, brotherly

fratricida, -i, -e [fratri't∫ida] AGG fratricidal; **guerra fratricida** civil war ♦ SM, SF fratricide (*person*)

frattaglie [frat'taʎʎe] SFPL (*Culin: gen*) offal *sg*; (: *di pollo*) giblets

frattanto [frat'tanto] AVV meanwhile, in the meantime

frattempo [frat'tɛmpo] **nel frattempo** AVV in the meantime, meanwhile

frattura [frat'tura] SF (*Med, Geol*) fracture; (*fig: dissenso*) split, break; **una grave frattura** a serious fracture; **ha una frattura alla gamba** he's broken his leg

fratturare [frattu'rare] /72/ VT (*Med*) to fracture, break; **fratturarsi un braccio/una gamba** to break one's arm/one's leg; **fratturarsi** VIP (*Med*) to fracture, break; (*partito, gruppo*) to split

fraudolento, -a [fraudo'lento] AGG fraudulent

frazionamento [frattsjona'mento] SM division, splitting up

frazionare [frattsjo'nare] /72/ VT to divide, split up

frazione [frat'tsjone] SF 1 (*gen, anche Mat*) fraction; **una frazione di secondo** a fraction of a second 2 (*borgata*) ≈ hamlet

freccia, -ce ['frett∫a] SF 1 (*di arco*) arrow; **entrare/uscire come una freccia** o shoot in/out 2 (*Aut*) indicator; **mettere la freccia (a destra/sinistra)** to indicate that one is turning (right/left); **ha messo la freccia per voltare a destra** he indicated he was turning right 3 (*segnale stradale*) signpost

frecciata [fret't∫ata] SF: **lanciare una frecciata** to make a cutting remark

freddare [fred'dare] /72/ VT (*minestra*) to cool; (*fig: entusiasmo*) to put a damper on; (*uccidere*) to kill, shoot dead; **fai freddare la minestra** let the soup cool; **freddare qn con lo sguardo** to silence sb with an icy stare; **freddarsi** VIP to cool, become cold

freddezza [fred'dettsa] SF 1 (*indifferenza*) coldness, coolness; **accogliere qn/qc con freddezza** to greet sb/sth coolly 2 (*autocontrollo*) sang-froid; **la sua freddezza ha evitato il peggio** her cool-headedness prevented anything worse happening

freddo, -a ['freddo] AGG (*gen*) cold; (*accoglienza*) cool, cold; **la ministra è fredda** the soup is cold; **a mente fredda capì di avere torto** when he had cooled down he realized that he was wrong; **la macchina è ancora fredda** the engine is still cold ♦ SM 1 (*gen*) cold; **aver freddo** to be cold; **hai freddo?** are you cold?; **prendere freddo** to catch cold; **soffrire il freddo** to feel the cold; **sudare freddo** to be in a cold sweat; **fa freddo** it's cold; **c'è stata un'ondata di freddo** there's been a cold spell 2 **a freddo** (*lavare*) in cold water; (*fig*) deliberately; **a freddo ha poi negato di averlo detto** when he had cooled down, he denied having said it

freddoloso, -a [freddo'loso] AGG: **essere freddoloso** to feel o be sensitive to the cold

freddura [fred'dura] SF dry comment, pun

freezer ['frizə] SM INV fridge-freezer

fregare [fre'gare] /80/ VT 1 (*sfregare*) to rub; (*per pulire*) to polish; **fregarsi le mani/gli occhi** to rub one's hands/one's eyes; **si fregava le mani** he was rubbing his hands 2 (*fig: fam*): **fregare qn** (*imbrogliare*) to cheat sb, rip sb off, take sb in; **ha cercato di fregarmi** he tried to cheat me; **mi frega sempre a carte** (*vincere*) he always beats me at cards 3

(*rubare*): **fregare qc a qn** to steal o lift sth from sb; **mi ha fregato il ragazzo** she stole my boyfriend; **mi ha fregato il portafoglio** he lifted my wallet 4 (*fig: fam*): **fregarsene** (*di qc/qn*) (*infischiarsene*) not to give a damn (about sth/sb); **non gliene frega niente** he doesn't give a damn; **me ne frego** I don't give a damn; **che ti frega?** none of your business!; **chi se ne frega?** who cares?

fregata¹ [fre'gata] SF 1 (*vedi vb a*) rub; polish; **dare una fregata a qc** to rub sth, polish sth 2 (*fam*) = fregatura

fregata² [fre'gata] SF (*Naut*) frigate

fregatura [frega'tura] SF (*fam: imbroglio*) rip-off, con; **mi hanno tirato una fregatura** they ripped me off; **è stata una fregatura** (*delusione*) it's been a let-down

fregherò ecc [frege'rɔ] VB *vedi* fregare

fregio, -gi ['fredʒo] SM (*gen*) decoration, ornament; (*Archit*) frieze

fremere ['fremere] /29/ VI (*aus avere*) to shake, tremble; **fremere di** to tremble o quiver with; **fremere d'impazienza** to be champing at the bit

fremito ['fremito] SM shudder, shiver; (*di passione*) wave; **ebbe un fremito d'ira** he shook with anger

frenare [fre'nare] /72/ VT (*veicolo*) to slow down; (*progresso, avanzata*) to hold up; (*gioia, evoluzione*) to check; (*cavallo*) to rein in; **frenare la lingua** to hold one's tongue; **frenare le lacrime** to hold back one's tears; **misure per frenare l'inflazione** measures to curb inflation ♦ VI (*aus avere*) (*Aut*) to brake; (*Sci*) to slow down; **ha frenato per evitare un cane** he braked to avoid a dog; **frenarsi** VR to restrain o.s., stop o.s., control o.s.

frenata [fre'nata] SF braking; **fare una brusca frenata** to brake suddenly, hit the brakes; **ha fatto una brusca frenata** he braked suddenly

frenesia [frene'zia] SF frenzy; **con frenesia** frenziedly

frenetico, -a, -ci, -che [fre'netiko] AGG frenetic

freno ['freno] SM (*Aut*) brake; (*di cavallo*) bit; (*fig*) restraint; **bloccare i freni, azionare i freni** to apply the brakes; **freno a disco** disc brake; **freno a mano** handbrake, parking brake (*USA*); **tira il freno a mano** put the handbrake on 2 (*fraseologia*): **mettere o porre un freno a** (*inflazione, tendenza*) to put a brake on, keep in check; **tenere a freno** (*passioni*) to restrain; **tenere a freno la lingua** to hold one's tongue; **agire da freno** to act as a restraint

frequentare [frekwen'tare] /72/ VT (*scuola, corso*) to attend; (*persona*) to see (regularly o often); (*locale, casa, bar*) to go to, frequent; **frequentare cattive compagnie** to keep bad company; **frequento un corso di inglese** I go to English classes; **non li frequento più** I don't see them any more; **la frequento poco** I don't see much of her; **non mi piace la gente che frequenta** I don't like the people he mixes with; **è un locale mal frequentato** you get some shady types at that place o in that bar; **frequentarsi** (*uso reciproco*) to see each other (regularly); **si frequentano da anni** they have been seeing each other for years

frequentato, -a [frekwen'tato] AGG (*locale*) busy; **è la pizzeria più frequentata della città** it's the most popular pizzeria in town

frequente [fre'kwente] AGG frequent; **di frequente** frequently

frequenza [fre'kwentsa] SF (*gen, anche Fis, Radio, Elettr*) frequency; (*Scol*) attendance; **frequenza respiratoria** breathing rate; **con sempre maggiore frequenza** with increasing frequency

fresare [fre'zare] /72/ VT (*Tecn*) to mill

freschezza [fres'kettsa] SF (*gen*) freshness; (*di serata*) coolness

fresco, -a, -schi, -sche ['fresko] AGG (*gen*) fresh; (*temperatura, clima*) fresh, cool; (*vernice*) wet; (*traccia, notizia, ferita*) recent, new; **frutta fresca** fresh fruit; **"vernice fresca"** "wet paint"; **fresco e riposato** (*completamente*) refreshed; **fresca come una rosa** as fresh as a daisy; **bere qc di fresco** to have a cold drink; **fresco di bucato** freshly laundered, newly washed; **fresco di studi** (*fam*) fresh out of university o school; **se continui così stai fresco** (*fig*) if you go on like this you'll be in trouble ♦ SM (*temperatura*) cool; **è o fa fresco** it is cool; **mettere/tenere al fresco** (*fig: persona: in prigione*) to put/keep inside o in the cooler; **mettere in fresco** to put in the fridge; **metti il vino in fresco** put the wine in the fridge;

fatto di fresco newly done; **godersi il fresco** to enjoy the cool air

frescura [fres'kura] SF cool; **la frescura della sera** the cool of the evening

fresia ['frɛzja] SF freesia

fretta ['fretta] SF hurry, haste; **in fretta** in a hurry; **fallo in fretta** do it quickly; **fai in fretta!** hurry up!; **in tutta fretta** hurriedly, quickly; **in fretta e furia** in a great o tearing hurry, in a mad rush; **avere fretta (di fare qc)** to be in a hurry (to do sth); **scusa ma ho un po' di fretta** I'm sorry but I'm in a bit of a hurry; **aveva fretta di andarsene** he was in a hurry to leave; **fare qc in fretta** (velocemente) to do sth quickly, hurry up with sth; (troppo velocemente) to do sth in a hurry; **l'ho fatto un po' troppo in fretta** I did it in too much of a hurry; **far fretta a qn** to hurry sb; **non farmi fretta** don't hurry me; **che fretta c'è?** what's the hurry?

frettolosamente [frettolosa'mente] AVV hurriedly, in a rush; **salutò frettolosamente e se ne andò** he said a hurried goodbye and left

frettoloso, -a [fretto'loso] AGG (persona) in a hurry; (lavoro) hurried, rushed; **diede una scorsa frettolosa al libro** he flicked through the book; **è un po' troppo frettoloso in quello che fa** he tends to rush things

friabile [fri'abile] AGG (roccia: terreno) friable; (biscotto) crumbly

friggere ['friddʒere] VB IRREG /56/ VT to fry; **mandare qn a farsi friggere** to tell sb to get lost; **vai a farti friggere!** (fam) get lost! ♦ VI (aus avere) (grasso, olio) to sizzle; (fig): **friggere dalla rabbia** to seethe with rage; **friggere d'impazienza** to fume with impatience

frigidità [fridʒidi'ta] SF INV frigidity

frigido, -a ['fridʒido] AGG frigid

frignare [friɲ'ɲare] /15/ VI (aus avere) to whine, snivel

frignone, -a [friɲ'ɲone] SM, SF whiner, sniveller

frigo, -ghi ['frigo] SM fridge

frigobar [frigo'bar] SM INV minibar

frigorifero, -a [frigo'rifero] AGG refrigerated; **cella frigorifera** cold store ♦ SM refrigerator

fringuello [frin'gwello] SM chaffinch

frissi ecc ['frissi] VB vedi friggere

frittata [frit'tata] SF (Culin) omelette, omelet (USA); **la frittata è fatta!** (fig) that's torn it!, the damage is done

frittella [frit'tella] SF (Culin) fritter

fritto, -a ['fritto] PP di friggere ♦ AGG (patatine, pesce) fried; **pollo fritto** fried chicken; **patate fritte** chips (Brit), (French) fries (USA); **ormai siamo fritti!** (fig: fam) now we've had it!; **è un argomento fritto e rifritto** that's old hat ♦ SM fried food; **odore di fritto** smell of frying; **fritto misto** mixed fried fish

frittura [frit'tura] SF (cibo) fried food; **frittura di pesce** mixed fried fish

friulano, -a [friu'lano] AGG of o from Friuli, Friulian ♦ SM, SF inhabitant o native of Friuli

frivolezza [frivo'lettsa] SF frivolity

frivolo, -a ['frivolo] AGG frivolous

frizione [frit'tsjone] SF 1 (massaggio) rubbing, massage; **fare delle frizioni con una pomata** to rub in an ointment 2 (lozione) lotion 3 (tensione) friction 4 (Aut) clutch 5 (Fis) friction

frizzante [frid'dzante] AGG (gen) fizzy, sparkling; (vino) sparkling; (persona) effervescent, bubbly (fam); **acqua minerale frizzante** sparkling mineral water

frizzo ['friddzo] SM witticism

frodare [fro'dare] /72/ VT to defraud, cheat; **frodare il fisco** to evade tax

frode ['frode] SF (Dir) fraud; **frode fiscale** tax evasion

frodo ['frodo] SM: **di frodo** illegal, contraband; **pescatore/cacciatore di frodo** poacher; **pescare/cacciare di frodo** to poach

frogia, -gie o **, -ge** ['frodʒa] SF (di cavallo) nostril

frollo, -a ['frollo] AGG (Culin: carne) high; **pasta frolla** short(crust) pastry; (fig: persona) soft

fronda¹ ['fronda] SF (Bot) leafy branch; (spec al pl) foliage sg

fronda² ['fronda] SF (fig, o Pol) rebellion, internal opposition

frontale [fron'tale] AGG (Anat, Mil) frontal; **scontro frontale** (Aut) head-on collision; **lezione frontale** traditional lesson with the teacher teaching the whole class; **insegnamento frontale** whole class teaching

fronte ['fronte] SF 1 (Anat) brow, forehead; **a fronte alta** (anche fig) with one's head held high; **col sudore della fronte** by the sweat of one's brow; **gli ha dato un bacio in fronte** she gave him a kiss on the forehead 2 **di fronte** (dirimpetto) opposite; **l'edificio di fronte** the building opposite; **abita qui di fronte** he lives in the house opposite; **di fronte a** opposite, facing, in front of; (a paragone di) compared with; **si è seduto di fronte a me** he sat down opposite me; **la casa di fronte alla mia** the house opposite mine; **testo a fronte** parallel text; **vista di fronte la casa è più bella** seen from the front the house looks much more attractive ♦ SM (Mil, Pol, Meteor) front; **partì per il fronte a diciotto anni** he left for the front when he was eighteen; **far fronte a** (nemico, problema) to confront; (responsabilità) to face up to; (spese) to meet

fronteggiare [fronted'dʒare] /62/ VT (affrontare: nemico, problema, avversità) to face, confront, stand up to; (sostenere: spese) to meet

frontespizio, -zi [frontes'pittsjo] SM (di libro) title page

frontiera [fron'tjɛra] SF frontier, border; (fig) frontier; **zona di frontiera** frontier o border area; **guardia di frontiera** border guard; **polizia di frontiera** border police

frontone [fron'tone] SM pediment

fronzolo ['frondzolo] SM frill; **senza fronzoli** (fig) without (any) frills, plainly

frotta ['frotta] SF crowd; **in frotta, a frotte** in their hundreds, in droves

frottola ['frottola] SF (fam: bugia) lie, fib; **raccontare un sacco di frottole** to tell a pack of lies; **questa è una frottola** that's a lie

frugale [fru'gale] AGG frugal

frugare [fru'gare] /80/ VT to search; **frugarsi le tasche** to search through one's pockets; **ho frugato nelle tasche** I searched my pockets ♦ VI (aus avere) **frugare in** to search, rummage around in

frugherò ecc [fruge'rɔ] VB vedi frugare

fruitore, -trice [frui'tore] SM user

fruizione [fruit'tsjone] SF use

frullare [frul'lare] /72/ VT (gen) to blend; (frutta) to blend, liquidize; (uova) to whisk ♦ VI (aus avere) (uccelli) to flutter, whirr; **cosa ti frulla in mente?** (fig) what is going on in that mind of yours?

frullato [frul'lato] SM (Culin) milk shake (made with fresh fruit, cocoa etc)

frullatore [frulla'tore] SM blender, liquidizer; **frullatore a immersione** hand-held liquidizer

frullino [frul'lino] SM whisk

frumento [fru'mento] SM grain, wheat

frusciare [fruʃ'ʃare] /14/ VI (aus avere) to rustle

fruscio, -scii [fruʃ'ʃio] SM rustling, rustle

frusta ['frusta] SF 1 (per cavalli) whip; **colpo di frusta** whiplash 2 (Culin) whisk

frustare [frus'tare] /72/ VT to whip

frustata [frus'tata] SF lash

frustino [frus'tino] SM riding crop

frustrare [frus'trare] /72/ VT to frustrate

frustrato, -a [frus'trato] AGG frustrated ♦ SM, SF frustrated person

frustrazione [frustrat'tsjone] SF frustration

frutta ['frutta] SF fruit; (portata) dessert; **frutta fresca** fresh fruit; **vuoi della frutta?** would you like some fruit?; **mi piace molto la frutta** I love fruit; **torta alla frutta** fruit gateau; **gelato alla frutta** fruit-flavoured ice cream; **essere alla frutta** to be finished o done; **frutta candita** candied fruit; **frutta sciroppata** fruit in heavy syrup; **frutta secca** (fichi ecc) dried fruit; (noci, mandorle ecc) nuts

fruttare [frut'tare] /72/ VT: **il mio deposito in banca (mi) frutta il 5%** I get 5% interest on my bank deposits; **quella gara gli fruttò la medaglia d'oro** he won the gold medal in that competition ♦ VI (aus avere) (investimenti, deposito) to bear dividends, give a return; **questo investimento ha fruttato poco** this investment did not give much of a return o gave a poor yield

frutteto [frut'teto] SM orchard

frutticoltura [frutikol'tura] SF fruit growing

fruttifero, -a [frut'tifero] AGG 1 (*albero*) fruit-bearing 2 (*fig: che frutta*) fruitful, profitable; **deposito fruttifero** interest-bearing deposit

fruttivendolo, -a [frutti'vendolo] SM, SF fruiterer, greengrocer (*Brit*), produce dealer (*USA*); **dal fruttivendolo** at the fruit shop o greengrocer's o fruiterer's

frutto ['frutto] SM (*anche fig*) fruit; **un frutto tropicale** a tropical fruit; **dare frutti** (*anche fig*) to bear fruit; **raccogliere i frutti di qc** (*fig*) to reap the rewards of sth; **essere frutto di** (*fig*) to be the fruit of; **è frutto della tua immaginazione** it's a figment of your imagination; **il frutto del mio lavoro** (*fig*) the fruits of my labour; **senza alcun frutto** (*fig*) fruitlessly, in vain; **frutti di bosco** berries; **frutti di mare** shellfish sg o pl, seafood sg

fruttuoso, -a [fruttu'oso] AGG fruitful, profitable

FS ['effe'esse] SIGLA F (= *Ferrovie dello Stato*) Italian railways

f.t. ABBR = **fuori testo**

f.to ABBR (= *firmato*) signed

fu [fu] (*3a pers sg del passato remoto di* **essere**) ♦ AGG INV (*defunto*): **il fu Mario Rossi** the late Mario Rossi

fucilare [futʃi'lare] /72/ VT to shoot o execute (by firing squad)

fucilata [futʃi'lata] SF (*rifle*) shot; **fu ucciso da una fucilata alla schiena** it was a bullet in the back which killed him

fucilazione [futʃilat'tsjone] SF execution (by firing squad)

fucile [fu'tʃile] SM rifle, gun; **fucile da caccia** shotgun; **fucile a canne mozze** sawn-off shotgun; **fucile subacqueo** (underwater) spear gun

fucina [fu'tʃina] SF (*Tecn*) forge; (*fig: di ingegni*) breeding ground

fuco, -chi ['fuko] SM (*ape*) drone

fucsia ['fuksja] SF (*Bot*) fuchsia ♦ SM, AGG (*colore*) fuchsia

fuga, -ghe ['fuga] SF 1 escape; (*letter*) flight; **mettere qn in fuga** to put sb to flight; **tentare la fuga** to try to escape 2 (*perdita: di gas, notizie*) leak; **fuga di capitali** flight of capital; **fuga di cervelli** brain drain 3 (*Mus*) fugue 4 (*Sport*) breakaway

fugace [fu'gatʃe] AGG fleeting, transient

fugare [fu'gare] /80/ VT (*dubbi, incertezze*) to dispel, drive out

fuggevole [fud'dʒevole] AGG fleeting

fuggiasco, -a, -schi, -sche [fud'dʒasko] AGG runaway attr ♦ SM, SF fugitive; (*Mil*) deserter

fuggifuggi [fuddʒi'fuddʒi] SM INV stampede

fuggire [fud'dʒire] /31/ VT (*anche fig*) to avoid, shun ♦ VI (*aus* essere) (*ladro*) to run away, flee (*frm*); (*prigioniero*) to escape; (*fig: vita*) to fly o slip by; **è fuggito di prigione** he escaped from jail; **è fuggita di casa** she ran away from home; **il tempo fugge** time flies

fuggitivo, -a [fuddʒi'tivo] AGG 1 (*in fuga*) fleeing, escaping 2 (*fugace*) fleeting ♦ SM, SF fugitive; (*Mil*) deserter

fui ecc ['fui] VB *vedi* **essere**

fulcro ['fulkro] SM (*Tecn*) fulcrum; (*fig: di discussione, teoria*) central o key point

fulgore [ful'gore] SM brilliance; (*fig*) splendour (*Brit*), splendor (*USA*)

fuliggine [fu'liddʒine] SF soot

fulminare [fulmi'nare] /72/ VB IMPERS: **fulmina** there is lightning ♦ VT 1 **essere fulminato** (*da fulmine*) to be struck (by lightning); (*da elettricità*) to be electrocuted 2 (*fig: uccidere*) to shoot dead; **mi fulminò con uno sguardo** he looked daggers at me; **fulminarsi** VIP (*lampadina*) to go, blow

fulmine ['fulmine] SM bolt of lightning; **fulmini** lightning sg; **tuoni e fulmini** thunder and lightning; **come un fulmine** like lightning; **fulmine a ciel sereno** bolt from the blue; **un colpo di fulmine** (*fig*) love at first sight; **è stato colpito da un fulmine** he was struck by lightning

fulmineo, -a [ful'mineo] AGG (*fig: scatto*) rapid; (*minaccioso: sguardo*) threatening; **una morte fulminea** a sudden death

fulvo, -a ['fulvo] AGG tawny

fumaiolo [fuma'jɔlo] SM (*gen*) chimney; (*Naut, Ferr*) funnel

fumante [fu'mante] AGG (*piatto*) steaming

fumare [fu'mare] /72/ VT (*sigaretta, pipa*) to smoke ♦ VI (*aus* avere) (*esalare: fumo*) to smoke; (: *vapore*) to steam; **smettere di fumare** to give up smoking; **ha smesso di fumare** she's given up smoking; **fumare come un turco** to smoke like a chimney; **"vietato fumare"** "no smoking"

fumario, -ria, -ri, -rie [fu'marjo] AGG: **canna fumaria** flue

fumata [fu'mata] SF 1 (*il fumare*): **farsi una fumata** to have a smoke 2 (*emissione di fumo*) cloud of smoke; **fumata bianca/nera** (*in Vaticano*) signal that a new pope has/has not been elected

fumatore, -trice [fuma'tore] SM, SF smoker; **è un forte fumatore** he's a heavy smoker; **uno scompartimento fumatori** a smoking compartment

fumetto [fu'metto] SM 1 (*nuvoletta con parole*) bubble 2 (*storia a vignette*) cartoon, comic strip; **giornale a fumetti** comic (*Brit*), comic book (*USA*); **le piacciono i fumetti** she likes comics

fummo ecc ['fummo] VB *vedi* **essere**

fumo ['fumo] SM 1 (*di fuoco, sigaretta*) smoke; (*vapore*) steam; **fare fumo** (*camino ecc*) to smoke; **i fumi industriali** industrial fumes; **sento odore di fumo** I can smell smoke; **essere in preda ai fumi dell'alcol** (*fig*) to be under the influence of alcohol 2 (*il fumare*) smoking; **il fumo fa male** smoking is bad for you; **fumo passivo** passive smoking 3 (*fam: hascish*) dope 4 (*fraseologia*): **andare in fumo** to go up in smoke; **è solo fumo** it's worthless; **è tutto fumo e niente arrosto** there's no substance to it; **gettare fumo negli occhi a qn** to pull the wool over sb's eyes; **lo vedo come il fumo negli occhi** I can't stand him; **vendere fumo** to deceive, cheat ♦ AGG INV: **grigio fumo** smoky grey

fumogeno, -a [fu'mɔdʒeno] AGG (*candelotto*) smoke attr; **cortina fumogena** smoke screen ♦ SM smoke bomb

fumoso, -a [fu'moso] AGG 1 (*ambiente, stanza*) smoky 2 (*fig: idee*) woolly; (: *progetto*) muddled

funambolo, -a [fu'nambolo] SM, SF tightrope walker

fune ['fune] SF rope, cord; (*più grossa*) cable; **hanno tirato con forza e la fune si è spezzata** they pulled hard and the rope broke

funebre ['funebre] AGG (*gen, corteo, cerimonia*) funeral attr; (*atmosfera*) gloomy, funereal; (*voce, sguardo*) funereal, mournful

funerale [fune'rale] SM funeral; **una faccia da funerale** a long face

funesto, -a [fu'nesto] AGG (*incidente*) fatal; (*errore, decisione*) fatal, disastrous; (*atmosfera*) gloomy, dismal

fungere ['fundʒere] /5/ VI IRREG (*aus* avere) **fungere da** to act as

fungo, -ghi ['fungo] SM 1 (*commestibile*) mushroom; **fungo velenoso** toadstool; **funghi secchi** dried mushrooms; **andare a** o **per funghi** to go mushrooming; **crescere come i funghi** (*fig*) to spring up overnight; **fungo atomico** mushroom cloud 2 (*Med*) fungus 3 (*di annaffiatoio*) rose

funicolare [funiko'lare] SF funicular railway

funivia [funi'via] SF cablecar

funsi ecc ['funsi] VB *vedi* **fungere**

funto, -a ['funto] PP *di* **fungere**

funzionare [funtsjo'nare] /72/ VI (*aus* avere) 1 (*gen*) to work, function; (*sistema*) to function; **funziona a benzina** it runs on petrol; **far funzionare** to operate; **come funziona?** how does it work?; **il telefono non funziona** the telephone is out of order 2 **funzionare da** to act as

funzionario, -ria, -ri, -rie [funtsjo'narjo] SM, SF (*Amm: dirigente*) official; (: *impiegato*) employee; **funzionario dell'amministrazione comunale** local authority employee; **un funzionario del Parlamento Europeo** an official from the European Parliament; **funzionario statale** civil servant

funzione [fun'tsjone] SF 1 (*gen, anche Gramm, Mat*) function; **in funzione** (*macchina*) in operation; **essere in funzione** to be on; **non si apre quand'è in funzione** it won't open when it's on; **mettere in funzione** to switch on; **la funzione principale di...** the main function of...; **vive in funzione dei figli/della carriera** he lives for his children/his job; **participio usato in funzione di aggettivo** participle used as an adjective 2 (*carica*) post, office, position; **cessare dalle funzioni** to leave office; **far funzione di sindaco** to act as mayor; **non il presidente ma il facente funzione** not the president but his deputy; **nell'esercizio delle sue funzioni** in the performance of his duties **3** (*Rel*) service, religious ceremony

fuoco, -chi [ˈfwɔko] SM **1** fire; **vicino al fuoco** by the fire; **prendere fuoco** to catch fire; **la tenda ha preso fuoco subito** the curtain caught fire immediately; **dare fuoco a qc** to set fire to sth; **ha dato fuoco alla casa** he set fire to the house; **al fuoco!** fire!; **scherzare col fuoco** (*fig*) to play with fire; **soffiare sul fuoco** (*fig*) to add fuel to the flames **2** (*Culin: fornello*) ring; **mettere qc sul fuoco** to put sth on the stove; **cuocere a fuoco lento/vivo** to cook over a low/high heat **3** (*Mil: sparo*) fire; **far fuoco** to fire; **cessare/aprire il fuoco** to cease/open fire; **fuoco incrociato** crossfire; **fuoco amico** (*Mil*) friendly fire **4** (*ardore, vivacità*) fire; **parole di fuoco** heated words **5** (*Mat, Ottica*) focus; **mettere a fuoco** to focus; (*fig: problema*) to clarify **6** (*fraseologia*): **fare fuoco e fiamme (per fare)** 4 (*ardore, vivacità*) to do sth; **mettere la mano sul fuoco per qc** to stake one's life on sth ♦ AGG INV: **rosso fuoco** flame red ♦ **fuoco d'artificio** firework; **fuoco fatuo** will-o'-the-wisp; **fuoco di paglia** flash in the pan; **fuoco sacro** o di Sant'Antonio (*Med: fam*) shingles pl

fuorché [fwor'ke] CONG, PREP except, apart from

fuori [ˈfwɔri] AVV **1** (*gen*) outside; (*all'aperto*) outdoors, outside; (*fuori casa*) out; (*all'estero*) abroad; **era lì fuori ad aspettarmi** he was outside waiting for me; **ti aspetto fuori** I'll wait for you outside; **fuori è ancora buio** it's still dark outside; **cosa fai là fuori?** what are you doing out there?; **ceniamo fuori?** (*all'aperto*) shall we eat outside?; (*al ristorante*) shall we go out for a meal?, shall we eat out?; **mandali a giocare fuori** send them out to play; **mio marito è fuori** my husband is out o is not at home; **ho vissuto in Italia e fuori** I've lived in Italy and abroad; **tiralo fuori dalla scatola** take it out of the box **2** (*fraseologia*): **fuori (di qui)!** get out (of here)!; **fuori i soldi!** hand over your money!; **essere di fuori** to be a stranger; **essere in fuori** (*sporgere*) to stick out; (*denti, occhi*) to be prominent; **ha i denti in fuori** her teeth stick out; **finalmente ne sono fuori** (*da un vizio*) I've managed to break the habit; **far fuori** (*fam: soldi*) to spend; (: *cioccolatini*) to eat up; (: *rubare*) to nick; **far fuori qn** (*fam*) to do sb in; **lasciare/mettere fuori** to leave/put out; **essere tagliato fuori** (*da un gruppo, ambiente*) to be excluded; **mi sento tagliato fuori qui** I feel cut off here; **uscire fuori** to come out; **andare/venire fuori** to go/come out; **giocare fuori** (*Sport*) to play away ♦ PREP **1** **fuori (di)** out of, outside; **è fuori città** he's out of town; **abita fuori Roma** he lives outside Rome; **fuori da** outside; **c'era molta gente fuori dal teatro** there were lots of people outside the theatre **2** (*fraseologia*): **è fuori di sé (dalla gioia/rabbia)** he's beside himself (with joy/anger); **è fuori commercio** it's not for sale; **fuori fase** (*motore*) out of phase; **fuori mano** (*casa, paese*) out of the way, remote; **abitare fuori mano** to live in an out-of-the-way place; **fuori luogo** (*osservazione*) out of place, uncalled for; **fuori orario** outside working hours; **fuori pasto** between meals; **fuori pericolo** out of danger; **fuori dai piedi!** get out of the way!; **fuori programma** unscheduled; **è fuori questione** o **discussione** it's out of the question; **fuori servizio** out of order; **fuori stagione** out of season; **la macchina è andata fuori strada** the car left the road; **essere fuori tempo** (*Mus*) to be out of time; **è arrivato fuori tempo massimo** he arrived outside the time limit; **illustrazione fuori testo** plate; **fuori uso** out of use; **essere fuori** (*fam*) to be nuts o crazy ♦ SM outside; **dal di fuori** from the outside

fuoribordo [fwori'bordo] SM INV (*Naut: imbarcazione*) outboard, speedboat (with outboard motor); (: *motore*) outboard motor

fuoribusta [fwori'busta] SM INV unofficial payment

fuoriclasse [fwori'klasse] AGG INV unrivalled, unequalled ♦ SM INV, SF INV undisputed champion

fuoricorso [fwori'korso] AGG INV **1** (*moneta*) no longer in circulation **2** (*Univ*): (*studente*) **fuoricorso** student who takes longer than normal to complete his or her university degree

fuorigioco [fwori'dʒoko] SM INV (*Sport*): **in fuorigioco** offside; **quando ha segnato era in fuorigioco** he was offside when he scored

fuorilegge [fwori'leddʒe] SM INV, SF INV outlaw

fuoriprogramma [fworipro'gramma] SM INV (*TV, Radio*) unscheduled programme; (*fig*) change of plan o programme

fuoriserie [fwori'sɛrje] AGG INV (*macchina*) specially built; (*fig: eccezionale*) outstanding ♦ SF INV custom-built car

fuoristrada [fwori'strada] SM INV (*Aut*) jeep; **fare del fuoristrada** to drive cross-country

fuoriuscita [fworiuʃ'ʃita]**, fuoruscita** [fworuʃ'ʃita] SF (*di gas*) leakage, escape; (*di sangue, linfa*) seepage

fuoriuscito, -a [fworiuʃ'ʃito]**, fuoruscito, -a** [fworuʃ'ʃito] SM, SF exile, refugee

fuorviare [fworvi'are] /60/ VI = **forviare**

furbacchione, -a [furbak'kjone] SM, SF cunning o crafty old devil

furbizia [fur'bittsja] SF (*vedi agg*) cleverness; cunning; **una furbizia** a cunning trick

furbo, -a [ˈfurbo] AGG clever, smart; (*pegg*) cunning, sly; **un ragazzo furbo** a clever boy ♦ SM, SF clever person, cunning person; **fare il furbo** to (try to) be clever o smart; **fatti furbo!** show a bit of sense!

furente [fu'rente] AGG: **furente (contro)** furious (with)

fureria [fure'ria] SF (*Mil*) orderly room

furetto [fu'retto] SM ferret

furfante [fur'fante] SM, SF rascal, scoundrel

furgoncino [furgon'tʃino] SM small van

furgone [fur'gone] SM van

furia [ˈfurja] SF **1** (*ira, furore*) fury, rage; (*velocità*) hurry, haste; **andare** o **montare su tutte le furie** to get into a towering rage, fly into a rage o frenzy; **la furia del vento** the violence of the wind; **a furia di fare qc** by constantly doing sth; **si è fatto largo nella folla a furia di spinte** he shoved his way through the crowd; **perderai la voce a furia di gridare** you'll lose your voice if you shout so much **2** (*Mitol*): **le Furie** the Furies

furibondo, -a [furi'bondo] AGG furious

furiere [fu'rjere] SM quartermaster

furioso, -a [fu'rjoso] AGG (*gen*) furious; (*vento, assalto*) violent, raging; **è un pazzo furioso** he is a raving lunatic

furono [ˈfurono] VB *vedi* **essere**

furore [fu'rore] SM fury; **nel furore della battaglia** in the heat of the battle; **a furore di popolo** by popular acclaim; **far furore** to be all the rage

❏ furore non si traduce mai con la parola inglese *furore*

furtivamente [furtiva'mente] AVV (*vedi agg*) furtively

furtivo, -a [fur'tivo] AGG (*sguardo*) furtive; (*passo*) stealthy

furto [ˈfurto] SM theft; **commettere un furto** to commit a robbery; **vorrei denunciare un furto** I'd like to report a theft; **furto con scasso** (*Dir*) burglary; **furto di identità** identity theft

fusa [ˈfusa] SFPL: **fare le fusa** to purr

fuscello [fuʃ'ʃello] SM twig; **magro come un fuscello** thin as a lath

fuseaux [fu'zo] SMPL leggings

fusi ecc [ˈfuzi] VB *vedi* **fondere**

fusibile [fu'zibile] SM (*Elettr*) fuse

fusione [fu'zjone] SF **1** (*gen, anche Fis*) fusion; (*di metalli*) melting; (*fig: di idee*) merging, blending **2** (*Comm*) merger, amalgamation

fuso¹, -a [ˈfuzo] PP *di* **fondere**

fuso² [ˈfuzo] SM **1** (*Tessile*) spindle; **diritto come un fuso** as straight as a ramrod **2** **fuso orario** time zone; **non ho tenuto conto del fuso orario** I forgot about the time difference

fusoliera [fuzo'ljera] SF (*Aer*) fusillage

fustagno [fus'taɲɲo] SM fustian, corduroy

fustella [fus'tella] SF (*su scatola di medicinali*) tear-off tab

fustigare [fusti'gare] /80/ VT (*frustare*) to flog; (*fig: costumi*) to censure, denounce

fustino [fus'tino] SM (*di detersivo*) tub

fusto [ˈfusto] SM **1** (*Anat, Bot: di albero*) trunk; (: *di pianta*) stem; (: *colonna*) shaft **2** (*recipiente: di metallo*) drum **3** (*fam*) he-man

futile [ˈfutile] AGG futile, vain

futilità [futili'ta] SF INV futility

futurismo [futu'rizmo] SM futurism

futuro, -a [fu'turo] AGG future ♦ SM future; **futuro anteriore** future perfect

Gg

G, g [dʒi] SF INV, SM INV (lettera) G, g; **G come Genova** ≈ G for George

g ABBR (= grammo, grammi) g

gabardine [gabar'din] SM (tessuto) gabardine; (soprabito) gabardine raincoat

gabbare [gab'bare] /72/ VT to deceive, trick, dupe

gabbia [ˈgabbja] SF 1 (gen) cage; (da imballaggio) crate; **la gabbia degli accusati** (Dir) the dock; **gabbia di matti** (fig) madhouse; **gabbia toracica** (Anat) rib cage 2 (Equitazione: ostacolo) double

gabbiano [gab'bjano] SM (sea)gull; **gabbiano comune** black-headed gull; **gabbiano reale** herring gull

gabinetto [gabi'netto] SM 1 (WC) lavatory, toilet; **dov'è il gabinetto?** where's the toilet?; **posso andare al gabinetto?** can I go to the toilet, please? 2 (di medico) surgery, consulting room 3 (Pol: ministero) ≈ ministry; (: di ministro) advisers pl

Gabon [ɡa'bon] SM Gabon

gaelico, -a, -ci, -che [ɡa'eliko] AGG, SM Gaelic

gaffe [ɡaf] SF INV blunder, goof; **fare una gaffe** to put one's foot in it (fam); **ho fatto una gaffe** I've put my foot in it

gagliardo, -a [ɡaʎ'ʎardo] AGG strong, robust

gaiezza [ɡa'jettsa] SF (di persona) gaiety, cheerfulness; (di colori) brightness

gaio, -aia, -ai, -aie [ˈgajo] AGG (persona) cheerful, happy; (colore) bright, gay

gala [ˈgala] SF 1 (ornamento) bow 2 serata di gala gala evening; **uniforme di gran gala** full-dress uniform; **pranzo di gala** banquet ♦ SM gala, festivity

galante [ɡa'lante] AGG 1 (cortese) gallant, chivalrous 2 (amoroso) romantic; **avventura galante** love affair ♦ SM gallant

galanteria [ɡalante'ria] SF gallantry

galantuomo [ɡalan'twɔmo] SM (pl -uomini) gentleman

Galapagos [ɡa'pagos] SFPL (anche: le isole Galapagos) the Galápagos Islands

galassia [ɡa'lassja] SF galaxy

galateo [ɡala'tɛo] SM etiquette

galeotto [ɡale'ɔtto] SM (Storia) galley slave; (carcerato) convict

galera [ɡa'lɛra] SF 1 (fam) prison, gaol; **ha fatto due anni di galera** he spent two years in prison; **avanzo di galera** criminal type; **vita da galera** (fig) dog's life 2 (Naut) galley

galla [ˈgalla] SF **a galla** AVV afloat; **stare a galla** to float; (fig) to keep one's head above water; **venire a galla** to surface, come to the surface; (fig: verità) to come out, come to light

galleggiamento [ɡaleddʒa'mento] SM floating; **linea di galleggiamento** (di nave) waterline

galleggiante [ɡalled'dʒante] AGG floating ♦ SM (Tecn, Aer, Pesca) float; (natante) barge; (boa) buoy

galleggiare [ɡalled'dʒare] /62/ VI (aus avere) to float

galleria [ɡalle'ria] SF 1 (traforo) tunnel; **la galleria del Monte Bianco** the Mont Blanc tunnel; **galleria del vento** o **aerodinamica** (Aer) wind tunnel 2 (Archit: d'arte) gallery; (strada coperta con negozi) arcade; (Cine) balcony; (Teatro) circle; **due poltrone in galleria** two seats in the circle

Galles [ˈgalles] SM Wales; **mi è piaciuto molto il Galles** I really liked Wales; **andremo in Galles quest'estate** we're going to Wales this summer

gallese [ɡal'lese] AGG Welsh; **la squadra gallese** the Welsh team ♦ SM, SF Welshman o Welshwoman o **i gallesi** the Welsh ♦ SM (lingua) Welsh

galletta [ɡal'letta] SF cracker

galletto [ɡal'letto] SM young cock, cockerel; (fig) cocky young man; **fare il galletto** to show off in a cocky manner

Gallia [ˈgallja] SF Gaul

gallina [ɡal'lina] SF hen; **gallina lessa** boiled chicken; **andare**

a letto con le galline to go to bed early; **la gallina dalle uova d'oro** the goose that lays the golden eggs; **gallina vecchia fa buon brodo** (Proverbio) an old hen makes good broth

gallismo [ɡal'lizmo] SM machismo

gallo [ˈgallo] SM cock; **al canto del gallo** at daybreak, at cock-crow; **fare il gallo** to show off in a cocky manner; **gallo cedrone** capercaillie; **gallo da combattimento** fighting cock ♦ AGG INV (Pugilato): **peso gallo** bantamweight

gallone[1] [ɡal'lone] SM 1 (Mil) stripe; **guadagnarsi i galloni** to be promoted; **perdere i galloni** to lose one's stripes 2 (ornamento) braid, piece of braid

gallone[2] [ɡal'lone] SM (unità di misura) gallon

galoppare [ɡalop'pare] /72/ VI (aus avere) (cavallo) to gallop; (fig: correre affannosamente) to rush about; (: fantasia, immaginazione) to run wild, run riot; **sua madre lo fa galoppare!** his mother runs him off his feet!

galoppino [ɡalop'pino] SM 1 errand boy 2 (Pol) canvasser

galoppo [ɡa'lɔppo] SM gallop; **piccolo galoppo** canter; **al galoppo** (anche fig) at a gallop; **andare al galoppo** to gallop; **partire al galoppo** to set off at a gallop; (fig) to rush off o away

galvanizzare [ɡalvanid'dzare] /72/ VT (Med, Tecn, anche fig) to galvanize

gamba [ˈgamba] SF (Anat: di mobile) leg; (di lettera, nota musicale) tail; **mi fa male la gamba** my leg hurts; **le gambe del tavolo** the table legs; **con le proprie gambe** on one's own two feet; **essere di buona gamba** o **di gamba lesta** to be a good walker; **scappare a gambe levate** o **in spalla** to take to one's heels; **darsela a gambe** to take to one's heels; **gambe!** scatter!; **andare a gambe all'aria** to fall headlong; (fig: progetto) to fall through; **prendere qc sotto gamba** to treat sth too lightly; **prendere qn sotto gamba** not to take sb seriously; **in gamba** (capace, sveglio) bright, smart, clever; (sul lavoro) good; **abbiamo un professore molto in gamba** our teacher's very good

gambale [ɡam'bale] SM (of boot) leg

gamberetto [ɡambe'retto] SM shrimp

gambero [ˈgambero] SM (di mare) prawn; (di fiume) crayfish; **fare come il gambero** to go backwards; **rosso come un gambero** as red as a beetroot (o lobster)

Gambia [ˈgambja] SM: **il Gambia** the Gambia

gambizzare [ɡambid'dzare] /72/ VT to kneecap

gambo [ˈgambo] SM (di fiore, bicchiere) stem; (di frutta, fungo) stalk; **gambo della punteria** (Aut) push rod

gamella [ɡa'mella] SF mess tin

gamma[1] [ˈgamma] AGG INV: **raggi gamma** gamma rays

gamma[2] [ˈgamma] SF (Mus) scale; (fig) range; **gamma d'onda** (Radio) waveband; **una vasta gamma di articoli sportivi** a wide range of sports goods; **gamma di prodotti** product range

ganascia, -sce [ɡa'naʃʃa] SF (Zool, Tecn) jaw; (Aut: del freno) brake shoes; **mangiare a quattro ganasce** to eat like a horse

gancio, -ci [ˈgantʃo] SM (gen, anche Pugilato) hook; **le chiavi erano appese ad un gancio** the keys were hanging on a hook

Gange [ˈgandʒe] SM: **il Gange** the Ganges

ganghero [ˈgangero] SM (di porta) hinge; **uscire dai gangheri** (fig) to lose one's temper, go off at the deep end, fly into a rage; **essere fuori dai gangheri** (fig) to be beside o.s. with rage

gangrena [ɡan'grena] SF = **cancrena**

gara [ˈgara] SF 1 (concorso) competition, contest; (di velocità) race; **gara di canto/nuoto/tiro** singing/swimming/shooting competition; **gare automobilistiche/ciclistiche** car/cycle races; **entrare in gara** to enter a competition (o race); **essere in gara** to be competing; **partecipare a una gara** to take part in a competition; **facciamo a gara a chi arriva primo!** I'll race you!; **hanno fatto a gara a chi riusciva meglio** they competed *o* vied with each other to see who could do it best **2** (*Comm, Econ*): **gara d'appalto** call for bids

garage [ga'raʒ] SM INV (*autorimessa*) garage; **hai messo la macchina in garage?** have you put the car in the garage?

garante [ga'rante] AGG: **farsi garante di** *o* **per qc** to vouch for sth, guarantee sth; **farsi garante di** *o* **per qn** to stand surety for sb ♦ SM, SF guarantor

garantire [garan'tire] /55/ VT (*gen*) to guarantee; (*dare per certo*) to assure; **ti garantisco che sarà pronto domani** I guarantee that/assure you that it will be ready tomorrow; **questo televisore è garantito per tre anni** this television is guaranteed for three years; **garantire un debito** to stand surety for a debt; **garantirsi** VIP: **garantirsi da** *o* **contro to** insure o.s. against

garantismo [garan'tizmo] SM protection of civil liberties

garantista, -i, -e [garan'tista] AGG protecting civil liberties ♦ SM, SF civil libertarian

garanzia [garan'tsia] SF (*gen, anche Comm*) guarantee; (*pegno*) security, surety; **in garanzia** under guarantee; **l'orologio è ancora in garanzia** the watch is still under guarantee; **questa persona non dà alcuna garanzia** this person is not to be trusted, this person is unreliable

garbare [gar'bare] /72/ VI (*aus essere*) **non mi garba** I don't like it (*o* him *ecc*)

garba'tezza [garba'tettsa] SF courtesy, politeness

garbato, -a [gar'bato] AGG (*cortese*) courteous, polite; (*gentile*) kind

garbo [ˈgarbo] SM **1** (*grazia*) grace; **muoversi con garbo/ senza garbo** to move gracefully/awkwardly **2** (*gentilezza*) politeness, courtesy; **una persona di garbo** a well-mannered person

garbuglio, -gli [gar'buʎʎo] SM tangle; (*fig*) muddle, mess

gareggiare [gared'dʒare] /62/ VI (*aus avere*) **gareggiare in qc** to compete in sth; **gareggiare con qn** to compete *o* vie with sb

garganella [garga'nɛlla] SF: **a garganella** from the bottle

gargarismo [garga'rizmo] SM gargle; **fare un gargarismo** *o* **i gargarismi** to gargle

garitta [ga'ritta] SF (*di caserma*) sentry box

garofano [ga'rɔfano] SM carnation

garretto [gar'retto] SM hock

garrire [gar'rire] /55/ VI (*aus avere*) (*uccelli*) to chirp

garrulo, -a [ˈgarrulo] AGG **1** (*uccello*) chirping **2** (*loquace*) garrulous, talkative

garza [ˈgardza] SF (*tessuto, anche Med*) gauze; **una garza** (*Med*) a gauze bandage

garzone [gar'dzone] SM (*di negozio*) boy; **il garzone del macellaio** the butcher's boy

gas [gas] SM INV **1** gas; **l'uomo del gas** the gasman; **hai spento il gas?** have you turned off the gas?; **scaldabagno/stufa a gas** gas boiler/heater **2** (*Aut*): **dare gas** to step on the gas, accelerate; **a tutto gas** at full speed; **è partito a tutto gas** he roared off ♦ **gas asfissiante** poison gas; **gas di città** *o* **illuminante** town gas; **gas esilarante** laughing gas; **gas inerti** *o* **nobili** inert gases; **gas lacrimogeno** tear gas; **gas liquido** liquid gas; **gas naturale** natural gas

gasare [ga'zare] /72/ VT = **gassare; gasarsi** VR (*fam*) to get excited; (*montarsi*) to become too full of o.s.

gasato, -a [ga'zato] AGG **1** (*bibita*) = **gassato 2** (*fam: persona*) excited; (: *montato*) big-headed ♦ SM, SF (*fam: persona*) big-head

gasdotto [gaz'dotto] SM gas pipeline

gasolio [ga'zɔljo] SM diesel (oil)

gassare [gas'sare] /72/ VT **1** (*liquido*) to aerate, make fizzy **2** (*uccidere col gas*) to gas

gassato, -a [gas'sato] AGG (*bibita*) fizzy; **acqua minerale gassata** sparkling mineral water

gassoso, -a [gas'soso] AGG gaseous

gastrico, -a, -ci, -che [ˈgastriko] AGG gastric

gastrite [gas'trite] SF gastritis

gastroenterite [gastroente'rite] SF gastroenteritis

gastronomia [gastrono'mia] SF gastronomy

gastronomo, -a [gas'trɔnomo] SM, SF gourmet, gastronome

gatta [ˈgatta] SF female cat; **una gatta da pelare** (*fam*) a thankless task; **qui gatta ci cova!** I smell a rat!, there's something fishy going on here!

gattabuia [gatta'buja] SF (*fam, scherz: prigione*) clink

gattino, -a [gat'tino] SM, SF kitten

gatto [ˈgatto] SM (*gen*) cat; (*maschio*) tomcat; **siamo rimasti in quattro gatti** there were only a few of us left; **quando il gatto non c'è i topi ballano** (*Proverbio*) when the cat's away the mice will play ♦ **gatto delle nevi** (*Sci*) snowcat; **gatto a nove code** cat-o'-nine-tails; **gatto selvatico** wildcat

gattopardo [gatto'pardo] SM: **gattopardo africano** serval; **gattopardo americano** ocelot

gattuccio, -ci [gat'tuttʃo] SM dogfish

gaudente [gau'dente] SM, SF pleasure-seeker; **fare la vita del gaudente** to live like a lord

gaudio, -di [ˈgaudjo] SM joy, happiness

gavetta [ga'vetta] SF (*Mil*) mess tin; **venire dalla gavetta** (*fig*) to rise from the ranks

gazza [ˈgaddza] SF magpie

gazzarra [gad'dzarra] SF racket, din; **fare gazzarra** to make a din

gazzella [gad'dzɛlla] SF **1** (*Zool*) gazelle **2** (*auto dei Carabinieri*) (high-speed) police car

gazzetta [gad'dzetta] SF gazette; **Gazzetta Ufficiale** *official publication containing the text of new laws*

Gazz. Uff. ABBR = **Gazzetta Ufficiale**

GB SIGLA (= *Gran Bretagna*) GB

GE SIGLA = Genova

gel [dʒɛl] SM INV gel

gelare [dʒe'lare] /72/ VT to freeze; **mi ha gelato il sangue** (*fig*) it made my blood run cold ♦ VI (*aus essere*) to freeze; **il lago è gelato** the lake has frozen over; **chiudi la porta, si gela!** close the door, it's freezing! ♦ VB IMPERS to freeze; **gela** it's freezing

gelata [dʒe'lata] SF frost

gelataio, -aia, -ai, -aie [dʒela'tajo] SM, SF (*venditore*) ice-cream seller; (*produttore*) ice-cream maker

gelateria [dʒelate'ria] SF ice-cream shop, ice-cream parlour (*USA*)

gelatina [dʒela'tina] SF (*gen, anche Culin*) gelatine; **gelatina esplosiva** gelignite; **gelatina di frutta** fruit jelly

gelatinoso, -a [dʒelati'noso] AGG gelatinous

gelato, -a [dʒe'lato] AGG frozen; **ho le mani gelate** my hands are frozen (stiff) ♦ SM ice-cream; **gelato di fragola/di crema** strawberry/vanilla ice cream

gelido, -a [ˈdʒɛlido] AGG (*aria, vento*) icy, freezing; (*mani, acqua*) freezing, ice-cold; (*fig: accoglienza, espressione, sguardo*) icy, frosty

gelo [ˈdʒɛlo] SM (*temperatura*) intense cold; (*brina*) frost; (*fig: inverno*) cold weather; **il gelo invernale** the cold winter weather; **sentirsi il gelo nelle ossa** to feel a chill of fear; **il gelo della morte** the chill hand of death

gelone [dʒe'lone] SM chilblain

gelosia [dʒelo'sia] SF (*sentimento*) jealousy; **conservare qc con gelosia** to guard sth jealously

geloso, -a [dʒe'loso] AGG jealous; **è geloso del fratellino** he's jealous of his baby brother

gelso [ˈdʒɛlso] SM mulberry (tree); **gelso nero** black mulberry

gelsomino [dʒelso'mino] SM jasmine

gemellaggio, -gi [dʒemel'laddʒo] SM twinning

gemellare [dʒemel'lare] /72/ AGG twin attr ♦ VT (*città*) to twin

gemello, -a [dʒe'mello] AGG (*fratelli, letti*) twin attr ♦ SM, SF (*persona*) twin; **Rossana ha avuto due gemelli** Rossana had twins ♦ **gemelli** SMPL **1** (*di camicia*) cufflinks; **un paio di gemelli d'oro** a pair of gold cufflinks **2** (*Astrol*): **Gemelli** Gemini; **essere dei Gemelli** to be Gemini

gemere [ˈdʒɛmere] /29/ VI (*aus avere*) (*ferito*) to groan (with); (*cane*) to whine; (*piccione, tortora: tubare*) to coo; (*fig: cigolare*) to creak

gemito [ˈdʒɛmito] SM groan, moan

gemma [ˈdʒɛmma] SF **1** (*Bot*) bud **2** (*gioiello*) gem, jewel

Gen. ABBR (*Mil:* = *generale*) Gen.

gen. ABBR (= *generale, generalmente*) gen.

gendarme [dʒenˈdarme] SM **1** policeman; **essere un gendarme** (*fig*) to be a martinet **2** (*Alpinismo*) gendarme

gene [ˈdʒɛne] SM gene

genealogia, -gie [dʒenealoˈdʒia] SF genealogy

genealogico, -a, -ci, -che [dʒeneaˈlɔdʒiko] AGG genealogical; **albero genealogico** family tree

generale¹ [dʒeneˈrale] AGG general; **nell'interesse generale** in the interest of everyone, for the common good; **un quadro generale della situazione** a general *o* overall view of the situation; **l'opinione generale** public opinion; **direttore generale** managing director; **console generale** consul general; **in generale** generally, in general; (*parlare*) in general terms; **in generale sto bene** on the whole I am quite well; **mantenersi** *o* **stare sulle generali** to stick to generalities

generale² [dʒeneˈrale] SM general; **generale di brigata** brigadier

generalità [dʒeneraliˈta] SF INV **1** (*qualità*) generality **2** (*maggioranza*) majority; **nella generalità dei casi** in most cases **3** (*dati anagrafici*): **generalità** SFPL particulars; **fornire le proprie generalità** give one's name and address

generalizzare [dʒeneralidˈdzare] /**72**/ VT, VI (*aus* avere) to generalize

generalizzazione [dʒeneraliddzatˈtsjone] SF generalization

generalmente [dʒeneralˈmente] AVV generally, usually

generare [dʒeneˈrare] /**72**/ VT **1** (*dar vita, anche fig*) to give birth to **2** (*produrre: Tecn*) to generate, produce; (*: Geom*) to generate, form **3** (*causare: sospetti*) to arouse; (*: confusione*) to create

generatore [dʒeneraˈtore] SM (*Elettr*) generator

generazione [dʒeneratˈtsjone] SF generation; **la nuova generazione** the new *o* younger generation

genere [ˈdʒɛnere] SM **1** kind, type, sort; **è il genere di musica che preferisco** it's the kind of music I like best; **oggetti di ogni genere** all kinds of things; **cose del** *o* **di questo genere** such things; **qualcosa del genere** something like that; **non ho mai visto una cosa del genere!** I've never seen anything like it!; **non farmi più uno scherzo del genere!** don't ever play such a trick on me again!; **è bravo nel suo genere** in his own way he is quite good; **questo vaso è bello, nel suo genere** this is a nice vase of its kind; **in genere** generally, usually, as a rule; **in genere mi alzo alle sette** I usually get up at seven; **i documentari non sono il mio genere** documentaries aren't my cup of tea **2** (*prodotti*): **generi** SMPL article, product; **generi alimentari** foodstuffs; **generi di consumo** consumer goods; **generi di prima necessità** basic essentials **3** (*Bio, Zool, Bot*) genus; **il genere umano** mankind, the human race **4** (*Gramm*) gender **5** (*Letteratura, Arte*) genre

generico, -a, -ci, -che [dʒeˈnɛriko] AGG **1** generic; (*vago: descrizione, accuse*) vague, imprecise **2** (*non specializzato*): **medico generico** general practitioner, GP ♦ SM generality; **i suoi discorsi non escono dal generico** his speeches never get beyond generalities

genero [ˈdʒɛnero] SM son-in-law

generosità [dʒenerosiˈta] SF INV generosity; **è un uomo di grande generosità** he's a very generous man

generoso, -a [dʒeneˈroso] AGG generous; **un'offerta generosa** a generous offer; **non è generoso da parte tua** that's not very nice of you; **un vino generoso** a full-bodied wine

genesi [ˈdʒɛnezi] SF genesis; (*Bibbia*) **la Genesi** Genesis

genetico, -a, -ci, -che [dʒeˈnɛtiko] AGG genetic

gengiva [dʒenˈdʒiva] SF gum

genia [dʒeˈnia] SF (*pegg*) mob, gang

geniale [dʒeˈnjale] AGG (*persona, artista*) of genius; (*idea, soluzione*) brilliant, inspired; **ho avuto un'idea geniale** I've had a brilliant idea

❑ **geniale** non si traduce mai con la parola inglese *genial*

genio¹, -ni [ˈdʒɛnjo] SM **1** (*persona*) genius; **sei un genio!** you're a genius!; **essere un genio in matematica** he is a mathematical genius *o* wizard; **essere un genio incompreso** to be a misunderstood genius; **avere un lampo di genio** to have a brainwave **2** (*talento*): **avere il genio degli affari** to have a genius *o* flair for business **3** (*gusto*):

andare a genio a qn to be to sb's liking; **non mi va a genio** I am not very keen on it (*o* him *ecc*) **4** (*Mitol: gen*) spirit; (*: arabo*) genie

genio² [ˈdʒɛnjo] SM **1** (*Mil*): **il genio (militare)** the Engineers *pl* **2 genio civile** civil engineers *pl*

genitale [dʒeniˈtale] AGG genital ♦ **genitali** SMPL genitals

genitore, -trice [dʒeniˈtore] SM, SF parent, father (*o* mother); **genitori** SMPL parents

genn. ABBR (= *gennaio*) Jan

gennaio [dʒenˈnajo] SM January; *vedi* luglio

genocidio, -di [dʒenoˈtʃidjo] SM genocide

Genova [ˈdʒɛnova] SF Genoa; **domani vado a Genova** I'm going to Genoa tomorrow; **abitiamo a Genova** we live in Genoa

genovese [dʒenoˈvese] AGG, SM, SF Genoese *pl inv*

gentaglia [dʒenˈtaʎʎa] SF (*pegg*) rabble, scum

gente [ˈdʒɛnte] SF people *pl*; **c'era tanta gente** there were lots of people there; **gente di campagna** country people; **gente di città** townspeople; **gente di mare** seafaring folk; **è brava gente** they are nice people; **aspetto gente** I'm waiting for somebody; **ho gente a cena** I've got people to dinner; **le genti anglosassoni** (*letter: popolazioni*) the Anglo-Saxon peoples; **diritto delle genti** law of nations

gentildonna [dʒentilˈdɔnna] SF gentlewoman, lady

gentile [dʒenˈtile] AGG **1** (*buono*) kind; (*garbato*) courteous, polite; **è molto gentile da parte sua** it's very kind *o* nice of you; **vuoi essere tanto gentile da...?** would you be so kind as to ...?; **i commessi sono sempre così gentili** the shop assistants are always so helpful **2** (*delicato: lineamenti*) fine; (*: profumo*) delicate; **il gentil sesso** the fair sex **3** (*nelle lettere*): **Gentile Signore** Dear Sir; (*sulla busta*): **Gentile Signor Fernando Villa** Mr Fernando Villa

❑ **gentile** non si traduce mai con la parola inglese *gentle*

gentilezza [dʒentiˈlettsa] SF **1** (*bontà*) kindness; (*garbatezza*) courtesy; **gentilezze** SFPL acts of kindness; **fare una gentilezza a qn** to do sb a favour; **fammi la gentilezza di chiudere la porta** be so kind as to close the door; **per gentilezza** (*per favore*) please **2** (*grazia: di lineamenti*) delicacy; (*: di movimento*) grace

gentiluomo [dʒentiˈlwɔmo] SM (*pl* **-uomini**) gentleman

genuflessione [dʒenufleˈsjone] SF genuflection, genuflexion (*Brit*)

genuino, -a [dʒenuˈino] AGG (*prodotto*) natural; (*persona, sentimento*) genuine, sincere; (*risata*) natural, unaffected; **ha una genuina vocazione** he has a true *o* real vocation

geografia [dʒeograˈfia] SF geography

geografico, -a, -ci, -che [dʒeoˈgrafiko] AGG geographical; **atlante geografico** atlas; **carta geografica** map

geografo, -a [dʒeˈografo] SM, SF geographer

geologia [dʒeoloˈdʒia] SF geology

geologico, -a, -ci, -che [dʒeoˈlɔdʒiko] AGG geological

geometra, -i, -e [dʒeˈmetra] SM, SF surveyor

geometria [dʒeomeˈtria] SF geometry

geometrico, -a, -ci, -che [dʒeoˈmetriko] AGG geometric(al)

geopolitico, -a, -ci, -che [dʒeopoˈlitiko] AGG geopolitical

Georgia [dʒeˈordʒa] SF (*in USA, Europa*) Georgia

georgiano, -a [dʒeorˈdʒano] (*in Europa, USA*) AGG, SM, SF Georgian

geranio, -ni [dʒeˈranjo] SM geranium

gerarca, -chi [dʒeˈrarka] SM (*Storia: nel fascismo*) party official

gerarchia [dʒerarˈkia] SF hierarchy; **le più alte gerarchie** the upper echelons

gerarchico, -a, -ci, -che [dʒeˈrarkiko] AGG hierarchical

gerente [dʒeˈrente] SM, SF manager (manageress)

gerenza [dʒeˈrentsa] SF management

gergale [dʒerˈgale] AGG (*vedi sm*) slang *attr*; jargon *attr*

gergo [ˈdʒergo] SM (*gen*) slang; (*professionale*) jargon; **gergo della malavita** criminals' slang

geriatria [dʒerjaˈtria] SF geriatrics *sg*

geriatrico, -a, -ci, -che [dʒeˈrjatriko] AGG geriatric

gerla [ˈdʒerla] SF conical wicker basket

Germania [dʒerˈmanja] SF Germany; **mi è piaciuta molto la**

Germania I really liked Germany; **andremo in Germania quest'estate** we're going to Germany this summer

germe [ˈdʒɛrme] SM (*gen*) germ; (*fig*) seed; **germi dell'influenza** flu germs; **i germi della ribellione** the seeds of rebellion; **germi di grano** wheatgerm *sg*

germinazione [dʒerminatˈtsjone] SF germination

germogliare [dʒermoʎˈʎare] /27/ VI (*aus* **avere** *o* **essere**) (*germinare*) to germinate; (*emettere germogli*) to sprout

germoglio, -gli [dʒerˈmoʎʎo] SM (*gen*) shoot; (*gemma*) bud

geroglifico, -ci [dʒeroˈɡlifiko] SM hieroglyphic

gerontologo, -a, -gi, -ghe [dʒeronˈtologo] SM, SF specialist in geriatrics

gerundio, -di [dʒeˈrundjo] SM gerund

Gerusalemme [dʒeruzaˈlemme] SF Jerusalem

gesso [ˈdʒɛsso] SM (*gen*) chalk; (*minerale*) gypsum; (*Scultura, Med, Edil*) plaster; (*statuetta*) plaster figure; **mi hanno tolto il gesso** (*Med*) they've taken off my plaster (cast)

gesta [ˈdʒɛsta] SFPL (*letter*) deeds, feats

gestante [dʒesˈtante] SF expectant mother

gestazione [dʒestatˈtsjone] SF gestation; **il progetto è ancora in gestazione** (*fig*) the project is still at the planning stage

gesticolare [dʒestikoˈlare] /72/ VI (*aus* **avere**) to gesticulate

gestionale [dʒestjoˈnale] AGG management *attr*

gestione [dʒesˈtjone] SF management; **gestione finanziaria** financial management

gestire [dʒesˈtire] /55/ VT to manage, run

gesto [ˈdʒɛsto] SM gesture; **ha fatto un gesto di rabbia** he made an angry gesture; **non mi ha fatto un gesto per aiutarmi** he didn't lift a finger to help me

gestore [dʒesˈtore] SM manager

Gesù [dʒeˈzu] SM Jesus; **Gesù Bambino** the Christ Child, baby Jesus (*fam*)

gesuita, -i [dʒezuˈita] SM Jesuit

gettare [dʒetˈtare] /72/ VT 1 (*lanciare*) to throw; (*con forza*) to fling, hurl; (*in aria*) to toss; **gettare (via)** (*liberarsi di*) to throw away; **gettare qc a qn** to throw sth to sb; **gettare qc addosso a qn** to throw sth at sb; (*acqua, sabbia*) to throw sth over sb; **ha gettato il libro dalla finestra** he threw the book out of the window; **non gettare il giornale per terra** don't throw the paper on the floor; **si gettò un mantello sulle spalle** he threw a coat round his shoulders; **gettare a terra qn** to throw sb to the ground; **gettare le braccia al collo di qn** to throw *o* fling one's arms round sb's neck; **gettare la colpa addosso a qn** to cast the blame on sb; **gettare qc in faccia a qn** (*anche fig*) to throw sth in sb's face; **gettò un rapido sguardo intorno** he had a quick look round; **gettare l'ancora** (*Naut*) to drop anchor; **gettare le reti** to cast the nets; **gettare a mare** (*fig: persona*) to abandon; **quella notizia l'ha gettato nella disperazione** he was plunged into despair at the news 2 (*metalli, cera*) to cast; (*fondamenta*) to lay; **gettare un ponte su un fiume** to throw a bridge over a river 3 (*emettere: acqua*) to spout; (: *grido*) to utter, give 4 (*fraseologia*): **gettare le armi** (*anche fig*) to throw down one's weapons; **gettare la spugna** to throw in the sponge; **gettare la polvere negli occhi a qn** (*fig*) to throw dust in sb's eyes; **gettare luce su qc** to shed light on sth ♦ VI (*aus* **avere**) (*pianta*) to sprout; **gettarsi** VR 1 **gettarsi in un'impresa** to throw o.s. into an enterprise; **gettarsi nella mischia** to hurl o.s. into the fray; **gettarsi in acqua** to jump into the water; **gettarsi contro** *o* **addosso a qn** to hurl o.s. at sb; **gettarsi sulla preda** to pounce on one's prey; **gettarsi ai piedi di qn** to throw o.s. at sb's feet 2 (*fiume*): **gettarsi in** to flow into

gettata [dʒetˈtata] SF 1 (*di cemento, bronzo, reti*) cast 2 (*in balistica*) range 3 (*diga*) jetty

gettito [ˈdʒɛttito] SM (*Econ: rendita, introito*) yield, revenue

getto [ˈdʒɛtto] SM 1 (*azione*) throwing; (*risultato*) throw, cast 2 (*di acqua*) jet; **di getto** (*scrivere*) in one go, straight off; **a getto continuo** in a continuous stream, uninterruptedly; **scrive novelle a getto continuo** he writes one short story after another, he produces a constant stream of short stories; **a getto d'inchiostro** (*stampante*) ink-jet 3 (*Bot*) shoot 4 (*Metallurgia, Edil*) casting

gettone [dʒetˈtone] SM (*gen*) token; (*per giochi*) counter; (*roulette*) chip; **gettone di presenza** attendance fee; **gettone del telefono** telephone token

gettoniera [dʒettoˈnjera] SF token vending machine

geyser [ˈɡaizə] SM INV geyser

Ghana [ˈɡana] SM: **il Ghana** Ghana

ghenga, -ghe [ˈɡenɡa] SF (*fam*) gang, crowd

ghepardo [ɡeˈpardo] SM cheetah

ghermire [ɡerˈmire] /55/ VT to grasp, clasp, clutch

ghetta [ˈɡetta] SF (*gambale*) gaiter

ghettizzare [ɡettidˈdzare] /72/ VT to confine to a ghetto; (*fig: isolare*) to ghettoize

ghetto [ˈɡetto] SM ghetto

ghiacciaia [ɡjatˈtʃaja] SF (*anche fig*) icebox

ghiacciaio, -ai [ɡjatˈtʃajo] SM glacier; **ghiacciaio continentale** ice sheet

ghiacciare [ɡjatˈtʃare] /14/ VI (*aus* **essere**) to freeze; (*lago, fiume*) to ice over, freeze (over); **mi si è ghiacciato il sangue** my blood ran cold; **questa notte è ghiacciato** there was a frost last night ♦ VT to freeze ♦ VB IMPERS to freeze

ghiacciato, -a [ɡjatˈtʃato] AGG (*gen*) frozen; (*bevanda*) ice-cold; (*una birra ghiacciata* an ice-cold beer; **avevo le mani ghiacciate** my hands were frozen

ghiaccio [ˈɡjattʃo] SM ice; **un cubetto di ghiaccio** an ice cube; **hai le mani di ghiaccio** your hands are like ice; **restare di ghiaccio** to be dumbfounded; **rompere il ghiaccio** (*fig*) to break the ice; **ghiaccio secco** dry ice

ghiacciolo [ɡjatˈtʃɔlo] SM 1 (*formazione di ghiaccio*) icicle 2 (*gelato*) ice lolly (*Brit*), popsicle (*USA*); **un ghiacciolo al limone** a lemon ice lolly

ghiaia [ˈɡjaja] SF gravel

ghianda [ˈɡjanda] SF (*Bot*) acorn

ghiandola [ˈɡjandola] SF 1 (*Anat*) gland; **ghiandole endocrine** *o* **a secrezione interna** endocrine *o* ductless glands; **ghiandole esocrine** *o* **a secrezione esterna** exocrine glands

ghiandolare [ɡjandoˈlare] AGG glandular

ghigliottina [ɡiʎʎotˈtina] SF guillotine

ghignare [ɡiɲˈɲare] /15/ VI (*aus* **avere**) to sneer, laugh derisively

ghigno [ˈɡiɲɲo] SM (*espressione*) sneer; (*risata*) mocking laugh

ghingheri [ˈɡinɡeri] SMPL: **in ghingheri** all dolled up; **mettersi in ghingheri** to dress up to the nines

ghiotto, -a [ˈɡjotto] AGG (*persona*): **ghiotto (di)** greedy (for); (*cibi*) appetizing, delicious; (*fig: notizia*) juicy

ghiottone, -a [ɡjotˈtone] SM, SF 1 (*persona*) glutton 2 (*Zool*) wolverine

ghiottoneria [ɡjottoneˈria] SF (*di persona*) greed, gluttony; (*cibo*) delicacy

ghirigoro [ɡiriˈɡɔro] SM (*scarabocchio*) doodle, scribble; (*arabesco*) flourish

ghirlanda [ɡirˈlanda] SF garland, wreath

ghiro [ˈɡiro] SM dormouse; **dormire come un ghiro** to sleep like a log *o* top

ghisa [ˈɡiza] SF cast iron

GI ABBR = **giudice istruttore**

già [dʒa] AVV 1 (*gen*) already; **te l'ho già detto** I have already told you; **ho finito — di già?** I've finished — (*bevanda*) so already?; **sei già di ritorno?** are you back already?; **già che ci sei...** while you are at it ...; **è successo già da molto tempo** it happened a long time ago; **ma non ci conosciamo già?** haven't we met before?; **fra qualche anno sarà già un pianista famoso** in just a few years he will be a famous pianist; **già da bambino amava la musica** even as a child he loved music; **già sua madre lo faceva** his mother used to do it too 2 (*ex*) formerly; **lo Zimbabwe, già Rodesia** Zimbabwe, formerly Rhodesia 3 (*naturalmente*) of course, naturally; **già, avrei dovuto saperlo!** of course, I should have known!

giacca, -che [ˈdʒakka] SF jacket; **una giacca sportiva** a sports jacket; **giacca a vento** windcheater (*Brit*), windbreaker (*USA*), anorak

giacché [dʒakˈke] CONG since, as

giacchetta [dʒakˈketta] SF (*light*) jacket

giaccio *ecc* [ˈdʒattʃo] VB *vedi* **giacere**

giaccone [dʒakˈkone] SM heavy jacket

giacenza [dʒaˈtʃɛntsa] SF **1** (*Comm*): **merce in giacenza** (*non reclamata*) unclaimed goods; (*non recapitata*) undelivered goods; **giacenze di cassa** cash on *o* in hand; **giacenze di magazzino** unsold stock **2** (*Fin*): **capitale in giacenza** uninvested *o* idle capital

giacere [dʒaˈtʃere] /57/ VI IRREG (*aus essere*) (*gen*) to lie; (*Fin*: *capitale*) to lie idle; **il paese giace ai piedi della montagna** the village lies *o* is situated at the foot of the mountain; **giacere nell'ozio** to live in idleness; **la mia domanda giace ancora negli uffici del consolato** my application is still buried somewhere in the consulate

giacimento [dʒatʃiˈmento] SM (*Mineralogia*) deposit; **giacimento petrolifero** oil field

giacinto [dʒaˈtʃinto] SM hyacinth

giaciuto, -a [dʒaˈtʃuto] PP *di* giacere

giacqui ecc [ˈdʒakkwi] VB *vedi* giacere

giada [ˈdʒada] SF jade

giaggiolo [dʒadˈdʒɔlo] SM iris

giaguaro [dʒaˈgwaro] SM jaguar

giallastro, -a [dʒalˈlastro] AGG yellowish; (*carnagione*) sallow

giallo, -a [ˈdʒallo] AGG **1** (*colore*) yellow; (*carnagione*) sallow; **una sciarpa gialla** a yellow scarf **2 film/libro giallo** detective film/novel ♦ SM **1** (*colore*) yellow; (*di semaforo*) amber (*Brit*), yellow (*USA*); **non attraversare con il giallo** do not cross when the light is yellow; **dipingere qc di giallo** to paint sth yellow; **il giallo dell'uovo** (egg) yolk **2** (*romanzo*) detective story; (*film*) thriller

giallognolo, -a [dʒalˈloɲɲolo] AGG yellowish, dirty yellow

Giamaica [dʒaˈmaika] SF Jamaica

giamaicano, -a [dʒamaiˈkano] AGG, SM, SF Jamaican

giammai [dʒamˈmai] AVV never

Giappone [dʒapˈpone] SM Japan; **mi è piaciuto molto il Giappone** I really liked Japan; **andremo in Giappone quest'estate** we're going to Japan this summer

giapponese [dʒappoˈnese] AGG, SM, SF Japanese *inv*; **i giapponesi** the Japanese ♦ SM (*lingua*) Japanese; **parla giapponese** she speaks Japanese

giara [ˈdʒara] SF earthenware vessel

giardinaggio [dʒardiˈnaddʒo] SM gardening

giardinetta [dʒardiˈnetta] SF estate car (*Brit*), station wagon (*USA*)

giardiniere, -a [dʒardiˈnjere] SM, SF gardener

giardino [dʒarˈdino] SM garden; **sono in giardino** they're in the garden; **giardino d'infanzia** nursery school, kindergarten; **giardino pensile** roof garden; **giardino pubblico** public gardens *pl*, (public) park; **giardino zoologico** zoo

giarrettiera [dʒarretˈtjera] SF garter; **Ordine della Giarrettiera** Order of the Garter

Giava [ˈdʒava] SF Java

giavellotto [dʒavelˈlɔtto] SM javelin; **lancio del giavellotto** throwing the javelin

gibboso, -a [dʒibˈboso] AGG (*superficie*) bumpy; (*naso*) crooked

Gibilterra [dʒibilˈtɛrra] SF Gibraltar

giga [ˈdʒiga] SM INV = gigabyte

gigabyte [dʒigaˈbait] SM INV (*Inform*) gigabyte

gigante [dʒiˈgante] AGG gigantic, giant; **un cavolfiore gigante** a giant cauliflower; **confezione/formato gigante** (*Comm*) giant-size ♦ SM giant; **gigante della letteratura** literary giant; **compiere passi da gigante** (*scienza*) to make huge strides

gigantesco, -a, -schi, -sche [dʒiganˈtesko] AGG gigantic, huge

gigantografia [dʒigantograˈfia] SF (*Fot*) blow-up

giglio, -gli [ˈdʒiʎʎo] SM lily

gilè [dʒiˈle] SM INV (*panciotto*) waistcoat; (*fatto a maglia*) sleeveless cardigan

gin [dʒin] SM INV gin

gincana [dʒinˈkana] SF gymkhana

ginecologia [dʒinekoloˈdʒia] SF gynaecology (*Brit*), gynecology (*USA*)

ginecologo, -a, -gi, -ghe [dʒineˈkɔlogo] SM, SF gynaecologist (*Brit*), gynecologist (*USA*)

ginepro [dʒiˈnepro] SM juniper

ginestra [dʒiˈnestra] SF (*Bot*) broom

Ginevra [dʒiˈnevra] SF Geneva; **domani vado a Ginevra** I'm going to Geneva tomorrow; **abitano a Ginevra** they live in Geneva; **il lago di Ginevra** Lake Geneva

gingillarsi [dʒindʒilˈlarsi] /72/ VIP **1** (*perdere tempo*) to fritter away one's time **2** (*trastullarsi*): **gingillarsi con** to fiddle with

gingillo [dʒinˈdʒillo] SM (*ninnolo*) knick-knack, trinket; (*balocco*) plaything

ginnasio, -si [dʒinˈnazjo] SM *the first and second year of* liceo classico (*secondary school specializing in classics*)

ginnasta, -i, -e [dʒinˈnasta] SM, SF gymnast

ginnastica [dʒinˈnastika] SF (*disciplina*) gymnastics *sg*; (*educazione fisica*) physical education; **fare ginnastica** (*Scol*) to do gym; **dovresti fare un po' di ginnastica** you should take some exercise; **vado a fare ginnastica due volte alla settimana** I go to the gym twice a week; **ginnastica artistica** gymnastics; **ginnastica dolce** low-impact exercise; **ginnastica riabilitativa** physiotherapeutic exercise

ginnico, -a, -ci, -che [ˈdʒinniko] AGG gymnastic

ginocchio [dʒiˈnɔkkjo] (*pl f* ginocchia) SM knee; **al ginocchio** (*lunghezza*) knee-length; **in ginocchio** on one's knees, kneeling; **mettersi in ginocchio** to kneel (down); **mettere qn in ginocchio** (*vincere*) to bring sb to his knees; **sedersi sulle ginocchia di qn** to sit on sb's lap

ginocchioni [dʒinokˈkjoni] AVV on one's knees; **cadere ginocchioni** to fall to one's knees

giocare [dʒoˈkare] /20/ VI (*aus avere*) **1** (*gen, anche Sport*) to play; **giocare a scacchi/ai soldatini/al pallone** to play (at) chess/soldiers/football; **giocava con l'accendino** (*trastullarsi*) he was toying *o* playing with the lighter; **giocare in Nazionale** (*Calcio*) to play for Italy; **il Milan gioca in casa** Milan is playing at home; **giocare i minuti di recupero** (*Calcio*) to play injury time **2** (*scommettere*: *anche*: **giocare d'azzardo**) to gamble; **giocare in Borsa** to speculate *o* gamble on the Stock Exchange; **giocare alla roulette** to play roulette; **giocare ai cavalli** to bet on the horses **3** (*intervenire*: *fattore*) to matter, count, come into play; **ciò ha giocato a suo favore** that worked in his favour; **qui gioca l'elemento sorpresa** this is where the surprise element counts **4** (*muoversi liberamente*: *meccanismo*) to play freely **5** (*fraseologia*): **a che gioco giochiamo?** what are you playing at?; **giocare a carte scoperte** to act openly; **giocare sul sicuro** to play safe; **giocare d'astuzia** to be crafty ♦ VT **1** (*partita, carta*) to play; **giocare l'atout** to play trumps; **giocare l'ultima carta** (*fig*) to play one's last card **2** (*scommettere*): **giocare (su)** (*Casinò*) to stake (on), wager (on); (*Corse*) to bet (on); **giocare forte** to gamble heavily; **giocarsi una cena** to play for a meal; **si è giocato anche la camicia** he has gambled away his last penny; **ci giocherei l'anima** I'd stake my life on it; **giocarsi tutto** to risk everything; **si sta giocando la carriera** he's putting his career at risk **3** (*imbrogliare*) to deceive, trick, take in; **ci hanno giocato un brutto tiro** they played a dirty trick on us

giocatore, -trice [dʒokaˈtore] SM, SF **1** (*gen, anche Sport*) player; **un giocatore di scacchi** a chess player **2** (*d'azzardo*) gambler

giocattolo [dʒoˈkattolo] SM toy

giocherellare [dʒokerelˈlare] /72/ VI (*aus avere*) **giocherellare con** (*giocattolo*) to play with; (*distrattamente*) to fiddle with

giocherò ecc [dʒokeˈrɔ] VB *vedi* giocare

giochetto [dʒoˈketto] SM **1** (*gioco*) game; **è un giochetto** (*cosa molto facile*) it's child's play, it's a piece of cake **2** (*tranello*) trick

gioco, -chi [ˈdʒɔko] SM **1** (*gen*) game; **facciamo un gioco** let's play a game; **il gioco degli scacchi/delle bocce** (the game of) chess/bowls *sg*; **gioco d'abilità** game of skill; **gioco d'azzardo** game of chance; **gioco di pazienza** puzzle; **gioco di ruolo** roleplaying game; **gioco di società** parlour game; **gioco da tavolo** board game **2** (*Sport*: *partita, modo di giocare*) game; **gioco di squadra** team game; **due giochi a uno** (*Tennis*) two games to one; **i giochi olimpici** the Olympic Games **3** (*Carte*: *mano*) hand; **non avere gioco** to have a poor hand **4** (*il gioco*) (*Casinò*) gambling; (*Corse*) betting; **avere il vizio del gioco** to be a gambler; **casa/tavolo da gioco** gaming house/table; **fortunato al gioco, sfortunato in amore** lucky at cards, unlucky in love **5** (*Tecn*) play; **lo sterzo ha troppo gioco** there is too much play in the steering wheel **6 giochi di luce** play of light and shade; **giochi d'acqua** play of water **7** (*fraseologia*): **gioco di parole** play on words, pun; **è un gioco da ragazzi** it's child's play; **ho deciso di fare il suo gioco** I've decided to play his game; **entrano in gioco diversi fattori** various factors come into play; **essere in gioco** to be at stake; **è in gioco la mia reputazione** my reputation is at stake; **stare al gioco di qn** to play along with sb; **scoprire il proprio gioco** to show one's hand; **prendersi gioco di qn** to pull sb's leg; **per gioco** in *o* for fun; **far buon viso a cattivo gioco** to make the best of a bad job; **fare il doppio gioco con qn** to double-cross sb; **gioco al massacro** character assassination **8** (*Proverbi*): **un bel gioco dura poco** never take a joke too far; **gioco di mano, gioco di villano** never use your fists; **il gioco non vale la candela** the game's not worth the candle

giocoforza [dʒoko'fɔrtsa] SM: **essere giocoforza** to be inevitable

giocoliere [dʒoko'ljɛre] SM juggler

giocoso, -a [dʒo'koso] AGG playful, jocular

giogaia [dʒo'gaja] SF (*Geog*) range of mountains

giogo, -ghi [dʒogo] SM (*Agr, anche fig*) yoke; (*di montagna*) range; (*di bilancia*) beam; **sotto il giogo di** under the yoke of

gioia¹ [dʒɔja] SF **1** (*felicità*) joy, delight; **essere pazzo di gioia** to be beside o.s. with joy, be overjoyed; **darsi alla pazza gioia** to live it up; **le gioie della vita** the joys of life **2** (*fig*): **gioia mia!** darling!; **è la nostra gioia** he's the light of our life

gioia² [dʒɔja] SF (*pietra preziosa*) jewel, precious stone

gioielleria [dʒojelle'ria] SF **1** (*negozio*) jeweller's (*Brit*) *o* jeweler's (*USA*) (shop) **2** (*arte*) jeweller's (*Brit*) *o* jeweler's (*USA*) craft

gioielliere [dʒojel'ljɛre] SM, SF jeweller (*Brit*), jeweler (*USA*)

gioiello [dʒo'jɛllo] SM jewel, piece of jewellery (*Brit*) *o* jewelry (*USA*); (*fig*) jewel, treasure; **i gioielli di mia madre** my mother's jewellery

gioioso, -a [dʒo'joso] AGG joyful, cheerful

Giordania [dʒor'danja] SF Jordan

Giordano [dʒor'dano] SM: **il Giordano** the Jordan

giordano, -a [dʒor'dano] AGG, SM, SF Jordanian

giornalaio, -aia, -ai, -aie [dʒorna'lajo] SM, SF newsagent (*Brit*), newsdealer (*USA*)

giornale [dʒor'nale] SM **1** (news)paper; (*periodico*) journal; **l'ho letto sul giornale** I read it in the newspaper; **lo dicono i giornali, è sui giornali** it's in the papers; **giornale a fumetti** comic; **giornale murale** wall poster; **il giornale radio** the (radio) news; **giornale di strada** *newspaper o magazine sold on the streets by immigrants* **2** (*diario*) diary, journal; **giornale di bordo** (*Naut*) logbook, ship's log

giornaletto [dʒorna'letto] SM (*fam*) (children's) comic

giornaliero, -a [dʒorna'ljɛro] AGG daily ♦ SM **1** (*operaio*) day labourer (*Brit*) *o* laborer (*USA*) **2** (*abbonamento*) day pass, day ticket

giornalino [dʒorna'lino] SM (*fam*) children's comic

giornalismo [dʒorna'lizmo] SM journalism

giornalista, -i, -e [dʒorna'lista] SM, SF journalist; **fa la giornalista** she's a journalist

giornalistico, -a, -ci, -che [dʒorna'listiko] AGG (*stile*) journalistic

giornalmente [dʒornal'mente] AVV daily

giornata [dʒor'nata] SF **1** day; **bella giornata, vero?** lovely day, isn't it?; **durante la giornata** during the day; **durante la giornata di ieri** yesterday; **in giornata** by the end of the day; **fresco di giornata** (*uovo*) new-laid; **è una giornata di cammino/macchina** it's a day's walk/drive away; **come stai?** — mah, va a giornate how are you? — well, a bit up and down; **vivere alla giornata** to live one day to the next; **è proprio la mia giornata!** (*iro*) it's not my day today!; **giornata lavorativa** working day **2** (*paga*) day's wages, day's pay; **lavorare/pagare a giornata** to work/pay by the day

giorno [dʒorno] SM **1** (*periodo di luce*) day(light), day(time); **giorno e notte** day and night; **si fa giorno** it's getting light; **è già giorno** it's daylight; **di giorno** by day, during the

day(time); **preferisco guidare di giorno** I prefer driving during the day; **in pieno giorno** in full daylight; **ci corre come dal giorno alla notte** there's absolutely no comparison **2** (*periodo di tempo*) day; **giorno feriale** weekday; **giorno festivo** holiday; **giorno di paga** payday; **prendere un giorno di ferie** to take a day off; **che giorno è oggi?** what day is it today?; **tutti i giorni** every day; **tutti i santi giorni** every blessed day; **tutto il santo giorno** all day long; **fra 2 giorni** in 2 days' time; **uno di questi giorni** one of these days; **il giorno prima** the day before, the previous day; **il giorno dopo** the day after, the next day, the following day; **a giorni alterni** every other day; **un giorno sì e uno no** on alternate days; **due giorni fa** two days ago; **fra quindici giorni** in a fortnight, in two weeks' time; **al giorno** a *o* per day, per day; **tre volte al giorno** three times a day; **giorno per giorno** day by day; **a giorni** *o* **da un giorno all'altro** any day now **3** (*periodo indeterminato*): **al giorno d'oggi** nowadays; **ha i giorni contati** his days are numbered; **mettere fine ai propri giorni** to put an end to one's life; **passare i propri giorni a fare qc** to spend one's time doing sth; **il giorno dei Morti** All Souls' Day (*Nov 2nd: relatives visit the graves of loved ones to lay flowers*)

giostra [dʒɔstra] SF **1** (*nei luna-park*) merry-go-round **2 le giostre** SFPL the funfair *sg* **3** (*Storia*) joust

giostrare [dʒos'trare] /72/ VI (*aus avere*) (*Storia*) to joust, tilt; **giostrarsi** VIP to manage; **giostrarsi fra i creditori** to manage one's creditors

giov. ABBR (= *giovedì*) Thurs.

giovamento [dʒova'mento] SM benefit, help; **trarre giovamento da qc** to benefit from sth; **non ho avuto nessun giovamento dalla cura** the treatment hasn't done me any good

giovane [dʒovane] AGG (*gen*) young; (*aspetto*) youthful; **non è più tanto giovane** he is not as young as he was; **è più giovane di me** he is younger than me; **è il più giovane della squadra** he's the youngest in the team; **vestirsi giovane** to wear young styles; **è morto in giovane età** he died young; **giovane di spirito** young at heart; **è giovane del mestiere** he's new to the job ♦ SM youth, young man; **i giovani** the young, young people; **giovane di bottega** apprentice; **da giovane** when I was young ♦ SF girl, young woman

giovanetto, -a [dʒova'netto] SM, SF young man *o* woman

giovanile [dʒova'nile] AGG (*aspetto*) youthful; (*scritti*) early; (*errore*) of youth

giovanotto [dʒova'nɔtto] SM young man

giovare [dʒo'vare] /72/ VI (*aus avere o essere*) (*essere utile*) to be useful to; (*far bene*) to be good for; **nascondere la verità non ti gioverà di sicuro** it certainly won't do you any good to conceal the truth; **lavorare fino a tardi non ti giova** working late isn't good for you ♦ VB IMPERS (*essere bene, utile*) to be useful; **a che giova prendersela?** what's the point of getting upset?; **giova sapere che...** it's useful to know that ...; **giovarsi** VIP: **giovarsi di qn/qc** to make use of sb/sth

Giove [dʒɔve] SM (*Mitol*) Jove; (*Astron*) Jupiter

giovedì [dʒove'di] SM INV Thursday; *vedi* **martedì**

giovenca, -che [dʒo'venka] SF heifer

gioventù [dʒoven'tu] SF **1** (*gen*) youth; **errori di gioventù** errors of youth; **in gioventù** in one's youth, in one's younger days **2** (*persone*) young (people); **la gioventù del giorno d'oggi** young people today; **libri per la gioventù** books for the young

gioviale [dʒo'vjale] AGG jolly, jovial

giovinastro [dʒovi'nastro] SM young thug

giovincello [dʒovin'tʃɛllo] SM young lad

giovinezza [dʒovi'nettsa] SF (*gen*) youth; (*di spirito*) youthfulness; **godersi la giovinezza** to enjoy one's youth

GIP, gip [dʒip] ABBR SM INV (*Dir.* = *giudice per le indagini preliminari*)

giradischi [dʒira'diski] SM INV record player

giraffa [dʒi'raffa] SF (*Zool*) giraffe; (*TV, Cine, Radio*) boom

giramento [dʒira'mento] SM: **giramento di testa** fit of dizziness; **mi è venuto un giramento di testa** I feel dizzy

giramondo [dʒira'mondo] SM INV, SF INV globetrotter

girandola [dʒi'randola] SF (*fuochi artificiali*) Catherine wheel; (*giocattolo*) toy windmill; (*banderuola*) weathervane, weathercock

girante [dʒi'rante] SM, SF (*chi gira un assegno*) endorser

girare [dʒi'rare] /72/ VT **1** (*ruota, chiave, sguardo*) to turn; (*pagina*) to turn (over); **ha girato la testa dall'altra parte** he looked the other way; **girare l'angolo** to turn the corner; **ha girato la domanda al presidente** he referred the question to the president; **non girare il discorso** don't change the subject; **girala come ti pare** (*fig*) look at it whichever way you like **2** (*museo, città, negozio*) to go round; **ha girato il mondo** he has travelled the world; **ho girato tutta la città** I've been all over town; **ho girato tutta Londra per trovarlo** I searched all over London for it **3** (*cambiale, assegno*) to endorse **4** (*Cine, TV: scena*) to shoot, film; (: *film: fare le riprese*) to shoot; (*esserne il regista*) to make ♦ VI (*aus* **avere** *o* **essere**) **1** (*gen*) to turn; (*trottola*) to spin; (*ruota*) to revolve; (*tassametro*) to tick away; **girare su se stesso** (*persona*) to turn right round (*rapidamente*) to spin round; **la terra gira intorno al proprio asse** the earth turns on its axis; **continuavano a girare intorno allo stesso argomento** they kept on discussing the same topic; **gli gira intorno da mesi** she's been hanging round him for months; **la strada gira intorno al lago** the road goes round the lake **2** (*errare*) to go round, wander round; **girare per i negozi** to go *o* wander round the shops **3** (*voltare*) to turn; **giri subito a destra** take the first turning on the right **4** (*denaro, notizie*) to circulate; **girano troppi drogati** there are too many drug addicts about **5** (*fraseologia*): **mi gira la testa** I feel dizzy, my head's spinning; **gira al largo!** keep your distance!; **gira e rigira...** after a lot of driving (*o* walking) about ...; (*fig*) whichever way you look at it ...; **cosa ti gira?** (*fam*) what's got into you?; **mi ha fatto girare le scatole** (*fam*) he drove me crazy *o* round the bend; **girarsi** VR (*voltarsi*) to turn (round); (*nel letto*) to turn over; **si è girata e mi ha guardato** she turned round and looked at me; **si girava e rigirava nel letto** he tossed and turned in bed; **non so più da che parte girarmi** (*fig*) I don't know which way to turn

girarrosto [dʒirar'rosto] SM (*Culin*) spit

girasole [dʒira'sole] SM sunflower

girata [dʒi'rata] SF (*di cambiale, assegno*) endorsement

giratario, -ria, -ri, -rie [dʒira'tarjo] SM, SF endorsee

giravolta [dʒira'volta] SF turn, twirl; (*di strada*) sharp bend; (*fig*) about-face, about-turn

giretto [dʒi'retto] SM (*passeggiata*) walk, stroll; (*in macchina*) drive, spin; (*in bicicletta*) ride

girevole [dʒi'revole] AGG (*sedia*) swivel *attr*; (*porta, piattaforma*) revolving

girino [dʒi'rino] SM tadpole

giro ['dʒiro] SM **1** (*circuito, cerchio*) circle; (*di manovella, chiave*) turn; (*Tecn*) revolution; **3000 giri al minuto** 3000 revolutions *o* revs per minute; **compiere un intero giro** to go full circle; **un giro di vite** a turn of the screw; **dare un giro di vite** (*fig*) to put the screws on, put pressure on; **essere nel giro** to belong to a circle (of friends); **un giro di parole** (*fig*) a circumlocution; **essere giù di giri** (*fig*) to be depressed; **essere su di giri** (*fig*) to be on top of the world; **giro d'affari** (*Comm*) turnover **2** (*passeggiata*) walk, stroll; (*in macchina*) drive; (*in bicicletta, a cavallo*) ride; (*viaggio*) tour, trip; (*percorso intorno a*): **fare il giro di** (*parco, città*) to go round; **abbiamo dovuto fare un giro intorno all'isolato** we had to go round the block; **abbiamo dovuto fare un lungo giro** we had to take the long way round; **fare un giro in centro** to have a look round the city centre; **abbiamo fatto un giro in campagna** we went for a walk (*o* a drive *o* a ride) in the country; **giro turistico della città** sightseeing tour of the city; **fare il giro del mondo** to go round the world; **giro d'ispezione** tour of inspection; **il medico sta facendo il giro dei malati** the doctor is doing his rounds **3** (*Sport: di pista*) lap; (*Carte*) hand; **sono al primo giro** they are on the first lap; **giro di Francia** Tour de France; **giro d'onore** lap of honour; **giro di prova** (*Aut*) test lap **4** (*di parte del corpo*) measurement; **giro manica** armhole; **giro vita** waist measurement **5** (*di tempo*): **nel giro di** in the course of; **nel giro di un mese** in a month's time; **a** (*stretto*) **giro di posta** by return of post **6** (*cerchia, ambiente*): **non ti preoccupare, è del nostro giro** don't worry, he's one of us; **essere nel** *o*

del giro to be one of a circle; **entrare in un giro** to become one of a group; **essere fuori dal giro** to be no longer part of a group **7** **in giro, guardarsi in giro** to look around; **andare in giro** to wander about, go about, walk around; **sono stato in giro tutto il giorno** I've been on the go all day; **non trovo la penna, ma dev'essere in giro** I can't find my pen, but it must be around somewhere; **prendere in giro qn** (*stuzzicare*) to pull sb's leg, make fun of sb; (*imbrogliare*) take sb for a ride; **lo prendono in giro perché è grassottello** they make fun of him because he's chubby; **ma va', mi stai prendendo in giro!** come on, you're pulling my leg!; **lascia sempre tutto in giro** he always leaves everything lying about; **mettere in giro** (*voci, denaro*) to circulate; **c'è parecchio denaro falso in giro** there is a lot of counterfeit money in circulation

girocollo [dʒiro'kɔllo] SM: **a girocollo** crewneck *attr*

giroconto [dʒiro'konto] SM (*Fin*) giro credit transfer

girone [dʒi'rone] SM **1** (*dantesco*) circle **2** (*Sport*) series of games; **girone di andata/ritorno** first/second half of the season

gironzolare [dʒirondzo'lare] /72/ VI (*aus* **avere**) to wander *o* stroll about; **gironzolare intorno a qn** (*pegg: importunare*) to hang around sb

girotondo [dʒiro'tondo] SM ring-a-ring-o'roses (*Brit*), ring-around-the-rosey (*USA*); (*Pol*) protest where the protesters *join hands in a circle*

girovagare [dʒirova'gare] /80/ VI (*aus* **avere**) to wander about

girovago, -a, -ghi, -ghe [dʒi'rovago] AGG wandering, strolling; **vita girovaga** itinerant life ♦ SM, SF (*vagabondo*) tramp; (*venditore*) peddler

gita ['dʒita] SF trip, outing; **andare in gita, fare una gita** to go on an outing, go on a trip; **gita in barca** boat trip; **gita scolastica** school trip

gitano, -a [dʒi'tano] AGG, SM, SF gipsy

gitante [dʒi'tante] SM, SF member of a tour

giù [dʒu] AVV **1** (*gen*) down; (*dabbasso*) downstairs; **è sceso giù in giardino** he's gone down to the garden; **scese giù per le scale** he came down the stairs; **è giù in cantina** he's down in the cellar; **scendi giù dal tavolo!** get down off the table!; **mi tiri giù quella scatola** can you get that box down for me?; **vieni giù un minuto** come down a minute; **è venuto giù il tetto** the roof came down; **veniva giù un'acqua!** it was pouring with rain!; **fagli mettere giù quel libro** make him put that book down; **due isolati più in giù** two blocks further down; **spostalo più in giù** move it further down; **la mia casa è un po' più in giù** my house is a bit further on; **cadere a testa in giù** to fall head first; **vai giù di là** go down that way **2** (*al di sotto di*) below; **bambini dai 6 anni in giù** children aged 6 and under; **ce n'erano 30 o giù di lì** there were about 30, there were 30 or thereabouts **3** (*nelle esclamazioni*): **giù!** down!; **giù le mani!** hands off!; **giù di lì!** get down from there!; **e giù botte!** and the fists flew! **4** (*fraseologia*): **essere giù** (*persona: di morale*) to be depressed; (: *di salute*) to be run down; **oggi sono un po' giù** I'm a bit down today; **quel tipo non mi va giù** I can't stand that bloke (*Brit*) *o* guy; **non riesco a mandarla giù** (*fig*) it really sticks in my throat; **buttare giù** *vedi* **buttare** 3

giubba [dʒubba] SF tunic

giubbotto [dʒub'bɔtto] SM jerkin; **giubbotto antiproiettile** bulletproof vest; **giubbotto salvagente** life jacket

giubilare [dʒubi'lare] /72/ AGG jubilee *attr* ♦ VI (*aus* **avere**) to rejoice

giubilo ['dʒubilo] SM rejoicing; **grida di giubilo** shouts of joy

giudicare [dʒudi'kare] /20/ VT **1** (*Dir: causa*) to judge; (: *lite*) to arbitrate in; (: *accusato*): **giudicare (per)** to try (for); **l'hanno giudicato e l'hanno trovato colpevole** they tried him and found him guilty; **l'hanno giudicato colpevole** they found him guilty; **il caso verrà giudicato il prossimo anno** the case will be heard next year **2** (*valutare*) to judge; **non giudicarla con tanta severità** don't judge her so harshly; **giudicare qn abile alla leva/idoneo ad un lavoro** to judge sb fit for military service/suitable for a job **3** (*stimare*) **giudicare qn capace di fare qc** to consider sb capable of doing sth; **anche se mi giudicherai pazzo** even though you think I'm mad; **giudicare qn bene/male** to think well/badly of sb; **giudicare opportuno fare** to consider it advisable to do ♦ vi (*aus* avere) (*dare un giudizio*): **giudicare di** to judge; **se devo giudicare in base alla mia esperienza** judging by my experience; **a giudicare da ciò che dice** judging by what he says; **giudicare dalle apparenze** to judge *o* go by appearances; **sta a voi giudicare** it's up to you to decide *o* judge

giudicato [dʒudiˈkato] SM (*Dir*): **passare in giudicato** to pass final judgment

giudice [ˈdʒuditʃe] SM (*gen*) judge; **farsi giudice** *o* **erigersi a giudice di qc** to set o.s. up as a judge of sth; **giudice collegiale** member of the court; **giudice conciliatore** magistrate, justice of the peace; **giudice di gara** (*Sport*) umpire; **giudice per le indagini preliminari** magistrate in charge of preliminary investigations; **giudice istruttore** examining (*Brit*) *o* committing (*USA*) magistrate; **giudice di linea** (*Tennis*) linesman; **giudice popolare** member of a jury

giudiziale [dʒudit'tsjale] AGG judicial

giudiziario, -ria, -ri, -rie [dʒudit'tsjarjo] AGG legal, judicial

giudizio, -zi [dʒu'dittsjo] SM **1** (*opinione*) judgment, opinion; **dare** *o* **esprimere un giudizio su qn/qc** to express an opinion on sb/sth; **non vorrei esprimere un giudizio troppo affrettato** I wouldn't like to pass judgment *o* to judge too hastily; **a giudizio di qn** in sb's opinion; **a mio giudizio** in my opinion; **chiedere il giudizio di qn** to ask sb's opinion **2** (*discernimento*) judgment; **essere privo di giudizio** to lack judgment; **l'età del giudizio** the age of reason; **denti del giudizio** wisdom teeth; **fai giudizio!** be good! **3** (*Dir: processo*) trial; (: *verdetto*) judgment, verdict; (: *in processi civili*) decision; **essere in attesa di giudizio** to be awaiting trial; **l'imputato è stato rinviato a giudizio** the accused has been committed for trial; **citare in giudizio** to summons **4** (*Rel*) judgment; **il giudizio universale** the Last Judgment

giudizioso, -a [dʒudit'tsjoso] AGG judicious

giuggiola [ˈdʒuddʒola] SF: **andare in brodo di giuggiole** (*fam*) to be over the moon

giugno [ˈdʒuɲɲo] SM June; *vedi* **luglio**

giulivo, -a [dʒuˈlivo] AGG (*letter*) merry

giullare [dʒulˈlare] SM (*Storia*) jester

giumenta [dʒuˈmenta] SF mare

giunco, -chi [ˈdʒunko] SM (*Bot*) rush

giungere [ˈdʒundʒere] VB IRREG /5/ VI (*aus* essere) **giungere a** to arrive at, reach; **giungere all'orecchio di qn** to come to sb's attention *o* notice; **giungere nuovo a qn** to come as news to sb; **giungere alla meta** to achieve one's aim; **giungere in porto** to reach harbour; (*fig*) to have a successful outcome ♦ VT (*unire*) to join

giungla [ˈdʒungla] SF jungle

giunsi [ˈdʒunsi] VB *vedi* **giungere**

giunto, -a [ˈdʒunto] PP *di* giungere ♦ SM (*Tecn*) coupling, joint; **giunto cardanico** universal joint; **giunto elastico** flexible joint

giuntura [dʒunˈtura] SF **1** (*Cucito*) seam **2** (*Anat*) joint

giuocare ecc [dʒwoˈkare] /20/ VT, VI = **giocare**

giuramento [dʒuraˈmento] SM oath; **fare** *o* **prestare un giuramento** to take *o* swear an oath; **venir meno a un giuramento** to break an oath

giurare [dʒuˈrare] /72/ VT to swear; **è vero, te lo giuro!** it's true, I swear!; **giurare di fare qc** to swear to do sth; **giurare fedeltà a qn** to swear *o* pledge loyalty to sb; **giurare il falso** to commit perjury; **ti giuro che non sono stato io** I swear it wasn't me; **ti giuro che non ne posso più** I swear I've had more than I can take; **giurerei di averlo visto prima** I'd swear I have seen him somewhere before; **mi pare che fosse lui, ma non potrei giurarci** I think it was him, but I couldn't swear to it; **io non ci giurerei** I wouldn't swear to it; **gliel'ho giurata** I swore I would get even with him ♦ VI (*aus* avere)) to swear, take an oath; **giurare su qc** to swear on sth; **giurare su qn** to swear by sb

giurato, -a [dʒuˈrato] AGG sworn; **nemico giurato** sworn enemy ♦ SM, SF juror

giuria [dʒuˈria] SF (*Dir*) jury; (*di gara, concorso*) (panel of) judges

giuridico, -a, -ci, -che [dʒuˈridiko] AGG legal

giurisdizione [dʒurizditˈtsjone] SF jurisdiction

giurisprudenza [dʒurispruˈdentsa] SF jurisprudence

giurista, -i, -e [dʒuˈrista] SM, SF jurist

giustapporre [dʒustapˈporre] /77/ VT IRREG to juxtapose

giustapposizione [dʒustappozitˈtsjone] SF juxtaposition

giustapposto, -a [dʒustapˈposto] PP *di* giustapporre

giustificare [dʒustifiˈkare] /20/ VT (*gen*) to justify; (*Amm: spese*) to account for; **il fine giustifica i mezzi** the end justifies the means; **posso giustificarlo** I can understand why he did it; **non lo giustifico, però capisco perché l'ha fatto** I don't excuse him but I understand why he did it; **giustificare il proprio ritardo** to give a reason for one's lateness; **giustificarsi** VR: **giustificarsi per il ritardo** to excuse one's lateness; **si è giustificato dicendo che era stanco** his excuse was that he was tired

giustificativo, -a [dʒustifikaˈtivo] AGG (*Amm*): **nota** *o* **pezza giustificativa** receipt

giustificazione [dʒustifikatˈtsjone] SF **1** (*spiegazione*) justification, explanation; (*prova*) proof; (*Scol*) excuse note, (note of) excuse; **non c'è alcuna giustificazione per quello che hai fatto** there's no excuse for what you did **2** (*Tip*) justification

giustizia [dʒusˈtittsja] SF **1** (*gen*) justice; **in questo mondo non c'è giustizia!** there's no justice in this world!; **render giustizia a qn** to do sb justice; **farsi giustizia (da sé)** (*vendicarsi*) to take the law into one's own hands; **con giustizia** justly, with justice **2** (*autorità*) law; **ricorrere alla giustizia** to have recourse to the law; **affidarsi alla giustizia** to give o.s. up

giustiziare [dʒustitˈtsjare] /19/ VT to execute, put to death

giustiziere [dʒustitˈtsjere] SM executioner

giusto, -a [ˈdʒusto] AGG **1** (*persona, sentenza*) just, fair; **per essere giusto verso di lui** *o* **nei suoi confronti** in fairness to him, to be fair to him; **non mi sembra giusto** it doesn't seem fair to me; **non è giusto!** vince sempre lui it's not fair! he always wins; **il giusto prezzo** the right price; **il giusto mezzo** the happy medium **2** (*calcolo, risposta*) right, correct; (*ragionamento*) sound; (*osservazione*) apt; (*misura, peso, ora*) correct, exact; **dobbiamo aspettare il momento giusto** we'll have to wait for the right moment; **non trovo la parola giusta** I can't find the right word; **tre ore giuste** exactly three hours; **i tuoi stivali mi stanno giusti** your boots fit me perfectly; **queste scarpe mi sono un po' troppo giuste** these shoes are a bit tight on me; **giusto di sale** with enough *o* the right amount of salt; **giusto di cottura** well-cooked ♦ SM **1** righteous person; **i giusti** SMPL the just; (*Rel*) the righteous **2** (*il dovuto*): **chiedere/dare il giusto** ask for/give what's right ♦ AVV **1** (*proprio*) just, exactly; **arrivare giusto in tempo** to arrive just in time; **sono arrivato giusto in tempo** I arrived just in time; **volevo giusto te** you're just *o* exactly the person I wanted; **saranno state giusto le quattro quando mi sono svegliato** it must have been exactly four o'clock when I woke up; **ho finito giusto adesso** I've only just finished; **è andato via giusto adesso** he's just left; **giusto!** right!, of course!; (*a proposito*) that reminds me!; **giusto a me dovevi dare questo lavoro** why did you have to give this job to me? **2** (*rispondere, capire*) correctly; (*indovinare*) rightly; **mirare giusto** to aim straight

glabro, -a [ˈglabro] AGG hairless

glaciale [glaˈtʃale] AGG icy, freezing; (*fig*) icy, frosty; **periodo glaciale** (*Geol*) glacial period, Ice Age

gladiolo [glaˈdiolo] SM gladiolus

glandola [ˈglandola] SF = **ghiandola**

glassa [ˈglassa] SF (*Culin*) icing; **glassa alla vaniglia** vanilla icing

glaucoma [glauˈkɔma] SM glaucoma

gli¹ [ʎi] ART DET MPL *vedi* **il**

gli² [ʎi] PRON PERS **1** (*a lui*) (to) him; (*a esso: riferito ad animale*) (to) it, (to) him; **dagli qualcosa da mangiare** (*persona*) give him something to eat; (*animale*) give it something to eat; **gli ho detto tutto** I told him everything; **scrivigli!** write to him!; **gli sembrava una buona idea** it seemed a good idea to him; **gli ha sorriso** he smiled at him; **dagli una lucidata** give it a polish; **aggiungigli un po' di sale** add a bit of salt to it; **dagli un'occhiata** have a look at it **2** (*in coppia con lo, la, li, le, ne: a lui, a lei, a loro, a esso ecc*): **Gabriele lo sa? — sì, gliel'ho detto** does Gabriele know? — yes, I've told him;

dagliela give it to him (*o* her *o* them); **glieli hai promessi** you promised them to him (*o* her *o* them); **glielo ha detto** he told him (*o* her *o* them); **gliele ha spedite** he sent them to him (*o* her *o* them); **gliene ho parlato** I spoke to him (*o* her *o* them) about it

glicemia [glitʃeˈmia] SF (*Med*) glycaemia

glicerina [glitʃeˈrina] SF glycerine

glicine [ˈglitʃine] SM wistaria

gliela *ecc vedi* **gli²**

globale [gloˈbale] AGG (*gen*) overall, inclusive; (*spesa, reddito*) total; (*visione*) global

globo [ˈglɔbo] SM globe; **globo oculare** eyeball; **il globo terrestre** the globe

globulo [ˈglɔbulo] SM globule; (*Anat*): **globulo bianco/rosso** white/red corpuscle, white/red blood cell

gloria [ˈglɔrja] SF 1 (*fama*) glory, fame; **coprirsi di gloria** to cover o.s. in glory; **lavorare per la gloria** (*iro*) to work for peanuts 2 (*vanto*) pride; **farsi gloria di qc** to pride o.s. on sth, take pride in sth

gloriarsi [gloˈrjarsi] /72/ VIP: **gloriarsi di qc** to glory in sth

glorificare [glorifiˈkare] /20/ VT to glorify

glorioso, -a [gloˈrjoso] AGG glorious

glossario, -ri [glosˈsarjo] SM glossary

glucosio [gluˈkɔzjo] SM glucose

gluteo [ˈgluteo] SM gluteus (*Anat*); **glutei** SMPL buttocks

GM ABBR = **genio militare**

gnocco, -chi [ˈɲɔkko] SM 1 (*Culin*) small dumpling made of potato or semolina 2 (*fig: fam*) dolt, idiot

gnomo [ˈɲɔmo] SM gnome

gnorri [ˈɲɔrri] SM INV, SF INV: **non fare lo gnorri!** stop acting as if you didn't know anything about it!

GO SIGLA = **Gorizia**

goal [ˈgoul] SM INV = **gol**

gobba [ˈgɔbba] SF (*Anat, Zool*) hump; (*di terreno, naso*) bump

gobbo, -a [ˈgɔbbo] AGG (*che ha una gobba*) hunchbacked; (*ricurvo*) bent ♦ SM, SF hunchback

Gobi [ˈgɔbi] SM: **il Deserto dei Gobi** the Gobi Desert

goccia, -ce [ˈgottʃa] SF (*gen*) drop; (*di sudore*) bead; **goccia a goccia** drop by drop; **goccia di rugiada** dewdrop; **le prime gocce di pioggia** the first drops *o* spots of rain; **gocce per il naso/gli occhi** nose/eyedrops; **una goccia d'olio** a drop of oil; **orecchini a goccia** drop earrings; **somigliarsi come due gocce d'acqua** to be as like as two peas in a pod; **avere la goccia al naso** to have a runny nose; **è la goccia che fa traboccare il vaso!** it's the last straw!

goccio, -ci [ˈgottʃo] SM drop, spot; **vuoi un goccio di vino?** would you like some wine?, would you like a drop of wine?

gocciolare [gottʃoˈlare] /72/ VI (*aus avere o essere*) to drip; **mi gocciola il naso** I've got a runny nose, my nose is running; **l'acqua gocciola dal rubinetto, il rubinetto gocciola** the tap's dripping; **l'acqua gocciola dal soffitto** there's water coming in through the ceiling ♦ VB IMPERS to drizzle

gocciolio, -lii [gottʃoˈlio] SM dripping

godere [goˈdere] VB IRREG /58/ VT 1 (*gustare: pace, fresco*) to enjoy; (: *bene, rendita*) to enjoy, benefit from 2 **godersi il sole** to soak up the sun; **godersi la vita** to enjoy life; **godersela** to enjoy o.s., have a good time; **si è goduta sua suocera per due mesi** (*iro*) she had the pleasure of her mother-in-law's company for two months ♦ VI (*aus avere*) 1 (*essere felice*): **godere di** to enjoy, rejoice at *o* in, be delighted (at); **godere nel fare qc** to enjoy *o* delight in doing sth; **godere delle disgrazie altrui** to take pleasure in other people's misfortunes; **godere della compagnia di qn** to enjoy sb's company; **godere all'idea che...** to rejoice at the thought of ... 2 (*possedere*): **godere di** (*buona salute, reputazione*) to enjoy; **gode di buona salute** she enjoys good health; **godere di riduzioni speciali** to benefit from special reductions

godimento [godiˈmento] SM 1 (*piacere*) pleasure, enjoyment 2 (*Dir*) enjoyment, possession

godrò *ecc* [goˈdrɔ] VB *vedi* **godere**

goffaggine [gofˈfaddʒine] SF clumsiness

goffo, -a [ˈgɔffo] AGG (*persona, gesto*) clumsy, awkward; (*vestito*) inelegant; **è un po' goffo** he's a bit clumsy; **è la persona più goffa che abbia mai conosciuto** he's the clumsiest person I've ever met

gogna [ˈgoɲɲa] SF pillory; **mettere qn alla gogna** (*anche fig*) to pillory sb

gol [gɔl] SM INV (*Sport*) goal; **segnare un gol** to score a goal; **il gol del pareggio** the equalizer

gola [ˈgola] SF 1 (*Anat*) throat; **avere mal di gola** to have a sore throat; **tagliare la gola a qn** to cut sb's throat; **ricacciare il pianto** *o* **le lacrime in gola** to swallow one's tears 2 (*golosità*) gluttony, greed; **fare gola a qn** to tempt sb 3 (*di montagna*) gorge 4 (*di camino*) flue

goletta [goˈletta] SF (*Naut*) schooner

golf¹ [gɔlf] SM (*sport*) golf; **giocare a golf** to play golf; **campo da golf** golf course; **giocatore di golf** golfer

golf² [gɔlf] SM INV jumper; (*con bottoni*) cardigan

golfo [ˈgolfo] SM gulf; **il golfo del Messico** the Gulf of Mexico; **il golfo di Napoli** the Bay of Naples; **il golfo Persico** the Gulf

goliardico, -a, -ci, -che [goˈljardiko] AGG (*canto, vita*) student *attr*

goloso, -a [goˈloso] AGG greedy; **è golosa di dolci** she has a sweet tooth

golpe [ˈgolpe] SM INV (*Pol*) coup

gomitata [gomiˈtata] SF: **dare una gomitata a qn** to nudge sb; (*per zittire ecc*) to nudge sb; **mi ha dato una gomitata nello stomaco** he elbowed me in the stomach; **farsi avanti a (forza** *o* **furia di) gomitate** to elbow one's way through; **fare a gomitate per qc** to fight to get sth

gomito [ˈgomito] SM (*Anat*) elbow; (*di tubatura*) bend; **a gomito** (*tubo, giunto*) L-shaped; **curva a gomito** hairpin bend; **gomito a gomito** shoulder to shoulder; **alzare il gomito** (*fig*) to drink too much

gomitolo [goˈmitolo] SM (*di lana, filo*) ball

gomma [ˈgomma] SF 1 (*Bot*) gum; (*caucciù*) rubber; (*per cancellare*) rubber (*Brit*), eraser; **mi presti la gomma?** can I borrow your eraser?; **gomma arabica** gum arabic; **gomma da masticare** chewing gum 2 (*pneumatico*) tyre (*Brit*), tire (*USA*); **avere una gomma a terra** to have a flat tyre; **trasporto su gomma** road transport; **gomma rigenerata** (*Aut*) remould

gommino [gomˈmino] SM (*gen*) rubber tip; (*rondella*) rubber washer

gommista, -i, -e [gomˈmista] SM, SF tyre (*Brit*) *o* tire (*USA*) specialist; (*rivenditore*) tyre *o* tire merchant

gommone [gomˈmone] SM rubber dinghy

gommoso, -a [gomˈmoso] AGG rubbery

gondola [ˈgondola] SF 1 gondola 2 (*Aer*): **gondola del motore** engine pod

gondoliere [gondoˈljɛre] SM gondolier

gonfalone [gonfaˈlone] SM (*Storia*) banner

gonfiare [gonˈfjare] /19/ VT 1 (*palloncino*) to blow up, inflate; (*con pompa*) to inflate, pump up; (*le guance*) to puff out, blow out; **devo gonfiare le gomme della bici** I need to pump up the tyres on my bike 2 (*fiume, vele*) to swell; (*fig: lo stomaco*) beer makes me feel bloated 3 (*fig: notizia, fatto*) to exaggerate; **gonfiarsi** VIP (*gen*) to swell (up); (*fiume*) to rise; **mi si è gonfiata la caviglia** my ankle is swollen

gonfio, -fia, -fi, -fie [ˈgonfjo] AGG 1 (*occhi, piedi*) swollen; (*fiume*) swollen; (*vela*) full; (*stile*) bombastic, wordy; **gonfio di orgoglio** (*persona*) puffed up (with pride); **aveva il cuore gonfio (di dolore)** her heart was heavy; **aveva gli occhi gonfi per il pianto** her eyes were puffy with crying; **ho il piede gonfio** my foot's swollen; **mi sento gonfio** I feel bloated; **avere il portafoglio gonfio** to have a bulging wallet 2 (*palloncino, gomme*) inflated, blown up; (*con pompa*) inflated, pumped up

gonfiore [gonˈfjore] SM swelling

gongolare [gongoˈlare] /72/ VI (*aus avere*) **gongolare (per)** to look pleased with o.s. (about); **gongolare di gioia** to be overjoyed

gonna [ˈgonna] SF skirt; **una gonna lunga** a long skirt; **stare attaccato alle gonne della madre** to cling to one's mother's apron strings; **gonna pantalone** culottes *pl*

gonzo [ˈgondzo] SM simpleton, dolt, fool

goo'glare [guˈglare] /72/ VT (*Inform*) to google

gorgheggiare [gorgedˈdʒare] /62/ VI (*aus avere*) (*cantante*) to trill; (*uccello*) to warble

gorgheggio, -gi [gor'geddʒo] SM (*Mus*) trill; (*di uccello*) warbling

gorgo, -ghi ['gorgo] SM whirlpool; **essere preso nel gorgo della passione** to be in the grip of passion

gorgogliare [gorgoʎ'ʎare] /27/ VI (*aus* **avere**) to gurgle

gorgoglio, -glii [gorgoʎ'ʎio] SM gurgling

gorilla [go'rilla] SM INV 1 (*Zool*) gorilla 2 (*fig: guardia del corpo*) bodyguard

gotico, -a, -ci, -che ['gɔtiko] AGG, SM (*scrittura, architettura*) Gothic

gotta ['gotta] SF gout

governante¹ [gover'nante] SM ruler

governante² [gover'nante] SF (*donna di servizio*) housekeeper; (*di bambini*) governess

governare [gover'nare] /72/ VT 1 (*stato, nazione*) to govern, rule 2 (*barca, nave*) to steer; (*bestiame*) to look after, tend

governativo, -a [governa'tivo] AGG (*politica, decreto*) government *attr*, governmental; (*stampa*) pro-government

governatore, -trice [governa'tore] SM, SF governor; (*di Regione*) directly elected leader of an Italian region

governo [go'verno] SM 1 (*regime*) government; (*gabinetto*) Cabinet, Government; **il governo britannico** the British government; **crisi di governo** Government crisis; **governo ponte** caretaker government; **i partiti al governo** the parties in power *o* in office 2 (*di cavallo*) grooming

gozzo ['gottso] SM (*di uccello*) crop; (*Med*) goitre; (*fig: fam*) throat; **restare sul gozzo** (*fig*) to stick in one's throat; **se hai qualcosa sul gozzo sarà meglio che parli** if something is bothering you, you'd better spit it out

gozzovigliare [gottsoviʎ'ʎare] /27/ VI (*aus* **avere**) to make merry, carouse

GPL [dʒipi'elle] SIGLA M (= *Gas di Petrolio Liquefatto*) LPG (= *Liquefied Petroleum Gas*)

gpm ABBR (= *giri per minuto*) rpm

GPS [dʒipi'esse] SIGLA M GPS (= *Global Positioning System*)

GR [dʒi'erre] SIGLA = **Grosseto** ◆ SIGLA M INV = **giornale radio**

gracchiare [grak'kjare] /19/ VI (*aus* **avere**) (*cornacchia*) to caw, croak; (*telefono, radio*) to crackle; (*persona*) to croak

gracidare [gratʃi'dare] /72/ VI (*aus* **avere**) (*rana*) to croak

gracidio, -dii [gratʃi'dio] SM croaking

gracile ['gratʃile] AGG (*persona, costituzione*) delicate, frail; (*braccia, gambe*) slender

gradasso [gra'dasso] SM braggart, boaster; **che gradasso!** what a loudmouth!

gradatamente [gradata'mente] AVV gradually, by degrees

gradazione [gradat'tsjone] SF (*sfumatura*) gradation; **gradazione alcolica** alcoholic content *o* strength

gradevole [gra'devole] AGG agreeable, pleasant

gradimento [gradi'mento] SM pleasure, satisfaction; **non è di mio gradimento** it's not my taste *o* liking

gradinata [gradi'nata] SF (*scalinata*) (flight of) steps *pl*; (*di stadio*) terraces (*Brit*) *pl*, terracing (*Brit*); (*in anfiteatro*) tiers *pl*; **abbiamo seguito la partita dalla gradinata** we watched the match from the terraces

gradino [gra'dino] SM (*gen*) step; (*Alpinismo*) foothold; "**attenti al gradino**" "mind the step"; **è salito di un gradino nella carriera** he has taken a step forward in his career; **è l'ultimo gradino della scala sociale** it's the bottom rung of the social ladder

gradire [gra'dire] /55/ VT 1 (*accogliere, ricevere con piacere*) to accept (with pleasure); **gradire un dono/un invito** to accept a gift/an invitation with pleasure; **ho gradito molto il vostro regalo** I was delighted with your present; **...tanto per gradire** I shouldn't, but ...; **gradisca i miei omaggi** please accept my best wishes; **ho gradito la sua visita** I enjoyed your visit 2 (*frm: desiderare*) to like, want, wish; **gradisce un caffè?** would you like a coffee?; **gradirei avere un po' di pace** I should like some peace and quiet

gradito, -a [gra'dito] AGG welcome

grado¹ ['grado] SM: **di buon grado** willingly

grado² ['grado] SM 1 (*gen*) degree; (*livello*) degree, level; (*Alpinismo*) grade; **per gradi** by degrees; **un cugino di primo/secondo grado** a first/second cousin; **essere in grado di fare qc** to be able to do sth; **presto sarà in grado di camminare di nuovo** he'll soon be able to walk again; **non sono**

in grado di farlo da solo I can't do it by myself; **cinque gradi sotto zero** five degrees below zero; **subire il terzo grado** (*anche fig*) to be given the third degree 2 (*Mil: sociale*) rank; **salire di grado** to be promoted; **perdere i gradi** to lose one's stripes

graduale [gradu'ale] AGG gradual

graduare [gradu'are] /72/ VT (*scala, termometro*) to graduate; (*difficoltà*) to increase by degrees

graduato, -a [gradu'ato] AGG (*scala, termometro*) graduated; (*esercizi*) graded ◆ SM (*Mil*) non-commissioned officer
☐ **graduato** non si traduce mai con la parola inglese *graduate*

graduatoria [gradua'torja] SF (*di concorso*) list; (*per promozione*) order of seniority

graffa ['graffa] SF (*Tip: parentesi*) brace; (*punto metallico*) staple

graffetta [graf'fetta] SF (*fermaglio*) paper clip; (*punto metallico*) staple

graffiare [graf'fjare] /19/ VT to scratch; **il gatto mi ha graffiato la mano** the cat scratched my hand; **graffiarsi** VIP to get scratched; **il CD si è graffiato** the CD got scratched

graffiatura [graffja'tura] SF scratch

graffio, -fi ['graffjo] SM scratch

graffiti [graf'fiti] SMPL graffiti *sg*

grafia [gra'fia] SF (*di parola*) spelling; (*scrittura*) handwriting

grafico, -a, -ci, -che ['grafiko] AGG graphic ◆ SM 1 (*diagramma*) graph; **il grafico illustra il calo nelle vendite** the graph shows the drop in sales 2 (*disegnatore*) commercial artist, graphic designer; **fa il grafico** he's a graphic designer; **grafico industriale** draughtsman (*Brit*), draftsman (*USA*)

gramigna [gra'miɲɲa] SF (*Bot*) couch grass; (*erbaccia*) weed

grammatica, -che [gram'matika] SF grammar; **un errore di grammatica** a grammatical error; **libro di grammatica** grammar book

grammaticale [grammati'kale] AGG grammatical

grammo ['grammo] SM gram, gramme (*Brit*)

grammofono [gram'mɔfono] SM gramophone

gramo, -a ['gramo] AGG (*vita*) wretched

gran [gran] AGG *vedi* **grande**

grana¹ ['grana] SF grain; **di grana grossa** coarse-grained

grana² ['grana] SF (*fam: seccatura*) trouble; **avere delle grane** to have problems; **piantare grane** to stir up trouble

grana³ ['grana] SM INV *cheese similar to Parmesan*

grana⁴ ['grana] SF INV (*fam*) cash; **essere pieno di grana** to be rolling in it, be stinking rich

granaglie [gra'naʎʎe] SFPL corn seed *sg*, corn *sg*

granaio, -ai [gra'najo] SM barn, granary

granata¹ [gra'nata] SF (*Mil*) grenade

granata² [gra'nata] SF (*Bot*) pomegranate ◆ AGG (*colore*) garnet(-coloured)

granatiere [grana'tjere] SM (*Mil*) grenadier; (*fig*) fine figure of a man

Gran Bretagna [granbre'taɲɲa] SF Great Britain

grancassa [gran'kassa] SF (*Mus*) bass drum

granchio, -chi ['grankjo] SM (*Zool*) crab; (*fig: errore*) blunder; **prendere un granchio** (*fig*) to blunder

grandangolo [gran'dangolo], **grandangolare** [grandango'lare] SM (*Fot*) wide-angle lens *sg*

PAROLA CHIAVE

grande ['grande] AGG *a volte* gran + *consonante*, grand' + *vocale*

1 (*gen*) big; (*quantità*) large; (*alto*) tall; (*montagna*) high; (*largo*) wide, broad; (*lungo*) long; (*forte: rumore*) loud; (*: vento*) strong, high; (*: pioggia*) heavy; (*: caldo*) intense; (*: affetto, bisogno*) great; (*: sospiro*) deep; **è grande per la sua età** he's big for his age; **un ragazzo grande e grosso** a big strong boy; **un grande invalido** a seriously disabled person; **la gran maggioranza degli italiani** the great *o* vast majority of Italians; **ha una grande opinione di sé** he has a high opinion of himself; **il gran pubblico** the general public; **una taglia più grande** a larger *o* bigger size

2 (*di età*): **sei abbastanza grande per capire** you're big *o* old enough to understand; **farsi grande** to grow up; **hanno due figli grandi** they have two grown-up children; **mio fratello**

più grande my big *o* older brother; **è più grande di me** he's older than me
3 (*importante, rilevante*) great; (*illustre, nobile*) noble, great; **è arrivato il gran giorno** the great day dawned; **un grande musicista** a great musician; **un grande poeta** a great poet; **le grandi potenze** (*Pol*) the major powers; **è un gran signore** he's a real gentleman; **ha fatto grandi spese** he's been spending his money
4 (*rafforzativo: lavoratore*) hard; (: *bevitore*) heavy; (: *amico, bugiardo*) great; **è un gran bellguaio** it's one big mess; **una gran bella vita** a great life; **oggi fa un gran caldo** it's extremely hot today; **di gran classe** (*prodotto*) high-class; **la famiglia al gran completo** the entire family; **è un gran cretino** he's an utter fool; **per sua gran fortuna non c'era la polizia** he was really lucky that the police weren't around; **oggi fa un gran freddo** it's extremely cold today; **in gran parte** to a large extent, mainly; **ha fatto una gran risata** he laughed loudly; **con mia gran sorpresa** to my great surprise
5 (*fraseologia*): **ti farà un gran bene** it'll do you good; **non ci ho fatto gran caso** I didn't really notice; **non ne so (un) gran che** I don't know very much about it; **non è** *o* **non vale (un) gran che** it (*o* he *ecc*) is nothing special; **quel quadro non è poi (una) gran cosa** that painting's nothing special
♦ SM, SF
1 (*persona adulta*) adult, grown-up; **cosa farai da grande?** what will you be *o* do when you grow up?
2 (*persona importante*) great person; **fare il grande** (*strafare*) to act big; **Pietro il Grande** Peter the Great
♦ SM: **fare le cose in grande** to do things on a grand scale, do things in style

grandeggiare [grandedˈdʒare] /62/ VI (*aus* avere) **1** **grandeggiare (su)** to tower (over) **2** (*darsi arie*) to put on airs, give *o.s.* airs

grandezza [granˈdettsa] SF **1** (*dimensione*) size; (*Astron*) magnitude; (*Mat, Fis*) quantity; **di media grandezza** of average size; **a** *o* **in grandezza naturale** life-size(d) **2** (*fig: qualità*) greatness; **grandezza d'animo** nobility of soul **3** (*fasto*) grandeur; **manie di grandezza** delusions of grandeur

grandinare [grandiˈnare] /72/ VB IMPERS to hail; **ieri è grandinato** it hailed yesterday ♦ VI (*aus* essere) (*fig: bombe, proiettili*) to hail down

grandine [ˈgrandine] SF hail; **un chicco di grandine** a hailstone

grandioso, -a [granˈdjoso] AGG grandiose, magnificent; **dalle idee grandiose** with grandiose ideas; **avere un'idea grandiosa** to have a great idea

granduca, -chi [granˈduka] SM grand duke
granducato [granduˈkato] SM grand duchy
granduchessa [granduˈkessa] SF grand duchess
granello [graˈnello] SM (*di sabbia, sale*) grain; (*di polvere*) speck; **un granello di pepe** a peppercorn
granita [graˈnita] SF *kind of water ice*
granito [graˈnito] SM (*Geol*) granite
grano [ˈgrano] SM **1** (*Bot*) grain, wheat **2** (*chicco: gen*) grain; (: *di rosario*) bead; **un grano di pepe** a peppercorn; **pepe in grani** peppercorns
granturco [granˈturko] SM (*Bot*) maize (*Brit*), (Indian) corn (*USA*); **pannocchia di granturco** corncob
granulo [ˈgranulo] SM granule; (*Med*) pellet
grappa [ˈgrappa] SF grappa
❑ **grappa** non si traduce mai con la parola inglese *grape*
grappolo [ˈgrappolo] SM bunch, cluster; **un grappolo d'uva** a bunch of grapes
grassetto [grasˈsetto] SM (*Tip*) bold (type) (*Brit*), bold face
grasso, -a [ˈgrasso] AGG **1** (*gen*) fat; (*cibo*) fatty; (*pelle, capelli*) greasy; (*terreno*) rich, fertile; **un signore grasso** a fat man; **cucina grassa** oily cooking; **dovresti evitare i cibi grassi** you should avoid fatty food; **formaggio grasso** full-fat cheese; **un'annata grassa** (*Agr*) a good year; **pianta grassa** succulent plant **2** (*volgare*) lewd, coarse; **una grassa risata** a coarse laugh ♦ SM (*adipe, anche Culin*) fat; (*unto*) grease; **una macchia di grasso** a grease stain; **grassi animali e vegetali** animal and vegetable fats; **senza grassi** fat free; **grasso per**

cucinare cooking fat; **grasso (per lubrificare)** (lubricating) grease; **grasso di balena** blubber
grassoccio, -cia, -ci, -ce [grasˈsɔttʃo] AGG plump, podgy
grassone, -a [grasˈsone] SM, SF (*fam: persona*) dumpling
grata [ˈgrata] SF grating
graticcio, -ci [graˈtittʃo] SM (*di vimini ecc*) trellis; (*stuoia*) mat
graticola [graˈtikola] SF (*Culin*) grill
gratifica, -che [graˈtifika] SF bonus
gratificazione [gratifikatˈtsjone] SF (*soddisfazione*) satisfaction, reward
gratinare [gratiˈnare] /72/ VT (*Culin*) to cook au gratin
gratis [ˈgratis] AVV (*viaggiare*) free; (*lavorare*) for nothing; **i bambini viaggiano gratis** children travel free; **me l'ha riparato gratis** he repaired it for me for nothing; **biglietto gratis** free ticket; **ingresso gratis** admission free
gratitudine [gratiˈtudine] SF gratitude
grato, -a [ˈgrato] AGG (*riconoscente*) grateful; **ti sono molto grato** I am very grateful to you
grattacapo [grattaˈkapo] SM worry, headache (*fig*)
grattacielo [grattaˈtʃelo] SM skyscraper
gratta e 'sosta SM INV *scratch card used to pay for parking*
gratta e 'vinci [ˈgratta e ˈvintʃi] SM INV (*biglietto*) scratchcard; (*lotteria*) scratchcard lottery
grattare [gratˈtare] /72/ VT **1** to scratch; **grattar via** (*vernice*) to scrape off; **grattarsi la testa** to scratch one's head; **si grattava la schiena** he was scratching his back; **grattarsi la pancia** (*fig*) to twiddle one's thumbs; **grattare il violino** (*fam*) to scrape on the violin **2** (*grattugiare*) to grate **3** (*fam: rubare*) to steal, nick (*Brit*) ♦ VI (*aus* avere) (*stridere*) to grate; (*Aut: marcia*) to grind; **grattarsi** VR to scratch (o.s.); **smettila di grattarti!** stop scratching!
grattata [gratˈtata] SF **1** (*alla testa*) scratch; **darsi una grattata alla testa** to scratch one's head **2** (*Aut: fam*): **fare una grattata** to grind the gears
grattugia, -gie [gratˈtudʒa] SF grater
grattugiare [grattuˈdʒare] /62/ VT to grate; **pane grattugiato** breadcrumbs *pl*
gratuità [gratuiˈta] SF (*anche fig*) gratuitousness
❑ **gratuità** non si traduce mai con la parola inglese *gratuity*
gratuito, -a [graˈtuito] AGG **1** (*gratis*) free; **l'ingresso è gratuito** admission is free **2** (*fig: critiche, commenti*) gratuitous, uncalled-for
gravame [graˈvame] SM: **gravame fiscale** tax
gravare [graˈvare] /72/ VT: **gravare di** (*responsabilità, imposte*) to burden with ♦ VI (*aus* essere) **gravare su** to weigh on, lie heavy on
grave [ˈgrave] AGG **1** (*pericolo, errore*) grave, serious; (*responsabilità*) heavy, grave; (*contegno*) grave, solemn; **una malattia grave** a serious illness; **un malato grave** a seriously ill patient, a person who is seriously ill; **non è grave** it's not serious; **non è niente di grave** it's nothing serious **2** (*suono, voce*) deep, low-pitched **3** (*Gramm*) **accento grave** grave accent ♦ SM (*Fis*) (heavy) body
gravemente [graveˈmente] AVV (*in modo solenne*) gravely, solemnly; (*seriamente*) seriously, gravely; **è rimasto gravemente ferito** he was seriously injured
gravidanza [graviˈdantsa] SF pregnancy; **una gravidanza difficile** a difficult pregnancy
gravido, -a [ˈgravido] AGG pregnant; **gravido di minaccia** fraught with *o* full of menace
gravità [graviˈta] SF INV **1** (*di errore, situazione, malattia*) seriousness, gravity; (*di comportamento, occasione*) solemnity, gravity; (*di punizione*) severity **2** (*Fis*) gravity; **la legge di gravità** the law of gravity; **la forza di gravità** gravity
gravitare [graviˈtare] /72/ VI (*aus* avere) (*Fis, anche fig*): **gravitare intorno a** to gravitate round; **gravitare verso** to gravitate towards
gravoso, -a [graˈvoso] AGG (*tasso, imposta*) heavy, onerous; **un compito gravoso** a hard *o* onerous task
grazia [ˈgrattsja] SF **1** (*di persona*) grace; **la grazia di una ballerina** the grace of a ballerina; **piena di grazia** graceful; **muoversi con grazia** to move gracefully; **di buona/mala grazia** with good/bad grace **2** (*favore, benevolenza*) favour (*Brit*), favor (*USA*); **entrare nelle grazie di qn** to win sb's

favo(u)r; **essere nelle grazie di qn** to be in sb's good graces *o* books; **di grazia** (*iro*) if you please; **troppa grazia!** (*iro*) you're too generous! **3** (*misericordia*) mercy; (*Dir*) pardon; **concedere la grazia a qn** to pardon sb; **ottenere la grazia** to be pardoned; **Ministero di Grazia e Giustizia** Ministry of Justice, ≈ Lord Chancellor's Office (*Brit*), ≈ Department of Justice (*USA*) **4** (*Rel*) grace; **quanta grazia di Dio!** what abundance! **5** (*Mitol*): **le tre Grazie** the three Graces **6** (*titolo*): **Sua Grazia** Your Grace

graziare [grat'tsjare] /19/ ντ (*Dir*) to pardon

grazie ['grattsje] ESCL thank you, thanks; **vuole un caffè? —** (**sì**) **grazie/no grazie** would you like some coffee? — yes, please/no, thank you; **hai trovato i libri? — sì grazie** did you find the books? — yes, thanks; **mille** *o* **tante grazie!** many thanks!; **Marco non è mai stanco — grazie al cavolo** *o* **grazie tante, lui non fa mai niente!** Marco is never tired — and neither he should be, since he never does a thing! ◆ **grazie a** PREP thanks to; **grazie a lui** thanks to him; **grazie a Dio!** thank God! ◆ SM INV thank you; **non ho avuto neanche un grazie** I did not get a word of thanks; **dille un grazie da parte mia** thank her for me

grazioso, -a [grat'tsjoso] AGG (*piacevole*) delightful, charming; (*gentile*) kind, gracious

Grecia ['gretʃa] SF Greece; **mi piace la Grecia** I like Greece; **andremo in Grecia quest'estate** we're going to Greece this summer

greco, -a, -ci, -che ['grɛko] AGG, SM, SF Greek ◆ SM (*lingua*) Greek; **greco antico/moderno** Ancient/Modern Greek

gregario, -ria, -ri, -rie [gre'garjo] AGG (*Bot, Zool*) gregarious ◆ SM (*Ciclismo*) supporting rider; (*Pol*) follower, supporter

gregge ['greddʒe] (*pl f* **greggi**) SM (*gen, anche fig*) flock; **un gregge di pecore** a flock of sheep

greggio, -gia, -gi, -ge ['greddʒo] AGG (*materia*) raw, unrefined; (*petrolio*) crude; (*diamante*) rough, uncut; (*cuoio*) untanned, untreated; (*tessuto*) unbleached ◆ SM crude oil

grembiule [grem'bjule] SM apron; (*sopravveste*) overall (*Brit*), work coat (*USA*)

grembo ['grembo] SM **1** (*ginocchia*) lap; **tenere qn in grembo** to have sb on one's knee *o* in one's arms **2** (*ventre materno*) womb; **in grembo alla famiglia** in the bosom of one's family

gremito, -a [gre'mito] AGG: **gremito di** packed *o* crowded *o* crammed with

greto ['greto] SM (exposed) gravel bed of a river

gretto, -a ['gretto] AGG **1** (*meschino*) petty, narrow-minded **2** (*avaro*) mean, stingy

greve ['grɛve] AGG heavy

grezzo, -a ['greddzo] AGG **1** = **greggio 2** (*poco raffinato*) coarse, rough

gridare [gri'dare] /72/ VI (*aus avere*) (*gen*) to shout, cry (out); (*strillare*) to scream, yell; (*animale*) to call; **smettila di gridare!** stop shouting!; **gridare a squarciagola** to yell at the top of one's voice; **gridare di dolore** to cry out *o* scream out in pain ◆ VT to shout (out), yell (out); **gridare aiuto** to cry *o* shout for help; **abbiamo sentito qn che gridava aiuto** we heard someone shouting for help; **gridare qc ai quattro venti** to shout *o* cry sth from the rooftops; **gridare vendetta** to cry out for vengeance

grido ['grido] SM **1** (*pl f* **grida**) (*gen*) shout, cry; (*strillo*) scream, yell; **le grida dei bambini** the children's shouts; **un grido di dolore** a cry of pain; **un grido di aiuto** a cry for help; **i soccorritori hanno sentito le sue grida di aiuto** the rescuers heard his cries for help; **lanciare grida di gioia** to shout for joy; **un cantante di grido** a famous singer; **è l'ultimo grido (della moda)** it's the latest fashion; **vestito all'ultimo grido** dressed in the latest style **2** (*pl m* **gridi**): *di animale:* cry

  ❑ **grido** non si traduce mai con la parola inglese *grid*

grigio, -gia, -gi, -gie ['gridʒo] AGG grey (*Brit*), gray (*USA*); (*fig*) dull, boring; **ha i capelli grigi** she's got grey hair; **materia grigia** (*Anat*) grey matter ◆ SM grey (*Brit*), gray (*USA*); **grigio argento** silver grey

griglia ['griʎʎa] SF **1** (*Culin*) grill (*Brit*), broiler (*USA*); **alla griglia** grilled (*Brit*), broiled (*USA*); **una bistecca alla**

griglia a grilled steak **2** (*di stufa, focolare*) grate; (*di apertura*) grating **3** (*Aut*) grille **4** (*Elettr*) grid

grigliata [griʎ'ʎata] SF (*Culin*) grill; **fare una grigliata sulla spiaggia** to have a beach barbecue; **grigliata mista** mixed grill

grilletto [gril'letto] SM trigger; **premere il grilletto** to pull the trigger

grillo ['grillo] SM **1** (*Zool*) cricket **2** (*fig*) whim; **gli è saltato il grillo di...** he's taken it into his head to ...; **ha dei grilli per la testa** his head is full of nonsense **3** (*Naut*) shackle

grimaldello [grimal'dɛllo] SM picklock

grinfia ['grinfja] SF: **cadere nelle grinfie di qn** to fall into sb's clutches

grinta ['grinta] SF (*di persona*) determination; (*nello Sport*) pluck; **avere molta grinta** to be very determined; **una macchina che ha grinta** a car with aggressive acceleration

grintoso, -a [grin'toso] AGG (*persona*) forceful; (*nello Sport*) plucky, combative

grinza ['grintsa] SF (*di pelle*) wrinkle; (*di stoffa*) wrinkle, crease; **il tuo ragionamento non fa una grinza** your argument is faultless

grinzoso, -a [grin'tsoso] AGG (*vedi sf*) wrinkled; creased

grippare [grip'pare] /72/ VI (*aus avere*), **gripparsi** VIP (*Tecn*) to seize (up), jam

grissino [gris'sino] SM bread-stick

groenlandese [groenlan'dese] SM, SF Greenlander ◆ AGG Greenland *attr*

Groenlandia [groen'landja] SF Greenland

gronda ['gronda] SF eaves *pl*

grondaia [gron'daja] SF gutter

grondante [gron'dante] AGG dripping; **un impermeabile grondante di pioggia** a soaking wet *o* dripping raincoat; **grondante di sudore** *o* dripping with sweat

grondare [gron'dare] /72/ VI (*aus essere*) to pour; **il sudore gli grondava dalla fronte** the sweat was pouring down his face ◆ VT to drip with

groppa ['grɔppa] SF (*di quadrupede*) back, rump; (*fam: di persona*) back, shoulders *pl*; **salire in groppa a un cavallo** to mount a horse

groppo ['grɔppo] SM (*groviglio*) tangle; **avere un groppo alla gola** (*fig*) to have a lump in one's throat

grossa ['grɔssa] SF (*unità di misura*) gross

grossezza [gros'settsa] SF (*dimensione*) size; (*spessore*) thickness

grossista, -i, -e [gros'sista] SM, SF (*Comm*) wholesaler

grosso, -a ['grɔsso] AGG **1** (*gen*) big, large; (*spesso*) thick; (*pesante*) heavy; **un grosso macigno** a big rock; **una grossa fune** a thick rope **2** (*fig: errore, rischio*) serious, great; (*: patrimonio*) large; (*: tempo, mare*) rough; **una grossa somma** a large sum; **un pezzo grosso** (*fig*) a big shot; **un grosso industriale** a business magnate **3** (*non raffinato: sale, anche fig*) coarse **4** (*fraseologia*): **avere il fiato grosso** to be short of breath; **fare la voce grossa** to raise one's voice; **farla grossa** to do something very stupid; **questa volta l'hai fatta grossa!** now you've done it!; **dirla** *o* **spararla grossa** to shoot a line, to tell tall stories (*Brit*) *o* tales (*USA*); **sbagliarsi di grosso** to be completely wrong *o* mistaken; **ti sbagli di grosso** you're very much mistaken; **questa è grossa!** that's a good one!; **dormire della grossa** to sleep like a log; **grosso modo = grossomodo** ◆ SM: **il grosso del lavoro è fatto** the bulk *o* the main part of the work is over; **il grosso dell'esercito** the main body of the army

  ❑ **grosso** non si traduce mai con la parola inglese *gross*

grossolanità [grossolani'ta] SF INV coarseness

grossolano, -a [grosso'lano] AGG (*gen*) coarse; (*lavoro*) roughly done; (*linguaggio*) coarse, crude; (*errore*) stupid, gross

grossomodo [grosso'mɔdo] AVV roughly

grotta ['grɔtta] SF cave

grottesco, -a, -schi, -sche [grot'tesko] AGG grotesque ◆ SM: **il suo atteggiamento ha del grottesco** his attitude is somewhat ridiculous

groviera [gro'vjera] SM INV, SM INV gruyère (cheese)

groviglio, -gli [gro'viʎʎo] SM (*di fili, lana*) tangle; (*fig: di idee*) muddle

gru [gru] SF INV (*Zool, Tecn*) crane

gruccia, -ce [ˈgruttʃa] SF 1 (*stampella*) crutch 2 (*per abiti*) coat hanger

grugnire [gruɲˈɲire] /55/ VI (*aus* avere) (*maiale*) to grunt; (*fig: persona*) to grumble, growl ♦ VT to mutter, growl out

grugnito [gruɲˈɲito] SM grunt

grugno [ˈgruɲɲo] SM (*di maiale*) snout; (*fam: faccia*) mug; **rompere il grugno a qn** to smash sb's face in

grullo, -a [ˈgrullo] AGG stupid, silly ♦ SM, SF fool, idiot

grumo [ˈgrumo] SM (*di sangue, latte*) clot; (*di farina*) lump; **c'erano dei grumi nella besciamella** there were lumps in the béchamel sauce

grumoso, -a [gruˈmoso] AGG lumpy

gruppo [ˈgruppo] SM 1 group; **suddividere in gruppi di 10** to divide into groups of 10; **arrivare a gruppi di 3** to arrive in groups of 3 *o* in threes; **un gruppo di turisti** a group *o* party of tourists; **un gruppo letterario** a literary circle *o* group; **gruppo elettrogeno** generating set; **gruppo sanguigno** blood group 2 (*Ciclismo*) pack

gruviera [gruˈvjɛra] SF INV, SM INV = **groviera**

gruzzolo [ˈgruttsolo] SM (*di denaro*) hoard; **ha messo da parte un bel gruzzolo** he has saved a fair bit

GSM [dʒiesseˈemme] SIGLA M GSM (= *Global System for Mobile Communication*)

GT ABBR (*Aut: = gran turismo*) GT

guadagnare [gwadaɲˈɲare] /15/ VT 1 (*stipendio, percentuale, anche fig*) to earn; **guadagna bene** he earns a lot; **quanto guadagni al mese?** how much do you earn per month?; **guadagnarsi la vita/il pane** to earn one's living/one's bread and butter 2 (*conquistare*) to win; **guadagnare la fiducia/l'affetto di qn** to win sb's confidence/affection 3 (*ottenere*) to gain; **guadagnare tempo** (*temporeggiare*) to gain time; (*risparmiare*) to save time; **l'ha detto per guadagnare tempo** he said it to gain time; **guadagnare terreno** (*Mil, anche fig*) to gain ground; **e io che cosa ci guadagno?** what's in it for me?; **che cosa ci guadagni a fare cosi?** what will you gain by doing that?; **in tutti i casi ci guadagni** you can't lose; **tanto di guadagnato!** so much the better! 4 (*raggiungere: riva, porto*) to reach

guadagno [gwaˈdaɲɲo] SM 1 (*gen*) earnings *pl*; (*Comm*) profit; **guadagno lordo/netto** gross/net earnings *pl*; **fare grossi guadagni** to earn a packet; (*Comm*) to make a large profit 2 (*fig: vantaggio*) advantage, gain

guado [ˈgwado] SM ford; **passare a guado** to ford

guai [ˈgwai] ESCL: **guai a te** (*o lui ecc*)! woe betide you (*o him ecc*)!; **guai a te se lo fai un'altra volta!** don't you dare do that again!; **se non lo fai subito guai!** there will be trouble if you don't do it straight away!

guaina [gwaˈina] SF 1 (*fodero*) sheath 2 (*busto*) girdle

guaio [ˈgwajo] SM trouble, difficulty; (*inconveniente*) trouble, snag; **essere nei guai** to be in trouble *o* in a mess; **sono in un bel guaio** I'm in a real mess; **mettersi o ficcarsi nei guai** (*fam*) to get into trouble, get into a spot of bother; **andare a caccia di guai** (*fam*) to go looking for trouble; **il guaio è che...** the trouble *o* snag is that ...; **il guaio è che sono già partiti** the trouble is that they've already left

guaire [gwaˈire] /55/ VI (*aus* avere) (*cane*) to yelp, to whine; (*persona*) to whine

guaito [gwaˈito] SM (*di cane*) yelp, whine; (*il guaire*) yelping, whining

guancia, -ce [ˈgwantʃa] SF cheek; **porgere l'altra guancia** to turn the other cheek

guanciale [gwanˈtʃale] SM pillow; **dormire fra due guanciali** (*fig*) to sleep easy, have no worries

guanto [ˈgwanto] SM glove; **un paio di guanti di lana** a pair of woollen gloves; **trattare qn con i guanti** (*fig*) to handle sb with kid gloves; **gettare/raccogliere il guanto** (*fig*) to throw down/take up the gauntlet; **guanto da forno** oven glove; **guanto di spugna** (*per lavarsi*) wash glove

guantone [gwanˈtone] SM boxing glove

guardaboschi [gwardaˈbɔski] SM INV forester

guardacaccia [gwardaˈkattʃa] SM INV gamekeeper

guardacoste [gwardaˈkɔste] SM INV (*persona*) coastguard; (*nave*) coastguard patrol vessel

guardalinee [gwardaˈlinee] SM INV (*Sport*) linesman

guardamacchine [gwardaˈmakkine] SM INV, SF INV car-park (*Brit*) *o* parking lot (*USA*) attendant

guardare [gwarˈdare] /72/ VT 1 (*oggetto, paesaggio*) to look at; (*persona, cosa in movimento*) to watch; **guardare la televisione** to watch television; **hai guardato la partita ieri sera?** did you watch the match last night?; **guarda chi c'è** *o* **chi si vede!** look who's here!; **guarda cos'hai combinato!** look what you've done!; **e guarda caso...** as if by coincidence ... 2 (*rapidamente*) to glance at; (*a lungo*) to gaze at; **guardare di sfuggita** to steal a glance at; **guardare con diffidenza** to look warily at; **guardare di traverso** to scowl *o* frown at; **guardare fisso** to stare at; **guardare qc di buon/mal occhio** to look on *o* view sth favourably (*Brit*) *o* favorably (*USA*) *o* unfavorably (*USA*); **cos'hai da guardare?** what are you looking at?; **guardare qn dall'alto in basso** to look down on sb; **guardare qn in faccia** to look sb in the face; **non guardare in faccia a nessuno** (*fig*) to have no regard for anybody 3 (*esaminare*) to (have a) look at, check; **guardare una parola sul dizionario** to look sth up *o* check a word in the dictionary 4 (*custodire*) to look after, take care of; (*proteggere*) to guard; **guardare a vista qn** (*prigioniero*) to keep a close watch on sb; **chi guarda i bambini?** who is looking after the children?; **Dio me ne guardi!** God forbid! ♦ VI (*aus* avere) 1 **guardare di** to try to; **guarda di non arrivare in ritardo** try not to be late 2 (*badare*): **guardare a** to mind, be careful about, pay attention to; **comprare qc senza guardare a spese** to buy sth without worrying about the expense; **per il matrimonio di sua figlia non ha guardato a spese** he spared no expense when his daughter got married 3 (*essere rivolto*): **guardare a** to face; **guardare su** to give *o* look onto 4 (*fraseologia*): **guardare dalla finestra** to look out of the window; **guarda un po' lì** (*cerca*) take a look over there; **ma guarda un po'!** good heavens!; **guardarsi** VR 1 (*uso reciproco*) to look at each other; **si guardavano negli occhi** they were looking into each other's eyes 2 (*in vetrina, specchio*) to look at o.s.; **guardarsi allo specchio** to look at o.s. in the mirror 3 **guardarsi da** (*astenersi*) to refrain from; (*stare in guardia*) to be wary of, beware of; **guardarsi dal fare qc** to take care *o* be careful not to do sth

□ **guardare** non si traduce mai con la parola inglese *guard*

guardaroba [gwardaˈrɔba] SM INV 1 (*armadio*) wardrobe (*Brit*) *o* closet (*USA*); (*locale*) cloakroom, checkroom (*USA*); **ho lasciato l'impermeabile al guardaroba** I left my raincoat in the cloakroom

guardarobiere, -a [gwardaroˈbjɛre] SM/F 1 (*in albergo, grande casa*) housekeeper 2 (*in locale pubblico*) cloakroom *o* checkroom (*USA*) attendant

guardasigilli [gwardasiˈdʒilli] SM INV 1 (*Storia*) keeper of the seals 2 (*ministro*) ≈ Lord Chancellor (*Brit*), ≈ Attorney General (*USA*)

guardia [ˈgwardja] SF 1 (*individuo, corpo*) guard; **il cambio della guardia** the changing of the guard; **essere della vecchia guardia** to be one of the old guard; **giocare a guardie e ladri** to play cops and robbers 2 (*sorveglianza: gen: Naut*) watch; (*Mil: servizio*) guard duty, sentry duty; **lasciare qn a guardia di qc** to leave sb to look after sth, leave sb to keep an eye on sth, leave sth in sb's care; **fare la guardia** to keep watch; **stavo facendo la guardia** I was keeping watch; **fare la guardia a qn/qc** to guard sb/sth; **essere di guardia** to be on duty; **il medico di guardia** the doctor on call; **al cancello c'era un poliziotto di guardia** there was a policeman on duty at the gate; **il fiume ha raggiunto il livello di guardia** the river has reached the high-water mark; **cane da guardia** guard dog 3 (*Pugilato, Scherma*) guard; (*di spada*) hilt; **in guardia!** on guard!; **stare in guardia** (*fig*) to be on one's guard; **mettersi in guardia** to take one's guard; **mettere qn in guardia contro** (*fig*) to put sb on his guard against ♦ **guardia carceraria** (prison) warder (*Brit*) *o* guard (*USA*); **guardia del corpo** bodyguard; **guardia di finanza** (*corpo*) customs *pl*; (*persona*) customs officer; **guardia forestale** forest ranger; **guardia giurata** security guard; **guardia medica** emergency doctor service; **guardia municipale** town policeman; **guardia notturna** night security guard; **guardia di pubblica sicurezza** policeman

guardiacaccia [gwardjaˈkattʃa] SM INV = **guardacaccia**

guardiano [gwarˈdjano] SM (*di carcere*) warder (*Brit*), guard

(USA); (di stabilmento, villa) caretaker; (di faro, zoo) keeper; (di museo) attendant; (Rel: anche: **padre guardiano**) Father Guardian; **guardiano dei porci** swineherd; **un guardiano notturno** a night watchman

guardina [gwar'dina] SF cell

guardingo, -a, -ghi, -ghe [gwar'dingo] AGG wary, cautious

guardiola [gwar'djɔla] SF porter's lodge

guarigione [gwari'dʒone] SF recovery; **auguri di pronta guarigione!** best wishes for a speedy recovery!; **essere in via di guarigione** to be on the way o road to recovery

guarire [gwa'rire] /55/ VT (anche fig) to cure; (ferita) to heal; **guarire qn da qc** to cure sb of sth; **i medici non sono riusciti a guarirlo** the doctors couldn't cure him ♦ VI (aus essere) (persona) to recover; (ferita) to heal (up); **spero che tu guarisca presto** I hope you'll be better soon; **non sono ancora completamente guarito** I'm not completely better yet; **la ferita guarirà in dieci giorni** the wound will heal up in ten days; **far guarire qn** to cure sb; **è guarito dal vizio del fumo** he is cured of smoking

guarnigione [gwarni'dʒone] SF (Mil) garrison

guarnire [gwar'nire] /55/ VT (ornare: abiti) to trim; (: Culin) to garnish

guarnizione [gwarnit'tsjone] SF 1 (vedi vb) trimming; garnish 2 (di rubinetto) washer; (Aut) gasket; **guarnizione della testata** cylinder head gasket; **guarnizioni dei freni** brake linings; **cambiare le guarnizioni dei freni** to reline the brakes

guastafeste [gwasta'fɛste] SM INV, SF INV spoilsport; **non fare il guastafeste!** don't be such a killjoy!

guastare [gwas'tare] /72/ VT (danneggiare: gen) to spoil, ruin; (: meccanismo) to break; (: cibo) to spoil; **guastarsi** VIP (meccanismo) to break down; (cibo) to go bad, go off; (tempo, persona) to change for the worse

guasto, -a ['gwasto] AGG 1 (non funzionante: gen) broken; (: telefono, distributore) out of order; **il mio televisore è guasto** my television isn't working; **"guasto"** "out of order" 2 (andato a male) bad, rotten; (dente) decayed, bad; (fig: corrotto) depraved; **quella mela è guasta** that apple is bad ♦ SM (rottura completa) breakdown; (avaria) failure; **guasto al motore** engine failure; **l'aereo è precipitato per un guasto al motore** the plane crashed because of engine failure; **il meccanico ha riparato un guasto al motore** the mechanic repaired a fault in the engine

Guatemala [gwate'mala] SM Guatemala

guatemalteco, -a, -chi, -che [gwatemal'tɛko] AGG, SM, SF Guatemalan

guercio, -cia, -ci, -ce ['gwertʃo] AGG cross-eyed ♦ SM, SF cross-eyed person

guerra ['gwerra] SF (conflitto) war; (tecnica bellica) warfare; **corrispondente di guerra** war correspondent; **in guerra con** at war with o against; **fare la guerra (a)** to wage war (against); **essere sul piede di guerra** to be on a war footing; **la grande guerra** the First World War; **la prima/seconda guerra mondiale** the First/Second World War, World War I/II; **ha fatto la prima guerra mondiale** he fought in World War I; **sembra che abbia fatto la guerra** (fig) it looks as if it has been in the wars; **tra di loro ormai è guerra aperta** there is open war between them now; **guerra batteriologica** germ warfare; **guerra chimica** chemical warfare; **guerra fredda** cold war; **guerra mondiale** world war; **guerra preventiva** preventive war

guerrafondaio, -ai [gwerrafon'dajo] SM warmonger

guerreggiare [gwerred'dʒare] /62/ VI (aus avere) guerreggiare (contro) to wage war (on, against)

guerresco, -a, -schi, -sche [gwer'resko] AGG (di guerra) war attr; (bellicoso) warlike

guerriero, -a [gwer'rjero] AGG warlike ♦ SM warrior

guerriglia [gwer'riʎʎa] SF guerrilla warfare

guerrigliero, -a [gwerriʎ'ʎero] SM, SF guerrilla

gufo ['gufo] SM owl; **gufo comune** long-eared owl; **gufo reale** eagle-owl

guglia ['guʎʎa] SF (Archit) spire; (di roccia) needle

Guiana [gu'jana] SF: **la Guiana francese** French Guiana

guida ['gwida] SF 1 (manuale) guide, manual; **guida telefonica** telephone directory, phone book 2 (capo) guide;

(direzione) guidance, direction; **sotto la guida di qn** with sb's guidance; **essere alla guida di** (governo) to head; (spedizione, paese) to lead; **far da guida a qn** (mostrare la strada) to show sb the way; (in una città) to show sb (a) round; **guida alpina** mountain guide; **guida turistica** (persona) guide; (libro) guide(book) 3 (Aut) driving; **ha preso la multa per guida in stato di ebbrezza** he was fined for drink-driving; **avere guida a destra/sinistra** to be a right-/left-hand drive; **lezioni di guida** driving lessons; **patente di guida** driving licence (Brit), driver's license (USA); **posto di guida** driving seat 4 (tappeto, cassetto) runner; (Tecn) runner, guide 5 (scout) (girl) guide (Brit), girl scout

guidare [gwi'dare] /72/ VT 1 (gen) to guide; (capeggiare) to lead; **ha guidato una spedizione in Antartide** he led an expedition to Antarctica; **lasciarsi guidare dal proprio istinto** to let o.s. be guided by one's instincts, follow one's instincts; **guidare qn sulla retta via** (fig) to steer sb in the right direction; **guidare una spedizione** to lead an expedition; **guidare la classifica** (Sport) to head the table 2 (auto) to drive; **guidare bene/male** to drive well/badly; **sa guidare?** can you drive?; **ha guidato tutta la notte** she drove all night; **ha mai guidato in Gran Bretagna?** have you ever driven in Britain?

guidatore, -trice [gwida'tore] SM, SF (conducente) driver

Guinea [gwi'nea] SF: **la Guinea Equatoriale** Equatorial Guinea; **la (Repubblica di) Guinea** (Republic of) Guinea

guinzaglio, -gli [gwin'tsaʎʎo] SM lead (Brit), leash (USA: frm); **un cane al guinzaglio** a dog on a lead; **tenere qn al guinzaglio** (fig) to keep sb on a tight rein

guisa ['gwisa] SF manner, way; **a guisa di** like, in the manner of; **in tal guisa** in such a way

guizzare [gwit'tsare] /72/ VI (aus essere) 1 (pesce, serpente) to dart; (fiamma) to flicker 2 (balzare) to leap, slip; **mi guizzò via dalle mani** it leapt o slipped out of my hands; **il ladro riuscì a guizzare via** the thief managed to slip away

guizzo ['gwittso] SM (di animale) dart; (di fulmine) flash; (di persona) spring, leap

guru ['guru] SM INV (Rel, anche fig) guru

guscio, -sci ['guʃʃo] SM shell; **uscire dal proprio guscio** (fig) to come out of one's shell; **chiudersi nel proprio guscio** (fig) to retreat into one's shell; **guscio di noce** nutshell; (fig: barca) cockleshell

gustare [gus'tare] /72/ VT 1 (assaggiare) to taste 2 to enjoy, savour (Brit), savor (USA); (fig: apprezzare) to relish, enjoy, appreciate ♦ VI (aus avere) **gustare (a qn)** to please (sb); **non mi gusta affatto** I don't like it at all

gustativo, -a [gusta'tivo] AGG (Anat): **papille gustative** taste buds

gusto ['gusto] SM 1 (senso) taste; (sapore) taste, flavour (Brit), flavor (USA); **disponibile in tre nuovi gusti** available in three new flavours; **ha un gusto amaro/di lampone** it tastes bitter/of raspberries, it has a bitter/a raspberry taste; **al gusto di fragola** strawberry-flavo(u)red; **privo di gusto** tasteless, flavo(u)rless 2 (senso estetico) taste; **con gusto** tastefully; **veste con gusto** she's got good taste in clothes; **di buon/cattivo gusto** in good/bad taste; **uno scherzo di cattivo gusto** a joke in bad taste; **abbiamo gli stessi gusti** we like the same things, we have the same tastes; **abbiamo gusti diversi in fatto di musica** we have different tastes in music; **non è di mio gusto** it is not my taste; **per i miei gusti tu corri un po' troppo** you drive too fast for my liking 3 (piacere): **fare qc di o con gusto** to do sth with pleasure; **lo fa per il gusto di farlo** he does it for the fun of it; **mangiare/ridere di gusto** to eat/laugh heartily; **prendere gusto a qc/a fare qc** to get a taste for sth/for doing sth, get to like sth/doing sth; **ci ha preso gusto** he's acquired a taste for it, he's got to like it; **non c'è gusto a...** there's no pleasure in...; **tutti i gusti sono gusti** there is no accounting for taste 4 (stile) style; **di gusto barocco** in the baroque style

❏ **gusto** non si traduce mai con la parola inglese *gust*

gustoso, -a [gus'toso] AGG (piatto) tasty; (romanzo, commedia) enjoyable, agreeable; **la carne è più gustosa cucinata così** meat is tastier when it's cooked like this

gutturale [guttu'rale] AGG guttural

Guyana [gu'jana] SF = **Guiana**

Hh

H, h [ˈakka] SF INV, SM INV *(lettera)* H, h; **H come hotel** ≈ H for Harry *(Brit)*, ≈ H for How *(USA)* ♦ ABBR **1** = ora **2** = altezza
ha¹ ABBR (= *ettaro*) ha
ha² [a] VB *vedi* **avere**
hacker [ˈhækəʳ] SM INV, SF INV *(Inform)* hacker
Haiti [aˈiti] SF Haiti
haitiano,-a [aiˈtjano] AGG, SM, SF Haitian
hall [hɔːl] SF INV *(di albergo)* hall, foyer
hamburger [amˈburger] SM INV hamburger
handicap [ˈhændikap] SM INV *(Sport, anche fig)* handicap
handicappato, -a [andikapˈpato] AGG handicapped ♦ SM, SF handicapped person, disabled person; **gli handicappati** the handicapped
hanno *ecc* [ˈanno] VB *vedi* **avere**
hard 'disk [arˈdisk] SM INV hard disk
hardware [ˈardwer] SM INV hardware
hascisc [aʃˈʃiʃ] SM INV hashish
'hashtag [aˈʃteg] SM INV *(Inform)* hashtag
hawaiano,-a [avaˈjano] AGG, SM, SF Hawaiian
Hawaii [ɔˈwaːiː] SFPL Hawaii *sg*
help [ɛlp] SM INV: "Help" *(Inform)* "Help"

Helsinki [ˈɛlsinki] SF Helsinki
herpes [ˈɛrpes] SM *(Med)* herpes *sg*; **herpes zoster** shingles *sg*
hg ABBR (= *ettogrammo*) hg
hi-fi [ˈhaifai] SM INV, AGG INV hi-fi
Himalaia [imaˈlaja] SM: **l'Himalaia** the Himalayas *pl*
hl ABBR (= *ettolitro*) hl
ho *ecc* [ɔ] VB *vedi* **avere**
hobby [ˈhɔbi] SM INV hobby
hockey [ˈhɔki] SM hockey; **hockey su ghiaccio** ice hockey; **hockey su prato** field hockey, hockey *(Brit)*
holding [ˈhouldiŋ] SF INV holding company
home page [homˈpeidʒ] SF INV *(Inform)* home page
Honduras [onˈduras] SM Honduras
Hong Kong [ongˈkɔng] SF Hong Kong
Honolulu [onoˈlulu] SF Honolulu
hot dog [ˈhɔtdɔg] SM INV **1** *(panino)* hot dog **2** *(Sport: sci acrobatico)* hot-dogging
hotel [oˈtɛl] SM INV hotel
humour [ˈhjuːmə] SM (sense of) humour
humus [ˈumus] SM humus
husky [ˈaski] SM INV *(cane)* husky
Hz ABBR (= *hertz*) Hz

Ii

I, i [i] SF INV, SM INV (*lettera*) I, i; **I come Imola** ≈ I for Isaac (*Brit*), ≈ I for Item (*USA*)

i [i] ART DET MPL *vedi* **il**

iato [i'ato] SM hiatus

iberico, -a, -ci, -che [i'beriko] AGG Iberian; **la penisola iberica** the Iberian Peninsula

ibernare [iber'nare] /72/ VI (*aus* **avere**) to hibernate ♦ VT (*Med*) to induce hypothermia in

ibernazione [ibernat'tsjone] SF hibernation

ibid. ABBR (= *ibidem*) ib(id).

ibrido, -a ['ibrido] AGG hybrid; **auto ibrida** hybrid car ♦ SM hybrid

IC ABBR = intercity

icona [i'kɔna] SF (*Rel, Inform, o fig*) icon

id. ABBR (= *idem*) do.

Iddio [id'dio] SM God

idea [i'dɛa] SF **1** (*gen*) idea; **non ne ho la minima** *o* **più pallida idea** I haven't the faintest *o* foggiest idea; **farsi un'idea di qc** to get an idea of sth; **non hai idea di quanto sia difficile** you have no idea how difficult it is; **non hai idea del traffico che c'era** you've no idea how much traffic there was; **un'idea geniale** a brilliant *o* clever idea; **chissà che idea gli è saltata in mente adesso?** who knows what idea he may have got into his head now?; **tremo solo all'idea che possa venire** just the thought that he might come is enough to terrify me; **ho idea che…** I have an idea *o* a feeling that …; **nemmeno neanche** *o* **neppure per idea!** not on your life!, certainly not!, no way!; **pensi di andarci? — neanche per idea!** are you thinking of going? — no way!; **dare l'idea di** to seem, look like; **idea fissa** obsession **2** (*opinione*) opinion, view; **avere le idee chiare** to know one's mind; **cambiare idea** to change one's mind; **ho cambiato idea** I've changed my mind; **essere dell'idea (che)** to be of the opinion (that), think (that) **3** (*intenzione*): **avere una mezza idea di fare qc** to have half a mind to do sth; **la mia idea era di andare al cinema** I had thought of going to the movies **4** (*ideale*) ideal; **l'idea del bello/della pace** the ideal of beauty/of peace

ideale [ide'ale] AGG ideal; **secondo me è la soluzione ideale** in my opinion it's the ideal solution ♦ SM ideal; **l'ideale sarebbe andarsene** the best thing would be to leave; **il mio ideale di casa** my ideal home; **hanno fatto sacrifici per i loro ideali** they have made sacrifices for their ideals

idealismo [idea'lizmo] SM idealism

idealista, -i, -e [idea'lista] SM, SF idealist

idealistico, -a, -ci, -che [idea'listiko] AGG idealistic

idealizzare [idealid'dzare] /72/ VT to idealize

ideare [ide'are] /72/ VT (*escogitare: scherzo*) to think of; (: *piano*) to think out, conceive; (*progettare: congegno*) to invent

ideatore, -trice [idea'tore] SM, SF (*di piano*) originator; (*di metodo*) inventor

identico, -a, -ci, -che [i'dɛntiko] AGG: **identico (a)** identical (to); **è identico al mio** it's exactly the same as mine; **è la stessa identica cosa** it's exactly the same thing

identificare [identifi'kare] /20/ VT to identify; **identificarsi** VR: **identificarsi con** to identify o.s. with

identificazione [identifikat'tsjone] SF identification

identità [identi'ta] SF INV identity; **carta d'identità** identity card

ideologia, -gie [ideolo'dʒia] SF ideology

ideologico, -a, -ci, -che [ideo'lɔdʒiko] AGG ideological

idilliaco, -a, -ci, -che [idil'liako], **idillico, -a, -ci, -che** [i'dilliko] AGG idyllic

idillio, -li [i'dilljo] SM idyll; **tra di loro è nato un idillio** they have fallen in love

idioma, -i [i'djɔma] SM language

idiomatico, -a, -ci, -che [idjo'matiko] AGG idiomatic; **frase idiomatica** idiom

idiosincrasia [idjosinkra'zia] SF **1** (*avversione*) dislike; **avere un'idiosincrasia per qc** to dislike sth **2** (*Med*) idiosyncrasy

idiota, -i, -e [i'djɔta] AGG (*Med*) idiotic; (*fig*) idiotic, stupid ♦ SM, SF idiot

idiozia [idjot'tsia] SF (*Med*) idiocy; (*fig*) idiocy, stupidity; (*atto, discorso*) idiotic thing to do (*o* say)

idolatra, -i, -e [ido'latra] AGG idolatrous ♦ SM, SF idolater (idolatress)

idolatrare [idola'trare] /72/ VT (*divinità*) to worship; (*fig: persona*) to idolize

idolatria [idola'tria] SF idolatry

idolo ['idolo] SM (*Rel, anche fig*) idol

idoneità [idonei'ta] SF suitability, fitness; **esame di idoneità** qualifying examination

idoneo, -a [i'dɔneo] AGG: **idoneo (a)** suitable (for), fit (for); **idoneo all'insegnamento** qualified to teach; **fare qn idoneo (al servizio militare)** to pass sb as fit (for military service)

idrante [i'drante] SM hydrant

idratante [idra'tante] AGG (*crema*) moisturizing; **crema idratante** moisturizing cream ♦ SM moisturizer

idratare [idra'tare] /72/ VT (*pelle*) to moisturize

idratazione [idratat'tsjone] SF (*della pelle*) moisturizing

idraulico, -a, -ci, -che [i'drauliko] AGG hydraulic ♦ SM plumber; **fa l'idraulico** he's a plumber

idrico, -a, -ci, -che [i'driko] AGG water attr

idrocarburo [idrokar'buro] SM hydrocarbon

idroelettrico, -a, -ci, -che [idroe'lettriko] AGG hydroelectric

idrofilo, -a [i'drɔfilo] AGG hydrophilic; **cotone idrofilo** cotton wool (*Brit*), absorbent cotton (*USA*)

idrofobia [idrofo'bia] SF (*Med*) rabies sg

idrofobo, -a [i'drɔfobo] AGG rabid; (*fig*) furious

idrogeno [i'drɔdʒeno] SM hydrogen

idrolipidico, -a, -ci, -che [idroli'pidiko] AGG hydrolipid

idrorepellente [idrorepel'lente] AGG water-repellent ♦ SM water-repellent substance

idroscalo [idros'kalo] SM (*Aer*) seaplane base

idrovolante [idrovo'lante] SM seaplane

iella ['jɛlla] SF bad luck; **essere perseguitato dalla iella** to be plagued by bad luck

iellato, -a [jel'lato] AGG plagued by bad luck

iena ['jɛna] SF hyena; (*fig: persona crudele*) nasty piece of work

ieratico, -a, -ci, -che [je'ratiko] AGG (*Rel: scrittura*) hieratic; (*fig: atteggiamento*) solemn

ieri ['jɛri] AVV yesterday; **l'altro ieri** *o* **ieri l'altro** the day before yesterday; **ieri mattina** yesterday morning; **ieri sera** yesterday evening, last night; **ieri notte** last night; **sono tornato ieri** I got back yesterday; **non sono nato ieri** I wasn't born yesterday ♦ SM yesterday; **il giornale di ieri** yesterday's paper

iettatore, -trice [jetta'tore] SM, SF jinx; **smettila di fare lo iettatore!** stop trying to put a jinx on things!

igiene [i'dʒɛne] SF hygiene; **igiene del corpo** personal hygiene; **norme d'igiene** sanitary regulations; **igiene mentale** mental health; **igiene pubblica** public health

igienico, -a, -ci, -che [i'dʒɛniko] AGG (*gen*) hygienic; (*salubre: clima*) healthy; **carta igienica** toilet paper; **impianto igienico** sanitary fittings

igloo ['iglu] SM INV igloo; (*tenda*) dome tent

ignaro, -a [iɲ'ɲaro] AGG: **ignaro (di)** unaware (of), ignorant (of)

ignifugo, -a [iɲ'ɲifugo] AGG flame-resistant, fireproof

ignobile [iɲ'ɲɔbile] AGG vile, despicable

ignominia [iɲɲoˈminja] SF ignominy; **questo monumento è un'ignominia!** (*scherz*) this monument is a disgrace!

ignorante [iɲɲoˈrante] AGG ignorant; **non ho fatto domande per paura di sembrare ignorante** I didn't ask any questions for fear of appearing ignorant; **come sei ignorante!** don't you know anything! ♦ SM, SF ignoramus; (*villano*) boor

ignoranza [iɲɲoˈrantsa] SF ignorance; **è di un'ignoranza spaventosa** he is appallingly ignorant

ignorare [iɲɲoˈrare] /72/ VT 1 (*non conoscere*) to be ignorant *o* unaware of, not to know; **ignoravo che...** I was unaware that ..., I was ignorant of the fact that ...; **ignoravo che tu fossi qui** I was unaware *o* I didn't know that you were here 2 (*fingere di non conoscere*) to ignore; **ha ignorato la mia domanda** he ignored my question; **mi ha ignorato completamente** she completely ignored me

ignoto, -a [iɲˈɲɔto] AGG unknown; **figlio di genitori ignoti** child of unknown parentage; **il Milite Ignoto** the Unknown Soldier ♦ SM, SF stranger, unknown person ♦ SM: **l'ignoto** the unknown

il [il] ART DET M *pl*(m) i; *diventa* **lo** (*pl* **gli**) *dav s impura, gn, pn, ps, x, z; f* **la** (*pl* **le**) 1 (*determinazione*) the; **il bambino ha la febbre** the baby has a temperature; **le donne non sono arrivate** the women aren't here yet; **i figli dell'architetto** the architect's children; **lo zio di Roberta** Roberta's uncle; **gli studenti del primo anno** first-year students; **l'ora di cena** dinner time 2 (*generalizzazione, astrazione*) gen non tradotto; **l'uomo è un animale sociale** man is a social animal; **i cavalli dormono in piedi** horses sleep on their feet; **l'oro è un metallo prezioso** gold is a precious metal; **la leucemia** leukemia; **lo zucchero caria i denti** sugar causes tooth decay; **mi piace la musica classica** I like classical music; **non sopporto il rumore** I can't stand noise; **il bello** the beautiful; **i poveri** the poor 3 (*tempo*) the (*spesso omesso*); **siamo arrivati il lunedì di Pasqua** we arrived on Easter Monday; **la settimana prossima** next week; **l'inverno scorso** last winter; **il venerdì** ecc (*abitualmente*) on Fridays ecc; (*quel giorno*) on (the) Friday ecc; **riceve il venerdì** he sees people on Fridays *o* on a Friday; **la sera** in the evening; **verso le 6** at about 6 o'clock; **è partito il 20 luglio** he left on the 20th of July *o* on July the 20th (*lingua parlata*), he left on July 20th (*lingua scritta*) 4 (*distributivo*) a, an; **costano 2 euro il chilo** they cost 2 euros a *o* per kilo; **li vendono a 70 euro il paio** they are sold at 70 euros a *o* per pair; **120 km l'ora** 120 km an *o* per hour; **ne abbiamo fatto la metà** we have done half of it 5 (*partitivo*) some, any; **hai messo lo zucchero?** have you put sugar in it?; **hai comprato il pane?** did you buy (some *o* any) bread? 6 (*possesso*): **ha aperto gli occhi** he opened his eyes; **mi fa male la gamba** my leg is hurting; **prendo il caffè senza zucchero** I take my coffee without sugar; **avere i capelli neri/il naso rosso** to have dark hair/a red nose 7 (*con nomi propri*): **Plinio il giovane** Pliny the Younger; **il Petrarca** Petrarch; **il Presidente Chirac** President Chirac; **sono arrivati i Martinoni** the Martinonis have arrived; **le sorelle Clari** the Clari sisters; **ma dov'è finito il Cozzi?** whatever happened to the Cozzi boy? 8 (*con nomi geografici*): **il Tevere** the Tiber; **i Pirenei** the Pyrenees; **l'Everest** Everest; **l'Italia** Italy; **il Regno Unito** the United Kingdom

ilare [ˈilare] AGG cheerful

ilarità [ilariˈta] SF hilarity, mirth

ill. ABBR (= *illustrazione, illustrato*) ill.

illanguidire [illaŋɡwiˈdire] /55/ VT to weaken ♦ VI (*aus essere*) to grow weak *o* feeble

illazione [illatˈtsjone] SF inference, deduction

illecito, -a [ilˈletʃito] AGG illicit

illegale [illeˈɡale] AGG illegal, unlawful

illegalità [illeɡaliˈta] SF illegality, unlawfulness

illeggibile [illedˈdʒibile] AGG (*scrittura*) illegible; (*romanzo*) unreadable

illegittimità [illedʒittimiˈta] SF illegitimacy

illegittimo, -a [illeˈdʒittimo] AGG illegitimate

illeso, -a [ilˈlɛzo] AGG unharmed, unhurt; **è uscito illeso dall'incidente** he escaped unhurt from the accident

illetterato, -a [illetteˈrato] AGG, SM, SF illiterate

illibatezza [illibaˈtettsa] SF (*verginità*) virginity; (*purezza*) purity

illibato, -a [illiˈbato] AGG (*vergine*) virgin; (*puro*) pure

illimitato, -a [illimiˈtato] AGG (*gen*) unlimited, boundless; (*fiducia*) absolute; (*congedo, visto*) indefinite

illividire [illiviˈdire] /55/ VI (*aus essere*) (*volto, mani*) to go blue; (*cielo*) to grow leaden

ill.mo ABBR = illustrissimo

illogico, -a, -ci, -che [ilˈlɔdʒiko] AGG illogical

illudere [ilˈludere] VB IRREG /35/ VT to deceive, fool, delude; **non voglio illuderti** I don't want to deceive you; **illudersi** VR to deceive o.s., delude o.s.; **illudersi sul conto di qn** to be mistaken about sb; **si illuse di poter cambiare tutto** he flattered himself that he could change everything; **ti illudi se pensi di riavere i soldi** you're deceiving yourself if you think you'll get the money back; **si illudeva di trovare qn pronto ad aiutarlo** he mistakenly thought he might find sb ready to help (him)

illuminare [illumiˈnare] /72/ VT 1 (*strada, stanza*) to light; (*volto*) to illuminate; **la stanza era illuminata da un'unica lampada** the room was lit by a single lamp; **illuminare a giorno** (*con riflettori*) to floodlight; **lo stadio era illuminato a giorno** the stadium was floodlit 2 (*fig: informare*) to enlighten; **illuminarsi** VIP (*stanza*) to grow lighter; (*volto*) to light up

illuminato, -a [illumiˈnato] AGG (*fig: sovrano, spirito*) enlightened

illuminazione [illuminatˈtsjone] SF 1 (*vedi vb*) lighting, illumination; floodlighting; enlightenment 2 (*lampo di genio*) flash of inspiration

illuminismo [illumiˈnizmo] SM (*Storia*): **l'Illuminismo** the Enlightenment

illusi ecc [ilˈluzi] VB *vedi* illudere

illusione [illuˈzjone] SF illusion; **illusione ottica** optical illusion; **farsi illusioni** to deceive *o* delude o.s.; **non farti illusioni** don't delude yourself, don't kid yourself (*fam*); **ha perso ogni illusione** he has become thoroughly disillusioned

illusionismo [illuzjoˈnizmo] SM conjuring

illusionista, -i, -e [illuzjoˈnista] SM, SF conjurer

illuso, -a [ilˈluzo] PP *di* illudere ♦ AGG deluded ♦ SM, SF: **sei un illuso!** you're fooling yourself!

illusorio, -ria, -ri, -rie [illuˈzɔrjo] AGG illusory

illustrare [illusˈtrare] /72/ VT to illustrate

illustrativo, -a [illustraˈtivo] AGG illustrative; **un catalogo illustrativo** a descriptive catalogue

illustrazione [illustratˈtsjone] SF illustration

illustre [ilˈlustre] AGG eminent, renowned, illustrious

ILOR [ˈilor] SIGLA F = imposta locale sui redditi

IM SIGLA = Imperia

imbaccucare [imbakukˈkare] /20/ VT to wrap up; **imbaccucarsi** VR to wrap (o.s.) up

imbaldanzire [imbaldanˈtsire] /55/ VT to give confidence to; **imbaldanzirsi** VIP to grow bold, get cocky (*fam*)

imballaggio, -gi [imballˈladdʒo] SM 1 (*gen*) packing *no pl*; **cassa da imballaggio** packing case; **carta da imballaggio** brown paper 2 (*costo*) cost of packing

imballare¹ [imbalˈlare] /72/ VT to pack

imballare² [imbalˈlare] /72/ VT (*Aut: motore*) to race, rev up (*fam*); **imballarsi** VIP (*Aut*) to race

imbalsamare [imbalsaˈmare] /72/ VT to embalm; (*animale*) to stuff

imbalsamato, -a [imbalsaˈmato] AGG embalmed

imbambolato, -a [imbamboˈlato] AGG (*sguardo, espressione*) vacant, blank

imbandire [imbanˈdire] /55/ VT: **imbandire un banchetto** to prepare a lavish feast

imbandito, -a [imbanˈdito] AGG: **tavola imbandita** lavishly *o* sumptuously decked table

imbarazzante [imbaratˈtsante] AGG embarrassing, awkward; **una domanda imbarazzante** an awkward question; **una situazione imbarazzante** an embarrassing situation

imbarazzare [imbaratˈtsare] /72/ VT 1 (*mettere a disagio*) to embarrass 2 (*ostacolare: movimenti*) to hamper; (*ingombrare: stanza*) to clutter up; (*appesantire: stomaco*) to lie heavily on; **imbarazzarsi** VIP to become embarrassed

imbarazzato, -a [imbaratˈtsato] AGG (*persona*) embarrassed; **avere lo stomaco imbarazzato** to have an upset stomach; **ero così imbarazzato che non sapevo cosa dire** I was so embarrassed I didn't know what to say

imbarazzo [imba'rattso] SM 1 (disagio) embarrassment; **essere** o **trovarsi in imbarazzo** to be in an awkward situation o predicament; **mettere in imbarazzo** to embarrass; **la sua domanda mi ha messo in imbarazzo** her question embarrassed me; **non è riuscito a mascherare il suo imbarazzo** he couldn't hide his embarrassment 2 (perplessità) bewilderment, puzzlement; **avere solo l'imbarazzo della scelta** to be spoilt for choice; **non hai che l'imbarazzo della scelta** you are spoilt for choice 3 (pesantezza): **imbarazzo di stomaco** indigestion

imbarbarimento [imbarbari'mento] SM (di civiltà, costumi) barbarization

imbarcadero [imbarka'dero] SM landing stage

imbarcare [imbar'kare] /20/ VT (passeggeri) to embark; (merci) to load; **imbarcare acqua** (Naut) to ship water; **imbarcarsi** VR 1 **imbarcarsi su** (nave) to board, embark on; (altro veicolo) to board; **imbarcarsi per l'America** to sail for America 2 (fig): **imbarcarsi in** (affare ecc) to embark on

imbarcazione [imbarkat'tsjone] SF (small) boat, (small) craft pl inv; **imbarcazione da pesca** fishing boat

imbarco [im'barko] SM 1 (di persone) embarkation, boarding; (di merci) loading; **carta d'imbarco** boarding card; **è già cominciato l'imbarco del mio volo?** has boarding started for my flight yet? 2 (banchina) embarkation point, departure point

imbastardire [imbastar'dire] /55/ VT to bastardize, debase; **imbastardirsi** VIP to degenerate, become debased

imbastire [imbas'tire] /55/ VT (Cucito) to baste, to tack; (fig: piano) to sketch out, outline

imbattersi [im'battersi] /72/ VIP: **imbattersi in** to bump o run into

imbattibile [imbat'tibile] AGG unbeatable, invincible

imbavagliare [imbava'ʎʎare] /27/ VT (anche fig) to gag; **l'hanno legato e imbavagliato** they bound and gagged him

imbeccare [imbek'kare] /20/ VT (uccelli) to feed; (fig) to prompt, put words into sb's mouth

imbeccata [imbek'kata] SF (di uccelli) beakful of food; (Teatro) prompt; **dare l'imbeccata a qn** (Teatro) to prompt sb; (fig) to give sb their cue

imbecille [imbe'tʃille] AGG (Psic) imbecilic; (fig) idiotic, stupid ♦ SM, SF (Psic) idiot, imbecile; **fare l'imbecille** to play the fool

imbecillità [imbetʃilli'ta] SF INV (Med, anche fig) imbecility, idiocy; **dire imbecillità** to talk nonsense

imbellettare [imbellet'tare] /72/ VT (viso) to make up, put make-up on; **imbellettarsi** VR to make o.s. up, put on one's make-up

imbellire [imbel'lire] /55/ VT to adorn, embellish VI (aus essere), **imbellirsi** VIP to grow more beautiful

imberbe [im'berbe] AGG beardless; **un giovanotto imberbe** a callow youth

imbestialire [imbestja'lire] /55/ VT to infuriate; **imbestialirsi** VIP to become infuriated, fly into a rage

imbevere [im'bevere] /16/ VT: **imbevere qc di** to soak sth in; **imbeversi** VIP (anche fig): **imbeversi di** to soak up, absorb

imbevuto, -a [imbe'vuto] AGG (spugna): **imbevuto (di)** soaked (in): (fig: nozioni): **imbevuto di** imbued with

imbiancare [imbjan'kare] /20/ VT (gen) to whiten; (muro: con il bianco di calce) to whitewash; (: con qualsiasi pittura) to paint; **sepolcro imbiancato** (fig) whited sepulchre VI (aus essere), **imbiancarsi** VIP to turn white, go white

imbiancatura [imbjanka'tura] SF (di muro: con bianco di calce) whitewashing; (: con altre pitture) painting

imbianchino [imbjan'kino] SM (house) painter, painter and decorator; **fa l'imbianchino** he's a painter and decorator

imbiondire [imbjon'dire] /55/ VT (capelli) to lighten; (Culin: cipolla) to brown VI (aus essere), **imbiondirsi** VIP (capelli) to lighten, bleach; (messi) to turn golden, ripen

imbizzarrire [imbiddzar'rire] /55/ VI (aus essere), **imbizzarrirsi** VIP (cavallo) to become frisky, get excited

imboccare [imbok'kare] /20/ VT 1 (bambino) to feed 2 (tromba) to put to one's mouth 3 (entrare in: strada) to turn into, enter

imboccatura [imbokka'tura] SF (di grotta, galleria, fiume)

mouth; (di strada, porto) entrance 2 (Mus) mouthpiece; (per cavallo) bit

imbocco, -chi [im'bokko] SM (di autostrada, galleria) entrance; (di valle) mouth

imbonitore [imboni'tore] SM (di spettacolo, circo) barker

imborghesire [imborge'zire] /55/ VI (aus essere), **imborghesirsi** VIP to become bourgeois

imboscare [imbos'kare] /20/ VT (nascondere) to hide; **imboscarsi** VR (Mil) to evade military service, dodge the draft (USA); **quei due si sono imboscati di nuovo** (fig) those two have disappeared again

imboscata [imbos'kata] SF ambush; **tendere un'imboscata** to lay an ambush; **l'hanno ucciso in un'imboscata** he was killed in an ambush

imboscato [imbos'kato] SM draft dodger (USA)

imboschimento [imboski'mento] SM afforestation

imbottigliare [imbottiʎ'ʎare] /27/ VT (vino) to bottle 2 (Mil: nemico) to hem in, bottle up; (: porto) to blockade; **siamo rimasti imbottigliati** we got stuck in a traffic jam; **imbottigliarsi** VIP to get o be stuck in a traffic jam

imbottire [imbot'tire] /55/ VT (sedia, cuscino) to stuff; (giacca) to pad; (panino) to fill; **gli hanno imbottito la testa di idee strane** they filled his head with silly notions; **imbottirsi** VR (coprirsi) to wrap o.s. up; (rimpinzarsi): **imbottirsi di** to stuff o.s. with

imbottito, -a [imbot'tito] AGG (sedia) upholstered; (giacca) padded; **panino imbottito** filled roll; **un reggiseno imbottito** a padded bra

imbottitura [imbotti'tura] SF (vedi vb) stuffing; padding; filling

imbracciare [imbrat'tʃare] /14/ VT (fucile) to shoulder; (scudo) to grasp

imbranato, -a [imbra'nato] (fam) AGG clumsy, awkward ♦ SM, SF clumsy person

imbrattacarte [imbratta'karte] SM, SF (pegg) scribbler

imbrattare [imbrat'tare] /72/ VT: **imbrattare (di)** to dirty (with), smear (with), daub (with); **imbrattarsi** VR: **imbrattarsi (di)** to dirty o.s. (with)

imbrattatele [imbratta'tele] SM, SF (pegg) dauber

imbrigliare [imbriʎ'ʎare] /27/ VT (cavallo) to bridle; (acque) to dam; (passioni) to curb

imbroccare [imbrok'kare] /20/ VT (bersaglio) to hit; (fig: risposta) to guess correctly; **non riesco mai ad imbroccarne una!** I never manage to get anything right!

imbrogliare [imbroʎ'ʎare] /27/ VT 1 (ingannare) to trick, deceive; (in gioco) to cheat; **non imbrogliare!** don't cheat! 2 (confondere: documenti) to muddle up; (: idee) to confuse, muddle, mix up; (fili) to tangle up; **e per imbrogliare la faccenda...** and to complicate matters ...; **imbrogliare le carte** to confuse the issue 3 (Naut: vele) to clew up; **imbrogliarsi** VIP (vedi vt b) to become muddled up; to become confused, become muddled, get mixed up; to get tangled up; **s'imbrogliò nel parlare** his speech became confused

imbroglio, -gli [im'brɔʎʎo] SM 1 (truffa) swindle, con (fam); **niente imbrogli!** no cheating! 2 (groviglio) tangle; (fig: situazione confusa) confusion; **cacciarsi in un imbroglio** to get into a mess

imbroglione, -a [imbroʎ'ʎone] SM, SF cheat, swindler ♦ AGG dishonest; **un affarista imbroglione** a dishonest businessman

imbronciato, -a [imbron'tʃato] AGG (persona) sulky; (cielo) cloudy, threatening

imbrunire [imbru'nire] /55/ VI (aus essere), VB IMPERS to grow dark ♦ SM: **all'imbrunire** at dusk

imbruttire [imbrut'tire] /55/ VT to make ugly VI (aus essere), **imbruttirsi** VIP to grow ugly

imbucare [imbu'kare] /20/ VT to post, mail (USA); **imbucarsi** VR (fam) to gate-crash

imburrare [imbur'rare] /72/ VT to butter; (stampo, teglia) to grease

imbutiforme [imbuti'forme] AGG funnel-shaped

imbuto [im'buto] SM funnel

imene [i'mene] SM hymen

imitare [imi'tare] /72/ VT (gen) to imitate; (Teatro) to impersonate, do an impression of; (gesti) to mimic; (firma) to forge;

un materiale che imita il cuoio a material which looks like leather

imitatore, -trice [imita'tore] SM, SF (gen) imitator; (Teatro) impersonator, impressionist

imitazione [imitat'tsjone] SF (vedi vb) imitation, impersonation, impression; mimicry; forgery

immacolato, -a [immako'lato] AGG immaculate, spotless; l'Immacolata Concezione (Rel) the Immaculate Conception

immagazzinare [immagaddzi'nare] /72/ VT (merce, energia) to store; (nozioni, idee) to accumulate

immaginabile [immadʒi'nabile] AGG conceivable, imaginable

immaginare [immadʒi'nare] /72/ VT 1 (credere, supporre) to imagine, suppose; **immaginare che** to imagine o think that; **me lo immaginavo più giovane** I'd thought he was younger; **me lo immaginavo** I thought as much; **me lo immaginavo!** I thought so!; **dovevo immaginarmelo** I should have expected it; **non riesco ad immaginarlo** I can't imagine it; **immagina di essere su un'isola deserta...** imagine you're on a desert island ... 2 (in espressioni di cortesia): **s'immagini!** don't mention it!, not at all!; **grazie mille! - S'immagini!** thank you very much! - Don't mention it!

immaginario, -ria, -ri, -rie [immadʒi'narjo] AGG imaginary; (mondo) make-believe; **un malato immaginario** a hypochondriac ♦ SM: **l'immaginario collettivo** the collective imagination

immaginativa [immadʒina'tiva] SF imagination; **mancare d'immaginativa** to lack imagination

immaginazione [immadʒinat'tsjone] SF imagination; **è frutto della tua immaginazione** it's a figment of your imagination

immagine [im'madʒine] SF (gen, anche Fis) image; (rappresentazione, fotografia) picture; **una bella immagine** a nice picture; **è l'immagine della salute** he's the picture of health; **è l'immagine di suo padre** he's the image of his father; **avere nella mente l'immagine di qn/qc** to have a mental picture of sb/sth; **diritto all'immagine** (Dir) right to privacy (prohibiting unauthorised publication of photographs of a person); **salvaguardare la propria immagine pubblica** to safeguard one's public image; **immagine dell'azienda** (Comm) corporate image o identity

immaginoso, -a [immadʒi'noso] AGG (linguaggio, stile) full of imagery

immalinconire [immalinko'nire] /55/ VT to sadden, depress; **immalinconirsi** VIP to become depressed, become melancholy

immancabile [imman'kabile] AGG unfailing; **ecco l'immancabile Giovanna** here comes Giovanna as usual

immancabilmente [immankabil'mente] AVV without fail, unfailingly

immane [im'mane] AGG (smisurato) huge; (spaventoso, inumano) terrible

immanente [imma'nente] AGG (Filosofia) inherent, immanent

immangiabile [imman'dʒabile] AGG (non commestibile) inedible; (ripugnante) uneatable, unpalatable; **il cibo era immangiabile** the food was inedible; **è immangiabile** I can't stomach it

immatricolare [immatriko'lare] /72/ VT (veicolo) to register; **immatricolarsi** VR (Univ) to matriculate, enrol

immatricolazione [immatrikolat'tsjone] SF (vedi vb) registration; matriculation, enrolment

immaturità [immaturi'ta] SF immaturity

immaturo, -a [imma'turo] AGG (frutto) unripe; (persona) immature; (neonato) premature; **una ragazza immatura** an immature girl

immedesimarsi [immedezi'marsi] /72/ VR: **immedesimarsi in** to identify with; **immedesimarsi nella parte** (Cine, Teatro) to get into a part, live a part

immediatamente [immedjata'mente] AVV (subito) immediately, at once; (direttamente) immediately; **vai immediatamente dal medico!** go and see the doctor immediately!

immediatezza [immedja'tettsa] SF immediacy

immediato, -a [imme'djato] AGG (gen) immediate; (intervento) prompt

immemorabile [immemo'rabile] AGG immemorial; **da tempo immemorabile** from time immemorial

immemore [im'memore] AGG (letter): **immemore di** forgetful of

immensità [immensi'ta] SF immensity

immenso, -a [im'menso] AGG (gen) immense, huge; (spazio) boundless; (folla) huge, enormous; (fig: dolore, tristezza) immense; **odio immenso** deep hatred; **c'era un giardino immenso** there was a huge garden

immergere [im'merdʒere] VB IRREG /59/ VT (gen) to immerse, plunge; **immergere in acqua** (mani) to put in water; (stoffa) to soak in water; **ha immerso il metallo incandescente nell'acqua** he plunged the red-hot metal into the water; **immerso nello studio** immersed o absorbed in one's studies; **immergersi** VR to plunge; (sommergibile) to dive, submerge; **immergersi in** (fig) to immerse o.s. in, become absorbed in

immeritato, -a [immeri'tato] AGG (non meritato) undeserved, unmerited; (ingiusto) unjust

immeritevole [immeri'tevole] AGG undeserving, unworthy

immersione [immer'sjone] SF 1 (gen) immersion; (di sommergibile) submersion, dive; (Sport) diving; (di palombaro) dive; **navigare in immersione** to sail underwater; **linea di immersione** (Naut) water line 2 (Geol) hade

immerso, -a [im'merso] PP di **immergere**

immesso, -a [im'messo] PP di **immettere**

immettere [im'mettere] /63/ VT IRREG: **immettere (in)** (gen) to introduce (into); **immettere aria nei polmoni** to take air into the lungs; **immettere dati in un computer** to feed information into a computer, enter data on a computer

immigrante [immi'grante] AGG, SM, SF immigrant

immigrare [immi'grare] /72/ VI (aus essere) to immigrate

immigrato, -a [immi'grato] AGG, SM, SF immigrant

immigrazione [immigrat'tsjone] SF immigration

imminente [immi'nente] AGG imminent

imminenza [immi'nentsa] SF imminence

immischiare [immis'kjare] /19/ VT to involve; **immischiare qn in** to involve sb in; **trovarsi immischiato in uno scandalo** to find o.s. mixed up o involved in a scandal; **immischiarsi** VIP: **immischiarsi in** to interfere o meddle in

immiserimento [immizeri'mento] SM impoverishment

immiserire [immize'rire] /55/ VT to impoverish

immissario, -ri [immis'sarjo] SM (Geog) affluent, tributary

immissione [immis'sjone] SF (gen) introduction; (Tecn, Med) intake; **immissione di dati** (Inform) data entry

immobile [im'mobile] AGG motionless, stationary, still; **è rimasto lì, immobile** he stood there, motionless ♦ SM item of real estate; **(beni) immobili** real estate sg

immobiliare [immobi'ljare] AGG property attr; **patrimonio immobiliare** real estate; **agenzia immobiliare** estate agent's (Brit), realtor (USA); **società immobiliare** property company ♦ SF = società immobiliare

immobilismo [immobi'lizmo] SM (Pol) opposition to progress

immobilità [immobili'ta] SF immobility; **immobilità politica** political inertia

immobilizzare [immobilid'dzare] /72/ VT (gen) to immobilize; (Econ: capitali) to lock up

immobilizzo [immobi'liddzo] SM: **spese d'immobilizzo** capital expenditure

immodestia [immo'destja] SF immodesty

immodesto, -a [immo'desto] AGG immodest, conceited

immolare [immo'lare] /72/ VT: **immolare (a)** to sacrifice (to); **immolarsi** VR: **immolarsi per** to sacrifice o.s. for

immondezzaio, -ai [immondet'tsajo] SM rubbish dump

immondizia [immon'dittsja] SF (spazzatura) rubbish no pl, refuse no pl, trash no pl (USA)

immorale [immo'rale] AGG immoral

immoralità [immorali'ta] SF immorality

immortalare [immorta'lare] /72/ VT to immortalize; **immortalarsi** VIP to win immortality for o.s.

immortale [immor'tale] AGG immortal

immortalità [immortali'ta] SF immortality

immune [im'mune] AGG: **immune da** (esente) exempt from; (Med) immune to; (Dir) immune from

immunità [immuniˈta] SF (*Med*, *Dir*) immunity; **immunità diplomatica** diplomatic immunity; **immunità parlamentare** ≈ parliamentary privilege

immunizzare [immunidˈdzare] /72/ VT: **immunizzare contro** to immunize against; **immunizzarsi** VR (*fig*): **immunizzarsi contro** to become immune to

immunizzazione [immuniddzatˈtsjone] SF immunization

immunodeficienza [immunodefiˈtʃɛntsa] SF: **sindrome da immunodeficienza acquista** acquired immunodeficiency syndrome

immunologico, -a, -ci, -che [immunoˈlɔdʒiko] AGG immunological

immutabile [immuˈtabile] AGG (*gen*) unchanging; (*decreto*, *decisione*) immutable

impaccare [impakˈkare] /20/ VT to pack

impacchettare [impakketˈtare] /72/ VT to wrap up, parcel up; **devo impacchettare il regalo** I've got to wrap up the present

impacciare [impatˈtʃare] /14/ VT to hamper, hinder; **impacciare qn nei movimenti** to hamper sb's movements

impacciato, -a [impatˈtʃato] AGG 1 (*imbarazzato*) embarrassed; **mi sentivo un po' impacciato** I felt a bit awkward 2 (*goffo*) awkward, clumsy

impaccio, -ci [imˈpattʃo] SM 1 (*imbarazzo*) embarrassment; (*situazione imbarazzante*) awkward situation; **trarsi d'impaccio** to get out of an awkward situation 2 (*ostacolo*) obstacle; **essere d'impaccio a qn** to be in sb's way

impacco, -chi [imˈpakko] SM (*Med*) compress; **dovrai fare degli impacchi freddi** you'll have to apply cold compresses

impadronirsi [impadroˈnirsi] /55/ VIP: **impadronirsi di** (*città*, *ricchezze*) to seize, take possession of; (*fig*: *lingua*) to master

impagabile [impaˈgabile] AGG priceless

impaginare [impadʒiˈnare] /72/ VT (*Tip*) to make up

impaginazione [impadʒinatˈtsjone] SF (*Tip*) make-up

impagliare [impaʎˈʎare] /27/ VT 1 (*animale*: *imbalsamare*) to stuff (with straw) 2 **impagliare una sedia** to cane a chair

impalato, -a [impaˈlato] AGG (*fig*) stock-still; **non startene lì impalato, fai qualcosa!** don't just stand there, do something!

impalcatura [impalkaˈtura] SF scaffolding; (*fig*) framework, structure

impallidire [impalliˈdire] /55/ VI (*aus essere*) to turn pale; (*colore*, *ricordo*) to fade; **è impallidito per la paura** he went pale with fear

impallinare [impalliˈnare] /72/ VT to riddle with shot

impalpabile [impalˈpabile] AGG impalpable

impanare [impaˈnare] /72/ VT 1 (*Culin*) to roll (*o* coat) in breadcrumbs, bread (USA) 2 (*Tecn*: *vite*) to thread

impanato, -a AGG (*Culin*) coated in breadcrumbs

impantanarsi [impantaˈnarsi] /72/ VIP to sink into mud; (*fig*) to get bogged down; **la nostra macchina si è impantanata** our car got stuck in the mud

impaperarsi [impapeˈrarsi] /72/ VIP to stumble over a word

impappinarsi [impappiˈnarsi] /72/ VIP to falter, stammer

imparare [impaˈrare] /72/ VT to learn; **imparare a fare qc** to learn to do sth; **sto imparando a suonare la chitarra** I'm learning to play the guitar; **imparare qc a memoria** to learn sth (off) by heart; **l'ha imparata a memoria** he's learnt it by heart; **imparare qc a proprie spese** to learn sth to one's cost; **così impari!** that'll teach you!; **sbagliando s'impara** (*Proverbio*) practice makes perfect

imparaticcio, -ci [imparaˈtittʃo] SM half-baked notions *pl*

impareggiabile [impareɡˈdʒabile] AGG incomparable

imparentare [imparenˈtare] /72/ VT (*famiglie*) to ally by marriage; **imparentarsi** VIP: **imparentarsi con** to marry into, become related by marriage to

impari [ˈimpari] AGG INV (*disuguale*) unequal

impartire [imparˈtire] /55/ VT (*ordine*) to give; (*benedizione*) to bestow

imparziale [imparˈtsjale] AGG impartial, unbiased

imparzialità [impartsjaliˈta] SF impartiality

impassibile [impasˈsibile] AGG impassive

impastare [impasˈtare] /72/ VT (*pane*) to knead; (*cemento*, *malta*) to mix

impasticcarsi [impastikˈkarsi] /20/ VR (*fam*) to pop pills

impasto [imˈpasto] SM 1 (*l'impastare*: *di pane*) kneading; (*: cemento*) mixing 2 (*pasta*) dough; (*miscuglio*, *anche fig*) mixture, blend

impatto [imˈpatto] SM (*urto*, *effetto*) impact; **impatto ambientale** impact on the environment

impaurire [impauˈrire] /55/ VT to frighten, scare; **mi hai impaurito** you frightened me; **impaurirsi** VIP to get *o* grow scared *o* frightened

impavido, -a [imˈpavido] AGG intrepid, fearless

impaziente [impatˈtsjente] AGG impatient; **impaziente di fare qc** eager to do sth

impazienza [impatˈtsjentsa] SF (*vedi agg*) impatience; eagerness

impazzata [impatˈtsata] **all'impazzata** AVV (*correre*) at breakneck speed; (*colpire*) wildly

impazzire [impatˈtsire] /55/ VI (*aus essere*) 1 to go mad; **impazzire per qn/qc** to be mad *o* crazy about sb/sth; **impazzire per lo sport/il gelato** to be mad about sport/ice cream; **impazzire per il dolore** to go mad with grief; **far impazzire qn** to drive sb mad; **questo compito mi fa impazzire** this homework's driving me mad; **impazzisco d'amore per te** I'm mad *o* crazy about you; **ma sei impazzito?** have you gone mad?; **sono impazzito a cercare un taxi** I nearly went crazy trying to find a taxi; **ho un mal di testa da impazzire** I've got a splitting headache; **ho un prurito da impazzire** I've got an itch that's driving me mad 2 (*Culin*: *salsa*, *maionese*) to curdle

impeccabile [impekˈkabile] AGG impeccable; **ha un gusto impeccabile** she's got impeccable taste; **in modo impeccabile** impeccably; **si veste sempre in modo impeccabile** he's always impeccably dressed

impedimento [impediˈmento] SM 1 (*ostacolo*) obstacle, hindrance; **essere un impedimento** *o* **d'impedimento a qc/qn** to stand in the way of sth/sb 2 (*Dir*) impediment

impedire [impeˈdire] /55/ VT 1 (*proibire*): **impedire a qn di fare qc** to prevent *o* stop sb (from) doing sth; **il rumore mi ha impedito di dormire** the noise stopped me sleeping; **l'hanno messo per impedire alle macchine di parcheggiare** they put it there to stop cars parking; **chi ti impedisce di farlo?** who's stopping you? 2 (*ostruire*) to obstruct 3 (*impacciare*) to hamper, hinder; **la vista le era impedita dalla nebbia** her ability to see was hampered by the fog.

impegnare [impeɲˈɲare] /15/ VT 1 (*dare in pegno*) to pawn 2 (*vincolare*) to bind 3 (*sogg*: *lavoro*) to keep busy; **quel compito di matematica ha impegnato tutta la classe** the mathematics exercise kept the whole class busy 4 (*Mil*) to engage; (*Sport*) to put under pressure; **impegnarsi** VR (*vincolarsi*): **impegnarsi a fare qc** to undertake to do sth; **impegnarsi con un contratto** to enter into a contract; **impegnarsi con qn** (*accordarsi*) to come to an agreement with sb; **impegnarsi in qc** (*dedicarsi*) to devote o.s. to sth

impegnativo, -a [impeɲɲaˈtivo] AGG (*lavoro*) demanding; (*promessa*) binding; **un lavoro impegnativo** a demanding job

impegnato, -a [impeɲˈɲato] AGG 1 (*persona*: *occupata*) busy; **sono già impegnato** I have a prior engagement; **oggi sono molto impegnato** I'm very busy today; **mi sembra che sia più impegnato di te** I think he's busier than you; **essere impegnato con** (*lavoro*) to be busy with; (*ditta*) to be involved with 2 (*gioielli*) pawned 3 (*fig*: *romanzo*, *autore*, *film*) serious, engagé

impegno [imˈpeɲɲo] SM 1 (*obbligo*) obligation; (*promessa*) promise, pledge; (*compito*, *di scrittore*) commitment; **assumere un impegno** to take on a commitment; **penso di venire, ma senza impegno** I'll probably come but I can't promise; **domani non posso, ho un impegno** I can't tomorrow, I've got something on; **ha molti impegni di lavoro** she has a lot of work commitments 2 (*affare*, *incombenza*) engagement, appointment; **un impegno precedente** a previous engagement 3 (*zelo*) enthusiasm, diligence; **studiare con impegno** to study hard

impegolarsi [impegoˈlarsi] /72/, **impelagarsi** [impelaˈgarsi] VR: **impegolarsi in** to get heavily involved in

impellente [impel'lɛnte] AGG pressing, urgent; **un bisogno impellente** an urgent need

impenetrabile [impene'trabile] AGG (*volto*) inscrutable; (*mistero*) complete; (*segreto*) closely-guarded; (*bosco*) impenetrable

impennare [impen'nare] /72/ VT (*Aer*): **far impennare l'aereo** to go into a climb; **impennarsi** VIP 1 (*aereo*) to go into a climb; (*cavallo*) to rear (up) 2 (*fig: arrabbiarsi*) to flare up

impennata [impen'nata] SF 1 (*di cavallo*) rearing (up); (*di aereo*) climb, nose-up; (*di motociclo*) wheelie 2 (*fig: scatto d'ira*) burst of anger 3 (*rialzo: di prezzi, valuta*) sharp rise

impensabile [impen'sabile] AGG (*inaccettabile*) unthinkable; (*difficile da concepire*) inconceivable

impensato, -a [impen'sato] AGG unexpected, unforeseen

impensierire [impensje'rire] /55/ VT to worry; **impensierirsi** VIP: **impensierirsi (per)** to worry (about)

imperante [impe'rante] AGG (*tendenza, moda*) prevailing

imperare [impe'rare] /72/ VI (*aus* avere) (*anche fig*) to rule, reign

imperativo, -a [impera'tivo] AGG (*tono, discorso*) commanding; (*Gramm*) imperative ♦ SM (*Gramm*): **l'imperativo** the imperative

imperatore, -trice [impera'tore] SM, SF emperor (empress)

impercettibile [impertʃet'tibile] AGG imperceptible

imperdonabile [imperdo'nabile] AGG unforgivable, unpardonable

imperfetto, -a [imper'fetto] AGG (*gen, anche Gramm*) imperfect; (*difettoso*) faulty, defective; (*incompleto*) unfinished ♦ SM (*Gramm*): **l'imperfetto** the imperfect (tense)

imperfezione [imperfet'tsjone] SF (*gen*) imperfection; (*di gioiello*) flaw; (*della pelle*) blemish, imperfection

imperiale [impe'rjale] AGG imperial

imperialismo [imperja'lizmo] SM imperialism

imperialista, -i, -e [imperja'lista] AGG, SM, SF imperialist

imperioso, -a [impe'rjoso] AGG (*autoritario: persona, tono*) imperious; (*motivo, esigenza*) urgent, pressing

imperituro, -a [imperi'turo] AGG (*letter*) everlasting

imperizia [impe'rittsja] SF inexperience, lack of experience

impermalire [imperma'lire] /55/ VT: **far impermalire qn** to offend sb; **impermalirsi** VIP: **impermalirsi (per)** to take offence o umbrage (at)

impermeabile [imperme'abile] AGG (*terreno, roccia*) impermeable; (*tessuto*) waterproof; (*orologio*) water-resistant; **essere impermeabile alle offese** to be thick-skinned, have a thick skin; **tessuto impermeabile** waterproof material ♦ SM (*indumento*) raincoat, mac (Brit)

imperniare [imper'njare] /19/ VT: **imperniare qc su** to hinge sth on; (*fig: discorso, relazione*) to base sth on; **il mio discorso è imperniato su un unico concetto** my talk hinges on one basic concept; **imperniarsi** VIP (*fig*): **imperniarsi su** to be based on

impero [im'pero] SM empire; **l'impero della ragione** (*fig*) the rule of reason; **impero romano** Roman Empire; **impero romano d'oriente** Eastern Roman Empire ♦ AGG INV Empire *attr*

imperscrutabile [imperskru'tabile] AGG inscrutable

impersonale [imperso'nale] AGG impersonal

impersonare [imperso'nare] /72/ VT 1 (*qualità, concetto astratto*) to personify 2 (*Teatro*) to play (the part of), act (the part of); **impersonarsi** VIP (*incarnarsi*): **in lei s'impersona la cupidigia** she is the personification of greed

❏ **impersonare** non si traduce mai con la parola inglese *impersonate*

imperterrito, -a [imper'territo] AGG unperturbed; **continuare imperterrito (a fare qc)** to carry on (doing sth) regardless o unperturbed; **è rimasto imperterrito quando gliel'ho detto** he was unperturbed when I told him

impertinente [imperti'nɛnte] AGG impertinent

impertinenza [imperti'nɛntsa] SF impertinence

imperturbabile [impertur'babile] AGG imperturbable

imperversare [imperver'sare] /72/ VI (*aus* avere) (*persona, tempesta, malattia*) to rage; (*scherz: moda, costumi*) to be all the rage

impervio, -via, -vi, -vie [im'pervjo] AGG (*luogo*) inaccessible; (*strada*) impassable

❏ **impervio** non si traduce mai con la parola inglese *impervious*

impeto ['impeto] SM (*moto, forza*) force, impetus; (*assalto*) onslaught; (*fig: d'odio, amore*) surge; **lo uccise in un impeto d'ira** he killed him in a fit of rage; **agire d'impeto** to act on impulse; **con impeto** (*parlare*) forcefully, energetically

impettito, -a [impet'tito] AGG: **essere tutto impettito** to be as stiff as a ramrod; **camminare impettito** to strut

impetuoso, -a [impetu'oso] AGG (*gen*) impetuous; (*vento, corrente*) raging, strong

impiantare [impjan'tare] /72/ VT (*installare*) to install; (*avviare: azienda*) to set up, establish

impiantistica [impjan'tistika] SF plant design and installation

impianto [im'pjanto] SM 1 (*installazione*) installation; **spese d'impianto** installation costs 2 (*Anat: di embrione*) implantation 3 (*apparecchiature*) plant; (*sistema*) system; **impianti di risalita** (*Sci*) ski lifts; **impianto elettrico** wiring; **impianto industriale** plant; **impianto di raffreddamento** cooling system; **impianto di riscaldamento** heating system; **impianto sportivo** sports complex; **impianto stereo** stereo system

impiastrare [impjas'trare] /14/, **impiastricciare** [impjastrit'tʃare] VT: **impiastrare di** (*fango ecc*) to dirty with; (*pittura, trucco*) to smear with

impiastro [im'pjastro] SM 1 (*Med*) poultice 2 (*fig: fam: persona*) nuisance

impiccagione [impikka'dʒone] SF hanging

impiccare [impik'kare] /20/ VT to hang; **l'hanno impiccato** he was hanged; **questo colletto m'impicca** (*fig*) this collar's choking me; **non lo farò nemmeno se m'impicchi!** there's no way I'll do that!; **impiccarsi** VR to hang o.s.; **si è impiccato** he hanged himself; **impiccati!** (*fam*) go to hell!

impicciare [impit'tʃare] /14/ VT (*sogg: persona, tavolo*) to be in the way of, get in the way of; (: *abiti*) to hinder, hamper; **impicciarsi** VIP to meddle, interfere; **impicciarsi di o in qc** to interfere o meddle in sth; **impicciati degli affari tuoi!** mind your own business!

impiccio, -ci [im'pittʃo] SM 1 (*ostacolo*) hindrance; (*seccatura*) trouble, bother; **essere d'impiccio** to be in the way 2 (*affare imbrogliato*) mess *no pl*; **cavare o togliere qn dagli impicci** to get sb out of trouble

impiccione, -a [impit'tʃone] SM, SF busybody; **essere impiccione** to be a busybody

impiegare [impje'gare] /80/ VT 1 (*utilizzare*) to use, employ; (*tempo*) to spend; (*metterci: tempo*) to take; (*investire: denaro*) to invest; **impiega il tempo libero a dipingere** he spends his free time painting; **impiego un quarto d'ora per andare a casa** it takes me o I take a quarter of an hour to get home; **ho impiegato più di due ore a fare i compiti** it took me more than two hours to do my homework; **quanto ci impieghi per arrivare a scuola?** how long does it take you to get to school? 2 (*lavoratore*) to employ; **impiegarsi** VR to get a job, obtain employment

impiegatizio, -zia, -zi, -zie [impjega'tittsjo] AGG clerical, white-collar *attr*; **il ceto impiegatizio** clerical o white-collar workers *pl*

impiegato, -a [impje'gato] SM, SF employee; **impiegato di banca** bank clerk; **impiegato statale** state employee

impiego, -ghi [im'pjɛgo] SM 1 (*gen*) use; (*Econ*) investment 2 (*occupazione*) employment; (*posto di lavoro*) post, (regular) job; **un impiego fisso** a permanent job; **pubblico impiego** public sector

impietosire [impjeto'sire] /55/ VT to move (to pity); **impietosirsi** VIP to be moved (to pity)

impietoso, -a [impje'toso] AGG pitiless, cruel

impietrire [impje'trire] /55/ VT (*anche fig*) to petrify

impigliare [impiʎ'ʎare] /27/ VT to catch, entangle; **impigliarsi** VIP: **impigliarsi (in qc)** to get caught o entangled (in sth)

impigrire [impi'grire] /55/ VT to make lazy VI (*aus* essere), **impigrirsi** VIP to get o grow lazy

impinguare [impin'gware] /72/ VT (*fig: tasche, casse dello Stato*) to fill; (*maiale*) to fatten

impiombare [impjom'bare] /**72**/ vt **1** (*saldare: tubo ecc*) to seal (with lead); (*sigillare: baule, cassa*) to seal **2** (*dente*) to fill

implacabile [impla'kabile] AGG implacable

implementare [implemen'tare] /**72**/ vt (*Inform*) to implement; (*progetto*) to carry out

implicare [impli'kare] /**20**/ vt **1** (*sottintendere*) to imply; (*comportare*) to entail **2** (*coinvolgere*): **implicare qn (in)** to involve sb (in), **implicate sb (in), essere implicato in un omicidio** to be involved in a murder; **implicarsi** vr: **implicarsi (in)** to get o become involved in (in)

implicazione [implikat'tsjone] SF implication

implicito, -a [im'plitʃito] AGG implicit

implorare [implo'rare] /**72**/ vt to implore, beseech

implorazione [implorat'tsjone] SF plea, entreaty

impollinare [impolli'nare] /**72**/ vt to pollinate

impollinazione [impollinat'tsjone] SF pollination

impolverare [impolve'rare] /**72**/ vt to cover with dust; **impolverarsi** vip to get dusty

impomatare [impoma'tare] /**72**/ vt (*capelli*) to pomade; (*baffi*) to wax; (*pelle*) to put ointment on; **impomatarsi** vr (*fam*) to get spruced up

imponderabile [imponde'rabile] AGG, SM imponderable

impone ecc [im'pone] vB vedi **imporre**

imponente [impo'nente] AGG (*persona, monumento*) imposing, impressive; **un edificio imponente** an impressive building

impongo ecc [im'pongo] vB vedi **imporre**

imponibile [impo'nibile] AGG taxable; **reddito imponibile** taxable income ♦ SM taxable income

impopolare [impopo'lare] AGG unpopular; **un provvedimento impopolare** an unpopular measure

impopolarità [impopolari'ta] SF unpopularity

imporre [im'porre] vB IRREG /**77**/ vt (*gen*) to impose; (*compito*) to set, impose; (*condizioni*) to impose, lay down; **imporre qc a qn** to impose sth on sb; **imporre a qn di fare qc** to oblige o force sb to do sth, make sb do sth; **imporre la propria autorità** to assert one's authority, make one's authority felt; **imporre la propria volontà** to have one's way; **imporsi qc** to impose sth on o.s.; **imporsi di fare qc** to make o.s. do sth, force o.s. to do sth; **imporsi** vr **1** (*farsi valere*) to assert o.s., make o.s. respected; **si è imposto sugli altri per la sua competenza** he commanded the others' respect because of his ability **2** (*aver successo: musicista, attore, sportivo*) to come to the fore, become popular; (*moda*) to become popular, come into the public eye ♦ **imporsi** vip **1** (*diventare necessario*) to become necessary; **s'impone una scelta** a choice is called for **2** (*avere successo: moda*) to become established, become popular

importante [impor'tante] AGG (*gen*) important; (*fatti*) important, significant; (*somma*) sizeable; **questo è molto importante** this is very important; **una partita importante** a big match; **poco importante** of little importance o significance; **è importante che ci sia anche lui** it is important that he should be there too ♦ SM: **l'importante è...** the important thing is ..., what is important is ...; **l'importante è arrivare entro domani** the important thing is to get there by tomorrow

importanza [impor'tantsa] SF (*vedi agg*) importance; significance; size; **di una certa importanza** of considerable importance; **della massima importanza** of the utmost importance; **un fatto della massima importanza** a matter of the greatest importance; **avere importanza** to be important; **che importanza ha sapere chi è stato?** what does it matter who it was?; **assumere importanza** to become more important; **dare importanza a qc** to attach importance to sth; **danno molta importanza all'abbigliamento** they think clothes are very important; **dare troppa importanza a qc** to make too much of sth, attach too much importance to sth; **darsi importanza** (*darsi arie*) to give o.s. airs

importare¹ [impor'tare] /**72**/ vt (*introdurre dall'estero*) to import; **la vodka viene importata dalla Russia** vodka is imported from Russia

importare² [impor'tare] /**72**/ vi, vB IMPERS (*aus essere*) (*essere importante*) to matter, be important; **le tue ragioni non mi importano** your reasons aren't important to me, I don't care about your reasons; **sembra che non gli importi degli esami** he doesn't seem to care about the exams; **ciò che importa di più è...** the most important thing is ...; **non importa!** it doesn't matter!, never mind!; **oggi o domani non importa** today or tomorrow, it doesn't matter; **non preoccuparti, non importa** don't worry, it doesn't matter; **non m'importa niente** I couldn't care less, I don't care; **non m'importa niente di quello che pensano** it doesn't matter to me what they think; **che importa?** what does it matter?; **non importa cosa/quando/dove** it doesn't matter what/when/where

importatore, -trice [importa'tore] AGG importing; **la ditta importatrice di questo prodotto** the firm that imports this product ♦ SM, SF importer

importazione [importat'tsjone] SF (*operazione*) importation; (*merci importate*) imports pl; **merci/prodotti d'importazione** imported goods/products

importo [im'porto] SM (total) amount

importunare [importu'nare] /**72**/ vt **1** (*disturbare*) to bother, disturb; **non vorrei importunarti con le mie richieste** I don't want to bother you with my requests **2** (*molestare*) to pester, annoy; (*sessualmente*) to harass

importuno, -a [impor'tuno] AGG (*visita*) inopportune, ill-timed; (*persona*) irksome, annoying ♦ SM, SF troublesome individual

imposi ecc [im'posi] vB vedi **imporre**

imposizione [impozit'tsjone] SF **1** (*atto*) imposition **2** (*ordine*) order, command; **non accetto imposizioni da nessuno** I don't take orders from anyone **3** (*onere, imposta*) tax

impossessarsi [imposses'sarsi] /**72**/ vip: **impossessarsi di** (*terreno, beni*) to seize, take possession of; (*segreto*) to get hold of; **si è impossessato della mia stanza** (*fig*) he has taken over my room

impossibile [impos'sibile] AGG impossible; **mi è impossibile farlo** it's impossible for me to do it, I can't (possibly) do it; **ma va', è impossibile!** come off it, it's impossible!; **è impossibile che lo sappia** she can't know about it ♦ SM: **fare l'impossibile** to do one's utmost, do all one can

impossibilità [impossibili'ta] SF impossibility; **essere o trovarsi nell'impossibilità di fare qc** to be unable o find it impossible to do sth

impossibilitato, -a [impossibili'tato] AGG: **essere impossibilitato a fare qc** to be unable to do sth

imposta¹ [im'posta] SF (*di finestra*) shutter

imposta² [im'posta] SF (*tassa*) tax; **imposte dirette/indirette** direct/indirect taxation sg; **ufficio imposte** tax office; **imposta indiretta sui consumi** excise duty o tax; **imposta locale sui redditi** tax on unearned income; **imposta patrimoniale** property tax; **imposta sul reddito** income tax; **imposta sul reddito delle persone fisiche** personal income tax; **imposta di successione** capital transfer tax (*Brit*), inheritance tax (*USA*); **imposta sugli utili** tax on profits; **imposta sul valore aggiunto** value added tax (*Brit*), sales tax (*USA*)

impostare¹ [impos'tare] /**72**/ vt **1** (*servizio, organizzazione*) to set up; (*lavoro*) to organize, plan; (*resoconto, rapporto*) to plan; (*questione, problema*) to formulate, set out; (*Tip: pagina*) to lay out, make up **2** (*Mus*): **impostare la voce** to pitch one's voice

impostare² [impos'tare] /**72**/ vt (*lettera*) to post (*Brit*), mail (*USA*)

impostazione¹ [impostat'tsjone] SF (*di problema, questione*) formulation, statement; (*di lavoro*) organization, planning; (*di attività*) setting up; (*Mus: di voce*) pitch

impostazione² [impostat'tsjone] SF (*di lettera*) posting (*Brit*), mailing (*USA*)

imposto, -a [im'posto] PP di **imporre**

impostore, -a [impos'tore] SM, SF impostor

impotente [impo'tente] AGG **1** (*persona, governo*) impotent, powerless; **essere impotente di fronte a qc** to be powerless in the face of sth; **sentirsi impotente** to feel helpless **2** (*Med: incapace sessualmente*) impotent ♦ SM (*Med*) impotent man

impotenza [impo'tentsa] SF (*debolezza*) impotence, powerlessness; (*Med*) impotence

impoverire [impove'rire] /**55**/ vt to impoverish vi (*aus essere*), **impoverirsi** vip to become poor(er)

impraticabile [imprati'kabile] AGG (*strada*) impassable; (*Sport: campo*) unfit for play, unplayable

impratichirsi [imprati'kirsi] VIP (*fare pratica*) to get practice, gain experience; **impratichirsi in qc** to gain experience in (doing) sth

imprecare [impre'kare] /20/ VI (*aus avere*) to curse, swear; **imprecare contro** to hurl abuse at

imprecazione [imprekat'tsjone] SF abuse, curse; **lanciare un'imprecazione** to curse

imprecisato, -a [impretʃi'zato] AGG **1** (*non preciso: quantità, numero*) indeterminate **2** (*non chiaro: dettagli, particolari*) unclear; **per motivi imprecisati** for reasons which are not clear; **ad un'ora imprecisata** at an unspecified time

imprecisione [impretʃi'zjone] SF (*vedi agg*) imprecision; inaccuracy

impreciso, -a [impre't'fizo] AGG (*definizione, descrizione*) imprecise, vague; (*calcolo*) inaccurate; **è impreciso nel suo lavoro** he's a careless worker

impregnare [impreɲ'ɲare] /15/ VT: **impregnare (di)** (*imbevere*) to soak o impregnate (with); (*riempire, anche fig*) to fill (with); **impregnarsi** VIP: **impregnarsi di** (*vedi vt*) to become impregnated with; to become filled with

imprenditore [imprendi'tore] SM (*industriale*) entrepreneur; (*appaltatore*) contractor; **piccolo imprenditore** small businessman; **imprenditore edile** building contractor

imprenditoria [imprendito'ria] SF enterprise; (*imprenditori*) entrepreneurs *pl*

imprenditoriale [imprendito'rjale] AGG (*ceto, classe*) entrepreneurial

impreparato, -a [imprepa'rato] AGG: **impreparato (a)** (*gen*) unprepared (for); (*lavoratore*) untrained (for); **quel professore di matematica è impreparato** that mathematics teacher has a poor knowledge of his subject; **cogliere qn impreparato** to catch sb unawares

impreparazione [impreparat'tsjone] SF lack of preparation

impresa [im'presa] SF **1** (*iniziativa*) enterprise, undertaking; **abbandonare un'impresa** to abandon an enterprise o an undertaking; **è un'impresa!** that's quite an undertaking!; **sarà un'impresa riuscire a convincerlo!** it'll be hard work persuading him! **2** (*azione gloriosa*) feat, exploit **3** (*ditta, azienda*) firm, concern; **mettere su un'impresa** to set up a business; **lavora nell'impresa del padre** he works in his father's business; **le piccole e medie imprese** small and medium-sized businesses; **un'impresa edile** a building firm; **impresa familiare** family firm; **impresa pubblica** state-owned enterprise

impresario, -ria, -ri, -rie [impre'sarjo] SM, SF (*Teatro*) theatre manager; (*di teatri maggiori, o più teatri*) impresario; **impresario di pompe funebri** funeral director

imprescindibile [impreʃʃin'dibile] AGG (*necessità*) inescapable, unavoidable; (*condizione*) essential; (*obbligo*) binding

impressi ecc [im'pressi] VB *vedi* **imprimere**

impressionante [impressjo'nante] AGG **1** (*che suscita turbamento*) disturbing, upsetting; **una scena impressionante** a terrible scene **2** (*che suscita sensazione*) impressive; **una velocità impressionante** an amazing speed

impressionare [impressjo'nare] /72/ VT **1** (*turbare*) to upset; (*colpire*) to impress; **l'incidente mi ha impressionato moltissimo** the accident upset me a lot; **mi ha impressionato il numero dei partecipanti** I was struck by the number of participants; **mi impressiono alla vista del sangue** I can't stand the sight of blood **2** (*Fot*) to expose; **impressionarsi** VIP (*spaventarsi*) to get o be upset; **non impressionarti!** don't get upset!

impressione [impres'sjone] SF **1** (*sensazione*) impression, sensation, feeling; **ho l'impressione che mi nasconda qualcosa** I have the feeling that he's hiding something from me; **ho avuto l'impressione che non si fidasse di me** I had the feeling that she didn't trust me; **far impressione a qn** (*colpire*) to impress sb; (*turbare*) to upset sb, frighten sb; **il sangue mi fa impressione** I can't stand the sight of blood; **fare una buona/cattiva o brutta impressione a qn** to make a good/bad impression on sb; **che impressione ti ha fatto?** what was your impression of it (o him *ecc*)?, what did you make of it (o him *ecc*)?; **che impressione!** how awful!, how ghastly! **2** (*Tip: stampa*) printing; (: *ristampa*) impression

impresso, -a [im'presso] PP *di* **imprimere**

imprestare [impres'tare] /72/ VT (*fam*): **imprestare qc a qn** to lend sth to sb

imprevedibile [impreve'dibile] AGG (*destino, futuro*) unforeseeable; (*cambiamento*) unexpected; (*persona, risultato*) unpredictable

imprevidente [imprevi'dente] AGG lacking in foresight, improvident

imprevidenza [imprevi'dentsa] SF lack of foresight, improvidence

imprevisto, -a [impre'visto] AGG (*arrivo, cambiamento*) unexpected; (*circostanza*) unforeseen, unexpected; **una spesa imprevista** an unexpected expense ◆ SM unexpected o unforeseen event; **salvo imprevisti** unless anything unexpected happens

impreziosire [imprettsjo'sire] /55/ VT: **impreziosire con** to embellish with

imprigionamento [impridʒona'mento] SM imprisonment

imprigionare [impridʒo'nare] /72/ VT (*chiudere in prigione*) to imprison; (*rinchiudere: in casa ecc*) to shut up, confine; (*fig: intrappolare*) to trap; **la nave era imprigionata nel ghiaccio** the ship was icebound

imprimere [im'primere] VB IRREG /50/ VT **1** (*marchio*) to impress, stamp; **imprimersi qc nella mente** to fix sth firmly in one's mind; **mi è rimasto impresso ciò che hai detto** I have never forgotten what you said **2** (*trasmettere*): **imprimere (un) movimento a** to impart o transmit movement to; **imprimersi** VIP (*fig: ricordo*) to stamp itself, imprint itself

improbabile [impro'babile] AGG improbable, unlikely; **è improbabile che venga** he's unlikely to come

improbo, -a [im'probo] AGG (*letter: fatica, lavoro*) gruelling (*Brit*), grueling (*USA*), laborious

improduttivo, -a [improdut'tivo] AGG (*investimento*) unprofitable; (*terreno*) unfruitful; (*fig: sforzo*) fruitless, futile

impronta [im'pronta] SF **1** (*di piede, mano*) print; (*fig: di genio, maestro*) mark, stamp; **lasciare la propria impronta in qc** (*fig*) to leave one's mark on sth; **impronta del piede** footprint; **impronta di carbonio** carbon footprint; **rilevamento delle impronte genetiche** genetic fingerprinting; **impronte digitali** fingerprints **2** (*di moneta*) impression

improperio, -ri [impro'perjo] SM (*insulto*) insult; **lanciare un improperio** to swear; **coprire qn d'improperi** to hurl abuse at sb

improponibile [impropo'nibile] AGG (*idea, patto, accordo*) which cannot be proposed o suggested

improprio, -ria, -ri, -rie [im'proprjo] AGG (*non corretto: uso*) incorrect, improper; (*sconveniente: tono, abbigliamento*) improper, inappropriate; **arma impropria** something used as a weapon

improrogabile [improro'gabile] AGG (*termine*) that cannot be extended

improvvisamente [improvviza'mente] AVV suddenly, unexpectedly; **improvvisamente si è messo a piovere** it suddenly started to rain; **è arrivato improvvisamente** he arrived unexpectedly

improvvisare [improvvi'zare] /72/ VT (*gen*) to improvise; (*cena, piatto*) to knock up, throw together, improvise; **improvvisare una festa** to hold an impromptu party; **abbiamo improvvisato una cenetta alla buona** we put together a simple meal; **improvvisarsi** VR to act as; **si è improvvisato cuoco per l'occasione** he took on the role of chef on that occasion

improvvisata [improvvi'zata] SF (pleasant) surprise; **fare un'improvvisata a qn** to give sb a surprise

improvvisazione [improvvizat'tsjone] SF improvisation; **spirito d'improvvisazione** spirit of invention; **capacità d'improvvisazione** ability to improvise

improvviso [improv'vizo] AGG (*inaspettato: arrivo ecc*) unexpected; (*subitaneo: simpatia, cambiamento d'umore*) sudden; **all'improvviso, d'improvviso** (*inaspettatamente*) unexpectedly; (*tutto d'un tratto*) suddenly; **all'improvviso si è spalancata la porta** the door suddenly opened; **è partita all'improvviso** she left suddenly; **un improvviso cambiamento di programma** a sudden change of plan

imprudente [impru'dente] AGG (*gen*) careless, foolish,

imprudent; (*osservazione*) unwise; **un guidatore imprudente** a careless driver ♦ SM, SF imprudent person

imprudenza [impru'dentsa] SF (*qualità*) carelessness, foolishness, imprudence; (*azione*): **è stata un'imprudenza** that was a rash *o* an imprudent thing to do

impudente [impu'dɛnte] AGG impudent, cheeky ♦ SM, SF impudent person

impudenza [impu'dɛntsa] SF impudence, cheek; **avere l'impudenza di fare qc** to have the cheek to do sth

impudicizia [impudi't∫ittsja] SF immodesty

impudico, -a, -chi, -che [impu'diko] AGG immodest

impugnare [impuɲ'ɲare] /15/ VT 1 (*arma*) to grasp, seize 2 (*Dir: sentenza*) to contest

impugnatura [impuɲɲa'tura] SF (*di coltello, frusta*) handle; (*di spada*) hilt; (*di remo, racchetta*) grip; **impugnatura a due mani** (*Tennis*) two-handed grip *o* grasp

impulsività [impulsivi'ta] SF impulsiveness; **fare qc per impulsività** to do sth impulsively

impulsivo, -a [impul'sivo] AGG impulsive; **ha un carattere impulsivo** he's got an impulsive nature ♦ SM, SF impulsive person

impulso [im'pulso] SM 1 (*Fis: moto istintivo*) impulse; **agire d'impulso** to act on impulse; **ho agito d'impulso** I acted on impulse; **sentì l'impulso di picchiarlo** he was seized with an urge to hit him; **impulso sessuale** sex drive 2 (*fig: spinta*) boost; **dare un impulso alle vendite** to boost sales

impunemente [impune'mente] AVV with impunity; **fare qc impunemente** to get away with sth

impunità [impuni'ta] SF impunity

impuntarsi [impun'tarsi] /72/ VIP (*cavallo, asino*) to jib, refuse to budge; (*fig: ostinarsi*) to dig one's heels in, be obstinate

impuntura [impun'tura] SF stitching

impurità [impuri'ta] SF INV impurity

impuro, -a [im'puro] AGG impure; **esse impura** (*Fonetica*) "s" impure ("*s*" + *consonant*)

imputare [impu'tare] /72/ VT 1 (*Dir*): **imputare qn di** to charge sb with, accuse sb of 2 **imputare qc a** (*attribuire*) to attribute *o* ascribe sth to; (*Contabilità*) to charge sth to

imputato, -a [impu'tato] SM, SF (*Dir*) defendant, accused

imputazione [imputat'tsjone] SF (*Dir*) charge; **capo d'imputazione** charge, count (of indictment); **imputazione delle spese generali** (*Contabilità*) allocation of overheads

imputridire [imputri'dire] /55/ VT to rot ♦ VI (*aus essere*) to putrefy, rot

---

<u>**PAROLA CHIAVE**</u>

in [in] PREP *in* + *il* = nel, *in* + *lo* = nello, *in* + *l'* = nell', *in* + *la* = nella, *in* + *i* = nei, *in* + *gli* = negli, *in* + *le* = nelle

1 (*stato in luogo*) in; (*all'interno*) inside; **sono rimasto in casa** I stayed at home, I stayed indoors; **è nell'editoria/nell'esercito** he is in publishing/in the army; **è nel fondo all'armadio** it is at the back of the wardrobe; **è bravo in latino** he's good at Latin; **dottore in legge** doctor of law; **in lei ho trovato una sorella** I found a sister in her; **in lui non c'era più speranza** there was no hope left in him; **nell'opera di Shakespeare** in Shakespeare's works; **vivo in Scozia** I live in Scotland; **aveva le mani in tasca** he had his hands in his pockets; **il pranzo è in tavola** lunch is on the table; **se fossi in te** if I were you; **un giornale diffuso in tutta Italia** a newspaper read all over *o* throughout Italy

2 (*moto a luogo*) to; (*dentro*) into; **andare in campagna/in montagna** to go into the country/to the mountains; **andrò in Francia** I'm going to France; **entrare in casa** to go into the house; **entrare in macchina** to get into the car; **gettare qc in acqua** to throw sth into the water; **inciampò in una radice** he tripped over a root; **l'ho messo là in alto/basso** I put it up/down there; **spostarsi di città in città** to move from town to town

3 (*moto per luogo*): **il corteo è passato in piazza** the procession passed through the square; **sta facendo un viaggio in Egitto** he's travelling in *o* around Egypt

4 (*tempo*) in; **negli anni ottanta** in the eighties; **nel 1960** in 1960; **è cambiata molto in un anno** she has changed a lot in a year; **in autunno** in autumn; **di giorno in giorno** from day to day; **in gioventù** in one's youth; **in questo istante** at

the moment; **in luglio, nel mese di luglio** in July; **lo farò in settimana** I'll do it within the week

5 (*mezzo*) by; **mi piace viaggiare in aereo** I like travelling by plane, I like flying; **pagare in contanti/in dollari** to pay cash/in dollars; **ci andremo in macchina** we'll go there by car, we'll drive there; **siamo andati in treno** we went by train

6 (*modo, maniera*) in; **in abito da sera** in evening dress; **tagliare in due** to cut in two; **in fiamme** on fire, in flames; **in gruppo** in a group; **in guerra** at war; **tradurre in italiano** to translate into Italian; **parlare in italiano** to speak Italian; **nell'oscurità** in the darkness; **in piedi** standing, on one's feet; **in prosa** in prose; **in silenzio** in silence; **scrivere in stampatello** to write in block letters; **in versi** in verse; **Maria Bianchi in Rossi** Maria Rossi née Bianchi

7 (*materia*) made of; **in marmo** made of marble, marble *attr*; **braccialetto in oro** gold bracelet; **lo stesso modello in seta** the same model in silk

8 (*fine, scopo*): **spende tutto in divertimenti** he spends all his money on entertainment; **me lo hanno dato in dono** they gave it to me as a gift; **in favore di** in favour of; **in onore di** in honour of

9 (*misura*) in; **in altezza** in height; **arrivarono in gran numero** they arrived in large numbers; **in lunghezza** in length; **siamo in quattro** there are four of us; **in tutto** in all

10 (*con infinito*): **ha sbagliato nel rispondere male** he was wrong to be rude; **si è fatto male nel salire sull'autobus** he hurt himself as he was getting onto the bus; **nell'udire la notizia** on hearing the news

♦ AVV: **essere in** (*di moda, attuale*) to be in

♦ AGG INV: **la gente in** the in-crowd

inabile [i'nabile] AGG (*fisicamente, anche Mil*): **inabile (a)** unfit (for); (*per infortunio*) disabled; **inabile al servizio militare** unfit for military service

inabilità [inabili'ta] SF (*fisica, anche Mil*): **inabilità (a)** unfitness (for); (*per infortunio*) disablement

inabissare [inabis'sare] /72/ VT (*nave*) to sink; **inabissarsi** VIP to sink, go down

inabitabile [inabi'tabile] AGG uninhabitable

inabitato, -a [inabi'tato] AGG uninhabited

inaccessibile [inatt∫es'sibile] AGG (*luogo*) inaccessible; (*spesa*) prohibitive; (*persona*) unapproachable; (*mistero*) unfathomable; (*teoria*) incomprehensible

inaccettabile [inatt∫et'tabile] AGG unacceptable

inacerbire [inat∫er'bire] /55/ VT to exacerbate; **inacerbirsi** VIP (*persona*) to become embittered

inacidire [inat∫i'dire] /55/ VT (*persona, carattere*) to embitter VI (*aus essere*), **inacidirsi** VIP (*latte*) to go sour; (*fig: persona, carattere*) to become sour, become embittered

inadatto, -a [ina'datto] AGG: **inadatto (a)** (*persona*) unsuited (to), unfit (for); (*luogo, costruzione, lavoro*) unsuitable (for); (*parole, azione*) inappropriate (to); **le sue scarpe sono inadatte a camminare** her shoes are unsuitable for walking

inadeguato, -a [inade'gwato] AGG: **inadeguato (a)** (*non sufficiente*) inadequate (for); (*inadatto*) not suitable (for)

inadempiente [inadem'pjente] AGG defaulting ♦ SM, SF defaulter

inadempienza [inadem'pjentsa] SF: **inadempienza a un contratto** non-fulfilment of a contract; **dovuto alle inadempienze dei funzionari** due to negligence on the part of the officials

inadempimento [inadempi'mento] SM non-fulfilment

inafferrabile [inaffer'rabile] AGG (*ladro, criminale*) elusive; (*fig: concetto, significato*) incomprehensible, difficult to grasp

inaffidabile [inaffi'dabile] AGG (*persona*) untrustworthy

inalare [ina'lare] /72/ VT to inhale

inalatore [inala'tore] SM inhaler

inalazione [inalat'tsjone] SF inhalation

inalberare [inalbe'rare] /72/ VT (*bandiera, insegna*) to hoist, run up, raise; **inalberarsi** VIP (*fig: arrabbiarsi*) to flare up, fly off the handle

inalterabile [inalte'rabile] AGG (*colore*) permanent, fast; (*prezzo, qualità*) stable; (*amicizia*) steadfast; (*affetto*) unchanging, constant; **i termini del contratto sono inalterabili** the terms of the contract cannot be changed

inalterato, -a [inalte'rato] AGG (*prezzi*) stable; (*affetto, amicizia, termini di contratto*) unaltered, unchanged

inamidare [inami'dare] /72/ VT to starch

inamidato, -a [inami'dato] AGG (*colletto, camicia*) starched

inammissibile [inammis'sibile] AGG (*comportamento, reazione*) intolerable; (*Dir: prova*) inadmissible

inanimato, -a [inani'mato] AGG (*gen*) inanimate; (*svenuto*) unconscious; (*morto*) lifeless

inappagabile [inappa'gabile] AGG (*desiderio*) insatiable

inappellabile [inappel'labile] AGG (*decisione*) final, irrevocable; (*Dir*) not open to appeal, final

inappetenza [inappe'tentsa] SF lack of appetite; **soffrire di inappetenza** to have no appetite

inappuntabile [inappun'tabile] AGG (*persona*) irreproachable; (*contegno*) faultless, irreproachable; (*eleganza*) faultless, impeccable

inarcare [inar'kare] /20/ VT (*schiena*) to arch; (*sopracciglia*) to raise; **inarcarsi** VIP (*legno*) to warp; (*schiena*) to arch

inaridimento [inaridi'mento] SM (*anche fig*) drying up

inaridire [inari'dire] /55/ VT (*terreno*) to parch, dry up; (*fig: vena poetica*) to dry up; (*: persona*) to sour VI (*aus essere*), **inaridirsi** VIP (*anche fig*) to dry up, become arid; (*persona*) to become soured

inarrestabile [inarres'tabile] AGG **1** (*processo*) irreversible; (*emorragia*) that cannot be staunched **2** (*corsa del tempo*) relentless

inascoltato, -a [inaskol'tato] AGG unheeded, unheard; **rimanere inascoltato** to go unheeded *o* unheard

inaspettatamente [inaspettata'mente] AVV unexpectedly

inaspettato, -a [inaspet'tato] AGG unexpected; **una visita inaspettata** an unexpected visit

inasprire [inas'prire] /55/ VT (*disciplina*) to tighten up, make harsher; (*persona, carattere*) to embitter, sour; (*rapporti*) to make worse; **inasprirsi** VIP (*vedi vt*) to become harsher; to become bitter; to become worse; **si sono inasprite le ostilità** hostilities have intensified

inattaccabile [inattak'kabile] AGG (*fortezza, castello*) unassailable, impregnable; (*fig: alibi*) cast-iron; (*: posizione*) unassailable; **inattaccabile dagli acidi** proof against acids

inattendibile [inatten'dibile] AGG (*versione dei fatti*) unreliable; (*testimone*) unreliable, untrustworthy

inatteso, -a [inat'teso] AGG unexpected

inattivo, -a [inat'tivo] AGG (*persona*) idle, inactive; (*vulcano*) inactive, dormant; (*Chim*) inactive

inattuabile [inattu'abile] AGG impracticable

inaudito, -a [inau'dito] AGG (*crudeltà, ferocia*) unheard-of, unprecedented; (*somma, prezzo*) outrageous; **è inaudito!** it's outrageous!

inaugurale [inaugu'rale] AGG inaugural; **la fase inaugurale** the opening stages

inaugurare [inaugu'rare] /72/ VT (*scuola, linea ferroviaria*) to open, inaugurate; (*mostra*) to open; (*monumento*) to unveil; (*era, periodo*) to usher in, inaugurate; (*sistema*) to inaugurate; (*scherz: scarpe, vestito*) to christen; **il nuovo stadio sarà inaugurato domani** the new stadium is being opened tomorrow; **oggi ho inaugurato le scarpe nuove** I wore my new shoes for the first time today

inaugurazione [inaugurat'tsjone] SF (*vedi vt*) opening, inauguration; unveiling; **fare l'inaugurazione di** to inaugurate, open; **l'inaugurazione di una mostra** the opening of an exhibition

inavveduto, -a [inavve'duto] AGG (*gesto*) inadvertent, unintentional, careless

inavvertenza [inavver'tentsa] SF carelessness, inadvertence

inavvertitamente [inavvertita'mente] AVV inadvertently, unintentionally

inavvicinabile [inavvitʃi'nabile] AGG unapproachable

Inca ['inka] AGG, SM INV, SF INV Inca

incagliarsi [inkaʎ'ʎarsi] VIP (*nave, barca*) to run aground; (*fig: trattative*) to become bogged down, grind to a halt

incalcolabile [inkalko'labile] AGG incalculable

incallito, -a [inkal'lito] AGG **1** (*mani*) calloused **2** (*fig: ladro*) hardened; (*: bugiardo*) inveterate; (*: fumatore, bevitore*) heavy; **è un incallito rubacuori** he's a real heartbreaker

incalzante [inkal'tsante] AGG (*richiesta*) urgent, insistent; (*crisi*) imminent

incalzare [inkal'tsare] /72/ VT (*inseguire*) to pursue, follow closely; (*fig*) to press ♦ VI (*urgere: tempo*) to be pressing; (*essere imminente: pericolo*) to be imminent

incamerare [inkame'rare] /72/ VT (*Dir*) to expropriate, confiscate

incamminarsi [inkammi'narsi] VIP to set forth, set out; **incamminarsi verso** to set out for, head for; (*fig*) to head for; **ci siamo incamminati verso la spiaggia** we set off towards the beach

incanalare [inkana'lare] /72/ VT (*acque*) to canalize; (*traffico, folla*) to direct, channel; **incanalarsi** VIP: **incanalarsi verso** (*folla*) to converge on

incancrenire [inkankre'nire] /55/ VI (*aus essere*), **incancrenirsi** VIP to become gangrenous

incandescente [inkandeʃ'ʃente] AGG incandescent, white-hot

incantare [inkan'tare] /72/ VT (*per magia, anche fig: persona*) to enchant, bewitch; (*serpente*) to charm; **non m'incanti con le tue chiacchiere!** you don't fool me with your fine words!; **incantarsi** VIP (*bloccarsi: meccanismo*) to stick, jam; (*: persona*) to be spellbound, be in a daze; **incantarsi nel parlare** to hesitate and stare in one's speech; **incantarsi a guardare qn/qc** to stop and stare at sb/sth

incantatore, -trice [inkanta'tore] AGG enchanting, bewitching ♦ SM, SF enchanter (enchantress); **incantatore di serpenti** snake charmer

incantesimo [inkan'tezimo] SM spell, charm; **rompere l'incantesimo** (*anche fig*) to break the spell

incantevole [inkan'tevole] AGG enchanting, delightful, lovely; **c'era un paesaggio incantevole** the scenery was lovely; **è ancora più incantevole del solito** it's even lovelier than usual

incanto¹ [in'kanto] SM (*incantesimo*) spell, charm, enchantment; **quella persona/quel paese è un incanto** that person/village is enchanting; **sei un incanto stasera** you look enchanting this evening; **l'incanto della montagna** the magic of the mountains; **come per incanto** as if by magic; **l'eczema è scomparso come per incanto** the eczema disappeared as if by magic; **ti sta d'incanto!** (*vestito ecc*) it really suits you!

incanto² [in'kanto] SM (*asta*) auction; **vendita all'incanto** sale by auction; **mettere all'incanto** to put up for auction

incanutire [inkanu'tire] /55/ VI (*aus essere*) to go white

incapace [inka'patʃe] AGG incapable; **essere incapace (di fare qc)** to be incapable (of doing sth); **è incapace di mentire** she's incapable of lying ♦ SM, SF **essere un incapace** to be useless, be a dead loss: (*fam*): **solo un incapace poteva...** only an idiot could ...

incapacità [inkapatʃi'ta] SF **1** (*inabilità*) incapability, inability; **incapacità a fare qc** inability to do sth **2** (*Dir*) incapacity; **incapacità d'intendere e di volere** diminished responsibility

incaponirsi [inkapo'nirsi] /55/ VIP (*ostinarsi*) to be set on; **incaponirsi a fare qc** to insist on doing sth

incappare [inkap'pare] /72/ VI (*aus essere*) **incappare in** (*problema, guaio*) to run into, get into; (*persona*) to run into

incappucciare [inkapput'tʃare] /14/ VT to put a hood on; **la neve incappuccia le cime dei monti** snow covers the mountain tops; **incappucciarsi** VR (*persona*) to put on a hood

incapricciarsi [inkaprit'tʃarsi] /14/ VIP: **incapricciarsi di** to take a fancy to

incapsulare [inkapsu'lare] /72/ VT (*Med: dente*) to crown

incarcerare [inkartʃe'rare] /72/ VT to imprison, jail

incaricare [inkari'kare] /20/ VT: **incaricare qn di fare qc** to give sb the responsibility of doing sth, ask sb to do sth; **mi hanno incaricato di rispondere al telefono** they asked me to answer the phone; **incaricarsi** VIP: **incaricarsi di fare qc** to take it upon o.s. to do sth; **me ne incarico io** I'll see to it

incaricato, -a [inkari'kato] AGG: **incaricato (di)** in charge (of), responsible (for); **docente incaricato** (*Univ*) lecturer without tenure ♦ SM, SF representative; **l'incaricato** the person in charge; **incaricato d'affari** (*Pol*) chargé d'affaires

incarico, -chi [in'kariko] SM **1** (*gen, compito*) task, job; **dare un incarico a qn** to give sb a task *o* job to do; **ricevere un incarico** to be given a task *o* job to do; **avere l'incarico di fare qc** to have the job of doing sth; **per incarico di qn** on sb's behalf; **un incarico importante** an important job; **chi aveva l'incarico di comprare i biglietti?** who was supposed to get the tickets? **2** (*Scol, Univ*) temporary post

incarnare [inkar'nare] /72/ VT (*rappresentare*) to embody; **incarnarsi** VIP (*Rel*) to become incarnate; (*concretarsi*) to be embodied

incarnazione [inkarnat'tsjone] SF (*Rel*) incarnation; (*fig*) embodiment; **è l'incarnazione della virtù** he (*o* she) is the embodiment of virtue; **sembra l'incarnazione di suo nonno** he (*o* she) is the image of his (*o* her) grandfather

incartamento [inkarta'mento] SM dossier, file

incartapecorito, -a [inkartapeko'rito] AGG (*pelle*) wizened, shrivelled (*Brit*), shriveled (*USA*)

incartare [inkar'tare] /72/ VT to wrap (in paper); **devo ancora incartare i regali** I still have to wrap the presents; **me lo incarta, per favore?** could you wrap it for me please?

incasellare [inkasel'lare] /72/ VT (*posta*) to sort; (*fig: nozioni*) to pigeonhole

incassare [inkas'sare] /72/ VT **1** (*Comm: denaro*) to take, receive; (*: assegno, cambiale*) to cash; **puoi incassare l'assegno in qualunque banca** you can cash the cheque at any bank **2** (*Pugilato: colpi*) to take, stand up to; (*fig: offese*) to take **3** (*montare: pietra preziosa*) to set; (*: mobile*) to build in **4** (*imballare: merce*) to pack (in cases)

incasso [in'kasso] SM **1** (*somma incassata*) takings pl; (*per un incontro sportivo*) take; **incasso giornaliero/mensile** daily/ monthly takings; **fare un buon incasso** to take a lot of cash *o* money; **i ladri sono fuggiti con l'incasso della giornata** the thieves escaped with the day's takings; **il film ha battuto ogni record d'incasso** the film has been a great box office success **2** (*cavità*) **frigorifero da incasso** fitted refrigerator

incastonare [inkasto'nare] /72/ VT to set

incastonatura [inkastona'tura] SF setting

incastrare [inkas'trare] /72/ VT **1** (*gen, far combaciare*) to fit in, insert **2** (*intrappolare*) to catch; (*con false accuse*) to frame; **era ovvio che l'avevano incastrato** it was obvious that he had been framed; **incastrarsi** VIP **1** (*combaciare: pezzi meccanici*) to fit together; **questo pezzo s'incastra qui** this part fits here **2** (*rimanere bloccato*) to get stuck; **la chiave si è incastrata nella serratura** the key got stuck in the lock

incastro [in'kastro] SM (*punto di unione*) joint; (*scanalatura*) slot, groove; **gioco a incastro** interlocking puzzle; **sistema a incastro** interlocking system; **incastro a coda di rondine** dovetail joint

incatenare [inkate'nare] /72/ VT: **incatenare qc/qn a qc** to chain sth/sb to sth; **i prigionieri venivano incatenati al muro** the prisoners were chained to the wall; **incatenarsi** VR: **incatenarsi a qc** to chain o.s. to sth

incatramare [inkatra'mare] /72/ VT to tar

incattivire [inkatti'vire] /55/ VT to make wicked VI (*aus essere*), **incattivirsi** VIP to turn nasty

incauto, -a [in'kauto] AGG imprudent, rash

incavare [inka'vare] /72/ VT to hollow out

incavato, -a [inka'vato] AGG (*gen*) hollow; (*occhi*) sunken

incavo [in'kavo] SM hollow; (*solco*) groove

incavolarsi [inkavo'larsi] /72/ VIP (*fam*) to lose one's temper, fly off the handle; **incavolarsi per** *o* **a causa di qc** to get annoyed about sth, lose one's temper over sth; **incavolarsi con qn** to get annoyed *o* lose one's temper with sb; **non t'incavolare con me!** don't get angry with me!

incazzarsi [inkat'tsarsi] /72/ VIP (*fam!*) to get pissed off (*fam!*); **mi sono incazzato da morire!** I was really pissed off!

incedere [in't∫edere] /29/ VI (*aus avere*) to advance solemnly ♦ SM solemn gait

incendiare [int∫en'djare] /19/ VT (*gen*) to set fire to; (*fig: animi*) to fire; **dei vandali hanno incendiato la scuola** vandals set fire to the school; **incendiarsi** VIP to catch fire, burst into flames

incendiario, -ria, -ri, -rie [int∫en'djarjo] AGG incendiary ♦ SM, SF arsonist

incendio, -di [in't∫endjo] SM fire; **provocare l'incendio di** to set fire to; **i vigili del fuoco hanno domato l'incendio** the firemen have got the fire under control; **incendio doloso** arson

incenerire [int∫ene'rire] /55/ VT (*gen*) to incinerate; (*casa, albero*) to burn (down), burn to ashes; **incenerire qn con uno sguardo** to give sb a withering look; **incenerirsi** VIP to be burnt to ashes

inceneritore [int∫eneri'tore] SM incinerator

incenso [in't∫enso] SM incense; **odore d'incenso** smell of incense; **bastoncini d'incenso** joss sticks

incensurato, -a [int∫ensu'rato] AGG (*Dir*): **essere incensurato** to have a clean record

incentivare [int∫enti'vare] /72/ VT (*produzione, vendite*) to boost; (*dipendente*) to motivate

incentivo [int∫en'tivo] SM incentive

incentrarsi [int∫en'trarsi] /72/ VIP: **incentrarsi su** (*fig*) to centre (*Brit*) *o* center (*USA*) on

inceppare [int∫ep'pare] /72/ VT (*fig: operazione*) to obstruct, hamper; **incepparsi** VIP (*fucile ecc*) to jam

incerata [int∫e'rata] SF (*impermeabile*) oilskins pl; (*tela*) oilcloth, tarpaulin; (*da letto*) waterproof sheet

incertezza [int∫er'tettsa] SF **1** (*di notizie, fonti*) uncertainty, doubtful nature **2** (*esitazione*) uncertainty, hesitation; **un momento d'incertezza** a moment's uncertainty *o* hesitation; **ha avuto un momento d'incertezza nel rispondere** he hesitated for a moment before answering; **rispondere con incertezza** to answer hesitantly **3** (*insicurezza, instabilità*) uncertainty, doubt; **essere nell'incertezza** to be in a state of uncertainty; **tenere qn nell'incertezza** to keep sb in suspense; **vivere nell'incertezza** to live in a state of uncertainty; **un periodo di incertezza politica** a period of political uncertainty

incerto, -a [in't∫erto] AGG (*esito, risultato*) uncertain, doubtful; (*tempo*) uncertain; (*persona*) undecided, hesitating; **essere incerto su qc** to be uncertain *o* unsure about sth; **essere incerto sul da farsi** not to know what to do, be uncertain what to do; **camminare con passo incerto** to walk unsteadily; **la situazione è ancora incerta** the situation is still uncertain; **ero incerto se dirglielo o no** I was uncertain whether to tell him or not ♦ SM uncertainty; **lasciare il certo per l'incerto** to shun the unknown, leave certainty behind one; **gli incerti del mestiere** the risks of the job

incespicare [int∫espi'kare] /20/ VI (*aus avere*) **incespicare (in qc)** to trip (over sth); **incespicare nel parlare** to stumble over one's words

incessante [int∫es'sante] AGG (*gen*) unceasing, incessant; (*serie*) never-ending

incesto [in't∫esto] SM incest

incestuoso, -a [int∫estu'oso] AGG incestuous

incetta [in't∫etta] SF buying up, hoarding; **fare incetta di** (*prodotti, merce*) to stockpile, buy up; **cercare di fare incetta di voti** to try to get as many votes as possible

inchiesta [in'kjesta] SF (*gen, anche Dir*) inquiry, investigation; (*giornalistica*) report; **fare un'inchiesta su qc** to investigate sth, carry out an investigation *o* inquiry into sth; **to report on** sth; **è stata aperta un'inchiesta** an inquiry has been opened; **un'inchiesta sui giovani e la droga** a special report on young people and drugs; **inchiesta parlamentare** ≈ parliamentary inquiry (*Brit*), ≈ congressional investigation (*USA*)

inchinare [inki'nare] /72/ VT (*schiena*) to bend; (*testa, fronte*) to bow; **inchinarsi** VR to bend down; (*per riverenza*) to bow; (*donna*) to curts(e)y; **inchinarsi davanti a qn** to bow (*o* curts(e)y) to sb; **m'inchino davanti alla tua bravura** I take off my hat to you

inchino [in'kino] SM (*gen*) bow; (*di donna*) curts(e)y; **fare un inchino** to bow; to curts(e)y

inchiodare [inkjo'dare] /72/ VT to nail (down); **inchiodare qc a qc** to nail sth to sth; **ha inchiodato il coperchio alla cassa** he nailed the lid onto the crate; **il lavoro lo inchioda al tavolino** his work keeps him chained to his desk; **sta tutto il giorno inchiodato davanti alla TV** he spends all day glued to the TV; **con queste prove lo hanno inchiodato** they nailed him with this evidence; **inchiodare la macchina** to jam on the brakes; **inchiodarsi** VIP (*fermarsi di colpo*) to stop dead

inchiostro [in'kjostro] SM ink; **una macchia d'inchiostro** an ink blot; **inchiostro di china** Indian ink; **inchiostro simpatico** invisible ink

inciampare [intʃam'pare] /72/ VI (*aus* avere *o* essere) to trip, stumble; **inciampare in** (*gradino, pietra*) to trip over; (*fig: persona*) to run into; **sono inciampato nel tappeto** I tripped over the carpet; **far inciampare qn** to trip sb (up)

inciampo [in'tʃampo] SM obstacle; **proseguire senza inciampi** to proceed smoothly

incidentale [intʃiden'tale] AGG 1 (*casuale*) accidental 2 (*secondario*) incidental; **questione incidentale** (*Dir*) interlocutory matter; **proposizione incidentale** (*Gramm*) parenthetical clause

incidentalmente [intʃidental'mente] AVV (*per caso*) by chance; (*per inciso*) incidentally, by the way

incidente [intʃi'dente] SM 1 (*disgrazia*) accident; **incidente aereo** plane crash; **è il terzo incidente aereo in un mese** it's the third plane crash in a month; **incidente d'auto** car crash *o* accident; **sono rimasti feriti in un incidente d'auto** they were injured in a car accident; **incidente ferroviario** train crash; **incidente mortale** fatal accident; **incidente stradale** road accident 2 (*episodio*) incident; **e con questo l'incidente è chiuso** and that is the end of the matter; **incidente diplomatico** diplomatic incident 3 (*Dir*): **incidente pre-trial** investigation

incidenza [intʃi'dentsa] SF 1 (*fig: effetto*): **avere una forte incidenza su qc** to affect sth greatly, have a considerable effect on sth 2 (*Mat*): **angolo di incidenza** angle of incidence

incidere¹ [in'tʃidere] /34/ VT IRREG 1 (*tagliare: corteccia, legno*) to cut into, carve; (*scolpire: pietra*) to engrave; **incidere un'iscrizione su** to engrave an inscription on; **incidere ad acquaforte** to etch; **incidere una ferita** (*Med*) to lance a wound 2 (*canzone*) to record; **incidere un disco** to make a record

incidere² [in'tʃidere] /34/ VI IRREG (*aus* avere) (*influire*): **incidere su** to influence, affect, have a bearing upon; **le spese di riscaldamento incidono molto sull'economia domestica** heating costs are an important item of household expenditure

incinta [in'tʃinta] AGG F pregnant; **restare** *o* **rimanere incinta** to become *o* get pregnant; **è rimasta incinta** she became pregnant; **incinta di 5 mesi** 5 months pregnant

incipiente [intʃi'pjente] AGG incipient

incipriare [intʃi'prjare] /19/ VT to powder; **andare ad incipriarsi il naso** (*euf*) to go and powder one's nose; **incipriarsi** VR to powder one's face

incirca [in'tʃirka] AVV: **all'incirca** approximately, more or less, very nearly; **è grande all'incirca così** it's about this big; **saranno all'incirca le tre** it must be about three

incisi ecc [in'tʃizi] VB *vedi* incidere¹, incidere²

incisione [intʃi'zjone] SF 1 (*taglio*) cut; (*Med*) incision 2 (*Arte*) engraving; **incisione ad acquaforte** etching; **incisione su legno** woodcut; **incisione su rame** copperplate engraving 3 (*registrazione*) recording; **sala d'incisione** recording studio; **incisione su nastro** tape recording

incisivo, -a [intʃi'zivo] AGG 1 (*Anat*): (**dente**) **incisivo** incisor 2 (*fig: parole, stile*) incisive

inciso, -a [in'tʃizo] PP *di* incidere¹, incidere² ♦ SM (*Gramm*) parenthesis; **per inciso** incidentally, by the way

incisore [intʃi'zore] SM (*Arte*) engraver

incitamento [intʃita'mento] SM incitement; **essere d'incitamento per** *o* **a** to be an incitement to

incitare [intʃi'tare] /72/ VT: **incitare qn a (fare) qc** to incite sb to (do) sth

incivile [intʃi'vile] AGG (*popolazione, costumi*) uncivilized; (*fig: persona, comportamento*) rude, impolite; **una persona incivile** a rude person; **che modi incivili!** what bad manners! ♦ SM, SF boor

incivilire [intʃivi'lire] /55/ VT to civilize; **incivilirsi** VIP to become civilized

inciviltà [intʃivil'ta] SF 1 (*di popolazione*) barbarism 2 (*fig: di trattamento*) barbarity; (*: maleducazione*) incivility, rudeness

incl. ABBR (= *incluso*) encl.

inclemente [inkle'mente] AGG (*fig: clima*) harsh; (*: tempo*) inclement; (*: giudice, critica*) severe, harsh

inclemenza [inkle'mentsa] SF (*vedi agg*) harshness; inclemency; severity

inclinabile [inkli'nabile] AGG (*schienale*) reclinable

inclinare [inkli'nare] /72/ VT (*recipiente*) to tilt, tip; (*schienale*) to tilt (back), recline; **inclinare il busto in avanti** to bend forward, lean forward; **inclina un po' il tavolo** tilt the table a bit ♦ VI (*aus* avere) **inclinare a qc/a fare** to incline towards sth/doing, tend towards sth/to do; **inclinarsi** VIP (*barca*) to list, heel; (*aereo*) to bank; (*ago magnetico*) to dip

inclinato, -a [inkli'nato] AGG (*recipiente*) tilted; (*strada*) sloping; **piano inclinato** (*Mat*) inclined plane

inclinazione [inklinat'tsjone] SF 1 (*pendenza: di strada*) gradient; (*: di superficie*) slope; (*: di tetto*) slope, pitch; (*: di retta, piano*) inclination 2 (*fig: tendenza*) inclination, bent, tendency; **seguire le proprie inclinazioni** to follow one's inclinations

incline [in'kline] AGG: **essere incline a pensare che...** to be inclined to think that ...; **essere incline alla collera** to be prone to anger, be irascible

includere [in'kludere] /3/ VT IRREG: **includere (in)** (*accludere*) to enclose (in); (*comprendere*) to include (in)

inclusione [inklu'zjone] SF inclusion

inclusivo, -a [inklu'zivo] AGG: **inclusivo di** inclusive of

incluso, -a [in'kluzo] PP *di* includere ♦ AGG 1 (*accluso*) attached, enclosed 2 (*compreso*) inclusive, included; **fino a giovedì incluso** up to and including Thursday; **leggere da pagina cinque a pagina sette inclusa** read from the beginning of page five to the end of page seven; **incluso mio cugino** including my cousin, my cousin included; **è inclusa la colazione?** is breakfast included?; **spese incluse** inclusive of expenses

incoerente [inkoe'rente] AGG 1 (*terreno, materiali*) loose 2 (*fig: confuso*) incoherent; (*: illogico*) inconsistent

incoerenza [inkoe'rentsa] SF (*vedi agg*) looseness; incoherence; inconsistency

incognito, -a [in'kɔɲɲito] AGG unknown ♦ SM: **mantenere l'incognito** to remain incognito; **in incognito** incognito; **viaggiare in incognito** to travel incognito

incollare [inkol'lare] /72/ VT (*gen*) to stick, gum; (*legno, porcellana*) to glue, stick; **incollare un'etichetta ad una busta** to put *o* stick a label on an envelope; **incollare insieme dei cartoncini** to stick *o* glue pieces of card together; **incollare gli occhi addosso a qn** to fix one's eyes on sb; **incollarsi** VIP (*gen*): **incollarsi (a)** to stick (to); **incollarsi a qn** (*fig*) to stick close to sb; **le pagine si sono incollate** the pages have stuck together; **la camicia bagnata gli si incollò addosso** his wet shirt stuck to him

incollatura [inkolla'tura] SF (*Ippica*): **vincere/perdere di un'incollatura** to win/lose by a head

incolonnare [inkolon'nare] /72/ VT (*cifre*) to put in columns; (*Mil: truppe*) to draw up in columns; (*Tip*) to set up in columns; (*valori*) to tabulate; **incolonnarsi** VIP (*truppe*) to draw up in columns

incolore [inko'lore] AGG (*senza colore*) colourless (*Brit*), colorless (*USA*); (*monotono*) dull

incolpare [inkol'pare] /72/ VT (*gen*): **incolpare (di)** to blame (for); **hanno incolpato me** they blamed me; **incolpare qn di aver fatto qc** to accuse sb of having done sth; **mi ha incolpato di avergli rotto il motorino** he accused me of damaging his moped; **incolpare l'inesperienza** to blame one's inexperience

incolto, -a [in'kolto] AGG 1 (*terreno*) uncultivated 2 (*trascurato: barba*) neglected; (*ignorante: persona*) uneducated

incolume [in'kɔlume] AGG unhurt, safe and sound; **è uscito incolume dall'incidente** he escaped from the accident unhurt

incolumità [inkolumi'ta] SF safety; **attentato all'incolumità di qn** attempt on sb's life

incombente [inkom'bente] AGG (*pericolo*) imminent, impending

❏ **incombente** non si traduce mai con la parola inglese *incumbent*

incombenza [inkom'bentsa] SF duty, task

incombere [in'kombere] /29/ VI *vb dif*: **incombere su** (*sovrastare minacciando*) to hang over, threaten

incominciare [inkomin't∫are] /14/ VT to begin, start; incominciare a fare qc to begin o start doing sth; **ha incominciato a ridere** she started to laugh; **ha incominciato a piangere** she started crying ♦ VI (aus essere) to begin, start; **la partita incomincia alle sette** the match starts at seven; **la prima parola incomincia per F** the first word starts with F

incomodare [inkomo'dare] /72/ VT to trouble, inconvenience; **incomodarsi** VR to put o.s. out

incomodo [in'kɔmodo] AGG: **fare il terzo incomodo** to play gooseberry (Brit) to be a fifth wheel (USA) ♦ SM trouble, inconvenience, bother; **prendersi l'incomodo di fare qc** to take the trouble to do sth; **essere d'incomodo a qn** to be in sb's way; **togliere l'incomodo** (andarsene) to take o.s. off

incomparabile [inkompa'rabile] AGG incomparable

incompatibile [inkompa'tibile] AGG (inconciliabile) incompatible

incompatibilità [inkompatibili'ta] SF incompatibility; **incompatibilità di carattere** (mutual) incompatibility

incompetente [inkompe'tente] AGG (gen, anche Dir) incompetent; **essere incompetente in qc** to be incompetent o useless (fam) at sth ♦ SM, SF incompetent person; **è un incompetente** he is incompetent

incompetenza [inkompe'tentsa] SF incompetence

incompiuto, -a [inkom'pjuto] AGG unfinished, incomplete; **rimanere incompiuto** to be left unfinished; **una sinfonia incompiuta** an unfinished symphony

incompleto, -a [inkom'pleto] AGG incomplete

incomprensibile [inkompren'sibile] AGG (gen) incomprehensible

incomprensione [inkompren'sjone] SF 1 (mancanza di comprensione) lack of understanding, incomprehension 2 (malinteso) misunderstanding

incompreso, -a [inkom'preso] AGG misunderstood, not understood; **sono un genio incompreso** (scherz) I'm a misunderstood genius ♦ SM, SF: **è un incompreso** people don't understand him

inconcepibile [inkont∫e'pibile] AGG (impensabile) inconceivable, unthinkable; (assurdo) incredible; **è inconcepibile!** it's incredible!

inconciliabile [inkont∫i'ljabile] AGG irreconcilable

inconcludente [inkonklu'dente] AGG (persona) ineffectual; (sforzi) unavailing; (discorso: sconclusionato) disconnected

incondizionato, -a [inkondittsjo'nato] AGG (approvazione ecc) unconditional; (fiducia) unquestioning, complete; **resa incondizionata** (anche fig) unconditional surrender

inconfessabile [inkonfes'sabile] AGG (pensiero, peccato) unmentionable

inconfondibile [inkonfon'dibile] AGG unmistakable; **il suo stile è inconfondibile** his style is unmistakable

inconfutabile [inkonfu'tabile] AGG irrefutable

incongruente [inkongru'ente] AGG inconsistent

incongruenza [inkongru'entsa] SF inconsistency

incongruo, -a [in'kɔngruo] AGG insufficient, inadequate

inconsapevole [inkonsa'pevole] AGG: **inconsapevole di** unaware of, ignorant of

inconsapevolezza [inkonsapevo'lettsa] SF ignorance, lack of awareness

inconscio, -scia, -sci, -sce [in'kɔn∫o] AGG (desiderio, impulso) unconscious ♦ SM: **l'inconscio** (Psic) the unconscious

inconsistente [inkonsis'tente] AGG (dubbio) unfounded; (ragionamento, prove) tenuous, flimsy
❑ **inconsistente** non si traduce mai con la parola inglese *inconsistent*

inconsistenza [inkonsis'tentsa] SF (di dubbio) lack of foundation; (di ragionamento, prove) flimsiness
❑ **inconsistenza** non si traduce mai con la parola inglese *inconsistency*

inconsolabile [inkonso'labile] AGG inconsolable

inconsueto, -a [inkonsu'eto] AGG unusual

inconsulto, -a [inkon'sulto] AGG (gesto, azione) rash, impetuous

incontenibile [inkonte'nibile] AGG (rabbia) uncontrollable; (entusiasmo) irrepressible

incontentabile [inkonten'tabile] AGG (desiderio, avidità)

insatiable; (persona: capriccioso) hard to please, very demanding

incontestabile [inkontes'tabile] AGG incontrovertible, indisputable

incontestato, -a [inkontes'tato] AGG undisputed

incontinenza [inkonti'nentsa] SF (Med) incontinence

incontrare [inkon'trare] /72/ VT 1 (gen) to meet; (in riunione) to have a meeting with; (difficoltà, pericolo) to meet with, run into, come up against; **incontrare qn per caso** to run o bump into sb; **l'ho incontrato ad una festa** I met him at a party; **ho incontrato Maurizio per strada** I bumped into Maurizio in the street; **incontrare il favore del pubblico** (attore, prodotto ecc) to find favour with o be popular with the public 2 (Sport: squadra) to meet, play (against); (: pugile) to meet, fight; **l'Inter incontrerà la Juve domenica prossima** Inter Milan are playing Juventus next Sunday; **incontrarsi** VR (uso reciproco) 1 (trovarsi: su appuntamento) to meet (each other); (: in riunione) to have a meeting; **incontriamoci davanti al cinema** let's meet in front of the cinema 2 (Sport) to meet

incontrario [inkon'trarjo] **all'incontrario** AVV (sottosopra) upside down; (alla rovescia) back to front; (all'indietro) backwards; (nel senso contrario) the other way round

incontrastabile [inkontras'tabile] AGG incontrovertible, indisputable

incontrastato, -a [inkontras'tato] AGG (successo, vittoria, verità) undisputed

incontro¹ [in'kontro] SM 1 (gen) meeting; (fortuito) encounter; **un incontro al vertice** a summit (meeting); **un incontro casuale** a chance meeting; **a tarda notte si possono fare brutti incontri** you can have some unpleasant encounters late at night 2 (Sport) match; **incontro di calcio** football match (Brit), soccer game (USA); **incontro di pugilato** boxing match

incontro² [in'kontro] **incontro a** PREP (verso) towards; **mi è venuto sorridente** he came towards me smiling; **andare incontro a qn** to go to meet sb; (fig: aiutare) to meet sb halfway; **andare incontro a** (brutte sorprese) to come up against, meet; (spese) to incur; **andare incontro alla morte** to go to one's death; **stiamo ormai andando incontro alla primavera** we're moving towards spring now, it'll soon be spring; **venire incontro a** (richieste, esigenze) to comply with

incontrollabile [inkontrol'labile] AGG uncontrollable

inconveniente [inkonve'njente] SM 1 (difficoltà) setback, mishap; **ho avuto degli inconvenienti con la macchina** I had some problems with the car 2 (svantaggio) drawback, disadvantage, snag; **ha un unico inconveniente: è troppo piccolo** it's only got one drawback: it's too small
❑ **inconveniente** non si traduce mai con la parola inglese *inconvenient*

incoraggiamento [inkoradd3a'mento] SM encouragement; **premio d'incoraggiamento** consolation prize

incoraggiare [inkorad'd3are] /62/ VT (esortare) to encourage; **incoraggiare qn a fare qc** to encourage sb to do sth; **i suoi l'hanno incoraggiato a studiare musica** his parents encouraged him to study music; **incoraggiare qn allo studio** to encourage sb to study

incornare [inkor'nare] /72/ VT to gore; (Calcio) to head

incorniciare [inkorni't∫are] /14/ VT to frame; **ho incorniciato la foto** I've framed the photo; **i lunghi capelli le incorniciavano il volto** her long hair framed her face

incoronare [inkoro'nare] /72/ VT (anche fig) to crown

incoronazione [inkoronat'tsjone] SF coronation

incorporare [inkorpo'rare] /72/ VT: **incorporare (in)** (gen, anche Comm) to incorporate (into); (sostanza) to mix (in); **"incorporare gli albumi nell'impasto"** (Culin) "fold the egg whites into the mixture"

incorreggibile [inkoredd3ibile] AGG (gen) incorrigible; (giocatore) inveterate

incorrere [in'korrere] /28/ VI IRREG (aus essere) **incorrere in** (pericolo, guaio) to run into, come up against, meet with

incorruttibile [inkorrut'tibile] AGG (funzionario) incorruptible; (fig: fede) unshakeable; (: bellezza) unfading

incorso, -a [in'korso] PP di **incorrere**

incosciente [inko∫'∫ente] AGG 1 (irresponsabile) reckless, thoughtless; **un automobilista incosciente** a reckless driver **2** (*privo di sensi*) unconscious; **è rimasto incosciente per alcuni minuti** he was unconscious for several minutes ♦ SM, SF reckless person, thoughtless person

incoscienza [inkoʃˈʃentsa] SF (*vedi* **agg**) recklessness, thoughtlessness; unconsciousness

incostante [inkosˈtante] AGG (*studente, impiegato*) inconsistent; (*carattere*) fickle, inconstant; (*rendimento*) sporadic

incostanza [inkosˈtantsa] SF inconstancy, fickleness

incostituzionale [inkostituttsjoˈnale] AGG unconstitutional

incredibile [inkreˈdibile] AGG incredible, unbelievable; **è incredibile!** that's incredible!

incredulità [inkreduliˈta] SF incredulity

incredulo, -a [inˈkredulo] AGG incredulous, disbelieving

incrementare [inkremenˈtare] /72/ VT (*aumentare: vendite, produzione*) to increase; (*dar sviluppo a: commercio*) to promote

incremento [inkreˈmento] SM: **incremento (di)** (*aumento numerico*) increase (in), growth (in); (*sviluppo*) development; **un incremento del numero di macchine** an increase in the number of cars; **incremento demografico** population rise *o* growth

increscioso, -a [inkreʃˈʃoso] AGG (*spiacevole*) unpleasant; **incidente increscioso** regrettable incident

increspare [inkresˈpare] /72/ VT (*capelli*) to curl; (*stoffa*) to gather; (*superficie: del mare*) to ripple; **incresparsi** VIP (*superficie: di mare, lago*) to ripple

incriminare [inkrimiˈnare] /72/ VT (*Dir*): **incriminare qn per qc** to charge sb with sth

incriminazione [inkriminatˈtsjone] SF (*atto d'accusa*) indictment, charge; **non c'erano prove sufficienti per la sua incriminazione** there wasn't sufficient evidence to charge him

incrinare [inkriˈnare] /72/ VT (*vetro, specchio, vaso*) to crack; (*fig: rapporti, amicizia*) to spoil, create a rift in; **non l'ho rotto, l'ho solo incrinato** I didn't break it, I just cracked it; **incrinarsi** VIP (*vetro, ghiaccio, roccia*) to crack; (*rapporti, amicizia*) to deteriorate

incrinatura [inkrinaˈtura] SF (*crepa*) crack; (*fig: di rapporti*) rift

incrociare [inkroˈtʃare] /14/ VT **1** (*gen*) to cross; (*strada, linea*) to cut across; **incrociare le gambe** to cross one's legs; **incrociare le braccia** to fold one's arms; (*fig*) to down tools, refuse to work; **ha incrociato le braccia** he crossed his arms **2** (*autoveicolo, persona*) to meet; **l'ho incrociato per strada** I met him in the street **3** (*animali, piante*) to cross ♦ VI (*aus avere*) (*Naut, Aer*) to cruise; **incrociarsi** VR (*uso reciproco: strade, rette*) to cross, intersect; (: *persone, veicoli*) to pass each other; (*fig: sguardi*) to meet; (: *battute*) to fly thick and fast; **ci siamo incrociati nel corridoio** we met in the corridor

incrociatore [inkrotʃaˈtore] SM (*Naut*) cruiser

incrocio, -ci [inˈkrotʃo] SM **1** (*di strade*) crossroads, junction; (*Ferr*) crossing; **all'incrocio gira a destra** turn right at the junction **2** **l'incrocio dei pali** (*Calcio*) the top corner of the goalposts **3** (*Zool, Bot*) **un incrocio tra un collie e un labrador** a cross between a collie and a labrador

incrollabile [inkrolˈlabile] AGG (*fede*) unshakeable, firm

incrostare [inkrosˈtare] /72/ VT to encrust; **incrostarsi** VIP: **incrostarsi di** to become encrusted with

incrostazione [inkrostatˈtsjone] SF incrustation, encrustation; (*di calcare*) scale; (*nelle tubature*) scale, fur (*Brit*)

incruento, -a [inkruˈento] AGG (*battaglia*) without bloodshed, bloodless

incubatrice [inkubaˈtritʃe] SF incubator

incubazione [inkubatˈtsjone] SF incubation

incubo [ˈinkubo] SM (*anche fig*) nightmare; **stanotte ho avuto un incubo** I had a nightmare last night; **ho l'incubo degli esami** exams are a nightmare for me

incudine [inˈkudine] SF anvil; **trovarsi** *o* **essere tra l'incudine e il martello** (*fig*) to be between the devil and the deep blue sea, to be between a rock and a hard place

inculcare [inkulˈkare] /20/ VT: **inculcare qc in qn** to inculcate sth into sb, instil sth into sb

incuneare [inkuneˈare] /72/ VT to wedge; **incunearsi** VIP to slot in

incupire [inkuˈpire] /55/ VT (*rendere scuro*) to darken; (*fig:*

intristire) to fill with gloom VI (*aus* **essere**), **incupirsi** VIP (*vedi vt*) to darken; to become gloomy

incurabile [inkuˈrabile] AGG, SM, SF incurable; **un male incurabile** an incurable disease

incurante [inkuˈrante] AGG: **incurante (di)** heedless (of), careless (of)

incuria [inˈkurja] SF negligence

incuriosire [inkurjoˈsire] /55/ VT to arouse the curiosity of, make curious; **incuriosirsi** VIP to become curious

incursione [inkurˈsjone] SF (*Mil, Aer*) incursion, foray, raid; (*di ladri ecc*) raid; **un'incursione aerea** an air raid

incurvare [inkurˈvare] /72/ VT (*piegare*) to curve, bend; **non incurvare la schiena!** sit *o* stand up straight!; **il lavoro a tavolino gli ha incurvato la schiena** *o* **le spalle** deskwork has made him round-shouldered *o* has given him a stoop; **incurvarsi** VIP to bend; (*legno*) to warp; (*persona*) to develop a stoop, become bent

incusso, -a [inˈkusso] PP *di* **incutere**

incustodito, -a [inkustoˈdito] AGG (*bagaglio*) unattended, unguarded; **passaggio a livello incustodito** unmanned level crossing; **il parcheggio è incustodito** the car park is unattended; **non lasciare il bagaglio incustodito** don't leave your luggage unattended

incutere [inˈkutere] /40/ VT IRREG: **incutere rispetto a qn** to command sb's respect; **incutere paura a qn** to strike fear into sb; **incutere soggezione a qn** to cow sb

indaco, -chi [ˈindako] AGG INV, SM indigo

indaffarato, -a [indaffaˈrato] AGG: **indaffarato (a fare qc)** busy (doing sth); **era indaffarato a riparare la bici** he was busy mending his bike

indagare [indaˈgare] /80/ VI (*aus avere*) **indagare su** to investigate; **la polizia sta indagando sul delitto** the police are investigating the crime; **indagare sul conto di qn** to investigate sb, make enquiries about sb; **è meglio non indagare** it's better not to enquire too closely ♦ VT to investigate, look into

indagatore, -trice [indagaˈtore] AGG (*sguardo, domanda*) searching; (*mente*) inquiring; **rivolgere a qn uno sguardo indagatore** to give sb a searching look

indagine [inˈdadʒine] SF **1** (*inchiesta*) investigation, inquiry, enquiry; **fare** *o* **svolgere un'indagine (su)** to carry out an investigation *o* inquiry (into); **le indagini della polizia** police investigations **2** (*ricerca*) research, study; **fare** *o* **svolgere un'indagine su** to carry out *o* do research into, make a study of; **indagine su campione** sample survey; **indagine demoscopica** public opinion poll; **indagine di mercato** market survey

indebitamente [indebitaˈmente] AVV (*immeritatamente*) undeservedly; (*erroneamente*) wrongfully

indebitare [indebiˈtare] /72/ VT: **indebitare qn** to get sb into debt; **indebitarsi** VR: **si è indebitato fino al collo** he is up to his eyes in debt; **indebitarsi con qn/con la banca** to owe money to sb/to the bank

indebito, -a [inˈdebito] AGG (*onori, accuse*) undeserved; **appropriazione indebita** embezzlement

indebolimento [indeboliˈmento] SM **1** weakening **2** (*debolezza*) weakness

indebolire [indeboˈlire] /55/ VT to weaken VI (*aus* **essere**), **indebolirsi** VIP (*persona*) to grow weak; (*vista*) to deteriorate

indecente [indeˈtʃente] AGG indecent; **in quel ristorante il servizio è indecente** (*inaccettabile*) the service is disgraceful at that restaurant; **un'immagine indecente** an indecent image

indecenza [indeˈtʃentsa] SF indecency; **è un'indecenza!** (*vergogna*) it's scandalous!, it's a disgrace!

indecifrabile [indetʃiˈfrabile] AGG (*scrittura*) illegible, indecipherable; (*messaggio, testo*) incomprehensible

indecisione [indetʃiˈzjone] SF indecision, indecisiveness

indeciso, -a [indeˈtʃizo] AGG (*persona: titubante*) indecisive; (: *che non ha ancora deciso, questione, risultato*) undecided; (*tempo*) unsettled; (*colore, forma*) indistinct; **sono indeciso tra questi due** I can't decide between these two; **era indeciso su cosa regalarle** he couldn't decide what to give her

indecoroso, -a [indekoˈroso] AGG (*comportamento*) indecorous, unseemly

indefesso, -a [inde'fesso] AGG indefatigable, untiring
indefinibile [indefi'nibile] AGG indefinable
indefinito, -a [indefi'nito] AGG (*indeterminato, anche Gramm*) indefinite; (*impreciso*) undefined; (*irrisolto: questione, controversia*) unresolved
indeformabile [indefor'mabile] AGG crushproof
indegno, -a [in'deɲɲo] AGG (*atto*) shameful; (*persona*) unworthy; **è indegno di tanta ammirazione** he doesn't deserve so much admiration
indelebile [inde'lebile] AGG indelible, permanent
indelicatezza [indelika'tettsa] SF tactlessness; **è stata un'indelicatezza da parte sua** it was tactless of him
indelicato, -a [indeli'kato] AGG (*domanda*) indiscreet, tactless
indemoniato, -a [indemo'njato] AGG possessed (by the devil); **quel ragazzino è indemoniato** (*fig*) that boy is a little demon ♦ SM, SF person possessed by the devil; **gridare come un indemoniato** to shout like one possessed
indenne [in'denne] AGG (*illeso*) unscathed, unharmed, unhurt
indennità [indenni'ta] SF INV (*rimborso: di spese*) reimbursement; (: *di perdita*) indemnity, compensation; **indennità di contingenza** cost-of-living allowance; **indennità di fine rapporto** severance payment; **indennità parlamentare** member of parliament's salary; **indennità di trasferta** travel allowance, travel expenses *pl*
indennizzare [indenniđ'dzare] /72/ VT to indemnify, compensate
indennizzo [inden'niddzo] SM (*somma*) indemnity, compensation
inderogabile [indero'gabile] AGG binding
indescrivibile [indeskri'vibile] AGG indescribable
indesiderabile [indeside'rabile] AGG undesirable; **persona indesiderabile** persona non grata
indesiderato, -a [indeside'rato] AGG unwanted
indeterminatezza [indetermina'tettsa] SF vagueness
indeterminativo, -a [indetermina'tivo] AGG (*Gramm*) indefinite; **articolo indeterminativo** indefinite article
indeterminato, -a [indetermi'nato] AGG (*tempo*) unspecified, indefinite; (*quantità, spazio*) indeterminate; **rimandare qc a tempo indeterminato** to postpone sth indefinitely
indetto, -a [in'detto] PP *di* indire
India ['indja] SF India; **le Indie occidentali** the West Indies; **mi è piaciuta molto l'India** I really liked India; **andremo in India quest'estate** we're going to India this summer
indiano, -a [in'djano] AGG Indian; **un ristorante indiano** an Indian restaurant; **l'oceano Indiano** the Indian Ocean ♦ SM, SF (*dell'India*) Indian; (*dell'America*) (American) Indian, Native American; **gli indiani** the Indians; **fare l'indiano** (*fig*) to feign ignorance
indiavolato, -a [indjavo'lato] AGG (*persona: arrabbiato*) furious; (: *vivace, violento*) wild; (: *bambino*) high-spirited; (: *chiasso*) terrible, awful; (: *danza, ritmo*) frenzied
indicare [indi'kare] /20/ VT 1 (*mostrare*) to show, indicate; (*col dito*) to point to, point out; **indicare qc a qn** to show sb sth; **indicare la strada a qn** to show sb the way; **gli indicherò la strada** I'll show him the way; **indicare qn col dito** to point to o at sb; **m'indicò l'uscita** he showed me where the exit was; **la lancetta grande indica i minuti** the big hand shows the minutes; **cosa indica questo segnale?** what does this signal mean?; **le varie tappe erano indicate sulla carta** the various stops were indicated o shown o marked on the map; **i risultati indicano che...** the results indicate o show that ... 2 (*consigliare*) to suggest, recommend; **mi indicò un medico** he recommended a doctor to me
indicativo, -a [indika'tivo] AGG (*gen, anche Gramm*) indicative; (*prezzo*) approximate; **a titolo puramente indicativo** just as an indication ♦ SM (*Gramm*) indicative (mood)
indicato, -a [indi'kato] AGG (*consigliato*) advisable; (*adatto*): **indicato per** suitable for, appropriate for; **questa cura non è indicata in caso di gravidanza** this treatment is not advisable during pregnancy
indicatore, -trice [indika'tore] AGG indicating; **cartello indicatore** sign ♦ SM (*Tecn*) gauge, indicator; (*Chim*) indicator; **indicatore della benzina** fuel gauge, petrol (*Brit*) o gas (*USA*) gauge; **indicatore ecologico** indicator species; **indicatore di radiazioni** radiation detector; **indicatore di**

velocità (*Aut*) speedometer; (*Aer*) airspeed indicator; **indicatori di direzione** (*Aut*) indicator lights
indicazione [indikat'tsjone] SF (*gen*) indication; (*istruzione*) instruction, direction; (*informazione*) piece of information; **indicazioni** SFPL (*Med*) directions; **non è stato in grado di fornirmi indicazioni utili** he was unable to give me any useful information; **mi ha dato le indicazioni sbagliate per arrivare lì** he didn't tell me the right way to get there
indice ['inditʃe] SM 1 (*Anat*) index finger, forefinger 2 (*indicatore*) needle, pointer; (*fig: indizio*) sign; **tale comportamento è indice d'ignoranza/di pigrizia** such behaviour is a sign of ignorance/laziness 3 (*di libro*) (table of) contents *pl*; **indice analitico** index 4 (*Rel*): **l'Indice** (dei libri proibiti) the Index; **mettere all'indice** (*fig*) to blacklist 5 (*Mat, Statistica: rapporto*) index; **indice azionario** (*Borsa*) share index; **indice di gradimento** (*Radio, TV*) popularity rating; **indice dei prezzi al consumo** ≈ retail price index (*Brit*), ≈ consumer price index (*USA*); **indice di produzione** production index; **indice di rifrazione costante** (*Fis*) refractive constant ♦ AGG: **dito indice** index finger, forefinger
indicherò ecc [indike'rɔ] VB *vedi* indicare
indicibile [indi'tʃibile] AGG inexpressible, unspeakable
indicizzare [indititʃid'dzare] /72/ VT (*salari*) to index-link (*Brit*), index (*USA*)
indicizzato, -a [indititʃid'dzato] AGG (*polizza, salario ecc*) index-linked (*Brit*), indexed (*USA*)
indicizzazione [indititʃiddzat'tsjone] SF indexing
indietreggiare [indjetred'dʒare] /62/ VI (*aus avere o essere*) (*anche fig*) to draw back, retreat; (*Mil*) to retreat
indietro [in'djetro] AVV 1 (*stato, tempo*) behind; **essere indietro negli studi** to be behind in one's studies; **rimanere indietro** (*persona: di proposito*) to stay back o behind; (: *proprio malgrado*) to drop o lag behind, be left behind; **mentre dettava sono rimasto indietro** while he was dictating I got behind, I couldn't keep up with his dictation; **mettere indietro l'orologio** to put one's watch back; **bisogna mettere l'orologio indietro di un'ora** the clock has to be put back an hour; **essere indietro** (*orologio*) to be slow; (*persona: col lavoro*) to be behind; **il mio orologio è indietro** my watch is slow; **essere indietro con i pagamenti** to be behind o in arrears with one's payments 2 (*moto*) back, backwards; **tornare indietro** to go back; **torniamo indietro?** shall we turn back?; **mandare o rimandare qc indietro** to send sth back; **andare avanti e indietro** to walk up and down; **non vado né avanti né indietro** (*fig*) I'm not getting anywhere, I'm getting nowhere; **voltarsi indietro** to look back, look round; **farsi indietro** to move back; **fare un passo indietro** to take a step back o backwards; **facciamo un passo indietro negli anni venti** let's go back o cast our minds back to the twenties; **ho fatto un passo indietro** I took a step back; (*state*) **indietro!** get back! 3 **dare qc indietro a qn** (*restituire*) to give sth back to sb; **ha voluto indietro i soldi** she wanted her money back 4 **all'indietro** backwards; **camminare all'indietro** to walk backwards; **cadere all'indietro** to fall over backwards; **è caduta all'indietro** she fell backwards
indifeso, -a [indi'feso] AGG (*città, confine*) undefended; (*persona*) helpless, defenceless (*Brit*), defenseless (*USA*); **un povero bambino indifeso** a poor defenceless child
indifferente [indiffe'rente] AGG 1 indifferent (a): indifferent (to); **lasciare indifferente** to leave cold; **la notizia mi ha lasciato del tutto indifferente** the news left me completely cold; **mi è indifferente** I don't mind, it's all the same to me; **quell'uomo mi è indifferente** that man means nothing to me, I feel quite indifferent towards that man; **a piedi o in auto è indifferente** on foot or by car, it's all the same to me 2 **non indifferente** (*notevole: somma, spesa*) sizeable, not inconsiderable ♦ SM: **fare l'indifferente** to pretend to be indifferent, to o act casual; (*fingere di non vedere o sentire*) to pretend not to notice; **cerca di fare l'indifferente, sta venendo da questa parte** try to act casual, she's coming this way; **non fare l'indifferente, sto parlando di te** don't pretend you don't understand, I'm talking about you
indifferenza [indiffe'rentsa] SF indifference
indigeno, -a [in'didʒeno] AGG indigenous, native ♦ SM, SF native

indigente [indiˈdʒɛnte] AGG destitute, poverty-stricken ♦ SM, SF pauper; **gli indigenti** the poor o needy

indigenza [indiˈdʒɛntsa] SF extreme poverty, destitution; **vivere nell'indigenza** to live in extreme poverty

indigestione [indidʒesˈtjone] SF indigestion; **fare indigestione di qc** to eat too much of sth; (fig: di romanzi, film) to have a surfeit of sth, be sick of; **ho fatto un'indigestione di dolci** I've eaten too many cakes

indigesto, -a [indiˈdʒɛsto] AGG indigestible; (fig: persona, libro) unbearable; **il latte mi è indigesto** I find milk indigestible

indignare [indiɲˈɲare] /15/ VT: **indignare qn** to make sb indignant o angry, fill sb with indignation; **il suo comportamento mi ha indignato** his behaviour made me angry; **indignarsi** VIP: **indignarsi per** to be (o get) indignant about o at

indignazione [indiɲɲatˈtsjone] SF indignation; **con sua grande indignazione** much to his indignation

indimenticabile [indimentiˈkabile] AGG unforgettable; **una vacanza indimenticabile** an unforgettable holiday

indio, -dia, -di, -die [ˈindjo] AGG, SM, SF (South American) Indian

indipendente [indipenˈdɛnte] AGG (gen, anche Pol, Gramm): **indipendente (da)** independent (of); **è indipendente dalla mia volontà** it is beyond my control; **"affittasi camera con ingresso indipendente"** "room to let with independent access"; **ha un carattere molto indipendente** she's got a very independent nature; **essere economicamente indipendente** to be financially independent; **non sono ancora economicamente indipendente** I'm not yet financially independent ♦ SM, SF (Pol) independent

indipendentemente [indipendenteˈmente] AVV 1 (in modo libero) independently 2 (a prescindere da): **verrò indipendentemente dal fatto che lui venga o meno** I'll come anyway, whether he comes or not; **indipendentemente dal fatto che gli piaccia o meno, verrà!** whether he likes it or not, he's coming!, he's coming, whether he likes it or not!

indipendenza [indipenˈdɛntsa] SF independence

indire [inˈdire] /38/ VT IRREG (concorso) to announce; (elezioni) to call

indiretto, -a [indiˈrɛtto] AGG (gen) indirect; **per vie indirette** indirectly; **discorso indiretto** indirect speech

indirizzare [indiritˈtsare] /72/ VT (lettera, osservazione, richiesta) to address; **la lettera era indirizzata a me** the letter was addressed to me; **indirizzare la parola a qn** to address sb; **mi hanno indirizzato qui** they sent me here; **un libro indirizzato ai ragazzi** a book intended o written for young people; **indirizzare i propri sforzi verso** to direct one's efforts towards; **l'hanno indirizzato alla segretaria del personale** he was referred to the personnel officer; **indirizzarsi** VR (rivolgersi): **indirizzarsi a qn** to speak to sb

indirizzario, -ri [indiritˈtsarjo] SM mailing list

indirizzo [indiˈrittso] SM 1 (di domicilio) address; **sbagliare indirizzo** to have the wrong address; **se vieni da me in cerca di aiuto, hai sbagliato indirizzo** if you're looking for help from me, you've come to the wrong person; **mi dai il tuo indirizzo?** can I have your address? 2 (fig: direzione) direction, course; (: tendenza) trend; **mutare indirizzo** to change course o direction; **stanno seguendo l'indirizzo giusto** they're on the right lines, they're going in the right direction; **l'attuale indirizzo politico** the present political trend 3 (Inform): **indirizzo assoluto** absolute address; **indirizzo relativo** relative address

indisciplina [indiʃʃiˈplina] SF indiscipline, lack of discipline

indisciplinato, -a [indiʃʃipliˈnato] AGG undisciplined, unruly

indiscreto, -a [indisˈkreto] AGG indiscreet; **se non sono indiscreto...** if you don't mind my asking ...

indiscrezione [indiskretˈtsjone] SF 1 (qualità) indiscretion 2 (azione) indiscretion; (fuga di notizie) unconfirmed report

indiscriminato, -a [indiskrimiˈnato] AGG indiscriminate

indiscusso, -a [indisˈkusso] AGG (autorità, campione) undisputed

indiscutibile [indiskuˈtibile] AGG indisputable, unquestionable

indispensabile [indispenˈsabile] AGG (essenziale) essential, indispensable; (necessario) necessary; **rendersi indispensabile** to make o.s. indispensable; **è uno strumento indispensabile** it's an essential tool; **non è indispensabile che ci sia anche tu** it's not essential for you to be there ♦ SM: **porterò con me solo l'indispensabile** I'll take the absolute minimum with me; **ho l'indispensabile per il picnic** I've got everything I need for the picnic

indispettire [indispetˈtire] /55/ VT to irritate, annoy VI (aus essere), **indispettirsi** VIP to get o grow irritated o annoyed

indisponente [indispoˈnɛnte] AGG irritating, annoying

indisporre [indisˈporre] /77/ VT IRREG to antagonize; **il suo modo di fare mi indispone** I find his manner irritating

indisposizione [indispozitˈtsjone] SF (slight) indisposition

indisposto, -a [indisˈposto] PP di **indisporre** ♦ AGG indisposed (frm), unwell; **essere indisposto** to be unwell

indissolubile [indissoˈlubile] AGG indissoluble

indissolubilmente [indissolubilˈmente] AVV indissolubly

indistintamente [indistintaˈmente] AVV 1 (senza distinzioni) indiscriminately, without exception 2 (in modo indefinito): **vedere, sentire)** vaguely, faintly

indistinto, -a [indisˈtinto] AGG (gen) indistinct; (colori) vague

indistruttibile [indistrutˈtibile] AGG indestructible

indivia [inˈdivja] SF endive

individuale [individuˈale] AGG (gen) individual; (libertà) personal; (qualità) distinctive; **libertà individuale** personal freedom; **lezioni individuali** individual tuition

individualismo [individuaˈlizmo] SM individualism

individualista, -i, -e [individuaˈlista] SM individualist

individualità [individualiˈta] SF (unicità) individuality; (personalità) personality

individualmente [individualˈmente] AVV individually

individuare [individuˈare] /72/ VT 1 (determinare) to identify; (posizione) to locate 2 (riconoscere) to pick out, single out; **sono riuscito ad individuarlo tra la folla** I managed to pick him out in the crowd ♦ **individuarsi** VIP (assumere forma distinta) to be characterized

individuo [indiˈviduo] SM (gen) individual; (pegg: uomo) character, fellow; **un losco individuo** a shady character

indivisibile [indiviˈzibile] AGG (Mat) indivisible; **quei due sono indivisibili** those two are inseparable

indiziare [inditˈtsjare] /19/ VT: **indiziare qn** to cast suspicion on sb; **essere indiziato di qc** to be suspected of sth

indiziato, -a [inditˈtsjato] AGG suspected ♦ SM, SF suspect

indizio, -zi [inˈdittsjo] SM (segno) indication, sign; (traccia) clue; (Dir) piece of evidence; **la polizia non ha trovato alcun indizio** the police haven't found any clues

Indocina [indoˈtʃina] SF Indochina

indole [ˈindole] SF nature, character; **di indole buona** good-natured

indolente [indoˈlɛnte] AGG indolent, lazy

indolenza [indoˈlɛntsa] SF indolence, laziness

indolenzire [indolenˈtsire] /55/ VT (gambe, braccia ecc) to make stiff, cause to ache; (intorpidire) to numb VI (aus essere), **indolenzirsi** VIP (vedi vt) to become stiff; to go numb

indolenzito, -a [indolenˈtsito] AGG stiff, aching; (intorpidito) numb; **sono tutto indolenzito** I'm aching all over

indolore [indoˈlore] AGG (anche fig) painless

indomani [indoˈmani] SM: **l'indomani** the next day, the following day; **ha detto che sarebbe tornata l'indomani** she said she'd come back the next day

Indonesia [indoˈnɛzja] SF Indonesia

indonesiano, -a [indoneˈzjano] AGG, SM, SF Indonesian

indorare [indoˈrare] /72/ VT (rivestire in oro) to gild; (Culin) to dip in egg yolk; **indorare la pillola** (fig) to sugar the pill

indossare [indosˈsare] /72/ VT (mettere indosso) to put on; (avere indosso) to wear, have on

indossatore, -trice [indossaˈtore] SM, SF model; **fare l'indossatore** to be a model; **fa l'indossatrice** she's a model; **indossatrice volante** freelance model

indotto, -a [inˈdɔtto] PP di **indurre** ♦ SM (Econ) components industry and services connected to a major industry

indottrinare [indottriˈnare] /72/ VT to indoctrinate

indovinare [indoviˈnare] /72/ VT 1 (gen) to guess; (il futuro) to predict, foretell; **tirare a indovinare** to hazard a guess, to guess; **non lo sapevo, quindi ho tirato a indovinare** I didn't know, so I had a guess; **indovina chi viene a cena! ** guess who's coming to dinner!; **indovina chi ho incontrato ieri!** guess who I met yesterday! **2** (*azzeccare: risposta*) to get right; **non ne indovini una** you never get anything right; **bravo, hai indovinato!** well done, you've got it right!

indovinato, -a [indovi'nato] AGG successful; (*scelta*) inspired; **una festa indovinata** a successful party

indovinello [indovi'nɛllo] SM riddle; **sai risolvere questo indovinello?** do you know the answer to this riddle?

indovino, -a [indo'vino] SM, SF fortune-teller, soothsayer

indù [in'du] AGG, SM, SF Hindu

indubbiamente [indubbja'mente] AVV undoubtedly; **sarai a Parigi per la fine del mese?** — **indubbiamente** will you be in Paris by the end of the month? — definitely; **è indubbiamente uno dei migliori** it's definitely one of the best

indubbio, -bia, -bi, -bie [in'dubbjo] AGG undoubted, undeniable; **è indubbio che...** there is no doubt that ...

induco ecc [in'duko] VB *vedi* **indurre**

indugiare [indu'dʒare] /62/ VI (*aus* avere) (*attardarsi*) to take one's time, delay; **non ha indugiato ad accettare l'invito** he wasted no time in accepting the invitation

indugio, -gi [in'dudʒo] SM (*ritardo*) delay; **senza indugio** without delay, straight away

indulgente [indul'dʒente] AGG (*gen*) indulgent; (*giudice*) lenient

indulgenza [indul'dʒentsa] SF **1** (*vedi agg*) indulgence; leniency **2** (*Rel*) indulgence; **indulgenza plenaria** plenary indulgence

indulgere [indul'dʒere] /54/ VI IRREG (*aus* avere) **indulgere a qc** (*abbandonarsi*) to indulge in sth; (*accondiscendere*) to comply with sth

indulto [in'dulto] PP *di* **indulgere** ♦ SM (*Dir*) pardon

indumento [indu'mento] SM garment, article of clothing; **un indumento pesante** a warm garment; **un negozio di indumenti usati** a secondhand clothes shop; **ha preso alcuni indumenti e se n'è andata** she took some clothes and left; **indumenti intimi** underwear *sg*, underclothing *sg*, underclothes *pl*

indurimento [induri'mento] SM hardening

indurire [indu'rire] VB IRREG /55/ VT (*anche fig: cuore*) to harden; **viene usato per indurire l'acciaio** it's used to harden steel VI (*aus* essere), **indurirsi** VIP to harden, become hard; **il terreno si è indurito** the ground has gone hard

indurre [in'durre] /90/ VT IRREG **indurre qn a fare qc** to induce *o* persuade sb to do sth; **indurre con lusinghe qn a fare qc** to cajole sb into doing sth; **indurre in errore** to mislead, lead astray; **indurre in tentazione** to lead into temptation

indussi ecc [in'dussi] VB *vedi* **indurre**

industria [in'dustrja] SF **1** (*attività*) industry; **industria pesante/leggera** heavy/light industry; **la piccola/grande industria** small/big business **2** (*impresa*) factory, industrial concern; **industria di assemblaggio** assembly industry; **industria automobilistica** motor industry; **lavora nell'industria automobilistica** he works in the car industry; **industria tessile** textile industry

industriale [indus'trjale] AGG industrial; **una città industriale** an industrial town ♦ SM, SF industrialist; **è un industriale** he is an industrialist

industrializzare [industrjalid'dzare] /72/ VT to industrialize

industrializzazione [industrjaliddzat'tsjone] SF industrialization

industriarsi [indus'trjarsi] /19/ VIP to do one's best, try hard

industrioso, -a [indus'trjoso] AGG industrious, hard-working

induzione [indut'tsjone] SF induction

inebetito, -a [inebe'tito] AGG dazed, stunned

inebriare [inebri'are] /19/ VT (*anche fig*) to intoxicate; **inebriarsi** VIP to become intoxicated; **inebriarsi alla vista di qc** to go into raptures at the sight of sth

ineccepibile [inettʃe'pibile] AGG (*comportamento*) exemplary, unexceptionable

inedia [i'nɛdja] SF starvation; **morire d'inedia** to starve to death

inedito, -a [i'nɛdito] AGG (*non pubblicato*) unpublished; **notizia inedita** fresh piece of news ♦ SM unpublished work

ineffabile [inef'fabile] AGG ineffable

inefficace [ineffi'katʃe] AGG ineffective

inefficacia [ineffi'katʃa] SF inefficacy, ineffectiveness

inefficiente [ineffi'tʃɛnte] AGG inefficient

inefficienza [ineffi'tʃɛntsa] SF inefficiency

ineguagliabile [inegwaʎ'ʎabile] AGG incomparable, matchless

ineguaglianza [inegwaʎ'ʎantsa] SF (*sociale*) inequality; (*di trattamento*) disparity; (*di superficie, livello*) unevenness

ineguale [ine'gwale] AGG (*non uguale*) unequal; (*irregolare*) uneven

ineluttabile [inelut'tabile] AGG inescapable

ineluttabilità [ineluttabili'ta] SF inescapability

inenarrabile [inenar'rabile] AGG unutterable

inequivocabile [inekwivo'kabile] AGG unequivocal

inerente [ine'rɛnte] AGG: **inerente a** concerning, regarding

inerme [i'nerme] AGG unarmed, defenceless (*Brit*), defenseless (*USA*)

inerpicarsi [inerpi'karsi] /72/ VIP: **inerpicarsi (su** *o* **per)** (*persona*) to clamber (up); **la strada si inerpicava fino in cima al colle** the road wound steeply up to the top of the hill

inerte [i'nɛrte] AGG **1** (*corpo*) lifeless; (*persona*) inactive; **peso inerte** (*anche fig*) dead weight **2** (*Chim*) inert

inerzia [i'nertsja] SF (*gen, anche Fis*) inertia; (*inoperosità*) inactivity; **per forza d'inerzia** (*anche fig*) through inertia

inesattezza [inezat'tettsa] SF inaccuracy

inesatto[1], -a [ine'zatto] AGG (*impreciso*) inaccurate, inexact; (*erroneo*) incorrect

inesatto[2], -a [ine'zatto] AGG (*Amm: non riscosso*) uncollected

inesauribile [inezau'ribile] AGG inexhaustible

inesistente [inezis'tɛnte] AGG non-existent

inesorabile [inezo'rabile] AGG (*destino, nemico, ostilità*) inexorable, relentless; (*giudice*) inflexible

inesorabilmente [inezorabil'mente] AVV inexorably, relentlessly

inesperienza [inespe'rjentsa] SF inexperience; **un errore dovuto all'inesperienza** a mistake caused by inexperience

inesperto, -a [ines'pɛrto] AGG inexperienced; **un giovane medico inesperto** an inexperienced young doctor

inesplicabile [inespli'kabile] AGG inexplicable

inesplorato, -a [inesplo'rato] AGG unexplored

inesploso, -a [ines'plɔzo] AGG unexploded

inespressivo, -a [inespres'sivo] AGG (*viso*) expressionless, inexpressive

inespresso, -a [ines'presso] AGG unexpressed

inesprimibile [inespri'mibile] AGG inexpressible

inespugnabile [inespuɲ'ɲabile] AGG (*fortezza, torre*) impregnable

inestetismo [ineste'tizmo] SM beauty problem, (slight) blemish; **combatte gli inestetismi della cellulite** combats the signs of cellulite

inestimabile [inesti'mabile] AGG (*bene, qualità*) inestimable; (*valore*) incalculable; **un quadro di valore inestimabile** a priceless painting

inestirpabile [inestir'pabile] AGG ineradicable

inestricabile [inestri'kabile] AGG (*anche fig*) impenetrable

inettitudine [inetti'tudine] SF ineptitude

inetto, -a [i'nɛtto] AGG (*incapace*) incompetent; (*sciocco*) inept ♦ SM, SF incompetent

inevaso, -a [ine'vazo] AGG (*pratica*) pending; (*corrispondenza*) unanswered

inevitabile [inevi'tabile] AGG (*ostacolo*) unavoidable; (*risultato*) inevitable; **era inevitabile!** it was inevitable!, it was bound to happen!; **era inevitabile che lo scoprisse** he was bound to discover it ♦ SM: **l'inevitabile** the inevitable

inevitabilmente [inevitabil'mente] AVV inevitably

inezia [i'nettsja] SF trifle, bagatelle, thing of no importance

infagottare [infagot'tare] /72/ VT to bundle up, wrap up; **essere infagottato** to be well wrapped up; **infagottarsi** VR to wrap (o.s.) up

infallibile [infal'libile] AGG infallible; **nessuno è infallibile**

nobody is infallible; **un rimedio infallibile contro il raffreddore** an excellent remedy for colds

infallibilità [infallibili'ta] SF infallibility

infamante [infa'mante] AGG (*accusa*) defamatory, slanderous

infamare [infa'mare] /72/ VT to defame

infame [in'fame] AGG (*persona*) wicked; (*calunnia*) vile; (*fig: pessimo*) awful, dreadful

infamia [in'famja] SF 1 (*disonore*) infamy 2 (*azione*) infamous deed, vile deed

infangare [infan'gare] /80/ VT to cover with mud; (*fig: reputazione, nome*) to sully; **infangarsi** VIP to get covered in mud; (*fig*) to be sullied

infantile [infan'tile] AGG 1 (*per bambini*) child *attr*; (*malattia*) childhood *attr*; (*di bambino: grazia, ingenuità*) childlike; **asilo infantile** nursery school; **psicologia infantile** child psychology; **letteratura infantile** children's books *pl* 2 (*immaturo: adulto, azione*) childish, infantile; **comportamento infantile** childish behaviour

infanzia [in'fantsja] SF 1 (*periodo*) childhood; **prima infanzia** infancy, babyhood 2 (*bambini*) children *pl*; **l'infanzia abbandonata** abandoned children

infarinare [infari'nare] /72/ VT to cover with (*o* sprinkle with *o* dip in) flour; **infarinare di zucchero** to sprinkle with sugar

infarinatura [infarina'tura] SF (*fig: conoscenza superficiale*) smattering; **ho solo un'infarinatura di informatica** I only know a bit about computing

infarto [in'farto] SM (*Med*): **infarto (cardiaco)** heart attack; **ha avuto un infarto** he had a heart attack

infastidire [infasti'dire] /55/ VT to annoy, irritate; **infastidirsi** VIP to get annoyed *o* irritated

infaticabile [infati'kabile] AGG indefatigable, tireless, untiring

infatti [in'fatti] CONG as a matter of fact, in fact, actually; **mi aveva promesso un regalo e infatti me l'ha portato** she'd promised me a present and she brought me one; **penso che sia uscito — infatti non risponde nessuno** I think he's out — yes, no one's answering; **ha detto che avrebbe telefonato — sì, infatti...** she said she'd phone — yes, well ...

infatuarsi [infatu'arsi] /72/ VIP: **infatuarsi di** to become infatuated with

infatuazione [infatuat'tsjone] SF infatuation; **avere un'infatuazione per qn** to be infatuated with sb

infausto, -a [in'fausto] AGG (*infelice*) unhappy, unpropitious, unfavourable (*Brit*), unfavorable (*USA*); **presagio infausto** ill omen; **prognosi infausta** (*Med*) fatal prognosis

infecondità [infekondi'ta] SF infertility

infecondo, -a [infe'kondo] AGG (*anche fig*) infertile

infedele [infe'dele] AGG unfaithful; **essere infedele a qn** to be unfaithful to sb ♦ SM, SF (*Storia*) infidel

infedeltà [infedel'ta] SF INV infidelity

infelice [infe'litʃe] AGG 1 (*persona, sguardo, vita*) unhappy; (*incontro, osservazione, posizione*) unfortunate; **una frase infelice** an unfortunate choice of words; **il giorno più infelice della mia vita** the unhappiest day of my life 2 (*mal riuscito: traduzione, lavoro*) bad, poor; **esito infelice** unsuccessful outcome ♦ SM, SF poor wretch

infelicità [infelitʃi'ta] SF (*gen*) unhappiness; (*inopportunità*) inopportuneness

infeltrire [infel'trire] /55/ VI (*aus essere*), **infeltrirsi** VIP (*lana*) to become matted

inferenza [infe'rentsa] SF inference

inferiore [infe'rjore] AGG (*parte, rango, velocità*) lower; (*quantità, numero*) smaller; (*qualità, intelligenza*) inferior; **il labbro inferiore** the lower lip; **un prodotto di qualità inferiore** a product of inferior quality; **inferiore alla media** below average; **il piano inferiore** the next floor down, the floor below; **inferiore a** (*numero, quantità*) less *o* smaller than, below; (*meno buono*) inferior to; **i bambini di età inferiore ai cinque anni** children under five ♦ SM, SF inferior

inferiorità [inferjori'ta] SF inferiority; **complesso di inferiorità** inferiority complex

inferire [infe'rire] /55/ VT IRREG (*dedurre*) to infer, deduce

infermeria [inferme'ria] SF (*gen*) infirmary; (*di scuola, nave*) sick bay

infermiera, -e, -e, -i [infer'mjera] SF (hospital) nurse; **fa l'infermiere** he's a nurse

infermità [infermi'ta] SF INV (*stato*) infirmity; (*malattia*) illness; **infermità mentale** mental illness; (*Dir*) insanity

infermo, -a [in'fermo] AGG (*fisicamente debole*) infirm; (*malato*) ill; **infermo di mente** mentally ill; (*Dir*) insane ♦ SM, SF invalid

infernale [infer'nale] AGG (*gen*) infernal; (*complotto, proposito*) diabolical; **fa un caldo infernale** (*fam*) it's roasting; **un tempo infernale** (*fam*) hellish weather

inferno [in'ferno] SM hell; **la mia vita è un inferno** my life is hell; **mandare qn all'inferno** to tell sb to go to hell; **soffrire le pene dell'inferno** to go through hell

inferocire [infero'tʃire] /55/ VT to make fierce VI (*aus essere*), **inferocirsi** VIP to become fierce

inferriata [infer'rjata] SF grating

infervorare [infervo'rare] /72/ VT to arouse enthusiasm in; **infervorarsi** VIP: **infervorarsi (per qc)** to get excited (about sth), get carried away (by sth); **infervorarsi in una discussione** to get carried away in a discussion

infestare [infes'tare] /72/ VT to infest; **infestato dai topi** infested with *o* overrun by mice; **le erbacce infestavano il giardino** the garden was full of *o* overgrown with weeds

infettare [infet'tare] /72/ VT (*acqua, aria*) to pollute, contaminate; **infettarsi** VIP to become infected

infettivo, -a [infet'tivo] AGG infectious; **malattia infettiva** infectious disease

infetto, -a [in'fetto] AGG (*ferita*) infected; (*acque, aria*) polluted, contaminated

infezione [infet'tsjone] SF infection

infiacchire [infjak'kire] /55/ VT (*anche fig*) to weaken, exhaust VI (*aus essere*), **infiacchirsi** VIP to grow weak

infiammabile [infjam'mabile] AGG, SM inflammable

infiammare [infjam'mare] /72/ VT (*gen*) to set fire to, set alight; (*Med: ferita, organo*) to inflame; **il suo discorso infiammò gli animi dei rivoltosi** his speech inflamed the rebels; **infiammarsi** VIP (*gen*) to catch fire; (*Med*) to become inflamed; **infiammarsi d'amore** to be fired with love

infiammazione [infjammat'tsjone] SF inflammation

infiascare [infjas'kare] /20/ VT (*vino, olio*) to bottle

inficiare [infi'tʃare] /14/ VT (*Dir: testimonianza, dichiarazione*) to invalidate

infido, -a [in'fido] AGG unreliable, treacherous

infierire [infje'rire] /55/ VI (*aus avere*) 1 (*comportarsi con ferocia*): **infierire su** (*fisicamente*) to attack furiously; (*verbalmente*) to rage at 2 (*imperversare: epidemia, peste*) to rage *o* sweep through

infiggere [in'fiddʒere] /104/ VT IRREG: **infiggere qc in** to thrust *o* drive sth into

infilare [infi'lare] /72/ VT 1 (*introdurre: moneta, chiave*) to insert; **infilò le mani in tasca** he put *o* slipped his hands into his pockets; **le infilò un anello al dito** he put *o* slipped a ring on her finger; **infilò la mano nel cassetto** he slid his hand into the drawer; **puoi infilare anche questo nella busta?** can you put this in the same envelope?; **ho infilato la chiave nella serratura** I put the key into the lock; **riesci ad infilarci ancora qualcosa?** (*in borsa, valigia*) can you squeeze anything else in? 2 (*ago, perle*) to thread 3 (*indossare: vestito*) to slip *o* put on; **infilarsi la giacca** to put on one's jacket; **si è infilato la giacca ed è uscito** he put on his jacket and went out 4 (*imboccare: strada*) to turn into, take; **infilò la porta e se ne andò** he slipped through the door and off he went 5 (*far seguire in successione*): **infilare uno sbaglio dopo l'altro** to make one mistake after the other; **infilare sette vittorie consecutive** to win seven matches *o* times on the trot; **abbiamo infilato cinque semafori verdi** we met five green lights in succession; **infilarsi** VR (*introdursi*): **infilarsi in** to slip into; **infilarsi tra la folla** to merge into the crowd; **il gatto si è infilato lì sotto e non riesco a prenderlo** the cat slipped under there and I can't get at it; **infilarsi a letto** to slip into bed; **infilarsi in un taxi** to jump into a taxi

infiltrarsi [infil'trarsi] /72/ VIP (*persona*) **infiltrarsi in** to infiltrate; (*fumo, gas, luce*) to penetrate into, filter into; (*umidità, liquido*) to penetrate, seep (into)

infiltrato, -a [infil'trato] SM, SF infiltrator

infiltrazione [infiltrat'tsjone] SF (*vedi vb*) infiltration; penetration; seepage

infilzare [infil'tsare] /72/ vt (*trafiggere*) to run through, pierce; (*sullo spiedo*) to skewer; (*infilare*) to string together; **infilzare un pollo sullo spiedo** to spit a chicken

infimo, -a ['infimo] AGG (*qualità*) very poor, lowest; **un albergo di infimo ordine** a third-rate hotel; **un impiegato di infimo grado** an employee of the lowest grade

infine [in'fine] AVV (*alla fine*) finally; (*per concludere*) in short; **vorrei dire, infine...** finally I would like to say ...

infingardo, -a [infin'gardo] AGG slothful ♦ SM, SF sluggard

infinità [infini'ta] SF infinity; **un'infinità di** an infinite number of; **ho un'infinità di cose da fare** I have masses of things to do

infinitesimale [infinitezi'male] AGG infinitesimal

infinito, -a [infi'nito] AGG (*gen*) infinite; **con infinito rammarico** with deep regret; **con infinita gioia** with great pleasure; **grazie infinite!** many thanks! ♦ SM **1** (*Filosofia*): **l'infinito** the infinite; (*Mat, Fot*) infinity; **all'infinito** (*senza fine*) endlessly; (*Mat*) to infinity; **te l'ho ripetuto all'infinito!** I've told you a thousand times! **2** (*Gramm*) infinitive; **all'infinito** in the infinitive

infinocchiare [infinok'kjare] /19/ vt (*fam*) to hoodwink, bamboozle

infiorescenza [infjoreʃ'ʃentsa] SF inflorescence

infirmare [infir'mare] /72/ vt (*Dir*) to invalidate

infischiarsi [infis'kjarsi] /19/ vip: **infischiarsi di** not to care about; **me ne infischio!** I couldn't care less!; **mi infischio di quello che pensa** I don't care what he thinks

infisso [in'fisso] PP *di* **infiggere** ♦ SM (*di porta, finestra*) frame

infittire [infit'tire] /55/ vt to thicken VI (*aus* **essere**), **infittirsi** VIP to become thicker, thicken

inflazionare [inflattsjo'nare] /72/ vt (*Econ*) to inflate; **inflazionare un'espressione** to overwork an expression; **un titolo di studio inflazionato** an overrated qualification

inflazione [inflat'tsjone] SF **1** (*Econ*) inflation; **il tasso di inflazione** the rate of inflation; **inflazione galoppante** galloping inflation; **inflazione strisciante** creeping inflation **2** (*pegg: quantità esagerata*) proliferation; **un'inflazione di telefonini** a proliferation of mobile phones; **un'inflazione di laureati in medicina** an over-abundance of people graduating in medicine

inflazionistico, -a, -ci, -che [inflattsjo'nistiko] AGG (*Econ*) inflationary

inflessibile [infles'sibile] AGG (*gen*) inflexible; (*carattere*) unyielding; (*volontà*) iron *attr*

inflessione [infles'sjone] SF inflexion

infliggere [in'fliddʒere] /104/ vt IRREG (*pena, castigo*) to inflict; (*multa*) to impose

inflissi *ecc* [in'flissi] VB *vedi* **infliggere**

inflitto, -a [in'flitto] PP *di* **infliggere**

influente [influ'ente] AGG influential

influenza [influ'entsa] SF **1** (*ascendente, peso*) influence; **è una persona che ha influenza** he's an influential person; **avere influenza su qn/qc** to have an influence over sb/sth; **subire l'influenza di qn/qc** to be influenced by sb/sth; **zona** *o* **sfera d'influenza** (*Pol*) sphere of influence **2** (*Med*) influenza, flu; **prendere l'influenza** to catch *o* get (the) flu; **ho l'influenza** I've got the flu

influenzare [influen'tsare] /72/ vt to influence, have an influence on; **lasciarsi** *o* **farsi influenzare** to be (easily) influenced; **si lascia influenzare troppo dagli amici** she's too easily influenced by her friends

influire [influ'ire] /55/ VI (*aus* **avere**) **influire su** to influence, affect; **non ha influito sulla sua decisione** it didn't influence his decision

influsso [in'flusso] SM influence

❏ **influsso** non si traduce mai con la parola inglese *influx*

infocato, -a [info'kato] AGG = **infuocato**

infognarsi [infoɲ'ɲarsi] /15/ VIP (*fam*) to get into a mess; **infognarsi in un mare di debiti** to be up to one's *o* the eyes in debt

infoltire [infol'tire] /55/ vt to thicken, make thicker VI (*aus* **essere**), **infoltirsi** VIP to become thicker, thicken

infondato, -a [infon'dato] AGG unfounded, groundless; **un sospetto infondato** an unfounded suspicion

infondere [in'fondere] /25/ vt IRREG: **infondere qc in qn** to instil (*Brit*) *o* instill (*USA*) sth in sb; **infondere fiducia in qn** to inspire sb with confidence

inforcare [infor'kare] /20/ vt **1** (*prendere con la forca*) to fork (up) **2** (*bicicletta, cavallo*) to mount, get on; (*occhiali*) to put on

informale [infor'male] AGG informal

informare [infor'mare] /72/ vt to inform, tell; **informare qn di qc** to inform sb of *o* about sth, tell sb of *o* about sth; **avete informato la polizia?** have you informed the police?; **informarsi** VIP to make inquiries; **informarsi di** *o* **su** to inquire about, ask about, find out about; **mi sono informato sugli orari dei treni** I asked about train times; **un'altra volta informati!** next time make sure you're better informed!

informatico, -a, -ci, -che [infor'matiko] AGG (*settore*) computer *attr*

informativo, -a [informa'tivo] AGG informative; **a titolo informativo** for information only

informatizzare [informatid'dzare] vt to computerize

informato, -a [infor'mato] AGG informed; **tienimi informato** keep me informed; **è sempre informato sulle novità discografiche** he always knows about the latest releases; **tenersi informato** to keep o.s. (well-)informed

informatore, -trice [informa'tore] AGG informative ♦ SM, SF (*della polizia*) informer; **informatore medico scientifico** representative (*of pharmaceutical company*)

informazione [informat'tsjone] SF **1** (*ragguaglio*) piece of information; **può darmi un'informazione?** can you give me some information?; **mi ha dato un'informazione utile** he gave me some useful information; **chiedere un'informazione** to ask for (some) information; **ho chiesto un'informazione ad un poliziotto** I asked a policeman for information; **chiedere/prendere informazioni sul conto di qn** to ask for/get information about sb, to make inquiries about sb; **a titolo d'informazione** for information; **per ulteriori informazioni telefonare al numero...** for further information call ...; **informazione** *o* **inquiry of office; dov'è l'ufficio informazioni?** where's the information office? **2** (*Inform*) information; **teoria dell'informazione** information theory **3** (*Dir*): **informazione di garanzia** = **avviso di garanzia; informazione genetica** (*Bio*) genetic code

informe [in'forme] AGG formless, shapeless

informicolarsi [informiko'larsi] /72/, **informicolirsi** [informiko'lirsi] VIP: **mi si è informicolata una gamba** I've got pins and needles in my leg

infornare [infor'nare] /72/ vt to put in the oven

infornata [infor'nata] SF (*anche fig*) batch

infortunarsi [infortu'narsi] /72/ VIP to injure o.s., have an accident

infortunato, -a [infortu'nato] AGG injured, hurt ♦ SM, SF injured person

infortunio, -ni [infor'tunjo] SM accident; **infortunio sul lavoro** industrial accident, accident at work; **ha avuto un infortunio sul lavoro** he had an accident at work

infortunistica [infortu'nistika] SF study of (industrial) accidents

infossarsi [infos'sarsi] /72/ VIP (*terreno*) to sink; (*guance*) to become hollow

infossato, -a [infos'sato] AGG (*guance*) hollow; (*occhi*) deepset; (*per malattia*) sunken

infradiciare [infradi'tʃare] /14/ vt (*inzuppare*) to soak, drench; (*marcire*) to rot; **infradiciarsi** VIP (*vedi vt*) to get soaked, get drenched; to rot

infradito [infra'dito] SM INV (*calzatura*) flip flop (*Brit*), thong (*USA*)

infrangere [in'frandʒere] VB IRREG /37/ vt (*legge, patto*) to violate, break; (*vetro, vaso*) to smash; **infrangersi** VIP (*onde*) to break, smash; **le onde s'infrangevano sugli scogli** the waves were breaking on the rocks

infrangibile [infran'dʒibile] AGG unbreakable

infranto, -a [in'franto] PP *di* **infrangere** ♦ AGG (*anche fig: cuore*) broken

infrarosso, -a [infra'rosso] AGG, SM infrared
infrasettimanale [infrasettima'nale] AGG midweek *attr*
infrastruttura [infrastrut'tura] SF infrastructure
infrazione [infrat'tsjone] SF infringement; **infrazione a violation of; infrazione al codice della strada** traffic offence
infreddatura [infredda'tura] SF slight cold
infreddolito, -a [infreddo'lito] AGG cold, chilled; **sono tutto infreddolito** I'm chilled to the bone; **sono un po' infreddolito** I'm a bit cold
infrequente [infre'kwente] AGG infrequent, rare
infrollire [infrol'lire] /55/ VT (*aus* essere), **infrollirsi** VIP (*selvaggina*) to become high
infruttuoso, -a [infruttu'oso] AGG (*anche fig*) unfruitful, fruitless
infuocato, -a [infwo'kato] AGG (*metallo*) red-hot; (*sabbia*) burning; (*discorso*) heated, passionate
infuori [in'fwori] AVV **1 infuori, all'infuori** (*sporgere*) out, outwards; **avere i denti/gli occhi infuori** to have prominent *o* protuberant teeth/eyes; **sporge un po' infuori** it sticks out a bit **2 all'infuori di** (*eccetto*) except, apart from, with the exception of; **lo sapevano tutti all'infuori di lui** they all knew except him; **non so altro all'infuori di questo** that's all I know
infuriare [infu'rjare] /19/ VT to enrage, make furious ♦ VI (*aus* avere) (*tempesta, vento*) to rage; **infuriarsi** VIP to fly into a rage
infusione [infu'zjone] SF (*operazione*) infusion; (*infuso*) infusion, herb tea; **lasciare in infusione** to leave to infuse
infuso, -a [in'fuzo] PP *di* infondere ♦ AGG: **scienza infusa** (*anche iro*) innate knowledge ♦ SM infusion, herb tea; **infuso di camomilla** camomile tea
Ing. ABBR = **ingegnere**
ingabbiare [ingab'bjare] /19/ VT (*animali*) to (put in a) cage; (*fig: persona*) to cage in
ingaggiare [ingad'dʒare] /62/ VT (*assumere: operai*) to take on, hire; (: *Sport: giocatore*) to sign; **essere ingaggiato** to sign; **è stato ingaggiato per la prossima stagione** he's signed for next season; **ingaggiare battaglia** (*Mil*) to engage the enemy
ingaggio, -gi [in'gaddʒo] SM (*di operaio*) taking on, hiring; (*Sport*) signing; (*somma*) signing-on fee
ingagliardire [ingaʎʎar'dire] /55/ VT to strengthen, invigorate VI (*aus* essere), **ingagliardirsi** VIP to grow stronger
ingannare [ingan'nare] /19/ VT (*imbrogliare*) to deceive; (*tradire: moglie, marito*) to cheat on, be unfaithful to; **mi hai ingannato!** you deceived me!; **non lasciarti ingannare dalla sua aria innocente** don't be taken in by his air of innocence; **le apparenze spesso ingannano** appearances are often deceptive; **ingannare il tempo** to while away the time; **abbiamo giocato a carte per ingannare l'attesa** while we waited we played cards to kill time; **ingannarsi** VIP to be mistaken, be wrong; **ingannarsi sul conto di qn** to be mistaken *o* wrong about sb
ingannatore, -trice [inganna'tore] AGG (*gen*) deceptive; (*persona, sguardo*) deceitful
ingannevole [ingan'nevole] AGG (*gen*) deceptive; (*consiglio*) misleading
inganno [in'ganno] SM (*imbroglio*) deceit, deception; (*menzogna, frode*) con, swindle; (*insidia*) trick; (*illusione*) illusion; **trarre in inganno** to deceive, mislead; **con l'inganno** by a trick; **inganno dei sensi** sensory illusion
ingarbugliare [ingarbuʎ'ʎare] /27/ VT (*fili, corde*) to tangle; (*fig: situazione*) to muddle, confuse; **ingarbugliarsi** VIP (*fili, corde, capelli*) to get tangled; (*fig: situazione*) to become confused *o* muddled
ingarbugliato, -a [ingarbuʎ'ʎato] AGG (*vedi vb*) tangled; muddled, confused
ingegnarsi [indʒeɲ'ɲarsi] /15/ VIP to use one's ingenuity; **non avevamo l'occorrente ma ci siamo ingegnati** we didn't have what we needed but we made do; **ingegnarsi per vivere** to live by one's wits; **basta ingegnarsi un po'** you just need a bit of ingenuity
ingegnere [indʒeɲ'ɲere] SM engineer; **fa l'ingegnere** he is an engineer; **ingegnere civile** civil engineer; **ingegnere navale** naval engineer

ingegneria [indʒeɲɲe'ria] SF engineering; **è laureata in ingegneria** she's got a degree in engineering; **ingegneria chimica** chemical engineering; **ingegneria civile** civil engineering; **ingegneria elettrica** electrical engineering; **ingegneria meccanica** mechanical engineering
ingegno [in'dʒeɲɲo] SM **1** (*intelligenza*) intelligence, brains *pl*; (*attitudine, talento*) talent; (*ingegnosità*) ingenuity; **avere dell'ingegno** to have a creative mind; **aguzzare l'ingegno** to sharpen one's wits; **un'alzata d'ingegno** (*anche iro*) a bright idea **2** (*persona*) mind; **è un bell'ingegno** he has a good brain; **i più grandi ingegni del secolo** the greatest minds of the century
ingegnosità [indʒeɲɲosi'ta] SF ingenuity
ingegnoso, -a [indʒeɲ'ɲoso] AGG ingenious, clever
ingelosire [indʒelo'sire] /55/ VT to make jealous VI (*aus* essere), **ingelosirsi** VIP to become jealous
ingente [in'dʒente] AGG huge, enormous
ingentilire [indʒenti'lire] /55/ VT to refine, civilize; **ingentilirsi** VIP to become more refined *o* civilized
ingenuità [indʒenui'ta] SF naïvety, ingenuousness
ingenuo, -a [in'dʒenuo] AGG naïve, ingenuous; **è molto ingenua** she's very naïve; **ma come fai ad essere così ingenuo?** how can you be so naïve? ♦ SM, SF: **è un ingenuo** he is naïve; **fare l'ingenuo** to act the innocent; **non fare l'ingenuo, sai benissimo di cosa parlo** don't act the innocent, you know perfectly well what I'm talking about
ingerenza [indʒe'rentsa] SF interference
ingerire [indʒe'rire] /55/ VT to ingest
ingessare [indʒes'sare] /72/ VT to put in plaster; **gli hanno ingessato il braccio** they put his arm in plaster
ingessatura [indʒessa'tura] SF plaster (cast); **mi hanno tolto l'ingessatura** they took off the plaster
Inghilterra [ingil'terra] SF England; **mi è piaciuta molto l'Inghilterra** I really liked England; **andrò in Inghilterra quest'estate** I'm going to England this summer
inghiottire [ingjot'tire] /17/ VT (*anche fig*) to swallow; **la barca fu inghiottita dai flutti** the boat was swallowed up *o* engulfed by the waves; **essere inghiottito dal buio** to be swallowed up by the darkness; **ne ha inghiottite tante nella vita** (*fig: dispiaceri*) he's had so much to put up with in life
inghippo [in'gippo] SM trick
ingiallire [indʒal'lire] /55/ VT to turn yellow VI (*aus* essere), **ingiallirsi** VIP to (turn *o* go) yellow
ingigantire [indʒigan'tire] /55/ VT (*immagine*) to enlarge, magnify; (*fig: problema*) to exaggerate VI (*aus* essere), **ingigantirsi** VIP to become gigantic *o* enormous
inginocchiarsi [indʒinok'kjarsi] /19/ VIP to kneel (down); **si è inginocchiato accanto al cane** he knelt down beside the dog; **essere inginocchiato** to be kneeling down, be on one's knees
inginocchiatoio, -oi [indʒinokkja'tojo] SM prie-dieu
ingioiellare [indʒojel'lare] /72/ VT to bejewel, adorn with jewels; **ingioiellarsi** VR to put on one's jewels
ingiù [in'dʒu] AVV down, downwards; **con la testa all'ingiù** head downwards; (*capovolto*) upside down
ingiungere [in'dʒundʒere] /5/ VT IRREG: **ingiungere a qn di fare qc** to enjoin *o* order sb to do sth
ingiunto, -a [in'dʒunto] PP *di* ingiungere
ingiunzione [indʒun'tsjone] SF injunction, command; **ingiunzione di pagamento** final demand
ingiuria [in'dʒurja] SF (*insulto*) insult; **coprire qn di ingiurie** to heap abuse on sb; **le ingiurie del tempo** the ravages of time
   ❑ **ingiuria** non si traduce mai con la parola inglese *injury*
ingiuriare [indʒu'rjare] /19/ VT to insult, abuse
   ❑ **ingiuriare** non si traduce mai con la parola inglese *injure*
ingiurioso, -a [indʒu'rjoso] AGG insulting, abusive
ingiustamente [indʒusta'mente] AVV unjustly
ingiustificabile [indʒustifi'kabile] AGG unjustifiable
ingiustificato, -a [indʒustifi'kato] AGG unjustified; **assenza ingiustificata** unexplained absence; (*Scol*) absence without permission; (*Mil*) absence without leave

ingiustizia [indʒusˈtittsja] SF injustice; **ha commesso un'ingiustizia** he was unjust, he acted unjustly; **è un'ingiustizia! that's not fair!**

ingiusto, -a [inˈdʒusto] AGG unjust, unfair; **essere ingiusto con qn** to be unfair o unjust to sb; **questo è profondamente ingiusto** this is utterly unfair; **è ingiusto nei miei confronti** it's unfair to me

inglese [inˈɡlese] AGG English; **andarsene** o **filarsela all'inglese** to take French leave (to leave without saying goodbye); **la squadra inglese** the English team ♦ SM, SF Englishman o Englishwoman **gli Inglesi** the English, English people ♦ SM (lingua) English; **parlare (l')inglese** to speak English; **parli inglese?** do you speak English?

inglorioso, -a [inɡloˈrjoso] AGG (privo di gloria) inglorious; (ignominioso) ignominious

ingobbire [inɡobˈbire] /55/ VI (aus essere), **ingobbirsi** VIP to become stooped

ingoiare [inɡoˈjare] /19/ VT (inghiottire) to swallow; (in fretta) to gulp (down); (fig) to swallow (up); **se l'ingoiò in un boccone** he swallowed it in one go; **furono ingoiati dai flutti** they were swallowed up o engulfed by the waves; **è stato un boccone amaro da ingoiare** (fig) it was a bitter pill to swallow; **ha dovuto ingoiare tante amarezze** he has had to endure so many disappointments; **ha dovuto ingoiare il rospo** he had to accept the situation, whether he liked it or not

ingolfare [inɡolˈfare] /72/ VT (Aut) to flood; **ingolfarsi** VIP (Aut) to flood; **ingolfarsi nei debiti** to get up to one's o the ears in debt

ingolosire [inɡoloˈsire] /55/ VT: **ingolosire qn** to make sb's mouth water; (fig) to attract sb VI (aus essere), **ingolosirsi** VIP to become greedy

ingombrante [inɡomˈbrante] AGG cumbersome; **una valigia ingombrante** a cumbersome case

ingombrare [inɡomˈbrare] /72/ VT (strada) to block, obstruct; (stanza, tavolo) to clutter up; **si prega di non ingombrare il corridoio** please don't block the corridor; **i bagagli ingombravano la stanza** the room was full of luggage

ingombro¹, -a [inˈɡombro] AGG: **ingombro di** (strada) blocked by; (stanza) cluttered up with

ingombro² [inˈɡombro] SM 1 obstacle; **essere d'ingombro** to be in the way; **per ragioni di ingombro** for reasons of space 2 (di auto) overall dimensions pl

ingordigia [inɡorˈdidʒa] SF: **ingordigia (di)** (vedi agg) greed (for); avidity (for)

ingordo, -a [inˈɡordo] AGG: **ingordo (di)** (cibo) greedy (for); (fig: denaro) greedy o avid (for); **non essere ingordo!** don't be greedy!; **è più ingordo di me** he's greedier than me ♦ SM, SF glutton

ingorgare [inɡorˈɡare] /80/ VT to block; **ingorgarsi** VIP to get blocked

ingorgo, -ghi [inˈɡorɡo] SM 1 (di tubo) blockage, obstruction 2 (anche: ingorgo stradale) hold-up; **c'era un ingorgo all'incrocio** there was a hold-up at the junction

ingozzare [inɡotˈtsare] /72/ VT (animali) to fatten; **ingozzare (di cibo)** (persona) to stuff (with food); **ingozzarsi** VR: **ingozzarsi (di qc)** to stuff o.s. with

ingranaggio, -gi [inɡraˈnaddʒo] SM (Tecn) gear; (di orologio) mechanism; **gli ingranaggi della burocrazia** the bureaucratic machinery; **essere preso nell'ingranaggio** (fig) to be caught in the system

ingranare [inɡraˈnare] /72/ VI (aus avere) (Tecn) to engage, mesh; **non riesco ad ingranare nel nuovo lavoro** I can't seem to get into my stride in the new job; **gli affari cominciano ad ingranare** business is beginning to move ♦ VT: **ingranare la marcia** (Aut) to engage gear, get into gear; **non riesco a ingranare la marcia** I can't get into gear

ingrandimento [inɡrandiˈmento] SM (di città, azienda) development, growth, expansion; (di casa) extension; (di strada) widening; (Ottica, Fis) magnification; (Fot) enlargement; **lente d'ingrandimento** magnifying glass; **vorrei un ingrandimento di questa foto** I'd like an enlargement of this photo; **far fare un ingrandimento** to get an enlargement

ingrandire [inɡranˈdire] /55/ VT (azienda, città) to develop, expand; (locale) to extend; (strada) to widen; (Ottica) to magnify; (Fot) to enlarge; (fig: storia: esagerare) to embroider;

ho deciso di ingrandire la casa I've decided to extend my house VI (aus essere), **ingrandirsi** VIP (gen) to get larger o bigger; (azienda, città) to grow, expand; (strada) to get wider; (potere) to grow, increase; (problema) to become more serious o worse; **la città si sta ingrandendo** the town is getting bigger

ingranditore [inɡrandiˈtore] SM (Fot) enlarger

ingrassaggio, -gi [inɡrasˈsaddʒo] SM greasing

ingrassare [inɡrasˈsare] /72/ VT 1 (animali) to fatten (up); (persone) to make fat; **ingrassare di** to put on; **sono ingrassato di due chili** I've put on two kilos; **far ingrassare** to be fattening; **i dolci fanno ingrassare** puddings are fattening 2 (lubrificare) to grease 3 (concimare: terreno) to manure VI (aus essere), **ingrassarsi** VIP to get fat, put on weight; **sei un po' ingrassata** you've put on a bit of weight; **sei molto ingrassato** you've put on a lot of weight; **ingrassarsi alle spalle altrui** (fig) to thrive at the expense of others

ingratitudine [inɡratiˈtudine] SF ingratitude, ungratefulness

ingrato, -a [inˈɡrato] AGG (persona) ungrateful; (lavoro) thankless, unrewarding ♦ SM, SF ungrateful person; **sei un ingrato!** you're an ungrateful wretch!

ingraziarsi [inɡratˈtsjarsi] VT: **ingraziarsi qn** to ingratiate o.s. with sb

ingrediente [inɡreˈdjente] SM ingredient

ingresso [inˈɡresso] SM 1 (porta) entrance, entry; (atrio) hall; **non stare lì nell'ingresso, accomodati** don't stand there in the doorway, come in; **ingresso principale** main entrance; **l'ingresso principale è sulla via laterale** the main entrance is in the side street; **ingresso di servizio** service entrance 2 (accesso) admission; **fare il proprio ingresso** to make one's entrance; **vietato l'ingresso** no admittance; **ingresso libero** admission free; **biglietto d'ingresso** admission ticket, entrance ticket; **prezzo d'ingresso** cost of admission

ingrossare [inɡrosˈsare] /72/ VT (spessore, patrimonio) to increase; (fiume, folla) to swell; (muscoli) to develop; **ingrossare le file** (Mil, anche fig) to swell the ranks; **quest'abito ti ingrossa** this dress makes you look fat VI (aus essere), **ingrossarsi** VIP (vedi vt) to increase; to swell; to develop; (persona) to put on weight

ingrosso [inˈɡrosso] AVV: **all'ingrosso** (Comm) wholesale; (all'incirca) roughly, about; **prezzo all'ingrosso** wholesale price; **vendere all'ingrosso, effettuare vendite all'ingrosso** to sell wholesale ♦ SM: **un ingrosso di calzature** a shoe wholesaler

ingrugnato, -a [inɡruɲˈɲato] AGG grumpy

inguaiare [inɡwaˈjare] (fam) /19/ VT to get (sb) into trouble; **inguaiarsi** VR to get into trouble

inguainare [inɡwaiˈnare] /72/ VT to sheathe

ingualcibile [inɡwalˈtʃibile] AGG crease-resistant

inguaribile [inɡwaˈribile] AGG (anche fig) incurable

inguine [ˈinɡwine] SM (Anat) groin; **ho uno strappo all'inguine** I've strained my groin

ingurgitare [inɡurdʒiˈtare] /72/ VT to gulp down

inibire [iniˈbire] /55/ VT to inhibit

inibito, -a [iniˈbito] AGG inhibited; **non pensavo che fossi così inibito** I didn't think you were so inhibited! ♦ SM, SF inhibited person

inibitorio, -ria, -ri, -rie [inibiˈtɔrjo] AGG (Psic) inhibitory, inhibitive; (Dir: provvedimento, misure) restrictive

inibizione [inibitˈtsjone] SF inhibition

iniettare [injetˈtare] /72/ VT to inject; **iniettare qc a qn** to inject sb with sth; **iniettare una sostanza stupefacente** to inject o.s. with a drug; **con gli occhi iniettati di sangue** with bloodshot eyes; **iniettarsi** VIP: **iniettarsi di sangue** (occhi) to become bloodshot

iniettore [injetˈtore] SM (Tecn) injector

iniezione [injetˈtsjone] SF 1 (Med) injection; **fare** o **farsi fare un'iniezione** to get an injection; **fare un'iniezione (a qn)** to give (sb) an injection; **mi hanno fatto un'iniezione di penicillina** they gave me an injection of penicillin; **dare un'iniezione di fiducia a qn** to boost sb's morale o confidence 2 (Aut): **motore a iniezione** injection engine

inimicare [inimiˈkare] /20/ VT to alienate, make hostile; **si è inimicato gli amici di un tempo** he has alienated his old friends; **inimicarsi** VIP: **inimicarsi con qn** to fall out with sb

inimicizia [inimi'tʃittsja] SF enmity, animosity

inimitabile [inimi'tabile] AGG inimitable

inimmaginabile [inimmadʒi'nabile] AGG unimaginable

ininfiammabile [ininfjam'mabile] AGG non-flammable

inintelligibile [intelli'dʒibile] AGG unintelligible

ininterrottamente [ininterrotta'mente] AVV non-stop, continuously; **è piovuto ininterrottamente per 2 settimane** it rained non-stop *o* continuously for 2 weeks; **ha parlato ininterrottamente per tre ore** he talked non-stop for three hours

ininterrotto, -a [ininter'rotto] AGG (*fila*) continuous, unbroken; (*viavai, rumore*) constant

iniquità [inikwi'ta] SF INV (*qualità*) iniquity; (*atto*) wicked action

iniquo, -a [i'nikwo] AGG iniquitous

iniziale [init'tsjale] AGG initial; **fase iniziale** initial phase; **stipendio iniziale** starting salary ♦ SF initial; **iniziali** to initial; **un accendino con le sue iniziali** a lighter with his initials

inizializzare [inittsjalid'dzare] /72/ VT (*Inform: diskette*) to initialize; (*: computer*) to boot

inizialmente [inittsjal'mente] AVV initially, at first

iniziare [init'tsjare] /19/ VT 1 (*cominciare*) to begin, start; (*dibattito, ostilità*) to open; **iniziare a fare qc** to start doing sth; **hai iniziato a cucinare?** have you started cooking? 2 (*persona: a un culto*) to initiate into; (*: a un'attività*) to introduce to ♦ VI (*aus essere*) to begin, start; **il film sta per iniziare** the film is about to start

iniziativa [inittsja'tiva] SF (*gen*) initiative; **di propria iniziativa** on one's own initiative; **è venuta di propria iniziativa** she came on her own initiative; **spirito d'iniziativa** spirit of initiative, drive; **prendere l'iniziativa** to take the initiative; **se vuoi rivederla, devi prendere tu l'iniziativa** if you want to see her again, you'll have to take the initiative; **una serie di iniziative culturali** a series of arts events; **iniziativa privata** (*Comm*) private enterprise

iniziatore, -trice [inittsja'tore] SM, SF initiator

inizio [i'nittsjo] SM beginning, start; **fin dall'inizio** from the beginning; **all'inizio** at the beginning, at the start; **all'inizio pensavo che scherzasse** at first I thought he was joking; **all'inizio di** at the beginning of; **il pareggio è arrivato all'inizio del secondo tempo** the equalizer came at the beginning of the second half; **essere agli inizi** (*progetto, lavoro ecc*) to be in the initial stages; **dare inizio a qc** to start sth, get sth going; **avere inizio** to begin; **il film ha inizio con una scena d'azione** the film begins with an action scene; **ho riletto l'inizio della lettera dieci volte** I read the beginning of the letter ten times; **l'inizio dei lavori è previsto per la fine del mese** work will begin at the end of the month

innaffiare ecc [innaf'fjare] = **annaffiare**

innalzare [innal'tsare] /72/ VT (*gen, sollevare*) to raise; (*costruire: monumento*) to erect; **innalzare gli occhi al cielo** to raise one's eyes to heaven; **innalzare al trono** to raise to the throne; **innalzarsi** VIP to rise

innamoramento [innamora'mento] SM falling in love

innamorare [innamo'rare] /72/ VT to enchant, charm; **un viso che innamora** an enchanting *o* a delightful face; **innamorarsi** VR (*uso reciproco*) to fall in love (with each other) ♦ VIP: **innamorarsi (di)** to fall in love (with)

innamorato, -a [innamo'rato] AGG: **innamorato (di)** (*anche fig: di lavoro ecc*) in love (with), very fond (of); **essere innamorato di qn** to be in love with someone; **sei innamorato di lei?** are you in love with her?; **è innamorato del suo bambino** he dotes on his child; **è innamorata persa** she's madly in love ♦ SM, SF boyfriend *o* girlfriend; (*anche scherz*) sweetheart

innanzi [in'nantsi] AVV 1 (*stato in luogo*) in front, ahead; (*moto a luogo*) forward, on; **stare** *o* **essere innanzi** to be in front *o* ahead; **farsi innanzi** to step forward; **a 2** (*tempo*) before, earlier; **il giorno innanzi** the day before; **d'ora innanzi** from now on ♦ PREP 1 (*davanti*): **innanzi a** in front of, before; **lo giuro innanzi a Dio** I swear before God 2 (*prima*) before; **innanzi tempo** ahead of time; **morire innanzi tempo** to die before one's time

innanzitutto [innantsi'tutto] AVV (*soprattutto*) above all; (*per prima cosa*) first of all; **innanzitutto bisogna informarsi degli orari** first of all you need to check the times

innato, -a [in'nato] AGG innate, inborn

innaturale [innatu'rale] AGG unnatural

innegabile [inne'gabile] AGG undeniable

inneggiare [inned'dʒare] /62/ VI (*aus avere*) **inneggiare a** to sing hymns to; (*fig*) to sing the praises of

innervosire [innervo'sire] /55/ VT: **innervosire qn** (*rendere nervoso*) to make sb nervous; (*irritare*) to get on sb's nerves, annoy sb; **il traffico mi innervosisce** the traffic gets on my nerves; **innervosirsi** VIP (*vedi vt*) to become nervous; to get irritated *o* upset; **si è innervosito per il rumore** the noise got on his nerves

innescare [innes'kare] /20/ VT 1 (*ordigno esplosivo*) to prime; (*fig: serie di eventi ecc*) to trigger off 2 (*amo*) to bait

innesco, -schi [in'nesko] SM primer, fuse

innestare [innes'tare] /72/ VT (*Agr, Med*) to graft; (*Tecn*) to engage; (*Elettr: presa*) to put in

innesto [in'nesto] SM (*Agr, Med*) graft; (*azione*) grafting *no pl*; (*Tecn*) clutch; (*Elettr*) connection

inno ['inno] SM (*anche fig*) hymn; **inno nazionale** national anthem

innocente [inno'tʃente] AGG 1 (*gen*) innocent; (*scherzo*) harmless; **uno scherzo innocente** a harmless joke 2 (*Dir*) not guilty; **dichiararsi innocente** to maintain one's innocence; **si è sempre dichiarato innocente** he has always maintained his innocence; **secondo me è innocente** in my opinion he's innocent ♦ SM, SF innocent person; (*bambino*) innocent

innocenza [inno'tʃentsa] SF innocence

innocuo, -a [in'nɔkuo] AGG innocuous, harmless

innominato, -a [innomi'nato] AGG unnamed

innovare [inno'vare] /72/ VT to make changes to

innovativo, -a [innova'tivo] AGG innovative

innovazione [innovat'tsjone] SF innovation

innumerevole [innume'revole] AGG innumerable, countless

inoculare [inoku'lare] /72/ VT (*Med*) to inoculate

inodore [ino'dore], **inodoro, -a** [ino'dɔro] AGG (*gen*) odourless (*Brit*), odorless (*USA*); (*fiore*) scentless; **un gas inodore** an odourless gas

inoffensivo, -a [inoffen'sivo] AGG harmless

inoltrare [inol'trare] /72/ VT (*Amm: pratica*) to pass on, forward; (*lettera*) to send on, forward; **inoltrarsi** VIP: **inoltrarsi (in)** to advance (into), go forward (into)

inoltrato, -a [inol'trato] AGG: **a notte inoltrata** late at night; **a primavera inoltrata** late in the spring

inoltre [i'noltre] AVV besides, moreover

inoltro [i'noltro] SM (*Amm*) forwarding

inondare [inon'dare] /72/ VT (*anche fig*) to flood; (*mercato*): **inondare (di)** to flood (with); **la folla inondava la piazza** the crowd flooded into the square; **il sole inondava la stanza** the sun flooded into the room; **le lacrime le inondavano il viso** her face was bathed in tears

inondazione [inondat'tsjone] SF flood, flooding *no pl*

inoperoso, -a [inope'roso] AGG idle, inactive

inopinato, -a [inopi'nato] AGG (*letter*) unexpected

inopportuno, -a [inoppor'tuno] AGG (*poco adatto*) inappropriate; (*intempestivo*) untimely, ill-timed; **è arrivato in un momento inopportuno** he arrived at an awkward *o* inopportune moment

inoppugnabile [inoppuɲ'ɲabile] AGG incontrovertible

inorganico, -a, -ci, -che [inor'ganiko] AGG inorganic

inorgoglire [inorgoʎ'ʎire] /55/ VT to make proud VI (*aus essere*), **inorgoglirsi** VIP to become proud; **inorgoglirsi per qc** to pride o.s. on sth

inorridire [inorri'dire] /55/ VT to horrify; **far inorridire qn** to horrify sb ♦ VI (*aus essere*) to be horrified; **ero inorridito** I was horrified

inospitale [inospi'tale] AGG inhospitable

inosservante [inosser'vante] AGG: **essere inosservante di** to fail to comply with

inosservato, -a [inosser'vato] AGG (*non notato*) unobserved, unnoticed; (*non rispettato*) not observed, not kept; **passare**

inosservato to go unobserved, escape notice; **l'errore non è passato inosservato** the mistake didn't go unnoticed

inossidabile [inossi'dabile] AGG (*acciaio*) stainless; **acciaio inossidabile** stainless steel

INPS ['inps] SIGLA M (= *Istituto Nazionale Previdenza Sociale*) social security service

inquadrare [inkwa'drare] /72/ VT **1** (*foto, immagine*) to frame; **inquadrare un autore nel suo periodo** to place an author in his historical context; **l'ho inquadrato appena l'ho visto** I recognized his sort as soon as I saw him **2** (*Mil*) to regiment; (*personale*) to organize; **inquadrarsi** VIP (*collocarsi*): **inquadrarsi in** to fit in

inquadratura [inkwadra'tura] SF (*Cine, Fot*: *atto*) framing; (: *immagine*) shot; (: *sequenza*) sequence

inqualificabile [inkwalifi'kabile] AGG unspeakable

inquietante [inkwje'tante] AGG disturbing, worrying

inquietare [inkwje'tare] /72/ VT (*preoccupare*) to disturb, worry; (*irritare*) to upset; **inquietarsi** VIP (*vedi vt*) to worry, to get upset

inquieto, -a [in'kwjeto] AGG (*agitato*) restless; (*preoccupato*) worried, anxious; (*arrabbiato*) upset

inquietudine [inkwje'tudine] SF anxiety, worry

inquilino, -a [inkwi'lino] SM, SF tenant

inquinamento [inkwina'mento] SM pollution; **inquinamento acustico** noise pollution; **inquinamento luminoso** light pollution; **inquinamento delle prove** (*Dir*) tampering with the evidence

inquinare [inkwi'nare] /72/ VT to pollute; (*prove*) to contaminate; **le fabbriche hanno inquinato il mare** the factories have polluted the sea

inquirente [inkwi'rente] AGG (*Dir*): **magistrato inquirente** examining (*Brit*) o committing (*USA*) magistrate; **commissione inquirente** commission of inquiry

inquisire [inkwi'zire] /55/ VT, VI (*aus avere*) to investigate

inquisito, -a AGG (*persona*) under investigation ♦ SM person under investigation

inquisitore, -trice [inkwizi'tore] AGG (*sguardo*) inquiring ♦ SM inquisitor

inquisizione [inkwizit'tsjone] SF inquisition

insabbiamento [insabbja'mento] SM (*fig: di pratica*) shelving

insabbiare [insab'bjare] /19/ VT (*fig: pratica*) to shelve; **insabbiarsi** VIP (*barca*) to run aground; (*fig: pratica*) to be shelved

insaccare [insak'kare] /20/ VT (*grano, farina ecc*) to bag, put into sacks; (*carne*) to put into sausage skins

insaccati [insak'kati] SMPL sausages

insalata [insa'lata] SF (*pianta*) lettuce (*or other green-leaf vegetable*); (*piatto*) salad; **hai lavato l'insalata?** have you washed the lettuce?; **insalata di mare** seafood salad; **insalata mista** mixed salad; **insalata di pomodori** tomato salad; **insalata russa** Russian salad; **insalata verde** green salad

insalatiera [insala'tjera] SF salad bowl

insalubre [insa'lubre] AGG insalubrious (*frm*), unhealthy

insanabile [insa'nabile] AGG (*piaga*) that will not heal; (*fig: situazione*) irremediable; **fra di loro si è creata una rottura insanabile** a rift has developed between them which cannot be healed

insanguinare [insangwi'nare] /72/ VT to stain with blood; **arrivò tutto insanguinato** he arrived all covered in blood; **una feroce rivolta insanguinò la Francia** France was plunged into a bloody revolution; **insanguinarsi** VR to get covered in blood

insania [in'sanja] SF (*letter*) insanity

insano, -a [in'sano] AGG (*letter*: *gesto, proposito*) insane

insaponare [insapo'nare] /72/ VT to soap; (*con sapone da barba*) to lather; **insaponarsi le mani** to soap one's hands

insaponata [insapo'nata] SF: **dare un'insaponata a qc** to give sth a (quick) soaping

insapore [insa'pore], **insaporo, -a** [insa'poro] AGG tasteless, insipid

insaporire [insapo'rire] /55/ VT to flavour (*Brit*) o flavor (*USA*); (*con spezie*) to season; **insaporirsi** VIP to gain flavo(u)r

insaputa [insa'puta] SF: **all'insaputa di qn** without sb's knowledge, unbeknown to sb, without sb knowing; **l'ha comprato all'insaputa dei suoi** she bought it without her parents' knowledge

insaziabile [insat'tsjabile] AGG insatiable

inscatolare [inskato'lare] /72/ VT (*frutta, carne*) to can

inscenare [inʃe'nare] /72/ VT (*Teatro*) to stage, put on; (*fig: protesta, sciopero*) to stage; **inscenare una commedia** (*fig*) to put on an act

inscindibile [inʃin'dibile] AGG (*fattori*) inseparable; (*legame*) indissoluble

insecchire [insek'kire] /55/ VT (*seccare*) to dry up; (*piante*) to wither VI (*aus essere*), **insecchirsi** VIP (*vedi vt*) to dry up, become dry; to wither

insediamento [insedja'mento] SM **1** (*Amm: in carica, ufficio*) installation **2** (*villaggio, colonia*) settlement

insediare [inse'djare] /19/ VT (*Amm*) to install; **insediarsi** VIP **1** (*Amm*) to take up office **2** (*colonia, profughi ecc*) to settle; (*Mil*) to take up positions

insegna [in'seɲɲa] SF **1** (*stradale, di negozio*) sign; **insegna al neon** neon sign **2** (*bandiera*) flag, banner; (*emblema*) emblem, sign; **insegne** SFPL (*decorazioni*) insignia *pl*; **un'estate all'insegna del maltempo** a summer marked by bad weather

insegnamento [inseɲɲa'mento] SM teaching; **il suo metodo d'insegnamento** her way of teaching; **che ti serva da insegnamento** let this be a lesson to you; **trarre insegnamento da un'esperienza** to learn from an experience

insegnante [inseɲ'ɲante] AGG teaching *attr* ♦ SM, SF teacher; **fare l'insegnante** to be a teacher; **fa l'insegnante** she's a teacher; **insegnante d'inglese** English teacher; **insegnante di storia** History teacher; **insegnante di sostegno** support teacher

insegnare [inseɲ'ɲare] /15/ VT to teach; **insegnare alle elementari** to be a primary school teacher; **insegnare a qn qc/a fare qc** to teach sb sth/(how) to do sth; **ha insegnato ai bambini i nomi delle piante** she taught the children the names of plants; **mi ha insegnato a suonare la chitarra** she taught me to play the guitar; **vi insegno io a comportarvi bene!** I'll teach you how to behave!; **come lei ben m'insegna...** (*iro*) as you will doubtless be aware ...

inseguimento [insegwi'mento] SM pursuit, chase; **darsi all'inseguimento di qn** to give chase to sb; (*gara di*) **inseguimento** (*Ciclismo*) pursuit (race)

inseguire [inse'gwire] /45/ VT (*anche fig*) to pursue, chase; **la polizia ha inseguito i rapinatori** the police chased the robbers

inseguitore, -trice [insegwi'tore] SM, SF pursuer; (*Ciclismo*) track rider

insellare [insel'lare] /72/ VT (*curvare*) to curve; **insellarsi** VIP (*curvarsi*) to sag

inselvatichire [inselvati'kire] /55/ VT (*persona*) to make unsociable VI (*aus essere*), **inselvatichirsi** VIP (*giardino, animale domestico*) to grow wild; (*persona*) to become unsociable

inseminazione [inseminat'tsjone] SF insemination; **inseminazione artificiale** artificial insemination; **inseminazione artificiale eterologa** AID; **inseminazione artificiale omologa** AIH

insenatura [insena'tura] SF inlet, creek

insensato, -a [insen'sato] AGG senseless, stupid

insensibile [insen'sibile] AGG (*anche fig*) insensitive; **è insensibile al freddo** he doesn't feel the cold; **insensibile ai complimenti** indifferent to compliments

❏ **insensibile** non si traduce mai con la parola inglese *insensible*

insensibilità [insensibili'ta] SF insensitivity, insensibility

inseparabile [insepa'rabile] AGG inseparable

insepolto, -a [inse'polto] AGG unburied

inserimento [inseri'mento] SM (*gen*) insertion; **ha avuto problemi di inserimento nella nuova scuola** he has had problems settling in at his new school

inserire [inse'rire] /55/ VT (*introdurre*) to insert; (*Elettr: spina*) to insert, put in; (*allegare*) to enclose; **bisogna inserire la vite nel foro** you need to put the screw in the hole; **inserire la spina della TV** to plug in the TV; **inserire un annuncio sul giornale** to put o place an advertisement in the newspaper; **inserire un apparecchio in un circuito elettrico** to connect a machine to an electrical circuit; **inserirsi** VR: **inserirsi in** (*ambiente*) to fit into, become part of; **inserirsi** VIP: **inserirsi in** (*contesto*) to be a part of, be included in; **non si è ancora inserito bene nella nuova scuola** he hasn't settled into his new school yet

inserto [in'serto] SM (*pubblicazione*) insert, supplement; **inserto filmato** (*film*) clip

inservibile [inser'vibile] AGG useless

inserviente [inser'vjɛnte] SM, SF attendant

inserzione [inser'tsjone] SF (*aggiunta*) insertion; (*avviso*) advertisement, ad; **mettere un'inserzione sul giornale** to put *o* place an advertisement in the newspaper; **ho messo un'inserzione sul giornale** I put an advert in the paper

inserzionista, -i, -e [insertsjo'nista] SM, SF advertiser

insetticida, -i, -e [insetti'tʃida] AGG, SM insecticide; **una bomboletta d'insetticida** a can of insecticide

insetto [in'setto] SM insect; **è un insetto** (*pegg: persona*) he's a louse

insicurezza [insiku'rettsa] SF insecurity

insicuro, -a [insi'kuro] AGG insecure

insidia [in'sidja] SF (*pericolo*) hidden danger; (*inganno*) trap, snare; **tendere un'insidia a qn** to lay *o* set a trap for sb

insidiare [insi'djare] /19/ VT 1 (*Mil*) to harass 2 **insidiare la vita di qn** to make an attempt on sb's life

insidioso, -a [insi'djoso] AGG insidious

insieme [in'sjɛme] AVV 1 together; **tutti insieme** all together; **stanno bene insieme** (*persone*) they get on well together; (*colori*) they go well together; **quei due stanno proprio bene insieme** (*coppia*) those two make a nice couple; **da quanto tempo state insieme?** how long have you been together?; **stanno insieme da due anni** they have been (going out) together for two years; **si sono messi insieme due anni fa** they started going out together two years ago; **questo libro non sta più insieme** this book is falling apart 2 (*contemporaneamente*) at the same time; **abbiamo finito insieme** we finished together *o* at the same time; **l'ha bevuto tutto insieme** (*in una volta*) he drank it at one go *o* in one draught; **forza, spingete tutti insieme!** come on, everyone push together!; **non parlate tutti insieme, per favore** don't all speak at the same time, please ♦ **insieme a** PREP (together) with; **ha cenato insieme a noi** he had dinner with us; **bevilo insieme al succo di frutta** take it with a drink of fruit juice; **mettilo insieme al mio** put it along with mine ♦ SM 1 (*totalità*) whole; **l'insieme degli elettori** the whole electorate; **l'insieme dei cittadini/degli edifici** all the citizens/buildings; **nell'insieme** on the whole; **nell'insieme mi sembra buono** it seems okay on the whole; **bisogna considerare la cosa nell'insieme** *o* **nel suo insieme** we will have to take an overall view of the matter; **d'insieme** (*sguardo, veduta*) overall, general 2 (*Mat: assortimento*) set; (*Moda*) outfit, ensemble; **nella stanza c'era uno strano insieme di persone/oggetti** there was a strange collection of people/objects in the room

insigne [in'siɲɲe] AGG (*persona*) distinguished, eminent; (*città, monumento*) notable

insignificante [insiɲɲifi'kante] AGG (*gen*) insignificant; (*somma*) trifling, insignificant; **un particolare insignificante** an insignificant detail

insignire [insiɲ'ɲire] /55/ VT: **insignire qn di** to honour (*Brit*) *o* honor (*USA*) sb with, decorate sb with; **insignire qn del titolo di cavaliere** to knight sb

insincero, -a [insin'tʃero] AGG insincere

insindacabile [insinda'kabile] AGG unquestionable, unchallengeable; **la decisione è insindacabile** (*di giuria*) the decision is final

insinuante [insinu'ante] AGG (*osservazione, sguardo*) insinuating; (*maniere*) ingratiating

insinuare [insinu'are] /72/ VT 1 (*introdurre*): **insinuare qc in** to slip *o* slide sth into 2 (*alludere*) to insinuate, imply; **cosa vorresti insinuare?** what are you trying to insinuate?; **insinuarsi** VIP (*umidità, acqua*): **insinuarsi (in qc)** to seep in(to sth), penetrate (sth); **insinuarsi in** to creep into; **insinuarsi** VR (*persona*): **insinuarsi in** to worm one's way into, insinuate o.s. into

insinuazione [insinuat'tsjone] SF insinuation, innuendo; **fare insinuazioni su qn** to make insinuations about sb

insipido, -a [in'sipido] AGG (*anche fig*) insipid

insistente [insis'tɛnte] AGG (*che insiste*) insistent; (*pioggia, dolore*) persistent

insistentemente [insistente'mente] AVV repeatedly, persistently

insistenza [insis'tɛntsa] SF (*vedi agg*) insistence; persistence; **chiedere con insistenza** to ask insistently

insistere [in'sistere] /11/ VI IRREG (*aus* avere) insistere (su qc/a fare qc) to insist (on sth/on doing sth); **insistere (in qc/a fare qc)** (*perseverare*) to persist in sth/in doing sth; se proprio insisti, vengo if you really insist, I'll come; **non insistere, tanto non te lo presto** don't keep on, I'm not going to lend it to you; **è inutile insistere su quell'argomento** there's no point keeping on about this

insistito, -a [insis'tito] PP *di* insistere

insito, -a [in'sito] AGG: **insito (in)** inherent (in)

insoddisfatto, -a [insoddis'fatto] AGG (*persona*) dissatisfied; (*desiderio*) unfulfilled, unsatisfied; **essere insoddisfatto di qc** to be dissatisfied with sth

insoddisfazione [insoddisfat'tsjone] SF dissatisfaction

insofferente [insoffe'rɛnte] AGG (*impaziente*) impatient; (*irrequieto*) edgy

insofferenza [insoffe'rɛntsa] SF impatience

insolazione [insolat'tsjone] SF (*Med*) sunstroke; **prendere un'insolazione** to get sunstroke; **ho preso un'insolazione** I got sunstroke

insolente [inso'lɛnte] AGG insolent ♦ SM, SF insolent person

insolentire [insolen'tire] /55/ VI (*aus* essere) to grow insolent ♦ VT to insult, be rude to

insolenza [inso'lɛntsa] SF (*arroganza*) insolence; (*osservazione*) insolent remark; **è stata un'insolenza da parte sua** (*azione*) that was a piece of insolence on his part

insolito, -a [in'sɔlito] AGG unusual, out of the ordinary, strange

insolubile [inso'lubile] AGG 1 (*problema*) insoluble, insolvable 2 (*sostanza*) insoluble

insoluto, -a [inso'luto] AGG (*problema*) unsolved; (*debito*) unpaid, outstanding

insolvente [insol'vɛnte] AGG (*Dir*) insolvent

insolvenza [insol'vɛntsa] SF (*Dir*) insolvency

insolvibile [insol'vibile] AGG (*Dir*) insolvent

insomma [in'somma] AVV (*in breve, in conclusione*) in short, all in all; (*dunque*) well; **insomma, sei pronta o no?** well, are you ready or not?; **insomma, cosa ti hanno detto?** well, what did they say to you?; **era sporco, scomodo e caro, insomma un disastro!** it was dirty, uncomfortable and expensive - all in all, a disaster! ♦ ESCL: **insomma!** for heaven's sake!; **come stai? — insomma...!** how are you? — not too bad; **insomma, basta!** that's enough!

insondabile [inson'dabile] AGG unfathomable

insonne [in'sonne] AGG (*notte*) sleepless

insonnia [in'sɔnnja] SF insomnia, sleeplessness; **soffrire d'insonnia** (*Med*) to suffer from insomnia; **da un po' di tempo soffro d'insonnia** I haven't been able to sleep lately

insonnolito, -a [insonno'lito] AGG sleepy, drowsy; **è sempre più insonnolito** he's getting sleepier and sleepier

insonorizzazione [insonoriddzat'tsjone] SF soundproofing

insopportabile [insoppor'tabile] AGG unbearable; **c'è una puzza insopportabile qui dentro** there's a horrible smell in here

insopprimibile [insoppri'mibile] AGG unsuppressible, insuppressible

insorgenza [insor'dʒɛntsa] SF (*di malattia*) onset

insorgere [in'sordʒere] /109/ VI IRREG (*aus* essere) 1 (*ribellarsi*): **insorgere (contro)** to rise up (against), rebel (against) 2 (*manifestarsi improvvisamente*) to arise, come *o* crop up

insormontabile [insormon'tabile] AGG (*ostacolo*) unsurmountable, insurmountable, insuperable

insorsi ecc [in'sorsi] VB *vedi* insorgere

insorto, -a [in'sorto] PP *di* insorgere ♦ AGG: **il popolo insorto** the rebels, the insurgents ♦ SM, SF rebel, insurgent

insospettabile [insospet'tabile] AGG 1 (*al di sopra di ogni sospetto*) above suspicion 2 (*inatteso*) unsuspected

insospettire [insospet'tire] /55/ VT to make suspicious, arouse suspicions in; **il suo atteggiamento mi ha insos-pettito** her behaviour made me suspicious VI *(aus* **essere)**, **insospettirsi** VIP: **insospettirsi (per/di qc)** to become suspicious (because of/about sth); **si è insospettito e ha chiamato la polizia** he became suspicious and called the police

insostenibile [insoste'nibile] AGG 1 *(posizione, teoria)* untenable 2 *(dolore, situazione)* intolerable, unbearable; **le spese di manutenzione sono insostenibili** the maintenance costs are prohibitive

insostituibile [insostitu'ibile] AGG *(persona)* irreplaceable; *(aiuto, presenza)* invaluable

insozzare [insot'tsare] /**72**/ VT 1 *(pavimento)* to (make) dirty 2 *(fig: reputazione, memoria di qn)* to tarnish, sully; **insozzarsi** VR, VIP to get dirty

insperabile [inspe'rabile] AGG: **la guarigione/salvezza era insperabile** there was no hope of a cure/of rescue; **abbiamo ottenuto risultati insperabili** the results we achieved were beyond our expectations

insperato, -a [inspe'rato] AGG unhoped-for

inspiegabile [inspje'gabile] AGG inexplicable

inspirare [inspi'rare] /**72**/ VT to inhale, breathe in

instabile [in'stabile] AGG *(carico, carattere, situazione)* unstable; *(tempo)* unsettled, changeable; *(umore)* uncertain, changeable; *(equilibrio)* unsteady; **la situazione politica è un po' instabile** the political situation is rather unstable; **il tempo è ancora instabile** the weather is still unsettled; **la sedia è un po' instabile** the chair is a bit unsteady

instabilità [instabili'ta] SF *(gen)* instability; *(del tempo)* changeability; *(di umore)* inconstancy

installare [instal'lare] /**72**/ VT *(impianto, telefono)* to install, put in; **installarsi** VR: **installarsi in** *(sistemarsi)* to set up house, settle in; **si è installata in casa mia** *(scherz)* she has taken up residence at my house

installazione [installat'tsjone] SF 1 *(di telefono ecc)* installation 2 *(impianto)* system; **installazioni di bordo** *(Aer, Naut)* on-board equipment

instancabile [instan'kabile] AGG tireless, untiring

instaurare [instau'rare] /**72**/ VT *(regola, sistema)* to establish, institute; *(moda ecc)* to introduce; **instaurarsi** VIP to be o become established

instaurazione [instaurat'tsjone] SF *(vedi vt)* establishment, institution; introduction

instillare [instil'lare] /**72**/ VT to instil

instradare [instra'dare] /**72**/ VT = **istradare**

insù [in'su] AVV up, upwards; **guardare all'insù** to look up o upwards; **naso all'insù** turned-up nose

insubordinazione [insubordinat'tsjone] SF insubordination

insuccesso [insut'tʃesso] SM failure, flop

insudiciare [insudi'tʃare] /**14**/ VT to dirty, soil; *(fig: reputazione, nome)* to sully, tarnish; **insudiciarsi i vestiti** to get one's clothes dirty, dirty one's clothes; **insudiciarsi** VR, VIP to get dirty

insufficiente [insuffi'tʃente] AGG 1 **insufficiente a** o **per** *(quantità)* insufficient (for); *(qualità)* inadequate (for); **il cibo è insufficiente** there's not enough food; **200 sterline al mese sono insufficienti per vivere** £200 a month is not enough o sufficient to live on 2 *(Scol: voto)* unsatisfactory; *(: compito)* below standard

insufficienza [insuffi'tʃentsa] SF 1 *(di denaro, viveri)* shortage; *(di tempo, spazio)* lack; *(di preparazione)* inadequacy; *(Med)* insufficiency; **insufficienza di prove** *(Dir)* lack of evidence; **l'hanno assolto per insufficienza di prove** he was acquitted because of lack of evidence 2 *(Scol)* fail; **prendere un'insufficienza in** to fail; **ho preso un'insufficienza in chimica** I got a fail in chemistry

insulare [insu'lare] AGG island *attr*

insulina [insu'lina] SF *(Chim)* insulin

insulso, -a [in'sulso] AGG *(persona)* dull, insipid; *(osservazione)* inane, silly; *(film, romanzo)* crass, silly; **fa discorsi sempre più insulsi** the things he says get sillier and sillier; **è una delle persone più insulse che abbia mai conosciuto** he's one of the dullest people I've ever met

insultare [insul'tare] /**72**/ VT to insult

insulto [in'sulto] SM insult, affront; **coprire qn di insulti** to hurl abuse at sb, heap abuse on sb

insuperabile [insupe'rabile] AGG 1 *(ostacolo, difficoltà)* insuperable, unsurmountable, insurmountable 2 *(eccellente: qualità, prodotto)* unbeatable; *(: persona, interpretazione)* unequalled

insuperbire [insuper'bire] /**55**/ VT to make proud, make arrogant; **il successo lo ha insuperbito** success has gone to his head VI *(aus* **essere)**, **insuperbirsi** VIP to become arrogant

insurrezione [insurret'tsjone] SF insurrection, revolt

insussistente [insussis'tente] AGG *(accusa, paura)* unfounded, groundless; *(pericolo)* non-existent

intaccare [intak'kare] /**20**/ VT 1 *(sogg: ruggine)* to corrode; *(: acido)* to eat into; **non vorrei intaccare i miei risparmi** I wouldn't want to break into my savings 2 *(fare tacche in)* to cut into, nick 3 *(infettare, anche fig: reputazione)* to affect, damage

intagliare [intaʎ'ʎare] /**27**/ VT *(pietre)* to engrave, carve; *(legno)* to carve

intagliatore, -trice [intaʎʎa'tore] SM, SF engraver

intaglio, -gli [in'taʎʎo] SM intaglio

intangibile [intan'dʒibile] AGG 1 *(eredità, patrimonio)* tied-up 2 *(fig: diritto)* inviolable; *(: differenza)* intangible

intanto [in'tanto] AVV *(nel frattempo)* meanwhile, in the meantime; *(per cominciare)* just to begin with; **intanto che** while; **intanto che aspetti leggiti questo** you can read this while you're waiting; **intanto prendi questo, poi ti darò il resto** take this for now o the time being and I'll give you the rest later; **sì, sì, intanto tocca sempre a me farlo!** yes, yes, but it's always me who has to do it!; **mettiti il cappotto, io intanto chiamo un taxi** put on your coat while I get a taxi

intarsiare [intar'sjare] /**19**/ VT to inlay

intarsio, -si [in'tarsjo] SM *(arte, tecnica)* inlaying *no pl*, marquetry *no pl*; *(parte lavorata)* marquetry, inlay; **mobili lavorati a intarsio** inlaid furniture

intasamento [intasa'mento] SM *(ostruzione)* blockage, obstruction; *(Aut: ingorgo)* traffic jam

intasare [inta'sare] /**72**/ VT *(tubo)* to block (up); *(traffico)* to hold up; **ho il naso intasato** I've got a blocked o stuffed-up nose; **intasarsi** VIP to become choked o blocked

intascare [intas'kare] /**20**/ VT *(denaro, premio)* to pocket

intatto, -a [in'tatto] AGG *(gen)* intact; *(puro)* unsullied; **la neve era intatta** there were no footprints in the snow

intavolare [intavo'lare] /**72**/ VT *(discussione, trattative)* to open, start, enter into

integerrimo, -a [inte'dʒerrimo] AGG honest, upright; **è un uomo integerrimo** he's a man of the utmost integrity

integrale [inte'grale] AGG 1 *(gen)* complete; *(rimborso)* full; *(pane, farina)* wholemeal *(Brit)*, wholewheat *(USA)*; **pane integrale** wholemeal bread; **abbronzatura integrale** all-over tan; **edizione integrale** unabridged edition; **film in versione integrale** uncut version of a film; **auto a trazione integrale** four-wheel drive vehicle 2 *(Mat)* integral ♦ SM *(Mat)* integral

integrante [inte'grante] AGG: **essere parte integrante di** to be an integral part of

integrare [inte'grare] /**72**/ VT 1 *(completare)* to complete; *(personale)* to bring up to strength; *(stipendio, dieta ecc)* to supplement; **integra il proprio stipendio dando lezioni private** he supplements his income by giving private lessons 2 *(Sociol, Mat)* to integrate; **integrarsi** VIP *(Sociol)* to become integrated

integrativo, -a [integra'tivo] AGG *(assegno)* supplementary; *(Scol)*: **esame integrativo** assessment sat when changing schools; **pensione integrativa** personal pension

integratore [integra'tore] SM: **integratori alimentari** nutritional supplements

integrazione [integrat'tsjone] SF integration

integrità [integri'ta] SF 1 *(interezza: di patrimonio)* intact state; **tutelare l'integrità fisica dei prigionieri** to guarantee the physical well-being of (the) prisoners 2 *(onestà)* integrity, honesty, uprightness

integro, -a ['integro] AGG 1 *(intero)* intact, complete, whole 2 *(onesto)* honest, upright

intelaiatura [intelaja'tura] SF *(Edil)* skeleton, framework, frame; *(fig: economica, sociale)* framework, structure

intelletto [intel'letto] SM intellect; **perdere il ben dell'intelletto** (*impazzire*) to go out of one's mind

intellettuale [intellettu'ale] AGG intellectual; **sforzo intellettuale** mental effort ♦ SM, SF intellectual

intellettualoide [intellettua'lɔide](*pegg*) AGG (*atteggiamento*) highbrow, pseudo-intellectual ♦ SM, SF pseudo-intellectual, would-be intellectual

intelligente [intelli'dʒente] AGG (*gen*) intelligent; (*brillante*) clever, bright; (*capace*) clever, able; **missile intelligente** smart missile

intelligenza [intelli'dʒentsa] SF intelligence; **ha un'intelligenza viva** he's got a quick *o* sharp mind; **è una bella intelligenza** he has a fine mind *o* a good brain; **un lavoro fatto con intelligenza** a clever piece of work; **giocato con intelligenza** cleverly played; **intelligenza artificiale** artificial intelligence

intellighenzia [intelli'gentsia] SF intelligentsia

intelligibile [intelli'dʒibile] AGG intelligible; **ripetilo in modo chiaro e intelligibile** repeat it loudly and clearly; **un messaggio poco intelligibile** an unclear message; **ha una scrittura chiara e intelligibile** he has clear, legible handwriting

intemerato, -a [inteme'rato](*letter*) AGG (*persona, vita*) blameless, irreproachable; (*coscienza*) clear; (*fama*) unblemished

intemperante [intempe'rante] AGG intemperate, immoderate

intemperanza [intempe'rantsa] SF (*qualità*) intemperance; **intemperanze** (*eccessi*) excesses

intemperie [intem'pɛrje] SFPL bad weather *sg*; **esposto alle intemperie** exposed to the elements; **resistente alle intemperie** weatherproof

intempestivo, -a [intempes'tivo] AGG (*intervento*) untimely, ill-timed

intendente [inten'dente] SM: **intendente di Finanza** inland (*Brit*) *o* internal (*USA*) revenue officer

intendenza [inten'dentsa] SF: **intendenza di Finanza** inland (*Brit*) *o* internal (*USA*) revenue office

intendere [in'tendere] VB IRREG /120/ VT 1 (*avere intenzione*): **intendere fare qc** to intend *o* mean to do sth, have the intention of doing sth; **non intendo farlo** I have no intention of doing it, I don't intend to do it 2 (*significare*) to mean; **cosa intendevi (dire)?** what did you mean?; **dipende da cosa intendi per "giustizia"** it depends what you mean by "justice" 3 (*capire*) to understand; **mi ha dato a intendere che...** he led me to believe that ...; **ha lasciato intendere che...** he gave (me *o* us) to understand that ...; **ma io non la intendo così** I don't see things that way; **puoi intenderla come vuoi** you can take it how you like; **non riesce a farsi intendere** he cannot make himself understood; **s'intende!** naturally!, of course!; **s'intende che verrai anche tu!** you'll be coming too, of course! 4 (*udire*) to hear; **ho inteso dire che...** I've heard (it said) that ...; **non vuole intendere ragione** he won't listen to reason; **intendersi** VR (*uso reciproco*: *capirsi*) to understand each other, get on (well); **intendersi con qn su qc** (*accordarsi*) to come to an agreement with sb about sth; **intendiamoci** let's get it quite clear; **ci siamo intesi?** is that clear?, is that understood?; **cominciamo a intenderci** we're beginning to understand each other; **intendersi** VIP 1 (*conoscere bene*): **intendersi di qc** to know a lot about sth (*cibi, vini*) to be a connoisseur of sth; **si intende di fotografia** she knows about photography; **me ne intendo poco** I know very little about it 2 (*avere una relazione amorosa*): **intendersela (con qn)** to have an affair with sb

intendimento [intendi'mento] SM (*proposito*) intention

intenditore, -trice [intendi'tore] SM, SF expert; (*di vini, cibi*) connoisseur; **a buon intendítor poche parole** (*Proverbio*) a word to the wise ...; **un intenditore di vini** a connoisseur of wine

intenerire [intene'rire] /55/ VT (*commuovere*) to touch, move (to pity); **intenerirsi** VIP to be touched, be moved

intensificare [intensifi'kare] /20/ VT, **intensificarsi** VIP to intensify, increase

intensità [intensi'ta] SF INV (*gen, anche Fis*) intensity; (*del vento*) force, strength

intensivo, -a [inten'sivo] AGG intensive

intenso, -a [in'tenso] AGG (*gen*) intense; (*profumo*) strong; (*luce*) bright; (*colore*) intense, deep; **un calore intenso** intense heat; **una luce intensa** a bright light; **il traffico è più intenso attorno alle otto** the traffic is heaviest around eight; **ho avuto un pomeriggio intenso** I had a busy afternoon

intentare [inten'tare] /72/ VT (*Dir*): **intentare causa a** *o* **contro qn** to start *o* institute proceedings against sb

intentato, -a [inten'tato] AGG: **non lasciare nulla d'intentato** to leave no stone unturned, try everything

intento¹, -a [in'tento] AGG intent; **essere intento a qc/a fare qc** to be intent on sth/absorbed in doing sth

intento² [in'tento] SM intention, aim, purpose; **fare qc con l'intento di** to do sth with the intention of; **riuscire nell'intento** to achieve one's aim

intenzionale [intentsjo'nale] AGG (*gen*) intentional, deliberate; (*Dir*: *omicidio*) premeditated; **fallo intenzionale** (*Sport*) deliberate foul

intenzionato, -a [intentsjo'nato] AGG: **essere intenzionato a fare qc** to intend *o* do sth, have the intention of doing sth; **ben intenzionato** well-meaning, well-intentioned; **mal intenzionato** ill-intentioned

intenzione [inten'tsjone] SF intention; **avere (l')intenzione di fare qc** to intend *o* do sth, have the intention of doing sth; **avevo intenzione di andare ma poi ho cambiato idea** I meant to go but then I changed my mind; **non avevo intenzione di offenderti** I didn't mean to offend you; **è mia intenzione farlo** I intend to do it; **non era mia intenzione offenderti** I didn't mean to offend you; **è l'intenzione che conta** it's the thought that counts; **non so quali sono le sue intenzioni** I don't know what her intentions are; **con intenzione** intentionally, deliberately; **senza intenzione** unintentionally; **secondo l'intenzione** *o* **le intenzioni di qn** in accordance with sb's wishes; **animato dalle migliori intenzioni** with the best of intentions

interagire [intera'dʒire] /55/ VI (*aus* avere) to interact

interamente [intera'mente] AVV entirely, completely

interattivo, -a [interat'tivo] AGG interactive

interazione [interat'tsjone] SF interaction

intercalare [interka'lare] /72/ VT: **intercalare a, intercalare in** (*testo, discorso ecc*) to insert into ♦ SM pet phrase, stock phrase; **il suo intercalare preferito è "cioè"** one of his favourite expressions is "cioè"

intercapedine [interka'pedine] SF gap, cavity

intercedere [inter't∫edere] /29/ VI (*aus* avere) intercedere (**presso/in favore di**) to intercede (with/on behalf of)

intercessione [intert∫es'sjone] SF intercession

intercettare [intert∫et'tare] /72/ VT (*gen, anche Sport, Telec*) to intercept

intercettazione [intert∫ettat'tsjone], **intercettamento** [intert∫etta'mento] SF interception; **intercettazione ambientale** electronic surveillance; **intercettazione telefonica** telephone tapping

intercity [inter'siti] SM INV (*Ferr*) ≈ intercity (train)

interconnettere [interkon'nettere] /63/ VT IRREG to interconnect

intercorrere [inter'korrere] /28/ VI IRREG (*aus* essere) 1 (*passare*: *tempo*) to elapse 2 (*esserci*) to exist; **fra loro intercorrono ottimi rapporti** they are on the very best of terms

intercorso, -a [inter'korso] PP *di* intercorrere

❏ **intercorso** non si traduce mai con la parola inglese *intercourse*

interdetto, -a [inter'detto] PP *di* interdire ♦ AGG (*sconcertato*) dumbfounded; **rimanere interdetto** to be taken aback; **lasciare qn interdetto** to take sb aback, dumbfound ♦ SM (*Rel, Dir*) interdict

interdire [inter'dire] /38/ VT IRREG (*gen, vietare*) to forbid, ban, prohibit; (*Rel*) to interdict; (*Dir*) to deprive of civil rights; **interdire qn dai pubblici uffici** to ban *o* debar sb from public office

interdizione [interdit'tsjone] SF (*divieto*) prohibition, ban; (*Rel*) interdict; (*Dir*) debarment; **interdizione legale** deprivation of civil rights

interessamento [interessa'mento] SM (*interesse*) interest; (*intervento*) intervention, good offices *pl*; **grazie al suo**

interessamento sono riuscito ad avere il lavoro it was thanks to his good offices that I managed to get the job

interessante [interes'sante] AGG (gen) interesting; **essere in stato interessante** (fam) to be expecting (a baby)

interessare [interes'sare] /72/ VI (aus essere) **interessare (a qn)** to interest (sb); **forse ti interesserà sapere che...** perhaps you might be interested to know that ...; **se ti interessa ti posso dare il suo indirizzo** if you are interested I can give you his address; **non m'interessa!** I'm not interested!; **a lui non interessano che i suoi libri** he's only interested in his books; **ci interessa che tutto vada bene** what matters to us is that everything should go o goes well ♦ VT **1** (suscitare interesse) to interest; **interessare qn a qc** to interest sb in sth **2** (riguardare) to affect, concern; **la notizia interesserà gli appassionati di cinema** the news will interest cinema fans; **precipitazioni che interessano le regioni settentrionali** rainfall affecting the north; **un provvedimento che interessa gli automobilisti** a regulation affecting o concerning motorists **3** (Comm): **interessare qn in** (utili) to give sb a share o an interest in; **interessarsi** VIP **1** (mostrare curiosità): **interessarsi (a)** to show interest (in); **si è interessato molto a quel progetto** he showed a lot of interest in the project **2** (occuparsi): **interessarsi di** o **a** (politica, pittura ecc) to be interested in, take an interest in; **non mi interesso di politica** I'm not interested in politics; **si sono interessati al suo caso** they took up his case; **si è interessato alla mia promozione** he helped me get a promotion; **si è interessato di farmi avere quei biglietti** he took the trouble to get me those tickets; **interessati degli affari tuoi!** mind your own business!

interessato, -a [interes'sato] AGG **1** (coinvolto) interested, involved; **le parti interessate** the interested parties; **le regioni interessate dal maltempo** the regions affected by the bad weather **2** (pegg): **essere interessato** to act out of self-interest ♦ SM, SF (coinvolto) person concerned; **a tutti gli interessati** to all those concerned, to all interested parties

interesse [inte'resse] SM **1** (gen) interest; **ho sempre avuto un certo interesse per...** I've always had a certain interest in ..., I've always been rather interested in ...; **ha ascoltato con grande interesse** she listened with great interest **2** (affare, attività): **badare ai propri interessi** to look after one's own interests o affairs; **ha degli interessi in quell'azienda** he has a financial interest in that company; **curare gli interessi del proprio cliente** (avvocato) to act in the interests of one's client; **interesse privato in atti di ufficio** (Amm) abuse of public office **3** (tornaconto): **fare qc per interesse** to do sth out of self-interest; **non pensa che a fare il proprio interesse** he only thinks of his own interests; **nell'interesse dell'umanità** in the interests of mankind; **agire nell'interesse comune** to act for the common good o in the common interest; **non ho alcun interesse a farlo, non è nel mio interesse farlo** it is not in my interest to do it; **lo dico nel tuo interesse** I'm saying this for your own good; **quando c'è di mezzo l'interesse...** when personal interests are involved ... **4** (Fin, Comm) interest; **un interesse del 5%** 5% interest; **interesse composto** compound interest; **interesse maturato** accrued interest; **interesse semplice** simple interest

interessenza [interes'sentsa] SF (Econ) profit-sharing

interfaccia [inter'fatt∫a] SF INV (Inform) interface; **interfaccia utente** user interface

interfacciare [interfat't∫are] /14/ VT (Inform) to interface

interferenza [interfe'rentsa] SF (gen, anche Tecn) interference; **ci sono delle interferenze nella linea** (Telec) there is interference on the line

interferire [interfe'rire] /55/ VI (aus avere) **interferire (in)** to interfere (in); **non interferire in questa faccenda!** don't interfere in this!

interfono [inter'fono] SM intercom (fam); (in una casa) house phone, internal phone

interiezione [interjet'tsjone] SF (Gramm) interjection, exclamation

interim ['interim] SM INV **1** (periodo) interim, interval; **ministro ad interim** acting o interim minister **2** (incarico) temporary appointment

interinale [interi'nale] AGG: **lavoro interinale** temporary work (through an agency)

interiora [inte'rjora] SFPL entrails pl

interiore [inte'rjore] AGG **1** (interno) inner attr; **parte interiore** inside **2** (fig: vita, mondo) inner attr

interiorità [interjori'ta] SF inner being

interiorizzare [interjorid'dzare] /72/ VT to internalize

interlinea [inter'linea] SF **1** (Dattilografia) line spacing; **interlinea doppia** double spacing **2** (Tip) lead, leading

interlocutore, -trice [interloku'tore] SM, SF speaker; **il suo interlocutore** the person he was speaking to

interlocutorio, -ria, -ri, -rie [interloku'torjo] AGG interlocutory

interludio, -di [inter'ludjo] SM (Mus, anche fig) interlude

intermediario, -ria, -ri, -rie [interme'djarjo] AGG intermediary ♦ SM, SF intermediary, go-between; (Comm, Econ) middleman

intermediazione [intermedjat'tsjone] SF mediation

intermedio, -dia, -di, -die [inter'mεdjo] AGG intermediate attr

intermezzo [inter'mεddzo] SM (intervallo) interval; (breve spettacolo) interlude

interminabile [intermi'nabile] AGG interminable, endless, never-ending

intermittente [intermit'tente] AGG intermittent

intermittenza [intermit'tentsa] SF: **ad intermittenza** intermittent

internamento [interna'mento] SM (vedi vb) internment; confinement (to a psychiatric hospital)

internare [inter'nare] /72/ VT (Pol) to intern; (Med) to confine to a psychiatric hospital

internato[1], -a [inter'nato] (vedi vb) AGG interned; confined (to a psychiatric hospital) ♦ SM, SF internee; inmate (of a psychiatric hospital)

internato[2] [inter'nato] SM **1** (collegio) boarding school **2** (di medico) period as a houseman (Brit) o an intern (USA)

internauta, -i, -e [inter'nauta] SM, SF web o net surfer

internazionale [internattsjo'nale] AGG international ♦ SF: **l'Internazionale** (Pol: associazione) the International; (: inno) the Internationale

internet ['internet] SM internet; **in internet** on the internet

internista, -i, -e [inter'nista] SM, SF internist

interno, -a [in'terno] AGG (gen, anche Med) internal; (tasca) inside attr; (regione, navigazione, mare) inland attr; (politica, commercio) domestic; **alunno interno** boarder; **la politica interna** domestic policy; **commissione interna** (Scol) internal examination board; **la tasca interna della giacca** the inside pocket of the jacket; **i confini interni dell'Unione europea** the internal borders of the European Union ♦ SM **1** (di edificio) inside, interior; (di scatola) inside; (di cappotto: fodera) lining; **dall'interno** from the inside; **all'interno (della casa)** inside (the house); **c'erano ancora venti persone all'interno della discoteca** there were still twenty people inside the club; **l'interno della scatola è rosso** the inside of the box is red **2** (Cine): **interni** SM interior shots; **girare gli interni** to film the indoor shots **3** (di paese) interior; **regioni dell'interno** inland areas, areas of the interior; **notizie dall'interno** (Stampa) home news; **Ministero degli Interni** Ministry of the Interior, ≈ Home Office (Brit), ≈ Department of the Interior (USA) **4** (di telefono) extension; (di appartamento) flat (Brit) o apartment (USA) (number); **vorrei l'interno trentadue** can I have extension thirty two, please?; **abita in Via Mangili 6, 2° piano, interno 5** he lives at number 6 Via Mangili, 2nd floor, flat 5 ♦ SM, SF (Scol) boarder

intero, -a [in'tero] AGG **1** (gen) whole, entire; (quantità) whole, full; (Mat: numero) whole; **latte intero** full-cream milk; **ti ho aspettato per un'ora intera** I waited for you for a whole o full hour; **ho trascorso l'intera settimana a studiare** I spent the whole week studying; **a prezzo intero** at full price; **pagare il prezzo intero** to pay the full price; **ha ingoiato una prugna tutta intera** he swallowed a plum whole; **ho trascorso l'intera settimana a studiare** I spent the whole o entire week studying; **ha girato il mondo intero** he's travelled all over the world; **è rimasto intero** it remained intact; **ho 500 euro interi, me li cambi?** I have a 500 euro note, can you give me change for it? ◆ SM (*anche Mat*) whole; **scrivere per intero qc** to write sth in full

interpellanza [interpel'lantsa] SF (*Pol: anche:* **interpellanza parlamentare**) (parliamentary) question; **presentare un'interpellanza** to ask a (parliamentary) question

interpellare [interpel'lare] /72/ VT (*consultare*) to consult, ask; (*Pol*) to question

Interpol [inter'pɔl] SF Interpol

interporre [inter'porre] VB IRREG /77/ VT **1** (*ostacoli, difficoltà*): **interporre qc a qc** to put sth in the way of sth; (*influenza*) to use; **ha interposto i suoi buoni uffici per aiutarlo** he used his good offices to help him **2 interporre appello** (*Dir*) to appeal; **interporsi** VIP (*intervenire*) to intervene; **interporsi fra** (*mettersi in mezzo*) to come between

interposto, -a [inter'posto] PP *di* **interporre** ◆ AGG: **per interposta persona** through a third party

interpretare [interpre'tare] /72/ VT **1** (*gen, spiegare, tradurre, capire*) to interpret; **interpretare male** to misinterpret; **forse hai interpretato male quello che ha detto** perhaps you misunderstood what he said; **non so come interpretare il suo comportamento** I don't know how to interpret his behaviour **2** (*Mus, Teatro*) to perform; (*personaggio, sonata*) to play; (*canzone*) to sing; **ha interpretato il ruolo di Robin Hood** he played the part of Robin Hood

interpretariato [interpreta'rjato] SM interpreting

interpretazione [interpretat'tsjone] SF interpretation

interprete [in'terprete] SM, SF **1** (*traduttore*) interpreter; (*portavoce*): **farsi interprete di** to act as a spokesman for; **fa l'interprete** she is an interpreter **2** (*Teatro, Cine*) performer, actor (actress); (*Mus*) performer

interpunzione [interpun'tsjone] SF punctuation; **segni di interpunzione** punctuation marks

interrare [inter'rare] /72/ VT **1** (*seme, pianta*) to plant; (*tubature, cavi*) to lay underground; (*Mil: pezzo d'artiglieria*) to dig in **2** (*riempire di terra: canale*) to fill in

interregionale [interredʒo'nale] SM *train that travels between two or more regions of Italy, stopping frequently*

interrogare [interro'gare] /80/ VT (*gen*) to question; (*Dir*) to examine; (*Scol*) to examine, test; **essere interrogato** to have an oral test; **sono stato interrogato in storia oggi** I had an oral test in history today; **mi ha interrogato in matematica** he examined me in math(s); **l'insegnante di inglese mi ha interrogato sul futuro** the English teacher tested me on the future tense; **la polizia vuole interrogarlo** the police want to question him; **lo interrogarono in merito agli ultimi avvenimenti** they questioned him regarding recent events; **interrogare gli astri** (*Astrol*) to consult the stars

interrogativo, -a [interroga'tivo] AGG (*sguardo, espressione*) questioning, inquiring; (*Gramm*) interrogative; **punto interrogativo** (*anche fig*) question mark ◆ SM question; (*fig: persona, futuro*) mystery; **porsi un interrogativo** to ask o.s. a question

interrogatorio, -ri [interroga'tɔrjo] SM questioning *no pl*; (*più severo*) interrogation; **subire un interrogatorio** to be questioned; (*anche fig*) to be interrogated

interrogazione [interrogat'tsjone] SF **1** (*Scol*): **interrogazione (di)** (oral) examination (in), oral test (in); **interrogazione ciclica** (*Inform*) polling **2** (*Pol*): **interrogazione (parlamentare)** (parliamentary) question

interrompere [inter'rompere] VB IRREG /97/ VT (*viaggio, studi, trattative*) to interrupt, break off; (*conversazione*) to interrupt; (*gravidanza*) to terminate; (*Elettr: circuito*) to break; **interrompere l'erogazione del gas/dell'acqua** to cut off the gas/water supply; **le comunicazioni con il nord sono interrotte** the north is cut off; **scusa se t'interrompo** excuse me for interrupting; **non interrompere!** don't interrupt!; **interrompersi** VIP (*gen*) to break off, stop; (*corrente, linea telefonica*) to be cut off; (*circuito elettrico*) to be broken; (*trasmissione*) to be interrupted

interrotto, -a [inter'rotto] PP *di* **interrompere**

interruttore [interrut'tore] SM switch; **l'interruttore della luce** the light switch

interruzione [interrut'tsjone] SF (*azione*) interruption; (*stato*) break, interruption; **senza interruzione** (*lavorare*) without a break; (*dormire, parlare*) non-stop; **interruzione di gravidanza** termination of pregnancy

intersecare [interse'kare] /20/ VT, **intersecarsi** VR (*uso reciproco*) to intersect

interstizio, -zi [inter'stittsjo] SM interstice

interurbano, -a [interur'bano] AGG intercity *attr*; (*Telec: telefonata*) long-distance *attr* ◆ SF (*Telec*) long-distance call

intervallo [inter'vallo] SM **1** (*di tempo: Teatro, Cine, Mus*) interval; (*a scuola*) break; (*in ufficio*) (tea *o* coffee) break; (*Sport: fra due tempi*) half-time; **nell'intervallo** in the interval; at half-time; during break; **fare un intervallo di 10 minuti** to have a 10-minute break; **a intervalli regolari** at regular intervals **2** (*di spazio*) space, gap; **a intervalli di 10 cm** at intervals of 10 cm, every 10 cm

intervenire [interve'nire] /128/ VI IRREG (*aus* **essere**) **1 intervenire (in)** (*discussione*) to intervene (in); **è intervenuto nella discussione** he intervened in the discussion; **intervenire** (*riunione, cerimonia, manifestazione*) to take part in; **tutti possono intervenire alla riunione** everybody can take part in the meeting; **hanno dovuto far intervenire l'esercito** the army had to be brought in; **i vigili del fuoco sono intervenuti immediatamente** the firemen took immediate action **2** (*insorgere: nuovi elementi*) to arise **3** (*Med: operare*) to operate; **intervenire d'urgenza su un paziente** to perform emergency surgery on a patient

interventista, -i, -e [interven'tista] AGG, SM, SF interventionist

intervento [inter'vento] SM **1** (*gen, anche Pol, Mil*) intervention; **politica del non intervento** policy of non-intervention; **l'intervento militare americano** the American military intervention; **hanno chiesto l'intervento della polizia** they asked for police assistance, they asked the police to intervene; **un intervento falloso** (*Sport*) a foul **2** (*breve discorso*) speech; (*partecipazione*) participation; **fare un intervento nel corso di** (*dibattito, programma*) to take part in; **un intervento interessante** an interesting speech **3** (*Med*) operation; **subire un intervento** to be operated on, have an operation; **ha subito un intervento delicato** he's had a complicated operation

intervenuto, -a [interve'nuto] PP *di* **intervenire** ◆ SM, SF: **gli intervenuti** those present

intervista [inter'vista] SF interview; **fare un'intervista a qn** to interview sb; **non concede interviste** she doesn't give interviews

intervistare [intervis'tare] /72/ VT to interview; **è stato intervistato alla TV** he was interviewed on TV

intervistatore, -trice [intervista'tore] SM, SF interviewer

inteso, -a [in'teso] PP *di* **intendere** ◆ AGG **1** (*pattuito*) agreed; (*capito*) understood; **resta inteso che...** it is understood that ...; **non darsi per inteso di qc** to take no notice of sth; **siamo intesi?** ok? **2** (*destinato*): **inteso a fare qc** intended to do sth

intessere [in'tessere] /1/ VT to weave together; (*fig: trama, storia*) to weave; **intessere lodi a qn** to sing sb's praises

intestare [intes'tare] /72/ VT **1** (*lettera, busta*) to address **2** **intestare a** (*casa, proprietà*) to register in the name of; **a chi è intestata la macchina?** whose name is the car registered in?; **intestare un assegno a qn** to make out a cheque to sb

intestatario, -ria, -ri, -rie [intesta'tarjo] SM, SF holder

intestato, -a [intes'tato] AGG (*proprietà, casa, conto*) in the name of; (*assegno*) made out to; **carta intestata** headed paper; **la macchina è intestata a lui** the car is registered in his name

intestazione [intestat'tsjone] SF (*gen*) heading; (*su carta da lettere*) letterhead; **qual è l'intestazione dell'assegno?** who is the cheque made out to?

intestinale [intesti'nale] AGG intestinal

intestino, -a [intes'tino] AGG (*lotte*) internal; **guerra intestina** civil war ◆ SM (*Anat*) intestine; **intestino tenue/crasso** small/large intestine

intiepidire [intjepi'dire] /55/ VT (*riscaldare*) to warm (up); (*raffreddare*) to cool (down); (*fig: amicizia ecc*) to cool; **intiepidirsi** VIP (*vedi vt*) to warm (up); to cool (down); to cool

Intifada [inti'fada] SF Intifada

intimamente [intima'mente] AVV intimately; **sono intimamente convinto che...** I'm firmly *o* deeply convinced that ...; **i due fatti sono intimamente connessi** the two events are closely connected

intimare [inti'mare] /72/ VT (*ordinare*) to order, command;

(*notificare*) to give notice of; **intimare a qn di fare qc** to order sb to do sth; **intimare la resa a qn** (*Mil*) to call upon sb to surrender; **intimare l'alt** to order sb to stop *o* halt; **intimare lo sfratto a qn** (*Dir*) to serve an eviction notice *o* order on sb

❑ **intimare** non si traduce mai con la parola inglese *intimate*

intimazione [intimat'tsjone] SF order, command; **intimazione di sfratto** (*Dir*) eviction notice *o* order

❑ **intimazione** non si traduce mai con la parola inglese *intimation*

intimidatorio, -ria, -ri, -rie [intimida'tɔrjo] AGG threatening; **sparare (in aria) a scopo intimidatorio** to fire warning shots

intimidazione [intimidat'tsjone] SF intimidation; **vittima di intimidazioni** victim of intimidation *o* threats

intimidire [intimi'dire] /55/ VT to intimidate VI (*aus* **essere**), **intimidirsi** VIP to become *o* grow shy

intimità [intimi'ta] SF (*vita privata*) privacy; (*familiarità*) familiarity; (*di rapporto*) intimacy; **nell'intimità della propria casa** in the privacy of one's own home

intimo, -a ['intimo] AGG (*amico*) close, intimate; (*affetti, vita*) private; (*gioia, dolore*) deep; (*cerimonia*) quiet; (*atmosfera*) cosy, intimate; (*igiene*) personal; **amico intimo** close friend; **biancheria intima** underwear; **parti intime** (*genitali*) private parts; **rapporti intimi** (*sessuali*) intimate relations; **una cenetta intima** an intimate dinner ♦ SM **1** (*persona*) close friend **2 nell'intimo della sua coscienza** deep down in his conscience; **nell'intimo del suo cuore** in his heart of hearts **3** (*biancheria intima*) underwear; (*per donna*) lingerie; **saldi del 30% sull'intimo uomo** 30% reductions on men's underwear

intimorire [intimo'rire] /55/ VT to frighten, make afraid; **intimorirsi** VIP to become frightened

intingere [in'tindʒere] /37/ VT IRREG (*biscotto, pane*) to dunk; (*penna, pennello*) to dip

intingolo [in'tingolo] SM (*sugo*) sauce; (*pietanza*) tasty dish

intinto, -a [in'tinto] PP *di* **intingere**

intirizzire [intirid'dzire] /55/ VT to numb VI (*aus* **essere**), **intirizzirsi** VIP to grow numb (with cold)

intirizzito, -a [intirid'dzito] AGG numb (with cold)

intitolare [intito'lare] /72/ VT **1** (*dare un titolo a*) to entitle, give a title to; **come ha intitolato il suo ultimo romanzo?** what title has he given to his latest book?; **ho intitolato questo quadro "Mattina e Sera"** I've called this picture "Morning and Evening" **2** (*dedicare: chiesa, monumento*) to dedicate; **intitolarsi** VIP (*libro, film*) to be called; **come s'intitola il film?** what's the film called?

intollerabile [intolle'rabile] AGG intolerable, unbearable

intollerante [intolle'rante] AGG **intollerante (di)** intolerant (of) ♦ SM, SF intolerant person

intolleranza [intolle'rantsa] SF intolerance

intonacare [intona'kare] /20/ VT to plaster

intonaco, -ci [in'tonako] SM plaster

intonare [into'nare] /72/ VT (*Mus: canzone*) to sing the opening phrases of; (*fig: armonizzare*) to match; **intonare a** *o* **con** to tone in with, match with; **intonare due colori tra di loro** to match two colours; **intonarsi** VIP (*colori*) to go together; **intonarsi a** *o* **con** (*circostanza, carnagione*) to suit; (*abito*) to match, go with

intonazione [intonat'tsjone] SF (*nel cantare*) pitch; (*nel parlare*) intonation

intontire [inton'tire] /55/ VT (*sogg: botta*) to stun, daze; (: *gas, alcolici*) to make dizzy, make woozy (*fam*) VI (*aus* **essere**), **intontirsi** VIP to be stunned *o* dazed

intontito, -a [inton'tito] AGG (*persona: da botta*) stunned, dazed; (: *da gas, alcolici*) dizzy, woozy (*fam*); (*sguardo*) glazed; **intontito dal sonno** befuddled with sleep

intoppo [in'toppo] SM (*ostacolo*) hitch, stumbling block, obstacle; (*difficoltà*) difficulty

intorbidare [intorbi'dare] /72/, **intorbidire** [intorbi'dire] VT (*liquido*) to make turbid; (*mente*) to cloud; **intorbidare le acque** (*fig*) to muddy the waters VI (*aus* **essere**), **intorbidarsi** VIP (*vedi vt*) to become turbid; to cloud, become confused

intorno [in'torno] AVV around, round; **qui/lì intorno** round

here/there; **qui intorno non c'è neanche un giornalaio** there's isn't even a newspaper agent round here; **c'è un castello e tutt'intorno un giardino** there is a castle with a garden surrounding it; **un giardino con una siepe intorno** a garden with a hedge round it ♦ **intorno a** PREP **1** (*attorno a, circa*) (a)round about; **smettila di girarmi intorno** stop hanging around me; **erano seduti intorno al tavolo** they were sitting round the table; **successe intorno al 1910** it happened (a)round about 1910 **2** (*riguardo*) about

intorpidire [intorpi'dire] /55/ VT (*membra*) to numb; (*mente*) to slow down, make sluggish VI (*aus* **essere**), **intorpidirsi** VIP (*membra*) to grow numb; (*mente, persona*) to become sluggish

intossicare [intossi'kare] /20/ VT to poison; **intossicarsi** VR: **intossicarsi (con)** to poison o.s. (with)

❑ **intossicare** non si traduce mai con la parola inglese *intoxicate*

intossicazione [intossikat'tsjone] SF poisoning; **intossicazione alimentare** food poisoning

intraducibile [intradu'tʃibile] AGG untranslatable

intralciare [intral'tʃare] /14/ VT to hamper, hinder, hold up

intralcio, -ci [in'traltʃo] SM hitch; **essere d'intralcio** to be in the way

intrallazzare [intrallat'tsare] /72/ VI (*aus* **avere**) to intrigue, scheme

intrallazzo [intral'lattso] SM (*Pol*) intrigue, manoeuvre (*Brit*), maneuver (*USA*); (*traffico losco*) racket

intramontabile [intramon'tabile] AGG timeless

intramuscolare [intramusko'lare] AGG intramuscular

intranet ['intranet] SF intranet

intransigente [intransi'dʒɛnte] AGG uncompromising, intransigent; **è piuttosto intransigente in fatto di amicizie** he's rather choosy about who he makes friends with

intransigenza [intransi'dʒɛntsa] SF intransigence

intransitivo, -a [intransi'tivo] AGG, SM (*Gramm*) intransitive

intrappolare [intrappo'lare] /72/ VT to trap; **rimanere intrappolato** to be trapped; **farsi intrappolare** to get caught

intraprendente [intrapren'dɛnte] AGG (*che si dà da fare*) enterprising, go-ahead; (*audace*) forward, bold; **un giovane intraprendente** an enterprising young man

intraprendenza [intrapren'dentsa] SF (*spirito d'iniziativa*) initiative; (*audacità*) audacity, boldness

intraprendere [intra'prɛndere] /81/ VT IRREG (*riforme*) to undertake; (*carriera*) to embark (up)on; **intraprendere una spedizione** to set out on an expedition

intrapreso, -a [intra'preso] PP *di* **intraprendere**

intrattabile [intrat'tabile] AGG intractable; **il capo oggi è intrattabile** the boss is impossible today; **oggi sei proprio intrattabile** you're being really awkward today

intrattenere [intratte'nere] VB IRREG /121/ VT **1** (*divertire*) to entertain; (*chiacchierando*) to engage in conversation **2** (*rapporti*) to have, maintain; **intrattenersi** VIP (*fermarsi: con ospiti*) to linger; **intrattenersi su** (*argomento, questione*) to dwell on

intrattenimento [intratteni'mento] SM entertainment

intravedere [intrave'dere] /127/ VT IRREG **1** (*vedere appena*) to make out, catch a glimpse of; **l'ho intravisto tra la folla** I caught sight of him in the crowd **2** (*presagire: difficoltà, pericoli*) to foresee; (: *verità*) to have an inkling of

intrecciare [intret'tʃare] /14/ VT (*gen*) to plait, braid; (*intessere*) to weave, interweave, intertwine; **intrecciare una relazione amorosa** to begin an affair; **intrecciarsi** VIP (*rami, corde*) to become interwoven, intertwine

intreccio, -ci [in'trettʃo] SM **1** (*di tessuto*) weave; (*di paglia*) plaiting **2** (*fig: trama*) plot, story

intrepido, -a [in'trɛpido] AGG intrepid, dauntless, fearless

intricare [intri'kare] /20/ VT (*fili*) to tangle; (*fig: faccenda*) to complicate; **intricarsi** VIP (*vedi vt*) to become tangled; to become complicated

intrico, -chi [in'triko] SM (*anche fig*) tangle

intrigante [intri'gante] AGG (*persona: imbroglione*) scheming; (*misterioso: sorriso, sguardo*) enigmatic; (: *romanzo*) intriguing ♦ SM, SF schemer, intriguer

intrigare [intri'gare] /80/ VT (*affascinare*) to intrigue ♦ VI (*aus* **avere**) to scheme, intrigue, manoeuvre (*Brit*), maneuver (*USA*)

intrigo, -ghi [in'trigo] SM (*complotto*) intrigue, scheme, plot; (*situazione complicata*) tricky situation

intrinseco, -a, -ci, -che [in'trinseko] AGG intrinsic

intriso, -a [in'trizo] AGG: **intriso di** (*inzuppato*) soaked with; **un film intriso di sentimentalismo** a film dripping with sentimentality

intristire [intris'tire] /55/ VI (*aus* **essere**) (*persona: diventare triste*) to grow sad; (*pianta*) to wilt

introdotto, -a [intro'dotto] PP *di* **introdurre** ♦ AGG: **essere bene introdotto** to know all the right people

introdurre [intro'durre] VB IRREG /90/ VT (*gen*) to introduce; (*moneta, chiave*) to insert, put in; (*descrizione, elemento*) to introduce, bring in; (*persona*) to show in; **gli ospiti venivano introdotti in sala** the guests were shown o ushered into the room; **introdurre prodotti di contrabbando** to smuggle in goods; **introdurre la moneta nella fessura** put the coin in the slot; **ha introdotto subito l'argomento** he immediately raised the subject; **introdursi** VIP (*penetrare*): **introdursi in** to enter, get into (*furtivamente*) to sneak in, slip in; (*moda, tecniche*) to be introduced

introduzione [introdut'tsjone] SF introduction; **dobbiamo leggere solo l'introduzione** we only have to read the introduction

introito [in'trɔito] SM (*Comm: entrata*) revenue, income

intromesso, -a [intro'messo] PP *di* **intromettersi**

intromettersi [intro'mettersi] /63/ VR IRREG (*immischiarsi*) to interfere, meddle; (*in conversazione*) to intervene

intromissione [intromis'sjone] SF (*vedi vb*) interference, meddling; intervention

introspezione [introspet'tsjone] SF introspection

introvabile [intro'vabile] AGG (*persona, oggetto*) who (o which) cannot be found; (*libro*) unobtainable

introverso, -a [intro'verso] AGG introverted ♦ SM, SF introvert

intrufolarsi [intrufo'larsi] /72/ VR: **intrufolarsi (in)** (*stanza, casa*) to sneak in(to), slip in(to)

intruglio, -gli [in'truʎʎo] SM concoction

intrusione [intru'zjone] SF intrusion, interference; **scusate l'intrusione...** forgive the intrusion ...

intruso, -a [in'truzo] SM, SF (*estraneo*) intruder; (*ad un ricevimento*) gatecrasher; **mi trattano come un intruso** they treat me as if I had no right to be there

intuire [intu'ire] /55/ VT (*presentire, accorgersi*) to realize; (*capire*) to know intuitively; (*indovinare*) to guess; **ha intuito la verità** she realized the truth; **ho intuito subito che c'era qualcosa che non andava** I realized at once that something was wrong

intuito [in'tuito] SM (*intuizione*) intuition; (*perspicacia*) perspicacity; **per intuito** intuitively; **capire per intuito** to know intuitively

intuizione [intuit'tsjone] SF intuition

inturgidire [inturdʒi'dire] /55/ VI (*aus* **essere**), **inturgidirsi** VIP to swell

inumanità [inumani'ta] SF inhumanity

inumano, -a [inu'mano] AGG inhuman

inumare [inu'mare] /72/ VT (*seppellire*) to bury, inter

inumazione [inumat'tsjone] SF burial, interment

inumidire [inumi'dire] /55/ VT (*labbra*) to moisten; (*biancheria*) to dampen; **inumidirsi le labbra** to moisten one's lips; **inumidirsi** VIP to get damp o wet

inurbamento [inurba'mento] SM urbanization

inusitato, -a [inuzi'tato] AGG unusual

inutile [i'nutile] AGG (*che non serve*) useless; (*superfluo*) needless, unnecessary; **un aggeggio inutile** a useless gadget; **mi sento inutile qui** I feel useless here; **è inutile insistere** o **che tu insista** it's no use o no good insisting, there's no point in insisting; **è stato tutto inutile!** it was all in vain!; **è inutile, tanto non lo convinci** it's pointless, you won't persuade him; **è inutile arrabbiarsi!** there's no point getting angry!

inutilità [inutili'ta] SF (*vedi agg*) uselessness; needlessness

inutilizzabile [inutilid'dzabile] AGG unusable

inutilmente [inutil'mente] AVV (*senza risultato*) fruitlessly; (*senza utilità, scopo*) unnecessarily, needlessly; **l'ho cercato inutilmente** I looked for him in vain; **ti preoccupi inutilmente** you're worrying unnecessarily, there's no need for you to worry

invadente [inva'dente] AGG interfering; **non vorrei essere invadente** I don't want to interfere; **un vicino di casa invadente** an interfering neighbour ♦ SM, SF interfering person, busybody

invadenza [inva'dentsa] SF intrusiveness

invadere [in'vadere] /52/ VT IRREG (*gen*) to invade; (*affollare*) to overrun, swarm into; (*sogg: acque*) to flood; **i tifosi hanno invaso il campo** the fans invaded the pitch; **le auto giapponesi hanno invaso il mercato** Japanese cars have flooded the market; **invadere la privacy di qn** to invade sb's privacy

invaghirsi [inva'girsi] /55/ VIP: **invaghirsi di** to take a fancy to

invalicabile [invali'kabile] AGG (*montagna*) impassable; (*fig: difficoltà*) insurmountable; **limite invalicabile** (*zona militare*) no unauthorised access

invalidare [invali'dare] /72/ VT to invalidate

invalidità [invalidi'ta] SF INV (*vedi agg*) disablement, disability; infirmity; invalidity

invalido, -a [in'valido] AGG 1 (*inabile*) disabled; (*malato*) infirm 2 (*Dir: nullo*) invalid ♦ SM, SF (*inabile*) disabled person; (*malato*) invalid; **invalido di guerra** disabled ex-serviceman; **invalido del lavoro** industrially disabled person

invalso, -a [in'valso] AGG (*diffuso*) established

invano [in'vano] AVV in vain

invariabile [inva'rjabile] AGG invariable

invariato, -a [inva'rjato] AGG unchanged

invasare [inva'zare] /72/ VT (*pianta*) to pot

invasato, -a [inva'zato] AGG possessed (by the devil) ♦ SM, SF person possessed by the devil; **urlare come un invasato** to shout like one possessed

invasione [inva'zjone] SF invasion

invaso, -a [in'vazo] PP *di* **invadere**

invasore [inva'zore] AGG invading ♦ SM invader

invecchiamento [invekkja'mento] SM (*di persona*) ageing; **questo whisky ha un invecchiamento di 12 anni** this whisky has been matured for 12 years

invecchiare [invek'kjare] /19/ VI (*aus* **essere**) (*diventare vecchio*) to grow old; (*sembrare più vecchio*) to age; (*vino*) to age; **lo trovo invecchiato** I think he has aged; **molti hanno paura di invecchiare** a lot of people are afraid of getting old ♦ VT (*persona*) to make look older, age, put years on; (*vino*) to age

invece [in'vetʃe] AVV (*gen*) instead; (*ma*) but; **credevo di aver ragione e invece no** I thought I was right but I wasn't; **io preferisco i romanzi, Peter invece i gialli** I like novels but Peter prefers detective stories; **invece di qc** o **che fare qc** instead of sth/of doing sth; **potresti aiutarmi invece di stare lì a guardare la TV** you could help me instead of sitting there watching TV; **potresti venire con me invece che startene a casa** you could come with me instead of staying home; **preferisco lavorare in Italia invece che all'estero** I prefer to work in Italy rather than abroad; **prendo un tè invece del caffè** I'll have tea instead of coffee

inveire [inve'ire] /55/ VI (*aus* **avere**) **inveire contro** to rail against

invelenire [invele'nire] /55/ VT to embitter VI (*aus* **essere**), **invelenirsi** VIP to become bitter

invenduto, -a [inven'duto] AGG unsold ♦ SM (*Comm*): **rendere l'invenduto** to return unsold goods

inventare [inven'tare] /72/ VT (*gen*) to invent; (*metodo*) to invent, devise; (*gioco, scusa*) to invent, make up, think up; **ho inventato una scusa per uscire prima** I made up an excuse to leave early; **ha inventato un nuovo gioco** he invented a new game; **lui ne inventa di tutti i colori!** what will he think up next!; **se l'è inventata di sana pianta** he made the whole thing up

inventariare [inventa'rjare] /19/ VT to make an inventory of, inventory

inventario, -ri [inven'tarjo] SM (*gen*) inventory; (*Comm: registro*) stock list; (: *operazione*) stocktaking *no pl*; **inventario fisico** physical stocktaking; **fare l'inventario di** to make an inventory of; **mi ha fatto l'inventario delle sue malattie** (*fig*) he regaled me with his medical history

inventivo, -a [inven'tivo] AGG inventive

inventore, -trice [inven'tore] AGG inventive ♦ SM, SF inventor

invenzione [inven'tsjone] SF (*gen*) invention; **è tutta**

un'**invenzione** it's pure invention; **una ricetta di mia invenzione** a recipe I made up myself

inverecondia [invere'kondja] SF shamelessness, immodesty

invernale [inver'nale] AGG (*gen*) winter *attr*; (*simile all'inverno*) wintry; **una giornata invernale** a winter's day

inverno [in'vɛrno] SM winter; **d'inverno** in (the) winter; **essere in pieno inverno** to be in the depths of winter

inverosimile [invero'simile] AGG (*racconto*) unlikely, improbable; (*scusa*) far-fetched ♦ SM: **l'inverosimile** the improbable; **ha dell'inverosimile** it's hard to believe, it's incredible

inversione [inver'sjone] SF inversion; **inversione di tendenza** (*fig*) radical change of direction; (*pegg, spec Pol*) U-turn; **"divieto d'inversione"** (*Aut*) "no U-turns"; **inversione di marcia** (*Aut*) U-turn

inverso, -a [in'vɛrso] AGG 1 (*direzione*) opposite; **in ordine inverso** in reverse order; **si è scontrato con una macchina che veniva in senso inverso** he collided with a car coming in the opposite direction 2 (*Mat*) inverse; **in ragione inversa** (*Mat*) in inverse ratio ♦ SM: **l'inverso** the opposite, the reverse, the contrary; **capisce tutto all'inverso** he always gets hold of the wrong end of the stick; **fa tutto all'inverso** he does everything the wrong way round

invertebrato, -a [inverte'brato] AGG, SM invertebrate

invertire [inver'tire] /45/ VT (*gen*) to invert; (*disposizione, posti*) to change; (*ruoli*) to exchange; **invertire la marcia** (*Aut*) to do a U-turn; **invertire la rotta** (*Naut*) to go about; (*fig*) to do a U-turn

invertito, -a [inver'tito] AGG (*Chim*): **zucchero invertito** invert sugar

investigare [investi'gare] /80/ VT (*indagare*) to investigate; (*analizzare*) to examine ♦ VI (*aus* avere) **investigare su** to investigate

investigativo, -a [investiga'tivo] AGG: **squadra investigativa** detective squad; **agente investigativo** detective

investigatore, -trice [investiga'tore] SM, SF investigator, detective; **investigatore privato** private detective, private investigator

investigazione [investigat'tsjone] SF investigation, inquiry

investimento [investi'mento] SM 1 (*Econ*) investment; **un buon investimento** a good investment 2 (*di pedone*) running down, knocking down; (*di veicolo*) collision, crash

investire [inves'tire] /45/ VT 1 (*Econ*) to invest; **ha investito i suoi risparmi in titoli di stato** he has invested his savings in government bonds 2 (*sogg: veicolo: pedone*) to run over, knock down; (: *altro veicolo*) to crash into, hit; **è stato investito da un camion** he was run over by a truck 3 (*apostrofare*) to assail; **investire qn di** *o* **con qc** (*domande*) to besiege sb with sth; (*ingiurie, insulti*) to heap sth on sb 4 (*Dir, Amm: incaricare*): **investire qn di** (*poteri*) to invest sb with; (*incarico*) to appoint sb to; **investirsi** VR (*fig*): **investirsi di una parte** to enter thoroughly into a role

investitore, -trice [investi'tore] SM, SF driver responsible for an accident; (*Econ*) investor; **investitore istituzionale** corporate acquirer

investitura [investi'tura] SF (*Amm, Pol*) appointment, nomination; (*Rel*) investiture

inveterato, -a [invete'rato] AGG (*abitudine, vizio*) ingrained; (*giocatore, bugiardo*) inveterate

invettiva [invet'tiva] SF invective; **lanciare invettive contro qn/qc** to hurl abuse at sb/sth

inviare [invi'are] /60/ VT (*gen*) to send; (*merce*) to dispatch

inviato, -a [invi'ato] SM, SF (*Pol*) envoy; (*Stampa*) correspondent; **un inviato speciale** a special correspondent

invidia [in'vidja] SF envy; **fare invidia a qn** to make sb envious; **farebbe invidia ai migliori ristoranti** it would be the envy of the best restaurants; **avere** *o* **provare invidia per qn/qc** to be envious of sb/sth; **per invidia** out of envy; **morire d'invidia** to be green with envy; **sta morendo d'invidia** he's green with envy; **degno d'invidia** enviable; **che invidia!** how I envy you!; **è tutta invidia, la tua** you're just jealous

invidiabile [invi'djabile] AGG enviable

invidiare [invi'djare] /19/ VT: **invidiare qc a qn** to envy sb sth; **invidiare qn per qc** to envy sb for sth; **l'ha sempre invidiato** he's always envied him; **non aver nulla da invidiare a nessuno** to be as good as the next one

invidioso, -a [invi'djoso] AGG envious; **è invidioso perché io ce l'ho e lui no** he's jealous because I've got one and he hasn't

❏ **invidioso** non si traduce mai con la parola inglese *invidious*

invincibile [invin't'ʃibile] AGG (*esercito, nemico*) invincible; (*fig: antipatia, timidezza*) insurmountable

invio, -vii [in'vio] SM 1 (*vedi vb*) sending; dispatching; **chiedere l'invio di qc** to ask for sth to be sent (*o* dispatched) 2 (*insieme di merci*) consignment 3 (*tasto*) Return (key), Enter (key)

inviolabile [invio'labile] AGG inviolable

inviolato, -a [invio'lato] AGG 1 (*diritto, segreto*) inviolate 2 (*foresta*) virgin *attr*; (*montagna, vetta*) unscaled

inviperire [invipe'rire] /55/ VI (*aus* essere), **inviperirsi** VIP to become furious, fly into a temper; **mi ha fatto inviperire** he made me furious

inviperito, -a [invipe'rito] AGG furious

invischiare [invis'kjare] /19/ VT (*fig*): **invischiare qn in qc** to involve sb in sth, mix sb up in sth; **invischiarsi** VIP: **invischiarsi con qn/in qc** to get mixed up *o* involved with sb/ in sth

invisibile [invi'zibile] AGG (*gen, anche Econ*) invisible; **rendersi invisibile** (*scherz*) to make o.s. scarce

inviso, -a [in'vizo] AGG: **inviso a** unpopular with

invitante [invi'tante] AGG (*proposta, odorino*) inviting; (*sorriso*) appealing, attractive

invitare [invi'tare] /72/ VT (*gen*) to invite; **invitare qn a fare qc** to invite sb to do sth; **invitare a cena gli amici** to invite *o* ask friends to dinner; **invitare qn a ballare** to ask someone to dance; **mi hanno invitato ad una festa** they've invited me to a party; **furono invitati a entrare** they were invited *o* asked in; **è stato invitato a dimettersi** he was asked to resign; **è una giornata che invita a uscire** it's the sort of day that tempts one to go out; **invitarsi** VR: **si invita sempre da solo** he always invites himself along

invitato, -a [invi'tato] SM, SF guest

invito [in'vito] SM invitation; **fare un invito a qn** to extend an invitation to sb; **su** *o* **dietro invito di qn** at sb's invitation; **hai ricevuto l'invito?** did you get the invitation?

invocare [invo'kare] /20/ VT (*aiuto, pietà*) to beg for, cry out for; (*Dio*) to invoke, call upon, appeal to; (*articolo*) to cite, appeal to

invogliare [invoʎ'ʎare] /27/ VT (*stimolare*) to encourage; (*invitare*) to tempt, entice; **invogliare qn a fare qc** to tempt sb to do sth, induce sb to do sth; **bisognerebbe invogliarlo a studiare** we should encourage him to study; **la giornata di sole invogliava ad uscire** the sunny weather tempted one out of doors

involontario, -ria, -ri, -rie [involon'tarjo] AGG (*movimento, muscolo*) involuntary; (*offesa, errore*) unintentional

involtino [invol'tino] SM (*Culin*) roulade

involto [in'volto] SM (*fagotto*) bundle; (*pacco*) parcel

involucro [in'vɔlukro] SM (*rivestimento*) covering, cover; (*confezione*) wrapping

involutivo, -a [involu'tivo] AGG: **subire un processo involutivo** to regress

involuto, -a [invo'luto] AGG (*stile*) convoluted

involuzione [involut'tsjone] SF 1 (*di stile*) convolutedness 2 (*regresso*): **subire un'involuzione** to regress

invulnerabile [invulne'rabile] AGG invulnerable

inzaccherare [intsakke'rare] /72/ VT to spatter with mud; **inzaccherarsi** VR, VIP to get muddy

inzuppare [intsup'pare] /72/ VT (*gen*): **inzuppare qc (di)** to soak sth (in); **inzuppò i biscotti nel latte** he dipped the biscuits in the milk; **abiti inzuppati di pioggia** rain-soaked clothes; **inzupparsi** VIP to get soaked, get drenched

io [io] PRON PERS I; **sono io** it's me; (*più formale*) it is I; **chi è? — sono io, apri** who's that? — it's me, open the door; **io e te** you and I, you and me (*fam*); **il mio amico ed io ci andremo** my friend and I will go; **io ci vado, tu fai come vuoi** I'm going, you do what you like; **pronto, c'è Paola? — sì, sono io** hello, is Paola there? — yes, speaking; **ho fame** — **anch'io** I'm hungry — so am I; **vengo anch'io** I'll come too; **non lo sapevo nemmeno io** I didn't even know it myself; **lo farò**

io, IO lo farò I'LL do it; **io stesso(a)** I myself ♦ SM INV: **l'io** the self, the ego

iodio [ˈjɔdjo] SM iodine

ione [ˈjone] SM ion; **ione idrogeno** hydrogen ion; **ioni complessi** complex ions

Ionio [ˈjɔnjo] SM: **lo Ionio, il mar Ionio** the Ionian (Sea)

ionizzatore [jonidzzaˈtore] SM ionizer

iosa [ˈjɔsa] **a iosa** AVV in abundance, in great quantity; **ce ne sono a iosa** there are thousands of them; **avere matite a iosa** to have pencils galore

iperbole [iˈperbole] SF (*Letteratura*) hyberbole; (*Mat*) hyperbola

iperbolico, -a, -ci, -che [iperˈbɔliko] AGG (*Letteratura, Mat*) hyperbolic(al); (*fig: esagerato*) exaggerated

ipermercato [ipermerˈkato] SM hypermarket

ipersensibile [ipersenˈsibile] AGG (*persona*) hypersensitive; (*Fot: lastra, pellicola*) hypersensitized

ipertecnologico, -a, -ci, -che [iperteknoˈlodʒiko] AGG hi-tech

ipertensione [ipertenˈsjone] SF (*Med*) high blood pressure, hypertension (*termine tecn*)

ipertesto [iperˈtesto] SM (*Inform*) hypertext

ipertestuale [ipertesˈtwale] AGG (*Inform*) hypertext attr

ipnosi [ipˈnɔzi] SF INV hypnosis

ipnotico, -a, -ci, -che [ipˈnɔtiko] AGG, SM hypnotic

ipnotismo [ipnoˈtizmo] SM hypnotism

ipnotizzare [ipnotidˈdzare] /72/ VT to hypnotize; **l'hanno ipnotizzato** he was hypnotized

ipoallergenico, -a, -ci, -che [ipoallerˈdʒeniko], **ipoallergico, -a, -ci, -che** [ipoalˈlɛrdʒiko] AGG (*crema, sapone, rossetto*) hypoallergenic

ipocondria [ipokonˈdria] SF hypochondria

ipocondriaco, -a, -ci, -che [ipokonˈdriako] AGG, SM, SF hypochondriac

ipocrisia [ipokriˈzia] SF hypocrisy; **è stata un'ipocrisia da parte sua** that was sheer hypocrisy on his part

ipocrita, -i, -e [iˈpɔkrita] AGG hypocritical ♦ SM, SF hypocrite

iposodico, -a, -ci, -che [ipoˈsɔdiko] AGG (*sale*) low sodium attr

ipoteca, -che [ipoˈtɛka] SF mortgage; **fare** o **mettere un'ipoteca su qc** to mortgage sth, raise a mortgage on sth; **la squadra ha messo una seria ipoteca sullo scudetto** the team has practically put its name on the cup

ipotecare [ipoteˈkare] /20/ VT (*Dir, anche fig*) to mortgage

ipotenusa [ipoteˈnuza] SF hypotenuse

ipotesi [iˈpɔtezi] SF INV hypothesis; **le ipotesi sono due** there are two possibilities; **facciamo l'ipotesi che...**, **ammettiamo per ipotesi che...** let's suppose o assume that ...; **facciamo l'ipotesi che non venga** supposing he doesn't come; **nella peggiore/migliore delle ipotesi** at worst/best; **nella migliore delle ipotesi lo finirò sabato** at best I'll finish it on Saturday; **nell'ipotesi che venga** should he come, if he comes; **se per ipotesi io partissi...** just supposing I were to leave ...

ipotetico, -a, -ci, -che [ipoˈtetiko] AGG (*gen*) hypothetical; (*guadagni, profitti*) theoretical, hypothetical; (*mondo*) imaginary; **nel caso ipotetico che tu non arrivi in tempo** should you not arrive in time; **periodo ipotetico** (*Gramm*) conditional clause

ipotizzare [ipotidˈdzare] /72/ VT: **ipotizzare che** to form the hypothesis that, hypothesize

ippico, -a, -ci, -che [ˈippiko] AGG horse attr; **un concorso ippico** a horse race

ippocastano [ippokasˈtano] SM horse chestnut (tree)

ippodromo [ipˈpɔdromo] SM racecourse, racetrack

ippopotamo [ippoˈpɔtamo] SM hippopotamus

ipsilon [ˈipsilon] SF INV, SM INV (*lettera*) Y, y; (*dell'alfabeto greco*) upsilon; **si scrive con la "i"** o **con la "ipsilon"?** do you spell it with an "i" or with a "y"?

IR ABBR (*Ferr*) = interregionale

IRA [ˈira] SIGLA F (= *Irish Republican Army*) IRA

ira [ˈira] SF anger, fury, wrath; **l'ira di Dio** the wrath of God; **costa un'ira di Dio** it costs a king's ransom; **farsi prendere dall'ira** to lose one's temper

iracheno, -a [iraˈkɛno] AGG, SM, SF Iraqi

Iran [ˈiran] SM Iran

iraniano, -a [iraˈnjano] AGG, SM, SF Iranian

I'raq SM: **l'Iraq** Iraq

irascibile [iraʃˈʃibile] AGG irascible, quick-tempered

iride [ˈiride] SF **1** (*Anat*) iris **2** (*arcobaleno*) rainbow

iris [ˈiris] SM INV iris

Irlanda [irˈlanda] SF Ireland; **il mar d'Irlanda** the Irish Sea; **la Repubblica d'Irlanda** Eire, the Republic of Ireland; **l'Irlanda del Nord** Northern Ireland, Ulster; **mi è piaciuta molto l'Irlanda** I really liked Ireland; **andremo in Irlanda quest'estate** we're going to Ireland this summer

irlandese [irlanˈdese] AGG Irish; **la squadra irlandese** the Irish team ♦ SM, SF Irishman o Irishwoman; **gli Irlandesi** the Irish

ironia [iroˈnia] SF irony; **fare dell'ironia su qc** to be sarcastic about sth; **l'ironia della sorte** the irony of fate

ironico, -a, -ci, -che [iˈrɔniko] AGG ironic(al); **un sorrisetto ironico** an ironic little smile

ironizzare [ironidˈdzare] /72/ VT, VI (*aus avere*) **ironizzare su** to be ironical about

iroso, -a [iˈroso] AGG (*sguardo, tono*) angry, wrathful; (*persona*) irascible

irpino, -a [irˈpino] AGG of o from Irpinia ♦ SM, SF inhabitant o native of Irpinia

irradiare [irraˈdjare] /19/ VT **1** (*illuminare, anche fig*) to light up **2** (*diffondere: calore, energia*) to radiate ♦ VI (*aus essere*) to radiate; **irradiarsi** VIP: **irradiarsi (da)** (*strade, rette*) to radiate (from)

irradiazione [irradjatˈtsjone] SF (*di calore, energia*) radiation

irraggiungibile [irraddʒunˈdʒibile] AGG unreachable; (*fig: meta*) unattainable

irragionevole [irradʒoˈnevole] AGG (*privo di ragione*) irrational; (*fig: persona, pretese, prezzo*) unreasonable

irrazionale [irrattsjoˈnale] AGG (*gen, anche Mat*) irrational

irreale [irreˈale] AGG unreal

irrealizzabile [irrealidˈdzabile] AGG (*sogno, desiderio*) unattainable, unrealizable; (*progetto*) unworkable, impracticable

irrealtà [irrealˈta] SF unreality

irrecuperabile [irrekupeˈrabile] AGG (*gen*) irretrievable; (*fig: persona*) irredeemable

irrecusabile [irrekuˈzabile] AGG **1** (*prova*) indisputable, irrefutable **2** (*offerta*) which cannot be refused, not to be refused

irredentista, -i, -e [irredenˈtista] AGG, SM, SF (*Storia*) Irredentist

irrefrenabile [irrefreˈnabile] AGG uncontrollable

irrefutabile [irrefuˈtabile] AGG irrefutable

irregolare [irregoˈlare] AGG (*gen*) irregular; (*terreno*) uneven; (*sonno*) fitful; (*risultati, sviluppo*) erratic; **un verbo irregolare** an irregular verb; **lineamenti irregolari** irregular features ♦ SM (*Mil*) irregular

irregolarità [irregolariˈta] SF INV **1** (*vedi agg*) irregularity; unevenness no pl; fitfulness; erratic nature **2** (*azione irregolare*) irregularity; (*Sport*) foul

irremovibile [irremoˈvibile] AGG (*fig*) unshakable, unyielding; **essere irremovibile in qc** to be adamant about sth

irreparabile [irrepaˈrabile] AGG irreparable

irreperibile [irrepeˈribile] AGG who (o which) cannot be found, nowhere to be found

irreprensibile [irreprenˈsibile] AGG irreproachable

irrequieto, -a [irreˈkwjeto] AGG (*agitato*) restless; (*vivace*) lively

irresistibile [irresisˈtibile] AGG irresistible

irresoluto, -a [irresoˈluto] AGG irresolute, indecisive

irrespirabile [irrespiˈrabile] AGG (*aria*) unbreathable; (*malsano*) unhealthy; (*fig: opprimente*) stifling, oppressive

irresponsabile [irresponˈsabile] AGG irresponsible ♦ SM, SF irresponsible person

irrestringibile [irrestrinˈdʒibile] AGG unshrinkable, nonshrink (*Brit*)

irretire [irreˈtire] /55/ VT to seduce

irreversibile [irreverˈsibile] AGG irreversible

irrevocabile [irrevoˈkabile] AGG irrevocable
irriconoscibile [irrikonoʃˈʃibile] AGG unrecognizable
irriducibile [irriduˈtʃibile] AGG (frazione, cifra) irreducible; (fig: avversario) indomitable, unshakable; (: ostinazione) unyielding
irriflessivo, -a [irriflesˈsivo] AGG thoughtless
irrigare [irriˈgare] /80/ VT (Agr, Med) to irrigate
irrigazione [irrigatˈtsjone] SF (Agr, Med) irrigation
irrigidimento [irridʒidiˈmento] SM (di muscoli) stiffening; (fig: di disciplina) tightening; (: di posizione, atteggiamento) hardening
irrigidire [irridʒiˈdire] /55/ VT (gen) to stiffen; (fig: disciplina) to tighten; **irrigidirsi** VIP to stiffen; **irrigidirsi sulle proprie posizioni** to become entrenched in one's position
irriguardoso, -a [irrigwarˈdoso] AGG disrespectful
irrilevante [irrileˈvante] AGG (trascurabile) insignificant
irrimediabile [irrimeˈdjabile] AGG: **un errore irrimediabile** a mistake which cannot be rectified; **danneggiato in modo irrimediabile** irreparably o irremediably damaged; **non è irrimediabile!** we can do something about it!
irrinunciabile [irrinunˈtʃabile] AGG (bene, diritto) that cannot be renounced, which cannot be abandoned
irripetibile [irripeˈtibile] AGG unrepeatable
irrisolto, -a [irriˈsolto] AGG (problema) unresolved
irrisorio, -ria, -ri, -rie [irriˈzɔrjo] AGG ridiculous
irrispettoso, -a [irrispetˈtoso] AGG disrespectful
irritabile [irriˈtabile] AGG irritable
irritante [irriˈtante] AGG (atteggiamento) irritating, annoying; (Med) irritant
irritare [irriˈtare] /72/ VT 1 (infastidire) to irritate, annoy; **irritare qn** to get on sb's nerves; **il suo modo di ridere mi irrita** his laugh gets on my nerves 2 (pelle, occhi) to irritate; **irritarsi** VIP 1 **irritarsi per qc/con qn** (infastidirsi) to get irritated o annoyed at sth/with sb; **si irrita moltissimo se qn lo interrompe** he gets very annoyed if anyone interrupts him 2 (infiammarsi: pelle, occhi) to become irritated
irritazione [irritatˈtsjone] SF (fastidio) irritation, annoyance; (Med) irritation
irriverente [irriveˈrente] AGG irreverent
irrobustire [irrobusˈtire] /55/ VT (persona) to make stronger, make more robust; (muscoli) to strengthen; **irrobustirsi** VIP to become stronger
irrompere [irˈrompere] /97/ VI vb dif: **irrompere in** to burst into
irrorare [irroˈrare] /72/ VT (bagnare) to bathe; (Agr) to spray
irruente [irruˈente] AGG (impetuoso) impetuous; (chiassoso) boisterous
irruenza [irruˈentsa] SF impetuousness; **con irruenza** impetuously
irruppi ecc [irˈruppi] VB vedi **irrompere**
irruvidire [irruviˈdire] /55/ VT to roughen VI (aus essere), **irruvidirsi** VIP to become rough
irruzione [irrutˈtsjone] SF: **fare irruzione in** (sogg: polizia) to raid, burst into; **i tifosi hanno fatto irruzione nel campo** the fans invaded the pitch
irsuto, -a [irˈsuto] AGG (petto) hairy; (barba) bristly
irto, -a [ˈirto] AGG (barba) bristly; **irto di** (anche fig) bristling with
Is. ABBR (= isola) I.
ISBN ABBR (= International Standard Book Number) ISBN
iscrissi ecc [isˈkrissi] VB vedi **iscrivere**
iscritto¹, -a [isˈkritto] PP di **iscrivere** ♦ SM, SF registered member (o student o candidate); **gli iscritti alla gara** the competitors; **gli iscritti al primo anno di università** first year university students
iscritto² [isˈkritto] **per iscritto** AVV in writing; **mettere per iscritto** to put sth in writing
iscrivere [isˈkrivere] VB IRREG /105/ VT 1 (Scol) **iscrivere (a)** to register (in), enrol (in); (all'anagrafe) to register; **iscrivere qn a un club** to enrol sb as a member of a club 2 (Comm) to enter; **iscrivere una spesa nel bilancio** to enter an item on the balance sheet; **iscriversi** VR: **iscriversi a** (partito, club) to join; (gara) to enter; (concorso) to register o enter for; (corso) to enrol for; (università) to register o enrol at

iscrizione [iskritˈtsjone] SF 1 (epigrafe) inscription 2 (a scuola, università) enrolment; (all'anagrafe) registration; **chiedere/fare l'iscrizione a un club** to apply for membership of/join a club; **tassa di iscrizione** (a una gara) entry fee; (a un circolo) membership fee; (a università) registration fee 3 (Comm) entering
Islam [izˈlam] SM: **l'Islam** Islam
islamico, -a, -ci, -che [izˈlamiko] AGG Islamic
Islanda [izˈlanda] SF Iceland
islandese [izlanˈdese] AGG Icelandic ♦ SM, SF Icelander ♦ SM (lingua) Icelandic
isola [ˈizola] SF island; **le Isole britanniche** the British Isles; **un'isola deserta** a desert island; **isola pedonale** (Aut) pedestrian precinct; **isola spartitraffico** o **salvagente** traffic island
isolamento [izolaˈmento] SM 1 (gen) isolation; (solitudine) loneliness, solitude; **reparto d'isolamento** (in ospedale) isolation ward; **è ricoverata nel reparto d'isolamento** she's been admitted to the isolation ward; **mettere qn in cella di isolamento** to put sb in solitary confinement 2 (Tecn, Elettr) insulation; **isolamento acustico** soundproofing; **isolamento termico** thermal insulation
isolano, -a [izoˈlano] AGG island attr ♦ SM, SF islander
isolante [izoˈlante] AGG insulating ♦ SM insulator
isolare [izoˈlare] /72/ VT 1 (gen) to isolate; **la neve ha isolato il paese dal resto del mondo** snow has cut the village off from the rest of the world 2 (Tecn, Elettr) to insulate; (acusticamente) to soundproof 3 (Bio: virus) to isolate; **isolarsi** VR to isolate o.s., cut o.s. off; **non isolarti, frequenta un po' di gente** don't cut yourself off, go out and meet people
isolato¹, -a [izoˈlato] AGG (gen) isolated; (luogo) lonely, remote; **c'è stato un caso isolato di epatite** there was an isolated case of hepatitis; **vivono isolati, in campagna** they live in a remote place in the country; **rimanere isolato** to be cut off; **il paese è rimasto isolato a causa della neve** the village was cut off by the snow
isolato² [izoˈlato] SM (gruppo di palazzi) block; **fare il giro dell'isolato** to walk round the block; **ho fatto il giro dell'isolato** I went round the block; **il cinema è a due isolati da qui** the cinema is two blocks from here
isolazionismo [izolattsjoˈnizmo] SM isolationism
isotopo, -a [iˈzɔtopo] AGG isotopic ♦ SM isotope
ispessimento [ispessiˈmento] SM thickening
ispessire [ispesˈsire] /55/ VT to thicken; **ispessirsi** VIP to get thicker, thicken
ispettorato [ispettoˈrato] SM inspectorate
ispettore, -trice [ispetˈtore] SM, SF (Amm) inspector; **ispettore di polizia** police inspector; **ispettore di reparto** shop walker (Brit), floor walker (USA); **ispettore alle vendite** (Comm) supervisor; **ispettore di zona** (Comm) area supervisor o manager
ispezionare [ispettsjoˈnare] /72/ VT to inspect
ispezione [ispetˈtsjone] SF inspection
ispido, -a [ˈispido] AGG (barba) bristly, shaggy; (fig: carattere) prickly, touchy
ispirare [ispiˈrare] /72/ VT (gen) to inspire; **ispirare fiducia a qn** to inspire sb with confidence; **non mi ha ispirato fiducia** he didn't inspire confidence; **è un tipo/un'idea che non mi ispira** o **che mi ispira poco** I'm not all that keen on him/the idea; **l'idea m'ispira** the idea appeals to me; **ispirarsi** VIP 1 **ispirarsi a** (prendere ispirazione) to be inspired by, draw one's inspiration from; **per il romanzo si è ispirato a un fatto di cronaca** he got the idea for the novel from a news story 2 (conformarsi): **ispirarsi a qc** to be based on sth
ispiratore, -trice [ispiraˈtore] AGG inspiring ♦ SM, SF inspirer
ispirazione [ispiratˈtsjone] SF inspiration; **secondo l'ispirazione del momento** according to the mood of the moment; **mi è venuta l'ispirazione di telefonargli** I suddenly thought of phoning him
Israele [izraˈele] SM Israel; **andremo in Israele quest'estate** we're going to Israel this summer
israeliano, -a [izraeˈljano] AGG, SM, SF Israeli
israelita, -i, -e [izraeˈlita] SM, SF Jew; (Storia) Israelite
israelitico, -a, -ci, -che [izraeˈlitiko] AGG Jewish
issare [isˈsare] /72/ VT (bandiera, vela) to hoist; (oggetto) to

hoist, haul up; **issare l'ancora** to weigh anchor; **issare qn in spalla** to lift sb onto one's shoulders

Istanbul [istan'bul] SF Istanbul

istantaneo, -a [istan'taneo] AGG (gen) instantaneous; (che dura un istante) momentary

istante [is'tante] SM moment, instant; **all'istante, sull'istante** at once, immediately, instantly; **in un istante** in a flash; **fra un istante, tra qualche istante** in a moment o minute; **sarò pronta tra un istante** I'll be ready in a moment; **abbiamo saputo proprio in questo istante che...** we have just (this moment) heard that ...; **l'aereo dovrebbe essere atterrato proprio in questo istante** the plane should be landing at this very moment; **in quell'istante** at that very o precise moment; **in quell'istante è entrata Paola** at that moment Paola came in

istanza [is'tantsa] SF (richiesta: Amm, Dir) request, petition; **fare** o **presentare un'istanza a qn** to present a petition to sb; **su istanza di qn** at sb's request; **giudice di prima istanza** (Dir) judge of the court of first instance; **giudizio di seconda istanza** judg(e)ment on appeal; **in ultima istanza** (fig) finally; **istanza di divorzio** petition for divorce

isterico, -a, -ci, -che [is'teriko] AGG hysterical ♦ SM, SF (Med) hysteric; (pegg) hysterical type

isterilire [isteri'lire] /55/ VT (terreno) to render infertile; (fig: fantasia) to dry up ♦ **isterilirsi** VIP (vedi vt) to become infertile; to dry up

isterismo [iste'rizmo] SM hysteria

istigare [isti'gare] /80/ VT: **istigare qn a (fare) qc** to incite sb to (do) sth

istigazione [istigat'tsjone] SF incitement, instigation; **su istigazione di qn** (up)on sb's instigation; **istigazione a delinquere** (Dir) incitement to crime

istintivo, -a [istin'tivo] AGG instinctive ♦ SM, SF: **essere un istintivo** to be guided by one's instincts

istinto [is'tinto] SM instinct; **istinto di conservazione** instinct of self-preservation; **per** o **d'istinto** instinctively; **ho seguito il mio istinto** I followed my instinct

istituire [istitu'ire] /55/ VT (gen) to institute; (borsa di studio) to found, endow; (commissione d'inchiesta) to set up; (stabilire: parallelo) to establish

istituto [isti'tuto] SM 1 (gen) institute; (Univ) department; (Scol) college, school, institute; **istituto di francese/storia** (Univ) French/history department; **capo d'istituto** head-teacher 2 (istituzione) institution ♦ **istituto d'arte** art school; **istituto di bellezza** beauty salon; **istituto di credito** bank, banking institution; **istituto magistrale** teacher training school; **istituto tecnico commerciale** school specializing in commercial subjects; **istituto tecnico industriale statale** ≈ technical college

istitutore, -trice [istitu'tore] SM, SF 1 (fondatore) founder 2 (precettore) tutor (governess)

istituzione [istitut'tsjone] SF 1 (atto) institution, founding 2 (ente, tradizione) institution; **essere un'istituzione** (fig) to be an institution 3 (stato): **istituzioni** SFPL state institutions

istmo ['istmo] SM isthmus

istogramma, -i [isto'gramma] SM (Statistica) histogram

istradare [istra'dare] /72/ VT (fig: persona): **istradare (in** o **verso)** to guide sb's steps (in o towards); **istradare qn nella via del bene** to set sb on the right path

istriano, -a [istri'ano] AGG, SM, SF Istrian

istrice ['istritʃe] SM (Zool) porcupine; (fig: persona): **essere un istrice** to be prickly

istrione [istri'one] SM (Teatro, anche fig) ham (actor); **fare l'istrione** to ham

istruire [istru'ire] VB IRREG /55/ VT 1 (dare un'istruzione a) to educate; (Mil) to drill 2 (dare istruzioni a): **istruire qn sul da farsi** to instruct o tell sb what to do 3 (Dir): **istruire una causa** o **un processo** to prepare a case; **istruirsi** VR (informarsi): **istruirsi su qc** to find out about sth

istruito, -a [istru'ito] AGG educated; **una persona molto istruita** a very well-educated person

istruttivo, -a [istrut'tivo] AGG (esempio) instructive; (libro, film, discussione) informative

istruttore, -trice [istrut'tore] AGG: **giudice istruttore** (Dir) examining (Brit) o committing (USA) magistrate ♦ SM, SF instructor; **istruttore di nuoto** swimming instructor; **istruttore di scuola guida** driving instructor; **istruttore di volo** flying instructor

istruttoria [istrut'tɔrja] SF (Dir) (preliminary) investigation and hearing; **formalizzare un'istruttoria** to proceed to a formal hearing

istruzione [istrut'tsjone] SF 1 (gen) training, instruction; (Mil) training; (Scol) education; **Ministero della pubblica istruzione** Ministry of Education; **ha avuto una buona istruzione** he had a good education 2 **istruzioni** SFPL (direttive, avvertenze) instructions, directions; **siamo in attesa di istruzioni** we're waiting for instructions; **istruzioni per l'uso** instructions (for use) 3 (Dir) investigation

istupidire [istupi'dire] /55/ VT (sogg: colpo) to stun, daze; (: droga, stanchezza) to stupefy VI (aus essere), **istupidirsi** VIP to become stupid

Italia [i'talja] SF Italy; **in Italia** in Italy; **ti è piaciuta l'Italia?** did you like Italy?; **verranno in Italia quest'estate** they're coming to Italy this summer

italiano, -a [ita'ljano] AGG Italian; **all'italiana** in the Italian style ♦ SM, SF (abitante) Italian; **gli Italiani** the Italians ♦ SM (lingua) Italian; **parlare (l')italiano** to speak Italian; **parli italiano?** do you speak Italian?; **l'insegnante di italiano** the Italian teacher

ITC [iti'tʃi] SIGLA M = istituto tecnico commerciale

iter ['iter] SM passage, course; **iter burocratico** bureaucratic process; **iter parlamentare** parliamentary procedure

itinerante [itine'rante] AGG wandering, itinerant; **spettacolo itinerante** touring show, travelling (Brit) o traveling (USA) show; **mostra itinerante** touring exhibition

itinerario, -ria, -ri, -rie [itine'rarjo] SM (percorso) route, itinerary; (Alpinismo) route; **itinerario turistico** tourist route

itterizia [itte'rittsja] SF (Med) jaundice

ittico, -a, -ci, -che ['ittiko] AGG fish attr; **industria ittica** fishing industry

IUD ['jud] SIGLA M INV IUD (= intrauterine device)

Iugoslavia [jugoz'lavja] SF = Jugoslavia

iugoslavo, -a [jugoz'lavo] = jugoslavo

iuta ['juta] SF jute

IVA ['iva] SIGLA F (= Imposta sul Valore Aggiunto) V.A.T. (Brit)

ivi ['ivi] AVV (letter) therein; (nelle citazioni) ibid

Jj

J, j [iˈlunga] SM INV, SF INV (*lettera*) J, j; **J come Jersey** ≈ J for Jack (*Brit*), ≈ J for Jig (*USA*)
jazz [dʒaz] SM INV jazz ♦ AGG INV jazz *attr*
jazzista, -i, -e [dʒadˈdzista] SM, SF jazz player
jeans [dʒinz] SMPL jeans
jeep [dʒip] SF INV jeep
jersey [ˈdʒɛrzi] SM INV jersey (cloth); **jersey di lana/cotone** jersey wool/cotton
jockey [ˈdʒɔki] SM INV (*fantino*) jockey

jogging [ˈdʒɔɡiŋ] SM INV jogging; **fare jogging** to go jogging
jolly [ˈdʒɔli] SM INV joker ♦ AGG: **caratteri jolly** wild cards
joystick [dʒoisˈtik] SM INV joystick
jr. ABBR (= *junior*) Jr., jr.
judo [dʒuˈdɔ] SM judo; **fare judo** to do judo
Jugoslavia [jugozˈlavja] SF: **la ex Jugoslavia** the former Yugoslavia
jugoslavo, -a [jugozˈlavo] AGG, SM, SF Yugoslav(ian)
jukebox [ˈdʒukˈbɔks] SM INV jukebox

Kk

K, k [ˈkappa] SF INV, SM INV (*lettera*) K, k; **K come Kursaal** ≈ K for King
kamikaze [kamiˈkaddze] SM INV kamikaze; **una politica economica da kamikaze** (*fig*) a suicidal economic policy ♦ AGG INV (*terrorista, commando, missione*) kamikaze *attr*
Kampala [kamˈpala] SF Kampala
karaoke [karaˈoke] SM INV karaoke
karatè [karaˈtɛ] SM INV karate; **fare karatè** to do karate
Kashmir [kaʃˈmir] SM Kashmir
kayak [kaˈjak] SM INV kayak
Kazakistan [kaˈdzakistan] SM Kazakhstan
kazako, -a [kaˈdzako] SM, SF, AGG Kazakh
keniota, -i, -e [keˈnjɔta], **keniano, -a** [keˈnjano] AGG, SM, SF Kenyan
Kenya [ˈkɛnja] SM Kenya
kerosene [keroˈzɛne] SM INV = cherosene
kg ABBR (= *chilogrammo*) kg
kibbutz [kibˈbuts] SM INV kibbutz
Kilimangiaro [kilimanˈdʒaro] SM: **il Kilimangiaro** Kilimanjaro
kilo *ecc* [ˈkilo] = chilo

kilt [kilt] SM INV kilt
kimono [kiˈmɔno] SM INV = chimono
kirghiso, -a [kirˈɡiso] SM, SF, AGG Kyrgyz
Kirghizistan [kirˈɡizistan] SM Kyrgyzstan
kitsch [kitʃ] SM INV, AGG INV kitsch; **arredamento kitsch** (*pegg*) tacky furniture
kiwi [ˈkiwi] SM INV 1 (*frutto*) kiwi (fruit) 2 (*uccello*) kiwi
km ABBR (= *chilometro*) km
kmq ABBR (= *chilometro quadrato*) km²
KO [kappaˈo], **k.o.** = knock out AVV: **mettere qn k.o.** to knock sb out ♦ SM INV KO, k.o.; **ha vinto per k.o. tecnico** he won on a technical knockout
koala [koˈala] SM INV koala (bear)
kosovaro, -a [kosoˈvaro] AGG, SM, SF Kosovan
Kosovo [ˈkosovo] SM Kosovo
KR SIGLA = Crotone
krapfen [ˈkrapfən] SM INV ≈ doughnut
Kuala Lumpur [ˈkwala ˈlumpur] SF Kuala Lumpur
Kuwait [kuˈvait] SM Kuwait
kW ABBR (= *kilowatt*) kW
kWh ABBR (= *kilowattora*) kW/h

L l

L¹, l¹ [ˈɛlle] SF INV, SM INV (*lettera*) L, l; **L come Livorno** ≈ L for Lucy (*Brit*), ≈ L for Love (*USA*)

L², l² ABBR (= *lira*) L, l

L³ [ˈɛlle] SIGLA F (*taglia*) L (= *large*)

l ABBR (= *litro*) L, l

l' *vedi* **il, la², lo²**

la¹ [la] ART DET F *vedi* **il**

la² [la] PRON *dav vocale* l' **1** (*oggetto: riferito a persona*) her; (: *riferito a cosa*) it; *vedi* **lo² 2** (*oggetto: forma di cortesia: anche:* **La**) you; **in attesa di risentirla I** (*o we*) look forward to hearing from you; **molto lieto di conoscerla** pleased to meet you

la³ [la] SM INV (*Mus*) A; (*solfeggiando la scala*) lah

là [la] AVV **1** there; **mettilo là** put it there; **eccolo là!** there he (*o it*) is; **resta là dove sei** stay where you are; **là dentro/fuori/sopra/sotto ecc** in/out/up (*o* on)/under there *ecc*; **più in là** (*spazio*) further on; (*tempo*) later on; **la mia casa è un po' più in là** my house is a bit further on; **potresti sederti un po' più in là?** could you move along a bit?; **deciderò più in là** I'll decide later on; **chi va là?** who goes there?; **alto là!** halt. **2 di là, di là dal fiume** beyond the river, on the other side of the river; **vieni via di là** come away from there; **mia madre è di là** my mother's in the other room; **al di là di** beyond; **per di là** (*andare, passare*) that way; **se vai per di là allunghi** if you go that way it'll take you longer; **non passo mai per di là** I never go that way; **essere più di là che di qua** to be more dead than alive; **cerca di guardare al di là del fatto in sé** try to look beyond the event itself **3** (*fraseologia*): **là per là** (*sul momento*) there and then; **va' là!** come off it!; **stavolta è andato troppo in là** this time he's gone too far; **essere in là con gli anni** to be getting on (in years)

labbro [ˈlabbro] SM **1** (*Anat: pl f*) **labbra** lip; **leccarsi le labbra** to lick one's lips; **mordersi le labbra** (*fig*) to bite one's tongue; **parlare a fior di labbra** to murmur; **sorridere a fior di labbra** to smile faintly; **pendere dalle labbra di qn** to hang on sb's every word **2** (*pl m* **labbri**): *di ferita, vaso*: lip

labile [ˈlabile] AGG fleeting, ephemeral; **avere una memoria labile** to have a poor memory

labirinto [labiˈrinto] SM (*Mitol*) labyrinth; (*di stradine*) maze

laboratorio, -ri [laboraˈtɔrjo] SM **1** (*di ricerca*) laboratory; **esperimento di** *o* **da laboratorio** laboratory experiment; **laboratorio linguistico** language laboratory **2** (*per lavori manuali*) workshop; (*stanza*) workroom; **laboratorio fotografico** photo lab

laborioso, -a [laboˈrjoso] AGG (*operoso*) industrious, hard-working; (*faticoso*) laborious, difficult

laburista, -i, -e [labuˈrista] AGG Labour *attr* (*Brit*) ♦ SM, SF Labour Party member (*Brit*)

lacca, -che [ˈlakka] SF (*per mobili*) varnish, lacquer; (*per capelli*) (hair) lacquer, hair spray; (*per unghie*) nail polish, nail varnish (*Brit*)

laccare [lakˈkare] /20/ VT (*mobili*) to varnish, lacquer

laccio [ˈlattʃo] SM lace, string; **lacci delle scarpe** shoelaces; **laccio emostatico** (*Med*) tourniquet

lacerante [latʃeˈrante] AGG (*suono*) piercing, shrill

lacerare [latʃeˈrare] /72/ VT (*vestiti, stoffa*) to rip, tear; (*fare a pezzi*) to tear *o* rip to shreds; (*Med, fig*) to lacerate; **un grido lacerò il silenzio** a piercing cry broke the silence; **lacerato dai dubbi/dal rimorso/dal dolore** racked by doubt/remorse/pain; **lacerarsi** VIP to tear, rip

lacerazione [latʃeratˈtsjone] SF (*anche Med*) tear

lacero, -a [ˈlatʃero] AGG **1** (*abiti*) ripped, torn, tattered; (*persona*) ragged, in rags **2** (*Med*) lacerated; **ferita lacero-contusa** injury with lacerations and bruising

laconico, -a, -ci, -che [laˈkɔniko] AGG laconic

lacrima [ˈlakrima] SF **1** tear; **con le lacrime agli occhi** with tears in one's eyes; **mi ha guardato con le lacrime agli occhi** he looked at me with tears in his eyes; **essere/scoppiare in lacrime** to be in/burst into tears; **quando ha visto la foto è scoppiata in lacrime** when she saw the photo she burst into tears; **lacrime di coccodrillo** crocodile tears **2** (*goccia*) drop

lacrimare [lakriˈmare] /72/ VI (*aus avere*) (*occhi*) to water; (*persona*) to cry, weep

lacrimevole [lakriˈmevole] AGG heart-rending, pitiful

lacrimogeno, -a [lakriˈmɔdʒeno] AGG: **gas lacrimogeno** tear gas ♦ SM tear-gas grenade; **hanno lanciato dei lacrimogeni** they fired tear gas

lacrimoso, -a [lakriˈmoso] AGG (*viso, occhi*) tearful; (*commovente: storia, film*) moving

lacuna [laˈkuna] SF (*vuoto*) gap; (*in un testo*) blank (space); (*di memoria*) lapse; **colmare una lacuna** to fill a gap

lacustre [laˈkustre] AGG lake *attr*

laddove [ladˈdove] CONG whereas

ladro, -a [ˈladro] AGG thieving; **governo ladro!** (*fam*) damned government! ♦ SM, SF thief; (*di case*) burglar; **al ladro!** stop thief!; **l'occasione fa l'uomo ladro** (*Proverbio*) opportunity makes the thief

ladrocinio, -ni [ladroˈtʃinjo] SM theft, robbery

ladruncolo, -a [laˈdrunkolo] SM, SF petty thief

laggiù [ladˈdʒu] AVV (*in basso*) down there; (*di là*) down *o* over there

lagna [ˈlaɲɲa] SF (*fam: persona, cosa*) drag, bore; **lagne** SFPL whining *sg*, moaning *sg*; **fare la lagna** to whine, moan

lagnanza [laɲˈɲantsa] SF complaint

lagnarsi [laɲˈɲarsi] /15/ VIP: **lagnarsi (di** *o* **per)** to complain (about), grumble (about)

lago, -ghi [ˈlago] SM lake; **il lago di Garda** Lake Garda; **un lago di sangue** a pool of blood; **lago vulcanico** (*Geol*) crater lake

Lagos [ˈlagos] SF Lagos

lagrima *ecc* [ˈlagrima] = **lacrima**

laguna [laˈguna] SF lagoon

lagunare [laguˈnare] AGG lagoon *attr* ♦ SM: **i lagunari** SMPL ≈ the marines

laico, -a, -ci, -che [ˈlaiko] AGG (*Rel*) lay *attr*; (*stato, potere*) secular; (*scuola*) non-denominational ♦ SM, SF layman *o* lay-woman ♦ SM (*frate converso*) lay brother

laido, -a [ˈlaido] AGG filthy, foul; (*osceno*) obscene, filthy

lama¹ [ˈlama] SM INV (*Rel*) lama

lama² [ˈlama] SM INV (*animale*) llama

lambiccare [lambikˈkare] /20/ VT to distil; **lambiccarsi il cervello** to rack one's brains

lambire [lamˈbire] /55/ VT (*fig: acqua*) to lap; (: *fiamme*) to lick

lambretta [lamˈbretta] (*Marchio registrato*) (motor)scooter

lamella [laˈmella] SF **1** (*di metallo*) thin sheet **2** (*Bio*) lamella; (*di fungo*) gill, lamella (*termine tecn*)

lamentare [lamenˈtare] /72/ VT to lament; **si lamentano gravi perdite** heavy losses are reported; **lamentarsi** VIP **1** (*gemere*) to moan, groan **2** (*lagnarsi*): **lamentarsi (di)** to complain (about); **non mi lamento!** I can't complain!

lamentela [lamenˈtela] SF complaint; **lamentele** SFPL complaining *sg*, grumbling *sg*; **smettila con queste lamentele!** stop grumbling!; **ci sono state molte lamentele sul servizio** there have been a lot of complaints about the service

lamentevole [lamenˈtevole] AGG (*voce*) plaintive, mournful, complaining; (*stato*) lamentable, pitiful

lamento [laˈmento] SM (*gemito*) groan, moan; (*per la morte di qn*) lament

lamentoso, -a [lamenˈtoso] AGG plaintive, mournful

lametta [laˈmetta] SF (*da rasoio*) razor blade

lamiera [laˈmjɛra] SF (*Tecn*) sheet (metal); **lamiera di ferro/d'acciaio** sheet iron/steel; **lamiera ondulata** corrugated iron

lamina ['lamina] SF (di metallo) thin layer o sheet o plate; (di sci) edge; (Bot, Anat) lamina; **lamina d'oro** gold leaf o foil

laminare [lami'nare] /72/ VT to laminate

laminato [lami'nato] SM (metallico) rolled section; **laminato plastico** laminated plastic ♦ AGG laminated

lampada ['lampada] SF light, lamp; **lampada abbronzante** tanning lamp; **lampada alogena** halogen lamp; **lampada a gas** gas lamp; **lampada al neon** neon light; **lampada a petrolio** oil lamp; **lampada da scrivania** reading lamp; **lampada di sicurezza** safety lamp; **lampada a spirito** blowlamp (Brit), blowtorch; **lampada a stelo** standard lamp (Brit), floor lamp (USA); **lampada da tavolo** table lamp

lampadario, -ri [lampa'darjo] SM chandelier

lampadina [lampa'dina] SF (Elettr) (light) bulb; **una lampadina da 100 watt** a 100 watt bulb; **lampadina tascabile** torch (Brit), flashlight (USA)

lampante [lam'pante] AGG 1 (fig: evidente) blindingly obvious, crystal clear; **prova lampante** clear proof 2 **olio lampante** lamp oil

lampara [lam'para] SF (lampada) fishing lamp; (barca) boat for fishing by lamplight in Mediterranean

lampeggiare [lamped'dʒare] /62/ VI (aus avere) (luce, occhi) to flash; (Aut) to flash one's lights ♦ VB IMPERS: **lampeggia** it is lightning

lampeggiatore [lampeddʒa'tore] SM (Aut) indicator; (Fot) flash(gun)

lampione [lam'pjone] SM street light o lamp (Brit); (palo) lamppost

lampo ['lampo] SM (gen) flash; (Meteor) flash of lightning; **lampi** SMPL (Meteor) lightning sg; **un lampo di luce** a flash of light; **tuoni e lampi** thunder and lightning; **in un lampo** in a flash; **passare come un lampo** to flash past o in a flash; **lampo di speranza** glimmer of hope; **lampo di genio** flash of genius, sudden inspiration; **lampo al magnesio** (Fot) magnesium flash ♦ AGG INV (cerimonia: anche Mil: operazione) lightning attr; **la (cerniera) lampo** zip (fastener) (Brit), zipper (USA); **guerra lampo** blitzkrieg; **visita lampo** flying visit

lampone [lam'pone] SM (Bot) raspberry

lana ['lana] SF wool; **di lana** wool, woollen (Brit), woolen (USA); **un maglione di lana** a wool sweater; **pura lana vergine** pure new wool; **essere una buona lana** (fig) to be a scoundrel o rogue; **lana d'acciaio** steel wool; **lana di cammello** camel hair; **lana di vetro** fibreglass (Brit), fiberglass (USA), glass wool

❏ **lana** non si traduce mai con la parola inglese lane

lancetta [lan'tʃetta] SF (di orologio) hand; (di barometro) needle, pointer

lancia¹, -ce [lantʃa] SF (arma) lance, spear; (Pesca) harpoon; (di pompa antincendio) nozzle; **spezzare una lancia in favore di qn** to come to sb's defence; **partire lancia in resta** (fig) to set off ready for battle

lancia², -ce [lantʃa] SF (Naut) launch; **lancia di salvataggio** lifeboat

lanciabombe [lantʃa'bombe] SM INV (Mil) mortar

lanciafiamme [lantʃa'fjamme] SM INV (Mil) flame-thrower

lanciamissili [lantʃa'missili] AGG INV missile-launching ♦ SM INV missile launcher

lanciarazzi [lantʃa'raddzi] AGG INV rocket-launching ♦ SM INV rocket launcher

lanciare [lan'tʃare] /14/ VT 1 (gen) to throw; (con forza) to hurl, fling; (bombe) to drop; (missili, siluri) to launch; **lanciare una bomba** to drop a bomb; **lanciare qc a qn** to throw sth to sb; (per colpirlo) to throw sth at sb; **lanciare qc in aria** to throw sth into the air; **lanciare una moneta in aria** to toss a coin; **lanciare il peso** (Sport) to put the shot; **lanciare il disco** (Sport) to throw the discus 2 (emettere: grido) to give out; (: invettiva) to hurl; (: S.O.S.) to send out; **mi ha lanciato un'occhiataccia** he flashed me a nasty look; **ha lanciato un urlo** he let out a yell; **ha lanciato un grido di dolore** he let out a cry of pain 3 (introdurre: idea, nave, prodotto, moda) to launch; **fu quel regista a lanciarla** it was that director who started her on her career; **hanno lanciato una nuova moda** they've started a new fashion 4 (far andare veloce: macchina) to get up to top speed; **lanciare un cavallo** to set a horse off (at a gallop); **lanciarsi** VR 1 (gen): **lanciarsi in**

qc (anche fig) to throw o.s. into sth; **lanciarsi contro qn** to hurl o fling o.s. at sb; **lanciarsi nella mischia** to throw o.s. into the fray; **lanciarsi all'inseguimento di qn** to set off in pursuit of sb; **lanciarsi col paracadute** to parachute 2 (fig: fare il primo passo): **lanciarsi in** to launch into, embark upon o on; **che aspetti? — lanciati!** what are you waiting for? — off you go!

lanciato, -a [lan'tʃato] AGG 1 (affermato: attore, prodotto) well-known, famous 2 (veicolo) speeding o racing along; **lanciato a tutta velocità** racing along at top speed; **chilometro lanciato** (Sport) flying start kilometre

lancinante [lantʃi'nante] AGG (dolore) stabbing, shooting; (grido) piercing

lancio, -ci ['lantʃo] SM 1 (vedi vt a, c) throwing no pl; hurling no pl, flinging no pl; dropping no pl; launching no pl 2 (Sport) throw; **lancio di corda** (Alpinismo) lassoing; **lancio del disco** the discus; **lancio del giavellotto** the javelin; **lancio del peso** the shot put

landa ['landa] SF (terreno) moor

languido, -a ['langwido] AGG (voce) languid; (sguardo, atteggiamento) languishing

languire [lan'gwire] /17/ VI (aus avere) 1 (struggersi) to pine, languish; **languire d'amore** to be languishing with love 2 (perdere forza: persona) to languish; (: conversazione) to flag; (: affari, commercio) to be slack; **languire in carcere** to languish in prison

languore [lan'gwore] SM 1 (debolezza) weakness, faintness; **sento un languore allo stomaco** I'm feeling a bit peckish 2 (comportamento) languor

laniero, -a [la'njero] AGG (industria, commercio) wool attr, woollen (Brit), woolen (USA)

lanificio, -ci [lani'fitʃo] SM wool mill, woollen (Brit) o woolen (USA) mill

lanolina [lano'lina] SF (Chim) lanolin(e)

lanoso, -a [la'noso] AGG woolly (Brit), wooly (USA)

lanterna [lan'terna] SF (lume, anche Archit) lantern; (faro) lighthouse; **lanterna magica** (Cine) magic lantern

lanternino [lanter'nino] SM: **cercarsele col lanternino** (fig) to be asking for trouble

lanugine [la'nudʒine] SF down

Laos ['laos] SM Laos

lapalissiano, -a [lapalis'sjano] AGG self-evident

La Paz [la'pats] SF La Paz

lapidare [lapi'dare] /72/ VT to stone (to death); (fig) to tear to pieces

lapidario, -ria, -ri, -rie [lapi'darjo] AGG (arte) lapidary; (fig: stile) succinct, terse

lapide ['lapide] SF (di sepolcro) tombstone; (lastra commemorativa) memorial stone, plaque

lapin [la'pɛ̃] SM INV rabbit fur, cony

lapis ['lapis] SM INV pencil

lappone [lap'pone] AGG Lappish, Lapp ♦ SM, SF Laplander, Lapp ♦ SM (lingua) Lapp, Lappish

Lapponia [lap'ponja] SF Lapland

lapsus ['lapsus] SM INV (parlando) slip (of the tongue); (scrivendo) slip (of the pen); **lapsus freudiano** Freudian slip

laptop ['lɛptɔp] SM INV laptop (computer)

lardo ['lardo] SM (per cucinare) lard; (da affettare) pork fat (salted or smoked)

larghezza [lar'gettsa] SF 1 (Mat: misura) width, breadth; (di barca) beam; **larghezza: 20 cm** width: 20 cm; **una stanza della larghezza di 3 metri** a room 3 metres wide 2 (generosità) generosity; **larghezza di vedute** (fig) broad-mindedness

largire [lar'dʒire] /55/ VT (letter) to give generously

largo, -a, -ghi, -ghe ['largo] AGG 1 (dimensione, misura) wide, broad; **un cappello a larghe falde** a wide-brimmed hat; **un uomo largo di spalle** o **dalle spalle larghe** a broad-shouldered man; **ha le spalle larghe** he's got broad shoulders; **ha i fianchi larghi** he's got broad hips; **a gambe larghe** with legs wide apart; **un corridoio largo 2 metri** a corridor 2 metres wide 2 (abiti) loose; (maniche) wide; **questa gonna mi sta larga** this skirt is loose on me; **questa giacca mi sta larga alle spalle** this jacket is too big around the shoulders for me 3 (ampio: parte, percentuale) large, big; **in larga misura** to a great o large extent; **su larga scala** on a large scale; **di larghe vedute** (*fig: liberale*) broad-minded; **di manica larga** (*fig*) generous, open-handed ♦ SM **1 fate largo!** make room *o* way!; **farsi largo tra la folla** to make *o* push one's way through the crowd; **si è fatta largo tra la folla ed è salita sul palco** she pushed her way through the crowd and went up on the stage; **farsi largo a gomitate** to elbow one's way **2** (*piazzetta*) (small) square **3** (*Naut*) open sea; **andare al largo** to sail on the open sea; **non andare al largo** (*nuotando*) don't go too far out; **prendere il largo** to put out to sea; (*fig*) to make off, escape; **al largo di Genova** off (the coast of) Genoa **4** (*Mus*) largo ♦ SF: **stare** *o* **tenersi alla larga (da qn/qc)** to keep one's distance (from sb/sth), keep away (from sb/sth); **stai alla larga da casa mia!** keep away from my house!

larice ['lariʧe] SM (*albero*) larch

laringe [la'rindʒe] SF larynx

laringite [larin'dʒite] SF laryngitis

laringoiatra, -i, -e [laringo'jatra] SM, SF (*medico*) throat specialist

larva ['larva] SF (*Zool, Bio*) larva; (*fig: pegg: apatico*) zombie; **essere** (ridotto a) **una larva** (*fig*) to be (all) skin and bone(s)

lasagne [la'zaɲɲe] SFPL lasagna *sg*; **lasagne al forno** baked lasagna *sg*

lasciapassare [laʃʃapas'sare] SM INV pass, permit

lasciare [laʃ'ʃare] /14/ VT **1** (*gen*) to leave; **lasciare qc a qn** to leave sb sth *o* sth to sb; **ha lasciato Roma nel '76** he left Rome in '76; **ho lasciato i soldi a casa** I've left my money at home; **devo lasciare l'università** I've have to leave university, I have to give up university; **ha lasciato la scuola a 16 anni** he left school at 16; **lasciare la stanza** to vacate the room; **lasciare la porta aperta** to leave the door open; **lasciare qn solo (a casa)** to leave sb (at home) alone; **ha lasciato la moglie** he's left his wife; **lascia la moglie e due bambini** he leaves a wife and two children; **lasciare qn erede** to make sb one's heir; **lasciare qn perplesso/confuso** to leave sb perplexed/confused **2** (*permettere*): **lasciare qn fare qc** *o* **che qn faccia qc** to let sb do sth, allow sb to do sth; **mio padre non mi lascia uscire fino a tardi** my father doesn't let me stay out late; **lascia fare a me** let me do it; **lascia stare** *o* **correre** *o* **perdere** let it drop, forget it **3** (*deporre: cose*) to leave, deposit; (: *persone*) to leave, drop (off); **ti lascio all'angolo** I'll drop you off at the corner **4** (*dare, concedere*) to give, let have; **mi puoi lasciare la macchina oggi?** can you let me have the car today?; **lasciami il tempo di farlo** give me time to do it **5** (*omettere*) to leave out, forget; **non lasciare tutti i particolari interessanti** don't leave out all the interesting bits **6** (*serbare*) to leave, keep; **lasciami un po' di vino** leave some wine for me **7 lasciare stare qn** to let sb be, leave sb alone; **lasciare stare qc** to leave sth alone; **lascia stare quel povero gatto!** leave that poor cat alone!; **lascia stare, ci penso io** leave it, I'll see to it; **lascia stare, offro io** it's all right, I'm paying *o* it's on me; **è meglio lasciar stare certi argomenti** it's better not to bring up certain subjects; **volevo insistere ma poi ho lasciato stare** I was going to insist but then I decided to let it go **8 lasciarsi sfruttare** to let o.s. be exploited; **lasciarsi andare** to let o.s. go **9** (*fraseologia*): **lasciare in bianco** to leave blank; **lasciare (molto) a desiderare** to leave much *o* a lot to be desired; **lasciare detto** *o* **scritto (a qn)** to leave word (for sb); **lasciare qn indifferente** to leave sb unmoved; **non lascia mai niente al caso** he never leaves anything to chance; **lasciami in pace** leave me alone *o* in peace; **lasciare la presa** to lose one's grip; **lasciare il segno (su qc)** to mark (sth); (*fig*) to leave one's *o* a mark (on sth); **ci ha lasciato la vita** it cost him his life; **lasciarsi** VR (*uso reciproco*) to part (from each other); (*coniugi*) to leave each other, split up; **si sono lasciati all'aeroporto** they left each other at the airport, they said goodbye at the airport; **ci siamo lasciati un anno fa** we split up a year ago

lascito [laʃ'ʃito] SM (*Dir*) legacy, bequest

lascivia [laʃ'ʃivja] SF lust, lasciviousness

lascivo, -a [laʃ'ʃivo] AGG lascivious, wanton

laser ['lazer] SM INV, AGG INV: **(raggio) laser** laser (beam); **una stampante laser** a laser printer

lassativo, -a [lassa'tivo] AGG, SM laxative

lassismo [las'sizmo] SM laxity

lasso ['lasso] SM: **lasso di tempo** interval, lapse of time

lassù [las'su] AVV (*in alto*) up there; (*in paradiso*) in heaven above

lastra ['lastra] SF **1** (*di marmo, pietra*) slab; (*di vetro, ghiaccio*) sheet; (*di finestra*) pane; (*di metallo*) plate **2** (*Fot*) plate; (*Med*) X-ray; **fare le lastre a qn** (*fam*) to X-ray sb; **ho fatto una lastra alla gamba** I had my leg X-rayed

lastricare [lastri'kare] /20/ VT to pave

lastricato [lastri'kato] SM paving(stone)

lastrico, -ci *o* **, -chi** ['lastriko] SM paving; **essere sul lastrico** to be penniless; **gettare qn sul lastrico** to leave sb destitute

lastrone [las'trone] SM (*di pietra*) slab; (*Alpinismo*) sheer rock face

latente [la'tɛnte] AGG latent

laterale [late'rale] AGG (*gen*) side *attr*, lateral; (*uscita, ingresso, linea*) side *attr*; **rimessa laterale** throw-in ♦ SM (*Calcio: anche*: **mediano laterale**) halfback

lateralmente [lateral'mente] AVV sideways

laterizio, -zi [late'rittsjo] SM (perforated) brick

latifondista, -i, -e SM, SF large agricultural landowner

latifondo [lati'fondo] SM large (agricultural) estate

latino, -a [la'tino] AGG Latin ♦ SM (*lingua*) Latin

latino-americano, -a [la'tino ameri'kano] AGG, SM, SF Latin-American

latitante [lati'tante] AGG: **essere latitante** (*persona*) to be in hiding *o* on the run; (*fig*) to be an absent force; (*potere, governo*) to be inactive ♦ SM, SF fugitive (from justice)

latitanza [lati'tantsa] SF (*fig: assenza*) absence; **darsi alla latitanza** (*nascondersi*) to go into hiding

latitudine [lati'tudine] SF latitude

lato¹ ['lato] SM (*gen*) side, part; (*Mat, Geom*) side; (*fig: di problema*) aspect; **l'altro lato della strada** the other side of the street; **da ogni lato, da tutti i lati** from all sides; **dal lato opposto (di)** from the other *o* opposite side (of); **d'altro lato** (*d'altra parte*) on the other hand; **da un lato... dall'altro lato...** on the one hand ... on the other hand ...; **l'altro lato della medaglia** (*fig*) the other side of the coin

lato² ['lato] AGG: **in senso lato** broadly speaking

latrare [la'trare] /72/ VI (*aus* **avere**) to bark

latrato [la'trato] SM howling

latrina [la'trina] SF (public) lavatory (*Brit*), rest room (*USA*)

latrocinio, -ni [latro'ʧinjo] SM = **ladrocinio**

latta ['latta] SF (*sostanza*) tin (plate); (*recipiente*) tin (*Brit*), can

lattaio, -aia, -ai, -aie [lat'tajo] SM, SF (*commerciante*) dairy farmer; (*distributore*) milkman *o* milkwoman; **vado dal lattaio** I'm going to the dairy

lattante [lat'tante] AGG unweaned ♦ SM, SF unweaned baby

latte ['latte] SM milk; **al latte** milk *attr*; **dare il latte (a un bambino)** (*al seno*) to (breast)feed (a baby); (*con il biberon*) to (bottle-)feed (a baby); **avere ancora il latte alla bocca** (*fig*) to be still wet behind the ears; **tutto latte e miele** (*fig*) all smiles ♦ **latte di bellezza** beauty lotion; **latte di cocco** coconut milk; **latte condensato** condensed milk; **latte detergente** cleansing milk *o* lotion; **latte di gallina** eggnog; **latte intero** full-cream milk; **latte a lunga conservazione** long-life milk, UHT milk; **latte magro** *o* **scremato** skimmed milk; **latte materno** mother's milk, breast milk; **latte parzialmente scremato** semi-skimmed milk; **latte in polvere** dried *o* powdered milk

latteo, -a ['latteo] AGG (*di latte*) milk *attr*; (*colore*) milky (-white); **la Via Lattea** the Milky Way

latteria [latte'ria] SF dairy

latticino [latti'ʧino] SM dairy product

lattina [lat'tina] SF can; **una lattina di birra** a can of beer

lattuga, -ghe [lat'tuga] SF lettuce

laurea ['laurea] SF degree (*gained after 4-6 years' study and the presentation of a dissertation*); **prendere** *o* **conseguire la laurea** to take *o* obtain one's degree, graduate; **ha preso la laurea in legge** he graduated *o* got a degree in law; **laurea breve** *university degree awarded at the end of a two or three year course*

laureando, -a [laure'ando] AGG final year *attr* (*Brit*), senior (*USA*) ♦ SM, SF final-year student (*Brit*), senior (*USA*)

laureare [laure'are] /72/ VT to confer a degree on; **laurearsi** VIP to graduate; **si è laureato in legge** he graduated in law

laureato, -a [laureˈato] AGG graduate *attr* ♦ SM, SF graduate
lauro [ˈlauro] SM (*Bot*) laurel; **il lauro della vittoria** the laurels of victory
lauto, -a [ˈlauto] AGG (*pranzo, mancia*) lavish; **lauti guadagni** handsome profits
lava [ˈlava] SF lava
lavabiancheˈria [lavabjankeˈria] SF INV washing machine
lavabo [laˈvabo] SM washbasin (*Brit*), washbowl (*USA*)
lavaggio, -gi [laˈvaddʒo] SM (*gen*) washing *no pl*; **lavaggio auto** car wash; **lavaggio del cervello** brainwashing; **gli hanno fatto il lavaggio del cervello** he's been brainwashed; **lavaggio a secco** dry cleaning
lavagna [laˈvaɲɲa] SF 1 (*nelle scuole*) blackboard, chalkboard (*USA*); **scrivere alla lavagna** to write on the blackboard *o* chalkboard; **lavagna bianca** whiteboard; **lavagna interattiva multimediale** (interactive) whiteboard; **lavagna luminosa** overhead projector 2 (*minerale*) slate
lavanda[1] [laˈvanda] SF (*gen*) washing; (*Med*) lavage; **fare una lavanda gastrica a qn** to pump sb's stomach
lavanda[2] [laˈvanda] SF (*Bot*) lavender
lavandaia [lavanˈdaja] SF launderer
lavanderia [lavandeˈria] SF (*di ospedale, caserma*) laundry; (*negozio*) laund(e)rette (*Brit*), laundromat (*USA*); (*lavanderia a secco*) dry-cleaner's
lavandino [lavanˈdino] SM (*del bagno*) washbasin (*Brit*), washbowl (*USA*); (*della cucina*) sink
lavapiatti [lavaˈpjatti] SM INV, SF INV (*persona*) dishwasher ♦ SF INV (*macchina*) dishwasher, dishwashing machine
lavare [laˈvare] /72/ VT 1 (*gen*) to wash; **lava la macchina tutte le domeniche** she washes her car every Sunday; **lavare a mano** to wash by hand, handwash; **lavare a secco** to dry-clean; **lavare i piatti** to wash the dishes, do the washing up, wash up; **lavare la testa a qn** to wash sb's hair 2 (*fig: purificare*) to cleanse, purify 3 **lavarsi le mani/i capelli** to wash one's hands/hair; **lavarsi i denti** to clean *o* brush one's teeth; **me ne lavo le mani** (*fig*) I wash my hands of it; **lavarsi** VR to wash o.s., have a wash
lavasecco [lavaˈsekko] SM INV (*negozio*) dry-cleaner's ♦ SF INV dry-cleaning machine
lavastoviglie [lavastoˈviʎʎe] SF INV dishwasher
lavata [laˈvata] SF wash; **dare una lavata a qc** to give sth a wash; **dare una lavata di capo a qn** (*fig*) to give sb a good telling-off
lavativo [lavaˈtivo] SM (*buono a nulla*) good-for-nothing, idler
lavatoio, -oi [lavaˈtojo] SM (public) washhouse
lavatrice [lavaˈtritʃe] SF washing machine
lavatura [lavaˈtura] SF 1 (*atto*) washing *no pl* 2 (*liquido*) dirty water; **lavatura di piatti** dishwater; **questa minestra è lavatura di piatti** this soup is like dishwater
lavello [laˈvello] SM (kitchen) sink
lavina [laˈvina] SF snowslide
lavorante [lavoˈrante] SM, SF worker
lavorare [lavoˈrare] /72/ VI (*aus avere*) 1 (*persona*) to work; **lavoro dalle otto alle cinque** I work from eight to five; **andare a lavorare** to go to work; **vado a lavorare alle sette** I go to work at seven; **va a lavorare!** go and get on with your work!; **lavorare duro** *o* **sodo** to work hard; **lavorare in proprio** to work for o.s., be self-employed; **lavorare a maglia/ad ago** to knit/do needlework; **lavorare a qc** to work on sth; **lavorare di fantasia** (*suggestionarsi*) to imagine things; (*fantasticare*) to let one's imagination run free 2 (*funzionare: macchinari*) to work, run, operate; (*negozi, uffici: far affari*) to do well, do good business; **quel bar non lavora molto** that bar isn't doing very well; **far lavorare il cervello** to use one's brains ♦ VT (*creta, ferro*) to work; (*legno*) to carve; (*Culin: pane, pasta*) to work, knead; (: *burro*) to beat; (*Agr: terra*) to work, cultivate; **lavorarsi qn** (*fig: convincere*) to work on sb
lavorativo, -a [lavoraˈtivo] AGG (*giorno, capacità*) working *attr*; **attività lavorativa** occupation
lavoratore, -trice [lavoraˈtore] AGG working *attr*; **la classe lavoratrice** the working class ♦ SM, SF worker; **è un gran lavoratore** he's a hard worker
lavorazione [lavoratˈtsjone] SF 1 (*gen*) working; (*di legno, pietra*) carving; (*di film*) making; (*del terreno*) cultivation; (*di pane, pasta*) working, kneading; (*di prodotto*) manufacture;

lavorazione della carta paper making; "**lavorazione a mano**" "handmade"; **lavorazione a macchina** machine production; **lavorazione in serie** mass production 2 (*modo di esecuzione*) workmanship
lavorio, -rii [lavoˈrio] SM intense activity
lavoro [laˈvoro] SM 1 (*attività*): **il lavoro** work; **lavoro manuale/dei campi** manual/farm work; **avere molto/poco lavoro** to have a lot of/little work to do; **essere al lavoro (su qc)** to be at work (on sth); **mettersi al lavoro** to set to *o* get down to work 2 (*compito*) job, task, work *no pl*; **è un lavoro da specialisti** it's a skilled job, it's a job for a professional; **sta svolgendo un lavoro di ricerca** he is carrying out *o* doing research work; **è un lavoro da niente!** it's no job at all!; **eseguire** *o* **fare (bene/male) un lavoro** to do a job (well/badly) 3 (*posto, impiego*): **il lavoro** work; **un lavoro** a job, an occupation; **avere un buon lavoro** to have a good job; **essere senza lavoro** to be out of work *o* unemployed; **i senza lavoro** the jobless, the unemployed; **ha perso il lavoro** he's lost his job; **dar lavoro a** to employ; **l'azienda dà lavoro a 50 dipendenti** the company employs 50 people; **incidente sul lavoro** industrial accident, accident at work; **Ministero del Lavoro e della Previdenza Sociale** ≈ Department of Employment (*Brit*), ≈ Department of Labor (*USA*); **lavoro d'équipe** teamwork; **lavoro interinale** *o* **in affitto** *temporary work*; **lavoro nero** moonlighting (*Brit*), double-dipping (*USA*); **lavoro ripartito** job share; **lavoro straordinario** overtime 4 **lavori** SMPL work *sg*; **lavori scientifici/di ricerca** scientific/research work; **lavori pesanti/leggeri** heavy/light work *o* jobs; **(fare) i lavori di casa** (to do) the housework; **far fare dei lavori in casa** to have some work done in the house; **aprire/chiudere i lavori del parlamento** to open/close the parliamentary session; **il convegno conclude domani i suoi lavori** the conference comes to an end tomorrow; **lavori di scavo** (*Archeol*) excavation works; **Ministero dei Lavori Pubblici** Ministry of Public Works; "**lavori in corso**" "work in progress"; (*segnale stradale*) "roadworks (ahead)"; **questi lavori non si fanno!** you just don't do these things!; **lavori forzati** hard labour *sg* 5 (*opera*) piece of work; (*artistica*) work 6 (*Econ*) labour (*Brit*), labor (*USA*) 7 (*Fis*) work
laziale [latˈtsjale] AGG *o* from Lazio ♦ SM, SF inhabitant *o* native of Lazio
lazzaretto [laddzaˈretto] SM leper hospital
lazzarone [laddzaˈrone] SM scoundrel
lazzo [ˈladdzo] SM jest
LC SIGLA = Lecco
LE SIGLA = Lecce
le[1] [le] ART DET FPL *vedi* **il**
le[2] [le] PRON PERS 1 (*complemento oggetto*) them; *vedi anche* **lo**[2] 2 (*complemento di termine: a lei*) (to) her; **le ho detto tutto** I told her everything; **le appartiene** it belongs to her; **dalle qualcosa da mangiare** give her something to eat; **le ho già scritto** I've already written to her; **le ho spiegato il motivo** I explained the reason to her; **le ha sorriso** he smiled at her 3 (*forma di cortesia: anche:* **Le**: *complemento di termine*) (to) you; **le posso dire una cosa?** may I tell you something?; **le dispiace attendere?** would you mind waiting?; **le posso offrire qualcosa da bere?** can I get you something to drink?; **le chiedo scusa** I beg your pardon; **le ho prenotato una stanza nello stesso albergo** I've booked you a room at the same hotel
leale [leˈale] AGG (*fedele*) loyal, faithful; (*onesto*) fair, honest
lealista, -i, -e [leaˈlista] SM, SF loyalist
lealtà [lealˈta] SF 1 (*fedeltà*) loyalty, faithfulness 2 (*onestà*) fairness, honesty; **comportarsi con lealtà** to behave fairly
leasing [ˈliːziŋ] SM INV (*Comm*) leasing
lebbra [ˈlebbra] SF leprosy
lecca lecca [ˈlekka ˈlekka] SM INV lollipop, lolly
leccapiedi [lekkaˈpjedi] SM INV, SF INV (*pegg*) bootlicker
leccare [lekˈkare] /20/ VT to lick; **leccarsi le labbra** *o* **i baffi/le dita** to lick one's lips/fingers; **leccarsi le ferite** (*anche fig*) to lick one's wounds; **leccare (i piedi a) qn** (*fig*) to suck up to sb; **leccarsi** VR (*fig*) to preen o.s.
leccato, -a [lekˈkato] AGG affected
leccherò *ecc* [lekkeˈrɔ] VB *vedi* **leccare**
leccio, -ci [ˈlettʃo] SM (*albero*) holm oak, ilex
leccornia [lekkorˈnia] SF delicacy, titbit

lecito, -a ['lɛtʃito] AGG (*domanda, comportamento*) permissible; (*Dir*) lawful, legal; **ti par** *o* **sembra lecito che...?** does it seem right to you that ...?; **crede che tutto gli sia lecito** he thinks he can do whatever he likes; **mi sia lecito far presente che...** may I point out that ...?; **se mi è lecito** if I may ♦ SM (what is) right

ledere ['lɛdere] /81/ VT IRREG to damage; **ledere gli interessi di qn** to prejudice sb's interests

lega¹, -ghe ['lega] SF 1 (*Pol, Calcio*) league; **lega doganale** customs union; **far lega (con qn) contro qn/qc** to be in league (with sb) against sb/sth; **la Lega delle Nazioni** the League of Nations 2 (*Chim*) alloy; **metallo di bassa lega** base metal; **gente di bassa lega** (*fig*) common *o* vulgar people

lega², -ghe ['lega] SF (*misura*) league

legaccio, -ci [le'gattʃo] SM lace, string

legale [le'gale] AGG (*gen*) legal; **medicina legale** forensic medicine; **studio legale** lawyer's office; **numero legale** quorum; **corso legale delle monete** official exchange rate ♦ SM, SF lawyer

legalità [legali'ta] SF lawfulness, legality

legalizzare [legalid'dzare] /72/ VT 1 (*rendere legale*) to legalize 2 (*autenticare*) to authenticate

legalizzazione [legaliddzattsjone] SF (*vedi vb*) legalization; authentication

legame [le'game] SM 1 (*gen, anche fig*) tie, bond; **c'è un legame molto forte tra di loro** they're very close; **legame di sangue/di parentela** blood/family tie; **legame di amicizia** bond of friendship; **rompere i legami con qn/qc** to break one's ties with sb/sth 2 (*rapporto logico*) link, connection; **dev'esserci un legame tra i due episodi** there must be a link between the two events 3 (*Chim*) bond

legamento [lega'mento] SM (*Anat*) ligament

legare [le'gare] /80/ VT 1 (*gen*) to bind, tie (up); (*Tip: libro*) to bind; **i rapinatori lo hanno legato ad una sedia** the robbers tied him to a chair; **legare le mani a qn** (*anche fig*) to tie sb's hands; **è pazzo da legare** (*fam*) he should be locked up 2 (*persone: unire*) to bind (together), unite; (*vincolare*) to bind; **sono legati da amicizia** they are friends; **siamo legati da questioni di interesse** we have financial interests in common; **questo posto è legato ai ricordi della mia infanzia** this place is bound up with memories of my childhood; **legarsela al dito** (*fig*) to bear a grudge 3 (*connettere*) to connect, link up; **questi due fatti sono strettamente legati** these two facts are closely linked *o* connected 4 (*Culin: ingredienti, salsa*) to bind; (: *arrosto, pollo*) to truss ♦ VI (*aus avere*) 1 (*persone*) to get on; **non hanno mai legato** they've never got on; **non ho mai legato con lui** I've never been very friendly with him 2 (*metalli*) to alloy 3 (*Culin*) to bind; **legarsi** VR 1 (*fig*): **legarsi (a qn)** to become attached (to sb) 2 (*Alpinismo*): **legarsi in cordata** to rope up

legatario, -ria, -ri, -rie [lega'tarjo] SM, SF (*Dir*) legatee

legato¹ [le'gato] SM: **legato pontificio** papal legate

legato² [le'gato] SM (*Dir*) legacy, bequest

legatoria [legato'ria] SF (*attività*) bookbinding; (*negozio*) bookbinder's

legatura [lega'tura] SF (*di libri*) binding; (*Tip, Mus*) ligature

legazione [legat'tsjone] SF legation

legenda [le'dʒɛnda] SF *vedi* **leggenda 2**

legge ['lɛddʒe] SF (*gen*) law; (*Parlamento*) act; **una nuova legge** a new law; **studia legge** he's studying law; **a norma** *o* **termini di legge** according to the law; **per legge** by law; **la legge è uguale per tutti** everybody is equal before the law; **la legge del più forte** law of survival of the fittest; **ogni suo desiderio è legge** your wish is my command; **la sua parola è legge** his word is law; **le leggi della società** the rules *o* laws of society; **legge marziale** martial law

leggenda [led'dʒɛnda] SF 1 (*mito*) legend; (*diceria*) old wives' tale; **leggenda metropolitana** urban myth 2 (*iscrizione: di moneta*) legend 3 (*chiave di lettura*) key

leggendario, -ria, -ri, -rie [leddʒen'darjo] AGG legendary

leggere ['lɛddʒere] /61/ VT IRREG (*gen, anche Mus*) to read; (*discorso, comunicato*) to read (out); **non ho ancora letto quel libro** I haven't read that book yet; **leggere ad alta voce** to read aloud; **l'ho letto sul giornale** I read (about) it in the

newspaper; **leggere nel futuro** (*chiromante*) to read the future; **leggere la mano a qn** to read sb's palm; **leggere qc negli occhi di qn** to see sth in sb's eyes; **leggere nel pensiero a qn** to read sb's mind *o* thoughts; **leggere fra le righe** (*fig*) to read between the lines; **letto e approvato** read and approved

leggerezza [leddʒe'rettsa] SF 1 (*gen*) lightness; (*di ballerina*) lightness, nimbleness 2 (*sconsideratezza*) thoughtlessness; (*volubilità*) fickleness; **con leggerezza** (*agire*) thoughtlessly

leggero, -a [led'dʒɛro] AGG (*gen*) light; (*agile*) light, nimble, agile; (*rumore, dolore*) slight; (*malattia, punizione*) mild, slight; (*cibo, vino*) light; (*caffè, tè*) weak; **un pacco leggero** a light parcel; **un pasto leggero** a light meal; **leggero come una piuma** light as a feather; **avere il sonno leggero** to be a light sleeper; **a passi leggeri** with a light step; **avere un leggero accento straniero** to have a slight foreign accent; **ho un leggero mal di testa** I've got a slight headache; **ha avuto la malattia in forma leggera** she had a mild form of the illness; **fanteria/cavalleria leggera** light infantry/cavalry; **una persona leggera** (*fig*) a flirt; **prendere le cose alla leggera** to take things lightly; **a cuor leggero** light-heartedly

leggiadro, -a [led'dʒadro] AGG (*gen*) lovely, pretty; (*stile, movimenti*) elegant, graceful

leggibile [led'dʒibile] AGG (*calligrafia*) legible; (*libro*) readable

leggio, -gii [led'dʒio] SM (*per libri*) bookrest; (*Mus*) music stand; (*in chiesa: Univ*) lectern

legherò ecc [lege'rɔ] VB *vedi* **legare**

leghismo [le'gizmo] SM (*Pol*) *in Italy, political movement with federalist tendencies*

legiferare [ledʒife'rare] /72/ VI (*aus avere*) to legislate

legionario, -ri [ledʒo'narjo] SM (*volontario*) legionnaire; (*Storia*) legionary

legione [le'dʒone] SF (*Mil*) legion; (*fig*) host, multitude; **la Legione straniera** the Foreign Legion

legislativo, -a [ledʒizla'tivo] AGG legislative

legislatore [ledʒizla'tore] SM legislator

legislatura [ledʒizlas'tura] SF legislature

legislazione [ledʒizlat'tsjone] SF legislation

legittimare [ledʒitti'mare] /72/ VT (*figlio*) to legitimize; (*giustificare: comportamento*) to justify

legittimità [ledʒittimi'ta] SF legitimacy

legittimo, -a [le'dʒittimo] AGG (*figlio*) legitimate; (*orgoglio*) justifiable; (*dubbio, desiderio*) reasonable; (*fondato: paura, sospetto*) justified; **per legittima difesa** in self-defence (*Brit*), in self-defense (*USA*); **legittimo sospetto** (*Dir*) transfer of a case to a different court because the impartiality of the judge is in doubt

legna ['leɲɲa] SF (fire)wood; **legna da ardere** firewood; **stufa a legna** wood stove; **far legna** to gather firewood; **mettere legna al fuoco** (*fig*) to add fuel to the fire

legnaia [leɲ'ɲaja] SF woodshed

legnaiolo [leɲɲa'jɔlo] SM woodcutter

legname [leɲ'ɲame] SM timber, wood

legnata [leɲ'ɲata] SF blow with a stick; **dare a qn un sacco di legnate** to give sb a good hiding

legno ['leɲɲo] SM 1 (*gen*) wood; **di legno** wood *attr*, wooden; **un tavolo di legno** a wooden table; **legno stagionato** seasoned wood; **legno dolce/duro** soft/hardwood; **testa di legno** (*fig*) blockhead 2 (*pezzo di legno*) piece of wood 3 (*fig: nave*) sailing ship 4 (*Mus*): **i legni** SMPL the woodwind *sg o pl*

legnoso, -a [leɲ'ɲoso] AGG (*di legno*) woody; (*come legno: movimenti*) stiff, wooden

legume [le'gume] SM pulse; **legumi** SMPL pulses

lei¹ ['lɛi] PRON PERS F 1 (*complemento: dopo prep, con valore enfatico*) her; **sono venuto con lei** I came with her; **dimmi qualcosa di lei** tell me something about her; **senza di lei** without her; **se non fosse per lei** if it were not for her; **hanno accusato lei, non me** they accused her, not me; **chiedilo a lei** ask her; **lei qui non la voglio** I don't want her here 2 (*sogg: al posto di 'ella', con valore enfatico*) she; **lei è meglio di te** she is better than you; **prendetela, è lei** catch her, she's the one; **è lei, apri la porta** it's her, open the door; **è stata lei a dirmelo** she told me herself, it was she who told me; **ha ragione lei, non tu** she's right, not you; **viene anche lei?** is she coming too?; **neanche lei ha tutti i torti** even she isn't completely in the wrong; **non lo sapeva nemmeno lei** she didn't even know it herself **3** (*nelle comparazioni: sogg*) she, her; (: *complemento*) her; **ne so quanto lei** I know as much as she does, I know as much as her ♦ SF INV (*scherz*): **la mia lei** my beloved

lei² ['lɛi] PRON PERS (*anche: forma di cortesia*) Lei) **1** you; **lei per cortesia venga con noi** be so good as to come with us; **senza di lei** without you; **riconosco lei senz'altro** I certainly recognize you; **posso venire con lei?** may I come with you? **2** (*nelle comparazioni*) you; **farò come lei** I'll do the same as you (do) ♦ SM: **dare del lei a qn** to address sb as 'lei'
❑ The third person singular pronoun **lei** is used when speaking to adults with whom you do not have a close relationship, as a sign of respect. In some parts of southern Italy, "voi" is still used as a respectful form of address. "Tu" is used when speaking to friends, relatives and children.

lembo ['lembo] SM (*orlo*) hem; (*striscia: di stoffa, fig: di terra*) strip
❑ **lembo** non si traduce mai con la parola inglese *limb*

lemma, -i ['lemma] SM **1** (*di dizionario*) headword; (*di enciclopedia*) (main) entry **2** (*Mat, Filosofia*) lemma

lemme lemme ['lemme 'lemme] AVV (*fam*) (very) very slowly

lena ['lena] SF: **di buona lena** (*lavorare, camminare*) at a good pace

lenire [le'nire] /55/ VT to soothe, relieve

lentamente [lenta'mente] AVV slowly

lente ['lɛnte] SF (*Ottica, Fot*) lens; **lente d'ingrandimento** magnifying glass; **lenti a contatto) morbide** soft lenses; **lenti (a contatto) rigide** hard lenses; **lenti a contatto** contact lenses; **portare le lenti (a contatto)** to wear contacts o contact lenses

lentezza [len'tettsa] SF slowness; (*di mente*) slowwittedness; **con lentezza** slowly

lenticchia [len'tikkja] SF (*Bot*) lentil; **per un piatto di lenticchie** (*fig*) for nothing, for peanuts

lentiggine [len'tiddʒine] SF freckle

lento, -a ['lɛnto] AGG **1** (*gen*) slow; **il mio computer è troppo lento** my computer is too slow; **lento a** o **nel fare qc** slow in doing sth; **a passi lenti** slowly, with a slow step; **il bambino è un po' lento** (*fig*) the child is a bit slow; **cuocere a fuoco lento** to cook over a low heat **2** (*allentato*) loose; (*fune*) slack ♦ SM (*ballo*) slow dance

lenza ['lɛntsa] SF (*fishing*) line

lenzuolo [len'tswɔlo] (*pl f* **lenzuola**, *pl m* **lenzuoli**) SM sheet; **lenzuolo (di) sopra/sotto** top/bottom sheet; **lenzuolo funebre** shroud

leoncino [leon'tʃino] SM lion cub

leone [le'one] SM **1** (*Zool*) lion; **fare la parte del leone** (*fig*) to take the lion's share; **leone marino** sea-lion **2** (*Astrol*): **Leone** Leo; **essere del Leone** to be Leo

leopardo [leo'pardo] SM leopard

leporino, -a [lepo'rino] (*Med*): **labbro leporino** harelip

lepre ['lɛpre] SF hare; **lepre delle nevi** mountain o blue hare

lercio, -cia, -ci, -ce ['lɛrtʃo] AGG filthy, foul

lerciume [ler'tʃume] SM filth

lesbica ['lɛzbika] SF lesbian

lesinare [lezi'nare] /72/ VI (*aus avere*) **lesinare (su)** to skimp (on), be stingy (with) ♦ VT: **lesinare la lira** to count the pennies

lesione [le'zjone] SF **1** (*danno*) damage; **lesione personale** (*Dir*) personal injury **2** (*Med*) lesion; **lesioni interne** internal injuries **3** (*Edil*) crack

lesivo, -a [le'zivo] AGG: **lesivo (di)** detrimental (to), damaging (to)

leso, -a ['lɛzo] PP *di* **ledere** ♦ AGG (*Dir*): **parte lesa** injured party; **lesa maestà** lese-majesty

Lesotho [le'sɔto] SM Lesotho

lessare [les'sare] /72/ VT (*Culin*) to boil

lessi *ecc* ['lɛssi] VB *vedi* **leggere**

lessicale [lessi'kale] AGG lexical

lessico, -ci ['lɛssiko] SM (*Ling*) lexis, vocabulary; (*dizionario*) lexicon

lessicografia [lessikogra'fia] SF lexicography

lessicografo, -a [lessi'kɔgrafo] SM, SF lexicographer

lesso, -a ['lɛsso] (*Culin*) AGG boiled ♦ SM (*gen*) boiled meat; (*manzo*) boiled beef

lesto, -a ['lɛsto] AGG quick, fast; **lesto di mano** (*fig: per rubare*) light-fingered; (: *per picchiare*) free with one's fists

lestofante [lesto'fante] SM swindler, con man

letale [le'tale] AGG lethal, deadly

letamaio, -ai [leta'majo] SM dung o manure heap; (*fig*) pigsty

letame [le'tame] SM manure, dung; (*fig*) filth, muck

letargo [le'targo] SM **1** (*di animale*) hibernation; **essere/andare** o **cadere in letargo** to be in/go into hibernation **2** (*di persona, Med, anche fig*) lethargy

letizia [le'tittsja] SF joy, happiness

lettera ['lɛttera] SF **1** (*dell'alfabeto*) letter; **scrivere qc con lettere maiuscole/minuscole** to write sth in capitals o capital letters/in small letters; **scrivere un numero in lettere** to write out a number in full; **prendere qc alla lettera** to take sth literally; **eseguire qc alla lettera** (*legge, ordine*) to carry out sth to the letter; **restar lettera morta** (*consiglio, invito*) to go unheeded; **diventar lettera morta** (*legge*) to become a dead letter; **lettere maiuscole** capitals o capital letters; **lettere minuscole** small letters **2** (*missiva*) letter; **hai ricevuto la mia lettera?** did you get my letter?; **lettera d'affari/d'amore** business/love letter **3** **lettere** SFPL (*letteratura*) literature *sg*; **fa lettere all'università** he is doing an arts degree; **lettere antiche** classics *sg*; **un uomo di lettere** a man of letters ♦ **lettera di accompagnamento** cover letter; **lettera assicurata** registered letter; **lettera di cambio** (*Comm*) bill of exchange; **lettera di credito** (*Comm*) letter of credit; **lettera di intenti** (*Comm*) letter of intent; **lettera di presentazione** letter of presentation; **lettera raccomandata** recorded delivery (*Brit*) o certified (*USA*) letter

letterale [lette'rale] AGG literal

letteralmente [letteral'mente] AVV literally

letterario, -ria, -ri, -rie [lette'rarjo] AGG literary

letterato, -a [lette'rato] AGG cultured ♦ SM, SF scholar

letteratura [lettera'tura] SF literature

lettiga, -ghe [let'tiga] SF **1** (*barella*) stretcher **2** (*portantina*) litter

lettino [let'tino] SM (*anche:* **lettino solare**) sunbed; (*per bambini*) cot (*Brit*), crib (*USA*)

letto¹, -a ['lɛtto] PP *di* **leggere**

letto² ['lɛtto] SM (*gen, di fiume, lago*) bed; **(ri)fare il letto** to make the bed; **essere a letto** to be in bed; **andare a letto, mettersi a letto** to go to bed; **ieri sera sono andato a letto molto tardi** I went to bed very late last night; **andare a letto con qn** to go to bed with sb, sleep with sb; **a letto, bambini!** bedtime, children!; **figlio di primo/secondo letto** child by one's first/second marriage; **sul letto di morte** on one's deathbed; **letti a castello** bunk beds; **letti gemelli** twin beds; **letto matrimoniale** o **a due piazze** double bed; **letto a una piazza** single bed

lettone ['lɛttone] AGG, SM, SF Latvian ♦ SM (*lingua*) Latvian, Lettish

Lettonia [let'tɔnja] SF Latvia

lettorato [letto'rato] SM **1** (*Univ*) lectorship, assistantship **2** (*Rel*) lectorate, lectorship

lettore, -trice [let'tore] SM, SF **1** (*gen*) reader; **sono un avido lettore di fantascienza** I'm an avid reader of science fiction; **il pubblico dei lettori** the reading public **2** (*Univ*) lector, assistant ♦ SM **1** (*Rel*) lector **2** **lettore CD** CD player; **lettore DVD** DVD player; **lettore di e-book** e-reader; **lettore MP3** MP3 player; **lettore ottico** (*Inform*) optical character reader

lettura [let'tura] SF (*gen*) reading; **un libro di piacevole lettura** a very readable book; **un libro di facile lettura** an easy book to read; **libro di lettura** (*Scol*) reading book; **letture obbligatorie** (*Scol*) set books
❑ **lettura** non si traduce mai con la parola inglese *lecture*

leucemia [leutʃe'mia] SF leukaemia (*Brit*), leukemia (*USA*)

leva¹ ['lɛva] SF (*anche fig*) lever; **far leva su qc** to lever sth up; (*fig*) to take advantage of sth; **far leva su qn** to work on sb; **leva del freno a mano** handbrake (lever); **avere in mano le**

leve del comando (*fig*) to hold the reins; **leva del cambio** gear lever *o* stick (*Brit*), gear shift (*USA*); **leva di comando** control lever

leva² ['leva] SF (*Mil*) conscription, call-up (*Brit*), draft (*USA*); **essere di leva** to be due for call-up *o* draft; (*in servizio*) to be a conscript; **le nuove leve** (*fig*) the younger generation

levante [le'vante] SM (*Geog*) east; (*vento*) east wind; (*nel Mediterraneo*) levanter; **il Levante** the Levant

levare [le'vare] /72/ VT 1 (*gen*: *togliere*) to remove, take away; (: *coperchio*) to take off; (: *tassa*) to abolish; (: *dente*) to take out; (*Mat*) to subtract, take away; **leva i tuoi libri dal tavolo** take your books off the table; **levare la sete** to quench one's thirst; **levare qn/qc di torno** *o* **di mezzo** to get rid of sb/sth; **levare l'assedio** (*Mil*) to raise the siege; **levare un divieto** to lift a ban; **levare le tende** (*fig*) to pack up and leave 2 (*sollevare*: *occhi, testa*) to lift (up), raise; **levare l'ancora** (*Naut*) to lift *o* weigh anchor; **levare un grido** to let out a cry 3 **levarsi qc** (*vestito*) to take sth off, remove sth; **si è levato le scarpe** he took off his shoes; **levarsi il pensiero** to put one's mind at rest; **levarsi** VR (*persona*: *alzarsi*) to get up; **levati di mezzo** *o* **di lì** *o* **di torno!** get out of the *o* my way!; **levarsi** VIP (*vento, burrasca, sole*) to rise

levata [le'vata] SF 1 (*della posta*) collection; **una levata di scudi** concerted opposition 2 (*Mil*) reveille

levataccia, -ce [leva'tattʃa] SF: **fare una levataccia** to get up at an ungodly hour

levatoio, -oi [leva'tojo] AGG: **ponte levatoio** drawbridge

levatrice [leva'tritʃe] SF midwife

levatura [leva'tura] SF intellect, intellectual capacity

levigare [levi'gare] /80/ VT (*gen*) to smooth; (*marmo*) to polish; (*con carta vetrata*) to sand; (*fig*: *discorso*) polish

levigato, -a [levi'gato] AGG (*superficie*) smooth; (*fig*: *stile*) polished; (: *pelle*) flawless

levità [levi'ta] SF (*letter*) lightness

levriere [le'vrjere] SM greyhound

lezione [let'tsjone] SF (*Scol*) lesson; (*Univ*) lecture; **ora di lezione** (*Scol*) period; **far lezione (a qn)** to teach (sb), give lessons (to sb); (*Univ*) to give a lecture (to sb); **una lezione di generosità** a lesson in generosity; **servire di lezione a qn** to be a lesson to sb; **lezione privata** private lesson; **do lezioni private** I give private lessons

lezioso, -a [let'tsjoso] AGG (*stile*) affected; (*sorriso*) simpering

lezzo ['leddzo] SM stink, stench

LI SIGLA = Livorno

li [li] PRON PERS PL them; *vedi anche* **lo²**

lì [li] AVV 1 there; **mettilo lì** put it there; **eccolo lì!** there he (*o* it) is!; **è rimasto lì dov'era** he stayed where he was; **lì dentro/fuori/sopra/sotto** *ecc* in/out/on (*o* up)/under there *ecc*; **di** *o* **da lì** from there; **vieni via di lì** come away from there; **da lì non si entra** you can't come in that way; **per di lì** that way; **di lì a pochi giorni** a few days later; **la discussione è finita lì** the discussion ended there; **fin lì** tutto sembrava normale up until then everything seemed normal; *vedi anche* **quello 2** (*fraseologia*): **lì per lì** (*sul momento*) there and then, then and there; (*dapprima*) at first; **è arrabbiato, tutto lì** he's angry, that's all; **essere lì (lì) per fare qc** to be on the point of doing sth, be about to do sth

libagione [liba'dʒone] SF libation

libanese [liba'nese] AGG, SM, SF Lebanese *inv*

Libano ['libano] SM the Lebanon; **andremo in Libano** we're going to Lebanon

libbra ['libbra] SF pound

libeccio, -ci [li'bettʃo] SM libeccio, libecchio, *south-west wind*

libello [li'bello] SM libel

libellula [li'bellula] SF dragonfly

liberale [libe'rale] AGG (*gen, anche Pol*) liberal ♦ SM, SF (*Pol*) Liberal

liberalizzare [liberalid'dzare] /72/ VT to liberalize

liberare [libe'rare] /72/ VT 1 (*rendere libero*: *prigioniero*) to release; (: *popolo*) to free, liberate, free; **hanno curato il cigno e poi l'hanno liberato** they treated the swan and then set it free; **liberaci dal male** (*Rel*) deliver us from evil 2 (*sgombrare*: *passaggio*) to clear; (: *stanza*) to vacate; **dobbiamo liberare la stanza entro le undici** we have to vacate the room by eleven 3 (*produrre*: *energia*) to release; **liberarsi** VR to get free; è

riuscito a liberarsi ed è scappato he managed to get free and escaped; **liberarsi di qn/qc** to get rid of sb/sth; **finalmente mi sono liberata di lui** I finally got rid of him; **liberarsi dagli impegni** to free o.s. from one's commitments; **riesco a liberarmi per le 5...** if I can manage to be free by 5 o'clock ...; **liberarsi** VIP (*stanza*) to become vacant; (*telefono, posto*) to become free

liberatore, -trice [libera'tore] AGG liberating; **guerra liberatrice** war of liberation ♦ SM, SF liberator

liberazione [liberat'tsjone] SF 1 (*di prigioniero*) release; (*di popolo*) liberation; **è stata una liberazione per lui** (*sollievo*) it was a release for him; **che liberazione!** what a relief! 2 **la Liberazione** *national holiday that falls on April 25*

libercolo [li'berkolo] SM (*pegg*) worthless book

Liberia [li'berja] SF Liberia

liberiano, -a [libe'rjano] AGG, SM, SF Liberian

liberismo [libe'rizmo] SM (*Econ*) laissez-faire

libero, -a ['libero] AGG 1 (*senza costrizioni*) free; (*persona*: *non sposata*) unattached; **sei libero domani sera?** are you free tomorrow evening?; **tenersi libero per domani/lunedì** to keep tomorrow/Monday free; **libero da** (*legami, preoccupazioni*) free of *o* from; **essere libero di fare qc** to be free to do sth; **sei libero di rifiutare** you're free *o* at liberty to refuse; **siete liberi di andarvene** you're free to go; **dar libero corso a** to give free rein to; **dar libero sfogo a** to give vent to; **libera discussione** free *o* open discussion; **"ingresso libero"** (*gratuito*) "entrance *o* admission free" 2 (*non occupato*: *posto*) free; (: *passaggio*) clear; (: *posto*) vacant, free; (: *linea telefonica*) free; **finalmente è libero!** the line is free at last!; **è libero questo posto?** is this seat free?; **avete una camera libera per questa sera?** have you a room available for tonight?; **non ha mai un momento libero** he never has a free moment; **cosa fai nel tempo libero?** what do you do in your free *o* spare time?; **la strada è libera** the road is clear; **via libera!** all clear!; **avere via libera** to have a free hand; **dare via libera a qn** to give sb the go-ahead ♦ SM (*Calcio*: *anche*: **battitore libero**) sweeper ♦ **libera professione** self-employment; **libera uscita** (*Mil*) leave; (*in Marina*) liberty; **libero arbitrio** free will; **libero professionista** self-employed (professional) person; (*che lavora per varie aziende*) freelance, freelancer; **libero scambio** free trade

liberoscambismo [liberoskam'bizmo] SM (*Econ*) free trade

libertà [liber'ta] SF INV 1 (*gen*) freedom, liberty; **combattere per la libertà** to fight for freedom; **il ladro è ancora in libertà** the thief is still at large; **nei momenti di libertà** (*tempo libero*) in one's free time; **le libertà civili** civil liberties; **libertà di espressione** freedom of expression; **libertà di pensiero** freedom of thought; **libertà di scelta** freedom of choice; **libertà di stampa** freedom of the press 2 (*Dir*) freedom, liberty; **concedere la libertà a qn** to release sb; **rimettere qn in libertà** to set sb free, release sb; **essere in libertà provvisoria** to be released on (*o* without) bail; **essere in libertà vigilata** to be on probation 3 (*licenza*) liberty; **prendersi la libertà di** to take the liberty of; **prendersi delle libertà** to take liberties

libertario, -ria, -ri, -rie [liber'tarjo] AGG libertarian

libertino, -a [liber'tino] AGG, SM, SF libertine

liberty [li'berti] AGG INV, SM INV *art nouveau*

Libia ['libja] SF Libya

libico, -a, -ci, -che ['libiko] AGG, SM, SF Libyan

libidine [li'bidine] SF lust, lechery

libidinoso, -a [libidi'noso] AGG lustful, lecherous, libidinous

libido [li'bido] SF INV (*Psic*) libido

libraio, -ai [li'brajo] SM bookseller

librario, -ria, -ri, -rie [li'brarjo] AGG book *attr*

librarsi [li'brarsi] /72/ VR to hover; **librarsi in volo** to soar

libreria [libre'ria] SF 1 (*negozio*) bookshop 2 (*mobile*) bookcase 3 (*Inform*) library

libretto [li'bretto] SM booklet; (*Mus*) libretto ♦ **libretto degli assegni** chequebook (*Brit*), checkbook (*USA*); **libretto di banca** bank book; **libretto di circolazione** (*Aut*) registration document (*Brit*), logbook (*Brit*), registration (*USA*); **libretto di garanzia** user's manual, instruction booklet; **libretto di lavoro** booklet showing a person's current and previous employment; **libretto di risparmio** bankbook (*Brit*), passbook; **libretto universitario** *booklet showing a university student's academic record*

libro ['libro] SM **1** (*gen*) book; **essere sul libro nero di qn** to be in sb's bad books; **essere un libro aperto** (*fig: persona*) to be an open book; **a libro** (*scala*) folding; **Libro bianco** (*Pol*) white paper (*Brit*); **libro di consultazione** reference book; **libro di cucina** cookery book, cookbook; **libro elettronico** electronic book; **libro giallo** detective story, thriller; **libro tascabile** paperback; **libro di testo** textbook; **libro usato** second-hand book; **Libro verde** (*Pol*) Green Paper **2** (*registro*) book, register; **tenere i libri** to keep the books; **libri contabili** (account) books; **libri sociali** company records; **libro di cassa** cash book; **libro mastro** ledger; **libro paga** payroll

licantropo [li'kantropo] SM werewolf

liceale [lit∫e'ale] AGG secondary school *attr: Brit*), high school *attr* (*USA*) ♦ SM, SF secondary school (*Brit*) *o* high school (*USA*) pupil

licenza [li't∫entsa] SF **1** (*gen*, *permesso*) permission, leave; **chiedere/dare licenza di fare qc** to ask/give permission to do sth; **prendersi la licenza di fare qc** to take the liberty of doing sth **2** (*autorizzazione*) licence (*Brit*), license (*USA*), permit; **licenza di caccia/di pesca/ matrimoniale** hunting/fishing/marriage licence; **licenza di esportazione/ importazione** export/import licence; **licenza di fabbricazione** manufacturer's licence; **su licenza di...** (*Comm*) under licence from ... **3** (*Scol*) school-leaving certificate **4** (*Mil: documento*) pass; **essere/andare in licenza** to be/go on leave **5** (*sfrenatezza*) licence (*Brit*), license (*USA*), licentiousness; **licenza poetica** poetic licence

licenziamento [lit∫entsja'mento] SM dismissal; (*per esubero di personale*) redundancy; **licenziamento ingiustificato** unfair dismissal; **licenziamento in massa** mass dismissals *pl o* redundancies *pl*

licenziare [lit∫en'tsjare] /19/ VT **1** to dismiss, sack (*Brit*), fire (*fam*); (*per esubero di personale*) to make redundant; **ha minacciato di licenziarla** he threatened to sack her; **mio padre è stato licenziato dopo trent'anni di lavoro** my father was made redundant after working there for thirty years **2** (*Scol*) to award a school-leaving certificate to; **licenziarsi** VR **1** (*andare via*) to take one's leave; (*dal lavoro*) to resign, hand in one's notice, give up one's job **2** (*Scol*) to obtain one's school-leaving certificate

licenziosità [lit∫entsjosi'ta] SF licentiousness

licenzioso, -a [lit∫en'tsjoso] AGG licentious

liceo [li't∫ɛo] SM ≈ secondary school (*Brit*), ≈ high school (*USA*); **liceo classico/scientifico** *secondary or high school specializing in classics/scientific subjects*

lichene [li'kɛne] SM (*Bot*) lichen

lido ['lido] SM (*spiaggia*) beach; (*letter: paese*) shore; **il lido di Venezia** the Venice Lido

Liechtenstein ['likten∫tain] SM Liechtenstein

lieto, -a ['ljɛto] AGG glad, happy; **a lieto fine** with a happy ending; **lieto evento** happy event; **molto lieto (di fare la sua conoscenza)** pleased to meet you

lieve ['ljɛve] AGG (*tocco, brezza*) soft, light, faint; (*ferita*) slight

lievitare [ljevi'tare] /72/ VI (*aus essere*) (*pane, pasta, anche fig*) to rise ♦ VT to leaven

lievito ['ljɛvito] SM yeast; **lievito di birra** brewer's yeast; **lievito in polvere** baking powder

ligio, -a, -gi, -gie *o* , **-ge** ['lidʒo] AGG: **ligio (a)** faithful (to), loyal (to); **ligio al dovere** devoted to duty

lignaggio, -gi [liɲ'naddʒo] SM descent, lineage

ligure ['ligure] AGG, SM, SF Ligurian; **la Riviera Ligure** the Italian Riviera

Likud ['likud] SM Likud

lilla ['lilla] AGG INV, SM INV (*colore*) lilac

Lima ['lima] SF Lima

lima ['lima] SF file; **lima per le unghie** nailfile

limaccioso, -a [limat't∫oso] AGG muddy

limare [li'mare] /72/ VT (*superficie, unghie*) to file; (*fig: scritti*) to polish, perfect

limbo ['limbo] SM (*Rel, anche fig*) limbo

limetta [li'metta] SF **1** (*per le unghie*) nailfile **2** (*Bot*) lime (*fruit*)

limitare [limi'tare] /72/ VT **1** (*circoscrivere*) to bound, mark

the bounds of, surround **2** (*contenere*): **limitare (a)** to limit (to), restrict (to); **dobbiamo cercare di limitare le spese** we must try to control our spending; **limitarsi** VR: **limitarsi a qc/a fare qc** to limit *o* confine o.s. to sth/to doing sth; **mi sono limitato a consigliarle di stare attenta** I confined myself to advising her to be careful; **limitarsi nel fumare** to limit one's smoking; **limitarsi nel bere** to drink moderately; **mi limiterò a dire che...** all I'm prepared to say *o* all I'll say is that ...

limitatamente [limitata'mente] AVV to a limited extent; **limitatamente alle mie possibilità** in so far as I am able

limitato, -a [limi'tato] AGG (*ristretto*) limited, restricted; (*scarso*) scarce, limited; **persona di idee limitate** narrow-minded person

limitazione [limitat'tsjone] SF (*gen*) limitation, restriction; **limitazione degli armamenti** arms limitation *o* control

limite ['limite] SM (*gen, anche fig*) limit; (*confine*) boundary, limit, border; **c'è un limite a tutto!, tutto ha un limite!** there are limits!; **senza limite** *o* **limiti** boundless, limitless; **conoscere i propri limiti** to know one's limitations; **nei limiti del possibile** as far as possible; **ti aiuterò nei limiti del possibile** I'll help you as far as possible; **passare il** *o* **ogni limite** to go too far; **hai passato ogni limite!** you've gone too far!; **entro certi limiti** within certain limits; **al limite** if the worst comes to the worst (*Brit*), if worst comes to worst (*USA*), if necessary; **non portare l'ombrello - al limite te ne presto uno** don't bring your umbrella - if necessary I'll lend you one; **limite d'età** age limit; **limite delle nevi perenni** snow line; **limite di rottura** breaking point; **limite di tempo** time limit; **limite della vegetazione arborea** tree line; **limite di velocità** speed limit ♦ AGG INV: **caso limite** extreme case

limitrofo, -a [li'mitrofo] AGG neighbouring (*Brit*), neighboring (*USA*)

limo ['limo] SM (*fango*) mud, slime; (*Geog*) silt

limonata [limo'nata] SF lemonade (*Brit*), (lemon) soda (*USA*); (*spremuta*) lemon squash (*Brit*), lemonade (*USA*)

limone [li'mone] SM (*frutto*) lemon; (*albero*) lemon (tree); **l'hanno spremuto come un limone e poi l'hanno licenziato** they worked him to death and then sacked him

limpidezza [limpi'dettsa] SF (*di acqua, cielo*) clearness; (*di discorso*) clarity

limpido, -a ['limpido] AGG (*acqua*) limpid, clear; (*cielo*) clear; (*fig: discorso*) clear, lucid

lince ['lint∫e] SF lynx; **avere un occhio di lince** to be eagle-eyed

linciaggio, -gi [lin't∫addʒo] SM lynching

linciare [lin't∫are] /14/ VT to lynch

lindo, -a ['lindo] AGG (*casa, stanza*) neat and tidy, spick and span; (*biancheria, abiti*) clean

linea ['linea] SF **1** (*gen, anche Mat*) line; **a grandi linee** in outline; **in linea di massima** on the whole; **in linea di massima penso che tu abbia ragione** on the whole I think you're right; **in linea d'aria, il paese dista dieci chilometri da qui** in linea d'aria the village is ten kilometres from here as the crow flies; **avere qualche linea di febbre** to have a slight temperature; **linea di confine** boundary line; **linea continua** solid line; **linea punteggiata** dotted line; **linea tratteggiata** broken line **2** (*fig: direzione*) line; **linea d'azione/ di condotta** line of action/of conduct; **rimanere in linea col proprio partito** to toe the party line **3** (*figura: di persona*) figure; (*: Moda, Aut*) line; **mantenere la linea** to keep one's figure; **la linea Dior** (*collezione*) the Dior collection; **una giacca di linea classica** a classically styled jacket **4** (*Ferr, Aer*) line; **linea d'autobus** (*percorso*) bus route; (*servizio*) bus service; **aereo di linea** airliner; **volo di linea** scheduled flight; **linea aerea** airline; **linea di navi** (ocean) liner **5** (*Elettr*) line; **linee di alta tensione** high tension cables **6** (*Telec*) line; **la linea è occupata** the line is engaged (*Brit*) *o* busy (*USA*); **è caduta la linea** (*o you ecc*) have been cut off **7** (*Mil*) line; **essere in prima linea** to be in the front line; **linea di mira/tiro** line of sight/fire **8** (*Sport*) line; **linea d'arrivo** finishing line; **linea di fondo** (*Calcio*) goal line; **linea laterale** sideline; **linea di massima pendenza** (*Sci*) fall line; **linea di metà campo** (*Calcio*) halfway line; **linea di pallone morto** (*Rugby*) dead-ball line; **linea di partenza** starting line

lineamenti [linea'menti] SMPL (*di volto*) features; (*fig: elementi essenziali*): **lineamenti di fisica** introduction *sg* to physics

lineare [line'are] AGG (*Mat: disegno*) linear; (*fig*) consistent, coherent, logical

lineetta [line'etta] SF (*trattino*) dash; (*in composti, a fine riga*) hyphen

linfa ['linfa] SF (*Bot*) sap; (*Anat*) lymph; **linfa vitale** (*fig*) lifeblood

lingotto [lin'gotto] SM ingot, bar

lingua ['lingwa] SF 1 (*Anat, Culin, fig*) tongue; **mostrare la lingua a qn** to stick *o* put out one's tongue at sb; **avere qc sulla punta della lingua** (*fig*) to have sth on the tip of one's tongue; **ce l'ho sulla punta della lingua** it's on the tip of my tongue; **avere la lingua sciolta** to have the gift of the gab; **avere una lingua velenosa** (*fig*) to have a nasty tongue; **tenere a freno la lingua** to hold one's tongue; **avere la lingua lunga** (*fig*) to talk too much; **la lingua batte dove il dente duole** (*Proverbio*) it is human nature to dwell on one's misfortunes; **lingua di bue** (*Culin*) ox tongue; **lingue di gatto** (*biscotti*) langues de chat 2 (*linguaggio*) language, tongue; **parla tre lingue** he speaks three languages; **lingua viva/morta** living/dead language; **la lingua italiana** the Italian language; **paesi di lingua inglese** English-speaking countries; **non parliamo la stessa lingua** (*anche fig*) we don't talk the same language; **studiare lingue** to study languages; **studio lingue all'università** I'm studying languages at university; **lingua franca** lingua franca; **lingua madre** mother tongue 3 **lingua di fuoco** tongue of flame; **lingua di terra** spit of land

linguaccia [lin'gwattʃa] SF (*pegg: persona*) spiteful gossip

linguacciuto, -a [lingwat'tʃuto] AGG gossipy ♦ SM, SF gossip

linguaggio, -gi [lin'gwaddʒo] SM language; **linguaggio infantile** baby talk; **linguaggio di programmazione** programming language

linguetta [lin'gwetta] SF (*di scarpe*) tongue; (*di busta*) flap; (*di strumento*) reed

linguista, -i, -e [lin'gwista] SM, SF linguist

linguistico, -a, -ci, -che [lin'gwistiko] AGG linguistic ♦ SM (*anche: liceo linguistico*) secondary or high school specializing in modern languages

linimento [lini'mento] SM liniment

lino ['lino] SM (*pianta*) flax; (*tessuto*) linen; **seme di lino** linseed; **una giacca di lino** a linen jacket

linoleum [li'nɔleum] SM INV linoleum, lino (*Brit*)

liofilizzare [liofilid'dzare] /72/ VT to freeze-dry

liofilizzato, -a [liofilid'dzato] AGG freeze-dried; **caffè liofilizzato** instant coffee ♦ SM freeze-dried food

Lione [li'one] SF Lyons

liposuzione [liposut'tsjone] SF liposuction

liquame [li'kwame] SM liquid sewage

liquefare [likwe'fare] VB IRREG /41/ VT (*render liquido*) to liquefy; (*fondere*) to melt; **liquefarsi** VIP to liquefy; (*burro, ghiaccio*) to melt

liquefatto, -a [likwe'fatto] PP *di* **liquefare**

liquidare [likwi'dare] /72/ VT 1 (*debiti*) to settle, pay off; (*società*) to wind up, liquidate; (*merci*) to sell off, clear; (*pensione*) to pay 2 (*fig: sbarazzarsi di: persona*) to get rid of; (*: uccidere*) to kill, liquidate; **liquidare una questione** to settle a matter once and for all

liquidazione [likwidat'tsjone] SF 1 (*pagamento*) settlement, payment; (*di società*) liquidation; (*di merci*) clearance; **vendita/prezzi di liquidazione** clearance sale/prices; **ho comprato questa gonna in liquidazione** I bought this skirt in a sale 2 (*Amm*) severance pay

liquidità [likwidi'ta] SF INV liquidity

liquido, -a ['likwido] AGG (*gen, anche Comm, Fonetica*) liquid; (*Culin*) runny; (*gas*) liquid gas; **denaro liquido** cash, ready money ♦ SM 1 (*corpo liquido*) liquid, fluid 2 (*Econ: denaro contante*) ready money *o* cash

liquirizia [likwi'rittsja] SF liquorice

liquore [li'kwore] SM liqueur; **liquori** SMPL (*bevande alcoliche*) spirits

liquoroso, -a [likwo'roso] AGG: **vino liquoroso** dessert wine

lira¹ ['lira] SF (*unità monetaria*) lira; **non vale una lira** it's worthless; **non avere una lira** to be penniless; **lira sterlina** pound sterling

lira² ['lira] SF 1 (*Mus*) lyre 2 (*anche: uccello lira*) lyrebird

lirico, -a, -ci, -che ['liriko] AGG 1 (*poesia*) lyric; (*impeto, descrizione*) lyrical 2 (*Mus*) opera *attr*; **musica lirica** opera; **una cantante lirica** an opera singer; **la stagione lirica** the opera season ♦ SM lyric poet

lirismo [li'rizmo] SM lyrisism

Lisbona [lis'bona] SF Lisbon; **andrò a Lisbona quest'estate** I'm going to Lisbon this summer; **abita a Lisbona** he lives in Lisbon

lisca, -sche ['liska] SF (*fish*)bone

lisciare [liʃ'ʃare] /14/ VT (*gen*) to smooth; (*fig: adulare*) to flatter; **lisciarsi i capelli** to smooth (down) one's hair; **lisciarsi** VR (*fig*) to preen o.s.

liscio, -scia, -sci, -sce ['liʃʃo] AGG (*pelo, capelli*) sleek; (*pelle*) smooth; (*affare, faccenda*) simple, straightforward; (*liquore*) neat, straight; **avere i capelli lisci** to have straight hair; **un whisky, per favore — liscio o con ghiaccio?** a whisky, please — straight or with ice?; **è andato tutto liscio** it all went off smoothly *o* without a hitch; **passarla liscia** to get away with it; **non la passerà liscia** he won't get away with it; **com'è andata?** — **liscia come l'olio** how did it go? — it went like a dream

liso, -a ['lizo] AGG worn(-out), threadbare

lista ['lista] SF 1 (*gen, elenco*) list; (*menù*) menu; **lista della spesa/degli invitati** shopping/guest list; **fare la lista di qc** to make a list of sth; **mettersi in lista per** to put one's name down for *o* on the list for; **lista elettorale** electoral roll *o* register; **lista nera** (*fig*) blacklist; **lista di nozze** wedding list; **lista delle vivande** menu 2 (*striscia*) strip

listare [lis'tare] /72/ VT 1 **listare (di)** to border (with), edge (with) 2 (*Inform*) to list

listato [lis'tato] SM (*Inform*) list, listing

listino [lis'tino] SM list; **prezzo di listino** list price; **listino di borsa** (*Fin*) Stock Exchange listing; **listino dei cambi** (*Fin*) (foreign) exchange rate; **listino dei prezzi** price list

litania [lita'nia] SF (*Rel*) litany; (*fig: di nomi, titoli*) string

lite ['lite] SF 1 (*gen*) quarrel, argument; **attaccar lite (con qn)** to pick a fight (with sb) 2 (*Dir*) lawsuit

litigare [liti'gare] /80/ VI (*aus avere*) (*gen*) to quarrel, argue; (*Dir*) to litigate; **ho litigato con il mio capo** I had an argument with my boss

litigio, -gi [li'tidʒo] SM quarrel, dispute

litigioso, -a [liti'dʒoso] AGG (*gen*) quarrelsome; (*Dir*) litigious, contentious

litografia [litogra'fia] SF (*metodo*) lithography; (*stampa*) lithograph; (*stabilimento*) lithographic printing works *sg*

litografico, -a, -ci, -che [lito'grafiko] AGG lithographic

litorale [lito'rale] SM coast ♦ SM coastal, coast *attr*

litoraneo, -a [lito'raneo] AGG coastal

litro ['litro] SM litre (*Brit*), liter (*USA*)

littorio, -ria, -ri, -rie [lit'torjo] AGG (*Storia romana*) lictorial; **fascio littorio** (*anche Fascismo*) fasces *pl*

Lituania [litu'anja] SF Lithuania

lituano, -a [litu'ano] AGG, SM, SF Lithuanian

liturgia, -gie [litur'dʒia] SF liturgy

liuto [li'uto] SM lute

livella [li'vella] SF (*Tecn*) level; **livella a bolla (d'aria)** spirit level

livellare [livel'lare] /72/ VT (*anche fig*) to level; **livellarsi** VIP to become level; (*fig*) to level out, balance out

livellatrice [livella'tritʃe] SF steamroller

livello [li'vello] SM 1 (*di olio, acqua*) level; **allo stesso livello** at the same level; **a livello della strada** at street *o* ground level; **livello di guardia** (*anche fig*) danger level; **sotto il/sul livello del mare** (*Geog*) below/above sea level 2 (*grado*) standard; (*intellettuale, sociale*) level; **un alto livello di vita** a high standard of living; **una conferenza ad alto livello** high-level *o* top-level talks; **contatti ad alto livello** high-level contacts; **allo stesso livello** at the same level; **non è al tuo livello** he is not on the same level as you; **a livello economico/politico** at an economic/a political level; **a livello mondiale** worldwide ♦ **livello impiegatizio** employment grading; **livello**

di magazzino stock level; **livello occupazionale** level of employment; **livello retributivo** salary grade

livido, -a ['livido] AGG (*bluastro*) livid; (*per percosse*) bruised, black and blue; (*plumbeo: cielo*) leaden; **labbra livide dal freddo** lips blue with cold; **livido di collera** *o* **rabbia** livid with rage; **livido di invidia** green with envy ♦ SM bruise

livore [li'vore] SM venom

Livorno [li'vorno] SF Livorno, Leghorn

livrea [li'vrɛa] SF (*uniforme*) livery; (*di animale*) coat; (*di uccello*) plumage

lizza ['littsa] SF: **entrare** *o* **scendere in lizza** (*anche fig*) to enter the lists; **essere in lizza per** (*fig*) to be competing for, compete for; **rimanere in lizza** (*fig*) to still be in the running

lo¹ [lo] ART DET M *vedi* **il**

lo² [lo] PRON (*dav vocale* **l'**) **1** (*riferito a persona*) him; (*riferito ad animale*) it; (: *affettuosamente*) him; (*riferito a cosa*) it; **lo vuoi conoscere?** *o* **vuoi conoscerlo?** would you like to meet him?; **Paolo lo conosco bene, ma Giovanna no** I know Paolo well, but not Giovanna; **lo chiamerò domani mattina** I'll call him tomorrow morning; **lo compro** I'll buy it; **guardalo!** look at him (*o* it)! **2** (*con valore neutro: spesso non tradotto*): **vieni? — non lo so** are you coming? — I don't know; **te lo dicevo io!** I told you so!; **non lo vedi che stai sbagliando?** can't you see you're wrong; **può sembrare innocuo ma non lo è** he may look harmless but he's not

LO SIGLA = Lodi

lobbista, -i, -e [lob'bista] SM, SF lobbyist

lobby ['lɔbi] SF INV lobby

lobo ['lɔbo] SM (*Anat, Bot*) lobe; **lobo dell'orecchio** ear lobe

locale [lo'kale] AGG local; (*treno*) stopping (*Brit*), local (*USA*) ♦ SM **1** (*stanza*) room; (*luogo pubblico*) place, premises *pl*; **non si servono alcolici in questo locale** no alcohol is served on the premises; **è un locale molto costoso** it's a very expensive place; **locale caldaie** boiler room; **locale (notturno)** (night)club **2** (*anche: treno locale*) stopping train (*Brit*), local train (*USA*)

località [lokali'ta] SF INV locality; **località balneare/di villeggiatura** seaside/holiday resort

localizzare [lokalid'dzare] /72/ VT (*individuare*) to locate, place; (*circoscrivere: epidemia, incendio*) to confine, localize; **localizzarsi** VIP: **localizzarsi in** to become localized in

locanda [lo'kanda] SF inn

locandiere, -a [lokan'djere] SM, SF landlord *o* landlady

locandina [lokan'dina] SF poster

locare [lo'kare] /20/ VT (*Dir*) to rent out, let

locatario, -ria, -ri, -rie [loka'tarjo] SM, SF (*di casa, appartamento*) tenant; (*di camera*) lodger

locativo, -a [loka'tivo] AGG (*Dir*): **valore locativo** rental value

locatore, -trice [loka'tore] SM, SF landlord *o* landlady

locazione [lokat'tsjone] SF **1** (*da parte del locatario*) renting; (*da parte del locatore*) renting out, letting; **dare in locazione** to rent out, let **2** (*anche: contratto di locazione*) lease; **canone di locazione** rent

locomotiva [lokomo'tiva] SF locomotive, engine

locomotore [lokomo'tore] SM , **locomotrice** [lokomo'tritʃe] SF (electric) locomotive, engine

locomozione [lokomot'tsjone] SF locomotion; **mezzi di locomozione** means of transport

loculo ['lɔkulo] SM burial recess

locusta [lo'kusta] SF locust

locuzione [lokut'tsjone] SF phrase, locution, expression

lodare [lo'dare] /72/ VT to praise; **lodare qn per qc/per aver fatto qc** to praise sb for sth/for having done sth; **sia lodato Dio!** God be praised!

lode ['lɔde] SF praise; **degno di lode** praiseworthy; **tessere le lodi di qn** to sing sb's praises; **in lode di** in praise of; **torna a sua lode** it's to his credit; **laurearsi con 110 e lode** (*Univ*) ≈ to graduate with first-class honours *o* a first-class honours degree (*Brit*), ≈ to graduate summa cum laude (*USA*)

loden ['lɔdan] SM INV (*stoffa*) loden; (*cappotto*) loden overcoat

lodevole [lo'devole] AGG praiseworthy

logaritmo [loga'ritmo] SM (*Mat*) logarithm

log'garsi /72/ VR (*Inform*) to log in

loggia, -ge ['lɔddʒa] SF (*Archit*) loggia; (*circolo massonico*) lodge

loggione [lod'dʒone] SM (*Teatro*): **il loggione** the gods *sg*

logicamente [lodʒika'mente] AVV naturally, obviously

logicità [lodʒitʃi'ta] SF logicality

logico, -a, -ci, -che ['lɔdʒiko] AGG logical; **quello che dici non è molto logico** what you're saying isn't very logical ♦ SM logician

logistica [lo'dʒistika] SF logistics *sg*

logo ['lɔgo] SM INV logo

logoramento [logora'mento] SM (*di vestiti*) wear

logorante [logo'rante] AGG exhausting; (*attesa, giornata*) wearing

logorare [logo'rare] /72/ VT (*abiti, scarpe*) to wear out; (*scalini, pietra*) to wear away; (*occhi, salute*) to ruin; (*nervi, resistenza*) to wear down; (*persona*) to wear out, exhaust; (*volto*) to line, mark; **logorarsi l'anima** *o* **la vita su qc** to wear o.s. out over sth; **logorarsi la vista** to ruin one's eyesight; **logorarsi** VIP (*abiti, scarpe*) to wear out; (*occhi*) to become ruined; (*nervi*) to go; **logorarsi** VR (*persona*) to wear o.s. out

logorio, -rii [logo'rio] SM wear and tear, strain; **il logorio della vita moderna** the stresses and strains of life today

logoro, -a ['logoro] AGG (*scarpe*) worn (out); (*abiti, tappeto*) worn out, threadbare, shabby; (*fig: occhi, vista*) ruined; (: *aspetto*) worn out, exhausted; **indossava un cappotto logoro** he was wearing a shabby overcoat

Loira ['lɔira] SF: **la Loira** the Loire

lombaggine [lom'baddʒine] SF (*Med*) lumbago

Lombardia [lombar'dia] SF Lombardy

lombardo, -a [lom'bardo] AGG, SM, SF Lombard

lombare [lom'bare] AGG (*Anat, Med*) lumbar

lombata [lom'bata] SF (*Culin*) loin

lombo ['lombo] SM (*Anat, Culin*) loin

lombrico, -chi [lom'briko] SM earthworm

londinese [londi'nese] AGG London *attr*; **il traffico londinese** London traffic; **la vita londinese** life in London ♦ SM, SF Londoner

Londra ['londra] SF London; **domani vado a Londra** I'm going to London tomorrow; **abita a Londra** he lives in London

longanime [lon'ganime] AGG forbearing

longevità [londʒevi'ta] SF longevity

longevo, -a [lon'dʒevo] AGG long-lived

longilineo, -a [londʒi'lineo] AGG long-limbed

longitudine [londʒi'tudine] SF longitude

lontanamente [lontana'mente] AVV remotely; **non ci pensavo neppure lontanamente** I didn't even occur to me

lontananza [lonta'nantsa] SF (*distanza*) distance; (*assenza*) absence; **in lontananza** in the distance; **vedo una macchina in lontananza** I can see a car in the distance; **la lontananza da casa lo faceva soffrire** being away from home made him unhappy

lontano, -a [lon'tano] AGG **1** (*nello spazio, nel tempo*) distant, faraway, far-off; (*di parentela*) distant; **paesi lontani** distant countries; **sento delle voci lontane** I can hear distant voices; **lontano da** far from, a long way from; **essere ben lontano dal pensare che...** to be far from thinking that ...; **tenere qn lontano** to keep sb at a distance; **tenersi lontano da** to keep one's distance from; **lontano dagli occhi lontano dal cuore** (*Proverbio*) out of sight out of mind; **il giorno della sua partenza non era lontano** the day when he was due to leave was not far off *o* away; **amici lontani** absent friends; **siamo parenti alla lontana** we're distantly related; **i nostri ricordi più lontani** our earliest memories; **i tempi lontani dell'università** those far-off days at university; **terre lontane** faraway places **2** (*vago*) vague, slight ♦ AVV far; **è lontano** it's a long way; **il mare non è lontano da qui** the sea isn't far from here; **è lontano 10 chilometri** it's 10 kilometres away; **la città è ancora molto lontana** the city is still a long way off; **più lontano** farther, further; **la città più lontana dal mare** the city farthest from the sea; **è più lontano di quanto pensassi** it's farther than I thought; **è meno lontano di quello che pensi** it's not as far as you think; **abita lontano** he lives a long way away, he lives a long way from here; **abiti lontano dalla scuola?** do you live far from school?; **da lontano** from a distance; **da lontano mi sembravi tuo fratello** from a distance you looked like your brother; **vengo da lontano** I've come quite a distance; **lontano nel passato** far back in the past; **lontano nel futuro** in the distant future; **andar lontano** (*anche fig*) to go far; **mirare lontano** (*fig*) to aim high; **vedere lontano** (*fig*) to see far ahead

lontra ['lontra] SF otter

loquace [lo'kwatʃe] AGG talkative, loquacious; (*fig: occhiata, gesto*) expressive, eloquent

loquacità [lokwatʃi'ta] SF talkativeness, loquacity

lordo, -a ['lordo] AGG 1 (*Comm: peso, stipendio*) gross 2 (*sporco*) dirty, filthy; **lordo di sangue** bloody ♦ SM: **al lordo d'imposta** before tax

Lorena [lo'rena] SF Lorraine

loro[1] ['loro] PRON PERS PL 1 (*complemento*) them; **chiedi (a) loro** ask them; **disse loro che non sarebbe venuto** he told them he wouldn't be coming; **ho spedito loro una cartolina** I sent them a postcard; **sono venuto con loro** I came with them; **dimmi qualcosa di loro** tell me something about them; **senza di loro** without them; **loro qui non li voglio** I don't want them here 2 (*sogg: al posto di "essi", "esse", con valore enfatico*) they; **loro abitano qui** they live here; **loro sono meglio di te** they are better than you; **vengono anche loro?** are they coming too?; **prendeteli, sono loro** catch them, they're the ones; **sono loro, apri la porta** it's them, open the door; **sono stati loro a dirmelo** they told me themselves, it was they (*frm*) o them who told me; **hanno ragione loro, non tu** they are right, not you; **neanche loro hanno tutti i torti** even they aren't completely in the wrong; **non lo sapevano nemmeno loro** they didn't even know it themselves 3 (*nelle comparazioni: sogg*) they, them; (*: complemento*) them; **ne so quanto loro** I know as much as they do, I know as much as them

loro[2] ['loro] PRON PERS PL (*anche: (forma di cortesia*) Loro) 1 you; **loro capiscono quanto ciò sia penoso** you are aware of how distressing that is; **chiedo lor signori di seguirmi** be so good as to follow me, (if you would) gentlemen 2 (*nelle comparazioni*) you

loro[3] ['loro] AGG POSS INV: **il(la) loro, i(le) loro** 1 their; **i loro amici** their friends; **un loro amico** a friend of theirs; **verranno con la loro macchina** they'll come in their car; **è colpa loro** it's their fault 2 (*forma di cortesia: anche:* Loro) your ♦ PRON POSS INV: **il(la) loro, i(le) loro** 1 theirs; **questi libri sono i loro** those books are theirs; **di chi è questo?** — **è loro** whose is this? — it's theirs; **la nostra casa è più grande della loro** our house is bigger than theirs 2 (*forma di cortesia: anche:* Loro) yours 3 **vivono del loro** they live on what they have; **i loro** (*famiglia*) their family; (*amici*) their own people; **siamo dei loro, stiamo dalla loro** (*parte*) we're on their side, we're with them; **vogliono sempre dire la loro** they've always got something to say; **ne hanno fatto un'altra delle loro** they've (gone and) done it again

losanga, -ghe [lo'zanga] SF lozenge

Losanna [lo'zanna] SF Lausanne

losco, -a, -schi, -sche ['losko] AGG 1 (*occhiata, aspetto*) sullen, surly 2 (*fig: equivoco: persona, affare*) shady, suspicious; **un tipo losco** a shady character ♦ SM: **qui c'è del losco** I smell a rat

lotta ['lɔtta] SF (*combattimento*) fight, struggle; (*conflitto*) conflict; (*Sport*) wrestling; **essere in lotta (con)** to be in conflict (with); **fare la lotta (con)** to wrestle (with); **lotta all'ultimo sangue** (*anche fig*) fight to the death; **lotta mortale** mortal combat ♦ **lotta armata** armed struggle; **lotta di classe** (*Pol*) class struggle; **lotta contro la droga** war against drugs; **lotta corpo a corpo** hand-to-hand combat; **lotta libera** (*Sport*) all-in wrestling, freestyle; **lotta per la sopravvivenza** struggle o fight for survival

lottare [lot'tare] /72/ VI (*aus* avere) **lottare (con** o **contro)** to fight (with o against), struggle (with o against); (*Sport*) to wrestle; **dobbiamo lottare per i nostri diritti** we must fight for our rights; **ha sempre lottato contro il razzismo** she's always fought against racism; **lottare contro il sonno** to struggle to keep awake; **lottare con la morte** to battle against death

lottatore, -trice [lotta'tore] SM, SF fighter; (*Sport*) wrestler

lotteria [lotte'ria] SF lottery; (*di gara ippica*) sweepstake; **vincere alla lotteria** to win the lottery; **lotteria istantanea** instant lottery

lottizzare [lottid'dzare] /72/ VT (*terreno*) to divide into plots; (*fig*) to share out

lottizzazione [lottiddzat'tsjone] SF (*di terreno*) division into plots; (*fig*) share-out

lotto[1] ['lɔtto] SM (*gen*) lot; (*di terreno*) plot; **lotto fabbricabile** o **edificabile** building lot

lotto[2] ['lɔtto] SM (*gioco*) (state) lottery; **vincere un terno al lotto** (*anche fig*) to hit the jackpot

lozione [lot'tsjone] SF lotion

LT SIGLA = Latina

LU SIGLA = Lucca

lubrificante [lubrifi'kante] AGG lubricating ♦ SM lubricant

lubrificare [lubrifi'kare] /20/ VT to lubricate

lucano, -a [lu'kano] AGG of o from Lucania ♦ SM, SF inhabitant o native of Lucania

lucchetto [luk'ketto] SM padlock

luccicare [luttʃi'kare] /20/ VI (*aus* avere) (*gen*) to sparkle; (*stella*) to twinkle; (*oro*) to glitter; (*occhi*) to glisten; **non è tutt'oro quel che luccica** (*Proverbio*) all that glitters is not gold

luccichio, -chii [luttʃi'kio] SM (*vedi vb*) sparkling; twinkling; glittering; glistening

luccicone [luttʃi'kone] SM: **avere i lucciconi agli occhi** to have tears in one's eyes

luccio, -ci ['luttʃo] SM (*pesce*) pike

lucciola ['luttʃola] SF 1 (*Zool*) firefly, glow-worm; **prendere lucciole per lanterne** to get hold of the wrong end of the stick 2 (*euf: prostituta*) prostitute

luce ['lutʃe] SF 1 (*gen*) light; **alla luce del giorno** in daylight; **luce del sole/della luna** sun/moonlight; **accendere/spegnere la luce** to turn o switch the light on/off; **fare luce su qc** (*fig*) to shed o throw light on sth; **mettere in luce** (*fig*) to spotlight, highlight; **mettere qn in buona/cattiva luce** (*fig*) to put sb in a good/bad light; **fare qc alla luce del sole** (*fig*) to do sth in the open; **dare alla luce** (*bambino*) to give birth to; **venire alla luce** (*fatto*) to come to light; (*bambino*) to come into the world; **alla luce di questi fatti** in light of this; **luci della ribalta** (*Teatro*) footlights 2 (*Aut*): **luci di arresto** brake lights; **luci di emergenza** hazard warning lights; **luci di posizione** sidelights (*Brit*), parking lights (*USA*); **luci di retromarcia** reversing lights 3 (*Archit: di ponte, arco*) span; (*finestra*) window; **negozio a una luce** shop with one window

lucente [lu'tʃente] AGG shining

lucentezza [lutʃen'tettsa] SF shine

lucerna [lu'tʃerna] SF oil lamp

lucernario, -ri [lutʃer'narjo] SM skylight

lucertola [lu'tʃertola] SF (*animale*) lizard; (*pellame*) lizardskin

lucidare [lutʃi'dare] /72/ VT 1 (*mobili, scarpe, pavimenti*) to polish 2 (*ricalcare: disegno*) to trace

lucidatrice [lutʃida'tritʃe] SF floor polisher

lucidità [lutʃidi'ta] SF lucidity

lucido, -a ['lutʃido] AGG 1 shining, bright; **occhi lucidi di pianto/per la febbre** eyes bright with tears/with fever; **una camicia di raso nero lucido** a shiny black satin blouse 2 (*pavimento, argento, scarpe*) polished; **è lucido come uno specchio** you can see your face in it 3 (*mente, discorso*) lucid, clear; (*malato*) lucid; **è ancora lucido** he's still lucid ♦ SM 1 (*lucentezza*) shine, lustre (*Brit*), luster (*USA*); **perdere il lucido** to lose its shine 2 (*sostanza*) polish; **lucido da scarpe** shoe polish 3 (*disegno, ricalco*) tracing; **carta da lucido** tracing paper

lucignolo [lu'tʃiɲɲolo] SM wick

lucrare [lu'krare] /72/ VT to make money (out of)

lucrativo, -a [lukra'tivo] AGG lucrative; **organizzazione non lucrativa** non-profit organization

lucro ['lukro] SM profit, gain; **a scopo di lucro** for gain; **organizzazione a scopo di lucro** profit-making organization

lucroso, -a [lu'kroso] AGG lucrative, profitable

luculliano, -a [lukul'ljano] AGG (*pasto*) sumptuous

ludibrio [lu'dibrjo] SM 1 (*scherno*) mockery, scorn 2 (*zimbello*) laughing stock

lue ['lue] SF (*Med*) syphilis

luglio ['luλλo] SM July; **nel mese di luglio** in July o in the month of July; **il primo luglio** the first of July; **arrivare il**

2 luglio to arrive on the 2nd of July; **all'inizio/alla fine di luglio** at the beginning/at the end of July; **durante il mese di luglio** during July; **a luglio del prossimo anno** in July (of) next year; **ogni anno a luglio** every July; **che fai a luglio?** what are you doing in July?; **è piovuto molto a luglio** quest'anno July was very wet this year

lugubre ['lugubre] AGG gloomy, dismal; **un'atmosfera lugubre** a gloomy atmosphere

lui ['lui] PRON PERS M 1 (complemento: dopo prep, con valore enfatico) him; **sono venuto con lui** I came with him; **dimmi qualcosa di lui** tell me something about him; **senza di lui** without him; **se non fosse per lui** if it were not for him; **hanno accusato lui, non me** they accused him, not me; **chiedilo a lui** ask him; **lui qui non lo voglio** I don't want him here 2 (sogg: al posto di 'egli', con valore enfatico) he; **lui è meglio di te** he is better than you; **viene anche lui?** is he coming too?; **prendetelo, è lui** catch him, he's the one; **è lui, apri la porta** it's him, open the door; **è stato lui a dirmelo** he told me himself, it was he who told me; **ha ragione lui, non tu** he's right, not you; **neanche lui ha tutti i torti** even he isn't completely in the wrong; **non lo sapeva nemmeno lui** he didn't even know it himself 3 (nelle comparazioni: sogg) he, him; **ne so quanto lui** I know as much as he does, I know as much as him ♦ SM INV (scherz): **il mio lui** my beloved

lumaca, -che [lu'maka] SF (Zool) slug; (fam: chiocciola) snail; (: fig) slowcoach (Brit), slowpoke (USA); **a passo di lumaca** at a snail's pace

lumacone [luma'kone] SM (Zool) (large) slug; (fig) slowcoach (Brit), slowpoke (USA)

lume ['lume] SM 1 (gen) light; **a lume di candela** by candlelight; **a lume di naso** by rule of thumb; **chiedere lumi a qn** (fig) to ask sb for advice; **perdere il lume della ragione** to be blinded by rage 2 (lampada) lamp; **lume a olio** oil lamp

lumicino [lumi't∫ino] SM small o faint light; **essere (ridotto) al lumicino** to be at death's door

luminaria [lumi'narja] SF (per feste) illuminations pl

luminescente [lumine∫'∫ente] AGG luminescent

lumino [lu'mino] SM small light; **lumino da notte** nightlight; **lumino per i morti** candle for the dead

luminosità [luminosi'ta] SF brightness; (fig: di sorriso, volto) radiance; **c'è una luminosità diffusa sopra la città** there's a hazy glow over the city

luminoso, -a [lumi'noso] AGG 1 (gen) luminous; (sorgente) of light, light attr; (fig: sorriso, volto) radiant; **insegna luminosa** neon sign 2 (cielo, occhi, avvenire, idea) bright; (sorriso, viso) bright, radiant; **il soggiorno è molto luminoso** the living room is very bright

lun. ABBR (= lunedì) Mon.

luna ['luna] SF moon; **una notte di luna** a moonlit night; **avere la luna** to be in a bad mood; **svegliarsi con la luna** (fig) to get out of bed on the wrong side; **chiedere la luna** to ask for the moon; **luna di miele** honeymoon; **luna nuova** new moon; **luna piena** full moon

luna park ['luna 'park] SM INV amusement park, funfair

lunare [lu'nare] AGG lunar, moon attr; **paesaggio lunare** (fig) lunar landscape

lunario, -ri [lu'narjo] SM almanac; **sbarcare il lunario** (fig) to make ends meet; **riesco a malapena a sbarcare il lunario** I can only just make ends meet

lunatico, -a, -ci, -che [lu'natiko] AGG quirky, temperamental ♦ SM, SF temperamental person
❑ **lunatico** non si traduce mai con la parola inglese lunatic

lunedì [lune'di] SM INV Monday; **lunedì dell'Angelo** Easter Monday; vedi **martedì**

lungaggine [lun'gaddʒine] SF slowness; **le lungaggini della burocrazia** red tape sg

lungamente [lunga'mente] AVV (a lungo) for a long time; (diffusamente) at length; **un figlio lungamente atteso** a long-awaited child; **dopo aver lungamente sofferto** after long suffering

lungarno [lun'garno] SM embankment along the Arno

lunghezza [lun'gettsa] SF length; **lunghezza: 20 cm** length:

20 cm; **il lungomare si estende per una lunghezza di 5 km** the promenade stretches for 5 km; **nel senso della lunghezza** lengthways, along its length; **vincere per una lunghezza** (cavallo) to win by a length; **lunghezza d'onda** wavelength

lungi ['lundʒi] **lungi da** PREP far from; **lungi da me l'idea di offenderti!** far be it from me to offend you!; **lungi dall'essere** far from being

lungimirante [lundʒimi'rante] AGG far-sighted

lungo, -a, -ghi, -ghe ['lungo] AGG 1 (gen) long; (persona) tall; (viaggio) lengthy; **è lungo quattro metri** it's four metres long; **questa gonna è troppo lunga** this skirt is too long; **hanno fatto una lunga passeggiata** they went for a long walk; **una fila di macchine lunga 2 km** a tailback of cars 2 km long; **amici di lunga data** long-standing o old friends; **lo conosco da lungo tempo** I've known him for a long time; **un discorso lungo 2 ore** a 2-hour speech 2 (lento: persona) slow; **essere lungo a** o **nel fare qc** to be slow at doing sth, take a long time to do sth; **essere lungo come la fame** to be a slowcoach (Brit) o slowpoke (USA) 3 (diluito: caffè) weak, watery; (brodo) thin 4 (fraseologia): **avere la barba lunga** to be unshaven; **avere le mani lunghe** to be light-fingered; **fare il passo più lungo della gamba** to bite off more than one can chew; **cadere lungo disteso** to measure one's length on the ground; **fare la faccia lunga** o **il muso lungo** o **il viso lungo** to pull a long face; **a lunga gittata** (Mil) long-range; **saperla lunga** (fam) to know a thing or two, know what's what; **a lunga scadenza** long term; **a lungo andare** in the long run, in the end; **a lungo andare si stuferà** he'll get fed up with it in the end ♦ SM length; **per il lungo** along its length, lengthways; **in lungo e in largo** (girare, cercare) far and wide, everywhere; **l'ho cercato in lungo e in largo** I looked for it everywhere; **a lungo** (aspettare) for a long time; (spiegare) in great detail; **abbiamo parlato a lungo** we talked for a long time ♦ SF: **di gran lunga** far and away; **è di gran lunga il migliore** it's far and away the best, it's the best by far; **andare per le lunghe** to drag on; **alla lunga** in the long run, in the end; **alla lunga si stuferà** he'll get fed up with it in the end ♦ PREP (spazio) along, beside; (tempo) during; **camminare lungo il fiume** to walk along o beside the river; **lungo il corso dei secoli** throughout the centuries, in the course of the centuries; **lungo il viaggio** during the journey

lungofiume [lungo'fjume] SM embankment

lungolago [lungo'lago] SM road round a lake

lungomare [lungo'mare] SM promenade

lungometraggio, -gi [lungome'traddʒo] SM (Cine) feature film

lungotevere [lungo'tevere] SM embankment along the Tiber

lunotto [lu'nɔtto] SM (Aut) rear o back window; **lunotto termico** heated rear window

luogo, -ghi ['lwɔgo] SM 1 (gen) place; **in ogni luogo** everywhere; **in qualsiasi luogo** anywhere; **in qualsiasi luogo vada** wherever you go; **in nessun luogo** nowhere; **sul luogo** on the spot; **fuori luogo** (fig) out of place, inopportune; **uno del luogo** a native, a local 2 (fraseologia): **aver luogo** to take place; **l'incontro ha avuto luogo a maggio** the meeting took place in May; **far luogo a** to give way to, make room for; **dar luogo a** (critiche, dubbi) to give rise to; **in luogo di** in place of, instead of; **in primo/secondo luogo** in the first/second place; **non luogo a procedere** (Dir) nonsuit ♦ **luogo comune** commonplace, cliché; **luogo del delitto** scene of the crime; **luogo geometrico** locus; **luogo di nascita** (gen) birthplace; (Amm) place of birth; **luogo di origine** o **di provenienza** place of origin; **luogo di pena** penitentiary (USA), prison; **luogo pubblico** public place

luogotenente [lwogote'nente] SM (Mil, anche fig) lieutenant

lupacchiotto [lupak'kjɔtto] SM (Zool) (wolf) cub

lupara [lu'para] SF (fucile) sawn-off shotgun

lupetto [lu'petto] SM (Zool) (wolf) cub; (negli scouts) cub (scout)

lupo ['lupo] SM wolf; **cane lupo** alsatian (Brit), German shepherd; **avere una fame da lupi** to be ravenous o famished; **gridare al lupo** to cry wolf; **tempo da lupi** filthy weather; **in bocca al lupo!** good luck!; **il lupo perde il pelo ma non il vizio** (Proverbio) the leopard cannot change its spots; **lupo**

mannaro (*licantropo*) werewolf; **lupo di mare** (*fig*) old salt, sea dog

luppolo [ˈluppolo] SM (*pianta*) hop

lurido, -a [ˈlurido] AGG (*anche fig*) filthy, foul
❑ **lurido** non si traduce mai con la parola inglese *lurid*

luridume [luriˈdume] SM filth

lusinga, -ghe [luˈzinga] SF flattery; **con la lusinga di un lauto stipendio** with the promise of a high salary; **non mi convincerai con le lusinghe** flattery will get you nowhere

lusingare [luzinˈgare] /80/ VT (*adulare*) to flatter; **si è fatto lusingare dalle promesse di una brillante carriera** he let himself be swayed by promises of a brilliant career; **lusingatissimo!** (*onorato*) I'm honoured!

lusinghiero, -a [luzinˈgjero] AGG flattering

lussare [lusˈsare] /72/ VT (*Med*) to dislocate

lussazione [lussatˈtsjone] SF (*Med*) dislocation

lussemburghese [lussemburˈgese] AGG of *o* from Luxembourg ♦ SM, SF native *o* inhabitant of Luxembourg

Lussemburgo [lussemˈburgo] SM (*stato*) Luxembourg ♦ (*città*) Luxembourg

lusso [ˈlusso] SM luxury; **di lusso** (*macchina, appartamento*) luxury *attr*; (*prodotto*) de luxe *attr*; **non posso permettermi il lusso di una vacanza** I can't afford the luxury of a vacation; **andare di lusso** (*fam*) to go like a dream

lussuoso, -a [lussuˈoso] AGG luxurious; **un albergo lussuoso** a luxury hotel

lussureggiare [lussuredˈdʒare] /62/ VI (*aus* **avere**) to be luxuriant

lussuria [lusˈsurja] SF lust
❑ **lussuria** non si traduce mai con la parola inglese *luxury*

lussurioso, -a [lussuˈrjoso] AGG lascivious, lustful
❑ **lussurioso** non si traduce mai con la parola inglese *luxurious*

lustrare [lusˈtrare] /72/ VT (*mobili, pavimenti*) to polish; (*scarpe*) to polish, shine

lustrascarpe [lustrasˈkarpe] SM INV, SF INV shoeshine

lustrino [lusˈtrino] SM sequin

lustro, -a [ˈlustro] AGG (*superficie*) shiny; (*capelli, pelo*) glossy; (*occhi*) moist ♦ SM 1 shine, gloss 2 (*fig: gloria*) prestige, glory 3 (*quinquennio*) five-year period

luterano, -a [luteˈrano] AGG, SM, SF Lutheran

lutto [ˈlutto] SM (*gen*) mourning; (*perdita*) loss, bereavement; **essere in/portare il lutto** to be in/wear mourning; **un lutto nazionale** an occasion for national mourning; **è stato un grave lutto per il paese** it was a great loss to the country

Mm

M¹, m¹ [ˈemme] SF INV, SM INV (*lettera*) M, m; **M come Milano** ≈ M for Mary (*Brit*), ≈ M for Mike (*USA*)

M² [ˈemme] SIGLA F (*taglia*) M (= *medium*)

m. ABBR = **mese miglio¹**

ma [ma] CONG but; (*tuttavia*) yet, still, but; (*comunque*) however; **mi piacerebbe venire ma non posso** I would love to come but I can't; **hanno fatto quel che potevano ma non sono riusciti a salvarlo** they did what they could, but they couldn't save him; **non se lo merita ma dovremmo cercare di capirlo** even though he doesn't deserve it, we should try to understand him; **ma non se lo merita** he doesn't deserve it though; **incredibile ma vero** incredible but true; **ma si può sapere che cosa vuoi?** just what do you want?; **ma smettila!** give over!, stop it!; **ma va'?** (*dubitativo*) really?; (*esclamazione*) surely not!; **ma davvero?** really?; **ma sì!** (*certo*) yes, of course!; **ma no!** of course not!; **ti dispiace? — ma no!** do you mind? — of course I don't!; **ma insomma!** for goodness sake!; **ma insomma, vuoi smetterla?** stop it, for heaven's sake! ♦ SM INV but; **ci sono ancora dei ma** there are still some uncertainties; **non c'è ma che tenga** I'm not going to take no for an answer

macabro, -a [ˈmakabro] AGG macabre, gruesome ♦ SM: **il gusto del macabro** a taste for the macabre

macaco, -chi [maˈkako] SM (*Zool*) macaque; (*fig: fam*) clod

macché [makˈke] ESCL (*fam*) certainly not!, you must be joking!

maccheroni [makkeˈroni] SMPL macaroni *sg*; **sono buoni i maccheroni?** is the macaroni nice?

macchia¹ [ˈmakkja] SF 1 (*chiazza*) mark, spot; (*sulla pelle*) blotch, mark; (*sul pelo*) patch; (*di sporco*) stain, mark; **macchie di colore** splashes of colour; **coprirsi di macchie** (*pelle*) to come out in a rash; **a macchie** spotted; **estendersi a macchia d'olio** (*fig: rivolta, epidemia*) to spread rapidly; (: *città*) to grow rapidly; **macchia di caffè** coffee stain; **macchia di grasso** greasy mark, grease stain; **macchia d'inchiostro** ink stain; (*su foglio*) (ink) blot; **macchia di sangue** bloodstain; **macchia di vino** wine stain; **macchie solari** (*Astron*) sunspots 2 (*fig: su reputazione*) blot, stain

macchia² [ˈmakkja] SF (*boscaglia*) scrub; **darsi/vivere alla macchia** (*fig*) to go into/live in hiding

macchiare [makˈkjare] /19/ VT 1 (*sporcare: tovaglia, camicia*) to stain; (*con inchiostro: quaderno*) to blot; (*fig: reputazione*) to sully, tarnish; **hai macchiato la tovaglia di caffè** you've got coffee on the tablecloth; **la birra non macchia** beer doesn't stain *o* leave a mark; **mi sono macchiata il vestito** I've got a stain on my dress 2 **macchiare il caffè (col latte)** to add a drop of milk to (one's) coffee; **macchiarsi** VIP (*persona*) to get stains *o* marks on one's clothes, get o.s. dirty; (: *tessuto*) to get stained *o* marked; **ti sei macchiato tutto!** you've got yourself all dirty!; **macchiarsi di un delitto** to be guilty of a crime

macchiato, -a [makˈkjato] AGG 1 (*gen*): **macchiato (di)** stained (with); **caffè macchiato** espresso coffee with a dash of milk; **i suoi vestiti erano macchiati di fango** his clothes were stained with mud 2 (*pelo*) spotted

macchietta [makˈkjetta] SF 1 (*piccola macchia*) spot 2 (*vignetta, anche Teatro*) caricature; (*fig: persona*) character

macchina [ˈmakkina] SF 1 (*automobile*) car; **salire in macchina** to get into the car; **andare/venire in macchina** to go/come by car; **ci andate in macchina o in treno?** are you going there by car or by train? 2 (*gen, anche fig*) machine; (*motore, locomotiva*) engine; **sala macchine** (*Naut*) engine room; **la macchina funziona premendo il pulsante** the machine works when you press the button; **la macchina burocratica** the bureaucratic machinery; **scrivere a macchina** to type; **macchina bellica** war machine; **andare in macchina** (*Stampa*) to go to press ♦ **macchina per caffè** espresso

(machine); **macchina da corsa** racing car; **macchina da cucire** sewing machine; **macchina fotografica** camera; **macchina da presa** cine *o* movie camera; **macchina da scrivere** typewriter; **macchina utensile** machine tool; **macchina a vapore** steam engine

macchinalmente [makkinalˈmente] AVV mechanically

macchinare [makkiˈnare] /72/ VT to plot

macchinario, -ri [makkiˈnarjo] SM machinery; **macchinari** SMPL machinery *no pl*

macchinazione [makkinatˈtsjone] SF plot, machination

macchinetta [makkiˈnetta] SF (*fam: caffettiera*) espresso coffee maker; (: *accendino*) lighter; (: *per il taglio dei capelli*) hair clippers; (: *per i denti*) brace; **parlare come una macchinetta** (*fig*) to talk nineteen to the dozen

macchinista, -i [makkiˈnista] SM (*di treno*) engine-driver; (*di nave*) engineer; (*Teatro, Cine, TV*) stagehand

macchinoso, -a [makkiˈnoso] AGG complex, complicated

macedone [maˈtʃedone] SM, SF, AGG Macedonian

Macedonia [matʃeˈdɔnja] SF Macedonia

macedonia [matʃeˈdɔnja] SF (*Culin*) fruit salad

macellaio, -ai [matʃelˈlajo] SM (*anche fig*) butcher

macellare [matʃelˈlare] /72/ VT (*anche fig*) to slaughter, butcher

macellazione [matʃellatˈtsjone] SF slaughtering, butchering

macelleria [matʃelleˈria] SF butcher's (shop); **sono andato in macelleria** I went to the butcher's

macello [maˈtʃello] SM 1 (*mattatoio*) slaughterhouse, abattoir (*Brit*) 2 (*azione, o fig*) slaughter, massacre; **mandare al macello** (*soldati*) to send to their deaths 3 (*fig: fam: disordine*) mess, shambles *sg*; (: *disastro*) disaster; **è un macello!** it's a disaster!

macerare [matʃeˈrare] /72/ VT (*canapa, carta*) to macerate; (*Culin*) to marinate; **macerarsi** VR (*consumarsi*): **macerarsi nel rimorso** to be consumed with remorse

macerazione [matʃeratˈtsjone] SF maceration

macerie [maˈtʃerje] SFPL rubble *sg*, debris *sg*

macero [ˈmatʃero] SM (*operazione*) pulping; (*stabilimento*) pulping mill; **carta da macero** paper for pulping

machiavellico, -a, -ci, -che [makjaˈvelliko] AGG (*anche fig*) Machiavellian

macigno [maˈtʃiɲɲo] SM (*masso*) rock, boulder; **duro come un macigno** as hard as rock

macilento, -a [matʃiˈlento] AGG emaciated

macina [ˈmatʃina] SF (*pietra*) millstone; (*macchina*) grinder

macinacaffè [matʃinakafˈfɛ] SM INV coffee grinder, coffee mill

macinapepe [matʃinaˈpepe] SM INV pepper mill

macinare [matʃiˈnare] /72/ VT (*grano, caffè*) to grind; (*carne*) to mince (*Brit*), grind (*USA*); **caffè macinato** ground coffee; **carne macinata** mince; **macinare i chilometri** to eat up the miles

macinato [matʃiˈnato] SM 1 (*cereali, farina*) meal 2 (*carne*) mince, minced (*Brit*) *o* ground (*USA*) meat

macinino [matʃiˈnino] SM 1 (*per caffè*) mill, coffee grinder; (*per pepe*) mill, pepper mill 2 (*scherz: macchina*) old banger (*Brit*), clunker (*USA*)

maciullare [matʃulˈlare] /72/ VT (*canapa, lino*) to brake; (*fig: braccio ecc*) to crush

macro- [ˈmakro] PREF macro-

macrobiotico, -a, -ci, -che [makrobiˈɔtiko] AGG (*dieta, alimenti*) macrobiotic

maculato, -a [makuˈlato] AGG (*pelo*) spotted

madama [maˈdama] SF 1 (*scherz*) madam 2 (*gergo: polizia*) cops *pl*

made in Italy SM: **il made in Italy** Italian exports *pl* (*especially fashion goods*)

Madera [maˈdɛra] SF (*Geog*) Madeira ♦ SM INV (*vino*) Madeira

madido, -a [ˈmadido] AGG (*letter*): **madido (di)** wet *o* moist (with); **madido di sudore** bathed in sweat

madonna [maˈdɔnna] SF (*Rel*): **Madonna** Our Lady; (*Arte*) madonna; (*letter: Storia*) my lady, madam; **madonna!** (*fam*) good God!

madornale [madorˈnale] AGG enormous, huge; **un errore madornale** a huge mistake

madre [ˈmadre] SF **1** mother; **mia madre** my mother; **la madre dei due bambini** the mother of the two children; **la madre di Matteo** Matteo's mother; **senza madre** motherless; **la madre di tutte...** (*fig*) the mother of all ...; **madre adottiva** adoptive mother; **madre coraggio** Mother Courage (*mother who defies the mafia, state etc to defend her child*); **madre di famiglia** mother; **madre natura** Mother Nature; **madre superiora** (*Rel*) mother superior **2 madre dell'aceto** mother of vinegar **3** (*matrice di bolletta*) counterfoil ♦ AGG INV mother *attr*; **casa madre** (*Rel*) mother house; **ragazza madre** unmarried mother; **regina madre** queen mother; **scena madre** (*Teatro*) principal scene

madrelingua [madreˈlingwa] SF mother tongue, native language; **non è di madrelingua inglese** English isn't his mother tongue ♦ SM INV, SF INV (*persona*) native speaker; **un madrelingua inglese** an English native speaker

madrepatria [madreˈpatrja] SF mother country, native land

madreperla [madreˈperla] SF mother-of-pearl

Madrid [maˈdrid] SF Madrid

madrigale [madriˈgale] SM madrigal

madrileno, -a [madriˈlɛno] AGG of *o* from Madrid ♦ SM, SF native *o* inhabitant of Madrid

madrina [maˈdrina] SF (*di bambino*) godmother; (*di nave*) christener

maestà [maesˈta] SF INV (*gen*) majesty; **Sua Maestà il Re** His Majesty the King; **Sua Maestà la Regina** Her Majesty the Queen

maestosità [maestosiˈta] SF majesty

maestoso, -a [maesˈtoso] AGG majestic

maestra [maˈestra] SF maestra; **maestra di scuola** primary school teacher; **maestra d'asilo** nursery school teacher; **scusi, signora maestra...** miss ...; *vedi anche* **maestro**

maestrale [maesˈtrale] SM northwest wind, northwesterly ♦ AGG northwest *attr*, northwesterly

maestranze [maesˈtrantse] SFPL workforce *sg*, workers

maestria [maesˈtria] SF mastery, skill

maestro, -a [maˈestro] SM, SF **1** (*anche:* **maestro di scuola** *o* **elementare**) primary (*Brit*) *o* grade school (*USA*) teacher; **scusi, signor maestro...** sir ... **2** (*fig: esperto*) expert; **è maestra nella cucina** she's an expert cook; **è stato un colpo da maestro** (*fig*) that was a masterstroke ♦ SM **1** (*artigiano*) master; **i Maestri del Rinascimento** the Masters of the Renaissance **2** (*Mus*) maestro **3** (*vento*) northwest wind ♦ AGG (*di grande abilità*) masterly, skilful (*Brit*), skillful (*USA*); **albero maestro** (*Naut*) main mast; **muro maestro** main wall; **strada maestra** main road ♦ **maestra d'asilo** nursery teacher; **maestro di ballo** dancing master; **maestro di cerimonie** master of ceremonies; **maestro d'orchestra** conductor, director (*USA*); **maestro di piano** piano teacher; **maestro di scherma** fencing master; **maestro di sci** ski *o* skiing instructor

mafia [ˈmafja] SF Mafia

mafioso, -a [maˈfjoso] AGG mafia *attr* ♦ SM, SF member of the Mafia

maga, -ghe [ˈmaga] SF sorceress

magagna [maˈgaɲɲa] SF **1** (*anche fig*) defect, flaw, blemish **2** (*noia, guaio*) problem

magari [maˈgari] ESCL (*esprime desiderio*): **magari fosse vero!** if only it were true!; **ti piacerebbe andare in Italia? — magari!** would you like to go to Italy? —certainly would! *o* you bet!; **hai avuto l'aumento? — sì, magari!** did you get the increase? — I should have been so lucky! ♦ AVV (*anche*) even; (*forse*) perhaps; **saremo in 5, magari in 6** there will be 5 of us, or maybe 6

magazzinaggio, -gi [magaddziˈnaddʒo] SM storage; (**spese di**) **magazzinaggio** storage charges *pl*, warehousing charges *pl*

magazziniere [magadzziˈnjere] SM warehouseman

magazzino [magadˈdzino] SM **1** (*deposito*) warehouse; **lo tengono in un magazzino** they keep it in a warehouse; **avere merci in magazzino** to have goods in stock; **fondi di magazzino** unsold stock; **magazzino doganale** bonded warehouse **2 grande magazzino** department store

maggio [ˈmaddʒo] SM May; *vedi* **luglio**

maggiorana [maddʒoˈrana] SF (*Bot*) (sweet) marjoram

maggioranza [maddʒoˈrantsa] SF (*gen*) majority; **partito di maggioranza** majority party; **eletto con una maggioranza di** elected by a majority of; **essere in maggioranza** to be in the majority; **nella maggioranza dei casi** in most cases; **la maggioranza di** most; **la maggioranza degli italiani** most Italians, the majority of Italians; **la maggioranza silenziosa** the silent majority; **maggioranza assoluta/relativa** absolute/relative majority; **maggioranza qualificata** qualified majority

maggiorare [maddʒoˈrare] /72/ VT (*Comm: prezzo, conto*): **maggiorare (di)** to increase (by)

maggiorazione [maddʒoratˈtsjone] SF (*Comm*) rise, increase

maggiordomo [maddʒorˈdɔmo] SM butler

maggiore [madˈdʒore] AGG *comp di* **grande 1** (*più grande*) bigger, larger; (*di quantità*) greater; **le spese sono state maggiori del previsto** expenses were higher than expected; **con maggiore entusiasmo** with more *o* greater enthusiasm; **ha dimostrato maggior entusiasmo di te** he showed greater enthusiasm than you; **a maggior ragione dovresti parlargli tu** all the more reason for you to speak to him yourself **2** (*più importante*) more important; (*di notevole rilevanza*) major; **opere maggiori** major works **3** (*più anziano: sorella, fratello*) elder, older; **il mio fratello maggiore** my older brother **4** (*di grado*): **sergente maggiore** sergeant major; **Stato Maggiore** (*Mil*) general staff **5** (*Mus*) major; **do maggiore** C major; **in re maggiore** in D major ♦ AGG *superl di* **grande**(*vedi agg comp 1,2,3*) biggest, largest; greatest; most important; eldest, oldest; **la maggior parte di** most of; **la maggior parte dei miei amici** most of my friends; **la maggior parte della gente** most people, the majority (of people); **andare per la maggiore** (*cantante, attore ecc*) to be very popular, be "in"; **la maggiore età** majority; **raggiungere la maggior età** to reach the age of majority; **la maggiore industria automobilistica d'Italia** the biggest car maker in Italy; **il maggiore poeta francese del secolo** the most important French poet of the century ♦ SM, SF **1** (*grado: Mil*) major; (: *Aer*) squadron leader **2** (*d'età: tra due*) older, elder; (: *tra più di due*) oldest, eldest; **la maggiore delle due sorelle** the older of the two sisters; **il maggiore dei tre fratelli** the oldest of the three brothers

maggiorenne [maddʒoˈrenne] AGG of age ♦ SM, SF person who has come of age; **diventare maggiorenne** to come of age, reach one's majority; **adesso sono maggiorenne** now I'm of age; **quando sarai maggiorenne...** when you're eighteen ...

maggioritario, -ria, -ri, -rie [maddʒoriˈtarjo] AGG majority *attr* ♦ SM (*Pol: anche:* **sistema maggioritario**) first-past-the-post system

maggiormente [maddʒorˈmente] AVV more; **impegnandoti maggiormente supereresti l'esame** if you were to work harder you'd pass the exam; **l'artista che lo ha maggiormente influenzato è Rembrandt** the artist who most influenced him was Rembrandt

magia [maˈdʒia] SF magic; **come per magia** as if by magic, like magic; **scomparve come per magia** it disappeared as if by magic

magico, -a, -ci, -che [ˈmadʒiko] AGG magic; (*fig: serata, incontro*) magical; (: *sorriso*) charming; **pronunciare la formula magica** to say the magic words

magio, -gi [ˈmadʒo] SM (*Rel*): **i re Magi** the Magi, the Three Wise Men

magistero [madʒisˈtero] SM: **Facoltà di Magistero** ≈ teacher(s') training college

magistrale [madʒisˈtrale] AGG **1** (*Scol*) primary (*Brit*) *o* grade school (*USA*) teachers', primary *o* grade school teaching *attr*; **abilitazione magistrale** *teaching diploma for primary teachers*; **istituto magistrale** *secondary school for the training of primary teachers: attended by students aged 14 - 18*

2 (*abile: colpo, intervento*) masterly, skilful (*Brit*), skillful (*USA*) ♦ **magistrali** SFPL = **istituto magistrale**

magistrato [madʒis'trato] SM magistrate

magistratura [madʒistra'tura] SF: **la magistratura** the magistracy, the magistrature

maglia [ˈmaʎʎa] SF **1** (*punto*) stitch; **avviare/calare le maglie** to cast on/off; **maglia dritta** plain; **maglia rovescia** purl; **lavora una maglia dritta, una rovescia** knit one, purl one **2** (*lavoro ai ferri*) knitting *no pl*; **lavorare a maglia, fare la maglia** to knit; **mi piace lavorare a maglia** I like knitting **3** (*indumento intimo*) vest; (*Sport: maglione, tessuto*) jersey; (*Storia: di armatura*) coat of mail; **indossa la maglia iridata** (*Ciclismo*) he's the world cycling champion **4** (*di catena*) link; (*di armatura*) coat of mail; (*di rete: Tecn*) mesh; **una rete a maglie fitte/grosse** a fine-/wide-mesh net; **passare per le maglie della rete** (*anche fig*) to slip through the net

maglieria [maʎʎeˈria] SF **1** (*indumenti*) knitwear; **macchina per maglieria** knitting machine **2** (*negozio*) knitwear shop

maglietta [maʎˈʎetta] SF (*con maniche*) T-shirt; (*canottiera*) vest

maglificio, -ci [maʎʎiˈfitʃo] SM knitwear factory

maglina [maʎˈʎina] SF (*tessuto*) jersey

maglio, -gli [ˈmaʎʎo] SM (*martello*) mallet; (*Tecn: macchina*) power hammer

maglione [maʎˈʎone] SM jersey, sweater

magma, -i [ˈmagma] SM (*Geol*) magma; **allo stato di magma** (*fig*) inchoate

magnaccia [maɲˈɲattʃa] SM INV (*pegg*) pimp

magnanimità [maɲɲanimiˈta] SF magnanimity

magnanimo, -a [maɲˈɲanimo] AGG magnanimous

magnate [maɲˈɲate] SM tycoon, magnate

magnesia [maɲˈɲezja] SF magnesia

magnesio [maɲˈɲezjo] SM magnesium; **al magnesio** (*lampada, flash*) magnesium *attr*

magnete [maɲˈɲete] SM (*calamita*) magnet; (*Elettr, Aut*) magneto

magnetico, -a, -ci, -che [maɲˈɲetiko] AGG (*anche fig*) magnetic

magnetismo [maɲɲeˈtizmo] SM (*anche fig*) magnetism; **il magnetismo terrestre** the earth's magnetism

magnetizzare [maɲɲetidˈdzare] /72/ VT (*Fis*) to magnetize; (*fig*) to mesmerize

magnificamente [maɲɲifikaˈmente] AVV magnificently, extremely well

magnificenza [maɲɲifiˈtʃɛntsa] SF magnificence, splendour (*Brit*), splendor (*USA*)

magnifico, -a, -ci, -che [maɲˈɲifiko] AGG (*gen*) magnificent, splendid; (*serata*) marvellous, wonderful; (*tempo*) gorgeous, superb; **domani si parte — magnifico!** we're setting off tomorrow — terrific!; **uno scenario magnifico** wonderful scenery

magno, -a [ˈmaɲɲo] AGG: **aula magna** main hall

magnolia [maɲˈɲolja] SF magnolia

mago, -ghi [ˈmago] SM (*stregone*) magician, wizard; (*illusionista*) magician; (*fam: persona abilissima*) wizard

magrezza [maˈgrettsa] SF (*di persona, corpo*) thinness; (*di risorse*) scarcity

magro, -a [ˈmagro] AGG **1** (*persona, corpo*) thin, skinny (*pegg*); (*viso*) thin; **è alta e magra** she's tall and thin; **è più magra di me** she's thinner than me **2** (*latte*) skimmed; (*carne*) lean; (*formaggio*) low-fat **3** (*stipendio, guadagno*) poor, meagre (*Brit*), meager (*USA*); (*profitti*) small, slim; (*annata, raccolto*) poor; (*scusa*) poor, lame; (*soddisfazione, consolazione*) scant; (*cena, pasto*) skimpy ♦ SM **1** (*carne*) lean meat **2** (*Rel*): **giorno di magro** day of abstinence; **mangiare di magro** not to eat meat ♦ SM, SF (*persona magra*) slim person

mai [ˈmai] AVV **1** (*negativo*) never, not ...ever; **non esce mai** she never goes out; **non l'ho mai visto** I've never seen it; **non lo aveva mai visto nessuno** nobody had ever seen it; **non sono mai stato in Russia** I've never *o* I haven't ever been to Russia; **non me ne dimenticherò mai** I'll never *o* won't ever forget it; **non avrei mai detto che...** I would never have said that ...; **non le ha mai più telefonato** he never phoned her again, he has never phoned her since; **non si sa mai** you never can tell; **mai e poi mai!** no way!; **mai più**

never again; **non lo farò mai più** I'll never do it again; **mai e poi mai** never ever; (*assolutamente no*) no way; **quasi mai** hardly ever, practically never; **non esco quasi mai** I hardly ever go out; **mai, o quasi mai** never, or hardly ever; **ora o mai più** it's now or never; **più che mai** more than ever **2** (*con tempi indefiniti*) ever; **l'hai mai visto prima?** have you ever seen him before?; **il più bello che abbia mai visto** the best I've ever seen; **sei mai in ufficio il sabato?** are you ever in the office on Saturdays?; **se mai ne trovassi uno te lo farei sapere** if I ever found one I would let you know; **i prezzi delle case sono più alti che mai** house prices are higher than ever; **caso mai si mettesse a piovere** in case it starts raining, should it start to rain; **se mai direi che ha sbagliato lui** if anything, I would say that he was in the wrong; **caso mai ti telefono domenica** I might phone you on Sunday; **come mai?** why?, why (*o* how) on earth?; **come mai sei arrivato in ritardo?** why were you late?; **come mai non ci hai avvisato?** why (on earth) didn't you let us know?; **hai fatto molti errori nel tema, come mai?** you made a lot of mistakes in your essay, why was that?; **che dici mai?** what (on earth) are you saying?; **chi/dove/quando mai?** whoever/ wherever/whenever?; **quando mai ho detto una cosa simile?** when did I ever say any such thing?

maiale [maˈjale] SM **1** (*Zool, o fig: pegg*) pig; **mangiare come un maiale** to eat like a pig; **sei proprio un maiale!** you're a real pig! **2** (*Culin*) pork; **una cotoletta di maiale** a pork chop

mail [ˈmeil] SF INV (*messaggio di posta elettronica*) email

maiolica [maˈjɔlika] SF majolica

maionese [majoˈnese] SF mayonnaise

Maiorca [maˈjɔrka] SF Majorca

mais [ˈmais] SM (*coltura*) maize (*Brit*), corn (*USA*); (*in scatola*) sweetcorn

maiuscolo, -a [maˈjuskolo] AGG capital; **a lettere maiuscole** in capital letters ♦ SM capital letters *pl*; (*Tip*) upper case; **in maiuscolo** in capital letters; **scrivere tutto in maiuscolo** to write everything in capitals *o* in capital letters

mal [ˈmal] AVV, SM *vedi* **male**

mala [ˈmala] SF (*gergo*) underworld

malaccorto, -a [malakˈkɔrto] AGG rash, careless

malafede [malaˈfede] SF bad faith; **è sicuramente in malafede** he's certainly not sincere; **questo dimostra la tua malafede** this shows you aren't sincere

malaffare [malafˈfare] **di malaffare** AGG (*gente*) shady, dishonest; **donna di malaffare** prostitute

malagevole [malaˈdʒevole] AGG difficult, hard

malagrazia [malaˈgrattsja] SF: **con malagrazia** with bad grace, impolitely

malalingua [malaˈlingwa] SF (*pl* **malelingue**) gossip (*person*)

malamente [malaˈmente] AVV (*gen*) badly; (*sgarbatamente*) rudely; **finire malamente** (*persona*) to come to a bad end

malandato, -a [malanˈdato] AGG (*persona: di salute*) in poor health, in a bad way; (*: di condizioni finanziarie*) badly off; (*trascurato: persona*) shabby; (*: cosa*) dilapidated

malanimo [maˈlanimo] SM ill will, malevolence; **di malanimo** unwillingly, grudgingly

malanno [maˈlanno] SM **1** (*disgrazia*) misfortune **2** (*malattia*) ailment; **prendersi un malanno** to catch something; **mi devo essere preso un malanno** I must have caught something

malapena [malaˈpena] **a malapena** AVV hardly, scarcely; **ti sento a malapena** I can hardly hear you; **ci vedo a malapena** I can hardly see

malaria [maˈlarja] SF malaria

malarico, -a, -ci, -che [maˈlariko] AGG malarial

malasorte [malaˈsɔrte] SF bad luck, ill luck

malaticcio, -cia, -ci, -ce [malaˈtittʃo] AGG sickly

malato, -a [maˈlato] AGG (*persona*) ill, sick, unwell; (*organo, pianta*) diseased; **mio nonno è molto malato** my grandfather is very ill; **un bambino malato** a sick child; **ho una gamba malata** I've got a bad leg; **essere malato di cuore** to have heart trouble *o* a bad heart; **essere malato di mente** mentally ill; **è malato di cancro** he's got cancer; **tu sei malato al cervello!** (*fig*) you're off your head!; **una mente/fantasia malata** a sick mind/morbid imagination; **darsi malato** (*sul* *lavoro ecc*) to say one is sick; **essere malato d'amore** to be lovesick ♦ SM, SF (*infermo*) sick person; (*paziente*) patient; **i malati** the sick; **un malato grave** a person who is seriously ill; **un malato di cancro** a cancer patient

malattia [malat'tia] SF 1 (*Med*) illness, disease; (*di pianta*) disease; (*cattiva salute*) illness, sickness; **è morto dopo una lunga malattia** he died after a long illness; **una malattia infettiva** an infectious disease; **malattie nervose** nervous system diseases; **malattie del lavoro** industrial diseases; **mettersi in malattia** to go on sick leave; **fare una malattia di qc** (*fig: disperarsi*) to get in a state about sth 2 (*fissazione*) mania; **ha la malattia del gioco** he's addicted to gambling, he's hooked on gambling

malaugurato, -a [malaugu'rato] AGG ill-fated, unlucky

malaugurio, -ri [malau'gurjo] SM bad *o* ill omen; **uccello del malaugurio** bird of ill omen; (*fig*) jinx, Jonah

malavita [mala'vita] SF underworld; **darsi alla malavita** to turn to crime

malavitoso, -a [malavi'toso] SM, SF gangster

malavoglia [mala'vɔʎʎa] **di malavoglia** AVV reluctantly, un-willingly; **lo fece di malavoglia** she did it reluctantly

Malawi [ma'lawi] SM Malawi

Malaysia [ma'laizja] SF Malaysia

malaysiano, -a [malai'zjano] AGG, SM, SF Malaysian

malcapitato, -a [malkapi'tato] AGG unlucky, unfortunate ♦ SM, SF unfortunate person

malconcio, -cia, -ci, -ce [mal'kontʃo] AGG (*abiti, persona*) in a sorry state; **uscire malconcio da qc** (*fig*) to come out of sth badly

malcontento, -a [malkon'tento] AGG: **malcontento (di)** dis-satisfied (with) ♦ SM (*sentimento*) discontent

malcostume [malkos'tume] SM corruption

maldestro, -a [mal'dɛstro] AGG (*goffo*) clumsy, awkward; (*persona: inesperto*) inexperienced, inexpert; **è la persona più maldestra che conosca** he's the clumsiest person I know

maldicente [maldi'tʃente] SM, SF gossip

maldicenza [maldi'tʃentsa] SF malicious gossip; **è solo una maldicenza, sono solo maldicenze** it's just gossip

maldisposto, -a [maldis'posto] AGG: **maldisposto (verso)** ill-disposed (towards)

Maldive [mal'dive] SFPL: **le Maldive** the Maldives, the Mal-dive Islands

male [ˈmale] AVV 1 (*in modo insoddisfacente*) badly; (*in modo errato*) badly, wrongly; **oggi ho giocato male** I played bad-ly today; **male! non avresti dovuto farlo** that was wrong of you - you shouldn't have done it; **questa porta chiude male** this door doesn't shut properly; **scrivere/comportarsi male** to write/behave badly; **pronunciare male una parola** to pronounce a word wrongly; **rispondere male** (*in modo errato*) to answer wrongly *o* incorrectly; (*in modo sgarbato*) to answer back; **riuscire male** to turn out badly; **qui si mangia molto male** the food is very bad here; **pensi che abbia fatto male ad andare?** do you think it was wrong of him to go?; **parlar male di qn** to speak ill of sb, say bad things about sb; **mi ha parlato male di te** he said bad things about you; **trat-tar male qn** to ill-treat sb 2 **sentirsi/star male** (*di salute*) to feel/be ill; **mi sono sentita male** I fell ill 3 (*fraseologia*): **gli è andata male di nuovo** he failed again; **per male che vada** however badly things go; **capire male** to misunderstand; **hai capito male** you've misunderstood; **le cose si stanno mettendo male** things are taking a turn for the worse; **ha preso molto male la cosa** he took it very badly; **restare** *o* **rimanere male** (*deluso*) to be disappointed; (*dispiaciuto*) to be sorry; (*offeso*) to be hurt *o* offended; **sta male compor-tarsi così** that's no way to behave; **quell'abito le sta pro-prio male** that dress just doesn't suit her, that dress looks terrible on her; **il giallo sta male con il rosa** yellow looks awful with pink; **la vedo male** things look bad (to me), it doesn't look good to me; **bene o male ce la farò** one way or the other I'll manage; **niente male quel ragazzo** that boy's not bad, that boy's a bit of alright (*fam*); **di male in peggio** from bad to worse; **non faresti male a dirglielo** it wouldn't be a bad idea to tell him ♦ SM 1 (*ciò che è ingiusto, disonesto*) evil; **il male** evil; **il bene e il male** good and evil; **un male necessario** a necessary evil; **le forze del male** the forces of evil; **il minore dei due mali** the lesser of two evils;

mali sociali social evils 2 (*danno*) harm; **fare del male a qn** to harm *o* hurt sb; **le sigarette fanno male** cigarettes are bad for you; **che c'è di male?** what's the harm in that?; **che c'è di male se esco con lui?** what harm is there in my going out with him?; **non ho fatto niente di male** I haven't done anything wrong; **non sarebbe (un) male se gliene parlassi** it wouldn't do any harm to talk to him about it; **non fareb-be (del) male a una mosca** he wouldn't hurt a fly; **non gli voglio male** I don't bear him ill-will 3 (*dolore*) pain, ache; (*malattia*) illness, disease; **far male** to hurt; **mi fa male una gamba** my leg hurts, I've got a pain in my leg; **mi fa male** it hurts; **farsi male** to hurt o.s.; **fare (del) male a qn** to hurt *o* harm sb; **ahi! mi hai fatto male!** ouch! you've hurt me!; **far male alla salute** to be bad for one's health; **fumare fa male** smoking is bad for you; **avere un brutto male** (*euf: cancro*) to have cancer; **i mali della vecchiaia** the infirmities of old age; **mal d'aria** air sickness; **mal d'auto** car sickness; **mal di denti** toothache; **mal di gola** sore throat; **mal di mare** sea-sickness; **mal di schiena** backache; **mal di stomaco** stomach ache; **mal di testa** headache; **avere mal di testa/di stomaco** to have a headache/stomach ache; **aver mal di denti/d'orec-chi/di gola** to have a toothache/earache/sore throat; **avere mal di cuore/di fegato** to have a heart/liver complaint; **avere il mal di mare** to be seasick; **soffrire di mal d'auto** to get car sick 4 (*fraseologia*): **andare a male** (*carne*) to go off *o* bad; (*latte*) to go off; **non avertene a male, non prender-tela a male** don't take it to heart; **come va? — non c'è male** how are you? — not bad *o* O.K. (*fam*); **mal comune mezzo gaudio** (*Proverbio*) a trouble shared is a trouble halved; **a mali estremi, estremi rimedi** (*Proverbio*) desperate circum-stances call for desperate remedies; **non tutto il male vien per nuocere** (*Proverbio*) it's an ill wind that blows nobody any good, every cloud has a silver lining

maledetto, -a [male'detto] PP *di* **maledire** ♦ AGG 1 (*dannato*) accursed; (*nelle imprecazioni*) cursed, damned 2 (*fig: fam*) damned, blasted, confounded; **avere una fame maledetta** to be damned hungry; **spegni quella maledetta radio!** turn off that damn radio!; **ho una paura maledetta dei ragni** I'm scared stiff of spiders

maledire [male'dire] /38/ VT IRREG to curse

maledizione [maledit'tsjone] SF (*condanna, imprecazione*) curse; **maledizione!** damn!; **devo avere la maledizione addosso!** I must be fated!; **la maledizione del faraone** the curse of the Pharaoh

maleducato, -a [maledu'kato] AGG (*persona*) rude, ill-man-nered ♦ SM, SF ill-mannered person; **fare il maleducato** to be rude

maleducazione [maledukat'tsjone] SF rudeness; **è maledu-cazione parlare con la bocca piena** it's bad manners to speak with your mouth full

malefatta [male'fatta] SF misdeed

maleficio, -ci [male'fitʃo] SM evil spell, witchcraft

malefico, -a, -ci, -che [ma'lɛfiko] AGG (*influsso*) evil; (*clima*) harmful, bad

malese [ma'lese] AGG, SM, SF Malaysian ♦ SM (*lingua*) Malay

Malesia [ma'lɛzja] SF Malaysia

malessere [ma'lessere] SM 1 (*indisposizione*) indisposition, slight illness; **ha avuto un leggero malessere** he didn't feel quite right 2 (*fig: disagio*) disquiet, uneasiness

malevolenza [malevo'lentsa] SF malevolence

malevolo, -a [ma'levolo] AGG malevolent

malfamato, -a [malfa'mato] AGG of ill repute, notorious; **un quartiere malfamato** a rough area

malfatto, -a [mal'fatto] AGG (*lavoro*) badly done; (*oggetto*) badly made; (*persona, corpo*) deformed

malfattore, -trice [malfat'tore] SM, SF wrongdoer; **è una banda di malfattori!** they're a bunch of crooks!

malfermo, -a [mal'fermo] AGG (*voce, mano*) shaky; (*passo*) unsteady; (*salute*) poor, delicate; **essere malfermo sulle gambe** to be unsteady on one's legs; **è sempre più malfer-mo sulle gambe** he's getting increasingly unsteady on his feet

malformazione [malformat'tsjone] SF (*Med*) malformation

malga, -ghe [ˈmalga] SF Alpine hut

malgoverno [malgo'vɛrno] SM (*Pol*) mismanagement, mis-rule

malgrado [mal'grado] PREP in spite of, despite; **malgrado tutto le sono ancora amico** we are still friends in spite of *o* despite everything; **mio** (*o* **tuo** *ecc*) **malgrado** against my (*o* your *ecc*) will; **suo malgrado ha dovuto fare il lavoro** he had to do the work much against his will ♦ CONG even though, although; **malgrado fosse tardi...** although it was late ...; **malgrado fossi in ritardo sono riuscito a prendere il treno** even though I was late I managed to get the train

malia [ma'lia] SF (*incantesimo*) spell; (*fig: fascino*) charm

maliardo, -a [mali'ardo] AGG (*occhi, sorriso*) bewitching

malignamente [maliɲɲa'mente] AVV maliciously

malignare [maliɲ'ɲare] /15/ VI (*aus* avere) **malignare su** to malign, speak ill of

malignità [maliɲɲi'ta] SF INV 1 (*qualità*) malice, spite; **con malignità** spitefully, maliciously 2 (*osservazione*) spiteful remark

maligno, -a [ma'liɲɲo] AGG 1 (*persona, parole*) malicious; **spirito maligno** evil spirit; **delle insinuazioni maligne** malicious gossip 2 (*Med*) malignant; **un tumore maligno** a malignant tumour ♦ SM, SF malicious person

malinconia [malinko'nia] SF melancholy, gloom

malinconico, -a, -ci, -che [malin'kɔniko] AGG melancholy, sad; **cantava una canzone malinconica** she was singing a sad song; **è sempre più malinconico** he's getting sadder and sadder

malincuore [malin'kwɔre] **a malincuore** AVV reluctantly, unwillingly; **gliel'ho dato a malincuore** I gave it to him reluctantly

malinformato, -a [malinfor'mato] AGG misinformed

malintenzionato, -a [malintentsjo'nato] AGG ill-intentioned ♦ SM, SF ill-intentioned person; **è stato aggredito da un malintenzionato** he was attacked by a mugger

malinteso [malin'teso] AGG (*riguardo, senso del dovere*) mistaken, misguided ♦ SM misunderstanding

malizia [ma'littsja] SF (*cattiveria*) malice, spite; (*furbizia*) mischievousness; (*astuzia*) clever trick; **con malizia** maliciously, spitefully; mischievously; cleverly

malizioso, -a [malit'tsjoso] AGG (*cattivo*) malicious, spiteful; (*vivace, birichino*) mischievous; (*astuto*) clever

malleabile [malle'abile] AGG malleable

malloppo [mal'lɔppo] SM (*fam: refurtiva*) loot

malmenare [malme'nare] /72/ VT to beat up

malmesso, -a [mal'messo] AGG (*persona*) in a difficult situation; (*vestito male*) poorly dressed, shabby; (*economicamente*) badly off; (*casa, macchina*) in a poor state of repair

malnutrito, -a [malnu'trito] AGG undernourished

malnutrizione [malnutrit'tsjone] SF malnutrition

malo, -a ['malo] AGG: **in malo modo** badly; (*sgarbatamente*) rudely; **essere a mal partito** to be in an awkward situation; **mala lingua = malalingua; mala sorte = malasorte; mala voglia = malavoglia**

malocchio [ma'lɔkkjo] SM evil eye; **guardare di malocchio** to look at with disfavour

malora [ma'lora] SF (*fam*): **andare in malora** to go to the dogs; **alla malora!** hell!; **va in malora!** go to hell!; **è un tirchio della malora!** he's a bloody miser!

malore [ma'lore] SM sudden illness; **venire** *o* **essere colto da malore** to be suddenly taken ill; **è stato colto da malore** he was suddenly taken ill

malridotto, -a [malri'dotto] AGG (*abiti, scarpe, persona*) in a sorry state; (*casa*) dilapidated; (*macchina*) in a poor state of repair

malsano, -a [mal'sano] AGG unhealthy; **il clima è più malsano qui** the climate is unhealthier here

malsicuro, -a [malsi'kuro] AGG (*scala, edificio*) unsafe

Malta ['malta] SF Malta

malta ['malta] SF (*Edil*) mortar

maltempo [mal'tempo] SM bad weather

malto ['malto] SM malt

maltolto [mal'tɔlto] SM: **restituire il maltolto** to give back one's ill-gotten gains

maltrattamento [maltratta'mento] SM ill-treatment; **subire maltrattamenti** to be ill-treated; **maltrattamento di animali** cruelty to animals

maltrattare [maltrat'tare] /72/ VT to ill-treat, abuse; **gli ostaggi non sono stati maltrattati** the hostages weren't ill-treated

malumore [malu'more] SM (*irritabilità*) bad temper, ill humour; (*discordia*) ill feeling; **di malumore** in a bad mood; **oggi il capo è di malumore** the boss is in a bad mood today

malva ['malva] SF (*Bot*) mallow ♦ SM INV (*colore*) mauve ♦ AGG INV mauve

malvagio, -gia, -gi, -gie [mal'vadʒo] AGG (*uomo, azione*) evil, wicked; **non è malvagio** (*fig: vino, cibo*) it's not unpleasant *o* bad; (: *spettacolo, film*) it's not bad ♦ SM, SF wicked person

malvagità [malvadʒi'ta] SF INV (*qualità*) wickedness; (*azione*) wicked deed

malvasia [malva'zia] SF Italian dessert wine

malversazione [malversat'tsjone] SF (*Dir*) embezzlement

malvestito, -a [malves'tito] AGG badly dressed, ill-clad

malvisto, -a [mal'visto] AGG (*persona, idea, proposta*): **malvisto (da)** unpopular (with)

malvivente [malvi'vente] SM, SF criminal

malvolentieri [malvolen'tjɛri] AVV unwillingly, reluctantly

malvolere [malvo'lere] /131/ VT **farsi malvolere (da)** to make o.s. unpopular (with); **essere malvoluto da qn** to be disliked by sb; **prendere qn a malvolere** to take a dislike to sb

malware ['malwer] SM INV (*Inform*) malware (program)

mamma ['mamma] SF (*fam*) mum(my) (*Brit*), mom (*USA*); **me l'ha detto la mamma** mum told me that; **la mamma mia** my mum; **come l'ha fatto mamma** in one's birthday suit; **mamma mia!** good heavens!, my goodness!

mammario, -ria, -ri, -rie [mam'marjo] AGG (*Anat*) mammary

mammella [mam'mella] SF (*di donna*) breast; (*di animale*) udder

mammifero, -a [mam'mifero] AGG (*Zool*) mammalian ♦ SM (*Zool*) mammal

mammismo [mam'mizmo] SM *excessive attachment to one's mother*

mammola ['mammola] SF (*Bot*) violet; **è una mammoletta** (*fig: scherz*) he's a shrinking violet

manager ['mænidʒə] SM INV, SF INV manager

manageriale [manadʒe'rjale] AGG managerial

manata [ma'nata] SF (*colpo*) slap; (*quantità*) handful; **a manate** by the handful

manca ['manka] SF left (hand); **a destra e a manca** left, right and centre, on all sides

mancamento [manka'mento] SM (*di forze*) (feeling of) faintness, weakness

mancanza [man'kantsa] SF 1 **mancanza di** (*assenza*) lack of; (*carenza*) shortage of, scarcity of; **mancanza di rispetto** lack of respect; **mancanza di soldi** lack (*o* shortage) of money; **in mancanza di vino berremo acqua** as there is no wine we'll drink water; **in mancanza d'altro/di meglio** for want *o* lack of anything else/better; **per mancanza di tempo** through lack of time; **sentire la mancanza di qn/qc** to miss sb/sth; **sento la tua mancanza** I miss you 2 (*fallo*) fault; (*difetto*) failing, shortcoming; **commettere una mancanza** to commit an error

mancare [man'kare] /20/ VI (*aus* essere) 1 (*far difetto*) to be lacking; **mancano i fondi per la ricerca** there aren't the funds to do research; **manca sempre il tempo** there's never enough time; **mi mancano le parole per esprimerti la mia gratitudine** I can't find words to express my gratitude to you; **ci manca il pane** we've run out of bread, we don't have *o* haven't got any bread; **fammi sapere se ti manca qualcosa** let me know if you need anything; **i suoi non gli fanno mancar niente** his family doesn't let him want for anything; **gli sono venuti a mancare i soldi** his money ran out, he ran out of money; **quanto manca all'arrivo del treno?** how long before the train arrives?; **manca un quarto alle 6** it's a quarter to (*Brit*) *o* of (*USA*) 6; **mancano cinque minuti alla fine del film** there's five minutes to go to the end of the film 2 (*non esserci*) to be missing, not to be there; (*persona: essere assente*) to be absent; **mancano ancora 10 sterline** we're still £10 short; **quanti pezzi mancano?** how many pieces are missing?; **mancavi solo tu** you were the only one missing, you were the only one who wasn't there;

mi manchi I miss you; **mancano prove** there's not enough evidence; **mancare da casa** to be away from home; **mancare all'appello** (*persona*) to be absent from roll call; (*cose*) to be missing **3** (*venir meno: coraggio, forze*) to fail; (*morire*) to die; **gli è mancato il coraggio** his courage failed him; **gli sono mancate le parole** words failed him; **sentirsi mancare** to feel faint; **gli sono venuti a mancare i genitori** he lost his parents; **è mancata la luce** the electricity went off **4** (*aus avere; essere in errore*) to be wrong, make a mistake; **mi dispiace se ho mancato** I'm sorry if I was wrong **5** (*aus avere*) **mancare di** (*coraggio, giudizio*) to lack, be lacking in; (*risorse, soldi*) to be short of, lack; **mancare di rispetto a qn** to be lacking in respect towards sb, be disrespectful towards sb; **mancare di parola** not to keep one's word, go back on one's word; **non mancherò di salutarlo da parte tua** of course I'll give him your regards; **non mancherò** I won't forget, I'll make sure I do **6** (*doveri*) to neglect; (*promessa*) to fail to keep; (*appuntamento*) to miss; **mancare alla parola data** to break one's promise **7** (*fraseologia*): **ci mancherebbe altro!** of course I (*o* ecc) will!; **ci mancava solo questa!, ci mancava anche questo!** that's all we need!; **c'è mancato poco** it was a near thing; **c'è mancato poco** *o* **poco è mancato che si facesse male** he very nearly hurt himself; **gli manca una rotella** (*fig*) he's got a screw loose; **a questo cane manca solo la parola** that dog is almost human ♦ vt (*bersaglio*) to miss; **ha mancato la presa ed è caduto** he lost his grip and fell

mancato, -a [man'kato] AGG (*tentativo*) abortive, unsuccessful; (*appuntamento*) missed; (*occasione*) lost, wasted; (*artista*) failed; **è un dottore mancato** (*fallito*) he's a failure as a doctor; (*non realizzato*) he should have been a doctor; **mancato pagamento** non-payment; **mancato arrivo** failure to arrive

manche [mãʃ] SF INV (*Sport*) heat

mancherò ecc [manke'rɔ] VB *vedi* mancare

manchevole [man'kevole] AGG (*insufficiente*) inadequate, insufficient

manchevolezza [mankevo'lettsa] SF (*scorrettezza*) fault, shortcoming; **è stata una manchevolezza non invitarlo** it was remiss of us not to invite him

mancia, -ce [ˈmantʃa] SF tip; **dare una mancia a qn** to tip sb, give sb a tip; **ha dato la mancia al cameriere** he tipped the waiter; **mancia competente** reward

manciata [man'tʃata] SF handful; **a manciate** by the handful

mancino, -a [man'tʃino] AGG (*persona*) left-handed; (*calciatore*) left-footed; (*pugile*) southpaw attr; (*fig*): **tiro mancino** dirty trick ♦ SM, SF left-handed person, left-hander

manco [ˈmanko] AVV (*fam: nemmeno*) not even; **manco per sogno!, manco per idea!** not on your life!, (I) wouldn't dream of it!

mandante [man'dante] SM, SF (*Dir*) principal; (*istigatore*) instigator

mandarancio, -ci [manda'rantʃo] SM clementine

mandare [man'dare] /72/ VT **1** (*gen*) to send; **mandare qc a qn** to send sb sth; **manderò una mail a Loredana** I'll send Loredana an email; **mi puoi mandare un po' di denaro?** can you send me some money?; **glielo manderò** I'll send it to him; **mando sempre una mail a tutti i miei amici** I always send emails to all my friends; **mandare qc per posta/per via aerea** to send sth through the *o* by post/by air; **mandare a chiamare qn** to send for sb; **mandare a dire (a qn)** to send word (to sb); **mandare due righe a qn** to drop sb a line; **mandare qn in prigione** to send sb to prison; **mandare un bacio a qn** to blow sb a kiss; **mandare in pezzi** (*vaso, vetro*) to shatter; **mandare in rovina** to ruin; **che Dio ce la mandi buona!** God help us! **2 mandare avanti** (*persona*) to send ahead; (*fig: famiglia*) to provide for; (*: ditta, azienda, attività*) to keep going, run; (*: pratica*) to attend to; **mandare giù** (*persona*) to send down; (*cibo, fig*) to swallow; **mandare via** (*persona*) to send away (*licenziare*) to sack, fire **3** (*emettere: segnali*) to send out; (*: odori*) to give, utter, let out; **mandare in onda** (*Radio, TV*) to broadcast

mandarino¹ [manda'rino] SM (*Bot*) mandarin (orange)

mandarino² [manda'rino] SM (*in Cina*) mandarin

mandata [man'data] SF **1** (*di chiave*) turn; **chiudere a doppia mandata** to double-lock **2** (*quantità*) consignment, lot, batch

mandatario, -ri [manda'tarjo] SM (*Dir*) representative, agent

mandato [man'dato] SM **1** (*incarico: di deputato*) mandate; (*durata dell'incarico*) term of office; **su mandato di** by order of **2** (*Dir. penale*) warrant; **mandato d'arresto** *o* **di cattura** warrant for arrest; **mandato di comparizione** summons sg; **mandato di perquisizione** search warrant **3** (*Dir. civile*) mandate **4 mandato di pagamento** postal *o* money order

mandibola [man'dibola] SF (*Anat*) jaw, mandible

mandolino [mando'lino] SM (*Mus*) mandolin(e)

mandorla [ˈmandorla] SF (*frutto*) almond; **occhi a mandorla** almond(-shaped) eyes

mandorlato [mandor'lato] SM nut brittle

mandorlo [ˈmandorlo] SM almond tree

mandria [ˈmandrja] SF herd

mandriano [mandri'ano] SM cowherd, herdsman

mandrino [man'drino] SM (*Tecn*) mandrel

maneggevole [maned'dʒevole] AGG easy to handle; **poco maneggevole** difficult to handle

maneggiare [maned'dʒare] /62/ VT (*utensili, arnesi*) to handle, use; (*cera, creta*) to work; (*fig: persone, denaro*) to handle, deal with; **"maneggiare con cura"** "handle with care"

maneggio, -gi [ma'neddʒo] SM **1** (*Equitazione: scuola*) riding school; (*: pista*) ring; **maneggio coperto/all'aperto** indoor/outdoor riding school **2** (*fig: di denaro, affari*) management, handling **3** (*fig: manovra, intrigo*) scheme, ploy

manesco, -a, -schi, -sche [ma'nesko] AGG ready with one's fists; **una mamma manesca** a mother who smacks a lot

manette [ma'nette] SFPL handcuffs; **mettere le manette a qn** to handcuff sb

manganello [manga'nɛllo] SM club, cudgel; (*della polizia*) truncheon, night stick (*USA*)

manganese [manga'nese] SM manganese

mangereccio, -cia, -ci, -ce [mandʒe'rettʃo] AGG edible

mangiabile [man'dʒabile] AGG edible, eatable

mangiadischi [mandʒa'diski] (*Marchio registrato*) portable record player

mangiare [man'dʒare] /62/ VT **1** (*gen*) to eat; **non mangio carne** I don't eat meat; **vuoi mangiare qualcosa?** would you like something to eat?; **mangiare di tutto** to eat anything *o* everything; **qui si mangia bene/male** the food is good/bad here; **non avere da mangiare** not to have enough to eat; **dare da mangiare a qn** to give sb something to eat; **fare da mangiare** to cook; **la mamma sta facendo da mangiare** mum is cooking; **farsi qc da mangiare** to make o.s. sth to eat; **mangiare fuori** to eat out, have a meal out; **resta a mangiare un boccone con noi** stay and have a bite with us; **allora, si mangia?** is it ready then?; **si mangiano questi funghi?** are these mushrooms edible?; **mangiare per due/quattro** (*fig*) to eat enough for two/like a horse; **mangiare come un uccellino** (*fig*) to eat like a bird; **mangiare alle spalle di qn** (*fig*) to live off sb; **sembrava volesse mangiarmi** (*fig*) I thought he was going to kill me; **mangiarsi qn con gli occhi** to devour sb with one's eyes; **mangiarsi qn di baci** to smother sb with kisses; **mangiarsi il patrimonio** to squander one's inheritance; **mangiarsi il fegato** (*fig*) to be consumed with rage; **mi sarei mangiato le mani** I could have kicked myself; **mangiarsi le parole** to mumble; **mangiarsi le unghie** to bite one's nails; **questo mobile è mangiato dai tarli** this piece of furniture has woodworm; **esser mangiato vivo dalle zanzare** to be eaten alive by mosquitoes **2** (*Carte, Scacchi*) to take ♦ SM (*cibo*) food; **essere difficile nel mangiare** to be a fussy eater; **il mangiare è pronto** lunch/breakfast/dinner is ready

mangiasoldi [mandʒa'soldi] AGG INV (*fam*): **macchinetta mangiasoldi** one-armed bandit

mangiatoia [mandʒa'toja] SF (feeding-)trough

mangime [man'dʒime] SM (*foraggio*) fodder; (*becchime*) birdseed

mangiucchiare [mandʒuk'kjare] /19/ VT to nibble

mango, -ghi [ˈmango] SM (*frutto*) mango; (*albero*) mango tree

mania [ma'nia] SF (*Psic*) mania; (*fissazione*) obsession; (*abitudine*) odd *o* strange habit; **gli è presa la mania dei francobolli** his latest craze is stamp collecting; **una delle sue manie** one of his funny habits; **ha la mania della**

puntualità/della pulizia he's obsessively punctual/clean; **avere la mania di fare qc** to have a habit of doing sth; **mania di grandezza** delusions *pl* of grandeur; **mania di persecuzione** persecution complex *o* mania

maniacale [mania'kale] AGG (*Psic*) maniacal; (*fanatico*) fanatical; **è un igienista maniacale** (*fig*) he's fanatical about hygiene

maniaco, -a, -ci, -che [ma'niako] AGG (*Med: stato*) maniac; (: *persona*) suffering from a mania; **essere maniaco dell'ordine** (*fig*) to be obsessively tidy ♦ SM, SF (*Med*) maniac; (*fanatico*) fanatic; **un maniaco sessuale** (*anche scherz*) sex maniac; **è un maniaco del calcio** he's football mad *o* crazy

manica, -che ['manika] SF **1** sleeve; **le maniche sono troppo corte** the sleeves are too short; **con le maniche lunghe** long-sleeved; **una maglia con le maniche lunghe** a long-sleeved sweater; **senza maniche** sleeveless; **una maglia senza maniche** a sleeveless sweater; **essere in maniche di camicia** to be in (one's) shirt sleeves; **manica (a) kimono** bat sleeve; **essere di manica larga** (*prodigo*) to be free with one's money; (*indulgente*) to be easy-going; **essere di manica stretta** (*tirchio*) to be stingy, be tight (*fam*); (*rigoroso*) to be strict **2** (*fig: banda*) gang; **una manica di delinquenti** a bunch of criminals; **una manica di ladri** a pack of thieves **3** (*Geog*): **la Manica, il Canale della Manica** the (English) Channel **4 manica** (*Aer*) wind sock; (*Naut*) ventilator

manicaretto [manika'retto] SM delicious dish

manichetta [mani'ketta] SF (*Tecn*) hose

manichino [mani'kino] SM (*di sarto, vetrina*) dummy

manico, -ci *o* , **-chi** ['maniko] SM (*gen*) handle; (*di strumento musicale*) neck; **manico di scopa** broomstick

manicomio, -mi [mani'kɔmjo] SM psychiatric hospital; (*fig*) madhouse; **è roba da manicomio!** this is complete lunacy!

manicotto [mani'kotto] SM (*di pelliccia*) muff; (*Tecn*) sleeve, coupling; (*Aut*) hose

manicure [mani'kure] SM INV, SF INV manicure; **farsi il** *o* **la manicure** to do one's nails, give o.s. a manicure ♦ SF INV (*persona*) manicurist

maniera [ma'njɛra] SF **1** (*modo*) way, manner; **maniera di vivere/di parlare** way of life/of speaking; **in maniera strana** in an odd way; **fare qc alla propria maniera** to do sth one's own way; **in una maniera o nell'altra** one way or another; **in qualche maniera** somehow or other; **in maniera che** so that; **in maniera da** so as to; **fa' in maniera che sia tutto pronto per domani** see to it that everything's ready for tomorrow; **dobbiamo fare in maniera da non ripetere gli stessi errori** we must see that we don't make the same mistakes again; **in tutte le maniere** (*a tutti i costi*) at all costs; **usare le maniere forti** to take tough action; **in nessuna maniera** in no way **2** (*Arte: stile*) style, manner; **alla maniera di** *in* *o* after the style of; **è un Picasso prima maniera** it's an early Picasso **3** (*comportamento*): **maniere** SFPL manners; **usare buone maniere con qn** to be polite to sb; **non conosce le buone maniere** her manners are awful; **non mi piacciono le sue maniere** I don't like the way he behaves

manierato, -a [manje'rato] AGG (*affettato*) affected; (*Arte*) mannered

maniero [ma'njɛro] SM manor

manifattura [manifat'tura] SF (*stabilimento*) factory; (*lavorazione*) manufacture

manifatturiero, -a [manifattu'rjɛro] AGG manufacturing *attr*

manifestante [manifes'tante] SM, SF demonstrator

manifestare [manifes'tare] /72/ VT (*gen*) to show, display; (*opinioni, intenzioni*) to reveal, disclose; **manifestare il desiderio di fare qc** to express a desire to do sth, indicate one's wish to do sth ♦ VI (*aus avere*) **manifestare contro/a favore di** to demonstrate against/in favour of; **manifestarsi** VR: **si è manifestato per quello che è** he has shown his true colours; **manifestarsi contrario a un progetto** to reveal one's opposition to a plan; **manifestarsi amico/nemico** to prove to be a friend/an enemy; **manifestarsi** VIP (*sintomi, malattia*) to appear

manifestazione [manifestat'tsjone] SF **1** (*di opinione, sentimento*) expression; (*di entusiasmo*) demonstration; (*di malattia: comparsa*) manifestation; (: *sintomo*) sign, symptom **2** (*spettacolo*) event, show, display; (*Pol*) demonstration; **manifestazione sportiva** sporting event; **una manifestazione**

contro il governo a demonstration against the government

manifestino [manifes'tino] SM leaflet

manifesto, -a [mani'festo] AGG (*errore, verità*) obvious, manifest; (*fatto*) well-known; **i giornali hanno reso manifesto il suo rapporto con la mafia** the newspapers have uncovered his links with the Mafia ♦ SM **1** (*Letteratura, Arte, Pol*) manifesto **2** (*cartellone*) poster, bill; **manifesto pubblicitario** advertising poster

maniglia [ma'niʎʎa] SF (*di porta, cassetta*) handle; (*sostegno: in autobus*) strap; (*fig: fam: appoggio influente*) help from a highly-placed friend; (*Naut*) shackle; **maniglie dell'amore** (*fig*) love handles, spare tyre *sg*

Manila [ma'nila] SF Manila

manipolare [manipo'lare] /72/ VT **1** (*gen*) to manipulate, handle; (*creta, cera*) to work, fashion **2** (*alterare: elezione*) to rig; (: *conti*) to falsify, doctor, fiddle (*fam: notizia, informazioni*) to manipulate; (: *vino*) to adulterate

manipolazione [manipolat'tsjone] SF (*gen, anche Med*) manipulation; (*di conti*) falsification, fiddling (*fam*)

manipolo [ma'nipolo] SM **1** (*drappello*) handful **2** (*Storia, Rel*) maniple

maniscalco, -chi [manis'kalko] SM blacksmith, farrier (*Brit*)

manna ['manna] SF (*Rel*) manna; **è una manna dal cielo!** (*fig*) it is a godsend!

mannaia [man'naja] SF (*del boia*) (executioner's) axe *o* ax; (*per carni*) cleaver

mannaro [man'naro] AGG: **lupo mannaro** werewolf

mano, -i ['mano] SF **1** hand; **dare la mano a qn** to give sb one's hand; (*camminando*) to hold sb's hand; (*per salutare*) to shake hands with sb; **darsi** *o* **stringersi la mano** to hold hands; (*per salutarsi*) to shake hands; **i due ministri si strinsero la mano** the two ministers shook hands; **tenersi per mano** to hold hands; **si tenevano per mano** they were holding hands; **mano nella mano** hand in hand; **battere le mani** to clap (one's hands); **mani in alto!** hands up!; **mi sono scottato la mano** I've burnt my hand; (*cadere*) **nelle mani di qn** (*fig*) to fall into sb's hands; **mani pulite** *the judicial operation which brought to trial politicians and industrialists implicated in corruption scandals* **2** (*locuzioni*): **di seconda mano** second-hand; **ha comprato una macchina di seconda mano** she bought a second-hand car; **di prima mano** (*notizia*) first-hand; **a portata di mano** within reach; **tienilo sempre a portata di mano** always keep it within reach; **sotto mano** (*vicino*) to hand; (*furtivamente*) secretly; **ce l'hai sotto mano?** have you got it to hand?; **fuori mano** out of the way; **in mani fidate** in safe hands; **in buone mani** in good hands; **a mani vuote** empty-handed; **rapina a mano armata** armed robbery; **recapitato a mano** (*lettera, pacco*) (delivered) by hand; **fatto a mano** handmade; **cucito a mano** hand-sewn; **bagaglio a mano** hand luggage; **alla mano** (*persona*) easy-going; **con i soldi alla mano** cash in hand; **con i fatti alla mano** with his (*o* her *ecc*) facts at the ready; **a mano a mano che** (*mentre*) as; **man mano** (*gradualmente*) little by little, gradually **3** (*locuzioni verbali*): **andare contro mano** (*Aut*) to go against the (flow of) traffic; **ho le mani legate** (*fig*) my hands are tied; **restare a mani vuote** to be left empty-handed; **avere le mani bucate** to spend money like water; **avere mani di fata** to have a light touch; **aver le mani in pasta** to have a finger in the pie; **avere qc per le mani** (*progetto, lavoro*) to have sth in hand; **alzare le mani su qn** to raise one's hand to sb; **dammi una mano a qn** to lend sb a hand, to give sb a hand; **dammi una mano, per favore** give me a hand, please; **gli dai una mano e si prende il braccio** give him an inch and he'll take a mile; **fare man bassa di qc** to run off with sth; **forzare la mano** to go too far; **sai com'è, una mano lava l'altra...** you know how it is - you scratch my back and I'll scratch yours ...; **mettere la mano sul fuoco per qc** (*fig*) to stake one's life on sth; **mettere le mani su qc** to lay one's hands on sth; **mettere mano a qc** to have a hand in sth; **mettere le mani avanti** to safeguard o.s.; **mettere le mani addosso a qn** to lay hands on sb; (*molestare*) to touch sb up; **mettersi una mano sulla coscienza** to examine one's conscience; **ci ho preso la mano** I've got the hang of it; **starsene con le mani in mano** to twiddle one's thumbs; **venire alle mani** to come to blows **4** (*strato*) coat; **dare una mano di vernice a qc** to give sth a coat of paint **5** (*Carte*) hand; **facciamo ancora una mano** let's play one more hand

manodopera [manoˈdɔpera] SF manpower, labour (*Brit*), labor (*USA*)

manomesso, -a [manoˈmesso] PP *di* **manomettere**

manometro [maˈnɔmetro] SM manometer

manomettere [manoˈmettere] /63/ VT IRREG (*alterare: documento, prove*) to tamper with; (*aprire indebitamente: lettera*) to open (without permission); (: *serratura*) to force; (: *cassaforte*) to break open; **la serratura sembrava manomessa** the lock looked as though it had been tampered with

manomissione [manomisˈsjone] SF (*di prove*) tampering; (*di lettera*) (unauthorized) opening

manopola [maˈnɔpola] SF **1** (*di televisore, radio*) knob; (*impugnatura*) hand-grip; (*sostegno: su autobus, vetture*) strap; **girò la manopola per cercare il canale** he turned the knob to find the station **2** (*di armatura*) gauntlet; (*guanto*) mitten, mitt; (*di spugna*) wash mitt

manoscritto, -a [manosˈkritto] AGG handwritten ♦ SM manuscript

manovalanza [manovaˈlantsa] SF (*lavoratori*) unskilled workers *pl*; **la manovalanza mafiosa** (*criminali*) mafia henchmen *pl*, small-time *Mafiosi who do the dirty work*

manovale [manoˈvale] SM unskilled worker, labourer (*Brit*), laborer (*USA*)

manovella [manoˈvella] SF (*gen*) handle; (*Tecn*) crank; **manovella alzacristalli** (window) winder; **manovella d'avviamento** starting handle; **dare il primo giro di manovella** (*Cine*) to begin filming

manovra [maˈnɔvra] SF **1** (*Mil, anche fig*) manoeuvre (*Brit*), maneuver (*USA*); (*Pol, Econ*) measures *pl*; **la nuova manovra fiscale** the new tax(ation) measures; **manovra di accerchiamento** encircling movement; **grandi manovre** army manoeuvres *o* exercises; **manovre di corridoio** lobbying **2** (*Ferr*) shunting; **fare manovra** (*Aut*) to manoeuvre; **fare manovra di parcheggio** to park; **mentre faceva manovra di parcheggio** while parking; **manovra di atterraggio** landing **3** **manovre** SFPL (*Naut*) rigging *sg*; **manovre fisse/correnti** standing/running rigging

manovrare [manoˈvrare] /72/ VT (*veicolo*) to manoeuvre (*Brit*), maneuver (*USA*); (*macchinario*) to operate, work; (*fig: persona*) to manipulate ♦ VI (*aus avere*) manovrare per parcheggiare l'auto to pull (*o* back) into a parking space; **mentre manovrava per entrare nel parcheggio** while parking

manrovescio, -sci [manroˈveʃʃo] SM slap, back hander

mansarda [manˈsarda] SF attic

mansione [manˈsjone] SF duty, job, task; **non rientra nelle mie mansioni** it's not part of my job; **quali sono le sue mansioni?** what are his duties?; **svolgere** *o* **esplicare le proprie mansioni** to carry out one's duties

❑ **mansione** non si traduce mai con la parola inglese *mansion*

mansueto, -a [mansuˈeto] AGG (*animale*) tame; (*persona*) gentle, docile

mansuetudine [mansueˈtudine] SF (*vedi agg*) tameness; gentleness, docility

mantello [manˈtello] SM **1** (*cappotto*) cloak; (*Zool*) coat; (*fig: di neve*) blanket, mantle **2** (*Tecn: rivestimento*) casing, shell **3** (*Geol*) mantle

mantenere [manteˈnere] VB IRREG /121/ VT **1** (*gen*) to keep; (*decisione*) to stand by, abide by; (*promessa*) to keep, maintain; (*tradizione*) to maintain, uphold; (*edificio*) to maintain; **mantenere l'equilibrio/la linea** to keep one's balance/one's figure; **mantenere qn in vita** to keep sb alive; **mantenere i prezzi bassi** to hold prices down; **mantenere i contatti con qn** to keep in touch with sb; **mantenere l'ordine** (*Polizia*) to maintain law and order; (*in assemblea ecc*) to keep order; **pensi che manterrà la promessa?** do you think she'll keep her promise?; **cerca di mantenere la calma** try to keep calm **2** (*famiglia*) to maintain, support; **ha una famiglia da mantenere** he's got a family to support; **mantenersi** VR **1** (*conservarsi*): **mantenersi calmo/giovane** to stay *o* keep *o* remain calm/young; **mantenersi bene** to look good for one's age **2** (*sostentarsi*) to keep o.s.; **si mantiene da anni** he has supported himself financially for years; **lavora per**

mantenersi he works for a living; **si mantiene facendo la cameriera** (*studentessa*) she supports herself by waitressing; **mantenersi** VIP (*cibi*) to keep; **il tempo si mantiene bello** the weather is holding

mantenimento [manteniˈmento] SM (*gen*) maintenance; **provvedere al mantenimento della famiglia** to provide for one's family

mantenuto [manteˈnuto] SM (*pegg*) gigolo

mantice [ˈmantitʃe] SM bellows *pl*; **sbuffare** *o* **soffiare come un mantice** to puff like a grampus

manto [ˈmanto] SM (*cappotto*) cloak; (*Zool*) coat; (*fig: di neve*) blanket, mantle; **manto stradale** road surface

Mantova [ˈmantova] SF Mantua; **abito a Mantova** I live in Mantua

mantovano, -a [mantoˈvano] AGG of *o* from Mantua ♦ SM, SF native *o* inhabitant of Mantua

manuale [manuˈale] AGG (*lavoro*) manual ♦ SM (*libro*) manual, handbook; **il manuale di istruzioni** the instruction manual; **un caso di manuale** (*fig*) a textbook example

manualistico, -a, -ci, -che [manuaˈlistiko] AGG: **cultura manualistica** (*pegg*) superficial knowledge

manualmente [manualˈmente] AVV manually, by hand

manubrio, -ri [maˈnubrjo] SM (*gen*) handle; (*di bicicletta*) handlebars *pl*; (*attrezzo da ginnastica*) dumbbell

manufatto [manuˈfatto] SM manufactured article; **manufatti** SMPL manufactured goods

manutenzione [manutenˈtsjone] SF (*gen*) maintenance; (*di edifici, locali*) upkeep; (*d'impianti*) maintenance, servicing

manzo [ˈmandzo] SM (*animale*) steer, bullock; (*carne*) beef; **uno spezzatino di manzo** a beef stew

Maometto [maoˈmetto] SM Muhammad

mappa [ˈmappa] SF map

mappamondo [mappaˈmondo] SM (*globo*) globe; (*carta*) map of the world

marasma, -i [maˈrazma] SM (*fig*) decline, decay; **un marasma generale** (*fig: disordine*) chaos

maratona [maraˈtona] SF (*Sport, anche fig*) marathon; **maratona TV** telethon

marca, -che [ˈmarka] SF **1** (*Comm: di sigarette, caffè*) brand; (: *di scarpe, vestito*) make; (*marchio di fabbrica*) trademark; **di che marca è il tuo stereo?** what make is your stereo?; **capi di marca** designer clothes; **prodotti di (gran) marca** high-class products **2** (*bollo*) stamp; **marca da bollo** official stamp **3** (*contrassegno, scontrino*) ticket, check

❑ **marca** non si traduce mai con la parola inglese *mark*

marcare [marˈkare] /20/ VT **1** (*segnare*) to mark; (*a fuoco: animale*) to brand; (*biancheria*) to mark; **marcare visita** (*Mil*) to report sick **2** (*accentuare*) to stress **3** (*Sport: gol*) to score; (: *avversario*) to mark; **devi marcare il numero otto** mark number eight; **la squadra ha marcato all'ultimo minuto** the team scored in the final minute

marcato, -a [marˈkato] AGG (*lineamenti, accento*) pronounced

Marche [ˈmarke] SFPL: **le Marche** the Marches (*region of central Italy*)

marcherò ecc [markeˈrɔ] VB *vedi* **marcare**

marchese [marˈkeze] SM marquis, marquess

marchiano, -a [marˈkjano] AGG (*errore*) glaring, gross

marchiare [marˈkjare] /19/ VT (*bestiame*) to mark; **marchiare a fuoco** to brand; **marchiare a vita** (*fig*) to brand for life

marchigiano, -a [markiˈdʒano] AGG of *o* from the Marches ♦ SM, SF inhabitant *o* native of the Marches

marchio, -chi [ˈmarkjo] SM **1** (*Comm*) mark; **marchio depositato** registered trademark; **marchio di fabbrica** trademark; **marchio registrato** registered trademark **2** (*per bestiame: segno*) brand; (: *strumento*) branding iron; **ha il marchio di bugiardo** he has been branded a liar

marcia, -ce [ˈmartʃa] SF **1** (*gen, anche Mil, Mus*) march; **marcia forzata** forced march; **marcia funebre** funeral march **2** **mettersi in marcia** to get moving *o* going; **mettiamoci in marcia** let's get going; **mettere in marcia** (*veicolo*) to start (up); (*apparecchio*) to start; **essere in marcia verso** to be marching towards **3** (*Aut*) gear; **cambiare marcia** to change gear; **fare marcia indietro** to reverse; (*fig*) to back-pedal, backtrack **4** (*Sport*) walking

marciapiede [martʃaˈpjɛde] SM (di strada) pavement (Brit), sidewalk (USA); (Ferr) platform

marciare [marˈtʃare] /14/ VI (aus avere) 1 (Mil) to march; (Sport) to walk; **far marciare dritto qn** (fig) to make sb toe the line 2 (veicolo) to go, travel; (fig: funzionare) to run, work; **il treno marcia a 70 km/h** the train goes o travels at 70 km/h; **la ditta marcia bene** the firm is running smoothly

marcio, -cia, -ci ce [ˈmartʃo] AGG (uovo, legno) rotten; (foglie) rotting; (frutta) rotten, bad; (ferita, piaga) festering; (fig: corrotto) corrupt, rotten; **avere torto marcio** to be utterly wrong ♦ SM (di frutto ecc) rotten o bad part; **c'è del marcio in questa storia** there's something fishy about this business

marcire [marˈtʃire] /55/ VI (aus essere) (cibi, frutta) to go rotten o bad; (cadaveri, legno, foglie) to rot; (ferita) to fester; **marcire in prigione** (fig) to rot in prison ♦ VT to rot

marciume [marˈtʃume] SM 1 (parte guasta: di cibi) rotten part, bad part 2 (di radice, pianta) rot; (fig: corruzione) rottenness, corruption

marco, -chi [ˈmarko] SM (moneta) mark

mare [ˈmare] SM 1 (gen) sea; **mare interno** inland sea; **mare calmo/mosso/grosso** calm/rough/heavy sea; **per mare** by sea; **sul mare** (barca) on the sea; (villaggio, località) by o beside the sea; **in mare** at sea; **è morto in mare** he died at sea; **una casa al mare** a house at the seaside; **una vacanza al mare** a vacation beside o by the sea, a seaside vacation; **andare al mare** (in vacanza) to go to the seaside; **mettersi in mare** to put out to sea; **c'è un po' di mare oggi** there's a bit of a swell today; **uomo in mare!** man overboard!; **di mare** (brezza, acqua, uccelli, pesce) sea attr; **essere in alto mare** (fig) to have a long way to go; **è una goccia nel mare** (fig) it's a drop in the ocean 2 (gran quantità di: lettere, lamentele) flood; (: gente, problemi, difficoltà) host; (: lavoro) pile; **ho un mare di cose da fare** I've got stacks of things to do; **essere in un mare di guai** to be surrounded by problems; **essere in un mare di lacrime** to be in floods of tears; **promettere mari e monti a qn** to promise sb the earth ♦ **il Mar Adriatico** the Adriatic; **il mar Caspio** the Caspian Sea; **il mare del Nord** the North Sea; **il mar Morto** the Dead Sea; **il mar Nero** the Black Sea; **il mar Rosso** the Red Sea; **il mar dei Sargassi** the Sargasso Sea; **i mari del Sud** the South Seas; **il mare della Tranquillità** (sulla luna) the Sea of Tranquillity; **il mar Mediterraneo** the Mediterranean Sea

❑ mare non si traduce mai con la parola inglese *mare*

marea [maˈrea] SF 1 tide; **alta/bassa marea** high/low tide; **c'era bassa marea** it was low tide; **marea calante/montante** ebb/flood o rising tide 2 (fig) flood; **una marea di gente** hordes of people

mareggiata [maredˈdʒata] SF rough seas (inshore)

maremma [maˈremma] SF (Geog) maremma, swampy coastal area

maremmano, -a [maremˈmano] AGG 1 (zona, macchia) swampy 2 (della Maremma) of o from the Maremma ♦ SM, SF inhabitant o native of the Maremma

maremoto [mareˈmɔto] SM seaquake

maresciallo [mareʃˈʃallo] SM (Mil) marshal; (sottufficiale) warrant officer

marezzato, -a [maredˈdzato] AGG (seta) watered, moiré; (legno) veined; (carta) marbled

margarina [margaˈrina] SF margarine

margherita [margeˈrita] SF 1 (Bot) oxeye daisy, marguerite 2 (di stampante) daisy wheel 3 **la Margherita** (Pol) the Daisy (centre-left political grouping)

margheritina [margeriˈtina] SF (Bot) daisy

marginale [mardʒiˈnale] AGG marginal ♦ SM, SF socially excluded person

margine [ˈmardʒine] SM (gen) margin; (di bosco, via) edge; **al margine di** on the edge of; **ai margini della società** on the fringes of society; **note in** o **a margine** notes in the margin; **avere un buon margine di tempo/denaro** to have plenty of time/money (to spare) ♦ **margine di errore** margin of error; **margine di guadagno** o **di utile** profit margin; **margine operativo** operating margin; **margine sul prezzo** mark-up; **margine di sicurezza** safety margin

marijuana [mæriˈwanə] SF marijuana

marina [maˈrina] SF 1 (costa) coast; (quadro) seascape 2 (Mil) navy; **marina mercantile** merchant navy (Brit) o marine (USA); **marina militare** ≈ Royal Navy (Brit), ≈ United States Navy (USA)

marinaio, -ai [mariˈnajo] SM sailor; **marinaio di acqua dolce** (pegg) landlubber

marinare [mariˈnare] /72/ VT 1 (Culin) to marinate; **aringhe marinate** soused o pickled herring 2 (disertare): **marinare la scuola** to play truant, play hooky (spec USA)

marinaro, -a [mariˈnaro] AGG (tradizione, popolo) seafaring; **borgo marinaro** fishing village/town; **alla marinara** (vestito, cappello) sailor attr; (Culin) with seafood

marinata [mariˈnata] SF (Culin) marinade

marino, -a [maˈrino] AGG (aria, fondali) sea attr; (fauna) marine; (città, colonia) seaside attr

marionetta [marjoˈnetta] SF puppet, marionette; (fig: persona debole) puppet; **teatrino/spettacolo di marionette** puppet theatre/show

maritare [mariˈtare] /72/ VT to marry, give in marriage; **maritarsi** VR: **maritarsi (a** o **con qn)** to get married (to sb), marry (sb)

maritato, -a [mariˈtato] AGG married

marito [maˈrito] SM husband; **suo marito** her husband; **il marito di mia sorella** my sister's husband; **prendere marito** to get married

marittimo, -a [maˈrittimo] AGG (gen) maritime, sea attr; (città) coastal; **linee marittime** shipping lines ♦ SM seaman

marmaglia [marˈmaʎʎa] SF (gente ignobile) riff-raff, mob; (ragazzacci) gang of kids

marmellata [marmelˈlata] SF jam; (di agrumi) marmalade; **marmellata di fragole** strawberry jam

marmitta [marˈmitta] SF 1 (Aut) silencer; **marmitta catalitica** catalytic converter 2 (recipiente) cauldron 3 (Geol) pothole

marmo [ˈmarmo] SM marble; **di marmo** marble attr, made of marble; **una statua di marmo** a marble statue; **avere un cuore duro come il marmo** to have a heart of stone

marmocchio, -chi [marˈmɔkkjo] SM (fam) (tiny) tot, (little) kid

marmotta [marˈmɔtta] SF (Zool) marmot; (fig: persona lenta) slowcoach

marocchino, -a [marokˈkino] AGG, SM, SF Moroccan ♦ SM (cuoio) morocco (leather)

Marocco [maˈrɔkko] SM Morocco

maroso [maˈroso] SM breaker

marra [ˈmarra] SF (Agr) hoe; (Naut) fluke

Marrakesh [marraˈkeʃ] SF Marrakesh

marrone [marˈrone] AGG INV brown ♦ SM 1 (colore) brown 2 (Bot) chestnut

❑ marrone non si traduce mai con la parola inglese *maroon*

marsala [marˈsala] SM INV (vino) Marsala

Marsiglia [marˈsiʎʎa] SF Marseilles

marsina [marˈsina] SF tails pl, tail coat

marsupio, -pi [marˈsupjo] SM 1 (Zool) pouch, marsupium (termine tecn) 2 (per neonati) sling; (per denaro) bum-bag

mart. ABBR (= martedì) Tues.

Marte [ˈmarte] SM (Astron, Mitol) Mars

martedì [marteˈdi] SM INV Tuesday; **oggi è martedì 3 aprile** (the date) today is Tuesday, April 3rd; **martedì stavo male** I wasn't well on Tuesday; **l'ho vista martedì** I saw her on Tuesday; **ogni martedì, tutti i martedì** every Tuesday, on Tuesdays; **di** o **il martedì** on Tuesdays; **vado in piscina di martedì** I go swimming on Tuesdays; **un martedì sì un martedì no** every other Tuesday; **martedì scorso/prossimo** last/next Tuesday; **il martedì successivo, il martedì dopo** the following Tuesday; **2 settimane fa, di martedì** a fortnight ago on Tuesday; **martedì fra una settimana/quindici giorni** a week/fortnight on Tuesday, Tuesday week/fortnight; **martedì mattina/pomeriggio/sera** Tuesday morning/afternoon/evening; **il film del martedì** the Tuesday film; **il giornale di martedì** Tuesday's newspaper; **martedì grasso** Shrove Tuesday

martellante [martelˈlante] AGG (fig: dolore) throbbing; **una martellante campagna elettorale** a high-pressure electoral campaign

martellare [martel'lare] /**72**/ VT (*gen*) to hammer; **martellare qn di domande** to fire questions at sb ♦ VI (*aus avere*) (*pulsare: tempie*) to throb; (: *cuore*) to thump

martelletto [martel'letto] SM (*di pianoforte*) hammer; (*di macchina da scrivere*) typebar; (*di giudice, nelle vendite all'asta*) gavel; (*Med*) percussion hammer

martello [mar'tello] SM (*gen, anche Sport, Anat*) hammer; **battere col martello** to hit with a hammer, hammer; **piantare un chiodo col martello** to hammer, in a nail; **lancio del martello** (*Sport*) hammer throw; **suonare a martello** (*fig: campane*) to sound the tocsin; **martello pneumatico** pneumatic drill

martinetto [marti'netto] SM (*Tecn*) jack

martingala [martin'gala] SF (*di giacca*) half-belt; (*di cavallo*) martingale

martire ['martire] SM, SF (*anche fig*) martyr; **fare il o atteggiarsi a martire** to play the martyr

martirio, -ri [mar'tirjo] SM martyrdom; (*fig*) agony, torture; **lavorare per quel tipo è un martirio** working for that guy is hell

martoriare [marto'rjare] /**19**/ VT to torment, torture

marxismo [mark'sizmo] SM Marxism

marxista, -i, -e [mark'sista] AGG, SM, SF Marxist

marzapane [martsa'pane] SM marzipan

marziale [mar'tsjale] AGG martial

marzo ['martso] SM March; *vedi* **luglio**

marzolino, -a [martso'lino] AGG March *attr*

mascalzonata [maskaltso'nata] SF dirty trick

mascalzone [maskal'tsone] SM (*anche scherz*) rascal, scoundrel

mascara [mas'kara] SM INV mascara

mascarpone [maskar'pone] SM *soft cream cheese often used in desserts*

mascella [ma∫'∫ella] SF (*Anat*) jaw

maschera ['maskera] SF 1 (*gen*) mask; (*costume*) fancy dress; **in maschera** (*mascherato*) masked; **una maschera di carnevale** a carnival mask; **mettersi o vestirsi in maschera** to put on o wear fancy-dress; **una maschera fancy-dress ball**; **gettare la maschera** (*fig*) to reveal o.s.; **giù la maschera!** (*fig*) stop acting! 2 (*Cine*) usher (usherette) 3 (*Teatro*) stock character 4 (*per nuotare*) mask; **ho comprato la maschera e le pinne** I bought a mask and flippers ♦ **maschera antigas** gas mask; **maschera di bellezza** face pack; **maschera ad ossigeno** oxygen mask; **maschera subacquea** diving mask

mascherare [maske'rare] /**72**/ VT (*viso*) to mask; (*entrata, fig: sentimenti, intenzioni*) to hide, conceal; (*Mil*) to camouflage; **mascherare i bambini per una festa** to get the children into fancy dress for a party; **mascherarsi** VR: **mascherarsi (da)** (*travestirsi*) to disguise o.s. (as); (*per un ballo*) to dress up (as)

mascherina [maske'rina] SF 1 (*bambino in maschera*) child in fancy dress; (*piccola maschera*) mask; (*di animale*) patch; (*di scarpe*) toe-cap 2 (*Aut*) radiator grille

maschile [mas'kile] AGG (*gen, anche Gramm*) masculine; (*sesso, popolazione*) male *attr*; (*abiti*) men's; (*per ragazzi: scuola*) boys'; **un nome maschile** a masculine noun; **sesso: maschile** sex: male; **una voce maschile** a male voice ♦ SM (*Gramm*): **il maschile** the masculine

maschilista, -i, -e [maski'lista] AGG, SM, SF (*uomo*) (male) chauvinist, sexist; (*donna*) sexist

maschio, -chia, -chi, -chie ['maskjo] AGG (*figlio*) male; (*comportamento, atteggiamento*) male, masculine; (*volto, voce*) masculine ♦ AGG INV (*animale*) male; **una tigre maschio** a male tiger; **i miei colleghi maschi** my male colleagues ♦ SM (*gen, anche Tecn, Bio, Zool*) male; (*uomo*) man; (*ragazzo*) boy; (*figlio*) son; **hanno un maschio e una femmina** they've got a boy and a girl; **un maschio bianco** a white male; **i maschi** the men; **il maschio della tigre** the male tiger; **maschio della vite** screw tap

mascolino, -a [masko'lino] AGG masculine

mascotte [mas'kɔt] SF INV mascot

masochismo [mazo'kizmo] SM masochism

masochista, -i, -e [mazo'kista] AGG masochistic ♦ SM, SF masochist

massa ['massa] SF 1 (*volume, anche Fis*) mass; **massa critica**

(*Fis*) critical mass; **massa d'acqua** body of water; **massa atomica** atomic mass; **massa cerebrale** brain, cerebral mass 2 (*Sociol*): **la massa, le masse** the masses *pl*; **la massa dei cittadini** the majority of the townspeople; **di massa** mass; **manifestazione/cultura di massa** mass demonstration/ culture; **turismo di massa** mass tourism 3 **una massa di** (*oggetti*) heaps of, loads of; (*errori*) masses of; (*persone*) crowds of, masses of; **siete una massa di idioti!** (*fam*) you're a bunch of idiots! 4 **produzione in massa** mass production; **produrre in massa** to mass-produce; **vendere in massa** (*Comm*) to sell in bulk; **esecuzioni in massa** mass executions; **arrivare in massa** to arrive en masse 5 (*Elettr*) earth; **collegare a massa** to earth

massacrante [massa'krante] AGG exhausting, gruelling

massacrare [massa'krare] /**72**/ VT (*uccidere*) to massacre, slaughter; (*animali*) to slaughter; (*fig: avversario*) to make mincemeat of; (: *brano musicale*) to murder

massacro [mas'sakro] SM massacre, slaughter; (*fig*) disaster, mess; **fare un massacro** to carry out a massacre; **all'esame i professori hanno fatto un massacro** the lecturers were failing exam candidates left, right and centre

massaggiare [massad'dʒare] /**62**/ VT to massage; **farsi massaggiare** to have a massage

massaggiatore, -trice [massaddʒa'tore] SM, SF masseur (masseuse) ♦ SM (*apparecchio*) massager

massaggio, -gi [mas'saddʒo] SM massage; **massaggio cardiaco** heart massage

massaia [mas'saja] SF housewife

masseria [masse'ria] SF large farm

masserizie [masse'rittsje] SFPL (household) furnishings

massicciata [massit't∫ata] SF (*di strada, ferrovia*) ballast

massiccio, -cia, -ci, -ce [mas'sitt∫o] AGG 1 (*mobile, edificio*) massive, solid; (*corporatura*) stout 2 **oro/legno massiccio** solid gold/wood 3 (*fig: attacco*) massive; (: *dose*) heavy, massive ♦ SM (*Geog*) massif

massima ['massima] SF 1 (*motto*) maxim 2 (*Meteor*) maximum temperature 3 **in linea di massima** generally speaking

massimale [massi'male] SM (*Assicurazione*) maximum sum payable by insurers

massimo, -a ['massimo] AGG *superl* **di grande**; (*gen*) greatest; (*temperatura, livello, prezzo*) maximum, highest; (*importanza, cura*) utmost, greatest; **è una questione della massima importanza** it's a question of the greatest importance; **è della massima importanza che tu ci sia** it is of the utmost importance o it is vital that you be o are there; **è il massimo poeta del secolo** he is the greatest poet of the century; **erano presenti le massime autorità** all the most important dignitaries were there; **al massimo grado** to the highest degree; **stupido al massimo grado** stupid beyond belief; **ha la mia massima stima/il mio massimo rispetto** I have the highest regard/greatest respect for him; **ottenere il massimo effetto con la minima spesa** to get the best results at the least cost; **in massima parte** for the most part, mainly; **arrivare entro il tempo massimo** to arrive within the time limit; **il tempo massimo concesso** the maximum time allowed; **la velocità massima che questa macchina può raggiungere è...** the top o maximum speed of this car is ...; **la velocità massima permessa nei centri abitati** the speed limit in built-up areas ♦ SM (*gen*) maximum; **è il massimo che io possa fare** it's the most I can do; **è il massimo della avidità** (*persona*) you can't get much more greedy than him; **è il massimo della stupidità** (*gesto*) it's the height of stupidity; **è il massimo!** (*colmo*) that's the limit o end!; **può portare al massimo cinque persone** it can take five people at the most; **cerca di impegnarti al massimo** try to do your best; **costerà al massimo 5 sterline** it'll cost 5 pounds at (the) most; **lavorare al massimo** to work flat out; **sfruttare qc al massimo** to make full use of sth; **al massimo finiamo lunedì** we'll finish on Monday at the outside/by the latest; **arriverò al massimo alle 5** I'll arrive at 5 at the latest; **ottenere il massimo dei voti** (*Scol*) to get full marks; (*in votazione*) to be accepted unanimously; **il massimo della pena** (*Dir*) the maximum penalty

massivo, -a [mas'sivo] AGG (*intervento*) en masse; (*emigrazione*) mass; (*emorragia*) massive

masso ['masso] SM rock, boulder; **caduta (di) massi** (*cartello*) (beware!) falling rocks; **dormire come un masso** to sleep like a log; **masso erratico** (*Geol*) erratic

massone [mas'sone] SM freemason

massoneria [massone'ria] SF freemasonry

massonico, -a, -ci, -che [mas'soniko] AGG masonic

mastello [mas'tello] SM tub

masterizzare [masterid'dzare] /72/ VT (*CD, DVD*) to burn

masterizzatore [masteriddza'tore] SM CD burner *o* writer

masticare [masti'kare] /20/ VT to chew, masticate (*frm*); (*tabacco, gomma*) to chew; **gomma da masticare** chewing gum; **mastico un po' di inglese** I have a smattering of English

mastice ['mastitʃe] SM (*resina*) mastic; (*per vetri*) putty

mastino [mas'tino] SM mastiff

mastodontico, -a, -ci, -che [masto'dontiko] AGG (*fig*) gigantic, colossal

masturbare [mastur'bare] /72/ VT , **masturbarsi** VR to masturbate

masturbazione [masturbat'tsjone] SF masturbation

matassa [ma'tassa] SF (*gen*) skein, hank; **venire a capo della matassa** (*fig*) to unravel the problem; **ingarbugliare** *o* **imbrogliare la matassa** (*fig*) to confuse the issue

matematico, -a, -ci, -che [mate'matiko] AGG mathematical; **avere la certezza matematica che** to be absolutely certain that ♦ SM, SF mathematician

materassino [materas'sino] SM mat; **materassino gonfiabile** air bed

materasso [mate'rasso] SM mattress; **materasso ad acqua** water bed; **materasso di gommapiuma** foam mattress; **materasso a molle** spring *o* interior-sprung mattress

materia [ma'terja] SF (*gen, anche Filosofia, Fis*) matter; (*Scol: argomento*) subject matter, material; (*disciplina*) subject; (*sostanza*) Tecn, Comm) material, substance; **è una materia difficile** it's a difficult subject; **prima di entrare in materia...** before discussing the matter in hand ...; **un esperto in materia** (*di musica ecc*) an expert on the subject (of music *ecc*); **sono ignorante in materia** I know nothing about it ♦ **materia cerebrale** cerebral matter; **materia grassa** fat; **materia grigia** (*anche fig*) grey matter; **materie plastiche** plastics; **materie prime** raw materials

materiale [mate'rjale] AGG (*interessi, necessità, danni*) material; (*persona: materialista*) materialistic; **non ho avuto il tempo materiale di farlo** I simply haven't had the time to do it; **non ha avuto la possibilità materiale di evitarlo** he just couldn't avoid it ♦ SM (*gen*) material; (*insieme di strumenti*) equipment *no pl*; **di che materiale è fatto?** what is it made of?; **sto raccogliendo materiale per il mio progetto** I'm collecting material for my project; **hai il materiale per scrivere?** have you got pen and paper? ♦ **materiale bellico** war materiel *o* matériel; **materiale da costruzione** building materials *pl*; **materiale rotabile** rolling stock; **materiale di scarto** waste material

materialista, -i, -e [materja'lista] AGG materialistic ♦ SM, SF materialist

materializzarsi [materjalid'dzarsi] /72/ VIP to materialize

materialmente [materjal'mente] AVV: **è materialmente impossibile farlo** it's a physical impossibility

maternità [materni'ta] SF INV 1 (*condizione*) motherhood; **essere in (congedo di) maternità** to be on maternity leave; **maternità surrogata** *o* **sostitutiva** surrogate motherhood, surrogacy 2 (*clinica*) maternity hospital; **reparto maternità** maternity ward

materno, -a [ma'terno] AGG (*gen*) maternal; (*amore, cura*) motherly, maternal; (*nonno*) maternal; (*lingua, terra*) mother *attr*; **scuola materna** nursery school (*attended by children aged 3*); **l'istinto materno** the maternal instinct; **i miei nonni materni** my maternal grandparents; **la mia lingua materna** my mother tongue

matita [ma'tita] SF pencil; **scrivere a matita** to write in pencil; **scrivi le note a matita** write your notes in pencil; **disegno a matita** pencil drawing ♦ **matita emostatica** styptic pencil; **matita per (gli) occhi** eyeliner (pencil); **matita per (le) labbra** lip liner; **matite colorate** coloured pencils

matrice [ma'tritʃe] SF 1 (*Bio, Mat, Tip, Tecn*) matrix; (*per duplicatore*) stencil 2 (*Comm*) counterfoil; (*di assegno*) (cheque) stub 3 (*fig: origine*) background; **l'attentato è di chiara matrice fascista** the fascists are undoubtedly behind this bombing

matricola [ma'trikola] SF 1 (*registro*) register 2 (*anche: numero di matricola*) registration number; (*Mil*) regimental number; (*Tecn*) part number 3 (*studente: nell'università*) freshman, fresher (*Brit fam*)

matrigna [ma'triɲɲa] SF stepmother

matrimoniale [matrimo'njale] AGG (*gen*) matrimonial, marriage *attr*; (*rapporto*) marital; (*vita*) married; (*anello*) wedding *attr*; **camera/letto matrimoniale** double room/bed

matrimonio, -ni [matri'monjo] SM (*unione*) marriage; (*cerimonia*) wedding; (*durata*) marriage, married life; **dopo 5 anni di matrimonio** after 5 years of marriage; **pubblicazioni di matrimonio** (marriage) banns; **non mi hanno invitato al matrimonio** they didn't invite me to the wedding; **matrimonio religioso/civile** religious/civil wedding; **matrimonio d'amore** love match; **matrimonio di convenienza** marriage of convenience

matrona [ma'trona] SF (*fig*) matronly woman

mattatoio, -oi [matta'tojo] SM slaughterhouse, abattoir (*Brit*)

mattina [mat'tina] SF morning; **la** *o* **alla** *o* **di mattina** in the morning; **alle sette di mattina** at seven in the morning; **di mattina** in the morning; **prima mattina, la mattina presto** early in the morning; **domani mattina** tomorrow morning; **ogni mattina** every morning; **la mattina prima/dopo** the previous/following morning; **la mattina prima di...** the morning before ...; **dalla mattina alla sera** (*continuamente*) from morning to night; (*improvvisamente: cambiare*) overnight; **alle due di mattina** at 2 a.m.

mattinata [matti'nata] SF 1 morning; **in mattinata** in the course of the morning; **sarà pronto in mattinata** it will be ready before noon; **nella mattinata** in the morning; **nella tarda mattinata** at the end of the morning; **nella tarda mattinata di sabato** late on Saturday morning 2 (*spettacolo*) matinée, afternoon performance

mattiniero, -a [matti'njero] AGG: **essere mattiniero** to be an early riser

mattino [mat'tino] SM morning; **di buon mattino** early in the morning; **sul far del mattino** at daybreak; **il mattino ha l'oro in bocca** (*Proverbio*) the early bird catches the worm

matto, -a [matto] AGG 1 (*gen, anche fig*) mad, crazy; (*Med*) insane; **sei matto!** you're mad!; **sempre più matto** madder and madder; **diventare matto** to go mad; **sto diventando matta!** I'm going mad!; **far diventare matto qn** to drive sb mad *o* crazy; **mi ha fatto diventar matto** he drove me mad; **andare matto per qc** to be crazy *o* mad about sth; **va matta per il calcio** she's mad about football; **quella testa matta ne ha combinato un'altra** that lunatic has done it again; **matto da legare** as mad as a hatter; **fossi matto!** (*neanche per sogno*) not on your life!; **avere una voglia matta di** (*cibo, cioccolato*) to have a craving for; **ho una voglia matta di incontrarlo** I'm dying to meet him, I can't wait to meet him 2 (*falso*): **oro matto** imitation gold 3 (*opaco*) matt ♦ SM, SF madman *o* madwoman, lunatic; **ridere come un matto** to laugh hysterically; **fare il matto** to act the fool; **mi piace da matti la tua giacca** I just love your jacket; **roba da matti!** it's unbelievable!; **una gabbia di matti** (*fig*) a madhouse

mattone [mat'tone] SM 1 brick; **una casa di mattoni** a brick house; **un muro di mattoni** a brick wall; **color mattone, rosso mattone** brick red 2 (*fig*): **questo libro/film è un mattone** this book/film is really heavy going; **ho un mattone sullo stomaco** I feel as though I've got a lead weight in my stomach

mattonella [matto'nella] SF 1 (*piastrella*) tile; **a mattonelle** tiled 2 (*di carbone*) briquette 3 (*del biliardo*) cushion

mattutino, -a [mattu'tino] AGG morning *attr*; **il sole mattutino** the morning sun

maturare [matu'rare] /72/ VT (*frutta*) to ripen; (*fig: persona*) to (make) mature; **maturare una decisione** to come to a decision VI (*aus essere*), **maturarsi** VIP (*frutta, grano*) to ripen; (*ascesso*) to come to a head; (*fig: persona, idea: Econ: interessi*) to mature

maturità [maturi'ta] SF 1 maturity; **se avessi un minimo di maturità** if you were a responsible adult 2 (*Scol: anche:*

esame di maturità) school-leaving examination, ≈ G.C.E.A levels (Brit), ≈ (high-school) graduation (USA)

maturo, -a [ma'turo] AGG 1 (frutto) ripe, mature; **troppo maturo** overripe; **una pesca matura** a ripe peach 2 (persona) mature; **è molto matura per la sua età** she's very mature for her age; **è un uomo maturo** he's middle-aged; **i tempi sono maturi per agire** the time is ripe for action 3 (Scol: studente) student who has gained A levels (Brit), ≈ high-school graduate (USA)

matusa [ma'tuza] SM INV, SF INV (scherz) old fogey

Mauritania [mauri'tanja] SF Mauritania

Maurizio [mau'rittsjo] SF: (l'isola di) **Maurizio** Mauritius

mausoleo [mauzo'lɛo] SM mausoleum

max. ABBR (= massimo) max.

maxi- ['maksi] PREF maxi-

maxiprocesso [maksipro'tʃɛsso] SM trial involving a large number of accused

maxischermo [maksis'kermo] SF: giant screen

mazza ['mattsa] SF (bastone) club; (Mil) baton; (nelle cerimonie) mace; (martello) sledgehammer; (Sport: da golf) (golf) club; (: da baseball, cricket) bat

mazzata [mat'tsata] SF (anche fig) heavy blow

mazzetta [mat'tsetta] SF (di banconote) bundle; (fig) rake-off; (tangente) bribe

mazzo ['mattso] SM 1 (di fiori, chiavi) bunch 2 (di carte da gioco) pack; **tenere il mazzo** to be dealer; **fare il mazzo** (mescolare) to shuffle the cards 3 (fam!: culo): **farsi un o il mazzo** (faticare molto) to work bloody hard, work one's guts out

MC SIGLA = Macerata

mcm ABBR (= minimo comune multiplo) lcm

ME SIGLA = Messina

me [me] PRON PERS 1 (forma tonica) me; **parlavate di me?** were you talking about me?; **vieni con me?** are you coming with me?; **dietro di me** behind me; **senza di me** without me; **lo ha dato a me, non a te** he gave it to me o ME, not to you o YOU; **dopo di me tocca a te** it's your turn after me; **vieni da me?** are you coming to my place?; **l'ho fatto da me** I did it (all) by myself; **il dolce l'ho fatto da me** I made the cake myself; **pensavo tra me e me...** I was thinking to myself that ...; **se fossi in me cosa faresti?** what would you do if you were me? o if you were in my position? 2 (nelle comparazioni) I, me; (in espressioni esclamative) me; **è alta come me** she's as tall as I am o as me; **fai come me** do the same as me, do as I do; **sei bravo quanto me** you are as clever as I (am) o as me; **è più giovane di me** he's younger than I (am) o than me; **povero me!** poor me! 3 vedi **mi¹**

meandro [me'andro] SM (di fiume) meander; **si è perso nei meandri del palazzo** he lost his way in the building's maze of corridors; **i meandri del pensiero** the mind's meanderings

MEC [mɛk] SIGLA M = Mercato Comune Europeo

mecca ['mekka] SF (Geog): **la Mecca** Mecca; **la mecca del cinema** (fig) the mecca of the film world

meccanicamente [mekkanika'mente] AVV mechanically

meccanico, -a, -ci, -che [mek'kaniko] AGG (anche fig) mechanical; **officina meccanica** garage ♦ SM mechanic

meccanismo [mekka'nizmo] SM mechanism

meccanizzare [mekkanid'dzare] /72/ VT to mechanize

meccanizzazione [mekkaniddzat'tsjone] SF mechanization

meccanografia [mekkanogra'fia] SF (mechanical) data processing

meccanografico, -a, -ci, -che [mekkano'grafiko] AGG: **centro meccanografico** data processing department

mecenate [metʃe'nate] SM, SF patron

mèche [mɛʃ] SF INV streak; **farsi le mèche** to have one's hair streaked

medaglia [me'daʎʎa] SF (gen) medal; (distintivo) badge; **il rovescio della medaglia** (fig) the other side of the coin; **medaglia d'oro: ha vinto una medaglia d'oro** he won a gold medal; (oggetto) gold medal; (atleta) gold medallist (Brit) o medalist (USA)

medaglione [medaʎ'ʎone] SM 1 (Arte) medallion; (Culin) médaillon 2 (gioiello) locket

medesimo, -a [me'dezimo] AGG 1 (identico, uguale) same; **mi ha detto le medesime cose** he said the same things to me;

sono della medesima taglia they are the same size 2 (enfatizzato) very; **arrivò il medesimo giorno in cui io dovevo partire** he arrived the very day I was due to leave; **è la stessa medesima cosa** it's the very same thing; **le regole medesime del gioco impongono ciò** the very rules of the game require this 3 (in persona): **io medesimo/tu medesimo** I myself/you yourself; **il presidente medesimo** the president herself ♦ PRON: **il (la) medesimo(a)** the same one

media ['mɛdja] SF 1 (valore intermedio) average; **al di sopra/sotto della media** above/below average; **in media** on average; **questa macchina fa in media i 120 km/h** this car has an average speed of 120 km/h; **abbiamo fatto in media settanta chilometri all'ora** we did an average of seventy kilometres an hour; **viaggiare ad una media di...** to travel at an average speed of ...; **riceve in media 1000 euro al mese** he earns 1000 euros per month on average, he has an average income of 1000 euros per month 2 (Scol: voto) end-of-term average; **fu promosso con la media del 7** he passed with an average of 7 out of 10; **ha avuto una media molto bassa** his average marks were very low, he had a very low average mark 3 **medie** SFPL = **scuola media**; vedi **medio** 4 (Mat) mean; **media aritmetica/geometrica** arithmetic/geometric mean

mediamente [medja'mente] AVV on average

mediano, -a [me'djano] AGG (Geom) median ♦ SM (Calcio) half-back; **mediano sinistro/destro** left/right half; **mediano di mischia** (Rugby) scrum half ♦ SF (Geom) median

mediante [me'djante] PREP (per mezzo di) by (means of)

mediare [me'djare] /19/ VT (fare da mediatore) to act as mediator in, mediate

mediato, -a [me'djato] AGG indirect

mediatore, -trice [medja'tore] SM, SF (gen, anche Pol) mediator; (Comm) middleman, agent; **fare da mediatore tra** to mediate between; **mediatore d'affari** business agent; **mediatore culturale** person who helps immigrants with integration into society

mediazione [medjat'tsjone] SF (gen, anche Pol) mediation; (Industria) arbitration; (Comm: azione, compenso) brokerage

medicamento [medika'mento] SM medicament

medicare [medi'kare] /20/ VT (paziente) to treat; (ferita) to dress; **la medicò e la rimandò a casa** he treated her and sent her home; **medicarsi un piede ferito** to dress one's injured foot; **gli medicò la ferita** she dressed his wound

medicato, -a [medi'kato] AGG (garza, shampoo) medicated

medicazione [medikat'tsjone] SF (di ferita) dressing; **fare una medicazione a qn** to dress sb's wounds; **togliere/cambiare la medicazione** to remove/change the dressings

medicina [medi'tʃina] SF 1 (scienza, preparato medicinale) medicine; **una medicina contro la tosse** a cough medicine; **il tempo è la miglior medicina** (fig) time is the best cure; **medicina legale** forensic medicine 2 (Univ: anche: facoltà di medicina) medical faculty/school; **studente in medicina** medical student; **laurea in medicina** degree in medicine; **voglio studiare medicina** I want to study medicine

medicinale [meditʃi'nale] AGG medicinal ♦ SM medicine, drug

medico, -a, -ci, -che ['mɛdiko] AGG (gen) medical; (sostanza, erba) medicinal; **ricetta medica** prescription; **cure mediche** medical treatment; **visita medica** medical (examination); **fare una visita medica** to have a medical examination ♦ SM (gen) doctor; **chi è il tuo medico curante?** who's your doctor o GP?; (in ospedale) which doctor is in charge of your case?; **medico di bordo** ship's doctor; **medico chirurgo** surgeon; **medico di famiglia** family doctor; **medico fiscale** doctor who checks that the sick leave given to patients by GPs is reasonable; **medico generico o di base** general practitioner; **medico legale** forensic scientist

medievale [medje'vale] AGG (anche fig) medi(a)eval

medio, -dia, -di, -die ['mɛdjo] AGG (gen) average; (misura, corporatura) average, medium; (peso, ceto) middle; **persona di statura media** person of average o medium height; (dito) **medio** middle finger; **scuola media** school for pupils aged 11 - 14 education beyond this level is not compulsory; **licenza media** leaving certificate at the end of 3 years of secondary education; **il Medio Oriente** the Middle East ♦ SM (dito) middle finger

mediocre [me'djɔkre] AGG (gen) mediocre; (qualità, stipendio) poor; (persona, impiego) mediocre, second-rate; **il suo ultimo album è mediocre** his latest album is mediocre; **un prodotto di qualità mediocre** a poor quality product

mediocrità [medjokri'ta] SF (vedi agg) mediocrity; poorness

Medioevo [medjo'evo] SM: **il Medioevo** the Middle Ages pl

meditabondo, -a [medita'bondo] AGG meditative, thoughtful

meditare [medi'tare] /72/ VT to ponder over, meditate on; (progettare) to plan, think out; **meditare di fare qc** to contemplate doing sth; (pianificare) to plan to do sth ♦ VI (aus avere) **meditare (su)** to meditate (on/upon), think (about)

meditato, -a [medi'tato] AGG (gen) meditated; (parole) carefully-weighed; (vendetta) premeditated; **ben meditato** (piano) well worked-out, neat

meditazione [meditat'tsjone] SF meditation; **dopo lunga meditazione si risolse a partire** after much thought he decided to leave

mediterraneo, -a [mediter'raneo] AGG Mediterranean ♦ SM: **il (mare) Mediterraneo** the Mediterranean (Sea)

medium ['mɛdjum] SM INV, SF INV medium

medusa [me'duza] SF (Zool) jellyfish

mega ['mega] SM INV (Inform) = megabyte

megabyte [mega'bait] SM INV (Inform) megabyte

megafono [me'gafono] SM megaphone

megalomane [mega'lɔmane] AGG, SM, SF megalomaniac

megera [me'dʒɛra] SF (pegg: donna) shrew

meglio ['mɛʎʎo] COMP, SUPERL di bene ♦ AVV **1** better; **sto meglio** I feel better; **gioca meglio di lui** she plays better than he does; **è cambiato in meglio** he has changed for the better, he has improved; **meglio non passare per quella strada** it's better not to take that road **2** (con senso superlativo) best; **i meglio allenati** the best trained **3** **meglio che mai** better than ever; **meglio tardi che mai** better late than never; **meglio poco che niente** half a loaf is better than no bread; **faresti meglio ad andartene** you had better leave; **andare di bene in meglio, andare sempre meglio** to get better and better ♦ AGG INV **1** better; **questa casa è meglio dell'altra** this house is better than the other one; **è meglio che tu te ne vada** you'd better leave; **è meglio per te** it would be better for you to go; **è meglio non raccontargli niente** it would be better not to tell him anything o if you didn't tell him anything; **è molto meglio così** it's much better like this; **ha trovato di meglio da fare** he's found something better to do **2 alla meglio** as best one can; **alla bell'e meglio** somehow or other ♦ SM best; **al meglio delle proprie possibilità** as best one can, to the best of one's ability; **è il meglio che io possa fare** it's the best I can do; **fare del proprio meglio** to do one's best; **le cose si sono messe per il meglio** things turned out for the best; **essere al meglio della forma** to be in top form ♦ SF: **avere la meglio** to come off best; **aver la meglio su qn** to get the better of sb

mela ['mela] SF apple; **torta di mele** apple tart; **mele cotte** stewed apples; **mela cotogna** quince; **mela selvatica** crab apple

melagrana [mela'grana] SF pomegranate

melanzana [melan'dzana] SF aubergine (Brit), eggplant (USA)

melassa [me'lassa] SF (Culin) treacle, molasses sg (USA)

melatonina [melato'nina] SF melatonin

melenso, -a [me'lɛnso] AGG dull, stupid

melissa [me'lissa] SF (lemon) balm

mellifluo, -a [mel'lifluo] AGG (pegg) sugary, honeyed

melma ['melma] SF slime

melo ['melo] SM apple tree

melodia [melo'dia] SF (Mus) melody; (aria) melody, tune; **cantare una melodia** to hum a tune

melodico, -a, -ci, -che [me'lɔdiko] AGG melodic

melodioso, -a [melo'djoso] AGG melodious, tuneful

melodramma, -i [melo'dramma] SM (Teatro, anche pegg) melodrama

melone [me'lone] SM (musk) melon

membrana [mem'brana] SF membrane

membro ['membro] SM **1** (pl m membri) (persona: Mat, Gramm) member; **diventare membro di** to become a

member of; **diventò membro del partito socialista** he became a member of the Socialist Party **2** (pl f membra): (Anat) limb; **riposare le stanche membra** to rest one's weary limbs **3** (pl m membri); **membro (virile)** male sexual organ

memorabile [memo'rabile] AGG memorable

memorandum [memo'randum] SM INV memorandum

memore ['mɛmore] AGG (letter): **memore di** (ricordando) mindful of; (riconoscere) grateful for

memoria [me'mɔrja] SF **1** (gen, anche Inform) memory; **avere molta memoria** to have a good memory; **non avere memoria** to have a bad memory; **non ho molta memoria** I haven't got a good memory; **avere una memoria fotografica** to have a photographic memory; **ho una buona memoria** I've got a good memory; **imparare/sapere qc a memoria** to learn/know sth by heart; **ha imparato a memoria la poesia** she learnt the poem by heart; **frugare nella memoria** to search one's memory; **mi è rimasto impresso nella memoria** it was imprinted in my memory; **se la memoria non m'inganna** if I remember correctly **2** (ricordo) recollection, memory; **non resta memoria di quel fatto** no one remembers that event; **fatto degno di memoria** memorable deed; **a memoria d'uomo** within living memory; (da tempo immemorabile) from time immemorial; **in** o **alla memoria di** in (loving) memory of; **medaglia alla memoria** commemorative medal **3 memorie** SFPL (opera autobiografica) memoirs **4** (Inform) memory; **il mio computer non ha abbastanza memoria** my computer hasn't got enough memory; **memoria di cache** (Inform) cache memory; **memoria flash** flash drive; **memoria permanente** nonvolatile memory; **memoria di sola lettura** read-only memory; **memoria tampone** buffer; **memoria volatile** volatile memory

memoriale [memo'rjale] SM (raccolta di memorie) memoirs pl

memorizzare [memorid'dzare] /72/ VT (gen) to memorize; (Inform) to store

memorizzazione [memoriddzat'tsjone] SF (vedi vb) memorization; storage; **memorizzazione transitoria** (Inform) buffering

menadito [mena'dito] a **menadito** AVV perfectly, thoroughly; **sapere** o **conoscere qc a menadito** to know sth inside out

menagramo [mena'gramo] SM INV, SF INV jinx, Jonah

menare [me'nare] /72/ VT **1** (letter: condurre) to take, lead; **qual buon vento ti mena?** what brings you here?; **menare qn per il naso** (fig) to lead sb by the nose; **menare il can per l'aia** (fig) to beat about (Brit) o around (USA) the bush; **menare qc per le lunghe** to drag sth out; **menar vanto di qc** to boast about sth **2** (picchiare): **menare qn** to hit o beat sb; **menare le mani** (essere manesco) to be free with one's fists; (picchiarsi) to come to blows; **menare calci** to kick; **menare colpi** to deal blows **3 menarla a qc** (fam: infastidire) to bore sb, drone on to sb; **menarsi** VR (uso reciproco) to come to blows

mendicante [mendi'kante] SM, SF beggar

mendicare [mendi'kare] /20/ VT (anche fig) to beg for; **mendicare qc da qn** to beg sb for sth, beg sth from sb ♦ VI (anche fig) to beg

menefreghismo [menefre'gizmo] SM (fam) couldn't-care-less attitude; **il suo è menefreghismo bello e buono!** he simply doesn't give a damn!

meninge [me'nindʒe] SF (Anat) meninx; **spremersi le meningi** to rack one's brains

meningite [menin'dʒite] SF (Med) meningitis

menisco [me'nisko] SM (Anat, Mat, Fis) meniscus

PAROLA CHIAVE

meno ['meno] AVV
1 less; **meno caro** less expensive, cheaper; **è meno alto di suo fratello/di quel che pensavo** he's not as tall as his brother/as I thought, he is less tall than his brother/than I thought; **ha due anni meno di me** he's two years younger than me; **dovresti mangiare meno** you should eat less, you shouldn't eat so much; **meno ne discutiamo, meglio è** the less we talk about it, the better; **deve avere non meno di trent'anni** he must be at least thirty; **meno fumo più mangio** the less I smoke the more I eat; **andare all'università diventa sempre meno facile** it's getting less and less easy to

go to university; **ho speso (di) meno** I spent less; **arrivo tra meno di un'ora** I'll be there in less than *o* in under an hour **2** (*con senso superlativo*) least; **è il meno dotato dei miei studenti** he's the least gifted of my pupils; **è quello che leggo meno spesso** it's the one I read least often

3 (*sottrazione: Mat*) minus, less; **5 meno 2** 5 minus 2, 5 take away 2; **sono le otto meno un quarto** it's a quarter to eight (*Brit*) *o* of eight (*USA*); **mi hai dato due carte di meno** you gave me two cards too few; **eh, se avessi dieci anni di meno!** oh, if only I were ten years younger!; **ho una sterlina in meno** I am one pound short; **ci sono meno 25°** it's minus 25°, it is 25° below (zero); **ha preso sette meno** ≈ he got (a) B minus

4 (*fraseologia*): **non è da meno di lui** she is (every bit) as good as he is; **non voglio essere da meno di lui** I don't want to be outdone by him; **fare a meno di** to do *o* manage without; **se non c'è zucchero ne faremo a meno** if there isn't any sugar we'll do without; **potresti fare a meno di fumare in macchina?** would you mind not smoking in the car?; **non ho potuto fare a meno di ridere** I couldn't help laughing; **in men che non si dica** in less than no time, quick as a flash; **meno male!** good!, thank goodness!, just as well!; **meno male che sei arrivato** it's a good thing that you have come; **men che meno gli inglesi** least of all the English; **fammi sapere se verrai o meno** let me know if you are coming or not; **quanto meno poteva avvertire** he could at least have let us know; **non mi piace come scrive e tanto meno come parla** I don't like the way he writes let alone the way he talks

♦ AGG INV (*acqua, lavoro, soldi*) less; (*persone, libri, errori*) fewer; **meno persone ci sono, meglio è** the fewer people there are the better; **meno storie!** stop messing around!; **meno tempo** less time; **meno turisti** fewer tourists

♦ SM INV

1 (*la minor cosa*): **il meno** the least; **era il meno che ti potesse capitare** (*rimprovero*) you were asking for it; **parlare del più e del meno** to talk about this and that; **per lo meno = perlomeno**; **i meno** (*la minoranza*) the minority **2** (*Mat*) minus (sign)

♦ PREP (*fuorché, eccetto che*) except (for); **a meno che non faccia caldo** unless it is hot; **a meno di prendere un giorno di ferie** unless I (*o* you *ecc*) take a day off; **ci siamo tutti meno lui** we are all here except (for) him; **tutti meno uno** all but one

menomare [meno'mare] /72/ VT to maim, disable

menomato, -a [meno'mato] AGG (*persona*) disabled ♦ SM, SF disabled person

menomazione [menomat'tsjone] SF disablement

menopausa [meno'pauza] SF menopause; **essere in menopausa** to be going through the menopause

mensa ['mɛnsa] SF **1** (*locale*) canteen; (*Mil*) mess; (*nelle università*) refectory **2** (*fig*) table; **i piaceri della mensa** the pleasures of the table

mensile [men'sile] AGG monthly; **un abbonamento mensile** a monthly ticket ♦ SM (*periodico*) monthly (magazine); (*stipendio*) monthly salary

mensilmente [mensil'mente] AVV (*ogni mese*) every month; (*una volta al mese*) monthly

mensola ['mɛnsola] SF (*supporto*) bracket; (*ripiano*) shelf; (*Archit*) corbel; **mensola del camino** mantelpiece; **mensola portaspezie** spice rack

menta ['menta] SF (*Bot*) mint; (*caramella*) mint, peppermint; (*bibita*) peppermint cordial; **alla menta, di menta** mint *attr*; **una caramella alla menta** a mint; **menta di giardino** *o* **comune** *o* **verde** spearmint; **menta piperita** peppermint

mentale [men'tale] AGG mental

mentalità [mentali'ta] SF INV mentality; **mentalità aperta/ristretta** open/narrow mind; **ha una mentalità aperta** he's open-minded; **ha una mentalità ristretta** he's narrow-minded

mentalmente [mental'mente] AVV mentally

mente ['mente] SF **1** (*gen, anche fig*) mind; **mente aperta/lucida** open/clear mind; **mente agile/acuta** quick/sharp mind; **ha una mente logica** he's got a logical mind; **mente malata** sick mind; **malato di mente** mentally ill; **avevo la mente altrove** my mind was elsewhere, I was miles away **2** (*fraseologia*): **a mente fredda** objectively; **rivedere qc a**

mente fresca to take another look at sth when one's mind is fresh; **a mente serena** calmly; **avere in mente qc/qn** to have sth/sb in mind; **ha qualcosa in mente** he's got something in mind; **ha la mente sempre in mente** she's always thinking of him; **avere in mente di fare qc** to intend to do sth; **lasciami fare mente locale** let me think; **fare venire in mente qc a qn** to remind sb of sth; **mettersi in mente di fare qc** to make up one's mind to do sth; **gli è passato di mente** he forgot about it; **mi è scappato di mente ciò che ti volevo dire** I've forgotten what I was going to say to you; **volevo farlo ma mi è scappato di mente** I meant to do it, but it went out of my head *o* slipped my mind; **ma cosa ti salta in mente?** what are you thinking of?, you must be crazy!; **tenere a mente qc** to bear sth in mind; **toglitelo dalla mente** forget about it, put it out of your mind; **mi è tornato in mente quell'indirizzo** that address has come back to me, I've remembered that address; **mi è venuto in mente che...** it occurred to me that ...; **non mi passa neppure per la mente** I wouldn't even consider it

mentecatto, -a [mente'katto] AGG half-witted ♦ SM, SF half-wit, imbecile

mentire [men'tire] /17/ VI (*aus* avere) **mentire (a qn su qc)** to lie (to sb about sth); **mente** he's lying; **non saper mentire** to be a poor liar; **mentire spudoratamente** to lie through *o* in one's teeth

mentito, -a [men'tito] AGG: **sotto mentite spoglie** under false pretences (*Brit*) *o* pretenses (*USA*)

mento ['mento] SM chin; **doppio mento** double chin

mentolo [men'tolo] SM menthol

mentre ['mentre] CONG **1** (*temporale*) while, as; **è successo mentre ero fuori** it happened while I was out; **l'ho incontrato mentre entravo nel negozio** I met him as I was going into the shop **2** (*avversativo*) whereas, while; **lui è biondo mentre sua sorella è mora** he's blond while his sister is dark ♦ SM: **in quel mentre** at that very moment

menu [me'nu] SM INV **1** (*Culin*) (set) menu; **menu turistico** tourists' menu **2** (*Inform*) menu; **menu a tendina** (*Inform*) pull-down menu

menzionare [mentsjo'nare] /72/ VT to mention

menzione [men'tsjone] SF mention; **fare menzione di** to mention; **degno di menzione** worthy of note

menzogna [men'tsoɲɲa] SF lie, falsehood; **dire menzogne** to tell lies

menzognero, -a [mentsoɲ'ɲero] AGG (*scuse*) false, untrue; (*persona*) lying

meraviglia [mera'viʎʎa] SF **1** (*stupore*) amazement, wonder; **non ti nascondo la mia meraviglia** you can imagine my surprise; **con mia (grande) meraviglia** to my amazement, to my great surprise; **suscitare gran meraviglia** to cause quite a stir; **mi fa meraviglia che...** I'm amazed that ...; **quest'abito ti sta a meraviglia** you look wonderful in that dress; **tutto va a meraviglia** everything is going perfectly **2** (*persona, cosa*) marvel, wonder; **hai un bimbo che è una meraviglia** isn't your baby gorgeous!; **il panorama è una meraviglia!** it's a wonderful view!; **le sette meraviglie del mondo** seven Wonders of the World

meravigliare [meraviʎ'ʎare] /27/ VT to amaze, surprise, astonish; **sono rimasto meravigliato** I was amazed *o* astonished; **mi meraviglierebbe se...** I'd be surprised if ..., it would surprise me if ...; **meravigliarsi** VIP: **meravigliarsi (di** *o* **per)** (*stupirsi*) to be amazed (at), be astonished (at); **mi meraviglio di te!** I'm surprised at you!; **non c'è da meravigliarsi** it's not surprising

meraviglioso, -a [meraviʎ'ʎoso] AGG wonderful, marvellous (*Brit*), marvelous (*USA*)

merc. ABBR (= *mercoledì*) Wed.

mercante [mer'kante] SM dealer, trader; (*ant*) merchant; **mercante d'arte** art dealer; **mercante di cavalli** horse dealer

mercanteggiare [merkanted'dʒare] /62/ VI (*aus* avere) to bargain, haggle; **mercanteggiare sul prezzo** to haggle over the price ♦ VT (*pegg: onore, voto*) to sell

mercantile [merkan'tile] AGG (*gen*) mercantile, commercial; (*marina, nave*) merchant *attr* ♦ SM (*nave*) merchantman

mercanzia [merkan'tsia] SF (*pegg*) stuff

mercatino [merka'tino] SM **1** (*rionale*) local street market **2** (*Econ*) unlisted securities market

mercato [mer'kato] SM **1** (*luogo*) market; **giorno di mercato** market day; **mercato ortofrutticolo/del pesce** fruit/ fish market; **mercati generali** wholesale market *sg*; **vado al mercato** I'm going to the market; **mercato delle pulci** flea market **2** (*Econ, Fin*) market; **mettere** *o* **lanciare qc sul mercato** to put sth on the market; **a buon mercato** (*agg*) cheap; (*avv*) cheaply; **di mercato** (*economia, prezzo, ricerche*) market *attr* ♦ **mercato dei cambi** exchange market; **mercato dei capitali** capital market; **il Mercato Comune (Europeo)** the (European) Common Market; **mercato interno** *o* **nazionale** domestic market; **mercato del lavoro** labour market, job market; **mercato libero** free market; **mercato nero** black market; **mercato al rialzo** (*Borsa*) bull market; **mercato al ribasso** (*Borsa*) bear market; **mercato a termine** forward *o* futures market; **mercato dei valori** stock market

merce ['mɛrtʃe] SF goods *pl*, merchandise *no pl*; **merce in conto vendita** sale or return goods; **merce deperibile** perishable goods *pl*

mercé [mer'tʃe] SF mercy; **essere alla mercé di qn** to be at sb's mercy

mercenario, -ria, -ri, -rie [mertʃe'narjo] AGG, SM, SF mercenary

merceria [mertʃe'ria] SF (*articoli*) haberdashery (*Brit*), notions *pl* (*USA*); (*bottega*) haberdasher's shop (*Brit*), notions store (*USA*)

mercoledì [merkole'di] SM INV Wednesday; **mercoledì delle Ceneri** Ash Wednesday; *vedi* **martedì**

mercurio [mer'kurjo] SM mercury

merda ['merda] SF (*fam!*) shit (*fam!*); **che giornata di merda!** what a lousy/shitty day!

merenda [me'renda] SF snack; **far merenda** to have a snack; **ragazzi, venite a fare merenda** children, come and have a snack

merendina [meren'dina] SF snack, *prepacked cakes etc sold as snacks for children*

meridiano, -a [meri'djano] AGG (*di mezzogiorno*) midday *attr*, noonday *attr* ♦ SM (*Geog, Agopuntura*) meridian; **meridiano terrestre** meridian

meridionale [meridjo'nale] AGG (*gen*) southern; (*dell'Italia*) Southern Italian ♦ SM, SF (*gen*) southerner; (*dell'Italia*) Southern Italian; **i meridionali** people from Southern Italy

meridione [meri'djone] SM: **il meridione** the South; (*dell'Italia*) the South of Italy, Southern Italy

meringa, -ghe [me'ringa] SF meringue

meritare [meri'tare] /72/ VT **1** (*premio, stima*) to deserve; **(si) merita un premio/un ceffone** he deserves a prize/a smack; **si è meritato la stima di tutti** he earned everybody's respect; **è una persona che merita** he deserves our respect (*o affection ecc*); **se l'è proprio meritato!** it serves him right **2** (*richiedere*): **meritare attenzione/considerazione** to require *o* need attention/consideration **3** (*valere*) to be worth; **questo pranzo non merita il prezzo** this meal's not worth the money ♦ VB IMPERS (*valere la pena*): **merita andare** it's worth going; **non merita neanche parlarne** it's not worth talking about; **per quel che merita** for what it's worth

meritevole [meri'tevole] AGG: **meritevole (di)** (*di lode, biasimo*) worthy (of); **è più meritevole di te** he's worthier than you

merito ['merito] SM **1** (*gen*) worth; (*valore*) worth; **dare (il) merito a qn di qc/di aver fatto qc** to give sb credit for sth/ for doing sth; **è merito mio se hai avuto quel lavoro** it's thanks to me that you got that job; **è merito suo se hanno vinto** it's thanks to him that they won; **Dio ve ne renda merito!** may God reward you!; **finire a pari merito** to finish joint first (*o second ecc*); **le due squadre hanno finito a pari merito** the two teams tied; **medaglia al merito** (*Mil*) medal for bravery **2** (*argomento*): **entrare nel merito di una questione** to go into a matter; **non so niente in merito** I don't know anything about it; **in merito a** as regards, with regard to; **in merito a ciò di cui si è parlato** with reference to what was discussed

meritocrazia [meritokrat'tsia] SF meritocracy

meritorio, -ria, -ri, -rie [meri'tɔrjo] AGG praiseworthy

merletto [mer'letto] SM lace

merlo¹ ['merlo] SM **1** (*Zool*) blackbird; **merlo acquaiolo** dipper; **merlo dal petto bianco** ring ouzel **2** (*sciocco*) fool, idiot

merlo² ['mɛrlo] SM (*Archit*) battlement

merluzzo [mer'luttso] SM cod

mescere ['meʃʃere] /29/ VT to pour (out)

meschinità [meskini'ta] SF (*grettezza*) meanness, pettiness, narrow-mindedness; (*spilorceria*) stinginess; **è stata una meschinità** it was a mean *o* petty trick

meschino, -a [mes'kino] AGG (*avaro*) mean; (*gretto*) narrow-minded, mean, petty; (*scarso: guadagno*) meagre (*Brit*), meager (*USA*); **fare una figura meschina** to cut a poor figure, look silly ♦ SM, SF: **non fare il meschino** (*gretto*) don't be so petty

mescita ['meʃʃita] SF wine bar

mesciuto, -a [meʃ'ʃuto] PP *di* **mescere**

mescolanza [mesko'lantsa] SF (*gen*) mixture; (*di ingredienti*) blend, mixture; **una mescolanza di gente/di idee** a mix of people/ideas

mescolare [mesko'lare] /72/ VT (*gen, anche Culin*) to mix; (*col cucchiaio*) to stir; (*vini, colori*) to blend; (*mettere in disordine: fogli, schede*) to mix up, muddle up; (*carte*) to shuffle; **mescolate la farina e lo zucchero** mix the flour and sugar; **mescolarsi** VR: **mescolarsi alla folla** to mingle with the crowd; **mescolarsi** VIP (*Culin*) to mix; (*vini, colori*) to blend; (*fogli, schede*) to get mixed up

mese ['mese] SM month; **fra un mese** in a month('s time); **un mese di vacanza** a month's holiday; **un mese di sciopero** a month-long strike; **il mese scorso** last month; **il corrente mese** this month; **alla fine del mese** at the end of the month; **guadagna 2000 euro al mese** she earns 2000 euros a *o* per month; **tre mesi d'affitto** three months' rent; **un bambino di sei mesi** a six-month-old baby; **è al settimo mese (di gravidanza)** she's in the seventh month of her pregnancy

messa¹ ['messa] SF (*Rel*) mass; **andare** *o* **alla messa** to go to mass; **andiamo a messa di domenica** we go to Mass on Sundays; **dire la messa** (*celebrarla*) to say mass; **messa nera** black *o* Satanic mass

❏ **messa** non si traduce mai con la parola inglese *mess*

messa² ['messa] SF (*il mettere*): **messa a fuoco** focusing; **messa in moto** starting-up; **messa in opera** installation; **messa in orbita** launching; **messa in piega** set; **messa in posizione** installation; **messa a punto** (*termine tecn*) adjustment; (*Aut*) tuning; (*di progetto*) finalization; **messa in scena** (*Teatro*) production; **messa a terra** earthing

messaggerie [messadʤe'rie] SFPL (*ditta: di distribuzione*) distributors; (: *di trasporto*) freight company *sg*

messaggero, -a [messad'dʤero] SM, SF messenger

messaggiare [messad'dʤare] /62/ VI (*fam*) to message ♦ VT to message; **messaggiare con qn** to message sb; **messaggiare qn su Facebook** to facebook sb

messaggi'arsi [messad'dʤarsi] /72/ VR to text; **messaggiamoci** we'll text each other

messaggino [messad'dʤino] SM (*di telefonino*) text (message)

messaggio, -gi [mes'saddʤo] SM message; **il messaggio augurale del capo dello stato** ≈ the Queen's Christmas message; **vuole lasciare un messaggio?** would you like to leave a message?; **messaggio di errore** (*Inform*) error message; **messaggio di posta elettronica** e-mail; **messaggio istantaneo** instant message

messaggistica [messad'dʤistika] SF: **messaggistica immediata** (*Inform*) instant messaging; **programma di messaggistica immediata** instant messenger

messale [mes'sale] SM (*Rel*) missal

messe ['mɛsse] SF (*letter*) harvest; **fare messe di** (*fig: lodi, consensi*) to win

messia [mes'sia] SM INV messiah; **il Messia** the Messiah

messicano, -a [messi'kano] AGG, SM, SF Mexican

Messico ['messiko] SM Mexico; **Città del Messico** Mexico City; **mi è piaciuto molto il Messico** I really liked Mexico; **quest'estate andremo in Messico** we're going to Mexico this summer

messinscena [messin'ʃena] SF INV (*Teatro*) production; (*fig*) performance; **è tutta una messinscena** it's all an act

messo¹ ['messo] SM messenger

messo², -a ['messo] PP *di* **mettere** ♦ AGG: **essere ben/mal**

messo (*economicamente*) to be well-/badly-off; (*di salute*) to be in good/bad health

mestierante [mestjeˈrante] SM, SF (*pegg*) money-grubber; (*scrittore*) hack

mestiere [mesˈtjere] SM (*gen: lavoro*) job; (: *manuale*) trade; (: *artigianale*) craft; (*fig: abilità nel lavoro*) skill, technique; **di mestiere** by trade; **un mestiere difficile** a difficult job; **cosa fa tuo padre di mestiere?** what does your father do?; **fa il mestiere di calzolaio** he is a shoemaker; **imparare un mestiere** to learn a trade; **essere del mestiere** to be in the trade; (*fig*) to be an expert; **conoscere i trucchi del mestiere** to know the tricks of the trade; **essere padrone del mestiere** to know one's job

mestizia [mesˈtittsja] SF sadness, melancholy

mesto, -a [ˈmesto] AGG sad, melancholy

mestolo [ˈmestolo] SM ladle

mestruale [mestruˈale] AGG menstrual

mestruazione [mestruatˈtsjone] SF menstruation; **avere le mestruazioni** to have one's period

meta [ˈmeta] SF 1 (*destinazione*) destination; (*fig: scopo*) aim, goal; **finalmente giunsero alla meta** they finally reached their destination; **vagare senza meta** to wander aimlessly; **vagava senza meta** he was wandering aimlessly 2 (*Rugby*) try; **segnare una meta** to score a try

metà [meˈta] SF INV 1 half; **dividere qc a metà** to divide sth in half *o* into two halves, halve sth; **fare a metà di qc con qn** to go halves with sb in sth; **facciamo a metà** let's go halves; **dammene la metà** give me half (of it); **ho impiegato la metà del tempo** it only took me half the time; **siamo arrivati a metà del concerto** we arrived halfway through the concert; **dire le cose a metà** to leave some things unsaid; **fare le cose a metà** to leave things half-done; **la mia dolce metà** (*fam, scherz*) my better half; **a metà prezzo** at half price, half-price; **a metà strada** halfway 2 (*punto di mezzo*) middle; **tagliare una pagina per metà** to cut a page down the middle; **a metà settimana** mid-week; **verso la metà del mese** halfway through the month, towards the middle of the month

metabolismo [metaboˈlizmo] SM metabolism; **metabolismo basale** basal metabolism

metadone [metaˈdone] SM methadone

metafisica [metaˈfizika] SF metaphysics *sg*

metafora [meˈtafora] SF metaphor; **parlare per metafore** to speak metaphorically; **fuor di metafora** without beating about the bush

metaforico, -a, -ci, -che [metaˈfɔriko] AGG metaphorical

metallico, -a, -ci, -che [meˈtalliko] AGG (*simile al metallo*) metallic; (*di metallo*) metal *attr*

metallizzato, -a [metalliˈdzato] AGG (*vernice*) metallic

metallo [meˈtallo] SM metal; **di metallo** metal *attr*; **una scultura di metallo** a metal sculpture

metallurgia [metallurˈdʒia] SF metallurgy

metalmeccanico, -a, -ci, -che [metalmekˈkaniko] AGG engineering *attr*; **l'industria metalmeccanica** the engineering industry ♦ SM, SF engineering worker

metamorfosi [metaˈmorfozi] SF INV metamorphosis

metano [meˈtano] SM methane; **riscaldamento a metano** gas heating

meteora [meˈteora] SF meteor; **quell'attore è passato come una meteora** that actor's success was a flash in the pan

meteorite [meteoˈrite] SF meteorite

meteorologia [meteorolɔˈdʒia] SF meteorology

meteorologico, -a, -ci, -che [meteorolɔˈdʒiko] AGG (*fenomeno*) meteorological; (*previsione, stazione, carta*) weather *attr*; **bollettino meteorologico** weather report; **ufficio meteorologico dell'Aeronautica** Airforce Meteorological Office

meteorologo, -a, -gi, -ghe [meteoˈrɔlogo] SM, SF meteorologist

meticcio, -cia, -ci, -ce [meˈtittʃo] AGG (*persona*) half-caste (*offensivo*); (*animale*) crossbreed ♦ SM, SF half-caste, half-breed (*offensivo*)

meticolosità [metikolosiˈta] SF INV meticulousness

meticoloso, -a [metikoˈloso] AGG meticulous

metodico, -a, -ci, -che [meˈtɔdiko] AGG methodical

metodo [ˈmetodo] SM (*procedimento*) method; (*manuale*) tutor (*Brit*), manual; **far qc con/senza metodo** to do sth methodically/unmethodically; **aver il proprio metodo per fare qc** to have one's own way *o* method of doing sth

metraggio, -gi [meˈtraddʒo] SM 1 (*Sartoria*) length; **vendere a metraggio** to sell by the metre 2 (*Cine*) footage; (**film a) lungo metraggio** feature film; (**film a) corto metraggio** short (film)

metratura [metraˈtura] SF length

metrico, -a, -ci, -che [ˈmetriko] AGG metric; (*Poesia*) metrical; **il sistema metrico decimale** the metric system

metro [ˈmetro] SM (*gen*) metre (*Brit*), meter (*USA*); (*strumento: a nastro*) tape measure; (: *ad asta*) (metre) rule; (*fig: criterio*) yardstick; **metro cubo/quadrato** cubic/square metre; **i cento metri** (*Sport*) the hundred metres (race)

metrò [meˈtro] SM INV underground (*Brit*), subway (*USA*)

metronotte [metroˈnotte] SM INV night security guard

metropoli [meˈtrɔpoli] SF INV metropolis

metropolitano, -a [metropoliˈtano] AGG metropolitan; **leggende metropolitane** urban myths

mettere [ˈmettere] VB IRREG /63/ VT 1 (*porre*) to put; **dove hai messo la mia penna?** where did you put my pen?; **guarda dove metti i piedi** be careful where you step; **gli ha messo una mano sulla spalla** he put *o* laid a hand on his shoulder; **mettere qc diritto** to put *o* set sth straight; **mettere un bambino a letto** to put a child to bed; **mettere un annuncio sul giornale** to put an advert in the paper; **mettere il lavoro al di sopra di tutto** to put work before all else; **quando si mette una cosa in testa...** when he gets an idea into his head ...; **mettere qn sulla strada giusta** (*fig*) to set sb right 2 (*infondere*): **mettere fame/allegria/malinconia a qn** to make sb (feel) hungry/happy/sad 3 (*anche: mettersi: abito: indossare*) to put on; (: *portare*) to wear; **mettiti il maglione** put your jumper on; **si mise le scarpe** he put his shoes on; **non metto più quelle scarpe** I've stopped wearing those shoes, I don't wear those shoes any more; **mettersi il cappello** to put on one's hat; **non so cosa mettermi** I don't know what to wear; **ma che cosa ti sei messo?** what on earth have you got on? 4 (*installare: telefono, gas, finestre*) to put in; (*acqua*) to lay on, install 5 (*sveglia, allarme*) to set; **hai messo la sveglia?** have you set the alarm?; **hai messo la sicura?** (*Aut*) have you locked the door? 6 (*supporre*): **mettiamo che...** let's suppose *o* say that ... 7 **metterci, metterci molta cura/molto tempo** to take a lot of care/a lot of time; **quanto tempo ci hai messo?** how long did it take you?; **ci ho messo 3 ore per venire** it's taken me 3 hours to get here; **mettercela tutta** to do one's utmost *o* very best 8 (*fraseologia*): **mettere a confronto** to compare; **mettere in conto** (*somma ecc*) to put on account; **mettere qn contro qn** (*fig*) to turn sb against sb; **mettere qn al corrente di qc** to let someone know about sth, to bring someone up to speed about sth; **mettere dentro qn** (*fam: imprigionare*) to put sb inside; **mettere in giro** (*pettegolezzi, voci*) to spread; **mettere insieme** (*gen*) to put together; (*organizzare: spettacolo, gruppo*) to organize, get together; (*soldi*) to save; **mettere in luce** (*problemi, errori*) to show up, highlight; **mettere qn a sedere** to sit sb down; **mettere sotto** (*sopraffare*) to get the better of; **mettere su il caffè** (*fam*) to put the coffee on; **mettere su casa** to set up house; **mettere su un negozio** to start a shop; **mettere su pancia** to develop a paunch; **mettere su peso** to put on weight; **mettere a tacere qn/qc** to keep sb/sth quiet; **mettere via** to put away; **mettersi** VR 1 to put o.s.; **non metterti là** (*seduto*) don't sit there; (*in piedi*) don't stand there; **mettiti là e aspetta** wait there; **mettersi a sedere** to sit down; **mettersi a letto** to go to bed; (*malato*) to take to one's bed 2 (*vestirsi*): **mettersi in costume** to put on one's swimming things; **ti dispiace se mi metto in maniche di camicia?** do you mind if I take off my jacket? 3 (*in gruppo*): **mettersi in società** to set up in business; **si sono messi insieme** (*coppia*) they've started going out together (*Brit*) *o* dating (*USA*); **mettersi** VIP 1 (*incominciare*): **mettersi a fare qc** to start to do sth; **mettersi a piangere/ridere** to start crying/laughing, start *o* begin to cry/laugh; **mettersi a bere** to take to drink; **mettersi al lavoro** to set to work 2 (*prendere un andamento*): **si mette al bello** (*tempo*) the weather's turning fine; **mettersi bene/male** (*faccenda*) to turn out well/badly; **vediamo come si mettono le cose** let's see how things go

mezzadro [med'dzadro] SM (*Agr*) sharecropper

mezzaluna [meddza'luna] SF (*pl* **mezzelune**) half-moon; (*dell'islamismo*) crescent; (*coltello*) (semicircular) chopping knife

mezzanino [meddza'nino] SM mezzanine (floor)

mezzano, -a [med'dzano] AGG (*medio*) average, medium; (*figlio*) middle *attr*; (*vela*) mizzen *attr* ♦ SM, SF (*intermediario*) go-between; (*ruffiano*) procurer ♦ SF (*Naut*): **albero di mezzana** mizzen mast

mezzanotte [meddza'nɔtte] SF midnight; **a mezzanotte** at midnight

mezzo¹ ['mɛddzo] SM 1 (*strumento*) means *sg*; (*metodo*) means, way; **mezzi di produzione** means of production; **per mezzo di** by means of, through; **per mezzo della nuova tecnologia** by means of new technology; **a mezzo corriere** by carrier; **cercherò di ottenere il posto con qualsiasi mezzo** I'll try to get the job by whatever means; **non c'è mezzo di fermarlo** there's no way of stopping him; **ci siamo arrangiati con mezzi di fortuna** we managed as best we could; **mezzi di comunicazione** media *pl*; **mezzi di comunicazione di massa** mass media *pl* 2 (*veicolo*) vehicle; **mezzi pubblici** public transport *sg*; **mezzi di trasporto** means of transport; **un mezzo di trasporto** a means of transport 3 **mezzi** SMPL (*possibilità economiche*) means; **è una persona che ha molti mezzi** he has a large income, one's very well off; **farcela con i propri mezzi** to manage on one's own; **fare una vita al di sopra dei propri mezzi** to live beyond one's means 4 (*Fis*) medium

mezzo², -a ['meddzo] AGG 1 half; **mezza bottiglia di vino** half a bottle of wine; **una mezza bottiglia di vino** a half-bottle of wine; **una mezza dozzina di uova** half a dozen eggs; **ha lasciato mezzo panino** he left half of his sandwich; **c'era mezza città al concerto** half the town was at the concert; **mi ha fatto una mezza promessa** he half-promised me; **aver una mezza idea di fare qc** to have half a mind to do sth; **è venuto mezzo mondo** just about everybody was there; **è stato un mezzo scandalo** it almost caused a scandal; **me l'ha detto a mezza voce** he said it to me in an undertone; **non mi piacciono le mezze misure** I don't like half measures; **mezz'ora** = **mezzora** 2 (*medio*): **di mezza età** middle-aged; **un uomo di mezza età** a middle-aged man; **un soprabito di mezza stagione** a spring (*o* autumn) coat ♦ AVV half-; **mezzo pieno/vuoto** *ecc* half-full/ empty *ecc*; **mezzo morto** half-dead ♦ SM 1 (*metà*) half; **un chilo e mezzo** a kilo and a half, one and a half kilos; **è l'una e mezza/a** it's half past one; **una volta e mezzo più grande** one and a half times bigger 2 (*parte centrale*) middle; **nel mezzo della piazza** in the middle of the square; **il sedile di mezzo** the middle seat; **la porta di mezzo** the middle door; **in mezzo a** in the middle of; (*folla*) in the midst of; **era in mezzo alla strada** he was in the middle of the road; **nel bel mezzo (di)** right in the middle (of) 3 (*fraseologia*): **esserci di mezzo** (*ostacolo*) to be in the way; **quando ci sono di mezzo i numeri non ci capisco più niente** when numbers are involved I get completely lost; **non voglio andarci di mezzo** I don't want to suffer for it; **mettersi di mezzo** to interfere; **non mettermi in mezzo!** don't drag me into it!; **è meglio non porre tempo in mezzo** it'd be better not to delay; **togliere di mezzo** (*persona, cosa*) to get rid of; (*fam: uccidere*) to bump off; **levarsi** *o* **togliersi di mezzo** to get out of the way; **il giusto mezzo** the happy medium; **non c'è una via di mezzo** there's no middle course

mezzogiorno [meddzo'dʒorno] SM 1 (*ora*) midday, noon; **a mezzogiorno** at 12 (o'clock) *o* midday *o* noon; **a mezzogiorno e mezzo/a** at half past twelve 2 (*Geog*) south; **il Mezzogiorno (d'Italia)** the South of Italy, Southern Italy

mezzora, mezz'ora [med'dzora] SF an hour, half-hour; **ti aspetterò una mezzora** I'll wait for you for half an hour; **la prima mezzora** the first half-hour

MI SIGLA = Milano

mi¹ [mi] PRON PERS *dav* **lo, la, li, le, ne diventa me** 1 (*ogg diretto*) me; **mi aiuti?** will *o* could you help me?; **mi scusi!** excuse me!; **mi chiamava** he was calling to me; **aspettami!** wait for me! 2 (*complemento di termine*) (to) me; **mi dai il libro?** will

you give me the book?; **mi compri il libro?** will you buy me the book?, will you buy the book for me?; **puoi prestarmi la penna?** could you lend me your pen?; **me ne ha parlato** he spoke to me about it, he told me about it; **mi sembrava una buona idea** it seemed a good idea to me; **mi ha sorriso** he smiled at me 3 (*riflessivo*) myself; **mi servo da solo** I'll help myself; **mi sono pettinato** I combed my hair; **mi sono lavato i denti** I brushed my teeth; **mi sono divertita** I enjoyed myself; **mi sono fatto male** I've hurt myself; **mi guardai allo specchio** I looked at myself in the mirror

mi² [mi] SM INV (*Mus*) E; (*solfeggiando la scala*) mi

mia ['mia] *vedi* **mio**

miagolare [mjago'lare] /72/ VI (*aus avere*) to miaow, mew

MIB [mib] SIGLA M, AGG (= *Milano Indice Borsa*) Milan Stock Exchange; **l'indice MIB** the Milan (Stock Exchange) index

mica ['mika] AVV: **non...mica** not ... at all; **non ci credo mica!** I don't believe that for a minute!; **non ci crederai mica!** you won't believe it!; **non sarà mica partito?** he wouldn't have left, would he?; **non sono mica stanco** I'm not at all tired; **mica male!** not bad (at all)!

mica² ['mika] SF (*minerale*) mica

miccia, -ce ['mittʃa] SF fuse; **accendere la miccia** to light the fuse

micidiale [mitʃi'djale] AGG (*letale*) fatal, deadly; (*fig: musica*) excruciating; (*liquore*) deadly; **fa un caldo micidiale oggi** it's terribly hot today

micio, -cia, -ci, -cie ['mitʃo] SM, SF (*fam*) pussy (cat)

microbiologia [mikrobiolo'dʒia] SF microbiology

micro'blog [mikro'blɔg] SM INV microblog

microbo ['mikrobo] SM microbe

microcircuito [mikrotʃir'kuito] SM microcircuit

microfibra [mikro'fibra] SF microfibre

microfilm [mikro'film] SM INV microfilm

microfono [mi'krɔfono] SM microphone

microinformatica [mikroinfor'matika] SF microcomputing

microonda [mikro'onda] SF microwave; **forno a microonde** microwave (oven)

microprocessore [mikroprotʃes'sore] SM microprocessor

microscopico, -a, -ci, -che [mikros'kɔpiko] AGG microscopic; **un microscopico bikini** (*scherz*) a microscopic bikini

microscopio, -pi [mikros'kɔpjo] SM microscope; **microscopio elettronico** electron microscope; **microscopio ottico** light microscope

microsolco, -chi [mikro'solko] SM (*solco*) microgroove; (*disco a 33 giri*) long-playing record, LP

microspia [mikros'pia] SF hidden microphone, bug (*fam*)

midollo [mi'dollo] SM (*pl f* **midolla**) (*Anat*) marrow; (*Bot*) pith; **bagnarsi fino alle midolla** *o* **al midollo** (*fig*) to get soaking wet *o* drenched; **midollo allungato** medulla oblongata; **midollo osseo** bone marrow; **midollo spinale** spinal cord

mie ['mie] *vedi* **mio**

miele ['mjɛle] SM honey; **color miele** honey-coloured

mietere ['mjɛtere] /29/ VT (*Agr, anche fig*) to reap, harvest; **l'epidemia ha mietuto molte vittime** the epidemic has claimed many victims

mietitrebbiatrice [mjetitrebbja'tritʃe] SF combine harvester

mietitrice [mjeti'tritʃe] SF (*macchina*) harvester

mietitura [mjeti'tura] SF (*raccolto*) harvest; (*lavoro*) harvesting; (*tempo*) harvest time

migliaio [miʎ'ʎajo] SM (*pl f* **migliaia**) thousand; **un migliaio (di)** about a thousand, a thousand or so; **un migliaio di persone** about a thousand people; **due migliaia di persone** about two thousand people; **a migliaia** by the thousand, in thousands; **poche migliaia di persone** a few thousand people; **centinaia di migliaia di persone** hundreds of thousands of people; **parecchie migliaia di copie** several thousand copies; **l'ho fatto migliaia di volte** I've done it thousands of times

miglio¹ [miʎ'ʎo] SM (*pl f* **miglia**) mile; **camminò per miglia e miglia** she walked for miles and miles; **si vede lontano un miglio che è falso** you can see a mile off that it's a fake; **miglio inglese** *o* **terrestre** (= *1609,33 metri*) mile; **miglio marino** *o* **nautico** (= *1852,28 metri*) nautical mile

miglio² ['miʎʎo] SM (*Bot*) millet

miglioramento [miʎʎora'mento] SM improvement; **non c'è ancora nessun miglioramento** there hasn't been any improvement yet

migliorare [miʎʎo'rare] /72/ VT, VI (*aus essere*; *riferito a persone, anche* avere) to improve; **partiremo domani, se il tempo migliora** we'll set off tomorrow, if the weather improves; **fa un corso per migliorare il suo inglese** he's taking a course to improve his English; **migliorarsi** VR to improve o.s.

migliore [miʎ'ʎore] COMP, SUPERL *di* buono¹ ♦ AGG (*comparativo*) better; (*superlativo*) best; **migliore (di)** better (than); **il libro è migliore del film** the book is better than the film; **molto migliore** much better; **rendere migliore** to make better, improve; **i migliori auguri** best wishes; **la cosa migliore sarebbe partire subito** the best thing would be to leave immediately ♦ SM, SF: **il/la migliore** (*comparativo*) the better (one); (*superlativo*) the best (one); **il migliore dei due** the better of the two; **il migliore della classe** the best in the class; **questo è il miglior ristorante della città** this is the best restaurant in town; **nella migliore delle ipotesi** at best; **vinca il migliore** let the best man/woman win

miglioria [miʎʎo'ria] SF improvement; **fare** *o* **apportare delle migliorie** to make *o* carry out improvements

mignolo ['miɲnolo] SM (*di mano*) little finger, pinkie (*fam*); (*di piede*) little toe

migrare [mi'grare] /72/ VI (*aus essere*) to migrate

migrazione [migrat'tsjone] SF migration

mila ['mila] (*in combinazione con* due, tre *ecc*) *vedi* mille

milanese [mila'nese] AGG Milanese; **cotoletta alla milanese** Wiener schnitzel; **risotto alla milanese** *risotto with saffron* ♦ SM, SF inhabitant *o* native of Milan; **i milanesi** the Milanese

Milano [mi'lano] SF Milan; **domani vado a Milano** I'm going to Milan tomorrow; **abitiamo a Milano** we live in Milan

miliardario, -ria, -ri, -rie [miljar'darjo] AGG, SM, SF ≈ billionaire; **è miliardario** he's a billionaire

miliardo [mi'ljardo] SM thousand million, billion; **un miliardo di euro** one thousand million euros, a billion euros; **tre miliardi di euro** three thousand million euros, three billion euros; **miliardi di persone** millions of people

miliare [mi'ljare] AGG: **pietra miliare** (*anche fig*) milestone

milionario, -ria, -ri, -rie [miljo'narjo] AGG, SM, SF millionaire

milione [mi'ljone] SM million; **un milione di dollari** one million dollars; **due milioni di sterline** two million pounds; **parecchi milioni di euro** several million euros; **milioni di persone** millions of people

militante [mili'tante] AGG, SM, SF militant

militanza [mili'tantsa] SF militancy

militare¹ [mili'tare] /72/ VI (*aus* avere) **militare in** (*partito, gruppo*) to be active in; (*marina, aeronautica*) to serve in; **militare in una squadra** (*Sport*) to play for/in a team; **una squadra che milita in serie A** ≈ a team (which plays) in the Premier division

militare² [mili'tare] /72/ AGG army *attr*, military; **governo militare** military government; **il servizio militare** military service; **un ufficiale militare** an army officer ♦ SM serviceman; **fare il militare** to do one's military service; **non ho fatto il militare** I didn't do my military service; **militare di carriera** regular (soldier)

militaresco, -a, -schi, -sche [milita'resko] AGG (*portamento*) military *attr*, soldierly

milite ['milite] SM (*soldato*) soldier; **il Milite ignoto** the Unknown Soldier *o* Warrior

milizia [mi'littsja] SF militia

miliziano [milit'tsjano] SM militiaman

millantatore, -trice [millanta'tore] SM, SF boaster

millanteria [millante'ria] SF (*qualità*) boastfulness; **queste sono millanterie** that's just boasting

mille ['mille] AGG INV *a o* one thousand; **mille persone** a thousand people; **duemila** two thousand; **tremila** three thousand; **milleuno** *a o* one thousand and one; **mille grazie** thanks a lot, thank you very much; **a mille (a mille)** in their thousands ♦ SM INV *a o* one thousand; **nel mille d.C.** in one thousand A.D.

millefoglie [mille'fɔʎʎe] SM INV (*Culin*) millefeuille

millennio, -ni [mil'lɛnnjo] SM millennium

millepiedi [mille'pjedi] SM INV millipede

millesimo, -a [mil'lezimo] AGG, SM thousandth

milligrammo [milli'grammo] SM milligram(me)

millilitro [mil'lilitro] SM millilitre (*Brit*), milliliter (*USA*)

millimetro [mil'limetro] SM millimetre (*Brit*), millimeter (*USA*)

milza ['miltsa] SF (*Anat*) spleen

mimetico, -a, -ci, -che [mi'metiko] AGG (*arte*) mimetic; **tuta mimetica** (*Mil*) camouflage

mimetismo [mime'tizmo] SM (*Bio, Mil*) camouflage

mimetizzare [mimetid'dzare] /72/ VT to camouflage; **mimetizzarsi** VR to camouflage o.s.

mimica ['mimika] SF 1 (*arte*) mime 2 (*insieme di gesti*) gestures *pl*; **mimica facciale** facial expressions

mimo ['mimo] SM 1 (*attore, spettacolo*) mime 2 (*Zool*) mocking bird

mimosa [mi'mosa] SF mimosa

min. ABBR (= *minuto, minimo*) min.

mina ['mina] SF 1 (*ordigno*) mine; **mina terrestre** landmine; **mina vagante** time bomb 2 (*di matita*) lead

minaccia, -ce [mi'nattʃa] SF threat; **è una grave minaccia per la nazione** it is a serious threat to the nation; **una minaccia per l'ambiente** a threat to the environment; **fare delle minacce a qn** to threaten sb; **in segno di minaccia** as a threat; **sotto la minaccia di** under threat of

minacciare [minat'tʃare] /14/ VT to threaten; **minacciare qn di morte** to threaten sb with death, threaten to kill sb; **minacciare qn con una pistola** to threaten sb with a gun; **lo sciopero minaccia di durare** the strike looks set to continue; **ha minacciato di andarsene** he threatened to leave; **minaccia di piovere** it looks like rain; **minaccia tempesta** there's a storm brewing

minaccioso, -a [minat'tʃoso] AGG threatening, menacing

minare [mi'nare] /72/ VT (*ponte*) to mine; (*fig: salute, reputazione*) to undermine; **questo campo è minato** this field has been mined; **ha la salute minata dall'alcol** his health has been ruined by drink

minatore [mina'tore] SM miner

minatorio, -ria, -ri, -rie [mina'tɔrjo] AGG threatening

minchione, -a [min'kjone] (*fam*) AGG idiotic ♦ SM, SF idiot

minerale [mine'rale] AGG mineral ♦ SM mineral; **minerale di ferro** iron ore ♦ SF (*anche:* acqua minerale) mineral water

mineralogia [mineralo'dʒia] SF mineralogy

minerario, -ria, -ri, -rie [mine'rarjo] AGG (*delle miniere*) mining *attr*; (*dei minerali*) ore *attr*

minestra [mi'nɛstra] SF soup; **"minestre"** (*sul menu*) "first courses"; **è sempre la solita minestra** (*fig*) it's always the same old story; **o mangi questa minestra o salti dalla finestra** (*Proverbio*) take it or leave it; **minestra in brodo** noodle soup; **minestra di verdura** vegetable soup

minestrone [mines'trone] SM (*Culin*) minestrone (*thick vegetable and pasta soup*); (*fig*) mix-up, confusion

mingherlino, -a [minɡer'lino] AGG skinny

mini ['mini] AGG INV mini ♦ SF INV (*Moda*) miniskirt, mini

miniatura [minja'tura] SF (*dipinto*) miniature; (*arte, genere*) miniature painting; **in miniatura** in miniature; **una città/un giardino in miniatura** a model town/garden

minibar [mini'bar] SM INV minibar

minielaboratore [minielabora'tore] SM minicomputer

miniera [mi'njera] SF mine; **una miniera di informazioni** (*fig*) a mine of information; **miniera di carbone** (*gen*) coal mine; (*impresa*) colliery (*Brit*), coalmine; **miniera a cielo aperto** open-cast mine; **miniera d'oro** gold mine; **miniera sotterranea** pit, mine

minigonna [mini'gonna] SF miniskirt

minimalista, -i, -e [minima'lista] AGG, SM, SF (*Arte, Letteratura*) minimalist

minimizzare [minimid'dzare] /72/ VT to minimize

minimo, -a ['minimo] AGG (*il più piccolo*) least, slightest; (*piccolissimo*) very small, slight; (*il più basso*) lowest, minimum; **la temperatura minima** the minimum temperature; **a un costo minimo** at a minimal cost; **non c'è la minima differenza** there isn't the slightest difference; **la differenza è minima** the difference is minimal *o* very small *o* slight, there's hardly any difference; **non c'è stato il minimo cambiamento** there hasn't been the slightest change; **il prezzo minimo è 100 euro** the lowest *o* minimum price is 100 euros; **gli effetti collaterali della medicina sono minimi** the drug's side effects are minimal; **non ne ho la minima idea** I haven't the slightest idea; **ridurre una frazione ai minimi termini** (*Mat*) to reduce a fraction to its lowest terms; **queste scarpe sono ridotte ai minimi termini** (*fig: molto consumate*) these shoes are completely worn out ♦ SM **1** minimum; **è il minimo che tu possa fare** it's the least you can do; **non ha un minimo di comprensione** he is totally lacking in understanding; **gli hanno dato il minimo della pena** they gave him the minimum sentence; **come minimo avrebbe potuto dirmelo** he could at least have told me; **il minimo indispensabile** the bare minimum **2** (*Aut*): **girare al minimo** to idle; **questo motore ha il minimo basso** this engine has a low idling speed

ministero [minisˈtɛro] SM **1** (*Pol*) ministry, department (*spec USA*); ministero delle Finanze Ministry of Finance, ≈ Treasury **2** (*Dir*): **pubblico ministero** State Prosecutor **3** (*Rel*) ministry

ministro [miˈnistro] SM **1** (*Pol*) minister, secretary (*spec USA*); **il Primo ministro** the Prime Minister; **ministro delle Finanze** Minister of Finance, ≈ Chancellor of the Exchequer (*Brit*); **ministro degli Interni** Minister of the Interior, ≈ Home Secretary (*Brit*), ≈ Secretary of the Interior (*USA*) **2** (*Rel*) minister

minoranza [minoˈrantsa] SF (*gen*) minority; (*gruppo*) minority (group); **essere in minoranza** to be in the minority

minorato, -a [minoˈrato] AGG handicapped ♦ SM, SF physically (*o* mentally) handicapped person

minorazione [minoratˈtsjone] SF handicap

Minorca [miˈnɔrka] SF Minorca

minore [miˈnore] AGG *comp di* piccolo **1** less; (*più piccolo*) smaller; (*più breve*) shorter; (*meno grave*) lesser; (*numero*) lower; **con minore entusiasmo** with less enthusiasm; **un numero minore di studenti** a smaller number of students; **le vendite sono state minori del previsto** sales were less *o* lower than expected; **questo è il male minore** this is the lesser evil; **vocabolario in edizione minore** shorter *o* concise edition of a dictionary; **in misura minore** to a lesser extent **2** (*meno importante*) less important; (*inferiore*) lower, inferior; (*di poco rilievo*) minor; **opere minori** minor works; **le opere minori di Shakespeare** Shakespeare's minor works; **di minor pregio** of inferior quality **3** (*più giovane*) younger; **il mio fratello minore** my younger brother **4** (*Mus*) minor; **(in) do minore** (in) C minor ♦ AGG *superl di* piccolo (*vedi agg comp 1, 2, 3*) least; smallest; shortest; lowest; least important; youngest; **la minore delle due sorelle** the younger of the two sisters; **il minore dei tre fratelli** the youngest of the three brothers ♦ SM, SF **1** (*d'età: tra due*) younger; (: *tra più di due*) youngest **2** (*minorenne*) minor, person under age; **minore non accompagnato** unaccompanied minor; **spettacolo vietato ai minori** no admittance to persons under the age of 18 (*to film, show ecc*); "*vietato ai minori di 18 anni*" "18 certificate"

minorenne [minoˈrenne] AGG under age; **mia sorella è minorenne** my sister is under 18 ♦ SM, SF minor, person under age; **tribunale dei minorenni** (*Dir*) juvenile court

minorile [minoˈrile] AGG juvenile; **carcere minorile** young offenders' institution; **delinquenza minorile** juvenile delinquency

minoritario, -ria, -ri, -rie [minoriˈtarjo] AGG minority *attr*

minuscolo, -a [miˈnuskolo] AGG **1** (*piccolissimo*) tiny, minuscule, minute; **un appartamento minuscolo** a tiny apartment **2** (*lettera*) small; **a lettere minuscole** in small letters ♦ SM small letters *pl*; (*Tip*) lower case; **in minuscolo** in small letters; **scrivere tutto (in) minuscolo** to write everything in small letters

minuta [miˈnuta] SF rough copy, draft

minuto¹, -a [miˈnuto] AGG tiny, minute; (*pioggia*) fine; (*corporatura*) delicate, fine; (*lavoro, descrizione*) detailed; **spese minute** minor expenses; **al minuto** (*Comm*) retail; **comprare al minuto** to buy at retail prices, buy retail

minuto² [miˈnuto] SM (*gen*) minute; (*momento*) moment, minute; **all'ultimo minuto** at the (very) last minute *o* moment;

a minuti, da un minuto all'altro any second *o* minute now; **in un minuto** in one minute; (*fig: rapidamente*) in a flash; **tra pochi minuti** in a few minutes, in a few minutes' time; **avere i minuti contati** to have very little time; **spaccare il minuto** (*fig: persona*) to be (always) on the dot; (: *orologio*) to be accurate to a split second; **minuti di recupero** (*Calcio*) injury time

minuzia [miˈnuttsja] SF (*cura*) meticulousness; (*particolare*) detail; **perdersi in minuzie** to waste one's time with trifling details

minuziosamente [minuttsjosaˈmente] AVV (*vedi agg*) meticulously; in minute detail

minuzioso, -a [minutˈtsjoso] AGG (*persona*) meticulous; (*descrizione*) detailed; (*esame*) minute

mio, -a [ˈmio] (*pl* miei, mie) AGG POSS: **il mio, la mia** *ecc* my; **il mio cane** my dog; **mia madre** my mother; **i miei libri** my books; **un mio amico** a friend of mine; **è colpa mia** it's my fault; **è casa mia, è la mia casa** it's my house; **di chi è questo? — è mio** whose is this? — it's mine; **per amor mio** for my sake ♦ PRON POSS: **il mio, la mia** *ecc* mine, my own; **la sua barca è più lunga della mia** his boat is longer than mine; **la tua casa è più grande della mia** your house is bigger than mine; **è questo il mio?** is this mine?; **è questo il tuo cappotto? — no, il mio è nero** is this your coat? — no, mine's black; **il mio è stato solo un errore** it was simply an error on my part ♦ PRON POSS M **1 ho speso del mio** I spent my own money; **vivo del mio** I live on my own income **2 i miei** (*genitori*) my parents; (*famiglia*) my family; (*amici*) my side; **vivo con i miei** I live with my parents; **lui è dei miei** he is on my side ♦ PRON POSS F: **la mia** (*opinione*) my view; **è dalla mia** she is on my side; **non riuscita a dire la mia** I managed to say my piece; **anch'io ho avuto le mie** (*disavventure*) I've had my problems too; **ne ho fatta una delle mie!** (*sciocchezze*) I've done it again!; **cerco di stare sulle mie** I try to keep myself to myself

miope [ˈmiope] AGG short-sighted, myopic, (*fig*) short-sighted ♦ SM, SF myopic *o* short-sighted person

miopia [mioˈpia] SF short-sightedness, myopia; (*fig*) short-sightedness

mira [ˈmira] SF (*anche fig*) aim; **prendere la mira** to take aim; **prendere di mira qn** (*fig*) to pick on sb, target sb; **avere una buona/cattiva mira** to be a good/bad shot

mirabile [miˈrabile] AGG admirable, wonderful

miracolo [miˈrakolo] SM (*anche fig*) miracle; (*persona*) wonder, prodigy; **miracolo economico** economic miracle; **fare miracoli** to perform *o* do miracles; (*fig*) to work wonders; **sapere vita, morte e miracoli di qn** to know everything there is to know about sb; **per miracolo** by a miracle

miracoloso, -a [mirakoˈloso] AGG miraculous, prodigious; **non c'è niente di miracoloso** there's nothing extraordinary about it ♦ SM *no pl* **la sua guarigione ha del miracoloso** his recovery is well nigh miraculous

miraggio, -gi [miˈraddʒo] SM (*anche fig*) mirage

mirare [miˈrare] /72/ (*us* avere) mirare (a) (*anche fig*) to aim (at); **mirai al bersaglio e sparai** I aimed at the target and fired; **ha sempre mirato a diventare presidente** it has always been his aim to become president; **mirare al potere** to aspire to power; **mirarsi** VR: **mirarsi allo specchio** to look at o.s. in the mirror

mi'rato, -a, mirata AGG targeted

miriade [miˈriade] SF myriad, host

mirino [miˈrino] SM (*di arma da fuoco, strumento ottico*) sight; (*Fot*) viewfinder, viewer; **essere nel mirino della Mafia** (*fig*) to be a target of the Mafia

mirtillo [mirˈtillo] SM bilberry (*Brit*), blueberry (*USA*)

mirto [ˈmirto] SM myrtle

misantropo, -a [miˈzantropo] AGG misanthropic ♦ SM, SF misanthrope, misanthropist

miscela [miʃˈʃela] SF mixture; (*di caffè, tè, tabacco*) blend; (*per motorino*) petrol and oil mixture; **miscela pronta** (*per dolci*) cake mix; **miscela carburante** mixture

miscellanea [miʃʃelˈlanea] SF miscellany

mischia [ˈmiskja] SF (*rissa, zuffa*) scuffle, brawl; (*Rugby*) scrum, scrummage; **stare al di fuori della mischia** (*fig*) to stay out of the fray; **mischia aperta/chiusa** (*Rugby*) loose/set scrum

mischiare [mis'kjare] /19/ vt (gen) to mix; (caffè, tè) to blend; (carte) to shuffle; **mischiarsi** vip (liquidi ecc) to mix, blend

misconoscere [misko'noʃʃere] /26/ vt irreg (qualità, coraggio ecc) to fail to appreciate

miscredente [miskre'dɛnte] sm, sf (Rel) heretic; (indifferente) unbeliever ♦ agg (vedi sm/f) heretical; unbelieving

miscuglio, -gli [mis'kuʎʎo] sm (gen) mixture; (accozzaglia) jumble, hotchpotch

mise ecc vb vedi **mettere**

miserabile [mize'rabile] agg 1 (pietoso: vita, condizioni) miserable, wretched, pitiful; (: persona) pitiful, wretched 2 (povero) poor, destitute, poverty-stricken; **vivere in condizioni miserabili** to live in abject poverty; **una somma miserabile** a miserable o paltry sum of money 3 (spregevole: azione, persona) mean, wretched ♦ sm, sf (persona spregevole) wretch

miseria [mi'zɛrja] sf 1 (povertà) (extreme) poverty, destitution; **cadere in miseria** to become destitute; **ridursi in miseria** to be reduced to poverty; **vivere nella miseria più nera** to live in dire poverty; **piangere miseria** to plead poverty; **porca miseria!** (fam) (bloody) hell! 2 (somma): **comprare qc per una miseria** to buy sth for next to nothing o for a song; **costare una miseria** to cost next to nothing; **lo pagano una miseria** they pay him a pittance 3 **miserie** sfpl (brutture) misfortunes, troubles; **le miserie del mondo** the wretchedness of this world 4 (Bot) wandering Jew

misericordia [mizeri'kɔrdja] sf mercy, pity; **avere misericordia di qn** to have pity on sb; **misericordia divina** Divine mercy; **invocare la misericordia di qn** to beg sb for mercy; **misericordia!** my goodness!

misericordioso, -a [mizerikor'djoso] agg merciful

misero, -a ['mizero] agg 1 (pietoso: vita, condizioni) miserable, wretched, pitiful; (: persona) pitiful, wretched; **fare una misera figura** to cut a poor figure 2 (povero) poor, poverty-stricken; **una misera somma** a miserable o paltry sum 3 (spregevole, meschino) mean, wretched; **ho preso un misero 22 all'esame** ≈ I didn't get a very good pass in the exam; **è un misero impiegatuccio** he's a miserable pen-pusher; **una misera scusa** a lame excuse

misfatto [mis'fatto] sm (cattiva azione) misdeed; (delitto) crime

misi ecc vb vedi **mettere**

misogino, -a [mi'zɔdʒino] agg misogynous ♦ sm misogynist

missile ['missile] sm missile; **missile cruise** o **da crociera** cruise missile; **missile teleguidato** guided missile; **missile terra-aria** surface-to-air missile

missionario, -ria, -ri, -rie [missjo'narjo] agg, sm, sf missionary

missione [mis'sjone] sf mission; **essere/partire in missione** to be/leave on a mission; **missione compiuta** mission accomplished

misterioso, -a [miste'rjoso] agg mysterious ♦ sm, sf: **fare il misterioso** to act mysterious

mistero [mis'tero] sm mystery; **fare mistero di qc** to make a mystery out of sth; **non se ne fa un mistero** there's no mystery about it; **quanti misteri!** why all the mystery?

mistico, -a, -ci, -che ['mistiko] agg mystic(al) ♦ sm mystic

mistificare [mistifi'kare] /20/ vt 1 (dato, fatti) to falsify 2 (ingannare) to fool, take in

misto, -a ['misto] agg (tutti i sensi) mixed; (classe) mixed, co-educational; **un'insalata mista** a mixed salad; **una griglia mista** a mixed grill; **una scuola mista** a mixed school; **misto a qc** mixed with sth; **un tessuto in misto lino** a linen mix; **cane di razza mista** a mixed breed of dog, crossbreed dog ♦ sm mixture
   ❑ **misto** non si traduce mai con la parola inglese mist

mistura [mis'tura] sf (miscuglio) mixture

misura [mi'zura] sf 1 (Mat) measure; **unità di misura** unit of measurement; **misura di capacità** unit of capacity; **misura di lunghezza** unit of length 2 (dimensione) measurement; (taglia) size; **prendere le misure a qn** to take sb's measurements; **può prendermi la misura?** can you take my measurements?, measure sb; **prendere le misure di qc** to measure sth; **di misura grande/piccola** (scarpe, abito) in a

large/small size; **ha una misura più piccola?** have you got a smaller size?; (fatto) **su misura** made-to-measure; **un completo fatto su misura** a made-to-measure suit; **a misura d'uomo** on a human scale; **l'episodio dà la misura del livello di corruzione raggiunto** the affair gives an indication of the prevailing level of corruption 3 (proporzione): **in misura di** in accordance with, according to; **i prezzi aumenteranno in misura del 5%** prices will increase by 5% 4 (provvedimento) measure, step; **ho preso le mie misure** I've taken the necessary steps; **mezze misure** (fig) half measures; **misure di prevenzione** precautionary measures; **misure di sicurezza** safety measures 5 (Mus) time; (gruppo di note) bar 6 (Poesia) measure, metre 7 (fraseologia): **in ugual misura** equally, in the same way; **non ha il senso della misura** he doesn't know when to stop; **passare la misura** to overstep the mark, go too far; **bere senza misura** to drink to excess; **oltre misura** beyond measure, excessively; **vincere di stretta misura** to win by a narrow margin

misurare [mizu'rare] /72/ vt 1 (gen) to measure; (vista, udito) to test; (valore) to estimate; (capacità) to judge; (terreno) to survey; **misurare a occhio** to measure roughly, give a rough estimate; **misura la distanza fra questi due punti** measure the distance between these two points; **misurare a passi una stanza** to pace out a room 2 (fig: limitare: spese) to limit; **misurare le parole** to weigh one's words 3 (provare): **misurare** o **misurarsi qc** (abito, scarpe, cappotto) to try sth on ♦ vi (aus avere) to measure; **quanto misura questa stanza?** how big is this room?, what are the measurements of this room?; **misurarsi** vr 1 (contenersi, regolarsi): **misurarsi nel bere** to control one's drinking 2 (provare le proprie forze): **misurarsi con qn** to compete with sb, pit o.s. against sb

misurato, -a [mizu'rato] agg (ponderato) measured; (prudente) cautious; (moderato) moderate

misurazione [mizurat'tsjone] sf measuring, measurement; (di terreno) surveying

mite ['mite] agg (tempo, persona) mild; (condanna) lenient; (animale) meek

mitico, -a, -ci, -che ['mitiko] agg mythical; (leggendario) legendary; (fam): **Mitico!** Fantastic!, Brilliant!

mitigare [miti'gare] /80/ vt (gen) to mitigate, lessen; (dolore) to soothe, relieve; (sapore) to sweeten; **mitigarsi** vip (dolore) to lessen; (odio) to subside; (clima) to become milder

mitilo [mi'tilo] sm mussel

mito ['mito] sm myth; **far crollare un mito** to explode a myth; **sei un mito!** (fam) you're a star!; **quel cantante è un mito!** that singer's fantastic!

mitologia, -gie [mitolo'dʒia] sf mythology

mitologico, -a, -ci, -che [mitolɔ'dʒiko] agg mythological

mitra[1] ['mitra] sm inv (arma) sub-machine gun

mitra[2] ['mitra] sf (Rel) mitre (Brit), miter (USA)

mitragliare [mitraʎ'ʎare] /27/ vt to machine-gun; **mitragliare qn di domande** (fig) to fire questions at sb, bombard sb with questions

mitragliatore, -trice [mitraʎʎa'tore] agg: **fucile mitragliatore** sub-machine gun

mitteleuropeo, -a [mitteleuro'pɛo] agg Central European

mittente [mit'tente] sm, sf sender; "**rispedire al mittente**" "return to sender"

ml abbr (= millilitro) ml

mm abbr (= millimetro) mm

M.M. abbr (= marina militare) ≈ RN (Brit) (= Royal Navy)

mms [emmeemme'esse] sigla m inv (servizio) MMS (= Multimedia Messaging Service); (messaggio) MMS message

MN sigla = Mantova

M/N, m/n abbr (= motonave) MV (= motor vessel)

MO[1] sigla = Modena

MO[2] abbr = Medio Oriente

mo' [mɔ] prep as; **a mo' di** like; **a mo' di esempio** by way of example

mobile ['mɔbile] agg 1 (gen) mobile; (parte di meccanismo) moving; (Rel: festa) movable; **beni mobili** (Fin) movable property 2 (occhi) darting ♦ sm (per arredamento) piece of furniture; **mobili** furniture sg; **un negozio di mobili** a furniture shop; **mobile componibile** unit 2 (Fin); **mobili** smpl movable property, movables ♦ sf: **la (squadra) mobile** the flying squad

mobilia [mo'bilja] SF furniture
mobiliare [mobi'ljare] AGG (*credito*) personal; (*beni*) movable
mobilio [mo'biljo] SM furniture
mobilità [mobili'ta] SF (*gen*) mobility; **mobilità del lavoro** *o* **della manodopera** labour mobility; **lista di mobilità** redeployment list
mobilitare [mobili'tare] /72/ VT (*Mil, anche fig*) to mobilize; **mobilitare l'opinione pubblica** to mobilize public opinion; **mobilitarsi** VR: **mobilitarsi per fare qc** to go into action to do sth
mobilitazione [mobilitat'tsjone] SF mobilization
mocassino [mokas'sino] SM moccasin
moccioso, -a [mot't∫oso] SM, SF (*bambino piccolo*) little kid; (*pegg*) snotty-nosed kid
moccolo ['mɔkkolo] SM **1** (*di candela*) candle end; **reggere il moccolo** (*fig*) to play gooseberry (*Brit*), to be a fifth wheel **2** (*fam: bestemmia*): **tirare** *o* **mandare un moccolo** to curse, swear **3** (*fam: moccio*) snot
moda ['mɔda] SF (*gen*) fashion; (*pegg*) craze; **l'alta moda** haute couture; **la moda pronta** ready-to-wear (clothes); **essere alla moda** (*persona*) to be fashionable; **seguire la moda** to follow fashion; **essere di moda, andare di moda** (*abbigliamento, acconciatura ecc*) to be fashionable, be in fashion; **è di moda il nero** black is in fashion; **veste sempre all'ultima moda** she's always dressed in the latest fashion; **è tornata di moda la mini** the mini is back in fashion; **essere fuori moda** to be out of fashion; **non è più di moda, è fuori moda** it's (gone) out of fashion, it's no longer fashionable; **è diventato una moda** it has become the fashion; **rivista di moda** fashion magazine; **sfilata di moda** fashion show
modalità [modali'ta] SF INV (*procedura*) formality; **secondo le modalità previste dalla legge** in accordance with what is laid down by the law; **modalità di pagamento** method of payment; **modalità d'uso** instructions; **seguire attentamente le modalità d'uso** to follow the instructions carefully
modella [mo'della] SF model
modellare [model'lare] /72/ VT (*creta, statua*) to model, mould; **modellare qc su qc** (*fig: opera, stile ecc*) to model sth on sth; **un vestito che modella la figura** a figure-hugging dress; **modellarsi** VR: **modellarsi su qn/qc** to model o.s. on sb/sth, take sb/sth as a model
modello [mo'dello] SM **1** (*gen, anche fig*) model; (*stampo*) mould (*Brit*), mold (*USA*); **un modello in cera** a wax model; **ha comprato l'ultimo modello della FIAT** he's bought the latest Fiat; **prendere a modello** (*fig*) to take as one's model; **modello di serie/in scala** production/scale model **2** (*Sartoria*) model, style; (*forma*) style; **gli ultimi modelli di Armani** the latest Armani models *o* styles **3** (*Amm*) form ♦ AGG INV (*madre, marito, ospedale ecc*) model *attr*
modem ['mɔdem] SM INV modem
modenese [mode'nese] AGG *of o* from Modena ♦ SM, SF inhabitant *o* native of Modena
moderare [mode'rare] /72/ VT (*gen*) to moderate, curb; **moderare la velocità** to reduce speed; **moderare i termini** to weigh one's words; **moderarsi** VR to restrain o.s.; **moderarsi nel mangiare/nelle spese** to control one's eating/one's spending
moderato, -a [mode'rato] AGG **1** (*gen, anche Pol*) moderate **2** (*Mus*) moderato ♦ SM (*Pol*) moderate
moderatore, -trice [modera'tore] SM, SF **1** (*in una discussione*) moderator; **fare da moderatore** to act as moderator **2** (*Fis*) moderator
moderazione [moderat'tsjone] SF (*vedi vb*) moderation; restraint; **bere con moderazione** to drink in moderation; **usare moderazione** (*nel bere, nello spendere*) to be moderate
modernizzare [moderniddzare] /72/ VT to bring up to date, modernize; **modernizzarsi** VR to get up to date
moderno, -a [mo'dɛrno] AGG (*gen*) modern; **una mamma moderna** an up-to-date young mother; **a modern mum** ♦ SM **1** (*stile*) modern style **2 gli antichi e i moderni** ancient and (the) modern
modestia [mo'dɛstja] SF modesty; **modestia a parte...** in all modesty ..., though I say it myself ...; **certo non pecca di modestia** modesty isn't one of his faults

modesto, -a [mo'desto] AGG modest; **di modeste origini** from humble origins; **una casa modesta** a modest house *o* home
modico, -a, -ci, -che ['mɔdiko] AGG (*gen*) modest, moderate; **prezzi modici** low prices
modifica, -che [mo'difika] SF (*a motore*) adjustment; (*ad abito*) alteration; (*a piano*) modification; **fare una modifica** to make an adjustment (*o* alteration *o* modification); **subire delle modifiche** (*cambiamenti*) to undergo some modifications; (*miglioramenti*) to be revamped
modificabile [modifi'kabile] AGG modifiable
modificare [modifi'kare] /20/ VT to modify, alter; **modificarsi** VIP to alter, change
modista [mo'dista] SF milliner
modo ['mɔdo] SM **1** (*maniera*) way, manner; **allo stesso modo** in the same way; **in modo strano** strangely, in a strange way, in an odd way; **in modo eccessivo** excessively; **a** *o* **in questo/quel modo** (in) this/that way; **fallo in questo modo** do it this way; **va fatto in questo modo** it should be done this way *o* like this; **in nessun modo** in no way; **fare a modo proprio** to do as one likes; **lo farò a modo mio** I'll do it my own way; **non è il modo di comportarsi** this is no way to behave; **un modo di dire** a turn of phrase, an expression; **per modo di dire** so to speak, as it were; **per modo di dire** in a manner of speaking; **non mi piace il suo modo di fare** I don't like the way he goes about things; **non c'è modo di convincerlo** there's no way of persuading him; **c'è modo e modo di farlo** there's a right way and a wrong way of doing it; **aver modo di fare qc** to have the opportunity *o* chance of doing sth; **trovare il modo di fare qc** to find a way *o* the means of doing sth; **ad** *o* **in ogni modo** anyway; **ad ogni modo, non ha importanza** anyway, it doesn't matter; **in qualche modo** somehow (or other); **in qualche modo riuscirò a farlo** I'll manage it somehow; **in un certo qual modo** in a way, in some ways; **in tutti i modi** at all costs; (*comunque sia*) anyway; (*in ogni caso*) in any case; **di** *o* **in modo che** so that; **dovrò fare in modo che non mi vedano** I'll have to make sure they don't see me; **in modo da** so as to, in such a way as to; **entrai in punta di piedi in modo da non disturbarlo** I went in on tiptoe so as not to disturb him; **fare in modo di** to try to; **fate in modo di tornare per le cinque** try and be back for 5 o'clock **2** (*misura, regola*): **oltre modo** extremely; **fare le cose a modo** to do things properly; **una persona a modo** a well-mannered person **3 modi** SMPL (*maniere*) manners; **che modi!** what bad manners!; **ha dei modi molto brutti** he has dreadful manners **4** (*Gramm*) mood; **modo congiuntivo/indicativo** subjunctive/indicative mood **5** (*Mus, Inform*) mode; **modo conversazionale** (*Inform*) conversation mode
modulare¹ [modu'lare] /72/ VT (*voce, anche Fis*) to modulate
modulare² [modu'lare] /72/ AGG modular
modulazione [modulat'tsjone] SF modulation; **modulazione di frequenza** frequency modulation
modulo ['mɔdulo] SM **1** (*modello*) form; **riempire un modulo** to fill in a form; **riempite il modulo in stampatello** fill in the form in block letters; **modulo continuo** continuous stationery; **modulo di domanda** application form; **modulo d'iscrizione** enrolment form; **modulo di versamento** deposit slip **2** (*Archit, Aer*) model; **modulo di comando/lunare** command/lunar module **3** (*Mat*) modulus **4** (*Calcio*) plan
Mogadiscio [moga'diʃʃo] SF Mogadishu
mogano ['mɔgano] SM mahogany
mogio, -a, -gi, -ge *o* **, -gie** ['mɔdʒo] AGG down in the dumps, dejected; **se n'è andato mogio mogio** he went off with his tail between his legs
moglie ['moʎʎe] SF wife; **questa è mia moglie Anna** this is my wife Anna; **prendere moglie** to get married, take a wife
mohair [mɔ'er] SM mohair
moine [mo'ine] SFPL (*carezze*) endearments; (*lusinghe*) flattery *sg*, cajolery *sg*; (*smancerie*) affectation *sg*; **fare un sacco di moine a qn** to be all over sb; **non mi convincerai le tue moine** you're not going to sweet-talk me into it
mola ['mɔla] SF (*di mulino*) millstone; (*per utensili ecc*) grindstone
molare¹ [mo'lare] /72/ AGG, SM (*dente*) molar

molare[2] [mo'lare] /72/ VT to grind, polish

molare[3] [mo'lare] /72/ AGG (Chim, Fis) molar

mole ['mɔle] SF (gen) massive shape; (dimensioni) size; (Chim) mole; **una mole di lavoro** masses (Brit fam) o loads of work; **una mole di lavoro arretrato** a massive backlog of work
❏ **mole** non si traduce mai con la parola inglese mole

molecola [mo'lɛkola] SF molecule

molestare [moles'tare] /72/ VT (infastidire) to annoy, bother; (sessualmente) to harass; **non molestare quel povero cane** don't torment that poor dog

molestia [mo'lɛstja] SF (noia, fastidio) annoyance, bother; **molestie** SFPL trouble sg, bother sg; **molestie sessuali** sexual harassment sg

molesto, -a [mo'lɛsto] AGG annoying

molisano, -a [moli'zano] AGG o from Molise ♦ SM, SF inhabitant o native of Molise

molla ['mɔlla] SF 1 (Tecn) spring; (fig: incentivo) motivating force; **molla elicoidale** helical spring, coil spring; **molla di orologio** watch spring; **materasso a molle** spring mattress; **a molla** (giocattolo) clockwork; **i soldi sono la molla che lo spinge ad agire** money is the driving force as far as he's concerned 2 (per camino): **molle** SFPL tongs; **prendere qn con le molle** to treat sb with kid gloves

mollare [mol'lare] /72/ VT (gen) to let go; (far cadere) to drop; **mollare la presa** to let go; **mollare gli ormeggi** (Naut) to cast off; **mollare un pugno a qn** (fig: fam) to punch sb; **mollare uno schiaffo a qn** (fig: fam) to slap sb, give sb a slap; **ha mollato il lavoro** she's chucked her job; **ha mollato il suo ragazzo** she's ditched o dumped her boyfriend; **ha mollato il pacco qua e se n'è andato** he dumped the parcel here and left; **mi ha mollato i soldi per il cine** he let me have the money to go to the cinema ♦ VI (aus avere) (cedere, arrendersi) to give in o up; (fig: fam: smettere) stop; **non mollare proprio adesso!** don't give up now!

molle ['mɔlle] AGG 1 (gen) soft; (muscoli) flabby 2 (fig: debole) weak, feeble

molleggiato, -a [molled'dʒato] AGG (letto) sprung; (auto) with good suspension; (passo, camminata) springy

molleggio, -gi [mol'leddʒo] SM 1 (per veicoli) suspension; (per letti) springs pl 2 (elasticità) springiness 3 (Ginnastica) knee-bends pl

molletta [mol'letta] SF (per capelli) hairgrip, hairclip; (per panni) clothes peg (Brit) o pin (USA); **mollette** SFPL (per zucchero, ghiaccio) tongs

mollezza [mol'lettsa] SF 1 (fig: di carattere) weakness, feebleness 2 **mollezze** SFPL (agi, comodità) luxury sg; **vivere nelle mollezze** to live in the lap of luxury

mollica, -che [mol'lika] SF soft part of loaf; **molliche** SFPL (briciole) crumbs

molliccio, -cia, -ci, -ce [mol'littʃo] AGG 1 (terreno, impasto) soggy; (frutta) soft 2 (floscio: mano) limp; (: muscolo) flabby

mollusco, -schi [mol'lusko] SM (Zool) mollusc

molo ['mɔlo] SM jetty, pier; **attraccare al molo** to dock

molteplice [mol'teplitʃe] AGG (formato di più elementi) complex; **molteplici** (svariati: interessi, attività ecc) numerous, various

molteplicità [molteplitʃi'ta] SF multiplicity; **una molteplicità di interessi** a wide range of interests

moltiplicare [moltipli'kare] /20/ VT (anche fig) to multiply; **moltiplicare 5 per 3** to multiply 5 by 3; **moltiplicarsi** VIP (gen) to multiply; (spese, richieste) to increase

moltiplicazione [moltiplikat'tsjone] SF multiplication

moltitudine [molti'tudine] SF 1 **una moltitudine di** a vast number o a multitude of 2 (letter: folla) multitude

---

PAROLA CHIAVE

molto, -a ['molto] AVV

1 a lot, (very) much, a great deal; **non legge molto** he doesn't read much o a great deal; **ha viaggiato molto** he has travelled a lot o a great deal; **ti è piaciuto?** — **sì, molto** did you like it? — yes, very much; **questo libro è molto meglio dell'altro** this book is a lot o much better than the other one; **ci vorranno a dir molto 3 giorni** it will take 3 days at the most

2 (con aggettivi, avverbi) very; (con participio passato) (very) much; **l'ha fatto molto bene** he did it very well; **molto lodato** highly o (very) much praised; **sono molto stanco** I'm very tired

3 (distanza, tempo): **c'è ancora molto da camminare** there's still a long way to go; **ci vuole molto?** (tempo) will it take long?; **non la vedo da molto** I haven't seen her for quite a while o for a long time; **ne hai ancora per molto?** will you be much longer?; **arriverà fra non molto** he'll arrive soon

♦ AGG (quantità) a great deal of, a lot of, lots of, much (in domande e con negazioni); (numero) a lot of, lots of, many (in domande e con negazioni); **molta gente** a lot of people, many people; **molti libri** a lot of books, many books; **c'è molta neve** there's a great deal of o a lot of snow; **non c'è molta pane** there isn't a lot of bread, there isn't (very) much bread; **non ho molto tempo** I don't have o haven't got much time; **non c'erano molti turisti** there weren't many tourists

♦ PRON much, a lot; **molti, molte** many, a lot; **c'è pane?** — **sì, molto** is there any bread? — yes plenty o lots (fam); **molti pensano che sia giusto** many (people) think it's right; **molti di noi** many of o a lot of us

momentaneamente [momentanea'mente] AVV at the moment, at present; **è momentaneamente assente** she's not here at the moment

momentaneo, -a [momen'taneo] AGG (gioia, dolore) momentary; (assenza, scarsità) temporary

momento [mo'mento] SM 1 (gen) moment; **in questo momento** at the moment, at present; **in questo momento è al telefono** he's on the phone at the moment; **la situazione non è rosea in questo momento** o **al momento** things don't look too rosy at the moment o at present; **da un momento all'altro** any moment now, at any moment; (all'improvviso) suddenly; **può arrivare da un momento all'altro** he'll be here any moment now; **il tempo è cambiato da un momento all'altro** the weather changed suddenly; **per il momento** for the time being; **sul momento** there and then; **fino a questo momento** up till now, until now; **in qualunque momento** at any time; **un momento prego!** just a moment, please!; **proprio in quel momento** at that very moment, just at that moment; **non sta fermo un momento** he can't keep still; **posso parlarti un momento?** could I have a word with you?; **dal momento che** given that, since 2 (contingenza) time; (occasione) opportunity; **sono momenti difficili, è un momento difficile** it's a difficult time o moment; **aspettare il momento favorevole** to wait for the right moment; **è successo al momento sbagliato** it came at the wrong time; **momento culminante** climax; **abbiamo passato momenti bellissimi insieme** we had some great times together; **verremo in un altro momento** we'll come another time; **è l'uomo del momento** he's the man of the moment; **non è il momento di scherzare** this is no time to joke; **al momento di pagare...** when it came to paying ...; **al momento di partire mi sono accorto che...** just as I was leaving, I realised ... 3 **a momenti** (da un momento all'altro) any time o moment now; (quasi) nearly; **arriverà a momenti** he should arrive any time now; **a momenti cadevo** I nearly fell 4 (Fis) moment

monaca, -che ['mɔnaka] SF (Rel) nun; **farsi monaca** to become a nun

Monaco ['mɔnako] SF: (Principato di) Monaco Monaco; **Monaco (di Baviera)** Munich

monaco, -ci ['mɔnako] SM monk

monarca, -chi [mo'narka] SM monarch

monarchia [monar'kia] SF monarchy

monarchico, -a, -ci, -che [mo'narkiko] AGG (stato, autorità) monarchic; (partito, fede) monarchist attr ♦ SM, SF monarchist

monastero [monas'tero] SM (di monaci) monastery; (di monache) convent

monastico, -a, -ci, -che [mo'nastiko] AGG monastic

monco, -a, -chi, -che ['monko] AGG maimed, mutilated; (fig) incomplete; **monco di un braccio** one-armed ♦ SM, SF maimed o mutilated person

moncone [mon'kone] SM stump

mondana [mon'dana] SF (euf) prostitute

mondanità [mondani'ta] SF INV 1 (frivolezza) worldliness 2 **le mondanità** SFPL (piaceri) worldly pleasures

mondano, -a [mon'dano] AGG (*Rel: terrestre*) worldly, earthly; (*riunione, cronaca, vita*) society *attr*; (*obblighi*) social

mondare [mon'dare] /72/ VT (*piselli*) to shell; (*frutta, patate*) to peel; (*grano*) to winnow; (*fig: anima*) to cleanse

mondezzaio, -ai [mondet'tsajo] SM rubbish (*Brit*) *o* garbage (*USA*) dump; (*fig*) tip (*Brit*)

mondiale [mon'djale] AGG (*gen*) world *attr*; (*crisi, successo*) world-wide; **di fama mondiale** world famous; **la prima guerra mondiale** the First World War; **su scala mondiale** on a world-wide scale ♦ SM world championship; **i mondiali di calcio** the World Cup

mondo ['mondo] SM 1 (*gen, anche fig*) world; **in tutto il mondo** all over the world, throughout the world; **il migliore del mondo** the best in the world; **nessuno al mondo** no-one in the world; **essere solo al mondo** to have no family; **il mondo dell'aldilà** the next life, the after life; **il gran** *o* **bel mondo** high society; **il mondo del teatro** the world of the theatre 2 (*fraseologia*): **ti faccio un mondo di auguri, ti auguro un mondo di bene** all the best!; **ti voglio un mondo di bene** I really love you!; **gli voglio tutto il bene di questo mondo ma...** I'm very fond of him but ...; **per niente al mondo, per nessuna cosa al mondo** not for all the world; **da che mondo è mondo** since time *o* the world began; **(sono) cose dell'altro mondo!** it's incredible!; **non è poi la fine del mondo se non vengo** it won't be the end of the world if I can't make it; **una moto che è la fine del mondo** one hell of a motorbike; **mettere/venire al mondo** to bring/come into the world; **com'è piccolo il mondo!** it's a small world!; **è un uomo di mondo** he's a man of the world; **così va il mondo** that's life; **vivere fuori dal mondo** to be out of touch with the real world; **ma in che mondo vivi?** what planet are you living on?; **vive in un mondo tutto suo** he lives in a world of his own; **mandare qn all'altro mondo** to kill sb; **il mondo è bello perché è vario** (*Proverbio*) variety is the spice of life; (*fam*) **mondo cane!** bloody hell!

monegasco, -a, -schi, -sche [mone'gasko] AGG Monegasque ♦ SM, SF native *o* inhabitant of Monaco

monelleria [monelle'ria] SF prank, naughty trick; **fare una monelleria** to play a trick *o* prank

monello, -a [mo'nello] SM, SF (*ragazzo di strada*) (street) urchin; (*ragazzo vivace*) rascal, scamp

moneta [mo'neta] SF 1 (*pezzo*) coin; **una moneta da due euro** a two euro coin; **ripagare qn della stessa moneta** (*fig*) to pay sb back in his own coin 2 (*denaro*) money; (*spiccioli*) (small) change; **non ho moneta** I haven't (got) any change; **moneta cartacea** paper money 3 (*valuta*) currency; **la sterlina è una moneta forte** the pound is a strong currency; **moneta corrente** currency; **moneta debole/forte** weak/ strong currency; **moneta estera** foreign currency; **moneta legale** legal tender; **moneta unica (europea)** single (European) currency

monetario, -ria, -ri, -rie [mone'tarjo] AGG monetary

mongolfiera [mongol'fjera] SF hot-air balloon

Mongolia [mon'golja] SF Mongolia

mongolico, -a, -ci, -che [mon'goliko] AGG Mongolian

mongolo, -a ['mongolo] AGG, SM, SF Mongolian, Mongol ♦ SM (*lingua*) Mongolian, Mongol

monito ['monito] SM warning; **che ti serva di monito!** let this be a lesson to you!

monitor ['monitor] SM INV monitor

monitoraggio, -gi [monito'raddʒo] SM monitoring

monitorare [monito'rare] /72/ VT to monitor

monocolo [mo'nokolo] SM monocle, eyeglass

monocolore [monoko'lore] SM (*Pol: anche:* **governo monocolore**) one-party government

monogamia [monoga'mia] SF monogamy

monogamo, -a [mo'nogamo] AGG monogamous ♦ SM, SF monogamist

monografia [monogra'fia] SF monograph

monogramma, -i [mono'gramma] SM monogram

monolingue [mono'lingwe] AGG monolingual ♦ SM (*dizionario*) monolingual dictionary

monolocale [monolo'kale] SM studio apartment

monologo, -ghi [mo'nologo] SM monologue; **il monologo di**

Amleto Hamlet's soliloquy; **monologo interiore** (*Letteratura*) interior monologue

monopattino [mono'pattino] SM scooter

monopolio, -li [mono'poljo] SM (*Econ, anche fig*) monopoly; **monopolio di stato** state monopoly

monopolizzare [monopolid'dzare] /72/ VT (*Comm, anche fig*) to monopolize

monosillabo, -a [mono'sillabo] AGG monosyllabic ♦ SM monosyllable; **rispondere a monosillabi** (*fig*) to answer in monosyllables

monotonia [monoto'nia] SF monotony, dullness

monotono, -a [mo'notono] AGG (*gen*) monotonous; (*vita*) humdrum; (*lavoro*) dull, monotonous

monouso [mono'uzo] AGG INV (*siringa*) disposable

monovolume [monovo'lume] AGG INV, SF INV: (**automobile**) **monovolume** people carrier, people mover

Mons. ABBR (= *Monsignore*) Mgr

monsignore [monsiɲ'ɲore] SM 1 (*titolo ecclesiastico*) monsignor 2 (*titolo: parlando a arcivescovo, vescovo*) Your Grace; (: *parlando di terzi*) His Grace

monsone [mon'sone] SM monsoon

montacarichi [monta'kariki] SM INV goods lift, service elevator (*USA*)

montaggio, -gi [mon'taddʒo] SM 1 (*di macchina, telaio, mobile*) assembly; **scatola/catena di montaggio** assembly kit/ line 2 (*Cine*) editing

montagna [mon'taɲɲa] SF 1 (*monte*) mountain; **una montagna di** (*fig: gran quantità*) a mountain *o* pile *o* heap of; **il Ben Nevis è la montagna più alta della Scozia** Ben Nevis is the highest mountain in Scotland; **montagne russe** (*giostra*) roller coaster *sg*, big dipper *sg* (*Brit*) 2 (*zona, regione*): **la montagna** the mountains *pl*; **andare in montagna** to go to the mountains; **andremo in vacanza in montagna** we're going to the mountains for our holiday; **casa di montagna** house in the mountains; **aria/strada di montagna** mountain air/road; **un paesino di montagna** a mountain village; **mi piace la montagna** I like the mountains; **ha una casa in montagna** he's got a house in the mountains

montagnoso, -a [montaɲ'ɲoso] AGG mountainous

montanaro, -a [monta'naro] AGG mountain *attr* ♦ SM, SF (*persona*) mountain dweller

montano, -a [mon'tano] AGG mountain *attr*

montante [mon'tante] SM 1 (*di porta*) jamb; (*di finestra*) upright; (*Calcio: palo*) post 2 (*Pugilato*) upper cut 3 (*Comm*) total amount

montare [mon'tare] /72/ VI (*aus essere*) 1 (*salire*) to go (*o* come) up; **montare in bicicletta/macchina/in treno** to get on a bicycle/into a car/on a train; **montare su una scala** to climb a ladder; **montare in cima a** to climb to the top of; **montare su tutte le furie** (*fig*) to lose one's temper 2 (*cavalcare*): **montare bene/male** to ride well/badly; **montare a cavallo** to mount *o* get on a horse 3 (*aumentare: vento, marea*) to rise ♦ VT 1 (*salire*) to go (*o* come) up; **montare le scale** to go upstairs, climb the stairs 2 (*cavallo*) to ride 3 (*Zool*) to cover 4 **montare la guardia** (*Mil*) to mount guard 5 (*costruire: macchina, mobile ecc*) to assemble; (*tenda*) to pitch; (*film*) to edit; (*gioielli*) to set; (*fotografia*) to mount; (*Aut: gomma*) to put on; **ha montato l'armadio da solo** he assembled the wardrobe himself; **montarono la tenda vicino al lago** they pitched their tent near the lake 6 (*fig: esagerare: notizia*) to blow up, exaggerate 7 (*fig*): **montare la testa a qn** to turn sb's head; **montarsi la testa** to get *o* become big-headed; **si è montato la testa** he's got big-headed 8 (*Culin: panna*) to whip; (: *albume*) to whisk; **montare a neve** to whisk until stiff; **montate a neve gli albumi** whisk the egg whites until stiff; **montarsi** VIP (*insuperbirsi*) to become big-headed

montatura [monta'tura] SF (*di gioiello*) setting; (*di occhiali*) frames *pl*; (*fig: esagerazione*) exaggeration; **una montatura pubblicitaria** (*fig*) a publicity stunt

montavivande [montavi'vande] SM INV dumbwaiter

monte ['monte] SM 1 mountain; **qual è il monte più alto d'Europa?** which is the highest mountain in Europe?; **a monte (di)** (*fiume*) upstream (from); (*vallata*) at the head (of); **un monte di** (*gran quantità*) a mountain *o* pile *o* heap of; **il problema è a monte** (*fig*) the problem goes back to the early stages; **andare a monte** (*fig*) to come to nothing; **mandare a monte** (*fig: piano, progetto*) to put paid to, to put an end to; **fu quel fatto a mandare a monte il matrimonio** that's what caused the wedding to be called off; **il Monte Bianco** Mont Blanc; **il Monte Everest** Mount Everest; **il Monte degli Ulivi** the Mount of Olives **2 monte di pietà** pawnbroker's, pawnshop; **portare qc al monte di pietà** (*impegnare*) to pawn sth

Montecitorio [montetʃiˈtorjo] SM *building which houses the Italian Parliament*

montenegrino,-a [monteneˈgrino] SM, SF, AGG Montenegrin

Montenegro [monteˈnegro] SM Montenegro

montgomery [mɔntˈgʌmɛri] SM INV duffle *o* duffel coat

montone [monˈtone] SM **1** (*Zool*) ram; **carne di montone** mutton **2** (*anche:* **giacca di montone**) sheepskin (jacket)

montuosità [montuosiˈta] SF mountainous nature

montuoso,-a [montuˈoso] AGG mountainous

monumento [monuˈmento] SM monument; **visitare i monumenti** to go sightseeing; **un monumento ai caduti** a war memorial; **ti farei un monumento!** (*fig*) you deserve a medal!

moquette [mɔˈket] SF INV fitted carpet

mora¹ [ˈmɔra] SF (*Bot: di gelso*) mulberry; (: *di rovo*) blackberry

mora² [ˈmɔra] SF (*Dir*) **1** delay **2** (*somma dovuta*) arrears *pl*

morale [moˈrale] AGG (*gen*) moral ♦ SF **1** (*norme, consuetudini*) morals *pl*, morality; (*Filosofia*) moral philosophy, ethics *sg*; **non hanno morale** they haven't got any morals; **la morale corrente** current moral standards *pl* **2** (*insegnamento*) moral; **la morale della favola** the moral of the story; **così, morale della favola, siamo rimasti a casa** and the result was that we stayed at home ♦ SM (*stato d'animo*) morale; **essere giù di morale** to be feeling down; **sono giù di morale** I'm feeling down; **su col morale!** cheer up!; **aver il morale alto/a terra** to be in high/low spirits; **bisogna tener alto il morale delle truppe** we must keep the troops' morale high

moralista,-i,-e [moraˈlista] AGG moralistic ♦ SM, SF moralist

moralità [moraliˈta] SF **1** (*norme di vita, morale*) morality, morals *pl*, moral standards *pl*; **una persona di alta moralità** a person of high moral standards **2** (*di comportamento*) morality

moralizzare [moralidˈdzare] /72/ VT (*costumi, vita pubblica*) to set moral standards for ♦ VI (*aus* avere), **moralizzare (su)** to moralize (on, about)

moralizzazione [moraliddzatˈtsjone] SF setting of moral standards

moratoria [moraˈtɔrja] SF (*Dir*) moratorium

morbidezza [morbiˈdettsa] SF (*vedi agg*) softness; tenderness; smoothness

morbido,-a [ˈmɔrbido] AGG (*gen*) soft; (*carne*) tender; (*pelle*) soft, smooth; **pelle morbida** soft skin
❏ **morbido** non si traduce mai con la parola inglese *morbid*

morbillo [morˈbillo] SM measles *sg*; **Giorgio ha il morbillo** Giorgio has got measles

morbo [ˈmɔrbo] SM (*Med*) disease; (*epidemia*) epidemic

morboso,-a [morˈboso] AGG (*Med, anche fig*) morbid; **una gelosia morbosa** pathological jealousy

morchia [ˈmɔrkja] SF sludge, oily deposit

mordente [morˈdente] SM **1** (*Chim*) mordant **2** (*fig: di satira, critica, stile*) bite; (: *di persona*) drive

mordere [ˈmɔrdere] /64/ VT IRREG (*sogg: persona, cane, insetto*) to bite; (*addentare: mela, panino*) to bite into; **mordere la gamba a qn** to bite sb's leg, bite sb in the leg; **il cane mi ha morso la gamba** the dog bit my leg; **mordersi le labbra/la lingua** (*anche fig*) to bite one's lips/one's tongue; **mordere il freno** (*anche fig*) to champ at the bit; **mordere l'asfalto** (*Aut*) to grip the road; **mi sarei morso le mani** I could have kicked myself; **can che abbaia non morde** (*Proverbio*) his (*o* her *ecc*) bark is worse than his (*o* her *ecc*) bite

mordicchiare [mordikˈkjare] /19/ VT (*gen*) to chew at; **mordicchiarsi le labbra** to bite one's lips

morente [moˈrente] AGG dying ♦ SM, SF (*persona*) dying person; **i morenti** the dying

morfina [morˈfina] SF morphine

moria [moˈria] SF (*di bestiame*) disease; (*Bot*) blight

moribondo, -a [moriˈbondo] AGG (*persona*) dying ♦ SM, SF dying person

morigerato, -a [moridʒeˈrato] AGG (*persona, vita*) moderate, sober

morire [moˈrire] /65/ VI IRREG (*aus* essere) **1** (*gen*) to die; **morì nel 1857** he died in 1857; **morire di malattia** to die after an illness; **morire di morte violenta/naturale** to die a violent/ natural death; **morire di stenti** to die from hardship; **morire in guerra** to die in battle; **morire assassinato** to be murdered; **morire di dolore** to die of a broken heart; **morire di fame** to starve to death, die of hunger; (*fig*) to be starving, be famished; **morire di freddo** to freeze to death; (*fig*) to be frozen (stiff); **morire di sete** (*anche fig*) to die of thirst; **muoio di sete** I'm dying of thirst **2** (*fig*): **morire d'invidia** to be green with envy; **morire di noia** to be bored to death *o* to tears; **morire di paura** to be scared to death; **morire dalle risate** *o* **dal ridere** to kill o.s. laughing, die laughing; **morire di sonno** to be dead *o* dog tired; **morire dalla voglia di fare qc** to be dying to do sth; **moriva dalla voglia di raccontarle tutto** he was dying to tell her everything; **fa un caldo da morire** it's terribly hot; **ho un caldo da morire** I'm terribly hot; **mi fa male da morire questo braccio** my arm is killing me; **bella da morire** stunning; **chi non muore si rivede!** (*scherz*) fancy meeting you! (after all this time) **3** (*luce, giorno*) to fade, die; (*fiamma*) to die down; (*fuoco, tradizione, civiltà*) to die out; **il blu sul nero muore un po'** blue doesn't show up well on a black background

mormorare [mormoˈrare] /72/ VI (*aus* avere) **1** (*gen*) to murmur; (*sussurrare: persona, vento*) to murmur, whisper; (*brontolare*) to grumble, mutter; **si mormora che...** it's rumoured (*Brit*) *o* rumored (*USA*) that ... **2** (*parlare male*): **mormorare sul conto di qn** to speak ill of sb; **la gente mormora** people are talking ♦ VT (*parole d'amore ecc*) to whisper, murmur

mormorio,-rii [mormoˈrio] SM (*di persone, vento, acque*) murmur, murmuring; (*di foglie, fronde*) rustling

moro, -a [ˈmɔro] AGG **1** (*Storia*) Moorish **2** (*persona: dai capelli scuri*) dark, dark-haired; (: *di carnagione scura*) dark, dark-skinned ♦ SM, SF (*vedi agg*) Moor; dark-haired person; (*offensive*) dark-skinned person; **i Mori** (SMPL: *Storia*) the Moors

moroso, -a [moˈroso] AGG (*Dir*) defaulting, in arrears ♦ SM, SF (*fam: innamorato*) sweetheart
❏ **moroso** non si traduce mai con la parola inglese *morose*

morsa [ˈmɔrsa] SF (*Tecn*) vice (*Brit*), vise (*USA*); (*fig: stretta*) grip; **stretto in una morsa d'acciaio** (*fig*) held in an iron grip

morsetto [morˈsetto] SM (*Tecn*) clamp; (*Elettr*) terminal; **morsetto della batteria** (*Aut*) battery lead connection

morsicare [morsiˈkare] /20/ VT to bite

morso,-a [ˈmɔrso] PP *di* **mordere** ♦ SM **1** (*di insetto*) sting; **dare un morso a qn** to bite sb; **dare un morso a qc** to bite sth; (*mangiare un pezzetto*) to bite into sth; **diede un morso al panino** he bit into his roll; **mi dai un morso di panino?** can I have a bite of your sandwich?; **i morsi della fame** hunger pangs **2** (*parte della briglia*) bit

mortadella [mortaˈdella] SF (*Culin*) mortadella (*type of salted pork meat*)

mortaio,-ai [morˈtajo] SM mortar

mortale [morˈtale] AGG **1** (*vita, uomo*) mortal **2** (*veleno*) deadly; (*ferita, incidente*) fatal; **un colpo mortale** a deadly *o* fatal blow; **peccato mortale** (*Rel*) mortal sin ♦ SM, SF mortal

mortalità [mortaliˈta] SF **1** (*l'essere mortale*) mortality **2** (*Statistica*) mortality, death rate; **mortalità infantile** infant mortality

morte [ˈmorte] SF **1** (*gen*) death; (*fig: fine, rovina*) death, end; **morte clinica** brain death; **alla morte di sua madre** on the death of his mother; **in punto di morte** at death's door; **in punto di morte ha confessato** he confessed on his deathbed; **essere tra la vita e la morte** to be fighting for one's life; **ferito a morte** (*soldato*) mortally wounded; (*in incidente*) fatally injured; **condannare qn a morte** to sentence sb to death; **pena di/condanna a morte** death penalty/sentence **2** (*fraseologia*): **è questione di vita o di morte** it's a matter of life or death; **essere annoiato a morte** to be bored to death *o* to tears; **avercela a morte con qn** to hate sb like poison; **si odiano a morte** they can't stand the sight of each other; **avere la morte nel cuore** to have a heavy heart; **così facendo ha firmato la sua condanna a morte** by doing that he signed his own death warrant

mortificare [mortifi'kare] /20/ VT to mortify; **mortificarsi** VR (*Rel*) to mortify o.s.; **mortificarsi** VIP (*vergognarsi, spiacersi*) to feel mortified

morto, -a ['mɔrto] PP *di* **morire** ♦ AGG (*gen, o fig*) dead; **il loro fratello** dead their dead brother; **sono morto di freddo** I'm frozen stiff; **sono stanco morto** I'm dead tired, I'm knackered (*fam!*); **sono morto di paura** I'm scared to death; **l'inverno è una stagione morta per noi** winter is our slack season; **morto e sepolto** (*fig*) dead and buried ♦ SM, SF **1** dead person; **i morti** the dead; **il due novembre commemoriamo i morti** we remember the dead on November the second; **ci sono stati tre morti nella sparatoria** three people were killed in the shooting; **fare il morto** (*in acqua*) to float on one's back; **un morto di fame** (*fig: pegg*) a down-and-out; **sembri un morto che cammina** you look like death warmed up; **le campane suonavano a morto** the funeral bells were tolling; **giorno dei morti** All Souls' Day; **il regno dei morti** the world beyond the grave **2** (*Carte*) dummy

mortorio, -ri [mor'tɔrjo] SM (*fig: cerimonia, festa*): **quella festa è stata un mortorio** that party was more like a funeral *o* wake

mosaico, -ci [mo'zaiko] SM **1** (*Arte*) mosaic; **pavimento a mosaico** mosaic floor; **l'ultimo tassello del mosaico** (*fig*) the final piece of the puzzle **2** (*fig: di lingue, popoli*) mixture

Mosca ['moska] SF Moscow; **vado a Mosca** I'm going to Moscow; **abitano a Mosca** they live in Moscow

mosca ['moska] SF (*pl* **mosche**) **1** (*Zool, Pesca*) fly; **mosca della carne** bluebottle, blowfly; **mosca cavallina** horsefly; **mosca tse-tse** tsetse fly **2** (*fraseologia*): **non farebbe male a una mosca** he wouldn't hurt a fly; **morire come mosche** to die like flies; **non si sentiva volare una mosca** you could have heard a pin drop; **gli è saltata la mosca al naso** he lost his temper; **giocare a mosca cieca** to play blindman's buff; **essere una mosca bianca** to be like hen's teeth; **rimanere** *o* **restare con un pugno di mosche** (*fig*) to be left empty-handed **3** (*barba*) goatee ♦ AGG INV (*Pugilato*): **peso mosca** flyweight

moscato, -a [mos'kato] AGG (*uva*) muscat ♦ SM (*uva*) muscat grape; (*vino*) muscatel, muscat

moscerino [moʃʃe'rino] SM midge, gnat

moschea [mos'kɛa] SF mosque

moschetto [mos'ketto] SM musket

moschettone [mosket'tone] SM (*gancio*) spring clip; (*Alpinismo*) karabiner, snaplink; (*Naut*) snapshackle

moschicida, -i, -e [moski'tʃida] SM flykiller ♦ AGG: **carta moschicida** flypaper

moscio, -scia, -sci, -sce ['moʃʃo] AGG **1** (*cappello*) soft; (*fig: persona*) lifeless, dull **2 ha la 'r' moscia** he can't roll his 'r's

moscone [mos'kone] SM **1** (*insetto*) bluebottle **2** (*pattino*) pedalo; (*a remi*) pedalo with oars **3** (*corteggiatore*) suitor

moscovita, -i, -e [mosko'vita] AGG, SM, SF Muscovite

mossa ['mɔssa] SF **1** (*gen, movimento*) movement; **prendere le mosse da qc** to come about as the result of sth; **datti una mossa!** (*fig*) get a move on! **2** (*Scacchi, Dama, fig*) move; **fare una mossa sbagliata** (*anche fig*) to make a bad move; **ha fatto una mossa sbagliata** he made a bad move

mossi *ecc* ['mɔssi] VB *vedi* **muovere**

mosso, -a ['mɔsso] PP *di* **muovere** ♦ AGG **1** (*mare*) rough; (*capelli*) wavy; (*fotografia*) blurred; **oggi c'è mare mosso** the sea's rough today; **ha i capelli mossi** he's got wavy hair; **la fotografia è un po' mossa** the photo is a bit blurred **2** (*Mus*) mosso

mostarda [mos'tarda] SF (*Culin*) mustard; **mostarda di Cremona** pickled fruit with mustard

mosto ['mosto] SM must

mostra ['mostra] SF **1** (*di oggetti*) exhibition; (*di animali, fiori*) show; **fare una mostra** to put on an exhibition *o* a show; **il negozio ha messo in mostra gli ultimi arrivi** the shop has put its latest stock on display; **essere in mostra** to be on show; **mostra d'arte** art exhibition; **mostra canina** dog show **2** (*locale*) exhibition hall **3** (*fraseologia*): **far mostra di**

sé to show off; **fare mostra di fare qc** (*fingere*) to pretend to do sth; **mettersi in mostra** to draw attention to o.s.; **mettere qc in bella mostra** to show sth off

mostrare [mos'trare] /72/ VT: **mostrare (qc a qn)** to show (sb sth), show (sth to sb); **ho mostrato le foto a Paolo** I showed Paolo the photos; **le ho mostrato il mio vestito nuovo** I showed her my new dress; **mi mostri come si fa?** will you show me how to do it?; **ha mostrato un notevole coraggio** he displayed great courage; **mostrare i denti** (*anche fig*) to bare one's teeth; **mostrare la lingua** to stick out one's tongue; **mi ha mostrato la lingua** he stuck his tongue out at me; **mostrare i pugni a qn** to shake one's fist at sb; **ha mostrato di non conoscermi** he pretended not to know me; **mostrarsi** VR **1** (*dimostrarsi*) to appear; **si è mostrato felice** he appeared *o* looked happy **2** (*comparire*) to appear, show o.s.; **mostrarsi in pubblico** to appear in public

mostro ['mostro] SM (*anche fig*) monster; **sei un mostro di bravura!** you're a genius!; **i mostri sacri del cinema italiano** the giants of the Italian cinema

mostruoso, -a [mostru'oso] AGG (*anche fig*) monstrous; **un delitto mostruoso** a terrible crime; **ha una cultura mostruosa** she knows an awful lot

motel [mo'tɛl] SM INV motel

motivare [moti'vare] /72/ VT **1** (*giustificare*) to give reasons for **2** (*causare*) to cause **3** (*stimolare*) to motivate

motivazione [motivat'tsjone] SF (*ragione*) justification; (*stimolo*) motivation

motivo [mo'tivo] SM **1** (*causa, ragione*) reason, grounds *pl*, cause; **senza motivo** for no reason; **qual è il motivo del tuo ritardo?** what is the reason for your lateness?; **avere un motivo valido per fare qc** to have a valid reason for doing sth; **ho un motivo valido per andarmene** I've got a good reason for leaving; **per motivi di salute** for health reasons, on health grounds; **motivi personali** personal reasons; **si è dimesso per motivi personali** he resigned for personal reasons; **per quale motivo?** why?, for what reason?; **per questo motivo** for this reason, therefore; **mia madre sta male, motivo per cui non potrò venire** my mother is ill so I won't be able to come **2** (*Mus*) motif; (*di opera letteraria*) (central) theme; (*disegno*) design, pattern

moto¹ ['mɔto] SM **1** (*di mare, macchina, pianeti*) movement; (*Fis, Tecn*) motion; **quantità di moto** (*Fis*) momentum; **moto armonico semplice** (*Fis*) simple harmonic motion; **verbi di moto** verbs of motion; **mettere in moto qc** (*anche fig*) to set sth in motion; (*motore, macchina*) to start sth (up); **mettersi in moto** (*macchina*) to start; (*persona*) to set off **2** (*esercizio fisico*) exercise; **fare del moto** to take some exercise; **devi fare un po' di moto** you should take some exercise **3** (*gesto*) movement; **un moto d'impazienza** an impatient gesture **4** (*rivolta*) rising, revolt

moto² ['mɔto] SF INV (*fam*) (motor)bike; **vado a scuola in moto** I go to school on my motorbike; **moto d'acqua** personal watercraft

motocarro [moto'karro] SM three-wheeler van

motocicletta [mototʃi'kletta] SF motorcycle

motociclismo [mototʃi'klizmo] SM motorcycling, motorcycle racing

motociclista, -i, -e [mototʃi'klista] SM, SF motorcyclist

motonave [moto'nave] SF motor vessel

motopeschereccio, -ci [motopeske'rettʃo] SM trawler

motore, -trice [mo'tore] AGG **1** (*Anat: organo*) motor *attr* **2** (*Tecn*) driving; **albero motore** drive shaft; **forza motrice** driving force ♦ SM **1** (*Tecn*) engine, motor; (*di macchina, treno, nave*) engine; **a motore** power-driven, motor *attr*; **una barca a motore** a motor boat; **spegni il motore** switch off the engine; **motore a 2/4 tempi** 2-/4-stroke engine; **motore diesel** diesel engine; **motore a iniezione** fuel-injection engine; **motore a reazione** jet engine; **motore a scoppio** internal combustion engine; **motore turbo** turbo(-charged) engine **2** (*Filosofia*) mover; **il primo motore** the Prime Mover **3 motore di ricerca** (*Inform*) search engine

motorino [moto'rino] SM **1** (*Aut*): **motorino d'avviamento** starter(-motor) **2** (*fam: ciclomotore*) moped; **vado a scuola in motorino** I go to school on my moped

motorizzato, -a [motorid'dzato] AGG: **reparto motorizzato**

(*Mil*) motorized division; **sei motorizzato?** have you got transport?

motorizzazione [motoriddzat'tsjone] SF (*ufficio tecnico e organizzativo*): **(ufficio della) motorizzazione** road traffic office

motoscafo [motos'kafo] SM motorboat

motovedetta [motove'detta] SF (*motor*) patrol vessel

motrice [mo'tritʃe] SF (*Tecn*) engine, motor

motteggio, -gi [mot'teddʒo] SM (*letter*) banter

motto ['mɔtto] SM (*detto arguto*) witty remark; (*massima*) motto, maxim; **il mio motto è...** my motto is ...

mountain bike ['mauntin 'baik] SF INV mountain bike

mouse SM INV mouse *inv*; **mouse incorporato** touchpad

movente [mo'vɛnte] SM (*Dir*) motive; **avevano un movente per ucciderlo** they had a motive for killing him

movenza [mo'ventsa] SF movement; **sciolto nelle movenze** graceful in one's movements

movimentare [movimen'tare] /72/ VT to liven up

movimentato, -a [movimen'tato] AGG (*festa, partita*) lively; (*riunione*) animated; (*strada, vita*) busy; (*soggiorno*) eventful

movimento [movi'mento] SM (*gen, anche Pol, Letteratura*) movement; (*Mus: grado di velocità*) tempo; (: *parte*) movement; (*fig: animazione*) activity, hustle and bustle; **un movimento politico** a political movement; **un movimento brusco** a sudden movement; **un movimento di rotazione/rivoluzione** a rotation/revolution; **essere sempre in movimento** to be always on the go; **è vietato salire sul treno in movimento** do not get on the train while it is in motion; **fare un movimento falso** to make an awkward movement; **fece un movimento all'indietro** he stepped back; **fare un po' di movimento** (*esercizio fisico*) to take some exercise; **c'è molto movimento in città** the town is very busy ♦ **movimento di capitali** movement of capital; **movimento di conto** (*Banca*) (bank) account transaction; **movimento passeggeri e merci** passenger and freight traffic; **movimento di truppe** troop movement

moviola [mo'vjɔla] SF moviola; **rivedere qc alla moviola** to see an action (*Brit*) *o* instant (*USA*) replay of sth

Mozambico [mottsam'biko] SM Mozambique

mozione [mot'tsjone] SF (*Pol*) motion; **mozione d'ordine** point of order

mozzafiato [mottsa'fjato] AGG INV breathtaking

mozzare [mot'tsare] /72/ VT (*testa*) to cut off; (*coda*) to dock; **mozzare il fiato** *o* **il respiro a qn** (*fig*) to take sb's breath away

mozzarella [mottsa'rella] SF mozzarella

mozzicone [mottsi'kone] SM (*di sigaretta*) stub, end, butt; (*di candela*) end; (*di matita*) stub

mozzo¹, -a ['mottso] AGG (*testa*) cut off; (*coda*) docked

mozzo² ['mottso] SM 1 (*Naut*) ship's boy 2 **mozzo di stalla** stable boy

mq ABBR (= *metro quadro*) sq.m.

MS SIGLA = Massa Carrara

mucca, -che ['mukka] SF cow; (*morbo della*) **mucca pazza** mad cow disease, BSE; **l'emergenza mucca pazza** the mad cow crisis

mucchio, -chi ['mukkjo] SM (*gen*) heap, pile; **a mucchi** in piles; **un mucchio di** (*molto*) heaps *pl* of, lots *pl* of, piles *pl* of; **un mucchio di sassi** a heap of stones; **ho un mucchio di cose da fare** I've got loads of things to do; **ha detto un mucchio di sciocchezze** he talked a load of rubbish

mucillagine [mutʃil'ladʒine] SF (*Bot*) mucilage (*termine tecn*), green slime *produced by plants growing in water*

muco ['muko] SM (*Med*) mucus

mucosa [mu'kosa] SF (*Anat*) mucous membrane

muffa ['muffa] SF (*biancastra*) mildew; (*verdognola*) mould (*Brit*), mold (*USA*); **fare la muffa** to go mouldy (*Brit*) *o* moldy (*USA*); **non ho intenzione di restare a casa a fare la muffa** (*fig*) I'm not going to moulder (*Brit*) *o* molder (*USA*) away at home; **avere odore di muffa** to smell mouldy

mugghiare [mug'gjare] /19/ VI (*aus avere*) (*letter, fig: mare, tuono*) to roar; (: *vento*) to howl

muggire [mud'dʒire] /55/ VI (*aus avere*) (*bovini*) to low; (*vacca*) to moo, low; (*toro*) to bellow; (*fig*) to roar

muggito [mud'dʒito] SM (*vedi vb*) lowing; mooing; bellow; roar; **i muggiti del bestiame** the lowing of the cattle

mughetto [mu'getto] SM 1 (*Bot*) lily of the valley 2 (*Med*) thrush

mugnaio, -aia, -ai, -aie [muɲ'ɲajo] SM, SF miller

mugolare [mugo'lare] /72/ VI (*aus avere*) (*cane*) to whimper, whine; **mugolare (di)** (*fig: persona*) to moan (in *o* with) ♦ VT (*borbottare*) to mutter

mugugnare [muguɲ'ɲare] /15/ VI (*aus avere*) (*fam*) to mutter, mumble

mulattiera [mulat'tjɛra] SF mule track

mulinare [muli'nare] /72/ VI (*aus avere*) to whirl, spin (round and round)

mulinello [muli'nɛllo] SM 1 (*di vento, acqua*) eddy 2 (*di canna da pesca*) reel 3 (*Naut*) windlass

mulino [mu'lino] SM mill; **lottare** *o* **combattere contro i mulini a vento** (*fig*) to tilt at windmills; **mulino ad acqua** water mill; **mulino a vento** windmill

mulo ['mulo] SM mule; **testardo** *o* **ostinato** *o* **cocciuto come un mulo** as stubborn as a mule

multa ['multa] SF fine; **fare** *o* **dare una multa a qn** to fine sb; **il controllore le ha dato la multa** the inspector fined her; **ho preso una multa di 100 euro** I was fined 100 euros, I got a 100 euro fine; **ho preso una multa per divieto di sosta** I got a parking ticket

multare [mul'tare] /72/ VT to fine

multicolore [multiko'lore] AGG multicoloured (*Brit*), multicolored (*USA*)

multietnico, -a, -ci, -che [multi'ɛtniko] AGG multiethnic

multiforme [multi'forme] AGG (*interessi*) varied; (*ingegno*) versatile

multimediale [multime'djale] AGG multimedia *attr*

multinazionale [multinattsjo'nale] AGG, SF multinational; **forza multinazionale di pace** multinational peace-keeping force

multiplo, -a ['multiplo] AGG multiple ♦ SM (*Mat*): **multiplo (di)** multiple (of); **minimo comune multiplo** lowest common multiple

multirazziale [multirat'tsjale] AGG multiracial

multisala [multi'sala] AGG INV (*cinema*) multi-screen *attr*

multiutenza [multiu'tentsa] SF (*Inform*) time sharing

multivitaminico, -a, -ci, -che [multivita'miniko] AGG: **complesso multivitaminico** multivitamin

mummia ['mummja] SF mummy; (*fig: persona*) old fogey

mungere ['mundʒere] /5/ VT IRREG (*anche fig*) to milk

mungitura [mundʒi'tura] SF milking

municipale [munitʃi'pale] AGG (*gen*) municipal; **palazzo municipale** town hall; **autorità municipali** local authority *sg* (*Brit*), local government *sg*

municipio, -pi [muni'tʃipjo] SM (*comune*) town council; (*palazzo*) town hall; **sposarsi in municipio** ≈ to get married in a registry office (*Brit*)

munificenza [munifi'tʃentsa] SF munificence, generosity

munifico, -a, -ci, -che [mu'nifiko] AGG magnificent, generous

munire [mu'nire] /55/ VT: **munire di** (*fortificare: città*) to fortify with; (*equipaggiare: persona, stanza ecc*) to equip with; **munire una nave di uomini** to man a ship; **munire di firma** (*documento*) to sign; **munirsi di: munirsi di** (*gen, denaro, documenti*) to provide o.s. with; (*armi*) to arm o.s. with; **munirsi di coraggio/pazienza** to arm o.s. with courage/patience

munizioni [munit'tsjoni] SFPL ammunition *sg*

munsi *ecc* ['munsi] VB *vedi* **mungere**

munto, -a ['munto] PP *di* **mungere**

muoio *ecc* ['mwɔjo] VB *vedi* **morire**

muovere ['mwɔvere] VB IRREG /66/ VT 1 (*gen*) to move; (*macchina, ruota*) to drive; **non riesco a muovere la gamba** I can't move my leg; **il cane muoveva festosamente la coda** the dog was joyfully wagging its tail; **muovere i primi passi** to take one's first steps; (*fig*) to be starting out; **mosse un passo verso di me** he took a step towards me; **non muove un passo senza interpellare la moglie** (*fig*) he never does anything without asking his wife; **non ha mosso un dito per aiutarmi** he didn't lift a finger to help me; **muovere mari e monti** to move heaven and earth 2 (*fig: sollevare*): **muovere un'accusa a** *o* **contro qn** to make an accusation against sb; **muovere causa a qn** (*Dir*) to take legal action against sb; **muovere guerra a** *o* **contro qn** to wage war

against sb; **muovere un'obiezione** to raise an objection **3**
(*commuovere*): **muovere a compassione** to move to pity;
muovere al pianto to move to tears **4** (*Scacchi*) to move;
tocca a te muovere it's your move ♦ vi (*aus avere o essere*)
1 (*gen*) to move; **muovere verso, muovere in direzione di**
to move towards **2** (*derivare*): **muovere da** to derive from;
le sue osservazioni muovono da una premessa errata his
comments are based on a mistaken *o* wrong assumption;
muoversi vr **1** to move; **non si muove** it won't move; **muoversi in aiuto di qn** to go to sb's aid; **non si muove dalle
sue posizioni** (*fig*) he won't budge **2** (*sbrigarsi*) to hurry up,
get a move on; **muoviti!** hurry up!; **muoviti, o perdiamo il
treno!** hurry up, or we'll miss the train!; **muoviti, cammina!**
hurry up and get moving!; **muoversi** vip **1** (*commuoversi*):
muoversi a compassione *o* **pietà** to be moved to pity **2** (*essere in movimento*) to move; **finalmente qualcosa si è mosso**
(*fig*) at last things are moving

mura ['mura] sfpl *di muro*; **le mura della città** the city walls

muraglia [mu'raʎʎa] sf (high) wall; **la grande muraglia cinese** the Great Wall of China

murale [mu'rale] agg wall *attr*; (*Arte*) mural *attr*; **carta murale** wall map; **pittura murale** mural ♦ sm (*Arte*) mural

murare [mu'rare] /72/ vt (*porta, finestra*) to wall up; (*mensola*)
to embed into a wall; **murare qn vivo** to wall sb up; **murarsi** vr: **murarsi in casa** (*fig: rinchiudersi*) to shut o.s. away
at home

murario, -ria, -ri, -rie [mu'rarjo] agg (*tecnica*) building *attr*;
arte muraria masonry; **opera muraria** piece of masonry
work

muratore [mura'tore] sm (*che costruisce con pietre*) mason;
(*che costruisce con mattoni*) bricklayer

muratura [mura'tura] sf **1** (*atto del murare*) walling (up) **2**
(*lavoro murario: con pietra*) masonry; (*: con mattoni*) brick-
laying; **casa in muratura** (*di pietra*) stonebuilt house; (*di
mattoni*) brick house

muro ['muro] sm (*anche fig*) wall; **un muro alto** a high wall;
armadio a muro built-in cupboard; **il muro di Berlino** the
Berlin Wall; **alzare un muro** to build a wall; **attaccare qc
al muro** to hang sth on the wall; **chiudere qc con un muro**
(*campo, giardino*) to build a wall around sth; **mettere al
muro** (*fucilare*) to shoot *o* execute (by firing squad); **è come
parlare al muro** it's like talking to a brick wall; **tra noi c'è
un muro** (*fig*) there's a barrier between us; **un muro d'incomprensione** a total lack of understanding; **mura** sfpl (*di
città, castello*) walls; **chiudersi fra quattro mura** (*fig*) to shut
o.s. up at home ♦ **muro di cinta** surrounding wall; **muro
divisorio** dividing wall; **muro di gomma** (*fig: indifferenza*)
the wall of indifference; **muro maestro** main *o* supporting
wall; **muro di mattoni** brick wall; **muro a secco** dry-stone
wall; **muro del suono** (*Fis*) sound barrier

musa ['muza] sf (*Mitol*) Muse; (*fig*) muse, inspiration

muschio¹, -chi ['muskjo] sm (*profumo*) musk

muschio², -chi ['muskjo] sm (*Bot*) moss

muscolare [musko'lare] agg (*Anat: tessuto, fascio*) muscular,
muscle *attr*; **strappo muscolare** torn muscle

muscolatura [muskola'tura] sf musculature; **muscolatura
atletica** athletic build

muscolo ['muskolo] sm **1** (*Anat*) muscle; **scaldare i muscoli**
to warm up; **è tutto muscoli e niente cervello** (*fig*) he's all
brawn and no brains; **muscolo involontario** involuntary
muscle; **muscolo volontario** voluntary muscle **2** (*Culin*)
lean meat **3** (*Zool*) mussel

muscoloso, -a [musko'loso] agg muscular

museo [mu'zɛo] sm museum; **un pezzo da museo** (*fig*) a museum piece

museruola [muze'rwɔla] sf (*per cani*) muzzle; **mettere la
museruola a un cane** to muzzle a dog; **mettere la museruola a qn** (*fig*) to muzzle sb, shut sb up; **i cani devono
avere la museruola** dogs have to be muzzled

musica ['muzika] sf (*gen, anche fig*) music; **musica di sottofondo** background music; **un pezzo** *o* **brano di musica** a
piece of music; **mi piace la musica classica** I like classical
music; **mettere in musica** to set to music; **è sempre la stessa musica** (*fig*) it's always the same old story; **è ora di cambiare musica** (*fig*) it's time you changed your tune; **musica**

classica classical music; **musica da ballo** dance music; **musica da camera** chamber music; **musica disco** (o) **da discoteca** disco music; **musica leggera** light music; **musica pop**
pop music; **musica popolare** folk music

musicale [muzi'kale] agg musical; **avere orecchio musicale**
to have an ear for music

musicassetta [muzikas'setta] sf (pre-recorded) cassette

musicista, -i, -e [muzi'tʃista] sm, sf musician; **fa il musicista**
he's a musician; **uno dei musicisti dell'orchestra** one of the
players in the orchestra

musicomane [muzi'kɔmane] sm, sf music lover

muso ['muzo] sm (*di animale*) muzzle; (*fig: di persona*) face;
(*: pegg*) mug; (*: di aereo*) nose; (*: di auto, moto*) front (end);
rompere il muso a qn to smash sb's face in; **gli diede un
pugno sul muso** he punched him in the face; **mettere** *o*
fare il muso to sulk *o* pout; **tenere il muso** to sulk; **tenere il muso a qn** to be in a huff with sb; **ha storto il muso
quando gliene ho parlato** he didn't look at all pleased
when I mentioned it; **gliel'ho detto sul muso** I told him
so to his face

musone, -a [mu'zone] sm, sf sulky person

mussola ['mussola] sf muslin

musulmano, -a [musul'mano], **mussulmano, -a** [mus-
sul'mano] agg, sm, sf Muslim

muta [mu'ta] sf **1** (*di animali*) moulting (*Brit*), molting
(*USA*) **2** (*di serpenti*) sloughing **3** (*per immersioni subacquee*)
diving suit **4** (*gruppo di cani*) pack

mutabile [mu'tabile] agg changeable

mutamento [muta'mento] sm change

mutande [mu'tande] sfpl (*da uomo*) underpants, pants; (*da
donna*) panties

mutandine [mutan'dine] sfpl pants; **mutandine da bagno**
swimming trunks

mutare [mu'tare] /72/ vt **1** (*gen*) to change; (*opinione, carattere*) to change, alter; **mutare qc in** to change sth into
2 (*Zool: sogg: rettili*) to slough; (*: animali*): **mutare il pelo**
to moult ♦ vi (*aus essere*) to change; **mutare di colore**
to change colour; **qualcosa è mutato in lui** there's something different about him; **mutare in meglio/in peggio** to
change for the better/for the worse; **mutarsi** vip: **mutarsi in**
to change into, turn into; **il ghiaccio si mutò in acqua** the
ice turned to water; **mutarsi d'abito** to change one's clothes

mutazione [mutat'tsjone] sf change, alteration; (*Bio*) muta-
tion

mutevole [mu'tevole] agg changeable; **umore mutevole**
moodiness

mutilare [muti'lare] /72/ vt (*gen, anche fig*) to mutilate; (*persona*) to maim; (*statua*) to deface; **la fresatrice gli ha mutilato la mano** the milling machine chopped off his hand

mutilato, -a [muti'lato] agg (*vedi vb*) mutilated; maimed; defaced ♦ sm, sf disabled person (*through loss of limbs*); **mutilato di guerra** disabled ex-serviceman (*Brit*) *o* war veteran
(*USA*)

mutilazione [mutilat'tsjone] sf (*vedi vb*) mutilation; maim-
ing; defacement

mutismo [mu'tizmo] sm **1** (*Med*) muteness, mutism **2** (*atteggiamento*) (stubborn) silence; **chiudersi in un mutismo
ostinato** to maintain a stubborn silence

muto, -a ['muto] agg (*Med*) unable to speak; (*Ling*) silent,
mute; (*Geog: cartina, atlante*) blank; **la h è muta** the h is silent; **il cinema muto** the silent cinema; **muto per lo stupore**
ecc speechless with amazement *ecc*; **ha fatto scena muta** he
didn't utter a word; **giuro che sarò muto come un pesce**
I swear I won't say a word; **un muto rimprovero** a silent
reproach ♦ sm, sf (*Med*) mute

mutua ['mutua] sf: **medico della mutua** ≈ National Health
Service doctor (*Brit*); **cassa mutua** health insurance scheme

mutuare [mutu'are] /72/ vt (*fig*) to borrow

mutuato, -a [mutu'ato] sm, sf *person contributing to sickness
benefit fund*

mutuo¹, -a ['mutuo] agg (*reciproco*) mutual

mutuo² ['mutuo] sm (long-term) loan; **mutuo ipotecario**
mortgage; **fare un mutuo** to take out a mortgage; **ho dovuto fare un mutuo per comprare la casa** I had to take out a
mortgage to buy the house

Nn

N¹, n¹ [ˈɛnne] SF INV, SM INV (*lettera*) N, n; **N come Napoli** ≈ N for Nellie (*Brit*), ≈ N for Nan (*USA*)

N² ABBR (= *Nord*) N

n. ABBR (= *numero*) no.

NA SIGLA = Napoli

nababbo [naˈbabbo] SM (*anche fig*) nabob

nacchere [ˈnakkere] SFPL castanets

nadir [naˈdir] SM (*Astron*) nadir

nafta [ˈnafta] SF (*Chim*) naphtha; (*carburante*) diesel oil; **motore a nafta** diesel engine

naftalina [naftaˈlina] SF (*Chim*) naphthalene; (*tarmicida*) mothballs *pl*

naia [ˈnaja] SF (*Mil: fam*) national service (*Brit*), draft (*USA*)

naïf [naˈif] AGG INV naïve; **un pittore naïf** a primitive painter

nailon [ˈnailon] SM = nylon

Nairobi [naiˈrɔbi] SF Nairobi

nanna [ˈnanna] SF (*fam*) bye-byes (*Brit*), beddy-byes (*USA*); **andare a nanna** to go bye-byes *o* beddy-byes; **andiamo a nanna** let's go bye-byes; **fare la nanna** to sleep; **fai la nanna, ora** go to sleep now

nano, -a [ˈnano] SM, SF dwarf ♦ AGG dwarf *attr*

napoletano, -a [napoleˈtano] AGG, SM, SF Neapolitan; **un ragazzo napoletano** a boy from Naples

Napoli [ˈnapoli] SF Naples; **domani vado a Napoli** I'm going to Naples tomorrow; **abitiamo a Napoli** we live in Naples

nappa [ˈnappa] SF **1** (*ornamento per tende*) tassel **2** (*pelle*) nappa, soft leather

narciso [narˈtʃizo] SM (*Bot*) narcissus

narcodollari [narkoˈdɔllari] SMPL drug money *sg*

narcos [ˈnarkos] SM INV (*colombiano*) Colombian drug trafficker

narcosi [narˈkɔzi] SF INV (*Med*) general anaesthesia (*Brit*) *o* anesthesia (*USA*), narcosis; **essere sotto narcosi** to be under general anaesthetic (*Brit*) *o* anesthetic (*USA*)

narcotico, -a, -ci, -che [narˈkɔtiko] AGG, SM narcotic

narcotrafficante [narkotraffiˈkante] SM, SF drug trafficker

narcotraffico [narkoˈtraffiko] SM drug trade

narice [naˈritʃe] SF nostril

narrare [narˈrare] /72/ VT to tell, narrate, recount; **narrare una storia** to tell a story ♦ VI (*aus avere*) **narrare di** to tell the story of

narrativo, -a [narraˈtivo] AGG narrative

narratore, -trice [narraˈtore] SM, SF narrator

narrazione [narratˈtsjone] SF **1** (*di fatto, avvenimento*) narration, account **2** (*storia, racconto*) story, tale

NASA [ˈnaza] SIGLA F (= *National Aeronautics and Space Administration*) NASA

nasale [naˈsale] AGG (*Anat, Fonetica*) nasal ♦ SF nasal consonant

nascente [naʃˈʃente] AGG (*sole, luna*) rising

nascere [ˈnaʃʃere] /67/ VI IRREG (*aus essere*) **1** (*bambino, animale*) to be born; (*pianta*) to come *o* spring up; **è nato nel 1977** he was born in 1977; **sono nata il 28 aprile** I was born on the 28th of April; **l'uomo nasce libero** man is born free; **nascono più femmine che maschi** there are more girls being born than boys; **è appena nato** he's a newborn baby; **nascere da genitori ricchi/poveri** to be born of rich/poor parents; **essere nato per qc/per fare qc** (*fig*) to be destined for sth/to do sth; **non sono nato ieri** I wasn't born yesterday **2** (*fiume*) to rise, have its source; (*sole*) to rise; (*giorno*) to break; (*dente*) to come through; (*idea, speranza*) to be born; (*difficoltà, dubbio*) to arise; (*industria, movimento*) to set up; **il sole nasce ad oriente** the sun rises in the east; **far nascere** (*industria*) to create; (*sospetto, desiderio*) to arouse; **nascere da** (*fig: derivare, conseguire*) to arise from, be born out of; **l'odio che nasce da tali conflitti** the hatred which springs

from such conflicts; **nasce spontanea la domanda...** the question which springs to mind is ...; **da cosa nasce cosa** one thing leads to another; **la rivolta è stata stroncata sul nascere** the revolt was nipped in the bud

nascita [ˈnaʃʃita] SF birth; **di nascita** by birth; **dopo la nascita della bambina** after the baby's birth; **nobile di nascita** of noble birth; **dalla nascita** from birth

nascituro, -a [naʃʃiˈturo] ·SM, SF future child; **come si chiamerà il nascituro?** what's the baby going to be called?

nascondere [nasˈkondere] VB IRREG /68/ VT (*gen*) to hide, conceal; **dove hai nascosto la lettera?** where have you hidden the letter?; **nascondere il viso tra le mani** to bury one's face in one's hands; **nascondere qc alla vista di qn** to hide sth from sb; **nascondere la verità a qn** to hide *o* keep the truth from sb; **non nascondo che mi farebbe molto piacere** I make no secret of the fact that I would like it; **nascondersi** VR to hide; **nascondersi alla vista di qn** to hide from sb, keep out of sb's sight; **dove si è nascosto?** where is he hiding?, where has he got to?; **si è nascosto dietro al divano** he hid behind the sofa; **dovresti nasconderti** you had better hide; (*fig*) you should be ashamed of yourself

nascondiglio, -gli [naskonˈdiʎʎo] SM hiding place

nascondino [naskonˈdino] SM: **giocare a nascondino** to play hide-and-seek *o* hide-and-go-seek (*USA*)

nascosi *ecc* [nasˈkosi] VB *vedi* nascondere

nascosto, -a [nasˈkosto] PP *di* nascondere ♦ AGG hidden; **un pericolo nascosto** a hidden danger; **tenere nascosto qc** to keep sth hidden; **gli hanno tenuto nascosta la notizia** they concealed *o* kept the news from him; **di nascosto** secretly; **fare qc di nascosto** to do sth secretly; **andarsene di nascosto** to slip away

nasello [naˈsello] SM (*pesce*) hake

naso [ˈnaso] SM nose; **si è soffiato il naso** he blew his nose; **parlare col naso** to talk through one's nose; **torcere *o* arricciare il naso (di fronte a qc)** to turn up one's nose (at sth); **avere naso per gli affari** to have a flair for business; **ha naso per gli affari** he has a flair for business; **mettere il naso negli affari altrui** to poke one's nose into other people's business

Nassau [nasˈsau] SF Nassau

nastro [ˈnastro] SM (*gen, di macchina da scrivere*) ribbon; (*Tecn, Sport*) tape; **un nastro di seta** a silk ribbon; **ha fatto tornare indietro il nastro** he rewound the tape; **a nastro** (*fam*) without a break, non-stop; **nastro adesivo** adhesive tape; **nastro isolante** insulating tape; **nastro magnetico** magnetic tape; **nastro trasportatore** conveyor belt

nasturzio, -zi [nasˈturtsjo] SM cress; **nasturzio indiano** nasturtium

natale [naˈtale] AGG (*paese, città*) native, of one's birth; **la sua città natale** his native city; **natali** SMPL: **di illustri/umili natali** of noble/humble birth

natalità [nataliˈta] SF birth rate

natalizio, -zia, -zi, -zie [nataˈlittsjo] AGG (*del Natale*) Christmas *attr*; **gli addobbi natalizi** Christmas decorations

natante [naˈtante] SM craft *inv*, boat

natica, -che [ˈnatika] SF (*Anat*) buttock

natio, -tia, -tii, -tie [naˈtio] AGG native

Natività [nativiˈta] SF INV (*Rel*) Nativity

nativo, -a [naˈtivo] AGG, SM, SF (*gen*) native

NATO [ˈnato] SIGLA F NATO (= *North Atlantic Treaty Organization*)

nato, -a [ˈnato] PP *di* nascere ♦ AGG **1** (*artista ecc*) born; **un attore nato** a born actor **2** (*di donna, prima di sposarsi*): **la sig.ra Rossi, nata Bianchi** Mrs Rossi, née Bianchi ♦ SM: **un nuovo nato** a newborn child; **i nati del *o* nel 1960** those born in 1960

natura [naˈtura] SF **1** (*mondo naturale*): **la natura** nature; **gli**

amanti della natura nature lovers; **il mondo della natura** the world of nature; **vivere a contatto con la natura** to live close to nature; **questa sostanza non esiste in natura** this substance does not exist naturally; **contro natura** unnatural **2** (*carattere*) nature; **la natura umana** human nature; **è nella natura delle cose** it's in the nature of things; **è allegro di natura** he's naturally cheerful; **non è nella sua natura fare così** he's not the sort of person who would do that; **i nostri rapporti sono di natura professionale** our relationship is of a professional nature **3** (*tipo*) nature, kind; **scritti di varia natura** writings of various kinds; **pagare in natura** to pay in kind **4** (*Pittura*): **natura morta** still life

naturale [natu'rale] AGG (*gen*) natural; **è naturale che sia così** it's natural that it should be so; **gli viene naturale comportarsi così** it comes naturally to him to behave like that; **(ma) è naturale!** (*in risposte*) of course!; **posso venire anch'io? — naturale!** can I come with you? — of course!; **a grandezza naturale** life-size; **figlio naturale** natural child; **risorse naturali** natural resources; **acqua minerale naturale** still mineral water; **i suoi capelli sono biondi naturali** her hair is naturally blonde ♦ SM: **al naturale** (*alimenti*) served plain; (*ritratto*) life-size; **tonno al naturale** tuna in brine; **pesche/fragole al naturale** peaches/strawberries in fruit juice

naturalezza [natura'lettsa] SF naturalness; **con naturalezza** naturally

naturalista, -i, -e [natura'lista] SM, SF naturalist

naturalizzare [naturalid'dzare] /72/ VT to naturalize; **naturalizzarsi** VIP to become naturalized; **si è naturalizzato italiano** he's become a naturalized Italian

naturalmente [natural'mente] AVV naturally; **vieni? — naturalmente** are you coming? — of course *o* naturally

naturismo [natu'rizmo] SM naturism, nudism

naturista, -i, -e [natu'rista] AGG, SM, SF naturist, nudist

naufragare [naufra'gare] /80/ VI (*aus avere o essere*) (*nave*) to be wrecked; (*persona*) to be shipwrecked; (*fig: progetto, disegno*) to fall through; **la nave è naufragata a causa della tempesta** the ship was wrecked in the storm; **naufragarono poco lontano dall'isola** they were shipwrecked not far from the island; **tutte le nostre speranze naufragarono** all our hopes were dashed

naufragio, -gi [nau'fradʒo] SM shipwreck; (*fig*) ruin, failure; **fare naufragio** to be shipwrecked; (*fig*) to fail, fall through

naufrago, -a, -ghi, -ghe ['naufrago] SM, SF shipwrecked person, shipwreck victim; (*su un'isola*) castaway

nausea ['nauzea] SF (*Med*) nausea; **avere la nausea** to feel sick (*Brit*) *o* sick to one's stomach (*USA*); **avevo un po' di nausea** I felt a bit sick; **mi dai la nausea!** (*fig*) you make me sick!; **fino alla nausea** ad nauseam; **ho bevuto fino alla nausea** I drank till I felt sick (to my stomach)

nauseabondo, -a [nauzea'bondo], **nauseante** [nauze'ante] AGG nauseating, sickening

nauseare [nauze'are] /72/ VT to nauseate, make (feel) sick (*Brit*) *o* sick to one's stomach (*USA*); **ho mangiato tanti funghi che ora ne sono nauseato** I've eaten so many mushrooms that now I'm sick of them; **il suo comportamento mi ha nauseato** his behaviour sickened me

nautico, -a, -ci, -che ['nautiko] AGG (*gen*) nautical; **carta nautica** chart; **salone nautico** (*mostra*) boat show; **sci nautico** water-skiing

navale [na'vale] AGG (*gen*) naval; **battaglia navale** naval battle; (*gioco*) battleships *sg*; **cantiere navale** shipyard

navata [na'vata] SF: **navata centrale** nave; **navata laterale** aisle

nave ['nave] SF ship, vessel; **nave ammiraglia** flagship; **nave da carico** cargo ship, freighter; **nave cisterna** tanker; **nave da crociera** cruise liner; **nave da guerra** warship; **nave di linea** liner; **nave mercantile** merchant ship; **nave passeggeri** passenger ship; **nave portaerei** aircraft carrier; **nave scuola** training ship; **nave spaziale** spaceship; **nave da trasporto** cargo ship; **nave a vapore** steamship; **nave a vela** sailing ship

❑ **nave** non si traduce mai con la parola inglese *nave*

navetta [na'vetta] SF **1** (*di telaio*) shuttle **2** (*servizio di collegamento*) shuttle (service)

navicella [navi't'ʃella] SF **1** (*di pallone, dirigibile*) gondola; **navicella spaziale** spaceship **2** (*per l'incenso*) incense boat

navigabile [navi'gabile] AGG (*canale, fiume*) navigable

navigante [navi'gante] SM sailor, seaman

navigare [navi'gare] /80/ VI (*aus avere*) to sail; **suo marito naviga** her husband is a sailor; **navigarono per tre mesi prima di raggiungere la costa** they sailed for three months before they reached land; **navigare in cattive acque** (*fig: finanziariamente*) to be hard up; **navigare in internet** to surf the internet

navigato, -a [navi'gato] AGG (*fig: esperto*) experienced

navigatore, -trice [naviga'tore] SM, SF (*gen*) navigator; (*Inform*) surfer; **navigatore satellitare** satellite navigator; **navigatore solitario** single-handed sailor

navigazione [navigat'tsjone] SF (*Naut, Aer*) navigation; (*Inform*) surfing; **la storia della navigazione** the history of navigation; **navigazione aerea/interna/fluviale** air/inland/ river navigation; **compagnia di navigazione** shipping company; **durante la navigazione** during the (sea *o* river) voyage; **dopo una settimana di navigazione** after a week at sea

naviglio, -gli [na'viʎʎo] SM **1** (*letter: imbarcazione*) ship; (: *flotta*) fleet, ships *pl*; **naviglio da pesca** fishing fleet **2** (*canale artificiale*) canal; (*canale navigabile*) (navigable) canal

nazionale [nattsjo'nale] AGG (*gen*) national; (*arrivi, passeggeri, economia*) domestic; **l'inno nazionale** the national anthem; **un parco nazionale** a national park ♦ SF (*Sport*) national team; **la nazionale azzurra** the Italian team

nazionalismo [nattsjona'lizmo] SM nationalism

nazionalista, -i, -e [nattsjona'lista] AGG, SM, SF nationalist

nazionalità [nattsjonali'ta] SF INV nationality; **nazionalità: italiana** nationality: Italian; **è di nazionalità britannica** she's British

nazionalizzare [nattsjonalid'dzare] /72/ VT to nationalize

nazionalizzazione [nattsjonaliddzat'tsjone] SF nationalization

nazione [nat'tsjone] SF nation

naziskin ['na:tsi skin] SM INV, SF INV skinhead (*belonging to extreme right-wing group*)

nazismo [nat'tsizmo] SM Nazism

nazista, -i, -e [nat'tsista] AGG, SM, SF Nazi *inv*

NB, n.b. ABBR (= *nota bene*) N.B.

NE ABBR (= *Nord-Est*) NE

ne [ne] PRON **1** (*di lui, lei, loro*) of him (*o* her *o* them); about him (*o* her *o* them); **ne riconosco la voce** I recognize his (*o* her) voice; **non lo vedo da anni, parlamene** I haven't seen him for years, tell me about him **2** (*con valore partitivo*) of it; of them (*spesso omesso*); **ne voglio ancora un po'** I want some more (of it *o* them); **ne voglio ancora un po'** I want a bit more; **dammene un po'** give me some; **dammene uno, per favore** give me one, please; **hai dei libri? — sì, ne ho** have you got any books? — yes I have; **hai del pane? — no, non ne ho** have you got any bread? — no I haven't; **quanti anni hai? — ne ho 17** how old are you? — I'm 17 **3** (*riguardo*) about it; about them; **non me ne importa niente** I couldn't care less about it; **cosa ne pensi?** what do you think (about it)?; **cosa ne faremo?** what will we do with it (*o* them)?; **non parliamone più!** let's not talk about it any more! **4** (*da ciò*): **ne deduco che l'avete trovato** I gather you've found it; **ne consegue che...** it follows therefore that ... ♦ AVV (*moto da luogo: da lì*) from there; (*da qui*) from here; **ne vengo ora** I've just come from there; **è meglio che tu te ne vada** you'd better leave; **me ne vado immediatamente** I'm leaving (here) right away; **siamo arrivati al teatro alle 7 e ne siamo venuti via alle 10** we got to the theatre at 7 and left at 10

né [ne] CONG: **né... né...** neither ... nor ...; **non verranno né Chiara né Donatella** neither Chiara nor Donatella are coming; **né mio padre né mia madre parlano l'italiano** neither my father nor my mother speaks Italian; **non parla né l'italiano né il tedesco** he speaks neither Italian nor German, he doesn't speak either Italian or German; **non voglio discutere con lui né con mio fratello** I don't want to quarrel with him or with my brother; **non l'ho più vista né sentita** I didn't see or hear from her again; **non voglio né posso accettare** I neither wish to nor can accept; **non piove né nevica** it isn't raining or snowing; **né da una parte**

né dall'altra on neither side; **né più né meno** no more no less; **né l'uno né l'altro** neither of them, neither the one nor the other; **né l'uno né l'altro lo vuole** neither of them wants it; **né l'uno né l'altro gioca a tennis** neither of them plays tennis; **non conosco né l'uno né l'altro** I don't know either of them

neanche [ne'anke] AVV not even; **non mi ha neanche pagato** he didn't even pay me; **non ci vado — neanch'io** I'm not going — neither o nor am I; **non l'ho visto — neanch'io** I didn't see him — neither did I o I didn't either; **non ne ero sicuro — neanche lei** I wasn't sure — neither was she; **neanche lui lo farebbe** not even he would do it, even he wouldn't do it; **neanche un bambino ci crederebbe** not even a child would believe it; **non ho neanche un soldo** I haven't got a single penny; **non ci penso neanche!** I wouldn't dream of it!; **neanche per idea** o **per sogno!** certainly not!, not on your life!; **se ne è partito senza neanche salutare** he went off without even saying goodbye; **non parlo spagnolo — e lui?** — **neanche** I don't speak Spanish — what about him? — he doesn't either o neither does he; **lui non è inglese e neanche sua moglie** he isn't English and neither is his wife ♦ CONG not even; **neanche a pagarlo lo farebbe** he wouldn't do it even if you paid him; **non... neanche** not even...; **non mi ha neanche pagato** she didn't even pay me; **neanche se** even if; **non potrebbe venire neanche se volesse** he couldn't come even if he wanted to; **neanche se volesse potrebbe venire** he couldn't come even if he wanted to

nebbia ['nebbja] SF (densa) fog; (foschia) mist; **odio la nebbia** I hate fog; **oggi c'è nebbia** it's foggy today

nebbioso, -a [neb'bjoso] AGG (vedi sf) foggy; misty

nebulizzatore [nebuliddza'tore] SM atomizer

nebulosa [nebu'losa] SF nebula

nebulosità [nebulosi'ta] SF haziness

nebuloso, -a [nebu'loso] AGG (atmosfera, cielo) hazy; (fig) hazy, vague

nécessaire [nese'ser] SM INV: **nécessaire da cucito** sewing kit; **nécessaire da toilette** make-up bag o case; **nécessaire da viaggio** overnight case o bag

necessariamente [netʃessarja'mente] AVV necessarily

necessario, -ria, -ri, -rie [netʃes'sarjo] AGG (gen) necessary; (persona) indispensable; **è necessario che tu vada** you will have to go, you must go; **è necessario far presto** we've got to hurry, it is necessary for you to go; **non è necessario che ti fermi** you don't need to stay; **non ho avuto il tempo necessario** I didn't have enough o sufficient time; **se necessario** if need be, if necessary; **rendersi necessario** (persona) to make o.s. indispensable; **si rende necessario partire** it has become necessary for me (o you ecc) to leave; **portami i documenti necessari** bring me the necessary documents ♦ SM: **fare il necessario** to do what is necessary; **lo stretto necessario** the bare essentials; **ha messo in valigia lo stretto necessario** she packed the bare essentials; **hanno appena il necessario per vivere** they have barely enough to live on; **non ho con me il necessario** I haven't got what I need with me; **hai tutto il necessario per scrivere?** have you got all your writing materials?; **lavorare/preoccuparsi più del necessario** to work/worry more than is necessary o more than one has to

necessità [netʃessi'ta] SF INV (bisogno) necessity, need; (povertà) poverty; **per necessità** out of need o necessity; **l'ho fatto per necessità** I did it because I had to; **di necessità** (necessariamente) of necessity; **in caso di necessità** if need be, if necessary; **non è un lusso, è una necessità** it isn't a luxury, it's a necessity; **non vedo la necessità di andare tutti quanti** I don't see any necessity for us all to go; **trovarsi nella necessità di fare qc** to be forced o obliged to do sth, have to do sth; **fare di necessità virtù** to make a virtue of necessity

necessitare [netʃessi'tare] /72/ VI (aus essere) (aiuto, intervento) to be necessary, be needed, be required; **necessita il vostro aiuto** your help is needed o necessary o required; **necessitare di** (aver bisogno) to need; **necessita di un'attenzione maggiore** it requires greater attention o care; **prima di essere pronto necessita di molte altre cose** a lot of other things are needed before it will be ready ♦ VT to need, require

necrologio, -gi [nekro'lɔdʒo] SM (annuncio) obituary notice; (registro) register of deaths

nefando, -a [ne'fando] AGG vile

nefasto, -a [ne'fasto] AGG (giorno) fateful, fatal; (segno, presagio) inauspicious, ill-omened; (fam: persona) full of gloom and doom

negare [ne'gare] /80/ VT (gen) to deny; (rifiutare) to deny, refuse; **negare qc/di aver fatto qc** to deny sth/having done sth; **non puoi negarlo** you can't deny it; **ha negato di aver preso i soldi** he denied taking the money; **negare qc a qn** to refuse to give sb sth; **mi ha negato il suo appoggio** he refused to give me his support; **negare a qn il permesso (di fare qc)** to refuse sb permission (to do sth); **negare a qn la possibilità di fare qc** to deny sb the possibility of doing sth; **mi hanno negato un aumento** they turned down my request for a (Brit) o raise; **negare obbedienza a qn** to refuse to obey sb

negativamente [negativa'mente] AVV negatively; **rispondere negativamente** to give a negative response, reply in the negative

negativo, -a [nega'tivo] AGG negative; **il risultato del test è stato negativo** the result of the test was negative ♦ SM (Fot) negative

negazione [negat'tsjone] SF negation

negherò ecc [nege'rɔ] VB vedi negare

negletto, -a [ne'gletto] AGG (trascurato) neglected

negli ['neʎʎi] PREP + ART vedi in

négligé [negli'ʒe] SM INV negligee

negligente [negli'dʒente] AGG (gen) negligent; (non diligente) careless

negligenza [negli'dʒentsa] SF (vedi agg) negligence; carelessness

negoziabile [negot'tsjabile] AGG negotiable

negoziante [negot'tsjante] SM, SF shopkeeper (Brit), storekeeper (USA)

negoziare [negot'tsjare] /19/ VT to negotiate ♦ VI (aus avere) **negoziare in** to trade o deal in

negoziato [negot'tsjato] SM negotiation; **negoziati per la pace** peace talks o negotiations

negoziatore, -trice [negottsja'tore] SM, SF negotiator

negozio, -zi [ne'gɔttsjo] SM 1 (bottega) shop (Brit), store (USA); **andare per negozi** to go shopping; **negozio di scarpe** shoe shop o store 2 (Dir): **negozio giuridico** legal transaction

negriere, -a [ne'grjere], **negriero, -a** [ne'grjɛro] SM (Storia) slaver, slave-trader ♦ SM, SF (fig: pegg) slave-driver

negro, -a ['negro] AGG SPESSO (offensivo) (razza, popolo) black ♦ SM, SF SPESSO (offensivo) black person

negromante [negro'mante] SM, SF necromancer

negromanzia [negroman'tsia] SF necromancy

nei ['nei] PREP + ART vedi in

nembo ['nembo] SM (Meteor) nimbus

nemico, -a, -ci, -che [ne'miko] SM, SF enemy; **ha molti nemici** he's got a lot of enemies ♦ AGG (Mil) enemy attr; (ostile) hostile; **farsi nemico qn** to make an enemy of sb; **essere nemico di qc** to be strongly averse o opposed to sth; **il gelo è nemico delle piante** frost is harmful to plants; **territorio nemico** enemy territory

nemmeno [nem'meno] AVV, CONG = **neanche**

nenia ['nɛnja] SF (canto) dirge; (motivo monotono) monotonous tune; (fig: discorso) tale of woe

neo ['nɛo] SM (gen) mole; (sul viso) beauty spot; (fig: imperfezione) (slight) flaw; (: di persona) slight defect

neo- ['nɛo] PREF neo-

neofascista, -i, -e [neofaʃ'ʃista] AGG, SM, SF neofascist

neologismo [neolo'dʒizmo] SM neologism

neon ['nɛon] SM INV (Chim) neon; (lampadario) neon lamp; **luce al neon** neon light

neonato, -a [neo'nato] AGG newborn ♦ SM, SF newborn baby

neozelandese [neoddzelan'dese] AGG New Zealand attr; **la squadra neozelandese** the New Zealand team ♦ SM, SF New Zealander

Nepal ['nepal] SM Nepal

nepotismo [nepo'tizmo] SM nepotism

neppure [nep'pure] AVV, CONG = **neanche**

nerbata [ner'bata] SF (*colpo*) blow; (*sferzata*) whiplash

nerbo ['nerbo] SM whip, lash; (*fig: di esercito*) backbone

nerboruto, -a [nerbo'ruto] AGG brawny, muscular; (*robusto*) robust

neretto [ne'retto] SM **1** (*Tip*) bold (type) (*Brit*), bold face **2** (*articolo di giornale*) article in bold type *o* face

nero, -a ['nero] AGG **1** (*colore*) black; (*scuro*) dark; (*pelle: abbronzata*) tanned; **ha i capelli neri** she's got black hair; **mettere qc nero su bianco** to put sth down in black and white; **nero come il carbone/la pece** as black as coal/pitch **2** (*negro: razza*) black **3** (*fig: disperazione, futuro*) black; (: *giornata*) awful; **essere (di umore) nero** to be in a filthy mood; **oggi sono di umore nero** I'm in a very bad mood today; **sono in un periodo nero** I'm going through a bad time; **vedere tutto nero** to look on the black side (of things); **vivono nella miseria più nera** they live in utter *o* abject poverty **4** (*illegale*): **lavoro nero** work in the black economy; **mercato nero** black market; **fondi neri** slush fund *sg* ◆ SM (*colore*) black; **vestirsi di** *o* **in nero** to dress in black; **è vestita di nero** she's dressed in black; **essere pagato in nero** to be paid in cash (*to evade payment of taxes*); **lavorare in nero** to moonlight (*Brit*) *o* double-dip (*USA: without statutory deductions of payment of taxes*) ◆ SM, SF (*persona*) black person

nerofumo [nero'fumo] SM lampblack

nervatura [nerva'tura] SF (*Anat*) nerves *pl*, nervous system; (*Bot*) veining; (*Archit, Tecn*) rib

nervo ['nervo] SM **1** (*Anat*) nerve; (*Bot*) vein; **nervo ottico** optic nerve **2 avere i nervi** to be very irritable; **avere i nervi a fior di pelle** to be on edge, be edgy; **avere i nervi saldi** to be calm; **ho i nervi scossi** my nerves are shattered; **far venire i nervi a qn**, **dare sui nervi a qn** to get on sb's nerves; **quando fa così mi dà proprio sui nervi** it really gets on my nerves when he does that; **avere i nervi saldi** to be calm; **che nervi!** damn (it)!

nervosismo [nervo'sizmo] SM (*Psic*) nervousness; (*irritazione*) irritability; **farsi prendere dal nervosismo** to let one's nerves get the better of one

nervoso, -a [ner'voso] AGG **1** (*tensione, sistema*) nervous; (*centro*) nerve *attr*; **esaurimento nervoso** nervous breakdown **2** (*agitato*) nervous, tense; (*irritabile*) irritable, touchy; **è sempre nervoso e si arrabbia spesso** he's always irritable and often loses his temper; **sono sempre un po' nervoso prima di un compito in classe** I'm always a bit nervous before a test at school **3** (*gambe, corpo*) sinewy ◆ SM: **far venire il nervoso a qn** (*fam*) to get on sb's nerves; **farsi prendere dal nervoso** to let o.s. get irritated

nespola ['nespola] SF (*frutto*) medlar; (*fig*) blow, punch

nespolo ['nespolo] SM medlar (tree)

nesso ['nesso] SM connection, link

nessuno, -a [nes'suno] AGG *dav sm:* nessun + *consonante, vocale*, nessuno + *s impura, gn, pn, ps, x, z,*; *dav sf:* nessuna + *consonante*, nessun' + *vocale* **1** (*non uno*) no, not any; (*espressione negativa*) + any; **nessun uomo è immortale** no man is immortal; **nessun altro** no-one else, nobody else; **nessun altro ti crederà** no one else will believe you; **nessun altro voleva andarci** no one else wanted to go; **non ho incontrato nessun altro** I didn't meet anyone else; **non ho nessun dubbio** I have no doubts; **non ha fatto nessun commento** he didn't make any comment; **non c'è nessun bisogno** there's no need, there isn't any need; **in nessun caso** under no circumstances; **in nessun luogo** nowhere; **da nessuna parte** not... anywhere; **non riesco a trovarlo da nessuna parte** I can't find it anywhere; **nessun'altra cosa** nothing else; **per nessuna cosa nel mondo** not for anything in the world **2** (*qualche*) any; **nessuna obiezione?** any objections? ◆ PRON **1** (*non uno*) no-one, nobody, (*espressione negativa*) + anyone; (*cosa*) none, (*espressione negativa*) + any; **nessuno di** (*riferito a persone, cose*) none of; **nessuno mi crede** no-one believes me; **nessuno si muova!** nobody move!; **non c'era nessuno** there was no-one there, there wasn't anyone there; **non è venuto nessuno** nobody came; **non dirlo a nessuno** don't tell that to anybody; **nessuno di loro/dei presenti** none of them/of those present; **non è venuto nessuno di loro** none of them came; **non è venuto nessuno dei due** neither of them came; **non mi fido di nessuno dei due** I

don't trust either of them; **ha molti libri ma non me ne piace nessuno** he has lots of books but I don't like any of them; **non ne ho letto nessuno** I haven't read any of them, I have read none of them **2** (*qualcuno*) anyone, anybody; **ha telefonato nessuno?** did anyone phone?; **hai visto nessuno?** did you see anyone? ◆ SM (*pegg: nullità*) nobody, nonentity; **e io chi sono, nessuno?** and who am I then, nobody?; **con tutte quelle arie resta comunque un nessuno** despite his airs and graces, he's still a nobody

nettamente [netta'mente] AVV (*chiaramente*) clearly; (*decisamente*) decidedly

nettare¹ [net'tare] /72/ VT to clean

nettare² [net'tare] /72/ SM nectar

nettezza [net'tettsa] SF **1** (*pulizia*) cleanness, cleanliness; **nettezza urbana** cleansing department (*Brit*), department of sanitation (*USA*) **2** (*chiarezza*) clarity

netto, -a ['netto] AGG **1** (*pulito*) clean **2** (*chiaro: contorni, immagine*) clear, sharp, clear-cut; (*deciso: rifiuto, vittoria*) clear, definite; **la squadra ha riportato una netta vittoria** the team won a clear victory; **tagliare qc di netto** to cut sth clean off; **taglio netto** clean cut; **un taglio netto col passato** a clean break with the past **3** (*stipendio, peso*) net; **peso netto** net weight ◆ SM: **al netto delle tasse** after tax, net of tax ◆ AVV: **chiaro e netto** plainly

netturbino [nettur'bino] SM dustman (*Brit*), dustbin man (*Brit*), garbage collector (*USA*) trash collector (*USA*)

neuro- ['neuro] PREF neuro-

neurochirurgia [neurokirur'dʒia] SF neurosurgery

neurologia [neurolo'dʒia] SF neurology

neurologico, -a, -ci, -che [neuro'lɔdʒiko] AGG neurological; **clinica neurologica** neurological clinic

neurologo, -a, -gi, -ghe [neu'rɔlogo] SM, SF neurologist

neurosi [neu'rɔzi] SF INV = **nevrosi**

neutrale [neu'trale] AGG, SM neutral

neutralità [neutrali'ta] SF neutrality

neutralizzare [neutralid'dzare] /72/ VT (*gen, anche Chim*) to neutralize

neutro, -a ['neutro] AGG (*gen*) neutral; (*Gramm, Zool*) neuter ◆ SM (*Gramm*) neuter

neutrone [neu'trone] SM neutron

nevaio, -ai [ne'vajo] SM snowfield

neve ['neve] SF snow; **mi piace camminare sulla neve** I like walking in the snow; **è caduta tanta neve ieri** it snowed a lot yesterday; **c'era un tempo da neve** it was snowy; **montare a neve** (*Culin*) to whip up; **neve carbonica** dry ice

nevicare [nevi'kare] /20/ VB IMPERS to snow, be snowing; **nevica** it's snowing

nevicata [nevi'kata] SF snowfall

nevischio, -chi [ne'viskjo] SM sleet

nevoso, -a [ne'voso] AGG (*montagna*) snow-covered; (*tempo, inverno*) snowy; **manto nevoso** blanket of snow

nevralgia [nevral'dʒia] SF neuralgia; **ho una terribile nevralgia** I've got awful neuralgia

nevralgico, -a, -ci, -che [ne'vraldʒiko] AGG: **punto nevralgico** (*Med*) nerve centre (*Brit*) *o* center (*USA*); (*fig*) crucial point; **è un punto nevralgico del traffico** it is one of the main areas of traffic congestion

nevrastenico, -a, -ci, -che [nevras'teniko] AGG (*Med*) neurasthenic; (*fig*) hot-tempered ◆ SM, SF (*vedi agg*) neurasthenic; hot-tempered person

nevrosi [ne'vrɔzi] SF INV neurosis

nevrotico, -a, -ci, -che [ne'vrɔtiko] AGG, SM, SF (*anche fig*) neurotic

Niagara [nja'gara] SM: **le cascate del Niagara** the Niagara Falls

nibbio, -bi ['nibbjo] SM (*uccello*) kite

Nicaragua [nika'ragwa] SM Nicaragua

nicaraguese [nikara'gweze], **nicaraguense** [nikara'gwɛnse] AGG, SM, SF Nicaraguan

nicchia ['nikkja] SF (*gen, anche fig*) niche; (*naturale*) cavity, hollow; **nicchia ecologica** niche; **nicchia di mercato** (*Comm*) niche market

nicchiare [nik'kjare] /19/ VI (*aus avere*) to shilly-shally, hesitate

nichel ['nikel] SM nickel

nichilismo [niki'lizmo] SM nihilism

Nicosia [niko'zia] SF Nicosia

nicotina [niko'tina] SF nicotine

nidiata [ni'djata] SF (*di uccelli, anche fig: di bambini*) brood; (*di altri animali*) litter

nidificare [nidifi'kare] /20/ VI (*aus avere*) to nest

nido ['nido] SM (*Zool*) nest; (*fig: casa*) nest, home; **a nido d'ape** (*tessuto, ricamo*) honeycomb *attr* ♦ AGG INV: **asilo nido** crèche (*Brit*), day-care center (*USA*)

niente ['njɛnte] PRON (*nessuna cosa*) nothing; (*qualcosa*) anything; **non... niente** nothing, (*espressione negativa*) + anything; **niente lo fermerà** nothing will stop him; **non ho visto niente** I saw nothing, I didn't see anything; **non è successo niente** nothing happened; **cos'hai comprato? — niente** what did you buy? — nothing; **hai bisogno di o ti serve niente?** do you need anything?; **cosa c'è? — niente** what's the matter? — nothing; **niente di grave/nuovo** nothing serious/new; **non gli va bene niente** he's never satisfied; **un uomo da niente** a nobody, a nonentity; **una cosa da niente** a trivial thing; **non fa niente!** it doesn't matter!; **fa niente se non vengo?** does it matter if I don't come?; **non mi sono fatto niente** I haven't hurt myself at all; **la cura non gli ha fatto niente** the treatment hasn't done anything for him; **non ho niente a che fare con lui** I have nothing to do with him; **ha niente in contrario se...?** would you object if ...?; **come se niente fosse** as if nothing had happened; **niente al mondo** nothing on earth *o* in the world; **niente di niente** absolutely nothing; **nessuno fa niente per niente** no one does anything for nothing; **ho parlato per niente** I spoke to no purpose, I wasted my breath; **sono venuto per niente** there was no point in my coming; **si arrabbia per niente** he gets annoyed at the slightest thing; **nient'altro** nothing else; **nient'altro?** (*in negozio*) is that all?, will that be all?; **nient'altro che** nothing but; (*solamente*) just, only; **so poco o niente di lui** I know next to nothing about him; **non so niente di niente** I know nothing at all; **grazie — di niente** thanks — you're welcome; **quel brodo non sa di niente** that soup is tasteless; **niente meno = nientemeno** ♦ AGG: **non ho niente voglia di farlo** I'm not at all keen to do it; **niente paura!** don't worry!; **e niente scuse!** don't try to make excuses!; **niente male!** not bad at all! ♦ SM nothing; **si è fatto dal niente** he's a self-made man; **il mondo è stato creato dal niente** the world was created out of nothing; **un bel niente** absolutely nothing; **si è ridotto al niente** he has lost everything; **si è ridotto a un niente** he's just skin and bone ♦ AVV (*in nessuna misura*): **non... niente** not ... at all; **non è niente buono** it's not good at all; **non... per niente** (*affatto*) not ...at all; **non si è visto per niente** he hasn't been seen at all; **non mi sono divertito per niente** I didn't enjoy it at all; **non è per niente vero** it's not true at all; **niente affatto** not at all, not in the least; **le dispiace se fumo? — niente affatto** do you mind if I smoke? — not at all; **poco o niente** next to nothing

nientedimeno [njentedi'meno], **nientemeno** [njɛnte'meno] AVV (*addirittura*) actually, even; **è diventata nientedimeno che amministratore delegato** she has become managing director, no less ♦ ESCL really!, you don't say!

Niger ['nidʒer] SM (*stato*) Niger; (*fiume*) the Niger

Nigeria [ni'dʒerja] SF Nigeria

nigeriano, -a [nidʒe'rjano] AGG, SM, SF Nigerian

Nilo ['nilo] SM: **il Nilo** the Nile

nimbo ['nimbo] SM halo

ninfa ['ninfa] SF nymph

ninfea [nin'fɛa] SF water lily

ninfomane [nin'fɔmane] SF nymphomaniac

ninnananna [ninna'nanna] SF lullaby

ninnolo ['ninnolo] SM (*gingillo*) knick-knack; (*balocco*) plaything

nipote [ni'pote] SM, SF (*di nonni*) grandchild, grandson *o* granddaughter; (*di zii*) nephew *o* niece; **nipotini** SMPL (*maschi e femmine*) grandchildren; **il nonno con i nipotini** grandad with his grandchildren; **un regalo della zia Lucia ai nipoti** (*maschi e femmine*) a present from aunt Lucia for her nephews and nieces

nipponico, -a, -ci, -che [nip'pɔniko] AGG Japanese, Nipponese

nitidezza [niti'dettsa] SF (*gen*) clearness; (*di stile*) clarity; (*Fot, TV: di immagine*) sharpness

nitido, -a ['nitido] AGG (*gen*) clear; (*immagine*) sharp, well-defined; **un'immagine nitida** a sharp image

nitrato [ni'trato] SM nitrate

nitrico, -a, -ci, -che ['nitriko] AGG nitric

nitrire [ni'trire] /55/ VI (*aus avere*) to neigh

nitrito¹ [ni'trito] SM (*di cavallo*) neigh; **nitriti** SMPL neighing *no pl*

nitrito² [ni'trito] SM (*Chim*) nitrite

nitroglicerina [nitroglitʃe'rina] SF nitroglycerine

niveo, -a ['niveo] AGG snow-white, snowy

Nizza ['nittsa] SF Nice

nn ABBR (= *numeri*) nos

NO SIGLA = Novara ♦ ABBR (= *Nord-Ovest*) NW

no [nɔ] AVV **1** no; **vieni? — no** are you coming? — no (I'm not); **la conosce? — no** does he know her? — no (he doesn't); **lo conosciamo? — tu no ma io sì** do we know him? — you don't but I do; **ti piace? — no** do you like it? — no, I don't; **ne vuoi ancora? — no, grazie** would you like some more? — no thank you; **verrai, no?** you'll come, won't you?; **hai finito, no?** you've finished, haven't you?; **può venire, no?** he can come, can't he?; **vieni anche tu, no?** you're coming too, aren't you? **2** (*con avverbio, congiunzione*) not; **perché no?** why not?; **no di certo!** certainly not!; **vieni? — come no!** are you coming? — of course! *o* certainly!; **come no?** what do you mean, no?; **vieni o no?** are you coming or not?; **simpatico o no lo devo sopportare** (whether he's) nice or not, I'll have to put up with him **3** **credo di no** I think not, I don't think so; **spero di no** I hope not; **sembra di no** apparently not; **direi di no** I don't think so; **ha detto di no** he said no ♦ SM no; **da lui un no non me l'aspettavo** I didn't expect him to say no; **ci sono stati molti no** (*voti, pareri contrari*) there were a lot of votes against, there were a lot of noes

nobildonna [nobil'dɔnna] SF noblewoman

nobile ['nɔbile] AGG noble; **nobili sentimenti** noble sentiments; **di animo nobile** noble-hearted; **una famiglia nobile** an aristocratic family ♦ SM, SF nobleman, nobleman *o* noblewoman; **i nobili** the nobility, the aristocracy

nobiliare [nobi'ljare] AGG noble

nobilitare [nobili'tare] /72/ VT (*anche fig*) to ennoble; **nobilitarsi** VR (*rendersi insigne*) to distinguish o.s.

nobiltà [nobil'ta] SF INV (*condizione, classe sociale*) nobility; (*fig: di azione, animo*) nobleness

nobiluomo [nobil'wɔmo] SM (*pl* nobiluomini) nobleman

nocca, -che ['nɔkka] SF (*Anat*) knuckle; (*di cavallo*) fetlock

noccio ecc ['nɔttʃo] VB *vedi* nuocere

nocciola [not'tʃɔla] SF hazelnut; **gelato alla nocciola** hazelnut ice cream ♦ AGG INV (*anche:* color nocciola) hazel, light brown

nocciolina [nottʃo'lina] SF (*anche:* nocciolina americana) peanut

nocciolo¹ [ˈnɔttʃolo] SM (*di frutto*) stone; (*fig*) heart, core; **veniamo al nocciolo!** let's get to the point!; **nocciolo duro** hard core

nocciolo² [not'tʃɔlo] SM (*albero*) hazel

noce [ˈnotʃe] SM (*albero*) walnut (tree); (*legno*) walnut ♦ SF **1** (*frutto*) walnut; **noce di cocco** coconut; **noce moscata** nutmeg **2** **una noce di burro** (*Culin*) a knob of butter (*Brit*), a dab of butter (*USA*); **noce di manzo/vitello** beef/veal fillet

nocepesca, -sche [notʃe'peska] SF nectarine

nocevo ecc [no'tʃevo] VB *vedi* nuocere

nociuto [no'tʃuto] PP *di* nuocere

nocivo, -a [no'tʃivo] AGG (*gen*) harmful; (*fumi*) noxious; **non contiene sostanze nocive** it doesn't contain any harmful substances; **insetti nocivi** pests

nocqui ecc [ˈnɔkkwi] VB *vedi* nuocere

nodo ['nɔdo] SM **1** (*gen, di cravatta, fune*) knot; (*fig: legame*) bond, tie; (: *pendenza-commerciale*) heart, crux; (*Med, Astron, Bot*) node; **fare/sciogliere un nodo** to tie/untie a knot; **avere i capelli pieni di nodi** to have tangles in one's hair; **avere un nodo alla gola** to have a lump in one's throat; **fare un nodo al fazzoletto** (*fig*) to tie a knot in one's handkerchief; **tutti i nodi vengono al pettine** (*Proverbio*) your sins will find you out; **nodo d'amore** love knot; **nodo scorsoio** slipknot **2** (*Aut, Ferr: incrocio*) junction; **nodo ferroviario** railway junction **3** (*Naut: velocità*) knot

nodoso, -a [no'doso] AGG (*tronco, mani*) gnarled

nodulo ['nɔdulo] SM (*Anat, Bot*) nodule

no-global [no'global] SM, SF anti-globalization protester ♦ AGG (*movimento, manifestante*) anti-globalization

noi ['noi] PRON PERS **1** (*soggetto*) we; **noi andiamo al cinema** we're going to the cinema; **noi stessi(e)** we ourselves; **non lo sapevamo nemmeno noi** we didn't even know it ourselves; **tutti noi pensiamo che sia giusto** we all think it's right, all of us think it's right; **noi italiani** we Italians; **siamo stati noi a dirglielo** it was us who told him, we were the ones to tell him; **noi accettare? non sia mai detto!** us accept that? never! **2** (*oggetto: per dare rilievo, con preposizione*) us; **noi stessi(e)** ourselves; **chi è?** — **siamo noi** who is it? — it's us; **vuol vedere proprio noi** it's us he wants to see; **dice a noi?** is he talking to us?; **tocca a noi** is it our turn?; **chi viene con noi?** who's coming with us?; **da noi** (*nel nostro paese*) in our country, where we come from; (*a casa nostra*) at our house **3** (*comparazioni*) we, us; **vanno veloce come noi** they are going as fast as we are, they are going as fast as us; **fate come noi** do as we do, do the same as us; **sono più giovani di noi** they are younger than we are *o* than us

noia ['nɔja] SF (*tedio*) boredom; (*disturbo, impaccio*) bother *no pl*, trouble *no pl*; (*fastidio*) nuisance; **morire di noia** to die of boredom; **stavano morendo di noia** they were dying of boredom; **mi è venuto a noia** I'm tired of it; **dare noia a qn** to bother *o* annoy sb; **finiscila di dar noia a tua sorella** stop bothering your sister; **le dà noia se fumo?** do you mind if I smoke?; **avere qn/qc a noia** not to like sb/sth; **avere (delle) noie con la polizia** to be in trouble with the police; **che noia!** what a bore!; (*fastidio*) what a nuisance!; **che noia, quel film!** the film was so boring!

noialtri, -e [no'jaltri] PRON PERS we

noioso, -a [no'joso] AGG (*tedioso*) boring; (*fastidioso*) tiresome, annoying

❏ **noioso** non si traduce mai con la parola inglese *noisy*

noleggiare [noled'dʒare] /62/ VT (*auto, bicicletta: prendere a noleggio*) to hire (*Brit*), rent; (: *dare a noleggio*) to hire out (*Brit*), rent out; (: *aereo, nave*) to charter; **dove possiamo noleggiare una macchina?** where can we hire a car?; **noleggiano biciclette ai turisti** they hire out bikes to tourists

noleggiatore, -trice [noledd'ʒatore] SM, SF (*vedi vb*) hirer (*Brit*), renter; charterer

noleggio, -gi [no'leddʒo] SM (*di auto, bicicletta*) hire (*Brit*), rental; (*di nave, barca*) charter; **prendere/dare a noleggio** to hire/hire out) *o* rent/rent out; **prenderemo gli sci a noleggio** we're going to hire skis; **contratto di noleggio** (*Naut*) charter party (contract); **c'è un noleggio di biciclette?** is there a place where you can hire *o* rent bikes?

nolente [no'lente] AGG: **volente o nolente** whether one likes it or not, willy-nilly

nolo ['nɔlo] SM (*di auto*) hire (charge) (*Brit*), rental (charge); (*di nave*) charter (fee); (*per trasporto merci*) freight (charge); **prendere/dare a nolo qc** to hire *o* rent/rent out

nomade ['nɔmade] AGG nomadic ♦ SM, SF nomad

nomadismo [noma'dizmo] SM nomadism

nome ['nome] SM (*gen*) name; **che bel nome!** what a nice name!; **un uomo di nome Giovanni** a man by the name of John, a man called John; **a nome di** (*per conto di*) on behalf of; **parlo a nome dei miei colleghi** I'm speaking on behalf of my colleagues; **tanti saluti anche a nome di mia moglie** my wife asked me to give you her regards; **solo di nome** in name only; **in nome della legge** in the name of the law; **in nome del cielo!** in heaven's name!; **sotto il nome di** under the name of; **sotto falso nome** under an assumed name *o* an alias; **chiamare qn per nome** to call sb by name; **posso chiamarla per nome?** can I call you by your first name?; **li conosce tutti per nome** she knows them all by name; **lo conosco solo di nome** I know him only by name; **fare il nome di qn** to name sb; **faccia pure il mio nome** feel free to mention my name; **farsi un buon/cattivo nome** to get a good/bad name; **ormai si è fatto un nome** he has made a name for himself now; **porta** *o* **gli hanno dato il nome di suo nonno**

he is named after his grandfather; **senza nome** nameless ♦ **nome d'arte** stage name; **nome astratto** (*Gramm*) abstract noun; **nome di battaglia** nom de guerre; **nome di battesimo** Christian name; **nome comune** (*Gramm*) common noun; **nome depositato** trade name; **nome di dominio** (*Inform*) domain name; **nome di famiglia** surname; **nome del file** (*Inform*) file name; **nome proprio** (*Gramm*) proper noun; **nome da ragazza** maiden name; **nome da sposata** married name; **nome utente** (*Inform*) username

nomea [no'mɛa] SF notoriety

nomenclatura [nomenkla'tura] SF nomenclature

nomenklatura [nomenkla'tura] SF (*di partito, di stato*) nomenclature

nomignolo [no'miɲɲolo] SM nickname

nomina ['nɔmina] SF appointment; **conferire una nomina a qn** to appoint sb; **ottenere la nomina a presidente** to be appointed president

nominale [nomi'nale] AGG (*gen*) nominal; (*Gramm*) noun *attr*; **valore nominale** face *o* nominal value

nominare [nomi'nare] /72/ VT (*citare*) to mention; (*per nome*) to name; (*eleggere*) to appoint; **l'ha nominata nel suo discorso** he mentioned her in his speech; **non l'ho mai sentito nominare** I've never heard of it (*o* him); **l'hanno nominato segretario generale** he has been appointed secretary-general

nomination [nomi'neʃʃon] SF INV (*in reality show*) nomination

nominativo, -a [nomina'tivo] AGG (*Gramm*) nominative; (*Comm*) registered; **elenco nominativo** list of names ♦ SM **1** (*Gramm: anche:* **caso nominativo**) nominative (case) **2** (*Comm, Amm: nome*) name

non [non] AVV **1** not; **non sono inglesi** they are not *o* aren't English; **non ne ho** I haven't (got) any; **non avresti dovuto farlo** you shouldn't have done that; **non devi farlo** you must not *o* mustn't do it; **non puoi venire** you cannot *o* can't come; **non vieni?** aren't you coming?; **non parli francese?** don't you speak French?; **la legge non è stata ancora approvata** the law has not yet been passed; **Mario non c'è** Mario isn't here; **non è venuto nessuno** nobody came; **non andarci!** don't go!; **non ci sono andato** I didn't go; **non l'ho mai visto** I have never seen it *o* him; **non lo so** I don't know; **non lo capisco affatto** I do not *o* don't understand him *o* it at all; **non più di 5 minuti** no more than 5 minutes; **non oltre il 15 luglio** no later than (the) 15th (of) July; **grazie** — **non c'è di che** thank you — don't mention it **2** (*con sostantivo, aggettivo, pronome, avverbio*) not; **un guadagno non indifferente** a not inconsiderable gain; **non pochi sono d'accordo** not a few are in agreement, many are in agreement; **non uno dei presenti si è alzato** not one of those present stood up **3** (*con valore rafforzativo*): **non puoi non vederlo** you can't not see him, you'll have to see him; **finché non torno** until I get back; **per poco non cadevo in acqua** I almost fell into the water ♦ PREF non-, un-

nonché [non'ke] CONG **1** (*tanto più, tanto meno*) let alone **2** (*e inoltre*) as well as; **lo ricorderò a lui, nonché a suo fratello** I'll remind him as well as his brother

nonconformista, -i, -e [nonkonfor'mista] AGG, SM, SF nonconformist

noncurante [nonku'rante] AGG: **noncurante (di)** indifferent (to), careless (of); **con fare noncurante** with a nonchalant *o* casual air

noncuranza [nonku'rantsa] SF carelessness, indifference; **assumere un'aria di noncuranza** to put on a nonchalant air

nondimeno [nondi'meno] CONG (*tuttavia*) however; (*nonostante*) nevertheless

nonno, -a ['nɔnno] SM, SF grandfather *o* grandmother; (*in senso più familiare*) grandad (*o* grandpa) *o* grandma; **nonni** SMPL grandparents

nonnulla [non'nulla] SM INV: **un nonnulla** nothing, a trifle; **se la prende per un nonnulla** he gets annoyed over the slightest thing

nono, -a ['nɔno] AGG, SM, SF ninth

nonostante [nonos'tante] PREP in spite of, notwithstanding; **ci è riuscita nonostante tutto** she succeeded in spite of everything ♦ CONG even though, although, in spite of the fact that; **nonostante fosse notte fonda** in spite of the fact that it was late at night; **nonostante piovesse** even though o in spite of the fact that it was raining; **ciò nonostante** nevertheless

non plus ultra ['non plus 'ultra] SM INV: **il non plus ultra (di)** the last word (in)

nontiscordardimé [nontiskordardi'me] SM INV (Bot) forget-me-not

nord [nɔrd] SM north; **piove di più a nord** it rains more in the north; **la sua famiglia è del nord** his family comes from the north; **a nord (di)** north (of); **si trova a nord della città** it's north of the city; **si è diretto a nord** he headed north; **esposto a nord** north-facing; **verso nord** northward(s), north; **il mare del Nord** the North Sea; **l'America del Nord** North America; **l'Italia del nord** northern Italy ♦ AGG INV (gen) north; (regione) northern; **è partito in direzione nord** he set off northwards o in a northward direction

nord-est [nor'dest] SM northeast; **vento di nord-est** north-easterly wind

nordico, -a, -ci, -che ['nɔrdiko] AGG Nordic; (sci) nordic ♦ SM, SF Northern European

nordista, -i, -e [nor'dista] AGG, SM, SF Yankee

nord-ovest [nor'dɔvest] SM northwest; **vento di nord-ovest** northwesterly wind

Norimberga [norim'bɛrga] SF Nuremberg; **il processo di Norimberga** the Nuremberg trials

norma ['nɔrma] «SF (principio) norm; (regola) regulation, rule; (consuetudine) custom, rule; **scostarsi dalla norma** to diverge from the norm; **al di sopra della norma** above average, above the norm; **di norma** normally, as a rule; **di norma chiudo a chiave la porta** I lock the door as a rule; **a norma di legge** in accordance with the law, according to the law, as laid down by law; **per tua norma e regola** for your information; **proporsi una norma di vita** to set o.s. rules to live by; **le norme sociali** social norms; **norme per l'uso** instructions for use; **norme di sicurezza** safety regulations

normale [nor'male] AGG normal; (solito) usual, normal; **ma tu non sei normale!** there must be something wrong with you!; **è normale che sia così** it is quite normal for it to be like that ♦ SM: **più di del normale** taller than average; **ha un'intelligenza al di sopra del normale** he is of above average intelligence ♦ SF (Mat) normal

normalità [normali'ta] SF normality

normalizzare [normalid'dzare] /72/ VT to bring back to normal, normalize; (Pol, Mat) normalize; **normalizzarsi** VIP to return to normal

normalmente [normal'mente] AVV (in modo normale) normally; (abitualmente) normally, usually, ordinarily

Normandia [norman'dia] SF Normandy

normanno, -a [nor'manno] AGG, SM, SF Norman

normativo, -a [norma'tivo] AGG normative

norvegese [norve'dʒese] AGG, SM, SF Norwegian; **i norvegesi** the Norwegians ♦ SM (lingua) Norwegian; **parla norvegese** he speaks Norwegian

Norvegia [nor'vɛdʒa] SF Norway; **ti è piaciuta la Norvegia?** did you like Norway?; **andremo in Norvegia quest'estate** we're going to Norway this summer

nosocomio, -mi [nozo'kɔmjo] SM hospital

nostalgia [nostal'dʒia] SF (di casa, paese) homesickness; (del passato) nostalgia; **soffrire di nostalgia** to be homesick; **aver nostalgia di casa** to be homesick; **ho nostalgia di casa** I'm homesick; **ho nostalgia dei vecchi tempi** I'm nostalgic for the good old days

nostalgico, -a, -ci, -che [nos'taldʒiko] AGG (vedi sf) homesick; nostalgic ♦ SM, SF (Pol) person who hopes for the return of Fascism

nostrano, -a [nos'trano] AGG (gen) local; (pianta, frutta) home-grown

nostro, -a ['nɔstro] AGG POSS: **il(la) nostro(a)** ecc our; **il nostro giardino** our garden; **la nostra macchina** our car; **i nostri libri** our books; **nostra madre** our mother; **un nostro amico** a friend of ours; **è colpa nostra** it's our fault; **a casa nostra** at our house, at home ♦ PRON POSS: **il(la) nostro(a)** ecc ours, our own; **la vostra barca è più lunga della nostra** your boat is longer than ours; **il nostro è stato solo un errore** it was simply an error on our part; **è questa la vostra macchina?**

— **no, la nostra è nera** is this your car? — no, ours is black; **le sue foto sono più belle delle nostre** his pictures are better than ours; **di chi è questo?** — **è nostro** whose is this? — it's ours ♦ PRON POSS M **1 abbiamo speso del nostro** we spent our own money; **viviamo del nostro** we live on our own income **2 i nostri** (famiglia) our family; (amici) our own people, our side; **è dei nostri** he's one of us ♦ PRON POSS F: **la nostra** (opinione) our view; **è dalla nostra** (parte) he's on our side; **anche noi abbiamo avuto le nostre** (disavventure) we've had our problems too; **alla nostra!** (brindisi) to us!

nostromo [nos'trɔmo] SM boatswain

nota ['nɔta] SF **1** (gen, anche Mus) note; **leggi la nota a pagina cinquantasei** read the note on page fifty-six; **prendere nota di qc** to note sth, make a note of sth, write sth down; **ho preso nota di tutto quello che ha detto** I made a note of everything she said; (fig: fare attenzione) to note sth, take note of sth; **degno di nota** noteworthy, worthy of note; **una nota di tristezza/allegria** a note of sadness/happiness; **nota fondamentale** (Mus) tonic; **note caratteristiche** (di carattere, stile) distinguishing marks o features; **note a piè di pagina** footnotes **2** (fattura) bill; (elenco) list; **nota di addebito** debit note; **nota della spesa** shopping list; **nota spese** list of expenses

notabile [no'tabile] AGG (letter: mutamento, avvenimento) notable; (persona) important ♦ SM notable

notaio, -ai [no'tajo] SM notary (public)

notare [no'tare] /72/ VT (rilevare, osservare) to notice, note; (segnare: errori) to mark; (registrare) to note (down), write down; **hai notato com'era strano?** did you notice how strange he was?; **vi faccio notare che...** I would have you note o I wish to point out that ...; **gli ho fatto notare che l'errore era suo** I pointed out it was his mistake; **notare qc a margine** to write sth in the margin; **farsi notare** to get o.s. noticed, draw attention to o.s.

notarile [nota'rile] AGG: **studio notarile** notary's office; **atto notarile** legal document (authorized by a notary)

notazione [notat'tsjone] SF (Mus) notation

notevole [no'tevole] AGG (talento) notable, remarkable; (peso) considerable; **si tratta di una somma notevole** it's a considerable sum; **quell'anello ha un valore notevole** that ring is very valuable

notifica, -che [no'tifika] SF notification

notificare [notifi'kare] /20/ VT (Dir): **notificare qc a qn** to notify sb of sth, give sb notice of sth

notificazione [notifikat'tskjone] SF notification

notizia [no'tittsja] SF (piece of) news sg; (informazione) piece of information; **notizie** SFPL news sg, information sg; **avere una bella/brutta notizia** to have some good/bad news; **ho delle buone notizie per te** I've got some good news for you; **brutte notizie, purtroppo!** bad news, unfortunately!; **aver notizie di qn** to hear from sb; **non abbiamo sue notizie da un anno** it's a year since we had any news of her; **fammi avere tue notizie!** keep in touch!

❑ notizia non si traduce mai con la parola inglese notice

notiziario, -ri [notit'tsjarjo] SM (Radio, TV, Stampa) news sg; **l'hanno dato al notiziario delle otto** it was on the eight o'clock news

noto, -a ['nɔto] AGG (well-)known; **noto a tutti** (well) known to everybody; **rendere noto qc** to make sth known; **uomo politico** a well-known politician; **suo fratello è più noto** his brother is better known ♦ SM: **il noto e l'ignoto** the known and the unknown

notorietà [notorje'ta] SF fame; (pegg) notoriety

notorio, -ria, -ri, -rie [no'tɔrjo] AGG **1** well-known; (pegg) notorious **2** (Dir): **atto notorio = atto notarile**; vedi notarile

nottambulo, -a [not'tambulo] SM, SF night owl (fig), nighthawk (USA, fig)

nottata [not'tata] SF night; **ho passato la nottata in piedi** I was up all night

notte ['nɔtte] SF night; (oscurità) darkness, night; (periodo) night, night-time; **buona notte** goodnight; **dare la buona notte** to say goodnight; **di notte** at night; (durante la notte) in the night, during the night; **è meglio non uscire di notte** it's better not to go out at night; **è successo di notte** it happened during the night; **la notte è meglio dormire** it's better to sleep at night; **la notte di sabato, sabato notte** (on) Saturday night; **questa notte** (*quella passata*) last night; (*quella che viene*) tonight; **rientrare prima di notte** to come back home before dark; **col favore della notte** under cover of darkness; **nella notte dei tempi** in the mists of time; **come va? — peggio che andare di notte** how are things? — worse than ever; **camicia da notte** nightgown; **portiere di notte** night porter; **notte bianca** *o* **in bianco** sleepless night

nottetempo [notte'tempo] AVV at night, during the night

nottola ['nɔttola] SF (*pipistrello*) noctule

notturno, -a [not'turno] AGG (*locale, servizio, guardiano*) night *attr*; (*Zool, fig*) nocturnal; **non c'è un servizio notturno** there is no night service ♦ SM (*Mus*) nocturne ♦ SF (*Sport*) evening match *o* fixture (*Brit*); **in notturna** (*partita*) under floodlights

nov. ABBR (= *novembre*) Nov

novanta [no'vanta] AGG INV, SM INV ninety

novantenne [novan'tɛnne] AGG, SM, SF ninety-year-old

novantesimo, -a [novan'tezimo] AGG, SM ninetieth

novantina [novan'tina] SF: **una novantina (di)** about ninety

nove ['nɔve] AGG INV, SM INV nine

novecentesco, -a, -schi, -sche [novetʃen'tesko] AGG twentieth-century

novecento [nove'tʃɛnto] AGG INV nine hundred ♦ SM INV nine hundred; (*secolo*): **il Novecento** the twentieth century

novella [no'vɛlla] SF (*Letteratura*) short story
❏ **novella** non si traduce mai con la parola inglese *novel*

novellino, -a [novel'lino] SM, SF beginner, greenhorn ♦ AGG (*pivello*) green, inexperienced

novellista, -i, -e [novel'lista] SM, SF short-story writer

novellistica [novel'listika] SF (*arte*) short-story writing; (*insieme di racconti*) short stories *pl*

novello, -a [no'vello] AGG (*piante, patate*) new; (*insalata, verdura*) early; (*sposo*) newly-married; **pollo novello** spring chicken

novembre [no'vembre] SM November; *vedi* **luglio**

novembrino, -a [novem'brino] AGG November *attr*

novemila [nove'mila] AGG INV, SM INV nine thousand

novennale [noven'nale] AGG (*che dura 9 anni*) nine-year *attr*; (*ogni 9 anni*) nine-yearly

novilunio, -ni [novi'lunjo] SM (*Astron*) new moon

novità [novi'ta] SF INV 1 (*originalità*) novelty; (*innovazione*) innovation; (*cosa originale, insolita*) something new; (*libro*) new publication; **questa è una novità!** that's new!; **le novità della moda francese** the latest French fashions; **l'ultima novità in fatto di lettori CD** the latest thing in CD players 2 (*notizia*) (piece of) news *sg*; **che novità ci sono?** what's the news?; **ci sono novità?** is there any news?

noviziato [novit'tsjato] SM (*Rel*) novitiate; (*tirocinio*) apprenticeship

novizio, -zia, -zi, -zie [no'vittsjo] SM, SF (*Rel*) novice; (*tirocinante*) beginner, apprentice

nozione [not'tsjone] SF notion, idea; **nozioni** SFPL (*rudimenti*) basic knowledge *sg*, rudiments; **la nozione del tempo e dello spazio** the notion of time and space; **ho perso la nozione del tempo** I've lost all notion of time; **le prime nozioni di matematica** the first elements of mathematics; **non ha che alcune nozioni di filosofia** he only has a vague notion of philosophy; **"nozioni di algebra"** "algebra for beginners"

nozionismo [nottsjo'nizmo] SM superficial knowledge

nozionistico, -a, -ci, -che [nottsjo'nistiko] AGG superficial

nozze ['nɔttse] SFPL wedding *sg*, marriage *sg*; **regalo di nozze** wedding present; **viaggio di nozze** honeymoon; **dove andrete in viaggio di nozze?** where are you going on your honeymoon?; **offrendomi quel lavoro mi hanno invitato a nozze** (*fig*) when they offered me that job it was just what I wanted; **nozze d'argento** silver wedding *sg*; **nozze d'oro** golden wedding *sg*

ns. ABBR (*Comm*) = **nostro**

NU SIGLA = Nuoro ♦ ABBR (= *Nazioni Unite*) UN; (= *Nettezza Urbana*) *vedi* **nettezza**

nube ['nube] SF (*anche fig*) cloud

nubifragio, -gi [nubi'fradʒo] SM cloudburst

nubile ['nubile] AGG (*donna*) unmarried, single ♦ SF single *o* unmarried woman

nuca, -che ['nuka] SF nape (of the neck)

nucleare [nukle'are] AGG nuclear; **l'energia nucleare** nuclear energy ♦ SM: **il nucleare** nuclear energy

nucleo ['nukleo] SM (*Bio, Fis*) nucleus; (*Geog*) core; (*fig: parte centrale*) core, nucleus; (*gruppo*) unit, group, team; (*Mil, Polizia*) unit, squad; **il nucleo familiare** the family unit; **nucleo antidroga** anti-drugs squad

nudismo [nu'dizmo] SM nudism

nudista, -i, -e [nu'dista] SM, SF nudist

nudità [nudi'ta] SF INV (*di persona*) nudity, nakedness *sg*; (*parti nude del corpo*) nakedness; (*di paesaggio*) bareness *sg*; **le proprie nudità** one's nakedness

nudo, -a ['nudo] AGG (*persona, membra*) bare, naked, nude; (*albero, parete, montagna*) bare; (*verità*) plain, naked; **un uomo nudo** a naked man; **era completamente nuda** she was completely naked; **mezzo/tutto nudo** half-/stark-naked; **a piedi nudi** barefoot; **camminava a piedi nudi in giardino** he was walking barefoot in the garden; **a occhio nudo** to the naked eye; **è invisibile a occhio nudo** it's not visible to the naked eye; **gli ha detto nudo e crudo che...** he said to him bluntly that ...; **questa è la verità nuda e cruda** this is the plain, unvarnished truth; **mettere a nudo** (*cuore, verità*) to lay bare ♦ SM (*Arte*) nude

nugolo ['nugolo] SM: **un nugolo di** a whole host of

nulla ['nulla] PRON, AVV = **niente** ♦ SM 1 **il nulla** nothing, nothingness; **Dio creò il mondo dal nulla** God created the world out of nothing; **svanire nel nulla** to vanish into thin air 2 (*minima quantità*): **basta un nulla per farlo arrabbiare** he gets annoyed over the slightest thing; **te lo cedo per (un) nulla** I am giving it to you for a song *o* for next to nothing

nullaosta [nulla'ɔsta] SM INV authorization, permission

nullatenente [nullate'nɛnte] AGG: **essere nullatenente** to own nothing ♦ SM, SF person with no property

nullità [nulli'ta] SF INV 1 (*Dir*) nullity; (*di idea, ragionamento*) invalidity 2 (*persona*) nonentity

nullo, -a ['nullo] AGG (*tentativo, sforzo*) vain, pointless; (*Dir*) null (and void); **scheda nulla** (*Pol*) spoiled vote; **incontro nullo** (*Sport*) draw; **colpo nullo** (*Tennis*) let

numerale [nume'rale] AGG, SM numeral

numerare [nume'rare] /72/ VT to number

numeratore [numera'tore] SM 1 (*Mat*) numerator 2 (*macchina*) numbering device

numerazione [numerat'tsjone] SF numbering; **numerazione araba** arabic numerals *pl*; **numerazione romana** roman numerals *pl*

numerico, -a, -ci, -che [nu'mɛriko] AGG numerical

numero ['numero] SM 1 (*gen*) number; (*arabo, romano*) numeral; **i Numeri** (*Bibbia*) the Book of Numbers; **dodici di numero** twelve in number; **abito al numero 6** I live at number 6; **ha tutti i numeri per riuscire** he's got what it takes to succeed; **dare i numeri** (*farneticare*) to be not all there; **tanto per fare numero** invitiamo anche lui why don't we invite him to make up the numbers?; **che numero tuo fratello!** your brother is a real character!; **numero chiuso** (*Univ*) selective entry system; **numero civico** house number; **numero legale** quorum; **numero di scarpe** shoe size; **che numero di scarpe porti?** what size (of) shoe do you take? 2 (*Telec: anche:* **numero di telefono**) (tele)phone number; **qual è il tuo numero di telefono?** what's your phone number?; **numero verde** (*Telec*) ≈ Freephone *o* Freefone number (*Brit*), ≈ toll-free number (*USA*); **fare un numero** to dial a number 3 (*di giornale, rivista*) issue, number; **numero arretrato** back number; **numero doppio** issue with supplement 4 (*di spettacolo*) act, turn; **il suo numero è stato molto divertente** his act was very entertaining 5 (*Chim, Fis*) number; **numero di massa** mass number

numeroso, -a [nume'roso] AGG 1 numerous, many; **ci sono stati numerosi casi di morbillo quest'anno** there have been numerous cases of measles this year; **le personalità sono intervenute numerose** celebrities were present in large numbers 2 (*folla, famiglia*) large; **ha una famiglia numerosa** he's got a large family

numismatica [numiz'matika] SF numismatics sg, coin collecting

nunzio, -zi ['nuntsjo] SM (*Rel*) nuncio

nuoccio *ecc* ['nwɔttʃo] VB *vedi* **nuocere**

nuocere ['nwɔtʃere] /69/ VI IRREG (*aus* avere) nuocere a to harm, damage, be bad for; **il fumo nuoce alla salute** smoking is bad for your health; **tentar non nuoce** (*Proverbio*) there's no harm in trying

nuociuto, -a [nwo'tʃuto] PP *di* nuocere

nuora ['nwɔra] SF daughter-in-law

nuotare [nwo'tare] /72/ VI (*aus* avere) to swim; (*galleggiare: oggetti*) to float; **sai nuotare?** can you swim?; nuotare a rana/sul dorso to do the breaststroke/backstroke; **nuotare nell'oro** to be rolling in money ♦ VT to swim

nuotata [nwo'tata] SF swim

nuotatore, -trice [nwota'tore] SM, SF swimmer; **è un bravo nuotatore** he's a good swimmer

nuoto ['nwɔto] SM swimming; **una gara di nuoto** a swimming gala (*Brit*), meet (*USA*); **attraversare la Manica a nuoto** to swim (across) the Channel; **nuoto pinnato** fin swimming; **nuoto sincronizzato** synchronized swimming

nuova ['nwɔva] SF news sg; **che nuove ci sono?** is there any news?; **nessuna nuova buona nuova** (*Proverbio*) no news is good news

nuovamente [nwɔva'mente] AVV again; **si è nuovamente ammalato** he's ill again

Nuova York ['nwɔva 'jork] SF New York

Nuova Zelanda ['nwɔva dze'landa] SF New Zealand; **ti è piaciuta la Nuova Zelanda?** did you like New Zealand?; **andremo in Nuova Zelanda** we're going to New Zealand

nuovo, -a ['nwɔvo] AGG **1** (*gen*) new; (*originale: idea*) novel, new; (: *metodo*) new, up-to-date; **un vestito nuovo** a new dress; **nuovo fiammante, nuovo di zecca** brand-new; **ha una macchina nuova di zecca** he's got a brand-new car; **il nuovo presidente** the new *o* newly-elected president; **sono nuovo del mestiere** I am new to this job; **sono nuova di qui/di Glasgow** I am new here/to Glasgow; **il suo volto non mi è nuovo** I know his face; **come nuovo** as good as new; **sembra nuovo** it looks like new **2** (*altro, secondo*) new, fresh;

(*diverso*) new, different; **usa un foglio nuovo** take a fresh sheet of paper; **hai letto il suo nuovo libro?** have you read his new *o* latest book?; **fino a nuovo ordine** until further notice; **c'è stata una nuova serie di scosse** there has been a new *o* further series of tremors; **fare un nuovo tentativo** to make another attempt; **anno nuovo, vita nuova!** it's time to turn over a new leaf! **3 di nuovo** again; **di nuovo tu?** (is that) you again?; **è successo di nuovo** it happened again ♦ SM: **che c'è di nuovo?** what's the news?, what's new?; **non c'è niente di nuovo** there's no news *o* nothing new; **rimettere a nuovo** (*cosa, macchina*) to do up like new; **questa cura mi ha rimesso a nuovo** this treatment has given me a new lease of life

nutrice [nu'tritʃe] SF wet nurse

nutriente [nutri'ente] AGG nutritious, nourishing; (*balsamo*) nourishing; **crema nutriente** (*Cosmetica*) nourishing cream

nutrimento [nutri'mento] SM nourishment, food

nutrire [nu'trire] /45/ VT to feed; (*fig: sentimenti*) to harbour (*Brit*), harbor (*USA*); (: *risentimento, rancore*) to nurse, feel; **la madre nutriva i piccoli** the mother was feeding her young; **nutrivo profonda stima per lui** I felt great respect for him ♦ VI (*aus* avere) (*cibo*) to be nourishing; **nutrirsi** VR: **nutrirsi di** to feed on, eat; **i leoni si nutrono esclusivamente di carne** lions only eat meat

nutritivo, -a [nutri'tivo] AGG (*proprietà*) nutritional; (*sostanza*) nutritious

nutrito, -a [nu'trito] AGG **1 ben/mal nutrito** well/poorly fed **2** (*numeroso*) large; (*fitto*) heavy

nutrizione [nutrit'tsjone] SF (*atto*) feeding, nutrition; (*dieta*) nutrition; **una scarsa nutrizione** a poor diet

nuvolo, -a ['nuvolo] AGG cloudy

nuvolosità [nuvolosi'ta] SF INV cloudiness; **nuvolosità persistente** persistent cloud cover

nuvoloso, -a [nuvo'loso] AGG (*tempo*) cloudy; (*cielo*) cloudy, overcast; **oggi è più nuvoloso di ieri** it's cloudier today than it was yesterday

nuziale [nut'tsjale] AGG wedding *attr*, nuptial; **la cerimonia nuziale** the wedding ceremony

nylon ['nailɔn] (*Marchio registrato*) nylon

Oo

O¹, o¹ [ɔ] SF INV, SM INV (*lettera*) O, o; **O come Otranto** ≈ O for Oliver (*Brit*), ≈ O for Oboe (*USA*)

O² ABBR (= *Ovest*) W

o [o] *dav vocale talvolta* od CONG **1** (*gen*) or; **o... o...** either ... or ...; **o meglio** or rather; **due o tre volte** two or three times; **oggi o domani** (either) today or tomorrow; **lo farò o oggi o domani** I'll do it either today or tomorrow; **(o) l'uno o l'altro** either (of them); **sono decisa: o lui o nessuno** I've made up my mind: it's him or nobody **2** (*altrimenti*) (or) else; **sbrigati o faremo tardi** hurry up or (else) we'll be late

oasi [ˈɔazi] SF INV (*anche fig*) oasis; **oasi di pace** haven of peace

obbediente *ecc* [obbeˈdjɛnte] *vedi* **ubbidiente**

obbiettare *ecc vedi* **obiettare**

obbligare [obbliˈɡare] /80/ VT: **obbligare qn a fare qc** (*sogg: circostanza, persona*) to force *o* oblige sb to do sth, make sb do sth; (*legalmente*) to require sb to do sth; (*Dir*) to bind sb to do sth; **mi ha obbligato a fare i compiti** she made me do my homework; **essere obbligato a fare qc** to have to do sth; **sono obbligato (a farlo)** I have to (do it); **non sei obbligato a farlo** you don't have to do it; **e chi ti obbliga?** who's forcing you (to do it)?; **la mia coscienza mi obbligò a tacere** I was bound by conscience to remain silent; **l'influenza lo obbliga a letto** he's confined to bed with flu; **obbligarsi** VR **1** (*Dir*): **obbligarsi per qn** to stand surety for sb, act as guarantor for sb **2** (*impegnarsi*): **obbligarsi a fare qc** to undertake to do sth

obbligatissimo, -a [obbligaˈtissimo] AGG: **obbligatissimo!** (*ringraziamento*) much obliged!

obbligato, -a [obbliˈɡato] AGG **1** (*riconoscente*): **obbligato verso qn** obliged *o* indebted to sb; **le sono molto obbligato!** I'm much obliged! **2** (*imposto: percorso, tappa*) set, fixed; **passaggio obbligato** (*fig*) essential requirement; **è stata una scelta obbligata** I (*o tu ecc*) had no choice

obbligatorio, -ria, -ri, -rie [obbligaˈtɔrjo] AGG (*assicurazione, esame*) compulsory; (*clausola*) (legally) binding

obbligazione [obbligatˈtsjone] SF **1** (*gen, anche Dir*) obligation **2** (*Fin*) bond, debenture; **obbligazione al portatore** bearer bond; **obbligazione dello Stato** government bond; **obbligazioni convertibili** convertible loan stock *sg*, convertible debentures

obbligazionista, -i, -e [obbligattsjoˈnista] SM, SF bondholder

obbligo, -ghi [ˈobbligo] SM obligation; (*dovere*) obligation, duty; **avere degli obblighi con** *o* **verso qn** to have obligations to sb; (*essere riconoscente*) to be indebted to sb; **ho degli obblighi nei confronti dei miei genitori** I've got obligations to my parents; **sentire/avere l'obbligo di fare qc** to feel/be obliged to do sth, feel/be under an obligation to do sth; **mi sono sentito in obbligo (di farlo)** I felt obliged to (do it); **non ho l'obbligo di timbrare il cartellino al lavoro** I don't have to clock in at work; **i libri vengono dati in prestito con l'obbligo di restituirli entro 15 giorni** books are lent on condition that they are returned within a fortnight; **essere d'obbligo** (*discorso, applauso*) to be called for; **fare una visita d'obbligo** to make a duty call; **le formalità d'obbligo** the necessary formalities; **frasi d'obbligo** civilities; "**è d'obbligo l'abito scuro**" "black tie"; **scuola dell'obbligo** compulsory education; **obblighi militari** compulsory military service *sg*

obb.mo ABBR = **obbligatissimo**

obbrobrio, -bri [obˈbrɔbrjo] SM **1** (*infamia*) disgrace, shame **2** (*fig: cosa brutta*) mess, eyesore; **quel palazzo è un obbrobrio** that building's an eyesore

obelisco, -schi [obeˈlisko] SM obelisk

oberato, -a [obeˈrato] AGG: **oberato di** (*lavoro*) overloaded *o* overburdened with; **oberato di** *o* **da debiti** crippled with debts

obesità [obesiˈta] SF obesity

obeso, -a [oˈbeso] AGG obese

obiettare [objetˈtare] /72/ VT: **obiettare che...** to object that ...; **non ho nulla da obiettare** I have no objection (to make), I haven't got any objections; **ha obiettato che non aveva tempo** he pleaded lack of time; **obiettare su qc** to object to sth, raise objections concerning sth

obiettivamente [objettivaˈmente] AVV objectively

obiettività [objettiviˈta] SF objectivity

obiettivo, -a [objetˈtivo] AGG objective ♦ SM **1** (*scopo*) objective, aim; **il suo obiettivo è quello di vincere la gara** his aim is to win the competition **2** (*Ottica, Fot*) lens *sg*, objective; **obiettivo a fuoco fisso** fixed-focus lens; **obiettivo grandangolare** wide-angle lens

obiettore [objetˈtore] SM objector; **obiettore di coscienza** conscientious objector

obiezione [objetˈtsjone] SF objection; **fare** *o* **muovere** *o* **sollevare un'obiezione** to make *o* raise an objection, object; **ci sono obiezioni?** any objections?; **obiezione accolta/respinta** (*Dir*) objection sustained/overruled

obitorio, -ri [obiˈtɔrjo] SM mortuary, morgue
  ❑ **obitorio** non si traduce mai con la parola inglese *obituary*

obliquo, -a [oˈblikwo] AGG (*gen, anche Mat*) oblique; (*calligrafia, raggi*) slanting; (*fig*) devious, underhand; **una linea obliqua** an oblique line

obliterare [obliteˈrare] /72/ VT (*francobollo*) to cancel; (*biglietto: con timbro*) to stamp; (: *con foratura*) to punch

obliteratrice [obliteraˈtritʃe] SF (*anche: macchina obliteratrice: vedi vb*) cancelling machine; stamping machine; punch

oblò [oˈblɔ] SM INV (*Naut*) porthole

oblungo, -a, -ghi, -ghe [oˈblungo] AGG oblong

oboe [ˈɔboe] SM oboe

obolo [ˈɔbolo] SM (*elemosina*) (small) offering, mite

obsolescenza [obsoleʃˈʃɛntsa] SF (*Econ*) obsolescence

obsoleto, -a [obsoˈleto] AGG obsolete

OC ABBR (= *onde corte*) SW (= *short wave*)

oca [ˈɔka] SF (*pl* **oche**) (*Zool*) goose; (*fig: pegg: anche*: **un'oca giuliva**) silly goose; **gioco dell'oca** ≈ snakes and ladders; **oca maschio** gander

ocaggine [oˈkaddʒine] SF silliness, stupidity

occasionale [okkazjoˈnale] AGG (*incontro*) chance attr; (*cliente, guadagni*) casual, occasional

occasione [okkaˈzjone] SF **1** (*opportunità*) opportunity; (*caso favorevole*) chance; **sarebbe l'occasione buona per fare...** it would be an ideal opportunity to do ...; **avere occasione di fare qc** to have the chance *o* opportunity of doing sth; **alla prima occasione** at the first opportunity; **lo farò alla prima occasione** I'll do it at the first opportunity; **all'occasione** should the need arise **2** (*circostanza*) occasion; **in occasione di** on the occasion of; **in occasione del suo compleanno** on the occasion of his birthday; **a seconda delle occasioni** depending on circumstances *o* on the situation **3** (*motivo, pretesto*) occasion, cause; **dare occasione a** to cause, give rise to **4** (*buon affare*) bargain; **compralo! è un'occasione** buy it! it's a bargain; **d'occasione** (*a buon prezzo*) bargain attr; (*di seconda mano*) secondhand; **comprare qc d'occasione** to get sth cheap

occhiaia [okˈkjaja] SF **1** (*orbita*) eye socket **2** **occhiaie** SFPL: **avere le occhiaie** to have bags under one's eyes

occhiali [okˈkjali] SMPL (*da vista*) glasses, spectacles; (*di protezione*) goggles; **occhiali da sole** sunglasses; **porto gli occhiali** I wear glasses

occhiata [okˈkjata] SF look, glance; **dare un'occhiata a** (*guardare*) to have a look at, glance at; (*badare*) to keep an eye on; **vorrei dare un'occhiata a quel libro** I'd like to have a look at that book; **potresti dare un'occhiata alle mie valigie?** could you keep an eye on my cases?; **un'occhiata d'intesa** a knowing look *o* glance

occhieggiare [okkjed'dʒare] /62/ vi (*aus* avere) (*apparire qua e là*) to appear here and there, peep out

occhiello [ok'kjɛllo] sm 1 (*asola*) buttonhole; (*di scarpe*) eyelet 2 (*Tip*) half-title

occhio, -chi ['ɔkkjo] sm 1 (*Anat*) eye; **avere gli occhi azzurri** to have blue eyes; **dagli occhi castani** brown-eyed; **avere occhi buoni** to have good eyesight; **logorarsi gli occhi** to strain one's eyes; **fare un occhio nero a qn** to give sb a black eye; **a occhio nudo** with the naked eye; **visibile a occhio nudo** visible to the naked eye 2 (*sguardo, espressione*) look; **alzò gli occhi dal libro** he looked up from *o* raised his eyes from his book; **cercare qn con gli occhi** to look *o* glance around for sb; **ha l'occhio smorto oggi** he's looking rather bleary-eyed today 3 (*accortezza, capacità di giudicare*): **avere occhio** to have a good eye; **ci vuole occhio per fare questo lavoro** this job requires a good eye; **vedere di buon/mal occhio qn/qc** to view sb/sth favourably/unfavourably, look favourably/unfavourably on sb/sth 4 (*attenzione*): **occhio!** look out!, watch out!, careful!; **occhio alla borsa!** watch your bag!, keep an eye on your bag!; **essere tutt'occhi** to be all eyes 5 (*cosa a forma d'occhio: di ciclone, patata*) eye; **occhio magico** (*su porta*) peephole 6 (*fraseologia*): **a occhio** (**e croce**) roughly, round about; **a occhio e croce costerà cento euro** it'll cost round about one hundred euros; **tieni gli occhi aperti per...** keep an eye out for ...; **non riuscivo a tener gli occhi aperti** I couldn't keep my eyes open; **non ho chiuso occhio stanotte** I didn't sleep a wink last night; **aprire gli occhi a qn su qc** to open sb's eyes to sth; **chiudere un occhio** (**su**) (*fig*) to turn a blind eye (to), shut one's eyes (to); **per qualche volta chiuderò un occhio** I'll turn a blind eye this once; **sognare a occhi aperti** to daydream; **a occhi chiusi** (*anche fig*) with one's eyes shut; **costare un occhio della testa** to cost a fortune, cost an arm and a leg; **costa un occhio della testa** it costs an arm and a leg; **darei un occhio per sapere** I'd give my eyeteeth to know; **dare nell'occhio** to attract attention; (*spiccare*) to stand out a mile; (*vestito, colore*) to be loud *o* gaudy; **dare all'occhio o nell'occhio a qn** to catch sb's eye; **tenere d'occhio qn/qc** to keep an eye on sb/sth; **per favore, tieni d'occhio le mie valigie** please could you keep an eye on my cases?; **fare l'occhio a qc** to get used to sth; **fare gli occhi dolci a qn** to make sheep's eyes at sb; **guardare con tanto d'occhi** to gaze wide-eyed at; **lasciare gli occhi su qc** to set one's heart on sth; **mettere gli occhi addosso a qn/su qc** to have got one's eyes on sb/sth; **a quattr'occhi** privately, in private; **ce l'hai sotto gli occhi** it's right there in front of you; **mi è capitato sott'occhio un articolo interessante** I happened to see an interesting article; **occhio per occhio, dente per dente** (*Proverbio*) an eye for an eye, a tooth for a tooth; **lontano dagli occhi lontano dal cuore** (*Proverbio*) out of sight, out of mind

occhiolino [okkjo'lino] sm: **fare l'occhiolino a qn** to wink at sb; **le fece l'occhiolino** he winked at her

occidentale [ottʃiden'tale] agg (*Geog*) western, west; (*vento*) westerly; (*cultura, paesi*) Western; **i paesi occidentali** Western countries; **la costa occidentale della Francia** the west coast of France ♦ sm, sf Westerner

occidente [ottʃi'dente] sm west; **a occidente** in the west; **a occidente di** (to the) west of; **il sole tramonta a occidente** the sun sets in the west; **l'Occidente** (*Pol*) the West

occipite [ot'tʃipite] sm back of the head, occiput (*Anat*)

occludere [ok'kludere] /3/ vt irreg to block, occlude (*Med*)

occlusione [okklu'zjone] sf blockage, obstruction, occlusion (*Med*)

occluso, -a [ok'kluzo] pp *di* occludere

occorrente [okkor'rɛnte] agg necessary ♦ sm all that is necessary; **porta con te tutto l'occorrente** bring everything you need; **l'occorrente per scrivere/disegnare** writing/drawing materials *pl*

occorrenza [okkor'rɛntsa] sf 1 (*evenienza*) eventuality 2 (*bisogno*) necessity, need; **all'occorrenza** if need be, if necessary, in case of need

❏ **occorrenza** non si traduce mai con la parola inglese *occurrence*

occorrere [ok'korrere] /28/ vi irreg (*aus* essere) (*essere necessario*) to be needed, be required; **ti occorre qc?** do you need anything?; **mi occorre del denaro** I need some money; **mi occorrono 2 mila euro** I need 2 thousand euros; **mi occorre un'ora per arrivarci** it takes me *o* I need an hour to get there ♦ vb impers: **occorre farlo** it must be done; **occorre far presto** we'll (*o* you'll *ecc*) have to hurry; **non occorre che gli scriva subito** there's no need to write to him at once; **non occorre che mi telefoni** you don't need to phone me

❏ **occorrere** non si traduce mai con la parola inglese *occur*

occorso, -a [ok'korso] pp *di* occorrere

occultamento [okkulta'mento] sm concealment

occultare [okkul'tare] /72/ vt to hide, conceal; **occultarsi** vr: **occultarsi (a)** to hide (from), conceal *o.s.* (from)

occulto, -a [ok'kulto] agg (*segreto*) hidden, secret, concealed; (*arcano*) occult; **le scienze occulte** the occult *sg*, the occult sciences ♦ sm: **il vuole occulto** the occult

occupante [okku'pante] agg (*Mil*) occupying ♦ sm, sf (*di casa*) occupier, occupant; **occupante abusivo** squatter

occupare [okku'pare] /72/ vt (*gen, anche Mil*) to occupy; (*spazio, tempo*) to occupy, take up; (*casa*) to live in; (*carica*) to hold; (*manodopera*) to employ; **l'esercito ha occupato il paese** the army has occupied *o* taken over the country; **la città è stata occupata durante la guerra** the city was occupied during the war; **l'armadio occupa tutta la parete** the cupboard takes up the whole wall; **lo sport mi occupa tutto il tempo libero** sport takes up all my spare time; **gli studenti hanno occupato la scuola** the students have occupied the school; **la casa è stata occupata (abusivamente)** the house has been taken over by squatters; **occuparsi** vip 1 **occuparsi di** (*interessarsi*) to be interested in, take an interest in; (*prendersi cura*) to take care of, look after; (*impicciarsi*) to interfere in, meddle in; **potresti occuparti dei bambini?** could you look after the children?; **si occupa di assicurazioni he's** in insurance; **occupati dei fatti tuoi!** mind your own business! 2 **occuparsi in** (*impiegarsi*) to get a job in

occupato, -a [okku'pato] agg (*telefono, gabinetto*) engaged; (*posto, sedia*) taken, occupied; (*zona, fabbrica, scuola*) occupied; (*persona: affaccendato*) busy; **è occupato quel posto?** is that seat taken?; **la toilette è occupata** the toilet is engaged; **non riesco a telefonargli; è sempre occupato** I can't get through to him; the line's always engaged; **la scuola è ancora occupata** the school is still occupied; **una città occupata** an occupied city; **in questo momento il signor Rossi è molto occupato** Mr Rossi is very busy at the moment; **domani sarò ancora più occupato** I'll be even busier tomorrow; **essere occupato a fare qc** to be busy doing sth ♦ sm: **gli occupati e i disoccupati** the employed and the unemployed

occupazionale [okkupattsjo'nale] agg employment *attr*, of employment

occupazione [okkupat'tsjone] sf 1 (*Mil: di fabbrica, scuola*) occupation; (*di casa*) occupancy, occupation; (*interesse, attività*) occupation; **occupazione abusiva** squatting 2 (*gen*) employment; (*impiego, lavoro*) job, occupation; **sto cercando un'occupazione** I'm looking for a job; **occupazione: infermiere** occupation: nurse; **la piena occupazione** full employment

Oceania [otʃe'anja] sf Oceania

oceano [o'tʃɛano] sm ocean

ocra ['ɔkra] sf, agg inv ochre

oculare [oku'lare] agg (*bulbo, lenti*) ocular, eye *attr*; **testimone oculare** eyewitness

oculatezza [okula'tettsa] sf (*vedi agg*) caution; shrewdness

oculato, -a [oku'lato] agg (*attento*) cautious, prudent; (*accorto*) shrewd

oculista, -i, -e [oku'lista] sm, sf eye specialist, ophthalmologist; **devo andare dall'oculista** I need to go to the eye specialist

od [od] cong *vedi* o

ode¹ ['ɔde] sf *vedi* ode

ode² ['ɔde] vb *vedi* udire

odiare [o'djare] /19/ vt to hate, detest, loathe; **ti odio!** I hate you!; **odio le persone egoiste** I hate selfish people; **odiare**

fare qc to hate doing sth; **odio alzarmi presto al mattino** I hate getting up early in the morning; **odiarsi** VR to hate o.s.; (uso reciproco) to hate each other; **Marco e Matteo si odiano** Marco and Matteo hate each other

odierno, -a [oˈdjɛrno] AGG (di oggi) today's, of today; (attuale) present, current; **in data odierna** (frm) today

odio, odi [ˈɔdjo] SM hatred, hate; **avere in odio qn/qc** to hate o; detest sb/sth; **prendere in odio qn/qc** to take a strong dislike to sb/sth

odioso, -a [oˈdjoso] AGG (detestabile) hateful, odious; (antipatico) unpleasant, obnoxious; **sei odioso** you're horrible; **rendersi odioso (a)** to make o.s. thoroughly unpopular (with)

odo ecc [ˈɔdo] VB vedi udire

odontoiatra, -i, -e [odontoˈjatra] SM, SF dentist, dental surgeon

odontoiatria [odontojaˈtria] SF dentistry

odontotecnico, -ci [odontoˈtekniko] SM dental technician

odorare [odoˈrare] /72/ VT (anche fig) to smell; (profumare) to perfume, scent ♦ VI (aus avere) (anche fig): **odorare (di)** to smell (of); **questi fiori non odorano** these flowers don't have any smell o perfume; **odorare di pulito/fresco** to smell clean/fresh; **odorare di muffa/d'aglio** to smell mouldy/of garlic

odorato [odoˈrato] SM sense of smell

odore [oˈdore] SM 1 (gen) smell, odour (Brit), odor (USA); (fragranza) scent, fragrance; **un buon odore** a nice smell; **un cattivo odore** a bad smell; **senza odore** odo(u)rless; **sentire odore di qc** to smell sth; **sento odore di pesce** I can smell fish; **avere buon/cattivo odore** to smell nice/bad, have a nice o good/bad smell; **ha un buon/cattivo odore** it smells nice/bad; **odore di cucina** smell of cooking; **morire in odore di santità** (Rel) to die in the odo(u)r of sanctity 2 **odori** SMPL (Culin) (aromatic) herbs

odoroso, -a [odoˈroso] AGG sweet-smelling

offendere [ofˈfɛndere] VB IRREG /36/ VT 1 (persona, morale pubblica, senso estetico) to offend; (ferire) to hurt; **offendere qn nell'onore** to offend sb's honour (Brit) o honor (USA); **offendere la vista** (fig) to offend the eye 2 (insultare) to insult, offend; **non avevo intenzione di offenderti** I didn't mean to insult you 3 (violare: libertà, diritti) to violate; (: legge) to break; **offendere i diritti di qn** to infringe on sb's rights; **offendersi** VR (uso reciproco) to insult each other; **offendersi** VIP (risentirsi): **offendersi (per)** to take offence (Brit) o offense (USA) (at), be offended (by); **se non vieni mi offendo** I'll be offended if you don't come; **si è offeso per non essere stato invitato** he took offence because they didn't invite him

offensivo, -a [offenˈsivo] AGG (parole) offensive, insulting; (armi) offensive

offensore [offenˈsore] SM (Mil) aggressor

offerente [offeˈrɛnte] PART PRES di offrire ♦ SM, SF (ad un'asta) bidder; **vendere al migliore offerente** to sell to the highest bidder

offerto, -a [ofˈfɛrto] PP di offrire

offeso, -a [ofˈfeso] PP di offendere ♦ AGG 1 (nei sentimenti) offended, hurt; (fisicamente) hurt, injured; **è offesa per quello che hai detto** she's offended about what you said; **sei ancora offeso con me?** are you still annoyed with me? 2 (Dir): **la parte offesa** the plaintiff ♦ SM, SF: **fare l'offeso** to go into a huff

officiare [offiˈtʃare] /14/ VI (aus avere) (Rel) to officiate

officina [offiˈtʃina] SF workshop; **officina meccanica** (Aut) garage; **devo portare la macchina in officina** I have to take the car to the garage

offrire [ofˈfrire] VB IRREG /70/ VT 1 (sigaretta, lavoro, merce, aiuto) to offer; (preghiere, messa) to offer (up); (ad un'asta) to bid; **offrire qc a qn** to offer sth to sb, offer sb sth; **mi ha offerto un passaggio** he offered me a lift; **le hanno offerto un lavoro** they've offered her a job; **mi offri una sigaretta?** can I have a cigarette?; **ti offro da bere** I'll buy you a drink; **offro io (da bere)** the drinks are on me; **offro io, questa volta!** I'll pay this time!; **le offre la casa** it's on the house; **ti va una pizza?** offro io do you feel like a pizza? my treat 2 (regalare): **offrire a** to give to; **offrire qc in dono a qn** to present sb with sth 3 (opportunità, vantaggio) to offer, present; **offrire il fianco alle critiche** to expose o.s. to criticism; **"offresi posto di segretaria"** "secretarial vacancy", "vacancy

for secretary"; **offrirsi** VR: **offrirsi volontario** to offer (o.s.), volunteer; **nessuno si è offerto volontario** nobody volunteered; **offrirsi di fare qc** to offer o volunteer to do sth; **si è offerto di aiutarci** he offered to help us; **"segretaria offresi"** "secretary seeks post" ♦ VIP (presentarsi: occasione) to present itself, arise; **una vista stupenda si offrì ai loro occhi** a wonderful view lay before them

offuscare [offusˈkare] /20/ VT (cielo) to darken; (sole) to obscure; (fig: fama) to obscure, overshadow; (: mente) to dim, cloud; **offuscarsi** VIP (vedi vt) to darken, grow dark; to become obscured; to grow dim; (fig: sguardo) to cloud over

oftalmico, -a, -ci, -che [ofˈtalmiko] AGG ophthalmic

oggettività [oddʒettiviˈta] SF objectivity

oggettivo, -a [oddʒetˈtivo] AGG objective; **proposizione oggettiva** (Gramm) object clause

oggetto [odˈdʒɛtto] SM 1 (cosa, articolo) object, thing; **un oggetto rotondo** a round object; **oggetti preziosi** valuables, articles of value; **oggetti smarriti** lost property sg (Brit), lost-and-found sg (USA); **dov'è l'ufficio oggetti smarriti?** where's the lost property office? 2 (di disputa, discorso, studio) subject; (di sogni, pensieri) object; **essere oggetto di** (critiche, controversia) to be the subject of; (odio, pietà) to be the object of; **essere oggetto di scherno** to be a laughing stock; **essere oggetto di persecuzione** to be subjected to persecution 3 (di attività, contratto) object, purpose 4 (in lettere commerciali): **oggetto... re ...**; **in oggetto** a quanto detto as regards the (matter mentioned) above 5 (Gramm, Filosofia) object

oggi [ˈɔddʒi] AVV today; (al presente, al giorno d'oggi) today, nowadays, these days; **oggi è venerdì** it's Friday today; **il giornale di oggi** today's paper; **oggi stesso** today, this very day; **lo farò oggi stesso** I'll do it today; **oggi nel pomeriggio** this afternoon; **oggi (a) otto** a week today, today week; **quanti ne abbiamo oggi?** what's the date today?; **oggi come oggi** at present, as things stand; **oggi qui, domani là** (fig) here today, gone tomorrow; **oggi o domani** (fig) sooner or later; **oggi a me, domani a te** (fig) your day will come; **dagli oggi, dagli domani** in the long run, over time ♦ SM today; **dall'oggi al domani** from one day to the next; **potrebbe cambiare tutto dall'oggi al domani** everything could change from one day to the next; **a tutt'oggi** up till now, till today; **le spese a tutt'oggi sono... expenses to date are ...

oggigiorno [oddʒiˈdʒorno] AVV nowadays, these days ♦ SM today

ogiva [oˈdʒiva] SF ogive, pointed arch

OGM [odʒiˈemme] SIGLA MPL (= Organismi Geneticamente Modificati) GMOs (= Genetically Modified Organisms)

ogni [ˈoɲɲi] AGG 1 (ciascuno) every, each; (tutti) all; **ogni passeggero** every o each passenger; **ogni cosa** everything; **lo vedo ogni giorno** I see him every day; **ogni sorta di articoli** all sorts pl of goods 2 (qualsiasi) any, all; **ad ogni costo** at any price, at all costs; **gente d'ogni tipo** people of all sorts; **c'era gente di ogni tipo** there were all sorts of people 3 (con valore distributivo) every; **ogni due giorni** every two days, every other day; **viene ogni due giorni** he comes every two days; **l'autobus passa ogni 20 minuti** the bus comes past every 20 minutes; **una persona ogni cento** one person in every hundred 4 (fraseologia): **in ogni caso** at any rate, in any case, anyway; **penso che dovresti telefonargli in ogni caso** I think you should phone him anyway; **in ogni luogo** everywhere; **da ogni parte** from everywhere; **in o ad ogni modo** anyway, anyhow; **ogni tanto** every so often, every now and then; **ogni tanto le scrivo** I write to her every so often; **ogni volta che** every time (that), whenever

Ognissanti [oɲɲisˈsanti] SM All Saints' Day

ognuno [oɲˈɲuno] PRON (tutti) everybody, everyone; (ciascuno) each (one); **ognuno di noi sa quello che vuole** each of us knows what he wants, we all know what we want; **ad ognuno di voi verrà dato un questionario** each of you will be given a questionnaire

ohi [ˈɔi] ESCL (esprime disappunto, spesso ripetuto) oh!; (esprime dolore) ow!; **ohi la!** hey there!

ohimè [oiˈmɛ] ESCL oh dear!

OIL [ˈɔil] SIGLA F (= Organizzazione Internazionale del Lavoro) ILO (= International Labour Organisation)

OL ABBR (= onde lunghe) LW (= long wave)

Olanda [o'landa] SF Holland; **mi è piaciuta molto l'Olanda** I liked Holland very much; **andrò in Olanda in giugno** I'm going to Holland in June

olandese [olan'dese] AGG Dutch ♦ SM, SF Dutchman o Dutchwoman; **gli Olandesi** the Dutch ♦ SM 1 (*lingua*) Dutch; **parla olandese** he speaks Dutch 2 (*formaggio*) Dutch cheese

oleandro [ole'andro] SM oleander

oleato, -a [ole'ato] AGG: **carta oleata** greaseproof paper (*Brit*), wax paper (*USA*)

oleodotto [oleo'dɔtto] SM oil pipeline

oleoso, -a [ole'oso] AGG oily; (*che contiene olio*) oil *attr*

olezzo [o'leddzo] SM fragrance; (*scherz*: *puzzo*) aroma

olfatto [ol'fatto] SM sense of smell

oliare [ol'jare] /19/ VT (*meccanismo*) to oil, lubricate; (*Culin*) to grease

oliatore [olja'tore] SM (*recipiente*) oilcan; (*dispositivo*) oiler

oliera [ol'jɛra] SF oil and vinegar cruet

oligarchia [oligar'kia] SF oligarchy

Olimpiadi [olim'piadi] SFPL: **le Olimpiadi** the Olympics, the Olympic games

olimpico, -a, -ci, -che [o'limpiko] AGG Olympic

olio, oli [ˈɔljo] SM 1 oil; **sott'olio** (*Culin*) in oil; **tonno/funghi sott'olio** tuna/mushrooms in oil; **il mare è un olio** the sea is like a millpond; **gettare olio sul fuoco** (*fig*) to add fuel to the flames; **una lampada ad olio** an oil lamp; **oli essenziali** essential oils; **olio essenziale di timo** thyme essential oil; **olio di fegato di merluzzo** cod-liver oil; **olio dei freni** (*Aut*) brake fluid; **olio di lino** linseed oil; **olio lubrificante** lubricating oil; **olio d'oliva** olive oil; **olio di semi** vegetable oil; **olio solare** suntan oil 2 (*Rel*): **olio santo** holy oil; **dare l'olio santo a qn** to give sb Extreme Unction 3 (*Pittura*): **un** (*quadro a*) **olio** an oil painting; **dipingere a olio** to paint in oils

oliva [o'liva] SF olive ♦ AGG INV (*colore*) olive(-green)

olivastro, -a [oli'vastro] AGG (*colore*) olive-greenish, olive (-coloured) (*Brit*), olive(-colored) (*USA*); (*carnagione*) olive

oliveto [oli'veto] SM olive grove

olivo [o'livo] SM olive tree

olmo [ˈɔlmo] SM elm

olocausto [olo'kausto] SM (*Rel, anche fig*) sacrifice; (*genocidio*) holocaust

OLP [ɔlp] SIGLA F (= *Organizzazione per la Liberazione della Palestina*) PLO (= *Palestine Liberation Organization*)

oltraggiare [oltrad'dʒare] /62/ VT to offend, insult

oltraggio, -gi [ol'traddʒo] SM 1 (*insulto*) insult, offence (*Brit*), offense (*USA*); **fare un oltraggio a** to offend, insult; **subire un oltraggio** to suffer an affront 2 (*Dir*): **accusato di oltraggio a pubblico ufficiale** charged with insulting a public official; **oltraggio alla corte** contempt of court; **oltraggio al pudore** indecent exposure

oltraggioso, -a [oltrad'dʒoso] AGG (*offensivo*) insulting, offensive

oltralpe [ol'tralpe] AVV on the other side of the Alps, beyond the Alps; **un paese d'oltralpe** a country beyond the Alps

oltranza [ol'trantsa] SF: **a** o **ad oltranza** to the (bitter) end; **continueremo ad oltranza** we'll go on to the bitter end; **sciopero ad oltranza** all-out strike

oltranzismo [oltran'tsismo] SM (*Pol*) extremism

oltranzista, -i, -e [oltran'tsista] SM, SF (*Pol*) extremist

oltre [ˈoltre] AVV 1 (*di luogo: più in là*) farther, further; (: *fig*) further; **andare troppo oltre** (*fig*) to go too far 2 (*di tempo: di più*): **non...oltre** no more, no longer; **non posso aspettare oltre** I can't wait any longer 3 (*di età*) over; **persone di oltre trent'anni** people over thirty (years of age); **gli uomini oltre i cinquant'anni** men over fifty ♦ PREP 1 (*di luogo: di là da*) on the other side of, beyond, over; **l'ho gettato oltre il muro** I threw it over the wall; **sono passati oltre i confini** they crossed the border 2 (*di tempo, quantità: più di*) more than, over; **sono oltre 3 mesi che non ti vedo** I haven't seen you for more than o for over three months; **non oltre il 10 febbraio** not later than 10th February 3 (*in aggiunta a*): **oltre a o che** besides, as well as; **è anche piccola, oltre ad essere cara** it's small as well as being expensive; **oltre che piovere fa freddo** it's cold as well as wet; **oltre a tutto** on top of all

that 4 (*all'infuori di, eccetto*): **oltre a** besides, except, apart from; **oltre a te non voglio vedere nessuno** apart from you, I don't want to see anyone

oltrecortina [oltrekor'tina] AVV behind the Iron Curtain; **paesi d'oltrecortina** Iron Curtain countries

oltremanica [oltre'manika] AVV across the Channel

oltremare [oltre'mare] AVV overseas; **paesi d'oltremare** overseas countries

oltremodo [oltre'mɔdo] AVV extremely, greatly

oltreoceano [oltreo'tʃeano] SM: **paesi d'oltreoceano** overseas countries

oltrepassare [oltrepas'sare] /72/ VT (*varcare*) to cross, go beyond; (*superare*) to exceed, go over; **oltrepassarono il confine** they crossed the border; **oltrepassare i limiti** o **la misura** (*fig*) to go too far; **questa volta hai oltrepassato ogni limite!** this time you've gone too far!

oltretomba [oltre'tomba] SM: **l'oltretomba** the hereafter

OM ABBR 1 (= *onde medie*) MW (= *medium wave*) 2 (*Mil*: = *ospedale militare*)

omaggio, -gi [o'maddʒo] SM 1 (*segno di rispetto*) homage, tribute; **rendere omaggio a** to pay homage o tribute to 2 (*dono*) gift; (*Comm*): **fare omaggio di un libro** to give a presentation copy of a book; **copia in omaggio** presentation o complimentary copy; **biglietto in omaggio** complimentary ticket, free ticket; **è un omaggio della ditta** it's a present from the firm; **"in omaggio"** "free gift" 3 **omaggi** SMPL (*ossequi*) respects, regards; **presentare i propri omaggi a qn** (*frm*) to pay one's respects to sb ♦ AGG INV free

Oman [o'man] SM Oman

ombelicale [ombeli'kale] AGG umbilical; **cordone ombelicale** umbilical cord

ombelico, -chi [ombe'liko] SM navel

ombra [ˈombra] SF 1 (*sagoma scura*) shadow; (*zona non assolata*) shade; (*oscurità*) darkness; **l'ombra di un grattacielo** the shadow of a skyscraper; **sedersi all'ombra (di)** to sit in the shade (of); **mi sedetti all'ombra** I sat down in the shade; **dare ombra a qn** (*fig*) to put sb in the shade; **essere l'ombra di se stesso** to be a shadow of one's former self; **aver paura della propria ombra** to be afraid of one's own shadow 2 (*fantasma*) shade (*letter*), ghost 3 (*fig: oscurità*) obscurity; **nell'ombra** (*tramare, agire*) secretly; **restare nell'ombra** (*persona*) to remain in obscurity 4 (*parvenza, traccia*): **non c'è ombra di verità in quello che dice** there isn't a grain of truth in what he says; **senza ombra di dubbio** without a shadow of a doubt; **un'ombra di burro** a hint o touch of butter ♦ AGG INV: **bandiera ombra** flag of convenience; **governo ombra** (*Pol*) shadow cabinet

ombreggiare [ombred'dʒare] /62/ VT to shade

ombrello [om'brɛllo] SM (*anche fig*) umbrella; **ombrello da sole** parasol, sunshade

ombrellone [ombrel'lone] SM (*da spiaggia*) beach umbrella; (*di caffè, bar*) sunshade

ombretto [om'bretto] SM eyeshadow

ombroso, -a [om'broso] AGG 1 (*bosco, viale*) shady, shaded 2 (*fig: cavallo*) skittish, nervous; (: *persona*) touchy, easily offended

OMC [oemme't∫i] SIGLA F (= *Organizzazione Mondiale del Commercio*) WTO (= *World Trade Organization*)

omelette [ɔmɔ'lɛt] SF INV omelette (*Brit*), omelet (*USA*); **un'omelette al prosciutto** a ham omelette

omelia [ome'lia] SF (*Rel*) homily, sermon

omeopata [ome'ɔpata] SM, SF homoeopath (*Brit*), homeopath (*USA*)

omeopatia [omeopa'tia] SF homoeopathy (*Brit*), homeopathy (*USA*)

omeopatico, -a, -ci, -che [omeo'patiko] AGG homoeopathic (*Brit*), homeopathic (*USA*)

omertà [omer'ta] SF conspiracy of silence

omesso, -a [o'messo] PP *di* **omettere**

omettere [o'mettere] /63/ VT IRREG to leave out, omit; **ho omesso un piccolo particolare** I left out one small detail; **omettere di fare qc** to neglect o omit o fail to do sth

omicida, -i, -e [omi't∫ida] AGG (*maniaco, istinto, furia*) homicidal; (*sguardo, intenzione*) murderous ♦ SM, SF murderer (murderess)

omicidio, -di [omi'tʃidjo] SM murder, homicide (USA); **commettere un omicidio** to commit a murder; **omicidio colposo** (Dir) manslaughter, second-degree murder (USA); **omicidio premeditato** (Dir) murder, first-degree murder (USA)

omisi ecc [o'mizi] VB vedi **omettere**

omissione [omis'sjone] SF 1 (non inclusione) omission; **nell'elenco c'erano molte omissioni** there were a lot of omissions from the list; **salvo errori e omissioni** errors and omissions excepted 2 (Dir): **reato d'omissione** criminal negligence; **omissione di atti d'ufficio** negligence (by a public employee); **omissione di denuncia** failure to report a crime; **omissione di soccorso** failure to stop and give assistance

omogeneizzato, -a [omodʒeneid'dzato] AGG homogenized ♦ SM (per bambini) baby food

omogeneo, -a [omo'dʒɛneo] AGG (gen) homogeneous; (fig: insieme di colori) harmonious

omologare [omolo'gare] /80/ VT (Dir) to approve, sanction; (ratificare) to ratify; **macchina omologata per 5 persone** car authorized to carry 5 people

omologazione [omologat'tsjone] SF (vedi vb) approval, sanction; ratification

omologo, -a, -ghi, -ghe [o'mɔlogo] AGG homologous, corresponding; (Chim) homologous; **inseminazione artificiale omologa** AIH ♦ SM, SF opposite number, counterpart

omonimo, -a [o'mɔnimo] AGG (persone, cose) with the same name; **il film Lolita, tratto dall'omonimo romanzo** the film "Lolita", adapted from the book of the same name ♦ SM, SF (persona) namesake; **è un mio omonimo** he's got the same name as me ♦ SM (Gramm) homonym

omosessuale [omosessu'ale] AGG, SM, SF homosexual

OMS [o'emme'esse] SIGLA F = Organizzazione Mondiale della Sanità) WHO (= World Health Organization)

On. ABBR (Pol) = **onorevole**

oncia, -ce ['ontʃa] SF (unità di misura) ounce

onda ['onda] SF 1 (flutto, anche fig) wave; **si è tuffato tra le onde** he dived into the waves; **un'onda di commozione** a wave o surge of excitement; **capelli a onde** wavy hair; **onda lunga** roller; **onda verde** (Aut) synchronized traffic lights pl 2 (Fis) wave; **andare in onda** (Radio, TV) to go on the air, be broadcast, be on; **il programma va in onda alle sei** the programme is on at six o'clock; **mettere** o **mandare in onda** (Radio, TV) to broadcast; **onde corte** short wave sg; **onde lunghe** long wave sg; **onde medie** medium wave sg

ondata [on'data] SF (flutto) wave; (fig) wave, surge; **a ondate** (muovere, avanzare) in waves; **un'ondata di turisti** an influx of tourists; **un'ondata di entusiasmo** a wave o surge of enthusiasm; **un'ondata di caldo** a heatwave; **un'ondata di freddo** a cold spell o snap

onde ['onde] CONG (frm: affinché: con l'infinito) in order to, so as to; (: con il congiuntivo) so that, in order that

ondeggiare [onded'dʒare] /62/ VI (us avere) (acqua, superficie, grano) to ripple; (bandiera) to flutter; (muoversi sulle onde: barca) to rock, roll; (fig: folla, alberi, edificio) to sway; (: persona: essere incerto) to waver, hesitate

ondoso, -a [on'doso] AGG (moto) of the waves

ondulato, -a [ondu'lato] AGG (capelli) wavy; (terreno) undulating; **cartone ondulato** corrugated paper; **lamiera ondulata** sheet of corrugated iron

ondulatorio, -ria, -ri, -rie [ondula'tɔrjo] AGG (movimento) undulating; (Fis) undulatory attr

ondulazione [ondulat'tsjone] SF undulation; (di capelli) wave

onerato, -a [one'rato] AGG: **onerato di** burdened with, loaded with

onere ['ɔnere] SM (peso) burden; (responsabilità) responsibility; **onere finanziario** financial burden; **oneri fiscali** taxes

oneroso, -a [one'roso] AGG (compito) onerous; (tasse, pena) heavy; (condizioni di contratto) hard

onestà [ones'ta] SF (vedi agg) honesty; fairness; virtue; chastity

onestamente [onesta'mente] AVV (vedi agg) honestly; fairly; virtuously; (in verità) honestly, frankly

onesto, -a [o'nɛsto] AGG (probo, retto) honest; (giusto: persona, prezzi) fair; (virtuoso, pudico) virtuous; (casto) chaste; **è una**

persona onesta he's an honest person; **mi sembra un prezzo onesto** it seems a fair price; **con intenzioni poco oneste** with dubious intentions

ONG [ɔenne'dʒi] SIGLA F INV (= Organizzazione Non Governativa) NGO (= Non-Governmental Organization)

onice ['ɔnitʃe] SF onyx

onirico, -a, -ci, -che [o'niriko] AGG dreamlike, dream attr

onnipotente [onnipo'tɛnte] AGG omnipotent, all-powerful; **Dio onnipotente** Almighty God ♦ SM: **l'Onnipotente** (Rel) the Almighty

onnipresente [onnipre'zɛnte] AGG (of God) omnipresent; (fig) ubiquitous

onnisciente [onniʃ'ʃɛnte] AGG omniscient

onniveggente [onnived'dʒɛnte] AGG all-seeing

onomastico, -ci [ono'mastiko] SM name day; **oggi è il mio onomastico** today's my name day

onomatopea [onomato'pɛa] SF onomatopoeia

onomatopeico, -a, -ci, -che [onomato'pɛiko] AGG onomatopoeic

onoranze [ono'rantse] SFPL honours (Brit), honors (USA); **onoranze funebri** funeral hono(u)rs

onorare [ono'rare] /72/ VT (gen) to honour (Brit), honor (USA); (far onore a) to be a credit to, do credit to; **onorare qn con** o **di qc** to hono(u)r sb with sth; **onorare una cambiale** (Comm) to hono(u)r a bill; **onorarsi** VR: **onorarsi di qc/di fare qc** to feel hono(u)red by sth/to do sth

onorario, -ria, -ri, -rie [ono'rarjo] AGG honorary ♦ SM fee

onoratissimo, -a [onora'tissimo] AGG (in presentazioni): **onoratissimo!** delighted to meet you!

onorato, -a [ono'rato] AGG (reputazione, famiglia, carriera) distinguished; **onorare** to have the honour (Brit) o honor (USA) to do sth o of doing sth; **onorare** (it is) a pleasure to meet you

onore [o'nore] SM 1 (reputazione, integrità) honour (Brit), honor (USA); **giuro sul mio onore che...** I swear on my hono(u)r that ... 2 (omaggio) hono(u)r; **rendere onore a qn/qc** to hono(u)r sb/sth 3 (privilegio) hono(u)r, privilege; **è un onore per me** it's an hono(u)r for me; **aver l'onore di** to have the hono(u)r of; **posto d'onore** place of hono(u)r 4 (merito) credit; **fare onore ai genitori** to be a credit to one's parents; **farsi onore** to distinguish oneself; **si è fatto onore agli esami** he distinguished himself in the exams 5 **onori** SMPL (onorificenze) hono(u)rs 6 (Carte) hono(u)r (card) 7 (fraseologia): **in onore di** in hono(u)r of; **a onor del vero** to tell the truth; **fare onore alla tavola** to do justice to the dinner; **fare gli onori di casa** to play host (o hostess), act as host; **Paolo ha fatto gli onori di casa** Paolo acted as host

onorevole [ono'revole] AGG honourable (Brit), honorable (USA); (Pol: titolo): **l'Onorevole...** the Honourable ... ♦ SM, SF (Pol) : **Onorevole** ≈ Member of Parliament (Brit), ≈ Congressperson, member of Congress (USA)

onorificenza [onorifi'tʃentsa] SF honour (Brit), honor (USA); (decorazione) decoration

onorifico, -a, -ci, -che [ono'rifiko] AGG honorary

onta ['onta] SF 1 (vergogna) shame, disgrace; (affronto) insult, affront 2 **ad onta di** despite, notwithstanding

ontano [on'tano] SM alder

ONU ['ɔnu] SIGLA F (= Organizzazione delle Nazioni Unite) UN, UNO (= United Nations (Organization))

OPA ABBR = offerta pubblica d'acquisto

opaco, -a, -chi, -che [o'pako] AGG (vetro, corpo) opaque; (carta) matt; (metallo, colore, fig: voce, sguardo, mente) dull

opale [o'pale] SM, SF opal

OPEC ['opek] SIGLA F OPEC (= Organization of Petroleum Exporting Countries)

opera ['ɔpera] SF 1 (attività, lavoro) work; (azione rilevante) action, deed, work; **mettersi/essere all'opera** to get down to/be at work; **vedere qn all'opera** to see sb in action; **abbiamo ottenuto quell'aumento per opera sua** it was thanks to him that we got the rise; **fare opera di persuasione presso qn** to try to convince sb; **fare opere buone** o **di carità** to do good works o works of charity 2 (lavoro materiale) work, piece of work; **opera di scavo** excavation work sg; **opere pubbliche** (Amm) public works; **opere di restauro** restoration work sg 3 (produzione artistica: nell'insieme) works pl;

(: *libro, quadro*) work; **le opere più importanti di Dante** Dante's most important works; **opera d'arte** work of art   **4** (*ente*) foundation, institution, organization; **opera pia** religious charity **5** (*Mus*) opus; (*melodramma*) opera; (*teatro*) opera (house); **opera buffa** comic opera; **opera lirica** (grand) opera **6** (*Naut*): **opera** topsides *pl*; **opera viva** bottom

operaio, -aia, -ai, -aie [ope'rajo] AGG **1** (*movimento, partito*) workers' *attr*; (*prete*) worker *attr*; **classe operaia** working class; **movimento operaio** labour movement; **quartiere operaio** working-class district **2** (*Zool: ape, formica*) worker *attr* ♦ SM, SF worker; **operaio di fabbrica** factory worker; **operaio a giornata** day labourer (*Brit*) *o* laborer (*USA*); **operaio non specializzato** semi-skilled worker; **operaio qualificato** *o* **specializzato** skilled worker

operare [ope'rare] /72/ VT **1** (*riforma*) to carry out, make; (*effetto*) to produce; **operare miracoli** to work wonders **2** (*Med*) to operate on; **il chirurgo ha operato Mario di appendicite** the surgeon operated on Mario for appendicitis; **Matteo è stato operato allo stomaco** Matteo had an operation on his stomach; **operare qn d'urgenza** to perform an emergency operation on sb ♦ VI (*aus* avere) **1** (*agire*) to act, work; (*Mil, Comm*) to operate **2** (*Med*) to operate; **hanno dovuto operare d'urgenza** they had to do an emergency operation; **operarsi** VIP **1** (*verificarsi*) to take place, occur **2** (*Med*) to have an operation; **dovrò operarmi la prossima settimana** I'm going to have an operation next week; **operarsi d'ernia** to have a hernia operation; **operarsi d'appendicite** to have one's appendix out; **si è operato d'appendicite** he had his appendix out

operativo, -a [opera'tivo] AGG operative, operating; **piano operativo** (*Mil*) plan of operations

operato, -a [ope'rato] SM (*comportamento*) actions *pl* ♦ SM, SF (*Med*) patient (*who has undergone an operation*) ♦ AGG (*tessuto*) diapered; (*carta*) embossed; (*cuoio*) tooled

operatore, -trice [opera'tore] SM, SF **1** (*TV, Cine*) camera operator; (*Inform*) operator; **operatore cinematografico** projectionist; **operatore ecologico** refuse collector; **operatore del suono** sound recordist **2** (*Econ*) agent; **gli operatori economici del settore** those with commercial interests in that sector; **aperto solo agli operatori** (*Comm*) open to the trade only; **operatore di borsa** dealer on the stock exchange; **operatore economico** agent, broker; **operatore turistico** tour operator

operatorio, -ria, -ri, -rie [opera'torjo] AGG (*Med*) operating

operazione [operat'tsjone] SF (*gen, anche Med, Mil, Mat*) operation; (*Econ*) transaction

operetta [ope'retta] SF (*Mus*) operetta, light opera

operosità [operosi'ta] SF industry, industriousness

operoso, -a [ope'roso] AGG (*attivo*) industrious, hard-working

opificio, -ci [opi'fitʃo] SM (*ant*) factory, works *pl*

opinabile [opi'nabile] AGG (*discutibile*) debatable, questionable; **è opinabile** it is a matter of opinion

opinione [opi'njone] SF opinion; **vorrei sapere qual è la tua opinione su di lui** I'd love to hear your opinion of him; **secondo la mia opinione** in my opinion; **avere il coraggio delle proprie opinioni** to have the courage of one's convictions; **l'opinione pubblica** public opinion

opinionista, -i, -e [opinjo'nista] SM, SF (political) columnist

op là [op'la] ESCL (*per far saltare*) hup!; (*un bimbo che è caduto*) upsy-daisy!

oppio ['ɔppjo] SM opium

oppiomane [op'pjɔmane] SM, SF opium addict

opponente [oppo'nɛnte] SM, SF opponent ♦ AGG opposing

oppongo ecc [op'pongo] VB *vedi* opporre

opporre [op'porre] VB IRREG /77/ VT **1** (*ragioni, argomenti*) to put forward; **opporre resistenza** to put up a struggle; **si sono arresi senza opporre resistenza** they surrendered without putting up a struggle; **opporre un netto rifiuto** to give a clear-cut refusal to **2** (*obiettare*) to object; **non ho nulla da opporre** I have no objection; **opporsi** VR (*fare opposizione*): **opporsi (a)** (*nemico*) to oppose; (*proposta*) to object (to); **ci siamo opposti alla proposta** we objected to the proposal; **mi oppongo alla sua idea** I am opposed to *o* against his idea

opportunista, -i, -e [opportu'nista] SM, SF opportunist; **è un opportunista** he's an opportunist

opportunità [opportuni'ta] SF INV **1** (*convenienza*) opportuneness, timeliness; **avere il senso dell'opportunità** to have a sense of timing **2** (*occasione*) opportunity; **una grossa opportunità** a big opportunity; **avere l'opportunità di fare qc** to have the opportunity of *o* for doing *o* to do sth; **non ho avuto l'opportunità di parlargli** I didn't have the opportunity to speak to him; **Commissione per le Pari Opportunità** Equal Opportunities Commission

opportuno, -a [oppor'tuno] AGG (*adatto, conveniente*) opportune, timely; (*giusto*) right, appropriate; **non era il momento opportuno per parlarne** it wasn't the right moment to talk about it; **a tempo opportuno** at the right *o* the appropriate time; **ritengo opportuno che tu gli scriva** I think you should write to him, I think it would be advisable for you to write to him

opposi ecc [op'posi] VB *vedi* opporre

oppositore, -trice [oppozi'tore] SM, SF opponent, opposer ♦ AGG opposing

opposizione [oppozit'tsjone] SF **1** (*resistenza*) opposition; (*Pol*): **l'Opposizione** the Opposition; **i partiti dell'opposizione** the opposition parties; **fare opposizione a qn/qc** to oppose sb/sth **2** (*contrasto*) opposition; **essere in netta opposizione** (*idee, opinioni*) to clash, be in complete opposition **3** (*Dir*) objection

opposto, -a [op'posto] PP *di* opporre ♦ AGG **1** (*direzione, lato*) opposite; **veniva dalla direzione opposta** she was coming from the opposite direction **2** (*contrario: idee, vedute*) opposite, conflicting; **le sue idee sono opposte alle mie** his ideas conflict with mine, his ideas are the opposite of mine; **hanno opinioni opposte** they have very different ideas ♦ SM: **l'opposto** the opposite, the contrary; **all'opposto** on the contrary; **io, all'opposto di te, non li approvo** unlike you, I don't approve of them

oppressione [oppres'sjone] SF (*Pol*) oppression; (*fisica, morale*) feeling of oppression

oppressivo, -a [oppres'sivo] AGG oppressive

oppresso, -a [op'presso] PP *di* opprimere ♦ AGG oppressed ♦ **gli oppressi** SMPL the oppressed

oppressore [oppres'sore] SM oppressor ♦ AGG oppressive

opprimente [oppri'mente] AGG (*caldo, noia*) oppressive; (*persona: deprimente*) depressing; (*fidanzato: soffocante*) possessive

opprimere [op'primere] /50/ VT IRREG **1** (*sogg: caldo, afa*) to suffocate, oppress; **cibo che opprime lo stomaco** food that lies heavy on the stomach **2** (*sogg: ansia, lavoro*) to weigh down, weigh heavily on; **il lavoro mi opprime** my work is getting me down **3** (*tiranneggiare: popolo*) to oppress

oppugnare [oppuɲ'ɲare] /15/ VT (*letter, fig: dottrina*) to refute

oppure [op'pure] CONG (*o invece*) or; (*altrimenti*) otherwise, or (else); **possiamo guardare la TV oppure noleggiare un video** we can watch TV or rent a video

optare [op'tare] /72/ VI (*aus* avere) **optare per** (*scegliere*) to opt for, decide upon; (*Borsa*) to take (out) an option on

optimum ['ɔptimum] SM INV optimum

opulento, -a [opu'lento] AGG (*ricco: paese, società*) rich, wealthy, affluent; (: *stile letterario*) opulent

opulenza [opu'lentsa] SF (*vedi agg*) richness, wealth, affluence; opulence

opuscolo [o'puskolo] SM (*letterario, scientifico*) booklet, pamphlet; (*pubblicitario*) brochure, leaflet

OPV ABBR = offerta pubblica di vendita

opzionale [optsjo'nale] AGG optional

opzione [op'tsjone] SF (*gen, anche Comm*) option; **diritto di opzione** (*Borsa*) (right of) option

OR SIGLA = Oristano

ora ['ora] SF **1** (*unità di tempo, durata*) hour; **tre ore e mezza** three and a half hours; **mezz'ora** half an hour; **durante le ore d'ufficio** during office hours; **è a un'ora di cammino/d'auto dalla stazione** it's an hour's walk/drive from the station; **aspetto da un'ora** I've been waiting for an hour; **pagare a ore** to pay by the hour; **sono pagati a ore** they're paid by the hour; **all'ora** an hour; **lo pagano 30 euro all'ora** they pay him 30 euros an hour; **70 km all'ora** 70 km an hour **2** (*parte della giornata*): **che ora è?, che ore sono? — sono le**

4 what time is it? — it's 4 (o'clock); **che ora fai?** what time do you make it?; **a che ora ci vediamo?** what time *o* when shall we meet?; **a che ora parti?** what time are you leaving?; **ora legale** summer time (*Brit*), daylight saving time (*USA*); **ora locale** local time **3** (*momento*) time; **domani a quest'ora** this time tomorrow; **l'ora di pranzo** lunchtime; **l'ora dei pasti** mealtimes; **è ora di partire** it's time to go; **era ora!** about time too!; **le notizie dell'ultima ora** the latest news; **ora di punta** (*Aut*) rush hour; **il traffico dell'ora di punta** the rush hour traffic; **l'ora X** zero hour **4** (*fraseologia*): **non vedo l'ora di finire** I'm looking forward to finishing; (*excitement, frustration*) I can't wait to finish; **non vedo l'ora di dirglielo** I can't wait to tell him; **non vedevo l'ora che arrivasse l'estate** I couldn't wait for summer (to come); **fare le ore piccole** to stay up till the early *o* small hours (of the morning); **di buon'ora** early; **alla buon'ora!** at last!; **di ora in ora** hourly, hour by hour ♦ AVV **1** (*adesso*) now; **ora sto meglio** I'm better now; **ora non posso uscire** I can't go out (just) now; **ora sono molto occupata** I'm very busy at the moment; **d'ora in avanti** *o* **poi** from now on; **ora come ora** right now, at present; **per ora** for now **2** (*poco fa*): **è uscito (proprio) ora** he's just gone out; **or ora** just now, a moment ago; **10 anni or sono** 10 years ago **3** (*tra poco*) in a moment, presently, in a minute; **ora arrivo** I'm just coming, I'll be right there **4** (*correlativo*): **ora... ora...** now ..., now ...; **ora qui ora lì** now here now there; **ora piange ora ride** one minute he's crying, the next he's laughing ♦ CONG now; **ora che** now (that)

oracolo [oˈrakolo] SM oracle

orafo, -a [ˈɔrafo] SM goldsmith ♦ AGG (*arte*) goldsmith's *attr*, of a goldsmith

orale [oˈrale] AGG, SM oral; **un esame orale** an oral exam

oralmente [oralˈmente] AVV orally

oramai [oraˈmai] AVV = **ormai**

orario, -ria, -ri, -rie [oˈrarjo] AGG (*cambiamento, media*) hourly; (*velocità*) per hour; (*fuso, segnale*) time *attr*; **disco orario** parking disc; **segnale orario** time signal; **tariffa oraria** hourly rate; **in senso orario** clockwise ♦ SM **1** (*di ufficio, visite*) hours *pl*, time(s *pl*); **qual è l'orario delle visite?** when's visiting time?; **fare l'orario ridotto** to be on short time; **in orario** on time; **orario di apertura** opening time; **orario di chiusura** closing time; **orario flessibile** (*Industria*) flexitime; **orario di lavoro** working hours *pl*; **orario di sportello** (*Banca*) bank opening hours *pl*; **orario d'ufficio** office hours *pl*, business hours *pl* **2** (*tabella*) timetable, schedule; **orario ferroviario** railway timetable

orata [oˈrata] SF (*pesce*) sea bream

oratore, -trice [oraˈtore] SM, SF (*public*) speaker, orator

oratorio, -ria, -ri, -rie [oraˈtɔrjo] AGG oratorical ♦ SM **1** (*cappella*) oratory **2** (*Mus*) oratorio ♦ SF (*arte*) oratory

orazione [oratˈtsjone] SF **1** (*preghiera*) prayer **2** (*discorso*) oration, speech; **orazione funebre** funeral oration

orbene [orˈbene] CONG (*letter*) well (then), so

orbita [ˈɔrbita] SF **1** (*Anat*) (eye-)socket; **aveva gli occhi fuori dalle orbite** (*fig*) his eyes were popping out of his head **2** (*Astron, Fis*) orbit; **mettere in orbita** to put into orbit; **il razzo fu lanciato in orbita** the rocket was launched into orbit **3** (*fig: ambito d'influenza*) sphere of influence

orbitare [orbiˈtare] /72/ VI (*aus* **essere**) to orbit

orbo, -a [ˈɔrbo] AGG (*scherz*) blind; **e giù botte da orbi** and the fists were flying

Orcadi [ˈɔrkadi] SFPL: **le (isole) Orcadi** the Orkney Islands, the Orkneys

orchestra [orˈkestra] SF (*complesso di musicisti, strumenti musicali*) orchestra; (*da ballo, jazz*) band; (*Teatro: spazio*) orchestra pit

orchestrale [orkesˈtrale] AGG orchestral ♦ SM, SF member of an orchestra, orchestra player

orchestrare [orkesˈtrare] /72/ VT (*Mus, anche fig*) to orchestrate

orchidea [orkiˈdɛa] SF orchid

orcio, orci [ˈɔrtʃo] SM (earthenware) pot

orco, -chi [ˈɔrko] SM (*in fiabe*) ogre

orda [ˈɔrda] SF (*Storia, anche fig*) horde

ordigno [orˈdiɲɲo] SM: **ordigno esplosivo** explosive device

ordinale [ordiˈnale] AGG ordinal ♦ SM ordinal (number)

ordinamento [ordinaˈmento] SM (*organizzazione*) order, arrangement; (*regolamento*) regulations *pl*, rules *pl*; **ordinamento giuridico** legal system; **ordinamento scolastico** education system

ordinanza [ordiˈnantsa] SF **1** (*Dir*) order **2** (*Amm: decreto*) decree; **ordinanza municipale** by(e-)law **3** (*Mil*) order; (*prescrizione*) regulation; (*anche*: **soldato d'ordinanza**) batman, orderly; **d'ordinanza** (*pistola, divisa*) regulation *attr*

ordinare [ordiˈnare] /72/ VT **1** (*mettere in ordine*) to organize, put in order, arrange **2** (*comandare*) to order; (*prescrivere: cura, medicina*) to prescribe; (*merce, pranzo*) to order; **hai già ordinato?** have you already ordered?; **ordinare che...** to order that ...; **ordinare a qn di fare qc** to order sb to do sth; **gli hanno ordinato di andarsene subito** they ordered him to leave immediately; **il medico mi ha ordinato di riposare** the doctor told me to rest **3** (*Rel: sacerdote*) to ordain; **ordinarsi** VR (*disporsi*): **ordinarsi in fila/in colonna** to line up/ form a column

ordinario, -ria, -ri, -rie [ordiˈnarjo] AGG **1** (*consueto, normale*) ordinary, usual; (*tariffa, spedizione, seduta*) ordinary; **spese ordinarie** ordinary expenses; **di statura ordinaria** of average height; **di ordinaria amministrazione** (*fig*) routine *attr* **2** (*rozzo: persona*) common, coarse; (*scadente: materiale, stoffa*) poor-quality **3** (*professore: Scol*) permanent; (*: Univ*) full ♦ SM **1** **l'ordinario** the ordinary; **fuori dall'ordinario** out of the ordinary; **d'ordinario** usually, as a rule **2** (*Scol*) permanent teacher; (*Univ*) (full) professor

ordinativo, -a [ordinaˈtivo] AGG governing, regulating ♦ SM (*Comm*) order

ordinato, -a [ordiˈnato] AGG (*casa, persona*) tidy, orderly; (*vita*) well-ordered; (*impiegato*) methodical; (*corteo*) orderly; **è la persona più ordinata che abbia mai conosciuto** he's the tidiest person I've ever met

ordinazione [ordinatˈtsjone] SF **1** (*Comm*) order; **fare un'ordinazione di qc** to put in an order for sth, order sth; **eseguire qc su ordinazione** to make sth to order **2** (*Rel*) ordination

ordine [ˈordine] SM **1** (*disposizione, sequenza*) order; **in ordine alfabetico** in alphabetical order; **in ordine di anzianità/ importanza** in order of seniority/importance; **in ordine di battaglia** (*Mil*) in battle order; **ritirarsi in buon ordine** (*Mil*) to retreat in good order; (*fig*) to back down gracefully; **ciò è nell'ordine naturale delle cose** it's in the nature of things **2** (*di persona, camera*) tidiness, orderliness; **in ordine** (*documenti*) in order; (*casa*) tidy, orderly; **essere/tenere in ordine** to be/keep in order; **la casa è in ordine** the house is tidy; **mettere in ordine** to tidy (up), put in order; **stavano mettendo in ordine la loro camera** they were tidying up their room; **mettersi in ordine** to tidy (o.s.) up **3** (*categoria: Archit, Bio*) order **4** (*associazione*) association, order; (*Rel*) order; **l'ordine degli avvocati** ≈ the Bar; **l'ordine dei medici** ≈ the British *o* American Medical Association **5** (*carattere*): **questioni di ordine pratico/generale** questions of a practical/general nature; **un affare dell'ordine di 20 milioni** a deal of the order of 20 million; **di prim'ordine** (*albergo, merce*) first-class; **non rientra nel mio ordine di idee** that's not the way I see things **6** (*principio d'organizzazione*) order; **richiamare all'ordine** to call to order; **le forze dell'ordine** the police; **l'ordine pubblico** law and order, public order; **l'ordine costituito** the established order **7** **ordini** SMPL (*Rel*) (Holy) Orders; **ordini minori/maggiori** minor/ major orders **8** (*comando*) order, command; **ho l'ordine di non farvi entrare** I've been told not to let you in; **dare (l') ordine di fare qc** to give the order to do sth; **essere agli ordini di qn** (*Mil*) to be under sb's command; (*fig*) to be at sb's beck and call; **per ordine del preside** by order of the headmaster; **fino a nuovo ordine** until further orders **9** (*Comm, Fin*) order; **pagabile all'ordine di** payable to the order of; **ordine d'acquisto** purchase order; **ordine di pagamento** standing order (*Brit*), automatic payment (*USA*); **ordine di prova** trial order **10** **l'ordine del giorno** (*in riunioni*) the agenda; (*Mil*) the order of the day

ordire [orˈdire] /55/ VT (*tessuto*) to warp; (*fig*) to plot, scheme; **ordire una congiura** *o* **una trama** to hatch a plot, plot

ordito [orˈdito] SM (*di tessuto*) warp

orecchiabile [orek'kjabile] AGG (*canzone*) catchy
orecchino [orek'kino] SM earring; **un paio di orecchini d'oro** a pair of gold earrings
orecchio, -chi [o'rekkjo] SM 1 (*Anat*) (*pl f* **orecchie**) ear; **farsi fare i buchi nelle orecchie** to have one's ears pierced; **mi sono fatta fare i buchi nelle orecchie** I've had my ears pierced; **mi fa male un orecchio** I've got an earache; **mi fischiano le orecchie** (*lett*) my ears are singing; (*fig*) my ears are burning; **essere tutto orecchi** to be all ears; **venire all'orecchio di qn** to come to sb's attention; **te lo dico in un orecchio** this is for your ears only; **tapparsi** *o* **turarsi le orecchie** to put one's fingers in one's ears; **fare orecchie da mercante (a)** to turn a deaf ear (to); **tirare le orecchie a qn** to tweak sb's ears; (*fig*) to tell sb off, give sb an earful 2 (*udito*) hearing; **essere debole d'orecchio** to be hard of hearing; **avere orecchio** to have a good ear (for music); **ha orecchio** he's got a good ear; **a orecchio** by ear; **cantare/suonare a orecchio** to sing/play by ear
orecchioni [orek'kjoni] SMPL (*Med*): **gli orecchioni** (the) mumps *sg*
orefice [o'refit∫e] SM, SF (*negoziante*) jeweller (*Brit*), jeweler (*USA*); (*artigiano*) goldsmith
oreficeria [orefit∫e'ria] SF (*negozio*) jeweller's (shop) (*Brit*), jewelry store (*USA*); (*arte*) goldsmith's (*o* silversmith's) art *o* craft (*gioielli*) jewellery (*Brit*), jewelry (*USA*)
orfano, -a ['ɔrfano] AGG orphan(ed); **rimanere orfano** to be orphaned; **è rimasto orfano a dieci anni** he was orphaned at the age of ten; **essere orfano di madre/padre** to be motherless/fatherless, have lost one's mother/father; **è orfano di madre** he has lost his mother ♦ SM, SF orphan
orfanotrofio, -fi [orfano'trɔfjo] SM orphanage
organetto [orga'netto] SM (*strumento a manovella*) barrel organ, street organ; (*fam: armonica a bocca*) mouth organ; (: *fisarmonica*) accordion
organico, -a, -ci, -che [or'ganiko] AGG (*Chim, Med, Dir*) organic ♦ SM (*personale*) staff, personnel; (*Mil*) cadre; **essere nell'organico** to be on the permanent staff
organigramma, -i [organi'gramma] SM (*diagramma gerarchico*) organization chart; (*Inform*) computer flow chart
organismo [orga'nizmo] SM (*vegetale, animale*) organism; (*Anat, Amm*) body, organism; **organismi geneticamente modificati** genetically modified organisms
organista, -i, -e [orga'nista] SM, SF organist
organizzare [organid'dzare] /72/ VT to organize, arrange; **hanno organizzato un concerto** they organized a concert; **abbiamo organizzato una gita in campagna** we've arranged a trip to the country; **organizzarsi** VR to organize o.s., get (o.s.) organized
organizzativo, -a [organiddza'tivo] AGG organizational
organizzatore, -trice [organiddza'tore] AGG organizing ♦ SM, SF organizer
organizzazione [organiddzat'tsjone] SF 1 (*azione*) organizing, organization, arranging; (*risultato*) organization, arrangement; **ci occuperemo dell'organizzazione della festa** we'll organize the party 2 (*associazione*) organization; **un'organizzazione studentesca** a student organization
organo ['ɔrgano] SM (*Anat, Mus: pubblicazione*) organ; (*di congegno*) part; (*Amm*) organ, body; **suona l'organo** she plays the organ; **trapianto d'organi** organ transplants; **organi di comando** (*Tecn*) controls; **organi di trasmissione** (*Tecn*) transmission (unit) *sg*
orgasmo [or'gazmo] SM 1 (*Fisiologia*) orgasm, climax 2 (*fig: agitazione, ansia*) anxiety, agitation; **essere/mettersi in orgasmo** to be/get in a state
orgia, -ge ['ɔrdʒa] SF orgy; **un'orgia di** a profusion *o* riot of; **un'orgia di colori** an orgy of colour (*Brit*) *o* color (*USA*)
orgoglio [or'ɡoʎʎo] SM pride
orgoglioso, -a [orɡoʎ'ʎoso] AGG proud; **sono orgogliosa di te** I'm proud of you
orientabile [orjen'tabile] AGG adjustable
orientale [orjen'tale] AGG (*paese, regione*) eastern; (*civiltà, lingua, tappeto*) oriental; **l'Europa orientale** eastern Europe; **la costa orientale della Gran Bretagna** the east coast of Britain; **un tappeto orientale** an oriental carpet ♦ SM, SF Asian

orientamento [orjenta'mento] SM 1 (*azione: vedi vt*) positioning; orientation; directing 2 (*direzione*) direction; **senso di** *o* **dell'orientamento** sense of direction; **perdere l'orientamento** to lose one's bearings; **ho perso l'orientamento** I've lost my bearings 3 (*tendenza: di partito, rivista*) tendencies *pl*, leanings *pl*; (: *di scienze*) trends *pl*; (: *di ricerche*) direction; **orientamento professionale** careers guidance
orientare [orjen'tare] /72/ VT 1 (*disporre: antenna, ventilatore*) to position; (*carta, bussola*) to orientate 2 (*fig: dirigere: ricerche, persona*) to direct; **hanno orientato la conversazione su un tema d'attualità** they steered the conversation round to a topical subject; **orientarsi** VR 1 (*viaggiatore*) to find one's bearings; (*fig: raccapezzarsi*) to find one's way; **in questa faccenda non riesco a orientarmi** I can't make head nor tail of this business 2 **orientarsi per** *o* **verso** (*fig: indirizzarsi*) to take up, go in for; (: *propendere*) to lean towards, tend towards; **mi sto orientando verso l'acquisto di una casa** I'm coming round to the idea of buying a house
orientativo, -a [orjenta'tivo] AGG indicative, approximate; **a scopo orientativo** for information
oriente [o'rjente] SM (*levante*) east; **l'Oriente** the East, the Orient; **a oriente** in the east; **il Medio/l'Estremo Oriente** the Middle/Far East
orificio, -ci [ori'fit∫o], **orifizio, -zi** [ori'fittsjo] SM (*apertura*) opening; (*di tubo*) mouth; (*Anat*) orifice
origano [o'riɡano] SM (*Bot*) oregano
originale [oridʒi'nale] AGG (*gen*) original; (*nuovo*) new, original; (*bizzarro*) eccentric, odd; **un'idea originale** an original idea; **è un tipo originale** he's a bit eccentric ♦ SM (*opera, documento*) original; **vuoi una copia o l'originale?** do you want a copy, or the original?; **originale radiofonico** radio play; **originale televisivo** television play ♦ SM, SF eccentric; **il tuo amico è un bell'originale!** your friend is a real character!
originalità [oridʒinali'ta] SF 1 (*vedi agg*) originality; eccentricity, oddness 2 (*atto da originale*) eccentric behaviour
originare [oridʒi'nare] /72/ VT to cause, give rise to, bring about, produce ♦ VI (*aus essere*) **originare da** to arise *o* spring from
originario, -ria, -ri, -rie [oridʒi'narjo] AGG 1 **essere originario di** (*persona*) to be a native of, be from; (*animale, pianta*) to be indigenous to, be native to; **è originario di Roma** he is a native of Rome, he's from Rome 2 (*primitivo, originale*) original
origine [o'ridʒine] SF (*gen*) origin; (*provenienza: di persona, famiglia*) origin, extraction; (: *di cosa*) origin, provenance; (: *di fiume*) source; (*causa*) origin, cause; **luogo/paese d'origine** place/country of origin; **di origine italiana** of Italian extraction *o* origin; **risalire alle origini** *o* **all'origine di qc** to go back to the origins *o* the beginning of sth; **cominciare dalle origini** to start at the beginning; **dare origine a** to give rise to; **avere origine da** to originate from; **all'origine** originally
origliare [oriʎ'ʎare] /27/ VI (*aus avere*) **stava origliando alla porta** he was eavesdropping at the door ♦ VT to eavesdrop (on)
orina [o'rina] SF urine
orinale [ori'nale] SM chamberpot
orinare [ori'nare] /72/ VI (*aus avere*) to pass water, urinate ♦ VT: **orinare sangue** to pass blood
orinatoio, -oi [orina'tojo] SM (*public*) urinal
oriundo, -a [o'rjundo] AGG: **essere oriundo di Milano** to be of Milanese extraction *o* origin ♦ SM, SF person of foreign extraction *o* origin; **negli Stati Uniti ci sono molti oriundi italiani** in the United States there are many people of Italian extraction *o* origin ♦ SM (*Sport: in Italia*) foreign player of Italian extraction
orizzontale [oriddzon'tale] AGG horizontal ♦ SF (*di cruciverba*) clue (*o* word) across
orizzonte [orid'dzonte] SM 1 horizon; **all'orizzonte** (*apparire*) on the horizon; (*sparire*) below the horizon; **improvvisamente comparve un'isola all'orizzonte** suddenly an island appeared on the horizon 2 (*fig: prospettiva*) horizon; **l'orizzonte politico** the political scene; **fare un giro d'orizzonte** (*di situazione*) to examine the main aspects
ORL [ɔrl] SIGLA F (*Med: = otorinolaringoiatria*) ENT (= *ear, nose and throat*)
orlare [or'lare] /72/ VT (*gen*) to hem; (*con fettucce, nastri*) to edge, trim

orlatura [orla'tura] SF (*orlo*) hem; (*azione*) hemming *no pl*

orlo ['orlo] SM **1** (*di marciapiede*) edge; (*di recipiente*) rim, brim; (*di precipizio*) brink, edge; **la macchina era sull'orlo del precipizio** the car was on the edge of the precipice; **ha riempito il bicchiere fino all'orlo** she filled the glass to the brim; **pieno fino all'orlo** full to the brim, brimful; **sull'orlo della pazzia/della rovina** on the brink *o* verge of madness/ruin **2** (*ripiegatura: di vestiti*) hem; **l'orlo della tovaglia si è scucito** the hem of the tablecloth has come unstitched; **orlo a giorno** hemstitch

orma ['orma] SF (*di persona*) footprint; (*di animale*) track; (*fig: impronta, traccia*) trace, mark; **segui le orme della volpe** follow the fox's tracks; **la polizia ha trovato delle orme in giardino** the police found footprints in the garden; **seguire** *o* **calcare le orme di qn** to follow in sb's footsteps; **ha seguito le orme del padre** he followed in his father's footsteps

ormai [or'mai] AVV **1** (*riferito al presente*) by now, by this time; (*a questo punto*) now; **ormai è tardi** it's late now; **ormai dovrebbe essere partito** he must have left by now **2** (*allora*) by then **3** (*riferito al futuro: quasi*) almost, nearly; **ormai siamo arrivati** we're nearly *o* almost there

ormeggiare [ormed'dʒare] /62/ VT , **ormeggiarsi** VR to moor

ormeggio, -gi [or'meddʒo] SM (*atto*) mooring *no pl*; (*luogo*) moorings *pl*; **ormeggi** SMPL (*cavi e catene*) moorings; **le navi erano all'ormeggio** the ships were at their moorings; **posto d'ormeggio** berth

ormonale [ormo'nale] AGG (*disfunzione*) hormonal, hormone *attr*; (*cura*) hormone *attr*; **terapia ormonale** hormone therapy

ormone [or'mone] SM hormone

ornamentale [ornamen'tale] AGG ornamental, decorative

ornamento [orna'mento] SM (*gen*) ornament, decoration; (*azione*) adornment, decoration; (*Archit, Arte*) embellishment; **privo di ornamenti** (*stile, vestito, stanza*) plain, unadorned

ornare [or'nare] /72/ VT **1** (*tavola, vestito*): **ornare (di** *o* **con)** to decorate (with), adorn (with); (*fig: discorso*) to embellish (with) **2** (*sogg: affresco, statua*) to adorn, decorate; **ornarsi** VR: **ornarsi (di)** to deck o.s. (out) (with)

ornato, -a [or'nato] AGG **1** (*adorno*): **ornato di** adorned with, decorated with; **un cappello ornato di piume** a hat trimmed with feathers **2** (*stile*) ornate, florid ♦ SM (*Archit*) embellishment

ornitologia [ornitolo'dʒia] SF ornithology

ornitologo, -a, -gi *o* **, -ghi, -ghe** [orni'tɔlogo] SM, SF ornithologist

oro ['ɔro] SM **1** gold; **bracciale in oro** *o* **d'oro** gold bracelet; **oro nero** (*petrolio*) black gold; **oro zecchino** pure gold **2 ori** SMPL (*oggetti d'oro*) gold sg; (*gioielli*) jewellery sg (*Brit*), jewelry sg (*USA*); (*Carte*) suit in Neapolitan pack of cards **3** *d'oro* (*oggetto*) gold; (*colore, occhio*) golden; (*persona*) wonderful, marvellous (*Brit*), marvelous (*USA*); **un orologio d'oro** a gold watch; **ha vinto la medaglia d'oro** he won the gold medal; **un'occasione d'oro** a golden opportunity; **un affare d'oro** a real bargain; **fare affari d'oro** to do excellent business; **avere un cuore d'oro** to have a heart of gold **4** (*fraseologia*): **nuotare nell'oro** to be rolling in money; **prendere qc per oro colato** to take sth as gospel (truth); **non lo farei per tutto l'oro del mondo** I wouldn't do it for all the money in the world; **quell'uomo vale tanto oro quanto pesa** that man is worth his weight in gold; **non è tutt'oro quel che luccica** all that glitters is not gold

orologeria [orolodʒe'ria] SF (*arte, industria*) watchmaking *no pl*; (*negozio*) watchmaker's (shop); clockmaker's (shop); (*meccanismo*) clockwork; **bomba a orologeria** time bomb

orologiaio, -ai [orolo'dʒajo] SM watchmaker; clockmaker

orologio, -gi [oro'lɔdʒo] SM (*da muro, a pendolo*) clock; (*da tasca, polso*) watch; **il mio orologio va avanti/indietro** my watch is fast/slow; **una mezz'ora di orologio** exactly half an hour; **andare** *o* **funzionare come un orologio** (*meccanismo*) to run like clockwork; **orologio analogico** analogue watch *o* clock; **orologio biologico** biological clock; **orologio digitale** digital watch *o* clock; **orologio da polso** wristwatch; **orologio da tasca** pocket watch; **orologio al quarzo** quartz watch; **orologio solare** sundial

oroscopo [o'rɔskopo] SM horoscope

orrendo, -a [or'rendo] AGG (*spaventoso*) horrible, horrendous; (*bruttissimo*) hideous; (*cattivo*) awful, terrible, dreadful; (*ripugnante*) revolting

orribile [or'ribile] AGG (*brutto*) horrible; (*pessimo*) awful, dreadful; (*ripugnante*) revolting

orrido, -a [ˈɔrrido] AGG horrid, dreadful, fearful

orripilante [orripi'lante] AGG horrifying, hair-raising

orrore [or'rore] SM (*gen*) horror; (*ribrezzo*) disgust, loathing; **avere orrore di qc** to loathe *o* detest sth; **avere in orrore qn/qc** to loathe *o* detest sb/sth; **i ragni mi fanno orrore** I have a horror of spiders, I loathe spiders; **gli orrori della guerra** the horrors of war; **che orrore!** how awful *o* dreadful!; **quel quadro è un orrore** that painting is hideous; **film dell'orrore** horror film (*Brit*) *o* movie (*USA*)

orsacchiotto [orsak'kjɔtto] SM (*cucciolo*) bear cub; (*giocattolo*) teddy bear

orso ['orso] SM (*Zool, anche fig*) bear; **orso bianco** polar bear; **orso bruno** brown bear

orsù [or'su] ESCL (*letter*) come now!

ortaggio, -gi [or'taddʒo] SM vegetable

ortensia [or'tɛnsja] SF hydrangea

ortica [or'tika] SF (stinging) nettle; **mi sono punto con le ortiche** I stung myself on the nettles; **falsa ortica** dead-nettle

orticaria [orti'karja] SF nettle rash

orticoltura [ortikol'tura] SF horticulture

orto ['ɔrto] SM vegetable garden, kitchen garden; (*Agr*) market garden (*Brit*), truck farm (*USA*); **orto botanico** botanical garden(s *pl*)

ortodosso, -a [orto'dɔsso] AGG, SM, SF orthodox

ortofrutticolo, -a [ortofrut'tikolo] AGG fruit and vegetable *attr*

ortogonale [ortogo'nale] AGG perpendicular, orthogonal

ortografia [ortogra'fia] SF spelling, orthography; **errori di ortografia** spelling mistakes

ortolano, -a [orto'lano] SM, SF (*negoziante*) greengrocer (*Brit*), produce dealer (*USA*)

ortopedia [ortope'dia] SF orthopaedics sg (*Brit*), orthopedics sg (*USA*)

ortopedico, -a, -ci, -che [orto'pɛdiko] AGG orthopaedic (*Brit*), orthopedic (*USA*) ♦ SM, SF orthopaedic specialist (*Brit*), orthopedist (*USA*)

orzaiolo, -a [ordza'jɔlo] , **orzaiuolo** SM (*Med*) sty(e)

orzata¹ [or'dzata] SF (*bevanda*) barley water; (*sciroppo*) almond-based cordial

orzata² [or'dzata] SF (*Naut*): **fare un'orzata** to head up

orzo ['ɔrdzo] SM barley

osare [o'zare] /72/ VT **1 osare (fare)** to dare (do) *o* (to do); **non osava domandargli** he didn't dare (to) ask him; **ha osato sfidarlo** she dared to defy him; **non osavo dirlo** I didn't dare to say it...; **oserei dire che...** I dare say that ...; **come osi?** how dare you? **2** (*tentare*) to attempt; (*arrischiare*) to risk

oscenità [oʃʃeni'ta] SF INV obscenity

osceno, -a [oʃ'ʃeno] AGG (*indecente*) obscene; (*bruttissimo*) dreadful, awful; (*ripugnante*) ghastly

oscillare [oʃʃil'lare] /72/ VI (*aus avere*) (*Fis*) to oscillate; (*pendolo*) to swing; (*fiamma*) to flicker; (*dondolare: al vento*) to rock; (*prezzi, temperatura*): **oscillare (fra)** to fluctuate (between); (*persona: essere indeciso*) to waver (between)

oscillazione [oʃʃillat'tsjone] SF (*Fis*) oscillation; (*di prezzi, temperatura*) fluctuation

oscuramento [oskura'mento] SM **1** (*cielo*) darkening; (*sole*) obscuring; (*vista*) dimming **2** (*in tempo di guerra*) blackout

oscurare [osku'rare] /72/ VT **1** (*rendere scuro*) to darken, obscure; (*offuscare: sole, veduta*) to obscure; (*schermare: lampada*) to shade **2** (*fig*) to obscure; **oscurarsi** VIP **1** (*cielo*) to cloud over, darken, get *o* become darker **2** (*vista, mente*) to dim, grow dim; **si oscurò in volto** his face clouded (over)

oscurità [oskuri'ta] SF (*vedi agg*) darkness; obscurity; gloominess; **la stanza piombò nell'oscurità** the room was plunged into darkness

oscuro, -a [os'kuro] AGG (*scuro*) dark; (*fig: incomprensibile, sconosciuto*) obscure; (*: triste: pensiero*) gloomy, sombre; (*: umile:*

vita, natali) humble, obscure; **ci sono alcuni punti oscuri nel suo racconto** there are some unclear points in his account; **è morto in circostanze oscure** he died in mysterious circumstances ♦ sm darkness; **all'oscuro; all'oscuro di qn/essere all'oscuro di qc** to keep sb/be in the dark about sth; **mi hanno sempre tenuto all'oscuro della faccenda** they've always kept me in the dark about this

Oslo ['oslo] sf Oslo

ospedale [ospe'dale] sm hospital; **essere ricoverato in ospedale** to be admitted to the hospital; **essere all'ospedale** to be in the hospital; **Luigi è all'ospedale da una settimana** Luigi's been in the hospital for a week; **ospedale da campo** field hospital; **ospedale militare** military hospital

ospedaliero, -a [ospeda'ljero] agg hospital *attr*; **attrezzatura ospedaliera** hospital facilities *pl* ♦ sm, sf hospital worker

ospitale [ospi'tale] agg (*gente*) hospitable; (*casa, paese*) friendly

ospitalità [ospitali'ta] sf hospitality

ospitare [ospi'tare] /72/ vt 1 (*dare alloggio*) to put up; (*sogg: albergo*) to accommodate; **mi hanno ospitato per una settimana** they put me up for a week 2 (*accogliere: mostre, gare, avvenimenti*) to hold; (: *Sport*) to play at home to; **il Milan ospiterà la Juventus domenica prossima** Milan will play at home to Juventus next Sunday

ospite ['ospite] sm, sf (*persona ospitata*) guest; (*persona che ospita*) host (hostess); **ero l'unico ospite dell'albergo** I was the only guest at the hotel; **la stanza degli ospiti** the guest room ♦ agg: **squadra ospite** (*Calcio*) visiting team

ospizio, -zi [os'pittsjo] sm (*istituto di ricovero*) home; (*per anziani*) old people's home; (*per viaggiatori, pellegrini*) hospice

ossa ['ossa] sfpl *vedi* osso

ossario, -ri [os'sarjo] sm war memorial (*with burial place*)

ossatura [ossa'tura] sf (*di corpo*) bone structure, frame, skeletal structure; (*di edificio, ponte, romanzo*) framework; **è di ossatura robusta** he's strongly built

osseo, -a ['osseo] agg (*Anat, Med*) bone *attr*, bony

ossequente [osse'kwente], **ossequiente** [osse'kwjente] agg: **ossequente alle leggi** law-abiding

ossequio, -qui [os'sekwjo] sm 1 respect, deference; **in ossequio a** out of respect for 2 **ossequi** smpl (*saluto*) respects, regards; **ossequi alla signora!** (give my) respects to your wife!; **porgere i propri ossequi a qn** (*frm*) to pay one's respects to sb; **i miei ossequi** (*in una lettera*) sincere regards

ossequioso, -a [osse'kwjoso] agg (*rispettoso*) respectful; (*servile*) obsequious

osservanza [osser'vantsa] sf observance

osservare [osser'vare] /72/ vt 1 (*guardare*) to observe; (*attentamente: nemico*) to watch; (*al microscopio*) to examine; **osservava attentamente quello che stavo facendo** he was carefully watching what I was doing 2 (*notare, rilevare*) to notice, observe; (*far notare*) to point out, remark, observe; **far osservare qc a qn** to point sth out to sb; **vorrei farvi osservare alcune cose** I'd like to point out a few things to you; **ha osservato che...** (*ha detto*) he remarked that ...; (*ha obiettato*) he objected o made the objection that ...; **non ho nulla da osservare** I have no objections 3 (*rispettare: legge, regolamento*) to observe, respect; (*mantenere: silenzio*) to keep; **osservare il digiuno** to fast, keep the fast

osservatore, -trice [osserva'tore] agg observant ♦ sm, sf observer

osservatorio, -ri [osserva'torjo] sm (*Astron, Meteor*) observatory; (*Mil*) observation o look-out post

osservazione [osserva'tsjone] sf 1 observation; **tenere qn in o sotto osservazione** (*Med*) to keep sb under observation; **l'hanno tenuto sotto osservazione per due giorni** he was kept under observation for two days 2 (*considerazione critica*) comment, observation, remark; (*obiezione*) objection; (*rimprovero*) criticism, reproof; **nessuno ha delle osservazioni da fare?** has anyone got any comments?; **questa è un'osservazione molto acuta** that's a very intelligent remark; **fare un'osservazione** (*considerazione*) to make a remark; (*obiezione*) to raise an objection; **fare un'osservazione a qn** to criticise sb; **il professore mi ha fatto un'osservazione ingiusta** the teacher criticized me unfairly; **fare osservazione a qn** to reprimand sb

ossessionare [ossessjo'nare] /72/ vt (*tormentare: sogg: idea,*

ricordo) to obsess, haunt; (: *sogg: persona*) to torment, harass; (*infastidire*) to trouble, bother

ossessione [osses'sjone] sf 1 (*fissazione*) obsession; **aveva l'ossessione del denaro** he was obsessed with money 2 (*seccatura*) nuisance

ossessivo, -a [osses'sivo] agg obsessive, haunting; (*ricordo, idea: persona*) troublesome; **ma sei proprio ossessivo!** you really are a pest!

ossesso, -a [os'sesso] agg (*spiritato*) possessed ♦ sm, sf person possessed; (*fig*) **urlare come un ossesso** to shout like a maniac

ossia [os'sia] cong (*cioè*) that is, to be precise; (*o meglio*) or rather

ossibuchi [ossi'buki] smpl *di* ossobuco

ossidare [ossi'dare] /72/ vt, **ossidarsi** vip to oxidize

ossidazione [ossidat'tsjone] sf oxidization, oxidation

ossido ['ossido] sm oxide; **ossido di carbonio** carbon monoxide

ossigenare [ossidʒe'nare] /72/ vt 1 (*Chim*) to oxygenate; (*decolorare: capelli*) to bleach; **ossigenare i polmoni** to get some fresh air (into one's lungs) 2 (*fig*) to inject new life into; **ossigenarsi** vr 1 (*decolorarsi*) to bleach one's hair 2 (*ritemprarsi*) to get some fresh air

ossigeno [os'sidʒeno] sm oxygen; **dare l'ossigeno a qn** to give sb oxygen; **dare ossigeno a qn/qc** (*fig*) to give sb/sth a new lease on life

osso ['osso] sm 1 (*pl f* ossa *o pl m* ossi) bone; **le ossa della gamba** the bones of the leg; **d'osso** (*bottone, manico*) bone *attr*, of bone; **carne senza ossa** boneless o boned meat; **osso di balena** whalebone; **osso di seppia** cuttlebone 2 (*fam: di pesca*) stone 3 (*fraseologia*): **avere le ossa rotte** to be dead o dog tired; **bagnato fino all'osso** soaked to the skin; **rompersi l'osso del collo** to break one's neck; **rimetterci l'osso del collo** (*fig*) to ruin o.s., lose everything; **essere ridotto all'osso** (*fig: magro*) to be just skin and bone; (: *senza soldi*) to be in dire straits; **farsi le ossa** to gain experience; **un osso duro** (*persona*) a hard o tough nut, a tough cookie (*USA*); (*impresa*) a tall order

ossobuco [osso'buko] sm (*pl* ossibuchi) (*Culin*) marrowbone; (*piatto*) ossobuco, stew made with knuckle of veal in tomato sauce

ossuto, -a [os'suto] agg (*persona, viso*) angular; (*animale*) scraggy; (*mano*) bony

ostacolare [ostako'lare] /72/ vt (*persona, piano*) to hinder; **le gonne strette ostacolano i movimenti** tight skirts hinder one's movements; **Maurizio ha cercato di ostacolare il mio piano** Maurizio tried to spoil my plan; **hanno cercato di ostacolarmi** they tried to make things difficult for me; **ostacolare la giustizia** to obstruct justice

ostacolo [os'takolo] sm 1 (*anche fig*) obstacle, difficulty; **ha superato molti ostacoli** she has overcome many difficulties; **essere di ostacolo a qn/qc** (*fig*) to stand in the way of sb/sth 2 (*Atletica*) hurdle; (*Equitazione*) jump, fence; **i quattrocento metri a ostacoli** the four hundred meter hurdles

ostaggio, -gi [os'taddʒo] sm hostage; **prendere/tenere qn in ostaggio** to take/keep sb hostage

oste, ostessa ['oste] sm, sf innkeeper, landlord (landlady)

osteggiare [osted'dʒare] /62/ vt to oppose, be opposed to

ostello [os'tello] sm hostel; **ostello della gioventù** youth hostel

ostensorio, -ri [osten'sorjo] sm (*Rel*) monstrance

ostentare [osten'tare] /72/ vt (*ricchezze, bravura*) to show off, flaunt, make a show of; (*distacco, indifferenza*) to feign

ostentazione [ostentat'tsjone] sf ostentation, show; **con ostentazione** ostentatiously

osteria [oste'ria] sf ≈ pub (*Brit*), ≈ bar

ostetrico, -a, -ci, -che [os'tetriko] agg obstetric(al); **clinica ostetrica** maternity hospital o home ♦ sm, sf (*medico*) obstetrician ♦ sf (*levatrice*) midwife

ostia ['ostja] sf (*Rel*) host; (*per medicinali*) wafer

ostico, -a, -ci, -che ['ostiko] agg difficult, tough

ostile [os'tile] agg: **ostile (a)** hostile (to o towards)

ostilità [ostili'ta] sf inv (*stato, atteggiamento*) hostility; (*atto*) act of hostility; (*Mil*): **le ostilità** hostilities

ostinarsi [osti'narsi] /72/ vip 1 (*impuntarsi*): **ostinarsi su** o **in**

qc to insist on sth, dig one's heels in about sth; **ostinarsi a voler fare qc** to be determined to do sth **2** (*persistere*): **ostinarsi a fare qc** to persist (obstinately) in doing sth, keep on doing sth; **è inutile che ti ostini a negarlo** it's no use keeping on denying it

ostinato, -a [osti'nato] AGG (*persona, resistenza*) obstinate, stubborn; (*tenace*) determined; (*tosse, pioggia*) persistent ♦ SM, SF obstinate *o* stubborn person

ostinazione [ostinat'tsjone] SF (*di persone*) obstinacy, stubbornness; **ostinazione a fare qc** obstinate *o* stubborn determination to do sth

ostracismo [ostra't∫izmo] SM ostracism; **dare l'ostracismo a qn** to ostracize sb

ostrica, -che ['ostrika] SF oyster; **ostrica perlifera** pearl oyster
❏ **ostrica** non si traduce mai con la parola inglese *ostrich*

ostruire [ostru'ire] /55/ VT to obstruct, block; **c'è qualcosa che ostruisce il tubo** there's something blocking the pipe; **ostruirsi** VIP to become obstructed *o* blocked

ostruzione [ostrut'tsjone] SF **1** obstruction, blocking **2** (*effetto, cosa che ostruisce*) obstruction, blockage; (*Sport*) obstruction; **fare ostruzione** (*Calcio*) to obstruct

ostruzionismo [ostruttsjo'nizmo] SM (*Pol*) obstructionism; (*Sport*) obstruction; **fare ostruzionismo a** (*progetto, legge*) to obstruct

otite [o'tite] SF ear infection; **ho l'otite** I've got an ear infection

otorinolaringoiatra, -i, -e [otorinolaringo'jatra] SM, SF
otorino [oto'rino] SM ear, nose and throat specialist

otre ['otre] SM (*recipiente*) goatskin

ott. ABBR (= *ottobre*) Oct

ottagonale [ottago'nale] AGG octagonal, eight-sided

ottagono [ot'tagono] SM octagon

ottano [ot'tano] SM octane; **numero di ottani** octane rating *o* number; **benzina ad alto numero di ottani** high-octane petrol (*Brit*) *o* gasoline (*USA*)

ottanta [ot'tanta] AGG INV, SM INV eighty

ottantenne [ottan'tenne] AGG eighty-year-old ♦ SM, SF octogenarian

ottantesimo, -a [ottan'tezimo] AGG, SM, SF eightieth

ottantina [ottan'tina] SF: **una ottantina (di)** about eighty

ottavo, -a [ot'tavo] AGG, SM, SF eighth ♦ SM **1** (*frazione*) eighth **2** (*Tip*) octavo; **edizione in ottavo** octavo edition **3** (*Sport*): **entrare negli ottavi di finale** to get into the last sixteen; **superare gli ottavi di finale** to reach the quarterfinals ♦ SF (*Poesia, Mus, Rel*) octave

ottemperanza [ottempe'rantsa] SF (*Amm*): **in ottemperanza a** in accordance with, in compliance with

ottemperare [ottempe'rare] /72/ VI (*aus avere*) **ottemperare a** to comply with, obey

ottenebrare [ottene'brare] /72/ VT (*anche fig*) to cloud; (*sole*) to hide, obscure; **ottenebrarsi** VIP to cloud (over), darken

ottenere [otte'nere] /121/ VT IRREG (*risposta, laurea, permesso*) to obtain, get; **ha ottenuto il permesso di uscire** she got permission to go out; **ottenere una promozione** to get a promotion; **ha ottenuto di parlargli lunedì** he managed to arrange a meeting with him for Monday; **ha ottenuto che il ragazzo venisse ricoverato** he managed to get the boy admitted to the hospital **2** (*totale*) to reach, arrive at; (*risultato*) to achieve, obtain; (*premio, approvazione, fiducia*) to gain, win; **ottenere un buon successo** to have great success; **abbiamo ottenuto un buon risultato** we got a good result; **aggiungendo il giallo al blu si ottiene il verde** green is obtained *o* you get green by adding yellow to blue

ottico, -a, -ci, -che ['ottiko] AGG (*nervo*) optic; (*fenomeno, strumento*) optical; **un'illusione ottica** an optical illusion ♦ SM optician

ottimale [otti'male] AGG optimal, optimum

ottimamente [ottima'mente] AVV very well, excellently

ottimismo [otti'mizmo] SM optimism

ottimista, -i, -e [otti'mista] AGG optimistic ♦ SM, SF optimist

ottimizzare [ottimid'dzare] /72/ VT (*servizio, produzione*) optimize

ottimizzazione [ottimiddzat'tsjone] SF optimization

ottimo, -a ['ottimo] AGG superl di buono¹ very good, excellent; **risultati ottimi** excellent results; **la cena è stata ottima** the

dinner was delicious ♦ SM (*condizione ottimale*) peak; (*Scol*) top marks *pl*

otto ['otto] AGG INV eight ♦ SM INV (*numero, anche Canottaggio*) eight; (*tracciato*) figure of eight; **oggi (a) otto** in a week's time, today week; **otto volante** switchback

ottobre [ot'tobre] SM October; *vedi* luglio

ottobrino, -a [otto'brino] AGG October *attr*

ottocentesco, -a, -schi, -sche [ottot∫en'tesko] AGG nineteenth-century

ottocento [otto't∫ento] AGG INV, SM INV eight hundred ♦ SM INV eight hundred; (*secolo*): **l'Ottocento** the nineteenth century

ottomila [otto'mila] AGG INV, SM INV eight thousand

ottone [ot'tone] SM brass; **di** *o* **in ottone** brass *attr*; **un campanello di ottone** a brass bell; **gli ottoni** (*Mus*) the brass *sg*

ottuagenario, -a, -ri [ottuad3e'narjo] AGG, SM, SF octogenarian

ottundere [ot'tundere] /34/ VT IRREG (*fig: mente*) to dull

otturare [ottu'rare] /72/ VT (*chiudere: falla, apertura*) to stop up, close (up), seal; (*bloccare: lavandino*) to block (up); (*riempire: dente*) to fill; **bisogna otturare la falla** we need to seal the leak; **ci dev'essere qualcosa che ottura il lavandino** there must be something blocking the sink; **il dentista mi ha otturato due denti** the dentist has filled two of my teeth; **otturarsi** VIP (*bloccarsi*) to become *o* get blocked (up)

otturatore [ottura'tore] SM (*Fot*) shutter; (*nelle armi*) breechblock; (*Tecn*) valve

otturazione [otturat'tsjone] SF **1** (*vedi vb*) stopping up, closing (up), seal; (*bloccare: lavandino*) to block (up); (*riempire: dente*) to fill **2** (*di dente*) filling; **fare un'otturazione a qn** to give sb a filling

ottusità [ottuzi'ta] SF (*vedi agg*) obtuseness; dullness

ottuso, -a [ot'tuzo] PP *di* ottundere ♦ AGG (*Mat*) obtuse; (*fig*) obtuse, slow-witted; (*suono*) muffled, dull

ovaia [o'vaja] SF , **ovaio** [o'vajo] SM (*Anat*) ovary

ovale [o'vale] AGG, SM oval

ovarico, -a, -ci, -che AGG ovarian

ovatta [o'vatta] SF (*per medicazione*) cotton wool; (*per imbottiture*) padding, wadding

ovattare [ovat'tare] /72/ VT **1** (*imbottire*) to pad; **ambiente ovattato** (*fig*) cocoon-like environment **2** (*fig: smorzare*) to muffle

ovazione [ovat'tsjone] SF ovation

ovest ['ovest] SM INV west; **a ovest (di)** west (of); **si è diretto a ovest** he headed west; **il sole tramonta a ovest** the sun sets in the west; **l'Italia confina a ovest con la Francia** Italy has a border to the west with France; **si trova a ovest della città** it's west of the city; **il vento viene da ovest** the wind comes from the west; **verso ovest** westward(s) ♦ AGG INV (*gen*) west; (*regione*) western; **è partito in direzione ovest** he set off westwards *o* in a westward direction

ovile [o'vile] SM pen, (sheep)fold; **tornare all'ovile** (*fig*) to return to the fold

ovino, -a [o'vino] AGG (*specie*) ovine (*termine tecn*), sheep *attr*; (*mercato, allevamento*) sheep *attr*

ovulazione [ovulat'tsjone] SF ovulation

ovulo ['ovulo] SM (*Anat*) ovum; (*Bot*) ovule

ovunque [o'vunkwe] AVV = dovunque

ovvero [ov'vero] CONG (*o meglio*) or (rather); (*ossia*) that is, to be precise; (*oppure*) or (else)

ovviare [ovvi'are] /19/ VI (*aus avere*) **ovviare a** to remedy, get round; **ovviare all'inconveniente (di)** to get round the problem (of)

ovvio, -via, -vi, -vie ['ovvjo] AGG obvious; **è ovvio che...** obviously ..., it is obvious *o* clear that ...

oziare [ot'tsjare] /19/ VI (*aus avere*) to laze around

ozio, ozi ['ottsjo] SM **1** (*peccato*) sloth; (*inattività*) idleness; **stare in ozio** to be idle; **se ne sta tutto il giorno in ozio** he sits around doing nothing all day; **l'ozio è il padre dei vizi** (*Proverbio*) the Devil finds work for idle hands (to do) **2** (*riposo*): **ore d'ozio** leisure *o* spare time *sg*

ozioso, -a [ot'tsjozo] AGG **1** (*sfaccendato*) idle; (*inattivo: persona, giornata*) lazy; (: *per malattia*) inactive **2** (*fig: discorsi*) idle; (: *domanda*) pointless ♦ SM, SF layabout, idler

ozono [od'dzono] SM ozone; **il buco nell'ozono** the hole in the ozone layer; **la fascia** *o* **lo strato d'ozono** the ozone layer

ozonosfera [oddzonos'fera] SF ozonosphere, ozone layer

Pp

P¹, p¹ [pi] SF INV, SM INV (*lettera*) P, p; **P come Padova** ≈ P for Peter

P² ABBR 1 (= *peso*) wt (= *weight*) 2 (= *parcheggio*) P 3 (*Aut*: = *principiante*) L (= *learner*)

p. ABBR (= *pagina*) p (= *page*)

P2 [pi'due] SIGLA F: **la (loggia) P2** the P2 masonic lodge

PA SIGLA = Palermo ♦ ABBR = pubblica amministrazione

pacare [pa'kare] /20/ VT to calm; **pacarsi** VIP (*tempesta, disordini*) to subside

pacatezza [paka'tettsa] SF (*vedi agg*) placidness; quietness, calmness

pacato, -a [pa'kato] AGG (*carattere*) placid; (*voce, tono*) quiet, calm

pacca, -che ['pakka] SF slap; **gli ho dato una pacca sulla schiena** I gave him a pat on the back

pacchetto [pak'ketto] SM (*confezione*) parcel; (*di sigarette*) packet (*Brit*), pack (*USA*); **un pacchetto di sigarette** a packet of cigarettes; **le ho spedito un pacchetto** I sent her a parcel; **pacchetto applicativo** (*Inform*) applications package; **pacchetto azionario** (*Fin*) shareholding; **pacchetto software** (*Inform*) software package; **pacchetto turistico** package holiday (*Brit*) o tour

pacchiano, -a [pak'kjano] AGG (*colori*) garish; (*abiti, arredamento*) vulgar, garish; **un gusto veramente pacchiano** an extremely vulgar taste

pacco, -chi ['pakko] SM 1 package, parcel; (*di farina, zucchero*) bag; **un grosso pacco marrone** a large brown parcel; **c'era un grosso pacco per lui sotto l'albero** there was a big parcel for him under the tree; **un pacco di zucchero** a bag of sugar; **carta da pacchi** brown paper; (*da regalo*) wrapping paper; **pacco bomba** parcel bomb; **pacco postale** parcel 2 (*involto*) bundle 3 (*fam!: organo genitale maschile*) lunchbox

paccottiglia [pakkot'tiʎʎa] SF trash, junk

pace ['patʃe] SF (*gen*) peace; **trattato di pace** peace treaty; **firmare la pace** to sign a peace treaty; **fare (la) pace con qn** to make (it) up with sb; **ho fatto la pace con Luciana** I've made it up with Luciana; **far fare (la) pace a due persone** to make peace between two people; **non si dà pace per quello che è successo** she can't stop thinking about what happened; **non mi dà un momento di pace** he doesn't give me a moment's peace; **mettersi l'animo in pace, darsi pace** to resign o.s.; **lasciare qn in pace** to leave sb alone; **lasciami in pace!** leave me alone!; **riposare in pace** to rest in peace; **santa pace!** for heaven's sake!; **pace all'anima sua!** (*anche scherz*) may he rest in peace!; **pace!** (*fa niente*) never mind!

pachistano, -a [pakis'tano] AGG, SM, SF Pakistani; **i pachistani** the Pakistanis

pacificare [patʃifi'kare] /20/ VT (*riconciliare*) to reconcile, make peace between; (*mettere in pace*) to pacify; **riuscì a pacificare gli animi** he managed to pacify o mollify everyone

pacificazione [patʃifikat'tsjone] SF (*vedi vb*) reconciliation; pacification

pacifico, -a, -ci, -che [pa'tʃifiko] AGG 1 (*persona, carattere*) peaceable; (*vita, manifestazione*) peaceful 2 (*fig: indiscusso*) indisputable; (: *ovvio*) obvious, clear; **è pacifico che resterà in carica** it is obvious o it goes without saying that he will stay in office ♦ SM: **il Pacifico, l'Oceano Pacifico** the Pacific (Ocean)

pacifismo [patʃi'fizmo] SM pacifism

pacifista, -i, -e [patʃi'fista] AGG pacifist; **è pacifista** he's a pacifist ♦ SM, SF pacifist

PACS [paks] SIGLA MPL civil partnerships

padano, -a [pa'dano] AGG of the Po; **la pianura padana** the Lombardy plain

padella [pa'dɛlla] SF 1 (*Culin*) frying pan (*Brit*), skillet (*USA*); **cucinare in padella** to fry; **cadere dalla padella nella brace** (*fig*) to jump out of the frying pan into the fire 2 (*per infermi*) bedpan

padiglione [padiʎ'ʎone] SM 1 (*di mostra, ospedale*) pavilion; **padiglione di caccia** hunting lodge 2 (*Anat*): **padiglione auricolare** auricle, pinna

Padova ['padova] SF Padua

padovano, -a [pado'vano] AGG of o from Padua ♦ SM, SF inhabitant o native of Padova

padre ['padre] SM 1 father; **mio padre** my father; **il padre di Roberto** Roberto's father; **Rossi padre** Rossi senior; **di padre in figlio** from father to son; **per parte di padre** on my (o his *ecc*) father's side; **padre di famiglia** father, family man 2 (*antenati*): **padri** SMPL forefathers, ancestors 3 (*Rel*) father; **Padre mio** Father; **il Santo Padre** (*il Papa*) the Holy Father

Padreterno [padre'terno] SM: **il Padreterno** God the Father; **si crede un padreterno** (*fig*) he thinks he is God Almighty

padrino [pa'drino] SM (*di battesimo*) godfather; (*di cresima*) sponsor; (*di duello*) second

padronale [padro'nale] AGG (*scala, entrata*) main, principal; **casa padronale** country house

padronanza [padro'nantsa] SF (*dominio*) command, mastery; **padronanza di sé** self-control; **avere una buona padronanza dell'inglese** to have a good command of English

padronato [padro'nato] SM: **il padronato** the ruling class

padrone, -a [pa'drone] SM, SF 1 (*dominatore, anche fig*) master (mistress); (*proprietario*) owner; **chi è il padrone di questo cane?** who's the owner of this dog?; **essere padrone di sé** to be self-possessed; **non era più padrone di sé** he had lost his self-control; **sono padrone di fare ciò che voglio** I am my own master; **essere padrone di una lingua** to have mastered a language; **essere padrone della situazione** to be master of the situation, have the situation in hand; **padrona di casa** mistress of the house; (*per gli inquilini*) landlady; **padrone di casa** master of the house; (*per gli inquilini*) landlord 2 (*datore di lavoro*) employer, boss (*fam*); **essere sotto padrone** to be an employee

padroneggiare [padroned'dʒare] /62/ VT (*fig: istinti, sentimenti*) to control, master; (: *lingua, materia*) to master, know thoroughly; **padroneggiarsi** VR to control o.s.

paesaggio, -gi [pae'zaddʒo] SM (*panorama, anche Arte*) landscape; (*aspetto di un luogo*) scenery

paesaggista, -i, -e [paezad'dʒista] SM, SF (*pittore*) landscape painter

paesano, -a [pae'zano] AGG country *attr* ♦ SM, SF 1 (*campagnolo*) peasant, rustic; (*abitante di paese*) villager 2 (*concittadino*) fellow countryman o countrywoman

paese [pa'eze] SM 1 (*nazione*) country, nation; **i paesi in via di sviluppo** the developing countries o nations; **l'Iraq è il paese d'origine della mia famiglia** my family comes from Iraq 2 (*terra*) country, land; **vorrei visitare paesi lontani** I should like to visit far away places; **la Francia è un paese fertile** France is a fertile country o land 3 (*villaggio*) village; **vivo in un paese** I live in a village; **gente di paese** village people 4 (*fraseologia*): **paese che vai usanze che trovi** when in Rome do as the Romans do; **tutto il mondo è paese** people are the same the world over; **mandare qn a quel paese** (*fam*) to tell sb to get lost

paffuto, -a [paf'futo] AGG plump, chubby

paga, -ghe ['paga] SF (*gen*) pay; (*di operaio*) wages *pl*; (*fig: ricompensa*) reward, recompense; **la paga non è molto alta** the pay's not very good; **giorno di paga** payday

pagabile [pa'gabile] AGG payable; **pagabile alla consegna/a vista** payable on delivery/on demand

pagaia [pa'gaja] SF paddle

pagamento [paga'mento] SM payment; **non lo faccio nemmeno a pagamento** I won't do it even if they pay me; **la TV a pagamento** pay TV; **pagamento anticipato** payment in advance; **pagamento alla consegna** payment on delivery, cash on delivery; **pagamento in contanti** payment in cash; **pagamento all'ordine** cash with order

pagano, -a [pa'gano] AGG, SM, SF pagan

pagare [pa'gare] /80/ VT **1** (*somma, conto, operaio*) to pay; (*debito*) to pay, settle; **hai pagato il conto?** have you paid the bill?; **pagare una cambiale** to pay a bill, honour (*Brit*) o honor (*USA*) a bill; **pagare in contanti** to pay cash; **pagare con carta di credito** to pay by credit card; **posso pagare con la carta di credito?** can I pay by credit card? **2** (*merce, lavoro, anche fig: colpa*) to pay for; **quanto l'hai pagato?** how much did you pay for it?; **l'ho pagato 10 euro** I paid 10 euros for it; **pagare una macchina 20 mila euro** to pay 20 thousand euros for a car; **me l'ha fatto pagare 35 euro** he charged me 35 euros for it; **l'ho pagato caro/poco** I paid a lot/very little for it; **l'ho pagata cara** (*fig*) I paid dearly for it; **pagare qc salato** o **un occhio della testa** to pay through the nose for sth; **te la farò pagare!** (*fig*) I'll make you pay for it!, you'll pay for this!; **ha pagato con la vita** it cost him his life; **pagare di persona** (*fig*) to suffer the consequences; **pagare qc di tasca propria** to pay for sth out of one's own pocket; (*fig*) to learn sth to one's cost; **quanto non pagherei per sapere!** what wouldn't I give to know! **3** (*offrire*): **ti pago da bere** let me buy you a drink; **pago io** this is on me, I'll get it; **pago io questo giro** this is my round **4** (*contraccambiare*) to repay, pay back

pagella [pa'dʒɛlla] SF (*Scol*) school report (*Brit*), report card (*USA*)

paggio, -gi ['paddʒo] SM page(boy)

pagherò¹ [page'rɔ] VB *vedi* **pagare**

pagherò² [page'rɔ] SM INV IOU; **pagherò cambiario** promissory note

pagina ['padʒina] SF page; **a pagina 5** on page 5; **fate l'esercizio 2 a pagina 10** do exercise 2 on page 10; **andate a pagina 5** turn to page 5; **ha scritto un tema di tre pagine** he wrote a three-page essay; **le più belle pagine del Manzoni** Manzoni's finest passages; **Pagine bianche** phone book, telephone directory

paglia ['paʎʎa] SF straw; (*fam: sigaretta*) fag (*Brit*), cigarette; **cappello di paglia** straw hat; **tetto di paglia** thatched roof; **avere la coda di paglia** (*fig*) to have a guilty conscience; **fuoco di paglia** (*fig*) flash in the pan

pagliaccetto [paʎʎat'tʃetto] SM (*per bambini*) rompers *pl*; (*per signora*) camiknickers (*Brit*) *pl*

pagliacciata [paʎʎat'tʃata] SF farce

pagliaccio, -ci [paʎ'ʎattʃo] SM clown; **fare il pagliaccio** (*fig*) to play the fool

pagliaio, -ai [paʎ'ʎajo] SM haystack

pagliericcio, -ci [paʎʎe'rittʃo] SM straw mattress

paglierino, -a [paʎʎe'rino] AGG: **giallo paglierino** pale yellow

paglietta [paʎ'ʎetta] SF **1** (*cappello per uomo*) (straw) boater **2** (*per tegami ecc*) steel wool

pagliuzza [paʎ'ʎuttsa] SF (blade of) straw; (*d'oro ecc*) tiny particle, speck

pagnotta [paɲ'ɲɔtta] SF round loaf

pago, -a, -ghi, -ghe ['pago] AGG: **essere pago di** to be satisfied with

pagoda [pa'gɔda] SF pagoda

paillette [pa'jɛt] SF INV sequin

paio¹ ['pajo] VB *vedi* **parere²**

paio² ['pajo] SM (*pl f* **paia**) (*coppia*) pair; **un paio di** (*guanti, scarpe*) a pair of; (*alcuni*) a couple of; **un paio di occhiali** a pair of glasses; **un paio di giorni** a couple of days; **tra un paio di settimane** in a couple of weeks; **dare un paio di schiaffi a qn** to box sb's ears; **fanno il paio** they are two of a kind; **è un altro paio di maniche** that's another kettle of fish

paiolo [pa'jɔlo], **paiuolo** [pa'jwɔlo] SM (copper) pot

Pakistan [pakis'tan] SM Pakistan

pakistano, -a [pakis'tano] AGG, SM, SF = **pachistano**

pal. ABBR = **palude**

pala ['pala] SF **1** shovel; (*di remo, ventilatore, elica*) blade; (*di ruota*) paddle **2** (*Rel*): **pala d'altare** altar piece

palandrana [palan'drana] SF (*scherz: abito lungo e largo*) tent

palata [pa'lata] SF (*contenuto*) shovelful; **fa soldi a palate** he is making a mint

palatale [pala'tale] AGG, SF (*Anat, Ling*) palatal

palato [pa'lato] SM (*Anat*) palate; (*gusto*) palate, (sense of) taste; **gradevole al palato** palatable; **avere un palato fine** to have a refined palate

palazzo [pa'lattso] SM (*reggia*) palace; (*edificio*) building; **palazzo dei congressi** conference centre; **palazzo di giustizia** law courts *pl*, courthouse; **palazzo dello sport** indoor sports arena

palchetto [pal'ketto] SM shelf

palco, -chi ['palko] SM **1** (*tavolato*) platform, stand; (*ripiano*) layer **2** (*Teatro*) box; (*tribuna*) stand

palcoscenico [palkoʃ'ʃeniko] SM (*Teatro*) stage

palermitano, -a [palermi'tano] AGG of o from Palermo ♦ SM, SF inhabitant o native of Palermo

Palermo [pa'lermo] SF Palermo

palesare [pale'zare] /72/ VT to reveal, disclose; **palesarsi** VIP (*sentimento*) to reveal o show itself

palese [pa'leze] AGG clear, evident; **rendere palesi le proprie intenzioni** to make one's intentions clear

Palestina [pales'tina] SF Palestine

palestinese [palesti'nese] AGG, SM, SF Palestinian

palestra [pa'lestra] SF (*luogo*) gymnasium, gym; (*esercizio atletico*) exercise, training; (*fig*) training ground, school; **vado in palestra due volte alla settimana** I go to the gym twice a week; **fare palestra** to work out; **fa palestra un'ora al giorno** he works out for an hour every day; **devo fare un po' di palestra** I must take a bit of exercise; **la scuola è palestra di vita** school is a preparation for life

paletot [pal'to] SM INV = **paltò**

paletta [pa'letta] SF (*giocattolo*) spade; (*per il focolare*) shovel; (*del capostazione, vigile*) signalling disc; (*Culin: da dolce*) cake slice

paletto [pa'letto] SM (*picchetto*) stake, peg; (*spranga*) bolt; (*Sci*) pole (*marking run*)

palinsesto [palin'sesto] SM (*TV, Radio*) schedule; (*Storia*) palimpsest

palio, -li ['paljo] SM (*Storia: drappo*) (prize) banner; **il Palio di Siena** horse race in which the different districts of Siena compete; **mettere qc in palio** (*fig*) to offer sth as a prize

palissandro [palis'sandro] SM rosewood

palizzata [palit'tsata] SF palisade

palla ['palla] SF ball; (*pallottola*) bullet; **giocare a palla** to play (with a) ball; **sei una palla al piede!** you are a drag!; **prendere la palla al balzo** (*fig*) to seize one's opportunity; **rompere le palle a qn** (*fam!*) to be a bloody nuisance to sb; **che palle!** (*fam*) what a pain!; **palla gol** scoring opportunity; **a palla** (*al massimo: di volume*) full blast; (: *di velocità*) flat out; **palla da golf** golf ball; **palla di neve** snowball; **palla da tennis** tennis ball

pallacanestro [pallaka'nestro] SF basketball

pallamano [palla'mano] SF handball

pallanuoto [palla'nwɔto] SF water polo

pallavolo [palla'vɔlo] SF volleyball

palleggiare [palled'dʒare] /62/ VI (*aus* avere) (*Calcio*) to practise (*Brit*) o practice (*USA*) with the ball; (*Tennis*) to knock up; (*Basket*) to dribble; **palleggiarsi** VR (*uso reciproco*): **si stanno palleggiando le responsabilità** each is trying to shift the responsibility onto the other

palliativo [pallja'tivo] SM (*Med*) palliative; (*fig*) stopgap measure

pallido, -a ['pallido] AGG (*gen*) pale; (*malaticcio*) pallid; (*ricordo*) faint; (*sorriso*) faint, wan; **sei pallida** you're pale; **è diventata pallida** she paled, she turned pale; **non ho la più pallida idea** I haven't the faintest o foggiest (idea)

pallina [pal'lina] SF (*bilia*) marble

pallino [pal'lino] SM **1** (*pois*) dot; **bianco a pallini blu** white with blue dots **2** (*Biliardo*) cue ball; (*Bocce*) jack **3** (*proiettile*) pellet **4** (*idea fissa*) craze, obsession; **avere il pallino di** to be crazy about; **ha il pallino della matematica** he has a passion for mathematics

palloncino [pallon'tʃino] SM (*giocattolo*) balloon; (*lampioncino*) Chinese lantern

pallone [pal'lone] SM **1** (*palla*) ball; (*Calcio*) football; **giocare**

a pallone to play football; **gioco del pallone** football; **essere un pallone gonfiato** (fig) to be full of o.s. **2** (aerostato) balloon; **pallone sonda** weather balloon **3** (Chim) flask

pallore [pal'lore] SM pallor, paleness

pallottola [pal'lɔttola] SF **1** (proiettile) bullet; (di fucile da caccia) pellet **2** (di carta) ball; **c'erano delle pallottole di carta nel cestino** there were some bits of screwed-up paper in the wastepaper basket

palma¹ ['palma] SF (Anat) palm

palma² ['palma] SF (Bot) palm; **riportare/vincere la palma** (fig) to walk off with/win the prize; **palma da datteri** date palm

palmato, -a [pal'mato] AGG (Zool: piede) webbed; (Bot) palmate

palmipede [pal'mipede] AGG web-footed

palmizio, -zi [pal'mittsjo] SM (palma) palm tree; (ramo) palm

palmo ['palmo] SM (misura) handbreadth; **palmo a palmo** inch by inch; **hanno ispezionato la stanza palmo a palmo** they searched the room inch by inch; **un palmo di polvere sul tavolo** (fig) a layer of dust on the table; **restare con un palmo di naso** (fig) to be badly disappointed; **essere alto un palmo** (fig) to be tiny

palo ['palo] SM (legno appuntito) stake; (sostegno) pole; (Calcio) goalpost; **fare da** o **il palo** (fig) to act as look-out; **saltare di palo in frasca** (fig) to jump from one topic to another; **palo della luce** lamppost; **palo del telegrafo** telegraph pole

palombaro [palom'baro] SM (deep-sea) diver

palombo [pa'lombo] SM (pesce) dogfish; (colombo) wood pigeon

palpare [pal'pare] /72/ VT (tastare) to feel, finger; (Med) to palpate

palpebra ['palpebra] SF eyelid

palpitare [palpi'tare] /72/ VI (aus avere) (cuore) to beat; (più forte) to pound, throb; (fremere) to quiver; **palpitare di paura** to tremble with fear; **palpitare di gioia** to quiver with delight

palpitazione [palpitat'tsjone] SF (Med): **avere le palpitazioni** to have palpitations

palpito ['palpito] SM (del cuore) beat; (fig: d'amore) throb

paltò [pal'tɔ] SM INV overcoat

palude [pa'lude] SF marsh, swamp

paludoso, -a [palu'doso] AGG swampy, marshy

palustre [pa'lustre] AGG marsh attr, swamp attr

pampino ['pampino] SM vine leaf

panacea [pana'tʃea] SF panacea

Panama ['panama] SF Panama; **il canale di Panama** the Panama Canal

panamense [pana'mɛnse] AGG, SM, SF Panamanian

panca, -che ['panka] SF bench

pancarré [pankar're] SM INV sliced bread

pancetta [pan'tʃetta] SF **1** (Culin) bacon; **pancetta affumicata** smoked streaky bacon **2** (fam: ciccia) belly; **mio padre ha un po' di pancetta** my dad's got a bit of a belly

panchetto [pan'ketto] SM (sgabello) stool

panchina [pan'kina] SF garden seat; (di giardino pubblico) (park) bench; (Sport) substitutes' bench

pancia, -ce ['pantʃa] SF belly, stomach; **aver la pancia** to have a potbelly; **aver la pancia piena** to be full; **aver mal di pancia** to have a stomach ache o a sore stomach; **mettere su pancia** to develop o be getting a paunch; **non star lì a grattarti la pancia!** don't sit (o stand) there doing nothing!

panciera [pan'tʃera] SF corset

panciolle [pan'tʃɔlle] AVV: **stare in panciolle** to lounge about (Brit) o around

panciotto [pan'tʃɔtto] SM waistcoat

panciuto, -a [pan'tʃuto] AGG (persona) potbellied; (vaso, bottiglia) rounded

pancreas ['pankreas] SM INV pancreas

panda ['panda] SM INV panda

pandemia [pande'mia] SF pandemic

pandemonio, -ni [pande'mɔnjo] SM pandemonium

pandoro [pan'dɔro] SM type of sponge cake eaten at Christmas

pane ['pane] SM (gen) bread; (pagnotta) loaf (of bread); (di cera) bar; (di burro) block; **il pane quotidiano** one's daily

bread; **guadagnarsi il pane** to earn one's living; **mangiare (il) pane a tradimento** to sponge, scrounge; **rendere pan per focaccia** to give tit for tat; **dire pane al pane, vino al vino** to call a spade a spade; **essere buono come il pane** to have a heart of gold; **per un pezzo di pane** (comprare, vendere) for a song ♦ **pane a** o **in cassetta** sliced bread; **pane bianco** white bread; **pane casereccio** homemade bread; **pane integrale** o **nero** wholemeal bread; **pane al latte** milk bread; **pane di segale** rye bread; **pane tostato** toast; **una fetta di pane tostato** a slice of toast; **pan di Spagna** sponge cake; **pan di zucchero** sugar loaf

panegirico, -ci [pane'dʒiriko] SM panegyric; **fare un panegirico di qn** to sing sb's praises

panetteria [panette'ria] SF (forno) bakery; (negozio) baker's (shop), bakery; **la panetteria all'angolo** the bakery on the corner; **vado in panetteria** I'm going to the baker's

panettiere, -a [panet'tjere] SM, SF baker; **fa il panettiere** he's a baker

panettone [panet'tone] SM panettone, a kind of spiced brioche with sultanas, eaten at Christmas; (di cemento) bollard

panfilo ['panfilo] SM yacht

panforte [pan'fɔrte] SM Sienese nougat-type delicacy

pangrattato [pangrat'tato] SM breadcrumbs pl

panico, -a, -ci, -che ['paniko] SM panic; **essere in preda al panico** to be panic-stricken; **farsi prendere dal panico** to panic; **si è fatta prendere dal panico** she panicked ♦ AGG panic attr

paniere [pa'njere] SM basket

panificatore, -trice [panifika'tore] SM, SF bread-maker, baker

panificio, -ci [pani'fitʃo] SM (forno) bakery; (negozio) baker's (shop), bakery

panino [pa'nino] SM roll; **un panino al prosciutto** a ham roll; **panino imbottito** filled roll

paninoteca, -che [panino'teka] SF ≈ café

panna ['panna] SF (Culin) cream; **panna acida** sour(ed) cream; **panna da cucina** long-life cream used for cooking; **panna montata** whipped cream

panne ['pan] SF INV (Aut) breakdown; **la macchina è in panne** the car has broken down; **rimanere in panne** to break down; **siamo rimasti in panne sull'autostrada** we broke down on the motorway

pannello [pan'nello] SM panel; **pannello di controllo** control panel; **pannello divisorio** partition; **pannello fonoisolante** acoustic screen; **pannello solare** solar panel

panno ['panno] SM **1** (tessuto, straccio) cloth; **un panno umido** a damp cloth **2** (vestiti): **panni** SMPL clothes; **panni da lavare** laundry, washing; **mettiti nei miei panni** put yourself in my shoes; **non stava più nei panni dalla gioia** he was beside himself with joy

pannocchia [pan'nɔkkja] SF (di granturco) corncob; **non ho mai mangiato le pannocchie** I've never eaten corn on the cob

pannolino [panno'lino] SM (per bambini) nappy (Brit), diaper (USA); (assorbente) sanitary towel; **pannolino mutandina** disposable nappy o diaper

pannolone [panno'lone] SM (per adulti) incontinence pad

panorama, -i [pano'rama] SM panorama; **che bel panorama!** what a lovely view!

panoramico, -a, -ci, -che [pano'ramiko] AGG (gen) panoramic; **strada panoramica** scenic route; **rassegna panoramica** overall view

pantacollant [pantakol'lan] SM INV leggings pl

pantaloni [panta'loni] SMPL trousers (Brit), pants (USA); **un paio di pantaloni** a pair of trousers o pants

pantano [pan'tano] SM marsh, bog

pantera [pan'tɛra] SF **1** (Zool) panther **2** (fam: auto della polizia) (high-speed) police car

pantheon ['panteon] SM INV pantheon

pantofola [pan'tɔfola] SF slipper

pantomima [panto'mima] SF pantomime

panzana [pan'tsana] SF tall story

paonazzo, -a [pao'nattso] AGG purple

papa, -i ['papa] SM pope; **ad ogni morte di papa** once in a blue moon; **morto un papa se ne fa un altro** nobody's indispensable; **vivere come un papa** to live like a Lord

papà [pa'pa] SM INV daddy, dad; **il mio papà** my dad; **il papà di Claudio** Claudio's father; **figlio di papà** spoilt young man

papale [pa'pale] AGG papal

papato [pa'pato] SM papacy

papavero [pa'pavero] SM poppy

papero, -a ['papero] SM, SF (*Zool*) gosling

papillon [papi'jɔ] SM INV bow tie

papiro [pa'piro] SM papyrus

pappa ['pappa] SF (*per bambini*) pap; (*pegg: poltiglia*) mush; **hai sempre avuto la pappa pronta** (*fig*) you've never had to stand on your own two feet; **pappa reale** royal jelly

pappagallo [pappa'gallo] SM (*Zool*) parrot; (*fig: pegg: uomo*) wolf; **ripetere tutto a pappagallo** to repeat everything parrot-fashion

pappagorgia, -ge [pappa'gɔrdʒa] SF double chin

pappardella [pappar'della] SF (*Culin*) *wide strip of pasta*; (*fig: tiritera*) rigmarole

pappare [pap'pare] /72/ VT (*fam: anche: papparsi*) (*mangiare*) to gobble up; (*appropriarsi di: soldi*) to walk off with

par. ABBR (= *paragrafo*) par. (= *paragraph*)

para ['para] SF: **suole di para** crepe soles

parà [pa'ra] SM INV para

parabola¹ [pa'rabola] SF (*Mat*) parabola

parabola² [pa'rabola] SF (*Rel*) parable

parabolico, -a, -ci, -che [para'bɔliko] AGG parabolic; **antenna parabolica** (satellite) dish

parabrezza [para'breddza] SM INV (*Aut*) windscreen (*Brit*), windshield (*USA*)

paracadutare [parakadu'tare] /72/ VT , **paracadutarsi** VR to parachute

paracadute [paraka'dute] SM INV parachute

paracadutismo [parakadu'tizmo] SM parachuting

paracadutista, -i [parakadu'tista] SM parachutist; (*Mil*) paratrooper

paracarro [para'karro] SM kerbstone (*Brit*), curbstone (*USA*)

paradisiaco, -a, -ci, -che [paradi'ziako] AGG heavenly

paradiso [para'dizo] SM (*anche fig*) paradise, heaven; **sentirsi in paradiso** to be in seventh heaven; **paradisi artificiali** drug-induced fantasies; **paradiso fiscale** tax haven; **il Paradiso terrestre** the Garden of Eden, the Earthly Paradise

paradossale [parados'sale] AGG paradoxical

paradosso [para'dɔsso] SM paradox

parafango, -ghi [para'fango] SM (*di auto*) mudflap (*Brit*) o splashguard (*USA*); (*di bicicletta*) mudguard (*Brit*) o fender (*USA*)

paraffina [paraf'fina] SF paraffin (wax)

parafrasare [parafra'zare] /72/ VT to paraphrase

parafrasi [pa'rafrazi] SF INV paraphrase

parafulmine [para'fulmine] SM lightning conductor

paraggi [pa'raddʒi] SMPL: **nei paraggi (di)** in the vicinity (of), near, in the neighbourhood (*Brit*) o neighborhood (*USA*) (of); **nei paraggi della stazione** near the station; **dev'essere qui nei paraggi** it's around here somewhere; **in questi paraggi** in this neighbo(u)rhood, somewhere around here

paragonare [parago'nare] /72/ VT to compare; **paragonate le due frasi** compare the two sentences; **paragonare a/con** to compare to/with; **lo paragona sempre al fratello** she's always comparing him with his brother; **paragonarsi** VR: **paragonarsi a/con** to compare o.s. to/with

paragone [para'gone] SM comparison; (*esempio analogo*) analogy, parallel; **fare un paragone tra** to compare; **se facciamo un paragone tra le due macchine...** if we compare the two cars...; **a paragone di** as compared to, in comparison with; **il paragone non regge** the two just can't be compared; **non regge al paragone** it doesn't stand o bear comparison; **senza paragone** incomparable, peerless

❑ **paragone** non si traduce mai con la parola inglese *paragon*

paragrafo [pa'ragrafo] SM (*Gramm, anche fig*) paragraph

paraguaiano, -a [paragwa'jano] AGG, SM, SF Paraguayan

Paraguay [para'gwai] SM Paraguay

paralisi [pa'ralizi] SF INV (*Med, anche fig*) paralysis

paralitico, -a, -ci, -che [para'litiko] AGG, SM, SF paralytic

paralizzare [paralid'dzare] /72/ VT (*Med, anche fig*) to paralyze

parallelamente [parallela'mente] AVV: **parallelamente (a)** (*gen*) parallel (to); (*contemporaneamente*) at the same time (as), in parallel (with)

parallelismo [paralle'lizmo] SM (*Mat*) parallelism; (*fig: corrispondenza*) similarities *pl*

parallelo, -a [paral'lɛlo] AGG (*gen, anche Inform*) parallel; **interfaccia parallela** (*Inform*) parallel interface ♦ SM (*Geog, anche fig*) parallel; **fare un parallelo tra** (*comparazione*) to draw a parallel between

paralume [para'lume] SM lampshade

paramedico, -a, -ci, -che [para'mɛdiko] AGG paramedical; **il personale paramedico** the paramedics *pl* ♦ SM, SF paramedic

paramenti [para'menti] SMPL (*Rel*) vestments

parametro [pa'rametro] SM parameter

paramilitare [paramili'tare] AGG paramilitary

paranco, -chi [pa'ranko] SM hoist

paranoia [para'nɔja] SF (*Psic*) paranoia; **andare/mandare in paranoia** (*fam*) to freak/be freaked out

paranoico, -a, -ci, -che [para'nɔiko] AGG, SM, SF paranoid; (*fam*) freaked (out)

paranormale [paranor'male] AGG paranormal

paraocchi [para'ɔkki] SMPL (*anche fig*) blinkers (*Brit*), blinders (*USA*)

paraolimpiadi [paraolim'piadi] SFPL paralympics

parapetto [para'petto] SM parapet

parapiglia [para'piʎʎa] SM INV uproar, commotion

parapsicologia [parapsikolo'dʒia] SF parapsychology

parare [pa'rare] /72/ VT 1 (*addobbare*) to adorn, deck (out) 2 (*proteggere: occhi*) to shield, protect 3 (*scansare: colpo: anche fig*) to parry; (: *goal, tiro*) to save; **ha parato il rigore** he saved the penalty ♦ VI (*aus avere*) **dove vuoi andare a parare?** what are you driving at?; **pararsi** VR (*presentarsi*) to present o.s., appear

parascolastico, -a, -ci, -che [parasko'lastiko] AGG (*attività*) extracurricular

parasole [para'sole] SM INV parasol, sunshade

parassita, -i [paras'sita] (*anche fig*) AGG parasitic ♦ SM parasite

parassitario, -ria, -ri, -rie [parassi'tarjo] AGG parasitic

parastatale [parasta'tale] AGG state-controlled

parastato [paras'tato] SM *employees in the state-controlled sector*

parata¹ [pa'rata] SF (*Sport*) save; **parata in due tempi** (*Calcio*) double save

parata² [pa'rata] SF (*Mil*) review, parade

parati [pa'rati] SMPL hangings; **carta da parati** wallpaper

paratia [para'tia] SF (*Naut*) bulkhead

paraurti [para'urti] SM INV (*Aut*) bumper

paravento [para'vento] SM folding screen; **fare da paravento a qn** (*fig*) to shield sb

parcella [par'tʃella] SF fee

❑ **parcella** non si traduce mai con la parola inglese *parcel*

parcheggiare [parked'dʒare] /62/ VT to park

parcheggiatore, -trice [parkeddʒa'tore] SM, SF parking attendant

parcheggio, -gi [par'keddʒo] SM (*luogo*) car park (*Brit*), parking lot (*USA*); (*azione*) parking *no pl*; (*singolo posto*) parking space; **hanno costruito un nuovo parcheggio** a new car park has been built; **non riesco a trovare parcheggio** I can't find a parking space; **qui c'è divieto di parcheggio** you can't park here; **"divieto di parcheggio"** "no parking"

parchimetro [par'kimetro] SM parking meter

parco¹, -chi ['parko] SM 1 (*giardino*) park; **parco dei divertimenti** amusement park, funfair; **parco giochi** (children's) playground; **parco nazionale** national park; **parco a tema** theme park 2 (*insieme di veicoli*) fleet; **parco macchine** car fleet; **parco rotabile** (*Ferr*) rolling stock 3 (*spazio per deposito*) depot

parco², -a, -chi, -che ['parko] AGG: **parco (in)** (*sobrio*) moderate (in); (*avaro*) sparing (with)

parcometro [par'kɔmetro] SM (Aut) (Pay and Display) ticket machine

parecchio, -a, -chi [pa'rekkjo] AGG INDEF 1 quite a lot of; c'è **parecchio vino** there is quite a lot of wine; c'**era parecchia gente** there were quite a lot of o several people; **ho parecchia fame** I am quite hungry; **parecchio tempo** quite a lot of time, a long time; **non lo vedo da parecchio tempo** I haven't seen him for ages o for a long time; è **parecchio tempo che ti aspetto** I have been waiting for you for ages; **parecchio tempo fa** a long time ago, long ago 2 **parecchi(e)** several, quite a lot of; **parecchie persone/volte/cose** several o a number of people/times/things; **ho avuto parecchi guai** I have had quite a lot of trouble ♦ PRON INDEF quite a lot, quite a bit; **parecchi(e)** several, quite a lot; c'**è del pane?** — **parecchio** is there any bread? — yes, quite a lot; **ce n'è parecchio** there's quite a lot; **quanto tempo hai aspettato?** — **parecchio** how long did you wait? — quite a long time o quite a while; **ci ho pensato parecchio** I gave it quite a lot of thought; **parecchi dicono...** a lot of people o a number of people say ...; **eravamo in parecchi** there were quite a few of us; **parecchi di noi** several of us, quite a few of us ♦ AVV 1 (seguito da agg) quite, rather; è **parecchio intelligente** he is quite intelligent 2 (preceduto da vb) quite a lot, quite a bit; **mangia parecchio** he eats quite a lot; è **dimagrito parecchio** he has lost quite a lot of weight; **mi è costato parecchio** it cost me quite a lot

pareggiare [pared'dʒare] /62/ VT (gen) to make equal; (terreno) to level, make level; (bilancio, conti) to balance ♦ VI (aus avere) (Sport: durante la partita) to equalize; (: risultato) to draw; **hanno pareggiato due a due** they drew two all

pareggio, -gi [pa'reddʒo] SM (Sport) draw; (Econ) balance

parentado [paren'tado] SM relatives pl, relations pl; **alla festa** c'**era tutto il parentado** the whole family was at the party

parente [pa'rente] SM, SF relative, relation; è **un mio parente** he's a relative of mine

❏ **parente** non si traduce mai con la parola inglese parent

parentela [paren'tɛla] SF (vincolo di sangue, anche fig) relationship; (insieme dei parenti) relations pl, relations pl

parentesi [pa'rentezi] SF INV (segno grafico) bracket, parenthesis; (digressione) digression, parenthesis; **tra parentesi** in brackets; (fig) incidentally; **fare una parentesi** (fig) to digress; **dopo la parentesi estiva** after the summer break; **parentesi graffe** curly braces o brackets; **parentesi quadre** square brackets; **parentesi tonde** round brackets

parere¹ [pa'rere] /71/ SM (opinione) opinion; (consiglio) advice; **a mio parere** in my opinion

parere² [pa'rere] /71/ VI IRREG (aus essere) 1 (apparire) to look, seem, appear; **pare onesto** he looks o seems o appears honest; **pare impossibile ma è così** it doesn't seem possible and yet it's true; **pare di sì/no** it seems/doesn't seem so; **non mi pare vero!** I can scarcely believe it!; **pare che...** it seems o appears that ..., apparently; **pare che voglia cambiare squadra** apparently he wants to change teams; **pare che sia stato lui** it seems it was him; **a quanto pare se n'è andato** he seems to have left, he has apparently left 2 (essere dell'opinione): **mi pare che...** I think (that) ..., it seems to me (that) ...; **mi pare che sia già arrivato** I think he's already here; **mi pare di sì/no** I think/don't think so; **che te ne pare?** what do you think?; **che te ne pare del mio libro?** what do you think of my book?; **che te ne pare di andare al cinema?** how about going to the cinema?, how do you fancy going to the cinema?; è **ora di andare, non ti pare?** don't you think it's time we left?; **disturbo? — ma le pare!** am I disturbing you? — not at all!; **fai come ti pare!** do what o as you like!

parete [pa'rete] SF (muro) wall; (di montagna) face; **fra le pareti domestiche** at home, within one's own four walls; **parete cellulare** (Bio) cell wall

pargolo, -a ['pargolo] SM, SF (letter, anche scherz) child

pari¹ ['pari] AGG INV 1 (uguale) equal, (the) same; **hanno pari diritti e doveri** they have equal rights and duties; **essere pari a qn in qc** to be equal to sb in sth; **essere pari di grado** to have the same rank; **essere pari in bellezza/intelligenza** to be equally beautiful/intelligent; **andare di pari passo (con)** to proceed at the same rate (as); **hanno vinto a pari**

merito they were joint winners; **pari opportunità** equal opportunities 2 (piano) level; **una superficie pari** a level o even surface; **saltare qc a piè pari** (fig: omettere) to skip sth 3 (Mat: numero) even; **numeri pari** even numbers 4 (in giochi) equal, drawn, tied; **la partita è pari** (Sport) the match is a draw; **siamo pari, vuoi la rivincita?** it's a draw, do you want a decider?; **siamo pari** (fig) we are quits o even ♦ SM (numero) even number; (parità): **rimettersi in pari (con)** to catch up (with); **cercherò di rimettermi in pari** I'll try to catch up; **essere intelligente al pari di qn** to be as intelligent as sb; **comportarsi al pari di qn** to behave like sb ♦ SM, SF peer, equal ♦ AVV 1 **copiato pari pari dal libro** copied word for word from the book 2 **alla pari** on the same level; (Borsa) at par; **mettersi alla pari con** to place o.s. on the same level as

pari² ['pari] SM INV (Pol: in Gran Bretagna) peer; **pari a vita** life peer

parificare [parifi'kare] /20/ VT (scuola) to recognize officially

parificato, -a [parifi'kato] AGG: **scuola parificata** officially recognized private school

Parigi [pa'ridʒi] SF Paris; **vado a Parigi quest'estate** I'm going to Paris this summer; **vive a Parigi** he lives in Paris

parigino, -a [pari'dʒino] AGG, SM, SF Parisian

pariglia [pa'riʎʎa] SF 1 (tiro di cavalli) pair 2 (fig): **rendere la pariglia** to give tit for tat

parità [pari'ta] SF INV parity, equality; **a parità di condizioni** all things being equal; **trattamento di parità** equal treatment; **un risultato di parità** (Sport) a draw, a tie; **finire in parità** to end in a draw

paritetico, -a, -ci, -che [pari'tetiko] AGG: **rapporto paritetico** equal relationship; **commissione paritetica** joint committee

parlamentare¹ [parlamen'tare] /72/ AGG parliamentary ♦ SM, SF ≈ Member of Parliament (Brit), ≈ Congressperson, member of Congress

parlamentare² [parlamen'tare] /72/ VI (aus avere) to negotiate, parley

parlamento [parla'mento] SM parliament; **il Parlamento europeo** the European Parliament

parlantina [parlan'tina] SF (fam) talkativeness; **avere una buona parlantina** to have the gift of the gab

parlare [par'lare] /72/ VI (aus avere) 1 (facoltà) to talk; (modo) to talk, to speak; **il bambino non sa ancora parlare** the baby can't talk yet; **non parlate tutti insieme** don't all talk at once; **si parlavano a gesti** they were using sign language; **parla piano/più forte** talk o speak quietly/louder; **non riusciva a parlare per la gioia** he was speechless with joy; **parla bene!** talk properly!; **parlare tra i denti** to mutter; **parlare come un libro stampato** to talk like a book; **ha occhi che parlano** he has expressive eyes 2 (esprimere il proprio pensiero) to speak; **parlare chiaro** to speak one's mind; **voglio parlare con il direttore** I want to speak to the manager!; **parlare a caso** o **a vanvera** to ramble on; **parlare bene/male di qn/qc** to say nice/nasty things about sb/sth; **fallo** o **lascialo parlare** give him a chance to speak, let him have his say; **con rispetto parlando** with respect; **i dati parlano chiaro** the facts speak for themselves 3 (conversare) to talk; **abbiamo parlato per ore** we talked for hours; **parlare a/con qn di qc** to talk o speak to/with sb about o of sth; **lascia che gli parli io** let me talk to him; **gli parlerò di te** I'll talk to him about you; **di che cosa avete parlato?** what did you talk about?; **parlare di lavoro** o **d'affari** to talk shop; **non ci parliamo più** we're not on speaking terms; **parlare del più e del meno** to talk about this and that; è **come parlare al vento** o **a un muro** it's like talking to a brick wall; **senti, ne parliamo a quattrocchi** look, we'll discuss it o talk about it in private; **parliamone** let's talk about it; **non parliamone più** let's just forget about it; **non ne voglio più sentir parlare** let's hear no more about it; **far parlare di sé** to get o.s. talked about; **parlano di matrimonio** they are talking about getting married, they are discussing marriage; **per ora non se ne parla** there's nothing doing for the moment 4 (Telec): **sta parlando al telefono** he's on the phone; **pronto? chi parla?** hello, who's speaking?; **parla Bianchi** Bianchi here o speaking; **posso parlare con il Sig. Rossi?** may I speak to Mr Rossi? 5 **parlare di** (far cenno a) to mention; (trattare di: argomento) to be about, deal with; **per non parlare di...**

not to mention ...; **ne ho sentito parlare** I've heard of it (*o* him *o* her *ecc*); **ne parlano tutti i giornali** it's in all the newspapers; **il libro parla del problema della droga** the book deals with the drug problem; **di cosa parla il suo ultimo romanzo?** what is his latest novel about? **6** (*confessare*) to talk; **far parlare un prigioniero** to make a prisoner talk ♦ VT (*una lingua*) to speak; **sai parlare l'inglese?** can you speak English?; **per me parla arabo** (*fig*) it's all Greek to me ♦ SM (*dialetto*) dialect

parlata [par'lata] SF (*dialetto*) dialect

parlatore, -trice [parla'tore] SM, SF (*oratore*) speaker

parlatorio, -ri [parla'torjo] SM (*di carcere*) visiting room; (*di collegio, convento*) parlour (*Brit*), parlor (*USA*)

parlottare [parlot'tare] /72/ VI (*aus* avere) to mutter

parmigiano, -a [parmi'dʒano] AGG Parma *attr, of o* from Parma; **alla parmigiana** (*Culin*) with Parmesan cheese ♦ SM, SF inhabitant *o* native of Parma ♦ SM (*grana*) Parmesan (cheese)

parodia [paro'dia] SF parody

parodiare [paro'djare] /19/ VT to parody

parola [pa'rɔla] SF **1** (*facoltà*) speech; **ha perso la parola** he's lost the power of speech; **rimanere senza parole** to be speechless; **a quel cane manca solo la parola** that dog is almost human; **avere la parola facile** to have the gift of the gab **2** (*vocabolo*) word; **una parola difficile** a difficult word; **rivolgere la parola a qn** to speak to sb; **mi hai tolto la parola di bocca** you have taken the words right out of my mouth; **mettere una buona parola per qn** to put in a good word for sb; **non è detta l'ultima parola** that's not the end of the matter; **non farne parola a nessuno!** don't breathe a word to anyone!; **è una parola!** it's easier said than done!; **non ho parole per ringraziarti** I don't know how to thank you; **passare dalle parole ai fatti** to get down to business; **in parole povere** in plain English; **parola d'ordine** password; **parole incrociate** crossword (puzzle) *sg*; **sta facendo le parole incrociate** she's doing the crossword **3 parole** SFPL (*di canzone*) words, lyrics; (*chiacchiere*) talk *sg* **4** (*promessa*) word; **dare la propria parola a qn** to give sb one's word; **gli ho dato la mia parola** I gave him my word; **mantenere la parola** to keep one's word; **ho mantenuto la parola** I've kept my word; **è una persona di parola** he is a man of his word; **rimangiarsi la parola** to go back on one's word, break one's promise; **si è rimangiato la parola** he broke his promise; **parola chiave** keyword; **parola d'onore** word of honour **5** (*in dibattiti*): **diritto di parola** right to speak; **chiedere la parola** to ask permission to speak; **prendere la parola** to take the floor; **dare la parola a qn** to call on sb to speak

parolaccia, -ce [paro'lattʃa] SF bad word, swearword; **dire le parolacce** to swear

parossismo [paros'sizmo] SM (*Med*) paroxysm; (*fig: di amore, odio*) height; **amare/odiare fino al parossismo** to be beside o.s. with love/hate

parquet [par'kɛ] SM INV parquet (flooring)

parrò *ecc* [par'rɔ] VB *vedi* parere²

parrocchia [par'rɔkkja] SF (*suddivisione*) parish; (*chiesa*) parish church

parrocchiano, -a [parrok'kjano] SM, SF parishioner

parroco, -ci ['parroko] SM parish priest

parrucca, -che [par'rukka] SF wig

parrucchiere [parruk'kjɛre] SM (*per uomo*) barber; (*per signora*) hairdresser; **fa la parrucchiera** she's a hairdresser; **devo andare dal parrucchiere** I need to go to the hairdresser's

parruccone [parruk'kone] SM (*pegg*) old fogey

parsimonia [parsi'mɔnja] SF parsimony, frugality, thrift

parsimonioso, -a [parsimo'njoso] AGG frugal, thrifty

parso, -a ['parso] PP *di* parere²

parte ['parte] SF **1** (*gen*) part; (*quota spettante a ciascuno*) share; **la prima parte del libro** the first part of the book; **parte del libro non mi è piaciuta** I didn't like some *o* part of the book; **ognuno ebbe la sua parte** everyone had their share; **una parte di noi** some of us; **gran *o* la maggior parte degli spettatori** most of the audience; **in parte** in part, partly; **fare le parti di qc** to divide sth up; **fare la parte del leone** to take the lion's share **2** (*partecipazione*): **fare parte di qc** to belong to sth; **fa parte di un club sportivo** he belongs to a sports club; **prendere parte a** (*dibattito,*

conversazione) to take part in, participate in; (*lutto*) to share in; **non ha preso parte alla discussione** he didn't take part in the discussion; **mettere qn a parte di qc** to inform sb of sth, tell sb about sth **3** (*lato, anche fig*) side; (*direzione*) direction; **la parte destra del corpo** the right-hand side of the body; **dall'altra parte della strada** on the other side of the road; **veniva dall'altra parte** he was coming from the opposite direction; **da parte a parte** right through; **essere dalla parte della ragione** to be in the right; **non sapeva da che parte voltarsi** (*fig*) he didn't know which way to turn; **stare dalla parte di qn** to be on sb's side; **prendere le parti di qn** to take sb's side, side with sb; **hanno preso le sue parti** they sided with him; **mettere da parte qc** to save up, put sth aside; **ha messo da parte un bel po' di denaro** he's saved up quite a lot of money **4** (*luogo, regione*) da qualche parte somewhere; **da tutte le parti** everywhere; **da questa parte** (*in questa direzione*) this way; **da che parte è andato?** which way did he go?; **da ogni parte** (*stato in luogo*) everywhere, on all sides; (*moto da luogo*) from all sides; **da nessuna parte** nowhere, not... anywhere; **non riesco a trovarlo da nessuna parte** I can't find it anywhere; **da queste parti** (*qui vicino*) around here; **dalle mie parti** where I come from; **abita dalle mie parti** he lives in the same area as I do; **dalle parti di Main Street** in the vicinity of Main Street **5** (*fazione, partito*) group, faction; (*Dir*) party; **la parte avversaria** the opposing party; **uomo di parte** partisan; **la parte lesa** (*Dir*) the injured party; **costituirsi parte civile contro qn** (*Dir*) to associate in an action with the public prosecutor against sb; **le parti in causa** the parties concerned; **parti sociali** *representatives of workers and employers* **6** (*Teatro*) part, role; **avere una parte secondaria** to have a minor role; **fare la parte dello stupido/della vittima** (*fig*) to act the fool/the martyr **7** (*fraseologia*): **a parte** (*con funzione di agg*) separate; (*con funzione di avv*) separately; **fatto a parte** done separately; **pagare qc a parte** to pay for sth separately; **inviare a parte** (*campioni*) to send under separate cover; **scherzi a parte** joking aside, but, seriously; **a parte ciò** apart from that; **da un anno a questa parte** for about a year now; **da parte** (*in disparte*) to one side, aside; **da parte mia** as far as I'm concerned, as for me; **da parte di** (*per conto di*) on behalf of; (*regalo, saluti*) from; **questo è da parte di Giorgio** this is from Giorgio; **da parte di madre** on his (*o* her *ecc*) mother's side; **d'altra parte** on the other hand

partecipante [partetʃi'pante] AGG: **partecipante a** taking part in, participating in ♦ SM, SF: **partecipante (a)** (*riunione, dibattito*) participant (in); (*gara sportiva*) competitor (in); (*concorso*) entrant (to); **i partecipanti alla cerimonia** those taking part in the ceremony; **tutti i partecipanti alla riunione** everyone who attended the meeting

partecipare [partetʃi'pare] /72/ VI (*aus* avere) **partecipare a** to take part in, participate in; (*utili*) to share in; (*spese*) to contribute to; (*dolore, successo di qn*) to share (in); **parteciperai alla gara?** are you going to take part in the competition?; **posso partecipare alle spese?** can I help pay? ♦ VT: **partecipare le nozze (a)** to announce one's wedding (to)

partecipazione [partetʃipat'tsjone] SF **1** partecipazione (a) (*dibattito, cerimonia*) participation (in); (*spettacolo*) appearance (in); (*complotto*) involvement (in); **partecipazione a banda armata** (*Dir*) belonging to an armed gang; **partecipazione di nozze** wedding announcement card **2** (*Econ*) sharing, interest; **ministro delle Partecipazioni statali** *minister responsible for companies in which the state has a financial interest*; **partecipazione di maggioranza** controlling interest; **partecipazione di minoranza** minority interest; **partecipazione agli utili** profit-sharing

partecipe [par'tetʃipe] AGG participating; **essere partecipe del dolore/della gioia di qn** to share in sb's sorrow/joy

parteggiare [parted'dʒare] /62/ VI (*aus* avere) **parteggiare per** to side with, be on the side of, support

partenza [par'tentsa] SF **1** (*gen*) departure; **dopo la mia partenza si deciderà** things will be decided after I leave *o* after my departure; **il tabellone delle partenze** the departure board; **essere in partenza** (*treno, aereo, nave*) to be about to leave; **fa' presto, il treno è in partenza** hurry up, the train is about to leave; **prenderò il primo treno in partenza per Milano** I'll catch the first train for Milan; **"il treno per Roma è in partenza dal binario 15"** "the Rome train is leaving from platform 15"; **passeggeri in partenza per** passengers travelling (*Brit*) *o* traveling (*USA*) to; **siamo tornati al punto di partenza** (*fig*) we are back where we started, we are back to square one **2** (*Sport*) start; **segnale di partenza** start, starting signal; **linea di partenza** start, starting line; **falsa partenza** (*anche fig*) false start

particella [parti'tʃɛlla] SF (*Gramm*, *Fis*) particle; **particelle alfa/beta** (*Fis*) alpha/beta particles

participio, -pi [parti'tʃipjo] SM (*Gramm*) participle; **participio passato** past participle; **participio presente** present participle

particolare [partiko'lare] AGG **1** (*specifico*) particular; (*caratteristico*) distinctive; (*speciale*) special, particular; **in questo caso particolare** in this particular case, in this specific instance; **ha un sapore particolare** it has a distinctive flavour; **in particolare** in particular, particularly **2** (*strano*) peculiar, odd **3** (*insolito*) unusual; **l'ho fatto con cura particolare** I took particular care over it **4** (*privato: udienza, ragioni*) private, personal ♦ SM detail; **vorrei sapere i particolari** I'd like to know the details; **raccontare un fatto in tutti i particolari** to give all the details *o* particulars of an occurrence; **entrare nei particolari** to go into details

particolareggiato, -a [partikolared'dʒato] AGG (extremely) detailed

particolarità [partikolari'ta] SF INV **1** (*carattere eccezionale*) peculiarity; **data la particolarità del caso** given the peculiarity of the case **2** (*dettaglio*) detail, particularity **3** (*caratteristica specifica*) (distinctive) feature, characteristic

partigiano, -a [parti'dʒano] AGG partisan ♦ SM (*Storia*) partisan; (*fautore*) supporter, champion

partire [par'tire] /45/ VI (*aus essere*) **1** (*gen*) to go, leave; (*lasciare un luogo*) to leave; (*mettersi in cammino*) to set off, set out; (*allontanarsi*) to go away, go off; **partire da/per** to leave from/for; **sono partita da Roma alle 7** I left Rome at 7; **partire in treno/in macchina** to go by train/car; **partire come una freccia** to be off like a shot; **non dargli troppo da bere perché lui parte subito** (*fam*) don't give him too much to drink because it goes straight to his head **2** (*cominciare: Sport, fig*): **partire (da)** to start (from); **la corsa parte dal nord della città** the race leaves from the north of the town; **la loro è una storia partita male** theirs is a relationship which got off to a bad start **3** (*motore*) to start; (*aereo*) to take off; (*treno*) to leave; **la macchina non parte** the car won't start; **il volo parte da Linate** the flight leaves from Linate; **a che ora parte il treno?** what time does the train leave?; **partire in quarta** to drive off at top speed; (*fig*) to be very enthusiastic; **far partire la macchina** to start (up) the car **4** (*colpo di arma da fuoco, petardo*) to go off; (*tappo*) to pop out, shoot out; **è partito un colpo** the gun went off **5** **a partire da** from; **a partire da oggi** from today onwards; **a partire da ora** from now on; **la seconda a partire/partendo da destra** the second from the right; **a partire da 20 euro** from 20 euros

partita [par'tita] SF **1** (*Comm*) lot, consignment **2** (*Contabilità*) entry, item; **partita doppia** double-entry book-keeping; **partita IVA** VAT registration number (*Brit*); **partita semplice** single-entry book-keeping **3** (*gioco, anche Carte*) game; (*Sport*) match, game; **sono andata alla partita di calcio ieri** I went to the football match yesterday; **una partita a carte** a game of cards; **facciamo una partita a tennis** let's have a game of tennis; **dare partita vinta a qn** to admit defeat (by sb); **partita amichevole** friendly (match) **4** (*escursione*): **partita di caccia** hunting party

partito [par'tito] SM **1** (*Pol*) party **2** (*decisione*): **per partito preso** on principle; **non saprei che partito prendere** I wouldn't know what to do; **mettere la testa a partito** to settle down **3** (*persona da sposare*): match; **è un buon partito** (*uomo*) he's a very eligible young man, he's a good match **4** (*condizione*): **essere ridotto a mal partito** to be in desperate straits

partitocrazia [partitokrat'tsia] SF *hijacking of institutions by the party system*

partitura [parti'tura] SF (*Mus*) score

parto [ˈparto] SM (*Med*) labour (*Brit*), labor (*USA*); **durante il parto** during labo(u)r; **i dolori del parto** labo(u)r pains; **sala parto** labo(u)r room; **è stato un parto difficile** it was

a difficult birth; **al momento del parto il bambino stava bene** at birth the child was in good health; **morire di parto** to die in childbirth; **parto cesareo** Caesarean (section); **parto naturale** natural childbirth; **parto pilotato** induced labo(u)r; **parto plurigemellare** multiple birth; **parto podalico** breech delivery; **parto prematuro** premature birth *o* delivery

partoriente [parto'rjɛnte] SF woman in labour (*Brit*) *o* labor (*USA*)

partorire [parto'rire] /55/ VT to give birth to; (*fig: invenzione*) to produce

parvenza [par'vɛntsa] SF semblance

parvi ecc [ˈparvi] VB *vedi* **parere**[2]

parziale [par'tsjale] AGG (*limitato*) partial; (*non obiettivo*) biased, partial; **un successo parziale** a partial success

parzialità [partsjali'ta] SF INV **1** **parzialità (a favore di qn)** partiality (for sb), bias (towards sb); **parzialità (contro qn)** bias (against sb) **2** (*azione*) unfair action

pascere [ˈpaʃʃere] VB IRREG /29/ VI (*aus avere*) to graze ♦ VT (*brucare*) to graze on; **pascersi** VR: **pascersi di** (*erba, anche fig: illusioni*) to feed on

pasciuto, -a [paʃˈʃuto] PP *di* **pascere** ♦ AGG: **ben pasciuto** plump

pascolare [pasko'lare] /72/ VT, VI (*aus avere*) to graze

pascolo [ˈpaskolo] SM (*luogo*) pasture; **diritto di pascolo** grazing rights *pl*

Pasqua [ˈpaskwa] SF **1** Easter; **la domenica di Pasqua** Easter Sunday; **cosa fai per Pasqua?** what are you doing at Easter?; **le vacanze di Pasqua** the Easter holidays; **il lunedì di Pasqua** Easter Monday; **un uovo di Pasqua** an Easter egg **2 isola di Pasqua** Easter Island

pasquale [pas'kwale] AGG Easter *attr*

pasquetta [pas'kwetta] SF Easter Monday

passabile [pas'sabile] AGG fairly good, passable

passaggio, -gi [pas'saddʒo] SM **1** (*atto del passare*) passage, passing *no pl*; (*traversata*) crossing *no pl*; **guardare il passaggio degli uccelli** to watch the birds fly past; **essere di passaggio** to be passing through; **sono qui solo di passaggio** I'm just passing through **2** (*trasferimento: di poteri, diritti, calciatore*) transfer; **il passaggio dall'infanzia all'adolescenza** the transition from childhood to adolescence; **il passaggio dal giorno alla notte** the change from day to night; **passaggio di proprietà** transfer *o* change of ownership **3** (*luogo*) passage; (*cammino*) way, passage; (*itinerario*) route; **uno stretto passaggio tra le rocce** a narrow passage between the rocks; **impedire il passaggio a qn** to block *o* stand in sb's way; **passaggio a livello** level (*Brit*) *o* grade (*USA*) crossing; **passaggio pedonale** pedestrian crossing; **"passaggio di servizio"** "staff only" **4** (*traffico*): **c'è molto passaggio** there's a lot of traffic; **luogo di passaggio** thoroughfare **5** (*Aut*) lift (*Brit*), ride; **dare un passaggio a qn** to give sb a lift; **puoi darmi un passaggio?** can you give me a lift? **6** (*brano*) passage; **un passaggio da "I Promessi Sposi"** a passage from "I Promessi Sposi" **7** (*Sport*) pass; **passaggio in avanti/indietro** forward/back pass; **passaggio in profondità** (*Calcio*) long pass

passamaneria [passamane'ria] SF braid, trimming

passamontagna [passamon'taɲɲa] SM INV balaclava

passante [pas'sante] SM, SF passer-by ♦ SM (*di cintura*) loop; (*raccordo: stradale*) road link; (: *ferroviario*) (high-speed) rail link

passaporto [passa'pɔrto] SM passport

passare [pas'sare] /72/ VI (*aus essere*) **1** (*persona, veicolo*) to go by, pass (by); **l'autobus passa davanti a casa nostra** the bus goes past our house; **siamo passati davanti a casa tua** we went past your house, we walked (*o* drove) past your house; **non è passata neanche una macchina** not one car went by; **passare dall'altra parte della strada** to cross (over) to the other side of the street **2** (*fare una breve sosta*) to call in; (*presso amico*) to call *o* drop in; (*postino*) to come, call; **passa quando vuoi** call in whenever you like; **passare a casa di qn** to call *o* drop in on sb; **passo da te dopo cena** I'll call in after dinner; **passare a trovare/salutare qn** to drop by to see sb/say "hello" to sb; **passare a prendere qc/qn** to come and pick sth/sb up; **ti passo a prendere alle otto** I'll come and pick you up at eight o'clock; **passare in**

banca/ufficio to call in at the bank/office; **devo passare in banca** I've got to call in at the bank **3** (*filtrare attraverso: aria, sole, luce*) to pass, get through; (: *acqua*) to seep through **4** (*trasferirsi*): **passare da...a** to pass from ... to; **passare di mano in mano** to be passed *o* handed round; **passare di padre in figlio** to be handed *o* passed down *o* from father to son; **passare da un argomento ad un altro** to go from one subject to another; **passare ad altro** to change the subject; (*in una riunione*) to discuss the next item; **passiamo ad altro!** let's go on!; **passare al nemico** to go over to the enemy; **passare alla storia** to pass into history; (*fig*) to become a legend; **passare di moda** to go out of fashion; **passare a miglior vita** (*euf*) to pass away **5** (*trascorrere: giorni, tempo*) to pass, go by; **sono passati molti anni dalla fine della guerra** many years have passed since the end of the war **6** (*allontanarsi: temporale, dolore, voglia*) to pass, go away; **il peggio è passato** the worst is over; **far passare a qn la voglia di qc/di fare qc** to stifle sb's desire for sth/to do sth; **ti è passato il mal di testa?** has your headache gone?; **gli passerà!** he'll get over it! **7** (*essere accettato: proposta di legge*) to be passed; (: *candidato*) to pass; **passare a un esame** to go up (to the next class) after an exam; **passare di grado** to be promoted **8** (*Culin*): **passare di cottura** to be overdone **9** (*Carte*) to pass **10** **30 anni e passa** well over 30 years ago; **c'erano 100 persone e passa** there were well over a 100 people **11** (*esistere*): **ci passa una bella differenza tra i 2 quadri** there's a big difference between the 2 pictures **12** **passare per uno stupido/un genio** to be taken for a fool/a genius; **passare per buono** to be taken as valid, be accepted; **passare inosservato** to go unnoticed; **farsi passare per** to pass o.s. off as, pretend to be **13** **passare attraverso, per** (*anche fig*) to go through; **passare sopra** *o* above; (*fig: lasciar correre*) to pass over, overlook; **passare sotto** to pass below; **cosa ti passa per la testa?** (*a che pensi?*) what is going through your mind?; (*come puoi pensarlo?*) what are you thinking of!; **per dove si passa per arrivare in centro?** which way do I (*o* we) go to get into town?; **lasciar passare qn/qc** to let sb/sth through; **non mi hanno lasciato passare** they didn't let me through; **far passare qn per** *o* **da** to let sb in (*o* out) by; **far passare avanti qn** to let sb get past *o* by; **questa volta non ci passo sopra** I'm not prepared to overlook it this time ♦ **vt 1** (*attraversare*) to cross **2** (*esame*) to pass; (*dogana*) to go through, clear; (*visita medica*) to have; **hai passato l'esame?** did you pass the exam? **3** (*approvare*) to pass, approve **4** (*trafiggere*): **passare qn/qc da parte a parte** to pass right through sb/sth **5** (*trascorrere*) to spend; **passare le vacanze in montagna** to spend one's holidays in the mountains; **ho passato due giorni a Parigi** I spent two days in Paris; **non passerà la notte** he (*o* she) won't survive the night; **non passa giorno che non ne combini una delle sue** hardly a day goes by without him getting up to something **6** (*oltrepassare, sorpassare*) to go beyond; (*fig: andare oltre i limiti*) to exceed, go beyond; **ha passato la quarantina** he (*o* she) is over 40 **7** (*dare: oggetto*) to pass, give, hand; (*Sport: palla*) to pass; **passare qc a qn** to pass sth to sb, pass sb sth; (*trasmettere: messaggio*) to pass sth (on) to sb; **ha passato la palla a Enrico** he passed the ball to Enrico; **potresti passarmi il sale?** could you pass me the salt, please?; **mi hai passato l'influenza** you gave me the flu; **passare indietro qc** to pass *o* give *o* hand sth back; **i miei genitori mi passano 300 euro al mese** my parents give me 300 euros a month; **mi passi Maria?** (*al telefono*) can I speak to Maria?; **le passo il signor Rossi** I'm putting you through to Mr Rossi, here's Mr Rossi **8** (*brodo, verdura*) to strain **9** **passare lo straccio per terra** to give the floor a wipe; **passare l'aspirapolvere** to hoover (*Brit*), vacuum (*USA*); **passare una mano di vernice su qc** to give sth a coat of paint **10** (*fraseologia*): **passarsela bene/male** to get on well/badly; (*economicamente*) to manage well/badly; **come te la passi?** how are you getting on *o* along?; **passarla liscia** to get away with it; **ne ha passate tante** he's been through a lot, he's had some difficult times ♦ **sm:** **col passare del tempo...** with the passing of time ...; **col passare degli anni** (*riferito al presente*) as time goes by; (*riferito al passato*) as time passed *o* went by

passata [pas'sata] SF **1** **dare una passata a qc** (*spolverata*) to dust sth quickly; (*pulita*) to give sth a wipe; (*stirata*) to

give sth a quick iron; **dare una passata di vernice a qc** to give sth a coat of paint **2** (*occhiata*) glance, look; **dare una passata al giornale** to skim through *o* have a glance at the paper

passatempo [passa'tempo] SM pastime, hobby; **per passatempo** as a hobby

passato, -a [pas'sato] AGG **1** (*scorso*) last; **l'anno passato** last year; **nel corso degli anni passati** over the past years **2** (*finito: gloria, generazioni*) past; (*usanze*) out of date; (*sfiorito*) faded; **passato di moda** out of fashion; **sono cose ormai passate** that's all over now; **nei tempi passati** in the past; **è acqua passata** it's over and done with, it's water under the bridge **3** (*superato*): **sono le 8 passate** it's past *o* after 8 o'clock; **ha 40 anni passati** he's over 40 ♦ SM **1** past; **ha un passato di droga e furti** he has a history of drugs and theft; **in passato** in the past **2** (*Gramm*) past (tense); **il participio passato** the past participle; **passato prossimo** present perfect; **passato remoto** simple past **3** (*Culin*): **passato di verdura** vegetable purée

passaverdura [passaver'dura] SM INV vegetable mill

passeggero, -a [passed'dʒero] AGG (*malessere, nuvola, temporale*) passing; (*bellezza, benessere*) transient ♦ SM, SF passenger; **passeggero in arrivo/in partenza/in transito** arriving/departing/transit passenger

passeggiare [passed'dʒare] /62/ VI (*aus* avere) to stroll, walk; **passeggiava nervosamente nel corridoio** he was pacing nervously up and down the corridor

passeggiata [passed'dʒata] SF **1** (*a piedi*) walk; (*in macchina*) drive; **fare una passeggiata** to go for a walk; (*in veicolo*) to go for a drive **2** (*luogo*) promenade

passeggino [passed'dʒino] SM pushchair (*Brit*), stroller (*USA*)

passeggio [pas'seddʒo] SM walk, stroll; (*luogo*) promenade; **andare a passeggio** to go for a walk *o* a stroll; **guardare il passeggio** to watch people out for a stroll

passerella [passe'rella] SF (*gen, di aereo*) footbridge; (*di nave*) gangway, gangplank; (*pedana: per sfilate*) catwalk

passero ['passero] SM sparrow

passibile [pas'sibile] AGG: **passibile di** liable to; **passibile di aumento** liable to go up *o* increase

passionale [passjo'nale] AGG (*temperamento*) passionate; **delitto passionale** crime of passion

passione [pas'sjone] SF passion; **amore e passione** love and passion; **il giardinaggio è la mia più grande passione** gardening is my greatest pleasure; **aver la passione di** *o* **per** to have a passion for; **domenica di Passione** Passion Sunday

passività [passivi'ta] SF INV **1** (*qualità*) passivity, passiveness **2** (*Econ*) liability; **passività a breve termine** current liabilities *pl*

passivo, -a [pas'sivo] AGG passive; **fumo passivo** passive smoking ♦ SM **1** (*Gramm*) passive **2** (*Econ*) debit; (*complesso dei debiti*) liabilities *pl*

passo¹ ['passo] SM **1** (*gen*) step; (*rumore*) (foot)step; (*orma*) footprint; **a due passi da qui** a stone's throw from here; **passo (a) passo** step by step; **seguire qn passo passo** to follow close on sb's heels; **fare i primi passi** (*anche fig*) to take one's first steps; **fare due** *o* **quattro passi** to go for a short walk; **fare un passo avanti/indietro** (*anche fig*) to take a step forward/back; **fai un passo avanti** take a step forward; **mi è sembrato di sentire dei passi** I thought I heard footsteps; **ha fatto passi da gigante in spagnolo** his Spanish has improved by leaps and bounds; **fare il gran passo** to take the plunge; **fare un passo falso** to make a wrong move; **fare i passi necessari** to take the necessary steps; **fare il passo più lungo della gamba** to bite off more than one can chew; **tornare sui propri passi** (*anche fig*) to retrace one's steps; **non ho intenzione di tornare sui miei passi** (*fig*) I have no intention of starting all over again **2** (*andatura*) pace; (*Mil, Danza*) step; (*Equitazione*) walk; **fare il passo dell'oca** to goosestep; **un passo di danza** a dance step; **passo di pattinaggio** (*Sci*) skating turn; **allungare il passo** to quicken one's pace; **avere il passo lento** to walk slowly, be a slow walker; **camminava con passo veloce** he was walking fast; **di buon passo** at a good *o* brisk pace; **marciare al passo** to march; **mettere il cavallo al passo** to walk one's horse; **a passo d'uomo** at walking pace; (*Aut*) dead slow; **le macchine andavano**

a passo d'uomo the cars were crawling along; **andare al passo coi tempi** to keep up with the times; **di questo passo** (*fig*) at this rate; **di questo passo non finiremo mai** we'll never finish at this rate 3 (*brano*) passage 4 (*Cine*) gauge

passo² [ˈpasso] SM 1 (*passaggio*): **cedere il passo a qn** to give way to sb; **sbarrare il passo a qn** to bar sb's way; **uccelli di passo** birds of passage, migratory birds; **"passo carrabile** *o* **carraio"** "vehicle entrance — keep clear" 2 (*valico*) pass

pasta [ˈpasta] SF 1 (*Culin: impasto per pane*) dough; (: *impasto per dolce*) pastry; (: *anche:* **pastasciutta**) pasta; (*pasticcino*) cake, pastry; **lavorare la pasta** to knead the dough; **spianare la pasta** to roll pastry; **pasta in brodo** noodle soup; **pasta fatta in casa** home-made pasta; **pasta frolla** shortcrust pastry; **hai le mani di pasta frolla!** what a butterfingers you are!; **pasta sfoglia** puff pastry; **pasta all'uovo** egg pasta 2 (*sostanza pastosa*) paste; **pasta di acciughe** anchovy paste; **pasta dentifricia** toothpaste; **pasta di mandorle** almond paste 3 (*fig: indole*) nature; **sono tutt'e due della stessa pasta** they're both cast in the same mould (*Brit*) *o* mold (*USA*)

pastasciutta [pastaʃˈʃutta] SF pasta

pasteggiare [pastedˈdʒare] /62/ VI (*aus* avere) **pasteggiare a vino/champagne** to have wine/champagne with one's meal

pastella [pasˈtella] SF batter

pastello [pasˈtello] SM pastel ♦ AGG INV pastel *attr*

pastetta [pasˈtetta] SF (*Culin*) = **pastella**

pasticca, -che [pasˈtikka] SF pastille, lozenge

pasticceria [pastittʃeˈria] SF 1 (*negozio*) cake shop 2 (*pasticcini*) pastries *pl*, cakes *pl* 3 (*arte*) confectionery

pasticciare [pastitˈtʃare] /14/ VT to mess up, make a mess of

pasticciere, -a [pastitˈtʃɛre] SM, SF pastry-cook; (*gestore di pasticceria*) confectioner

pasticcino [pastitˈtʃino] SM petit four

pasticcio, -ci [pasˈtittʃo] SM 1 (*Culin*) pie; **un pasticcio di carne** a meat pie 2 (*lavoro disordinato, imbroglio*) mess; **è proprio un bel pasticcio** it's a real mess; **cacciarsi nei pasticci** to get into trouble

pastificio, -ci [pastiˈfitʃo] SM pasta factory

pastiglia [pasˈtiʎʎa] SF 1 (*Med*) pastille, lozenge; **pastiglie per la gola** throat lozenges *o* pastilles; **pastiglie per la tosse** cough drops *o* pastilles 2 (*Aut*): **pastiglie dei freni** brake lining *sg*

pastina [pasˈtina] SF *small pasta shapes used in soup*

pasti'naca, -che, pastinache SF parsnip

pasto [ˈpasto] SM meal; **saltare i pasti** to skip meals; **da prendersi prima dei pasti** to be taken before meals; **non mangiare fuori pasto** *o* **fuori dei pasti** don't eat between meals; **vino da pasto** table wine; **la notizia fu data in pasto al pubblico** the news was made common knowledge; **lo diedero in pasto ai leoni** (*anche fig*) he was thrown to the lions

pastoia [pasˈtoja] SF (*fig*): **pastoia burocratica** red tape

pastone [pasˈtone] SM (*per animali*) mash; (*pegg: cibo*) overcooked stodge

pastorale [pastoˈrale] AGG (*gen*) pastoral ♦ SF 1 (*Rel: lettera del vescovo*) pastoral (letter) 2 (*Mus*) pastoral(e) ♦ SM (*Rel: bastone*) crook, crosier

pastore [pasˈtore] SM 1 (*anche Rel*) shepherd; (*sacerdote*) minister, pastor; **il buon Pastore** (*Rel*) the Good Shepherd 2 (*anche:* **cane (da) pastore**) sheepdog; **pastore scozzese** collie; **pastore tedesco** Alsatian (*Brit*), German shepherd

pastorizia [pastoˈrittsja] SF sheep-rearing, sheep farming

pastorizzare [pastoridˈdzare] /72/ VT to pasteurize; **latte pastorizzato** pasteurized milk

pastoso, -a [pasˈtoso] AGG 1 (*miscuglio*) doughy; (*più liquido*) pasty 2 (*fig: colore, voce*) mellow, soft; (*vino*) mellow

pastrano [pasˈtrano] SM greatcoat

patacca, -che [paˈtakka] SF 1 (*distintivo*) medal, decoration; 2 (*fig: macchia*) grease spot, grease mark; (: *oggetto senza valore*) piece of rubbish; **li vendono solo patacche** they just sell junk there

patata [paˈtata] SF potato; **che spirito di patata!** (*fam*) some joke that! (*iro*); **patata americana** *o* **dolce** sweet potato, batata, yam (*USA*); **patate arrosto** roast potatoes; **patate fritte** chips (*Brit*), French fries (*USA*)

patatine [pataˈtine] SFPL chips (*Brit*), French fries (*USA*); (*confezionate*) (potato) crisps (*Brit*) *o* chips (*USA*)

patatrac [pataˈtrak] SM INV (*fig: disastro*) disaster; (: *dissesto economico*) crash

pâté [paˈte] SM INV pâté; **pâté di fegato d'oca** pâté de foie gras

patella [paˈtella] SF (*Zool*) limpet

patema, -i [paˈtema] SM: **patema (d'animo)** anxiety, worry

patentato, -a [patenˈtato] AGG 1 (*munito di patente*) licensed, certified 2 (*fig: scherz: qualificato*) utter, thorough; **un cretino patentato** an utter fool; **un ladro patentato** an out and out thief

patente [paˈtente] SF (*anche:* **patente di guida**) driving licence (*Brit*), driver's license (*USA*), **ho perso la patente** I've lost my driving licence; (*me l'hanno ritirata*) I've had my driving licence taken away; **mio fratello non ha la patente** my brother doesn't drive; **patente a punti** *driving licence with penalty points*

❏ **patente** non si traduce mai con la parola inglese *patent*

patentino [patenˈtino] SM temporary licence (*Brit*) *o* license (*USA*)

paternalismo [paternaˈlizmo] SM paternalism

paternalista, -i, -e [paternaˈlista] AGG paternalistic ♦ SM, SF paternalist

paternalistico, -a, -ci, -che [paternaˈlistiko] AGG paternalistic

paternità [paterniˈta] SF INV (*gen*) fatherhood; (*Dir*) paternity; **hanno rivendicato la paternità dell'attentato** (*fig*) they've claimed responsibility for the bombing

paterno, -a [paˈterno] AGG (*autorità*) paternal; (*benevolo: affetto, consigli*) fatherly; **lasciare la casa paterna** to leave one's father's house

patetico, -a, -ci, -che [paˈtɛtiko] AGG (*gen, anche Anat: pegg*) pathetic; (*commovente*) moving, touching; **non essere patetico!** don't be pathetic! ♦ SM sentimentalism; **cadere nel patetico** to become (over)sentimental

pathos [ˈpatos] SM INV pathos

patibolo [paˈtibolo] SM scaffold, gallows *sg*; **pare che vada al patibolo!** (*fig*) you'd think his hour had come!

patimento [patiˈmento] SM suffering

patina [ˈpatina] SF (*su rame*) patina; (*su medaglie*) coat; (*sulla lingua*) fur, coating

patire [paˈtire] /55/ VT (*ingiurie, offese*) to suffer; (*fame, sete*) to suffer (from); (*ingiustizie*) to endure ♦ VI (*aus* avere) (*di*) to suffer (from); **patire di cuore** to have a weak heart; **ha finito di patire** his sufferings are over

patito, -a [paˈtito] AGG (*sofferente*) run-down; (*volto*) wan ♦ SM, SF: **essere un patito di** (*musica, sport*) to be a fan *o* lover of; **è un patito del calcio** he's a football fan; **un patito di musica classica** a classical music lover

patologia [patoloˈdʒia] SF (*Med*) pathology

patologico, -a, -ci, -che [patoˈlɔdʒiko] AGG (*Med, anche fig*) pathological

patologo, -a, -gi, -ghe [paˈtɔlogo] SM, SF (*Med*) pathologist

patria [ˈpatrja] SF (*paese*) homeland, fatherland; (*fig: città o luogo natale*) birthplace; **Vienna, la patria del walzer** Vienna, the home of the waltz; **tornare in patria** to return to one's own country; **amor di patria** patriotism

patriarca, -chi [patriˈarka] SM patriarch

patrigno [paˈtriɲɲo] SM stepfather

patrimoniale [patrimoˈnjale] AGG patrimonial; **rendita patrimoniale** income from property; **imposta patrimoniale** property tax ♦ SF (*imposta*) property tax

patrimonio, -ni [patriˈmɔnjo] SM 1 estate, property; **mi è costato un patrimonio** (*fig*) it cost me a fortune, I paid a fortune for it; **patrimonio pubblico** public property 2 (*fig: eredità*) heritage; **il nostro patrimonio artistico** our artistic heritage; **patrimonio culturale** cultural heritage; **patrimonio ereditario** hereditary characteristics *pl*; **patrimonio spirituale** spiritual heritage

patrio, -ria, -rii, -rie [ˈpatrjo] AGG 1 (*di patria*) of one's country, native *attr*; **amor patrio** love of one's country 2 (*Dir*): **patria potestà** parental authority

patriota, -i, -e [patriˈɔta] SM, SF patriot

patriottico, -a, -ci, -che [patriˈɔttiko] AGG patriotic

patriottismo [patriot'tizmo] SM patriotism
patrocinare [patrotʃi'nare] /72/ VT (Dir) to defend; (fig: candidatura: appoggiare) to support; (: finanziariamente) to sponsor
patrocinio, -nii [patro'tʃinjo] SM (vedi vb) defence (Brit), defense (USA); support; sponsorship, patronage
patronato [patro'nato] SM 1 (patrocinio) patronage 2 (istituzione benefica) charitable institution o society
patrono [pa'trono] SM 1 (Rel) patron saint 2 (benefattore) patron 3 (Dir) counsel
patta ['patta] SF (di tasca) flap; (dei pantaloni) fly
patteggiamento [patteddʒa'mento] SM (Dir: anche: patteggiamento della pena) plea bargaining
patteggiare [patted'dʒare] /62/ VT (negoziare: resa, tregua) to negotiate; (Dir): patteggiare la pena to plea-bargain ♦ VI (aus avere) patteggiare con qn (scendere a patti) to negotiate with sb; (scendere a compromessi) to come to a compromise with sb
pattinaggio [patti'naddʒo] SM skating; fare pattinaggio to go skating; pattinaggio artistico figure skating; pattinaggio sul ghiaccio ice skating; pattinaggio a rotelle roller skating
pattinare [patti'nare] /72/ VI (aus avere) 1 (Sport) to skate; pattinare sul ghiaccio/a rotelle to ice-/roller-skate 2 (Aut: scivolare) to skid
pattinatore, -trice [pattina'tore] SM, SF skater
pattino[1] ['pattino] SM 1 (Sport) skate; pattini da ghiaccio ice skates; pattini in linea Rollerblades (Marchio registrato); pattini a rotelle roller skates 2 (Tecn) sliding block; (Aer) skid; (di slitta) runner
pattino[2] [pat'tino] SM (barca) kind of pedalo with oars
pattista, -i, -e [pat'tista] AGG (Pol) of Patto per l'Italia ♦ SM, SF (Pol) member (o supporter) of Patto per l'Italia
patto ['patto] SM 1 (accordo) pact, agreement; fare un patto to make a pact o an agreement; il Patto di Varsavia the Warsaw Pact; patto di non aggressione non-aggression pact; il Patto per l'Italia (Pol) centrist party 2 (condizione) condition, term; a nessun patto under no circumstances; venire o scendere a patti (con) to come to an agreement (with), come to terms (with); a patto che on condition that
pattuglia [pat'tuʎʎa] SF (Mil) patrol; essere di pattuglia to be on patrol
pattugliare [pattuʎ'ʎare] /27/ VT to patrol
pattuire [pattu'ire] /55/ VT to reach an agreement on
pattumiera [pattu'mjɛra] SF (dust)bin (Brit), garbage can (USA), trashcan (USA)
paura [pa'ura] SF fear; stava tremando dalla paura she was trembling with fear; aver paura di/di fare/che... to be scared o frightened o afraid of/of doing/that ...; avevo molta paura I was really scared; ha paura di volare he's scared of flying; ho paura di uscire da sola la sera I'm afraid to go out alone at night; ho paura dei ragni I'm scared of spiders; hai paura del buio? are you afraid of the dark?; fare o mettere paura a qn to frighten sb; mi hai fatto paura you frightened me; era morto di paura he was scared to death o frightened out of his wits; che paura! how scary!; ho paura di sì/no I am afraid so/not; ho paura che non venga o che non verrà I'm afraid he won't come; non aver paura, tutto si risolverà don't worry, everything will work out in the end; niente paura, ci penso io don't worry, I'll see to it; per paura di/che... for fear of/that ...; parlava piano per paura di svegliarlo she spoke quietly so as not to wake him; è magro da far paura he is terribly thin; ha una faccia da far paura he looks terrible; piove da far paura it's bucketing down
pauroso, -a [pau'roso] AGG 1 (che incute paura) frightening; (fig: straordinario) awful, dreadful; un pauroso incidente stradale an awful road accident 2 (che ha paura) timid, fearful, timorous; essere pauroso to get scared easily; è pauroso he gets scared easily
pausa ['pauza] SF (sosta) break; (nel parlare: Mus) pause; fare una pausa di 10 minuti to have a 10-minute break; facciamo una pausa let's have a break; dopo una pausa after a pause; fece una pausa e poi riprese a parlare he paused then began speaking again
paventato, -a [paven'tato] AGG much-feared

pavese [pa'vese] AGG of o from Pavia ♦ SM, SF inhabitant o native of Pavia
pavido, -a ['pavido] AGG (letter) fearful
pavimentare [pavimen'tare] /72/ VT (stanza) to floor; (strada) to pave
pavimentazione [pavimentat'tsjone] SF (vedi vb) flooring; paving
pavimento [pavi'mento] SM floor
  ❏ pavimento non si traduce mai con la parola inglese pavement
pavone [pa'vone] SM peacock
pavoneggiarsi [pavoned'dʒarsi] /62/ VIP to strut about, show off
'paywall ['peiwol] SM INV paywall
pazientare [pattsjen'tare] /72/ VI (aus avere) to be patient
paziente [pat'tsjɛnte] AGG patient ♦ SM, SF (Med) patient
pazienza [pat'tsjɛntsa] SF patience; aver pazienza to be patient; perdere la pazienza to lose (one's) patience; alla fine ha perso la pazienza e se n'è andato finally he lost patience and left; pazienza! never mind!; santa pazienza! (God) give me patience!
pazzamente [pattsa'mente] AVV madly; essere pazzamente innamorato to be madly in love
pazzesco, -a, -schi, -sche [pat'tsesko] AGG (assurdo: persona, comportamento) crazy, daft, mad; (incredibile: scena) incredible; un'idea pazzesca a crazy idea; una somma pazzesca an incredible amount of money; ad una velocità pazzesca at breakneck speed; ha una cultura pazzesca she's incredibly knowledgeable; pazzesco! incredible!
pazzia [pat'tsia] SF (Med) madness, lunacy, insanity; (di azione, decisione) madness, folly; dar segni di pazzia to show signs of madness; mi sento in vena di far pazzie I feel like doing something crazy; ho paura che possa fare una pazzia I'm afraid he'll do something crazy; è stata una pazzia! it was sheer madness!
pazzo, -a ['pattso] AGG (Med) mad, insane, crazy; (strano: persona, idea) wild, mad; è pazzo! he's crazy!; essere pazzo da legare to be raving mad o a raving lunatic; essere pazzo di (gioia, dolore) to be beside o.s. with, to be mad o crazy with; essere pazzo di gelosia to be insanely jealous; essere innamorato pazzo di to be madly in love with; è pazzo per lei he's crazy about her; pazzo per qn/qc mad o crazy about sb/sth; va pazza per il cioccolato she adores chocolate; prova un gusto pazzo a prendere in giro la gente he thoroughly enjoys taking people for a ride; andava a pazza velocità he was going at breakneck speed ♦ SM, SF lunatic, madman o madwoman; urlava come un pazzo he was shouting his head off, he was shouting like a lunatic; dovremo lavorare come pazzi per finire in tempo we'll have to work like mad to finish in time
PC SIGLA = Piacenza ♦ ABBR (Comm: = polizza di carico) ♦ [pi'tʃi] SIGLA M INV (= personal computer) PC
p.c. ABBR 1 = per condoglianze 2 (= per conoscenza) cc
p.c.c. ABBR (= per copia conforme) cc
PE SIGLA = Pescara
pecca, -che ['pɛkka] SF defect, flaw, fault
peccaminoso, -a [pekkami'noso] AGG sinful, wicked
peccare [pek'kare] /20/ VI (aus avere) 1 (Rel) to sin; (fig) to err; peccare di superbia (anche fig) to be guilty of pride; peccare per troppa bontà to be too kind 2 (difettare): peccare di to lack, be lacking in; peccare di modestia to be lacking in modesty; quel romanzo pecca nella struttura that novel lacks structure
peccato [pek'kato] SM (Rel) sin; un peccato di gioventù (fig) a youthful error o indiscretion; che peccato! what a shame o pity!; è un peccato che sia finita così it's a shame that it had to end like that; è un peccato che non sia potuto venire it's a shame that he couldn't come; peccato di gola gluttony; peccato mortale mortal sin; peccato originale original sin; peccato veniale venial sin
peccatore, -trice [pekka'tore] SM, SF sinner
peccherò ecc [pekke'rɔ] VB vedi peccare
pece [pet'ʃe] SF pitch
pechinese [peki'nese] AGG, SM, SF Pekin(g)ese inv ♦ SM (anche: cane pechinese) Pekin(g)ese inv, Peke (fam)

Pechino [pe'kino] SF Beijing, Peking (ant)

pecora ['pekora] SF (gen, anche fig) sheep inv; (femmina) ewe; c'erano solo due pecore nel campo there were only two sheep in the field; **latte di pecora** sheep's milk; **pecora nera** (fig) black sheep; **la pecora nera della famiglia** the black sheep of the family

pecoraio, -ai [peko'rajo] SM shepherd

pecorella [peko'rɛlla] SF lamb; **la pecorella smarrita** the lost sheep; **cielo a pecorelle** (fig: nuvole) mackerel sky

pecorino [peko'rino] SM (anche: **formaggio pecorino**) pecorino, cheese made from sheep's milk

peculato [peku'lato] SM (Dir) embezzlement

peculiare [peku'ljare] AGG **peculiare di** peculiar to

peculiarità [pekuljari'ta] SF INV peculiarity

pecuniario, -ria, -ri, -rie [peku'njarjo] AGG financial, monetary, money attr

pedaggio, -gi [pe'daddʒo] SM toll

pedagogia [pedago'dʒia] SF pedagogy, pedagogics sg, educational methods pl

pedagogico, -a, -ci, -che [peda'gɔdʒiko] AGG pedagogic(al)

pedagogo, -a, -ghi, -ghe [peda'gɔgo] SM, SF pedagogue

pedalare [peda'lare] /72/ VI (aus avere) to pedal; (andare in bicicletta) to cycle

pedale [pe'dale] SM (gen) pedal; (di macchina da cucire) treadle

pedana [pe'dana] SF 1 (gen) footboard; **pedana della cattedra** platform, dais 2 (Sport: nel salto) springboard; (: nella scherma) piste; (: nel lancio del disco) throwing circle

pedante [pe'dante] AGG pedantic ♦ SM, SF pedant

pedanteria [pedante'ria] SF pedantry

pedata [pe'data] SF (colpo) kick; (impronta) footprint; **dare una pedata a qn** to kick sb, give sb a kick; **mi ha dato una pedata** he kicked me; **prendere a pedate qn/qc** to kick sb/sth

pederasta, -i [pede'rasta] SM pederast

pedestre [pe'dɛstre] AGG pedestrian

pediatra, -i, -e [pe'djatra] SM, SF paediatrician (Brit), pediatrician (USA); **fa il pediatra** he's a p(a)ediatrician

pediatria [pedja'tria] SF paediatrics sg (Brit), pediatrics sg (USA)

pediatrico, -a, -ci, -che [pe'djatriko] AGG paediatric (Brit), pediatric (USA), children's attr

pedicure [pedi'kure] SM INV, SF INV chiropodist (Brit), podiatrist (USA)

pedigree ['pidigri] SM INV pedigree

pediluvio, -vi [pedi'luvjo] SM footbath

pedina [pe'dina] SF (Dama) draughtsman (Brit), draftsman (USA); (Scacchi, fig) pawn

pedinare [pedi'nare] /72/ VT to shadow, tail; **far pedinare qn** to have sb followed, put a tail on sb

pedofilo, -a [pe'dɔfilo] AGG, SM, SF paedophile (Brit), pedophile (USA), paedophiliac (Brit), pedophiliac (USA)

pedonale [pedo'nale] AGG (passaggio, isola, traffico ecc) pedestrian attr; **una zona pedonale** a pedestrian precinct

pedone [pe'done] SM 1 (persona) pedestrian 2 (Scacchi) pawn

peeling ['pilin] SM INV (Cosmetica) exfoliation

peggio ['pɛddʒo] COMP, SUPERL di male ♦ AVV 1 (con senso comparativo) worse; **gioca peggio di lui** she plays worse than he does, she's a worse player than he is; **andare peggio** to be worse; **gli affari vanno peggio che mai** business is worse than ever; **Luca è andato peggio di me all'esame** Luca did worse than me in the exam; **cambiare in peggio** to get o become worse, change for the worse; **si comporta sempre peggio** his behaviour gets worse and worse; **sta sempre peggio** he's getting worse and worse; **peggio per te!** that's your lookout!; **non vuoi venire? peggio per te** you don't want to come? that's your loss; **peggio di così si muore** things couldn't be worse; **è peggio che andar di notte!** it's worse than ever!; **non c'è niente di peggio che...** there's nothing worse than ... 2 (con senso superlativo) worst; **i peggio allenati** the worst trained; **la peggio pagata** the worst paid ♦ AGG INV (con senso comparativo) worse; **è peggio di suo fratello** she's worse than her brother ♦ SM worst; **il peggio è che...** the worst thing o the worst of it is that ... ♦ SF 1 **avere la peggio** to come off worse, get the worst of it; **hanno**

litigato e Gigi ha avuto la peggio they had an argument and Gigi came off worst 2 **alla peggio** if the worst comes to the worst, at worst; **tirare avanti alla meno peggio** to get along as best one can

peggioramento [peddʒora'mento] SM (gen, di malattia) worsening; (di rapporti) worsening, deterioration; **portare un peggioramento in, portare ad un peggioramento** di to worsen, lead to a worsening in; **ci sarà un peggioramento** (Meteor) the weather will deteriorate o become worse

peggiorare [peddʒo'rare] /72/ VT to worsen, to make worse ♦ VI (aus essere) to worsen, become o grow worse

peggiorativo, -a [peddʒora'tivo] AGG pejorative

peggiore [ped'dʒore] AGG (comparativo) worse; (superlativo) worst; **peggiore (di)** worse (than); **è peggiore di lui** she's worse than him; **molto peggiore** much worse; **nel peggiore dei casi** if the worst comes to the worst; **le cose non potevano concludersi in modo peggiore** things couldn't have come to a worse end; **ho conosciuto tempi peggiori** I've been through worse ♦ SM, SF: **il/la peggiore** the worst one, the worst (person); **il peggiore dei due** the worse of the two; **il peggiore della classe** the worst in the class

pegno ['peɲɲo] SM 1 (Dir) pledge, security; **dare in pegno qc** to pawn sth, leave sth as security; **posso darle in pegno l'orologio** I can leave you my watch as security; **banco dei pegni** pawnshop 2 (fig: segno) token, pledge; (nei giochi di società) forfeit; **un pegno d'amore** a love token; **in pegno d'amicizia** as a token of friendship

pelapatate [pelapa'tate] SM INV potato peeler

pelare [pe'lare] /72/ VT (spennare) to pluck; (spellare) to skin; (sbucciare) to peel; **ti hanno pelato!** (di capelli) they've scalped you!; **in quel negozio ti pelano** they make you pay through the nose in that shop

pelato, -a [pe'lato] AGG 1 (sbucciato) peeled 2 (calvo) bald; **è pelato** he's bald ♦ **pelati** SMPL (anche: **pomodori pelati**) peeled tomatoes

pellame [pel'lame] SM (di animali) skins pl, hides pl

pelle ['pɛlle] SF 1 (gen) skin; **avere la pelle delicata** to have sensitive skin; **pelle grassa** greasy skin; (Cosmetica) oily skin; **pelle mista** combination skin; **pelle secca** dry skin 2 (di animale) skin, hide; (di rettile) skin; (conciata) leather; **borsa/giacca di pelle** leather handbag/jacket; **pelle di camoscio** suede; **pelle di daino** shammy (leather); **pelle di foca** (Sci) skins; **pelle di montone** sheepskin 3 (buccia) skin, peel 4 (fraseologia): **avere la pelle dura** (fig) to be tough; **avere la pelle d'oca** to have goose pimples (Brit) o goose flesh (Brit) o goose bumps (USA); **mi ha fatto venire la pelle d'oca** (paura, disgusto) it made my flesh creep; **avere i nervi a fior di pelle** to be on edge; **essere pelle ed ossa** to be skin and bone; **non stare più nella pelle dalla gioia** to be beside o.s. with delight; **lasciarci la pelle** to lose one's life; **salvare la pelle** to save one's skin; **vendere cara la pelle** to put up a fierce struggle; **amici per la pelle** firm o close friends

pellegrinaggio, -gi [pellegri'naddʒo] SM pilgrimage; **andare in pellegrinaggio** to go on a pilgrimage

pellegrino, -a [pelle'grino] SM, SF pilgrim

pelletteria [pellette'ria] SF 1 (negozio) leather goods shop; **articoli di pelletteria** leather goods 2 (industria) leather trade o industry

pellicano [pelli'kano] SM pelican

pellicceria [pellittʃe'ria] SF 1 (negozio) furrier's (shop) 2 (pellicce) furs pl

pelliccia, -ce [pel'littʃa] SF 1 (mantello di animale) fur, coat 2 (indumento) fur (coat); **pelliccia ecologica** fake fur; **pelliccia di visone** mink coat

pellicciaio, -ciai [pellit'tʃajo] SM furrier

pellicola [pel'likola] SF 1 (membrana) film, layer; **pellicola trasparente** (Culin) cling film (Brit), plastic wrap (USA) 2 (Fot, Cine) film

pelo ['pelo] SM 1 (gen) hair; **ho tanti peli sulle gambe** I've got a lot of hair o hairs on my legs; **non aver peli sulla lingua** to speak one's mind; **cercare il pelo nell'uovo** to pick holes, split hairs; **per un pelo** nearly; **per un pelo non ho perso il treno** I very nearly missed the train; **l'ha mancato per un pelo** he just missed it; **per un pelo non s'ammazzava** he almost o nearly killed himself; **ha perso per un pelo**

he lost but only just; **c'è mancato un pelo che affogasse** he narrowly escaped drowning; **è un pelo più grande** (*un po'*) it's a shade bigger **2** (*di animale: pelame*) coat, fur; (*: peli*) hair; (*: pelliccia*) fur; **il gatto ha il pelo morbido** the cat has soft fur *o* a soft coat; **impermeabile con l'interno di pelo** fur-lined raincoat; **pelliccia a pelo lungo** long-haired fur coat; **essere di primo pelo** to be wet behind the ears; **fare il pelo e il contropelo a qn** to give sb a good dressing-down; **il lupo perde il pelo ma non il vizio** (*Proverbio*) the leopard cannot change its spots **3** (*di tappeto*) pile; (*di tessuto*) pile, nap; **tappeto a pelo lungo** thick pile carpet **4** (*superficie: di liquido*) surface; **il pelo dell'acqua** the surface of the water

peloso, -a [pe'loso] AGG hairy

peltro ['peltro] SM pewter

peluche [pɔ'lyʃ] SM (*tessuto*) plush; **giocattoli di peluche** soft *o* cuddly toys; **un cane di peluche** a fluffy dog

peluria [pe'lurja] SF down

pelvi ['pɛlvi] SF INV pelvis

pelvico, -a, -ci, -che ['pɛlviko] AGG pelvic

pena ['pena] SF **1** (*dolore*) sorrow, sadness *no pl*; (*angoscia*) worry, anxiety; **essere** *o* **stare in pena (per qn/qc)** to worry *o* be anxious (about sb/sth); **ero in pena per te** I was worried about you; **le pene dell'inferno** the torments of hell; **ha passato le pene dell'inferno** (*fig*) she went through hell **2** (*pietà*) pity; **far pena** to be pitiful; **mi fa pena** I feel sorry for him; **fa pena vederlo così** it is pitiful to see him like this; **quel cappello fa pena** (*fig*) that hat is a disgrace **3** (*Dir*) sentence; (*punizione*) penalty, punishment; **fu condannato ad una pena di 5 anni** he was sentenced to 5 years' imprisonment; **scontare una pena** to serve a term of imprisonment; **pena capitale** capital punishment; **pena di morte** death sentence *o* penalty; **sono contrario alla pena di morte** I'm against the death penalty; **è stato condannato alla pena di morte** he was sentenced to death; **pena pecuniaria** fine **4** (*fatica*) trouble *no pl*, effort; (*difficoltà*) difficulty; **prendersi** *o* **darsi la pena di fare qc** to go to the trouble of doing sth, take the trouble to do sth; **valere la pena** to be worth it; **vale la pena farlo** it's worth doing, it's worth it; **non ne vale la pena** it's not worth the effort *o* worth it

penale [pe'nale] AGG (*Dir*) criminal, penal; **codice penale** penal code; **causa penale** criminal trial; **diritto penale** criminal law; **precedenti penali** criminal record ♦ SF (*anche:* **clausola penale**) penalty clause; **pagare la penale** to pay the penalty

penalista, -i, -e [pena'lista] SM, SF (*avvocato*) criminal lawyer

penalità [penali'ta] SF INV penalty

penalizzare [penalid'dzare] /72/ VT (*Sport*) to penalize

penalizzazione [penaliddzat'tsjone] SF (*Sport*) penalty

penare [pe'nare] /72/ VI (*patire*) to suffer; (*faticare*) to struggle; **ha finito di penare** his sufferings are over; **penare a fare qc** to have difficulty in doing sth; **lo fecero senza penare troppo** they did it without too much difficulty

pendente [pen'dɛnte] AGG **1** (*appeso*) hanging; (*inclinato*) leaning **2** (*Dir: causa, lite*) pending ♦ SM (*pendaglio*) pendant; (*orecchino*) drop earring

pendenza [pen'dɛntsa] SF **1** slope, slant; (*grado d'inclinazione*) gradient; **in pendenza** (*tetto*) sloping; (*strada, terreno*) on a slope; **essere in leggera pendenza** to slope (down) gently; **una strada con una pendenza del 20%** a road with a 1 in 5 gradient **2** (*Dir*) pending suit **3** (*Comm*) outstanding account

pendere ['pɛndere] /8/ VI (*aus avere*) **1** (*essere appeso*): **pendere (da)** to hang (from); **la lampada che pende dal soffitto** the lamp that hangs from the ceiling; **pendere dalle labbra di qn** to hang on sb's every word **2** (*Dir: causa*) to be pending **3** (*essere inclinato: superficie*) to slope, slant; (*: palo, edificio*) to lean; (*: nave*) to list; **pendere da una parte** to slope to one side; **pendere dalla parte di qn** (*fig*) to be inclined to take sb's part; **la bilancia pende in suo favore** things are in his favour **4** (*fig: incombere*): **pendere su** to hang over

pendice [pen'ditʃe] SF (*di monte*) slope

pendio, -dii [pen'dio] SM **1** (*luogo in pendenza*) slope **2** (*pendenza*) slope, slant

pendola ['pendola] SF pendulum clock

pendolare [pendo'lare] AGG (*moto*) pendular, pendulum *attr* ♦ SM, SF (*lavoratore*) commuter; **fare il pendolare** to commute

pendolarismo [pendola'rizmo] SM commuting

pendolino [pendo'lino] SM tilting train, pendolino

pendolo ['pendolo] SM (*peso*) pendulum; (*anche:* **orologio a pendolo**) pendulum clock

pene ['pene] SM (*Anat*) penis

penetrante [pene'trante] AGG (*freddo*) biting, piercing; (*odore*) penetrating; (*sguardo*) penetrating, piercing

penetrare [pene'trare] /72/ VI (*aus essere*) **1** (*gen*): **penetrare (in qc)** to penetrate (sth), enter (sth); **i ladri sono penetrati in casa di notte** the thieves entered the house at night; **penetrò in casa di nascosto** he entered the house by stealth, he stole into the house **2** (*freddo*) to come *o* get in; (*liquido*) to soak in; **penetrare nella parete** (*chiodo*) to penetrate the wall; (*acqua*) to soak into the wall; **il sole penetrò nella stanza** the sun shone into the room; **il proiettile gli è penetrato nel cuore** the bullet went into his heart; **il freddo mi penetrava nelle ossa** the cold went right through me; **far penetrare** (*aria, luce*) to let in ♦ VT (*gen, anche fig*) to penetrate; (*sogg: proiettile*) to penetrate; (*: acqua, aria*) to go *o* come into; **penetrare un mistero** to get to the bottom of a mystery

penetrazione [penetrat'tsjone] SF penetration

penicillina [penitʃil'lina] SF penicillin

peninsulare [peninsu'lare] AGG peninsular; **l'Italia peninsulare** mainland Italy

penisola [pe'nizola] SF peninsula; **la penisola italiana** the Italian mainland

penitente [peni'tɛnte] SM, SF, AGG penitent

penitenza [peni'tɛntsa] SF **1** (*Rel: pentimento*) repentance, penitence; (*: pena*) penance; **far penitenza** to do penance **2** (*nei giochi*) forfeit

penitenziario, -ri [peniten'tsjarjo] SM prison, penitentiary (*USA*)

penna ['penna] SF **1** (*di uccello*) feather; **mettere le penne** to grow feathers; **lasciarci** *o* **rimetterci le penne** (*fig*) to get one's fingers burnt; **le penne nere** (*Mil*) the Italian Alpine troops **2** (*per scrivere*) pen, ballpoint (*USA*); **penna luminosa** *o* **ottica** light pen; **penna d'oca** quill; **penna a sfera** ballpoint pen; **penna stilografica** fountain pen **3** (*Culin*): **penne** SFPL quills (*type of pasta*) **4** (*Mus*) pick

pennacchio, -chi [pen'nakkjo] SM (*ornamento*) plume; **un pennacchio di fumo** (*fig*) a plume *o* spiral of smoke

pennarello [penna'rɛllo] SM felt(-tip) pen

pennellare [pennel'lare] /72/ VI (*aus avere*) to paint

pennellata [pennel'lata] SF (*di vernice*) brush stroke; **dare le ultime pennellate a qc** (*anche fig*) to give the finishing touches to sth

pennello [pen'nɛllo] SM (*gen*) brush; (*di pittore, imbianchino*) (paint)brush; **a pennello** (*perfettamente*) to perfection, perfectly; **quel vestito ti sta a pennello** that dress fits you perfectly; **pennello da barba** shaving brush

Pennini [pen'nini] SMPL: **i Pennini** the Pennines

pennino [pen'nino] SM (*pen*) nib

pennone [pen'none] SM **1** (*Naut*) yard **2** (*bandiera*) banner, standard

pennuto, -a [pen'nuto] AGG feathered ♦ SM bird

penombra [pe'nombra] SF half-light, dim light; **in penombra** in the half-light; **mi è sembrato di vedere qualcuno nella penombra** I thought I saw someone in the half-light

penoso, -a [pe'noso] AGG (*doloroso: esperienza, compito*) painful, distressing; (*angoscioso: attesa*) anxious; (*faticoso: lavoro, viaggio*) difficult, tiring; (*patetico: scena, scusa*) pathetic; **un penoso silenzio** a painful silence

pensare [pen'sare] /72/ VI (*aus avere*) **1** to think; **pensare a** to think of; (*amico, vacanze*) to think of *o* about; (*problema*) to think about; **a chi stai pensando?** who are you thinking about?; **pensava al tempo passato** he was remembering days gone by; **vorrei pensarci su** I would like to think it over *o* give it some thought; **penso di sì** I think so; **penso di no** I don't think so; **a pensarci bene...** on second thoughts (*Brit*) *o* thought (*USA*) ...; **pensare con la propria testa** to think for o.s.; **pensa a come sarebbe bello** think how lovely it would be; **prima di parlare pensa** think before you speak; **se solo ci avessi pensato** if only I had thought about it; **non voglio nemmeno pensarci** I don't even want to think about it; **ciò mi dà da pensare** that gives me something to think about; **pensare bene/male di qn** to think well/badly of sb, have a good/bad opinion of sb; **ma pensa un po'!** just think of that! **2** (*provvedere*): **pensare a qc** to see to sth, take care of sth; **ci penso io** I'll see to *o* take care of it; **ha altro a cui pensare ora** he's got other *o* more important things to think about now; **pensa ai fatti tuoi!** mind your own business! ♦ VT **1** (*gen*) to think; **che stai pensando?** what are you thinking?; **cosa ne pensi?** what do you think of it?, how do you feel about it?; **penso che sia colpa sua** I think it is his fault *o* that he is to blame; **ciò mi fa pensare che...** that makes me think that ...; **il suo comportamento farebbe pensare che...** his behaviour would lead you to suppose that ..., his behaviour would make you think that ...; **non avrei mai pensato finisse così** I would never have believed it would end like this; **ti pensavo più furbo** I thought you were smarter than that; **chi l'avrebbe mai pensato?** who would have thought it?; **e pensare che...** and to think that ... **2** (*prendere in considerazione*) to realize; **devi pensare che ha appena iniziato** you must realize *o* remember that he's only just started; **non pensa che quello che fa può danneggiare gli altri** he doesn't realize that what he does may harm others **3** (*avere intenzione*): **pensare di fare qc** to think of doing sth; **pensavo di invitare anche lui** I was thinking of inviting him too; **penso di partire in serata** I'm thinking of leaving in the course of the evening **4** (*inventare, escogitare*) to think out; **ne pensa sempre una nuova** he's always got something new up his sleeve; **l'ha pensata bella** he had a bright idea; **una ne fa e cento ne pensa** he's always up to something

pensata [pen'sata] SF (*trovata*) idea, thought; **ma che bella pensata!** (*anche iro*) what a good idea!

pensatore, -trice [pensa'tore] SM, SF thinker

pensierino [pensje'rino] SM **1** (*pensiero*): **ci farò un pensierino** I'll think about it **2** (*dono*) little gift

pensiero [pen'sjɛro] SM **1** thought; **riandare col pensiero a** to remember, think back to; **leggere il pensiero di qn** to read sb's thoughts *o* mind; **essere assorto nei propri pensieri** to be deep *o* lost in thought; **un pensiero gentile** (*anche fig: dono*) a kind thought; **libertà di pensiero** freedom of thought **2** (*preoccupazione*) worry, care, trouble; **ha tanti pensieri** he has so many worries; **stare in pensiero per qn/qc** to be worried about sb/sth; **darsi pensiero per qc** to worry about sth; **è un tipo senza pensieri** he's a carefree chap **3** (*modo di pensare, dottrina*) thinking *no pl*; **il pensiero di Hegel** Hegelian thinking

pensieroso, -a [pensje'roso] AGG pensive, thoughtful

pensile ['pensile] AGG hanging, suspended; **giardino pensile** hanging garden

pensilina [pensi'lina] SF projecting roof; (*di stazione*) platform roof

pensionamento [pensjona'mento] SM retirement; **pensionamento anticipato** early retirement

pensionante [pensjo'nante] SM, SF (*presso una famiglia*) lodger; (*in albergo*) resident, guest

pensionato[1] [pensjo'nato] SM (*istituto: per studenti*) hostel; (*: per anziani*) rest home

pensionato[2]**, -a** [pensjo'nato] SM, SF pensioner

pensione [pen'sjone] SF **1** (*rendita*) pension; **andare in pensione** to retire; **essere in pensione** to be retired; **pensione di anzianità** occupational pension (*paid after a certain number of years of employment*); **pensione baby** *pension paid to someone who has worked for only a short time, usually 15-20 years*; **pensione di guerra** war pension; **pensione d'invalidità** disability pension; **pensione di reversibilità** spouse's pension; **pensione sociale** minimum state pension (*payable to those on low incomes*); **pensione di vecchiaia** old-age pension (*payable to those who have made sufficient contributions*) **2** (*albergo*) boarding house; (*vitto e alloggio*) board and lodging; **essere a pensione da qn** to board with sb; **tenere a pensione qn** to have sb as a lodger; **mezza pensione** half board; **pensione completa** full board

pensionistico, -a, -ci, -che [pensjo'nistiko] AGG pension *attr*; **fondo pensionistico** pension fund

pensoso, -a [pen'soso] AGG thoughtful, pensive

pentagono [pen'tagono] SM **1** (*Geom*) pentagon **2** (*Pol*) : **il Pentagono** the Pentagon

pentagramma, -i [penta'gramma] SM (*Mus*) staff, stave

pentapartito [pentapar'tito] SM (*Pol*) five-party coalition government

pentathlon ['pentatlon] SM INV pentathlon

Pentecoste [pente'kɔste] SF Pentecost, Whit Sunday (*Brit*)

pentimento [penti'mento] SM repentance, contrition; (*rimpianto*) regret

pentirsi [pen'tirsi] /45/ VIP (*Rel*) to repent; **pentirsi dei propri peccati** to repent of one's sins; **pentirsi di qc/di aver fatto qc** (*rimpiangere*) to regret sth/doing sth; **mi pento di averglielo detto** I regret telling him; **se segui i miei consigli non te ne pentirai** if you follow my advice you won't regret it; **vieni con noi e non te ne pentirai** if you come with us you won't regret it

pentitismo [penti'tizmo] SM *the phenomenon of criminals or terrorists who decide to collaborate with the police*

pentito, -a [pen'tito] AGG (*gen, persona, sguardo ecc*) penitent, repentant ♦ SM, SF (*terrorista, mafioso*) ≈ supergrass (*Brit*), *terrorist/criminal who turns police informer*

pentola ['pentola] SF (*recipiente*) pot; (*contenuto*) pot(ful); **metti la pentola sul fuoco** put the pot on the gas; **qualcosa bolle in pentola** (*fig*) there's something brewing; **pentola a pressione** pressure cooker

penultimo, -a [pe'nultimo] AGG penultimate, last but one (*Brit*), next to last; **è arrivato penultimo** he arrived second from last ♦ SM, SF: **il(la) penultimo(a)** the last but one (*Brit*)

penuria [pe'nurja] SF shortage

❑ **penuria** non si traduce mai con la parola inglese *penury*

penzolare [pendzo'lare] /72/ VI (*aus* avere) (*pendere*) to hang loosely, dangle

penzoloni [pendzo'loni] AVV (*anche:* **a penzoloni**) hanging down, dangling; **se ne stava con le braccia penzoloni** he stood there with his arms dangling

pepato, -a [pe'pato] AGG **1** (*condito con pepe*) peppery, hot **2** (*fig: pungente*) sharp

pepe ['pepe] SM pepper; **è tutta pepe** (*fig*) she's full of life; **pepe bianco** white pepper; **pepe della Giamaica** allspice; **pepe in grani** whole pepper, peppercorns; **pepe macinato** ground pepper; **pepe nero** black pepper

peperonata [pepero'nata] SF (*Culin*) *stewed peppers, tomatoes and onions*

peperoncino [peperon'tʃino] SM chilli pepper

peperone [pepe'rone] SM capsicum; **rosso come un peperone** as red as a beetroot (*Brit*) *o* beet (*USA*); **peperone rosso** red pepper, capsicum; **peperone verde** green pepper, capsicum; **peperoni ripieni** stuffed peppers

pepita [pe'pita] SF nugget

PAROLA CHIAVE

per [per] PREP

1 (*direzione*) for, to; **l'autobus per Milano** the Milan bus, the bus for *o* to Milan; **quando parti per Parigi?** when are you leaving for *o* are you off to Paris?; **proseguire per Londra** to go on to London

2 (*verso, nei confronti di*) for, towards; **il suo grande amore per la sorella** his great love for *o* of his sister; **ha una passione per la musica** he is passionately fond of music

3 (*moto attraverso luogo*) through; **l'ho cercata per tutta la casa** I searched the whole house *o* I searched all over the house for it; **ti ho cercato per mari e per monti** I looked everywhere for you; **l'ho incontrato per le scale** I met him on the stairs; **sono passata per Roma** I came through *o* via Rome; **il maestro è passato per i banchi** the teacher went along the rows of desks; **i ladri sono passati per la finestra** the thieves got in (*o* out) through the window

4 (*stato in luogo*): **seduto/sdraiato per terra** sitting/lying on the ground

5 (*tempo*) for; **per anni** for years; **per tutta l'estate** all summer long, all through the summer, throughout the summer; **per tutta la giornata** all day long; **per giorni e giorni** for days on end; **giorno per giorno** day by day; **dobbiamo**

finirlo per lunedì we must get it finished by *o* for Monday; **ci rivedremo per Pasqua** we'll see one another again at Easter; **è piovuto per tutta la settimana** it has rained all week long; **per molto tempo** for a long time; **sarò di ritorno per le tre** I'll be back by three o'clock **6** (*mezzo, maniera*) by; **per ferrovia** by rail *o* train; **l'ha fatto per gioco** he did it as a joke; **per lettera** by letter; **l'ha presa per mano** he took her by the hand; **chiamare qn per nome** to call sb by name; **l'ha fatto per scherzo** he did it as a joke; **non mi piace parlare per telefono** I don't like using the phone *o* speaking on the phone; **per via aerea** by air; **per vie legali** through legal channels **7** (*causa*) for, because of, owing to; (*scopo*) for; **per abitudine** out of habit, from habit; **è morto per avvelenamento** he died from poisoning; **le tende per la cucina** the kitchen curtains, the curtains for the kitchen; **per un errore** through *o* by error; **per il freddo** because of the cold; **non stare in pena per lui** don't worry about him; **pastiglie per il mal di gola** throat pastilles *o* lozenges; **chiuso per malattia** closed because of *o* on account of illness; **assentarsi per malattia** to be off because of *o* through *o* owing to illness; **questo lavoro non fa per me** this isn't the right job for me; **per motivi di salute** for health reasons; **condannato per omicidio** convicted of murder; **non l'ha fatto per pigrizia** he didn't do it out of laziness; **processato per rapina a mano armata** tried for armed robbery **8** (*prezzo, misura*) for; **assicurato per un milione** insured for 1 million euros; **l'ho comprato per 500 euro** I bought it for 500 euros; **per miglia e miglia non si vedeva nulla** you couldn't see anything for miles; **il terreno si estende per molti chilometri** the land extends for several kilometres; **lo vendo per poco** I'm selling it for very little, I'm selling it cheap **9** (*limitazione*) for; **è troppo difficile per lui** it's too hard for him; **per me è come una madre** she's like a mother to me; **per quel che mi riguarda** as far as I'm concerned; **per questa volta ci passerò sopra** I'll forget about it this time **10** (*distributivo*): **un interesse del 5 per cento** 5 per cent interest; **dividere 12 per 4** to divide 12 by 4; **2 per 3 fa 6** 2 times 3 equals 6; **in fila per tre!** line up in threes!; **moltiplicare 9 per 3** to multiply 9 by 3; **ce n'è una per parte** there's one on each side; **750 euro per persona** 750 euros per person *o* a head *o* apiece; **vi interrogo uno per uno** I'll question you one by one; **entrate uno per volta** come in one at a time **11** (*in qualità di*) as; (*al posto di*) for; **te lo dico per certo** I tell you it's gospel; **me l'hanno venduto per lana** they sold it to me as (if it were) wool; **lo hanno dato per morto** he was given up for dead; **ha avuto suo padre per professore** he had his father as one of his teachers, he was taught by his father; **prendere qn per uno sciocco** to take sb for a fool; **ti ho preso per tuo fratello** I (mis)took you for your brother **12** (*introduce proposizione finale*) to, in order to; **per fare qc** (so as) to do sth, in order to do sth; **l'ho fatto per aiutarti** I did it to help you; **dicevo così per scherzare** I said it as a joke *o* in fun **13** (*introduce proposizione causale*) for; **per aver fatto qc** for doing sth; **è stato punito per aver picchiato suo fratello** he was punished for hitting his brother; **è morta per aver ingerito troppi barbiturici** she died from *o* of an overdose of barbiturates **14** (*introduce proposizione concessiva*): **per poco che sia** however little it is *o* it may be, little though it is *o* it may be; **per quanto si dia da fare...** however hard he tries ...; **per quanto io sappia** as far as I know

pera ['pera] SF **1** pear; **pere cotte** stewed pears; **cadere come una pera cotta** (*fig: innamorarsi*) to fall head over heels in love **2 pera di gomma** (*Med: per clistere*) rubber syringe **3 farsi una pera** (*fig: fam*) to shoot up

peraltro [pe'raltro] AVV (*per di più*) moreover, what's more; (*comunque*) however

perbacco [per'bakko] ESCL by Jove!

perbene [per'bene] AGG INV (*ammodo*) respectable, decent; **gente perbene** respectable people ♦ AVV (*con cura*) well, properly

perbenismo [perbe'nizmo] SM (so-called) respectability

percentuale [pert∫entu'ale] AGG percentage *attr* ♦ SF per-centage; (*provvigione*) commission; **percepisce una percentuale del 20% su ciò che vende** he receives a commission of 20% on what he sells

percepire [pert∫e'pire] /**55**/ VT **1** (*sentire, intuire*) to perceive **2** (*ricevere: somma, compenso*) to receive

percettibile [pert∫et'tibile] AGG perceptible; **un suono appena percettibile** a barely audible sound

percezione [pert∫et'tsjone] SF perception

perché [per'ke] AVV why; **non so perché** I don't know why; **perché no?** why not?; **perché non vuoi andarci?** why don't you want to go?; **perché l'hai fatto?** why did you do it?; **spiegami perché l'hai fatto** tell me why you did it; **vorrei sapere perché non te ne vai** I'd like to know why you don't leave ♦ CONG **1** (*causale: poiché*) because; **non posso uscire perché ho molto da fare** I can't go out because *o* as I've a lot to do **2** (*finale: affinché*) so (that), in order that; **te lo do perché tu lo legga** I'm giving it to you so you can read it; **ho telefonato perché non si preoccupasse** I phoned so that they wouldn't worry **3** (*consecutivo: cosicché*): **l'ostacolo era troppo alto perché si potesse scavalcarlo** the obstacle was too high to climb over; **è troppo forte perché si possa vincerlo** he's too strong to be beaten *o* for anyone to beat him ♦ SM INV (*motivo*) reason; **non c'è un vero perché** there's no real reason for it; **vorrei sapere il perché di un simile atteggiamento da parte sua** I'd like to know the reason for his attitude; **i perché sono tanti** there are many reasons for it; **voglio sapere il perché e il percome** I want to know the whys and wherefores

perciò [per't∫ɔ] CONG therefore, so, for this (*o* that) reason

percorrere [per'korrere] /**28**/ VT IRREG (*distanza, circuito, territorio*) to cover; (*strada*) to follow; (*luogo*) to go all over; (*paese*) to travel up and down, go all over; **abbiamo percorso venti chilometri al giorno** we covered twenty kilometres a day; **percorrere un paese in lungo e in largo** to travel all over a country

percorribile [perkor'ribile] AGG (*strada*) which can be followed

percorso, -a [per'korso] PP *di* percorrere ♦ SM (*distanza*) distance; (*tragitto*) journey; (*itinerario*) route; (*Sport*) course; **ho seguito il percorso più breve** I took the shortest route; **lungo il percorso** along the way; **percorso netto** (*Ippica*) clear round; **percorso obbligato** (*Sport*) set course

percosso, -a [per'kɔsso] PP *di* percuotere

percuotere [per'kwɔtere] /**106**/ VT IRREG (*gen*) to beat, hit, strike; **percuotersi il petto** to beat one's breast

percussione [perkus'sjone] SF percussion; **strumenti a percussione** (*Mus*) percussion instruments

perdente [per'dente] AGG losing ♦ SM, SF loser

perdere ['perdere] VB IRREG /**73**/ VT **1** (*gen*) to lose; (*abitudine*) to get out of; **ho perso il portafoglio** I've lost my wallet; **perdere di vista qn** (*anche fig*) to lose sight of sb; **l'ho perso di vista dopo mezz'ora** I lost sight of him after half an hour; **perdere la speranza/l'appetito/la vista** to lose hope/one's appetite/one's sight; **perdere i capelli** to lose one's hair, go bald; **gli alberi perdono le foglie** the trees are losing *o* shedding their leaves; **perdere al gioco** to lose money gambling; **saper perdere** to be a good loser; **lascia perdere!** (*non insistere*) forget it!, never mind!; **lascialo perdere!** (*non ascoltarlo*) don't listen to him!; **non ho niente da perdere** I've got nothing to lose **2** (*lasciar sfuggire: treno, autobus*) to miss; **ho perso il treno** I've missed the train; **è un'occasione da non perdere** it's a wonderful opportunity; (*affare*) it's a great bargain **3** (*sprecare: tempo, denaro*) to waste; **ho perso tempo e denaro** you've wasted time and money; **ho perso l'intera giornata a cercarlo** I wasted the whole day looking for it; **è falsa presa** it's a waste of effort **4** (*lasciar uscire: sangue*) to lose; **il rubinetto perde** (*acqua*) the tap is leaking; **la stufa perde gas** the gas fire is leaking **5** (*rimetterci*): **hanno alzato i prezzi per non perderci** they put up their prices so as not to make a loss; **non hai perso niente a non vedere quel film** you haven't missed anything by not seeing that film; **ci perdi a non venire** you are missing out by not coming ♦ VI (*aus avere*) **perdere di**, (*diminuire*) **perdere di autorità/importanza** to lose authority/importance; **perdere di valore** to go down in value; **perdersi** VIP **1** (*smarrirsi*) to lose one's way, get lost; **ci siamo persi** we got lost; **perdersi in un bicchiere d'acqua** to be unable to cope with the slightest problem; **perdersi in chiacchiere** to waste time talking; **perdersi dietro a qn** to waste one's time with *o* on sb; **non perderti in queste sciocchezze** don't waste your time with this nonsense **2** (*scomparire*: *oggetto*) to disappear, vanish; (: *suono*) to fade away; **perdersi alla vista** to disappear from sight **3** (*uso reciproco*): **perdersi di vista** to lose sight of each other; (*fig*) to lose touch; **dopo la scuola si sono persi di vista** they lost touch after leaving school

perdifiato [perdi'fjato] **a perdifiato** AVV (*correre*) at breathtaking speed; (*gridare*) at the top of one's voice

perdigiorno [perdi'dʒorno] SM INV, SF INV idler, loafer, waster

perdita ['perdita] SF **1** (*gen*) loss; (*di persona*: *morte*) loss, death; **è una grave perdita** it's a great loss; **a perdita d'occhio** as far as the eye can see; **perdite** casualties **2** (*Econ*) loss, deficit; (*spreco*) waste; **è una perdita di tempo** it's a waste of time **4** (*spandimento*: *di rubinetto*) leak; (: *di sangue*) loss; **le perdite bianche** (*Med*) the whites

perditempo [perdi'tempo] SM INV, SF INV waster, idler

perdizione [perdit'tsjone] SF (*Rel*) perdition, damnation; **luogo di perdizione** place of ill repute

perdonare [perdo'nare] /72/ VT **1** to forgive, pardon; **perdonare a qn qc/di aver fatto qc** to forgive sb (for) sth/for doing *o* having done sth; **mi perdoni?** will you forgive me?; **non gliel'ha mai perdonata** he has never forgiven him for that; **non glielo perdonerò mai** I'll never forgive him for that; **non me lo perdonerò mai** I'll never forgive myself **2** (*scusare*) to excuse, pardon; **perdona la domanda** if you don't mind my asking ...; **vogliate perdonare il (mio) ritardo** my apologies for being late; **perdona la mia ignoranza** forgive my ignorance ♦ VI (*aus avere*) to forgive; **un male che non perdona** an incurable disease; **un uomo che non perdona** an unforgiving man

perdono [per'dono] SM (*gen*) forgiveness; **chiedere perdono a qn (per)** to ask for sb's forgiveness (for); (*scusarsi*) to apologize to sb (for); **l'ho urtata?** **chiedo perdono** was that you I hit? I do beg your pardon *o* I do apologize; **perdono giudiziale** (*Dir*) pardon

perdurare [perdu'rare] /72/ VI (*aus avere*) (*continuare*) to go on, last; (*perseverare*: *aus essere*) to persist; **il cattivo tempo perdura** the bad weather continues; **perdurare nei propositi di vendetta** to persist in seeking revenge

perdutamente [perduta'mente] AVV desperately, passionately; **amare perdutamente qn** to be desperately in love with sb

perduto, -a [per'duto] PP *di* **perdere** ♦ AGG (*gen*) lost; **sentirsi** *o* **vedersi perduto** (*fig*) to realize the hopelessness of one's position

peregrinare [peregri'nare] /72/ VI (*aus avere*) to wander, roam

perenne [pe'renne] AGG (*Bot*) perennial; (*gloria, ricordo*) everlasting; **nevi perenni** perpetual snow *sg*

perentorio, -ria, -ri, -rie [peren'tɔrjo] AGG (*tono, ordine*) peremptory; (*definitivo*) final

perfettamente [perfetta'mente] AVV perfectly; **funziona perfettamente** it works perfectly; **sai perfettamente che...** you know perfectly well that ...

perfetto, -a [per'fetto] AGG (*gen*) perfect; (*silenzio, accordo*) complete, total; **è un perfetto cretino** he's an utter *o* a perfect idiot ♦ SM (*Gramm*) perfect (tense)

perfezionamento [perfettsjona'mento] SM (*vedi vb*): **perfezionamento (di)** perfection (of); improvement (in); **un corso di perfezionamento di inglese** a course to improve one's English

perfezionare [perfettsjo'nare] /72/ VT (*rendere perfetto*) to perfect; (*migliorare*) to improve; **perfezionarsi** VIP (*tecnica*) to improve; **perfezionarsi in inglese** to improve one's English

perfezione [perfet'tsjone] SF perfection; **alla** *o* **a perfezione** to perfection

perfezionismo [perfettsjo'nizmo] SM perfectionism

perfezionista, -i, -e [perfettsjo'nista] SM, SF perfectionist

perfidia [per'fidja] SF perfidy

perfido, -a ['perfido] AGG perfidious, treacherous

perfino [per'fino] AVV even; **perfino lui si è commosso** even he was moved; **è un peccato perfino pensarlo** you should be ashamed to even think of such a thing

perforare [perfo'rare] /72/ VT (*gen*) to pierce; (*banda, schede*) to punch; (*trivellare*) to drill; (*Med*) to perforate; **ulcera perforata** (*Med*) perforated ulcer

perforatore, -trice [perfora'tore] SM, SF (*Inform*: *persona*) punch-card operator ♦ SM (*macchina*) punch; **perforatore di schede** (*Inform*) card punch ♦ SF (*Tecn*) boring *o* drilling machine; (*Inform*) card punch

perforazione [perforat'tsjone] SF **1** (*di sottosuolo*) boring, drilling; (*Inform*: *atto*) punching; (: *foro*) punch **2** (*Med*) perforation

pergamena [perga'mena] SF parchment

pergola ['pergola] SF , **pergolato** [pergo'lato] SM pergola

pericolante [periko'lante] AGG (*muro, edificio*) unsafe; (*fig*: *economia*) shaky, precarious

pericolo [pe'rikolo] SM danger; **essere/trovarsi in pericolo** to be/find o.s. in danger; **mettere in pericolo** to endanger, put in danger; **essere fuori pericolo** to be out of danger; (*Med*) to be off the danger list; **"pericolo di morte"** (*su centralina elettrica*) ≈ "danger: high voltage"; **è un pericolo pubblico** (*fig*: *persona*) he's a public menace; **non c'è pericolo che rifiuti** (*iro*) there's no chance of his refusing, there's no fear that he'll refuse

pericoloso, -a [periko'loso] AGG (*gen*) dangerous; (*impresa*) hazardous, risky; **zona pericolosa** danger zone

periferia [perife'ria] SF (*anche fig*) periphery; (*di città*) outskirts *pl*, suburbs *pl*; **la periferia di Milano** the outskirts of Milan; **vivere in periferia** to live on the outskirts *o* on the edge of town; **vivo in periferia** I live on the edge of town

periferico, -a, -ci, -che [peri'feriko] AGG (*Anat, Inform*) peripheral; (*zona*) outlying

perifrasi [pe'rifrazi] SF INV circumlocution

perimetro [pe'rimetro] SM (*gen, anche Mat*) perimeter

periodico, -a, -ci, -che [peri'ɔdiko] AGG periodic(al); (*Mat*) recurring ♦ SM (*pubblicazione*) periodical

periodo [pe'riodo] SM (*gen*) period; **un periodo di tre anni** a period of three years; **durante il periodo elettorale** at election time; **durante il periodo estivo** during the summer (period); **periodo contabile** accounting period; **periodo di prova** trial period

peripezie [peripet'tsie] SFPL vicissitudes, ups and downs

periplo ['periplo] SM circumnavigation

perire [pe'rire] /55/ VI (*aus essere*) to perish, die

periscopio, -pi [peris'kɔpjo] SM periscope

perito, -a [pe'rito] SM (*esperto*) expert; (*Edil, Agr, Naut*) surveyor; (*Assicurazione*) loss adjuster; **è perito chimico/agrario** (*Scol*) he has a qualification *o* diploma in chemistry/agriculture ♦ AGG expert, skilled

peritonite [perito'nite] SF peritonitis

perizia [pe'rittsja] SF **1** (*maestria*) skill, ability; **un lavoro fatto con perizia** a skilful piece of work **2** (*Dir*: *giudizio tecnico*) expert opinion; (: *scritto*) expert's report; (: *stima*) appraisal, valuation; **perizia psichiatrica** psychiatrist's report

perizoma, -i [perid'dzɔma] SM (*di popolazioni primitive*) loincloth; (*indumento intimo*) thong; (*di spogliarellista*) G-string

perla ['perla] SF pearl; **una collana di perle** a pearl necklace; **Venezia, la perla dell'Adriatico** Venice, the jewel of the Adriatic; **una perla di marito** a gem of a husband; **perla coltivata** cultured pearl ♦ AGG INV (*colore*) pearl *attr*; **grigio perla** pearl grey

perlina [per'lina] SF bead

perlinato [perli'nato] SM matchboarding

perlomeno [perlo'meno] AVV (*almeno*) at least

perlopiù [perlo'pju] AVV (*quasi sempre*) in most cases, usually

perlustrare [perlus'trare] /72/ VT to patrol, reconnoitre

perlustrazione [perlustrat'tsjone] SF patrol, reconnaissance; **andare in perlustrazione** to go on patrol

permaloso, -a [perma'loso] AGG touchy ♦ SM, SF touchy person

permanente [perma'nente] AGG (*gen*) permanent; (*esercito, commissione*) standing ♦ SF (*acconciatura*) permanent wave, perm; **ha la permanente** she's got a perm; **farsi fare la permanente** to have one's hair permed; **mi sono fatta fare la permanente** I had my hair permed

permanenza [perma'nentsa] SF 1 (*presenza continua*) permanence 2 (*soggiorno*) stay, sojourn; **buona permanenza!** enjoy your stay!

permanere [perma'nere] /93/ VI IRREG (*aus* essere) (*rimanere*) to remain; **il cattivo tempo permane sulla Scozia** the bad weather conditions persist over Scotland

permango *ecc* [per'mango] VB *vedi* **permanere**

permasi *ecc* [per'masi] VB *vedi* **permanere**

permeabile [perme'abile] AGG permeable

permeare [perme'are] /72/ VT (*anche fig*): **permeare (di)** to permeate (with)

permesso, -a [per'messo] PP *di* **permettere** ♦ SM 1 (*autorizzazione*) permission; **chiedere il permesso di fare qc** to ask permission to do sth; **ho chiesto il permesso di uscire** I asked permission to leave the room *o* go out 2 (*Amm, Mil*) leave (of absence); **andare in permesso** to go on leave 3 (*documento*) permit, licence (*Brit*), license (*USA*); (*Mil*) pass; **permesso di lavoro** work permit; **permesso di soggiorno** residence permit

permettere [per'mettere] /63/ VT IRREG 1 (*gen, consentire*) to allow, permit; **permettere a qn di fare qc** (*autorizzare*) to allow *o* permit sb to do sth, let sb do sth; (*dare la possibilità*) to enable sb to do sth; (*dare il diritto*) to entitle sb to do sth; **crede che tutto gli sia permesso** he thinks he can do just as he likes; **i miei impegni non me lo permettono** I'm too busy to be able to do it; **non mi ha permesso di vederla** he didn't allow me to see her; **ci andremo, tempo permettendo** we'll go, weather permitting; **non permetto che mi si tratti così** I will not tolerate being treated in this way 2 **permettersi qc/di fare qc** (*concedersi*) to allow o.s. sth/to do sth; (*avere la possibilità*) to afford sth/to do sth; (*osare*) to dare (to) do sth; **non possono permettersi una casa più grande** they can't afford a bigger house; **non posso permettermi di perdere neanche un minuto** I can't afford to waste a minute; **come ti permetti?** how dare you? 3 (*fraseologia*): **è permesso?** (*posso entrare?*) may I come in?; **scusi, permesso...** (*posso passare?*) excuse me, can I get by *o* past?; **se permetti avrei un'obiezione** if you don't mind I have an objection to raise; **mi sia permesso di sottolineare che...** may I take the liberty of pointing out that ...; **permettete che mi presenti** let me introduce myself, may I introduce myself?

permisi *ecc* [per'mizi] VB *vedi* **permettere**

permissivo, -a [permis'sivo] AGG permissive

permuta ['permuta] SF (*Dir*) transfer; **valore di permuta** (*di macchina*) trade-in value; **accettare qc in permuta** to take sth as a trade-in

permutare [permu'tare] /72/ VT to exchange; (*Mat*) to permute

pernacchia [per'nakkja] SF (*fam*) raspberry; **fare una pernacchia** to blow a raspberry

pernice [per'nitʃe] SF partridge; **pernice bianca** ptarmigan

perno ['perno] SM (*anche fig*) pivot; **fare perno su qc** to pivot on sth

pernottamento [pernotta'mento] SM overnight stay

pernottare [pernot'tare] /72/ VI (*aus* avere) to spend the night, stay overnight

pero ['pero] SM (*Bot*) pear (tree)

però [pe'rɔ] CONG (*ma*) (and) yet, but (nevertheless); (*tuttavia*) nevertheless, however; **però non è giusto che...** and yet *o* but nevertheless it's not fair that ...; **però avresti potuto dirmelo** you could have told me nevertheless; **mi piace, però è troppo caro** I like it, but it's too expensive; **sono stanco, non tanto però da non poter finire** I'm tired, but not so tired as not to be able to finish

perorare [pero'rare] /72/ VT (*Dir, anche fig*): **perorare la causa di qn** to plead sb's case

perpendicolare [perpendiko'lare] AGG perpendicular ♦ SF (*Mat*) perpendicular (line)

perpendicolo [perpen'dikolo] SM: **a perpendicolo** perpendicularly

perpetrare [perpe'trare] /72/ VT to perpetrate, commit

perpetuare [perpetu'are] /72/ VT to perpetuate

perpetuo, -a [per'petuo] AGG (*gen*) perpetual; (*rendita*) life attr

perplessità [perplessi'ta] SF INV perplexity

perplesso, -a [per'plɛsso] AGG perplexed, puzzled; **lasciare qn perplesso** to perplex *o* puzzle sb

perquisire [perkwi'zire] /55/ VT to search; **all'aeroporto siamo stati perquisiti** we were searched at the airport

perquisizione [perkwizit'tsjone] SF search; **mandato di perquisizione** search warrant; **fare una perquisizione (di)** to carry out a search (of)

persecutore, -trice [perseku'tore] SM, SF persecutor

persecuzione [persekut'tsjone] SF persecution; **mania di persecuzione** (*Psic*) persecution complex

perseguibile [perse'gwibile] AGG (*reato*) prosecutable

perseguire [perse'gwire] /45/ VT 1 (*scopo, intento*) to pursue 2 (*Dir*) to prosecute

perseguitare [persegwi'tare] /72/ VT (*anche fig*) to persecute; **essere perseguitato dalla sfortuna** to be dogged by ill luck

perseverante [perseve'rante] AGG persevering

perseveranza [perseve'rantsa] SF perseverance

perseverare [perseve'rare] /72/ VI (*aus* avere) to persevere; **perseverare in qc/nel fare qc** to persevere in sth/in doing sth

persi *ecc* ['persi] VB *vedi* **perdere**

Persia ['persja] SF Persia

persiano, -a [per'sjano] AGG, SM, SF Persian ♦ SM 1 (*lingua*) Persian 2 (*Zool: gatto*) Persian (cat) 3 (*pelliccia*) Persian lamb

persico, -a, -ci, -che ['persiko] AGG: **il golfo Persico** the Persian Gulf; **pesce persico** perch

persino [per'sino] AVV = **perfino**

persistente [persis'tɛnte] AGG persistent

persistenza [persis'tentsa] SF persistence

persistere [per'sistere] /11/ VI IRREG (*aus* avere) to persist; **persistere in qc/a fare qc** to persist in sth/in doing sth; **persiste nella sua opinione** he is sticking to his opinion

persistito, -a [persis'tito] PP *di* **persistere**

perso, -a ['perso] PP *di* **perdere** ♦ AGG (*smarrito, anche fig*) lost; (*sprecato*) wasted; **questo è tempo perso** this is a waste of time; **fare qc a tempo perso** to do sth in one's spare time; **dipinge a tempo perso** she paints in her spare time; **perso per perso** I've (*o* we've *ecc*) got nothing left *o* more to lose; **andare perso** to get lost; **il libro è andato perso** the book got lost; **dare per perso** to give up for lost

persona [per'sona] SF 1 (*essere umano*) person; **una persona intelligente** an intelligent person; **persone** SFPL people *pl*; **c'erano molte persone** there were a lot of people; **tre persone** *o* persons (*USA*); **a/per persona** (*a testa*) per head *o* person, a head; **3 euro a persona** three euros a head; **per interposta persona** through a third party *o* an intermediary; **prima persona plurale** (*Gramm*) first person plural; **seconda persona singolare** (*Gramm*) second person singular; **persona giuridica** (*Dir*) legal person; **persona di servizio** domestic servant 2 (*corpo*): **aver cura della propria persona** to look after o.s.; **in persona, di persona** in person; **ci andrò di persona** I'll go there personally *o* in person; **è l'onestà in persona** he is honesty personified 3 (*Gramm*): **alla terza persona singolare** in the third person singular; **vivere qc in prima persona** (*fig*) to experience sth personally 4 (*qualcuno*): **una persona** somebody, someone; **c'era una persona che ti cercava** somebody was looking for you

personaggio, -gi [perso'naddʒo] SM 1 (*celebrità*) personage; (*persona ragguardevole*) personality; (*scherz: individuo*) character, individual; **un importante personaggio politico** an important political figure 2 (*di romanzo*) character; (*di quadro*) figure; **i personaggi del romanzo** the characters in the novel

personale [perso'nale] AGG personal ♦ SF (*mostra*) one-man (*o* one-woman) exhibition ♦ SM 1 (*complesso di dipendenti*) personnel, staff; **il personale dell'azienda** the staff of the company; **ufficio personale** personnel office; **personale di terra** (*Aer*) ground personnel 2 (*corpo, figura*) build; **un bel personale** a lovely figure

personalità [personali'ta] SF INV (*gen*) personality; **ha una forte personalità** he's got a strong personality; **personalità giuridica** (*Dir*) legal status; **personalità multipla** (*Psic*) multiple personality

personalizzare [personalid'dzare] /72/ vt (arredamento, stile) to personalize; (auto, accessorio) to customize

personalizzato, -a [personalid'dzato] AGG (vedi vb) personalized; customized

personalmente [personal'mente] AVV personally

personificare [personifi'kare] /20/ vt (rappresentare) to personify; (simboleggiare) to embody

personificazione [personifikat'tsjone] SF (vedi vb) personification; embodiment; **essere la personificazione della gentilezza** to be kindness itself

perspicace [perspi'katʃe] AGG discerning, shrewd

perspicacia [perspi'katʃa] SF perspicacity, shrewdness

persuadere [persua'dere] vb IRREG /88/ vt to persuade, convince; **persuadere qn di qc/a fare qc** to persuade o convince sb of sth/to do sth; **lasciarsi persuadere** to let o.s. be convinced; **ne sono persuaso** I'm quite sure o convinced (of it); **persuadersi** vr to convince o.s.

persuasione [persua'zjone] SF (gen) persuasion; (credenza) conviction, belief

persuasivo, -a [persua'zivo] AGG persuasive, convincing

persuaso, -a [persu'azo] PP di **persuadere**

pertanto [per'tanto] CONG (quindi) therefore, so

pertica, -che ['pertika] SF (bastone) pole, rod; (Sport) pole; (fig: persona alta e magra) beanpole

pertinace [perti'natʃe] AGG pertinacious

pertinente [perti'nente] AGG: **pertinente (a)** pertinent (to), relevant (to); **un'osservazione pertinente** a pertinent remark

pertinenza [perti'nentsa] SF 1 (attinenza) pertinence, relevance 2 (competenza): **essere di pertinenza di qn** to be sb's business; **è di pertinenza del tribunale di Napoli** it comes under the jurisdiction of the Naples courts

pertosse [per'tosse] SF (Med) whooping cough

pertugio, -gi [per'tudʒo] SM opening, hole

perturbare [pertur'bare] /72/ vt (persona) to upset, disturb, perturb; **perturbarsi** VIP to become o get upset

perturbazione [perturbat'tsjone] SF (Meteor, Astron) disturbance

Perù [pe'ru] SM Peru

perugino, -a [peru'dʒino] AGG of o from Perugia ♦ SM, SF inhabitant o native of Perugia

peruviano, -a [peru'vjano] AGG, SM, SF Peruvian

pervadere [per'vadere] /52/ vt IRREG to pervade, permeate

pervaso, -a [per'vazo] PP di **pervadere**

pervenire [perve'nire] /128/ vi IRREG (aus essere) 1 **pervenire a** to reach, arrive at, come to; **far pervenire qc a qn** to have sth sent to sb; **ci sono pervenute migliaia di lettere** we have received thousands of letters 2 (venire in possesso): **gli pervenne una fortuna** he inherited a fortune

pervenuto, -a [perve'nuto] PP di **pervenire**

perversione [perver'sjone] SF perversion

perversità [perversi'ta] SF INV perversity

perverso, -a [per'verso] AGG perverted

pervertire [perver'tire] /55/ vt to pervert

pervertito, -a [perver'tito] AGG perverted ♦ SM, SF pervert

pervicace [pervi'katʃe] AGG stubborn, obstinate

pervicacia [pervi'katʃa] SF stubbornness, obstinacy

pervinca, -che [per'vinka] SF (Bot) periwinkle ♦ SM INV (colore) periwinkle (blue)

p.es. ABBR (= per esempio) e.g.

pesa ['pesa] SF (azione) weighing no pl; (luogo) weigh-house; (apparecchiatura: per merci) weighing machine; (: per autoveicoli) weighbridge; (: per animali) cattle-weighing platform

pesante [pe'sante] AGG (gen) heavy; (cibo) heavy, rich; (sonno) heavy, deep; (droga) hard; (fig: stile) ponderous; (: battuta) crass; (noioso: conferenza) dull, boring; (: persona) tedious, boring; **quella valigia è troppo pesante** that suitcase is too heavy; **questo libro è pesante** (fig) this book is heavy going; **il film era un po' pesante** I found the film rather heavy going; **ho gli occhi pesanti** I can't keep my eyes open; **è andata giù pesante** (ha esagerato) she was rather heavy-handed; **avere l'alito pesante** to have bad breath; **atletica pesante** weightlifting and wrestling; **droghe pesanti** hard drugs; **gioco pesante** (Sport)

physical game; **terreno pesante** (Sport: per pioggia) water-logged pitch

pesantezza [pesan'tettsa] SF (anche fig) heaviness; **avere pesantezza di stomaco** to feel bloated

pesapersone [pesaper'sone] AGG INV, SF INV: **(bilancia) pesapersone** (weighing) scales pl; (automatica) weighing machine

pesare [pe'sare] /72/ vt to weigh; (fig: valutare) to weigh (up); **pesare i pro e i contro** to weigh up the pros and cons; **pesare le parole** to weigh one's words; **pesarsi** to weigh o.s. ♦ vi (aus avere) 1 (avere un peso) to weigh; (essere pesante) to be heavy; (fig) to carry weight; **quanto pesi?** how much do you weigh?; **come pesa!** it weighs a ton!; **l'ho già pesato** I've already weighed it; **pesare sulla coscienza/sullo stomaco** to lie heavy on one's conscience/on one's stomach; **tutta la responsabilità pesa su di lui** all the responsibility rests on his shoulders; **la responsabilità gli pesa** the responsibility weighs heavy on him 2 (dispiacere): **mi pesa partire** I don't want to leave; **mi pesa dirti di no** I regret having to say no to you; **mi pesa sgridarlo** I find it hard to scold him; **è una situazione che mi pesa** it's a difficult situation for me 3 (contare) to carry weight, count; **il suo parere pesa molto** his opinion counts for a lot o carries a lot of weight

pesca¹, -sche ['peska] SF (frutto) peach

pesca² ['peska] SF 1 (Sport) fishing; **andare a pesca** to go fishing; **pesca con la lenza** angling; **pesca subacquea** underwater fishing 2 (pesce pescato) catch; **avete fatto una buona pesca?** did you get a good catch? 3 (lotteria): **pesca di beneficenza** lucky dip

pescaggio, -gi [pes'kadd3o] SM (Naut) draught (Brit), draft (USA)

pescare [pes'kare] /20/ vt (essere pescatore di) to fish for; (prendere) to catch; (molluschi) to gather; (recuperare qc nell'acqua) to fish out; (fig: trovare) to get hold of, find; **ti insegnerò a pescare** I'll teach you how to fish; **ho pescato un pesce enorme** I caught an enormous fish; **pescare nel torbido** (fig) to fish in troubled waters; **ma dove le vai a pescare queste idee?** where on earth do you get hold of such ideas?; **dove hai pescato questo cappello?** where on earth did you get that hat?; **l'hanno pescato le mani nel sacco** they caught him red-handed ♦ vi (aus avere) (Naut) to draw

pescatore [peska'tore] SM fisherman; (con lenza) angler; **un paesino di pescatori** a fishing village

pesce ['peʃʃe] SM 1 fish (gen inv): **c'erano molti pesci** there were a lot of fishes; **ho pescato due pesci** I caught two fish; **ti piace il pesce?** do you like fish? 2 (Astrol): **Pesci** SMPL Pisces; **essere dei Pesci** to be Pisces 3 (Tip) omission 4 (fraseologia): **sano come un pesce** as fit as a fiddle; **buttarsi a pesce su un'offerta** to jump at an offer; **sentirsi un pesce fuor d'acqua** to feel like a fish out of water; **prendere qn a pesci in faccia** to treat sb like dirt; **non saper che pesci prendere** not to know which way to turn; **hanno preso solo i pesci piccoli** they only caught the small fry; **chi dorme non piglia pesci** (Proverbio) the early bird catches the worm ♦ **pesce d'aprile** April Fool; **pesce azzurro** mackerel, sardines and anchovies; **pesce gatto** catfish; **pesce martello** hammerhead; **pesce ragno** weever; **pesce rosso** goldfish; **pesce spada** swordfish

pescecane [peʃʃe'kane] SM (pl pescecani o pescicani) (Zool) shark; (fig: profittatore) shark, profiteer

peschereccio, -a, -ci, -ce [peske'rettʃo] SM fishing boat

pescheria [peske'ria] SF fishmonger's (shop) (Brit), fish shop

pescherò ecc [peske'rɔ] VB vedi **pescare**

peschiera [pes'kjera] SF fish farm, fishery

pescivendolo, -a [peʃʃi'vendolo] SM, SF fishmonger (Brit), fish merchant (USA); (negozio) fishmonger's (shop) (Brit), fish shop (USA); **andare dal pescivendolo** to go to the fishmonger's

pesco, -schi ['pesko] SM (Bot) peach (tree)

pescoso, -a [pes'koso] AGG teeming with fish

peseta [pe'zeta] SF peseta

peso ['peso] SM 1 (gen) weight; **comprare a peso** to buy by weight; **rubare sul peso** to give short weight; **eccesso di peso** excess weight; **metter su peso** to put on weight;

piegarsi sotto il peso di (*sogg: trave*) to bend under the weight of; **lo portarono via di peso** they carried him away bodily; **avere due pesi e due misure** (*fig*) to have double standards; **peso lordo** gross weight; **peso morto** dead load *o* weight; **peso netto** net weight; **peso specifico** (*Fis*) specific gravity **2** (*fig: onere*) weight; **il peso degli anni** the weight of years; **avere un peso sullo stomaco** to have something lying heavy on one's stomach; **mi sono liberato di un peso** (*preoccupazione*) that's a load off my mind; **togliersi un peso dalla coscienza** to take a load off one's conscience; **essere di peso a qn** to be a burden to sb; **non voglio essere di peso a nessuno** I don't want to be a burden to anybody; **piegarsi sotto il peso di** (*dispiaceri, problemi*) to be weighed down by **3** (*fig: importanza*) weight, importance; **una questione di un certo peso** a matter of some weight *o* importance; **dar peso a qc** to attach importance to sth; **non ho dato molto peso alle sue parole** I didn't attach much importance to his words **4** (*Sport*) shot; **lancio del peso** putting the shot, the shot put; **sollevamento pesi** weightlifting; **fare pesi** to do weight training; **peso gallo** bantamweight; **peso massimo** heavyweight; **peso medio** middleweight; **peso mosca** flyweight; **peso piuma** featherweight

pessimismo [pessi'mizmo] SM pessimism

pessimista, -i, -e [pessi'mista] AGG pessimistic ♦ SM, SF pessimist

pessimo, -a ['pessimo] AGG *superl di* **cattivo 1** (*gen*) awful, dreadful, very bad; **abbiamo fatto un pessimo viaggio** we had a dreadful *o* an awful *o* an appalling journey; **c'è un pessimo odore in questa stanza** there's an awful *o* a dreadful smell in this room; **ha fatto un tempo pessimo** the weather has been dreadful; **è un pessimo insegnante** he is a very bad teacher; **di pessima qualità** of very poor quality, very shoddy; **essere di pessimo umore** to be in a foul *o* a terrible mood; **hai un pessimo aspetto** *o* **una pessima cera** you look awful *o* dreadful; **quello scherzo è di pessimo gusto** that joke is in very bad taste **2** (*molto riprovevole*) very wicked, nasty

pestare [pes'tare] /72/ VT **1** (*calpestare*) to tread on, trample on; **pestare un piede a qn** to tread on sb's foot; **pestare i piedi** to stamp one's feet; **pestare i piedi a qn** (*dare fastidio*) to tread on sb's toes; **pestare qn** (*picchiarlo*) to beat sb up **2** (*frantumare: uva, aglio*) to crush; (*: pepe*) to grind

peste ['peste] SF (*Med*) plague; (*fig: persona*) pest, nuisance; **sei una peste!** you're a pest!; **dire peste e corna di qn** to tear sb to bits

pestello [pes'tello] SM pestle

pesticida, -i [pesti't∫ida] SM pesticide

pestifero, -a [pes'tifero] AGG (*anche fig*) pestilential, pestiferous; (*odore*) noxious

pestilenza [pesti'lɛntsa] SF (*peste*) plague, pestilence; (*fetore*) stench

pesto, -a ['pesto] AGG: **occhio pesto** black eye; **avere gli occhi pesti** (*per la stanchezza*) to have bags under one's eyes; **era buio pesto** it was pitch-black ♦ SM (*Culin*) pesto, *sauce made with basil, garlic, cheese and oil*

petalo ['petalo] SM petal

petardo [pe'tardo] SM firecracker, banger (*Brit*); (*Ferr*) detonator, torpedo (*USA*)

petizione [petit'tsjone] SF (*Dir*) petition; **fare una petizione a** to petition

peto ['peto] SM: **fare un peto** to break wind

petrodollaro [petro'dollaro] SM petrodollar

petrolchimica [petrol'kimika] SF petrochemical industry

petroliera [petro'ljera] SF (*nave*) (oil) tanker (*ship*)

petroliere [petro'ljere] SM **1** (*industriale*) oilman **2** (*tecnico*) worker in the oil industry

petroliero, -a [petro'ljero] AGG oil *attr*

petrolifero, -a [petro'lifero] AGG (*industria, pozzo*) oil *attr*; **l'industria petrolifera** the oil industry

petrolio [pe'trɔljo] SM oil, petroleum; (*per lampada, fornello*) paraffin (*Brit*), kerosene (*USA*); **lume a petrolio** oil *o* paraffin *o* kerosene lamp; **petrolio grezzo** crude oil

❑ **petrolio** non si traduce mai con la parola inglese *petrol*

pettegolare [pettego'lare] /72/ VI (*aus avere*) to gossip

pettegolezzo [pettego'leddzo] SM gossip *no pl*, piece of gossip; **non mi piacciono i pettegolezzi** I don't like gossip; **sono solo pettegolezzi** it's just gossip; **vuoi sentire un pettegolezzo?** do you want to hear a bit of gossip?; **fare pettegolezzi** to gossip

pettegolo, -a [pet'tegolo] AGG gossipy; **è pettegolo di carattere** he is given to gossip ♦ SM, SF gossip; **Lucia è una pettegola** Lucia is a bit of a gossip

pettinare [petti'nare] /72/ VT (*capelli*) to comb; (*tessuto*) to comb, tease; **le ho pettinato con cura i capelli** I combed her hair carefully; **pettinarsi** VR to comb one's hair, do one's hair; **ti sei pettinata?** have you combed your hair?

pettinatura [pettina'tura] SF **1** (*acconciatura*) hairstyle, hairdo **2** (*di tessuto*) carding, combing

pettine ['pettine] SM **1** comb **2** (*Zool*) scallop

pettirosso [petti'rosso] SM robin

petto ['petto] SM **1** (*Anat*) chest; (*seno*) breast, bust; **ho un dolore al petto** I've got a pain in my chest; **battersi** *o* **picchiarsi il petto** to beat one's breast; **prendere qn/qc di petto** to face up to sb/sth; **giacca a doppio petto** double-breasted jacket **2** (*Culin: di pollo*) breast; **punta di petto** (*carne bovina*) brisket **3** (*Mus*): **voce di petto** chest voice

pettorale [petto'rale] AGG, SM pectoral

pettorina [petto'rina] SF (*di grembiule*) bib

pettoruto, -a [petto'ruto] AGG (*uomo*) broad-chested; (*donna*) full-breasted

petulante [petu'lante] AGG insolent

petunia [pe'tunja] SF petunia

pezza ['pettsa] SF **1** (*rotolo di tessuto*) bolt of cloth **2** (*toppa*) patch; (*cencio*) rag, cloth; **ha una pezza sui pantaloni** he has a patch on his trousers; **bambola di pezza** rag doll; **mettere una pezza su qc** (*vestito, camera d'aria*) to patch sth; **trattare qn come una pezza da piedi** to treat sb like a doormat **3** (*Amm*): **pezza d'appoggio** *o* **giustificativa** voucher

pezzato, -a [pet'tsato] AGG piebald ♦ SM (*anche:* **cavallo pezzato**) piebald (horse)

pezzente [pet'tsɛnte] SM, SF (*accattone*) beggar, wretch; (*fig: tirchio*) miser

pezzo ['pettso] SM **1** (*gen*) piece; (*brandello, frammento*) piece, bit; **un pezzo di pane** a piece of bread; **ne vuoi ancora un pezzo?** (*di torta, pane*) would you like a bit more *o* another piece?; **ci ha accompagnato per un bel pezzo di strada** he came quite a long way with us; **andare in pezzi** to shatter; **fare a pezzi qc** to pull sth to pieces; **andare a pezzi** to break into pieces; **essere a pezzi** (*oggetto*) to be in pieces *o* bits; (*fig: persona*) to be shattered; **ho lavorato tutto il giorno e sono a pezzi** I've been working all day and I'm shattered; **ha i nervi a pezzi** his nerves are shattered **2** (*oggetto, negli scacchi*) piece; (*Mil*) gun; **da vendersi al pezzo** to be sold separately *o* individually; **2 euro al pezzo** 2 euros each *o* apiece; **un due pezzi** (*costume*) a bikini; **un servizio da 24 pezzi** (*piatti*) a 24-piece dinner service **3** (*di macchina, arnese*) part; **ha cambiato un pezzo** he's replaced a part; **smontare qc pezzo per pezzo** to dismantle sth piece by piece *o* bit by bit; **pezzo di ricambio** spare part **4** (*brano: Mus*) piece; (*: scritto*) piece, passage; (*: Stampa*) article; **pezzo di cronaca** (*Stampa*) report; **pezzo forte** pièce de résistance **5** (*tempo*): **da un pezzo** for a while; **è qui da un pezzo** he has been here for a while; **resterà per un bel pezzo** he'll stay for quite a long time; **è un pezzo che non lo vedo** I haven't seen him for a while; **aspettare un pezzo** to wait quite a while *o* some time **6** (*fraseologia*): **un pezzo grosso** a big shot, a bigwig; **un (bel) pezzo d'uomo** a fine figure of a man; **essere tutto d'un pezzo** to be a man of integrity

PG SIGLA = **Perugia** ♦ [pi'dʒi] SIGLA M = **procuratore generale**

pH [pi'akka] SIGLA M (*Chim*) pH

PI SIGLA = **Pisa** ♦ ABBR (= *Pubblica Istruzione*) *vedi* **istruzione**

piaccio *ecc* ['pjatt∫o] VB *vedi* **piacere²**

piacente [pja't∫ɛnte] AGG attractive

piacere¹ [pja't∫ere] /74/ SM **1** (*gen*) pleasure; **i piaceri della vita** the pleasures of life; **fare qc per il piacere di farlo** to do sth for the sake of doing it; **ho il piacere di annunciare che...** it gives me great pleasure to tell you that ...; **mi fa piacere per lui** I'm pleased for him; **è un piacere averti qui** it's a pleasure to have you here; **che piacere vederti!** how nice to see you!; **piacere!, è un piacere conoscerla** pleased to meet you; **mi farebbe piacere rivederlo** I would like to see him again; **se ti fa piacere** if you like; **con piacere** with pleasure, certainly; **fare qc con piacere** to be happy *o* glad to do sth; **ho saputo con piacere che ti sposi** I was delighted to hear you're getting married; **un viaggio di piacere** a pleasure trip; **è un viaggio d'affari o di piacere?** is this trip for business or for pleasure?; **potevi averne a piacere** (*volontà*) you could take as many as you wanted; **tanto piacere!** (*iro*) so what? **2** (*favore*) favour (*Brit*), favor (*USA*); **fare un piacere a qn** to do sb a favo(u)r; **mi faresti un piacere?** would you do me a favo(u)r?; **mi fai il piacere di smetterla?** would you kindly stop that?; **per piacere** please; **per piacere, potresti...?** could you please ...?; **su, mangia la minestra, fammi il piacere** come on, eat your soup like a good boy (*o* girl); **ma fammi il piacere!** for heaven's sake!

piacere² [pja'tʃere] /74/ vi IRREG (*aus* essere) (*persona*): **piacere a qn** to be liked by sb; **mi piace** (*lavoro, film*) I like *o* enjoy it; (*progetto*) it suits me; (*sport, attività*) I enjoy it; **quei ragazzi non mi piacciono** I don't like those boys; **mi piace molto questo quadro** I like this picture very much; **non credo gli piaccia** I don't think he likes it; **mi piace di più così** I like it better this way; **un gusto che piace** a pleasant *o* agreeable flavour; **il suo discorso è piaciuto molto** his speech was well received; **che ti piaccia o no, ti piaccia o non ti piaccia** whether you like it or not; **che cosa ti piacerebbe fare?** what would you like to do?, what do you fancy doing?; **gli piacerebbe andare al cinema** he would like to go to the cinema; **mi sarebbe piaciuto andarci** I would have liked to go; **fa' come ti pare e piace** do as you please *o* like; **a Dio piacendo** God willing

piacevole [pja'tʃevole] AGG pleasant, nice, agreeable

piacimento [pjatʃi'mento] SM: **a piacimento** (*a volontà*) as much as one likes, at will; **lo farà a suo piacimento** he'll do it when it suits him

piaciuto, -a [pja'tʃuto] PP *di* piacere²

piacqui *ecc* [pi'akkwi] VB *vedi* piacere²

piaga, -ghe [pi'aga] SF **1** (*Med*) sore; (*ferita, o fig*) wound; (*fig: flagello*) scourge, curse; **mettere un dito sulla piaga** to touch a sore point; **rigirare il coltello nella piaga** to twist the knife (in the wound); **le piaghe d'Egitto** the plagues of Egypt; **piaghe da decubito** bedsores **2** (*fig: pegg: persona*) nuisance, pain in the neck, pest

piagnisteo [pjaɲis'teo] SM whining, whimpering

piagnucolare [pjaɲɲuko'lare] /72/ VI (*aus* avere) to whine, whimper

piagnucolio, -lii [pjaɲɲuko'lio] SM whimpering, whining

piagnucoloso, -a [pjaɲɲuko'loso] AGG whiny, whimpering, moaning

pialla ['pjalla] SF (*arnese*) plane

piallare [pjal'lare] /72/ VT to plane

piallatrice [pjalla'tritʃe] SF planing machine

piana ['pjana] SF stretch of level ground; (*più estesa*) plain

pianeggiante [pjaned'dʒante] AGG flat, level

pianerottolo [pjane'rɔttolo] SM landing

pianeta, -i [pja'neta] SM (*Astron*) planet

piangere ['pjandʒere] VB IRREG /75/ VI (*aus* avere) (*gen*) to cry, weep; (*occhi*) to water; **piangere di gioia** to weep for joy; **piangere a calde lacrime** to cry one's heart out; **mi piange il cuore** (*iro*) my heart bleeds; **mi piange il cuore a buttare via tanta roba** I hate having to throw away so much stuff; **è inutile piangere sul latte versato** it's no use crying over spilt milk ♦ VT **1** to weep **2** (*lamentare*) to bewail, lament; **piangere la morte di qn** to mourn sb's death; **sta sempre piangendo miseria** he's always claiming he has no money

pianificare [pjanifi'kare] /20/ VT to plan

pianificazione [pjanifikat'tsjone] SF (*Econ*) planning; **pianificazione aziendale** corporate planning; **pianificazione familiare** family planning

pianista, -i, -e [pja'nista] SM, SF pianist; (*Pol*) *deputy who votes on behalf of absent colleagues by pressing the voting buttons*

piano¹, -a ['pjano] AGG **1** (*piatto*) flat, level; (*senza asperità*) smooth; (*Mat*) plane *attr*; **geometria piana** plane geometry; **corsa piana** (*Sport*) flat race **2** (*facile*) straightforward, simple; (*chiaro*) clear, plain ♦ AVV (*lentamente*) slowly; (*con cautela*) carefully, slowly; (*a basso volume o voce*) softly, quietly;

la macchina andava piano the car was travelling slowly; **vai piano!** (*in macchina*) drive slowly!; **vacci piano!** (*fig: non esagerare: nel bere*) take it easy with that!; (*: nelle minacce*) calm down!; (*: nel lodarsi*) come off it!; **attento, fai piano!** (*fa' meno rumore*) don't make so much noise!; (*sta' attento*) watch out!, be careful!; **parla più piano** (*lentamente*) speak more slowly; (*a bassa voce*) lower your voice, keep your voice down; **pian piano** (*lentamente*) very slowly; (*poco a poco*) little by little; **pian piano** *o* **pian piano siamo arrivati** slowly but surely we got there; **pian pianino** *o* **pian piano ha acquistato una certa esperienza** he gradually acquired experience ♦ SM **1** (*Geom*) level, plane; (*superficie*) top, surface; (*fig: livello*) level, plane; (*Geog: pianura*) plain; **mettere tutto sullo stesso piano** to lump everything together, give equal importance to everything; **quei due alunni sono sullo stesso piano** those two pupils are at the same level *o* are on a par; **piano inclinato** inclined plane; **piano di lavoro** (*in cucina*) worktop; **piano stradale** road surface **2** (*di edificio*) floor, storey (*Brit*), story (*USA*); (*di autobus*) deck; **una casa di 3 piani** a 3-storey (*Brit*) *o* 3-storied (*USA*) house; **abito al terzo piano** I live on the third floor; **al piano di sopra/di sotto** on the floor above/below; **all'ultimo piano** on the top floor; **al piano terra** on the ground floor (*Brit*) *o* first floor (*USA*); **un autobus a due piani** a double-decker (bus) **3** (*Fot, Cine, Arte*): **primo piano** foreground; **secondo piano** background; **in primo/secondo piano** in the foreground/background; **una figura in primo piano** a figure in the foreground; **fare un primo piano** to take a close-up; **in primissimo piano** right in the foreground; **di primo piano** (*fig*) prominent, high-ranking; **uno scrittore di primo piano** a major author; **mettere qc in secondo piano** to consider sth of secondary importance; **un fattore di secondo piano** a secondary *o* minor factor; **passare in secondo piano** (*questione*) to become less important

piano² ['pjano] SM (*progetto: anche Mil*) plan; (*: industriale*) design; (*: programma*) work plan; **un piano di pace** a peace plan; **facciamo un piano** let's draw up a plan; **non era nei nostri piani** we hadn't intended to do it, we hadn't planned on doing so; **tutto va secondo i piani** everything's going according to plan ♦ **piano di battaglia** (*Mil*) battle plan; **piano di guerra** (*Mil*) plan of campaign; **piano regolatore** (*Urbanistica*) town-planning scheme; **piano di studi** (*Univ*) study programme (*Brit*) *o* program (*USA*), study plan; **piano di volo** (*Aer*) flight plan

piano³ ['pjano] SM (*Mus*) piano

pianoforte [pjano'fɔrte] SM piano, pianoforte

pianoterra [pjano'terra] SM INV ground floor (*Brit*), first floor (*USA*); **al pianoterra** on the ground *o* first floor

piansi *ecc* ['pjansi] VB *vedi* piangere

pianta ['pjanta] SF **1** (*Bot*) plant; **pianta d'appartamento** house plant; **pianta grassa** succulent (plant) **2** (*Anat: anche: pianta del piede*) sole (of the foot) **3** (*disegno*) plan; (*cartina topografica*) map, plan; **una pianta della città** a map of the city; **pianta stradale** street map *o* plan **4** (*fraseologia*): **l'ha inventato di sana pianta** he made the whole thing up; **in pianta stabile** on the permanent staff

piantagione [pjanta'dʒone] SF plantation

piantagrane [pjanta'grane] SM INV, SF INV troublemaker

piantare [pjan'tare] /72/ VT **1** (*pianta*) to plant, put in; **ho piantato un albero in giardino** I've planted a tree in the garden **2** **piantare (in)** (*chiodo*) to hammer in(to), knock in(to); (*paletto*) to drive in(to); (*ago*) to stick in(to); **piantare una tenda** to put up a tent, pitch a tent; **piantare grane** to cause trouble **3** (*fig: lasciare: moglie, figli*) to leave, abandon, desert; **ha piantato il suo ragazzo** she's dumped her boyfriend; **piantare qn in asso** to leave sb in the lurch; **mi ha piantata in asso** he left me in the lurch; **piantala!** stop it!, cut it out!; **piantarsi** VR (*persona*): **mi si piantò davanti, si piantò davanti a me** he planted himself in front of me; **piantarsi** VIP (*proiettile*): **piantarsi in** to enter; **mi si è piantata una scheggia nel dito** I've got a splinter in my finger

piantato, -a [pjan'tato] AGG: **ben piantato** (*persona*) well-built

piantatore [pjanta'tore] SM (*persona*) planter

pianterreno [pjanter'reno] SM ground floor (*Brit*), first floor (*USA*)

piantina [pjan'tina] SF **1** (*di edificio, città*) (small) map **2** (*Bot*) (small) plant

pianto, -a ['pjanto] PP *di* **piangere** ♦ SM crying, weeping, tears *pl*; **scoppiò in un pianto dirotto** she burst into tears; **è uno che ha il pianto facile** he cries easily

piantonare [pjanto'nare] /72/ VT to guard, watch over

piantone [pjan'tone] SM **1** (*soldato*) orderly; (*vigilante*) sentry, guard **2** (*Aut*) steering column

pianura [pja'nura] SF (*Geog*) plain

piastra ['pjastra] SF **1** (*di metallo*) sheet, plate; (*di cemento, pietra*) slab; (*Elettr, Fot: di rivestimento*) plate; (*di cucina*) hotplate; **piastra di registrazione** tape deck **2** (*moneta*) piastre

piastrella [pjas'trella] SF tile

piastrellare [pjastrel'lare] /72/ VT to tile

piastrina [pjas'trina] SF **1** (*Anat*) platelet **2 piastrina di riconoscimento** (*Mil*) name tag, identity disc (*Brit*) *o* tag (*USA*)

piattaforma [pjatta'forma] SF (*pl* **piattaforme**) (*gen, anche fig: Pol*) platform; (*per tuffi*) board; **piattaforma continentale** (*Geog*) continental shelf; **piattaforma girevole** (*Tecn*) turntable; **piattaforma di lancio** (*Mil*) launch(ing) pad; **piattaforma rivendicativa** *document setting out claims of the unions in an industry*

piattello [pjat'tello] SM **1** (*bersaglio*) clay pigeon; **tiro al piattello** clay-pigeon shooting, skeet shooting, trapshooting **2** (*Sci: di skilift*) disc

piattino [pjat'tino] SM (*di tazza*) saucer

piatto, -a ['pjatto] AGG (*gen*) flat; (*fig: scialbo*) flat, dreary, dull; **questa zona è più piatta** this area is flatter; **piatto come una tavola** as flat as a pancake ♦ SM **1** (*recipiente*) dish, plate; (*quantità*) plate(ful); **metti più pasta nel mio piatto** put more pasta on my plate; **lavo io i piatti** I'll wash the dishes; **un piatto di minestra** a plate *o* bowl of soup; **piatto fondo** soup plate *o* dish; **piatto da frutta** side plate; **piatto piano** dinner plate; **piatto di portata** serving dish **2** (*Culin: portata*) course; **primo/secondo piatto** first/second course; **un piatto tipico spagnolo** a traditional Spanish dish; **piatto forte** main course; **piatto freddo** cold dish (*meat, cheese, pickles ecc*); **piatto del giorno** dish of the day, plat du jour; **piatti già pronti** ready-cooked dishes **3** (*Tecn*) plate; **piatto della bilancia** scale pan; **piatto del giradischi** turntable **4** (*Mus*); **piatti** SMPL cymbals **5** (*parte piana*) flat (part)

piazza ['pjattsa] SF **1** (*Archit*) square; (*Comm*) market; **piazza San Marco** St Mark's Square; **piazza del mercato** market place; **scendere in piazza** (*dimostrare*) to take to the streets, demonstrate; **gli operai sono scesi in piazza** the workers took to the streets; **vendere sulla pubblica piazza** to sell in the market place; **fare piazza pulita** to make a clean sweep; **mettere in piazza** (*rendere pubblico*) to make public **2** (*Mil*): **piazza** parade ground **3** (*di letto, lenzuolo*): **a una piazza** single *attr*; **a due piazze** double *attr* **4 Piazza Affari** *the Italian stock exchange in Milan*

piazzaforte [pjattsa'forte] SF (*pl* **piazzeforti**) (*Mil*) fortified town; (*fig*) stronghold

piazzale [pjat'tsale] SM (*piazza*) (large) square; (*di autostrada, stazione*) service area

piazzamento [pjattsa'mento] SM (*Sport*) place, placing

piazzare [pjat'tsare] /72/ VT **1** (*mettere: gen*) to place, put; (: *colpo*) to land, place **2** (*Comm: vendere*) to place, sell, market; **piazzarsi** VR **1** (*Sport*) be placed; **piazzarsi bene** to finish with the leaders *o* in a good position; **piazzarsi male** to do badly (in a race) **2** (*fig: piantarsi*): **si è piazzato di fronte a me** he planted himself in front of me

piazzista, -i, -e [pjat'tsista] SM, SF (*Comm*) travelling salesperson

piazzola [pjat'tsola] SF **1** (*Aut*) lay-by (*Brit*), (roadside) stopping place **2** (*Mil*) (gun) emplacement **3** (*di tenda*) pitch

picca, -che ['pikka] SF (*arma*) pike; **picche** SFPL spades; **rispondere picche a qn** (*fig*) to give sb a flat refusal

piccante [pik'kante] AGG (*sapore*) spicy, hot; (*fig: sconcio: barzelletta*) risqué, racy; (: *dettaglio*) titillating, juicy; **è molto piccante?** is it very hot?; **a me piace più piccante** I like it hotter

piccarsi [pik'karsi] /20/ VIP **1** (*pretendere*): **piccarsi di fare qc** to pride o.s. on one's ability to do sth **2** (*impermalirsi*): **piccarsi per qc** to take offence (*Brit*) *o* offense (*USA*) at sth

picchettaggio, -gi [pikket'taddʒo] SM picketing

picchettare [pikket'tare] /72/ VT **1** (*piantare paletti*) to stake out **2** (*fare picchettaggio*) to picket

picchetto [pik'ketto] SM **1** (*paletto*) stake, peg **2** (*Mil*) picket; **essere di picchetto** to be on picket duty; **ufficiale di picchetto** orderly officer **3** (*di scioperanti*) picket

picchiare [pik'kjare] /19/ VT **1** (*persona: colpire*) to hit, strike; (: *dar botte a*) to beat (up), thrash; **è lui che mi ha picchiato!** it was him who hit me!; **lo picchiarono selvaggiamente** they gave him a savage beating; **picchiare qn a sangue** to beat sb black and blue **2** (*battere*) to beat; (*sbattere*) to bang, knock; **picchiare i pugni sul tavolo** to bang *o* beat one's fists on the table; **ho picchiato la testa contro il muro** I banged my head against *o* on the wall ♦ VI (*aus* avere) **1** (*bussare*) to knock; (*con forza*) to bang; **picchiare alla porta di qn** to knock at *o* on sb's door; **qualcuno picchiava alla porta** somebody was knocking at the door **2** (*colpire*) to hit, strike; **ha picchiato sodo** he hit out hard; **il sole picchiava forte** the sun was beating down; **picchiare in testa** (*Aut*) to knock; **picchia e ripicchia** by dint of perseverance

picchiata [pik'kjata] SF **1** (*bussata*) knock; (*più forte*) bang; (*percosse*) beating, thrashing **2** (*Aer*) (nose-)dive; **scendere in picchiata** to (nose-)dive

picchiettare [pikkjet'tare] /72/ VI (*aus* avere) (*gen*) to tap; (*pioggia*) to patter ♦ VT (*punteggiare*) to spot, dot, fleck; (*colpire*) to tap

picchio, -chi ['pikkjo] SM (*Zool*) woodpecker; **picchio muratore** nuthatch

piccino, -a [pit'tʃino] AGG little, tiny, (very) small ♦ SM, SF (*bambino*) small child, little boy (girl); **è uno spettacolo per grandi e piccini** the show is suitable for all ages

picciolo [pit'tʃɔlo] SM (*Bot*) stalk

piccionaia [pittʃo'naja] SF **1** pigeon loft **2** (*soffitta*) loft **3** (*Teatro: loggione*): **la piccionaia** the gods *sg* (*Brit*), the gallery

piccione [pit'tʃone] SM pigeon; **prendere due piccioni con una fava** to kill two birds with one stone; **piccione viaggiatore** carrier pigeon

picco, -chi ['pikko] SM (*cima*) peak, summit; (*valore più alto: in diagramma*) peak; **a picco** vertically; **una roccia a picco sul mare** a sheer cliff; **colare a picco** (*Naut, anche fig*) to sink

piccolezza [pikko'lettsa] SF **1** (*dimensione*) smallness; (*fig: grettezza*) meanness, pettiness **2** (*fig: inezia*) trifle; **è inutile che ti arrabbi per delle piccolezze simili** there's no point in getting annoyed over such trifles

piccolo, -a ['pikkolo] AGG **1** (*oggetto, misura*) small; (*vezzeggiativo*) little; **ho una macchina molto piccola** I have a very small car; **me ne dia uno più piccolo** give me a smaller one; **qual è la stanza più piccola della casa?** which is the smallest room in the house?; **una piccola casetta in campagna** a little house in the country; **è piccolo di statura** he is small, he is of small stature; **è più piccolo di me** he is smaller than me; **com'è piccolo il mondo!** it's a small world! **2** (*giovane*) young, small, little; (*vezzeggiativo*) little; **un bambino piccolo** a little boy; **è ancora troppo piccolo** he's still too young; **bambini piccoli** young children; **mio fratello più piccolo** my younger *o* little brother; **Paolo è il più piccolo dei fratelli** Paolo is the youngest of the brothers **3** (*di poco conto: difetto*) slight; (: *regalo*) little; (: *dettaglio*) minor **4** (*breve: viaggio, lettera*) short **5** (*modesto*) small; (*fig: pegg: meschino*) petty, mean; **piccolo possidente** smallholder; **la piccola borghesia** the lower middle-classes *pl*; (*pegg*) the petty bourgeoisie; **farsi piccolo** (*umile*) to make o.s. small, to cower ♦ SM, SF (*bambino*) (small) child, small boy (girl); (*vezzeggiativo*) little one; **da piccolo** as a child; **da piccola ero molto timida** I was very shy as a child ♦ SM **1 in piccolo** in miniature; **mi sembra il Colosseo in piccolo** it's like a miniature version of the Colosseum; **nel mio piccolo** in my own small way **2** (*di animale*): **piccoli** SMPL young *pl*; **la gatta e i suoi piccoli** the cat and her kittens; **la volpe e i suoi piccoli** the vixen and her young *o* cubs

piccone [pik'kone] SM pick, pickaxe (*o* pickax)

piccozza [pik'kɔttsa] SF ice axe (*o* ice ax)

picnic [pik'nik] SM INV picnic; **fare un picnic** to have a picnic

pidiessino, -a [pidies'sino] AGG (*Pol*) *o* belonging to the P.D.S. (*successor to Italian communist party*) ♦ SM, SF (*Pol*) member *o* supporter of the P.D.S.

pidocchio, -chi [pi'dɔkkjo] SM 1 (*Zool*) louse; **pieno di pidocchi** crawling with lice 2 (*fig: persona gretta*) mean person

pidocchioso, -a [pidok'kjoso] AGG 1 (*infestato*) lousy, full of lice 2 (*fig: taccagno*) mean, stingy, tight

piduista, -i, -e [pidu'ista] AGG P2 *attr* (*masonic lodge*) ♦ SM *member of the P2 masonic lodge*

piè [pjɛ] **a ogni piè sospinto** (*fig*) at every step; **saltare a piè pari** (*omettere*) to skip; **a piè di pagina** at the foot of the page; **note a piè di pagina** footnotes

piede ['pjede] SM 1 (*gen*) foot; **mi fanno male i piedi** my feet are sore; **a piedi nudi** barefoot; **avere i piedi piatti** to have flat feet, be flat-footed; **essere o stare in piedi** to stand, be standing; **stava in piedi in un angolo** he was standing in a corner; **alzarsi in piedi** to get to one's feet, stand up; **andare a piedi** to walk; **ci andrò a piedi** I'll walk; **essere a piedi** to be on foot; **rimanere a piedi** to be without transport; **ai piedi della montagna/del letto** at the foot o bottom of the mountains/of the bed; **da capo a piedi** from head to foot, from top to bottom 2 (*di mobile*) leg; (*di lampada*) base 3 **piede di porco** (*Tecn*) crowbar; (*per forzare serrature*) jemmy (*Brit*), jimmy (*USA*); (*Culin*) pig's trotter 4 (*Poesia*) foot 5 (*fraseologia*): **avere tutti ai propri piedi** to have the world at one's feet; **essere sul piede di guerra** to be ready for action; **fare qc con i piedi** to do sth badly; **ragionare con i piedi** to reason like a fool; **fuori dai piedi!** get out of the way!; **levarsi o togliersi dai piedi** to get out from under sb's feet; **tra i piedi** in the way; **è sempre tra i piedi** he's always in the way; **a piede libero** (*Dir*) on bail; **io non ci ho mai messo piede** I've never set foot in there; **mettere i piedi in testa a qn** to walk all over sb; **mettere qn sotto i piedi** to push sb around; **mettere qc in piedi** (*azienda*) to set sth up; **prendere piede** (*teoria, tendenza*) to gain ground, catch on; **puntare i piedi** to dig one's heels in; **sentirsi mancare la terra sotto i piedi** to feel completely lost; **su due piedi** (*rispondere, accettare*) on the spot, at once; **tenere in piedi** (*persona*) to keep on his (o her) feet; **tra i piedi** (*persona*) to keep going; **non sta in piedi** (*persona*) he can't stand; (*fig: scusa*) it doesn't hold water

piedipiatti [pjedi'pjatti] SM INV, SF INV (*fam: poliziotto*) cop

piedistallo [pjedis'tallo], **piedestallo** [pjedes'tallo] SM (*anche fig*) pedestal

piega, -ghe ['pjega] SF 1 (*gen, anche Geol*) fold; (*Cucito: di gonna*) pleat; (*: di pantaloni*) crease; (*: grinza*) wrinkle, crease; (*della pelle*) (skin) fold; **è tutto pieno di pieghe** (*spiegazzato*) it's all creased; **prendere una brutta o cattiva piega** (*fig: persona*) to get into bad ways; (*: situazione*) to take a turn for the worse; **non fa una piega** (*fig: ragionamento*) it's faultless; **non ha fatto una piega** (*fig: persona*) he didn't bat an eye(lid) (*Brit*) o an eye(lash) (*USA*) (*acconciatura*) set; **farsi (fare) la messa in piega** to have one's hair set

piegamento [pjega'mento] SM 1 (*vedi vt*) folding; bending 2 (*Ginnastica*): **piegamento sulle gambe** kneebend

piegare [pje'gare] /80/ VT 1 (*ripiegare: vestito, tovagliolo, foglio*) to fold (up); (*: sedia, tavola*) to fold up; **piega la cartina e mettila via** fold the map and put it away 2 (*curvare: ramo, schiena, braccia*) to bend; **piegare il capo di fronte a qn** (*fig*) to bow to sb; **piegare qn alla propria volontà** to bend sb to one's will; **piegarsi** VR (*curvarsi: persona*) to bend (over); (*fig: cedere*): **piegarsi (a)** to yield (to), submit (to); **piegarsi in due dalle risate/dal dolore** to double up with laughter/with pain; **piegarsi** VIP (*asse, superficie*) to sag; (*sedia, tavolo*) to fold (up)

piegatura [pjega'tura] SF (*vedi vt*) 1 folding *no pl*; bending *no pl* 2 (*piega*) fold; bend

piegherò ecc [pjege'rɔ] VB *vedi* **piegare**

pieghettare [pjeget'tare] /72/ VT to pleat

pieghevole [pje'gevole] AGG 1 (*ripiegabile: porta, sedia*) folding 2 (*flessibile*) pliable, bendable, flexible; (*fig*) pliable, yielding, docile

Piemonte [pje'monte] SM Piedmont

piemontese [pjemon'tese] AGG, SM, SF Piedmontese

piena ['pjena] SF 1 (*di corso d'acqua*) flood, spate; **essere in piena** to be in flood o in spate; **il fiume è in piena** the river is in flood 2 (*fig: calca*) crowd, throng

pienezza [pje'nettsa] SF fullness

pieno, -a ['pjeno] AGG 1 (*gen*) full; (*giornata, vita*) full, busy; **pieno di** (*gen*) full of; (*idee*) bursting with; (*macchie*)

covered in o with; **la mia valigia è piena** my suitcase is full; **una borsa piena di libri** a bag full of books; **un bicchiere pieno d'acqua** a glass full of water o filled with water; **avere la pancia piena** to be full; **il cinema era pieno zeppo (di gente)** the cinema was packed; **luna piena** full moon 2 (*completo: successo, fiducia*) total, complete; **a tempo pieno** full-time; **cerco un lavoro a tempo pieno** I'm looking for a full-time job; **avere pieni poteri** to have full powers; **nel pieno possesso delle sue facoltà** in full possession of his faculties 3 (*muro, mattone*) solid 4 (*fraseologia*): **a piene mani** abundantly; **è una persona che dà a piene mani** he (o she) is very generous; **a pieni voti** (*eleggere*) unanimously; **laurearsi a pieni voti** *to graduate with full marks*; **pieno di sé** full of oneself, self-important; **essere pieno di lavoro** to have a lot of work to do; **essere in piena forma** to be in top form; **pieno come un uovo** full to overflowing; **in pieno** (*completamente: sbagliare*) completely; (*: colpire, centrare*) bang o right in the middle; **in pieno giorno** in broad daylight; **in pieno inverno** in the depths of winter; **in piena notte** in the middle of the night; **in piena stagione** at the height of the season ♦ SM 1 **fare il pieno (di benzina)** (*Aut*) to fill up (with petrol (*Brit*) o gas (*USA*)); **il pieno, per favore** fill her up, please 2 (*colmo*) height, peak; **arrivò nel pieno della festa** he arrived when the party was in full swing

pienone [pje'none] SM: **c'era un tale pienone a teatro!** the theatre was packed!

piercing ['pirsin(g)] SM piercing; **farsi il piercing all'ombelico** to have one's navel pierced

pietà [pje'ta] SF INV (*gen*) pity, compassion; (*Rel*) piety; **non voglio la vostra pietà** I don't want your pity; **sentire o provare pietà per qn** to pity sb, feel pity for sb; **avere pietà di** (*compassione*) to pity, feel pity for; (*misericordia*) to have pity o mercy on; **muovere qn a pietà** to move sb to pity; **senza pietà** (*agire*) ruthlessly; (*persona*) pitiless, ruthless; **far pietà** to arouse pity; (*pegg*) to be terrible o awful; **come pianista fa pietà** he's a terrible o an awful pianist

pietanza [pje'tantsa] SF course, dish

pietoso, -a [pje'toso] AGG 1 (*che prova pietà*) compassionate, pitying 2 (*che fa pietà*) pitiful; **uno spettacolo pietoso** a pitiful sight; **essere ridotto in uno stato pietoso** to be reduced to a pitiful o sorry state; **ho fatto una figura pietosa** I made an awful fool of myself

pietra ['pjetra] SF stone; **di pietra** stone *attr*; **una casa di pietra** a stone house; **avere un cuore di pietra** to be hard-hearted; **porre la prima pietra** (*fondare*) to set up; **scagliare la prima pietra** to cast the first stone; **mettiamoci una pietra sopra** let bygones be bygones ♦ **pietra dura** semiprecious stone; **pietra focaia** flint(stone); **pietra di paragone** (*fig*) touchstone; **pietra pomice** pumice stone; **pietra preziosa** precious stone, gem; **pietra dello scandalo** cause of scandal

pietraia [pje'traja] SF (*mucchio*) pile of stones; (*terreno*) stony ground; (*cava*) stone quarry

pietrificare [pjetrifi'kare] /20/ VT to petrify; (*fig*) to petrify, transfix, paralyze; **pietrificarsi** VIP (*anche fig*) to be petrified, be turned to stone

pietrina [pje'trina] SF (*per accendino*) flint

pietrisco, -schi [pje'trisko] SM crushed stone; road metal

pieve ['pjeve] SF parish church

piffero ['piffero] SM (*Mus*) pipe, fife

pigiama, -i [pi'dʒama] SM pyjamas *pl* (*Brit*), pajamas *pl* (*USA*); **questo pigiama mi è un po' stretto** these pyjamas are a bit tight on me; **essere in pigiama** to be in one's pyjamas; **sei ancora in pigiama?** are you still in your pyjamas?

pigia pigia ['pidʒa 'pidʒa] SM INV throng, crowd, press

pigiare [pi'dʒare] /62/ VT (*pulsante*) to press; (*uva*) to tread

pigiatrice [pidʒa'tritʃe] SF (*macchina*) wine press

pigione [pi'dʒone] SF rent

pigliare [piʎ'ʎare] /27/ VT (*fam*) = **prendere**

piglio [piʎ'ʎo] SM (*aspetto*) look, countenance, expression

pigmento [pig'mento] SM pigment

pigmeo, -a [pig'mɛo] AGG, SM, SF pigmy

pigna ['piɲɲa] SF (*Bot*) pine cone

pignoleria [piɲɲole'ria] SF fastidiousness, fussiness

pignolo, -a [piɲˈɲɔlo] AGG pernickety, fussy; **è più pignolo di me** he's fussier than me ♦ SM, SF fussy person

pignorare [piɲɲoˈrare] /72/ VT (Dir) to distrain

pigolare [pigoˈlare] /72/ VI (aus avere) to cheep, chirp

pigolio, -lii [pigoˈlio] SM cheeping no pl, chirping no pl

pigramente [pigraˈmente] AVV lazily

pigrizia [piˈgrittsja] SF laziness; **non l'ho fatto per pigrizia** I didn't do it out of laziness

pigro, -a [ˈpigro] AGG (persona) lazy, idle; (fig: mente) slow, dull; (andatura) lazy; (stomaco) sluggish; **è il ragazzo più pigro che abbia mai conosciuto** he's the laziest boy I've ever known; **in un pigro pomeriggio d'agosto** on a lazy August afternoon

PIL [pil] SIGLA M (= Prodotto Interno Lordo) GDP (= Gross Domestic Product)

pila [ˈpila] SF 1 (mucchio) pile 2 (Elettr) battery; **una pila di libri** a pile of books; **a pila, a pile** battery-operated; **funziona a pile** it works on batteries; **pila atomica** nuclear reactor 3 (fam: torcia) torch (Brit), flashlight (spec USA)

pilastro [piˈlastro] SM (Archit) pillar, pilaster; (Alpinismo) pillar; (fig: sostegno) pillar, mainstay

pile [ˈpail] SM INV (materiale, maglia) fleece

pillola [ˈpillola] SF (pill); **la pillola (anticoncezionale)** the pill; **prendere la pillola** to be on the pill; **pillola del giorno dopo** morning-after pill

pilone [piˈlone] SM 1 (di linea elettrica) pylon; (di ponte) pier 2 (Rugby) prop

pilota, -i, -e [piˈlɔta] SM, SF (Naut, Aer) pilot; (Aut) driver; **secondo pilota** co-pilot; **pilota automatico** automatic pilot ♦ AGG INV pilot attr

pilotaggio [piloˈtaddʒo] SM: **cabina di pilotaggio** flight deck

pilotare [piloˈtare] /72/ VT (Aer, Naut) to pilot; (Aut) to drive

piluccare [pilukˈkare] /20/ VT to nibble at; **smettila di piluccare** stop nibbling (at) your food

pimento [piˈmento] SM pimento, allspice

pimpante [pimˈpante] AGG lively, full of beans

pinacoteca, -che [pinakoˈteka] SF art gallery

pineta [piˈneta] SF pinewood, pine forest

ping-pong [ping ˈpɔng] SM INV table tennis

pingue [ˈpingwe] AGG (grasso) fat, corpulent; (fertile) rich, fertile; (fig: abbondante: guadagno) huge

pinguedine [pinˈgwedine] SF (adiposità) fatness, corpulence

pinguino [pinˈgwino] SM 1 (Zool) penguin 2 (gelato) chocolate-coated ice cream on a stick

pinna [ˈpinna] SF 1 (di pesce) fin; (di cetacei) flipper 2 (per nuotare) flipper 3 (Naut) stabilizer; (Aer) fin 4 (Anat): **pinna nasale** ala of the nose

pinnacolo [pinˈnakolo] SM pinnacle

pino [ˈpino] SM (albero) pine (tree); (legno) pine(wood); **pino silvestre o di Scozia** Scots pine

pinolo [piˈnɔlo] SM (seme) pine kernel

pinta [ˈpinta] SF pint

pinza [ˈpintsa] SF 1 (gen) pliers pl; (tanaglia) pincers pl; (molle) tongs pl 2 (Med) forceps pl 3 (di granchio) pincer

pinzette [pinˈtsette] SFPL tweezers

pio, pia, pii, pie [ˈpio] AGG (devoto) pious, devout; (misericordioso: opere, istituzione) charitable, charity attr

pioggerella [pjoddʒeˈrella] SF drizzle

pioggia, -ge [ˈpjoddʒa] SF 1 rain; **sorpreso dalla pioggia** caught in the rain; **sotto la pioggia** in the rain; **pioggia fine** drizzle; **pioggia scrosciante** driving rain; **pioggia acida** acid rain 2 (fig: di regali, fiori) shower; (di insulti) hail

piolo [piˈɔlo] SM peg, stake; (di scala) rung; **un piolo rotto** a broken rung; **scala a pioli** ladder

piombare¹ [pjomˈbare] /72/ VI (aus essere) 1 (cadere) to fall heavily; **piombare su** (sogg: tigre, leone) to pounce on; (: rapaci) to swoop down on; (: esercito nemico) to swoop down on, pounce on; **il falco piombò sulla preda** the hawk swooped (down) on its prey; **gli sono piombati addosso** they swooped down on him, they pounced on him; **piombò nella più cupa disperazione** he plunged o sank into blackest despair; **piombare a terra** to crash to the ground; **piombare nel vuoto** to fall downwards 2 (arrivare) to arrive

unexpectedly, turn up; **è piombato qui alle 2 di mattina** he turned up here at 2 in the morning

piombare² [pjomˈbare] /72/ VT (pacco) to seal (with lead); (dente) to fill

piombatura [pjombaˈtura] SF 1 vedi **piombare²** sealing; filling 2 (sigillo) seal; (di dente) filling

piombino [pjomˈbino] SM (sigillo) (lead) seal; (Pesca) sinker (weight); (del filo a piombo) plummet

piombo [ˈpjombo] SM 1 (metallo) lead; (Pesca) sinker; (Tip) type; (sigillo) (lead) seal; (proiettile) (lead) shot; **di piombo** (tubo) lead attr; (fig: cielo) leaden; **soldatino di piombo** tin soldier; **senza piombo** (benzina) unleaded, lead-free; **gli anni di piombo** era of terrorist outrages 2 (fraseologia): **gli a piombo** (muro) plumb; (cadere) straight down; **non essere a piombo** to be out of plumb; **cadere di piombo** to fall suddenly; **andare con i piedi di piombo** to tread carefully; **avere/sentirsi addosso una cappa di piombo** to have/feel a great weight on one's shoulders; **riempire qn di piombo** to fill sb with lead ♦ AGG INV (colore) leaden, lead-coloured; **grigio piombo** lead grey

pioniere, -a [pjoˈnjere] SM, SF pioneer

pioppo [ˈpjɔppo] SM poplar; **pioppo bianco** white poplar; **pioppo nero** black poplar; **pioppo tremolo** aspen, trembling poplar

piovano, -a [pjoˈvano] AGG: **acqua piovana** rainwater

piovere [ˈpjɔvere] /76/ VB IMPERS to rain; **piove** it's raining; **piove a dirotto o a catinelle** it's pouring (buckets); **mi piove in casa** the rain comes in through my roof; **su questo non ci piove** (fig: fam) there's no doubt about it ♦ VI IRREG (aus essere) (scendere dall'alto) to rain down; (fig: lettere, regali) to pour in; (: persona: arrivare all'improvviso) to turn up, arrive unexpectedly

piovigginare [pjoviddʒiˈnare] /72/ VB IMPERS to drizzle

piovosità [pjovosiˈta] SF INV (Meteor) rainfall

piovoso, -a [pjoˈvoso] AGG rainy, wet

piovra [ˈpjovra] SF octopus

piovve ecc [ˈpjovve] VB vedi **piovere**

pipa [ˈpipa] SF pipe; (quantità di tabacco) pipe(ful); **fumare la pipa** to smoke a pipe

pipì [piˈpi] SF INV (fam) wee(-wee), pee; **fare (la) pipì** to have a pee, have a wee(-wee)

pipistrello [pipisˈtrello] SM 1 (Zool) bat 2 (mantello) cloak

piramide [piˈramide] SF pyramid; **a piramide** pyramid-shaped

piranha [piˈraɲa] SM INV piranha

pirata, -i [piˈrata] SM pirate; (fig: ladro) swindler, shark; **pirata dell'aria** hijacker; **pirata informatico** hacker; **pirata della strada** hit-and-run driver ♦ AGG INV pirate attr; **una cassetta pirata** a pirate tape

Pirenei [pireˈnɛi] SMPL: **i Pirenei** the Pyrenees

piretro [piˈretro] SM (Bot) pyrethrum

pirico, -a, -ci, -che [ˈpiriko] AGG: **polvere pirica** gunpowder

pirite [piˈrite] SF pyrite

piroetta [piroˈetta] SF pirouette

pirofilo, -a [piˈrɔfilo] AGG heat-resistant

piroga, -ghe [piˈrɔga] SF dugout (canoe)

piromane [piˈrɔmane] SM, SF pyromaniac, arsonist

piroscafo [piˈrɔskafo] SM steamship, steamer

Pisa [ˈpisa] SF Pisa

pisano, -a [piˈsano] AGG Pisan, of o from Pisa ♦ SM, SF inhabitant o native of Pisa

pisciare [piʃˈʃare] /14/ VI (aus avere) (fam) to piss

piscina [piʃˈʃina] SF (swimming pool); (pubblica, comunale) (swimming) baths pl; **piscina coperta** indoor swimming pool; **piscina scoperta** open-air o outdoor swimming pool

pisello [piˈsello] SM (Bot) pea; (fam: pene) willie (Brit), peter (USA)

pisolino [pizoˈlino] SM nap, snooze; **fare un pisolino** to have a nap

pista [ˈpista] SF 1 (traccia) track, trail; **siamo su una buona pista** we are on the right track; **la polizia sta seguendo una pista** the police are following a lead; **pista!** get out of the way! 2 (Radio) (sound)track; (Inform) track; **registrato a doppia pista** double-tracked 3 (di circo) ring; (di stadio) track; (Sci) (ski) run, piste; (Pattinaggio) rink; (Ippica) course;

(*Aer*) runway; **i corridori erano in pista** the runners were on the track ♦ **pista artificiale** (*Sci*) dry ski slope; **pista (da ballo)** (dance) floor; **pista ciclabile** cycle track; **pista da fondo** (*Sci*) (cross-country) trail; **pista di lancio** launch(ing) pad; **pista per principianti** (*Sci*) nursery slope; **pista di rullaggio** (*Aer*) taxiway; **pista di volo** (*Aer*) runway

pistacchio, -chi [pisˈtakkjo] SM (*albero*) pistachio (tree); (*seme*) pistachio (nut)

pistillo [pisˈtillo] SM (*Bot*) pistil

pistola [pisˈtɔla] SF pistol, gun; **sotto la minaccia della pistola** at gunpoint; **pistola ad acqua** water pistol; **pistola automatica** automatic (pistol); **pistola a spruzzo** (*per vernice*) spray gun; **pistola a tamburo** revolver

pistone [pisˈtone] SM (*Tecn*) piston; (*Mus*) valve

pitocco, -a, -chi, -che [piˈtɔkko] AGG mean, stingy ♦ SM, SF miser, skinflint

pitone [piˈtone] SM python

pittima [ˈpittima] SF (*fig: persona*) bore

pittore, -trice [pitˈtore] SM, SF 1 (*artista*) painter 2 (*imbianchino*) (house) painter, decorator

pittoresco, -a, -schi, -sche [pittoˈresko] AGG (*veduta, paesaggio*) picturesque; (*modo di parlare*) colourful, vivid

pittorico, -a, -ci, -che [pitˈtɔriko] AGG pictorial, painting *attr*, of painting

pittura [pitˈtura] SF 1 (*arte*) painting; (*dipinto*) painting, picture; **la pittura astratta** abstract painting; **pittura murale** mural 2 (*vernice*) paint; **pittura fresca** wet paint

pitturare [pittuˈrare] /72/ VT to paint; **pitturarsi le labbra** to put on lipstick; **pitturarsi le unghie** to paint one's nails; **pitturarsi** VR (*fam: truccarsi*) to make o.s. up, put on make-up

---

PAROLA CHIAVE

più [pju] AVV

1 (*tempo: usato al negativo*): **non... più** no longer, no more, not ... any more; **non lavora più** he doesn't work any more, he no longer works; **non ha detto una parola** he didn't say another word; **non c'è più bisogno che...** there's no longer any need for ...; **non riesco più a sopportarla** I can't stand her any more *o* any longer; **non ne posso più!** I can't take any more!; **non ritornerò mai più** I'll never come back; **non è più così giovane** he is not as young as he was

2 (*quantità: usato al negativo*): **non...più** no more; **non abbiamo più vino/soldi** we have no more wine/money, we haven't got any wine/money (left); **non ce n'è più** there isn't any left; **non ce n'è quasi più** there's hardly any; **non c'è più nessuno** there's no one left; **non c'è più niente da fare** there's nothing else to do, there's nothing more to be done

3 (*uso comparativo*) more, (*aggettivo corto*) +...er; **più bello** more beautiful; **più elegante** smarter, more elegant; **parla più forte!** speak up!; **e chi più ne ha, più ne metta!** and so on and so forth!; **è più furbo che capace** he's cunning rather than able; **è più che intelligente** he's clever to say the least; **noi lavoriamo più di loro** we work more *o* harder than they do; **mi piace più di ogni altra cosa al mondo** I like it better *o* more than anything else in the world; **non guadagna più di me** he doesn't earn any more than me; **è più intelligente di te** he is more intelligent than you (are); **è più povero di te** he is poorer than you (are); **cammina più veloce di me** he walks more quickly than me *o* than I do; **non ce n'erano più di 15** there were no more than 15; **ha più di 70 anni** she is over 70; **è a più di 10 km da qui** it's more than *o* over 10 km from here; **più di uno gli ha detto che...** several people have told him that ...; **si fa sempre più difficile** it is getting more and more difficult; **due volte più grande del mio** twice as big as mine

4 **di più, in più,** more; **ne voglio di più** I want some more; **3 ore/litri di più che** 3 hours/litres more than; **una volta di più** once more; **ci sono 3 persone in più** there are 3 more *o* extra people; **mi ha dato 3 pacchetti in più** he gave me 3 more *o* extra packets; (*troppi*) he gave me 3 packets too many; **e in più fa anche...** and in addition to *o* on top of that he also ...

5 (*uso superlativo*) most, (*aggettivo corto*) +...est; **la più bella del mondo** the most beautiful in the world; **il più bravo di tutta la classe** the best in the class; **il più veloce di tutti** the fastest of all; **è ciò che ho di più caro** it's the thing I

hold dearest; **è quello che mi piace di più** it's the one I like the most *o* best; **ciò che mi ha colpito di più** the thing that struck me most; **fare qc il più in fretta possibile** to do sth as quickly as possible; **è il programma che guardo più spesso** it's the programme I watch most often

6 (*Mat*) plus; **2 più 2 fa 4** 2 plus 2 equals 4; **più due** (*gradi*) plus two, two degrees above freezing *o* above zero

7 (*fraseologia*): **a più non posso** as much as possible; **urlava a più non posso** she was shouting at the top of her voice; **al più presto** as soon as possible; **al più tardi** at the latest; **più che altro** above all; **più che mai** more than ever; **chi più chi meno hanno tutti contribuito** everybody made a contribution of some sort; **più o meno** more or less; **avrà più o meno 30 anni** he must be about 30; **sarò lì più o meno alle 4** I'll be there about 4 o'clock; **minuto più minuto meno** give or take a minute; **né più né meno** no more, no less; **né più né meno come sua madre** just like her mother; **e per di più** (*inoltre*) and what's more, moreover; **tanto più che non sai neppure parlare l'inglese** all the more so as you can't even speak English

♦ AGG

1 (*comparativo*) more; (*superlativo*) the most; **chi ha più voti di tutti?** who has the most votes?; **più gente viene meglio è** the more the merrier; **ci sono più macchine** there are more cars; **ci vuole più sale** it needs more salt

2 (*molti, parecchi*) several; **abbiamo discusso per più ore** we argued for several hours

♦ PREP plus; **i genitori, più i figli** parents plus *o* and their children

♦ SM INV

1 (*Mat*) plus (sign)

2 (*la parte maggiore*): **il più** the most; **ottenere il più possibile** to get the best possible; **tutt'al più** *o* **al più possiamo andare al cinema** if the worst comes to the worst we can always go to the cinema; **il più delle volte** more often than not, generally; **il più ormai è fatto** the worst is over, most of it is already done; **parlare del più e del meno** to talk about this and that; **per lo più** = **perlopiù**

3 **i più** the majority; **i più pensano così** most people think so; **la reazione dei più** the reaction of the majority

piucheperfetto [piukkeperˈfetto] SM past perfect (tense), pluperfect (tense)

piuma [ˈpjuma] SF (*di uccello*) feather; (*ornamento*) feather, plume; **piume** SFPL down *sg*; (*piumaggio*) plumage, feathers *pl*; **leggero/morbido come una piuma** light/soft as a feather; **guanciale di piume** feather pillow; **cappello con le piume** plumed hat

piumaggio [pjuˈmaddʒo] SM plumage, feathers *pl*

piumino [pjuˈmino] SM (*per letto*) eiderdown; (*tipo danese*) duvet, continental quilt (*Brit*); (*giacca*) quilted jacket *o* down jacket (*with goose-feather padding*); (*per cipria*) powder puff; (*per spolverare*) feather duster

piuttosto [pjutˈtosto] AVV 1 (*preferibilmente*) rather; **prenderei piuttosto un'acqua minerale** I'd rather have some mineral water; **piuttosto che** (*anziché*) rather than; **piuttosto che studiare farebbe di tutto** he'd do anything rather than study; **qui piove in primavera piuttosto che in autunno** here it rains in the spring rather than *o* instead of in the autumn; **piuttosto la morte!** I'd rather die! 2 (*alquanto*) quite, rather; **fa piuttosto freddo** it's rather *o* fairly cold; **sono piuttosto stanco** I'm quite *o* rather tired; **siamo piuttosto indietro con il lavoro** we're rather *o* somewhat behind with the work

piva [ˈpiva] SF: **tornarsene con le pive nel sacco** (*fig*) to return empty-handed

pivello, -a [piˈvello] SM, SF (*fam*) greenhorn

pizza [ˈpittsa] SF 1 (*Culin*) pizza; (*fig: persona o cosa noiosa*) bore; **che pizza!** what a bore! 2 (*Cine*) reel

pizzeria [pittseˈria] SF pizzeria (*place where pizzas are made, sold o eaten*)

pizzicagnolo, -a [pittsiˈkaɲɲolo] SM, SF delicatessen owner

pizzicare [pittsiˈkare] /20/ VT 1 (*stringere*) to nip; (*con pinze*) to pinch; (*pungere: sogg: ape*) to sting; (: *zanzara, pulce*) to bite; (: *sostanza*) to sting; **gli ho pizzicato un braccio** I pinched his arm; **ha un sapore che ti pizzica la gola** the taste makes your mouth tingle; **mi sono pizzicato un dito**

I've nipped my finger; **mi sono pizzicato un dito nella porta** I caught my finger in the door **2** (*fig: acciuffare*) to nab, pinch; (*fig: rubare*) to pinch **3** (*Mus*) to pluck ♦ VI (*aus avere*) **1** (*prudere*) to itch, be itchy; **mi pizzica il naso** my nose is itching **2** (*essere piccante*) to be spicy, be hot

pizzicheria [pittsike'ria] SF (*negozio*) delicatessen

pizzico, -chi ['pittsiko] SM (*pizzicotto*) pinch, nip; (*piccola quantità*) pinch, dash; (*puntura: di ape, vespa*) sting; (: *di zanzara*) bite; **un pizzico di sale** a pinch of salt; **non ha un pizzico di pudore** he hasn't an ounce of common decency

pizzicotto [pittsi'kɔtto] SM pinch, nip

pizzo ['pittso] SM **1** (*merletto*) lace **2** (*barbetta*) goatee (beard) **3** (*cima*) peak **4** (*tangente*) protection money

placare [pla'kare] /20/ VT (*persona*) to calm down, pacify; (*desiderio*) to placate, assuage; (*dolore, eccitazione*) to soothe; (*coscienza*) to salve; (*scrupoli*) to allay; **placare la fame** to satisfy one's hunger; **placare la sete** to quench one's thirst; **placare gli animi** to appease the crowd; **placarsi** VIP (*rivolta, tempesta*) to die down; (*persona*) to calm down

placca, -che ['plakka] SF **1** (*gen, anche Elettr*) plate; (*con iscrizione*) plaque **2** (*Med: anche:* **placca dentaria**) (dental) plaque **3** (*Culin*): **placca da forno** baking sheet

placcare [plak'kare] /20/ VT **1** to plate; **placcato in oro/argento** gold-/silver-plated **2** (*Rugby*) to tackle, bring down

placenta [pla'tʃɛnta] SF placenta

placidità [platʃidi'ta] SF calm, peacefulness

placido, -a ['platʃido] AGG (*persona*) placid, calm; (*acque, vento, sera*) calm

plafoniera [plafo'njɛra] SF ceiling light

plagiare [pla'dʒare] /62/ VT **1** (*copiare*) to plagiarize **2** (*Dir: influenzare*) to coerce

plagio, -gi ['pladʒo] SM **1** (*di opera*) plagiarism **2** (*Dir*) duress

plaid [plɛd] SM INV (*travelling*) rug (*Brit*), lap robe (*USA*)

planare [pla'nare] /72/ VI (*aus avere*) (*Aer*) to glide; (*Naut*) to skim

plancia, -ce ['plantʃa] SF **1** (*Naut*) bridge; (*passerella*) gangway **2** (*Aut: cruscotto*) dashboard

plancton ['plankton] SM INV plankton

planetario, -ria, -ri, -rie [plane'tarjo] AGG planetary ♦ SM **1** (*Astron: locale*) planetarium **2** (*Aut*) crown wheel

planisfero [planis'fɛro] SM planisphere

plantare [plan'tare] SM orthopaedic (*Brit*) o orthopedic (*USA*) insole, arch support

plasma ['plazma] SM plasma

plasmare [plaz'mare] /72/ VT (*anche fig*) shape, to mould (*Brit*), mold (*USA*)

plastico, -a, -ci, -che ['plastiko] AGG plastic; **in materiale plastico** plastic o plastic ♦ SM **1** (*Topografia*) plastic model, relief model **2** (*esplosivo*) plastic explosive; **bomba al plastico** plastic bomb

platano ['platano] SM plane tree

platea [pla'tɛa] SF **1** (*Teatro*) stalls *pl* (*Brit*), orchestra (*USA*); (*pubblico*) audience; **un posto in platea** a seat in the stalls; **la platea ha applaudito** the audience applauded **2** (*Geol*) shelf

plateale [plate'ale] AGG (*gesto, atteggiamento*) theatrical

platealmente [plateal'mente] AVV theatrically

platino ['platino] SM platinum

platonico, -a, -ci, -che [pla'tɔniko] AGG platonic ♦ SM Platonist

plaudire [plau'dire] /45/ VI (*aus avere*) (*frm*): **plaudire a** (*progetto, iniziativa*) to applaud

plausibile [plau'zibile] AGG plausible

plauso ['plauzo] SM (*fig*) approbation, approval

playback ['pleibæk] SM INV: **cantare in playback** to mime

playboy ['pleibɔi] SM INV playboy

playmaker ['pleimeika] SM INV, SF INV (*Sport*) playmaker

play-off ['plei'ɔf] SM INV (*Sport*) play-off

plebaglia [ple'baʎʎa] SF (*pegg*) rabble, riffraff *sg* o *pl*

plebe ['plebe] SF common people *pl*; (*pegg*) rabble, riffraff *sg* o *pl*

plebeo, -a [ple'bɛo] AGG plebeian; (*volgare*) coarse, common ♦ SM, SF plebeian

plebiscito [plebiʃ'ʃito] SM plebiscite

plenario, -ria, -ri, -rie [ple'narjo] AGG plenary; **in sessione plenaria** in plenary session

plenilunio, -ni [pleni'lunjo] SM full moon

plenipotenziario, -ria, -ri, -rie [plenipoten'tsjarjo] AGG, SM plenipotentiary

plenum ['plɛnum] SM INV plenum

plettro ['plɛttro] SM plectrum

pleura ['plɛura] SF (*Anat*) pleura

pleurite [pleu'rite] SF pleurisy

plico, -chi ['pliko] SM (*pacco*) parcel; **in plico a parte** under separate cover; **plico bomba** letter bomb

plissé [pli'se] AGG INV, SM INV = **plissettato**

plissettato, -a [plisset'tato] AGG: **tessuto plissettato** plissé *attr* ♦ SM plissé

plotone [plo'tone] SM (*Mil*) platoon; **plotone d'esecuzione** firing squad

plug-in [plʌ'gin] AGG (*Inform*) plug-in

plumbeo, -a ['plumbeo] AGG (*colore, cielo*) leaden

plurale [plu'rale] AGG plural ♦ SM plural; **mettere al plurale** to put into the plural, pluralize

pluralismo [plura'lizmo] SM pluralism

pluralità [plurali'ta] SF plurality; (*maggioranza*) majority

plusvalenza [pluzva'lentsa] SF capital gain

plusvalore [pluzva'lore] SM (*Econ*) surplus (value)

plutonio [plu'tɔnjo] SM plutonium

pluviale [plu'vjale] AGG rain *attr*

pluviometro [plu'vjɔmetro] SM rain gauge

PM [pi'emme] SIGLA M (*Dir*) = **Pubblico Ministero** ♦ ABBR (= *Polizia Militare*) MP (= *Military Police*)

PN SIGLA = **Pordenone**

pneumatico, -a, -ci, -che [pneu'matiko] AGG (*Tecn*) pneumatic; (*gonfiabile*) inflatable ♦ SM (*Aut*) tyre (*Brit*), tire (*USA*); **pneumatico chiodato** studded tyre o tire; **pneumatico da neve** snow tyre o tire; **pneumatico rigenerato** remould

PNL [pi'enne'elle] SIGLA M (= *Prodotto Nazionale Lordo*) GNP (= *Gross National Product*)

PO SIGLA = **Prato** ♦ ABBR = **Posta Ordinaria**

Po [pɔ] SM: **il Po** the Po

po' [pɔ] AVV *vedi* **poco**

pochezza [po'kettsa] SF insufficiency, shortage; (*fig: meschinità*) meanness, smallness

---

PAROLA CHIAVE

poco, -a, -chi, -che ['pɔko] AVV

1 (*piccola quantità*) little, (*negazione*) + much; **si accontenta di poco** he's easily satisfied; **c'è poco da ridere** there's nothing to laugh about; **guadagna poco** he doesn't earn much, he earns little; **dorme troppo poco** she doesn't get enough sleep

2 (*con aggettivo, avverbio*) (a) little, (*negazione*) + very; **sta poco bene** he's not very well; **è poco più alta di lui** she's a little o slightly taller than him; **è poco probabile** it's not very likely; **è poco socievole** he's not very sociable

3 (*tempo*): **poco dopo** shortly after(wards); **il film dura poco** the film doesn't last long; **poco fa** a short while o time ago; **fra poco** in a little while; **manca poco alla fine** it's almost o nearly finished, it's more or less finished; **poco prima** shortly before; **ci vediamo poco** we hardly ever see each other

4 un po' a little, a bit; **è un po' corto** it's a little o bit short; **sono un po' stanco** I'm a bit tired; **zoppica un po'** he limps a bit, he has a slight limp; **arriverà tra un po'** he'll arrive shortly o in a little while; **un po' prima del solito** a little earlier than usual; **ha dormito un bel po'** he slept for quite a while; **fammi un po' vedere** let me have a look

5 (*fraseologia*): (a) **poco a poco** bit by bit, little by little; **a dir poco** to say the least; **eravamo in 30 a dir poco** there were at least 30 of us; **è una cosa da poco** it's nothing, it's of no importance; **una persona da poco** a worthless individual; **ha vinto di poco** he just won; **poco male** never mind, it doesn't matter; **per poco non cadevo** I almost o nearly fell

♦ AGG INDEF

1 (*quantità*) little, (*negazione*) + (very) much; (*numero*) few,

(negazione) + (very) many; **poco denaro** little *o* not much money; **poco vino** little *o* not much wine; **poche persone** few *o* not many people; **poche idee** few *o* not many ideas; **c'era poca gente** there were only a few people; **è un tipo di poche parole** he's a man of few words; **a poco prezzo** at a low price, cheap; **con poca spesa** for a small outlay **2** *(in espressioni ellittiche: tempo)* a short time, a little while; (: *quantità*) (a) little; **ci vediamo fra poco** see you soon *o* shortly; **l'ha comprato per poco** he bought it cheap; **ne abbiamo ancora per poco** we'll only be a little longer; **basta poco per farlo contento** it doesn't take much to make him happy
♦ PRON
1 (a) little; **c'è chi ha molto tempo e chi ne ha poco** there are those who have a lot of time and those who have little **2** *(persone)*: **pochi, poche** few (people); **pochi la pensano come lui** few people think as he does; **pochi di noi** few of us
♦ SM
1 little; **il poco che guadagno...** what little I earn ...; **vive del poco che ha** she lives on the little she has; *vedi anche* **buono**[1] **2** **un po'** a little; **un po' di soldi** a little money; **un po' di pane** a little bread; **un po' di zucchero** a little sugar; **un po' di silenzio!** let's have a bit of quiet!; **ha un po' di mal di testa** he has a slight headache; **ha un po' d'influenza** she has a touch of flu; **un bel po' di denaro** quite a lot of money, a tidy sum; **facciamo un po' per uno** let's do a bit each **3 po' po'**, **che po' po' di coraggio!** what courage!; **niente po' po' di meno che il presidente in persona!** no less than the president himself!

podcast ['pɔdkast] SM podcast
podere [po'dere] SM *(Agr)* farm
poderoso, -a [pode'roso] AGG powerful
podestà [podes'ta] SM INV *(nel fascismo)* mayor, podestà
podio, -di ['pɔdjo] SM *(gen)* podium, dais; *(Mus)* platform
podismo [po'dizmo] SM *(Sport: marcia)* walking; (: *corsa*) running
podista, -i, -e [po'dista] SM, SF *(vedi sm)* walker; runner
poema, -i [po'ema] SM poem; **conciato così sei un poema** *(iro)* you look a pretty sight like that; **è tutto un poema!** *(complicato)* it's a real palaver!
poesia [poe'zia] SF *(Arte: produzione poetica)* poetry; *(singolo componimento)* poem; *(fig: di incontro)* magic; **una poesia di Foscolo** a poem by Foscolo; **la poesia e la prosa** poetry and prose; **scrivere poesie** to write poetry
poeta, -i [po'eta] SM poet
poetare [poe'tare] /72/ VI *(aus avere)* to write poetry, write verse
poetico, -a, -ci, -che [po'etiko] AGG poetic(al); **la produzione poetica di Dante** Dante's poetical works
poggiare [pod'dʒare] /62/ VT to lean, rest; *(posare)* to lay, place; *(mettere)* to put; **puoi poggiare il pacco sul tavolo** you can put the parcel on the table; **non poggiare i gomiti sulla tavola** don't put your elbows on the table; **poggia la scala al muro** lean the ladder against the wall; **poggiarsi a qc** to lean against sth; **si è dovuto poggiare al muro per sostenersi** he had to lean against the wall for support ♦ VI *(aus avere)* **1** *(anche fig)* to stand, rest **2** *(Naut)* to bear away
poggiatesta [poddʒa'testa] SM INV *(Aut)* headrest
poggio, -gi ['pɔddʒo] SM hill, hillock, knoll
poggiolo [pod'dʒɔlo] SM balcony
poi ['pɔi] AVV **1** *(gen)* then; *(più tardi)* later (on); *(alla fine)* finally, at last; **e poi cos'è successo?** and then what happened?; **e poi** *(inoltre)* and besides; **non ne ho voglia e poi sono stanco** I can't feel like it and what's more I'm tired; **devi poi sapere che...** you should also know that ...; **prima o poi** sooner or later; **poi te lo dico** I'll tell you later (on); **a poi** till later; **d'ora in poi** from now on; **da domani in poi** from tomorrow onwards **2** *(enfatico)*: **lui, poi, non c'entra proprio** he simply doesn't come into it, it's nothing at all to do with him; **questa poi non me l'aspettavo** I just wasn't expecting this at all; **questa poi (è bella)!** *(iro)* that's a good one! ♦ SM: **il poi** the future; **pensare al poi** to think of the future
poiana [po'jana] SF buzzard
poiché [poi'ke] CONG since, as

pois [pwa] SM INV (polka) dot; **a pois** spotted, dotted; **bianco a pois rossi** white with red dots
poker ['pɔker] SM INV poker; **un poker d'assi** four aces; **giocare a poker** to play poker
polacco, -a, -chi, -che [po'lakko] AGG Polish ♦ SM, SF *(persona)* Pole; **i polacchi** the Poles ♦ SM *(lingua)* Polish; **parli polacco?** do you speak Polish?
polare [po'lare] AGG polar; **la stella polare** the Pole Star
polarizzare [polarid'dzare] /72/ VT *(Fis)* to polarize; *(fig: attrarre)* to attract; **polarizzare la propria attenzione su** to focus one's attention on; **polarizzarsi** VIP *(attenzione, sguardo)*: **polarizzarsi su** to focus on
polca ['pɔlka] SF = polka
polemico, -a, -ci, -che [po'lɛmiko] AGG *(gen)* controversial, polemic(al); *(pegg)* contentious
polemizzare [polemid'dzare] /72/ VI *(aus avere)* **polemizzare (su qc)** to argue (about sth)
polenta [po'lenta] SF *(Culin)* polenta, *sort of thick porridge made with maize flour*; *(fig: persona lenta)* slowcoach *(Brit)*, slowpoke *(USA)*
polentone, -a [polen'tone] SM, SF slowcoach *(Brit)*, slowpoke *(USA)*
polesano, -a [pole'zano] AGG of *o* from Polesine *(area between the Po and the Adige)* ♦ SM, SF inhabitant *o* native of Polesine
POLFER ['pɔlfer] SIGLA F = polizia ferroviaria
poli- ['pɔli] PREF poly-
poliambulatorio, -ri [poliambula'tɔrjo] SM *(Med)* ≈ health centre *(Brit)*
policlinico, -ci [poli'kliniko] SM *(Med)* general hospital
poliedro [poli'edro] SM *(Mat)* polyhedron
poliestere [poli'estere] SM polyester
poligamia [poliga'mia] SF polygamy
poliglotta [poli'glɔtta] AGG, SM, SF polyglot
poligono [po'ligono] SM **1** *(Mat)* polygon **2 poligono di tiro** rifle range
Polinesia [poli'nɛzja] SF Polynesia
polinesiano, -a [poline'zjano] AGG, SM, SF Polynesian ♦ SM *(lingua)* Polynesian
polio ['pɔljo] SF polio
polipo ['pɔlipo] SM *(Zool, Med)* polyp
polistirolo [polisti'rɔlo] SM polystyrene
politecnico, -a, -ci, -che [poli'tekniko] AGG polytechnic ♦ SM *university institution providing courses in science, technology and engineering*
politica, -che [po'litika] SF **1** *(scienza, carriera)* politics *sg*; **si interessa di politica** he's interested in politics; **fare politica** *(militante)* to be a political activist; *(come professione)* to be in politics; **darsi alla politica** to go into politics **2** *(linea di condotta)* policy; *(modo di governare)* policies *pl*; **la politica del governo** the government's policies; **la politica economica del governo** the government's economic policy; **politica aziendale** company policy; **politica estera** foreign policy; **politica dei prezzi** prices policy; **politica dei redditi** incomes policy
politicamente [politika'mente] AVV politically; **politicamente corretto** politically correct
politicante [politi'kante] SM, SF *(pegg)* petty politician
politicizzare [politit∫id'dzare] /72/ VT to politicize
politico, -a, -ci, -che [po'litiko] AGG political; **la situazione politica** the political situation; **uomo politico** politician; **scienze politiche** political sciences; **elezioni politiche** parliamentary *(Brit)* o congressional *(USA)* election(s) ♦ SM politician
polivalente [poliva'lɛnte] AGG *(Chim)* polyvalent; *(fig)* multi-purpose
polizia [polit'tsia] SF **1** *(Amm)* police (force); *(poliziotti)* police *pl*; **è arrivata la polizia?** have the police arrived?; **chiama la polizia!** call the police!; **agente di polizia** policeman; **polizia ferroviaria** railway *(Brit)* o railroad *(USA)* police; **polizia fluviale** river police; **polizia giudiziaria** ≈ Criminal Investigation Department *(Brit)*, ≈ Federal Bureau of Investigation *(USA)*; **polizia sanitaria** health inspectorate; **polizia stradale** traffic police *(Brit)*, state highway patrol *(USA)*; **polizia tributaria** tax inspectorate *(commissariato)* police station

poliziesco, -a, -schi, -sche [polit'tsjesko] AGG (*indagine*) police *attr*; (*film, libro*) detective *attr*; (*pegg: modi*) bullying; **un film poliziesco** a detective film

poliziotto [polit'tsjɔtto] SM police officer; **poliziotto di quartiere** local police officer ♦ AGG INV: **cane poliziotto** police dog

polizza ['pɔlittsa] SF 1 (*Assicurazione*) policy; **polizza di assicurazione** insurance policy; **polizza casco** comprehensive insurance policy 2 (*Comm*) bill, voucher; **polizza di carico** bill of lading; **polizza di pegno** pawn ticket

pollaio, -ai [pol'lajo] SM (*edificio*) henhouse; (*recinto*) chicken run

pollaiolo, -a [polla'jɔlo] SM, SF poulterer (*Brit*), poultryman/woman

pollame [pol'lame] SM poultry

pollastra [pol'lastra] SF pullet; (*fam: ragazza*) chick, bird (*Brit*)

pollastro [pol'lastro] SM (*Zool*) cockerel, young cock; (*fig: persona ingenua*) sucker (*fam*)

pollice ['pɔllitʃe] SM 1 (*Anat*) thumb; **avere il pollice verde** to have green fingers (*Brit*) o a green thumb (*USA*); **girarsi i pollici** to twiddle one's thumbs 2 (*unità di misura*) inch; **uno schermo a 17 pollici** a 17-inch screen

polline ['pɔlline] SM pollen; **sono allergico al polline** I suffer from hay fever

pollo ['pollo] SM 1 chicken; (*fig: persona ingenua*) sucker (*fam*) 2 (*fraseologia*): **conoscere i propri polli** to know who one is dealing with; **far ridere i polli** (*situazione, persona*) to be utterly ridiculous

polmonare [polmo'nare] AGG lung *attr*, pulmonary

polmone [pol'mone] SM lung; **avere buoni polmoni** to have a good pair of lungs; **gridare a pieni polmoni** to shout at the top of one's voice; **respirare a pieni polmoni** to take deep breaths, breathe deeply; **polmone d'acciaio** iron lung

polmonite [polmo'nite] SF (*Med*) pneumonia; **polmonite atipica** SARS

Polo ['pɔlo] SM the Pole (*centre right political grouping*)

polo¹ ['pɔlo] SM (*Fis, Mat, Geog*) pole; **abitiamo ai poli opposti della città** we live at opposite ends of the city; **il Polo nord** the North Pole; **il Polo sud** the South Pole

polo² ['pɔlo] SM (*Sport*) polo

polo³ ['pɔlo] SF INV (*maglietta*) polo shirt

Polonia [po'lɔnja] SF Poland; **ti è piaciuta la Polonia?** did you like Poland?; **sei mai stato in Polonia?** have you ever been to Poland?

polpa ['polpa] SF 1 (*di frutto*) pulp, flesh 2 (*di carne*) lean meat

polpaccio, -ci [pol'pattʃo] SM (*Anat*) calf

polpastrello [polpas'trello] SM fingertip

polpetta [pol'petta] SF (*in tegame*) meatball; (*fritta*) rissole; **far polpette di qn** to make mincemeat of sb

polpettone [polpet'tone] SM (*Culin*) meatloaf; **questo film/libro è un polpettone** this film/book is far too long and involved

polpo ['polpo] SM octopus

polposo, -a [pol'poso] AGG fleshy

polsino [pol'sino] SM cuff

polso ['polso] SM 1 (*Anat*) wrist; (*di camicia*) cuff; (*Med: pulsazione*) pulse; **ha un braccialetto al polso** she's got a bracelet on her wrist; **orologio da polso** wristwatch; **con le manette ai polsi** in handcuffs 2 (*fig: forza*) drive, vigour (*Brit*), vigor (*USA*); **avere polso** to be strong o firm; **un uomo di polso** a strong o firm man

poltiglia [pol'tiʎʎa] SF (*miscuglio*) paste, mush; (*cibo stracotto*) mush, pulp; (*di fango e neve*) slush; **il riso si era ridotto in poltiglia** the rice had cooked to a mush; **ridurre qn in poltiglia** to make mincemeat of sb

poltrire [pol'trire] /55/ VI (*aus avere*) (*rimanere a letto*) to have a lie(-in); (*oziare*) to loaf about, laze about, idle

poltrona [pol'trona] SF armchair; (*Teatro*) seat in the front stalls (*Brit*) o the orchestra (*USA*); **starsene in poltrona** to laze about; **aspirare alla poltrona di direttore generale** to aspire to the managing directorship; **poltrona letto** put-you-up (*Brit*), sofa bed (*USA*)

poltroncina [poltron'tʃina] SF (*Teatro*) seat in the back stalls (*Brit*) o the orchestra (*USA*)

poltrone, -a [pol'trone] SM, SF loafer, idler ♦ AGG lazy, idle

polvere ['polvere] SF (*gen, sostanza ridotta minutissima*) powder, dust; (*pulviscolo*) dust; **c'è uno strato di polvere sul tavolo** there's a layer of dust on the table; **caffè in polvere** instant coffee; **latte in polvere** dried o powdered milk; **sapone in polvere** soap powder; **fare polvere** to raise clouds of dust; **ridurre in polvere** to pulverize; **buttare o gettare la polvere negli occhi a qn** (*fig*) to pull the wool over sb's eyes; **far mangiare la polvere a qn** (*fig*) to leave sb far behind; **polvere di ferro** iron filings *pl*; **polvere d'oro** gold dust; **polvere pirica o da sparo** gunpowder; **polvere di stelle** stardust; **polveri sottili** particulates

polveriera [polve'rjɛra] SF (*Mil*) (gun)powder magazine; (*fig: zona calda*) powder keg

polverina [polve'rina] SF (*gen, anche Med*) powder; (*gergo: cocaina*) snow

polverizzare [polverid'dzare] /72/ VT (*legno, ferro*) to pulverize; (*liquido*) to atomize; (*fig: nemico*) to crush, pulverize; (: *record*) to smash; **polverizzarsi** VIP to turn to dust

polverone [polve'rone] SM thick cloud of dust; **sollevare un polverone** (*fig*) to raise a stink

polveroso, -a [polve'roso] AGG dusty, covered with dust

pomata [po'mata] SF ointment

pomello [po'mello] SM 1 (*impugnatura*) knob 2 (*gota*) cheek

pomeridiano, -a [pomeri'djano] AGG afternoon *attr*; **nelle ore pomeridiane** in the afternoon

pomeriggio, -gi [pome'riddʒo] SM afternoon; **il o di pomeriggio** in the afternoon; **nel primo/tardo pomeriggio** in the early/late afternoon; **alle 2 di o del pomeriggio** at 2 o'clock in the afternoon, at 2 pm; **tutti i pomeriggi** every afternoon; **tutte le domeniche pomeriggio** every Sunday afternoon; **domani/sabato pomeriggio** tomorrow/Saturday afternoon

pomice ['pomitʃe] SF: (**pietra**) **pomice** pumice (stone)

pomiciare [pomi'tʃare] /14/ VI (*aus avere*) (*fam: sbaciucchiarsi*) to neck

pomo ['pomo] SM (*frutto*) apple; (*oggetto sferico*) knob; (*di sella*) pommel; **pomo d'Adamo** (*Anat*) Adam's apple; **pomo della discordia** (*Mitol*) apple of discord; (*fig*) bone of contention

pomodoro [pomo'dɔro] SM (*frutto*) tomato; (*pianta*) tomato plant; **spaghetti al pomodoro** spaghetti with tomato sauce

pompa¹ ['pompa] SF 1 (*fasto*) pomp (and ceremony); **mettersi in pompa magna** to get all dressed up; **accogliere qn in grande pompa** to roll out the red carpet for sb 2 (*impresa*) **pompe funebri** undertaker's *sg*, funeral director's *sg* (*Brit*), funeral parlor o home (*USA*), mortician's (*USA*)

pompa² ['pompa] SF (*Tecn*) pump; **una pompa da bicicletta** a bicycle pump; **pompa antincendio** fire hose; **pompa di benzina** petrol (*Brit*) o gas (*USA*) pump; (*distributore*) filling o gas (*USA*) station; **pompa idraulica** hydraulic pump; (*Aut: dei freni*) master cylinder

pompare [pom'pare] /72/ VT to pump; (*estrarre*) to pump out; (*gonfiare d'aria*) to pump up; (*fig: esagerare*) to exaggerate, blow up; **devo pompare il materassino** I need to pump up my airbed

pompeiano, -a [pompe'jano] AGG o from Pompeii ♦ SM, SF inhabitant o native of Pompeii

pompelmo [pom'pelmo] SM (*frutto*) grapefruit; (*albero*) grapefruit (tree)

pompiere [pom'pjɛre] SM fireman, firefighter; **fa il pompiere** he's a fireman; **i pompieri** the fire brigade; **chiamare i pompieri** to call the fire brigade (*Brit*) o fire department (*USA*)

pompon [pom'pɔn] SM INV pompom, pompon

pomposo, -a [pom'poso] AGG (*cerimonia*) full of pomp (and circumstance); (*fig: discorso, atteggiamento*) pompous

ponderare [ponde'rare] /72/ VT to ponder (over), think over, consider carefully; **ponderare i pro ed i contro** to weigh up the pros and cons; **fu una decisione ben ponderata** it was a carefully considered decision

ponderoso, -a [ponde'roso] AGG (*anche fig*) weighty

ponente [po'nɛnte] SM (*direzione*) west; (*vento*) west wind

pongo *ecc* ['pongo] VB *vedi* **porre**
poni *ecc* ['poni] VB *vedi* **porre**
ponte ['ponte] SM (*Edil, Med, Mil*) bridge; (*Naut*) deck; (*anche:* **ponte di comando**) bridge; (*Aut*) axle; (*impalcatura*) scaffold; **è dell'altra parte del ponte** it's across the bridge; **vivere sotto i ponti** to be a tramp; **tagliare** *o* **rompere i ponti con qn** to break off relations with sb; **fare il ponte** to take the extra day off (*between 2 public holidays*); **abbiamo fatto un ponte di 3 giorni** we had 3 days off; **ponte aereo** airlift, air bridge (*Brit*); **ponte di barche** pontoon bridge; **ponte di coperta** (*Naut*) upper deck; **ponte levatoio** drawbridge; **ponte radio** radio link; **ponte (sollevatore)** (*Aut*) hydraulic ramp; **ponte sospeso** suspension bridge ♦ AGG INV: **governo ponte** caretaker *o* interim government; **legge ponte** interim law
pontefice [pon'tefitʃe] SM (*Rel*) pontiff
ponticello [ponti'tʃello] SM (*di occhiali, anche Mus*) bridge
pontificare [pontifi'kare] /20/ VI (*aus* avere) (*anche fig*) to pontificate
pontificato [pontifi'kato] SM (*Rel*) papacy, pontificate
pontificio, -cia, -ci, -cie [ponti'fitʃo] AGG pontifical, papal; **Stato pontificio** Papal State
pontile [pon'tile] SM jetty
pony ['poni] SM INV pony
pool [puːl] SM INV (*consorzio*) consortium; (*organismo internazionale*) pool; (*di esperti, ricercatori*) team; (*antimafia, antidroga*) working party
pop [pɔp] AGG INV pop *attr*
popcorn ['pɔpkɔːn] SM INV popcorn
popeline [pɔpə'lin] SF INV poplin
popò [po'pɔ] (*linguaggio infantile*) SM INV (*sedere*) botty, bum (*fam*) ♦ SF INV (*cacca*) pooh, poop
popolano, -a [popo'lano] AGG of the people, popular; **saggezza popolana** popular lore ♦ SM, SF man *o* woman of the people
popolare¹ [popo'lare] /72/ VT (*rendere abitato*) to populate; **popolarsi** VIP (*diventare popolato*) to become populated; (*affollarsi*): **popolarsi di** to become crowded with
popolare² [popo'lare] /72/ AGG 1 (*gen, anche fig*) popular; (*quartiere, clientela*) working-class; **un cantante molto popolare** a very popular singer; **canzone popolare** folk song; **case popolari** council houses (*Brit*), subsidized housing (*USA*); **manifestazione popolare** mass demonstration; **repubblica popolare** people's republic 2 (*Pol*) of P.P.I. ♦ SM, SF (*Pol*) member (*o supporter*) of P.P.I.
popolarità [popolari'ta] SF popularity
popolazione [popolat'tsjone] SF population
popolo ['popolo] SM (*gen*) people; (*classe*): **il popolo** the (common) people; **il popolo italiano** the Italian people, the Italians *pl*; **il popolo della notte** clubbers; **il popolo di Seattle** *the anti-globalization movement*; **a furor di popolo** by popular acclaim
popoloso, -a [popo'loso] AGG densely populated, populous
popone [po'pone] SM melon
poppa¹ ['poppa] SF (*Anat*) breast
poppa² ['poppa] SF (*Naut*) stern; **a poppa** aft, astern; **andare a poppa** to go aft; **andare col vento in poppa** to sail before the wind
poppante [pop'pante] SM, SF unweaned infant; (*fig: inesperto*) whippersnapper
poppare [pop'pare] /72/ VT to suck
poppata [pop'pata] SF (*allattamento*) feed; **l'ora della poppata** feeding time
poppatoio, -toi [poppa'tojo] SM (baby's) bottle, feeding bottle (*Brit*), baby bottle (*USA*)
populista, -i, -e [popu'lista] AGG populist
porcaio, -ai [por'kajo] SM (*anche fig*) pigsty
porcata [por'kata] SF (*libro, piatto*) load of rubbish; **fare una porcata a qn** to play a dirty trick on sb
porcellana [portʃel'lana] SF porcelain, china; (*oggetto*) piece of porcelain
porcellino [portʃel'lino] SM piglet; **porcellino d'India** guinea pig
porcheria [porke'ria] SF (*gen*) dirt, muck, filth; (*azione disonesta*) dirty trick; (*oscenità*) obscenity; (*cosa fatta male*) (load of) rubbish *o* trash; **mangia un sacco di porcherie** he

eats a lot of rubbish; **non si fanno queste porcherie!** you shouldn't behave like that!
porchetta [por'ketta] SF (*Culin*) roast sucking pig
porcile [por'tʃile] SM (*anche fig*) pigsty
porcino, -a [por'tʃino] AGG of pigs, pork *attr*; **occhi porcini** (*fig*) piggy eyes ♦ SM (*anche:* **fungo porcino**) cep
porco, -a, -ci, -che ['porko] SM (*Zool*) pig; (*Culin*) pork; **gettare le perle ai porci** (*fig*) to cast pearls before swine ♦ SM, SF (*pegg*) pig; **un vecchio porco** a dirty old man ♦ AGG (*fam*): **porca miseria!, porco Giuda!** bloody hell! (*Brit*)
porcospino [porkos'pino] SM porcupine; (*fig: persona*): **è chiuso come un porcospino** he doesn't come out of his shell easily
porfido ['porfido] SM porphyry
porgere ['pordʒere] /115/ VT IRREG to hand, give; (*tendere*) to hold out; **porgere la mano a qn** to hold out one's hand to sb; (*fig*) to give sb a helping hand, lend sb a hand; **porgere l'altra guancia** to turn the other cheek; **porgere orecchio** *o* **ascolto** to pay attention, listen
porno ['porno] (*fam*) AGG INV porno; **film porno** porn film (*Brit*) *o* movie (*USA*) ♦ SM INV (*pornografia*) porn
pornografia [pornogra'fia] SF pornography
pornografico, -a, -ci, -che [porno'grafiko] AGG pornographic
poro ['poro] SM (*Anat*) pore; (*forellino*) hole
poroso, -a [po'roso] AGG porous
porpora ['porpora] AGG, SM (*colore*) crimson ♦ SF (*stoffa, simbolo*) purple
porre ['porre] VB IRREG /77/ VT 1 (*mettere*) to put; (*collocare*) to place; (*posare*) to lay (down), put (down); **porre le fondamenta di** (*edificio*) to lay the foundations of; **porre le basi di** (*fig*) to lay the foundations of, establish; **abbiamo posto le basi per una futura collaborazione** we have laid the foundations for future cooperation; **fu posto al comando del reggimento** he was placed in command of the regiment; **porre la propria fiducia in qn** to place one's trust in sb; **porre fine** *o* **termine a qc** to put an end *o* a stop to sth 2 (*condizioni*) to lay down, set out, state; (*problema*) to pose; (*questione*) to raise; **porre una domanda a qn** to ask sb a question, put a question to sb 3 (*supporre*) to suppose; **poniamo (il caso) che...** let's suppose that ...; **posto che...** supposing that ..., on the assumption that ...; **porsi** VR: **porsi in cammino** to set out *o* forth; **porsi al lavoro** to get down to work; **porsi a sedere** to sit down; **porsi in salvo** to save o.s.
porro ['porro] SM 1 (*Bot*) leek; **una minestra di porri** leek soup 2 (*Med*) wart
porsi *ecc* ['porsi] VB *vedi* **porgere**
porta ['porta] SF (*gen*) door; (*soglia*) doorstep; (*apertura*) doorway; (*di fortezza: Sci*) gate; (*Calcio, Rugby*) goal; (*Inform*) port; (*di città*): **porte** SFPL gates; **chiudi la porta, per favore** close the door, please; **a tre/cinque porte** (*automobile*) three/five door; **abitare porta a porta con qn** to live right next door to sb; **vendere porta a porta** to sell from door to door; **vendita porta a porta** door-to-door selling; **indicare la porta a qn** (*fig*) to show sb the door; **mettere qn alla porta** (*anche fig*) to throw sb out; **lo hanno messo alla porta** they threw him out; **prendere la porta** ed andarsene to walk out the door; **sbattere** *o* **chiudere la porta in faccia a qn** (*anche fig*) to slam the door in sb's face; **suonare alla porta** to ring the (door)bell; **suonano alla porta** there's somebody at the door; **trovare tutte le porte chiuse** (*fig*) to find the way barred; **a porte chiuse** (*processo*) in camera; **cacciamo questo problema dalla porta e rientra dalla finestra** there's no getting rid of this problem; **esce dalla porta e rientra dalla finestra** there's no getting rid of him; **l'inverno è alle porte** winter is upon us; **tirare in porta** (*Sport*) to take a shot at goal; **porta blindata** reinforced door; **porta parallela** (*Inform*) parallel port; **porta seriale** (*Inform*) serial port; **porta di servizio** tradesman's entrance; **porta di sicurezza** emergency exit; **porta stagna** watertight door; **porta USB** (*Inform*) USB port
portabagagli [portaba'gaʎʎi] SM INV 1 (*facchino*) porter 2 (*Aut*) boot (*Brit*), trunk (*USA*); (*sul tetto*) roof rack; (*in treno, corriera: anche:* **rete portabagagli**) luggage rack
portabandiera [portaban'djera] SM INV, SF INV (*anche fig*) standard bearer

portaborse [porta'borse] SM INV, SF INV (pegg) lackey

portabottiglie [portabot'tiʎʎe] SM INV (scaffale) bottle rack; (per trasporto) bottle carrier; (da tavola) wine cooler

porta-CD [portat∫i'di] SM INV CD rack; (astuccio) CD holder

portacenere [porta't∫enere] SM INV ashtray

portachiavi [porta'kjavi] SM INV (anello) key ring; (astuccio) key case

portacipria [porta't∫ipria] SM INV (powder) compact

portaerei [porta'erei] SF INV (anche: nave portaerei) aircraft carrier ◆ SM INV (aereo) aircraft transporter

portafinestra [portafi'nestra] SF (pl portefinestre) French window o door (USA)

portafoglio, -gli [porta'fɔʎʎo] SM 1 (per soldi) wallet, billfold (USA); (cartella) briefcase; **mettere mano al portafoglio** (fig) to put one's hand in one's pocket; **gonna a portafoglio** wrapover skirt 2 (Fin, Pol) portfolio; **ministro senza portafoglio** minister without portfolio; **portafoglio titoli** investment portfolio

portafortuna [portafor'tuna] SM INV (amuleto) lucky charm; (persona, animale) mascot ◆ AGG INV lucky

portagioie [porta'dʒɔje] SM INV, **portagioielli** [portadʒo'jɛlli] SM INV jewellery (Brit) o jewelry (USA) box

portale [por'tale] SM (Archit, Inform) portal

portalettere [porta'lettere] SM INV, SF INV postal worker, mail carrier

portamento [porta'mento] SM bearing, carriage

portamonete [portamo'nete] SM INV purse (Brit), change purse (USA)

portante [por'tante] AGG (muro) load-bearing, supporting

portantina [portan'tina] SF 1 (sedia) sedan chair 2 (barella) stretcher

portaoggetti [portaod'dʒetti] AGG INV: **vano portaoggetti** (Aut) glove compartment

portaombrelli [portaom'brelli] SM INV umbrella stand

portapacchi [porta'pakki] SM INV (di moto, automobile) luggage rack

portapenne [porta'penne] SM INV pen holder; (astuccio) pencil case

portare [por'tare] /72/ VT 1 (sostenere, sorreggere: peso, bambino, pacco) to carry; **portava il sacco sottobraccio** he was carrying the parcel under his arm; **questa macchina porta 4 persone** this car can carry 4 people; **puoi portarmi la valigia?** can you carry my case for me?; **si porta dietro un sacco di roba** he carries masses of stuff round with him; **portare via** to take away; (rubare) to take; **schedare questi documenti porta via molto tempo** filing these documents takes (up) a lot of time; **porta bene i suoi anni** he's wearing well, he doesn't look his age; **ognuno ha la propria croce da portare** we all have our cross to bear 2 (consegnare, recare): **portare qc (a qn)** to take (o bring) sth (to sb); **porta il libro in cucina!** (vicino a chi parla) bring the book into the kitchen!; (lontano da chi parla) take the book into the kitchen!; **portami un bicchiere!** bring me a glass!; **portalo qui** bring it here; **porta questa lettera a Lucia** take this letter to Lucia; **posso portarli a casa?** can I bring (o take) them home?; **portare qc alla bocca** to lift o put sth to one's lips; **il suo intervento ha portato dei vantaggi** his intervention has brought certain advantages; **portare fortuna/sfortuna a qn** to bring (good) luck/bad luck to sb 3 (condurre) to take; (sogg: strada) to take, lead; (fig: indurre): **portare qn a (fare) qc** to lead sb to (do) sth; **dove porta questa strada?** where does this road lead?, where does this road take you?; **portare i bambini a spasso** to take the children for a walk; **sta portando i bambini a scuola** she's taking the children to school; **il vento ci sta portando al largo** the wind is carrying us out to sea; **dove ti porterà tutto questo?** where will all this lead you?; **portare qn alla disperazione** to drive sb to despair; **stiamo portando avanti il discorso sul disarmo** we are pursuing the topic of disarmament 4 (indossare: scarpe, vestito, occhiali) to wear, have on; **portava un bel vestito** she was wearing a beautiful dress; **non porta più queste scarpe** I don't wear these shoes any more; **porta i capelli lunghi** he wears his hair long, he has long hair 5 (avere: nome, titolo, firma) to have, bear; (fig: sentimenti) to bear; **porta il nome di suo nonno** he is called after his grandfather; **il documento porta la tua firma** the document has o bears your signature; **Firenze porta ancora**

i segni dell'alluvione Florence still bears the signs of the flood; **non gli porto rancore** I don't bear him a grudge; **portarsi** VIP (recarsi) to go; **la polizia si è portata sul luogo del disastro** the police went to the scene of the disaster; **portarsi al tiro** (Calcio, Basket) to move into a scoring position

portaritratti [portari'tratti] SM INV photo(graph) frame

portariviste [portari'viste] SM INV magazine rack

portasapone [portasa'pone] SM INV soap dish

portasigarette [portasiga'rette] SM INV cigarette case

portaspilli [portas'pilli] SM INV pincushion

portata [por'tata] SF 1 (Culin) course; **un pranzo di 7 portate** a 7-course lunch; **la portata principale** the main course 2 (di veicolo) carrying (o loading) capacity 3 (di arma) range; (fig: limite) scope, capability; **a/fuori portata (di)** within/out of reach (of); **a portata di mano** within (arm's) reach; (prezzo) within everybody's means 4 (fig: importanza) importance, significance; **di grande portata** of great importance 5 (volume d'acqua) (rate of) flow

portatile [por'tatile] AGG portable; **una TV portatile** a portable TV

portato, -a [por'tato] AGG (incline): **portato a** inclined o apt to; **essere portato per** (studio, matematica) to have a bent o a gift for; **è portato per le lingue** he has a gift for languages

portatore, -trice [porta'tore] SM, SF 1 (di messaggio, assegno) bearer; **pagabile al portatore** payable to the bearer 2 (Med) carrier; **portatore di handicap** disabled person; **portatore sano** (symptomless) carrier 3 (Alpinismo) porter

portatovagliolo [portatovaʎ'ʎɔlo] SM (anello) napkin ring; (busta) napkin holder

portauova [porta'wɔva] SM INV, **portauovo** [porta'wɔvo] SM INV egg cup; (scatola) egg box

portavoce [porta'vot∫e] SM INV, SF INV spokesperson

portello [por'tɛllo] SM (di portone, aereo) door; (Naut) hatch

portellone [portel'lone] SM (Aer, Naut) hold door; (Aut) tailgate

portento [por'tɛnto] SM wonder, marvel

portentoso, -a [porten'toso] AGG wonderful, marvellous (Brit), marvelous (USA)

porticato [porti'kato] SM portico

portico ['portiko] SM (Archit) porch, portico; (riparo) lean-to; **i portici** the arcades

portiera [por'tjera] SF (Aut) door

portiere, -a [por'tjere] SM, SF 1 (portinaio) concierge, caretaker, janitor (USA); (di hotel) porter 2 (Sport) goalkeeper

portinaio, -naia, -nai, -naie [porti'najo] SM, SF concierge, caretaker, janitor (USA)

portineria [portine'ria] SF caretaker's lodge

porto¹ ['porto] SM port, harbour (Brit), harbor (USA); **un porto riparato** a sheltered harbo(u)r; **andare o giungere in porto** (fig) to come to a successful conclusion; **condurre qc in porto** (fig) to bring sth to a successful conclusion; **questa casa è un porto di mare** people are always coming and going in this house; **porto fluviale** river port; **porto franco** free port; **porto marittimo** seaport; **porto militare** naval base; **porto di scalo** port of call

porto² ['porto] SM 1 (Comm: spesa di trasporto) carriage; **franco di porto** carriage free 2 **porto d'armi** gun licence (Brit) o license (USA)

porto³ ['porto] SM INV (vino) port (wine)

porto⁴, -a ['porto] PP di **porgere**

Portogallo [porto'gallo] SM Portugal; **ti è piaciuto il Portogallo?** did you like Portugal?; **sei mai stato in Portogallo?** have you ever been to Portugal?

portoghese [porto'gese] AGG Portuguese ◆ SM, SF 1 (abitante, nativo) Portuguese inv; **i portoghesi** the Portuguese 2 (spettatore senza biglietto) gate-crasher ◆ SM (lingua) Portuguese

portone [por'tone] SM main entrance

portoricano, -a [portori'kano] AGG, SM, SF Puerto Rican

Portorico [porto'riko] SM Puerto Rico

portuale [portu'ale] AGG port attr, dock attr, harbour attr (Brit), harbor attr (USA); **lavoratori portuali** dockers, dock workers, longshoremen (USA) ◆ SM docker, dock worker, longshoreman (USA)

porzione [por'tsjone] SF (gen) portion, share; (di cibo) helping, portion; **una porzione abbondante** a big portion

posa ['pɔsa] SF **1** (atteggiamento: di modello) pose; (affettato) posing; **teatro di posa** photographic studio; **mettersi in posa** to pose; **assumere pose da grandonna** to act the lady; **è tutta una posa** it's just an act **2** (Fot) exposure; **un rullino a 24 pose** a 24 exposure film **3** (riposo): **lavorare senza posa** to work without a break **4** (collocazione) laying, placing

posacenere [posa'tʃenere] SM INV ashtray

posare [po'sare] /72/ VT (gen) to put (down); (piatto, vassoio) to lay o put (down); (fondamenta, cavo) to lay; **ha posato la penna sul tavolo** he put the pen on the table; **posare gli occhi su** to gaze at; (con mire particolari) to set one's sights on; **posalo contro il muro** put it against the wall ♦ VI (aus avere) **1** (ponte, edificio, teoria): **posare su** to rest on **2** (Fot, Arte) to pose, sit; (atteggiarsi) to pose; **posa a grande scrittore** (fig) he poses as a great writer; **posarsi** VIP (polvere) to settle; (uccello) to alight; (ape, mosca) to land; (aereo) to land, touch down; (sguardo) to settle, fix

posata [po'sata] SF piece of cutlery o flatware (USA); **posate** SFPL cutlery sg, flatware sg

posatezza [posa'tettsa] SF (di persona) composure; (di discorso) balanced nature

posato, -a [po'sato] AGG (persona) steady, level-headed; (comportamento) steady, sober; (discorso) balanced

poscritto [pos'kritto] SM postscript

posi ecc ['pɔsi] VB vedi **porre**

positivamente [pozitiva'mente] AVV positively; (rispondere) in the affirmative, affirmatively

positivo, -a [pozi'tivo] AGG, SM positive

posizione [pozit'tsjone] SF (gen, anche fig) position; **una posizione scomoda** an uncomfortable position; **prendere posizione a favore di/contro** to take up a position in favour (Brit) o favor (USA) of/against; **devi prendere una posizione** you must take a stand; **farsi una posizione** to make one's way in the world; **si è fatto una posizione** he's done well; **è arrivato in prima/seconda posizione** (Sport) he arrived first/second; **posizione di attesa** (Tennis) ready position; **posizione dei piedi** stance; **luci di posizione** (Aut) sidelights (Brit), parking lights (USA)

posologia [pozolo'dʒia] SF dosage, directions pl for use

posporre [pos'porre] /77/ VT IRREG **1** (rimandare) to postpone, defer **2** (subordinare) to subordinate, place after

posposto, -a [pos'posto] PP di **posporre**

possedere [posse'dere] /107/ VT IRREG (gen) to have; (qualità, virtù, fortuna) to possess; (casa, terreno) to own; (diploma) to hold; (sogg: ira) to possess; **quasi tutti possiedono una macchina** most people have a car; **possiede una casa in campagna** she owns a house in the country; **era posseduto dal demone** he was possessed by the Devil

possedimento [possedi'mento] SM **1** (proprietà terriera) property, estate **2** (di uno Stato: territorio) possession

possente [pos'sente] AGG strong, powerful

possessivo, -a [posses'sivo] AGG (gen, anche Gramm) possessive

possesso [pos'sesso] SM **1** (gen, anche Dir) possession; **essere in possesso di qc** to be in possession of sth; **prendere possesso di qc** to take possession of sth; **entrare in possesso dell'eredità** to come into one's inheritance **2** (possedimenti): **possessi** SMPL property sg

possessore [posses'sore], **posseditrice** [posseditri'tʃe] SM, SF possessor, owner; (di carica, diploma) holder

possibile [pos'sibile] AGG (gen) possible; (fattibile: progetto, piano) feasible; **non mi sarà possibile farlo** I won't be able to do it; **pensi che sia possibile?** do you think it's possible?; **è possibile che arrivi più tardi** he may o might arrive later; **cerca di venir presto, se possibile** try to come early, if possible o if you can; **ha trovato tutte le scuse possibili e immaginabili per non venire** he came up with every excuse imaginable for not coming; **il più presto possibile** as soon as possible; **vieni prima possibile** come as soon as possible; **fallo meglio possibile** do it as best you can; **porta meno roba possibile** bring as little as possible; **non è possibile!** (irrealizzabile) it's not possible!; (falso) that can't be true!; **possibile?** (sorpresa) well I never! ♦ SM: **fare il possibile** to

do everything possible o everything in one's power; **nei limiti del possibile** as far as possible

possibilista, -i, -e [possibi'lista] AGG: **essere possibilista** to keep an open mind

possibilità [possibili'ta] SF INV **1** (gen) possibility; **c'è sempre la possibilità che cambi idea** there's always the possibility o chance that he'll change his mind; **ci sono varie possibilità** there are various possibilities; **avere la possibilità di fare qc** (facoltà) to be in a position to do sth; (opportunità) to have the opportunity to do; **non ha avuto la possibilità di andare all'università** he didn't have the opportunity to go to university; **non ha possibilità di salvezza** there's no hope of escape for him; **nella mia posizione non ho avuto la possibilità di aiutarlo** in my position I couldn't assist him o I had no means of assisting him **2** (mezzi): **possibilità** SFPL means; **vivere secondo le proprie possibilità** (finanziarie) to live according to one's means; **nei limiti delle nostre possibilità** in so far as we can

possibilmente [possibil'mente] AVV if possible; **ti telefono possibilmente domani** I'll phone you tomorrow if I can

□ **possibilmente** non si traduce mai con la parola inglese possibly

possidente [possi'dente] SM, SF property owner, landowner

possiedo ecc [pos'sjedo] VB vedi **possedere**

posso ecc ['pɔsso] VB vedi **potere²**

post- [pɔst] PREF post-

posta ['pɔsta] SF **1** (corrispondenza) post (Brit), mail (USA); (servizio) postal service, mail service, post; (ufficio) post office; **poste** SFPL (amministrazione) post office; **c'è posta per me?** are there any letters for me?, is there any post o mail for me?; **perché non lo mandi per posta?** why don't you send it by post o mail?; **sto andando alla posta** I'm going to the post office; **impiegato delle poste** post office clerk; **piccola posta** (su giornale) letters to the editor, letters page; **posta aerea** airmail; **posta elettronica** electronic mail, e-mail; **posta ordinaria** ≈ second-class post o mail; **posta prioritaria** first class (post); **Poste e Telecomunicazioni** postal and telecommunications service; **ministro delle Poste e Telecomunicazioni** Postmaster General **2** (Giochi: somma in palio) stake(s); **la posta in gioco è troppo alta** (fig) there's too much at stake **3** (Caccia) hide (Brit), blind (USA); **fare la posta a qn** (fig) to lie in wait for sb **4** (apposta): **a bella posta** on purpose

postagiro [posta'dʒiro] SM post office cheque (Brit) o check (USA), postal giro (Brit)

postale [pos'tale] AGG (servizio, vaglia) postal attr (Brit), mail attr (USA); (casella, impiegato) post office attr; (nave, treno) mail attr; **timbro postale** postmark ♦ SM (treno) mail train; (nave) mail boat; (furgone) mail van

postazione [postat'tsjone] SF (Mil) emplacement

postbellico, -a, -ci, -che [post'belliko] AGG postwar attr

postdatare [postda'tare] /72/ VT to postdate

posteggiare [posted'dʒare] /62/ VT, VI (aus avere) to park

posteggiatore, -trice [posteddʒa'tore] SM, SF car-park attendant (Brit), parking-lot attendant (USA)

posteggio, -gi [pos'teddʒo] SM **1** car park (Brit), parking lot (USA); **un posteggio gratuito** a free car park; **non riesco a trovare posteggio** I can't find a parking space; **posteggio custodito** attended car park o parking lot; **posteggio di taxi** taxi rank (Brit), taxi stand (USA) **2** (di rivenditore) pitch

postelegrafonico, -a, -ci, -che [postelegra'fɔniko] AGG postal and telecommunications attr

poster ['poster] SM INV poster

posteri ['pɔsteri] SMPL posterity sg; **i nostri posteri** our descendants

posteriore [poste'rjore] AGG **1** (dietro: parte di oggetto) back attr, rear attr; (zampe) hind attr; **il sedile posteriore** the back seat **2** (tempo) later; **questi avvenimenti sono posteriori alla mia partenza** these events occurred after my departure ♦ SM (euf, fam: sedere) behind, bottom

posteriori [poste'rjori] : **a posteriori** AGG INV after the event (dopo sostantivo) ♦ AVV looking back

posticcio, -a, -ci, -ce [pos'tittʃo] AGG (capelli, barba, denti) false ♦ SM hairpiece

posticipare [postit∫i'pare] /72/ vt to defer, postpone; **posticipare di 3 giorni** to postpone for 3 days; **la riunione è stata posticipata a sabato** the meeting has been postponed until Saturday

postilla [pos'tilla] sf marginal note

postino, -a [pos'tino] sm, sf postal worker, mail carrier

posto¹, -a ['posto] pp *di* **porre**

posto² ['posto] sm **1** (*luogo*) place; **è un posto magnifico** it's a beautiful place; **non è un posto adatto ai bambini** it's no place for children; **sul posto** on the spot; **i pompieri sono accorsi sul posto** the firemen rushed to the spot; **lo faremo sul posto** *o* **quando saremo sul posto** we'll do it when we get there; **la gente del posto** the local people; **posto di polizia** police station; **un incontro in un posto pubblico** an encounter in a public place; **posto di villeggiatura** holiday (*Brit*) *o* tourist spot, resort **2** (*spazio libero*) room, space; (*sedile: al teatro, in treno*) seat; (*di parcheggio*) space; **non c'è più posto in macchina** there's no more room in the car; **fate posto!** make way!; **prender posto** to take a seat; **ci sono 20 posti letto in quell'albergo** they can sleep 20 in that hotel; **vorrei prenotare due posti** I'd like to book two seats; **vai pure al posto** (*scolaro*) go and sit down; **mi tieni il posto in fila?** will you keep my place in the queue?; **una macchina a 5 posti** a 5-seater car; **posti in piedi** (*Teatro: in autobus*) standing room; **posto a sedere** seat **3** (*impiego*) job, post; **ha un posto di segretaria** she works as *o* has a job as a secretary, she has a secretarial post; **posto di lavoro** job **4** (*posizione in classifica*): **primo/secondo posto** first/second place; **arrivare al primo posto** to come first; **è arrivato al primo posto** he came first **5** (*Mil*) post; **tutti ai posti di combattimento!** action stations!; **posto di blocco** (*di polizia*) roadblock; (*alla frontiera*) frontier post **6** (*fraseologia*): **al posto di** in place of, instead of; **c'è un film al posto della partita** there's a film in place of the match; **andrò io al suo posto** I'll go instead of him; **l'hanno assunto al posto tuo** they employed him instead of you; **al posto tuo ci andrei** I'd go if I were you; **essere a posto** (*in ordine: stanza*) to be tidy; (: *persona*) to be neat and tidy; (*fig: questione*) to be settled; (: *persona*) to be OK; **tutto a posto?** is everything OK?; **è gente a posto** they are very respectable (people); **mettere a posto** (*riordinare*) to tidy (up), put in order; (*faccende: sistemare*) to straighten out; **metti a posto la tua camera** tidy your room; **rimetti il libro al suo posto** put the book back in its place; **mettere a posto qn** to sort sb out; **sa stare al suo posto** he knows his place; **tenere la lingua a posto** to hold one's tongue; **tieni le mani a posto!** keep your hands to yourself!; **per me non ha la testa tanto a posto!** I don't think he's all there!; **sarebbe ora che mettessi la testa a posto** it's time you got yourself sorted out

postoperatorio, -ria, -ri, -rie [postopera'tɔrjo] AGG (*Med*) postoperative

postribolo [pos'tribolo] sm (*letter*) brothel

postscriptum [post'skriptum] sm INV postscript

postumo, -a ['postumo] AGG posthumous; (*tardivo*) belated
♦ **postumi** SMPL (*conseguenze*) consequences, after-effects; **soffrire i postumi della sbornia** to have a hangover

potabile [po'tabile] AGG drinkable; **acqua potabile** drinking water

potare [po'tare] /72/ vt (*albero da frutta*) to prune; (*siepe*) to trim

potassio [po'tassjo] sm potassium

potatura [pota'tura] sf pruning

potente [po'tente] AGG (*gen*) powerful; (*nazione*) strong; (*efficace: medicina, veleno*) potent, strong; (*argomenti*) potent, forceful; **un motore potente** a powerful engine; **è potente all'interno dell'azienda** he has a lot of influence in the company ♦ SMPL: **i potenti** the mighty, the powerful

potentino, -a [poten'tino] AGG of *o* from Potenza ♦ SM, SF inhabitant *o* native of Potenza

Potenza [po'tɛntsa] sf Potenza

potenza [po'tɛntsa] sf **1** (*potere, influenza*) power, influence; (*forza: fisica, psicologica*) strength; (*efficacia: di medicina, veleno*) potency; (*di argomenti, onde, pugni, armi*) force; **la potenza della stampa** the power of the press; **le Grandi Potenze** the Great Powers; **potenza militare** military might *o* strength **2** (*Fis, Mat*) power; **all'ennesima potenza** to the nth degree; **è un idiota all'ennesima potenza** he's a complete and utter idiot

potenziale [poten'tsjale] AGG, SM potential

potenziamento [potentsja'mento] SM development

potenziare [poten'tsjare] /19/ vt to develop

potere¹ [po'tere] /78/ SM (*gen*) power; **una lotta per il potere** a power struggle; **avere il potere di fare qc** (*capacità*) to have the power *o* ability to do sth; (*autorità*) to have the authority *o* power to do sth; **ha il potere di rovinare sempre tutto** he always manages to ruin everything; **il quarto potere** (*stampa*) the fourth estate; **non ho nessun potere su di lui** I have no power *o* influence over him; **essere al potere** (*Pol*) to be in power *o* in office; **potere d'acquisto** purchasing power; **potere esecutivo** executive power

potere² [po'tere] /78/ VB AUS IRREG (*nei tempi composti prende l'ausiliare del verbo che accompagna*) **1** (*possibilità, capacità*) can; (*sogg: persona*) can, to be able to; **non posso venire** I can't come; **non è potuto venire** he couldn't come, he was unable to come; **potresti aprire la finestra?** could you open the window?; **non potrò venire domani** I won't be able to come tomorrow; **dovresti potercela fare da solo** you should be able to do it by yourself; **non potrà mai farlo da solo** he'll never be able to do it alone; **non ho potuto farlo** I couldn't *o* wasn't able *o* was unable to do it; **come hai potuto fare una cosa simile?** how could you do a thing like that?; **a più non posso** (*correre*) as fast as one can; (*urlare*) as loud as one can **2** (*permesso*) can, may; **posso?** may I?; **posso entrare?** can *o* may I come in?; **potrei parlarti?** could I have a word with you?; **si può sapere dove sei stato?** where on earth have you been?; **si può visitare il castello tutti i giorni dell'anno** you can visit the castle any day of the year **3** (*eventualità*) can; **può anche esser vero** it may *o* might *o* could even be true; **può aver avuto un incidente** he may have had an accident; **può darsi che non venga** he may not *o* might not come; **può essere che non voglia** he may not *o* might not want to; **può accadere di tutto** anything can happen; **potrebbe avere trent'anni** he must be about thirty; **si può fare** it can be done; **può darsi** perhaps; **pensi di andarci? —** **può darsi** do you think you'll go? — perhaps **4** (*augurio*): **potessimo trovare un po' di pace!** if only we could get a little peace! **5** (*rimprovero*): **potresti almeno ringraziare!** you could *o* might at least say thank you!; **avresti potuto dirmelo!** you could *o* might have told me! ♦ VT IRREG: **puoi molto per me** you can do a lot for me; **non ha potuto niente** he could do nothing; **non ne posso più!** I can't take any more!

potestà [potes'ta] SF INV (*Dir: potere*) power, authority

potrò [po'trɔ] VB *vedi* **potere²**

poveraccio, -a, -ci, -ce [pove'ratt∫o] SM, SF poor devil

povero, -a ['pɔvero] AGG **1** (*gen*) poor; (*stile, scusa*) weak; (*raccolto*) poor, scanty; (*vegetazione*) sparse; (*vestito*) poor; (*stanza*) bare; **sono molto poveri** they're very poor; **povero di** lacking in, having little; **minerale povero di ferro** ore with a low iron content; **aria povera di ossigeno** air low in oxygen; **paese povero di risorse** country short of *o* lacking in resources **2** (*fraseologia*): **essere povero in canna** to be as poor as a church mouse; **povero illuso!** poor fool!; **povera piccola!** poor little thing!; **sei un povero stupido!** you're a stupid fool!; **povera me!** poor me!; **in parole povere** in plain language; **povero di spirito** half-wit; **povero te se lo fai!** just you dare!; **il mio povero marito** my poor (late) husband ♦ SM, SF poor person; **i poveri** the poor

povertà [pover'ta] SF (*vedi agg*) poverty; weakness; scantiness; sparseness

pozione [pot'tsjone] SF potion

pozza ['pɔttsa] SF (*pozzanghera*) puddle; **una pozza di sangue** a pool of blood

pozzanghera [pot'tsangera] SF puddle

pozzo ['pɔttso] SM (*di acqua, petrolio*) well; (*di miniera*) shaft; (*cava: di carbone*) pit; **essere un pozzo di scienza** to be a walking encyclopaedia *o* a mine of information; **essere un pozzo senza fondo** (*ghiottone*) to be a bottomless pit; **pozzo nero** cesspit; **pozzo petrolifero** oil well

pp. ABBR (= *pagine*) pp

p.p. ABBR (= *per procura*) pp

PPI [pipi'i] SIGLA M (*Pol:* = *Partito Popolare Italiano*) *party originating from DC*

PP.TT. ABBR = Poste e Telecomunicazioni

PR [pi'ɛrre] SIGLA = Parma ♦ SIGLA M (*Pol*: = Partito Radicale) ♦ ABBR 1 = piano regolatore 2 = procuratore della Repubblica

PRA [pra] SIGLA M (= *Pubblico Registro Automobilistico*) ≈ DVLA (*Brit*) (= *Driver and Vehicle Licensing Agency*)

Praga ['praga] SF Prague

pragmatico, -a, -ci, -che [prag'matiko] AGG pragmatic

prammatica [pram'matika] SF custom; **essere di prammatica** to be customary

pranoterapia [pranotera'pia] SF faith healing

pranzare [pran'dzare] /72/ VI (*aus* avere) to (have) lunch; **abbiamo appena pranzato** we've just had lunch; **pranzare fuori** to go out for lunch; **siamo andati a pranzare fuori** we went out for lunch

pranzo ['prandzo] SM (*a mezzogiorno*) lunch; **vieni a pranzo da me?** will you come and have lunch with me?; **pranzo di lavoro** business lunch; **pranzo di nozze** wedding breakfast

prassi ['prassi] SF normal procedure

pratica, -che ['pratika] SF 1 (*attività*) practice; **la pratica e la teoria** practice and theory; **in pratica** (*praticamente*) in practice; **mettere in pratica qc** to put sth into practice; **ho messo in pratica i tuoi consigli** I have acted on your advice; **cercate di mettere in pratica questa idea** try to put this idea into practice 2 (*esperienza*) (practical) experience; (*conoscenza*) knowledge, familiarity; (*tirocinio*) training; **far pratica presso un avvocato** to be articled to a solicitor (*Brit*) o lawyer (*USA*); **acquistare pratica** to gain experience; **ha fatto pratica presso un altro falegname** he was trained by another carpenter; **devi solo fare un po' di pratica** you only need a bit of practice; **non ho molta pratica di queste cose** I haven't got much experience in these things 3 (*Amm: incartamento*) file, dossier; (: *affare*) matter, case; **può cercarmi quella pratica?** can you get that file for me?; **fare le pratiche per** to do the paperwork for 4 (*usanza*) practice; **pratica restrittiva** restrictive practice; **pratiche illecite** (*abortive*) dishonest practices; **pratiche religiose** religious practices

praticabile [prati'kabile] AGG (*progetto*) practicable, feasible; (*luogo*) passable, practicable

praticamente [pratika'mente] AVV 1 (*quasi*) practically, almost 2 (*in modo pratico*) in a practical way, practically

praticante [prati'kante] AGG practising (*Brit*), practicing (*USA*) ♦ SM, SF apprentice, trainee; (*Rel*) (regular) churchgoer

praticare [prati'kare] /20/ VT 1 (*esercitare: arte, medicina*) to practise (*Brit*), practice (*USA*); (*Sport: calcio, tennis*) to play; (: *nuoto, scherma*) to go in for, do; **pratica molti sport** he does a lot of different sports 2 (*frequentare: persona*) to associate with, mix with; (: *luogo*) to frequent 3 (*eseguire: apertura, incisione*) to make; **praticare uno sconto** to give a discount

praticità [pratitʃi'ta] SF practicality, practicalness; **per praticità** for practicality's sake

pratico, -a, -ci, -che ['pratiko] AGG 1 (*non teorico, realista*) practical; **avere senso pratico** to be practical; **all'atto pratico** in practice 2 (*comodo: gen*) practical; (: *strumento*) handy; **un metodo pratico** a practical method; **un aggeggio molto pratico** a very handy tool; **mi è più pratico venire di pomeriggio** it's more convenient for me to come in the afternoon; **è pratico avere i negozi così vicino** it's handy o convenient to have the shops so near 3 **pratico di** (*esperto*) experienced o skilled in; (*familiare*) familiar with; **è pratico di motori** he's good with engines; **è pratico del mestiere** he knows his trade; **è pratica del luogo** she knows the place well; **non sono pratica di queste parti** I don't know this area very well

prato ['prato] SM meadow; (*di giardino*) lawn; **prato all'inglese** lawn

preallarme [preal'larme] SM warning (signal)

Prealpi [pre'alpi] SFPL: **le Prealpi** (the) Pre-Alps

prealpino, -a [preal'pino] AGG of the Pre-Alps

preambolo [pre'ambolo] SM preamble; **senza tanti preamboli** without beating about (*Brit*) o around (*USA*) the bush

preannunciare [preannun'tʃare] /19/, **preannunziare** [preannun'tsjare] VT to give advance notice of; **le nubi preannunziavano la tempesta** the clouds heralded the storm

preavvisare [preavvi'zare] /72/ VT to give advance notice of

preavviso [preav'vizo] SM (*advance*) notice; (*Dir*) notice; **senza preavviso** without notice; **3 giorni di preavviso** 3 days' notice; **telefonata con preavviso** personal o person-to-person call

prebellico, -a, -ci, -che [pre'belliko] AGG prewar *attr*

precariato [preka'rjato] SM temporary employment

precarietà [prekarje'ta] SF precariousness

precario, -ria, -ri, -rie [pre'karjo] AGG 1 precarious; **in precarie condizioni economiche** in a precarious financial state 2 (*Scol*) temporary, without tenure ♦ SM, SF (*Scol*) temporary member of staff

precauzionale [prekauttsjo'nale] AGG precautionary

precauzione [prekaut'tsjone] SF 1 (*cautela*) caution, care 2 (*misura*) precaution; **prendere precauzioni** to take precautions

precedente [pretʃe'dente] AGG previous; **il giorno precedente** the previous day, the day before; **il discorso/ film precedente** the previous o preceding speech/film ♦ SM precedent; **senza precedenti** unprecedented; **precedenti penali** (*Dir*) criminal record *sg*

precedentemente [pretʃedente'mente] AVV previously, before

precedenza [pretʃe'dentsa] SF 1 (*priorità*) priority, precedence; **dare precedenza assoluta a qc** to give sth top priority 2 (*Aut*): **avere la precedenza** to have right of way; **dare la precedenza** to give way 3 **in precedenza** (*precedentemente*) previously, before

precedere [pre'tʃedere] /29/ VT to precede, go (o come) before

precettare [pretʃet'tare] /72/ VT (*Mil*) to call up (*Brit*), draft (*USA*); (*scioperanti*) to order back to work (*via an injunction*)

precettazione [pretʃettat'tsjone] SF (*di scioperanti*) labour (*Brit*) o labor (*USA*) injunction *calling off industrial action*; (*alle armi*) call-up (*Brit*), draft (*USA*)

precetto [pre'tʃetto] SM (*gen*) precept; (*Mil*) call-up papers *pl* (*Brit*), draft notice (*USA*)

precettore [pretʃet'tore] SM (private) tutor

precipitare [pretʃipi'tare] /72/ VT (*gettare dall'alto in basso*) to hurl down, fling down; (*fig: affrettare*) to hurry, rush; **precipitare una decisione** to make a hasty decision; **non precipitiamo le cose** let's not rush o precipitate things ♦ VI (*aus* essere) 1 (*cadere*) fall (headlong); (*aereo*) to crash; **precipitare da una rupe/in un burrone** to fall off a cliff/down a ravine; **la situazione sta precipitando** the situation is getting out of control 2 (*Chim*) to precipitate; **precipitarsi** VIP (*affrettarsi*) to rush; **precipitarsi** VR (*gettarsi*): **precipitarsi da, in** to hurl o fling o.s. from, into

precipitato, -a [pretʃipi'tato] AGG hasty ♦ SM (*Chim*) precipitate

precipitazione [pretʃipitat'tsjone] SF (*Meteor*) precipitation; (*fig*) haste; **con precipitazione** hastily

precipitoso, -a [pretʃipi'toso] AGG (*fig: affrettato*) hasty, rushed; (: *avventato*) rash, reckless; **è un po' troppo precipitoso** he's a bit too rash

precipizio, -zi [pretʃi'pittsjo] SM precipice; **cadere da un precipizio** to fall over a precipice; **scogli a precipizio sul mare** cliffs rising sheer from the sea; **essere sull'orlo del precipizio** (*fig*) to be on the edge of a precipice; **correre a precipizio** (*fig*) to run headlong

precipuo, -a [pre'tʃipuo] AGG main, principal

precisamente [pretʃiza'mente] AVV (*gen*) precisely; (*con esattezza*) exactly; **è precisamente quello che intendevo** that's precisely what I meant

precisare [pretʃi'zare] /72/ VT to clarify; (*spiegare*) to explain (in detail); **vi preciseremo la data in seguito** we'll let you know the exact date later; **tengo a precisare che...** I must point out that ...; **vorrei precisare che...** I'd like to point out that ...

precisazione [pretʃizat'tsjone] SF clarification

precisione [pretʃi'zjone] SF (*esattezza*) precision; (*accuratezza*) accuracy; **ci vuole molta precisione** great accuracy is needed; **strumenti di precisione** precision instruments

preciso, -a [pre't∫izo] AGG 1 (*esatto*) precise; (*accurato*) accurate, precise; (*ben determinato: ordine, idee, piano*) precise, definite; **in quel preciso istante** at that precise *o* very moment; **queste sono le sue precise parole** these were his very words; **sono le 4 precise** it's exactly 4 o'clock; **non ho un'idea precisa di come funzioni** I don't know precisely how it works; **è molto preciso nel suo lavoro** he's very careful in his work 2 (*uguale*): **2 vestiti precisi** 2 dresses exactly the same; **il tuo cappello è preciso al mio** your hat is exactly the same as *o* identical to mine

precludere [pre'kludere] /3/ VT IRREG to preclude

precluso, -a [pre'kluzo] PP *di* precludere

precoce [pre'kɔt∫e] AGG (*stagione*) early; (*bambino*) precocious; (*vecchiaia*) premature; (*morte*) untimely; (*decisione*) hasty, premature

precocità [prekot∫i'ta] SF (*di morte*) untimeliness; (*di bambino*) precociousness, precocity

preconcetto [prekon't∫etto] AGG preconceived ♦ SM preconceived idea, prejudice

precorrere [pre'korrere] /28/ VT IRREG to anticipate; **precorrere i tempi** to be ahead of one's time

precorritore, -trice [prekorri'tore] SM, SF precursor, forerunner

precorso, -a [pre'korso] PP *di* precorrere

precursore [prekur'sore] SM precursor, forerunner

preda ['preda] SF (*animale, anche fig*) prey; (*bottino*) booty; **uccello da preda** bird of prey; **essere preda di** to fall prey to; **essere in preda a** (*paura, terrore*) to be prey to; **era in preda all'ira** he was beside himself with rage; **era in preda al panico** he was in a panic, he was panicking

predare [pre'dare] /72/ VT to plunder

predatore, -trice [preda'tore] AGG predatory ♦ SM, SF (*Zool*) predator; (*predone*) plunderer

predecessore, -a [predet∫es'sore] SM, SF predecessor

predella [pre'della] SF (*di cattedra*) platform, dais; (*di altare*) predella, altar-step

predestinare [predesti'nare] /72/ VT to predestine

predestinazione [predestinat'tsjone] SF predestination

predetto, -a [pre'detto] PP *di* predire ♦ AGG aforesaid, aforementioned

predica, -che ['predika] SF (*Rel*) sermon; (*fig*) lecture, talking-to; **fare una predica** to preach a sermon; **fare una predica a qn** (*fig*) to give sb a lecture o a talking-to

predicare [predi'kare] /20/ VT to preach ♦ VI (*aus avere*) (*anche fig*) to preach; **predica bene e razzola male** he doesn't practise what he preaches

predicativo, -a [predika'tivo] AGG predicative

predicato [predi'kato] SM (*Gramm*) predicate; **in funzione di predicato** predicatively

prediletto, -a [predi'letto] PP *di* prediligere ♦ AGG (*figlio, allievo*) favourite (*Brit*), favorite (*USA*); (*amico*) best, closest ♦ SM, SF favourite (*Brit*), favorite (*USA*); **il prediletto della mamma** mummy's pet

predilezione [predilet'tsjone] SF partiality, predilection, fondness; **avere una predilezione per qc/qn** to be partial to sth/fond of sb

prediligere [predi'lidʒere] /117/ VT IRREG to prefer, have a preference *o* a predilection for; **queste sono le piante che prediligo** these are the plants I like best

predire [pre'dire] /38/ VT IRREG to predict, foretell; **aveva predetto che sarebbe successo** he had predicted it would happen; **predire il futuro** to tell *o* predict the future

predisporre [predis'porre] VB IRREG /77/ VT to get ready, prepare; **predisporre qn a qc** to prepare sb for sth; **predisporsi** VR: **predisporsi a qc** to prepare o.s. for sth

predisposizione [predisposit'tsjone] SF (*Med*) predisposition; (*attitudine*) bent, aptitude; **avere predisposizione alla musica** to have a bent *o* gift for music

predisposto, -a [predis'posto] PP *di* predisporre ♦ AGG (*gen*) prepared; **le misure predisposte per prevenire gli incidenti stradali...** the measures which have been drawn up to prevent road accidents ...; **predisposto alle malattie** (*persona*) prone to illness

predizione [predit'tsjone] SF prediction

predominante [predomi'nante] AGG predominant

predominare [predomi'nare] /72/ VI (*aus avere*) (*prevalere*) to predominate; (*eccellere*) to excel

predominio [predo'minjo] SM (*il prevalere*) predominance; (*supremazia*) supremacy; (*dominio*) domination; (*fig*) sway; **avere il predominio** (*prevalere*) to be predominant

preesistente [preezis'tɛnte] AGG pre-existent

preesistere [pree'zistere] /11/ VI IRREG (*aus essere*) to pre-exist

preesistito, -a [preezis'tito] PP *di* preesistere

prefabbricato, -a [prefabbri'kato] AGG (*Edil*) prefabricated ♦ SM prefab, prefabricated house

prefazione [prefat'tsjone] SF preface, foreword

preferenza [prefe'rɛntsa] SF preference; **di preferenza** preferably, by preference; **a preferenza di** rather than; **dare la preferenza a qn/qc** to prefer sb/sth; **non ho preferenze** I have no preference either way, I don't mind; **qui non si fanno preferenze** there is no favouritism here

preferenziale [preferen'tsjale] AGG preferential; **corsia preferenziale** (*Aut*) bus and taxi lane; (*fig*) fast track

preferibile [prefe'ribile] AGG: **preferibile (a)** preferable (to), better (than); **sarebbe preferibile andarsene** it would be better if we left

preferibilmente [preferibil'mente] AVV preferably

preferire [prefe'rire] /55/ VT to prefer, like better; **preferisco la città alla campagna** I prefer the town to the countryside; **preferisce spendere i suoi soldi in vestiti** he prefers to spend his money on clothes; **preferirei lavorare a casa** I'd rather work at home; **preferisco non parlarne** I'd rather not talk about it; **preferirei non farlo** I'd rather not do it, I'd prefer not to do it; **preferirei morire piuttosto che...** I'd rather die than ...; **cosa preferisci, tè o caffè?** what would you like, tea or coffee?; **preferire il caffè al tè** to prefer coffee to tea, like coffee better than tea; **preferirei un'insalata** I'd rather have a salad

prefetto [pre'fetto] SM prefect

prefettura [prefet'tura] SF prefecture

prefiggere [pre'fiddʒere] /79/ VT IRREG: **prefiggersi qc** (*scopo, meta*) to set o.s. sth

prefigurare [prefigu'rare] /72/ VT (*simboleggiare*) to foreshadow; (*prevedere*) to foresee

prefisso, -a [pre'fisso] PP *di* prefiggere ♦ SM (*Telec*) dialling (*Brit*) *o* dial (*USA*) code; (*Gramm*) prefix; **qual è il prefisso di Londra?** what's the code for London?

pregare [pre'gare] /80/ VT (*Rel*) to pray to; (*supplicare*) to beg; (*chiedere*): **stava pregando** she was praying; **pregare qn di fare qc** to ask sb to do sth; **l'ho pregata di venire** I asked her to come; **i passeggeri sono pregati di...** passengers are requested to ...; **farsi pregare** to need coaxing *o* persuading; **non si fa pregare due volte** he doesn't wait to be asked twice; **ti prego!** please!; **ti prego, lasciami in pace** please leave me alone!; **la prego, stia comodo** please don't get up

pregevole [pre'dʒevole] AGG (*persona, azione*) praiseworthy; (*oggetto, opera*) valuable

pregherò ecc [prege'rɔ] VB *vedi* pregare

preghiera [pre'gjɛra] SF (*Rel*) prayer; (*richiesta*) request; (*supplica*) plea, entreaty

pregiarsi [pre'dʒarsi] /62/ VR (*frm*): **pregiarsi di fare qc** to be honoured to do sth; **mi pregio di farle sapere che...** I am pleased *o* honoured to inform you that ...

pregiatissimo, -a [predʒa'tissimo] AGG (*in lettere*): **pregiatissimo Signor G. Agelli** G. Agelli, Esq(uire)

pregiato, -a [pre'dʒato] AGG (*opera*) valuable; (*tessuto*) fine; (*valuta*) strong; **un tappeto pregiato** a valuable carpet; **vino pregiato** vintage wine

pregio, -gi ['predʒo] SM (*valore*) worth, value; (*qualità*) (good) quality, merit; (*frm: stima*) esteem, regard; **avere molti pregi** (*persona*) to have a lot of good qualities; **i pregi artistici di un'opera** the artistic merit of a work; **il pregio di questo sistema è...** the merit of this system is ...; **i pregi e i difetti** the good points and the bad points; **oggetto di pregio** valuable object

pregiudicare [predʒudi'kare] /20/ VT (*compromettere*): **pregiudicare qc** to jeopardize sth, put sth in jeopardy, prejudice sth; **pregiudicare la propria salute** to endanger one's health

pregiudicato, -a [predʒudiˈkato] SM, SF (*Dir*) person with a criminal record

pregiudizio, -zi [predʒuˈdittsjo] SM 1 (*opinione errata*) prejudice; (*superstizione*) superstition; **avere dei pregiudizi contro** o **nei confronti di qn** to be prejudiced o biased against sb; **è un pregiudizio largamente diffuso** it's a widely held superstition; **pregiudizio razziale** racial prejudice 2 (*danno*) harm *no pl*; **essere di pregiudizio a** to be detrimental to; **con pregiudizio della sua salute** to the detriment of his health

Preg.mo ABBR = **pregiatissimo**

pregnante [preɲˈɲante] AGG (*fig: frasi, parole*) pregnant, meaningful

pregno, -a [ˈpreɲɲo] AGG 1 (*gravido: animale*) pregnant 2 **pregno di** (*odio, passione*) filled with, full of

prego [ˈprego] ESCL (*a chi ringrazia*) don't mention it!, you're welcome!, not at all!; (*invitando qn ad accomodarsi*) please sit down!; (*invitando qn ad andare prima*) after you!; **prego, si accomodi** (*entri*) please come in; (*si sieda*) please take a seat; **posso prenderlo? — prego!** can I take it? — please do!; **prego? pardon?, sorry?** (*Brit*)

pregustare [preguˈstare] /72/ VT to look forward to; **pregustava il piacere della vendetta** he savoured the idea of vengeance

preistoria [preisˈtɔrja] SF prehistory; **fin dalla preistoria** from time immemorial

preistorico, -a, -ci, -che [preisˈtɔriko] AGG prehistoric; (*fig: scherz*) antediluvian

prelato [preˈlato] SM prelate

prelavaggio [prelaˈvaddʒo] SM prewash

prelazione [prelatˈtsjone] SF (*Dir*) pre-emption; **avere il diritto di prelazione su qc** to have the first option on sth

prelevamento [prelevaˈmento] SM (*Banca*) withdrawal; (*di merce*) picking up, collection

prelevare [preleˈvare] /72/ VT (*Banca*) to withdraw; (*campione di sangue*) to take; (*merce*) to collect, to pick up; (*sogg: polizia*) to arrest; **vorrei prelevare 150 sterline** I'd like to withdraw 150 pounds, please

prelievo [preˈljevo] SM (*Banca*) withdrawal; (*di merce*) collection; (*di tasse*) levying; **fare un prelievo di sangue** to take a blood sample

preliminare [preliɱiˈnare] AGG preliminary ♦ **preliminari** SMPL preliminaries; (*in rapporto sessuale*) foreplay *sg*

preludere [preˈludere] /35/ VI IRREG (*aus avere*) **preludere a** (*preannunciare: crisi, guerra, temporale*) to herald, be a sign of 2 (*introdurre: dibattito*) to introduce, be a prelude to

preludio, -di [preˈludjo] SM (*Mus, anche fig*) prelude; (*introduzione*) introduction

preluso, -a [preˈluzo] PP di **preludere**

pre-maman [premaˈmã] AGG INV maternity *attr* ♦ SM INV maternity dress

prematrimoniale [prematrimoˈnjale] AGG premarital

prematuro, -a [premaˈturo] AGG (*gen*) premature; (*morte*) untimely ♦ SM, SF premature baby

premeditare [premediˈtare] /72/ VT to premeditate, plan; **omicidio premeditato** premeditated murder

premeditazione [premeditatˈtsjone] SF (*Dir*) premeditation; **con premeditazione** with intent

premere [ˈpremere] /29/ VT (*gen*) to press; **premere il grilletto** to pull the trigger; **premi forte!** press hard! ♦ VI (*aus avere*) 1 **premere su** (*gen*) to press on; (*pedale*) to press down on; (*fig*) to put pressure on 2 (*fig: stare a cuore*): **è una faccenda che mi preme molto** it's a matter which I am very concerned about; **gli premeva (di) terminare il lavoro** he was anxious to finish the job

premesso, -a [preˈmesso] PP di **premettere**

premettere [preˈmettere] /63/ VT IRREG 1 (*dire prima*) to start by saying, state first; **vorrei premettere alcune considerazioni di carattere generale** I should like to begin by making a few general points; **premetto che...** I must say first of all that ...; **premesso che...** given that ...; **ciò premesso...** that (having been) said ... 2 (*porre prima*) to put before; **premettere una prefazione ad un'opera** to preface a work

premiare [preˈmjare] /19/ VT (*atleta, studente*) to give a prize to, award a prize to; (*libro, film*) to award a prize to;

(*fig: merito, onestà*) to reward; **il preside ha premiato due studenti** the head gave prizes to two students; **il film è stato premiato** the film won a prize; **è stata premiata con una medaglia** she was awarded a medal

premiazione [premjatˈtsjone] SF prize-giving

premier [ˈpremjer] SM INV (*Pol*) premier

preminente [premiˈnente] AGG prominent, pre-eminent

premio, -mi [ˈpremjo] SM 1 (*gen*) prize; (*ricompensa*) reward; **ho ricevuto un premio** I was given a prize; **in premio per** as a prize (o reward) for; **premio di consolazione** consolation prize; **premio Nobel** Nobel prize 2 (*Fin, Assicurazione*) premium 3 (*indennità speciale*) bonus; **premio d'ingaggio** (*Sport*) signing-on fee; **premio di produzione** productivity bonus ♦ AGG INV: **vincere una vacanza premio** to win a holiday

premisi ecc [preˈmizi] VB vedi **premettere**

premonitore, -trice [premoniˈtore] AGG premonitory

premonizione [premonitˈtsjone] SF premonition

premunire [premuˈnire] /55/ VT: **premunire (contro)** (*nemico, influenza*) to protect (against); **premunire qn contro i rischi della droga** to make sb aware of the dangers of drugs; **premunirsi** VR: **premunirsi (di** o **con)** to arm o.s. (with); **premunirsi (contro)** to protect o.s. (from), guard o.s. (against)

premura [preˈmura] SF 1 (*fretta*) haste, hurry; **aver premura** to be in a hurry; **svelto, che ho premura!** quick, I'm in a hurry!; **far premura a qn** to hurry sb; **mi dispiace farti premura, ma devo andare** I'm sorry to hurry you, but I have to go 2 (*riguardo*) attention, care; **usare ogni premura nei riguardi di qn**, **circondare qn di premure** to make a fuss of sb

premuroso, -a [premuˈroso] AGG attentive, thoughtful, considerate; **un padre premuroso** a devoted father

prenatale [prenaˈtale] AGG antenatal, prenatal

prendere [ˈprendere] VB IRREG /81/ VT 1 (*gen*) to take; (*portare: cosa*) to get, fetch; (: *persona*) to pick up, fetch; **ha preso il libro dal tavolo** he picked up o took the book from the table; **l'ho preso dal cassetto** I took o got it out of the drawer; **l'ha preso per mano** she took his hand o took him by the hand; **hai preso l'ombrello?** have you taken your umbrella?; **prendi quella borsa** take that bag; **prendere qc in spalla** to shoulder sth; **prendere qc per il manico** to take sth by the handle; **andare a prendere qc** to go and get sth; **vai a prendermi gli occhiali** go and get my glasses; **venire a prendere qn** to come and get sb; **potresti venire a prendermi alla stazione?** could you come and get me from the station?; **abbiamo preso una casa** (*affittare*) we have rented a house; (*comprare*) we have bought a house 2 (*afferrare*) to seize, grab; (*catturare: ladro, pesce*) to catch; (: *fortezza*) to take; **prendere qn per i capelli** to grab sb by the hair; **è stato preso dalla polizia** he was caught by the police; **l'ho preso mentre tentava di scappare** I caught him trying to escape; **ho preso un grosso pesce** I caught a huge fish; **la cintura mi è rimasta presa nella porta** my belt got caught in the door 3 (*direzione, scorciatoia, mezzo pubblico*) to take; **non so che strada prendere** I don't know which road to take; **ha preso il treno** he took the train, he went by train; **ha preso il treno delle 10** he took o caught the 10 o'clock train; **preferisco prendere l'aereo anziché il treno** I prefer to go by plane rather than by train; **la nave ha preso il largo** the ship put out to sea 4 (*registrare*) to take (down); **prendere le misure di qn** to take sb's measurements; **prendere le generalità di qn** to take down sb's particulars; **prendere nota di** to take note of 5 (*guadagnare*) to get, earn; (*chiedere: somma, prezzo*) to charge, ask; **quanto prende al mese?** how much does he earn a month?; **prende 2000 euro al mese** he makes o earns 2000 euros a month; **quanto prende per un taglio di capelli?** how much do you charge for a haircut? 6 (*ricevere: colpi, schiaffi, sgridata*) to get; (*subire: malattia*) to catch; **le ha prese** he got a good hiding; **ho preso uno spavento** I got such a fright; **ho preso freddo** I've caught a chill; **ho preso l'influenza** I've caught (the) flu; **ho preso un bel voto** I got a good mark; **non so come la prenderà** I don't know how he'll take the news 7 (*ingoiare: pasto, panino, tè*) to have; (: *medicina*) to take; **non prendo nulla fuori pasto** I don't eat between meals; **prendi qualcosa?** (*da bere, da mangiare*) would you like something to eat (o drink)?; **prendo un caffè** I'll have a coffee; **prendi pure** help yourself **8** (*assumere: collaboratore, dipendente*) to take on, hire; (: *responsabilità*) to take on, assume; (: *tono, aria*) to put on; (: *colore*) to take on; (*decisione*) to take, make, come to; **prendere un impegno** to take on a commitment; **ha preso uno strano odore** it smells funny; **prendere l'abitudine di** to get into the habit of **9** (*pervadere*): **essere preso dai rimorsi** to be full of remorse; **essere preso dal panico** to be panic-stricken; **cosa ti prende?** what's got into you?; **quel film mi ha preso** that film caught my imagination **10** (*scambiare*): **prendere qn/qc per** to mistake sb/sth for; **mi ha preso per mio fratello** he mistook me for my brother; **ha preso le mie parole per** *o* **come un'offesa** he took offence at my words; **per chi mi prendi?** who do you think I am?, what do you take me for? **11** (*trattare: persona*) to handle; **prendere qn per il verso giusto** to handle sb the right way; **prendere qn con le buone/cattive** to handle sb tactfully/rudely; **so come prenderlo** I know how to handle him **12** (*occupare: spazio, tempo*) to take up; **il tavolo prende poco posto** the table doesn't take up much room; **questo lavoro mi sta prendendo troppo tempo** this work is taking up too much of my time **13** (*cominciare*): **prendere a fare qc** to begin to do sth, start doing sth **14 prendersela** (*adirarsi*) to get annoyed; (*preoccuparsi*) to get upset, worry; **prendersela a male** to take offence; **prendersela con qn** to get angry with sb; **perché te la prendi sempre con me?** why do you always pick on me?; **prendersela comoda** to take it easy **15** (*fraseologia*): **prendere da qn** (*assomigliare*) to take after sb; **prendere a calci qn** to kick sb; **prendere qn per fame** to starve sb into submission; **prendere o lasciare** take it or leave it; **prendersi la soddisfazione (di)** to have the satisfaction (of); **prendersi una vacanza** to take a holiday; **prendersi cura di qn/qc** to look after sb/sth; **prendersi gioco di qn** to mock sb; **prendere parte a** to take part in; **prendere fuoco** to catch fire ♦ **vi** (*aus* **avere**) **1** (*far presa: colla, cemento*) to set; (: *piante*) to take (root); (: *fuoco*) to catch **2** (*andare*): **prendere a destra** *o* **a** turn right; **prendere per i campi** to go across the fields **3** (*fraseologia*): **mi è preso un colpo** I got such a fright; **mi è preso freddo** I started feeling cold; **mi è presa la voglia di andare al mare** I feel like going to the seaside; **prendersi vr** (*uso reciproco: afferrarsi*) to grab each other, seize each other; **prendersi a pugni** to come to blows, punch each other; **prendersi a calci** to kick each other

prendisole [prendi'sole] SM INV sundress

prenotare [preno'tare] /72/ VT (*posto, tavolo*) to book, reserve; (*camera*) to book; **prenotarsi** VR: **prenotarsi per qc** to put one's name down for sth

prenotazione [prenotat'tsjone] SF booking, reservation; **fare una prenotazione** to make a booking *o* reservation

prensile ['prensile] AGG prehensile

preoccupante [preokku'pante] AGG worrying

preoccupare [preokku'pare] /72/ VT (*impensierire*) to worry; **ciò che mi preoccupa è il viaggio** what's worrying *o* bothering me is the journey; **Giovanna mi preoccupa, sono preoccupato per Giovanna** I am worried about Giovanna; **la sua salute mi preoccupa** I'm concerned *o* anxious about his health; **preoccuparsi** VIP: **preoccuparsi (per qn/qc)** to worry (about sb/sth), be anxious (about sb/sth); **non preoccuparti** don't worry

❏ **preoccupare** non si traduce mai con la parola inglese *preoccupy*

preoccupazione [preokkupat'tsjone] SF (*problema*) worry; (*inquietudine*) anxiety, worry; **è pieno di preoccupazioni** he has lots of worries *o* problems; **la sua unica preoccupazione è vestirsi bene** his only concern *o* preoccupation is to dress well

preordinato, -a [preordi'nato] AGG preordained

preparare [prepa'rare] /72/ VT **1** (*gen*) to prepare; (*pranzo*) to make, prepare; (*letto*) to make; (*tavola*) to lay; (*valigia*) to get ready, pack; (*esame, concorso*) to prepare for, study for; **preparare da mangiare** to prepare a meal; **preparare il terreno** (*anche fig*) to prepare the ground; **chissà cosa ci prepara il futuro!** who knows what the future has in store for us! **2** **preparare qn a** (*esame*) to prepare *o* coach sb for; (*notizia*) to prepare sb for; **preparare qn per un intervento**

to get sb ready for an operation; **prepararsi** VR (*vestirsi*) to get ready; (*atleta: allenarsi*) to train; **prepararsi a qc/a fare qc** to get ready *o* prepare (o.s.) for sth/to do sth; **prepararsi ad un esame** to prepare for *o* study for an exam

preparativi [prepara'tivi] SMPL: **preparativi (per)** preparations (for); **stanno facendo i preparativi per la festa** they're making preparations for the party

preparato, -a [prepa'rato] AGG (*gen*) prepared; (*pronto*) ready; **uno studente preparato** a student who has worked hard; **scusi professore ma non sono preparato** sorry, Sir, I haven't done the work ♦ SM (*prodotto*) preparation

preparatorio, -ria, -ri, -rie [prepara'tɔrjo] AGG preparatory

preparazione [preparat'tsjone] SF (*gen*) preparation; (*Sport*) training; **preparazione atletica** physical training; **iniziare la preparazione per gli esami** to begin preparation for the exams; **non ha la necessaria preparazione per svolgere questo lavoro** he doesn't have either the knowledge or the experience necessary for the job

prepensionamento [prepensjona'mento] SM early retirement

preponderante [preponde'rante] AGG predominant

preporre [pre'porre] /77/ VT IRREG **1** (*porre innanzi*) to place before; (*fig: preferire*) to prefer, put before **2** (*mettere a capo*): **preporre qn a qc** to put sb in charge of sth; **l'ufficiale preposto al comando del reggimento** the officer in command of the regiment

preposizione [preposit'tsjone] SF (*Gramm*) preposition

preposto, -a [pre'posto] PP *di* **preporre**

prepotente [prepo'tente] AGG (*persona*) overbearing, arrogant, domineering; (*fig: desiderio, bisogno*) overwhelming, pressing; **un prepotente desiderio di qc/di fare qc** an overwhelming desire for sth/to do sth; **quel bambino è molto prepotente** that child is a real bully ♦ SM, SF bully; **è un prepotente** he's a bully

prepotenza [prepo'tentsa] SF (*arroganza*) arrogance; (*comportamento*) arrogant behaviour (*Brit*) *o* behavior (*USA*); **agire con prepotenza** to behave arrogantly; **è stata una prepotenza da parte tua** it was very high-handed of you

prepuzio, -zi [pre'puttsjo] SM (*Anat*) foreskin

prerogativa [preroga'tiva] SF **1** (*privilegio*) prerogative **2** (*peculiarità*) property, quality

presa ['presa] SF **1** (*gen*) grip; (*appiglio*) hold; (*Lotta*) grip, hold; **allentare la presa (di qc)** to loosen one's grip *o* hold (on sth); **ha allentato la presa** he loosened his grip; **avere una presa forte** to have a strong grip; **venire alle prese con qc** (*fig*) to come to grips with sth; **essere alle prese con qc** (*fig*) to be struggling with sth; **di forte presa** (*fig*) with wide appeal; **a presa rapida** (*cemento*) quick-setting; **far presa** (*colla*) to set; **ha fatto presa sul pubblico** (*fig*) it caught the public's imagination; **in presa diretta** direct transmission **2** (*conquista: di città*) taking *no pl*, capture; (*Carte*) trick **3** (*pizzico: di sale, tabacco*) pinch **4** (*Cine*): **macchina da presa** cine camera (*Brit*), movie camera (*USA*) ♦ **presa dell'acqua** water (supply) point; **presa d'aria** air inlet *o* intake; **presa di corrente** (*Elettr*) socket (*al muro*) point; **presa diretta** (*Aut*) direct drive; **presa del gas** gas (supply) point; **presa in giro** leg-pull (*Brit*), joke; **presa multipla** (*Elettr*) multiple socket; **presa di posizione** stand; **presa di possesso** taking possession; **presa SCART** SCART socket

presagio, -gi [pre'zadʒo] SM omen, sign; (*presentimento*) premonition, presentiment

presagire [preza'dʒire] /55/ VT (*prevedere*) to predict, foresee; (*presentire*) to have a premonition of

presalario [presa'larjo] SM (*Univ*) grant

presbite ['prezbite] AGG long-sighted

presbiteriano, -a [prezbite'rjano] AGG, SM, SF Presbyterian

presbiterio, -ri [prezbi'tɛrjo] SM presbytery

prescindere [preʃ'ʃindere] /102/ VI IRREG (*aus* **avere**) **prescindere da** to leave aside, leave out of consideration; **prescindendo da, a prescindere da** leaving aside, apart from

prescisso, -a [preʃ'ʃisso] PP *di* **prescindere**

prescolastico, -a, -ci, -che [presko'lastiko] AGG preschool *attr*; **bambini in età prescolastica** children not yet of school age

prescritto, -a [pres'kritto] PP *di* **prescrivere**

prescrivere [pres'krivere] /105/ VT IRREG (*Med, Dir*) to prescribe; **prescrivere una medicina a qn** to prescribe medicine for sb

prescrizione [preskrit'tsjone] SF (*Med, Dir*) prescription; (*norma*) rule, regulation; **cadere in prescrizione** (*Dir*) to become statute-barred

prese *ecc* ['prese] VB *vedi* **prendere**

presentare [prezen'tare] /72/ VT **1** (*gen*) to present; (*documento*) to present, show, produce; (*proposta, conti, bilancio*) to present, submit; (*domanda, reclamo*) to put in; **ha presentato domanda di assunzione** he put in a job application **2** (*nuovo modello*) to present; (*spettacolo*) to present, host; (*persona*) to introduce; **presentare qn (a)** to introduce sb (to); **l'ha presentata ai suoi amici** he introduced her to his friends; **presentare qn in società** to introduce sb into society; **presentare qc in un'esposizione** to show *o* display sth at an exhibition; **chi ha presentato lo spettacolo?** who presented the show? **3** (*dono*) to present, give; (*omaggi*) to present, pay; **presentare le armi** (*Mil*) to present arms; **presentarsi** VR **1** (*recarsi, farsi vedere*) to present o.s., appear; **presentarsi davanti al tribunale** to appear before the court; **è così che ti presenti?** is this any way to be seen?; **presentarsi bene/male** to have a good/poor appearance **2** (*farsi conoscere*) to introduce o.s. **3** (*candidato*) to come forward; **presentarsi a** (*elezione*) to stand for (*Brit*), run for (*USA*); (*concorso*) to enter for; (*esame*) to sit, take; **presentarsi** VIP **1** (*capitare: occasione, caso strano*) to occur, arise; **se mi si presenterà una simile occasione** should a similar opportunity occur *o* arise; **presentarsi alla mente** (*idea*) to come *o* spring to mind **2** (*apparire*) to look, seem; **la situazione si presenta difficile** things aren't looking too good, things look a bit tricky

presentazione [prezentat'tsjone] SF (*gen*) presentation; (*di persona*) introduction; **fare le presentazioni** to make the introductions

presente[1] [pre'zɛnte] AGG (*gen*) present; (*questo*): **la presente lettera** this letter; **essere presente a una riunione** to be present at *o* attend a meeting; **erano tutti presenti alla lezione** everybody was present at the class; **presente! here!**; **avere presente qn/qc** to know sb/sth; **hai presente la casa rossa vicino alla mia?** you know the red house near mine?; **tener presente qn/qc** to bear sb/sth in mind; **tieni presente che non ho molto tempo libero** bear in mind (that) I don't have much spare time ♦ SM, SF person present; **i presenti** those present; **esclusi i presenti** present company excepted ♦ SM (*Gramm*) present tense; (*tempo attuale*): **il presente** the present; **per il presente** for the present; **al presente** at present ♦ SF (*Comm: lettera*): **con la presente vi comunico...** this is to inform you that ...

presente[2] [pre'zɛnte] SM (*regalo*) present, gift

presentimento [presenti'mento] SM premonition, presentiment; **ho il presentimento che...** I've a feeling that...

presenza [pre'zɛntsa] SF (*gen*) presence; (*Scol*) attendance; **fare atto di presenza** to put in an appearance; **in presenza di** in (the) presence of; **di bella presenza** of good appearance; **presenza di spirito** presence of mind

presenziare [prezen'tsjare] /19/ VI (*aus* avere) **presenziare a** to be present at, attend

presepio, -pi [pre'zɛpjo], **presepe** [pre'zɛpe] SM nativity scene

preservare [preser'vare] /72/ VT to protect; **preservare qn da qc** to protect sb from *o* against sth; **preservare la salute** to protect one's health

preservativo [preserva'tivo] SM (*profilattico*) condom, sheath (*Brit*)

❏ **preservativo** non si traduce mai con la parola inglese *preservative*

presi *ecc* ['presi] VB *vedi* **prendere**

preside ['preside] SM, SF (*Scol*) headmaster/headmistress (*Brit*), head (teacher) (*Brit*), principal (*USA*); **preside di facoltà** (*Univ*) dean of faculty

presidente, -essa [presi'dɛnte] SM (*di nazione, club*) president; (*di assemblea, riunione, società commerciale*) chairperson, chair; (*Dir*) presiding judge *o* magistrate; **Presidente della Camera (dei Deputati)** (*Pol*) ≈ Speaker; **Presidente della commissione** (*Scol*) chief examiner; **Presidente del Consiglio (dei Ministri)** (*Pol*) ≈ Prime Minister; **Presidente della Repubblica** (*Pol*) President of the Republic

presidentessa SF **1** president **2** (*moglie*) president's wife, first lady (*USA*) **3** (*di assemblea, o Comm*) chairwoman

presidenza [presi'dɛntsa] SF **1** *vedi* **presidente** presidency, office of president **2** chairmanship; **essere alla presidenza** to be president; to be chairperson; **assumere la presidenza** to become president; to take the chair; **candidato alla presidenza** presidential candidate; candidate for the chairmanship **3** (*di preside: carica*) headship (*Brit*), post of principal (*USA*); (: *ufficio*) headmaster's/headmistress's office *o* study (*Brit*), principal's office (*USA*)

presidenziale [presiden'tsjale] AGG presidential

presidiare [presi'djare] /19/ VT (*Mil*) to garrison; (*casa, fabbrica*) to guard

presidio, -di [pre'sidjo] SM (*Mil: guarnigione*) garrison; (: *comando territoriale*) command; (: *ufficio*) area recruitment office

presiedere [pre'sjedere] VB IRREG /29/ VT (*assemblea, riunione*) to preside over, chair; **presiedere la Camera dei Deputati** (*Pol*) ≈ he (*o* she) is Speaker of the House of Commons ♦ VI (*aus* avere) **presiedere a** (*discussione, riunione*) to preside over, chair; (*realizzazione, svolgimento*) direct, be in charge of

preso, -a ['preso] PP *di* **prendere**

pressa ['pressa] SF (*Tecn*) press

pressante [pres'sante] AGG (*bisogno*) urgent, pressing; (*richiesta*) urgent

pressappoco [pressap'pɔko] AVV about, roughly, approximately; **sono pressappoco uguali** they are more or less the same; **ha pressappoco quarant'anni** he's about forty

pressare [pres'sare] /72/ VT (*Tecn, anche fig: schiacciare*) to press; **pressare qn con richieste di aiuti** to press sb for assistance

pressione [pres'sjone] SF **1** (*gen, anche Fis, Med*) pressure; **mettere sotto pressione** (*Tecn*) to pressurize; **la macchina del caffè non è ancora in pressione** there isn't enough steam in the espresso machine yet; **pentola a pressione** pressure cooker; **avere la pressione alta/bassa** (*Med*) to have high/low blood pressure; **pressione atmosferica** atmospheric pressure; **pressione sanguigna** blood pressure; **ha la pressione alta** he's got high blood pressure **2** (*fig: sollecitazione*) pressure; **far pressione su qn** to put pressure on sb; **subire forti pressioni** to be under strong pressure; **essere/mettere qn sotto pressione** to be/put sb under pressure; **gruppo di pressione** pressure group

presso ['presso] AVV **1** (*vicino*) nearby, near, close at hand; **abitava lì presso** he lived nearby *o* near there **2** **di** *o* **da presso** (*incalzare*) closely; **da presso** (*esaminare*) closely; **a un di presso** about, approximately ♦ PREP **1** (*vicino a*) close to, near (to); (*accanto a*) beside, next to; **presso a** near (to), by; **stava presso la finestra** she was standing near the window **2** **presso qn** (*in casa di*) at sb's home; **abita presso una zia** he lives with an aunt; **lavora presso di noi** (*alle dipendenze di*) he works for *o* with us; **'presso'** (*su busta, cartolina*) 'care of', 'c/o'; **Lucia Micoli, presso fam. Bianchi** Lucia Micoli, c/o Mr and Mrs Bianchi; **ambasciatore presso la Santa Sede** ambassador to the Holy See **3** (*nell'ambiente di*) among; **diffuso presso le popolazioni primitive** common among primitive peoples; **ha avuto grande successo presso i giovani** it has been a hit with young people ♦ SMPL: **nei pressi di** near, in the vicinity of; **nei pressi di Londra** near London

pressoché [presso'ke] AVV nearly, almost

pressurizzare [pressurid'dzare] /72/ VT to pressurize

prestabilire [prestabi'lire] /55/ VT to arrange beforehand, arrange in advance; **era già tutto prestabilito** everything had already been arranged

prestanome [presta'nome] SM INV, SF INV (*Dir*) nominee; (*pegg*) front man

prestante [pres'tante] AGG good-looking; **un uomo prestante** a fine figure of a man

prestanza [pres'tantsa] SF (*robust*) good looks *pl*

prestare [pres'tare] /72/ VT to lend; **prestare qc a qn** to lend sb sth, lend sth to sb; **mi ha prestato 25 euro** he lent me 25 euros; **gliel'ho prestato** I lent it to him; **farsi prestare qc da qn** to borrow sth from sb; **mi sono fatto prestare una**

penna da Luca I borrowed a pen from Luca; **prestare aiuto a qn** to give sb a helping hand, lend sb a hand; **prestare soccorso a** to give assistance to; **prestare ascolto** o **orecchio a** to listen to; **prestare attenzione a** to pay attention to; **prestare fede a** to give credence to; **prestare giuramento** to take an oath; **prestarsi** VR (offrirsi): **prestarsi (a fare qc)** to offer (to do sth); **si presta sempre volentieri** he's always willing to lend a hand; **prestarsi** VIP (essere adatto): **prestarsi per** o **a** to lend itself to, be suitable for; **la frase si presta a molteplici interpretazioni** the phrase lends itself to numerous interpretations

prestazione [prestat'tsjone] SF 1 (Tecn, Sport) performance 2 (opera, servizio): **prestazioni** SFPL services

prestigiatore, -trice [prestidʒa'tore] SM, SF conjurer

prestigio [pres'tidʒo] SM 1 (fama, autorità) prestige; **di prestigio** prestigious; **è una questione di prestigio** it's a matter of prestige 2 (illusione): **gioco di prestigio** conjuring trick

prestigioso, -a [presti'dʒoso] AGG prestigious

prestito ['prestito] SM loan; **prendere qc in prestito da qn** to borrow sth from sb; **ha preso in prestito 100 euro da sua madre** she borrowed 100 euros from her mother; **dare qc in prestito a qn** to lend sth to sb, lend sb sth; **gli ho dato in prestito la mia bici** I lent him my bike; **mi fai un prestito?** can I borrow some money from you?, will you lend me some money?; **prestito bancario** (Banca) bank loan; **prestito linguistico** loan word; **prestito pubblico** (Fin) public borrowing

presto ['presto] AVV 1 (fra poco) soon; **ci rivedremo presto** we'll see one another soon; **arriverà presto** he'll be here soon; **presto o tardi** sooner or later; **a presto** see you soon; **arrivederci a presto!** goodbye for now!, see you soon!; **il più presto possibile** as soon as possible; **se non la smette, presto avrà dei guai** if he doesn't stop that he'll be in for it 2 (in fretta) quickly, fast; **fai presto!** hurry up!, be quick (about it)!; **fai presto che è già buio** come on - it's already dark; **più presto che puoi** as quickly o fast as you can; **fare presto a fare qc** to hurry up and do sth; (con facilità) to have no trouble doing sth; **ha fatto presto a sbrigare quel lavoro** he got through that job quickly; **si fa presto a criticare** it's easy to criticize; **presto detto** it's easier said than done 3 (di buon'ora) early; **mi alzo sempre presto** I always get up early; **mi alzo più presto di te** I get up earlier than you; **sono arrivato troppo presto all'appuntamento** I arrived too early for the appointment; **è ancora presto per decidere** it's still too early o soon to decide

presumere [pre'zumere] /12/ VT IRREG 1 (ritenere, credere): **presumere che...** to presume o imagine that ...; **presumo che venga** I presume he'll come 2 (pretendere, avere la presunzione di) to presume, assume; **e tu presumi di potermi criticare?** you have the nerve to think you can criticize me; **presume di sapere più degli altri** he thinks he knows more o better than everybody else

presumibile [prezu'mibile] AGG (dati, risultati) likely

presunsi ecc [pre'zunsi] VB vedi presumere

presunto, -a [pre'zunto] PP di presumere ♦ AGG: **il presunto colpevole** the alleged culprit

presuntuoso, -a [prezuntu'oso] AGG presumptuous, conceited ♦ SM: **fare il presuntuoso** to be cocksure

presunzione [prezun'tsjone] SF 1 (congettura) presumption 2 (immodestia) presumptuousness; **peccare di presunzione** to be presumptuous

presupporre [presup'porre] /77/ VT IRREG 1 (immaginare, prevedere) to assume, suppose 2 (implicare) to presuppose

presupposto, -a [presup'posto] PP di **presupporre** ♦ SM (premessa) supposition, premise; **partendo dal presupposto che...** assuming that ...; **mancano i presupposti necessari** the necessary conditions are lacking

prete ['prɛte] SM priest; **scherzo da prete** (fig: fam) nasty trick; **prete operaio** worker-priest

pretendente [preten'dɛnte] SM, SF 1 (aspirante): **pretendente (a)** pretender (to) 2 (corteggiatore) suitor

pretendere [pre'tɛndere] /120/ VT IRREG 1 (esigere) to demand, require; (aspettarsi) to expect; **pretendo un po' di rispetto** I demand some respect; **pretendo la mia parte** I demand o claim my share; **pretende di essere pagato in anticipo** he expects to be paid in advance; **pretendi troppo**

da lui you expect too much of him 2 (sostenere, presumere): **pretendere (che...)** to claim (that ...); **pretende di aver sempre ragione** he thinks he's always right

pretenzioso, -a [preten'tsjoso] AGG pretentious

preterintenzionale [preterintentsjo'nale] AGG (Dir): **omicidio preterintenzionale** manslaughter

preteso, -a [pre'teso] PP di pretendere

pretesto [pre'testo] SM excuse, pretext; **con il pretesto di** on the pretext of; **mi ha fornito il pretesto per agire** he has provided me with a pretext for taking action

pretestuoso, -a [pretestu'oso] AGG (data, motivo) used as an excuse

pretore [pre'tore] SM (Dir) magistrate

pretura [pre'tura] SF (Dir: sede) magistrate's court (Brit), circuit o superior court (USA); (: insieme dei pretori) magistracy

prevalente [preva'lɛnte] AGG prevalent, prevailing

prevalentemente [prevalente'mente] AVV predominantly, mainly, for the most part; **in quella zona si parla prevalentemente il tedesco** German is the main o predominant language in that area

prevalenza [preva'lɛntsa] SF predominance; **in prevalenza** predominantly, mainly

prevalere [preva'lere] /126/ VI IRREG (aus avere o essere) to prevail; **prevalere su tutti per intelligenza** to surpass everyone in intelligence

prevalso, -a [pre'valso] PP di prevalere

prevaricare [prevari'kare] /20/ VI (aus avere) (abusare del potere) to abuse one's power

prevaricazione [prevarikat'tsjone] SF (abuso di potere) abuse of power

❏ **prevaricazione** non si traduce mai con la parola inglese prevarication

prevedere [preve'dere] /82/ VT IRREG 1 (avvenimento, conseguenza) to foresee, anticipate; (tempo) to forecast; **prevedere il futuro** to foretell the future; **era da prevedere** it was to be expected; **non si sarebbe potuto prevedere** that couldn't have been foreseen; **nulla lasciava prevedere che...** there was nothing to suggest o to make one think that ...; **non possiamo prevedere tutto** we can't think of everything; **non possiamo prevedere cosa succederà** we can't foresee what will happen; **come previsto** as expected; **spese previste** anticipated expenditure; **tempo previsto per domani** weather forecast for tomorrow; **è previsto maltempo per il fine settimana** bad weather is forecast for the weekend 2 (programmare) to plan; **prevedere di fare qc** to plan to do sth; **avevamo previsto di partire oggi** we had planned to leave today; **all'ora prevista** at the appointed o scheduled time; **previsto per martedì** scheduled o planned for Tuesday 3 (sogg: contratto, legge) to make provision for, provide for; **questo caso non è previsto dalla legge** the law makes no provision for such a case

prevedibile [preve'dibile] AGG predictable; **non era assolutamente prevedibile che...** no one could have foreseen that ...

prevedibilmente [prevedibil'mente] AVV as one would expect o have expected

prevenire [preve'nire] /128/ VT IRREG 1 (anticipare: domanda) to anticipate; (: obiezione) to forestall 2 **prevenire qn (di)** (preavvertire) to inform sb in advance (of); (mettere sull'avviso) to warn sb (of); **ti hanno prevenuto contro di me** they have already warned you about me 3 (evitare: malattia, disgrazia) to prevent; **gli incidenti si possono prevenire** accidents can be prevented

preventivare [preventi'vare] /72/ VT (Comm: spesa) to estimate; (: mettere in bilancio) to budget for; **non avevamo preventivato un figlio** we hadn't reckoned on having a child

preventivo, -a [preven'tivo] AGG (intervento, cura) preventive; **carcere preventivo** custody (pending trial); **bilancio preventivo** (Comm) budget ♦ SM (Comm) estimate; **fare un preventivo** to give an estimate

prevenuto, -a [preve'nuto] PP di prevenire ♦ AGG (mal disposto): **prevenuto (contro qn/qc)** prejudiced (against sb/sth)

prevenzione [preven'tsjone] SF 1 prevention; **prevenzione degli infortuni** prevention of accidents 2 (preconcetto) prejudice; **avere prevenzioni contro qn/qc** to be prejudiced against sb/sth

previdente [previ'dɛnte] AGG prudent, showing foresight; **essere previdente** to think ahead

previdenza [previ'dɛntsa] SF prudence, foresight; **istituto di previdenza** provident institution; **previdenza sociale** social security (*Brit*), welfare (*USA*)

previdi *ecc* [pre'vidi] VB *vedi* **prevedere**

previo, -a, -vi ['prɛvjo] AGG (*Comm*): **previo avviso** upon (prior) notice; **previo pagamento** upon payment

previsione [previ'zjone] SF (*gen*) prediction; (*attesa*) expectation; **tutto è andato secondo le previsioni** everything went according to expectation(s); **in previsione di** in anticipation of; **previsioni del tempo** *o* **meteorologiche** weather forecast *sg*

previsto, -a [pre'visto] PP *di* **prevedere** ♦ SM: **più/meno del previsto** more/less than expected; **prima del previsto** earlier than expected

prezioso, -a [pret'tsjoso] AGG (*gen*) precious; (*documento*) valuable; (*testimonianza, aiuto, consiglio*) invaluable; **una pietra preziosa** a precious stone; **il loro consiglio mi è stato prezioso** their advice was invaluable to me ♦ SM 1 (*gioiello*) jewel; (*oggetto di valore*) valuable; **le hanno rubato tutti i preziosi** they stole all her valuables 2 (*fig: persona*): **fare il prezioso** to play hard to get; **fa il prezioso perché è diventato importante** he puts on airs and graces because he has become important

prezzemolo [pret'tsemolo] SM (*Bot*) parsley; **essere come il prezzemolo** (*fig*) to turn up everywhere

prezzo ['prɛttso] SM price; **a buon prezzo** cheaply, at a good price; **a prezzo di costo** at cost, at cost price (*Brit*); **a metà prezzo** at half price; **menu a prezzo fisso** set price menu; **il prezzo della benzina** the price of petrol (*Brit*), gasoline (*USA*); **il prezzo pattuito è 5000 euro** the agreed price is 5000 euros; **tirare sul prezzo** to bargain, haggle; **ti faccio un prezzo d'amico** *o* **di favore** I'll let you have it at a reduced price; **pagare qc a caro prezzo** (*fig*) to pay dearly for sth; **la libertà non ha prezzo** you can't put a price on freedom; **è una cosa di poco prezzo** it's of little value, it's not worth much ♦ **prezzo d'acquisto** purchase price; **prezzo per contanti** cash price; **prezzo di fabbrica** factory price; **prezzo di listino** list price; **prezzo di mercato** market price; **prezzo scontato** reduced price; **prezzo unitario** unit price; **prezzo di vendita** selling price; **prezzo di vendita al dettaglio** retail price

prigione [pri'dʒone] SF (*luogo*) prison, jail; (*pena*) imprisonment; **andare/mettere in prigione** to go/send to prison; **scontare un anno di prigione** to spend a year in prison

prigionia [pridʒo'nia] SF imprisonment

prigioniero, -a [pridʒo'njɛro] AGG captive; **essere prigioniero** to be a prisoner; **essere prigioniero di un ricordo** to be tormented by a memory ♦ SM, SF prisoner; **fare/tenere qn prigioniero** to take/hold sb prisoner

prima¹ ['prima] AVV 1 (*in precedenza*) before; (*una volta*) once, formerly; **prima non lo sapevo** I didn't know that before; **due giorni prima** two days before *o* earlier; **ne so quanto prima** I know as much as I did before, I'm none the wiser; **amici come prima!** let's make it up *o* let's be friends again!; **prima non si faceva così** people used not to do that; **usanze di prima** former customs; **non è più la stessa di prima** she's not the same as she was 2 (*in anticipo*) beforehand, in advance; **un'altra volta dimmelo prima** next time let me know in advance 3 (*più presto*) sooner, earlier; **prima o poi** sooner or later; **prima possibile** as soon as possible; **credevo di fare prima** I thought I'd be finished sooner *o* earlier; **domani devo alzarmi un po' prima** tomorrow I have to get up a bit earlier; **è arrivato prima del previsto** he arrived earlier than expected; **prima lo farai prima sarai libero di uscire** the sooner you do it, the sooner you can go out; **chi arriva prima compra i biglietti** whoever arrives first gets the tickets 4 (*innanzi*) before; (*in primo luogo*) first; **prima la famiglia** family first; **prima di tutto** first of all; **prima il dovere e poi il piacere** duty before pleasure ♦ **prima di** PREP (*tempo, spazio*) before; **prima del suo arrivo** before his arrival; **sono andati via prima di noi** they left before us; **mi sono alzato prima delle sette** I got up before seven;

prima d'ora before now; **c'è un cinema prima del semaforo** there's a cinema before the lights ♦ **prima di, prima che** CONG before; **prima di fare/che tu faccia** before doing/ you do; **pensaci prima che sia troppo tardi** give it some thought before it is too late; **dobbiamo decidere prima che Luca parta** we must decide before Luca leaves

prima² ['prima] SF 1 (*gen*) first; (*Teatro*) opening night; (*Cine*) première; (*Ferr*) first class; (*Aut*) first gear; **viaggiare in prima** to travel first class; **ingranare la prima** to engage first gear 2 (*Scol*) first year(*prima elementare*) ≈ year two (*Brit*), ≈ first grade (*USA*); (*prima media*) ≈ year seven (*Brit*), ≈ sixth grade (*USA*); (*prima superiore*) ≈ year ten (*Brit*), ≈ tenth grade (*USA*)

primario, -ria, -ri, -rie [pri'marjo] AGG 1 (*funzione, motivo, scopo*) main, chief, primary 2 (*Geol*): **roccia primaria** primary rock 3 (*medico*) head *o* chief physician

primate [pri'mate] SM (*Rel, Zool*) primate

primatista, -i, -e [prima'tista] SM, SF (*Sport*) record holder; **il primatista mondiale del salto in lungo** the world record holder for the long jump

primato [pri'mato] SM 1 (*in campo industriale, artistico*) supremacy; **l'Italia ha il primato nel campo della moda** Italy is the leader *o* holds the lead in the world of fashion 2 (*Sport*) record

primavera [prima'vera] SF spring; **in primavera** in spring

primaverile [primave'rile] AGG spring *attr*

primeggiare [primed'dʒare] /62/ VI (*aus avere*) primeggiare (in) to excel (in), be one of the best (in)

primitivo, -a [primi'tivo] AGG (*società, popolazione, usanza*) primitive; (*significato*) original ♦ SM, SF (*della preistoria, arcaico*) primitive; (*fig: zotico*) uncivilized person

primizia [pri'mittsja] SF 1 (*Agr*): **primizie** SFPL early fruit and vegetables, early produce *sg* 2 (*notizia inedita*): **ho una primizia per il tuo giornale** I've got a scoop for your paper

primo, -a ['primo] AGG 1 (*gen*) first; (*impressione*) first, initial; (*infanzia*) early; (*Mat: numero*) prime; **le prime 20 pagine** the first 20 pages; **dalla prima all'ultima pagina** from beginning to end; **in prima pagina** (*Stampa*) on the front page; **i suoi primi quadri** his early paintings; **questo quadro è un Michelangelo prima maniera** this is an early Michelangelo; **questo film è di Fellini prima maniera** this film is in Fellini's early style; **di prima mattina** early in the morning; **le prime ore del mattino** the early hours of the morning; **posare la prima pietra** to lay the foundation stone; **ai primi freddi** at the first sign of cold weather; **ustioni di primo grado** first-degree burns 2 (*in un ordine*) first; **preferisco il primo pittore al secondo** I prefer the former painter to the latter; **essere primo in classifica** (*squadra*) to be top of the league; (*disco*) to be number one in the charts; **essere in prima posizione** to be in the lead; **sul primo scaffale in alto/in basso** on the top/bottom shelf; **prima classe** first class; **un biglietto di prima classe** a first class ticket; **viaggiare in prima classe** to travel first-class; **di prim'ordine** *o* **prima qualità** first-class, first-rate; **è un attore di prim'ordine** he is a first-rate actor 3 (*prossimo*) first, next; **prendi la prima (strada) a destra** take the first *o* next (street) on the right; **scendo alla prima fermata I am getting off at the next stop** 4 (*principale*) main, principal; **il primo attore** the leading man; **la causa prima** the main reason 5 (*fraseologia*): **in primo caso** firstly; **in primo luogo** in the first place, first of all; **in un primo tempo** *o* **momento** at first; **fin dal primo momento** from the very first; **amore a prima vista** love at first sight; **fare i primi passi** to take one's first steps; **fare il primo passo** (*fig*) to make the first move ♦ SM, SF first (one); **è stata la prima a farlo** she was the first to do it; **fu tra i primi ad arrivare** he was among the first to arrive; **è la prima della classe** she is the top of the class; **non sposerò il primo venuto** I won't marry just anyone ♦ SM (*gen*) first; (*piano*) first floor (*Brit*), second floor (*USA*); (*Culin*) first course; **il primo luglio** the first of July; **il primo d'Aprile** April Fools' Day; **il primo dell'anno** New Year's Day; **i primi del Novecento** the early twentieth century; **ai primi del mese** at the beginning of the month; **ai primi di maggio** at the beginning of May

primogenito, -a [primo'dʒenito] SM, SF first *o* eldest child, firstborn ♦ AGG firstborn

primordi [pri'mɔrdi] SMPL beginnings; **ai primordi della storia** at the dawn of history

primordiale [primor'djale] AGG (*era, scienza*) primordial

primula ['primula] SF primula, primrose; **la primula rossa** (*fig*) the most wanted man

principale [printʃi'pale] AGG (*strada, motivo*) main, principal; (*opera*) major; **è questa la strada principale?** is this the main road?; **proposizione principale** (*Gramm*) main clause; **sede principale** head office ♦ SM, SF (*fam*) boss; **il principale ti vuole parlare** the boss wants to speak to you

principalmente [printʃipal'mente] AVV mainly, principally

principato [printʃi'pato] SM (*titolo nobiliare*) princedom; (*Stato*) principality

principe [principe] SM (*titolo nobiliare*) prince; **il principe di Galles** the Prince of Wales; **stare come un principe** (*fig*) to live like a lord; **principe azzurro** (*fig*) prince charming; **principe consorte** prince consort; **principe ereditario** crown prince

principesco, -a, -schi, -sche [printʃi'pesko] AGG (*anche fig*) princely

principessa [printʃi'pessa] SF princess

principiante [printʃi'pjante] SM, SF beginner; **un lavoro da principianti** (*pegg*) an amateur job

principiare [printʃi'pjare] (*frm*) /19/ VT (*discorso, trattative, lavoro*) to start, begin ♦ VI (*persona: aus avere; tempo, aus essere*) to start, begin; **a principiare da qc** to begin *o* start doing *o* to do sth; **a principiare da oggi/domani** starting from today/tomorrow; **a principiare da te/noi** starting with you/us

principio, -pi [prin'tʃipjo] SM 1 (*inizio*) beginning, start; **ricominciare dal principio** to start from the beginning again, go back to square one; **fin dal principio** right from the start; **al** *o* **in principio** at first, at the beginning; **dal principio alla fine** from beginning to end, from start to finish 2 (*concetto, norma*) principle; **essere senza principi** to have no principles; **una questione di principio** a matter of principle; **per principio** on principle; **principio precauzionale** precautionary principle 3 (*Mat*) principle 4 (*Chim*): **principio attivo** active ingredient

priore [pri'ore] SM (*Rel, Storia*) prior

priori [pri'ori] **a priori** AGG INV prior, a priori ♦ AVV at first glance; (*giudicare, valutare*) initially; (*dedurre, ragionare*) a priori

priorità [priori'ta] SF priority; **avere la priorità (su)** to have priority (over)

prioritario, -ria, -ri, -rie [priori'tarjo] AGG having priority, of utmost importance; **posta prioritaria** first-class mail *o* post

prisma, -i ['prizma] SM prism

privare [pri'vare] /72/ VT: **privare qn di qc** to deprive sb of sth; **privare qn della vita** to take sb's life; **non mi ha privato di niente** he didn't deny me anything; **privarsi** VR: **privarsi di qc** to do *o* go without sth; **non privarsi di niente** to deny o.s. nothing

privativa [priva'tiva] SF (*Econ*) monopoly

privatizzare [privatid'dzare] /72/ VT to privatize

privatizzazione [privatiddzat'tsjone] SF privatization

privato, -a [pri'vato] AGG (*gen*) private; **diritto privato** (*Dir*) civil law; **proprietà privata** private property; **privato cittadino** private citizen; **ritirarsi a vita privata** to withdraw from public life; **discutere** *o* **parlare in privato** to talk in private ♦ SM 1 (*cittadino*) private citizen; (*persona singola*) member of the public; **un'azienda gestita da privati** a privately owned business; **"non vendiamo a privati"** "wholesale only" 2 (*vita privata*) private life

privazione [privat'tsjone] SF 1 (*di diritti, genitori*) loss 2 (*sacrificio: spec pl*) hardship, privation

privilegiare [privile'dʒare] /62/ VT to favour (*Brit*), favor (*USA*)

privilegiato, -a [privile'dʒato] AGG 1 (*individuo, classe*) privileged; (*trattamento*) preferential 2 (*Comm: credito*) preferential; **azioni privilegiate** preference shares (*Brit*), preferred stock *sg* (*USA*) ♦ SM, SF privileged person

privilegio, -gi [privi'ledʒo] SM privilege; **godere di/concedere un privilegio** to enjoy/grant a privilege; **avere il privilegio di fare** to have the privilege of doing, be privileged to do

privo, -a ['privo] AGG: **privo di** (*senza*) without; (*carente in*) lacking in; **privo di scrupoli** without scruples; **è privo di scrupoli** he's got no scruples; **privo di coraggio** lacking in courage; **privo di sensi** unconscious; **parole prive di significato** meaningless words

pro¹ [prɔ] PREP (*in favore di*) for, in favour (*Brit*) *o* favor (*USA*) of, on *o* in (*USA*) behalf of; **pro patria** patriotic; **raccolta pro rifugiati** collection for refugees; **sei pro o contro?** are you for or against?

pro² [prɔ] SM *no pl* (*vantaggio*) good; (*utilità*) advantage, benefit; **a che pro?** what's the use?; **a che pro l'hai fatto?** why did you do it?; **tutta questa fatica, e a che pro?** all this work, and for what?; **buon pro ti faccia!** much good may it do you!; **i pro e i contro** the pros and cons

probabile [pro'babile] AGG likely, probable; **è probabile che venga** he will probably come, he is likely to come

probabilità [probabili'ta] SF INV 1 probability, likelihood; (*possibilità*) chance; **quali** *o* **che probabilità ci sono?** what chances are there?; **che probabilità hanno di vincere?** what are their chances of winning?; **ha buone probabilità di ottenere il lavoro** he's got a good chance of getting the job; **una probabilità su due** a fifty-fifty chance; **c'è una probabilità su mille** there's a one in a thousand chance; **con molta probabilità** very probably, in all probability 2 (*Mat*) probability

probabilmente [probabil'mente] AVV probably; **probabilmente verrà** he'll probably come

probante [pro'bante] AGG convincing

problema, -i [pro'blema] SM (*gen, anche Mat*) problem; (*questione*) issue

problematico, -a, -ci, -che [proble'matiko] AGG (*situazione*) problematic; (*intesa, esito*) doubtful

proboscide [pro'bɔʃʃide] SF (*di elefante*) trunk; (*di insetto*) proboscis

procacciare [prokat'tʃare] /14/ VT to get, obtain; **procacciarsi un lavoro** to get o.s. a job; **procacciarsi il pane** *o* **da vivere** to earn one's living

procacciatore [prokattʃa'tore] SM: **procacciatore d'affari** wheeler-dealer (*fam*)

procace [pro'katʃe] AGG (*aspetto*) provocative

procedere [pro'tʃɛdere] /29/ VI (*aus avere; nel senso 1 essere*) 1 (*aus essere*) (*avanzare*) to proceed, advance; (*continuare*) to proceed, go on; **procedere oltre** to go on ahead; **prima di procedere oltre** before going any further; **procedere con lentezza** (*veicolo*) to drive along slowly; (*trattative*) to proceed slowly; **procediamo con ordine** let's do this in an orderly fashion; **gli affari procedono bene** business is going well; **come procede il lavoro?** how's the work going?; **procede nella ricerca scientifica** he is continuing his scientific research 2 (*passare a*): **procedere a** to start, begin; **procediamo alla discussione** let's begin the discussion 3 (*agire*) to proceed; (*comportarsi*) to behave; **non mi piace il suo modo di procedere** I don't like the way he behaves; **bisogna procedere con cautela** we have to proceed cautiously 4 (*Dir*): **procedere contro qc** to start *o* take proceedings against sb; **non luogo a procedere** nonsuit

procedimento [protʃedi'mento] SM 1 (*svolgimento*) course 2 (*metodo*) procedure; (*Tecn*) process; **il procedimento usato per la fabbricazione** the manufacturing process 3 (*Dir*) proceedings *pl*; **procedimento penale** criminal proceedings *pl*

procedura [protʃe'dura] SF (*gen, anche Dir*) procedure; **seguire** *o* **osservare la procedura** to follow procedure

processare [protʃes'sare] /72/ VT (*Dir*): **processare qn (per)** to try sb (for)

processione [protʃes'sjone] SF (*gen*) procession

processo [pro'tʃɛsso] SM 1 (*gen, anche Chim, Med, Tecn*) process; **processo di fabbricazione** manufacturing process; **processo di pace** peace process 2 (*Dir: civile*) (legal) proceedings *pl*; (*court*) action, lawsuit; (: *penale*) trial; **un processo per omicidio** a murder trial; **essere sotto processo** to be on trial; **mettere sotto processo** (*anche fig*) to put on trial; **fare il processo alle intenzioni di qn** to question sb's motives

processuale [protʃessu'ale] AGG (*Dir*): **atti processuali** records of a trial; **spese processuali** legal costs

Proc. Gen. ABBR = procuratore generale

procinto [pro't∫into] SM: **in procinto di fare qc** about to do sth, on the point of doing sth; **ero in procinto di partire** I was about to leave o on the point of leaving

proclama, -i [pro'klama] SM (*bando, appello*) proclamation

proclamare [prokla'mare] /72/ VT (*legge*) to promulgate; (*stato d'assedio, guerra, pace*) to declare; **proclamare qn vincitore** to declare sb the winner; **proclamare la propria innocenza** to proclaim one's innocence

proclamazione [proklamat'tsjone] SF (*dichiarazione*) declaration; (*affermazione*) proclamation

procrastinare [prokrasti'nare] /72/ VT (*data*) to postpone; (*pagamento*) to defer

procreare [prokre'are] /72/ VT to procreate

procura [pro'kura] SF (*Dir*) 1 proxy, power of attorney; **per procura** by proxy 2 (*ufficio*): **la procura della Repubblica** the Public Prosecutor's office

procurare [proku'rare] /72/ VT 1 (*fornire*): **procurare qc a qn** to get o obtain sth for sb, provide sb with sth; **procurare danni** to cause damage; **procurare noie a qn** to cause sb trouble; **hai procurato i biglietti?** did you get the tickets? 2 (*fare in modo di*): **procurare di fare qc** to try to do sth

procuratore, -trice [prokura'tore] SM, SF (*Dir*) ≈ solicitor (*Brit*), ≈ lawyer (*USA*); (*chi è munito di procura*) holder of power of attorney; **procuratore generale** (*in corte d'appello*) public prosecutor; (*in corte di cassazione*) Attorney General; **procuratore legale** ≈ solicitor (*Brit*), ≈ lawyer (*USA*); **procuratore della Repubblica** (*in corte d'assise, tribunale*) public prosecutor

prodigare [prodi'gare] /80/ VT (*lodi, affetto*) to lavish, be lavish with; **gli prodiga tutte le sue cure** she lavishes all her care on him; **prodigarsi** VR: **prodigarsi per qn** to do all one can for sb

prodigio, -gi [pro'didʒo] SM (*miracolo*) wonder, marvel; (*fig: persona*) prodigy; **i prodigi della tecnica/scienza** the wonders of technology/science; **fare prodigi** to work wonders ♦ AGG INV: **bambino prodigio** child prodigy

prodigioso, -a [prodi'dʒoso] AGG wonderful, marvellous (*Brit*), marvelous (*USA*), prodigious; (*fenomenale*) phenomenal

prodigo, -a, -ghi, -ghe ['prɔdigo] AGG: **essere prodigo (di)** (*consigli, attenzioni*) to be lavish (with); (*denaro*) to be extravagant (with); **il figliol prodigo** (*Rel, anche fig*) the prodigal son

prodotto, -a [pro'dotto] PP *di* **produrre** ♦ SM (*gen, anche Mat*) product; (*fig: risultato*) result, fruit, product; **è un buon prodotto** it's a good product; **prodotti agricoli** farm produce *sg*; **prodotti alimentari** foodstuffs; **prodotti di bellezza** cosmetics; **prodotti chimici** chemicals; **prodotto di base** primary product; **prodotto finale** end product; **prodotto interno lordo** (*Econ*) gross domestic product; **prodotto nazionale lordo** (*Econ*) gross national product

produco *ecc* [pro'duko] VB *vedi* **produrre**

produrre [pro'durre] /90/ VT IRREG 1 (*gen, anche Cine*) to produce; (*calore*) to generate; (*fabbricare*) to manufacture, make, produce; **produrre in serie** to mass-produce 2 (*causare: angoscia, timori*) to cause, give rise to

produssi *ecc* [pro'dussi] VB *vedi* **produrre**

produttività [produttivi'ta] SF productivity

produttivo, -a [produt'tivo] AGG (*lavoro, investimento*) productive; (*metodo, ciclo*) of production, production *attr*

produttore, -trice [produt'tore] SM, SF (*gen, anche Cine, Agr*) producer ♦ AGG (*gen, anche Agr*) producing *attr*; **paese produttore di petrolio** oil-producing country

produzione [produt'tsjone] SF 1 (*gen, anche Cine, TV*) production; **articolo di produzione italiana** article of Italian manufacture; **produzione in serie** mass production 2 (*quantità prodotta*) production, output; (*Agr*) production, yield

proemio, -mi [pro'emjo] SM introduction, preface

Prof. ABBR (= *professore*) Prof.

profanare [profa'nare] /72/ VT (*Rel*) to profane, to desecrate; (*tomba*) to violate; (*fig: nome, ricordo*) to defile

profano, -a [pro'fano] AGG (*non sacro*) secular, profane; (*sacrilego*) profane; (*fig: orecchio, occhio*) untrained ♦ SM,

SF (*gen*) layman, lay person ♦ SM: **il profano** the profane, the secular

proferire [profe'rire] /55/ VT IRREG (*parola, nome*) to utter; (*giudizio, desiderio*) to express

professare [profes'sare] /72/ VT (*opinione, dottrina*) to profess; (*medicina, avvocatura*) to practise (*Brit*), practice (*USA*); **professarsi** VR: **professarsi innocente** to declare o.s. innocent

professionale [professjo'nale] AGG (*gen*) professional; (*malattia*) occupational; **istituto professionale** training college (*Brit*), vocational school (*USA*)

professione [profes'sjone] SF (*gen*) occupation, profession; (*manuale*) trade; **la professione medica** the medical profession; **libera professione** profession; **fare qc di professione** to do sth for a living; **di professione** professional, by profession; **professione: infermiera** occupation: nurse; **professione di fede** profession of faith

professionista, -i, -e [professjo'nista] AGG professional; **un fotografo professionista** a professional photographer ♦ SM, SF (*gen, anche Sport*) professional; **libero professionista** (*gen*) self-employed; (*avvocato, medico*) professional person; **i liberi professionisti** the self-employed

professore, -essa [profes'sore] SM, SF (*Scol*) teacher; (*Univ*) ≈ lecturer; (*titolare di cattedra*) professor; **professore d'orchestra** member of an orchestra

profeta, -i [pro'feta] SM prophet

profetico, -a, -ci, -che [pro'fetiko] AGG prophetic

profetizzare [profetid'dzare] /72/ VT to prophesy

profezia [profet'tsia] SF prophecy

proficuo, -a [pro'fikuo] AGG profitable, useful

profilare [profi'lare] /72/ VT 1 (*descrivere in breve*) to outline 2 (*ornare: vestito*) to edge 3 (*Tecn: barra metallica*) to shape; **profilarsi** VIP (*figura*) to stand out, be outlined, be silhouetted; (*soluzione, problemi*) to emerge; (*minaccia, crisi*) to loom up; **profilarsi all'orizzonte** (*anche fig*) to appear on the horizon

profilassi [profi'lassi] SF INV (*Med*) preventive treatment, prophylaxis

profilattico, -a, -ci, -che [profi'lattiko](*Med*) AGG prophylactic ♦ SM (*anticoncezionale*) condom, sheath (*Brit*)

profilo [pro'filo] SM (*gen, anche fig*) profile; (*breve descrizione*) sketch, outline; **di profilo** in profile; **mettersi di profilo** to turn sideways (on); **considerare qc sotto il profilo giuridico** to consider the legal aspects of sth; **una figura di scarso profilo** an insignificant character

profittare [profit'tare] /72/ VI (*aus avere*) **profittare di** (*situazione*) to profit by o from; (*pegg: persona*) to take advantage of

profitto [pro'fitto] SM (*gen, anche Econ*) profit; (*fig: progresso*) progress; **ricavare un profitto da** to make a profit from o out of; **un profitto di 8000 euro** an 8000 euro profit; **vendere con profitto** to sell at a profit; **conto profitti e perdite** profit and loss account; **trarre profitto da** (*lezione, esperienza*) to learn from; (*problemi altrui*) to take advantage of; (*invenzione*) to turn to good account; (*tempo libero*) to make the most of

profondere [pro'fondere] VB IRREG /25/ VT (*lodi*) to lavish; (*denaro*) to squander; **profondersi** VIP: **profondersi in** (*scuse, ringraziamenti*) to be profuse in

profondità [profondi'ta] SF INV 1 depth; **scavare in profondità** to dig deep; **avere 10 metri di profondità, avere una profondità di 10 metri** to be 10 metres deep o in depth; **il fiume qui ha una profondità di 5 metri** the river here is 5 metres deep; **le profondità del mare** the depths of the sea 2 (*di persona, osservazione*) profundity; (*di sentimento, rispetto*) depth 3 (*Cine, Fot*): **profondità di campo** depth of field

profondo, -a [pro'fondo] AGG 1 (*gen*) deep; **poco profondo** shallow; **profondo 5 metri** 5 metres deep 2 (*fig: notte, colore, voce*) deep; (*: sospiro*) deep, heavy; (*: sonno*) deep, sound; (*: silenzio, mistero*) total, profound; (*: interesse, sentimento, meditazione*) profound; (*: inchino*) deep, low; (*: causa, significato*) underlying, deeper; (*: tendenza*) deep-seated, underlying ♦ SM depth, depths *pl*, bottom; **nel profondo del mare** in the depths of the sea, at the bottom of the sea; **dal profondo del cuore** from the bottom of one's heart; **nel profondo del cuore** o **dell'animo** in one's heart of hearts

proforma [pro'forma] AGG routine *attr* ♦ AVV: **fare qc proforma** to do sth as a formality ♦ SM INV formality

profugo, -a, -ghi, -ghe ['prɔfugo] SM, SF refugee

profumare [profu'mare] /72/ VI (*aus* avere) to smell good, be fragrant; **profumare di pulito/fresco** to smell clean/ fresh ♦ VT 1 (*sogg: fiori*) to perfume, scent; (*fazzoletto*) to put perfume *o* scent on; **l'aroma del caffè profumava l'aria** the smell of coffee filled the air 2 **profumarsi** (*pelle, capelli*) to put perfume *o* scent on; **profumarsi** VR to put on perfume *o* scent

profumatamente [profumata'mente] AVV: **pagare qc profumatamente** to pay through the nose for sth; **pagare qn profumatamente** to pay sb handsomely

profumato, -a [profu'mato] AGG (*fiore, aria*) fragrant; (*fazzoletto, saponetta*) scented; (*pelle*) sweet-smelling; (*persona*) with perfume on

profumeria [profume'ria] SF perfumery

profumo [pro'fumo] SM (*sostanza*) perfume, scent; (*fragranza*) scent, fragrance; (*di caffè*) aroma; **mettersi il profumo** to put perfume *o* scent on; **avere un buon profumo** to smell nice; **questi fiori hanno un buon profumo** these flowers smell lovely; **senti che profumo!** what a lovely smell!; **questa saponetta ha profumo di limone** this soap smells of lemon

profusione [profu'zjone] SF profusion; **a profusione** in plenty

profuso, -a [pro'fuzo] PP *di* profondere

progenitore, -trice [prodʒeni'tore] SM, SF ancestor

progettare [prodʒet'tare] /72/ VT (*ponte, casa*) to plan, design; (*vacanza, fuga, rapina*) to plan; **progettare di fare qc** to plan to do sth

progettazione [prodʒettat'tsjone] SF planning; **in corso di progettazione** at the planning stage

progettista, -i, -e [prodʒet'tista] SM, SF designer

progetto [pro'dʒetto] SM 1 (*Archit*) plan; (*idea*) plan, project; **il progetto della casa** the plan of the house; **fare il progetto di una casa** to design a house; **i miei progetti per il futuro** my plans for the future; **fare progetti per il futuro** to make plans for the future; **avere in progetto di fare qc** to be planning to do sth 2 (*Pol*): **progetto di legge** bill

prognosi ['prɔɲɲozi] SF INV (*Med*) prognosis; **essere in prognosi riservata** to be on the danger list; **sciogliere la prognosi su qn** to take sb off the danger list

programma, -i [pro'gramma] SM 1 (*Pol, Econ, TV, Radio*) programme (*Brit*), program (*USA*); (*Inform*) program; **programma applicativo** (*Inform*) application program 2 (*progetto*) plan; **fare programmi** to plan; **avere in programma di fare qc** to be planning to do sth; **hai qualcosa in programma per la serata?** have you anything planned for this evening? 3 (*Scol*): **libri in programma** syllabus, curriculum

programmare [program'mare] /72/ VT (*gen*) to plan; (*Inform*) to program; (*Cine: presentare*) to screen; (*TV, Radio*) to put on; **programmare di fare qc** to plan to do sth

programmatore, -trice [programma'tore] SM, SF (*Inform*) (computer) programmer (*Brit*) *o* programer (*USA*)

programmazione [programmat'tsjone] SF (*Econ*) planning; (*Inform*) programming (*Brit*), programing (*USA*); **in programmazione all'Odeon** (*film*) now showing at the Odeon; **linguaggio di programmazione** (*Inform*) progra(m)ming language

progredire [progre'dire] /55/ VI (*persona, aus* essere; *cosa, aus* avere) (*migliorare*) to progress, make progress; **progredire in qc** to make progress in sth

progressione [progres'sjone] SF progression; **progressione aritmetica** (*Mat*) arithmetic progression; **progressione geometrica** geometric progression

progressista, -i, -e [progres'sista] AGG, SM, SF progressive

progressivamente [progressiva'mente] AVV progressively

progressivo, -a [progres'sivo] AGG progressive

progresso [pro'gresso] SM (*gen*) progress *no pl*; **i progressi della scienza** scientific progress; **fare progressi** to make progress; **sta facendo progressi in matematica** she's making progress in math(s)

proibire [proi'bire] /55/ VT 1 (*vietare*) to forbid, prohibit; (*per legge, regola*) to prohibit; **proibire a qn di fare qc** to forbid sb to do sth; **mi ha proibito di uscire** she has forbidden

me to go out; **gli fu proibito di entrare** he was refused admission 2 (*impedire*): **proibire a qn di fare qc** to prevent sb from doing sth

proibitivo, -a [proibi'tivo] AGG (*prezzo*) prohibitive; (*condizioni del tempo*) adverse

proibito, -a [proi'bito] AGG forbidden; **"è proibito l'accesso"** "no admittance"; **"è proibito fumare"** "no smoking"; **sogni proibiti** impossible dreams; **frutto proibito** (*Rel, anche fig*) forbidden fruit

proibizione [proibit'tsjone] SF prohibition

proibizionismo [proibittsjo'nizmo] SM prohibition

proiettare [projet'tare] /72/ VT 1 (*gen, anche Geom*) to project; (*Cine: riprodurre su schermo*) to project; (*ombra, luce*) to cast, throw, project 2 (*gettare*) to throw (out); **furono proiettati fuori dalla vettura** they were thrown out of the car 3 (*protendere*): **proiettare le proprie speranze nel futuro** to pin one's hopes on the future

proiettile [pro'jettile] SM (*pallottola*) bullet (*o* shell); (*corpo lanciato in aria*) projectile; **a prova di proiettile** bulletproof

proiettore [projet'tore] SM 1 (*Cine, Fot*) projector 2 (*in stadio*) floodlight; (*Aut*) headlight, headlamp; (*Mil*) searchlight

proiezione [projet'tsjone] SF (*gen, anche Geom, Cine*) projection; **cabina di proiezione** (*Cine*) projection room

prole ['prɔle] SF children *pl*, offspring; **senza prole** childless

proletariato [proleta'rjato] SM proletariat

proletario, -ria, -ri, -rie [prole'tarjo] AGG, SM, SF proletarian

proliferare [prolife'rare] /72/ VI (*aus* avere) (*anche fig*) to proliferate

prolifico, -a, -ci, -che [pro'lifiko] AGG prolific

prolisso, -a [pro'lisso] AGG verbose

prologo, -ghi ['prɔlogo] SM prologue

prolunga, -ghe [pro'lunga] SF (*di cavo elettrico, telefono*) extension

prolungamento [prolunga'mento] SM (*gen*) extension; (*di strada*) continuation

prolungare [prolun'gare] /80/ VT (*discorso, attesa*) to prolong; (*linea, termine*) to extend; (*strada, muro*) to extend, continue; (*vacanza*) to prolong, extend; **prolungarsi** VIP (*film, discussione*) to go on; (*effetto*) to last; **la vacanza si è prolungata di alcuni giorni** we (*o they ecc*) extended our (*o their ecc*) holiday (*Brit*) *o* vacation (*USA*) by a few days

promemoria [prome'mɔrja] SM INV memorandum, memo

promessa [pro'messa] SF promise; **fare/mantenere una promessa** to make/keep a promise; **gli ha fatto la promessa di tornare** she promised him that she would come back; **è una giovane promessa del teatro** he (*o* she) is a promising young actor (*o* actress); **ogni promessa è debito!** I'll hold you to that!

promesso, -a [pro'messo] PP *di* promettere ♦ AGG: **la terra promessa** the promised land; **sposi promessi** betrothed couple *sg* ♦ SM, SF (*fidanzato*) betrothed

promettente [promet'tente] AGG promising

promettere [pro'mettere] /63/ VT IRREG to promise; **te lo prometto** I promise (you); **promettere a qn di fare qc** to promise sb that one will do sth; **ha promesso di venire** *o* **che sarebbe venuto** he promised to come *o* that he would come; **promettimi che scriverai** promise me that you'll write; **promettere mari e monti a qn** to promise sb the earth; **promettere bene** (*tempo*) to be *o* look promising; (*studente, attore*) to show promise, be very promising; **il tempo promette male** *o* **non promette niente di buono** the weather doesn't look very promising

prominente [promi'nente] AGG prominent

prominenza [promi'nentsa] SF prominence

promiscuità [promiskui'ta] SF promiscuity, promiscuousness

promiscuo, -a [pro'miskuo] AGG 1 **matrimonio promiscuo** mixed marriage 2 (*Gramm*): **nome promiscuo** common-gender noun

promisi *ecc* [pro'mizi] VB *vedi* promettere

promontorio, -ri [promon'tɔrjo] SM (*Geog*) promontory, headland

promosso, -a [pro'mɔsso] PP *di* promuovere

promotore, -trice [promo'tore] SM, SF (*di iniziativa, campagna*) promoter, organizer ♦ AGG: **comitato promotore** organizing committee

promozionale [promottsjo'nale] AGG promotional; "**vendita promozionale**" "special offer"

promozione [promot'tsjone] SF (gen, anche Comm, Sport) promotion; **avere la promozione a** to be promoted to; **promozione delle vendite** sales promotion

promulgare [promul'gare] /80/ VT to promulgate

promulgazione [promulgat'tsjone] SF promulgation

promuovere [pro'mwɔvere] /66/ VT IRREG (gen) to promote; **promuovere qn (a)** to promote sb (to); **è stata promossa a vicedirettrice** she was promoted to assistant manager; **essere promosso agli esami** to pass one's exams; **lo studente è stato promosso** the student passed (his exams)

pronipote [proni'pote] SM, SF (di nonni) great-grandchild, great-grandson (-granddaughter); (di zii) great-nephew (-niece); **pronipoti** SMPL descendants

pronome [pro'nome] SM pronoun

pronominale [pronomi'nale] AGG pronominal

pronosticare [pronosti'kare] /20/ VT to predict, forecast, foretell

pronostico, -ci [pro'nɔstiko] SM forecast

prontezza [pron'tettsa] SF (vedi agg) readiness; quickness, promptness; **prontezza di mente** readiness of mind; **prontezza di riflessi** quick reflexes pl; **prontezza di spirito** readiness of wit

pronto, -a ['pronto] AGG 1 (gen) ready; **è pronto il pranzo?** is lunch ready?; **essere pronto a tutto** to be ready for anything; **essere pronto a fare qc** to be ready to do sth; **tieni pronto a partire** be ready to leave; **pronto all'ira** quick-tempered 2 (intervento: rapido) quick, prompt, fast; **ha sempre la risposta pronta** she's always got an answer; **a pronta cassa** (Comm) cash (Brit) o collect (USA) on delivery; **pronta consegna** (Comm) prompt delivery; **pronti contro termine** (Fin) repurchase agreement; **pronto soccorso** (trattamento) first aid; (reparto) A&E (Brit), ER (USA) ♦ ESCL (al telefono) hello; (in gara, gioco): **pronti! via!** ready! steady o set! go!

prontuario, -ri [prontu'arjo] SM manual, handbook

pronuncia [pro'nuntʃa] SF (articolazione di suono) pronunciation; (Dir) judgment; **difetto di pronuncia** speech defect

pronunciare [pronun'tʃare] /14/ VT (parola) to pronounce; (nome) to utter; (discorso) to deliver; **pronunciare male qc** to mispronounce sth; **pronunciare una sentenza** (Dir) to pass sentence; **pronunciarsi** VIP: **pronunciarsi (su qc)** (dare un'opinione) to give one's opinion (on sth), comment (on sth); **pronunciarsi a favore/contro** to pronounce o.s. in favour (Brit) o favor (USA) of/against; **non mi pronuncio** I don't want to comment

pronunciato, -a [pronun'tʃato] AGG 1 (accento, tendenza) pronounced, marked 2 (lineamenti) prominent; (mento) protruding

pronunzia ecc [pro'nuntsja] = **pronuncia**

propaganda [propa'ganda] SF propaganda; **fare propaganda per qn/qc** to push sb/sth

propagandare [propagan'dare] /72/ VT (idea) to propagandize; (prodotto, invenzione) to push

propagare [propa'gare] /80/ VT (Fis, Bio) to propagate; (notizia, idea, contagio) to spread; **propagarsi** VIP (gen) to spread; (Fis: onde) to travel; (Bio: specie) to propagate

propagazione [propagat'tsjone] SF (vedi vb) propagation; spreading

propedeutico, -a, -ci, -che [prope'dɛutiko] AGG (corso, trattato) introductory

propendere [pro'pendere] /8/ VI IRREG (aus avere) **propendere per** to favour (Brit), favor (USA), lean towards; **propendere a fare qc** to be inclined to do sth; **propendere per il sì** to be in favo(u)r; **propendere per il no** not to be in favo(u)r

propensione [propen'sjone] SF 1 inclination; **avere propensione a credere che...** to be inclined to think that ... 2 (disposizione) bent; **avere propensione per la matematica** to have a bent for mathematics

propenso, -a [pro'penso] PP di **propendere** ♦ AGG: **essere propenso a qc** to be in favour (Brit) o favor (USA) of sth; **essere propenso a fare qc** to be inclined to do sth

propinare [propi'nare] /72/ VT (scherz: pietanza) to serve up;

(: storia, discorso) to inflict, foist; **propinare veleno a qn** to slip poison to sb; **ci ha propinato tutte le foto di famiglia** he dragged out all the family photographs for us

propizio, -zia, -zi, -zie [pro'pittsjo] AGG: **propizio (per) (gen)** favourable (Brit) o favorable (USA) (to); (momento) opportune (for)

proporre [pro'porre] VB IRREG /77/ VT 1 (suggerire) to suggest, propose; (soluzione, candidato) to put forward; (legge, brindisi) to propose; **proporre qc a qn** to suggest o propose sth to sb; **proporre di fare qc** to suggest o propose doing sth; **gli ho proposto di venire** I suggested that he should come; **ho proposto di andare al cinema** I suggested going to the cinema 2 (offrire: aiuto, prezzo) to offer; **proporre qc a qn** to offer sth to sb, offer sb sth; **proporre di fare qc** to offer to do sth 3 (proposi qc (obiettivo, meta) to set o.s. sth; **proporsi di fare qc** to propose o intend to do sth; **proporsi** VR: **proporsi come candidato** to put o.s. forward as a candidate

proporzionale [proportsjo'nale] AGG proportional; **proporzionale a** proportional to, proportionate to; **sistema proporzionale** (Pol) proportional representation system

proporzionato, -a [proportsjo'nato] AGG: **proporzionato a** proportionate to, proportional to; **ben proporzionato** well-proportioned

proporzione [propor'tsjone] SF (gen, anche Mat) proportion; **in proporzione (a)** in proportion (to); **in proporzione diretta/inversa** in direct/inverse proportion o ratio; **mancare di proporzione** to be out of proportion; **un movimento di grandi proporzioni** (fig) an important movement

proposito [pro'pɔzito] SM 1 (intenzione) intention, aim; **avere il proposito di fare qc** to intend to do sth; **fare qc di proposito** to do sth deliberately o on purpose; **l'ha fatto di proposito** he did it on purpose; **essere pieno di buoni propositi** to be full of good intentions 2 (argomento): **a questo proposito** on this subject; **a quale proposito voleva vedermi?** what did he want to see me about?; **a proposito della tua ragazza...** speaking of your girlfriend ...; **a proposito di** (in lettera) regarding, with regard to; **le scrivo a proposito dell'inserzione** I am writing to you with reference to the advertisement; **a proposito, come sta tua madre?** by the way, how's your mother?; **a proposito, sai dirmi...** by the way, can you tell me ...; **capitare o arrivare a proposito** (cosa, persona) to turn up at the right time

proposizione [propozit'tsjone] SF 1 (Gramm) clause; (periodo) sentence; **proposizione principale** main clause; **proposizione secondaria** subordinate clause 2 (Mat) proposition

proposto, -a [pro'posto] PP di **proporre**

propriamente [proprja'mente] AVV (correttamente) properly, correctly; (in modo specifico) specifically; **propriamente detto** in the strict sense of the word; **subito dopo l'ingresso propriamente detto** immediately beyond the hall itself

proprietà [proprje'ta] SF INV 1 (caratteristica, qualità) property 2 (possedimento: casa) property; (: terreno) property, land; (: beni mobili e immobili) property gen no pl estate; **avere delle proprietà** to own property; **essere di proprietà di qn** to belong to sb; **proprietà privata** private property 3 (correttezza: nel parlare, nello scrivere) correctness; **proprietà di linguaggio** correct use of language

proprietario, -ria, -ri, -rie [proprje'tarjo] SM, SF (gen) owner; (di pensione) landlord (landlady); (di albergo) proprietor (proprietress), owner; **piccolo proprietario** (Agr) smallholder; **proprietario terriero** landowner

proprio, -pria, -pri, -prie ['prɔprjo] AGG 1 (possessivo) own; (impersonale) one's; **l'ha visto con i (suoi) propri occhi** he saw it with his own eyes; **ognuno è arrivato con la propria macchina** everybody arrived in their own car; **ognuno è tornato a casa propria** everybody went back home; **per motivi miei propri** for my own o for personal reasons; **fare qc per conto proprio** to do sth for oneself 2 (tipico, caratteristico): **proprio di** peculiar to, characteristic of; **è proprio dei mammiferi** it's peculiar to o characteristic of mammals; **è un atteggiamento proprio di quel tipo di persona** it's an attitude characteristic o typical of that kind of person 3 (esatto) proper, exact, correct; **senso proprio di un termine** exact o proper meaning of a term; **è stata una vera e propria sciocchezza** it was pure foolishness 4 (Gramm):

nome proprio proper noun ♦ PRON one's own; **ognuno si prenda il proprio** everybody take their own ♦ SM: **mettersi in proprio** (*Comm*) to set up one's own business, set up on one's own; **si è messo in proprio** he set up his own business; **perderci del proprio** to be out of pocket ♦ AVV **1** (*precisamente*) exactly, just; **proprio così!** exactly!; **le cose sono andate proprio così** that's just how things went **2** (*veramente*) really; **oggi mi sento proprio bene** I feel really fit today; **sono proprio stanco** I'm really tired; **ma sei proprio certo?** are you really sure?, are you a hundred per cent certain? **3** (*affatto*): **non...proprio** not ... at all; **non mi piace proprio** I don't like it at all; **quel tipo non mi piace proprio** I really can't stand that (type of) man; **non voleva proprio farlo** he really didn't want to do it, he didn't want to do it at all

propugnare [propuɲˈɲare] /15/ VT to support

propulsione [propulˈsjone] SF (*Tecn, Aer, Naut*) propulsion; **a propulsione atomica** atomic-powered

propulsore [propulˈsore] SM (*Tecn*) propeller

prora [ˈprɔra] SF (*Naut: prua*) bow, bows *pl*, prow; **vento di prora** headwind

proroga, -ghe [ˈprɔroga] SF (*vedi vb*) extension; deferment, postponement

prorogare [proroˈgare] /80/ VT (*durata*) to extend; (*scadenza, termine*) to defer, postpone

prorompere [proˈrompere] /97/ VI IRREG (*aus avere*) (*fiume, torrente*): **prorompere dagli argini** to burst its banks; **prorompere in pianto/in una risata** to burst into tears/out laughing

prorotto, -a [proˈrotto] PP *di* **prorompere**

proruppi *ecc* [proˈruppi] VB *vedi* **prorompere**

prosa [ˈprɔza] SF **1** (*Letteratura*) prose; **la prosa e la poesia** prose and poetry; **scrivere in prosa** to write in prose; **opera in prosa** prose work **2** (*Teatro*): **la stagione della prosa** the theatre season; **attore di prosa** theatre actor; **compagnia di prosa** theatrical company

prosaico, -a, -ci, -che [proˈzaiko] AGG prosaic, mundane

prosciogliere [proʃˈʃɔʎʎere] /103/ VT IRREG: **prosciogliere qn (da)** (*obbligo, giuramento*) to release sb (from); (*Dir: da accusa*) to acquit sb (of)

proscioglimento [proʃʃɔʎʎiˈmento] SM (*vedi vb*): **proscioglimento (da)** release (from); acquittal (of)

prosciolto, -a [proʃˈʃɔlto] PP *di* **prosciogliere**

prosciugare [proʃʃuˈgare] /80/ VT (*asciugare: naturalmente*) to dry up; (*: artificialmente*) to drain; (*: bonificare*) reclaim; **prosciugarsi** VIP to dry up

prosciutto [proʃˈʃutto] SM ham; **prosciutto affumicato** smoked ham; **prosciutto cotto** cooked *o* boiled ham; **prosciutto crudo** cured ham; **prosciutto di Parma** Parma ham

proscritto, -a [prosˈkritto] PP *di* **proscrivere** ♦ SM, SF (*fuorilegge*) outlaw; (*esule*) exile

proscrivere [prosˈkrivere] /105/ VT IRREG (*Storia*) to proscribe; (*esiliare*) to exile, banish; (*fig: abolire*) to ban

proscrizione [proskritˈtsjone] SF (*vedi vb*) proscription; banishment; banning

prosecuzione [prosekutˈtsjone] SF continuation

proseguimento [prosegwiˈmento] SM (*gen*) continuation; **buon proseguimento!** (*a chi viaggia*) enjoy the rest of your journey!; (*a chi festeggia*) enjoy the rest of the party!; (*a chi cena*) enjoy the rest of your meal!

proseguire [proseˈgwire] /45/ VT (*studi, viaggio*) to continue, carry on with; (*lavoro*) to continue with; **proseguire il cammino** to continue on one's way; **proseguì dicendo che...** he went on to say that ...; **proseguì la lettura del libro** he carried on reading the book; **decise di proseguire il viaggio** he decided to continue his journey ♦ VI (*aus avere*) (*sogg: persona*) to carry on, go on; (*: lavoro, viaggio*) to continue, go on; **proseguire negli studi** to continue *o* pursue one's studies; **come prosegue?** (*lavoro*) how is it coming along?; **la polizia prosegue nelle ricerche** the police are pursuing their inquiries

proselito, -a [proˈzelito] SM, SF (*Rel, Pol*) convert

prosperare [prospeˈrare] /72/ VI (*aus avere*) (*commercio, salute*) to flourish; (*finanze*) to thrive; (*paese, commerciante*) to prosper

prosperità [prosperiˈta] SF prosperity

prospero, -a [ˈprɔspero] AGG (*commercio, salute*) flourishing; (*finanze*) thriving; (*paese, commerciante*) prosperous, affluent

prosperoso, -a [prospeˈroso] AGG (*commercio, salute*) flourishing; (*regione*) prosperous, affluent; (*formosa*) buxom

prospettare [prospetˈtare] /72/ VT (*possibilità*) to indicate; (*affare*) to outline; (*ipotesi*) to advance; **prospettarsi** VIP (*possibilità*) to present itself; (*situazione, futuro*) to look, seem; **la vacanza si prospetta bene** it looks like being an enjoyable holiday

prospettiva [prospetˈtiva] SF **1** (*Disegno*) perspective; (*veduta*) view; **in prospettiva** in perspective **2** (*fig: previsione, possibilità*) prospect; **che prospettive hai?** what are your prospects?; **non ci sono molte prospettive di lavoro** there aren't many job prospects

prospetto [prosˈpetto] SM **1** (*Disegno*) elevation; (*veduta*) view, prospect; **guardare qc di prospetto** to get a front view of sth **2** (*facciata*) front, façade **3** (*tabella*) table, schedule; (*sommario*) summary; **prospetto delle lezioni** course timetable; **prospetto dei verbi** verb table

prospiciente [prospiˈtʃɛnte] AGG: **prospiciente qc** (*casa*) facing sth; (*terrazza*) overlooking sth

prossimamente [prossimaˈmente] AVV soon; **"prossimamente su questi schermi"** (*Cine*) "coming shortly to your screens"

prossimità [prossimiˈta] SF proximity, nearness; **in prossimità di** near (to), close to; **in prossimità delle feste natalizie** as Christmas approaches

prossimo, -a [ˈprɔssimo] AGG **1** (*successivo: in tempo, spazio*) next; **nei prossimi giorni** in the next few days; **scendo alla prossima fermata** I get off at the next stop; **la prossima volta stai attento!** next time be careful!; **venerdì prossimo** next Friday; **venerdì prossimo venturo** (*frm: Amm*) next Friday **2** (*vicino: gen*) near; (*: parente*) close; **in un prossimo futuro** in the near future; **prossimo a** near (to), close to; **essere prossimo alla laurea** *o* **a laurearsi** to be about to graduate; **è prossimo alla fine** (*fig: morte*) he is close to death **3** (*Gramm*): **passato prossimo** present perfect; **trapassato prossimo** past perfect ♦ SM **1** (*Rel*) neighbour (*Brit*), neighbor (*USA*), fellow man **2 avanti il prossimo!** (*a sportello ecc*) next please!

prostata [ˈprɔstata] SF (*Anat*) prostate (gland)

prostituire [prostituˈire] /55/ VT to prostitute; **prostituirsi** VR to prostitute o.s.

prostituta [prostiˈtuta] SF prostitute

prostituzione [prostitutˈtsjone] SF prostitution

prostrare [prosˈtrare] /72/ VT (*sogg: malattia*) to debilitate seriously; (*fig: nel morale*) to exhaust, wear out; **prostrato dal dolore** overcome *o* prostrate with grief; **prostrarsi** VR to prostrate o.s.; (*fig*) to humble o.s.; **prostrarsi ai piedi di qn/ davanti a qn** to bow down at sb's feet/before sb

prostrazione [prostratˈtsjone] SF prostration

protagonista, -i, -e [protagoˈnista] SM, SF protagonist

proteggere [proˈteddʒere] VB IRREG /83/ VT (*gen*) to protect; (*moralmente*) to guard, shield; (*fig: artista, arte*) to be a patron of; **proteggersi** VR to protect o.s.

proteggi-slip [proˈteddʒiˈzlip] SM INV pantyliner

proteico, -a, -ci, -che [proˈteiko] AGG protein *attr*; **altamente proteico** high in protein

proteina [proteˈina] SF protein

protendere [proˈtɛndere] VB IRREG /120/ VT to stretch out; **protendersi** VR to stretch forward; **protendersi dalla finestra** to lean out of the window

protesi [ˈprɔtezi] SF INV (*Med*) prosthesis; **protesi dentaria** dentures *pl*

proteso, -a [proˈteso] PP *di* **protendere**

protesta [proˈtesta] SF protest; **fare una protesta contro** to protest against; **di protesta** (*marcia, sciopero*) protest *attr*

protestante [protesˈtante] AGG, SM, SF Protestant

protestare [protesˈtare] /72/ VT to protest; **protestare la propria innocenza** to protest one's innocence ♦ VI (*aus avere*) to protest; **protestarsi** VR: **protestarsi innocente** to protest one's innocence

protesto [proˈtesto] SM (*Dir*) protest; **mandare una cambiale in protesto** to dishonour (*Brit*) *o* dishonor (*USA*) a bill

protettivo, -a [protetˈtivo] AGG protective

protetto, -a [pro'tetto] PP *di* **proteggere** ♦ AGG (*porto, baia*) sheltered; **una specie protetta** a protected species ♦ SM, SF protégé(e); (*fig: favorito*) favourite (*Brit*), favorite (*USA*)

protettorato [protetto'rato] SM (*Pol*) protectorate

protettore, -trice [protet'tore] SM, SF (*difensore*) protector, guardian; (*di artista, arte*) patron ♦ SM (*di prostituta*) pimp ♦ AGG **1** (*Rel*): **santo protettore** patron saint **2 società protettrice degli animali** animal protection society

protezione [protet'tsjone] SF (*difesa*) protection; (*di arte, artista*) patronage; **misure di protezione** protective measures; **prendere qn sotto la propria protezione** to give sb one's patronage; **protezione civile** civil defence (*Brit*) *o* defense (*USA*)

protezionismo [protettsjo'nizmo] SM protectionism

protocollare [protokol'lare] /72/ VT (*Amm*) to register ♦ AGG of protocol

protocollo [proto'kɔllo] SM **1** (*registro*) register of documents; **numero di protocollo** reference number **2** (*accordo internazionale, cerimoniale*) protocol ♦ AGG INV: **foglio protocollo** foolscap

protone [pro'tone] SM proton

prototipo [pro'tɔtipo] SM prototype; **il prototipo dell'americano** your typical American

protrarre [pro'trarre] VB IRREG /123/ VT (*prolungare*) to prolong; **ha deciso di protrarre il suo soggiorno di un mese** he decided to stay on a month longer; **protrarsi** VIP to go on, continue

protratto, -a [pro'tratto] PP *di* **protrarre**

protuberanza [protube'rantsa] SF (*gen*) bulge, protuberance; (*Anat*) swelling

Prov. ABBR (= *provincia*) Prov.

prova ['prɔva] SF **1** (*esperimento*) test, trial; **essere in prova** (*persona: per lavoro*) to be on probation; **assumere in prova** (*per lavoro*) to employ on a trial basis; **mettere alla prova** to put to the test; **sta mettendo a dura prova la mia pazienza** he is trying my patience severely; **sottoporre ad una prova** to test; **a prova di bomba** bombproof; (*fig*) indestructible; **a prova di proiettile** bulletproof; **la prova del fuoco** (*fig*) the acid test; **circuito/volo di prova** test track/flight; **giro di prova** (*Sport*) test *o* trial run; **prova su pista** (*Ciclismo*) track race **2** (*dimostrazione, anche Mat*) proof *no pl*; (*Dir*) proof *no pl*, evidence *no pl*; **dare prova di** to give proof of; **hai le prove di ciò che dici?** can you prove what you're saying?; **ho la prova che è stato lui** I've got proof that it was him; **avevo ragione e tutto ciò ne è la prova** I was right and this all goes to prove it; **fino a prova contraria** until (it's) proved otherwise; **fino a prova contraria questa è casa mia!** until I hear differently this is my house!; **una prova** (*Dir*) a piece of evidence; **non ci sono abbastanza prove per incriminarlo** there isn't enough evidence to charge him; **assolto per insufficienza di prove** (*Dir*) acquitted because of lack of evidence; **prova a carico** (*Dir*) evidence for the prosecution; **prova a discarico** (*Dir*) evidence for the defence; **prova documentale** (*Dir*) documentary evidence; **prova del nove** (*Mat*) casting out nines; (*fig*) acid test; **prova testimoniale** (*Dir*) testimonial evidence **3** (*tentativo*) attempt, try; **fare una prova** to make an attempt, have a try; **facciamo una prova** let's try it **4** (*Scol*) exam, test; **prova orale/scritta** oral/written exam *o* test **5** (*Teatro, Mus*) rehearsal; **fare le prove** to rehearse; **prova generale** dress rehearsal **6** (*di abito*) fitting

provare [pro'vare] /72/ VT **1** (*tentare*) to try, attempt; (*nuova medicina, macchina, freni*) to try out, test; (*scarpe, abito*) to try on; (*assaggiare*) to try, taste; **ho provato una nuova crema** I've tried a new cream; **prova questo gelato, ti piacerà** try this ice cream, you'll like it; **ho provato il suo motorino** I tried out his moped; **provare a fare qc** to try *o* attempt to do sth; **prova tu se ci riesci!** you try and see if you can do it!; **perché non provi a parlargli?** why don't you try talking to him?; **provaci e vedrai!** just you try it!; **provarsi una gonna** to try on a skirt; **provati questo maglione** try this jumper on **2** (*dimostrare: verità, teoria: Dir*) to prove **3** (*mettere alla prova: coraggio ecc*) to put to the test; **posso provare che era a casa** I can prove I was at home; **è molto provato da quell'esperienza** the experience has left its mark on him **4** (*sentimento*) to feel; (*sensazione*) to experience; **ho provato**

rabbia quando l'ho saputo I felt angry when I found out **5** (*Teatro, Mus*) to rehearse; **provarsi** VIP: **provarsi a fare qc** to try *o* attempt to do sth

provenienza [prove'njentsa] SF (*origine*) origin; (*fonte*) source; **luogo di provenienza** place of origin; **controlla la provenienza della notizia** check the source of the news

provenire [prove'nire] /128/ VI IRREG (*aus* **essere**) **provenire da** (*per nascita*) to come from; (*essere causato*) to be due to, be the result of

proventi [pro'venti] SMPL revenue *sg*, proceeds

provenuto, -a [prove'nuto] PP *di* **provenire**

Provenza [pro'ventsa] SF Provence

provenzale [proven'tsale] AGG, SM Provençal

proverbio, -bi [pro'verbjo] SM proverb; **come dice il proverbio** as the proverb says, as the saying goes

provetta [pro'vetta] SF (*Chim*) test tube; **bambino in provetta** test-tube baby

provetto, -a [pro'vetto] AGG skilled, experienced

provider [pro'vaider] SM INV (*Inform*) service provider

provincia, -ce *o* **, -cie** [pro'vintʃa] SF province; **gente/vita di provincia** provincial people/life; **venire dalla provincia** to come from the provinces

provinciale [provin'tʃale] AGG (*anche pegg*) provincial ♦ SM, SF (*anche pegg*) provincial ♦ SF (*anche*: **strada provinciale**) main road (*Brit*), highway (*USA*)

provino [pro'vino] SM (*Cine*) screen test; (*anteprima*) trailer; (*campione*) specimen; **fare un provino** (*Cine*) to do a screen test; **ha fatto un provino** she did a screen test

provocante [provo'kante] AGG (*attraente*) provocative

provocare [provo'kare] /20/ VT (*incidente, rivolta, risata*) to cause, bring about; (*persona*) to provoke; (*collera, curiosità*) to arouse; **la nebbia ha provocato molti incidenti** the fog caused a lot of accidents; **non provocarmi!** don't provoke me!

provocatore, -trice [provoka'tore] SM, SF (*di rivolta*) agitator ♦ AGG: **agente provocatore** agent provocateur

provocatorio, -ria, -ri, -rie [provoka'tɔrjo] AGG provocative

provocazione [provokat'tsjone] SF provocation

provvedere [provve'dere] VB IRREG /82/ VI (*aus* **avere**) **1** **provvedere a** (*famiglia*) to provide for **2** (*prendere provvedimenti*) to take steps, act; **hanno provveduto a mandare rinforzi** they arranged for reinforcements to be sent **3** **provvedere a** (*occuparsi di*) to look after, take charge of; **provvedere alla spesa** *o* **a fare la spesa** to do the shopping; **l'azienda che provvede alla raccolta dei rifiuti urbani** the company responsible for refuse collection ♦ VT: **provvedere qn di qc** to provide *o* supply sb with sth; **provvedersi** VR: **provvedersi di** to provide o.s. with

provvedimento [provvedi'mento] SM measure, step; (*di previdenza*) precaution; **provvedimento disciplinare** disciplinary measure

provveditorato [provvedito'rato] SM (*Amm*): **provveditorato agli studi** education offices *pl*

provveditore [provvedi'tore] SM (*Amm*): **provveditore agli studi** director (*Brit*) *o* commissioner (*USA*) of education

provvidenza [provvi'dentsa] SF: **la provvidenza** providence; **un dono della provvidenza** a godsend; **ti ha mandato la provvidenza!** you're a godsend!

provvidenziale [provviden'tsjale] AGG (*arrivo, pioggia*) providential; **il tuo arrivo è stato provvidenziale!** your coming here was a godsend!

provvigione [provvi'dʒone] SF (*Comm*) commission; **lavoro/stipendio a provvigione** job/salary on a commission basis

provvisorio, -ria, -ri, -rie [provvi'zɔrjo] AGG (*riparo, lavoro*) temporary; (*governo*) provisional, interim; **orario provvisorio** provisional timetable; **un governo provvisorio** a provisional government

provvista [prov'vista] SF supply, stock; **fare provvista di** to stock up with; **fare provviste** to take in supplies; **provviste alimentari** provisions

provvisto, -a [prov'visto] PP *di* **provvedere**

prozia [prot'tsia] SF great-aunt

prozio [prot'tsio] SM great-uncle

prua ['prua] SF (*Naut*) bow, bows *pl*, prow

prudente [pru'dente] AGG (*attento*) cautious, prudent;

(*assennato*) wise, sensible; **un automobilista prudente** a careful driver; **sarebbe prudente che tu lo facessi** you would be well advised to do it; **non è prudente guidare quando si è stanchi** it's not a good idea to drive when you're tired; **è più prudente aspettare qui** it would be better to wait here; **sii prudente!** be careful!, take care!

prudenza [pru'dɛntsa] SF (*vedi agg*) caution, prudence; wisdom; **guida con prudenza!** drive carefully!; **per prudenza** as a precaution, to be on the safe side; **ha avuto la prudenza di non dire niente** he had the good sense *o* he was wise enough to keep quiet

prudere ['prudere] /29/ VI *vb dif* to be itchy, itch; **mi prude un orecchio** my ear is itchy *o* itching

prugna ['pruɲɲa] SF (*Bot*) plum; **prugna secca** prune

pruriginoso, -a [pruridʒi'noso] AGG itchy

prurito [pru'rito] SM (*anche fig*) itch, itchiness *no pl*; **ho prurito alla mano** my hand is itchy *o* itching

PS SIGLA = Pesaro ♦ [pi'ɛsse] SIGLA F = **Pubblica Sicurezza** ♦ [pi'ɛsse] ABBR 1 (= *Postscriptum*) P.S. 2 (*Contabilità*: = **partita semplice**)

pseudonimo [pseu'dɔnimo] SM (*gen*) assumed name; (*di scrittore*) pen name, pseudonym; (*di attore*) stage name

PSI [pi'ɛsse'i] SIGLA M (*Pol*: = **Partito Socialista Italiano**)

psicanalisi [psika'nalizi] SF INV psychoanalysis

psicanalista, -i, -e [psikana'lista] SM, SF psychoanalyst

psicanalizzare [psikanalid'dzare] /72/ VT to psychoanalyse (*Brit*) *o* psycoanalyze (*USA*)

psiche ['psike] SF psyche

psichedelico, -a, -ci, -che [psike'dɛliko] AGG (*Psic*: luci) psychedelic

psichiatra, -i, -e [psi'kjatra] SM, SF psychiatrist

psichiatria [psikja'tria] SF psychiatry

psichiatrico, -a, -ci, -che [psi'kjatriko] AGG (*caso*) psychiatric; (*reparto, ospedale*) psychiatric, mental

psichico, -a, -ci, -che ['psikiko] AGG psychological

psicofarmaco, -ci [psiko'farmako] SM (*Med*) *drug used in treatment of mental conditions*

psicologia [psikolo'dʒia] SF psychology

psicologico, -a, -ci, -che [psiko'lɔdʒiko] AGG psychological

psicologo, -a, -gi, -ghe [psi'kɔlogo] SM, SF psychologist

psicopatico, -a, -ci, -che [psiko'patiko] AGG psychopathic ♦ SM, SF psychopath

psicosi [psi'kɔzi] SF INV (*Med*) psychosis; (*fig*) obsessive fear

psicosomatico, -a, -ci, -che [psikoso'matiko] AGG psychosomatic

PT SIGLA = Pistoia ♦ ABBR 1 (= *Poste e Telecomunicazioni*) ≈ PO (= *post office*) 2 (*Fisco*: = **polizia tributaria**)

Pt.a ABBR (*Geog*: = *Punta*) Pt.

pubblicare [pubbli'kare] /20/ VT to publish

pubblicazione [pubblikat'tsjone] SF 1 (*gen*) publication; **pubblicazione periodica** periodical 2 (*di matrimonio*): **pubblicazioni** SFPL (marriage) banns; **fare le pubblicazioni** to publish the (marriage) banns

pubblicista, -i, -e [pubbli'tʃista] SM, SF 1 (*giornalista*) freelance journalist 2 (*Dir*) expert in public law

pubblicità [pubblitʃi'ta] SF INV 1 (*Comm*: *professione*) advertising; **fare pubblicità a qc** to advertise sth; **fa pubblicità ad uno shampoo** she advertises a shampoo; **si occupa di pubblicità** he's in advertising 2 (*annunci in giornali, TV*) advertisements *pl*, ads *pl*, adverts *pl*; **c'è troppa pubblicità in TV** there are too many ads on TV; **ho visto la pubblicità sul giornale** I saw the advert in the paper 3 (*diffusione*) publicity; **fare molta pubblicità a qc** to give sth a lot of publicity

pubblicitario, -ria, -ri, -rie [pubblitʃi'tarjo] AGG (*campagna, agenzia*) advertising *attr*; (*film, trovata*) publicity *attr*; **cartello pubblicitario** advertising poster; **annuncio** *o* **avviso pubblicitario** advertisement ♦ SM, SF advertising agent

pubblico, -a, -ci, -che ['pubbliko] AGG (*gen*) public; (*statale*: *scuola*) state *attr*; **la scuola pubblica** state school; **funzionario pubblico** civil servant; **la pubblica amministrazione** public administration; **un pubblico esercizio** a catering (*o* hotel *o* entertainment) business; **pubbliche relazioni** public relations; **la Pubblica Sicurezza** the police; **Pubblico Ministero** Public Prosecutor's Office ♦ SM (*gen*) public; (*spettatori*: *Cine, Teatro*) audience, public; (: *di partita*)

spectators *pl*; **è aperto al pubblico di domenica** it's open to the public on Sundays; **il pubblico dei lettori** the reading public; **un libro destinato al grande pubblico** a book written for the general public; **in pubblico** in public

pube ['pube] SM (*Anat*) pubis

pubertà [puber'ta] SF puberty

pudico, -a, -ci, -che [pu'diko] AGG modest

pudore [pu'dore] SM (sense of) modesty; (*vergogna*) shame; (*riservatezza*) discretion; **falso pudore** false modesty; **oltraggio al pudore** (*Dir*) indecent behaviour

puericultura [puerikul'tura] SF paedology (*Brit*), pedology (*USA*), infant care

puerile [pue'rile] AGG (*anche pegg*) childish, puerile

puerpera [pu'ɛrpera] SF *woman who has just given birth*

pugilato [pudʒi'lato] SM boxing; **un incontro di pugilato** a boxing match

pugile ['pudʒile] SM boxer

pugliese [puʎ'ʎese] AGG *of o from Puglia* ♦ SM, SF inhabitant *o* native of Puglia

pugnalare [puɲɲa'lare] /72/ VT to stab; **pugnalare qn alle spalle** (*anche fig*) to stab sb in the back

pugnale [puɲ'ɲale] SM dagger; **colpo di pugnale** stab; **uccidere con un pugnale** to stab to death

pugno ['puɲɲo] SM 1 (*mano*) fist; **a pugni stretti** with clenched fists; **con la pistola in pugno** with one's gun in one's hand; **scrivere qc di proprio pugno** to write sth in one's own hand; **mostrare i pugni a qn** to shake one's fist at sb; **ormai ha la vittoria in pugno** he now has victory within his grasp; **tenere la situazione in pugno** to have control of the situation; **avere qn in pugno** to have sb in the palm of one's hand; **ormai lo abbiamo in pugno** (*con ricatto, minacce*) we've got him in our power now; (*criminale*) we've got him now 2 (*colpo*) punch; **dare un pugno a qn** to punch sb; **gli ha dato un pugno in un occhio** he punched him in the eye; **fare a pugni** to fight; (*fig*: *colori*) to clash; **essere un pugno in un occhio** (*fig*) to be an eyesore; **pugno di ferro** (*tirapugni*) knuckleduster (*Brit*), brass knuckles *pl* (*USA*) 3 (*manciata*): **un pugno di** a handful of; **due pugni di riso** two handfuls of rice; **un pugno di uomini** a handful of men; **rimanere con un pugno di mosche** to be left empty-handed

pulce [pul'tʃe] SF flea; **mercato delle pulci** flea market; **il gioco delle pulci** tiddlywinks *sg*; **mi hai messo una pulce nell'orecchio** (*fig*: *insospettire*) you've aroused my suspicions; **pulce di mare** sand hopper

pulcino [pul'tʃino] SM (*Zool*) chick; (*vezzeggiativo*) pet; **timido come un pulcino** as shy as a mouse; **bagnato come un pulcino** soaked to the skin

puledro [pu'ledro] SM colt

puleggia, -ge [pu'leddʒa] SF (*Tecn*) pulley

pulire [pu'lire] /55/ VT 1 (*gen*) to clean; (*giardino*) to clear; (*cassetto*) to clear out; (*lucidare*) to polish; **stava pulendo l'interno della macchina** she was cleaning the inside of the car; **pulire a secco** to dry-clean; **far pulire qc** to have sth cleaned; **ho fatto pulire la macchina** I had my car cleaned; **pulire il piatto** (*fig*) to clear one's plate 2 **pulirsi** (*mani*) to clean; (*naso, bocca*) to wipe; **pulirsi i denti** to brush *o* clean one's teeth; **pulisciti i piedi** wipe your feet; **pulirsi** VR to clean o.s. (up)

pulito, -a [pu'lito] AGG (*gen*) clean; (*ordinato*) neat, tidy; (*fig*: *lavoro, persona*) honest; **un pavimento pulito** a clean floor; **avere la coscienza pulita** to have a clear conscience

pulitura [puli'tura] SF cleaning; **pulitura a secco** dry cleaning

pulizia [pulit'tsia] SF (*condizione*) cleanliness, cleanness; (*atto*) cleaning; **fare le pulizie** (*gen*) to do the cleaning, do the housework; **fare le pulizie di primavera** to spring-clean; **far pulizia** (*fig*: *portarsi via tutto*) to make a clean sweep; **pulizia etnica** ethnic cleansing

❑ pulizia non si traduce mai con la parola inglese *polish*

pullman ['pulman] SM INV (*per escursioni*) coach (*Brit*), bus (*USA*)

pullover [pul'lɔver] SM INV pullover, sweater, jumper (*Brit*)

pullulare [pullu'lare] /72/ VI (*aus avere*) (*pesci*) to teem; (*insetti*) to swarm; **il fiume pullula di pesci** the river is teeming with fish; **la piazza pullulava di turisti** the square was swarming with tourists

pulmino [pul'mino] SM minibus

pulpito ['pulpito] SM pulpit; **senti da che pulpito viene la predica!** look who's talking!

pulsante [pul'sante] AGG pulsating ♦ SM (push) button; **premi il pulsante** press the button

pulsare [pul'sare] /72/ VI (aus avere) (cuore) to beat, pulsate; (vena) to throb

pulsazione [pulsat'tsjone] SF (di cuore) beat; (di vena) throbbing; (Fis) pulsation; **(numero di) pulsazioni** (Med) pulse rate

pulviscolo [pul'viskolo] SM fine dust; **pulviscolo atmosferico** specks pl of dust

puma ['puma] SM INV puma

pungente [pun'dʒɛnte] AGG (frutto, arbusto, spina) prickly; (odore) pungent; (fig: freddo, vento) biting; (: ironia, critica) biting, pungent

pungere ['pundʒere] VB IRREG /84/ VT 1 (sogg: spina, ago) to prick; (: insetto, ortica) to sting; (: freddo) to bite; **l'ha punto una vespa** a wasp stung him; **pungere qn sul vivo** to cut sb to the quick; **essere punto dal rimorso** to be stricken with remorse 2 **pungersi un dito/una mano** to prick one's finger/one's hand; **pungersi** VR (con ago, spina) to prick o.s.

pungiglione [pundʒiʎ'ʎone] SM sting

pungolare [pungo'lare] /72/ VT (anche fig: spingere) goad; **pungolare qn a fare qc** to goad sb into doing sth

punire [pu'nire] /55/ VT to punish

punitivo, -a [puni'tivo] AGG punitive

punizione [punit'tsjone] SF punishment; (Sport) penalty; **una punizione severa** a harsh punishment; **calcio di punizione** free kick; **dare una punizione a qn** to punish sb; **dare una punizione esemplare a qn** to make an example of sb; **per punizione** as a punishment

punsi ecc ['punsi] VB vedi **pungere**

punta¹ ['punta] SF 1 (di matita, ago, coltello) point; (di trapano) drill; (di perforatrice) bit; (di parte del corpo) tip; (di capelli, coda) tip, end; (di campanile, albero) top; (di monte) top, peak; **fare la punta a una matita** to sharpen a pencil; **le punte degli alberi** the treetops; **punta della freccia** arrowhead; **in punta di piedi** on tiptoe; **camminare in punta di piedi** to walk on tiptoe, tiptoe; **ballare sulle punte** (Danza) to dance on point; **a punta** pointed; **un paio di scarpe a punta** a pair of pointed shoes; **doppie punte** (di capelli) split ends; **avere qc sulla punta delle dita** (fig) to have sth at one's fingertips; **avere qc sulla punta della lingua** (fig) to have sth on the tip of one's tongue; **prendere qc di punta** (fig) to meet sth head on; **uomo di punta** (Sport, Pol) front-rank o leading man 2 (fig: pizzico: di zucchero, farina) touch; (: di sale) pinch; (: d'invidia: rancore) touch, hint; (: traccia) trace; **c'è una punta d'acido nel latte** the milk tastes slightly sour; **una punta di invidia** a touch of envy 3 (Geog) promontory 4 (massima frequenza o intensità) peak; **ore di punta** peak hours; **il traffico delle ore di punta** rush-hour traffic; **punta massima/minima** highest/lowest level 5 (Calcio) centre forward

punta² ['punta] SF: **cane da punta** pointer

puntare [pun'tare] /72/ VT 1 (arma) to point, aim; (cannocchiale, dito) to point; **puntare un fucile contro qn** to point a gun at sb; **puntare il dito verso qn/qc** to point (one's finger) at sb/sth; **puntare l'attenzione su qn/qc** to turn one's attention to sb/sth; **puntare gli occhi su qn** to fix one's eyes on sb 2 (piantare: gomiti, piedi) to plant; **puntare i piedi** (fig) to dig one's heels in 3 (nei giochi): **puntare su** to bet on; **ha puntato su quel cavallo** he bet on that horse 4 (sogg: cane) to point to ♦ VI (aus avere) 1 **puntare su, puntare verso** (aereo, nave) to make for, head for; **puntare a qc/a fare qc** (mirare) to aim for sth/to do sth 2 (contare): **puntare su qn/qc** to rely on sb/sth, count on sb/sth

puntaspilli [puntas'pilli] SM INV = **portaspilli**

puntata¹ [pun'tata] SF 1 (in scommessa, gioco) bet; **fare una puntata** to place a bet 2 (fig: breve visita) short trip; **fare una puntata a casa** to pop home; **farò una puntatina a Parigi** I'll pay a flying visit to Paris

puntata² [pun'tata] SF (di romanzo) instalment (Brit),

installment (USA); (di sceneggiato) episode; **hai visto la prima puntata?** did you see the first episode?; **romanzo a puntate** serial; **pubblicare a puntate** to serialize

punteggiare [punted'dʒare] /62/ VT to punctuate

punteggiatura [punteddʒa'tura] SF punctuation

punteggio, -gi [pun'teddʒo] SM (in gara) score; (in esame) mark; **qual è il punteggio?** what's the score?; **sistema di punteggio** scoring system; **totalizzare il punteggio massimo** to score maximum points

puntellare [puntel'lare] /72/ VT (ponte, muro) to shore (up); (porta, finestra) to prop up; (fig: ipotesi) to back up, support

puntello [pun'tello] SM prop, support

punteruolo [punte'rwɔlo] SM (Tecn) punch; (per stoffa) bodkin

puntiglio [pun'tiʎʎo] SM (ostinazione) obstinacy, stubbornness; **fare qc per puntiglio** to do sth out of sheer obstinacy

puntiglioso, -a [puntiʎ'ʎoso] AGG punctilious

puntina [pun'tina] SF 1 (da disegno) drawing pin (Brit), thumb tack (USA) 2 (del giradischi) stylus 3 (Aut); **puntine** SFPL points

puntino [pun'tino] SM (di punteggiatura) dot; **mettere i puntini sulle "i"** (fig) to dot the i's and cross the "t"s; **fare le cose a puntino** to do things perfectly; **cotto a puntino** cooked to a turn o to perfection; **arrivare a puntino** to arrive at just the right moment; **puntini di sospensione** suspension points

punto¹, -a ['punto] PP di **pungere**

punto² ['punto] SM 1 (gen) point; (luogo) spot, point, place; (grado) point, stage; **ha segnato tre punti** he scored three points; **la casa è in un bel punto** the house is in a nice spot; **a questo punto, al punto in cui siamo** at this stage; **a che punto sei?** (con lavoro) where have you got to?; (nel prepararsi) how are you getting on?; **ad un certo punto** at a certain point; **ad un certo punto uno si chiede...** there comes a time when one asks oneself ...; **fino ad un certo punto** to a certain extent; **non si può essere ingenui fino a questo o tal punto** one cannot be as naïve as that; **era arrabbiato a tal punto che...** he was so angry that ...; **lo odia al punto tale che...** she hates him so much that ...; **passiamo al prossimo punto** (in discorso) let's move on to the next item o point; **punto per punto** point by point; **di punto in bianco** (improvvisamente) all of a sudden; (inaspettatamente) out of the blue; **sono le 5 in punto** it's exactly 5 o'clock; **alle 6 in punto** at 6 o'clock sharp o on the dot; **vestito di tutto punto** all dressed up; **sul punto di fare qc** (just) about to do sth 2 (Aer, Naut: posizione) position; **fare il punto** to take a bearing; **fare il punto della situazione** (analisi) to take stock of the situation; (riassunto) to sum up the situation 3 (in alfabeto, in morse, su 'i') dot; (punteggiatura) full stop (Brit), period (USA); (di indirizzo e-mail) dot; **punto e basta!** that's it!, that's enough!; **due punti** colon; **punto e a capo** new paragraph; **punti di sospensione** suspension points; **punto esclamativo** exclamation mark (Brit) o point (USA); **punto interrogativo o di domanda** question mark; **punto e virgola** semicolon 4 (Cucito, Maglia, Med) stitch 5 (Tecn): **mettere a punto** (gen) to adjust; (motore) to tune; (cannocchiale) to focus; (Inform) to debug; (fig: questione) to define, settle; (: progetto) to finalize ♦ **punto d'appoggio** (Alpinismo) point of contact; **punto d'arrivo** arrival point; **punto caldo** (Mil) trouble spot; (d'attualità) major issue; **punto cardinale** cardinal point, point of the compass; **punto critico** (anche fig) critical point; **punto debole** weak spot, weak point; **punto (di) vendita** retail outlet; **punto di ebollizione** boiling point; **punto d'incontro** meeting place, meeting point; **punto d'intersezione** (Geom) point of intersection; **punto morto** standstill; **punto nero** (comedone) blackhead; **punto nevralgico** (anche fig) nerve centre (Brit) o center (USA); **punto d'onore** point of honour (Brit) o honor (USA); **punto di partenza** (anche fig) starting point; **punto di riferimento** landmark; (fig: per persona) point of reference, point of view ♦ AVV: **non...punto** not ... at all

puntuale [puntu'ale] AGG punctual; **essere puntuale** to be punctual, be on time; **è sempre puntuale** he's always punctual; **arrivare puntuale** to arrive on time; **essere puntuale nei pagamenti** to pay on time

puntualità [puntuali'ta] SF punctuality

puntualizzare [puntualid'dzare] /72/ VT to make clear

puntualmente [puntual'mente] AVV (gen) on time; (iro: al solito) as usual

puntura [pun'tura] SF 1 (di insetto) sting; (di zanzara, ragno) bite; (di spillo) prick; (dolore) sharp pain 2 (Med: iniezione) injection; **fare una puntura a qn** to give sb an injection; **gli ha fatto una puntura sul braccio** she gave him an injection in his arm; **puntura lombare** lumbar puncture

punzecchiare [puntsek'kjare] /19/ VT to prick; (fig: molestare) to tease; **punzecchiarsi** VR (uso reciproco) to tease each other

punzonare [puntso'nare] /72/ VT (Tecn) to stamp

punzone [pun'tsone] SM (per metalli) stamp, die

può [pwɔ], **-puoi** [pwɔi] VB vedi potere²

pupa ['pupa] SF 1 (bambola: anche fam: ragazza) doll 2 (Zool) pupa

pupazzo [pu'pattso] SM puppet; **pupazzo di neve** snowman

pupillo, -a [pu'pillo] SM, SF (prediletto) pet, favourite (Brit), favorite (USA); (Dir) ward

purché [pur'ke] CONG (a patto che) as long as, provided that, on condition that; **verrò con te purché non ci sia molto da aspettare** I'll come with you as long as we don't have to wait long; **verrò con te purché non piova** I'll come with you as long as it doesn't rain; **purché sia vero!** if only it were true!

pure ['pure] AVV 1 (anche) too, as well, also; (in proposizioni negative) either; **viene suo fratello e pure sua sorella** his brother is coming as is his sister, his brother is coming and his sister is too o as well; **siamo stati a Zurigo e pure a Lucerna** we went to Zurich and to Lucerne as well; **è venuto pure lui** he came too; **pure lei non lo sa fare** she can't do it either 2 (con valore concessivo): **faccia pure!** please do!, by all means!, go ahead!; **te l'avevo pur detto di non andarci** I did tell you not to go ♦ CONG 1 (tuttavia, nondimeno) but, and yet, nevertheless; **non è facile, pure bisogna riuscirci** it's not easy and yet we have to succeed; **è giovane, pure ha buon senso** he's young but he's sensible 2 (anche se, sebbene) even though; **pur non volendolo, ho dovuto farlo** I had to do it even though I didn't want to; **pur essendo fuori mano** even though it is out of the way 3 (con valore finale): **pur di vederlo contento farebbe di tutto** she would do anything to make him happy

purè [pu're] SM INV , **purea** [pu'rea] SF (Culin) purée; **purè di patate** mashed potatoes pl

purezza [pu'rettsa] SF (gen) purity; (di colore) clarity

purga, -ghe ['purga] SF (Med) purging no pl, purge; (Pol) purge

purgante [pur'gante] SM (Med) purge, purgative ♦ AGG (Med) purgative

purgare [pur'gare] /80/ VT (Med: malato) to purge, give a purgative to; (: sangue, aria) to purify; (fig: testo, discorso) to expurgate; **purgarsi** VR (fig): **purgarsi dei peccati** to purge o.s. of one's sins

purgatorio [purga'tɔrjo] SM (Rel, anche fig) purgatory

purificare [purifi'kare] /20/ VT (gen) to purify, cleanse; (metalli) to refine; **purificarsi** VIP to cleanse o.s.

purificazione [purifikat'tsjone] SF (vedi vb) purification, cleansing; refinement

puritano, -a [puri'tano] AGG (Rel) Puritan; (fig) puritanical ♦ SM, SF (Rel) Puritan; (fig) puritan

puro, -a ['puro] AGG (gen) pure; (acqua) clear, limpid; (vino) undiluted; (aria) pure, clean; (fig: ragazza) chaste, pure; **di razza pura** thoroughbred; **è pazzia pura** it's sheer madness; **è la pura verità** that's the simple truth; **per pura curiosità** out of sheer curiosity; **per puro caso** by sheer chance, purely by chance; **pura lana vergine** pure new wool

purosangue [puro'sangwe] AGG INV (cavallo) thoroughbred; **un inglese purosangue** a full-blooded Englishman ♦ SM INV, SF INV (cavallo) thoroughbred

purtroppo [pur'trɔppo] AVV unfortunately

pus [pus] SM (Med) pus; **fare pus** to ooze pus

pusillanime [puzil'lanime] AGG cowardly ♦ SM, SF coward

pustola ['pustola] SF (Med) pustule; (foruncolo) pimple

putacaso [puta'kazo] AVV just supposing, suppose; **metti, putacaso, che arrivi anche lui** just supposing o suppose he comes too

putiferio [puti'fɛrjo] SM row, rumpus; **fare/scatenare un putiferio** to kick up a row

putrefare [putre'fare] VB IRREG /41/ VI (aus essere), **putrefarsi** VIP to putrefy, rot

putrefatto, -a [putre'fatto] PP di putrefare ♦ AGG (carne, legno) rotten; (cadavere) putrid, decayed

putrefazione [putrefat'tsjone] SF putrefaction

putrido, -a ['putrido] AGG (acqua) putrid; (carne) rotten

puttana [put'tana] SF (fam!) whore (fam!); **figlio di puttana** (fig) son of a bitch

putto ['putto] SM cupid

puzza ['puttsa] SF = puzzo

puzzare [put'tsare] /72/ VI (aus avere) puzzare (di) to smell (of), stink (of); **puzza di fumo** it stinks of smoke; **gli puzza l'alito** his breath stinks, he's got very bad breath; **la faccenda puzza (d'imbroglio)** there's something fishy about the whole thing, the whole business stinks; **mi puzza!** it smells fishy to me!

puzzo ['puttso] SM stink, foul smell; **puzzo di bruciato** smell of burning; **puzzo di fritto** stink of fried food; **sento puzzo** there's a horrible smell; **c'è puzzo d'imbroglio** it smells fishy

puzzola ['puttsola] SF (Zool) polecat, skunk

puzzolente [puttso'lɛnte] AGG smelly, stinking

PV SIGLA = Pavia

p.v., p/v ABBR (Amm: = prossimo venturo)

PVC [pivi't ʃi] SIGLA M (= polivinilcloruro) PVC

PZ SIGLA = Potenza

p.zza ABBR = piazza

Qq

Q, q [ku] SF INV, SM INV (*lettera*) Q, q; **Q come Quarto** ≈ Q for Queen

q ABBR (= *quintale*) q

Qatar ['katar] SM Qatar

qb ABBR (*Culin:* = *quanto basta*) as required; **zucchero qb** sugar to taste

QG ABBR = **quartier generale**

QI ['ku'i] SIGLA M (= *quoziente d'intelligenza*) IQ

qua [kwa] AVV **1** here; **vieni qua** come here; **eccomi qua!** here I am!; **qua dentro/sotto** in/under here; **le penne e le matite sono qua dentro** the pens and pencils are in here; **qua sotto c'è la tua camicia** your shirt is under here; **abita qua sotto** she lives (in the apartment) downstairs; **da o di qua non mi muovo!** I'm not budging from here!; **da o di qua la vista è stupenda** the view is fantastic from here; **(al) di qua del fiume** on this side of the river; **passavo (per) di qua** I was just passing; **(per) di qua non si passa** you can't get through here o this way; **vieni più in qua** come closer **2** (*temporale*): **da un anno in qua** since last year, for a year now; **da quando in qua?** since when?; **da quando in qua ti interessi di musica classica?** since when have you been interested in classical music? **3** (*fraseologia*): **ecco qua cosa succede a non fare attenzione!** just look what happens when you don't pay attention!; **prendi qua questi soldi** here, take this money; **(dammi) qua, ci penso io!** just give it to me, I'll see to it!; **dammi qua, è mio** give it here, it's mine; **guarda qua che confusione!** just look at this mess!; **qua la mano** let's shake on it; **che diavolo vuole questo qua?** what on earth does he want?

quacchero, -a ['kwakkero] SM, SF Quaker

quaderno [kwa'derno] SM (*per scuola*) exercise book; **quaderno a quadretti** arithmetic exercise book; **quaderno a righe** lined exercise book

quadrangolo [kwa'drangolo] SM (*Geom*) quadrangle

quadrante [kwa'drante] SM **1** (*dell'orologio*) face **2** (*Naut, Geom*) quadrant

quadrare [kwa'drare] /72/ VT **1** (*Geom*) to square **2** (*Contabilità*) to balance, tally; **quadrare il bilancio** to balance the books ♦ VI (*aus avere o essere*) (*Contabilità: conti, bilancio*) to tally, balance; (*fig: corrispondere*): **quadrare (con)** to correspond (with); **qui c'è qualcosa che non quadra** there's something here that doesn't add up, there's something wrong here; **quel tipo non mi quadra** (*fam*) there's something fishy o I don't like about that guy

quadrato, -a [kwa'drato] AGG **1** (*Mat: tavolo, tovaglia*) square; **metro/chilometro quadrato** square metre/kilometre; **radice quadrata** (*Mat*) square root **2** (*equilibrato*) sensible, level-headed ♦ SM **1** (*gen, anche Mat*) square; **un quadrato rosso** a red square; **elevare al quadrato** (*Mat*) to square; **6 al quadrato** 6 squared **2** (*Pugilato*) ring **3** (*Naut*) officers' mess

quadrettato, -a [kwadret'tato] AGG (*foglio*) squared; (*tessuto*) checked

quadretto [kwa'dretto] SM **1** (*fig: scena, spettacolo*) picture; **siete un bel quadretto!** you make a lovely picture! **2 a quadretti** (*stoffa*) checked; (*foglio*) squared

quadriennale [kwadrien'nale] AGG (*che dura 4 anni*) four-year attr; (*che avviene ogni 4 anni*) four-yearly

quadrifoglio, -gli [kwadri'fɔʎʎo] SM **1** (*Bot*) four-leaf clover **2 raccordo a quadrifoglio** (*Aut*) cloverleaf

quadrimestre [kwadri'mestre] SM (*periodo*) four-month period; (*Scol*) term

quadro[1] [kwa'dro] AGG (*quadrato*) square; **parentesi quadra** square bracket; **essere una testa quadra** (*fig: pegg: ostinato*) to be pig-headed; (*tonto*) to be a blockhead

quadro[2] ['kwadro] SM **1** (*Arte*) picture, painting; **un quadro di Van Gogh** a painting by Van Gogh; **dipingere un quadro** to paint a picture, to do a painting; **quadro a olio** oil painting **2** (*quadrato*) square; **a quadri** (*disegno*) checked; **una giacca a quadri** a checked jacket **3** (*fig: descrizione*) outline, description; (*scena*) sight; **fare un quadro della situazione** to outline the situation; **questo ci fornisce un quadro completo della situazione** this gives us a complete picture of the situation; **quadro clinico** (*Med*) case history **4** (*Tecn*) panel, board; **quadro di comando** control panel; **quadro di distribuzione** (*Elettr*) switchboard; **quadro degli strumenti** instrument panel **5** (*fig: tabella di dati*) table, chart **6** (*Teatro*) scene; **quadro!** (*Cine*) focus! **7 quadri** SMPL (*Mil: di partito, organizzazione*) upper echelons, cadres; (*Comm*) managerial staff sg o pl, (senior) management sg o pl; **quadri intermedi** (*Comm*) middle management sg o pl **8 quadri** SMPL (*Carte*) diamonds

quadrupede [kwa'drupede] (*Zool*) SM quadruped ♦ AGG (*animale*) four-footed

quadruplicare [kwadrupli'kare] /20/ VT, VI (*aus essere*), **quadruplicarsi** VIP to quadruple, increase fourfold

quadruplo, -a ['kwadruplo] AGG quadruple; **il lavoro è quadruplo rispetto a quello iniziale** the workload is four times what it was originally ♦ SM (*Mat*) quadruple; **vorrei il quadruplo del denaro che ho ora** I would like four times as much money as I have now

quaggiù [kwad'dʒu] AVV (*gen*) down here; (*al sud*) here in the south; (*sulla terra*) in this life

quaglia ['kwaʎʎa] SF quail

qualche ['kwalke] AGG INDEF

1 (*alcuni, non molti*) a few; **per qualche giorno** for a few days; **ho comprato qualche libro** I've bought some o a few books; **fra qualche mese** in a few months; **qualche volta** sometimes; **l'ho incontrato qualche volta** I've met him a few times o once or twice

2 (*con valore indeterminato: in frasi affermative*) some; (: *in frasi negative e domande*) any; **sai se passa qualche autobus da questa parte?** do you know if any buses go this way?; **in qualche modo** somehow; **l'ho già visto da qualche parte** I've already seen him somewhere; **hai qualche sigaretta?** have you any cigarettes?; **hai qualche soldo da prestarmi?** can you lend me some money?

3 (*un certo*) some; **c'è qualche fondamento di verità** there's an element of truth in it; **ci vuole qualche tempo per abituarsi** it takes some o a little time to get used to it; **un personaggio di qualche rilievo** a person of some importance; **non senza qualche esitazione** not without some hesitation; **ci dev'essere una qualche spiegazione** there must be some explanation; **qualche cosa** = **qualcosa**

qualcheduno [kwalke'duno] PRON INDEF = **qualcuno**

qualcosa [kwal'kɔsa] PRON INDEF (*in frasi affermative*) something; (*in domande*) anything; **ci dev'essere qualcosa che non va** there must be something wrong o the matter; **è già qualcosa** that's something; **ho qualcosa da parte** (*soldi*) I've got a little something put aside; **qualcosa mi dice che...** something tells me that ...; **è medico, o qualcosa di simile o del genere** he's a doctor or something like that; **bevi qualcosa?** would you like something to drink?; **posso fare qualcosa per te?** can I do anything for you?; **c'è qualcos'altro che desideri?** do you want anything else?; **fammi sapere se hai bisogno di qualcosa** let me know if you need anything; **posso chiederti qualcos'altro?** can I ask you something else?; **voglio fare qualcos'altro** I'd like to do something else; **c'è qualcosa che non va?** is there something o anything wrong?

qualcuno [kwal'kuno] PRON INDEF **1** (*in frasi affermative*) somebody, someone; (*in domande, in proposizioni condizionali e dubitative*) anybody, anyone; **ho visto qualcuno là**

fuori I saw somebody out there; **ha telefonato qualcuno per te** somebody phoned for you; **qualcuno ha perso la borsa** somebody has lost their bag; **c'è qualcuno alla porta** there's someone at the door; **qualcuno ha visto il mio ombrello?** has anyone seen my umbrella?; **aspetti qualcuno?** are you waiting for somebody?; **c'è qualcuno in casa?** is (there) anybody at home? **2** (*con valore partitivo: affermazioni*) some; (: *domande*) any; **qualcuno di noi** some of us; **qualcuno di voi vuol venire?** do any of you want to come?; **se ti piacciono, prendine qualcuna in più** if you like them, take some *o* a few more; **hai visto i suoi film?** — **ne ho visto qualcuno** have you seen his films? — I've seen some of them; **qualcun altro** somebody *o* someone else; **chiedilo a qualcun altro** ask somebody else; **ne avresti qualcun altro da prestarmi?** have you got any more you could lend me?; **viene qualcun altro?** is anybody else coming?; **ce n'è rimasto qualcuno?** are there any left? **3** (*persona importante, di prestigio*) somebody; **diventerà qualcuno nella vita** he'll become somebody, he'll make something of his life

quale ['kwale] AGG
1 (*interrogativo*) what; **a quale conclusione è giunta?** what conclusion did she reach?; **in quale giorno vi siete incontrati?** when did you meet?; **quali sono i tuoi programmi?** what are your plans?; **per quale ragione?** why?
2 (*scegliendo tra due o più cose o persone*) which; **quale stanza preferisci?** which room do you prefer?
3 (*esclamazioni*) what; **quale onore!** what an honour!
4 **è tale e quale suo padre** he's just *o* exactly like his father; **è tale quale l'avevo lasciato** it's just *o* exactly as I left it
5 (*con valore relativo: qualunque*): **quale che** whatever; **accetterò quali che siano le condizioni** I'll accept whatever conditions
6 (*fraseologia*): **per la qual cosa** for which reason; **in un certo qual modo** in some way or other, somehow or other
♦ PRON INTERROG (*scegliendo tra due o più cose o persone*) which; **quale dei due scegli?** which of the two do you want?
♦ PRON REL
1 (*soggetto: persona*) who; (: *cosa*) which, that; **a tutti coloro i quali fossero interessati...** to whom it may concern ...; **suo padre, il quale è avvocato** his father, who is a lawyer
2 (*con preposizioni*): **l'albergo al quale ci siamo fermati** the hotel where we stayed *o* which we stayed at; **il signore con il quale parlavi** the gentleman to whom you were talking; **la collina della quale si vede la cima** the hill whose summit you can see; **la ragione per la quale sono qui** the reason why I am here
3 (*in elenchi*) such as, like; **piante quali l'edera e le rose** plants like *o* such as ivy and roses; **pittori quali Raffaello e Leonardo** painters like *o* such as Raphael and Leonardo
4 **per la quale**, (*fam*) non mi sembra una persona troppo per la quale he doesn't inspire me with confidence; **è stata una cena proprio per la quale** it was everything a dinner party should be
♦ AVV (*in veste di: in qualità di*) as; **quale legale della signora** as the woman's lawyer; **lo hanno assunto quale direttore** they employed him as manager

qualifica, -che [kwa'lifika] SF qualification; **ha la qualifica di insegnante** he has a teaching qualification, he is a qualified teacher; **sono stato assunto con la qualifica di meccanico** I was taken on as a mechanic
qualificare [kwalifi'kare] /20/ VT **1** (*giudicare: persona, lavoro*) to judge **2** (*definire*) to define, describe; **qualificare qn/qc come** to describe sb/sth as; **il suo gesto lo qualifica per quello che è** by doing that he shows the kind of person he is; **qualificarsi** VR **1** (*presentarsi*): **qualificarsi come** to describe o.s. as **2** (*ottenere una qualifica*) to qualify; **qualificarsi a un concorso** to pass an exam (*to obtain a post*); **qualificarsi per le semifinali** (*Sport*) to qualify for the semifinals
qualificativo, -a [kwalifika'tivo] AGG (*Gramm*): **aggettivo qualificativo** qualifying adjective
qualificato, -a [kwalifi'kato] AGG (*dotato di qualifica*) qualified; (*esperto, abile*) skilled; **operaio qualificato** skilled worker; **è un medico molto qualificato** he is a very distinguished

doctor; **non mi ritengo qualificato per quel lavoro** I don't think I'm qualified for that job
qualificazione [kwalifikat'tsjone] SF **1** (*qualifica*) qualification; **corso di qualificazione professionale** vocational training course **2** (*Sport: anche:* **gara di qualificazione**) qualifying event; **lottare per la qualificazione** to fight to qualify
qualità [kwali'ta] SF INV **1** (*gen*) quality; (*di suolo, clima*) nature; **di ottima** *o* **prima qualità** top quality; **è una stoffa di ottima qualità** it's top-quality fabric; **prodotto di qualità** quality product; **un vino di pessima qualità** a very poor wine; **controllo (di) qualità** quality control; **ci interessa la qualità non la quantità** we are interested in quality not quantity; **la qualità della vita** the quality of life **2** (*dote, pregio*) quality; **ha molte qualità** she has many good qualities **3** (*genere, tipo*) kind, type; **fiori di varie qualità** flowers of various kinds; **abbiamo sigarette di ogni qualità** we have cigarettes of every kind; **articoli di ogni qualità** all sorts of goods **4** (*veste, carica*): **in qualità di** in one's capacity as; **in qualità di avvocato** in my (*o* your *ecc*) capacity as a lawyer; **in qualità di amica** as a friend
qualitativo, -a [kwalita'tivo] AGG qualitative
qualora [kwa'lora] CONG in case, if; **qualora cambiassi idea** should you (happen to) change your mind
qualsiasi [kwal'siasi] AGG INDEF **1** (*tra molti*) any; **mettiti un vestito qualsiasi** wear anything you like; **in qualsiasi momento** at any time; **qualsiasi cosa** anything; **per lui farei qualsiasi cosa** I'd do anything for him; **a qualsiasi costo** at any cost, whatever the cost, no matter what; **ci riuscirò a qualsiasi costo** I'll manage it no matter what **2** (*tra due*) either; **prendine uno qualsiasi** take either of them **3** (*pegg*) ordinary, indifferent; **non è uno qualsiasi** he's not just anybody; **non voglio un vino qualsiasi** I don't want any old wine; **quale vuoi?** — **uno qualsiasi** which do you want? — any old one *o* whichever **4** (*Rel*) whatever; **qualsiasi cosa accada** whatever happens; **qualsiasi cosa dica** whatever he says; **qualsiasi favore tu mi chieda** whatever you ask of me
qualunquista, -i, -e [kwalun'kwista] SM, SF (*pegg*) politically apathetic person
quando ['kwando] AVV when; **quando arriverà?** when is he arriving?, when will he arrive?; **quando vai in vacanza?** when are you going on holiday?; **passerò a trovarti, ma non so quando** I'll come and see you, but I don't know when; **non so quando abbia telefonato** I don't know when he phoned; **da quando** since; **da quando sei qui?** how long have you been here?; **di quando è quel giornale?** which day's paper is that?; **fino a quando continuerà così?** how long will it go on *o* continue like this?; **quando mai avrei detto una cosa del genere?** whenever did I say anything of the kind?; **di quando in quando** from time to time; **ci penso di quando in quando** I think about it from time to time; **a quando i confetti?** when are we going to be hearing wedding bells? ♦ CONG when; **ti raggiungo quando ho finito** I'll join you when I've finished; **da quando sono arrivato** (ever) since I arrived; **abita lì da quando era piccola** she has lived there since she was a child; **chiamami quando vuoi** call me whenever you like; **quando fa così non lo sopporto** I can't stand him when he does that; **quand'anche tu volessi parlargli...** even if you wanted to speak to him ...
quantificare [kwantifi'kare] /20/ VT to quantify
quantità [kwanti'ta] SF INV **1** (*entità misurabile*) quantity, amount; **preferisco la qualità alla quantità** I prefer quality to quantity **2** (*gran numero*): **una quantità di** (*denaro, acqua*) a great deal of, a lot of; (*gente, cose*) a great many, a lot of, lots of, a great number of; **hanno invitato una quantità di gente** they invited lots of people; **ho una quantità di cose da fare** I have a lot of things to do; **in grande quantità** in large quantities; **c'è frutta in quantità** there is plenty of fruit **3** (*Mat: di vocale*) quantity
quantitativo, -a [kwanti'tativo] AGG quantitative ♦ SM (*Comm: di merce*) amount, quantity

quanto¹, -a ['kwanto] AGG
1 (*interrogativo: quantità*) how much; (: *numero*) how many; **quanti anni hai?** how old are you?; **quanti metri desidera?** how many metres would you like?; **quanti soldi ti hanno**

chiesto? how much did they ask you (for it)?; **quanta stoffa ti serve?** how much material do you need?; **quanto tempo?** how long?, how much time?; **quanto tempo ci metti da qui all'ufficio?** how long does it take you from here to the office?; **quante volte?** how often?, how many times? **2** (*esclamativo*): **quante storie!** what a fuss!; **quanto tempo sprecato!** what a waste of time!

3 (*relativo*) (*quantità*) as much as; (*numero*) as many as; **ti darò quanto denaro ti serve** I'll give you as much money as you need; **prendi quanti libri vuoi** take as many books as you want; **fermati quanto tempo vuoi** stay as long as you want

♦ PRON

1 (*interrogativo*) (*quantità*) how much; (*numero*) how many; **quanto costa?** how much does it cost?; **quanto credi costerà?** how much do you think it will cost?; **quanto è da qui al negozio?** how far is it from here to the shop?; **quanti di loro?** how many of them?; **quanto ci hai messo a farlo?** how long did it take you to do it?; **quanti ne desidera?** how many do you want?; **quanti ne abbiamo oggi?** what's the date today?; **quanto stai via?** how long will you be away?; **so che devo prendere del pane, ma non so quanto** I know I must get some bread, but I don't know how much; **quant'è?** how much is it?

2 (*esclamativo*): **vedi quanti hanno accettato!** see how many have accepted!; **quante me ne ha dette!** (*insulti*) the way he insulted me!; (*bugie*) the number of lies he told me!

3 (*relativo*: *quantità*) as much as; (: *numero*) as many as; **gli darò quanto chiede** I'll give him what *o* as much as he asks for; **è quanto di meglio potessi trovare** it's the best you could find; **a quanto dice lui** according to him; **in risposta a quanto esposto nella sua lettera...** in answer to the points raised in your letter ...; **saranno scelti quanti hanno fatto domanda in tempo** all (those) whose applications arrived in time will be selected; **per quanto ne so** as far as I know; **faremo quanto potremo per aiutarti** we'll do all we can *o* as much as we can to help you; **era tanto felice quanto non lo era mai stato** he was happier than he had ever been; **spende tanto denaro quanto ne guadagna** he spends all that *o* every penny he earns, he spends as much as he earns; **fanne venire quanti vuoi** get as many as you like to come

PAROLA CHIAVE

quanto² [ˈkwanto] AVV

1 (*quantità*) how much; (*numero*) how many; **sapessi quanto abbiamo camminato!** if you knew how far we have walked!; **quanto fumi al giorno?** how many (cigarettes) do you smoke a day?; **Dio solo sa quanto mi sono arrabbiato!** God only knows how angry I was!; **quanto pesi?** how much do you weigh?; **quanto sono felice!** how happy I am!

2 (*nella misura o quantità che*) as much; **aggiungere brodo quanto basta** add sufficient *o* enough stock, add as much stock as is necessary; **dovrai aspettare quanto è necessario** you'll have to wait as long as is necessary

3 (*come*): **siamo ricchi quanto loro** we are as rich as they are; **mi sono riposato quanto mai in questi ultimi tempi** I've had more rest than ever recently; **è famoso non tanto per i romanzi quanto per le poesie** he's famous not so much for his novels as for his poetry; **è tanto sciocco quanto cafone** he is as stupid as he is rude, he is both stupid and rude; **quanto è vero Iddio...!** I swear to God ...!

4 in quanto (*in qualità di*) as; (*perché, per il fatto che*) as, since; **in quanto insegnante** as a teacher; **non ho suonato in quanto temevo di svegliarti** I didn't ring as *o* since I was afraid I would wake you; **in quanto a** (*per ciò che riguarda*) as for; **in quanto ai soldi che mi devi...** as for the money you owe me ..., as far as the money you owe me is concerned ...

5 per quanto (*nonostante, anche se*) however; (*tuttavia*) although; **per quanto si sforzi, non riesce** however hard he tries he can't do it; **per quanto sembri complicato** however complicated it may seem; **cercherò di fare qualcosa per lui, per quanto non se lo meriti** I'll try and do something for him although *o* even though he doesn't deserve it

6 quanto meno the less; **quanto meno uno insiste tanto più gli viene offerto** the less one demands the more one is offered; **quanto più mi sforzo di ricordare tanto meno ci riesco** the harder *o* the more I try to remember the less

I succeed; **quanto più** the more; **quanto più presto potrò** as soon as I can; **verrò quanto prima** I'll come as soon as *o* early as possible

quantunque [kwanˈtunkwe] CONG (*sebbene*) although, even though; **quantunque mi piaccia non ci vivrei mai** even though I like the place I'd never live there; **accetto quantunque non convinto del tutto** I accept although *o* even though I'm not totally convinced

quaranta [kwaˈranta] AGG INV, SM INV forty

quarantena [kwaranˈtɛna] SF quarantine; **essere in quarantena** to be in quarantine; **mettere in quarantena** to quarantine

quarantenne [kwaranˈtenne] AGG, SM, SF forty-year-old

quarantennio, -ni [kwaranˈtɛnnjo] SM (period of) forty years

quarantesimo, -a [kwaranˈtɛzimo] AGG, SM, SF fortieth

quarantina [kwaranˈtina] SF: **una quarantina (di)** about forty

quarantotto [kwaranˈtɔtto] AGG INV forty-eight ♦ SM INV forty-eight; **fare un quarantotto** (*fam*) to raise hell

Quaresima [kwaˈrɛzima] SF (*Rel*): **la Quaresima** Lent; **osservare** *o* **fare la Quaresima** to keep Lent

quarta [ˈkwarta] SF (*gen*) fourth; (*Aut*) fourth gear; (*Scol*) fourth year; (*quarta elementare*) ≈ year five (*Brit*), ≈ fourth grade (*USA*); (*quarta superiore*) ≈ upper sixth (*Brit*), ≈ twelfth grade (*USA*); **mettere la quarta** to go into fourth (gear); **partire in quarta** (*fig*) to take off at top speed

quartetto [kwarˈtetto] SM (*Mus*) quartet(te); **che bel quartetto!** just look at the four of them!

quartiere [kwarˈtjɛre] SM **1** (*di città*) district, area; **la gente del quartiere** the local people; **lo conoscono tutti nel quartiere** everybody in the neighbourhood knows him; **un quartiere malfamato** a rough area *o* neighbourhood; **quartiere dormitorio** commuter area; **quartiere residenziale** residential area *o* district; **i quartieri alti** the exclusive areas; **i quartieri bassi** the poor areas **2** (*Mil*) quarters *pl*; **quartier generale** headquarters *pl* **3 lotta senza quartiere** (*fig*) unrelenting struggle

quarto, -a [ˈkwarto] AGG, SM, SF fourth; **quarta malattia** fourth disease; **quarto potere** fourth estate; **quarto uomo** (*Calcio*) fourth official ♦ SM **1** (*frazione*) quarter; **un quarto di vino** a quarter-litre (*Brit*) *o* quarter-liter (*USA*) bottle of wine; **un quarto di pollo** a quarter chicken; **primo/ultimo quarto** (*della luna*) first/last quarter; **un chilo e un quarto** a kilo and a quarter **2** (*ora*): **un quarto d'ora** a quarter of an hour; **tre quarti d'ora** three quarters of an hour; **tre ore e un quarto** three and a quarter hours; **le sei e un quarto** (a) quarter past six; **le otto e tre quarti, le nove meno un quarto** (a) quarter to (*Brit*) *o* of (*USA*) nine; **passare un brutto quarto d'ora** (*fig*) to have a bad *o* nasty time of it **3 quarti di finale** (*Sport*) quarterfinals **4** (*Naut*) watch; **il primo quarto** the first watch **5** (*Tip*) quarto

quarzo [ˈkwartso] SM quartz; **orologio al quarzo** quartz watch; **quarzo rosa** rose quartz

quasi [ˈkwazi] AVV (*gen*) almost, nearly; (*restrittivo*) hardly, scarcely; **ha quasi 30 anni** he's almost *o* nearly 30 (years old); **quasi niente** hardly *o* scarcely anything; **non sento quasi niente** I can hardly hear anything; **non è venuto quasi nessuno** hardly anybody came; **quasi mai** hardly ever; **non lo vedo quasi mai** I hardly ever see him; **quasi cadevo** I almost *o* nearly fell; **è quasi un fratello per me** he's like a brother to me; **oserei quasi dire che...** I'd almost say that ...; **quasi quasi me ne vado** I've half a mind to leave; **quasi quasi è meglio così** it may even be better this way ♦ CONG (*come se*) as if; **urla quasi fosse lui il padrone** he shouts as if he were the boss; **non si è fatto vivo, quasi sospettasse qualcosa** he hasn't been in touch, as if he suspected something

quassù [kwasˈsu] AVV up here

quatto, -a [ˈkwatto] AGG: **stare quatto quatto** to keep as quiet as a mouse; **entrare quatto quatto in una stanza** to creep stealthily into a room; **uscire quatto quatto** to slip away

quattordicenne [kwattordiˈtʃɛnne] AGG, SM, SF fourteen-year-old

quattordici [kwatˈtorditʃi] AGG, SM INV fourteen

quattrino [kwatˈtrino] SM **1 non avere un quattrino** *o* il becco di un quattrino (*fam*) to be penniless *o* broke **2 quattrini** SMPL money *sg*, cash *sg*; **fare quattrini** to make money; **essere pieno di quattrini** to be rolling in money; **quattrini a palate** piles of money; **costare fior di quattrini** to cost a fortune

quattro [ˈkwattro] AGG INV **1** four; **c'erano quattro persone** there were four people there **2** (*fig: pochi*): **fare quattro passi** to take a stroll, go for a little walk; **facciamo quattro passi** let's go for a little walk; **c'erano quattro gatti allo spettacolo** there was only a handful of people at the show; **fare quattro salti** to go dancing; **fare quattro chiacchiere** to have a chat; **lo pagano quattro soldi** they pay him peanuts *o* a pittance; **a quattr'occhi** (*tra 2 persone*) face to face; (*privatamente*) in private; **a quattro a quattro** four at a time; **a quattro zampe** on all fours ♦ SM INV four; **dirne quattro a qn** to give sb a piece of one's mind; **farsi in quattro per qn** to go out of one's way for sb, put o.s. out for sb; **fare il diavolo a quattro** to kick up a rumpus; **in quattro e quattr'otto** in less than no time, in no time at all; *vedi* **cinque**

quattrocchi [kwatˈtrɔkki] SM INV (*fig: fam: persona con occhiali*) four-eyes

quattrocentesco, -a, -schi, -sche [kwattrotʃenˈtesko] AGG fifteenth-century *attr*

quattrocento [kwattroˈtʃento] AGG INV four hundred ♦ SM INV four hundred; (*secolo*): **il Quattrocento** the fifteenth century

quattromila [kwattroˈmila] AGG INV, SM INV four thousand

PAROLA CHIAVE

quello, -a [ˈkwello] *davanti a sm* quel + *consonante*, quell' + *vocale*, quello + *s impura, gn, pn, ps, x, z; pl* quei + *consonante*, quegli + *vocale o s impura, gn, pn, ps, x, z; davanti a sf* quella + *consonante*, quell' + *vocale; pl* quelle AGG DIMOSTR **1** that, those *pl*; **mi passi quel libro?** could you pass me that book?; **voglio quella camicia lì** *o* **là** I want that shirt there; **dove hai comprato quei quadri?** where did you buy those paintings?; **dove metto quello scatolone?** where shall I put that box?; **chi sono quegli uomini?** who are those men? **2** (*seguito da proposizione relativa*): **con quel poco che abbiamo** with what *o* the little we have; **dov'è quel maglione che mi dicevi?** where's the *o* that jumper you were telling me about? **3** (*enfatico*): **ho una di quelle paure!** I'm scared stiff!; **ne ha fatte di quelle!** (*sciocchezze*) he did some really stupid things!; **una di quelle** (*euf: prostituta*) prostitute; **in quello stesso istante** at that very moment

♦ PRON DIMOSTR **1** that (one), those (ones) *pl*; **quale vuoi? — quello bianco** which do you want? — the white one; **il tuo nome e quello di Roberta** your name and Roberta's; **quello di Giovanna è il voto migliore** Giovanna's is the best mark, Giovanna has the best mark; **prendiamo quello là** we'll take that one there; **chi è quello lì?** who is that (person)?; **e quello cos'è?** and what is that?; **quelle sono le mie scarpe** those are my shoes; **ho incontrato quelli della festa** I met the people from the party; **a che ora viene quello dell'ufficio ispezioni ristoranti?** when does the restaurant inspector come? **2** (*egli*) he; (*ella*) she; (*essi, esse*) they; **sarebbe un'occasione d'oro e quelli non vogliono accettare** it's a golden opportunity but they don't want to accept **3** (*in proposizione relativa*): **quello(a) che** (*persona*) the one (who); (*cosa*) the one (which) *o* (that); **quelli(e) che** (*persone*) those who; (*cose*) those which *o* that; **quello che hai comprato tu è più bello** the one (which) you bought is nicer; **quello che hai visto è il padre** the person *o* the one you saw is the father; **quella che hai incontrato è la seconda moglie** the one *o* woman you met is his second wife; **chiedi a quelli che l'hanno conosciuto** ask those who knew him **4** (*ciò*): **quello che** the what; (*tutto*) all (that), everything; **ho detto quello che sapevo** I've told you all I know; **ho fatto quello che potevo** I did what I could; **nega, e quel che è peggio, ci scherza sopra** he denies it, and what is worse, jokes about it; **da quello che ho sentito** from what I've heard **5** (*fraseologia*): **in quel di Milano** in the Milan area *o* region; **in quel mentre** at that very moment

quercia, -ce [ˈkwertʃa] SF **1** (*albero*) oak (tree); (*legno*) oak; **quercia rossa** red oak; **forte come una quercia** as strong as an ox **2 la Quercia** (*Pol*) *symbol of P.D.S.*

querela [kweˈrɛla] SF (*Dir*) (legal) action; **sporgere querela contro qn** to bring an action against sb; **querela per diffamazione** libel action

querelare [kwereˈlare] /72/ VT (*Dir*) to bring an action against

quesito [kweˈsito] SM question, query; **porre un quesito (a)** to put a question (to)

questi [ˈkwesti] PRON DIMOSTR (*letter*) this person

questionario, -ri [kwestjoˈnarjo] SM questionnaire

questione [kwesˈtjone] SF **1** (*problema, faccenda*) question, matter, problem; (*controversia*) issue; **si tratta di una questione delicata/personale** it's a delicate/personal matter; **è una questione politica** it's a political question *o* matter; **è una questione di vita o di morte** it's a question *o* matter of life and death; **il nocciolo della questione** the heart of the matter; **ne ha fatto una questione** he made an issue out of it; **è sorta una questione in merito** they made an issue out of it; **comporre una questione** (*Dir*) to settle an issue; **il caso in questione** the matter at hand; **la persona in questione** the person involved; **non voglio essere chiamato in questione** I don't want to be involved; **è questione di tempo** it's a matter *o* question of time **2** (*dubbio*): **mettere qc in questione** to question sth; **è fuori questione** it's out of the question

PAROLA CHIAVE

questo, -a [ˈkwesto] AGG DIMOSTR **1** this, these *pl*; **in questi ultimi giorni** these last few days; **questo libro qui o qua** this book (here); **questo lunedì** this Monday; **ti piace questo maglione?** do you like this jumper?; **quest'oggi** nowadays, today; **questa sera** this evening; **di questi tempi** in times like these **2** (*enfatico*): **con questo caldo** in this heat; **non fatemi più prendere queste paure** don't give me such a fright again

♦ PRON DIMOSTR **1** this (one), these (ones) *pl*; **prendo questo qui o qua** I'll take this one; **questo è il tuo posto** this is your place; **questo cosa significa?** what does this mean?; **questo è troppo!** this is too much *o* the limit!; **questo mi fa piacere** I am pleased about that **2** (*egli*) he; (*ella*) she; (*essi, esse*) they; **e questo mi guarda e ride!** and this guy just looks at me and laughs!; **una tale occasione, e questi che fanno?** - **rifiutano** such a great opportunity, and what do they do? - they refuse **3 questo... quello...** (*il primo... il secondo...*) the former ... the latter ...; (*l'uno... l'altro...*) the one ... the other ...; **questi... quelli** some ... others; **questi gridavano, quelli ridevano** some were shouting, others were laughing; **preferisci questo o quello?** do you prefer this one or that one? **4** (*fraseologia*): **e con questo?** so what?; **e con questo se n'è andato** and with that he left; **con tutto questo** in spite of this, despite all this; **è per questo che sono venuto** this is why I came; **questo poi!** I don't believe it!; **questo è quanto** that's all; **questo sì che è il colmo!** this is the limit!; **questa non me la dovevi fare** you shouldn't have done this to me

questore [kwesˈtore] SM (*Polizia*) public official in charge of the police in the provincial capital, reporting to the prefetto, ≈ chief constable (*Brit*), ≈ police commissioner (*USA*)

questua [ˈkwestua] SF collection (of alms)

questura [kwesˈtura] SF (*organo*) police force; (*edificio*) police headquarters *pl*

questurino [kwestuˈrino] SM (*fam: poliziotto*) cop

qui [kwi] AVV **1** here; **vieni qui** come here; **eccomi qui!** here I am!; **qui dentro/sopra/sotto/vicino** in/up/under/near here; **non c'è molto spazio qui dentro** there's not much room in here; **qui sotto c'è la tua camicia** your shirt's under here; **abita qui sotto** she lives (in the apartment) downstairs; **da o di qui from here**; **da o di qui non mi muovo** I'm not budging from here!; **da qui la vista è stupenda** the view is fantastic from here; **di qui non si passa** you can't get through here o this way **2** (*temporale*): **da qui in avanti** from now on; **di qui a poco/una settimana** in a little while/a week's time **3** (*fraseologia*): (**dammi**) **qui, ci penso io!** just give it to me, I'll see to it!; **fin qui tutto bene** so far so good; **ah, qui ti voglio!** that's the problem!; **non è di qui** he's not from around here; **che diavolo vuole questo qui?** what on earth does he want?

quiescenza [kwjeʃˈʃɛntsa] SF **1** (*di vulcano*) dormancy **2** (*Amm*): **trattamento di quiescenza** retirement package; **porre qn in quiescenza** to retire sb

quietanza [kwjeˈtantsa] SF (*Comm*) receipt

quietare [kwjeˈtare] /72/ VT to soothe, calm; **quietarsi** VIP (*mare*) to become calm; (*vento*) to die down; (*bambino*) to calm down

quiete [ˈkwjɛte] SF **1** (*silenzio*) quiet, stillness, quietness; (*tranquillità*) peace, calmness; **la quiete che precede la tempesta** the calm before the storm; **aver bisogno di quiete** (*riposo*) to need peace and quiet; **la quiete della campagna** the tranquillity *o* peace of the countryside; **turbare la quiete pubblica** (*Dir*) to disturb the peace **2** (*Fis*): **stato di quiete** state of rest

quieto, -a [ˈkwjɛto] AGG (*gen*) quiet; (*notte*) quiet, still; (*mare*) calm; **l'ho fatto per il quieto vivere** I did it for a quiet life

quindi [ˈkwindi] CONG (*perciò*) therefore, so; **avevo freddo e quindi mi sono messo il maglione** I was cold, so I put on a sweater ♦ AVV (*in seguito*) then; **devi continuare diritto, quindi girare a destra** you should carry straight on, then turn right; **ho cenato e quindi sono andato al cinema** I had dinner and then went to the cinema

quindicenne [kwindiˈtʃɛnne] AGG, SM, SF fifteen-year-old

quindici [ˈkwinditʃi] AGG INV fifteen; **quindici giorni** two weeks, a fortnight (*Brit*); **oggi a quindici** two weeks *o* a fortnight (*Brit*) today; **tra quindici giorni** in two weeks *o* a fortnight (*Brit*) ♦ SM INV fifteen

quindicina [kwindiˈtʃina] SF: **una quindicina (di)** about fifteen; (*fra*) **una quindicina di giorni** (in) two weeks *o* a fortnight (*Brit*); **la seconda quindicina di marzo** the second half of March

quindicinale [kwinditʃiˈnale] AGG fortnightly (*Brit*), semimonthly (*USA*) ♦ SM (*rivista*) fortnightly magazine (*Brit*), semimonthly (*USA*)

quinquennale [kwinkwenˈnale] AGG (*che dura 5 anni*) five-year attr; (*che avviene ogni 5 anni*) five-yearly

quinquennio, -ni [kwinˈkwɛnnjo] SM (period of) five years, quinquennial

quinta [ˈkwinta] SF **1** (*gen*) fifth; (*Aut*) fifth gear; (*Scol*) fifth year; (*quinta elementare*) ≈ year six (*Brit*), ≈ fifth grade (*USA*); (*quinta superiore*) ≈ first year (at college) (*Brit*), ≈ freshman year (at college) (*USA*) **2 le quinte** (*Teatro*) the wings; **tra** *o* **dietro le quinte** (*fig*) behind the scenes

quintale [kwinˈtale] SM quintal (= *100 kg*); **pesa un quintale** (*fig*) it weighs a ton

quintetto [kwinˈtetto] SM (*Mus*) quintet(te)

quinto, -a [ˈkwinto] AGG fifth; **la quinta parte di** a fifth of; **la quinta volta** the fifth time; **al quinto piano** on the fifth (*Brit*) *o* sixth (*USA*) floor; **è arrivato quinto nella gara** he came fifth in the competition; **essere al quinto posto in classifica** to be fifth in the championship; **in quinta pagina** on the fifth page, on page five; **quinta colonna** (*fig*) fifth column; **quinta malattia** fifth disease; **quinto potere** fifth estate (*USA*), television, seen as a source of influence and propaganda ♦ SM, SF fifth; **sei la quinta a cui faccio la domanda** you are the fifth person I have asked; **il quinto da destra** the fifth from the right; **il quinto arrivato vincerà una macchina fotografica** whoever comes fifth will win a camera ♦ SM (*frazione*) fifth; **un quinto della popolazione** a fifth of the population; **tre quinti** three fifths

qui pro quo [ˈkwiprɔˈkwɔ] SM INV misunderstanding

Quirinale [kwiriˈnale] SM *one of the seven hills of Rome*

quiz [kwidz] SM INV **1** (*domanda*) question; **risolvere un quiz** to answer a question **2** (*anche: gioco a quiz*) quiz game; **quiz televisivo** television quiz

quorum [ˈkwɔrum] SM INV quorum

quota [ˈkwɔta] SF **1** (*parte*) quota, share; **la sua quota di azioni** his quota of shares; **le quote del totalizzatore** (*Ippica*) the odds; **quota fissa** fixed amount *o* sum; **quota imponibile** (*Fisco*) taxable income; **quota d'iscrizione** (*Univ*) enrolment fee; (*a gara*) entry fee; (*a club*) membership fee; **quota di mercato** market share; **quota non imponibile** (*Fisco*) personal allowance; **quote latte** milk quotas **2** (*altitudine*) altitude, height; **l'aereo volava a bassa quota** the plane was flying low; **di alta quota** high-altitude attr; **a quota zero** at sea level; **a quota 750 metri** 750 metres above sea level; **prendere/perdere quota** (*Aer*) to gain/lose height *o* altitude

quotare [kwoˈtare] /72/ VT **1** (*Fin, Borsa*) to quote; **la sterlina è quotata a 1 euro e 50** the pound is quoted at 1,50 euros; **queste azioni sono quotate in Borsa** these shares are quoted on the Stock Exchange **2** (*valutare, anche fig*) to value; **questo quadro è stato quotato 15 mila euro** this painting was valued at 15 thousand euros; **è un pittore molto quotato** he is rated highly as a painter, he is a highly rated painter

quotazione [kwotatˈtsjone] SF (*Fin*) quotation; (*fig: di artista*) rating

quotidianamente [kwotidjanaˈmente] AVV daily, every day

quotidiano, -a [kwotiˈdjano] AGG (*di ogni giorno*) daily; (*normale*) everyday; **la vita quotidiana** daily life ♦ SM (*giornale*) daily (paper)

quoziente [kwotˈtsjɛnte] SM **1** (*Mat*) quotient **2** (*tasso*) rate; **quoziente di crescita zero** zero growth rate; **quoziente d'intelligenza** intelligence quotient, IQ

Rr

R¹, r¹ [ˈɛrre] SF INV, SM INV (*lettera*) R, r; **R come Roma** ≈ R for Robert (*Brit*), R for Roger (*USA*)

R² ABBR 1 (*Posta*) = **raccomandata** 2 (*Ferr*) = **regionale**

RA SIGLA = Ravenna

rabarbaro [raˈbarbaro] SM (*Bot*) rhubarb; (*liquore*) rhubarb liqueur

Rabat [raˈbat] SF Rabat

rabberciare [rabberˈtʃare] /14/ VT (*anche fig*) to patch up

rabbia [ˈrabbja] SF 1 (*ira*) anger, rage; (*fig: di onde, vento*) fury; **essere fuori di sé dalla rabbia** to be beside o.s. with rage; **farsi prendere dalla rabbia** to fly into a rage; **fare qc con rabbia** to do sth angrily; **mi fai una rabbia!** you make me so angry!; (*scherz: invidia*) you make me so jealous!; **che rabbia!** what a damned nuisance! 2 (*Med: idrofobia*) rabies sg

rabbino [rabˈbino] SM rabbi

rabbioso, -a [rabˈbjoso] AGG 1 (*discorso, tono, sguardo*) furious, angry; (*fig: vento, odio*) raging, furious 2 (*Med*) rabid, mad

rabbonire [rabboˈnire] /55/ VT, **rabbonirsi** VIP to calm down; **l'ha rabbonita** he calmed her down

rabbrividire [rabbriviˈdire] /55/ VI (*aus essere*) (*per il freddo*) to shiver, shudder; (*fig: per paura*) to shudder; **rabbrividire al solo pensiero di qc/di fare qc** to shudder at the mere thought of sth/of doing sth

rabbuiare [rabbuˈjare] /19/ VI (*aus essere*), **rabbuiarsi** VIP to grow dark, darken; **si rabbuiò in viso** his (*o* her) face darkened

rabdomante [rabdoˈmante] SM water diviner

racc. ABBR (*Posta*) = **raccomandata**

raccapezzarsi [rakkapetˈtsarsi] /72/ VIP: to find one's way; **non raccapezzarsi** to be at a loss; **c'è tanta confusione che non mi raccapezzo più** things are in such a mess that I can't make head nor tail of anything

raccapricciante [rakkapritˈtʃante] AGG horrifying; **una scena raccapricciante** a horrifying scene

raccapriccio [rakkaˈpritˈtʃo] SM horror

raccattapalle [rakkattaˈpalle] SM INV (*spec Tennis*) ballboy

raccattare [rakkatˈtare] /72/ VT (*raccogliere, anche fig: voti*) to pick up

racchetta [rakˈketta] SF (*da tennis*) racket; (*da ping-pong*) bat; **racchetta da neve** snowshoe; **racchetta da sci** ski pole

racchio, -chia, -chi, -chie [ˈrakkjo] AGG (*fam*) ugly

racchiudere [rakˈkjudere] /22/ VT IRREG to contain

racchiuso, -a [rakˈkjuso] PP di **racchiudere**

raccogliere [rakˈkoʎʎere] VB IRREG /23/ VT 1 (*raccattare*) to pick up; **puoi raccogliere i tuoi giocattoli?** can you pick up your toys?; **mi ero chinato a raccogliere la penna** I had bent down to pick up the pen; **non ha raccolto il guanto** (*fig*) he didn't take up the gauntlet; **non ha raccolto** (*allusione*) he didn't take the hint; (*frecciata*) he took no notice of it 2 (*frutta, fiori*) to pick, pluck; (*Agr*) to harvest; (*fig: onori, successo*) to reap; (: *approvazione, voti*) to win; **abbiamo raccolto un mazzetto di fiori** we picked a bunch of flowers; **raccogliere il grano** to harvest the wheat; **raccogliere l'uva** to pick grapes; **raccogliere i frutti del proprio lavoro** (*fig*) to reap the benefits of one's work 3 (*radunare: persone*) to assemble; (*notizie, denaro, firme*) to gather, collect; **stiamo raccogliendo libri usati per la biblioteca** we're collecting second-hand books for the library; **raccogliere fondi** to raise funds; **ho raccolto le mie cose e me ne sono andata** I took my things and went; **raccogliere le idee** (*fig*) to gather *o* collect one's thoughts 4 (*collezionare: francobolli, monete, cartoline*) to collect 5 (*ripiegare: ali*) to fold; (: *gambe*) to draw up; (: *vele*) to furl; (: *capelli*) to put up; **raccogliersi** VIP (*radunarsi*) to gather

raccoglimento [rakkoʎʎiˈmento] SM meditation; **un minuto di raccoglimento** a minute's silence

raccoglitore [rakkoʎʎiˈtore] SM (*cartella*) folder, binder; (*per francobolli*) album; **raccoglitore a fogli mobili** loose-leaf binder

raccolta [rakˈkɔlta] SF 1 (*gen*) collection, collecting no pl; **la mia raccolta di CD** my CD collection; **fare (la) raccolta di qc** to collect sth; **faccio raccolta di cartoline** I collect postcards; **raccolta dei rifiuti** refuse *o* rubbish (*Brit*) *o* garbage (*USA*) collection; **raccolta differenziata** (*dei rifiuti*) separate collection of different kinds of household waste 2 (*Agr*) harvesting no pl, gathering no pl; **fare la raccolta della frutta** to pick fruit 3 (*di persone*) gathering; **chiamare a raccolta** to gather together 4 **raccolta di fondi** fund-raising

raccolto, -a [rakˈkɔlto] PP di **raccogliere** ♦ AGG 1 (*persona: assorto*) thoughtful; **raccolto in preghiera** absorbed in prayer 2 (*luogo: appartato*) secluded, quiet 3 (*gambe*) drawn up; **raccolto su se stesso** curled up ♦ SM (*Agr*) crop, harvest; (*periodo*) harvest time

raccomandabile [rakkomanˈdabile] AGG (highly) commendable; **è un tipo poco raccomandabile** he is not to be trusted

raccomandare [rakkomanˈdare] /72/ VT 1 (*consigliare*) to recommend; **l'albergo è raccomandato dalla guida** the hotel is recommended by the guide; **te lo raccomando, quello!** (*iro*) watch out for that one!; **raccomandare a qn di fare qc** to recommend that sb do sth; **ti raccomando questo libro/di leggere questo libro** I recommend this book to you/that you read this book; **raccomandare a qn di non fare qc** (*esortare*) to tell *o* warn sb not to do sth; **ti raccomando di non fare tardi** now remember, don't come in late 2 (*affidare*) to entrust; **raccomandare qn a qn/alle cure di qn** to entrust sb to sb/to sb's care 3 (*appoggiare*) to recommend; **raccomandare qn per un lavoro** to recommend sb for a job; **raccomandarsi** VR: **raccomandarsi a qn** to implore sb's help; **raccomandarsi alla pietà di qn** to implore sb's pity; **mi raccomando!** don't forget!; **mi raccomando, scrivimi!** please write to me!; **mi raccomando! non perderlo** please don't lose it!; **mi raccomando! studia bene** be sure and study hard!

raccomandato, -a [rakkomanˈdato] AGG 1 (*lettera, pacco*) recorded-delivery (*Brit*), certified (*USA*) 2 (*candidato*) recommended ♦ SM, SF: **essere un raccomandato di ferro** to have friends in high places

raccomandazione [rakkomandatˈtsjone] SF 1 (*appoggio*) recommendation; **lettera di raccomandazione** letter of introduction; **qui ci vuole la raccomandazione di qualcuno** we need somebody to pull a few strings here 2 (*esortazione*) piece of advice; **mi ha fatto mille raccomandazioni** he gave me lots of advice

raccomodare [rakkomoˈdare] /72/ VT (*riparare*) to repair, mend

raccontare [rakkonˈtare] /72/ VT (*storia, bugie*) to tell; (*avventure*) to tell about; **raccontare qc a qn** to tell sb sth; **mi ha raccontato una barzelletta molto divertente** he told me a very funny joke; **non raccontarlo a nessuno** don't tell anyone about it; **raccontano che sia fuggito** they say that he escaped; **nel libro racconta delle sue avventure** in the book he speaks of his adventures; **dai, raccontami tutto** come on, tell me all about it; **a me non la racconti** don't try and kid me; **raccontala a qualcun altro!** try and pull the wool over somebody else's eyes!; **a me lo vieni a raccontare!** don't tell me!; **se ne raccontano delle belle su di lui** I've heard a few stories about him; **cosa mi racconti di nuovo?** what's new?

racconto [rakˈkonto] SM 1 (*narrazione*) account, telling no pl, relating no pl; (*fatto raccontato*) story, tale; **il suo racconto dell'avventura** his account of the adventure 2 (*genere letterario*) short story; **racconti per bambini** children's stories

raccorciare [rakkorˈtʃare] /14/ VT to shorten; **raccorciarsi**

VIP to become shorter; **le giornate si stanno raccorciando** the days are drawing in *o* getting shorter

raccordare [rakkor'dare] /72/ VT (*collegare*) to link up, join (up)

raccordo [rak'kɔrdo] SM (*Tecn: giunzione*) joint, connection; (*di autostrada*) slip road (*Brit*), entrance (*o* exit) ramp (*USA*); (*Ferr*) siding; **raccordo anulare** (*Aut*) ring road (*Brit*), beltway (*USA*)

rachitico, -a, -ci, -che [ra'kitiko] AGG (*Med*) suffering from rickets; (*fig: pianta*) spindly; (: *persona*) scrawny ♦ SM, SF person who suffers from rickets

rachitismo [raki'tizmo] SM (*Med*) rickets *sg*

racimolare [ratʃimo'lare] /72/ VT (*denaro*) to scrape together; (*fig: notizie*) to glean

rada ['rada] SF (natural) harbour (*Brit*) *o* harbor (*USA*)

radar ['radar] SM INV radar ♦ AGG INV (*segnale, avvistamento*) radar *attr*; **uomini radar** air traffic controllers

raddolcire [raddol'tʃire] /55/ VT (*persona, carattere*) to soften; **raddolcirsi** VIP (*tempo*) to grow milder; (*persona*) to soften, mellow

raddoppiamento [raddoppja'mento] SM (*gen*) doubling

raddoppiare [raddop'pjare] /19/ VI (*aus essere*) to double; (*aus avere*) (*Calcio*) to score a second goal; **il prezzo del biglietto è raddoppiato** the price of the ticket has doubled ♦ VT to double

raddoppio, -pi [rad'doppjo] SM (*gen*) doubling; (*Biliardo*) double; (*Calcio*) second goal; (*Equitazione*) gallop

raddrizzare [raddrit'tsare] /72/ VT 1 (*mettere dritto*) to straighten; (*fig: correggere*) to put straight, correct 2 (*Elettr*) to rectify; **raddrizzarsi** VR (*persona*) to straighten (o.s.) up

radere ['radere] VB IRREG /85/ VT 1 (*barba*) to shave off; (*mento*) to shave; **radere i capelli a zero** to shave one's hair off; **s'è fatto radere i capelli a zero** he's had his head shaved 2 (*fig: sfiorare*) to graze, skim 3 (*abbattere*): **radere al suolo** to raze to the ground; **radersi** VR to shave (o.s.); **si rade ogni mattina** he shaves every morning

radiale [ra'djale] AGG, SM (*Anat, Geom, Aut*) radial

radiante [ra'djante] AGG (*superficie, pannello*) radiant ♦ SM (*Mat*) radian

radiare [ra'djare] /19/ VT (*da scuola, partito*) to expel; (*dall'esercito*) to dismiss; (*da albo professionale: medico*) to strike off; (*avvocato*) to disbar

radiatore [radja'tore] SM radiator

radiazione [radjat'tsjone] SF 1 (*Fis*) radiation; **radiazione nucleare** nuclear radiation 2 (*cancellazione*) striking off; (*espulsione*) expulsion

radica ['radika] SF (*per pipe*) briar, briarwood; **pipa in radica** briar-pipe; **radica di noce** walnut (wood)

radicale [radi'kale] AGG (*gen, anche Pol*) radical; (*Ling*) root *attr*; **un cambiamento radicale** a radical change ♦ SM, SF (*Pol*) radical ♦ SM (*Mat, Chim*) radical; (*Ling*) root; **radicali liberi** free radicals

radicato, -a [radi'kato] AGG (*pregiudizio, credenza*) deep-seated, deeply-rooted

radicchio [ra'dikkjo] SM radicchio, *variety of chicory*

radice [ra'ditʃe] SF (*gen, anche Mat, Anat, Ling, fig*) root; **segno di radice** (*Mat*) radical sign; **colpire alla radice** (*fig*) to strike at the root; **mettere radici** (*idee, odio*) to take root; (*persona*) to put down roots; **radice quadrata** (*Mat*) square root

radio¹ ['radjo] SF INV 1 (*apparecchio*) radio (set); **radio portatile** portable radio; **radio ricevente** receiver; **radio a transistor** transistor (radio); **radio trasmittente** transmitter 2 (*radiodiffusione*): **la radio** (the) radio; **l'ho sentito alla radio** I heard it on the radio; **trasmettere via radio a qn** (*messaggio*) to radio to sb; **trasmettere per radio** to broadcast ♦ AGG INV radio *attr*; **stazione /ponte radio** radio station/link

radio², -di ['radjo] SM (*Anat*) radius

radio³ ['radjo] SM (*Chim*) radium

radioabbonato, -a [radjoabbo'nato] SM, SF radio subscriber

radioamatore, -trice [radjoama'tore] SM, SF amateur radio operator

radioascoltatore, -trice [radjoaskolta'tore] SM, SF (radio) listener

radioattività [radjoattivi'ta] SF radioactivity

radioattivo, -a [radjoat'tivo] AGG radioactive; **scorie radioattive** radioactive waste

radiocomandare [radjokoman'dare] /72/ VT to operate by remote control

radiocomandato, -a [radjokoman'dato] AGG remote-controlled

radiocomando [radjoko'mando] SM remote control

radiocomunicazione [radjokomunikat'tsjone] SF radio message

radiocronaca, -che [radjo'krɔnaka] SF radio commentary; **la radiocronaca della partita** the radio commentary on the match

radiocronista, -i, -e [radjokro'nista] SM, SF radio commentator

radiodiffusione [radjodiffu'zjone] SF (radio) broadcasting

radiofonico, -a, -ci, -che [radjo'fɔniko] AGG radio *attr*

radiografare [radjogra'fare] /72/ VT to X-ray

radiografia [radjogra'fia] SF (*procedimento*) radiography; (*foto*) X-ray (photograph)

radiolina [radjo'lina] SF portable radio, transistor (radio)

radiologia [radjolo'dʒia] SF radiology

radiologo, -a, -gi, -ghe [ra'djɔlogo] SM, SF (*medico*) radiologist; (*tecnico*) radiographer

radioricevente [radjoritʃe'vɛnte] SF (*anche:* **apparecchio radioricevente**) receiver

radioso, -a [ra'djoso] AGG (*anche fig*) radiant

radiostazione [radjostat'tsjone] SF radio station

radiosveglia [radjoz'veʎʎa] SF radio alarm

radiotaxi [radjo'taksi], **radiotassì** [radjotas'si] SM INV radio taxi

radiotecnico, -a, -ci, -che [radjo'tɛkniko] AGG radio engineering *attr* ♦ SM radio engineer

radiotelegrafista, -i, -e [radjotelegra'fista] SM, SF radiotelegrapher

radioterapia [radjotera'pia] SF radiotherapy

radiotrasmittente [radjotrazmit'tɛnte] AGG (radio) broadcasting *attr* ♦ SF (radio) broadcasting station

rado, -a ['rado] AGG (*capelli*) sparse, thin; (*visite*) infrequent; **di rado** rarely; **vanno di rado al ristorante** they rarely go to a restaurant; **non di rado** not uncommonly

radunare [radu'nare] /72/ VT (*persone*) to gather, assemble; (*Mil: truppe*) to rally; (*oggetti*) to collect, gather together; **radunarsi** VIP to gather, assemble

radunata [radu'nata] SF (*Mil*) muster; (*Dir*): **radunata sediziosa** seditious assembly (*o* gathering)

raduno [ra'duno] SM gathering, meeting

radura [ra'dura] SF clearing

rafano ['rafano] SM (*Bot*) horseradish

raffazzonare [raffattso'nare] /72/ VT (*riparare*) to patch up; (*mettere insieme alla meglio*) to throw together

raffermo, -a [raf'fermo] AGG stale

raffica, -che ['raffika] SF (*Meteor*) gust (of wind); **raffica di mitra** burst of machine-gun fire; **il vento soffiava a raffiche** the wind was very blustery; **raffica di insulti** (*fig*) avalanche of insults; **raffica di domande** (*fig*) barrage of questions

raffigurare [raffigu'rare] /72/ VT (*rappresentare*) to depict, to represent; (*simboleggiare*) to represent, symbolize; **il quadro raffigura la presa della Bastiglia** the picture shows the storming of the Bastille; **non riesco a raffigurarmelo** I can't picture it

raffigurazione [raffigurat'tsjone] SF depiction, representation

raffinare [raffi'nare] /72/ VT (*zucchero, petrolio, anche fig*) to refine; **raffinarsi** VIP (*fig*) to become refined

raffinatezza [raffina'tettsa] SF refinement; **arredato con raffinatezza** tastefully furnished

raffinato, -a [raffi'nato] AGG (*zucchero, sale*) refined; (*persona*) cultivated, polished, refined; (*modi*) polished, sophisticated; (*crudeltà, astuzia*) refined, subtle; (*pranzo*) formal; **una donna raffinata** a sophisticated woman; **cibi raffinati** delicacies ♦ SM, SF refined person

raffinazione [raffinat'tsjone] SF (*di sostanza*) refining; **raffinazione del petrolio** oil refining

raffineria [raffine'ria] SF refinery

rafforzare [raffor'tsare] /72/ VT (*gen, anche Mil*) to reinforce;

rafforzarsi VIP to strengthen, grow stronger; **i miei dubbi su di lui si sono rafforzati** my doubts about him have grown

rafforzativo, -a [raffortsa'tivo](*Gramm*) AGG intensifying ♦ SM intensifier

raffreddamento [raffredda'mento] SM (*anche fig*) cooling; **c'è stato un raffreddamento nei loro rapporti** (*fig*) their relationship has cooled; **raffreddamento ad acqua** (*Aut*) water-cooling; **raffreddamento ad aria** (*Aut*) air-cooling

raffreddare [raffred'dare] /72/ VT to cool (down); (*fig: entusiasmo*) to have a cooling effect on, dampen; **lascia raffreddare la minestra** leave the soup to cool (down); **raffreddarsi** VIP 1 (*caffè, minestra ecc*) to cool down; (*aria*) to become cooler, become colder; (*fig: entusiasmo, relazione*) to cool (off); **non lasciare che la minestra si raffreddi** don't let the soup get cold; **aspetta che si raffreddi** wait till it cools down 2 (*prendere un raffreddore*) to catch a cold

raffreddato, -a [raffred'dato] AGG (*Med*): **essere raffreddato** to have a cold; **sono raffreddata** I've got a cold

raffreddore [raffred'dore] SM (*Med*) cold; **prendere/avere il raffreddore** to catch/have a cold; **raffreddore da fieno** hay fever

raffrontare [raffron'tare] /72/ VT to compare

raffronto [raf'fronto] SM comparison

rafia ['rafja] SF (*fibra*) raffia

rafting ['raftin(g)] SM (*Sport*) rafting

raganella [raga'nɛlla] SF (*Zool*) tree frog

ragazza [ra'gattsa] SF (*gen*) girl; (*giovane donna*) young woman; (*fidanzata*) girlfriend; **è la mia ragazza** she's my girlfriend; **nome da ragazza** maiden name; **da ragazza faceva la commessa** when she was younger she worked as a shop (*Brit*) *o* sales (*USA*) assistant; **ragazza madre** unmarried mother; **ragazza alla pari** au pair; **ragazza squillo** prostitute (*fam!*)

ragazzo [ra'gattso] SM 1 (*gen*) boy; (*giovanotto*) young man; (*fidanzato*) boyfriend; (*garzone*) boy; **fin da quando era ragazzo** since he was a boy; **da ragazzo faceva il commesso** when he was younger he worked as a shop (*Brit*) *o* sales (*USA*) assistant; **ragazzo padre** unmarried father; **ragazzo di strada** street urchin; **ragazzo di vita** rent boy (*Brit*), hustler (*USA*) 2 **ragazzi** SMPL (*bambini, figli*) children; (*amici*) folks (*fam*), guys (*USA*); **è in vacanza con sua moglie e i ragazzi** he's on vacation with his wife and children; **andiamo ragazzi!** let's go guys (*o* people)!; **film/libro per ragazzi** children's film (*Brit*) *o* movie (*USA*) /book

raggelare [raddʒe'lare] /72/ VI (*aus essere*), **raggelarsi** VIP to freeze; **si sentì raggelare all'idea** his blood froze *o* ran cold at the idea ♦ VT to freeze; **raggelare una conversazione** to stop a conversation dead

raggiante [rad'dʒante] AGG (*sorriso, espressione*) beaming, radiant; **raggiante di gioia** beaming *o* radiant with joy

raggiera [rad'dʒɛra] SF (*di ruota*) spokes *pl*; **a raggiera** with a sunburst pattern

raggio, -gi ['raddʒo] SM 1 (*gen, anche Fis, fig*) ray, beam; **un raggio di sole** (*anche fig*) a ray of sunshine; **raggio di luna** moonbeam; **raggio di speranza** (*fig*) ray *o* gleam of hope; **raggio laser** laser beam; **raggi X** X-rays 2 (*di ruota*) spoke 3 (*Mat, anche fig*) radius; **nel raggio di 20 km** within a radius of 20 km *o* a 20-km radius; **a largo raggio** (*esplorazione, incursione*) wide-ranging, extensive in scope; **raggio d'azione** (*di proiettile*) range; (*fig*) range, scope

❏ **raggio** non si traduce mai con la parola inglese *rage*

raggirare [raddʒi'rare] /72/ VT to deceive, take in, trick; **si è lasciato raggirare dai suoi discorsi** he was taken in by his arguments

raggiro [rad'dʒiro] SM trick, swindle; **non farti invischiare nei suoi raggiri** don't let yourself get mixed up in his schemes

raggiungere [rad'dʒundʒere] /5/ VT IRREG 1 (*persona*): **raggiungere qn** to catch sb up, catch up with sb (*telefonicamente*) to get in touch with sb, reach sb; **li abbiamo raggiunti per strada/alla stazione** we caught up with them on the way/ at the station; **vi raggiungo più tardi** I'll catch up with you later, I'll join you later 2 (*luogo, oggetto posto in alto*) to reach; (*obiettivo*) to reach, achieve; **la temperatura ha raggiunto i trenta gradi** the temperature has reached thirty degrees; **la**

criminalità sta raggiungendo livelli preoccupanti crime is reaching worrying levels; **raggiungere il proprio scopo** to reach one's goal, achieve one's aim; **raggiungere un accordo** to come to *o* reach an agreement

raggiunto, -a [rad'dʒunto] PP *di* **raggiungere**

raggomitolare [raggomito'lare] /72/ VT (*avvolgere*) to wind up; **raggomitolarsi** VR (*fig: rannicchiarsi*) to curl up

raggranellare [raggranel'lare] /72/ VT (*soldi*) to scrape together

raggrinzire [raggrin'tsire] /55/, **raggrinzare** [raggrin'tsare] VT to crease VI (*aus essere*), **raggrinzarsi** VIP (*stoffa*) to wrinkle (up); (*viso, pelle*) to become wrinkled

raggrumare [raggru'mare] /72/ VT, **raggrumarsi** VIP (*sangue, latte*) to clot

raggruppamento [raggruppa'mento] SM 1 (*azione*) grouping 2 (*gruppo*) group; (*Mil*) unit

raggruppare [raggrup'pare] /72/ VT (*in un unico gruppo*) to group (together); (*in molti gruppi*) to organize into groups; **raggrupparsi** VR (*in un unico gruppo*) to group (together); (*in molti gruppi*) to form into groups; **raggrupparsi intorno a qn** to gather around sb

ragguagliare [raggwaʎ'ʎare] /27/ VT 1 (*informare*): **ragguagliare (su)** to inform (about) 2 (*confrontare*): **ragguagliare qc a qc** to compare sth with sth

ragguaglio, -gli [rag'gwaʎʎo] SM 1 (*informazione*) piece of information; **fornire ragguagli su qc** to provide information about sth 2 (*paragone*) comparison

ragguardevole [raggwar'devole] AGG (*persona*) notable, distinguished; (*somma*) considerable, sizeable; (*successo*) remarkable

ragia ['radʒa] SF: **acqua ragia = acquaragia**

ragionamento [radʒona'mento] SM (*facoltà*) reasoning *no pl*; (*argomentazione*) argument, reasoning; **un ragionamento sbagliato** faulty reasoning; **ci sono arrivato con il ragionamento** I got there through reasoning, I reasoned it out; **è un ragionamento logico** it's a logical argument; **il tuo ragionamento fila** your argument makes sense

ragionare [radʒo'nare] /72/ VI (*aus avere*) 1 (*pensare*) to reason, think; **ragionaci su!** think about it!, think it over!; **cerca di ragionare** try and be reasonable; **non c'è modo di farla ragionare** you can't make her think clearly (*o* use her head); **quando ho fame non ragiono più** I can't think straight when I'm hungry 2 (*discutere*): **ragionare di** to discuss, talk over

ragione [ra'dʒone] SF 1 (*facoltà*) reason; **perdere il lume della ragione** to lose one's reason, take leave of one's senses 2 (*motivo*) reason, cause, motive; (*argomentazione*) argument; (*diritto*) right; **avrà le sue buone ragioni per dire di no** he must have his reasons for refusing; **non è una buona ragione!** that's no excuse *o* reason!; **ragione di più per fare così** all the more reason for doing so; **... ragion per cui sarebbe meglio partire** ...that's why it would be better to leave; **a maggior ragione dovresti fare qualcosa** all the more reason why you should do something; **a** *o* **con ragione** with good reason, rightly, justly; **senza ragione** for no reason; **a torto o a ragione** rightly or wrongly; **per ragioni di famiglia** for family reasons; **a ragion veduta** after due consideration; (*intenzionalmente*) deliberately; **far valere le proprie ragioni** to assert one's rights 3 (*Mat*) proportion, ratio; **in ragione di 2 euro per articolo** at the rate of 2 euros per item 4 (*fraseologia*): **aver ragione (a fare)** to be right (in doing *o* to do); **sì, hai perfettamente ragione** yes, you're quite right; **aver ragione di qn/qc** to get the better of sb/ sth; **avere ragione da vendere** to be absolutely right, be dead right (*fam*); **dare ragione a qn** (*sogg: persona*) to side with sb; (*: fatto*) to prove sb right; **farsi una ragione di qc** to accept sth, come to terms with sth; **non sentire ragioni** to refuse to listen to reason; **picchiare qn di santa ragione** to give sb a good hiding ♦ **ragione di scambio** (*Econ*) terms *pl* of trade; **ragione sociale** (*Comm*) corporate name; **ragion d'essere** raison d'être; **ragion di stato** reason of State

ragioneria [radʒone'ria] SF (*scienza*) accountancy; (*ufficio*) accounts department; (*scuola*) commercial school, institute of commerce

ragionevole [radʒo'nevole] AGG 1 (*sensato: persona*) reasonable, sensible; (*: consiglio*) sensible, sound; **sii ragionevole!**

be sensible! 2 (*giusto: prezzo*) reasonable, fair; **il prezzo mi sembra ragionevole** the price seems reasonable 3 (*fondato: timore, sospetto*) well-founded

ragioniere, -a [radʒoˈnjere] SM, SF accountant; **fa il ragioniere** he is an accountant

ragliare [raʎˈʎare] /27/ VI (*aus* avere) to bray

ragnatela [raɲɲaˈtela] SF (spider's) web, cobweb; **la casa era piena di ragnatele** the house was full of cobwebs; **una ragnatela d'intrighi** (*fig*) a web of intrigue

ragno [ˈraɲɲo] SM spider; **non cavare un ragno dal buco** (*fig*) to draw a blank, get nowhere

ragù [raˈgu] SM INV (*Culin*) meat sauce; **spaghetti al ragù** spaghetti with meat sauce

RAI-TV [ˈraitiˈvu] SIGLA F (= *Radio televisione italiana*) Public Italian Broadcasting Company

rallegramenti [rallegraˈmenti] SMPL congratulations

rallegrare [realleˈgrare] /72/ VT (*persona*) to cheer up; (*stanza, atmosfera*) to brighten up; **la notizia ha rallegrato tutti** the news cheered everyone up; **quel bel tappeto giallo rallegra la stanza** that lovely yellow carpet brightens up the room; **rallegrarsi** VIP 1 (*diventare allegro*) to cheer up; (*provare allegrezza*) to rejoice; **si rallegrò solo a vederlo** he was glad just to see him 2 (*congratularsi*): **rallegrarsi con qn per qc** to congratulate sb on sth

rallentamento [rallentaˈmento] SM (*di produzione*) slowing down, slackening; (*del traffico*) slowing down; **subire un rallentamento** to slow down, slacken

rallentare [rallenˈtare] /72/ VT (*gen*) to slow down; **rallentare il ritmo** to slow down; **rallentare il passo** to slacken one's pace ♦ VI (*aus* essere) to slow down

❏ **rallentare** non si traduce mai con la parola inglese *relent*

rallentatore [rallentaˈtore] SM (*Cine*) slow-motion camera; **al rallentatore** (*anche fig*) in slow motion

ramanzina [ramanˈdzina] SF lecture, telling-off; **fare una bella ramanzina a qn** to give sb a lecture, give sb a good talking-to

ramare [raˈmare] /72/ VT 1 (*superficie*) to copper, coat with copper 2 (*Agr: vite*) to spray with copper sulphate

ramarro [raˈmarro] SM green lizard

ramato, -a [raˈmato] AGG (*oggetto: rivestito di rame*) copper-coated, coppered; (*capelli, barba*) coppery, copper-coloured (*Brit*), copper-colored (*USA*)

rame [ˈrame] SM copper; **di rame** copper *attr*; **incisione su rame** copperplate

ramificare [ramifiˈkare] /20/ VI (*aus* avere) (*Bot*) to put out branches; **ramificarsi** VIP (*diramarsi, anche fig*) to branch out; (*Med: tumore, vene*) to ramify; **ramificarsi in** (*biforcarsi*) to branch into

ramificazione [ramifikatˈtsjone] SF ramification

ramingo, -a, -ghi, -ghe [raˈmingo] AGG (*letter*): **andare ramingo** to go wandering, wander

ramino [raˈmino] SM (*Carte*) rummy

rammaricare [rammariˈkare] /20/ VT to grieve; **rammaricarsi** VIP: **rammaricarsi di** *o* **per qc** (*dispiacersi*) to regret sth, be sorry about sth; (*lamentarsi*) to complain about sth; **è inutile rammaricarsi** there is no point in feeling sorry

rammarico, -chi [ramˈmariko] SM regret

rammendare [rammenˈdare] /72/ VT to mend, darn

rammendo [ramˈmendo] SM (*azione*) darning *no pl*, mending *no pl*; (*risultato*) darn, mend; **fare un rammendo** to darn, mend

rammentare [rammenˈtare] /72/ VT to remember, recall; **rammentare qc a qn** to remind sb of sth; **rammentarsi** VIP: **rammentarsi (di qc)** to remember (sth)

rammollire [rammolˈlire] /55/ VT to soften VI (*aus* essere), **rammollirsi** VIP to soften, grow *o* go soft

rammollito, -a [rammolˈlito] AGG weak ♦ SM, SF weakling

ramo [ˈramo] SM (*gen, anche fig*) branch; (*branca: di una scienza*) branch; (*: di commercio*) field; **non è il mio ramo** it's not my field *o* line; **i due rami del parlamento** the two chambers of parliament

❏ **ramo** non si traduce mai con la parola inglese *ram*

ramoscello [ramoʃˈʃello] SM twig

rampa [ˈrampa] SF 1 (*anche:* **rampa di scale**) flight (of stairs) 2 (*breve salita*) slope; **rampa d'accesso** (*in autostrada*) slip road (*Brit*), entrance (*o* exit) ramp (*USA*); (*in marciapiede*) ramp; **rampa di lancio** (*Aer*) launching pad

rampicante [rampiˈkante](*Bot*) AGG climbing ♦ SM creeper, climber

rampino [ramˈpino] SM (*gancio*) hook; (*Naut*) grapnel

rampollo [ramˈpollo] SM (*discendente*) descendant; (*scherz: figlio*): **è tutto orgoglioso del suo rampollo** he's very proud of his son and heir

rampone [ramˈpone] SM (*fiocina*) harpoon; (*Alpinismo*) crampon

rana [ˈrana] SF frog; **nuoto a rana** breaststroke; **nuotare a rana** to do the breaststroke; **uomo rana** frogman; **rana pescatrice** angler fish

rancido, -a [ˈrantʃido] AGG rancid ♦ SM: **odore di rancido** rank odour; **ha odore di rancido** it smells rancid; **sa di rancido** it tastes rancid

rancio, -ci [ˈrantʃo] SM (*Mil*) mess; **ora del rancio** mess time

rancore [ranˈkore] SM resentment, rancour (*Brit*), rancor (*USA*); **senza rancore?** no hard feelings?; **dimentichiamo i vecchi rancori** let bygones be bygones; **serbare rancore a qn**, **nutrire rancore contro** *o* **verso qn** to bear sb a grudge

randagio, -a, -gi, -gie *o* **, -ge** [ranˈdadʒo] AGG (*gatto, cane*) stray *attr*

randello [ranˈdello] SM cudgel, club

rango, -ghi [ˈrango] SM 1 (*grado*) rank; (*condizione sociale*) station, social standing; **avere il rango di** to hold the rank of; **gli alti ranghi** the upper ranks; **persone di rango inferiore** people of lower standing 2 (*Mil: schiera*) rank; (*: fila*) line; **rientrare nei ranghi** to fall in; (*fig*) to fall into line; **uscire dai ranghi** to fall out; (*fig*) to step out of line

Rangoon [ranˈgun] SF Rangoon

rannicchiarsi [rannikˈkjarsi] /19/ VR to crouch, huddle

rannuvolare [rannuvoˈlare] /72/ VT to darken; **rannuvolarsi** VIP (*cielo*) to cloud over, become overcast; (*fig: viso*) to darken

ranocchio, -chi [raˈnɔkkjo] SM (*edible*) frog

rantolare [rantoˈlare] /72/ VI (*aus* avere) (*respirare affannosamente*) to wheeze; **si sentiva il moribondo rantolare** you could hear the man's death rattle

rantolio, -lii [rantoˈlio] SM (*il respirare affannoso*) wheezing; (*di agonizzante*) death rattle

rantolo [ˈrantolo] SM (*respiro affannoso*) wheeze; (*di agonizzante*) death rattle

ranuncolo [raˈnunkolo] SM (*Bot*) buttercup

rapa [ˈrapa] SF turnip; **cime di rapa** turnip tops; **testa di rapa** (*fig*) fathead, idiot; **è come voler cavar sangue da una rapa** it's like trying to get blood out of a stone

❏ **rapa** non si traduce mai con la parola inglese *rape*

rapace [raˈpatʃe] AGG (*animale*) predatory; (*fig: avido*) rapacious, grasping ♦ SM bird of prey

rapare [raˈpare] /72/ VT (*capelli*) to crop, cut very short; **ti hanno rapato (i capelli) a zero** they have scalped you; **raparsi (i capelli) a zero** to get scalped; **raparsi** VR to have one's head shaved (*o* cropped)

rapidamente [rapidaˈmente] AVV quickly, rapidly, fast; **l'incendio si è esteso rapidamente** the fire spread quickly

rapidità [rapidiˈta] SF speed, rapidity; **ha colpito con rapidità** he was quick to strike

rapido, -a [ˈrapido] AGG (*gen*) fast; (*esame, occhiata*) quick, rapid; **gli ho dato solo una rapida occhiata** I just had a quick look at it; **è rapido nell'agire** he is quick to act ♦ SM (*Ferr*) express (train) (*on which supplement must be paid*)

rapimento [rapiˈmento] SM 1 (*di persona*) kidnapping, abduction; **il rapimento è avvenuto in pieno giorno** the kidnapping happened in broad daylight 2 (*Rel*) ecstasy; (*fig*) rapture; **fu preso da rapimento** he went into ecstasies *o* raptures; **con rapimento** rapturously, ecstatically

rapina [raˈpina] SF robbery; **rapina in banca** bank robbery; **rapina a mano armata** armed robbery

rapinare [rapiˈnare] /72/ VT to rob; **quella banca è stata rapinata tre volte in un mese** that bank has been robbed three times in a month

rapinatore, -trice [rapina'tore] SM, SF robber; **i rapinatori sono fuggiti a piedi** the robbers ran away
rapire [ra'pire] /55/ VT 1 (*persona*) to kidnap, abduct; **l'hanno rapito due mesi fa** he was kidnapped two months ago 2 (*fig: mandare in estasi*) to enrapture, delight
❑ **rapire** non si traduce mai con la parola inglese *rape*
rapito, -a [ra'pito] AGG 1 (*persona*) kidnapped 2 (*fig: in estasi*): **ascoltare rapito qn** to be captivated by sb's words; **guardava rapito il quadro** he gazed at the painting, entranced ♦ SM, SF kidnapped person
rapitore, -trice [rapi'tore] SM, SF kidnapper; **i rapitori hanno minacciato di uccidere l'ostaggio** the kidnappers threatened to kill the hostage
rappacificare [rappat͡ʃifi'kare] /20/ VT (*riconciliare*) to reconcile; **rappacificarsi** VR (*uso reciproco*) to become reconciled, make (it) up
rappacificazione [rappat͡ʃifikat'tsjone] SF reconciliation
rappezzare [rappet'tsare] /72/ VT to patch; **rappezzare un discorso** (*fig*) to cobble together a speech
rapportare [rappor'tare] /72/ VT 1 **rapportare qc a qc** (*confrontare*) to compare sth with sth 2 (*riprodurre disegno*): **rapportare su scala più grande** to reproduce on a larger scale; **rapportarsi** VIP: **rapportarsi a** to be related to
rapporto [rap'porto] SM 1 (*legame*) connection, relationship, link; **non avere alcun rapporto con qc** to have nothing to do with sth, be unrelated to sth; **in rapporto a quanto è successo** with regard to *o* in relation to what happened 2 (*relazione*) relationship; **abbiamo un ottimo rapporto** we have a very good relationship; **i rapporti tra loro sono piuttosto tesi** relations between them are rather strained; **essere in buoni/cattivi rapporti con qn** to be on good/bad terms with sb; **rapporti diplomatici** diplomatic relations; **rapporti prematrimoniali** sex *sg* before marriage, premarital sex; **rapporto d'affari** business relations *pl*; **rapporto coniugale** marital relationship; **rapporto intimo** sexual intercourse; **rapporto di lavoro** employer-employee relationship; **indennità di fine rapporto (di lavoro)** severance pay; **rapporto sessuale** (sexual) intercourse *sg*; **avere rapporti sessuali** to have intercourse 3 (*resoconto*) report; **scrivi un rapporto sulla situazione** write a report on the situation; **fare rapporto a qn su qc** to report sth to sb; **chiamare qn a rapporto** (*Mil*) to summon sb; **andare a rapporto da qn** to report to sb 4 (*Mat, Tecn*) ratio; (*di bicicletta*) gear; **in rapporto di 1 a 10** in a ratio of 1 to 10; **rapporto di compressione** (*Tecn*) pressure ratio; **rapporto di distanza** (*Fis*) distance ratio; **rapporto di trasmissione** (*Tecn*) gear
rapprendersi [rap'prɛndersi] /81/ VIP IRREG (*sangue*) to coagulate, clot; (*latte*) to curdle
rappresaglia [rappre'saʎʎa] SF reprisal, retaliation; **per rappresaglia** in reprisal *o* retaliation
rappresentante [rapprezen'tante] SM, SF (*gen, anche Pol, Comm*) representative; **il rappresentante di classe** the class representative; **rappresentante di commercio** sales representative, sales rep (*fam*); **rappresentante sindacale** union delegate *o* representative
rappresentanza [rapprezen'tantsa] SF 1 (*gen, anche Pol*) representation; (*gruppo*) delegation, deputation; **in rappresentanza di qn** on behalf of sb; **spese di rappresentanza** entertainment expenses; **macchina di rappresentanza** official car 2 (*Comm*) agency; **avere la rappresentanza di** to be the agent for; **rappresentanza esclusiva** sole agency; **avere la rappresentanza esclusiva** to be sole agent
rappresentare [rapprezen'tare] /72/ VT 1 (*sogg: pittore, romanziere, quadro*) to depict, portray; (: *fotografia*) to show; **il quadro rappresenta una scena rurale** the painting depicts a rural scene 2 (*simboleggiare, significare*) to represent; **ciò rappresenta un grave pericolo per la nazione** this represents a serious threat to the nation 3 (*Teatro: recitare*) to perform, play; (: *mettere in scena*) to perform, put on; **hanno intenzione di rappresentare la Carmen** they intend to stage *o* put on Carmen 4 (*agire per conto di*) to represent; **farsi rappresentare dal proprio legale** to be represented by one's lawyer
rappresentativo, -a [rapprezenta'tivo] AGG (*gen*) representative; (*tipico*) typical

rappresentazione [rapprezentat'tsjone] SF 1 (*raffigurazione*) representation; (*di società, paesaggio*) portrayal 2 (*spettacolo*) performance; **prima rappresentazione assoluta** world première; **sacra rappresentazione** religious play
rappreso, -a [rap'preso] PP *di* **rapprendersi** ♦ AGG (*sangue*) coagulated, clotted; (*latte*) curdled
rapsodia [rapso'dia] SF rhapsody
raptus ['raptus] SM INV: **raptus di follia** fit of madness
raramente [rara'mente] AVV seldom, rarely; **ci vediamo raramente** we rarely see each other
rarefare [rare'fare] VB IRREG /41/ VT , **rarefarsi** VIP to rarefy
rarefatto, -a [rare'fatto] AGG rarefied
rarefazione [rarefat'tsjone] SF rarefaction
rarità [rari'ta] SF INV 1 (*scarsezza: di oggetto, malattia*) rarity; (: *di visite*) infrequency 2 (*oggetto*) rarity; (*avvenimento*) rare occurrence, unusual occurrence
raro, -a ['raro] AGG 1 (*poco comune*) rare; **è un caso molto raro** it's a very unusual *o* rare case; **è una bestia rara** (*fig*) he's a rare breed 2 (*poco numeroso*) few, rare; **le rare persone che passavano** the few people that went by; **c'era qualche rara nuvola** there was the odd cloud; **i clienti sono diventati rari** customers have become scarce *o* few and far between
rasare [ra'sare] /72/ VT (*barba, capelli*) to shave off; (*siepi, erba*) to trim, cut; **rasarsi** VR to shave (o.s.)
rasato, -a [ra'sato] AGG (*erba*) trimmed, cut; (*tessuto*) smooth; **avere la barba rasata, essere ben rasato** to be clean-shaven
rasatura [rasa'tura] SF (*atto*) shaving; (*effetto*) shave
raschiamento [raskja'mento] SM (*Med*) curettage; **raschiamento uterino** D and C
raschiare [ras'kjare] /19/ VT to scrape; **raschiare (via) qc** to scrape sth off; **raschiarsi la gola** to clear one's throat
rasentare [razen'tare] /72/ VT (*muro*) to hug, keep close to; (*terra*) to skim along (*o* over); (*fig: sfiorare*) to border on; **questo rasenta la pazzia!** this is bordering on insanity!; **rasentare la cinquantina** to be getting on for fifty (years of age)
rasente [ra'zɛnte] PREP: **rasente (a)** close to, very near; **camminare rasente il** *o* **al muro** to hug the wall
raso, -a ['raso] PP *di* **radere** ♦ AGG 1 (*liscio*): **a pelo raso** (*pelliccia*) short-haired; (*tessuto*) smooth 2 (*con misure di capacità*) level *attr*; (*pieno: bicchiere*) full to the brim; **un cucchiaio raso** a level spoonful ♦ PREP: **raso terra** close to the ground; **volare raso terra** to hedgehop ♦ SM (*tessuto*) satin
rasoio, -oi [ra'sojo] SM razor; **rasoio elettrico** electric shaver *o* razor; **rasoio a lama** cut-throat *o* straight razor; **rasoio radi e getta** disposable *o* throwaway razor
raspare [ras'pare] /72/ VT 1 (*levigare*) to rasp 2 (*grattare: sogg: gallina, cane*) to scratch; (: *cavallo*) to paw ♦ VI (*aus avere*) to scrape, scratch
raspo ['raspo] SM (*di uva*) grape stalk
rassegna [ras'seɲɲa] SF 1 (*Mil*) inspection, review; **passare in rassegna** (*Mil, anche fig*) to review 2 (*resoconto*) review, survey; (*rivista*) review; (*mostra*) exhibition, show; **una rassegna del cinema latino-americano** a season of Latin American films
rassegnare [rasseɲ'ɲare] /15/ VT: **rassegnare le dimissioni** to resign, hand in one's resignation; **rassegnarsi** VIP: **rassegnarsi (a qc)** to resign o.s. (to sth); **bisogna rassegnarsi all'idea** we (*o* you *ecc*) will have to accept *o* get used to the idea; **mai rassegnarsi!** never give up!
rassegnazione [rasseɲɲat'tsjone] SF resignation; **accettare qc con rassegnazione** to resign o.s. to sth
rasserenare [rassere'nare] /72/ VT (*Meteor*) to clear up, brighten up ♦ VT (*persona*) to cheer up; **rasserenarsi** VIP (*Meteor*) to brighten up, clear up; (*persona*) to cheer up
rassettare [rasset'tare] /72/ VT to tidy up, put in order; **rassettarsi** VR to tidy o.s. up
rassicurante [rassiku'rante] AGG reassuring
rassicurare [rassiku'rare] /72/ VT to reassure; **ho cercato di rassicurarla, ma non è servito** I tried to reassure her, but with no success; **rassicurarsi** VIP to take heart, recover one's confidence
rassicurazione [rassikurat'tsjone] SF reassurance
rassodare [rasso'dare] /72/ VT (*muscoli*) to harden, strengthen; (*tessuti*) to firm (up); (*fig: amicizia*) to strengthen,

consolidate; **il nuoto aiuta a rassodare i muscoli** swimming helps to tone the muscles; **rassodarsi** VIP (*muscoli*) to harden, strengthen; (*tessuti*) to firm (up)

rassomiglianza [rassomiʎˈʎantsa] SF resemblance

rassomigliare [rassomiʎˈʎare] /27/ VI (*aus avere o essere*) **rassomigliare a** to resemble, look like; **rassomigli molto a tua madre** you look very like your mother; **rassomigliarsi** VR (*uso reciproco*) to look alike, resemble each other; **vi rassomigliate moltissimo** you look very much alike

rastrellamento [rastrellaˈmento] SM (*di erba, fieno*) raking; (*Mil: di polizia*) (thorough) search; **stanno facendo un rastrellamento nella zona** they are combing the area

rastrellare [rastrelˈlare] /72/ VT (*erba, fieno*) to rake; (*fig: perlustrare*) to comb

rastrelliera [rastrelˈljera] SF (*per fieno*) hayrack; (*per fucili, biciclette*) rack; (*per piatti*) dish rack

rastrello [rasˈtrɛllo] SM rake

rata [ˈrata] SF instalment (*Brit*), installment (*USA*); **pagare a rate** to pay by instal(l)ments *o* on hire purchase (*Brit*); **comprare/vendere a rate** to buy/sell on hire purchase (*Brit*) *o* on the installment plan (*USA*)

rateale [rateˈale] AGG: **pagamento rateale** payment by instal(l)ments; **vendita rateale** hire purchase (*Brit*), installment plan (*USA*)

rateare [rateˈare] /72/ VT to divide into instal(l)ments

rateazione [rateatˈtsjone] SF division into instal(l)ments

rateizzare [rateidˈdzare] /72/ VT = **rateare**

rateo [ˈrateo] SM (*Econ*) accrual

ratifica, -che [raˈtifika] SF ratification

ratificare [ratifiˈkare] /20/ VT (*gen*) to approve, ratify; (*Amm, Dir*) to ratify

ratto¹ [ˈratto] SM (*Storia, Dir*) abduction

ratto² [ˈratto] SM (*Zool*) rat; **ratto comune** black rat

rattoppare [rattopˈpare] /72/ VT to patch

rattoppo [ratˈtoppo] SM (*risultato*) patch; (*azione*) patching *no pl*; **fare un rattoppo a** *o* **su qc** to patch sth

rattrappire [rattrapˈpire] /55/ VT (*piedi, mani*) to make stiff; **rattrappirsi** VIP to become stiff

rattristare [rattrisˈtare] /72/ VT (*addolorare*) to sadden; **rattristarsi** VIP to grow *o* become sad

raucedine [rauˈtʃedine] SF hoarseness; **ho un po' di raucedine** I am a little hoarse

rauco, -a, -chi, -che [ˈrauko] AGG hoarse

ravanello [ravaˈnɛllo] SM radish

ravennate [ravenˈnate] AGG *di o* from Ravenna ♦ SM, SF inhabitant *o* native of Ravenna

ravioli [raviˈɔli] SMPL (*Culin*) ravioli *sg*

ravvedersi [ravveˈdersi] /82/ VIP IRREG to mend one's ways

ravviare [ravviˈare] /60/ VT (*capelli*) to tidy; **ravviarsi i capelli** to tidy one's hair

ravvicinamento [ravvitʃinaˈmento] SM (*tra persone*) reconciliation; (*Pol: tra paesi*) rapprochement

ravvicinare [ravvitʃiˈnare] /72/ VT (*oggetti*) to bring closer together; (*fig: persone*) to reconcile, bring together again; **ravvicinarsi** VR to be reconciled; **si è ravvicinato alla famiglia** he is now reconciled with his family

ravvisare [ravviˈzare] /72/ VT to recognize

ravvivare [ravviˈvare] /72/ VT (*fuoco, sentimento*) to revive, rekindle; (*fig: rallegrare*) to brighten up; **ravvivarsi** VIP (*fuoco, sentimento*) to be rekindled *o* revived; (*persona, ambiente*) to brighten up

Rawalpindi [rawalˈpindi] SF Rawalpindi

raziocinio [rattsjoˈtʃinjo] SM (*facoltà di ragionare*) reasoning *no pl*; (*buon senso*) common sense; **essere dotato di raziocinio** to be able to reason, possess the faculty of reason

razionale [rattsjoˈnale] AGG (*gen, anche Mat*) rational; **ci dev'essere una spiegazione razionale** there must be a rational explanation; **un razionale sfruttamento dello spazio** an intelligent use of space ♦ SM: **il razionale** the rational

razionalità [rattsjonaliˈta] SF rationality; (*buon senso*) common sense; (*funzionalità*) functionality, practicalness; **con razionalità** rationally, intelligently

razionalizzare [rattsjonalidˈdzare] /72/ VT (*metodo, lavoro,*

programma) to rationalize; (*problema, situazione*) to approach rationally

razionamento [rattsjonaˈmento] SM rationing; **il razionamento dell'acqua** water rationing

razionare [rattsjoˈnare] /72/ VT to ration; **stanno razionando l'acqua** water is being rationed

razione [ratˈtsjone] SF (*gen*) ration; (*di soldato*) rations *pl*; (*fig: porzione*) share

razza [ˈrattsa] SF 1 (*etnica*) race; (*Zool*) breed; **di razza** (*gen*) pedigree, purebred; (*cavallo*) thoroughbred; **di che razza è il tuo cane?** what breed is your dog?; **razza da latte** (*bovini*) dairy breed; **razza da macello** *o* **da carne** (*bovini*) beef breed; **essere di buona razza** to come of good stock 2 (*specie, tipo*) sort, kind; **che razza di discorso è?** what sort of argument is that?; **che razza di mascalzone!** what a scoundrel!

razzia [ratˈtsia] SF raid, foray; **fare razzia in un pollaio** to raid a henhouse; **ha fatto razzia nel frigorifero** he raided the refrigerator

razziale [ratˈtsjale] AGG racial; **pregiudizi razziali** racial prejudice *sg*

razzismo [ratˈtsizmo] SM racism, racialism; (*intolleranza*) prejudice

razzista, -i, -e [ratˈtsista] AGG, SM, SF racist, racialist

razzo [ˈraddzo] SM rocket; **lanciare un razzo** to send up *o* fire a rocket; **veloce come un razzo** as quick as lightning; **partire come un razzo** to be off like a shot; **razzo di segnalazione** flare; **razzo vettore** vector rocket

razzolare [rattsoˈlare] /72/ VI (*aus avere*) (*galline*) to scratch about

RC [ˈɛrreˈtʃi] SIGLA F 1 (= *Responsabilità Civile*): **RC-auto** (*assicurazione*) car insurance (*minimum liability*) 2 (= *Rifondazione Comunista*) Communist Refoundation (*Italian left-wing political party*) ♦ SIGLA = **Reggio Calabria**

RDT [ˈɛrreˈdiˈti] SIGLA F 1 (= *Rappresentanze Sindacali di Base*) trades union organization 2 (= *Repubblica Democratica Tedesca*) GDR

RE SIGLA = **Reggio Emilia**

re¹ [re] SM INV (*gen*) king; (*fig: magnate*) tycoon, magnate; **re Artù** king Arthur; **i Re Magi** the Three Wise Men, the Magi; **Cristo re** Christ the King; **fare una vita da re** (*fig*) to live like a king

re² [re] SM INV (*Mus*) D; (*solfeggiando la scala*) re

reagente [reaˈdʒente] AGG reacting ♦ SM reagent

reagire [reaˈdʒire] /55/ VI (*aus avere*) (*gen, anche Chim*) to react; **reagire** (**a/contro**) to react (to/against); **come ha reagito alla notizia?** how did she react to the news?; **il paziente reagisce bene alle cure** the patient is responding well to treatment

reale¹ [reˈale] AGG (*gen, anche Mat*) real; (*piacere, miglioramento*) real, genuine; (*Fin: valore, salario*) real, actual; **è basato su un fatto reale** it's based on a true story; **nella vita reale** in real life ♦ SM: **il reale** reality

reale² [reˈale] AGG (*di, da re*) royal; **la famiglia reale** the royal family ♦ SMPL: **i Reali** the Royal family *sg o pl*

realismo [reaˈlizmo] SM realism; **con realismo** realistically

realista¹, -i, -e [reaˈlista] AGG (*gen*) realistic; (*Arte, Letteratura*) realist ♦ SM, SF realist

realista², -i, -e [reaˈlista] AGG, SM, SF (*Pol*) royalist

realistico, -a, -ci, -che [reaˈlistiko] AGG realistic

reality [riˈaliti] SM INV reality show

realizzare [realidˈdzare] /72/ VT 1 (*opera, progetto*) to carry out, realize; (*scopo*) to achieve; (*sogno, desiderio*) to achieve, fulfil (*Brit*), fulfill (*USA*), realize; **ho realizzato il mio sogno di viaggiare** I've achieved my ambition to travel 2 (*fig: capire*) to realize; **quando Luca ha realizzato quello che era successo...** when Luca realized what had happened ... 3 (*Fin: capitale*) to realize; **abbiamo realizzato 2000 euro dalla vendita della macchina** we made 2000 euros from the sale of the car 4 (*Sport: goal*) to score; **realizzarsi** VIP (*sogno, speranza*) to come true, be realized; **realizzarsi** (*persona*) to fulfil (*Brit*) *o* fulfill (*USA*) o.s.; **non mi sento realizzata nel mio lavoro** I don't feel fulfilled in my job

realizzazione [realiddzatˈtsjone] SF 1 (*di libro, opera*) realization; (*di sogno*) fulfil(l)ment; (*di persona*) self-fulfil(l)ment

2 (*opera, creazione*) achievement; (*Cine, Teatro*) production; **realizzazione scenica** stage production 3 (*Fin*) realization

realizzo [rea'liddzo] SM 1 (*conversione in denaro*) conversion into cash 2 (*vendita forzata*) clearance sale

realmente [real'mente] AVV (*in realtà*) really; (*effettivamente*) actually; **è un fatto realmente accaduto? did it really happen?**

realtà [real'ta] SF INV reality; **la realtà era molto diversa** the reality was very different; **la dura realtà** harsh reality; **diventare realtà** to come true; **il suo sogno è diventato realtà** his dream has become (a) reality *o* has come true; **in realtà** (*in effetti*) in fact; (*a dire il vero*) really; **sembra un ragazzino, in realtà ha quasi quarant'anni** he looks very young, but in fact he's nearly forty; **realtà virtuale** virtual reality

reame [re'ame] SM kingdom, realm; (*fig*) realm

reato [re'ato] SM (*Dir*) crime, offence (*Brit*), offense (*USA*)

reattore [reat'tore] SM (*Aer: aereo*) jet; (: *motore*) jet engine; **reattore nucleare** nuclear reactor

reazionario, -ria, -ri, -rie [reattsjo'narjo] AGG, SM, SF reactionary

reazione [reat'tsjone] SF 1 (*gen*) reaction; **la sua prima reazione è stata scappare** her immediate reaction was to run away; **motore/aereo a reazione** jet engine/plane; **reazione a catena** (*anche fig*) chain reaction; **reazione fisica** physical change; **reazione chimica** chemical reaction 2 (*Pol*) reaction, repression; **forze della reazione** reactionary forces

rebbio, -bi [ˈrebbjo] SM prong

rebus [ˈrebus] SM INV (*gioco enigmistico*) rebus; (*fig: persona*) enigma; (: *situazione, comportamento*) puzzle

recapitare [rekapi'tare] /72/ VT to deliver

recapito [re'kapito] SM 1 (*indirizzo*) address; **puoi lasciarmi il tuo recapito?** can you give me your address?; **recapito telefonico** telephone number; **ha un recapito telefonico?** do you have a telephone number where you can be reached? 2 (*consegna*) delivery; **recapito a domicilio** home delivery (service)

recare [re'kare] /20/ VT 1 (*portare*) to bear, carry; (*contenere*) to bear; **le recò in dono un anello** he brought her a ring as a gift; **il telegramma reca la data di ieri** the telegram bears yesterday's date 2 (*causare, arrecare: gioia, piacere*) to give, bring; (: *danno*) to cause, bring; **non voglio recarvi disturbo** I don't want to cause any inconvenience to you, I don't want to disturb you; **recare danno a qn** to harm sb, cause harm to sb; **recarsi** VIP to go; **recarsi in città/a scuola** to go into town/to school

recedere [re'tʃedere] /29/ VI (*aus avere*) (*ritirarsi, anche Dir*): **recedere (da)** to withdraw (from)

recensione [retʃen'sjone] SF review; **il film ha avuto delle ottime recensioni** the film has had excellent reviews; **fare la recensione di qc, scrivere una recensione su qc** to review sth

recensire [retʃen'sire] /55/ VT to review

recensore [retʃen'sore] SM reviewer

recente [re'tʃɛnte] AGG recent; **una scoperta recente** a recent discovery; **più recente** latest, most recent; **di recente** recently; **questo ristorante è stato aperto di recente** this restaurant opened recently

recentemente [retʃente'mente] AVV recently; **ha cominciato a lavorare lì solo recentemente** she started working there only recently

recepire [retʃe'pire] /55/ VT take in

recessione [retʃes'sjone] SF recession

recesso [re'tʃɛsso] SM 1 (*Dir*) withdrawal 2 (*luogo*) recess; **i recessi della mente** (*fig*) the recesses of the mind

recherò ecc [reke'rɔ] VB *vedi* **recare**

recidere [re'tʃidere] /34/ VT IRREG to cut off, chop off

recidivo, -a [retʃi'divo] AGG, SM, SF (*Dir*) recidivist, second (*o* habitual) offender

recintare [retʃin'tare] /72/ VT to enclose, fence off, put a fence round; **hanno recintato il giardino** they've put a fence round the garden

recinto [re'tʃinto] SM 1 (*gen*) enclosure; (*per animali*) pen; (*per cavalli*) paddock 2 (*staccionata*) fence; (*in muratura*) surrounding wall 3 **recinto delle grida** (*Borsa*) floor

recinzione [retʃin'tsjone] SF 1 (*azione*) enclosure, fencing-

off 2 (*recinto: di legno*) fence; (: *di mattoni*) wall; (: *reticolato*) wire fencing; (: *a sbarre*) railings *pl*

recipiente [retʃi'pjɛnte] SM container; **i recipienti di plastica sono più pratici** plastic containers are more practical
❑ **recipiente** non si traduce mai con la parola inglese *recipient*

reciproco, -a, -ci, -che [re'tʃiproko] AGG (*gen*) reciprocal; (*sentimento, interesse*) mutual; **è chiaro che la adora, e l'affetto è reciproco** he obviously adores her, and the affection is mutual ♦ SM (*Mat*) reciprocal

reciso, -a [re'tʃizo] PP *di* **recidere** ♦ AGG (*risposta*) sharp, curt

recita [ˈretʃita] SF (*Teatro*) performance; (*di poesie*) recital

recital [retʃi'tal] SM INV recital

recitare [retʃi'tare] /72/ VI (*Teatro, anche fig*) to act; **non sa recitare** he can't act; **mi piace recitare** I like acting; **recita molto bene** he's a very good actor ♦ VT (*dramma*) to perform; (*poesia, lezione*) to recite; (*ruolo*) to play *o* act (the part of); **recitare una parte** to play a part; **ha recitato la parte di Giulietta** she played the part of Juliet

recitazione [retʃitat'tsjone] SF (*di poesia*) recitation; (*modo di recitare: di attore*) acting; **scuola di recitazione** drama school

reclamare [rekla'mare] /72/ VI (*aus avere*) **reclamare (contro/presso qn)** to complain (about/to sb) ♦ VT (*diritto*) to demand; **reclamare giustizia** to demand justice

réclame [re'klam] SF INV (*pubblicità*) advertising *no pl*; (*annuncio*) advertisement; **fare la réclame di qc, fare réclame a qc** to advertise sth

reclamizzare [reklamid'dzare] /72/ VT to advertise

reclamo [re'klamo] SM complaint; **sporgere reclamo presso** to complain to, make a complaint to; **ufficio reclami** complaints department

reclinabile [rekli'nabile] AGG (*sedile*) reclining

reclinare [rekli'nare] /72/ VT (*capo*) to bow, lower; (*sedile*) to tilt

reclusione [reklu'zjone] SF (*Dir*) imprisonment; **10 anni di reclusione** 10 years' imprisonment; **l'hanno condannato a un anno di reclusione** he was sentenced to a year in prison

recluso, -a [re'kluzo] AGG (*in prigione*) imprisoned ♦ SM, SF (*prigioniero*) prisoner; **fare vita di recluso** (*fig*) to lead the life of a recluse

recluta [ˈrekluta] SF (*Mil, anche fig*) recruit

reclutamento [rekluta'mento] SM recruitment; **ufficio (di) reclutamento** recruiting office

reclutare [reklu'tare] /72/ VT (*Mil, anche fig*) to recruit

recondito, -a [re'kondito] AGG (*letter: luogo*) hidden, secluded; (*fig: significato*) secret, hidden

record [ˈrekord] SM INV (*Sport, Inform*) record; **a tempo di record** in record time; **detenere il record di** to hold the record for; **record mondiale** world record; **ha battuto il record mondiale del salto in alto** he beat the world record for the high jump ♦ AGG INV record *attr*; **in tempo record** in record time

recriminare [rekrimi'nare] /72/ VI (*aus avere*) **recriminare (su qc)** to complain (about sth)

recriminazione [rekriminat'tsjone] SF recrimination

recrudescenza [rekrudeʃ'ʃentsa] SF (*di malattia*) fresh outbreak; (*fig: di violenza, scontri*) fresh wave

recuperare [rekupe'rare] /72/ VT = **ricuperare**

redarguire [redar'gwire] /55/ VT to rebuke, reproach

redassi ecc [re'dassi] VB *vedi* **redigere**

redatto, -a [re'datto] PP *di* **redigere**

redattore, -trice [redat'tore] SM, SF (*Stampa: chi cura*) editor; (: *chi scrive: articolo*) writer; (: *dizionario, enciclopedia*) compiler; **redattore capo** chief editor

redazione [redat'tsjone] SF 1 (*Stampa: messa a punto*) editing; (: *stesura: di articolo*) writing; (: *di dizionario, enciclopedia*) compilation 2 (*personale*) editorial staff; (*ufficio*) editorial office(s) 3 (*versione*) version

redditizio, -zia, -zi, -zie [reddi'tittsjo] AGG profitable; **un'attività redditizia** a profitable business

reddito [ˈreddito] SM (*privato*) income; (*statale*) revenue; (*di capitale*) yield; **reddito complessivo** gross income; **reddito fisso** fixed income; **reddito imponibile** taxable income; **reddito da lavoro** earned income; **reddito nazionale** national income; **reddito non imponibile** non-taxable income; **reddito pubblico** public revenue

redensi ecc [re'dɛnsi] VB vedi **redimere**

redento, -a [re'dento] PP di **redimere** ♦ SMPL: **i redenti** the redeemed

redentore, -trice [reden'tore] AGG redeeming ♦ SM: **il Redentore** the Redeemer

redenzione [reden'tsjone] SF redemption

redigere [re'didʒere] /47/ VT IRREG (lettera, articolo) to write; (contratto, verbale) to draft, draw up; (dizionario) to compile

redimere [re'dimere] VB IRREG /86/ VT to redeem; **redimersi** VR to redeem o.s.

redini ['rɛdini] SFPL (anche fig) reins; **tenere le redini** to hold the reins; **tiene le redini dell'azienda** he holds the reins of the company

redivivo, -a [redi'vivo] AGG restored to life; **sembri tua madre rediviva** you're the living image of your mother

reduce ['rɛdutʃe] AGG (gen, anche Mil): reduce da returning from, back from; **essere reduce da** (esame, colloquio) to have been through; (malattia) to be just over ♦ SM, SF (sopravvissuto) survivor; (veterano) veteran

refe ['refe] SM (filo) thread; (più grosso) yarn

referendum [refe'rɛndum] SM INV referendum; **fare un referendum** to hold a referendum

referenza [refe'rɛntsa] SF reference; **avere buone referenze** (impiegato ecc) to have good references

referto [re'fɛrto] SM: **referto medico** medical report

refettorio, -ri [refet'tɔrjo] SM (in convento) refectory; (Scol) dining hall

refezione [refet'tsjone] SF (Scol) school meal

refrattario, -ria, -ri, -rie [refrat'tarjo] AGG (materiale, o Med) refractory; (fig: scherz: persona): **refrattario (a)** indifferent (to); **essere refrattario alla matematica** to have no aptitude for mathematics

refrigerante [refridʒe'rante] AGG (Tecn) cooling, refrigerating ♦ SM (Chim: fluido) coolant; (Tecn: apparecchio) refrigerator

refrigerare [refridʒe'rare] /72/ VT to refrigerate

refrigerazione [refridʒerat'tsjone] SF refrigeration; (Tecn) cooling

refrigerio, -ri [refri'dʒɛrjo] SM: **trovare refrigerio** to find somewhere cool

refurtiva [refur'tiva] SF stolen goods pl

Reg. ABBR 1 (= reggimento) Regt 2 (Amm) = **regolamento**

regalare [rega'lare] /72/ VT: **regalare qc** to give sth (as a present), make a present of sth; (fig: vendere a poco prezzo) to give sth away; **cosa gli regali per il compleanno?** what are you giving him for his birthday?

❏ **regalare** non si traduce mai con la parola inglese regale

regale [re'gale] AGG royal; (fig: portamento) regal

regalo [re'galo] SM present, gift; **regali di Natale** Christmas presents; **ho ricevuto un sacco di regali** I got lots of presents; **"articoli da regalo" "gifts"; fare un regalo a qn** to give sb a present; **"con bagnoschiuma in regalo"** "with a free gift of bubble bath" ♦ AGG INV: **libro regalo** free book; **mi può fare una confezione regalo?** could you gift-wrap it for me?

regata [re'gata] SF regatta

reggente [red'dʒɛnte] AGG 1 (sovrano) reigning; **principe reggente** prince regent 2 (Gramm: proposizione) main ♦ SM, SF regent ♦ SF (Gramm) main clause

reggenza [red'dʒɛntsa] SF regency

reggere ['reddʒere] VB IRREG /87/ VT 1 (tenere: persona) to hold up, support; (: pacco, valigia, timone) to hold; **le gambe non lo reggevano più** his legs could carry him no longer; **reggi questa borsa, per favore** hold this bag, please 2 (sopportare: peso) to bear, carry; (: fig: situazione) to stand, bear; **reggere l'alcol** to hold one's drink; **non lo reggo più** (fig: persona) I can't put up with him any more 3 (Gramm: sogg: proposizione) to govern, take, be followed by; **reggere il dativo** to take the dative 4 (essere a capo di: Stato) to govern, rule; (: ditta) to run, manage ♦ VI (aus avere) 1 (resistere) to hold on; **reggere a** (peso, pressione) to bear; (urto) to stand up to; **reggere alla tentazione** to resist temptation; **non regge al paragone** it (o he ecc) doesn't stand comparison; **non ha retto a tali minacce** he was unable to hold

out against such threats 2 (durare: bel tempo, situazione) to last 3 (fig: stare in piedi: teoria) to hold up, hold water; **è un discorso che non regge** the argument doesn't hold water; **reggersi** VR 1 (stare dritto) to stand; (fig: dominarsi) to control o.s.; (tenersi): **reggersi a** to hold on to; **reggersi su** to be based on; **reggersi sulle gambe o in piedi** to stand up; **non si reggeva in piedi** he could barely stand; **non mi reggo più dalla stanchezza** I'm so tired that I can barely stand; **reggiti a me** hold on to me; **reggiti forte** hold on tight 2 (uso reciproco): **reggersi a vicenda** to support each other

reggia, -ge ['rɛddʒa] SF royal palace; (fig) palace

reggicalze [reddʒi'kaltse] SM INV suspender (Brit) o garter (USA) belt

reggimento [reddʒi'mento] SM regiment; (fig) horde

reggipetto [reddʒi'petto], **reggiseno** [reddʒi'seno] SM bra

regia, -gie [re'dʒia] SF (Teatro) production; (TV, Cine) direction; **regia di Fellini** directed by Fellini

regime [re'dʒime] SM 1 (Pol, anche pegg) regime; **un regime totalitario** a totalitarian regime 2 (sistema) system; regime (monetario) aureo (Fin) gold standard; **regime tributario** tax system 3 (regola): **regime dietetico** diet; **essere a regime** to be on a diet; **regime vegetariano** vegetarian diet 4 (di fiume, torrente) flow 5 (Tecn) (engine) speed; **funzionare a pieno regime** to run at top revs; **regime di giri** (di motore) revs pl per minute

regina [re'dʒina] SF (Pol, Scacchi, Carte: fig) queen; **la regina Elisabetta** Queen Elizabeth; **la regina madre** the Queen Mother; **la regina della festa** the belle of the ball

regio, -gia, -gi, -gie ['rɛdʒo] AGG royal

regionale [redʒo'nale] AGG regional ♦ SM (treno) slow local train

regione [re'dʒone] SF 1 (gen) region; (fig: zona) area, region 2 (istituzione) administrative unit

regista, -i, -e [re'dʒista] SM, SF (Teatro) producer; (TV, Cine) director

registrare [redʒis'trare] /72/ VT 1 (Amm: nascita, morte, veicolo) to register; (Comm: fattura, ordine) to enter; **registrare i bagagli** (Aer) to check in one's luggage 2 (notare, constatare) to report, note; (sogg: termometro, apparecchio) to record, register; **è stato registrato un aumento della domanda** an increase in demand has been reported 3 (su nastro) to (tape-)record; (su disco) to record; **voglio registrare questo programma** I want to record this programme 4 (Tecn: mettere a punto) to adjust, regulate; **registrare i freni** to adjust the brakes

registratore [redʒistra'tore] SM (per incidere) tape recorder; (per misurare) register, recorder; **registratore di cassa** (Comm) till, cash register; **registratore a cassette** cassette recorder; **registratore di volo** (Aer) flight recorder

registrazione [redʒistrat'tsjone] SF (vedi vb) registration; entry; check-in; reporting; recording; adjustment

registro [re'dʒistro] SM 1 (gen) register; **registro di bordo** log (Brit), logbook (USA); **registro di classe** class register; **registro** (di cassa) (Comm) ledger 2 (Amm, Dir) registry; **ufficio del registro** registrar's office; (pubblico) **registro automobilistico** motor registration office; **registro immobiliare** land register 3 (Tecn: di orologio) regulator; (: di treno) adjuster 4 (Mus: di voce) range, register; (: di strumento) register 5 (Ling) register

regnante [reɲ'ɲante] AGG reigning, ruling ♦ SM, SF ruler

regnare [reɲ'ɲare] /15/ VI (aus avere) (anche fig) to reign; (predominare) to rule; **regnava il silenzio** silence reigned

regno ['reɲɲo] SM 1 (periodo) reign; **durante il regno di** during the reign of 2 (luogo) kingdom; **il regno della fantasia** the realm of fantasy; **il regno animale** the animal kingdom; **il regno vegetale** the vegetable o plant kingdom

regola ['rɛgola] SF 1 (gen) rule; **di regola** as a rule; **essere in regola** (dipendente) to be a registered employee; (documenti) to be in order; **proporsi una regola di vita** to set o.s. rules to live by; **le regole del gioco** (anche fig) the rules of the game; **a regola d'arte** (lavoro) expert, professional; **per tua (norma e) regola** for your information; **avere le carte in regola** (gen) to have one's papers in order; (fig: essere adatto) to be the right person; **fare le cose in regola** to do things properly; **un'eccezione alla regola** an exception to the rule 2 (Rel) rule

regolabile [rego'labile] AGG adjustable

regolamentare [regolamen'tare] /72/ AGG (*distanza, velocità*) regulation *attr*; (*disposizione*) statutory; **lunghezza regolamentare** regulation length; **entro il tempo regolamentare** within the time allowed, within the prescribed time ♦ VT (*gen*) to control

regolamento [regola'mento] SM 1 (*norme*) regulations *pl*; **regolamento scolastico** school rules *pl*; **è proibito dal regolamento scolastico** it's against the school rules 2 (*atto del regolare: di debito*) settlement; **un regolamento di conti** (*fig*) a settling of scores

regolare¹ [rego'lare] /72/ AGG 1 (*senza variazioni: gen, Gramm, Mat*) regular; (*: velocità*) steady; (*: superficie*) even; (*: passo*) steady, even; **a intervalli regolari** at regular intervals 2 (*in regola: documento, permesso*) in order; **presentare regolare domanda** to apply through the proper channels; **esercito regolare** regular army; **è tutto regolare!** everything is in order!; **tutto ciò non è regolare** that's entirely irregular

regolare² [rego'lare] /72/ VT (*gen*) to regulate, control; (*questione, debito, conto*) to settle; (*apparecchio*) to adjust, regulate; (*orologio*) to set; **non riesco a regolare il volume** I can't adjust the sound; **regolare i conti** (*fig*) to settle old scores; **regolarsi** VR 1 (*moderarsi*): **regolarsi nel bere/nello spendere** to watch o control one's drinking/spending 2 (*comportarsi*) to behave, act; **non so come regolarmi** I don't know what to do; (*nell'usare ingredienti*) I don't know what quantities to add; **regolati come meglio credi** do as you think best

regolarità [regolari'ta] SF 1 (*vedi agg a*) regularity; steadiness; evenness 2 (*nel pagare*) punctuality

regolarizzare [regolarid'dzare] /72/ VT (*posizione*) to regularize; (*debito*) to settle

regolata [rego'lata] SF (*fig*): **darsi una regolata** to pull one's socks up, pull o.s. together

regolatezza [regola'tettsa] SF (*ordine*) orderliness; (*moderazione*) moderation

regolato, -a [rego'lato] AGG (*ordinato*) orderly; (*moderato*) moderate

regolatore, -trice [regola'tore] AGG (*principio*) controlling *attr*; **piano regolatore** (*Amm*) town-planning scheme ♦ SM (*Tecn*) regulator; **regolatore di frequenza** frequency control; **regolatore di tensione** voltage regulator; **regolatore di volume** volume control

regolo ['regolo] SM ruler; **regolo calcolatore** slide rule

regredire [regre'dire] /55/ VI (*aus* essere) to regress; **regredire negli studi** to fall behind in one's studies

regressione [regres'sjone] SF regression

regresso [re'gresso] SM (*fig: declino*) decline

reietto, -a [re'jetto] SM, SF outcast

reincarnazione [reinkarnat'tsjone] SF reincarnation

reintegrare [reinte'grare] /72/ VT (*produzione*) to restore; (*energie*) to recover; (*dipendente*) to reinstate; **reintegrare qn in una carica** to reinstate sb in a post

reintegrazione [reintegrat'tsjone] SF (*di produzione*) restoration; (*di dipendente*) reinstatement

relativamente [relativa'mente] AVV relatively; **relativamente a** as regards

relatività [relativi'ta] SF relativity

relativo, -a [rela'tivo] AGG (*gen, anche Gramm, Mat*) relative; (*attinente*) relevant; (*rispettivo*) respective; **relativo a** (*che concerne*) relating to, concerning; (*proporzionato*) in proportion to

relatore, -trice [rela'tore] SM, SF (*gen*) spokesperson; (*Univ: di tesi*) supervisor

relax [re'laks] SM relaxation

relazione [relat'tsjone] SF 1 (*legame, nesso*) relationship; **non c'è relazione tra le due cose** there's no connection between the two things, the two things are in no way related; **essere in relazione** to be connected; **mettere in relazione** (*fatti, elementi*) to make the connection between; **in relazione a quanto detto prima** with regard to what has already been said 2 (*rapporto con persone*) relationship; **essere in buone relazioni con qn** to be on good terms with sb; **relazione (sentimentale)** (love) affair; **relazione extraconiugale** extramarital affair; **ha scoperto che il marito ha una relazione** she's discovered that her husband is having an affair; **relazioni** SFPL (*conoscenze*) connections; **pubbliche relazioni** public relations; **relazioni sindacali** labour relations 3 (*resoconto*) report, account; **fare una relazione** to make a report, give an account; **devo scrivere una relazione sulla visita al museo** I've got to write a report on our visit to the museum

relegare [rele'gare] /80/ VT (*allontanare*) to banish; (*fig*) to relegate

religione [reli'dʒone] SF (*gen, anche fig*) religion; (*fede*) religious faith; **religione di Stato** state religion; **non c'è più religione!** (*fig*) what's the world coming to!

religioso, -a [reli'dʒoso] AGG (*gen*) religious; (*arte*) sacred; (*scuola, matrimonio, musica*) church *attr*; **in religioso silenzio** in reverent silence ♦ SM, SF monk (nun)

reliquia [re'likwja] SF (*Rel, anche fig*) relic; **tenere qc come una reliquia** (*fig*) to treasure sth

relitto [re'litto] SM (*gen, anche fig*) wreck; (*persona*) down-and-out

remainder [ri'meində] SM INV (*libro*) remainder

remake ['riː'meik] SM INV (*Cine, Teatro*) remake

remare [re'mare] /72/ VI (*aus* avere) to row; **ora tocca a te remare** it's your turn to row now

reminiscenza [reminiʃ'ʃentsa] SF reminiscence

remissione [remis'sjone] SF 1 (*di peccato, malattia*) remission; **remissione del debito** (*Dir*) remission of debt; **remissione di querela** (*Dir*) withdrawal of an action 2 (*sottomissione*) submissiveness, compliance

remissività [remissivi'ta] SF submissiveness

remissivo, -a [remis'sivo] AGG submissive, compliant

remo ['remo] SM oar; **barca a remi** rowing boat; **tirare i remi in barca** (*anche fig*) to rest on one's oars

remora ['remora] SF (*letter: indugio*) hesitation; **non avere remore!** don't hesitate!

remoto, -a [re'moto] AGG 1 (*lontano*) remote 2 (*Gramm*): **passato remoto** past definite; **trapassato remoto** pluperfect

remunerare ecc [remune'rare] = rimunerare

rena ['rena] SF sand

renale [re'nale] AGG kidney *attr*

rendere ['rendere] VB IRREG /88/ VT 1 (*ridare*) to give back, return; **potresti rendermi la penna?** could you give me back my pen?; **gli sarà resa la libertà quanto prima** he will be released as soon as possible; **rendere la visita** to pay a return visit; **"vuoto a rendere"** (*bottiglia*) "please return empties"; **a buon rendere!** (*anche iro*) my turn next time!; **rendere l'anima a Dio** (*euf*) to breathe one's last 2 (*dare*): **rendere grazie a qn** to thank sb; **rendere omaggio a qn** to honour sb; **rendere un servizio a qn** to do sb a service; **rendere una testimonianza** to give evidence; **rendersi conto di qc** to realize sth; **forse non ti rendi conto di quanto sia pericoloso** maybe you don't realize how dangerous it is 3 (*fruttare*) to yield, bring in; (*uso assoluto: sogg: ditta*) to be profitable; (*: investimento, campo*) to yield, be productive; **rendere il 10%** to yield 10%; **una ditta che non rende** an unprofitable firm 4 (*esprimere, tradurre*) to render; **rendere l'idea** to give the idea; **non so se rendo l'idea** I don't know if I'm making myself clear! 5 (+ *agg: far diventare*) to make; **il suo intervento ha reso possibile l'affare** his intervention made the whole affair possible; **un po' di diplomazia renderebbe tutto più facile** a bit of diplomacy would make everything easier; **l'hai resa felice** you made her happy; **rendere la vita impossibile a qn** to make life impossible for sb; **rendersi** VR (+ *agg: apparire*) to make o.s. (+ *agg*); **rendersi antipatico/ridicolo/utile** to make o.s. unpleasant/ridiculous/useful; **posso rendermi utile?** can I make myself useful?

rendiconto [rendi'konto] SM (*resoconto*) report, account; (*Amm, Comm*) statement (of accounts)

rendimento [rendi'mento] SM (*di manodopera, anche Fis*) efficiency; (*di industria: produttività*) productivity; (*di motore, studente*) performance; (*di podere*) yield; **avere un buon rendimento** (*atleta*) to perform well; (*studente*) to do well

rendita ['rendita] SF (*di individuo*) private o unearned income; (*Comm*) revenue; **vivere di rendita** to have private means; (*fig: studente*) to survive on one's past results; **rendita annua** annuity; **rendita vitalizia** life annuity

rene ['rene] SM kidney

reni ['reni] SFPL (*schiena*) back *sg*; **spezzare le reni a qn** (*fig*) to annihilate sb

renitente [reni'tente] AGG: **renitente (a)** unwilling (to), reluctant (to), loath (to); **renitente ai consigli di qn** unwilling to follow sb's advice; **essere renitente alla leva** (*Mil*) to fail to report for military service

renna ['renna] SF reindeer *inv*; **di renna** suede *attr*; **una giacca di renna** a suede coat

Reno ['reno] SM: **il Reno** the Rhine

reo, -a ['reo] AGG: **reo (di)** guilty (of) ♦ SM, SF (*Dir*) offender; **reo confesso** confessed criminal

reparto [re'parto] SM (*di ospedale*) ward; (*di ufficio, negozio*) department, section; (*Mil*: *di esercito*) unit, detachment; **reparti d'assalto** (*Mil*) assault troops; **reparto acquisti** purchasing office; **reparto d'attacco** (*Sport*) attack; **reparto maternità** maternity ward; **reparto uomo** (*in negozio*) men's department

repellente [repel'lente] AGG 1 (*che ripugna*) repulsive 2 (*Chim*: *insettifugo*): **liquido repellente** (liquid) repellent

repentaglio [repen'taʎʎo] SM: **mettere a repentaglio** to put at risk, jeopardize, endanger

repentino, -a [repen'tino] AGG (*gesto, decisione*) sudden, unexpected

reperibile [repe'ribile] AGG (*articolo, prodotto*) available; **non è reperibile** (*persona*) he can't be reached

reperire [repe'rire] /55/ VT to find, trace

reperto [re'perto] SM (*Archeol*) find; (*anche*: **reperto giudiziario**) exhibit; (*Med*) report

repertorio, -ri [reper'tɔrjo] SM (*Teatro*) repertoire, repertory; (*di canzoni*: *fig*) repertoire; **immagini di repertorio** (*Cine, TV*) archive footage *sg*

replica, -che ['replika] SF 1 (*risposta*: *gen, Pol*) reply, answer; (*: obiezione*) objection 2 (*ripetizione*: *gen*) repetition; (*: TV, Teatro, Cine*) repeat performance; **domani trasmettono la replica dell'ultima puntata** the repeat of the final episode is on tomorrow; **avere molte repliche** to have a long run 3 (*copia*) replica

replicare [repli'kare] /20/ VT 1 (*rispondere*) to reply, answer 2 (*Teatro, Cine*) to repeat

reportage [rəpɔr'taʒ] SM INV (*Stampa*) report

repressione [repres'sjone] SF repression

repressivo, -a [repres'sivo] AGG repressive

represso, -a [re'presso] PP *di* **reprimere** ♦ AGG repressed ♦ SM, SF (*persona*) repressed person

reprimere [re'primere] /50/ VT IRREG (*gen*) to suppress, repress; (*sommossa*) to put down, suppress; (*sentimenti*) to repress, hold back

repubblica, -che [re'pubblika] SF republic; **la Prima/Seconda Repubblica** terms used to refer to Italy before and after the political changes resulting from the 1994 elections

repubblicano, -a [repubbli'kano] AGG, SM, SF republican

reputare [repu'tare] /72/ VT to consider, judge; **reputare qn intelligente** to consider *o* judge sb (to be) intelligent; **reputo che si possa fare** I think it can be done; **se lo reputerai opportuno** if you think it advisable; **reputarsi** VR to consider o.s.

reputazione [reputat'tsjone] SF (*gen*) reputation; (*buon nome*) reputation, good name; **avere una buona/cattiva reputazione** to have a good/bad reputation; **farsi una cattiva reputazione** to get o.s. a bad name; **rovinarsi la reputazione** to ruin one's reputation

requie ['rekwje] SF rest; **dare requie a qn** to give sb some peace; **non dare requie a qn** to give sb no quarter *o* peace; **senza requie** unceasingly

requiem ['rekwjem] SM INV, SF INV (*preghiera*) requiem, prayer for the dead ♦ SM INV (*Mus*) Requiem; (*fig*: *ufficio funebre*) requiem; **messa di requiem** Requiem (mass)

requisire [rekwi'zire] /55/ VT to requisition

requisito [rekwi'zito] SM (*gen*) requirement; **uno dei requisiti era la conoscenza del tedesco** one of the requirements was a knowledge of German; **non aveva i requisiti necessari per il lavoro** he didn't have the necessary qualifications for the job

requisitoria [rekwizi'tɔrja] SF (*Dir*) closing speech (for the prosecution)

requisizione [rekwizit'tsjone] SF requisition

resa ['resa] SF 1 (*l'arrendersi*) surrender 2 (*rendimento*: *di podere*) yield; (*: di operaio*) productivity 3 **resa dei conti** rendering of accounts; **è venuto il momento della resa dei conti** (*fig*) the day of reckoning has arrived 4 (*Comm*: *restituzione*) repayment; (*: merce restituita*) unsold goods

rescindere [reʃ'ʃindere] /102/ VT IRREG (*Dir*) to rescind, annul

rescisso, -a [reʃ'ʃisso] PP *di* **rescindere**

resettare [reset'tare] /72/ VT (*Inform*: *macchina, computer*) to reset

resi ecc ['resi] VB *vedi* **rendere**

residente [resi'dɛnte] AGG, SM, SF resident; **è residente a Londra** he lives in London; **sono residenti all'estero** they live abroad; **per i residenti dell'Unione europea** for the residents of the European Union

residenza [resi'dɛntsa] SF 1 (*soggiorno*) stay 2 (*indirizzo, sede*) residence; **la residenza del Primo Ministro** the Prime Minister's residence; **cambiare residenza** to change one's address

residenziale [residen'tsjale] AGG residential; **un quartiere residenziale** a residential area

residuale [residu'ale] AGG residual

residuo, -a [re'siduo] AGG (*rimanente*) remaining; (*Chim*) residual ♦ SM (*gen*) remainder; (*Chim*: *fig*) residue; **residui industriali** industrial waste *sg*

resina ['rezina] SF resin

resistente [resis'tente] AGG (*persona, oggetto*) strong, tough; (*pianta*) hardy; (*tessuto*) strong, hard-wearing; (*colore*) fast; (*metallo*) strong, resistant; **resistente all'acqua** waterproof; **resistente al calore** heat-resistant; **resistente al fuoco** fireproof; **resistente al gelo** frost-resistant

resistenza [resis'tentsa] SF 1 (*gen*) resistance; (*fisica*) stamina, endurance; (*mentale*) endurance, resistance; **opporre resistenza (a)** to offer *o* put up resistance (to); (*decisione, scelta*) to show opposition (to); **prova di resistenza** endurance test; **resistenza passiva** passive resistance; **resistenza a pubblico ufficiale** (*Dir*) use of force or threats against a public official 2 (*Elettr, Tecn, Fis*) resistance; (*Elettr*: *apparecchio*) resistor; **coefficiente di resistenza** drag coefficient; **resistenza di attrito** frictional resistance 3 (*Pol*) : **la Resistenza** the Resistance (those who fought against the Nazis and the Fascists during World War II)

resistere [re'sistere] /11/ VI IRREG (*aus* avere) **resistere a** (*gen*) to resist; (*fatica, siccità*) to stand up to, withstand; (*peso*) to take; (*dolore*) to stand; (*tentazione*) to resist; (*tortura*) to endure; (*attacco*) to hold out against; **resistere al calore** to be heat-resistant; **resistere al fuoco** to be fireproof; **resistere alla prova del tempo** to stand the test of time; **resistere alla corrente di un fiume** to hold one's own against the current of a river; **colori che resistono al lavaggio** colours which are fast in the wash; **resistere al peso della responsabilità** to cope with the responsibility; **non ho saputo resistere alla tentazione** I couldn't resist the temptation!; **resisti!** hold on!; **non ho resistito e gliel'ho detto** I couldn't contain myself any longer and I told him; **non resisterà molto in quell'ufficio** he won't last long in that office; **nessuno sa resistergli** no one can resist him; **nessuno sa resistere al suo fascino** everybody succumbs to his charm

resistito, -a [resis'tito] PP *di* **resistere**

reso, -a ['reso] PP *di* **rendere**

resoconto [reso'konto] SM (*gen*) account; (*di giornalista*) report, account; (*di seduta, assemblea*) minutes *pl*; **fare il resoconto di** to give an account of; to give a report of; to take the minutes of

respingente [respin'dʒente] SM (*Ferr*) buffer

respingere [res'pindʒere] /114/ VT IRREG 1 (*attacco, nemico*) to drive back, repel; **respingere la palla** (*Calcio*) to kick the ball back; (*Pallavolo*) to return the ball 2 (*rifiutare*: *pacco, lettera*) to return; (*: invito*) to refuse; (*: proposta*) to reject, turn down; (*: persona*) to reject; **la sua domanda è stata respinta** his application was rejected 3 (*Scol*: *studente*) to fail

respinto, -a [res'pinto] PP *di* **respingere** ♦ SM, SF (*Scol*) failed candidate

respirare [respi'rare] /72/ VI (*aus* avere) (*gen*) to breathe; (*inspirare*) to breathe in, inhale; (*fig*: *distendersi*) to get one's breath (back); (*: rassicurarsi*) to breathe again; **non riuscivo**

a respirare I couldn't breathe; non respiri! (*dal medico*) hold your breath! ♦ VT: respirare un po' d'aria fresca (*anche fig*) to get a breath of fresh air; si respira un'aria di rinnovamento there is a feeling of renewal in the air

respiratore [respira'tore] SM (*Med*) respirator; (*di subacqueo*) breathing apparatus

respiratorio, -ria, -ri, -rie [respira'tɔrjo] AGG respiratory

respirazione [respirat'tsjone] SF breathing; esercizi di respirazione breathing exercises; respirazione artificiale artificial respiration; respirazione bocca a bocca mouth-to-mouth resuscitation, kiss of life (*fam*)

respiro [res'piro] SM breathing *no pl*; (*singolo atto*) breath; (*fig*) respite, rest; avere il respiro pesante to breathe heavily; trattenere il respiro to hold one's breath; esalare l'ultimo respiro to breathe one's last; godere di un momento di respiro to enjoy a moment's rest; lavorare senza respiro to work non-stop; dammi un attimo di respiro give me a break; di ampio respiro (*opera, lavoro*) far-reaching

responsabile [respon'sabile] AGG 1 (*gen, anche fig*): responsabile (di) responsible (for); (*danni*) liable (for), responsible (for); è un tipo molto responsabile he's a very responsible person; si sente responsabile dell'accaduto she feels responsible for what happened; sentirsi responsabile di fronte a qn (*moralmente*) to feel responsible to sb, hold o.s. accountable to sb 2 (*incaricato*): responsabile (di) responsible (for), in charge (of) ♦ SM, SF 1 responsabile (di) (*danni, delitto*) person responsible (for) 2 responsabile (di) (*sezione, ufficio*) person in charge (of), manager (of); vorrei parlare con il responsabile I'd like to speak to the person in charge

responsabilità [responsabili'ta] SF INV: responsabilità (di) (*gen*) responsibility (for); (*Dir*) liability (for); non voglio responsabilità I don't want responsibilities; assumersi la responsabilità di to take on the responsibility for; affidare a qn la responsabilità di qc to make sb responsible for sth; avere la responsabilità di to be responsible for, have responsibility for; fare qc sotto la propria responsabilità to do sth on one's own responsibility; responsabilità civile civil liability; responsabilità patrimoniale debt liability; responsabilità penale criminal liability

responsabilizzare [responsabilid'dzare] /72/ VT: responsabilizzare qn to make sb feel responsible; responsabilizzarsi VIP to become responsible

responso [res'ponso] SM (*risposta*) answer, reply; (*Dir*) verdict

ressa ['ressa] SF crowd, throng; c'è troppa ressa it's too crowded; quanta ressa! what a crush!; far ressa intorno a qn to throng round sb

ressi ecc ['ressi] VB *vedi* reggere

restare [res'tare] /72/ VI (*aus essere*) 1 (*in luogo*) to stay, remain; restare a casa to stay *o* remain at home; restare a letto to stay *o* remain in bed; restare a cena to stay for dinner; restare a guardare la televisione to stay and watch television; dai, resta ancora un po' go on, stay a bit longer; che resti tra di noi (*fig: segreto*) this is just between ourselves 2 (*in una condizione*) to stay, remain; restare zitto to remain *o* keep *o* stay silent; restare sorpreso to be surprised; restare orfano to become *o* be left an orphan; restare cieco to become *o* be left blind; restare in piedi (*non sedersi*) to remain standing; (*non coricarsi*) to stay up; restare amici to remain friends; restare in buoni rapporti to remain on good terms; restare senza parole to be left speechless 3 (*sussistere*) to be left, remain; non restano che poche pietre there are only a few stones left; è l'unico parente che le resta he's her only remaining relative; coi pochi soldi che mi restano with what little money I have left; restano da fare 15 km there are still 15 km to go; ne resta ancora un po' there's still some left; ne restano solo due there are only two left; resta ancora molto da fare there's still a lot to do; non ti resta altro (da fare) che accettare all you can do is accept; mi resti solo tu you're all I have left; mi resta ben poco da dire se non... I've little left to say except ...; non resta più niente there's nothing left

❑ restare non si traduce mai con la parola inglese *rest*

restaurare [restau'rare] /72/ VT to restore; stanno restaurando il quadro the painting is being restored

restauratore, -trice [restaura'tore] SM, SF restorer

restaurazione [restaurat'tsjone] SF (*Pol*) restoration

restauro [res'tauro] SM (*Archit, Arte*) restoration; in restauro under repair; sotto restauro (*dipinto*) being restored; chiuso per restauro closed for repairs

restio, -tia, -tii, -tie [res'tio] AGG (*riluttante*): restio a reluctant to

restituire [restitu'ire] /55/ VT: restituire qc (a) (*gen*) to return sth (to), give sth back (to); (*colore, forma, forza*) to restore sth (to); me lo presti? te lo restituisco domani will you lend it to me? I'll give it back to you tomorrow; mi ha restituito i soldi oggi he paid me back today; restituire un favore to return a favour

restituzione [restitut'tsjone] SF (*gen*) return; (*di soldi*) repayment

resto ['resto] SM 1 (*gen*) rest; (*di soldi*) change; (*Mat*) remainder; dove mettiamo il resto della roba? where shall we put the rest of the stuff?; tu porta il vino, al resto penso io you bring the wine, and I'll see to the rest; tenga pure il resto keep the change; "il resto alla prossima puntata" "to be continued"; del resto besides, moreover; del resto, cos'altro potevo fare? after all, what else could I do? 2 resti SMPL (*di cibo*) leftovers; (*di civiltà*) remains; resti mortali (mortal) remains

restringere [res'trindʒere] VB IRREG /117/ VT (*strada*) to narrow; (*abito, gonna*) to take in; restringersi VIP (*contrarsi*) to contract; (*farsi più stretto: strada, fiume*) to narrow; (: *tessuto*) to shrink; il campo si restringe (*fig: di ipotesi, possibilità*) the field is narrowing

restrittivo, -a [restrit'tivo] AGG restrictive

restrizione [restrit'tsjone] SF restriction

resurrezione [resurret'tsjone] SF = risurrezione

resuscitare [resuʃʃi'tare] /72/ VT, VI = risuscitare

retata [re'tata] SF 1 (*Pesca*) haul, catch 2 (*Polizia*): fare una retata (di) to round up

rete ['rete] SF 1 (*tessuto, anche Pesca*) net; (*di equilibristi*) safety net; (*per bagagli*) (luggage) rack; (*di recinzione*) wire netting; (*maglia metallica, di plastica*) mesh; la pallina ha toccato la rete the ball touched the net; finire nella rete (*fig: trappola*) to be caught in the trap; calze a rete fishnet tights *o* stockings; rete del letto (sprung) bed base; rete da pesca fishing net 2 (*sistema*) network; la Rete the Web; collegarsi in Rete to get connected to the Net; rete di distribuzione distribution network; rete elettrica (*nazionale*) (electricity) grid; rete ferroviaria railway network; rete di spionaggio spy network; rete stradale road network; rete sociale (*Inform*: *sito internet*) social networking site; rete (televisiva) (*sistema*) network; (*canale*) channel 3 (*Sport*) net; segnare una rete (*Calcio*) to score a goal; tirare in rete (*Calcio*) to take a shot at goal

reticente [reti'tʃɛnte] AGG reticent

reticenza [reti'tʃɛntsa] SF reticence; parlare senza reticenze to speak out

reticolato [retiko'lato] SM (*gen*) grid; (*recinto*) wire netting; (*Mil*) barbed wire (fence)

retina ['retina] SF (*Anat*) retina

retorico, -a, -ci, -che [re'tɔriko] AGG rhetorical; domanda retorica rhetorical question; figura retorica rhetorical device

retribuire [retribu'ire] /55/ VT (*gen*) to pay; retribuire il lavoro di qn to pay sb for his (*o* her) work; un lavoro mal retribuito a poorly-paid job

retributivo, -a [retribu'tivo] AGG pay *attr*

retribuzione [retribut'tsjone] SF (*stipendio*) pay, remuneration

retrivo, -a [re'trivo] AGG, SM, SF reactionary

retro¹ ['retro] SM (*gen*) back; (*di auto*) rear, back; sul retro c'è un giardino there's a garden at the back ♦ AVV: "vedi retro" "see over(leaf)"

retro² [re'tro] AGG INV: la moda retro retro fashion

retroattività [retroattivi'ta] SF (*Dir*) retroactivity

retroattivo, -a [retroat'tivo] AGG (*Dir: legge*) retroactive

retrobottega, -ghe [retrobot'tega] SF back shop

retrocedere [retro'tʃɛdere] VB IRREG /29/ VT (*Mil*) to demote; (*Sport*) to relegate ♦ VI (*aus essere*) (*gen*) to move back; (*esercito*) to retreat; (*fig: di fronte a minacce*) to back down; retrocedere in serie B (*Calcio*) to be relegated to the second division

retrocessione [retrotʃesˈsjone] SF (*Mil: di impiegato*) demotion; (*Sport*) relegation

retrocesso, -a [retroˈtʃɛsso] PP *di* retrocedere

retrodatare [retrodaˈtare] /72/ VT (*Amm*) to backdate

retrogrado, -a [reˈtrɔgrado] AGG 1 (*retrivo: persona, idee*) reactionary, backward-looking 2 (*Astron: moto*) retrograde, backward ♦ SM, SF reactionary

retroguardia [retroˈgwardja] SF (*anche fig*) rearguard

retromarcia [retroˈmartʃa] SF (*Aut*) reverse; (*dispositivo*) reverse (gear); **mettere la retromarcia** to go into reverse; **ha messo la retromarcia** he went into reverse; **andare in retromarcia, fare retromarcia** to reverse; **ho sbattuto facendo retromarcia** I bumped the car when I was reversing

retroscena [retroˈʃɛna] SF INV (*Teatro*) backstage ♦ SM INV (*fig*) behind-the-scenes activity

retrospettivo, -a [retrospetˈtivo] AGG retrospective ♦ SF (*Arte*) retrospective (exhibition)

retrostante [retrosˈtante] AGG: **retrostante (a)** at the back (of)

retroterra [retroˈtɛrra] SM INV 1 (*zona*) hinterland 2 (*sfondo*): **retroterra culturale/storico** historical/cultural background

retrovia [retroˈvia] SF (*Mil*) zone behind the front; **mandare nelle retrovie** to send to the rear

retrovisore [retroviˈzore] SM (*Aut: anche*: **specchietto retrovisore**) rear-view mirror; (: *laterale*) wing (*Brit*) *o* side (*USA*) mirror

retta [ˈrɛtta] SF 1 (*Geom*) straight line 2 (*di collegio, convitto*) fee, charge for bed and board 3 (*fig: ascolto*): **dare retta a** to pay attention to, listen to; **non dargli retta, quello s'inventa le cose!** don't listen to him, he makes things up!; **dammi retta, non vale la pena** listen to me, it's not worth it

rettangolare [rettangoˈlare] AGG rectangular

rettangolo, -a [retˈtangolo] AGG right-angled ♦ SM rectangle

rettifica, -che [retˈtifika] SF correction, rectification; **pubblicare una rettifica** (*su giornale*) to publish a retraction; **rettifica delle valvole** (*Aut*) valve grinding

rettificare [rettifiˈkare] /20/ VT 1 (*gen*) to rectify, correct 2 (*Chim, Elettr, Mat*) to rectify

rettile [ˈrɛttile] SM reptile

rettilineo, -a [rettiˈlineo] AGG (*gen, anche Mat*) rectilinear; (*strada*) straight ♦ SM (*di strada*) straight; **in rettilineo** on the straight; **rettilineo d'arrivo** (*Sport*) home straight

rettitudine [rettiˈtudine] SF rectitude, uprightness

retto, -a [ˈrɛtto] PP *di* reggere ♦ AGG 1 (*gen, linea*) straight; **angolo retto** right angle 2 (*fig: onesto*) honest, upright; **abbandonare la retta via** (*fig*) to stray from the straight and narrow; **seguire la retta via** (*fig*) to keep to the straight and narrow ♦ SM (*Anat*) rectum

rettore [retˈtore] SM 1 (*Univ*) ≈ chancellor 2 (*Rel*) rector

reumatismo [reumaˈtizmo] SM rheumatism *sg*; **soffre di reumatismi** she suffers from rheumatism

Rev. ABBR (= *Reverendo*) Rev(d).

reverendo [reveˈrendo] AGG, SM Reverend

reverente [reveˈrɛnte] AGG = riverente

reverenza [reveˈrɛntsa] SF = riverenza

reversibile [reverˈsibile] AGG (*gen*) reversible; (*Econ*) convertible, negotiable; (*Dir*) revertible

revisionare [revizjoˈnare] /72/ VT (*Aut*) to service, overhaul; (*Fin: conti*) to audit

revisione [reviˈzjone] SF (*di contratto, processo, sentenza*) review; (*di macchina*) servicing *no pl*, overhaul; (*di conti*) auditing *no pl*; (*di testo*) revision; **revisione di bilancio** audit; **revisione di bozze** proofreading; **revisione contabile interna** internal audit; **revisione dello stipendio** salary review

revisore [reviˈzore] SM: **revisore di bozze** proofreader; **revisore dei conti** auditor

revival [riˈvaival] SM INV revival; **un revival degli anni settanta** a Seventies revival

revoca, -che [ˈrɛvoka] SF (*Dir*) repeal, revocation

revocare [revoˈkare] /20/ VT (*gen*) to revoke, repeal; (*licenza*) to revoke

revolver [reˈvolver] SM INV revolver

revolverata [revolveˈrata] SF revolver shot

Reykjavik [ˈreikjavik] SF Reykjavik

RFT [ˈɛrreˈɛffeˈti] SIGLA F (= *Repubblica Federale Tedesca*) FRG

riabbia ecc [riˈabbja] VB *vedi* riavere

riabilitare [riabiliˈtare] /72/ VT (*gen*) to rehabilitate; (*fig*) to restore to favour (*Brit*) *o* favor (*USA*); **quel gesto lo ha riabilitato ai miei occhi** his action restored my good opinion of him; **riabilitarsi** VR to be rehabilitated; **riabilitarsi agli occhi di qn** to redeem o.s. in sb's eyes

riabilitazione [riabilitatˈtsjone] SF rehabilitation

riaccendere [riatˈtʃɛndere] VB IRREG /2/ VT (*sigaretta, fuoco, gas*) to light again; (*luce*) to switch on again; (*fig: sentimenti, interesse*) to rekindle, revive; **riaccendersi** VIP (*fuoco*) to catch again; (*luce, radio, TV*) to come back on again; (*fig: sentimenti, interesse*) to revive, be rekindled

riacceso, -a [riatˈtʃeso] PP *di* riaccendere

riacquistare [riakkwisˈtare] /72/ VT (*gen*) to buy again; (*ciò che si era venduto*) to buy back; (*fig: buonumore, sangue freddo, libertà*) to regain; **riacquistare la salute** to recover (one's health); **riacquistare le forze** to regain one's strength

Riad [riˈad] SF Riyadh

riaddormentare [riaddormenˈtare] /72/ VT to put to sleep again; **riaddormentarsi** VIP to fall asleep again

riallacciare [riallatˈtʃare] /14/ VT (*cintura, cavo*) to refasten, tie up *o* fasten again; (*cappotto*) to do up again; (*fig: rapporti, amicizia*) to resume, renew; **riallacciarsi il cappotto** to do one's coat up again; **riallacciarsi** VIP (*fig: ricollegarsi*): **riallacciarsi a** to draw on, have links with; **ricollegarsi** VR: **mi riallaccio a quello che ha detto il mio collega...** to go back to what my colleague was saying ...

rialzare [rialˈtsare] /72/ VT to raise, lift; (*fondo stradale, superficie*) to make higher, raise, heighten; (*prezzi*) to increase, put up, raise ♦ VI (*aus essere*) (*prezzi, azioni, febbre*) to rise, go up; **rialzarsi** VR (*persona*) to get up

rialzato, -a [rialˈtsato] AGG: **piano rialzato** mezzanine

rialzista, -i, -e [rialˈtsista] SM, SF (*Borsa*) bull

rialzo [riˈaltso] SM 1 (*Econ*): **rialzo (di)** rise (in), increase (in); **essere in rialzo** (*azioni, prezzi*) to be up; **giocare al rialzo** (*Borsa*) to bull; **tendenza al rialzo** (*Borsa*) upward trend, bullish tendency 2 (*rilievo: di terreno*) rise

riandare [rianˈdare] /6/ VI IRREG (*aus essere*) **riandare (in)** *o* (**a**) to go back (to), return (to); **riandare con la memoria a qc** (*fig*) to reminisce about sth, think back to sth

rianimare [rianiˈmare] /72/ VT (*Med*) to resuscitate; (*fig: rallegrare*) to cheer up; (: *dar coraggio*) to give heart to; **rianimare una festa** to liven up a party; **rianimarsi** VIP (*vedi vt*) to recover consciousness; to cheer up; to take heart; to liven up; **d'estate il paesino si rianima** the village comes to life in the summer

rianimazione [rianimatˈtsjone] SF (*Med*) resuscitation; (**centro di**) **rianimazione** intensive care (unit); **in rianimazione** in intensive care

riaperto, -a [riaˈpɛrto] PP *di* riaprire

riapertura [riaperˈtura] SF reopening

riapparire [riappaˈrire] /7/ VI IRREG (*aus essere*) to reappear

riapparso, -a [riapˈparso] PP *di* riapparire

riappendere [riapˈpɛndere] /8/ VT IRREG to hang up again, rehang; (*Telec*) to hang up

riaprire [riaˈprire] VB IRREG /9/ VT , **riaprirsi** VIP to reopen, open again; **quando riaprono le scuole?** when do the schools reopen?; **il cinema ha riaperto dopo l'incendio** the cinema has reopened after the fire

riarmo [riˈarmo] SM (*Mil*) rearmament

riarso, -a [riˈarso] AGG (*terreno*) arid; (*gola*) parched; (*labbra*) dry

riassettare [riassetˈtare] /72/ VT (*stanza*) to rearrange

riassetto [riasˈsetto] SM (*di sistema*) reorganization

riassumere [riasˈsumere] /12/ VT IRREG 1 (*ricapitolare: storia, racconto*) to summarize; **riassumere un articolo** to summarize an article 2 (*operaio, impiegato, domestico*) to re-employ 3 (*riprendere: attività, funzione*) to resume

riassunto, -a [riasˈsunto] PP *di* riassumere ♦ SM summary

riattaccare [riattakˈkare] /20/ VT 1 (*attaccare di nuovo*): **riattaccare (a)** (*manifesto, francobollo*) to stick back (on); (*bottone*) to sew back (on); (*quadro*) to hang back up (on); **riattaccare (il telefono o il ricevitore)** to hang up (the receiver); **ha riattaccato senza lasciarmi finire** he hung up without letting me finish 2 (*riprendere*): **riattaccare discorso con qn** to begin talking to sb again; **riattaccare a fare qc** to begin doing sth again

riattivare [riatti'vare] /72/ vт 1 (*strada, linea ferroviaria*) to reopen 2 (*Med*) to stimulate; (*Cosmetica*) to reactivate; **riattivare la circolazione del sangue** to get the circulation going again 3 (*macchina, motore*) to start up again

riavere [ria'vere] vв irreg /13/ vт 1 (*gen*) to have again; **oggi ho riavuto la nausea** I felt sick again today 2 (*recuperare*: *soldi, libro ecc*) to get back; **far riavere qn** (*da svenimento*) to bring sb round; **riaversi** vip (*da svenimento, stordimento*) to come round; **riaversi dallo stupore** to recover from one's surprise

ribadire [riba'dire] /55/ vт to reaffirm, confirm

ribalta [ri'balta] sf 1 (*Teatro: proscenio*) front of the stage; (*apparecchio d'illuminazione*) footlights *pl*; **essere/venire alla ribalta** (*fig*) to be in/come into the limelight; **tornare alla ribalta** (*personaggio*) to make a comeback; (*problema*) to come up again 2 (*piano, sportello*) flap; (*mobile*) bureau (*Brit*)

ribaltabile [ribal'tabile] agg (*sedile*) tip-up *attr*

ribaltare [ribal'tare] /72/ vт (*rovesciare*) to overturn, tip over; (*fig: situazione*) to reverse; (: *questione*) to turn round vı (*aus essere*), **ribaltarsi** vip to overturn, tip over

ribassare [ribas'sare] /72/ vт (*prezzi*) to lower, bring down; **hanno ribassato il prezzo dei CD** they've cut the price of CDs ♦ vı (*aus essere*) to fall, come down

ribassista, -i, -e [ribas'sista] sm,sf (*Borsa*) bear

ribasso [ri'basso] sm (*Econ*): **ribasso (di)** fall *o* reduction (in); **essere in ribasso** (*azioni, prezzi*) to be down; (*fig: popolarità*) to be on the decline; **giocare al ribasso** (*Borsa*) to bear; **tendenza al ribasso** (*Borsa*) downtrend, bearish tendency

ribattere [ri'battere] /1/ vт 1 (*controbattere a: accuse*) to refute; **ribattere che...** to retort that ... 2 (*battere di nuovo*) to beat again; (*con macchina da scrivere*) to type again; **ribattere (una palla)** to return a ball

ribattezzare [ribatted'dzare] /72/ vт to rename

ribellarsi [ribel'larsi] vip: **ribellarsi (a o contro)** to rebel (against); **si è ribellato alla decisione del padre** he rebelled against his father's decision

ribelle [ri'bɛlle] agg (*soldati, truppe*) rebel; (*carattere, ragazzo*) rebellious; (*capelli*) unruly ♦ sm,sf rebel

ribellione [ribel'ljone] sf: **ribellione (a o contro)** rebellion (against)

ribes ['ribes] sm inv (*Bot*) currant; **ribes nero** blackcurrant; **ribes rosso** redcurrant

ribollire [ribol'lire] /17/ vı (*aus avere*) (*liquido*) to bubble, boil; (*mare*) to seethe; (*vino*) to ferment; **scene che fanno ribollire il sangue** (*fig*) scenes which make one's blood boil

ribrezzo [ri'breddzo] sm disgust, repugnance, loathing; **avere ribrezzo di qc, provare ribrezzo per qc** to be disgusted at *o* by sth; **far ribrezzo a qn** to disgust sb

ributtante [ribut'tante] agg disgusting, revolting

ricacciare [rikat'tʃare] /14/ vт (*respingere*) to drive back; **ricacciare fuori qn** to throw sb out; **ricacciare un urlo in gola** to smother/stifle a cry

ricadere [rika'dere] /18/ vı irreg (*aus essere*) 1 (*cadere di nuovo*) to fall again; (*fig*): **ricadere nel vizio** to fall back into bad habits; **ricadere nell'errore** to lapse into error 2 (*riversarsi: responsabilità, colpa*): **ricadere su** to fall on 3 (*scendere*) to fall, drop; **i capelli le ricadevano sulle spalle** her hair hung down over her shoulders

ricaduta [rika'duta] sf 1 (*Med, anche fig*) relapse; **avere una ricaduta** to relapse 2 (*Fis*): **ricaduta radioattiva** fallout

ricalcare [rikal'kare] /20/ vт (*Disegno*) to trace; (*fig: imitare*) to follow closely *o* faithfully; **ricalcare le orme di qn** (*fig*) to follow in sb's footsteps

ricalcitrare [rikaltʃi'trare] /72/ vı (*aus avere*) (*cavallo, asino, mulo*) to kick; (*fig: persona*): **recalcitrare (di fronte a)** to be recalcitrant (to)

ricamare [rika'mare] /72/ vт (*anche fig*) to embroider; **ci ha ricamato su** (*fig*) he's exaggerated it

ricambiare [rikam'bjare] /19/ vт (*contraccambiare*) to return; **bisogna ricambiare il favore** we must return the favor

ricambio, -bi [ri'kambjo] sm 1 (*di biancheria, abiti*) change; **una camicia di ricambio** a spare shirt; **pezzi di ricambio** (*Tecn*) spare parts 2 (*Fisiologia*) metabolism 3 **ricambio del lavoro** (labour (*Brit*) *o* labor (*USA*)) turnover; **ricambio di magazzino** stock turnover

ricamo [ri'kamo] sm embroidery; **da ricamo** embroidery *attr*; **senza ricami** (*fig*) without frills

ricapitolare [rikapito'lare] /72/ vт to recapitulate, sum up; **ricapitolando..., per ricapitolare...** to sum up ...

ricapitolazione [rikapitolat'tsjone] sf recapitulation, summary

ricaricare [rikari'kare] /20/ vт (*arma, macchina fotografica*) to reload; (*orologio, giocattolo*) to rewind; (*penna*) to refill; (*batteria*) to recharge

ricattare [rikat'tare] /72/ vт to blackmail; **lo stavano ricattando** they were blackmailing him

ricattatore, -trice [rikatta'tore] sm, sf blackmailer

ricatto [ri'katto] sm blackmail; **ma questo è un ricatto!** this is blackmail!; **fare un ricatto a qn** to blackmail sb; **subire un ricatto** to be blackmailed; **ricatto morale** emotional blackmail

ricavare [rika'vare] /72/ vт 1 (*estrarre*): **ricavare (da)** to extract (from) 2 (*ottenere*): **ricavare (da)** to get (from), obtain (from); **ricavare una gonna da un taglio di stoffa** to make a skirt out of a piece of material; **ricavare un profitto** to make a profit; **cosa ne ricavo io?** what do I get out of it?; **dalla vendita ha ricavato ben poco** he made very little on the sale

ricavato [rika'vato] sm (*di vendite*) proceeds *pl*

ricavo [ri'kavo] sm (*gen*) proceeds *pl*; (*Contabilità*) revenue

ricchezza [rik'kettsa] sf 1 (*di persona, paese*) wealth; (*di terreno, colori*) richness; (*fig: abbondanza*) abundance; **ricchezza di particolari** in great detail; **in questa zona c'è ricchezza di carbone** there's an abundance of coal in this area 2 **ricchezze** sfpl (*averi*) wealth *sg*, riches; (*tesori*) treasures; **ricchezze naturali** natural resources

riccio¹, -cia, -ci, -ce ['rittʃo] agg (*capelli*) curly; (*persona*) curly-haired, with curly hair ♦ sm 1 (*di capelli*) curl; **farsi i ricci** to curl one's hair 2 (*di legno, metallo*) shaving; (*di burro*) curl

riccio², -ci ['rittʃo] sm 1 (*Zool*) hedgehog; (*anche*: **riccio di mare**) sea urchin 2 (*Bot*) chestnut husk

ricciolo ['rittʃolo] sm curl

ricciuto, -a [rit'tʃuto] agg (*testa*) curly; (*persona*) curly-haired

ricco, -a, -chi, -che ['rikko] agg 1 (*gen, anche fig*) rich; (*facoltoso*) rich, wealthy; (*fertile: terra*) rich, fertile; **è di famiglia ricca** he comes from a rich family; **essere ricco sfondato** to be rolling in money; **un piatto molto ricco** a very rich dish; **una ricca mancia** a large tip; **una ricca documentazione** a wealth of documentation 2 **ricco di** (*illustrazioni, idee*) full of; (*fauna, risorse, proteine, calorie*) rich in; **alimento ricco di vitamine** food rich in vitamins; **un ragazzo ricco di fantasia** a boy with a fertile imagination ♦ sm, sf rich person; **i ricchi** the rich, the wealthy

ricerca, -che [ri'tʃerka] sf 1 **ricerca (di)** (*gen*) search (for); (*piacere, gloria*) pursuit (of); (*perfezione*) quest (for); **mettersi alla ricerca di** to go in search of, look *o* search *o* hunt for; **essere alla ricerca di** to be searching *o* looking for; **mia sorella è alla ricerca di un lavoro** my sister is looking for a job; **fare delle ricerche** (*inchiesta*) to make inquiries; **hanno abbandonato le ricerche** the search has been abandoned; **dopo anni di ricerche hanno ritrovato il bambino** after years of searching they found the child; **ricerca di mercato** to market research; **ricerca operativa** operational research 2 (*Univ*): **la ricerca** research; **lavoro di ricerca** piece of research; **la ricerca scientifica** scientific research; **fare delle ricerche su un argomento** to carry out *o* do research into a subject

ricercare [ritʃer'kare] /20/ vт (*onore, gloria*) to seek; (*successo, piacere*) to pursue; (*motivi, cause*) to look for, try to determine; **è ricercato dalla polizia** he's wanted by the police

ricercatezza [ritʃerka'tettsa] sf (*raffinatezza*) refinement; (*pegg*) affectation

ricercato, -a [ritʃer'kato] agg 1 (*latitante*): **è ricercato dalla polizia** he's wanted by the police 2 (*molto richiesto*) in great demand, much sought-after 3 (*raffinato: qualità, gusti, stile*) refined; (*pegg: affettato*) affected; (: *stile*) studied ♦ sm, sf (*criminale*) wanted person

ricercatore, -trice [ritʃerka'tore] SM, SF (*Univ*) researcher

ricetrasmettitore [ritʃetrazmetti'tore] SM, **ricetrasmittente** [ritʃetrazmit'tente] SF transceiver, two-way radio

ricetta [ri'tʃetta] SF 1 (*Med*) prescription; (*fig: antidoto*): **ricetta contro** remedy *o* cure *o* recipe for; **fare una ricetta a qn** to make out a prescription for sb 2 (*Culin*) recipe; **mi dai la ricetta della torta di mele?** could I have the recipe for apple cake?

ricettacolo [ritʃet'takolo] SM (*luogo di raccolta*): **un ricettacolo per i microbi** a breeding-ground for germs; (*pegg: luogo malfamato*) den

ricettario, -ri [ritʃet'tarjo] SM 1 (*Med*) prescription pad 2 (*Culin*) recipe book

ricettatore, -trice [ritʃetta'tore] SM, SF (*Dir*) receiver (of stolen goods)

ricettazione [ritʃettat'tsjone] SF (*Dir*) receiving (stolen goods)

ricettivo, -a [ritʃet'tivo] AGG receptive

ricevente [ritʃe'vente] AGG (*Radio, TV*) receiving ♦ SM, SF (*Comm*) receiver

ricevere [ri'tʃevere] /29/ VT 1 (*gen*) to receive, get; (*voto*) to get; **cara Denise, ho ricevuto ieri la tua lettera...** dear Denise, I got your letter yesterday ...; **non ha ancora ricevuto lo stipendio** he hasn't got his pay yet; **ricevere uno schiaffo** to get *o* be given a slap; **ricevere un rifiuto** to meet with a refusal; **confermiamo di aver ricevuto la merce** (*Comm*) "we acknowledge receipt of the goods" 2 (*accogliere*) to welcome, receive; (*ammettere alla propria presenza*) to see, receive; **ricevere visite** to have visitors; **il dottore riceve il venerdì** the doctor has his surgery (*Brit*) *o* sees patients (*USA*) on Fridays; **il dottore la riceverà subito** the doctor will see you at once; **mi hanno ricevuto in salotto** they showed me into the living room 3 (*TV, Radio*) to pick up, receive

ricevimento [ritʃevi'mento] SM 1 (*festa*) reception; **ricevimento di nozze** wedding reception; **dare un ricevimento** to hold a reception *o* party 2 (*il ricevere*) receiving *no pl*, receipt; **al ricevimento della merce** on receipt of the goods

ricevitore [ritʃevi'tore] SM 1 (*Telec, Radio, Tecn*) receiver 2 **ricevitore delle imposte** tax collector; **ricevitore del lotto** receiver for the State lottery; **ricevitore del totocalcio** football pools collector (*Brit*)

ricevitoria [ritʃevito'ria] SF: **ricevitoria delle imposte** ≈ Inland Revenue (*Brit*) *o* Internal Revenue (*USA*) Office; **ricevitoria del lotto** state lottery office; **ricevitoria del totocalcio** football pools office (*Brit*)

ricevuta [ritʃe'vuta] SF (*gen, anche Comm*) receipt; **mi dà la ricevuta, per favore?** could you give me a receipt please?; **accusare ricevuta di qc** to acknowledge receipt of sth; **ricevuta fiscale** official receipt (for tax purposes); **ricevuta di ritorno** (*Posta*) advice of receipt; **ricevuta di versamento** receipt of payment

ricezione [ritʃet'tsjone] SF (*Radio, TV*) reception

richiamare [rikja'mare] /72/ VT 1 (*gen, al telefono*) to call back; (*Mil, Inform*) to recall; **richiamare qn indietro** to call sb back; **richiamare le truppe** to withdraw the troops; **richiamare qn alla realtà** to bring sb back to earth; **richiamare qn in vita** to bring sb back to life; **richiamerò tra un quarto d'ora** I'll call back in a quarter of an hour 2 (*attrarre: folla*) to attract, draw; **richiamare l'attenzione di qn** to draw sb's attention; **desidero richiamare la vostra attenzione su...** I should like to draw your attention to ... 3 (*ricordare*): **richiamare qc alla memoria di qn** (*sogg: avvenimento*) to remind sb of sth; **è un colore che richiama il verde** it's a greenish colour 4 (*rimproverare*) to reprimand; **richiamare qn all'ordine** to call sb to order; **richiamarsi** VIP: **richiamarsi a** (*riferirsi a*) to refer to

richiamo [ri'kjamo] SM 1 (*di truppe*) recall 2 (*voce, segno*) call; **il richiamo della foresta/della natura** the call of the wild/of nature; **uccello da richiamo** decoy; **servire da richiamo** (*fig: attrazione*) to act as a decoy 3 (*ammonimento*) reprimand; **richiamo all'ordine** call to order 4 (*Med: di vaccinazione*) booster 5 (*rimando*) cross-reference

richiedente [rikje'dente] SM, SF applicant

richiedere [ri'kjedere] /21/ VT IRREG 1 (*chiedere: di nuovo*) to ask again; **richiedere qc** (*in restituzione*) to ask for sth back

2 (*chiedere: prestito, aiuto*) to ask for; (: *passaporto, licenza*) to apply for; **ha richiesto il passaporto più d'un mese fa** he applied for a passport more than a month ago; **hanno richiesto il suo intervento** they asked him to intervene; **tutto ciò non è richiesto** all that is not necessary; **il tuo intervento non era richiesto** no-one asked you to intervene; **essere molto richiesto** to be in great demand 3 (*necessitare*) to need, require; **tutto ciò richiede tempo e pazienza** all this requires time and patience; **un lavoro che richiede molta concentrazione** a job that requires a lot of concentration

richiesto, -a [ri'kjesto] PP di **richiedere**

riciclaggio, -gi [ritʃi'kladdʒo] SM (*di carta, vetro*) recycling; **riciclaggio di denaro sporco** money laundering

riciclare [ritʃi'klare] /72/ VT (*carta, vetro*) to recycle; (*denaro sporco*) to launder

ricino [ri'tʃino] SM (*Bot*) castor-oil plant; **olio di ricino** castor oil

ricognitore [rikoɲɲi'tore] SM (*Aer*) reconnaissance aircraft *pl inv*

ricognizione [rikoɲɲit'tsjone] SF 1 (*Mil*) reconnaissance; **uscire in ricognizione** to reconnoitre 2 (*Dir*) recognition, acknowledgement

ricollegare [rikolle'gare] /80/ VT 1 (*collegare nuovamente: gen*) to join *o* link again 2 (*connettere: fatti*): **ricollegare (a, con)** to connect (with), associate (with); **ricollegarsi** VIP: **ricollegarsi a** (*sogg: fatti: connettersi*) to be connected to, be associated with; **ricollegarsi** VR (*persona: riferirsi*) to refer to

ricolmo, -a [ri'kolmo] AGG: **ricolmo (di)** (*bicchiere*) full to the brim (with); (*stanza, armadio*) full (of); **ricolmo di gioia** overflowing with joy

ricominciare [rikomin'tʃare] /14/ VT to start again, begin again; **ho dovuto ricominciare tutto da capo** I had to start all over again; **ricominciare a fare qc** to begin doing *o* to do sth again, start doing *o* to do sth again; **ha ricominciato a fumare** he's started smoking again; **ah, si ricomincia!** here we go again!; **ha ricominciato con la mania dei francobolli** he's off on his stamp craze again ♦ VI (*aus avere o essere*) (*spettacolo*) to start, begin; **è ricominciato l'inverno** winter is here again; **ricomincia a piovere** it's raining again

ricompensa [rikom'pensa] SF reward

ricompensare [rikompen'sare] /72/ VT to reward

ricomporre [rikom'porre] VB IRREG /77/ VT 1 (*viso, lineamenti*) to recompose 2 (*Tip*) to reset; **ricomporsi** VR to compose o.s., regain one's composure

ricomposto, -a [rikom'posto] PP di **ricomporre**

riconciliare [rikontʃi'ljare] /19/ VT to reconcile; **riconciliarsi** VR 1 **riconciliarsi con qn** to make it up with sb, make one's peace with sb 2 (*uso reciproco*) to be reconciled; (*amici*) to make friends again, make it up again, make peace

riconciliazione [rikontʃiljat'tsjone] SF reconciliation

ricondotto, -a [rikon'dotto] PP di **ricondurre**

ricondurre [rikon'durre] /90/ VT IRREG (*gen*) to bring (*o* take) back

riconferma [rikon'ferma] SF reconfirmation

riconfermare [rikonfer'mare] /72/ VT to reconfirm

ricongiungimento [rikondʒundʒi'mento] SM (*di famiglia, coniugi*) reconciliation; **ricongiungimento familiare** (*Dir: di immigrati*) family reunification

riconoscente [rikonoʃ'ʃente] AGG grateful

riconoscenza [rikonoʃ'ʃentsa] SF gratitude

riconoscere [riko'noʃʃere] VB IRREG /26/ VT 1 (*identificare*) to recognize; (*cadavere, salma*) to identify; **l'ho riconosciuto dalla voce** I recognized him by his voice; **per non farsi riconoscere** so as not to be recognized; **farsi riconoscere** (*esibendo documento*) to provide identification 2 (*ammettere: gen*) to recognize; (: *errore, torto*) to admit, acknowledge; (: *superiorità*) to acknowledge; **devo riconoscere che hai ragione** I must admit you're right; **riconoscere i propri limiti** to recognize one's own limitations; **riconoscere a qn il diritto di fare qc** to acknowledge sb's right to do sth 3 (*Dir*): **riconoscere un figlio** to acknowledge a child; **riconoscere qn colpevole** to find sb guilty; **riconoscersi** VR 1 (*ammettere*): **riconoscersi colpevole** to admit one's guilt; **si riconobbe sconfitto** he admitted he was beaten 2 (*uso reciproco*) to recognize each other

riconoscimento [rikonoʃʃiˈmento] SM (gen, di diritti) recognition; (Dir: di figlio) acknowledgement; (di cadavere, salma) identification; **documento di riconoscimento** means pl of identification; **a riconoscimento dei servizi resi** in recognition of services rendered; **segno di riconoscimento** distinguishing mark; **riconoscimento di caratteri** (Inform) character recognition

riconosciuto, -a [rikonoʃˈʃuto] PP di **riconoscere** ♦ AGG recognized

riconquistare [rikonkwisˈtare] /72/ VT (Mil) to reconquer, recapture; (libertà, stima) to win back

ricoperto, -a [rikoˈperto] PP di **ricoprire** ♦ SM (gelato): **un ricoperto (al cioccolato)** choc-ice (Brit) o ice cream bar (USA) on a stick

ricopiare [rikoˈpjare] /19/ VT to copy; **ricopiare qc in bella (copia)** to make a fair copy of sth

ricoprire [rikoˈprire] VB IRREG /9/ VT 1 (gen): **ricoprire (di)** to cover (with); (divano, poltrona) to re-cover (with); (fig: persona: di gentilezze) to shower (with); **ricoprire un dente** to cap a tooth 2 (carica) to hold; **ricoprirsi** VIP: **ricoprirsi di** (polvere) to become covered in; **il cielo si è ricoperto di nuvole** the sky clouded over; **il prato si è ricoperto di fiori** the field is covered with flowers

ricordare [rikorˈdare] /72/ VT 1 (nome, persona, fatto) to remember, recall; **il mio numero è facile da ricordare** my number is easy to remember; **ricordare di fare qc** to remember to do sth; **ricordare di aver fatto qc** to remember having done o doing sth; **se ben ricordo** if I remember rightly; **ti ricordo con affetto** (nella corrispondenza) I often think of you 2 (far presente ad altri): **ricordare a qn qc/di fare qc** to remind sb of sth/to do sth; **ricordami di spedire la lettera** remind me to post the letter; **ti ricordo che c'ero prima io** I'd like to remind you that I was here first; **scene che ricordano il passato** scenes which recall the past; **mi ricorda molto suo padre** he reminds me a lot of his father 3 (menzionare) to mention 4 (commemorare) to commemorate; **ricordarsi** VIP: **ricordarsi (di)** to remember; **non mi ricordo** I can't remember; **ricordarsi di fare qc** to remember to do sth; **ricordarsi di avere fatto qc** to remember having done o doing sth; **ti ricordi di me?** do you remember me?; **non si è più ricordato di darmi il libro** he forgot to give me the book; **non si ricorda dal naso alla bocca** (fig: fam) he would forget his own name

❏ **ricordare** non si traduce mai con la parola inglese record

ricordo [riˈkɔrdo] SM 1 (memoria) memory; **ho dei bellissimi ricordi dell'Irlanda** I have very happy memories of Ireland; **non ho che un vago ricordo di quella giornata** I have only a vague recollection of that day, I only remember that day vaguely; **vivere di ricordi** to live in the past 2 (oggetto) keepsake; (turistico) souvenir; **prendere/dare qc per o in ricordo** to take/give sth as a keepsake; **questo è un ricordo del viaggio in Marocco** this is a souvenir of my trip to Morocco; **un ricordo di famiglia** a family heirloom ♦ AGG INV (foto) souvenir attr

ricorrente [rikorˈrente] AGG recurring, recurrent ♦ SM, SF (Dir) plaintiff

ricorrenza [rikorˈrentsa] SF 1 (il ricorrere) recurrence 2 (anniversario) anniversary

ricorrere [rikorˈrere] /28/ VI IRREG (aus essere) 1 (ripetersi periodicamente) to recur; **oggi ricorre il 5° anniversario di...** today is the 5th anniversary of ...; **è un elemento che ricorre in tutta la sua poesia** it's a recurring element in all his poetry 2 (far ricorso a): **ricorrere a** (persona) to turn to; (forza, stratagemma) to resort to; **ricorrere alle vie legali** to take legal action 3 (Dir): **ricorrere contro una sentenza** to appeal against a sentence; **ricorrere in appello** to lodge an appeal

ricorso, -a [riˈkorso] PP di **ricorrere** ♦ SM 1 **fare ricorso a** (persona) to turn to; (mezzo, cosa) to resort to; **dovette far ricorso a tutto il suo coraggio** he had to summon all his courage 2 (Dir) appeal; **fare ricorso (contro)** to appeal (against) 3 (il ricorrere) recurrence; **un tipico esempio dei corsi e ricorsi della storia** a typical example of history repeating itself

ricostituente [rikostituˈente] AGG (Med): **cura ricostituente** tonic treatment ♦ SM (Med) tonic

ricostituire [rikostituˈire] /55/ VT (società) to build up again; (governo, partito) to re-form; **ricostituirsi** VIP (gruppo, partito) to re-form

ricostruire [rikostruˈire] /55/ VT (edificio) to rebuild, reconstruct; (testo, fatti, delitto) to reconstruct

ricostruzione [rikostrutˈtsjone] SF (di edificio) reconstruction, rebuilding no pl; (di testo, fatti, delitto) reconstruction

ricotta [riˈkotta] SF ricotta, soft white unsalted cheese made from sheep's milk

ricoverare [rikoveˈrare] /72/ VT (Med): **ricoverare qn in ospedale** to admit sb to the hospital; **far ricoverare qn in ospedale** to have sb admitted to the hospital; **è stato ricoverato d'urgenza (in ospedale)** he has been rushed to the hospital

❏ **ricoverare** non si traduce mai con la parola inglese recover

ricoverato, -a [rikoveˈrato] SM, SF patient

ricovero [riˈkovero] SM 1 (rifugio) shelter, refuge 2 (Med) admission (to the hospital); **foglio di ricovero** admission sheet

❏ **ricovero** non si traduce mai con la parola inglese recovery

ricreare [rikreˈare] /72/ VT 1 (creare di nuovo) to recreate 2 (fig: svagare) to cheer, amuse; **ricreare lo spirito** to restore one's spirits; **ricrearsi** VR (fig: svagarsi, divertirsi) to enjoy o.s.

ricreativo, -a [rikreaˈtivo] AGG recreational; **circolo ricreativo** (per adulti) social club; (per giovani) youth club

ricreazione [rikreatˈtsjone] SF 1 (Scol) break; (alle elementari) break, playtime 2 (svago) recreation, entertainment

ricredersi [riˈkredersi] /29/ VR: **ricredersi (su qc/qn)** to change one's mind (about sth/sb); **mi sono ricreduto sul suo conto** I've changed my mind about him

ricuperare [rikupeˈrare] /72/ VT 1 (gen) to recover; (soldi) to get back; (peso) to put back on; **parte della refurtiva è stata ricuperata** some of the stolen goods have been recovered; **ricuperare il tempo perduto** to make up for lost time; **ricuperare la salute/le forze** to recover (one's health)/one's strength; **ricuperare lo svantaggio** (anche Sport) to close the gap 2 (da naufragio, incendio: persone) to rescue; (: salme) to recover; (: oggetti, relitto) to salvage 3 (disadattato, ex detenuto) to rehabilitate 4 (usare di nuovo: cascami, rottami) to re-use 5 (Sport): **ricuperare una partita** to play a match which had been postponed

ricupero [riˈkupero] SM (gen) recovery; (di relitto) salvaging; (di disadattato, ex detenuto) rehabilitation; **di ricupero** (merce, materiali) salvage attr; **capacità di ricupero** resilience; **partita di ricupero** (Sport) postponed match; **minuti di ricupero** (Sport) injury time; **ricupero (di) crediti** (Comm) debt collection

ricusare [rikuˈzare] /72/ VT 1 (offerta, carica) to decline, to refuse 2 (Dir): **ricusare un giudice** to challenge a judge

ridacchiare [ridakˈkjare] /19/ VI (aus avere) to snigger

ridare [riˈdare] /33/ VT IRREG (oggetto) to give back, return; (salute, felicità) to restore; **me lo presti? te lo ridò domani** will you lend it to me? I'll give it back to you tomorrow

ridda [ˈridda] SF (di pensieri) jumble

ridente [riˈdente] AGG (occhi, volto) smiling; (paesaggio) delightful

ridere [ˈridere] VB IRREG /89/ VI (aus avere) (gen) to laugh; (deridere, beffare): **ridere di** to laugh at, make fun of; **perché ridi?** why are you laughing?; **ridere alle spalle di qn, ridere dietro a qn** to laugh behind sb's back; **ridere in faccia a qn** to laugh in sb's face; **ridere sotto i baffi** to laugh up one's sleeve; **ridere a denti stretti** to give a forced laugh; **cerchiamo di riderci sopra** let's try and see the funny side of it; **ridendo e scherzando si è fatto tardi** (fig) what with one thing and another, it got late; **ridere di cuore** o **di gusto** to laugh heartily; **ridere fino alle lacrime** to laugh till one cries; **far ridere qn** to make sb laugh; **ma non farmi ridere!** don't be ridiculous!, don't make me laugh!; **non c'è niente da ridere, c'è poco da ridere** it's not a laughing matter, it's not funny; **che c'è da ridere?** what's so funny?; **tutti sono scoppiati a ridere** they all burst out laughing; **lo ha detto per ridere** he was only joking, he said it in fun; **si fa così per ridere** we're just joking; **è roba da ridere** (facile) it's nothing, it's dead easy (*fam*); **che ridere!** what a laugh!; **c'è da morire dal ridere!** it's hilarious!, it's really funny!; **le ridevano gli occhi** her eyes sparkled; **ride bene chi ride ultimo** (*Proverbio*) he who laughs last laughs longest (*Brit*) *o* (*USA*) best; **ridersi** VIP: **ridersela (di qc)** to laugh (at sth); **se la rideva** he had a laugh to himself

ridestare [rides'tare] /72/ VT (*fig: ricordi, passioni*) to reawaken; **ridestarsi** VIP (*fig: odio*) to be roused again; (*amore, speranza*) to be rekindled

ridetto, -a [ri'detto] PP *di* **ridire**

ridicolaggine [ridiko'laddʒine] SF (*di situazione*) absurdity; (*cosa detta o fatta*) nonsense *no pl*

ridicolizzare [ridikolid'dzare] /72/ VT to ridicule

ridicolo [ri'dikolo] AGG (*gen*) ridiculous, absurd; **non essere ridicolo! io non c'entro niente!** don't be ridiculous! it's nothing to do with me!; **rendersi ridicolo** to make a fool of o.s. ♦ SM: **il ridicolo della situazione** the absurdity of the situation; **il ridicolo della storia era che...** the ridiculous *o* absurd thing about it was ...; **cadere nel ridicolo** to become ridiculous; **mettere in ridicolo** to ridicule; **coprirsi di ridicolo** to make a laughing stock of o.s.

ridimensionamento [ridimensjona'mento] SM reorganization; (*di fatto storico*) reappraisal

ridimensionare [ridimensjo'nare] /72/ VT (*ditta, industria*) to reorganize; (*fig: problema, autore, fatto storico*) to put in perspective, see in the right perspective; **ridimensionarsi** VIP (*sogni, ambizioni*) to become more realistic

ridire [ri'dire] /38/ VT IRREG 1 (*ripetere, riferire*) to repeat; **te l'ho detto e ridetto mille volte** I've told you over and over again 2 (*criticare*): **trovare da ridire (su qc/qn)** to find fault (with sth/sb), criticize (sb/sth); **trova sempre da ridire sui miei amici** she's always criticizing my friends; **che c'è da ridire?** what's your objection?

ridondante [ridon'dante] AGG (*linguaggio, frase*) flowery; (*discorso*) bombastic; **uno stile ridondante** (*gonfio*) a pompous style

ridosso [ri'dɔsso] **a ridosso di** AVV (*dietro*) behind; (*contro*) against; **costruire una casa a ridosso di una montagna** to build a house in the shelter of a mountain

ridotto, -a [ri'dotto] PP *di* **ridurre** ♦ AGG (*misura, formato*) small; (*versione, edizione*) abridged; (*tariffa*) cheap; (*prezzo*) reduced, cut; **marcia ridotta** (*Aut*) low gear ratio ♦ SM (*Teatro*) foyer

riduco *ecc* [ri'duko] VB *vedi* **ridurre**

ridurre [ri'durre] VB IRREG /90/ VT 1 (*gen, anche Mat*) to reduce; (*prezzo*) to reduce, cut, bring down; (*pressione*) to lessen; (*produzione*) to cut (back), lower; (*spese*) to cut down on, cut back on; **hanno ridotto il prezzo da 50 a 35 sterline** the price was cut from 50 pounds to 35; **ho dovuto ridurre il tema a 60 righe** I had to cut the essay to 60 lines 2 (*opera letteraria: per la radio, TV*) to adapt; (: *accorciare*) to abridge; (: *brano musicale*) to arrange 3 (*fraseologia*): **ridurre qc in cenere** to reduce sth to ashes; **ridurre qn in poltiglia** (*fig*) to make mincemeat of sb; **è proprio ridotto male** *o* **mal ridotto** (*oggetto*) it's really in bad condition; (*persona*) he's really in a bad way ♦ **ridursi** VIP 1 (*quantità*): **ridursi (a)** to be reduced (to); (*fig: questione, problema*) to come down (to); **il livello si è ridotto di un decimo** the level dropped by a tenth 2 (*persona*): **ridursi male** to be in a bad state *o* way; **ridursi pelle e ossa** to be reduced to skin and bone; **ridursi a uno straccio** to be washed out; **si è ridotto a mendicare** he was reduced to begging; **come ti sei ridotto!** what a state you're in!

ridussi *ecc* [ri'dussi] VB *vedi* **ridurre**

riduttore [ridut'tore] SM (*Tecn, Chim, Elettr*) reducer

riduzione [ridut'tsjone] SF 1 (*diminuzione: di salario, personale*): **riduzione (di)** reduction (in), cut (in) 2 (*sconto*) reduction, discount; **una riduzione del 10%** a 10% reduction *o* discount 3 (*di opera letteraria: adattamento*) adaptation; (: *accorciamento*) abridgement; **riduzione televisiva a cura di...** adapted for television by ... 4 (*Mat, Chim, Med*) reduction

riebbi *ecc* [ri'ebbi] VB *vedi* **riavere**

riecheggiare [rieked'dʒare] /62/ VI (*aus essere*) to re-echo; **in questi versi riecheggiano motivi leopardiani** in these lines we find echoes of Leopardi

rieducare [riedu'kare] /20/ VT (*persona, arto*) to re-educate; (*malato*) to rehabilitate

rieducazione [riedukat'tsjone] SF (*vedi vb*) re-education; rehabilitation; **centro di rieducazione** rehabilitation centre

rieleggere [rie'leddʒere] /61/ VT IRREG to re-elect

rieletto, -a [rie'letto] PP *di* **rieleggere**

riempimento [riempi'mento] SM filling (up); (*Edil*): **materiali di riempimento** filling *sg*

riempire [riem'pire] VB IRREG /91/ VT (*gen, anche fig*): **riempire (di)** to fill *o* fill up (with); (*Culin: farcire*) to stuff (with); **ho riempito il termos di caffè, va bene?** I've filled the flask with coffee, okay?; **riempire un modulo** to fill in *o* out a form; **riempirsi le tasche di** to fill one's pockets with; **gli hanno riempito la testa di sciocchezze** they filled his head with nonsense; **riempirsi** VIP (*gen*): **riempirsi (di)** to fill *o* fill up (with); **quel quadro si è riempito di polvere** that painting is covered in dust; **riempirsi** VR: **riempirsi di** (*cibo*) to stuff o.s. with

riempitivo [riempi'tivo] AGG filling ♦ SM (*anche fig*) filler

rientranza [rien'trantsa] SF (*di costruzione*) recess; (*di costa*) indentation

rientrare [rien'trare] /72/ VI (*aus essere*) 1 (*entrare di nuovo*) to come (*o* go) back in 2 (*ritornare*) to return, get back; **rientrare (a casa)** to get back home; **sono rientrato molto tardi** I got back very late; **no, Daniela non è ancora rientrata** no, Daniela isn't back yet; **rientrare alla base** (*Mil*) to return to base; **rientrare in possesso di qc** to regain possession of sth 3 (*fig: far parte di, essere incluso*): **rientrare in** to be included among, form part of; **non rientra nei miei doveri** it isn't my duty; **non rientriamo nelle spese** we are not within our budget 4 (*superficie, linea*) to curve inwards, go in; (*costa*) to be indented

rientro [ri'entro] SM (*gen, ritorno*) return; (*di astronave*) re-entry; **l'ora del rientro** (*dal lavoro*) the evening rush hour; **è cominciato il grande rientro (dalle vacanze)** everyone is coming back from holiday

riepilogare [riepilo'gare] /80/ VT (*discorso, fatti*) to summarize; **dunque, riepilogando...** to sum up, then ...

riepilogo, -ghi [rie'pilogo] SM recapitulation; **fare un riepilogo di qc** to summarize sth

riesame [rie'zame] SM re-examination

riesaminare [riezami'nare] /72/ VT to re-examine

riesco *ecc* [ri'esko] VB *vedi* **riuscire**

riessere [ri'essere] /51/ VI (*aus essere*) **ci risiamo!** (*fam*) we're back to this again!, here we go again!

rievocare [rievo'kare] /20/ VT (*passato*) to recall; (*commemorare: figura, meriti*) to commemorate

rievocazione [rievokat'tsjone] SF (*vedi vb*) recalling; commemoration

rifacimento [rifatʃi'mento] SM (*di film*) remake; (*di opera letteraria*) rehashing

rifare [ri'fare] VB IRREG /53/ VT (*ricominciare*) to redo, do again; (*ricostruire*) to make again; (*nodo*) to tie again, do up again; **lo devo rifare da capo** I've got to do it all over again; **è tutto da rifare!** it will have to be completely redone!; **stai tranquillo, non lo rifarà** don't worry, she won't do it again; **rifarsi la bocca** (*anche fig*) to take away a bad taste; **rifarsi il naso** to have a nose job; **rifarsi gli occhi** to look at something pleasant for a change; **rifare il letto** to make the bed; **rifarsi il trucco** to touch up one's make-up; **rifarsi una vita** to make a new life for o.s.; **rifarsi una verginità** to try to clear one's name; **rifarsi** VIP 1 **rifarsi vivo** to re-appear, turn up again 2 (*ricuperare*): **rifarsi di** (*perdita, spesa*) to recover from; **rifarsi del tempo perduto** to make up for lost time; **rifarsi di qc su qn** (*vendicarsi*) to get one's own back on sb for sth, get even with sb for sth 3 (*riferirsi*): **rifarsi a** (*periodo, fenomeno storico*) to go back to; (*stile, autore*) to follow

rifatto, -a [ri'fatto] PP *di* **rifare**

riferimento [riferi'mento] SM reference; **in** *o* **con riferimento a, facendo riferimento a** with reference to; **in riferimento alla Vostra del...** with reference to your letter of...; **far riferimento a** to refer to; **nell'articolo si fa riferimento al recente scandalo** there's a reference in the article to the recent scandal; **punto di riferimento** (*anche fig*) reference point

riferire [rife'rire] /55/ VT 1 (*raccontare, riportare*) to report; **andare a riferire qc a qn** to go and tell sb sth; **è andato a riferire tutto al professore** he went and told the teacher everything; **riferirò** I'll pass on the message 2 (*attribuire*):

riferire qc a to attribute sth to ♦ VI (aus avere) **riferire (su qc)** to make o do a report (on sth); **riferirsi** VIP: **riferirsi a** to refer to; **non ho capito a cosa si riferisse** I didn't understand what he was referring to

rifilare [rifi'lare] /72/ VT 1 (fam: affibbiare): **rifilare qc a qn** to palm sth off on sb; **gli ho rifilato un ceffone** I gave him a slap 2 (tagliare a filo) to trim

rifinire [rifi'nire] /55/ VT (lavoro) to finish off; (opera d'arte, vestito) to put the finishing touches to

rifinitura [rifini'tura] SF (gen) finishing touch; (di mobile, auto) finish no pl

rifiutare [rifju'tare] /72/ VT (gen) to refuse; (invito, offerta) to turn down, decline; (pretendente) to turn down; **rifiutare qc a qn** to deny sb sth; **rifiutare di fare qc** to refuse to do sth; **ha rifiutato di pagare la sua parte** he refused to pay his share; **rifiutarsi** VIP: **rifiutarsi di fare qc** to refuse to do sth

rifiuto [ri'fjuto] SM 1 (diniego) refusal; **opporre un secco rifiuto** to flatly refuse 2 (scarto) waste; **rifiuti** SMPL (immondizie) refuse sg, rubbish (Brit) sg, garbage (USA), trash (USA); **i rifiuti della società** (fig) the dregs of society; **rifiuti solidi urbani** solid urban waste

riflessione [rifles'sjone] SF 1 (meditazione) reflection, meditation, thought; (osservazione) observation, remark; **dopo matura riflessione** after due consideration; **ha risposto dopo un attimo di riflessione** she replied after a moment's thought; **ha fatto delle interessanti riflessioni** he made some interesting observations 2 (Fis) reflection

riflessivo, -a [rifles'sivo] AGG 1 (persona) thoughtful, reflective 2 (Gramm) reflexive

riflesso, -a [ri'flesso] PP di **riflettere** ♦ AGG (immagine) reflected; (atto) reflex attr ♦ SM 1 (di luce) reflection; (di capelli: naturale) light; (: artificiale) highlight; (fig: ripercussione) effect, repercussion; **il riflesso della luna sul mare** the reflection of the moon in the sea; **di riflesso** indirectly 2 (Fisiologia) reflex; **avere i riflessi pronti** to have quick reflexes; **quando si beve non si hanno i riflessi pronti** your reflexes are slower when you've been drinking; **riflesso condizionato** conditioned reflex

riflessologia [riflessolod'ʒia] SF: **riflessologia (plantare)** reflexology

riflettere [ri'flettere] VB IRREG /92/ VI (aus avere) **riflettere (su qc)** (meditare) to reflect (upon sth); (pensare) to think (over sth); **se ti fermi a riflettere** if you stop and think; **agire senza riflettere** to act without thinking; **ci ho riflettuto su e ho deciso di accettare** I've thought about it and have decided to accept; **riflettendoci su...** on reflection ... ♦ VT (Fis, fig) to reflect; **riflettersi** VR 1 (rispecchiarsi, anche fig) to be reflected 2 (ripercuotersi): **riflettersi su** to have repercussions on

riflettore [riflet'tore] SM 1 (Fis, Elettr) reflector; (Teatro, TV) spotlight; (proiettore) floodlight; (Mil) searchlight; **essere sotto i riflettori** (fig) to be in the limelight 2 (telescopio) reflecting telescope

riflusso [ri'flusso] SM (gen) flowing back; (di sangue) flow; (di acqua, marea) ebb; **flusso e riflusso** ebb and flow; **un'epoca di riflusso** an era of nostalgia

rifocillarsi [rifotʃil'larsi] /72/ VR to take refreshment

rifondazione [rifondat'tsjone] SF refounding

rifondere [ri'fondere] /25/ VT IRREG 1 (rimborsare) to refund, reimburse; **rifondere le spese a qn** to refund sb's expenses; **rifondere i danni a qn** to compensate sb for damages 2 (metalli, cera) to remelt, melt down again

riforma [ri'forma] SF 1 (gen) reform; (Rel): **la Riforma** the Reformation; **la riforma del sistema sanitario** the reform of the health service 2 (Mil: di recluta) declaration of unfitness for service; (: di soldato) discharge (on health grounds)

riformare [rifor'mare] /72/ VT 1 (formare di nuovo) to form again, re-form 2 (Rel, Pol) to reform; (Mil: recluta) to declare unfit for military service; (: soldato) to discharge, invalid out; **riformarsi** VIP (formarsi di nuovo) to form again, re-form

riformatore, -trice [riforma'tore] AGG reforming ♦ SM, SF reformer

riformatorio, -ri [riforma'tɔrjo] SM community home (Brit), reformatory (USA)

riformista, -i, -e [rifor'mista] AGG, SM, SF reformist

rifornimento [riforni'mento] SM 1 (operazione) supplying, providing; (di carburante) refuelling; **fare rifornimento di** (viveri) to stock up with; (benzina) to fill up with; **stazione di rifornimento** filling o petrol (Brit) o gas (USA) station 2 **rifornimenti** SMPL (scorte) stocks, supplies, provisions

rifornire [rifor'nire] /55/ VT: **rifornire di** to supply o provide with; **rifornirsi** VR: **rifornirsi di** (provviste) to get in a supply of, stock up with; (benzina) to re-fuel (with), fill up (with)

rifrangere [ri'frandʒere] VB IRREG /37/ VT (Fis) to refract; **rifrangersi** VIP to be refracted

rifratto, -a [ri'fratto] PP di **rifrangere**

rifrazione [rifrat'tsjone] SF (Fis) refraction

rifuggire [rifud'dʒire] /31/ VI (aus essere) **rifuggire da qc** to be averse to sth, shun sth

rifugiarsi [rifu'dʒarsi] /62/ VIP: **rifugiarsi in**; (gen, anche fig) to take refuge in; (da pioggia, freddo) to (take) shelter in

rifugiato, -a [rifu'dʒato] SM, SF refugee

rifugio, -gi [ri'fudʒo] SM (gen) shelter, refuge; (in montagna) shelter; (fig) refuge; **cercare rifugio in qc/presso qn** to seek refuge in sth/with sb; **rifugio antiaereo** air-raid shelter; **rifugio antiatomico** fallout shelter

rifuso, -a [ri'fuzo] PP di **rifondere**

riga, -ghe ['riga] SF 1 (linea) line; (striscia) stripe; **a righe** (foglio) lined; (tessuto) striped; **giallo a righe rosse** yellow with red stripes 2 (scritta) line; **ne ho letto solo poche righe** I just read a few lines; **buttare giù due righe** (note) to jot down a few notes; **mandami due righe appena arrivi** drop me a line as soon as you arrive 3 (Mil, Scol: fila) line, row; (Sport) line; **rompete le righe!** break ranks!; **mettersi in riga** to line up; **mettere qn in riga** (fig) to make sb toe the line; **rimettersi in riga** (fig) to get back into line; **sopra le righe** (fig) over the top 4 (righello) ruler 5 (scriminatura) parting; **farsi la riga in mezzo/da una parte** to put one's hair in a middle parting/side parting

rigagnolo [ri'gaɲɲolo] SM rivulet

rigare [ri'gare] /80/ VT (pagina, foglio) to rule; (superficie: sfregiare) to score; **col volto rigato di lacrime** with a tearstained face ♦ VI (aus avere) (fig): **rigare dritto** to toe the line, behave; **ti conviene rigare dritto!** you'd better behave!

rigatoni [riga'toni] SMPL (Culin) rigatoni, short, ridged pasta shapes

rigattiere [rigat'tjere] SM junk dealer, secondhand dealer

rigatura [riga'tura] SF (di pagina, quaderno) lining, ruling; (di fucile) rifling

rigenerare [ridʒene'rare] /72/ VT (gen, anche Tecn) to regenerate; (forze) to restore; (gomma) to retread, remould (Brit), recap (USA); **gomma rigenerata** retread, remould, recap; **rigenerarsi** VIP (gen) to regenerate; (ramo, tumore) to regenerate, grow again

rigenerazione [ridʒenerat'tsjone] SF regeneration

rigettare [ridʒet'tare] /72/ VT 1 (gettare: di nuovo) to throw again; (: indietro) to throw back 2 (respingere: proposta) to reject, turn down; (: Bio, Med) to reject 3 (vomitare) to vomit, bring o throw up; **rigettarsi** VR: **rigettarsi in acqua** to jump back into the water

rigetto [ri'dʒetto] SM (gen, anche Med) rejection; **crisi di rigetto** (Med) rejection crisis; (fig) total rejection

righello [ri'gello] SM ruler

righerò ecc [rige'rɔ] VB vedi **rigare**

rigidezza [ridʒi'dettsa], **rigidità** [ridʒidi'ta] SF (gen) rigidity; (di membra) stiffness; (fig: di clima) harshness, severity, rigours pl (Brit), rigors pl (USA); (: severità) strictness, sternness; **rigidità cadaverica** rigor mortis

rigido, -a ['ridʒido] AGG (gen) rigid; (membra, berretto, colletto) stiff; (fig: clima, inverno) harsh, severe; (: disciplina, principi) strict

rigirare [ridʒi'rare] /72/ VT (gen) to turn; **rigirare il discorso** to change the subject; **rigirare qc tra le mani** to turn sth over in one's hands; **rigirarsi** VR (voltarsi: di nuovo) to turn round; (: nel letto) to turn over; **girarsi e rigirarsi nel letto** to toss and turn in bed

rigo, -ghi ['rigo] SM (linea) line; (Mus) staff, stave

rigoglioso, -a [rigoʎ'ʎoso] AGG (pianta, giardino) luxuriant; (fig: commercio, sviluppo) thriving

rigonfiamento [rigonfja'mento] SM (gonfiore: su parte del corpo) swelling; (: su legno, intonaco) bulge

rigonfio, -fia, -fi, -fie [riˈɡonfjo] AGG (*vela*) full; (*grembiule, sporta*): **rigonfio di** bulging with

rigore [riˈɡore] SM **1** (*di sentenza, legge*) severity; (*di disciplina*) strictness, severity; (*di clima*) severity, harshness, rigours *pl* (*Brit*), rigors *pl* (*USA*); **punire qn con rigore** to punish sb severely; **mettere qn in cella di rigore** (*Mil*) to put sb in solitary confinement; **essere di rigore** (*d'obbligo*) to be compulsory; **"è di rigore l'abito da sera"** "evening dress"; **a rigor di termini** *o* **di logica** strictly speaking; **i rigori dell'inverno** the rigo(u)rs of winter **2** (*Calcio: anche*: **calcio di rigore**) penalty; **battere un rigore** to take a penalty; **segnare un rigore** to score from a penalty; **area di rigore** penalty area *o* box; **vincere ai rigori** to win on penalties

rigorosità [riɡorosiˈta] SF (*precisione: di conclusioni*) rigour (*Brit*), rigor (*USA*); (*severità: di costumi*) strictness

rigoroso, -a [riɡoˈroso] AGG (*definizione, logica*) rigorous, exact; (*punizione*) severe, harsh; (*persona, ordine*) strict

rigovernare [riɡoverˈnare] /72/ VT (*piatti, stoviglie*) to wash (up); **non ho ancora rigovernato** I haven't done the washing-up yet

riguardare [riɡwarˈdare] /72/ VT **1** (*concernere*) to concern, regard; **per quel che mi riguarda** as far as I'm concerned; **per quel che mi riguarda la faccenda è chiusa** as far as I'm concerned the matter is closed; **è un problema che ci riguarda tutti** it's a problem which concerns us all; **è un libro che riguarda la vita dei contadini** it's a book which deals with *o* looks at the life of country people; **sono affari che non ti riguardano** it's none of your business **2** (*curare, tenere da conto*) to look after, take care of **3** (*guardare di nuovo*) to look at again, take another look at; (*controllare*) to check; **riguardarsi** VR (*aver cura di sé*) to look after o.s., take care of o.s.; **ti devi riguardare dalle correnti d'aria** you should stay out of draughts (*Brit*) *o* drafts (*USA*)

riguardo [riˈɡwardo] SM **1** (*rispetto*) respect; (*considerazione*) consideration, regard; **non ha alcun riguardo per gli altri** he has no consideration for other people; **per riguardo a** out of respect for; **trattare qn col massimo riguardo** to treat sb with the greatest respect; **mancare di riguardo verso** *o* **a qn** to be disrespectful towards sb; **ospite/persona di riguardo** very important guest/person; **aver riguardo delle cose altrui** to respect other people's property; **agire/parlare senza (tanti) riguardi** to act/speak freely **2 riguardo a** (*a proposito di*) regarding, concerning, as regards, with regard to, about; **cos'hai deciso di fare riguardo all'offerta di lavoro?** what have you decided to do about the job offer?; **riguardo a me** as far as I'm concerned

riguardoso, -a [riɡwarˈdoso] AGG (*rispettoso*) respectful; (*premuroso*) considerate, thoughtful

rigurgitare [riɡurdʒiˈtare] /72/ VI (*aus* **essere**) **rigurgitare da** to gush out from ♦ VT (*vomitare*) to bring up

rigurgito [riˈɡurdʒito] SM (*Med*) regurgitation; (*fig: ritorno, risveglio*) revival

rilanciare [rilanˈtʃare] /14/ VT (*lanciare di nuovo: gen*) to throw again; (: *moda*) to bring back; (: *prodotto*) to relaunch; (*Carte*) to raise; **rilanciare un'offerta** (*asta*) to make a higher bid

rilancio, -ci [riˈlantʃo] SM (*di prodotto*) relaunching; (*Carte: di offerta*) raising

rilasciare [rilaʃˈʃare] /14/ VT **1** (*Amm: passaporto, certificato*) to issue; (*intervista*) to give; **rilasciare una dichiarazione** to make a statement **2** (*persona, prigioniero*) to release; **gli ostaggi sono stati rilasciati ieri** the hostages were released yesterday **3** (*muscoli, tensione, nervi*) to relax; **rilasciarsi** VIP to relax

rilascio, -sci [riˈlaʃʃo] SM (*di documento*) issue; (*di prigioniero*) release

rilassamento [rilassaˈmento] SM (*gen, anche Med*) relaxation

rilassare [rilasˈsare] /72/ VT (*distendere: nervi, muscoli*) to relax; (: *persona*) to help to relax; **rilassarsi** VR (*gen*) to relax; **rilassarsi** VIP (*fig: disciplina*) to become slack

rilassatezza [rilassaˈtettsa] SF (*fig: di costumi, disciplina*) laxity

rilassato, -a [rilasˈsato] AGG (*persona, muscoli*) relaxed; (*disciplina, costumi*) lax

rilegare [rileˈɡare] /80/ VT (*libro, volume*) to bind

rilegatura [rileɡaˈtura] SF binding

rileggere [riˈleddʒere] /61/ VT IRREG (*leggere di nuovo*) to read

again, reread; (*per correggere*) to read over; **l'ho letto e riletto cento volte** I've read it over and over again

rilento [riˈlento] **a rilento** AVV slowly; **gli affari vanno a rilento** business is slow

riletto, -a [riˈletto] PP *di* **rileggere**

rilettura [riletˈtura] SF (*vedi vt*) rereading; reading over; (*nuova interpretazione*) new interpretation

rilevamento [rilevaˈmento] SM (*topografico, statistico, geologico*) survey; (*Naut*) bearing

rilevante [rileˈvante] AGG (*notevole*) remarkable, considerable; (*importante*) important
❏ **rilevante** non si traduce mai con la parola inglese *relevant*

rilevanza [rileˈvantsa] SF importance

rilevare [rileˈvare] /72/ VT **1** (*notare*) to notice; **dai sintomi non si rileva alcun pericolo immediato** going by the symptoms, there is no immediate danger; **rilevo con soddisfazione che...** I note with satisfaction that ...; **far rilevare a qn che...** to point out to sb that ... **2** (*raccogliere: dati*) to gather, collect; (*Topografia*) to survey; (*Naut: posizione*) to plot; **la polizia non ha potuto rilevare alcun indizio** the police have been unable to find any evidence **3** (*Comm: negozio, ditta*) to take over **4** (*Mil: sentinella*) to relieve **5** (*levare di nuovo*) to take off again

rilevazione [rilevatˈtsjone] SF survey

rilievo [riˈljevo] SM **1** (*gen, anche Arte, Geog*) relief; **alto/basso rilievo** high/bas-relief; **i rilievi alpini** the Alps; **in rilievo** (*gen*) in relief; (*ricamo*) raised; **carta in rilievo** relief map **2** (*importanza*) importance; **dar rilievo a** *o* **mettere in rilievo qc** (*fig*) to stress *o* highlight sth, bring sth out; **di poco/nessun rilievo** (*fig*) of little/no importance; **un personaggio di rilievo** an important person **3** (*osservazione*) point, remark **4** (*Topografia, Statistica*) survey

riluttante [rilutˈtante] AGG reluctant; **essere riluttante a fare qc** to be reluctant to do sth

riluttanza [rilutˈtantsa] SF (*gen*) reluctance; **con riluttanza** reluctantly

rima [ˈrima] SF (*gen*) rhyme; (*verso*) verse; **far rima con** to rhyme with; **"head" fa rima con "red"** "head" rhymes with "red"; **mettere in rima** to put into rhyme; **rispondere a qn per le rime** (*fig*) to give as good as one gets; **rima baciata** rhyming couplet; **rime alternate** alternate rhymes

rimandare [rimanˈdare] /72/ VT **1** (*mandare: di nuovo*) to send again; (: *indietro*) to send back, return; **rimandare qn a** (*fig: far riferimento*) to refer sb to **2** (*posporre: partenza, appuntamento*): **rimandare (a)** to postpone (till), put off (till); **abbiamo dovuto rimandare la gita di qualche giorno** we had to put off the trip for a few days; **non rimandare a domani quel che puoi fare oggi** (*Proverbio*) don't put off till tomorrow what you can do today **3** (*Scol, Brit*): **rimandare qn (a settembre)** to make sb resit (in September); **essere rimandato** to have to resit one's exams

rimando [riˈmando] SM (*in testo*) cross-reference; **di rimando** (*fig*) in return

rimaneggiare [rimaneddʒare] /62/ VT (*testo*) to reshape, recast; (*ministero*) to reshuffle

rimanente [rimaˈnente] AGG remaining ♦ SM (*resto*): **il rimanente** the rest, the remainder; **i** (*o* **le**) **rimanenti** (*persone*) the rest *pl* (of them), the others

rimanenza [rimaˈnentsa] SF (*gen*) rest, remainder; **rimanenze di magazzino** (*Comm*) left-over stock *sg*, unsold stock *sg*

rimanere [rimaˈnere] /93/ VI IRREG (*aus* **essere**) **1** (*in luogo*) to stay, remain; **mi piacerebbe rimanere qualche altro giorno** I'd like to stay a few more days; **rimanere a casa/a letto** to stay *o* remain at home/in bed; **rimanere a cena** to stay for dinner; **rimanere a guardare la televisione** to stay and watch television; **che rimanga tra noi** (*fig: segreto*) this is just between ourselves; **dove eravamo rimasti?** (*fig*) where were we? **2** (*in una condizione*) to stay, remain; **rimanere in piedi** (*non sedersi*) to remain standing; (*non coricarsi*) to stay up; **rimanere senza benzina/pane** to run out of petrol (*Brit*) *o* gas (*USA*)/bread; **rimanere al buio/senz'acqua** to have one's electricity *o* water cut off; **rimanere indietro** to be left behind; **rimanere indietro col lavoro/con l'affitto** (*fig*) to fall behind with one's work/with the rent; **rimaniamo**

d'accordo così that's agreed then, that's settled then; **rimanere amici** to remain friends; **rimanere in buoni rapporti** to remain on good terms; **rimanere senza parole** to be (left) speechless; **sono rimasto senza parole** I was speechless; **rimanere o rimanerci male** to be hurt o offended; **c'è rimasta molto male** she was really hurt; **rimanere o rimanerci secco** (fam: morire) to drop dead; **rimanere sorpreso** to be surprised **3** (divenire): **rimanere orfano** to become o be left an orphan; **rimanere vedovo** to be left a widower; **rimanere incinta** to get pregnant; **rimanere ferito** to be injured; **è rimasto ferito in un incidente d'auto** he was injured in a car accident **4** (sussistere) to be left, remain; **è l'unico parente che le rimane** he's her only remaining relative; **coi pochi soldi che mi rimangono** with what little money I have left; **rimangono da fare 15 km** there are still 15 km to go; **ne è rimasto solo uno** there's only one left; **ne rimane ancora un po'** there's still some left; **non rimane più niente** there's nothing left; **rimane ancora molto da fare** there's still a lot to do; **non ti rimane altro (da fare) che accettare** all you can do is accept; **mi rimani solo tu** you're all I have left; **mi rimane ben poco da dire se non...** I've little left to say except ...; **rimane da vedere se...** it remains to be seen whether ...

rimangiare [riman'dʒare] /62/ vᴛ to eat again; **rimangiarsi la parola/una promessa** (fig) to go back on one's word/ one's promise

rimango ecc [ri'mango] vʙ vedi **rimanere**

rimare [ri'mare] /72/ vᴛ, vɪ (aus avere) to rhyme

rimarginare [rimardʒi'nare] /72/ vᴛ, vɪ (aus essere) to heal; **rimarginarsi** vɪᴘ to heal

rimasto, -a [ri'masto] ᴘᴘ di **rimanere**

rimasuglio, -gli [rima'suʎʎo] ꜱᴍ (di stoffa) remnant; **rimasugli** ꜱᴍᴘʟ leftovers pl

rimbalzare [rimbal'tsare] /72/ vɪ (aus avere o essere) **rimbalzare (su)** (pavimento) to bounce (off); (muro) to rebound (off), bounce back; (sogg: proiettile) to ricochet (off); **far rimbalzare una palla** to bounce a ball

rimbalzo [rim'baltso] ꜱᴍ (di palla) bounce; (di proiettile) ricochet; **di rimbalzo** (on the rebound; (fig) indirectly

rimbambire [rimbam'bire] /55/ vɪ (aus essere), **rimbambirsi** vɪᴘ to become stupid, grow foolish; **rimbambire o rimbambirsi con l'età** to become senile

rimbambito, -a [rimbam'bito] ᴀɢɢ (pegg) senile

rimbeccare [rimbek'kare] /20/ vᴛ (persona) to answer back; (offesa) to return; **rimbeccarsi** vʀ (uso reciproco: litigare) to bicker

rimbecillire [rimbetʃil'lire] /55/ vᴛ, vɪ, vɪᴘ = **rincretinire**

rimboccare [rimbok'kare] /20/ vᴛ (orlo) to turn up; (coperta) to tuck in; (pantaloni) to turn o roll up; **rimboccarsi le maniche** (anche fig) to roll up one's sleeves

rimbombare [rimbom'bare] /72/ vɪ (aus avere o essere) (suono, passi) to resound; (tuono) to roar, rumble; (cannonata) to roar, thunder; (voce) boom

rimbombo [rim'bombo] ꜱᴍ (suono) sound; (di voce) boom; (di tuono) roar, rumble; (di cannonata) roar, thunder

rimborsare [rimbor'sare] /72/ vᴛ (persona) to pay back, reimburse; (spese, biglietto) to refund, reimburse; **rimborsare qc a qn** to reimburse sb for sth; **mi hanno rimborsato il prezzo del biglietto** they refunded the price of the ticket

rimborso [rim'borso] ꜱᴍ repayment, reimbursement; (di spese, biglietto) refund; **rimborso d'imposta** tax rebate

rimboschimento [rimboski'mento] ꜱᴍ re(af)forestation

rimboschire [rimbos'kire] /55/ vᴛ to re(af)forest

rimbrottare [rimbrot'tare] /72/ vᴛ to reproach

rimbrotto [rim'brɔtto] ꜱᴍ reproach; **fare un rimbrotto a qn** to reproach sb

rimediare [rime'djare] /19/ vɪ (gen) to remedy; **rimediare a qc** to remedy sth; **e adesso come si rimedia?** what can we do about it now?; **ha cercato di rimediare al male fatto** he tried to make amends for the wrong he had done ♦ vᴛ (fam: procurarsi) to scrape up o together

rimedio, -di [ri'mɛdjo] ꜱᴍ (gen) remedy; (cura) remedy, cure; **un ottimo rimedio contro il raffreddore** an excellent cure for a cold; **un rimedio per tutti i mali** a panacea, a cure-all; **porre rimedio a qc** to remedy sth; **occorre porre rimedio**

alla situazione we must remedy the situation; **non c'è rimedio** there's no way out, there's nothing to be done about it; **è una situazione senza rimedio** it's a situation which cannot be remedied

rimescolare [rimesko'lare] /72/ vᴛ to mix well, stir well; (carte) to shuffle; **sentirsi rimescolare il sangue** (per paura) to feel one's blood run cold; (per rabbia) to feel one's blood boil

rimessa [ri'messa] ꜱꜰ **1** (per veicoli) garage; (per aerei) hangar **2** (Comm: di merce) shipment, consignment; (: di denaro) remittance **3** (Tennis) return **4** (Sport): **rimessa in gioco laterale** (Calcio) throw-in; **rimessa in gioco dal fondo** (Calcio) goal kick; (Rugby) drop-out

rimesso, -a [ri'messo] ᴘᴘ di **rimettere**

rimestare [rimes'tare] /72/ vᴛ (mescolare) to mix well, stir well; (fig: passato) to drag up again

rimettere [ri'mettere] vʙ ɪʀʀᴇɢ /63/ vᴛ **1** (mettere: di nuovo) to put back; (indossare) to put back on; **l'ho rimesso subito sul tavolo** I put it back on the table immediately; **rimettere mano a qc** to take up sth again; **rimettere a nuovo** (casa ecc) to do up (Brit) o over (USA) (: affidare: decisione): **rimettere a qn** to refer to sb, leave to sb; **rimettere l'anima a Dio** to entrust one's soul to God **3** (perdonare: peccato) to forgive; (condonare: pena) to quash; (: debito) to remit **4** (inviare: merce) to deliver; (: somma) to remit **5** (Sport: pallone) to throw in; (Tennis) to return **6** (vomitare) to bring up **7** (perdere): **rimetterci** to lose; **quando l'ho venduto ci ho rimesso un sacco di soldi** when I sold it I lost a lot of money; **rimetterci di tasca propria** to be out of pocket; **rimetterci la salute** to ruin one's health; **rimetterci la pelle** to lose one's life; **cosa ci rimetti?** what have you got to lose?; **rimettersi** vɪᴘ **1** (mettersi di nuovo): **rimettersi a fare qc** to start doing sth again; **rimettersi in cammino** to set off again; **dopo una breve sosta ci siamo rimessi in cammino** after a short stop we set off again; **rimettersi al lavoro** to start working again; **rimettersi a dormire** to go back to sleep; **rimettersi con qn** to get back together with sb **2** (affidarsi): **rimettersi a** to trust **3** (riprendersi) to recover; **non si è ancora rimesso dall'operazione** he hasn't yet recovered from the operation; **rimettersi in forze** to regain o recover one's strength; **rimettersi in salute** to get better, recover one's health; **rimettersi da uno shock** to recover from a shock; **il tempo si è rimesso al bello** the weather has cleared up; **rimettersi** vʀ (uso reciproco): **rimettersi insieme** to get back together

riminese [rimi'nese] ᴀɢɢ di o from Rimini ♦ ꜱᴍ, ꜱꜰ inhabitant o native of Rimini

rimisi ecc [ri'mizi] vʙ vedi **rimettere**

rimodernamento [rimoderna'mento] ꜱᴍ modernization

rimodernare [rimoder'nare] /72/ vᴛ (gen) to modernize; (vestito) to remodel

rimonta [ri'monta] ꜱꜰ (Sport: gen) recovery; **fare una rimonta in classifica** to climb back up the league

rimontare [rimon'tare] /72/ vᴛ **1** (montare di nuovo: meccanismo) to reassemble, put back together again; (: tenda) to put up again **2** (risalire): **rimontare la corrente** to go upstream ♦ vɪ (aus essere) **1** rimontare in (macchina, carrozza) to get back into; **rimontare a cavallo, rimontare in sella** to remount; **rimontare su una bici** to get back on a bike **2** (Sport) to close the gap

rimorchiare [rimor'kjare] /19/ vᴛ (veicolo) to tow; (nave) to tug; **ci può rimorchiare fino all'officina?** could you tow us to the garage?; **rimorchiare qn** (fig: fam) to pick sb up

rimorchiatore [rimorkja'tore] ꜱᴍ (Naut) tug(boat)

rimorchio, -chi [ri'mɔrkjo] ꜱᴍ **1** (operazione) towing; **cavo da rimorchio** towrope; **andare a rimorchio** to be towed; **prendere a rimorchio** to tow **2** (veicolo trainato) trailer; **autocarro con rimorchio** articulated lorry (Brit), semi(trailer) (USA)

rimorso, -a [ri'mɔrso] ᴘᴘ di **rimordere** ♦ ꜱᴍ remorse; **non ha dimostrato alcun rimorso** he showed no remorse; **essere preso dai rimorsi** to be stricken with remorse; **avere il rimorso di aver fatto qc** to deeply regret having done sth

rimosso, -a [ri'mɔsso] ᴘᴘ di **rimuovere**

rimostranza [rimos'trantsa] ꜱꜰ protest, complaint; **fare le proprie rimostranze a qn** to remonstrate with sb

rimozione [rimot'tsjone] SF 1 (gen) removal; (di veicolo) towing away; "rimozione forzata" "illegally parked vehicles will be towed away"; "zona rimozione" "vehicles will be towed away" 2 (da incarico) dismissal 3 (Psic) repression

rimpastare [rimpas'tare] /72/ VT 1 (pasta lievitata) to knead again; (cemento) to mix again 2 (Pol: governo) to reshuffle

rimpasto [rim'pasto] SM (Pol) reshuffle; rimpasto ministeriale cabinet reshuffle

rimpatriare [rimpa'trjare] /19/ VT to repatriate; sono stati rimpatriati they have been repatriated ♦ VI (aus essere) to return to one's country

rimpatrio, -tri [rim'patrio] SM repatriation; ottenere il rimpatrio to be repatriated

rimpiangere [rim'pjandʒere] /75/ VT IRREG (gen) to regret; (passato, giovinezza) to look back on with regret; rimpiangere di (non) aver fatto qc to regret (not) having done sth; ora rimpiange di non essere andato all'università he regrets not having gone to university

rimpianto, -a [rim'pjanto] PP di rimpiangere ♦ AGG (persona, periodo) sadly missed ♦ SM regret; non aver rimpianti to have no regrets

rimpiattino [rimpjat'tino] SM (gioco) hide-and-seek, hide-and-go-seek (USA)

rimpiazzare [rimpjat'tsare] /72/ VT to replace

rimpicciolire [rimpittʃo'lire] /55/ VT to make smaller VI (aus essere), rimpicciolirsi VIP to become smaller

rimpinzare [rimpin'tsare] (fam) /72/ VT: rimpinzare (di) to cram o stuff with; rimpinzarsi VR: rimpinzarsi (di) to stuff o.s. (with)

rimproverare [rimprove'rare] /72/ VT (figlio, scolaro) to scold, tell off, rebuke; (dipendente) to reprimand; l'hanno rimproverato perché era tornato tardi he was told off for coming home late; rimproverare qc a qn to reproach sb with sth; non ho niente da rimproverarmi I've nothing to reproach myself with

rimprovero [rim'provero] SM reproach; fare un rimprovero a qn to reproach sb; (bambino) to tell sb off; di rimprovero (tono, occhiata) reproachful; (parole) of reproach

rimuginare [rimudʒi'nare] /72/ VT: rimuginare qc to turn sth over in one's mind; che starà rimuginando? what can he be brooding over o about?

rimunerare [rimune'rare] /72/ VT (retribuire) to remunerate; un lavoro ben rimunerato a well-paid job

rimunerativo, -a [rimunera'tivo] AGG (lavoro, attività) remunerative, profitable

rimunerazione [rimunerat'tsjone] SF (retribuzione) remuneration; (ricompensa) reward

rimuovere [ri'mwovere] /66/ VT IRREG 1 (gen, anche Med) to remove; (fig: dubbio) to remove, eliminate; (: ostacolo) to eliminate; (: ostacolo) to get rid of; rimuovere qn da una carica to dismiss sb; rimuovere qn da un proposito to deter sb from a purpose 2 (Psic) to repress

rinascimentale [rinaʃʃimen'tale] AGG Renaissance attr, of the Renaissance

Rinascimento [rinaʃʃi'mento] SM: il Rinascimento the Renaissance

rinascita [ri'naʃʃita] SF (fig) rebirth, revival

rincalzare [rinkal'tsare] /72/ VT (coperte, lenzuola) to tuck in; (palo, albero) to prop up, support

rincalzo [rin'kaltso] SM 1 (sostegno) prop, support; (Mil): truppe di rincalzo reserves 2 (Sport: giocatore) reserve (player)

rincarare [rinka'rare] /72/ VT (prezzi) to raise, put up; (prodotto) to raise o increase the price of; rincarare la dose (fig) to pile it on ♦ VI (aus essere) (prezzo) to go up, rise; (prodotto) to go up (in price), become more expensive; la benzina è rincarata petrol has gone up

rincaro [rin'karo] SM: rincaro (di) (prezzi, costo della vita) increase (in); (prodotto) increase in the price (of)

rincasare [rinka'sare] /72/ VI (aus essere) to return home, go (o come) back home; è rincasato molto tardi he got home very late; no, Maria non è ancora rincasata no, Maria isn't back yet

rinchiudere [rin'kjudere] VB IRREG /22/ VT: rinchiudere (in) (gen) to shut up (in); (persona: in prigione) to shut o lock up

(in); far rinchiudere qn in prigione to have sb put away in prison; rinchiudersi VR: rinchiudersi in (stanza) to shut o.s. up in (a chiave) to lock o.s. up in; rinchiudersi in un convento/monastero to withdraw into a convent/monastery; rinchiudersi in se stesso to withdraw into o.s.; si è rinchiuso in un mutismo assoluto he maintained a stubborn silence

rinchiuso, -a [rin'kjuso] PP di rinchiudere

rincitrullirsi [rintʃitrul'lirsi] /55/ VR to grow foolish

rincorrere [rin'korrere] VB IRREG /28/ VT to chase, run after; (fig: sogno, chimere) to pursue; l'ho rincorso ma non sono riuscito ad acchiapparlo I ran after him but I couldn't catch him; rincorrersi VR (uso reciproco) to run after each other; giocare a rincorrersi to play tag

rincorso, -a [rin'korso] PP di rincorrere

rincrescere [rin'kreʃʃere] /30/ VB IMPERS IRREG: mi rincresce che... I'm sorry that ...; I regret that ...; mi rincresce che tu non stia bene I'm sorry you're not well; mi rincresce di non poterlo fare I'm sorry I can't do it, I regret being unable to do it; se non ti rincresce vorrei pensarci su if you don't mind I'd like to think it over

rincrescimento [rinkreʃʃi'mento] SM regret; con mio grande rincrescimento much to my regret

rincresciuto, -a [rinkreʃ'ʃuto] PP di rincrescere

rinculare [rinku'lare] /72/ VI (aus avere) (arma) to recoil

rinfacciare [rinfat'tʃare] /14/ VT: rinfacciare qc a qn to cast sth up at sb, throw sth in sb's face

rinfocolare [rinfoko'lare] /72/ VT (fig: odio, passioni) to rekindle; (: risentimento, rabbia) to stir up

rinforzare [rinfor'tsare] /72/ VT (muro, argomento, gruppo) to reinforce; (muscoli, posizione, prestigio) to strengthen; (presa, nodo) to tighten VI (aus essere), rinforzarsi VIP (persona) to become o grow stronger; (amicizia, legame) to strengthen

rinforzo [rin'fortso] SM 1 mettere un rinforzo a (gen) to strengthen; di rinforzo (asse, sbarra) strengthening; (esercito) supporting; (personale) extra, additional 2 (Mil): rinforzi SMPL reinforcements

rinfrancare [rinfran'kare] /20/ VT (persona) to encourage, reassure; (spirito) to cheer; rinfrancarsi VIP to be reassured

rinfrescante [rinfres'kante] AGG (bibita) refreshing

rinfresciare [rinfres'kare] /20/ VT (gen) to cool (down); (aria) to cool, freshen; (fig: pareti, soffitto, abiti) to freshen up; il temporale ha rinfrescato l'aria the storm freshened the air; rinfrescarsi la gola to quench one's thirst; rinfrescarsi il viso to splash one's face; rinfrescare la memoria a qn to refresh sb's memory ♦ VI (aus essere) (tempo) to grow o get cooler; rinfrescarsi VR (persona: con bibita) to have something to drink; (: con doccia, ecc.) to freshen up; vorrei rinfrescarmi un po' I'd like to freshen up a bit

rinfresco, -schi [rin'fresko] SM 1 (ricevimento) reception; (festa) party 2 rinfreschi SMPL (cibi e bevande) refreshments

rinfusa [rin'fuza] alla rinfusa AVV higgledy-piggledy, in confusion

ringhiare [rin'gjare] /19/ VI (aus avere) to growl, snarl

ringhiera [rin'gjera] SF (di balcone) railing; (di scale) banisters pl

ringhio, -ghi [rin'gjo] SM growl, snarl

ringhioso, -a [rin'gjoso] AGG growling, snarling

ringiovanire [rindʒova'nire] /55/ VT: ringiovanire qn (sogg: vestito, acconciatura) to make sb look younger; (: vacanze) to rejuvenate sb; quel taglio la ringiovanisce molto that hair style makes her look much younger VI (aus essere), ringiovanirsi VIP to become (o look) younger; sembra ringiovanita di dieci anni she looks ten years younger

ringraziamento [ringrattsja'mento] SM thanks pl; gli ho mandato i miei ringraziamenti I sent him my thanks; lettera/biglietto di ringraziamento thank-you letter/card/ note; bel ringraziamento! (iro) thanks for nothing!; il giorno del Ringraziamento (negli USA) Thanksgiving (Day)

ringraziare [ringrat'tsjare] /19/ VT to thank; ringraziare qn di qc/per aver fatto qc to thank sb for sth/for doing sth; vi ringrazio per avermi ospitato a Copenaghen thank you for putting me up in Copenhagen; ti ringrazio thank you; non so come ringraziarti I don't know how to thank you; se n'è andato senza neppure ringraziare he left without even saying thank you o without as much as a thank you; sia ringraziato il Cielo! thank heavens!

rinnegare [rinne'gare] /80/ vt (fede, idee, partito) to renounce; (famiglia, figlio, origini) to disown, repudiate

rinnegato, -a [rinne'gato] AGG, SM, SF renegade

rinnovabile [rinno'vabile] AGG renewable

rinnovamento [rinnova'mento] SM (morale, civile) renewal; (economico) revival

rinnovare [rinno'vare] /72/ vt (gen, anche fig) to renew; **devo rinnovare l'abbonamento ferroviario** I need to renew my rail pass; **quest'anno non gli hanno rinnovato il contratto** his contract hasn't been renewed this year; **rinnovare l'arredamento** to buy new furnishings; **l'intero personale è stato rinnovato** the entire staff has been replaced; **rinnovarsi** VIP (ripetersi: fenomeno, occasione) to be repeated, recur
□ **rinnovare** non si traduce mai con la parola inglese renovate

rinnovo [rin'novo] SM (di contratto) renewal; "**chiuso per rinnovo (dei) locali**" (negozio) "closed for alterations"

rinoceronte [rinot∫e'ronte] SM rhinoceros

rinomato, -a [rino'mato] AGG (specialista, ristorante) renowned, famous, celebrated; (marca) well-known

rinsaldare [rinsal'dare] /72/ vt (fig: vincoli, amicizia) to strengthen; **rinsaldarsi** VIP to get stronger, be strengthened

rinsavire [rinsa'vire] /55/ vi (aus essere) (anche fig) to come to one's senses

rinsecchito, -a [rinsek'kito] AGG (vecchio, albero) thin, gaunt

rintanarsi [rinta'narsi] /72/ VIP (animale) to go into its den; (persona: nascondersi) to hide; **rintanarsi in casa** to shut o.s. up in the house

rintoccare [rintok'kare] /20/ vi (aus avere) (campana) to toll; (ora, orologio) to strike

rintocco, -chi [rin'tokko] SM toll; **i rintocchi della campana** the tolling of the bell

rintracciare [rintrat't∫are] /14/ vt (selvaggina, ladro, persona assente) to track down; (persona scomparsa, documento) to trace; **la polizia sta cercando di rintracciare i testimoni** the police are trying to trace the witnesses

rintronare [rintro'nare] /72/ vt (fam: cervello) to stun; (: orecchi) to deafen ♦ vi (aus avere o essere) (tuono, cannone) to boom, roar; **la casa rintronava sotto i colpi** the blows echoed round the house

rintuzzare [rintut'tsare] /72/ vt (ribattere) to refute

rinuncia, -ce [ri'nunt∫a] SF (gen, anche Rel) renunciation; **rinuncia a** (carica) resignation from; (eredità) relinquishment of; **rinuncia agli atti del giudizio** (Dir) abandonment of a claim; **una vita di rinunce** a life of sacrifice

rinunciare [rinun't∫are] /14/ vi (aus avere) **rinunciare a** to give up, renounce; (incarico) to turn down; (trono, eredità) to renounce; **ho dovuto rinunciare al viaggio in Giappone** I had to give up my trip to Japan; **rinunciare a fare qc** to give up doing sth; **rinunciò a presentarsi come candidato** he decided not to stand as a candidate; **ci rinuncio!** I give up!

rinunciatario, -ria, -ri, -rie [rinunt∫a'tarjo] AGG renunciatory, defeatist

rinunzia ecc [ri'nuntsja] SF = rinuncia

rinvenimento [rinveni'mento] SM 1 (ritrovamento) recovery; (scoperta) discovery 2 (dopo svenimento) coming to, recovery

rinvenire [rinve'nire] vb IRREG /128/ vt (trovare) to discover, find out; (oggetto smarrito) to recover, find ♦ vi (aus essere) (persona) to come round, regain consciousness; (fiori) to revive; **far rinvenire** (funghi secchi) to reconstitute

rinvenuto, -a [rinve'nuto] PP di rinvenire

rinverdire [rinver'dire] /55/ vi (aus essere) (bosco, ramo) to become green again

rinviare [rinvi'are] /60/ vt 1 (mandare indietro: pacco) to send back, return; (: persona) to send away; (Sport: pallone) to return 2 (differire): **rinviare (a/di)** (partenza, manifestazione) to put off (till/for), postpone (till/for); (seduta) to adjourn (till/for); **rinviare una riunione ad altra data** to put off o postpone a meeting till a later date 3 (in testo, regolamento): **rinviare qn a** to refer sb to 4 (Dir): **rinviare a giudizio** to indict

rinvigorire [rinvigo'rire] /55/ vt to reinvigorate, strengthen vi (aus essere) , **rinvigorirsi** VIP to regain strength

rinvio, -vii [rin'vio] SM 1 (gen) postponement; (restituzione) return; (Dir) adjournment; **rinvio a giudizio** (Dir)

indictment 2 (in testo: rimando) cross-reference 3 (Sport: di pallone) clearance

riò ecc [ri'ɔ] VB vedi riavere

Rio de Janeiro [rio de dʒa'neiro] SF Rio de Janeiro

rionale [rio'nale] AGG (mercato, cinema) local, district attr

rione [ri'one] SM district, neighbourhood, quarter

riordinamento [riordina'mento] SM (di ente, azienda) reorganization

riordinare [riordi'nare] /72/ vt (armadio, casa, scaffali) to tidy up; (finanze, amministrazione) to reorganize; **dero riordinare la camera** I must tidy my room

riorganizzare [riorganid'dzare] /72/ vt to reorganize; **riorganizzarsi** VR to reorganize o.s.

riorganizzazione [riorganiddzat'tsjone] SF reorganization

ripagare [ripa'gare] /80/ vt 1 (ricompensare) to repay; **ripagare qn di qc** to repay sb for sth; **ripagare qn con la stessa moneta** (fig) to pay sb back in his (o her) own coin, give sb tit for tat 2 (pagare di nuovo) to pay again

riparare [ripa'rare] /72/ vt 1 (aggiustare) to repair; **me l'ha riparato in un attimo** he repaired it for me in no time; **portare qc a riparare** to take sth to be repaired; **far riparare qc** to have sth repaired; **ho fatto riparare il videoregistratore** I got the video repaired 2 (proteggere): **riparare (da)** to protect (from); **ripararsi gli occhi dalla luce** to shield one's eyes from the light 3 (rimediare): **riparare (a)** (offesa, gaffe) to make up (for); (errore) to put right 4 (Scol, Brit): **riparare (una materia) a settembre** to resit an exam in September vi (aus essere), **ripararsi** VR (rifugiarsi) to take refuge o shelter; **ripararsi dalla pioggia** to shelter from the rain

riparato, -a [ripa'rato] AGG (posto) sheltered; **stare o tenersi riparato** to shelter

riparazione [riparat'tsjone] SF 1 (di guasto) repairing no pl; (risultato) repair 2 **riparazione (di)** (di torto, offesa) reparation (for); (di danno) compensation (for)

riparo [ri'paro] SM (gen) shelter, protection; **dobbiamo trovare un riparo** we need to find shelter; **al riparo da** (sole, vento) sheltered from; **ormai siamo al riparo** (al sicuro) we're safe now; **mettersi al riparo** to take shelter; **sparano, mettiti al riparo!** they're shooting, take cover!; **correre ai ripari** (fig) to take remedial action

ripartire¹ [ripar'tire] /45/ vi (aus essere) (partire di nuovo: persona) to leave again; (: motore, macchina) to start again; **quando riparti?** when are you leaving?; **non riesco a far ripartire la macchina** I can't get the car to start

ripartire² [ripar'tire] /45/ vt (dividere): **ripartire (in)** (somma, lavoro) to divide up (into); **ripartire (tra)** to share out (among), distribute (among); **ripartire la posta** to sort the mail; **si sono ripartiti il lavoro** they shared out the work

ripartizione [ripartit'tsjone] SF 1 (vedi vt) division; sharing out, distribution 2 (Amm: dipartimento) department

ripassare [ripas'sare] /72/ vt 1 (lezione) to revise (Brit), review (USA), go over again; **devo ripassare, domani ho l'esame** I've got to revise o go over (my notes), I've got the exam tomorrow 2 (varcare di nuovo: confine) to cross again 3 (passare di nuovo: gen) to pass again; **mi puoi ripassare Francesco?** (al telefono) can I speak to Francesco again? 4 (stirare): **ripassare qc** to give sth a quick iron ♦ vi (aus essere) (ritornare) to call again; **ripasserò da lui più tardi** I'll call on him again later; **pensavo di ripassare in quel negozio** I was thinking of calling in at that shop again; **ripassiamo per Pisa?** are we going back via Pisa?; **può ripassare più tardi?** can you call back later?

ripasso [ri'passo] SM (di lezione) revision (Brit), review (USA)

ripensamento [ripensa'mento] SM change of mind, second thoughts pl; **avere un ripensamento** to have second thoughts, change one's mind

ripensare [ripen'sare] /72/ vi 1 (riflettere): **ripensare a qc** to think sth over; **ripensaci!** think it over!; **a ripensarci...** on thinking it over ... 2 (ricordare): **ripensare a** to recall; **quando ci ripenso mi vergogno un po'** when I think about it I feel rather ashamed 3 (cambiare idea): **ripensarci** to change one's mind; **ci ho ripensato, non vengo** I've changed my mind, I'm not coming; **però, ripensandoci...** on second thoughts (Brit) o thought (USA), however ...

ripercorrere [riper'korrere] /28/ vt IRREG (itinerario) to travel over again; (*strada*) to go along again; (*fig: ricordi, passato*) to go back over

ripercorso, -a [riper'korso] PP *di* **ripercorrere**

ripercosso, -a [riper'kɔsso] PP *di* **ripercuotersi**

ripercuotersi [riper'kwɔtersi] /106/ VIP IRREG (*luce*) to be reflected; (*suono*) to reverberate; (*fig: avere effetto*): **ripercuotersi su** to have repercussions on

ripercussione [riperkus'sjone] SF (*di luce*) reflection; (*di suono*) reverberation; (*fig*) repercussions *pl*; **avere una ripercussione** *o* **delle ripercussioni su** to have repercussions on

ripescare [ripes'kare] /20/ VT 1 (*pesce*) to catch again; (*recuperare: persona, cosa*) to fish out; (*fig*) to dig out; **ripescare qn a fare qc** (*fig: sorprendere*) to catch sb doing sth again 2 (*riproporre: candidato, progetto*) to re-propose

ripetente [ripe'tente] SM, SF student repeating the year, repeater (*USA*)

ripetere [ri'petere] /1/ VT (*parole, tentativo*) to repeat; **gliel'ho ripetuto cento volte!** I've told him dozens of times!; **non se l'è fatto ripetere due volte** he didn't need to be asked twice; **dopo ripetuti tentativi** after repeated attempts; **scusi, può ripetere?** excuse me, could you repeat that?; **continua a ripetere le stesse cose** he keeps repeating the same things; **ripetere qc a memoria** to recite sth by heart; **ripetere una lezione** (*studiarla*) to go over a lesson; **ripetere l'anno (scolastico)** to repeat the (school) year; **ripetersi** VR (*persona*) to repeat o.s.; **ripetersi** VIP (*avvenimento, fenomeno*) to recur, happen again; **che non si ripeta più!** don't let this happen again!

ripetitore [ripeti'tore] SM (*Radio, TV*) relay

ripetizione [ripetit'tsjone] SF 1 (*gen*) repetition; **fucile a ripetizione** repeating rifle 2 (*Scol: ripasso*) revision (*Brit*), review (*USA*); (: *lezioni private*) private tutoring *o* coaching *sg*; **dare** *o* **fare ripetizioni a qn** to give sb private lessons; **Malcolm dà ripetizioni di inglese** Malcolm gives private English lessons; **andare a ripetizione** to have private lessons

ripetutamente [ripetuta'mente] AVV repeatedly, again and again

ripiano [ri'pjano] SM (*di mobile*) shelf; (*di terreno*) terrace; **l'ho messo sull'ultimo ripiano** I put it on the top shelf

ripicca [ri'pikka] SF: **per ripicca** out of spite

ripido, -a [ri'pido] AGG steep; **c'è una salita ripida per andare al castello** it's a steep climb up to the castle

ripiegamento [ripjega'mento] SM (*Mil*) retreat

ripiegare [ripje'gare] /80/ VT 1 (*piegare: di nuovo*) to fold (again), refold; (: *più volte*) to fold up 2 (*reclinare: capo*) to lower ♦ VI (*aus avere*) (*Mil*) to retreat, fall back; **ripiegare su** (*fig*) to make do with, fall back on; **era troppo caro, ho ripiegato su uno più economico** it was too expensive, I made do with a cheaper one; **ripiegarsi** VIP (*ramo ecc*) to bend

ripiego, -ghi [ri'pjego] SM expedient; **una soluzione di ripiego** a makeshift solution

ripieno, -a [ri'pjeno] AGG: **ripieno (di)** full (of); (*panino*) filled (with); (*tacchino, peperoni*) stuffed (with) ♦ SM (*Culin*) stuffing

ripone [ri'pone], **ripongo** ecc [ri'pongo] VB *vedi* **riporre**

riporre [ri'porre] /77/ VT IRREG 1 (*mettere via*) to put away; (*dov'era prima*) to put back, replace; **riporre qc al suo posto** to put sth where it belongs 2 **riporre qc in qn** (*fiducia, speranza*) to place *o* put sth in sb

riportare [ripor'tare] /72/ VT 1 (*portare di nuovo: gen*) to take back; (: *verso chi parla*) to bring back; **tieni, ti ho riportato il CD here**, I've brought you back your CD; **mi ha riportato a casa** he took me back home; **riportalo in cucina** take it back to the kitchen; **la scena lo riportò col pensiero all'infanzia** the scene took him back to his childhood 2 (*ottenere*) to receive, get; (*vittoria*) to carry off, win; (*successo*) to have; **ha riportato gravi ferite** he was seriously injured; (*soldato*) he was seriously wounded; **ha riportato una frattura al braccio** he received a fracture to his arm; **la casa ha riportato gravi danni** the house has suffered serious damage, the house has been seriously damaged 3 (*riferire: notizie*) to report; (*citare*) to quote 4 (*Mat*) to carry (forward); **scrivo 5 e riporto 3** put down 5 and carry 3; **riportarsi** VIP: **riportarsi a** (*anche fig*) to go back to; (*riferirsi a*) to refer to

riporto [ri'porto] SM 1 (*Mat*) amount carried over; **col riporto di 1** carry 1 2 (*Sartoria*) appliqué; (*fam: di capelli*) combover 3 (*Caccia*): **cane da riporto** retriever

riposante [ripo'sante] AGG (*gen*) restful; (*musica, colore*) soothing

riposare [ripo'sare] /72/ VT 1 (*dare sollievo a: occhi, membra*) to rest; **per riposare un po' la mente** to give one's mind a rest 2 (*posare di nuovo*) to put down again ♦ VI (*aus avere*) 1 (*gen*) to rest; (*dormire*) to sleep; **è andato a riposare** he's having a rest; (*a letto*) he has gone to lie down; **avete riposato bene?** did you sleep well?; **riposi in pace** (*defunto*) may he rest in peace; **qui riposa...** (*su tomba*) here lies ... 2 (*Culin: pasta, liquido*) to stand; (*vino*) to settle; (*terra*) to lie fallow; **riposarsi** VIP to rest; (*dormire*) to sleep; **vado a riposarmi** I'm going to have a rest; (*a letto*) I'm going to lie down; **cerca di riposarti un po'** try to rest

riposato, -a [ripo'sato] AGG (*viso, aspetto*) rested; (*mente*) fresh

riposi ecc [ri'posi] VB *vedi* **riporre**

riposo [ri'poso] SM 1 (*gen*) rest; **eterno riposo** (*morte*) eternal rest; **casa di riposo** (*per anziani*) rest-home; **prendersi un giorno/un mese di riposo** (*da lavoro*) to take a day/a month off; **buon riposo!** sleep well!; **cinque minuti di riposo** five minutes' rest; **senza un attimo di riposo** without a moment's rest; **riposo!** (*Mil, Sport*) at ease!; **"oggi riposo"** (*Cine, Teatro*) "no performance today"; (*ristorante*) "closed today" 2 (*pensione*): **andare a riposo** to go into retirement, retire; **generale a riposo** retired general 3 (*Mus*) rest

ripostiglio, -gli [ripos'tiʎʎo] SM (*stanzino*) lumber room (*Brit*), storage room (*USA*)

riposto, -a [ri'posto] PP *di* **riporre** ♦ AGG (*letter: nascosto: senso, significato*) hidden

riprendere [ri'prendere] VB IRREG /81/ VT 1 (*prendere di nuovo: gen*) to take again; (: *prigioniero*) to recapture; (: *città*) to retake; (: *impiegato*) to take on again, re-employ; (: *raffreddore*) to catch again; (: *velocità*) to pick up again; (: *quota*) to regain; **riprendere moglie/marito** to get married again; **riprendere i sensi** to recover consciousness, come to *o* round; **riprendere sonno** to go back to sleep, get back to sleep; **non sono riuscito a riprendere sonno** I couldn't get back to sleep; **fu ripreso dal desiderio di vederla** again he felt the desire to see her; **fu ripreso dai dubbi** he began to have doubts again 2 (*riavere*) to get back; (*ritirare: oggetto riparato*) to collect; **riprenditi le tue cose** take your things; **passo a riprendere Francesco/l'impermeabile più tardi** I'll call by to pick up Francesco/the raincoat later; **si è interessato alle sue fotografie** he took his photos back; **puoi riprenderlo, non mi serve più** you can have it back, I don't need it any more 3 (*ricominciare: viaggio, lavoro*) to resume, start again; **riprendere a fare qc** to start doing sth again; **riprendere il cammino** to set off again; **riprendere una conversazione** to continue a conversation; **riprendi tutta la storia dall'inizio** start your story all over again; **"dunque", riprese, "dove eravamo?"** "so", he continued, "where were we?" 4 (*Cine, TV*) to shoot; **riprendere un attore in primo piano** to shoot a close-up of an actor; **questa foto li riprende in un atteggiamento affettuoso** this photo shows them in an affectionate pose 5 (*rimproverare*) to reprimand 6 (*restringere: abito*) to take in 7 (*Sport: raggiungere*) to catch up with; **riprendersi** VIP 1 (*riaversi*) to recover; (*pianta*) to revive; **si è appena ripreso dalla polmonite** he's just recovered from pneumonia; **era emozionato ma si è ripreso** he was nervous but he pulled himself together 2 (*correggersi*) to correct o.s.

ripresentare [riprezen'tare] /72/ VT (*certificato*) to submit again; (*domanda*) to put forward again; (*persona*) to introduce again; **ripresentarsi** VR (*ritornare: persona*) to come back; **ripresentarsi a** (*esame*) to sit (*Brit*) *o* take (*USA*) (an exam) again; (*concorso*) to enter again; **ripresentarsi come candidato** (*Pol*) to stand (*Brit*) *o* run (*USA*) again (as a candidate); **ripresentarsi** VIP (*occasione*) to arise again

ripreso, -a [ri'preso] PP *di* **riprendere**

ripristinare [ripristi'nare] /72/ VT (*gen*) to restore; (*Inform*) to reset; (*tradizione*) to revive, bring back into use; (*legge*) to bring back into force

ripristino [ri'pristino] SM (*gen*) restoration; (*di tradizioni*) revival

riprodotto, -a [ripro'dotto] PP *di* **riprodurre**

riprodurre [ripro'durre] VB IRREG /90/ VT to reproduce; **riprodursi** VIP (*moltiplicarsi*) to reproduce; (*ripetersi: situazione, fenomeno*) to occur *o* happen again, recur

riproduttivo, -a [riprodut'tivo] AGG reproductive

riproduttore, -trice [riprodut'tore] AGG (*organo*) reproductive ♦ SM: **riproduttore acustico** pick-up

riproduzione [riprodut'tsjone] SF (*gen*) reproduction; **"riproduzione vietata"** "all rights reserved", "copyright"

ripromesso, -a [ripro'messo] PP *di* **ripromettersi**

ripromettersi [ripro'mettersi] /63/ VIP IRREG: **ripromettersi di fare qc** to intend to do sth

riproporre [ripro'porre] VB IRREG /77/ VT (*soluzione*) to put forward again; (*legge*) to propose again; **riproporre di fare qc** to suggest doing sth again; **riproporsi** VIP 1 (*intendere*): **riproporsi di fare qc** to intend to do sth; **si è riproposto una lunga vacanza** he's thinking of having a long holiday 2 (*ripresentarsi: problema, situazione*) to come up again, arise again; **riproporsi** VR: **riproporsi come candidato** to propose oneself as candidate again

riproposto, -a [ripro'posto] PP *di* **riproporre**

riprova [ri'prɔva] SF confirmation; **a riprova di** as confirmation of

riprovare [ripro'vare] /72/ VT (*provare di nuovo: gen*) to try again; (: *vestito*) to try on again; (: *sensazione*) to experience again ♦ VI (*aus avere*) (*tentare*): **riprovare (a fare qc)** to try (to do sth) again; **riproverò più tardi** I'll try again later; **guai a lui se ci riprova!** God help him if he tries that again!

riprovevole [ripro'vevole] AGG reprehensible

ripudiare [ripu'djare] /19/ VT (*moglie, marito*) to repudiate; (*famiglia, patria*) to disown; (*principi, idee*) to reject

ripudio, -di [ri'pudjo] SM (*vedi vb*) repudiation; disowning; rejection

ripugnante [ripuɲ'ɲante] AGG repulsive, disgusting

ripugnanza [ripuɲ'ɲantsa] SF repugnance, disgust; **provare ripugnanza per qc/qn** to loathe sth/sb; **avere ripugnanza a fare qc** to loathe doing sth

ripugnare [ripuɲ'ɲare] /15/ VI (*aus avere*) **ripugnare a qn** to repel *o* disgust sb; **la sola idea mi ripugna** I find the very idea of it disgusting; **non ti ripugna fare una cosa del genere?** don't you loathe doing such a thing?

ripulire [ripu'lire] /55/ VT 1 (*pulire: di nuovo*) to clean again; (: *a fondo*) to clean up; **ripulire il giardino dalle foglie secche** to clear the garden of dead leaves; **ha ripulito il frigorifero** (*fig*) he finished off *o* polished off everything in the refrigerator; **gli hanno ripulito le tasche** (*fig*) they cleaned him out 2 (*perfezionare*) to polish, refine; **ripulirsi** VR to clean o.s. up

ripulsione [ripul'sjone] SF repulsion

riquadro [ri'kwadro] SM (*gen, spazio*) square; (*di parete, soffitto, mobile*) panel

risacca, -che [ri'sakka] SF backwash

risaia [ri'saja] SF paddy field

risalire [risa'lire] /98/ VT (*salire di nuovo: gen*) to go up again; (*scale*) to climb again; **risalire la corrente** to go upstream ♦ VI (*aus essere*) 1 (*gen, livello, prezzi*) to go up again, rise again; **risalire a cavallo** to remount; **risalire in macchina** to get back into the car; **risalire al piano di sopra** to go back upstairs; **risalire in classifica** to climb back (up) to the top of the league 2 **risalire a** (*data, periodo*) to date back to *o* from, go back to); **il palazzo risale al Cinquecento** the palace dates from the sixteenth century 3 (*ritornare*): **risalire a** to go back to; **risalire alle fonti** to go back to source material

risalita [risa'lita] SF: **impianti di risalita** (*Sci*) ski lifts

risaltare [risal'tare] /72/ VI (*aus avere o essere*) (*anche fig*): **risaltare (su/fra)** to stand out (against/among); (*colore*) to show up (against/among)

risalto [ri'salto] SM (*rilievo*) prominence; (*enfasi*) emphasis; **dar risalto a qc** to give prominence to sth, lay emphasis on sth; **mettere *o* porre in risalto qc** to make sth stand out

risanamento [risana'mento] SM 1 (*economico*) improvement; **risanamento del bilancio** reorganization of the budget 2 (*bonifica*) reclamation; **risanamento edilizio** urban redevelopment

risanare [risa'nare] /72/ VT 1 (*economia*) to improve; (*bilancio*) to reorganize 2 (*palude*) to reclaim; (*quartiere*) to redevelop 3 (*guarire*) to heal, cure VI (*aus essere*), **risanarsi** VIP (*guarire, anche fig*) to heal

risapere [risa'pere] /99/ VT to come to know of; **è risaputo che...** everyone knows that ..., it's common knowledge that ...

risaputo, -a [risa'puto] AGG: **sono cose risapute** it's common knowledge

risarcimento [risartʃi'mento] SM: **risarcimento (di)** compensation (for); **ha ricevuto un risarcimento di 10.000 euro** he got 10,000 euros compensation; **chiedere il risarcimento** to claim compensation; **aver diritto al risarcimento dei danni** to be entitled to damages

risarcire [risar'tʃire] /55/ VT (*compensare: cose*) to pay compensation for; (: *persona*): **risarcire qn di qc** to compensate sb for sth; **risarcire i danni a qn** to pay sb damages

risata [ri'sata] SF laugh; **che risate!** what a laugh!, how we laughed!; **farsi una bella risata** to have a good laugh

riscaldamento [riskalda'mento] SM 1 (*di casa, auto*) heating; **il riscaldamento non funziona** the heating isn't working; **riscaldamento autonomo** central heating (*for one home only*); **riscaldamento centrale** central heating (*serving an entire block of apartments*); **riscaldamento globale** global warming 2 (*Sport*) warm-up; **prima della partita facciamo riscaldamento** we do a warm-up before a match

riscaldare [riskal'dare] /72/ VT 1 (*scaldare: stanza, acqua*) to heat; (: *mani, persona*) to warm; **un caminetto riscaldava la stanza** the room was heated by an open fire; **riscaldarsi le mani/i piedi** to warm one's hands/feet 2 (*scaldare di nuovo*) to heat up, reheat; **il pollo dev'essere solo riscaldato** the chicken just needs warming up ♦ VI (*aus avere*) (*stufa*) to heat up; **il motore riscalda troppo** the engine overheats; **riscaldarsi** VIP (*persona*) to get warm, warm o.s. up; (*atleta*) to warm up; (*fig: infervorarsi*) to get worked up, get excited; (*adirarsi*) to get angry

riscaldo [ris'kaldo] SM (*fam*) (slight) inflammation; **ha un po' di riscaldo** (*brufoletti*) he's got a bit of a rash

riscattare [riskat'tare] /72/ VT (*Dir, anche fig*) to redeem; (*prigioniero*) to ransom, pay a ransom for; **riscattarsi** VR (*fig*) to redeem o.s.

riscatto [ris'katto] SM (*Dir, anche fig*) redemption; (*di rapimento*) ransom

rischiarare [riskja'rare] /72/ VT (*gen*) to light up; (*colore*) to make lighter; **rischiararsi la voce** to clear one's throat VI (*aus essere*), **rischiararsi** VIP (*cielo*) to clear; (*fig: volto*) to brighten up; (*liquido*) to become clear; **si rischiarò in volto** his face lit up; **rischiara, si sta rischiarando** (*tempo, cielo*) it's clearing up

rischiare [ris'kjare] /19/ VT to risk; **ha rischiato la vita** he risked his life; **rischiare il tutto per tutto** to risk everything ♦ VI (*aus avere*) **rischiare di fare qc** to risk doing sth, run the risk of doing sth; **non voglio rischiare di arrivare in ritardo** I don't want to risk arriving late; **ha rischiato di cadere** he nearly fell

rischio, -chi [ˈriskjo] SM risk; **a rischio di fare qc** at the risk of doing sth; **a proprio rischio e pericolo** at one's own risk; **correre il rischio di fare qc** to run the risk of doing sth; **mettere a rischio qc** to put sth at risk; **un rischio calcolato** a calculated risk; **c'è il rischio che questo viaggio non si possa fare** there is a danger that we (*o* you *ecc*) won't be able to make this trip; **soggetto/categoria a rischio** subject/group at risk; **capitale di rischio** (*Fin*) risk *o* venture capital; **rischio del mestiere** occupational hazard

rischioso, -a [ris'kjoso] AGG risky, dangerous, hazardous; **un'impresa rischiosa** a risky enterprise

risciacquare [riʃʃak'kware] /72/ VT (*panni, stoviglie*) to rinse; **risciacquarsi la bocca** to rinse one's mouth out

risciacquo [riʃ'ʃakkwo] SM rinse

riscontrare [riskon'trare] /72/ VT 1 (*rilevare*) to notice, find; **non ho riscontrato errori** I haven't found *o* noticed any mistakes 2 (*confrontare*) to compare; (*controllare: conti, motore*) to check, inspect; **riscontrare la copia con l'originale** to compare the copy with the original; (*Tip*) to read against copy

riscontro [ris'kontro] SM 1 (*conferma*) confirmation; **le sue osservazioni non trovano riscontro nella realtà** his remarks are not borne out by the facts 2 (*confronto*) comparison; (*controllo*) check; **mettere a riscontro** to compare, check; **fare il riscontro della copia con l'originale** to compare the copy with the original; (*Tip*) to read against copy;

un avvenimento che non ha avuto riscontro in passato an event which had no parallel in the past **3** (*Comm: risposta per iscritto*) reply; **in attesa di un vostro cortese riscontro** we look forward to your reply

riscoperto, -a [risko'perto] PP *di* riscoprire

riscoprire [risko'prire] /9/ VT IRREG to rediscover

riscossione [riskos'sjone] SF collection

riscosso, -a [ris'kɔsso] PP *di* riscuotere

riscrivibile [riskri'vibile] AGG: **CD riscrivibile** rewriteable CD, CD-RW

riscuotere [ris'kwɔtere] VB IRREG /106/ VT (*stipendio, pensione*) to draw; (*tasse, affitto*) to collect; (*fig: applausi, approvazione, successo*) to win, earn; **riscuotere un assegno** to cash a cheque (*Brit*) o check (*USA*); **riscuotersi** VIP: **riscuotersi (da)** (*fig*) to rouse o.s. (from), shake o.s. (out of)

rise *ecc* ['rise] VB *vedi* ridere

risentimento [risenti'mento] SM resentment; **provare** o **avere del risentimento verso** o **contro qn** to feel resentful towards sb

risentire [risen'tire] /45/ VT (*sentire di nuovo*) to hear again; (*disco*) to listen to again ♦ VI: **risentire di** (*esperienza, trauma*) to feel the effects of (*portarne i segni*) to show the effects of; **risentire dell'influenza di** to show traces of the influence of; **le piante hanno risentito del freddo** the plants have felt the cold; **risentirsi** VR (*offendersi*) to take offence (*Brit*) o offense (*USA*); **risentirsi di** o **per qc** to resent sth, take offence o offense at sth

risentito, -a [risen'tito] AGG resentful

riserbo [ri'serbo] SM reserve; **è una persona di grande riserbo** he's a very reserved person; **senza riserbo** unreservedly; **mantenere un assoluto riserbo (su qc)** to maintain a complete silence (about sth)

riserva [ri'serva] SF **1** (*provvista, scorta*) reserve; **fare riserva di** (*acqua, cibo*) to get in a supply of, stock up on; **tenere di riserva** to keep in reserve; **entrare in riserva, essere in riserva** (*Aut*) to be nearly out of petrol (*Brit*) o gas (*USA*); **di riserva** (*gen*) reserve *attr*; (*aereo, corriera*) back-up *attr*; **riserva aurea** gold reserves *pl* **2** (*Mil, Sport*) reserve; **domenica scorsa ho giocato come riserva** last Sunday I played as reserve; **(giocatore di) riserva** reserve (player); (*Calcio*) substitute; **truppe della riserva** reserves **3** (*limitazione: anche*: **riserva mentale**) reservation; **con le dovute riserve** with certain reservations; **ha accettato con la riserva di potersi ritirare** he accepted with the proviso that he could pull out; **senza riserve** (*incondizionatamente*) unreservedly **4** (*territorio*): **riserva di caccia/pesca** hunting/fishing preserve; **riserva indiana** Indian reservation; **riserva naturale** nature reserve

riservare [riser'vare] /72/ VT **1** (*tenere da parte*) to keep aside; (*mettere da parte*) to put aside; **riservare una sorpresa a qn** to have a surprise in store for sb; **cosa ci riserva il destino?** what has destiny in store for us?; **riservarsi di fare qc** to intend to do sth; **riservarsi il diritto di fare qc** to reserve the right to do sth **2** (*prenotare*) to book, reserve; **vorrei riservare un tavolo per stasera** I'd like to book a table for this evening

riservatezza [riserva'tettsa] SF (*vedi agg a*) confidential nature; reserve; discretion

riservato, -a [riser'vato] AGG **1** (*lettera, informazione*) confidential; (*persona, carattere*) reserved; (*discreto*) discreet **2** (*prenotato*) reserved, booked

risi *ecc* ['risi] VB *vedi* ridere

risibile [ri'sibile] AGG laughable

risicato, -a [rizi'kato] AGG (*maggioranza*) very narrow

risiedere [ri'sjedere] /29/ VI **1** (*vivere*): **risiedere in** o **a** to reside in **2** (*consistere, stare*): **risiedere in** to lie in; **il motivo del suo successo risiede nel suo senso dell'umorismo** the reason for his success is his sense of humour

risma [ˈrizma] SF **1** (*di carta*) ream **2** (*fig: pegg: tipo*) kind, sort; **essere della stessa risma** to be all of a kind

riso¹ [ˈriso] PP *di* ridere ♦ SM (*pl f* **risa**) (*il ridere*) laughter; (*risata*) laugh; **il riso e il pianto** laughter and tears; **uno scoppio di risa** a burst of laughter; **risa allegre** cheerful laughter; **non riusciva a trattenere il riso** he couldn't help laughing; **sbellicarsi** o **crepare dalle risa** (*fam*) to split one's sides laughing; **il riso fa buon sangue** laughter is the best medicine

riso² [ˈriso] SM (*Bot*) rice; **riso in brodo** consommé with rice;

riso in bianco rice with butter; **riso integrale** brown rice; **carta di riso** (*Arte*) rice paper

risolino [riso'lino] SM (*di scherno, ironico*) snigger

risollevare [risolle'vare] /72/ VT (*sollevare di nuovo: testa*) to raise again, lift up again; (*fig: questione*) to raise again, bring up again; (: *morale*) to raise; **risollevare le sorti di qc** to improve the chances of sth; **risollevarsi** VR (*da terra*) to rise again; (*fig: da malattia*) to recover

risolsi *ecc* [ri'sɔlsi] VB *vedi* risolvere

risolto, -a [ri'sɔlto] PP *di* risolvere

risolutezza [risolu'tettsa] SF decisiveness, resolution, determination

risolutivo, -a [risolu'tivo] AGG (*determinante*) decisive; **arrivare ad una formula risolutiva** (*che risolve*) to come up with a formula to resolve a situation

risoluto, -a [riso'luto] AGG resolute, determined; **essere risoluto a fare qc** to be determined to do sth

risoluzione [risolut'tsjone] SF **1** (*soluzione, anche Mat*) solution **2** (*decisione*) resolution **3** (*Dir: di contratto*) annulment, cancellation **4** (*Chim*) resolution **5** (*di schermo*) resolution

risolvere [ri'sɔlvere] VB IRREG /94/ VT **1** (*problema, anche Mat*) to solve, work out; (*mistero, indovinello*) to solve; (*difficoltà, faccenda, controversia*) to resolve, sort out; **cosa risolvi facendo così?** what do you solve by doing that? **2** (*decidere*) to decide, resolve; **abbiamo risolto di partire al più presto** we've decided to leave as soon as possible **3** (*Dir: contratto*) to annul, cancel **4** (*Chim*) to break down; **risolversi** VIP **1** (*andare a finire*): **risolversi in bene** to end well, turn out well; **risolversi in nulla** to come to nothing; **l'operazione si è risolta in un fiasco** the operation turned out to be a disaster **2** (*decidersi*): **risolversi a fare qc** to make up one's mind to do sth **3** (*malattia*) to clear up

risolvibile [risol'vibile] AGG solvable

risonanza [riso'nantsa] SF (*Fis*) resonance; (*fig: eco*) interest; **suscitare una grande risonanza** to arouse great interest; **aver vasta risonanza** (*fatto, vicenda*) to be known far and wide; **risonanza magnetica** magnetic resonance

risonare [riso'nare] /72/ VT, VI = risuonare

risorgere [ri'sɔrdʒere] /109/ VI IRREG (*aus essere*) (*Rel, anche fig*) to rise again; **risorgeva in lui la speranza** his hopes were revived

risorgimentale [risɔrdʒimen'tale] AGG of the Risorgimento

risorgimento [risɔrdʒi'mento] SM (*di arte, cultura*) revival; **il Risorgimento** movement that led to the unification of Italy

risorsa [ri'sorsa] SF (*gen*) resource; **è l'ultima risorsa** it's the last resort; **una persona piena di risorse** a resourceful person; **risorse umane** human resources

risorsi *ecc* [ri'sorsi] VB *vedi* risorgere

risorto, -a [ri'sorto] PP *di* risorgere

risotto [ri'sɔtto] SM (*Culin*) risotto

risparmiare [rispar'mjare] /19/ VT **1** (*denaro, cibo, tempo*) to save; (*gas, elettricità*) to economize on, save on; **sto risparmiando per comprare un lettore di MP3** I'm saving up to buy an MP3 player; **risparmiare fatica/fiato** to save one's energy/breath; **risparmiati il disturbo** o **la fatica** (*anche iro*) save yourself the trouble; **risparmiare qc a qn** (*fig: evitare*) to spare sb sth; **ti risparmio i particolari** I'll spare you the details **2** (*non uccidere, non colpire*) to spare; **risparmiare la vita a qn** to spare sb's life ♦ VI (*aus avere*) **risparmiare su qc** to economize on sth, save on sth; **risparmiarsi** VR to spare oneself

risparmiatore, -trice [risparmja'tore] SM, SF saver

risparmio, -mi [ris'parmjo] SM **1** (*azione*) saving; **un grosso risparmio di tempo** a big saving in time; **ci riuscimmo con un risparmio di tempo e denaro** we succeeded and saved time and money into the bargain; **senza risparmio di forze** sparing no effort **2** **risparmi** SMPL (*denaro risparmiato*) savings *pl*; **ha speso tutti i suoi risparmi** he spent all his savings

rispecchiare [rispek'kjare] /19/ VT to reflect; **rispecchiarsi** VR to be reflected; **è così lucido che ti ci puoi rispecchiare** it's so shiny that you can see your face in it

rispedire [rispe'dire] /55/ VT to send back; **rispedire qc a qn** to send sth back to sb

rispettabile [rispet'tabile] AGG **1** (*persona*) respectable **2** (*considerevole: somma*) sizeable, considerable

rispettare [rispet'tare] /72/ VT (*persona, idea*) to respect, have respect for; (*legge*) to obey, comply with, abide by; (*promessa*) to keep; **bisogna rispettare le opinioni altrui** you have to respect other people's opinions; **farsi rispettare da qn** to command sb's respect; **far rispettare la legge** to enforce the law; **rispettare l'ordine alfabetico** to maintain alphabetical order; **rispettare i tempi (stabiliti)** to keep to schedule; **rispettare le distanze** to keep one's distance; **ogni medico che si rispetti** every self-respecting doctor; **rispettarsi** VR to respect o.s.

rispettivamente [rispettivaˈmente] AVV respectively

rispettivo, -a [rispetˈtivo] AGG respective

rispetto [risˈpɛtto] SM **1 rispetto (di** o **per)** (*gen*) respect (for); . (*norme, leggi*) observance (of), compliance (with); **portare rispetto a qn/qc** to have o feel respect for sb/sth; **mancare di rispetto a qn** to be disrespectful to sb; **non ha alcun rispetto per le cose altrui** she has no respect for other people's property; **con rispetto** (*nelle lettere*) respectfully yours; **con rispetto parlando** if you will excuse my saying so, with respect **2 rispetti** SMPL (*frm: omaggi*): **(porga) i miei rispetti alla signora** my regards to your wife **3** (*riguardo, relazione*): **rispetto a** (*in confronto*) compared to, in comparison with; (*riguardo a*) as regards, with respect to, regarding, as for; **sotto questo rispetto** from this point of view; **sotto ogni rispetto** in every respect

rispettoso, -a [rispetˈtoso] AGG respectful; **essere rispettoso verso qn** to be respectful to sb, show respect to sb; **essere rispettoso di qc** to have respect for sth

risplendente [rispleⁿˈdɛnte] AGG (*sole*) bright, shining; (*occhi*) sparkling; **risplendente di gioia** (*viso*) shining with joy

risplendere [risˈplɛndere] /29/ VI (*gen*) to shine; (*luccicare*) to sparkle, glitter

rispondente [rispoⁿˈdɛnte] AGG: **rispondente a** in accordance with, in keeping o conformity with

rispondenza [rispoⁿˈdɛntsa] SF correspondence

rispondere [risˈpondere] VB IRREG /95/ VI (*aus* avere) **1 rispondere a** (*domanda*) to reply to, answer; (*persona*) to answer; (*invito*) to reply to; **ha risposto alla tua lettera?** has he answered your letter?; **rispondere al telefono** to answer the telephone; **ho telefonato ma non ha risposto nessuno** I phoned, but nobody answered; **rispondere di sì/di no** to say yes/no; **cosa vuoi che ti risponda?** what can I say?; **rispondere bene** to give the right o correct answer; **rispondere male** (*sgarbatamente*) to answer back, answer rudely; (*in modo errato*) to give the wrong answer; **rispondere al nome di** to answer to the name of **2** (*rimbeccare*): **rispondere (a qn)** to answer (sb) back; **rispondere per le rime** (*fig*) to give sb as good as one gets **3** (*reagire: veicolo, freni*) to respond **4** (*corrispondere*): **rispondere a** to correspond to (*speranze, bisogno*) to answer; **rispondere alle esigenze di** to meet the needs of **5** (*garantire*): **rispondere di qn** to answer for sb, be responsible for sb, vouch for sb; (*essere responsabile*): **rispondere di qc** to be accountable for sth;: **rispondere a qn di qc** to be answerable to sb for sth; **non rispondo più di me stesso** o **delle mie azioni** I can't answer for my actions **6** (*Carte*) to follow, reply ♦ VT **1 rispondere che...** to answer that ..., reply that ... **2 rispondere picche** (*fig*) to give a flat refusal, refuse flatly

risposare [rispoˈzare] /72/ VT to marry again, remarry; **risposarsi** VIP to get married again, remarry

risposto, -a [risˈposto] PP *di* **rispondere**

rissa [ˈrissa] SF fight, brawl

rissoso, -a [risˈsoso] AGG quarrelsome

rist. ABBR = **ristampa**

ristabilire [ristabiˈlire] /55/ VT **1** (*gen*) to re-establish; (*servizio*) to put back in operation; (*ordine, istituzione*) to restore **2** (*sogg: riposo ecc*): **ristabilire qn** to restore sb to health; **ristabilirsi** VIP (*persona*) to recover, get better; **ristabilirsi da** to recover from

ristagnare [ristaˈɲɲare] /15/ VI (*aus* avere) (*acqua*) to be stagnant; (*sangue*) to cease flowing; (*fig: affari, industria*) to stagnate

ristagno [risˈtaɲɲo] SM (*anche fig*) stagnation; **c'è un ristagno delle vendite** business is slack

ristampa [risˈtampa] SF (*il ristampare*) reprinting *no pl*; (*opera ristampata*) reprint

ristampare [ristamˈpare] /72/ VT to reprint

ristorante [ristoˈrante] SM restaurant; **abbiamo mangiato al ristorante** we ate in a restaurant; **ristorante della stazione** station buffet ♦ AGG INV restaurant *attr*

ristorare [ristoˈrare] /72/ VT to revive, refresh; **ristorare le forze** to restore one's strength; **ristorarsi** VR (*rifocillarsi*) to have something to eat and drink; (*riposarsi*) to rest, have a rest

ristoratore, -trice [ristoraˈtore] AGG refreshing, reviving ♦ SM, SF restaurateur

ristoro [risˈtoro] SM (*bevanda, cibo*) refreshment; **posto di ristoro** refreshment bar, buffet, snack bar; **servizio di ristoro** (*Ferr*) refreshments *pl*

ristrettezza [ristretˈtettsa] SF **1** (*scarsità*) shortage, lack, scarcity; **ristrettezza di idee** narrow-mindedness **2 ristrettezze** SFPL poverty *sg*, straitened circumstances

ristretto, -a [risˈtretto] PP *di* **restringere** ♦ AGG **1** (*limitato*) limited, restricted; (*angusto*) narrow; (*racchiuso*) enclosed, hemmed in; **ristretto a** restricted o limited to; **di idee ristrette** (*fig*) narrow-minded **2** (*concentrato: brodo*) thick; (: *caffè*) extra strong

ristrutturare [ristruttuˈrare] /72/ VT (*appartamento*) to do up; (*ridipingere ecc*) to redecorate; (*edificio*) to restore; (*azienda*) to reorganize; (*pelle, capelli*) to repair

ristrutturazione [ristrutturatˈtsjone] SF (*vedi vb*) alteration; redecoration; restoration; reorganization; repair

risucchiare [risukˈkjare] /19/ VT (*sogg: vortice*) to swallow up

risucchio, -chi [riˈsukkjo] SM (*di acqua*) undertow, pull; (*di aria*) suction

risultare [risulˈtare] /72/ VI (*aus* essere) **1** (*rivelarsi*) to prove to be, turn out to be; (*essere accertato*) to be clear, emerge; (*essere noto*) to appear, seem; **la tue previsioni sono risultate errate** your predictions proved to be wrong; **dalle indagini è risultato che...** it emerged from the inquiry that ...; **risulta appartenere ad un determinato gruppo politico** he's known to belong to a specific political group; **è risultato vincitore** he emerged as the winner **2 mi risulta che...** I understand that ..., as far as I know ...; **(ne) risulta che...** it follows that ...; **non mi risulta** not as far as I know; **ti risulta che sia ancora qui?** do you know whether he's still here?; **non mi risulta che sia partito** I don't think he's left

risultato [risulˈtato] SM (*gen, anche Mat, Sport*) result; **domani sapremo il risultato degli esami** we'll get the exam results tomorrow; **risultati parziali** (*Sport*) half-time results

risuonare [riswoˈnare] /72/ VI **1** (*gen*) to resound; **un grido risuonò nel silenzio** a scream pierced the silence; **mi risuonano nella mente le sue parole** his words still echo in my mind **2** (*Fis*) to resonate ♦ VT (*suonare di nuovo: musica*) to play again; (: *campanello*) to ring again

risurrezione [risurretˈtsjone] SF (*Rel*) resurrection

risuscitare [risuʃʃiˈtare] /72/ VT to resuscitate, restore to life; (*fig*) to revive, bring back; **risuscitare qn dalla morte** to raise sb from the dead; **questo vino farebbe risuscitare un morto** (*fig: scherz*) this wine would revive the dead ♦ VI (*aus* essere) to rise from the dead; (*fig: riprendere vigore*) to revive

risvegliare [rizveʎˈʎare] /27/ VT (*gen*) to wake up, waken; (*fig: dall'inerzia*): **risvegliare qn (da)** to rouse sb (from); (*fig: interesse*) to stir up, arouse; (: *curiosità*) to arouse; **risvegliare l'appetito** to whet one's appetite; **risvegliare i ricordi** to bring back old memories; **risvegliarsi** VIP to wake up, awaken; (*fig: interesse, curiosità*) to be aroused; **il vulcano si è risvegliato** the volcano has become active again

risveglio, -gli [rizˈveʎʎo] SM (*azione*) awakening, waking up; (*fig: di arte, cultura: interesse*) revival; **il risveglio della coscienza nazionale** the awakening of national consciousness; **al risveglio** when he (o she ecc) woke up

risvolto [rizˈvɔlto] SM **1** (*di giacca*) lapel; (*di manica*) cuff; (*di pantaloni*) turn-up (*Brit*), cuff (*USA*); (*di tasca*) flap; (*di libro*) inside flap **2** (*fig: aspetto secondario*) implication

ritagliare [ritaʎˈʎare] /27/ VT (*tagliare via*): **ritagliare (da)** to cut out (of); **ho ritagliato l'articolo dal giornale** I cut the article out of the paper

ritaglio, -gli [riˈtaʎʎo] SM (*di giornale*) cutting, clipping; (*di stoffa*) remnant, scrap; **nei ritagli di tempo** in one's spare time

ritardare [ritarˈdare] /72/ VT **1** (*differire*) to delay, hold up; **ha ritardato la partenza di un'ora** he delayed the departure by an hour; **ritardare il pagamento** to defer payment

2 (*rallentare: sviluppo, processo*) to slow down ♦ vi (*aus con soggetto inanimato* essere; *con soggetto animato* avere) (*persona, treno*) to be late; (*orologio*) to be slow; **ritardare a fare qc** to be late in doing sth; **ritardare di un quarto d'ora** to be fifteen minutes late

ritardatario, -ria, -ri, -rie [ritarda'tarjo] SM, SF latecomer

ritardato, -a [ritar'dato] AGG (*Psic*) retarded

ritardo, -a [ri'tardo] SM **1** (*di treno, posta*) delay; (*di persona*) lateness *no pl*; **essere in ritardo** to be late; **un ritardo di 2 ore** a 2-hour delay; **il volo ha avuto un ritardo di due ore** the flight was two hours late; **arrivò con 2 ore di ritardo** it (*o* he *ecc*) arrived 2 hours late; **scusa il ritardo** sorry I'm late **2** (*mentale*) backwardness, retardation

ritegno [ri'teɲɲo] SM restraint; **abbi un po' di ritegno!** restrain yourself; **senza ritegno** unrestrained, without restraint

ritemprare [ritem'prare] /72/ VT (*forze, spirito*) to restore

ritenere [rite'nere] VB IRREG /121/ VT **1** (*considerare*) to think, believe, consider; **lo ritengo un ottimo insegnante** I think he's an excellent teacher; **ritenere opportuno fare qc** to think it opportune to do sth; **ho ritenuto che fosse opportuno fare così** I felt it opportune to do so; **ritengo di sì** I think so; **ritengo di no** I don't think so; **si ritiene che l'uomo sia fuggito in macchina** they think that the man escaped by car **2** (*trattenere: denaro*) to withhold, deduct; (: *nozioni, concetti*) to retain; **gli hanno ritenuto due giorni di paga** they withheld 2 days' pay **3** (*umidità, liquidi*) to retain; **ritenersi** VR to consider o.s.; **si ritiene un genio** he thinks he's a genius

ritengo [ri'tengo], **-ritenni** [ri'tenni] VB *vedi* ritenere

ritentare [riten'tare] /72/ VT to try again, make another attempt at

ritenuta [rite'nuta] SF deduction; **ritenuta sulla paga** deduction from one's pay; **ritenuta d'acconto** advance tax deduction; **ritenuta alla fonte** taxation at source

riterrò *ecc* [riter'rɔ] VB *vedi* ritenere

ritirare [riti'rare] /72/ VT **1** (*mano, braccio*) to pull back; (*candidatura*) to withdraw; (*soldi*) to withdraw, take out; (*certificato, bagaglio*) to collect, pick up; (*bucato*) to bring in; **ha ritirato dei soldi** he took out some money; **ritirare (lo stipendio)** to get paid; **appena ritiro (lo stipendio) ti restituisco i soldi** as soon as I get paid I'll pay you back; **dove si ritirano i bagagli?** where is the baggage reclaim?; **ritirare il passaporto a qn** to withdraw sb's passport; **gli hanno ritirato la patente** they took away his licence (*Brit*) *o* license (*USA*); **ritiro quello che ho detto** I take back what I said **2** (*cambiale*) to retire **3** (*tirare di nuovo*) to pull again; (*lanciare di nuovo*) to throw again; **ritirarsi** VR (*Mil*) to retreat, withdraw; (*persona: da un'attività*) to retire; (: *appartarsi*) to withdraw, retire; **si ritirò nella sua stanza** he withdrew *o* retired to his room; **ritirarsi a vita privata** to withdraw from public life; **ritirarsi** VIP **1** (*retrocedere: acque*) to recede, subside **2** (*tessuto*) to shrink

ritirata [riti'rata] SF **1** (*Mil*) retreat, withdrawal; (*in caserma*) tattoo; **suonare la ritirata** to sound the retreat (*o* the tattoo); **essere in ritirata** to be in retreat **2** (*latrina*) lavatory (*Brit*), toilet (*Brit*), bathroom (*USA*)

ritirato, -a [riti'rato] AGG secluded; **fare vita ritirata** to live in seclusion

ritiro [ri'tiro] SM **1** (*il ritirare: di truppe, candidatura, soldi*) withdrawal; (: *di biglietti, pacchi*) collection; (: *di passaporto*) confiscation; (*Rel*) retreat; **la ricevuta vi verrà consegnata al momento del ritiro della merce** you will be given the receipt on collection of the goods; **"per il ritiro dei vaglia postali rivolgersi a..."** "postal orders are issued at ..." **2** (*il ritirarsi: Mil*) withdrawal, retreat; (: *di acque*) subsidence; **dopo il suo ritiro dal mondo dello spettacolo** after retiring from show business **3** (*luogo appartato, anche Rel*) retreat; **in ritiro** in retreat

ritmato, -a [rit'mato] AGG rhythmic(al)

ritmico, -a, -ci, -che [ˈritmiko] AGG rhythmic(al)

ritmo [ˈritmo] SM **1** (*gen*) rhythm; **ballare al ritmo di valzer** to waltz **2** (*fig: velocità*) speed, rate; **al ritmo di** at a speed *o* rate of; **a questo ritmo** at this rate

rito [ˈrito] SM (*Rel*) rite; (*cerimonia*) ritual; **di rito** customary, usual

ritoccare [ritok'kare] /20/ VT (*disegno, foto, trucco*) to touch up; (*testo, prezzi*) to alter

ritocco, -chi [ri'tokko] SM (*di disegno, trucco*) touching up *no pl*; (*di testo*) alteration; **dare un ritocco a qc** to touch sth up; alter sth

ritorcere [ri'tɔrtʃere] VB IRREG /106/ VT (*filato*) to twist; (*fig: accusa, insulto*) to throw back; **ritorcersi** VIP (*tornare a danno di*): **ritorcersi contro** to turn against

ritornare [ritor'nare] /72/ VI (*aus* essere) = tornare ♦ VT (*restituire*): **ritornare qc a qn** to return sth to sb, give sth back to sb

ritornello [ritor'nello] SM (*Mus, Poesia*) refrain; (*fig: storia*) story; **è sempre il solito ritornello** it's always the same old story

ritorno [ri'torno] SM **1** (*gen*) return; **essere di ritorno** to be back; **sarò di ritorno venerdì prossimo** I'll be back next Friday; **far ritorno** to return; **al ritorno** (*tornando*) on the way back; **al ritorno siamo passati per Bristol** we went through Bristol on the way back; **al mio/tuo ritorno** on my/your return; **il viaggio di ritorno** the return journey; **il viaggio di ritorno è stato più breve** the return journey was shorter; **durante il (viaggio di) ritorno** on the return trip, on the way back; **due ore andata e ritorno** two hours there and back; **un biglietto di andata e ritorno** a return (*Brit*), round-trip (*USA*) ticket; **girone di ritorno** (*Sport*) second half of the season; **avere un ritorno di fiamma** (*Aut*) to backfire; **hanno avuto un ritorno di fiamma** (*fig*) they're back in love again **2** (*in restituzione*): **fammelo avere di ritorno entro la fine del mese** let me have it back by the end of the month

ritorsione [ritor'sjone] SF (*rappresaglia*) retaliation

ritorto, -a [ri'tɔrto] PP *di* ritorcere ♦ AGG (*cotone, corda*) twisted

ritrarre [ri'trarre] VB IRREG /123/ VT **1** (*Pittura, anche fig*) to portray, depict **2** (*tirare indietro*) to withdraw; **ritrarsi** VR to move back

ritrattare [ritrat'tare] /72/ VT **1** (*dichiarazione*) to retract, withdraw, take back **2** (*trattare nuovamente*) to deal with again, cover again

ritrattazione [ritrattat'tsjone] SF withdrawal

ritrattista, -i, -e [ritrat'tista] SM, SF portrait painter

ritratto, -a [ri'tratto] PP *di* ritrarre ♦ SM portrait; **essere il ritratto della salute** to be the picture of health; **è il ritratto di suo padre** he's his father's image

ritrosia [ritro'sia] SF (*riluttanza*) reluctance, unwillingness; (*timidezza*) shyness

ritroso, -a [ri'troso] AGG **1** (*timido*) shy, bashful **2** (*restio*): **ritroso a fare qc** reluctant to do sth ♦ **a ritroso** AVV (*indietro*) backwards

ritrovamento [ritrova'mento] SM (*di cadavere, oggetto smarrito*) finding; (*oggetto ritrovato*) find

ritrovare [ritro'vare] /72/ VT **1** (*ricuperare: oggetto, persona*) to find; (*pace*) to find again; (*forza*) to find again, recover; **ho ritrovato il telefonio** I've found my phone **2** (*rincontrare*) to meet again; (*per caso*) to run into; **ritrovarsi** VIP **1** (*in una situazione*) to find o.s., end up; **si ritrovò solo/a fare i lavori più umili** he ended up alone/doing the most menial tasks; **ci ritrovammo al punto di partenza** we ended up where we started **2** (*possedere: fam, scherz*): **con la fortuna che si ritrova...** with his luck ... **3** (*incontrarsi*): **ritrovarsi con** (*amici*) to meet

ritrovato [ritro'vato] SM discovery

ritrovo [ri'trɔvo] SM (*punto d'incontro*) meeting place; **ritrovo notturno** night club

ritto, -a [ˈritto] AGG (*in piedi: persona*) upright, on one's feet; **non riusciva a star ritto** he couldn't stand upright; **aveva i capelli ritti** his hair was standing on end

rituale [ritu'ale] AGG (*di rito*) ritual; (*fig: solito*) customary, usual ♦ SM (*Rel*) ritual

ritwit'tare [ritwit'tare] /72/ VT (*su Twitter*) to retweet

riunione [riu'njone] SF (*adunanza*) meeting; (*riconciliazione*) reunion; **una riunione familiare** a family gathering; **essere in riunione** to be in a meeting

riunire [riu'nire] /55/ VT **1** (*mettere insieme: oggetti*) to gather together, collect; (: *persone*) to assemble, get together; (: *fig: riconciliare*) to bring together (again), reunite; **siamo qui riuniti per festeggiare...** we are gathered here to celebrate ... **2** (*ricongiungere*) to put together, join together; **riunirsi**

VIP (*radunarsi*) to meet; (*tornare insieme*) to come together again, be reunited

riuscire [riuʃˈʃire] /125/ VI IRREG (*aus* essere) 1 (*aver successo*): riuscire (in qc/a fare qc) to succeed (in sth/in doing sth), be successful (in sth/in doing sth); il tentativo non è riuscito the attempt was unsuccessful; riuscire negli studi to do well at school (*o* at university) 2 (*essere capace*) to be able, manage; riuscire a fare qc to manage *o* be able to do sth; siamo riusciti a convincerla we managed to persuade her; non riesco a farlo I can't do it, I am unable to do it; non mi riesce di farlo I can't (manage to) do it; non ci riesco I can't 3 (*essere, risultare*) to be, prove (to be); ti riuscirà più facile dopo un po' di pratica it'll be easier *o* you'll find it easier after a bit of practice; mi riesce antipatico I don't like him; mi riesce difficile I find it difficult 4 (*uscire di nuovo*) to go out again, go back out

riuscita [riuʃˈʃita] SF (*esito*) result, outcome; (*buon esito*) success; fare *o* avere una buona riuscita to be a success, be successful

riutilizzare [riutilidˈdzare] /72/ VT to use again, reuse

riva [ˈriva] SF (*di mare, lago*) shore; (*di fiume*) bank; in riva al mare on the (sea) shore

rivale [riˈvale] AGG rival *attr*; appartengono a bande rivali they belong to rival gangs ♦ SM, SF rival; non avere rivali (*anche fig*) to be unrivalled; come stilista non ha rivali as a designer he has no rivals

rivaleggiare [rivaledˈdʒare] /62/ VI (*aus* avere) to compete, vie; rivaleggiare con qn per qc to vie with sb for sth; nessuno può rivaleggiare con lui he is unrivalled

rivalità [rivaliˈta] SF INV rivalry

rivalsa [riˈvalsa] SF 1 (*risarcimento*) compensation 2 (*rivincita*) revenge; prendersi una rivalsa su qn to take revenge on sb

rivalutare [rivaluˈtare] /72/ VT (*Econ*) to revalue; (*fig*) to re-evaluate

rivalutazione [rivalutatˈtsjone] SF (*Econ*) revaluation; (*fig*) re-evaluation

rivangare [rivanˈgare] /80/ VT (*ricordi*) to dig up (again) ♦ VI (*aus* avere) rivangare nel passato to dig up the past again

rivedere [riveˈdere] VB IRREG /127/ VT 1 (*vedere di nuovo: film ecc*) to see again; (: *persona*) to see again, meet again; dalla scorsa estate non li ho più rivisti I haven't seen them since last summer; guarda chi si rivede! look who it is! 2 (*verificare, correggere*) to revise, check; rivedere le bozze to proofread; rivedersi VR (*uso reciproco*) to see each other again, meet (again)

rivedrò ecc [riveˈdrɔ] VB *vedi* rivedere

rivelare [riveˈlare] /72/ VT (*svelare*) to reveal; (*segreto*) to disclose, reveal; (*dimostrare: capacità*) to reveal, display, show; non ha voluto rivelare il nome dell'informatore she wouldn't reveal the name of her informant; rivelarsi VIP (*tendenza, talento*) to be revealed, reveal itself; rivelarsi VR to prove to be; rivelarsi onesto to prove to be honest; si è rivelato un ottimo portiere he proved to be an excellent goalkeeper

rivelatore, -trice [rivelaˈtore] AGG revealing ♦ SM (*Tecn*) detector; (*Fot*) developer

rivelazione [rivelatˈtsjone] SF (*gen*) revelation; (*di segreto, notizia*) disclosure; quell'attore è stato la rivelazione dell'anno that actor was the discovery of the year

rivendere [riˈvendere] /29/ VT (*vendere: di nuovo*) to resell, sell again; (: *al dettaglio*) to retail, sell retail

rivendicare [rivendiˈkare] /20/ VT to claim, demand

rivendicazione [rivendikatˈtsjone] SF claim; rivendicazioni salariali wage claims; rivendicazioni sindacali union demands

rivendita [riˈvendita] SF (*negozio*) retailer's (shop); rivendita di tabacchi tobacconist's (shop) (*Brit*), tobacco *o* smoke shop (*USA*)

rivenditore, -trice [rivendiˈtore] SM, SF retailer; rivenditore autorizzato authorized dealer

riverberare [riverbeˈrare] /72/ VT (*luce, calore*) to reflect; (*suono*) to reverberate

riverbero [riˈverbero] SM (*vedi vb*) reflection; reverberation

riverente [riveˈrente] AGG reverent, respectful

riverenza [riveˈrentsa] SF 1 (*rispetto*) reverence, respect 2

(*inchino*) bow; (*di donna*) curtsey; fece una profonda riverenza he bowed low

riverire [riveˈrire] /55/ VT (*rispettare*) to revere, respect; la riverisco, professore (*salutando*) my respects, professor

riversare [riverˈsare] /72/ VT 1 (*versare*) to pour; (*di nuovo*) to pour again; (*fig: amore, affetto*) riversare su to shower on, lavish on; ha riversato tutte le sue energie in quel lavoro he threw himself into that job 2 (*Inform*) to dump; riversarsi VIP to pour (out); la folla si riversò nelle strade the crowd poured into the streets

❏ riversare non si traduce mai con la parola inglese *reverse*

rivestimento [rivestiˈmento] SM (*azione, materiale*) covering; (*strato: di vernice*) coating, veneer

rivestire [rivesˈtire] /45/ VT 1 (*ricoprire: gen*): rivestire (di) to cover (with); (*con vernice*) to coat (with); rivestire in stoffa l'interno di una scatola to line a box with material; rivestire di piastrelle to tile 2 (*carica*) to hold; rivestire un grado elevato to be high-ranking 3 (*vestire di nuovo*) to dress again; rivestirsi VR to get dressed (again)

rividi ecc [riˈvidi] VB *vedi* rivedere

riviera [riˈvjera] SF 1 coast; la Riviera Ligure the Italian Riviera 2 (*Equitazione: ostacolo*) water jump

rivincita [riˈvintʃita] SF (*Sport*) return match; (*Carte*) return game; (*fig*) revenge; prendersi la rivincita (su qn) to take *o* get one's revenge (on sb)

rivissuto, -a [rivisˈsuto] PP *di* rivivere

rivista [riˈvista] SF 1 (*periodica*) magazine; (*letteraria*) review; (*Tecn, Med*) journal; una rivista di moda a fashion magazine 2 (*Teatro, TV*) revue, variety show 3 (*Mil*) inspection; passare in rivista to review

rivisto, -a [riˈvisto] PP *di* rivedere

rivitalizzante [rivitalidˈdzante] AGG (*prodotti cosmetici*) revitalizing

rivitalizzare [rivitalidˈdzare] /72/ VT to revitalize

rivivere [riˈvivere] VB IRREG /130/ VT: rivivere qc (*avventura, esperienza*) to live through sth again ♦ VI (*aus* essere) (*vivere di nuovo*) to live again; (*prendere vigore*) to come to life again; (*tradizioni*) to be revived; far rivivere (*resuscitare*) to bring back to life; (*rinvigorire*) to revive, put new life into; (*epoca, moda*) to revive

rivo [ˈrivo] SM (*di lava, lacrime*) stream

rivolgere [riˈvoldʒere] VB IRREG /96/ VT (*indirizzare: attenzione, sguardo, proiettore*) to turn, direct; (: *parole*) to address; rivolgere un'arma contro qn to point a weapon at sb; rivolgere lo sguardo verso qn to turn *o* direct one's gaze towards sb; le rivolse uno sguardo di rimprovero he gave her a disapproving look; rivolgere un'accusa/una critica a qn to accuse/criticize sb; rivolgere la propria attenzione a un problema to turn one's attention to a problem; rivolgere la parola a qn to talk *o* speak to sb, address sb; non si rivolgono più la parola they are no longer on speaking terms; rivolgere un saluto a qn to greet sb, say hello to sb; rivolgersi VR 1 rivolgersi a (*per informazioni*) to go and see, go and speak to, go and ask; dovrebbe rivolgersi all'impiegato laggiù you should go and ask the man over there; rivolgersi all'ufficio competente to apply to the office concerned; non mi rivolgevo a te I wasn't talking to you; si rivolse a lei dicendo... he turned to her and said ... 2 rivolgersi verso (*girarsi*) to turn to

rivolgimento [rivoldʒiˈmento] SM upheaval

rivolsi ecc [riˈvolsi] VB *vedi* rivolgere

rivolta [riˈvolta] SF revolt, rebellion; in rivolta (contro) in revolt (against)

rivoltante [rivolˈtante] AGG revolting, disgusting

rivoltare [rivolˈtare] /72/ VT 1 (*voltare: di nuovo*) to turn again; (: *pagine, carte*) to turn over again; (: *vestito*) to turn inside out; (: *bistecca, frittata*) to turn over 2 (*disgustare*) to revolt, disgust; una scena che fa rivoltare lo stomaco a scene which turns one's stomach; rivoltarsi VR (*rigirarsi*) to turn; rivoltarsi nel letto to toss and turn (in bed); rivoltarsi VIP (*ribellarsi*): rivoltarsi (a) to revolt *o* rebel (against)

rivoltella [rivolˈtella] SF (*gen*) pistol; (*a tamburo*) revolver

rivolto, -a [riˈvolto] PP *di* rivolgere

rivoltoso, -a [rivolˈtoso] AGG rebellious ♦ SM, SF rebel

rivoluzionare [rivoluttsjo'nare] /72/ VT (*anche fig*) to revolutionize; (*fig: mettere sottosopra*) to turn upside down `

rivoluzionario, -ria, -ri, -rie [rivoluttsjo'narjo] AGG, SM, SF revolutionary

rivoluzione [rivolut'tsjone] SF (*gen, anche Pol, Mat, Astron*) revolution; (*fig: scompiglio*) mess; **rivoluzione industriale** industrial revolution

rizzare [rit'tsare] /72/ VT (*palo*) to erect; (*tenda*) to pitch; (*coda*) to raise, lift; (*orecchie*) to prick up; **è roba da far rizzare i capelli** it's enough to make your hair stand on end; **rizzarsi** VR to stand up; **rizzarsi in piedi** to stand up, get to one's feet; **rizzarsi a sedere** to sit up; **rizzarsi** VIP: **gli si sono rizzati i capelli** his hair stood on end

RN SIGLA = Rimini

RNA ['erre'enne'a] SIGLA M RNA (= *ribonucleic acid*)

RO SIGLA = Rovigo

roba ['rɔba] SF 1 (*gen*) things *pl*, stuff; (*cose proprie*) belongings *pl*, things *pl*, possessions *pl*; **roba da lavare** washing; **posso mettere la mia roba da lavare in lavatrice?** can I put my washing in the machine?; **roba da mangiare** food, things to eat; **c'era un sacco di roba da mangiare** there was lots of food; **roba da stirare** ironing; **roba usata** secondhand goods; **roba di valore** valuables; **ho un sacco di roba da fare** I've got a lot to do, I've got lots of things to do; **ha ancora qui tutta la sua roba?** has he still got all his things here?; **che roba è questa?** what is this?; **cos'è quella roba sul tavolo?** what's that stuff on the table?; **e chiami whisky questa roba?** and you call this stuff whisky? 2 (*faccenda, affare*) affair, matter; **non è roba che ti riguardi** this doesn't concern you 3 (*fraseologia*): **bella roba!** (*iro: che gran cosa!*) so what!; (: *che mascalzonata!*) that's nice, isn't it!; **roba da matti** *o* **pazzi!** it's sheer madness *o* lunacy!, it's just incredible

❑ **roba** non si traduce mai con la parola inglese *robe*

robivecchi [robi'vekki] SM INV, SF INV junk dealer

robot ['rɔbot] SM INV robot; **robot di** *o* **da cucina** foodprocessor

robotica [ro'botika] SF robotics *sg*

robustezza [robus'tettsa] SF (*di persona, pianta*) robustness, sturdiness; (*di edificio, ponte*) soundness

robusto, -a [ro'busto] AGG (*persona, pianta*) robust, sturdy; (*euf: persona: grasso*) well-built; (*edificio, ponte*) sound, solid; (*corda, catena*) strong; (*appetito*) healthy; (*vino*) full-bodied; (*voce*) powerful

rocca, -che ['rɔkka] SF fortress; **la Rocca di Gibilterra** the Rock of Gibraltar

roccaforte [rokka'fɔrte] SF (*pl* **roccheforti**) (*anche fig*) stronghold

rocchetto [rok'ketto] SM 1 (*di filo*) spool 2 (*Cine*) reel 3 (*Elettr*) coil

roccia, -ce ['rɔttʃa] SF (*gen, anche Geol*) rock; (*sport*) rock climbing; **fare roccia** to go rock climbing

rocciatore, -trice [rottʃa'tore] SM, SF rock climber

roccioso, -a [rot'tʃoso] AGG rocky; **le Montagne Rocciose** the Rocky Mountains

roco, -a, -chi, -che ['rɔko] AGG hoarse

rodaggio, -gi [ro'daddʒo] SM (*Aut*) running (*Brit*) *o* breaking (*USA*) in; **la macchina è ancora in rodaggio** the car is still being run *o* broken in; **periodo di rodaggio** (*fig*) period of adjustment

Rodano ['rɔdano] SM: **il Rodano** the Rhone

rodare [ro'dare] /72/ VT (*Aut, Tecn*) to run (*Brit*) *o* break (*USA*) in

rodeo [ro'dɛo] SM rodeo

rodere ['rɔdere] VB IRREG /49/ VT (*rosicchiare*) to gnaw (at); (*corrodere*) to corrode; **rodersi il fegato** (*fig*) to torment o.s.; **rodersi** VR: **rodersi dal rimorso/dall'invidia** to be consumed with remorse/with envy

Rodi ['rɔdi] SF Rhodes *sg*

roditore [rodi'tore] SM (*Zool*) rodent

rododendro [rodo'dɛndro] SM (*Bot*) rhododendron

rogito ['rɔdʒito] SM (*Dir*) (notary's) deed

rogna ['rɔɲɲa] SF (*Med*) scabies *sg*; (*di animale*) mange; (*fig: guaio*) trouble, bother, nuisance; **cercar rogne** to be looking for trouble, to be asking for it; **ha avuto rogne con la polizia** he got into trouble with the police

rognone [roɲ'ɲone] SM (*Culin*) kidney

rognoso, -a [roɲ'ɲoso] AGG (*persona*) scabby; (*animale*) mangy; (*fig*) troublesome

rogo, -ghi ['rɔgo] SM (*funebre*) funeral pyre; (*supplizio*): **il rogo** the stake; **mandare qn al rogo** to condemn sb to be burned at the stake; **la casa era ormai un rogo** the house was now a mass of flames

rollare [rol'lare] /72/ VI (*aus* avere) (*Naut, Aer*) to roll
♦ VT (*fam: sigaretta*) to roll (up)

rollino [rol'lino] SM = **rullino**

rollio, -lii [rol'lio] SM (*Naut, Aer*) roll, rolling

Roma ['roma] SF Rome; **domani andremo a Roma** we're going to Rome tomorrow; **abita a Roma** she lives in Rome

romagnolo, -a [romaɲ'ɲɔlo] AGG of *o* from Romagna ♦ SM, SF inhabitant *o* native of Romagna

romanesco, -sca, -schi, -sche [roma'nesko] AGG Roman
♦ SM Roman dialect

Romania [roma'nia] SF Romania

romanico, -a, -ci, -che [ro'maniko] AGG, SM (*Arte*) Romanesque

romano, -a [ro'mano] AGG Roman; **la Chiesa romana** the Roman Catholic Church; **fare** *o* **pagare alla romana** to go Dutch ♦ SM, SF Roman

romanticheria [romantike'ria] SF sentimentality

romanticismo [romanti'tʃizmo] SM romanticism

romantico, -a, -ci, -che [ro'mantiko] AGG, SM, SF romantic

romanza [ro'mandza] SF (*Mus, Letteratura*) romance

romanzare [roman'dzare] /72/ VT to romanticize

romanzesco, -a, -schi, -sche [roman'dzesko] AGG (*stile, personaggi*) fictional; (*fig: amori, vicende*) fantastic, storybook *attr* ♦ SM: **avere del romanzesco** to sound like something out of a novel

romanziere, -a [roman'dzjere] SM, SF novelist

romanzo [ro'mandzo] SM (*gen*) novel; **leggo soprattutto romanzi** I mainly read novels; **romanzo d'amore** love story; **romanzo d'appendice** serial novel, serial (story); **romanzo d'avventure** adventure story; **romanzo cavalleresco** tale of chivalry; **romanzo di fantascienza** science-fiction novel *o* story; **romanzo fiume** saga; **romanzo giallo** detective story; **romanzo poliziesco** detective story; **romanzo rosa** romantic novel; **romanzo sceneggiato** novel adapted for television ♦ AGG (*lingua*) Romance *attr*

rombare [rom'bare] /72/ VI (*aus* avere) to roar, rumble, thunder

rombo¹ ['rombo] SM (*rumore*) roar, rumble, thunder

rombo² ['rombo] SM (*Geom*) rhombus

rombo³ ['rombo] SM (*pesce*) turbot

romeno, -a [ro'mɛno], **rumeno, -a** [ru'mɛno] AGG, SM, SF Romanian ♦ SM (*lingua*) Romanian

rompere ['rompere] VB IRREG /97/ VT (*gen, anche fig*) to break; (*sfasciare*) to smash up; (*scarpe, calzoni*) to split; (*fidanzamento, negoziati*) to break off; **ho rotto un bicchiere!** I've broken a glass!; **rompere qc in testa a qn** to break sth over sb's head; **il fiume ha rotto gli argini** the river burst its banks; **rompere un contratto** to break a contract; **rompere il silenzio/il ghiaccio** to break the silence/the ice; **rompere gli indugi** (*fig*) to take action; **rompere le scatole a qn** (*fam*) to get on sb's nerves; **hai proprio rotto (le scatole)!** (*fam*) knock it off!; **uffa quanto rompi!** (*fam*) what a pain in the neck you are!; **rompere (i rapporti) con qn** to break off with sb; **un rumore che rompe i timpani** a deafening noise; **rompersi una gamba/l'osso del collo** to break a leg/one's neck; **rompersi la testa** (*fig*) to rack one's brains; **rompersi la schiena** (*fig*) to work hard; **rompersi** VIP (*gen*) to break

❑ **rompere** non si traduce mai con la parola inglese *romp*

rompicapo [rompi'kapo] SM (*problema*) worry, headache; (*gioco enigmistico*) brain-teaser, puzzle

rompicollo, -ci [rompi'kɔllo] SM daredevil

rompighiaccio, -ci [rompi'gjattʃo] SM icebreaker

rompiscatole [rompis'katole] SM INV, SF INV (*fam*) nuisance, pain in the neck; **è un vero rompiscatole!** he's a real pain!

ronda ['ronda] SF (*Mil*) rounds *pl*; (*Polizia*) beat, patrol, rounds *pl*; (*pattuglia*) patrol; **fare la ronda** to be on one's rounds (*o* on patrol); **essere di ronda** to be on patrol duty

rondella [ron'della] SF (*Tecn*) washer

rondine ['rondine] SF (*uccello*) swallow; **una rondine non fa primavera** (*Proverbio*) one swallow doesn't make a summer; **rondine di mare** tern

rondone [ron'done] SM (*uccello*) swift

ronfare [ron'fare] /72/ VI (*aus avere*) (*persona: russare*) to snore; (*gatto: far le fusa*) to purr

ronzare [ron'dzare] /72/ VI (*aus avere*) to buzz, hum; **ronzare intorno a qn** (*fig*) to hang about sb; **quell'idea continuava a ronzargli in testa** that idea was still buzzing around in his head; **mi ronzano le orecchie** my ears are buzzing

ronzino [ron'dzino] SM (*pegg: cavallo*) nag

ronzio, -ii [ron'dzio] SM (*di insetti*) buzzing, humming; (*del motore*) humming; (*di orecchie*) buzzing, ringing; **ronzio auricolare** (*Med*) tinnitus *sg*

rosa ['rɔza] AGG INV (*colore*) pink; (*sentimentale: letteratura, romanzo*) romantic; **stampa rosa** women's magazines; **vedere tutto rosa** to see everything through rose-coloured spectacles ♦ SF **1** (*Bot*) rose; **non sono tutte rose e fiori** (*fig*) it's not all a bed of roses; **se son rose fioriranno** (*fig*) the proof of the pudding is in the eating; **non c'è rosa senza spine** (*Proverbio*) there's no rose without a thorn; **rosa canina** dog rose; **rosa di Natale** Christmas rose **2** (*fig: gruppo*): **rosa dei candidati** list of candidates **3 rosa dei venti** wind rose ♦ SM INV (*colore*) pink

rosaio, -ai [ro'zajo] SM (*pianta*) rosebush, rose tree; (*giardino*) rose garden; (*aiuola*) rosebed

rosario, -ri [ro'zarjo] SM (*Rel*) rosary; **dire** *o* **recitare il rosario** to say *o* recite the rosary

rosato, -a [ro'zato] AGG (*colore*) pinkish, rosy; (*vino*) rosé ♦ SM INV (*vino*) rosé (wine)

roseo, -a ['rɔzeo] AGG (*colorito*) pinkish, rosy; (*fig: ottimistico*) rosy, bright

roseto [ro'zeto] SM rose garden

rosetta [ro'zetta] SF **1** (*diamante*) rose-cut diamond **2** (*Tecn: rondella*) washer **3** (*pane*) kind of roll

rosi *ecc* ['rɔsi] VB *vedi* **rodere**

rosicchiare [rosik'kjare] /19/ VT (*rodere*) to gnaw (at); (*mangiucchiare*) to nibble (at); **rosicchiarsi le unghie** to bite one's nails

rosmarino [rozma'rino] SM (*Bot*) rosemary

roso, -a ['rɔso] PP *di* **rodere**

rosolare [rozo'lare] /72/ VT (*Culin*) to brown

rosolia [rozo'lia] SF (*Med*) German measles *sg*, rubella (*termine tecn*)

rosone [ro'zone] SM (*finestra: su chiese*) rose window; **rosone da soffitto** ceiling rose

rospo ['rɔspo] SM (*Zool*) toad; **è un rospo** (*pegg: persona*) she (*o* he) is hideous; **ingoiare un** *o* **il rospo** (*fig*) to swallow a bitter pill; **sputa il rospo!** out with it!

rossetto [ros'setto] SM lipstick

rossiccio, -cia, -ci, -ce [ros'sittʃo] AGG reddish

rosso, -a ['rosso] AGG (*gen*) red; **ha i capelli rossi** she's got red hair; **diventare rosso (per la vergogna)** to blush *o* go red (with *o* for shame); **rosso come un gambero** *o* **un peperone** (*per la vergogna*) as red as a beetroot (*Brit*) *o* beet (*USA*); (*per il sole*) as red as a lobster; **l'Armata Rossa** the Red Army; **il mar Rosso** the Red Sea ♦ SM (*colore*) red; (*di roulette*) rouge, red; (*di semaforo*) red light; (*d'uovo*) yolk; (*vino*) red wine; **rosso di sera bel tempo si spera** (*Proverbio*) red sky at night shepherd's delight; **rosso di mattina maltempo s'avvicina** (*Proverbio*) red sky at dawning shepherd's warning; **essere in rosso** (*Banca*) to be in the red ♦ SM, SF (*che ha i capelli rossi*) redhead; (*fig: Pol*) Red; (*persona di sinistra*) red, left-winger

rossore [ros'sore] SM (*per infiammazione*) redness; (*delle guance*) flush; (*per vergogna*) blush; **sentirsi salire il rossore alle guance** (*per vergogna, pudore*) to begin to blush, feel one's cheeks go red

rosticceria [rostittʃe'ria] SF *shop selling roast meat and other prepared food*

rostro ['rɔstro] SM (*di rapace*) beak; (*sulle navi*) rostrum

rotabile [ro'tabile] AGG: **strada rotabile** carriageway, roadway; **materiale rotabile** (*Ferr*) rolling stock

rotaia [ro'taja] SF (*Ferr*) rail; (*guida metallica*) rut, track

rotare [ro'tare] /72/ VT, VI (*aus avere*) to rotate

rotativo, -a [rota'tivo] AGG rotating, rotation *attr*

rotazione [rotat'tsjone] SF rotation; **rotazione delle colture** (*Agr*) crop rotation

roteare [rote'are] /72/ VT (*spada, bastone*) to whirl; (*occhi*) to roll ♦ VI (*aus essere*) (*uccello rapace*) to circle

rotella [ro'tella] SF (*gen*) small wheel; (*di pattini*) roller; (*di mobili*) castor; (*ingranaggio*) cog wheel; (*Culin: per la pasta*) pastry wheel; **una valigia con le rotelle** a case with wheels; **pattini a rotelle** roller skates; **gli manca una rotella** (*fig: fam*) he's got a screw loose

rotocalco, -chi [roto'kalko] SM (*rivista*) illustrated magazine; (*Tip*) rotogravure

rotolare [roto'lare] /72/ VT, VI (*aus essere*) to roll; **il pallone è rotolato giù per le scale** the ball rolled down the steps; **rotolarsi** VR to roll (about); **rotolarsi per terra** to roll about on the floor; **rotolarsi nell'erba** to roll (about) on the grass; **rotolarsi (per terra) dalle risate** to roll about laughing

rotolio, -lii [roto'lio] SM rolling

rotolo ['rɔtolo] SM (*di carta, stoffa*) roll; (*di corda*) coil; (*di documenti*) scroll; **un rotolo di carta igienica** a roll of toilet paper; **andare a rotoli** (*fig*) to go to rack and ruin; **mandare a rotoli** (*fig*) to ruin

rotondo, -a [ro'tondo] AGG (*circolare*) round; (*paffuto: viso*) round, full

rotore [ro'tore] SM (*Tecn*) rotor

rotta[1] ['rɔtta] SF (*Aer, Naut*) route, course; **essere in rotta per** *o* **in** en route for; **fare rotta su** *o* **per** *o* **verso** to head for *o* towards; **cambiare rotta** (*anche fig*) to change course; **in rotta di collisione** on a collision course; **ufficiale di rotta** navigator, navigating officer

rotta[2] ['rɔtta] SF **1** (*fig: rottura*): **essere in rotta con qn** (*fig*) to be on bad terms with sb; **a rotta di collo** at breakneck speed **2** (*disfatta*): **mettere in rotta il nemico** to rout the enemy

rottamare [rotta'mare] /72/ VT (*auto*) *to scrap an old vehicle in return for incentives*

rottamazione [rottamat'tsjone] SF *the scrapping of old vehicles in return for incentives*

rottame [rot'tame] SM **1** (*pezzo di ferro*) piece of scrap iron; **rottami** SMPL (*di nave, auto, aereo*) wreckage *sg*; **rottami di ferro** scrap iron *sg* **2** (*fig: pegg: persona, macchina*) wreck

rotto, -a ['rotto] PP *di* **rompere** ♦ AGG (*gen*) broken; (*braccio, gamba*) broken, fractured; **avere le ossa rotte** (*fig*) to ache all over; **rotto a** (*persona: abituato*) accustomed *o* inured to; **è rotto ad ogni esperienza** (*fig*) he's seen it all, he's been through it all ♦ SM: **per il rotto della cuffia** by the skin of one's teeth ♦ SMPL: **30 euro e rotti** 30 odd euros

❏ **rotto** non si traduce mai con la parola inglese *rotten*

rottura [rot'tura] SF (*azione*) breaking *no pl*; (*di rapporti*) breaking off *no pl*; (*fra amici*) split-up, break-up; (*di negoziati*) breakdown; (*di contratto*) breach; **è una tale rottura!** (*fam: persona*) he's such a pain (in the neck)!; (*: situazione*) it's such a drag *o* bore!; **rottura delle acque** (*Med*) breaking of the waters

roulotte [ru'lɔt] SF INV caravan (*Brit*), trailer (*USA*)

rovente [ro'vente] AGG (*ferro, carbone*) red-hot; (*fig: sabbia, sole*) burning

rovere ['rovere] SM, SF (*albero*) English oak ♦ SM (*legno*) oak; **una botte di rovere** an oak barrel

rovesciare [roveʃ'ʃare] /14/ VT (*far cadere: gen*) to knock over; (*: liquido: intenzionalmente*) to pour; (*: accidentalmente*) to spill; (*capovolgere: barca*) to capsize, turn upside down; (*fig: situazione*) to reverse; (*: governo*) to overthrow; **mi sono alzato di scatto e ho rovesciato la sedia** I got up in a hurry and knocked over the chair; **rovesciare qc addosso a qn** to pour sth over sb; **ha rovesciato tutto il latte per terra** she spilled all the milk on the floor; **rovesciare la testa all'indietro** to throw one's head back; **rovesciarsi** VIP (*sedia, macchina*) to overturn; (*barca*) to capsize; (*liquido*) to spill; (*fig: situazione*) to be reversed; **si è rovesciato tutto per terra** everything fell to the floor; (*liquido*) it all spilled onto the floor; **la folla si rovesciò nella piazza** the crowd poured into the square

rovescio, -scia, -sci, -sce [ro'veʃʃo] AGG (*Maglia*) purl *attr*

♦ SM 1 (*lato: di stoffa, indumento*) wrong side, other side; (*: di medaglia*) reverse; **stirala dal rovescio** iron it inside out; **il rovescio della medaglia** (*fig*) the other side of the coin 2 (*Meteor*) downpour, heavy shower 3 (*fig*): **rovescio di fortuna** setback 4 (*Maglia: anche: punto rovescio*) purl (stitch) 5 (*Tennis*) backhand (stroke); **ha un rovescio potentissimo** she has a very powerful backhand ♦ **a rovescio, alla rovescia** AVV (*con il davanti dietro*) back to front; (*sottosopra*) upside down; (*con l'esterno all'interno*) inside out; **oggi mi va tutto alla rovescia** everything is going wrong (for me) today; **capisce sempre tutto alla rovescia** he always gets things the wrong way round, he always gets the wrong end of the stick

rovina [ro'vina] SF (*gen, anche fig*) ruin; **in rovina** (*palazzo*) in ruins; **rovina finanziaria** financial ruin; **mandare in rovina** to ruin; **andare in rovina** (*andare a pezzi*) to collapse; (*fig*) to go to rack and ruin; **sull'orlo della rovina** on the brink of ruin

rovinare [rovi'nare] /72/ VT (*oggetto, persona, anche fig*) to ruin; (*fig: atmosfera, festa*) to ruin, spoil; **si è rovinata il vestito** she has ruined her dress ♦ VI (*aus essere*) (*crollare*) to collapse, fall down; (*precipitare*) to fall; **rovinarsi** VR (*persona*) to be ruined, ruin o.s.; **mi voglio rovinare!** (*fig: sogg: venditore*) I'm giving it away!; **rovinarsi** VIP (*oggetto*) to get o be ruined

rovinato, -a [rovi'nato] AGG (*oggetto*) ruined, damaged; (*fig: persona*) ruined

rovinoso, -a [rovi'noso] AGG ruinous

rovistare [rovis'tare] /72/ VT (*casa*) to ransack; (*tasche*) to rummage in (o through), search thoroughly

rovo ['rovo] SM (*Bot*) blackberry bush, bramble bush; (*cespugli spinosi*) briar

rozzezza [rod'dzettsa] SF (*vedi agg*) roughness; coarseness

rozzo, -a ['roddzo] AGG (*gen*) rough; (*persona, modi*) uncouth, coarse

RP ['erre'pi] SIGLA FPL (= *Relazioni Pubbliche*) PR

RR ABBR (*Posta*: = *ricevuta di ritorno*)

RSVP ABBR (= *répondez s'il vous plaît*) RSVP

ruba ['ruba] SF: **andare a ruba** to sell like hot cakes

rubacuori [ruba'kwɔri] SM INV, SF INV heart-breaker, charmer

rubare [ru'bare] /72/ VT: **rubare (qc a qn)** (*gen*) to steal (sth from sb); (*fig: idea, affetti, posto*) to steal (sth from sb), take (sth from sb); **gli hanno rubato tutto** they robbed him of everything; **a Londra mi hanno rubato la macchina fotografica** my camera was stolen in London; **rubare il mestiere a qn** to do sb out of a job; **posso rubarti un minuto?** can I steal a minute of your time?; **mi hai rubato le parole di bocca** you've taken the words right out of my mouth

rubicondo, -a [rubi'kondo] AGG ruddy

rubinetto [rubi'netto] SM tap (*Brit*), faucet (*USA*)

rubino [ru'bino] SM ruby

rubizzo, -a [ru'bittso] AGG lively, sprightly

rublo ['rublo] SM rouble

rubrica, -che [ru'brika] SF 1 (*quaderno*) index notebook; (*per indirizzi e numeri di telefono*) address book 2 (*di giornale: colonna*) column; (*: pagina*) page; **rubrica sportiva** sports page 3 (*Radio, TV: parte di un programma*) spot, time; "**rubrica sportiva**" "sports time"

rude ['rude] AGG (*duro, brusco*) tough; (*rozzo*) rough, coarse

rudere ['rudere] SM (*rovina*) ruins *pl*; (*fig: persona*) wreck

rudimentale [rudimen'tale] AGG rudimentary, basic

rudimenti [rudi'menti] SMPL (*di disciplina*) rudiments; (*di teoria*) (basic) principles

ruffiano, -a [ruf'fjano] SM, SF pander, pimp; (*fig: leccapiedi*) bootlicker

❑ **ruffiano** non si traduce mai con la parola inglese *ruffian*

ruga, -ghe ['ruga] SF wrinkle

ruggine ['ruddʒine] SF (*Chim, Bot: colore*) rust; (*fig: rancore*): **fra di loro c'è della vecchia ruggine** there's bad blood between them ♦ AGG INV (*colore*) rust, rust-coloured

ruggire [rud'dʒire] /55/ VI (*aus avere*) to roar

ruggito [rud'dʒito] SM roar

rugiada [ru'dʒada] SF dew

rugoso, -a [ru'goso] AGG (*pieno di rughe*) wrinkled; (*scabro: superficie*) rough

rullare [rul'lare] /72/ VT (*spianare con il rullo*) to roll ♦ VI (*aus avere*) 1 (*tamburo*) to roll 2 (*Aer*) to taxi

rullino [rul'lino] SM (*Fot*) roll of film, spool; **un rullino da ventiquattro foto** a twenty-four exposure film

rullio, -lii [rul'lio] SM (*di tamburi*) roll

rullo ['rullo] SM 1 (*di tamburo*) roll 2 (*Tecn, Tip*) roller; (*di stampante, macchina da scrivere*) platen; (*Cine*) reel; **rullo compressore** steam-roller

rum [rum] SM INV rum

rumeno, -a [ru'mɛno] AGG, SM, SF Romanian

ruminante [rumi'nante] SM (*Zool*) ruminant

ruminare [rumi'nare] /72/ VT (*Zool*) to ruminate; (*fig*) to ruminate on o over, chew over

rumore [ru'more] SM (*gen*) noise; (*di treno*) rumble; (*di motore*) sound; (*di piatti, stoviglie*) clatter; **cos'è questo rumore?** what's that noise?; **un rumore sordo** a thud; **un rumore stridente** a shrill noise; **un rumore di passi** the sound of footsteps; **rumore di sottofondo** background noise; **fare rumore** to make a noise; **cerca di non far rumore, dormono tutti** try not to make a noise, everybody's asleep; **senza far rumore** quietly; **non si sentiva alcun rumore** not a sound could be heard; **la notizia ha fatto molto rumore** (*fig*) the news aroused great interest

rumoreggiare [rumored'dʒare] /62/ VI (*aus avere*) (*tuono*) to rumble; (*fig: folla*) to clamour (*Brit*), clamor (*USA*)

rumoroso, -a [rumo'roso] AGG (*gen*) noisy; (*voce, risata*) loud, noisy; **una strada rumorosa** a noisy street

ruolo ['rwɔlo] SM 1 (*gen, anche Cine, Teatro*) role, part; **recita nel ruolo di Capitan Uncino** he's playing the part of Captain Hook; **avere un ruolo di primo piano in qc** (*anche fig*) to play a leading role o part in sth 2 (*elenco*) roll, register, list; **ruolo d'imposta** (*Fisco*) tax-list, tax-roll 3 **di ruolo** (*personale, insegnante*) permanent, on the permanent staff; **professore di ruolo** (*Univ*) ≈ lecturer with tenure; **fuori ruolo** (*personale, insegnante*) temporary

ruota ['rwɔta] SF (*gen*) wheel; (*di ingranaggio*) cog (wheel); **fare la ruota** (*Ginnastica*) to do a cartwheel; **gonna a ruota** flared skirt; **a ruote** wheeled; **veicolo a due ruote** two-wheeled vehicle; **auto a 4 ruote motrici** 4-wheel-drive car; **ruote in lega leggera** light alloy wheel; **la ruota della fortuna** the wheel of fortune; **andare a ruota libera** to freewheel; **parlare a ruota libera** (*fig*) to speak freely; **essere l'ultima ruota del carro** (*fig*) to count for nothing; **ruota anteriore** front wheel; **ruota posteriore** back wheel; **ruota di scorta** spare wheel; **ruota di stampa** (*su stampante*) print wheel; **ruota del timone** (*Naut*) (steering) wheel, helm

ruotare /72/ VT, VI to rotate

rupe ['rupe] SF cliff, rock

rupestre [ru'pestre] AGG rocky

rupia [ru'pia] SF (*moneta*) rupee

ruppi ecc ['ruppi] VB *vedi* rompere

rurale [ru'rale] AGG rural, country *attr*

ruscello [ruʃ'ʃɛllo] SM stream, brook

ruspa ['ruspa] SF excavator

ruspante [rus'pante] AGG (*pollo*) free-range

russare [rus'sare] /72/ VI (*aus avere*) to snore

Russia ['russja] SF Russia

russo, -a ['russo] AGG, SM, SF Russian

rustico, -a, -ci, -che ['rustiko] AGG (*gente*) country *attr*, rural; (*arredamento*) rustic; (*fig: modi*) rough, unrefined ♦ SM (*Edil*) shell, carcass; (*deposito per attrezzi*) shed; (*alloggio di contadini*) farm labourer's (*Brit*) o farmhand's cottage

ruta ['ruta] SF (*Bot*) rue

ruttare [rut'tare] /72/ VI (*aus avere*) to belch, to burp

rutto ['rutto] SM belch; **fare un rutto** to belch, to burp

ruvido, -a ['ruvido] AGG (*gen, anche fig*) rough, coarse

ruzzolare [ruttso'lare] /72/ VI (*aus essere*) to roll down, tumble down

ruzzolone [ruttso'lone] SM tumble, fall; **un gran ruzzolone** a heavy fall; **ha fatto un ruzzolone per le scale** he tumbled down the stairs

ruzzoloni [ruttso'loni] AVV: **venir giù ruzzoloni** to fall head over heels; **fare le scale ruzzoloni** to tumble down the stairs

Ss

S¹, s¹ [ˈesse] SF INV, SM INV (*lettera*) S, s; **S come Savona** ≈ S for Sugar ♦ SIGLA F (*taglia*) S (= *small*)
S² ABBR (= *Sud*) S
S. ABBR (= *san(to)*) St
SA SIGLA = **Salerno** ♦ ABBR = **Società Anonima**
sa *ecc* [sa] VB *vedi* **sapere**
sab. ABBR (= *sabato*) Sat.
sabato [ˈsabato] SM Saturday; (*Rel*) sabbath; **Sabato Santo** (*Rel*) Holy Saturday; *vedi* **martedì**
sabbia [ˈsabbja] SF sand; **sulla sabbia** on the sand; **sabbie mobili** quicksand *sg*, quicksands *pl*
sabbiatura [sabbjaˈtura] SF 1 (*Med*) sand bath; **fare le sabbiature** to take sand baths 2 (*Tecn*) sandblasting
sabbioso, -a [sabˈbjoso] AGG sandy
sabotaggio, -gi [saboˈtaddʒo] SM (*Mil, Pol, fig*) sabotage; (*atto*) act of sabotage
sabotare [saboˈtare] /72/ VT to sabotage
sabotatore, -trice [sabotaˈtore] SM, SF saboteur
sacca, -che [ˈsakka] SF 1 (*borsa*) bag; **sacca portabiancheria** laundry bag; **sacca da viaggio** travelling bag 2 (*di fiume*) inlet 3 (*di pus*) pocket; **sacca d'aria** air pocket
saccarina [sakkaˈrina] SF saccharin(e)
saccente [satˈtʃɛnte] AGG presumptuous, conceited ♦ SM, SF know-all (*Brit*), know-it-all (*USA*)
saccheggiare [sakkedˈdʒare] /62/ VT (*Mil*) to sack, plunder; (*fig*) to raid
saccheggio, -gi [sakˈkeddʒo] SM (*Mil*) plundering, sacking; (*fig*) plundering
sacchetto [sakˈketto] SM 1 (*piccolo sacco*) (small) bag; **sacchetto di carta/di plastica** paper/plastic bag 2 (*quantità*) bag(ful)
sacco, -chi [ˈsakko] SM 1 (*contenitore*) sack, bag; (*quantità*) sack(ful); (*fig*) lots of, heaps of; **un sacco di patate** a sack of potatoes; **un sacco di** a lot of; **un sacco di gente** lots of people; **colazione al sacco** packed lunch; **sacco custodia** (*per vestiti*) clothes bag; **sacco da montagna** rucksack; **sacco per i rifiuti** bin bag (*Brit*), garbage bag (*USA*); **sacco postale** mailbag; **cogliere** *o* **prendere qn con le mani nel sacco** to catch sb red-handed; **vuotare il sacco** to confess, spill the beans (*fam*); **mettere qn nel sacco** to cheat sb; **sacco a pelo** sleeping bag 2 (*tessuto*) sacking 3 (*Anat, Bio*) sac 4 (*saccheggio*) plundering, sack(ing)
sacerdote, -essa [satʃerˈdɔte] SM, SF priest (priestess)
sacerdozio, -zi [satʃerˈdɔttsjo] SM priesthood
Sacra Corona Unita [ˈsakra koˈrona uˈnita] SF the Mafia in Puglia
sacramento [sakraˈmento] SM (*Rel*) sacrament
sacrario, -ri [saˈkrarjo] SM memorial chapel
sacrestano [sakresˈtano] SM = **sagrestano**
sacrestia [sakresˈtia] SF = **sagrestia**
sacrificare [sakrifiˈkare] /20/ VT (*gen*) to sacrifice; **sacrificarsi** VR to sacrifice o.s.
sacrificato, -a [sakrifiˈkato] AGG (*gen, anche Rel*) sacrificed; (*fig: sprecato, sciupato*) wasted; **una vita sacrificata** a life of hardship
sacrificio, -ci [sakriˈfitʃo] SM (*Rel, anche fig*) sacrifice; **fare un sacrificio** to make a sacrifice
sacrilegio, -gi [sakriˈlɛdʒo] SM (*Rel, anche fig*) sacrilege; **fare sacrilegio, commettere un sacrilegio** to commit sacrilege
sacrilego, -a, -ghi, -ghe [saˈkrilego] AGG (*Rel*) sacrilegious
sacro, -a [ˈsakro] AGG 1 (*Rel*) holy, sacred; (*arte, diritto*) sacred; **il Sacro Cuore (di Gesù)** the Sacred Heart (of Jesus); **musica sacra** church music 2 (*Anat*): **osso sacro** sacrum ♦ SM the sacred
sacrosanto, -a [sakroˈsanto] AGG sacrosanct
sadico, -a, -ci, -che [ˈsadiko] AGG sadistic ♦ SM, SF sadist

sadismo [saˈdizmo] SM sadism; **trattare qn con sadismo** to treat sb sadistically
sadomasochismo [sadomazoˈkizmo] SM sadomasochism
saetta [saˈetta] SF (*fulmine*) thunderbolt; **essere (veloce come) una saetta** (*fig*) to be as quick as lightning
safari [saˈfari] SM INV safari
sagace [saˈgatʃe] AGG sagacious, shrewd
sagacia [saˈgatʃa] SF sagacity, shrewdness
saggezza [sadˈdʒettsa] SF wisdom
saggiare [sadˈdʒare] /62/ VT (*metalli preziosi*) to assay; (*fig: mettere alla prova*) to test
saggio¹, -gia, -gi, -ge [ˈsaddʒo] AGG wise ♦ SM wise man; (*Storia*) sage
saggio², -gi [ˈsaddʒo] SM 1 (*prova: di abilità, forza*) proof; **dare saggio di** to give proof of; **saggio di ginnastica** gymnastics display; **saggio di musica** recital 2 (*campione*) sample; (*di libro*) sample copy; **in saggio** as a sample 3 (*scritto: letterario*) essay; (: *Scol*) written test 4 (*di metalli preziosi*) assay; **un saggio su Dante** an essay on Dante
saggistica, -che [sadˈdʒistika] SF (*attività*) essay writing; (*produzione*) essays *pl*
Sagittario, -ri [sadʒitˈtarjo] SM Sagittarius; **essere del Sagittario** to be Sagittarius
sagoma [ˈsagoma] SF 1 (*profilo, linea*) outline, profile; (*forma*) shape, form; (*modello in cartone, legno*) template; (*nel tiro al bersaglio*) target; **da lontano si vedeva la sagoma di una nave** in the distance we saw the outline of a ship; **ha una sagoma irregolare** it has an irregular shape 2 (*fig: persona*) character; **è una sagoma!** he's a scream!
sagra [ˈsagra] SF festival, feast
sagrato [saˈgrato] SM churchyard
sagrestano [sagresˈtano] SM sexton, sacristan
sagrestia [sagresˈtia], **sagristia** [sagrisˈtia] SF sacristy
Sahara [saˈara] SM: **il (deserto del) Sahara** the Sahara (Desert)
sahariana [saaˈrjana] SF bush jacket
sai *ecc* [ˈsai] VB *vedi* **sapere**
saio, sai [ˈsajo] SM (*Rel*) habit; **prendere** *o* **vestire il saio** to take the habit
sala [ˈsala] SF 1 (*gen*) room; (*molto grande*) hall; (*salotto*) living room; (*Cine: di proiezione*) cinema; **c'era un tavolo rotondo in mezzo alla sala** there was a round table in the middle of the room; **l'enorme sala era piena zeppa** the enormous hall was packed; **il cinema ha tre sale** the cinema has three screens; **sala d'aspetto** *o* **d'attesa** waiting room; **sala da ballo** dance hall; **sala da biliardo** (*pubblica*) billiard hall; (*privata*) billiard room; **sala dei concerti** concert hall; **sala per conferenze** (*Univ*) lecture hall; (*in aziende*) conference room; **sala (dei) comandi** control room; **sala corse** betting shop; **sala giochi** amusement arcade; **sala di lettura** reading room; **sala macchine** (*Naut*) engine room; **sala di montaggio** (*Cine*) cutting room; **sala operatoria** (*Med*) operating theatre (*Brit*) *o* room (*USA*); **sala partenze** departure lounge; **sala da pranzo** dining room; **sala professori** staff room; **sala per ricevimenti** banqueting hall; **sala delle udienze** (*Dir*) courtroom
salace [saˈlatʃe] AGG (*spinto, piccante*) salacious, saucy; (*mordace*) cutting, biting
salamandra [salaˈmandra] SF (*Zool*) salamander
salame [saˈlame] SM (*cibo*) salami *no pl*, salami sausage; (*fig: persona sciocca*) dope
salamoia [salaˈmɔja] SF (*Culin, Chim*) brine; **olive in salamoia** olives in brine
salare [saˈlare] /72/ VT 1 (*condire*) to salt, add salt to 2 (*mettere sotto sale: senza acqua*) to salt; (: *con acqua*) to brine
salariale [salaˈrjale] AGG wage *attr*, pay *attr*; **aumento salariale** wage *o* pay increase (*Brit*) *o* raise (*USA*)

salariato, -a [sala'rjato] AGG wage-earning ♦ SM, SF wage-earner

salario, -ri [sa'larjo] SM pay, wage, wages pl; **un aumento di salario** a pay rise; **salario base** basic wage; **salario minimo garantito** guaranteed minimum wage

salassare [salas'sare] /72/ VT (Med) to bleed; (fig) to bleed dry o white

salasso [sa'lasso] SM (Med) bleeding, bloodletting; (fig: forte spesa) drain

salatino [sala'tino] SM cracker, salted biscuit

salato, -a [sa'lato] AGG (sapore, cibo) salty; (acqua) salt attr; (burro) salted; (fig: costoso) expensive, costly; (: prezzo) stiff, steep; (: mordace: discorso) sharp, cutting; **è troppo salato** it's too salty; **preferisco le cose salate** I prefer savoury things; **pagare qc salato** (acquisto) to pay through the nose for sth; **l'ha pagata salata** (fig) he paid dearly for it

saldare [sal'dare] /72/ VT 1 (Tecn: gen) to join; (con saldatore) to solder; (con saldatura autogena) to weld 2 (conto) to settle, pay; (fattura, debito) to pay; **devo saldare il conto** I must settle the bill; **saldare un conto (con qn)** to settle an account (with sb); (fig) to settle a score (with sb); **saldarsi** VIP (ferita) to heal

saldatore [salda'tore] SM 1 (operaio: vedi vt) solderer; welder 2 (utensile) soldering iron

saldatrice [salda'tritʃe] SF (macchina) welder, welding machine; **saldatrice ad arco** arc welder

saldatura [salda'tura] SF (vedi vt: azione) soldering; welding; (: punto saldato) soldered joint; weld; **saldatura ad arco** arc welding; **saldatura autogena** welding

saldezza [sal'dettsa] SF firmness, strength

saldo¹, -a [ˈsaldo] AGG (gen) steady, firm, stable; (fig: rapporto) sound; (: principi) sound; **non è più molto saldo sulle gambe** he's not very steady on his feet any more

saldo² [ˈsaldo] SM 1 (pagamento) settlement, payment; (somma residua da pagare) balance; **pagare a saldo** to pay in full; **saldo attivo** credit; **saldo passivo** deficit; **saldo riportato** balance brought forward 2 (svendita): **saldi estivi** summer sale

sale [ˈsale] SM 1 (gen) salt; **c'è troppo sale** there's too much salt in it; **conservare sotto sale** to salt; **sotto sale** salted; **acciughe sotto sale** salted anchovies; **restare di sale** (fig) to be dumbfounded; **avere molto sale in zucca** to have a lot of good sense; **non ha molto sale in zucca** he doesn't have much sense 2 **sali** SMPL (Med: da annusare) smelling salts ♦ **sale da cucina** cooking salt; **sale fino** table salt; **sale grosso** coarse salt; **sale da tavola** table salt; **sali da bagno** bath salts; **sali minerali** mineral salts; **sali e tabacchi** tobacconist's (shop) sg

❏ **sale** non si traduce mai con la parola inglese sale

salgemma [sal'dʒemma] SM rock salt

salgo ecc [ˈsalgo] VB vedi salire

salice [ˈsalitʃe] SM (Bot) willow; **salice bianco** white willow; **salice piangente** weeping willow

saliente [sa'ljɛnte] AGG salient, main

saliera [sa'ljɛra] SF (Culin) saltcellar

salino, -a [sa'lino] AGG saline

salire [sa'lire] VB IRREG /98/ VT (scale, pendio) to climb, go (o come) up ♦ VI (aus essere) 1 (gen) to go (o come) up; (aereo) to climb, go up; **sali tu o vengo giù io?** are you coming up or shall I come down?; **è appena salito in camera sua** he's just gone up to his room; **saliva le scale** he was going up the stairs; **salimmo a piedi/con la bicicletta fino in cima** we walked/cycled up to the top; **la strada sale per 2 km** the road climbs for 2 km; **sull'albero** he climbed the tree; **salire in quota** (Aer) to gain altitude 2 **salire in macchina** to get into the car; **salire sull'autobus/sul treno** to get on the bus/on the train; **salire a bordo di** to (get on) board; **salire a cavallo** to mount; **salire su una** o **in bicicletta** to get on a bicycle; **salire in sella** to get into the saddle 3 (prezzo, temperatura) to rise, go up; (marea) to come in; (fiumo) to rise; **i prezzi sono saliti** prices have gone up; **la temperatura sta salendo** the temperature is rising 4 (fraseologia): **salire in cielo** o **paradiso** to go to heaven; **salire al potere** to rise to power; **salire al trono** to ascend the throne; **salire alle stelle** (prezzi) to rocket; **salire nella stima di qn** to rise in sb's estimation

saliscendi [saliʃ'ʃendi] SM INV latch

salita [sa'lita] SF 1 (azione) climb, ascent; **salita a spina di pesce** (Sci) herringbone climb; **la salita è stata molto faticosa** the climb was very tiring; **abbiamo dovuto fermarci a metà della salita** we had to stop halfway up the hill 2 (strada) hill, slope; **strada in salita** road going uphill

saliva [sa'liva] SF saliva

salma [ˈsalma] SF body (of dead person)

salmastro, -a [sal'mastro] AGG (acqua) salt attr; (sapore) salty ♦ SM (sapore) salty taste; (odore) salty smell

salmì [sal'mi] SM INV (Culin) salmi; **lepre in salmì** salmi of hare

salmo [ˈsalmo] SM (Rel) psalm

salmone [sal'mone] SM salmon

salmonella [salmo'nɛlla] SF salmonella

Salomone [salo'mɔne] SFPL: **le (isole) Salomone** the Solomon Islands

salone [sa'lone] SM 1 (stanza) living room, sitting room (Brit), lounge (Brit); (di ricevimento) reception room; (su nave) lounge, saloon 2 (mostra) show, exhibition; **salone dell'automobile** motor show 3 (negozio: di parrucchiere) hairdresser's (salon); **salone di bellezza** beauty salon

salopette [salɔ'pɛt] SF INV dungarees o overalls pl; (Sci) salopettes pl

salottiero, -a [salot'tjero] AGG mundane

salotto [sa'lotto] SM 1 (stanza) living room, sitting room (Brit), lounge (Brit); (mobilio) lounge suite 2 (circolo letterario) salon; **chiacchiere da salotto** (fig) society gossip sg

salpare [sal'pare] (Naut) /72/ VT: **salpare l'ancora** to weigh anchor ♦ VI (aus essere) to set sail

salsa [ˈsalsa] SF sauce; **in tutte le salse** (fig) in all kinds of ways; **salsa di pomodoro** tomato sauce; **spaghetti con salsa di pomodoro** spaghetti with tomato sauce; **salsa verde** savoury sauce made with parsley, anchovies, onion, olive oil and garlic

salsedine [sal'sedine] SF (del mare, vento) saltiness; (incrostazione) (dried) salt

salsiccia, -ce [sal'sittʃa] SF (pork) sausage

salsiera [sal'sjera] SF gravy boat, sauceboat (Brit)

salso [ˈsalso] SM (salsedine) saltiness

saltare [sal'tare] /72/ VT (siepe, ostacolo) to jump (over), leap (over); (fig: capitolo, pasto) to skip, miss (out); **ho saltato una riga** I've skipped a line; **hai saltato il pranzo oggi?** did you skip lunch today? ♦ VI (aus avere o essere) 1 (gen) to jump, leap; (saltellare) to skip; (su un piede solo) to hop; **saltare su/ sopra qc** to jump on/over sth; **il gatto è saltato sul tavolo** the cat jumped on the table; **saltare giù to jump down; saltare giù da qc** to jump off sth, jump down from sth; **è saltato giù dal treno** he jumped off the train; **saltare addosso a qn** (aggredire) to attack sb; **saltare con la corda** to skip; **salta su!** (in macchina) jump in!; (su moto, bici) jump on!; **è saltato su e mi ha detto che...** he jumped up and told me that ...; **saltare a terra** to jump down; **saltare dal letto/dalla finestra** to jump out of bed/out of the window; **saltare al collo di qn** (in segno di affetto) to throw one's arms round sb's neck; (per strangolarlo) to grab sb by the neck; **saltare da un argomento all'altro** to jump from one subject to another; **saltare dalla gioia** to jump for joy; **salta agli occhi** it's obvious; **ma che ti salta in mente?** what on earth are you thinking of?; **far saltare un bimbo sulle ginocchia** to bounce a child on one's knees 2 (bottone) to pop off; (bomba) to explode, blow up; (ponte, ferrovia) to blow up; (valvola) to blow; (fig: impiegato) to be fired; (: corso) to be cancelled; **saltare in aria** to blow up 3 **far saltare** (treno, ponte) to blow up; (fusibile) to blow; (mina) to explode; (serratura: forzare) to break; (: con esplosivo) to blow; (: lezione, appuntamento) to cancel; **i terroristi hanno fatto saltare in aria l'edificio** terrorists blew up the building; **far saltare il banco** (Giochi) to break the bank; **farsi saltare le cervella** to blow one's brains out 4 **saltare fuori** (apparire improvvisamente) to jump out, leap out; (venire trovato) to turn up; **saltare fuori con** (dire improvvisamente) to come out with; **dall'auto sono saltati fuori due ladri** two thieves jumped o leapt out of the car; **quel libro è finalmente saltato fuori** that book finally turned up; **da dove salta fuori questa camicia?** where has this shirt appeared from?; **da dove salti fuori?** where did you spring from? 5 (Culin) to sauté

saltellare [saltel'lare] /72/ vı (aus avere) to skip; (su un solo piede) to hop

saltello [sal'tɛllo] sм little jump; (su un solo piede) hop

saltimbanco, -a, -chi, -che [saltim'banko] sм, sf (acrobata) acrobat; (pegg) charlatan, fraud

salto ['salto] sм **1** (gen) jump, leap; **un salto in avanti** a jump forward; **fare un salto** to jump, leap; (per la paura) to start; **fare un salto a Milano** to pop over to Milan; **fare un salto da qn** to drop in on sb; **fare un salto da un amico** to drop in on a friend; **faccio un salto da te questo pomeriggio** I'll drop in on you this afternoon; **fare i salti dalla gioia** to jump for joy; **un salto nel buio** (fig) a leap in the dark **2** (Sport): **salto in alto** high jump; **salto con l'asta** pole vault; **salto in lungo** long jump; **salto mortale** somersault; **ho fatto i salti mortali per arrivare qui in tempo** (fig) I almost killed myself trying to get here on time; **salto dal trampolino** (Sci) ski jumping; **salto triplo** triple jump **3** (dislivello, anche Alpinismo) drop; **un salto di qualità** a difference in quality; (miglioramento: nel lavoro, in condizioni) a step up the ladder

saltuario, -ria, -ri, -rie [saltu'arjo] AGG occasional; **lavoro saltuario** occasional work

salubre [sa'lubre] AGG healthy, salubrious (frm); **l'aria qui è molto più salubre** the air here is much healthier

salume [sa'lume] sм (Culin) cured pork; **salumi** sмPL cured pork meats

salumeria [salume'ria] sf ≈ delicatessen

salumiere, -a [salu'mjɛre] sм, sf ≈ delicatessen owner

salumificio, -ci [salumi'fitʃo] sм cured pork meat factory

salutare¹ [salu'tare] /72/ AGG healthy, salutary, beneficial

salutare² [salu'tare] /72/ vт **1** (incontrandosi) to greet; (congedandosi) to say goodbye to; (trasmettere i saluti) to give o send one's regards to; **non mi saluta mai** he never says hello to me; **è uscito senza salutare nessuno** he left without saying goodbye to anybody; **è andata a salutarlo alla stazione** she went to see him off at the station; **salutare qn con la mano** to wave to sb; **mi saluti sua moglie** please give my regards to your wife; **salutami Giulia** say hello to Giulia for me **2** (Mil) to salute; **salutare la bandiera** to salute the flag; **salutarsi** vr (uso reciproco: incontrandosi) to greet each other; (: congedandosi) to say goodbye (to each other)

salute [sa'lute] sf health; **fumare fa male alla salute** smoking is bad for your health; **per motivi di salute** for health reasons; **godere di buona salute** to be healthy, to be in good health; **avere una salute di ferro** to have an iron constitution; **bere alla salute di qn** to drink (to) sb's health ♦ ESCL (a chi starnutisce) bless you!; (nei brindisi) your health!, cheers!
❑ salute non si traduce mai con la parola inglese *salute*

saluto [sa'luto] sм **1** (incontrandosi) greeting; (congedandosi) goodbye, farewell; **rivolgere il saluto a qn** to greet sb; **gli ha tolto il saluto** he no longer says hello to him; **tanti saluti, cari saluti** best regards, best wishes; **cordiali saluti, distinti saluti** yours truly, yours faithfully, yours sincerely **2** (gesto: del capo) nod; (: con la mano) wave; **mi fece un cenno di saluto** he nodded to me; he waved to me **3** (Mil) salute

salva ['salva] sf salvo; **sparare a salva** to fire a salute

salvacondotto [salvakon'dotto] sм (Mil) pass, safe-conduct

salvadanaio, -ai [salvada'najo] sм moneybox, piggy bank

salvadoregno, -a [salvado'reɲɲo] AGG, sм, sf Salvadorean

salvagente [salva'dʒɛnte] sм **1** (Naut: gen) life buoy; (: ciambella) life belt; (: per bambini) rubber ring; (: giubbotto) lifejacket (Brit), life preserver (USA); **sai nuotare senza il salvagente?** can you swim without a rubber ring? **2** (stradale: pl inv) traffic island

salvaguardare [salvagwar'dare] /72/ vт to safeguard, protect

salvaguardia [salva'gwardja] sf safeguard; **a salvaguardia di** for the safeguard of

salvare [sal'vare] /72/ vт (gen, anche Inform) to save; (portare soccorso) to rescue; **lo salvarono da morte sicura** they saved him from certain death; **la cintura di sicurezza lo ha salvato** the seat belt saved him; **i pompieri hanno salvato due bambini** the firemen rescued two children; **hanno salvato poche persone dal naufragio** they rescued few people from the shipwreck; **salvare la vita a qn** to save sb's life;

una volta mi ha salvato la vita he once saved my life; **mi hai salvato!** (anche fig) you saved me!; **hanno salvato poche cose dall'incendio** they salvaged very few items from the fire; **salvare la faccia** (fam) to save face; **salvare le apparenze** to keep up appearances; **salvare capra e cavoli** to have the best of both worlds; **Dio salvi la regina!** God save the Queen!; **salvarsi** vr (salvare la propria vita) to save o.s.; **non si è salvato nessuno nell'incidente** nobody survived the accident; **si salvi chi può** every man for himself; **non si è salvato nulla** everything was destroyed

salvaschermo [salvas'kermo] sм (Inform) screen saver

salvataggio, -gi [salva'taddʒo] sм rescue; **c'è stato un ferito durante le operazioni di salvataggio** one person was injured during the rescue operation; **cintura di salvataggio** lifebelt; **giubbotto di salvataggio** life jacket; **scialuppa di salvataggio** lifeboat

salvatore, -trice [salva'tore] sм, sf rescuer, saviour (Brit), savior (USA); (Rel): **il Salvatore** the Saviour

salvazione [salvat'tsjone] sf (Rel) salvation

salve ['salve] ESCL (ciao) hello!, hi!

salvezza [sal'vettsa] sf salvation; **cercare salvezza nella fuga** to seek safety in flight

salvia ['salvja] sf (Bot) sage

salvietta [sal'vjetta] sf napkin, serviette (Brit); (di spugna) hand towel; **salviette umidificate** wet wipes; **salviette umidificate per bambini** baby wipes

salvo¹, -a ['salvo] AGG (persona) safe, unhurt, unharmed; (fuori pericolo) safe, out of danger; **sono salvo!** I'm safe!; **uscir salvo da qc** to come out of sth safely; **avere salva la vita** to have one's life spared ♦ sм: **essere in salvo** (persona, cosa) to be safe; **non preoccuparti, ora sei in salvo** don't worry, you're safe now; **mettere qc in salvo** to put sth in a safe place; **mettersi in salvo** to reach safety; **portare qn in salvo** to lead sb to safety

salvo² ['salvo] PREP **1** (eccetto) except (for); **è aperto tutti i giorni salvo il lunedì** it's open every day with the exception of o except Monday; **vennero tutti salvo lui** everybody came except him; **salvo errori, la somma ammonta a...** unless I am (o we are ecc) mistaken, it amounts to ...; **salvo imprevisti** all being well; **ci vediamo domani, salvo imprevisti** I'll see you tomorrow, all being well; **salvo errori e omissioni** errors and omissions excepted; **salvo contrordini** barring instructions to the contrary **2** salvo che (eccetto che) except (that); (a meno che) unless; **sono soddisfatto salvo che per una cosa** I'm quite satisfied except for one thing; **lo farò salvo che tu non voglia farlo** I'll do it unless you would rather do it

sambuca [sam'buka] sf (liquore) sambuca (type of anisette)

sambuco, -chi [sam'buko] sм (Bot) elder (tree)

sanare [sa'nare] /72/ vт (malato) sм to heal, cure; (economia) to cure, put right, restore

sanatoria [sana'tɔrja] sf (Dir) act of indemnity

sanatorio, -ri [sana'tɔrjo] sм sanatorium (Brit), sanitarium (USA)

sancire [san'tʃire] /55/ vт (sanzionare) to sanction; (ratificare) to ratify

sandalo ['sandalo] sм **1** (calzatura) sandal **2** (Bot) sandalwood

sangria [san'gria] sf (bibita) sangria

sangue ['sangwe] sм blood; **devo fare le analisi del sangue** I've got to have a blood test; **animale a sangue caldo/freddo** warm-/cold-blooded animal; **uccidere a sangue freddo** to kill in cold blood; **all'ultimo sangue** (duello, lotta) to the death; **il sangue gli sali alla testa** the blood rushed to his head; **non corre buon sangue tra di loro** there's bad blood between them; **ha la musica nel sangue** music is in his blood; **sentirsi gelare il sangue nelle vene** to feel one's blood run cold; **farsi cattivo sangue per qc** to get worked up about sth; **buon sangue non mente!** blood will tell!; **il sangue non è acqua** blood is thicker than water; **al sangue** (Culin) rare; **una bistecca al sangue** a rare steak; **sangue freddo** (fig) sang-froid, calm; **avere sangue freddo** to stay calm

sanguigno, -a [san'gwiɲɲo] AGG (gruppo, pressione, vaso) blood attr; (fig: collerico) bad-tempered; (color rosso intenso) blood-red; **vasi sanguigni** blood vessels

sanguinante [sangwi'nante] AGG bleeding

sanguinare [sangwi'nare] /72/ VI (aus avere) (anche fig) to bleed

sanguinario, -ria, -ri, -rie [sangwi'narjo] AGG bloodthirsty

sanguinoso, -a [sangwi'noso] AGG bloody

sanguisuga, -ghe [sangwi'suga] SF (Zool) leech; (fig) leech, bloodsucker

sanità [sani'ta] SF 1 (gen) health; **Ministero della Sanità** ≈ Department of Health (Brit), ≈ Department of Health and Human Services (USA) 2 (Mil) army medical corps sg o pl

sanitario, -ria, -ri, -rie [sani'tarjo] AGG (servizio, misure) health attr; (condizioni) sanitary; **Ufficiale Sanitario** Health Officer; (impianti) **sanitari** bathroom o sanitary fittings ♦ SM (Amm: medico) doctor

San Marino [san ma'rino] SF: (**la Repubblica di**) **San Marino** (the Republic of) San Marino

sanno ecc ['sanno] VB vedi **sapere**

sano, -a ['sano] AGG (persona, fisico, denti) healthy; (alimento) healthy, wholesome; (frutto) sound; (fig: politica, ambiente) good; **un bambino sano** a healthy child; **un'alimentazione sana** a healthy diet; **sano e salvo** safe and sound; **è tornata a casa sana e salva** she got home safe and sound; **sano di mente** sane; **di sani principi** of sound principles; **una sana educazione** a good education; **essere sano come un pesce** to be (as) fit as a fiddle; **di sana pianta** completely, entirely

San Silvestro ['san sil'vestro] SM (giorno) New Year's Eve; **cosa fai per San Silvestro?** what are you doing on New Year's Eve?

Santiago [santi'ago] SF: **Santiago (del Cile)** Santiago (de Chile)

santificare [santifi'kare] /20/ VT (dichiarare santo) to sanctify, hallow; (feste) to observe

santino [san'tino] SM holy picture

santissimo, -a [san'tissimo] AGG 1 **il Santissimo Sacramento** the Blessed Sacrament; **il Padre Santissimo** (papa) the Holy Father 2 (fig): **fammi il santissimo piacere di star zitto!** do me a favour and keep quiet! ♦ SM (Rel): **il Santissimo** the Blessed Sacrament

santità [santi'ta] SF INV (Rel) sanctity, holiness; (fig) sanctity; **Sua/Vostra Santità** His/Your Holiness

santo, -a ['santo] AGG 1 (sacro) holy; **Venerdì Santo** Good Friday; **la Santa Sede** the Holy See; **santo cielo!** good heavens!; **Dio santo!** good God! 2 seguito da sm: **san** + consonante, **sant'** + vocale, **santo** + s impura, gn, pn, ps, x, z seguito da sf: **santa** + consonante, **sant'** + vocale santo; **San Pietro** (apostolo) Saint Peter; (chiesa) Saint Peter's 3 (fig) saint; è **una santa donna** she's a saint; **quel sant'uomo di tuo nonno** (defunto) your sainted grandfather; **parole sante!** very true!; **vuoi farmi il santo piacere di uscire?** would you do me a favour and get out?; **tutto il santo giorno** the whole blessed day, all day long ♦ SM, SF (anche fig) saint; **non sono una santa** I'm no saint; **qualche santo provvederà** something will turn up; **non c'è santo che tenga!** that's no excuse!; **quella santa di sua moglie** his wife, saint that she is ♦ **santi** SMPL. **Santi** SMPL: **i Santi** (Ognissanti) All Saints' Day

santone [san'tone] SM holy man

santuario, -ri [santu'arjo] SM sanctuary

sanzionare [santsjo'nare] /72/ VT to sanction

sanzione [san'tsjone] SF 1 (approvazione) sanction, approval 2 (punizione) sanction, penalty; **sanzioni economiche** economic sanctions

sapere [sa'pere] VB IRREG /99/ VT 1 (conoscere: lezione, nome) to know; (venire a sapere: notizia) to hear; **sai dove abita?** do you know where he lives?; **sai se torna?** do you know if o whether he is coming back?; **lo so** I know; **lo so, non è colpa tua** I know, it's not your fault; **non ne so nulla** I don't know anything about it; **sa quattro lingue** he knows o can speak four languages; **non sa l'inglese** he doesn't speak English; **non ne vuole più sapere di lei** he doesn't want to have anything more to do with her; **come l'ha saputo?** how did he find out o hear about it?; **ho saputo che ti sei sposato** I hear you got married; **vuoi sapere la verità?** do you want to know o hear the truth?; **far sapere qc a qn** to let sb know (about) sth, inform sb about sth; **fagli sapere che lo sto cercando** let him know I'm looking for him; **venire a sapere qc (da qn)** to find out o hear about sth (from sb) 2 (essere capace di)

to know how to; **non sa far niente** he can't do anything; **sai nuotare?** do you know how to swim?, can you swim?; **è utile saper guidare** it's useful to be able to drive; **non so guidare** I can't drive; **non sapeva andare in bicicletta** he couldn't ride a bike; **sa (come) cavarsela** he can manage 3 (rendersi conto) to know; **non sa cosa dice** he doesn't know o realize what he's saying; **sa quello che fa** he knows what he's doing; **so com'è difficile parlargli** I know how difficult it is to talk to him; **senza saperlo** without realizing it, unwittingly 4 (fraseologia): **è difficile, e io ne so qualcosa** it's difficult and don't I know it; **e chi lo sa?** who knows?; **si sa che...** it's well known that ..., everybody knows that ...; **non si sa mai** you never know; **non saprei** I don't o wouldn't know; **non saprei dire** I couldn't say; **mi dispiace, non so che farci** I'm sorry, I don't see what I can do about it; **averlo saputo!** had I (o we ecc) known!, if only I (o we ecc) had known!; **ci sa fare con le persone/macchine** he has a way with people/cars; **lui sì che ci sa fare** he's very good at it ♦ VI (aus avere) 1 **sapere di** (aver sapore) to taste of; (aver odore) to smell of; (fig) to smack of, resemble; **sa di fragola** it tastes of strawberries; **sa di pesce** it smells of fish; **è un film che non sa di niente** it's a very dull film 2 **mi sa che...** (credo) I think (that) ...; **mi sa che non viene** I don't think he's coming ♦ SM knowledge

sapiente [sa'pjente] AGG (dotto) learned; (che rivela abilità) masterly; **con mano sapiente** with a skilful hand ♦ SM, SF scholar

sapientone, -a [sapjen'tone] SM, SF (pegg) know-all (Brit), know-it-all (USA)

sapienza [sa'pjentsa] SF (saggezza) wisdom; (conoscenza) knowledge, learning

sapone [sa'pone] SM soap; **sapone da barba** shaving soap; **sapone da bucato** washing soap (Brit), laundry detergent (USA); **sapone liquido** liquid soap; **sapone in scaglie** soapflakes pl

saponetta [sapo'netta] SF bar o cake of soap

sapore [sa'pore] SM (anche fig) flavour (Brit), flavor (USA); **avere un buon sapore** to taste good; **non ha alcun sapore** it doesn't taste of anything, it doesn't have any flavo(u)r; **è ciò che dà sapore alla vita** this is what makes life worth living; **parole di sapore amaro** words with a bitter ring to them

saporito, -a [sapo'rito] AGG (cibo) tasty; (fig: battuta) witty; **un piatto saporito** a tasty dish; **è più saporito cucinato così** it's tastier when it's cooked like this; **poco saporito** tasteless; **farsi una dormita saporita** (fig) to sleep soundly

sappiamo ecc [sap'pjamo] VB vedi **sapere**

saprò ecc [sa'prɔ] VB vedi **sapere**

saputello, -a [sapu'tello] SM, SF know-all (Brit), know-it-all (USA)

sarà ecc [sa'ra] VB vedi **essere**

sarabanda [sara'banda] SF (fig) uproar

saracinesca, -sche [saratʃi'neska] SF rolling shutter

sarcasmo [sar'kazmo] SM (ironia) sarcasm; (commento) sarcastic remark; **fare del sarcasmo** to be sarcastic, make sarcastic remarks

sarcastico, -a, -ci, -che [sar'kastiko] AGG sarcastic

sarcofago, -gi o **, -ghi** [sar'kɔfago] SM sarcophagus

Sardegna [sar'deɲɲa] SF Sardinia; **mi è piaciuta molto la Sardegna** I really liked Sardinia; **andrò in Sardegna quest'estate** I'm going to Sardinia this summer

sardina [sar'dina] SF sardine; **pigiati come sardine** (fig) packed like sardines

sardo, -a ['sardo] AGG, SM, SF Sardinian

sardonico, -a, -ci, -che [sar'dɔniko] AGG sardonic

sarei ecc [sa'rɛi] VB vedi **essere**

SARS [sars] SIGLA F (Med) SARS (= Severe Acute Respiratory Syndrome)

sarta ['sarta] SF dressmaker

sartia ['sartja] SF (Naut) stay

sarto ['sarto] SM tailor; (d'alta moda) couturier; **sarto da donna** ladies' tailor

sartoria [sarto'ria] SF 1 (attività: di sarto) tailoring...; (: di sarta) dressmaking; **sartoria d'alta moda** haute couture 2 (laboratorio: di sarto) tailor's (shop); (: di sarta) dressmaker's (shop); (: d'alta moda) couturier's, fashion house

sassaiola [sassaˈjɔla] SF hail of stones

sassata [sasˈsata] SF blow with a stone; **infranse il vetro con una sassata** he broke the pane with a stone; **tirare una sassata contro** *o* **a qn/qc** to throw a stone at sb/sth

sasso [ˈsasso] SM (*pietra*) stone; (*ciottolo*) pebble; (*roccia*) rock; **restare** *o* **rimanere di sasso** (*fig*) to be dumbfounded; **è una cosa che fa piangere i sassi** (*fig: penoso*) it's pitiful

sassofonista, -i, -e [sassofoˈnista] SM, SF saxophonist

sassofono [sasˈsɔfono] SM saxophone

sassone [ˈsassone] AGG, SM, SF Saxon

sassoso, -a [sasˈsoso] AGG (*vedi sm*) stony; pebbly; rocky

Satana [ˈsatana] SM Satan

satanico, -a, -ci, -che [saˈtaniko] AGG satanic; (*fig*) diabolical, devilish, fiendish

satellitare [satelliˈtare] AGG satellite *attr*; **antenna satellitare** satellite aerial; **televisione satellitare** satellite television

satellite [saˈtellite] SM, AGG INV (*anche fig*) satellite; **la TV via satellite** satellite TV

satira [ˈsatira] SF satire; **fare la satira di qn/qc** to satirize sb/sth

satireggiare [satiredˈdʒare] /62/ VT to satirize ♦ VI (*aus avere*) (*fare della satira*) to be satirical; (*scrivere satire*) to write satires

satirico, -a, -ci, -che [saˈtiriko] AGG satiric(al)

satollo, -a [saˈtollo] AGG full, replete

saturare [satuˈrare] /72/ VT (*Fis, Chim*) to saturate; (*fig: riempire*) to fill, stuff; **saturarsi** VIP (*Fis, Chim*) to become saturated; (*fig: riempirsi*) to fill, stuff

saturazione [saturatˈtsjone] SF (*Fis, Chim*) saturation; **aver raggiunto il punto di saturazione** to have reached saturation point; (*fig*) to have had more than enough *o* as much as one can take

saturo, -a [ˈsaturo] AGG (*gen*) saturated; **saturo (di)** (*fig*) full (of); **saturo d'acqua** (*terreno*) waterlogged

SAUB SIGLA F (= *Struttura Amministrativa Unificata di Base*) state welfare system

sauna [ˈsauna] SF sauna; **fare la sauna** to have *o* take a sauna; **abbiamo fatto la sauna** we had a sauna

savana [saˈvana] SF savannah

savio, -via, -vi, -vie [ˈsavjo] AGG wise, sensible ♦ SM wise man

Savoia [saˈvoja] SF Savoy

savoiardo, -a [savoˈjardo] AGG of Savoy, Savoyard ♦ SM (*Culin*) sponge finger

saziare [satˈtsjare] /19/ VT (*anche fig*) to satisfy, satiate; **saziarsi** VIP: **saziarsi (di)** to eat one's fill (of); **non si sazia di viaggiare** (*fig*) he never tires of travel(l)ing

sazietà [sattsjeˈta] SF satiety, satiation; **mangiare a sazietà** to eat one's fill; **ce ne sono a sazietà** there are more than enough

sazio, -zia, -zi, -zie [ˈsattsjo] AGG: **sazio (di)** sated (with), full (of); **no, grazie, sono sazio** no thanks, I've had enough; **sono sazio di questi discorsi** (*fig*) I'm fed up with this talk

sbadataggine [zbadaˈtaddʒine] SF (*sventatezza*) carelessness; (*azione*) oversight

sbadato, -a [zbaˈdato] AGG careless, inattentive

sbadigliare [zbadiˈʎʎare] /27/ VI (*aus avere*) to yawn

sbadiglio, -gli [zbaˈdiʎʎo] SM yawn; **fare uno sbadiglio** to yawn

sbafo [ˈzbafo] SM: **a sbafo** at somebody else's expense

sbagliare [zbaʎˈʎare] /27/ VT (*gen*) to make a mistake in, get wrong; (*bersaglio*) to miss; **ha sbagliato tutto** he got everything wrong; **ha sbagliato tutto (nella vita)** he has made a mess of his life; **sbagliare la mira** to miss one's aim; **sbagliare strada** to take the wrong road; **sbagliare treno** to get *o* take the wrong train; **scusi, ho sbagliato numero** (*al telefono*) sorry, I've got the wrong number; **sbagliò porta** he opened the wrong door; **sbagli tattica** you're going the wrong way about it; **sbagliare una mossa** (*al gioco*) to make a wrong move ♦ VI (*aus avere*) to make a mistake; **mi dispiace, ho sbagliato** I'm sorry, I've made a mistake; **ha sbagliato nel ricopiare il numero** he made a mistake in *o* when copying down the number; **potrei sbagliare ma...** I might be mistaken but ...; **ha sbagliato nei suoi confronti** he behaved badly towards her; **sbagliando s'impara** you

learn by your mistakes; **sbagliarsi** VIP (*fare errori*) to make a mistake (*o* mistakes); (*ingannarsi*) to be wrong, be mistaken; **pensavo fosse lei, ma mi sono sbagliato** I thought it was her, but I was wrong; **si è sbagliato nel ricopiare** he made a mistake in *o* when copying; **non c'è da sbagliarsi** there can be no mistake

sbagliato, -a [zbaʎˈʎato] AGG (*gen*) wrong; (*compito*) full of mistakes; (*conclusione*) erroneous

sbaglio, -gli [ˈzbaʎʎo] SM mistake, error; **fare uno sbaglio** to make a mistake; **è stato uno sbaglio** it was a mistake; **ci deve essere uno sbaglio** there must be some mistake; **ha pagato per lo sbaglio commesso** he's paid for his mistake

sbalestrato, -a [zbalesˈtrato] AGG (*persona: scombussolato*) unsettled

sballare [zbalˈlare] /72/ VT (*merce*) to unpack ♦ VI (*aus essere*) **1** (*nel fare un conto*) to overestimate **2** (*Carte*) to go out **3** (*fam*) to be high (on drugs)

sballato, -a [zbalˈlato] AGG (*calcolo*) wrong; (*fam: ragionamento, persona*) screwy ♦ SM, SF (*fam: spostato*) misfit; (: *drogato*) junkie

sballo [ˈzballo] SM (*fam*) **1** (*droga*) trip **2 che sballo di macchina!** what a totally amazing car!; **un film da sballo** a knockout film

sballottare [zballotˈtare] /72/ VT to toss (about), throw (about)

sbalordire [zbalorˈdire] /55/ VT to stun, amaze, astound; **la notizia mi ha sbalordito** I was stunned by the news ♦ VI (*aus avere*) to be stunned, be amazed, be astounded

sbalorditivo, -a [zbalordiˈtivo] AGG (*abilità, memoria*) amazing, astounding; (*prezzo, affitto*) incredible, absurd

sbalzare [zbalˈtsare] /72/ VT **1** (*scaraventare*) to throw, hurl; **è stato sbalzato fuori dall'auto** he was thrown out of the car; **è stato sbalzato a 10 metri di distanza** he was thrown 10 metres **2** (*rimuovere: da una carica, sede*) to remove, dismiss ♦ VI (*aus essere*) (*temperatura: alzarsi bruscamente*) to jump, rise; (: *abbassarsi bruscamente*) to fall, plummet

sbalzo [ˈzbaltso] SM (*sussulto*) start; **a sbalzi** jerkily; (*fig*) in fits and starts; **procedere a sbalzi** (*macchina*) to jolt along; **uno sbalzo di temperatura** a sudden change in temperature

sban'care /20/ VT **1** (*nei giochi*) to break the bank at (*o* of) **2** (*fig*) to ruin, bankrupt

sbandamento [zbandaˈmento] SM (*di veicolo*) skid; (*Naut*) list; (*fig: di persona*) confusion; **ha avuto un periodo di sbandamento** he went off the rails for a bit

sbandare [zbanˈdare] /72/ VI (*aus avere*) (*Aut*) to skid; (*Naut*) to list; **sbandarsi** VIP (*folla*) to disperse; (*truppe*) to scatter; (*fig: famiglia*) to break up

sbandata [zbanˈdata] SF (*Aut*) skid; (*Naut*) list; **prendere** *o* **prendersi una sbandata per qn** (*fig*) to fall for sb

sbandato, -a [zbanˈdato] SM, SF mixed-up person

sbandierare [zbandjeˈrare] /72/ VT (*bandiere*) to wave; (*fig: ostentare*) to show off, flaunt, parade

sbando [ˈzbando] SM: **essere allo sbando** (*fig*) to drift

sbaraccare [zbarakˈkare] /20/ VT (*fam: libri, piatti*) to clear (up); **sarà meglio sbaraccare** it's time we cleared out

sbaragliare [zbaraʎˈʎare] /27/ VT (*Mil*) to rout; (*in gare sportive*) to beat, defeat

sbaraglio [zbaˈraʎʎo] SM: **andare** *o* **buttarsi allo sbaraglio** (*soldato*) to throw o.s. into the fray; (*fig: rischiare*) to risk everything

sbarazzare [zbaratˈtsare] /72/ VT to clear; **sbarazzarsi** VR: **sbarazzarsi di qn/qc** to get rid of sb/sth, rid o.s. of sb/sth

sbarazzino, -a [zbaratˈtsino] AGG impish, cheeky ♦ SM scamp, imp

sbarbare [zbarˈbare] /72/ VT, **sbarbarsi** VR to shave

sbarbatello [zbarbaˈtello] SM novice, greenhorn

sbarcare [zbarˈkare] /20/ VT (*merci*) to unload; (*passeggeri: da nave, aereo*) to disembark, land; (: *da autobus, macchina*) to put down; **sbarcare il lunario** (*fig*) to make ends meet ♦ VI (*aus essere*) **sbarcare da** (*aereo, nave*) to get off, disembark; **i passeggeri stavano sbarcando** the passengers were disembarking; **sbarcare (da un treno)** to get off (a train), alight (from a train)

sbarco, -chi [ˈzbarko] SM **1** (*vedi vb*) unloading; disembarkation, landing; putting down; **allo sbarco** on disembarking

2 (*Mil*): **forza da sbarco** landing party; **testa di sbarco** beachhead

sbarra [ˈzbarra] SF **1** (*gen, anche Sport*) bar; (*di passaggio a livello*) barrier; (*di timone*) tiller; **dietro le sbarre** (*fig: in prigione*) behind bars; **presentarsi alla sbarra** (*Dir: in tribunale*) to appear in court; **mettere alla sbarra** (*fig*) to put on trial **2** (*lineetta*) stroke

sbarramento [zbarraˈmento] SM (*di strada, passaggio*) barrier; (*diga*) dam, barrage; (*Mil*) barrage; (*Pol*) cut-off point (*level of support below which a political party is excluded from representation in Parliament*)

sbarrare [zbarˈrare] /72/ VT **1** (*bloccare*) to block, bar; **sbarrare la strada a qn** (*anche fig*) to block *o* bar sb's way; **una macchina della polizia gli ha sbarrato la strada** a police car blocked his way **2** (*spalancare*): **sbarrare gli occhi** to open one's eyes wide **3** (*cancellare*) to cross out, strike out; **sbarrare un assegno** to endorse a cheque (*Brit*), to endorse a check "for deposit only" (*USA*)

sbarrato, -a [zbarˈrato] AGG **1** (*porta*) barred; (*passaggio*) blocked, barred; (*strada*) blocked, obstructed **2** (*occhi*) staring **3** (*assegno*) crossed (*Brit*), endorsed "for deposit only" (*USA*)

sbattere [ˈzbattere] /1/ VT **1** (*gen*) to beat; (*uova*) to beat, whisk; (*panna*) to whip; (*ali*) to beat, flap; (*porta*) to slam, bang; **sbattere un ginocchio contro qc** to bang one's knee on sth; **ho sbattuto il ginocchio** I banged my knee; **sbattere un pugno sul tavolo** to thump the table; **sbattere la porta in faccia a qn** (*anche fig*) to slam the door in sb's face; **se n'è andato sbattendo la porta** he went out slamming the door; **non sapevo dove sbattere la testa** (*fig*) I didn't know which way to turn; **sbattere la testa contro un muro** (*fig*) to bang one's head against a brick wall; **finché non ci sbatte la testa contro non capirà** he'll find out the hard way **2** (*buttare*) to throw; **sbattere qc per terra** to throw sth to the ground; **sbattere qn fuori/in galera** to throw sb out/into prison; **sbattere via** to throw away *o* out; **sbattilo pure lì** just throw it over there; **sbattere una notizia in prima pagina** to splash a piece of news across the front page **3** (*fam!: possedere sessualmente*) to fuck (*fam!*) ♦ VI (*aus avere*) (*porta, finestra*) to bang; (*vele, ali*) to flap; **la finestra sbatte per il vento** the window is banging in the wind; **sbattere contro qc** to knock against sth **2** (*fam*): **sbattersene** not to give a damn; **me ne sbatto!** I don't give a damn!

sbattuto, -a [zbatˈtuto] AGG **1** (*uovo*) beaten **2** (*fig: persona*) worn out, dejected; (: *pallido*) peaked; **avere un'aria sbattuta** to look worn out

sbavare [zbaˈvare] /72/ VI (*aus avere*) **1** (*gen*) to dribble **2** (*colore*) to run; (*rossetto, inchiostro*) to smudge, smear ♦ VT: **sbavare qc** to dribble over sth; **sbavarsi** VR to dribble down o.s.

sbavatura [zbavaˈtura] SF (*di persone*) dribbling; (*di lumache*) slime; (*di rossetto, vernice*) smear

sbellicarsi [zbelliˈkarsi] /20/ VIP: **sbellicarsi dalle risa** to split one's sides laughing

sberla [ˈzberla] SF slap; **dare una sberla a qn** to slap *o* hit sb

sberleffo [zberˈleffo] SM: **fare uno sberleffo a qn** to make a face at sb; **fare gli sberleffi** to pull faces, grimace

sbiadire [zbjaˈdire] /55/ VI (*aus essere*) to fade; **ricordi che sbiadiscono col tempo** memories which fade with time ♦ VT to (cause to) fade

sbiadito, -a [zbjaˈdito] AGG (*scolorito*) faded; (*fig: stile*) colourless (*Brit*), colorless (*USA*), dull

sbiancare [zbjanˈkare] /20/ VI (*aus essere*), **sbiancarsi** VIP (*persona*): **sbiancare** *o* **sbiancarsi in viso** to pale, blanch, grow pale *o* white ♦ VT to whiten

sbieco, -chi [ˈzbjɛko] AGG (*muro*) at an angle; (*pavimento*) sloping, slanting; **tagliare una stoffa di sbieco** to cut material on the bias; **guardare qn di sbieco** (*fig*) to look askance at sb ♦ SM (*Cucito*) bias

sbigottire [zbigotˈtire] /55/ VT to dismay, dumbfound VI (*aus essere*), **sbigottirsi** VIP to be dismayed, be dumbfounded

sbilanciare [zbilanˈtʃare] /14/ VT to throw off balance; **sbilanciarsi** VIP (*perdere l'equilibrio*) to lose one's balance, overbalance; (*fig: compromettersi*) to compromise o.s.

sbilenco, -a, -chi, -che [zbiˈlɛnko] AGG (*sedia, tavolino*)

rickety; (*persona*) crooked, misshapen; (*fig: idea, ragionamento*) twisted

sbirciare [zbirˈtʃare] /14/ VT to peep at, cast sidelong glances at, eye

sbirciata [zbirˈtʃata] SF: **dare una sbirciata a qc** to glance at sth, have a look at sth

sbirro [ˈzbirro] SM (*pegg*) cop

sbizzarrirsi [zbiddzarˈrirsi] /55/ VIP (*sfogare i propri desideri*) to indulge one's whims; (*fare pazzie*) to go wild; **sbizzarrirsi a fare qc** to indulge o.s. in doing sth

sbloccare [zblokˈkare] /20/ VT (*gen*) to unblock, free; (*passaggio, strada*) to clear, unblock; (*affitti*) to free from controls; (*freno*) to release; **sbloccare la situazione** to get things moving again; **sbloccarsi** VIP (*gen*) to become unblocked; (*passaggio, strada*) to clear, become unblocked; (*Psic: persona*) to free o.s. from a psychological block; **la situazione si è sbloccata** things are moving again

sblocco, -chi [ˈzblɔkko] SM (*vedi vt*) unblocking; clearing; **dopo lo sblocco degli affitti** after the lifting of rent controls

sboccare [zbokˈkare] /20/ VI (*aus essere*) **sboccare in** (*fiume*) to flow into; (*strada*) to lead (in)to; (*valle*) to open into; (*persona*) to emerge into, come (out) into; (*fig: concludersi*) to end (up) in ♦ VT (*rompere: vaso, brocca*) to chip

sboccato, -a [zbokˈkato] AGG (*fig: persona*) foul-mouthed; (: *linguaggio*) coarse, foul

sbocciare [zbotˈtʃare] /14/ VI (*aus essere*) (*fiori*) to bloom, flower, open (out); (*fig: nascere*) to blossom

sbocco, -chi [ˈzbɔkko] SM **1** (*di fiume*) mouth; (*di tubazione*) outlet; (*di strada*) end; **una strada senza sbocco** a dead end; **siamo in una situazione senza sbocco** *o* **sbocchi** there's no way out of this for us **2** (*Comm*) outlet

sbocconcellare [zbokkontʃelˈlare] /72/ VT: **sbocconcellare (qc)** to nibble (at sth)

sbollentare [zbollenˈtare] /72/ VT (*Culin*) to parboil

sbollire [zbolˈlire] /55/ VI (*aus essere*) (*fig: calmarsi*) to cool down

sbornia [ˈzbɔrnja] SF (*fam*): **prendersi una sbornia** to get plastered; **smaltire la sbornia** to sober up

sborsare [zborˈsare] /72/ VT to fork out, shell out

sbottare [zbotˈtare] /72/ VI (*aus essere*) **sbottare in una risata** to burst out laughing; **alla fine sono sbottato** in the end I couldn't keep quiet any longer

sbottonare [zbottoˈnare] /72/ VT to unbutton, undo; **si è sbottonato la camicia** he unbuttoned his shirt; **sbottonarsi** VR to undo one's buttons; (*fig: fam: confidarsi*) to unburden o.s.

sbracato, -a [zbraˈkato] AGG (*fam: sciatto*) dishevelled, slovenly

sbracciarsi [zbratˈtʃarsi] /14/ VIP to wave (one's arms about)

sbracciato, -a [zbratˈtʃato] AGG (*persona*) with bare arms, bare-armed; (*indumento: senza maniche*) sleeveless; (: *a maniche corte*) short-sleeved

sbraitare [zbraiˈtare] /72/ VI (*aus avere*) to shout, yell, bawl

sbranare [zbraˈnare] /72/ VT to tear to pieces; **sbranarsi** VR (*uso reciproco, anche fig*) to tear each other to pieces

sbriciolare [zbritʃoˈlare] /72/ VT to crumble; **sbriciolarsi** VIP to crumble; **la pietra mi si è sbriciolata in mano** the stone crumbled in my hand; **la torta s'è tutta sbriciolata** the cake is all crumbly

sbrigare [zbriˈgare] /80/ VT (*lavoro, pratiche*) to deal with, get through; (*clienti*) to attend to, see to, deal with; **ho ancora alcune faccende da sbrigare** I've still got a few things to do; **sbrigare le faccende domestiche** to do the housework; **se la sa sbrigare da solo** he can manage *o* do it by himself; **sbrigarsi** VIP (*fare in fretta*) to hurry (up), get a move on; **devi sbrigarti se non vuoi perdere il treno** you'll have to hurry if you don't want to miss the train; **sbrigatevi!** hurry up!

sbrigativo, -a [zbrigaˈtivo] AGG (*persona, modi*) quick, expeditious; (*pegg*) abrupt, brusque; (*giudizio*) hasty; **è un piatto sbrigativo** it's a quick dish

sbrinamento [zbrinaˈmento] SM defrosting

sbrinare [zbriˈnare] /72/ VT to defrost

sbrindellato, -a [zbrindelˈlato] AGG tattered, in tatters

sbrodolare [zbrodo'lare] /72/ vт to stain, dirty; **sbrodolarsi** vʀ to stain o.s., dirty o.s.; **ti sei tutto sbrodolato** you've spilt food all down yourself

sbronza ['zbrontsa] sꜰ (fam) = **sbornia**

sbronzarsi [zbron'tsarsi] /72/ vʀ (fam) to get plastered

sbruffone, -a [zbruf'fone] sм, sꜰ boaster, braggart

sbucare [zbu'kare] /20/ vι (aus essere) **sbucare da** to pop out of o from; **sbucare fuori** to appear (from nowhere); **un ragazzino è sbucato fuori all'improvviso** a little boy suddenly appeared from nowhere; **da dove è sbucato quel libro?** where did that book spring from?

sbucciare [zbut'tʃare] /14/ vт (gen) to peel; (piselli) to shell; **sbucciarsi un ginocchio** to graze one's knee; **mi sono sbucciato un ginocchio** I grazed my knee

sbucherò ecc [zbuke'rɔ] vʙ vedi **sbucare**

sbudellare [zbudel'lare] /72/ vт to disembowel; **sbudellarsi** vʀ: **sbudellarsi dalle risate** (fig) to split one's sides laughing

sbuffare [zbuf'fare] /72/ vι (aus avere) (gen) to puff, pant; (con impazienza) to snort, fume; (cavallo) to snort; (treno) to puff; **saliva le scale sbuffando per la fatica** he was panting with the effort of climbing the stairs; **sbuffa sempre quando deve lavare i piatti** he always grumbles when he has to wash the dishes

sbuffo ['zbuffo] sм **1** (di vento) gust; (di aria, fumo, vapore) puff **2 maniche a sbuffo** puff(ed) sleeves

sc. ABBR (Teatro: = scena) sc.

scabbia ['skabbja] sꜰ (Med) scabies sg

scabro, -a ['skabro] ᴀɢɢ (superficie) rough; (fig: stile) concise, terse

scabroso, -a [ska'broso] ᴀɢɢ (fig: difficile) difficult, thorny; (: imbarazzante) embarrassing; (: sconcio) indecent

scacchiera [skak'kjera] sꜰ (Scacchi) chessboard; (Dama) draughtboard (Brit), checkerboard (USA)

scacchiere [skak'kjere] sм **1** (Mil) sector **2** (Pol: in Gran Bretagna): **Cancelliere dello Scacchiere** Chancellor of the Exchequer

scacciacani [skattʃa'kani] sм ɪɴᴠ, sꜰ ɪɴᴠ pistol with blanks

scacciapensieri [skattʃapen'sjeri] sм ɪɴᴠ (Mus) jew's-harp

scacciare [skat'tʃare] /14/ vт (mandar via) to chase away o out, drive away o out; (buttar fuori) to throw out, turn out; (fig: malinconia, noia) to overcome; (: sospetto, dubbio) to dispel; **scacciare qn di casa** to turn sb out of the house

scacco, -chi ['skakko] sм **1** (pezzo del gioco) chess piece, chessman; (riquadro) square; **scacchi** sᴍᴘʟ chess sg; **giocare a scacchi** to play chess; **dare scacco al re** to check the king; **subire uno scacco** (fig: sconfitta) to suffer a setback; **scacco matto** checkmate; **dare scacco matto a qn** (anche fig) to checkmate sb **2** (quadretto) square, check; **tessuto a scacchi** check(ed) material

scaccomatto sм checkmate; **dare scaccomatto a qn** (anche fig) to checkmate sb

scaddi ecc ['skaddi] vʙ vedi **scadere**

scadente [ska'dente] ᴀɢɢ (qualità) poor, shoddy; (voto) unsatisfactory; (prodotto) poor-quality attr; (film, libro) poor

scadenza [ska'dentsa] sꜰ (di documento) expiry; (su documento) sell-by date; (di cambiale, contratto) maturity; **data di scadenza** expiry date; (su prodotto) sell-by date; **con scadenza il 24 maggio** (pagamento) (which falls) due on the 24th of May; (documento) expiring on the 24th of May; **a breve/lunga scadenza** (progetto, piano) short-/long-term

scadere [ska'dere] /18/ vι ɪʀʀᴇɢ (aus essere) **1** (perdere valore, stima) to decline, go down; **scadere agli occhi di qn, scadere nella stima di qn** to go down in sb's estimation **2** (perdere validità: documento, contratto) to expire; (: cambiale, termine di pagamento) to fall due

scafandro [ska'fandro] sм (di palombaro) diving suit; (di astronauta) spacesuit

scaffalatura [skaffala'tura] sꜰ shelving, shelves pl

scaffale [skaf'fale] sм (ripiano) shelf; (mobile) set of shelves

scafista, -i [ska'fista] sꜰ (di immigrati) people smuggler (by boat)

scafo ['skafo] sм (Naut) hull

scagionare [skadʒo'nare] /72/ vт to exonerate, free from blame; **scagionarsi** vʀ to exonerate o.s., free o.s. from blame

scaglia ['skaʎʎa] sꜰ (squama) scale; (di metallo, pietra) splinter, chip; (di sapone) flake

scagliare [skaʎ'ʎare] /27/ vт (anche fig) to throw, hurl, fling; **scagliarsi** vʀ: **scagliarsi contro qn, scagliarsi addosso a qn** to fling o.s. at sb, hurl o.s. at sb; (fig: inveire) to rail at sb

scaglionamento [skaʎʎona'mento] sм (Mil) arrangement in echelons

scaglionare [skaʎʎo'nare] /72/ vт (truppe) to echelon; (pagamenti) to space out, spread out

scaglione [skaʎ'ʎone] sм (Mil) echelon; (Geol) terrace; **a scaglioni** (fig) in groups

scagnozzo [skaɲ'ɲɔttso] sм (pegg) lackey, hanger-on

Scala ['skala] sꜰ: **la Scala** theatre in Milan

scala ['skala] sꜰ **1** (in edificio) stairs pl, staircase; (all'esterno) steps pl; **salire/scendere le scale** to go upstairs/downstairs, go up/down the stairs; **fece le scale in fretta** he hurried up (o down) the stairs; **una scala di corda** a rope ladder; **una scala di marmo** a marble staircase; **scala a chiocciola** spiral staircase; **scala a libretto** stepladder; **scala mobile** escalator, moving staircase; **scala a pioli** ladder; **scala di servizio** backstairs pl; **scala di sicurezza** (antincendio) fire escape **2** (Econ, Fis, Mat, Geog) scale; **riproduzione in scala** reproduction to scale; **in scala di 1 a 100.000** on a scale of 1 to 100,000; **su larga/piccola scala** on a large/small scale; **su scala nazionale/mondiale** on a national/worldwide scale; **scala Celsius/Fahrenheit** Celsius/Fahrenheit scale; **scala cromatica** (Mus) chromatic scale; **scala di misure** system of weights and measures; **scala mobile (dei salari)** index-linked pay scale; **scala termometrica** scale of temperatures **3** (Mus) scale; **scala maggiore/minore** major/minor scale **4** (Carte) straight; **scala reale** straight o royal flush

scalare [ska'lare] /72/ vт **1** (Alpinismo: muro) to climb, scale **2** (ridurre): **scalare un debito** to pay off a debt in instalments; **questa somma vi viene scalata dal prezzo originale** this sum is deducted from the original price **3** (capelli) to layer

scalata [ska'lata] sꜰ **1** (azione) scaling, climbing **2** (arrampicata, anche fig) climb; (Alpinismo) climb, ascent; **scalata al potere** climb to power

scalatore, -trice [skala'tore] sм, sꜰ climber

scalcagnato, -a [skalkaɲ'ɲato] ᴀɢɢ (logoro) worn; (persona) shabby

scalciare [skal'tʃare] /14/ vι (aus avere) to kick

scalcinato, -a [skaltʃi'nato] ᴀɢɢ (fig: pegg) shabby

scaldabagno [skalda'baɲɲo] sм (per casa) water heater

scaldare [skal'dare] /72/ vт **1** (latte, stanza) to heat (up); **scalda un po' di latte** heat some milk; **scaldare i muscoli** to warm up, do warming-up exercises; **scaldare il motore** to warm up the engine; **scaldare la sedia** (fig) to twiddle one's thumbs **2 scaldarsi le mani/i piedi** to warm one's hands/feet; **scaldarsi** vʀ to warm up; **scaldarsi al fuoco** to warm o.s. by the fire; **scaldarsi** (vip) (stanza) to heat up; (fig: arrabbiarsi) to get excited, get worked up

❏ **scaldare** non si traduce mai con la parola inglese scald

scaldavivande [skaldavi'vande] sм ɪɴᴠ dish warmer

scaldino [skal'dino] sм (per mani) hand-warmer; (per piedi) foot-warmer; (per letto) bedwarmer

scalfire [skal'fire] /55/ vт (superficie) to scratch; (fig: sicurezza) to undermine

scalfittura [skalfit'tura] sꜰ scratch

scalinata [skali'nata] sꜰ (interna) staircase, (flight of) stairs pl; (esterna) (flight of) steps pl

scalino [ska'lino] sм (gen, anche fig) step; (di scala a pioli) rung

scalmana [skal'mana] sꜰ (hot) flush

scalmanarsi [skalma'narsi] /72/ vɪᴘ (affaticarsi) to rush about, rush around; (agitarsi, darsi da fare) to get all hot and bothered; (arrabbiarsi) to get excited, get steamed up; **non scalmanarti a cercarlo** don't wear yourself out trying to find him

scalmanato, -a [skalma'nato] sм, sꜰ hothead

scalo ['skalo] sм **1** (per varo) slipway, slips pl **2** (fermata: Naut, Aer) stop; **fare scalo (a)** (Naut) to call (at), put in (at); (Aer) to make a stopover (at), land (at); **scalo tecnico** (Aer) technical stop o landing; **volo senza scalo** non-stop flight **3** (luogo: Naut) port of call; (: Aer) stopover **4** (Ferr): **scalo merci** goods (Brit) o freight (USA) yard

scalogna [ska'loɲɲa] SF (*fam*) bad.luck

scalognato, -a [skaloɲ'ɲato] AGG (*fam*) unlucky

scaloppina [skalop'pina] SF (*Culin*) escalope; **una scaloppina di vitello** a veal escalope

scalpello [skal'pɛllo] SM (*gen*) chisel; (*Med*) scalpel; (*per pozzi petroliferi*) drill

scalpitare [skalpi'tare] /72/ VI (*aus* avere) (*cavallo*) to paw the ground; (*fig: persona*) to champ at the bit

scalpore [skal'pore] SM sensation; **fare** *o* **suscitare scalpore** to cause a sensation *o* a stir

scaltro, -a ['skaltro] AGG shrewd, astute; (*pegg*) sly, cunning

scalzare [skal'tsare] /72/ VT (*pianta*) to bare the roots of; (*muro: fig*) to undermine

scalzo, -a ['skaltso] AGG barefoot(ed); **era scalzo** he was barefoot

scambiare [skam'bjare] /19/ VT 1 (*confondere*): **scambiare qn/qc per** to take *o* mistake sb/sth for; **l'ho scambiato per suo fratello** I mistook him for his brother; **scusa, l'ho scambiato per il mio** sorry, I thought it was mine 2 (*barattare*): **scambiare qc per** to exchange sth for; **ho scambiato un quadro con una bicicletta** I exchanged a painting for a bicycle 3 (*conversare*): **scambiare due parole** to exchange a few words; **scambiarsi** VR (*uso reciproco*) to exchange; **scambiarsi gli auguri di Natale** to wish each other a Happy Christmas; **si scambiarono un'occhiata** they exchanged looks

scambievole [skam'bjevole] AGG mutual, reciprocal

scambio, -bi ['skambjo] SM 1 (*di persone, cose*) exchange; **uno scambio di prigionieri** an exchange of prisoners; **scambi culturali** cultural exchanges; **uno scambio di opinioni** an exchange of views; **fare (uno) scambio** to swap; **facciamo uno scambio?** shall we swap? 2 (*Comm*) trade; **libero scambio** free trade; **scambi con l'estero** foreign trade 3 (*Ferr*) points *pl* (*Brit*), switches (*USA*) 4 (*Calcio*) pass; (*Tennis*) shot and return 5 (*Chim*): **scambio ionico** ion exchange

scamosciato, -a [skamoʃ'ʃato] AGG suede

scampagnata [skampaɲ'ɲata] SF trip to the country, outing to the country; **fare una scampagnata** to go for a day out in the country

scampanare [skampa'nare] /72/ VI (*aus* avere) to peal ♦ VT (*gonna*) to flare

scampare [skam'pare] /72/ VT (*pericolo*) to escape; **scampare la morte** to escape death; **scamparla bella** to have a lucky *o* narrow escape; **Dio ci scampi e liberi!** God forbid! ♦ VI (*aus* essere) **scampare (a qc)** (*pericolo, morte*) to survive (sth), escape (sth); **pochi scamparono alla strage** few escaped (from) the massacre; **pochi scamparono al disastro** few people were untouched by the disaster

scampo¹ ['skampo] SM (*salvezza*) escape, way out; **non c'è (via di) scampo** there's no way out; **cercare scampo nella fuga** to seek safety in flight

scampo² ['skampo] SM (*Zool*) (Dublin Bay) prawn

scampolo ['skampolo] SM remnant

scanalatura [skanala'tura] SF (*azione*) grooving; (*incavo*) groove, channel; (*Archit*) fluting

scandagliare [skandaʎ'ʎare] /27/ VT (*mare*) to sound, fathom; (*fig: indagare*) to sound out; (: *anima, sentimenti, intenzioni*) to probe

scandalistico, -a, -ci, -che [skanda'listiko] AGG (*settimanale*) sensational, sensationalist *attr*

scandalizzare [skandalid'dzare] /72/ VT to scandalize, to shock; **scandalizzarsi** VIP to be scandalized, be shocked; **si scandalizza per un nonnulla** she's easily shocked

scandalo ['skandalo] SM scandal; **il loro comportamento è motivo di scandalo** their behaviour is scandalous; **dare scandalo** to cause a scandal

scandaloso, -a [skanda'loso] AGG scandalous, shocking, outrageous

Scandinavia [skandi'navja] SF Scandinavia

scandinavo, -a [skandi'navo] AGG, SM, SF Scandinavian

scandire [skan'dire] /55/ VT (*versi*) to scan; (*parole*) to articulate, pronounce clearly *o* distinctly; **scandire il tempo** (*Mus*) to beat time

scannare [skan'nare] /72/ VT (*animale*) to butcher, slaughter; (*persona*) to cut *o* slit the throat of

scanner ['skanner] SM INV (*Inform*) scanner

scannerare [skanne'rare] /72/, **scannerizzare** [skanner-id'dzare] VT (*Inform*) to scan

scanno ['skanno] SM seat, bench

scansafatiche [skansafa'tike] SM INV, SF INV idler, loafer

scansare [skan'sare] /72/ VT 1 (*spostare*) to move (aside), shift 2 (*evitare: colpo*) to dodge; (: *pericolo*) to avoid; **scansarsi** VR (*spostarsi*) to get out of the way, move out of the way; (*per evitare un colpo*) to dodge

scansia [skan'sia] SF (*ripiano*) shelf; (*mobile*) bookcase, shelves *pl*

scanso ['skanso] SM avoidance: **a scanso di** in order to avoid, as a precaution against; **a scanso di equivoci** to avoid (any) misunderstanding

scantinato [skanti'nato] SM basement

scantonare [skanto'nare] /72/ VI (*aus* avere) 1 (*per non essere visto*) to duck round the corner 2 (*fig*) to become irrelevant

scanzonato, -a [skanzo'nato] AGG easy-going

scapaccione [skapat'tʃone] SM blow, slap; **dare uno scapaccione a qn** to clout sb; **prendere qn a scapaccioni** to slap sb about

scapestrato, -a [skapes'trato] AGG loose-living, dissolute ♦ SM, SF dissolute person

scapito ['skapito] SM: **a scapito di** to the detriment of

scapola ['skapola] SF (*Anat*) shoulder blade

scapolo ['skapolo] SM bachelor

scappamento [skappa'mento] SM (*Aut*) exhaust; **tubo di scappamento** exhaust pipe

scappare [skap'pare] /72/ VI (*aus* essere) 1 (*gen*): **scappare (da)** (*città, stato, stanza*) to escape (from); **i ladri sono scappati** the thieves got away; **scappare di prigione** to escape from prison; **scappare di casa** to run away from home; **far scappare qn** (*mettere in fuga*) to scare sb away; (*aiutare a fuggire*) to help sb to escape; **scappar via** to run away, escape; **scappare all'estero** to flee the country; **scusa, devo scappare** I'm sorry, but I must dash; **scappare a gambe levate** to take to one's heels 2 (*sfuggire*): **mi è scappato di mano** it slipped out of my hands; **mi è scappato di mente** it slipped my mind; **mi è scappato da ridere** I burst out laughing; **mi scappa la pipì** I'm bursting 3 lasciarsi **scappare** (*occasione, affare*) to miss, let go by; (*dettaglio*) to overlook; (*parola*) to let slip; (*prigioniero*) to let escape; **non lasciarti scappare l'occasione** don't miss this opportunity

scappata [skap'pata] SF (*breve visita*): **fare una scappata da qn** to call *o* drop *o* in on sb; **farò una scappata a Parigi/a casa tua** I'll pop over to Paris/to your place; **faccio una scappata in centro** I'm just going to pop into town

scappatella [skappa'tɛlla] SF escapade

scappatoia [skappa'toja] SF (*gen*) way out; (*nella burocrazia*) loophole

scarabeo [skara'bɛo] SM (*Zool*) scarab (beetle)

scarabocchiare [skarabok'kjare] /19/ VT (*fare scarabocchi*) to scribble, doodle, scrawl; (*scrivere svogliatamente*) to scribble off

scarabocchio, -chi [skara'bɔkkjo] SM (*sgorbio*) scribble, scrawl; (*disegno*) doodle; (*fig: pegg: quadro*) daub; (*macchia d'inchiostro*) blot

scarafaggio, -gi [skara'faddʒo] SM (*Zool*) cockroach

scaramanzia [skaraman'tsia] SF: **per scaramanzia** for luck; **incrocia le dita per scaramanzia** cross your fingers for luck; **non gliel'ho ancora detto per scaramanzia** I haven't told him yet, just in case

scaramuccia, -ce [skara'muttʃa] SF skirmish

scaraventare [skaraven'tare] /72/ VT to fling, hurl; **scaraventarsi** VR: **scaraventarsi contro qn/qc** to fling o.s. at sb/sth

scarcerare [skartʃe'rare] /72/ VT to release (from prison)

scarcerazione [skartʃerat'tsjone] SF release (from prison)

scardinare [skardi'nare] /72/ VT to take off its hinges

scarica, -che ['skarika] SF 1 (*di arma*) shot; (*fig: di insulti*) flood; (: *di sassi, pugni*) hail, shower; **una scarica di mitra** a burst of machine-gun fire 2 (*Elettr*): **scarica (elettrica)** discharge (of electricity)

scaricare [skari'kare] /20/ VT (*merce, veicolo*) to unload; (*passeggeri*) to set down; (*Inform*) to download; (*batteria*) to cause to run down, cause to go flat (Brit) o dead (USA); (fig: coscienza) to unburden, relieve; (: fam: fidanzata, amico) to drop; **stanno scaricando il camion** they're unloading the truck; **ci vuole un'ora per scaricare il file** it takes an hour to download the file; **scaricare qc in** (sogg: fabbrica) to discharge sth into; (: corso d'acqua) to empty sth into, pour sth into; **il canale scarica i rifiuti in mare** the canal deposits the rubbish in the sea; **scaricare un'arma** (togliendo la carica) to unload a gun; (sparando) to discharge a gun; **scaricare le proprie responsabilità su qn** to off-load one's responsibilities onto sb; **scaricare la colpa addosso a qn** to blame sb else; **scaricare la tensione** (fig: rilassarsi) to unwind; (: sfogarsi) to let off steam; **scaricarsi** VIP (molla, orologio) to run o wind down, stop; (batteria) to go flat (Brit) o dead (USA); **la batteria si è scaricata** the battery is flat; **il fulmine si scaricò su un albero** the lightning struck a tree; **scaricarsi** VR (fig: persona) to unwind; (: sfogarsi) to let off steam; **scaricarsi di ogni responsabilità** to relieve o.s. of all responsibilities

scaricatore [skarika'tore] SM: **scaricatore di porto** docker

scarico¹, -a, -chi, -che [ˈskariko] AGG (fucile) unloaded, empty; (orologio) wound down; (batteria) run down, flat (Brit), dead (USA)

scarico², -chi [ˈskariko] SM (di merci, materiali) unloading; (di immondizie) dumping, tipping (Brit); (luogo) refuse o rubbish (Brit) o garbage (USA) dump; (Tecn: deflusso) draining; (: dispositivo) drain; (Aut) exhaust; **scarico del lavandino** washbasin outlet

scarlattina [skarlat'tina] SF scarlet fever

scarlatto, -a [skar'latto] AGG, SM scarlet

scarno, -a [ˈskarno] AGG (persona) lean, bony; (volto) gaunt; (mano) thin, bony; (fig: insufficiente) meagre (Brit), meager (USA); (: spoglio: stile) bare

scarpa [ˈskarpa] SF shoe; **un paio di scarpe** a pair of shoes; **mettiti le scarpe** put on your shoes; **fare le scarpe a qn** (fig) to double-cross sb; **essere una scarpa** (fig: fam) to be useless; **scarpe coi tacchi (alti)** high-heeled shoes; **scarpe col tacco basso** low-heeled shoes; **scarpe da ginnastica** gym shoes, sneakers; **scarpe senza tacco** flat shoes; **scarpe sportive** trainers (Brit), sneakers (USA); **scarpe da tennis** tennis shoes

scarpata [skar'pata] SF escarpment

scarpiera [skar'pjera] SF shoe rack

scarpone [skar'pone] SM boot; **scarponi da montagna** climbing boots; **scarponi da sci** ski boots

scarrozzare [skarrot'tsare] /72/ VT to drive around

scarseggiare [skarsed'dʒare] /62/ VI (aus avere) (viveri, risorse) to be scarce, be lacking; **i viveri scarseggiavano** food was in short supply; **cominciano a scarseggiare i medicinali** supplies of medicine are starting to run low; **scarseggiare di qc** to lack sth, be short of sth

scarsezza [skar'settsa] SF shortage, lack, scarcity

scarso, -a [ˈskarso] AGG (raccolto) poor, lean; (risorse) meagre (Brit), meager (USA); (qualità) poor; (alunno, voto) mediocre; **è un chilo/metro scarso** it's just under a kilo/metre; **le porzioni erano scarse** the portions were rather small; **di scarso interesse** of little interest; **hanno scarse risorse a disposizione** they have few resources at their disposal; **scarsa visibilità** poor visibility; **ha dimostrato scarsa maturità/intelligenza** he showed little maturity/intelligence; **scarso di** lacking in

scartabellare [skartabel'lare] /72/ VT to skim through, glance through

scartafaccio, -ci [skarta'fattʃo] SM notebook

scartamento [skarta'mento] SM (Ferr) gauge; **a scartamento ridotto** narrow-gauge

scartare¹ [skar'tare] /72/ VT (regalo, caramella) to unwrap; **hai scartato i regali?** have you unwrapped your presents?

scartare² [skar'tare] /72/ • VT 1 (Carte) to discard 2 (fig: possibilità, idea) to reject; **hanno scartato tutte le mie proposte** they rejected all my suggestions 3 (concorrente) to reject, eliminate; (Mil) to declare unfit for military service

scartare³ [skar'tare] /72/ VI (aus avere) (deviare) to swerve; **scartare a sinistra** to swerve to the left ♦ VT (Calcio) to dodge (past); (Equitazione): **scartare (l'ostacolo)** to run out

scarto¹ [ˈskarto] SM 1 (prodotto, oggetto scartato) reject 2 (Carte) discard

scarto² [ˈskarto] SM 1 (movimento brusco) swerve; (Equitazione) run-out; **fare uno scarto** to swerve; to run out 2 (differenza) gap, difference; **scarto salariale** wage differential

scartoffie [skar'tɔffje] SFPL (pegg) papers

scassare [skas'sare] /72/ VT 1 (fam: rompere) to wreck, smash 2 (dissodare) to plough up; **scassarsi** VIP (rompersi) to be wrecked

scassinare [skassi'nare] /72/ VT to force, break open

scasso [ˈskasso] SM (Dir) breaking and entering; **furto con scasso** burglary

scatenare [skate'nare] /72/ VT (reazione, rabbia) to provoke; (rivolta) to spark off; (guai) to stir up; **scatenarsi** VIP (temporale) to break; (rivolta) to break out; (persona): **scatenarsi contro qn** to rage at sb

scatenato, -a [skate'nato] AGG wild

scatola [ˈskatola] SF (gen) box; (di latta) tin (Brit), can (USA); **cibo in scatola** tinned (Brit) o canned (USA) foods; **una scatola di sardine** a tin o can of sardines; **una scatola di cioccolatini** a box of chocolates; **comprare qc a scatola chiusa** to buy sth sight unseen; **accettare qc a scatola chiusa** (fig) to accept sth blindly; **avere le scatole piene (di qn/qc)** (fam) to be fed up to the back teeth (with sb/sth); **rompere le scatole a qn** (fam) to get on sb's nerves; **levati** o **togliti dalle scatole!** get out of the way! ♦ **scatola di cartone** cardboard box; **scatola cranica** cranium; **scatola del differenziale** (Aut) differential housing; **scatola di fiammiferi** (vuota) matchbox; (piena) box of matches; **scatola dei fusibili** fuse box; **scatola nera** (Aer) black box

scatolone [skato'lone] SM cardboard box

scattante [skat'tante] AGG (svelto) quick off the mark; (agile) agile

scattare [skat'tare] /72/ VI (aus essere) (molla) to be released; (grilletto, interruttore) to spring back; (serratura: aprirsi) to click open; (: chiudersi) to click shut; (iniziare: legge, provvedimento) to come into effect; (Sport) to put on a spurt; **è scattato l'allarme** the alarm went off; **far scattare** to release; **ha fatto scattare l'allarme** he set the alarm off; **scattare in piedi** to spring o leap to one's feet; **sono scattati in piedi** they sprang to their feet; **scattare sull'attenti** to spring o leap to attention; **scatta per niente** (si arrabbia) he flies off the handle at the slightest provocation; **domani scatta l'ora legale** tomorrow the clocks go forward (o back) ♦ VT (Fot): **scattare una foto** to take a photograph o a photo o a picture

scatto [ˈskatto] SM 1 (congegno) release; (di arma da fuoco) trigger mechanism; (rumore) click; **serratura a scatto** spring lock; **ho sentito lo scatto della serratura** I heard the lock click, I heard the click of the lock; **scatto automatico** automatic release; (Fot) (automatic) timer 2 (Telec) unit 3 (Sport) spurt; **ha sorpassato gli altri corridori con uno scatto** he put on a spurt and overtook the other runners 4 (di persona) jump, start; **muoversi a scatti** to move jerkily; **ha avuto uno scatto (d'ira)** he flew off the handle; **di scatto** suddenly; **si alzò di scatto** he sprang o leapt to his feet 5 (aumento): **scatto d'anzianità** long service bonus; **scatto di stipendio** increment

scaturire [skatu'rire] /55/ VI (aus essere) (liquido): **scaturire (da)** to spurt (from), gush (from); (fig: avere origine) to derive (from)

scavalcare [skaval'kare] /20/ VT (ostacolo, anche fig) to pass (o climb) over; (fig: concorrenti) to overtake, get ahead of; (: collega) to be promoted over (the head of); **abbiamo scavalcato il muretto** we climbed over the wall

scavare [ska'vare] /72/ VT (gen, terreno) to dig; (trincea: Archeol) to dig, excavate; (pozzo, galleria) to bore; (tronco, pietra: renderlo cavo) to hollow (out); **scavarsi la fossa** (fig) to dig one's own grave; **un volto scavato dalla stanchezza** a haggard face; **scavare nell'animo di qn** to search sb's soul; **scavare nel passato di qn** to dig into sb's past

scavatrice [skava'tritʃe] SF (macchina) excavator

scavezzacollo, -a [skavettsa'kɔllo] SM, SF daredevil

scavo [ˈskavo] SM (luogo) excavation; (azione) excavating no pl; **fare degli scavi in una zona** to excavate an area

scazzottare [skattsot'tare] (fam) /72/ VT to beat up, give a thrashing to; **scazzottarsi** VR (uso reciproco) to beat each other up

scegliere [ˈʃeʎʎere] /100/ VT IRREG (gen) to choose; (prodotto, *candidato*) to select, choose; **hai scelto il suo regalo?** have you chosen her present?; **scegliere di fare qc** to choose to do sth; **scegliere il campo** (*Sport*) to toss for ends

sceicco, -chi [ʃeˈikko] SM sheik

scelgo *ecc* [ˈʃelgo] VB *vedi* **scegliere**

scellerato, -a [ʃelleˈrato] AGG wicked, evil ♦ SM, SF villain

scellino [ʃelˈlino] SM (*inglese, austriaco*) schilling

scelto, -a [ˈʃelto] PP *di* **scegliere** ♦ AGG (*gruppo*) carefully selected; (*frutta, verdura*) top-quality, choice; **brani scelti** selected passages; **una compagnia scelta** a distinguished company; **pubblico scelto** select audience; **tiratore scelto** crack shot, highly skilled marksman

scemare [ʃeˈmare] /72/ VI (*aus* **essere**) (*rumore, applausi, interesse*) to lessen; (*forze*) to decline; (*vento*) to drop, abate

scemenza [ʃeˈmɛntsa] SF stupidity *no pl*; **dire scemenze** to talk nonsense *o* rubbish; **ha fatto una scemenza** he behaved foolishly *o* stupidly; **è stata una scemenza** it was sheer stupidity

scemo, -a [ˈʃemo] AGG stupid, foolish, silly ♦ SM, SF idiot, fool; **fare lo scemo** to play the fool

scempio, -pi [ˈʃempjo] SM (*strage*) massacre, slaughter; (*deturpazione*) destruction; **fare scempio di qc** (*fig*) to destroy sth, wreak havoc with sth, ruin sth; **lo scempio dei centri storici** the destruction of historic town centres; **quel viadotto è uno scempio** that viaduct is an eyesore

scena [ˈʃena] SF 1 (*gen, anche Teatro, Cine*) scene; **nella prima scena** in the first scene, in scene one; **la scena si svolge a Parigi** the action takes place in Paris, the scene is set in Paris; **cambiamento di scena** scene change; **una scena di caccia** a hunting scene; **sulla scena internazionale** on the international scene; **ho assistito a tutta la scena** I was present at *o* during the whole scene; **fare una scena** (*fig*) to make a scene; **ha fatto una scena orribile** it was a horrible sight; **ha fatto scena muta** (*fig*) he didn't open his mouth 2 (*palcoscenico*) stage; **entrare in scena** to come on stage; (*fig*) to come on the scene; **uscire di scena** to leave the stage; (*fig*) to leave the scene; **mettere in scena** (*personaggio*) to present on the stage; (*commedia*) to stage, direct

scenario, -ri [ʃeˈnarjo] SM (*Teatro*) scenery, set; (*fig: sfondo*) backdrop

scenata [ʃeˈnata] SF row, scene; **fare una scenata (a qn)** to make a scene; **Sandra ha fatto una scenata al ristorante** Sandra made a scene at the restaurant

scendere [ˈʃendere] VB IRREG /101/ VT (*scale, sentiero*) to go (*o* come) down, descend ♦ VI (*aus* **essere**) 1 (*gen*) to go (*o* come) down, descend; (*fiume, torrente*) to flow down; (*strada*) to slope down, descend; (*aereo*) to come down, descend; **scendere con l'ascensore** to go (*o* come) down in the lift (*Brit*) *o* elevator (*USA*); **scendere in città** to go into town; **scendere in strada** to go down into the street; **scendere in piazza** (*folla, manifestanti*) to take to the streets; **scendere in sciopero** to come out on strike; **scendere a piedi/correndo** to walk/run down; **scendere ad aprirgli il portone** I'll go down and open the door for him; **sali tu o scendo io?** are you coming up or shall I come down?; **scendo subito!** I'm just coming!; **siamo scesi in mezz'ora** (*da collina*) we got down in half an hour; **i capelli le scendevano sulle spalle** her hair fell to her shoulders; **scendere a terra** (*sbarcare*) to go ashore; **scendere da un albergo** to put up *o* stay at a hotel 2 **scendere da** (*macchina, treno*) to get out of; (*nave*) to disembark from, get off; (*aereo, autobus, bici*) to get off; **scendere da cavallo** to dismount, get off one's horse; **scendere dal letto** to get out of bed; **scendere dalle scale** to go (*o* come) down the stairs; **scendo alla prossima fermata** I'm getting off at the next stop; **scendi da quell'albero!** come down from that tree! 3 (*prezzi, temperatura*) to fall, drop; (*livello*) to fall, drop, go down; (*marea*) to go out; (*notte, oscurità*) to fall; (*sole, strada*) to go down; (*nebbia*) to come down; **la temperatura è scesa di due gradi** the temperature fell by two degrees

sceneggiato [ʃenedˈdʒato] SM (*TV*) television drama

sceneggiatore, -trice [ʃenedʒaˈtore] SM, SF scriptwriter

sceneggiatura [ʃenedʒaˈtura] SF (*Teatro*) scenario; (*Cine*) screenplay, scenario

scenico, -a, -ci, -che [ˈʃeniko] AGG stage *attr*

scenografia [ʃenograˈfia] SF (*Teatro*) stage design; (*Cine*) set design; (*elementi scenici*) scenery

scenografo, -a [ʃeˈnɔɡrafo] SM, SF set designer

sceriffo [ʃeˈriffo] SM sheriff

scervellarsi [ʃervelˈlarsi] /72/ VIP: **scervellarsi (su qc)** to rack one's brains (over sth)

scervellato, -a [ʃervelˈlato] SM, SF half-wit, idiot ♦ AGG feather-brained, scatterbrained

sceso, -a [ˈʃeso] PP *di* **scendere**

scetticismo [ʃettiˈtʃizmo] SM scepticism (*Brit*), skepticism (*USA*)

scettico, -a, -ci, -che [ˈʃettiko] AGG sceptical (*Brit*), skeptical (*USA*) ♦ SM, SF sceptic (*Brit*), skeptic (*USA*)

scettro [ˈʃettro] SM sceptre (*Brit*), scepter (*USA*)

scheda [ˈskeda] SF (*di schedario*) (index) card; (*di elezioni*) ballot paper; (*in libro*) inset; (*servizio televisivo*) brief report; **scheda audio** (*Inform*) sound card; **scheda bianca/nulla** (*Pol*) unmarked/spoiled ballot paper; **scheda madre** (*Inform*) motherboard; **scheda perforata** punch card; **scheda ricaricabile** (*Telec*) top-up card; **scheda telefonica** phonecard; **scheda video** (*Inform*) video card

schedare [skeˈdare] /72/ VT (*dati*) to file; (*registrare su scheda*) to card-index; (*libri*) to catalogue; (*della polizia*) to put on record

schedario, -ri [skeˈdarjo] SM card index, file; (*mobile*) filing cabinet

schedato, -a [skeˈdato] AGG with a (police) record ♦ SM, SF person with a (police) record

schedina [skeˈdina] SF ≈ pools coupon (*Brit*); **giocare la schedina** to do the football pools

scheggia, -ge [ˈskeddʒa] SF (*gen*) splinter; (*di vetro*) splinter, sliver; (*di porcellana*) chip; **scheggia impazzita** (*fig*) loose cannon

scheletrico, -a, -ci, -che [skeˈletriko] AGG (*anche Anat*) skeletal; (*fig: essenziale*) skeleton *attr*

scheletro [ˈskeletro] SM (*Anat*) skeleton; (*fig: struttura*) frame, framework; (: *di trama*) outline; **essere ridotto a uno scheletro** to be all skin and bone; **avere uno scheletro nell'armadio** (*fig*) to have a skeleton in the closet *o* cupboard (*Brit*)

schema, -i [ˈskema] SM 1 (*gen*) outline; (*diagramma*) diagram, sketch; **ha disegnato lo schema alla lavagna** he drew the diagram on the board; **schema riassuntivo** outline of the main points; **schema di legge** bill 2 (*fig: modello*): **ribellarsi agli schemi** to rebel against traditional values; **secondo gli schemi tradizionali** in accordance with traditional values

schematico, -a, -ci, -che [skeˈmatiko] AGG schematic

schematizzare [skematidˈdzare] /72/ VT to schematize

scherma [ˈskerma] SF (*Sport*) fencing; **faccio scherma** I do fencing; **tirare di scherma** to fence

schermaglia [skerˈmaʎʎa] SF (*fig*) skirmish

schermata [skerˈmata] SF (*Inform*) 1 screen 2 screenshot

schermire [skerˈmire] /55/ VT to protect, shield; **schermirsi** VR to defend o.s., protect o.s.

schermo [ˈskermo] SM 1 (*gen*) screen; **farsi schermo con la mano** (*per proteggersi dalla luce*) to shield one's eyes with one's hand 2 (*TV, Cine*): **il piccolo/grande schermo** the small/big screen; **divo dello schermo** screen star; **a schermo panoramico** (*TV*) widescreen

schermografia [skermograˈfia] SF X-rays *pl*

schernire [skerˈnire] /55/ VT to mock, sneer at

scherno [ˈskerno] SM scorn; **farsi scherno di** to sneer at; **essere oggetto di scherno** to be a laughing stock; **di scherno** (*parole*) scornful, sneering; (*gesto*) scornful; **grida di scherno** jeers

scherzare [skerˈtsare] /72/ VI (*aus* **avere**) (*gen*) to joke; **stavo scherzando** I was only joking *o* kidding; **è meglio non scherzare su queste cose** it's better not to joke about these things; **quello è un tipo che non scherza** he is not a man to be trifled with; **c'è poco da scherzare!** it's no laughing matter!, it's no joke!; **scherzare con i sentimenti altrui** to trifle with other people's feelings; **non scherzare col fuoco!** (*fig*) you shouldn't play with fire!

scherzo [ˈskertso] SM 1 (*gen*) joke; (*burla*) (practical) joke, prank; **fare uno scherzo a qn** to play a (practical) joke *o* prank *o* trick on sb; **facciamo uno scherzo a Daniele!** let's play a trick on Daniele!; **per scherzo** as *o* for a joke, for a laugh, for fun; **fare un brutto scherzo a qn** to play a nasty trick on sb; **neppure per scherzo** not even in fun; **non sa stare allo scherzo** he can't take a joke; **scherzi a parte** seriously, joking apart; **...e niente scherzi!** ...and no funny business!; **uno scherzo da prete** a dirty trick; **è uno scherzo!** (*facile*) it's child's play!, it's easy!; **scherzi d'acqua** waterworks; **scherzi di luce** effects of the light **2** (*Mus*) scherzo

scherzoso, -a [sker'tsoso] AGG (*tono, gesto*) playful; (*osservazione*) facetious; **è un tipo scherzoso** he likes *o* is fond of a joke

schiaccianoci [skjattʃa'notʃi] SM INV nutcracker

schiacciante [skjat'tʃante] AGG overwhelming

schiacciare [skjat'tʃare] /14/ VT **1** (*gen*) to squash, crush; (*patate*) to mash; (*aglio*) to crush; (*noce*) to crack; (*mozzicone*) to stub out; **la macchina gli ha schiacciato un piede** the car crushed his foot; **schiacciare la palla** (*Tennis, Pallavolo*) to smash the ball; **schiacciare un sonnellino** to take *o* have a nap; **schiacciarsi un dito nella porta** to shut one's finger in the door **2** (*pulsante*) to press; (*pedale*) to press down **3** (*fig: opposizione, nemico*) to crush; (: *squadra avversaria*) to hammer; **era schiacciato da un senso di colpa** he was weighed down by feelings of guilt; **schiacciarsi** VIP to get squashed, get crushed

schiaffeggiare [skjaffed'dʒare] /62/ VT to smack, slap

schiaffo ['skjaffo] SM slap (in the face); **dare uno schiaffo a qn** to slap sb; **prendere qn a schiaffi** to slap sb about *o* around; **uno schiaffo morale** a slap in the face, a rebuff; **avere una faccia da schiaffi** to look impudent

schiamazzare [skjamat'tsare] /72/ VI (*aus* avere) (*galline, oche*) to squawk, cackle; (*fig: persone*) to make a din, make a racket

schiamazzo [skja'mattso] SM (*fig: chiasso*) din, racket

schiantare [skjan'tare] /72/ VT (*spezzare*) to break, tear apart; **il fulmine ha schiantato l'albero** the lightning split the tree; **schiantarsi** VIP (*macchina*): **schiantarsi contro** to crash into; (*aereo*): **schiantarsi al suolo** to crash (to the ground)

schianto ['skjanto] SM (*rumore*) crash; **di schianto** (*improvvisamente*) all of a sudden; **quella macchina è uno schianto!** (*fam*) that car's great

schiarire [skja'rire] /55/ VT (*gen*) to lighten, make lighter; (*Fot*) to make brighter; (*tende, tessuto: far sbiadire*) to fade; **schiarirsi la gola** *o* **la voce** to clear one's throat; **schiarirsi i capelli** to dye one's hair blonde; **si è schiarita i capelli** she's dyed her hair blonde; **schiarire le idee a qn** (*fig*) to put sb straight VI (*aus* essere), **schiarirsi** VIP (*cielo, tempo*) to clear up; (*colore*) to become lighter; (*sbiadire*) to fade

schiarita [skja'rita] SF (*Meteor*) bright spell; (*fig*) improvement, turn for the better

schiattare [skjat'tare] /72/ VI (*aus* essere) (*fig: scoppiare*) to burst; **schiattare d'invidia** to be green with envy; **schiattare di rabbia** to be beside o.s. with rage

schiavitù [skjavi'tu] SF slavery; **ridurre in schiavitù** to subject, subjugate

schiavizzare [skjavid'dzare] /72/ VT (*anche fig*) to reduce to slavery, enslave; (*dipendenti, figli*) to tyrannize over

schiavo, -a ['skjavo] AGG enslaved; **essere schiavo delle proprie abitudini** to be a slave to habit ♦ SM, SF slave

schiena ['skjena] SF back; **soffrire di mal di schiena** to have a bad back; **avere mal di schiena, avere la schiena a pezzi** to have backache, have a pain in one's back; **ho mal di schiena** I've got backache; **avere la schiena curva** (*con le spalle curve*) to be round-shouldered; (*con la spina dorsale curva*) to have a stoop; **voltare la schiena a qn** (*fig*) to turn one's back on sb; **mi ha voltato la schiena proprio quando avevo bisogno di lui** he turned his back on me just when I needed him; **rompersi la schiena** to break one's back; (*fig: lavorare sodo*) to work one's fingers to the bone; **visto di schiena** seen from behind *o* from the back; **a schiena di mulo** (*ponte*) humpback; (*strada*) steeply cambered

schienale [skje'nale] SM **1** (*di poltrona, sedia*) back **2** (*di animale macellato*) saddle

schiera ['skjera] SF (*Mil: linea*) rank; **le schiere dei nemici** the enemy forces; **una schiera di persone** a crowd of people; **arrivarono a schiere** they arrived in their hundreds; **villetta a schiera** ≈ terraced house

schieramento [skjera'mento] SM (*Mil*) (rank) formation; (*Sport*) formation; (*fig*) alliance

schierare [skje'rare] /72/ VT (*Mil*) to draw up, line up, marshal; **schierarsi** VR (*Mil*) to draw up; (*fig*): **schierarsi con** *o* **dalla parte di/contro qn** to side with/oppose sb

schietto, -a ['skjetto] AGG frank, straightforward

schifare [ski'fare] /72/ VT to disgust; **schifarsi** VIP to be disgusted

schifezza [ski'fettsa] SF: **essere una schifezza** (*cibo, bibita*) to be disgusting; (*film, libro*) to be dreadful; **mangia un sacco di schifezze** he eats a lot of rubbish

schifiltoso, -a [skifil'toso] AGG fussy, difficult; **fare lo schifiltoso** to be fussy

schifo ['skifo] SM (*sensazione*) disgust; **è uno schifo!** it's disgusting!; **fare schifo** (*cibo, insetto*) to be disgusting; (*libro, film*) to be dreadful *o* awful; **mi fai schifo** you make me sick; **la nostra squadra fa schifo** our team was useless

schifoso, -a [ski'foso] AGG (*che fa ribrezzo*) disgusting, revolting; (*pessimo*) dreadful, awful; **hai avuto una fortuna schifosa** (*fam*) you've been terribly lucky

schioccare [skjok'kare] /20/ VT (*frusta*) to crack; (*dita*) to snap, click; (*lingua*) to click; (*labbra*) to smack; **le schioccò un bacio** he gave her a smacker (*fam*)

schioppettata [skjoppet'tata] SF gunshot

schioppo ['skjoppo] SM rifle, gun; **essere a un tiro di schioppo da** to be a stone's throw from

schiudere ['skjudere] VB IRREG /22/ VT to open; **schiudersi** VIP (*fiore*) to open, come out

schiuma ['skjuma] SF (*gen*) foam; (*di bevande*) froth; (*di sapone*) lather; **avere la schiuma alla bocca** (*fig: arrabbiato*) to be foaming at the mouth; **schiuma da barba** shaving foam

schiumare [skju'mare] /72/ VT (*brodo*) to skim ♦ VI (*aus* avere) to foam; **schiumare di rabbia** to foam at the mouth

schiuso, -a ['skjuso] PP *di* **schiudere**

schivare [ski'vare] /72/ VT (*colpo, proiettile*) to dodge, avoid; (*persona, pericolo*) to avoid; (*domanda*) to evade

schivo, -a ['skivo] AGG (*ritroso*) reserved; (*timido*) shy

schizofrenia [skiddzofre'nia] SF schizophrenia

schizofrenico, -a, -ci, -che [skiddzo'freniko] AGG, SM, SF schizophrenic

schizzare [skit'tsare] /72/ VT **1** (*gen*) to squirt; (*inzuppare*) to splash; (*macchiare*) to spatter; **mi ha schizzato d'acqua** he splashed water over me, he splashed me with water; **finiscila di schizzarmi** stop splashing me; **ha schizzato inchiostro sulla tovaglia** he spattered ink on the tablecloth, he spattered the tablecloth with ink; **ti sei schizzato la giacca di vino** you've got wine on your jacket **2** (*disegnare*) to sketch ♦ VI (*aus* essere) (*liquido*) to squirt; (*con violenza*) to gush, spurt; **schizzare via** (*animale, persona*) to dart away; (*macchina, moto*) to speed off; **schizzare fuori** (*persona*) to dash out; **schizzare fuori dal letto** to leap *o* jump out of bed; **gli occhi gli schizzarono dalle orbite** (*fig*) his eyes nearly popped out of his head

schizzinoso, -a [skittsi'noso] AGG fussy, difficult, finicky; **è più schizzinosa di me** she's fussier than me ♦ SM, SF fussy person, difficult person; **non fare lo schizzinoso!** don't be so fussy!

schizzo ['skittso] SM **1** (*di liquido*) squirt, splash; (*macchia*) stain, spot; **uno schizzo d'acqua** a splash of water **2** (*abbozzo*) sketch

sci [ʃi] SM INV (*Sport: attività*) skiing; (: *attrezzo*) ski; **sci a monte** uphill ski; **un paio di sci** a pair of skis; **una gara di sci** a ski race; **lo sci mi piace molto** I love skiing; **fare dello sci** to ski; **sci acrobatico** hot-dogging, free-styling; **sci alpinismo** *o* **d'alta quota** ski mountaineering; **sci alpino** alpine skiing; **sci di fondo** cross-country skiing, ski touring (*USA*); **sci nautico** water-skiing; **sci nordico** Nordic skiing

scia ['ʃia] SF (*di imbarcazione*) wake; (*fig: di fumo, profumo*) trail

scià [ʃa] SM INV shah

sciabola ['ʃabola] SF sabre (*Brit*), saber (*USA*)

sciacallo [ʃa'kallo] SM (*Zool*) jackal; (*fig: pegg: profittatore*) shark, profiteer; (: *ladro*) looter

sciacquare [ʃak'kware] /72/ VT (*mani, capelli*) to rinse; (*panni*) to rinse (out); **sciacquarsi la bocca** to rinse one's mouth

sciagura [ʃa'gura] SF disaster, calamity; **una sciagura aerea** an air disaster

sciagurato, -a [ʃaguˈrato] AGG (*disgraziato*) wretched, unfortunate; (*malvagio*) wicked ♦ SM, SF wretch

scialacquare [ʃalakˈkware] /72/ VT to squander

scialare [ʃaˈlare] /72/ VI (*aus* avere) throw one's money around; **c'è poco da scialare** there's little money to spare

scialbo, -a [ˈʃalbo] AGG (*colore*) pale, dull; (*fig: persona*) dull, colourless (*Brit*), colorless (*USA*)

scialle [ˈʃalle] SM shawl

scialo [ˈʃalo] SM squandering, waste; **fare scialo di qc** to squander sth (away)

scialuppa [ʃaˈluppa] SF (*Naut*) sloop; **scialuppa di salvataggio** lifeboat

sciamare [ʃaˈmare] /72/ VI (*aus* avere *o* essere) to swarm

sciame [ˈʃame] SM swarm; (*fig: di persone*) crowd, swarm

sciancato, -a [ʃanˈkato] AGG (*persona*) crippled, lame; (*fig: mobile*) rickety

sciare [ʃiˈare] /60/ VI (*aus* avere) to ski; **sai sciare?** can you ski?; **andare a sciare** to go skiing

sciarpa [ˈʃarpa] SF scarf

sciatore, -trice [ʃiaˈtore] SM, SF skier

sciattezza [ʃatˈtettsa] SF slovenliness

sciatto, -a [ˈʃatto] AGG (*persona*) slovenly, unkempt; (*lavoro*) sloppy, careless

scibile [ˈʃibile] SM knowledge

scientifico, -a, -ci, -che [ʃenˈtifiko] AGG (*gen*) scientific; (*materia, insegnamento*) science *attr*; **la ricerca scientifica** scientific research; **una materia scientifica** a science subject; **ha scelto il ramo scientifico** he chose science; **la (polizia) scientifica** the forensic department

scienza [ˈʃentsa] SF 1 (*gen*) science; **scienze** SFPL (*Scol*) science *sg*; **la scienza e la tecnologia** science and technology; **scienze della comunicazione** (*Univ*) media studies; **scienze motorie** (*Univ*) sports science; **scienze naturali** natural sciences; **scienze occulte** occult sciences; **scienze politiche** political science *pl*; **scienze sociali** (*Univ*) social sciences 2 (*conoscenza*) knowledge, learning

scienziato, -a [ʃenˈtsjato] SM, SF scientist

Scilly [ˈʃilli] SFPL: **le (isole) Scilly** the Scilly Isles

scimmia [ˈʃimmja] SF (*Zool*) monkey; (*più grande*) ape; (*fig: persona brutta*) horror; **avere la scimmia** (*fam: dipendenza da droga*) to have a monkey on one's back (*USA*)

scimmiottare [ʃimmjotˈtare] /72/ VT (*beffeggiare*) to mock, make fun of; (*imitare*) to mimic, ape

scimpanzé [ʃimpanˈtse] SM INV chimpanzee

scimunito, -a [ʃimuˈnito] AGG idiotic, stupid, silly ♦ SM, SF fool, idiot

scindere [ˈʃindere] VB IRREG /102/ VT to split (up), divide; **scindersi** VIP to split (up), break up; **scindersi in** to split into

scintilla [ʃinˈtilla] SF (*anche fig*) spark; **fare scintille** to give off sparks, spark

scintillare [ʃintilˈlare] /72/ VI (*aus* avere) to give off sparks, spark; (*acqua, occhi*) to sparkle, glitter; **gli occhi le scintillavano di gioia** her eyes were sparkling with joy

scintillio, -lii [ʃintilˈlio] SM sparkling, glittering

scioccare [ʃokˈkare] /20/ VT to shock

sciocchezza [ʃokˈkettsa] SF 1 (*qualità*) foolishness *no pl*, silliness *no pl*, stupidity *no pl*; **fare una sciocchezza** to do something silly; **mi raccomando, non fare sciocchezze!** make sure you don't do anything silly!; **è stata una sciocchezza** it was really foolish; **per me ha fatto una sciocchezza** I think it was very foolish *o* silly of him to do that; **dire sciocchezze** to talk nonsense; **ha detto un sacco di sciocchezze** he talked a load of nonsense; **sciocchezze!** nonsense! 2 **l'ho pagato una sciocchezza** I hardly paid anything for it; **è solo una sciocchezza** (*regalo*) it's only a trifle

sciocco, -a, -chi, -che [ˈʃokko] AGG silly, foolish, stupid; **è l'idea più sciocca che abbia mai sentito** it's the silliest idea I've ever heard; (*insipido*) tasteless ♦ SM, SF fool

sciogliere [ˈʃoʎʎere] VB IRREG /103/ VT 1 (*liquefare*) to melt; (*nell'acqua: zucchero*) to dissolve; (*neve*) to melt, thaw; **il sole ha sciolto la neve** the sun has melted the snow; **sciogliere il ghiaccio** (*fig*) to break the ice 2 (*disfare: nodo*) to undo, untie; (: *capelli*) to loosen 3 (*slegare: persona, animale*) to set free, release, untie; (*fig: persona: da obbligo*) to absolve, release; (: *contratto*) to cancel, annul; (: *parlamento, matrimonio*)

to dissolve; (: *riunione*) to break up, bring to an end; (: *società*) to dissolve, wind up; **sciogliere le vele** (*Naut*) to set sail; **sciogliere i muscoli** to limber up; **esercizi per sciogliere i muscoli** warm-up exercises; **(far) sciogliere la lingua a qn** to loosen sb's tongue; **sciogliere un mistero** to solve *o* unravel a mystery; **sciogliersi** VIP 1 (*vedi vt a*) to melt; to dissolve; to thaw; **questa carne si scioglie in bocca** this meat melts in the mouth; **sciogliersi in lacrime** to burst into tears 2 (*assemblea, corteo, duo*) to break up; **sciogliersi** VR (*liberarsi*) to free o.s., release o.s.; **sciogliersi dai legami** (*fig*) to free o.s. from all ties

scioglilingua [ʃoʎʎiˈlingwa] SM INV tongue-twister

sciolgo ecc [ˈʃolgo] VB *vedi* sciogliere

scioltezza [ʃolˈtettsa] SF (*agilità*) agility, nimbleness, suppleness; (*disinvoltura*) ease, smoothness; (*nel parlare*) fluency, ease

sciolto, -a [ˈʃolto] PP *di* sciogliere ♦ AGG 1 (*persona: agile*) agile, nimble; (: *disinvolto*) easy-going, free and easy; **essere sciolto nei movimenti** to be supple; **avere la lingua sciolta** to have the gift of the gab 2 (*Comm: sfuso*) loose 3 (*in poesia*): **versi sciolti** blank verse

scioperante [ʃopeˈrante] AGG on strike ♦ SM, SF striker

scioperare [ʃopeˈrare] /72/ VI (*aus* avere) (*fare sciopero*) to strike, go on strike; (*entrare in sciopero*) to go on strike

sciopero [ˈʃopero] SM strike; **essere in sciopero, fare sciopero** to be on strike; **entrare in sciopero** to go on *o* come out on strike; **sciopero bianco** work-to-rule (*Brit*), slowdown (*USA*); **sciopero della fame** hunger strike; **sta facendo lo sciopero della fame** he is on a hunger strike; **sciopero selvaggio** wildcat strike; **sciopero a singhiozzo** on-off strike; **sciopero di solidarietà** sympathy strike

sciorinare [ʃoriˈnare] /72/ VT 1 (*ostentare*) to show off, display 2 (*dire con disinvoltura: consigli, citazioni*) to rattle off; **sciorinare bugie** to tell one lie after another 3 (*bucato*) to hang out

sciovia [ʃioˈvia] SF ski tow

sciovinismo [ʃoviˈnizmo] SM chauvinism

sciovinista, -i, -e [ʃoviˈnista] SM, SF chauvinist

scipito, -a [ʃiˈpito] AGG insipid

scippare [ʃipˈpare] /72/ VT: **scippare qn** to snatch sb's bag; **mi hanno scippato** my bag was snatched

scippatore [ʃippaˈtore] SM bag-snatcher

scippo [ˈʃippo] SM bag-snatching; **ci sono stati troppi scippi ultimamente** there's been a lot of bag-snatching lately

scirocco [ʃiˈrokko] SM sirocco

sciroppo [ʃiˈroppo] SM syrup; **sciroppo per la tosse** cough syrup, cough mixture

scisma, -i [ˈʃizma] SM (*Rel, Pol*) schism

scissione [ʃisˈsjone] SF (*Fis, Bio*) fission; (*di gruppo, partito*) splitting (up), division, split; **ha causato una scissione nel partito** it caused a split in the party

scisso, -a [ˈʃisso] PP *di* scindere

sciupare [ʃuˈpare] /72/ VT 1 (*rovinare*) to ruin, spoil 2 (*sprecare: tempo, denaro*) to waste, throw away; (: *occasione*) to miss; **sciuparsi** VIP (*rovinarsi*) to get spoiled *o* ruined; **le scarpe nuove si sono sciupate** my new shoes were ruined; **l'ho visti molto sciupati** they looked very run down when I saw them

scivolare [ʃivoˈlare] /72/ VI (*aus* essere) (*cadere*) to slip; **scivolare sul ghiaccio** (*persona*) to slip on the ice (*per ghiaccio*) to slide on the ice; (*macchina*) to skid on the ice; **è scivolato giù dalle scale** he slipped and fell down the stairs; **attento, si scivola** be careful, it's slippery; **il vaso gli scivolò dalle mani** the vase slipped out of his hands; **scivolò via non visto** he slipped away unseen; **l'uomo scivolò silenziosamente nella stanza** the man slipped silently into the room; **gli fece scivolare il biglietto in tasca** he slipped the note into his pocket; **scivolare su una buccia di banana** (*anche fig*) to slip on a banana skin

scivolo [ˈʃivolo] SM (*gioco*) slide; (*Tecn*) chute

scivoloso, -a [ʃivoˈloso] AGG slippery

sclerosi [skleˈrɔzi] SF INV (*Med*) sclerosis; **sclerosi multipla** multiple sclerosis

scoccare [skokˈkare] /20/ VT 1 (*freccia*) to shoot 2 (*ore*) to strike; **l'orologio scoccò le 8** the clock struck 8 3 **scoccare**

un bacio a qn to give sb a smacker ♦ vi (aus essere) **1** (freccia) to shoot out; (scintilla) to fly up **2** (ore) to strike; **scoccavano le 11** it was striking 11

scoccherò ecc [skokke'rɔ] vb vedi **scoccare**

scocciare [skot'tʃare] /14/ vt to annoy, bother; **le sue continue lamentele mi hanno scocciato** his constant complaints have annoyed me; **mi hai scocciato** (stufato) I'm fed up with you; (seccato) I'm annoyed with you; **se non ti scoccia** if it doesn't bother you, if you don't mind; **ti scoccia se...?** do you mind if ...?; **e ancora faceva lo scocciato** and he still wasn't happy; **scocciarsi** vip (stufarsi) to get fed up; (seccarsi) to get annoyed; **si è un po' scocciato** he was rather annoyed

scocciatore, -trice [skottʃa'tore] sm, sf nuisance, pest (fam)

scocciatura [skottʃa'tura] sf nuisance, bore; **che scocciatura!** what a nuisance!

scodella [sko'dɛlla] sf (ciotola) bowl; (piatto fondo) soup plate

scodinzolare [skodintso'lare] /72/ vi (aus avere) (cane) to wag its tail; **il cane scodinzola** the dog is wagging its tail

scogliera [skoʎ'ʎɛra] sf (scogli) rocks pl, reef; (rupe) cliff; **le bianche scogliere di Dover** the white cliffs of Dover; **la nave è finita sulla scogliera** the ship went onto the rocks

scoglio, -gli ['skɔʎʎo] sm rock; (fig: ostacolo) difficulty, stumbling block

scoglioso, -a [skoʎ'ʎoso] agg rocky

scoiattolo [sko'jattolo] sm (Zool) squirrel; **agile come uno scoiattolo** (fig) agile as a monkey

scolapasta [skola'pasta] sm inv colander

scolapiatti [skola'pjatti] sm inv (del lavandino) draining board; (rastrelliera) plate rack

scolare¹ [sko'lare] /72/ vt to drain; **puoi scolare la pasta per favore?** can you drain the pasta, please?; **si è scolato una bottiglia!** he's drained o downed a bottle! ♦ vi (aus essere) to drip

scolare² [sko'lare] /72/ agg: **in età scolare** school-age attr

scolaresca, -sche [skola'reska] sf schoolchildren pl, pupils pl

scolaro, -a [sko'laro] sm, sf pupil, schoolboy o schoolgirl; (discepolo) disciple, follower

❏ **scolaro** non si traduce mai con la parola inglese scholar

scolastico, -a, -ci, -che [sko'lastiko] agg (gen) scholastic; (libro, anno, divisa) school attr; (pegg: cultura) superficial; (francese, inglese, ecc) basic; **l'anno scolastico** the school year

scollare [skol'lare] /72/ vt to unstick, unglue; **scollarsi** vip to come unstuck, come off o away

scollato, -a [skol'lato] agg (vestito) low-cut, low-necked; **un vestito scollato** a low-cut dress

scollatura [skolla'tura] sf, **scollo** sm neckline, neck; **scollo a barchetta** boat neck

scollegare /80/ vt (fili, apparecchi) to disconnect; **scollegarsi** vr **1** (da internet) to disconnect **2** (da chat-line) to log off

scolo ['skolo] sm **1** (condotto) drainage; (sbocco) drain; **canale di scolo** drain; **tubo di scolo** drainpipe **2** (acqua) waste water

scolorare [skolo'rare] /55/, **scolorire** [skolo'rire] vt to discolour (Brit), discolor (USA); (sbiadire) to fade; **scolorarsi**, **scolorirsi** vip (vestito) to become discolo(u)red; to fade, become faded; (impallidire) to turn pale

scolpire [skol'pire] /55/ vt (pietra) to sculpt, sculpture; (legno) to carve; (metallo) to engrave; **quelle parole rimasero scolpite nella sua memoria** (fig) those words were engraved on his memory

scombinare [skombi'nare] /72/ vt (scomporre) to mess up, ruin, upset; (mandare a monte) to break off, cancel

scombinato, -a [skombi'nato] agg confused, muddled

scombussolare [skombusso'lare] /72/ vt (persona) to upset, disturb; (piani) to upset, mess up

scommesso, -a [skom'messo] pp di **scommettere**

scommettere [skom'mettere] /63/ vt irreg to bet; **scommettere 20 euro** to bet o wager 20 euros; **scommettere su un cavallo** to bet on a horse; **scommettiamo?** do you want to (take a) bet on it?; **non ci scommetterei** I wouldn't bet on it; **ci avrei scommesso!** I would have put money on it!; **puoi scommetterci** you can count on it; **quanto scommettiamo che...?** what's the betting that ...?

scomodare [skomo'dare] /72/ vt to disturb, bother, trouble; (fig: nome famoso) to involve, drag in; **scomodarsi** vr to bother, trouble (o.s.), put o.s. out; **scomodarsi a fare qc** to go to the bother of doing sth

scomodità [skomodi'ta] sf inv (di sedia, letto) discomfort; (di orario, sistemazione) inconvenience

scomodo, -a ['skɔmodo] agg (sedia, letto, posizione) uncomfortable; (orario, turno, sistemazione, posto) inconvenient, awkward; **stare scomodo** to be uncomfortable; **mi è scomodo venire la sera** it's inconvenient for me to come in the evening; **l'orario della banca mi è scomodo** the opening hours of the bank are inconvenient for me; **è scomodo da portare** it's difficult to carry, it's cumbersome

scompaginare [skompadʒi'nare] /72/ vt to upset, throw into disorder; **scompaginarsi** vip to be thrown into disorder

scompagnato, -a [skompaɲ'ɲato] agg (scarpe, calzini) odd

scomparire [skompa'rire] /7/ vi (aus essere) (sparire) to disappear, vanish; (fig: non risaltare) to look (o be) insignificant; **la nave è scomparsa all'orizzonte** the ship disappeared over the horizon; **dov'eri scomparso?** where did you get to?

scomparso, -a [skom'parso] pp di **scomparire**

scompartimento [skomparti'mento] sm **1** (sezione) division **2** (Ferr) compartment

scomparto [skom'parto] sm division, compartment

scompenso [skom'penso] sm imbalance, lack of balance; (Med) decompensation

scompigliare [skompiʎ'ʎare] /27/ vt to mess up, muddle up; (capelli) to mess up, ruffle; (fig: piani) to upset; (: idee) to mess up, confuse

scompiglio, -gli [skom'piʎʎo] sm confusion, chaos; **portare lo scompiglio in** to cause confusion in

scomporre [skom'porre] vb irreg /77/ vt (parola, numero) to break up; (Chim) to decompose ♦ **scomporsi** vip **1** (Chim) to decompose **2** (fig: turbarsi) to lose one's composure, get upset; **senza scomporsi** unperturbed

scomposto, -a [skom'posto] pp di **scomporre** ♦ agg **1** (parola, numero) broken up **2** (persona: sguaiato) unseemly **3** (capelli, vestiti: in disordine) dishevelled, in a mess

scomunica, -che [sko'munika] sf (Rel) excommunication

scomunicare [skomuni'kare] /20/ vt (Rel) to excommunicate

sconcertante [skontʃer'tante] agg disconcerting

sconcertare [skontʃer'tare] /72/ vt to disconcert, bewilder; **sconcertarsi** vip to be disconcerted

sconcio, -cia, -ci, -ce ['skontʃo] agg (osceno) obscene, indecent; (parole) rude, dirty; **una barzelletta sconcia** a dirty joke ♦ sm (cosa mal fatta) disgrace

sconclusionato, -a [skonkluzjo'nato] agg incoherent, illogical

sconfessare [skonfes'sare] /72/ vt (ritrattare) to renounce, retract; (smentire) to repudiate

sconfiggere [skon'fiddʒere] /104/ vt irreg (gen, anche Pol, Sport) to defeat, overcome

sconfinare [skonfi'nare] /72/ vi to cross the border; (da proprietà) to trespass; (involontariamente) to stray; (fig: uscire dai limiti fissati) to stray from; **sconfinare da** (verità, sentiero) to stray from; (tema, argomento) to digress from, stray from

sconfinato, -a [skonfi'nato] agg (spazio) limitless, boundless; (fig: conoscenza, pazienza) unlimited

sconfitto, -a [skon'fitto] pp di **sconfiggere**

sconfortante [skonfor'tante] agg discouraging, disheartening

sconfortare [skonfor'tare] /72/ vt to discourage, dishearten; **sconfortarsi** vip to become discouraged, become disheartened, lose heart

sconforto [skon'fɔrto] sm dejection, despondency; **essere in preda allo sconforto** to be dejected

scongelare [skondʒe'lare] /72/ vt to defrost

scongiurare [skondʒu'rare] /72/ vt **1** (supplicare) to beg, implore, beseech; **ti scongiuro, aiutami** I beg you, help me **2** (allontanare) to avert, ward off; **il pericolo è scongiurato** we're out of danger

scongiuro [skon'dʒuro] sm (esorcismo) exorcism; (formula) spell, charm; **fare gli scongiuri** to touch wood (*Brit*), knock on wood (*USA*)

sconnesso, -a [skon'nɛsso] AGG (*staccato*) disconnected; (*fig: sconclusionato*) incoherent, disconnected, rambling

sconosciuto, -a [skonoʃ'ʃuto] AGG unknown; **un attore sconosciuto** an unknown actor; **è una zona sconosciuta** it's a little-known area; **una gioia sconosciuta** a strange joy; **il suo viso mi è sconosciuto** his face is new to me ♦ SM, SF unknown person, stranger; **non parlare agli sconosciuti** don't talk to strangers

sconquassare [skonkwas'sare] /72/ VT to shatter, smash

sconquasso [skon'kwasso] SM (*danno*) damage; (*fig*) confusion

sconsiderato, -a [skonside'rato] AGG thoughtless, inconsiderate, rash ♦ SM, SF thoughtless person, inconsiderate person

sconsigliare [skonsiʎ'ʎare] /27/ VT: **sconsigliare qc a qn** to advise sb against sth; **sconsigliare a qn di fare qc** to advise sb not to do sth; **ti avevo sconsigliato di telefonarle** I advised you not to phone her; **ti sconsiglio di provarci** I advise you against trying; **quel ristorante? te lo sconsiglio!** that restaurant? I wouldn't recommend it!; **volevo andare ma mi hanno sconsigliato** I wanted to go but they advised me not to

sconsolato, -a [skonso'lato] AGG disconsolate

scontare [skon'tare] /72/ VT 1 (*Comm: detrarre*) to deduct, discount; **scontare una cambiale** to discount a bill of exchange; **scontare un debito** to pay off a debt in instalments 2 (*peccato, colpa*) to pay for, suffer for; (*Dir: pena*) to serve; **scontare 5 anni di prigione** to serve 5 years in prison

scontato, -a [skon'tato] AGG 1 (*prezzo, merce*) discounted, at a discount; **tutto a prezzi scontati** everything at reduced prices 2 (*previsto*) foreseen, taken for granted; **il finale del film era scontato** the ending of the film was predictable; **era scontato che finisse così** it was bound to end that way; **dare qc per scontato** to take sth for granted

scontentare [skonten'tare] /72/ VT to displease, dissatisfy

scontentezza [skonten'tettsa] SF displeasure, dissatisfaction

scontento, -a [skon'tento] AGG dissatisfied, displeased; **è sempre scontento** he's always unhappy; **essere scontento di qc** to be displeased o dissatisfied with sth ♦ SM discontent, dissatisfaction

sconto ['skonto] SM (*Comm*) discount; **fare** o **concedere uno sconto** to give a discount; **mi ha fatto uno sconto** he gave me a discount; **uno sconto del 10%** a 10% discount; **sconto (sulla) quantità** quantity o volume discount

scontrarsi [skon'trarsi] /72/ VR 1 (*veicolo, persona*): **scontrarsi con** to collide with; **la macchina si è scontrata con un autobus** the car crashed into a bus 2 (*uso reciproco: veicoli, persone*) to collide, to crash; (*Mil: fig: opinioni*) to clash

scontrino [skon'trino] SM (*biglietto*) ticket (*Brit*), check (*USA*); (*di cassa*) receipt

scontro ['skontro] SM (*di veicoli*) collision, crash; (*Mil*) clash, engagement; (*fig: litigio*) disagreement; **è rimasto ferito nello scontro** he was injured in the crash; **uno scontro frontale** a head-on collision; **ci sono stati scontri tra polizia e dimostranti** there were clashes between police and demonstrators, police and demonstrators clashed; **scontro a fuoco** shoot-out

scontroso, -a [skon'troso] AGG (*poco socievole*) surly, sullen; (*permaloso*) touchy

sconveniente [skonve'njɛnte] AGG 1 (*comportamento, modi*) unseemly; (*osservazione, proposta*) improper 2 (*prezzo, affare*) disadvantageous, unattractive

sconvolgente [skonvol'dʒɛnte] AGG (*notizia, brutta esperienza*) upsetting, disturbing; (*bellezza*) amazing; (*passione*) overwhelming

sconvolgere [skon'vɔldʒere] VB IRREG /96/ VT (*persona*) to upset, disturb; (*piani*) to upset; **la notizia mi ha sconvolto** the news upset me; **sconvolgere l'opinione pubblica** to shock o shake public opinion; **la notizia ha sconvolto il mondo intero** the news shook the whole world; **la zona sconvolta dal terremoto** the area hit o affected by the earthquake; **le campagne sconvolte dall'alluvione** the flooded countryside, the countryside devastated by the floods ♦ **sconvolgersi** VIP to become upset

sconvolto, -a [skon'vɔlto] PP di **sconvolgere** ♦ AGG (*persona*)

distraught, very upset; (*mente*) disturbed, deranged; **era sconvolto per la morte dell'amico** he was devastated by the death of his friend; **una faccia sconvolta** a ravaged face; **sconvolto dal dolore** beside o.s. with grief

scooter ['skuter] SM INV scooter

scopa¹ ['skopa] SF broom; **sembra un manico di scopa** (*fig*) he's as thin as a rake

scopa² ['skopa] SF *Italian card game*

scopare [sko'pare] /72/ VT 1 (*spazzare*) to sweep 2 (*fam*) to bonk (*Brit*), to boink, to screw (*USA*) ♦ VI (*aus avere*) (*fam*) to bonk (*Brit*)

scopata [sko'pata] SF 1 sweep; **dare una scopata a qc** to give sth a sweep, sweep sth out; **dare una scopata a qn** to hit sb with a broom 2 (*fam*) bonk (*Brit*), boink, screw (*USA*)

scoperchiare [skoper'kjare] /19/ VT (*pentola, vaso*) to take the lid off, uncover; (*casa*) to take the roof off

scoperto, -a [sko'pɛrto] PP di **scoprire** ♦ AGG 1 (*pentola*) uncovered, with the lid off; (*macchina*) open; (*spalle, braccia*) bare, uncovered; (*Mil*) exposed, without cover; **a capo scoperto** bare-headed; **dormire scoperto** to sleep uncovered; **giocare a carte scoperte** (*anche fig*) to put one's cards on the table 2 (*Banca*): **assegno scoperto** dud cheque (*Brit*), rubber check (*USA*); **conto scoperto** overdrawn account; **avere un conto scoperto** to be overdrawn ♦ SM **1 allo scoperto** (*dormire*) out in the open; **è uscito allo scoperto** (*fig*) he came out into the open 2 (*Banca*): **scoperto di conto** bank overdraft

scopo ['skɔpo] SM aim, purpose; **lo scopo di questo studio** the aim of this research; **allo scopo di fare qc** in order to do sth; **cercare uno scopo nella vita** to look for an aim o a purpose in life; **senza scopo** (*fare, cercare*) pointlessly; **la sua vita è senza scopo** his life is pointless; **a scopo di lucro** for gain o money; **adatto allo scopo** fit for its purpose; **a che scopo?** what for?; **a che scopo lavori tanto?** what are you working so hard for?

❑ *scopo* non si traduce mai con la parola inglese *scope*

scoppiare [skop'pjare] /19/ VI (*aus essere*) 1 (*bomba, serbatoio*) to explode; (*pneumatico, palloncino*) to burst; (*fig: rivolta, guerra, epidemia*) to break out; **la bomba è scoppiata alle 11 precise** the bomb went off at exactly 11 o'clock; **la guerra è scoppiata nel 1939** war broke out in 1939; **mi è scoppiata una gomma sull'autostrada** my tyre burst on the motorway; **la notizia fece scoppiare uno scandalo** the news caused a scandal 2 (*fraseologia*): **scoppiare dal caldo** to be boiling; **scoppiare dall'invidia** to be dying of envy; **scoppiare a piangere** o **in lacrime** to burst into tears; **scoppiare a ridere** to burst out laughing; **scoppiare di salute** to be the picture of health; **scoppiare dalla voglia di fare qc** to be dying o longing to do sth; **a quel punto sono scoppiato** (*dalla rabbia, dal ridere*) at that point I couldn't contain myself any longer

scoppiettare [skoppjet'tare] /72/ VI (*aus avere*) (*fuoco*) to crackle; (*motore*) to chug

scoppio, -pi ['skɔppjo] SM (*esplosione*) explosion; (*di pneumatico*) bang; (*di tuono, arma*) crash; (*fig: di rivolta, guerra, epidemia*) outbreak; **bomba a scoppio ritardato** delayed-action bomb; **reazione a scoppio ritardato** delayed o slow reaction; **uno scoppio di risa** a burst of laughter; **uno scoppio di collera** an explosion of anger

scoprire [sko'prire] VB IRREG /9/ VT 1 (*trovare*) to discover; (*causa, verità*) to discover, find out; **ha scoperto la verità** he's found out the truth; **scoprire che.../come ...** to find out o discover that .../how ...; **ha scoperto di avere uno zio in India** he found out o discovered he has an uncle in India; **chi ha scoperto l'America?** who discovered America?; **hai scoperto l'America!** (*iro*) you mean you've only just found out about it! 2 (*pentola*) to take the lid off; (*statua*) to unveil; (*rovine, cadaveri*) to uncover; (*spalle, braccia*) to bare, uncover; **una camicetta che scopre la schiena** a blouse with a low-cut back; **scoprirsi il capo** to take off one's hat, bare one's head; **scoprirsi il fianco** (*fig*) to leave one's flank exposed; **scoprirsi** VR (*esporsi: Sport, fig*) to expose o.s.; (*fig: rivelare le proprie idee*) to betray o.s., give o.s. away; **non scoprirti che fa freddo** keep well wrapped up because it's cold

scopritore, -trice [skopri'tore] SM, SF discoverer

scoraggiare [skorad'dʒare] /62/ vt to discourage; **scoraggiarsi** vip to become discouraged, become disheartened, lose heart

scorbutico, -a, -ci, -che [skor'butiko] AGG (fig) peevish, cantankerous

scorciatoia [skortʃa'toja] SF (anche fig) short cut; **ho preso una scorciatoia** I took a short cut

scorcio, -ci ['skortʃo] SM 1 (Arte) foreshortening 2 (di paesaggio) glimpse; (fig: di secolo, periodo) end, close

scordare [skor'dare] /72/ vt (gen) to forget; (appuntamento, preoccupazione) to forget (about); **ho scordato il suo numero di telefono** I've forgotten his phone number; **ho scordato a casa l'ombrello** I left my umbrella at home; **scordare di fare qc** to forget to do sth; **scordavo di avertelo già chiesto** I forgot that I had already asked you; **scordarsi** vip: **scordarsi di qc/di fare qc** to forget sth/to do sth; **mi sono scordato di telefonargli** I forgot to phone him; **scordarsi di qn** to forget about sb

scoreggia, -ge [sko'reddʒa], **scorreggia, -ge** [skor'reddʒa] SF (fam!) fart

scoreggiare [skored'dʒare] /62/, **scorreggiare** [skorred'dʒare] vi (aus avere) (fam!) to fart

scorgere ['skordʒere] /59/ vt IRREG to see, catch sight of; (fig: accorgersi di) to become aware of, realize; **senza farsi scorgere** unnoticed, without being seen

scoria ['skorja] SF (di metalli) slag; (vulcanica) scoria; **scorie radioattive** (Fis) radioactive waste sg

scorno ['skorno] SM humiliation, ignominy, disgrace

scorpacciata [skorpat'tʃata] SF big feed; **farsi una scorpacciata (di qc)** to stuff o.s. (with sth)

scorpione [skor'pjone] SM 1 (Zool) scorpion 2 (Astrol): **Scorpione** Scorpio; **essere dello Scorpione** to be Scorpio

scorporo [skor'poro] SM (Pol) transfer of votes aimed at increasing the chances of representation for minority parties

scorrazzare [skorrat'tsare] /72/ vi (aus avere) to run about, romp about

scorrere ['skorrere] VB IRREG /28/ vi (aus essere) (liquido, fiume) to run, flow; (fune) to run; (cassetto, porta) to slide easily; (tempo) to pass (by); (traffico) to flow; **lascia scorrere l'acqua** let the water run, leave the water running; **il tempo scorre lento** time passes slowly; **ha uno stile che scorre** he (o it ecc) has a flowing style ♦ vt (leggere) to glance through, run one's eye over

scorreria [skorre'ria] SF raid, incursion

scorrettezza [skorret'tettsa] SF (vedi agg) incorrectness; lack of politeness, rudeness; unfairness; **scorrettezza nel gioco** foul play no pl; **con scorrettezza** (sgarbatamente) rudely, impolitely; **è stata una scorrettezza da parte sua** it was rude of him, it was bad manners on his part; **commettere una scorrettezza** (essere sleale) to be unfair

scorretto, -a [skor'retto] AGG (traduzione, uso) incorrect; (persona: sgarbato) impolite, rude; (: sleale) unfair; (: gioco) foul; **un uso scorretto** an incorrect use; **è stato scorretto da parte tua** it was unfair of you

scorrevole [skor'revole] AGG (porta) sliding; (nastro) moving; (fig: stile) flowing, fluent

scorribanda [skorri'banda] SF (Mil) raid, incursion; (escursione) trip, excursion

scorsi ecc ['skorsi] VB vedi **scorgere**

scorso, -a ['skorso] PP di **scorrere** ♦ AGG last; **lo scorso mese** last month

scorsoio, -oia, -oi, -oie [skor'sojo] AGG: **nodo scorsoio** slipknot, noose

scorta ['skorta] SF 1 (gen, di personalità, convoglio: Mil) escort; **il ministro è arrivato con la scorta** the minister arrived with a police escort; **fare la scorta a qn** to escort sb; **sotto la scorta di due agenti** escorted by two policemen 2 (provvista) supply, stock; **fare scorta di** to stock up with, get in a supply of; **di scorta** (materiali) spare; **ruota di scorta** spare wheel

scortare [skor'tare] /72/ vt to escort

scortese [skor'tese] AGG impolite, discourteous, rude; **in modo scortese** rudely

scortesia [skorte'zia] SF (qualità) impoliteness, discourtesy, rudeness; (azione) discourtesy

scorticare [skorti'kare] /20/ vt (animali) to skin, flay; **scorticarsi un gomito** to skin o graze one's elbow

scorto, -a ['skorto] PP di **scorgere**

scorza ['skordza] SF (di albero) bark; (di agrumi) peel, skin; **avere la scorza dura** (fig: persona) to be thick-skinned; **sotto la scorza c'è un animo gentile** he's kind-hearted beneath his crusty exterior

scosceso, -a [skoʃ'ʃeso] AGG steep; **sempre più scosceso** steeper and steeper

scosso, -a ['skosso] PP di **scuotere** ♦ AGG (persona) shaken, upset; **sono ancora scosso** I'm still shaken; **ho i nervi scossi** my nerves are shattered

scossone [skos'sone] SM: **dare uno scossone a qn** to give sb a shake; **procedere a scossoni** (auto) to jolt o jerk along

scostante [skos'tante] AGG (persona, modi) unpleasant, off-putting

scostare [skos'tare] /72/ vt to push aside, move aside; **far scostare qn** to push aside; **scosta la poltrona dal muro** move the armchair away from the wall; **scostarsi** vr to move aside; **scostati dal muro** move away from the wall

scostumato, -a [skostu'mato] AGG (immorale) immoral, dissolute; (maleducato) bad-mannered, boorish ♦ SM (vedi agg) dissolute person; boor

scotch [skotʃ] SM INV (whisky) Scotch

scottante [skot'tante] AGG (urgente) pressing; (delicato) delicate

scottare [skot'tare] /72/ vt (gen) to burn; (con liquido, vapore) to scald, burn; (Culin: in acqua) to scald; (: friggendo) to sear; **scottarsi una mano** to burn one's hand; **sono già stato scottato una volta** (fig) I've already burnt my fingers once ♦ vi (aus avere) (gen) to be very hot; (sole, sabbia) to be burning, be scorching; **attento che scotta** be careful, it's hot; **il sole scotta in agosto** the sun is hot in August; **è roba che scotta** (fig: refurtiva) it's hot; **sono argomenti che scottano** (fig: delicati) these are delicate issues; **gli scotta la terra sotto ai piedi** (fig) he's itching to be off; **scottarsi** VR to burn o.s.; (con liquido, vapore) to scald o.s., burn o.s.; (al sole) to get burnt

scottatura [skotta'tura] SF (gen) burn; (con liquido, vapore) scald, burn

scotto¹, -a ['skotto] AGG (Culin) overcooked, overdone

scotto² ['skotto] SM (fig: punizione): **pagare lo scotto** to pay the consequences

scovare [sko'vare] /72/ vt (Caccia) to drive out, flush out, put up; (fig) to unearth, find, discover

Scozia ['skottsja] SF Scotland; **mi è piaciuta molto la Scozia** I really liked Scotland; **andremo in Scozia quest'estate** we're going to Scotland this summer

scozzese [skot'tese] AGG (gen) Scottish; (whisky) Scotch; **tessuto scozzese** tartan; **gonna scozzese** kilt; **le isole scozzesi** the Scottish islands ♦ SM, SF Scot, Scotsman o Scotswoman; **gli scozzesi** the Scots

screanzato, -a [skrean'tsato] AGG ill-mannered ♦ SM, SF boor

screditare [skredi'tare] /72/ vt to discredit; **screditarsi** vip to be discredited

screen saver ['skrin'seiver] SM INV (Inform) screen saver

scremare [skre'mare] /72/ vt to skim

scremato, -a [skre'mato] AGG skimmed; **parzialmente scremato** semi-skimmed

screpolare [skrepo'lare] /72/ vt (pelle, labbra) to chap, crack; (mani) to chap; (intonaco) to crack; **screpolarsi** vip (vedi vt) to chap; to crack

screpolato, -a [skrepo'lato] AGG (vedi vt) chapped; cracked

screpolatura [skrepola'tura] SF (su pelle, labbra, mani) chap; (su intonaco) crack, cracking no pl

screziato, -a [skret'tsjato] AGG (striato) streaked

screzio, -zi ['skrettsjo] SM friction, disagreement; **hanno avuto degli screzi** there was some friction between them

scribacchino [skribak'kino] SM (pegg: impiegato) penpusher; (: scrittore) hack

scricchiolare [skrikkjo'lare] /72/ vi (aus avere) to creak, squeak

scricchiolio, -lii [skrikkjo'lio] SM creaking

scricciolo ['skritt'tʃolo] SM (uccello) wren; **è uno scricciolo** (fig: persona gracile) she's like a little bird

scrigno [ˈskriɲɲo] SM casket
scriminatura [skriminaˈtura] SF (di capelli) parting
scrissi ecc [ˈskrissi] VB vedi **scrivere**
scritto, -a [ˈskritto] PP di **scrivere** ♦ AGG (lingua, esame) written ♦ SM 1 (lettera) letter, note; **per o in scritto** in writing 2 (opera) work; **gli scritti di** the works o the writings of
scrittoio, -oi [skritˈtojo] SM (writing-)desk
scrittore, -trice [skritˈtore] SM, SF writer, author
scrittura [skritˈtura] SF 1 (calligrafia) (hand)writing; **non riesco a leggere la sua scrittura** I can't read his writing; **avere una bella/brutta scrittura** to have good/bad handwriting 2 (Rel): **la Sacra Scrittura** the Scriptures pl 3 (Cine, Teatro, TV: contratto) contract 4 (Dir) document; **scrittura privata** parol, contract 5 (Comm); **scritture** SFPL accounts, books; **scritture contabili** (account) books
scritturare [skrittuˈrare] /72/ VT 1 (Cine, Teatro, TV) to engage, sign on o up 2 (Comm) to enter
scrivania [skrivaˈnia] SF (writing-)desk
scrivano [skriˈvano] SM (amanuense) scribe; (impiegato) clerk
scrivente [skriˈvɛnte] SM, SF writer
scrivere [ˈskrivere] /105/ VT IRREG (gen) to write; **scrivere qc a qn** to write sth to sb; **ho scritto una lettera a Luca** I wrote Luca a letter; **scrivo sempre biglietti di Natale a tutti i miei amici** I always write Christmas cards to all my friends; **scrivimi presto** write to me soon; **scrivere a penna/matita** to write in pen/pencil; **scrivere qc maiuscolo/minuscolo** to write sth in capital/small letters; **scrivere alla lavagna** to write on the blackboard; **come si scrive questa parola?** how do you write o spell this word?; **si scrive con la K** it's spelled with a K; **era scritto che dovesse succedere** (fig) it was fated o bound to happen
scroccare [skrokˈkare] /20/ VT (fam) to scrounge, cadge
scroccone, -a [skrokˈkone] SM, SF (fam) scrounger, sponger
scrofa [ˈskrɔfa] SF (Zool) sow
scrollare [skrolˈlare] /72/ VT 1 (scuotere) to shake; **scrollare la testa** to shake one's head; **ha scrollato la testa** he shook his head; **scrollare le spalle** to shrug one's shoulders 2 **scrollarsi qc di dosso** to shake sth off; (fig: malinconia, stanchezza) to shrug sth off; **scrollarsi** VIP to shake o.s.; (fig) to stir o.s., give o.s. a shake
scrollata [skrolˈlata] SF shake; **dare una scrollata a qc** to give sth a shake; **scrollata di spalle** shrug (of one's shoulders)
scrosciante [skroʃˈʃante] AGG (pioggia) pouring; (fig: applausi) thunderous
scrosciare [skroʃˈʃare] /14/ VI (aus avere o essere) (pioggia) to pelt down, pour down; (torrente) to thunder, roar; **gli applausi scrosciavano** there was thunderous applause
scroscio, -sci [ˈskrɔʃʃo] SM (di torrente, cascata) roar; (di applausi) thunder; **sentivamo lo scroscio della pioggia** we could hear the rain pelting down
scrostare [skrosˈtare] /72/ VT (vernice, intonaco) to scrape off, strip (off); (tubo) to descale; **scrostare una ferita** to remove the scab (from a wound); **scrostarsi** VIP (vernice, intonaco) to peel off, flake off
scrupolo [ˈskrupolo] SM (morale) scruple; (diligenza) care, conscientiousness; **scrupolo morale, scrupolo di coscienza** scruple; **essere senza scrupoli** to be unscrupulous; **non farti tanti scrupoli con lui** I wouldn't have any scruples about him if I were you; **non mi farei degli scrupoli a chiederglielo** I wouldn't have any scruples about asking him; **lavoro fatto con scrupolo** a conscientious piece of work; **è onesto fino allo scrupolo** he's scrupulously honest
scrupoloso, -a [skrupoˈloso] AGG (onesto) scrupulous; (diligente) conscientious
scrutare [skruˈtare] /72/ VT (orizzonte, vallata) to scan; (cielo, volto) to search; (persona) to scrutinize; (intenzioni, causa) to examine, scrutinize
scrutatore, -trice [skrutaˈtore] AGG (sguardo) searching ♦ SM, SF (di votazione) scrutineer
scrutinare [skrutiˈnare] /72/ VT (voti) to scrutinize, count
scrutinio, -ni [skruˈtinjo] SM 1 (votazione) ballot; (insieme delle operazioni) poll; **scrutinio segreto** secret ballot 2 (Scol) (meeting for) assignment of marks at end of a term o year
scucire [skuˈtʃire] /31/ VT (abito, tasca) to unstitch, unpick, undo; (fam: soldi) to fork out; **scucirsi** VIP to come unstitched

scuderia [skudeˈria] SF (stalla) stable; (Aut) team
scudetto [skuˈdetto] SM (Sport) (championship) shield; **vincere lo scudetto** to win the championship; **il Milan ha vinto lo scudetto** Milan has won the championship
scudiscio, -sci [skuˈdiʃʃo] SM (riding) crop, (riding) whip
scudo [ˈskudo] SM (gen) shield; **farsi scudo di o con qc** to shield o.s. with sth; **scudo aereo** air defence (Brit) o defense (USA); **scudo missilistico** missile defence (Brit) o defense (USA); **scudo termico** heat shield
sculacciare [skulatˈtʃare] /14/ VT to spank
sculacciata [skulatˈtʃata] SF, **sculaccione** [skulatˈtʃone] SM spanking; **dare una sculacciata a qn** to spank sb, give sb a spanking
scultore, -trice [skulˈtore] SM, SF (di pietra) sculptor (sculptress); (di legno) woodcarver
scultura [skulˈtura] SF (di pietra) sculpture; (di legno) woodcarving
scuola [ˈskwɔla] SF 1 (istituzione, edificio) school; **andare a scuola** to go to school; **non c'è scuola domani** there's no school tomorrow; **ci vediamo dopo la scuola** see you after school; **scuola guida** driving school; **scuola dell'infanzia** nursery school; **scuola dell'obbligo** compulsory education; **scuola primaria** primary (Brit) o grade (USA) school; **scuola privata** private school; **scuola secondaria di primo grado** lower secondary school; **scuola pubblica** state school (Brit), public school (USA); **scuola secondaria di secondo grado** secondary school; **scuola serale** night school 2 (Arte) school; **un artista che ha fatto scuola** an artist who has developed a following ♦ AGG INV: **nave scuola** training ship
scuotere [ˈskwɔtere] VB IRREG /106/ VT 1 (anche fig) to shake; **scuotere la testa** to shake one's head; **ha scosso la testa** he shook his head; **scuotere le spalle** to shrug one's shoulders; **cercò di scuoterlo dalla sua apatia** he tried to shake him out of o rouse him from his apathy 2 **scuotersi di dosso qc** to shake sth off; (fig: malinconia, stanchezza) to shrug off; **scuotersi** VIP to shake o.s.; (fig) to stir o.s.; **scuotersi dall'apatia** to rouse o.s. from one's apathy
scure [ˈskure] SF axe (Brit), ax (USA)
scurire [skuˈrire] /55/ VT to darken, make darker VI (aus essere), **scurirsi** VIP to darken, become dark, grow dark
scuro¹, -a [ˈskuro] AGG (colore, vestito, capelli) dark; **una gonna verde scuro** a dark green skirt; **avere una faccia scura** to have a grim expression on one's face ♦ SM (colore) dark colour (Brit) o color (USA); **vestire di scuro** to wear dark colo(u)rs
scuro² [ˈskuro] SM (di finestra) (window) shutter
scurrile [skurˈrile] AGG scurrilous
scusa [ˈskuza] SF 1 (gen) apology; **vi prego di accettare le mie scuse** please accept my apologies; **chiedere scusa a qn per qc** to apologize to sb for sth; **devi chiedere scusa all'insegnante** you must apologize to the teacher; **chiedo o domando scusa** I apologize, I beg your pardon; **fare/presentare le proprie scuse** to make/give one's apologies; **una lettera di scuse** a letter of apology 2 (pretesto) excuse; **era solo una scusa per andarsene** it was just an excuse to leave; **cercare una scusa/delle scuse** to look for an excuse/excuses; **questa è una scusa bella e buona!** that's a real excuse!; **non c'è scusa che tenga!** there's no possible excuse!
scusare [skuˈzare] /72/ VT (gen) to excuse; (perdonare) to forgive; **scusare qn di o per qc** to forgive sb for sth; **scusami, scusa, mi scusi** (I'm) sorry; (più formale) I beg your pardon; **scusa il ritardo** I'm sorry I'm late; **tutto questo non ti scusa** this is no excuse; **scusi, sa dirmi dove...?** excuse me, can you tell me where ...?; **scusate un attimo, torno subito** excuse me, I'll be back in a minute; **scusarsi** VR to apologize; **scusarsi con qn di o per qc** to apologize to sb for sth; **ti sei scusato con lui?** did you apologize to him?; **si è scusato del ritardo** he apologized for being late
SCV SIGLA = Stato della Città del Vaticano
sdebitarsi [zdebiˈtarsi] /72/ VR: **sdebitarsi (con qn di o per qc)** (anche fig) to repay (sb for sth)
sdegnare [zdeɲˈɲare] /15/ VT (disprezzare) to scorn, despise; **sdegnarsi** VIP (arrabbiarsi): **sdegnarsi (con)** to get angry (with)
sdegnato, -a [zdeɲˈɲato] AGG indignant, angry

sdegno [ˈzdeɲɲo] SM (*disprezzo*) scorn, disdain; (*indignazione*) indignation

sdegnosamente [zdeɲɲosaˈmente] AVV scornfully, contemptuously, disdainfully

sdegnoso, -a [zdeɲˈɲoso] AGG scornful, contemptuous, disdainful

sdilinquirsi [zdilinˈkwirsi] /55/ VIP (*illanguidirsi*) to become sentimental

sdoganare [zdogaˈnare] /72/ VT (*Comm*) to clear through customs

sdolcinato, -a [zdoltʃiˈnato] AGG (*persona*) gushing; (*parole*) sugary; (*modi*) affected; (*film, libro*) oversentimental, mawkish

sdoppiamento [zdoppjaˈmento] SM (*Chim*: *di composto*) splitting; (*Psic*): **sdoppiamento della personalità** split personality

sdoppiare [zdopˈpjare] /19/ VT , **sdoppiarsi** VIP to divide *o* split in two

sdraiare [zdraˈjare] /19/ VT to lay down; **sdraiare qn a terra/sul letto** to lay sb down on the ground/on the bed; **sdraiarsi** VR to lie down; **sdraiarsi a terra/sul letto** to lie down on the ground/on the bed; **sdraiarsi al sole** to stretch out in the sun

sdraio, -ai [ˈzdrajo] SM (*anche*: **sedia a sdraio**) deckchair

sdrammatizzare [zdrammatidˈdzare] /72/ VT to play down, minimize

sdrucciolare [zdruttʃoˈlare] /72/ VI (*aus* avere *o* essere) (*persona*) to slip, slide

sdrucciolevole [zdruttʃoˈlevole] AGG slippery

sdrucito, -a [zdruˈtʃito] AGG (*strappato*) torn; (*logoro*) threadbare

SE ABBR **1** (= *Sud-Est*) SE **2** (= *Sua Eccellenza*) HE

PAROLA CHIAVE

se¹ [se] CONG

1 (*condizionale, concessiva*) if; **se fosse più furbo verrebbe** if he were smarter he would come; **se fosse stato interessato sarebbe venuto** if he had been interested he would have come; **se fossi in te** if I were you; **deve essere così se lo dice lui** it must be so if he says so; **se nevica non vengo, se nevicherà non verrò** I won't come if it snows; **se invece preferisci questo...** should you *o* if you prefer this one ...

2 (*dubitativa, in domande indirette*) whether, if; **mi chiedevo se avesse capito** I wondered whether he had understood; **guarda lì se c'è** look and see whether *o* if it's there; **non so se scrivere o telefonare** I don't know whether *o* if I should write or phone; **lo so se mi manca** I know how much I miss him

3 (*ottativa*) if only; **se (solo) me l'avesse detto prima!** if only he had told me earlier!; **se ci fosse ancora lui!** if only he were still here!

4 (*fraseologia*): **come se** as if; **come se non lo sapesse!** as if he didn't know!; **e se andassimo in montagna?** how about going to the mountains?; **ma se l'ho visto io!** but I saw it myself!; **se mai passassi per di qua** should you ever *o* if ever you pass this way; **lascialo nell'atrio se mai** leave it in the hall if necessary; **siamo noi se mai che le siamo grati** it is we who should be grateful to you; **se no** (*altrimenti*) or (else), otherwise; **non fiatare, se no vedi!** don't breathe a word or else!; **mangia, se no non reggi fino a stasera** eat up, otherwise *o* else you'll be starving by this evening; **scappo se no perdo l'autobus** I must dash or I'll miss the bus; **se non** (*anzi*) if not; (*tranne*) except; **costa lo stesso, se non meno** it costs the same, if not less; **non lo darò a nessuno se non a lui** I won't give it to anybody except *o* other than *o* but him; **se non altro** if nothing else, at least; **se non altro non disturba** at least he's no trouble; **se poi decidesse di restare** should he decide *o* were he to decide to stay; **e se poi se ne accorge?** and what if he notices?; **se pure** = **seppure**

♦ SM if; **c'è solo un grosso se** there's just one big if

se² [se] *vedi* **si¹**

sé [se] PRON RIFLESSIVO (*gen*) oneself; (*maschile*) himself; (*femminile*) herself; (*neutro*) itself; (*pl*) themselves; **l'ha fatto da sé** he did it (all) by himself; **lo portò con sé** he took it with him; **pensa solo a sé** *o* **se stesso** he thinks only of himself; **è piena di sé** she's full of herself; **hanno tenuto la notizia**

per sé they kept the news to themselves; **di per sé non è un problema** it's no problem in itself; **parlare tra sé e sé** to talk to oneself; **tornare in sé** to come to (one's senses); **va da sé che...** it goes without saying that ..., it's obvious that ..., it stands to reason that ...; **è un caso a sé (stante)** it's a special case; **si chiude da sé** (*porta*) it closes automatically; **un uomo che s'è fatto da sé** a self-made man; **chi fa da sé fa per tre** (*Proverbio*) if you want something done well *o* properly do it yourself

sebbene [sebˈbene] CONG (even) though, although; **sebbene non sia colpa sua...** although *o* (even) though it is not his fault ...; **lo farò, sebbene mi pesi molto** I'll do it, even though I'm not very happy about it

sebo [ˈsebo] SM sebum

sec ABBR (= *secolo*) c. (= *century*)

secca, -che [ˈsekka] SF (*Naut*) bank, shallows *pl*; **andare in secca** to run aground

seccamente [sekkaˈmente] AVV (*rispondere, rifiutare*) sharply, curtly

seccare [sekˈkare] /20/ VT **1** (*gen*) to dry; (*prosciugare*) to dry (up); (*fiori: far appassire*) to wither; **il vento secca la pelle** wind dries the skin **2** (*infastidire*) to annoy, bother; **smettila di seccarmi!** stop bothering me!; **questa volta mi hai proprio seccato** I've had enough of you this time; **ti secca se aspetto qui?** do you mind if I wait here?; **se ti secca chiederglielo lo faccio io** if you don't like to ask him I'll do it; **mi secca fare tutta questa fila** it annoys me having to queue like this ♦ VI (*aus* essere) to dry (up); **seccarsi** VIP **1** (*diventar secco: gen*) to dry (up); (*pelle*) to become dry; (*fiori*) to wither **2** (*infastidirsi*) to become annoyed, grow annoyed, get annoyed; **si è seccato molto** he got very annoyed

seccato, -a [sekˈkato] AGG (*fig: infastidito*) bothered, annoyed; (: *stufo*) fed up

seccatore, -trice [sekkaˈtore] SM, SF nuisance, bother

seccatura [sekkaˈtura] SF nuisance, bother *no pl*, trouble *no pl*; **che seccatura!** what a nuisance!; **non voglio seccature!** I don't want any bother!

seccherò ecc [sekkeˈrɔ] VB *vedi* **seccare**

secchia [ˈsekkja] SF bucket, pail

secchiello [sekˈkjɛllo] SM (*per bambini*) bucket, pail; **secchiello del ghiaccio** ice bucket

secchio, -chi [ˈsekkjo] SM bucket, pail; **un secchio d'acqua** a bucket of water; **secchio della spazzatura** *o* the immondizie dustbin (*Brit*), garbage can (*USA*), trash can (*USA*)

secco, -a, -chi, -che [ˈsekko] AGG **1** (*gen*) dry; (*terreno*) arid, dry; (*uva, fichi, pesce*) dried; (*foglie, rami*) withered; (*fig: risposta*) sharp; **ho la pelle molto secca** I've got very dry skin; **avere la gola secca** to feel dry, be parched; **potrei avere qualcosa da bere? ho la gola secca** could I have something to drink please? I'm parched; **un no secco** a curt no; **un colpo secco** a sharp blow; **frutta secca** (*noci, mandorle ecc*) nuts; (*fichi, datteri ecc*) dried fruit **2** (*persona: magro*) thin, skinny; **secco come un chiodo** as thin as a rake **3** (*fraseologia*): **fare secco qn** (*assassinare*) to knock sb off; **ci è rimasto secco** (*fig: morto*) it killed him ♦ SM **1** (*di clima*) dryness; (*siccità*) drought **2** (*fraseologia*): **lavare a secco** to dry-clean; **devo far lavare a secco la giacca** I need to get my jacket dry-cleaned; **tirare a secco** (*barca*) to beach; **essere a secco** (*di soldi*) to be broke; **rimanere a secco di benzina** to run out of petrol (*Brit*) *o* gas (*USA*)

secentesco, -a, -schi, -sche [setʃenˈtesko] AGG seventeenth-century

secernere [seˈtʃɛrnere] /29/ VT to secrete

secolare [sekoˈlare] AGG **1** (*antico*) centuries-old, age-old **2** (*laico*) secular, lay *attr*; **clero secolare** lay clergy

secolo [ˈsekolo] SM **1** century; (*epoca*) century, age; **nel terzo secolo a.C.** in the third century B.C.; **nel nostro secolo** this century; **l'avvenimento del secolo** the event of the century; **il secolo della Ragione** the Age of Reason; **per tutti i secoli dei secoli** (*Rel*) forever and ever; **Giovanni Paolo II, al secolo Carol Wojtyla** John Paul II, whose original name was Carol Wojtyla **2** (*fig*): **è un secolo che non ti vedo** I haven't seen you in ages; **è un secolo che aspetto** I've been waiting for ages

seconda [seˈkonda] SF **1** (*Aut*) second (gear); **mettere in seconda** to go into second gear **2** (*Scol*) second year; (*seconda* *elementare*) ≈ year three (*Brit*), ≈ second grade (*USA*); (*seconda media*) ≈ year eight (*Brit*), ≈ seventh grade (*USA*); (*seconda superiore*) ≈ year eleven (*Brit*), ≈ tenth grade (*USA*) **3** (*Ferr*) second class; **viaggiare in seconda** to travel second class; **un biglietto di seconda** a second-class ticket **4 comandante in seconda** second-in-command **5 a seconda di** PREP according to, in accordance with; **le tariffe cambiano a seconda dell'ora** charges vary according to the time of day

secondariamente [sekondarja'mente] AVV secondly

secondario, -ria, -ri, -rie [sekon'darjo] AGG secondary, minor; **di secondaria importanza** of secondary *o* minor importance; **scuola/istruzione secondaria** secondary school/education

secondino [sekon'dino] SM prison officer, warder (*Brit*), prison guard (*USA*)

secondo¹, -a [se'kondo] AGG (*gen*) second; **in seconda fila** in the second row; **in secondo luogo** in the second place; **prendi la seconda strada a destra** take the second street on the right; **si è classificato al secondo posto** he came second; **il suo disco è secondo in classifica** his record is number two in the charts; **figlio di seconde nozze** son by a second marriage; **passare a seconde nozze** to remarry, marry for a second time; **elevare alla seconda (potenza)** (*Mat*) to raise to the power of two; **Carlo secondo** Charles the Second; **è un secondo Picasso** he's another *o* a second Picasso; **un albergo di second'ordine** a second-class hotel; **un biglietto di seconda classe** a second class ticket; **viaggiare in seconda classe** to travel second-class; **di seconda mano** (*oggetto, informazione*) second-hand; **una moto di seconda mano** a second-hand motorbike; **avere un secondo fine** to have an ulterior motive ♦ SM **1** (*tempo*) second; **un minuto e dieci secondi** one minute and ten seconds; **aspetta un secondo!** wait a moment!; **un secondo, arrivo subito!** I won't be a minute! **un secondo, arrivo subito!** I won't be a minute! **(anche: secondo piatto)** main course, second course; **come secondo vorrei del salmone alla griglia** I'd like grilled salmon for my main course ♦ SM, SF second (person); **sei il secondo che me lo dice** you're the second person to tell me that

secondo² [se'kondo] PREP **1** (*in base a, nell'opinione di*) according to; (*nel modo prescritto da, stando a*) in accordance with; **secondo lui** according to him, in his opinion; **secondo me** in my opinion; **secondo me dovresti scrivergli** in my opinion you should write to him; **secondo il giornale quel film è da non perdere** according to the paper that film shouldn't be missed; **secondo le mie possibilità** according to my means; **tutto sta andando secondo i piani** everything's going according to plan; **il Vangelo secondo Matteo** the Gospel according to St Matthew; **secondo la legge/quanto si era deciso** in accordance with the law/the decision taken; **agire secondo coscienza** to follow one's conscience **2** (*in direzione di: vento, corrente*) with; (*: linea*) along

secondogenito, -a [sekondo'dʒenito] SM, SF second-born

secrezione [sekret'tsjone] SF (*Bio*) secretion

sedano ['sedano] SM celery; **sedano rapa** celeriac

sedare [se'dare] /72/ VT **1** (*dolore*) to soothe **2** (*rivolta*) to put down, suppress

sedativo, -a [seda'tivo] AGG, SM (*Med*) sedative

sede ['sede] SF **1** (*luogo di residenza*) (place of) residence; **prendere sede** to take up residence; **cambiare sede** to change one's residence **2** (*di società: principale*) head office; (*: secondaria*) branch (office); (*: di partito*) headquarters *pl*; (*: di governo, parlamento*) seat; (*: Rel*) seat; **la Santa Sede** the Holy See; **un'azienda che diverse sedi in città** a firm with several branches in the city; **il presidente è fuori sede** the chairman is not in the office; **sede sociale** registered office **3** (*località*) site; **Londra sarà sede di un'importante mostra** London will be the site of an important exhibition **4 in sede di** (*in occasione di*) during; **in sede d'esame** during the exam; **in sede di discussione** during the discussion; **in sede legislativa** in legislative sitting; **in altra sede** on another occasion

sedentario, -ria, -ri, -rie [seden'tarjo] AGG sedentary

sedere [se'dere] VB IRREG /107/ VI (*aus essere*) **1** (*essere seduto*) to be sitting, be seated; **sedeva a tavola** he was sitting at table; **era seduta accanto a me** she was sitting beside me; **posto a sedere** seat; **siede in Parlamento** he has a seat in

Parliament **2** (*mettersi seduto*) to sit (down); **siedi qui** sit here; **mettiti a sedere** sit down, take a seat; **sieda per cortesia** please sit down, please take a seat; **mettersi seduto** (*da posizione orizzontale*) to sit up; **sedersi** VIP to sit (down); **sono così stanca che non vedo l'ora di sedermi!** I'm so tired I can't wait to sit down!; **siediti qui** sit down (here); **sedersi per terra** (*in casa*) to sit on the floor; (*all'esterno*) to sit on the ground

sedia ['sɛdja] SF chair; **sedia elettrica** electric chair; **sedia pieghevole** folding chair; **sedia a rotelle** wheelchair

sedicenne [sedi'tʃɛnne] AGG, SM, SF sixteen-year-old

sedicente [sedi'tʃɛnte] AGG self-styled

sedicesimo, -a [sedi'tʃɛzimo] AGG, SM, SF **1** sixteenth **2** (*Tip*): **in sedicesimo** sexto decimo; *vedi* **quinto**

sedici ['seditʃi] AGG INV, SM INV sixteen

sedile [se'dile] SM (*in automezzi*) seat

sedimentare [sedimen'tare] /72/ VI (*aus avere o essere*) to leave *o* deposit a sediment

sedimento [sedi'mento] SM sediment

sedizione [sedit'tsjone] SF uprising, insurrection

sedizioso, -a [sedit'tsjoso] AGG seditious ♦ SM, SF insurrectionist

sedotto, -a [se'dotto] PP *di* **sedurre**

seducente [sedu'tʃɛnte] AGG (*donna*) seductive; (*proposta*) very attractive

sedurre [se'durre] /90/ VT IRREG **1** (*abusare di*) to seduce **2** (*affascinare*) to charm, captivate; (*sogg: idea*) to appeal to

seduta [se'duta] SF (*gen*) session, sitting; **una seduta del parlamento** a parliamentary sitting; **essere in seduta** to be in session, be sitting; **seduta stante** (*fig: immediatamente*) straight away, immediately; **seduta spiritica** seance

seduttore, -trice [sedut'tore] SM, SF seducer (seductress)

seduzione [sedut'tsjone] SF (*vedi vb*) seduction; charm; appeal

sega, -ghe ['sega] SF (*Tecn*) saw; **sega circolare** circular saw; **sega a mano** handsaw; (*fam!*) wank

segala [se'gala], **segale** [se'gale] SF (*Bot*) rye

segare [se'gare] /80/ VT to saw; (*in più parti*) to saw up; (*fam: bocciare*) to flunk; **segare via** to saw off; **segare in due** to saw in two VIP *aus essere* to mastrubate (*fam!*)

segatura [sega'tura] SF sawdust

seggio, -gi ['sɛddʒo] SM **1** (*gen*) seat **2 seggio elettorale** polling station

❑ **seggio** non si traduce mai con la parola inglese *siege*

seggiola ['sɛddʒola] SF chair

seggiolino [seddʒo'lino] SM seat; (*per bambini*) child's chair; **seggiolino di sicurezza** (*su auto*) child safety seat

seggiolone [seddʒo'lone] SM (*per bambini*) highchair

seggiovia [seddʒo'via] SF chair lift

segheria [sege'ria] SF sawmill

segherò *ecc* [sege'rɔ] *vb vedi* **segare**

seghettato, -a [seget'tato] AGG serrated

seghetto [se'getto] SM hacksaw

segmento [seg'mento] SM segment

segnalare [seɲɲa'lare] /72/ VT (*essere segno di*) to indicate, be a sign of; (*avvertire*) to signal; (*menzionare*) to indicate, point out; (*fatto, risultato, anomalo, guasto*) to report; (*errore, dettaglio*) to point out; **ho segnalato il fatto alla polizia** I reported the incident to the police; **segnalare una svolta a sinistra** (*Aut*) to indicate *o* signal a left turn; **segnalare la posizione di una nave** to signal the position of a ship; **niente da segnalare** nothing to report; **potresti segnalarci un buon albergo?** could you recommend a good hotel?; **l'insegnante ha segnalato alcuni nomi per la borsa di studio** the teacher suggested a few names for the scholarship; **segnalare qn a qn** (*per lavoro*) to bring sb to sb's attention; **segnalarsi** VR (*distinguersi*) to distinguish o.s.

segnalazione [seɲɲalat'tsjone] SF **1** (*azione*) signalling; (*segnale*) signal; **segnalazioni acustiche** acoustic *o* sound signals; **segnalazioni stradali** road signs **2** (*annuncio*) report; (*raccomandazione*) recommendation

segnale [seɲ'ɲale] SM (*gen*) signal; **al mio segnale spegnete la luce** when I give the signal switch the light off; **segnale**

acustico acoustic o sound signal; **lasciate un messaggio dopo il segnale acustico** please leave a message after the tone; (di segreteria telefonica) tone; **segnale d'allarme** alarm; (sui treni) communication cord (Brit); **segnale di linea libera** (Telec) dialling (Brit) o dial (USA) tone; **segnale luminoso** light signal; **segnale di occupato** (Telec) engaged tone (Brit), busy signal (USA); **segnale orario** (Radio, TV) time signal; **segnale stradale** road sign

segnaletica [seɲɲaˈletika] SF: **segnaletica (stradale)** road signs pl, traffic signs pl

segnalibro [seɲɲaˈlibro] SM (anche Inform) bookmark

segnapunti [seɲɲaˈpunti] SM INV, SF INV scorer, scorekeeper ♦ SM INV scorecard

segnare [seɲˈɲare] /15/ VT 1 (fare un segno: gen) to mark; (scalfire) to score, mark, cut into; (graffiare) to scratch; **segnare il passo** (Mil, anche fig) to mark time; **è molto segnato da quell'esperienza** that experience has left its mark on him; **aveva il volto segnato dalla stanchezza** his face was drawn and tired 2 (annotare) to make a note of, jot down, note; **segna quanto ti devo** make a note of what I owe you 3 (indicare) to show, indicate, mark; **non segna la velocità giusta** it's not showing the right speed; **quella lancetta serve a segnare le ore** that hand shows o indicates the hours; **il mio orologio segna le 5** my watch says 5 o'clock; **gli errori sono segnati in rosso** the mistakes are marked in red; **segnare a dito** to point at; **essere segnato a dito** (fig) to be talked about 4 (Sport) to score; **segnare di testa** (Calcio) to score with a header; **segnare un rigore** to score a penalty; **segnare su rigore** to score with a penalty; **ha segnato nella ripresa** he scored in the second half; **segnarsi** VR (Rel) to cross o.s., make the sign of the cross

segno [ˈseɲɲo] SM 1 (gen) sign; (traccia) mark, sign; (graffio) scratch; (indizio) sign, indication; **lasciare un segno** (anche fig) to leave a mark; **non c'era segno di vita** there was no sign of life; **non ha dato segni di vita** he gave no sign of life; **è brutto segno** it's a bad sign; **in** o **come segno d'amicizia** as a mark o token of friendship; **diede segno di voler andare** he indicated that he wanted to leave; **perdere il segno** (leggendo) to lose one's place; **il segno dei suoi passi** his footprints pl; **fare segno di sì** to nod; **fare segno di no** to shake one's head; **fare segno con la mano** to make a sign with one's hand; **mi fece segno di spostarmi/avvicinarmi/fermarmi** he made a sign to me to move/come nearer/stop; **di che segno sei?** what sign are you?; **essere del segno dell'Acquario** ecc to be an Aquarian ecc 2 (bersaglio) target; **tiro a segno** target shooting; **cogliere** o **colpire nel segno** to hit the target o mark; (fig) to hit the bullseye, hit the nail on the head ♦ **"segni particolari"** (su documento) "distinguishing marks"; **il segno della croce** (Rel) the sign of the cross; **segno meno** (Mat) minus sign; **segno più** plus sign; **segno zodiacale** sign of the zodiac

segregare [segreˈgare] /80/ VT (gen) to segregate; (prigioniero) to confine; **segregarsi** VIP (fig: isolarsi): **segregarsi in casa** to shut o.s. up in the house

segregazione [segregatˈtsjone] SF segregation

segreta [seˈgreta] SF dungeon

segretario, -ria, -ri, -rie [segreˈtarjo] SM, SF (gen) secretary; **segretaria di direzione** personal assistant; **segretario comunale** town clerk; **segretario del partito** party leader

segreteria [segreteˈria] SF 1 (ufficio) secretary's office; (in enti) secretarial offices pl 2 (Pol: carica) secretaryship, office of Secretary; (: segretariato) secretariat 3 **segreteria telefonica** answering machine

segretezza [segreˈtettsa] SF secrecy; **notizie della massima segretezza** highly confidential information sg; **in tutta segretezza** in secret; (confidenzialmente) in confidence

segreto, -a [seˈgreto] AGG (gen) secret; (documenti) confidential, secret; **tenere segreto qc** to keep sth secret; **passaggio segreto** secret passage ♦ SM (gen) secret; **in segreto** in secret, secretly; (in confidenza) in confidence; **mantenere** o **tenere un segreto** to keep a secret; **sai mantenere un segreto?** can you keep a secret?; **il segreto professionale** professional secrecy; **un segreto professionale** a professional secret; **il segreto di Pulcinella** an open secret; **il segreto del successo** the secret of o key to success; **nel segreto dell'animo** in the depths of one's soul, deep down

seguace [seˈgwatʃe] SM, SF (Rel: gen) disciple, follower

seguente [seˈgwɛnte] AGG following, next; **il giorno seguente** the next o following day; **i seguenti candidati sono pregati di farsi avanti** would the following candidates please come forward; **nel modo seguente** as follows, in the following way

segugio, -gi [seˈgudʒo] SM 1 (Zool) hound, hunting dog 2 (fig) private eye, sleuth

seguire [seˈgwire] /45/ VT 1 (gen) to follow; **seguire qn come un'ombra** to follow sb about like a shadow; **segui quella macchina!** follow that car!; **mi ha seguita fino a casa** he followed me home; **ha fatto seguire la moglie** he had his wife followed; **mi segua, la prego** this way o follow me, please; **segui la statale per 15 km** follow o keep to the main road for 15 km; **seguire una cura** to follow a course of treatment; **seguire i consigli di qn** to follow o take sb's advice; **perché non segui i miei consigli?** why don't you take my advice?; **seguire una dieta** to be on a diet; **far seguire una dieta a qn** to put sb on a diet; **le cose seguono il loro corso** things are taking o running their course; **seguire un programma alla TV** to watch a programme on TV; **seguire un alunno** (fig) to follow the progress of a pupil; **seguire gli avvenimenti di attualità** to follow o keep up with current events 2 (capire: persona, argomento) to follow; **scusa, non ti seguo** I'm sorry, I don't follow you; **mi hai seguito o vado troppo veloce?** are you following me or am I going too fast? 3 (corso, lezione: gen) to follow, take; (: essere presente a) to attend, go to; **seguire un corso per corrispondenza** to follow o take a correspondence course; **non è obbligatorio seguire le lezioni** attendance at lessons is not compulsory ♦ VI 1 (venir dopo, anche fig: derivare) to follow; **come segue** as follows; **a Pio XI seguì Pio XII** Pius XI was succeeded by Pius XII; **a ciò seguì un aumento dei prezzi** this was followed by a rise in prices 2 (continuare) to continue; **"segue"** "to be continued"

seguitare [segwiˈtare] /72/ VT to continue, carry on with; **seguitare a fare qc** to continue doing sth ♦ VI (aus essere o avere) to continue, carry on

seguito [seˈgwito] SM 1 (di persone) retinue, suite; (discepoli, ammiratori) followers pl; **essere al seguito di qn** to be among sb's suite, be one of sb's retinue 2 (continuazione: di film) sequel; (: nuovo episodio) continuation; (: resto) remainder, rest; **il seguito la settimana prossima** to be continued next week; **manca il seguito** the rest is missing 3 (conseguenze): **non aver seguito** to have no repercussions 4 **in seguito** then, later on; **ora leggete; in seguito vi farò delle domande** now read it, then I'll ask you some questions; **in seguito a, a seguito di** following; **facciamo seguito alla lettera del...** further to o in answer to your letter of ...; **di seguito** at a stretch, on end; **è piovuto per tre settimane di seguito** it rained non-stop for three weeks; **tre volte di seguito** three times in a row

sei¹ [ˈsei] AGG INV, SM INV six

sei² [ˈsei] VB vedi essere

Seicelle [seiˈtʃelle] SFPL: **le (isole) Seicelle** the Seychelles

seicentesco, -a, -schi, -sche [seitʃenˈtesko] AGG seventeenth-century

seicento [seiˈtʃento] AGG INV six hundred ♦ SM INV six hundred; (secolo): **il Seicento** the seventeenth century

seimila [seiˈmila] AGG INV, SM INV six thousand

selce [ˈseltʃe] SF flint, flintstone

selciato [selˈtʃato] SM cobbled surface; **si sentirono i suoi passi sul selciato** you could hear his footsteps on the cobbles

selettivo, -a [seletˈtivo] AGG selective

selettore [seletˈtore] SM (Tecn) selector; **selettore dei canali** (TV) channel selector

selezionare [selettsjoˈnare] /72/ VT to select, choose

selezione [seletˈtsjone] SF selection, choice; **fare una selezione** to make a selection o choice; **selezione naturale** (Bio) natural selection

sella [ˈsella] SF saddle; **montare in sella** to mount, get into the saddle

sellare [selˈlare] /72/ VT to saddle, put a saddle on

sellino [selˈlino] SM saddle

seltz [selts] SM INV soda (water)

selva [ˈselva] SF (*letter*: *bosco*) wood; (: *foresta*) forest; (*fig*: *di gente, capelli*) mass

selvaggina [selvadˈdʒina] SF game

selvaggio, -gia, -gi, -ge [selˈvaddʒo] AGG (*gen*) wild; (*incontrollato*: *fenomeno, aumento*) uncontrolled; (*tribù*) savage, primitive, uncivilized; (*pegg*: *omicidio*) savage, ferocious; (: *torture*) brutal, cruel; **sciopero selvaggio** wildcat strike; **inflazione selvaggia** runaway inflation ♦ SM, SF savage

selvatico, -a, -ci, -che [selˈvatiko] AGG (*animali, fiori*) wild; (*fig*: *persona*: *timido*) unsociable ♦ SM (*di selvaggina*): **sapere di selvatico** to taste gamy; **puzzare di selvatico** to smell high o gamy

S.Em. ABBR (= *Sua Eminenza*) HE

semaforo [seˈmaforo] SM (*Aut*) traffic lights *pl*; (*Ferr*) signal; **attento! il semaforo è rosso** watch out! the traffic light is red

semantico, -a, -ci, -che [seˈmantiko] AGG semantic

sembianza [semˈbjantsa] SF (*poet*) 1 (*aspetto*) appearance 2 **sembianze** SFPL (*lineamenti*) features; (*fig*: *falsa apparenza*) semblance *sg*

sembrare [semˈbrare] (*aus essere*) /72/ VI (*gen*) to seem; **sembra simpatico** he seems o appears (to be) nice; **sembrava più giovane** he seemed o looked younger; **sembra una ragazzina** she looks like a young girl; **sembra suo padre** he looks like his father; **sembra caffè** it tastes like coffee; **al tocco sembrava seta** it felt like silk; **sembra odore di bruciato** it smells as if something is burning ♦ VB IMPERS: **sembra che** it seems that; **mi sembra che...** (*ho l'impressione*) it seems to me that ..., it looks to me as though ...; (*penso*) I think (that) ..., I have a feeling that ...; **non è facile come sembra** it's not as easy as it seems; **ti sembra giusto?** do you think it's fair?; **non gli sembrava onesto farlo** he didn't think it was honest to do it; **fai come ti sembra** do as you please o as you see fit; **non mi sembra vero!** I can't believe it!

seme [ˈseme] SM 1 (*gen*) seed; (*di agrumi, mela, pera*) pip; (*di ciliegia, pesca*) stone; **gettare il seme della discordia** to sow the seeds of discord; **olio di semi** vegetable oil 2 (*Anat*: *sperma*) semen 3 (*Carte*) suit

semente [seˈmente] SF seed

semestrale [semesˈtrale] AGG (*che dura 6 mesi*) six-month *attr*; (*che avviene ogni 6 mesi*) six-monthly

semestre [seˈmestre] SM (*gen*) six months *pl*, six-month period, half-year; (*Scol*) semester; **nel primo semestre dell'anno** in the first half of the year

semi- [ˈsemi] PREF semi-

semicerchio, -chi [semiˈtʃerkjo] SM semicircle

semiconduttore [semikondutˈtore] SM semiconductor

semidetenzione [semidetenˈtsjone] SF *custodial sentence of a minimum 10 hours per day in prison*

semifinale [semifiˈnale] SF (*Sport*) semifinal

semifreddo [semiˈfreddo] SM (*Culin*) *chilled dessert made with ice cream*

semilibertà [semiliberˈta] SF *custodial sentence allowing part-time study or work outside prison*

semina [ˈsemina] SF (*Agr*) sowing; **periodo della semina** sowing time

seminare [semiˈnare] /72/ VT 1 (*Agr*) to sow; (*fig*: *vestiti, libri*) to scatter, leave lying around; **chi non semina non raccoglie** (*Proverbio*) as you sow, so shall you reap 2 (*inseguitore*) to lose, shake off

seminario, -ri [semiˈnarjo] SM 1 (*Rel*) seminary 2 (*Scol*) seminar; **ho seguito un seminario di storia** I attended a history seminar; **seminario online** webinar

seminato [semiˈnato] SM: **uscire dal seminato** (*fig*) to wander off the point

seminterrato [seminterˈrato] SM (*piano*) basement; (*appartamento*) basement flat (*Brit*) o apartment (*USA*)

semiologo, -a, -gi, -ghe [seˈmjɔlogo] SM, SF semiologist

semiotica [seˈmjɔtika] SF semiotics *sg*

semitico, -a, -ci, -che [seˈmitiko] AGG Semitic

semivuoto, -a [semiˈvwɔto] AGG half empty

semmai [semˈmai] = **se mai**; *vedi* **se**[1]

semola [ˈsemola] SF bran; **semola di grano duro** durum wheat

semolato [semoˈlato] AGG: **zucchero semolato** caster sugar

semolino [semoˈlino] SM semolina

semplice [ˈsemplitʃe] AGG 1 (*gen, non complicato*) simple; (*persona, modi*: *non affettato*) simple, unaffected; (: *ingenuo*) simple, ingenuous; **l'esercizio è molto semplice** the exercise is very simple; **conduce una vita semplice** he lives a simple life; **è semplice da capire** it's easy o simple to understand; **una visione della vita un po' semplice** a simplistic view of life; **è una semplice formalità** it's a mere formality; **è una semplice questione d'orgoglio** it's simply a matter of pride; **è pazzia pura e semplice** it's sheer madness; **acqua semplice** tap water 2 (*Gramm*) simple 3 (*Mil*): **marinaio semplice** ordinary seaman; **soldato semplice** private

semplicemente [semplitʃeˈmente] AVV 1 (*in maniera semplice*) simply, in a simple way; **parla semplicemente e lentamente** speak slowly and simply 2 (*solamente*) only, merely, simply; **desidero semplicemente la verità** I merely want the truth; **è semplicemente ridicolo** it's simply ridiculous 3 (*con modestia*) simply, modestly; **vive molto semplicemente** he lives very simply

semplicistico, -a, -ci, -che [sempliˈtʃistiko] AGG simplistic

semplicità [semplitʃiˈta] SF simplicity, simpleness

semplificare [semplifiˈkare] /20/ VT to simplify

semplificazione [semplifikatˈtsjone] SF simplification; **fare una semplificazione di** to simplify

sempre [ˈsempre] AVV 1 (*continuità*) always; (*eternamente*) always, forever; **viene sempre alle 5** he always comes at 5 o'clock; **è sempre in ritardo** he's always late; **ti amerò sempre** I'll always love you, I'll love you for ever; **come sempre** as usual; **è la persona di sempre** he's the same as ever, he's his usual self; **sei il buffone di sempre, sei sempre il solito buffone** you're as funny as ever; **per sempre** forever; **la situazione non durerà per sempre** the situation won't last for ever; **da sempre** always; **lo so da sempre** I've always known it; **una volta per sempre** once and for all; **arriva sempre a disturbarmi** he's always o forever coming to disturb me; **è sempre nevicato** it snowed all the time; **è un abito che puoi indossare sempre** it's a dress you can wear any time o on any occasion; **è rimasto sempre lì fermo** he stayed there, immobile 2 (*ancora, comunque*) still; **esci sempre con lui?** are you still going out with him?; **c'è sempre la possibilità che...** there's still a chance that ..., there's always the possibility that ...; **è (pur) sempre tuo fratello** he is still your brother (however); **è sempre meglio che niente** it's better than nothing; **posso sempre tentare** I can always o still try 3 **sempre che** as long as, provided (that); **sempre che non piova** as long as o provided that it doesn't rain, unless it rains; **sempre che tu non cambi idea** as long as you don't change your mind, unless you change your mind 4 (*rafforzativo*): **sempre più** more and more; **diventa sempre più difficile** it's getting more and more difficult; **sempre meno** less and less; **l'attività è sempre meno redditizia** the business is getting less and less profitable; **va sempre meglio** things are getting better and better; **diventa sempre più raro** it's getting rarer and rarer

sempreverde [sempreˈverde] AGG, SM, SF (*Bot*) evergreen

sen. ABBR (= *senatore*) Sen.

senape [ˈsenape] SF (*Bot, Culin*) mustard ♦ AGG INV (*colore*) mustard-coloured, mustard *attr*

senato [seˈnato] SM 1 (*Storia*) senate 2 **il Senato** upper chamber of the Italian parliament

senatore, -trice [senaˈtore] SM, SF senator

Senegal [ˈsenegal] SM Senegal

senegalese [senegaˈlese] AGG, SM, SF Senegalese *inv*

senese [seˈnese] AGG Sienese, of o from Siena ♦ SM, SF inhabitant o native of Siena

senile [seˈnile] AGG senile

Senna [ˈsenna] SF: **la Senna** the Seine

senno [ˈsenno] SM judgment, good sense, (common) sense; **uscire di senno** to lose one's mind o wits, go mad; **col senno di poi** with hindsight; **del senno di poi son piene le fosse** (*Proverbio*) it's easy to be wise after the event

sennò [senˈnɔ] AVV (= *se no*) *vedi* **se**[1]

seno[1] [ˈseno] SM 1 (*Anat*) bosom; (*mammella*) breast; (*grembo*) womb; **portare un figlio in seno** to carry a child (in one's womb); **in seno alla famiglia** in the bosom of the family; **in seno al partito/all'organizzazione** within the party/

the organization **2** (*Anat, Zool: cavità*) sinus **3** (*Geog*) inlet, creek

seno² [ˈseno] SM (*Mat*) sine

sensale [senˈsale] SM (*Comm*) agent

sensatezza [sensaˈtettsa] SF good sense, good judgment

sensato, -a [senˈsato] AGG sensible

sensazionale [sensattsjoˈnale] AGG sensational, exciting

sensazione [sensatˈtsjone] SF feeling, sensation; **ho la sensazione di averlo già incontrato** I have a feeling I've met him before; **fare sensazione** (*interesse, stupore*) to cause a sensation, create a stir; **essere a caccia di nuove sensazioni** to be after new thrills *o* experiences

sensibile [senˈsibile] AGG **1** (*gen*) sensitive; (*obiettivo: Mil*) high-risk; **è un ragazzo sensibile** he's a sensitive boy; **ha un animo sensibile** he's tender-hearted; **essere sensibile a** (*freddo, caldo*) to be sensitive to; (*complimenti, adulazioni, fascino*) to be susceptible to; *vedi anche* **sensibile a**; (*notevole: progresso, differenze*) appreciable, noticeable; **c'è stato un sensibile aumento della temperatura** there's been a considerable rise in the temperature **3** (*Fot: pellicola*) sensitive
❏ **sensibile** non si traduce mai con la parola inglese *sensible*

sensibilità [sensibiliˈta] SF sensitivity, sensitiveness

sensibilizzare [sensibilidˈdzare] /72/ VT (*fig*) to make aware, awaken; **sensibilizzare l'opinione pubblica su qc** to raise public awareness of sth

senso [ˈsenso] SM **1** (*istinto, coscienza*) sense; **i 5 sensi** the 5 senses; **perdere/riprendere i sensi** to lose/regain consciousness; **senso d'orientamento** sense of direction; **avere senso pratico** to be practical; **ha molto senso pratico** she's very practical; **senso del dovere/dell'umorismo** sense of duty/humour; **avere un sesto senso** to have a sixth sense; **i piaceri dei sensi** (*della sensualità*) sensual pleasures, the pleasures of the senses **2** (*sensazione*) feeling, sense, sensation; **un senso di angoscia** a feeling *o* sense of anxiety; **provare un senso di inquietudine** to feel anxious; **fare senso (a qn)** (*ribrezzo*) to disgust (sb), repel (sb); **mi fa senso** it disgusts me; **senso di colpa** sense of guilt **3** (*significato*) meaning, sense; **nel senso letterale/figurato** in the literal/figurative sense; **senza** *o* **privo di senso** meaningless; **un discorso senza senso** a meaningless speech; **in un certo senso ha ragione lui** in a way *o* sense he's right; **nel senso che...** in the sense that ...; **che senso ha?** where's the sense in that?; **(per me) non ha senso** it doesn't make (any) sense (to me); **nel vero senso della parola** in the true sense of the word **4** (*direzione*) direction; **in senso opposto** in the opposite direction; **nel senso della lunghezza** lengthwise, lengthways; **nel senso della larghezza** widthwise; **io venivo in senso contrario** I was coming from the opposite direction; **in senso orario** clockwise; **in senso antiorario** anticlockwise (*Brit*), counterclockwise (*USA*); **ho dato disposizioni in quel senso** I've given instructions to that end *o* effect **5** (*Aut*): **a senso unico** (*strada*) one-way; **una via a senso unico** a one-way street; **"senso vietato"** "no entry" **6** (*Dir*): **ai sensi di legge** in compliance with the law

sensuale [sensuˈale] AGG (*persona, sguardo*) sensual; (*voce*) sensuous

sensualità [sensualiˈta] SF (*vedi agg*) sensuality; sensuousness

sentenza [senˈtentsa] SF **1** (*Dir*) sentence; **pronunciare una sentenza di morte contro qn** to sentence sb to death **2** (*massima*) maxim; **sputar sentenze** (*fig*) to moralize

sentenziare [sententˈsjare] (*Dir*) /19/ VT: **sentenziare che...** to rule that ...; **sentenziare la pena di morte** to pass the death sentence ♦ VI (*aus avere*) to pass judgment

sentiero [senˈtjero] SM path

sentimentale [sentimenˈtale] AGG (*gen*) sentimental; (*pegg*) soppy; **vita sentimentale** love life ♦ SM, SF sentimentalist

sentimento [sentiˈmento] SM (*gen*) feeling; **aveva sempre nascosto i suoi sentimenti per lei** he had always hidden his feelings for her; **una persona di nobili sentimenti** a person of noble sentiments; **urtare i sentimenti di qn** to hurt sb's feelings

sentinella [sentiˈnella] SF (*Mil*) sentry, guard; **essere di sentinella** to be on guard *o* sentry duty

sentire [senˈtire] /45/ VT **1** (*percepire: gen: al tatto*) to feel;

sentire freddo/caldo to feel cold/hot; **sentire dolore** to feel pain; **sento un gran male qui** I've got a terrible pain here; **senti quanto pesa** feel how heavy it is; **non sento niente** I can't feel a thing; **il caldo si fa sentire** the heat is oppressive; **la sua assenza si fa sentire** his absence is noticeable **2** (*emozione*) to feel; **sentire un profondo affetto per qn** to feel deep affection for sb; **non sento niente per lui** I don't feel anything for him; **sentire la mancanza di qn** to miss sb; **sento che succederà qualcosa** I've got a feeling that something is going to happen; **dice sempre quello che sente** he always says what he feels **3** (*al gusto*) to taste; (*all'olfatto*) to smell; **senti se ti piace questa salsa** taste this sauce to see if you like it; **senti se ti piace questo profumo** smell this perfume to see if you like it; **sento odore di pesce** I can smell fish; **ho il raffreddore e non sento gli odori/i sapori** I've got a cold and I can't smell/taste anything **4** (*udire*) to hear; (*ascoltare*) to listen to; **mi sentite?** can you hear me?; **sento dei passi** I can hear footsteps; **mi piace sentire la musica** I like listening to music; **stare a sentire** to listen; **hai sentito l'ultima?** have you heard the latest?; **senti, mi presti quel libro?** listen, will you lend me that book?; **ho sentito dire che...** I have heard that ...; **stammi a sentire!** listen to me!; **stammi bene a sentire!** just you listen to me!; **a sentir lui...** to hear him talk ...; **farsi sentire** to make o.s. heard; **fatti sentire** keep in touch; **non ci sente** (*sordo*) he's deaf, he can't hear; **non ci sente da quell'orecchio** (*fig*) he always turns a deaf ear to things like that; **senti quello che ti dice l'avvocato** go and ask your lawyer for advice; **intendo sentire il mio legale/il parere di un medico** I'm going to consult my lawyer/a doctor; **senti cosa vuole** see what he wants; **ma senti un po'!** just fancy that!; **senti questa!** just listen to this!; **per sentito dire** by hearsay; **sentirsi** VR **1** (*gen*) to feel; **sentirsi bene/male** to feel well/unwell *o* ill; **come ti senti?** how are you?, how do you feel?; **sentirsi svenire** to feel faint **2** (*essere disposto*): **sentirsi di fare qc** to feel like doing sth; **non me la sento** I don't feel like it; **proprio non se la sente di continuare** he doesn't feel like carrying on **3** (*uso reciproco*) to hear from each other, be in touch; **ci sentiamo spesso** (*al telefono*) we often talk on the phone; **si sono sentiti di recente** they were in touch (with each other) recently

sentitamente [sentitaˈmente] AVV sincerely; **ringraziare sentitamente** to thank sincerely

sentito, -a [senˈtito] AGG (*ringraziamenti, condoglianze*) sincere, deep; **le mie più sentite scuse** my most sincere apologies

sentore [senˈtore] SM talk, rumour (*Brit*), rumor (*USA*); **aver sentore di qc** to hear about sth

senza [ˈsentsa] PREP without; **uscì senza ombrello** he went out without an *o* his umbrella; **non so cosa farei senza il suo aiuto** I don't know what I'd do without his help; **non senza alcune riserve** not without some reservations; **senza di te** without you; **non posso stare senza di te** I can't live without you; **siamo rimasti senza zucchero/tè** we've run out of sugar/tea, we have no sugar/tea left; **forza, senza tante chiacchiere** come on, stop the talking and let's get on with it; **senza casa** homeless; **senza padre** fatherless; **senza amici** friendless; **senza preoccupazioni** carefree; **senza scrupoli** unscrupulous; **senza impegno** without obligation; **un dettato senza errori** an error-free dictation; **un discorso senza senso** a meaningless speech; **i senza lavoro** the jobless, the unemployed; **senz'altro** of course, certainly; **mi scriverai? - senz'altro!** will you write to me? - of course!; **lo farò senz'altro domani** I'll do it tomorrow without fail; **senza dubbio** no doubt ♦ CONG without; **senza batter ciglio** without batting an eyelid; **ho trascorso tutta la notte senza chiudere occhio** I didn't sleep a wink all night, I didn't get a wink of sleep all night; **senza dire niente** without saying a thing; **è andato via senza dire niente** he left without saying anything; **parlò senza riflettere** he spoke without thinking; **senza che tu lo sapessi** without your knowing about it; **senza dire che...** not to mention (the fact) that ...; **senza contare che...** without considering that ...

senzatetto [sentsaˈtetto] SM INV, SF INV homeless person; **i senzatetto** the homeless ♦ AGG INV homeless

separare [sepaˈrare] /72/ VT (*gen*) to separate; (*litiganti*) to pull apart, part; (*aspetti, problemi*) to distinguish between; **le Alpi separano la Svizzera dall'Italia** the Alps divide *o* separate Italy from Switzerland; **separare il bene dal male** to distinguish between good and evil; **solo pochi chilometri lo separavano da casa** only a few kilometres separated him from home *o* stood between him and home; **separarsi** VR **1** (*lasciare*): **separarsi da** (*persona*) to leave; (*oggetto*) to part with; **gli dispiaceva separarsi dai propri cari/da quegli oggetti cari** he didn't want to leave his loved ones/to part with those dear objects; **si è separata dal marito** she has left her husband **2** (*staccarsi*): **separarsi da** to split off from, separate off from **3** (*uso reciproco: gen*) to part; (: *coniugi, soci*) to part, split up, separate; **dopo 2 ore di cammino si separarono** after 2 hours' walk they parted (company); **i miei genitori si sono separati quando ero piccolo** my parents split up when I was little

separatamente [separata'mente] AVV separately

separato, -a [sepa'rato] AGG (*gen*) separate; **abbiamo chiesto conti separati** we asked for separate bills; **i miei genitori sono separati** my parents are separated; **vivono separati** (*coniugi*) they have separated; **in separata sede** (*privatamente*) in private

separazione [separat'tsjone] SF (*gen, anche Dir*) separation; **dopo la separazione** (*di coniugi*) after they parted; **separazione dei beni** (*Dir*) division of property

séparé [sepa're] SM INV screen

sepolcro [se'polkro] SM sepulchre (*Brit*), sepulcher (*USA*); **il Santo Sepolcro** the Holy Sepulchre *o* Sepulcher

sepolto, -a [se'polto] PP *di* **seppellire** ♦ AGG (*gen, anche fig*) buried; **morto e sepolto** (*anche fig*) dead and buried; **sepolto nel profondo del cuore** buried deep in one's heart

sepoltura [sepol'tura] SF burial; **dare sepoltura a qn** to bury sb

seppellire [seppel'lire] VB IRREG /55/ VT (*gen*) to bury; (*fig: passato, ricordi*) to bury, forget; **il villaggio era sepolto dalla neve** the village was buried under the snow; **seppellire antichi rancori** to bury the hatchet, let bygones be bygones; **seppellirsi** VR (*fig: isolarsi*) to shut o.s. off, cut o.s. off; **seppellirsi tra i libri** to bury o.s. in one's books

seppi etc ['seppi] VB *vedi* **sapere**

seppia ['seppja] SF (*Zool*) cuttlefish; **nero di seppia** sepia

seppure [sep'pure] CONG even if

sequela [se'kwɛla] SF (*di avvenimenti*) series *inv*, sequence; (*di offese, ingiurie*) string

sequenza [se'kwɛntsa] SF sequence

sequenziale [sekwen'tsjale] AGG sequential

sequestrare [sekwes'trare] /72/ VT **1** (*gen*) to confiscate; (*Dir: beni*) to sequestrate; (*film, libri*) to impound **2** (*rapire*) to kidnap

sequestro [se'kwɛstro] SM **1** (*gen*) confiscation, seizure; (*Dir*) sequestration, impounding **2** (*anche: sequestro di persona*) kidnapping

sequoia [se'kwɔja] SF sequoia; **sequoia gigante** giant sequoia; **sequoia sempreverde** redwood

sera ['sera] SF evening; **si fa sera** it's getting dark, night is falling; **di sera** in the evening; **alle 6 di sera** at 6 o'clock in the evening, at 6 p.m.; **alle 11 di sera** at 11 o'clock at night, at 11 p.m.; **domani sera** tomorrow evening; **questa sera** this evening, tonight; **dalla mattina alla sera** from morning to night

serale [se'rale] AGG evening *attr*; **scuola serale** evening classes *pl*, night school

serata [se'rata] SF **1** (*sera*) evening; **grazie per la bella serata** thanks for the lovely evening **2** (*ricevimento*) soirée, party; **serata danzante** dance **3** (*Teatro*) evening performance; **serata di gala/d'addio** gala/farewell performance

serbare [ser'bare] /72/ VT (*tenere*) to keep; (*mettere da parte*) to put aside, keep; **serbare rancore a qn** to bear *o* harbour a grudge against sb

serbatoio, -oi [serba'tojo] SM (*gen*) tank; (*cisterna*) cistern; **serbatoio (della benzina)** (*Aut*) (petrol) (*Brit*) *o* (gas) (*USA*) tank

Serbia SF: **la Serbia** Serbia

serbo¹ ['serbo] SM: **in serbo** (*sorpresa*) in store; **te lo tengo in serbo** I'll put it aside for you

serbo², -a ['serbo] AGG Serbian ♦ SM, SF Serbian, Serb *attr* ♦ SM (*lingua*) Serbian

serbocroato, -a [serbokro'ato] AGG, SM, SF Serbo-Croat

serenamente [serena'mente] AVV (*guardare*) serenely, calmly; (*giudicare*) dispassionately; (*vivere*) quietly

serenata [sere'nata] SF serenade; **fare la serenata a qn** to serenade sb, sing sb a serenade, sing a serenade to sb

serenità [sereni'ta] SF peace, tranquillity, serenity; **serenità d'animo** peace of mind

sereno, -a [se'reno] AGG (*tempo, cielo*) clear, serene; (*volto, persona*) calm, serene; (*giudizio*) dispassionate; (*vita*) quiet; **un fulmine a ciel sereno** (*fig*) a bolt from the blue ♦ SM (*tempo*) good weather

serg. ABBR (= *sergente*) Sgt.

sergente [ser'dʒɛnte] SM (*Mil*) sergeant; **sergente maggiore** sergeant major

seriale [se'rjale] AGG (*Inform*) serial

seriamente [serja'mente] AVV (*gen*) **1** (*con serietà*) seriously, earnestly; **sto parlando seriamente!** I'm serious!; **lavorare seriamente** to take one's job seriously **2** (*gravemente*) seriously, gravely; **è seriamente malato** he's seriously ill

serie ['sɛrje] SF INV **1** (*gen*) series *inv*; (*di numeri*) series, sequence; (*di chiavi*) set; **tutta una serie di problemi** a whole string *o* series of problems; **una serie di furti** a series of robberies **2** (*Sport*) division; **serie A/B** ≈ first/second division; (*Calcio*) ≈ Premier League (*England*), ≈ Premier Division (*Scotland*); (*fig*) first/second class **3** (*Comm*): **produzione in serie** mass production; **produrre in serie** to mass-produce; **modello di serie/fuori serie** (*Aut*) standard/custom-built model

serietà [serje'ta] SF (*vedi agg*) seriousness; earnestness; reliability

serio, -ria, -ri, -rie ['sɛrjo] AGG (*gen*) serious; (*persona, conversazione*) serious, earnest; (*persona, ditta: affidabile*) reliable, responsible, dependable; **è una ditta seria** it's a reliable firm; **è una faccenda seria** it's a serious matter; **restare serio** to keep a straight face; **sii serio!** be serious!; **aveva una faccia seria** he looked serious ♦ SM: **sul serio** seriously, in earnest; **sul serio ti ha invitato?** did he really invite you?; **sul serio vuoi andarci?** do you really want to go?; **non facevo sul serio, non dicevo sul serio** I wasn't being serious; **faccio sul serio** I mean it; **prendere qn/qc sul serio** to take sb/sth seriously; **prende lo studio molto sul serio** he takes his schoolwork very seriously

serioso, -a [se'rjoso] AGG (*persona, modi*): **un po' serioso** a bit too serious

sermone [ser'mone] SM (*Rel*) sermon; (*fig*) lecture, sermon; **fare un sermone a qn** (*fig*) to give sb a lecture *o* sermon

serpe ['sɛrpe] SF snake; (*fig: pegg*) viper; **scaldare** *o* **allevare una serpe in seno** to nurse a viper in one's bosom

serpeggiare [serped'dʒare] /62/ VI (*aus avere*) (*strada, fiume*) to wind, snake, twist; (*fig: malcontento, rivolta*) to spread (insidiously)

serpente [ser'pɛnte] SM **1** (*Zool*) snake, serpent; **serpente a sonagli** rattlesnake **2** (*pelle*) snakeskin **3** (*Fin*): **il serpente monetario** (the currency) snake

serra¹ ['sɛrra] SF (*Agr*) greenhouse; (*riscaldata*) hothouse; **l'effetto serra** the greenhouse effect

serra² ['sɛrra] SF (*Geog*) sierra

serramanico [serra'maniko] SM: **coltello a serramanico** flick-knife, clasp knife

serranda [ser'randa] SF (rolling *o* roller) shutter

serrare [ser'rare] /72/ VT (*chiudere*) to close, shut; (*stringere*) to shut tightly; **serrare i pugni/i denti** to clench one's fists/teeth; **serrare le file** (*anche fig*) to close ranks; **serrare il nemico** to close in on the enemy

serrata [ser'rata] SF (*Industria*) lockout

serrato, -a [ser'rato] AGG **1** (*porta, finestra*) closed, shut; (*pugni, denti*) clenched; (*occhi*) tightly closed **2** (*stringato*) logical, coherent **3** (*veloce*): **a ritmo serrato** quickly, fast

❏ **serrato** non si traduce mai con la parola inglese *serrated*

serratura [serra'tura] SF lock

serva ['sɛrva] SF *vedi* **servo**

server ['sɛrver] SM INV (*Inform*) server

servigio, -gi [ser'vidʒo] SM favour (*Brit*), favor (*USA*), service

servire [ser'vire] /45/ VT **1** (*essere al servizio di*) to serve; **servire qn** (*in negozio*) to attend to *o* serve sb; (*al ristorante*) to wait on *o* serve sb; **gli piace farsi servire** he likes to be waited on; **in cosa posso servirla?** (*negozio*) can I help you?; **adesso ti servo io!** (*iro*) now I'll show you!; **servire la Messa/la Patria** to serve Mass/one's country **2** (*piatto*) to serve; **servire qc a qn** to serve sb with sth, help sb to sth; "**servire ghiacciato**" "serve chilled"; **servire a tavola** to wait on table; **servire da bere a qn** to serve a drink to sb; **il pranzo è servito** dinner is served; **dopo la cena ha servito il caffè** after dinner she served coffee **3** (*Carte*) to deal **4** (*Calcio: giocatore*) to pass the ball to ♦ VI **1** (*aus essere*) **servire a (fare) qc** (*essere utile*) to be used for (doing) sth, be for sth; **servire a qn** to be of use to sb; **a che cosa serve?** what's it for?; **a cosa serve questo aggeggio?** what is this gadget (used) for?; **serve a tagliare la frutta** it's for cutting fruit; **questa stanza serve da studio** this room is used as a study; **che ti serva da lezione** let that be a lesson to you; **ha insistito ma non è servito (a niente)** he insisted but to no purpose; **mi serve un paio di forbici** I need a pair of scissors; **non mi serve più** I don't need it any more; **te lo presto, se ti serve** I'll lend it to you, if you need it; **non serve a niente** it's not of any use; **piangere non serve a niente** it's no use crying, crying doesn't help; **a che serve lamentarsi?** what would be the point of complaining? **2** (*Tennis*) to serve; **servirsi** VIP **1** (*fare uso*): **servirsi di** to make use of, use **2** (*a tavola*) to help o.s.; **serviti pure!** help yourself! **3 servirsi da** (*negoziante*) to shop at, be a regular customer at, go to

servitù [servi'tu] SF INV **1** (*condizione*) slavery, bondage, servitude; **servitù della gleba** (*Storia*) serfdom **2** (*domestici*) servants *pl*, domestic staff *sg o pl* **3** (*Dir*): **servitù di passaggio** right of way

servizievole [servit'tsjevole] AGG obliging, helpful, willing to help

servizio, -zi [ser'vittsjo] SM **1** (*lavoro*) duty; **essere di** *o* **in servizio** to be on duty; **non bevo in servizio** I don't drink on duty; **prendere servizio** to come on duty; **avere 20 anni di servizio** to have done *o* completed 20 years' service **2** (*come domestico*) (domestic) service; **andare/essere a servizio** to go into/be in service; **entrata di servizio** service *o* tradesman's (*Brit*) entrance **3 servizio civile** community service (*chosen instead of military service, especially by conscientious objectors*); **il servizio militare** military service; **prestare servizio militare** to do one's military *o* national service; **servizio d'ordine** (*Polizia*) police patrol; (*di manifestanti*) team of stewards (*for crowd control*); **servizio segreto** secret service; **servizi di sicurezza** security forces **4** (*istituzioni pubbliche*) service; **servizio postale/telefonico** postal/telephone service; **servizio sanitario nazionale** ≈ National Health Service (*Brit*), ≈ Medicaid/Medicare (*USA*) **5** (*funzionamento*) service; **fuori servizio** out of order; **rimettere in servizio** to put *o* bring back into service **6** (*favore*) service, favour (*Brit*), favor (*USA*); (*prestazioni*): **servizi** services; **offrire i propri servizi a qn** to offer sb one's services, offer one's services to sb; **bel servizio mi hai fatto!** (*iro*) you've been a real help!; **sono al suo servizio** I am at your service **7** (*al ristorante*) service; (*sul conto*) service (charge); **servizio a bordo** (*Aer*) in-flight service; **servizio compreso/escluso** service included/not included; **il servizio è compreso?** is service included? **8** (*TV, Radio, Stampa*) report; **un servizio sul terremoto in Afghanistan** a report on the earthquake in Afghanistan; **servizio in diretta** live coverage; **servizio fotografico** (*Stampa*) photo feature **9** (*Rel*) service **10** (*Tennis*) service; **ha un servizio potentissimo** she has a very powerful serve; **al servizio Sampras** Sampras to serve; **servizio vincente** ace **11** (*insieme di oggetti*): **servizio all'americana** tablemat and napkin set; **servizio da tè** tea set; **servizio di cristallo** set of crystal glassware; **servizio di posate** set of cutlery **12 i servizi** SMPL (*di casa*) kitchen and bathroom; **casa con doppi servizi** house with two bathrooms **13** (*Econ*): **servizi** SMPL services

servo, -a ['servo] SM, SF servant, manservant (maidservant)

servofreno [servo'freno] SM (*Aut*) servo brake

servosterzo [servos'tertso] SM (*Aut*) power steering

sesamo ['sɛzamo] SM (*Bot*) sesame; **apriti sesamo!** open sesame!

sessanta [ses'santa] AGG INV, SM INV sixty

sessantenne [sessan'tenne] AGG, SM, SF sixty-year-old

sessantesimo, -a [sessan'tɛzimo] AGG, SM, SF sixtieth

sessantina [sessan'tina] SF: **una sessantina (di)** about sixty

sessantottino, -a [sessantot'tino] SM, SF (*fam*) *a person who took part in the events of 1968* (*sessantotto*)

sessantotto [sessan'tɔtto] SM (*fam*): **il sessantotto** *student protest movement of 1968*

sessione [ses'sjone] SF session

sesso ['sɛsso] SM sex; **il sesso debole/forte** the weaker/stronger sex; **fare sesso** to have sex; **sesso sicuro** safe sex

sessuale [sessu'ale] AGG (*gen*) sexual; (*vita, organo, educazione*) sex *attr*, sexual

sessualità [sessuali'ta] SF sexuality

sessuologo, -a, -gi, -ghe [sessu'ɔlogo] SM, SF sexologist, sex specialist

sestante [ses'tante] SM (*Naut*) sextant

sesto¹, -a ['sɛsto] AGG, SM, SF (*numerale*) sixth; **sesta malattia** sixth disease; **sesto senso** sixth sense

sesto² ['sɛsto] SM: **rimettere in sesto** (*aggiustare*) to put back in order; (*fig: persona*) to put back on his (*o* her) feet; **rimettersi in sesto** (*riprendersi*) to recover, get well; (*riassettarsi*) to tidy o.s. up

seta ['seta] SF silk; **una camicia di seta** a silk shirt

setacciare [setat't ʃare] /14/ VT (*farina*) to sift, sieve; (*fig: zona*) to search, comb

setaccio, -ci [se'tatt ʃo] SM sieve; **passare al setaccio** (*fig*) to search, comb

sete ['sete] SF (*anche fig*) thirst; **avere sete** to be thirsty; **soffrire la sete** to suffer from thirst; **morire di sete** to die of thirst; **muoio di sete** I'm dying of thirst; **sete di potere** thirst for power

setificio, -ci [seti'fit ʃo] SM silk factory

setola ['setola] SF bristle

sett. ABBR (= *settembre*) Sept.

setta ['setta] SF (*Rel*) sect

settanta [set'tanta] AGG INV, SM INV seventy

settantenne [settan'tenne] AGG, SM, SF seventy-year-old

settantesimo, -a [settan'tɛzimo] AGG, SM, SF seventieth

settantina [settan'tina] SF: **una settantina (di)** about seventy

settare [set'tare] /72/ VT to set

sette ['sette] AGG INV, SM INV seven

settecentesco, -a, -schi, -sche [settetʃen'tesko] AGG eighteenth-century

settecento [sette'tʃento] AGG INV seven hundred ♦ SM INV seven hundred; **il Settecento** (*secolo*) the eighteenth century

settembre [set'tembre] SM September; *vedi* **luglio**

sette'mila AGG INV, SM INV seven thousand

settentrionale [settentrjo'nale] AGG northern; **Italia settentrionale** Northern Italy; **vento settentrionale** north *o* northerly wind ♦ SM, SF northerner, person from the north

settentrione [setten'trjone] SM north; **del settentrione** north(ern), of the north; (*vento*) north(erly)

settico, -a, -ci, -che [settiko] AGG septic

settimana [setti'mana] SF **1** week; **una volta/due volte alla settimana** once/twice a week; **questa settimana** this week; **la settimana scorsa/prossima** last/next week; **a metà settimana** in the middle of the week; **2 settimane fa** 2 weeks ago; **fra 2 settimane** in 2 weeks' time, in 2 weeks; **prendere 3 settimane di ferie** to take 3 weeks' holiday; **settimana dopo settimana** week after week, week in, week out; **una settimana sì, una no** every other week; **settimana lavorativa** working week; **settimana bianca** winter-sports holiday; **settimana santa** Holy Week **2** (*paga*) week's pay, wages *pl*; (*per bambini*) pocket money (*Brit*), allowance (*USA*)

settimanale [settima'nale] AGG weekly ♦ SM (*rivista*) weekly (publication)

settimo, -a ['settimo] AGG, SM, SF seventh; **essere al settimo cielo** (*fig*) to be in seventh heaven

settore [set'tore] SM (*Econ, Geom, Mil*) sector; (*fig*) area; **settore primario/secondario/terziario** primary/secondary/tertiary sector; **settore privato/pubblico** private/public sector

Seul [se'ul] SF Seoul

severità [severi'ta] SF (*vedi agg*) severity; strictness

severo, -a [se'vero] AGG (*gen*) severe; (*padre, insegnante, giudice*) strict

seviziare [sevit'tsjare] /19/ ᴠᴛ (*torturare*) to torture; (*picchiare*) to beat up

sevizie [se'vittsje] sꜰᴘʟ torture *sg*

sexy ['seksi] ᴀɢɢ ɪɴᴠ sexy

sez. ᴀʙʙʀ = sezione

sezionare [settsjo'nare] /72/ ᴠᴛ (*gen*) to divide up, cut up, divide into sections; (*Med*) to dissect

sezione [set'tsjone] sꜰ (*gen, anche Geom, Archit, Tecn*) section; (*di ufficio*) department; (*a scuola*) ≈ class; (*Med*) dissection

sfaccendato, -a [sfattʃen'dato] ᴀɢɢ lazy, idle ♦ sᴍ, sꜰ idler, loafer

sfaccettatura [sfattʃetta'tura] sꜰ (*azione*) faceting; (*parte sfaccettata, fig*) facet

sfacchinare [sfakki'nare] /72/ ᴠɪ (*aus avere*) (*fam*) to toil, drudge

sfacchinata [sfakki'nata] sꜰ (*fam*) toil *no pl*, chore, drudgery *no pl*; è stata una bella sfacchinata! it was really exhausting!

sfacciataggine [sfattʃa'taddʒine] sꜰ insolence, cheek; ma che sfacciataggine! what a cheek *o* nerve!; avere la sfacciataggine di fare qc to have the nerve *o* cheek to do sth

sfacciato, -a [sfat'tʃato] ᴀɢɢ insolent, cheeky, impudent

sfacelo [sfa'tʃelo] sᴍ (*fig: di famiglia, organizzazione*) breakup; andare in sfacelo (*costruzione*) to fall to pieces; (*piani*) to be ruined

sfaldarsi [sfal'darsi] /72/ ᴠɪᴘ (*rocce*) to exfoliate

sfalsare [sfal'sare] /72/ ᴠᴛ to stagger

sfamare [sfa'mare] /72/ ᴠᴛ (*nutrire*) to feed; (*soddisfare la fame*): sfamare qn to satisfy sb's hunger; sfamarsi ᴠʀ to satisfy one's hunger, fill o.s. up

sfarfallio, -lii [sfarfal'lio] sᴍ (*Cine, TV*) flickering

sfarzo ['sfartso] sᴍ pomp, splendour (*Brit*), splendor (*USA*), magnificence

sfarzoso, -a [sfar'tsoso] ᴀɢɢ splendid, magnificent

sfasamento [sfaza'mento] sᴍ (*Elettr*) phase displacement; (*fig*) confusion, bewilderment

sfasato, -a [sfa'zato] ᴀɢɢ (*Elettr: motore*) out of phase; (*fig: persona*) confused, bewildered

sfasciare¹ [sfaʃ'ʃare] /14/ ᴠᴛ (*togliere una fascia*) to unbandage

sfasciare² [sfaʃ'ʃare] /14/ ᴠᴛ (*macchina*) to smash, wreck; (*vaso*) to smash, shatter; (*letto, sedia*) to wreck, break; sfasciarsi ᴠɪᴘ (*macchina*) to be smashed, be wrecked; (*vaso*) to shatter, smash; (*letto, sedia*) to fall to pieces

sfatare [sfa'tare] /72/ ᴠᴛ (*leggenda, mito*) to explode

sfaticato, -a [sfati'kato] ᴀɢɢ lazy, idle ♦ sᴍ, sꜰ idler, loafer

sfatto, -a ['sfatto] ᴘᴘ *di* sfare ♦ ᴀɢɢ (*letto*) unmade; (*orlo*) undone; (*gelato, neve*) melted; (*frutta*) overripe; (*riso, pasta*) overdone, overcooked; (*fam: persona, corpo*) flabby

sfavillare [sfavil'lare] /72/ ᴠɪ (*aus avere*) (*diamante, occhi*) to sparkle; (*fiamma*) to flicker, spark, send out sparks

sfavore [sfa'vore] sᴍ disfavour (*Brit*), disfavor (*USA*), disapproval

sfavorevole [sfavo'revole] ᴀɢɢ unfavourable (*Brit*), unfavorable (*USA*)

sfegatato, -a [sfega'tato] ᴀɢɢ (*anche pegg*) fanatical

sfera ['sfera] sꜰ (*anche fig*) sphere; sfera di cristallo crystal ball; penna a sfera ballpoint pen; sfera d'influenza sphere of influence

sferico, -a, -ci, -che ['sferiko] ᴀɢɢ spherical

sferrare [sfer'rare] /72/ ᴠᴛ (*fig: attacco*) to launch; sferrare un colpo a qn to hit out at sb, lash out at sb (with one's fist); sferrare un calcio a qn to kick out at sb, lash out at sb (with one's foot); sferrarsi ᴠɪᴘ: sferrarsi contro qn (*lanciarsi*) to hurl *o* fling o.s. at sb

sferzante [sfer'tsante] ᴀɢɢ (*critiche, parole*) stinging

sferzare [sfer'tsare] /72/ ᴠᴛ (*gen*) to whip; (*sogg: vento*) to lash; (: *onde*) to lash against, break on; (: *fig*) to lash out at

sfiancare [sfjan'kare] /20/ ᴠᴛ to wear out, exhaust; sfiancarsi ᴠɪᴘ to exhaust o.s., wear o.s. out

sfiatare [sfja'tare] /72/ ᴠɪ (*aus avere*) to allow air *o* gas to escape

sfiatatoio, -oi [sfjata'tojo] sᴍ 1 (*Tecn*) vent 2 (*Zool*) blowhole

sfibrante [sfi'brante] ᴀɢɢ exhausting, energy-sapping

sfibrare [sfi'brare] /72/ ᴠᴛ (*indebolire*) to exhaust, enervate

sfibrato, -a [sfi'brato] ᴀɢɢ exhausted, worn out

sfida ['sfida] sꜰ challenge; lanciare una sfida a qn to challenge sb; uno sguardo di sfida (*fig*) a defiant look

sfidante [sfi'dante] ᴀɢɢ challenging ♦ sᴍ, sꜰ challenger

sfidare [sfi'dare] /72/ ᴠᴛ 1 (*avversario*) to challenge; l'ho sfidato a scacchi I challenged him to a game of chess; sfidare qn a duello to challenge sb to a duel; sfidare qn a fare qc to challenge sb to do sth 2 (*fig: affrontare*) to defy, brave; sfidare la morte to defy death; sfidare un pericolo to brave a danger 3 (*fraseologia*): sfido io! naturally!, of course!, no wonder!; sfidarsi ᴠʀ (*uso reciproco*) to challenge each other

sfiducia [sfi'dutʃa] sꜰ distrust, mistrust; avere sfiducia in qn/qc to distrust sb/sth; voto di sfiducia (*Pol*) vote of no confidence

sfiduciato, -a [sfidu'tʃato] ᴀɢɢ discouraged, disheartened

sfigato, -a [sfi'gato] (*fam*) ᴀɢɢ (*sfortunato*) unlucky ♦ sᴍ, sꜰ (*fallito, sfortunato*) loser; (*fuori moda ecc*) dork

sfigurare [sfigu'rare] /72/ ᴠᴛ (*persona*) to disfigure; (*quadro, statua*) to deface; ha sfigurato il quadro he defaced the picture; l'incidente lo ha sfigurato the accident left him disfigured ♦ ᴠɪ (*aus avere*) to make a bad impression, cut a poor figure; non vorrei sfigurare I don't want to make a bad impression

sfilacciare [sfilat'tʃare] /14/ ᴠᴛ, ᴠɪ (*aus essere*) sfilacciarsi ᴠɪᴘ to fray

sfilare¹ [sfi'lare] /72/ ᴠᴛ 1 (*orlo, tessuto*) to pull the threads out of; (*perle*) to unstring; (*ago*) to unthread 2 (*togliere: stivali, scarpe*) to take off, slip off; gli sfilò il portafoglio he pinched *o* lifted his wallet; sfilarsi il vestito/le scarpe to take one's dress/shoes off; gli ho sfilato le scarpe I took his shoes off; sfilarsi ᴠɪᴘ (*orlo, tessuto*) to fray; (*calza*) to ladder, run; (*perle*) to come unstrung

sfilare² [sfi'lare] /72/ ᴠɪ (*aus avere o essere*) (*truppe*) to parade, march past; (*manifestanti*) to march; (*modelle*) to parade

sfilata [sfi'lata] sꜰ (*Mil*) parade; (*di manifestanti*) march; sfilata (di moda) fashion show

sfilza ['sfiltsa] sꜰ (*di case*) row; (*di errori*) series *inv*

sfinge ['sfindʒe] sꜰ sphinx

sfinimento [sfini'mento] sᴍ exhaustion

sfinito, -a [sfi'nito] ᴀɢɢ exhausted, worn out

sfiorare [sfjo'rare] /72/ ᴠᴛ (*acqua, cime di alberi*) to skim (over); (*volto, guancia*) to brush (against); qualcosa mi ha sfiorato la gamba something brushed against my leg; il proiettile l'ha solo sfiorato the bullet only grazed him; sfiorare un argomento to touch on *o* upon a subject; non ha neppure sfiorato l'argomento he didn't even touch on the subject; è un'idea che non mi sfiora nemmeno it's an idea which hasn't even crossed my mind; non ti ha mai sfiorato il dubbio che possa rifiutare? has it never occurred to you *o* has it never crossed your mind that he might refuse?; sfiorare la velocità di 150 km/h to touch 150 km/h

sfiorire [sfjo'rire] /55/ ᴠɪ (*aus essere*) (*fiore, pianta*) to wither, fade; (*fig: bellezza*) to fade

sfitto, -a ['sfitto] ᴀɢɢ vacant, empty

sfocato, -a [sfo'kato] ᴀɢɢ (*Fot*) blurred, out of focus; (*fig: ricordo, immagine*) vague, dim

sfociare [sfo'tʃare] /14/ ᴠɪ (*aus essere*) (*fiume*): sfociare in to flow into; il malcontento sfociò in una rivolta (*fig*) the discontent developed into open rebellion

sfoderato, -a [sfode'rato] ᴀɢɢ (*vestito*) unlined

sfogare [sfo'gare] /80/ ᴠᴛ (*gioia, tristezza*) to give vent to; (*energia*) to work off; sfogare la propria rabbia su qn to vent one's anger on sb ♦ ᴠɪ (*aus essere*) (*liquido*) to flow out; (*gas*) to escape; (*malattia, febbre*) to run its course; sfogarsi ᴠʀ (*persona*) to give vent to one's feelings; (*liberarsi di un peso*) to get a load off one's chest; sfogarsi con qn (*confidarsi*) to unburden o.s. *o* open one's heart to sb, pour out one's feelings to sb; non sfogarti su di me! don't take it out on me!

sfoggiare [sfod'dʒare] /62/ ᴠᴛ to show off; voglio sfoggiare il mio vestito nuovo I want to show off my new dress

sfoggio, -gi ['sfɔddʒo] sᴍ show, display; fare sfoggio di to show off, display

sfogherò ecc [sfoge'rɔ] VB vedi **sfogare**

sfoglia ['sfɔʎʎa] SF (gen) thin layer; (Culin) sheet of pasta dough; **pasta sfoglia** puff pastry

sfogliare [sfoʎ'ʎare] /27/ VT (libro, rivista) to leaf through; **stava sfogliando una rivista** she was leafing through a magazine

sfogo, -ghi ['sfogo] SM 1 (di liquido, gas) outlet; (di aria) vent; (fig: di rabbia) outburst; **dare sfogo a** (fig) to give vent to 2 (eruzione cutanea) rash

sfolgorante [sfolgo'rante] AGG (luce) blazing; (fig: vittoria) brilliant

sfolgorare [sfolgo'rare] /72/ VI (aus avere) to blaze

sfollagente [sfolla'dʒente] SM INV truncheon (Brit), nightstick (USA), billy club (USA)

sfollare [sfol'lare] /72/ VT (piazza, strada) to clear, empty; (edificio) to evacuate, empty ♦ VI (aus essere) (gente, dimostranti) to disperse; **sfollare da una città** to evacuate a town

sfollato, -a [sfol'lato] AGG evacuated ♦ SM, SF evacuee

sfoltire [sfol'tire] /55/ VT, **sfoltirsi** VIP to thin (out)

sfondare [sfon'dare] /72/ VT (porta) to break down; (parete) to break down, knock down; (pavimento) to break through; (scarpe) to wear through, wear a hole in; (sedia, barca) to knock the bottom out of; (scatola) to burst, knock the bottom out of; **ha sfondato la porta** he broke down the door; **sfondare le linee nemiche** (Mil) to break through the enemy lines; **sfondare il tetto di** (fig) to go beyond the limit of ♦ VI (aus avere) (fig: attore, scrittore: avere successo) to make a name for o.s.; **è difficile sfondare nel cinema** it's difficult to be successful in the film world; **sfondarsi** VIP (porta, sedia, pavimento) to give way; (parete) to fall down; (scarpe) to wear out; (scatola) to burst

sfondato, -a [sfon'dato] AGG (scarpe) worn out; (scatola) burst; (sedia) broken, damaged; **essere ricco sfondato** to be rolling in it

sfondo ['sfondo] SM (gen, anche Pittura, Fot) background; (di film, libro) background, setting; **sullo sfondo** in the background; **bianco su sfondo rosso** white on a red background

sforare [sfo'rare] /72/ VI (aus avere) (TV, Radio) to overrun

sformare [sfor'mare] /72/ VT 1 to put out of shape, knock out of shape 2 (dolce, budino) to turn out; **sformarsi** VIP to lose shape, get out of shape

sformato¹, -a [sfor'mato] AGG (che ha perso forma) shapeless

sformato² [sfor'mato] SM (Culin) type of soufflé

sfornare [sfor'nare] /72/ VT (Culin) to take out of the oven; (fig: libri, film) to churn out

sfornito, -a [sfor'nito] AGG: **sfornito di** lacking in, without; (negozio) out of

sfortuna [sfor'tuna] SF misfortune, bad o ill luck no pl; **avere sfortuna** to be unlucky; **ho avuto sfortuna ieri sera, non ho vinto niente** I was unlucky last night, I didn't win anything; **che sfortuna!** what bad luck!; **portare sfortuna** to be unlucky; **passare sotto una scala porta sfortuna** it's unlucky to walk under a ladder; **per sfortuna** unfortunately

sfortunato, -a [sfortu'nato] AGG (persona, numero) unlucky; (impresa, film) unsuccessful

sforzare [sfor'tsare] /72/ VT (gen) to force; (voce, occhi) to strain; **sforzare qn a fare qc** to force sb to do sth; **sforzarsi** VIP: **sforzarsi (a fare qc)** (costringersi) to force o.s. to do sth; (fare uno sforzo) to make an effort (to do sth); **sforzarsi di fare qc** to try to do sth; **sforzati di ricordare!** try to remember!

sforzo ['sfɔrtso] SM (gen) effort; (Tecn) stress, strain; **fare uno sforzo** to make an effort; **essere sotto sforzo** (motore, macchina, anche fig: persona) to be under stress; **che o bello sforzo!** (iro) that didn't take much effort!

sfottere ['sfottere] /1/ VT (fam) to tease

sfracellare [sfratʃel'lare] /72/ VT to smash; **sfracellarsi** VIP to smash; **sfracellarsi al suolo** to crash to the ground

sfrattare [sfrat'tare] /72/ VT to evict

sfratto ['sfratto] SM eviction; **dare lo sfratto a qn** to give sb notice to quit; **ci hanno dato lo sfratto** we've been given notice to quit

sfrecciare [sfret'tʃare] /14/ VI (aus essere) to shoot o flash past

sfregare [sfre'gare] /80/ VT (strofinare) to rub; (graffiare) to scratch; **sfregare un fiammifero** to strike a match; **sfregarsi le mani** to rub one's hands; **si sfregava gli occhi** he was rubbing his eyes

sfregiare [sfre'dʒare] /62/ VT to slash, gash; (volto) to disfigure, slash; (quadro) to deface, slash; **sfregiarsi** VIP to be disfigured

sfregio ['sfredʒo] SM 1 (cicatrice) scar; (ferita) gash; (graffio) scratch 2 (fig: offesa) affront, insult

sfrenato, -a [sfre'nato] AGG (persona) wild, uncontrolled; (dissoluto) dissolute; (passioni) unbridled, unrestrained; (bambino) unruly; **essere sfrenato nel bere/nel mangiare** to drink/eat excessively; **vivere in un lusso sfrenato** to live in unrestrained luxury

sfrondare [sfron'dare] /72/ VT (albero) to prune, thin out; (fig: discorso, scritto) to prune (down)

sfrontatezza [sfronta'tettsa] SF impudence, cheek; **avere la sfrontatezza di fare qc** to have the cheek to do sth

sfrontato, -a [sfron'tato] AGG impudent, cheeky; **è sempre più sfrontato** he's getting cheekier and cheekier

sfruttamento [sfrutta'mento] SM exploitation

sfruttare [sfrut'tare] /72/ VT (terreno) to overwork, exhaust; (miniera) to exploit, work; (operaio) to exploit; (occasione, momento) to make the most of, take advantage of; **dobbiamo sfruttare lo spazio che abbiamo** we have to make the most of the space we have

sfruttatore, -trice [sfrutta'tore] SM, SF exploiter

sfuggente [sfud'dʒente] AGG (fig: sguardo) elusive; (mento, fronte) receding

sfuggire [sfud'dʒire] /31/ VI (aus essere) (gen) to escape; **sfuggire alla polizia** to escape from the police; **sfuggire alla morte/alla cattura** to escape death/capture; **il sapone mi è sfuggito di mano** the soap slipped out of my hands; **mi sfugge il nome** his name escapes me; **mi è sfuggito di mente** it slipped my mind; **non ti sfugge niente** nothing escapes you, you don't miss a thing; **lasciarsi sfuggire un'occasione** to let an opportunity go by, miss an opportunity; **non lasciarti sfuggire l'occasione** don't miss this opportunity; **sfuggire al controllo** (macchina) to go out of control; (situazione) to get out of control

sfuggita [sfud'dʒita] SF: **di sfuggita** (notare, salutare) in passing; **vedere di sfuggita** to catch a glimpse of

sfumare [sfu'mare] /72/ VT (colore: schiarire) to soften, shade off; (suono) to fade out; (capelli) to taper ♦ VI (aus essere) (colore): **sfumare in** to fade into, shade off into; (fig: speranza) to vanish, disappear, come to nothing

sfumatura [sfuma'tura] SF 1 (azione: vedi vt) softening, shading off; fading out; tapering 2 (di colore) shade, tone; **diverse sfumature di significato** different shades of meaning, different nuances; **una sfumatura d'ironia** a hint of irony

sfuocato, -a [sfwo'kato] AGG = **sfocato**

sfuriata [sfu'rjata] SF outburst of rage, fit of rage o anger; **fare una sfuriata a qn** to give sb a good telling off

sfuso, -a ['sfuso] AGG (caramelle) loose, unpacked; (vino) unbottled; (birra) draught (Brit), draft (USA)

sg. ABBR = **seguente**

sgabello [zga'bello] SM stool

sgabuzzino [zgabud'dzino] SM lumber room (Brit), storage room (USA)

sgambettare [zgambet'tare] /72/ VI (aus avere) to kick (one's legs) about; (bambino) to toddle

sgambetto [zgam'betto] SM: **fare lo sgambetto a qn** to trip sb up; (fig) to oust sb

sganasciarsi [zganaʃ'ʃarsi] /14/ VIP: **sganasciarsi dalle risate** o **dal ridere** to roar with laughter

sganciare [zgan'tʃare] /14/ VT (gen) to unhook; (chiusura) to unfasten, undo; (treno) to uncouple; (bombe) to drop, release; (fig: fam: soldi) to fork out; **sganciarsi** VIP (gen) to come unhooked; (chiusura) to come unfastened, come undone; (treno) to come uncoupled; **sganciarsi da** (fig: persona) to get away from

sgangherato, -a [zgange'rato] AGG (porta) unhinged, off its hinges; (auto) ramshackle, rickety; (risata) wild, boisterous

sgarbato, -a [zgar'bato] AGG rude, ill-mannered, impolite

sgarbo ['zgarbo] SM: **fare uno sgarbo a qn** to be rude to sb

sgargiante [zgarˈdʒante] AGG gaudy, showy

sgarrare [zgarˈrare] /72/ VI (aus avere) (persona) to step out of line; (orologio: essere avanti) to gain; (: essere indietro) to lose; **e guarda di non sgarrare!** watch your step!; **l'orologio sgarra di 2 minuti** the clock is 2 minutes fast (o slow)

sgarro [ˈzgarro] SM (mancanza di correttezza) mistake, inaccuracy; **non ammetto sgarri** I won't allow anyone to step out of line

sgattaiolare [zgattajoˈlare] /72/ VI (aus essere) **sgattaiolare fuori** to slip out, sneak out; **sgattaiolare via** to sneak away o off

sgelare [zdʒeˈlare] /72/ VT, VI (aus essere), **sgelarsi** VIP to melt, thaw

sghembo, -a [ˈzɡembo] AGG (storto) crooked; **di sghembo** (storto) crookedly; (obliquamente) on the slant

sghignazzare [zɡiɲɲatˈtsare] /72/ VI (aus avere) to laugh scornfully, sneer

sghignazzata [zɡiɲɲatˈtsata] SF scornful laugh, sneer

sgobbare [zɡobˈbare] /72/ VI (aus avere) (fam: lavorare) to slog, slave; (: a scuola) to swot (Brit), cram (USA); **sgobbare sui libri** to slog away at one's books

sgocciolare [zgottʃoˈlare] /72/ VT (acqua) to drip; (cosa immersa in un liquido) to drain ♦ VI (aus essere) to drip

sgoccioli [ˈzgottʃoli] SMPL: **essere agli sgoccioli** (lavoro, provviste) to be nearly finished; (periodo) to be nearly over; **siamo agli sgoccioli** we've nearly finished, the end is in sight

sgolarsi [zgoˈlarsi] /72/ VIP to become hoarse, talk (o shout o sing) o.s. hoarse; (fig: parlare inutilmente) to waste one's breath

sgomberare [zgombeˈrare] /72/ VT (stanza, aula, strada) to clear; (alloggio) to move out of, vacate; (zona: evacuare) to evacuate; **stanno sgomberando la stanza** they're clearing the room ♦ VI (aus avere) (traslocare) to move; **dobbiamo sgomberare entro lunedì** we have to move out by Monday

sgombero [ˈzgombero] SM (di strada, stanze) clearing; (di città) evacuation; (trasloco) moving

sgombro¹, -a [ˈzgombro] AGG (gen) clear, empty ♦ SM = sgombero

sgombro² [ˈzgombro] SM (pesce) mackerel

sgomentare [zgomenˈtare] /72/ VT to dismay, alarm; **sgomentarsi** VIP to be dismayed, be alarmed

sgomento, -a [zgoˈmento] AGG dismayed, alarmed ♦ SM dismay, alarm; **farsi prendere dallo sgomento** to be filled with dismay, be alarmed

sgominare [zgomiˈnare] /72/ VT (nemico) to rout; (avversario) to defeat; (fig: epidemia) to overcome

sgonfiare [zgonˈfjare] /19/ VT (pneumatico) to deflate, let the air out, let down; (fig: persona) to bring down a peg or two; **sgonfia il materassino** let down the airbed; **sgonfiarsi** VIP **1** (gen) to deflate; (pneumatico) to go flat; (fig: persona) to be deflated **2** (Med) to go down; **la caviglia si è sgonfiata** my ankle is no longer swollen

sgonfio, -fia, -fi, -fie [ˈzgonfjo] AGG **1** (pneumatico, pallone) flat; **hai una gomma sgonfia** you've got a flat tyre (Brit) o tire (USA) **2** (Med) no longer inflamed o swollen

sgorbio, -bi [ˈzgɔrbjo] SM (macchia) blot; (scarabocchio) scrawl, scribble; (pegg: quadro) daub; (fam: persona brutta) fright

sgorgare [zgorˈgare] /80/ VI (aus essere) (gen) to gush (out), spurt (out); (lacrime) to pour, flow; **il sangue sgorgava dalla ferita** the blood gushed o spurted from the wound

sgozzare [zgotˈtsare] /72/ VT to cut the throat of; (macellare, anche fig) to slaughter

sgradevole [zgraˈdevole] AGG unpleasant; (voce, odore) unpleasant, disagreeable

sgradito, -a [zgraˈdito] AGG unwelcome

sgraffignare [zgraffiɲˈɲare] /15/ VT (fam) to pinch, swipe

sgrammaticato, -a [zgrammatiˈkato] AGG ungrammatical

sgranare [zgraˈnare] /72/ VT (fagioli) to shell; (pannocchia) to remove the corn from; **sgranare gli occhi** (fig) to open one's eyes wide

sgranchire [zgranˈkire] /55/ VT to stretch; **sgranchirsi le gambe** to stretch one's legs

sgranocchiare [zgranokˈkjare] /19/ VT to munch, crunch

sgrassare [zgrasˈsare] /72/ VT to remove the grease from

sgravio, -vi [ˈzgravjo] SM: **sgravio fiscale** o **contributivo** tax relief

sgraziato, -a [zgratˈtsjato] AGG ungraceful, awkward, clumsy, ungainly

sgretolare [zgretoˈlare] /72/ VT (roccia) to split; (intonaco) to cause to flake off; **sgretolarsi** VIP (muro, creta, gesso) to crumble; (roccia) to split

sgridare [zgriˈdare] /72/ VT: **sgridare qn** to tell sb off, scold sb; **perché mi sgridi?** why are you telling me off?

sgridata [zgriˈdata] SF telling off, scolding

sguaiato, -a [zgwaˈjato] AGG coarse, vulgar; **una risata sguaiata** a guffaw

sguainare [zgwaiˈnare] /72/ VT to draw, unsheathe

sgualcire [zgwalˈtʃire] /55/ VT to crumple (up), crease; **attenta a non sgualcire il vestito** mind you don't crease your dress; **sgualcirsi** VIP to become o get crumpled, become o get creased

sgualdrina [zgwalˈdrina] SF (spesso offensivo: fam!) whore, slut, trollop

sguardo [ˈzgwardo] SM **1** (occhiata) glance, look; **dare uno sguardo a qc** to glance at sth, cast a glance o an eye over sth; **lanciare uno sguardo di rimprovero a qn** to give sb a reproachful look; **mi ha lanciato uno sguardo d'intesa** he gave me a knowing look **2** (espressione) expression, look (in one's eye); **avere lo sguardo fisso** to have a fixed expression; **ha uno sguardo intelligente** he has an intelligent expression; **aveva lo sguardo triste** he looked sad **3** (occhi): **alzare** o **sollevare lo sguardo** to raise one's eyes, look up; **abbassare lo sguardo** to lower one's eyes, look down; **cercare qn/qc con lo sguardo** to look (a)round for sb/sth; **distogliere lo sguardo da qn/qc** to take one's eyes off sb/sth; **fissare lo sguardo su qn/qc** to stare at sb/sth; **soffermarsi con lo sguardo su qn/qc** to let one's eyes rest on sb/sth; **volgere lo sguardo altrove** to look elsewhere; **attirare gli sguardi** (fig: attenzione) to attract (people's) attention

sguattero, -a [zgwattero] SM scullery boy (maid)

sguazzare [zgwatˈtsare] /72/ VI (aus avere) (in acqua) to splash (about); (nel fango) to wallow; (fig: trovarsi a proprio agio) to be in one's element; **sguazzare nell'oro** to be rolling in money

sguinzagliare [zgwintsaʎˈʎare] /27/ VT (cane) to let off the leash; (fig: persona): **sguinzagliare qn dietro a qn** to set sb on sb

sgusciare¹ [zguʃˈʃare] /14/ VT (uovo, piselli) to shell

sgusciare² [zguʃˈʃare] /14/ VI (aus essere) to slip; **sgusciare di mano** to slip out of one's hand; **sgusciare via** (scappare) to escape, slip o slink away

shaker [ˈʃeikə] SM INV (cocktail) shaker

shampoo [ˈʃampuː] SM INV shampoo

shiatsu, shiatzu [ʃiˈatsu] SM INV, AGG INV shiatsu

shoccare [ʃɔkˈkare] /20/ VT = scioccare

shock [ʃɔk] SM INV (gen, anche Med) shock; **sotto shock** in a state of shock

shockare [ʃɔkˈkare] /72/ VT = scioccare

SI SIGLA = Siena

PAROLA CHIAVE

si¹ [si] PRON davanti la, li, le, ne diventa se

1 (in verbi riflessivi: impersonale) oneself; (: maschile) himself; (: femminile) herself; (: plurale) themselves; (in verbi intransitivi pronominali) itself; **si crede importante** he (o she) thinks a lot of himself (o herself); **se ne è dimenticata** she forgot about it; **si è dimenticato di me** he has forgotten me; **l'orologio si è fermato** the clock has stopped; **si guardava allo specchio** he was looking at himself in the mirror; **lavarsi** to wash (oneself); **si nascosero** they hid; **pettinarsi** to comb one's hair; **si è rotto** it has broken; **digli di sbrigarsi** tell him to hurry up; **sporcarsi** to get dirty; **si è tagliato** he's cut himself

2 (con complemento oggetto): **si è tolto il cappello** he took off his hat; **lavarsi le mani** to wash one's hands; **si è sporcato i pantaloni** he got his trousers (Brit) o pants (USA) dirty; **se l'è ricordato** he remembered it; **si godette la vacanza** he (o she) enjoyed his (o her) holiday

3 (uso reciproco) each other, one another; **si baciarono** they kissed; **si incontrarono alle 5** they met at 5 o'clock; **si odiano** they hate each other o one another

4 (*passivo*): **dove si parla russo** where Russian is spoken, where they speak Russian; **si ripara facilmente** it can easily be repaired; **si vende al chilo** it is sold by the kilo **5** (*impersonale*): **si dice che...** it is said that ..., people say that ...; **si dice che...** I am told that ...; **non si risponde così!** that's no way to answer somebody!; **non si sa mai** you never can tell, you never know; **si vede che è nuovo** one (*o* you) can tell it's new

si² [si] SM INV (*Mus*) B; (*solfeggiando la scala*) ti

sì¹ [si] AVV **1** yes; **hai finito? — sì** have you finished? — yes (I have); **sei sicuro? — sì, certo** are you sure? — yes, of course (I am); **vuoi un caffè? - sì, grazie** would you like a coffee? - yes, please; **siete andati al cinema ieri? - sì** did you go to the cinema yesterday? - yes, we did; **ma sì!** yes, of course!, I should say so!; **sì e no** yes and no; **avrà sì e no 10 anni** he must be about 10 years old; **saranno stati sì e no in 20** there must have been about 20 of them; **uno sì e uno no** every other one; **un giorno sì e uno no** every other day; **sì, domani!, sì, proprio!** (*iro*) you'll be lucky!, fat chance of that! **2** (*rafforzativo*): **allora vieni, sì o no?** are you coming or not?; **questa sì che è bella!** that's a good one! **3** **dire di sì** to say yes; **spero/penso di sì** I hope/think so; **forse (che) sì, forse (che) no** maybe, maybe not; **fece di sì col capo** he nodded (his head); **vieni! se sì ci vediamo dopo** are you coming? if so I'll see you later; **e sì che...** and to think that ... ♦ SM yes; **non mi aspettavo un sì** I didn't expect him (*o* her *ecc*) to say yes; **sono tra il sì e il no** I'm uncertain, I can't make up my mind; **per me è sì** I should think so, I expect so

sì² [si] AVV = **così**

sia¹ ['sia] CONG **1** **sia... sia..., sia... che...** (*tanto... quanto...*) both ... and ...; **sia Franco sia Mario hanno accettato, sia Franco che Mario hanno accettato** both Franco and Mario have accepted **2** **sia che... sia che...** (*o... o...*) whether ...or ...; **sia che accetti sia che non accetti** whether he accepts or not

sia² ['sia] VB *vedi* **essere**

Siam ['siam] SM Siam

siamese [sia'mese] AGG Siamese; **gatto siamese** Siamese (cat); **fratelli siamesi** Siamese twins ♦ SM, SF Siamese *inv* ♦ SM (*lingua*) Siamese

siamo ['sjamo] VB *vedi* **essere**

Siberia [si'bɛrja] SF Siberia

siberiano, -a [sibe'rjano] AGG, SM, SF Siberian

sibilare [sibi'lare] /72/ VI (*aus* avere) (*serpente*) to hiss; (*vento*) to whistle

sibilo ['sibilo] SM (*di serpente*) hiss(ing); (*di vento*) whistling, whistle

sicario, -ri [si'karjo] SM hired assassin *o* killer

sicché [sik'ke] CONG (*così che*) so (that), therefore; (*allora*) (and) so

siccità [sittʃi'ta] SF drought

siccome [sik'kome] CONG since, as; **siccome era tardi ho deciso di tornare a casa** since it was late I decided to go home

Sicilia [si't∫ilja] SF Sicily; **mi è piaciuta molto la Sicilia** I really liked Sicily; **vado in Sicilia quest'estate** I'm going to Sicily this summer

siciliano, -a [sit∫i'ljano] AGG, SM, SF Sicilian

sicomoro [siko'mɔro] SM sycamore

siculo, -a [si'kulo] AGG, SM, SF Sicilian

sicura [si'kura] SF (*di arma, di spilla*) safety catch; (*di portiera*) safety lock

sicuramente [sikura'mente] AVV (*con sicurezza: comportarsi, dichiarare*) confidently; (*certamente*) undoubtedly, certainly

sicurezza [siku'rettsa] SF **1** (*immunità*) safety; **una campagna per la sicurezza stradale** a road safety campaign; **di sicurezza** (*dispositivo, margine*) safety *attr*; **cintura di sicurezza** seat belt **2** (*salvaguardia di diritti*) security; **per la sicurezza nazionale** for national security; (*forze di*) **Pubblica Sicurezza** police (force) **3** (*certezza*) certainty; **avere la sicurezza di qc** to be sure *o* certain of sth; **lo so con sicurezza** I am quite certain **4** (*fiducia, tranquillità*) confidence; **sicurezza (di sé)** self-confidence, self-assurance; **ha risposto con molta sicurezza** he answered very confidently; **per sicurezza** just in case; **per sicurezza portati l'ombrello** take your umbrella, just in case

sicuro, -a [si'kuro] AGG **1** (*senza pericolo*) safe; (*ben difeso*) safe, secure; **non è sicuro qui** it isn't safe here; **sentirsi sicuro** to feel safe *o* secure; **non mi sento sicuro qui** I don't feel safe here **2** (*certo*) certain, sure; **la vittoria è sicura** victory is assured; **essere sicuro di qc/che...** to be sure of sth/that ...; **sono sicuro che ce la farai** I'm sure you'll manage it; **ne ero sicuro!** I knew it!; **ne sei proprio sicuro?** are you sure *o* certain? **3** (*fiducioso, tranquillo*) (self-)confident, sure of o.s.; **essere sicuro di sé** to be self-confident, be sure of o.s.; **è molto sicuro di sé** he's very self-confident **4** (*attendibile*) reliable, sure; (*rimedio*) sure, safe; (*esperto*) skilled; **da fonte sicura** from a reliable source; **l'ho saputo da fonte sicura** I heard about it from a reliable source **5** (*saldo*) firm, steady; **con mano sicura** with a steady hand ♦ AVV of course, certainly; **verrai? - sicuro!** will you come? - of course I will!; **di sicuro** (*senz'altro*) certainly; (*con certezza*) for sure; **non sappiamo di sicuro cosa sia successo** we don't know for sure what happened ♦ SM **1** (*cosa certa*): **dare qc per sicuro** to be sure about sth; **dare per sicuro che...** to be sure that ... **2** (*luogo sicuro*): **essere al sicuro** to be safe, be in a safe place; **non preoccuparti, qui siamo al sicuro** don't worry, we're safe here; **mettersi al sicuro** to take cover; **mettere qc al sicuro** to put sth away (in a safe place); **ho messo il tuo anello al sicuro** I've put your ring in a safe place **3** (*non rischiare*) **andare sul sicuro** to play safe

siderurgia [siderur'dʒia] SF iron and steel industry

siderurgico, -a, -ci, -che [side'rurdʒiko] AGG iron and steel *attr*

sidro ['sidro] SM cider

siedo *ecc* ['sjɛdo] VB *vedi* **sedere**

siepe ['sjɛpe] SF hedge; (*Sport*) hedge, hurdle

siero ['sjɛro] SM serum; **siero antivipera** snake bite serum; **siero del latte** whey; **siero della verità** truth serum *o* drug

sieronegatività [sjeronegativi'ta] SF HIV-negative status

sieronegativo, -a [sjeronega'tivo] AGG HIV-negative ♦ SM, SF HIV-negative person

sieropositività [sjeropozitivi'ta] SF HIV-positive status

sieropositivo, -a [sjeropozi'tivo] AGG HIV-positive ♦ SM, SF HIV-positive person

sierra ['sjɛrra] SF (*Geog*) sierra

Sierra Leone ['sjɛrra le'one] SF Sierra Leone

siesta ['sjɛsta] SF siesta, (afternoon) nap; **fare la siesta** to have a nap *o* siesta

siete ['sjɛte] VB *vedi* **essere**

sifilide [si'filide] SF syphilis

sifone [si'fone] SM (*Tecn*) siphon; (*per seltz*) (soda) siphon (*Brit*), soda-water siphon (*USA*)

Sig. ABBR (= *signore*) Mr

sigaretta [siga'retta] SF cigarette

sigaro ['sigaro] SM cigar

Sigg. ABBR (= *signori*) Messrs

sigillare [sidʒil'lare] /72/ VT to seal

sigillo [si'dʒillo] SM seal; **mettere** *o* **porre i sigilli a qc** to seal sth, put seals on sth; **anello con sigillo** signet ring

sigla ['sigla] SF **1** (*abbreviazione*) acronym, abbreviation; (*iniziali*) initials *pl*; (*monogramma*) monogram; **sigla automobilistica** abbreviation of province on vehicle number (*Brit*) *o* license (*USA*) plate **2** **sigla musicale** signature tune

siglare ['sigla] /72/ VT to initial

Sig.na ABBR (= *signorina*) Miss, Ms

significare [siɲɲifi'kare] /20/ VT **1** (*aver senso*) to mean; **cosa significa?** what does this mean?; **cosa significa questa parola?** what does this word mean? **2** (*avere importanza*) to mean, matter; **tu significhi molto per me** you mean a lot to me

significativo, -a [siɲɲifika'tivo] AGG significant

significato [siɲɲifi'kato] SM meaning, sense; (*valore, importanza*) importance; **senza significato** meaningless; **non ha alcun significato per me** it doesn't mean anything to me

signora [siɲ'ɲora] SF **1** (*donna*) lady; (*moglie*) wife; **ti cercava una signora** there was a lady looking for you; **è una signora molto simpatica** she's a very nice lady; **vive da signora** she leads a life of luxury; **le presento la mia signora** may I introduce my wife?; **il signor Rossi e signora** Mr Rossi and his wife; **Signore e Signori!** Ladies and Gentlemen!;

Nostra Signora (*Rel*) Our Lady **2** (*rivolgendosi a qualcuno*): **buon giorno signora** good morning; (*deferente*) good morning Madam; (*quando si conosce il nome*) good morning Mrs (*o* Ms) X; **signora maestra!** please Mrs (*o* Ms) X!, please Miss! **3** (*parlando di qualcuno*): **la signora Rossi sta male** Mrs (*o* Ms) Rossi is ill; **lo dirò alla signora** I'll let Mrs (*o* Ms) X know **4** (*in lettere*): **Gentile Signora** Dear Madam; **Gentile** (*o* **Cara**) **Signora Rossi** Dear Mrs (*o* Ms) Rossi; **Gentile Signora Anna Rossi** (*sulle buste*) Mrs (*o* Ms) Anna Rossi

signore [siɲˈɲore] SM **1** (*uomo*) gentleman; **c'è un signore che ti cerca** there's a gentleman looking for you; **è un signore molto simpatico** he's a very nice man; **è un vero signore** he's a real gentleman; **fa una vita da (gran) signore** lives like a lord; **fanno una vita da signori** they lead a life of luxury; **il Signore** (*Rel*) the Lord; **oh Signore!** oh Lord!, oh God! **2** (*rivolgendosi a qualcuno*): **buon giorno signore** good morning; (*deferente*) good morning Sir; (*quando si conosce il nome*) good morning Mr X; **signor maestro!** please Mr X!, please Sir!; **signor Presidente** Mr Chairman **3** (*parlando di qualcuno*): **il signor Rossi sta male** Mr Rossi is ill; **lo dirò al signore** I'll let Mr X know; **i signori Bianchi** (*coniugi*) Mr and Mrs Bianchi **4** (*in lettere*): **Gentile Signore** Dear Sir; **Gentile** (*o* **Caro**) **Signor Rossi** Dear Mr Rossi; **Gentile Signor Paolo Rossi** (*sulle buste*) Mr Paolo Rossi

signoria [siɲɲoˈria] SF (*Storia*) seignory, signoria

signorile [siɲɲoˈrile] AGG (*distinto*) refined, distinguished; (*quartiere*) exclusive; (*da signore*) gentlemanly, gentlemanlike; (*da signora*) ladylike

signorilità [siɲɲoriliˈta] SF (*raffinatezza*) refinement; (*eleganza*) elegance

signorina [siɲɲoˈrina] SF **1** (*giovane donna*) young woman; **è la signorina che abita al piano di sotto** she's the young woman who lives downstairs **2** (*rivolgendosi a qualcuno*): **buon giorno signorina** good morning; (*deferente*) good morning Madam; (*quando si conosce il nome*) good morning Miss (*o* Ms) X **3** (*parlando di qualcuno*): **la signorina Rossi sta male** Miss (*o* Ms) Rossi is ill **4** (*in lettere*): **Gentile signorina Rossi** Dear Madam; **Gentile** (*o* **Cara**) **Signorina Rossi** Dear Miss (*o* Ms) Rossi; **Gentile Signorina Anna Rossi** (*sulle buste*) Miss (*o* Ms) Anna Rossi

signorino [siɲɲoˈrino] SM young master

Sig.ra ABBR (= *signora*) Mrs, Ms

silenziatore [silentsjaˈtore] SM (*di arma, anche Tecn*) silencer

silenzio, -zi [siˈlentsjo] SM **1** (*gen*) silence; **fare silenzio** to be quiet, stop talking; **fate silenzio!** be quiet!; **restare in silenzio** to keep quiet; **in silenzio** in silence; **ascoltavano in silenzio** they listened in silence; **far passare qc sotto silenzio** to keep quiet about sth, hush sth up; **silenzio assenso** mechanism by which an official request is considered to have been granted if no answer is received within a certain period; **silenzio stampa** press blackout **2** (*calma, pace*) silence, still(ness), quiet; **nel silenzio della notte** in the still of the night **3** (*Mil*) lights out

silenzioso, -a [silenˈtsjoso] AGG (*gen*) silent, quiet; (*motore*) quiet; **è un ragazzo silenzioso** he's a quiet boy

silice [ˈsilitʃe] SF silica

silicio [siˈlitʃo] SM silicon

silicone [siliˈkone] SM silicone

sillaba [ˈsillaba] SF syllable; **dividere in sillabe** to divide into syllables; **non ho capito una sillaba di quello che hai detto** I haven't understood a single word of what you've said; **senza cambiare una sillaba** word for word

silurare [siluˈrare] /72/ VT (*Mil, anche fig: legge*) to torpedo; (: *progetto*) wreck; (: *persona di comando*) to remove from power, dismiss

siluro [siˈluro] SM (*Mil*) torpedo

SIM [sim] SIGLA F INV **1** (= *Società di Intermediazione Mobiliare*) brokerage company **2 SIM card** SIM card

simbiosi [simbiˈozi] SF INV (*Bio, anche fig*) symbiosis

simboleggiare [simboledˈdʒare] /62/ VT to symbolize, represent

simbolico, -a, -ci, -che [simˈboliko] AGG symbolic(al)

simbolismo [simboˈlizmo] SM symbolism

simbolo [ˈsimbolo] SM (*gen, anche Mat, Chim*) symbol; **simbolo di successo** status symbol

similare [simiˈlare] AGG similar

simile [ˈsimile] AGG **1** (*gen, analogo*) similar; **simile a** like, similar to; **hai la gonna simile alla mia** you've got a skirt like mine; **avevo un vestito simile una volta** I had a dress like that once; **abbiamo gusti simili** we have similar tastes **2** (*pegg: tale*) such; **una cosa simile** such a thing; **un uomo simile** such a man, a man like this **3 di simile, non ho mai visto niente di simile** I've never seen anything of the sort *o* like that; **è insegnante o qualcosa di simile** he's a teacher or something like that ♦ SM, SF **1** (*spec al pl: persona*) fellow being; **i suoi simili** one's fellow men; (*pari*) one's peers **2** (*oggetti*): **vendono vasi e simili** they sell vases and things like that

similitudine [similiˈtudine] SF **1** (*Retorica*) simile **2** (*Mat*) similarity

simmetria [simmeˈtria] SF symmetry

simmetrico, -a, -ci, -che [simˈmetriko] AGG symmetric(al)

simpatia [simpaˈtia] SF (*qualità*) pleasantness; (*inclinazione*) liking; **è di una simpatia!** she's extremely nice *o* pleasant!; **con simpatia** (*su lettera*) with much affection; **avere** *o* **provare simpatia per qn** to like sb, have a liking for sb; **prendere qn in simpatia** to take (a liking) to sb; **guadagnarsi la simpatia di qn** to gain sb's affection; **avere una simpatia per qn** (*esserne attratto*) to feel attracted to sb
❏ **simpatia** non si traduce mai con la parola inglese *sympathy*

simpatico, -a, -ci, -che [simˈpatiko] AGG **1** (*persona*) nice, pleasant, likeable; (*appartamento, albergo*) nice, pleasant; **è una ragazza simpatica** she's a nice girl; **è molto simpatico** I like him very much, I really like him; **non è simpatico quando succedono queste cose** it's not very nice when these things happen; **un modo di fare simpatico** a friendly manner **2 inchiostro simpatico** invisible ink
❏ **simpatico** non si traduce mai con la parola inglese *sympathetic*

simpatizzante [simpatidˈdzante] SM, SF sympathizer

simpatizzare [simpatidˈdzare] /72/ VI (*aus avere*) **simpatizzare con** to take a liking to
❏ **simpatizzare** non si traduce mai con la parola inglese *sympathize*

simposio, -si [simˈpɔzjo] SM symposium

simulacro [simuˈlakro] SM (*statua, immagine*) image, simulacrum; (*fig: traccia, parvenza*) semblance

simulare [simuˈlare] /72/ VT (*gen, anche Tecn*) to simulate; (*sentimento*) to fake, feign; **simulare uno svenimento** to pretend to faint; **simulare una malattia** to pretend to be ill, feign *o* fake illness

simulazione [simulatˈtsjone] SF (*vedi vb*) simulation; faking, feigning; **fu tutta una simulazione** it was all a pretence

simultaneo, -a [simulˈtaneo] AGG simultaneous

sin. ABBR (= *sinistra*) L

sinagoga [sinaˈgoga] SF synagogue

sinceramente [sintʃeraˈmente] AVV (*gen*) sincerely; (*francamente*) honestly, sincerely; **lo credo sinceramente** I honestly believe this; **sinceramente non riesco a capirti** I really don't understand you

sincerarsi [sintʃeˈrarsi] /72/ VIP: **sincerarsi (di qc)** to make sure (of sth)

sincerità [sintʃeriˈta] SF (*vedi agg*) sincerity; genuineness; **con tutta sincerità** in all sincerity, honestly

sincero, -a [sinˈtʃero] AGG **1** (*onesto*) sincere, honest; **essere sincero con qn** to be honest with sb; **sii sincero con me** be honest with me; **per essere sincero** to be honest, honestly **2** (*genuino*) real, genuine, true; **un amico sincero** a real friend

sincope [ˈsinkope] SF (*Ling*) syncope; (*Med*) fainting fit, blackout; (*Mus*) syncopation

sincronia [sinkroˈnia] SF (*di movimento*) synchronism

sincronico, -a, -ci, -che [sinˈkroniko] AGG synchronic

sincronizzare [sinkronidˈdzare] /72/ VT to synchronize

sindacale [sindaˈkale] AGG (*legge, lotta, riunione*) (trade) union attr; (*dottrina*) unionist; **una riunione sindacale** a trade-union meeting

sindacalista, -i, -e [sindakaˈlista] SM, SF trade unionist

sindacare [sinda'kare] /20/ VT 1 (controllare) to inspect 2 (fig: criticare) to criticize
sindacato [sinda'kato] SM (di lavoratori) (trade) union; (di datori di lavoro) association
sindaco, -ci ['sindako] SM mayor
sindrome ['sindrome] SF (Med) syndrome; **sindrome da affaticamento cronico** chronic fatigue syndrome, ME; **sindrome da immunodeficienza acquisita** acquired immune deficiency syndrome, AIDS; **sindrome di Peter Pan** Peter Pan syndrome; **sindrome di Stoccolma** Stockholm syndrome
sinergia, -gie [siner'dʒia] SF (anche fig) synergy
sinfonia [sinfo'nia] SF symphony
sinfonico, -a, -ci, -che [sin'fɔniko] AGG symphonic; (orchestra) symphony attr
singalese [singa'lese] AGG, SM, SF Sin(g)halese inv
Singapore [singa'pore] SF Singapore
singhiozzare [singjot'tsare] /72/ VI (aus avere) 1 (piangere) to sob 2 (avere il singhiozzo) to hiccup
singhiozzo [sin'gjottso] SM 1 (Med) hiccup; **avere il singhiozzo** to have (the) hiccups; **a singhiozzo** o **singhiozzi** (fig) by fits and starts; **sciopero a singhiozzo** on-off strike; **la macchina andava a singhiozzi** the car jolted o jerked along 2 (di pianto) sob; **scoppiare in singhiozzi** to burst into tears; **addormentarsi tra i singhiozzi** to sob o.s. to sleep
single ['siŋgol] SM INV, SF INV, AGG INV single
singolare [singo'lare] AGG 1 (Gramm) singular; **1ª persona singolare** 1st person singular 2 (insolito, particolare) remarkable, singular; (strano) strange, peculiar, odd ♦ SM 1 (Gramm) singular; **al singolare** in the singular 2 (Tennis): **un singolare** a singles (match)
singolarmente [singolar'mente] AVV 1 (separatamente) individually, one at a time 2 (in modo strano) strangely, peculiarly, oddly
singolo, -a ['singolo] AGG (gen) single, individual; **ogni singolo caso** every single case, each case; **ogni singolo individuo** each individual; **camera singola** single room ♦ SM 1 (individuo) individual 2 (Tennis): **un singolo** a singles (match); **il singolo maschile** the men's singles
sinistrato, -a [sinis'trato] AGG damaged; **zona sinistrata** disaster area ♦ SM, SF (vittima di catastrofe) disaster victim
sinistro, -a [si'nistro] AGG 1 (mano, piede) left; (parte, lato) left(-hand) 2 (bieco) sinister ♦ SM 1 (incidente) accident 2 (Pugilato) left; (Calcio): **tirare di sinistro** to kick with one's left foot
sino ['sino] PREP = **fino²**
sinonimo [si'nɔnimo] SM synonym ♦ AGG synonymous; **un nome che è sinonimo di qualità** a name which is synonymous with good quality
sintassi [sin'tassi] SF INV syntax
sintattico, -a, -ci, -che [sin'tattiko] AGG syntactic
sintesi ['sintezi] SF INV 1 (Chim, Filosofia) synthesis 2 (riassunto) summary, résumé; **fare la sintesi di qc** to make a summary of sth; **in sintesi** in brief, in short
sintetico, -a, -ci, -che [sin'tetiko] AGG 1 (conciso) brief, concise 2 (fibre, materiale) synthetic
sintetizzare [sintetid'dzare] /72/ VT (Bio, Chim) to synthesize; (riassumere: testo) to summarize
sintetizzatore [sintetiddza'tore] SM (Mus) synthesizer
sintomatico, -a, -ci, -che [sinto'matiko] AGG (Med, anche fig) symptomatic
sintomo ['sintomo] SM (Med, anche fig) symptom; **presentare i sintomi di** to show symptoms of
sintonia [sinto'nia] SF (Radio) tuning; **essere in sintonia con qn** (fig) to be on the same wavelength as sb
sintonizzare [sintonid'dzare] /72/ VT to tune (in); **sintonizzarsi** VIP: **sintonizzarsi su** to tune in to
sintonizzatore [sintoniddza'tore] SM tuner
sinuoso, -a [sinu'oso] AGG (gen) sinuous; (fiume, strada) winding, sinuous
sinusite [sinu'zite] SF (Med) sinusitis
sipario, -ri [si'parjo] SM (Teatro) curtain; **calare il sipario su qc** (fig: concluderla) to bring the curtain down over sth
sirena¹ [si'rena] SF (Mitol, anche fig) mermaid, siren

sirena² [si'rena] SF (segnale: di polizia, ambulanza, pompieri) siren; (: di fabbrica) whistle; **sirena d'allarme** (per incendio) fire alarm; (per furto) burglar alarm
Siria ['sirja] SF Syria
siriano, -a [si'rjano] AGG, SM, SF Syrian
siringa, -ghe [si'ringa] SF 1 (Med) syringe 2 (Culin) ≈ piping o forcing bag
sisma, -i ['sizma] SM earthquake
SISMI ['sizmi] SIGLA M (= Servizio per l'informazione e la sicurezza militari) military security service
sismico, -a, -ci, -che ['sizmiko] AGG (gen) seismic; (zona) earthquake attr
sismografo [siz'mɔgrafo] SM seismograph
sissignore [sissi'ɲore] AVV (a un superiore) yes, sir; (enfatico) yes indeed, of course
sistema, -i [sis'tema] SM 1 (Anat, Mat, Filosofia) system; **sistema decimale/nervoso/solare** decimal/nervous/solar system; **sistema operativo** operating system; **sistema di sicurezza** security system; **sistema operativo** (Inform) operating system 2 (metodo) method, way; (procedimento) process; **è meglio seguire questo sistema** it's better to follow this method; **è un nuovo sistema per imparare le lingue** it's a new way to learn languages; **il suo sistema di vita** his way of life; **trovare il sistema per fare qc** to find a way to do sth; **non è questo il sistema di lavorare!** this is no way to work!; **ti suggerisco di cambiare sistema** I suggest you go about things in a different way; **bel sistema di trovare la soluzione!** (iro) that's some solution! 3 (Totocalcio) system
sistemare [siste'mare] /72/ VT 1 (mettere a posto: stanza) to tidy (up), put in order; (: arredamento) to arrange; **mi piace come hai sistemato la casa** I like the way you've got the house; **ha sistemato tutti i libri sullo scaffale** he arranged all the books on the shelf; **sistemarsi i capelli** to tidy one's hair; **sistemarsi i vestiti** to straighten one's clothes 2 **sistemare qn** (trovargli lavoro) to fix sb up with a job; (trovargli marito o moglie) to marry sb off; (fare i conti con) to fix sb; **sistemare qn in un albergo** to fix sb up with a hotel; **l'abbiamo sistemato da noi** we put him up; **sistemare qn per le feste** to beat sb up; **ti sistemo io!** I'll soon sort you out! 3 (questione, faccenda) to settle, sort out; **sistemo tutto io** I'll see to everything; **abbiamo ancora una questione da sistemare** we've still got one question to settle; **sistemarsi** VR (persona: trovare alloggio) to find accommodation (Brit) o accommodations (USA); (: trovarsi un lavoro) to find a job, to get fixed up with a job; (: sposarsi) to get married; **è ora che ti sistemi** it's time you settled down; **si è sistemato in un albergo** he found a room in a hotel, he fixed himself up with a hotel; **si sistemò sul divano** he slept on the sofa; **sistemarsi** VIP (problema, questione) to be settled; **vedrai, tutto si sistemerà** you'll see, everything will work out
sistematicamente [sistematika'mente] AVV systematically
sistematico, -a, -ci, -che [siste'matiko] AGG systematic, methodical
sistemazione [sistemat'tsjone] SF 1 (di stanza, casa: assetto) tidying up; (: disposizione) arrangement, layout, order 2 **cercare una sistemazione** (alloggio) to look for accommodation (Brit) o accommodations (USA); (lavoro) to look for work o employment; **è solo una sistemazione provvisoria** it's only temporary accommodation 3 (di problema, questione) settlement
sito, -a ['sito] AGG (Amm) situated ♦ SM 1 (archeologico, su internet) site; un **sito internet** a web site 2 (letter) place
situare [situ'are] /72/ VT (casa) to site, situate, locate; (film, romanzo) to set; **la casa è situata su una collina/in riva al mare** the house is situated on a hill/on the coast
situazione [situat'tsjone] SF situation; **vista la tua situazione familiare** given your family situation o circumstances; **nella tua situazione** in your position o situation; **mi trovo in una situazione critica** I'm in a very difficult situation o position
ski-lift ['skilift] SM INV ski tow
slacciare [zlat'tʃare] /14/ VT (nodo) to untie, undo, unfasten; (scarpa) to unlace; (bottoni) to unfasten; (abito, cravatta, cappotto) to undo; **slacciarsi** VIP (vedi vt) to come untied, come undone; to come unlaced; to come unfastened
slanciare [zlan'tʃare] /14/ VT to hurl, fling, throw; **slanciarsi**

VR to throw o.s., hurl o.s.; **slanciarsi contro qn** to throw o.s. on sb; **slanciarsi nella mischia** to throw o.s. into the fray

slanciato, -a [zlan't∫ato] AGG (*persona*) slender, slim; (*colonna*) slender

slancio, -ci [ˈzlant∫o] SM dash, leap; (*fig*) surge; **darsi** o **prendere lo slancio** (*da fermo*) to spring up; (*correndo*) to bound forward; **in uno slancio d'affetto** in a burst o rush of affection; **abbracciare qn con slancio** to hug sb enthusiastically; **agire di slancio** to act impetuously; **uno slancio di generosità** a fit of generosity

slavato, -a [zlaˈvato] AGG (*colore*) washed out, faded; (*persona*) mousy; (*viso*) pale, colourless (*Brit*), colorless (*USA*)

slavina [zlaˈvina] SF snowslide

slavo, -a [ˈzlavo] AGG Slav(onic); **lingue slave** slavonic languages ♦ SM, SF Slav ♦ SM (*lingua*) Slavonic

sleale [zleˈale] AGG (*persona: non leale*) disloyal; (*concorrenza*) unfair; **essere sleale con** to be disloyal towards; **gioco sleale** (*Sport*) foul play; **essere sleale al gioco** to cheat

slealtà [zlealˈta] SF (*vedi agg*) disloyalty; unfairness

slegare [zleˈgare] /80/ VT (*gen*) to untie; (*liberare*) to free, release; **slegarsi** VR (*vedi vt*) to untie o.s.; to free o.s.

slip [zlip] SM INV (*mutandine*) briefs pl; (*da bagno: per uomo*) (swimming) trunks pl; (*: per donna*) bikini briefs pl

slitta [ˈzlitta] SF (*gen*) sledge; (*trainata*) sleigh

slittamento [zlittaˈmento] SM (*vedi vb*) slipping; skidding; sliding; fall; postponement; **slittamento salariale** wage drift

slittare [zlitˈtare] /72/ VI (*gen*) to slip, slide; (*automobile*) to skid; (*fig: partito*) to slide; (*: valuta*) to fall; (*: incontro, conferenza*) to be put off, be postponed

s.l.m. ABBR (= *sul livello del mare*) a.s.l. (= *above sea level*)

slogare [zloˈgare] /80/ VT (*Med: caviglia, polso*) to sprain; (*: spalla*) to dislocate; **mi si è slogata la caviglia** I've sprained my ankle

slogatura [zlogaˈtura] SF (*di spalla*) dislocation; (*di caviglia, polso*) sprain

sloggiare [zlodˈdʒare] /62/ VT: **sloggiare (da)** (*nemico*) to dislodge (from), drive out (of); (*inquilino*) to turn out (of) ♦ VI (*aus avere*) **sloggiare (da)** to move out (of); **sloggia!** (*fam*) shove off!, clear off!

Slovacchia [zloˈvakkja] SF Slovakia

slovacco, -a, -ci, -che [zloˈvakko] AGG, SM, SF Slovak, Slovakian; **la Repubblica Slovacca** the Slovak Republic

Slovenia [zloˈvenja] SF Slovenia

sloveno, -a [zloˈveno] AGG, SM, SF Slovene, Slovenian ♦ SM (*lingua*) Slovene

SM ABBR 1 (*Mil*) = **Stato Maggiore** 2 (= *Sua Maestà*) HM

smaccato, -a [zmakˈkato] AGG (*fig*) excessive

smacchiare [zmakˈkjare] /19/ VT to remove stains from

smacchiatore [zmakkjaˈtore] SM stain remover

smacco, -chi [ˈzmakko] SM humiliating defeat; **subire uno smacco** to be humiliated

smagliante [zmaʎˈʎante] AGG (*anche fig*) dazzling, brilliant; **un sorriso smagliante** a dazzling smile

smagliare [zmaʎˈʎare] /27/ VT (*catena, rete*) to break; (*calze*) to ladder (*Brit*), get a run in (*USA*); **smagliarsi** VIP (*calze*) to ladder (*Brit*), run (*USA*)

smagliatura [zmaʎʎaˈtura] SF 1 (*su calza*) ladder (*Brit*), run (*USA*) 2 (*sulla pelle*) stretch mark

smagrire [zmaˈgrire] /55/ VT to make thin VI (*aus essere*), **smagrirsi** VIP to get o grow thin, lose weight

smagrito, -a [zmaˈgrito] AGG: **essere smagrito** to have lost a lot of weight

smaliziato, -a [zmalitˈtsjato] AGG shrewd, cunning

smaltare [zmalˈtare] /72/ VT to enamel; (*ceramica*) to glaze; **smaltarsi le unghie** to put on nail polish o varnish (*Brit*)

smaltimento [zmaltiˈmento] SM (*vedi vt*) digestion; loss; selling off; draining away o off; disposal; **smaltimento dei rifiuti** waste disposal

smaltire [zmalˈtire] /55/ VT 1 (*cibo*) to digest; (*fig: peso*) to lose; (*: rabbia*) to get over; **smaltire la sbornia** to get over one's hangover, sober up; (*dormendo*) to sleep it off 2 (*merce*) to sell off 3 (*acque di scarico*) to drain away o off 4 (*rifiuti*) to dispose of

smalto [ˈzmalto] SM 1 (*per metalli*) enamel; (*per ceramica*)

glaze; **smalto per le unghie** nail polish, nail varnish (*Brit*); **mettersi lo smalto** to put on nail polish o varnish (*Brit*); **mi sto mettendo lo smalto** I'm putting on my nail polish 2 (*Anat: di denti*) enamel

smancerie [zmantʃeˈrie] SFPL mawkishness sg

smania [ˈzmanja] SF (*agitazione*) agitation, restlessness; (*fig: di potere, ricchezze*): **smania di** craving for, thirst for; **ha una gran smania di andarsene** he's desperate to leave; **avere la smania addosso** to have the fidgets

smaniare [zmaˈnjare] /19/ VI (*aus avere*) to be agitated, be restless; **smaniare di fare qc** (*fig*) to long o yearn to do sth

smantellamento [zmantellaˈmento] SM (*anche fig*) dismantling

smantellare [zmantelˈlare] /72/ VT (*gen*) to dismantle; (*anche fig: demolire*) to demolish

smarcare [zmarˈkare] (*Sport*) /20/ VT: **smarcare qn** to help sb to get away from his (o her) marker; **smarcarsi** VIP (*Sport*) to escape one's marker

smargiasso [zmarˈdʒasso] SM show-off; **fare lo smargiasso** to show off

smarrimento [zmarriˈmento] SM 1 (*perdita*) loss 2 (*fig: turbamento*) confusion, bewilderment; (*: sgomento*) dismay; **avere un attimo di smarrimento** to be momentarily nonplussed o bewildered

smarrire [zmarˈrire] /55/ VT (*perdere*) to lose, mislay; **ho smarrito il portafoglio** I've lost my wallet; **smarrire la strada** to lose one's way; **smarrirsi** VIP to get lost, lose one's way; **si sono smarriti nel bosco** they got lost in the woods

smarrito, -a [zmarˈrito] AGG 1 (*oggetto*) lost; **ufficio oggetti smarriti** lost property office (*Brit*), lost and found (*USA*) 2 (*fig: confuso: persona*) bewildered, nonplussed; (*: sguardo*) bewildered

smascherare [zmaskeˈrare] /72/ VT (*colpevole*) to unmask; (*intrigo, complotto*) to uncover; **smascherarsi** VR to give o.s. away

SME [zme] ABBR = **Stato Maggiore Esercito** ♦ SIGLA M (= *Sistema Monetario Europeo*) EMS (= *European Monetary System*)

smembrare [zmemˈbrare] /72/ VT (*gruppo, partito*) to split; **smembrarsi** VIP to split up

smemorato, -a [zmemoˈrato] AGG forgetful, absent-minded ♦ SM, SF forgetful person, absent-minded person

smentire [zmenˈtire] /55/ VT (*notizie*) to deny; (*testimonianza*) to refute; **il ministro ha smentito le voci** the minister denied the rumours; **smentisco quello che afferma il testimone** I refute what the witness is saying; **smentirsi** VR to be inconsistent; **non ti smentisci mai** you're always the same

smentita [zmenˈtita] SF (*di notizie*) denial; (*di testimonianza*) refutation

smeraldo [zmeˈraldo] SM, AGG INV emerald; **un anello con smeraldo** an emerald ring

smerciare [zmerˈtʃare] /14/ VT (*gen*) to sell; (*rimanenze*) to sell off

smercio, -ci [ˈzmertʃo] SM sale; **avere poco/molto smercio** to have poor/good sales

smerigliato, -a [zmeriʎˈʎato] AGG: **carta smerigliata** emery paper; **vetro smerigliato** frosted glass

smeriglio, -gli [zmeˈriʎʎo] SM emery

smesso, -a [ˈzmesso] PP di **smettere** ♦ AGG: **abiti smessi** cast-offs

smettere [ˈzmettere] VB IRREG /63/ VT (*gen*) to stop; (*studi*) to give up; (*vestiti*) to stop wearing; **smettila!** stop it!; **smettila di urlare!** stop shouting! ♦ VI (*aus avere*) (*interrompersi*) to stop, cease; **smettere di fare qc** to stop doing sth; **quando sono entrato hanno smesso di parlare** when I came in they stopped talking; **smettere di fumare** to stop o give up smoking; **sta cercando di smettere di fumare** he's trying to stop smoking; **smise di piovere** it stopped raining; **a che ora smetti stasera?** when do you finish (work) this evening?

smidollato, -a [zmidolˈlato] AGG (*fig: persona*) spineless ♦ SM, SF spineless person

smilitarizzazione [zmilitariddzatˈtsjone] SF demilitarization

smilzo, -a [ˈzmiltso] AGG thin, lean

sminuire [zminuˈire] /72/ VT (*diminuire*) to diminish, lessen;

(fig) to belittle, make light of, minimize; **sminuire l'importanza di qc** to play sth down; **sminuirsi** VR *(fig)* to run o.s. down, belittle o.s.

sminuzzare [zminut'tsare] /72/ VT *(gen)* to break into small pieces; *(pane)* to crumble; *(carta)* to tear into small pieces

smisi *ecc* ['zmizi] VB *vedi* **smettere**

smistamento [zmista'mento] SM *(di posta)* sorting; *(Ferr)* shunting

smistare [zmis'tare] /72/ VT *(posta)* to sort; *(Ferr)* to shunt; **hanno smistato gli alunni in varie classi** they sorted the pupils into different classes

smisurato, -a [zmizu'rato] AGG enormous, immense; *(eccessivo)* excessive; *(senza limiti)* boundless, immeasurable

smitizzare [zmitid'dzare] /72/ VT to debunk

smobilitare [zmobili'tare] /72/ VT to demobilize

smobilitazione [zmobilitat'tsjone] SF demobilization

smobilizzo [zmobi'liddzo] SM *(Comm)* disinvestment

smodato, -a [zmo'dato] AGG excessive, unrestrained

smoderato, -a [zmode'rato] AGG *(gen)* immoderate; **smoderato nel bere** intemperate

smog [zmɔg] SM INV smog

smoking ['smoukiŋ] SM INV dinner jacket *(Brit)*, tuxedo *(USA)*
❏ **smoking** non si traduce mai con la parola inglese *smoking*

smontare [zmon'tare] /72/ VT *(gen)* to take to pieces; *(macchina, mobile)* to dismantle, take to pieces; *(motore)* to strip (down); *(fig: persona: scoraggiare)* to discourage, dishearten ♦ VI *(aus essere)* **smontare (da)** *(bicicletta, treno)* to get off; *(sedia)* to get down (from); *(macchina)* to get out (of); **smontare da cavallo** to dismount; **a che ora smonti?** *(fig: da lavoro)* when do you knock off?, when do you finish (work)?; **smontarsi** VIP *(fig: persona: scoraggiarsi)* to lose heart, lose one's enthusiasm

smorfia ['zmɔrfja] SF *(gen)* **1** grimace; **una smorfia di dolore** a grimace of pain; **fare una smorfia di dolore** to grimace with pain; **fare smorfie** *(boccacce)* to make faces **2** *(atteggiamento lezioso)* simpering

smorfioso, -a [zmor'fjoso] AGG simpering ♦ SM, SF: **non fare lo smorfioso** stop simpering; **fare la smorfiosa con qn** *(civettare)* to flirt with sb

smorto, -a ['zmɔrto] AGG *(viso)* pale, wan; *(colore, stile)* dull; *(voce, faccia)* expressionless, lifeless; **ci vuole un colore un po' più smorto** we need a colour that's not quite so bright

smorzare [zmor'tsare] /72/ VT *(suoni)* to muffle, deaden; *(colori)* to tone down; *(luce)* to dim; *(sete)* to quench; *(entusiasmo)* to dampen; **smorzarsi** VIP *(suoni)* to die down, fade; *(luce)* to fade; *(entusiasmo)* to dampen

smosso, -a ['zmɔsso] PP *di* **smuovere**

smottamento [zmotta'mento] SM landslide

sms [essemme'esse] SIGLA M INV *(messaggino: = short message service)* text (message)

smunto, -a ['zmunto] AGG haggard, pinched

smuovere ['zmwɔvere] VB IRREG /66/ VT *(oggetto)* to move, shift; *(fig: persona: scuotere)* to rouse, stir; *(: dissuadere)*: **smuovere qn da qc** to dissuade o deter sb from sth; **smuoversi** VIP *(fig: persona: scuotersi)* to rouse o.s.; *(: dissuadersi)*: **smuoversi da qc** to change one's mind about sth

smussare [zmus'sare] /72/ VT *(angolo)* to round off, smooth down; *(lama)* to blunt; *(fig: carattere)* to soften; **smussarsi** VIP *(lama)* to become blunt; *(fig: carattere)* to soften

s.n. ABBR = **senza numero**

snaturato, -a [znatu'rato] AGG cruel, heartless, inhuman; **una madre snaturata** a heartless mother

snazionalizzare [znattsjonalid'dzare] /72/ VT to denationalize

snellimento [znelli'mento] SM *(di traffico)* speeding up; *(di procedura)* streamlining

snellire [znel'lire] /55/ VT *(persona)* to make slim; *(traffico)* to speed up; *(procedura)* to streamline; **snellirsi** VIP *(persona)* to (get) slim; *(traffico)* to speed up

snello, -a ['znello] AGG *(slanciato)* slim, slender; *(fig: stile)* easy, flowing

snervante [zner'vante] AGG *(attesa, lavoro)* exhausting; **l'attesa è stata snervante** it was a strain having to wait

snervare [zner'vare] /72/ VT to wear out, enervate

snidare [zni'dare] /72/ VT *(selvaggina, anche fig)* to drive out, flush out; *(uccelli)* to flush (out)

sniffare [znif'fare] /72/ VT *(fam: cocaina)* to snort

snobbare [znob'bare] /72/ VT to snub

snobismo [zno'bizmo] SM snobbery

snocciolare [znottʃo'lare] /72/ VT *(frutta)* to stone; *(fig: bugie, lamentele)* to rattle off; *(: verità)* to blab; *(: fam: soldi)* to shell out

snodabile [zno'dabile] AGG *(lampada)* adjustable; *(tubo, braccio)* hinged; **rasoio con testina snodabile** swivel-head razor

snodare [zno'dare] /72/ VT *(nodo)* to untie, undo; *(membra)* to loosen (up), limber up; **snodarsi** VIP *(tubatura)* to be hinged; *(fig: strada, fiume)* to wind

snodato, -a, snodata AGG **1** *(articolazione, persona)* flexible **2** *(fune ecc)* undone

snowboard [zno'bord] SM INV snowboard

SO SIGLA = **Sondrio** ♦ ABBR *(= Sud-Ovest)* SW

so [so] VB *vedi* **sapere**

soave [so'ave] AGG *(voce, maniere)* gentle; *(volto)* delicate, sweet; *(musica)* soft, sweet; *(profumo)* delicate
❏ **soave** non si traduce mai con la parola inglese *suave*

soavità [soavi'ta] SF *(vedi agg)* gentleness; delicacy; sweetness; softness

sobbalzare [sobbal'tsare] /72/ VI *(aus avere)* *(veicolo)* to bump, jolt, jerk; *(persona: trasalire)* to jump, start

sobbalzo [sob'baltso] SM *(vedi vb)* bump, jolt, jerk; jump, start

sobbarcarsi [sobbar'karsi] /20/ VR: **sobbarcarsi a** to undertake, take on

sobborgo, -ghi [sob'borgo] SM suburb

sobillare [sobil'lare] /72/ VT to stir up, incite

sobrio, -ria, -ri, -rie ['sɔbrjo] AGG *(persona)* sober, moderate; *(non ubriaco)* sober; *(colore, stile)* sober, simple; *(vita)* moderate, simple; **vestire in modo sobrio** to dress soberly

Soc. ABBR *(= Società)* Soc.

socchiudere [sok'kjudere] /22/ VT IRREG *(occhi)* to half-close; *(porta, finestra)* to leave ajar; **ha socchiuso la porta** he left the door ajar; **ho socchiuso gli occhi** I half-closed my eyes

socchiuso, -a [sok'kjuso] PP *di* **socchiudere** ♦ AGG *(porta, finestra)* ajar; *(occhi)* half-closed; **lascia la porta socchiusa** leave the door ajar; **aveva gli occhi socchiusi** his eyes were half-closed

soccombere [sok'kombere] /29/ VI *vb dif* to succumb, give way

soccorrere [sok'korrere] /28/ VT IRREG to help, assist

soccorritore, -trice [sokkorri'tore] SM, SF rescuer

soccorso, -a [sok'korso] PP *di* **soccorrere** ♦ SM *(gen)* help, assistance, aid; *(di vittime di terremoto ecc)* rescue; **organizzare soccorsi per i terremotati** to organize relief o aid for the earthquake victims; **prestare soccorso a qn** to help o assist sb; **nessuno si è fermato a prestare soccorso** nobody stopped to help; **venire in soccorso di qn** to help sb, come to sb's aid; **operazioni di soccorso** rescue operations; **omissione di soccorso** failure to offer assistance; **pronto soccorso** *(assistenza)* first aid; *(reparto)* casualty; **soccorso stradale** breakdown service

socialdemocratico, -a, -ci, -che [sotʃaldemo'kratiko] AGG Social Democratic ♦ SM, SF Social Democrat

sociale [so'tʃale] AGG **1** *(gen)* social; **la realtà sociale** the reality of life **2** *(di ditta, società)* company *attr* **3** *(di associazione)* club *attr*, association *attr*

socialismo [sotʃa'lizmo] SM socialism

socialista, -i, -e [sotʃa'lista] AGG, SM, SF socialist

socializzare [sotʃalid'dzare] /72/ VI *(aus avere)* to socialize

società [sotʃe'ta] SF INV **1** *(comunità)* society; **vivere in società** to live in society; **l'alta società** high society; **la buona società** polite society; **la società dei consumi** the consumer society; **giochi di società** parlour games **2** *(associazione)* association, club, society; **una società segreta** a secret society; **società sportiva** sports club **3** *(Comm)* company, firm; **in società con qn** in partnership with sb; **mettersi in società con qn** to go into business with sb; **si è messo in società con suo fratello** he went into business with his brother; **società per azioni** joint-stock company; **società finanziaria** holding company; **società di intermediazione mobiliare**

brokerage company; **società in nome collettivo** unlimited company; **società a responsabilità limitata** *type of limited liability company*

socievole [soˈtʃevole] AGG sociable

socievolezza [sotʃevoˈlettsa] SF sociability, sociableness

socio, -ci [ˈsɔtʃo] SM 1 (*Comm*) partner, associate (*USA*); **socio non attivo** silent partner; **"Bianchi e Soci"** "Bianchi & Co" 2 (*membro*) member; (*di società scientifiche*) fellow; **farsi socio di un circolo** to become a member of a club

sociologia [sotʃoloˈdʒia] SF sociology

sociologo, -a, -gi, -ghe [soˈtʃɔlogo] SM, SF sociologist

soda [ˈsɔda] SF 1 (*Chim*) soda; **soda caustica** caustic soda 2 (*per bevande*) soda (water)

sodalizio, -zi [sodaˈlittsjo] SM association, society

soddisfacente [soddisfaˈtʃɛnte] AGG satisfactory

soddisfare [soddisˈfare] VB IRREG /41/ VT, VI (*aus avere*) **soddisfare (a)** (*gen*) to satisfy; (*impegno*) to fulfil; (*richiesta*) to comply with, meet; **il mio lavoro non mi soddisfa** my job doesn't satisfy me

soddisfatto, -a [soddisˈfatto] PP *di* **soddisfare** ♦ AGG satisfied, pleased; **essere soddisfatto di** to be satisfied *o* pleased with; **sono soddisfatto del risultato** I'm pleased with the result; **mostrarsi soddisfatto** to show one's satisfaction

soddisfazione [soddisfatˈtsjone] SF (*gen, di offesa*) satisfaction; **avere la soddisfazione di** to have the satisfaction of; **dare la soddisfazione a qn di** to give sb the satisfaction of; **la vita mi ha dato tante soddisfazioni!** life has given me so much satisfaction!

sodio [ˈsɔdjo] SM (*Chim*) sodium

sodo, -a [ˈsɔdo] AGG (*terreno*) hard, firm; (*corpo*) firm; **uova sode** hard-boiled eggs ♦ SM: **venire al sodo** to come to the point; **vieni al sodo!** come to the point! ♦ AVV: **picchiare sodo** to hit hard; **dormire sodo** to sleep soundly; **lavorare sodo** to work hard

sofà [soˈfa] SM INV sofa

sofferenza [soffeˈrɛntsa] SF 1 (*gen*) suffering; **dopo anni di sofferenze** (*povertà, stenti*) after years of hardship 2 (*Comm*): **in sofferenza** unpaid

sofferto, -a [sofˈfɛrto] PP *di* **soffrire** ♦ AGG (*vittoria*) hard-fought, hard-won; (*distacco*) painful; **una decisione sofferta** a painful decision; **ha un viso sofferto** she has the face of someone who has suffered

soffiare [sofˈfjare] /19/ VT 1 (*gen*) to blow; **soffiarsi il naso** to blow one's nose; **si è soffiata il naso rumorosamente** she blew her nose loudly; **soffiare il vetro** to blow glass 2 (*fig: fam: rubare*): **soffiare qn/qc a qn** to pinch *o* steal sb/sth from sb ♦ VI (*aus avere*) (*gen*) to blow; (*sbuffare*) to puff (and blow); **soffiava un forte vento** a strong wind was blowing; **soffiare sul fuoco** (*fig*) to fan the flames

soffiata [sofˈfjata] SF (*fam*) tip-off; **fare una soffiata alla polizia** to tip off the police

soffice [ˈsoffitʃe] AGG soft

soffietto [sofˈfjetto] SM 1 (*mantice per fuoco*) bellows *pl* 2 **porta a soffietto** folding door

soffio, -fi [ˈsoffjo] SM 1 (*di aria, vento*) breath; **non c'era neanche un soffio di vento** there wasn't a breath of wind; **in un soffio** (*fig*) in a flash; **per un soffio** (*fig*) by a hair's breadth 2 (*Med*) murmur; **soffio cardiaco** heart murmur

soffione [sofˈfjone] SM (*pianta*) dandelion

soffitta [sofˈfitta] SF (*solaio*) attic, loft; (*appartamento*) attic flat (*Brit*) *o* apartment (*USA*)

soffitto [sofˈfitto] SM ceiling

soffocante [soffoˈkante] AGG (*caldo, atmosfera*) suffocating, stifling; (*fig: persona*): **ma sei proprio soffocante!** you're stifling me!

soffocare [soffoˈkare] /20/ VT (*gen*) to suffocate; (*fiamme*) to smother, put out; (*fig: sommossa*) to suppress; (*sentimento*) to stifle, repress; (*sbadiglio*) to stifle; **ho rischiato di soffocare** I nearly suffocated; **qui dentro si soffoca** it's stifling in here; **soffocare qn di baci/d'affetto** to smother sb with kisses/ with affection

soffocazione [soffokatˈtsjone] SF (*gen*) suffocation; (*di sommossa*) suppression

soffriggere [sofˈfriddʒere] VB IRREG /56/ VT, VI (*aus avere*) to fry lightly

soffrire [sofˈfrire] VB IRREG /70/ VT 1 (*patire*) to suffer; **soffrire la fame/sete** to suffer (from) hunger/thirst; **soffrire le pene dell'inferno** (*fig*) to go through *o* suffer hell 2 (*sopportare*) to stand, bear; **non lo posso soffrire** I can't stand him ♦ VI (*aus avere*) 1 to suffer, be in pain; **sta soffrendo molto** he's suffering a lot; **la tua vita privata ne soffrirà** your private life will suffer 2 (*Med*): **soffrire di qc** to suffer from sth; **soffre di frequenti mal di testa** he suffers from frequent headaches

soffritto, -a [sofˈfritto] PP *di* **soffriggere** ♦ SM (*Culin*) fried mixture of herbs, bacon and onions

soffuso, -a [sofˈfuzo] AGG (*luce*) suffused, diffused

sofisticare [sofistiˈkare] /20/ VT (*vino*) to adulterate

sofisticato, -a [sofistiˈkato] AGG 1 (*vino*) adulterated 2 (*macchina, persona*) sophisticated

sofisticazione [sofistikatˈtsjone] SF (*di vino*) adulteration

software [ˈsɔftˈwɛə] SM INV: **software applicativo** applications package

soggettivo, -a [soddʒetˈtivo] AGG subjective

soggetto¹, -a [sodˈdʒɛtto] AGG: **soggetto a** (*a variazioni, danni*) subject *o* liable to; **soggetto a tassa** taxable; **andare** *o* **essere soggetto a frequenti mal di testa** to be prone to frequent headaches

soggetto² [sodˈdʒɛtto] SM 1 (*argomento*) subject, topic; **recitare a soggetto** (*Teatro*) to improvise 2 (*Gramm*) subject 3 (*persona: Med*) subject; (: *pegg*) sort; **è un cattivo soggetto** (*pegg*) he's a bad sort

soggezione [soddʒetˈtsjone] SF 1 (*imbarazzo, disagio*) uneasiness; **incutere soggezione a qn, mettere qn in soggezione** to make sb feel uneasy; **avere soggezione di qn** to feel uneasy with sb, be ill at ease in sb's presence, be in awe of sb; **aveva soggezione del fratello maggiore** he was in awe of his older brother 2 (*sottomissione*) subjection

sogghignare [soggiɲˈɲare] /15/ VI (*aus avere*) to sneer

sogghigno [sogˈɡiɲɲo] SM sneer

soggiacere [soddʒaˈtʃere] /57/ VI IRREG (*aus essere*) **soggiacere a** (*leggi*) to be subject to; (*essere sottomesso a*) to be subjected to, submit to

soggiogare [soddʒoˈɡare] /80/ VT to subdue, subjugate

soggiornare [soddʒorˈnare] /72/ VI (*aus avere*) to stay

soggiorno [sodˈdʒorno] SM 1 (*permanenza*) stay; **un soggiorno di due settimane a Londra** a two-week stay in London; **luogo di soggiorno** holiday (*Brit*) *o* vacation (*USA*) resort 2 (*stanza*) living room, sitting room (*Brit*), lounge (*Brit*) 3 (*mobili*) living-room suite

soggiungere [sodˈdʒundʒere] /5/ VT IRREG to add

soggiunto, -a [sodˈdʒunto] PP *di* **soggiungere**

soglia [ˈsɔʎʎa] SF 1 (*di porta*) doorstep; (*fig*) threshold; **varcare la soglia** to cross the threshold; **essere sulla soglia della vecchiaia** to be on the threshold of old age 2 (*Geol*) sill

sogliola [ˈsɔʎʎola] SF (*pesce*) sole

sognante [soɲˈɲante] AGG dreamy

sognare [soɲˈɲare] /15/ VT 1 **sognare qc** to dream of *o* about sth; **ho sognato di essere sulla luna** I dreamt I was on the moon; **stanotte ti ho sognato** I dreamt about you last night; **ha sempre sognato una casa così/di avere una casa così** he has always dreamt of a house like that/of having a house like that 2 (*fig: fam*): **non me lo sogno nemmeno!** I wouldn't dream of it!; **te lo puoi sognare!** you can forget it!, in your dreams!; **non te lo sono mica sognato!** I didn't dream it up! ♦ VI (*aus avere*) to dream; **sognare a occhi aperti** to daydream; **sognarsi** VIP: **sognarsi di qn/qc** to dream of sb/sth

sognatore, -trice [soɲɲaˈtore] SM, SF dreamer

sogno [ˈsoɲɲo] SM dream; **un brutto sogno** a bad dream; **fare un sogno** to have a dream; **ho fatto uno strano sogno** I had a strange dream; **un sogno ad occhi aperti** a daydream; **una crociera/casa di sogno** a dream cruise/house; **nemmeno** *o* **neanche per sogno!** not on your life!, no way!

soia [ˈsɔja] SF (*Bot*) soya

sol [sɔl] SM INV (*Mus*) G; (*solfeggiando la scala*) so(h)

solaio, -ai [soˈlajo] SM (*soffitta*) attic, loft

solamente [solaˈmente] AVV only, just

solare [soˈlare] AGG 1 (*Astron*) solar; (*crema*) sun *attr*; **crema**

solare sun cream; **energia solare** solar power; **luce solare** sunlight; **pannelli solari** solar panels; **plesso solare** (*Anat*) solar plexus **2** (*fig: ragionamento*) clear; **una persona solare** a sunny-natured person

solcare [sol'kare] /20/ VT (*terreno, anche fig: mari*) to plough (*Brit*), plow (*USA*)

solco, -chi ['solko] SM (*di aratro*) furrow; (*di ruota*) track, rut; (*di nave*) wake; (*su disco*) groove; (*sulla fronte*) wrinkle, furrow

soldato [sol'dato] SM soldier; **fare il soldato** to serve in the army; **andare (a fare il) soldato** to enlist (in the army); **soldato di leva** conscript; **soldato semplice** private

soldo ['soldo] SM **1** (*quattrino, moneta*) penny, cent (*USA*); **non ho un soldo** I haven't got a penny; **non vale un soldo bucato** it isn't worth a penny; **per quattro soldi** for next to nothing; **è roba da pochi soldi** it's cheap stuff **2 soldi** SMPL (*denaro*) money *sg*; **fare soldi** to make money; **essere pieno di soldi** to have lots of money; **buttare via i soldi** to throw one's money away; **avere un sacco di soldi** to be loaded, to be rolling in money

sole ['sole] SM (*astro*) sun; (*luce*) sun(light); (*calore*) sun(shine); **preferirei stare al sole** I'd rather stay in the sun; **c'è il sole** the sun is shining; **una giornata di sole** a sunny day; **prendere il sole** to sunbathe; **al calar del sole** at sunset; **al sorgere del sole** at sunrise; **il Sole che ride** (*Pol*) *symbol of the Italian Green Party*
❏ **sole** non si traduce mai con la parola inglese *sole*

soleggiato, -a [soled'dʒato] AGG sunny; **il mio appartamento è più soleggiato del suo** my apartment's sunnier than hers

solenne [so'lɛnne] AGG (*giuramento, voto*) solemn; (*scherz: ceffone*) almighty, sound

solennità [solenni'ta] SF **1** (*di cerimonia*) solemnity **2** (*festività*) holiday, feast day

solere [so'lere] *vb dif* /108/ VT: **solere fare qc** to be in the habit of doing sth; **soleva raccontare lunghe storie della guerra** he used to tell long stories about the war ♦ VB IMPERS (*aus essere*) **come suole accadere** as is usually the case, as usually happens; **come si suol dire** as they say

solerte [so'lɛrte] AGG diligent

solerzia [so'lertsja] SF diligence

soletta [so'letta] SF **1** (*per scarpe*) insole **2** (*di sci*) running surface **3** (*Edil*) slab

solfato [sol'fato] SM (*Chim*) sulphate (*Brit*), sulfate (*USA*); **solfato ferroso** iron sulphate *o* sulfate; **solfato di rame** copper sulphate *o* sulfate

solforico, -a, -ci, -che [sol'fɔriko] AGG (*Chim*) sulphuric (*Brit*), sulfuric (*USA*); **acido solforico** sulphuric *o* sulfuric acid

solfuro [sol'furo] SM (*Chim*) sulphur (*Brit*), sulfur (*USA*)

solidale [soli'dale] AGG in agreement; **essere solidale con qn** (*essere d'accordo*) to be in agreement with sb; (*appoggiare*) to be behind sb

solidarietà [solidarje'ta] SF solidarity

solidificare [solidifi'kare] /20/ VT, VI (*aus essere*), **solidificarsi** VIP to solidify

solidità [solidi'ta] SF (*vedi agg*) solidity; firmness; strength; soundness; reliability

solido, -a ['solido] AGG **1** (*non liquido*) solid **2** (*robusto: oggetto, muscoli, fede*) firm, strong; (*gambe, muri*) sturdy, sound; (*nervi, salute*) sound, strong; (*amicizia, matrimonio*) sound, solid; (*società*) reliable, sound ♦ SM (*Mat*) solid

soliloquio, -qui [soli'lɔkwjo] SM (*Teatro*) soliloquy; (*discorso tra sé e sé*) monologue

solista, -i, -e [so'lista] AGG solo ♦ SM, SF soloist

solitamente [solita'mente] AVV usually, generally, as a rule

solitario, -ria, -ri, -rie [soli'tarjo] AGG (*gen*) solitary; (*passante, navigatore*) lone, solitary; (*luogo, strada*) lonely, deserted, secluded; (*vita*) lonely, secluded; **una strada buia e solitaria** a dark, lonely road; **è un tipo solitario** he is a loner ♦ SM, SF (*persona*) solitary person, loner ♦ SM **1** (*brillante*) solitaire **2** (*Carte*) patience; **sto facendo un solitario** I'm playing patience

solito, -a ['solito] AGG usual; **essere solito fare qc** to be in the habit of doing sth; **è solito mangiare alle otto** he usually eats at eight o'clock, he is in the habit of eating at eight o'clock; **era solito passeggiare di notte** he used to go for

walks during the night; **è sempre la solita storia!** it's always the same old story!; **siamo alle solite!** (*fam*) here we go again! ♦ SM: **di solito** usually, generally, as a rule; **di solito mi alzo alle sette** I usually get up at seven o'clock; (**come**) **al solito** as usual; **più tardi del solito** later than usual

solitudine [soli'tudine] SF **1** (*tranquillità*) solitude; (*l'essere solo*) loneliness; (*di posto*) loneliness **2** (*luogo solitario*) solitude, wilderness

sollazzare [sollat'tsare] /72/ VT to entertain; **sollazzarsi** VIP to amuse o.s.

sollazzo [sol'lattso] SM amusement

sollecitare [sollet ʃi'tare] /72/ VT **1** (*affrettare: pratica, lavoro, telefonata*) to speed up; (: *persona*) to urge on; (: *chiedere con insistenza*) to press for, request urgently; **sollecitare qn perché faccia qc** to urge sb to do sth **2** (*stimolare: fantasia*) to stimulate, rouse **3** (*Tecn*) to stress

sollecitazione [sollet ʃitat'tsjone] SF **1** (*richiesta*) request, entreaty; (*fig: stimolo*) stimulus, incentive; **lettera di sollecitazione** (*Comm*) reminder **2** (*Tecn*) stress

sollecito, -a [sol'let ʃito] AGG prompt, quick; **essere sollecito nel fare qc** to be prompt in doing sth ♦ SM (*Comm*) reminder; **sollecito di pagamento** payment reminder

sollecitudine [sollet ʃi'tudine] SF promptness, speed

solleticare [solleti'kare] /20/ VT (*gen*) to tickle; (*fig: curiosità*) to arouse; (: *fantasia*) to excite; (: *appetito*) to whet

solletico [sol'letiko] SM tickling; **fare il solletico a qn** to tickle sb; **mi ha fatto il solletico** he tickled me; **soffrire il solletico** to be ticklish; **soffro molto il solletico** I'm very ticklish

sollevamento [solleva'mento] SM **1** (*gen*) raising, lifting; **c'è stato un sollevamento del terreno** (*Geol*) the ground has risen; **sollevamento pesi** (*Sport*) weightlifting **2** (*rivolta*) revolt, rebellion

sollevare [solle'vare] /72/ VT **1** (*peso, occhi, testa*) to lift, raise; (*polvere, sabbia*) to raise; (*con argani*) to hoist; **non riesco a sollevare la valigia** I can't lift the suitcase; **ha sollevato gli occhi dal libro** she raised her eyes from the book; **sollevare da terra** to lift up, lift off the ground; **il motoscafo sollevò delle onde** the motorboat made waves; **sollevare un'obiezione** (*fig*) to raise an objection **2** (*fig: dar conforto*) to comfort, cheer up; **sollevare il morale a qn** to raise sb's morale **3** (*rendere libero*): **sollevare qn da** (*incarico*) to dismiss sb from; (*fatica*) to relieve sb of; **sollevare qn da un peso** (*fig*) to take a load off sb's mind **4** (*fig: folla*) to rouse, stir up, stir (to revolt); **sollevarsi** VIP **1** (*persona*) to get up; **sollevati un po'** (*dal letto*) sit up a little; (*da una sedia*) stand up a minute; **sollevarsi da terra** (*persona*) to get up from the ground; (*aereo*) to take off **2** (*vento, polvere*) to rise; (*nebbia*) to lift, clear; **si sollevarono onde enormi** the sea became very rough **3** (*fig: riprendersi*) to feel better, recover; **sollevarsi da qc** (*malattia, spavento*) to get over sth; **sentirsi sollevato** to feel relieved **4** (*fig: truppe, popolo*) to rise up, rebel

sollievo [sol'ljevo] SM relief; (*conforto*) comfort; **con mio grande sollievo** to my great relief; **un sospiro di sollievo** a sigh of relief; **ho tirato un sospiro di sollievo** I heaved a sigh of relief

solo, -a ['solo] AGG **1** (*senza compagnia*) alone, on one's (*o* its *ecc*) own, by oneself (*o* itself *ecc*); (*isolato*) lonely; **da solo** (*senza aiuti*) by oneself (*o* himself *ecc*); **entra pure, sono solo** please come in, I'm alone *o* there's no-one with me; **vive (da) solo** he lives on his own; **è tanto solo** he's very lonely; **ci vado da sola** I'll go on my own; **riesci a farlo da solo?** can you do it by yourself?; **parlare da solo** to talk to oneself **2** (*senza altri*): **finalmente soli!** alone at last!; **vogliono stare sole** they want to be alone; **possiamo vederci da soli?** can I see you in private? **3** (*seguito da sostantivo*) only; **il solo motivo** the only reason; **c'è un solo libro** there is only one book; **ha un solo figlio maschio** she has only one son; **è il solo proprietario** he's the sole proprietor; **essi sono una persona sola** they are as one; **non si vive di solo pane** man does not live by bread alone; **l'incontrò due sole volte** he only met him twice; **la sola idea mi fa tremare** the very *o* mere thought of it is enough to make me tremble; **la mia sola speranza è che...** my only hope is that ...; **non un solo istante ho creduto che...** I didn't believe for a single moment that ... **4** (*con agg numerale*): **veniamo noi tre soli** just *o* only the three of us are coming ♦ AVV (*soltanto*) only, just; **resto solo un giorno** I'm only staying one day; **l'ho incontrato solo due volte** I've only met him twice; **mancavi solo tu** you were the only one missing, you were the only one who wasn't there; **non solo ha negato, ma...** not only did he deny it, but ... ♦ **solo che** CONG but; **l'ho visto, solo che non son riuscito a parlargli** I saw him, but I didn't get a chance to speak to him ♦ SM, SF: **sono il solo a poter giudicare** I'm the only one who can judge; **è la sola che ha chiesto notizie** she was the only one to ask for news ♦ **a solo** SM (*Mus*) = **assolo**

solstizio, -zi [sol'stittsjo] SM solstice

soltanto [sol'tanto] AVV (*gen*) only; **c'era soltanto lui** there was only him; **restano qui soltanto 2 giorni** they are only staying 2 days; **sono arrivato soltanto ieri** I only arrived yesterday; **chiedo soltanto questo!** that's all I ask! ♦ CONG but, only; **vorrei, soltanto (che) non posso** I would like to, but I can't; **ha la macchina, soltanto temo che non funzioni** he has a car, only *o* but I don't think it's working

solubile [so'lubile] AGG soluble; **caffè solubile** instant coffee

soluzione [solut'tsjone] SF (*gen, anche Mat, Chim*) solution; (*di indovinello*) answer; **non riesco a trovare una soluzione** I can't find a solution; **non c'è altra soluzione!** there's no alternative!; **senza soluzione di continuità** uninterruptedly

solvente [sol'vɛnte] AGG (*Chim*) solvent ♦ SM (*Chim*) solvent; **solvente per unghie** nail polish *o* nail varnish (*Brit*) remover; **solvente per vernici** paint remover *o* stripper

solvenza [sol'vɛntsa] SF (*Comm*) solvency

soma ['sɔma] SF burden, load; **bestia da soma** pack animal, beast of burden

Somalia [so'malja] SF Somalia

somalo, -a ['sɔmalo] AGG, SM, SF Somali, Somalian ♦ SM (*lingua*) Somali

somaro [so'maro] SM (*Zool*) donkey, ass; (*fig*) dunce; **sei un somaro!** you're an idiot!

somatico, -a, -ci, -che [so'matiko] AGG (*Bio*) somatic

somiglianza [somiʎ'ʎantsa] SF (*tra cose*) similarity; (*tra persone*) resemblance

somigliare [somiʎ'ʎare] /27/ VI (*aus avere*) **somigliare a** to resemble, look like, be like; **somiglia a sua sorella** she looks like *o* resembles her sister; **somiglio moltissimo a mia madre** I look very like my mother; **somiglia al mio** it looks like mine; **somigliarsi** VR (*uso reciproco*) to be alike, look alike, resemble each other; **non si somigliano affatto** they don't look at all like each other

somma ['somma] SF 1 (*Mat*) addition; (*risultato*) sum; (*fig: sostanza*) conclusion; **sai fare le somme?** can you add up?; **tirare le somme** (*fig*) to sum up; **tirate le somme** (*fig*) all things considered 2 (*di denaro*) amount, sum (of money); **una grossa somma di denaro** a large sum of money

sommare [som'mare] /72/ VT (*Mat*) to add up, add together; (*aggiungere*) to add; **somma i due numeri** add the two numbers together; **tutto sommato** (*fig*) all things considered, all in all; **tutto sommato sono contento di essere venuto** all in all I'm glad I came ♦ VI (*aus avere o essere*) (*ammontare*): **sommare a** to add up to, amount to

sommario, -ria, -ri, -rie [som'marjo] AGG 1 (*esame*) brief; (*lavoro*) rough; **racconto sommario** brief summary 2 (*Dir*) summary ♦ SM (*breve riassunto*) summary; (*compendio*) compendium; **sommario del telegiornale** (*TV*) news headlines *pl*

sommergere [som'mɛrdʒere] /59/ VT IRREG (*barca*) to submerge; **le onde hanno sommerso la barca** the waves swamped the boat; **sommergere qn di** (*doni, gentilezze*) to overwhelm sb with; (*baci*) to smother sb with

sommergibile [sommer'dʒibile] AGG submersible ♦ SM (*Naut*) submarine

sommerso, -a [som'mɛrso] PP *di* **sommergere** ♦ AGG (*tesori, città*) sunken; **l'economia sommersa** the black economy ♦ SM: **il sommerso** (*economia*) the black economy

sommesso, -a [som'messo] AGG soft, low, subdued

somministrare [somminis'trare] /72/ VT to give, administer

sommità [sommi'ta] SF INV summit, top; (*fig*) peak, height

sommo, -a ['sommo] AGG (*grado, livello*) highest; (*rispetto*) highest, greatest; (*poeta, artista*) great, outstanding; **il**

Sommo Pontefice the Supreme Pontiff; **per sommi capi** in short, in brief ♦ SM (*fig*) peak, height

sommossa [som'mɔssa] SF uprising, revolt

sommozzatore [sommottsa'tore] SM (deep-sea) diver; (*Mil*) frogman

sonaglio, -gli [so'naʎʎo] SM (*di mucche*) bell; (*per bambini*) rattle

sonante [so'nante] AGG: **denaro *o* moneta sonante** (ready) cash

sonare ecc [so'nare] = **suonare**

sonda ['sonda] SF (*Med, Meteor, Aer*) probe; (*Mineralogia*) drill ♦ AGG INV: **pallone sonda** weather balloon

sondaggio, -gi [son'daddʒo] SM (*vedi sb*) sounding; drilling, boring; probing; survey; **sondaggio d'opinioni** opinion poll

sondare [son'dare] /72/ VT (*Naut*) to sound; (*Mineralogia*) to drill, to bore; (*Meteor, Med*) to probe; (*fig: opinione*) to survey, poll

sonetto [so'netto] SM sonnet

sonnambulo, -a [son'nambulo] SM, SF somnambulist, sleepwalker

sonnecchiare [sonnek'kjare] /19/ VI (*aus avere*) to doze, drowse, nod

sonnellino [sonnel'lino] SM nap; **fare un sonnellino** to have a nap

sonnifero [son'nifero] SM (*pillola*) sleeping pill *o* drug; (*gocce*) sleeping draught (*Brit*) *o* draft (*USA*)

sonno ['sonno] SM 1 (*il dormire*) sleep; **avere il sonno pesante/leggero** to be a heavy/light sleeper; **parli durante il sonno** you talk in your sleep; **prendere sonno** to fall asleep; **ho perso 4 ore di sonno** I lost 4 hours' sleep; **il sonno eterno** (*euf*) eternal rest 2 (*bisogno di dormire*) sleepiness, sleep; **avere sonno** to be sleepy; **cascare dal sonno** to be asleep on one's feet; **far venire sonno a qn** (*fig*) to send sb to sleep

sonnolento, -a [sonno'lɛnto] AGG (*persona*) sleepy, drowsy; (*movimenti*) sluggish

sonnolenza [sonno'lɛntsa] SF sleepiness, drowsiness

sono ['sono] VB *vedi* **essere**

sonorizzare [sonorid'dzare] /72/ VT (*Ling*) to voice; (*Cine*) to add a soundtrack to

sonoro, -a [so'nɔro] AGG 1 (*ambiente*) resonant; (*voce*) sonorous; (*schiaffo, risata*) loud; (*fig: parole*) high-flown, high-sounding; **una risata sonora** a loud laugh 2 (*Cine*) sound *attr*; **colonna sonora di un film** soundtrack of a film; **il cinema sonoro** the talkies *pl* 3 (*Ling*) voiced ♦ SM: **il sonoro** (*cinema*) the talkies *pl*; (*parte sonora*) soundtrack

sontuoso, -a [sontu'oso] AGG sumptuous

sopire [so'pire] /55/ VT (*dolore, tensione*) to soothe

sopore [so'pore] SM drowsiness

soporifero, -a [sopo'rifero] AGG (*sostanza*) soporific; (*fig: discorso*) tedious, soporific

soppalco, -chi [sop'palko] SM mezzanine

sopperire [soppe'rire] /55/ VI (*aus avere*) **sopperire a** to provide for; **sopperire alla mancanza di qc** to make up for the lack of sth

soppesare [soppe'sare] /72/ VT to weigh in one's hand(s), feel the weight of; **soppesare i pro e i contro** to weigh up the pros and cons

soppiantare [soppjan'tare] /72/ VT to supplant

soppiatto [sop'pjatto] AVV: **di soppiatto** secretly, furtively; **se n'è andato di soppiatto** he stole off *o* away

sopportabile [soppor'tabile] AGG tolerable, bearable

sopportare [soppor'tare] /72/ VT 1 (*peso*) to support, bear 2 (*subire: perdita, spese*) to bear, sustain; (: *conseguenze, disagi*) to bear, suffer 3 (*tollerare: persona, comportamento*) to stand, put up with, bear, tolerate, endure; (: *temperatura, sforzo*) to take, stand, withstand; **non sopporto il pesce/il giallo** I can't stand fish/yellow; **non sopporto le persone disoneste!** I can't stand dishonest people!; **non lo sopporto** I can't stand him

sopportazione [sopportat'tsjone] SF patience; **avere spirito *o* capacità di sopportazione** to be long-suffering; **la mia sopportazione ha un limite** there is a limit to my patience; **ho raggiunto il limite della sopportazione** I am at the end of my tether

soppressione [soppres'sjone] SF 1 (*di legge*) abolition; (*di linea ferroviaria*) closure; (*di servizio*) withdrawal 2 (*uccisione*) elimination, liquidation

soppresso, -a [sop'presso] PP *di* **sopprimere**

sopprimere [sop'primere] /50/ VT IRREG 1 (*privilegi, carica*) to do away with, abolish; (*servizio*) to withdraw; (*giornale*) to suppress; (*clausola, parola, frase*) to cut out, delete; il servizio navetta è stato soppresso the shuttle service has been withdrawn 2 (*uccidere*) to eliminate, liquidate

sopra ['sopra] PREP 1 (*gen*) over; c'era un lampadario sopra il tavolo there was a chandelier over the table; indossava un golf sopra la camicetta she was wearing a sweater over her blouse; mettiti il cappotto sopra le spalle put your coat over your shoulders; costruirono un ponte sopra il fiume they built a bridge over the river; guadagna sopra i 2000 euro al mese he earns over 2000 euros a month; pesa sopra il chilo it weighs over *o* more than a kilo; persone sopra i 30 anni people over 30 (years of age); passar sopra a qc (*anche fig*) to pass over sth; sopra pensiero = soprappensiero 2 (*più in su di*) above; l'aereo volava sopra le nuvole the plane was flying above the clouds; 100 metri sopra il livello del mare 100 metres above sea level; 5 gradi sopra lo zero 5 degrees above zero; sopra l'orizzonte above the horizon; sopra l'equatore north of *o* above the equator; un paesino sopra Napoli a village north of Naples; abitano sopra di noi they live above us; ha un appartamento sopra il negozio he has a flat (*Brit*) *o* apartment (*USA*) over the shop; essere al di sopra di ogni sospetto to be above suspicion; amare qn sopra ogni cosa to love sb above all else 3 (*a contatto con*) on; (*moto*) on(to); (*in cima a*) on (top of); il libro è sopra il tavolo the book is on the table; il dizionario è sopra quella pila di libri the dictionary is on top of that pile of books; il gatto è salito sopra il tavolo the cat climbed onto the table; mettilo sopra l'armadio put it on top of the wardrobe (*Brit*) *o* closet (*USA*); si buttò sopra di lui he threw himself on him 4 (*intorno a, riguardo a*) about, on; un dibattito sopra la riforma carceraria a debate about *o* on prison reform; chiedere un parere sopra qc to ask for an opinion about *o* on sth ♦ AVV 1 (*su*) up; (*in superficie*) on top; là sopra up there; metti tutto lì *o* là sopra put everything up there; qua sopra up here; sopra è un po' rovinato (*libro, borsa*) it's a bit damaged on top; una torta con sopra la panna a cake topped with cream; un disegno con sopra la firma a signed drawing 2 (*al piano*) di sopra upstairs; abitano di sopra they live upstairs; vado di sopra a chiudere le finestre I'm just going upstairs to close the windows; la tua è la stanza di sopra yours is the upstairs room 3 (*prima*) above; per i motivi sopra illustrati for the above-mentioned reasons, for the reasons shown above; vedi/come sopra see/as above; mettilo nel cassetto sopra put it in the drawer above 4 pensaci sopra think it over; dormirci sopra (*fig*) to sleep on it ♦ SM top; il sopra del tavolo è in mogano the top of the table is mahogany; il di sopra the top, the upper part

soprabito [so'prabito] SM overcoat

sopraccennato, -a [soprattʃen'nato] AGG above-mentioned

sopracciglio [soprat'tʃiλλo] SM (*pl m* **sopraccigli**, *pl f* **sopracciglia**) eyebrow

sopraccoperta [soprakko'perta] SF (*di letto*) bedspread; (*di libro*) jacket ♦ AVV (*Naut*) on deck

sopraddetto, -a [soprad'detto] AGG aforesaid

sopraffare [sopraf'fare] /41/ VT IRREG to overwhelm, overpower, overcome

sopraffatto, -a [sopraf'fatto] PP *di* **sopraffare**

sopraffazione [sopraffat'tsjone] SF overwhelming, overpowering

sopraffino, -a [sopraf'fino] AGG (*olio*) extra fine; (*burro*) best-quality *attr*; (*pranzo, gusto*) excellent; (*fig: astuzia, mente*) masterly

sopraggiungere [soprad'dʒundʒere] /5/ VI IRREG (*aus essere*) (*persone, rinforzi*) to arrive (unexpectedly); (*fig: difficoltà, complicazioni*) to arise *o* occur (unexpectedly)

sopraggiunto, -a [soprad'dʒunto] PP *di* **sopraggiungere**

sopralluogo, -ghi [sopral'lwɔgo] SM (*di esperti*) inspection; (*di polizia*) on-the-spot investigation

soprammobile [sopram'mɔbile] SM ornament

soprannaturale [soprannatu'rale] AGG, SM supernatural

soprannome [sopran'nome] SM nickname

soprannominare [soprannomi'nare] /72/ VT to nickname

soprannumero [sopran'numero] AVV: in soprannumero in excess; in questa classe siamo in soprannumero there are too many in this class

soprano [so'prano] SM, SF (*pl m* **soprani**, *pl f* **soprano**) (*Mus*) soprano

soprappensiero [soprappen'sjero] AVV lost in thought

soprappiù [soprap'pju] SM surplus, extra; in soprappiù (*in eccesso*) extra, surplus; (*per giunta*) besides, in addition; l'offerta è in soprappiù rispetto alla domanda there is more supply than demand

soprassalto [sopras'salto] SM: di soprassalto with a jump, with a start; mi sono svegliata di soprassalto I woke up with a start

soprassedere [soprasse'dere] /107/ VI IRREG (*aus avere*) soprassedere a to put off, postpone, delay

soprattassa [soprat'tassa] SF (*Fin*) surtax

soprattutto [soprat'tutto] AVV 1 (*anzitutto*) above all; dipende soprattutto da lui it depends mainly on him 2 (*specialmente*) especially, particularly; Firenze è piena di turisti, soprattutto d'estate Florence is full of tourists, especially in the summer

sopravvalutare [sopravvalu'tare] /72/ VT (*persona, capacità*) to overestimate, overrate

sopravvenire [sopravve'nire] /128/ VI IRREG (*aus essere*) (*persone, macchine, rinforzi*) to arrive suddenly; (*difficoltà, complicazioni*) to arise, occur

sopravvento [soprav'vento] SM: avere/prendere il sopravvento su qn to have/get the upper hand over sb ♦ AVV windward; essere/mettersi sopravvento to be/get on the windward side

sopravvissuto, -a [sopravvis'suto] PP *di* **sopravvivere** ♦ SM, SF survivor

sopravvivenza [sopravvi'ventsa] SF survival

sopravvivere [soprav'vivere] /130/ VI IRREG (*aus essere*) to survive; riuscirà a sopravvivere? will he survive?; sopravvivere a (*incidente, guerra*) to survive; (*persona*) to outlive, survive; è sopravvissuto all'incidente he survived the accident

soprelevata [soprele'vata] SF (*di strada, ferrovia*) elevated section

soprintendente [soprinten'dente] SM, SF (*gen*) superintendent, supervisor; (*funzionario: di museo*) director, head

soprintendenza [soprinten'dentsa] SF 1 (*gen*) superintendence, supervision 2 (*ente statale*): Soprintendenza ai beni ambientali e architettonici government department responsible for the environment and historical buildings; Soprintendenza ai beni artistici e storici government department responsible for monuments and other treasures

soprintendere [soprin'tendere] /120/ VI IRREG: soprintendere a to superintend, supervise

soprinteso, -a [soprin'teso] PP *di* **soprintendere**

sopruso [so'pruzo] SM abuse (of power); subire un sopruso to be abused; questo è un sopruso! this is an outrage!

soqquadro [sok'kwadro] SM: mettere a soqquadro to turn upside-down

sorbetto [sor'betto] SM sorbet, water ice (*Brit*)

sorbire [sor'bire] /17/ VT to sip; sorbirsi qn/qc (*fig*) to put up with sb/sth

sorcio, -ci [sortʃo] SM mouse; far vedere i sorci verdi a qn (*fig*) to give sb a rough time

sordido, -a ['sɔrdido] AGG (*locale, appartamento*) sordid, squalid; (*fig: affare, storia*) sordid; (: *gretto*) mean, stingy

sordina [sor'dina] SF (*Mus*) mute; mettere la sordina a qc to mute sth; in sordina softly; cantare in sordina to hum softly; andarsene in sordina (*fig*) to sneak off

sordità [sordi'ta] SF deafness

sordo, -a ['sordo] AGG 1 (*persona*) deaf; essere sordo da un orecchio to be deaf in one ear; essere sordo come una campana to be as deaf as a post; sordo ai consigli deaf to advice 2 (*rumore, colpo*) muffled; (*dolore*) dull; (*odio, rancore*) veiled; (*lotta*) silent, hidden; un rumore sordo a dull sound 3 (*Fonetica*) voiceless ♦ SM, SF deaf person; i sordi the deaf; non fare il sordo! don't pretend you didn't hear me!

sordomuto, -a [sordo'muto] AGG unable to hear or speak ♦ SM, SF person who can neither hear nor speak

sorella [so'rella] SF (gen, anche Rel) sister; **mia sorella** my sister; **la sorella di Nadia** Nadia's sister; **è come una sorella per me** she's like a sister to me ♦ AGG (organizzazione, nave) sister attr

sorellastra [sorel'lastra] SF stepsister; (con genitore in comune) half sister

sorgente [sor'dʒɛnte] SF (fonte) spring; (di fiume, fig: Fis) source; **acqua di sorgente** spring water; **sorgente di calore** source of heat; **sorgente luminosa** source of light, light source; **sorgente termale** thermal spring

sorgere ['sordʒere] VB IRREG /109/ VI (aus essere) (gen) to rise; (fig: difficoltà) to arise; **mi sorge il dubbio che...** I am beginning to suspect that ...; **mi sorge un dubbio, forse ho lasciato il gas acceso** I wonder, did I leave the gas on? ♦ SM: **al sorgere del sole** at sunrise

soriano, -a [so'rjano] AGG, SM, SF tabby

sormontare [sormon'tare] /72/ VT (fig: ostacoli, difficoltà) to overcome, surmount

sornione, -a [sor'njone] AGG sly, crafty ♦ SM, SF sly one

sorpassare [sorpas'sare] /72/ VT (oltrepassare) to go past; (auto) to overtake; (fig) to surpass; (rivali) to surpass, outdo; **sorpassare qn in intelligenza** to be more intelligent o brighter than sb; **l'ha sorpassato in altezza** she has grown taller than him

sorpassato, -a [sorpas'sato] AGG (metodo, moda) outmoded, old-fashioned; (macchina) obsolete

sorpasso [sor'passo] SM overtaking; **fare un sorpasso** to overtake

sorprendente [sorpren'dɛnte] AGG surprising; (eccezionale, inaspettato) astonishing, amazing

sorprendere [sor'prɛndere] VB IRREG /81/ VT 1 (cogliere di sorpresa) to catch; (ladro) to surprise, catch in the act; **l'ha sorpreso a fumare** she caught him smoking; **furono sorpresi dalla bufera** they were caught in the storm 2 (fig: stupire) to surprise; **mi ha sorpreso molto la sua risposta** his answer really surprised me; **non mi sorprenderebbe affatto!** I wouldn't be at all surprised!; **sorprendersi** VIP 1 (meravigliarsi): **sorprendersi di qc** to be surprised about o at sth 2 (trovarsi): **sorprendersi a pensare a qn** to catch o find o.s. thinking of sb

sorpreso, -a [sor'preso] PP di sorprendere

sorreggere [sor'rɛddʒere] /87/ VT IRREG (malato, bambino) to support, hold up; (fig: sogg: fede, speranza) to sustain

sorretto, -a [sor'rɛtto] PP di sorreggere

sorridere [sor'ridere] /89/ VI IRREG (aus avere) to smile; **sorridere a qn** to smile at sb, give sb a smile; **mi sorrideva** she was smiling at me; **la vita ti sorride** life smiles on you; **mi sorride l'idea di rivederlo** the idea of seeing him again appeals to me

sorriso [sor'riso] PP di sorridere ♦ SM smile; **mi ha fatto un sorriso** he gave me a smile, he smiled at me; **un accenno di sorriso** a faint smile

sorsata [sor'sata] SF gulp; **bere a sorsate** to gulp

sorseggiare [sorsed'dʒare] /62/ VT to sip

sorsi ecc ['sorsi] VB vedi sorgere

sorso ['sorso] SM sip; **vuoi un sorso?** do you want a sip?; **ne ho bevuto solo un sorso** I only had a sip; **d'un sorso, in un sorso solo** at one gulp; **l'ho bevuto tutto d'un sorso** I drank it all in one gulp

sorta ['sorta] SF sort, kind; **ogni sorta di** all sorts pl of; **di ogni sorta** of every kind, of all sorts; **non voglio regali di sorta** I want no presents whatsoever o of any kind o at all

sorte ['sorte] SF (fato) fate, destiny; (caso) chance; **decidere della sorte di qn** to decide sb's fate; **tentare la sorte** to try one's luck; **tirare a sorte** to draw lots; **hanno tirato a sorte per decidere chi doveva andare per primo** they drew lots to decide who should go first; **non sappiamo quale sarà la sua sorte** we don't know what his fate will be; **la sua sorte è segnata** his fate is sealed

sorteggiare [sorted'dʒare] /62/ VT to draw for

sorteggio, -gi [sor'teddʒo] SM draw

sortilegio, -gi [sorti'lɛdʒo] SM spell, witchcraft no pl; **fare un sortilegio a qn** to cast o put a spell on sb

sortire [sor'tire] /55/ VT (ottenere) to produce; **sortire l'effetto contrario** to have the opposite effect

sortita [sor'tita] SF (Mil) sortie; (fig: battuta) witty remark

sorto, -a ['sorto] PP di sorgere

sorvegliante [sorveʎ'ʎante] SM, SF (di carcere) warder (Brit), guard (USA); (di fabbrica) supervisor; (notturno) night watchman

sorveglianza [sorveʎ'ʎantsa] SF (controllo) supervision, watch; (Polizia, Mil) surveillance; **fare sorveglianza agli esami** to invigilate (at) (Brit) o monitor (USA) the exams

sorvegliare [sorveʎ'ʎare] /27/ VT (detenuto, bambino, bagaglio) to watch, keep an eye on; (casa) to watch, keep watch on; (operai, lavori) to supervise, oversee; **la polizia sorveglia la casa notte e giorno** the police are watching the house night and day

sorvolare [sorvo'lare] /72/ VT, VI (aus avere) **sorvolare su** (territorio) to fly over; (fig: argomento, dettagli) to pass over, skim over, say nothing about; **sorvoliamo!** let's skip it!

SOS ['esse 'o 'esse] SIGLA M INV SOS, mayday; **lanciare un SOS** to send (out) an SOS

sosia ['sɔzja] SM INV, SF INV double; **è un tuo sosia!** he's your double!

sospendere [sos'pɛndere] /8/ VT IRREG 1 (appendere) to hang (up); **sospendere un lampadario al soffitto** to hang a chandelier from the ceiling 2 (interrompere: gen) to suspend; (: vacanze, trasmissione) to interrupt; (: seduta) to adjourn; **la partita è stata sospesa** the match was suspended 3 (funzionario, alunno) to suspend; **sospendere qn dal suo incarico** to suspend sb from office

sospensione [sospen'sjone] SF (gen, anche Aut, Chim) suspension; (rinvio: di processo) adjournment; (: di partita) postponement

sospeso, -a [sos'peso] PP di sospendere ♦ AGG (mano, braccio) raised; (vallata) hanging; (treno, autobus) cancelled; **ponte sospeso** suspension bridge; **col fiato sospeso** with bated breath; **tenere qn col fiato sospeso** to keep sb in suspense; **in sospeso** (pratica) pending; (discorso) unfinished; (conto) outstanding

sospettare [sospet'tare] /72/ VT to suspect; **nessuno sospettava niente** nobody suspected anything; **sospettare qn di qc** (furto, omicidio) to suspect sb of sth; **sospettare che...** to suspect (that) ...; **lo sospettavo!** I suspected as much! ♦ VI (aus avere) **sospettare (di qn)** to suspect (sb); (diffidare) to be suspicious (of sb); **la polizia sospettava di loro** the police suspected them; **non sospetta di niente** he doesn't suspect a thing

sospetto¹, -a [sos'pɛtto] AGG (individuo) suspicious; (affermazione) suspect

sospetto² [sos'pɛtto] SM suspicion; **destare i sospetti di qn** to arouse sb's suspicions; **destare sospetti** to give rise to suspicion, arouse suspicion; **avere dei sospetti** to have one's suspicions; **avevo dei sospetti su di lui** I had my suspicions about him; **ho il sospetto che...** I suspect (that) ...; **guardare qn con sospetto** to look suspiciously at sb

sospettoso, -a [sospet'toso] AGG suspicious

sospingere [sos'pindʒere] /114/ VT IRREG to push, to drive; (fig: incitare) to urge, impel; **il vento li sospinse al largo** the wind drove them out to sea

sospinto, -a [sos'pinto] PP di sospingere

sospirare [sospi'rare] /72/ VI (aus avere) to sigh ♦ VT to yearn for, long for; **fare sospirare qc a qn** to keep sb waiting o hanging around for sth

sospiro [sos'piro] SM sigh; **sospiro di sollievo** sigh of relief; **fare o trarre un sospiro** to sigh, heave a sigh; **ho tirato un sospiro di sollievo** I heaved a sigh of relief

sosta ['sɔsta] SF (fermata) stop, halt; (pausa, interruzione) pause, break; **fare una sosta** to stop; **abbiamo fatto una sosta a Torino** we stopped in Turin; **"divieto di sosta"** (Aut) "no parking"; **senza sosta** without a break, non-stop; **abbiamo lavorato senza sosta tutto il pomeriggio** we worked non-stop all afternoon; **avere un attimo di sosta** to have a moment's rest; **non dar sosta a qn** to give sb no peace, allow sb no respite

sostantivato, -a [sostanti'vato] AGG (Gramm): **aggettivo sostantivato** adjective used as a noun

sostantivo [sostanˈtivo] SM (*Gramm*) noun, substantive; **sostantivo in funzione di aggettivo** noun used as an adjective

sostanza [sosˈtantsa] SF **1** substance; **badare alla sostanza delle cose** to pay attention to essentials; **la sostanza del discorso** the essence of the speech; **in sostanza** in short, to sum up **2 sostanze** SFPL (*ricchezze*) wealth *sg*; (*beni*) property *sg*, possessions

sostanziale [sostanˈtsjale] AGG substantial

sostanzioso, -a [sostanˈtsjoso] AGG (*cibo, pasto*) nourishing, substantial; (*fig: patrimonio, resoconto*) substantial; **un libro sostanzioso** a book of substance

sostare [sosˈtare] /72/ VI (*aus* avere) (*fermarsi*) to stop; (*macchina*) to stop, park; (*fare una pausa*) to take a break; (*pernottare: in albergo*) to stay, stop (for a while); (*: in città*) to stop over; **sostare in preghiera/raccoglimento** to pause in prayer/in thought

sostegno [sosˈteɲɲo] SM support; **a sostegno di** in support of; **muro di sostegno** supporting wall

sostenere [sosteˈnere] VB IRREG /121/ VT **1** (*gen, tenere su*) to support, hold up; (*con medicina*) to sustain; **sostenere il peso di** (*anche fig*) to bear the weight of; **l'albero è sostenuto da una sbarra di ferro** the tree is supported by an iron bar **2** (*candidato, partito*) to support, back; (*famiglia*) to support; **il partito è sostenuto dall'industria** the party is supported by industry; **sostenere qn** (*moralmente*) to be a support to sb; (*difendere*) to stand up for sb, take sb's part **3** (*attacco, shock*) to stand up to, withstand; (*sguardo*) to bear, stand; (*sforzo*) to keep up, sustain; (*esame*) to take; **sostenere gli esami** to sit one's exams; **ho sostenuto gli esami in giugno** I sat my exams in June; **sostenere il confronto** to stand comparison; **sostenere delle spese** to meet *o* incur expenses; **sostenere un'ingente spesa** to have a large outlay **4** (*teoria*) to maintain, uphold; (*diritti*) to assert; (*innocenza*) to maintain; **la tesi da lui sostenuta è che...** he maintains that ...; **ha sempre sostenuto la propria innocenza** he's always maintained his innocence **5** (*Teatro, Cine*): **sostenere una parte** to play a role; **sostenere la parte di** to play the part of; **sostenersi** VR **1** (*tenersi su*) to hold o.s. up, support o.s.; (*con medicine*) to keep up one's strength up; **sostenersi al muro** (*appoggiarsi*) to hold on to the wall, lean on the wall **2** (*uso reciproco*) to hold each other up; (*fig: moralmente*) to stand by each other, support each other

sostenibile [sosteˈnibile] AGG (*tesi*) tenable; (*spese*) bearable; (*sviluppo, turismo*) sustainable

sostenitore, -trice [sosteniˈtore] SM, SF (*di partito, candidato*) supporter, backer; (*di tesi*) upholder, supporter, advocate

sostentamento [sostentaˈmento] SM sustenance, maintenance, support; **mezzi di sostentamento** means of support

sostenuto, -a [sosteˈnuto] AGG (*stile*) elevated; (*prezzo, velocità*) high; **lavora a ritmo sostenuto** she works very fast ♦ SM, SF: **fare il sostenuto** to be standoffish, keep one's distance

sostituire [sostituˈire] /55/ VT **1 sostituire (a/con)** to substitute (for/with); **sostituire il rosso col verde** to replace red with green; **sostituire un pezzo difettoso** to replace a faulty part; **devo sostituire la cartuccia** I need to change the cartridge **2** (*prendere il posto di: persona*) to replace, take the place of; (*: temporaneamente*) to stand in for; (*: cosa*) to take the place of; **era stanco e il suo collega l'ha sostituito** he was tired and his colleague took his place; **sostituirsi** VR: **sostituirsi a qn** to replace sb, take the place of sb

sostitutivo, -a [sostituˈtivo] AGG (*Amm: documento, certificato*) equivalent

sostituto, -a [sostiˈtuto] SM, SF substitute, deputy; **sostituto procuratore della Repubblica** (*Dir*) ≈ deputy public prosecutor (*Brit*), assistant district attorney (*USA*)

sostituzione [sostitutˈtsjone] SF substitution; **ha fatto una sostituzione all'ultimo minuto della partita** he made a substitution in the last minute of the game; **in sostituzione di** in place of, as a substitute for

sottaceto, sott'aceto [sottaˈtʃeto] (*Culin*) SM (*spec al pl*): **i sottaceti** pickles ♦ AGG INV (*cetriolini, cipolline*) pickled ♦ AVV: **mettere sottaceto** to pickle

sottana [sotˈtana] SF (*gonna*) skirt; (*Rel*) cassock, soutane; **stare sempre attaccato alla sottane della mamma** (*fig*) to be tied to one's mother's apron-strings

sottecchi [sotˈtekki] AVV: **guardare di sottecchi** to steal a glance at

sotterfugio, -gi [sotterˈfudʒo] SM subterfuge

sotterraneo, -a [sotterˈraneo] AGG underground; **un fiume sotterraneo** an underground river ♦ SM (*spec al pl*) vault, cellar

sotterrare [sotterˈrare] /72/ VT (*oggetto*) to bury; (*morto*) to bury, inter; **mi sarei sotterrato per la vergogna!** (*fig: fam*) I wished the ground would open up and swallow me!

sottigliezza [sottiʎˈʎettsa] SF **1** (*di spessore*) thinness; (*fig: acutezza*) subtlety **2 sottigliezze** SFPL: **perdersi in sottigliezze** to get bogged down in details; **non bado a certe sottigliezze** I don't care about such niceties

sottile [sotˈtile] AGG **1** (*fetta, corda, viso*) thin; (*figura, caviglia*) slim, slender; (*capelli*) fine; (*profumo*) delicate **2** (*fig: vista*) sharp, keen; (*: ragionamento, significato, ironia*) subtle; (*: mente*) subtle, shrewd; (*: differenza*) slight ♦ SM: **non andare troppo per il sottile** not to mince matters

sottilizzare [sottiliˈdzare] SF /72/ VI (*aus* avere) to split hairs

sottintendere [sottinˈtendere] /120/ VT IRREG (*implicare*) to imply; **è sottinteso che...** it is understood that ..., it goes without saying that ...; **lasciare sottintendere che...** to let it be understood that ...; **il soggetto è sottinteso** (*Gramm*) the subject is understood

sottinteso, -a [sottinˈteso] PP *di* sottintendere ♦ SM insinuation, allusion; **smetti di parlare per sottintesi, parla senza sottintesi** speak plainly, speak your mind

sotto [ˈsotto] PREP **1** (*posizione*) under, beneath, underneath; **dov'era? — sotto il giornale** where was it? — under *o* beneath *o* underneath the newspaper; **la cartina è sotto quel libro** the map is under that book; **si riparò sotto un albero** he sheltered under *o* beneath *o* underneath a tree; **sotto la superficie** under *o* beneath the surface; **si nascose sotto il letto** he hid under *o* underneath the bed; **sotto il soprabito indossava un vestito verde** she was wearing a green dress under her coat; **portare qc sotto il braccio** to carry sth under one's arm; **vieni sotto l'ombrello** come under the umbrella; **dormire sotto la tenda** to sleep under canvas *o* in a tent; **sotto la pioggia** in the rain; **camminare sotto la pioggia** to walk in the rain; **sotto il sole** in the sun; **finire sotto un treno** to get run over by a train; **infilarsi sotto le lenzuola** to get in between the sheets; **c'incontriamo sotto casa** we'll meet outside my house; **sotto le mura** (*di città*) beneath the walls **2** (*più in basso di*) below; (*a sud di*) south of, below; **sotto il livello del mare** below sea level; **sotto zero** below zero; **tutti quelli sotto i 18 anni** all those under 18 (years of age) (*Brit*) *o* under age 18 (*USA*); **questo giocattolo non è adatto ai bambini sotto i 3 anni** this toy is not suitable for children under 3; **quest'anno le gonne si portano sotto il ginocchio** this year skirts are being worn below the knee; **Palermo è sotto Napoli** Palermo is south of *o* below Naples; **sotto il chilo** under *o* less than a kilo; **abita sotto di noi** he lives below us **3** (*durante il governo di*) under; **l'Italia sotto Vittorio Emanuele** Italy under Victor Emmanuel; **sotto il regno di** during the reign of **4** (*soggetto a*) under; **ha 5 impiegati sotto di sé** he has 5 clerks under him; **sotto l'effetto dell'alcol** under the influence of alcohol; **sotto anestesia** under anaesthetic; **tenere qn sotto la propria protezione** to keep sb under one's wing; **tenere qn/qc sott'occhio** to keep an eye on sb/sth; **sotto l'alto patronato di** under the patronage of **5** (*tempo: in prossimità di*) near; **siamo sotto Natale/Pasqua** it's nearly Christmas/Easter **6** (*da*): **analizzare qc sotto un altro aspetto** to examine sth from another point of view; **sotto un certo punto di vista** in a sense **7** (*fraseologia*): **sotto forma di** in the form of; **sotto falso nome** under a false name; **non c'è niente di nuovo sotto il sole** there is nothing new under the sun; **avere qc sotto il naso/gli occhi** to have sth under one's nose/before one's eyes ♦ AVV **1** (*giù*) down; (*nella parte inferiore*) underneath, beneath; **qua/là sotto** down here/there; **qui/lì sotto** down here/there; **sotto c'è uno strato di cioccolato** there's a layer of chocolate underneath; **sotto, la scatola è rossa** underneath, the box is red; **sei sotto tu!** (*nei giochi*) you're it! **2** (*al piano di sotto*) downstairs; **ti aspetto** (*di*) **sotto** I'll wait for you downstairs; **quelli di sotto** the people who live downstairs **3** (*oltre*) below; **vedi sotto** see below; **la riga**

sotto the line below **4** (*addosso*) underneath; **cos'hai sotto?** what have you got on underneath? ♦ SM INV bottom; **il sotto della pentola** the bottom of the pan

sottobanco [sotto'banko] AVV (*di nascosto: vendere, comprare*) under the counter *o* table; (*agire*) in an underhand way; **passare una notizia sottobanco** to hush up a piece of news

sottobicchiere [sottobik'kjɛre] SM mat, coaster

sottobosco, -schi [sotto'bɔsko] SM undergrowth *no pl*

sottobraccio [sotto'brattʃo] AVV by the arm; **prendere qn sottobraccio** to take sb by the arm; **camminare sottobraccio a qn** to walk arm in arm with sb

sottochiave [sotto'kjave] AVV under lock and key

sottocoperta [sottoko'perta] AVV (*Naut*) below deck

sottocosto [sotto'kɔsto] AVV below cost (price)

sottocutaneo, -a [sottoku'taneo] AGG subcutaneous

sottoesposto, -a [sottoes'posto] PP *di* **sottoesporre** ♦ AGG (*fotografia, pellicola*) underexposed

sottofondo [sotto'fondo] SM background; **sottofondo musicale** background music

sottogamba [sotto'gamba] AVV: **prendere qn/qc sottogamba** (*con leggerezza*) not to take sb/sth seriously; (*sottovalutare*) to underestimate sb/sth

sottogonna [sotto'gonna] SF underskirt

sottogoverno [sottogo'vɛrno] SM political patronage

sottogruppo [sotto'gruppo] SM subgroup

sottolineare [sottoline'are] /72/ VT to underline; (*fig*) to underline, emphasize, stress; **hai sottolineato le parole che non conosci?** have you underlined the words you don't know?; **vorrei sottolineare l'importanza di quello che ha detto** I'd like to stress the importance of what he said

sottolio, -li, sott'olio [sot'tɔljo] SM: **sottoli** SMPL vegetables pickled in oil ♦ AGG INV (*funghetti, melanzane, tonno*) in oil ♦ AVV: **conservare sottolio** to bottle in oil

sottomano [sotto'mano] AVV **1** (*a portata di mano*) within reach, to *o* on *o* at hand **2** (*di nascosto*) secretly

sottomarino, -a [sottoma'rino] AGG (*flora, paesaggio*) submarine; (*cavo, galleria, navigazione*) underwater *attr* ♦ SM (*Naut*) submarine

sottomesso, -a [sotto'messo] PP *di* **sottomettere** ♦ AGG submissive

sottomettere [sotto'mettere] VB IRREG /63/ VT (*gen*) to subject; (*popolo, nemico*) to subjugate, subdue; **sottomettere qn alla propria volontà** to impose one's will on sb; **sottomettersi** VR to submit; **sottomettersi alla volontà di qn** to bow to sb's will

sottomissione [sottomis'sjone] SF submission

sottopassaggio, -gi [sottopas'saddʒo] SM (*per auto*) underpass; (*pedonale*) subway (*Brit*), underpass (*USA*)

sottoporre [sotto'porre] VB IRREG /77/ VT **1** (*costringere*): **sottoporre qn/qc a** to subject sb/sth to; **sottoporre ad un esame** to subject to an examination **2** (*fig: presentare*): **sottoporre qc a qn** *o* **all'attenzione di qn** to submit sth to sb, put sth to sb; **gli ho sottoposto la mia richiesta** I submitted my request to him; **sottoporsi** VR: **sottoporsi a** (*volontà*) to submit to; (*operazione*) to undergo

sottoposto, -a [sotto'posto] PP *di* **sottoporre**

sottoprodotto [sottopro'dotto] SM by-product

sottoproduzione [sottoprodut'tsjone] SF underproduction

sottoproletariato [sottoproleta'rjato] SM: **il sottoproletariato** the underclasses *pl*, the underprivileged classes *pl*

sottordine [sot'tordine] in sottordine AVV: **passare in sottordine** to become of minor importance ♦ SM (*Bot, Zool*) sub-order

sottoscala [sottos'kala] SM INV (*ripostiglio*) cupboard (*Brit*) *o* closet (*USA*) under the stairs; (*stanza*) room under the stairs

sottoscritto, -a [sottos'kritto] PP *di* **sottoscrivere** ♦ SM, SF: **il(la) sottoscritto(a)** the undersigned

sottoscrivere [sottos'krivere] VB IRREG /105/ VT (*firmare: atto, petizione*) to sign; (*titoli, azioni*) to underwrite; **sottoscrivere per 10 euro** (*contribuire*) to contribute 10 euros ♦ VI (*aus avere*) **sottoscrivere a** (*programma*) to subscribe to

sottoscrizione [sottoskrit'tsjone] SF **1** (*firma*) signing **2** (*raccolta di adesioni*) subscription; **è iniziata la sottoscrizione per il referendum** signatures in favour of a referendum are now being collected

sottosegretario, -ria, -ri, -rie [sottosegre'tarjo] SM, SF (*Pol*) undersecretary; **sottosegretario di stato** under-secretary of state (*Brit*), assistant secretary of state (*USA*)

sottosopra [sotto'sopra] AVV (*capovolto*) upside down, topsy-turvy; **mettere tutto sottosopra** to turn everything upside down; **hanno messo la casa sottosopra** they turned the house upside down; **sentirsi sottosopra, avere lo stomaco sottosopra** to feel queasy; **sentirsi sottosopra** (*turbato*) to be in a whirl

sottostante [sottos'tante] AGG (*piani*) lower; (*zona*) underlying; **la valle sottostante** the valley below

sottostare [sottos'tare] /116/ VI IRREG (*aus essere*) **sottostare a** (*assoggettarsi a*) to submit to *o* (*richieste*) to give in to; (*subire: prova*) to undergo

sottosuolo [sotto'swɔlo] SM subsoil

sottosviluppato, -a [sottozvilup'pato] AGG underdeveloped

sottosviluppo [sottozvi'luppo] SM underdevelopment

sottotenente [sottote'nɛnte] SM (*Mil*) second lieutenant

sottoterra [sotto'terra] AVV underground

sottotetto [sotto'tetto] SM attic

sottotitolo [sotto'titolo] SM subtitle

sottovalutare [sottovalu'tare] /72/ VT (*persona, prova*) to underestimate, underrate; (*Econ*) to undervalue; **sottovalutarsi** VR to underrate o.s.

sottovento [sotto'vɛnto] (*Naut*) AVV leeward(s) ♦ AGG INV (*lato*) leeward

sottoveste [sotto'vɛste] SF petticoat, slip

sottovoce [sotto'votʃe] AVV in a low voice, softly

sottovuoto [sotto'vwɔto] AVV: **confezionare sottovuoto** to vacuum-pack ♦ AGG INV: **confezione sottovuoto** vacuum pack

sottrarre [sot'trarre] VB IRREG /123/ VT **1** (*Mat*) to subtract, take away; (*dedurre*) to deduct; **sottratte le spese** once expenses have been deducted **2** (*portar via*): **sottrarre a** to take away from; (*liberare*): **sottrarre a** *o* **da** to save from, rescue from;: **sottrarre da** to remove from, steal from; **gli hanno sottratto il portafoglio** they stole his wallet; **sottrarre qn/qc alla vista di qn** to remove sb/sth from sb's sight; **sottrarsi** VR: **sottrarsi a** (*sfuggire*) to escape; (*evitare*) to avoid; **sottrarsi alle proprie responsabilità** to avoid one's responsibilities; **cerca di sottrarsi alle sue responsabilità** he's trying to avoid his responsibilities

sottratto, -a [sot'tratto] PP *di* **sottrarre**

sottrazione [sottrat'tsjone] SF (*Mat*) subtraction; (*furto*) removal

sottufficiale [sottuffi'tʃale] SM (*Mil*) non-commissioned officer; (*Naut*) petty officer

soufflé [su'fle] SM INV (*Culin*) soufflé

souvenir [suva'nir] SM INV souvenir

sovente [so'vɛnte] AVV (*letter*) frequently

soverchiare [sover'kjare] /19/ VT to overpower, overwhelm

soverchieria [soverkje'ria] SF (*prepotenza*) abuse (of power)

sovietico, -a, -ci, -che [so'vjɛtiko] AGG Soviet ♦ SM, SF Soviet citizen

sovrabbondante [sovrabbon'dante] AGG overabundant

sovrabbondanza [sovrabbon'dantsa] SF overabundance; **in sovrabbondanza** in excess

sovraccaricare [sovrakkari'kare] /20/ VT to overload; **sovraccaricare qn di lavoro** to overload sb with work

sovraccarico, -a, -chi, -che [sovrak'kariko] AGG: **sovraccarico (di)** overloaded (with); **sovraccarico di lavoro** overworked ♦ SM excess load; **sovraccarico di lavoro** extra work

sovraesposizione [sovraespozit'tsjone] SF (*Fot*) overexposure

sovraffollato, -a [sovraffol'lato] AGG overcrowded

sovranità [sovrani'ta] SF (*potere*) sovereignty; (*fig: superiorità*) supremacy

sovrannaturale [sovrannatu'rale] AGG = **soprannaturale**

sovrano, -a [so'vrano] AGG (*gen*) sovereign *attr*; (*fig: sommo*) supreme ♦ SM, SF sovereign

sovrappopolazi'one [sovrappopolat'tsjone] SF overpopulation

sovrapporre [sovrap'porre] VB IRREG /77/ VT (*gen*) to place on top of, put on top of; (*Fot, Geom*) to superimpose;

sovrapponili place *o* put them one on top of the other ♦
sovrapporsi VIP (*Fot*) to be superimposed; (*fig: aggiungersi*):
sovrapporsi a to arise in addition to
sovrapposizione [sovrapposit'tsjone] SF superimposition
sovrapposto, -a [sovrap'posto] PP *di* **sovrapporre**
sovrapproduzione [sovrapprodut'tsjone] SF overproduction
sovrastante [sovras'tante] AGG (*montagna*) dominating;
(*pericolo*) impending
sovrastare [sovras'tare] /72/ VT IRREG 1 (*sogg: montagna, fortezza*) to dominate; (: *nube*) to hang over; **è così alto che
sovrasta gli altri** he's so tall that he towers over the others;
il pericolo di un'epidemia sovrasta la città the danger of
an epidemic threatens the city 2 (*fig: superare*) to surpass
sovrastruttura [sovrastrut'tura] SF superstructure
sovreccitare [sovrett∫i'tare] /72/ VT to overexcite
sovrimpressione [sovrimpres'sjone] SF (*Fot, Cine*) superimposition; (*per errore*) double exposure; **immagini in sovrimpressione** superimposed images; **il numero in sovrimpressione** (*TV*) the number appearing on the screen
sovrintendente *ecc* [sovrinten'dεnte] = **soprintendente**
sovrumano, -a [sovru'mano] AGG superhuman
sovvenire [sovve'nire] /128/ VI IRREG (*aus essere*) (*letter: venire
in mente*): **sovvenire a** to occur to; **mi sovvenne che...** it occurred to me that ...
sovvenzionare [sovventsjo'nare] /72/ VT to subsidize; **sov-
venzionato dallo Stato** state-subsidized
sovvenzione [sovven'tsjone] SF subsidy, grant
sovversivo, -a [sovver'sivo] SM, SF, AGG subversive
sovvertimento [sovverti'mento] SM subverting, undermin-
ing
sovvertire [sovver'tire] /45/ VT (*Pol: ordine, stato*) to subvert,
undermine
sozzo, -a ['sottso] AGG filthy, dirty
SP SIGLA = **La Spezia**
S.P. ABBR (= *strada provinciale*) *vedi* **provinciale**
S.p.A. ['εssepi'a] SIGLA F = **società per azioni**
spaccare [spak'kare] /20/ VT (*rompere*) to break, split; (*legna*)
to chop; (*partito, maggioranza*) to split; **ti spacco il muso!** I'll
smash your face in!; **è caduto e si è spaccato la testa** he fell
and cut his head open; **o la va o la spacca** it's all or nothing; **quest'orologio spacca il minuto** this watch keeps perfect time; **c'è un sole che spacca le pietre** it's hot enough
to fry an egg; **una questione che ha spaccato l'opinione
pubblica** an issue which has split public opinion; **spaccarsi**
VIP (*rompersi*) to break, split; (*fig: scindersi: partito*) to split
spaccatura [spakka'tura] SF (*gen, anche fig*) split; (*in un muro*)
crack; (*nel terreno*) crack, fissure
spaccherò *ecc* [spakke'rɔ] VB *vedi* **spaccare**
spacciare [spat't∫are] /14/ VT (*merce rubata*) to traffic in;
(*droga*) to sell, push; (*denaro falso*) to pass; **spacciare per** (*far
passare per*) to pass off as; **l'ha spacciata per sua moglie** he
passed her off as his wife; **spacciarsi** VR (*farsi credere*): **spacciarsi per** to pass o.s. off as, pretend to be; **si è spacciata per
tua cugina** she pretended to be your cousin
spacciato, -a [spat't∫ato] AGG (*fam: malato, fuggiasco*): **essere
spacciato** to be done for
spacciatore, -trice [spatt∫a'tore] SM, SF (*di droga*) pusher; (*di
denaro falso*) dealer
spaccio, -ci [spatt∫o] SM 1 **spaccio (di)** (*merce rubata*) trafficking (in); (*denaro falso*) passing (of); **spaccio di droga**
drug dealing 2 (*negozio*) shop
spacco, -chi ['spakko] SM 1 (*incrinatura*) crack, split; (*strappo*)
tear 2 (*di gonna*) slit; (*di giacca*) vent
spaccone, -a [spak'kone] SM, SF (*fam*) boaster, braggart
spada ['spada] SF 1 sword 2 (*Carte*); **spade** SFPL *suit in Neapolitan pack of cards*
spadroneggiare [spadroned'dʒare] /62/ VI (*aus avere*) to
swagger; **pensa di poter spadroneggiare** he thinks he can
boss everyone about; **non ti permetto di spadroneggiare
in casa mia** I won't allow you to lord it in my house
spaesato, -a [spae'zato] AGG lost, disorientated; **si sentiva
spaesato nella grande città** he felt lost in the big city; **mi
sentivo spaesato tra di loro** I felt lost *o* out of my depth in
their company

spaghettata [spaget'tata] SF spaghetti meal
spaghetti [spa'getti] SMPL (*Culin*) spaghetti *sg*; **sono buoni
gli spaghetti?** is the spaghetti nice *o* good?
Spagna ['spaɲɲa] SF Spain; **mi è piaciuta molto la Spagna** I
really liked Spain; **andrò in Spagna quest'estate** I'm going
to Spain this summer
spagnolo, -a [spaɲ'ɲɔlo] AGG Spanish ♦ SM, SF (*abitante*)
Spaniard; **gli spagnoli** the Spanish ♦ SM (*lingua*) Spanish;
parli spagnolo? do you speak Spanish?; **un insegnante di
spagnolo** a Spanish teacher
spago, -ghi ['spago] SM string, twine; **un rotolo di spago** a
ball of string; **dare spago a qn** (*fig*) to let sb have his (*o* her)
way
spaiato, -a [spa'jato] AGG (*calza, guanto*) odd
spalancare [spalan'kare] /20/ VT to open wide; **spalancò la
porta** he flung the door open; **spalancarsi** VIP to open wide
spalare [spa'lare] /72/ VT (*terra, neve*) to shovel
spalla ['spalla] SF 1 (*Anat, Geog, Alpinismo*) shoulder; **mi fa
male una spalla** one of my shoulders hurts; **questa giacca mi sta grande di spalle** this jacket is too big across the
shoulders; **avere le spalle curve** to have round shoulders,
be round-shouldered; **avere le spalle larghe** (*anche fig*) to
have broad shoulders; **portare qn/qc in** *o* **a spalle** to carry
sb/sth on one's shoulders; **alzare le spalle** to shrug one's
shoulders; **avere la famiglia sulle spalle** to have a family
to support; **vivere alle spalle di qn** to live off sb, live at sb's
expense 2 (*schiena*) back; **seduto alle mie spalle** sitting
behind me; **voltare le spalle a qn/qc** (*fig*) to turn one's back
on sb/sth; **mi ha voltato le spalle proprio quando avevo
bisogno di lui** he turned his back on me just when I needed
him; **ridere alle spalle di qn** (*fig*) to laugh behind sb's back;
prendere/colpire qn alle spalle to take/hit sb from behind;
mettere qn con le spalle al muro (*fig*) to get sb with his (*o*
her) back to the wall 3 (*Teatro*) stooge; **fare da spalla a qn** to
act as sb's stooge
spallata [spal'lata] SF push (*o* shove) with the shoulder; **dare
una spallata a qc** to give sth a push (*o* a shove) with one's
shoulder
spalleggiare [spalled'dʒare] /62/ VT to support, back up
spalletta [spal'letta] SF parapet
spalliera [spal'ljεra] SF (*di sedia, poltrona*) back; (*di letto: alla
testa*) head(board); (: *ai piedi*) foot(board); (*Ginnastica*) wall
bars *pl*; (*Agr*) espalier
spallina [spal'lina] SF 1 (*di sottoveste, maglietta*) strap; **senza
spallina** strapless 2 (*anche*: **spallina imbottita**) shoulder
pad 3 (*Mil*) epaulette
spalmare [spal'mare] /72/ VT to spread; **spalmare il burro
sul pane**, **spalmare il pane di burro** to butter one's bread,
spread butter on one's bread; **spalmare una crema sulla
pelle** to rub a cream into one's skin; **stava spalmandosi
la crema sulle gambe** she was rubbing cream on her legs;
spalmarsi VR: **spalmarsi di** to cover o.s. with
spalti ['spalti] SMPL (*di stadio*) terraces (*Brit*), ≈ bleachers
(*USA*)
spamming ['spammin(ɡ)] SM (*Inform*) spamming
spandere ['spandere] VB IRREG /110/ VT 1 (*stendere: cera, crema*) to spread 2 (*spargere: liquido*) to pour (out); (: *polvere*) to
scatter; (: *calore, profumo*) to give off; (: *fig: notizie*) to spread;
spandere lacrime to shed tears; **spandersi** VIP to spread
spanto, -a ['spanto] PP *di* **spandere**
sparare [spa'rare] /72/ VT (*arma, colpo*) to fire; **sparare a bruciapelo** to shoot at point-blank range; **sparare un colpo** to
fire a shot; **si è sparato un colpo alla tempia** he shot himself in the head; **sparare fandonie** to talk nonsense; **sparar-
le grosse** to exaggerate; **ha sparato un prezzo assurdo** he
came out with a ridiculous price; **sparare calci** to kick out
♦ VI (*aus avere*) (*arma*) to fire; (*soldato, persona*) to shoot, fire;
sparare a qn/qc (*colpire*) to shoot sb/sth; (*mirare*) to fire at
sb/sth; **sparare a zero contro qn** (*fig*) to be ruthless with sb,
to show sb no pity
sparato [spa'rato] SM (*di camicia*) dicky *o* shirtfront
sparatore, -trice [spara'tore] SM (*fig*) gunman *o* gunwoman
sparatoria [spara'tɔrja] SF (*tra polizia e malviventi*) exchange
of shots; (*tra malviventi*) shoot-out
sparecchiare [sparek'kjare] /19/ VT: **sparecchiare (la tavola)**

to clear the table; **ti aiuto a sparecchiare?** shall I help you clear the table?

spareggio, -gi [spa'reddʒo] SM (*Sport*) play-off

spargere ['spardʒere] VB IRREG /111/ VT 1 (*spargliare*) to scatter; **i miei fogli erano sparsi sulla scrivania** my papers were scattered over the desk 2 (*versare: vino*) to spill; (: *sangue, lacrime*) to shed 3 (*diffondere: notizia*) to spread; (: *luce*) to give off (*o* out); **spargersi** VIP (*persone*) to scatter; (*voce, notizia*) to spread; **si è sparsa una voce sul suo conto** there is a rumour going round about him

spargimento [spardʒi'mento] SM: **spargimento di sangue** bloodshed

sparire [spa'rire] /112/ VI IRREG (*aus* essere) to disappear, vanish; **la nave sparì all'orizzonte** the ship disappeared over the horizon; **sparire dalla circolazione** (*fig: fam*) to lie low, keep a low profile; **far sparire** (*fig: rubare*) to steal, pinch; (: *mangiare*) to go through, put away; **far sparire qn** (*uccidere*) to kill sb, bump sb off (*fam*); **dov'è sparita la mia penna?** where has my pen gone?; **chissà dove è sparito il mio passaporto!** I wonder where my passport has got to!; **sparisci!** (*fig: fam*) scram!, beat it!

sparizione [spariti'tsjone] SF disappearance

sparlare [spar'lare] /72/ VI (*aus* avere) **sparlare di qn/qc** to run sb/sth down, bad-mouth sb/sth (*fam*)

sparo ['sparo] SM shot

sparpagliare [sparpaʎ'ʎare] /27/ VT , **sparpagliarsi** VIP to scatter

sparso, -a ['sparso] PP *di* spargere ♦ AGG (*fogli*) scattered; (*capelli*) loose; **in ordine sparso** (*Mil*) in open order

spartiacque [sparti'akkwe] SM INV (*Geog*) watershed; (*fig: divergenza*) basic difference

spartineve [sparti'neve] SM INV snowplough (*Brit*), snowplow (*USA*)

spartire [spar'tire] /55/ VT 1 (*denaro, eredità*) to share out; **non ho nulla da spartire con lui** (*fig*) I have nothing in common with him; **ci siamo spartiti il bottino** we split up the loot 2 (*separare: avversari*) to separate

spartito [spar'tito] SM (*Mus*) score

spartitraffico [sparti'traffiko] SM INV (*Aut: banchina: in città*) traffic island ♦ AGG INV: **aiuola spartitraffico** traffic island

spartizione [spartit'tsjone] SF division; **la spartizione dell'eredità** the dividing up of the inheritance

sparuto, -a [spa'ruto] AGG (*scarno: viso*) gaunt, haggard; (*esiguo: gruppo*) small, thin

sparviero [spar'vjero] SM (*Zool*) sparrowhawk

spasimante [spazi'mante] SM (*corteggiatore*) suitor; (*scherz: innamorato*) sweetheart, lover

spasimare [spazi'mare] /72/ VI (*aus* avere) to be in agony; **spasimare di fare** (*fig*) to long to do sth, be dying to do sth, yearn to do sth; **spasimare per qn** to be madly in love with sb

spasimo ['spazimo] SM pang; **morire tra atroci spasimi** to die in agony

spasmo ['spazmo] SM (*Med*) spasm

spasmodico, -a, -ci, -che [spaz'mɔdiko] AGG 1 (*affannoso: attesa, ricerca*) agonizing 2 (*Med*) spasmodic

spassarsi [spas'sarsi] VIP (*aus* essere) **spassarsela** to enjoy o.s., have a good time

spassionato, -a [spassjo'nato] AGG (*parere, consiglio*) impartial, dispassionate

spasso ['spasso] SM 1 (*divertimento*) amusement, enjoyment; **per spasso** for amusement; **che spasso!** what a laugh!; **sei uno spasso!** you're a scream! 2 (*passeggiata*) **andare a spasso** to go for a walk; **portare qn a spasso** to take sb for a walk; **portare a spasso il cane** to take the dog for a walk; **essere a spasso** (*fig*) to be unemployed *o* out of work; **mandare qn a spasso** (*fig: fam: licenziare*) to give sb the sack

spassoso, -a [spas'soso] AGG amusing, entertaining

spastico, -a, -ci, -che ['spastiko] AGG, SM, SF spastic

spatola ['spatola] SF 1 (*Med*) spatula (*Brit*), tongue depressor (*USA*); (*di muratore*) trowel; (*di decoratore*) putty knife; (*di sci*) tip; (*Culin*) spatula 2 (*uccello*) spoonbill

spauracchio, -chi [spau'rakkjo] SM (*spaventapasseri*) scarecrow; (*fig*) bogey, bugbear

spaurire [spau'rire] /55/ VT to frighten, terrify

spavalderia [spavalde'ria] SF cockiness

spavaldo, -a [spa'valdo] AGG cocky; **ora è più spavaldo che mai** now he's cockier than ever

spaventapasseri [spaventa'passeri] SM INV scarecrow

spaventare [spaven'tare] /72/ VT to frighten, scare; **l'idea mi spaventa un po'** the idea scares me a bit; **spaventarsi** VIP to become frightened, become scared, be scared; **si è spaventato molto vedendo la pistola** he was very scared when he saw the gun

spavento [spa'vento] SM fear, fright; **fare** *o* **mettere spavento a qn** to frighten *o* scare sb, give sb a fright; **morire di spavento** (*fig*) to be scared to death; **è uno spavento, è brutto da far spavento** he is terribly ugly

spaventoso, -a [spaven'toso] AGG (*sogno, avventura*) frightening; (*incidente, delitto*) horrifying, terrible; (*fig: fam: incredibile*) incredible; (: *tempesta*) terrible; (: *prezzi*) appalling; **ho una fame spaventosa** I'm ravenous; **ho fatto una figura spaventosa** I made an awful fool of myself

spaziale [spat'tsjale] AGG 1 (*volo, nave, tuta*) space attr 2 (*Archit, Geom*) spatial

spaziatura [spattsja'tura] SF (*Tip*) spacing

spazientirsi [spattsjen'tirsi] /55/ VIP to lose one's patience; **si è spazientito e se n'è andato** he lost patience and left

spazio, -zi ['spattsjo] SM (*gen, anche Fis, Mus, Tip*) space; (*posto*) room, space; **occupa molto spazio** it takes up a lot of room; **non c'è più spazio nell'armadio** there's no more room in the wardrobe; **fare spazio per qn/qc** to make room for sb/sth; **dare spazio a** (*fig*) to make room for; **ci manca lo spazio** we are short of room *o* space; **lo spazio tra le file** the space *o* gap between the rows; **grandi spazi aperti** wide open spaces; **nello spazio di un'ora** within an hour, in the space of an hour; **hanno lanciato un satellite nello spazio** they've launched a satellite into space; **spazio aereo** airspace; **spazio su disco** (*Inform*) disk space; **spazio vitale** living space

spazioso, -a [spat'tsjoso] AGG (*casa, macchina*) spacious, roomy; (*strada*) wide

spazzacamino [spattsaka'mino] SM chimney sweep

spazzaneve [spattsa'neve] SM INV (*spartineve, anche Sci*) snowplough (*Brit*), snowplow (*USA*)

spazzare [spat'tsare] /72/ VT (*pavimento, strada*) to sweep; (*foglie, polvere*) to sweep up; **spazzare via** to sweep away; (*fig: cibo*) to put away

spazzatura [spattsa'tura] SF (*immondizia*) rubbish (*Brit*), garbage (*USA*), trash (*USA*); **puoi portare fuori la spazzatura?** can you take the rubbish out?; **camion della spazzatura** dustcart (*Brit*), garbage truck (*USA*) ♦ AGG INV (*giornale, romanzo*) trashy; **posta-spazzatura** junk mail sg

spazzino, -a [spat'tsino] SM, SF roadsweeper (*Brit*), street sweeper (*USA*)

spazzola ['spattsola] SF brush; **capelli a spazzola** crew cut sg; **spazzola per abiti** clothes brush; **spazzola da bagno** back scrubber; **spazzola per capelli** hairbrush; **spazzola di ferro** wire brush; **spazzola per le scarpe** shoebrush; **spazzola rotante** (*Aut*) rotor arm

spazzolare [spattso'lare] /72/ VT to brush

spazzolino [spattso'lino] SM (small) brush; **spazzolino da denti** toothbrush; **spazzolino per unghie** nailbrush

specchiarsi [spek'kjarsi] /19/ VR to look at o.s. in a mirror; **il pavimento è così pulito che ti ci puoi specchiare** the floor is so clean you can see your face in it ♦ VIP: **le montagne si specchiano nel lago** the mountains are reflected in the lake

specchiera [spek'kjera] SF 1 (*specchio*) large mirror 2 (*mobile*) dressing table

specchietto[1] [spek'kjetto] SM (small) mirror; **specchietto per le allodole** (*Caccia*) lure; (*fig*) bait; **specchietto da borsetta** pocket mirror; **specchietto di cortesia** (*Aut*) vanity mirror; **specchietto laterale** wing mirror; **specchietto retrovisore** (*Aut*) rear-view mirror

specchietto[2] [spek'kjetto] SM (*tabella*) table, chart

specchio, -chi ['spekkjo] SM mirror; **mi sono guardata allo specchio** I looked at myself in the mirror; **la sua casa è uno specchio** her house is spotlessly clean; **il mare è uno specchio** the sea is as calm as a millpond; **uno specchio d'acqua** a sheet of water

speciale [spe't∫ale] AGG (gen) special; (specifico) particular; (singolare) peculiar, singular; **hai qualche motivo speciale per sospettare di lui?** do you have any particular reason to suspect him?; **ha un modo tutto speciale di parlare** he has a highly individual way of speaking; **questo arrosto è speciale** this roast is delicious; **in special modo** especially; **inviato speciale** (Radio, TV, Stampa) special correspondent; **offerta speciale** special offer; **treno speciale** special o extra train; **poteri/leggi speciali** (Pol) emergency powers/ legislation sg

specialista, -i, -e [spet∫a'lista] SM, SF (gen) expert, specialist; (Med) specialist

specialistico, -a, -ci, -che [spet∫a'listiko] AGG (conoscenza, preparazione) specialized; **devo fare una visita specialista** (Med) I have to see a specialist

specialità [spet∫ali'ta] SF INV 1 (prodotto tipico) speciality (Brit), specialty (USA) 2 (branca di studio) specialism

specializzare [spet∫alid'dzare] /72/ VT (industria) to make more specialized; **specializzarsi** VR: **specializzarsi (in)** (studio, professione) to specialize (in)

specializzato, -a [spet∫alid'dzato] AGG (manodopera) skilled; (elaboratore) dedicated; **operaio non specializzato** unskilled worker; **essere specializzato in** to be a specialist in

specializzazione [spet∫aliddzat'tsjone] SF specialization; **prendere la specializzazione in** to specialize in

specialmente [spet∫al'mente] AVV especially, particularly

specie ['spet∫e] SF INV 1 (Bio, Bot, Zool) species inv; **una specie in via di estinzione** an endangered species; **alcune specie rare di piante** some rare species of plants; **la specie umana** mankind 2 (tipo) sort, kind, variety; **una specie di** a kind of; **è una specie di piatto con grandi manici** it's a sort of dish with big handles; **gente di ogni specie** all kinds of people; **mi fa specie** it surprises me ♦ AVV especially, particularly

specifica, -che [spe't∫ifika] SF specification

specificare [spet∫ifi'kare] /20/ VT to specify, state (clearly)

specificatamente [spet∫ifikata'mente] AVV in detail

specifico, -a, -ci, -che [spe't∫ifiko] AGG (gen, anche Med) specific; **mi ha rivolto accuse specifiche** his accusations were very specific; **nel caso specifico** in this particular case

speck [∫pek] SM INV kind of smoked ham

speculare[1] [speku'lare] /72/ VI (aus avere) 1 (Comm) to speculate; (fig: approfittare) **speculare su** to take advantage of; **speculare in Borsa** to speculate on the Stock Exchange 2 (Filosofia): **speculare (su)** to speculate (on o about)

speculare[2] [speku'lare] /72/ AGG (immagine, scrittura) mirror attr

speculatore, -trice [spekula'tore] SM, SF (Comm) speculator

speculazione [spekulat'tsjone] SF speculation

spedire [spe'dire] /55/ VT (gen) to send, dispatch; (Comm) to dispatch, forward; **non ho ancora spedito la lettera** I haven't sent the letter yet; **spedire qc a qn** to send sb sth; **gli ho spedito una cartolina** I sent him a postcard; **gliel'ho già spedito** I've already sent it to him; **spedire per posta** to post (Brit), mail (USA); **spedire per mare** to ship; **spedire qn all'altro mondo** to send sb to meet his (o her) maker

❑ **spedire** non si traduce mai con la parola inglese *expedite*

speditamente [spedita'mente] AVV (lavorare) quickly; (parlare: veloce) quickly; (: con sicurezza) fluently; **camminare speditamente** to walk at a brisk pace

spedito, -a [spe'dito] AGG (gen) quick; **con passo spedito** at a brisk pace; **ha una pronuncia spedita** he has a fluent manner of speaking ♦ AVV = **speditamente**

spedizione [spedit'tsjone] SF 1 (atto) sending, posting; (Comm: gen) forwarding; (: via mare) shipping; (: collo, merce) consignment; (: via mare) shipment; **agenzia di spedizione** forwarding agency; **spese di spedizione** (gen) postal (Brit) o mail (USA) charges; (Comm) forwarding charges; **fare una spedizione** to send a consignment 2 (scientifica, anche Mil, Alpinismo) expedition; **una spedizione punitiva** a punitive raid

spedizioniere [spedittsjo'njere] SM forwarding agent, shipping agent

spegnere ['spe.ɲɲere] VB IRREG /113/ VT (fuoco, sigaretta) to

put out, extinguish; (apparecchio elettrico) to switch o turn off; (luce) to switch o turn off; (gas) to turn off; (fig: suoni, passioni) to stifle; (: debito) to extinguish; **spegnersi** VIP 1 (fuoco, sigaretta) to go out; (apparecchio elettrico, luce) to go off; (motore) to stall; (fig: passioni, suoni) to die down; (: ricordo) to fade; **la luce si è spenta all'improvviso** the light went off suddenly; **mi si è spenta la macchina al semaforo** the car stalled at the traffic lights 2 (euf: morire) to pass away

speleologia [speleolo'dʒia] SF (scienza) speleology; (pratica) potholing (Brit), spelunking (USA)

speleologo, -a, -gi, -ghe [spele'ɔlogo] SM, SF (vedi sf) speleologist; potholer (Brit), spelunker (USA)

spellare [spel'lare] /72/ VT 1 (coniglio) to skin; (fam: scorticare) to graze; **mi sono spellato il ginocchio** I grazed my knee 2 (fig: cliente) to fleece; **spellarsi** VIP (persona: per il troppo sole) to peel; (: scorticarsi) to graze o.s.; (rettile) to shed its skin

spendaccione, -a [spendat't∫one] SM, SF spendthrift

spendere ['spendere] /8/ VT IRREG (denaro, tempo) to spend; **quanto ti hanno fatto spendere?** how much did they charge you?; **quanto hai speso?** how much did you spend?; **quanto hai speso per quel vestito?** how much did you spend on o pay for that dress?; **si mangia bene e si spende poco** the food's good and it doesn't cost much; **spendere un occhio della testa** to spend a fortune; **spendere una buona parola per qn** to put in a good word for sb; **spendere e spandere** to squander one's money; **spendere la vita sui libri** to spend one's life studying

spengo ecc ['spengo] VB vedi **spegnere**

spennare [spen'nare] /72/ VT (gallina) to pluck; (fig: cliente) to fleece; **spennarsi** VIP to moult, lose its feathers

spensi ecc ['spensi] VB vedi **spegnere**

spensieratezza [spensjera'tettsa] SF carefreeness, lightheartedness

spensierato, -a [spensje'rato] AGG carefree, lighthearted

spento, -a ['spento] PP di **spegnere** ♦ AGG (luce, fuoco, sigaretta) out; (colore) dull, faded; (vulcano, civiltà) extinct; (persona, sguardo, festa) lifeless; (suono) muffled

speranza [spe'rantsa] SF hope; **nella speranza di rivederti** (in lettera) hoping to see o in the hope of seeing you again; **avere la speranza che...** to be hopeful that ...; **avere la speranza di qc/di fare qc** to be hopeful of sth/of doing sth; **hai qualche speranza di vincere?** have you any hope o chance of winning?; **hai qualche speranza di rivederlo?** do you have any hope of seeing him again?; **pieno di speranze** hopeful; **senza speranza** (situazione) hopeless; (amare) without hope; **quel giovane è una speranza dell'atletica** that boy is a promising athlete; **speranza di vita** life expectancy

speranzoso, -a [speran'tsoso] AGG hopeful

sperare [spe'rare] /72/ VT: **sperare qc/di fare qc** to hope for sth/to do sth; **spero che Luca arrivi in tempo** I hope Luca arrives in time; **spero di trovare un lavoro presto** I hope to find a job soon; **spero di sì** I hope so; **spero di no** I hope not; **speriamo bene!** let's hope so!; **lo spero** I hope so; **non speravo più di vederti** I'd given up hope of seeing you ♦ VI (aus avere) **sperare in** (successo) to hope for; **spero in Dio** to trust in God; **spero in te per risolvere la situazione** I'm counting on you to sort things out; **tutto fa sperare per il meglio** everything leads one to hope for the best

sperduto, -a [sper'duto] AGG (isolato: casa, villaggio) out-of-the-way; (persona: smarrito) lost; (: a disagio) ill at ease

spergiuro, -a [sper'dʒuro] AGG perjured ♦ SM, SF perjurer ♦ SM perjury

spericolato, -a [speriko'lato] AGG (gen) fearless, daring; (guidatore) reckless ♦ SM, SF daredevil

sperimentale [sperimen'tale] AGG experimental; **scuola sperimentale** pilot school; **fare qc in via sperimentale** to try sth out

sperimentare [sperimen'tare] /72/ VT 1 (nuovo farmaco) to experiment with, test; (metodo) to try out, test out; **sperimentare qc sugli animali** to test sth on animals 2 (fig: tentare) to try; (: mettere alla prova) to test, put to the test

sperimentazione [sperimentat'tsjone] SF experimentation; **sperimentazione sugli animali** animal testing

sperma ['sperma] SM sperm, semen

spermatozoo, -i [spermato'dzɔo] SM spermatozoon

sperone [spe'rone] SM (*di stivali, anche Geog*) spur; (*Naut: rostro*) ram; (*Archit*) buttress; (*Zool*) dew claw

sperperare [sperpe'rare] /72/ VT (*denaro*) to squander

sperpero ['sperpero] SM (*di denaro*) squandering, waste; (*di cibo, materiali*) waste

spesa ['spesa] SF 1 (*soldi spesi*) expense; (*uscita*) outlay, expenditure; (*costo*) cost; **una grossa spesa** a big expense; **la spesa è di 200 euro** it will cost 200 euros; **con la modica spesa di 1000 euro** for the modest sum *o* outlay of 1000 euros; **ridurre le spese** (*gen*) to cut down (on spending); (*Comm*) to reduce expenditure; **a spese della ditta** at the firm's expense; **sono andata a Parigi a spese della ditta** I went to Paris at the company's expense; **le spese ti verranno rimborsate** your expenses will be reimbursed; **a mie spese** (*fig*) at my expense; **fare le spese di qc** (*fig*) to pay the price for sth 2 (*acquisto*) buy, purchase; (*fam: compere*) shopping *no pl*; **fare la spesa** to do the shopping; **fare (delle) spese** to go shopping; **adoro fare spese** I love shopping ♦ **spesa pubblica** public expenditure; **spese in conto capitale** (*Comm*) capital expenditure *sg*; **spese fisse** (*di azienda*) fixed costs; **spese generali** (*Comm*) overheads; **spese di gestione** operating expenses; **spese d'impianto** (*Comm*) initial outlay *sg*; **spese legali** legal costs; **spese di manutenzione** maintenance costs; **spese postali** postage *o* postal (*Brit*) *o* mail (*USA*) charges; **spese di trasporto** handling charges; **spese straordinarie** extraordinary expenses; **spese di viaggio** travelling (*Brit*) *o* traveling (*USA*) expenses

spesare [spe'sare] /72/ VT: **sono spesato dalla società** the company pays my expenses; **un viaggio tutto spesato** an all-expenses-paid trip

speso, -a ['speso] PP *di* spendere

spesso¹ ['spesso] AVV often; **andiamo spesso al cinema** we often go to the cinema; **anche troppo spesso** all too often; **spesso e volentieri** very often

spesso², -a ['spesso] AGG (*nebbia, fumo*) thick, dense; (*stoffa*) heavy, heavyweight; (*carta*) thick, heavy; **spesso 40 mm** 40 mm thick

spessore [spes'sore] SM 1 thickness; (*fig: importanza: di ricerca*) significance; (: *di personaggio*) stature; **ha uno spessore di 20 cm** it is 20 cm thick 2 (*Tecn*) gauge

Spett. ABBR = **spettabile**

spettabile [spet'tabile] AGG (*Comm*) esteemed: **spettabile ditta X** (*sulla busta*) Messrs X and Co; (*inizio lettera*) Dear Sirs, ...; **avvertiamo la spettabile clientela...** we inform our customers ...

spettacolare [spettako'lare] AGG spectacular

spettacolo [spet'takolo] SM 1 (*Cine, TV, Teatro*) show, performance; **uno spettacolo televisivo** a TV show; **mettere su uno spettacolo** to put on a show; **gli spettacoli iniziano alle 20** performances begin at 8 pm; **primo/secondo spettacolo** (*Cine*) first/second showing; **andremo al primo spettacolo** we'll go to the first showing 2 (*vista, scena*) sight; **dare spettacolo di sé** to make an exhibition *o* a spectacle of o.s.

spettacoloso, -a [spettako'loso] AGG (*vista*) spectacular; (*fig*) amazing, incredible

spettanza [spet'tantsa] SF (*frm*) 1 (*competenza*) concern; **non è di mia spettanza** it's no concern of mine 2 (*somma dovuta*): **spettanze** SFPL amount due; **non ho ancora avuto le mie spettanze** I haven't yet received what is owing to me

spettare [spet'tare] /72/ VI (*aus essere*) **spettare a** (*decisione*) to be up to; (*stipendio*) to be due to; **spetta a te decidere** it's up to you to decide; **mi spetta una parte degli incassi** I'm due a share of the takings; **voglio solo quello che mi spetta** I only want what's due to me

spettatore, -trice [spetta'tore] SM, SF (*Cine, Teatro*) member of the audience; (*TV*) viewer; (*Sport*) spectator; (*di avvenimento*) witness; **è stato spettatore di un incidente** he witnessed an accident

spettegolare [spettego'lare] /72/ VI (*aus avere*) to gossip

spettinare [spetti'nare] /72/ VT: **spettinare qn** to ruffle sb's hair; **spettinarsi** VR to get one's hair in a mess

spettinato, -a [spetti'nato] AGG dishevelled; **sono tutta spettinata** my hair's in a mess

spettrale [spet'trale] AGG (*gen*) spectral, ghostly

spettro ['spεttro] SM 1 (*fantasma*) spectre (*Brit*), specter (*USA*), ghost 2 (*Fis*) spectrum

spezie ['spεttsje] SFPL (*Culin*) spices

spezzare [spet'tsare] /72/ VT (*rompere*) to break, snap; (*fig: interrompere*) to break up; **basta, mi spezzi il braccio!** stop it! you're breaking my arm!; **spezzare il cuore a qn** to break sb's heart; **spezzare il viaggio** to break one's journey; **mi spezza la giornata** it breaks up my day; **spezzarsi** VIP to break, snap; **la fune si è spezzata** the rope broke

spezzatino [spettsa'tino] SM (*Culin*) stew

spezzato, -a [spet'tsato] AGG (*unghia, ramo, braccio*) broken; **fare orario spezzato** to work a split shift ♦ SM (*abito maschile*) (coordinated) jacket and trousers (*Brit*) *o* pants (*USA*)

spezzettare [spettset'tare] /72/ VT to break up (*o* chop) into small pieces; **spezzettare il pane** to crumble bread

spezzino, -a [spet'tsino] AGG of *o* from La Spezia ♦ SM, SF inhabitant *o* native of La Spezia

spezzone [spet'tsone] SM (*Cine*) clip

spia ['spia] SF 1 (*gen*) spy; (*confidente della polizia*) informer; **non fare la spia** (*gen*) don't give me (*o* us *ecc*) away; (*di bambini*) don't be a telltale *o* a sneak 2 (*Elettr: anche:* **spia luminosa**) warning light, indicating light; (*di porta*) spyhole, peephole; (*fig: sintomo*) sign, indication; **spia dell'olio** (*Aut*) oil warning light

spiaccicare [spjatt∫i'kare] /20/ VT (*fam: schiacciare*) to squash, crush; **ti spiaccico al muro** I'll flatten you

spiacente [spja't∫ente] AGG sorry; **siamo spiacenti di non poter accettare** we regret being unable to accept, we are sorry we cannot accept; **siamo spiacenti di quanto è successo** we regret what happened, we are sorry about what happened; **siamo spiacenti di dovervi annunciare che...** we regret to inform you that ...; **sono molto spiacente ma...** I am extremely sorry, but ...

spiacevole [spja't∫evole] AGG (*compito*) unpleasant; (*incidente, equivoco*) regrettable

spiaggia, -ge ['spjaddʒa] SF beach; **una spiaggia sabbiosa** a sandy beach

spianare [spja'nare] /72/ VT (*terreno*) to level, make level; (*palazzo, città*) to raze to the ground; (*pasta*) to roll out; **spianare il fucile** to level one's gun; **spianare la strada** (*fig*) to prepare *o* clear the ground

spiano ['spjano] **a tutto spiano** AVV (*lavorare*) flat out; (*spendere*) lavishly

splantato, -a [spjan'tato] AGG penniless ♦ SM penniless person

spiare [spi'are] /60/ VT to spy on; **spiare le mosse di qn** to spy on sb's movements; **spiare l'occasione propizia** to wait for the right moment; **ci stava spiando da dietro la porta** he was spying on us from behind the door; **spiare attraverso il buco della serratura** to spy through the keyhole

spiata [spi'ata] SF tip-off

spiattellare [spjattel'lare] /72/ VT (*fam: verità, segreto*) to blurt out; **spiattellare tutto** to spill the beans

spiazzo ['spjattso] SM (*gen*) open space; (*radura*) clearing; **giocano in uno spiazzo davanti alla casa** they play on a piece of ground in front of the house; **si fermarono in uno spiazzo nel bosco** they stopped in a clearing in the forest

spiccare [spik'kare] /20/ VT 1 **spiccare un balzo** to jump, leap; **spiccare il volo** (*uccello*) to take wing; (*fig*) to spread one's wings 2 (*Dir, Comm: mandato, assegno*) to issue ♦ VI (*aus avere*) (*risaltare*) to stand out

spiccato, -a [spik'kato] AGG (*senso del dovere, dell'umorismo*) marked, strong; (*gusto*) definite, marked; (*accento*) broad; **ha una spiccata simpatia per lui** she is very fond of him

spiccherò *ecc* [spikke'rɔ] VB *vedi* spiccare

spicchio, -chi ['spikkjo] SM (*di agrumi*) segment; (*di aglio*) clove; (*di formaggio*) piece; **fare** *o* **tagliare a spicchi** to divide into segments

spicciare [spit't∫are] /14/ VT (*lavoro, faccenda*) to finish off; (*cliente*) to attend to; **spicciarsi** VIP to hurry up, get a move on

spiccio, -cia, -ci, -ce ['spitt∫o] AGG 1 (*faccenda*) quick; **andare per le spicce** not to waste time on niceties 2 **denaro spiccio** (small) change ♦ SMPL (*moneta*): **spicci** (small) change *sg*

spicciolata [spittʃoˈlata] AVV: **alla spicciolata** in dribs and drabs, a few at a time

spicciolo, -a [ˈspittʃolo] AGG: **denaro spicciolo, moneta spicciola** (small) change ♦ SM: **non ho uno spicciolo** I'm penniless; **hai degli spiccioli?** have you got any (small) change?

spicco [ˈspikko] SM: **fare spicco** to stand out; **di spicco** (*personaggio*) prominent; (*tema*) main, principal

spiedino [spjeˈdino] SM 1 (*utensile*) skewer 2 (*Culin: di carne, pesce*) kebab

spiedo [ˈspjɛdo] SM (*Culin*) spit; **allo spiedo** on a spit; **pollo allo spiedo** spit-roasted chicken

spiegamento [spjegaˈmento] SM (*Mil*): **spiegamento di forze** deployment of forces

spiegare [spjeˈgare] /80/ VT 1 (*significato, mistero*) to explain; **spiegare qc a qn** to explain sth to sb; **potresti spiegarci il motivo?** could you explain the reason to us?; **gli ho spiegato la situazione** I explained the situation to him; **farsi spiegare qc** to get *o* have sth explained 2 (*tovaglia*) to unfold; (*vele*) to unfurl; **a voce spiegata** at the top of one's voice; **a sirene spiegate** with sirens wailing 3 (*Mil*) to deploy; **spiegarsi** VR (*farsi capire*) to explain o.s., make o.s. clear; (*capire*) to understand; **era così agitato che non riusciva a spiegarsi** he was so upset that he couldn't make himself understood; **mi spiego?** do I make myself clear?, do you understand?; **non so se mi spiego** need I say more!; **spieghiamoci una volta per tutte!** let's get things straight once and for all!; **non mi spiego come...** I can't understand how ...; **non mi spiego come sia potuto accadere** I can't understand how it could have happened; **ora si spiega tutto!** now everything is clear!

spiegazione [spjegatˈtsjone] SF explanation; **avere una spiegazione con qn** to have it out with sb

spiegazzare [spjegatˈtsare] /72/ VT to crease, crumple

spiegherò ecc [spjegeˈrɔ] VB *vedi* spiegare

spietato, -a [spjeˈtato] AGG (*persona*) ruthless, pitiless; (*guerra*) cruel, bitter; (*fig: concorrenza*) fierce; **fare una corte spietata a qn** to chase (after) sb

spifferare [spiffeˈrare] /72/ VT (*fam*) to blurt out, blab

spiffero [ˈspiffero] SM (*fam: corrente d'aria*) draught (*Brit*), draft (*USA*); **questa stanza è piena di spifferi** this room is full of draughts

spiga, -ghe [ˈspiga] SF (*Bot: di grano*) ear

spigliato, -a [spiʎˈʎato] AGG (*persona*) self-confident, self-possessed; (*modi*) (free and) easy

spigolare [spigoˈlare] /72/ VT (*anche fig*) to glean

spigolo [ˈspigolo] SM (*di mobile, muro*) corner, edge; (*Geom*) edge; **smussare gli spigoli** (*fig*) to knock off the rough edges

spigoloso, -a [spigoˈloso] AGG (*mobile*) angular; (*persona, carattere*) difficult

spilla [ˈspilla] SF (*gen*) brooch; (*da cravatta, cappello*) pin; **spilla di sicurezza** *o* **da balia** safety pin

spillare [spilˈlare] /72/ VT 1 (*botte, vino, anche fig*) to tap; **spillare denaro/notizie a qn** to tap sb for money/information 2 (*fogli*) to clip together

spillo [ˈspillo] SM (*gen*) pin; (*da cappello*) hatpin; (*da cravatta*) tiepin; **tacco a spillo** stiletto heel (*Brit*), spike heel (*USA*); **valvola a spillo** needle valve

spilorceria [spilortʃeˈria] SF meanness, stinginess; **questa è una spilorceria!** that's really mean *o* stingy!

spilorcio, -cia, -ci, -ce [spiˈlortʃo] AGG mean, stingy, tight-fisted ♦ SM, SF miser, stingy person

spilungone, -a [spilunˈgone] SM, SF beanpole

spina [ˈspina] SF 1 (*Bot: di rosa*) thorn; **avere una spina nel cuore** to have a thorn in one's flesh *o* side; **stare sulle spine** (*fig*) to be on tenterhooks; **spina nel fianco** thorn in sb's side 2 (*Zool: di riccio, istrice*) spine, prickle; (: *di pesce*) bone; **a spina di pesce** (*tessuto*) herringbone; **spina dorsale** (*Anat*) backbone 3 (*Elettr*) plug; **staccare la spina** (*Elettr*) to pull out the plug; (*di malato terminale*) to turn off the life support; (*fig: interrompere un'attività*) to knock off 4 (*di botte*) bunghole; **birra alla spina** draught (*Brit*) *o* draft (*USA*) beer

spinacio, -ci [spiˈnatʃo] SM (*Bot*) spinach; **spinaci** SMPL spinach *sg*

spinale [spiˈnale] AGG (*Anat*) spinal

spinato, -a [spiˈnato] AGG 1 **filo spinato** barbed wire 2 (*tessuto*) herringbone *attr*

spinello [spiˈnɛllo] SM (*Droga*) joint

spingere [ˈspindʒere] VB IRREG /114/ VT 1 (*gen*) to push; (*premere*) to press, push; **non spingete** don't *o* shove; "**spingere**" "push"; **mi spingi?** (*sull'altalena*) can you give me a push?; **le onde ci hanno spinto contro gli scogli** the waves drove us onto the rocks; **spingere le cose all'eccesso** to take *o* carry things too far *o* to extremes; **spingere lo sguardo lontano** to look into the distance 2 (*fig: stimolare*): **spingere qn a fare qc** to urge *o* press sb to do sth; **spingere qn al delitto/suicidio** to drive sb to crime/suicide; **spinto dalla fame/disperazione** driven by hunger/despair; **è stato spinto dalla gelosia** he was driven by jealousy; **che cosa ti spinge a continuare?** what drives you on?; **spingersi** VR (*aus avere*) to push; **spingersi** VIP: **spingersi troppo lontano** (*anche fig*) to go too far; **ci siamo spinti fino al faro** we ventured as far as the lighthouse

spino [ˈspino] SM (*Bot*) thorn bush

spinoso, -a [spiˈnoso] AGG (*anche fig*) thorny, prickly

spinsi ecc [ˈspinsi] VB *vedi* spingere

spinterogeno [spinteˈrɔdʒeno] SM (*Aut*) ignition coil

spinto, -a [ˈspinto] PP *di* spingere ♦ AGG (*film, barzelletta*) risqué

spintonare [spintoˈnare] /72/ VT (*spingere*) to shove, push

spintone [spinˈtone] SM shove, push

spionaggio [spioˈnaddʒo] SM espionage, spying; **è stato accusato di spionaggio** he was accused of spying; **un film di spionaggio** a spy film

spioncino [spionˈtʃino] SM peephole, spyhole

spione, -a [spiˈone] SM, SF (*fam*) telltale, sneak

spionistico, -a, -ci, -che [spioˈnistiko] AGG (*organizzazione*) spy *attr*; **rete spionistica** spy ring

spiovere¹ [ˈspjɔvere] /76/ VB IMPERS (*aus avere o essere*) (*Meteor*) to stop raining

spiovere² [ˈspjɔvere] /76/ VI IRREG (*aus essere*) (*scorrere*) to flow down; (*ricadere: capelli*) to hang down, fall

spira [ˈspira] SF (*gen*) coil; (*di fumo*) curl

spiraglio, -gli [spiˈraʎʎo] SM (*fessura*) chink, narrow opening; (*raggio di luce, anche fig*) glimmer, gleam; **uno spiraglio di speranza** a glimmer of hope, a faint hope

spirale [spiˈrale] SF 1 spiral; **a spirale** spiral(-shaped); **molla a spirale** (*di orologio*) hairspring; **nebulosa a spirale** spiral nebula; **spirale inflazionistica** inflationary spiral 2 (*contraccettivo*) coil

spirare¹ [spiˈrare] /72/ VI (*aus avere*) (*vento*) to blow; (*odore: emanare*): **spirare da** to come from; **spira aria di burrasca** (*fig*) there's trouble brewing

spirare² [spiˈrare] /72/ VI (*aus essere*) (*morire*) to expire, pass away; (*scadere*) to expire

spiritato, -a [spiriˈtato] AGG (*occhi, espressione*) wild ♦ SM, SF person possessed by a devil; **come uno spiritato** like one possessed

❑ **spiritato** non si traduce mai con la parola inglese *spirited*

spiritismo [spiriˈtizmo] SM spiritualism

spirito [ˈspirito] SM 1 (*gen*) spirit; (*fantasma*) spirit, ghost; **lo Spirito Santo** the Holy Spirit *o* Ghost; **valori dello spirito** spiritual values; **aver paura degli spiriti** to be afraid of ghosts 2 (*intelletto*) mind; **uno dei più grandi spiriti della storia** one of the greatest minds in history 3 (*disposizione d'animo*) spirit, disposition; (*significato: di legge, epoca, testo*) spirit; **ha preso lo scherzo con lo spirito giusto** he took the joke in the right spirit; **per sollevarti lo spirito** to raise your spirits; **in buone condizioni di spirito** in the right frame of mind; **non ha spirito di parte** he never takes sides; **spirito di squadra** team spirit; **ha detto di no per spirito di contraddizione** he said no just to be awkward 4 (*arguzia*) wit; (*umorismo*) humour (*Brit*), humor (*USA*), wit; **battuta di spirito** joke; **è una persona di spirito** he has a sense of humo(u)r; **non fare dello spirito** don't try to be witty 5 (*Chim*) spirit, alcohol; **sotto spirito** preserved in alcohol

spiritosaggine [spiritoˈsaddʒine] SF (*qualità*) wittiness; (*battuta*) witticism

spiritoso, -a [spiriˈtoso] AGG witty; **è il più spiritoso del**

gruppo he's the wittiest in the group ♦ SM, SF wit, witty person; **non fare lo spiritoso!** don't try and be funny!

spirituale [spiritu'ale] AGG (*gen, anche Filosofia, Rel*) spiritual

splendente [splen'dɛnte] AGG (*giornata*) bright, sunny; (*occhi*) shining; (*pavimento*) shining, gleaming

splendere ['splɛndere] /29/ VI *vb* to shine; **il sole splende** the sun is shining

splendido, -a ['splɛndido] AGG (*gen*) magnificent, splendid; (*carriera*) brilliant; **una giornata splendida** a glorious day

splendore [splen'dore] SM splendour (*Brit*), splendor (*USA*); (*luce intensa*) brilliance, brightness; **gli splendori dell'antica Roma** the splendo(u)r of ancient Rome

spodestare [spodes'tare] /72/ VT (*sovrano*) to depose, dethrone; **spodestare da** to oust from

spoglia ['spɔʎʎa] SF 1 (*di rettile*) slough; **sotto mentite spoglie** (*fig*) in disguise 2 (*letter: salma*) remains *pl*

spogliare [spoʎ'ʎare] /27/ VT 1 (*svestire*) to undress; (*con la forza*) to strip; (*fig: privare: di autorità*) to divest, strip; (*: di tesori*) to strip; **spogliare qn di qc** (*derubare*) to strip *o* rob sb of sth 2 (*fare lo spoglio: di schede elettorali*) to count; **spogliarsi** VR (*persona*) to undress, get undressed, strip; (*serpente*) to slough (off) *o* shed its skin; **spogliarsi** VIP (*albero*) to shed its leaves; (*persona*): **spogliarsi di** (*fig: ricchezze*) to strip o.s. of; (*: pregiudizi*) to get rid of, rid o.s. of

spogliarello [spoʎʎa'rɛllo] SM striptease

spogliatoio, -oi [spoʎʎa'tojo] SM changing room

spoglio¹, -glia, -gli, -glie ['spɔʎʎo] AGG (*stanza*) empty, bare; (*terreno, albero*) bare; (*stile*) simple

spoglio², -gli ['spɔʎʎo] SM: **spoglio dei voti** counting of the votes

spola ['spɔla] SF (*Cucito: bobina*) spool; (*: navetta*) shuttle; **fare la spola (fra)** (*sogg: autobus, persona*) to go to and fro *o* shuttle (between)

spoletta [spo'letta] SF (*Cucito: bobina*) spool; (*di bomba*) fuse

spolpare [spol'pare] /72/ VT (*pollo*) to strip the flesh off; (*fig: fam: spennare*) to skin, fleece; **ci hanno spolpato con queste tasse** they have bled us white with these taxes

spolverare¹ [spolve'rare] /72/ VT (*mobile*) to dust; (*fig: mangiare*) to polish off ♦ VI (*aus avere*) to dust

spolverare² [spolve'rare] /72/ VT (*Culin*): **spolverare (di)** to sprinkle (with), dust (with)

spolverino [spolve'rino] SM (*soprabito*) dust coat, duster (*USA*)

sponda ['sponda] SF 1 (*di fiume*) bank; (*di mare, lago*) shore 2 (*bordo: di letto, carro*) side, edge

sponsorizzare [sponsorid'dzare] /72/ VT to sponsor

sponsorizzazione [sponsoriddzat'tsjone] SF sponsorship

spontaneamente [spontanea'mente] AVV (*agire*) naturally, spontaneously; (*reagire*) instinctively, spontaneously; (*pianta: crescere*) wild; **offrirsi spontaneamente di fare qc** to volunteer to do sth

spontaneo, -a [spon'taneo] AGG (*gen*) spontaneous; (*affetto, persona*) natural, unaffected; (*vegetazione*) wild; **è stato un gesto spontaneo da parte sua** it was a spontaneous gesture on his part; **di sua spontanea volontà** of his own free will; **viene spontanea la domanda...** the question springs to mind ...; **i bambini sono sempre spontanei** children always act naturally; **sii spontanea quando ti fanno una foto!** try to be natural when you're having your photo taken!

spopolare [spopo'lare] /72/ VT to depopulate ♦ VI (*aus avere*) (*fam: aver successo: cantante, attore*) to draw the crowds; **spopolarsi** VIP to become depopulated

sporadico, -a, -ci, -che [spo'radiko] AGG sporadic

sporcaccione, -a [sporkat't̬ʃone] AGG filthy, disgusting; (*sessualmente*): **un vecchio sporcaccione** a dirty old man ♦ SM, SF filthy person; (*sessualmente*) filthy beast, pig

sporcare [spor'kare] /20/ VT (*gen*) to dirty, make dirty; (*macchiare*) to stain; (*fig: reputazione*) to sully, soil; **attento a non sporcare il divano** mind you don't dirty the sofa; **mi sono sporcato la camicia riparando la moto** I got my shirt dirty when I was fixing the motorbike; **si è sporcata la camicia di sugo** she's got sauce on her shirt; **sporcarsi le mani** (*anche fig*) to dirty one's hands; **sporcarsi la reputazione** to sully one's reputation; **sporcarsi la fedina penale** to get a police record; **sporcarsi** VR to get dirty; **deve essersi sporcato in giardino** he must have got dirty in the garden

sporcizia [spor'tʃittsja] SF (*sudiciume*) filth, dirt; **c'era tanta di quella sporcizia per le strade** the streets were really filthy *o* dirty; **vivere nella sporcizia** to live in squalor

sporco, -a, -chi, -che ['sporko] AGG (*gen*) dirty, filthy; (*macchiato*) stained; (*fig: immorale*) dirty; (*: losco: politica, faccenda*) shady; (*: denaro*) dirty; **il fazzoletto è sporco** the handkerchief is dirty; **il fazzoletto è sporco di inchiostro/ sangue** there is ink/blood on the handkerchief; **hai le scarpe sporche di fango** there is mud on your shoes, your shoes are muddy; **una barzelletta sporca** a dirty *o* coarse joke; **avere la coscienza sporca** to have a guilty conscience; **avere la fedina penale sporca** to have a police record; **sporco bastardo!** dirty bastard! ♦ SM dirt, filth

sporgenza [spor'dʒɛntsa] SF (*su scogli: rocce*) projection; (*su parete*) bulge

sporgere ['spɔrdʒere] VB IRREG /115/ VT 1 (*braccio, testa*): **sporgere da** to put out of, stretch out of 2 (*Dir*): **sporgere querela contro qn** to take legal action against sb ♦ VI (*aus essere*) (*venire in fuori*) to stick out; (*protendersi: massi*) to jut out; **sporge un po' troppo** it sticks out a bit too much; **sporgersi** VR: **sporgersi da** to lean out of (*Brit*); **non sporgerti dal finestrino** don't lean out of the window

sporsi *ecc* ['spɔrsi] VB *vedi* **sporgere**

sport [spɔrt] SM INV sport; **fare dello sport** to do sport; **che sport fai?** what sports do you play?; **fa diversi sport** he does various sports; **fare qc per sport** to do sth for fun; **sport estremi** extreme sports

sporta ['spɔrta] SF (*borsa*) shopping bag; **dirne un sacco e una sporta a qn** (*insultare*) to give sb a mouthful

sportello [spor'tɛllo] SM 1 (*di veicolo, mobile*) door 2 (*di banca, ufficio*) counter, window; **sportello automatico** (*di banca*) cash dispenser (*Brit*), automated teller machine (*USA*)

sportivo, -a [spor'tivo] AGG (*gara, giornale, auto*) sports attr; (*persona, spirito, atteggiamento*) sporting; (*abito*) casual; **la pagina sportiva** the sports page; **è molto sportiva** she's very sporty; **abbigliamento sportivo** casual clothes; **giacca sportiva** sports (*Brit*) *o* sport (*USA*) jacket; **un atteggiamento molto poco sportivo** a very unsporting attitude; **campo sportivo** playing field ♦ SM, SF sportsman *o* sportswoman

sporto, -a ['spɔrto] PP *di* **sporgere**

sposa ['spɔza] SF (*nel giorno delle nozze*) bride; (*moglie*) wife; **abito** *o* **vestito da sposa** wedding dress; **dare qn in sposa a** to give sb in marriage to

sposalizio, -zi [spoza'littsjo] SM wedding (ceremony)

sposare [spo'zare] /72/ VT (*gen*) to marry; (*sogg: genitori*) to marry off; (*fig: idea, fede, causa*) to embrace, espouse; **le ha chiesto di sposarlo** he asked her to marry him; **sposarsi** VR (*uso reciproco*) to get married, marry; **si sono sposati a giugno** they got married in June; **sposarsi con qn** to marry sb, get married to sb; **si è sposato con Paola** he married Paola

sposato, -a [spo'zato] AGG married

sposo ['spɔzo] SM (*nel giorno delle nozze*) (bride)groom; (*marito*) husband; **gli sposi** the newlyweds; **viva gli sposi!** to the bride and groom!

spossante [spos'sante] AGG exhausting

spossatezza [spossa'tettsa] SF exhaustion

spossato, -a [spos'sato] AGG exhausted, worn-out

spostamento [sposta'mento] SM movement, change of position; **il mio lavoro mi costringe a continui spostamenti** I have to travel constantly for my work; **spostamento d'aria** blast

spostare [spos'tare] /72/ VT 1 (*gen*) to move; (*mobile*) to move, shift; **mi aiuti a spostare il tavolo?** can you help me move the table? 2 (*cambiare: orario, data*) to change; **hanno spostato la data** they've changed the date; **hanno spostato la partenza di qualche giorno** they postponed *o* put off their departure for a few days; **spostarsi** VR to move; **potresti spostarti più in là?** could you move along a bit?

spot [spɔt] SM INV 1 (*faretto*) spotlight, spot 2 (*TV*): **spot pubblicitario** advertisement, commercial

spranga, -ghe ['spranga] SF (*barra*) bar; (*catenaccio*) bolt

sprangare [spran'gare] /80/ VT (*con barra*) to bar; (*con catenaccio*) to bolt

spray [ˈsprai] SM INV (*dispositivo, sostanza*) spray ♦ AGG INV (*bombola, confezione*) spray *attr*

sprazzo [ˈsprattso] SM (*di luce, sole*) flash; (*fig: di gioia*) burst; (: *di intelligenza*) flash

sprecare [spreˈkare] /20/ VT (*gen, anche fig*) to waste; (*denaro*) to waste, squander; **è fatica sprecata!** it's a waste of effort!; **è fiato sprecato!** it's a waste of breath!; **stai sprecando tempo** you're wasting time; **sei sprecato qui!** your talents are wasted here!; **sprecarsi** VIP (*persona*) to waste one's energy; **non sprecarti!** (*iro: non affaticarti*) don't strain yourself!; **si sono sprecati!** (*iro*) they certainly didn't break the bank!

spreco, -chi [ˈspreko] SM waste; **che spreco!** what a waste!

spregevole [spreˈdʒevole] AGG contemptible, despicable

spregio, -gi [ˈspredʒo] SM (*disprezzo*) contempt, scorn, disdain

spregiudicato, -a [spredʒudiˈkato] AGG (*senza pregiudizi*) unprejudiced, unbiased; (*senza scrupoli*) unscrupulous

spremere [ˈspremere] /62/ VT (*agrumi*) to squeeze; (*olive*) to press; **spremere denaro a o da qn** to squeeze money out of sb; **spremersi le meningi** to rack one's brains

spremiagrumi [spremiaˈgrumi], **spremilimoni** [spremiliˈmoni] SM INV lemon squeezer

spremuta [spreˈmuta] SF freshly squeezed fruit juice; **spremuta d'arancia** freshly-squeezed orange juice

sprezzante [spretˈtsante] AGG (*sguardo, modi, parole*) contemptuous, scornful, disdainful

sprezzo [ˈsprettso] SM contempt, scorn, disdain; **con sprezzo del pericolo** without heeding the danger

sprigionare [spridʒoˈnare] /72/ VT (*calore, odore*) to give off, emit; (*gas tossici*) to release; (*fig: energia*) to unleash; **sprigionarsi** VIP: **sprigionarsi da** (*sogg: calore*) to emanate from, be given off by; (: *con impeto: gas*) to burst (out) from; (: *petrolio, acqua*) to gush out from

sprizzare [spritˈtsare] /72/ VI (*aus* essere) to spurt ♦ VT (*scaturire*) to spurt; (*fig: gioia, vitalità*) to be bursting with; **sprizza salute da tutti i pori** he's bursting with health

sprofondare [sprofonˈdare] /72/ VI (*aus* essere) (*casa, tetto*) to collapse; (*pavimento, terreno*) to subside, give way; (*nave*) to sink; **i suoi piedi sprofondavano nella neve** his feet sank into the snow; **sprofondò nel dolore** he was overcome with grief; **sprofondarsi** VR: **sprofondarsi in** (*poltrona*) to sink into; (*fig: studio, lavoro*) to become engrossed in

sproloquiare [sproloˈkwjare] /19/ VI (*aus* avere) to ramble on

sproloquio, -qui [sproˈlɔkwjo] SM rambling speech

spronare [sproˈnare] /72/ VT (*cavallo*) to spur (on); (*fig: persona*) to spur on, encourage; **spronare qn a fare qc** to encourage sb to do sth

sprone [ˈsprone] SM (*sperone*) spur; (*fig*) spur, incentive; **fuggire a spron battuto** to take to one's heels

sproporzionato, -a [sproportsjoˈnato] AGG (*gen*) disproportionate, out of all proportion; (*prezzo*) exorbitant; (*condanna*) excessive; **sproporzionato** (*rispetto*) **a** out of proportion to; **il suo peso è sproporzionato all'altezza** his (*o* her *o* its) weight is out of proportion to his (*o* her *o* its) height

sproporzione [sproporˈtsjone] SF disproportion

spropositato, -a [spropoziˈtato] AGG (*costo*) excessive; (*lettera, discorso*) full of mistakes

sproposito [sproˈpɔzito] SM (*azione sconsiderata*) blunder; **ho fatto uno sproposito** (*pazzia*) I did something silly; **non dire spropositi** don't talk nonsense *o* rubbish (*Brit*); **non farmi dire uno sproposito** don't make me say something I'll regret; **costa uno sproposito!** it costs a fortune!; **arrivare a sproposito** to arrive at the wrong time; **parlare a sproposito** to talk out of turn

sprovveduto, -a [sprovveˈduto] AGG inexperienced, naïve

sprovvisto, -a [sprovˈvisto] AGG **1** **sprovvisto di** lacking in, without; **passeggeri sprovvisti di passaporto** passengers without a passport; **siamo sprovvisti di bicchieri** we haven't enough glasses; **ne siamo sprovvisti** (*negozio*) we are out of it (*o* them) **2** **prendere qn alla sprovvista** to catch sb unawares

spruzzare [sprutˈtsare] /72/ VT (*nebulizzare*) to spray; (*aspergere*) to sprinkle; (*inzaccherare*) to splash

spruzzatore [spruttsaˈtore] SM (*per profumi*) spray, atomizer; (*per biancheria*) spray

spruzzo [ˈspruttso] SM splash; **verniciatura a spruzzo** spray painting

spudoratezza [spudoraˈtettsa] SF shamelessness

spudorato, -a [spudoˈrato] AGG shameless; **è stato così spudorato da venire a chiedermi aiuto** he had the cheek to come and ask me for help

spugna [ˈspuɲɲa] SF (*Zool*) sponge; (*tessuto*) (terry) towelling, terrycloth; **una spugna insaponata** a soapy sponge; **di spugna** towelling; **un accappatoio di spugna** a towelling bathrobe; **bere come una spugna** to drink like a fish; **gettare la spugna** (*Pugilato, anche fig*) to throw in the sponge *o* towel

spugnoso, -a [spuɲˈɲoso] AGG spongy

spulciare [spulˈtʃare] /14/ VT (*animali*) to rid of fleas; (*fig: testo, compito*) to examine thoroughly

spuma [ˈspuma] SF (*schiuma*) foam; (*bibita*) fizzy drink; (*Culin*) mousse

spumante [spuˈmante] SM sparkling wine

spumeggiante [spumedˈdʒante] AGG (*vino, anche fig*) sparkling; (*mare*) foaming

spumone [spuˈmone] SM (*dolce*) light, frothy dessert made with egg whites and cream; (*gelato*) soft ice cream made with whipped cream

spuntare[1] [spunˈtare] /72/ VT (*lapis, coltello*) to break the point of; (*capelli, baffi*) to trim; **spuntarla** (*fig: vincere*) to succeed, win (through); (: *averla vinta*) to get one's own way ♦ VI (*aus* essere) (*nascere: germogli*) to sprout; (: *capelli*) to begin to grow; (: *dente*) to come through; (*apparire: sole*) to rise; (: *giorno*) to dawn; **gli è spuntato un dente** he has cut a tooth; **è spuntato da chissà dove** (*fig*) he turned up from out of the blue; **spuntarsi** VIP to lose its point, become blunt ♦ SM: **allo spuntare del sole** at sunrise; **allo spuntare del giorno** at daybreak

spuntare[2] [spunˈtare] /72/ VT (*elenco*) to tick off (*Brit*), check off (*USA*)

spuntino [spunˈtino] SM snack; **fare uno spuntino** to have a snack

spunto [ˈspunto] SM (*Mus, Teatro*) cue; (*fig: base*) starting point; (: *idea*) idea; **dare o fornire lo spunto a qc** (*polemiche*) to give rise to sth; **ciò mi ha dato lo spunto per iniziare a dipingere** it started me painting; **prendere spunto da qc** to take sth as one's starting point, take inspiration from sth; **il regista ha preso spunto da un fatto realmente accaduto** the director took his inspiration from a real life story

spurgare [spurˈgare] /80/ VT (*fogna, canale*) to clear, clean; (*bronchi*) to clean; (*Aut: freni*) to bleed

sputare [spuˈtare] /72/ VT to spit (out); **mi ha fatto sputar sangue** (*fig*) he made me sweat blood; **sputare veleno** (*fig*) to talk spitefully; **sputa fuori!** (*anche fig*) spit it out!; **sputa l'osso!** (*fig*) out with it!; **è suo padre sputato** (*fam*) he's the spitting image of his father ♦ VI (*aus* avere) to spit; **sputare in faccia a qn** (*fig*) to spit in sb's face; **sputare addosso a qn** (*fig*) to despise sb; **non ci sputerei sopra** (*fam*) I wouldn't turn my nose up at it; **non sputare nel piatto in cui mangi** don't bite the hand that feeds you

sputo [ˈsputo] SM spittle *no pl*, spit *no pl*; **questo libro deve essere appiccicato con lo sputo** this book just comes apart in your hands

sputtanare [sputtaˈnare] (*fam*) /72/ VT (*sparlare*) to badmouth; (*sperperare*) to piss away (*fam!*); **sputtanarsi** VIP to make an arse of o.s. (*Brit fam!*)

squadra[1] [ˈskwadra] SF (*strumento*) (set) square; **a squadra** at right angles; **essere fuori squadra** (*gen*) to be crooked; (*fig: persona*) to be out of sorts

squadra[2] [ˈskwadra] SF (*gruppo*) team, squad; (*di operai*) gang, squad; (*Sport*) team; (*Mil*) squad; (*Aer, Naut*) squadron; **lavoro a squadre** teamwork; **squadra del buon costume** (*Polizia*) vice squad; **squadra mobile** flying squad (*Brit*); **squadra di soccorso** rescue party

squadrare [skwaˈdrare] /72/ VT to square, make square; **squadrare qn da capo a piedi** to look sb up and down

squadriglia [skwaˈdriʎʎa] SF (*Aer*) flight; (*Naut*) squadron

squadrone [skwaˈdrone] SM (*Mil*) squadron

squagliare [skwaʎ'ʎare] /27/ vT to melt; **squagliarsi** vip to melt; **squagliarsi, squagliarsela** (fig: fam) to sneak off

squalifica, -che [skwa'lifika] sf disqualification

squalificare [skwalifi'kare] /20/ vT (gen, anche Sport) to disqualify; (fig: screditare) to bring discredit on; **squalificarsi** vr to bring discredit on o.s.

squallido, -a ['skwallido] AGG (luogo) wretched, bleak; (vita) miserable; (vicenda) squalid, sordid; **una squallida stanza d'albergo** a dingy hotel room

squallore [skwal'lore] sM (vedi agg) wretchedness, bleakness; misery; squalor

squalo ['skwalo] sM shark

squama ['skwama] sf (scaglia) scale

squamare [skwa'mare] /72/ vT to scale; **squamarsi** vip (pelle: gen) to flake o peel (off); (: per malattia) to desquamate

squarciagola [skwartʃa'gola] a squarciagola AVV at the top of one's voice; **gridava a squarciagola** he was shouting at the top of his voice

squarciare [skwar'tʃare] /14/ vT (corpo) to rip open; (tessuto) to rip; (fig: tenebre, silenzio) to split; (: nuvole) to pierce; **squarciarsi** vip (vedi vt) to rip open; to rip; (nuvole) to part

squarcio, -ci [skwar'tʃo] sM 1 (ferita) gash; (in lenzuolo, abito) rip; (in nave) hole; **uno squarcio di sole** a burst of sunlight 2 (brano) passage, excerpt

squartare [skwar'tare] /72/ vT (animale macellato) to quarter, cut up; (persona) to dismember

squattrinato, -a [skwattri'nato] AGG penniless ♦ SM, SF (gen) penniless person

squilibrare [skwili'brare] /72/ vT to unbalance; (psicologicamente) to derange, unbalance; **squilibrare qn finanziariamente** to upset sb's bank balance

squilibrato, -a [skwili'brato] AGG (alimentazione) unbalanced; (mente) deranged, unbalanced; **una dieta squilibrata** an unbalanced diet ♦ SM, SF (anche: squilibrato mentale) deranged person

squilibrio, -ri [skwi'librjo] sM 1 (Psic: anche: squilibrio mentale) derangement 2 (Econ: differenza) imbalance

squillante [skwil'lante] AGG (suono) shrill, sharp; (voce) shrill; (fig: colore) loud

squillare [skwil'lare] /72/ vi (aus avere o essere) (campanello, telefono) to ring (out); (tromba) to blare

squillo ['skwillo] sM (di campanello) ring, ringing no pl; (di tromba) blast, blare; **il avverto con tre squilli di telefono** I'll let the phone ring three times to warn you ♦ SF INV (anche: **ragazza squillo**) prostitute (fam!)

squisito, -a [skwi'zito] AGG (gen) lovely, exquisite; (gusto, gioiello) exquisite; (persona) delightful; (modi) considerate; (cibo) delicious

squittire [skwit'tire] /55/ vi (aus avere) (uccello) to squawk; (topo) to squeak

SR SIGLA = Siracusa

sradicare [zradi'kare] /20/ vT (albero) to uproot; (erba) to root out; (fig: vizio) to eradicate; **sentirsi sradicato** to feel uprooted

sragionare [zradʒo'nare] /72/ vi (aus avere) (vaneggiare) to rave; (fare discorsi sconnessi) to talk nonsense

sregolatezza [zregola'tettsa] sf (nel mangiare, bere) lack of moderation; (di vita) dissoluteness, dissipation; **le sue sgregolatezze gli costeranno care** his excesses will cost him dear

sregolato, -a [zrego'lato] AGG (vita: senza ordine) disorderly; (: dissoluta) dissolute; **è sregolato nel mangiare** he has irregular eating habits

Sri Lanka [sri'lanka] sM Sri Lanka

S.r.l. ['esse 'erre 'elle] SIGLA F = **società a responsabilità limitata**

srotolare [zroto'lare] /72/ vT, **srotolarsi** vip to unroll

SS SIGLA = Sassari

S.S. ABBR 1 (Rel: = Sua Santità) 2 (Rel: = Santa Sede) 3 (Rel: = Santi, Santissimo) 4 (Aut) = **strada statale**; vedi **statale**

SSN ABBR (= Servizio Sanitario Nazionale) ≈ NHS (Brit), ≈ Medicaid (USA), ≈ Medicare (USA)

sta ecc [sta] VB vedi **stare**

stabbio, -bi ['stabbjo] sM 1 (recinto) pen, fold; (di maiali) pigsty 2 (letame) manure

stabile ['stabile] AGG (gen) stable, steady; (fondamenta) solid; (impiego) steady, permanent; (tempo) settled; **un'occupazione stabile** a steady job; **la scala non è stabile** the ladder is shaky; **il ponte non è stabile** the bridge is unstable; **essere stabile nei propri propositi** to stick to one's decisions, keep to one's plans; **compagnia stabile** (Teatro) resident company; **teatro stabile** civic theatre ♦ SM (edificio) building

stabilimento [stabili'mento] sM (fabbrica) plant, factory; **stabilimento balneare** bathing establishment; **stabilimento carcerario** prison; **stabilimento tessile** textile mill

stabilire [stabi'lire] /55/ vT (gen) to establish; (fissare: prezzi, data) to fix; (decidere) to decide; **hanno stabilito la chiusura di tutte le scuole** they decided to close all the schools; **stabilire un aumento dei prezzi** to decide on a price increase; **stabilire un collegamento** to establish contact; **resta stabilito che... it is agreed that ...; **stabilirsi** vr (prendere dimora) to settle; **si sono stabiliti qui tre anni fa** they settled here three years ago

stabilità [stabili'ta] sf stability

stabilizzare [stabilid'dzare] /72/ vT to stabilize; **stabilizzarsi** vip (situazione economica, malato) to become stable; (tempo) to become settled

stabilizzatore, -trice [stabiliddza'tore] AGG stabilizing ♦ SM (Aer, Naut, Chim) stabilizer; (Elettr): **stabilizzatore di tensione** voltage regulator

stabilizzazione [stabiliddzat'tsjone] sf stabilization

stacanovista, -i, -e [stakano'vista] sM, SF (scherz) eager beaver

staccare [stak'kare] /20/ vT 1 (togliere): **staccare (da)** to remove (from), take (from); (quadro) to take down (from); (foglio, pagina) to tear out (of), remove (from); **ha staccato una pagina dal quaderno** he tore a page out of the exercise book; **hai staccato l'etichetta dal dischetto?** did you remove the label from the disk?; **stacca la sedia dal muro** pull the chair away from the wall; **staccare la televisione/il telefono** to disconnect the television/the phone; **se non paghi ti staccheranno il telefono** if you don't pay they'll disconnect your phone; **ho staccato il telefono perché la bambina dormiva** I unplugged the phone because the baby was sleeping; **staccare un assegno** to write a cheque; **non riusciva a staccare gli occhi da quella scena** he could not take his eyes off the scene before him 2 (separare: anche fig) to separate, divide; (: buoi) to unyoke; (: cavalli) to unharness; **staccare la locomotiva dal treno** to uncouple the locomotive from the train; **staccare le parole** to pronounce one's words clearly; **staccare le note** (Mus) to play staccato 3 (Sport: distanziare) to leave behind ♦ vi (aus avere) 1 (risaltare) to stand out 2 (fam: finire di lavorare) to knock off; **staccarsi** vip 1 (venir via: bottone) to come off; (: foglio) to come out; (: sganciarsi) to break loose; **mi si è staccato un bottone della camicia** a button has come off my shirt 2 (persona): **staccarsi da** (allontanarsi) to move away from (dalla famiglia) to leave; **non si stacca mai dalla televisione** he's always glued to the television

staccionata [stattʃo'nata] sf fence

stacco, -chi ['stakko] sM 1 (intervallo) gap; (tra due scene) break; (differenza) difference; **fare uno stacco tra una parola e l'altra** to articulate one's words; **c'è troppo stacco tra i due colori** there's too much of a difference between the two colours; **fare stacco su** to stand out against 2 (Sport: nel salto) takeoff

stadera [sta'dera] sf lever scales pl

stadio, -di ['stadjo] sM 1 (Sport) stadium 2 (periodo, fase) stage, phase; **durante l'ultimo stadio della malattia** during the final stage of the illness; **a due/tre stadi** two-/three-stage attr

staffa ['staffa] sf 1 (gen, anche Tecn, Edil) stirrup; (Alpinismo) étrier (Brit), stirrup (USA); **perdere le staffe** (fig) to fly off the handle; **tenere il piede in due staffe** (fig) to run with the hare and hunt with the hounds 2 (Anat) stirrup bone

staffetta [staf'fetta] sf 1 (messo) courier, dispatch rider 2 (Sport) relay race

stagflazione [stagflat'tsjone] sf (Econ) stagflation

stagionale [stadʒo'nale] AGG seasonal; **"apertura stagionale"** "open during the tourist season" ♦ SM, SF seasonal worker

stagionare [stadʒo'nare] /72/ VT, VI (*aus* **essere**), **stagionarsi** VIP (*legno*) to season; (*formaggi*) to mature

stagionato, -a [stadʒo'nato] AGG (*vedi vb*) seasoned; matured; (*scherz: attempato*) getting on in years

stagione [sta'dʒone] SF season; **la bella stagione** the summer months; **la stagione delle piogge** the rainy season; **in questa stagione** at this time of year; **frutta di stagione** seasonal fruit; **saldi di fine stagione** end-of-season sales; **vestiti di mezza stagione** clothes for spring and autumn; **alta/bassa stagione** (*Turismo*) high/low *o* off-season

stagista, -i, -e [sta'dʒista] SM, SF trainee (*Brit*), intern (*USA*)

stagliarsi [staʎ'ʎarsi] /27/ VIP: **stagliarsi contro** *o* **su** to stand out against, be silhouetted against

stagnante [staɲ'ɲante] AGG (*anche fig*) stagnant

stagnare¹ [staɲ'ɲare] /15/ VT **1** (*ricoprire di stagno*) to tinplate; (*saldare*) to solder **2** (*rendere ermetico*) to make watertight

stagnare² [staɲ'ɲare] /15/ VI (*aus* **avere**) (*acqua, anche Econ*) to stagnate; **l'aria stagnava nella stanza** the air in the room was stale ♦ VT (*sangue*) to stop

stagnino [staɲ'ɲino] SM tinsmith

stagno¹ ['staɲɲo] SM (*Chim*) tin; (*per saldare*) solder

stagno² ['staɲɲo] SM (*acquitrino*) pond

stagno³, -a ['staɲɲo] AGG (*a tenuta d'acqua*) watertight; (*a tenuta d'aria*) airtight

stagnola [staɲ'ɲola] SF (*anche: carta stagnola*) tinfoil, aluminium foil (*USA*)

stalagmite [stalag'mite] SF stalagmite

stalattite [stalat'tite] SF stalactite

stalinismo [stali'nizmo] SM (*Pol*) Stalinism

stalla ['stalla] SF (*per bovini*) cowshed; (*per cavalli*) stable; (*fig: casa sporca*) pigsty; **passare dalle stelle alle stalle** (*fig*) to come down in the world

stalliere [stal'ljere] SM groom, stableboy

stallo ['stallo] SM **1** stall, seat **2** (*Scacchi*) stalemate; (*Aer*) stall; **situazione di stallo** (*fig*) stalemate

stallone [stal'lone] SM stallion

stamani [sta'mani], **stamattina** [stamat'tina] AVV this morning

stambecco, -chi [stam'bekko] SM (*Zool*) ibex

stamberga, -ghe [stam'berga] SF hovel

staminale [stami'nale] AGG (*Bio*): **cellula staminale** stem cell

stampa ['stampa] SF **1** (*Tip, Fot: tecnica*) printing; (: *riproduzione, copia*) print; (*insieme dei quotidiani, giornalisti*): **la stampa** the press; **stampa a diffusione nazionale** national press; **andare in stampa** to go to press; **mandare in stampa** to pass for press; **il libro è in stampa** the book is being printed; **fuori stampa** out of print; **dare alle stampe un'opera** to have a work published; **errore di stampa** printing error; **prova di stampa** print sample; **libertà di stampa** freedom of the press; **"stampe"** "printed matter" *sg* **2** (*Tecn: di plastica*) moulding (*Brit*), molding (*USA*); (*di metallo*) pressing; (*di tessuto*) printing

stampante [stam'pante] SF (*Inform*) printer; **stampante ad aghi** dot matrix printer; **stampante a getto d'inchiostro** ink jet printer; **stampante laser** laser printer; **stampante di linea** line printer; **stampante a margherita** daisy wheel printer

stampare [stam'pare] /72/ VT **1** (*gen, anche Tip, Fot*) to print; (*denaro*) to strike, coin; (*pubblicare*) to publish; **ce l'ho stampato nella memoria** it's engraved in my memory; **stampatelo bene in testa!** get it into your head!; **gli ha stampato un bacio in fronte** she planted a kiss on his forehead; **non li stampo mica i soldi** I am not made of money **2** (*Tecn: plastica*) to mould (*Brit*), to mold (*USA*); (: *metalli*) to press; (: *tessuti*) to print; **stamparsi** VIP: **stamparsi nella mente** *o* **nella memoria** to be imprinted in one's memory

stampatello [stampa'tello] SM block capitals *pl*, block letters *pl*; **scrivere in** *o* **a stampatello** to write in block capitals *o* letters; **devo scrivere il mio nome in stampatello?** shall I write my name in block letters?

stampato, -a [stam'pato] AGG printed ♦ SM (*opuscolo*) leaflet; (*modulo*) form; (*Inform*) hard copy

stampella [stam'pella] SF (*apparecchio ortopedico*) crutch

stampigliare [stampiʎ'ʎare] /27/ VT to stamp

stampigliatura [stampiʎʎa'tura] SF (*atto*) stamping; (*marchio*) stamp

stampo ['stampo] SM (*gen, anche Culin*) mould (*Brit*), mold (*USA*); (*Tecn*) mo(u)ld, die; (*fig: indole*) type, kind, sort; **di stampo antico** old-fashioned; **essere fatto con lo stampo** (*fig*) to be all the same; **stampo a cerniera** (*Culin*) spring-release tin; **stampo per plum-cake** (*Culin*) loaf tin
❑ **stampo** non si traduce mai con la parola inglese *stamp*

stanare [sta'nare] /72/ VT to drive out

stancare [stan'kare] /20/ VT (*spossare*) to tire, make tired; (*annoiare*) to bore; (*infastidire*) to annoy; **non stancare i bambini con troppi giochi** don't tire the children with too many games; **il viaggio lo ha stancato molto** the journey tired him out; **mi hai stancato con le tue lamentele** I'm fed up of your complaining; **stancarsi** VIP to get tired, tire *o.s.* out; **non stancarti troppo** don't get too tired; **stancarsi (di)** (*stufarsi*) to grow tired (of), get fed up (with), grow weary (of); **mi sono stancato di aspettare** I got tired of waiting

stanchezza [stan'kettsa] SF (*fisica*) fatigue, tiredness; (*mentale*) tiredness, weariness; (*fig: noia*) weariness, boredom; **dare segni di stanchezza** to show signs of tiredness; **che stanchezza!, ho una stanchezza addosso!** I'm dead beat!

stanco, -a, -chi, -che ['stanko] AGG tired; **sei stanco?** are you tired?; **stanco morto** dead tired; **con una voce stanca disse...** he said wearily ...; **stanco di** (*stufo*) tired of, fed up with; **sono stanco di ripetere la stessa cosa** I'm tired of repeating the same thing; **stanco di vivere** tired of life; **nato stanco** (*scherz*) born idle

stand [stænd] SM INV (*in fiera*) stand

standard ['standard] AGG INV standard ♦ SM INV standard; **standard di vita** standard of living

standardizzare [standardid'dzare] /72/ VT to standardize

standista, -i, -e [stan'dista] SM, SF (*in una fiera*) person responsible for a stand

stanga, -ghe ['stanga] SF (*gen*) bar; (*di carro*) shaft; (*fig: fam: persona alta*) beanpole

stangare [stan'gare] /80/ VT (*colpire*) to beat, thrash; (*fig: far pagare troppo*) to sting; (: *bocciare*) to fail

stangata [stan'gata] SF (*gen, anche fig*) blow; (*Calcio*) shot; **prendere una stangata** (*fam: pagare troppo*) to get stung; (: *agli esami*) to fail miserably; **stangata fiscale** tax hike

stanghetta [stan'getta] SF **1** (*di occhiali*) leg **2** (*Mus: di scrittura*) bar-line

stanno ['stanno] VB *vedi* **stare**

stanotte [sta'nɔtte] AVV (*nella notte in corso o che sta per venire*) tonight; (*nella notte appena passata*) last night; **stanotte ci saranno i fuochi d'artificio** there are going to be fireworks tonight; **stanotte non ho dormito bene** I didn't sleep well last night

stante ['stante] AGG: **a sé stante** (*appartamento, casa*) independent, separate; **seduta stante** (*fig: subito*) on the spot ♦ PREP owing to, because of

stantio, -tia, -tii, -tie [stan'tio] AGG (*anche fig*) stale; (*burro*) rancid; **sapere di stantio** to taste stale (*o* rancid); **idee stantie** old-fashioned ideas

stantuffo [stan'tuffo] SM piston

stanza ['stantsa] SF **1** (*vano*) room; **stanza da bagno** bathroom; **stanza dei bottoni** (*fig*) control room; **stanza da letto** bedroom **2** (*Poesia*) stanza **3** **essere di stanza a** (*Mil*) to be stationed in
❑ **stanza** non si traduce mai con la parola inglese *stance*

stanziamento [stantsja'mento] SM allocation

stanziare [stan'tsjare] /19/ VT **1** () to allocate **2** (*Fin*) to ring-fence; **stanziarsi** VIP (*gen*) to settle; (*Mil*) to be stationed

stanzino [stan'tsino] SM (*ripostiglio*) storeroom; (*spogliatoio*) changing room (*Brit*), locker room (*USA*)

stappare [stap'pare] /72/ VT (*bottiglia: con tappo di sughero*) to uncork; (: *con tappo a corona*) to uncap

star [star] SF INV (*attore, attrice*) star

stare ['stare] /116/ VI IRREG (*aus* **essere**) **1** (*rimanere*) to stay, be, remain; **stare in piedi** to stand; **stare fermo** to keep *o* stay still; **stare seduto** to sit, be sitting; **stare disteso** to lie; **stare zitto** to keep *o* be quiet; **stai dove sei!** stay where you are!;

stai ancora un po'! stay a bit longer!; **starò a Roma per qualche giorno** I'll stay *o* be in Rome for a few days; **stare a casa** to be *o* stay at home; **è stato su tutta la notte** he stayed up *o* was up all night; **stare in equilibrio** to keep one's balance **2** (*abitare: temporaneamente*) to stay; (: *permanentemente*) to live; **sta con i suoi** he lives with his parents; **sta da solo** he lives on his own; **dove stai di casa?** where do you live?; **sta in via Rossetti 5** he lives at No. 5 via Rossetti; **al momento sta con degli amici** he's staying with friends at the moment **3** (*essere, trovarsi*) to be, be situated; **la casa sta in cima al colle** the house is at the top of the hill; **stando così le cose** given the situation; **le cose stanno così** this is the situation; **non voglio stare da solo** I don't want to be on my own; **sei mai stato in Francia?** have you ever been to France?; **sono stato dal dentista** I've been to the dentist; **come stai?** how are you?; **sto bene, grazie** I'm fine, thanks; **sta bene!** (*d'accordo così*) that's fine!; **come mi sta?** how does it look?; **quel vestito ti sta bene/male** that dress suits/doesn't suit you; **queste scarpe mi stanno strette** these shoes are too tight for me; **questa giacca non mi sta** this jacket doesn't fit me; **gli sta bene!** (*così impara*) it serves him right!; **stai sicuro che non la passerà liscia!** rest assured he won't get away with it!; **stare al banco** (*cameriere*) to serve at the bar; **stare alla cassa** to work at the till; **stare a dieta** to be on a diet **4** (*seguito da gerundio*): **stavo andando a casa** I was going home; **cosa stai facendo?** what are you doing?; **sta studiando** he's studying; **stava piovendo** it was raining **5 stare per fare qc** to be about to do sth, be on the point of doing sth; **stavo per uscire quando ha squillato il telefono** I was about to go out when the phone rang; **stavi per rovinare tutto** you nearly spoiled *o* ruined everything **6 stare a sentire** to listen; **sta' a sentire** listen a minute; **stare ad insistere** to insist; **è inutile che stai a dirmi tutte queste cose** there's no good *o* use telling me all this; **sta a te decidere** it's up to you to decide; **stando a ciò che dice lui** according to him *o* to his version; **stando ai fatti, sembrerebbe che...** the facts would seem to indicate that ...; **staremo a vedere** let's wait and see; **stiamo a vedere cosa succede** let's wait and see (what happens) **7 starci,** (*essere contenuto*) **ci sta ancora qualcosa lì dentro?** is there room for anything else?; **nel bagagliaio non ci sta più niente** there's no room for anything more in the boot (*Brit*) *o* trunk (*USA*); **non credo ci stia tutta quella pasta** I don't think there's room for all that pasta; **non ci stanno più di 4 persone in quella macchina** there is only room for 4 in that car; **il 5 nel 25 ci sta 5 volte** 5 goes into 25 5 times **8 starci,** (*essere d'accordo*) **ci stai se andiamo** *o* **ad andare fuori a cena?** do you want to go out for a meal?; **ha detto che non ci sta** he said he didn't agree, he said he was against the idea; **OK, ci sto** OK, that's fine **9 starsene, se ne stava lì in un angolo** he was over in the corner; **se n'è stato zitto** he never opened his mouth; **non startene lì seduto, fa' qualcosa** don't just sit there, do something; **stasera me ne sto a casa** I'll be staying in tonight

❏ **stare** non si traduce mai con la parola inglese *stare*

starnazzare [starnat'tsare] /72/ vɪ (*aus* avere) to squawk; (*fig: far chiasso*) to make a din

starnutire [starnu'tire] /55/ vɪ (*aus* avere) to sneeze

starnuto [star'nuto] sᴍ sneeze; **fare uno starnuto** to sneeze

stasera [sta'sera] ᴀᴠᴠ this evening, tonight

stasi ['stazi] sꜰ (*Med, anche fig*) stasis

statale [sta'tale] ᴀɢɢ government *attr*, state *attr*; **bilancio statale** national budget; **impiegato statale** state employee, civil servant; **un'industria statale** a state-owned industry; **strada statale** ≈ main *o* trunk (*Brit*) road ♦ sᴍ, sꜰ (*impiegato*) state employee, ≈ civil servant ♦ sꜰ (*strada*) ≈ main *o* trunk (*Brit*) road

statalizzare [statalid'dzare] /72/ ᴠᴛ to nationalize, put under state control

statico, -a, -ci, -che ['statiko] ᴀɢɢ (*Elettr, anche fig*) static

statista, -i [sta'tista] sᴍ statesman

statistico, -a, -ci, -che [sta'tistiko] ᴀɢɢ statistical

stato¹, -a ['stato] ᴘᴘ *di* essere stare

stato² ['stato] sᴍ **1** (*condizione: gen*) state; (*di paziente*) condition; **la macchina è in buono stato** the car is in good condition; **stato d'animo** state of mind; **stato (di salute)** state

of health; **guarda in che stato si è ridotto!** look at the state it (*o* he) is in!; **vivere allo stato selvaggio** to live in the wild **2** (*fraseologia*): **essere in stato d'accusa** (*Dir*) to have been charged with an offence (*Brit*) *o* offense (*USA*), be committed for trial; **essere in stato d'arresto** (*Dir*) to be under arrest; **essere in stato d'assedio** to be under siege; **essere in stato d'emergenza** to be in a state of emergency; **essere in stato interessante** to be pregnant; **allo stato liquido/gassoso** in the liquid/gaseous state ♦ **stato civile** (*Amm*) marital status; **stato di famiglia** (*Amm*) *certificate giving details of a household and its dependents*; **Stato Maggiore** (*Mil*) general staff *sg o pl*; **stato patrimoniale** statement of assets and liabilities

stato³ ['stato] sᴍ (*Pol*) state; **di stato** state *attr*; **uno stato totalitario** a totalitarian state; **un capo di stato** a head of state; **stato assistenziale** (*pegg*) welfare state; **stato di diritto** legally constituted state; **stato sociale** welfare state; **gli Stati Uniti (d'America)** the United States (of America)

statua ['statua] sꜰ statue

statunitense [statuni'tɛnse] ᴀɢɢ United States *attr*, of the United States; **il governo statunitense** the government of the United States ♦ sᴍ, sꜰ American citizen, citizen of the United States

statura [sta'tura] sꜰ (*gen*) height; (*fig*) stature; **essere alto/basso di statura** to be tall/short; **un uomo politico della sua statura** (*fig*) a politician of his stature

statuto [sta'tuto] sᴍ statute; **regione a statuto speciale** *Italian region with political autonomy in certain matters*; **statuto della società** (*Comm*) articles *pl* of association

stavolta [sta'volta] ᴀᴠᴠ this time

stazionamento [stattsjona'mento] sᴍ (*Aut*) parking; (*sosta*) waiting; **freno di stazionamento** handbrake

stazionare [stattsjo'nare] /72/ vɪ (*aus* avere) (*veicolo*) to be parked

stazionario, -ria, -ri, -rie [stattsjo'narjo] ᴀɢɢ (*temperatura, condizioni di salute*) stable, unchanged

stazione [stat'tsjone] sꜰ **1** (*gen, anche Radio*) station; **stazione degli autobus** bus *o* coach (*Brit*) station; **stazione ferroviaria** railway (*Brit*) *o* railroad (*USA*) station; **stazione di lavoro** (*Inform*) work station; **stazione meteorologica** weather station; **stazione radio** radio station; **stazione di servizio** filling *o* petrol (*Brit*) *o* gas (*USA*) station; **stazione trasmittente** (*Radio, TV*) transmitting station **2** (*località*): **stazione seaside resort**; **stazione climatica** health resort; **stazione invernale** winter sports resort; **stazione sciistica** ski resort; **stazione termale** (*thermal*) spa **3** (*Rel*): **stazione della Via Crucis** Station of the Cross

stazza ['stattsa] sꜰ (*gen*) tonnage; (*di regata*) rating

st. civ. ᴀʙʙʀ = stato civile

stecca, -che ['stekka] sꜰ (*gen*) stick; (*di ombrello*) rib; (*da biliardo*) cue; (*Med*) splint; (*di sigarette*) carton; **prendere una stecca** (*fig: stonatura: cantando*) to sing a wrong note; (: *suonando*) to play a wrong note

steccato [stek'kato] sᴍ fence

stecchito, -a [stek'kito] ᴀɢɢ (*ramo*) dried up; (*persona*) skinny; **morto stecchito** stone dead; **lasciare qn stecchito** (*fig: sorpreso*) to leave sb flabbergasted

stella ['stella] sꜰ star; **stanotte si vedono le stelle** you can see the stars tonight; **senza stelle** starless; **alla luce delle stelle** by starlight; **dormire sotto le stelle** to sleep out under the stars; **vedere le stelle** (*per il dolore*) to see stars; **ringrazia la tua buona stella** thank your lucky stars; **nascere sotto una buona/cattiva stella** to be born under a lucky/an unlucky star; **i prezzi sono andati** *o* **saliti alle stelle** prices have gone sky-high; **portare alle stelle qn** to lavish praise on sb; **una stella del cinema** a film star; **la sua stella sta tramontando** his star is waning; **stella alpina** (*Bot*) edelweiss; **stella cadente** shooting star; **stella di mare** (*Zool*) starfish; **stella di Natale** (*Bot*) poinsettia; **stella polare** pole *o* north star; **stelle filanti** (*per carnevale*) streamers

stellato, -a [stel'lato] ᴀɢɢ (*cielo, notte*) starry

stelo ['stelo] sᴍ (*Bot*) stem; (*asta*) rod; **lampada a stelo** standard lamp (*Brit*), floor lamp (*USA*)

stemma, -i ['stemma] sᴍ coat of arms

❏ **stemma** non si traduce mai con la parola inglese *stem*

stemmo ecc [ˈstemmo] VB vedi **stare**

stemperare [stempeˈrare] /72/ VT (calce, colore) to dissolve

stempiato, -a [stemˈpjato] AGG with a receding hairline; **essere stempiato** to have a receding hairline

stempiatura [stempjaˈtura] SF receding hairline

stendardo [stenˈdardo] SM standard

stendere [ˈstendere] VB IRREG /120/ VT 1 (braccia, gambe) to stretch (out); (tovaglia) to spread (out); (bucato) to hang out; (spalmare) to spread; (pasta) to roll out 2 (persona: far giacere) to lay (down); (: gettare a terra, fig: vincere) to floor; (: uccidere) to kill; **far stendere qn** to lay sb down 3 (lettera, verbale) to draw up; **stendersi** VR (persona) to lie down; **stendersi a terra/sul letto** to lie down on the ground/on the bed; **si è steso sul letto** he lay down on the bed; **stendersi** VIP (pianura, vallata) to extend, stretch

stendibiancheria [stendibjankeˈria] SM INV clotheshorse

stenditoio, -oi [stendiˈtojo] SM (locale) drying room; (stendibiancheria) clotheshorse

stenodattilografia [stenodattilograˈfia] SF shorthand typing (Brit), stenography (USA)

stenodattilografo, -a [stenodattiˈlɔgrafo] SM, SF shorthand typist (Brit), stenographer (USA)

stenografare [stenograˈfare] /72/ VT to take down in shorthand

stenografia [stenograˈfia] SF shorthand, stenography (USA)

stenografo, -a [steˈnɔgrafo] SM, SF shorthand typist (Brit), stenographer (USA)

stentare [stenˈtare] /72/ VI (aus avere) **stentare a fare qc** to have difficulty in doing sth, find it hard to do sth; **stento a crederci** I find it hard to believe

stentato, -a [stenˈtato] AGG (compito, stile) laboured (Brit), labored (USA); (sorriso) forced

stento [ˈstento] SM 1 **stenti** SMPL (privazioni) hardship sg, privation sg; **una vita di stenti** a life of hardship o privation; **vivere tra gli stenti** to live a life of hardship o privation 2 **a stento** AVV with difficulty, barely; **capire qc a stento** to understand sth with difficulty; **riesco a stento a pagare l'affitto** I only just manage to pay the rent

steppa [ˈsteppa] SF steppe

sterco [ˈsterko] SM dung

stereo [ˈstereo] AGG INV, SM INV stereo

stereofonia [stereofoˈnia] SF stereophony

stereofonico, -a, -ci, -che [stereoˈfɔniko] AGG stereo(phonic)

stereotipato, -a [stereotiˈpato] AGG (anche fig) stereotyped

stereotipo [stereˈɔtipo] SM stereotype; **pensare per stereotipi** to think in clichés

sterile [ˈsterile] AGG (terreno) arid, barren; (persona) sterile; (fig: polemica) fruitless, futile

sterilità [steriliˈta] SF (vedi agg) barrenness; sterility; fruitlessness

sterilizzare [sterilidˈdzare] /72/ VT to sterilize

sterilizzazione [steriliddzatˈtsjone] SF sterilization

sterlina [sterˈlina] SF pound (sterling)

sterminare [stermiˈnare] /72/ VT to exterminate, wipe out

sterminato, -a [stermiˈnato] AGG immense, endless

sterminio, -ni [sterˈminjo] SM extermination, destruction; **campo di sterminio** death camp

sterno [ˈsterno] SM (Anat) breastbone, sternum (termine tecn)

steroide [steˈrɔide] SM steroid

sterpaglia [sterˈpaʎʎa] SF brushwood

sterpo [ˈsterpo] SM dry twig

sterrare [sterˈrare] /72/ VT to excavate

sterzare [sterˈtsare] /72/ VT, VI (aus avere) (Aut) to steer; (bruscamente) to swerve; (Pol): **sterzare a destra/a sinistra** to veer to the right/the left

sterzo [ˈstertso] SM (volante) steering wheel

steso, -a [ˈsteso] PP di **stendere**

stessi ecc [ˈstessi] VB vedi **stare**

stesso, -a [ˈstesso] AGG 1 (medesimo, identico) same; **aveva lo stesso vestito** she had the same dress; **abbiamo gli stessi gusti** we have the same tastes; **al tempo stesso** at the same time; **è sempre la stessa storia** it's always the same old thing 2 (esatto, preciso) very; **in quello stesso istante** at

that very moment; **quello stesso giorno** the very same day; **oggi stesso** today 3 (rafforzativo: dopo sostantivo): **il medico stesso lo sconsiglia** even the doctor o the doctor himself advises against it; **è venuto il ministro stesso ad inaugurarlo** the minister himself came to inaugurate it 4 (rafforzativo: dopo pron pers sogg): **l'ho visto io stesso** I saw him myself; **voi stessi sapete bene che...** you (yourselves) know very well that ...; **lei stessa è venuta a dirmelo** she came and told me herself, she herself came and told me 5 (rafforzativo: dopo pron rifl): **me stesso** myself; **te stesso** yourself; **se stesso** himself; (neutro) itself; (indef) oneself; **se stessa** herself; **noi stessi** ourselves; **voi stessi** yourselves; **loro stessi** themselves; **ama solo se stesso** he only loves himself; **di per sé stesso non ha un gran valore** it's not worth a lot in itself 6 (proprio) own; **l'ho visto con i miei stessi occhi** I saw it with my own eyes; **l'ho sentito con le mie stesse orecchie** I heard it with my own ears; **l'ha fatto con le sue stesse mani** he did it with his own hands ♦ PRON DIMOSTR **lo(la) stesso(a)** the same (one); **sei la stessa di sempre** you're the same as ever; **chi canta? — lo stesso di prima** who's singing? — the same singer as before; **per me fa lo stesso** it's all the same to me; **per me è lo stesso** it doesn't matter to me ♦ **lo stesso** AVV (comunque) all the same, even so; **parto lo stesso** I'm going all the same

stesura [steˈsura] SF (azione) drafting no pl, drawing up no pl; (documento) draft

stetoscopio, -pi [stetosˈkɔpjo] SM stethoscope

stetti ecc [ˈstetti] VB vedi **stare**

stia¹ [ˈstia] VB vedi **stare**

stia² [ˈstia] SF (chicken) coop

stigma, -i [ˈstigma] SM (Bot, Zool, anche fig) stigma

stigmate [ˈstigmate] SFPL (Rel) stigmata pl

stilare [stiˈlare] /72/ VT to draw up, draft

stile [ˈstile] SM (gen) style; (classe) style, class; (Nuoto): **gli stili architettonici** architectural styles; **bisogna ammettere che ha stile!** you have to admit he's got style!; **stile libero** freestyle, crawl; **sai nuotare a stile libero?** can you do the crawl?; **i cento metri stile libero** the hundred metres freestyle; **mobili in stile** period furniture; **in grande stile** in great style; **è proprio nel suo stile** (fig) it's just like him; **non è nel suo stile** (fig) it's not like him

stilismo SM concern for style

stilista, -i, -e [stiˈlista] SM, SF (Moda) designer

stilistico, -a, -ci, -che [stiˈlistiko] AGG stylistic

stilizzato, -a [stilidˈdzato] AGG stylized

stillare [stilˈlare] /72/ VT, VI (aus essere) (gocciolare) to drip; (trasudare) to ooze

stillicidio, -di [stilliˈtʃidjo] SM (fig): **uno stillicidio di rivelazioni** a steady stream of revelations

stilografica, -che [stiloˈgrafika] SF (anche: **penna stilografica**) fountain pen

Stim. ABBR = **stimato**

stima [ˈstima] SF 1 (buona opinione) respect, esteem; **avere stima di qn** to have respect for sb; **ho molta stima di lui** I have great respect for him; **godere della stima di qn** to enjoy sb's respect 2 (Econ, Fin) estimate, valuation, assessment; **fare la stima di qc** to estimate the value of sth; **la stima dei danni** estimate of the damage; **stima approssimativa** guesstimate (fam)

stimare [stiˈmare] /72/ VT 1 (persona) to respect, esteem, hold in high regard; **la stimo molto** I really respect her 2 (Econ, Fin) to assess the value of, estimate the value of, value

stimolante [stimoˈlante] AGG stimulating ♦ SM stimulant

stimolare [stimoˈlare] /72/ VT (gen) to stimulate; **stimolare qn a fare qc** (incitare) to spur sb on to do sth

stimolazione [stimolatˈtsjone] SF stimulation

stimolo [ˈstimolo] SM (anche fig) stimulus

stinco, -chi [ˈstinko] SM (Anat: persona) shinbone, shin; (: di animale) shank; **non essere uno stinco di santo** to be no saint

stingere [ˈstindʒere] VB IRREG /37/ VT, VI (aus essere), **stingersi** VIP to fade

stinto, -a [ˈstinto] PP di **stingere** ♦ AGG faded

stipare [stiˈpare] /72/ VT to cram, pack; **stiparsi** VIP (accalcarsi): **stiparsi in** to crowd into, throng

stipendiare [stipen'djare] /19/ VT (*pagare*) to pay (a salary to)
stipendiato, -a [stipen'djato] AGG salaried ♦ SM, SF salaried worker
stipendio, -di [sti'pendjo] SM salary
stipite ['stipite] SM (*di porta, finestra*) jamb
stipulare [stipu'lare] /72/ VT (*accordo, contratto*) to draw up
❑ **stipulare** non si traduce mai con la parola inglese *stipulate*
stipulazione [stipulat'tsjone] SF (*di contratto: stesura*) drafting; (*firma*) signing
stiracchiare [stirak'kjare] /19/ VT (*fig: significato di una parola*) to stretch, force; **stiracchiarsi** VR (*persona*) to stretch
stiramento [stira'mento] SM (*Med*) sprain
stirare [sti'rare] /72/ VT 1 (*con ferro da stiro*) to iron 2 (*distendere*) to stretch; (*Med*): **stirarsi un legamento** to pull a ligament; **stirarsi** VR to stretch (o.s.)
stiratura [stira'tura] SF 1 (*con ferro da stiro*) ironing 2 (*Med*) sprain
stirpe ['stirpe] SF 1 (*schiatta*) birth, stock; **di nobile stirpe** of noble descent 2 (*discendenti*) descendants *pl*
stitichezza [stiti'kettsa] SF constipation
stitico, -a, -ci, -che ['stitiko] AGG constipated
stiva ['stiva] SF (*di nave, aereo*) hold
stivale [sti'vale] SM boot; **quel medico dei miei stivali!** (*pegg*) that apology for a doctor!; **stivale da birra** boot-shaped beer glass; **stivali di gomma** wellingtons
stivaletto [stiva'letto] SM ankle boot
stivare [sti'vare] /72/ VT to stow, load
stizza ['stittsa] SF anger, vexation
stizzire [stit'tsire] /55/ VT to irritate; **stizzirsi** VIP to become irritated, become vexed
stizzoso, -a [stit'tsoso] AGG (*persona*) irascible, quick-tempered; (*risposta*) angry
stoccafisso [stokka'fisso] SM stockfish, dried cod
Stoccarda [stok'karda] SF Stuttgart
stoccata [stok'kata] SF (*Scherma*) thrust, stab; (*Calcio*) shot; (*fig: allusione*) gibe, cutting remark
Stoccolma [stok'kolma] SF Stockholm
stock [stok] SM INV (*Comm*) stock
stoffa ['stoffa] SF material, fabric; **avere della stoffa** (*fig*) to have what it takes; **avere la stoffa per diventare qc** to have the makings of sth
stoicismo [stoi'tʃizmo] SM stoicism
stoico, -a, -ci, -che ['stoiko] AGG, SM, SF (*anche fig*) stoic(al)
stoino [sto'ino] SM doormat
stola ['stola] SF (*gen, anche Rel*) stole
stoltezza [stol'tettsa] SF (*qualità*) stupidity; (*azione*) foolish action
stolto, -a ['stolto] AGG stupid, foolish ♦ SM, SF fool
stomaco, -chi ['stomako] SM stomach; **ho mal di stomaco** I've got a stomach ache; **dare di stomaco** to be sick; **avere qc sullo stomaco** to have sth lying on one's stomach; **quel tipo mi sta sullo stomaco** I can't stand that guy; **mi fa rivoltare lo stomaco** (*anche fig*) it makes me sick; **bisogna avere dello stomaco per fare quel lavoro** you need a strong stomach to do that kind of work
stonare [sto'nare] /72/ VT (*cantando*) to sing out of tune; (*suonando*) to play out of tune ♦ VI (*aus avere*) to be out of tune, sing *o* play out of tune; (*fig: colori*) to clash
stonato, -a [sto'nato] AGG (*persona, strumento*) off-key, out of tune; **c'era una nota stonata** (*fig*) something didn't ring true
stonatura [stona'tura] SF (*suono*) false note
stop [stop] SM INV 1 (*Aut: fanalino*) brake-light; (: *segnale stradale*) stop sign 2 (*Telegrafia*) stop
stoppa ['stoppa] SF tow; **come stoppa** (*capelli*) tow-coloured (*Brit*), tow-colored (*USA*); **essere come un pulcino nella stoppa** to look lost and helpless
stoppia ['stoppja] SF stubble
stoppino [stop'pino] SM (*di candela*) wick; (*miccia*) fuse
storcere ['stortʃere] VB IRREG /106/ VT (*gen*) to twist; **storcere il naso** (*fig*) to turn up one's nose; **storcersi la caviglia** to twist one's ankle; **storcersi** VIP to writhe, twist
stordimento [stordi'mento] SM (*gen*) daze; (*da droga*) stupefaction

stordire [stor'dire] /55/ VT (*sogg: colpo, notizia, droga*) to stun, daze; **stordirsi** VR (*fig*): **stordirsi col bere** to dull one's senses with drink, drink o.s. stupid
stordito, -a [stor'dito] AGG (*intontito*) dazed, stunned; (*sventato*) scatterbrained, heedless
storia ['storja] SF 1 (*scienza, materia, opera*) history; **l'insegnante di storia** the history teacher; **libro di storia** history book; **passare alla storia** to go down in history; **storia dell'arte** history of art 2 (*racconto, bugia*) story; (*pretesto*) excuse, pretext; **una storia d'amore** a love story; **è sempre la stessa storia** it's the same old story; **mi racconti una storia?** will you tell me a story?; **mi ha raccontato un sacco di storie** he told me a lot of nonsense *o* rubbish (*Brit*); **sono tutte storie!** it's all lies! 3 (*faccenda*) business; **non voglio saperne più di questa storia** I don't want to hear any more about this business; **è sempre la solita storia** it's always the same old story 4 **storie** SFPL (*capricci*) fuss *sg*; **non ha fatto storie** he didn't make a fuss; **senza tante storie!** don't make such a fuss! 5 (*relazione amorosa*) affair
storicità [storitʃi'ta] SF historical authenticity
storico, -a, -ci, -che ['storiko] AGG (*gen*) historical; (*memorabile*) historic; **un personaggio storico** a historical figure; **è stato un momento storico** it was a historic moment ♦ SM, SF historian
storiografia [storjogra'fia] SF historiography
storione [sto'rjone] SM (*Zool*) sturgeon
stormire [stor'mire] /55/ VI (*aus avere*) to rustle
stormo ['stormo] SM (*di uccelli*) flock
stornare [stor'nare] /72/ VT 1 (*Comm*) to transfer 2 (*fig: evitare: pericolo*) to avert
stornello [stor'nello] SM *kind of folk song*
storno ['storno] SM 1 (*Zool*) starling 2 (*Comm*) transfer
storpiare [stor'pjare] /19/ VT (*persona*) to cripple, maim; (*fig: parole*) to mangle; **storpiarsi** VIP to become crippled
storpiatura [storpja'tura] SF (*fig: di significato*) mangling
storpio, -pia, -pi, -pie ['storpjo] AGG crippled, maimed ♦ SM, SF cripple
storsi *ecc* ['storsi] VB *vedi* **storcere**
storto, -a ['storto] PP *di* **storcere** ♦ AGG (*tubo, chiodo*) twisted, bent; (*ruota*) buckled, warped; (*manubrio, quadro*) crooked; (*fig: ragionamento*) false, wrong; **avere le gambe storte** to have crooked legs; **avere gli occhi storti** to have a squint, be cross-eyed; **mi va tutto storto, mi vanno tutte storte** (*fam*) everything's going wrong ♦ AVV: **guardare storto qn** (*fig*) to look askance at sb
stoviglie [sto'viʎʎe] SFPL dishes
Str. ABBR (*Geog*) = **stretto**
strabico, -a, -ci, -che ['strabiko] AGG (*occhi*) squint; (*persona*): **essere strabico** to have a squint
strabiliante [strabi'ljante] AGG astonishing, amazing
strabiliare [strabi'ljare] /19/ VI (*aus avere*) to astonish, amaze
strabismo [stra'bizmo] SM squinting
strabuzzare [strabud'dzare] /72/ VT: **strabuzzare gli occhi** to open one's eyes wide
stracarico, -a, -chi, -che [stra'kariko] AGG overloaded
stracchino [strak'kino] SM *type of soft cheese*
stracciare [strat'tʃare] /14/ VT to tear up, rip up; **ho stracciato la lettera** I tore up the letter; **stracciare gli avversari** to wipe the floor with one's opponents; **stracciarsi** VIP to tear, rip
straccio, -cia, -ci, -ce ['strattʃo] AGG: **carta straccia** wastepaper ♦ SM (*gen*) rag; (*per pulire*) cloth, duster; (*fig: persona*) wretch; **non ho uno straccio di vestito** I haven't got a thing to wear
straccione, -a [strat'tʃone] SM, SF ragamuffin
straccivendolo [strattʃi'vendolo] SM ragman
stracco, -a, -chi, -che ['strakko] AGG: **stracco (morto)** exhausted, dead tired
stracotto, -a [stra'kotto] PP *di* **stracuocere** ♦ AGG overcooked ♦ SM (*Culin*) beef stew
strada ['strada] SF 1 (*gen*) road; (*di città*) street; **andare fuori strada** (*Aut*) to go off the road; **attraversare la strada** to cross the road; **tagliare la strada a qn** to cut across in front of sb; **l'uomo della strada** (*fig*) the man in the street; **donna di strada** (*fig: pegg*) streetwalker; **ragazzo di strada** (*fig: pegg*)

street urchin; **strada ferrata** railway (*Brit*), railroad (*USA*); **strada principale** main road; **strada a senso unico** one-way street; **strada senza uscita** dead end, cul-de-sac **2** (*percorso*) way; **qual è la strada per andare al cinema?** which is the way to the cinema?, how does one get to the cinema?; **mostrare la strada a qn** to show sb the way; **c'è tanta strada da fare?** is it a long way?; **tre ore di strada (a piedi)/(in macchina)** three hours' walk/drive; **non è sulla mia strada** it's not on my way; **facciamo la strada insieme?** shall we go along together?; **strada facendo** on the way **3** (*fig*) path, way, road; **essere sulla buona strada** (*nella vita*) to be on the right path; (*Polizia: ricerca*) to be on the right track; **essere fuori strada** (*Polizia*) to be on the wrong track; **portare qn sulla cattiva strada** to lead sb astray **4** (*fraseologia*): **fare** o **farsi strada** (*fig: persona*) to get on in life; **farsi strada tra la folla** to make one's way through the crowd; **trovarsi in mezzo ad una strada** to find o.s. out on the streets; **fare strada a qn** to show sb the way; **ti faccio strada** I'll show you the way

stradale [stra'dale] AGG (*gen*) road *attr*; (*polizia, regolamento*) traffic *attr*; **un cartello stradale** a road sign ♦ SF (*polizia*) traffic police

stradario, -ri [stra'darjo] SM street guide

stradino [stra'dino] SM road worker

strafalcione [strafal'tʃone] SM (*errore*) howler, blunder

strafare [stra'fare] /53/ VI IRREG (*aus* avere) to overdo it

strafatto, -a [stra'fatto] PP di **strafare**

straforo [stra'foro] **di straforo** AVV (*di nascosto*) on the sly

strafottente [strafot'tɛnte] AGG arrogant ♦ SM, SF arrogant person

strafottenza [strafot'tɛntsa] SF arrogance

strage ['stradʒe] SF massacre, slaughter; **fare una strage** to carry out a massacre o slaughter; **fare strage di** (*animali*) to slaughter; **fare strage di cuori** to be a heartbreaker

stragrande [stra'grande] AGG: **la stragrande maggioranza** the overwhelming majority

stralciare [stral'tʃare] /14/ VT to remove

stralcio, -ci ['straltʃo] SM (*Comm*): **vendere a stralcio** to sell off (at bargain prices), clear ♦ AGG INV: **legge stralcio** *abridged version of an act*

stralunato, -a [stralu'nato] AGG (*occhi*) staring; (*persona*) dazed, thunderstruck

stramazzare [stramat'tsare] /72/ VI (*aus* essere) to collapse, fall heavily; **stramazzare al suolo** to crash to the floor

stramberia [strambe'ria] SF eccentricity

strambo, -a ['strambo] AGG strange; **un tipo strambo** an odd person

strampalato, -a [strampa'lato] AGG odd, eccentric

stranamente [strana'mente] AVV (*comportarsi, vestirsi*) oddly, strangely; **e lui, stranamente, ha accettato** and, surprisingly, he agreed

stranezza [stra'nettsa] SF (*qualità*) strangeness; (*atto*): **le sue stranezze mi preoccupano** his strange behaviour (*Brit*) o behavior (*USA*) worries me

strangolare [strango'lare] /72/ VT to strangle ♦ VIP to choke

straniero, -a [stra'njero] AGG (*gen*) foreign; (*Amm*) alien; **un paese straniero** a foreign country ♦ SM, SF (*gen*) foreigner; (*Amm*) alien; **cacciare lo straniero** to drive out foreigners ❏ **straniero** non si traduce mai con la parola inglese *stranger*

stranito, -a [stra'nito] AGG (*sguardo, aria*) dazed

strano, -a ['strano] AGG (*gen*) strange; (*bizzarro*) strange, odd; **è strano che...** it is odd that ...; **e cosa strana...** strangely enough ...

straordinario, -ria, -ri, -rie [straordi'narjo] AGG (*gen*) extraordinary; (*treno, imposta*) special; (*impiegato*) temporary; **lavoro straordinario** overtime ♦ SM (*impiegato*) temporary employee; (*lavoro*) overtime; **ho fatto tre ore di straordinario** I did three hours' overtime

strapazzare [strapat'tsare] /72/ VT (*maltrattare: persona, oggetto*) to handle roughly, ill-treat; (*affaticare*) to tire out; **strapazzarsi** VR to tire o.s. out, overdo things

strapazzato, -a [strapat'tsato] AGG (*persona: affaticato*) worn out; **uova strapazzate** scrambled eggs

strapazzo [stra'pattso] SM **1** strain, fatigue **2 da strapazzo** (*fig: pegg: persona*) third-rate

strapieno, -a [stra'pjeno] AGG overflowing, full to overflowing; **essere** o **sentirsi strapieno** to be o feel full up

strapiombo [stra'pjombo] SM (*roccia*) overhanging rock; **a strapiombo** overhanging

strapotere [strapo'tere] SM excessive power

strappalacrime [strappa'lakrime] AGG INV (*fam*): **romanzo** (*o film*) **strappalacrime** tear-jerker

strappare [strap'pare] /72/ VT (*gen*) to tear, rip; (*pagina*) to tear off, tear out; (*erbacce*) to pull up; (*bottone*) to pull off; **ha strappato la lettera** she tore up the letter; **strappare qc di mano a qn** to snatch sth out of sb's hand; **mi ha strappato la borsa** he snatched the bag from me; **si strappò la gonna** she tore o ripped her skirt; **strapparsi i vestiti di dosso** to rip one's clothes off; **strapparsi i capelli** to tear one's hair; **strapparsi un muscolo** to tear a muscle; **strappare una promessa a qn** to extract a promise from sb; **strappare un segreto a qn** to wring a secret from sb; **strappare gli applausi del pubblico** to win the audience's applause; **strappare qn dal suo ambiente** to take sb away from his (*o her*) own environment; **una scena che strappa il cuore** a heart-rending scene; **strapparsi** VIP (*lacerarsi*) to tear, rip; **la camicia si è strappata sulla manica** the sleeve of the shirt is torn

strappato, -a [strap'pato] AGG (*lacerato*) torn, ripped

strappo ['strappo] SM **1** (*lacerazione*) tear, rip; **c'è uno strappo nella camicia** there's a tear in the shirt; **strappo muscolare** (*Med*) strain, tear, torn muscle **2** (*strattone*) tug, pull; **dare uno strappo a qc** to give sth a tug; **fare uno strappo alla regola** to make an exception to the rule **3** (*fig: fam: passaggio*) lift (*Brit*), ride (*USA*); **puoi darmi uno strappo (fino) in centro?** can you give me a lift o ride into town?

strapuntino [strapun'tino] SM (*sedile*) foldaway seat, jump seat

straripare [strari'pare] /72/ VI (*aus* avere o essere) (*fiume*) to overflow, burst its banks

Strasburgo [straz'burgo] SF Strasbourg

strascicare [straʃʃi'kare] /20/ VT (*trascinare*): **strascicare qc per terra** to drag sth along the ground, trail sth along the ground; **strascicare i piedi** to drag one's feet; **strascicare le parole** to drawl; **strascicare un lavoro** to drag out o draw out a piece of work; **strascicare una malattia** to be unable to shake off an illness ♦ VI (*aus* avere) to trail; **strascicarsi** VR (*trascinarsi*) to drag o.s. (along)

strascico, -chi ['straʃʃiko] SM **1** (*di abito*) train; **reggere lo strascico a qn** to carry sb's train; (*fig*) to lick sb's boots **2 rete a strascico** trawl (net); **pesca a strascico** trawling **3** (*fig: conseguenza*) after-effect

stratagemma, -i [strata'dʒemma] SM (*Mil, anche fig*) stratagem

stratega, -ghi [stra'tega] SM strategist

strategia, -gie [strate'dʒia] SF (*Mil, anche fig*) strategy

strategico, -a, -ci, -che [stra'tedʒiko] AGG (*Mil, anche fig*) strategic

strato ['strato] SM (*gen*) layer; (*di vernice*) coat, coating; (*Meteor*) stratus; (*Geol*) stratum; **uno strato di polvere** a layer of dust; **i vari strati della società** the various strata of society; **strato sociale** social stratum

stratosfera [stratos'fera] SF stratosphere

strattone [strat'tone] SM tug, jerk; **dare uno strattone a qc** to tug o jerk sth, give sth a tug o jerk

stravaccato, -a [stravak'kato] AGG sprawling

stravagante [strava'gante] AGG eccentric, odd

stravaganza [strava'gantsa] SF eccentricity

stravecchio, -chia, -chi, -chie [stra'vɛkkjo] AGG (*gen*) very old; (*vino*) mellow; (*formaggio*) very mature

stravedere [strave'dere] /127/ VI IRREG (*aus* avere) **stravedere per qn** to dote on sb

stravisto, -a [stra'visto] PP di **stravedere**

stravizio, -zi [stra'vittsjo] SM excess; **darsi agli stravizi** to lead a dissolute life

stravolgere [stra'voldʒere] /96/ VT IRREG (*persona*) to upset; (*volto*) to contort; (*organizzazione, sistema*) to shake, rock; (*significato*) to twist, distort

stravolto, -a [stra'volto] PP di **stravolgere** ♦ AGG (*persona: per stanchezza*) in a terrible state; (: *per sofferenza*) distraught;

era stravolto dalla stanchezza he was shattered; **aveva la faccia stravolta** he looked terrible

straziante [strat'tsjante] AGG (*scena*) harrowing; (*urlo*) blood-curdling; (*dolore*) excruciating

straziare [strat'tsjare] /19/ VT (*carni, corpo*) to torment, torture; **straziare il cuore a qn** to break sb's heart; **una musica che strazia le orecchie** an excruciating piece of music

strazio, -zi ['strattsjo] SM (*di torture*) torment; **fare strazio di** (*corpo, vittima*) to mutilate; **la scena era uno strazio** it was a harrowing scene; **questo libro è uno strazio!** this book is appalling!; **che strazio!** (*compito*) what a mess!; (*spettacolo*) what a disaster!

strega, -ghe ['strega] SF (*anche fig*: *donna malvagia*) witch; (*pegg*: *donna brutta*) old hag, old witch

stregare [stre'gare] /80/ VT (*anche fig*) to bewitch

stregone [stre'gone] SM (*in tribù*) witch doctor; (*mago*) sorcerer, wizard

stregoneria [stregone'ria] SF (*pratica*) witchcraft; (*incantesimo*) spell; **fare una stregoneria** to cast a spell

stregua ['stregwa] SF: **alla (stessa) stregua di** on a par with; **trattare tutti alla stessa stregua** to treat everybody in the same manner

stremare [stre'mare] /72/ VT to exhaust

stremo ['stremo] SM: **essere allo stremo (delle forze)** to be at the end of one's tether

strenna ['strenna] SF: **strenna natalizia** (*regalo*) Christmas present; (*libro*) book published for the Christmas market

strenuo, -a ['strenuo] AGG (*valoroso*) brave, courageous; (*infaticabile*) tireless

strepitare [strepi'tare] /72/ VI (*aus avere*) to yell and shout

strepito ['strepito] SM (*di voci, folla*) clamour (*Brit*), clamor (*USA*); (*di catene*) clanking, rattling; **fare strepito** (*notizia, scandalo*) to cause an uproar

strepitoso, -a [strepi'toso] AGG (*successo*) resounding; (*applauso*) clamorous, deafening

stressante [stres'sante] AGG stressful; **fa un lavoro stressante** he has a stressful job

stressare [stres'sare] /72/ VT to put under stress

stressato, -a [stres'sato] AGG under stress; **è un po' stressato ultimamente** he's been rather stressed lately

stretch [stretʃ] AGG INV stretch

stretta ['stretta] SF (*gen*) grip, firm hold; **una stretta di mano** a handshake; **dare una stretta di mano a qn** to shake hands with sb, shake sb's hand; **una stretta di spalle** a shrug (of one's shoulders); **una stretta al cuore** a sudden sadness; **essere alle strette** to be in a tight corner, have one's back to the wall; **mettere qn alle strette** to put sb in a tight corner, get sb with his (*o* her) back to the wall; **stretta creditizia** (*Econ*) credit squeeze

strettamente [stretta'mente] AVV 1 (*in modo stretto*) tightly 2 (*fig*: *rigorosamente*) strictly, closely; **attenersi strettamente alle regole** to keep strictly to the rules, stick closely to the rules

strettezza [stret'tettsa] SF 1 (*gen*) narrowness 2 **strettezze** SFPL poverty sg, straitened circumstances

stretto, -a ['stretto] PP *di* stringere ♦ AGG 1 (*corridoio, stanza, limiti*) narrow; (*gonna, scarpe, nodo*) tight; (*curva*) tight, sharp; **la strada diventa stretta in quel punto** the road gets narrow there; **questa camicia mi è stretta** this shirt is tight on me; **stavamo stretti in macchina** we were packed tight in the car; **tieni stretto!** hold on tight!; **tenere stretto qn/qc** to hold sb/sth tight; **a denti stretti** with clenched teeth 2 (*parente, amico*) close; **un parente stretto** a close relative 3 (*preciso, esatto*: *significato*) strict, exact; (*rigoroso*: *osservanza*: *rigoroso*) strict 4 (*soltanto*): **lo stretto necessario** the bare minimum ♦ SM (*di mare*) strait

strettoia [stret'toja] SF (*di strada*) bottleneck; (*fig*) tricky situation

striato, -a [stri'ato] AGG streaked

striatura [stria'tura] SF (*atto*) streaking; (*effetto*) streaks *pl*

stricnina [strik'nina] SF strychnine

stridente [stri'dente] AGG (*rumore*) strident; (*colori*) clashing

stridere ['stridere] /89/ VI *vb dif* (*porta*) to squeak; (*animale*) to screech, shriek; (*colori*) to clash

strido ['strido] SM (*pl f* **strida**) (*di animale*) screech, shriek; (*urlo*) scream

stridore [stri'dore] SM screeching, shrieking

stridulo, -a ['stridulo] AGG (*voce*) shrill

striglia ['striʎʎa] SF currycomb

strigliare [striʎ'ʎare] /27/ VT (*cavallo*) to curry

strigliata [striʎ'ʎata] SF (*di cavallo*) currying; (*fig*): **dare una strigliata a qn** to give sb a dressing-down

strillare [stril'lare] /72/ VI (*aus avere*) (*gridare*) to scream, shriek; **non strillare!** (*parla piano*) don't shout! ♦ VT: **strillare aiuto** to cry for help; **strillò arrivederci** he shouted goodbye

strillo ['strillo] SM scream, shriek; **fare uno strillo** to let out a scream

strillone [stril'lone] SM news vendor, newspaper seller

striminzito, -a [strimin'tsito] AGG (*misero*) shabby; (*molto magro*) skinny

strimpellare [strimpel'lare] /72/ VT (*chitarra*) to strum away on; (*pianoforte*) to plonk away on

stringa, -ghe ['stringa] SF (*cordoncino*) lace; (*Inform, Ling*) string; **stringhe per scarpe** shoelaces

stringare [strin'gare] /80/ VT (*fig*: *discorso*) to condense

stringato, -a [strin'gato] AGG (*fig*) concise

stringere ['strindʒere] VB IRREG /117/ VT 1 (*con la mano*) to grip, hold tight; **stringere il braccio di qn** to clasp sb's arm; **stringere la mano a qn** (*afferrarla*) to squeeze *o* press sb's hand; (*salutando*) to shake sb's hand, shake hands with sb; **si strinsero la mano** they shook hands; **stringere qn alla gola** to grab sb by the throat 2 (*pugno, mascella*) to clench; (*labbra*) to compress; **una scena che stringe il cuore** a scene which brings a lump to one's throat; **stringere i denti** to clench one's teeth; (*fig*) to grit one's teeth 3 (*gonna, vestito*) to take in 4 (*vite*) to tighten; (*rubinetto*) to turn tight; (*cintura, nodo*) to tighten, pull tight 5 (*avvicinare*: *oggetti*) to close up, put close together; (:: *persone*) squeeze together; **se vi stringete un po' posso sedermi anch'io** if you squeeze up a bit I'll be able to sit down 6 (*fraseologia*): **stringere qn tra le braccia** to clasp sb in one's arms; **stringere amicizia con qn** to make friends with sb; **stringere un patto** to conclude a treaty; **stringere un'alleanza** to form an alliance; **stringi stringi** in conclusion; **stringi!** get to the point!; **queste scarpe mi stringono** these shoes are tight on me; **il tempo stringe** time is short; **stringersi** VR (*persona*): **stringersi a** (*muro, parete*) to press o.s. up against; **si strinse a lui** she drew close to him

strinsi ecc ['strinsi] VB *vedi* stringere

striscia, -sce ['striʃʃa] SF (*di tessuto, carta, fumetto*) strip; (*riga*) stripe; **a strisce** striped; **una maglia a strisce blu e bianche** a blue and white striped jumper; **la striscia di Gaza** the Gaza strip; **strisce pedonali** zebra crossing *sg* (*Brit*), crosswalk *sg* (*USA*)

strisciante [striʃ'ʃante] AGG 1 (*fig*: *pegg*) unctuous 2 (*Econ*: *inflazione*) creeping

strisciare [striʃ'ʃare] /14/ VT (*piedi*) to drag; (*muro, macchina*) to scrape, graze ♦ VI (*aus avere*) (*gen*) to crawl, creep; **stava strisciando sul pavimento** he was crawling on the floor; **strisciare contro un muro** to sidle along a wall; **strisciare con la macchina contro il muro** to scrape one's car against the wall; **lo farò strisciare ai miei piedi** I'll make him crawl at my feet

striscio, -sci ['striʃʃo] SM 1 (*segno*) scratch; **colpire di striscio** to graze 2 (*Med*: *esame*) smear (test), pap smear (*USA*)

striscione [striʃ'ʃone] SM banner

stritolare [strito'lare] /72/ VT (*anche fig*) to crush, grind

strizzare [strit'tsare] /72/ VT (*panni*) to wring (out); **strizzare l'occhio (a qn)** to wink (at sb); **mi ha strizzato l'occhio** she winked at me

strizzata [strit'tsata] SF: **dare una strizzata a qc** to give sth a wring; **una strizzata d'occhio** a wink

strofa ['strɔfa] SF, **strofe** ['strɔfe] SF INV strophe

strofinaccio, -ci [strofi'nattʃo] SM (*gen*) duster, cloth; (*per piatti*) dishcloth; (*per pavimenti*) floorcloth

strofinare [strofi'nare] /72/ vt (gen) to rub; (lucidare) to polish; (pavimento) to wipe; **strofinarsi gli occhi/le mani** to rub one's eyes/one's hands; **strofinarsi** vr: **strofinarsi (contro)** to rub o.s. (against)

stroncare [stron'kare] /20/ vt (ramo) to break off; (fig: rivolta) to put down, suppress; (: libro, film) to pan, tear to pieces; **fu stroncato da un infarto** he was carried off by a heart attack

stronzo ['strontso] sm (fig: fam!: persona) shit (fam!), turd (fam!); (: sterco) turd

stropicciare [stropit't∫are] /14/ vt 1 (strofinare) to rub; **stropicciarsi gli occhi** to rub one's eyes 2 (spiegazzare) to crease

strozzare [strot'tsare] /72/ vt (persona) to choke, strangle; (sogg: cibo) to choke; (conduttura) to narrow; **strozzarsi** vip to choke

strozzatura [strottsa'tura] sf (di conduttura) narrowing; (di strada: fig) bottleneck

strozzino, -a [strot'tsino] sm, sf (usuraio) usurer; (fig) shark

struccare [struk'kare] /20/ vt to remove make-up from; **struccarsi** vr to remove one's make-up

struggere ['strudd3ere] vb irreg (letter) /39/ vt (sogg: amore) to consume; **struggersi** vip: **struggersi d'amore per qn** to be consumed with love for sb; **struggersi dal dolore** to be consumed with grief

struggimento [strudd3i'mento] sm (desiderio) yearning

strumentale [strumen'tale] agg (gen, anche Mus) instrumental; (Aer: volo) instrument attr; **fare uso strumentale di qc** to make (instrumental) use of sth

strumentalizzare [strumentalid'dzare] /72/ vt to exploit, use for one's own ends

strumentalizzazione [strumentaliddzat'tsjone] sf exploitation, use for one's own ends

strumentazione [strumentat'tsjone] sf 1 (Mus) orchestration 2 (Tecn) instrumentation

strumento [stru'mento] sm 1 (arnese) tool; **essere lo strumento di qn** (fig: persona) to be sb's tool; **strumenti di bordo** (Aer) flight instruments; (Naut) ship instruments; **strumenti di precisione** precision instruments 2 (Mus) instrument; **strumento ad arco** string(ed) instrument; **strumento a corda** string(ed) instrument; **strumento a fiato** wind instrument

strussi ecc ['strussi] vb vedi **struggere**

strutto ['strutto] sm (Culin) lard

struttura [strut'tura] sf (tutti i sensi) structure; **struttura portante** (Edil) supporting structure; **struttura sociale** social structure

strutturare [struttu'rare] /72/ vt to structure

struzzo ['struttso] sm (Zool) ostrich; **piume di struzzo** ostrich feathers; **fare lo struzzo, fare la politica dello struzzo** to bury one's head in the sand; **avere uno stomaco di struzzo** to have a cast-iron stomach

stuccare [stuk'kare] /20/ vt (muro) to plaster; (vetro) to putty; (decorare con stucchi) to stucco

stuccatore, -trice [stukka'tore] sm, sf (operaio) plasterer; (artista) stucco worker

stucchevole [stuk'kevole] agg (cibo) nauseating; (scena, spettacolo) tedious, boring

stucco, -chi ['stukko] sm (per muro) plaster; (per vetri) putty; (ornamentale) stucco; **una stanza piena di stucchi** a room full of stucco work; **rimanere di stucco** to be dumbfounded, be left speechless

studente, -essa [stu'dente] sm, sf (gen) student; (scolaro) pupil; (Univ) student, undergraduate; **uno studente di medicina** a medical student

studentesco, -a, -schi, -sche [studen'tesko] agg student attr

studiare [stu'djare] /19/ vt (gen) to study; (lezione) to learn; **studiare un sistema per fare qc** to try to find a way of doing sth; **una persona che studia i gesti/le parole** a person of studied manners/speech ♦ vi (aus avere) to study; **studiarsi** vr (osservarsi) to examine o.s. 2 (uso reciproco) to eye o weigh one another up

studiato, -a [stu'djato] agg (modi, sorriso) affected

studio, -di ['studjo] sm 1 (gen, azione) studying, study; **una giornata di studio** a day's studying; **ha interrotto gli studi**

per un anno he took a break from his studies for a year; **mantenersi agli studi** to pay one's way through college (o university); **fare studi letterari/scientifici** to study arts/ science; **alla fine degli studi** at the end of one's course (of studies) 2 (lavoro, ricerca, disegno) study; **fare uno studio o degli studi su qn/qc** to do research on sb/sth, make a study of sb/sth; **secondo recenti studi, appare che...** recent research indicates that ...; **ho letto uno studio recente sull'inquinamento** I read a recent piece of research on pollution; **uno studio critico** a critical study; **uno studio dal vero** a life study; **studio di settore** system for calculating the presumed income of particular categories of taxpayers, used by the tax authorities to combat tax evasion 3 (progettazione) project; **la proposta è allo studio** the proposal is under consideration 4 (stanza) study; (di professionista) office; (di medico) surgery (Brit), office (USA); **il nonno legge nello studio** grandpa's reading in the study; **studio fotografico** photographer's studio; **studio legale** lawyer's office 5 (TV, Cine) studio; **trasmettiamo dagli studi di Roma** we are broadcasting from our Rome studios

studioso, -a [stu'djoso] agg studious, hardworking ♦ sm, sf scholar

stufa ['stufa] sf (gen) stove; (elettrica) electric fire o heater; **stufa a legna/carbone** wood-burning/coal stove; **stufa a gas** gas heater

stufare [stu'fare] /72/ vt 1 (Culin) to stew 2 (fig: fam) to bore, weary; **mi avete proprio stufato con le vostre lamentele** I am really fed up with your moaning; **mi hai proprio stufato** I am really fed up with you; **stufarsi** vip: **stufarsi (di)** to grow weary (of); **mi sono stufato di loro** I got fed up with them; **si è stufato di ascoltarlo** he got fed up listening to him

stufato [stu'fato] sm (Culin) stew

stufo, -a ['stufo] agg (fam): **essere stufo (di)** to be fed up (with), be sick and tired (of); **sei già stufa?** are you fed up already?; **sono stufo di studiare** I'm fed up of studying

stuoia ['stwoja] sf (tappeto) mat; (tessuto) rush matting

stuolo ['stwolo] sm crowd, host

stupefacente [stupefa't∫ente] agg amazing, astounding; **sostanze stupefacenti** drugs ♦ sm drug, narcotic

stupefare [stupe'fare] /53/ vt irreg to stun, astound

stupefatto, -a [stupe'fatto] pp di **stupefare**

stupefazione [stupefat'tsjone] sf astonishment

stupendo, -a [stu'pendo] agg marvellous, wonderful

stupidaggine [stupi'dadd3ine] sf (qualità) stupidity, foolishness; (atto, discorso): **dire una stupidaggine** to say something stupid; **dire stupidaggini** to talk nonsense; **non dire stupidaggini!** don't talk nonsense!; **fare una stupidaggine** to do something stupid; **ho fatto una stupidaggine** I did something stupid; **ti ho preso una stupidaggine** (regalino) I bought you a little something

stupidità [stupidi'ta] sf (qualità) stupidity

stupido, -a ['stupido] agg stupid ♦ sm, sf fool, idiot; **fare lo stupido** to fool around

stupire [stu'pire] /55/ vt to amaze, stun; **la sua risposta mi ha stupito molto** his answer really amazed me vi (aus essere), **stupirsi** vip to be amazed (at), be stunned (by); **mi sono stupito del suo coraggio** I was amazed at his courage; **non c'è da stupirsi** it's not surprising

stupore [stu'pore] sm amazement, astonishment; **con mio grande stupore ho scoperto che...** much to my amazement I discovered that ...

❏ **stupore** non si traduce mai con la parola inglese **stupor**

stuprare [stu'prare] /72/ vt to rape

stupratore [stupra'tore] sm rapist

stupro ['stupro] sm rape

sturare [stu'rare] /72/ vt (lavandino) to unblock; (bottiglia) to uncork; **sturati le orecchie!** (fig) clean your ears out!

stuzzicadenti [stuttsika'denti] sm inv toothpick; (fig: persona magra) beanpole

stuzzicante [stuttsi'kante] agg (gen) stimulating; (appetitoso) appetizing; **che idea stuzzicante** what a nice idea

stuzzicare [stuttsi'kare] /20/ vt (ferita) to poke (at), prod (at); (fig: persona) to tease; (: appetito) to whet; (: curiosità) to stimulate; **smettila di stuzzicarlo** stop teasing him; **stuzzicarsi i denti** to pick one's teeth

---

PAROLA CHIAVE

su [su] PREP *su + il*=sul, *su + lo*=sullo, *su + l'*=sull', *su + la*=sulla, *su + i*=sui, *su + gli*=sugli, *su + le*=sulle

1 (*gen*) on; (*moto*) on(to); (*in cima a*) on (top of); **non è mai stato su un aereo** he's never been in a plane; **puntare una somma su un cavallo** to bet a sum on a horse; **è sulla destra** it's on the right; **conto su di te** I'm counting on you; **fa errori su errori** he makes one mistake after another; **fece fuoco sulla folla** he fired on the crowd; **la finestra dà sul giardino** the window looks onto the garden; **l'ho visto sul giornale** I saw it in the paper; **fecero rotta su Palermo** they set out towards Palermo; **gettarsi sulla preda** to throw o.s. on one's prey; **la marcia su Roma** the march on Rome; **mettilo sulla scrivania** put it on the desk; **ricamo su seta** embroidery on silk; **procedi sulla sinistra** keep on *o* to the left; **sta sulle sue** he keeps to himself; **il libro è sul tavolo** the book is on the table; **è salito sul tavolo** he got up on(to) the table; **olio su tela** oil on canvas; **basare un argomento su** to base an argument on

2 (*addosso*) over; **buttati uno scialle sulle spalle** throw a shawl over *o* round your shoulders; **sul vestito indossava un golf rosso** she was wearing a red sweater over her dress

3 (*da una parte all'altra*) over; **un ponte sul fiume** a bridge over the river; **un aereo passò sulle nostre teste** an aeroplane flew over our heads

4 (*autorità, dominio*) over; **non ha alcun potere su di lui** he has no power over him

5 (*più in alto di*) above; **100 metri sul livello del mare** 100 metres above sea level

6 (*argomento*) about, on; **discutere su un argomento** to discuss a subject; **un articolo sulla prima guerra mondiale** an article on *o* about the First World War; **una conferenza sulla pace nel mondo** a conference on *o* about world peace

7 (*circa*) about, around; **è costato sui due milioni** it cost about two million euros; **c'erano sulle 100 persone** there were about 100 people; **sarà sulla sessantina** he must be about sixty

8 (*proporzione*) out of, in; **50 su 100 hanno votato contro** 50 out of 100 voted against (it); **2 giorni su 3** 2 days out of 3, 2 days in 3; **uno su tre** one in three; **5 su 10** (*voto*) 5 out of 10

9 (*modo*) **scarpe su misura** handmade shoes; **spedire qc su richiesta** to send sth on request

♦ AVV

1 (*in alto, verso l'alto*) up; (*al piano superiore*) upstairs; **guarda su** look up; **lì su** up there; **su le mani!** hands up!; **qui su** up here; **era su che ci aspettava** he was waiting for us upstairs

2 (*in poi*) onwards; **dal numero 39 in su** from number 39 onwards; **dai 20 anni in su** from the age of 20 onwards; **prezzi dalle 50 euro in su** prices from 50 euros (upwards)

3 (*addosso*) on; **cos'hai su?** what have you got on?; **aveva su una strana tunica** she had a strange tunic on; **posso metterlo su?** can I put it on?

4 (*fraseologia*): **su coraggio!** come on, cheer up!; **andare su e giù** to go up and down; **andava su e giù per il corridoio** he paced up and down the corridor; **su per giù** = suppergiù; **su smettila!** come on, that's enough of that!; **su su non fare così!** now, now, don't behave like that!; **su svelto!** come on, hurry up!; **venir su dal niente** to rise from nothing

sua ['sua] *vedi* **suo**[1]

suadente [sua'dɛnte] AGG persuasive

sub [sub] SM INV, SF INV skin-diver ♦ SM (*sport*) skin diving

subacqueo, -a [su'bakkweo] AGG underwater *attr*; **esplorazione subacquea** underwater exploration; **una muta subacquea** a wetsuit ♦ SM skin-diver

subaffittare [subaffit'tare] /72/ VT to sublet

subaffitto [subaf'fitto] SM (*contratto*) sublet

subalterno, -a [subal'tɛrno] AGG, SM (*gen*) subordinate; (*Mil*) subaltern

subappaltare [subappal'tare] /72/ VT to subcontract

subappalto [subap'palto] SM subcontract

subbuglio [sub'buʎʎo] SM confusion, turmoil; **essere/mettere in subbuglio** to be in/throw into a turmoil

subconscio, -scia, -sci, -scie [sub'kɔnʃo], **subcosciente** [subkoʃ'ʃɛnte] AGG, SM subconscious

subdolo, -a ['subdolo] AGG sneaky, underhand

subentrare [suben'trare] /72/ VI (*aus* **essere**) (*prendere il posto di*) to replace: **è subentrato al padre nella direzione della ditta** he took over the management of the firm from his father; **alla sorpresa subentrò la paura** surprise gave way to fear; **sono subentrati altri problemi** other problems have arisen

subire [su'bire] /55/ VT (*gen*) to suffer, endure; (*operazione*) to undergo; **subire un interrogatorio** to undergo an interrogation, be interrogated; **subire una tortura** to be tortured; **ha subito un torto** he suffered an injustice; **dovrai subirne le conseguenze** you'll have to suffer the consequences; **ha dovuto subire e tacere** he had to suffer in silence

subissare [subis'sare] /72/ VT: **subissare qn di** (*domande, richieste*) to overwhelm with; (*doni, lodi*) to shower sb with

subitaneo, -a [subi'taneo] AGG sudden

subito ['subito] AVV immediately, at once, straight away; **è arrivato subito dopo di te** he arrived immediately after you; **fallo subito!** do it immediately!; **torno subito** I'll be right back; **è subito fatto** it's easily done

sublimare [subli'mare] /72/ VT (*Rel, anche fig*) to exalt; (*Psic*) to sublimate; (*Chim*) to sublime

sublime [su'blime] AGG, SM sublime

sublocare [sublo'kare] /20/ VT to sublease

sublocazione [sublokat'tsjone] SF sublease

subnormale [subnor'male] AGG subnormal

subodorare [subodo'rare] /72/ VT (*insidia*) to smell, suspect

subordinare [subordi'nare] /72/ VT to subordinate

subordinato, -a [subordi'nato] AGG (*gen, anche Gramm*) subordinate; (*dipendente*): **proposizione subordinata** subordinate clause; **subordinato a** dependent on, subject to

subordinazione [subordinat'tsjone] SF subordination

subordine [su'bordine] SM: **in subordine** secondarily

subprime [sab'praim] AGG INV subprime; **mutuo subprime** subprime mortgage ♦ SM subprime lending

suburbano, -a [subur'bano] AGG suburban

succedaneo, -a [suttʃe'daneo] AGG substitute *attr* ♦ SM substitute

succedere [sut'tʃedere] VB IRREG /118/ VI (*aus* **essere**) **1** (*accadere*) to happen; **sapessi cosa mi è successo!** wait till you hear what happened to me!; **cosa ti succede?** what's the matter with you?; **cos'è successo?** what happened?; **dev'essergli successo qualcosa** something must have happened to him; **sono cose che succedono** these things happen **2** (*succedere a*) (*seguire: persona*) to succeed; (*venire dopo*) to follow; **succedere al trono** to succeed to the throne; **succedersi** VIP to follow each other; **i mesi si succedevano lenti** the months dragged on

successione [suttʃes'sjone] SF succession; **imposta di successione** death duty (*Brit*), inheritance tax (*USA*)

successivamente [suttʃessiva'mente] AVV (*in seguito*) later, subsequently

successivo, -a [suttʃes'sivo] AGG (*continuo*) successive; (*che segue*) following; **il giorno successivo** the following *o* next day; **in un momento successivo** subsequently

successo, -a [sut'tʃɛsso] PP *di* **succedere** ♦ SM (*gen*) success; (*canzone*) hit; (*libro*) bestseller; (*film*) box-office success, hit; **è stato un successo!** it was a success!; **arrivare al successo** to become a success; **avere successo** (*persona*) to be successful; (*idea*) to be well received; **non ha avuto successo** I was unsuccessful; **ho provato, ma senza successo** I tried, but without success, I tried in vain; **di successo** (*attore, cantante*) successful; **un film di successo** a successful film; **canzone di successo** hit (song)

successore [suttʃes'sore] SM successive ♦ SM successor

succhiare [suk'kjare] /19/ VT (*gen*) to suck (up); **succhiare il sangue a qn** (*fig*) to bleed sb dry

succhiotto [suk'kjɔtto] SM (*tettarella*) dummy (*Brit*), pacifier (*USA*), comforter (*USA*); (*fam: segno sul collo*) lovebite, hickey (*USA*)

succinto, -a [sut'tʃinto] AGG (*discorso*) succinct; (*abito*) scanty

succo, -chi ['sukko] SM (*Anat: di frutto*) juice; (*fig: della conferenza*) gist; **il succo del discorso** (*fig*) the essence of the speech; **succo di frutta** fruit juice; **succo di pomodoro** tomato juice

succoso, -a [suk'koso] AGG juicy; (*fig*) pithy

succube ['sukkube] SM, SF victim; **essere succube di qn** to be dominated by sb, be under sb's thumb

succursale [sukkur'sale] SF branch (office)

sud [sud] SM south; **la sua famiglia è del sud** his family is from the south; **a sud (di)** south (of); **si trova a sud della città** it's south of the city; **la Svizzera confina a sud con l'Italia** to the south Switzerland has a border with Italy; **il vento viene da sud** the wind comes from the south; **esposto a sud** facing south; **verso sud** south, southwards; **si è diretto a sud** he headed south; **i mari del Sud** the South Seas; **l'Italia del Sud** Southern Italy; **l'America del Sud** South America ♦ AGG INV (*gen*) south; (*regione*) southern; **partirono in direzione sud** they set off southwards *o* in a southerly direction, they headed south

Sudafrica [su'dafrika] SM South Africa

sudafricano, -a [sudafri'kano] AGG, SM, SF South African

Sudamerica [suda'merika] SM South America

sudamericano, -a [sudameri'kano] AGG, SM, SF South American

Sudan [su'dan] SM: **(il) Sudan** (the) Sudan

sudanese [suda'nese] AGG, SM, SF Sudanese *inv*

sudare [su'dare] /72/ VI (*aus* avere) to perspire, sweat; **ho dovuto sudare per finire quella traduzione** (*fig*) I had to work hard to finish that translation; **mi ha fatto sudare** (*fig*) he made me work hard; **sudare freddo** (*anche fig*) to come *o* break out in a cold sweat ♦ VT to work hard for; **sudarsi il pane** to earn one's bread by the sweat of one's brow

sudato, -a [su'dato] AGG (*persona, mani*) sweaty; (*fig: denaro*) hard-earned; **una vittoria sudata** a hard-won victory

suddetto, -a [sud'detto] AGG above-mentioned *attr*

sudditanza [suddi'tantsa] SF subjection

suddito, -a ['suddito] SM, SF subject

suddividere [suddi'videre] /43/ VT IRREG to subdivide

suddivisione [suddivi'zjone] SF subdivision

suddiviso, -a [suddi'vizo] PP *di* suddividere

sud-est [su'dest] SM southeast; **vento di sud-est** southeasterly wind; **il sud-est asiatico** Southeast Asia

sudiceria [suditʃe'ria] SF (*qualità*) filthiness, dirtiness; (*cosa sporca*) dirty thing; **libro pieno di sudicerie** filthy *o* obscene book

sudicio, -cia, -ci, -ce ['suditʃo] AGG dirty, filthy; (*fig: indecente*) dirty, filthy, indecent; (: *disonesto*) dirty ♦ SM (*anche fig*) dirt, filth

sudiciume [sudi'tʃume] SM (*anche fig*) dirt, filth

su'doku SM INV sudoku

sudore [su'dore] SM perspiration, sweat; **si è asciugato il sudore dalla fronte** he wiped the sweat off his forehead; **essere in un bagno di sudore** to be bathed in sweat; **col sudore della propria fronte** (*fig*) with the sweat of one's brow

sud-ovest [su'dɔvest] SM southwest; **vento di sud-ovest** southwesterly wind

sue ['sue] *vedi* suo[1]

Suez ['suez] SF: **il canale di Suez** the Suez Canal

sufficiente [suffi'tʃente] AGG 1 (*adeguato*) sufficient, enough; (*abbastanza*) enough; (*voto*) satisfactory; **questo fu sufficiente a farlo tacere** that was enough to shut him up; **non c'è spazio sufficiente per tutti** there is not enough room for everyone; **pensi che il pane sia sufficiente?** do you think there's enough bread?; **credi tu sia sufficiente?** do you think that will do?; **è più che sufficiente** it is more than enough 2 (*borioso*) self-important ♦ SM: **avere il sufficiente per vivere** to have enough to live on

sufficientemente [suffitʃente'mente] AVV (*guadagnare, darsi da fare*) enough; **sufficientemente bene** well enough, sufficiently well

sufficienza [suffi'tʃentsa] SF 1 **a sufficienza** enough; **ne hai a sufficienza?** have you got enough?; **ne ho a sufficienza** I have had plenty; **ne ho avuto a sufficienza!** (*sono stufo*) I've had enough of this!; **ce ne sono a sufficienza** there are enough 2 **con un'aria di sufficienza** (*fig*) with a condescending air 3 (*Scol*) pass mark; **sono riuscito a prendere la sufficienza** I managed to get a pass mark

suffisso [suf'fisso] SM (*Gramm*) suffix

suffragare [suffra'gare] /80/ VT (*fig: affermazioni*) to support

suffragio [suf'fradʒo] SM 1 (*Pol: voto*) vote; **suffragio universale** universal suffrage 2 (*Rel*) intercession; **messa di suffragio** mass for somebody's soul

suggellare [suddʒel'lare] /72/ VT (*anche fig*) to seal

suggerimento [suddʒeri'mento] SM suggestion, hint; **qualcuno ha altri suggerimenti?** has anyone got any other suggestions?; **dietro suo suggerimento** on his advice

suggerire [suddʒe'rire] /55/ VT (*gen*) to suggest; (*soluzione*) to suggest, put forward; (*Teatro*) to prompt; **cosa suggerisci?** what do you suggest?; **suggerirei di trovarci lì** I'd suggest that we meet there, I'd suggest meeting there; **suggerire a qn di fare qc** to suggest to sb that he (*o* she) do (*o* should do) sth; **gli ho suggerito di dire tutto ai suoi genitori** I suggested he told his parents everything; **mi ha suggerito un periodo di riposo** he advised me to take some time off; **non suggerire!** (*in classe*) don't help!

suggeritore, -trice [suddʒeri'tore] SM, SF (*Teatro*) prompter

suggestionare [suddʒestjo'nare] /72/ VT to influence; **non lasciarti suggestionare da quello che dice** don't let yourself be influenced by what he says; **suggestionarsi** VIP to be influenced

suggestione [suddʒes'tjone] SF (*Psic*) suggestion; (*fascino*) fascination

suggestivo, -a [suddʒes'tivo] AGG (*paesaggio*) evocative; (*veduta*) enchanting; (*teoria*) interesting, attractive

sughero ['sugero] SM (*gen*) cork; (*albero*) cork oak; **tappo di sughero** cork

sugli ['suʎʎi] PREP + ART *vedi* su

sugo, -ghi ['sugo] SM (*succo*) juice; (*di carne*) gravy; (*per pastasciutta*) sauce; (*fig: del discorso*) essence; **senza sugo** (*fig: persona*) insipid, wishy-washy; (*discorso*) pointless, senseless

sugoso, -a [su'goso] AGG (*frutto*) juicy; (*fig: articolo*) pithy

sui ['sui] PREP + ART *vedi* su

suicida, -i, -e [sui'tʃida] AGG suicidal ♦ SM, SF suicide (*person*)

suicidarsi [suitʃi'darsi] /72/ VR to commit suicide

suicidio, -di [sui'tʃidjo] SM suicide (*action*)

suino, -a [su'ino] AGG: **carne suina** pork ♦ SM pig; **i suini** swine *pl*

sul [sul] PREP + ART *vedi* su

sulfamidico, -a, -ci, -che [sulfa'midiko] AGG, SM sulphonamide *attr*

sultanina [sulta'nina] SF: **(uva) sultanina** sultana

sultano, -a [sul'tano] SM, SF sultan (sultana)

Sumatra [su'matra] SF Sumatra

summit ['summit] SM INV summit

SUNIA [su'nia] SIGLA M (= *Sindacato Unitario Nazionale Inquilini e Assegnatari*) *national association of tenants*

sunnominato, -a [sunnomi'nato] AGG aforesaid *attr*

sunto ['sunto] SM summary; **fare il sunto di qc** to summarize sth

suo[1], **-a** ['suo] (*pl* **suoi**, **sue**) AGG POSS: **il(la) sua(a)** (*maschile*) his; (*femminile*) her; (*neutro*) its; **il cane dorme nella sua cuccia** the dog is sleeping in its kennel; **il suo giardino** his (*o* her) garden; **sua madre** his (*o* her) mother; **suo padre** his (*o* her) father; **un suo amico** a friend of his (*o* hers); **Luciana e le sue amiche** Luciana and her friends; **è colpa sua** it's his (*o* her) fault; **è casa sua, è la sua casa** it's his (*o* her) house; **per amor suo** for love of him (*o* her); **Sua Altezza His** (*o* Her) Highness ♦ PRON POSS: **il(la) suo(a)** (*maschile*) his, his own; (*femminile*) hers, her own; (*neutro*) its, its own; **la mia barca è più lunga della sua** my boat is longer than his (*o* hers); **è di Roberta questa macchina? - sì, è sua** is this Roberta's car? - yes, it's hers; **il suo** his (*o* her) own; it was simply an error on his (*o* her) part ♦ SM 1 **ha speso del suo** he (*o* she) spent his (*o* her) own money; **vive del suo** he (*o* she) lives on his (*o* her) own income 2 **i suoi** SMPL (*genitori*) his (*o* her) parents; (*famiglia*) his (*o* her) family; (*amici, alleati*) his (*o* her) own people, his (*o* her) side; **lui è dei suoi** he is on his (*o* her) side ♦ SF: **la sua** (*opinione*) his (*o* her) view; **è dalla sua** (*parte*) he's on his (*o* her) side; **anche lui ha avuto le sue** (*disavventure*) he's had his problems too; **sta sulle sue** he keeps himself to himself

suo[2], **-a** ['suo] (*pl* **suoi**, **sue**), (*forma di cortesia: Suo*) AGG POSS:

il(la) suo(a) your; **il suo ombrello, signore!** your umbrella, sir!; **Sua Altezza** Your Highness; **suo devotissimo** (*in lettere*) your devoted servant ♦ PRON POSS: **il(la) suo(a)** yours, your own; **scusi signore, è suo questo?** excuse me sir, is this yours?; **la sua è pura scortesia** that's sheer discourtesy on your part ♦ PRON POSS M: **ha speso del suo?** did you spend your own money? ♦ PRON POSS F: **la sua** (*opinione*) your view; **è dalla sua** he's on your side; **alla sua!** to your very good health!

suocera ['swɔtʃera] SF mother-in-law, (*fig: fam.!*) nagging woman

suocero ['swɔtʃero] SM father-in-law; **i suoceri** father- and mother-in-law; **i miei suoceri** my in-laws

suoi ['swɔi] *vedi* **suo**[1]

suola ['swɔla] SF (*di scarpa*) sole; **rifare le suole alle scarpe** to have one's shoes resoled

suolo ['swɔlo] SM (*terreno*) ground; (*terra*) soil; **studia gli effetti dell'inquinamento sul suolo** she's studying the effects of pollution on the soil; **cadde al suolo** he fell to the ground; **in suolo italiano** on Italian soil

suonare [swo'nare] /72/ VT (*strumento, pezzo musicale*) to play; (*campana, campanello*) to ring; (*clacson, allarme, ritirata*) to sound; **sai suonare la chitarra?** can you play the guitar?; **l'orologio ha suonato le cinque** the clock struck five; **suonare il clacson** to hoot, sound the horn; **gliele ho suonate** (*fam*) I gave him a thrashing ♦ VI (*aus avere*) (*musicista*) to play; (*campane, campanello, telefono*) to ring; (*ore*) to strike; (*fig: discorso*) to sound, ring; **sta suonando il telefono** the phone is ringing; **le campane suonano a morto** the bells are sounding a death knell; **mi suona strano** (*fig*) it sounds strange to me

suonato, -a [swo'nato] AGG 1 (*compiuto*): **ha cinquant'anni suonati** he is well over fifty 2 (*Pugilato*) punch-drunk; (*fig: fam: rimbambito*) soft in the head

suonatore, -trice [swona'tore] SM, SF player; **suonatore ambulante** street musician

suoneria [swone'ria] SF alarm; (*di telefono*) ring tone

suono ['swɔno] SM (*gen*) sound; (*di campane*) sound, ringing; **ballare al suono di un'orchestra** to dance to the music of an orchestra; **lo accolsero a suon di fischi** they booed and jeered him as he arrived

suora ['swɔra] SF (*Rel*) nun; **vuole farsi suora** she wants to become a nun; **Suor Maria** Sister Maria

super ['super] AGG INV: **(benzina) super** four-star (petrol) (*Brit*), premium (*USA*) ♦ PREF **super..., over...**

superamento [supera'mento] SM (*di ostacolo*) overcoming; (*di montagna*) crossing; **arrivare al superamento di** (*idee, dottrine*) to move on from

superare [supe'rare] /72/ VT (*limite, aspettative*) to exceed; (*traguardo, montagne*) to cross; (*esame*) to pass; (*muro*) to get over; (*fig: ostacolo, malattia, paura*) to overcome; (: *rivale*) to beat, surpass, outdo; (*fig: sorpassare*) to overtake; **il risultato ha superato le aspettative** the result exceeded expectations; **sono certo che riusciremo a superare queste difficoltà** I'm sure we can overcome these difficulties; **ha superato l'esame di guida** he's passed his driving test; **superare i limiti di velocità** to exceed *o* break the speed limit; **ha superato il limite di velocità** he broke the speed limit; **superare qn in altezza/peso** to be taller/heavier than sb; **ha superato la cinquantina** he's over fifty (years of age); **stavolta ha superato se stesso** this time he has surpassed himself

superato, -a [supe'rato] AGG outmoded

superattico, -ci [supe'rattiko] SM penthouse

superbia [su'perbja] SF pride

superbo, -a [su'perbo] AGG 1 (*persona*) proud, haughty 2 (*fig: grandioso, splendido*) superb, magnificent ♦ SM, SF haughty person

superconduttore [superkondut'tore] SM superconductor

superficiale [superfi'tʃale] AGG (*gen*) superficial; **fortunatamente è solo una ferita superficiale** fortunately, it's only a superficial wound; **è un po' superficiale** she's a bit superficial; **acque superficiali** surface water *sg* ♦ SM, SF superficial person

superficialità [superfitʃali'ta] SF superficiality

superficie [super'fitʃe] SF 1 (*di muro, specchio*) surface; **superficie terrestre** surface of the earth; **tornare in superficie**

(*a galla*) to return to the surface; (*fig: problemi*) to resurface; **non va mai oltre la superficie delle cose** he has a superficial approach 2 (*area*) surface area; **superficie alare** (*Aer*) wing area; **superficie velica** (*Naut*) sail area

superfluo, -a [su'perfluo] AGG (*gen*) superfluous; (*spese*) unnecessary; **peli superflui** unwanted hair *sg* ♦ SM surplus

superiora [supe'rjora] SF (*Rel: anche:* **madre superiora**) mother superior

superiore [supe'rjore] AGG 1 (*intelligenza, qualità*) superior; (*numero*) greater; (*quantità, somma*) larger; **intelligenza superiore alla media** above-average intelligence; **la temperatura è superiore alla media** the temperature is above average; **è superiore alle mie forze** it's beyond me; **sono superiore a queste cose** I'm above such things 2 (*che sta più in alto: rami, classe*) upper; (*livello*) higher; **la parte superiore del corpo** the upper part of the body; **il corso superiore di un fiume** the upper reaches *pl* of a river; **al piano superiore** on the upper floor; (*di edificio a più piani*) on the floor above; **scuola superiore, scuole superiori** ≈ secondary school (*Brit*), senior high (school) (*USA*); **istruzione superiore** higher education; **per ordine superiore** on orders from above ♦ SM superior; **è il mio superiore** he's my superior ♦ SFPL (*Scol*): **le superiori** ≈ secondary school (*Brit*), ≈ senior high (school) (*USA*)

superiorità [superjori'ta] SF INV superiority; **ha dimostrato una netta superiorità sull'avversario** he was clearly superior to his opponent; **aria di superiorità** air of superiority

superlativo, -a [superla'tivo] AGG, SM (*gen, anche Gramm*) superlative

superlavoro [superla'voro] SM overwork

supermercato [supermer'kato] SM , **supermarket** [super'market] SM INV supermarket

supernova, -ae [super'nɔva] SF (*Astron*) supernova

superpotenza [superpo'tentsa] SF (*Pol*) superpower

supersonico, -a, -ci, -che [super'sɔniko] AGG supersonic

superstite [su'perstite] AGG surviving ♦ SM, SF survivor

superstizione [superstit'tsjone] SF superstition

superstizioso, -a [superstit'tsjoso] AGG superstitious ♦ SM, SF superstitious person

superstrada [super'strada] SF ≈ motorway (*Brit*), ≈ expressway (*USA*)

supervisione [supervi'zjone] SF supervision

supervisore [supervi'zore] SM supervisor

supino, -a [su'pino] AGG supine; **dormire supino** to sleep on one's back; **accettazione supina** (*fig*) blind acceptance

suppellettile [suppel'lettile] SF (*gen*) ornaments *pl*; (*arredo*) furnishings *pl*; (*Archeol*) grave goods

suppergiù [supper'dʒu] AVV roughly, more or less, approximately

suppl. ABBR (= *supplemento*) supp(l)

supplementare [supplemen'tare] AGG 1 (*gen*) extra; (*entrate*) additional; (*treno*) relief *attr*; **tempi supplementari** (*Sport*) extra time *sg*; **hanno segnato nei tempi supplementari** they scored in extra time 2 (*Geom*) supplementary

supplemento [supple'mento] SM supplement

supplente [sup'plente] AGG (*insegnante*) supply *attr* (*Brit*), substitute *attr* (*USA*) ♦ SM, SF supply *o* substitute teacher

supplenza [sup'plentsa] SF (*Scol*): **fare supplenza** to do supply (*Brit*) *o* substitute (*USA*) teaching; **ha avuto una supplenza di un anno** he's been asked to do a year's supply *o* substitute teaching

suppletivo, -a [supple'tivo] AGG (*gen*) supplementary; (*sessione d'esami*) extra

supplica, -che ['supplika] SF (*Rel, anche fig*) supplication, plea; **con un tono di supplica** in an imploring voice

supplicare [suppli'kare] /20/ VT to implore, beseech; **ti supplico, non andartene** don't go, I beg you

supplichevole [suppli'kevole] AGG imploring

supplire [sup'plire] /45/ VT to stand in for, replace temporarily ♦ VI (*aus avere*) **supplire a** (*difetto, mancanza*) to make up for, compensate for

supplizio, -zi [sup'plittsjo] SM (*tortura*) torture; (*fig*) torment; **fu condotto al supplizio** (*a morte*) he was led to execution

suppongo [sup'pongo], **supponi** *ecc* [sup'poni] VB *vedi* **supporre**

supporre [sup'porre] /77/ VT IRREG (gen) to suppose; **supponiamo che...** let's o just suppose that ...; **suppongo che sia lo stesso** I imagine it's the same; **suppongo di sì/di no** I suppose so/not

supporto [sup'pɔrto] SM (sostegno) support; (struttura) stand, holder

supposizione [suppozit'tsjone] SF supposition; **le mie sono solo supposizioni** I'm only guessing; **è una supposizione infondata** it's a groundless assumption

supposta [sup'pɔsta] SF (Med) suppository

supposto [sup'posto] PP di **supporre ♦ supposto che...** CONG supposing that ...

suppurare [suppu'rare] /72/ VI (aus avere) to suppurate

supremazia [supremat'tsia] SF supremacy

supremo, -a [su'prɛmo] AGG (gen) supreme; **con supremo disprezzo** with the utmost contempt; **l'ora suprema** (fig) one's last hour; **il giudizio supremo** (Rel) the Last Judgement

surclassare [surklas'sare] /72/ VT to outclass

surgelare [surdʒe'lare] /72/ VT to (deep-)freeze

surgelato, -a [surdʒe'lato] AGG (deep-)frozen; **cibo surgelato** frozen food ♦ SMPL: **i surgelati** frozen food sg

surmenage [surmə'naʒ] SM INV (fisico) overwork; (mentale) mental strain; (Sport) overtraining

surplus [sur'plus] SM INV (Econ) surplus; **surplus di mano-dopera** overmanning

surreale [surre'ale] AGG surrealistic

surriscaldamento [surriskalda'mento] SM (gen, anche Tecn) overheating

surriscaldare [surriskal'dare] /72/ VT, VIP, **surriscaldarsi** VIP (gen, anche Tecn) to overheat

surrogato, -a [surro'gato] AGG, SM substitute attr

suscettibile [suʃʃet'tibile] AGG **1** (permaloso) touchy, sensitive; **è molto suscettibile** she's very touchy **2 suscettibile di** (cambiamento) subject to; **suscettibile di miglioramento** open to improvement

suscettibilità [suʃʃettibili'ta] SF touchiness; **urtare la suscettibilità di qn** to hurt sb's feelings

suscitare [suʃʃi'tare] /72/ VT (provocare) to cause, provoke; (destare: ira) to arouse; **suscitare uno scroscio di applausi** to provoke thunderous applause

susina [su'sina] SF plum

susino [su'sino] SM plum (tree)

susseguire [susse'gwire] /45/ VT, VI (aus essere) to follow; **da ciò che segue...** it follows that ...; **susseguirsi** VR (uso reciproco) to succeed each other, follow each other; **le sorprese continuavano a susseguirsi** there was a continual succession of surprises

sussidiario, -ria, -ri, -rie [sussi'djarjo] AGG (gen) subsidiary; (fermata) extra; (nave) supply attr

sussidio, -di [sus'sidjo] SM **1** (aiuto) aid; **sussidi audiovisivi** audiovisual aids; **sussidi didattici** teaching aids **2** (sovvenzione) subsidy; **sussidio di disoccupazione** unemployment benefit (Brit) o benefits pl (USA); **sussidio per malattia** sickness benefit

sussiego [sus'sjɛgo] SM haughtiness; **con aria di sussiego** haughtily

sussistenza [sussis'tentsa] SF **1** (esistenza) existence **2** (sostentamento) subsistence; **mezzi di sussistenza** means of subsistence **3** (Mil) provisioning

sussistere [sus'sistere] /11/ VI (aus essere) (esistere) to exist; (essere fondato: motivi) to be valid o sound

sussultare [sussul'tare] /72/ VI (aus avere) (per spavento) to start

sussulto [sus'sulto] SM start; **dare** o **avere un sussulto** to give a start, start

sussurrare [sussur'rare] /72/ VT to whisper; **gli sussurrò qualcosa all'orecchio** he whispered something in his ear; **si sussurra che...** it's rumoured (Brit) o rumored (USA) that ... ♦ VI (aus avere) (fronde) to rustle; (acque) to murmur

sussurro [sus'surro] SM (vedi vb) whisper; rustle; murmur

sutura [su'tura] SF (Med) suture

suturare [sutu'rare] /72/ VT (Med) to stitch up, suture

suvvia [suv'via] ESCL come on!

SV SIGLA = Savona ♦ ABBR = Signoria Vostra

svagare [zva'gare] /80/ VT (divertire) to amuse; (distrarre): **svagare qn** to take sb's mind off things; **svagarsi** VR (divertirsi) to amuse o.s.; (distrarsi) to take one's mind off things

svagato, -a [zva'gato] AGG (persona) absent-minded; (scolaro) inattentive

svago, -ghi [zvago] SM (riposo) relaxation; (passatempo) pastime, amusement; **l'ho fatto per svago** I did it just to pass the time

svaligiare [zvali'dʒare] /62/ VT (banca) to rob; (casa) burgle (Brit), burglarize (USA)

svaligiatore, -trice [zvalidʒa'tore] SM, SF (di banca) robber; (di casa) burglar

svalutare [zvalu'tare] /72/ VT (Econ) to devalue; (fig) to belittle; **svalutarsi** VIP (Econ) to be devalued

svalutazione [zvalutat'tsjone] SF (Econ) devaluation

svampito, -a [zvam'pito] AGG absent-minded ♦ SM, SF absent-minded person

svanire [zva'nire] /55/ VI (aus essere) (anche fig) to disappear, vanish; (rumore) to fade; **svanire nel nulla** to disappear o vanish completely

svanito, -a [zva'nito] AGG (fig: persona) absent-minded ♦ SM, SF absent-minded person

svantaggiato, -a [zvantad'dʒato] AGG at a disadvantage; **i bambini svantaggiati** disadvantaged children

svantaggio, -gi [zvan'taddʒo] SM disadvantage; (inconveniente) drawback, disadvantage; **i vantaggi e gli svantaggi della situazione** the advantages and disadvantages of the situation; **tornerà a suo svantaggio** it will work against you; **sono in svantaggio rispetto a te** you have an advantage over me; **essere in svantaggio di due gol** (Calcio) to be two goals down; **essere in svantaggio di due minuti** (Sport) to be two minutes behind

svantaggioso, -a [zvantad'dʒoso] AGG disadvantageous; **è un'offerta svantaggiosa per me** it is not in my interest to accept this offer; **è un prezzo svantaggioso** it is not an attractive price

svaporare [zvapo'rare] /72/ VI (aus essere) to evaporate

svaporato, -a [zvapo'rato] AGG (bibita) flat

svariato, -a [zva'rjato] AGG (numeroso) various; (vario, diverso) varied; **di questa macchina esistono svariati modelli** this car comes in a variety of models

svastica, -che ['zvastika] SF swastika

svedese [zve'dese] AGG **1** (della Svezia) Swedish; **il governo svedese** the Swedish government **2** (fiammiferi) svedesi safety matches ♦ SM, SF Swede; **gli svedesi** the Swedes ♦ SM (lingua) Swedish; **parla svedese** he speaks Swedish

sveglia ['zveʎʎa] SF **1** (azione) waking up; (Mil) reveille; **la sveglia è alle 7** we have to get up at 7; **mi svegli alla sveglia alle 9?** would you wake me up at 9?; **suonare la sveglia** (Mil) to sound the reveille **2** (orologio) alarm (clock); **hai puntato la sveglia?** have you set the alarm clock?; **non ho sentito la sveglia stamattina** I didn't hear the alarm clock this morning; **sveglia telefonica** alarm call

svegliare [zveʎ'ʎare] /27/ VT (persona) to wake (up), waken; (fig: sentimenti) to awaken, arouse; **svegliami alle 7** wake me up at 7; **la camminata ha svegliato il suo appetito** the walk gave him an appetite; **svegliarsi** VR to wake up; (fig) to waken o.s. up; **mi sveglio sempre presto** I always wake up early

sveglio, -glia, -gli, -glie ['zveʎʎo] AGG (gen) awake; (fig: attento, pronto) quick-witted, alert; (: furbo) smart; **sei sveglio?** are you awake?; **ero sveglio quando ha telefonato** I was awake when he phoned; **un ragazzo sveglio** a bright boy; **non è molto sveglio** he's not very bright

svelare [zve'lare] /72/ VT (segreto) to reveal; (mistero) to uncover; **svelarsi** VR to show o.s.; **con quell'azione si è svelato per quello che è** that action has shown him up for what he is

sveltezza [zvel'tettsa] SF (gen) speed; (mentale) quick-wittedness

sveltire [zvel'tire] /55/ VT (gen) to speed up; (procedura) to streamline; **sveltire il traffico** to speed up the flow of traffic; **sveltire il passo** to quicken one's pace; **sveltirsi** VR (fig: persona) to waken o.s. up

svelto, -a [zvelto] AGG (gen) quick; (passo) brisk; (fig: persona: sveglio) quick-witted, alert; (linea) slim, slender; **essere**

svelto di mano (*rubare*) to be light-fingered; (*picchiare*) to be free with one's hands *o* fists; **alla svelta** quickly; **facciamo alla svelta** let's get a move on; **svelto, vieni qua!** quick, come here!

svendere [ˈzvɛndere] /29/ vt to sell off, clear

svendita [ˈzvendita] sf (*Comm*) (clearance) sale; **una svendita di fine stagione** an end-of-season sale; **in svendita** in a sale; **ho comprato questo cappotto in svendita** I bought this coat on sale

svenevole [zveˈnevole] agg mawkish

svengo *ecc* [ˈzvɛngo] vb *vedi* **svenire**

svenimento [zveniˈmento] sm fainting fit, faint; **avere uno svenimento** to faint

svenire [zveˈnire] /128/ vi irreg (*aus* **essere**) to faint, pass out

sventare [zvenˈtare] /72/ vt to foil, thwart

sventatezza [zventaˈtettsa] sf (*qualità: distrazione*) absent-mindedness; (: *mancanza di prudenza*) rashness; **è stata una sventatezza da parte sua accettare...** it was rash of him to accept ...

sventato, -a [zvenˈtato] agg (*distratto*) scatterbrained; (*imprudente*) rash ♦ sm, sf scatterbrain

sventola [ˈzventola] sf **1** (*fig: sberla*) slap; **mollare una sventola a qn** to slap sb **2 orecchie a sventola** sticking-out ears

sventolare [zventoˈlare] /72/ vt (*bandiera*) to wave ♦ vi (*aus* avere) to flutter; **sulla torre del castello sventolavano delle bandiere** flags were waving on the castle tower

sventrare [zvenˈtrare] /72/ vt (*animale*) to disembowel; (*persona*) to rip open; (*fig: demolire*) **hanno completamente sventrato il centro medievale** they have demolished the medieval town centre

sventura [zvenˈtura] sf (*sorte avversa*) misfortune; (*disgrazia*) mishap; **per colmo di sventura** to crown it all; **è stata una sventura** it was a piece of bad luck; **compagno di sventura** (*scherz*) fellow sufferer

sventurato, -a [zventuˈrato] agg unlucky, unfortunate ♦ sm, sf (*sfortunato*) unlucky person; (*scherz*) poor unfortunate

svenuto, -a [sveˈnuto] pp *di* **svenire**

svergognare [zvergoɲˈɲare] /15/ vt to shame

svergognato, -a [zvergoɲˈɲato] agg (*privo di: pudore*) shameless, brazen; (: *ritegno*) impudent ♦ sm, sf (*vedi agg*) shameless person; impudent person

svernare [zverˈnare] /72/ vi (*aus* avere) to winter, spend the winter

sverrò *ecc* [zverˈrɔ] vb *vedi* **svenire**

svestire [zvesˈtire] /45/ vt to undress; **svestirsi** vr to get undressed

Svezia [ˈzvɛtsja] sf Sweden; **ti è piaciuta la Svezia?** did you like Sweden?; **andrò in Svezia quest'estate** I'm going to Sweden this summer

svezzare [zvetˈtsare] /72/ vt to wean

sviare [zviˈare] /60/ vt (*sospetti*) to divert; (*attenzione*) to distract; (*colpo*) to ward off; (*traviare*) to lead astray; **sviare le indagini della polizia** to put the police off the track; **sviare il discorso** to change the subject

svicolare [zvikoˈlare] /72/ vi (*aus* avere *o* essere) (*scantonare*) to slip down an alley; (*fig*) to sneak off

svignarsela [zviɲˈɲarsela] /72/ vip to slip away, sneak off

svilimento [zviliˈmento] sm debasement

svilire [zviˈlire] /55/ vt to debase

sviluppare [zvilupˈpare] /72/ vt (*gen, anche Fot, Mat*) to develop; (*commercio*) to expand; (*incendio*) to cause; (*gas*) to emit; **hai già fatto sviluppare le foto?** have you had the photos developed yet?; **svilupparsi** vip (*gen*) to develop; (*città*) to expand, grow; (*commercio*) to develop, expand

sviluppo [zviˈluppo] sm (*gen, anche Fot, Mat, Econ*) development; (*di città*) development, growth; (*di concetto, tema*) development, treatment; (*di industria*) expansion; **gli sviluppi della situazione** the developments in the situation; **in via di sviluppo** in the process of development; **paesi in via di sviluppo** developing countries; **sviluppo economico** economic growth; **sviluppo sostenibile** sustainable development

svincolare [zvinkoˈlare] /72/ vt (*da vincolo*) to free, release; (*Comm: merce*) to clear; **svincolarsi** vr to free o.s.

svincolo [ˈzvinkolo] sm **1** (*Aut*) motorway (*Brit*) *o* expressway (*USA*) intersection **2** (*Comm*) clearance

sviscerare [zviʃʃeˈrare] /72/ vt (*fig: argomento*) to examine *o* analyse in depth

sviscerato, -a [zviʃʃeˈrato] agg (*amore, odio*) passionate

svista [ˈzvista] sf oversight, slip

svitare [zviˈtare] /72/ vt to unscrew

Svizzera [ˈzvittsera] sf Switzerland; **ti è piaciuta la Svizzera?** did you like Switzerland?; **andrò in Svizzera quest'inverno** I'm going to Switzerland this winter

svizzero, -a [ˈzvittsero] agg, sm, sf Swiss *inv*; **il formaggio svizzero** Swiss cheese; **gli svizzeri** the Swiss

svogliatezza [zvoʎʎaˈtettsa] sf (*vedi agg*) listlessness; indolence

svogliato, -a [zvoʎˈʎato] agg (*senza entusiasmo*) listless; (*pigro*) lazy, indolent ♦ sm, sf lazybones *sg*

svolazzare [zvolatˈtsare] /72/ vi (*aus* avere) to flutter (about)

svolgere [ˈzvɔldʒere] vb irreg /96/ vt (*rotolo*) to unroll; (*gomitolo*) to unwind; (*fig: argomento, tema*) to discuss, develop; (: *piano, programma*) to carry out; **svolgere un tema** to write an essay; **che attività svolge?** what does she do?; **quale professione svolge?** what is your occupation?; **svolgersi** vip (*filo*) to unwind; (*rotolo*) to unroll; (*fig: vita, eventi: procedere*) to go on; (: *aver luogo: scena, film*) to be set, take place; **come si sono svolti veramente i fatti?** how did it actually happen?; **ecco come si sono svolti i fatti** this was the sequence of events; **tutto si è svolto secondo i piani** everything went according to plan

svolgimento [zvoldʒiˈmento] sm (*di tema*) discussion; (*di programma*) carrying out; **lo svolgimento dei fatti** the sequence of events

svolsi *ecc* [ˈzvɔlsi] vb *vedi* **svolgere**

svolta [ˈzvɔlta] sf (*curva*) turn, bend; (*fig: mutamento*) turning point; **divieto di svolta a sinistra** no left turn; **prendi la prima svolta a destra** take the first turning on your right; **svolta a destra/a sinistra** (*Pol*) swing to the right/to the left; **essere ad una svolta nella propria vita** to be at a crossroads in one's life

svoltare [zvolˈtare] /72/ vi (*aus* avere) to turn; **all'incrocio svolta a destra** turn right at the junction

svolto, -a [ˈzvɔlto] pp *di* **svolgere**

svuotare [zvwoˈtare] /72/ vt (*vuotare*) to empty (out); (*fig*): **svuotare di** to deprive of; **ho dovuto svuotare tutti i cassetti per trovarlo** I had to empty all the drawers to find it

Swaziland [ˈswadziland] sm Swaziland

Tt

T¹, t¹ [ti] SF INV, SM INV (*lettera*) T, t; **T come Taranto** ≈ T for Tommy

T² [ti] ABBR = **tabaccheria**

t [ti] ABBR 1 = **tara** 2 = **tonnellata**

TA SIGLA = Taranto

tabaccaio, -aia, -ai, -aie [tabak'kajo] SM, SF tobacconist (*Brit*), tobacco dealer (*USA*)

tabaccheria [tabakke'ria] SF tobacconist's (shop) (*Brit*), tobacco *o* smoke shop (*USA*)

tabacchiera [tabak'kjɛra] SF snuffbox

tabacco, -chi [ta'bakko] SM tobacco

tabella [ta'bɛlla] SF (*prospetto*) table, list; (*cartellone*) board; (*Inform*) array; **tabella di marcia** schedule; **tabella dei prezzi** price list

tabellone [tabel'lone] SM (*per pubblicità*) billboard; (*per informazioni*) notice board (*Brit*), bulletin board (*USA*); (*in stazione*) timetable board

tabernacolo [taber'nakolo] SM tabernacle

tabù [ta'bu] AGG INV, SM INV taboo; **un argomento tabù** a taboo subject

tabula rasa ['tabula 'raza] SF tabula rasa; **fare tabula rasa** (*fig*) to make a clean sweep; **ha fatto tabula rasa di tutti i dolci** he polished off all the cakes

tabulare [tabu'lare] /72/ VT (*compilare una tabella*) to tabulate

tabulato [tabu'lato] SM (*Inform*) printout

tabulatore [tabula'tore] SM (*anche: tasto tabulatore*) tabulator

TAC [tak] SIGLA F INV (*Med*) 1 (*esame: = Tomografia Assiale Computerizzata*) CT *o* CAT scan 2 (*apparecchiatura*) CT *o* CAT scanner

tacca, -che ['takka] SF (*gen*) notch; (*meno profondo*) nick; **di mezza tacca** (*fig: pegg*) mediocre

taccagneria [takkaɲɲe'ria] SF meanness, stinginess

taccagno, -a [tak'kaɲɲo] AGG mean, stingy ♦ SM, SF miser, mean *o* stingy person

taccheggio, -gi [tak'keddʒo] SM (*furto*) shoplifting

tacchino [tak'kino] SM turkey

taccia, -ce ['tattʃa] SF bad reputation

tacciare [tat'tʃare] /14/ VT: **tacciare qn di** (*vigliaccheria ecc*) to accuse sb of

taccio *ecc* ['tattʃo] VB *vedi* **tacere**

tacco, -chi ['takko] SM 1 (*di scarpe*) heel; **scarpe senza tacco** flat shoes; **coi tacchi bassi/alti** low-/high-heeled; **tacco a spillo** stiletto (heel) (*Brit*), spike heel (*USA*) 2 (*cuneo per fermare le ruote*) chock

taccuino [takku'ino] SM notebook

tacere [ta'tʃere] VB IRREG /119/ VI (*aus avere*) (*stare in silenzio*) to be silent *o* quiet; (*smettere di parlare*) to fall silent; **continuava a tacere** he remained silent; **taci!** be quiet!; **farlo tacere** make him be quiet; **tutto taceva** all was silent *o* quiet; **i cannoni tacquero** the cannons fell silent; **fatelo tacere qn** to silence sb; **mettere a tacere qc** to hush sth up ♦ VT (*particolare, accaduto*) to keep silent about, keep to oneself, say nothing about; **tacere la verità** to hold back the truth

tachicardia [takikar'dia] SF (*Med*) tachycardia

tachimetro [ta'kimetro] SM speedometer

tacito, -a ['tatʃito] AGG (*sottinteso*) tacit, unspoken; (*silenzioso*) silent

taciturno, -a [tatʃi'turno] AGG taciturn

taciuto, -a [ta'tʃuto] PP *di* **tacere**

tacqui *ecc* ['takkwi] VB *vedi* **tacere**

tafano [ta'fano] SM horsefly

tafferuglio, -gli [taffe'ruʎʎo] SM brawl, scuffle

taffettà [taffet'ta] SM INV taffeta

taglia ['taʎʎa] SF 1 (*misura: di abito*) size; **che taglia porti?** what size do you wear *o* take?; **taglia forte** outsize; **taglia unica** one size; **taglie forti** extra large sizes 2 (*misura: di animali*) size 3 (*su criminale*) reward; **c'è una taglia sulla sua testa** there is a price on his head

tagliaboschi [taʎʎa'boski] SM INV woodcutter

tagliacarte [taʎʎa'karte] SM INV paperknife

taglialegna [taʎʎa'leɲɲa] SM INV woodcutter, lumberjack (*USA*)

tagliando [taʎ'ʎando] SM 1 (*cedola*) coupon, voucher; **tagliando controllo bagaglio** (*Aer*) luggage (*Brit*) *o* baggage (*USA*) identification tag 2 (*Aut*): **fare il tagliando** to have one's car serviced

tagliare [taʎ'ʎare] /27/ VT 1 (*gen*) to cut; (*torta, salame*) to cut, slice; (*arrosto*) to carve; (*siepe*) to trim; (*fieno, prato*) to mow; (*grano*) to reap; (*albero*) to fell, cut down; **tagliare qc in due/in più parti** to cut sth in two/into several pieces; **tagliare la gola a qn** to cut *o* slit sb's throat; **tagliare il capo** *o* **la testa a qn** to behead sb, cut sb's head off; **mi tagli una fetta di torta?** would you cut me a slice of cake?; **tagliarsi** to cut oneself; **mi sono tagliato** I've cut myself; **mi sono tagliato un dito** I've cut my finger; **tagliarsi i capelli** to have one's hair cut; **devo tagliarmi i capelli** I need to get my hair cut; **ti sei tagliato i capelli?** have you had your hair cut?; **tagliarsi le unghie** to cut one's nails; **una lama che taglia** a sharp blade; **taglia e incolla** (*Inform*) cut and paste 2 (*articolo, scritto, scena*) to cut; (*acqua, telefono, gas*) to cut off; **mio padre mi ha tagliato i viveri** my father is refusing to support me any more 3 (*intersecare: sogg: strada*) to cut across; **tagliare la strada a qn** (*in macchina*) to cut in on sb; (*a piedi*) to cut across in front of sb 4 (*curva*) to cut; (*traguardo*) to cross; (*palla*) to put a spin on 5 (*carte*) to cut 6 (*vini*) to blend; (*droga*) to cut 7 (*fraseologia*): **tagliare la corda** to sneak off; **tagliare la testa al toro** to settle things once and for all; **tagliare corto** to cut short; **tagliare le gambe a qn** (*fig*) to make it impossible for sb to act, tie sb's hands; **un vino che taglia le gambe** a very strong wine; **tagliare i panni addosso a qn** (*sparlare*) to tear sb to pieces ♦ VI (*aus avere*) (*prendere una scorciatoia*) to take a short cut; **tagliare per i campi** to cut across the fields; **tagliamo per di là** let's cut across that way

tagliatelle [taʎʎa'telle] SFPL tagliatelle *sg*

tagliato, -a [taʎ'ʎato] AGG: **essere tagliato per qc** (*fig*) to be cut out for sth

tagliatrice [taʎʎa'tritʃe] SF (*Tecn*) cutter

tagliaunghie [taʎʎa'ungje] SM INV nail clippers *pl*

taglieggiare [taʎʎed'dʒare] /62/ VT to extort money from; (*Storia*) to exact a tribute from

tagliente [taʎ'ʎɛnte] AGG (*lama*) sharp; (*fig: tono, parole*) cutting, sharp

tagliere [taʎ'ʎɛre] SM (*gen*) chopping board; (*per il pane*) bread board, cutting board

taglio, -gli ['taʎʎo] SM 1 (*gen, atto*) cutting, cut; (*di capelli*) (hair)cut; (*di fieno, erba*) mowing; (*di vini*) blending; **vino da taglio** blending wine; **dare un taglio netto a qc** (*fig*) to make a clean break with sth; **taglio cesareo** (*Med*) Caesarean section 2 (*effetto*) cut; **farsi un taglio al dito** to cut one's finger; **ha un taglio sulla fronte** he's got a cut on his forehead; **taglio netto** clean cut; **c'erano dei tagli nel film/nel libro** cuts were made in the film (*Brit*) *o* movie (*USA*) in the book; **un taglio alla spesa pubblica** a cut in public spending 3 (*pezzo: di carne*) piece; (: *di stoffa*) length; **pizza al taglio** pizza by the slice; **banconote di piccolo/grosso taglio** small-/large-denomination notes 4 (*stile: di abito*) cut, style; (: *di capelli*) (hair)style; (: *di pietra preziosa*) cut; **questo taglio di capelli ti dona moltissimo** that hairstyle really suits you; **di taglio classico** with a classic cut; **scuola di taglio** dressmaking school 5 (*di lama*) cutting edge, edge;

colpire qc di taglio to hit sth on edge *o* edgeways **6** (*Sport*) spin; **dare il taglio alla palla** to put a spin on the ball

tagliola [taʎˈʎɔla] SF trap, snare

taglione [taʎˈʎone] SM: **la legge del taglione** the concept of an eye for an eye (and a tooth for a tooth)

tagliuzzare [taʎʎutˈtsare] /72/ VT to cut into small pieces

Tahiti [taˈiti] SF Tahiti

tailandese [tailanˈdese] AGG, SM, SF Thai ♦ SM (*lingua*) Thai

Tailandia [taiˈlandja] SF Thailand

tailleur [taˈjœr] SM INV (lady's) suit

talamo [ˈtalamo] SM (*letter*) bridal bed

talco, -chi [ˈtalko] SM talcum powder

PAROLA CHIAVE

tale [ˈtale] AGG DIMOSTR
1 (*simile, così grande*) such (a); **è di una tale arroganza** he is so arrogant; **tale articolo è in vendita presso tutte le nostre filiali** the above-mentioned article is on sale at all our branches; **tali discorsi sono inaccettabili** such talk is not acceptable; **non avevo mai visto un tale disordine** I had never seen such a mess; **cosa ti fa credere che nutra tali sentimenti?** what makes you think he feels like that?
2 (*nelle similitudini*): **tale... tale...** like ... like ...; **tale padre tale figlio** like father like son; **è tale quale suo nonno** he's the spitting image of *o* exactly like his grandfather; **il tuo vestito è tale quale il mio** your dress is just *o* exactly like mine; **hanno riportato una vittoria tale, quale non avevano sperato** they won an even greater victory than they had expected

♦ AGG INDEF
1 (*certo*): **quella tale persona desidera parlarti** that man (*o* woman) wants to speak with you; **ti cercava una tale Giovanna** somebody called Giovanna was looking for you; **ha detto che vedeva un amico, un tal Rossi** he said he was meeting a friend, a certain Rossi
2 (*persona o cosa indeterminata*) such-and-such; **il tale giorno alla tale ora** on such and such a day at such and such a time

♦ PRON INDEF
1 un (una) tale (*una certa persona*) someone; (*quella persona già menzionata*) the one, the person, that person, that man, that woman; **è fidanzata con un tale dell'ufficio contabilità** she's engaged to someone in accounts; **hai più visto quel tale di cui mi dicevi?** did you ever see that person *o* man you were telling me about again?; **ha telefonato di nuovo quella tale** that woman phoned again
2 il tal dei tali whatshisname; **la tal dei tali** whatshername; **diciamo che l'ho saputo dal tal dei tali** let's just say I had *o* heard it from you-know-who

---

talebano [taleˈbano] SM Taliban

talento [taˈlento] SM (*capacità*) talent; (*persona*) talented person; **avere talento per qc** to have a talent for sth; **essere privo/pieno di talento** to be untalented/very talented

talismano [talizˈmano] SM talisman

talk-show [ˈtɔːkʃou] SM INV chat (*Brit*) *o* talk (*USA*) show

tallonare [talloˈnare] /72/ VT (*inseguire*) to follow (hot) on the heels of, pursue; (*Sport*) to pursue; **tallonare il pallone** (*Rugby*) to heel the ball; (*Calcio*) to back-heel the ball

talloncino [tallonˈtʃino] SM stub, counterfoil (*Brit*); **talloncino del prezzo** (*di medicinali*) tear-off tag

tallone [talˈlone] SM heel; **tallone di Achille** Achilles' heel
❏ **tallone** non si traduce mai con la parola inglese *talon*

talmente [talˈmente] AVV (*così tanto*) so; **sono talmente contento!** I'm so happy!; **ero talmente emozionato che...** I was so excited that ...; **l'Irlanda mi è talmente piaciuta che ci tornerei domani** I liked Ireland so much that I'd go back there tomorrow; **è stato talmente ingenuo da cascarci** he was naïve enough to fall for it

talora [taˈlora] AVV = talvolta

talpa [ˈtalpa] SF (*Zool, anche fig*) mole; **cieco come una talpa** as blind as a bat

talvolta [talˈvɔlta] AVV sometimes, at times

tamburello [tambuˈrello] SM (*Mus*) tambourine; (*gioco*) *ball game played with tambourine-shaped bats*

tamburino [tambuˈrino] SM drummer boy

tamburo [tamˈburo] SM **1** (*Mus: strumento*) drum; (: *suonatore*) drummer; **a tamburo battente** (*fig*) immediately, at once **2** (*Tecn, Aut*) drum; (*di armi*) cylinder; (*di orologio*) barrel; **freni a tamburo** drum brakes; **pistola a tamburo** revolver

Tamigi [taˈmidʒi] SM: **il Tamigi** the Thames

tamponamento [tampona'mento] SM (*Aut*) collision; **tamponamento a catena** pile-up

tamponare [tampoˈnare] /72/ VT **1** (*urtare: macchina*) to go into the back of; **abbiamo tamponato un furgone** we went into the back of a van **2** (*otturare*) to plug

tampone [tamˈpone] SM **1** (*assorbente interno*) tampon **2** (*Med: gen*) plug; (: *di cotone*) wad; (: *per pulire una ferita*) swab; (: *per stendere un liquido*) pad **3** (*cuscinetto: per timbri*) ink-pad; (: *di carta assorbente*) blotter ♦ AGG INV: **provvedimento tampone** stopgap measure

tamtam, tam-tam [tamˈtam] SM INV (*Mus*) tomtom; (*fig*): **il tamtam dei carcerati** the prison grapevine

tana [ˈtana] SF (*gen*) lair, den; (*di coniglio*) burrow; (*fig: nascondiglio*) den, hideout

tanfo [ˈtanfo] SM stench

tanga [ˈtanga] SM INV tanga

tangente [tanˈdʒente] AGG (*Geom*): **tangente (a)** tangential (to) ♦ SF **1** (*Geom*) tangent; **filare per la tangente** (*fig: svignarsela*) to make one's getaway; **partire per la tangente** (*fig: divagare*) to go off at a tangent **2** (*pizzo*) protection money *sg*; (*bustarella*) kickback; **lo scandalo delle tangenti** the kickback scandal

tangentopoli [tandʒenˈtɔpoli] SF *corruption scandal involving government ministers, industrialists and businessmen: it began in 1992, in Milan, which was consequently dubbed Tangentopoli* (*Bribesville*)

tangenziale [tandʒenˈtsjale] AGG (*Geom*) tangential; **retta tangenziale** tangent ♦ SF (*anche*: **strada tangenziale**) bypass

Tangeri [ˈtandʒeri] SF Tangier(s)

tangibile [tanˈdʒibile] AGG tangible

tangibilmente [tandʒibilˈmente] AVV tangibly

tango, -ghi [ˈtango] SM tango

tanica, -che [ˈtanika] SF (*contenitore*) jerry can; (*Naut: serbatoio*) tank

tannino [tanˈnino] SM tannin

tantino [tanˈtino] **un tantino** AVV (*un po'*) a little, a bit; (*alquanto*) rather ♦ SM: **un tantino di** a little bit of

---

PAROLA CHIAVE

tanto, -a [ˈtanto] AGG INDEF
1 (*molto: quantità*) a lot of, much; (: *numero*) a lot of, many; (*così tanto: quantità*) so much, such a lot of; (: *numero*) so many, such a lot of; **ogni tanti chilometri/giorni** every so many kilometres/days; **tante persone, tante opinioni diverse** there are as many different opinions as there are people; **c'è ancora tanta strada da fare!** there's still a long way to go!; **tante volte** so many times; **tanta gente** so many people
2 (*rafforzativo*) such; **l'ha detto con tanta gentilezza** he said it with such kindness *o* so kindly; **ho aspettato per tanto tempo** I waited so long *o* for such a long time
3 tanto... quanto... (*quantità*) as much ... as ...; (*numero*) as many ... as ...; **ho tanta pazienza quanta ne hai tu** I am as patient as you are, I have as much patience as you (have); **ha tanti amici quanti nemici** he has as many friends as he has enemies; **ho tanti libri quanti ne ha lui** I have as many books as him *o* as he has

♦ PRON INDEF
1 (*molto*) much, a lot; (*così tanto*) so much, such a lot; (*plurale*): **tanti(e)** (*molti*) many, a lot; (*così tanti*) so many, such a lot; **è una ragazza come tante** she's like any other girl; **è solo uno dei tanti che...** he's just one of the many who ...; **credevo ce ne fosse tanto** I thought there was (such) a lot, I thought there was plenty; **se cerchi un bicchiere, lassù ce ne sono tanti** if you are looking for a glass there are a lot *o* lots up there; **tanti credono sia semplice farlo** many people believe it is easy to do
2 (*altrettanto*): **tanto quanto** as much as; (*plurale*): **tanti quanti** as many as; **tempo? ne ho tanto quanto basta** time? I have as much as I need

3 (*con valore indeterminato*): **riceve un tanto al mese** he receives so much a month; **costa un tanto al metro** it costs so much per *o* a metre; **della somma che ho a disposizione tanto andrà per il vitto, tanto per l'alloggio** of the money I've got so much will go on food and so much on accommodation; **nell'anno millecinquecento e tanti** in the year fifteen hundred and something

4 (*fraseologia*): **me ne ha dette tante!** he gave me a real mouthful!; **di tanto in tanto** every so often, (every) now and again; **è rimasto con tanto di naso** he was left feeling disappointed; **tanto di guadagnato!** so much the better!; **tanto meglio così!** so much the better!; **se tanto mi dà tanto** oh well, if that's the case ...; **guardare qc con tanto d'occhi** to gaze wide-eyed at sth; **ogni tanto** every so often, (every) now and then; **ascoltava con tanto d'orecchi** he was all ears; **tanto vale che...** you may *o* might as well ...

♦ AVV

1 (*così, in questo modo*: *con verbo*) so much, such a lot; (: *con avverbio, aggettivo*) so; (*così a lungo*) so long; **tanto... che...** so ... (that) ...; **è tanto bello che sembra finto** it's so beautiful (that) it seems unreal; **tanto... da...** so ... as ...; **saresti tanto gentile da prendermi una tazza?** would you be so kind as to get me a cup?; **è stato tanto idiota da crederci** he was stupid enough to believe it; **non lavorare tanto!** don't work so hard!; **stanno tanto bene insieme!** they go so well together!

2 (*nei comparativi*): **tanto... quanto...** as ... as ...; **è tanto gentile quanto discreto** he is as kind as he is discreet; **non è poi tanto difficile quanto sembra** it is not as difficult as it seems after all; **mi piace non tanto per l'aspetto quanto per il suo sapore** I like it not so much for its looks as for its taste; **conosco tanto Carlo quanto suo padre** I know both Carlo and his father

3 (*molto*) very; **un'ora a dir tanto** an hour at the most; **non ci vuole tanto a capirlo** it doesn't take much to understand it; **non è poi tanto giovane** he is not all that young after all; **l'ho visto tanto giù** he seemed *o* looked very down to me; **scusami tanto** I'm very sorry; **do excuse me; sono tanto tanto contento di vederti** I'm so very happy to see you; **vengo tanto volentieri** I'd love to come

4 (*a lungo*) (for) long; **starai via tanto?** will you be away (for) long?; **non stare fuori tanto** don't stay out for long

5 (*solamente*) just; **tanto per cambiare** (*anche iro*) just for a change; **parla tanto per parlare** he talks just for the sake of talking; **tanto per ridere** just for a laugh; **una volta tanto** just for once

6 (*con valore moltiplicativo*): **due volte tanto** twice as much; **tre volte tanto** three times as much

7 **tanto più insisti tanto più non mollerà** the more you insist the more stubborn he'll be; **tanto più lo vedo tanto meno mi piace** the more I see him the less I like him

♦ CONG **after all; lo farò, tanto non mi costa niente** I'll do it, after all it won't cost me anything; **fanne a meno, tanto a me non importa** do without then, I don't care; **tanto è inutile** in any case it's useless

Tanzania [tanˈdzanja] SF Tanzania

tapioca [taˈpjɔka] SF tapioca

tapiro [taˈpiro] SM tapir

tappa [ˈtappa] SF **1** (*luogo di sosta, fermata*) stop, halt; **la prima tappa del nostro viaggio sarà Pisa** the first stop on our journey will be Pisa; **far tappa a Pisa** to stop (off); **abbiamo fatto tappa a Bath** we stopped off in Bath **2** (*Sport: parte di percorso*) stage, leg; (*fig: stadio*) stage; **a tappe** in stages; **bruciare le tappe** (*fig*) to get there fast
❏ **tappa** non si traduce mai con la parola inglese *tap*

tappabuchi [tappaˈbuki] SM INV, SF INV stopgap; **fare da tappabuchi** to act as a stopgap

tappare [tapˈpare] /72/ VT (*otturare*) to plug, stop up; (*bottiglia*) to cork; **potresti tappare la bottiglia?** could you put the cork in the bottle, please?; **tapparsi il naso** to hold one's nose; **mi si è tappato il naso** my nose is blocked; **tapparsi le orecchie** to cover one's ears; **tappare un buco** (*fig*) to provide a short-term remedy; **tappare la bocca a qn** (*fig*) to shut sb up; **tapparsi le orecchie/gli occhi** (*fig*) to turn a

deaf ear/a blind eye; **tapparsi** VR: **tapparsi in casa** to shut o.s. up at home

tapparella [tappaˈrella] SF rolling shutter

tappetino [tappeˈtino] SM (*per auto*) car mat; **tappetino antiscivolo** (*da bagno*) non-slip mat; **tappetino del mouse** mouse pad

tappeto [tapˈpeto] SM (*gen*) carpet; (*piccolo*) rug; (*stuoia*) mat; (*per tavolo*) cloth; **un tappeto persiano** a Persian rug; **bombardamento a tappeto** carpet bombing; **andare al tappeto** (*Pugilato*) to go down for the count; (*fig*) to be floored; **mandare qn al tappeto** (*fig*) to floor sb; **mettere sul tappeto** (*fig: questione*) to table; **tappeto erboso** lawn; **tappeto verde** (*panno*) green baize (cloth); (*tavolo da gioco*) gaming table

tappezzare [tappetˈtsare] /72/ VT (*pareti*) to paper; (*divano, sedia*) to cover, to upholster; **tappezzare una stanza di manifesti** to cover a room with posters

tappezzeria [tappettseˈria] SF (*arredamento*) soft furnishings pl; (*carta da pareti*) wallpaper; (*tessuto*) wall covering; (*di automobile*) upholstery; **in camera da letto c'era la tappezzeria rosa** there was pink wallpaper in the bedroom; **fare da tappezzeria** (*fig*) to be a wallflower

tappezziere, -a [tappetˈtsjere] SM, SF upholsterer

tappo [ˈtappo] SM (*di bottiglia: in sughero*) cork; (: *in vetro, plastica*) stopper; (*di barattolo, serbatoio, radiatore*) cap; (*di penna*) top; (*di vasca, lavandino*) plug; (*scherz: persona bassa*) shorty; **tappi per le orecchie** earplugs; **tappo a corona** bottle top; **tappo salvagocce** dripless pour spout; **tappo di scarico della coppa** (*Aut*) drain plug; **tappo con serratura** (*Aut*) locking petrol cap; **tappo a vite** screw top

TAR [tar] SIGLA M = Tribunale Amministrativo Regionale

tara [ˈtara] SF **1** (*peso*) tare **2** (*Med*) hereditary defect; (*difetto*) flaw

tarantella [taranˈtɛlla] SF (*danza*) tarantella

tarantola [taˈrantola] SF tarantula

tarare [taˈrare] /72/ VT (*Comm*) to tare; (*Tecn*) to calibrate

tarato, -a [taˈrato] AGG **1** (*Comm*) tared; (*Tecn*) calibrated **2** (*Med*) with a hereditary defect; **ma tu sei tarato** (*scherz*) you're nuts

taratura [taraˈtura] SF (*Comm*) taring; (*Tecn*) calibration

tarchiato, -a [tarˈkjato] AGG stocky, thickset

tardare [tarˈdare] /72/ VI (*aus* avere) to be late; **ha tardato molto** he was very late; **come mai hai tardato tanto?** how come you're so late?; **tardare a fare qc** (*involontariamente*) to be late in doing sth; (*apposta*) to delay doing sth; **scusa se ho tardato a rispondere alla tua lettera, ma...** I'm sorry I've taken so long to reply to your letter, but ... ♦ VT (*consegna*) to delay

tardi [ˈtardi] AVV late; **ormai è troppo tardi** it's too late now; **alzarsi tardi** to get up late; **svegliarsi tardi** to wake up late, oversleep; **arrivare tardi** to arrive late; **lavorare fino a tardi** to work late; **fare tardi** (*essere in ritardo*) to be late; (*restare alzato*) to stay up late; **scusa se ho fatto tardi, ho perso l'autobus** I'm sorry I'm late, I missed the bus; **non devo fare tardi stasera, domani ho l'esame** I mustn't stay up late tonight, I've got an exam tomorrow; **meglio tardi che mai** better late than never; **più tardi** later (on); **vi raggiungo più tardi** I'll join you later; **a più tardi!** see you later!; **al più tardi** at the latest; **presto o tardi** sooner or later; **presto o tardi se ne pentirà** sooner or later he'll be sorry; **si è fatto tardi** it is late; **sul tardi** (*verso sera*) late in the day; **ci siamo incontrati sul tardi** we met quite late

tardivo, -a [tarˈdivo] AGG (*primavera, fioritura, sviluppo*) late; (*rimedio, pentimento*) belated

tardo, -a [ˈtardo] AGG (*lento, ottuso*) slow; (*avanzato: mattinata, primavera*) late; (*tardivo: pentimento*) belated; **nel tardo pomeriggio** late in the afternoon

tardona [tarˈdona] SF (*pegg*): **essere una tardona** to be mutton dressed as lamb (*Brit*), (*fam*) old girl

targa, -ghe [ˈtarga] SF (*gen*) plate; (*su una porta*) nameplate; (*Aut*) numberplate (*Brit*), license plate (*USA*); (*placca*) plaque

targare [tarˈgare] /80/ VT (*Aut*) to register

targhetta [tarˈgetta] SF (*con nome*) nameplate; (*on door*); (*su bagaglio*) name tag

tariffa [taˈriffa] SF (*gen*) rate, tariff; (*di trasporti*) fare; **la tariffa in vigore** the going rate; **tariffa inserzioni per pagina** (*Stampa*) page rate; **tariffa normale** (*gen*) standard rate; (*su mezzi di trasporto*) full fare; **tariffa professionale** fee; **tariffa ridotta: c'è una tariffa ridotta per i bambini** there are reduced fares for children; (*gen*) reduced rate; (*su mezzi di trasporto*) reduced *o* concessionary fare; **tariffa salariale** wage rate; **tariffa unica** flat rate; **tariffe doganali** customs rates *o* tariff *sg*; **tariffe ferroviarie** train fares; **tariffe postali** postal charges; **tariffe telefoniche** telephone charges

tariffario, -ria, -ri, -rie [tariffarjo] AGG: **aumento tariffario** increase in charges *o* rates ♦ SM tariff, table of charges

tarlo [ˈtarlo] SM **1** (*insetto*) woodworm **2** **il tarlo della gelosia** the pangs *pl* of jealousy; **il tarlo del dubbio lo assillava** doubts ate away at him

tarma [ˈtarma] SF moth

tarmicida, -i [tarmiˈtʃida] AGG, SM moth-killer

tarocco, -chi [taˈrɔkko] SM tarot card; **il gioco dei tarocchi** tarot

tarpare [tarˈpare] /72/ VT (*fig*): **tarpare le ali a qn** to clip sb's wings

tartagliare [tartaʎˈʎare] /27/ VI (*aus* **avere**) to stutter, stammer ♦ VT to mutter

tartaro, -a [ˈtartaro] AGG (*Storia*) Tartar; (*Culin*) tartar(e); **bistecca alla tartara** steak tartare ♦ SM, SF Tartar

tartaruga, -ghe [tartaˈruga] SF (*testuggine*) tortoise; (*di mare*) turtle; (*materiale*) tortoiseshell; **zuppa di tartaruga** turtle soup; **essere lento come una tartaruga** to be a slowcoach (*Brit*) *o* slowpoke (*USA*)

tartassare [tartasˈsare] /72/ VT (*fam*): **tartassare qn** to give sb the works; **tartassare qn a un esame** to give sb a grilling at an exam; **smettila di tartassare quel piano!** stop thumping on that piano!; **essere tartassato dal fisco** to be hard hit by the taxman

tartina [tarˈtina] SF canapé

tartufo [tarˈtufo] SM **1** (*fungo*) truffle; (*semifreddo*) individual filled chocolate ice-cream cake **2** **tartufo di mare** (*Zool*) Venus clam **3** (*naso di cane*) nose

tasca, -sche [ˈtaska] SF (*gen*) pocket; (*scomparto: di valigia*) compartment; (*Zool, Anat*) pouch; **l'ho messo nella tasca della giacca** I put it in my jacket pocket; **tasca dei pantaloni** trouser (*Brit*) *o* pants (*USA*) pocket; **da tasca** pocket *attr*; **non ho un soldo in tasca** (*al momento*) I haven't any money *o* a penny on me; (*essere al verde*) I'm broke; **riempirsi le tasche di qc** to fill one's pockets with sth; **non startene con le mani in tasca** (*fig*) don't just stand there with your hands in your pockets; **non me ne viene niente in tasca** I get nothing out of it; **che cosa me ne viene in tasca?** what's in it for me?; **fare i conti in tasca a qn** to meddle in sb's affairs; **conosco Roma come le mie tasche** I know Rome like the back of my hand; **averne le tasche piene di** to be fed up with; **tasca da pasticciere** piping bag

tascabile [tasˈkabile] AGG (*libro*) pocket *attr*; **una calcolatrice tascabile** a pocket calculator; **un'edizione tascabile** a pocket edition ♦ SM ≈ paperback

tascapane [taskaˈpane] SM haversack

taschino [tasˈkino] SM breast pocket

Tasmania [tazˈmanja] SF Tasmania

tassa [ˈtassa] SF (*imposta*) tax; (*doganale*) duty; (*Scol, Univ*) fee; **non aveva pagato le tasse** he hadn't paid his taxes; **soggetto a tasse** taxable; **tassa di circolazione** road tax (*Brit*), registration fee (*USA*); **tassa di soggiorno** tourist tax; **tasse scolastiche** school fees

tassametro [tasˈsametro] SM taximeter

tassare [tasˈsare] /72/ VT (*gen*) to tax; (*sogg: dogana*) to levy a duty on; **tassarsi** VR: **tassarsi per** to chip in, contribute

tassativo, -a [tassaˈtivo] AGG peremptory

tassazione [tassatˈtsjone] SF taxation; **soggetto a tassazione** taxable

tassello [tasˈsɛllo] SM (*pezzetto: di legno, pietra*) plug; (*per vestiti*) gusset; (*assaggio: di formaggio, cocomero*) wedge

tassì [tasˈsi] SM INV = **taxi**

tassista, -i, -e [tasˈsista] SM, SF taxi driver, cab driver; **fa il tassista** she's a taxi driver

tasso¹ [ˈtasso] SM (*di natalità, mortalità*) rate; **tasso agevolato** (*Banca*) special rate; **tasso di cambio** rate of exchange; **tasso di crescita** growth rate; **tasso glicemico** (*Med*) blood sugar level; **tasso d'inquinamento** pollution level; **tasso di interesse** rate of interest; **tasso ufficiale di sconto** (*Econ*) official discount rate

tasso² [ˈtasso] SM (*Bot*) yew

tasso³ [ˈtasso] SM (*Zool*) badger

tastare [tasˈtare] /72/ VT to feel; **tastare il polso a qn** to feel sb's pulse; **tastare il terreno** to test the ground; (*fig*) to see how the land lies

tastiera [tasˈtjera] SF (*gen, anche Mus, Inform*) keyboard; (*di strumenti a corda*) fingerboard; **apparecchio (telefonico) a tastiera** push-button phone

tastierino [tastjeˈrino] SM: **tastierino numerico** numeric keypad

tasto [ˈtasto] SM (*gen, anche Tecn, Mus*) key; (*tatto*) touch, feel; (*fig: argomento*) topic, subject; **toccare un tasto delicato** to touch on a delicate subject; **toccare il tasto giusto** (*fig*) to strike the right note; **tasto di controllo** (*Inform*) control key; **tasto funzione** (*Inform*) function key; **tasto delle maiuscole** (*su tastiera*) shift key; **tasto di ritorno a margine** (*Inform*) return key; **tasto di scelta rapida** (*Inform*) hot key; **tasto tabulatore** (*su tastiera*) tab (key)

❑ **tasto** non si traduce mai con la parola inglese *taste*

tastoni [tasˈtoni] AVV: **procedere (a) tastoni** to grope one's way forward

tata [ˈtata] SF (*linguaggio infantile*) nanny

tattico, -a, -ci, -che [ˈtattiko] AGG tactical ♦ SM (*Mil, anche fig*) tactician

tatto [ˈtatto] SM **1** (*senso*) touch; **duro al tatto** hard to the touch **2** (*diplomazia*) tact; **aver tatto** to be tactful, have tact; **essere privo di tatto, non avere tatto** to be tactless

tatuaggio, -gi [tatuˈaddʒo] SM (*operazione*) tattooing; (*disegno*) tattoo; **ha un tatuaggio sul braccio** he's got a tattoo on his arm

tatuare [tatuˈare] /72/ VT to tattoo; **tatuarsi** VR to have o.s. tattooed

taumaturgico, -a, -ci, -che [taumaˈturdʒiko] AGG (*fig*) miraculous

TAV [tav] SF INV, SM INV **1** (= *treno alta velocità*) high-speed train **2** (*sistema*) high-speed rail system

taverna [taˈverna] SF (*osteria*) tavern

tavola [ˈtavola] SF **1** (*mobile*) table; **a tavola!** come and eat!, dinner's ready!; **essere a tavola** to be having a meal; **preparare la tavola** to lay *o* set the table; **sedersi a tavola** to sit down to eat, sit down at the table; **ama i piaceri della tavola** he enjoys his food; **la buona tavola** good food **2** (*asse*) plank, board; **il mare è una tavola** the sea is like a millpond **3** (*tabella*) table; (*illustrazione*) plate; (*quadro su legno*) panel (*painting*) ♦ **tavola calda** snack bar; **tavola periodica degli elementi** (*Chim*) periodic table; **tavola pitagorica** multiplication table; **tavola reale** (*gioco*) backgammon; **tavola rotonda** (*anche fig*) round table; **tavola a vela** sailboard

tavolata [tavoˈlata] SF (*commensali*) table

tavolato [tavoˈlato] SM **1** (*gen*) planking, boarding; (*di palco*) boards *pl* **2** (*Geog*) plateau

tavoletta [tavoˈletta] SF (*di cioccolata*) bar; **andare a tavoletta** (*Aut*) to go flat out; **tavoletta grafica** (*Inform*) graphics tablet

tavolino [tavoˈlino] SM (*gen*) small table; (*scrittoio, banco*) desk; **un bar con i tavolini all'aperto** a café with outdoor tables; **mettersi a tavolino** to get down to work; **decidere qc a tavolino** (*fig*) to decide sth on a theoretical level *o* in theory; **il risultato della partita è stato deciso a tavolino** the result of the match was decided by the referee; **tavolino da gioco** card table; **tavolino da tè** coffee table

tavolo [ˈtavolo] SM (*gen*) table; (*scrittoio*) desk; **vieni a sedere al nostro tavolo** come and sit at our table; **da tavolo** table *attr*; **tavolo anatomico** mortuary slab; **tavolo da disegno** drawing board; **tavolo da lavoro** (*gen*) desk; (*Tecn*) workbench; **tavolo dei negoziati** negotiating table; **tavolo operatorio** operating table; **tavolo pieghevole** folding table; **tavolo da ping-pong** table-tennis table; **tavolo a ribalta** drop-leaf table

tavolozza [tavo'lɔttsa] SF (*Arte*) palette

taxi ['taksi] SM INV taxi

tazza ['tattsa] SF (*recipiente*) cup; (*contenuto*) cupful; (*fam: di gabinetto*) bowl, pan (*Brit*); **una tazza di caffè/tè** a cup of coffee/tea; **tazza da caffè** coffee cup; **tazza da tè** teacup

tazzina [tat'tsina] SF coffee cup

TBC [tibi't ʃi] SIGLA F (= *tubercolosi*) TB

TE SIGLA = Teramo

te [te] PRON PERS 1 (*dopo prep, accentato*) you; **lo ha dato a te**, **non a me** he gave it to you, not to me; **parlavamo di te** we were talking about you; **vengo con te** I'm coming with you; **dietro di te** behind you; **verrò da te** I'll come round to your place, I'll drop in and see you; **fallo da te** do it yourself; **se fossi in te** if I were you; **povero te!** poor you! 2 (*nelle comparazioni*) you; **è alto come te** he's as tall as you (are); **parla come te** she speaks like you (do); **è più giovane di te** he's younger than you (are) 3 *vedi* **ti**

tè [te] SM INV (*bevanda*) tea; (*pianta*) tea plant; (*trattenimento*) tea party; **da tè** tea *attr*; **vuoi un tè?** would you like a cup of tea?

teatrale [tea'trale] AGG (*spettacolo*) theatrical, stage *attr*; (*stagione, compagnia, attore*) theatre *attr* (*Brit*), theater *attr* (*USA*); (*fig: gesto, atteggiamento*) theatrical; **siamo andati a vedere uno spettacolo teatrale** we went to the theatre *o* theater

teatro [te'atro] SM 1 (*edificio*) theatre (*Brit*), theater (*USA*); (*pubblico*) house, audience; (*fig: luogo*) scene; **andare a teatro** to go to the theatre *o* theater; **qualche volta vanno a teatro** they sometimes go to the theatre; **il teatro era pieno** there was a full house; **il teatro delle operazioni** (*Mil*) the theatre *o* theater of operations; **la sua casa è stata teatro di un orrendo delitto** his house was the scene of a hideous crime; **teatro all'aperto** open-air theatre *o* theater; **teatro di posa** film studio; **teatro tenda** marquee (*used for pop concerts ecc*) 2 (*genere*) theatre (*Brit*), theater (*USA*); (*professione*) theatre (*Brit*), theater (*USA*), stage; **il teatro classico** classical theatre *o* theater *o* drama; **il teatro di Pirandello** Pirandello's plays *o* dramatic works, the theatre *o* theater of Pirandello; **interessarsi di teatro** to be interested in drama *o* the theatre *o* theater; **è un uomo di teatro** he's in the theatre *o* theater; **teatro comico** comedy; **teatro lirico** opera; **teatro di strada** street theatre

techno ['tekno] AGG INV (*musica*) techno

tecnico, -a, -ci, -che ['tɛkniko] AGG technical; **fa l'istituto tecnico** he goes to the technical college ♦ SM, SF (*gen*) technician; (*esperto*) expert; **è venuto il tecnico per riparare la TV** the repair man's come to fix the TV; **tecnico del suono** sound engineer; **tecnico della televisione** television engineer

tecnologia, -gie [teknolo'dʒia] SF (*scienza*) technology; (*tecnica*) technique; **alta tecnologia** high technology, hi-tech; **nuove tecnologie** new technology *sg*

tecnologico, -a, -ci, -che [tekno'lɔdʒiko] AGG technological

tedesco, -a, -schi, -sche [te'desko] AGG, SM, SF German; **è tedesca** she's German; **i tedeschi** the Germans ♦ SM (*lingua*) German; **parli tedesco?** do you speak German?

tediare [te'djare] /19/ VT (*infastidire*) to bother, annoy; (*annoiare*) to bore

tedio ['tɛdjo] SM tedium, boredom

tedioso, -a [te'djoso] AGG tedious, boring

tegame [te'game] SM (*Culin*) (frying) pan, skillet (*USA*); (*contenuto*) panful; **al tegame** fried

teglia ['teʎʎa] SF (*Culin: per dolci*) (baking) tin (*Brit*), cake pan (*USA*); (: *per arrosti*) roasting tin *o* pan

tegola ['tegola] SF (*roofing*) tile

Teheran [te'ran] SF Teh(e)ran

teiera [te'jɛra] SF teapot

teina [te'ina] SF (*Chim*) theine

tel. [tel] ABBR (= *telefono*) tel.

tela ['tela] SF 1 (*tessuto*) cloth; **una pezza di tela** a piece of cloth; **di tela** (*lenzuolo*) linen; (*pantaloni*) (heavy) cotton *attr*; (*scarpe, borsa*) canvas *attr*; **rilegato in tela** clothbound 2 (*Pittura: supporto*) canvas; (: *dipinto*) canvas, painting ♦ **tela cerata** oilcloth; **tela (da) vela** sailcloth; **tela di ragno** spider's web, cobweb; **tela di sacco** sackcloth, sacking

telaio, -ai [te'lajo] SM (*per tessere*) loom; (*struttura*) frame; (*Aut*) chassis; **telaio da ricamo** embroidery frame

Tel Aviv [tela'viv] SF Tel Aviv

tele- ['tɛle] PREF tele-

teleabbonato, -a [teleabbo'nato] SM, SF television *o* TV licence holder (*Brit*)

telecamera [tele'kamera] SF television *o* TV camera; **telecamera a circuito chiuso** CCTV camera

telecomandare [telekoman'dare] /72/ VT to operate by remote control

telecomando [teleko'mando] SM remote control

telecomunicazioni [telekomunikat'tsjoni] SFPL telecommunications

teleconferenza [telekonfe'rentsa] SF teleconference

telecronaca, -che [tele'krɔnaka] SF television *o* TV report; **telecronaca differita** (pre-)recorded (TV) report; **telecronaca diretta** live (TV) report

telecronista, -i, -e [telekro'nista] SM, SF (television) commentator

teleferica, -che [tele'fɛrika] SF cableway

telefilm [tele'film] SM INV television *o* TV film (*Brit*) *o* movie (*USA*)

telefonare [telefo'nare] /72/ VI (*aus* avere) (*gen*) to (tele)phone, ring; (*fare una chiamata*) to make a phone call; **stamattina ha telefonato tua madre** your mother phoned this morning; **telefonare a qn** to telephone sb, phone *o* ring *o* call sb (up); **ieri ho telefonato a Richard** I phoned Richard yesterday; **sta telefonando** he is on the phone ♦ VT to (tele)phone

telefonata [telefo'nata] SF (telephone) *o* (phone) call; **posso fare una telefonata?** can I make a phone call?; **telefonata a carico del destinatario** reverse charge (*Brit*) *o* collect (*USA*) call; **telefonata interurbana** long-distance call; **telefonata in teleselezione** STD (*Brit*) *o*, direct-dialing (*USA*) call; **telefonata urbana** local call

telefonicamente [telefonika'mente] AVV by (tele)phone

telefonico, -a, -ci, -che [tele'fɔniko] AGG (tele)phone *attr*; **cabina telefonica** phone box; **elenco telefonico** phone book; **scheda telefonica** phone card

telefonino [telefo'nino] SM mobile phone

telefonista, -i, -e [telefo'nista] SM, SF (*gen*) telephonist; (*di centralino*) switchboard operator

telefono [te'lɛfono] SM (*sistema*) telephone; (*apparecchio*) (tele)phone; **avere il telefono** to be on the (tele)phone; **al telefono** she's on the phone; **un colpo di telefono** a call, a ring; **ti do un colpo di telefono più tardi** I'll give you a ring *o* call later; **numero di telefono** phone number; **telefono amico** ≈ the Samaritans *pl*; **telefono azzurro** ≈ Childline; **telefono a disco** dial (tele)phone; **telefono fisso** landline; **telefono interno** internal phone; **telefono mobile** mobile (phone) (*Brit*), cellphone (*USA*); **telefono a monete** pay phone; **telefono pubblico** public (tele)phone; **telefono rosa** rape crisis line; **telefono satellitare** satellite phone; **telefono a scheda (magnetica)** cardphone (*Brit*); **telefono a tastiera** push-button phone

telegiornale [teledʒor'nale] SM (*notiziario*) (television) news *sg*; **l'hanno detto al telegiornale** it was on the news; **il telegiornale è alle otto** the news is at eight

telegrafare [telegra'fare] /41/ VT, VI (*aus* avere) to telegraph, cable

telegrafia [telegra'fia] SF telegraphy

telegrafico, -a, -ci, -che [tele'grafiko] AGG telegraph *attr*; (*fig: stile*) telegraphic

telegrafista, -i, -e [telegra'fista] SM, SF telegraphist, telegraph operator

telegrafo [te'lɛgrafo] SM (*apparecchio*) telegraph; (*ufficio*) telegraph office

telegramma, -i [tele'gramma] SM telegram

telelavoro [telela'voro] SM teleworking

telematica [tele'matika] SF (*servizio*) data transmission; (*disciplina*) telematics *sg*

telenovela [teleno'vela] SF soap opera

teleobiettivo [teleobjet'tivo] SM telephoto lens *sg*

telepatia [telepa'tia] SF telepathy

telequiz [tele'kwits] SM INV (TV) game show

teleschermo [teles'kɛrmo] SM television o TV screen
telescopio, -pi [teles'kɔpjo] SM telescope; **a telescopio** telescopic
telescrivente [teleskri'vɛnte] AGG teleprinting ♦ SF teleprinter (*Brit*), teletypewriter (*USA*)
teleselettivo, -a [teleselet'tivo] AGG: **prefisso teleselettivo** STD code (*Brit*), dialling code (*Brit*), dial code (*USA*)
teleselezione [teleselet'tsjone] SF ≈ subscriber trunk dialling (*Brit*), ≈ direct dialing (*USA*); **telefonata in teleselezione** STD (*Brit*) o direct-dialing (*USA*) call
telespettatore, -trice [telespetta'tore] SM, SF (television) viewer
televendita [tele'vendita] SF teleshopping
televisione [televi'zjone] SF (*gen*) television; (*televisore*) television (set); **alla televisione** on television; **l'ho visto alla televisione** I saw it on television
televisore [televi'zore] SM television (set); **un televisore a schermo piatto** a flat-screen television
telex ['tɛleks] AGG INV telex attr ♦ SM INV telex
telo ['tɛlo] SM length of cloth; **telo da bagno** bath towel; **telo cerato** (*per materasso*) rubber sheet; **telo da spiaggia** beach towel
telone [te'lone] SM 1 (*per copertura*) tarpaulin 2 (*sipario*) drop curtain
tema, -i ['tɛma] SM 1 (*argomento*) theme; (*di conversazione*) subject, topic; (*Mus*) theme, motif; (*Scol*) essay, composition; **ho consegnato il tema senza rileggerlo** I handed in my essay without reading it through; **il tema della lezione di oggi** the subject of today's lecture; **tema libero** (*Scol*) free composition; **andare fuori tema** to go off the subject 2 (*Ling*) theme, stem
tematica [te'matika] SF basic themes *pl*
temerario, -ria, -ri, -rie [teme'rarjo] AGG reckless, rash ♦ SM, SF reckless person
temere [te'mere] /29/ VT to be afraid of, fear; **temo il pericolo** I am afraid of danger; **non temo la sua reazione** I'm not afraid of his reaction; **temo che non venga** I am afraid he won't come; **temo che se ne sia andato** I'm afraid he's gone; **temo di non farcela** I am afraid I won't make it; **temere il peggio** to fear the worst; **temere una brutta sorpresa** to expect a nasty surprise; **mi hai fatto temere che...** you had me worried that ...; **temo di sì/no** I'm afraid so/not; **temere il freddo** (*pianta*) to be sensitive to cold ♦ VI (*aus avere*) to be afraid; **temere per** (*preoccuparsi*) to worry about; **non temere!** (*non aver paura*) don't be afraid!; (*non preoccuparti*) don't worry!
tempera ['tɛmpera] SF 1 (*Arte: colore, tecnica*) tempera; (: *dipinto*) painting in tempera; **colori a tempera** tempera *sg*; **dipingere a tempera** to paint in tempera 2 (*Tecn*) = **tempra**
temperama'tite SM INV pencil sharpener
temperamento [tempera'mento] SM (*carattere*) temperament, character; **è nervoso di temperamento** he has a nervous temperament o disposition o character; **avere del temperamento** to have a strong personality; **manca di temperamento** he's weak-willed
temperante [tempe'rante] AGG moderate
temperare [tempe'rare] /72/ VT 1 (*matita*) to sharpen 2 (*metalli*) to temper
temperato, -a [tempe'rato] AGG 1 (*moderato*) moderate, temperate; (*clima*) temperate 2 (*acciaio*) tempered
temperatura [tempera'tura] SF temperature; **temperatura ambiente** room temperature
temperino [tempe'rino] SM penknife
tempesta [tem'pesta] SF 1 (*Meteor*) storm; **il mare era in tempesta** the sea was stormy; **una tempesta in un bicchier d'acqua** a storm in a teacup (*Brit*), a tempest in a teapot (*USA*); **c'è aria di tempesta** (*fig*) there is a storm brewing; **tempesta magnetica** magnetic storm; **tempesta di neve** snowstorm; **tempesta di sabbia** sandstorm 2 (*fitta serie*): **una tempesta di pugni** a hail of blows; **una tempesta di domande** a barrage of questions
tempestare [tempes'tare] /72/ VT 1 **tempestare qn di colpi** to rain blows on sb; **tempestare qn di domande/telefonate** to bombard sb with questions/(phone)calls 2 (*ornare*) to stud

tempestività [tempestivi'ta] SF timeliness
tempestivo, -a [tempes'tivo] AGG timely, well-timed
tempestoso, -a [tempes'toso] AGG stormy
tempia ['tɛmpja] SF (*Anat*) temple
tempio, -pi ['tɛmpjo] SM (*Rel, anche fig*) temple
tempismo [tem'pizmo] SM sense of timing
tem'pistiche [tem'pistike] SFPL (*Comm*) time and motion
tempo ['tɛmpo] SM 1 (*gen*) time; **il tempo e lo spazio** time and space; **il tempo vola!** time flies!; **il tempo stringe** time is short; **ci vuole tempo** it takes time; **abbiamo tempo 3 giorni** we have 3 days; **scusa, adesso non ho tempo** sorry, I haven't got time at the moment; **c'è o abbiamo tempo** there is plenty of time; **rilassati, abbiamo ancora tempo!** relax, we've still got time!; **c'è sempre tempo** there is still time; **non c'è tempo da perdere** there is no time to lose; **perdere tempo** (*sprecare tempo*) to waste time; (*far tardi*) to lose time; **trovare il tempo di fare qc** to find the time to do sth; **col tempo** with time; **con l'andare del tempo** with the passing of time; **a tempo di record** in record time; **a tempo pieno** full time; **un lavoratore a tempo pieno** a full-time worker; **un impiego a tempo pieno** a full-time job; **nei ritagli di tempo, a tempo perso** in one's spare moments; **tempo libero** free o spare time 2 (*periodo*) time; **da tempo** for a long time now; **aspetto da tempo** I've been waiting for a long time; **da quanto tempo?** since when?; **tempo fa** some time ago; **poco tempo dopo** not long after; **per qualche tempo** for a while; **un po' di tempo** a while; **non lo vedo da un po' di tempo** I haven't seen him for a while; **era qui un po' di tempo fa** she was here a while ago; **dove sei stato tutto questo tempo?** where have you been all this time?; **a tempo e luogo** at the right time and place; **a suo tempo** in due course, at the appropriate time; **ogni cosa a suo tempo** we'll (o you'll *ecc*) deal with it in due course; **in tempo utile** in due time o course; **al tempo stesso, a un tempo** at the same time; **fare in tempo a fare qc** to manage to do sth; **farai in tempo a prendere il treno?** will you be in time for the train?; **arrivare/essere in tempo** to arrive/be in time; **per tempo** in good time, early; **un tempo** once 3 (*durata di un'operazione; anche: fase*) stage; **rispettare i tempi** to keep to the schedule o timetable; **stringere i tempi** to speed things up; **tempi di esecuzione** (*Comm*) time scale *sg*; **tempi di lavorazione** (*Industria*) throughput time *sg*; **tempi morti** (*Comm*) downtime *sg*, idle time *sg*; **tempo di accesso** (*Inform*) access time; **tempo di cottura** cooking time; **tempo reale** (*Inform, Comm*) real time 4 (*stagione*) season; **quando arriva il tempo delle ciliege** when the cherries ripen 5 (*epoca*) time, times *pl*; **al tempo della Rivoluzione Culturale** at the time of o in the days of the Cultural Revolution; **tempi duri** hard times; **altri tempi!** those were the days!; **con i tempi che corrono** these days; **andare al passo con i tempi** to keep pace o keep up with the times; **in tempo di pace** in peace time; **in questi ultimi tempi** of late; **ai miei tempi** in my day; **aver fatto il proprio tempo** to have had its (o his *ecc*) day 6 (*Meteor*) weather; **che tempo fa?** what's the weather like?; **fa bel/brutto tempo** the weather's fine/bad; **con questo tempo!** in this weather!; **tempo da lupi** o **da cani** foul weather; **condizioni del tempo** weather conditions; **previsioni del tempo** weather forecast *sg* 7 (*Mus*) time; (*battuta*) beat; (*grado di velocità*) tempo; (*movimento*) movement; **andare a tempo** to keep time; **essere fuori tempo** to be out of time; **battere o segnare il tempo** to mark time; **in tre tempi** in triple time 8 (*Gramm*) tense; **tempo presente** present tense 9 **primo/secondo tempo** (*Teatro, Cine*) first/second part; (*Sport*) first/second half; **il primo tempo era un po' noioso** the first part was a bit boring; **ha segnato nel secondo tempo** he scored in the second half; **tempi supplementari** (*Sport*) extra time *sg* 10 (*di motore a scoppio*) stroke; **motore a due tempi** two-stroke engine 11 (*fraseologia*): **dare tempo al tempo** to let matters take their course; **chi ha tempo non aspetti tempo** there's no time like the present; **il tempo è denaro** time is money; **senza tempo** timeless

temporale [tempo'rale] SM (*Meteor*) (thunder)storm
temporalesco, -a, -schi, -sche [tempora'lesko] AGG stormy
temporaneo, -a [tempo'raneo] AGG temporary; **una**

sistemazione temporanea temporary accommodation; (*lavoro, lavoratore*) temporary

temporeggiare [tempored'dʒare] /62/ vi (*aus* avere) to play for time, temporize

tempra ['tempra] SF **1** (*Tecn*: *atto*) tempering, hardening; (: *effetto*) temper **2** (*fig*: *costituzione fisica*) constitution; (: *intellettuale*) temperament

temprare [tem'prare] /72/ VT (*gen, anche Tecn*) to temper; (*fig*) to strengthen, toughen; **temprarsi** VR, VIP (*anche fig*) to become stronger *o* tougher

tenace [te'natʃe] AGG (*odio*) lasting; (*volontà*) strong, firm; (*persona*) tenacious

tenacia [te'natʃa] SF tenacity

tenaglie [te'naλλe] SFPL (*arnese, chele*) pincers *pl*; (*del dentista*) forceps *pl*

tenda ['tenda] SF **1** (*di finestra*) curtain; (*riparo: di negozio, terrazza*) awning; **tirare le tende** to draw the curtains *o* drapes (*USA*); **tenda per doccia** shower curtain **2** (*Mil: da campeggio*) tent; **piantare le tende** to pitch one's tent; (*fig*) to settle down; **è ora di levar le tende** (*fig*) it's time to hit the trail *o* pack up and go **3 tenda a ossigeno** oxygen tent

tendaggio [ten'daddʒo] SM curtaining, curtains *pl*, drapes *pl* (*USA*)

tendenza [ten'dɛntsa] SF (*gen*) tendency; (*inclinazione*) inclination; (*orientamento: Pol, Econ*) trend; **avere la tendenza a** to tend to; **ha tendenza ad arrossire** he tends to blush; **avere tendenza a** *o* **per qc** to have a bent for sth; **con tendenza al bello** (*Meteor*) tending to fair; **tendenza al rialzo** (*Borsa*) upward trend; **tendenza al ribasso** (*Borsa*) downward trend

tendenziosità [tendentsjosi'ta] SF tendentiousness

tendenzioso, -a [tenden'tsjoso] AGG tendentious, bias(s)ed

tendere ['tɛndere] VB IRREG /120/ VT **1** (*mettere in tensione: corda*) to tighten, pull tight; (: *elastico, muscoli*) to stretch; (: *tessuto*) to stretch, pull *o* draw tight; **hanno teso una corda tra due alberi** they stretched a rope between two trees; **tendere una trappola a qn** to set a trap for sb **2** (*sporgere: collo*) to crane; (: *mano*) to hold out; (: *braccio*) to stretch out; **tendere la mano** to hold out one's hand; (*fig: chiedere l'elemosina*) to beg; (: *aiutare*) to lend a helping hand; **tendere gli orecchi** (*fig*) to prick up one's ears ♦ vi (*aus* avere) **tendere a qc/a fare qc** (*aver la tendenza*) to tend towards sth/to do sth; (*mirare a*) to aim at sth/to do sth; **tutti i nostri sforzi sono tesi a...** all our efforts are geared towards ...; **tende al pessimismo** he tends to be pessimistic; **tendere a sinistra** (*Pol*) to have left-wing tendencies; **la situazione tende a migliorare** the situation is improving; **il tempo tende al bello** the weather is improving; **un blu che tende al verde** a greenish blue

tendina [ten'dina] SF curtain

tendine ['tɛndine] SM tendon, sinew

tendone [ten'done] SM (*da circo*) big top
❑ **tendone** non si traduce mai con la parola inglese *tendon*

tendopoli [ten'dɔpoli] SF INV (large) camp

tenebre ['tɛnebre] SFPL darkness *sg*, gloom *sg*

tenebroso, -a [tene'broso] AGG (*gen*) dark, gloomy; (*fig*) mysterious

tenente [te'nɛnte] SM lieutenant
❑ **tenente** non si traduce mai con la parola inglese *tenant*

tenere [te'nere] VB IRREG /121/ VT **1** (*reggere: in mano*) to hold; (: *in posizione*) to hold, keep; (: *in una condizione*) to keep; **tieni!** here!; **tieni, usa il mio** here, use mine; **tieni, questo è per te** here, this is for you; **non mi serve, puoi tenerlo** I don't need it, you can keep it; **tenere qn per mano** to hold sb by the hand; **tenere in braccio un bambino** to hold a baby; **tenere una pentola per il manico** to hold a pan by the handle; **tiene la racchetta con la sinistra** he holds the racket with his left hand; **tieni la porta aperta** hold the door open; **tengono sempre la porta aperta** they always keep their door open; **tiene sempre la camicia sbottonata** he always has his shirt unbuttoned; **tenere le mani in tasca** to keep one's hands in one's pockets; **tieni gli occhi chiusi** keep your eyes shut *o* closed; **un cappotto che tiene caldo** a warm coat; **tiene la**

casa molto bene her house is always tidy; **tenere presente qc** to bear sth in mind; **tenere la rotta** (*Naut*) to keep *o* stay on course; **il nemico teneva la città** the enemy had the city under its control *o* held the city; **tenere la destra/la sinistra** (*Aut*) to keep to the right/the left **2** (*dare: conferenza, lezione*) to give; (*organizzare: riunione, assemblea*) to hold **3** (*occupare: spazio*) to take up, occupy; **tenere il posto a qn** to keep sb's seat; **mi tieni il posto?** torno subito will you keep my seat for me? I'll be right back **4** (*contenere: sogg: recipiente*) to hold **5** (*resistere a*): **tenere il mare** (*Naut*) to be seaworthy; **tenere la strada** (*Aut*) to hold the road **6** (*considerare*): **tenere conto di qn/qc** to take sb/sth into account *o* consideration; **tenere in gran conto** *o* **considerazione qn** to have a high regard for sb, think highly of sb ♦ vi (*aus* avere) **1** (*resistere*) to hold out, last; (*chiusura, nodo*) to hold; **tiene quella scatola?** is that box strong enough?; **questa vite non tiene** this screw is loose; **non ci sono scuse che tengano** I'll take no excuses; **tenere duro** (*resistere*) to stand firm, hold out **2** (*parteggiare*): **tenere per qn/qc** to support sb/sth; **io tengo per lui** I am on his side **3 tenere a** (*reputazione, persona, vestiario*) to attach great importance to; **tiene molto all'educazione** he is a great believer in education **4** (*dare importanza*): **tenere a, tenerci a** to care about, attach great importance to; **tenere a fare** to want to do, be keen to do; **ci tengo ad ottenere la presidenza** it's important for me to become chairman; **ci tenevo ad andare** I was keen on going, I was keen to go; **ci tiene che lo sappia** he wants him to know; **non ci tengo** I don't care about it, it's not that important to me; **se ci tieni proprio!** if you really want!; **tenersi** VR **1** (*reggersi*): **tenersi a qn/qc** to hold onto sb/sth; **tieniti al corrimano** hold onto the rail; **tieniti forte!** hold on tight!; **tenersi per mano** (*uso reciproco*) to hold hands; **si tenevano per mano** they were holding hands; **tenersi in piedi** to stay on one's feet; **non si teneva più dal ridere** (*fig*) he couldn't help laughing, he couldn't keep from laughing **2** (*mantenersi*) to keep, be; **tenersi pronto a fare qc** to be ready (to do sth); **tieniti pronta per le cinque** be ready by five; **tenersi vicino al/lontano dal muro** to keep close to/away from the wall; **tenersi sulla corsia di destra** to stay in the right-hand lane; **tenersi a destra/sinistra** to keep right/left **3** (*attenersi*): **tenersi a** to comply with, stick to

tenerezza [tene'rettsa] SF tenderness; **che tenerezza che mi fa questo piccolino!** what a lovely little baby!; **non sono abituato a tutte queste tenerezze** I am not used to all this attention

tenero, -a ['tenero] AGG **1** (*carne, verdura*) tender; (*pietra, cera, colore*) soft; **grano tenero** soft wheat; **erba tenera** young grass; **è morto in tenera età** he died young; **alla sua tenera età** (*scherz*) at his tender age **2** (*indulgente*) soft, tender; (*che esprime tenerezza*) tender, loving; **un tenero padre** a loving father; **avere il cuore tenero** to be tender-hearted; **che tenero!** how lovely! ♦ SM **1** (*parte tenera*) tender part **2** (*affetto*): **tra quei due c'è del tenero** there's a romance budding between those two

tengo ecc ['tɛngo] VB *vedi* tenere

tenia ['tenja] SF tapeworm

tenni ecc ['tenni] VB *vedi* tenere

tennis ['tennis] SM INV tennis; **giocare a tennis** to play tennis; **giochi a tennis?** do you play tennis?; **da tennis** attr; **tennis da tavolo** table tennis

tennista, -i, -e [ten'nista] SM, SF tennis player

tenore [te'nore] SM **1** (*tono*) tone; **il tenore della sua lettera** the tone of his letter; **tenore di vita** (*modo di vivere*) way of life; (*livello*) standard of living **2** (*Mus*) tenor

tensione [ten'sjone] SF (*gen*) tension; (*Elettr*) tension, voltage; **ad alta tensione** (*Elettr*) high-voltage attr, high-tension attr; **c'è un po' di tensione** (*fig*) things are a bit tense

tentacolare [tentako'lare] AGG (*appendice, protuberanza*) tentacular; (*fig: città*) magnet-like

tentacolo [ten'takolo] SM (*anche fig*) tentacle

tentare [ten'tare] /72/ VT **1** (*provare*): **tentare qc/di fare qc** to attempt *o* try sth/to do sth; **ho tentato l'esame, ma non l'ho passato** I attempted the exam but I didn't pass it; **tenterà di battere il record mondiale** she's going to try to beat the world record; **tentare il suicidio** to attempt suicide, try to commit suicide; **tentato suicidio** attempted suicide; **tentare un nuovo metodo** (*sperimentare*) to try out a new method; **le ho tentate tutte per convincerli** I tried everything to persuade them; **tentare la sorte** to try one's luck; **tentar non nuoce** there's no harm in trying **2** (*cercare di corrompere, allettare*) to tempt; (*mettere alla prova*) to test; **non lo tentare** don't tempt him

tentativo [tenta'tivo] SM attempt; **fa' ancora un tentativo** try again

tentazione [tentat'tsjone] SF temptation; **non ho saputo resistere alla tentazione!** I couldn't resist the temptation!; **aver la tentazione di fare qc** to be tempted to do sth

tentennamento [tentenna'mento] SM (*fig*) hesitation, wavering; **dopo molti tentennamenti** after much hesitation

tentennare [tenten'nare] /**72**/ VI (*aus* avere) (*persona*) to totter, stagger; (*fig*) to hesitate, waver; **gli tentenna un dente** he's got a wobbly *o* loose tooth; **l'ubriaco uscì tentennando** the drunkard staggered out ♦ VT: **tentennare il capo** to shake one's head

tentoni [ten'toni] AVV (*anche fig*): **a tentoni** gropingly; **andare (a) tentoni** to grope one's way

tenue ['tɛnue] AGG **1** (*colore*) soft; (*voce*) feeble; (*luce*) faint; (*fig: speranza*) slender, slight **2** (*Anat*): **intestino tenue** small intestine

tenuta [te'nuta] SF **1** (*capacità*) capacity; **a tenuta d'aria** airtight; **tenuta di strada** (*Aut*) roadholding **2** (*divisa*) uniform; **in tenuta da lavoro** in one's work(ing) clothes; **in tenuta da sci** in a skiing outfit; **in tenuta da calciatore** in a football strip (*Brit*) **3** (*podere*) estate

teologia [teolo'dʒia] SF theology; **la teologia della liberazione** the liberation theology

teologico, -a, -ci, -che [teo'lɔdʒiko] AGG theological

teologo, -a, -gi, -ghe [te'ɔlogo] SM, SF theologian

teorema, -i [teo'rɛma] SM (*Mat*) theorem

teoria [teo'ria] SF theory; **in teoria** in theory, theoretically

teorico, -a, -ci, -che [te'ɔriko] AGG theoretic(al); **a livello teorico, in linea teorica** theoretically, in theory ♦ SM, SF theorist, theoretician

teorizzare [teorid'dzare] /**72**/ VT to theorize

tepido, -a ['tɛpido] AGG = **tiepido**

tepore [te'pore] SM warmth

teppa ['teppa] SF mob, hooligans *pl*

teppaglia [tep'paʎʎa] SF hooligans *pl*

teppismo [tep'pizmo] SM hooliganism

teppista, -i, -e [tep'pista] SM, SF hooligan

terapeutico, -a, -ci, -che [tera'pɛutiko] AGG therapeutic

terapia [tera'pia] SF (*Med*) therapeutics *sg*, therapy; (*cura*) therapy, treatment; **terapia di gruppo** group therapy; **terapia intensiva** intensive care; **terapia d'urto** massive-dose treatment; (*fig*) shock treatment *o* therapy

terapista, -i, -e [tera'pista] SM, SF therapist

tergicristallo [terdʒikris'tallo] SM windscreen (*Brit*) *o* windshield (*USA*) wiper; **tergicristallo (a funzionamento) intermittente** intermittent wiper

tergiversare [terdʒiver'sare] /**72**/ VI (*aus* avere) to beat about the bush, shilly-shally

tergo, -ghi ['tɛrgo] SM back; (*di moneta*) reverse; **a tergo** behind; **vedi a tergo** please turn over, see overleaf

termale [ter'male] AGG thermal; **sorgente termale** hot spring; **stazione termale** spa resort

terme ['tɛrme] SFPL (thermal) baths

termico, -a, -ci, -che ['tɛrmiko] AGG (*Fis*) thermic, thermal; **borsa termica** cool bag *o* box (*Brit*), cooler (*USA*); **centrale termica** thermal power station

terminale [termi'nale] AGG (*fase, parte*) final; (*Med*) terminal; **i malati terminali** the terminally ill *pl*; **tratto terminale** (*di fiume*) lower reaches *pl* ♦ SM terminal

terminare [termi'nare] /**72**/ VT (*gen*) to end; (*lavoro*) to finish; **dopo aver terminato l'università** after finishing university ♦ VI (*aus* essere) to end; **a che ora termina il film?** what time does the film finish?; **terminare a punta** to end in a point; **terminare in consonante** to end in *o* with a consonant; **dove termina la valle c'è un lago** there is a lake at the end of the valley

terminazione [terminat'tsjone] SF (*fine*) end; (*Gramm*) ending; **terminazioni nervose** (*Anat*) nerve endings

termine ['tɛrmine] SM **1** (*confine*) boundary, limit; (*punto estremo*) end; **al termine della strada** at the end of the road; **porre termine a qc** to put an end to sth; **avere termine** to end; **portare a termine qc** to bring sth to a conclusion **2** (*spazio di tempo*) stipulated period; (*scadenza*) deadline; **entro un termine di tre ore** within three hours; **fissare un termine** to set a deadline; **entro il termine convenuto** within the stipulated period; **qual è il termine per la presentazione delle domande?** what is the deadline for applications?; **a breve/lungo termine** short-/long-term; **contratto a termine** (*Dir*) fixed-term contract; (*Comm*) forward contract **3** (*termini*) (*condizioni*) terms; (*limiti*) limits; **ai termini di legge** by law; **questo contratto non è valido ai termini di legge** this contract is not valid under law; **fissare i termini della questione** to define the problem; **la questione sta in questi termini** this is how the matter stands; **essere in buoni/cattivi termini con qn** to be on good/bad terms with sb **4** (*Gramm, Mat*) term; **un termine tecnico/scientifico** a technical/scientific term; **ridurre ai minimi termini** (*Mat*) to reduce to the lowest terms; **termini di paragone** terms of comparison; **in altri termini** in other words; **modera i termini!** moderate your language!; **parlare senza mezzi termini** not to mince one's words

terminologia [terminolo'dʒia] SF terminology

termite ['tɛrmite] SF termite

termocoperta [termoko'pɛrta] SF electric blanket

termometro [ter'mɔmetro] SM (*anche fig*) thermometer

termonucleare [termonukle'are] AGG thermonuclear

termos ['tɛrmos] SM INV = **thermos**

termosifone [termosi'fone] SM (*radiatore*) radiator; (*sistema di riscaldamento*) central heating

termostato [ter'mɔstato] SM thermostat

terna ['tɛrna] SF (*gen*) set of three; (*lista di tre nomi*) list of three candidates; **terna arbitrale** (*Calcio*) referee and linesmen

terno ['tɛrno] SM (*al lotto*) (set of) three winning numbers; **vincere un terno al lotto** (*fig*) to hit the jackpot

terra ['tɛrra] SF **1 la Terra** (*pianeta*) the Earth; (*fig: mondo*) the world; **sulla faccia della terra** on the face of the Earth; **i piaceri di questa terra** the pleasures of this world **2** (*terreno, suolo*) ground; (*sostanza*) soil, earth; (*argilla*) clay; **la terra è bagnata** the ground's wet; **la pioggia laverà via la terra** the rain will wash away the soil; **per terra** (*appoggiare, sedersi*) on the ground; (*cadere*) to the ground; **il tesoro è sotto terra** the treasure is buried; **il fiume passa sotto terra** the stream runs underground; **strada in terra battuta** dirt track **3** (*distesa, campagna*) land *no pl*; **un pezzo di terra** (*gen*) a piece of land; (*fabbricabile, per orto*) a plot of land; **una lingua di terra** a strip of land; **le sue terre** (*possedimento*) his estate **4** (*terraferma*) land *no pl*; **scendere a terra** to go ashore; **via terra** (*viaggiare*) by land, overland **5** (*paese, regione*) land, country; **in terra straniera** in foreign parts; **la mia terra** my native land; **è della mia terra** he is a fellow countryman; **tattica della terra bruciata** (*Mil*) scorched earth policy **6** (*Elettr*) earth (*Brit*), ground (*USA*); **mettere a terra** to earth *o* ground **7** (*fraseologia*): **avere una gomma a terra** to have a flat tyre; **essere a terra** (*fig: depresso*) to be at rock bottom; **terra terra** (*fig: persona, argomento*) prosaic, pedestrian; **cercare qn/qc per mare e per terra** to look high and low for sb/sth; **non sta né in cielo né in terra** it is quite unheard of; **stare con i piedi per terra** (*fig*) to have both feet on the ground ♦ **terra di nessuno** no-man's-land; **la terra promessa** the Promised Land; **la Terra Santa** the Holy Land; **terra di Siena** sienna

terra-aria ['tɛrra 'arja] AGG INV (*Mil*) ground-to-air, surface-to-air

terracotta [terra'kɔtta] SF (*pl* terrecotte) terracotta *no pl*; **di terracotta** terracotta *attr*; **vasellame di terracotta** earthenware; **terracotta smaltata** glazed earthenware

terraferma [terra'ferma] SF (*terra emersa*) dry land, terra firma; (*continente*) mainland; **avvistare la terraferma** to sight land

terraglia [ter'raʎʎa] SF **1** pottery *sg* **2 terraglie** SFPL (*oggetti*) crockery *sg*, earthenware *sg*

Terranova [terra'nɔva] SF Newfoundland

terrapieno [terra'pjɛno] SM embankment, bank

terra-terra ['tɛrra 'tɛrra] AGG INV (*Mil*) ground-to-ground, surface-to-surface

terrazza [ter'rattsa] SF (*gen, anche Agr*) terrace; **erano seduti in terrazza** they were sitting on the terrace

terremotato, -a [terremo'tato] AGG (*zona*) devastated by an earthquake ♦ SM, SF earthquake victim

terremoto [terre'mɔto] SM earthquake; (*fig: scherz: bambino*) terror; (: *sconvolgimento*) havoc

terreno, -a [ter'reno] SM 1 (*gen*) ground; (*suolo*) soil, ground; **il terreno è bagnato** the ground's wet; **un terreno montuoso** a mountainous terrain; **dissodare il terreno** to till the soil; **preparare il terreno** (*fig*) to prepare the ground; **tastare il terreno** (*fig*) to see how the land lies; **terreno alluvionale** (*Geol*) alluvial soil 2 (*area coltivabile, edificabile*) land *no pl*, plot (of land); **hanno dei terreni in Toscana** they've got land in Tuscany; **ho comprato un terreno** I bought a piece *o* a plot of land; **una casa con 500 ettari di terreno** a house with 500 hectares of land 3 (*Mil: teatro di operazioni*) field; (: *guadagnato, perduto*) ground; **perdere terreno** (*anche fig*) to lose ground 4 (*Sport*): **terreno di gioco** field; **una partita sospesa a causa del terreno pesante** a match postponed because of waterlogged ground ♦ AGG 1 (*vita, beni*) earthly 2 (*a livello della strada*): **piano terreno** ground floor (*Brit*), first floor (*USA*)

terreo, -a ['tɛrreo] AGG (*viso, colorito*) wan

terrestre [ter'rɛstre] AGG (*della terra: superficie*) of the Earth, Earth's *attr*; (: *magnetismo*) terrestrial; (*di terra: battaglia, animale*) land *attr*; **un animale terrestre** a land animal; **il globo terrestre** the globe ♦ SM, SF earthling

terribile [ter'ribile] AGG (*orribile*) terrible, dreadful; (*nemico*) terrible; (*visione*) fearful; (*forza*) tremendous; (*fam: formidabile*) terrific, tremendous; **ho una fame terribile** I am terribly hungry

terriccio, -ci [ter'rittʃo] SM soil

terriero, -a [ter'rjero] AGG: **proprietà terriera** landed property; **proprietario terriero** landowner

terrificante [terrifi'kante] AGG terrifying
❑ **terrificante** non si traduce mai con la parola inglese *terrific*

terrina [ter'rina] SF (*zuppiera*) tureen; (*ciotola*) terracotta bowl; (*per paté*) terrine

territoriale [territo'rjale] AGG territorial

territorio, -ri [terri'tɔrjo] SM (*gen*) territory; (*di comune*) precinct; (*di giudice*) jurisdiction; **i Territori occupati** the Occupied Territories

terrone, -a [ter'rone] SM, SF *derogatory term used by Northern Italians to describe Southern Italians*

terrore [ter'rore] SM (*anche fig*) terror; **il Terrore** (*Storia*) the Reign of Terror; **incutere terrore a qn** to strike terror into sb's heart; **avere (il) terrore di qc/di fare qc** to be terrified of sth/of doing sth; **Anna ha il terrore dei ragni/di volare** Anna's terrified of spiders/of flying; **con terrore** in terror; **del terrore** (*film, racconto*) horror *attr*; **un film del terrore** a horror film

terrorismo [terro'rizmo] SM terrorism

terrorista, -i, -e [terro'rista] SM, SF terrorist

terrorizzare [terrorid'dzare] /72/ VT (*gen*) to terrify; (*popolazione*) to terrorize; **l'idea mi terrorizza** the idea terrifies me; **l'idea di viaggiare in aereo lo terrorizza** he is terrified of flying

terso, -a ['tɛrso] PP *di* **tergere** ♦ AGG clear

terza ['tɛrtsa] SF (*gen*) third; (*Aut*) third gear; (*Scol: terza elementare*) ≈ year four (*Brit*), ≈ third grade (*USA*); (: *terza media*) ≈ year nine (*Brit*), ≈ eighth grade (*USA*); (: *terza superiore*) ≈ lower sixth (*Brit*), ≈ eleventh grade (*USA*)

terzetto [ter'tsetto] SM (*Mus*) trio, terzetto; (*di persone*) trio

terziario, -ria, -ri, -rie [ter'tsjarjo] SM (*Geol, Econ*) tertiary ♦ SM 1 (*Geol*) tertiary period 2 (*Econ*) tertiary *o* service sector; **terziario avanzato** high-tech service sector ♦ SM, SF (*Rel*) tertiary

terzino [ter'tsino] SM (*Calcio*) fullback, back; **terzino destro/sinistro** right/left back; **gioca da terzino destro** he plays right back

terzo, -a ['tɛrtso] AGG third; **abito al terzo piano** I live on the third floor; **terzo, in terzo luogo** thirdly, in the third place; **di terz'ordine** third-rate; **il terzo mondo** the Third World; **la terza pagina** (*Stampa*) the Arts page; **la terza età** old age ♦ SM, SF 1 third 2 **terzi** SMPL (*altri*) others, other people *pl*; (*Dir*) third party *sg*; **agire per conto terzi** to act on behalf of a third party; **assicurazione contro terzi** third-party insurance (*Brit*), liability insurance (*USA*) ♦ SM (*frazione*) third

tesa ['tesa] SF (*di cappello*) brim; **a larghe tese** wide-brimmed

teschio, -chi ['teskjo] SM skull

tesi¹ ['tɛzi] SF INV (*gen*) thesis; (*Univ: anche:* **tesi di laurea**) (degree) thesis, dissertation; **presenterà una tesi su Jane Austen** he's going to do a dissertation on Jane Austen; **sostenere una tesi** to uphold a theory

tesi² ['tɛzi] VB *vedi* **tendere**

teso, -a ['teso] PP *di* **tendere** ♦ AGG (*corda*) taut, tight; (*nervi, volto*) tense; (*rapporti*) strained; (*braccia*) outstretched; **è molto teso in questi giorni** he's very tense these days; **con la mano tesa** with outstretched hand; **stava lì con le orecchie tese** he was all ears; **essere teso come una corda di violino** to be very tense

tesoreria [tezore'ria] SF treasury

tesoriere, -a [tezo'rjere] SM, SF treasurer

tesoro [te'zɔro] SM 1 (*gen, anche fig*) treasure; **far tesoro dei consigli di qn** to take sb's advice to heart; **sei un tesoro!** how nice of you!; **grazie tesoro!** thank you darling!; **caccia al tesoro** treasure hunt 2 (*Fin*): **il Tesoro** the Exchequer (*Brit*); **il ministero del Tesoro** the Treasury; **buono del Tesoro** Bond

tessera ['tɛssera] SF 1 (*di socio*) (membership) card; (*di abbonato*) season ticket; (*di giornalista*) pass, press card; **ho la tessera del Milan** I've got a season ticket for AC-Milan; **ha la tessera del partito** he's a party member; **tessera magnetica** swipe card; **tessera dell'autobus** bus pass; **tessera di riduzione ferroviaria** ≈ Railcard (*Brit*) 2 (*di mosaico*) tessera

tesserare [tesse'rare] /72/ VT (*iscrivere*) to give a membership card to; **tesserarsi** VIP to get one's membership card

tesserato, -a [tesse'rato] SM, SF (*di società sportiva*) (fully paid-up) member; (*Pol*) (card-carrying) member

tessere ['tɛssere] /1/ VT (*gen*) to weave; (*fig: inganni, tradimenti*) to plan, plot; **tessere le lodi di qn** to sing sb's praises

tessile ['tɛssile] AGG textile ♦ SM, SF textile worker

tessitore, -trice [tessi'tore] SM, SF weaver

tessitura [tessi'tura] SF (*operazione*) weaving; (*impianto*) weaving mill *o* factory

tessuto [tes'suto] SM 1 material, fabric; (*di lana*) cloth, material; **tessuti** SMPL textiles 2 (*Bio*) tissue

test ['tɛst] SM INV test

testa ['tɛsta] SF 1 (*gen, anche Anat*) head; **ho battuto la testa contro il pensile** I banged my head on the cupboard; **a testa alta** with one's head held high; **a testa bassa** (*correre*) headlong; (*con aria dimessa*) with head bowed; **gettarsi in qc a testa bassa** to rush headlong into sth; **cadere a testa in giù** to fall head first; **dalla testa ai piedi** from head to foot; **a testa** a head; **15 euro a testa** 15 euros apiece *o* a head *o* per person; **vincere di mezza testa** (*Ippica*) to win by half a head; **testa della racchetta** (*Tennis*) racket head; **una testa d'aglio** a bulb of garlic (*fig: cervello*) head, brain(s); **testa di rapa** blockhead; **che testa di cavolo!** what a moron!; **essere una testa calda** to be hot headed; **avere la testa dura** to be stubborn; **avere la testa vuota** to be empty-headed; **avere la testa tra le nuvole** to have one's head in the clouds; **non avere testa** to be scatterbrained; **usare la testa** to use one's head *o* brains; **ma dove hai la testa?** what on earth are you thinking of?; **ha poca testa per la matematica** he hasn't got much of a head for maths (*Brit*) *o* math (*USA*); **fare di testa propria** to do as one pleases; **far entrare qc in testa a qn** to din sth into sb's head; **mettersi in testa di fare qc** to take it into one's head to do sth; **che cosa gli hai messo in testa?** what ideas have you been putting into his head?; **non so che cosa gli sia passato per la testa** I don't know what's come over him 3 (*parte anteriore: di treno, processione*) front, head; (: *di colonna militare*) head; (: *di pagina, lista*) top, head; **le carrozze di testa** (*Ferr*) the front of the train; **essere in testa** (*pilota, ciclista*) to be in the lead, be the leader; **essere in testa alla classifica** (*pilota, ciclista*) to be number one; (*squadra*) to be top of the league; (*canzone*) to be top of the charts, be number one; **essere alla testa di qc**

(*società*) to be the head of; (*esercito*) to be at the head of; **testa di serie** (*Sport: giocatore*) seed, seeded player; (: *squadra*) top of the league **4** (*fraseologia*): **avere la testa sulle spalle** to have one's head screwed on; **dare alla testa** to go to one's head; **montarsi la testa** to become big-headed; **mettere la testa a posto** *o* **a partito** to settle down; **essere fuori** *o* **via di testa** to be off one's head; **perdere la testa per qn** to lose one's head over sb; **perdere la testa** (*per ira*) to lose one's head; **ci scommetterei la testa** I'd bet my boots; **tener testa a qn** (*nemico, avversario*) to stand up to sb; **lavata di testa** telling-off, ticking-off (*Brit*); **testa o croce?** heads or tails?; **fare a testa o croce** to toss (for sth); **facciamo a testa o croce?** shall we toss for it?

testa-coda [ˈtɛsta ˈkoda] SM INV (*Aut*) spin

testamentario, -ria, -ri, -rie [testamenˈtarjo] AGG (*Dir*) testamentary; **le sue disposizioni testamentarie** the provisions of his will

testamento [testaˈmento] SM **1** (*Dir*) will, testament; **fare testamento** to make one's will; **ha deciso di fare testamento** he decided to make his will; **testamento spirituale** (*fig*) spiritual testament; **testamento biologico** living will **2** (*Rel*): **l'Antico/il Nuovo Testamento** the Old/New Testament

testardaggine [testarˈdaddʒine] SF stubbornness, obstinacy

testardo, -a [tesˈtardo] AGG stubborn, obstinate ♦ SM, SF stubborn *o* obstinate person

testare [tesˈtare] /72/ VT to test

testata [tesˈtata] SF **1** (*di letto*) headboard **2** (*di giornale*) heading; (*il giornale stesso*) paper; **concentrazione delle testate** concentration of press ownership **3** (*Aut*) (cylinder) head; (*Aer: di missile*) head; **missile a testata nucleare** nuclear missile; **missile a testata convenzionale** missile with a conventional warhead **4** (*colpo: accidentale*) bang on the head; (: *intenzionale*) head butt; **dare una testata contro qc** to bang one's head on sth; **dare una testata a qn** to head-butt sb

teste [ˈtɛste] SM, SF (*Dir*) witness

testicolo [tesˈtikolo] SM testicle

testiera [tesˈtjɛra] SF **1** (*del letto*) headboard **2** (*di cavallo*) headpiece

testimone [testiˈmone] SM, SF witness; **non c'erano testimoni** there weren't any witnesses; **fare da testimone alle nozze di qn** to be a witness at sb's wedding; **queste rovine sono testimoni della grandezza di Roma** these ruins bear witness to the former greatness of Rome; **testimone di Geova** (*Rel*) Jehovah's Witness; **testimone oculare** eye witness ♦ SM (*Sport*) baton

testimonianza [testimoˈnjantsa] SF (*atto*) deposition; (*effetto*) evidence; (*fig: prova*) proof; **accusare qn di falsa testimonianza** to accuse sb of perjury; **rilasciare una testimonianza** to give evidence; **ne fanno testimonianza altri autori contemporanei** (*fig*) other contemporary authors testify to it; **ha dato testimonianza di grande fedeltà** he proved his great loyalty

testimoniare [testimoˈnjare] /19/ VT: **testimoniare che...** to testify that ..., give evidence that ...; **testimoniare il vero** to tell the truth; **testimoniare il falso** to perjure o.s.; **le impronte testimoniano la sua colpevolezza** the fingerprints are proof of his guilt; **testimoniare a favore di/contro qn** to testify for/against sb, give evidence for/against sb; **era disposta a testimoniare contro di lui** she was ready to give evidence against him; **è stato chiamato a testimoniare** he was called upon to give evidence ♦ VI (*aus avere*) to testify, give evidence; **non ha voluto testimoniare sull'accaduto** he didn't want to give evidence on *o* about what happened

testina [tesˈtina] SF (*di registratore, rasoio*) head; **testina di stampa** (*Inform*) print head

testo [ˈtɛsto] SM (*gen*) text; (*originale di traduzione*) original text; **un testo difficile** a difficult text; **libro di testo** (*Scol*) textbook; **fare testo** (*autore*) to be authoritative; (*opera*) be a standard work; **questo libro non fa testo** this book is not essential reading; **le sue parole fanno testo** his words carry weight

testosterone [testosteˈrone] SM testosterone

testuale [testuˈale] AGG textual; **le sue testuali parole furono...** his (*o* her) actual *o* exact words were ...

testuggine [tesˈtuddʒine] SF (*Zool*) tortoise; (*marina*) turtle

tetano [ˈtɛtano] SM (*Med*) tetanus

tetro, -a [ˈtɛtro] AGG (*anche fig*) gloomy; **era di umore tetro** he was gloomy *o* glum

tetta [ˈtɛtta] SF (*fam*) boob, tit

tettarella [tettaˈrɛlla] SF teat

tetto [ˈtɛtto] SM **1** (*gen*) roof; (*di veicolo*) roof, top; (*fig*) house, home; **restare senza tetto** to be homeless *o* without a roof over one's head; **abbandonare il tetto coniugale** to desert one's family; **tetto apribile** (*Aut*) sun roof; **tetto a cupola** dome; **tetto a terrazza** roof terrace **2** (*limite massimo: Econ*) (maximum) limit, ceiling; **porre un tetto alla spesa pubblica** to impose a limit on public spending

tettoia [tetˈtoja] SF (*gen*) canopy; (*di stazione*) roof

tet'tuccio [tetˈtuttʃo] SM: **tettuccio apribile** (*Aut*) sunroof

Tevere [ˈtevere] SM: **il Tevere** the Tiber

thermos [ˈtɛrmos] SM INV thermos (flask)

thriller [ˈθrilə] SM INV (*libro, film*) thriller

ti [ti] PRON PERS *dav* lo, la, li, le, ne *diventa* te **1** (*ogg diretto*) you; **non ti ascolta mai** he never listens to you; **non ti ho visto stamattina** I didn't see you this morning **2** (*complemento di termine*) (to) you; **ti dirò tutto** I'll tell you everything; **te lo ha dato?** did he give it to you?; **ti ha sorriso** he smiled at you; **ti piace?** do you like it? **3** (*riflessivo e medio*) yourself; **ti sei lavata?** have you washed (yourself)?; **ti sei pettinato?** have you combed your hair?; **ti sei divertito?** did you enjoy yourself?; **quando ti prendi una vacanza?** when are you going to have yourself a holiday?; **ti ricordi?** do you remember?

tiara [ˈtjara] SF tiara

Tibet [ˈtibet] SM Tibet

tibetano, -a [tibeˈtano] AGG, SM, SF Tibetan

tibia [ˈtibja] SF (*Anat*) tibia, shinbone

tic [tik] SM INV **1** (*gen*) click; (*di orologio*) tick **2** (*Med: anche:* **tic nervoso**) tic; (*fig*) mannerism

ticchettio, -tii [tikketˈtio] SM (*di macchina da scrivere*) clatter; (*di orologio*) ticking; (*di pioggia*) pattering, patter

ticchio, -chi [ˈtikkjo] SM (*tic*) tic; (*fig: capriccio*) whim; **mi è preso il ticchio di andare in Africa** I've taken a notion to visit Africa

ticket [ˈtikit] SM INV (*sui farmaci*) prescription charge (*Brit*); (*per prestazioni mediche*) medical charge

tiene ecc [ˈtjɛne] VB *vedi* **tenere**

tiepido, -a [ˈtjɛpido] AGG (*gen*) lukewarm, tepid; (*fig: accoglienza*) lukewarm; (: *entusiasmo*) half-hearted; **acqua tiepida** lukewarm water

tifare [tiˈfare] /72/ VI (*aus avere*) **tifare per** (*squadra*) to be a fan of, support; (*parteggiare*) to side with

tifo [ˈtifo] SM **1** (*Med*) typhus **2** (*Sport*): **fare il tifo per** to be a fan of, support; **faccio il tifo per la Juventus** I support Juventus

tifone [tiˈfone] SM (*Meteor*) typhoon

tifoso, -a [tiˈfoso] AGG: **essere tifoso di** to be a fan of; **sono tifoso del Milan** I'm a Milan supporter ♦ SM, SF (*Sport*) supporter, fan; **i tifosi del Liverpool** the Liverpool supporters

tight [ˈtait] SM INV morning suit

tigì [tidˈʒi] SM INV TV news

tiglio, -gli [ˈtiʎʎo] SM lime (tree), linden (tree)

tigna [ˈtiɲɲa] SF (*Med*) ringworm

tigrato, -a [tiˈgrato] AGG striped

tigre [ˈtigre] SF tiger; (*femmina*) tigress; **cavalcare la tigre** (*fig*) to have a tiger by the tail; **occhio di tigre** (*Mineralogia*) tiger's eye, tigereye; **tigre di carta** (*fig*) paper tiger

tilt [tilt] SM INV: **andare** *o* **essere in tilt** (*macchina*) to go/be on the blink; (*fig*) to go/be haywire

timballo [timˈballo] SM (*Culin*) timbale

timbrare [timˈbrare] /72/ VT (*gen*) to stamp; (*annullare: francobolli*) to postmark; **hai timbrato il biglietto?** have you stamped your ticket?; **timbrare il cartellino** to clock in

timbro [ˈtimbro] SM **1** (*strumento*) (rubber) stamp; (*su documento*) stamp; (*su francobollo*) postmark; **mettere il timbro su qc** to stamp sth; **gli hanno messo il timbro sul passaporto** they stamped his passport **2** (*Mus*) tone, timbre

timidezza [timiˈdettsa] SF shyness, timidity

timido, -a [ˈtimido] AGG (*persona, animale*) shy, timid; (*tentativo*) bashful ♦ SM, SF shy person

timo [ˈtimo] SM (*Bot*) thyme

timone [tiˈmone] SM (*Naut*) helm; (*parte sommersa*) rudder; (*Aer*) rudder; (*di carro*) shaft; **barra del timone** (*Naut*) tiller; **ruota del timone** (*Naut*) wheel; **essere al timone** (*anche fig*) to be at the helm; **prendere il timone** (*anche fig*) to take the helm; **timone di direzione** (*Aer*) rudder; **timone di profondità** (*Aer*) tail flap

timoniere [timoˈnjɛre] SM (*Naut*) helmsman; (*Canottaggio*) cox

timorato, -a [timoˈrato] AGG conscientious; **timorato di Dio** God-fearing

timore [tiˈmore] SM (*paura*) fear, dread; (*preoccupazione*) fear; (*rispetto*) awe; **avere timore di qn/qc** (*paura*) to be afraid of sb/sth; **ho il timore che non ci arriveremo** I fear we won't make it; **i miei timori si sono rivelati infondati** my fears proved to be unfounded

timoroso, -a [timoˈroso] AGG (*diffidente*) timid, timorous; (*pauroso*) frightened, afraid; (*preoccupato*) worried, afraid

timpano [ˈtimpano] SM 1 (*Anat*) tympanum, eardrum; **rompere i timpani a qn** to burst sb's eardrums 2 (*Mus*) kettledrum; **i timpani** the timpani

tinca, -che [ˈtinka] SF tench

tinello [tiˈnɛllo] SM small dining room

tingere [ˈtindʒere] VB IRREG /37/ VT (*stoffa, capelli*) to dye; **il tramonto tingeva il cielo di rosso** the sunset was reddening the sky *o* was turning the sky red; **tingersi** VIP: **il cielo si è tinto di rosso** the sky turned red

tino [ˈtino] SM vat

tinozza [tiˈnɔttsa] SF tub

tinsi ecc [ˈtinsi] VB *vedi* **tingere**

tinta [ˈtinta] SF 1 (*colore*) shade, colour (*Brit*), color (*USA*); **una tinta vivace** a bright colour; **una stoffa di tinta scura** a dark material; **una borsetta in tinta con le scarpe** a bag and matching shoes; **un vestito (in** *o* **a) tinta unita** a plain suit; **un vestito giallo in tinta unita** a plain yellow dress 2 (*per muri*) paint; (*per capelli*) dye; **un barattolo di tinta** a tin of paint; **dare una mano di tinta a qc** to give sth a coat of paint; **dipingere qc a tinte fosche** (*fig*) to paint a gloomy picture of sth; **un racconto a forti tinte** a dramatic story

tintarella [tintaˈrɛlla] SF (*fam*) (sun)tan; **prendere la tintarella** to get a tan

tintinnare [tintinˈnare] /72/ VI (*aus* avere) (*campanelle*) to tinkle; (*bicchieri*) to clink, tinkle

tintinnio, -nii [tintinˈnio] SM tinkling

tinto, -a [ˈtinto] PP *di* **tingere**

tintoria [tintoˈria] SF (*lavasecco*) dry cleaner's (shop); (*officina*) dyeworks *inv*; **devo portare il cappotto in tintoria** I need to take my coat to the dry cleaner's

tintura [tinˈtura] SF 1 (*operazione*) dyeing; (*soluzione colorante*) dye; **tintura per capelli** hair dye 2 (*Med*) tincture; **tintura di iodio** tincture of iodine

tipico, -a, -ci, -che [ˈtipiko] AGG typical; **un esempio tipico** a typical example; **un tipico pub inglese** a traditional English pub; **un tipico piatto scozzese** a traditional Scottish dish

tipo, -a [ˈtipo] SM 1 (*genere*) kind, sort, type; **vestiti di tutti i tipi** all kinds of clothes; **piante di tutti i tipi** all sorts of plants; **che tipo di bici hai?** what sort of bike have you got?; **sul tipo di questo** of this sort; **non è il mio tipo** he's not my type 2 (*modello*) type, model ♦ SM, SF (*fam: individuo*) character; **sei un bel tipo!** you're a fine one!; **chi era quel tipo?** who was that guy?; **mi sembra un tipo simpatico** he seems nice; **è una tipa molto sicura di sé** she's very self-confident ♦ AGG INV average, typical

tipografia [tipograˈfia] SF typography

tipografico, -a, -ci, -che [tipoˈɡrafiko] AGG typographic(al)

tipografo, -a [tiˈpɔɡrafo] SM, SF typographer

tip tap [tirkjeˈria] SM INV tap dancing

tira e molla [tiraeˈmɔlla] SM INV = **tiremmolla**

tiraggio, -gi [tiˈraddʒo] SM (*di camino*) draught (*Brit*), draft (*USA*)

Tirana [tiˈrana] SF Tirana

tiranneggiare [tiranneddˈdʒare] /62/ VT to tyrannize

tirannia [tiranˈnia] SF tyranny

tiranno, -a [tiˈranno] SM tyrant ♦ AGG tyrannical

tirante [tiˈrante] SM (*Naut: di tenda*) guy; (*Edil*) brace

tirapiedi [tiraˈpjɛdi] SM INV, SF INV hanger-on

tirapugni [tiraˈpuɲɲi] SM INV knuckle-duster (*Brit*), brass knuckles *pl* (*USA*)

tirare [tiˈrare] /72/ VT 1 (*gen*) to pull; (*slitta*) to pull, drag; (*rimorchio*) to tow; (*Culin: pasta*) to stretch; **tira! pull!**; **tirare qn per la manica** to tug at sb's sleeve; **tirare qn da parte** to take *o* draw sb aside; **tirare gli orecchi a qn** to tweak sb's ears; **mi ha tirato i capelli** she pulled my hair; **tirare qn per i capelli** to pull sb's hair; (*fig*) to force sb; **tirare qc per le lunghe** to drag sth out; **tirare le somme** (*fig*) to draw a conclusion; **tirare un sospiro di sollievo** to heave a sigh of relief; **una cosa tira l'altra** one thing leads to another; **tirare fuori** to pull out, take out; **il vigile mi fece tirare fuori i documenti** the policeman made me produce my identification papers; **alla fine ha tirato fuori tutta la verità** in the end he came out with the whole truth; **tirare giù** to pull down; **tirare su qn/qc** to pull sb/sth up; **tirare su qn** (*fig :rallegrare*) to cheer sb up; (: *allevare*) to bring sb up; **tirarsi dietro qn** to bring *o* drag sb along; **tirarsi su i capelli** to put one's hair up; **tirarsi addosso qc** to pull sth down on top of o.s.; (*fig*) to bring sth upon o.s. 2 (*chiudere: tende*) to draw, close, pull; **tirare la porta** to close the door, pull the door to 3 (*tracciare, disegnare*) to draw, trace; (*stampare*) to print 4 (*lanciare: sasso, palla*) to throw, fling; (: *colpo, freccia*) to fire; (: *fig: bestemmie, imprecazioni*) to hurl, let fly; **ha tirato un sasso e poi si è nascosto** he threw a stone and then hid; **tirami la palla!** throw me the ball!; **tirare un pugno a qn** to punch sb; **gli ho tirato un pugno** I punched him; **tirare uno schiaffo a qn** to slap sb; **gli ho tirato uno schiaffo** I slapped him; **tirare un calcio** to kick; **tirare calci** to kick; **tirare il pallone** (*Calcio*) to kick the ball ♦ VI (*aus* avere) (*sogg: pipa, camino*) to draw; (: *vestito, indumento*) to be tight; **tirare avanti** (*fig: vivere*) to get by; (: *proseguire*) to struggle on; **tirare diritto** to keep right on going; **tirare tardi/mattina** to stay up late/till the early hours *o* dawn; **tirare col fucile/con l'arco** to shoot with a rifle/with a bow and arrow; **tirava un forte vento** a strong wind was blowing; **che aria tira?** (*fig*) what are things like?, what's the situation like?; **tirare a campare** to keep going as best one can; **tirare a indovinare** to take a guess; **tirare sul prezzo** to bargain; **tirare di scherma** to fence; **tirare in porta** (*Calcio*) to shoot (at goal); **la fantascienza è genere che tira molto** science fiction is very popular; **il mercato/l'economia tira** the market/the economy is thriving; **tirarsi** VR: **tirarsi indietro** to draw *o* move back; (*fig*) to back out; **aveva promesso di aiutarmi ma poi si è tirato indietro** he promised to help me and then backed out; **tirarsi su** to pull o.s. up; (*fig*) to cheer o.s. up

tirato, -a [tiˈrato] AGG (*teso*) taut; (*stanco: viso, espressione*) drawn; (*avaro: persona*) stingy

tiratore, -trice [tiraˈtore] SM, SF shot; **un buon tiratore** a good shot; **franco tiratore** (*Mil*) irregular (*cecchino*) sniper; (*Pol*) ≈ rebel (*who votes against his/her own party in a secret ballot*); **tiratore scelto** marksman

tiratura [tiraˈtura] SF (*di giornali*) circulation; (*di libri*) printing, (print) run

tirchieria [tirkjeˈria] SF meanness, stinginess

tirchio, -chia, -chi, -chie [ˈtirkjo] AGG mean, stingy; **quant'è tirchio!** he's so mean! ♦ SM, SF miser

tiritera [tiriˈtera] SF (*fam*) drivel, hot air

tiro [ˈtiro] SM 1 (*di cavalli, buoi*) team; **tiro a quattro** coach and four; **cavallo da tiro** carthorse 2 (*di pistola, freccia, anche Calcio*) shooting *no pl*; (*colpo*) shot; **è stato un buon tiro** that was a good shot; **essere a tiro** to be in range; (*fig*) to be within reach; **se mi capita** *o* **viene a tiro!** if I get my hands on him (*o* her)!; **a un tiro di schioppo** a stone's throw away 3 (*lancio*) throwing *no pl*; (*effetto*) throw 4 (*fig*): **giocare un brutto tiro** *o* **un tiro mancino a qn** to play a dirty trick on sb 5 **mettersi in tiro** (*fam: vestirsi elegante*) to get dressed up ♦ **tiro al bersaglio** target shooting; **tiro alla fune** tug-of-war; **tiro con l'arco** archery; **tiro al piattello** clay pigeon shooting, skeet shooting (*USA*); **tiro al piccione** pigeon shooting; **tiro a segno** (*esercitazione*) target shooting; (*luogo*) shooting range

tirocinante [tirotʃiˈnante] AGG apprentice *attr*, trainee *attr* ♦ SM, SF apprentice, trainee

tirocinio, -ni [tiroˈtʃinjo] SM: **tirocinio (in)** (*di mestiere*) apprenticeship (in); (*di professione*) training (in); **fare il proprio tirocinio** to serve one's apprenticeship; to do one's training

tiroide [tiˈrɔide] SF (*Anat*) thyroid (gland)

tirolese [tiroˈlese] AGG, SM, SF Tyrolean, Tyrolese *inv*

Tirolo [tiˈrɔlo] SM: **il Tirolo** the Tyrol

tirrenico,-a,-ci,-che [tirˈreniko] AGG Tyrrhenian

Tirreno [tirˈreno] SM: **il (mar) Tirreno** the Tyrrhenian Sea

tisana [tiˈzana] SF herb tea, tisane

tisi [ˈtizi] SF (*Med*) consumption

tisico,-a,-ci,-che [ˈtiziko] AGG (*Med*) consumptive; (*fig: gracile*) frail ♦ SM, SF (*Med*) consumptive (person)

titanico, -a, -ci, -che [tiˈtaniko] AGG gigantic, enormous; **un'impresa titanica** an operation of titanic proportions

titano [tiˈtano] SM (*Mitol, anche fig*) titan

titolare [titoˈlare] AGG (*gen*) appointed; (*Univ*) with a full-time appointment; (*sovrano, vescovo*) titular ♦ SM, SF (*gen*) holder, incumbent; (*proprietario*) owner, proprietor; (*Sport: in squadra*) regular first-team player; (*: a livello nazionale*) regular member of the national team; **titolare di cattedra** (*Univ*) full professor

titolato,-a [titoˈlato] AGG (*persona*) titled

titolo [ˈtitolo] SM **1** (*di libro*) title; (*di giornale*) headline; **qual è il titolo di quella canzone?** what's the title of that song?; **titoli di coda** (*Cine, TV*) closing credits; **titoli di testa** (*Cine, TV*) opening credits **2** (*Fin: gen*) security; (*: azione*) share, stock; **titoli esteri** foreign securities; **titoli di stato** government securities *o* bonds; **titolo di credito** document of credit; **titolo obbligazionario** bond, share certificate; **titolo al portatore** bearer bond; **titolo di proprietà** title deed; **titolo spazzatura** junk bond **3** (*qualifica: nobiliare: Sport*) title; (*: di studio*) qualification; **titolo mondiale** (*Sport*) world title; **ha conservato il titolo mondiale** he retained the world title **4** (*fig: motivo*) why *o* for what reason have you come?; **a titolo di amicizia** for *o* out of friendship; **a titolo di curiosità** out of curiosity; **a titolo di prestito/favore** as a loan/favour (*Brit*) *o* favor (*USA*); **a titolo di cronaca** for your information

titubante [tituˈbante] AGG hesitant, undecided, irresolute; **è titubante per natura** he is a born ditherer

tivù [tiˈvu] SF INV (*fam*) TV, telly (*Brit*); **cosa c'è in tivù stasera?** what's on TV tonight?

tizio, -zia, -zi, -zie [ˈtittsjo] SM, SF character, individual; **chi era quel tizio?** who was that guy?; **chi era quella tizia?** who was that woman?; **Tizio, Caio e Sempronio** Tom, Dick and Harry

tizzone [titˈtsone] SM (*di legno*) (fire)brand; (*di carbone*) live coal

TMG [ˈtiˌɛmmeˈdʒi] SIGLA M (= *Tempo Medio di Greenwich*) GMT

TN SIGLA = Trento

TNT [tienneˈti] SIGLA M (*Chim: = trinitrotoluene*) TNT

TO SIGLA = Torino

toast [ˈtoust] SM INV toasted sandwich
❏ **toast** non si traduce mai con la parola inglese *toast*

toccante [tokˈkante] AGG (*commovente*) touching, moving

toccare [tokˈkare] /20/ VT **1** (*gen*) to touch; (*tastare*) to feel; (*fig: sfiorare: argomento, tema*) to touch on; **non toccare!** don't touch it!; **non toccare la mia roba** don't touch my things; **non ha toccato cibo** he hasn't touched his food; **non voglio toccare i miei risparmi** I don't want to touch my savings; **toccare un tasto delicato** to touch a sore point; **hai toccato il mio punto debole** you have hit on my weak point; **toccare con mano** (*fig*) to find out for o.s. **2** (*raggiungere*) to touch, reach; **si tocca?** (*in acqua*) can you touch the bottom?; **toccare il fondo** to touch the bottom; (*fig*) to touch rock bottom; **toccare terra** (*Naut*) to reach land; (*Aer*) to touch down; **abbiamo toccato diverse città** we stopped at a number of towns; **abbiamo toccato diversi porti** we put in at various ports; **ha appena toccato la cinquantina** he has just turned fifty **3** (*commuovere*) to touch, move; (*ferire*) to hurt, wound; **le tue allusioni non mi toccano** your remarks don't bother

me; **toccare qn sul vivo** to cut sb to the quick; **la vicenda ci tocca da vicino** the matter concerns *o* affects us closely ♦ VI (*aus essere*) **1** (*capitare*): **mi è toccata una bella fortuna** I've had great good fortune; **perché toccano sempre a me queste cose?** why is it always me who has to do these things?; **a chi tocca, tocca** that's life **2** (*essere costretto*): **mi tocca andare** I have to go; **che cosa mi tocca sentire!** what's this I hear?; **sai che cosa mi è toccato fare?** do you know what I had to do?; **mi è toccato pagare per tutti** I had to pay for everybody; **perché tocca sempre a me farlo?** why do I always have to do it? **3** (*spettare*): **toccare a** to be the turn of; **a chi tocca?** whose turn *o* go is it?; **tocca a me** it's my turn *o* go; **non tocca a me giudicare** it is not for me to judge; **tocca a te difenderci** it's up to you to defend us; **toccarsi** VR **1** (*masturbarsi*) to play with o.s. **2** (*uso reciproco*): **gli estremi si toccano** (*anche fig*) extremes meet

toccasana [tokkaˈsana] SM INV miracle cure

toccherò ecc [tokkeˈrɔ] VB *vedi* **toccare**

tocco¹,-a,-chi,-che [ˈtokko] AGG mad, touched

tocco²,-chi [ˈtokko] SM **1** (*gen, anche Mus*) touch; **gli ultimi tocchi** the finishing touches **2** (*colpo: di campana, orologio, pennello*) stroke

toeletta [toeˈletta] SF = **toilette**

toga,-ghe [ˈtɔga] SF (*di magistrato*) gown, robe; (*Storia*) toga

togliere [ˈtɔʎʎere] VB IRREG /122/ VT **1** (*gen*) to remove, take away *o* off; **togli il quadro dal muro** take the picture off the wall; **ho tolto il poster dalla parete** I took the poster off the wall; **mi hanno tolto due denti** I had two teeth taken out; **togliere le mani di tasca** to take one's hands out of one's pockets; **togliere qn di mezzo** (*allontanare*) to get rid of sb; (*uccidere*) to bump sb off; **togliere qc a qn** to take sth (away) from sb; **togliere la parola a qn** to interrupt sb; **togliere la parola di bocca a qn** to take the words out of sb's mouth; **togliere il saluto a qn** to ignore sb, snub sb; **mi hai tolto un peso** you've taken a weight off my mind; **volevo togliermi un peso (dalla coscienza)** I wanted to get it off my chest; **togliersi la vita** to take one's (own) life; **togliersi i guanti/il vestito/il trucco** to take off one's gloves/dress/make-up; **togliti il cappotto** take off your coat; **togliersi una voglia** to satisfy an urge *o* a whim; **togliersi la soddisfazione di** to have the satisfaction of; **ciò non toglie che...** that doesn't alter the fact that ..., nevertheless ..., be that as it may ... **2** (*Mat*) to take away, subtract; **togliere 3 da 7** to take 3 away from 7; **togliersi** VR: **togliersi di mezzo** to get out of the way; **togliti dai piedi!** get out of my way!

Togo [ˈtɔgo] SM Togo

toilette [twaˈlɛt] SF INV , **toletta** SF **1** (*gabinetto*) toilet (*Brit*), bathroom (*USA*); **dov'è la toilette?** where's the toilet? **2** (*abbigliamento*) gown, dress **3** (*mobile*) dressing table **4 fare toilette** to make o.s. beautiful

Tokyo [ˈtɔkjo] SF Tokyo

tolgo ecc [ˈtɔlgo] VB *vedi* **togliere**

tollerante [tolleˈrante] AGG tolerant

tolleranza [tolleˈrantsa] SF (*gen*) tolerance; (*Rel*) toleration; **non ha un minimo di tolleranza** he is completely intolerant; **casa di tolleranza** brothel

tollerare [tolleˈrare] /72/ VT **1** (*sopportare: ingiustizia, offese*) to tolerate, put up with; (*: alcolici*) to take; (*: persona*) to put up with, bear, stand; **tollerare il freddo/caldo** to stand *o* take the cold/the heat **2** (*ammettere*) to tolerate, allow; **non tollero repliche** I won't stand for objections; **non sono tollerati ritardi** lateness will not be tolerated

Tolosa [toˈloza] SF Toulouse

tolsi ecc [ˈtɔlsi] VB *vedi* **togliere**

tolto,-a [ˈtɔlto] PP *di* **togliere** ♦ PREP (*eccetto*) except for ♦ SM: **mal tolto** = **maltolto**

tomaia [toˈmaja] SF (*di scarpa*) upper

tomba [ˈtomba] SF (*gen*) grave; (*cappella sotterranea*) tomb; **è una tomba** (*fig: persona*) he won't give anything away; **non temere, sarò una tomba** don't worry, my lips are sealed; **nelle strade c'era un silenzio di tomba** it was as silent as the grave in the streets; **lo accolsero con un silenzio di tomba** he was greeted with a deathly hush; **avere un piede nella tomba** to have one foot in the grave

tombale [tomˈbale] AGG: **pietra tombale** tombstone, gravestone

tombino [tom'bino] SM (*pozzetto*) manhole; (*coperchio*) manhole cover

tombola¹ ['tombola] SF (*gioco*) tombola, bingo; **giocare a tombola** to play bingo

tombola² ['tombola] SF (*fam*: *caduta*) tumble; **tombola!** upsy-daisy!

tomo ['tomo] SM 1 (*volume*) volume, tome 2 (*persona*) odd duck

tomografia [tomogra'fia] SF (*Med*) tomography; **tomografia assiale computerizzata** computerised axial tomography

tonaca, -che ['tonaka] SF (*Rel*) habit; **indossare la tonaca** (*frate*) to take the habit; (*monaca*) to take the veil

tonare [to'nare] /72/ VI = **tuonare**

tondo, -a ['tondo] AGG (*circolare*) round; **un cuscino tondo** a round cushion; **fare cifra tonda** to round up (*o* down); **tre mesi tondi** exactly three months; **gli ho detto chiaro e tondo** I told him very clearly *o* bluntly; **parentesi tonde** round brackets ♦ SM (*cerchio*) circle; **scultura a tutto tondo** full-relief sculpture

tonfo ['tonfo] SM (*rumore sordo*) thud, thump; (*nell'acqua*) plop; **fare un tonfo** (*cadere*) to take a tumble

tonico, -a, -ci, -che ['toniko] AGG tonic ♦ SM 1 (*cosmetico*) toner 2 (*Med*) tonic

tonificante [toni'fikante] AGG invigorating, bracing

tonificare [tonifi'kare] /20/ VT (*gen*) to invigorate; (*muscoli, pelle*) to tone up

tonnara [ton'nara] SF tuna-fishing nets *pl*

tonnato, -a [ton'nato] AGG (*Culin*): **salsa tonnata** tuna fish sauce; **vitello tonnato** veal with tuna fish sauce

tonnellaggio [tonnel'laddʒo] SM (*Naut*) tonnage

tonnellata [tonnel'lata] SF ton; **questa valigia pesa una tonnellata!** this suitcase weighs a ton!

tonno ['tonno] SM tuna (fish); **un tramezzino al tonno** a tuna sandwich

tono ['tono] SM (*gen, anche Mus*) tone; (*di colore*) tone, shade; **parlare con tono minaccioso** to speak in a threatening tone *o* threateningly; **abbassa il tono (della voce)!** don't take that tone (of voice) with me!; **il tono della lettera/del discorso** the tone of the letter/speech; **dal tono si capiva che era seccata** you could tell she was annoyed by her tone of voice; **se la metti su questo tono...** if that's the way you want to put it ...; **rispondere a tono** (*a proposito*) to answer to the point; (*nello stesso modo*) to answer in kind; (*per le rime*) to answer back; **essere giù di tono** to be unwell *o* off-colour (*Brit*); **cercava di darsi un tono** she tried to act in a more refined way

tonsilla [ton'silla] SF (*Med*) tonsil; **farsi togliere le tonsille** to have one's tonsils out; **operarsi di tonsille** to have one's tonsils out

tonsillite [tonsil'lite] SF (*Med*) tonsillitis

tonsura [ton'sura] SF tonsure

tonto, -a ['tonto] AGG stupid, silly, dumb; **è un po' tonto** he's a bit thick ♦ SM, SF blockhead, dunce; **fare il finto tonto** to play dumb

top [top] SM INV (*vertice, anche Abbigliamento*) top

topaia [to'paja] SF (*casa*) hovel, dump; (*tana: di topo*) mousehole; (: *di ratto*) rat's nest

topazio, -zi [to'pattsjo] SM topaz

topicida, -i [topi'tʃida] SM rat poison

topless ['toplis] SM INV topless bathing costume

topo ['topo] SM 1 (*Zool*) mouse; (*ratto*) rat; **veleno per topi** rat poison; **color grigio topo** mousey grey; **topo campagnolo comune** fieldmouse; **topo delle chiaviche** brown rat; **topo domestico** house mouse; **topo muschiato** muskrat 2 (*persona*): **topo d'albergo** hotel thief; **topo d'auto** car thief; **topo di biblioteca** bookworm

topografia [topogra'fia] SF topography

topografico, -a, -ci, -che [topo'grafiko] AGG topographic(al)

toponimo [to'ponimo] SM place name

toppa ['toppa] SF 1 (*di stoffa*) patch; **mettere una toppa** (*fig*) to find a stopgap *o* short term solution 2 (*serratura*) keyhole

torace [to'ratʃe] SM (*Anat*) thorax, chest; (*Zool*) thorax

torba ['torba] SF peat

torbido, -a ['torbido] AGG (*liquido*) cloudy; (*fiume*) muddy; (*fig: pensieri*) dark, sinister ♦ SM: **qui c'è del torbido** there is

something fishy going on here; **pescare nel torbido** to fish in troubled waters

torcere ['tortʃere] VB IRREG /106/ VT 1 (*gen*) to twist; (*biancheria*) to wring (out); **torcere un braccio a qn** to twist sb's arm; **torcere il naso** (*per disgusto*) to wrinkle (up) one's nose; **avrei voluto torcergli il collo** I felt like wringing his neck; **non torcere un capello a qn** not to hurt a hair of sb's head; **dare del filo da torcere a qn** to make life *o* things difficult for sb 2 (*piegare*) to bend; **torcersi**: **torcersi dal dolore** to writhe in pain; **torcersi dalle risa** to double up laughing

torchiare [tor'kjare] /19/ VT (*olive*) to press; (*fig: fam: persona*) to grill

torchio, -chi ['torkjo] SM press; **mettere *o* tenere qn sotto il torchio** (*fig: fam: interrogare*) to grill sb

torcia, -ce ['tortʃa] SF (*fiaccola*) torch; **torcia elettrica** torch (*Brit*), flashlight (*USA*); **torcia umana** (*fig*) human torch

torcicollo [tortʃi'kɔllo] SM: **avere il torcicollo** to have a stiff neck; **ho il torcicollo** I've got a stiff neck

tordo ['tordo] SM thrush; **grasso come un tordo** fat as a pig; **tordo comune** song thrush

torero [to'rero] SM bullfighter, toreador

torinese [tori'nese] AGG of *o* from Turin ♦ SM, SF inhabitant *o* native of Turin

Torino [to'rino] SF Turin; **domani andremo a Torino** we're going to Turin tomorrow; **abita a Torino** she lives in Turin

tormenta [tor'menta] SF snowstorm, blizzard

tormentare [tormen'tare] /72/ VT (*gen*) to torment; (*fig: fastidire*) to bother, pester; **smettila di tormentare quel povero cane** stop tormenting that poor dog; **tormentarsi** VR to worry, torture o.s., fret

tormento [tor'mento] SM 1 (*dolore fisico, morale*) torment, agony; **morire fra atroci tormenti** to die in terrible agony 2 (*fastidio: di zanzare, caldo*) torment; (: *fam: persona*) pest

tornaconto [torna'konto] SM advantage, benefit; **pensa solo al proprio tornaconto** he thinks only of his own interest

tornado [tor'nado] SM tornado

tornante [tor'nante] SM hairpin bend (*Brit*) *o* curve (*USA*)

tornare [tor'nare] /72/ VI (*aus essere*) 1 (*a ritornare, go o come*) back; **quando sei tornato?** when did you get back?; **sono tornato domenica mattina** I got back on Sunday morning; **non sono ancora tornati dalle vacanze** they're not back from their holidays yet; **tornare a casa** to go (*o* come) home; **tornare da scuola** to come home from school; **a che ora torni da scuola?** what time do you get home from school?; **torno tra un attimo** I'll be back in a minute; **un'occasione così non torna più** such an opportunity won't repeat itself, you won't get another chance like this; **non torniamo più sull'argomento** let's drop the subject; **continua a tornare sull'argomento** he harps on about it; **è tornato alla carica con la sua idea di...** he's gone back to the old idea of ...; **è tornato a dire/a fare...** he's back to saying/doing ...; **mi è tornato alla mente** I've just remembered; **tornare al punto di partenza** to start again; **siamo tornati al punto di partenza** we are back where we started; **tornare in sé** (*dopo svenimento*) to regain consciousness, come to one's senses, come round; (*rinsavire*) to be back to one's old self; **tornare su** to come up; **la cipolla mi torna su** onions repeat on me (*Brit*) 2 (*ridiventare*) to become again; **tornare di moda** to become *o* be fashionable again, be back in fashion (again); **il cielo è tornato sereno** it's cleared up again 3 (*quadrare*) to be right, be correct; **i conti tornano** the accounts balance; (*fig*) it all falls into place; **qualcosa non torna in questa storia** there's something not quite right about this business 4 (*essere, risultare*) to turn out (to be), prove (to be); **tornare utile** to prove *o* turn out (to be) useful; **tornerà a tuo danno** it will come home to roost; **tornare a onore di qn** to be a credit to sb, do sb credit ♦ VT (*fam*): **tornare qc a qn** to return sth to sb, give sth back to sb

tornasole [torna'sole] SM INV litmus

torneo [tor'neo] SM (*Sport*) tournament, competition; (*Storia*) tournament; **un torneo di tennis** a tennis tournament

tornio, -ni ['tornjo] SM lathe; **tornio da vasaio** potter's wheel

tornire [tor'nire] /55/ VT (*Tecn*) to turn (on a lathe); (*fig*) to shape, polish

tornito, -a [tor'nito] AGG: **ben tornito** (*gambe, braccia*) well-shaped

toro ['tɔro] SM 1 (*Zool, anche fig*) bull; **essere forte come un toro** to be as strong as an ox; **prendere il toro per le corna** (*fig*) to take the bull by the horns 2 (*Astron, Astrol*): **Toro** Taurus; **essere del Toro** to be Taurus 3 (*Borsa*) bull

torpedine [tor'pɛdine] SF 1 (*Zool*) stingray 2 (*Mil: mina*) torpedo

torpediniera [torpedi'njera] SF (*Naut*) torpedo boat

torpore [tor'pore] SM torpor

torre ['torre] SF 1 (*di città, castello*) tower; (*di computer*) tower; **la torre pendente di Pisa** the Leaning Tower of Pisa; **torre d'avorio** (*fig*) ivory tower; **torre di controllo** (*Aer*) control tower; **torre di osservazione** lookout tower 2 (*Scacchi*) rook, castle

torrefazione [torrefat'tsjone] SF (*del caffè*) roasting

torreggiare [torred'dʒare] /62/ VI (*aus* avere) **torreggiare (su)** to tower (over)

torrente [tor'rente] SM torrent; (*fig*) flood, stream

torrenziale [torren'tsjale] AGG (*di torrente*) torrential

torrenziale [torren'tsjale] AGG (*pioggia*) torrential

torretta [tor'retta] SF (*gen, anche Mil*) turret; (*Naut*) tower; **torretta di comando** (*Naut*) conning tower

torrido, -a ['torrido] AGG scorching, torrid; **zona torrida** (*Geog*) Torrid Zone

torrione [tor'rjone] SM (*torre*) keep, tower; (*Naut*) conning tower

torrone [tor'rone] SM (*Culin*) kind of nougat

torsi *ecc* ['tɔrsi] VB *vedi* **torcere**

torsione [tor'sjone] SF (*gen*) twisting; (*Tecn*) torsion; (*Ginnastica*) twist

torso ['torso] SM (*Anat, Arte*) torso; (*di frutta*) core; **a torso nudo** bare-chested

torsolo ['torsolo] SM (*di cavolo*) stump; (*di mela*) core; **un torsolo di mela** an apple core

torta ['torta] SF (*Culin*) cake; **una fetta di torta** a slice of cake; **spartirsi la torta** (*fig*) to split the loot; **torta di mele** apple cake; (*tipo crostata*) apple tart (*Brit*) o pie (*USA*); **torta salata** savoury flan

tortellino [tortel'lino] SM (*Culin*) tortellino (*single piece of pasta*); **tortellini** SMPL (*piatto*) tortellini

tortelloni [tortel'loni] SMPL (*Culin*): **tortelloni di magro** ravioli-like pasta filled with cheese, eggs and spinach

tortiera [tor'tjera] SF cake tin (*Brit*), cake pan (*USA*)

torto¹, -a ['tɔrto] PP *di* **torcere**

torto² ['tɔrto] SM (*ingiustizia*) wrong; (*colpa*) fault; **fare un torto a qn** to wrong sb; **ricevere un torto** to be wronged; **avere torto** to be wrong; **mi dispiace ma hai torto** I'm sorry, but you're wrong; **hai torto marcio** you're dead wrong; **a torto** wrongly, unjustly; **a torto o a ragione** rightly or wrongly; **quest'azione ti fa torto** this action is unworthy of you; **gli ho dato torto** I said he was wrong; **i fatti gli hanno dato torto** the facts proved him wrong; **passare/essere dalla parte del torto** to be o put o.s./be in the wrong; **non ha tutti i torti** there's something in what he says

tortora ['tortora] SF (*Zool*) turtledove ♦ AGG INV: **grigio tortora** dove-grey

tortuoso, -a [tortu'oso] AGG (*strada*) winding; (*fig: discorso, ragionamento*) convoluted; (*: politica*) tortuous; **esprimersi in modo tortuoso** to express o.s. in a convoluted way

tortura [tor'tura] SF (*sevizia*) torment, torture; (*fig*) torment, torture; **sottoporre qn alla tortura** to torture sb

torturare [tortu'rare] /72/ VT to torture; (*fig*) to torment, torture; **smetti di torturare quel povero gatto!** stop tormenting that poor cat!; **torturarsi il cervello** to rack one's brains; **torturarsi** VR to torment o.s.

torvo, -a ['torvo] AGG (*occhi, sguardo*) surly, menacing, grim; **era torvo in viso** he looked grim; **guardare qn con occhi torvi** to give sb a surly look

tosaerba [toza'erba] SM INV (lawn)mower

tosare [to'zare] /72/ VT (*pecore*) to shear; (*cani*) to clip; (*siepi*) to trim, clip; **ti hanno tosato** (*scherz*) you've been scalped

tosatura [toza'tura] SF (*di pecore*) shearing; (*di cani*) clipping; (*di siepi*) trimming, clipping

Toscana [tos'kana] SF Tuscany; **andrò in Toscana** ques-

t'estate I'm going to Tuscany this summer; **ti è piaciuta la Toscana?** did you like Tuscany?

toscano, -a [tos'kano] AGG, SM, SF Tuscan ♦ SM (*anche:* **sigaro toscano**) *strong Italian cigar*

tosse ['tosse] SF cough; **colpo di tosse** fit of coughing; **avere la tosse** to have a cough; **ho la tosse** I've got a cough; **tosse asinina** o **canina** whooping cough

tossicità [tossitʃi'ta] SF toxicity

tossico, -a, -ci, -che ['tɔssiko] AGG toxic ♦ SM, SF (*fam: drogato*) junkie, druggie

tossicodipendente [tossikodipen'dɛnte] SM, SF drug addict

tossicodipendenza [tossikodipen'dɛntsa] SF drug addiction

tossicomane [tossi'kɔmane] SM, SF drug addict

tossicomania [tossikoma'nia] SF drug addiction

tossina [tos'sina] SF toxin

tossire [tos'sire] /55/ VI (*aus* avere) to cough

tostapane [tosta'pane] SM INV toaster

tostare [tos'tare] /72/ VT (*pane*) to toast; (*caffè, mandorle*) to roast

tostatura [tosta'tura] SF (*di pane*) toasting; (*di caffè*) roasting

tosto¹ ['tɔsto] AVV (*letter*) forthwith, immediately; **tosto che** as soon as

tosto², -a ['tɔsto] AGG **che faccia tosta!** what cheek!

totale [to'tale] AGG (*gen*) total; **la festa è stata un fallimento totale** the party was a total failure; **anestesia totale** general anaesthetic (*Brit*) o anesthetic (*USA*) ♦ SM total; **il totale è di sessanta sterline** the total is sixty pounds

totalità [totali'ta] SF totality, entirety; **nella totalità dei casi** in all cases; **la totalità dei presenti** all of those present

totalitario, -ria, -ri, -rie [totali'tarjo] AGG (*Pol*) totalitarian

totalitarismo [totalita'rizmo] SM (*Pol*) totalitarianism

totalizzare [totalid'dzare] /72/ VT to total, make a total of; (*Sport: punti*) to score

totalizzatore [totaliddza'tore] SM (*Tecn*) totalizator; (*Ippica*) totalizator, tote

totip [to'tip] SM *gambling pool based on horse racing*

totocalcio [toto'kaltʃo] SM ≈ (football) pools *pl* (*Brit*)

toupet [tu'pe] SM INV toupee

tour [tur] SM INV (*giro*) tour; (*Ciclismo: anche:* **tour de France**) tour de France

tour de force [turde'fɔrs] SM INV (*Sport, anche fig*) tremendous effort

tournée [tur'ne] SF INV tour; **essere in tournée** to be on tour; **sono in tournée in Italia** they're on tour in Italy

tovaglia [to'vaʎʎa] SF tablecloth

tovagliolo [tovaʎ'ʎɔlo] SM napkin, serviette (*Brit*); **tovagliolo di carta** paper napkin

tozzo¹, -a ['tɔttso] AGG (*persona*) stocky, thickset; (*cosa*) squat

tozzo² ['tɔttso] SM piece, morsel; **tozzo di pane** crust of bread; **per un tozzo di pane** (*fig*) for a song

TP SIGLA = Trapani

TR SIGLA = Terni

Tr ABBR (*Comm*) = tratta

tra [tra] PREP 1 (*fra due*) between; (*fra più di due*) among(st); **c'è un giardino tra le due case** there's a garden between the two houses; **era seduto tra il padre e lo zio** he was sitting between his father and his uncle; **era tra gente sconosciuta** he was among strangers; **tra i presenti c'era anche il sindaco** the mayor was also among those present; **tra i feriti c'era anche il pilota dell'aereo** the pilot of the plane was among the injured; **esitare tra il sì e il no** to hesitate between yes and no; **avrà tra i 15 e i 20 anni** he must be between 15 and 20 years old; **costerà tra i 20 e i 25 euro** it'll cost between 20 and 25 euros; **(sia) detto tra noi...** between you and me ...; **detto tra noi, non piace neanche a me** between you and me, I don't like it either; **mi raccomando, che resti tra noi** remember, that's between you and me; **tra sé e sé** (*parlare, riflettere*) to oneself; **scomparire tra la folla/gli alberi** to disappear into the crowd/among the trees; **tra una cosa e l'altra** what with one thing and another; **tra vitto e alloggio fanno 450 euro** food and accommodation together come to 450 euros; **tra casa mia e casa loro ci sono 10 minuti di strada** it's 10 minutes from my house to theirs 2 (*attraverso*) through; **il sole filtrava tra le persiane** the sun filtered through the shutters; **una strada tra i campi** a road through the fields; **farsi strada tra la folla** to make one's way through the crowd **3** (*in*); **prendere qn tra le braccia** to take sb in one's arms; **tra venti chilometri c'è un'area di servizio** it's twenty kilometres to the next service area **4** (*tempo*); in, within; **torno tra un'ora** I'll be back in an hour; **tra qualche giorno** in a few days; **tra 5 giorni** in 5 days' time; **tra poco** soon; **sarà qui tra poco** he'll be here soon *o* shortly; **tra breve** soon, shortly **5 tra l'altro** (*inoltre*) besides which, what is more; **tra tutti non saranno più di venti** there won't be more than twenty in all

traballante [trabal'lante] AGG (*mobile*) shaky

traballare [trabal'lare] /72/ VI (*aus* avere) (*persona*) to stagger, totter; (*mobile, fig: governo*) to be shaky

trabiccolo [tra'bikkolo] SM (*scherz: vecchia auto*) jalopy, old banger (*Brit*)

traboccare [trabok'kare] /20/ VI **1** (*aus* essere) (*liquido*): **traboccare (da)** to overflow (from) **2** (*aus* avere) (*contenitore*): **traboccare (di)** to overflow (with); **il teatro traboccava di gente** the theatre was full to bursting; **il suo cuore traboccava di felicità** his heart was bursting with happiness

trabocchetto [trabok'ketto] SM (*botola*) trap door; (*fig*) trap; **non cadere nel trabocchetto** don't fall into the trap; **tendere un trabocchetto a qn** to set a trap for sb ♦ AGG INV trap *attr*; **domanda trabocchetto** trick question

tracagnotto, -a [traka'ɲɲɔtto] AGG dumpy ♦ SM, SF dumpy person

tracannare [trakan'nare] /72/ VT to down, gulp down

traccia, -ce [trattʃa] SF **1** (*gen, anche fig: segno*) mark; (*di lumaca*) trace; (*di ruota*) track, trail; (*di animale*) tracks *pl*; (*di persona*) footprints *pl*; **sul bicchiere c'erano tracce di rossetto** there were traces of lipstick on the glass; **essere sulle tracce di qn** to be on sb's trail; **perdere le tracce di qn** to lose track of *o* lose the trail of sb; **seguire le tracce di qn** to follow sb's footprints *o* tracks; (*fig*) to follow in sb's footsteps; **la polizia sta chiaramente seguendo una falsa traccia** the police are clearly on the wrong track; **è sparito senza lasciare traccia** he vanished without a trace **2** (*residuo, vestigia di civiltà*) trace; (*indizio*) sign; **nella sua voce non c'è traccia di accento straniero** he speaks without a trace of a foreign accent; **hanno fatto sparire ogni traccia della loro presenza** they removed all sign of their presence **3** (*schema*) outline

tracciare [trat'tʃare] /14/ VT **1** (*percorso, strada*) to mark out, trace; (*confini*) to map out; (*rotta*) to plot **2** (*disegnare*) to sketch, draw; **tracciare una linea** to draw a line; **tracciare un arco** to describe a curve **3** (*fig*) to sketch out, outline; **tracciare un quadro della situazione** to outline the situation

tracciato [trat'tʃato] SM (*grafico*) layout, plan; **strada dal tracciato irregolare** winding road; **tracciato di gara** (*Sport*) (race) route

trachea [tra'kɛa] SF windpipe, trachea

tracolla [tra'kɔlla] SF shoulder strap; **portare qc a tracolla** to carry sth over one's shoulder; **borsa a tracolla** shoulder bag

tracollo [tra'kɔllo] SM (*fig*) collapse, ruin; **avere un tracollo** (*Med*) to have a setback; (*Fin*) to slip, fall; (*Comm*) to collapse; **tracollo finanziario** crash

tracotante [trako'tante] AGG arrogant, overbearing ♦ SM, SF arrogant person

tracotanza [trako'tantsa] SF arrogance

trad. ABBR = **traduzione**

tradimento [tradi'mento] SM (*gen*) betrayal; (*Dir, Mil*) treason; **lo considero un tradimento da parte sua** I consider it a betrayal on his part; **alto tradimento** high treason; **a tradimento** by surprise; **mangiare (il) pane a tradimento** to live off other people

tradire [tra'dire] /55/ VT **1** (*gen*) to betray; (*coniuge*) to cheat on, be unfaithful to; (*moglie*) **ha tradito suo marito** she was unfaithful to her husband; **tradire la fiducia di qn** to betray sb's trust; **hai tradito la mia fiducia** you betrayed my trust; **ha tradito le attese di tutti** he let everyone down; **se la memoria non mi tradisce** if my memory serves me well **2** (*rivelare: segreto*) to reveal, let out, give away; **tradirsi** VR to give o.s. away

traditore, -trice [tradi'tore] SM, SF traitor ♦ AGG treacherous

tradizionale [tradittsjo'nale] AGG traditional

tradizione [tradit'tsjone] SF tradition; **secondo la tradizione** traditionally, according to tradition

tradotto, -a [tra'dotto] PP *di* **tradurre**

tradurre [tra'durre] /90/ VT IRREG **1** (*testo: scritto, orale*) to translate; **tradurre dall'inglese in italiano** to translate from English into Italian; **tradurre alla lettera** to translate literally; **tradurre parola per parola** to translate word for word **2** (*esprimere*) to render, convey; **tradurre in parole povere** to explain simply; **tradurre in cifre** to put into figures; **tradurre in atto** (*fig*) to put into effect **3** (*Dir*): **tradurre qn in carcere/tribunale** to take sb to prison/court; **tradurre qn davanti al giudice** to bring sb before the court

traduttore, -trice [tradut'tore] SM, SF translator; **traduttore elettronico** hand-held electronic translator; **traduttore simultaneo** simultaneous interpreter

traduzione [tradut'tsjone] SF **1** (*di lingue*) translation; **traduzione assistita** computer-assisted translation; **traduzione simultanea** simultaneous interpreting **2** (*Dir*) transfer

trae ['trae] VB *vedi* **trarre**

traente [tra'ɛnte] SM, SF (*di assegno*) drawer

trafelato, -a [trafe'lato] AGG breathless, out of breath

trafficante [traffi'kante] SM, SF (*di droga*) trafficker

trafficare [traffi'kare] /20/ VI **1** (*commerciare*): **trafficare (in)** to traffic (in), deal *o* trade illicitly (in) **2** (*affaccendarsi*) to busy o.s. ♦ VT (*droga*) to traffic in

trafficato, -a [traffi'kato] AGG (*strada, zona*) busy

traffico ['traffiko] SM **1** (*stradale*) traffic; **c'è un traffico pazzesco** the traffic's terrible; **regolare il traffico** to control *o* regulate the traffic; **chiudere una strada al traffico** to close a road to traffic **2** (*movimento*) traffic; **traffico aereo** air traffic; **traffico ferroviario** rail traffic **3** (*commercio illecito*) traffic; **traffico di droga** drug trafficking

trafiggere [tra'fiddʒere] /104/ VT IRREG (*ferire*) to run through, stab; (*fig*) to pierce

trafila [tra'fila] SF procedure; **bisognerà seguire la solita trafila** we'll have to go through the usual routine *o* rigmarole

trafiletto [trafi'letto] SM (*di giornale*) short article

trafitto, -a [tra'fitto] PP *di* **trafiggere**

traforare [trafo'rare] /72/ VT (*gen*) to pierce; (*montagna*) to tunnel through, make a tunnel through; (*legno, metallo*) to drill, bore; **il proiettile gli ha traforato il cuore** the bullet pierced his heart

traforo [tra'foro] SM **1** (*operazione: vedi vb*) piercing; tunnelling; drilling, boring **2** (*galleria*) tunnel **3** lavoro di traforo (*su metallo, legno*) fretwork

trafugare [trafu'gare] /80/ VT to purloin

tragedia [tra'dʒɛdja] SF (*Teatro, anche fig: disastro*) tragedy; **tragedia greca/latina** Greek/Roman tragedy; **non farne una tragedia** don't make a fuss about it; **non è il caso di farne una tragedia!** there's no need to make such a fuss about it!

traggo ecc ['traggo] VB *vedi* **trarre**

traghettare [traget'tare] /72/ VT (*persone*) to ferry; (*fiume*) to cross by ferry

traghetto [tra'getto] SM (*trasporto*) ferrying, crossing; (*luogo*) ferry; (*mezzo*) ferry(boat); **siamo andati in Irlanda col traghetto** we went to Ireland by ferry ♦ AGG INV ferry *attr*

tragicità [tradʒitʃi'ta] SF tragedy

tragico, -a, -ci, -che ['tradʒiko] AGG tragic ♦ SM, SF (*tragediografo*) tragedian; **non fare il tragico** (*fig*) don't make a song and dance over it ♦ SM: **il tragico della faccenda è che...** the worst thing about it is...

tragicomico, -a, -ci, -che [tradʒi'kɔmiko] AGG tragicomic

tragitto [tra'dʒitto] SM **1** (*viaggio*) journey; **un breve tragitto** a short journey; **durante il tragitto** on the journey **2** (*tratto di strada*) way; **durante il tragitto** on the way

traguardo [tra'gwardo] SM (*Sport*) finish, finishing post; (*linea*) finishing line; (*fig*) aim, goal; **tagliare il traguardo** to cross the (finishing) line; **è stato il primo a tagliare il traguardo** he was the first to cross the finishing line; **raggiungere il traguardo** (*in gara*) to reach the finish; (*fig*) to reach one's goal

trai ecc ['trai] VB *vedi* **trarre**

traiettoria [trajet'tɔrja] SF trajectory

trainante [trai'nante] AGG (*cavo, fune*) towing; (*Econ: settore*) driving; (: *paese*) leading

trainare [trai'nare] /72/ VT (*carro*) to draw, pull, drag, haul; (*auto*) to tow; **il carro attrezzi ha trainato la macchina fino alla città più vicina** the breakdown van (*Brit*) *o* tow truck towed the car to the nearest town; **farsi trainare** (*fig*) to follow blindly

training ['treiniŋ] SM INV (*di personale*) training

traino ['traino] SM **1** (*operazione*) drawing, pulling; (*di auto*) towing; **al traino** on tow; **fare da traino** (*Econ*) to be a driving force **2** (*cosa trainata*) trailer load

tralasciare [tralaʃ'ʃare] /14/ VT **1** (*omettere: dettagli*) to leave out, omit; **tralasciamo i particolari** let's skip the details **2** (*trascurare: studi*) to neglect

tralcio, -ci ['traltʃo] SM shoot (*of a plant*)

traliccio, -ci [tra'littʃo] SM (*pilone*) pylon; (*struttura*) trellis

tram [tram] SM INV tram (*Brit*), streetcar (*USA*)

trama ['trama] SF **1** (*filo*) weft **2** (*di opera*) plot; (*inganno*) plot, conspiracy; **la trama del film è un po' complicata** the plot of the film is rather complicated; **ordire una trama ai danni di qn** to hatch a plot against sb

tramandare [traman'dare] /72/ VT to hand down, pass on

tramare [tra'mare] /72/ VT to plot, scheme; **tramare un complotto** to plot

trambusto [tram'busto] SM (*rumore*) racket; (*disordine*) turmoil

tramestio, -tii [trames'tio] SM bustle, bustling

tramezzino [tramed'dzino] SM sandwich; **un tramezzino al prosciutto** a ham sandwich

tramezzo [tra'meddzo] SM partition, dividing wall

tramite ['tramite] SM means *pl*; **agire/fare da tramite** to act as/be a go-between ♦ PREP (*per mezzo di: cosa*) by means of; (: *persona*) through

tramontana [tramon'tana] SF (*Meteor*) north wind; **perdere la tramontana** (*fig*) to lose one's bearings

tramontare [tramon'tare] /72/ VI (*aus essere*) (*astri*) to go down, set; (*fig: bellezza, gloria*) to fade

tramonto [tra'monto] SM (*del sole*) sunset; (*di astri*) setting; **è sul viale del tramonto** (*attore*) he has passed his peak

tramortire [tramor'tire] /55/ VT to knock out, knock unconscious, stun ♦ VI (*aus essere*) to pass out, faint, lose consciousness

trampolino [trampo'lino] SM (*Sport: per tuffi*) springboard; (: *in muratura*) diving board; (: *per lo sci*) ski jump; **servire da trampolino** (*fig*) to serve as a springboard

trampolo ['trampolo] SM stilt

tramutare [tramu'tare] /72/ VT: **tramutare in** to change *o* turn into; **tramutarsi** VR: **tramutarsi in** to change *o* turn into

trance ['tra:ns] SF INV trance; **in (stato di) trance** in a (state of) trance; **cadere in trance** to fall into a trance

trancia, -ce ['trantʃa] SF **1** (*Tecn*) shears *pl*, shearing machine **2** (*fetta*) slice; **trancia di salmone** (*Culin*) salmon steak; **a trance in slices**

tranciare [tran'tʃare] /14/ VT (*Tecn*) to shear

trancio, -ci ['trantʃo] SM = **trancia 2**

tranello [tra'nello] SM trap; **tendere un tranello a qn** to set a trap for sb; **cadere in un tranello** to fall into a trap

trangugiare [trangu'dʒare] /62/ VT to gulp down; (*fig: amarezze*) to swallow

tranne ['tranne] PREP (*eccetto*) except (for), but (for); **c'erano tutti tranne lui** they were all there except *o* but him; **tutti i giorni tranne il venerdì** every day except *o* with the exception of Friday; **ha invitato tutti tranne me** he invited everybody except me; **va d'accordo con tutti tranne che con me** he gets on with everybody except *o* but me ♦ **tranne che** CONG unless

tranquillante [trankwil'lante] SM (*Med*) tranquillizer

tranquillità [trankwilli'ta] SF (*stabilità*) tranquillity; (*immobilità*) calm, stillness; (*calma*) quietness; (*di animo*) peace of mind; **la tranquillità della campagna** the peace of the countryside; **è ritornata la tranquillità** the situation has returned to normal; **per mia tranquillità** to set my mind at ease; **con tranquillità** calmly; **gli ha risposto con molta tranquillità** she replied to him very calmly

tranquillizzare [trankwillid'dzare] /72/ VT to reassure; **l'ho detto per tranquillizzarla** I said it to reassure her; **tranquillizzarsi** VIP to calm down

tranquillo, -a [tran'kwillo] AGG **1** (*luogo*) calm, peaceful, quiet; **il mare è tranquillo** the sea is calm; **cerchiamo un angolo tranquillo** let's find a quiet corner **2** (*persona*) calm; (*sicuro*) sure, confident; **dormire sonni tranquilli** to sleep easy *o* peacefully; **avere la coscienza tranquilla** to have a clear conscience; **stai tranquillo — che ce la fa!** don't worry — he'll do it all right!

transatlantico, -a, -ci, -che [transat'lantiko] AGG transatlantic ♦ SM **1** (*Naut*) transatlantic liner **2** (*Pol*) *room in the Palazzo di Montecitorio*

transatto, -a [tran'satto] PP *di* **transigere**

transazione [transat'tsjone] SF (*Dir*) settlement; (*Comm*) transaction, deal

transenna [tran'senna] SF (*cavalletto*) barrier

transetto [tran'setto] SM (*Archit*) transept

transgenico, -a, -ci, -che [trans'dʒeniko] AGG genetically modified

transiberiano, -a [transibe'rjano] AGG trans-Siberian

transigere [tran'sidʒere] /47/ VI IRREG (*aus avere*) to compromise; **su queste cose non transigo** I don't compromise on these things; **è uno che non transige** he is intransigent; **in fatto di sincerità io non transigo** I won't put up with insincerity

transistor [tran'sistor] SM INV (*Elettr*) transistor; (*Radio*) transistor (radio)

transitabile [transi'tabile] AGG passable; **"strada transitabile solo con catene"** "road passable only with snow chains"

transitare [transi'tare] /72/ VI (*aus essere*) to pass

transitivo, -a [transi'tivo] AGG transitive

transito ['transito] SM transit; **"divieto di transito"** "no entry"; **"transito interrotto"** "road closed"; **stazione di transito** transit station

transitorio, -ria, -ri, -rie [transi'tɔrjo] AGG (*temporaneo: provvedimenti, disposizioni*) temporary, provisional; (: *gloria*) transitory, fleeting, transient

transizione [transit'tsjone] SF transition; **età/periodo di transizione** age/period of transition

tran tran [tran 'tran] SM INV routine; **il solito tran tran** the same old routine

tranvia [tran'via] SF tramway (*Brit*), streetcar line (*USA*)

tranviario, -ria, -ri, -rie [tran'vjarjo] AGG tram *attr* (*Brit*), streetcar *attr* (*USA*); **linea tranviaria** tramline, streetcar line

tranviere [tran'vjere] SM (*conducente*) tram driver (*Brit*), streetcar driver (*USA*); (*bigliettaio*) tram *o* streetcar conductor

trapanare [trapa'nare] /72/ VT to drill

trapano ['trapano] SM drill; **trapano da dentista** dentist's drill; **trapano elettrico** electric drill; **trapano a mano** hand drill

trapassare [trapas'sare] /72/ VT to go through, pierce ♦ VI (*aus essere*) (*fig: letter: morire*) to pass away

trapassato, -a [trapas'sato] SM (*Gramm*) past perfect

trapasso [tra'passo] SM **1** (*Dir: passaggio*): **trapasso di proprietà** (*di case*) conveyancing; (*di auto*) legal transfer **2 l'ora del trapasso** (*letter*) one's final hour

trapelare [trape'lare] /72/ VI (*aus essere*) (*luce*) to filter through; (*fig: segreto, indiscrezione*) to leak (out); **dal suo viso trapelava tutta la sua gioia** his face shone with joy

trapezio, -zi [tra'pettsjo] SM **1** (*Mat*) trapezium **2** (*Sport*) trapeze **3** (*Anat*) trapezius

trapezista, -i, -e [trapet'tsista] SM, SF trapeze artist

trapiantare [trapjan'tare] /72/ VT (*Bot, Med*) to transplant; (*fig: moda, usanza*) to introduce; **trapiantarsi** VIP to move; **ormai si sono trapiantati in Kenia** they have now settled in Kenya

trapianto [tra'pjanto] SM (*Med*) transplant; (*Bot*) transplanting

trappola ['trappola] SF **1** (*anche fig*) trap; **prendere qn/qc in trappola** (*anche fig*) to catch sb/sth in a trap; **cadere in trappola** (*anche fig*) to fall into a trap; **sono caduti nella trappola della polizia** they fell into the police trap; **tendere una trappola a qn** to set a trap for sb **2** (*pegg: auto*) old wreck

trapunta [tra'punta] SF quilt

trarre ['trarre] VB IRREG /123/ VT 1 to draw, pull; **trarre in inganno** to be misleading; **la sua aria innocente trae in inganno** his innocent appearance is misleading *o* deceptive; **sono stato tratto in inganno dal suo modo di fare** I was misled *o* deceived by his manner; **trarre qn d'impaccio** to get sb out of an awkward situation; **trarre in salvo** to rescue; **sono stati tratti in salvo dai vigili del fuoco** they were rescued by the fire brigade 2 (*estrarre*) to pull out, draw 3 (*derivare*) to obtain, get; **trarre guadagno** to make a profit; **trarre beneficio** *o* **profitto da qc** to benefit from sth; **trarre origine da qc** to have its origins *o* originate in sth; **trarre esempio da qn** to follow sb's example; **trarre un film da un libro** to make a film (*Brit*) *o* movie (*USA*) from a book; **un film tratto da un romanzo di A. Christie** a film based on a novel by A. Christie; **trarre le conclusioni** to draw one's own conclusions; **sta a te trarre le conclusioni** you can draw your own conclusions ♦ **trarsi** VR: **trarsi da** to get (o.s.) out of; **stai tranquillo che sa trarsi d'impaccio da solo** don't worry, he knows how to look after himself

trasalire [trasa'lire] /55/ VI (*aus* **avere** *o* **essere**) to jump, (give a) start; **fare trasalire qn** to make sb jump *o* start

trasandato, -a [trazan'dato] AGG (*persona, abito*) scruffy, shabby; **è trasandato nel vestire** he wears scruffy clothes

trasbordare [trazbor'dare] /72/ VT (*gen*) to transfer; (*Naut*) to tran(s)ship ♦ VI (*aus* **avere**) (*Naut*) to change ship; (*Aer*) to change plane; (*Ferr*) to change trains

trascendentale [traʃʃenden'tale] AGG (*Filosofia*) transcendental; (*fig*) **non è niente di trascendentale** it (*o* he *ecc*) is nothing exceptional

trascendere [traʃ'ʃendere] /101/ VT IRREG (*Filosofia, Rel*) to transcend; (*fig: superare*) to surpass, go beyond

trasceso, -a [traʃ'ʃeso] PP *di* **trascendere**

trascinare [traʃʃi'nare] /72/ VT (*gen*) to drag; **trascinare i piedi** to drag one's feet; **trascina una gamba** he has a stiff leg; **trascinare qn in tribunale** to take sb to court; **sa trascinare la folla** he knows how to carry the crowd; **la sua musica ti trascina** his music is enthralling; **trascinare qn sulla via del male** to lead sb astray; **trascinarsi** (*strisciare*) to drag o.s. (along); **trascinarsi** VIP (*controversia*) to drag on

trascorrere [tras'korrere] VB IRREG /28/ VT (*vacanze, giorni*) to spend, pass; **trascorrono sempre le vacanze al mare** they always spend their holidays at the seaside ♦ VI (*aus* **essere**) (*passare: ore, mesi, giorni*) to pass; **le ore trascorrevano lente** the hours dragged by; **sono trascorsi sei giorni da allora** six days have passed since then; **hai lasciato trascorrere troppo tempo** you've allowed too much time to pass

trascorso, -a [tras'korso] PP *di* **trascorrere** ♦ AGG past ♦ SM mistake; **non voglio conoscere i suoi trascorsi** I don't want to know about his past

trascritto, -a [tras'kritto] PP *di* **trascrivere**

trascrivere [tras'krivere] /105/ VT IRREG 1 (*citazioni, frasi, idee*) to write down, copy down 2 (*traslitterare*) to transliterate; (*sistema fonetico e delle note musicali*) to transcribe

trascrizione [traskrit'tsjone] SF (*gen*) writing down, copying down; (*di discorso*) transcript; (*traslitterazione*) transliteration; (*nel sistema fonetico e delle note musicali*) transcription

trascurare [trasku'rare] /72/ VT 1 (*studio, lavoro, famiglia*) to neglect 2 (*omettere*) to omit, skip, leave out 3 (*non tener conto di*) to ignore, overlook; (*non considerare*) to disregard; **trascurarsi** VR to neglect o.s.

trascuratezza [traskura'tettsa] SF (*negligenza*) carelessness, negligence; (*disordine*) untidiness

trascurato, -a [trasku'rato] AGG 1 (*sciatto*) slovenly 2 (*negligente*) careless, negligent 3 (*non curato*) neglected; **sentirsi trascurato** to feel neglected; **un'influenza trascurata può portare alla polmonite** if you neglect a bout of flu it can develop into pneumonia

trasecolato, -a [traseko'lato] AGG astounded, amazed, dumbfounded

trasferimento [trasferi'mento] SM 1 (*cambiamento di sede*) transfer; **ha chiesto il trasferimento** he's asked for a transfer 2 (*Dir: di titoli*) transfer; (*: di proprietà*) conveyancing 3 **trasferimento di chiamata** call diversion

trasferire [trasfe'rire] /55/ VT 1 (*sede, potere*) to transfer; **è stato trasferito a Milano** he's been transferred to Milan 2

(*Dir: titoli*) to transfer; (*: proprietà*) to transfer, convey; **trasferirsi** VIP to move; **il mese prossimo ci trasferiamo a Firenze** we're moving to Florence next month

trasferta [tras'fɛrta] SF 1 (*di funzionario*) temporary transfer; **essere in trasferta** to be on temporary transfer 2 (*anche:* **indennità di trasferta**) travel allowance, travel expenses *pl* 3 (*Sport*) away game; **giocare in trasferta** to play away (from home); **la prossima settimana giochiamo in trasferta** we're playing away from home next week

trasfigurare [trasfigu'rare] /72/ VT to transfigure; **trasfigurarsi** VIP to be transfigured

trasformare [trasfor'mare] /72/ VT 1 (*gen*) to change, alter; (*radicalmente*) to transform; **hanno trasformato la stalla in un ristorante** they converted the stable into a restaurant; **la strega trasformò il principe in un albero** the witch turned the prince into a tree; **quel vestito ti trasforma** that dress completely transforms you; **il soggiorno in America l'ha trasformato** his stay in America has transformed him 2 (*Rugby*) to convert; **trasformare un rigore** (*Calcio*) to score from a penalty; **trasformarsi** VIP (*embrione, larva*) to be transformed, transform itself; (*energia*) to be converted; (*persona, paese*) to change, alter; (*radicalmente*) to be transformed; **un tavolo che si trasforma in asse da stiro** a table that converts into an ironing board

trasformatore [trasforma'tore] SM (*Elettr*) transformer

trasformazione [trasformat'tsjone] SF (*vedi vb*) change, alteration; transformation; conversion

trasfusione [trasfu'zjone] SF (*Med*) transfusion

trasgredire [trazgre'dire] /55/ VT, VI (*aus* **avere**) **trasgredire a** (*legge, regola*) to break, infringe; (*ordini*) to disobey

trasgressione [trazgres'sjone] SF 1 (*vedi vb*) breaking, infringement; disobeying 2 (*anticonformismo*) transgression, rule-breaking

trasgressivo, -a [trazgres'sivo] AGG (*personaggio, atteggiamento*) rule-breaking *attr*

trasgressore [trazgres'sore], **trasgreditrice** [trazgredi'tritʃee] SM, SF (*Dir*) transgressor

traslato, -a [traz'lato] AGG metaphorical, figurative ♦ SM metaphor

traslocare [trazlo'kare] /20/ VT, VI (*aus* **avere**) to move

trasloco, -chi [traz'lɔko] SM removal; **una ditta di traslochi** a removal firm, a moving company; **fare un trasloco** to move house; **li ho aiutati a fare il trasloco** I helped them to move house

trasmesso, -a [traz'messo] PP *di* **trasmettere**

trasmettere [traz'mettere] VB IRREG /63/ VT 1 (*Telec*) to transmit; (*Radio, TV*) to broadcast; **trasmettere in diretta** to broadcast live; **trasmettere una partita in diretta** to broadcast a match live; **il concerto sarà trasmesso in diretta** the concert will be broadcast live; **trasmettono un western** (*TV*) they're showing a western 2 (*usanza, diritto, titolo*) to pass on; (*lettera, telegramma, notizia*) to send; **trasmettere una malattia a qn** to pass a disease on to sb; **trasmettersi** VIP (*usanza*) to be passed on; (*Med*) to be spread, be transmitted

trasmettitore, -trice [trazmetti'tore] AGG transmitting ♦ SM transmitter

trasmissione [trazmis'sjone] SF 1 (*gen*) transmission; (*di titolo, eredità*) passing on, handing down; **albero di trasmissione** (*Aut*) transmission shaft; **trasmissione (dei) dati** (*Inform*) data transmission; **trasmissione del pensiero** thought transference 2 (*Radio, TV: programma*) transmission, broadcast, programme (*Brit*), program (*USA*); **una trasmissione radiofonica** a radio programme; **le trasmissioni riprenderanno domani** program(me)s will resume tomorrow

trasmittente [trazmit'tente] AGG transmitting ♦ SF transmitter, transmitting *o* broadcasting station

trasognato, -a [trasoɲ'ɲato] AGG dreamy

trasparente [traspa'rente] AGG (*anche fig*) transparent; (*sottile*) wafer-thin ♦ SM transparency

trasparenza [traspa'rentsa] SF (*anche fig*) transparency; **guardare qc in trasparenza** to look at sth against the light

trasparire [traspa'rire] /112/ VI IRREG (*aus* **essere**) 1 to shine through; **lasciare trasparire la luce** to let the light shine through 2 (*vedersi*) to be visible, show (through); **sotto il**

vestito traspare la sottoveste her slip shows *o* can be seen through her dress; **dal suo volto traspariva la gioia** his face shone with joy; **la sua espressione non lasciava trasparire nulla** his face gave nothing away

trasparso, -a [tras'parso] PP *di* **trasparire**

traspirare [traspi'rare] /72/ VI (*aus* **essere**) (*sudare*) to perspire; (*fig: trapelare*) to leak out

traspirazione [traspirat'tsjone] SF (*sudorazione*) perspiration; (*Bot*) transpiration

trasporre [tras'porre] /77/ VT IRREG to transpose

trasportare [traspor'tare] /72/ VT 1 (*gen, anche fig*) to carry; (*con veicolo*) to carry, transport, convey; **il camion trasportava un carico di arance** the truck was carrying a load of oranges; **lo hanno trasportato d'urgenza in ospedale** they rushed him to (the) hospital; **questo libro ci trasporta al Rinascimento** this book takes us back to the Renaissance 2 **lasciarsi trasportare (da qc)** (*gioia, entusiasmo*) to let o.s. be carried away (by sth); **lasciarsi trasportare dall'ira** to lose one's temper 3 (*trascinare*) to carry off; **l'hanno trasportato in questura** they took him off to the police station

trasporto [tras'porto] SM 1 (*gen*) transport(ation); **danneggiato durante il trasporto** damaged in transit; **mezzi di trasporto** means of transport; **nave/aereo da trasporto** transport ship/aircraft *inv*; **compagnia di trasporto** carrier; (*per strada*) hauliers *pl* (*Brit*), haulers *pl* (*USA*); **i trasporti** transport *sg*; **un sistema di trasporti efficiente** an efficient transport system; **il ministero dei trasporti** ≈ the Department of Transport (*Brit*), ≈ the Department of Transportation (*USA*); **trasporti pubblici** public transport(ation) *sg*; **qui i trasporti pubblici funzionano molto bene** public transport(ation) is very efficient here; **trasporto aereo** air transport; **trasporto marittimo** sea transport; **trasporto stradale** (road) haulage 2 (*fig*) rapture, passion; **con trasporto** passionately; **un trasporto d'ira** a fit of anger

trasposto, -a [tras'posto] PP *di* **trasporre**

trassi *ecc* ['trassi] VB *vedi* **trarre**

trastullare [trastul'lare] /72/ VT (*bambino*) to play with, amuse; **trastullarsi** VR (*divertirsi*): **trastullarsi con qc** to amuse o.s. with sth; (*gingillarsi*) to fritter away one's time

trastullo [tras'tullo] SM game

trasudare [trasu'dare] /72/ VT to ooze with ♦ VI (*aus* **essere**) to ooze (out)

trasversale [trazver'sale] AGG (*taglio, sbarra*) cross *attr*; (*retta*) transverse; **via trasversale** side street; **motore trasversale** (*Aut*) transverse engine; **una camicia a righe trasversali** a shirt with horizontal stripes; **partito trasversale** (*fig*) unofficial grouping of diverse political interests

trasvolare [trazvo'lare] /72/ VT to fly across *o* over

tratta ['tratta] SF 1 (*traffico*): **la tratta degli schiavi** the slave trade; **la tratta delle bianche** the white slave trade 2 (*Comm*) draft; **tratta documentaria** documentary bill of exchange

trattamento [tratta'mento] SM 1 (*gen*) treatment; (*servizio in ristorante*) service; **trattamento di riguardo** special treatment; **ricevere un buon trattamento** (*cliente*) to get good service; **fare un trattamento di favore** to give special treatment 2 (*Tecn, Med*) treatment; **trattamento di bellezza** beauty treatment 3 (*Econ*) payment; **trattamento di fine rapporto** severance pay 4 (*Inform*): **trattamento testi** word processing

trattare [trat'tare] /72/ VT 1 (*discutere: tema, argomento*) to deal with, discuss; (*negoziare: pace, resa*) to negotiate; **trattare un affare** to negotiate a deal 2 (*comportarsi con*) to treat; **trattare bene/male qn** to treat sb well/badly; **trattare qn con i guanti** to handle *o* treat sb with kid gloves 3 (*Comm: vendere*) to deal in, handle 4 (*Tecn, Med*) to treat ♦ VI (*aus* **avere**) 1 (*libro, film*): **trattare di** to deal with, be about; **di cosa tratta il libro?** what's the book about? 2 (*avere relazioni*): **trattare con** to deal with; **con lui non si può trattare** he's impossible to deal with; **ho trattato direttamente con il proprietario** I dealt directly with the owner 3 (*forma impers*): **si tratta di sua moglie** it's about his wife; **si tratta di pochi minuti** it will only take a few minutes; **si tratterebbe solo di poche ore** it would just be a matter of a few hours; **di che si tratta?** what's it about?; **ti ha detto di cosa si tratta?** did he tell you what it's about?; **si tratta**

di vita o di morte it's a matter of life or death; **trattarsi** VR: **trattarsi bene** to look after o.s. (well)

trattativa [tratta'tiva] SF negotiation; **trattative** SFPL (*tra Stati, governi*) talks; **essere in trattativa con qn** to be in negotiation with sb

trattato, -a [trat'tato] SM 1 (*accordo*) treaty; **firmare/ratificare un trattato** to sign/ratify a treaty; **trattato commerciale** trade agreement; **trattato di pace** peace treaty 2 (*opera*) treatise ♦ AGG: **non trattato** (*prodotto, alimento*) untreated (with pesticides)

trattazione [trattat'tsjone] SF treatment

tratteggiare [tratted'dʒare] /62/ VT (*ombreggiare*) to hatch; (*abbozzare*) to sketch; (*fig: descrivere*) to outline; **linea tratteggiata** dotted line

tratteggio [trat'teddʒo] SM (*Disegno*) hatching

trattenere [tratte'nere] /121/ VT 1 (*fermare*) to keep back; (*in ospedale*) to keep; (*in carcere*) to detain; **trattenere qn dal fare qc** to restrain sb *o* hold sb back from doing sth; **trattenere in osservazione** (*in ospedale*) to keep in for observation; **ho cercato di trattenerlo** I tried to hold him back; **se non l'avessimo trattenuto l'avrebbe picchiato** if we hadn't held him back he would have hit him; **non ti tratterrò a lungo** I won't keep you long; **sono stato trattenuto in ufficio** I was delayed at the office; **mi hanno trattenuto a pranzo** they had me stay for lunch 2 (*lacrime, riso*) to hold back, keep back, restrain; (*respiro*) to hold; **prova a trattenere il respiro** try to hold your breath 3 (*detrarre*) to withhold, keep back, deduct; **trattenersi** VIP (*fermarsi*) to stay, remain; **quanto ti trattieni?** how long are you staying?; **mi sono trattenuto in ufficio** I stayed on at the office; **mi sono trattenuto a cena** I stayed for dinner; **trattenersi** VR (*astenersi*) to restrain o.s., stop o.s.; **trattenersi dal fare qc** to keep *o* stop o.s. from doing sth; **non sono più riuscito a trattenermi** I just couldn't stop myself

trattenimento [tratteni'mento] SM (*festa*) party; **trattenimento danzante** dance

trattenuta [tratte'nuta] SF (*anche*: **trattenuta sullo stipendio**) deduction

trattino [trat'tino] SM (*nelle parole composte*) hyphen; (*per iniziare il discorso diretto*) dash; **si scrive con il trattino** it's spelt with a hyphen

tratto¹, -a ['tratto] PP *di* **trarre**

tratto² ['tratto] SM 1 (*di penna, matita*) stroke; **disegnare a grandi tratti** to sketch; **descrivere qc a grandi tratti** to give an outline of sth 2 **tratti** SMPL (*caratteristiche*) features; **ha i tratti molto marcati** he has very prominent features; **i tratti essenziali del periodo/del suo carattere** the essential features of the period/his character 3 (*segmento*) part, section; (*di mare*) stretch, expanse; (*di strada*) stretch; **è un tratto di strada molto pericoloso** it's a very dangerous stretch of road; **dobbiamo fare ancora un bel tratto a piedi** we still have quite a long way to walk; **c'è ancora un bel tratto da fare** we've still got a long way to go; **alcuni tratti del suo romanzo** some parts of his novel 4 (*spazio di tempo*) time, period (of time); **a tratti** at times; **(tutto) ad un tratto, d'un tratto** (*all'improvviso*) suddenly; **tutt'a un tratto ha cominciato a piovere** it suddenly started to rain

trattore [trat'tore] SM tractor

trattoria [tratto'ria] SF trattoria, small restaurant

trauma, -i ['trauma] SM (*Med: anche*: **trauma psichico**) trauma; **la morte del padre è stata un trauma per lui** his father's death was a traumatic experience for him; **trauma cranico** concussion

traumatico, -a, -ci, -che [trau'matiko] AGG traumatic

traumatizzare [traumatid'dzare] /72/ VT (*Med*) to traumatize; (*fig: impressionare*) to shock; **è rimasto traumatizzato da quell'esperienza** he was traumatized by the experience; **le scene di violenza possono traumatizzare i bambini** scenes of violence can be traumatic for children

travaglio, -gli [tra'vaʎʎo] SM 1 (*sofferenza: mentale*) anguish, distress; (: *fisica*) pain, suffering 2 (*Med: anche*: **travaglio di parto**) labour (*Brit*) *o* labor (*USA*) pains *pl*

travasare [trava'zare] /72/ VT (*liquidi*) to pour; (*vino*) to decant

travaso [tra'vazo] SM (*vedi vb*) pouring; decanting

travatura [trava'tura] SF beams *pl*

trave ['trave] SF beam

traveggole [tra'veggole] SFPL: **avere le traveggole** to be seeing things

traversa [tra'versa] SF 1 (*trave trasversale*) crossbeam, crosspiece; (*Ferr*) sleeper (*Brit*), (railroad) tie (*USA*); (*Calcio, Rugby*) crossbar; **la palla ha colpito la traversa** the ball hit the crossbar 2 (*lenzuolo*) draw-sheet 3 (*via*) sideroad, sidestreet; **prendi la seconda traversa a destra** take the second right; **abita in una traversa di via Roma** she lives in a sidestreet off via Roma; **via Giotto è una traversa di via Rossetti** via Giotto is off Via Rossetti

traversare [traver'sare] /72/ VT (*attraversare*) to cross; **traversare un fiume a nuoto** to swim across a river

traversata [traver'sata] SF (*gen, anche Naut*) crossing; (*Aer*) flight, trip; **la traversata dell'Atlantico** the crossing of the Atlantic

traversie [traver'sie] SFPL hardships

traversina [traver'sina] SF (*Ferr*) sleeper (*Brit*), (railroad) tie (*USA*)

traverso, -a [tra'verso] AGG cross *attr*, transverse; **flauto traverso** (transverse) flute; **via traversa** sideroad; **ottenere qc per vie traverse** to obtain sth in an underhand way ♦ **di traverso** AVV sideways; **camminare di traverso** to walk sideways (on); **mettilo di traverso** put it sideways; **andare di traverso** (*cibo*) to go down the wrong way; **il latte mi è andato di traverso** the milk went down the wrong way; **guardare qn di traverso** to give sb a nasty look; **avere la luna di traverso** to be in a bad mood; **messo di traverso** sideways on

travestimento [travesti'mento] SM (*gen*) disguise; (*per carnevale*) costume

travestire [traves'tire] /45/ VT (*camuffare*) to disguise; (*in costume*) to dress up; **travestirsi** VR (*vedi vt*) to disguise o.s.; to dress up; **travestirsi da donna** to dress up as a woman

travestito [traves'tito] SM cross-dresser

traviare [travi'are] /19/ VT to lead astray; **traviarsi** VIP to go off the straight and narrow

travisare [travi'zare] /72/ VT to distort, misrepresent

travolgente [travol'dʒɛnte] AGG (*entusiasmo*) overwhelming; (*bellezza, fascino*) captivating; (*comicità, umorismo*) side-splitting; (*passione*) uncontrollable; (*amore*) passionate

travolgere [tra'vɔldʒere] /96/ VT (*sogg: piena, valanga*) to sweep away; (*fig*) to overwhelm; **è stato travolto da un'auto** he was run over by a car; **si è lasciato travolgere dalla passione** he was overwhelmed by passion

travolto, -a [tra'vɔlto] PP *di* travolgere

trazione [trat'tsjone] SF (*Med, Tecn*) traction; (*Aut*) drive; **a trazione integrale** (*Aut*) four wheel drive; **trazione anteriore** (*Aut*) front-wheel drive; **trazione posteriore** (*Aut*) rear-wheel drive

tre [tre] AGG INV three; **tre volte** three times ♦ SM INV three; **non c'è due senza tre** it never rains but it pours

trealberi [tre'alberi] SM INV (*Naut*) three-master

trebbia ['trebbja] SF (*Agr: operazione*) threshing; (*: stagione*) threshing season

trebbiare [treb'bjare] /19/ VT (*Agr*) to thresh

trebbiatrice [trebbja'tritʃe] SF (*Agr*) threshing machine

trebbiatura [trebbja'tura] SF threshing

treccia, -ce ['trettʃa] SF (*di capelli*) plait, braid; (*di tessuti, fili*) braid; **Anita ha le trecce** Anita has plaits; **lavorato a trecce** (*pullover*) cable-knit

trecentesco, -a, -schi, -sche [tretʃen'tesko] AGG fourteenth-century

trecento [tre'tʃɛnto] AGG INV three hundred ♦ SM INV three hundred; (*secolo*): **il Trecento** the fourteenth century

tredicenne [tredi'tʃɛnne] AGG, SM, SF thirteen-year-old

tredicesimo, -a [tredi'tʃɛzimo] AGG, SM, SF thirteenth

tredici ['treditʃi] AGG INV thirteen ♦ SM INV thirteen; **fare tredici** (*Totocalcio*) to win the pools (*Brit*)

tregua ['tregwa] SF (*Mil, Pol*) truce; (*fig*) rest, respite; **il dolore non gli dà tregua** the pain gives him no peace, he is in constant pain; **senza tregua** non-stop, without stopping, uninterruptedly

tremante [tre'mante] AGG trembling, shaking

tremare [tre'mare] /72/ VI (*aus avere*) 1 (*gen*) to tremble,

shake; (*fig: temere*) to be afraid; **tremare di** (*freddo*) to shiver *o* tremble with; (*paura, rabbia*) to shake *o* tremble with; **tremava di freddo** she was shivering with cold; **tremavo di paura** I was shaking with fear; **tremare come una foglia** to shake like a leaf; **mi tremano le gambe** my legs are shaking; **tremare per la sorte di qn** to fear for sb; **faceva tremare gli studenti** he made the students tremble with fear 2 (*oscillare: vetri*) to vibrate; (*: terra*) to shake; (*: voce*) to shake, tremble; (*: luce, candela*) to flicker; **mi trema la vista** I can't see straight

tremarella [trema'rella] SF shivers *pl*; **ho la tremarella** I have got the shivers; **mi ha fatto venire la tremarella** it gave me the shivers

tremendo, -a [tre'mɛndo] AGG (*in tutti i sensi*) terrible, awful, dreadful; **avere una fame tremenda** to be awfully *o* terribly hungry, be famished; **faceva un caldo tremendo** it was dreadfully *o* terribly hot; **aveva un mal di testa tremendo** he had a terrible headache

trementina [tremen'tina] SF turpentine

tremila [tre'mila] AGG INV, SM INV three thousand

tremito ['tremito] SM trembling *no pl*; **mi è venuto un tremito** I started to tremble

tremolare [tremo'lare] /72/ VI (*aus avere*) (*gen*) to tremble, shake; (*luci, candele*) to flicker; (*stelle*) to twinkle; (*foglie*) to quiver

tremolio, -lii [tremo'lio] SM (*gen*) trembling, shaking; (*di luci*) flickering

tremore [tre'more] SM tremor

treno ['trɛno] SM 1 (*Ferr*) train; **prendere/perdere il treno** to catch/miss the train; **ho perso il treno** I missed the train; **salire in/scendere dal treno** to get on/get off the train; **andare/viaggiare in treno** to go/travel by train; **siamo andati in treno** we went by train; **treno espresso** express train; **treno interregionale** long-distance train; **treno locale** stopping (*Brit*) *o* local (*USA*) train; **treno merci** goods (*Brit*) *o* freight (*USA*) train; **treno rapido** express (train); **treno regionale** stopping *o* local train; **treno straordinario** special train; **treno viaggiatori** passenger train 2 (*Aut*): **treno di gomme** set of tyres (*Brit*) *o* tires (*USA*)

trenta ['trɛnta] AGG INV thirty ♦ SM INV 1 thirty 2 (*Univ*): **trenta su trenta** full marks; **trenta e lode** full marks plus distinction *o* cum laude

trentenne [tren'tɛnne] AGG, SM, SF thirty-year-old

trentennio, -ni [tren'tɛnnjo] SM period of thirty years

trentesimo, -a [tren'tɛzimo] AGG, SM, SF thirtieth

trentina [tren'tina] SF about thirty, thirty or so

trentino, -a [tren'tino] AGG of *o* from Trento ♦ SM, SF inhabitant *o* native of Trento

trepidante [trepi'dante] AGG anxious

trepidare [trepi'dare] /72/ VI (*aus avere*) to be anxious; **trepidare per qn** to be anxious about sb

trepido, -a ['trepido] AGG (*letter*) anxious

treppiede [trep'pjɛde] SM (*per fotografia*) tripod; (*per cucina*) trivet

trequarti [tre'kwarti] SM INV 1 (*indumento*) three-quarter-length coat 2 (*Rugby*) three-quarter

tresca, -sche ['treska] SF (*relazione amorosa*) affair; (*intrigo*) intrigue, plot

trespolo ['trespolo] SM (*sostegno*) trestle; (*per uccelli*) perch

trevigiano, -a [trevi'dʒano], **trevisano, -a** [trevi'sano] AGG of *o* from Treviso ♦ SM, SF inhabitant *o* native of Treviso

triangolare [triango'lare] AGG triangular

triangolo [tri'angolo] SM (*gen, anche fig: Mat, Mus*) triangle; (*Aut*) warning triangle; **il solito** *o* **classico triangolo** (*fig*) the eternal triangle; **triangolo ottusangolo** obtuse-angled triangle; **triangolo rettangolo** right-angled triangle

tribolare [tribo'lare] /72/ VI (*aus avere*) (*patire*) to suffer; (*fare fatica*) to have a lot of trouble; **ha finito di tribolare** (*euf: è morto*) death has put an end to his suffering; **ha tribolato parecchio per ottenerlo** he went to a lot of trouble to get it

tribolazione [tribolat'tsjone] SF tribulation, suffering; **quel figlio è la mia tribolazione** that son of mine brings me nothing but suffering; **una vita di tribolazioni** a life of trials and tribulations

tribordo [tri'bordo] SM (*Naut*) starboard

tribù [tri'bu] SF INV tribe

tribuna [tri'buna] SF 1 (*per oratore*) platform 2 (*per il pubblico*) gallery; (*di stadio*) stand; (*di ippodromo*) grandstand; **tribuna della stampa/riservata al pubblico** press/public gallery 3 (*TV, Radio*): **tribuna politica** ≈ party political broadcast (*Brit*), ≈ paid political broadcast (*USA*)

tribunale [tribu'nale] SM (*Dir*) court; **chiamare in tribunale** to take to court; **presentarsi** o **comparire in tribunale** to appear in court; **tribunale amministrativo regionale** *regional administrative court*; **tribunale militare** military tribunal; **Tribunale penale internazionale** International Criminal Tribunal; **tribunale del riesame** *provincial court that re-examines cases of those who have been imprisoned and can order their release*

tributare [tribu'tare] /72/ VT to bestow; **tributare gli onori dovuti a qn** to pay tribute to sb

tributario, -ria, -ri, -rie [tribu'tarjo] AGG 1 (*Fisco*) tax *attr*, fiscal 2 (*Geog*): **fiume tributario** tributary

tributo [tri'buto] SM (*imposta*) tax; (*Storia, fig*) tribute

tricheco, -chi [tri'kɛko] SM walrus

triciclo [tri'tʃiklo] SM tricycle

tricolore [triko'lore] AGG three-coloured (*Brit*), three-colored (*USA*) ♦ SM (*bandiera*) tricolo(u)r; **il tricolore** the Italian flag

tridente [tri'dɛnte] SM (*gen*) trident; (*per fieno*) pitchfork

triennale [trien'nale] AGG (*che dura 3 anni*) three-year *attr*; (*che avviene ogni 3 anni*) three-yearly

triennio, -ni [tri'ennjo] SM (*period of*) three years

triestino, -a [tries'tino] AGG of o from Trieste ♦ SM, SF inhabitant o native of Trieste

trifase [tri'faze] AGG INV (*Elettr*) three-phase

trifoglio, -gli [tri'fɔʎʎo] SM clover; **trifoglio bianco** white clover; **trifoglio pratense** o **rosso** red clover

trifolato, -a [trifo'lato] AGG (*Culin*) *cooked in oil, garlic and parsley*

triglia ['triʎʎa] SF mullet; **fare gli occhi di triglia a qn** to make sheep's eyes at sb; **triglia di scoglio** red mullet

trigonometria [trigonome'tria] SF trigonometry

trillare [tril'lare] /72/ VI (*aus avere*) (*Mus*) to trill; (*campanello*) to ring

trillo ['trillo] SM (*Mus*) trill; (*di campanello*) ring

trimestre [tri'mestre] SM 1 (*periodo*) three months, period of three months, quarter; (*Scol*) term, quarter (*USA*) 2 (*rata*) quarterly payment

trimotore [trimo'tore] SM (*Aer*) three-engined plane

trina ['trina] SF lace

trincea [trin'tʃea] SF (*Mil*) trench; **guerra di trincea** trench warfare

trincerare [trintʃe'rare] /72/ VT (*Mil*) to entrench; **trincerarsi** VIP (*Mil*) to entrench o.s.; **trincerarsi nel silenzio** più **assoluto** to take refuge in silence; **trincerarsi dietro un pretesto** to hide behind an excuse

trinciare [trin'tʃare] /14/ VT 1 to cut up 2 (*fig*): **trinciare giudizi** (**su qn/qc**) to make rash judgments (about sb/sth)

Trinidad ['trinidad] SM: **Trinidad e Tobago** Trinidad and Tobago

trinità [trini'ta] SF trinity; **la (santissima) Trinità** the (Holy) Trinity

trio, trii ['trio] SM (*Mus, anche fig*) trio

trionfale [trion'fale] AGG (*arco, entrata*) triumphal; (*successo*) triumphant

trionfante [trion'fante] AGG triumphant

trionfare [trion'fare] /72/ VI (*aus avere*) 1 (*gen, anche Mil*) to triumph; (*commedia, film*) to be a great success; **la verità alla fine trionfa sempre** truth will out; **trionfare su** to triumph over, overcome; **trionfare sui nemici** to triumph over one's enemies 2 (*esultare*) to rejoice; **trionfare per qc** to rejoice at o over sth

trionfo [tri'onfo] SM (*gen*) triumph; (*morale*) (moral) victory; **il trionfo della nazionale italiana** the triumph of the Italian team; **in trionfo** in triumph

triplicare [tripli'kare] /20/ VT, VI (*aus essere*), **triplicarsi** VIP to treble, triple

triplice ['triplitʃe] AGG triple; **in triplice copia** in triplicate; **la Triplice Alleanza** the Triple Alliance

triplo, -a ['triplo] AGG triple, treble; **salto triplo** (*Sport*) triple jump; **la spesa è tripla** it costs three times as much ♦ SM: **il triplo (di)** three times as much (as); **guadagna il triplo di lei** he earns three times as much as her; **mi occorre il triplo** I need three times as much; **lavorare il triplo** to work three times as hard

tripode ['tripode] SM tripod

Tripoli ['tripoli] SF Tripoli

trippa ['trippa] SF (*Culin*) tripe; (*fig: pancia*) paunch

tripudio, -di [tri'pudjo] SM (*esultanza*) triumph, jubilation; (*fig: di colori*) galaxy

tris [tris] SM INV (*Carte*): **tris d'assi/di re** three aces/kings *pl*

triste ['triste] AGG (*gen*) sad; (*persona, destino*) unhappy, sad; (*sguardo*) sorrowful, sad; (*spettacolo, condizioni*) miserable; (*luogo*) gloomy, dismal, dreary; (*esperienza*) painful; **aveva un'aria molto triste** he looked very sad; **una stanzetta triste** a gloomy little room

tristezza [tris'tettsa] SF (*gen*) sadness; (*dolore*) sorrow; (*di paesaggio*) bleakness, dreariness; **che tristezza!** how sad!

tristo, -a ['tristo] AGG (*letter: cattivo*) wicked, evil; (: *meschino*) poor, mean, sorry

tritacarne [trita'karne] SM INV mincer, grinder (*USA*)

tritaghiaccio [trita'gjattʃo] SM INV ice crusher

tritare [tri'tare] /72/ VT (*carne*) to mince, grind (*USA*); (*verdura, cipolla*) to chop

tritatutto [trita'tutto] SM INV mincer, grinder (*USA*)

trito, -a ['trito] AGG (*carne*) minced, ground (*USA*) meat; **trito e ritrito** (*idee, argomenti, frasi*) trite, hackneyed ♦ SM: **fare un trito di cipolla** to chop an onion finely

tritolo [tri'tolo] SM trinitrotoluene

tritone [tri'tone] SM 1 (*Zool*) newt 2 (*Mitol*): **Tritone** Triton

trittico, -ci ['trittiko] SM triptych

triturare [tritu'rare] /72/ VT to grind

trivella [tri'vɛlla] SF (*Falegnameria*) auger; (*per miniera, pozzi*) drill

trivellare [trivel'lare] /72/ VT to drill

trivellazione [trivellat'tsjone] SF drilling; **torre di trivellazione** derrick

triviale [tri'vjale] AGG (*volgare*) coarse, crude, vulgar
❑ **triviale** non si traduce mai con la parola inglese *trivial*

trivialità [trivjali'ta] SF INV (*volgarità*) coarseness, crudeness; (*osservazione*) coarse o crude remark
❑ **trivialità** non si traduce mai con la parola inglese *triviality*

trofeo [tro'fɛo] SM trophy

trogolo ['trɔgolo] SM trough

troia ['trɔja] SF (*fam: scrofa*) sow; (*fam!, pegg*) whore

troll [trɔl] SM INV (*anche Inform*) troll

tromba ['tromba] SF 1 (*Mus*) trumpet; (*Aut*) horn; (*Mil*) bugle; **suono la tromba** I play the trumpet; **partire in tromba** (*fig*) to be off like a shot 2 (*suonatore*) trumpeter; (*Mil*) bugler ♦ **tromba d'aria** (*Meteor*) whirlwind; **tromba d'Eustachio** (*Anat*) Eustachian tube; **tromba di Falloppio** (*Anat*) Fallopian tube; **tromba marina** (*Meteor*) waterspout; **tromba delle scale** (*Archit*) stairwell

trombettista, -i, -e [trombet'tista] SM, SF trumpeter, trumpet (player)

trombone [trom'bone] SM 1 (*Mus: strumento*) trombone; (: *suonatore*) trombonist, trombone (player) 2 (*fig: persona*) windbag 3 (*Bot*) daffodil

trombosi [trom'bɔzi] SF INV thrombosis

troncare [tron'kare] /20/ VT 1 (*spezzare*) to break off; (*con cesoie, ascia*) to cut off 2 (*Ling*) to apocopate 3 (*amicizia, relazione*) to break off; (*carriera*) to ruin, cut short; **una salita che tronca le gambe** a tiring climb

tronco¹, -a, -chi, -che ['tronko] AGG (*colonna, parola*) truncated; **licenziare qn in tronco** to fire sb on the spot

tronco², -chi ['tronko] SM (*Bot, Anat*) trunk; (*d'albero tagliato*) log; (*fig: tratto: di strada, ferrovia*) section; **tronco di cono** (*Geom*) truncated cone

troneggiare [troned'dʒare] /62/ VI (*aus avere*) 1 (*sovra-*

stare): **troneggiare su qn/qc** to tower over *o* dominate sb/ sth **2** (*imporsi all'attenzione*): **troneggiare in mezzo a qc** to dominate sth; **un grosso brillante troneggiava al centro della vetrina** a large diamond dominated the window display

tronfio, -fia, -fi, -fie ['tronfjo] AGG conceited, pompous

trono ['trɔno] SM throne; **salire** *o* **ascendere al trono** to come to *o* ascend the throne

tropicale [tropi'kale] AGG tropical

tropico, -ci ['trɔpiko] SM tropic; **i tropici** the tropics; **tropico del Cancro** Tropic of Cancer; **tropico del Capricorno** Tropic of Capricorn

---

PAROLA CHIAVE

troppo, -a ['trɔppo] AGG INDEF (*quantità: tempo, acqua*) too much; (*numero: persone, promesse*) too many; **non vorrei causarvi troppo disturbo** I wouldn't like to put you to too much trouble; **c'era troppa gente** there were too many people

♦ PRON INDEF (*quantità eccessiva*) too much; (*numero eccessivo*) too many; **ha dettato anche troppo** he's said far too much *o* quite enough; **non ne prendo più, ne ho fin troppi** I won't take any more, I've got far too many; **eravamo in troppi** there were too many of us; **ne vorrei ancora un po', ma non troppo** I'd like a little more, but not too much though; **troppi la pensano come lui** too many (people) think like him ·

♦ AVV

1 (*con aggettivo, avverbio*) too; (*con verbo: gen*) too much; (: *aspettare, durare*) too long; **ho aspettato troppo** I've waited too long; **è troppo bello per essere vero** it's too good to be true; **fa troppo caldo** it's too hot; **fidarsi troppo di qn** to trust sb too much; **è fin troppo furbo!** he's too clever by half!; **troppo poco** too little; **sei arrivato troppo tardi** you arrived too late

2 (*rafforzativo*) too, so (very); **troppo buono da parte tua!** (*anche iro*) you're too kind!; **non ci sarebbe troppo da stupirsi se rifiutasse** I wouldn't be surprised if he refused; **non esserne troppo sicuro!** don't be too *o* so sure of that!; **non troppo volentieri** none too willingly

3 **di troppo** too much; **100 euro di troppo** 100 euros too much; **essere di troppo** to be in the way; **ha bevuto qualche bicchiere di troppo** he's had a few too many

---

trota ['trɔta] SF trout; **trota arcobaleno** *o* **iridea** rainbow trout; **trota di mare** sea trout; **trota salmonata** salmon trout

trottare [trot'tare] /72/ VI (*aus avere*) (*cavallo, cavaliere*) to trot; (*bambino, cucciolo*) to trot along

trotterellare [trotterel'lare] /72/ VI (*aus avere*) (*cavallo*) to jog along; (*cucciolo*) to trot along; (*bambino*) to trot along, toddle

trotto ['trɔtto] SM trot; **andare al trotto** to trot; **corse al trotto** trotting races

trottola ['trɔttola] SF (spinning) top

trovare [tro'vare] /72/ VT **1** (*gen*) to find; (*per caso*) to find, come upon *o* across; (*difficoltà*) to come up against, meet with; **trovare lavoro/casa** to find work *o* a job/a house; **ha trovato lavoro** she's found a job; **far trovare qc a qn** to help sb find sth; **non trovo le scarpe** I can't find my shoes; **non riesco a trovare le chiavi** I can't find my keys; **andare/venire a trovare qn** to go/come and see sb; **ieri sono andato a trovare Chris** I went to see Chris yesterday; **trovare la morte** to meet one's death **2** **trovare da ridire** (su tutto) to find sth to criticize (in everything); **trovare da dormire** to find somewhere to sleep **3** (*giudicare*): **trovare che...** to find *o* think that ...; **lo trovo un po' invecchiato** I think he has aged a bit; **l'ho trovato molto cambiato** I thought he'd changed a lot; **ti trovo dimagrito** you look thinner; **trovi?** do you think so?; **fa caldo, non trovi?** it's hot, don't you think?; **trovo giusto/sbagliato che...** I think/don't think it's right that ...; **lo trovo bello** *o* **buono** I like it; **trovare qn colpevole** to find sb guilty **4** (*cogliere*) to find, catch; **la notizia ci trovò impreparati** the news caught us unawares; **trovarsi** VIP **1** (*essere situato*) to be; **dove si trova la stazione?** where is the station?; **l'albergo si trova proprio al centro del hotel's right in the town centre; **in quel periodo mi trovavo a Londra** at that time I was in London **2** (*capitare*) to

---

find o.s.; **ci siamo trovati a Napoli** we found ourselves in Naples **3** (*essere*) to be; **trovarsi bene/male** to get on well/ badly; **mi sono trovata benissimo con i suoi** I got on very well with his parents; **trovarsi in pericolo/smarrito** to be in danger/lost; **trovarsi nell'impossibilità di rispondere** to be unable to answer; **trovarsi d'accordo con qn** to be in agreement with sb; **trovarsi a disagio** to feel ill at ease; **trovarsi solo** to find o.s. alone; **trovarsi nei pasticci** to find o.s. in trouble; **trovarsi con un pugno di mosche in mano** to be left empty-handed; **troviamoci alle cinque davanti al cinema** let's meet at five in front of the cinema; **si sono trovati in piazza** they met (each other) in the square

trovata [tro'vata] SF (*idea*) brainwave, stroke of genius; **trovata pubblicitaria** publicity stunt, (advertising) gimmick

trovatello, -a [trova'tɛllo] SM, SF foundling

truccare [truk'kare] /20/ VT **1** (*Sport: partita, incontro*) to fix, rig; (*carte da gioco*) to mark; (*dadi*) to load; (*Aut: motore*) to soup up **2** (*attore, viso, occhi*) to make up; **truccarsi il viso** to make up one's face; **truccarsi gli occhi** to put on eye make-up; **truccarsi** VR (*gen, anche Teatro, Cine*) to make o.s. up; **truccarsi da** to make o.s. up as

truccatore, -trice [trukka'tore] SM, SF make-up artist

trucco, -chi ['trukko] SM **1** (*cosmesi*) make-up **2** (*artificio*) trick; (*Cine*) effect, trick; **ti mostro un trucco che riesce sempre** I'll show you a trick that always works; **i trucchi del mestiere** the tricks of the trade

truce ['trutʃe] AGG (*viso, sguardo*) grim, cruel; (*tiranno*) cruel ❑ **truce** non si traduce mai con la parola inglese *truce*

trucidare [trutʃi'dare] /72/ VT to slay, massacre, slaughter

truciolo ['trutʃolo] SM (*di legno, metallo*) shaving; **trucioli di paglia/carta** straw/paper packing material *sg*

truffa ['truffa] SF (*Dir*) fraud; (*imbroglio*) swindle

truffare [truf'fare] /72/ VT to swindle, cheat; **sono stato truffato** I've been swindled

truffatore, -trice [truffa'tore] SM, SF swindler, cheat

truppa ['truppa] SF **1** (*Mil*) troop; (*soldati semplici*) troops *pl*; **truppe d'assalto** assault troops, shock troops **2** (*fig: di amici*) group, band, troop

TS SIGLA = Trieste

tu [tu] PRON PERS you; **tu faresti meglio a tacere!** you'd do better to keep quiet!; **questo lo dici tu!** that's what you say!; **proprio tu lo dici!** you're a right one to talk!; **sei tu quello che fa sempre storie** you're the one who always causes a fuss ♦ SM: **dare del tu a qn** to address sb as "tu", ≈ be on first-name terms with sb; **trovarsi a tu per tu con qn** to find o.s. face to face with sb; **perché non gli parli a tu per tu?** why don't you have a word with him in private?

tua ['tua] *vedi* **tuo**

tuba ['tuba] SF **1** (*Mus*) tuba **2** (*Anat*) tube **3** (*cappello*) top hat

tubare [tu'bare] /72/ VI (*aus avere*) (*colombi*) to coo; (*fig: innamorati*) to bill and coo

tubatura [tuba'tura], **tubazione** [tubat'tsjone] SF pipes *pl*, piping *no pl*

tubercolosi [tuberko'lɔzi] SF tuberculosis

tubero ['tubero] SM (*Bot*) tuber

tubetto [tu'betto] SM (*di dentifricio*) tube

tubino [tu'bino] SM **1** (*abito da donna*) sheath dress **2** (*cappello*) bowler (hat) (*Brit*), derby (*USA*)

tubo ['tubo] SM (*gen*) tube; (*per condutture*) pipe; **un tubo di cartone** a cardboard tube; **i tubi dell'acqua** the pipes; **non capisce/non sa un tubo** (*fam*) he doesn't understand/know a thing; **non me ne importa un tubo** (*fam*) I couldn't care less, I don't give a damn ♦ **tubo catodico** *o* **a raggi catodici** (*Fis*) cathode-ray tube; **tubo digerente** (*Anat*) digestive tract, alimentary canal; **tubo elettronico** (*Tecn*) electron tube; **tubo di scappamento** (*Aut*) exhaust (pipe); **tubo di scarico** waste pipe

tubolare [tubo'lare] AGG tubular; **elastico tubolare** elastic thread ♦ SM tubeless tyre (*Brit*) *o* tire (*USA*)

tue ['tue] *vedi* **tuo**

tuffare [tuf'fare] /72/ VT (*immergere*) to plunge; (*intingere*) to dip; **tuffarsi** VR (*gen*) to dive; **tuffarsi in mare** to dive *o* plunge into the sea; **tuffarsi nella mischia** to rush o dive into the fray; **tuffarsi nello studio** to bury o immerse o.s. in one's studies; **tuffarsi a capofitto in qc** to throw o.s. into sth

tuffatore, -trice [tuffaˈtore] SM, SF (*Sport*) diver

tuffo [ˈtuffo] SM (*gen*) dive; (*breve bagno*) dip; (*Calcio*) dive; (*Sport*): **tuffi** diving *no pl*; **fare un tuffo** to dive; **fare un tuffo nel passato** to jump back into the past; **ho provato un tuffo al cuore** my heart skipped o missed a beat

tugurio, -ri [tuˈgurjo] SM hovel

tulipano [tuliˈpano] SM tulip

tulle [ˈtulle] SM INV (*tessuto*) tulle

tumefare [tumeˈfare] VB IRREG /42/ VT to cause to swell; **tumefarsi** VIP to swell

tumido, -a [ˈtumido] AGG (*gonfio*) swollen; (*carnoso: labbra*) thick

tumore [tuˈmore] SM tumour (*Brit*), tumor (*USA*); **tumore benigno** benignant tumo(u)r; **tumore maligno** malignant tumo(u)r

tumulazione [tumulatˈtsjone] SF burial

tumulto [tuˈmulto] SM 1 (*di folla: rumore*) commotion, uproar; (: *agitazione*) turmoil, tumult; (: *sommossa*) riot 2 (*fig: di pensieri, desideri*) turmoil; **avere l'animo in tumulto** to be in a turmoil

tumultuoso, -a [tumultuˈoso] AGG (*folla*) turbulent, rowdy, unruly; (*assemblea*) stormy, turbulent; (*fiume*) turbulent; (*passione*) tumultuous, turbulent

tungsteno [tungˈsteno] SM tungsten

tunica, -che [ˈtunika] SF tunic

Tunisi [ˈtunizi] SF Tunis

Tunisia [tuniˈzia] SF Tunisia; **viene dalla Tunisia** he comes from Tunisia

tunisino, -a [tuniˈzino] AGG, SM, SF Tunisian

tunnel [ˈtunnel] SM INV tunnel

tuo, -a [ˈtuo] (*pl f* **tue,** *pl m* **tuoi**) AGG POSS: **il(la) tuo(a)** *ecc* your; **il tuo cane** your dog; **tuo padre** your father; **una tua amica** a friend of yours; **è colpa tua** it's your fault; **è casa tua, è la tua casa** it's your house; **per amor tuo** for love of you ♦ PRON POSS: **il(la) tuo(a)** *ecc* yours, your own; **la nostra barca è più lunga della tua** our boat is longer than yours; **la tua è più bella della mia** yours is nicer than mine; **è questo il tuo?** is this (one) yours?; **il tuo è stato solo un errore** it was simply an error on your part ♦ SM 1 **hai speso del tuo?** did you spend your own money?; **vivi del tuo?** do you live on your own income? 2 **i tuoi** (*genitori*) your parents; (*famiglia*) your family; (*amici*) your (own) people, your side; **cosa hanno detto i tuoi?** what did your parents say?; **è dei tuoi** he is on your side ♦ SF: **la tua** (*opinione*) your view; **è dalla tua** he is on your side; **ne hai fatta una delle tue!** (*sciocchezze*) you've done it again!; **anche tu hai avuto le tue** (*disavventure*) you've had your problems too; **alla tua!** (*brindisi*) your health!

tuonare [twoˈnare] /72/ VI (*aus avere*) (*fig: armi, voce*) to thunder, boom; **tuonare contro qn/qc** (*inveire*) to rage against sb/sth ♦ VB IMPERS (*aus avere* o *essere*) **sta tuonando** there is thunder, it is thundering

tuono [ˈtwono] SM (*anche fig*) thunder

tuorlo [ˈtworlo] SM yolk

turacciolo [tuˈrattʃolo] SM (*tappo*) stopper; (*di sughero*) cork

turare [tuˈrare] /72/ VT (*buco, falla*) to stop, plug; (*bottiglia*) to cork; **turarsi il naso** to hold one's nose; **ho il naso turato** my nose is blocked; **turarsi le orecchie** to stop one's ears

turba [ˈturba] SF 1 (*folla*) crowd, throng; (*pegg*) mob 2 (*Med*) disorder; **soffrire di turbe psichiche** to suffer from a mental disorder

turbamento [turbaˈmento] SM (*di animo*) anxiety, agitation; (*della pace, quiete*) disturbance; **provò un profondo turbamento** he was extremely upset

turbante [turˈbante] SM turban

turbare [turˈbare] /72/ VT to disturb, trouble; **le sue parole mi hanno turbato** her words upset me; **turbare la quiete pubblica** (*Dir*) to disturb the peace; **turbare l'opinione pubblica** to upset public opinion; **turbarsi** VIP to get upset

turbato, -a [turˈbato] AGG upset; (*preoccupato, ansioso*) anxious

turbina [turˈbina] SF turbine; **turbina eolica** wind turbine

turbinare [turbiˈnare] /72/ VI (*aus avere*) (*anche fig*) to whirl

turbine [ˈturbine] SM whirlwind; **il turbine della danza** the whirl of the dance; **il turbine della passione** the turmoil of passion; **turbine di neve** gust o swirl of snow; **turbine di polvere** dust storm; **turbine di sabbia** sandstorm

turbinoso, -a [turbiˈnoso] AGG (*vento, danza*) whirling

turbolento, -a [turboˈlento] AGG (*ragazzo*) boisterous, unruly; (*tempi, anni*) turbulent

turbolenza [turboˈlentsa] SF (*vedi agg*) boisterousness; turbulence

turboreattore [turboreatˈtore] SM turbojet engine

turchese [turˈkese] AGG, SM (*colore*) turquoise ♦ SF (*minerale*) turquoise

Turchia [turˈkia] SF Turkey; **andremo in Turchia quest'estate** we're going to Turkey this summer; **mi è piaciuta molto la Turchia** I really liked Turkey

turchino, -a [turˈkino] AGG, SM deep blue

turco, -a, -chi, -che [ˈturko] AGG Turkish; **è turca** she's Turkish; **bagno turco** Turkish bath; **ho fatto un bagno turco** (*fig*) I sweated like a pig (*fam*); **caffè alla turca** Turkish coffee ♦ SM, SF (*persona*) Turk; **i turchi** the Turks; **fumare come un turco** (*fig*) to smoke like a chimney; **bestemmiare come un turco** (*fig*) to swear like a trooper ♦ SM (*lingua*) Turkish; **parla turco?** does he speak Turkish?; **parlare turco** (*fig*) to talk double Dutch

turgido, -a [ˈturdʒido] AGG swollen

turismo [tuˈrizmo] SM tourism

turista, -i, -e [tuˈrista] SM, SF tourist

turistico, -a, -ci, -che [tuˈristiko] AGG tourist *attr*; **una località turistica** a tourist resort

turnista, -i, -e [turˈnista] SM, SF shift worker

turno [ˈturno] SM (*volta*) turn; (*di lavoro*) shift; **è il tuo turno** it's your turn; **essere di turno** (*soldato, medico, custode*) to be on duty; **qual è la farmacia di turno domenica?** which chemist (*Brit*) o drugstore (*USA*) will be open on Sunday?; **rispondere a turno** to answer in turn; **aspettare il proprio turno** to await one's turn; **fare a turno a fare qc** to take (it in) turns to do sth; **abbiamo fatto a turno a guidare** we took turns to drive; **un turno di sei ore** a six-hour shift; **turni articolati** split shifts; **turno di guardia** (*Mil*) sentry o guard duty; **turno di notte** night shift

turpe [ˈturpe] AGG (*voglia*) filthy; (*accusa*) foul, vile; (*persona*) vile, repugnant

turpiloquio, -qui [turpiˈlɔkwjo] SM obscene o foul language

tuta [ˈtuta] SF overalls *pl*; (*Sport*) tracksuit; (*Sci*) ski suit; **tuta mimetica** (*Mil*) camouflage clothing; **tuta spaziale** spacesuit; **tuta subacquea** wetsuit; **le tute blu** (*gli operai*) blue collar workers

tutela [tuˈtɛla] SF 1 (*Dir*) guardianship; **essere sotto la tutela di qn** to be sb's ward; **tutela di un minore** guardianship of a minor 2 (*protezione*) protection; **fare qc a tutela dei propri interessi** to do sth to protect one's interests; **tutela dell'ambiente** environmental protection; **tutela del consumatore** consumer protection

tutelare[1] [tuteˈlare] /72/ VT to protect, defend; **tutelarsi** VR to protect o.s.

tutelare[2] [tuteˈlare] /72/ AGG (*Dir*): **giudice tutelare** *judge with responsibility for guardianship cases*

tutore, -trice [tuˈtore] SM, SF (*Dir*) guardian; (*protettore*) protector, defender; **i tutori dell'ordine pubblico** the police *pl*

tuttavia [tuttaˈvia] CONG nevertheless, yet; **il compito era difficile, tuttavia ce l'ho fatta** the test was difficult, but I managed to do it

PAROLA CHIAVE

tutto, -a [ˈtutto] AGG

1 (*intero*) all (of), the whole (of); **ha letto tutto Dante** he has read all of Dante; **tutta l'Europa** the whole of o all Europe; **ho tutta la sua fiducia** I have his complete confidence; **ha studiato tutto il giorno** he studied the whole day o all day long; **famoso in tutto il mondo** world-famous, famous the world over; **rimanere sveglio tutta la notte** to stay awake all night (long); **a tutt'oggi** so far, up till now; **si diffuse in tutto il paese** it spread through the whole country; **sarò qui tutta la settimana** I'll be here all week o the whole week; **tutta una bottiglia** a whole bottle; **tutta la verità** the whole truth

2 (*proprio*): è tutt'altra cosa, è tutta un'altra cosa (*è ben diverso*) that's quite another thing; viaggiare in aereo è tutt'altra cosa (*è meglio*) travelling by plane is altogether different; è tutta sua madre she's just *o* exactly like her mother; è tutto l'opposto di... it's the exact opposite of ...
3 (*completamente*): era tutta contenta she was overjoyed; è tutta gambe e braccia she's all arms and legs; è tutto naso he's got a big nose; essere tutt'occhi to be all eyes; essere tutt'orecchi to be all ears; è tutta presa dal suo lavoro she's completely *o* entirely taken up by her work; era tutta sorrisi e sorrisetti she was all smiles; tremava tutto he was trembling all over; era tutta vestita di nero she was dressed all in black
4 (*plurale, collettivo*) all; tutti gli animali all animals; tutte queste cose all these things; in tutte le direzioni in all directions, in every direction; tutti e cinque all five of us (*o* them); tutti e due both *o* each of us (*o* them); con tutti i pensieri che ho worried as I am, with all my worries; tutti i posti erano occupati all the seats were *o* every seat was occupied; tutti i ragazzi all the boys; tutti gli uomini all men; una volta per tutte once and for all
5 (*qualsiasi*): a tutti i costi at all costs; in tutti i modi (*a qualsiasi costo*) at all costs; (*comunque*) anyway; telefona a tutte le ore she phones at all hours
6 (*ogni*): tutti gli anni every year; tutti i santi giorni every blessed day; tutti i venerdì every Friday; tutte le volte che every time (that)
7 (*fraseologia*): con tutta l'anima wholeheartedly; con tutto il cuore wholeheartedly; la sua fedeltà è a tutta prova his loyalty is unshakeable *o* will stand any test; per me è tutt'uno it's all one and the same to me; a tutta velocità at full *o* top speed; con tutta la mia buona volontà, non posso aiutarti however much I may want to, I can't help you

♦ PRON
1 (*ogni cosa*) everything, all; (*qualunque cosa*) anything; ha fatto (un po') di tutto he's done (a bit of) everything; essere capace di tutto to be capable of anything; mangia di tutto he eats anything; dimmi tutto tell me everything; tutto dipende da lui everything *o* it all depends on him; tutto è in ordine everything's in order; questo è tutto quello che ho this is all I have; tutto sta a vedere se... it all depends on whether or not ...; tutto sta nel cominciare the essential *o* important thing is to get started

2 (*fraseologia*): tutto compreso inclusive, all-in (*Brit*); questo è tutto that's all (I have to say); con tutto che (*malgrado*) although; tutto considerato all things considered; ...che è tutto dire ... and that's saying a lot; ecco tutto that's all (I have to say); in tutto (*complessivamente*) in all; in tutto sono 180 euro that's 180 euros in all; in tutto e per tutto (*completamente*); dipende in tutto e per tutto dai suoi he is entirely *o* completely dependent on his parents; innanzi tutto first of all; e non è tutto and that's not all; prima di tutto first of all; tutto sommato all things considered

♦ tutti(e) SMPL, SFPL (*tutte le persone*) all (of them); (*ognuno*) everybody; erano tutti presenti everybody was *o* they were all present; vengono tutti they are all coming, everybody's coming; tutti quanti all and sundry

♦ AVV
1 (*completamente*) entirely, quite, completely; è tutto il contrario it's quite *o* exactly the opposite; è tutto il contrario di ciò che credi it's not what you think at all; fa tutto il contrario di quello che gli dico he does the exact opposite of what I tell him to do; del tutto completely; non sono del tutto convinto/sicuro I'm not entirely convinced/sure; è tutto l'opposto it's quite *o* exactly the opposite
2 (*fraseologia*): saranno stati tutt'al più una cinquantina there were about fifty of them at (the very) most; tutt'al più possiamo prendere un treno if the worst comes to the worst we can catch a train; tutt'altro (*al contrario*) on the contrary; (*affatto*) not at all; tutt'altro che felice anything but happy; tutt'intorno all around; tutto a un tratto all of a sudden, suddenly

♦ SM (*l'insieme*): il tutto the whole lot, all of it; il tutto costa 550 euro the whole thing *o* lot costs 550 euros; vi manderemo il tutto nel corso della settimana we'll send you the (whole) lot during the course of the week; il tutto si è risolto in bene everything turned out for the best; rischiare il tutto per tutto to risk everything

tuttofare [tutto'fare] AGG INV: domestica tuttofare general maid; ragazzo tuttofare office boy ♦ SM INV, SF INV handyman, handywoman

tuttora [tut'tora] AVV still

tutù [tu'tu] SM INV tutu

TV [ti'vu] SF INV TV; l'hanno detto alla TV it was on TV; TV digitale digital TV; TV al plasma plasma screen TV; TV verità reality TV ♦ SIGLA = Treviso

Uu

U, u [u] SF INV, SM INV (*lettera*) U, u; **U come Udine** ≈ U for Uncle; **inversione ad U** U-turn

ubbia [ubˈbia] SF (*letter*) irrational fear

ubbidiente [ubbiˈdjɛnte] AGG obedient

ubbidienza [ubbiˈdjɛntsa] SF obedience

ubbidire [ubbiˈdire] /55/ VI (*aus* avere) **ubbidire a** to obey; (*sogg: veicolo, macchina*) to respond to; **ubbidire a qn** to obey sb; **farsi ubbidire** to enforce *o* compel obedience

ubicazione [ubikatˈtsjone] SF site, location

ubiquità [ubikwiˈta] SF ubiquity; **non ho il dono dell'ubiquità!** I can't be everywhere at once!

ubriacare [ubriaˈkare] /20/ VT: **ubriacare qn** (*sogg: persona*) to get sb drunk; (: *bevanda*) to make sb drunk, intoxicate sb; (: *con discorsi, promesse*) to intoxicate sb, make sb's head spin *o* reel; **ubriacarsi** VIP to get drunk

ubriachezza [ubriaˈkettsa] SF drunkenness; **essere arrestato per ubriachezza molesta** to be arrested for being drunk and disorderly; **guidare in stato di ubriachezza** to drive under the influence of alcohol

ubriaco, -a, -chi, -che [ubriˈako] AGG drunk; **era un po' ubriaco** he was a bit drunk; **essere ubriaco fradicio** to be blind *o* roaring drunk (*fam*); **ubriaco di stanchezza** reeling from tiredness; **ubriaco di gelosia** beside o.s. with jealousy ♦ SM, SF drunkard, drunk; **un ubriaco cantava a squarciagola** a drunk was singing at the top of his voice

ubriacone, -a [ubriaˈkone] SM, SF drunkard

uccellagione [uttʃellaˈdʒone] SF bird catching

uccelliera [uttʃelˈljɛra] SF aviary

uccellino [uttʃelˈlino] SM baby bird, chick

uccello [utˈtʃɛllo] SM 1 (*Zool*) bird; **uccello del malaugurio** (*fig*) bird of ill omen; **essere uccel di bosco** (*latitante*) to be nowhere to be found, have flown the coop 2 (*fam!: pene*) dick (*fam!*)

uccidere [utˈtʃidere] VB IRREG /34/ VT (*gen*) to kill; (*assassinare*) to murder, kill; (*sogg: malattia*) to carry off, kill; **uccidere a colpi d'arma da fuoco** to shoot dead; **uccidere a coltellate** to stab to death; **è rimasto ucciso in un incidente** he was killed in an accident; **il fumo uccide** smoking kills; **uccidere un uomo morto** (*fig*) to kick a man when he's down; **uccidersi** VR 1 (*uso reciproco*) to kill each other 2 (*suicidarsi*) to kill o.s.; **si è ucciso** he killed himself; **uccidersi col gas** to gas o.s.; **uccidersi** VIP (*perdere la vita*) to be killed

uccisione [uttʃiˈzjone] SF (*gen*) killing; (*assassinio*) murder

ucciso, -a [utˈtʃizo] PP *di* **uccidere** ♦ SM, SF person killed, victim; **gli uccisi** the dead

uccisore [uttʃiˈzore] SM killer

Ucraina [uˈkraina] SF Ukraine

ucraino, -a [uˈkraino] AGG, SM, SF Ukranian

UD SIGLA = Udine

udente [uˈdɛnte] SM, SF: **i non udenti** the hard of hearing

udibile [uˈdibile] AGG audible

udienza [uˈdjɛntsa] SF (*gen*) audience; (*Dir*) hearing; **dare udienza a** to grant an audience to; **udienza a porte chiuse** hearing in camera

udire [uˈdire] /124/ VT IRREG (*gen*) to hear; **l'abbiamo udita piangere** we heard her crying

uditivo, -a [udiˈtivo] AGG auditory

udito [uˈdito] SM (sense of) hearing
❑ **udito** non si traduce mai con la parola inglese *audit*

uditore, -trice [udiˈtore] SM, SF (*Univ*) unregistered student (*who is allowed to attend lectures* (Brit)), auditor (USA); **uditore giudiziario** (*Dir*) auditor

uditorio, -ri [udiˈtɔrjo] SM audience

UE [uˈe] SIGLA F (= *Unione Europea*) EU ♦ ABBR = **uso esterno**

UEFA [uˈefa] SIGLA F UEFA (= *Union of European Football Associations*)

UEM [wem] SIGLA F (= *Unione Economica e Monetaria*) EMU (= *Economic and Monetary Union*)

uf [uf], **uff** [uff], **uffa** [ˈuffa] ESCL (*con insofferenza*) oh; **uffa! sono stanco!** oh, I'm tired!; **uf(f)! che caldo!** phew! it's hot!

ufficiale [uffiˈtʃale] AGG (*gen*) official; **è in visita ufficiale in Italia** he's on an official visit to Italy ♦ SM 1 (*Mil, Naut*) officer; **un ufficiale di Marina** a naval officer; **primo ufficiale** (*Naut*) first mate; **ufficiale di marina** naval officer 2 (*Amm*) official, officer; **pubblico ufficiale** public official; **ufficiale giudiziario** (*Dir*) clerk of the court; **ufficiale sanitario** health inspector; **ufficiale di stato civile** registrar

ufficializzare [uffitʃalidˈdzare] /72/ VT to make official

ufficio, -ci [ufˈfitʃo] SM 1 (*luogo: gen*) office; (*organo*) office, bureau, agency; (*reparto*) department; **andare in ufficio** to go to the office; **oggi non è andata in ufficio** she didn't go to the office today; **ufficio brevetti** patent office; **ufficio di collocamento** employment office; **ufficio informazioni** information desk; **ufficio oggetti smarriti** lost property office (*Brit*), lost and found (*USA*); **ufficio del personale** personnel department; **ufficio postale** post office; **ufficio vendite** sales department 2 (*incarico*) office; (*dovere*) duty; (*mansione*) function, task, job; **l'ufficio di direttore generale** the office *o* position of general manager; **coprire/accettare un ufficio** to hold/accept a position; **provvedere d'ufficio** to act officially 3 (*Dir*): **difensore** *o* **avvocato d'ufficio** court-appointed counsel for the defence (*Brit*) *o* defense (*USA*); **convocare d'ufficio** to summons 4 (*intervento*): **grazie ai suoi buoni uffici** thanks to his good offices 5 (*Rel*) office, service

ufficioso, -a [uffiˈtʃoso] AGG unofficial
❑ **ufficioso** non si traduce mai con la parola inglese *officious*

UFO, ufo [ˈufo] SM INV UFO (= *unidentified flying object*)

ufo [ˈufo] **a ufo** AVV free, for nothing; **mangiare a ufo** to sponge a meal

Uganda [uˈganda] SF Uganda

uggia, -ge [ˈuddʒa] SF (*noia*) boredom; (*fastidio*) bore; **avere/prendere qn in uggia** to dislike/take a dislike to sb

uggioso, -a [udˈdʒoso] AGG (*gen*) tiresome; (*tempo*) dull, dreary

ugola [ˈugola] SF (*Anat*) uvula

uguaglianza [ugwaʎˈʎantsa] SF (*gen*) equality; (*Mat*) identity; **su una base di uguaglianza** on an equal footing, on equal terms; **segno di uguaglianza** (*Mat*) equals sign

uguagliare [ugwaʎˈʎare] /27/ VT 1 (*livellare: persone, stipendi*) to make equal; (: *siepe*) to straighten 2 (*raggiungere, essere uguale a*) to equal, be equal to; **uguagliare qn in bellezza/ bravura** to equal sb *o* be equal to sb in beauty/skill; **uguagliare un record** (*Sport*) to equal a record; **ha uguagliato il record mondiale** he equalled the world record; **in lui l'intelligenza uguaglia la bontà** he is as intelligent as he is good; **uguagliarsi** (*o: paragonarsi*): **uguagliarsi a** *o* **con qn** to compare o.s. to sb; **uguagliarsi** VIP to be equal

uguale [uˈgwale] AGG 1 (*avente il medesimo valore*) equal; (*identico*) identical, the same; **sono esattamente uguali** they're exactly the same; **di peso/valore uguale** of equal weight/value; **a uguale distanza da** equidistant from; **abbiamo stipendi uguali** our salaries are the same; **il tuo maglione è uguale al mio** your sweater is the same as mine; **due più due è uguale a quattro** two and two equals four; **per me è uguale** (*lo stesso*) it's all the same to me; **che venga oppure no, per me è uguale** it's all the same to me whether he comes or not; **decidi tu, per me è uguale** you decide, I don't mind 2 (*uniforme: superficie*) even, level; (: *andatura*) even; (: *voce*) steady ♦ AVV: **costano uguale** they cost the same; **siamo alti uguale** we are the same height; **sono bravi uguale** they're equally good ♦ SM, SF equal; **non ha uguali per ostinazione** when it comes to stubbornness there's no-one like him ♦ SM (*Mat*) equals sign

ugualmente [ugwal'mente] AVV **1** (*allo stesso modo*) equally; **sono ugualmente testardi** both of them are equally stubborn **2** (*lo stesso*) all the same, just the same; **ci siamo divertiti ugualmente** we enjoyed ourselves all the same; **lo farò ugualmente** I'm going to do it anyway

UI ABBR = **uso interno**

ulcera [ult'ʃera] SF ulcer; **avere l'ulcera** to have an ulcer

ulcerazione [ultʃerat'tsjone] SF ulceration

uliva *ecc* [u'liva] = **oliva**

ulteriore [ulte'rjore] AGG further

❏ **ulteriore** non si traduce mai con la parola inglese *ulterior*

ultimamente [ultima'mente] AVV lately, of late; **non hanno giocato bene ultimamente** they haven't been playing well lately

❏ **ultimamente** non si traduce mai con la parola inglese *ultimately*

ultimare [ulti'mare] /72/ VT to finish, complete

ultimatum [ulti'matum] SM INV ultimatum

ultimissime [ulti'missime] SFPL latest news *sg*; (*in corso di stampa*) stop press *sg*

ultimo, -a ['ultimo] AGG **1** (*di serie: gen*) last; (*: piano*) top; (*: fila*) back; (*: mano di vernice*) last, final; **l'ultimo scalino** (*in basso*) the bottom step; (*in alto*) the top step; **l'ultimo piano** the top floor; **abitare all'ultimo piano** to live on the top floor; **le ultime 20 pagine** the last 20 pages; **in ultima pagina** (*di giornale*) on the back page; **per ultimo** (*entrare, arrivare*) last; **arrivare per ultimo** to arrive last; **Marco è arrivato per ultimo alla festa** Marco arrived last at the party; **arrivare ultimo** to come last; **Chiara è arrivata ultima nella gara** Chiara came last in the competition **2** (*tempo: gen*) last; (*: più recente*) latest; (*: finale*) final; **negli ultimi tempi** recently; **gli ultimi giorni prima di partire** the last days before leaving; **l'ultima volta che l'ho visto** the last time I saw him; **quella è stata l'ultima volta che l'ho vista** that was the last time I saw her; **all'ultimo momento** at the last minute; **ha cambiato idea all'ultimo momento** he changed his mind at the last minute; **hai visto l'ultimo film di Spielberg?** have you seen Spielberg's latest film?; **il loro ultimo album è in testa alla classifica** their latest album is at the top of the charts; **ci vediamo poco, negli ultimi tempi** we haven't seen each other much recently; **l'ultimo anno** the final year; **fa l'ultimo anno dell'università** she is in her final year at university; **il termine ultimo** the deadline; **le ultime notizie** the latest news; **all'ultima moda** in the latest fashion; **...la vostra lettera del 7 aprile ultimo scorso ...** your letter of April 7th last **3** (*estremo: speranza, risorsa*) last, final; (*: più lontano*) farthest, utmost; **l'ultimo lembo di terra italiana** the farthest tip of Italy; **spendere fino all'ultimo centesimo** to spend every last penny; **dare un'ultima occhiata a qc** to have one last look at sth **4** (*per importanza*) last; **è l'ultimo film che vorrei andare a vedere** that's the last film I would want to go and see; **qual è l'ultimo prezzo (che mi può fare)?** what's the lowest you'll go? **5** (*Filosofia*) ultimate **6** (*fraseologia*): **in ultima analisi** in the final *o* last analysis; **in ultimo luogo** finally; **avere *o* dire l'ultima parola** to have the last word; **le ultime parole famose!** famous last words!; **esalare *o* rendere l'ultimo respiro** to breathe one's last ♦ SM, SF last (one); **questi sono gli ultimi** these are the last ones; **l'ultimo nato** the youngest (child); **l'ultimo ad entrare** the last (person) to come in; **gli ultimi arrivati** the last ones to arrive; **lei è stata l'ultima ad arrivare** she was the last one to arrive; **è l'ultima della classe** she's (at the) bottom of the class; **è l'ultima delle mie preoccupazioni** that's the least of my worries; **è l'ultimo degli ultimi** he's the lowest of the low; **quest'ultimo** (*tra due*) the latter; (*tra più di due*) this last, the last-mentioned ♦ SM: **l'ultimo del mese/dell'anno** the last day of the month/year; **l'ultimo dell'anno** New Year's Eve; **all'ultimo ho deciso di restare** in the end I decided to stay; **fino all'ultimo** to the last, till the end, until the end; **in ultimo, da ultimo** in the end, finally; **essere l'ultimo *o* agli ultimi** to be at death's

door ♦ SF (*notizia, barzelletta*): **hai sentito l'ultima?** have you heard the latest?; **questa è l'ultima (che mi combini)** that's the last time you'll play that trick on me

ultrà, ultra [ul'tra] SM INV, SF INV (*Pol*) extremist; (*Sport*): **gli ultrà della Juve** fanatical Juventus supporters

ultrasi'nistra SF (*Pol*) extreme left

ultrasuono [ultra'swɔno] SM ultrasound

ultravioletto, -a [ultravio'letto] AGG, SM ultraviolet

ululare [ulu'lare] /72/ VI (*aus* avere) to howl

ululato [ulu'lato] SM (*urlo*) howl; (*l'ululare*) howling *no pl*

umanamente [umana'mente] AVV (*con umanità*) humanely; (*nei limiti delle capacità umane*) humanly; **è umanamente impossibile** it's not humanly possible

umanesimo [uma'nezimo] SM humanism

umanità [umani'ta] SF (*gen*) humanity; **l'umanità** humanity, mankind

umanitario, -ria, -ri, -rie [umani'tarjo] AGG humanitarian; **aiuti umanitari** humanitarian aid *sg*

umanizzare [umanid'dzare] /72/ VT to humanize

umano, -a [u'mano] AGG (*gen*) human; (*comprensivo*) humane; **essere *o* mostrarsi umano (con qn)** to show humanity (towards sb), act humanely (towards sb); **errare è umano** to err is human; **un essere umano** a human being; **il corpo umano** the human body; **il genere umano** mankind; **è umano che si comporti così** it's quite normal to behave like that ♦ SM human

umbro, -a ['umbro] AGG, SM, SF Umbrian

umettare [umet'tare] /72/ VT (*labbra*) to moisten

umidiccio, -cia, -ci, -ce [umi'dittʃo] AGG (*terreno*) damp; (*mano*) moist, clammy

umidificare [umidifi'kare] /20/ VT to humidify

umidificatore [umidifika'tore] SM humidifier

umidità [umidi'ta] SF (*vedi agg*) dampness; moistness, clamminess; humidity; **proteggere qc dall'umidità** to protect sth from the damp; "**teme l'umidità**" (*su etichetta*) "to be kept dry"; **nella casa c'era molta umidità** the house was very damp

umido, -a ['umido] AGG (*gen*) damp; (*mano*) moist, clammy; (*clima: caldo*) humid; (*: freddo*) damp; **un clima caldo e umido** a hot, damp climate; **l'erba è un po' umida** the grass is a bit wet; **aveva gli occhi umidi di pianto** her eyes were moist with tears ♦ SM **1** (*umidità*) dampness, damp **2** (*Culin*): **carne in umido** stew

umile ['umile] AGG (*gen*) humble; **di umili origini** of humble origin(s); **i lavori più umili** the most menial tasks

umiliante [umi'ljante] AGG humiliating

umiliare [umi'ljare] /19/ VT (*gen*) to humiliate; **umiliare la carne** to mortify the flesh; **umiliarsi** VR: **umiliarsi (davanti a)** to humiliate *o* humble o.s. (before)

umiliazione [umiljat'tsjone] SF humiliation

umiltà [umil'ta] SF humility, humbleness; **con umiltà** humbly

umore [u'more] SM **1** (*indole*) temper, temperament; (*disposizione d'animo*) mood, humour (*Brit*), humor (*USA*); **una persona d'umore irascibile** an irascible *o* bad-tempered person; **di che umore è, oggi?** what mood is he in today?; **essere di buon umore** to be in a good mood; **essere di cattivo umore** to be in a bad mood; **di buon/cattivo umore** in a good/bad mood *o* humo(u)r **2** (*Bio*) humo(u)r

umorismo [umo'rizmo] SM humour (*Brit*), humor (*USA*); **senso dell'umorismo** sense of humo(u)r; **avere il senso dell'umorismo** to have a sense of humour; **ti sembra il momento di fare dell'umorismo?** this is no time to be funny!

umorista, -i, -e [umo'rista] SM, SF humorist

umoristico, -a, -ci, -che [umo'ristiko] AGG (*battuta, racconto*) humorous, funny; **un racconto più umoristico** a funnier story

un [un], **un'** [un], **una** ['una] *vedi* **uno**

unanime [u'nanime] AGG unanimous; **è stata una decisione unanime** it was a unanimous decision

unanimità [unanimi'ta] SF unanimity; **all'unanimità** unanimously

una tantum ['una 'tantum] AGG one-off *attr* ♦ SF INV (*imposta*) one-off tax

uncinato, -a [untʃi'nato] AGG (*amo*) barbed; (*ferro*) hooked; **croce uncinata** swastika

uncinetto [untʃiˈnetto] SM crochet hook; **lavorare all'uncinetto** to crochet; **lavoro all'uncinetto** crochet work

uncino [unˈtʃino] SM hook

undicenne [undiˈtʃɛnne] AGG, SM, SF eleven-year-old

undicesimo, -a [undiˈtʃɛzimo] AGG, SM, SF eleventh

undici [ˈunditʃi] AGG INV, SM INV eleven

UNESCO [uˈnɛsko] SIGLA F UNESCO (= *United Nations Educational, Scientific and Cultural Organization*)

ungere [ˈundʒere] VB IRREG /5/ VT (*macchina*) to oil, lubricate; (*teglia*) to grease; (*Rel*) to anoint; (*fig*) to flatter; **ungere le ruote a qn** (*fig: corrompere*) to grease sb's palm; **devo ungere la catena della bici** I need to oil the chain of my bike; **ungi bene la teglia** grease the tin well; **ungersi** VR: **ungersi con la crema** to put cream on; **ungersi** VIP (*macchiarsi*) to get covered in grease

ungherese [ungeˈrese] AGG, SM, SF Hungarian ♦ SM (*lingua*) Hungarian

Ungheria [ungeˈria] SF Hungary; **ti è piaciuta l'Ungheria?** did you like Hungary?; **andrò in Ungheria quest'estate** I'm going to Hungary this summer

unghia [ˈungja] SF 1 (*Anat*) nail; (*di animale*) claw; (*di rapace*) talon; (*di cavallo, bue*) hoof; **le unghie delle mani** the fingernails; **Marina si mangia le unghie** Marina bites her nails; **le unghie dei piedi** the toenails; **difendersi con le unghie e con i denti** to defend o.s. tooth and nail; **tirar fuori le unghie** (*anche fig*) to show one's claws; **pagare sull'unghia** to pay on the nail; **unghia incarnita** ingrown nail 2 (*di temperino*) groove 3 (*quantità*): **ce ne vuole un'unghia di più/di meno** a fraction more/less is needed

unghiata [unˈgjata] SF (*graffio*) scratch

unguento [unˈgwento] SM ointment

unicamente [unikaˈmente] AVV only

UNICEF [ˈunitʃɛf] SIGLA M UNICEF (= *United Nations International Children's Emergency Fund*)

unico, -a, -ci, -che [ˈuniko] AGG 1 (*solo*) only; (*esclusivo*) sole; **è la mia unica speranza** it's my only hope; **la mia unica speranza è che...** my one *o* only hope is that ...; **è stata l'unica volta che l'ho visto** it was the only time I saw him; **è figlio unico** he's an only child; **è l'unico esemplare in Italia** it's the only one of its kind in Italy; **due aspetti di un unico problema** two aspects of one and the same problem; **atto unico** (*Teatro*) one-act play; **agente unico** (*Comm*) sole agent; **binario unico** (*Ferr*) single track; **numero unico** (*di giornale*) special issue; **senso unico** (*Aut*) one way 2 (*eccezionale*) unique; **unico nel suo genere** unique of its kind; **unico al mondo** absolutely unique, the only one of its kind in the world; **sei unico!** you're priceless!; **è un tipo più unico che raro** he's one of a kind ♦ SM, SF the only one; **fu l'unica a capire** she was the only one who understood *o* to understand ♦ SF only thing to do; **l'unica è aspettare** the only thing to do is to wait, all we can do is wait

unicorno [uniˈkorno] SM unicorn

unificare [unifiˈkare] /20/ VT (*stato, leggi*) to unify, unite; (*standardizzare: prodotti*) to standardize

unificazione [unifikatˈtsjone] SF (*vedi vb*) unification; standardization; **dopo l'unificazione della Germania** after the unification of Germany

uniformare [uniforˈmare] /72/ VT (*terreno, superficie*) to level; **uniformare qc a** to adjust *o* relate sth to; **uniformarsi** VR: **uniformarsi a** to conform to

uniforme[1] [uniˈforme] AGG (*gen*) uniform; (*superficie*) even

uniforme[2] [uniˈforme] SF (*divisa*) uniform; **in uniforme** in uniform; **alta uniforme** dress uniform; **indossava l'uniforme della Marina** he was wearing naval uniform

uniformità [uniformiˈta] SF (*vedi agg*) uniformity; evenness

unilaterale [unilateˈrale] AGG (*Dir, Pol*) unilateral; (*fig*) one-sided

uninominale [uninomiˈnale] AGG (*Pol*): **collegio uninominale** single-member constituency

unione [uˈnjone] SF (*alleanza, matrimonio*) union; (*di colori*) combination, blending; (*di elementi*) cohesion; (*fig: concordia*) unity, harmony; **l'unione fa la forza** strength through unity; **l'Unione Europea** the European Union; **l'(ex) Unione Sovietica** the (former) Soviet Union; **unione sindacale** trade union (*Brit*), labor union (*USA*)

unire [uˈnire] /55/ VT 1 (*associare*) **unire (a)** to unite (with); **unire in matrimonio** to unite *o* join in matrimony; **il sentimento che li unisce** the feeling which binds them together *o* unites them 2 (*congiungere: città, linee*) to join, link, connect; (*mescolare: ingredienti*) to mix; **abbiamo deciso di unire i nostri sforzi** we decided to join forces; **se uniamo i due tavoli ci stiamo tutti** if we put the two tables together there'll be room for all of us 3 (*colori, suoni*) to combine; **unirsi** VR: **unirsi contro/a** to unite against/with; **unirsi in matrimonio** to be joined (together) in marriage; **unirsi** VIP: **unirsi a** to join; **unirsi a un gruppo** to join a group; **due ragazzi svizzeri si sono uniti a noi** two Swiss boys joined us

unisono [uˈnisono] **all'unisono** AVV (*Mus, anche fig*) in unison

unità [uniˈta] SF INV 1 (*unione*) unity; **un passo avanti verso l'unità europea** a step towards European unity 2 (*Mat, Comm: elemento*) unit; (*didattica*) unit; **unità di misura** unit of measurement; **unità monetaria** monetary unit 3 (*Mil*) unit; (*Naut*) (war)ship; (*Aer*) aeroplane 4 (*Inform*): **unità centrale (di elaborazione)** central processing unit; **unità disco** disk drive; **unità periferica** peripheral unit; **unità video** visual display unit

unitario, -ria, -ri, -rie [uniˈtarjo] AGG (*gen*) unitary; (*Pol, Rel*) unitarian; **prezzo** *o* **costo unitario** unit price, price per unit

unito, -a [uˈnito] AGG 1 (*gen*) united; (*amici, coppia*) close; (*famiglia*) close(-knit), united; **la mia è una famiglia molto unita** my family's very close 2 (*colore*) plain; **in tinta unita** plain, self-coloured (*Brit*), self-colored (*USA*); **una cravatta in tinta unita** a plain tie

universale [univerˈsale] AGG (*gen*) universal; (*plauso, consenso*) general; (*mente, genio*) wide-ranging; **il giudizio universale** (*Rel*) the Last Judgment; **suffragio universale** (*Pol*) universal suffrage; **erede universale** sole heir; **donatore universale** universal donor

universalità [universaliˈta] SF universality

universalmente [universalˈmente] AVV universally

università [universiˈta] SF INV university; **l'ho visto uscire dall'università** I saw him coming out of the university; **fa l'università** she's at university; **andrai all'università?** are you going to go to university?

universitario, -ria, -ri, -rie [universiˈtarjo] AGG (*gen*) university *attr*; (*studi*) university, academic; **uno studente universitario** a university student ♦ SM, SF (*studente*) university student; (*docente*) academic, university lecturer

universo [uniˈverso] SM universe

univoco, -a, -ci, -che [uˈnivoko] AGG unambiguous

PAROLA CHIAVE

uno, -a [ˈuno] (*davanti a sm* un *+ consonante, vocale,* uno *+ s impura, gn, pn, ps, x, z; davanti a sf* un' *+ vocale,* una *+ consonante* AGG one; **non ha una lira** he hasn't a penny, he's penniless; **ho comprato una mela e due pere** I bought one apple and two pears; **ho passato un mese in Italia** I spent one month in Italy; **una camera solo per una notte** a room for one night only

♦ ART INDET

1 a, an (*+ vocale*); **era una giornata splendida** it was a beautiful day; **un mio amico** a friend of mine; **è un artista** he's an artist; **un programma interessante** an interesting programme; **un giorno gli ho telefonato** one day I called him; **uno gnomo** a gnome; **dammene un po'** give me some; **è uno sciocco** he's a fool; **ho visto un uomo** I saw a man; **uno zingaro** a gypsy

2 (*intensivo*): **una noia!** such a bore!; **ho una paura!** I'm terrified!; **ma questo è un porcile!** it's an absolute pigsty in here!

3 (*circa*): **disterà un 10 km** it's round about 10 km away; **costerà un 300 euro** it'll cost round about 300 euros

♦ PRON

1 one; **me ne dai uno?** will you give me one (of them)?; **ne ho comprato uno stamattina** I bought one this morning; **ce n'è uno a testa** there's one each; **a uno a uno** one by one; **è uno dei più veloci** it's one of the fastest; **uno dei tanti** one of the many; **uno di noi** one of us; **facciamo metà per uno** let's go halves

2 (*un tale*) somebody, someone; **ho incontrato uno che ti conosce** I met someone who knows you; **c'era una al telefono**

there was a woman on the phone; **è una del mio paese** she's from the same village as I am

3 (*in costruzione impersonale*) one, you; **se uno vuole** if one wants, if you want; **se uno ha i soldi** if one has the money

4 (*con articolo determinativo*): **l'uno** one; **non confondere gli uni con gli altri** don't confuse one lot with the other; **abbiamo visto l'uno e l'altro** we've seen both of them; **sono entrati l'uno dopo l'altro** they came in one after the other; **si amano l'un l'altro** they love each other; **o l'uno o l'altro** either of them; **o l'uno o l'altro per me va bene** either of them will be fine; **né l'uno né l'altro** neither of them; **quale prendi? - Né l'uno né l'altro** which one are you going to take? - Neither of them; **non prendo né l'uno né l'altro** I'm not going to take either of them

5 ne ha detta una! you should have heard what he said!; **ne hai combinata una delle tue!** you've done it again, haven't you!; **ne vuoi sentire una?** do you want to hear a good one?; **non me ne va mai bene una** nothing ever goes right for me ♦ SM one; **uno più uno fa due** one plus one equals two ♦ SF (*ora*) one o'clock; **che ore sono? — è l'una** what time is it? — it's one (o'clock)

unsi *ecc* ['unsi] VB *vedi* **ungere**

unto, -a ['unto] PP *di* **ungere** ♦ AGG greasy, oily; **unto e bisunto** filthy dirty ♦ SM grease

untuoso, -a [untu'oso] AGG (*pelle*) greasy, oily; (*cibo*) oily; (*fig: persona*) unctuous, smooth

unzione [un'tsjone] SF: **l'Estrema Unzione** (*Rel*) Extreme Unction

uomo ['wɔmo] (*pl* **uomini**) SM (*gen*) man; (*specie umana*): **l'uomo** mankind, humanity; **da** *o* **per uomo** (*abito, scarpe*) men's, for men; **scarpe da uomo** men's shoes; **parlare da uomo a uomo** to have a man-to-man talk, talk man to man; **a memoria d'uomo** since the world began; **a passo d'uomo** at walking pace; **è un uomo finito** he's finished; **l'uomo della strada** the man in the street; **uomo avvisato mezzo salvato** (*Proverbio*) forewarned is forearmed; **un uomo di mezz'età** a middle-aged man; **c'erano due uomini nell'ufficio** there were two men in the office ♦ **uomo d'affari** businessman; **uomo d'azione** man of action; **uomo delle caverne** caveman; **uomini dell'equipaggio** the crew; **una nave con 30 uomini d'equipaggio** a ship with a crew of 30 men; **uomo di fatica** workhand; **uomo di fiducia** right-hand man; **uomo del gas** gasman; **uomo di mondo** man of the world; **uomo di paglia** stooge, figurehead; **uomo rana** frogman

uopo ['wɔpo] SM: **all'uopo** if necessary, in case of need; **è d'uopo far così** it is necessary to do this

uovo ['wɔvo] SM (*pl f* **uova**) **1** egg; **uovo fresco** new-laid *o* fresh egg; **uova strapazzate** scrambled eggs; **uovo affogato** *o* **in camicia** poached egg; **uovo bazzotto** soft-boiled egg; **uovo in cocotte** baked egg; **uovo alla coque** (soft-)boiled egg; **uovo all'ostrica** prairie oyster; **uovo di Pasqua** Easter egg; **uovo sodo** hard-boiled egg; **uovo al tegame** *o* **all'occhio di bue** *o* **fritto** fried egg **2** (*fraseologia*): **è l'uovo di Colombo!** it's as plain as the nose on your face!; **essere pieno come un uovo** to be full (up); **cercare il pelo nell'uovo** to split hairs; **rompere le uova nel paniere a qn** to upset sb's plans; **meglio un uovo oggi che una gallina domani** (*Proverbio*) a bird in the hand is worth two in the bush

uragano [ura'gano] SM hurricane; (*fig: di applausi, proteste*) storm

Urali [u'rali] SMPL: **gli Urali** the Urals; **i monti Urali** the Ural Mountains

uranio [u'ranjo] SM uranium; **uranio impoverito** depleted uranium

urbanista, -i, -e [urba'nista] SM, SF town planner

urbanistica [urba'nistika] SF town planning

urbanità [urbani'ta] SF urbanity

urbano, -a [ur'bano] AGG **1** (*gen, sviluppo ecc*) urban, city *attr*, town *attr*; (*telefonata*) local **2** (*cortese: modi, risposta*) urbane

urgente [ur'dʒɛnte] AGG urgent; **ha detto che era urgente** he said it was urgent

urgenza [ur'dʒɛntsa] SF (*di decisione, situazione*) urgency; **non c'è urgenza** there's no hurry; **fare qc d'urgenza** to do sth as a matter of urgency; **trasportare qn d'urgenza**

all'ospedale to rush sb to (the) hospital; **essere ricoverato d'urgenza** to be rushed into (the) hospital; **il direttore l'ha convocato d'urgenza** the director requested to see him urgently *o* immediately; **questo lavoro va fatto con urgenza** this work is urgent; **questo lavoro va fatto con molta urgenza** this work is very urgent; **chiamata/provvedimento d'urgenza** emergency call/measure; **diritto d'urgenza** (*Amm*) surtax paid for faster handling

urgere ['urdʒere] /5/ VI *vb dif*: **urge aiuto** help is needed urgently; **urge provvedere** something needs to be done urgently

urina [u'rina] SF urine

urlare [ur'lare] /72/ VI (*aus avere*) (*persona*) to scream, yell; (*animale, vento*) to howl; **non urlare, ti sento benissimo** there's no need to shout, I can hear you perfectly well; **ho dovuto urlare per farmi sentire** I had to shout to make myself heard; **urlare di dolore** to scream with pain ♦ VT: **urlare qc (a qn)** to scream *o* yell sth (at sb); **urlare a qn di fare qc** to scream at sb to do sth; **gliene ho urlate dietro di tutti i colori** I hurled abuse at him

urlo ['urlo] SM (*pl m* **urli**, *pl f* **urla**) (*di persona*) scream, yell; **urla di terrore** screams of terror; (*di animale, vento*) howl; (*di sirena*) wail; **lanciare un urlo (di)** to scream (with)

urna ['urna] SF **1** (*vaso*) urn **2** (*Pol*) : **urna (elettorale)** ballot box; **andare alle urne** to vote, go to the polls

urrà [ur'ra] ESCL hurrah!

URSS [urs] SIGLA F (= *Unione delle Repubbliche Socialiste Sovietiche*): **l'(ex) URSS** the (former) USSR

urtare [ur'tare] /72/ VT **1** (*persona, ostacolo*) to bump into, knock against; (*gomito, testa*) to knock, bump; **l'ha urtata e l'ha fatta cadere** he bumped into her and knocked her down **2** (*irritare*) to annoy, irritate; **urtare i nervi a qn** to get on sb's nerves ♦ VI (*aus avere*) **urtare contro** (*auto, barca*) to bump into; (*persona*) to bump into, knock against; **urtarsi** VR (*uso reciproco: scontrarsi*) to collide; (: *fig*) to clash; **urtarsi** VIP (*irritarsi*) to get annoyed, get irritated

❏ **urtare** non si traduce mai con la parola inglese *hurt*

urto ['urto] SM (*collisione*) crash, collision; (*colpo*) knock, bump; (*fig: contrasto*) clash; (*Mil*) attack; **nell'urto si è rotto il vetro** the impact of the crash broke the glass; **essere in urto con qn per qc** (*fig*) to clash with sb over sth; **terapia d'urto** (*Med*) massive-dose treatment; **dose d'urto** (*Med*) massive dose; **contingente d'urto** (*Mil*) shock troops *pl*

uruguaiano, -a [urugwa'jano] AGG, SM, SF Uruguayan

Uruguay [uru'gwai] SM Uruguay

u.s. ABBR = **ultimo scorso**

USA, U.S.A. ['uza] SIGLA MPL: **gli USA** the USA

usanza [u'zantsa] SF (*costume*) custom; **è l'usanza** it's the custom; **è un'usanza del posto** it's a local custom, it's what's done; **secondo l'usanza** according to custom, as is customary

usare [u'zare] /72/ VT **1** (*adoperare*) to use; **posso usare la tua macchina?** may I use your car?; **me lo fai usare?** will you let me use it?; **non mi lascia usare il suo computer** he doesn't let me use his computer; **come si usa questo coso?** how do you use this thing?; **sai usare** *o* **come si usa la lavatrice?** do you know how to use the washing machine?; **non usare tutta l'acqua** (*consumare*) don't use (up) all the water; **cerca di usare il cervello!** try to use your head!; **usa gli occhi/le orecchie!** use your eyes/ears!; **usare la forza** to use force; **usare violenza a qn** (*violentare*) to rape sb; **usare le mani** (*picchiare*) to use one's fists; **usare la massima cura nel fare qc** to exercise great care when doing sth; **dovresti usare un po' di comprensione** you should show a little understanding; **potresti usarmi la cortesia di spegnere la radio?** would you be so kind as to switch off the radio? **2** (*aver l'abitudine*): **usare fare qc** to be in the habit of doing sth, be accustomed to doing sth; **a casa nostra si usa fare così** this is how we do things at home ♦ VI (*aus avere*) **1** (*essere di moda*) to be fashionable, be in fashion; **si usano di nuovo i tacchi alti** high heels are fashionable again *o* are back in fashion; **quest'anno si usano le gonne lunghe** this year long skirts are in fashion **2** **usare di** (*servirsi di*) to use (*diritto*) to exercise ♦ VB IMPERS to be customary; **da queste**

parti usa così it's the custom round here, this is customary round here

usato, -a [uˈzato] AGG **1** (*logoro*) worn (out) **2** (*di seconda mano*) used, second-hand; **ha comprato una macchina usata** he bought a second-hand car ♦ SM (*gen*) second-hand goods *pl*; **il mercato dell'usato** the second-hand market

uscente [uʃˈʃɛnte] AGG (*Amm*) outgoing

usciere [uʃˈʃɛre] SM usher

uscio, -sci [ˈuʃʃo] SM door; **sull'uscio** on the doorstep

uscire [uʃˈʃire] /125/ VI IRREG (*aus* **essere**) **1** (*persona: andare fuori*) to go out, leave; (: *venire fuori*) to come out, leave; (: *a piedi*) to walk out; (: *a spasso, la sera*) to go out; **uscire in automobile** to go out in the car, go for a drive; **ieri sono uscita con degli amici** I went out with friends yesterday; **è uscito senza dire una parola** he went out without saying a word; **uscire a prendere il giornale** to go for the paper; **è uscita a comprare il giornale** she's gone for the paper; **lasciatemi** *o* **fatemi uscire!** let me out!; **uscite! get out!; uscire da** (*posto*) to go (*o* come) out of, leave (*carcere*) to get out of; **uscire da** *o* **di casa** to go out; **uscirà dall'ospedale domani** he's coming out of (the) hospital tomorrow **2** (*oggetto: gen*) to come out; **la merce che esce dal paese dev'essere dichiarata** goods leaving *o* going out of the country must be declared **3** (*giornale, libro*) to come out; (*CD, film*) to be released; (*numero alla lotteria*) to come up; **la rivista esce di lunedì** the magazine comes out on Mondays; **è appena uscito il loro ultimo album** their latest album has just come out **4** (*andar fuori, sconfinare*): **uscire dagli argini** (*fiume*) to overflow its banks; **uscire dai binari** (*treno*) to leave the rails; **uscire di strada** (*auto*) to go off *o* leave the road; **la macchina è uscita di strada** the car left the road; **l'acqua sta uscendo dalla vasca** the bath is overflowing; **uscire dall'ordinario** to be out of the ordinary **5** (*passare da una condizione a un'altra*): **uscire dall'adolescenza** to leave adolescence behind; **uscire da una brutta malattia** to recover from *o* get over a bad illness; **è uscito bene da quella storia** he came out of that business well; **è uscito illeso dall'incidente** he emerged from the accident unscathed **6** (*fraseologia*): **chissà cosa uscirà da tutta questa storia?** who knows what will come of all this?; **se ne uscì con una delle sue** he came out with one of his typical remarks; **uscire dai gangheri** to fly off the handle; **uscire di senno** *o* **di sé** to fly into a rage; **mi è uscito di mente** it slipped my mind; **uscire da un programma** (*Inform*) to quit a program

uscita [uʃˈʃita] SF **1** (*azione: di persona*) leaving, exit; **è l'ora dell'uscita degli scolari** school's over for the day, the children are coming out of school; **mia zia ha incontrato Claudia all'uscita di scuola** my aunt met Claudia as she was coming out of school; **un'uscita veloce** a quick exit; **sono in libera uscita** (*Mil*) I'm off duty **2** (*porta, passaggio*) exit, way out; (*Aer*) gate; **dov'è l'uscita?** where's the exit?; **"vietata l'uscita"** "no exit"; **uscita di sicurezza** emergency exit **3** (*passeggiata*) outing; (*Mil*) foray; **è la sua prima uscita dopo la malattia** it's his first day out since his illness **4** (*fig: battuta*) witty remark; **ha di quelle uscite** he comes out with some odd remarks **5** (*Comm*) outlay; **entrate ed uscite** income and expenditure *sg* **6** (*Elettr*) output

user'name [juzerˈneim] SM INV username

usignolo [uziɲˈɲɔlo] SM nightingale

uso [ˈuzo] SM **1** (*gen*) use; (*di parola*) usage; (*Dir*) exercise; **a uso di** for (the use of); **l'uso corretto di quell'espressione** the correct usage of that expression; **testo a uso delle elementari** book for use in primary (*Brit*) *o* elementary (*USA*) schools; **per uso esterno** (*Med*) for external use only; **per uso personale** for personal use; **fare buon/cattivo uso di qc** to make good/bad use of sth; **istruzioni per l'uso**

instructions; **fuori uso** out of use; **fare uso di qc** to use sth; **perdere l'uso della ragione** to go out of one's mind **2** (*esercizio*) practice; **con l'uso** with practice **3** (*abitudine*) usage, custom; **d'uso** (*corrente*) in use; **essere in uso** to be in common *o* current use; **gli usi e i costumi degli antichi romani** the customs of the ancient Romans

ustionare [ustjoˈnare] /72/ VT to burn; **ustionarsi** VR to burn o.s.

ustione [usˈtjone] SF burn; **ustioni di terzo grado** third-degree burns; **aveva ustioni di terzo grado** he had third-degree burns

usuale [uzuˈale] AGG (*frase*) everyday *attr*; (*oggetto*) everyday, ordinary, common

usufruire [uzufruˈire] /55/ VI (*aus* avere) **usufruire di** (*valersi di*) to take advantage of, make use of

usufrutto [uzuˈfrutto] SM (*Dir*) usufruct

usura¹ [uˈzura] SF usury; **prestare a usura** to lend at exorbitant interest

usura² [uˈzura] SF (*logoramento*) wear (and tear); **usura dei freni** wear on the brakes

usuraio, -aia, -ai, -aie [uzuˈrajo] SM, SF usurer

usurpare [uzurˈpare] /72/ (*trono, potere*) to usurp

usurpatore, -trice [uzurpaˈtore] SM, SF usurper

utensile [utenˈsile] AGG: **macchina utensile** machine tool ♦ SM tool, implement; **utensili da cucina** kitchen utensils

utensileria [utensileˈria] SF **1** (*utensili*) tools *pl* **2** (*reparto*) tool room

utente [uˈtente] SM, SF (*gen*) user; (*di gas*) consumer; (*del telefono*) subscriber; **utente finale** end user; **utente della strada** road user

utero [ˈutero] SM uterus, womb; **utero in affitto** host womb

utile [ˈutile] AGG (*gen*) useful; (*consiglio, persona*) helpful; **mi è stato molto utile** (*oggetto*) it came in very handy, it was very useful; **grazie per la guida, mi è stata molto utile** thanks for the guide book, it was very useful; **questo ti sarà utile** this will be of use to you; **posso esserle utile?** can I help you?, can I be of help?; **posso esserti utile?** can I do anything for you?; **in tempo utile per** in time for; **rendersi utile** to make o.s. useful; **posso rendermi utile?** can I make myself useful? ♦ SM **1 badare solo all'utile** to think only of what is useful; **unire l'utile al dilettevole** to combine business with pleasure **2** (*vantaggio*) advantage, benefit; (*Econ*) profit; **partecipare agli utili** to share in the profits; **non ha saputo trarne alcun utile** (*fig*) he couldn't get anything out of it

utilità [utiliˈta] SF usefulness; (*vantaggio*) benefit; **senza utilità pratica** without practical application, of no real use; **essere di grande utilità** to be very very useful

utilitario, -ria, -ri, -rie [utiliˈtarjo] AGG utilitarian

utilizzare [utilidˈdzare] /72/ VT to use, make use of, utilize; **l'ho fatto utilizzando ritagli di stoffa** I made it using scraps of material

utilizzazione [utiliddzatˈtsjone] SF use, utilization

utilizzo [utiˈliddzo] SM (*Amm*) utilization; (*Banca: di credito*) availment

utilmente [utilˈmente] AVV usefully, profitably

utopia [utoˈpia] SF utopia; **è pura utopia** that's sheer utopianism

utopistico, -a, -ci, -che [utoˈpistiko] AGG utopian

UVA [uviˈa] SIGLA MPL (= *ultravioletto prossimo*): **gli UVA** UVA ♦ AGG INV (*raggi*) UVA

uva [ˈuva] SF grapes *pl*; **un grappolo d'uva** a bunch of grapes; **uva passa** raisins *pl*; **uva spina** gooseberry; **uva sultanina** sultanas *pl*

UVB [uviˈbi] SIGLA MPL (= *ultravioletto lontano*): **gli UVB** UVB ♦ AGG INV (*raggi*) UVB

Vv

V¹, v¹ [vu, vi] SF INV, SM INV (*lettera*) V, v; **V come Venezia** ≈ V for Victor

V² ABBR (= *volt*) V

v. ABBR **1** (= *vedi*) v. (= *vide: see*) **2** (= *verso*) v. (= *verse*)

VA SIGLA = Varese

va, va' [va] VB *vedi* andare

vacante [va'kante] AGG vacant

vacanza [va'kantsa] SF **1** (*riposo, ferie*) holiday(s pl) (*Brit*), vacation (*USA*); (*giorno di permesso*) day off; **essere/andare in vacanza** to be/go on holiday *o* vacation; **dove andrai in vacanza quest'anno?** where are you going on holiday this year?; **prendersi una vacanza** to take a holiday *o* vacation; **un giorno/mese di vacanza** a day's/month's holiday *o* vacation; **far vacanza** to have a holiday *o* vacation; **ho fatto una lunga vacanza** I had a long holiday; **trascorriamo sempre le vacanze al mare** we always spend our holidays at the seaside; **vacanze** SFPL (*periodo di ferie*) holidays, vacation *sg*; **le vacanze di Pasqua** the Easter holidays; **le vacanze scolastiche** the school holidays; **vacanze estive** summer holiday(s) *o* vacation **2** (*l'essere vacante: di lavoro, cattedra ecc*) vacancy

vacca, -che ['vakka] SF **1** (*mucca*) cow; **tempo delle vacche grasse/magre** fat/lean years **2** (*pegg: sgualdrina*) slut

vaccinare [vattʃi'nare] /72/ VT (*Med*): **vaccinare qn contro qc** to vaccinate sb against sth; **farsi vaccinare** to have a vaccination, get vaccinated; **si è fatto vaccinare contro l'influenza** he got vaccinated against the flu

vaccinazione [vattʃinat'tsjone] SF vaccination

vaccino, -a [vat'tʃino] AGG: **latte vaccino** cow's milk ♦ SM vaccine; **fare un vaccino** to have a vaccination; **fare un vaccino a qn** to vaccinate sb

vacillante [vatʃil'lante] AGG (*edificio, vecchio*) shaky, unsteady; (*salute, memoria*) shaky, failing; (*fiamma*) flickering; **camminava con passo vacillante** he was walking shakily *o* unsteadily

vacillare [vatʃil'lare] /72/ VI (*aus avere*) **1** (*edificio, muro, ubriaco*) to sway (to and fro); **camminare vacillando** (*vecchio*) to totter along; (*ubriaco, persona stanca*) to stagger along; **il pugno lo fece vacillare** the punch made him reel **2** (*salute, memoria*) to be shaky, be failing; (*fiamma*) to flicker; (*trono, governo*) to be unstable; (*fede*) to waver, be shaky; (*coraggio*) to falter, waver, be failing

vacuo, -a ['vakuo] AGG vacuous, empty

vado ecc ['vado] VB *vedi* andare

vagabondaggio, -gi [vagabon'daddʒo] SM wandering, roaming; (*Dir*) vagrancy

vagabondare [vagabon'dare] /72/ VI (*aus avere*) to roam, wander; **vagabondare per le strade** to roam *o* wander (about) the streets

vagabondo, -a [vaga'bondo] AGG (*gente, vita*) wandering *attr*; (*fig: fannullone*) idle ♦ SM, SF (*gen*) vagrant, tramp, vagabond; (*fig: fannullone*) layabout, loafer, idler

vagare [va'gare] /80/ VI (*aus avere*) **vagare per** (*persona*) to wander around, roam around; (*animale*) to roam; **vagava senza meta per la città** he was wandering aimlessly around the town; **vagare con la mente** to let one's mind wander; **vagare con la fantasia** to give free rein to one's imagination, let one's imagination run away with one

vagheggiare [vaged'dʒare] /62/ VT (*letter: desiderare*) to long for, yearn for

vagherò ecc [vage'rɔ] VB *vedi* vagare

vaghezza [va'gettsa] SF vagueness

vagina [va'dʒina] SF vagina

vagire [va'dʒire] /55/ VI (*aus avere*) (*neonato*) to cry, wail

vagito [va'dʒito] SM (*di neonato*) crying, wailing

vaglia ['vaʎʎa] SM INV (*Comm*) money order; **vaglia bancario** bank draft; **vaglia cambiario** promissory note; **vaglia postale** postal order

vagliare [vaʎ'ʎare] /27/ VT (*sabbia*) to riddle, sift; (*grano*) to sift; (*fig: proposta, problema*) to weigh up

vaglio, -gli ['vaʎʎo] SM sieve; **passare al vaglio** (*fig*) to examine closely

vago, -a, -ghi, -ghe ['vago] AGG (*gen*) vague ♦ SM **1** vagueness; **tenersi nel vago** to keep it all rather vague, stick to generalities **2** (*Anat*) vagus (nerve)

vagone [va'gone] SM (*Ferr: per merci*) truck (*Brit*), wagon (*Brit*), freight car (*USA*); (: *per passeggeri*) carriage (*Brit*), car (*USA*); **vagone letto** sleeping car, sleeper; **vagone ristorante** restaurant *o* dining car

vai ecc ['vai] VB *vedi* andare

vaiolo [va'jɔlo] SM smallpox

val. ABBR = valuta

valanga, -ghe [va'langa] SF avalanche; (*fig: grande quantità: di lettere, regali*) flood; **arrivare/riversarsi a valanghe** (*fig: turisti*) to flood in/pour out

valente [va'lente] AGG able, talented

valenza [va'lentsa] SF (*fig: significato*) content; (*Chim*) valency (*Brit*), valence (*USA*)

valere [va'lere] VB IRREG /126/ VI (*aus essere*) **1** (*persona: contare*) to be worth; **come medico non vale molto** he's not much of a doctor; **vale tanto oro quanto pesa** she's worth her weight in gold; **far valere le proprie ragioni** to make o.s. heard; **far valere la propria autorità** to assert one's authority; **farsi valere** to make o.s. appreciated *o* respected **2** (*avere efficacia: documento*) to be valid; (*avere vigore*) to hold, apply; **questo vale anche per te** this applies to you, too **3** (*essere regolamentare: partita*) to be valid, count; **così non vale!** that's not fair! **4** (*giovare*) to be of use; **i suoi sforzi non sono valsi a niente** his efforts came to nought; **i tuoi consigli sono valsi a fargli cambiare idea** your advice convinced him to change his mind; **prima o poi lo verrà a sapere, tanto vale dirglielo subito** he'll find out sooner or later, so we (*o* you *ecc*) might as well tell him now; **tanto vale che te lo dica** I might as well tell you **5** (*equivalere*) to be equal to; (*essere comparabile a*) to be worth; (*significare*) to amount to; **l'uno vale l'altro** the one is as good as the other, they amount to the same thing; **valere la pena** to be worth the effort *o* worth it; **non ne vale la pena** it's not worth it; **non vale la pena arrabbiarsi tanto** it's not worth getting so angry; **vale a dire** that is to say **6** (*cosa: avere pregio*) to be worth; **l'auto vale tremila euro** the car is worth three thousand euros; **non valere niente** to be worthless; **non vale niente** it's worthless ♦ VT (*procurare*): **gli ha valso il primo premio** it earned him first prize; **ciò gli ha valso un esaurimento** that was what brought on *o* caused his nervous breakdown; **valersi** VIP: **valersi di** to take advantage of; **valersi dei consigli di qn** to take *o* act upon sb's advice

valeriana [vale'rjana] SF (*Bot, Med*) valerian

valevole [va'levole] AGG valid

valgo ['valgo] VB *vedi* valere

valicare [vali'kare] /20/ VT (*catena montuosa*) to cross

valico, -chi ['valiko] SM pass; **valico di frontiera** border crossing

validità [validi'ta] SF validity; **ha una validità di tre mesi** it is valid for three months

valido, -a ['valido] AGG **1** (*gen*) valid; **il suo passaporto non è più valido** your passport is no longer valid; **l'incontro non è valido per la finale** the match doesn't count for the final; **non è valido!** (*in giochi*) that doesn't count! **2** (*efficace: resistenza, rimedio*) effective; (: *aiuto*) real; (: *contributo*) substantial; (: *scusa, argomento*) valid; **essere di valido aiuto a qn** to be a great help to sb **3** (*persona: bravo*) worthy; (: *vigoroso*) healthy, strong; **uno dei registi più validi degli ultimi anni** one of the best directors of recent years

valigeria [validʒe'ria] SF (*assortimento*) leather goods pl; (*negozio*) leather goods shop; (*fabbrica*) leather goods factory

valigetta [validʒetta] SF: **valigetta ventiquattrore** overnight case, attaché case

valigia, -gie *o*, **-ge** [va'lidʒa] SF (suit)case; **fare le valigie** to pack (one's bags); (*fig*) to pack (up); **disfare le valigie** to unpack (one's bags); **valigia diplomatica** (*Pol*) diplomatic bag

vallata [val'lata] SF valley

valle ['valle] SF 1 valley; **a valle** (*di fiume*) downstream; **scendere a valle** to go downhill 2 **valli** SFPL (*tipo di laguna*) marshes

valletto [val'letto] SM 1 (*domestico*) valet 2 (*TV*) assistant

valligiano, -a [valli'dʒano] SM, SF inhabitant of a valley

valore [va'lore] SM 1 (*pregio: di merce*) value, worth; (*Fin: di moneta, titolo*) value, price; **il valore della merce** the value of the goods; **il valore di un anello** the value of a ring; **crescere/diminuire di valore** to go up/down in value, gain/lose in value; **è di gran valore** it's worth a lot, it's very valuable; **è un anello di gran valore** it's a very valuable ring; **senza valore** worthless 2 **valori** SMPL (*titoli*) securities; (*oggetti preziosi*) valuables; **Borsa Valori** Stock Exchange 3 (*di persona*) worth, merit; (*di opera*) merit, value; (*di vita, amicizia*) value; **artista di valore** artist of considerable merit; **valori morali/estetici** moral/aesthetic values; **scala dei valori** scale of values; **per te l'amicizia non ha alcun valore** friendship means nothing to you 4 (*significato*) meaning; (*funzione*) value; **le sue parole hanno** (il) **valore di una promessa** what he said amounts to *o* is tantamount to a promise; **il valore di un vocabolo** the exact meaning of a word; **qui il participio ha valore di aggettivo** the participle acts as *o* is used as an adjective here 5 (*coraggio*) courage, valour (*Brit*), valor (*USA*); **difendersi/combattere con gran valore** to defend o.s./fight with great courage; **medaglia al valor militare** medal for gallantry; **atti di valore** acts of bravery *o* gallantry 6 (*Dir: validità*): **questo documento non ha valore legale** this document has no legal validity; **valore aggiunto** (*lett, fig*) added value; **valore contabile** book value; **valore effettivo** real value; **valore facciale** nominal value; **valore di mercato** market value; **valore nominale** nominal value; **valore di realizzo** break-up value; **valore di riscatto** surrender value; **valori bollati** (revenue) stamps; **valori mobiliari** transferable securities

valorizzare [valorid'dzare] /72/ VT 1 (*prodotto*) to enhance the value of 2 (*mettere in risalto*) to set off, make the most of

valoroso, -a [valo'roso] AGG courageous, valorous

valso, -a ['valso] PP *di* valere

valuta [va'luta] SF 1 (*Fin: moneta*) currency, money; **valuta estera** foreign currency 2 (*Banca*): **con valuta 15 gennaio** interest to run from January 15th

valutare [valu'tare] /72/ VT 1 (*Econ: stimare: casa, gioiello*) to value; (: *danni, costo*) to assess, evaluate; (: *approssimativamente*) to estimate; (: *fig: capacità*) to appreciate; **la casa è stata valutata centomila euro** the house has been valued at a hundred thousand euros; **i danni sono valutati attorno a cinquecentomila euro** the damage has been assessed at about five hundred thousand euro 2 (*vagliare*) to weigh (up); **valutare i pro e i contro** to weigh up the pros and cons; **bisogna valutare i pro e i contro** we need to weigh up the pros and cons

valutario, -ria, -ri, -rie [valu'tarjo] AGG (*Fin: norme*) currency *attr*

valutazione [valutat'tsjone] SF (*vedi vb a*) valuation; assessment, evaluation; estimate; **stando alle prime valutazioni,...** going by initial estimates, ...; **valutazione di impatto ambientale** environmental impact assessment; **valutazione di rischio** risk assessment

valva ['valva] SF (*Zool, Bot*) valve

valvola ['valvola] SF (*gen, anche Anat*) valve; (*Elettr: fusibile*) fuse; **valvola a farfalla** (*Aut*) throttle; **valvola di sicurezza** (*anche fig*) safety valve; **valvola in testa** (*Aut*) overhead valve

valzer ['valtser] SM INV waltz; **sai ballare il valzer?** can you do the waltz?

vampata [vam'pata] SF (*fiammata*) blaze; (*di calore*) blast; (*fig: al viso*) flush

vampiro [vam'piro] SM (*gen*) vampire; (*Zool*) vampire bat

vanagloria [vana'glɔrja] SF boastfulness

vandalico, -a, -ci, -che [van'daliko] AGG vandal *attr*; **atto vandalico** act of vandalism

vandalismo [vanda'lizmo] SM vandalism; **un atto di vandalismo** an act of vandalism

vandalo, -a ['vandalo] SM, SF vandal

vaneggiamento [vanedddʒa'mento] SM raving, delirium

vaneggiare [vaned'dʒare] /62/ VI (*aus avere*) to rave, be delirious; **ma tu vaneggi!** you must be mad!

vanesio, -sia, -si, -sie [va'nezjo] AGG vain, conceited

vanga, -ghe ['vanga] SF spade

vangare [van'gare] /80/ VT to dig

vangelo [van'dʒelo] SM (*Rel, anche fig*) gospel; **per me è vangelo** (*fig*) it's gospel as far as I'm concerned

vanificare [vanifi'kare] /20/ VT to nullify

vaniglia [va'niʎʎa] SF vanilla; **un gelato alla vaniglia** a vanilla ice cream

vanigliato, -a [vaniʎ'ʎato] AGG: **zucchero vanigliato** (*Culin*) vanilla sugar

vanità [vani'ta] SF 1 (*vanagloria*) vanity, pride, conceit; **l'ha fatto per vanità** he did it out of vanity 2 (*futilità: di promessa*) emptiness, vanity; (: *di sforzo*) futility, fruitlessness

vanitoso, -a [vani'toso] AGG vain, conceited ♦ SM, SF vain person

vanno ['vanno] VB *vedi* andare

vano, -a ['vano] AGG 1 (*illusione, promessa*) vain, empty; (*fatiche*) vain, futile, fruitless; (*proteste, minacce*) idle; **vane speranze** vain hopes; **riuscire vano** to come to nothing; **tutti i nostri sforzi sono stati vani** all our efforts were useless 2 (*vanitoso*) vain, conceited ♦ SM 1 (*spazio vuoto*) space; **il vano della porta** the doorway; **vano portabagagli** (*Aut*) boot (*Brit*), trunk (*USA*); **vano portaoggetti** (*Aut*) glove compartment 2 (*stanza*) room; **un appartamento di quattro vani** a four-roomed flat (*Brit*) *o* apartment (*USA*)

vantaggio, -gi [van'taddʒo] SM 1 (*gen*) advantage; **avere il vantaggio** (**di**) to have the advantage (of); **i vantaggi e gli svantaggi di vivere in città** the advantages and disadvantages of living in a city 2 (*profitto*) benefit, advantage; **tornerà a tuo vantaggio** it will be to your advantage; **sei in una posizione di vantaggio** you're at an advantage; **trarre vantaggio da qc** to benefit from sth; **non trarre alcun vantaggio da qc** to get nothing out of sth 3 (*distacco*) start; (*Sport*) lead; (*Tennis*) advantage; **hanno un vantaggio di 3 ore su di noi** they have a 3-hour start on us; (*Sport*) they have a 3-hour lead over us; **essere/portarsi in vantaggio** (*Sport*) to be in/take the lead; **siamo in vantaggio** we're in the lead; **sono in vantaggio di due punti sugli avversari** they have a two-point lead over their opponents

vantaggioso, -a [vantad'dʒoso] AGG advantageous, favourable (*Brit*), favorable (*USA*); **mi ha fatto un'offerta molto vantaggiosa** he made me a very good offer; **un prezzo vantaggioso** a good price

vantare [van'tare] /72/ VT 1 (*lodare: persona, cosa, prodotto*) to speak highly of, praise; (*avere: qualità*) to boast, have 2 (*andare fiero di*) to boast of *o* about, vaunt; **vantarsi** VR: **vantarsi di qc/di aver fatto qc** to boast about sth/about having done sth; **non faccio per vantarmi** without false modesty, without wishing to boast *o* brag

vanteria [vante'ria] SF (*qualità*) boasting; (*atto, detto*) boast

vanto ['vanto] SM 1 **menar vanto di** to boast *o* brag about 2 (*merito*) merit, virtue 3 (*orgoglio*) pride; **è il vanto di sua madre** he's his mother's pride and joy

vanvera ['vanvera] **a vanvera** AVV haphazardly; **parlare a vanvera** to talk nonsense

vapore [va'pore] SM 1 (*Chim, Fis*) vapour (*Brit*), vapor (*USA*); **vapori** SMPL fumes; **vapore acqueo** steam, (water) vapour; **a vapore** (*ferro, locomotiva, turbina*) steam *attr*; **un ferro a vapore** a steam iron; **al vapore** (*Culin*) steamed; **verdure al vapore** steamed vegetables; **andare a tutto vapore** (*fig: persona, macchina*) to go at full speed 2 (*nave*) steamer

vaporetto [vapo'retto] SM steamer

vaporiera [vapo'rjera] SF steam engine

vaporizzare [vaporid'dzare] /72/ VT to vaporize; (*Cosmetica*) to steam

vaporizzatore [vaporiddza'tore] SM spray

vaporizzazione [vaporiddzat'tsjone] SF vaporization

vaporoso, -a [vapo'roso] AGG (*tessuto*) filmy; (*capelli*) soft and full

varare [va'rare] /72/ VT (*Naut, anche fig*) to launch; (*legge*) to pass; **varare una nave** to launch a ship; **varare una legge** to pass a law

varcare [var'kare] /20/ VT to cross; **varcare i limiti** to overstep *o* exceed the limits; **ha varcato l'ottantina** he's just over eighty

varco, -chi ['varko] SM passage; **aprirsi un varco tra la folla** to push one's way through the crowd; **aspettare qn al varco** (*fig*) to lie in wait for sb

varechina [vare'kina] SF bleach

variabile [va'rjabile] AGG (*gen*) variable; (*tempo*) changeable, unsettled, variable; (*umore*) changeable; **la qualità del prodotto è molto variabile** the quality of the product is very variable; **il tempo si manterrà variabile** the weather will continue unsettled ♦ SF (*Mat, Econ*) variable

variante [va'rjante] SF (*gen*) variation, change; (*di percorso*) alternative route; (*di piano, progetto*) modification; (*Ling*) variant

variare [va'rjare] /19/ VT to vary ♦ VI (*sogg: persona, aus essere; sogg: cosa, aus avere*) to vary; (*prezzi*) to range

variazione [varjat'tsjone] SF (*gen*) variation, change; (*Mat, Mus*) variation; **le variazioni della temperatura** variations in the temperature; **una variazione di programma** a change of plan; **variazioni sul tema** (*Mus, anche fig*) variations on a theme

varice [va'ritʃe] SF varicose vein

varicella [vari'tʃella] SF chickenpox

varicoso, -a [vari'koso] AGG: **vena varicosa** varicose vein

variegato, -a [varje'gato] AGG variegated

varietà [varje'ta] SF (*gen*) variety; **hanno una grande varietà di piatti** they have a great variety of dishes ♦ SM INV: (**spettacolo di**) **varietà** variety show

vario, -ria, -ri, -rie ['varjo] AGG 1 (*diversificato: stile, paesaggio*) varied; **il paesaggio è molto vario** the landscape is very varied 2 **vari(e)** (*parecchi: oggetti, argomenti*) various; **avere varie cose da fare** to have quite a few things to do; **devo vedere varie persone oggi** I've got to see various people today; **varie volte** several times 3 (*instabile: tempo*) unsettled; (: *umore*) changeable, uncertain ♦ PRON PL: **vari** several people ♦ SFPL: **varie ed eventuali** (*nell'ordine del giorno*) any other business

variopinto, -a [varjo'pinto] AGG multicoloured (*Brit*), multicolored (*USA*)

varo ['varo] SM (*Naut, anche fig*) launch, launching; (*di leggi*) passing

varrò *ecc* [var'rɔ] VB *vedi* **valere**

Varsavia [var'savja] SF Warsaw

vasaio, -aia, -ai, -aie [va'zajo] SM, SF potter

vasca, -sche ['vaska] SF 1 (*gen*) tub; (*per pesci*) tank; (*cisterna*) water butt; (*da bucato*) basin; (*anche*: **vasca da bagno**) bath(tub); **vasca dei pesci** fish tank 2 (*piscina*) (swimming) pool; (*lunghezza della vasca*) length; **fare una vasca** to swim a length

vascello [vaʃ'ʃello] SM (*Naut*) vessel, ship; **capitano di vascello** captain; **tenente di vascello** lieutenant

vaschetta [vas'ketta] SF (*per gelato*) tub; (*per sviluppare fotografie*) basin, dish; **una vaschetta di gelato** a tub of ice cream; **vaschetta per il ghiaccio** ice tray

vasellame [vazel'lame] SM (*stoviglie*) crockery; (*di porcellana*) china; (*d'oro, argento*) plate

vaso ['vazo] SM 1 (*recipiente: per fiori*) vase; (: *per piante*) flowerpot; (: *ornamentale*) vase, pot; (: *per conserve*) jar, pot; **vaso da notte** chamber pot; **vaso di Pandora** (*anche fig*) Pandora's box 2 (*Anat, Bot, Fis*) vessel; **vasi comunicanti** (*Fis*) communicating vessels; **vasi sanguigni** (*Anat*) blood vessels

vassallo [vas'sallo] SM vassal

vassoio, -oi [vas'sojo] SM tray

vastità [vasti'ta] SF vastness

vasto, -a ['vasto] AGG (*gen*) vast, huge, immense; **una vasta area** a vast area; **di vasta cultura** widely read; **di vaste proporzioni** (*incendio*) huge; (*fenomeno, rivolta*) widespread; **su vasta scala** on a vast *o* huge scale

vaticano, -a [vati'kano] AGG Vatican *attr* ♦ SM: **il Vaticano** the Vatican; **la Città del Vaticano** the Vatican City

VB SIGLA = **Verbano-Cusio-Ossola**

VC SIGLA = **Vercelli**

VE SIGLA = **Venezia** ♦ ABBR = **Vostra Eccellenza**

ve [ve] PRON, AVV *vedi* **vi**

vecchiaia [vek'kjaja] SF old age; **sarai il bastone della mia vecchiaia** you'll support me in my old age

vecchio, -chia, -chi, -chie ['vekkjo] AGG 1 (*gen*) old; **è più vecchio di me** he is older than me; **la casa più vecchia della via** the oldest house in the street; **è un mio vecchio amico** he's an old friend of mine; **ho una macchina vecchia** I've got an old car; **è una vecchia storia** it's an old story; **è un uomo vecchio stile** *o* **stampo** he's an old-fashioned man; **è vecchio del mestiere** he's an old hand at the job; **vecchia volpe** (*fig*) cunning *o* wily old fox; **vecchio come il mondo** as old as the hills 2 (*precedente*) old, former; **il vecchio sindaco** the old *o* former mayor; **la sua macchina vecchia** his old car 3 (*stagionato: vino, formaggio*) mature; (: *legno*) weathered; (: *stantio: pane*) stale ♦ SM old; **il contrasto tra il vecchio e il nuovo** the contrast between old and new ♦ SM, SF (*persona*) old person; **i vecchi** SMPL the old *o* aged, old *o* elderly people, old folk; **come stanno i tuoi vecchi?** (*fam: genitori*) how are your folks?; **il mio vecchio** (*padre*) the *o* my old man; **la mia vecchia** (*madre*) the *o* my old woman; **vecchio mio!** old man!, old chap!

vece ['vetʃe] SF (*funzione*) place, stead; **firma del padre o di chi ne fa le veci** signature of the father or guardian; **in vece mia/tua** in my/your place *o* stead

vedere [ve'dere] VB IRREG /127/ VT 1 to see; **senza occhiali, non ci vedo** I can't see without my glasses; **non si vede niente, non (ci) si vede** (*è buio*) you can't see a thing; **non si vede** (*non è visibile*) it doesn't show, you can't see it; **vedere qn non vale qc** to see sb do sth; **è una partita da vedere** it'll be a match worth seeing; **l'ho visto nascere** (*fig*) I've known him since he was born; **ho visto costruire questa casa** I saw this house being built 2 (*raffigurarsi*) to see; **vedere tutto nero** to take a bleak view of things; **non vedo una via d'uscita** I can see no way out; **modo di vedere** outlook, view of things 3 (*esaminare: libro, prodotto*) to see, look at; (: *conti*) to go over, check; **vedi pagina 8** see page 8; **mi fai vedere il vestito nuovo?** let me see *o* have a look at the new dress; **fammi vedere il tuo tema** let me see your essay 4 (*scoprire*) to see, find out; **vai a vedere cos'è successo** go and see *o* find out what has happened; **voglio vedere come vanno le cose/che possibilità ci sono** I want to see *o* find out how things are going/what opportunities there are; **vediamo se funziona** let's see if it works; **è da vedere se...** it remains to be seen whether ... 5 (*incontrare*) to see, meet; **non lo vedo da molto tempo** I haven't seen him for a long time; **guarda chi si vede!** look who it is!; **farsi vedere** to show one's face; **da quella volta non si è fatto più vedere** he hasn't shown his face since; **fatti vedere ogni tanto** come and see us (*o* me *ecc*) from time to time; **non farsi più vedere in giro** to disappear from the scene; **non la posso proprio vedere** (*fig*) I can't stand her 6 (*visitare: museo, mostra*) to visit; (*consultare: medico, avvocato*) to see, consult; **farsi vedere da un medico** to go and see a doctor 7 (*capire*) to see, grasp; **ho visto subito che...** I immediately realized that ...; **si vede!** that's obvious!; **si vede che sono stanchi** you can tell they are tired; **non vedo la ragione di farlo** I can't see any reason to do it *o* for doing it; **è triste ma non lo dà a vedere** he is sad but he isn't letting it show *o* he is hiding it 8 (*fare in modo*): **vedere di fare qc** to see (to it) that sth is done, make sure that sth is done; **vedi di non arrivare in ritardo** *o* make sure you don't arrive late; **vedi tu se ci riesci** see if you can do it; **vedi tu** (*decidi tu*) it's up to you 9 (*fraseologia*): **vedetevela voi** you see to it; **se l'è vista brutta** he thought his last hour had come; **essere ben/mal visto da qn** to be/ not to be well thought of by sb; **visto che...** seeing that ...; **non vedere qn di buon occhio** to disapprove of sb; **non avere niente a che vedere con qn/qc** to have nothing to do with sb/sth; **vedere la luce** (*nascere*) to come into being, see the light of day; **vedere le stelle** (*dal dolore*) to see stars; **vederci doppio** to see double; **vedere lontano** (*fig*) to be farsighted; **non vedere più lontano del proprio naso** to be unable to see beyond the end of one's nose; **chi s'è visto s'è visto!** and that's that!; **non vederci più dalla rabbia** to be beside o.s. with rage; **non vederci più dalla fame** to be ravenous o starving; **non vedere l'ora di fare qc** to look forward to doing sth; **non vedo l'ora che arrivino** I can't wait for them to arrive; **non vedo l'ora di conoscerlo** I can't wait to meet him; **a vederlo si direbbe che...** by the look of him you'd think that ...; **in vita mia ne ho viste di tutti i colori** I've been through a lot in my time; **ti faccio vedere io!** I'll show you!; **vedersi** VR 1 (*specchiarsi, raffigurarsi*) to see o.s. 2 **si vide perduto** he realized (that) he was lost; **si vide negare l'ingresso** he was refused admission; **si vide costretto a...** he found himself forced to ... 3 (*uso reciproco*) to see each other, meet; **ci vedremo da mio cugino** I'll see you at my cousin's; **ci vediamo domani!** see you tomorrow!

vedetta [ve'detta] SF 1 (*Mil: luogo, guardia*) lookout; **essere o stare di vedetta** to be on lookout duty 2 (*Naut*) patrol ship o boat

vedette [vɔ'dɛt] SF INV (*attore, attrice*) star

vedovo, -a ['vedovo] AGG widowed; **mio padre è vedovo** my father is a widower; **rimanere vedovo** to be widowed ♦ SM widower

vedrò ecc [ve'drɔ] VB *vedi* vedere

veduta [ve'duta] SF 1 (*panorama, rappresentazione di paesaggio*) view; **da quassù si ha una stupenda veduta sul mare** you get a wonderful view of the sea from up here 2 **vedute** SFPL (*fig*) views, opinions; **di larghe o ampie vedute** broad-minded; **di vedute ristrette o limitate** narrow-minded; **i miei sono di larghe vedute** my parents are broad-minded

veemente [vee'mente] AGG (*discorso, azione*) vehement; (*assalto*) vigorous; (*passione, desiderio*) overwhelming

veemenza [vee'mentsa] SF vehemence; **con veemenza** vehemently; **la veemenza dell'attacco** the force of the attack

vegetale [vedʒe'tale] AGG (*gen*) vegetable attr; (*organismo*) plant attr; **regno vegetale** plant o vegetable kingdom ♦ SM plant

vegetare [vedʒe'tare] /72/ VI (*aus* avere) 1 (*piante*) to grow 2 (*fig: persona*) to vegetate

vegetariano, -a [vedʒeta'rjano] AGG, SM, SF vegetarian

vegetativo, -a [vedʒeta'tivo] AGG vegetative

vegetazione [vedʒetat'tsjone] SF vegetation

vegeto, -a ['vedʒeto] AGG (*pianta*) thriving; (*persona*) strong, robust, vigorous; **vivo e vegeto** (*persona*) alive and kicking

veggente [ved'dʒɛnte] SM, SF (*indovino*) clairvoyant

veglia [ve'ʎʎa] SF 1 (*atto*) vigil, watch; **fare la veglia a un malato** to sit with a sick person; **veglia funebre** wake 2 **ha passato ore di veglia sui libri** he stayed up late working away at his books; **tra la veglia e il sonno** half awake

vegliardo, -a [veʎ'ʎardo] SM, SF elder, venerable old person

vegliare [veʎ'ʎare] /27/ VT (*malato, morto*) to watch over, sit up with ♦ VI (*aus* avere) 1 (*stare sveglio*) to stay up, sit up; **vegliare al capezzale di qn** to sit up with sb, watch by sb's bedside; **vegliare pregando** to pass the night in prayer 2 (*prendersi cura*): **vegliare su qn** to watch over sb

veglione [veʎ'ʎone] SM ball, dance; **veglione di Capodanno** New Year's Eve party; **veglione danzante** all-night dance

veicolo [ve'ikolo] SM 1 (*Tecn*) vehicle; **veicolo industriale** industrial vehicle; **veicolo a motore** motor vehicle; **veicolo spaziale** spacecraft inv 2 (*mezzo di diffusione: di idee, suoni*) vehicle, medium; (: *di malattia*) carrier; **veicolo pubblicitario** advertising medium

vela ['vela] SF 1 (*Naut*) sail; **una barca a vela** a sailing boat; **issare/spiegare/ammainare le vele** to hoist/unfurl/strike the sails; **far vela per** (*salpare*) to set sail for; **tutto va a gonfie vele** (*fig*) everything is going perfectly 2 (*Sport*) sailing; **andare a vela** to go sailing

velare [ve'lare] /72/ VT (*anche* fig) to veil, cover; **velarsi il volto** to cover one's face (with a veil); **le lacrime gli velarono gli occhi** his eyes were clouded with tears; **velarsi** VIP (*occhi, luna*) to mist over; (*voce*) to become husky; **gli occhi le si velarono di pianto** o **lacrime** her eyes clouded with tears; **lo sguardo le si velò** her eyes grew dim; **l'acqua si velò di ghiaccio** ice formed on the water

velato, -a [ve'lato] AGG (*anche* fig: *accenno*) veiled; **occhi velati di lacrime** eyes clouded with tears; **sorriso velato di**

tristezza smile tinged with sadness; **con la voce velata per l'emozione** in a voice thick with emotion; **calze velate** sheer stockings

velatura [vela'tura] SF (*Naut*) sails pl

veleggiare [veled'dʒare] /62/ VI (*aus* avere) 1 (*Naut*) to sail 2 (*aliante, deltaplano*) to soar, glide

veleno [ve'leno] SM (*sostanza tossica*) poison; (*di serpente*) venom; **gli alcolici sono un veleno per il fegato** alcohol poisons your liver; **parole piene di veleno** venomous words

velenoso, -a [vele'noso] AGG (*sostanza, fungo, animale*) poisonous; (*persona, lingua, risposta*) venomous

veletta [ve'letta] SF (*di cappello*) veil

veliero [ve'ljero] SM (*Naut*) sailing ship

velina [ve'lina] SF (*anche*: **carta velina**) (*per impacchettare*) tissue paper; (*per copie*) flimsy paper; (*copia*) carbon (copy)

velista, -i, -e [ve'lista] SM, SF yachtsman o yachtswoman

velivolo [ve'livolo] SM aircraft

velleità [vellei'ta] SF INV vain ambition, vain desire

velleitario, -ria, -ri, -rie [vellei'tarjo] AGG (*aspirazione*) fanciful, unrealistic; (*politica, tentativo*) unrealistic

vello ['vello] SM (*di pecora, montone*) fleece

vellutato, -a [vellu'tato] AGG (*stoffa, petalo, pesca, colore*) velvety; (*voce*) mellow

velluto [vel'luto] SM (*stoffa*) velvet; **velluto di cotone/seta** cotton/silk velvet; **di velluto** (*fig: pelle, guance*) velvety; **un paio di pantaloni di velluto** a pair of cords o corduroy trousers; **velluto a coste** corduroy, cord

velo ['velo] SM 1 (*gen*) veil; (*strato sottile*) film, layer; (*di nebbia*) layer, veil; **prendere il velo** (*Rel*) to take the veil; **un velo di ghiaccio** a film of ice; **nel suo sorriso c'era un velo di tristezza** there was a hint o touch of sadness in his smile; **senza veli** (*nudo*) without a stitch on; (*fig: esplicito*) explicit; **stendere un velo (pietoso) su qc** (*fig*) to draw a veil over sth; **velo nuziale** o **da sposa** bridal veil 2 (*tessuto*) voile 3 (*Anat*): **velo palatino** soft palate

veloce [ve'lotʃe] AGG (*gen*) quick, rapid; (*veicolo, cavallo, corridore*) fast; **è una macchina veloce** it's a fast car; **la mia moto è più veloce della tua** my motorbike is faster than yours; **è uno dei corridori più veloci del mondo** he's one of the fastest drivers in the world; **su, veloce, corri a casa!** quick, go home!; **il veloce scorrere del tempo** the swift passage of time; **veloce come un lampo** as quick as lightning; **più veloce della luce** (*fig*) as quick as a flash ♦ AVV fast, quickly; **guidi troppo veloce** you drive too fast

velocista, -i, -e [velo'tʃista] SM, SF (*Sport*) sprinter

velocità [velotʃi'ta] SF INV 1 (*gen, anche Fis*) speed, velocity; **la sua velocità nel reagire** the swiftness of his reaction; **a grande velocità** very quickly o fast; **a forte velocità** at high speed; **a tutta velocità** at full speed; **guidava a tutta velocità** he was driving at full speed; **aumentare la velocità** to accelerate; **diminuire** o **ridurre la velocità** to reduce speed; **prendere velocità** to gather speed; **viaggiava alla velocità di 130 chilometri all'ora** (*o* he) was travelling at a speed of 130 kilometres an hour; **a una velocità costante di 90 km/h** at a constant 90 kilometres per hour; **l'Europa a due velocità** two-speed Europe; **alta velocità** (*Ferr: servizio ferroviario*) high-speed rail service; **velocità di crociera** cruising speed; **velocità di fuga** (*Fis*) escape velocity; **velocità di reazione** (*Chim*) rate of reaction 2 (*Sport*): **gara** o **corsa di velocità** sprint, dash

velodromo [ve'lɔdromo] SM velodrome

ven. ABBR (= *venerdì*) Fri.

vena ['vena] SF 1 (*Anat*) vein; (*aurifera, di piombo*) vein, lode; (*di carbone*) seam; (*d'acqua*) spring; (*venatura: di marmo*) vein, streak; (: *di legno*) grain; **le vene e le arterie** veins and arteries; **tagliarsi le vene** to slash one's wrists; **una vena di tristezza** (*fig*) a hint of sadness 2 (*estro*) inspiration; (*disposizione*) mood; **essere/sentirsi in vena di fare qc** to be/feel in the mood to do sth; **oggi non sono in vena** I'm not in the mood today; **non sono in vena di scherzi** I'm not in the mood for jokes, I'm not in a joking mood

venale [ve'nale] AGG 1 (*Comm: valore*) market attr; (: *prezzo*) selling, market attr; **cose venali** (*fig*) material things 2 (*fig: persona*) venal; **ma come sei venale!** how mercenary you are!

venalità [venali'ta] SF venality

venato, -a [ve'nato] AGG (*marmo*) veined, streaked; (*legno*) grained

venatorio, -ria, -ri, -rie [vena'tɔrjo] AGG hunting *attr*; **la stagione venatoria** the hunting season

venatura [vena'tura] SF (*di marmo*) vein, streak; (*di legno*) grain *no pl*; **le venature del legno** the grain of the wood

vendemmia [ven'demmja] SF (*attività*) grape harvest, vintage; (*quantità d'uva*) grape crop, grapes *pl*; **fare la vendemmia** to pick *o* harvest the grapes

vendemmiare [vendem'mjare] /19/ VI (*aus* avere) to pick *o* harvest the grapes ♦ VT (*uva*) to pick, harvest

vendere ['vendere] /29/ VT to sell; **vendere qc a qn** to sell sb sth, sell sth to sb; **vendere qc a *o* per 20 sterline** to sell sth for 20 pounds; **l'ho venduto per tremila euro** I sold it for three thousand euros; **vendere all'ingrosso/al dettaglio *o* minuto** to sell wholesale/retail; **vendere a rate** to sell on hire purchase (*Brit*) *o* the instalment plan (*USA*); **una pubblicità che fa vendere** an advertisement which increases sales; **"vendesi", "for sale"; vendere all'asta** to auction, sell by auction; **questi articoli si vendono bene/male** these articles sell well/don't sell well; **vendere cara la pelle** (*fig*) to sell one's life dearly; **vendere l'anima al diavolo** to sell one's soul to the devil; **vendere il proprio corpo** (*prostituirsi*) to sell one's body; **vendere fumo** to talk hot air; **averne da vendere** (*fig*) to have enough and to spare; **vendere la pelle dell'orso prima di averlo ucciso** to count one's chickens before they're hatched; **vendersi** VR **1** (*tradire*): **vendersi al nemico** to sell out to the enemy **2** (*prostituirsi*) to prostitute o.s., sell o.s.

vendetta [ven'detta] SF revenge, vengeance; **prendersi una vendetta** to take one's revenge, wreak vengeance; **farsi vendetta** to take one's revenge; **ha deciso di farsi vendetta da solo** he decided to take his revenge; **essere assetato di vendetta** to thirst for revenge; **vendetta trasversale** (*della mafia*) *revenge against somebody by attacking their family or friends*

vendicare [vendi'kare] /20/ VT to avenge, revenge; **vendicarsi** VR: **vendicarsi (di qc)** to avenge *o* revenge o.s. (for sth); (*per rancore*) to take one's revenge (for sth); **vendicarsi su qn** to avenge *o* revenge o.s. on sb

□ **vendicare** non si traduce mai con la parola inglese *vindicate*

vendicativo, -a [vendika'tivo] AGG (*persona, carattere*) vindictive

vendita ['vendita] SF sale; **la vendita** (*attività*) selling; (*smercio*) sales *pl*; **contratto di vendita** sales agreement; **reparto vendite** sales department; **mettere in vendita** to put on sale; **hanno messo in vendita la casa** they have put their house up for sale; **in vendita presso** on sale at; **i biglietti saranno in vendita da venerdì** tickets will be on sale from Friday; **punto (di) vendita** retail outlet; **vendita all'asta** auction (sale), sale by auction; **vendita per corrispondenza** mail order; **vendita al dettaglio** retail; **vendita a domicilio** door-to-door selling; **vendita all'ingrosso** wholesale; **vendita al minuto** retail; **vendita porta a porta** door-to-door selling

venditore, -trice [vendi'tore] SM, SF seller, vendor, salesman *o* saleswoman; **venditore ambulante** hawker, pedlar; **venditore al dettaglio** retailer; **venditore all'ingrosso** wholesaler; **venditore al minuto** retailer

venduto, -a [ven'duto] AGG (*merce*) sold; (*fig: corrotto*) corrupt ♦ SM (*Comm*) goods *pl* sold

venefico, -a, -ci, -che [ve'nefiko] AGG poisonous; (*fig: insinuazione*) poisonous, venomous

venerabile [vene'rabile] , **venerando, -a** [vene'rando] AGG venerable

venerare [vene'rare] /72/ VT to venerate, revere

venerazione [venerat'tsjone] SF veneration, reverence

venerdì [vener'di] SM INV Friday; **venerdì santo** Good Friday; **gli manca qualche venerdì** (*fig*) he's got a screw loose; *vedi* **martedì**

Venere ['venere] SF (*Astron, Mitol*) Venus; **monte di Venere** (*Anat*) mons veneris

venereo, -a [ve'nɛreo] AGG venereal; **malattia venerea** venereal disease

veneto, -a ['veneto] AGG *of o* from the Veneto ♦ SM, SF inhabitant *o* native of the Veneto

Venezia [ve'nettsja] SF Venice; **abito a Venezia** I live in Venice; **domani vado a Venezia** I'm going to Venice tomorrow

veneziano, -a [venet'tsjano] AGG, SM, SF Venetian

Venezuela [venet'tswela] SM Venezuela

venezuelano, -a [venettsue'lano] AGG, SM, SF Venezuelan

vengo *ecc* ['vengo] VB *vedi* **venire**

veniale [ve'njale] AGG (*Rel: peccato*) venial

venire [ve'nire] VB IRREG **/128/** (*aus* essere) **1** to come; **verremo a salutarti** we'll come and say goodbye; **vieni a trovarci** come and see us; **è venuto in macchina/treno** he came by car/train; **sono venuto a piedi** I came on foot; **vieni di corsa** come quickly; **vengo!** I'm coming!, just coming!; **da dove vieni?** where do you come from? **2** (*giungere*) to come, arrive; **non è ancora venuto** he hasn't come *o* arrived yet; **prendere le cose come vengono** to take things as they come; **fallo come viene viene** do it any old how; **venire al mondo *o* alla luce** to come into the world; **venire a patti/alle mani** to come to an agreement/to blows; **venire a capo di qc** to unravel sth, sort sth out; **venire a sapere qc** to learn sth; **venire al dunque *o* nocciolo *o* fatto *o* sodo** to come to the point; **questo lavoro/quel tipo mi è venuto a noia** I'm fed up with this work/with that guy; **è venuto il momento di...** the time has come to ...; **è venuto il momento di dire la verità** the time has come to tell the truth; **negli anni a venire** in the years to come, in future; **sono cose di là da venire** these things are still a long way off; **mi è venuta un'idea** I've had an idea; **ma che ti viene in mente?** whatever are you thinking of?; **gli era venuto il dubbio *o* sospetto che...** he began to suspect that ...; **mi è venuto un dubbio** I began to have doubts; **mi è venuto il raffreddore** I've got a cold; **gli è venuto il mal di testa** he's got a headache; **mi viene da vomitare** I feel sick; **mi viene da piangere/ridere** I feel like crying/laughing; **ti venisse un colpo/accidente!** (*fam*) drop dead! **3** (*provenire*): **venire da** to come from **4** (*riuscire: lavoro*) to turn out; **venire bene/male** to turn out well/badly; **il dolce è venuto bene** the cake turned out well; **il maglione viene troppo lungo/stretto** the sweater is going to end up too long/tight; **non mi viene** (*problema, operazione, calcolo*) I can't get it to come out right **5** (*fam: raggiungere l'orgasmo*) to come **6** (*costare*) to cost; **quanto viene?** how much is it *o* does it cost? **7** (*essere sorteggiato*) to come up **8** (*con avv*): **venire fuori** to come out; **venire fuori con** (*battuta*) to come out with; **venire giù** to come down; **venire meno** (*svenire*) to faint; **venire meno a** (*promessa*) to break; (*impegno, dovere*) not to fulfil (*Brit*) *o* fulfill (*USA*); **venire su** (*crescere: persona*) to grow (up); (: *pianta*) to come up; **il bambino sta venendo su molto robusto** the baby's growing very strong; **venire via** to come away *o* off; (*macchia*) to come out **9** *far venire* (*medico*) to call, send for; **far venire qn** to call sb; **mi hai fatto venire per niente** you got me to come *o* you made me come for nothing; **mi fa venire il vomito** (*anche fig*) it (*o* he *ecc*) makes me sick; **mi fa venire i brividi** (*fig*) it (*o* he *ecc*) gives me the creeps **10** (*come ausiliare: essere*): **viene ammirato da tutti** he is admired by everyone; **venire stimato da tutti** to be respected by everybody; **viene venduto al chilo** it's sold by the kilo; **verrà giudicato in base al suo punteggio** he will be judged on his marks (*Brit*) *o* grades (*USA*); **venirsene** VIP: **venirsene via** to come away; **venirsene verso casa** to come home ♦ SM: **tutto quell'andare e venire mi rendeva nervoso** all that coming and going made me irritable

venni *ecc* ['venni] VB *vedi* **venire**

ventaglio, -gli [ven'taʎʎo] SM fan; **a ventaglio** fan-shaped; **disporsi a ventaglio** to fan out

ventata [ven'tata] SF (*folata*) gust (of wind); **come una ventata d'aria fresca** (*fig*) like a breath of fresh air; **una ventata di nazionalismo** a wave of nationalism

ventennale [venten'nale] AGG (*che dura 20 anni*) twenty-year *attr*; (*che ricorre ogni 20 anni*) which takes place every twenty years

ventenne [ven'tenne] AGG, SM, SF twenty-year-old

ventennio, -ni [ven'tennjo] SM period of twenty years; **il ventennio fascista** the Fascist period

ventesimo, -a [ven'tεzimo] AGG, SM, SF twentieth; **il ventesimo secolo** the twentieth century

venti ['venti] AGG INV, SM INV twenty

ventilare [venti'lare] /72/ VT **1** (*stanza*) to air, ventilate; (*fig*: *idea, proposta*) to air **2** (*Agr*) to winnow

ventilato, -a [venti'lato] AGG (*camera, zona*) airy; **poco ventilato** airless; **una zona troppo ventilata** a windy area

ventilatore [ventila'tore] SM (*per ambienti*) fan; (*Med*) ventilator

ventilazione [ventilat'tsjone] SF ventilation

ventina [ven'tina] SF: **una ventina (di)** around twenty, twenty or so, about twenty

ventiquattr'ore [ventikwat'trore] SFPL (*periodo*) twenty-four hours ♦ SF INV **1** (*valigetta*) overnight case, attaché case **2** (*Sport*) twenty-four-hour race

ventisette [venti'sette] AGG INV twenty-seven ♦ SM INV: **il ventisette** (*giorno di paga*) ≈ (monthly) pay day

ventitré [venti'tre] AGG INV, SM INV twenty-three ♦ SFPL: **portava il cappello sulle ventitré** he wore his hat at a jaunty angle

vento ['vento] SM wind; **un vento caldo** a warm wind; **c'è vento** it's windy; **un colpo di vento** a gust of wind; **a prova di vento** windproof; **contro vento** against the wind; **c'è una barca sopra/sotto vento** (*Naut*) there is a boat to windward/leeward of us; **con i capelli al vento** with windswept hair; **fatica buttata al vento** wasted effort; **parlare al vento** to waste one's breath; **non andare a dirlo ai quattro venti** don't go spreading it around; **un vento di rivolta** a wind of revolt; **qual buon vento ti porta?** to what do I (o we) owe the pleasure of seeing you?; **vento contrario** (*Naut*) headwind

❏ **vento** non si traduce mai con la parola inglese *vent*

ventola ['ventola] SF (*Aut, Tecn*) fan

ventosa [ven'tosa] SF (*di gomma*) suction cap o pad; (*Zool*) sucker; **funziona a ventosa** it works by suction

ventoso, -a [ven'toso] AGG windy; **questa zona è più ventosa** this area is windier

ventotto [ven'tɔtto] AGG INV, SM INV twenty-eight

ventre ['ventre] SM (*addome*) stomach; (*grembo*) womb; **avere dolori al ventre** to have (a) stomach ache; **sdraiato sul ventre** lying on one's (its) stomach o front; **il ventre della terra** (*fig*) the depths of the earth; **il basso ventre** lower abdomen; **colpire qn al basso ventre** to hit sb in the groin

ventriloquo, -a [ven'trilokwo] SM, SF ventriloquist

ventuno [ven'tuno] AGG INV, SM INV twenty-one

ventura [ven'tura] SF fortune, chance; **andare alla ventura** to trust to luck; **soldato di ventura** mercenary; **compagnia di ventura** company of mercenaries

venturo, -a [ven'turo] AGG next, coming

venuto, -a [ve'nuto] PP di *venire* ♦ SM, SF: **il primo venuto, la prima venuta** the first person who comes along

vera ['vera] SF wedding ring

verace [ve'ratʃe] AGG (*testimone*) truthful; (*testimonianza*) accurate, veracious; (*cibi*) real, genuine

veramente [vera'mente] AVV (*realmente*) really; **veramente?** really?; **è veramente bella** she's really beautiful; **è veramente cretino** he's a real idiot; **io, veramente, al posto tuo...** frankly, in your place, I ...; **veramente, non ne sapevo niente** actually, I didn't know anything about it

veranda [ve'randa] SF veranda(h)

verbale [ver'bale] AGG **1** (*orale*) verbal, spoken; **un accordo verbale** a verbal agreement **2** (*Gramm*) verbal ♦ SM (*di riunione*) minutes pl; (*Dir*) record; **le faccio il verbale** (*Polizia*) I'll have to report this; **mettere a verbale** to place in the minutes o on record

verbo ['verbo] SM **1** (*Gramm*) verb; **un verbo transitivo** a transitive verb **2** (*parola*) word; **il Verbo** (*Rel*) the Word

verboso, -a [ver'boso] AGG wordy, verbose

verdastro, -a [ver'dastro] AGG greenish

verde ['verde] AGG **1** (*colore*) green; **verde dalla bile** livid o white with rage; **verde d'invidia** green with envy **2** (*acerbo: frutta*) green, unripe; (*legna*) green; **gli anni verdi** youth **3** (*Telec*): **numero verde** freefone (line) (*Brit*), toll-free number (*USA*) **4** (*ecologista: associazione, gruppo*) green;

(*ecologico*) ecological, green; **benzina verde** lead-free o unleaded petrol ♦ SM **1** (*colore*) green; **essere al verde** to be broke; **una camicia verde scuro** a dark green shirt; **verde bottiglia** bottle green; **verde oliva** olive green; **verde pisello** pea green **2** (*vegetazione*) greenery; **c'è molto verde in questa città** this city has a lot of green space; **una casa immersa nel verde** a house surrounded by greenery; **ho bisogno di un po' di verde** I feel in need of country air **3** (*semaforo*) green (light) ♦ **i Verdi** SMPL (*Pol*) the Greens

verdeggiante [verded'dʒante] AGG green, verdant

verderame [verde'rame] SM (*Chim*) verdigris

verdetto [ver'detto] SM (*Dir: gen*) verdict

verdura [ver'dura] SF (*Culin*) vegetables pl; **non mi piace la verdura** I don't like vegetables; **minestra di verdura** vegetable soup; **negozio di frutta e verdura** fruit and vegetable shop, greengrocer's (*Brit*)

verecondia [vere'kondja] SF modesty

verecondo, -a [vere'kondo] AGG modest

verga, -ghe ['verga] SF (*bastone*) cane, rod; (*di pastore*) stick; **percuotere qn con la verga** to cane sb; **verga d'oro** (*lingotto*) gold bar; (*pianta*) goldenrod

vergato, -a [ver'gato] AGG: **carta vergata** laid paper

verginale [verdʒi'nale] AGG virginal, virgin *attr*

vergine ['verdʒine] SF **1** (*gen*) virgin; **la Vergine** the Virgin Mary o Mother **2** (*Astrol*): **Vergine** Virgo; **essere della Vergine** to be Virgo ♦ AGG (*persona, terra*) virgin *attr*; **essere vergine** to be a virgin; **foresta vergine** virgin forest; **pura lana vergine** pure new wool; **olio vergine d'oliva** virgin olive oil

verginità [verdʒini'ta] SF virginity; **rifarsi una verginità** (*fig*) to regain one's reputation, clear one's name

vergogna [ver'goɲɲa] SF **1** (*gen*) shame; (*timidezza*) shyness; (*imbarazzo*) embarrassment; **è arrossito per la vergogna** he went red with embarrassment; **provava vergogna per ciò che era successo** he felt ashamed about what had happened; **provo vergogna davanti a lui** he makes me feel shy; **vincere la propria vergogna** to overcome one's shyness; **non avere vergogna di nessuno** to be shameless; **sprofondare per la vergogna** to be overcome by embarrassment **2** (*onta, disonore*) disgrace; **è una vergogna!** it's a disgrace!; **è la vergogna della famiglia** he is a disgrace to his family

vergognarsi [vergoɲ'ɲarsi] /15/ VIP (*vedi sf a*): **vergognarsi (di)** to be o feel ashamed (of); to be o feel shy (about); be o feel embarrassed (about); **non ti vergogni di aver copiato all'esame?** aren't you ashamed that you copied in the exam?; **dai, suonaci qualcosa - no, mi vergogno** come on, play something - no, I'm embarrassed; **vergognati!** you should be ashamed of yourself!, shame on you!

vergognoso, -a [vergoɲ'ɲoso] AGG (*timido*) timid, shy; (*pieno di vergogna*) ashamed, embarrassed; (*che causa vergogna*) shameful; (*che causa disonore*) disgraceful; **è vergognoso che debbano ancora succedere cose simili!** it's outrageous that such things still happen!

veridicità [veridit'ʃi'ta] SF truthfulness; **nessuno mette in dubbio la veridicità delle sue parole** nobody doubts the truth of what he said

veridico, -a, -ci, -che [ve'ridiko] AGG truthful

verifica, -che [ve'rifika] SF **1** checking *no pl*; **fare una verifica di** (*freni, testimonianza, firma*) to check; **questo lavoro è una continua verifica delle proprie capacità** (*fig*) this work is a continual test of one's abilities **2** (*Fin*): **verifica contabile** audit

verificare [verifi'kare] /20/ VT **1** (*controllare: verità*) to check, verify **2** (*Fin*) to audit **3** (*Mat: teoria, postulato*) to prove; **verificarsi** (*accadere*) to happen, occur, take place; (*avverarsi*) to prove (to be)

verità [veri'ta] SF INV **1** (*gen*) truth; **hai detto la verità?** did you tell the truth?; **la pura verità** the absolute truth; **la verità nuda e cruda** the plain unvarnished truth; **è una verità sacrosanta** it's gospel; **travisare la verità** to distort the truth; **a dire la verità, per la verità** to tell the truth, actually; **macchina della verità** lie-detector; **siero della verità** truth serum **2** (*assioma*) truth; **le verità scientifiche** scientific truths

veritiero, -a [veri'tjεro] AGG (*conforme a verità*) true, accurate; (*che dice la verità*) truthful

verme [ˈvɛrme] SM (gen, anche fig) worm; (di frutto, formaggio) maggot; **nudo come un verme** stark naked; **mi sento un verme!** (fig) I could die!, I feel awful!; **verme solitario** tapeworm

vermicelli [vermiˈtʃɛlli] SMPL (pasta) vermicelli sg

vermiglio, -glia, -gli, -glie [verˈmiʎʎo] AGG, SM vermilion, scarlet

vermouth, vermut [ˈvɛrmut] SM INV vermouth

vernacolo, -a [verˈnakolo] AGG, SM vernacular

vernice [verˈnitʃe] SF 1 (trasparente) varnish; (pittura: lucida) gloss (paint); (: opaca) matt (paint); **vernice fresca** "wet paint" 2 (pelle) patent leather; **scarpe/borsa di vernice** patent leather shoes/bag

verniciare [verniˈtʃare] /14/ VT (con vernice trasparente) to varnish; (pitturare) to paint

verniciatura [vernitʃaˈtura] SF (con vernice trasparente) varnishing; (con vernice colorata) painting

vero, -a [ˈvero] AGG (gen) true; (reale) real; (autentico) genuine; **vero o falso?** true or false?; **questa è una storia vera** this is a true story; **incredibile ma vero** incredible but true; **vero e proprio** real; **questo è un vero e proprio affare** this is a real bargain; **un vero e proprio delinquente** a real criminal, an out and out criminal; **il suo vero nome è Giovanni** his real o true name is Giovanni; **ma è vero questo Modigliani?** is this a genuine o real Modigliani?; **perle vere** genuine pearls; **quei fiori sembrano veri** those flowers look real; **il vero problema è...** the real problem is ...; **fosse vero!** if only it were true!; **nulla di più vero!** you've said it!, how true!; **non mi pare vero!** it doesn't seem possible!; **come è vero Dio** I swear to God; **tant'è vero che...** so much so that ...; **vero?** isn't that right?; **hai tu il mio libro, vero?** you've got my book, haven't you?; **sei italiano, vero?** you're Italian, aren't you?; **questa è la tua macchina, vero?** this is your car, isn't it?; **è andata stamattina, vero?** she went this morning, didn't she?; **vorresti andare, vero?** you'd like to go, wouldn't you?; **ti piace la cioccolata, vero?** you like chocolate, don't you? ♦ SM (verità) truth; **c'è del vero in ciò che dice** there is some truth in what he says; **sto dicendo il vero** I am telling the truth; **a onor del vero, a dire il vero** to tell the truth; **è una copia dal vero** (disegno) it's a copy from life

Verona [veˈrona] SF Verona

veronese [veroˈnese] AGG, SM, SF Veronese inv

verosimile [veroˈsimile] AGG (racconto, ipotesi) likely, probable; (trama) plausible, convincing; **poco verosimile** (racconto) improbable, unlikely; (trama) implausible

verrò ecc [verˈrɔ] VB vedi venire

verruca, -che [verˈruka] SF (Med, Bot) verruca, wart

versamento [versaˈmento] SM 1 (gen) payment; (deposito in banca) deposit; **modulo o distinta di versamento** (Banca) pay-in slip 2 (Med) effusion

versante [verˈsante] SM (Geog) side, slopes pl; **sul versante del lavoro non ci sono novità** there's no news on the work front

versare¹ [verˈsare] /72/ VT 1 (liquido, polvere) to pour; (servire: caffè) to pour (out); **versare da bere a qn** to pour sb a drink; **mi versi un po' d'acqua?** can you pour me some water?; **versare la minestra** to serve (up) the soup; **versare a filo** (olio) to drizzle 2 (spargere: liquidi, polvere) to spill; (: lacrime, sangue) to shed; **mi sono versato il caffè addosso** I've spilt coffee over myself; **ho versato un po' di vino sulla tovaglia** I spilt some wine on the tablecloth; **versare acqua sul fuoco** (fig) to pour oil on troubled waters 3 **il Po versa le proprie acque nell'Adriatico** the Po flows into the Adriatic 4 (Econ: pagare) to pay; (: depositare) to deposit, pay in; **ho versato la somma sul mio conto** I paid the sum into my account; **ho depositato la somma sul mio conto** I deposited the sum into my account; **vorrei versare duecentocinquanta euro sul mio conto corrente** I'd like to pay two hundred and fifty euros into my current account; **versare una cauzione** to pay a deposit; **versarsi** VIP 1 (rovesciarsi) to spill; **il latte si è versato sul fuoco** the milk has boiled over 2 **versarsi in** (sogg: fiume) to flow into; (: folla) to pour into

versare² [verˈsare] /72/ VI (aus avere) **versare in fin di vita** to be dying; **versare in gravi difficoltà** to find o.s. with serious problems

versatile [verˈsatile] AGG versatile

versatilità [versatiliˈta] SF versatility

versato, -a [verˈsato] AGG: **essere versato in** to be (well-)versed in

versetto [verˈsetto] SM (di poesia) line; (Rel) verse

versione [verˈsjone] SF 1 (gen) version; **vorrei sentire la sua versione dell'accaduto** I'd like to hear her version of what happened; **una versione più aggiornata della guida** a more up-to-date edition of the guide; **in versione originale** (libro) in the original (version); (film) in the original language o version; **la versione cinematografica del suo ultimo libro** the film of his latest book; **versione lusso** (Aut) luxury model; **versione 4 porte** (Aut) 4-door model 2 (traduzione) translation

verso¹ [ˈverso] SM INV (di pagina) verso; (di moneta) reverse

verso² [ˈverso] SM 1 (di animale, uccello) call, cry; **qual è il verso del gatto?** what noise o sound does a cat make?; **che verso fa il maiale?** what noise does a pig make?; **verso di richiamo** call; **ha fatto un verso di dolore** she cried out in pain o gave a cry of pain; **smettila di fare tutti quei versi** stop making those noises; **fare il verso a qn** (imitare) to take sb off, mimic sb; **faceva il verso al professore** he mimicked the teacher 2 (riga: di poesia) line, verse; **versi** (poesia) verse sg; **in versi** in verse; **versi sciolti** blank verse sg 3 (direzione, anche Mat) direction; (di legno, stoffa) grain; **prendere qn/qc per il verso giusto** to approach sb/sth the right way; **non c'è verso di convincerlo** it is impossible to persuade him, there's no way of persuading him, he can't be persuaded; **non c'è verso di fargli cambiare idea** there's no way of making him change his mind; **per un verso o per l'altro** one way or another

verso³ [ˈverso] PREP 1 (in direzione di) toward(s), to; **andando verso la stazione** going towards the station; **stavo camminando verso la stazione quando l'ho visto** I was walking towards the station when I saw him; **è tardi, faremmo bene ad avviarci verso casa** it's late, we'd better head for home; **veniva verso di me** he was coming towards me; **verso l'alto** upwards; **verso il basso** downwards; **tirare l'anello verso il basso** pull the ring downwards; **guardare verso il cielo** to look heavenwards o skywards; **navigare verso sud** to sail south(wards) 2 (nei pressi di) near, around (about); **abito verso il centro** I live near the centre (Brit) o center (USA) 3 (in senso temporale) about, around; **arrivi verso che ora?** around o about what time will you arrive?; **arriverò verso le sette** I'll be there at around seven; **verso sera** towards evening; **verso la fine dell'anno** towards the end of the year; **ci rivediamo verso la fine di novembre** I'll see you around the end of November 4 (nei confronti di) for, towards; **dimostrare rispetto verso gli anziani** to show respect for o towards the elderly

vertebra [ˈvertebra] SF vertebra

vertebrale [verteˈbrale] AGG vertebral; **colonna vertebrale** spinal column, spine

vertebrato, -a [verteˈbrato] AGG, SM vertebrate

vertenza [verˈtentsa] SF (lite) lawsuit, case; (sindacale) dispute

verticale [vertiˈkale] AGG vertical; **in posizione verticale** in an upright position ♦ SF 1 (linea) vertical 2 (Ginnastica: sulle mani) handstand; (: sulla testa) headstand; **fare la verticale** to do a handstand (o headstand) 3 (di cruciverba) clue (o word) down

vertice [ˈvertitʃe] SM 1 (Geom) vertex 2 (vetta) summit, peak, top; (fig: punto più alto) peak, height; **il vertice della carriera** the peak of one's career 3 (Pol) summit; **incontro/conferenza al vertice** summit meeting/conference

vertigine [verˈtidʒine] SF giddiness no pl, dizziness no pl, dizzy spell; (Med) vertigo; **soffrire di vertigini** to be afraid of heights, have vertigo (termine tecn); **mi fa venire le vertigini** it makes my head spin; **avere le vertigini** to feel dizzy

vertiginoso, -a [vertidʒiˈnoso] AGG (altezza) dizzy; (velocità) breakneck attr; (danza) breathless; (cifra) exorbitant; (scollatura) plunging; **il ritmo vertiginoso della vita moderna** the frenetic pace of modern life

verza [ˈverdza] SF Savoy cabbage

vescica, -che [veʃˈʃika] SF 1 (Anat) bladder 2 (Med: bolla) blister; **ho una vescica sul piede** I've got a blister on my foot

vescovile [veskoˈvile] AGG episcopal

vescovo ['veskovo] SM bishop

vespa¹ ['vɛspa] SF (*Zool*) wasp; **ha un vitino di vespa** she's wasp-waisted

vespa² ['vespa] (*Marchio registrato*) (motor) scooter, Vespa (*Marchio registrato*)

vespaio, -ai [ves'pajo] SM wasps' nest; **suscitare un vespaio** (*fig*) to stir up a hornets' nest

vespasiano [vespa'zjano] SM urinal

vespro ['vespro] SM (*letter: sera*) evening; (*Rel*) vespers *pl*

vessare [ves'sare] /72/ VT (*letter*) to oppress

vessazione [vessat'tsjone] SF (*letter*) oppression

vessillo [ves'sillo] SM (*Mil*) standard; (*bandiera*) flag; (*fig*) banner, ensign; **il vessillo della libertà** the banner of freedom

vestaglia [ves'taʎʎa] SF dressing gown (*Brit*), bathrobe (*USA*)

veste ['veste] SF **1** (*gen*) garment; (*da donna*) dress; (*di monaco, suora*) habit; **vesti** SFPL clothes, clothing *sg*; **veste da camera** dressing gown (*Brit*), bathrobe (*USA*) **2** (*fig: di libro*): **veste editoriale** layout **3** (*funzione*) capacity; (*fig: apparenza*) appearance; **in veste di** (in one's capacity) as; **in veste ufficiale** in an official capacity; **si è presentato in veste di amico** he passed himself off as a friend

❏ **veste** non si traduce mai con la parola inglese *vest*

vestiario, -ri [ves'tjarjo] SM wardrobe, clothes *pl*; **capo di vestiario** article of clothing, garment

vestibolo [ves'tibolo] SM **1** (*ingresso*) (entrance) hall; (*Archeol*) vestibule **2** (*Anat*) vestibule

vestigia [ves'tidʒa] SFPL **1** (*tracce*) vestiges, traces **2** (*rovine*) ruins, remains

vestire [ves'tire] /45/ VT **1** (*gen*): **vestire (di)** to dress (in); (*mascherare*): **vestire da** to dress up as **2** (*provvedere degli indumenti necessari*) to clothe **3** (*indossare: stato*) to wear, have on; (: *atto*) to put on ♦ VI (*aus essere*) (*indossare*) to wear; (*abbigliarsi*) to dress; **vestire di bianco/a lutto** to wear white/mourning; **vestire con eleganza** to dress smartly; **questa giacca veste bene** this is a well-cut jacket; **vestirsi** VR (*gen*) to dress, get dressed; (*abbigliarsi*) to dress; **vestirsi da** (*negozio*) to buy *o* get one's clothes at; (*sarto*) to have one's clothes made at; **vestirsi da pirata/Peter Pan** to dress up as a pirate/Peter Pan; **si è vestito da donna** he dressed up as a woman; **vestirsi a festa** to wear one's Sunday best *o* one's best clothes; **vestirsi a lutto** to wear mourning; **vestirsi bene/con gusto** to dress well/tastefully; **vestiti, che usciamo** get dressed, we're going out; **si è vestito in fretta ed è uscito** he got dressed quickly and went out; **come mi devo vestire stasera?** what should I wear this evening?

vestito¹, -a [ves'tito] AGG dressed; **vestito di bianco** dressed in white; **vestito da** (*in maschera*) dressed up as; **vestito di tutto punto** all dressed up; **dormire vestito** to sleep in one's clothes

vestito² [ves'tito] SM (*gen*) garment; (*abito*) (*da donna*) dress; (*da uomo*) suit; **vestiti** SMPL clothes; **ho messo alcuni vestiti in valigia** I put some clothes in a suitcase; **cambiare vestiti** to change one's clothes; **farsi fare un vestito** to have a dress (*o* suit) made

Vesuvio [ve'zuvjo] SM Vesuvius

veterano, -a [vete'rano] SM (*Mil*) veteran ♦ SM, SF (*fig*) veteran, old hand

veterinario, -ria, -ri, -rie [veteri'narjo] AGG veterinary ♦ SM vet (*Brit*), veterinary surgeon (*Brit*), veterinarian (*USA*)

veto ['veto] SM (*Dir, anche fig*) veto; **diritto di veto** right of veto; **porre il veto a qc** to veto sth

vetraio, -ai [ve'trajo] SM (*gen*) glazier, glass-worker; (*chi soffia il vetro*) glass-blower, glassmaker

vetrato, -a [ve'trato] AGG glass *attr*; (*porta, finestra*) glazed; **carta vetrata** sandpaper

vetreria [vetre'ria] SF (*fabbrica*) glassworks *inv*; (*oggetti di vetro*) glassware *no pl*

vetrina [ve'trina] SF **1** (*di negozio*) (shop) window; **in vetrina** in the window; **c'è una gonna che mi piace in vetrina** there's a skirt I like in the window; **allestire una vetrina** to dress a window; **andare a guardare le vetrine** to go window-shopping; **mettersi in vetrina** (*fig*) to show off **2**

(*rassegna*) showcase **3** (*mobile: di museo*) showcase, display cabinet; (: *di negozio*) display cabinet

vetrinista, -i, -e [vetri'nista] SM, SF window dresser; **fa la vetrinista** she's a window dresser

vetrino [ve'trino] SM (*di microscopio*) slide

vetriolo [vetri'ɔlo] SM vitriol; **al vetriolo** (*fig: critica, risposta*) vitriolic

vetro ['vetro] SM **1** (*materiale*) glass; (*frammento*) piece of glass; (*scheggia*) splinter of glass; **un vaso di vetro** a glass vase; **lana di vetro** glass fibre (*Brit*) *o* fiber (*USA*); **fibra di vetro** fibreglass (*Brit*) *o* fiberglass (*USA*); **mettere qc sotto vetro** to put sth under glass **2** (*di finestra, porta*) (window) pane; (*di orologio*) watch glass; **devo pulire i vetri** I have to clean the windows; **porta a vetri** glass door **3** (*oggetto*): **i vetri di Murano** Murano glassware *sg* ♦ **vetro blindato** bulletproof glass; **vetro infrangibile** shatterproof glass; **vetro di sicurezza** safety glass; **vetro smerigliato** frosted glass

vetroso, -a [ve'troso] AGG vitreous

vetta ['vetta] SF (*di montagna*) top, summit, peak; (*di albero*) top; **abbiamo raggiunto la vetta in quattro ore** we reached the summit in four hours; **toccare le più alte vette del successo** to reach the top of the ladder; **essere in vetta alla classifica** (*squadra*) to be at the top of the league; (*canzone*) to be at the top of the charts

vettore [vet'tore] SM **1** (*Mat, Fis*) vector **2** (*trasportatore*) carrier ♦ AGG: **razzo vettore** booster rocket

vettovaglie [vetto'vaʎʎe] SFPL provisions, supplies

vettura [vet'tura] SF **1** (*carrozza*) coach, carriage; **vettura di piazza** hackney carriage **2** (*Ferr*) coach, carriage (*Brit*), car (*USA*); **in vettura!** all aboard! **3** (*auto*) car, automobile (*USA*); **vettura a noleggio senza autista** car for self-drive hire (*Brit*) *o* rent (*USA*)

vetturino [vettu'rino] SM coach driver, coachman

vezzeggiare [vettsed'dʒare] /62/ VT to make a fuss of

vezzeggiativo, -a [vettseddʒa'tivo] AGG of endearment ♦ SM term of endearment

vezzo ['vettso] SM **1** (*abitudine*) (affected) habit; **avere il vezzo di fare qc** to have the habit of doing sth **2** (*gesto affettuoso*) caress **3** **vezzi** SMPL (*moine*) affected ways; (*grazia*) charm *sg*, charms

vezzoso, -a [vet'tsoso] AGG **1** (*grazioso*) pretty, charming **2** (*lezioso*) affected ♦ SM, SF: **fare il(la) vezzoso(a)** to turn on the charm

VF ABBR = **vigili del fuoco**

V.G. ABBR = **Vostra Grazia**

VI SIGLA = **Vicenza**

vi [vi] *dav* **lo, la, li, le, ne** *diventa* **ve** PRON PERS **1** (*ogg diretto*) you; **vi stavo cercando** I was looking for you; **vorrei aiutarvi** I'd like to help you **2** (*complemento di termine*) (to) you; **ve l'hanno dato** they gave it to you; **vi darò un consiglio** I'll give you some advice; **vi scriverò** I'll write to you; **vi ha salutato?** did he say hello to you?; **ve lo do subito** I'll give it to you in a moment; **vi ha sorriso** he smiled at you **3** (*riflessivo*) yourselves; (*reciproco*) each other; **vestitevi** get dressed; **pettinatevi** comb your hair; **divertitevi** enjoy yourselves; **vi siete divertiti?** did you enjoy yourselves?; **vi siete fatti male?** did you hurt yourselves?; **ve ne pentirete** you'll regret it; **vi conoscete?** do you know each other? ♦ PRON DIMOSTR = **ci** ♦ AVV (*in questo luogo*) here; (*in quel luogo*) there; **vi sono stato parecchie volte** I've been there several times; **non vi erano che pochi turisti** there were only a few tourists there; **vi sono molti modi di farlo** there are many ways of doing it

via¹ ['via] SF **1** (*strada*) road; (*di città*) street, road; (*cammino*) way; (*percorso*) route; (*sentiero, pista*) path, track; **abito in una via molto stretta** I live in a very narrow street; **abito in via Manzoni 5** I live at number 5, Via Manzoni; **la via dell'oppio** the opium trail; **vie di comunicazione** communication routes; **che via fai di solito?** what route do you usually take?; **sulla via di casa** on one's way home; **hai via libera** (*a un incrocio*) the road is clear; **dare via libera a qc** (*fig*) to give the green light *o* the go-ahead; **allontanarsi dalla retta via** (*fig*) to stray from the straight and narrow; **in via di guarigione** on the road to recovery; **paese in via di sviluppo** developing country; **la sua laurea gli apre molte vie** his degree offers him many possibilities **2** (*mezzo*) way, means; (*procedimento*) channels *pl*; (*fig: modo*) way; **tentare tutte le vie** to try everything possible; **per vie traverse** by underhand means; **non avevo altra via** I had no alternative; **non c'è via di scampo** *o* **d'uscita** there's no way out; **via di mezzo** halfway; **è una via di mezzo tra…** it's halfway between…; **non c'è via di mezzo** there's no middle ground; **scegliere la via di mezzo** to compromise; **te lo dico in via privata** *o* **confidenziale** I'm telling you in confidence; (*ufficiosamente*) I'm telling you unofficially; **in via eccezionale** as an exception; **in via provvisoria** provisionally; **in via amichevole** in a friendly manner; **comporre una disputa in via amichevole** (*Dir*) to settle a dispute out of court; **adire le vie legali** to take legal proceedings; **le vie del Signore** the ways of the Lord; **passare alle vie di fatto** to resort to violence; **per via aerea** by air; **spedire per via aerea** to send by airmail; **via satellite** by satellite; **via Dover** via Dover; **per via di** because of, on account of 3 (*Anat*) tract; **le vie respiratorie** the respiratory tracts; **per via orale** (*Med*) orally 4 (*Astron*): **la Via Lattea** the Milky Way

via² [ˈvia] AVV 1 (*allontanamento*) away; (*temporaneo*) out; **buttare** *o* **gettare via qc** to throw sth away; **l'ho buttato via** I threw it away; **tagliare via** to cut off *o* away; **dare via qc** to give sth away; **è andato via** (*per poco tempo*) he has gone out; (*per molto tempo*) he has gone away; **sono stato via per 3 settimane** I was away for three weeks; **vai via!** go away!, clear off!; (*fam*); **questa macchia non va via** this mark won't come out 2 (*eccetera*): **e così via** and so on; **e via dicendo, e via di questo passo** and so on (and so forth) 3 **via via** (*pian piano*) gradually; **via via che** (*man mano*) as ♦ **da via** away from; **non andare via da me** don't leave me ♦ ESCL (*suvvia*) come on!; (*allontanati*) go away!; (*a un animale*) shoo!; **pronti, via!** ready, steady, go! ♦ SM (*Sport*) (signal to start) starting signal; **dare il via** to start the race, give the starting signal; **quando darai il via?** when are you going to give the starting signal?; **dare il via a un progetto** to give the green light to a project; **hanno dato il via ai lavori** they've begun *o* started work

viabilità [viabiliˈta] SF (*percorribilità*) practicability; (*rete stradale*) roads *pl*, road network; **la viabilità è interrotta a causa di una frana** the road is blocked because of a landslide; **un piano per migliorare la viabilità del centro** a plan to improve traffic circulation in the centre (*Brit*) *o* center (*USA*)

viadotto [viaˈdotto] SM viaduct

viaggiare [viadˈdʒare] /62/ VI (*aus avere*) 1 (*gen*) to travel; **mi piace viaggiare** I like travelling (*Brit*) *o* traveling (*USA*); **viaggi spesso per lavoro?** do you travel much for your job?; **viaggiare all'estero** to travel abroad; **viaggiare in treno/aereo** to travel by train/plane; **è uno che ha viaggiato molto** he's well-travel(l)ed, he has travel(l)ed a lot; **la macchina viaggiava a 50 chilometri all'ora** the car was travel(l)ing at (a speed of) 50 kilometres per hour; **il treno viaggia con 50 minuti di ritardo** the train is running 50 minutes late; **le merci viaggiano via mare** the goods go *o* are sent by sea 2 (*fare il commesso viaggiatore*): **viaggiare per una ditta** to be a travel(l)ing salesman *o* a sales representative for a company

viaggiatore, -trice [viaddʒaˈtore] AGG travelling (*Brit*), traveling (*USA*); **piccione viaggiatore** carrier pigeon; **commesso viaggiatore** travel(l)ing salesman ♦ SM, SF (*gen*) traveller (*Brit*), traveler (*USA*); (*passeggero*) passenger

viaggio, -gi [viˈaddʒo] SM (*gen*) travel, travelling (*Brit*), traveling (*USA*); (*tragitto*) journey, trip; (*in aereo*) flight; (*via mare*) voyage; **buon viaggio!** have a good trip!; **avete fatto buon viaggio?** did you have a good journey?; **è stato un viaggio molto faticoso** it was a very tiring journey; **vorrei fare un viaggio in Cina** I'd like to visit China; **è in viaggio** he's away; **agenzia di viaggi** travel agency; **spese di viaggio** travel(l)ing expenses; **ho dovuto fare due viaggi per portar su i libri** I had to make two trips to bring the books up; **fare un viaggio a vuoto** to make a wasted journey; **mi hanno rimborsato il viaggio** they gave me my travel(l)ing expenses; **viaggio d'affari** business trip; **papà è in viaggio d'affari** Dad's on a business trip; **viaggio di nozze** honeymoon; **dove andranno in viaggio di nozze?** where are they going on their honeymoon?; **viaggio organizzato** package tour *o* holiday; **sono andato a Praga con un viaggio organizzato** I went to Prague on a package tour; **viaggio di piacere** pleasure trip

viale [viˈale] SM 1·(*in città*) avenue 2 (*in parco*) path, walk 3 **è sul viale del tramonto** his star is on the wane

viandante [vianˈdante] SM, SF wayfarer

viatico, -ci [viˈatiko] SM (*Rel*) viaticum

viavai [viaˈvai] SM INV coming and going, bustle; **c'era un gran viavai** there was a lot of coming and going

vibrare [viˈbrare] /72/ VT (*dare con forza*): **vibrare un colpo a qn** to strike sb; **vibrare una coltellata a qn** to stab sb ♦ VI (*aus avere*) 1 (*gen, anche Fis*) to vibrate; **vibrare (di)** (*voce*) to quiver (with), be vibrant (with); **il suo cuore vibrava di emozione** her heart throbbed with emotion 2 (*risuonare*) to resound, ring

vibratore, -trice [vibraˈtore] AGG vibrating ♦ SM vibrator

vibrazione [vibratˈtsjone] SF vibration

vicario, -ri [viˈkarjo] SM (*Rel*) vicar

vice [ˈvitʃe] SM, SF deputy

viceconsole [vitʃeˈkɔnsole] SM vice-consul

vicedirettore, -trice [vitʃediretˈtore] SM, SF (*gen*) deputy manager (manageress), assistant manager (manageress); (*di giornale*) deputy editor; (*di scuola*) deputy headmaster/headmistress (*Brit*), vice-principal (*USA*)

vicenda [viˈtʃenda] SF 1 (*episodio*) event; **il libro parla delle vicende che hanno portato alla guerra** the book discusses the events that led up to the war; **è una vicenda estremamente complicata** it's an extremely complicated story 2 **vicende** (*sorte*) fortunes; **con alterne vicende** with mixed fortunes ♦ **a vicenda** AVV 1 (*reciprocamente*) each other, one another; **ci siamo aiutati a vicenda** we helped each other 2 (*alternativamente*) in turn(s)

vicendevole [vitʃenˈdevole] AGG mutual, reciprocal

vicentino, -a [vitʃenˈtino] AGG of *o* from Vicenza ♦ SM, SF inhabitant *o* native of Vicenza

vicepresidente [vitʃepresiˈdɛnte] SM (*di stato*) vice-president; (*di società*) vice-chairman

viceversa [vitʃeˈversa] AVV vice versa; **da Roma a Pisa e viceversa** from Rome to Pisa and back

vichingo, -a, -ghi, -ghe [viˈkingo] AGG, SM, SF Viking

vicinanza [vitʃiˈnantsa] SF 1 (*prossimità*) proximity, closeness, nearness 2 **vicinanze** SFPL (*paraggi*) vicinity *sg*; **nelle vicinanze ci sono due panettieri** there are two bakers in the vicinity *o* in the area

vicinato [vitʃiˈnato] SM (*zona*) neighbourhood (*Brit*), neighborhood (*USA*); (*vicini*) neighbo(u)rs *pl*; **avere rapporti di buon vicinato** to get on well with one's neighbo(u)rs

vicino, -a [viˈtʃino] AGG 1 (*a poca distanza*) near, nearby; (*paese*) neighbouring (*Brit*), neighboring (*USA*), nearby; **vicino a** near, close to; **un paese vicino** a nearby village; **l'interruttore della luce è vicino alla porta** the light switch is near the door; **la stazione è vicina** the station is near, the station is close (by); **dov'è il ristorante più vicino?** where is the nearest restaurant?; **quei quadri sono troppo vicini** those pictures are too close (together *o* to each other); **mi sono stati molto vicini** (*fig*) they were very supportive towards me 2 (*accanto*) next; **la mia stanza è vicina alla tua** my room is next to yours 3 (*nel tempo*) near, close at hand; **la fine è vicina** the end is near *o* imminent; **siamo vicini alla fine** we've almost *o* nearly finished; **le vacanze sono vicine** the holidays are (*Brit*) *o* the vacation is (*USA*) approaching; **è vicina ai trent'anni** she's almost thirty ♦ AVV 1 (*a poca distanza*) near, nearby, close (by); (*nel tempo*) near, close; **vieni più vicino** come closer; **abitiamo qui vicino** we live near here; **stai vicino!** stay close to me! 2 **da vicino** close to; (*esaminare, seguire*) closely; (*sparare*) at close quarters; **guardare qc da vicino** to take a close look at sth; **guardalo da vicino!** take a close look at it!; **da vicino è più viola** it looks more purple when you see it close up; **fai la fotografia da vicino** take the photograph close up 3 **vicino a** close to, near (to); (*accanto a*) beside, next to; **vivono vicino al mare** they live close to *o* near the sea; **era seduto vicino a me** he was sitting near me; (*accanto a*) he was sitting next to *o* beside me; **state vicino a vostro padre** (*anche fig*) stay close to your father; **ci sono andato vicino** (*fig: quasi indovinato*) I almost got it ♦ SM, SF neighbour (*Brit*), neighbor (*USA*); **i nostri vicini di casa** our next-door neighbo(u)rs; **il mio vicino di banco** the person at the desk next to mine, my neighbo(u)r

vicissitudini [vitʃissiˈtudini] SFPL trials and tribulations; **le vicissitudini della vita** the ups and downs of life

vicolo [ˈvikolo] SM alley; **vicolo cieco** blind alley

video [ˈvideo] SM INV 1 (*TV: schermo*) screen; **ci sono dei disturbi al video** the picture is not very good 2 (*Inform: schermo*) screen; (: *videoterminale*) visual display unit 3 (*video musicale*) video

videocamera [videoˈkamera] SF camcorder

videocassetta [videokasˈsetta] SF videocassette; **abbiamo noleggiato una videocassetta** we rented a video

videochia'mare [videokjaˈmare] /72/ VT to video call

videoclip [videoˈklip] SF INV video clip

videodipendente [videodipenˈdɛnte] SM, SF telly *o* television addict ♦ AGG: **un pigrone videodipendente** a couch potato

videofonino [videofoˈnino] SM video mobile

videogioco, -chi [videoˈdʒɔko] SM video game

videonoleggio [videonoleˈdʒo] SM video rental

videoregistratore [videoredʒistraˈtore] SM video (recorder)

videoteca, -che [videoˈtɛka] SF video shop

videotelefono [videoteˈlefono] SM videophone

videoterminale [videotermiˈnale] SM visual display unit

vidi ecc [ˈvidi] VB *vedi* **vedere**

vidimare [vidiˈmare] /72/ VT (*Amm*) to authenticate

vidimazione [vidimatˈtsjone] SF (*Amm*) authentication

Vienna [ˈvjenna] SF Vienna

viennese [vjenˈnese] AGG, SM, SF Viennese *inv*

vietare [vjeˈtare] /72/ VT (*proibire*) to forbid; (*Amm: importazione, sosta*) to prohibit, ban; (: *sciopero, manifestazione*) to ban, prohibit; **vietare a qn di fare qc** to forbid sb to do sth, prohibit sb from doing sth; **il dottore gli ha vietato di fumare** the doctor has forbidden him to smoke; **hanno vietato il passaggio dei camion in centro** trucks have been banned from *o* prohibited in the centre; **nulla ti vieta di farlo** there is nothing to prevent *o* stop you doing it; **nulla vieta che io lo faccia** there is nothing to stop me; **e chi te lo vieta?** who's stopping you?

vietato, -a [vjeˈtato] AGG (*vedi vb*) forbidden; prohibited; banned; **"vietato calpestare le aiuole"** "keep off the grass"; **"vietato fumare"** "no smoking"; **qui è vietato fumare** smoking is not allowed here; **"vietato sporgersi dal finestrino"** "do not lean out of the window"; **"senso vietato"** (*Aut*) "no entry"; **"sosta vietata"** (*Aut*) "no parking"; **"vietata l'affissione"** "post *o* stick no bills", "bill stickers will be prosecuted"; **"vietato ai minori di 14/18 anni"** "prohibited to children under 14/18"; **è un film vietato ai minori di 18 anni** you have to be eighteen to see that film

Vietnam [vjetˈnam] SM Vietnam

vietnamita, -i, -e [vjetnaˈmita] AGG, SM, SF Vietnamese *inv*

vieto, -a [ˈvjeto] AGG (*antiquato*) antiquated

vigente [viˈdʒɛnte] AGG (*Dir: legge*) in force; (*fig*) current, in use

vigere [ˈvidʒere] /29/ VI *vb dif* (*si usa solo alla terza persona*) to be in force; **in Italia vige ancora l'obbligo del servizio militare** in Italy national service is still compulsory; **in casa mia vige l'abitudine di...** at home we are in the habit of ...

vigilante [vidʒiˈlante] AGG vigilant, watchful ♦ SM, SF security guard

vigilanza [vidʒiˈlantsa] SF (*sorveglianza: di operai, alunni*) supervision; (: *di sospetti, criminali*) surveillance; **chiamate la vigilanza!** call security!; **occorre aumentare la vigilanza** we need to be more vigilant; **vigilanza notturna** night-watchman service

vigilare [vidʒiˈlare] /72/ VT (*sorvegliare: bambini*) to watch over, keep an eye on; (: *operai, studenti, lavori*) to supervise; (: *sospetti, criminali*) to keep under surveillance ♦ VI (*aus avere*) (*provvedere a*): **vigilare che...** to make sure that ..., see to it that ...

vigilato, -a [vidʒiˈlato] AGG (*Dir*): **essere in libertà vigilata** to be on probation ♦ SM, SF (*Dir*) person under police surveillance

vigilatrice [vidʒilaˈtritʃe] SF: **vigilatrice d'infanzia** nursery assistant, nursery nurse (*Brit*)

vigile [ˈvidʒile] AGG (*persona, occhio*) vigilant, watchful; (*cura*) vigilant ♦ SM, SF (*anche:* **vigile urbano**) (traffic) police officer; **i vigili urbani** municipal police; **vigile di quartiere** local police officer; **vigile del fuoco** firefighter ♦ SM: **i vigili del fuoco** the fire brigade; **chiamare i vigili del fuoco** to call the fire brigade (*Brit*) *o* department (*USA*)

vigi'lessa [vidʒiˈlessa] SF (traffic) policewoman

vigilia [viˈdʒilja] SF 1 (*giorno antecedente*) eve; **alla vigilia di** on the eve of; **alla vigilia degli esami** on the eve of the exams; **vigilia di Capodanno** New Year's Eve; **vigilia di Natale** Christmas Eve 2 (*Rel: digiuno*) fast 3 (*letter: veglia*) vigil

vigliaccheria [viʎʎakkeˈria] SF (*qualità*) cowardice; (*azione*) act of cowardice, cowardly action; **è stata una vigliaccheria da parte sua** it was contemptible of him

vigliacco, -a, -chi, -che [viʎˈʎakko] AGG (*persona, azione*) cowardly; (*spregevole*) contemptible ♦ SM, SF 1 (*codardo*) coward 2 (*profittatore*) rogue, scoundrel

vigna [ˈviɲɲa] SF vineyard

vignetta [viɲˈɲetta] SF (*disegno*) illustration; (*umoristica*) cartoon; (*bollino autostradale*) motorway pass (*used in countries such as Austria and Switzerland*)

vigogna [viˈɡoɲɲa] SF vicuña

vigore [viˈgore] SM 1 (*gen*) vigour (*Brit*), vigor (*USA*), strength; (*fig: forza*) vigo(u)r, force; **nel suo pieno vigore** in his prime, in the prime of life; **perdere vigore** (*persona*) to lose strength; (*campagna elettorale*) to lose impetus; (*discorso, stile*) to become less vigorous *o* energetic; **riacquistare vigore** (*persona*) to regain one's strength 2 (*Dir*): **essere in vigore** to be in force; **entrare in vigore** to come into force *o* effect; **non è più in vigore** it is no longer in force, it no longer applies

vigoroso, -a [vigoˈroso] AGG (*gen*) vigorous; (*membra*) strong, powerful; (*stile*) vigorous, energetic; (*resistenza*) vigorous, strenuous; **una vigorosa stretta di mano** a firm handshake

vile [ˈvile] AGG (*vigliacco*) cowardly; (*spregevole*) contemptible, base, low, mean; **una vile menzogna** a wicked lie; **il vile denaro** filthy lucre ♦ SM, SF coward

vilipendere [viliˈpendere] /8/ VT IRREG to despise, scorn

vilipendio, -di [viliˈpendjo] SM (*Dir*) contempt, scorn; **vilipendio alla bandiera** contempt for the national flag

vilipeso, -a [viliˈpeso] PP *di* **vilipendere**

villa [ˈvilla] SF (*in città*) detached house; (*in campagna*) country house; (*al mare*) villa

villaggio, -gi [vilˈladdʒo] SM village; **un villaggio africano** an African village; **villaggio globale** global village; **villaggio olimpico** Olympic village; **villaggio residenziale** commuter town; **villaggio turistico** holiday village (*Brit*) *o* town (*USA*)

villania [villaˈnia] SF (*sgarbataggine*) rudeness, bad manners *pl*, lack of manners; **è stata una villania da parte sua** it was very rude of him; **fare (o dire) una villania a qn** to be rude to sb

villano, -a [vilˈlano] AGG rude, ill-mannered; **modi villani** bad manners ♦ SM, SF 1 (*maleducato*) lout, boor 2 (*letter: contadino*) peasant; **un villano rifatto** (*pegg*) a nouveau riche, an upstart

❑ **villano** non si traduce mai con la parola inglese *villain*

villeggiante [villedˈdʒante] SM, SF holiday-maker (*Brit*), vacationer (*USA*), vacationist (*USA*)

villeggiare [villedˈdʒare] /62/ VI (*aus avere*) to holiday (*Brit*), spend one's holidays (*Brit*), vacation (*USA*)

villeggiatura [villeddʒaˈtura] SF holiday(s *pl*) (*Brit*), vacation (*USA*); **andare/essere in villeggiatura** to go/be on holiday *o* vacation; **luogo di villeggiatura** (holiday *o* vacation) resort

villetta [vilˈletta] SF , **villino** SM (*in città*) small (detached) house (*with a garden*); (*in campagna*) cottage; **villette a schiera** terraced houses

villoso, -a [vilˈloso] AGG hairy

viltà [vilˈta] SF INV cowardice *no pl*; **atto di viltà** act of cowardice, cowardly act

Viminale [vimiˈnale] SM *one of the Seven Hills of Rome*

vimine [ˈvimine] SM (*Bot*) osier; **di vimini** (*sedia*) wicker *attr*, wickerwork *attr*

vinaio, -ai [viˈnajo] SM wine merchant

vincere [ˈvintʃere] VB IRREG /129/ VT 1 (*gen*) to win; **vincere**

una causa (*Dir*) to win a case *o* suit; **vincere un premio** to win a prize; **ieri abbiamo vinto la partita** we won the match yesterday **2** (*sconfiggere: nemico*) to defeat, vanquish; (: *avversario*) to beat; **vincere qn a tennis** to beat sb at tennis **3** (*superare: sentimenti*) to overcome; (*avere ragione di*) to get the better of, outdo; **ho vinto la paura** I got over my fear; **fu vinto dalla stanchezza** tiredness overcame him; **lasciarsi vincere dalla tentazione** to succumb *o* yield to temptation; **vincere qn in** (*abilità*) to outdo *o* surpass sb in; (*bellezza*) to surpass sb in; **vuole sempre averla vinta** he always wants to have the upper hand ♦ VI (*aus* avere) **1** (*in gioco, battaglia*) to win; **vinca il migliore** may the best man win **2** (*prevalere*) to win, prevail; **vincersi** VR to control o.s.

vincita ['vintʃita] SF (*il vincere*) win, victory; (*cosa vinta*) winnings *pl*

vincitore, -trice [vintʃi'tore] AGG winning, victorious ♦ SM, SF (*in gara*) winner; (*in battaglia*) victor, winner

vincolante [vinko'lante] AGG binding

vincolare [vinko'lare] /72/ VT **1** (*Dir*) to bind; (*fig: sogg: famiglia, lavoro*) to tie down **2** (*Fin*): **vincolare una somma in banca** to place a sum on fixed deposit

vincolato, -a [vinko'lato] AGG (*vedi vt*) bound; tied; **deposito vincolato** fixed deposit

vincolo ['vinkolo] SM (*gen*) bond, tie; (*di sangue*) tie; (*Dir*) encumbrance, obligation; **libero da ogni vincolo** free from all ties; (*Dir*) unencumbered

vinicolo, -a [vi'nikolo] AGG wine *attr*; **regione vinicola** wine-producing area

vinificazione [vinifikat'tsjone] SF wine-making

vino ['vino] SM wine; **lista** *o* **carta dei vini** wine list; **vino bianco/rosso/rosato** white/red/rosé wine; (*fig*) **dire pane al pane, vino al vino** to call a spade a spade; **buon vino fa buon sangue** (*Proverbio*) good wine makes good cheer; **vin brûlé** mulled wine

❏ **vino** non si traduce mai con la parola inglese *vine*

vinsi *ecc* ['vinsi] VB *vedi* vincere

vinto, -a ['vinto] PP *di* vincere ♦ AGG **1** (*sconfitto*) defeated, beaten **2** (*oggetto*): **i soldi vinti al gioco** money won gambling; **darla vinta a qn** to let sb have his (*o* her) way; **darsi per vinto** to give up, give in; **vuol sempre avere partita vinta** he always wants to have the upper hand ♦ SM, SF (*gen*) loser; **i vinti** SMPL the defeated (side), the vanquished

viola¹ [vi'ɔla] SF (*Bot*) violet; **viola del pensiero** pansy ♦ SM INV (*colore*) violet, purple

viola² [vi'ɔla] SF (*Mus*) viola

violare [vio'lare] /72/ VT (*gen*) to violate; (*legge*) to violate, infringe, break; (*promessa*) to break; (*domicilio*) to break into; (*tempio*) to desecrate; (*donna*) to rape; **violare la privacy di qn** to invade sb's privacy

violazione [violat'tsjone] SF (*vedi vb*) violation; infringement, breach; breaking; breaking into; desecration; **violazione di domicilio** (*Dir*) unlawful entry

violentare [violen'tare] /72/ VT to use violence on; (*sessualmente*) to rape; (*fig: coscienza*) to outrage; **in questo modo violenti la sua volontà** you are forcing him to do it against his will

violento, -a [vio'lento] AGG (*gen*) violent; (*suono*) loud; (*luce*) blinding; (*colore*) loud, garish; (*incendio*) raging; **usare un tono violento** to express o.s. with violence; **usare modi violenti** to use violence; **morire di morte violenta** to die a violent death ♦ SM, SF violent person

violenza [vio'lentsa] SF (*gen*) violence; (*di vento, temporale*) violence, force; **ricorrere alla/far uso della violenza** to resort to/use violence

violetto, -a [vio'letto] AGG, SM (*colore*) violet

violinista, -i, -e [violi'nista] SM, SF violinist

violino [vio'lino] SM violin; **essere teso come una corda di violino** (*fig*) to be very tense; **primo violino** first violin; **chiave di violino** treble clef

violoncellista, -i, -e [violontʃel'lista] SM, SF cellist, cello player

violoncello [violon'tʃello] SM violoncello, cello

viottolo [vi'ɔttolo] SM path, track

VIP [vip] SM INV, SF INV (= *Very Important Person*) VIP

vipera ['vipera] SF (*Zool*) viper, adder; (*fig*) catty person

viraggio, -gi [vi'raddʒo] SM **1** (*Naut*) coming about; (*Aer*) turn **2** (*Fot*) toning

virale [vi'rale] AGG viral

virare [vi'rare] /72/ VI (*aus* avere) **1** (*Naut*) to come about; (*Aer*) to turn; **virare di bordo** to change course **2** (*Fot*) to tone

virata [vi'rata] SF (*vedi vb a*) coming about; turning; change of course; (*Sport: nuoto*) turn; **la virata del governo in materia fiscale** the government's U-turn on fiscal policy

virgola ['virgola] SF (*nella punteggiatura*) comma; (*Mat*) (decimal) point; **non c'è una virgola fuori posto** (*fig: in uno scritto*) it's an excellent piece of work; **non cambiare una virgola** (*fig*) don't change a thing; **punto e virgola** semicolon

virgolette [virgo'lette] SFPL quotation marks, inverted commas (*Brit*); **tra virgolette** in quotation marks *o* inverted commas; **una parola scritta tra virgolette** a word written in inverted commas

virile [vi'rile] AGG (*aspetto, voce*) masculine; (*atteggiamento, lineamenti*) manly, virile; (*bellezza*) male *attr*; (*stile*) vigorous, virile; (*linguaggio*) firm; **età virile** manhood

virilità [virili'ta] SF (*vedi agg*) masculinity; manliness; virility; vigour (*Brit*), vigor (*USA*); firmness

virtù [vir'tu] SF INV **1** (*Rel*) virtue; (*pregio, qualità*) virtue, quality; (*virtuosità, castità*) virtuousness; **un modello di virtù** a paragon of virtue; **fare di necessità virtù** to make a virtue of necessity **2** (*capacità: di persona*) ability; (*proprietà: di erbe, sostanze*) property; **in virtù di questa legge** by virtue of this law; **in virtù della nostra amicizia** for friendship's sake

virtuale [virtu'ale] AGG (*gen*) potential; (*Fis*) virtual; **realtà virtuale** virtual reality

virtuoso, -a [virtu'oso] AGG virtuous ♦ SM, SF (*del violino, pennello*) virtuoso, master (mistress)

virulento, -a [viru'lento] AGG virulent

virus ['virus] SM INV (*Med, Inform*) virus

visagista, -i, -e [viza'dʒista] SM, SF beautician

viscerale [viʃʃe'rale] AGG (*Med*) visceral; (*fig*) profound, deep-rooted

viscere [viʃʃere] SM (*Anat*) internal organ ♦ SFPL (*di animale*) entrails *pl*; (*fig*) depths *pl*, bowels *pl*; **nelle viscere della terra** in the bowels of the earth

vischio ['viskjo] SM **1** (*Bot*) mistletoe **2** (*pania*) birdlime

vischioso, -a [vis'kjoso] AGG (*colloso*) sticky; (*viscoso*) viscous

viscidità [viʃʃidi'ta] SF (*vedi agg*) sliminess; smarminess

viscido, -a [viʃʃido] AGG (*lumaca, pelle*) slimy; (*fig: persona*) smarmy

visconte, -essa [vis'konte] SM, SF viscount (viscountess)

viscosità [viskosi'ta] SF viscosity

viscoso, -a [vis'koso] AGG viscous

visibile [vi'zibile] AGG (*gen*) visible; (*imbarazzo*) obvious, evident, visible; (*progresso*) clear, perceptible

visibilio [vizi'biljo] SM: **andare in visibilio (per qc)** to go into ecstasies *o* raptures (over sth)

visibilità [vizibili'ta] SF visibility

visiera [vi'zjera] SF (*di cappello*) peak; (*di elmo, casco*) visor

visionare [vizjo'nare] /72/ VT (*gen*) to look at, examine; (*Cine*) to screen

visionario, -ria, -ri, -rie [vizjo'narjo] AGG, SM, SF visionary

visione [vi'zjone] SF **1** (*gen, anche Rel*) vision; (*scena*) sight; (*idea, concetto*) view; **hanno avuto una visione della Madonna** they had a vision of the Virgin Mary; **ma tu hai le visioni!** you must be seeing things!; **la mia visione della realtà** my view of reality; **avere una visione limitata della realtà** to have a narrow view of reality **2** (*atto del vedere*) vision, sight; **prendere visione di qc** to have a look at sth, examine sth, look sth over; **mandare qc in visione** (*Comm*) to send sth on approval; **prima/seconda visione** (*Cine*) first/second showing, first run/rerun; **trasmettiamo in prima visione il film...** we're showing the first screening of the film ...; **film in prima visione** newly released film; **cinema di prima visione** cinema where films are shown on first release

visita ['vizita] SF **1** (*gen*) visit; (*di amico, rappresentante*) visit, call; **far visita a qn, andare in visita da qn** to visit sb, pay sb a visit; **andiamo a fargli visita** let's go and visit him; **in visita ufficiale in Italia** on an official visit to Italy; **biglietto da visita** (visiting) card; **abbiamo visite** we have visitors *o* guests; **c'è una visita per te** you've got a visitor **2** (*turistica: di città*) tour; (: *di museo*) tour, visit; **la visita del castello dura 2 ore** the tour of the castle takes 2 hours, it takes 2 hours to go round the castle; **visita guidata** guided tour; **quanto costa la visita guidata della città?** how much is a guided tour of the city? **3** (*Med: esame*) examination; **il medico sta facendo il giro delle visite** the doctor is doing his rounds; **orario di visite** (*ospedale*) visiting hours; (*ambulatorio*) consulting *o* surgery (*Brit*) hours; **marcare visita** (*Mil*) to report sick; **visita di controllo** checkup; **ho fatto una visita di controllo** I had a check-up; **visita domiciliare** house call; **visita fiscale** *house call made on state employee by doctor to verify condition of patient*; **visita di leva** (*Mil*) medical (*Brit*) *o* physical (*USA*) examination

visitare [vizi'tare] /72/ VT **1** (*andare in visita*) to visit, call on, go and see; (*rappresentante*) to call on; **andare a visitare qn** to go and see *o* visit sb **2** (*museo*) to visit, go round; **ci ha fatto visitare la casa/il castello** he showed us round the house/castle; **hai già visitato la National Gallery?** have you visited the National Gallery?; **visitate il nostro sito internet** visit our website **3** (*Med*) to examine; **siamo rimasti con lei finché il dottore l'ha visitata** we stayed with her until the doctor examined her; **visitare i pazienti a casa** to see patients at home; **il medico sta visitando** the doctor is seeing *o* receiving patients now; **il medico visita solo il giovedì** the doctor only sees patients on Thursdays; **bisogna che mi faccia visitare** I must go and have a medical examination *o* a checkup

visitatore, -trice [vizita'tore] SM, SF **1** (*ospite*) visitor, guest **2** (*turista*) visitor, tourist

visivo, -a [vi'zivo] AGG visual; **memoria visiva** visual memory; **gli organi visivi** the eyes

viso ['vizo] SM face; **si è spalmata la crema sul viso** she rubbed the cream into her face; **crema per il viso** face cream; **guardare in viso qn** to look sb in the face, look straight at sb; **fare buon viso a cattivo gioco** to make the best of things; **a viso aperto** openly; **viso pallido** (*uomo bianco*) paleface

visone [vi'zone] SM (*Zool*) mink; (*pelliccia*) mink (coat); **una pelliccia di visone** a mink coat

visore [vi'zore] SM (*Fot*) viewer

vispo, -a ['vispo] AGG (*bambino*) lively; (*vecchietto*) sprightly; (*occhi*) bright

vissi *ecc* ['vissi] VB *vedi* **vivere**

vissuto, -a [vis'suto] PP *di* **vivere** ♦ AGG **1 storia di vita vissuta** story from real life **2** (*persona*) experienced, who has had many experiences

vista ['vista] SF **1** (*gen*) sight; (*capacità visiva*) eyesight, sight; **avere la vista buona** to have good eyesight; **avere la vista corta/lunga** to be short-/long-sighted; (*fig*) to be short-/far-sighted; **ho avuto un improvviso abbassamento della vista** my eyesight suddenly got worse; **la vista mi si sta indebolendo** my sight is deteriorating; **difetti della vista** eye problems; **esame della vista** eye test; **occhiali da vista** glasses; **sottrarsi alla vista di qn** to disappear from sb's sight; **mettersi in vista** to draw attention to o.s.; (*pegg*) to show off; **essere in vista** (*persona*) to be in the public eye; **terra in vista!** land ahoy!; **è in vista una ripresa economica** economic recovery is in sight; **a prima vista** at first sight; **è stato amore a prima vista** it was love at first sight; (*fig*) **conoscere qn di vista** to know sb by sight; **lo conosco solo di vista** I only know him by sight; **in vista di qc** in view of sth; **sparare a vista** to shoot on sight; **pagabile a vista** payable on demand; **avere in vista qc** to have sth in view; **a vista d'occhio** as far as the eye can see; (*fig*) before one's very eyes; **perdere qn di vista** (*anche fig*) to lose sight of sb; **correva così veloce che l'ho perso di vista** he was running so fast that I lost sight of him; **dopo aver finito l'università si sono persi di vista** they lost touch after they left university **2** (*veduta*) view; **una camera con vista sul lago** a room with a view of the lake

vistare [vis'tare] /72/ VT to approve; (*Amm: passaporto*) to visa

visto, -a ['visto] PP *di* **vedere** ♦ SM **1** (*segno*) tick (*Brit*), check (*USA*); (*Amm: approvazione*) approval **2** (*Amm*) visa; **visto d'ingresso** entry visa; **visto permanente** permanent visa; **visto di soggiorno** residence visa; **visto di transito** transit visa

vistoso, -a [vis'toso] AGG (*colore*) garish; (*bellezza*) flashy; (*scritta, insegna*) showy; (*aumento*) enormous, huge

visuale [vizu'ale] AGG visual ♦ SF (*gen*) view; (*Ottica*) line of vision; (*nel tiro*) line of sight; **togliere la visuale a qn** to block sb's view

visualizzare [vizualid'dzare] /72/ VT to visualize

visualizzatore [vizualiddza'tore] SM (*Inform*) display, visual display unit, VDU; **visualizzatore a cristalli liquidi** liquid crystal display

visualizzazione [vizualiddzat'tsjone] SF (*Inform*) display

vita¹ ['vita] SF **1** (*gen*) life; **essere in vita** to be alive; **quando sono arrivati era ancora in vita** when they got there he was still alive; **perdere la vita** to lose one's life; **far ritornare in vita qn** to bring sb back to life; **dare la vita per qn/qc** to give one's life for sb/sth; **ha rischiato la vita per aiutarla** he risked his life to help her; **pieno di vita** full of life; **ha dato un po' di vita alla festa** he livened up the party a bit **2** (*modo di vivere*) life, lifestyle; **nella vita quotidiana** *o* **di ogni giorno** in everyday life; **la vita da studente** life as a student; **la vita in Scozia** life in Scotland; **la vita degli animali** animal life; **condurre una vita attiva** to lead an active life; **avere una doppia vita** to lead a double life; **cambiare vita** to change one's way of life *o* one's lifestyle; **vita notturna** nightlife **3** (*mezzi di sussistenza*) living; **guadagnarsi la vita** to earn one's living; **il costo della vita** the cost of living; **la vita è cara a Parigi** it's expensive to live in Paris **4** (*durata*) life, lifetime; **ti amerò per tutta la vita** I'll love you for ever *o* all my life; **ho lavorato per tutta la vita** I've worked all my life; **una volta nella vita** once in a lifetime; **capita una volta sola nella vita** it only happens once in a lifetime; **mai... in vita mia** never; **non l'ho mai fatto in vita mia** I've never done it; **membro a vita** life member; **carcere a vita** life imprisonment; **avere sette vite** to have nine lives; **non basterebbe una vita per spiegartelo** it would take a lifetime to explain it to you; **vita media** average life expectancy **5** (*biografia*) life (story); **mi ha raccontato tutta la sua vita** she told me her life story *o* the story of her life **6** (*fraseologia*): **l'altra vita** the hereafter; **o la borsa o la vita!** your money or your life!; **ci metti una vita!** you are taking ages!; **da una vita** for a long time; **non lo vedo da una vita** I haven't seen him for a long time; **è la vita!** that's life!

vita² ['vita] SF (*Anat*) waist; **jeans a vita alta/bassa** jeans with a high/low waist; **mi è un po' largo in vita** it's a bit loose round the waist; **punto (di) vita** (*Sartoria*) waist

vitale [vi'tale] AGG **1** (*gen*) vital; (*vivace: persona*) lively, vital; **spazio vitale** living space **2** (*che può vivere*) viable

vitalità [vitali'ta] SF vitality, vigour (*Brit*), vigor (*USA*)

vitalizio, -zia, -zi, -zie [vita'littsjo] AGG life *attr* ♦ SM (*Dir*) life annuity

vitamina [vita'mina] SF vitamin

vite¹ ['vite] SF (*Bot*) (grape)vine; **vite del Canada** Virginia creeper

vite² ['vite] SF **1** (*Tecn*) screw; **giro di vite** (*anche fig*) turn of the screw; **tappo a vite** screw(-on) cap *o* top; **vite senza fine** endless screw **2** (*Aer*) (tail)spin

vitello [vi'tɛllo] SM **1** (*Zool*) calf **2** (*Culin*) veal; **una scaloppina di vitello** a veal escalope; **vitello tonnato** veal in tuna fish sauce **3** (*pelle*) calf(skin)

viticcio, -ci [vi'tittʃo] SM (*Bot*) tendril

viticoltore [vitikol'tore] SM vine grower

viticoltura [vitikol'tura] SF vine growing

vitreo, -a ['vitreo] AGG (*sostanza*) vitreous; (*occhio, sguardo*) glassy

vittima ['vittima] SF (*gen*) victim; (*di incidente*) casualty, victim; **fare la vittima** to play the martyr

vittimismo [vitti'mizmo] SM self-pity

vitto ['vitto] SM (*cibo*) food; (*in pensioni*) board; **vitto e alloggio** room and board, board and lodging

vittoria [vit'tɔrja] SF victory; **cantar vittoria** to crow (over one's victory)

vittoriano, -a [vitto'rjano] AGG, SM, SF Victorian

vittorioso, -a [vitto'rjoso] AGG victorious, triumphant

vituperare [vitupe'rare] /72/ VT (*letter*) to berate, rail at *o* against

viuzza [vi'uttsa] SF (*in città*) alley

viva [ˈviva] ESCL long live; **viva il re!** long live the king!; **viva il Milan!** three cheers for Milan!; **viva gli sposi!** to the bride and groom!; **viva l'Italia!** hooray for Italy!

vivacchiare [vivakˈkjare] /19/ VI (*aus* avere) to scrape a living

vivace [viˈvatʃe] AGG 1 (*gen*) lively; (*intelligenza*) lively, keen; (*colore*) vivid, brilliant, bright; **una persona vivace** a lively person; **è più vivace della sorella** she's livelier than her sister; **un colore vivace** a bright colour 2 (*Mus*) vivace

vivacità [vivatʃiˈta] SF (*vedi agg*) liveliness; keenness; vividness, brilliance, brightness

vivacizzare [vivatʃidˈdzare] /72/ VT to liven up

vivaio, -ai [viˈvajo] SM (*di piante*) nursery; (*di pesci*) fish farm, hatchery; (*fig*) breeding ground

vivamente [vivaˈmente] AVV (*commuoversi*) deeply, profoundly; (*ringraziare*) sincerely, warmly

vivanda [viˈvanda] SF (*cibo*) food *no pl*; (*piatto*) dish

vivavoce [vivaˈvɔtʃe] SM INV (*dispositivo*) loudspeaker; **mettere in vivavoce** to switch on the loudspeaker ♦ AGG INV: **telefono vivavoce** speakerphone

vivente [viˈvɛnte] AGG living, alive; **è il ritratto vivente del nonno** he is the spitting image of his grandfather; **l'autore è ancora vivente** the author is still alive; **è il massimo poeta vivente** he is the greatest living poet ♦ SMPL: **i viventi** the living

vivere [ˈvivere] VB IRREG /130/ VI (*aus* essere) 1 (*gen*) to live; (*essere vivo*) to live, be alive; **vivere fino a 100 anni** to live to be 100; **non gli resta molto da vivere** he hasn't long to live; **ha cessato di vivere** he is dead; **finché vivrò** as long as I live; **chi vivrà vedrà** only time will tell; **vivi e lascia vivere** live and let live; **vivere fuori dalla realtà** to live in another world, be out of touch with reality 2 (*abitare*) to live; **mi piacerebbe vivere in Scozia** I'd like to live in Scotland; **vivo in campagna** I live in the country; **viviamo insieme** we live together 3 (*sostentarsi*): **vivere (di)** to live (on); (*cibarsi*): **vivere di** to live on, feed on; **io vivo di poco o niente** I live on little or nothing; **ho giusto di che vivere** I have just enough to live on; **guadagnarsi da vivere** to earn one's living; **si guadagna da vivere dando lezioni di piano** she earns her living by giving piano lessons; **vivere d'aria e d'amore** to live on love alone; **vivere alla giornata** to live from day to day; **vivere nell'indigenza** to live in utter poverty; **vivere da signore** to live like a lord; **vivere nel lusso** to live a life of luxury; **vivere alle spalle di qn** to live off sb 4 (*comportarsi*) to live; **devi ancora imparare a vivere** you've still got a lot to learn about life; **modo di vivere** way of life 5 (*Tip*): **vive** stet ♦ VT (*vita*) to live; (*avvenimento, esperienza*) to live through, go through; **vivere una vita tranquilla** to lead a quiet life; **vivere giorni di dolore** to live through a sad period; **ha vissuto la scuola come una punizione** he hated his school days ♦ SM life; **lo faccio per il quieto vivere!** anything for a quiet life!

viveur [viˈvœr] SM INV pleasure-seeker

vivido, -a [ˈvivido] AGG (*ricordo*) vivid, very clear; (*luce*) bright, brilliant; (*colore*) bright, vivid; **di vivido ingegno** quick-witted, bright

vivificare [vivifiˈkare] /20/ VT (*materia*) to give life to, enliven; (*ravvivare: piante*) to revive, refresh; (*fig: racconto*) to bring to life

vivisezione [vivisetˈtsjone] SF vivisection

vivo, -a [ˈvivo] AGG 1 (*in vita*) alive, living; (*in uso: espressione, tradizione*) living; **è ancora vivo** he is still alive *o* living; **il pesce era ancora vivo** the fish was still alive; **esperimenti su animali vivi** experiments on live *o* living animals; **lingua viva** living language; **non c'era anima viva** there wasn't a (living) soul there; **me lo mangerei vivo!** (*fig*) I could eat him alive!, I could murder him!; **vivo o morto** dead or alive; **essere più morto che vivo** to be more dead than alive 2 (*intenso: ricordo*) vivid, very clear; (*: emozione*) intense; (*: luce*) brilliant, bright; (*: colore*) bright, vivid; **sguardo vivo** bright eyes; **viva commozione** intense emotion; **con vivo rammarico** with deep regret; **congratulazioni vivissime** sincerest *o* heartiest congratulations; **con i più vivi ringraziamenti** with deepest *o* warmest thanks; **cuocere a fuoco vivo** to cook on a high flame *o* at a high heat 3 (*vivace: persona*) lively, vivacious; (*: città, strada, discussione*) lively, animated;

ha un'intelligenza molto viva he has a very lively mind 4 (*fraseologia*): **farsi vivo** to keep in touch; **fatti vivo!** keep in touch!; **è tanto che non si fa vivo** he hasn't been in touch for ages; **spese vive** immediate *o* out-of-pocket expenses; **spigolo vivo** sharp edge; **l'ho sentito dalla sua viva voce** I heard it from the horse's mouth *o* from his own lips ♦ SM 1 (*essere*) living being; **i vivi** SMPL the living 2 **entrare nel vivo di una questione** to get to the heart of a matter; **registrazione dal vivo** live recording; **un programma dal vivo** a live program; **ritrarre dal vivo** to paint from life; **pungere** *o* **colpire qn nel vivo** to cut sb to the quick

vivrò ecc [viˈvrɔ] VB *vedi* vivere

viziare [vitˈtsjare] /19/ VT 1 (*persona*) to spoil 2 (*Dir*) to invalidate; (*rovinare: rapporti, ragionamento*) to ruin, spoil

viziato, -a [vitˈtsjato] AGG 1 (*persona*) spoilt; **un bambino viziato** a spoilt child 2 (*Dir*) invalid, invalidated; (*rapporti, ragionamento*) ruined, spoiled 3 (*aria*) stale, foul; **aria viziata** stale air

vizio, -zi [ˈvittsjo] SM 1 (*morale*) vice; (*cattiva abitudine*) bad habit; **vivere nel vizio** to live a life of vice; **i vizi e le virtù** vices and virtues; **ha il vizio del gioco** he's addicted to gambling; **il mio unico vizio è quello di mangiarmi le unghie** biting my nails is my only bad habit 2 (*Dir*) flaw, defect; **vizio di forma** legal flaw *o* irregularity; **vizio procedurale** procedural error 3 (*Med*): **vizio cardiaco** heart defect

vizioso, -a [vitˈtsjoso] AGG 1 (*corrotto*) depraved; **vita viziosa** life of vice 2 (*difettoso*) incorrect, wrong; **circolo vizioso** vicious circle ♦ SM, SF depraved person

V.le ABBR (= *Viale*) Ave. (= *Avenue*)

vocabolario, -ri [vokaboˈlarjo] SM (*dizionario*) dictionary; (*lessico personale*) vocabulary; **un vocabolario di italiano** an Italian dictionary; **il suo vocabolario è limitato** his vocabulary is limited

vocabolo [voˈkabolo] SM word

vocale¹ [voˈkale] AGG (*Anat, Mus*) vocal

vocale² [voˈkale] SF vowel

vocazione [vokatˈtsjone] SF (*anche Rel*) vocation; (*inclinazione naturale*) (natural) bent

voce [ˈvotʃe] SF 1 (*gen*) voice; **ho perso la voce** I've lost my voice; **la voce della coscienza** the voice of conscience; **parlare a alta/bassa voce** to speak loudly/quietly; **leggi il brano ad alta voce** read the passage aloud; **con un fil di voce** in a weak voice; **dar voce a qc** to voice *o* give voice to sth; **dare una voce a qn** to call sb, give sb a call; **fare la voce grossa** to raise one's voice; **a gran voce** in a loud voice, loudly; **l'hanno acclamato a gran voce** they greeted him with thunderous applause; **me l'ha detto a voce** he told me himself *o* in person; **te lo dico a voce** I'll tell you when I see you; **a una voce** unanimously 2 (*opinione*) opinion; (*diceria*) rumour (*Brit*), rumor (*USA*); **aver voce in capitolo** to have a say in the matter; **circolano delle voci secondo cui il governo si dimetterà** it is rumo(u)red *o* rumo(u)r has it that the government will resign; **voci di corridoio** rumo(u)rs; **sono solo voci di corridoio** they're only rumo(u)rs 3 (*Mus*) voice; **cantare a due voci** to sing in two parts 4 (*Gramm*) voice 5 (*vocabolo*) word; (*di elenco, bilancio*) item; (*di dizionario*) entry; **è una voce antiquata** it is an obsolete term *o* word

vociare [voˈtʃare] /14/ VI (*aus* avere) to shout, yell ♦ SM shouting

vocife'rante [votʃifeˈrante] AGG noisy

vocio [voˈtʃio] SM shouting

vodka [ˈvɔdka] SF INV vodka

voga¹ [ˈvoga] SF (*Naut*) rowing

voga² [ˈvoga] SF: **essere in voga** (*abito*) to be fashionable, be in fashion *o* in vogue; (*canzone*) to be popular

vogare [voˈgare] /80/ VI (*aus* avere) to row

vogatore, -trice [vogaˈtore] SM, SF oarsman *o* oarswoman ♦ SM rowing machine

vogherò ecc [vogeˈrɔ] VB *vedi* vogare

voglia [ˈvɔʎʎa] SF 1 (*desiderio*) wish, desire; (*di donna incinta*) craving; **aver voglia di qc/di fare qc** to feel like sth/like doing sth; (*più forte*) to want sth/to do sth; **morire dalla voglia di fare qc/di qc** to be dying *o* longing to do sth/for sth; **muoio dalla voglia di vederlo** I'm dying to see him; **adesso non ho voglia di mangiare** I don't feel like eating just now; **e chi ne ha voglia?** I don't feel like it at the moment;

hai voglia di gridare, tanto non ti sente! (*fam*) he can't hear you however much you shout 2 (*disposizione*) will; di buona voglia willingly; contro voglia, di mala voglia unwillingly 3 (*desiderio sessuale*) desire, lust 4 (*macchia della pelle*) birthmark

voglio ecc [ˈvoʎʎo] VB *vedi* volere

voglioso, -a [voʎˈʎoso] AGG (*sguardo*) longing; (*sessualmente*) full of desire

voi [ˈvoi] PRON PERS 1 (*soggetto*) you; **voi tutti lo sapete** all of you know, you all know; **voi che ne dite?** what do you think?; **io ci vado, voi fate come volete** I'm going, you do what you like; **venite anche voi?** are you coming too?; **voi italiani** you Italians; **voi stessi(e)** you yourselves; **siete stati voi a dirglielo** it was you who told him, you were the ones to tell him; **non lo sapevate nemmeno voi** you didn't even know it yourselves 2 (*oggetto: per dare rilievo, con preposizione*) you; **vuol vedere proprio voi** it's you he wants to see; **parlo a voi, non a lui** I'm talking to YOU, not to him; **tocca a voi** it's your turn; **da voi** (*nel vostro paese*) where you come from, in your country; (*a casa vostra*) at your house 3 (*comparazioni*) you; **sono come voi** they are as tall as you (are); **faremo come voi** we'll do as you do, we'll do the same as you; **sono più giovani di voi** they are younger than you

voialtri, -e [ˈvojaltri] PRON PERS you

vol. ABBR (= *volume*) vol.

volano [voˈlano] SM 1 (*palla*) shuttlecock; (*gioco*) badminton 2 (*Tecn*) flywheel

volant [voˈlã] SM INV frill

volante[1] [voˈlante] AGG (*gen*) flying; (*foglio*) loose; (*indossatrice*) freelance ♦ SF (*Polizia: anche*: **squadra volante**) flying squad

volante[2] [voˈlante] SM (*Aut*) (steering) wheel; **essere al volante** to drive, be at the wheel; **un asso del volante** ace driver

volantinaggio [volantiˈnaddʒo] SM leafleting

volantinare [volantiˈnare] /72/ (*aus avere*) to leaflet

volantino [volanˈtino] SM (*foglietto*) leaflet, pamphlet

volare [voˈlare] /72/ VI (*aus avere o essere*) 1 (*aereo, uccello, passeggero*) to fly; (*fig: tempo*) to fly, go by very quickly; (: *notizie*) to spread quickly; (: *pugni, insulti*) to fly; **quando ho sentito la notizia sono volato da lei** when I heard the news I rushed round to her place; **il pallone è volato fuori dal campo** the ball flew off the pitch; **volare in cielo o paradiso** (*euf: morire*) to go to heaven 3 (*allontanarsi*): **volare via** (*cappello, fogli*) to blow away, fly away o off; (*fig: tempo*) to fly; (*cadere*): **volare giù** (*vaso, persona*) to fall

volata [voˈlata] SF 1 (*fig: corsa*) rush; **faccio una volata a casa** I am just going to pop home; **passare di volata da qn** to drop in on sb briefly 2 (*Ciclismo*) final sprint; **vincere in volata** to sprint home to win 3 **volata di uccelli** (*stormo*) flock o flight of birds

volatile [voˈlatile] AGG (*Chim*) volatile ♦ SM (*uccello*) bird, winged creature

volatilizzare [volatilidˈdzare] /72/ VT (*Chim*) to volatilize; **volatilizzarsi** VIP (*Chim*) to volatilize; (*fig*) to vanish, disappear

volente [voˈlɛnte] AGG: **verrai volente o nolente** you'll come whether you like it or not

volenteroso, -a [volenteˈroso] AGG willing, keen; **un alunno volenteroso** a willing pupil

volentieri [volenˈtjɛri] AVV willingly, gladly; **l'ho fatto volentieri** I did it willingly; **spesso e volentieri** frequently, very often; **volentieri!** certainly!, of course!; **mi aiuti? - volentieri!** will you help me? - gladly!; **verresti a cena da noi stasera? - grazie, volentieri!** would you like to come to dinner with us this evening? - yes, I'd love to!

volere [voˈlere] VB IRREG /131/ VT (*nei tempi composti prende l'ausiliare del verbo che accompagna*)

1 (*gen*) to want; **voglio una risposta da voi** I want an answer from you; **voglio che ti lavi le mani** I want you to wash your hands; **che tu lo voglia o no** whether you like it or not; **vuol venire a tutti i costi** he wants to come at all costs; **quanto**

vuole per quel quadro? how much does he want for that painting?; **voglio comprare una macchina nuova** I want to buy a new car; **che cosa vuoi che faccia?** what do you want me to do?

2 (*desiderare*): **vorrei del pane** I would like some bread; **vorrei farlo/che tu lo facessi** I would like to do it/you to do it; **mi vorrebbero vedere sposato** they would like me to see married, they would like me to marry; **se volete, possiamo partire subito** if you like o want, we can leave right away; **come vuoi as you like; devo pagare subito o posso pagare domani? - come vuole** do I have to pay now or can I pay tomorrow? - as you prefer; **volevo parlartene** I meant to talk to you about it; **se volesse potrebbe farcela** he could do it if he wanted to; **vuole un po' di caffè?** would you like some coffee?; **adesso vorrei andarmene** I'd like to go now; **vorrebbe andare in America** she'd like to go to America

3 (*con funzione di richiesta o offerta*): **vuole o vorrebbe essere così gentile da...?** would you be so kind as to ...?; **vuoi chiudere la finestra?** would you mind closing the window?; **non vuole accomodarsi?** won't you sit down?; **vogliamo sederci?** shall we sit down?; **prendine quanto vuoi** help yourself, take as many (o much) as you like; **ne vuoi ancora?** would you like some more?; **vuoi che io faccia qualcosa?** would you like me to do something?, shall I do something?; **ma vuoi star zitto!** oh, do be quiet!

4 (*consentire*): **se la padrona di casa vuole, ti posso ospitare** if my landlady agrees I can put you up; **ho chiesto di parlargli, ma non ha voluto ricevermi** I asked to have a word with him but he wouldn't see me; **la macchina non vuole partire** the car won't start; **parla bene l'inglese quando vuole** he can speak English well when he has a mind to o when he feels like it

5 (*aspettarsi*) to want, expect; (*richiedere*) to want, require, demand; **che cosa vuoi da me?** what do you want from me?, what do you expect of me?; **la tradizione vuole che...** custom requires that ...; **vuole troppo dai suoi studenti** he expects too much of his students; **il verbo transitivo vuole il complemento oggetto** transitive verbs require a direct object

6 **volerne a qn** to have sth against sb, have a grudge against sb, bear sb a grudge; **me ne vuole ancora per quello che gli ho fatto** he still bears me a grudge for what I did to him; **non me ne volere** don't hold it against me

7 **voler dire (che)...** (*significare*) to mean (that) ...; **cosa vuol dire questa parola?** what does this word mean?; **se non puoi oggi vorrà dire che ci vediamo domani** if you can't make it today, I'll see you tomorrow; **vuoi dire che non parti più?** do you mean that you're not leaving after all?; **voglio dire...** (*per correggersi*) I mean ...; **volevo ben dire!** I thought as much!

8 (*ritenere*) to think; **la leggenda vuole che...** legend has it that ...; **si vuole che anche lui sia coinvolto nella faccenda** he is also thought to be involved in the matter

9 **volerci** (*essere necessario: materiale, attenzione*) to need; (: *tempo*) to take; **ci vuol ben altro per farmi arrabbiare** it'll take a lot more than that to make me angry; **quanto ci vuole per andare da Roma a Firenze?** how long does it take to go from Rome to Florence?; **quanta farina ci vuole per questa torta?** how much flour do you need to make this cake?; **ci vorrebbe un bel caffè** a nice cup of coffee is just what's needed; **è quel che ci vuole** it's just what is needed; **ce ne vuole per farglielo entrare nella zucca** it's not easy to get it into his thick skull; **per una giacca ci vogliono quattro metri di stoffa** you need four metres of material to make a jacket; **ci vuole il pane** we need bread

10 (*fraseologia*): **voler bene a qn** (*amore*) to love sb; (*affetto*) to be fond of sb, like sb very much; **volesse il cielo che...** God grant that ...; **se Dio vuole** God willing; **voler male a qn** to dislike sb; **sembra che voglia piovere** it looks like rain; **sembra che voglia mettersi al bello** the weather seems to be clearing up; **volere è potere** where there's a will there's a way; **qui ti voglio** that's the problem; **non vorrei sbagliarmi, ma...** I may be wrong, but ...; **senza volere** unwittingly, without meaning to, unintentionally; **l'ho spinto senza volere** I accidentally pushed him; **chi troppo vuole nulla stringe** (*Proverbio*) don't ask for too much or you may

come away empty-handed; **te la sei voluta** you asked for it; **voglio vedere se rifiuta** I bet she doesn't refuse; **vorrei proprio vedere!** I'm not at all surprised!, that doesn't surprise me in the slightest!; **vuoi... vuoi...** either ... or ...; **volersi** VR (*uso reciproco*): **volersi bene** (*amore*) to love each other; (*affetto*) to be fond of *o* like each other

♦ SM will, wish(es); **contro il volere di** against the wishes of; **per volere del padre** in obedience to his father's will *o* wishes

volgare [vol'gare] AGG **1** (*grossolano*) vulgar, coarse **2** (*comune*) common, popular ♦ SM vernacular

volgarità [volgari'ta] SF INV vulgarity

volgarizzare [volgarid'dzare] /72/ VT **1** (*divulgare*) to popularize **2** (*tradurre*) to translate into the vernacular

volgarmente [volgar'mente] AVV **1** (*in modo volgare*) vulgarly, coarsely **2** (*comunemente*) commonly, popularly

volgere ['voldʒere] VB IRREG /96/ VI (*aus* avere) **1 volgere a** (*piegare verso*) to turn to *o* towards, bend round to *o* towards; **la strada volge a destra** the road bends round to the right **2** (*avvicinarsi a*): **volgere al peggio** to take a turn for the worse; **volgere al termine** to draw to an end; **le vacanze volgono al termine** the holidays are coming to an end; **il giorno volge al termine** the day is drawing to its close; **il tempo volge al brutto/al bello** the weather is breaking/ is setting fair; **la situazione volge al peggio** the situation is deteriorating; **un rosso che volge al viola** a red verging on purple ♦ VT **1** (*voltare*) to turn; **volgere le spalle a qn** (*anche fig*) to turn one's back on sb **2** (*trasformare*) to turn; **volge sempre tutto in tragedia** he always turns everything into a tragedy; **volgersi** VR to turn; **si volse e mi guardò** he turned round and looked at me; **si volse verso di lui** he turned to *o* towards him; **la sua ira si volse contro di noi** he turned his anger on us

volgo, -ghi ['volgo] SM (*anche pegg*) common people *pl*

voliera [vo'ljera] SF aviary

volitivo, -a [voli'tivo] AGG wilful (*Brit*), willful (*USA*); (*persona*) wil(l)ful, strong-willed ♦ SM, SF strong-willed person

volli ecc ['volli] VB *vedi* volere

volo ['volo] SM **1** (*gen*) flight; **il tuo volo è alle tre** your flight leaves at three o'clock; **ci sono due ore di volo da Londra a Milano** it's a two-hour flight from London to Milan; **velocità/condizioni di volo** flying speed/conditions; **essere in volo** (*uccello*) to be in flight; (*Aer*) to be flying; **colpire un uccello in volo** to shoot a bird on the wing *o* in flight; **"volo cancellato"** "flight cancelled"; **"volo in chiusura"** "flight closing"; **volo di addestramento** training flight; **volo di andata** outward flight; **volo charter** charter flight; **volo di linea** scheduled flight; **volo di ritorno** return flight; **volo a vela** gliding **2** (*fraseologia*): **capire al volo** to understand straight away *o* straight away; **ha capito al volo la situazione** he understood the situation immediately; **prendere al volo** (*autobus, treno*) to only just catch; (*palla*) to catch as it flies past; (*fig: occasione*) to seize; **ho preso il treno al volo** I only just caught the train; **prendere il volo** (*aereo*) to take off; (*uccello*) to fly away; (*fig: giovane*) to leave home; (: *cosa: sparire*) to vanish; **fare un volo** (*cadere*) to go flying; **ha fatto un volo dalle scale** he went flying down the stairs; **veduta a volo d'uccello** bird's-eye view

volontà [volon'ta] SF INV **1** (*capacità di volere*) will; **ha molta volontà** he has a very strong will; **non ha volontà** he is weak-willed; **contro la sua volontà** against his will; **di sua spontanea volontà** of his own free will; **l'ha fatto di sua spontanea volontà** he did it of his own free will; **riuscire a forza di volontà** to succeed through sheer willpower *o* determination **2** (*disposizione*): **manifestare la volontà di fare qc** to show one's desire to do sth; **buona/cattiva volontà** goodwill/lack of goodwill; **ci ho messo tutta la mia buona volontà** I did it to the best of my ability; **a volontà** (*mangiare, bere*) as much as one likes; **ce ne sono a volontà** there are more than enough of them; **prendine a volontà** help yourself, take as much (*o* many) as you like; **"zuccherare a volontà"** "sugar to taste" **3** **le sue ultime volontà** (*testamento*) his last will and testament *sg*; **quali sono le sue ultime volontà?** what are his last wishes?

volontariamente [volontarja'mente] AVV voluntarily

volontariato [volonta'rjato] SM **1** (*Mil*) voluntary service **2** (*attività gratuita*) voluntary work

volontario, -ria, -ri, -rie [volon'tarjo] AGG (*gen*) voluntary; (*Mil*) volunteer *attr*; **esilio volontario** voluntary exile ♦ SM, SF (*gen, anche Mil*) volunteer; (*di organizzazione*) voluntary worker; **c'è qualche volontario?** are there any volunteers?; **lavoro come volontario** I'm a voluntary worker

volpe ['volpe] SF (*Zool*) fox; (*femmina*) vixen; (*pelliccia*) fox; (*fig*) sly fox, crafty person; (*ironico*) clever person, bright spark; **volpe della sabbia** *o* **del deserto** fennec

volpino, -a [vol'pino] AGG (*pelo, coda*) fox's *attr*; (*aspetto, astuzia*) fox-like ♦ SM (*cane*) Pomeranian

volpone, -a [vol'pone] SM, SF (*fig*): **un vecchio volpone** a crafty old fox

volsi ecc ['volsi] VB *vedi* volgere

volt [volt] SM INV (*Elettr*) volt

volta¹ ['volta] SF **1** (*gen*) time; **una volta** once; **una volta alla settimana** once a week; **due volte** twice; **gli ho telefonato due volte** I phoned him twice; **tre volte** three times; **una volta ogni due settimane** once every two weeks; **9 volte su 10** 9 times out of 10; **la prima/l'ultima volta che l'ho visto** the first/last time I saw him; **per questa volta passi** I'll let you off this time; **ci ho pensato due volte prima di decidere** I thought twice about it before making a decision; **tutto in una volta** all at once; **una volta per tutte** *o* **una buona volta** once and for all; **deciditi una volta per tutte** make up your mind once and for all; **una volta tanto** just for once; **una volta tanto potresti pagare tu** you could pay, just for once; **una volta ogni tanto** from time to time; **una volta sola** only once; **le ho scritto una volta sola** I wrote to her only once; **di volta in volta** as we go; **decideremo di volta in volta cosa fare** we'll decide what to do as we go; **delle** *o* **alle** *o* **certe volte, a volte** sometimes, at times; **certe volte sono un po' triste** I feel a bit down sometimes; **una volta** *o* **l'altra** one of these days; **una volta** *o* **l'altra glielo dirò** I'll tell him one of these days; **una cosa per volta** one thing at a time; **facciamo una cosa per volta** let's do one thing at a time; **te le darò volta per volta** (*istruzioni*) I'll give them to you a few at a time **2** (*tempo, occasione*): **c'era una volta...** once upon a time there was ...; **una volta** (*un tempo*) once, in the past; **una volta si camminava di più** people used to walk more in the past; **le cose di una volta** the things of the past; **una volta che sei partito** once *o* when you have left; **ti ricordi quella volta che...** do you remember (the time) when ...; **pensa a tutte le volte che...** think of all the occasions on which ...; **lo facciamo un'altra volta** we'll do it another time *o* some other time; **gli telefonerò un'altra volta, adesso non ne ho voglia** I'll phone him some other time, I don't feel like it now **3** (*Mat*): **3 volte 2** 3 times 2; **3 volte 4 fa 12** 3 times 4 makes 12; **4 volte di più** 4 times as much **4** (*fraseologia*): **a sua volta** (*in his* o *her ecc*) turn; **partire alla volta di** to set off for; **ti ha dato di volta il cervello?** have you gone out of your mind?

volta² ['volta] SF (*Archit, Anat*) vault; **la volta celeste** the vault of heaven

voltafaccia [volta'fattʃa] SM INV about-turn, volte-face

voltaggio [vol'taddʒo] SM voltage

voltare [vol'tare] /72/ VT (*girare*) to turn; (*moneta*) to turn over; (*rigirare*) to turn round; **voltate pagina** turn the page; **voltare pagina** (*fig*) to turn over a new leaf; **voltare le spalle a qn** (*anche fig*) to turn one's back on sb ♦ VI (*aus* avere) to turn; **voltare a destra/sinistra** to turn (to the) left/right; **volta a sinistra e poi va' dritto** turn left and then go straight on; **voltarsi** VR to turn; **voltarsi da un lato** to turn to one side; **voltarsi indietro** to turn back; **si è allontanato senza voltarsi indietro** he went off without looking back; **voltarsi dall'altra parte** to turn the other way; **non sapere da che parte voltarsi** (*fig*) not to know which way to turn

voltastomaco [volta'stomako] SM nausea; **dare il voltastomaco a qn** to make sb sick; **la sua ipocrisia mi dà il voltastomaco** his hypocrisy makes me sick

volteggiare [volted'dʒare] /62/ VI **1** (*volare girando: uccello, piuma*) to circle; **la ballerina volteggiava sul palco** the dancer twirled *o* spun across the stage **2** (*Ginnastica*) to vault; (*sul cavallo*) to do trick riding

volto¹, -a ['volto] PP *di* volgere ♦ AGG; **volto a 1** (*rivolto verso*:

casa) facing **2** (*inteso a*): **il mio discorso è volto a spiegare...** in my speech I intend to explain ...; **il corso è volto a introdurre gli studenti all'analisi matematica** the course is intended to introduce students to calculus

volto² ['volto] SM (*faccia*) face; (*fig*) face, nature

volubile [vo'lubile] AGG (*persona*) changeable, fickle; (*tempo*) changeable, variable

❏ **volubile** non si traduce mai con la parola inglese *voluble*

volume [vo'lume] SM (*gen*) volume; **potresti abbassare il volume?** could you turn down the volume, please?; **fa volume** (*oggetto*) it takes up a lot of space, it is very bulky; **volume delle vendite** (*Comm*) sales volume

voluminoso, -a [volumi'noso] AGG bulky, voluminous

voluta [vo'luta] SF (*gen*) spiral; (*Archit*) volute

voluttà [volut'ta] SF INV sensual pleasure *o* delight

voluttuoso, -a [voluttu'oso] AGG voluptuous, sensual

vomitare [vomi'tare] /72/ VT to vomit, throw up; **vomitare ingiurie** (*fig*) to spew out insults; **questo quadro mi fa vomitare** this painting makes me sick ♦ VI (*aus avere*) to be sick, vomit, throw up

vomito ['vomito] SM vomit; **ho il vomito** I feel sick; **mi fa venire il vomito** (*anche fig*) it makes me sick

vongola ['vongola] SF (*Zool*) clam

vorace [vo'ratʃe] AGG (*appetito*) voracious, greedy; **essere vorace** to have a huge appetite; **è un bambino vorace** this child has a voracious appetite

voracità [vorat'ʃita] SF voracity, voraciousness

voragine [vo'radʒine] SF chasm, abyss

vorrò *ecc* [vor'rɔ] VB *vedi* volere

vortice ['vortitʃe] SM whirl, vortex; (*fig*) vortex; **un vortice di vento** a whirlwind

vorticoso, -a [vorti'koso] AGG whirling

vostro, -a ['vostro] AGG POSS: **il(la) vostro(a)** your; **il vostro cane** your dog; **i vostri libri** your books; **un vostro conoscente** an acquaintance of yours; **un vostro amico** a friend of yours; **vostra zia** your aunt; **è colpa vostra** it's your fault; **a casa vostra** at your house ♦ PRON POSS: **il(la) vostro(a)** yours, your own; **la nostra casa è più grande della vostra** our house is bigger than yours; **la vostra è stata una brutta storia** your story is an unpleasant one; **di chi è questo?** - **è vostro** whose is this? - it's yours ♦ SM **1 avete speso del vostro?** did you spend your own money?; **ci potreste rimettere del vostro in quell'affare** you could well lose money in that business **2 i vostri** SMPL (*famiglia*) your family; **è dei vostri** he's on your side ♦ SF: **la vostra** (*opinione*) your view; **l'ultima vostra** (*Comm: lettera*) your most recent letter; **alla vostra!** (*brindisi*) here's to you!, your health!; **è dalla vostra** he's on your side

votante [vo'tante] SM, SF voter

votare [vo'tare] /72/ VI (*aus avere*) to vote ♦ VT **1** (*gen*) to vote for; (*sottoporre a votazione*) to take a vote on; (*approvare*) to pass; **ho votato per loro** I voted for them **2 votare**

a (*vita*) to devote to, dedicate to; **votarsi** VR: **votarsi a** to devote o.s. to

votazione [votat'tsjone] SF **1** (*gen, anche Pol: atto*) voting, vote; **alle votazioni** at the elections **2** (*Scol*) mark (*Brit*), grade (*USA*); **votazione finale** results *pl*

voto ['voto] SM **1** (*Scol*) mark (*Brit*), grade (*USA*); **ho preso un bel voto in matematica** I got a good mark in math(s); **laurearsi a pieni voti** ≈ to graduate with a first class degree (*Brit*) *o* summa cum laude (*USA*) **2** (*Pol*) vote; **hanno vinto per pochi voti** they won by a few votes; **mettere ai voti** to put to the vote; **voto di fiducia** vote of confidence; **voto di scambio** vote-buying **3** (*Rel*) vow; (*offerta*) votive offering; **prendere i voti** to take one's vows

VP ABBR (= *Vicepresidente*) VP

VR SIGLA = Verona

vs. ABBR (= *vostro*) yr (= *your*)

VT SIGLA = Viterbo

VU ABBR = vigile urbano

vulcanico, -a, -ci, -che [vul'kaniko] AGG volcanic; **ha una fantasia vulcanica** he has a fertile imagination

vulcanizzazione [vulkaniddzat'tsjone] SF (*Tecn*) vulcanization

vulcano [vul'kano] SM volcano; **quel ragazzo è un vulcano di idee** that boy is bursting with ideas

vulnerabile [vulne'rabile] AGG vulnerable

vulnerabilità [vulnerabili'ta] SF vulnerability

vuoi ['vwɔi], **vuole** ['vwɔle] VB *vedi* volere

vuotare [vwo'tare] /72/ VT (*bicchiere, stanza*) to empty; (*vasca, piscina*) to drain, empty; **vuotare il sacco** (*fig*) to confess, spill the beans (*fam*); **i ladri mi hanno vuotato la casa** the burglars cleaned out my house; **vuotarsi** VIP to empty

vuoto, -a ['vwɔto] AGG **1** (*gen*) empty; **a stomaco vuoto** on an empty stomach; **a mani vuote** empty-handed; **è arrivato a mani vuote** he arrived empty-handed **2** (*non occupato: posto*) vacant, free; (: *spazio*) empty; **un appartamento vuoto** an empty apartment **3** (*fig: discorso, persona*) shallow, superficial; **è una testa vuota** he's an empty headed person; **mi sento la testa vuota** my mind feels a complete blank ♦ SM **1** (*spazio*) void, empty space, gap; (*in bianco*) blank; (*fig: mancanza*) gap, void; (*Fis*) vacuum; **è rimasto sospeso nel vuoto** (*alpinista*) he was left hanging in mid-air; **aver paura del vuoto** to be afraid of heights; **guardare nel vuoto** to gaze into space; **fare il vuoto intorno a sé** to alienate o.s. from everybody; **ha lasciato un vuoto fra di noi** he has left a real gap; **ho un vuoto allo stomaco** my stomach feels empty; **sotto vuoto** = sottovuoto; **vuoto d'aria** (*Aer*) air pocket **2** (*bottiglia*) empty; **"vuoto a perdere"** "no deposit"; **"vuoto a rendere"** "returnable (bottle)" ♦ **a vuoto** AVV (*inutilmente*) vainly, in vain; (*senza effetto*) to no purpose; **parlare a vuoto** to waste one's breath; **ho fatto un viaggio a vuoto** I have had a wasted journey; **andare a vuoto** to come to nothing, fail; **assegno a vuoto** dud cheque (*Brit*), bad check (*USA*); **girare a vuoto** (*Aut*) to idle

W¹, w¹ [ˈdɔppjo vu] SF INV, SM INV (*lettera*) W, w; **W come Washington** ≈ W for William

W² [ˈdɔppjo vu] ABBR = **evviva**

wafer [ˈvafer] SM INV (*Culin, Elettr*) wafer

wagon-lit [vagɔˈli] SM INV (*Ferr*) sleeping car

water [ˈvater] SM INV toilet (bowl); **l'ho gettato nel water** I threw it in the toilet

water closet [ˈwɔːtə ˈklɔzit] SM INV toilet (*Brit*), lavatory (*Brit*), bathroom (*USA*)

watt [vat] SM INV (*Elettr*) watt

wattora [vatˈtora] SM INV (*Elettr*) watt-hour

WC [viˈtʃi] SM INV WC (*Brit*), bathroom (*USA*)

web [web] SM: **il web** the Web; **cercare nel web** to search the Web ♦ AGG: **pagina web** webpage

webcam [webˈkam] SF INV webcam

webinar [ˈwebinar] SM INV (*Inform*) webinar

webmail [webˈmeil] SF webmail

weekend [wiˈkɛnd] SM INV weekend

western [ˈwestern] AGG (*Cine*) cowboy *attr* ♦ SM INV (*Cine*) western, cowboy film (*Brit*) *o* movie (*USA*); **western all'italiana** spaghetti western

whisky [ˈwiski] SM INV whisky

Wi-Fi [uaiˈfai](*Inform*) SM INV Wi-Fi ♦ AGG INV Wi-Fi

wiki [ˈwiki] SM INV (*Inform*) wiki

windsurf [windˈserf] SM INV (*tavola*) windsurfer, windsurfing board, sailboard; (*sport*) windsurfing; **fare windsurf** to go windsurfing

würstel [ˈvyrstəl] SM INV frankfurter; **vorrei un würstel con la senape** I'd like a frankfurter with mustard

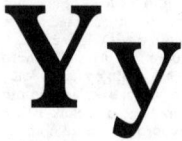

X, x [iks] SF INV, SM INV (*lettera*) X, x; **X come Xeres** ≈ X for Xmas

xenofobia [ksenofoˈbia] SF xenophobia

xenofobo, -a [kseˈnɔfobo] AGG xenophobic ♦ SM, SF xenophobe

xeres [ˈkseres] SM INV sherry

xerocopia [kseroˈkɔpja] SF photocopy

xerocopiare [kserokoˈpjare] /19/ VT to photocopy

xilofono [ksiˈlɔfono] SM xylophone

Yy

Y, y [ˈipsilon] SF INV, SM INV (*lettera*) Y, y; **Y come Yacht** ≈ Y for Yellow (*Brit*), ≈ Y for Yoke (*USA*)

yacht [jɔt] SM INV yacht

yankee [ˈjæŋki] SM INV, SF INV Yank, Yankee

Yemen [ˈjemen] SM: **lo Yemen** Yemen

yen [jen] SM INV (*moneta*) yen

yiddish [ˈjidiʃ] AGG INV, SM INV Yiddish

yoga [ˈjɔga] AGG INV, SM INV yoga *attr*; **fare yoga** to do yoga

yogurt [ˈjɔgurt] SM INV yog(h)urt; **uno yogurt alla fragola** a strawberry yoghurt

Zz

Z, z ['dzɛta] SF INV, SM INV (*lettera*) Z, z; **Z come Zara** ≈ Z for Zebra

zabaione [dzaba'jone], **zabaglione** [dzabaʎ'ʎone] SM zabaglione, *dessert made of egg yolks, sugar and marsala*

zaffata [tsaf'fata] SF (*di odore*) stench, stink

zafferano [dzaffe'rano] SM saffron

zaffiro [dzaf'firo] SM sapphire

zagara ['dzagara] SF orange blossom

zainetto [dzai'netto] SM (small) rucksack

zaino ['dzaino] SM rucksack (*Brit*), backpack (*USA*)

Zaire [dza'ire] SM Zaire

Zambia ['dzambja] SM Zambia

zampa ['tsampa] SF (*di animale*) leg; (*con artigli*) paw; (*di elefante, uccello*) foot; **pantaloni a zampa d'elefante** bell-bottom trousers, bell-bottoms; (*più larghi*) flares; **camminare a quattro zampe** to go on all fours; **giù le zampe!** (*fam*) paws off!; **zampe di gallina** (*rughe*) crow's feet; (*calligrafia*) scrawl sg

zampata [tsam'pata] SF (*di cane, gatto*) blow with a paw

zampettare [tsampet'tare] /72/ VI (*aus* avere) to scamper

zampillare [tsampil'lare] /72/ VI (*aus* avere) to gush, spurt

zampillo [tsam'pillo] SM gush, spurt

zampino [tsam'pino] SM paw; **ci ha messo lo zampino lui** (*fig*) he's had a hand in this; **zampino di coniglio** (*portafortuna*) lucky rabbit's foot

zampogna [tsam'poɲɲa] SF Italian bagpipes pl

zanna ['tsanna] SF (*di elefante, cinghiale*) tusk; (*di cane, lupo*) fang

zanzara [dzan'dzara] SF mosquito; **zanzara tigre** *type of striped mosquito*

zanzariera [dzandza'rjɛra] SF mosquito net

zappa ['tsappa] SF (*Agr*) hoe; **darsi la zappa sui piedi** (*fig*) to shoot o.s. in the foot

zappare [tsap'pare] /72/ VT (*Agr*) to hoe

zappatore [tsappa'tore] SM (*Agr*) hoer; (*Mil*) sapper (*Brit*)

zappatura [tsappa'tura] SF (*Agr*) hoeing

zapping ['dzappin(g)] SM (*TV*) channel hopping

zar [tsar] SM INV tsar

zattera ['tsattera] SF raft; **zattera di salvataggio** life raft

zavorra [dza'vɔrra] SF (*Naut, Aer*) ballast; (*fig*) junk; **gettare la zavorra** to dump ballast

zazzera ['tsattsera] SF shock of hair, mop

zebra ['dzebra] SF 1 (*Zool*) zebra 2 **le zebre** SFPL (*Aut*) zebra crossing sg (*Brit*), crosswalk sg (*USA*)

zebrato, -a [dze'brato] AGG with black and white stripes; **passaggio** o **attraversamento zebrato** (*Aut*) zebra crossing (*Brit*), crosswalk (*USA*)

zecca¹, -che ['tsekka] SF (*insetto*) tick

zecca² ['tsekka] SF (*di monete*) mint; **nuovo di zecca** brand-new

zecchino [tsek'kino] SM gold coin; **oro zecchino** pure gold

zelante [dze'lante] AGG zealous

zelo ['dzelo] SM zeal; **mostrare troppo zelo** to be overzealous

zenit ['dzenit] SM (*Astron*) zenith

zenzero ['dzendzero] SM ginger

zeppa ['tseppa] SF (*di mobili*) wedge; (*di scarpe*) platform

zeppo, -a ['tseppo] AGG: **zeppo** o **pieno zeppo (di)** jam-packed (with), crammed (with); **era zeppo di gente** it was crammed with people

zerbino [dzer'bino] SM (*door*)mat

zero ['dzero] SM 1 (*gen, anche Scol, Mat*) zero, nought (*Brit*); (*in un numero di telefono*) O; **zero virgola cinque** (zero o nought) point five; **2 gradi sopra zero** 2 degrees above freezing point o above zero; **3 gradi sotto zero** 3 degrees below zero; **zero in condotta** (*Scol*) bad marks for

behaviour (*Brit*); **ridursi a zero** (*fig*) to have nothing left, be at rock-bottom; **capelli tagliati a zero** close-cropped hair; **sparare a zero su qn/qc** (*fig*) to lay into sb/sth; **ricominciare da zero** to go back to square one; **partire da zero** to start from scratch 2 (*Calcio*) nil (*Brit*); (*Tennis*) love; **vincere per tre a zero** to win three-nil; **trenta a zero** thirty love ♦ AGG INV **zero** attr; **l'ora zero** zero hour; **a emissioni zero** zero-emission; **tolleranza zero** zero tolerance

zeta ['dzɛta] SM, SF (*pl f inv* zeta, *pl f* zete, *pl m inv* zeta) (*lettera*) zed (*Brit*), zee (*USA*), (the letter) z

zia ['tsia] SF aunt

zibellino [dzibel'lino] SM (*animale, pelliccia*) sable

zigano, -a [tsi'gano] AGG, SM, SF gypsy

zigomo ['dzigomo] SM cheekbone; **zigomi sporgenti** high cheekbones

zigrinare [dzigri'nare] /72/ VT (*gen*) to knurl; (*pellame*) to grain; (*monete*) to mill

Zimbabwe [dzim'babwe] SM Zimbabwe

zimbello [tsim'bello] SM (*Caccia*) decoy (bird); (*fig*) laughing stock

zinco ['tsinko] SM zinc

zingaresco, -a, -schi, -sche [tsinga'resko] AGG gypsy attr

zingaro, -a ['tsingaro] AGG, SM, SF gypsy

zio, zii ['tsio] SM uncle; **i miei zii** (*zio e zia*) my uncle and aunt; **zio d'America** (*fig*) rich uncle

zippare [dzip'pare] /72/ VT (*file*) to zip

zitella [tsi'tella] SF (*pegg*) spinster, old maid

zittire [tsit'tire] /55/ VT to silence, hush o shut up ♦ VI (*aus* avere) to hiss

zitto, -a ['tsitto] AGG quiet, silent; **zitto!** be quiet!, shut up! (*fam*); **stare zitto** to keep quiet, shut up (*fam*); **zitto zitto** (*di nascosto*) on the quiet

zizzania [dzid'dzanja] SF (*pianta*) darnel; (*fig*) discord; **seminare zizzania** to sow discord

zoccolo ['tsɔkkolo] SM 1 (*di cavallo*) hoof 2 (*calzatura*) clog 3 (*Archit*) plinth; (*di parete*) skirting (board) (*Brit*), baseboard (*USA*); (*di armadio*) base (support)

zodiacale [dzodia'kale] AGG of the zodiac, zodiac attr; **segno zodiacale** sign of the zodiac

zodiaco [dzo'diako] SM zodiac

zolfanello [tsolfa'nɛllo] SM (sulphur (*Brit*) o sulfur (*USA*)) match

zolfo ['tsolfo] SM sulphur (*Brit*), sulfur (*USA*)

zolla ['dzolla] SF (*di terra*) clod (of earth)

zolletta [dzol'letta] SF (*di zucchero*) (sugar) lump o cube

zona ['dzɔna] SF (*gen*) area, zone; (*regione*) area, region; (*di città*) district; **una zona malfamata** a rough area; **zona di depressione** (*Meteor*) trough of low pressure; **zona disco** (*Aut*) ≈ meter zone; **zona erogena** erogenous zone; **zona giorno** (*di casa*) living area; **zona di guerra** war zone; **zona industriale** industrial estate; **zona di interdizione del traffico aereo** no-fly zone; **zona notte** (*di casa*) sleeping area; **zona pedonale** pedestrian precinct (*Brit*) o mall (*USA*); **zona a traffico limitato** controlled traffic zone; **zona verde** (*Aut*) restricted parking zone o area; (*Urbanistica*) green area

zonzo ['dzondzo] **a zonzo** AVV: **andare a zonzo** to wander about, stroll about

zoo ['dzɔo] SM INV zoo

zoologia [dzoolo'dʒia] SF zoology

zoologico, -a, -ci, -che [dzoo'lɔdʒiko] AGG zoological; **giardino zoologico** zoological garden(s), zoo

zoologo, -a, -gi, -ghe [dzo'ɔlogo] SM, SF zoologist

zoosafari [dzoosa'fari] SM INV safari park

zootecnico, -a, -ci, -che [dzoo'tekniko] AGG zootechnical; **il patrimonio zootecnico di un paese** a country's livestock resources

zoppicare [tsoppi'kare] /20/ VI (*aus* **avere**) (*persona*) to
have a limp, walk with a limp, limp; (*essere zoppo*) to be
lame; (*fig*: *mobile*) to be shaky; **zoppica in matematica**
(*fig*) he's weak in maths (*Brit*) *o* math (*USA*), math(s)
isn't his strong point

zoppo, -a ['tsɔppo] AGG (*persona*) lame; (*mobile*) wobbly, shaky
♦ SM, SF lame person

zoti'cone [dzoti'kone] SM lout

ZTL [dzetati'elle] SIGLA F (= *Zona a Traffico Limitato*) *controlled
traffic zone*

zuava [dzu'ava] SF: **pantaloni alla zuava** knickerbockers

zucca ['tsukka] SF (*Bot*) pumpkin; (*di forma allungata*) marrow
(*Brit*), vegetable marrow; (*scherz*) head; **avere sale in zucca**
to be sensible, have sense; **non gli entra in zucca** it won't
enter his thick skull

zuccherare [tsukke'rare] /72/ VT to sugar, put sugar in, add
sugar to

zuccherato, -a [tsukke'rato] AGG sweet, sweetened; **non zuccherato** unsweetened

zuccheriera [tsukke'rjɛra] SF sugar bowl

zuccherificio, -ci [tsukkeri'fitʃo] SM sugar refinery

zuccherino, -a [tsukke'rino] AGG sweet, sugary ♦ SM piece of
sugar, lump of sugar

zucchero ['tsukkero] SM sugar; **zucchero di canna** cane sugar; **zucchero caramellato** caramel; **zucchero filato** candy
floss (*Brit*), cotton candy (*USA*); **zucchero in grani** crushed
sugar lumps; **zucchero in polvere** caster sugar; **zucchero
semolato** granulated sugar; **zucchero a velo** icing sugar
(*Brit*), confectioner's sugar (*USA*)

zuccheroso, -a [tsukke'roso] AGG sweet, sugary

zucchina [tsuk'kina] SF , **zucchino** [tsuk'kino] SM courgette
(*Brit*), zucchini (*USA*)

zuccotto [tsuk'kɔtto] SM (*Culin*) *dome-shaped dessert made of
sponge* (*cake*), *cream, chocolate and candied fruit*

zuffa ['tsuffa] SF fight, brawl

zufolare [tsufo'lare] /72/ VT, VI (*aus* **avere**) to whistle

zufolo ['tsufolo] SM (*Mus*) flageolet

zuppa ['tsuppa] SF soup; **una zuppa di verdura** a vegetable
soup; **se non è zuppa è pan bagnato** (*fig*) it's six of one
and half a dozen of the other; **zuppa inglese** (*Culin*) *li-
queur-soaked sponge* (*cake*) *with a filling of cream and chocolate*

zuppiera [tsup'pjɛra] SF (soup) tureen

zuppo, -a ['tsuppo] AGG: **zuppo (di)** soaked (with), drenched
(with); **sono zuppo** I'm soaked

Zurigo [dzu'rigo] SF Zurich

ENGLISH — ITALIAN

INGLESE — ITALIANO

Aa

A, a [eɪ] N **1** (*letter*) A, a *f inv*, m *inv*; **A for Andrew, A for Able** (*USA*) ≈ A come Ancona; **to know sth from A to Z** sapere *or* conoscere qc dalla a alla zeta; **to get from A to B** spostarsi da un punto all'altro **2** (*Mus*) la *m inv*; **it's in A flat** è in la bemolle **3** (*Scol: mark*) ≈ 10, ≈ ottimo; **I got an A for my essay** nel compito ho preso ottimo

<u>**KEYWORD**</u>

a [eɪ, ə] INDEF ART (*before vowel and silent h* **an** [æn, ən, n])
1 un *m*, uno (+ *s impure, gn, pn, ps, x, z*), una *f*, un' (*plus vowel*); **he's a friend** è un amico; **a herring** un'aringa; **an apple** una mela; **I haven't got a car** non ho la macchina; **a child is full of curiosity** i bambini sono molto curiosi; **he's a doctor** è medico, fa il medico; **a drink would be nice** berrei volentieri qualcosa; **half an hour** mezz'ora; **a hundred pounds** cento sterline; **as a young man** da giovane; **a mirror** uno specchio; **a Mr Smith called to see you** l'ha cercata un certo signor Smith; **what a surprise!** che sorpresa!
2 (*each*) a, per; **2 apples a head** 2 mele a testa *or* (per) ciascuno; **50 kilometres an hour** 50 chilometri all'ora; **3 times a month** 3 volte al mese; **£4 a person** *or* **a head** 4 sterline per *or* a persona; **£4 a pound** 4 sterline alla libbra

a. ABBR = **acre**
AA [eɪˈeɪ] N ABBR **1** (= *Alcoholics Anonymous*) AA *f* (= *Anonima Alcolisti*) **2** (*USA*: = *Associate in Arts*) ≈ laurea in lettere **3** (*Mil*) = **anti-aircraft**
AAA [ˌeɪeɪˈeɪ] N ABBR (= *American Automobile Association*) ≈ ACI *m* (= *Automobile Club d'Italia*)
AB [eɪˈbiː] N ABBR (*Canada*) = **Alberta**
aback [əˈbæk] ADV: **to be taken aback** essere colto(-a) *or* preso(-a) alla sprovvista, rimanere sconcertato(-a); **I was taken aback by his reaction** sono rimasto sconcertato dalla sua reazione
aba·cus [ˈæbəkəs] N (*pl* **abacuses** *or* **abaci** [ˈæbəsaɪ]) abaco, pallottoliere *m*
aban·don [əˈbændən] VT **1** (*desert*) abbandonare; **to aban-don ship** abbandonare la nave **2** (*give up: plan, hope, game*) abbandonare, rinunciare a; **to abandon o.s. to sth** abbandonarsi a qc, lasciarsi andare a qc ♦ N abbandono
aban·doned [əˈbændənd] ADJ (*unrestrained: manner*) disinvolto(-a), spontaneo(-a)
abase [əˈbeɪs] VT (*frm*) umiliare, mortificare; **to abase o.s.** umiliarsi, abbassarsi
abashed [əˈbæʃt] ADJ imbarazzato(-a)
abate [əˈbeɪt] VI (*frm: anger, enthusiasm, storm*) placarsi, calmarsi; (: *pain*) calmarsi; (: *fever*) abbassarsi, calare; (: *flood*) abbassarsi; (: *noise*) diminuire, affievolirsi
abate·ment [əˈbeɪtmənt] N (*frm: of pollution, noise*) soppressione *f*, eliminazione *f*
ab·at·toir [ˈæbətwɑːʳ] N (*Brit*) macello, mattatoio
ab·bey [ˈæbɪ] N abbazia, badia
ab·bot [ˈæbət] N abate *m*
ab·bre·vi·ate [əˈbriːvɪeɪt] VT abbreviare
ab·bre·vi·a·tion [əˌbriːvɪˈeɪʃən] N abbreviazione *f*
ABC [ˌeɪbiːˈsiː] N (*USA*: ABC's *npl*) abbicci *m inv*, alfabeto; **as easy as ABC** facile come bere un bicchier d'acqua
ab·di·cate [ˈæbdɪkeɪt] VI abdicare ♦ VT (*throne*) abdicare a; (*responsibility*) rinunciare a
ab·di·ca·tion [ˌæbdɪˈkeɪʃən] N (*of monarch*) abdicazione *f*
ab·do·men [ˈæbdəmən] N addome *m*
ab·domi·nal [æbˈdɒmɪnl] ADJ addominale
ab·duct [æbˈdʌkt] VT rapire
ab·duc·tion [æbˈdʌkʃən] N rapimento, sequestro di persona
ab·er·ra·tion [ˌæbəˈreɪʃən] N aberrazione *f*; **a youthful aberration** una follia *or* un errore giovanile
abet [əˈbet] VT (*Law*) *see* **aid**

abey·ance [əˈbeɪəns] N (*frm*): **to be in abeyance** (*law, custom*) essere in disuso; (*matter, plan*) essere in sospeso
ab·hor [əbˈhɔːʳ] VT aborrire, provare orrore per
ab·hor·rent [əbˈhɒrənt] ADJ odioso(-a), detestabile, ripugnante; **to be abhorrent to sb** ripugnare a qn
abide [əˈbaɪd] (*pt, pp* **abided**) VT (*only neg*) sopportare, soffrire; **I can't abide him** non lo posso soffrire *or* sopportare
▸ **abide by** VI + PREP (*rules*) rispettare, conformarsi a, attenersi a; (*consequences*) accettare; (*promise*) tener fede a, rispettare
abid·ing [əˈbaɪdɪŋ] ADJ (*memory etc*) duraturo(-a)
abil·ity [əˈbɪlɪtɪ] N capacità *f inv*, abilità *f inv*; **abilities** NPL capacità *fpl*, doti *fpl*; **to the best of my ability** con il massimo impegno; **a person of great abilities** una persona molto dotata
ab·ject [ˈæbdʒɛkt] (*frm*) ADJ (*poverty*) abietto(-a); (*apology*) umiliante; (*coward*) indegno(-a), vile
ablaze [əˈbleɪz] ADV, ADJ in fiamme; **the house was ablaze with light** (*fig*) la casa era tutta illuminata, la casa risplendeva di luci
able [ˈeɪbl] ADJ (*person*) capace, bravo(-a); (*piece of work*) abile, intelligente; **to be able to do sth** poter fare qc, essere in grado di fare qc; **he's not able to walk** non può *or* non è in grado di *or* non è in condizione di camminare; **those who are able to pay** coloro che sono in condizione *or* che possono permettersi di pagare
able-bodied [ˌeɪblˈbɒdɪd] ADJ robusto(-a), valido(-a); **able-bodied citizen** cittadino idoneo *or* abile (al servizio militare)
able-bodied seaman N (*Brit*) marinaio scelto
ably [ˈeɪblɪ] ADV abilmente
ABM [ˌeɪbiːˈɛm] N ABBR (*Mil*: = *antiballistic missile*) ABM *m inv* (= *missile antibalistico*)
ab·nor·mal [æbˈnɔːməl] ADJ anormale
ab·nor·mal·ity [ˌæbnɔːˈmælɪtɪ] N (*condition*) anormalità *f inv*; (*instance*) anomalia
aboard [əˈbɔːd] ADV (*Naut, Aer*) a bordo; **to go aboard** salire a bordo; **all aboard!** (*Rail*) (signori) in carrozza *or* in vettura!; (*Naut*) tutti a bordo! ♦ PREP: **aboard the ship** a bordo (della nave), sulla nave; **aboard the train** in *or* sul treno; **aboard the plane** a bordo (dell'aereo), sull'aereo
abode [əˈbəʊd] N (*old*) dimora; (*Law*) domicilio, dimora; **of no fixed abode** senza fissa dimora
abol·ish [əˈbɒlɪʃ] VT abolire
abo·li·tion [ˌæbəʊˈlɪʃən] N abolizione *f*
abomi·nable [əˈbɒmɪnəbl] ADJ (*detestable*) abominevole; (*unpleasant*) pessimo(-a), orrendo(-a), orribile
Abo·rigi·ne [ˌæbəˈrɪdʒɪnɪ] N aborigeno(-a) d'Australia
abort [əˈbɔːt] VI (*Med*) abortire; (*fig: plans, space mission*) fallire (prematuramente) ♦ VT **1** (*Med*: **to abort a baby** *or* **a pregnancy** interrompere una gravidanza **2** (*fig*) sospendere, rinunciare a portare a termine; (*Comput*) interrompere l'esecuzione di
abor·tion [əˈbɔːʃən] N (*Med*) aborto; **to have an abortion** (*termination*) abortire; (*miscarriage*) avere un aborto (spontaneo)
abor·tion·ist [əˈbɔːʃənɪst] N chi esegue aborti clandestini
abor·tive [əˈbɔːtɪv] ADJ (*Med*) abortivo(-a); (*fig: plan*) fallito(-a), mancato(-a); (: *attempt*) vano(-a), infruttuoso(-a)
abound [əˈbaʊnd] VI (*frm: exist in great quantity*) abbondare; (: *have in great quantity*): **to abound in** *or* **with** abbondare di, essere ricco(-a) di

<u>**KEYWORD**</u>

about [əˈbaʊt] ADV
1 (*place: here and there*) qua e là, in giro; **to be about again** (*after illness*) essere di nuovo in piedi; **we were about early**

eravamo in piedi presto; **is Paul about?** (*Brit*) hai visto Paul in giro?; **to look about** guardarsi intorno; **they left all their things lying about** hanno lasciato tutta la loro roba in giro; **to run about** (*Brit*) correre qua e là; **there's a lot of measles about** c'è molto morbillo in giro; **to walk about** camminare; **it's the other way about** (*Brit fig*) è il contrario, è viceversa

2 (*approximately*) circa, quasi, pressappoco; **she's about the same age as you** ha pressappoco la tua età; **it's just about finished** è quasi finito; **it takes about 10 hours** ci vogliono circa 10 ore; **(at) about 2 o'clock** verso le due; **it is about 2 o'clock** sono circa le due; **about 50 people** una cinquantina di persone; **that's about right** è più o meno giusto

3 to be about to do sth stare per fare qc; **he was about to cry** stava per piangere; **I'm not about to do all that for nothing** non ho intenzione di fare tutto questo per niente

♦ PREP

1 (*place*) intorno a; **somewhere about here** qui intorno da qualche parte; **he looked about him** si è guardato intorno; **to do jobs about the house** fare lavori in casa; **to wander about the town** andare in giro per la città

2 (*relating to*) su, a proposito di, riguardo a; **I'm phoning you about tomorrow's meeting** ti chiamo a proposito della riunione di domani; **do something about it!** fai qualcosa!; **how about coming with us?** che ne dici *or* diresti di venire con noi?; **how about a drink?** beviamo qualcosa?, e se bevessimo qualcosa?; **how about going to the cinema?** e se andassimo al cinema?; **there's something interesting about her** ha qualcosa di interessante; **we talked about it** ne abbiamo parlato; **a book about travel** un libro sui viaggi; **what is it about?** di che si tratta?; **what about me?** e io?; **what about it?** (*what do you say*) che te ne pare?, cosa ne pensi?; (*what of it*) e allora?

3 (*occupied with*) while you're about it ... già che ci sei...

about-face [ə,baʊt'feɪs], **about-turn** [ə,baʊt'tɜːn] N (*Mil, also fig*) dietro front *m inv*

above [ə'bʌv] ADV di sopra, al di sopra; (*in text*) prima, sopra; **mentioned above** summenzionato(-a); **from above** dall'alto; **the apartment above** l'appartamento di sopra *or* al piano di sopra; **the clouds above** le nuvole sovrastanti; **children of 7 years or above** ragazzi dai 7 anni in su *or* a partire dai 7 anni; **orders from above** ordini superiori *or* (che vengono) dall'alto; **the address above** l'indirizzo di cui sopra ♦ PREP sopra; **above all** soprattutto; **he raised his hands above his head** ha sollevato le mani sopra la testa; **above the clouds** al di sopra delle nuvole; **the Thames above London** il Tamigi a monte di Londra; **2000 metres above sea level** 2000 metri sopra il livello del mare; **he is above me in rank** ha un grado superiore al mio; **I couldn't hear above the din** non riuscivo a sentire in mezzo a *or* attraverso tutto quel frastuono; **she's above that sort of thing** è superiore a queste cose; **it's above me** è troppo complicato per me, è al di sopra delle mie possibilità; **to get above o.s.** montarsi la testa; **children above 7 years of age** ragazzi al di sopra dei 7 anni (di età); **costing above £10** più caro di 10 sterline

above-board [ə,bʌv'bɔːd] ADJ leale, onesto(-a); **are you sure this is aboveboard?** sei sicuro che sia una faccenda pulita?

abra·sion [ə'breɪʒən] N abrasione *f*; (*injury*) escoriazione *f*, abrasione *f*

abra·sive [ə'breɪsɪv] ADJ abrasivo(-a); (*fig: person, personality*) caustico(-a); (: *voice*) stridente; (: *manner*) brusco(-a) ♦ N abrasivo

abreast [ə'brest] ADV di fianco, fianco a fianco; **to march 4 abreast** marciare in riga per 4; **to come abreast of** affiancarsi a; **to keep abreast of the news/times** tenersi aggiornato(-a)

abridge [ə'brɪdʒ] VT ridurre

abroad [ə'brɔːd] ADV (*in foreign parts*) all'estero; **to go abroad** andare all'estero; **there is a rumour abroad that ...** (*fig: frm*) si sente dire in giro che..., circola la voce che...; **how did the news get abroad?** (*fig: frm*) come si è sparsa *or* diffusa la notizia?

ab·rupt [ə'brʌpt] ADJ (*halt, person*) brusco(-a); (*departure*) improvviso(-a); (*slope*) ripido(-a), erto(-a); (*style*) discontinuo(-a), sconnesso(-a); **his abrupt departure aroused suspicion** la sua improvvisa partenza ha sollevato dei sospetti;

he was a bit abrupt with me e' stato un po' brusco con me; **the film came to an abrupt end** il film terminò bruscamente

ab·scess ['æbses] N (*Med*) ascesso

ab·scond [əb'skɒnd] VI fuggire, scappare

ab·sence ['æbsəns] N (*of person*) assenza; (*of thing*) mancanza; **in the absence of** (*person*) in assenza di; (*thing*) in mancanza di; **in my absence** in mia assenza; **in the absence of any evidence** non essendoci prove; **absence of mind** distrazione *f*; **absence of proof** mancanza di prove

ab·sent [ADJ 'æbsənt, vb æb'sent] ADJ (*person*) assente; (*thing*) assente, mancante; (*fig: also:* **absent-minded**) distratto(-a); **to be absent without leave** (*Mil*) essere assente ingiustificato(-a) ♦ VT: **to absent o.s. from sth** non presentarsi a qc

ab·sen·tee [,æbsən'tiː] N assente *m/f*

ab·sen·tee·ism [,æbsən'tiːɪzəm] N assenteismo

absent-minded [,æbsənt'maɪndɪd] ADJ distratto(-a)

absent-mindedness [,æbsənt'maɪndɪdnɪs] N distrazione *f*

ab·so·lute ['æbsəluːt] ADJ (*gen*) assoluto(-a); (*support*) totale, completo(-a), senza riserve; (*proof*) inconfutabile; (*denial*) categorico(-a); (*lie*) bello(-a) e buono(-a); **he's an absolute idiot** è un perfetto idiota; **it's an absolute scandal** è un autentico scandalo ♦ N assoluto

ab·so·lute·ly ['æbsəluːtlɪ] ADV completamente, assolutamente; **absolutely!** altroché!; **do you think it's a good idea? — absolutely!** ti sembra una buona idea? — altroché!; **Jill's absolutely right** Jill ha assolutamente ragione

ab·solve [əb'zɒlv] VT: **to absolve sb (from or of)** (*sin etc*) assolvere qn (da); **to absolve sb from** (*oath*) sciogliere qn da; (*obligation etc*) liberare qn da

ab·sorb [əb'sɔːb] VT (*also fig*) assorbire; (*costs*) ammortizzare; (*information*) assimilare; **she was absorbed in a book** era immersa *or* assorta nella lettura di un libro

ab·sor·bent [əb'sɔːbənt] ADJ assorbente

absorbent cotton N (*USA*) cotone *m* idrofilo

ab·sorb·ing [əb'sɔːbɪŋ] ADJ avvincente, molto interessante

❑ **absorbing** is not translated by the Italian word *assorbente*

ab·sorp·tion [əb'sɔːpʃən] N **1** (*Physiology*) assorbimento; (*Aut*) ammortizzazione *f*; (*fig: of person into group*) integrazione *f* **2** (*fig*) concentrazione *f*; **his absorption in his work prevented him from noticing ...** era così assorto nel suo lavoro che non ha notato...

ab·stain [əb'steɪn] VI (*in election*): **to abstain (from)** astenersi (da); **to abstain from drinking/smoking** astenersi dal bere/ dal fumare; **three MPs abstained** tre deputati si sono astenuti

ab·ste·mi·ous [əb'stiːmɪəs] ADJ (*person: in eating, drinking*) moderato(-a)

❑ **abstemious** is not translated by the Italian word *astemio*

ab·sten·tion [əb'stenʃən] N astensione *f*

ab·sti·nence ['æbstɪnəns] N astinenza

ab·stract [*adj, n* 'æbstrækt, *vb* æb'strækt] ADJ astratto(-a) ♦ N (*summary*) riassunto, sommario; (*picture*) opera astratta; **in the abstract** in teoria, in astratto ♦ VT (*remove*) estrarre; (*summarize*) riassumere

ab·surd [əb'sɜːd] ADJ assurdo(-a); (*appearance, hat*) ridicolo(-a)

ab·surd·ity [əb'sɜːdɪtɪ] N **1** (*no pl: see adj*) assurdità, assurdo; ridicolaggine *f* **2** (*thing etc*) assurdità *f inv*; **the absurdities of life** le assurdità della vita

Abu Dha·bi [,æbuː'dɑːbɪ] N Abu Dhabi *f*

abun·dance [ə'bʌndəns] N abbondanza, gran quantità; **in abundance** in abbondanza, in gran quantità

abun·dant [ə'bʌndənt] ADJ (*crop, supply*) abbondante; (*proof*) ampio(-a)

abuse [*n* ə'bjuːs, *vb* ə'bjuːz] N **1** (*insults*) insulti *mpl*, ingiurie *fpl*, improperi *mpl*; **to heap abuse on sb** coprire qn di insulti **2** (*cruel treatment: of children*) abuso; (: *of patients, prisoners*) maltrattamento; **child abuse** violenza sui minori **3** (*misuse: of drugs, solvents*) abuso; **drug abuse** abuso di sostanze stupefacenti; **abuse of power** abuso di potere; **open to abuse** che si presta ad abusi ♦ VT **1** (*misuse: position, power*) abusare di; (: *drugs, solvents*) fare abuso di **2** (*revile*) insultare **3** (*maltreat: children*) approfittare sessualmente di; (: *patients, prisoners*) maltrattare; **to be abused** subire violenza

abu·sive [ə'juːsɪv] ADJ (*person*) offensivo(-a); (*language*) offensivo(-a), ingiurioso(-a)
❑ **abusive** is not translated by the Italian word *abusivo*

abys·mal [ə'bɪzməl] ADJ (*ignorance*) abissale, crasso(-a); (*result, food*) pessimo(-a); (*weather, job*) da cani

abyss [ə'bɪs] N (*liter*) abisso, baratro

AC [,eɪ'siː] N ABBR (*Elec*: = *alternating current*) c.a. (= *corrente alternata*)

a/c ABBR (*Banking, etc*: = *account, account current*) c

aca·dem·ic [,ækə'demɪk] ADJ **1** (*Scol*) accademico(-a), universitario(-a); (*intellectual*) intellettuale; **academic life** vita universitaria; **academic subjects** materie *fpl* umanistiche e scientifiche; **his academic performance** il suo rendimento scolastico **2** (*irrelevant*) puramente formale ♦ N (*teaching*) docente *m/f* universitario(-a); (*doing research*) studioso(-a)

academic year N (*Brit*) anno accademico

acad·emy [ə'kædəmɪ] N (*learned body*) accademia; (*school*) scuola privata; **academy of music** (*Brit*) conservatorio; **military/naval academy** accademia militare/navale

ac·cede [æk'siːd] (*frm*) VI: **to accede to** (*throne*) salire a, ascendere a; (*office, position*) accedere a; (*request*) aderire a, accedere a

ac·cel·er·ate [æk'seləreɪt] VT accelerare, affrettare ♦ VI (*Aut*) accelerare

ac·cel·era·tion [æk,selə'reɪʃən] N (*Aut, Phys*) accelerazione *f*

ac·cel·era·tor [æk'seləreɪtəʳ] N (*Aut, Tech*) acceleratore *m*

ac·cent ['æksənt] N (*all senses*) accento; **he hasn't got an accent** non ha alcun accento; **she spoke with a strong Spanish accent** parlava con un forte accento spagnolo

ac·cen·tu·ate [æk'sentjueɪt] VT (*syllable*) accentuare; (*need, difference etc*) accentuare, mettere in risalto *or* in evidenza

ac·cept [ək'sept] VT (*gen*) accettare; (*acknowledge*) ammettere; **to accept responsibility for something** assumersi la responsabilità di qualcosa; **he refused to accept defeat** non ha voluto ammettere la sua sconfitta; **I decided to accept the offer** ho deciso di accettare l'offerta

ac·cept·able [ək'septəbl] ADJ (*satisfactory*) accettabile; (*welcome: gift, offer*) gradito(-a); **tea is always acceptable** un tè è sempre ben accetto, un tè lo si beve sempre volentieri

ac·cept·ance [ək'septəns] N accettazione *f*; (*of person: by others*) accoglienza (favorevole); (*: for job, membership*) accettazione; (*: of proposal*) accoglimento; **I've received two acceptances** ho ricevuto due risposte positive; **to meet with general acceptance** incontrare il favore *or* il consenso generale

ac·cess ['ækses] N accesso; **wheelchair access** accesso per disabili; **to have/gain access to sb/sth** avere/ottenere libero accesso presso qn/a qc; **the burglars gained access through a window** i ladri sono penetrati da *or* attraverso una finestra; **we don't have access to a good sports complex** non abbiamo l'opportunità di frequentare un buon centro sportivo; **her ex husband has access to the children** suo marito ha diritto a vedere i bambini ♦ VT (*Comput*) accedere a

ac·ces·sible [æk'sesəbl] ADJ (*place*) accessibile, che si può raggiungere facilmente; (*person, information*) facilmente reperibile

ac·ces·sion [æk'seʃən] N (*addition*) aggiunta; (*to library*) accessione *f*, acquisto; (*of king*) ascesa *or* salita al trono

ac·ces·so·ry [æk'sesərɪ] N **1** (*gen pl*: *Dressmaking, Comm*) accessorio; **fashion accessory** accessorio di moda; **toilet accessories** (*Brit*) articoli *mpl* da toilette **2** (*Law*) complice *m/f*; **accessory to the crime** complice del delitto

access road N strada d'accesso; (*to motorway*) raccordo di entrata

access time N (*Comput*) tempo di accesso

ac·ci·dent ['æksɪdənt] N (*harmful*) incidente *m*, disgrazia; (*unexpected*) (puro) caso; **road accident** incidente stradale; **to meet with** *or* **to have an accident** avere un incidente; **accidents at work** infortuni *mpl* sul lavoro; **by accident** (*by chance*) per caso; (*unintentionally*) senza volere, per sbaglio; **they made the discovery by accident** lo hanno scoperto per caso; **accidents will happen** sono cose che capitano *or*

succedono; **the fog caused several accidents** la nebbia ha provocato diversi incidenti

ac·ci·den·tal [,æksɪ'dentl] ADJ (*by chance*) accidentale, fortuito(-a), casuale; (*unintentional*) involontario(-a); **accidental death** morte *f* accidentale

ac·ci·den·tal·ly [,æksɪ'dentəlɪ] ADV (*by chance*) per caso; (*unintentionally*) senza volere, inavvertitamente; **accidentally on purpose** (*fam*) di proposito, ma senza darlo a vedere

accident and emergency N (*Brit*) pronto soccorso

accident insurance N assicurazione *f* contro gli infortuni

accident-prone ['æksɪdənt,prəʊn] ADJ predisposto(-a) agli incidenti; **he's very accident-prone** gli succede sempre di tutto

acclaim [ə'kleɪm] VT acclamare ♦ N (*approval*) consenso; (*applause*) applauso

ac·cla·ma·tion [,æklə'meɪʃən] N (*approval*) acclamazione *f*; (*applause*) applauso; **by acclamation** per acclamazione

ac·cli·ma·tize [ə'klaɪmətaɪz], (*USA*) **ac·cli·mate** ['æklɪ,meɪt] VT acclimatare; **to acclimatize o.s.** (*to*) acclimatarsi (a), adattarsi (a); **to become acclimatized** acclimatarsi

ac·co·lade ['ækəleɪd] N (*frm: praise*) elogio, encomio; (*: award, honour*) onorificenza

ac·com·mo·date [ə'kɒmədeɪt] VT **1** (*lodge, have room for: person*) ospitare, alloggiare; (*: thing*) ospitare, accogliere; **the apartment can accommodate five people** ci si può stare in cinque nell'appartamento; **this car accommodates 4 people comfortably** quest'auto può trasportare comodamente 4 persone **2** (*oblige, help*) favorire; (*satisfy*) venire incontro a **3** (*differences*) conciliare **4** (*adjust to: idea, situation*): **accommodate o.s. to** venire incontro a, adattarsi a
❑ **accommodate** is not translated by the Italian word *accomodare*

ac·com·mo·dat·ing [ə'kɒmədeɪtɪŋ] ADJ (*easy to deal with*) accomodante, conciliante; (*willing to help*) gentile, premuroso(-a)

ac·com·mo·da·tion N [ə,kɒmə'deɪʃən], (*USA*) **ac·com·mo·da·tions** NPL **1** (*place to live*) sistemazione *f*, alloggio; (*space*) posto; **"accommodation to let"** "camere in affitto"; **have you any accommodation (available)?** avete posto?; **seating accommodation** (*Brit*) posti a sedere **2** (*frm: adjustment, adaptation*) adattamento **3** (*Anat*) accomodazione *f*
❑ **accommodation** is not translated by the Italian word *accomodamento*

ac·com·pa·ni·ment [ə'kʌmpənɪmənt] N (*also Mus*) accompagnamento

ac·com·pa·nist [ə'kʌmpənɪst] N (*Mus*) accompagnatore(-trice)

ac·com·pa·ny [ə'kʌmpənɪ] VT (*gen*) accompagnare; (*Mus*): **to accompany (on)** accompagnare (a)

ac·com·plice [ə'kʌmplɪs] N: **accomplice (in)** complice *m/f* (di)

ac·com·plish [ə'kʌmplɪʃ] VT (*task, mission*) compiere, portare a termine; (*one's design*) realizzare; (*purpose*) ottenere; **I don't think much will be accomplished** non credo si otterrà molto

ac·com·plished [ə'kʌmplɪʃt] ADJ (*pianist, cook*) esperto(-a)

ac·com·plish·ment [ə'kʌmplɪʃmənt] N (*completion*) realizzazione *f*, compimento, completamento; (*thing achieved*) risultato, impresa; **accomplishments** NPL (*skills*) doti *fpl*

ac·cord [ə'kɔːd] N (*harmony*) accordo; **of his own accord** spontaneamente, di sua iniziativa; **with one accord** all'unanimità, di comune accordo; **to be in accord with** essere d'accordo con ♦ VT accordare ♦ VI: **to accord (with)** andare d'accordo (con), accordarsi (con)

ac·cord·ance [ə'kɔːdəns] N: **in accordance with** secondo, in conformità di *or* a (or) con

ac·cord·ing [ə'kɔːdɪŋ] PREP: **according to** secondo, stando a; **according to him** secondo lui; **according to what he says** stando a quanto dice; **they will be punished according to the seriousness of their crimes** saranno puniti a seconda della gravità dei loro delitti; **it went according to plan** è andata secondo quanto previsto

ac·cord·ing·ly [ə'kɔːdɪŋlɪ] ADV (*all senses*) di conseguenza

ac·cor·di·on [əˈkɔːdɪən] N (*Mus*) fisarmonica

ac·cost [əˈkɒst] VT (*confront*) abbordare; (*approach*) avvicinare

ac·count [əˈkaʊnt] N 1 (*report*) resoconto, relazione *f*; **to give an account of sth** fare un resoconto di *or* una relazione su qc; **to keep an account of** tenere nota di; **to bring** *or* **call sb to account for sth/for having done sth** chiedere a qn di render conto di qc/per aver fatto qc; **by** *or* **from all accounts** a detta di tutti, a quanto si dice; **to give a good account of o.s.** farsi onore, dare un'ottima prova di sé 2 (*consideration*) considerazione *f*, conto; (*importance*) importanza, conto; **it's of no account** non importa; **of little account** di poca importanza; **on no account** per nessuna ragione, per nessun motivo, in nessun caso; **on account of** a causa di; **we couldn't go out on account of the bad weather** non siamo potuti uscire a causa del maltempo; **on his account** (*for his benefit*) per lui; **to take account of sth, take sth into account** tener conto di qc, prendere in considerazione qc; **to turn sth to good account** trarre profitto da qc 3 (*at shop, bank, also Comm*) conto; **a bank account** un conto in banca; **to open an account (with)** aprire un conto (presso); **"account payee only"** (*Brit: on cheque*) "non trasferibile"; **they have the Pirelli account** la Pirelli è fra i loro clienti; **your account is still outstanding** il suo conto non è ancora stato saldato; **to get £50 on account** ricevere 50 sterline come *or* in *or* di acconto, ricevere un acconto di 50 sterline; **to put £50 down on account** versare un acconto di 50 sterline; **to buy sth on account** comprare qc a credito 4 (*Comm*); **accounts** NPL conti *mpl*; **to keep/do the accounts** tenere la contabilità; **accounts department** ufficio *m* contabilità, *inv*

▸ **account for** VI + PREP 1 (*explain*) spiegare, giustificare; (*give reckoning of: actions, expenditure*) render conto di, rispondere di; **that accounts for it** questo spiega tutto; **all the children were accounted for** nessun ragazzo mancava all'appello; **there's no accounting for tastes** tutti i gusti son gusti 2 (*represent*) rappresentare 3 (*destroy, kill*) uccidere, distruggere

ac·count·abil·ity [əˌkaʊntəˈbɪlɪtɪ] N responsabilità

ac·count·able [əˈkaʊntəbl] ADJ: **to be accountable for sth** essere responsabile di qc; **to be accountable to sb** dover rendere conto a qn

ac·count·an·cy [əˈkaʊntənsɪ] N ragioneria

ac·count·ant [əˈkaʊntənt] N ragioniere(-a), contabile *m/f*; (*for personal finances*) ≈ commercialista *m/f*

ac·count·ing [əˈkaʊntɪŋ] N (*auditing*) contabilità; (*subject, field*) ragioneria

accounting period N esercizio finanziario, periodo contabile

account number N numero di conto

account payable N (*USA*) conto passivo

account receivable N (*USA*) conto da esigere

ac·cred·it·ed [əˈkredɪtɪd] ADJ (*authorized*) accreditato(-a)

ac·cre·tion [əˈkriːʃən] N (*frm: gen: Law*) accrescimento

ac·crue [əˈkruː] VI (*mount up*) aumentare; (*interest*) maturare; **to accrue to** derivare a

ac·cu·mu·late [əˈkjuːmjʊleɪt] VT accumulare; **to accumulate wealth** accumulare ricchezza ♦ VI accumularsi; **his debts are accumulating** i suoi debiti si stanno accumulando

ac·cu·mu·la·tion [əˌkjuːmjʊˈleɪʃən] N (*amassing*) accumulo, accumulazione *f*; (*mass, heap*) mucchio, cumulo

ac·cu·ra·cy [ˈækjʊrəsɪ] N (*see adj*) accuratezza; esattezza; precisione *f*; fedeltà

ac·cu·rate [ˈækjʊrɪt] ADJ (*description, report, assessment*) accurato(-a), esatto(-a), preciso(-a); (*observation, estimate*) accurato(-a); (*answer*) corretto(-a), esatto(-a); (*shot, instrument, worker*) preciso(-a); (*copy*) fedele

ac·cu·rate·ly [ˈækjʊrɪtlɪ] ADV (*see adj*) accuratamente; con esattezza; correttamente; con precisione; fedelmente

ac·cu·sa·tion [ˌækjʊˈzeɪʃən] N accusa

ac·cu·sa·tive [əˈkjuːzətɪv] ADJ (*Gram*) accusativo(-a) ♦ N (*Gram*) accusativo; in the accusative all'accusativo

ac·cuse [əˈkjuːz] VT: **to accuse sb (of)** accusare qn (di)

ac·cused [əˈkjuːzd] N (*Law*): **the accused** l'accusato(-a), l'imputato(-a)

ac·cus·er [əˈkjuːzəʳ] N accusatore(-trice)

ac·cus·tom [əˈkʌstəm] VT: **to accustom sb to sth/to doing**

sth abituare qn a qc/a fare qc; **to accustom o.s. to sth** abituarsi a qc

ac·cus·tomed [əˈkʌstəmd] ADJ (*usual*) abituale; **to be accustomed to sth** essere abituato(-a) a qc; **to get accustomed to sth/to doing sth** abituarsi *or* adattarsi a qc/a fare qc

ace [eɪs] N (*Cards, also fig: sportsman, driver*) asso; **to keep an ace up one's sleeve** avere un asso nella manica; **to serve an ace** (*Tennis*) effettuare un servizio vincente ♦ ADJ (*fam: excellent*) eccezionale; **to be ace at sth** essere bravissimo(-a) in *or* a qc

acer·bic [əˈsɜːbɪk] ADJ (*frm, also fig*) acido(-a)

ac·etate [ˈæsɪteɪt] N acetato

ache [eɪk] N (*pain*) dolore *m*, male *m*; **aches in your muscles** dolori ai muscoli; **stomach ache** mal *m* di stomaco; **I've got stomach ache** *or* (*USA*) **a stomach ache** ho mal di stomaco; **I'm full of aches and pains** mi fa male dappertutto, sono pieno di dolori ♦ VI (*hurt*) far male, dolere; **it makes my head ache** mi fa venire *or* mi dà il mal di testa; **my leg's aching** mi fa male la gamba; **I'm aching all over** sono tutto indolenzito, mi duole dappertutto; **it made her heart ache to see ...** (*fig*) le piangeva il cuore vedere... ♦ VT (*yearn*): **to ache to do sth** morire dalla voglia di fare qc

achieve [əˈtʃiːv] VT (*aim*) raggiungere; (*success, effect*) ottenere; (*victory*) riportare; (*result*) conseguire; **you won't achieve anything** non otterrai nulla ♦ VI (*be successful*) avere successo

achieve·ment [əˈtʃiːvmənt] N (*act*) realizzazione *f*, raggiungimento, compimento; (*thing achieved*) risultato, successo; **that's quite an achievement** è una bella impresa, è un bel successo; **it was a fantastic achievement for our team** è stato un risultato fantastico per la nostra squadra

Achilles heel N tallone *m* di Achille

acid [ˈæsɪd] N (*Chem: drug*) acido ♦ ADJ (*Chem*) acido(-a); (*sour*) acido(-a), acidulo(-a); (*fig: wit, remark*) caustico(-a); **acid salts** (*Chem*) sali *mpl* acidi; **acid oxides** (*Chem*) ossiacidi *mpl*

acid·ity [əˈsɪdɪtɪ] N acidità

acid rain N pioggia acida

acid test N prova del fuoco; (*of theory, idea*) prova del nove

ac·knowl·edge [əkˈnɒlɪdʒ] VT (*mistake*) riconoscere, ammettere; (*truth*) riconoscere; (*claim*) prendere atto di; (*letter: also:* **acknowledge receipt of**) accusare ricevuta di; (*help, present*) manifestare la propria gratitudine per; (*greeting*) rispondere a, ricambiare; **to acknowledge sb as leader** riconoscere qn come capo; **to acknowledge o.s. beaten** ammettere la propria sconfitta; **he won't acknowledge there's a problem** non vuole riconoscere che c'è un problema

ac·knowl·edge·ment [əkˈnɒlɪdʒmənt] N 1 (*admission*) ammissione *f*, riconoscimento; (*of letter*) conferma (di aver ricevuto); **in acknowledgement of** a riconoscimento di 2 **acknowledgements** NPL (*in book*) ringraziamenti *mpl*

ACLU [ˌeɪsiːelˈjuː] N ABBR (= *American Civil Liberties Union*) unione americana per le libertà civili

acme [ˈækmɪ] N (*frm*) culmine *m*, acme *f*

acne [ˈæknɪ] N acne *f*

acorn [ˈeɪkɔːn] N (*Bot*) ghianda

acous·tic [əˈkuːstɪk] ADJ acustico(-a)

acoustic coupler [əˈkuːstɪkˈkʌpləʳ] N (*Comput*) accoppiatore *m* acustico

acous·tics [əˈkuːstɪks] NSG (*Phys*) acustica ♦ NPL (*of room*) acustica *fsg*

ac·quaint [əˈkweɪnt] VT 1 (*inform*): **to acquaint sb with sth** informare qn di qc, far sapere qc a qn, mettere qn al corrente di qc; **he's already acquainted with the facts** è già informato *or* a conoscenza dei fatti; **to acquaint o.s. with sth** familiarizzarsi con qc, impratichirsi su qc 2 (*with person*): **to be acquainted with sb** conoscere (personalmente) qn; **to become acquainted with sb** fare la conoscenza di qn; **we became acquainted in Paris** ci siamo conosciuti a Parigi

ac·quaint·ance [əˈkweɪntəns] N 1 (*with person, subject etc*): **acquaintance (with)** conoscenza (di); **to make sb's acquaintance** fare la conoscenza di qn; **it improves on acquaintance** più lo si conosce e più lo si apprezza 2 (*person*) conoscente *m/f*, conoscenza; **a business acquaintance** una conoscenza di lavoro; **an acquaintance of mine** un mio conoscente

ac·qui·esce [ˌækwɪˈɛs] vi (*frm: agree*): **to acquiesce (to)** acconsentire (a)

ac·quire [əˈkwaɪəʳ] vt (*possessions, territory, knowledge*) acquisire; (*language*) apprendere; (*habit*) contrarre, prendere; (*reputation*) farsi; **to acquire a taste for** prender gusto a

ac·quired [əˈkwaɪəd] adj acquisito(-a); **it's an acquired taste** è una cosa che si impara ad apprezzare

ac·qui·si·tion [ˌækwɪˈzɪʃən] n acquisto

ac·quisi·tive [əˈkwɪzɪtɪv] adj (*person*) a cui piace accumulare; (*pej*) materialista

ac·quit [əˈkwɪt] vt 1 (*Law*): **to acquit sb (of)** assolvere qn (da) 2 **to acquit o.s.** (**well/badly**) (*frm*) cavarsela (bene/male)

ac·quit·tal [əˈkwɪtl] n (*Law*) assoluzione f

acre [ˈeɪkəʳ] n acro (= 4047 m²)

acre·age [ˈeɪkərɪdʒ] n superficie f in acri

ac·rid [ˈækrɪd] adj (*smell*) acre, pungente; (*fig*) pungente

ac·ri·mo·ni·ous [ˌækrɪˈməʊnɪəs] adj (*frm: remark*) astioso(-a), malevolo(-a); (: *argument*) aspro(-a)

ac·ro·bat [ˈækrəˌbæt] n acrobata m/f

ac·ro·bat·ic [ˌækrəʊˈbætɪk] adj acrobatico(-a)

ac·ro·bat·ics [ˌækrəʊˈbætɪks] npl acrobazie fpl

ac·ro·nym [ˈækrənɪm] n acronimo

Acropo·lis [əˈkrɒpəlɪs] n: **the Acropolis** l'Acropoli f

across [əˈkrɒs] prep 1 (*from one side to other of*) attraverso; **to go across a bridge** attraversare un ponte; **to run across the road** attraversare di corsa la strada; **to take sb across the road** far attraversare la strada a qn; **there was a motif printed across the front of his tee-shirt** c'era un disegno stampato sul davanti della sua maglietta; **a bridge across the river** un ponte sul fiume; **he gave interviews across the country** ha concesso delle interviste in tutto il paese 2 (*on the other side of*) dall'altra parte di, al di là di; **the shop across the road** il negozio sull'altro lato o dall'altra parte della strada; **across from** di fronte a; **across the street from our house** di fronte o dirimpetto a casa nostra; **he sat down across from her** si è seduto di fronte a lei 3 (*crosswise over*) di traverso a ♦ adv 1 (*direction*) dall'altra parte; **to jump across** saltare dall'altra parte, attraversare con un salto; **don't go round, go across** non fare il giro, attraversa *o* passa nel mezzo; **to cut sth across** tagliare qc per *o* di traverso; 3 **across** (*in crosswords*) 3 orizzontale; **to get sth across to sb** (*fig*) far capire qc a qn 2 (*measurement*) in larghezza; **the lake is 12 km across** il lago ha una larghezza di 12 km *o* è largo 12 km

acryl·ic [əˈkrɪlɪk] adj acrilico(-a) ♦ n acrilico

ACT n abbr (= *American College Test*) esame di ammissione ai college americani

act [ækt] vi 1 (*take action*) agire; **the police acted quickly** la polizia ha agito prontamente; **he acted to stop it** è intervenuto per fermarlo 2 (*function: thing, person*): **to act as** fungere da, fare da (*drug*) agire; **he acts as my assistant** mi fa da assistente; **acting in my capacity as chairman, I ...** in qualità di presidente, io...; **it acts as a deterrent** serve da deterrente; **to act for sb** agire in nome *or* per conto di qn; **who is acting for the defendant?** chi è l'avvocato difensore? 3 (*behave*) comportarsi; **to act like a fool** fare lo(-a) stupido(-a), comportarsi come uno(-a) stupido(-a); **she acted as if she was upset** si era mostrata contrariata 4 (*Theatre, Cine*) recitare; **he's only acting** sta solo facendo finta *or* recitando ♦ vt (*play*) rappresentare, mettere in scena; (*part*) recitare, interpretare; **to act Hamlet** recitare la parte di Amleto; **to act the fool** (*fig*) fare lo(-a) stupido(-a) *or* il, (la) cretino(-a) ♦ n 1 (*deed*) atto; **an act of kindness** un atto di gentilezza; **an act of folly** una pazzia, una follia; **I was in the act of writing to him** stavo (proprio) scrivendo a lui; **to catch sb in the act** cogliere qn in flagrante *or* sul fatto; **I caught him in the act of stealing** l'ho sorpreso a rubare 2 (*also: act of Parliament*) legge f 3 (*Theatre: of play*) atto; (*in circus, music-hall*) numero; (*fig: pretence*) scena, messinscena; **in the first act** nel primo atto; **it's only an act** è tutta scena, è solo una messinscena

▸ **act on, act upon** vi + prep (*advice*) seguire, agire in base a; (*order, instructions*) agire in base a, eseguire

▸ **act out** vt (*event*) ricostruire; (*fantasies*) mettere in atto

▸ **act up** vi + adv (*fam: person*) fare i capricci; (: *injury*) farsi sentire; (: *machine*) fare degli scherzi

act·ing [ˈæktɪŋ] adj che fa le funzioni di; **he is the acting manager** fa le veci del direttore ♦ n recitazione f; **to do some acting** fare del teatro (*or* del cinema); **the acting was marvellous** la recitazione è stata fantastica

ac·tion [ˈækʃən] n 1 (*doing*) azione f; (*deed*) fatto, azione; (*movement: of horse, athlete*) stile m; (*effect: of acid, drug etc*) azione, effetto; (*Mil*) azione, combattimento; (*Tech: of clock, machine*) meccanismo; **to take action** passare all'azione, agire; **to take firm action against** prendere misure energiche contro; **to put a plan into action** realizzare un piano; **to be out of action** essere fuori combattimento; (*machine etc*) non funzionare, essere fuori uso; **killed in action** (*Mil*) ucciso(-a) in combattimento; **the film was full of action** nel film c'erano molte scene d'azione 2 (*Law*) azione f legale, processo; **to bring an action against sb** (*Law*) intentare causa contro qn

ac·ti·vate [ˈæktɪveɪt] vt attivare; (*mechanism*) fare funzionare; (*Chem, Phys*) rendere attivo(-a)

ac·tive [ˈæktɪv] adj (*gen: also Gram: volcano*) attivo(-a); **to play an active part in** partecipare attivamente a, prendere parte attiva in; **we are giving it active consideration** lo stiamo considerando attentamente

ac·tive·ly [ˈæktɪvlɪ] adv attivamente; **to be actively involved in** prendere parte attiva in

active partner n (*Comm*) socio effettivo *or* accomandatario

active service, (*USA*) **active duty** n (*Mil*): **to be on active service** prestar servizio in zona di operazioni

ac·tiv·ist [ˈæktɪvɪst] n attivista m/f

ac·tiv·ity [ækˈtɪvɪtɪ] n (*gen*) attività f inv; (*of scene*) animazione f, movimento; **outdoor activities** attività all'aria aperta; **social activities** attività ricreative

ac·tor [ˈæktəʳ] n attore m

ac·tress [ˈæktrɪs] n attrice f

ac·tual [ˈæktjʊəl] adj (*amount, result*) reale, vero(-a), effettivo(-a); (*example*) concreto(-a); **what's the actual amount?** qual è la cifra effettiva?; **these stories are based on actual people, places and events** questi racconti sono basati su personaggi, luoghi e fatti reali; **in actual fact** in realtà; **what were his actual words?** cosa ha detto esattamente?

❏ **actual** is not translated by the Italian word *attuale*

ac·tu·al·ly [ˈæktjʊəlɪ] adv (*really*) veramente, davvero; (*even*) addirittura, perfino; **I'm not a student, I'm a doctor, actually** no sono uno studente, sono un medico; **I was so bored I actually fell asleep!** ero così annoiato che mi sono addormentato!; **you only pay for the electricity you actually use** si paga solo per l'elettricità effettivamente consumata; **that's not true, actually** questo non è affatto vero; **I wasn't actually there** o *per* dire la verità io non c'ero, veramente io non c'ero

❏ **actually** is not translated by the Italian word *attualmente*

ac·tu·ary [ˈæktjʊərɪ] n attuario(-a)

ac·tu·ate [ˈæktjʊeɪt] vt (*frm: person*) spingere; (*Tech: machine*) attivare; **actuated by** animato(-a) da

acu·ity [əˈkjuːɪtɪ] n (*frm*) acutezza

acu·men [ˈækjʊmɛn] n acume m, perspicacia; **business acumen** fiuto negli affari

acu·punc·ture [ˈækjʊpʌŋktʃəʳ] n agopuntura

acute [əˈkjuːt] adj (*eyesight, accent, angle*) acuto(-a); (*hearing, smell etc*) fine; (*pain, anxiety, joy*) intenso(-a); (*crisis, shortage*) grave; (*person, mind*) perspicace, dotato(-a) di acume

AD [ˈeɪˈdiː] adv abbr (= *Anno Domini*) d.C. ♦ n abbr (*USA Mil*) = **active duty**

ad [æd] n abbr (*fam*) = **advertisement**; (*on TV*) spot m inv (pubblicitario), pubblicità f inv; (*in newspaper*) inserzione f pubblicitaria, pubblicità; (*for jobs etc*) inserzione f, annuncio; **to put an ad in the paper** mettere un annuncio sul giornale; **an ad for soap powder** la pubblicità di un detersivo

ada·mant [ˈædəmənt] adj inflessibile, irremovibile

Adam's apple n pomo d'Adamo

a·dapt [əˈdæpt] vt (*machine*) modificare, fare delle modifiche a; (*building*) trasformare; (*text*) adattare; **to adapt o.s. to sth** adattarsi a qc ♦ VI: **to adapt (to)** adattarsi (a)

adapt·abil·ity [ə͵dæptə'bɪlɪtɪ] N adattabilità, capacità di adattamento

adapt·able [ə'dæptəbl] ADJ (*person: device*) adattabile, che sa adattarsi; (*device*) adattabile; **he's very adaptable** si adatta facilmente

ad·ap·ta·tion [͵ædæp'teɪʃən] N adattamento

adapt·er [ə'dæptə'], **adap·tor** [ə'dæptə'] N 1 (*Elec: for several plugs*) presa multipla; (: *for 2-pin to 3-pin system*) adattatore *m*, riduttore *m* 2 (*of novel*) chi cura un adattamento

ADC [͵eɪdiː'siː] N ABBR 1 (*Mil*) = aide-de-camp 2 (*USA:* = *Aid to Dependent Children*) sussidio per figli a carico 3 (= *analogue-digital converter*) convertitore *m* analogico-digitale

add [æd] VT: **to add (to)** aggiungere (a); (*Math*) sommare (a), addizionare (a); **he added that ...** ha aggiunto che...; **added to which ...** e per giunta..., e per di più...; **to add insult to injury** aggiungere al danno le beffe; **add a bit of sugar** aggiungi un po' di zucchero ♦ VI (*count*) fare le addizioni *or* le somme, addizionare
  ▸ **add in** VT + ADV aggiungere, includere
  ▸ **add on** VT + ADV aggiungere
  ▸ **add to** VI + PREP aumentare, accrescere
  ▸ **add up** VT + ADV (*figures*) addizionare, sommare; (*advantages etc*) mettere insieme ♦ VI + ADV: **it adds up to 25 la somma è 25; it doesn't add up** (*fig: fam*) non quadra, non ha senso; **it doesn't add up to much** (*fig*) non è un granché; **it's all beginning to add up** (*fig: fam*) tutto comincia a diventare chiaro

ad·der ['ædə'] N vipera

ad·dict ['ædɪkt] N tossicomane *m/f*, drogato(-a); (*fig*) fanatico(-a); **drug addict** tossicodipendente *m/f*, tossicomane *m/f*; **heroin addict** eroinomane *m/f*; **television addict** teledipendente *m/f*
  ❑ **addict** is not translated by the Italian word *addetto*

ad·dicted [ə'dɪktɪd] ADJ: **addicted (to)** (*drugs etc*) dipendente (da); (*fig*) fanatico(-a) (di), maniaco(-a) (di); **to be addicted to drugs** essere tossicodipendente; **to become addicted to cocaine** diventare cocainomane; **to be addicted to drink** essere dedito(-a) al bere; **to be addicted to chocolate** essere un(a) cioccolato-dipendente

ad·dic·tion [ə'dɪkʃən] N assuefazione *f*; (*Med*) tossicomania; **drug addiction** tossicodipendenza
  ❑ **addiction** is not translated by the Italian word *addizione*

ad·dic·tive [ə'dɪktɪv] ADJ che dà assuefazione

ad·ding ma·chine ['ædɪŋmə'ʃiːn] N addizionatrice *f*

Ad·dis Aba·ba ['ædɪs'æbəbə] N Addis Abeba *f*

ad·di·tion [ə'dɪʃən] N aggiunta; (*Math*) addizione *f*; **if my addition is correct** se ho fatto bene i conti; **there has been an addition to the family** la famiglia si è accresciuta; **in addition** to oltre a, in aggiunta a; **in addition, ...** inoltre,...

ad·di·tion·al [ə'dɪʃənl] ADJ supplementare

ad·di·tive ['ædɪtɪv] N additivo

ad·dress [ə'drɛs] N 1 (*of house etc*) indirizzo, recapito; (*on envelope: Comput*) indirizzo; **absolute/relative address** (*Comput*) indirizzo assoluto/relativo 2 (*talk*) discorso, allocuzione *f* 3 **form of address** (*gen*) formula di cortesia; (*in letters*) formula d'indirizzo *or* di intestazione; **the correct form of address for a bishop** la maniera corretta di rivolgersi ad un vescovo ♦ VT 1 (*direct: letter*) indirizzare; (: *write name etc on envelope*) mettere *or* scrivere l'indirizzo su; (: *remarks etc*) rivolgere; **this letter is wrongly addressed** l'indirizzo su questa lettera è sbagliato; **please address your complaints to the manager** (*frm*) per i reclami si rivolga al direttore; **to address o.s. to sth** (*frm*) indirizzare le proprie energie verso qc 2 (*person*) rivolgersi a; (*meeting*) parlare a, fare un discorso a; **she addressed him as "Your Lordship"** si rivolse a lui chiamandolo "Sua Eccellenza"; **the judge addressed the jury** il giudice si è rivolto alla giuria

address book N rubrica

ad·dressee [͵ædrɛ'siː] N destinatario(-a)

Aden ['eɪdn] N Aden *f*; **the Gulf of Aden** il golfo di Aden

ad·enoids ['ædɪnɔɪdz] NPL adenoidi *fpl*

adept ['ædɛpt] ADJ: **adept in** *or* **at sth/at doing sth** abile *or* esperto(-a) in qc/nel fare qc ♦ N: **adept (in, at)** esperto(-a) (in)

ad·equate ['ædɪkwɪt] ADJ (*amount, supply*): **adequate (for/to do sth)** sufficiente (a/per fare qc); (*reward, description, explanation*): **adequate (for)** adeguato(-a) (a); **adequate (to)** adatto(-a) (a); (*essay, performance*) passabile; (*person*) all'altezza; **to feel adequate to a task** sentirsi all'altezza di un compito

ad·equate·ly ['ædɪkwɪtlɪ] ADV (*heated, paid*) adeguatamente, sufficientemente; (*perform, answer*) convenientemente; **will he do it adequately?** sarà all'altezza?

ad·here [əd'hɪə'] VI: **to adhere to** (*surface, party, policy*) aderire a; (*belief*) rimanere fedele a; (*promise*) mantenere; (*rule, decision*) attenersi a, seguire

ad·he·sion [əd'hiːʒən] N (*Tech*) aderenza; (*fig: of supporters*) consenso

ad·he·sive [əd'hiːzɪv] ADJ adesivo(-a); **adhesive tape** (*Brit: for parcels etc*) nastro adesivo; (*USA: Med*) cerotto adesivo ♦ N adesivo

ad hoc [æd'hɒk] ADJ (*decision*) ad hoc *inv*; (*committee*) apposito(-a)

ad in·fi·ni·tum [͵ædɪnfɪ'naɪtəm] ADV all'infinito

ad·ja·cent [ə'dʒeɪsənt] ADJ: **adjacent (to)** adiacente (a)

ad·jec·tive ['ædʒektɪv] N aggettivo

ad·join [ə'dʒɔɪn] VT essere contiguo(-a) *or* attiguo(-a) a; **the room adjoining mine** la stanza accanto alla mia

ad·join·ing [ə'dʒɔɪnɪŋ] ADJ contiguo(-a), attiguo(-a), adiacente

ad·journ [ə'dʒɜːn] VT (*suspend*) aggiornare, rimandare, rinviare; **to adjourn a meeting till the following week** aggiornare *or* rinviare un incontro alla settimana seguente; **to adjourn a meeting for a month** rinviare un incontro di un mese ♦ VI 1 sospendere la seduta; (*Parliament*) sospendere i lavori 2 (*move*) spostarsi; **they adjourned to the pub** (*fam*) si sono trasferiti al pub

ad·journ·ment [ə'dʒɜːnmənt] N (*of meeting*) rinvio, aggiornamento

Adjt ABBR (*Mil*) = **adjutant**

ad·ju·di·cate [ə'dʒuːdɪkeɪt] VT (*contest*) giudicare; (*claim*) decidere su

ad·ju·di·ca·tion [ə'dʒuːdɪ'keɪʃən] N (*of contest*) giudizio; (*of claim*) decisione *f*

ad·just [ə'dʒʌst] VT (*instrument, tool, speed*) regolare; (*wages, prices*) modificare; (*aim, tie, dress*) aggiustare; **you can adjust the height of the seat** si può regolare l'altezza della sedia ♦ VI: **to adjust (to)** adattarsi (a)

ad·just·able [ə'dʒʌstəbl] ADJ regolabile; **adjustable pliers** pinza *fsg* regolabile; **the volume is adjustable** si può regolare il volume

ad·just·er [ə'dʒʌstə'] N = **loss adjuster**

ad·just·ment [ə'dʒʌstmənt] N (*of instrument*) regolazione *f*; (*of wages, prices*) modifica, aggiustamento; (*of person*) adattamento; **to make an adjustment to one's plans** modificare i propri piani

ad·ju·tant ['ædʒətənt] N (*Mil*) aiutante *m/f*

ad·lib [æd'lɪb] VT, VI improvvisare ♦ N improvvisazione *f* ♦ ADJ improvvisato(-a), estemporaneo(-a) ♦ ADV (*speak*) a piacere

ad·man ['ædmæn] N (*fam*) pubblicitario

ad·min ['ædmɪn] N ABBR (*fam:* = *administration*) amministrazione *f*; **her job is mostly admin** il suo lavoro è principalmente amministrativo

ad·min·is·ter [əd'mɪnɪstə'] VT 1 (*manage: company*) dirigere, gestire; (: *fund*) amministrare 2 (*dispense: medicine*) somministrare; (: *justice, laws*) amministrare; **to administer an oath to sb** far prestare giuramento a qn

ad·min·is·tra·tion [əd͵mɪnɪs'treɪʃən] N 1 (*of company*) direzione *f*, gestione *f*; (*of fund, justice*) amministrazione *f*; (*of medicine*) somministrazione *f* 2 (*USA Pol*) governo

ad·min·is·tra·tive [əd'mɪnɪstrətɪv] ADJ amministrativo(-a)

ad·min·is·tra·tor [əd'mɪnɪstreɪtə'] N amministratore(-trice); (*of will*) curatore(-trice)

ad·mi·rable ['ædmərəbl] ADJ ammirevole

ad·mi·ral ['ædmərəl] N ammiraglio

Ad·mi·ral·ty ['ædmərəltɪ] N (*Brit*): **the Admiralty** l'Ammiragliato

ad·mi·ra·tion [ˌædməˈreɪʃən] N ammirazione *f*

ad·mire [ədˈmaɪəʳ] VT ammirare

ad·mir·er [ədˈmaɪərəʳ] N ammiratore(-trice)

ad·mir·ing [ədˈmaɪərɪŋ] ADJ (*person*) pieno(-a) di ammirazione; (*look*) di ammirazione

ad·mis·sible [ədˈmɪsəbl] ADJ ammissibile

ad·mis·sion [ədˈmɪʃən] N 1 (*entry: to society, school etc*) ammissione *f*; (: *to exhibition, night club, building*) entrata, ingresso; (: *price*) prezzo del biglietto (d'ingresso); **"admission free"** *or* **"free admission"** "ingresso gratuito" 2 (*confession*) ammissione *f*, confessione *f*; **it would be an admission of defeat** sarebbe come dichiararsi sconfitto; **by his own admission** per sua ammissione

ad·mit [ədˈmɪt] VT 1 (*allow to enter*) lasciar entrare, far entrare; (*air, light*) lasciar passare; **children not admitted** vietato l'ingresso ai bambini; **this ticket admits two** questo biglietto è valido per due persone; **he was admitted to the hospital** è stato ricoverato all'ospedale 2 (*acknowledge*) ammettere, riconoscere; (*crime*) ammettere *or* confessare (di aver compiuto); **it is hard, I admit** è difficile, lo ammetto *or* devo ammetterlo; **I must admit that ...** devo ammettere *or* confessare che...; **he admitted that he'd done it** ha confessato di averlo fatto

  ▸ **admit of** VI + PREP (*frm*) dare adito a

  ▸ **admit to** VI + PREP riconoscere

ad·mit·tance [ədˈmɪtəns] N ingresso; **they refused me admittance** mi hanno rifiutato il permesso di entrare; **to gain admittance** riuscire a entrare; **"no admittance"** "vietato l'ingresso"

ad·mit·ted·ly [ədˈmɪtɪdlɪ] ADV bisogna ammettere *or* riconoscere (che), va detto (che)

ad·mon·ish [ədˈmɒnɪʃ] VT (*frm: reprimand*) ammonire; **to admonish sb (for)** riprendere qn (per)

ad nau·se·am [ædˈnɔːsɪæm] ADV fino alla nausea, a non finire

ado [əˈduː] N: **without (any) more ado** senza più indugi

ado·les·cence [ˌædəʊˈlɛsns] N adolescenza

ado·les·cent [ˌædəʊˈlɛsnt] ADJ, N adolescente *m/f*

adopt [əˈdɒpt] VT (*child, method*) adottare; (*report, suggestion*) approvare; (*Pol: candidate*) scegliere

adopt·ed [əˈdɒptɪd] ADJ adottivo(-a)

adop·tion [əˈdɒpʃən] N (*see vb*) adozione *f*; approvazione *f*; scelta

adore [əˈdɔːʳ] VT adorare

ador·ing [əˈdɔːrɪŋ] ADJ (*look, glance*) pieno(-a) di adorazione, adorante; **he has adoring parents** i suoi genitori lo adorano

ador·ing·ly [əˈdɔːrɪŋlɪ] ADV con adorazione, con venerazione

adorn [əˈdɔːn] VT (*liter*) abbellire, ornare

adorn·ment [əˈdɔːnmənt] N (*liter*) ornamento, decorazione *f*

adrena·lin [əˈdrɛnəlɪn] N adrenalina; **it gets the adrenalin going** ti dà una scarica di adrenalina

Adri·at·ic [ˌeɪdrɪˈætɪk] ADJ adriatico(-a) ◆ N: **the Adriatic (Sea)** l'Adriatico, il mare Adriatico

adrift [əˈdrɪft] ADV (*esp Naut*) alla deriva; **to come adrift** (*wire, rope etc*) essersi staccato(-a) *or* sciolto(-a)

adroit [əˈdrɔɪt] ADJ abile, destro(-a)

ADSL [ˌeɪdiːɛsˈɛl] N ABBR (= *asynchronous digital subscriber line*) ADSL *m*

ADT [ˌeɪdiːˈtiː] N ABBR (*USA:* = *Atlantic Daylight Time*) ora estiva nel fuso orario di New York

adult [ˈædʌlt] ADJ (*person, animal*) adulto(-a); (*behaviour*) da adulto; (*film, book*) per adulti ◆ N adulto(-a); **"adults only"** ≈ "vietato ai minori di 18 anni"

adult education N scuola per adulti

adul·ter·ate [əˈdʌltəreɪt] VT adulterare

adul·ter·er [əˈdʌltərəʳ] N adultero

adul·ter·ess [əˈdʌltərɪs] N adultera

adul·tery [əˈdʌltərɪ] N adulterio

adult·hood [əˈdʌlthʊd] N età adulta

ad·vance [ədˈvɑːns] VT 1 (*move forward: time, date*) anticipare; (*Mil: troops*) far avanzare; (*promote: interests*) favorire; (: *person: in career*) promuovere 2 (*idea, suggestion, claim*) avanzare ◆ VI (*move forward, also Mil*) avanzare; (*science, technology*) fare progressi,

progredire; (*civilization, mankind*) migliorare, fare progressi; **to advance on sb** (*threateningly*) avanzare contro qn; **technology has advanced a great deal** la tecnologia ha fatto grandi progressi ◆ N (*Mil*) avanzata; (*fig: progress*) passo (in) avanti, progresso; **the advance of old age** l'avanzare dell'età *or* degli anni; **recent advances in technology** i recenti progressi della tecnica; **to make advances to sb** (*gen*) tentare un approccio con qn; (*amorously*) fare le avances a qn; **in advance** in anticipo; **to arrive in advance of sb** arrivare in anticipo su qn *or* prima di qn; **to send sth a week in advance** spedire qc con una settimana di anticipo 2 (*loan*): **advance** (**on**) anticipo (su) (*from bank*) anticipazione *f* bancaria (su) ◆ ADJ (*payment, booking*) anticipato(-a); (*copy of book*) distribuito(-a) in anticipo; **we weren't given any advance warning of his visit** non ci avevano dato nessun preavviso del suo arrivo

❏ **advance** is not translated by the Italian word *avanzo*

ad·vanced [ədˈvɑːnst] ADJ (*ideas, civilization etc*) progredito(-a), avanzato(-a); (*Scol: studies*) superiore; (: *class*) avanzato(-a); (: *student*) di livello più avanzato; **of advanced years** avanti negli anni

ad·vance·ment [ədˈvɑːnsmənt] N (*improvement*) miglioramento; (*promotion*) promozione *f*, avanzamento; **career advancement** avanzamento di carriera

advance notice N preavviso

ad·van·tage [ədˈvɑːntɪdʒ] N (*gen, also Tennis*) vantaggio; **the plan has many advantages** il progetto presenta molti vantaggi; **it's to our advantage** è nel nostro interesse, torna a nostro vantaggio; **to have an advantage over sb** avere un vantaggio su qn; **to take advantage of** (*opportunity*) approfittare di, sfruttare; **to take advantage of sb** (*unfairly, sexually etc*) approfittare *or* approfittarsi di qn

ad·van·ta·geous [ˌædvənˈteɪdʒəs] ADJ: **advantageous (to)** vantaggioso(-a) (per)

Ad·vent [ˈædvɛnt] N (*Rel*) Avvento

ad·vent [ˈædvənt] N (*frm: arrival*) avvento

Advent calendar N calendario dell'Avvento

ad·ven·ture [ədˈvɛntʃəʳ] N avventura ◆ ADJ (*story, film*) di avventura

adventure playground N campo giochi attrezzato

ad·ven·tur·ous [ədˈvɛntʃərəs] ADJ avventuroso(-a)

ad·verb [ˈædvɜːb] N avverbio

ad·ver·sary [ˈædvəsərɪ] N avversario(-a), antagonista *m/f*

ad·verse [ˈædvɜːs] ADJ (*criticism, decision, effect*) sfavorevole; (*wind*) contrario(-a); **adverse to** contrario(-a) a; **adverse weather conditions** condizioni atmosferiche avverse; **in adverse circumstances** nelle avversità

ad·ver·sity [ədˈvɜːsɪtɪ] N avversità *f inv*

ad·vert [ˈædvɜːt] N ABBR (*Brit fam*) = **advertisement**; (*on TV*) spot *m inv* (pubblicitario), pubblicità *f inv*; (*in newspaper*) inserzione *f* pubblicitaria, pubblicità; (*for jobs etc*) inserzione *f*, annuncio; *see also* **advertisement**

ad·ver·tise [ˈædvətaɪz] VT (*Comm, etc*) fare pubblicità *or* réclame a, reclamizzare; **to advertise an apartment for sale** mettere un annuncio per vendere un appartamento; **they're advertising the new model** stanno facendo pubblicità per il nuovo modello ◆ VI fare (della) pubblicità *or* (della) réclame; **to advertise for** (*staff*) cercare tramite annuncio; **they're advertising for editors** cercano redattori; **to advertise on television** fare pubblicità in televisione

ad·ver·tise·ment [ədˈvɜːtɪsmənt] N (*Comm*) réclame *f inv*, pubblicità *f inv*; (*on TV*) spot *m inv*; (*in classified ads*) inserzione *f*, annuncio; **to put an advertisement in the paper** mettere un annuncio sul giornale; **an advertisement for soap** la réclame *or* la pubblicità di un sapone

❏ **advertisement** is not translated by the Italian word *avvertimento*

ad·ver·tis·er [ˈædvətaɪzəʳ] N azienda che reclamizza un prodotto; (*in newspaper*) inserzionista *m/f*

ad·ver·tis·ing [ˈædvətaɪzɪŋ] N pubblicità (commerciale); (*advertisements collectively*) pubblicità, réclame *f inv*; **my brother's in advertising** mio fratello lavora nel settore pubblicitario

advertising agency N agenzia pubblicitaria *or* di pubblicità

advertising campaign N campagna pubblicitaria
ad·vice [əd'vaɪs] N consiglio, consigli *mpl*; **a piece of advice** un consiglio; **some advice** dei consigli; **legal advice** consulenza legale; **to ask (sb) for advice** chiedere il consiglio (di qn), chiedere un consiglio (a qn); **to take sb's advice** seguire il consiglio *or* i consigli di qn
❑ **advice** is not translated by the Italian word *avviso*
ad·vis·able [əd'vaɪzəbl] ADJ consigliabile, raccomandabile; **I do not think it advisable for you to come** non le consiglierei di venire
ad·vise [əd'vaɪz] VT 1 (*counsel*): **to advise sb (on sth)** consigliare qn (a proposito di qc); **to advise sb to do sth** consigliare a qn di fare qc; **to advise sb against sth** sconsigliare qc a qn; **to advise against doing sth** sconsigliare a qn di fare qc; **he advises the President on foreign affairs** è il consigliere del Presidente in materia di affari esteri; **you would be well/ill advised to go** (*frm*) faresti bene/male ad andare 2 (*frm: inform*): **to advise sb of sth** avvisare qn di qc
ad·vis·ed·ly [əd'vaɪzɪdlɪ] ADV (*deliberately*) deliberatamente
ad·vis·er, ad·vis·or [əd'vaɪzə'] N (*in politics*) consigliere(-a); (*in business*) consulente *m/f*
ad·vi·so·ry [əd'vaɪzərɪ] ADJ (*body*) consultivo(-a); **in an advisory capacity** in veste di consulente ♦ N (*USA*) comunicato ufficiale
ad·vo·cate [*n* 'ædvəkɪt, *vb* 'ædvəkeɪt] N (*Scot: Law*) avvocato (difensore); (*fig*) sostenitore(-trice); **to be an advocate of** essere a favore di ♦ VT sostenere la validità di, propugnare
advt. ABBR = **advertisement**
Aegean [iː'dʒiːən] N: **the Aegean (Sea)** il mar *m* Egeo, l'Egeo
aegis ['iːdʒɪs] N (*frm*): **under the aegis of** sotto l'egida di
aeon, eon (*esp USA*) ['iːən] N eternità *f inv*
aer·i·al ['ɛərɪəl] ADJ aereo(-a); **aerial photograph** fotografia aerea; **aerial railway** teleferica, funivia ♦ N (*Brit: Radio, TV*) antenna
aero·bat·ics ['ɛərəʊ'bætɪks] NPL (*stunts*) acrobazie *fpl* aeree
aero·bics [ɛə'rəʊbɪks] NSG aerobica
aero·drome ['ɛərədrəʊm] N (*esp Brit*) aerodromo
aero·dy·nam·ic ['ɛərəʊdaɪ'næmɪk] ADJ aerodinamico(-a)
aero·naut·ics [ˌɛərə'nɔːtɪks] NSG aeronautica
aero·plane ['ɛərəˌpleɪn] N (*esp Brit*) aeroplano
aero·sol ['ɛərəˌsɒl] N (*can*) aerosol *m inv*
aero·space in·dus·try ['ɛərəʊspeɪs'ɪndəstrɪ] N industria aerospaziale
aes·thet·ic, es·thet·ic (*USA*) [iːs'θɛtɪk] ADJ estetico(-a)
afar [ə'fɑː'] ADV (*old, liter*) lontano; **from afar** da lontano
AFB [ˌeɪɛf'biː] N ABBR (*USA*: = **Air Force Base**)
AFDC [ˌeɪɛfdiː'siː] N ABBR (*USA*: = *Aid to Families with Dependent Children*) ≈ **AF** (= *assegni familiari*)
af·fable ['æfəbl] ADJ affabile
af·fair [ə'fɛə'] N 1 (*event*) faccenda, affare *m*; (*love affair*) relazione *f* (amorosa); (*brief*) avventura; **it will be a big affair** sarà un avvenimento; **the Watergate affair** il caso Watergate; **that's my affair** sono affari *or* fatti miei; **it's a bad state of affairs** è una brutta situazione; **the government has mishandled the affair** il governo ha gestito male la faccenda 2 **affairs** NPL (*business*) affari; **foreign affairs** affari esteri; **affairs of state** affari di stato
af·fect [ə'fɛkt] VT 1 (*have an effect on*) influire su, incidere su; (*concern*) riguardare, concernere; (*harm: health etc*) danneggiare; **it did not affect my decision** non ha influenzato la mia decisione, non ha influito sulla mia decisione; **these changes won't affect me** questi cambiamenti non avranno alcun impatto su di me; **millions have been affected by the drought** la siccità ha colpito milioni di persone 2 (*move emotionally*) colpire, toccare; **he seemed much affected** sembrava molto colpito; **the divorce affected him deeply** l'esperienza del divorzio l'ha segnato profondamente 3 (*feign*) fingere
af·fec·ta·tion [ˌæfɛk'teɪʃən] N affettazione *f*; **affectations** NPL modi *mpl* affettati, leziosaggini *fpl*
af·fect·ed [ə'fɛktɪd] ADJ affettato(-a)
af·fec·tion [ə'fɛkʃən] N affetto
af·fec·tion·ate [ə'fɛkʃənɪt] ADJ affettuoso(-a)

af·fec·tion·ate·ly [ə'fɛkʃənɪtlɪ] ADV affettuosamente
af·fi·da·vit [ˌæfɪ'deɪvɪt] N (*Law*) affidavit *m inv*
af·fili·ated [ə'fɪlɪeɪtɪd] ADJ: **affiliated (to** *or* **with)** affiliato(-a) (a), associato(-a) (a); **affiliated company** filiale *f*
af·fin·ity [ə'fɪnɪtɪ] N (*relationship*) affinità *f inv*; (*liking*) simpatia
af·firm [ə'fɜːm] VT affermare, asserire
af·fir·ma·tion [ˌæfə'meɪʃən] N affermazione *f*, asserzione *f*
af·firma·tive [ə'fɜːmətɪv] ADJ affermativo(-a) ♦ N: **to answer in the affirmative** rispondere affermativamente *or* di sì
af·fix [ə'fɪks] VT (*signature etc*) apporre; (*stamp*) attaccare
af·flict [ə'flɪkt] VT affliggere
af·flic·tion [ə'flɪkʃən] N (*suffering*) afflizione *f*, sofferenza; (*bodily*) infermità *f inv*
af·flu·ence ['æfluəns] N (*wealth*) ricchezza; (*plenty*) abbondanza
❑ **affluence** is not translated by the Italian word *affluenza*
af·flu·ent ['æfluənt] ADJ ricco(-a); **the affluent society** la società del benessere
af·ford [ə'fɔːd] VT 1 **to afford sth/to do sth** permettersi qc/di fare qc; **can we afford a car?** possiamo permetterci un'automobile?; **I can't afford the time** non ho proprio il tempo, non ho veramente tempo; **I can't afford not to do it** non mi posso permettere di non farlo; **an opportunity you cannot afford to miss** un'occasione che non puoi lasciarti sfuggire 2 (*frm: provide: opportunity*) offrire, fornire
af·ford·able [ə'fɔːdəbl] ADJ (*che ha un prezzo*) abbordabile
af·fray [ə'freɪ] N (*Law*) rissa
af·front [ə'frʌnt] N affronto ♦ VT fare un affronto a; **to be affronted (by)** offendersi (per)
Af·ghan ['æfɡæn] N (*person*) afgano(-a); (*language*) afgano; (*dog: also:* **Afghan hound**) levriero afgano ♦ ADJ afgano(-a)
Af·ghani·stan ['æfɡænɪˌstɑːn] N l'Afganistan *m*
afield [ə'fiːld] ADV: **far afield** lontano, distante
AFL-CIO [ˌeɪɛfɛlsiːaɪ'əʊ] N ABBR (= *American Federation of Labor and Congress of Industrial Organizations*) *confederazione sindacale*
afloat [ə'fləʊt] ADV, ADJ a galla; **to keep afloat** (*also fig*) rimanere a galla
afoot [ə'fʊt] ADJ, ADV in preparazione, in corso; **there's trouble afoot** ci sono guai in vista; **there is something afoot** si sta preparando qualcosa
afore·men·tioned [ə'fɔːˌmɛnʃənd], **afore·said** [ə'fɔːsɛd] ADJ (*Law*) suddetto(-a), summenzionato(-a)
afraid [ə'freɪd] ADJ impaurito(-a); **to be afraid** aver paura; **to be afraid for sb** temere per qn, preoccuparsi per qn; **to be afraid of sb/sth** aver paura di qn/qc; **I was afraid to ask** avevo paura di *or* non osavo domandare; **I'm afraid he's out** (*regret*) mi rincresce *or* dispiace, ma è fuori; **I'm afraid I have to go now** mi dispiace, ma adesso devo proprio andare; **I'm afraid so!** ho paura di sì!, temo proprio di sì!; **I'm afraid not,** mi dispiace, purtroppo no, temo di no; **I am afraid that I'll be late** mi dispiace, ma farò tardi
afresh [ə'frɛʃ] ADV da capo, di nuovo; **to start afresh** ricominciare (tutto) da capo
Af·ri·ca ['æfrɪkə] N Africa
Af·ri·can ['æfrɪkən] ADJ, N africano(-a)
African-American [ˌæfrɪkənə'mɛrɪkən] ADJ, N afroamericano(-a)
Af·ri·kaans [ˌæfrɪ'kɑːnz] N afrikaans *m*
Af·ri·kan·er [ˌæfrɪ'kɑːnə'] N africander *m/f inv*
Afro-American ['æfrəʊə'mɛrɪkən] ADJ, N afroamericano(-a)
Afro-Caribbean ['æfrəʊkærɪ'biːən] ADJ, N afrocaraibico(-a)
aft [ɑːft] ADV (*Naut*) a *or* verso poppa; **to go aft** andare a poppa
af·ter ['ɑːftə'] ADV (*afterwards*) dopo; **the day after** il giorno dopo *or* seguente ♦ PREP 1 (*time, order, place*) dopo; **day after day** giorno dopo giorno; **for kilometre after kilometre** per chilometri e chilometri; **you tell me lie after lie** mi stai dicendo una bugia dopo l'altra; **time after time** tantissime volte; **after dinner** dopo cena; **the day after tomorrow** dopodomani; **soon after eating it** poco dopo averlo mangiato; **after all** dopotutto, malgrado tutto; **half after two** (*USA*) le due e mezzo; **one after the other** uno(-a) dopo l'altro(-a);

shut the door after you chiudi la porta dietro di te; **after you!** prima lei!, dopo di lei! **2** (*in pursuit*) dietro; **he ran after me** mi è corso dietro, mi ha rincorso; **the police are after him** è ricercato dalla polizia; **what/who are you after?** (*fam*) (che) cosa/chi cerca? ♦ conj dopo che; **after he had eaten he went out** dopo aver mangiato *or* che ebbe mangiato uscì ♦ adj (*Naut*) poppiero(-a)

after·birth [ˈɑːftə,bɜːθ] n placenta (e membrane fetali)

after·care [ˈɑːftə,kɛə'] n (*Brit: of patients*) assistenza medica post-degenza; (: *of prisoners*) servizio di assistenza per ex-detenuti

after-effect [ˈɑːftərɪfekt] n (*of events*) ripercussione *f*, conseguenza; (*of drug*) reazione *f*; (*of illness, experience*) postumi *mpl*

after·life [ˈɑːftə,laɪf] n vita dell'al di là

after·math [ˈɑːftə,mæθ] n conseguenze *fpl*, strascichi *mpl*; **in the aftermath of** nel periodo dopo

after·noon [ˈɑːftəˈnuːn] n pomeriggio; **in the afternoon** nel *or* di pomeriggio; **at 3 o'clock in the afternoon** alle 3 del pomeriggio; **good afternoon!** buon giorno!

after-shave [ˈɑːftəˌʃeɪv], **after-shave lotion** n (lozione *f*) dopobarba, *m inv*

after·shock [ˈɑːftəˌʃɒk] n scossa di assestamento

after·sun [ˈɑːftəˌsʌn] adj: **aftersun (lotion/cream)** (lozione *f* /crema) doposole, *m inv*

after·taste [ˈɑːftəˌteɪst] n retrogusto

after·thought [ˈɑːftəˌθɔːt] n ripensamento; **it was very much an afterthought** è stata una cosa completamente improvvisata; **we added it as an afterthought** l'abbiamo aggiunto solo più tardi

after·wards [ˈɑːftəwədz] adv dopo, più tardi, in seguito; **soon afterwards** poco dopo

again [əˈɡɛn] adv ancora, di nuovo, un'altra volta; **to begin/ see again** ricominciare/rivedere; **he opened it again** l'ha aperto di nuovo, l'ha riaperto; **they're friends again** sono di nuovo amici; **come again soon!** torna presto!; **again and again** ripetutamente, tante volte; **I've told him again and again** gliel'ho detto e ripetuto; **never again!** mai più!; **not ...again** non... più; **I won't go there again** lì non ci torno più; **now and again** di tanto in tanto, a volte; **as much again** due volte tanto; **then again** (*on the other hand*) d'altra parte; (*moreover*) inoltre

against [əˈɡɛnst] prep **1** (*in contact with*) a, contro; **I was leaning against the desk** ero appoggiato alla scrivania; **he leaned the ladder against the wall** appoggiò la scala al *or* contro il muro **2** (*in opposition to*) contro; **I'm against nuclear testing** sono contro gli esperimenti nucleari; **he was against going** era contrario ad andare; **what have you got against me?** cos'hai contro di me?; **it's against the law** è contrario alla *or* contro la legge; **to run against sb** (*Pol*) contrapporre la propria candidatura a quella di qn **3** (*in contrast to*): **against the light** controluce; **a blue background** su uno sfondo azzurro **4** (*Brit: in comparisons*): **(as) against** in confronto a, contro

age [eɪdʒ] n **1** età *f inv*; (*of thing*) anni *mpl*; **old age** vecchiaia; **what's his age?** *or* **what age is he?** quanti anni ha?; **when I was your age** quando avevo la tua età; **he doesn't look his age** non dimostra la sua età *or* i suoi anni; **at the age of** all'età di; **to come of age** diventare maggiorenne, raggiungere la maggiore età **2** (*period*) epoca, era; **the Iron Age** l'età del ferro **3** (*fam: long time*): **we waited (for) ages** abbiamo aspettato per ore; **it's an age** *or* **ages since I saw him** sono secoli che non lo vedo ♦ vt fare invecchiare, invecchiare ♦ vi invecchiare

aged [eɪdʒd] adj **1** (*old*) anziano(-a), attempato(-a) **2** [eɪdʒd] dell'età di; **a boy aged 10** un ragazzo di 10 anni ♦ npl: **the aged** (*elderly*) gli anziani, i vecchi

age group n fascia d'età; **the 40 to 50 age group** le persone fra i 40 e i 50 anni

age·ing [ˈeɪdʒɪŋ] adj che diventa vecchio(-a)

age·less [ˈeɪdʒlɪs] adj (*eternal*) eterno(-a); (*always young*) senza età

age limit n limite *m* di età

agen·cy [ˈeɪdʒənsɪ] n **1** (*office*) agenzia; (*distributorship*) rappresentanza **2** (*instrumentality*): **through** *or* **by the agency of** grazie a, per mezzo *or* per opera di

agen·da [əˈdʒɛndə] n ordine *m* del giorno, agenda; **on the agenda** all'ordine del giorno

agent [ˈeɪdʒənt] n **1** (*Comm, Police, Theatre, etc*) agente *m/f*; (*representative*) rappresentante *m/f*; **to be sole agent for** avere la rappresentanza esclusiva per; **agent's commission** provvigione *f*; **he is not a free agent** (*fig*) non è padrone di fare quel che vuole; **an estate agent** un agente immobiliare; **a travel agent** un agente di viaggio **2** (*Chem*) agente *m*

ag·gra·vate [ˈæɡrəveɪt] vt aggravare, peggiorare; (*annoy*) esasperare, irritare

ag·gra·va·tion [ˌæɡrəˈveɪʃən] n (*of situation etc*) aggravamento, peggioramento; (*annoyance*) esasperazione *f*, irritazione *f*

ag·gre·gate [ˈæɡrɪɡɪt] n **1** (*total*) insieme *m*; **in the aggregate** nel complesso; **on aggregate** (*Sport*) con punteggio complessivo **2** (*Geol*) aggregato; (*Constr*) materiali *mpl* inerti ♦ adj complessivo(-a)

ag·gres·sion [əˈɡrɛʃən] n aggressione *f*; (*aggressiveness*) aggressività

ag·gres·sive [əˈɡrɛsɪv] adj aggressivo(-a); (*salesman, approach etc*) intraprendente

ag·gres·sive·ness [əˈɡrɛsɪvnɪs] n aggressività

ag·gres·sor [əˈɡrɛsə'] n aggressore (aggreditrice)

ag·grieved [əˈɡriːvd] adj: **aggrieved (at, by)** offeso(-a) (da), addolorato(-a) (da)

aghast [əˈɡɑːst] adj: **aghast (at)** (*shocked*) sbigottito(-a) (a); (*terrified*) inorridito(-a) (a), atterrito(-a) (a); **to be aghast at the idea of doing sth** essere atterrito(-a) all'idea di fare qc

ag·ile [ˈædʒaɪl] adj agile, svelto(-a)

agil·ity [əˈdʒɪlɪtɪ] n agilità *f inv*

agi·tate [ˈædʒɪteɪt] vt (*perturb*) turbare, mettere in (uno stato di) agitazione; (*shake*) agitare ♦ vi (*Pol*): **to agitate (for/ against)** fare un'agitazione (per/contro)

agi·tat·ed [ˈædʒɪteɪtɪd] adj agitato(-a), inquieto(-a)

agi·ta·tor [ˈædʒɪteɪtə'] n (*Pol, usu pej*) agitatore(-trice)

AGM [ˌeɪdʒiːˈɛm] n abbr = **annual general meeting**

ag·nos·tic [æɡˈnɒstɪk] adj, n agnostico(-a)

ago [əˈɡəʊ] adv: **a week ago** una settimana fa; **long ago** molto tempo fa; **not long ago** poco tempo fa; **as long ago as 1960** già nel 1960; **how long ago?** quanto tempo fa?; **how long ago was it?** quanto tempo fa è successo?, da quanto tempo è successo?

agog [əˈɡɒɡ] adj: **(all) agog (to hear sth)** ansioso(-a) *or* impaziente (di sentire qc); **agog with excitement** emozionato(-a), eccitato(-a)

ago·nize [ˈæɡənaɪz] vi: **to agonize (over)** angosciarsi (per)

ago·niz·ing [ˈæɡənaɪzɪŋ] adj (*cry, decision*) penoso(-a), angoscioso(-a); (*pain, death*) straziante

ago·ny [ˈæɡənɪ] n (*pain*) dolore *m* atroce; (*mental*) angoscia, tormento; **I am in agony** avevo dei dolori atroci; **it was agony!** è stata una tortura!, soffrivo atrocemente; **to suffer agonies of doubt** avere dei dubbi atroci

❏ **agony** is not translated by the Italian word *agonia*

agree [əˈɡriː] vi **1** (*be in agreement*): **to agree (with sb/sth)** essere *or* trovarsi d'accordo (con qn/qc); **to agree on/about sth** essere d'accordo su/riguardo a qc; **I quite agree** sono perfettamente d'accordo; **don't you agree?** non sei d'accordo? **2** (*come to terms*): **to agree (on sth)** mettersi d'accordo (su qc), accordarsi (su qc) **3** (*consent*): **to agree to sth** accettare qc, acconsentire a qc **4** (*be in harmony: things*) andare d'accordo, concordare; (: *persons: get on together*) andare d'accordo; (*Gram*) concordare **5** (*food*): **garlic doesn't agree with me** non riesco a digerire l'aglio, l'aglio mi rimane sullo stomaco ♦ vt **1** (*come to agreement*): **to agree (that)** essere d'accordo (sul fatto che); (*admit*) ammettere (che); **I agree that it's difficult** ammetto che è difficile; **it was agreed that ...** è stato deciso (di comune accordo) che...; **are we all agreed?** siamo tutti d'accordo?; **is that agreed?** (siamo) d'accordo?; **he'd prefer rimanere** ognuno della propria idea; **to agree a price** pattuire un prezzo **2** (*consent*): **to agree to do sth** accettare di fare qc, acconsentire a fare qc; **he agreed to go and pick her up** ha accettato di andare a prenderla

agree·able [əˈɡriːəbl] adj (*pleasing*) piacevole, gradevole;

(*willing*) disposto(-a); **to be agreeable to sth/to doing sth** essere ben disposto(-a) a qc/a fare qc; **if you are agreeable** se sei d'accordo; **are you agreeable to this?** è d'accordo con questo?

agreed [ə'griːd] ADJ (*time, place*) stabilito(-a); **at the agreed time** all'ora stabilita

agree·ment [ə'griːmənt] N (*gen*) accordo; (*consent*) consenso; **by mutual agreement** di comune accordo; **to come to an agreement** venire a un accordo, accordarsi; **in agreement** d'accordo; **to be in agreement with sb** essere *or* trovarsi d'accordo con qn

ag·ri·cul·tur·al [ˌægrɪ'kʌltʃərəl] ADJ (*gen*) agricolo(-a); (*college, studies*) agrario(-a); **agricultural expert** agronomo(-a)

ag·ri·cul·ture [ˈægrɪkʌltʃəʳ] N agricoltura; **commercial agriculture** agricoltura di mercato

aground [ə'graʊnd] ADV (*Naut*) in secca; **to run aground** arenarsi, incagliarsi

ahead [ə'hed] ADV 1 (*in space*) avanti, davanti; **she looked straight ahead** guardava dritto davanti a sé; **ahead of** davanti a; **they were (right) ahead of us** erano (proprio) davanti a noi; **to go ahead** andare avanti; **go ahead!** avanti!; (*fig*) fai pure!, prego!; **to get ahead of sb** superare qn; **go right** *or* **straight ahead!** vada diritto!; **to be ahead** (*in competition*) essere in vantaggio; **Italy is five points ahead** l'Italia è in vantaggio di cinque punti 2 (*in time: book, plan*) in anticipo; **ahead of time** in anticipo; **Italy is one hour ahead of Britain at the moment** attualmente l'Italia è un'ora avanti *or* avanti di un'ora rispetto all'Inghilterra; **he finished half an hour ahead of the others** ha finito con mezz'ora di anticipo sugli *or* rispetto agli altri, ha finito mezz'ora prima degli altri; **to look ahead** (*fig*) guardare avanti, pensare all'avvenire; **to plan ahead** pianificare; **to be ahead of one's time** precorrere i propri tempi

AI [ˌeɪˈaɪ] N ABBR 1 = **Amnesty International** 2 (*Comput*) = **artificial intelligence** 3 = **artificial insemination**

aid [eɪd] N aiuto, assistenza; **economic aid** aiuti *mpl* economici, assistenza economica; **humanitarian aid** aiuti umanitari; **with the aid of** con l'aiuto di; **in aid of** a favore di; **in aid of charity** a scopo di beneficenza; **to come to the aid of** venire in aiuto a ♦ VT (*person*) aiutare; (*progress, recovery*) contribuire a; **to aid sb to do sth** aiutare qn a fare qc; **to aid and abet sb** (*Law*) essere complice di qn

aide [eɪd] N (*person*) aiutante *m/f*; (*Mil*) aiutante *m* di campo, addetto (militare); (*Pol*) consigliere(-a), addetto(-a)

aide-de-camp [ˌeɪddə'kɒŋ] N (*Mil*) aiutante *m* di campo

AIDS [eɪdz] N ABBR (= *acquired immune deficiency syndrome*) AIDS *m, f*

ail·ing [ˈeɪlɪŋ] ADJ infermo(-a), sofferente; (*fig: economy, industry etc*) in difficoltà

ail·ment [ˈeɪlmənt] N malanno

❏ **ailment** is not translated by the Italian word *alimento*

aim [eɪm] N (*of weapon*) mira; (*fig: purpose, object*) scopo, proposito; **his aim is bad** non ha una buona mira; **to take aim** prendere la mira; **to take aim at sth/sb** mirare a qc/qn; **to have no aim in life** non avere un preciso scopo nella vita ♦ VT: **to aim (at)** (*gun*) puntare (su *or* contro); (*missile*) lanciare (contro); (*blow etc*) tirare (a); (*remark, criticism*) rivolgere (a); (*camera*) dirigere (verso); **he aimed the gun at me** mi ha puntato contro la pistola; **to aim to do sth** aspirare a fare qc; (*less formal*) avere l'intenzione di fare qc ♦ VI (*also:* **to take aim**) prendere la mira, mirare; **to aim at sth** (*also fig*) mirare a qc; **it's aimed at a young audience** è diretto ad un pubblico giovane; **to aim for the goal** (*Ftbl*) tirare in porta

aim·less [ˈeɪmlɪs] ADJ senza scopo

aim·less·ly [ˈeɪmlɪslɪ] ADV senza scopo

ain't [eɪnt] ABBR (*fam!: incorrect use*) = **am not; are not; is not; has not; have not**

air [ɛəʳ] N 1 aria; **in the open air** all'aria aperta, all'aperto; **by air** (*travel*) in aereo; (*Post*) per via *or* posta aerea; **to get some fresh air** andare a prendere una boccata d'aria (fresca); **to clear the air** (*fig*) chiarire la situazione; **there's something in the air** (*fig*) c'è qualcosa nell'aria; **our plans are up in the air** (*fig*) i nostri progetti non sono ancora ben definiti 2 (*Radio, TV*): **to be on the air** (*programme*) essere in onda;

(*station*) trasmettere; (*person*) parlare alla radio (*or* alla televisione); **we're now going off the air** la trasmissione si conclude qui 3 (*appearance*) aria, aspetto; **with a guilty air** con aria colpevole; **to give o.s. airs** darsi delle arie ♦ VT (*room, bed*) arieggiare; (*clothes*) far prendere aria a; (*idea, grievance*) esprimere pubblicamente, manifestare; (*views*) far conoscere ♦ ADJ (*current, bubble*) d'aria; (*pressure*) atmosferico(-a); (*Mil: base, attack etc*) aereo(-a)

air bag N airbag *m inv*

air base N base *f* aerea

air·borne [ˈɛəbɔːn] ADJ (*troops*) aerotrasportato(-a), aviotrasportato(-a); (*plane*) in volo; **as soon as the plane was airborne** appena l'aereo ebbe decollato; **suddenly we were airborne** in un attimo avevamo già preso quota

air cargo N carico trasportato per via aerea

air-conditioned [ˈɛəkənˌdɪʃnd] ADJ con *or* ad aria condizionata

air conditioning N aria condizionata, condizionamento d'aria

air-cooled [ˈɛəkuːld] ADJ raffreddato(-a) ad aria

air·craft [ˈɛəkrɑːft] N INV aeromobile *m*, apparecchio, velivolo; **there were two aircraft on the runway** c'erano due aerei sulla pista

aircraft carrier N portaerei *f inv*

air cushion N cuscino gonfiabile; (*Tech*) cuscino d'aria

air·field [ˈɛəfiːld] N campo d'aviazione

air force N aviazione *f* militare

air freight N (*mode of transport*) spedizione *f* merci per via aerea; (*goods*) carico spedito per via aerea ♦ ADV (*send*) per via aerea

air·gun [ˈɛəgʌn] N pistola ad aria compressa

air hostess N hostess *f inv*

airi·ly [ˈɛərɪlɪ] ADV con disinvoltura

air·ing [ˈɛərɪŋ] N: **to give an airing to** (*linen*) arieggiare, far prendere aria a; (*room*) arieggiare; (*fig: ideas etc*) ventilare

airing cupboard N armadio riscaldato per asciugare panni

air letter N aerogramma *m*

air·lift [ˈɛəlɪft] N ponte *m* aereo

air·line [ˈɛəlaɪn] N linea *or* compagnia aerea, aviolinea

air·lin·er [ˈɛəlaɪnəʳ] N aereo di linea

air·lock [ˈɛəlɒk] N (*in pipe*) bolla d'aria; (*in spacecraft etc*) camera d'equilibrio

air·mail [ˈɛəmeɪl] N posta aerea; **by airmail** per via *or* posta aerea

air mattress N materassino gonfiabile

air·plane [ˈɛəpleɪn] N (*USA*) aeroplano

air pocket N vuoto d'aria

air·port [ˈɛəpɔːt] N aeroporto ♦ ADJ (*staff*) aeroportuale; (*manager, security etc*) dell'aeroporto

air rage N comportamento aggressivo dei passeggeri di un aereo

air raid N incursione *f* aerea

air rifle N fucile *m* ad aria compressa

air·sick [ˈɛəsɪk] ADJ: **to be airsick** soffrire di mal d'aria *or* d'aereo

air·space [ˈɛəspeɪs] N spazio aereo

air·speed [ˈɛəspiːd] N velocità *f inv* di crociera (*Aer*)

air·strip [ˈɛəstrɪp] N pista d'atterraggio

air terminal N air-terminal *m inv*

air·tight [ˈɛətaɪt] ADJ (*container*) a chiusura ermetica; (*seal, cap*) ermetico(-a)

air time N (*Radio*) spazio radiofonico; (*TV*) spazio televisivo

air traffic control N controllo del traffico aereo

air traffic controller N controllore *m* del traffico aereo

air·way [ˈɛəweɪ] N 1 (*Aer*) rotta aerea 2 **the airways** NPL le vie *fpl* respiratorie

airy [ˈɛərɪ] ADJ (*comp* **-ier**, *superl* **-iest**) (*place*) arieggiato(-a); (*room*) arioso(-a); (*remark etc*) superficiale; (*manner*) spensierato(-a), noncurante

aisle [aɪl] N (*of church: lateral*) navata laterale; (*central*) navata centrale; (*of theatre, train, coach, plane*) corridoio; **an aisle seat** un posto sul corridoio; (*in supermarket*) passaggio; **it had them rolling in the aisles** li ha fatti rotolare (per terra) dalle risate

ajar [ə'dʒɑːʳ] ADV, ADJ socchiuso(-a)

AK ABBR (*USA Post* = Alaska)
aka [ˌeɪkeɪˈeɪ] ABBR (= *also known as*) alias
akin [əˈkɪn] ADJ: **akin to** (*similar to*) equivalente a, simile a; (*of same family as*) imparentato(-a) a
AL ABBR (*USA Post* = Alabama)
Ala. ABBR (*USA*: = Alabama)
A·la·ba·ma [ˌæləˈbæmə] l'Alabama
à la carte [ɑːlɑːˈkɑt] ADJ, ADV alla carta
alac·rity [əˈlækrɪtɪ] N: **with alacrity** prontamente
alarm [əˈlɑːm] N (*warning, signal*) allarme *m*; **fire alarm** allarme antincendio; **smoke alarm** rivelatore *m* di fumo; **to raise the alarm** dare l'allarme; **there's no need for any alarm** non c'è bisogno di allarmarsi ♦ VT allarmare, spaventare; **to be alarmed (at)** essere preoccupato(-a) (per) *or* allarmato(-a) (da)
alarm clock N sveglia
alarmed [əˈlɑːmd] ADJ (*person*) allarmato(-a); (*house, car etc*) dotato(-a) di allarme
alarm·ing [əˈlɑːmɪŋ] ADJ allarmante, preoccupante
alarm·ing·ly [əˈlɑːmɪŋlɪ] ADV in modo allarmante; **alarmingly close** pericolosamente vicino(-a)
alarm·ist [əˈlɑːmɪst] N allarmista *m/f*
alas [əˈlæs] EXCL (*frm*) ohimè!, ahimè!
Alas. ABBR (*USA*: = Alaska)
Alas·ka [əˈlæskə] N l'Alasca
Al·ba·nia [ælˈbeɪnɪə] N l'Albania
Al·ba·nian [ælˈbeɪnɪən] ADJ albanese ♦ N (*person*) albanese *m/f*; (*language*) albanese *m*
al·ba·tross [ˈælbətrɒs] N albatro
al·be·it [ɔːlˈbiːɪt] CONJ (*frm*) sebbene + *sub*, benché + *sub*
al·bum [ˈælbəm] N album *m inv*; (*L.P.*) 33 giri *m inv*, L.P. *m inv*; **photograph album** (*containing photos*) album di *or* delle fotografie; (*new*) album per fotografie
al·bu·men [ˈælbjʊmɪn] N albume *m*
al·che·my [ˈælkɪmɪ] N alchimia
al·co·hol [ˈælkəhɒl] N alcool *m inv*; **I never touch alcohol** non bevo (mai) alcolici
alcohol-free [ˈælkəhɒlˈfriː] ADJ analcolico(-a)
al·co·hol·ic [ˌælkəˈhɒlɪk] ADJ alcolico(-a); **alcoholic drinks** bevande alcoliche ♦ N alcolizzato(-a)
al·co·hol·ism [ˈælkəhɒlɪzəm] N alcolismo
al·cove [ˈælkəʊv] N alcova
Ald. ABBR = alderman
alderman [ˈɔːldəmən] N (*pl* -men) consigliere *m* comunale
ale [eɪl] N birra
alert [əˈlɜːt] ADJ (*acute, wide-awake*) sveglio(-a); (*watchful*) vigile; (*mind*) pronto(-a), agile, vivace; (*expression*) intelligente; **to be alert to sth** (*fact, danger*) essere consapevole di qc; **he's a very alert baby** è un bambino molto sveglio; **we must stay alert** dobbiamo stare all'erta ♦ N allarme *m*; **to be on the alert** (*person*) stare all'erta; (*troops*) essere in stato di allarme ♦ VT: **to alert sb (to sth)** avvisare qn (di qc), avvertire qn (di qc); **to alert sb to the dangers of sth** mettere qn in guardia contro qc
Aleu·tian Is·lands [əˈluːʃən ˈaɪləndz] NPL: **the Aleutian Islands** le isole *fpl* Aleutine
Al·ex·an·dria [ˌælɪɡˈzændrɪə] N Alessandria (d'Egitto)
al·fres·co [ælˈfreskəʊ] ADJ, ADV all'aperto
al·ge·bra [ˈældʒɪbrə] N algebra
Al·ge·ria [ælˈdʒɪərɪə] N Algeria
Al·ge·rian [ælˈdʒɪərɪən] ADJ, N algerino(-a)
Al·giers [ælˈdʒɪəz] N Algeri *fsg*
al·go·rithm [ˈælɡəˌrɪðəm] N (*Comput*) algoritmo
ali·as [ˈeɪlɪəs] N falso nome *m*, pseudonimo ♦ ADV alias, altrimenti detto(-a)
ali·bi [ˈælɪbaɪ] N alibi *m inv*
al·ien [ˈeɪlɪən] ADJ (*very different*): **alien to** estraneo(-a) (a), alieno(-a) (da); (*of foreign country*) straniero(-a), forestiero(-a) ♦ N (*foreigner*) straniero(-a), forestiero(-a); (*extra-terrestrial*) extraterrestre *m/f*, alieno(-a)
al·ien·ate [ˈeɪlɪəneɪt] VT alienare
al·iena·tion [ˌeɪlɪəˈneɪʃən] N alienazione *f*
alight¹ [əˈlaɪt] ADJ: **to be alight** (*building*) essere in fiamme; (*fire*) essere acceso(-a)

alight² [əˈlaɪt] VI (*from vehicle*): **to alight (from)** scendere (da); (*bird*): **to alight (on)** posarsi (su)
align [əˈlaɪn] VT allineare; **to align o.s. with** allinearsi con, schierarsi dalla parte di
align·ment [əˈlaɪnmənt] N (*Tech, Pol*) allineamento; (*Aut: also*: **wheel alignment**) assetto; **out of alignment (with)** non allineato(-a) (con); **a new alignment of political forces** un nuovo schieramento delle forze politiche
alike [əˈlaɪk] ADJ PRED simile, uguale; **to be alike** *or* **to look alike** assomigliarsi; **the two sisters look alike** le due sorelle si assomigliano; **you're all alike!** siete tutti uguali! ♦ ADV allo stesso modo; **winter and summer alike** sia d'estate che d'inverno
ali·mo·ny [ˈælɪmənɪ] N (*Law: payment*) alimenti *mpl*
alive [əˈlaɪv] ADJ (*living*) vivo(-a), in vita, vivente; (*fig: lively*) vivace, sveglio(-a); (: *active*) attivo(-a); **to stay alive** sopravvivere; **he was buried alive** è stato sepolto vivo; **it's good to be alive** essere vivi è una bella cosa; **he's the best footballer alive** è il miglior calciatore vivente *or* esistente; **to keep a tradition alive** mantener viva *or* in vita una tradizione; **to come alive** (*fig*) risvegliarsi, rianimarsi; **to be alive with** (*insects etc*) brulicare *or* pullulare di; **alive to** (*danger, honour*) conscio(-a) di
al·ka·li [ˈælkəlaɪ] N alcali *m inv*

---

all [ɔːl] ADJ tutto(-a), tutti(-e) *pl*; **all day** tutto il giorno; **all his life** tutta la sua vita; **all men** tutti gli uomini; **it's not as hard/bad as all that** non è mica così duro/cattivo; **all the books** tutti i libri; **all the country** tutto il paese; **all the time** tutto il tempo; **we can't be together all the time** non possiamo stare assieme tutto il tempo; **for all their efforts** nonostante tutti i loro sforzi; **all three** tutti(-e) e tre; **all three books** tutti e tre i libri
♦ PRON
1 tutto(-a); **he ate it all** l'ha mangiato tutto; **all is lost** tutto è perduto; **all of it** tutto(-a); **is that all?** non c'è altro?; (*in shop*) basta così?, altro?; **that's all I can remember** è tutto ciò che ricordo; **if that's all then it's not important** se è tutto lì allora non ha importanza
2 (*plural*) tutti(-e); **all of the girls** tutte le ragazze; **all of them** tutti(-e) (loro); **all of us went** ci siamo andati tutti; **we all sat down** ci sedemmo tutti quanti, noi tutti ci sedemmo
3 (*in phrases*): **above all** soprattutto, più di tutto; **after all** dopotutto; **not at all** (*in answer to question*) niente affatto, per niente; (*in response to thanks*) prego!, s'immagini!, si figuri!; **I'm not at all tired** non sono affatto *or* per niente stanco; **anything at all will do** andrà bene qualsiasi cosa; **for all I know** per quel che ne so io, per quanto ne so; **all in all** tutto sommato; **50 men in all** 50 uomini in tutto; **most of all** (*more than anybody*) più di chiunque altro, soprattutto; (*more than anything*) più di qualsiasi altra cosa, soprattutto
♦ ADV tutto; **all alone** tutto(-a) solo(-a); **all but** quasi, tutto(-) meno; **it's all dirty** è tutto sporco; **dressed all in black** vestito(-a) tutto(-a) di nero; **to be/feel all in** (*fam*) essere/sentirsi sfinito(-a) *or* distrutto(-a); **to go all out** mettercela tutta; **things aren't all that good/bad** le cose non vanno poi così bene/male; **the score is two all** il punteggio è di due a due; **all wrong** tutto sbagliato(-a)

Allah [ˈælə] N Allah *m*
al·lay [əˈleɪ] VT (*frm: fears*) dissipare
all clear N (*Mil*) cessato allarme *m inv*; (*fig*) okay *m*
al·le·ga·tion [ˌælɪˈɡeɪʃən] N accusa, asserzione *f*
al·lege [əˈledʒ] VT asserire, dichiarare; **he is alleged to have said ...** avrebbe detto che...
al·leged [əˈledʒd] ADJ presunto(-a); **the alleged crime** il presunto delitto
al·leg·ed·ly [əˈledʒɪdlɪ] ADV da quel che si dice, secondo quanto si asserisce
al·le·giance [əˈliːdʒəns] N fedeltà, lealtà; **to swear allegiance to** fare giuramento di fedeltà a
al·le·go·ry [ˈælɪɡərɪ] N allegoria
all-embracing [ˌɔːlɪmˈbreɪsɪŋ] ADJ che abbraccia tutto, universale
al·ler·gic [əˈlɜːdʒɪk] ADJ: **allergic to** allergico(-a) a
al·ler·gy [ˈælədʒɪ] N allergia

al·le·vi·ate [ə'li:vɪeɪt] VT alleviare

al·ley [ˈælɪ] N (between buildings) vicolo; (in garden, park) vialetto; (USA: Tennis) corridoio; **blind alley** vicolo cieco

alley·way [ˈælɪˌweɪ] N vicolo

al·li·ance [əˈlaɪəns] N (Pol) alleanza

allied [ˈælaɪd] ADJ alleato(-a)

al·li·ga·tor [ˈælɪgeɪtəʳ] N alligatore m

all-important [ˌɔːlɪmˈpɔːtənt] ADJ cruciale, fondamentale, importantissimo(-a)

all-in wrestling N lotta americana

al·lit·era·tion [əˌlɪtəˈreɪʃən] N allitterazione f

all-night [ˌɔːlˈnaɪt] ADJ (café, garage) aperto(-a) tutta la notte; (vigil, party) che dura (or è durato(-a) etc) tutta la notte

al·lo·cate [ˈæləʊkeɪt] VT (allot): **to allocate (to)** (duties, sum, time) assegnare (a) (in budget: money) stanziare (per); (distribute): **to allocate (among)** ripartire (fra), distribuire (fra)

al·lo·ca·tion [ˌæləʊˈkeɪʃən] N (see vb) assegnazione f, stanziamento; distribuzione f; **allocation of overheads** imputazione f delle spese generali

al·lot [əˈlɒt] VT **1** (assign: task, share, time): **to allot (to)** dare (a), assegnare (a) **2** (share among group) spartire (tra); **in the allotted time** nel tempo fissato or prestabilito

al·lot·ment [əˈlɒtmənt] N (Brit: land) piccolo lotto di terreno (dato in affitto per coltivazioni ad uso familiare); (share) spartizione f

all-out [ˌɔːlˈaʊt] ADJ (attack) con tutti i mezzi a disposizione; (effort etc) totale; **to make an all-out effort to do sth** impegnare tutte le proprie energie per fare qc

al·low [əˈlaʊ] VT **1** (permit): **to allow sb to do sth** permettere a qn di fare qc, autorizzare qn a fare qc; **smoking is not allowed** è vietato fumare, non è permesso fumare; **to be allowed to do something** avere il permesso di fare qc; **he is allowed to do it** lo può fare; **he's not allowed alcohol** gli hanno proibito l'alcol; **to allow sb in/out** etc lasciare entrare/uscire etc qn; **allow me!** mi permetta!, se mi permette!, prego! **2** (make provision for) tener conto di, calcolare; **we must allow 3 days for the journey** dobbiamo calcolare 3 giorni per il viaggio; **allow two hours for the paint to dry** lasciate asciugare la vernice per due ore; **allow 5 cm for them** lasciare 5 cm in più per il bordo **3** (grant: money, rations) concedere, accordare; (discount) riduzione f, sconto; (Law: claim, appeal) riconoscere, ammettere; (Sport: goal) convalidare; **to allow that** (frm: concede) ammettere che

  ▸ **allow for** VI + PREP tener conto di, calcolare

al·low·ance [əˈlaʊəns] N (payment) assegno; (for travelling, accommodation) indennità f inv; (ration) razione f; (Tax) detrazione f d'imposta; (discount) riduzione f, sconto; **travelling allowance** indennità di trasferta; **monthly clothing allowance** cifra mensile per il vestiario; **baggage allowance** bagaglio consentito; **family allowance** (old: child benefit) assegni mpl familiari; **to make allowance(s) for** (person) scusare; (allow for: shrinkage etc) tener conto di

al·loy [ˈælɔɪ] N lega; (fig) ombra ♦ ADJ: **alloy wheels** (Aut) cerchi mpl in lega

all right ADV (feel, work) bene; **all right!** va bene!; **everything turned out all right** tutto è andato bene; **to be all right** (well, safe) stare bene; (satisfactory) andare bene; **I'm all right** sto bene; **is that all right with you?** per te va bene?

all-round [ˈɔːlˈraʊnd] ADJ (athlete etc) completo(-a), versatile; (education) ampio(-a), completo(-a); **an all-round improvement** un miglioramento generale

all-rounder [ˈɔːlˈraʊndəʳ] N: **to be a good all-rounder** (Brit, esp Sport) essere bravo(-a) in tutto

all·spice [ˈɔːlˌspaɪs] N pepe m della Giamaica

all-time [ˈɔːlˈtaɪm] ADJ (record) senza precedenti, assoluto(-a)

al·lude [əˈluːd] VI: **to allude to** alludere a, fare allusione a

al·lur·ing [əˈljʊərɪŋ] ADJ allettante, seducente

al·lu·sion [əˈluːʒən] N accenno, allusione f; (Literature) riferimento

al·lu·vium [əˈluːvɪəm] N materiale m alluvionale

ally [n ˈælaɪ, vb əˈlaɪ] N alleato(-a) ♦ VT: **to ally o.s. with** allearsi con

al·mighty [ɔːlˈmaɪtɪ] ADJ onnipotente; (fam) enorme, colossale ♦ N: **the Almighty** l'Onnipotente

al·mond [ˈɑːmənd] N (nut) mandorla; (also: **almond tree**) mandorlo

al·most [ˈɔːlməʊst] ADV quasi; **he almost fell** per poco non è caduto

alms [ɑːmz] NPL (old) elemosina sg; **to give alms** fare l'elemosina

aloft [əˈlɒft] ADV in alto; (Naut) sull'alberatura

alone [əˈləʊn] ADJ, ADV (da) solo(-a); **all alone** tutto(-a) solo(-a); **leave me alone!** lasciami in pace!, lasciami stare!; **to let** or **leave sth alone** (object) lasciar stare qc; (business, scheme) non immischiarsi in qc; **leave my things alone!** lascia stare le mie cose!; **let alone ...** figuriamoci poi..., tanto meno...; **he can't read, let alone write** non sa leggere, figuriamoci scrivere; **you can't do it alone** non puoi farlo da solo; **she lives alone** vive da sola; **am I alone in thinking so?** sono il solo a pensarla così?; **the flight alone cost £600** il volo da solo costa 600 sterline, solo il volo costa 600 sterline

along [əˈlɒŋ] ADV: **to move along** (person, car) andare avanti; **he was hopping/limping along** veniva saltellando/zoppicando; **come along with me** vieni con me; **are you coming along?** vieni anche tu?; **move along there!** muovetevi, avanti!; (said by policeman) circolare!; **along with the others** con gli altri, insieme agli altri; **take it along** prendilo con te; **I knew all along** sapevo fin dall'inizio ♦ PREP lungo; **to walk along the street** camminare lungo la strada; **the trees along the path** gli alberi lungo il sentiero; **along here** per di qua; **somewhere along the way** (also fig) da qualche parte lungo la strada

along·side [əˈlɒŋˈsaɪd] ADV (Naut) sottobordo; **we brought our boat alongside** (of a pier/shore etc) abbiamo accostato la barca (al molo/alla riva etc) ♦ PREP (along) lungo; (beside) accanto a; **the railway runs alongside the beach** la ferrovia costeggia la spiaggia; **to come alongside the quay** accostare al molo; **to work alongside other people** lavorare assieme ad altre persone

aloof [əˈluːf] ADJ riservato(-a), distaccato(-a) ♦ ADV a distanza, in disparte; **to stand aloof (from)** tenersi a distanza (da) or in disparte (da)

aloof·ness [əˈluːfnɪs] N riserbo, distacco

aloud [əˈlaʊd] ADV ad alta voce, a voce alta

al·pha·bet [ˈælfəbet] N alfabeto

al·pha·beti·cal [ˌælfəˈbetɪkəl] ADJ alfabetico(-a); **in alphabetical order** in ordine alfabetico

al·pha·nu·mer·ic [ˌælfənjuːˈmerɪk] ADJ alfanumerico(-a)

al·pine [ˈælpaɪn] ADJ alpino(-a); (plant, pasture) alpestre; **alpine skiing** sci m alpino

Alps [ælps] NPL: **the Alps** le Alpi

al·ready [ɔːlˈredɪ] ADV già; **Liz had already gone** Liz se n'era già andata

al·right [ɔːlˈraɪt] ADJ = **all right**

Al·sa·tian [ælˈseɪʃən] N **1** (Brit: dog) pastore m tedesco, (cane m) lupo **2** (person) alsaziano(-a) ♦ ADJ alsaziano(-a)

also [ˈɔːlsəʊ] ADV **1** (too) anche, pure; **her cousin also came** è venuto anche suo cugino **2** (moreover) inoltre, anche; **also, I must explain ...** (e) inoltre devo spiegare..., devo anche spiegare...

Alta. ABBR (Canada: = **Alberta**)

al·tar [ˈɔːltəʳ] N altare m; **high altar** altar maggiore

al·ter [ˈɔːltəʳ] VT (gen) modificare, cambiare, alterare; (opinion: one's own) cambiare, mutare; (: sb else's) far cambiare or mutare; (garment, building) fare una modifica (or delle modifiche) a ♦ VI cambiare

al·tera·tion [ˌɔːltəˈreɪʃən] N (act: see vb) modifica, cambiamento; (in appearance) cambiamento, trasformazione f; **alterations** NPL (to garment, building) modifiche fpl; **timetable subject to alteration** orario soggetto a variazioni; **without any alteration** senza apportare modifiche; **to make alterations in sth** apportare delle modifiche a qc

al·ter·ca·tion [ˌɔːltəˈkeɪʃən] N (frm) alterco, litigio

al·ter·nate [adj ɪlˈtɜːnɪt, vb ˈɒltəneɪt] ADJ (alternating: layers) alternato(-a); (every other: days) alterni(-e) pl, uno(-a) e uno(-a) no; **on alternate days** ogni due giorni, a giorni alterni; **alternate angles** angoli alterni ♦ VI: **to alternate (with/between)** alternarsi (a/fra), avvicendarsi (a/fra) ♦ VT (crops) alternare, avvicendare

al·ter·nate·ly [ɒlˈtɜːnɪtlɪ] ADV alternatamente

al·ter·nat·ing cur·rent [ˈɒltəneɪtɪŋˈkʌrənt] N corrente *f* alternata

al·ter·na·tive [ɒlˈtɜːnətɪv] ADJ (*solutions*) alternativo(-a), altro(-a); (*medicine, energy*) alternativo(-a) ♦ N (*choice*) alternativa; **you have no alternative but to go** non hai altra alternativa che andare; **you have no alternative** non hai alternative; **there are several alternatives** ci sono diverse alternative *or* possibilità; **there is no alternative** non c'è altra alternativa *or* scelta

al·ter·na·tive·ly [ɒlˈtɜːnətɪvlɪ] ADV in alternativa, altrimenti; **alternatively, we could just stay at home** altrimenti potremmo semplicemente stare a casa

alternative medicine N medicina alternativa

al·ter·na·tor [ˈɒltəneɪtəʳ] N (*Elec, Aut*) alternatore *m*

al·though [ɔːlˈðəʊ] CONJ anche se, benché + *sub*, sebbene + *sub*; **although she was tired, she stayed up late** nonostante fosse stanca è rimasta alzata fino a tardi

al·ti·tude [ˈæltɪtjuːd] N altitudine *f*, altezza, quota; (*Geom*) altezza; **at these altitudes** a questa altezza; **to gain/lose altitude** (*Aer*) prendere/perdere quota

alto [ˈæltəʊ] N (*instrument*) contralto; (*male*) contraltino; (*female*) contralto

al·to·geth·er [ˌɔːltəˈgeðəʳ] ADV 1 (*in all*) in tutto, complessivamente; (*on the whole*) tutto considerato, tutto sommato, nel complesso, nell'insieme; **you owe me twenty pounds altogether** in tutto mi devi venti sterline; **altogether it was rather unpleasant** tutto sommato *or* in complesso è stato piuttosto spiacevole; **how much is that altogether?** quant'è in tutto? 2 (*entirely*) del tutto, completamente; **I'm not altogether sure** non sono del tutto *or* proprio sicuro

al·tru·ism [ˈæltrʊɪzəm] N altruismo

al·tru·is·tic [ˌæltrʊˈɪstɪk] ADJ altruistico(-a)

alu·min·ium [ˌæljʊˈmɪnɪəm], (*USA*) **alu·mi·num** [əˈluːmɪnəm] N alluminio

al·ways [ˈɔːlweɪz] ADV sempre; **as always** come sempre; **you can always go by train** puoi sempre prendere il treno

Alzheimer's [ˈæltshaɪməz] N (*also*: **Alzheimer's disease**) morbo di Alzheimer

AM [ˌeɪˈem] ABBR (= *amplitude modulation*) AM ♦ N ABBR (= *Assembly Member*) deputato gallese(-a)

am [æm] 1ST PERS SG PRESENT *of* be

a.m. [ˌeɪˈem] ADV ABBR (= *ante meridiem*) del mattino; **at four a.m.** alle quattro del mattino

AMA [ˌeɪemˈeɪ] N ABBR = **American Medical Association**

amalgam [əˈmælgəm] N amalgama *m*

amal·gam·ate [əˈmælgəmeɪt] VT (*metals, also fig*) amalgamare; (*Comm*) fondere ♦ VI (*metals, also fig*) amalgamarsi; (*Comm*) fondersi

amal·gama·tion [əˌmælgəˈmeɪʃən] N (*see vb*) amalgamazione *f*; fusione *f*

amass [əˈmæs] VT accumulare, ammassare

ama·teur [ˈæmətəʳ] N dilettante *m/f* ♦ ADJ (*player, painter*) dilettante; (*activity*) dilettantistico(-a), per dilettanti

ama·teur·ish [ˈæmətərɪʃ] ADJ (*pej*) dilettantesco(-a), da dilettanti

amaze [əˈmeɪz] VT stupire, sbalordire; **to be amazed (at)** essere sbalordito(-a) (da)

amazed ADJ sbalordito(-a), (sbalordita) **to be amazed (at)** essere sbalordito(-a) (da)

amaze·ment [əˈmeɪzmənt] N stupore *m*, meraviglia; **to my amazement ...** con mia grande sorpresa...; **he looked at me in amazement** mi guardò stupito

amaz·ing [əˈmeɪzɪŋ] ADJ sorprendente, sbalorditivo(-a); (*bargain, offer*) sensazionale; **that's amazing news!** è una notizia incredibile!

amaz·ing·ly [əˈmeɪzɪŋlɪ] ADV incredibilmente

Ama·zon [ˈæməzɒn] N 1 **the Amazon** (*river*) il Rio delle Amazzoni 2 (*Myth*) Amazzone *f* ♦ ADJ (*basin*) amazzonico(-a); **the Amazon rainforest** la foresta amazzonica

Ama·zo·nian [ˌæməˈzəʊnɪən] ADJ amazzonico(-a)

am·bas·sa·dor [æmˈbæsədəʳ] N ambasciatore(-trice)

am·ber [ˈæmbəʳ] N ambra ♦ ADJ (*colour*) ambra *inv*, ambrato(-a); (*Brit: traffic light*) giallo(-a)

am·bi·dex·trous [ˌæmbɪˈdɛkstrəs] ADJ ambidestro(-a)

am·bi·ence [ˈæmbrəns] N (*liter: atmosphere*) ambiente *m*; **the restaurant has a pleasant ambience** il ristorante ha un'atmosfera piacevole

am·bi·gu·ity [ˌæmbɪˈgjʊɪtɪ] N ambiguità *f inv*

am·bigu·ous [æmˈbɪgjʊəs] ADJ ambiguo(-a)

am·bi·tion [æmˈbɪʃən] N ambizione *f*, aspirazione *f*; **he has no ambition** non ha nessuna ambizione; **to achieve one's ambition** realizzare le proprie aspirazioni *or* ambizioni

am·bi·tious [æmˈbɪʃəs] ADJ ambizioso(-a); **to be ambitious for one's children** avere delle ambizioni per i propri figli

am·biva·lent [æmˈbɪvələnt] ADJ ambivalente

am·ble [ˈæmbl] VI (*also*: **to amble along** *or* **about**: *person*) camminare tranquillamente *or* senza fretta; **he ambled up to me** mi è venuto incontro senza fretta ♦ N (*of horse*) ambio

am·bu·lance [ˈæmbjʊləns] N ambulanza, autoambulanza ♦ ADJ: **ambulance driver** guidatore(-trice) d'ambulanza

am·bush [ˈæmbʊʃ] N (*attack*) imboscata, agguato; (*place*) agguato; **to lie in ambush** stare in agguato; **to lie in ambush for sb** tendere un'imboscata a qn ♦ VT tendere un'imboscata a qn

ame·ba [əˈmiːbə] N (*USA*) = **amoeba**

ame·lio·rate [əˈmiːlɪəreɪt] VT (*frm*) migliorare

amen [ˈɑːˈmen] EXCL così sia, amen

ame·nable [əˈmiːnəbl] ADJ: **amenable to** (*advice*) ben disposto(-a) verso; **amenable to flattery** sensibile alle lusinghe; **amenable to reason** ragionevole

amend [əˈmɛnd] VT (*law etc*) emendare; (*text*) correggere

amend·ment [əˈmɛndmənt] N (*see vb*) emendamento; correzione *f*

amen·ity [əˈmiːnɪtɪ] N (*facility*) struttura ricreativa o commerciale; **a house with all amenities** una casa con tutte le comodità

Ameri·ca [əˈmerɪkə] N America

Ameri·can [əˈmerɪkən] ADJ americano(-a) ♦ N (*person*) americano(-a); (*language: also*: **American English**) americano

American football N (*Brit*) football *m* americano

Ameri·can·ize [əˈmerɪkənaɪz] VT americanizzare

am·ethyst [ˈæmɪθɪst] N ametista

ami·able [ˈeɪmɪəbl] ADJ affabile, amabile

ami·cable [ˈæmɪkəbl] ADJ amichevole

ami·cably [ˈæmɪkəblɪ] ADV amichevolmente; **to part amicably** lasciarsi senza rancori; (*divorcing couple*) separarsi consensualmente

amid [əˈmɪd], **amidst** [əˈmɪdst] PREP (*frm, liter*) in mezzo a, fra, tra

amiss [əˈmɪs] ADJ, ADV: **there's something amiss** c'è qualcosa che non va; **don't take it amiss** non avertene a male

ammo [ˈæməʊ] N ABBR (*fam*) = **ammunition**: munizioni *fpl*

am·mo·nia [əˈməʊnɪə] N ammoniaca

am·mu·ni·tion [ˌæmjʊˈnɪʃən] N munizioni *fpl*; (*fig*) arma

ammunition dump N deposito di munizioni

am·ne·sia [æmˈniːzɪə] N amnesia

am·nes·ty [ˈæmnɪstɪ] N amnistia; **to grant an amnesty to** concedere l'amnistia a, amnistiare

Amnesty International N Amnesty International *f*

amoe·ba, ame·ba (*USA*) [əˈmiːbə] N ameba

amok [əˈmɒk] ADV = **amuck**

among [əˈmʌŋ], **amongst** [əˈmʌŋst] PREP tra, fra, in mezzo a; **among friends** tra amici; **he is among those who ...** fa parte di quelli che..., è uno di quelli che...; **share it among yourselves** dividetevelo tra (di) voi; **among other things** tra l'altro, tra le altre cose

amor·al [eɪˈmɒrəl] ADJ amorale

amo·rous [ˈæmərəs] ADJ amoroso(-a); (*stronger*) appassionato(-a)

amor·phous [əˈmɔːfəs] ADJ amorfo(-a)

amortization [əˌmɔːtaɪˈzeɪʃən] N (*Comm*) ammortamento

amount [əˈmaʊnt] N (*sum of money*) somma, cifra; (*of invoice, bill etc*) importo; (*quantity*) quantità *f inv*; **in small amounts** poco per volta; **the total amount** (*of money*) l'importo totale; (*of things*) la quantità totale; **a huge amount of rice** una grossa quantità di riso; **a large amount of money** una grossa somma di denaro; **he has any amount of time/money** ha tutto il tempo/tutti i soldi che vuole

▸ **amount to** VI + PREP (*total*) ammontare a; (*fig: be equivalent to*) equivalere a, non essere altro che; **he'll never amount to much** non conterà mai granché

amp [æmp], **am·père** [ˈæmpɛəʳ] N ampere *m inv*; **a 13 amp(ère) plug** una spina con fusibile da 13 ampere

am·per·sand [ˈæmpəˌsænd] N "e" *f* commerciale

am·pheta·mine [æmˈfetəmiːn] N anfetamina

am·phib·ian [æmˈfibɪən] N (*Bio: vehicle*) anfibio *m*

am·phibi·ous [æmˈfibɪəs] ADJ (*Bio: vehicle*) anfibio(-a)

am·phi·thea·tre, am·phi·thea·ter (*USA*) [ˈæmfɪˌθɪətəʳ] N anfiteatro

am·ple [ˈæmpl] ADJ (*comp* -er, *superl* -est) **1** (*large: trunk of car*) ampio(-a), spazioso(-a); (: *garment*) ampio(-a) **2** (*more than enough: money*) in abbondanza; (: *space, means, resources*) abbondante, ampio(-a); **we have ample reason to believe that ...** abbiamo parecchie ragioni per credere che...; **we have ample time to finish it** abbiamo tutto il tempo (necessario) per finirlo; **that should be ample** (*time, money etc*) dovrebbe essere più che sufficiente

am·pli·fi·er [ˈæmplɪfaɪəʳ] N amplificatore *m*

am·pli·fy [ˈæmplɪfaɪ] VT (*sound*) amplificare; (*statement etc*) ampliare

am·ply [ˈæmplɪ] ADV ampiamente

am·poule, am·pule (*USA*) [ˈæmpuːl] N (*Med*) fiala

am·pu·tate [ˈæmpjʊteɪt] VT amputare

am·pu·tee [æmpjʊˈtiː] N mutilato(-a) (*chi ha subito un'amputazione*)

Am·ster·dam [ˌæmstəˈdæm] N Amsterdam *f*

amt = amount

Amtrak [ˈæmtræk] (*USA*) N società ferroviaria americana

amuck [əˈmʌk], **amok** [əˈmɒk] ADV: **to run amuck** (*madman*) essere preso(-a) da follia omicida; (*children, fans*) scatenarsi; (*animals*) correre all'impazzata

amuse [əˈmjuːz] VT (*cause mirth*) divertire, far ridere; (*entertain*) (far) divertire; **to be amused at** essere divertito(-a) da; **he was most amused by the story** la storia lo diverti molto; **he was not amused** non l'ha trovato divertente; **to amuse o.s. with sth/by doing sth** divertirsi con qc/a fare qc; **run along and amuse yourselves** andate a divertirvi

amuse·ment [əˈmjuːzmənt] N **1** divertimento; **much to my amusement** con mio grande spasso; **a look of amusement** un'aria divertita **2** (*entertainment*) divertimento, svago; **they do it for amusement only** lo fanno solo per divertirsi *or* per svago

amusement arcade N sala *f* giochi, *inv*

amusement park N luna park *m inv*

amus·ing [əˈmjuːzɪŋ] ADJ divertente

an [æn, ən, n] INDEF ART *see* **a**

anach·ro·nism [əˈnækrənɪzəm] N anacronismo

anaemia, anemia (*USA*) [əˈniːmɪə] N anemia

anaemic, anemic (*USA*) [əˈniːmɪk] ADJ anemico(-a)

an·aes·thet·ic, an·es·thet·ic (*USA*) [ˌænɪsˈθetɪk] N anestetico; **under (the) anaesthetic** sotto anestesia; **local/general anaesthetic** anestesia locale/totale ♦ ADJ anestetico(-a)

anaes·the·tist, anes·the·tist (*USA*) [æˈniːsθɪtɪst] N anestetista *m/f*

ana·gram [ˈænəgræm] N anagramma *m*

anal [ˈeɪnəl] ADJ anale

an·alge·sic [ˌænælˈdʒiːzɪk] ADJ analgesico(-a) ♦ N analgesico

analo·gous [əˈnæləgəs] ADJ: **analogous (to, with)** analogo (a), affine (a)

ana·logue, ana·log (*USA*) [ˈænəlɒg] ADJ (*watch*) analogico(-a) ♦ N cosa analoga

anal·ogy [əˈnælədʒɪ] N analogia; **to draw an analogy between** fare un'analogia tra

ana·lyse [ˈænəlaɪz] VT (*Brit*) analizzare, fare l'analisi di

analy·sis [əˈnæləsɪs] N (*pl* analyses [əˈnæləsiːz]) analisi *f inv*; (*Psych*) (psic)analisi *f inv*; **in the last analysis** in ultima analisi

ana·lyst [ˈænəlɪst] N (*political, financial*) analista *m/f*; (*USA: also:* **psychoanalyst**) (psic)analista *m/f*

ana·lyze [ˈænəlaɪz] VT (*USA*) = analyse

an·ar·chic [æˈnɑːkɪk] ADJ anarchico(-a)

an·ar·chist [ˈænəkɪst] N, ADJ anarchico(-a); **to be an anarchist** essere anarchico(-a)

an·ar·chy [ˈænəkɪ] N anarchia

anath·ema [əˈnæθɪmə] N (*Rel, also fig*) anatema *m*; **it is anathema to him** non ne vuol neanche sentir parlare

ana·tomi·cal [ˌænəˈtɒmɪkəl] ADJ anatomico(-a)

anato·my [əˈnætəmɪ] N anatomia

an·ces·tor [ˈænsɪstəʳ] N antenato(-a), avo(-a)

an·ces·tral [ænˈsestrəl] ADJ (*of family*) avito(-a); (*of former times*) ancestrale, atavico(-a); **ancestral home** casa avita

an·ces·try [ˈænsɪstrɪ] N (*origin*) lignaggio, ascendenza, stirpe *f*; (*forebears*) antenati *mpl*

an·chor [ˈæŋkəʳ] N ancora; (*fig*) ancora di salvezza; (*of team, organization*) perno, pilastro; **to be (lying) at anchor** essere alla fonda; **to drop anchor** gettare l'ancora; **to weigh anchor** salpare *or* levare l'ancora ♦ VT (*also fig*) ancorare ♦ VI ancorarsi

an·chor·age [ˈæŋkərɪdʒ] N ancoraggio

anchor·man [ˈæŋkəmən] N (*pl* -men) (*Radio, TV*) anchor man *m inv*

anchor woman N (*TV, Radio*) anchorwoman *f inv*

an·cho·vy [ˈæntʃəvɪ] N acciuga, alice *f*

an·cient [ˈeɪnʃənt] ADJ (*old: classical*) antico(-a); (*fam: person*) decrepito(-a); (: *object*) vecchio(-a) come il cucco, vecchissimo(-a); **ancient monument** monumento storico; **ancient Rome** l'antica Roma; **an ancient record player** un vecchissimo giradischi

❏ **ancient** is not translated by the Italian word *anziano*

an·cil·lary [ænˈsɪlərɪ] ADJ ausiliario(-a)

and [ænd, ənd, nd, ən] CONJ e, ed (*often used before vowel*); **you and me** tu ed io; **one and a half** uno e mezzo; **three hundred and ten** trecentodieci; **faster and faster** sempre più veloce; **better and better** sempre meglio; **more and more** sempre di più; **without shoes and socks** senza scarpe né calze; **there are lawyers and lawyers** ci sono avvocati e avvocati!; **he talked and talked** (e) parlava (e) parlava; **try and do it** prova a farlo; **wait and see** aspetta e vedrai; **come and sit here** vieni a sedere qui; **and so on** e così via

An·des [ˈændiz] NPL: **the Andes** le Ande

An·dor·ra [ænˈdɔːrə] N Andorra

an·ec·dote [ˈænɪkdəʊt] N aneddoto

anemia *etc* [əˈniːmɪə] = **anaemia**

anemo·ne [əˈnemənɪ] N (*Bot*) anemone *m*; (*also:* **sea anemone**) anemone *m* di mare, attinia

an·es·thet·ic [ˌænɪsˈθetɪk] = **anaesthetic**

anew [əˈnjuː] ADV (*liter*) di nuovo; **to begin anew** ricominciare

an·gel [ˈeɪndʒəl] N angelo; **be an angel and fetch my gloves** se mi vai a prendere i guanti sei proprio un angelo

angel dust N *sedativo usato a scopo allucinogeno*

an·ger [ˈæŋgəʳ] N rabbia, collera; **red with anger** rosso(-a) per *or* dalla rabbia; **in anger** nell'impeto della collera ♦ VT far arrabbiare; **he is easily angered** si arrabbia facilmente

an·gi·na [ænˈdʒaɪnə] N angina

an·gle [ˈæŋgl] N **1** (*Geom*) angolo; **right angle** angolo retto; **at right angles to** ad angolo retto con, perpendicolare a; **at an angle of 80°** a un angolo di 80°; **at an angle** di sbieco; **to cut sth at an angle** tagliare qc di traverso **2** (*fig: point of view*) punto di vista; **from their angle** dal loro punto di vista; **to look at sth from a different angle** (*fig*) considerare qc da un altro punto di vista *or* sotto un altro aspetto

an·gle [ˈæŋgl] VI (*fish*) pescare (con l'amo); **to angle for** (*fig*) cercare di avere

an·gler [ˈæŋgləʳ] N pescatore *m* con la lenza

An·gli·can [ˈæŋglɪkən] ADJ, N anglicano(-a)

an·gli·cize [ˈæŋglɪsaɪz] VT anglicizzare

an·gling [ˈæŋglɪŋ] N pesca con la lenza

Anglo- [ˈæŋgləʊ] PREF anglo-

Anglo-Saxon [ˈæŋgləʊˈsæksən] ADJ, N anglosassone *m/f*

An·go·la [æŋˈgəʊlə] N Angola

An·go·lan [æŋˈgəʊlən] ADJ, N angolano(-a)

an·gri·ly [ˈæŋgrɪlɪ] ADV con rabbia

an·gry [ˈæŋgrɪ] ADJ (comp -ier, superl -iest) (gen) arrabbiato(-a), furioso(-a); (annoyed) irritato(-a); (wound) infiammato(-a); (sky) minaccioso(-a); **to be angry with sb/about** or **at sth** essere arrabbiato(-a) or in collera con qn/per qc; **to get angry** arrabbiarsi; **to make sb angry** far arrabbiare qn; **you won't be angry, will you?** non ti arrabbi, vero?; **he was angry at being treated so badly** era arrabbiato perché lo avevano trattato così male

an·guish [ˈæŋgwɪʃ] N angoscia; **to be in anguish** essere angosciato(-a)

an·guished [ˈæŋgwɪʃt] ADJ (expression, look) angosciato(-a); (cry) angoscioso(-a)

an·gu·lar [ˈæŋgjʊlə^r] ADJ angoloso(-a), spigoloso(-a); (measurement etc) angolare

ani·mal [ˈænɪməl] N animale m; (pej: person) bestia, bruto ♦ ADJ animale

animal rights NPL diritti mpl degli animali ♦ ADJ (organization, activist) animalista; **animal rights campaign** campagna animalista; **animal rights campaigner** or **activist** animalista m/f

ani·mate [adj ˈænɪmɪt, vb ˈænɪmeɪt] ADJ (animal, plants) vivente; (capable of movement) animato(-a) ♦ VT animare

ani·mat·ed [ˈænɪmeɪtɪd] ADJ animato(-a); **to become animated** animarsi

ani·ma·tion [ænɪˈmeɪʃən] N animazione f

ani·mos·ity [ænɪˈmɒsɪtɪ] N animosità

ani·seed [ˈænɪsiːd] N semi mpl di anice

An·ka·ra [ˈæŋkərə] N Ankara

an·kle [ˈæŋkl] N caviglia; **I've twisted my ankle** mi sono slogato la caviglia

ankle socks NPL calzini mpl

an·nex [vb əˈnɛks, n ˈænɛks] VT (territory): **to annex (to)** annettere (a) ♦ N (Brit: also: **annexe**) (edificio) annesso

an·nexa·tion [ænɛkˈseɪʃən] N annessione f

an·ni·hi·late [əˈnaɪəleɪt] VT annientare, annichilire; (argument) demolire

an·ni·hi·la·tion [əˌnaɪəˈleɪʃən] N annientamento

an·ni·ver·sa·ry [ænɪˈvɜːsərɪ] N anniversario; **it's their wedding anniversary** è il loro anniversario di matrimonio ♦ ADJ: **anniversary celebration** celebrazione f dell'anniversario; **anniversary dinner** pranzo per l'anniversario, cena commemorativa

an·no·tate [ˈænəʊteɪt] VT annotare

an·nounce [əˈnaʊns] VT (gen) annunciare; **to announce the marriage/death of sb** annunciare le nozze/la morte di qn; **he announced that he wasn't going** ha dichiarato che non (ci) sarebbe andato

an·nounce·ment [əˈnaʊnsmənt] N (declaration) comunicazione f, annuncio; (official: through media) comunicato; (private: in newspaper) annuncio; (letter, card) partecipazione f; **I'd like to make an announcement** ho una comunicazione da fare; **there's just been an announcement about our flight** c'è stato un annuncio riguardo al nostro volo un attimo fa

an·nounc·er [əˈnaʊnsə^r] N (Radio, TV: linking programmes) annunciatore(-trice); (: introducing people) presentatore(-trice)

an·noy [əˈnɔɪ] VT dare fastidio a, infastidire, dare noia a; **to be annoyed about sth** essere seccato(-a) per qc, essere contrariato(-a) or irritato(-a) da qc; **to be annoyed (at sth/with sb)** essere seccato(-a) or irritato(-a) (per qc/con qn); **he's just trying to annoy you** sta solo cercando di stuzzicarti; **to get annoyed** arrabbiarsi; **don't get so annoyed!** non prendertela tanto!

❏ **annoy** is not translated by the Italian word annoiare

an·noy·ance [əˈnɔɪəns] N (state) fastidio, irritazione f; (cause of annoyance) seccatura, noia; **to her annoyance** con suo gran dispetto

an·noy·ing [əˈnɔɪɪŋ] ADJ (person, habit, noise) irritante, seccante; **it's annoying to have to wait** è (una cosa) seccante dover aspettare

❏ **annoying** is not translated by the Italian word annoiato

an·nual [ˈænjʊəl] ADJ (income) annuo(-a); (event, plant) annuale ♦ N (book) pubblicazione f annuale, annuario; (children's comic book) almanacco; (Bot) pianta annuale

an·nual·ly [ˈænjʊəlɪ] ADV annualmente, ogni anno

annual report N relazione f annuale

an·nu·ity [əˈnjuːɪtɪ] N annualità f inv, rendita annuale; (also: **life annuity**) vitalizio; **pension annuity** (policy) ≈ polizza di pensione integrativa

an·nul [əˈnʌl] VT annullare; (law) rescindere

an·nul·ment [əˈnʌlmənt] N annullamento; (of law) rescissione f

an·num [ˈænəm] N see **per annum**

An·nun·cia·tion [əˌnʌnsɪˈeɪʃən] N: **the Annunciation** l'Annunciazione f

an·ode [ˈænəʊd] N anodo

anoint [əˈnɔɪnt] VT (Rel) ungere; **to anoint sb king** consacrare qn re

anoma·lous [əˈnɒmələs] ADJ anomalo(-a)

anoma·ly [əˈnɒmlɪ] N anomalia

anon. [əˈnɒn] ADJ ABBR = **anonymous**

ano·nym·ity [ænəˈnɪmɪtɪ] N anonimato

anony·mous [əˈnɒnɪməs] ADJ anonimo(-a); **to remain anonymous** mantenere l'anonimato

ano·rak [ˈænəræk] N (esp Brit) giacca a vento

ano·rexia [ænəˈrɛksɪə], **ano·rexia ner·vo·sa** [ænəˈrɛksɪə nɜːˈvəʊsə] N anoressia

ano·rex·ic [ænəˈrɛksɪk] ADJ, N anoressico(-a)

an·oth·er [əˈnʌðə^r] ADJ (additional) un altro (un'altra), ancora un(a); (different) un altro (un'altra); (second) un altro (un'altra), un(a) secondo(-a); **another book** (one more) un altro libro, ancora un libro; **I've got another T-shirt in my bag** ho un'altra maglietta nella borsa; **another drink?** bevi ancora qualcosa?; **in another 5 years** fra altri 5 anni; **without another word** senza aggiungere una sola or nemmeno una parola; **that's quite another matter** è tutt'un'altra cosa; **he's another Shakespeare** è un nuovo or altro Shakespeare ♦ PRON un altro (un'altra), ancora uno(-a); **from one town to another** da una città all'altra; **they love one another** si vogliono bene; see also **one**

an·swer [ˈɑːnsə^r] N 1 (reply) risposta; **in answer to your question** in risposta or per rispondere alla tua domanda; **to know all the answers** (fig) saper tutto, saperla lunga; **we need an answer by Tuesday** abbiamo bisogno di una risposta entro martedì 2 (solution) soluzione f; (Math, etc) soluzione, risposta; **the answer to the problem** la soluzione del problema; **there is no easy answer** non è un problema facile da risolvere ♦ VT 1 (reply to) rispondere a; **our prayers have been answered** le nostre preghiere sono state esaudite; **to answer the door** andare ad aprire (la porta); **to answer the phone** rispondere (al telefono) 2 (fulfil: needs) rispondere a, soddisfare; (: expectations, description) corrispondere a, rispondere a; (: purpose) servire a, rispondere a; (: problem) risolvere; (: prayer) esaudire ♦ VI rispondere

▸ **answer back** VI + ADV (fam): **to answer (sb) back** rispondere (a qn) (con impertinenza)

▸ **answer for** VI + PREP (action, crime) rispondere di; (sb's safety) essere responsabile di; (truth of sth) garantire; **he's got a lot to answer for** ci sono molte cose di cui deve render conto

▸ **answer to** VI + PREP (description) corrispondere a; (name) rispondere a

an·swer·able [ˈɑːnsərəbl] ADJ 1 (responsible) responsabile; **to be answerable (to sb for sth)** dover rispondere or render conto (a qn di qc); **I am answerable to no-one** non devo rispondere a nessuno 2 (question) (a) cui si può rispondere

an·swer·ing ma·chine [ˈɑːnsərɪŋˈʃiːn] N segreteria telefonica

ant [ænt] N formica

an·tago·nism [ænˈtægənɪzəm] N antagonismo

an·tago·nist [ænˈtægənɪst] N antagonista m/f

an·tago·nis·tic [ænˌtægəˈnɪstɪk] ADJ antagonistico(-a)

an·tago·nize [ænˈtægənaɪz] VT provocare l'ostilità di, inimicarsi; **I don't want to antagonize her** non voglio inimicarmela

Ant·arc·tic [æntˈɑːktɪk] ADJ antartico(-a) ♦ N: **the Antarctic** l'Antartico

Ant·arc·ti·ca [ænt'ɑːktɪkə] N Antartide f
Antarctic Circle N: **the Antarctic Circle** il Circolo polare antartico
Antarctic Ocean N: **the Antarctic Ocean** l'Oceano antartico
ante ['æntɪ] N (fam): **to up the ante** (in game, also fig) alzare la posta
ante– ['æntɪ] PREF anti-, ante-, pre-
ant·eater ['ænt,iːtəʳ] N formichiere m
ante·ced·ent [ænti'siːdənt] N antecedente m, precedente m; **antecedents** NPL (past history) antecedenti, precedenti; (ancestors) antenati mpl
ante·cham·ber ['ænti,tʃeɪmbəʳ] N anticamera
ante·lope ['æntɪləʊp] N antilope f
ante·na·tal ['ænti'neɪtl] ADJ prenatale
antenatal clinic N assistenza medica preparto
an·ten·na [æn'tenə] N (pl **antennae** [æn'teniː]) (Radio, TV, Zool) antenna
an·them ['ænθəm] N inno; **national anthem** inno nazionale
ant hill N formicaio
an·thol·ogy [æn'θɒlədʒɪ] N antologia
an·thrax ['ænθræks] N (Med) antrace m
an·thro·polo·gist [ænθrə'pɒlədʒɪst] N antropologo(-a)
an·thro·pol·ogy [,ænθrə'pɒlədʒɪ] N antropologia
anti– ['æntɪ] PREF anti-
anti·aircraft [ænti'ɛəkrɑːft] ADJ (gun) contraereo(-a), anti-aereo(-a)
anti·bal·lis·tic [ænti'bə'lɪstɪk] ADJ antibalistico(-a)
anti·bi·ot·ic ['æntɪbaɪ'ɒtɪk] N antibiotico ♦ ADJ antibiotico(-a)
anti·body ['ænti,bɒdɪ] N anticorpo
an·tici·pate [æn'tɪsɪpeɪt] VT 1 (expect: trouble) prevedere, aspettarsi; (: pleasure) pregustare, assaporare in anticipo; **this is worse than I anticipated** è peggio di quel che immaginavo or pensavo; **to anticipate that ...** prevedere che...; **I anticipate seeing him tomorrow** presumo or mi immagino che lo vedrò domani; **as anticipated** come previsto 2 (forestall: person) prevenire, precedere; (foresee: event) prevedere; (: question, objection, wishes) prevenire
an·tici·pa·tion [æn,tɪsɪ'peɪʃən] N: **in anticipation (of)** in previsione or attesa (di); **we waited in great anticipation** (excitement) abbiamo aspettato con grande impazienza; **in anticipation of an enjoyable week** pregustando una bella settimana; **thanking you in anticipation** vi ringrazio in anticipo
anti·cli·max ['ænti'klaɪmæks] N delusione f; **the game came as an anticlimax** la partita si rivelò una delusione
anti·clock·wise ['ænti'klɒkwaɪz] ADV, ADJ in senso antiorario
an·tics ['æntɪks] NPL (of clown etc) lazzi mpl, buffonerie fpl; (of child, animal etc) buffe acrobazie fpl; (pej) scherzetti mpl
anti·cy·clone ['ænti'saɪkləʊn] N anticiclone m
anti·dote ['æntɪdəʊt] N antidoto
anti·freeze ['ænti'friːz] N antigelo inv, anticongelante m
anti·globalization [,æntɪgləʊbəlaɪ'zeɪʃən] ADJ antiglobalizzazione inv
anti·his·ta·mine ['ænti'hɪstəmɪn] N antistaminico
An·til·les [æn'tɪliːz] NPL: **the Antilles** le Antille
an·tipa·thy [æn'tɪpəθɪ] N antipatia
anti·per·spi·rant [ænti'pɜːspɪrənt] N deodorante m (ad azione) antitraspirante
an·tipo·dean [æn,tɪpə'diːən] ADJ degli antipodi
An·tipo·des [æn'tɪpədiːz] NPL: **the Antipodes** gli antipodi
anti·quar·ian [,ænti'kwɛərɪən] ADJ: **antiquarian bookshop** libreria antiquaria ♦ N antiquario(-a)
anti·quat·ed ['æntɪkweɪtɪd] ADJ (pej) antiquato(-a), sorpassato(-a)
an·tique [æn'tiːk] ADJ (furniture etc) antico(-a), d'epoca ♦ N oggetto antico, pezzo d'antiquariato; **antiques** NPL antichità f inv; **he deals in antiques** commercia in antiquariato; **I bought an antique** ho comprato un pezzo d'antiquariato
antique dealer N antiquario(-a)
antique shop N bottega or negozio di antiquario, negozio d'antichità

an·tiq·uity [æn'tɪkwɪtɪ] N antichità; **of great antiquity** molto antico(-a)
anti-Semitic ['æntɪsɪ'mɪtɪk] ADJ antisemitico(-a), antisemita
anti-Semitism ['æntɪ'semɪtɪzəm] N antisemitismo
anti·sep·tic [æntɪ'septɪk] ADJ antisettico(-a) ♦ N antisettico
anti·so·cial ['æntɪ'səʊʃəl] ADJ (behaviour, tendency: against society) antisociale; (unsociable) scorbutico(-a), asociale
anti·tank [,ænti'tæŋk] ADJ anticarro inv
an·tith·esis [æn'tɪθɪsɪs] N (pl **antitheses** [æn'tɪθɪsiːz]) antitesi f inv; (contrast) carattere m antitetico
anti·trust [ænti'trʌst] ADJ (Comm): **anti-trust law/legislation** legge f /legislazione, f antitrust, inv
antiviral [ænti'vaɪrəl] ADJ (Med) antivirale
antivirus [ænti'vaɪərəs] ADJ (Comput) antivirus pl inv; **antivirus program** antivirus m inv
ant·ler ['æntləʳ] N palco; **antlers** NPL corna fpl
Ant·werp ['æntwɜːp] N Anversa
anus ['eɪnəs] N ano
an·vil ['ænvɪl] N incudine f
anxi·ety [æŋ'zaɪətɪ] N 1 ansia, ansietà f inv; **I have no anxieties about them** non sono in ansia per loro; **it is a great anxiety to me** è una grossa preoccupazione per me 2 (eagerness): **anxiety (to do sth)** smania (di fare qc)
anx·ious ['æŋkʃəs] ADJ 1 (worried) preoccupato(-a), ansioso(-a), in ansia, inquieto(-a); **I'm very anxious about you** sono molto preoccupato or in pensiero per te; **with an anxious glance** con uno sguardo pieno d'ansia 2 (causing worry: moment) angoscioso(-a) 3 (eager): **anxious for sth/to do sth** impaziente di qc/di fare qc; **I am anxious that she should do it** ci tengo moltissimo che lo faccia; **he is anxious for success** ha un grande desiderio di successo; **I'm not very anxious to go** ho poca voglia di andarci
anx·ious·ly ['æŋkʃəslɪ] ADV ansiosamente, con ansia

KEYWORD

any ['enɪ] ADJ
1 (in questions etc: some) del (dell', dello) m, della (dell') f, dei (degli) mpl, delle fpl, qualche; **is there any meat?** c'è (della) carne?; **have you any money?** hai (dei) soldi?, hai qualche soldo?; **are there any others?** ce ne sono (degli) altri?; **if there are any tickets left** se ci sono ancora (dei) biglietti, se c'è ancora qualche biglietto
2 (with negative) alcuno(-a), nessuno(-a); **I haven't any bread** non ho pane, sono senza pane; **I don't see any cows** non vedo alcuna or nessuna mucca, non vedo mucche; **I haven't any money** non ho soldi, sono senza soldi; **without any difficulty** senza (nessuna or alcuna) difficoltà; **I haven't any work** non ho lavoro, sono senza lavoro
3 (no matter which) (uno(-a)) qualsiasi, (uno(-a)) qualunque; (each and every) ogni inv, tutto(-a); **in any case** in ogni caso; **any excuse will do** (una) qualunque or qualsiasi scusa andrà bene, una scusa qualunque or qualsiasi andrà bene; **any farmer will tell you** qualunque or qualsiasi or ogni agricoltore te lo dirà; **wear any hat (you like)** mettiti un cappello qualsiasi or qualunque; **any time you like** quando vuoi; **at any moment** da un momento all'altro; **at any rate** ogni modo; **come (at) any time** vieni a qualsiasi ora
♦ PRON
1 (in negative and interrogative sentences): **are there any?** ce ne sono?; **are any of them coming?** viene qualcuno di loro?; **there aren't any left** non ce ne sono più; (emphatic) non ne è rimasto nemmeno uno; **can any of you sing?** c'è qualcuno che sa cantare?; **have you got any?** ne hai?; **I haven't got any (of them)** non ne ho
2 (whichever one) uno(-a) qualsiasi; (anybody) chiunque; **few, if any** pochi, sempre che ce ne siano; **take any of those books (you like)** prendi qualsiasi libro
♦ ADV (in negative sentences) per niente; (in interrogative sentences) un po'; **are you feeling any better?** ti senti un po' meglio?; **don't wait any longer** non aspettare più; **I can't hear him any more** non lo sento più; **do you want any more tea?** vuoi ancora un po' di tè?, vuoi ancora del tè?
any·body ['enɪbɒdɪ] PRON 1 (in interrogative sentences) qualcuno, nessuno; **has anybody got a pen?** qualcuno ha una penna?; **did you see anybody?** hai visto qualcuno or nessuno?; **is anybody in or home?** c'è nessuno (in casa)? 2 (in

negative sentences) nessuno; **I can't** *or* **don't see anybody** non vedo nessuno; **without anybody seeing him** senza che nessuno lo vedesse, senza esser visto da nessuno 3 (*no matter who*) chiunque, qualsiasi persona; **anybody will tell you the same** chiunque te lo dirà la stessa cosa; **anybody else would have laughed** chiunque altro avrebbe riso

any·how [ˈɛnɪˌhaʊ] ADV 1 (*at any rate*) ad *or* in ogni modo, comunque; **I'm going anyway** comunque; **he doesn't want to go out and anyhow he's not allowed** non vuole uscire e comunque non ha il permesso di farlo; **what business is it of yours, anyhow?** e tu di che t'impicci? 2 (*haphazard*) come capita, in qualsiasi modo; **do it anyhow you like** fallo come ti pare

any·one [ˈɛnɪˌwʌn] PRON = **anybody**

any·place [ˈɛnɪˌpleɪs] PRON (*USA fam*) = **anywhere**

any·thing [ˈɛnɪˌθɪŋ] PRON 1 (*in interrogative sentences*) niente, qualcosa; **do you need anything?** hai bisogno di niente?; **are you doing anything tonight?** fai qualcosa stasera?; **anything else?** (*in shop*) basta (così)?, nient'altro?, altro?; **is there anything else you want to tell me?** hai qualcos'altro *or* nient'altro da dirmi?; **can't anything be done?** (non) si può fare qualcosa *or* niente? 2 (*in negative sentences*) non... niente, non... nulla; **it wasn't anything serious** non era niente di serio; **I saw hardly anything** non ho visto quasi niente; **the bridge is anything but safe** il ponte non è affatto sicuro; **it isn't anything like as cold as it was** non è più così freddo come prima 3 (*no matter what*) qualsiasi cosa, qualunque cosa; **anything could happen** potrebbe succedere qualunque cosa; **you can say anything you like** puoi dire quello che vuoi; **anything but that** tutto tranne questo; **they'll eat anything** mangiano qualsiasi cosa *or* di tutto; **it can cost anything between £15 and £20** può costare qualcosa come 15 o 20 sterline; **if anything, I have more to do now** se mai *or* piuttosto adesso ho più da fare

any·time [ˈɛnɪˌtaɪm] ADV (*happen*) in qualunque momento; (*come*) a qualsiasi ora

any·way [ˈɛnɪˌweɪ] ADV 1 (*besides*) in ogni caso; **I forgot to buy cough sweets — they don't do much good anyway** ho dimenticato di comprare le caramelle per la tosse — tanto non servono un granché 2 (*just the same*) comunque; **thanks, anyway** grazie, comunque 3 (*at least, at any rate*) almeno; **everything is ok, as far as I know anyway** va tutto bene, per quel che ne so io 4 (*in narrative, conversation: well, then*) bene; **anyway, I've got to go be', devo andare; **it's a long story — anyway the upshot was that ...** è una lunga storia — a farla breve il risultato fu che...

any·where [ˈɛnɪˌwɛə] ADV 1 (*in interrogative sentences*) da qualche parte, in qualche posto; **can you see him anywhere?** lo vedi da qualche parte?; **anywhere else?** da qualche *or* nessun'altra parte?, in qualche *or* nessun altro posto? 2 (*in negative sentences*) da nessuna parte, in nessun posto; **I can't see him anywhere** non lo vedo da nessuna parte; **they never go anywhere else** non vanno mai da nessun'altra parte 3 (*no matter where*) da qualsiasi *or* qualunque parte, in qualunque *or* qualsiasi posto, dovunque; **anywhere in the world** dovunque nel mondo; **put the books down anywhere** metti i libri dove ti capita

apart [əˈpɑːt] ADV 1 (*separated*) a distanza, separatamente; **we live 3 miles apart** abitiamo a 3 miglia di distanza (l'uno dall'altro); **their birthdays are two days apart** i loro compleanni sono a distanza di due giorni l'uno dall'altro; **nothing will keep them apart** niente li terrà lontani l'uno dall'altro(-a); **she stood apart from the others** se ne stava *or* rimase in disparte; **to live apart** vivere separati; **he lives apart from his wife** vive separato da sua moglie; **I can't tell them apart** non li distinguo l'uno dall'altro; **joking apart** scherzi a parte, a parte gli scherzi; **these problems apart** a parte questi problemi; **apart from** a parte, eccetto; **apart from the fact that** a parte il fatto che; **apart from that, everything's fine** a parte quello, va tutto bene; **with one's legs apart** con le gambe divaricate 2 (*in pieces*) a pezzi; **to fall apart** cadere a pezzi, sfasciarsi; **to take sth apart** smontare qc

apart·heid [əˈpɑːteɪt] N apartheid *m*

apart·ment [əˈpɑːtmənt] N (*esp USA: flat*) appartamento; (*Brit: room in palace*) sala

apartment building N (*USA*) stabile *m*, caseggiato

apa·thet·ic [ˌæpəˈθɛtɪk] ADJ apatico(-a), indifferente

apa·thy [ˈæpəθɪ] N apatia, indifferenza

APB [ˌeɪpiːˈbiː] N ABBR (*USA: police expression: = all points bulletin*) espressione della polizia che significa "priorità assoluta: trovate..."

ape [eɪp] N (*esp anthropoid*) scimmia; **to go ape** (*USA fam*) diventare stupido(-a) ♦ VT scimmiottare

❑ *ape* is not translated by the Italian word *ape*

Ap·en·nines [ˈæpəˌnaɪnz] NPL: **the Apennines** gli Appennini *mpl*

ape·ri·tif [əˈpɛrɪtɪf] N aperitivo

ap·er·ture [ˈæpətʃʊə] N fessura; (*Phot*) apertura

apex [ˈeɪpɛks] N (*Geom*) vertice *m*; (*fig*) vertice *m*, apice *m*

aphid [ˈeɪfɪd] N afide *m*

aph·ro·dis·i·ac [ˌæfrəʊˈdɪzɪæk] N, ADJ afrodisiaco(-a)

apiece [əˈpiːs] ADV ciascuno(-a); **he gave them £10 apiece** ha dato loro dieci sterline (per) ciascuno; **these pens sell at 90p apiece** queste penne si vendono a 90 pence l'una

aplomb [əˈplɒm] N disinvoltura; **with great aplomb** senza scomporsi, con gran disinvoltura

APO [ˌeɪpiːˈəʊ] N ABBR (*USA: = Army Post Office*) *ufficio postale dell'esercito*

apoca·lypse [əˈpɒkəlɪps] N apocalisse *f*

apo·liti·cal [ˌeɪpəˈlɪtɪkəl] ADJ apolitico(-a)

apolo·get·ic [əˌpɒləˈdʒɛtɪk] ADJ (*look, remark, letter*) di scuse; **he was very apologetic about it/for not coming** si è scusato moltissimo di ciò/per *or* di non essere venuto

apolo·geti·cal·ly [əˌpɒləˈdʒɛtɪkəlɪ] ADV per scusarsi

apolo·gize [əˈpɒlədʒaɪz] VI: **to apologize (to sb for sth)** scusarsi (con qn per *or* di qc), chiedere scusa (a qn per *or* di qc); **I apologize!** Chiedo scusa!; **they apologized for being late** si sono scusati per il ritardo; **there's no need to apologize** non c'è bisogno che ti scusi

apol·ogy [əˈpɒlədʒɪ] N scuse *fpl*; **I demand an apology** esigo delle scuse; **I owe you an apology** ti devo delle scuse; **please accept my apologies** la prego di accettare le mie scuse; **an apology for a lunch** (*pej*) un tentativo mal riuscito di pranzo

apo·plec·tic [ˌæpəˈplɛktɪk] ADJ (*Med*) apoplettico(-a); **apoplectic with rage** (*fam*) livido(-a) per la rabbia

apo·plexy [ˈæpəplɛksɪ] N apoplessia

apos·tle [əˈpɒsl] N apostolo

apos·tro·phe [əˈpɒstrəfɪ] N (*Gram: sign*) apostrofo

ap·pal, ap·pall (*USA*) [əˈpɔːl] VT sconvolgere, atterrire; **to be appalled at** restare sconvolto(-a) davanti a

Ap·pa·la·chian Moun·tains [ˌæpəˈleɪʃən ˈmaʊntɪnz] NPL: **the Appalachian Mountains** (*also*: **the Appalachians**) i (monti) Appalachi

ap·pal·ling [əˈpɔːlɪŋ] ADJ (*ignorance, conditions, destruction*) spaventoso(-a), impressionante; (*fam: film, taste*) pessimo(-a), spaventoso(-a)

ap·pa·rat·us [ˌæpəˈreɪtəs] N (*for heating etc*) impianto; (*for filming, camping, in gym*) attrezzatura; (*in lab*) strumenti *mpl*; (*Anat*) apparato; (*system*) sistema *m*

ap·par·el [əˈpærəl] N (*frm*) abbigliamento, confezioni *fpl*

ap·par·ent [əˈpærənt] ADJ (*seeming*) apparente; (*clear*) evidente, ovvio(-a); **for no apparent reason** senza motivo apparente; **to become apparent** manifestarsi, rivelarsi; **it is apparent that** è evidente che; **it was becoming increasingly apparent to me that ...** stava diventando sempre più evidente per me che...

ap·par·ent·ly [əˈpærəntlɪ] ADV 1 (*it seems*) evidentemente; apparently... a quanto pare...; **did they give him the money? — apparently not** gli hanno dato i soldi? — no, a quanto pare 2 (*seemingly: unaffected, normal*) all'apparenza, apparentemente

ap·pa·ri·tion [ˌæpəˈrɪʃən] N fantasma *m*, apparizione *f*

ap·peal [əˈpiːl] VI 1 (*call, beg*): **to appeal (to sb)** implorare (qn), supplicare (qn); **to appeal for** chiedere (con insistenza); **to appeal for funds** lanciare un appello per ottenere dei fondi; **he appealed for silence** ha invitato al silenzio; **they appealed for help from the international community** hanno chiesto aiuto alla comunità internazionale 2

(*Law*): **to appeal (against sth/to sb)** appellarsi (contro qc/ presso qn), ricorrere in appello (contro qc/presso qn) **3** (*attract*) attirare, attrarre; **it doesn't appeal to me** mi dice poco; **Greece doesn't appeal to me** la Grecia non mi attira; **it appeals to the imagination** stimola la fantasia ♦ N **1** (*call*) appello; (*request*) richiesta; **an appeal for funds** una richiesta di aiuti economici *or* di fondi; **he made an appeal for calm** ha fatto appello alla calma **2** (*Law*) appello, ricorso (legale); **right of appeal** diritto d'appello **3** (*attraction*) attrattiva, fascino; **a book of general appeal** un libro di interesse generale

ap·peal·ing [əˈpiːlɪŋ] ADJ (*attractive*) attraente; (*pleading*) supplichevole

ap·pear [əˈpɪəʳ] VI **1** (*gen*) apparire, comparire; (*ghost*) apparire; **the bus appeared around the corner** l'autobus è apparso all'angolo della strada; **he appeared from nowhere** è saltato fuori all'improvviso **2** (*in public*) esibirsi; (*Theatre*) recitare; (*book etc*) uscire, essere pubblicato(-a); **to appear on TV** apparire in televisione; **to appear in Hamlet** recitare nell'Amleto **3** (*Law*) comparire, presentarsi; **who is appearing for the defendant?** chi è l'avvocato difensore? **4** (*seem*) sembrare, parere; **she appears to want to leave** sembra che voglia andarsene; **she appeared to be asleep** sembrava che dormisse; **the house appears to be empty** la casa sembra vuota; **he appears tired** sembra stanco, ha l'aria stanca; **it appears that ...** a quanto pare..., sembra che...; **it would appear that ...** sembrerebbe che; **so it would appear** pare proprio di sì

ap·pear·ance [əˈpɪərəns] N **1** (*act*) apparizione *f*; (*Theatre*) comparsa, apparizione; (*of book etc*) uscita, pubblicazione *f*; **in order of appearance** in ordine di apparizione; **to make one's first appearance** fare il proprio debutto, debuttare; **to put in** *or* **make an appearance** fare atto di presenza **2** (*look, aspect*) aspetto; **in appearance** a vedersi; **he was rather sickly in appearance** aveva un aspetto malaticcio *or* un'aria malaticcia; **appearances can be deceptive** non bisogna fidarsi delle apparenze, le apparenze ingannano; **to all appearances** a giudicar dalle apparenze; **to keep up appearances** salvare le apparenze

ap·pease [əˈpiːz] VT (*pacify*) placare; (*satisfy: curiosity*) appagare; (*: hunger*) calmare, soddisfare

ap·pease·ment [əˈpiːzmənt] N (*Pol*) appeasement *m inv*

ap·pend [əˈpend] VT (*frm: add: signature*) apporre; (*attach*) allegare; (*Comput*) aggiungere (in coda)

ap·pend·age [əˈpendɪdʒ] N (*frm: adjunct*) appendice *f*; (*Bot, Zool*) peduncolo

ap·pen·di·ci·tis [əˌpendɪˈsaɪtɪs] N appendicite *f*

ap·pen·dix [əˈpendɪks] N (*pl* **appendices** [əˈpendɪsiːz]) **1** (*Anat*) appendice *f*; **to have one's appendix out** operarsi *or* farsi operare di appendicite **2** (*to book etc*) appendice *f*

ap·pe·tite [ˈæpɪtaɪt] N: **appetite (for)** appetito (per); (*fig*) voglia (di), desiderio (di); **to have a good appetite** godere di *or* avere un ottimo appetito; **that walk has given me an appetite** la passeggiata mi ha messo *or* fatto venire appetito

ap·pe·tiz·er [ˈæpɪtaɪzəʳ] N (*food*) stuzzichino; (*drink*) aperitivo

ap·pe·tiz·ing [ˈæpɪtaɪzɪŋ] ADJ appetitoso(-a), invitante

ap·plaud [əˈplɔːd] VT applaudire; (*fig*) lodare, approvare ♦ VI applaudire

ap·plause [əˈplɔːz] N applauso; (*fig*) lode *f*, elogio; **a round of applause** un applauso

ap·ple [ˈæpl] N (*fruit*) mela; **the apple of one's eye** (*fam*) la pupilla dei propri occhi; **apple tree** melo

apple pie N crostata di mele ricoperta di pasta; **in apple-pie order** in ordine perfetto

apple turnover N sfogliatella alle mele

ap·pli·ance [əˈplaɪəns] N apparecchio; **electrical appliances** elettrodomestici *mpl*

ap·pli·ca·ble [əˈplɪkəbl] ADJ applicabile; **the law is applicable from January** la legge entrerà in vigore in gennaio; **to be applicable to** essere valido(-a) per

ap·pli·cant [ˈæplɪkənt] N (*for a post etc*) candidato(-a); (*Admin: for benefit, housing*) chi ha fatto domanda *or* richiesta; **there were a hundred applicants for that job** cento persone hanno fatto domanda per quel posto

ap·pli·ca·tion [ˌæplɪˈkeɪʃən] N **1** (*act of applying*) applica-

zione *f*; **for external application only** (*Med*) (solo) per uso esterno; **the practical application of the theory** l'applicazione pratica della teoria **2** (*request: for university place, grant etc*) domanda; **a job application** una domanda di lavoro; **application for a job** domanda di assunzione; **on application** su richiesta; **further details may be had on application to X** per informazioni più dettagliate rivolgersi a X **3** (*Comput*) applicazione *f* **4** (*diligence*) applicazione *f*, impegno

application form N modulo di domanda

application program N (*Comput*) programma *m* applicativo

applications package N (*Comput*) software *m inv* applicativo

ap·plied [əˈplaɪd] ADJ applicato(-a); **applied linguistics** linguistica applicata; **applied arts** arti *fpl* applicate

ap·ply [əˈplaɪ] VT: **to apply (to)** (*ointment*) applicare (su), spalmare (su); (*plaster*) mettere (su), applicare (su); (*paint*) dare (a), stendere (su); (*rule, law, theory*) applicare (a); **to apply one's knowledge to sth** servirsi delle proprie nozioni per qc; **to apply one's mind to a problem** concentrarsi su un problema; **to apply o.s. (to one's studies)** applicarsi (nello studio); **to apply the brakes** azionare i freni, frenare ♦ VI **1** (*be applicable*): **to apply (to)** applicarsi (a), essere valido(-a) (per); (*be suitable for, relevant to*) riguardare, riferirsi (a); **the law applies to everybody** la legge è valida *or* vale per tutti; **this rule doesn't apply** questa regola non vale; **this rule doesn't apply to us** questa norma non ci riguarda **2** (*request*) fare *or* presentare domanda; **to apply for a job** fare domanda d'impiego; **to apply for a visa** chiedere un visto; **to apply to a university** fare domanda d'ammissione all'università; **to apply to sb for sth** rivolgersi a qn per qc

ap·point [əˈpɔɪnt] VT **1** (*nominate*) nominare; **they appointed him chairman** lo hanno nominato presidente; **they appointed a new teacher** hanno assunto un nuovo insegnante **2** (*frm: time, place*) fissare, stabilire; **at the appointed time** all'ora stabilita **3 a well-appointed house** una casa ben attrezzata

❏ **appoint** is not translated by the Italian word *appuntare*

ap·poin·tee [əpɔɪnˈtiː] N incaricato(-a)

ap·point·ment [əˈpɔɪntmənt] N **1** (*arrangement to meet*) appuntamento; **by appointment** su *or* per appuntamento; **have you an appointment?** (*to caller*) ha un appuntamento?; **to keep an appointment** non mancare a un appuntamento; **she won't be able to keep the appointment** non potrà venire all'appuntamento; **to make an appointment with sb** prendere un appuntamento con qn; **I've got a dental appointment** ho un appuntamento dal dentista **2** (*to a job*) nomina; (*job*) posto, carica

ap·por·tion [əˈpɔːʃən] VT (*praise, blame*) attribuire

ap·prais·al [əˈpreɪzəl] N valutazione *f*, stima; (*fig*) giudizio

ap·praise [əˈpreɪz] VT (*value*) valutare, fare una stima di; (*fig*) dare *or* esprimere un giudizio su; (*situation*) fare il bilancio di

ap·pre·ci·able [əˈpriːʃəbl] ADJ (*increase, effect*) sensibile; (*change*) notevole

ap·pre·ci·ably [əˈpriːʃəblɪ] ADV (*increase*) sensibilmente; (*change*) notevolmente

ap·pre·ci·ate [əˈpriːʃɪeɪt] VT **1** (*be grateful for*) apprezzare, essere riconoscente di, essere grato(-a) per; **I appreciated your help** ti sono grato per l'aiuto **2** (*value*) apprezzare; **I am not appreciated here** qui nessuno mi apprezza abbastanza **3** (*understand: problem, difference*) rendersi conto di; **yes, I appreciate that** certo, me ne rendo conto ♦ VI (*Comm: property*) aumentare (di valore)

ap·pre·cia·tion [əˌpriːʃɪˈeɪʃən] N **1** (*understanding*) comprensione *f*; (*praise*) apprezzamento; (*gratitude*) riconoscimento; (*Art: critique*) critica; **as a token of my appreciation** in segno della mia gratitudine; **he has no appreciation of good music** non apprezza la buona musica **2** (*Comm: rise in value*) aumento (del valore)

ap·pre·cia·tive [əˈpriːʃɪətɪv] ADJ (*look*) di ammirazione; (*comment*) di elogio, elogiativo(-a); (*audience*) caloroso(-a); **he was very appreciative of what I had done** mi era molto grato di *or* ha dimostrato di apprezzare molto quello che avevo fatto

ap·pre·hend [ˌæprɪˈhɛnd] VT (*frm: arrest*) arrestare; (: *understand*) comprendere

❏ **apprehend** is not translated by the Italian word *apprendere*

ap·pre·hen·sion [ˌæprɪˈhɛnʃən] N 1 (*fear*) apprensione *f*, inquietudine *f*; **my chief apprehension is ...** la mia paura più grande è... 2 (*arrest*) arresto

ap·pre·hen·sive [ˌæprɪˈhɛnsɪv] ADJ (*person*) in apprensione; (*expression*) apprensivo(-a)

ap·pren·tice [əˈprɛntɪs] N apprendista *m/f*; **a plumber's apprentice** *or* **an apprentice plumber** un apprendista idraulico ♦ VT: **to apprentice to** mettere come apprendista presso; **to be apprenticed to** lavorare come apprendista presso

ap·pren·tice·ship [əˈprɛntɪsˌʃɪp] N apprendistato, tirocinio; **to serve one's apprenticeship** fare il proprio apprendistato *or* tirocinio

ap·proach [əˈprəʊtʃ] VT 1 (*come near: person*) avvicinarsi a, avvicinare; (: *animal*) avvicinarsi a; (: *place*) stare per arrivare a, avvicinarsi a; (: *fig: subject, problem, job*) impostare, affrontare; **he approached the house** si è avvicinato alla casa; **I'm not sure how to approach the problem** non so come affrontare il problema; **I approached it with an open mind** ho considerato la cosa senza pregiudizi; **he's approaching 50** si avvicina ai 50, va per i 50; **no other painter approaches him** (*fig*) nessun altro pittore lo uguaglia 2 (*with request etc*): **to approach sb about sth** rivolgersi a qn per qc ♦ VI avvicinarsi; **the approaching elections** le imminenti elezioni ♦ N 1 (*act*) l'avvicinarsi *m*, avvicinamento; **at the approach of night** all'avvicinarsi della notte 2 (*to problem, subject*) modo di affrontare, approccio 3 (*access*) accesso; **the northern approaches to the city** le vie d'accesso a nord della città 4 (*proposal, inquiry: about a job, project*) proposta; (: *to committee, department*) presa di contatto; **to make an approach to sb** contattare qn; **to make approaches to sb** (*amorous*) fare degli approcci *or* delle avances a qn ♦ ADJ di avvicinamento

ap·proach·able [əˈprəʊtʃəbl] ADJ (*person*) avvicinabile, accessibile

approach road N strada d'accesso

ap·pro·ba·tion [ˌæprəˈbeɪʃən] N (*frm*) approvazione *f*, benestare *m*

ap·pro·pri·ate [*adj* əˈprəʊprɪɪt, *vb* əˈprəʊprɪeɪt] ADJ (*moment, name*) adatto(-a), opportuno(-a); (*remark*) opportuno(-a); (*word*) giusto(-a), adatto(-a); (*authority*) competente; **appropriate for** *or* **to** adatto(-a) a, appropriato(-a) a, adeguato(-a) a; **an outfit appropriate to the job** un abbigliamento adatto al lavoro; **it would not be appropriate for me to comment** non sta a me fare dei commenti; **tick the appropriate box** barrare l'apposita casella; **whichever seems more appropriate** ciò che sembra più adatto; **appropriate behaviour** comportamento corretto; **he is the appropriate person to ask** è lui il competente in materia ♦ VT 1 (*take for one's own use*) appropriarsi di 2 (*frm: allocate*) destinare, stanziare

ap·pro·pri·ate·ly [əˈprəʊprɪtlɪ] ADV in modo adatto *or* appropriato; **he was appropriately insured** era assicurato in modo adeguato *or* convenientemente

ap·pro·pria·tion [əprəʊprɪˈeɪʃən] N (*taking for oneself*) appropriazione *f*; (*allocation*) stanziamento

ap·prov·al [əˈpruːvəl] N (*consent*) approvazione *f*, consenso; **on approval** (*Comm*) salvo vista e verifica, in esame; **to meet with sb's approval** essere di gradimento di qn, soddisfare qn

ap·prove [əˈpruːv] VT approvare
▸ **approve of** VI + PREP approvare; **I don't approve of his choice** non approvo la sua scelta; **I don't approve of kids going to pubs** non approvo *or* disapprovo che i ragazzi vadano al pub; **she doesn't approve of me** disapprova il mio modo di essere

ap·prov·ing·ly [əˈpruːvɪŋlɪ] ADV con approvazione

approx. ABBR = **approximately**

ap·proxi·mate [*adj* əˈprɒksɪmɪt, *vb* əˈprɒksɪmeɪt] ADJ approssimativo(-a), approssimato(-a) ♦ VI: **to approximate to** essere un'approssimazione di, avvicinarsi a

ap·proxi·mate·ly [əˈprɒksɪmətlɪ] ADV approssimativamente, pressappoco, circa

ap·proxi·ma·tion [əˈprɒksɪˈmeɪʃən] N approssimazione *f*

APR [ˌeɪpiːˈɑː] N ABBR (= *annual percentage rate*) tasso percentuale annuo

Apr. ABBR (= *April*) apr. (= *aprile*)

apri·cot [ˈeɪprɪˌkɒt] N (*fruit*) albicocca; **apricot tree** albicocco

April [ˈeɪprəl] N aprile *m*; *see* July

April Fool's Day N il primo d'aprile

apron [ˈeɪprən] N 1 (*gen: workman's*) grembiule *m* 2 (*Aer*) area di stazionamento

apse [æps] N (*Archit, Geom*) abside *f*

apt [æpt] ADJ (*comp* **-er**, *superl* **-est**) 1 (*suitable: remark*) appropriato(-a), adatto(-a), pertinente; (: *description*) felice, indovinato(-a), giusto(-a) 2 (*liable*): **to be apt to do sth** avere (la) tendenza a fare qc; **I am apt to be out on Mondays** generalmente di lunedì non ci sono; **we are apt to forget that ...** tendiamo a dimenticare che... 3 (*pupil, student: able*) dotato(-a), capace

apt. ABBR = **apartment**

ap·ti·tude [ˈæptɪtjuːd] N (*ability*) abilità *f inv*

aptitude test N test *m inv* attitudinale

apt·ly [ˈæptlɪ] ADV appropriatamente, in modo adatto; **she was aptly dressed for the occasion** aveva un vestito adatto all'occasione

aqua·lung [ˈækwəˌlʌŋ] N autorespiratore *m*

aquar·ium [əˈkwɛərɪəm] N acquario

Aquar·ius [əˈkwɛərɪəs] N Acquario

aquat·ic [əˈkwætɪk] ADJ acquatico(-a)

aque·duct [ˈækwɪˌdʌkt] N acquedotto

AR ABBR (*USA Post* = **Arkansas**)

Arab [ˈærəb] N (*person*) arabo(-a); (*horse*) cavallo arabo; **the Arabs** gli arabi ♦ ADJ arabo(-a)

Ara·bia [əˈreɪbɪə] N Arabia

Ara·bian [əˈreɪbɪən] ADJ arabo(-a), arabico(-a)

Arabian Desert N: **the Arabian Desert** il Deserto arabico

Arabian Sea N: **the Arabian Sea** il mare *m* Arabico

Ara·bic [ˈærəbɪk] N (*language*) arabo ♦ ADJ arabo(-a), arabico(-a)

Arabic numerals NPL numeri *mpl* arabi, numerazione *fsg* araba

ar·able [ˈærəbl] ADJ arabile, arativo(-a); **arable farming** coltura del terreno

ar·bi·ter [ˈɑːbɪtə] N (*frm*) arbitro

ar·bi·trary [ˈɑːbɪtrən] ADJ arbitrario(-a)

ar·bi·trate [ˈɑːbɪtreɪt] VI fare da arbitro, arbitrare

ar·bi·tra·tion [ˌɑːbɪˈtreɪʃən] N (*Law*) arbitrato; (*Industry*) arbitraggio; **the dispute went to arbitration** la controversia è stata sottoposta ad arbitrato

ar·bi·tra·tor [ˈɑːbɪtreɪtə] N arbitro

ARC [ɛːɑːsiː] N ABBR 1 (= *Aids Related Complex*) ARC *m* 2 (= *American Red Cross*) ≈ CRI *f*

arc [ɑːk] N arco

ar·cade [ɑːˈkeɪd] N (*passage with shops*) galleria; (*series of arches*) portico; (*round public square*) porticato, portici *mpl*; **shopping arcade** una galleria con negozi

arch[1] [ɑːtʃ] N (*Archit*) arco, arcata 2 (*of foot*) arco *or* arcata plantare ♦ VT (*back, body*) arcuare, inarcare; (*eyebrows*) inarcare

arch[2] [ɑːtʃ] ADJ grande (*before n*), per eccellenza; **an arch villain** un grande criminale; **the arch villain** il cattivo per eccellenza; **his arch rival** il suo rivale per eccellenza

ar·chaeo·logi·cal [ˌɑːkɪəˈlɒdʒɪkəl] ADJ archeologico(-a)

ar·chae·olo·gist [ˌɑːkɪˈɒlədʒɪst] N archeologo(-a)

ar·chae·ol·ogy [ˌɑːkɪˈɒlədʒɪ] N archeologia

ar·cha·ic [ɑːˈkeɪɪk] ADJ arcaico(-a)

arch·angel [ˈɑːkˌeɪndʒəl] N arcangelo

arch·bishop [ˈɑːtʃˈbɪʃəp] N arcivescovo

arched [ɑːtʃt] ADJ arcuato(-a)

arch·en·emy [ˈɑːtʃˈɛnɪmɪ] N 1 (*chief enemy*) nemico per eccellenza 2 (*Rel*): **the Arch-enemy** (*the Devil*) il diavolo

archeology *etc* [ˌɑːkɪˈɒlədʒɪ] (*esp USA*) = **archaeology**

arch·er [ˈɑːtʃə] N arciere *m*

ar·chery [ˈɑːtʃərɪ] N tiro con l'arco

ar·che·typ·al [ˌɑːkɪˈtaɪpəl] ADJ tipico(-a)
ar·che·type [ˈɑːkɪˌtaɪp] N (original) archetipo; (epitome) prototipo
archi·pela·go [ˌɑːkɪˈpelɪɡəʊ] N (pl **archipelagos** or **archipelagoes**) arcipelago
archi·tect [ˈɑːkɪˌtekt] N architetto
archi·tec·tur·al [ˌɑːkɪˈtektʃərəl] ADJ (plan, drawing) architettonico(-a); (practice, student) di architettura
archi·tec·ture [ˈɑːkɪˌtektʃəʳ] N architettura
archive file [ˈɑːkaɪv] N (Comput) file m inv di archivio
ar·chives [ˈɑːkaɪvz] NPL archivio msg, archivi mpl
archi·vist [ˈɑːkɪvɪst] N archivista m/f
arch·way [ˈɑːtʃweɪ] N (passage) (passaggio a) volta; (arch) arco, arcata
arc·tic [ˈɑːktɪk] ADJ artico(-a); (fig: very cold) polare ♦ N: **the Arctic** l'Artico
Arctic Circle N: **the Arctic Circle** il Circolo polare artico
Arctic Ocean N: **the Arctic Ocean** l'Oceano artico
ar·dent [ˈɑːdənt] ADJ (supporter) ardente, fervente; (desire, lover) ardente
ar·dour, ar·dor (USA) [ˈɑːdəʳ] N (frm) ardore m
ar·du·ous [ˈɑːdjʊəs] ADJ arduo(-a)
are [ɑːʳ, əʳ] 2ND PERS SG, 1ST PERS PL PRESENT, 2ND PERS PL PRESENT, 3RD PERS PL PRESENT of **be**
area [ˈɛərɪə] N **1** (surface extent) area, superficie f; (Geom) area; **the field has an area of 2000 square metres** il campo ha una superficie di 2000 metri quadrati **2** (region) zona; (district) zona, settore m; **the London area** la zona di Londra; **my favourite area of London is Chelsea** il quartiere londinese che preferisco è Chelsea **3** (fig: of knowledge) campo; (: of responsibility etc) sfera; **matters outside my area of responsibility** questioni che esulano dalla mia competenza; **in the area of £5000** sulle or intorno alle 5000 sterline
area code N (USA: Telec) prefisso
arena [əˈriːnə] N arena
aren't [ɑːnt] = **are not**
Ar·gen·ti·na [ˌɑːdʒənˈtiːnə] N l'Argentina
Ar·gen·tin·ian [ˌɑːdʒənˈtɪnɪən] ADJ, N argentino(-a)
ar·gu·able [ˈɑːɡjʊəbl] ADJ (rather doubtful) discutibile; (capable of being argued for): **it is arguable that ...** si può sostenere che...; **it is arguable whether ...** è una cosa discutibile se... + sub
ar·gu·ably [ˈɑːɡjʊəblɪ] ADV: **it is arguably ...** si può sostenere che sia...
ar·gue [ˈɑːɡjuː] VI **1** (dispute) litigare; **to argue about sth (with sb)** litigare per or a proposito di qc (con qn); **don't argue!** senza tante discussioni!, non discutere!; **they're always arguing** litigano sempre **2** (reason) ragionare; **to argue against/for** addurre degli argomenti contro/in favore di ♦ VT (debate: case, matter) dibattere, discutere; (persuade): **to argue sb into doing sth** persuadere or convincere qn a fare qc; **to argue that ...** (maintain) sostenere or affermare che...
ar·gu·ment [ˈɑːɡjʊmənt] N **1** (reasons) argomento, ragione f, motivo; **argument for/against** argomento a or in favore di/contro; **there are strong arguments against lowering the price** ci sono motivi validi per non abbassare il prezzo; **I don't follow your argument** non ti seguo **2** (discussion) discussione f, dibattito; (quarrel) litigio, lite f; **to have an argument** litigare; **to hear both sides of the argument** ascoltare entrambe le versioni
ar·gu·men·ta·tive [ˌɑːɡjʊˈmentətɪv] ADJ polemico(-a)
aria [ˈɑːrɪə] N aria
arid [ˈærɪd] ADJ arido(-a); (fig) piatto(-a)
arid·ity [əˈrɪdɪtɪ] N aridità
Aries [ˈɛərɪz] N Ariete m; **to be Aries** essere dell'Ariete
arise [əˈraɪz] (pt **arose**, pp **arisen** [əˈrɪzn]) VI **1** (occur: opportunity, problem) presentarsi, offrirsi; (result): **to arise (from)** derivare (da); **difficulties have arisen** sono sorte delle difficoltà; **should the need arise** dovesse presentarsi la necessità, in caso di necessità; **a storm arose** si scatenò una tempesta; **the question does not arise** la questione non si pone **2** (old: get up) levarsi (frm), alzarsi
ar·is·toc·ra·cy [ˌærɪsˈtɒkrəsɪ] N aristocrazia
aris·to·crat [ˈærɪstəˌkræt] N nobile m/f, aristocratico(-a)

aris·to·crat·ic [ˌærɪstəˈkrætɪk] ADJ aristocratico(-a)
arith·me·tic [n əˈrɪθmətɪk, adj ˌærɪθˈmetɪk] N aritmetica; **mental arithmetic** calcolo mentale ♦ ADJ aritmetico(-a); **arithmetic progression** progressione f aritmetica
arith·meti·cal [ˌærɪθˈmetɪkəl] ADJ aritmetico(-a)
Ariz. ABBR (USA: = Arizona)
A·ri·zo·na [ˌærɪˈzəʊnə] N l'Arizona
ark [ɑːk] N (Bible) arca; **Noah's Ark** l'arca di Noè; **it must have come out of the ark!** (hum, fam) sembra un reperto archeologico
Ark. ABBR (USA: = Arkansas)
Ar·kan·sas [ˈɑːkənsɔː] N l'Arkansas
arm [ɑːm] N (Anat) braccio; (of chair) bracciolo; **arm in arm** a braccetto, sottobraccio; **with open arms** (fig) a braccia aperte; **within arm's reach** a portata di mano; **to keep sb at arm's length** (fig) tenere qn a distanza; **to put one's arm round sb** mettere un braccio intorno alle spalle di qn; see also **arms** ♦ VT (person, ship) armare; **he armed himself with some good arguments** si è armato di validi argomenti
ar·ma·ments [ˈɑːməmənts] NPL (weapons) armamenti mpl
arm·band [ˈɑːmˌbænd] N bracciale m
arm·chair [ˈɑːmˌtʃɛəʳ] N poltrona
armed [ɑːmd] ADJ armato(-a); **armed to the teeth** armato(-a) fino ai denti; **she was armed with all the facts** aveva in mano tutti i fatti
armed forces NPL forze fpl armate
armed robbery N rapina a mano armata
Ar·me·nia [ɑːˈmiːnɪə] N Armenia
Ar·me·nian [ɑːˈmiːnɪən] ADJ armeno(-a) ♦ N (person) armeno(-a); (language) armeno
arm·ful [ˈɑːmfʊl] N bracciata
arm·i·stice [ˈɑːmɪstɪs] N armistizio
ar·mour, ar·mor (USA) [ˈɑːməʳ] N armatura; (also: armour-plating) corazza, blindatura; (Mil: tanks) mezzi mpl blindati
armoured car, armored car (USA) [ˈɑːməd ˈkɑːʳ] N autoblinda f inv
ar·moury, ar·mory (USA) [ˈɑːmərɪ] N arsenale m, armeria
arm·pit [ˈɑːmˌpɪt] N ascella
arm·rest [ˈɑːmˌrest] N bracciolo
arms [ɑːmz] NPL **1** (weapons) armi fpl; **to be up in arms** (fig) essere sul piede di guerra **2** (Heraldry: also: coat of arms) stemma m
arms control N controllo degli armamenti
arms race N corsa agli armamenti
army [ˈɑːmɪ] N (Mil, also fig) esercito; **to join the army** arruolarsi
aro·ma [əˈrəʊmə] N aroma m
aro·ma·thera·py [əˌrəʊməˈθerəpɪ] N aromaterapia
aro·mat·ic [ˌærəʊˈmætɪk] ADJ aromatico(-a)
arose [əˈrəʊz] PT of **arise**
around [əˈraʊnd] ADV **1** (place) attorno, intorno; **she ignored the people around her** ha ignorato la gente che aveva intorno; **around here** da queste parti; **is there a pharmacy around here?** c'è una farmacia da queste parti?; **for miles around** nel raggio di chilometri; **he must be somewhere around** dev'essere qui in giro or nei paraggi; **do you know your way around?** conosci il luogo?, sai come muoverti qui attorno? **2** (approximately) all'incirca, circa; **around 10 o'clock** verso le 10; **it costs around 100 pounds** costa circa 100 sterline ♦ PREP intorno a; **it's just around the corner** è appena girato l'angolo; **I've travelled around the country** ho girato tutto il paese
arous·al [əˈraʊzəl] N (sexual) eccitazione f; (awakening) risveglio
arouse [əˈraʊz] VT (awaken: sleeper) svegliare; (fig: person) eccitare, stimolare; (: feelings) suscitare
ar·range [əˈreɪndʒ] VT **1** (put into order: books, thoughts, furniture) sistemare, ordinare; (hair) acconciare; (flowers) sistemare; **the chairs were arranged in a circle** le sedie erano sistemate in cerchio **2** (Mus) adattare, arrangiare **3** (decide on: meeting) combinare, organizzare; (: date) stabilire, fissare; (: program) stabilire, preparare; **to arrange a time for** stabilire or fissare una data per; **everything is arranged** è tutto

a posto; **it was arranged that ...** è stato deciso or stabilito che...; **she arranged a trip to Scotland** ha organizzato un viaggio in Scozia; **what did you arrange with him?** per or su che cosa siete rimasti d'accordo?; **to arrange to do sth** mettersi d'accordo per fare qc; **they arranged to go out together on Friday** si sono messi d'accordo per uscire venerdì ♦ vi mettersi d'accordo, combinare; **to arrange for sth/for sb to do sth** organizzare or predisporre qc/che qn faccia qc; **we have arranged for a taxi to pick you up** la faremo venire a prendere da un taxi; **I have arranged for you to go** ho dato disposizione in modo che lei vada

ar·range·ment [əˈreɪndʒmənt] N 1 (order, act of ordering) sistemazione f, disposizione f; (Mus) arrangiamento; **a flower arrangement** una composizione floreale 2 (agreement) accordo; **to come to an arrangement (with sb)** venire a un accordo (con qn), mettersi d'accordo or accordarsi (con qn); **we have an arrangement** siamo d'accordo; **by arrangement** su richiesta; **by arrangement with the tour operator** secondo gli accordi con l'operatore turistico; **by arrangement with La Scala** con l'autorizzazione del Teatro della Scala 3 (plan) piano, programma m; **arrangements** NPL (preparations) preparativi mpl; **I'll make arrangements for you to be met** darò disposizioni or istruzioni perché ci sia qualcuno ad incontrarla; **we must make arrangements to help** dobbiamo organizzarci per dare un aiuto; **all the arrangements for the party are made** sono stati ultimati i preparativi per la festa

ar·rant [ˈærənt] ADJ: **arrant nonsense** colossali sciocchezze fpl

ar·ray [əˈreɪ] N 1 (of troops, police etc) schieramento; **in battle array** in ordine di battaglia; **a fine array of hats/cakes** tanti cappelli/tante torte in bella mostra 2 (Math) tabella; (Comput) array m inv, matrice f

ar·rears [əˈrɪəz] NPL (of money) arretrati mpl; **arrears of filing** pratiche fpl arretrate da archiviare; **in arrears** in arretrato; **to be in arrears with one's rent** essere in arretrato con l'affitto

ar·rest [əˈrest] N arresto; **to be under arrest** essere in (stato di) arresto; **to place sb under arrest** arrestare qn, mettere qn in stato di arresto; **you're under arrest!** la dichiaro in arresto! ♦ vt (criminal) arrestare; (attention, interest) fermare, attirare; (halt: progress, decay etc) arrestare, bloccare

ar·rest·ing [əˈrestɪŋ] ADJ (fig) che colpisce

ar·ri·val [əˈraɪvəl] N (gen) arrivo; (person) arrivato(-a); **a new arrival** (newcomer) un(a) nuovo(-a) venuto(-a); (baby) un(a) neonato(-a); **on arrival** all'arrivo

ar·rive [əˈraɪv] vi (gen) arrivare; (day, time) arrivare, giungere; **we arrived at eight** siamo arrivati alle otto
  ▸ **arrive at** vi + PREP (place, price) arrivare a; (decision, solution) arrivare a, giungere a

ar·ro·gance [ˈærəgəns] N arroganza

ar·ro·gant [ˈærəgənt] ADJ arrogante

ar·row [ˈærəʊ] N freccia

ar·senal [ˈɑːsnl] N arsenale m

ar·senic [ˈɑːsnɪk] N arsenico

ar·son [ˈɑːsn] N incendio doloso

art [ɑːt] N arte f; (craft) mestiere m; (Scol: subject) disegno e storia dell'arte; **to study art** studiare materie artistiche; **Greek art** l'arte greca; **he's good at art** è bravo nelle materie artistiche; **work of art** opera d'arte; see also **arts** ♦ ADJ d'arte

art college N scuola di belle arti

ar·te·fact, ar·ti·fact (USA) [ˈɑːtɪfækt] N manufatto

ar·te·rial [ɑːˈtɪərɪəl] ADJ (Anat) arterioso(-a); (road etc) di grande comunicazione; **arterial roads** le (grandi or principali) arterie

ar·tery [ˈɑːtərɪ] N (Anat, also fig) arteria

art·ful [ˈɑːtfʊl] ADJ (person) furbo(-a), abile; (trick) abile

art gallery N (museum) museo, galleria d'arte; (shop) galleria d'arte

ar·thri·tis [ɑːˈθraɪtɪs] N artrite f

ar·ti·choke [ˈɑːtɪtʃəʊk] N (globe artichoke) carciofo; (Jerusalem artichoke) topinambur m inv

ar·ti·cle [ˈɑːtɪkl] N 1 (Admin, Law, Comm, Gram) articolo; (object) oggetto; **articles of clothing** articoli mpl di vestiario, indumenti mpl 2 **articles** NPL (Brit Law, Admin) contratto di tirocinio; **to be in articles** fare il tirocinio

articles of association NPL (Comm) statuto sociale

ar·ticu·late [adj ɑːˈtɪkjʊlɪt, vb ɑːˈtɪkjʊleɪt] ADJ (account, diction) chiaro(-a); (person) che si esprime bene ♦ vt (words) articolare, pronunciare

ar·ticu·lated lor·ry [ɑːˈtɪkjʊleɪtɪdˈlɒrɪ] N (Brit) autoarticolato

ar·ti·fact [ˈɑːtɪfækt] N (USA) = **artefact**

ar·ti·fice [ˈɑːtɪfɪs] N (frm: cunning) abilità, destrezza; (: trick) artificio

ar·ti·fi·cial [ˌɑːtɪˈfɪʃəl] ADJ (synthetic) artificiale; (fig: pej: smile, manner) studiato(-a), affettato(-a); (: tears, situation) falso(-a)

artificial insemination N inseminazione f or fecondazione f artificiale

artificial intelligence N intelligenza artificiale

artificial respiration N respirazione f artificiale

ar·til·lery [ɑːˈtɪlərɪ] N artiglieria

ar·ti·san [ˈɑːtɪzæn] N artigiano(-a)

art·ist [ˈɑːtɪst] N artista m/f

ar·tis·tic [ɑːˈtɪstɪk] ADJ artistico(-a); **to be artistic** avere una sensibilità artistica

art·ist·ry [ˈɑːtɪstrɪ] N (skill) arte f, abilità artistica

art·less [ˈɑːtlɪs] ADJ ingenuo(-a), semplice

arts [ɑːts] NPL (Univ) lettere fpl, studi mpl umanistici; **the arts** le belle arti; **arts and crafts** artigianato; **Faculty of Arts** facoltà di Lettere; **you can study arts or science** si possono fare studi umanistici o scientifici

art school N scuola d'arte

art·work [ˈɑːtwɜːk] N materiale m illustrativo

KEYWORD

as [æz, əz] CONJ
1 (time) mentre, quando; **as I get older, I ...** con l'età io...; **as the years went by** col passare degli anni; **he came in as I was leaving** è arrivato nel momento in cui or quando stavo per andarmene; **as a child ...** da bambino...; **as or so long as** finché; **as soon as she arrived I left** me ne sono andato appena lei è arrivata
2 (because) visto che, poiché, dal momento che, siccome; **as he had been up since 4 a.m. he was exhausted** era esausto perché si era alzato alle 4
3 (although): **much as I like them, ...** per quanto mi siano simpatici, ...; **try as he might, he couldn't do it** malgrado i suoi sforzi, non ha potuto farlo; **young as he was he understood the situation perfectly** anche se giovane capì perfettamente la situazione
4 (way, manner: also preposition) come; **you've got plenty as it is** ne hai già abbastanza; **do as you wish** fa' come vuoi; **leave things as they are** lascia tutto così com'è; **as I've said before ...** come ho già detto...
5 (concerning): **as for, as regards, as to** per quanto or quello che riguarda, quanto a; **as for the children, they were exhausted** quanto ai bambini, erano sfiniti; **as to that I can't say** su quello non ti so dire
6 **as if, as though** come se + sub; **he fought as if his life depended on it** si battuto come se ne andasse della sua vita; **he got up as if to leave** si alzò come per andarsene; **he looked as if he was ill** aveva l'aria di star male
7 (providing): **as or so long as** purché
♦ ADV (in comparisons): **as big as** tanto grande quanto; **twice as big as** due volte più grande di; **this car will go as fast as 120 m.p.h.** questa macchina raggiunge le 120 miglia all'ora; **I didn't know it could go as fast as that** non sapevo che fosse così veloce; **as many (as)** tanti(-e) ... quanti(-e)); **you've got as much as she has** ne hai (tanto) quanto ne ha lei; **twice as old** due volte più vecchio(-a); **her coat cost twice as much as mine** il suo cappotto è costato il doppio del mio; **as pale as death** pallido(-a) come un morto; **as quickly as possible** il più rapidamente possibile; **as soon as possible** prima possibile; **as tall as him** alto(-a) come lui; **Peter's as tall as Michael** Peter è alto come Michael
♦ PREP
1 (in the capacity of) da; **he works as a waiter in the holidays** durante le vacanze lavora come cameriere; **disguised as a nun** travestito(-a) da suora; **he gave it to me as a**

present me lo ha regalato; **he succeeded as a politician** come politico ha avuto successo; **as such** come tale **2** (*time*): **as of** *or* **from tomorrow** (a partire *or* a cominciare) da domani; *see* **be, same, such, so, well**[2]

asap [ˌeɪeɪˈpiː] ADV ABBR (= *as soon as possible*) prima possibile

as·bes·tos [æsˈbestɒs] N amianto, asbesto

as·cend [əˈsend] VT (*frm: stairs*) salire; (*mountain*) scalare; (*throne*) salire a, ascendere a ♦ VI salire

as·cend·ancy [əˈsendənsı] N ascendente *m*

as·cend·ant [əˈsendənt] N: **to be in the ascendant** essere in auge

as·cen·sion [əˈsenʃən] N (*Rel*): **the Ascension** l'Ascensione *f* **Ascension Island** N isola dell'Ascensione

as·cent [əˈsent] N (*of mountain*) ascensione *f*, scalata; (*in plane*) salita; **we made a rapid ascent to our cruising altitude** siamo saliti rapidamente fino alla quota di crociera

as·cer·tain [ˌæsəˈteɪn] VT (*frm*) accertare; **have you ascertained her real name yet?** ha accertato quale sia il suo vero nome?

as·cet·ic [əˈsetɪk] ADJ ascetico(-a) ♦ N asceta *m*

as·ceti·cism [əˈsetɪsɪzəm] N ascetismo

ASCII [ˈæskı] N ABBR (= *American Standard Code for Information Interchange*) ASCII *m*

as·cribe [əˈskraɪb] VT: **to ascribe sth to sth/sb** attribuire qc a qc/qn

ash[1] [æʃ] N (*of cigarette*) cenere *f*; **ashes** NPL (*of fire*) cenere *f*; (*of dead*) ceneri *fpl*; **burnt to ashes** carbonizzato(-a)

ash[2] [æʃ] N (*Bot*) frassino

ashamed [əˈʃeɪmd] ADJ pieno(-a) di vergogna, vergognoso(-a); **to be** *or* **feel ashamed (of o.s.)** vergognarsi; **to be ashamed of sb/sth/to do sth** vergognarsi di qn/qc/di fare qc; **you ought to be ashamed of yourself!** dovresti vergognarti!, vergognati!; **it's nothing to be ashamed of** non è una cosa di cui ci si debba vergognare

ash·en [ˈæʃn] ADJ cinereo(-a); (*pale*) livido(-a)

ashore [əˈʃɔːʳ] ADV a terra; **to go ashore** scendere a terra, sbarcare

ash·tray [ˈæʃtreɪ] N portacenere *m inv*, posacenere *m inv*

Ash Wednesday N mercoledì *m inv* delle Ceneri

Asia [ˈeɪʃə] N Asia

Asia Minor N Asia minore

Asian [ˈeɪʃn], **Asi·at·ic** [ˌeɪʃɪˈætɪk] ADJ, N asiatico(-a)

aside [əˈsaɪd] ADV da parte; **to take sb aside** prendere qn da parte ♦ PREP: **aside from** (*as well as*) oltre a, a parte; (*except for*) a parte, salvo, eccetto ♦ N (*esp Theatre*) a parte *m inv*

ask [ɑːsk] VT **1** (*inquire*): **to ask sb sth** domandare qc a qn, chiedere qc a qn; **to ask sb a question** fare una domanda a qn; **to ask sb the time** chiedere l'ora a qn; **don't ask me!** (*fam*) non domandarlo a me!, a me lo chiedi?; **"have you finished?" she asked** "hai finito?" chiese; **she asked him about his father** gli domandò (notizie) di suo padre **2** (*request*): **to ask sb for sth/sb to do sth** chiedere qc a qn/a qn di fare qc; **to ask sb a favour** chiedere un piacere *or* un favore a qn; **how much are they asking for it?** quanto chiedono per quello?; **that's asking a lot!** questo è pretendere un po' troppo! **3** (*invite*): **to ask sb to sth/to do sth** invitare qn a qc/a fare qc; **have you asked Matthew to the party?** hai invitato Matthew alla festa?; **to ask sb to dinner** invitare qn a cena ♦ VI (*inquire*) chiedere; (*request*) chiedere; **to ask about sth** informarsi su *or* di qc; **I asked about train times to Leeds** mi sono informato sugli orari dei treni per Leeds; **you should ask at the information desk** dovresti rivolgerti all'ufficio informazioni; **it's yours for the asking** non hai che da chiederlo ♦ N: **it's a big** *or* **tough ask!** (*fam*) è domandare molto!

▸ **ask after** VI + PREP chiedere di, domandare *or* chiedere (notizie) di, informarsi di

▸ **ask for** VI + PREP (*person*) chiedere di, cercare; (*help, information, money*) chiedere, domandare; **he asked for a cup of tea** ha chiesto una tazza di tè; **I asked him for help** gli ho chiesto aiuto *or* di aiutarmi; **it's just asking for trouble** è proprio (come) andarsele a cercare

▸ **ask out** VI + ADV: **to ask sb out** chiedere a qn di uscire; **Peter asked her out** Peter le ha chiesto di uscire con lui

askance [əˈskɑːns] ADV: **to look askance at sb/sth** guardare qn/qc storto *or* di traverso

askew [əˈskjuː] ADV di traverso, storto

ask·ing price [ˈɑːskɪŋˈpraɪs] N prezzo

asleep [əˈsliːp] ADJ addormentato(-a); **to be asleep** dormire; **he's asleep** dorme; **to be fast asleep** dormire profondamente; **to fall asleep** addormentarsi; **I fell asleep in front of the TV** mi sono addormentato davanti alla TV; **my foot's asleep** mi si è addormentato *or* intorpidito il piede

AS level [ˈeɪˌes ˌlevl] N *qualifica intermedia di istruzione secondaria, tra GCSE e A level*

asp [æsp] N (*poisonous snake*) aspide *m*; (*Zool*) cobra *m inv* egiziano

as·para·gus [əsˈpærəgəs] N (*plant*) asparago; (*food*) asparagi *mpl*

asparagus tips NPL punte *fpl* d'asparagi

ASPCA [ˌeɪˌesˌpiːsiːˈeɪ] N ABBR (= *American Society for the Prevention of Cruelty to Animals*) ≈ ENPA *m* (= *Ente Nazionale Protezione Animali*)

as·pect [ˈæspekt] N **1** (*of person, situation*) aspetto; **to study all aspects of a question** esaminare una questione sotto tutti gli aspetti **2** (*of building etc*) esposizione *f*; **a house with a northerly aspect** una casa esposta a nord

As·per·ger's syndrome [ˈæspɜːdʒəsˌsɪndrəʊm] N sindrome *f* di Asperger (*tipo di autismo*)

as·per·sion [əsˈpɜːʃən] N (*frm*) calunnia, maldicenza; **to cast aspersions on sth/sb** (*often hum*) diffamare qc/qn

as·phalt [ˈæsfælt] N asfalto

as·phyxi·ate [æsˈfɪksɪeɪt] VT, VI asfissiare

as·phyxia·tion [æsˌfɪksɪˈeɪʃən] N asfissia

as·pi·ra·tion [ˌæspəˈreɪʃən] N aspirazione *f*

as·pire [əsˈpaɪəʳ] VI: **to aspire to** aspirare a, ambire a

as·pi·rin [ˈæsprɪn] N aspirina

as·pir·ing [əsˈpaɪərɪŋ] ADJ aspirante

ass[1] [æs] N (*Zool*) asino, somaro; (*fig: fam*) scemo(-a); **to make an ass of o.s.** rendersi ridicolo(-a)

ass[2] [æs] N (*USA fam!*) culo (*fam!*)

as·sail [əˈseɪl] VT: **to assail (with)** assalire (di)

as·sail·ant [əˈseɪlənt] N assalitore(-trice)

as·sas·sin [əˈsæsɪn] N assassino(-a)

as·sas·si·nate [əˈsæsɪneɪt] VT assassinare

as·sas·si·na·tion [əˌsæsɪˈneɪʃən] N assassinio

as·sault [əˈsɔːlt] N: **assault (on)** (*Mil*) assalto (a); (*Law*) aggressione *f* (a); **assault and battery** (*Law*) minacce *fpl* e vie, *fpl* di fatto ♦ VT (*Mil*) assaltare, assalire; (*Law*) aggredire; **to assault sexually** compiere atti di libidine violenta contro

as·sem·ble [əˈsembl] VT (*objects, ideas*) radunare, raccogliere; (*people*) radunare, riunire; (*Tech*) montare, assemblare ♦ VI radunarsi, riunirsi

as·sem·bly [əˈsemblɪ] N (*meeting*) assemblea; (*of machine, furniture*) assemblaggio, montaggio; (*Comput*) assemblaggio; **right of assembly** libertà di riunione; **the Welsh Assembly** *organo legislativo autonomo gallese*; **school assembly** riunione *f* mattutina

assembly language N (*Comput*) linguaggio assemblativo

assembly line N catena di montaggio

as·sent [əˈsent] N benestare *m*, assenso, consenso; **by common assent** di comune accordo ♦ VI assentire; **to assent (to sth)** approvare (qc)

as·sert [əˈsɜːt] VT (*declare*) affermare, asserire; (*insist on: rights*) far valere; **to assert o.s.** farsi valere

as·ser·tion [əˈsɜːʃən] N affermazione *f*, asserzione *f*

as·ser·tive [əˈsɜːtɪv] ADJ che sa imporsi

as·sess [əˈses] VT (*gen*) valutare; (*property, tax*) accertare l'imponibile di; (*damages*) valutare; (*fig: situation*) giudicare

as·sess·ment [əˈsesmənt] N (*of value, damages*) valutazione *f*; (*of property, tax*) accertamento *m*; (*judgment*): **assessment (of)** giudizio (su)

as·ses·sor [əˈsesəʳ] N **1** (*Scol*) consulente esterno incaricato *della valutazione di un curriculum o della preparazione degli studenti* **2** (*of taxes*) ≈ perito dell'ufficio del catasto **3** (*Law*) perito

as·set [ˈæset] N (*useful quality*) bene *m*, qualità *f inv*, vantaggio; (*person*) elemento prezioso; **assets** NPL (*Fin: of individual*) beni *mpl*, disponibilità *fpl*; (*of company*) attivo *msg*, attività *fpl*; **to be an asset for** essere prezioso per; **the film's chief asset is its cast** il cast è il punto di forza del film

as·set-stripping [ˈæsɛtˌstrɪpɪŋ] N (*Comm*) *acquisto di una società in fallimento allo scopo di rivenderne le attività*

as·sid·u·ous [əˈsɪdjʊəs] ADJ assiduo(-a)

as·sign [əˈsaɪn] VT: **to assign (to)** (*allot: task, room, resources*) assegnare (a); (*reason, cause, meaning*) dare (a), attribuire (a); (*Law: property*) cedere (a), trasferire (a); (*appoint*): **to assign sb to** dare a qn l'incarico di; **to assign a date to sth** fissare la data di qc; **she assigned us homework to be done by Friday** ci ha assegnato i compiti da fare per venerdì

as·sign·ment [əˈsaɪnmənt] N (*task*) incarico; (*Scol*) compito; **we have to do three written assignments** dobbiamo fare tre compiti scritti

as·simi·late [əˈsɪmɪleɪt] VT assimilare

as·simi·la·tion [əˌsɪmɪˈleɪʃən] N assimilazione *f*

as·sist [əˈsɪst] VT: **to assist sb (to do** *or* **in doing sth)** aiutare qn (a fare qc), assistere qn (a *or* nel fare qc); **can I assist in any way?** posso aiutare in qualche modo?; **we assisted him to his car** lo abbiamo aiutato a raggiungere la sua macchina ♦ VI (*help*): **to assist in sth** aiutare in qc, essere di aiuto in qc

as·sis·tance [əˈsɪstəns] N aiuto, assistenza; **can I be of any assistance?** posso esserle utile (in qualcosa)?; (*in shop*) desidera?; **to come to sb's assistance** venire in aiuto a qn

as·sis·tant [əˈsɪstənt] N aiutante *m/f*, assistente *m/f*; (*Brit: also:* **shop assistant**) commesso(-a) ♦ ADJ aiuto *inv*

assistant manager N vicedirettore(-trice)

as·sizes [əˈsaɪzɪz] NPL assise *fpl*

as·so·ci·ate [*vb* əˈsəʊʃɪeɪt, *n, adj* əˈsəʊʃɪt] VT associare, collegare; **to associate o.s. with** associarsi a, unirsi a; **I don't wish to be associated with it** non voglio che si pensi che io abbia a che fare con la cosa ♦ VI: **to associate with sb** frequentare qn ♦ N (*colleague*) collega *m/f*, socio(-a); (*accomplice*) complice *m/f*; (*member: of club*) socio(-a) aggregato(-a); (: *of learned society*) membro aggregato ♦ ADJ (*company*) consociato(-a); (*member*) aggregato(-a), aggiunto(-a)

as·so·ci·at·ed com·pa·ny [əˈsəʊsɪeɪtɪdˈkʌmpənɪ] N (*Comm*) consociata

associate director N amministratore(-trice) *m* aggiunto(-a)

as·so·ci·a·tion [əˌsəʊsɪˈeɪʃən] N (*most senses*) associazione *f*; **his association with her family** i suoi legami con la famiglia di lei; **in association with** in collaborazione con; **full of historic associations** ricco(-a) di reminiscenze storiche; **the name has unpleasant associations** il nome ha delle connotazioni negative

association football N (*Brit: frm*) (gioco del) calcio

as·sort·ed [əˈsɔːtɪd] ADJ assortito(-a); **in assorted sizes** in diverse taglie; **ill-/well-assorted** (*matched*) mal/ben assortito(-a)

as·sort·ment [əˈsɔːtmənt] N (*Comm: mixture*) assortimento; **there was a strange assortment of guests** c'era uno strano miscuglio di invitati

Asst. ABBR = **assistant**

as·suage [əˈsweɪdʒ] VT (*frm: feelings, pain*) attenuare, alleviare; (: *appetite*) placare

as·sume [əˈsjuːm] VT 1 (*suppose*) supporre, presumere, presupporre; **I assume so** suppongo di sì; **assuming that ...** supponendo che...; **I assumed he was coming** ho dato per scontato che venisse 2 (*power, control, attitude*) assumere, prendere; **to assume responsibility for** assumersi la responsabilità di

as·sumed name [əˈsjuːmdˈneɪm] N nome *m* falso; **under an assumed name** sotto falso nome

as·sump·tion [əˈsʌmpʃən] N 1 (*supposition*) supposizione *f*, ipotesi *f inv*; **on the assumption that** partendo dal presupposto che; **to work on the assumption that** partire dal presupposto che 2 **the Assumption** (*Rel*) l'Assunzione *f*

as·sur·ance [əˈʃʊərəns] N 1 (*guarantee*) assicurazione *f*, garanzia; **I can give you no assurances** non posso assicurarle *or* garantirle niente 2 (*confidence*) sicurezza, convinzione *f*; (*self-confidence*) fiducia in se stesso(-a), sicurezza di sé; **she spoke with assurance** ha parlato con convinzione 3 (*Brit*): **life assurance** assicurazione *f* sulla vita

as·sure [əˈʃʊəʳ] VT (*reassure*): **to assure sb (of sth)** assicurare qn (di qc); **I assured him of my support** gli ho assicurato il

mio appoggio; **he assured me he was coming** mi ha assicurato che sarebbe venuto

as·sured [əˈʃʊəd] ADJ (*confident*) sicuro(-a); (*certain: promotion*) assicurato(-a); **success was assured** il successo era garantito *or* assicurato

AST [ˌeɪesˈtiː] ABBR (*USA*: = *Atlantic Standard Time*) ora invernale nel fuso orario di New York

as·ter·isk [ˈæstərɪsk] N asterisco

astern [əˈstɜːn] ADV a poppa

as·ter·oid [ˈæstərɔɪd] N asteroide *m*

asth·ma [ˈæsmə] N asma

asth·mat·ic [æsˈmætɪk] ADJ, N asmatico(-a)

astig·ma·tism [æsˈtɪgmətɪzəm] N astigmatismo

astir [əˈstɜːʳ] ADJ (*out of bed*) in piedi; (*on the move*) in movimento

aston·ish [əˈstɒnɪʃ] VT stupire, meravigliare; **you astonish me!** ma chi l'avrebbe mai detto!; **I was astonished to learn that ...** fui sorpreso nell'apprendere che...

a·ston·ished [əˈstɒnɪʃt] ADJ stupito(-a), (stupita) sorpreso(-a), (sorpresa); **to be astonished (at)** essere stupito(-a), (stupita) (da)

aston·ish·ing [əˈstɒnɪʃɪŋ] ADJ sorprendente, stupefacente; **I find it astonishing that ...** mi stupisce che...

aston·ish·ing·ly [əˈstɒnɪʃɪŋlɪ] ADV straordinariamente, incredibilmente

aston·ish·ment [əˈstɒnɪʃmənt] N stupore *m*, meraviglia; **in astonishment** in modo attonito; **she gave me a look of astonishment** mi ha lanciato uno sguardo stupito; **to my astonishment** con mia gran meraviglia, con mio grande stupore

astound [əˈstaʊnd] VT sbalordire; **he was astounded to hear ...** è rimasto stupefatto *or* allibito nel sentire...

astray [əˈstreɪ] ADV: **to go astray** perdere la strada, smarrirsi, perdersi; (*morally*) mettersi su una cattiva strada, traviarsi; **to go astray in one's calculations** sbagliare i calcoli; **to lead sb astray** portare qn su una cattiva strada

astride [əˈstraɪd] PREP (*fence*) a cavalcioni di; (*animal*) a cavallo di; (*horse*) in sella a ♦ ADV a cavalcioni

as·trin·gent [əˈstrɪndʒənt] ADJ, N astringente *m*

as·trolo·ger [əˈstrɒlədʒəʳ] N astrologo(-a)

as·trol·ogy [əˈstrɒlədʒɪ] N astrologia

as·tro·naut [ˈæstrənɔːt] N astronauta *m/f*

as·trono·mer [əˈstrɒnəməʳ] N astronomo(-a)

as·tro·nomi·cal [ˌæstrəˈnɒmɪkəl] ADJ (*also fig*) astronomico(-a)

as·trono·my [əˈstrɒnəmɪ] N astronomia

as·tro·phys·ics [ˈæstrəʊˈfɪzɪks] NSG astrofisica

as·tute [əˈstjuːt] ADJ (*shrewd*) accorto(-a)

asun·der [əˈsʌndəʳ] ADV (*liter*): **to tear asunder** strappare

ASV [ˌeɪesˈviː] N ABBR (= *American Standard Version*) traduzione americana della Bibbia

asy·lum [əˈsaɪləm] N 1 (*refuge*) asilo, rifugio; **to seek political asylum** chiedere asilo politico; **seven per cent of asylum seekers** il sette per cent di chi chiede asilo politico 2 (*also:* **lunatic asylum** *pej*) manicomio (*pegg*)

asym·met·rical [ˌeɪsɪˈmetrɪkəl], **asym·met·ric** [ˌeɪsɪˈmetrɪk] ADJ asimmetrico(-a)

KEYWORD

at [æt] PREP

1 (*position*) a; (*direction*) verso; **to aim at the target** mirare al bersaglio; **at the bottom of the page** a fondo pagina; **at the desk** al banco; **to stand at the door** stare sulla porta; **at home** a casa; **at John's** da John, a casa di John; **at the office** in ufficio; **to look at sth** guardare qc; **at school** a scuola; **at the top** in cima

2 (*time*) **at Christmas** a *or* per Natale; **at night** di notte; **at 4 o'clock** alle quattro; **at a time like this** in un momento come questo; **at times** talvolta

3 (*rate*) a; **at 50p each** a 50 pence l'uno(-a); **two at a time** due alla *or* per volta

4 (*activity*): **to be good at sth** riuscire bene in qc, essere bravo(-a) in qc *or* a fare qc; **while you're at it** (*fam*) già che ci sei; **she's at it again** (*fam*) eccola che ricomincia, ci risiamo; **he's always (on) at me** (*fam*) mi tormenta continuamente; **to be at work** essere al lavoro, stare lavorando

5 (*manner*): **at 50 km/h** a 50 km/h; **at peace** in pace; **at a run** di corsa, correndo; **at full speed** a tutta velocità
6 (*cause*): **annoyed at** seccato(-a) per; **I was shocked at the news** sono rimasto colpito dalla notizia; **at his suggestion** dietro suo consiglio; **he was surprised at her reaction** lo stupì la sua reazione

ate [ɛt, ɛɪt] PT of **eat**

athe·ism ['eɪθɪɪzəm] N ateismo

athe·ist ['eɪθɪɪst] N ateo(-a); **to be an atheist** essere ateo(-a)

Athe·nian [ə'θiːnɪən] ADJ, N ateniese m/f

Ath·ens ['æθɪnz] N Atene f

ath·lete ['æθliːt] N atleta m/f

ath·let·ic [æθ'lɛtɪk] ADJ (*meeting etc*) di atletica, atletico(-a); (*person: muscular*) atletico(-a); (: *sporty*) sportivo(-a)

ath·let·ics [æθ'lɛtɪks] NSG atletica

At·lan·tic [ət'læntɪk] ADJ dell'Atlantico, atlantico(-a) ◆ N: **the Atlantic (Ocean)** l'(Oceano) Atlantico

at·las ['ætləs] N atlante m; **road atlas** carta stradale

Atlas Mountains NPL: **the Atlas Mountains** i Monti dell'-Atlante

ATM [ˌeɪtiːˈɛm] N ABBR (= *automated teller machine*) sportello automatico, Bancomat m inv

at·mos·phere ['ætməsˌfɪəʳ] N (*Geog, also fig*) atmosfera; (*air*) aria

at·mos·pher·ic [ˌætməsˈfɛrɪk] ADJ atmosferico(-a); (*music*) che crea un'atmosfera; (*film*) pieno(-a) di atmosfera

at·mos·pher·ics [ˌætməsˈfɛrɪks] NPL (*Radio*) scariche fpl elettriche

at·oll ['ætɒl] N atollo

atom ['ætəm] N atomo; (*fig*): **not an atom of truth** nemmeno un pizzico di verità

atom·ic [ə'tɒmɪk] ADJ atomico(-a)

atomic bomb, atom bomb N bomba atomica

at·om·iz·er ['ætəˌmaɪzəʳ] N atomizzatore m

atone [ə'təʊn] VI: **to atone for** (*frm: crime, sins*) espiare; (: *mistake, rudeness*) riparare a

atone·ment [ə'təʊnmənt] N (*frm*) espiazione f; (*Rel*) redenzione f; **to make atonement for a mistake** riparare ad un errore

ATP [ˌeɪtiːˈpiː] N ABBR (= *adenosine triphosphate*) ATP m

atro·cious [ə'trəʊʃəs] ADJ atroce, pessimo(-a)

atroc·ity [ə'trɒsɪtɪ] N atrocità f inv

at·ro·phy ['ætrəfɪ](*Med, fig*) N atrofia ◆ VT atrofizzare ◆ VI atrofizzarsi

attach [ə'tætʃ] **to attach (to)** VT **1** (*fasten, stick*) attaccare (a); (*tie*) legare (a); (*join*) annettere (a), attaccare (a); (*document, letter*) allegare (a); **please find attached ...** allego...; **the attached letter** la lettera acclusa or allegata; **they attached a rope to the car** hanno attaccato una corda alla macchina; **he attached himself to us** si è appiccicato a noi **2** (*Comput*) allegare **3** (*attribute: importance, value*) attribuire (a), dare (a) **4** (*assign: troops, employee*) assegnare (a) **5** (*Law: person*) trarre in arresto; (: *property*) sequestrare

at·ta·ché [ə'tæʃeɪ] N addetto (di ambasciata), attaché m inv; **cultural attaché** addetto culturale

attaché case N valigetta f portadocumenti, inv, valigetta (diplomatica)

attachment [ə'tætʃmənt] N **1** (*device*) accessorio **2** (*Comput*) allegato **3** (*affection*): **attachment (to)** attaccamento (a), affetto (per)

at·tack [ə'tæk] N **1** (*Mil, also fig*) attacco; (*on individual*) aggressione f; **a savage attack** una feroce aggressione; **surprise attack** attacco a sorpresa; **attack on sb's life** attentato alla vita di qn; **to be under attack (from)** essere attaccato(-a) (da); **to launch an attack (on)** (*Mil, Sport, fig*) sferrare un attacco (a) **2** (*Med*) attacco, accesso ◆ VT (*Mil, Med, fig*) attaccare; (*person*) aggredire, assalire; (*tackle: job, problem*) affrontare

at·tack·er [ə'tækəʳ] N aggressore m, assalitore(-trice)

at·tain [ə'teɪn] VT (*ambition*) realizzare; (*age, rank, happiness*) raggiungere, arrivare a

at·tain·ment [ə'teɪnmənt](*frm*) N (*of ambition*) realizzazione f; (*of position, happiness*) raggiungimento; (*achievement*) risultato ottenuto; **attainments** (*accomplishments*) cognizioni fpl (acquisite)

at·tempt [ə'tɛmpt] N (*try*) tentativo; **after several attempts** dopo diversi tentativi; **he made no attempt to help** non ha (neanche) tentato or cercato di aiutare; **to make an attempt on sb's life** attentare alla vita di qn ◆ VT: **to attempt sth/ to do sth** tentare qc/di fare qc; **he attempted the exam** ha tentato l'esame; **I attempted to write a song** ho tentato di scrivere una canzone; **attempted murder** (*Law*) tentato omicidio

at·tend [ə'tɛnd] VT **1** (*be present at: meeting etc*) andare a, assistere a, essere presente a; (*regularly: school, church*) frequentare; (: *course, classes*) seguire, frequentare; **the lecture was well attended** c'era molta gente alla conferenza **2** (*subj: bridesmaid, lady-in-waiting*) accompagnare; (: *doctor*) avere in cura, curare, assistere ◆ VI (*be present*) essere presente, esserci; (*pay attention to*) prestare attenzione, stare attento(-a)
  ▸ **attend to** VI + PREP (*needs, affairs*) prendersi cura di; (*customer, work*) occuparsi di; **are you being attended to?** (*in shop*) la stanno servendo?

at·tend·ance [ə'tɛndəns] N (*act*): **attendance (at)** presenza (a) (*regular*) frequenza (a); (*those present*) persone fpl presenti; **what was the attendance like at the meeting?** quanti erano i presenti alla riunione?; **there was a doctor in attendance on the queen** c'era un dottore al servizio della regina

at·tend·ant [ə'tɛndənt] N (*in car park, museum*) custode m/f; (*servant*) attendente m/f, persona di servizio ◆ ADJ (*frm*) concomitante

at·ten·tion [ə'tɛnʃən] N **1** attenzione f; **to call sb's attention to sth** richiamare qc all'attenzione di qn; **it has come to my attention that ...** sono venuto a conoscenza (del fatto) che...; **to pay attention (to)** stare attento(-a) (a), fare attenzione (a); **for the attention of** (*Admin*) all'attenzione di **2** (*Mil*): **attention!** attenti!; **to come to/stand at attention** mettersi/stare sull'attenti **3 attentions** NPL (*kindnesses*) attenzioni fpl, premure fpl

attention deficit disorder N (*Med*) disturbo dell'attenzione

attention deficit hyper·ac·tiv·ity disorder [-ˌhaɪpəˈræktɪvɪtɪ-] N (*Med*) disturbo dell'attenzione con iperattività

at·ten·tive [ə'tɛntɪv] ADJ (*audience*) attento(-a); (*escort*) premuroso(-a), sollecito(-a)

at·ten·tive·ly [ə'tɛntɪvlɪ] ADV attentamente

at·tenu·ate [ə'tɛnjʊeɪt](*frm*) VT ridurre, attenuare ◆ VI attenuarsi

at·test [ə'tɛst](*frm*) VT attestare; (*signature*) autenticare ◆ VI: **to attest to** testimoniare, attestare

at·tic ['ætɪk] N soffitta, solaio; (*room*) mansarda

at·tire [ə'taɪəʳ](*frm*) N tenuta, abbigliamento ◆ VT: **to attire (in)** abbigliare (con)
  ❏ **attire** is not translated by the Italian word *attirare*

at·ti·tude ['ætɪtjuːd] N (*view*) atteggiamento; (*posture*) posa; (*opinion*): **attitude (towards)** punto di vista (nei confronti di); **attitude of mind** modo di pensare; **if that's your attitude** se la prendi così
  ❏ **attitude** is not translated by the Italian word *attitudine*

at·tor·ney [ə'tɜːnɪ] N (*USA: lawyer*) avvocato; (*representative*) procuratore m; (*having proxy*) mandatario; **power of attorney** procura

Attorney General N (*Brit*) Procuratore m Generale; (*USA*) ≈ Ministro della Giustizia

at·tract [ə'trækt] VT (*subj: magnet*) attirare, attrarre; (*fig: interest, attention etc*) attirare, suscitare; **the Lake District attracts lots of tourists** la Regione dei Laghi attira molti turisti

at·trac·tion [ə'trækʃən] N attrazione f, fascino; (*pleasant feature*) attrattiva; **city life has no attraction for me** la vita di città non mi attira affatto; **one of the attractions was a free car** uno dei vantaggi era quello di una macchina gratis

at·trac·tive [ə'træktɪv] ADJ (*person, dress, place*) attraente, affascinante; (*idea, offer, price*) allettante, interessante

at·trib·ute [n 'ætrɪbjuːt, vb ə'trɪbjuːt] N attributo ◆ VT: **to attribute sth to** attribuire qc a

at·tri·tion [ə'trɪʃən] N usura (per attrito); **war of attrition** guerra di logoramento

Atty. Gen. ABBR = Attorney General

atypi·cal [eɪ'tɪpɪkəl] ADJ atipico(-a)

auber·gine ['əʊbəʒiːn] N (esp Brit) melanzana

auburn ['ɔːbən] ADJ (hair) ramato(-a), color rame inv

auc·tion ['ɔːkʃən] N (also: **sale by auction**) asta ♦ VT (also: **to sell by auction**) vendere all'asta; (also: **to put up for auction**) mettere all'asta

auc·tion·eer [ˌɔːkʃə'nɪəʳ] N banditore(-trice)

auction room N sala dell'asta

auda·cious [ɔː'deɪʃəs] ADJ (bold) audace; (impudent) sfrontato(-a)

audac·ity [ɔː'dæsɪtɪ] N (boldness) audacia; (impudence) sfacciataggine f, sfrontatezza

audible ['ɔːdɪbl] ADJ udibile, percettibile; **there was an audible sigh** si è chiaramente sentito un sospiro; **he was hardly audible** si riusciva a malapena a sentirlo

audi·ence ['ɔːdɪəns] N 1 (gathering) pubblico; (Radio) ascoltatori mpl; (TV) telespettatori mpl; (of speaker) uditorio; **a huge audience** un grandissimo pubblico; **there was a big audience at the theatre** c'erano molti spettatori or c'era un gran pubblico al teatro; **the concerts attracted huge audiences** i concerti hanno attirato tantissima gente 2 (formal interview) udienza; **an audience with the Queen** un'udienza con la Regina

audio-typist ['ɔːdɪəʊˌtaɪpɪst] N dattilografo(-a) che trascrive da nastro

audio-visual [ˌɔːdɪəʊ'vɪzjʊəl] ADJ audiovisivo(-a); **audiovisual aids** sussidi mpl audiovisivi

audit ['ɔːdɪt] N revisione f dei conti, verifica (ufficiale) dei conti ♦ VT (accounts) rivedere, verificare
❑ *audit* is not translated by the Italian word *udito*

audi·tion [ɔː'dɪʃən] N (Theatre) audizione f; (Cine) provino ♦ VT fare un'audizione (or un provino) a ♦ VI fare un'audizione (or un provino)

audi·tor ['ɔːdɪtəʳ] N revisore m dei conti

audi·to·rium [ˌɔːdɪ'tɔːrɪəm] N sala, auditorio

Aug. ABBR (= August) ago., ag. (= agosto)

aug·ment [ɔːɡ'mɛnt] VT, VI (frm) aumentare

augur ['ɔːɡəʳ] VI, VT (frm): **to augur well/ill** essere di buon/cattivo augurio or auspicio

August ['ɔːɡəst] N agosto; see July

august [ɔː'ɡʌst] ADJ (frm) augusto(-a)

aunt [ɑːnt] N zia; **my aunt and uncle** i miei zii, mia zia e mio zio

auntie, aunty ['ɑːntɪ] N (fam) zietta; **auntie Jane** zia Jane

au pair ['əʊ'pɛəʳ] N ragazza f alla pari, inv

aura ['ɔːrə] N aura

aus·pices ['ɔːspɪsɪz] NPL: **under the auspices of** sotto gli auspici di

aus·pi·cious [ɔːs'pɪʃəs] (frm) ADJ (sign) di buon augurio or auspicio; (occasion) propizio(-a), favorevole; **to make an auspicious start** iniziare sotto buoni auspici

aus·tere [ɒs'tɪəʳ] ADJ austero(-a)

aus·ter·ity [ɒs'tɛrɪtɪ] N austerità f inv

Aus·tral·asia [ˌɒstrə'leɪzɪə] N l'Australasia

Aus·tralia [ɒs'treɪlɪə] N l'Australia

Aus·tral·ian [ɒs'treɪlɪən] ADJ, N australiano(-a)

Aus·tria ['ɒstrɪə] N l'Austria

Aus·trian ['ɒstrɪən] ADJ, N austriaco(-a)

authen·tic [ɔː'θɛntɪk] ADJ autentico(-a)

authen·ti·cate [ɔː'θɛntɪkeɪt] VT (signature, document) autenticare; (statement, information) verificare, stabilire la veridicità di

au·then·tic·ity [ˌɔːθɛn'tɪsɪtɪ] N autenticità

author ['ɔːθəʳ] N autore(-trice)

authori·tar·ian [ˌɔːθɔrɪ'tɛərɪən] ADJ autoritario(-a)

authori·ta·tive [ɔː'θɔrɪtətɪv] ADJ (account, judgement) autorevole; (manner) autoritario(-a)

author·ity [ɔː'θɔrɪtɪ] N 1 (power) autorità f; (permission) autorizzazione f; **those in authority** i dirigenti, i governanti; **to be in authority over** dare gli ordini a; **to have authority to do sth** avere l'autorizzazione a fare or il diritto di fare

qc 2 **the authorities** NPL (government, council) le autorità; **the health authorities** l'autorità sg sanitaria 3 (expert): **he's an authority (on)** è un'autorità (in materia di); **I have it on good authority that ...** so da fonte sicura or autorevole che...

authori·za·tion [ˌɔːθəraɪ'zeɪʃən] N autorizzazione f

author·ize ['ɔːθəraɪz] VT: **to authorize sth/sb (to do sth)** autorizzare qc/qn (a fare qc)

author·ized capi·tal ['ɔːθəˌraɪzd'kæpɪtl] N (Fin) capitale m nominale

author·ship ['ɔːθəʃɪp] N paternità (letteraria etc)

autism ['ɔːtɪzm] N autismo

autis·tic [ɔː'tɪstɪk] ADJ autistico(-a)

auto ['ɔːtəʊ] N (USA) auto f inv

auto·bi·og·ra·phy [ˌɔːtəʊbaɪ'ɒɡrəfɪ] N autobiografia

auto·crat·ic [ˌɔːtəʊ'krætɪk] ADJ autocratico(-a)

auto·graph ['ɔːtəɡrɑːf] N autografo ♦ VT firmare

auto·im·mune [ˌɔːtəʊɪ'mjuːn] ADJ autoimmune

auto·mat ['ɔːtəˌmæt] N (vending machine) distributore m automatico; (USA: room) tavola calda fornita esclusivamente di distributori automatici

auto·mat·ed ['ɔːtəˌmeɪtɪd] ADJ automatizzato(-a)

auto·mat·ic [ˌɔːtə'mætɪk] ADJ automatico(-a) ♦ N (pistol) (pistola) automatica; (car) automobile f con cambio automatico; (washing machine) lavatrice f automatica

automatic data processing N elaborazione f automatica dei dati

auto·mat·i·cal·ly [ˌɔːtə'mætɪkəlɪ] ADV automaticamente

auto·ma·tion [ˌɔːtə'meɪʃən] N automazione f

automa·ton [ɔː'tɒmətən] N (pl **automatons** or **automata** [ɔː'tɒmətə]) automa m

auto·mo·bile ['ɔːtəmə,biːl] N (USA) automobile f

autono·mous [ɔː'tɒnəməs] ADJ autonomo(-a)

autono·my [ɔː'tɒnəmɪ] N autonomia

autop·sy ['ɔːtɒpsɪ] N autopsia

autumn ['ɔːtəm] N autunno; **in autumn** in autunno; **last autumn** lo scorso autunno ♦ ADJ autunnale

aux·ilia·ry [ɔːɡ'zɪlɪərɪ] ADJ ausiliario(-a); (Gram) ausiliare ♦ N (assistant) assistente m/f, aiuto; (verb) ausiliare m; **auxiliaries** NPL (Mil) truppe fpl ausiliarie

AV [ˌeɪ'viː] ABBR = audiovisual

Av., Ave. ABBR = Avenue

avail [ə'veɪl] N: **of no avail** inutile; **to no avail** invano, inutilmente ♦ VT: **to avail o.s. of** (opportunity) servirsi di, approfittare or approfittarsi di; (rights) (av)valersi di

avail·abil·ity [əveɪlə'bɪlɪtɪ] N disponibilità

avail·able [ə'veɪləbl] ADJ disponibile; **the amount of money available** la cifra disponibile; **to make sth available to sb** mettere qc a disposizione di qn; **is the manager available?** è libero il direttore?; **every available means** tutti i mezzi disponibili

ava·lanche ['ævəlɑːnʃ] N valanga

avant-garde ['ævɒŋ'ɡɑːd] N avanguardia ♦ ADJ d'avanguardia

ava·rice ['ævərɪs] N avarizia

ava·ri·cious [ˌævə'rɪʃəs] ADJ avaro(-a)

avdp. ABBR of avoirdupois

Ave. ABBR = Avenue

avenge [ə'vɛndʒ] VT vendicare; **to avenge o.s. (on sb)** vendicarsi (di qn)

av·enue ['ævənjuː] N viale m; (fig) strada, via

av·er·age ['ævərɪdʒ] ADJ medio(-a); (pej) qualsiasi inv, ordinario(-a); **the average price** il prezzo medio ♦ N media; **on average** in media; **above/below (the) average** sopra/sotto la media ♦ VT fare una media di
  ▸ **average out** VT (set of numbers) fare or calcolare la media fra
  ▸ **average out at** VI (reach an average of) aggirarsi in media su, essere in media di

averse [ə'vɜːs] ADJ: **averse to** (opposed) contrario(-a) a; (disinclined) restio(-a) a; **to be averse to sth/doing sth** essere contrario(-a) a qc/a fare qc; **I'm not averse to an occasional drink** non mi dispiace bere un bicchierino ogni tanto; **I wouldn't be averse to the idea** non avrei nulla in contrario all'idea

aver·sion [ə'vɜːʃən] N (*dislike*): **aversion (for** *or* **to)** avversione *f* (per); **spiders are his aversion** ha la fobia dei ragni; **my pet aversion** ciò che detesto di più; **to have an aversion to sb/sth** avere *or* nutrire un'avversione nei confronti di qn/qc

avert [ə'vɜːt] VT (*prevent: accident, danger*) evitare; (*turn away: eyes, thoughts*): **to avert (from)** distogliere (da), allontanare (da)

avian flu ['eɪvɪən-] N influenza aviaria

aviary ['eɪvɪərɪ] N voliera, uccelliera

avia·tion [ˌeɪvɪ'eɪʃən] N aviazione *f*

avid ['ævɪd] ADJ: **avid (for)** desideroso(-a) (di), avido(-a) (di); **an avid reader** un(a) accanito(-a) *or* appassionato(-a) lettore(-trice)

av·id·ly ['ævɪdlɪ] ADV avidamente

avo·ca·do [ˌævə'kɑːdəʊ] N (*Brit: also:* **avocado pear**) avocado *m inv*

avoid [ə'vɔɪd] VT (*obstacle*) scansare, schivare, evitare; (*argument etc*) (*danger*) sfuggire a; **to avoid doing sth** evitare di fare qc; **avoid going out on your own at night** evita di uscire da sola di sera; **try to avoid being seen** cerca di non farti vedere; **are you trying to avoid me?** stai cercando di evitarmi?

avoid·able [ə'vɔɪdəbl] ADJ evitabile

avoid·ance [ə'vɔɪdəns] N: **his avoidance of his duty** la sua mancanza al dovere

avowed [ə'vaʊd] ADJ dichiarato(-a)

await [ə'weɪt] VT aspettare, attendere; **long awaited** tanto atteso(-a); **awaiting attention** (*Comm: letter*) in attesa di risposta; (: *order*) in attesa di essere evaso(-a)

awake [ə'weɪk] ADJ sveglio(-a); **to be awake** essere sveglio(-a); **to lie awake** rimanere sveglio(-a) a letto; **coffee keeps me awake** il caffè mi fa star sveglio; **to be awake to** (*fig*) essere cosciente *or* conscio(-a) *or* consapevole di ♦ VT (*pt,* **awoke** *or* **awaked** *pp* **awoken** *or* **awaked**) svegliare; (*fig: emotions, memories*) risvegliare, ridestare; (: *suspicions*) destare ♦ VI svegliarsi; **to awake to sth** (*fig*) rendersi conto di qc, aprire gli occhi su qc

awak·en·ing [ə'weɪknɪŋ] N risveglio

award [ə'wɔːd] N (*prize*) premio; (*scholarship*) borsa di studio; (*Law: decision*) sentenza arbitrale, decreto; (: *sum*) ricompensa, risarcimento ♦ VT: **to award sb sth** *or* **to award sth to sb** (*prize*) assegnare qc a qn; (*medal*) conferire qc a qn, concedere; **to award sb damages** a qn il risarcimento dei danni

aware [ə'weə'] ADJ: **to be aware of** (*conscious*) rendersi conto di; (*informed*) essere al corrente di, essere conscio(-a) di; **to become aware of** accorgersi di; **not that I am aware of** non che io sappia; **I am fully aware that** mi rendo perfettamente conto che; **to make sb aware of sth** rendere qn consapevole di qc; **to be politically/socially aware** aver coscienza politica/sociale

aware·ness [ə'weənɪs] N (*consciousness*) coscienza; (*knowledge*) consapevolezza; **to develop people's awareness (of)** sensibilizzare la gente (su)

awash [ə'wɒʃ] ADJ: **awash (with)** inondato(-a) (da)

away [ə'weɪ] ADV **1** lontano; **away from** lontano da; **far away from home** molto lontano da casa; **the village is 3 miles away** il paese è a 3 miglia di distanza *or* è lontano 3 miglia; **two hours away by car** a due ore di distanza in macchina; **away in the distance** in lontananza; **the holiday was two weeks away** mancavano due settimane alle vacanze **2** (*absent*): **to be away** essere via; **Jason was away on a business trip** Jason era via per lavoro; **he's away in Milan** è (andato) a Milano; **he's away for a week** è andato via per una settimana; **go away!** vai via (di qui)!, via di qui!, vattene!; **to take away**

portare via **3 to turn away** girarsi, voltarsi; **to die away** (*sound*) spegnersi in lontananza; **the snow melted away** la neve si è completamente sciolta; **to play away** (*Sport*) giocare in trasferta *or* fuori casa; **to talk away** parlare in continuazione; **to work away** continuare a lavorare; **he was still working away in the library** stava ancora lavorando in biblioteca

away game, away match N (*Sport*) partita fuori casa *or* in trasferta

awe [ɔː] N timore *m* reverenziale; **to stand in awe of** aver soggezione di ♦ VT intimidire

awe-inspiring ['ɔːɪnˌspaɪərɪŋ], **awe·some** ['ɔːsəm] ADJ imponente

awe-struck ['ɔːstrʌk] ADJ sgomento(-a)

aw·ful ['ɔːfəl] ADJ terribile, orribile; **the weather's awful** il tempo è orribile; **I feel awful** mi sento malissimo; **an awful lot of** (*people, cars, dogs*) un numero incredibile di; (*jam, flowers*) una quantità incredibile di; **how awful!** che orrore!

aw·ful·ly ['ɔːflɪ] ADV (*very*) terribilmente; **thanks awfully** mille grazie; **I'm awfully sorry** sono terribilmente spiacente

awhile [ə'waɪl] ADV (per) un po'

awk·ward ['ɔːkwəd] ADJ **1** (*difficult: problem, question, situation, task*) delicato(-a), difficile; (*silence*) imbarazzante; (*Aut: corner*) brutto(-a); (*inconvenient*) scomodo(-a); (*time, moment*) poco opportuno(-a); (*tool*) poco maneggevole, scomodo(-a); (*shape*) difficile; **you've caught me at an awkward time** mi hai pescato in un momento poco opportuno; **Friday is awkward for me** venerdì mi riesce scomodo; **he's an awkward customer** è un tipo difficile **2** (*clumsy: person*) goffo(-a); (: *gesture, movement*) impacciato(-a); (: *style, phrasing*) contorto(-a); **the awkward age** l'età difficile

awk·ward·ness ['ɔːkwədnɪs] N (*of situation, problem*) difficoltà, delicatezza; (*of arrangement*) scomodità; (*of silence*) imbarazzo; (*of movement, behaviour*) goffaggine *f*; **the awkwardness of his prose style** lo stile contorto della sua prosa

awl [ɔːl] N punteruolo

awn·ing ['ɔːnɪŋ] N (*of shop, hotel etc*) tenda, tendone *m*; (*of tent*) veranda

awoke [ə'wəʊk] PT *of* **awake**

awok·en [ə'wəʊkən] PP *of* **awake**

AWOL ['eɪwɒl] ADJ ABBR (*Mil.: = absent without leave*) *see* **absent**

awry [ə'raɪ] ADV di traverso ♦ ADJ storto(-a); **to go awry** andare a monte

axe, ax (*USA*) [æks] N ascia, scure *f*; **to have an axe to grind** (*fig*) fare i propri interessi *or* il proprio tornaconto ♦ VT (*fig : expenditure*) ridurre drasticamente; (: *person*) liquidare (*per ragioni economiche*); (: *project etc*) annullare; (: *jobs*) sopprimere

axi·om ['æksɪəm] N assioma *m*

axio·mat·ic [ˌæksɪəʊ'mætɪk] ADJ assiomatico(-a)

axis ['æksɪs] N (*pl* **axes** ['æksiːz]) (*Geom: of the Earth*) asse *m*

axle ['æksl] N (*of wheel*) semiasse *m*; (*also:* **axletree**) asse *m*

aye, ay [aɪ] EXCL (*esp Scot: yes*) sì ♦ N voto favorevole

AZ ABBR (*USA Post* = Arizona)

azalea [ə'zeɪlɪə] N azalea

Azer·bai·jan [ˌæzəbaɪ'dʒɑːn] N Azerbaigian *m*

Azer·bai·ja·ni [ˌæzəbaɪ'dʒɑːnɪ], **Aze·ri** [ə'zeərɪ] ADJ azerbaigiano(-a) ♦ N azerbaigiano(-a), azero(-a); (*language*) azerbaigiano

Azores [ə'zɔːz] NPL: **the Azores** le Azzorre

AZT [ˌeɪzed'tiː] N ABBR (*= azidothymidine*) AZT *m*

Az·tec ['æztek] ADJ azteco(-a) ♦ N (*person*) azteco(-a); (*language*) azteco

az·ure ['eɪʒə'] ADJ azzurro(-a) ♦ N azzurro

Bb

B, b [biː] N **1** (*letter*) B, b *f inv*, *m inv* **2** (*Mus*) si *m* **3** (*Scol: mark*) ≈ 8 (*buono*); **B for Benjamin**, (*USA*) **B for Baker** ≈ B come Bologna

b. ABBR = **born**

BA [ˌbiːˈeɪ] N ABBR (= *Bachelor of Arts*) laurea in discipline umanistiche; **she's got a BA in History** ha una laurea in storia

bab·ble [ˈbæbl] N (*of voices*) mormorio; (*of baby*) balbettio; (*of stream*) gorgoglio; (*foolish*) ciance *fpl* ♦ VI (*indistinctly*) farfugliare; (*chatter*) cianciare; (*baby*) balbettare; (*stream*) gorgogliare

babe [beɪb] N (*old*) bimbo(-a), bebè *m inv*; (*esp USA: fam: endearment*) piccolo(-a), tesoro; **babe in arms** bimbo(-a) in fasce; (*fig*) ingenuo(-a)

ba·boon [bəˈbuːn] N babbuino

baby [ˈbeɪbɪ] N (*human*) bambino(-a), bimbo(-a); (*of animal*) piccolo; (*fam: as address: to woman*) piccola, bimba mia; (*: to man*) piccolo, bello; **a baby girl** una bambina piccola; **the baby of the family** il (la) piccolino(-a) di casa; **don't be such a baby!** non fare il bambino!; **to throw the baby out with the bathwater** (*fig*) buttar via il bambino con l'acqua sporca; **the new system was his baby** (*fam*) il nuovo sistema era la sua creatura ♦ ADJ (*clothes, food*) per la prima infanzia

baby carriage N (*USA*) carrozzina

baby grand N (*also: **baby grand piano**) pianoforte *m* a mezza coda

ba·by·hood [ˈbeɪbɪhʊd] N prima infanzia

ba·by·ish [ˈbeɪbɪʃ] ADJ puerile, infantile

baby-minder [ˈbeɪbɪˌmaɪndəʳ] N bambinaia (*per madri che lavorano*)

baby-sit [ˈbeɪbɪsɪt] VI: **to baby-sit (for sb)** guardare i bambini (a qn), fare il (*or* la) babysitter (per qn)

baby-sitter [ˈbeɪbɪˌsɪtəʳ] N baby-sitter *m/f inv*

baby wipe N salvietta umidificata

bach·elor [ˈbætʃələʳ] N scapolo

bach·elor·hood [ˈbætʃələhʊd] N celibato

bachelor party N (*USA*) festa di addio al celibato

Bachelor's Degree N *diploma di laurea che viene conferito a chi ha completato un corso di laurea di tre o quattro anni all'università*

back [bæk] N

1 (*of person*) schiena; (*of animal*) dorso, schiena; **he fell on his back** è caduto di schiena; **he's got a bad back** ha problemi alla schiena; **with one's back to the light** con la luce alle spalle; **seen from the back** visto(-a) di spalle; **back to back** di spalle (uno(-a) contro l'altro(-a)), schiena contro schiena; **on the horse's back** in groppa al cavallo; **behind sb's back** alle spalle di qn; (*fig*) alle spalle *or* dietro le spalle di qn; **to break one's back** rompersi la schiena; **to put one's back into it** (*fam*) mettercela tutta; **to have one's back to the wall** (*fig*) essere *or* trovarsi con le spalle al muro; **to put sb's back up** (*fam*) far irritare qn; **to get off sb's back** (*fam*) lasciare qn in pace

2 (*as opposed to front*) dietro; (*of cheque, envelope, medal, page*) retro, rovescio; (*of head*) nuca; (*of hand*) dorso; (*of hall, room*) fondo; (*of house, car*) parte *f* posteriore, dietro; (*of chair*) spalliera, schienale *m*; (*of train*) coda; **on the back of the cheque** sul retro dell'assegno; **at the back of the class** in fondo alla classe; **at the back of the house** sul retro della casa; **in the back of the car** sul sedile posteriore dell'auto; **back to front** all'incontrario; **at the back of my mind was the thought that ...** sotto sotto pensavo che...; **it's always there at the back of my mind** è sempre lì, non riesco a togliermelo dalla mente; **I know Naples like the back of my hand** conosco Napoli come il palmo della mia mano *or*

come le mie tasche; **he's at the back of all this** c'è lui dietro a questa storia

3 (*Sport*) terzino; **right/left back** terzino destro/sinistro

♦ ADJ ATTR

1 (*rear*) di dietro; (*wheel, seat*) posteriore; **the back seat** il sedile posteriore; **the back door** la porta sul retro; **back garden/room** giardino/stanza sul retro (della casa); **back cover** er retro della copertina; **back kitchen** retrocucina *m*; **back pass** (*Ftbl*) passaggio indietro; **on the back page** in ultima pagina; **to take a back seat** (*fig*) restare in secondo piano; **he's a back seat driver** sta sempre a criticare chi guida; **back street** vicolo; **he grew up in the back streets of Cardiff** è cresciuto nei bassifondi di Cardiff

2 (*overdue: rent*) arretrato(-a); **back payments** arretrati *mpl*

♦ ADV

1 (*again, returning: often* ri- + *verb*): **to give back** ridare; **to be back** essere tornato(-a); **when will you be back?** quando torni?; **he's not back yet** non è ancora tornato; **on the way back** al ritorno; **30 km there and back** 30 km fra andata e ritorno; **put it back on the shelf** rimettilo sullo scaffale; **I smiled back** ho ricambiato il sorriso; **throw the ball back** rilancia la palla; **he called back** ha richiamato; **can I have it back?** posso riaverlo?; **he ran back** tornò indietro di corsa; **we went there by bus and walked back** siamo andati in autobus e siamo ritornati a piedi

2 (*in distance*) indietro; **stand back!** indietro!; **back and forth** avanti e indietro; **a house set back from the road** una casa che non si affaccia sulla strada

3 (*in time*) **some months back** mesi fa *or* addietro; **as far back as the 13th century** già nel duecento

♦ VT

1 (*car*): **to back the car (into)** entrare (*or* uscire in) retromarcia (in); **he backed the car out of the garage** è uscito in retromarcia dal garage

2 (*support: plan, person, candidate*) appoggiare, sostenere, spalleggiare; (*: financially*) finanziare; **the union is backing his claim for compensation** il sindacato appoggia la sua domanda di indennizzo

3 (*bet on: horse*) puntare su; **I'm backing Red Rum at Epsom** ho puntato su Red Rum per la corsa di Epsom

♦ VI (*move: person*) indietreggiare; (*: car*) fare marcia indietro; **he backed into me** ha fatto un passo indietro e mi è venuto addosso; (*in car*) mi è venuto addosso a marcia indietro

▸ **back away** VI + ADV: **to back away (from)** indietreggiare (davanti a), tirarsi indietro (davanti a)

▸ **back down** VI + ADV (*fig*) abbandonare, arrendersi, fare marcia indietro

▸ **back off** VI + ADV tirarsi indietro

▸ **back on to** VI + ADV + PREP: **the house backs on to the golf course** il retro della casa dà sul campo da golf

▸ **back out** VI + ADV (*fig*) tirarsi indietro; **to back out of sth** (*undertaking*) sottrarsi a; (*deal*) ritirarsi da; **they promised to help us and then backed out** avevano promesso di aiutarci, ma si sono tirati indietro

▸ **back up** VT + ADV **1** (*support: person*) appoggiare, sostenere; (*: claim, theory*) confermare, avvalorare; **there's no evidence to back up his theory** non ci sono prove a sostegno della sua teoria **2** (*car*): **to back the car up** far marcia indietro **3** (*Comput*) copiare, fare una copia di riserva di ♦ VI + ADV **1** (*in car*) fare marcia indietro **2** (*USA: traffic*) ingorgarsi

back·ache [ˈbækeɪk] N mal *m* di schiena; **I've got an awful backache** ho un terribile mal di schiena

back·bencher [ˌbækˈbentʃəʳ] N deputato(-a) senza incarichi ufficiali

back·bit·ing [ˈbækˌbaɪtɪŋ] N maldicenze *fpl*

back·bone [ˈbækbəʊn] N (*also fig*) spina dorsale; **the**

backbone of the organization l'anima dell'organizzazione; **he's got no backbone** è uno smidollato

back·chat [ˈbækˌtʃæt] N (*Brit fam*) impertinenza

back·date [ˌbækˈdeɪt] VT (*arrangement, document*) retrodatare; **backdated pay rise** aumento (di stipendio) retroattivo

back·drop [ˈbækˌdrɒp] N = backcloth

back·er [ˈbækə'] N (*supporter*) fautore(-trice), sostenitore(-trice); (*Comm*) finanziatore(-trice)

back·fire [ˈbækˈfaɪə'] VI (*Aut*) avere un ritorno di fiamma; (*fig: plan, policy*) avere effetto contrario; **to backfire on sb** ritorcersi contro qn; **the trick backfired on him** lo scherzo gli si è ritorto contro

back·gam·mon [bækˈgæmən] N backgammon *m*, tavola reale

back·ground [ˈbækˌgraʊnd] N 1 (*gen*) sfondo; (*fig*) sfondo, scenario; **in the background** sullo sfondo; (*fig*) nell'ombra; **on a red background** su sfondo rosso; **a house in the background** una casa sullo sfondo 2 (*of person*) background *m inv*; (*basic knowledge*) base *f*; (*experience*) esperienza; (*of problem, event*) retroscena *m*, background *m inv*; **she comes from a wealthy background** è di famiglia ricca; **family background** ambiente familiare ♦ ADJ (*music, noise*) di fondo; (*Comput*) a bassa priorità; **background noise** rumori *mpl* di fondo

back·hand [ˈbækˌhænd] N (*Tennis: also:* backhand stroke) rovescio

back·hand·ed [ˌbækˈhændɪd] ADJ (*blow*) con il dorso della mano; (*Tennis: stroke*) di rovescio; **backhanded compliment** complimento ambiguo

back·hand·er [ˈbækˌhændə'] N (*Brit: bribe*) bustarella

back·ing [ˈbækɪŋ] N 1 (*support*) appoggio, sostegno; (*Comm*) finanziamento; **they promised their backing** hanno garantito il loro appoggio 2 (*Mus*) accompagnamento 3 (*protective layer of paper, cloth etc*) rivestimento, strato protettivo

back·lash [ˈbækˌlæʃ] N (*fig*) reazione *f* (violenta)

back·log [ˈbækˌlɒg] N: **backlog of work** lavoro arretrato; **the strike has resulted in a backlog of orders** a causa dello sciopero si sono accumulate le ordinazioni

back number N (*of magazine*) numero arretrato

back·pack [ˈbækˌpæk] N zaino

back·packer [ˈbækˌpækə'] N *chi viaggia con zaino e sacco a pelo*

back pay N arretrato di stipendio

back·pedal [ˌbækˈpɛdəl] VI (*on bicycle*) pedalare all'indietro; (*fig*) fare marcia indietro

back·seat driver [ˌbækˌsiːtˈdraɪvə'] N *passeggero che dà consigli non richiesti al guidatore*

back·side [ˌbækˈsaɪd] N (*fam*) didietro *m inv*, sedere *m*; **a kick in the backside** un calcio nel sedere

back·slash [ˈbækˌslæʃ] N (*Typ*) barra obliqua inversa

back·space [ˈbækˌspeɪs] VI (*in typing*) battere il tasto di ritorno

back·stage [ˌbækˈsteɪdʒ] ADV, ADJ dietro le quinte

back·street [ˈbækˌstriːt] N vicolo ♦ ADJ (*shop, factory*) situato(-a) in un vicolo; (*fig: shady*) losco(-a); **a backstreet cafe** un bar d'infima categoria; **backstreet abortionist** praticante *m/f* di aborti clandestini

back·stroke [ˈbækˌstrəʊk] N (*Swimming*) dorso

back·track [ˈbækˌtræk] VI (*retrace one's steps*) tornare indietro; (*fig: backpedal*) fare marcia indietro

back·up [ˈbækˌʌp] ADJ (*gen, also Comput*) di riserva ♦ N (*support*) sostegno, appoggio; (*substitute*) sostituto; (*Comput*) backup *m inv*; **a backup file** un file di backup; **they've got a generator as an emergency backup** hanno un generatore di riserva per le emergenze

back·ward [ˈbækwəd] ADJ 1 (*motion, glance*) all'indietro; **a backward step** un passo indietro 2 (*pupil*) che è indietro, tardivo(-a); (*pej: country*) arretrato(-a) 3 (*reluctant*): **backward (in doing sth)** restio(-a) (a fare qc)

back·wards [ˈbækwədz], (*USA*) **back·ward** [ˈbækwəd] ADV indietro; **he took a step backwards** ha fatto un passo indietro; **to walk backwards** camminare all'indietro; **to fall backwards** cadere all'indietro; **backwards and forwards** avanti e indietro; **to bend over backwards to do sth** (*fam*) farsi in quattro per fare qc; **to know sth backwards** (*fam*) sapere qc a menadito

back·water [ˈbækˌwɔːtə'] N acqua stagnante; (*fig: pej*) buco, angolo sperduto; **this town is a cultural backwater** questa città è culturalmente arretrata

back yard N (*Brit: paved area*) cortile *m* sul retro della casa; (*USA: garden*) giardino sul retro della casa

ba·con [ˈbeɪkən] N pancetta; **bacon and eggs** uova *fpl* con pancetta

bac·te·ria [bækˈtɪərɪə] NPL batteri *mpl*

bac·te·ri·ol·ogy [bækˌtɪərɪˈɒlədʒɪ] N batteriologia

bad [bæd] ADJ (*comp* worse, *superl* worst) 1 (*gen*) cattivo(-a); (*child*) cattivello(-a); (*habit*) cattivo(-a); (*news, weather*) brutto(-a); (*workmanship, film*) scadente, brutto(-a); (*mistake, illness, cut*) brutto(-a), grave; **bad language** parolacce *fpl*; **you bad boy!** (brutto) cattivo!; **he's in a bad mood** è di cattivo umore; **to be bad at sth** non essere bravo(-a) in qc; **he's bad at keeping appointments** non sa rispettare un impegno; **smoking is bad for you** il fumo fa male alla salute; **not bad** (*quite good*) non sarebbe una cattiva idea; **how are you feeling? — not bad** come si sente? — non c'è male; **not bad, eh?** mica male, eh?; **that wouldn't be a bad thing** non sarebbe una cattiva idea; **a bad accident** un grave incidente; **that's too bad** (*sympathetic*) che peccato; **that's just too bad** (*unsympathetic*) tanto peggio per te (or lei etc); **it's too bad of you** è poco carino da parte tua; **I feel bad about it** mi sento un po' in colpa; **business is bad** gli affari vanno male; **from bad to worse** di male in peggio; **to have a bad time of it** passarsela male; **to be in a bad way** (*in difficulties*) essere nei guai; (*ill*) stare molto male; **bad faith** malafede *f* 2 (*rotten: food*) guasto(-a), andato(-a) a male; (*: smell*) cattivo(-a); (*: tooth*) cariato(-a), guasto(-a); **to go bad** andare a male. 3 **to have a bad back/stomach** avere dei problemi alla schiena/allo stomaco; **his bad leg** la sua gamba malata; **to feel bad** (*sick*) sentirsi male; **I feel bad about it** (*guilty*) mi sento un po' in colpa; **there's no need for you to feel bad about it** non è il caso di prendersela

bad·die [ˈbædɪ] N (*fam*) cattivo

bade [bæd, beɪd] PT of **bid**

badge [bædʒ] N (*of policeman, also Scol*) distintivo; (*Mil*) mostrina; (*stick-on*) adesivo

badg·er [ˈbædʒə'] N (*Zool*) tasso ♦ VT tormentare

bad·ly [ˈbædlɪ] ADV (*comp* worse, *superl* worst) 1 (*work, dress*) male; **a badly behaved child** un(a) bambino(-a) maleducato(-a); **things are going badly** le cose vanno male; **to treat sb badly** trattar male qn; **badly paid** mal pagato(-a) 2 (*seriously: wounded*) gravemente; **badly hurt** gravemente ferito(-a) 3 (*very much*): **I need it badly** ne ho assolutamente bisogno; **I want it badly** lo voglio ad ogni costo; **it badly needs painting** ha proprio bisogno di una mano di vernice; **he needs help badly** ha urgente bisogno di aiuto

bad-mannered [ˌbædˈmænəd] ADJ maleducato(-a), sgarbato(-a)

bad·min·ton [ˈbædmɪntən] N badminton *m*

bad-tempered [ˌbædˈtɛmpəd] ADJ irascibile, irritabile; (*look*) antipatico(-a); **to be bad-tempered** (*always*) avere un brutto carattere; (*at a particular time*) essere di malumore

baf·fle [ˈbæfl] VT (*puzzle*) lasciare perplesso(-a), confondere; **it baffles me how she does it** non riesco a capire come faccia

baf·fling [ˈbæflɪŋ] ADJ sconcertante

bag [bæg] N (*gen*) borsa; (*paper bag, carrier*) sacchetto; (*handbag*) borsa, borsetta; (*suitcase*) valigia; (*of hunter*) carniere *m*; (*animals taken by hunter*) carniere, bottino di caccia; **I put it in my bag** l'ho messo in borsa; **to pack one's bags** fare le valigie; **it's in the bag** (*fam*) ce l'ho (or ce l'hai etc) in tasca, è cosa fatta; **bags under the eyes** borse sotto gli occhi; **bags of** (*fam: lots*) un sacco di ♦ VT (*fam: seat, place*) accaparrarsi
  ▸ **bag up** VT + ADV (*flour*) insaccare

bag·ful [ˈbægfʊl] N sacco (pieno)

bag·gage [ˈbægɪdʒ] N bagaglio, bagagli *mpl*; **where is your baggage?** dove sono i tuoi bagagli?; **a piece of baggage** un bagaglio

baggage car N (*USA*) bagagliaio

baggage reclaim N ritiro bagagli

bag·gy [ˈbægɪ] ADJ largo(-a), sformato(-a)

Bagh·dad [bægˈdæd] N Bagdad *f*

bag lady N (*fam*) stracciona, barbona
bag·pipes [ˈbæɡ͵paɪps] NPL (*in Scotland*) cornamusa *sg*; (*in Italy*) zampogna *sg*
bag-snatcher [ˈbæɡ͵snætʃəʳ] N (*Brit*) scippatore(-trice)
bag-snatching [ˈbæɡ͵snætʃɪŋ] N (*Brit*) scippo
Ba·ha·mas [bəˈhɑːməz] NPL: **the Bahamas** le Bahamas
Bah·rain, Bah·rein [bɑːˈreɪn] N il Bahrein *m*
bail¹ [beɪl] N (*Law*) cauzione *f*; **he was granted bail** ha ottenuto la libertà provvisoria su cauzione; **to stand bail for sb** rendersi garante di *or* per qn; **to be released on bail** essere rilasciato(-a) su cauzione
  ▸ **bail out** VT + ADV (*Law*) mettere in libertà provvisoria su cauzione; (*fig*) tirare fuori dai guai
bail² [beɪl] VT, VI *see* **bail out**
  ▸ **bail out** VT + ADV (*Naut: water*) vuotare; (: *boat*) sgottare, aggottare ♦ VI + ADV **1** (*Naut*) saltare in acqua **2** (*Aer*) gettarsi col paracadute
bail·iff [ˈbeɪlɪf] N (*Law*) ufficiale *m* giudiziario; (*on estate*) amministratore *m*, fattore *m*
bailout [ˈbeɪlaʊt] N ricapitalizzazione *f*; **government bailouts of large corporations** ricapitalizzazioni di grosse società da parte del governo
bait [beɪt] N (*also fig*) esca; **he didn't rise to the bait** (*fig*) non ha abboccato (all'amo) ♦ VT (*hook*) innescare; (*trap*) munire di esca; (*torment: person, animal*) stuzzicare, tormentare
bake [beɪk] VT (*bread, cake*) cuocere (al forno); (*bricks*) cuocere; **he baked a cake today** ha fatto un dolce oggi; **baked potatoes** patate *fpl* (con la buccia) cotte al forno ♦ VI cuocersi al forno
baked beans [ˈbeɪktˈbiːnz] NPL ≈ fagioli *mpl* all'uccelletto
bak·er [ˈbeɪkəʳ] N fornaio(-a), panettiere(-a); **baker's (shop)** panetteria, forno; **at/to the baker's** dal panettiere, dal fornaio
bak·ery [ˈbeɪkərɪ] N panetteria, forno
bak·ing [ˈbeɪkɪŋ] N cottura (al forno) ♦ ADJ (*fam: hot*): **it's baking in here** qui dentro è un forno, qui dentro si muore di caldo
baking powder N lievito (minerale) in polvere
baking sheet, baking tray N placca da forno, teglia
baking tin N stampo, tortiera
bala·cla·va [͵bæləˈklɑːvə] N (*also:* **balaclava helmet**) passamontagna *m inv*
bal·ance [ˈbæləns] N **1** (*equilibrium*) equilibrio; **to lose one's balance** perdere l'equilibrio; **to throw sb off balance** far perdere l'equilibrio a qn; (*fig*) sconcertare qn, far mancare la terra sotto i piedi a qn; **balance of power** equilibrio di potere; **to strike the right balance** trovare il giusto mezzo; **on balance** (*fig*) a conti fatti, tutto sommato; **a nice balance of humour and pathos** un'equilibrata combinazione di humour e pathos **2** (*scales*) bilancia; **to hang in the balance** (*fig*) essere incerto(-a) *or* in bilico **3** (*Comm*) bilancio; (*difference*) saldo; (*remainder*) resto; **balance brought or carried forward** saldo riportato, saldo da riportare ♦ VT **1** tenere in equilibrio *or* in bilico; (*Aut: wheel*) fare l'equilibratura di; (*fig: compare*) soppesare, valutare; (*make up for*) compensare; **the two things balance each other out** le due cose si compensano; **this must be balanced against that** nel considerare questo fattore bisogna tener presente l'altro **2** (*Comm: account*) saldare; (: *budget*) pareggiare, far quadrare; **to balance the books** fare il bilancio **3** (*Chem, Math: equations*) bilanciare ♦ VI **1** tenersi in equilibrio **2** (*accounts*) quadrare, essere in pareggio
bal·anced [ˈbælənst] ADJ (*views*) moderato(-a); (*personality, diet*) equilibrato(-a)
balance sheet N bilancio (di esercizio)
bal·co·ny [ˈbælkənɪ] N balcone *m*; (*Theatre*) prima galleria, balconata
bald [bɔːld] ADJ (*person*) calvo(-a); (*tyre* (*Brit*) *or* **tire** (*USA*)) liscio(-a); (*statement*) asciutto(-a); (*style*) spoglio(-a); **to go bald** perdere i capelli
bald·ness [ˈbɔːldnɪs] N calvizie *f sg*
bale [beɪl] N (*of cloth, hay*) balla
Bal·ear·ic [͵bælɪˈærɪk] ADJ: **the Balearic Islands** le (isole) Baleari
bale·ful [ˈbeɪlful] ADJ (*look*) malevolo(-a)

balk, baulk [bɔːk] VI: **to balk (at the idea of)** (*person*) recalcitrare (all'idea di), tirarsi indietro (davanti a); (*horse*) recalcitrare *or* impennarsi (di fronte a)
Bal·kan [ˈbɔːlkən] ADJ balcanico(-a)
ball¹ [bɔːl] N (*gen*) palla; (*inflated, Ftbl, etc*) pallone *m*; (*for golf etc*) pallina; (*of wool, string*) gomitolo; **pass the ball to me!** passami la palla!; **a tennis ball** una pallina da tennis; **a rugby ball** un pallone da rugby; **a glass ball** un globo di vetro; **he rolled the paper into a ball** ha appallottolato la carta; **the ball of the foot** la punta del piede; **the ball of the thumb** il polpastrello del pollice; **to be on the ball** (*fig: competent*) essere in gamba; (: *quick*) essere sveglio(-a); (: *alert*) stare all'erta; **to play ball (with sb)** (*fig*) stare al gioco (di qn); **to start the ball rolling** (*fig*) fare la prima mossa; **to keep the ball rolling** (*fig*) mandare avanti le cose; **the ball is in your court** (*fig*) tocca a te
ball² [bɔːl] N (*dance*) ballo; **a fancy dress ball** un ballo in maschera; **to have a ball** (*fig: fam*) divertirsi da matti, spassarsela
bal·lad [ˈbæləd] N ballata
bal·last [ˈbæləst] N zavorra
ball bearing N cuscinetto a sfere
ball cock [ˈbɔːl͵kɒk] N galleggiante *m* (*in serbatoio*)
bal·le·ri·na [͵bæləˈriːnə] N ballerina (classica)
bal·let [ˈbæleɪ] N (*dance*) balletto; (*art*) danza classica; **we went to a ballet** siamo andati a vedere un balletto; **ballet lessons** corso di danza classica
ballet dancer N ballerino(-a) (classico(-a))
bal·lis·tic [bəˈlɪstɪk] ADJ balistico(-a); **intercontinental ballistic missile** missile *m* a gettata intercontinentale
bal·lis·tics [bəˈlɪstɪks] NSG balistica
bal·loon [bəˈluːn] N (*toy*) palloncino; (*Aer*) pallone *m* aerostatico, mongolfiera; (*in comic strip*) fumetto ♦ VI gonfiarsi
bal·loon·ist [bəˈluːnɪst] N aeronauta *m/f*
bal·lot [ˈbælət] N votazione *f* (a scrutinio segreto); **on the first ballot** alla prima votazione ♦ VT (*members*) consultare tramite votazione
ballot box N urna (elettorale)
ballot paper N scheda (elettorale)
ball·park [ˈbɔːlpɑːk] N (*USA*) stadio di baseball
ballpark figure N (*fam*) cifra approssimativa
ball-point [ˈbɔːlpɔɪnt], **ball-point pen** [ˈbɔːlpɔɪntˈpɛn] N penna a sfera
ball·room [ˈbɔːlrum] N sala da ballo
balls [bɔːlz] (*fam!*) NPL coglioni *mpl* (*fam!*); (*fig: bullshit*) cazzate *fpl* (*fam!*)
balm [bɑːm] N (*also fig*) balsamo
balmy [ˈbɑːmɪ] ADJ **1** (*breeze, air*) balsamico(-a) **2** (*Brit fam*) = **barmy**
bal·sa [ˈbɔːlsə] N (*also:* **balsawood**) (legno di) balsa
bal·sam [ˈbɔːlsəm] N balsamo
Bal·tic [ˈbɔːltɪk] ADJ, N baltico(-a); **the Baltic (Sea)** il (mar) Baltico
bal·us·trade [͵bæləsˈtreɪd] N balaustrata
bam·boo [bæmˈbuː] N bambù *m inv* ♦ ADJ di bambù
bam·boo·zle [bæmˈbuːzl] VT (*fam*) abbindolare, infinocchiare
ban [bæn] N divieto, bando; **to put a ban on sth** proibire qc ♦ VT (*pt, pp* **banned**) (*alcohol, book, film*) proibire; **to ban sb from sth** proibire qc a qn; **to ban sb from doing sth** proibire a qn di fare qc; **to ban sb from a place** proibire a qn di andare in un posto; **they banned him from the competition** lo hanno escluso dalla gara; **arms sales were banned last year** la vendita di armi è stata vietata l'anno scorso; **he was banned from driving** (*Brit*) gli hanno tolto (*or* ritirato) la patente
ba·nal [bəˈnɑːl] ADJ banale
ba·na·na [bəˈnɑːnə] N (*fruit*) banana; (*tree*) banano
band¹ [bænd] N (*gen*) banda, striscia; (*of hat, cigar*) nastro
band² [bænd] N **1** (*Mus*) banda (musicale); (*jazz band, pop group*) complesso (musicale); (*Mil*) fanfara; **the procession was led by a band** la processione era preceduta da una banda; **he plays the guitar in a band** suona la chitarra in un gruppo **2** (*group of people*) banda
  ▸ **band together** VI + ADV mettersi in gruppo

band·age ['bændɪdʒ] N fascia, benda ♦ VT fasciare, bendare
B & B [ˌbiːənd'biː] N ABBR = **bed and breakfast**
ban·dit ['bændɪt] N bandito, brigante m
band·stand ['bænd,stænd] N palco coperto dell'orchestra (*in parco pubblico*)
band·wagon ['bænd,wægən] N: **to jump on the bandwagon** (*fig*) seguire la corrente
ban·dy ['bændɪ] VT (*jokes, insults*) scambiarsi
  ▸ **bandy about** VT + ADV (*word, phrase*) ripetere con insistenza; **to bandy sb's name about** parlare con insistenza di qn
bandy-legged ['bændɪ'lɛgɪd] ADJ dalle *or* con le gambe storte
bane [beɪn] N: **it** (*or he etc*) **is the bane of my life** è la mia rovina
bang [bæŋ] N (*noise: of explosion, gun*) scoppio, colpo; (: *of sth falling*) tonfo; (: *blow*) botta, colpo; **I heard a loud bang** ho sentito un forte scoppio; **he closed the door with a bang** ha sbattuto la porta; **a bang on the head** un colpo sulla testa; **it went with a bang** (*fam*) è stato una bomba ♦ ADV: **to go bang** esplodere, fare bang; **bang went £10** mi (*or gli etc*) sono volate 10 sterline ♦ VT (*thump*) battere, picchiare; (*hit, knock, slam*) sbattere, battere (violentemente); **he banged the receiver down** ha sbattuto giù il telefono; **I banged my head** ho sbattuto la testa; **to bang one's head against a wall** (*fig*) battere *or* picchiare la testa contro il muro ♦ VI (*explode*) scoppiare, esplodere; (*slam: door*) sbattere; **to bang at/on sth** picchiare a/su qc; **to bang at** *or* **on the door** picchiare alla porta; **to bang into sth** sbattere contro qc
  ▸ **bang about**(*fam*) VI + ADV sbatacchiare ♦ VI far rumore
bang·er ['bæŋə'] N (*Brit fam*) **1** (*sausage*) salsiccia; **bangers and mash** salsicce e purè di patate **2** (*firework*) mortaretto **3** (*old car*) macinino
Bang·kok [bæŋ'kɒk] N Bangkok f
Bang·la·desh [bæŋglə'dɛʃ] N il Bangladesh m
ban·gle ['bæŋgl] N braccialetto
ban·ish ['bænɪʃ] VT: **to banish (from)** (*person*) bandire (da), esiliare (da); (*thought, fear*) bandire (da)
ban·is·ters ['bænɪstəz] NPL ringhiera sg
ban·jo ['bændʒəʊ] N banjo m inv
bank [bæŋk] N **1** (*Fin, Med*) banca; (*Gambling*) banco; **the bank is closed** la banca è chiusa **2** (*of river*) sponda, riva; (*embankment*) argine m; (*of road, racetrack*) terrapieno; **we walked along the river bank** abbiamo camminato lungo la riva del fiume **3** (*heap: of earth, mud*) mucchio; (: *of snow*) cumulo; (: *of clouds, sand*) banco **4** (*Aer*) virata ♦ VT (*money*) depositare in banca ♦ VI **1** servirsi di una banca; **where do you bank?** qual è la sua banca? **2** (*Aer*) inclinarsi in virata
  ▸ **bank on** VI + PREP far conto su, contare su; **he was banking on a pay rise** contava su un aumento; **I wouldn't bank on it** non ci conterei
  ▸ **bank up** VT + ADV (*sand*) ammucchiare
bank account N (*gen*) conto in banca; (*frm*) conto bancario
bank balance N saldo; **a healthy bank balance** un solido conto in banca
bank card N = **cheque card**
bank draft N tratta bancaria
bank·er ['bæŋkə'] N banchiere m
bank holiday N (*Brit*) giorno di festa civile; **Monday's a bank holiday** lunedì è festa
bank·ing ['bæŋkɪŋ] N attività bancaria; **to study banking** fare studi bancari *or* di tecnica bancaria
banking hours NPL orario di sportello
bank loan N prestito bancario
bank manager N direttore(-trice) di banca
bank·note ['bæŋk,nəʊt] N banconota
bank rate N tasso ufficiale di sconto
bank·rupt ['bæŋkrʌpt] ADJ fallito(-a); (*fam: penniless*) senza una lira; **to go bankrupt** fallire, fare fallimento *or* bancarotta ♦ N fallito(-a) ♦ VT portare al fallimento
bank·rupt·cy ['bæŋkrəptsɪ] N fallimento, bancarotta; **bankruptcy proceedings** procedura fallimentare
bank statement N estratto m conto, inv

banned substance [ˌbænd'sʌbstəns] N (*Sport*) sostanza al bando
ban·ner ['bænə'] N stendardo, bandiera; (*with slogan*) striscione m
ban·nis·ters ['bænɪstəz] NPL = **banisters**
banns [bænz] NPL pubblicazioni fpl (di matrimonio); **to read** *or* **publish the banns** esporre le pubblicazioni
ban·quet ['bæŋkwɪt] N banchetto
bantam·weight ['bæntəm,weɪt] N (*Boxing*) peso gallo
ban·ter ['bæntə'] N scherzi mpl bonari
bap·tism ['bæptɪzəm] N battesimo
Bap·tist ['bæptɪst] ADJ, N (*Rel*) battista m/f; **St John the Baptist** San Giovanni Battista
bap·tize [bæp'taɪz] VT battezzare
bar¹ [bɑː'] N **1** (*pub*) bar m inv; (*counter: in pub*) banco **2** (*piece: of wood, metal etc*) sbarra, barra; (*of chocolate*) tavoletta; (*of electric fire*) elemento; **it's the most popular bar in town** è il locale più frequentato della città; **please order meals at the bar** si prega di ordinare le consumazioni al banco; **a bar of chocolate** una tavoletta di cioccolata; **bar of soap** saponetta **3** (*of window, cage*) sbarra; (*on door*) spranga; **bar (to)** (*fig: obstacle*) barriera (a), ostacolo (a); **behind bars** (*prisoner*) dietro le sbarre **4** (*Law: professional group*): **the Bar** l'ordine m degli avvocati; **the prisoner at the bar** (*area in court*) l'imputato(-a); **to be called to** *or* (*USA*) **admitted to the Bar** essere ammesso(-a) all'ordine degli avvocati **5** (*Mus*) battuta ♦ VT (*obstruct: way*) sbarrare; (*fasten: door, window*) sbarrare, sprangare; (*ban: person*) escludere; (*activity, thing*) proibire, interdire
bar² [bɑː'] PREP ad esclusione di, tranne; **the fastest sprinter bar none** il velocista più veloce in assoluto
Bar·ba·dos [bɑː'beɪdɒs] N Barbados fsg
bar·bar·ic [bɑː'bærɪk], **bar·ba·rous** [bɑːbərəs] ADJ (*cruelty, behaviour*) barbaro(-a); (*splendour*) barbarico(-a)
bar·becue ['bɑːbɪkjuː] N (*grill*) barbecue m inv; (*party*) grigliata all'aperto ♦ VT cuocere alla brace
barbed wire ['bɑːbd,waɪə'] N filo spinato
bar·ber ['bɑːbə'] N barbiere m; **to go to the barber's (shop)** andare dal barbiere
barber·shop ['bɑːbəˌʃɒp] N (*music*) barbershop m, tipo di musica melodica cantata senza strumenti d'accompagnamento; (*USA: shop*) barbiere m
bar·bi·tu·rate [bɑː'bɪtjʊrɪt] N barbiturico
Bar·ce·lo·na [bɑːsɪ'ləʊnə] N Barcellona
bar chart N diagramma m a colonna
bar code N codice m a barre
bare [bɛə'] ADJ **1** (*gen*) nudo(-a); (*arms, legs*) nudo(-a), scoperto(-a); (*head*) scoperto(-a); (*landscape*) spoglio(-a), brullo(-a); (*ground, tree, room*) nudo(-a), spoglio(-a); (*cupboard*) vuoto(-a); (*Elec: wire*) scoperto(-a); **there's a bare patch on the carpet** c'è un pezzo spelacchiato nella moquette; **with his bare hands** a mani nude; **the bare facts** i fatti nudi e crudi; **to lay bare** (*fig*) mettere a nudo, svelare **2** (*meagre: majority*) scarso(-a), striminzito(-a); **to strip sth down to the bare essentials** (*structure, narrative*) ridurre qc all'essenziale; **the bare necessities** lo stretto necessario; **to earn a bare living** guadagnare appena da vivere ♦ VT scoprire, denudare; (*teeth*) mostrare; **to bare one's heart** (*fig*) mettere a nudo il proprio animo
bare·back ['bɛəˌbæk] ADV senza sella
bare·faced ['bɛəˌfeɪst] ADJ sfacciato(-a), spudorato(-a)
bare·foot ['bɛəˌfʊt], **bare·footed** [ˌbɛə'fʊtɪd] ADJ, ADV scalzo(-a), a piedi nudi; **the children go around barefoot** i bambini vanno in giro scalzi
bare·headed [ˌbɛə'hɛdɪd] ADJ, ADV a capo scoperto
bare·ly ['bɛəlɪ] ADV appena; **they had barely enough money** avevano appena denaro a sufficienza; **he was so drunk he could barely stand** era così ubriaco che riusciva a malapena a stare in piedi; **I could barely hear what she was saying** sentivo a malapena quello che diceva
Bar·ents Sea ['bærənts,siː] N: **the Barents Sea** il mar di Barents
bar·gain ['bɑːgɪn] N **1** (*transaction*) affare m; **to make a bargain with sb** fare un patto con qn; (*business*) concludere un affare con qn; **it's a bargain!** affare fatto!; **you drive a**

hard bargain lei mi pone delle condizioni difficili; **into the bargain** (*fig*) per giunta, per di più **2** (*cheap thing*) affare *m*, occasione *f*; (*in sales*) occasione; **to get a bargain** fare un affare; **it's a (real) bargain** è un affarone, è un'occasione ◆ vi (*negotiate*) contrattare; (*haggle*) tirare sul prezzo
► **bargain for** vi + prep (*fam*): **to bargain for sth** aspettarsi qc; **he got more than he bargained for** non si aspettava quello che è successo

bar·gain·ing [ˈbɑːɡɪnɪŋ] adj: **bargaining position** posizione *f* di negoziato; **to be in a weak/strong bargaining position** non avere/avere potere contrattuale; (*fig*) non essere/essere nella posizione di poter trattare; **bargaining power** potere *m* contrattuale; **bargaining process** processo di negoziato ◆ n contrattazione *f*

barge [bɑːdʒ] n chiatta, barcone *m*; (*ceremonial*) lancia
► **barge in** vi + adv (*fam, pej: enter*) precipitarsi dentro, piombare dentro; (: *interrupt*) intromettersi
► **barge into** vi + prep (*fam: knock*) andare a sbattere contro, urtare contro; (: *enter*) piombare in; (: *interrupt*) intromettersi in

bari·tone [ˈbærɪtəʊn] n baritono
barium meal n (pasto di) bario
bark[1] [bɑːk] n (*of tree*) corteccia
bark[2] [bɑːk] n (*of dog*) latrato, abbaiare *m*; **his bark is worse than his bite** abbaia ma non morde ◆ vi: **to bark (at)** abbaiare a; **to be barking up the wrong tree** essere sulla strada sbagliata, sbagliarsi di grosso
► **bark out** vt + adv (*order*) urlare, abbaiare
bar·ley [ˈbɑːlɪ] n orzo
barley sugar n zucchero d'orzo
bar·maid [ˈbɑːˌmeɪd] n barista *f*
bar·man [ˈbɑːmən] n (*pl* barmen) barista *m*
bar·my [ˈbɑːmɪ] adj (*Brit fam*) tocco(-a), toccato(-a), suonato(-a)
barn [bɑːn] n fienile *m*, granaio; (*for animals*) stalla
bar·na·cle [ˈbɑːnəkl] n cirripede *m*
barn owl n barbagianni *m inv* nostrano
ba·rom·e·ter [bəˈrɒmɪtəʳ] n barometro
bar·on [ˈbærən] n barone *m*; (*fig*) magnate *m*; **the press barons** i baroni della stampa; **the oil barons** i magnati del petrolio
bar·on·ess [ˈbærənɪs] n baronessa
bar·on·et [ˈbærənɪt] n baronetto
bar·rack [ˈbærək] vt (*Brit*): **to barrack sb** subissare qn di grida e fischi
bar·racks [ˈbærəks] npl caserma *sg*; **confined to barracks** consegnato(-a) in caserma
❏ **barracks** is not translated by the Italian word *baracche*
bar·rage [ˈbærɑːʒ] n (*dam*) (opera di) sbarramento; (*Mil*) sbarramento; **a barrage of questions** una raffica di *or* un fuoco di fila di domande
bar·rel [ˈbærəl] n barile *m*; (*of gun*) canna; **a barrel of beer** un barile di birra
barrel organ n organetto
bar·ren [ˈbærən] adj (*land*) arido(-a), povero(-a); (*tree*) infruttuoso(-a); (*animal*) sterile
bar·ri·cade [ˌbærɪˈkeɪd] n barricata ◆ vt barricare
bar·ri·er [ˈbærɪəʳ] n barriera; (*Brit: also:* **crash barrier**) guardrail *m inv*; (*Rail: in station*) cancello; (*fig*) barriera, ostacolo
bar·ring [ˈbɑːrɪŋ] prep = **bar**[2]
bar·ris·ter [ˈbærɪstəʳ] n (*Brit*) avvocato (*con diritto di parlare davanti a tutte le corti*)
bar·row [ˈbærəʊ] n (*wheelbarrow*) carriola; (*market stall*) carretto, carrettino
bar·tender [ˈbɑːˌtɛndəʳ] n (*USA*) barista *m/f*
bar·ter [ˈbɑːtəʳ] vt: **to barter sth (for sth)** barattare qc (con qc) ◆ vi: **to barter with sb (for sth)** barattare (qc) con qn ◆ n baratto
base[1] [beɪs] n (*gen, also Mil*) base *f* ◆ vt (*troops*): **to base at** mettere di stanza a; (*opinion, relationship*): **to be on** basare su, fondare su; **the film is based on a play by Shakespeare** il film è basato su una commedia di Shakespeare; **I'm based in London** sono di base *or* ho base a Londra;

the job is based in London la sede di lavoro è a Londra; **a Paris-based firm** una ditta con sede centrale a Parigi; **coffee-based** a base di caffè
base[2] [beɪs] adj (*liter: action, motive*) basso(-a); (: *behaviour*) ignobile
base·ball [ˈbeɪsbɔːl] n baseball *m*; **a baseball cap** un berretto da baseball
baseball cap n berretto da baseball
base·board [ˈbeɪsbɔːd] n (*USA*) battiscopa *m inv*
base camp n campo *m* base, *inv*
Ba·sel [ˈbɑːzəl] n = **Basle**
base·line [ˈbeɪslaɪn] n (*Tennis*) linea di fondo; (*Baseball*) linea di base
base·ment [ˈbeɪsmənt] n (*of house*) seminterrato; (*of shop*) scantinato
❏ **basement** is not translated by the Italian word *basamento*
base rate n (*Fin*) tasso base
bases [ˈbeɪsiːz, ˈbeɪsɪz] npl **1** *of* **basis 2** *of* **base**[1]
bash [bæʃ](*fam*) n **1** (*blow*) botta; **the car has had a bash** la macchina ha preso una botta **2** (*fam: party*) festa ◆ vt (*fam: thing*) sbattere; (: *person*) picchiare, menare
► **bash in** vt + adv (*fam*) sfondare; **to bash sb's head in** spaccare la testa a qn; **bashed in** sfondato(-a)
► **bash on** vi + adv **to bash on with** andare avanti con
► **bash up** vt + adv (*fam: car*) sfasciare; (: *Brit: person*) riempire di botte
bash·ful [ˈbæʃfʊl] adj timido(-a)
bash·ing [ˈbæʃɪŋ] n: **to take a bashing** prendere una batosta; **union-bashing** denigrazione *f* sistematica dei sindacati
ba·sic [ˈbeɪsɪk] adj **1** (*fundamental: reason, problem*) fondamentale, base (*inv* (*after n*)); (*rudimentary: knowledge*) rudimentale; (: *equipment: essential*) essenziale; (*poor*) primitivo(-a); (*elementary: principles, precautions, rules*) elementare; (*salary*) base (*inv* (*after n*)); **it's one of the basic requirements** è uno dei requisiti basilari; **it's a basic model** è un modello base; **"Basic Italian"** "Italiano elementare"; **the accommodation is pretty basic** l'alloggio è piuttosto modesto **2** (*Chem: oxide, salt*) basico(-a)
ba·si·cal·ly [ˈbeɪsɪklɪ] adv fondamentalmente, sostanzialmente
basic rate n (*of tax*) aliquota minima
ba·sics [ˈbeɪsɪks] npl principi fondamentali
bas·il [ˈbæzl] n basilico
ba·sin [ˈbeɪsn] n (*Brit: for food*) terrina; (*washbasin*) lavabo, lavandino; (*Geog*) bacino
ba·sis [ˈbeɪsɪs] n (*pl* bases [ˈbeɪsiːz]) (*foundation*) base *f*, fondamento; **on the basis of what you've said** in base a quello che hai detto; **on a daily basis** quotidianamente; **on a regular basis** regolarmente
bask [bɑːsk] vi: **to bask in the sun** crogiolarsi al sole; **to bask in sb's favour** godere del favore di qn
basket [ˈbɑːskɪt] n (*gen: bread basket, wastepaper basket*) cestino; (*large*) cesto, cesta; (*shopping basket*) cestino della spesa; (*at supermarket*) cestello; (*wicker basket*) paniere *m*; (*Basketball*) canestro; (*Fin*) paniere *m*
basket·ball [ˈbɑːskɪtbɔːl] n pallacanestro *f*, basket *m*
basketball player n cestista *m/f*
Basle [bɑːl] n Basilea
bas·ma·ti rice [bæsˌmɑːtɪˈraɪs] n riso basmati, *varietà di riso usato nella cucina indiana*
Basque [bæsk] adj basco(-a) ◆ n (*person*) basco(-a); (*language*) basco
bass [beɪs](*Mus*) adj basso(-a) ◆ n (*voice*) voce *f* di basso; (*singer*) basso; (*double bass*) contrabbasso; (*guitar*) basso (elettrico); (*on hi-fi*) basso
bass clef [beɪs] n chiave *f* di basso
bas·soon [bəˈsuːn] n fagotto
bas·tard [ˈbɑːstəd] n bastardo(-a); (*fam!, pej*) figlio di puttana (*fam!*) ◆ adj (*child*) illegittimo(-a)
baste [beɪst] vt (*Culin*) ungere, inumidire col suo sugo; (*Sewing*) imbastire
bas·ti·on [ˈbæstɪən] n (*castle wall*) bastione *m*; (*stronghold, fig*) baluardo

bat¹ [bæt] N (*Cricket, Baseball*) mazza; (*Brit: Table-Tennis*) racchetta; **off one's own bat** (*fam*) di testa propria, di propria iniziativa ♦ VI (*Sport*) battere ♦ VT: **he didn't bat an eyelid** (*fam*) non ha battuto ciglio

bat² [bæt] N (*Zool*) pipistrello; **to have bats in the belfry** (*fig: fam*) essere picchiato(-a) *or* suonato(-a); **like a bat out of hell** come un fulmine

batch [bætʃ] N (*of applicants, letters*) gruppo; (*of work*) sezione *f*; (*of goods*) partita, lotto; (*of recruits*) contingente *m*; (*of bread*) infornata; (*of papers*) cumulo; **the next batch of students** il prossimo gruppo di studenti; **batch of statistics** insieme di dati

batch processing N (*Comput*) elaborazione *f* a blocchi

bat·ed [ˈbeɪtɪd] ADJ: **with bated breath** col fiato sospeso

bath [bɑːθ] N (*pl* **baths** [bɑːðz]) **1** (*tub*) vasca (da bagno); (*wash*) bagno; **room with bath** camera con vasca da bagno; **to have a bath** fare *or* farsi un bagno **2** (*esp pl*): **swimming baths** piscina ♦ VI fare *or* farsi un bagno ♦ VT fare il bagno a

bathe [beɪð] N (*in sea, pool*) bagno ♦ VI **1** (*swim*) fare i bagni, bagnarsi; **to go bathing** andare a fare il bagno *or* a nuotare; **it was too cold to bathe** era troppo freddo per fare il bagno **2** (*USA*) = **bath** VI ♦ VT (*wound*) lavare

bath·er [ˈbeɪðəʳ] N bagnante *m/f*

bath·ing [ˈbeɪðɪŋ] N bagni *mpl*; **"bathing is forbidden"** "è vietata la balneazione"

bathing cap N cuffia da bagno

bathing costume, bathing suit N costume *m* da bagno

bath·mat [ˈbɑːθˌmæt] N tappetino da bagno

bath·robe [ˈbɑːθˌrəʊb] N **1** (*towelling*) accappatoio **2** (*USA*) = **dressing gown**

bath·room [ˈbɑːθrʊm] N (stanza da) bagno; (*USA*) bagno, toilette *f inv*

baths [bɑːðz] NPL bagni *mpl* pubblici

bath towel N asciugamano da bagno

bath·tub [ˈbɑːθˌtʌb] N (*old*) vasca da bagno

bat·man [ˈbætˌmæn] N (*pl* **batmen**) (*Brit Mil*) attendente *m*

baton [ˈbætən] N (*Mus*) bacchetta; (*Mil*) bastone *m* di comando; (*of policeman*) sfollagente *m inv*, manganello; (*in race*) testimone *m*

bat·tal·ion [bəˈtælɪən] N battaglione *m*

bat·ten [ˈbætən] N listello di legno; (*Carpentry*) assicella, correntino; (*for flooring*) tavola; (*Naut*) serretta; (*on sail*) stecca
  ▸ **batten down** VT + ADV (*Naut*): **to batten down the hatches** chiudere i boccaporti; (*fig*) prepararsi per un'emergenza

bat·ter [ˈbætəʳ] N (*Culin*) pastella

bat·ter [ˈbætəʳ] VT (*person*) ridurre in cattivo stato; (*wife, baby*) maltrattare; (*subj: wind, waves*) colpire violentemente
  ▸ **batter down** VT + ADV abbattere, buttare giù

bat·tered [ˈbætəd] ADJ (*car, building*) malridotto(-a); (*baby, wife*) maltrattato(-a), vittima *inv* di maltrattamenti; (*hat*) sformato(-a); (*pan*) ammaccato(-a)

bat·ter·ing ram [ˈbætərɪŋˌræm] N ariete *m*

bat·tery [ˈbætərɪ] N (*Elec*) pila; (*Aut, Mil*) batteria; (*large number: of lights, tests*) batteria; (: *of questions*) pioggia, raffica

battery charger N caricabatterie *m inv*

battery farming N allevamento in batteria

bat·tle [ˈbætl] N (*Mil*) battaglia, combattimento; (*fig*) lotta, battaglia; **killed in battle** ucciso in combattimento; **I had quite a battle to get permission** ho dovuto lottare per ottenere il permesso; **a battle of wits** una gara d'ingegno; **half the battle** (*fam*) è già una mezza vittoria; **to fight a losing battle** (*fig*) battersi per una causa persa ♦ VI (*fig*): **to battle (for)** lottare (per), combattere (per); **he battled to retain his self-control** dovette fare uno sforzo per controllarsi; **to battle against the wind** lottare con *or* contro il vento

battle dress N uniforme *f* da combattimento

battle·field [ˈbætlˌfiːld], **battle·ground** [ˈbætlˌgraʊnd] N campo di battaglia

bat·tle·ments [ˈbætlmənts] NPL bastioni *mpl*

battle·ship [ˈbætlˌʃɪp] N nave *f* da guerra

bat·ty [ˈbætɪ] ADJ (*comp* **-ier**, *superl* **-iest**) (*fam: person*) svitato(-a), strambo(-a); (: *behaviour, idea*) strampalato(-a); **I must be going batty!** sto proprio rimbambendo!

bau·ble [ˈbɔːbl] N ninnolo

baud [bɔːd] N (*Comput*) baud *m inv*

baulk [bɔːk] VI = **balk**

baux·ite [ˈbɔːksaɪt] N bauxite *f*

Ba·varia [bəˈvɛərɪə] N Baviera

Ba·var·ian [bəˈvɛərɪən] ADJ, N bavarese *m/f*

bawdy [ˈbɔːdɪ] ADJ piccante, spinto(-a), salace; **bawdy song** canzonaccia

bawl [bɔːl] VI (*cry*) strillare; (*shout*) urlare, sbraitare
  ▸ **bawl out** VT + ADV **1** urlare (a squarciagola) **2** (*fam*): **to bawl sb out** fare una sfuriata *or* una lavata di testa a qn

bay¹ [beɪ] N (*Geog*) baia; **the Bay of Biscay** il golfo di Biscaglia

bay² [beɪ] N **1** (*Archit*) campata **2** (*Brit: for parking*) piazzola di sosta; (*for loading*) piazzale *m* di (sosta e) carico

bay³ [beɪ] N (*hound*) abbaiare, latrare ♦ VI (*bark*) latrato; **to keep sb/sth at bay** (*fig*) tenere a bada qn/qc

bay⁴ [beɪ] N (*also:* **bay tree**) alloro

bay leaf [ˈbeɪˌliːf] N foglia d'alloro

bayo·net [ˈbeɪənɪt] N baionetta ♦ VT infilzare con la baionetta

bay window N bovindo

ba·zaar [bəˈzɑːʳ] N (*sale of work*) vendita di beneficenza; (*Oriental market*) bazar *m inv*

ba·zoo·ka [bəˈzuːkə] N bazooka *m inv*

BBB [ˌbiːbiːˈbiː] N ABBR (*USA*: = *Better Business Bureau*) organismo per la difesa dei consumatori

BBC [ˌbiːbiːˈsiː] N ABBR (= *British Broadcasting Corporation*) BBC *f*

BC [ˌbiːˈsiː] ADV ABBR (= *before Christ*) a.C. ♦ ABBR = **British Columbia**

BCG [ˌbiːsiːˈdʒiː] N ABBR (= *Bacillus Calmette-Guérin*) vaccino antitubercolare

---

KEYWORD

be [biː] (*present* **am, is, are**, *pt* **was, were**, *pp* **been**) VI
  1 (*exist*) essere, esistere; **leave it as it is** lascialo così; **the best singer that ever was** il miglior cantante mai esistito; **how much was it?** quanto è costato?, quant'era?; **let me be!** lasciami in pace!; **so be it** sia pure, e sia; **be that as it may** sia come sia, comunque sia; **his wife to be** la sua futura moglie; **to be or not to be** essere o non essere
  2 (*in place*) essere, trovarsi; **she won't be here tomorrow** non ci sarà domani; **we've been here for ages** sono secoli che siamo qui; **Edinburgh is in Scotland** Edimburgo è *or* si trova in Scozia; **it's on the table** è *or* sta sul tavolo
  3 there is c'è; **there are** ci sono; **there were 3 of us** eravamo in 3; **there will be dancing** si ballerà; **there was once a house here** qua una volta c'era una casa; **let there be light** sia la luce
  4 (*presenting, pointing out*): **here is** *or* **here are** ecco; **there is** *or* **there are** (*over there*) ecco; **here you are (take it)** ecco qua (prendi); **there's the church** ecco la chiesa
  5 (*come, go: esp in perfect tense*): **I've been to China** sono stato in Cina; **where have you been?** dove sei stato?
  ♦ COPULATIVE VB
  1 essere; **2 and 2 are 4** 2 più 2 fa 4; **he's a pianist** è (un) pianista; **they're English** sono inglesi; **be good!** sii buono!; **I'm hot** ho caldo; **the book is in French** il libro è in francese; **I'm not Sue, I'm Mary** non sono Sue, sono Mary; **he's tall** è alto
  2 (*health*) stare; **I'm better now** ora sto meglio; **how are you?** come stai (*or* sta)?
  3 (*age*) **how old is she?** — **she's 9** quanti anni ha? — ne ha 9 *or* ha 9 anni
  ♦ IMPERS VB
  1 it is said that ... si dice che... + *sub*; **it is possible that ...** può darsi *or* essere che... + *sub*
  2 (*time*) essere; **it's the 3rd of May** è il 3 (di) maggio; **it's 8 o'clock** sono le 8
  3 (*measurement*): **it's 5 km to the village** da qui al paese sono 5 km
  4 (*weather*) fare; **it's too hot** fa troppo caldo
  5 (*emphatic*): **it's only me** sono solo io
  ♦ AUX VB
  1 (*with present participle: forming continuous tenses*): **they're coming tomorrow** vengono domani; **what are you doing?**

che fai?, che stai facendo?; **he's always grumbling** brontola sempre, non fa che brontolare; **I'll be seeing you** ci vediamo; **I've been waiting for her for 2 hours** l'aspetto da 2 ore **2** (*with past participle: forming passives*) essere; **what's to be done?** che fare?; **he is nowhere to be found** non lo si trova da nessuna parte; **to be killed** essere *or* venire ucciso(-a); **the box had been opened** la scatola era stata aperta **3** (*in tag questions*): **he's back again, is he?** così è tornato, eh?; **he's handsome, isn't he?** è un bell'uomo, vero?; **it was fun, wasn't it?** è stato bello, no?

4 (+ *to* + *infinitive*): **he's to be congratulated on his work** dobbiamo fargli i complimenti per il suo lavoro; **you're to do as I tell you** devi fare come ti dico; **he was to have come yesterday** sarebbe dovuto venire ieri; **he's not to open it** non deve aprirlo; **the car is to be sold** abbiamo (*or* hanno *etc*) intenzione di vendere la macchina; **am I to understand that ...?** devo dedurre che...?

5 (*modal: supposition*): **if it was** *or* **were to snow ...** (se) dovesse nevicare...; **if I were you ...** se fossi in te...

► **be in for** VI + ADV + PREP: **you'll only be in for a disappointment** non puoi che restare deluso; **we may be in for some trouble here** mi sa che qui potremmo avere delle grane

► **be on to** VI + ADV + PREP: **to be on to something** essere sulla pista giusta; **I think they're on to us** penso che abbiano dei sospetti su di noi

beach [biːtʃ] N spiaggia; **on the beach** in spiaggia ♦ VT tirare in secco

beach buggy N dune buggy *f inv*

beach·comber [ˈbiːtʃˌkəʊməʳ] N *persona che si aggira sulle spiagge alla ricerca di soldi, oggetti ecc*

beach·wear [ˈbiːtʃˌwɛəʳ] N abbigliamento da spiaggia

bea·con [ˈbiːkən] N (*fire*) fuoco di segnalazione; (*lighthouse*) faro, fanale *m*; (*radio beacon*) radiofaro; (*marker*) segnale *m*

bead [biːd] N perlina; (*of rosary*) grano; (*of dew, sweat*) goccia; **beads** NPL (*necklace*) collana; (*also*: **rosary beads**) corona (del rosario), rosario

beady [ˈbiːdɪ] ADJ: **beady eyes** occhi *mpl* piccoli e penetranti

bea·gle [ˈbiːgl] N bracchetto

beak [biːk] N becco

beak·er [ˈbiːkəʳ] N coppa; (*Chem*) becher *m inv*

beam [biːm] N **1** (*Archit*) trave *f* **2** (*Naut*) baglio **3** (*of light, sunlight*) raggio; (*of torch*) fascio (di luce); (*Radio*) fascio (d'onde); **to drive with headlights on full** *or* (*USA*) **high beam** guidare con gli abbaglianti accesi **4** (*smile*) sorriso raggiante ♦ VT (*Radio*) trasmettere con antenna direzionale a largo sorriso a qn ♦ VI (*smile*) sorridere radiosamente; **to beam at sb** fare un largo sorriso a qn

beam·ing [ˈbiːmɪŋ] ADJ (*sun*) splendente; (*face, smile*) raggiante

bean [biːn] N fagiolo; (*broad bean*) fava; (*runner bean*) fagiolino; (*of coffee*) grano, chicco; **green beans** fagiolini; **full of beans** (*fam: child*) che ha l'argento vivo addosso; (*: adult*) in gran forma

bean·pole [ˈbiːnˌpəʊl] N (*fam*) spilungone(-a)

bean·sprouts [ˈbiːnˌspraʊts], **bean·shoots** [ˈbiːnˌʃuːts] NPL germogli *mpl* di soia

KEYWORD

bear¹ [bɛəʳ] (*pt* **bore**, *pp* **borne**) VT
1 (*carry: burden, signature, date, name*) portare; (*: news, message*) recare; (*: traces, signs*) mostrare; **to bear some resemblance to** somigliare a; **he bore himself like a soldier** (*of posture*) aveva un portamento militare; (*of behaviour*) si comportò da soldato; **the love he bore her** l'amore che le portava; **to bear sb ill will** portare *or* serbare rancore a qn
2 (*support: weight*) reggere, sostenere; (*: cost*) sostenere; (*: responsibility*) assumere; (*: comparison*) reggere a; **the roof couldn't bear the weight of the snow** il tetto non ha retto il *or* al peso della neve
3 (*endure: pain*) sopportare; (*stand up to: inspection, examination*) reggere a; **he bore his sufferings bravely** ha sopportato con coraggio la sofferenza; **I can't bear it!** non lo sopporto!; **I can't bear him** non lo posso soffrire *or* sopportare; **I can't bear to look** non ho il coraggio di guardare; **it doesn't bear thinking about** non ci si può neanche pensare; **it**

won't bear close examination non bisogna guardarlo troppo da vicino
4 (*produce: fruit*) produrre, dare; (*: young*) partorire; (*: child*) generare, dare alla luce; (*Fin: interest*) fruttare
♦ VI
1 (*move*): **to bear right/left** andare a destra/sinistra, piegare a destra/sinistra; **to bear away** (*Naut*) poggiare
2 to bring sth to bear (on) (*influence, powers of persuasion*) esercitare qc (su); **to bring pressure to bear on sb** fare pressione su qn; **to bring one's mind to bear on sth** concentrarsi su qc

► **bear down** VI + ADV: **to bear down (on)** (*ship*) venire dritto (contro); (*person*) stare per piombare addosso (a)

► **bear on** VI + PREP (*frm*) essere in relazione con

► **bear out** VT + ADV (*theory, suspicion*) confermare, convalidare; (*person*) dare il proprio appoggio a

► **bear up** VI + ADV farsi coraggio; **he bore up well under the strain** ha sopportato bene lo stress

► **bear with** VI + PREP (*sb's moods, temper*) sopportare (con pazienza); **bear with me a minute** solo un attimo, prego; **if you'll bear with me ...** se ha la cortesia di aspettare (un attimo)...

bear² [bɛəʳ] N orso(-a); (*Stock Exchange*) ribassista *m/f*

bear·able [ˈbɛərəbl] ADJ sopportabile

beard [bɪəd] N barba ♦ VT: **to beard the lion in his den** (*hum*) affrontare il nemico in casa sua

beard·ed [ˈbɪədɪd] ADJ barbuto(-a)

bear·er [ˈbɛərəʳ] N (*of news, cheque*) portatore *m*; (*of passport*) titolare *m/f*

bear·ing [ˈbɛərɪŋ] N **1** (*of person*) portamento **2** (*relevance*): **bearing (on)** attinenza (con) **3** (*Tech*): **ball bearings** *npl* cuscinetti *mpl* a sfere **4** (*position*): **to take a compass bearing** effettuare un rilevamento con la bussola; **to take a ship's bearings** fare il punto nave; **to get** *or* **find one's bearings** orientarsi (*fig*); **to lose one's bearings** (*fig*) perdere l'orientamento

beast [biːst] N (*animal: also fam: disagreeable person*) bestia, animale *m*; (*cruel person*) bruto; **beast of burden** bestia da soma; **it's a beast of a job** (*fam*) è un lavoraccio

beast·ly [ˈbiːstlɪ] ADJ (*fam: person, behaviour*) insopportabile; (*: food*) orrendo(-a); (*: weather*) da cani

beat [biːt] (*pt* **beat**, *pp* **beaten**) N **1** colpo; (*of drum: single beat*) colpo; (*: repeated beating*) rullo; (*of heart*) battito; (*Mus: rhythm*) ritmo; (*: quaver, crotchet*) battuta; **to give the beat** dare il tempo **2** (*of policeman*) giro d'ispezione (a piedi), ronda; **on the beat** in giro d'ispezione, di ronda **3** (*Phys*) battimento ♦ VT **1** (*hit*) battere, picchiare; (*person: as punishment*) picchiare; (*: with stick*) bastonare; (*carpet*) battere, sbattere; (*drum*) suonare; **the bird beat its wings** l'uccello batteva le ali; **to beat time** (*Mus*) battere il tempo; **beat it!** (*fam*) fila!, aria! **2** (*defeat: team, army*) battere, sconfiggere; (*record*) battere; **we beat them three-nil** li abbiamo battuti tre a zero; **we were beaten** siamo stati battuti; **I beat him to it** (*fam*) ci sono arrivato prima di lui; **nothing beats a good cup of coffee** (*fam*) non c'è niente di meglio di un bel caffè; **that beats everything!** (*fam*) questo è il colmo!; **it beats me how they found out about it** (*fam*) non riesco a spiegarmi come l'abbiano scoperto; **it's got me beat(en)** (*fam*) devo arrendermi **3** (*Culin*) sbattere, battere ♦ VI (*heart*) battere, palpitare; (*drums*) rullare; **to beat on a door** picchiare a una porta; **the rain was beating against the windows** la pioggia batteva contro le finestre; **don't beat about the bush** non menare il can per l'aia ♦ ADJ **1** (*pred: fam: tired*) sfinito(-a) **2** (*usu attr: group, music*) beat *inv*

► **beat back, beat off** VT + ADV respingere

► **beat out** VT + ADV (*flames*) spegnere (battendo); (*dent*) ribattere, martellare; (*rhythm*) battere

► **beat down** VT + ADV (*door*) abbattere, buttare giù; (*price*) far abbassare; (*seller*) far scendere ♦ VI + ADV (*rain*) sgrosciare; (*sun*) picchiare

► **beat up** VT + ADV (*person*) picchiare, pestare; (*egg whites*) montare; **they beat him up** l'hanno picchiato

beat·er [ˈbiːtəʳ] N (*Culin*) frullino; (*carpet beater*) battipanni *m inv*

beat·ing [ˈbiːtɪŋ] N **1** (*punishment*) botte *fpl*; **to give sb a**

beating riempire qn di botte 2 (*defeat*) sconfitta, batosta; **to take a beating** prendere una (bella) batosta

beat-up [ˌbiːtˈʌp] ADJ (*fam*) scassato(-a)

beau·ti·cian [bjuːˈtɪʃən] N estetista *m/f*

beau·ti·ful [ˈbjuːtɪfʊl] ADJ bello(-a), splendido(-a); **thank you for the beautiful present** grazie del bel regalo; **a beautiful old watch** un bell'orologio antico; **a beautiful sapphire** un bello zaffiro; **thanks for the beautiful flowers** grazie dei bei fiori; **he's got beautiful eyes** ha begli occhi; **the weather was really beautiful** ha fatto bellissimo tempo

beau·ti·ful·ly [ˈbjuːtɪflɪ] ADV splendidamente, magnificamente

beau·ti·fy [ˈbjuːtɪfaɪ] VT abbellire

beau·ty [ˈbjuːtɪ] N (*concept*) bello; (*of person, thing*) bellezza; **beauty is in the eye of the beholder** non è bello ciò che è bello, è bello ciò che piace; **the beauty of it is that ...** il bello è che...; **his car's a beauty!** (*fam*) ha una macchina che è una meraviglia *or* una bellezza! ♦ ADJ (*consultant, counter*) di bellezza

beauty contest N concorso di bellezza

beauty parlour N istituto di bellezza

beauty salon N istituto di bellezza

beauty sleep N: **to get one's beauty sleep** (*hum*) farsi un sonno ristoratore

beauty spot N (*in country*) luogo di particolare bellezza; (*on face*) neo

bea·ver [ˈbiːvəʳ] N castoro

be·calmed [bɪˈkɑːmd] ADJ: **to be becalmed** essere fermo(-a) per mancanza di vento

be·came [bɪˈkeɪm] PT *of* become

be·cause [bɪˈkɒz] CONJ (*gen*) perché; **I ate it because I was hungry** l'ho mangiato perché ero affamato; **all the more surprising because** ancora più sorprendente dal momento che *or* poiché; **because of** a causa di

beck [bɛk] N: **to be at sb's beck and call** dover essere a completa disposizione di qn

beck·on [ˈbɛkən] VT, VI: **to beckon to sb** chiamare qn con un cenno; **he beckoned a waitress** ha chiamato una cameriera con un cenno; **he beckoned me in/over** mi ha fatto cenno di entrare/di avvicinarmi

be·come [bɪˈkʌm] (*pt* **became**, *pp* **become**) VI diventare, divenire; **to become famous** diventare famoso(-a); **to become fat/thin** ingrassare/dimagrire; **to become angry** arrabbiarsi; **to become accustomed to sth** abituarsi a qc; **to become a doctor** diventare medico; **it became increasingly difficult to cover costs** è diventato sempre più difficile far fronte ai costi; **it became known that** si è venuto a sapere che ♦ IMPERS VB: **what has become of him?** che ne è stato di lui?; **whatever can have become of that book?** dove sarà mai finito quel libro? ♦ VT: **it does not become her** (*dress etc*) non le sta bene; (*behaviour*) non le si addice

be·com·ing [bɪˈkʌmɪŋ] ADJ (*frm: clothes*) grazioso(-a), che dona; (: *behaviour, language*) adatto(-a), che si addice alla situazione

bed [bɛd] N 1 letto; **a single bed** un letto singolo; **a double bed** un letto matrimoniale; **to go to bed** andare a letto; **to go to bed with sb** andare a letto con qn; **to get out of bed** alzarsi dal letto; **to get out of bed on the wrong side** alzarsi col piede sbagliato; **to make the bed** (ri)fare il letto; **to put sb to bed** mettere qn a letto; **I was in bed** ero a letto; **could you give me a bed for the night?** puoi tenermi a dormire per stanotte?; **his life's not a bed of roses** la sua vita non è tutta rose e fiori 2 (*of sea, lake*) fondo; (*of river*) letto; **the river bed** il letto del fiume; **the sea bed** il fondo marino 3 (*flower bed*) aiuola; **oyster bed** banco di ostriche; **vegetable bed** orticello 4 (*layer: of coal, ore, clay*) strato; (: *in road building*) massicciata

▸ **bed out** VT + ADV (*plants*) piantare a intervalli regolari

▸ **bed down** VI + ADV sistemarsi (per dormire)

bed and breakfast N ≈ bed and breakfast *m inv*; **to book in for bed and breakfast** prenotare una camera con prima colazione

bed·bug [ˈbɛdˌbʌg] N cimice *f* (dei letti)

bed·clothes [ˈbɛdˌkləʊðz] NPL coperte e lenzuola *fpl*; **the bedclothes** la biancheria da letto

bed·cov·er [ˈbɛdˌkʌvəʳ] N copriletto

bed·ding [ˈbɛdɪŋ] N coperte e lenzuola *fpl*; (*for animal*) lettiera; **the bedding** la biancheria da letto

be·dev·il [bɪˈdɛvl] VT (*person*) affliggere, tormentare; (*enterprise*) intralciare, ostacolare continuamente

bed·fellow [ˈbɛdˌfɛləʊ] N: **they are strange bedfellows** (*fig*) fanno una coppia ben strana

bed·lam [ˈbɛdləm] N baraonda

bed linen N biancheria da letto

bed·pan [ˈbɛdˌpæn] N padella

bed·post [ˈbɛdˌpəʊst] N colonnina del letto

be·drag·gled [bɪˈdrægld] ADJ (*person, clothes*) sbrindellato(-a); (*hair*) scompigliato(-a); (*wet*) bagnato(-a) fradicio(-a)

bed·rid·den [ˈbɛdˌrɪdən] ADJ costretto(-a) *or* inchiodato(-a) a letto

bed·rock [ˈbɛdˌrɒk] N (*Geol*) basamento; (*fig*) fondamento, base *f*

bed·room [ˈbɛdˌrʊm] N camera (da letto), stanza da letto; **a three-bedroom house** una casa con tre camere da letto

bed settee N divano *m* letto, *inv*

bed·side [ˈbɛdˌsaɪd] N: **at his bedside** al suo capezzale ♦ ADJ: **to have a good bedside manner** (*doctor*) saper trattare i pazienti

bedside lamp N lampada da comodino, abat-jour *m inv*

bedside table N comodino

bed·spread [ˈbɛdˌsprɛd] N copriletto

bed·time [ˈbɛdˌtaɪm] N: **it's bedtime** è ora di andare a letto; **bedtime!** a nanna!; **ten o'clock is my usual bedtime** generalmente vado a letto alle dieci; **it's past your bedtime** a quest'ora dovresti già essere a letto ♦ ADJ: **will you tell me a bedtime story?** mi racconti una storia prima di dormire?

bee [biː] N (*Zool*) ape *f*; **to have a bee in one's bonnet (about sth)** avere la fissazione (di qc)

beech [biːtʃ] N faggio

beef [biːf] N (*Culin*) manzo; **roast beef** roast beef *m inv*, arrosto di manzo

▸ **beef up** VT + ADV (*fam*) rinforzare

beef·bur·ger [ˈbiːfˌbɜːgəʳ] N hamburger *m inv*

beef·eater [ˈbiːfˌiːtəʳ] N guardia della Torre di Londra

bee·hive [ˈbiːˌhaɪv] N alveare *m*

bee·keep·ing [ˈbiːˌkiːpɪŋ] N apicoltura

bee·line [ˈbiːˌlaɪn] N: **to make a beeline for sb/sth** (*fam*) andare diretto(-a) verso qn/qc

been [biːn] PP *of* be

beep [biːp] N (*of horn*) colpo di clacson; (*of phone etc*) segnale *m* (acustico), bip *m inv* ♦ VI (*horn*) suonare; (*computer, pager*) fare bip

beep·er [ˈbiːpəʳ] N cicalino; (*of doctor etc*) cercapersone *m inv*

beer [bɪəʳ] N birra

beer belly N (*fam*) stomaco da bevitore

beer can N lattina di birra

beet [biːt] N barbabietola

bee·tle [ˈbiːtl] N (*Zool*) coleottero; (*scarab*) scarabeo; (*black beetle*) scarafaggio

beet·root [ˈbiːtˌruːt] N (*Brit*) barbabietola

be·fall [bɪˈfɔːl] (*pt* **befell** [bɪˈfɛl], *pp* **befallen** [bɪˈfɔːlən]) VT accadere a

be·fit [bɪˈfɪt] IMPERS VB (*frm*): **to befit sb** addirsi a qn, confarsi a qn; **it ill befits you to speak in this way** non ti si addice *or* non ti si confà parlare così

be·fore [bɪˈfɔːʳ] PREP 1 (*in time*) prima di; **before 7 o'clock** prima delle 7; **before Tuesday** prima di martedì; **the day before last** *or* **yesterday** due giorni fa, l'altro ieri, ieri l'altro; **before Christ** avanti Cristo; **before long** fra poco, fra non molto 2 (*in place, rank, in the presence of*) davanti a; **a new life lay before him** una nuova vita si apriva davanti a lui; **to appear before a judge** comparire davanti *or* dinanzi a un giudice; **the question before us** la questione di cui ci dobbiamo occupare; **before my very eyes** proprio sotto i miei occhi; **ladies before gentlemen** prima le signore, la precedenza alle signore; **to put friendship before money** anteporre l'amicizia all'interesse ♦ ADV prima; **the day before** il giorno prima *or* precedente; **I've seen this film before** questo film l'ho già visto; **I've never seen it before** è la prima volta che lo vedo; **the week before** la settimana prima; **I knew long before that ...** sapevo da molto tempo che... ♦ CONJ (*time*) prima di + *infin*, prima che + *sub*; (*rather than*) piuttosto che; **before doing it you ...**, **before you do it, you ...** prima di farlo, tu..., prima che tu lo faccia, tu...

before·hand [bɪˈfɔːhænd] ADV prima, in anticipo; **let me know your plans beforehand** fammi sapere i tuoi piani in anticipo

be·friend [bɪˈfrɛnd] VT mostrare amicizia a

be·fud·dled [bɪˈfʌdld] ADJ confuso(-a)

beg [bɛɡ] VT **1** (*entreat*) supplicare, pregare; (*favour*) chiedere; (*subj: beggar: food, money*) mendicare; **he begged me for mercy** mi supplicava di aver pietà; **he begged me to help him** mi ha supplicato *or* pregato di aiutarlo; **to beg forgiveness** implorare perdono; **I beg your pardon** (*apologising*) mi scusi; (*not hearing*) scusi?; **I beg to differ** mi permetto di non essere d'accordo **2 this begs the question** questo dà per scontato ciò che dev'essere ancora dimostrato ♦ VI (*entreat*) supplicare, pregare; (*beggar*) chiedere l'elemosina *or* la carità; **there were a lot of people begging** c'era molta gente che chiedeva l'elemosina; **it's going begging** (*fam*) non lo vuole proprio nessuno
▸ **beg off** VI + ADV disdire

be·gan [bɪˈɡæn] PT *of* begin

beg·gar [ˈbɛɡəʳ] N mendicante *m/f*; **beggars can't be choosers** o mangiar questa minestra o saltar dalla finestra ♦ VT (*ruin*) ridurre sul lastrico *or* in miseria; **it beggars description** è indescrivibile

be·gin [bɪˈɡɪn] (*pt* began, *pp* begun) VT (*gen*) cominciare, incominciare, iniziare; (*originate: fashion*) lanciare; (: *custom*) inaugurare; (: *war*) scatenare; **to begin doing sth, to begin to do sth** incominciare *or* iniziare a fare qc; **it began to rain** ha cominciato *or* si è messo a piovere; **this skirt began life as an evening dress** questa gonna in origine era un abito da sera; **it doesn't begin to compare with ...** non c'è nemmeno da paragonarlo con...; **I can't begin to thank you** non so proprio come ringraziarti ♦ VI incominciare, cominciare; (*fashion, custom*) nascere; (*rumour*) spargersi; **to begin with sth/by doing sth** cominciare con qc/col fare qc; **to begin on sth** cominciare qc; **it began to rain** ha iniziato a piovere; **the match began at 10 a.m.** la partita è iniziata alle dieci del mattino; **the film has just begun** il film è appena iniziato; **let me begin by saying ...** permettetemi di cominciare col dire...; **to begin with, I'd like to know ...** tanto per cominciare vorrei sapere...; **to begin with there were only two of us** all'inizio eravamo solo in due; **beginning on Monday** a partire da lunedì; **the service began at 9 a.m.** la funzione ha avuto inizio alle 9

be·gin·ner [bɪˈɡɪnəʳ] N principiante *m/f*; **it's just beginner's luck** è la solita fortuna del principiante

be·gin·ning [bɪˈɡɪnɪŋ] N inizio, principio; **in the beginning** all'inizio; **at the beginning of the century** all'inizio *or* al principio del secolo; **right from the beginning** fin dal primo momento, fin dall'inizio; **start at the beginning and tell me all about it** raccontami tutto (cominciando *or* a partire) dall'inizio; **the beginning of the end** il principio della fine; **to make a beginning** cominciare; **the beginning of the world** le origini del mondo; **Buddhism had its beginnings ...** il buddismo nacque *or* ebbe origine...

be·grudge [bɪˈɡrʌdʒ] VT = grudge

be·guile [bɪˈɡaɪl] VT (*enchant*) incantare

be·guil·ing [bɪˈɡaɪlɪŋ] ADJ seducente; (*charming*) allettante

be·gun [bɪˈɡʌn] PP *of* begin

be·half [bɪˈhɑːf] N: **on behalf of** *or* (*USA*) **in behalf of** (*prep*) per conto di; (*thank, accept*) a nome di; **he spoke on my behalf** ha parlato a nome mio

be·have [bɪˈheɪv] VI (*also: behave o.s.*) (*conduct o.s.*) comportarsi; (*conduct o.s. well*) comportarsi bene; **he behaved like an idiot** si è comportato da stupido; **you behaved very wisely** hai agito saggiamente; **to behave well towards sb** comportarsi bene nei confronti di qn; **did the children behave themselves?** si sono comportati bene i bambini?; **behave (yourself)!** comportati bene!

be·hav·iour, **be·hav·ior** (*USA*) [bɪˈheɪvjəʳ] N comportamento; **to be on one's best behaviour** sforzarsi di comportarsi bene

be·head [bɪˈhɛd] VT decapitare

be·held [bɪˈhɛld] PT, PP *of* behold

be·hind [bɪˈhaɪnd] PREP dietro; (*time*) in ritardo con; **behind the sofa** dietro il divano; **look behind you!** guarda dietro di te!; **what's behind all this?** (*fig*) cosa c'è sotto?; **we're behind them in technology** (*fig*) siamo più indietro *or* più arretrati di loro nella tecnica; **his family is behind him** (*fig*) ha l'appoggio della famiglia; **behind the scenes** dietro le quinte ♦ ADV dietro; **to stay behind (to do sth)** fermarsi (a fare qc); **to leave sth behind** dimenticare di prendere qc; **to be behind with sth** essere indietro con qc; (*payments*) essere in arretrato con qc; **I'm behind with my work** sono indietro con il lavoro ♦ N (*fam*) didietro *m inv*

be·hold [bɪˈhəʊld] (*pt, pp* beheld) VT (*old, liter*) scorgere, vedere

beige [beɪʒ] ADJ, N beige *m inv*

Bei·jing [ˈbeɪˈdʒɪŋ] N Pechino *f*

be·ing [ˈbiːɪŋ] N **1** (*existence*) essere *m*, esistenza; **to come into being** nascere, essere creato(-a); **to bring sth into being** creare qc **2** (*creature*) essere *m*

Bei·rut [beɪˈruːt] N Beirut *f*

Belarus [ˈbelərʊs] N Bielorussia

be·lat·ed [bɪˈleɪtɪd] ADJ in ritardo; **his belated arrival** il suo ritardo

belch [bɛltʃ] N rutto ♦ VI ruttare ♦ VT (*also:* belch out: *smoke*) sputare (fuori); (*flames*) eruttare, vomitare

be·lea·guered [bɪˈliːɡəd] ADJ (*city*) assediato(-a); (*person*) assillato(-a); (*army*) accerchiato(-a); (*project, organization*) pieno(-a) di problemi

Bel·fast [ˈbelfɑːst] N Belfast *f*

bel·fry [ˈbelfrɪ] N campanile *m*

Bel·gian [ˈbeldʒən] ADJ, N belga *m/f*

Bel·gium [ˈbeldʒəm] N Belgio

Bel·grade [belˈɡreɪd] N Belgrado *f*

be·lie [bɪˈlaɪ] VT (*prove false*) smentire; (*give false impression of*) nascondere

be·lief [bɪˈliːf] N (*faith*) fede *f*; (*trust*) fiducia; (*tenet, doctrine, opinion*) convinzione *f*, opinione *f*; (*acceptance as true*) credenza; **belief in God** fede in Dio; **it's a belief held by all Christians** è credenza comune a tutti i cristiani; **it's beyond belief** è incredibile; **rich beyond belief** incredibilmente ricco(-a); **a man of strong beliefs** un uomo dalle ferme convinzioni; **it is my belief that** sono convinto che; **in the belief that** nella convinzione che

be·lieve [bɪˈliːv] VT (*story, person*) credere a; **to believe (that)** (*be of the opinion that*) credere (che); **I don't believe he'll come** non credo che verrà *or* che venga; **don't you believe it!** non crederci!; **I don't believe a word of it!** non credo a una parola di tutto questo!; **he is believed to be abroad** si pensa (che) sia all'estero ♦ VI credere; **to believe in** (*God*) credere in; (*ghosts*) credere a; (*method*) avere fiducia in; **do you believe in ghosts?** credi ai fantasmi?; **I don't believe in corporal punishment** sono contrario alle punizioni corporali

be·liev·er [bɪˈliːvəʳ] N (*Rel*) credente *m/f*; **to be a believer in** (*in idea, activity*) essere a favore di; **a great believer in** un(a) gran(de) sostenitore(-trice) di

be·lit·tle [bɪˈlɪtl] VT sminuire

Be·lize [beˈliːz] N Belize *m*

bell [bel] N (*small, on door, electric*) campanello; (*church bell*) campana; (*on cats, harness*) sonaglio; (*on cow*) campanaccio; (*of telephone*) soneria; **I rang the bell, but nobody came** ho suonato il campanello, ma non è arrivato nessuno; **the church bell** la campana della chiesa; **the bell goes at half past three** la campanella suona alle tre e mezza; **that rings a bell** (*fig*) mi ricorda qualcosa

bell-bottoms [ˈbelˌbɒtəmz] NPL pantaloni *mpl* a zampa d'elefante, pantaloni *mpl* a campana

bell·boy [ˈbelˌbɔɪ], (*USA*) **bell·hop** [ˈbelˌhɒp] N ragazzo d'albergo, fattorino d'albergo

bel·lig·er·ent [bɪˈlɪdʒərənt] ADJ (*at war*) belligerante; (*fig*) bellicoso(-a)

bel·low [ˈbeləʊ] N (*of bull etc*) muggito; (*of person*) urlo ♦ VI (*see n*) muggire; urlare (a squarciagola) ♦ VT (*also:* bellow out: *order, song*) urlare (a squarciagola)

bel·lows [ˈbɛləʊz] NPL (*of forge, organ*) mantice *m*; (*for fire*) soffietto

bell pepper N (*USA*) peperone *m*

bell push N bottone *m or* pulsante *m* del campanello

bel·ly [ˈbɛlɪ] N pancia

belly·ache [ˈbɛlɪˌeɪk](*fam*) N mal *m* di pancia ♦ VI (*fam*) mugugnare

belly·button [ˈbɛlˌbʌtn] N (*fam*) ombelico

bel·ly·ful [ˈbɛlɪˌfʊl] N (*fam*): **to have had a bellyful of sb/sth** aver fatto un'indigestione di qn/qc

be·long [bɪˈlɒŋ] VI **1 to belong to sb/sth** (*be the property of*) appartenere a qn/qc; **this ring belonged to my grandmother** quest'anello era di mia nonna; **who does this belong to?** questo di chi è?; **that belongs to me** è mio; **to belong to a club** essere socio(-a) di un club **2** (*have rightful place*): **put it back where it belongs** rimettilo al suo posto; **where does this belong?** dove va questo?; **it belongs on the shelf** va sullo scaffale; **I felt I didn't belong** mi sentivo un estraneo

be·long·ings [bɪˈlɒŋɪŋz] NPL ciò che si possiede, cose *fpl* (*fam*); **he lost all his belongings** ha perso tutto ciò che possedeva; **I collected my belongings and left** ho raccolto le mie cose e me ne sono andato; **personal belongings** effetti *mpl* personali

Be·lo·rus·sia [ˌbɛləʊˈrʌʃə] N = Byelorussia

Be·lo·rus·sian [ˌbɛləʊˈrʌʃən] ADJ, N = Byelorussian

be·lov·ed [bɪˈlʌvɪd] ADJ, N adorato(-a)

be·low [bɪˈləʊ] PREP sotto, al di sotto di; **ten degrees below freezing** dieci gradi sotto zero; **temperatures below normal** temperature al di sotto del normale; **on the floor below** al piano di sotto; **they live in the apartment below us** abitano nell'appartamento sotto al nostro ♦ ADV sotto, di sotto; **the mountains below** le montagne sottostanti; **the apartment below** l'appartamento al piano di sotto; **see below** (*on page*) vedi sotto *or* oltre

belt [bɛlt] N (*gen*) cintura; (*of trousers*) cintura, cinghia; (*Tech*) cinghia; (*Geog: zone*) zona, regione *f*; **industrial belt** zona industriale; **the cotton belt** la zona di coltivazione del cotone; **to tighten one's belt** (*fig*) tirare la cinghia; **that was below the belt** (*fig*) è stato un colpo basso ♦ VT (*fam: thrash*) usare la cinghia con, picchiare; **he belted me one** mi ha mollato un pugno ♦ VI (*fam: rush*): **to belt in/out** *etc* entrare/uscire *etc* di gran carriera; **he was belting up the motorway at 100 mph** filava sull'autostrada a 100 miglia all'ora

▸ **belt out** VT + ADV (*song*) cantare a squarciagola

▸ **belt up** VI + ADV (*fam: be quiet*) chiudere la boccaccia; **belt up!** chiudi quella boccaccia!

belt·way [ˈbɛltˌweɪ] N (*USA: Aut*) circonvallazione *f*; (*motorway*) raccordo anulare; **inside/outside the Beltway** (*USA*) all'interno/all'esterno di Washington DC

be·moan [bɪˈməʊn] VT lamentare

be·mused [bɪˈmjuːzd] ADJ perplesso(-a), stupito(-a)

bench [bɛntʃ] N (*seat: with back*) panchina; (: *without back*) panca; (: *in parliament, workbench*) banco; **to be on the Bench** (*Law*) essere giudice

bench·mark [ˈbɛntʃmɑːk] N (*Fin*) benchmark *m inv*, indice *m* di riferimento ♦ VT rapportare ad un indice di riferimento

bend [bɛnd] (*pt, pp* **bent**) N (*in road*) curva; (*in river*) ansa, gomito; (*in arm, knee*) piega; (*in pipe*) gomito; **he drives me round the bend!** (*fam*) mi fa diventare matto! ♦ VT (*wire etc*) curvare, piegare; (*knee*) flettere, piegare; (*arm*) piegare; (*head*) piegare, chinare; **I can't bend my arm** non riesco a piegare il braccio ♦ VI piegarsi, curvarsi; (*road*) fare una curva; (*river*) fare un gomito; (*person*) chinarsi; **it bends easily** si piega facilmente

▸ **bend down** VI + ADV chinarsi; **she bent down to pick a flower** si è chinata a raccogliere un fiore

▸ **bend over** VI + ADV chinarsi, piegarsi; **to bend over backwards** (*fig*) farsi in quattro

bends [bɛndz] NPL (*Med*): **the bends** un'embolia

be·neath [bɪˈniːθ] PREP sotto, al di sotto di; (*unworthy of*) indegno(-a) di; **it is beneath my notice** non è degno della mia attenzione; **it is beneath him to do such a thing** non si degnerebbe mai di fare una cosa del genere; **he thinks it's**

beneath him si ritiene superiore ♦ ADV sotto, di sotto; **the apartment beneath** l'appartamento al piano di sotto

ben·efac·tor [ˈbɛnɪfæktəʳ] N benefattore *m*

ben·efac·tress [ˈbɛnɪfæktrɪs] N benefattrice *f*

ben·efi·cial [ˌbɛnɪˈfɪʃəl] ADJ benefico(-a); **beneficial to** che giova a, che fa bene a; **vitamin A is beneficial to one's health** la vitamina A fa bene alla salute

bene·fi·ciary [ˌbɛnɪˈfɪʃərɪ] N (*Law*) beneficiario(-a)

benefit [ˈbɛnɪfɪt] N **1** vantaggio, beneficio; **the benefits of a good education** i vantaggi di una buona educazione; **the benefits of this treatment** i benefici di questa terapia; **it might be of some benefit to you** potrebbe giovarti; **for the benefit of one's health** per la propria salute; **to give sb the benefit of the doubt** concedere a qn il beneficio del dubbio **2** (*allowance*) indennità *f inv*, sussidio; **unemployment benefit** indennità di disoccupazione; **state benefits** sussidio dello Stato; **to live on benefit** vivere col sussidio dello Stato **3** manifestazione *f* di beneficenza; **a benefit concert** un concerto di beneficenza ♦ VI trarre vantaggio *or* profitto da; **he'll benefit from it** ne trarrà beneficio *or* profitto; **he'll benefit from the change** il cambiamento gli farà bene ♦ VT giovare a, far bene a; **a service which will benefit rich and poor** un servizio che gioverà sia ai ricchi che ai poveri; **the scheme benefits children** il programma si rivolge ai bambini

benefit performance N spettacolo di beneficenza

Bene·lux [ˈbɛnɪlʌks] ADJ: **the Benelux countries** i paesi del Benelux ♦ N il Benelux *m*

be·nevo·lent [bɪˈnɛvələnt] ADJ benevolo(-a)

be·nign [bɪˈnaɪn] ADJ benevolo(-a); (*Med*) benigno(-a); **the tumour was benign** il tumore era benigno

bent [bɛnt] PT, PP *of* **bend** ♦ ADJ **1** (*wire, pipe*) piegato(-a), storto(-a); (*fam: dishonest*) losco(-a) **2** (*fig: determined*): **to be bent on sth/on doing sth** essere deciso(-a) a qc/a fare qc; **to be bent on a quarrel** voler proprio litigare ♦ N (*aptitude*) inclinazione *f*, disposizione *f*; **to follow one's bent** seguire la propria inclinazione

be·queath [bɪˈkwiːð] VT: **to bequeath sth to sb** lasciare qc in eredità a qn

be·quest [bɪˈkwɛst] N lascito

be·reaved [bɪˈriːvd] ADJ in lutto ♦ **the bereaved** NPL i familiari in lutto

be·reave·ment [bɪˈriːvmənt] N lutto

be·ret [ˈbɛreɪ] N berretto

Bering Sea [ˈbɛərɪŋˈsiː] N: **the Bering Sea** il mare di Bering

Ber·lin [bɜːˈlɪn] N Berlino *f*; **East/West Berlin** Berlino est/ ovest

Ber·mu·da [bɜːˈmjuːdə] N: **the Bermudas** le Bermude

Bermuda shorts NPL bermuda *mpl*

Bern [bɜːn] N Berna *f*

ber·ry [ˈbɛrɪ] N bacca; **poisonous berries** bacche velenose; **brown as a berry** abbronzatissimo(-a)

ber·serk [bəˈsɜːk] ADJ: **to go berserk** dare in escandescenze; (*with anger*) andare *or* montare su tutte le furie, andare in bestia

berth [bɜːθ] N (*on ship, train*) cuccetta; (*Naut: place at wharf*) ormeggio; **to give sb a wide berth** (*fig*) tenersi alla larga da qn ♦ VI ormeggiare; (*in harbour*) entrare in porto

be·seech [bɪˈsiːtʃ] (*pt, pp* **besought**) VT (*liter*) implorare

be·set [bɪˈsɛt] (*pt, pp* **beset**) VT (*afflict*) assillare; (*attack*) assalire; **a policy beset with dangers** una politica irta *or* piena di pericoli

be·set·ting [bɪˈsɛtɪŋ] ADJ: **his besetting sin** il suo più grande difetto

be·side [bɪˈsaɪd] PREP (*at the side of*) accanto a, vicino a; (*compared with*) rispetto a, in confronto a; **beside the television** accanto al televisore; **to be beside o.s. (with)** (*anger, joy etc*) essere fuori di sé (da); **that's beside the point** questo non c'entra niente

be·sides [bɪˈsaɪdz] PREP (*in addition to*) oltre a; (*apart from*) all'infuori di, a parte; **besides, it's too expensive** e inoltre è troppo caro; **besides which ...** per di più... ♦ ADV (*in addition*) inoltre; (*anyway*) poi, del resto, per di più; **and more besides** e altro ancora

be·siege [bɪˈsiːdʒ] VT (*Mil, also fig*) assediare, assalire; **we**

were besieged with inquiries siamo stati tempestati di domande

be·sot·ted [bɪˈsɒtɪd] ADJ: **besotted with sb** infatuato(-a) di qn

be·sought [bɪˈsɔːt] PT, PP *of* beseech

be·spec·ta·cled [bɪˈspɛktɪkld] ADJ occhialuto(-a)

be·spoke [bɪˈspəʊk] ADJ (*Brit: garment*) su misura; **bespoke tailor** sarto (*che lavora su ordinazione*)

best [bɛst] ADJ *superl of* good migliore; **to be best** essere il (la) migliore; **he's the best player in the team** è il migliore giocatore della squadra; **the best pupil in the class** il (la) primo(-a) della classe; **in her best dress** vestita del suo abito migliore; **my best friend** il (la) mio(-a) migliore amico(-a); **the best thing about her is ...** la cosa più bella di lei è...; **the best thing to do is ...** la cosa migliore da fare *or* farsi è...; **for the best part of the year** per la maggior parte dell'anno; **may the best man win!** vinca il migliore! ♦ ADV *superl of* well[2] meglio; **Emma sings best** Emma canta meglio di tutti; **the best liked** il (la) più amato(-a); **the best dressed** il (la) più elegante; **as best I could** meglio che ho potuto; **you know best** tu sai meglio di chiunque; **John came off best** John ha avuto la meglio; **you had best leave now** faresti meglio ad andartene ora; **best before ...** da consumarsi preferibilmente entro... ♦ N il (la) migliore; **she's the best at drawing** disegna meglio di tutti; **he deserves the best** si merita quanto c'è di meglio; **at best** nella migliore delle ipotesi, tutt'al più; **he wasn't at his best** non era in vena *or* in piena forma; **he's not exactly patient at the best of times** non è mai molto paziente; **I acted for the best** ho agito per il meglio; **let's hope for the best** speriamo che tutto vada per il meglio; **to the best of my knowledge** per quel che ne so io; **I did it to the best of my ability** l'ho fatto come meglio ho potuto; **to do one's best** fare del proprio meglio; **it's not perfect, but I did my best** non è perfetto, ma ho fatto del mio meglio; **to look its best** (*house, apartment*) esser bello(-a) ed ordinato(-a); **to make the best of it** accontentarsi; **we'll have to make the best of it** dovremo accontentarci; **to make the best of a bad job** far buon viso a cattivo gioco; **all the best!** saluti!

best-before date N (*Comm*): **"best-before date: ..."** da consumarsi preferibilmente entro il...

best man N testimone *m* dello sposo

be·stow [bɪˈstəʊ] VT: **to bestow sth on sb** (*title*) conferire qc a qn; (*honour, affections*) accordare qc a qn

best·sell·er [ˌbɛstˈsɛlə[r]] N bestseller *m inv*

bet [bɛt] (PT, PP bet *or* betted) N scommessa; **to put a bet on** fare una scommessa su; **it's a safe bet** (*fig*) è molto probabile ♦ VI: **to bet (on)** scommettere (su); **to bet on a horse** scommettere *or* puntare su un cavallo; **are you going? — you bet!** (*fam*) ci vai? — ci puoi giurare!; **I'm not a betting man** non sono uno scommettitore ♦ VT scommettere; **he bet £5 on the favourite** ha giocato *or* puntato 5 sterline sul favorito; **I bet you a pound that ...** scommettiamo una sterlina che...; **I bet you he won't come** (*fam*) scommetti che non viene!; **you can bet your life that ...** (*fam*) puoi scommetterci la testa che...

Beth·le·hem [ˈbɛθlɪˌhɛm] N Betlemme *f*

be·tray [bɪˈtreɪ] VT (*also fig*) tradire; **he betrayed her trust** ha tradito la sua fiducia; **to betray sb to the enemy** consegnare qn nelle mani del nemico; **his face betrayed his surprise** il suo viso tradiva la sorpresa

be·tray·al [bɪˈtreɪəl] N tradimento

bet·ter [ˈbɛtə[r]] ADJ *comp of* good migliore; **this one's better than that one** questo è migliore di quello; **I'm better at German than French** riesco meglio in tedesco che in francese; **he's better than his brother at mending cars** è più bravo di suo fratello ad aggiustare le macchine; **are you better now?** (*in health*) stai meglio adesso?; **are you feeling better now?** ti senti meglio ora?; **to get better** migliorare; (*Med*) star meglio, rimettersi; **that's better!** così va meglio!; **it couldn't be better** non potrebbe andar meglio (di così); **it would be better to go now** sarebbe meglio andare adesso; **he's no better than a thief** non è né più né meno che un ladro; **it lasted the better part of a year** è durato quasi un anno ♦ ADV *comp of* well[2] meglio; **he speaks French better than Italian/his brother** parla il francese meglio

dell'italiano/di suo fratello; **better known** meglio *or* più conosciuto(-a); **so much the better, all the better** tanto meglio, meglio così; **he was all the better for it** ci ha guadagnato, gli ha fatto molto bene; **better still** meglio ancora; **you'd be better off staying where you are** faresti meglio a restare dove sei; **I had better go** dovrei andare; **hadn't you better ask him?** non sarebbe meglio se lo chiedessi a lui?; **to think better of it** cambiare idea ♦ N: **a change for the better** un cambiamento in meglio; **for better or worse** nella buona o nella cattiva sorte; **to get the better of sb** avere la meglio su qn; **one's betters** i propri superiori ♦ VT migliorare; **to better o.s.** migliorare la propria condizione

bet·ting [ˈbɛtɪŋ] N scommesse *fpl*; **what's the betting he'll be late?** (*fig*) quando scommettiamo che arriverà in ritardo?

betting shop N (*Brit*) ufficio dell'allibratore *m*

be·tween [bɪˈtwiːn] PREP (*gen*) tra, fra; **the road between here and London** la strada da qui a Londra; **a village between Florence and Pisa** un paese tra Firenze e Pisa; **between fifteen and twenty minutes** tra i quindici e i venti minuti; **between now and next week we must ...** da qui alla settimana prossima dobbiamo...; **I sat (in) between John and Sue** ero seduto (in mezzo) tra John e Sue; **it's between 5 and 6 metres long** è lungo fra i 5 e i 6 metri; **we shared it between us** ce lo siamo diviso tra di noi; **just between you and me *or* ourselves ...** (sia detto) tra me e te..., sia detto tra noi (due)...; **we only had £5 between us** fra tutti e due avevamo solo 5 sterline ♦ ADV (*also:* in between) (*of place*) in mezzo; (*of time*) nel frattempo; **few and far between** rarissimi

bev·el [ˈbɛvəl] N (*surface*) superficie *f* obliqua; (*bevel edge*) spigolo smussato ♦ VT smussare

bev·er·age [ˈbɛvərɪdʒ] N bevanda

bevy [ˈbɛvɪ] N banda; **a bevy of** una banda di

be·wail [bɪˈweɪl] VT lamentare

be·ware [bɪˈwɛə[r]] VI: **beware!** attento!; **to beware of sb/sth** stare attento(-a) a qn/qc, guardarsi da qn/qc; **you must beware of falling** devi stare attento a non cadere; **beware of the dog!** attenti al cane!

be·wil·dered [bɪˈwɪldəd] ADJ sconcertato(-a), disorientato(-a)

be·wil·der·ing [bɪˈwɪldərɪŋ] ADJ sconcertante, sbalorditivo(-a)

be·witch·ing [bɪˈwɪtʃɪŋ] ADJ (*fig: person*) affascinante, seducente; (: *smile, look*) ammaliatore(-trice)

be·yond [bɪˈjɒnd] PREP (*in place, time*) al di là di; (*further than*) più in là di; (*exceeding*) al di là di, al di sopra di; (*apart from*) oltre a; **I heard footsteps beyond the door** ho sentito dei passi oltre la porta; **the wheat fields and the mountains beyond ...** i campi di grano e le montagne più in là...; **beyond my reach** fuori della mia portata; **it would be unwise to delay it beyond 2008** sarebbe poco saggio rimandarlo oltre il 2008; **it's (almost) beyond belief** è incredibile; **that job is beyond him** quel lavoro è al di sopra delle sue capacità; **it's beyond me why ...** non arriverò mai a capire perché...; **beyond doubt** senza dubbio; **beyond repair** irreparabile ♦ ADV più oltre, più in là, più avanti

b/f ABBR = brought forward

bhp [ˌbiːeɪtʃˈpiː] N ABBR (*Aut:* = brake horsepower) ≈ CV (*potenza del freno*)

bi– [baɪ] PREF bi–

bi·an·nual [baɪˈænjʊəl] ADJ semestrale

bias [ˈbaɪəs] N 1 (*inclination*) bias (towards *or* in favour of) preferenza (per); **bias (against)** (*prejudice*) pregiudizio (contro); **her bias towards life in the city** la sua preferenza per la vita in città; **a right-wing bias** una tendenza di destra 2 (*of material*) sbieco; **to cut sth on the bias** tagliare qc in sbieco ♦ VT: **to bias sb towards** influenzare qn a favore di; **to bias sb against** prevenire qn contro

bi·ased, bi·assed [ˈbaɪəst] ADJ parziale; **to be biased against** essere prevenuto(-a) contro

bi·ath·lon [baɪˈæθlən] N biathlon *m inv*

bib [bɪb] N (*for child*) bavaglino; (*on dungarees*) pettorina; **in one's best bib and tucker** (*fam*) in ghingheri

Bi·ble [ˈbaɪbl] N: **the Bible** la Bibbia

bib·li·og·ra·phy [ˌbɪblɪˈɒɡrəfɪ] N bibliografia

bi·car·bo·nate of soda [baɪˈkɑːbənɪtəvˈsəʊdə] N bicarbonato (di sodio)

bi·cen·tenary [ˌbaɪsenˈtiːnərɪ], (*USA*) **bi·cen·ten·nial** [baɪsenˈtenɪəl] N, ADJ bicentenario

bi·ceps [ˈbaɪseps] NSG bicipite *m*

bick·er [ˈbɪkəʳ] VI bisticciare

bi·cy·cle [ˈbaɪsɪkl] N bicicletta; **to ride a bicycle** andare in bicicletta; **bicycle parts** ricambi *mpl* per bicicletta

bicycle pump N pompa della bicicletta

bicycle track N sentiero ciclabile

bid [bɪd] N offerta; (*Comm: tender*) offerta (di appalto); (*attempt*) tentativo; (*Cards*) dichiarazione *f*; **the highest bid** l'offerta più alta; **a rescue bid** un tentativo di salvataggio; **to make a bid for freedom/power** fare un tentativo per ottenere la libertà/per impadronirsi del potere ♦ VT 1 (*pt, pp* **bid**) offrire; **to bid £100 for** offrire 100 sterline per; **they bid 3 million pounds** hanno fatto un'offerta di 3 milioni di sterline 2 (*pt* **bade**, *pp* **bidden**): (*frm: order*): **to bid sb do sth** ingiungere a qn di fare qc 3 (*pt* **bade**, *pp* **bidden**): **to bid sb good morning/farewell** dare il buon giorno/l'addio a qn, dire buon giorno/addio a qn; **he bade me goodnight** mi ha augurato la buonanotte ♦ VI 1 (*pt, pp* **bid**): *gen*: **to bid (for)** fare un'offerta (per); (*Cards*) dichiarare; **to bid against sb** gareggiare contro qn 2 (*pt* **bade**, *pp* **bidden**): **to bid fair to be/do sth** promettere di essere/fare qc

bid·der [ˈbɪdəʳ] N offerente *m/f*; (*Cards*) chi fa la dichiarazione; **the highest bidder** il (la) miglior offerente

bid·ding [ˈbɪdɪŋ] N 1 (*at auction*) offerte *fpl*; (*Cards*) dichiarazioni *fpl*; **the bidding opened at £50** le offerte sono partite da 50 sterline 2 **I did his bidding** ho fatto ciò che voleva

bide [baɪd] VT: **to bide one's time** aspettare il momento giusto

bi·det [ˈbiːdeɪ] N bidè *m inv*

bi·di·rec·tion·al [ˌbaɪdɪˈrekʃənəl] ADJ bidirezionale

bi·en·nial [baɪˈenɪəl] ADJ biennale ♦ N (*plant*) biennale *f*

bier [bɪəʳ] N (*for coffin*) catafalco; (*for corpse*) feretro, bara

bi·fo·cals [baɪˈfəʊkəlz] NPL occhiali *mpl* bifocali

big [bɪg] ADJ (*comp* **-ger**, *superl* **-gest**) 1 (*in height, age: building, tree, person*) grande; (*in bulk, amount: parcel, lie, increase*) grosso(-a); (*important*) grande, importante; **a big house** una casa grande; **Taiwan's biggest companies** le più grosse aziende di Taiwan; **my big brother** mio fratello maggiore 2 **to make the big time** sfondare; **to earn big money** guadagnare forte; **to have big ideas** avere delle grandi idee; **to do things in a big way** fare le cose in grande; **he's too big for his boots** (*fam*) ha delle belle pretese; **why don't you keep your big mouth shut!** (*fam*) ma perché non tieni chiusa quella boccaccia?; **that's big of you!** (*iro*) che generosità!; **big deal!** (*iro*) capirai!; **it's no big deal** fa niente ♦ ADV (*fam*): **to talk big** dirne tante; **to think big** avere delle grandi idee

biga·my [ˈbɪgəmɪ] N bigamia

Big Apple N (*letteralmente*, "Grande Mela") città di New York

big dipper N montagne *fpl* russe

Big Dipper N (*costellazione*) il Grande Carro

big end N (*Aut*) testa di biella

big·gish [ˈbɪgɪʃ] ADJ *see* **big** piuttosto grande; piuttosto grosso(-a)

big·headed [bɪgˈhedɪd] ADJ (*fam*): **to be bigheaded** darsi un sacco di arie

big·hearted [ˌbɪgˈhɑːtɪd] ADJ generoso(-a), di buon cuore

big·ot [ˈbɪgət] N (*pej*) fazioso(-a)

big·ot·ed [ˈbɪgətɪd] ADJ (*pej*) fazioso(-a)

big·ot·ry [ˈbɪgətrɪ] N (*pej*) faziosità

big toe N alluce *m*

big top N (*circus*) circo; (*main tent*) tendone *m* del circo

big wheel N 1 (*at fair*) ruota (panoramica) 2 (*USA*) = **big noise**

big·wig [ˈbɪgwɪg] N (*fam*) pezzo grosso

bike [baɪk] N (*fam*) bici *f inv*; (*motorbike*) moto *f inv*; **can you ride a bike?** sai andare in bici?

bike lane N (*Brit*) pista ciclabile

bi·ki·ni [bɪˈkiːnɪ] N bikini *m inv*

bi·lat·er·al [baɪˈlætərəl] ADJ bilaterale

bile [baɪl] N (*Med, also fig*) bile *f*

bi·lin·gual [baɪˈlɪŋgwəl] ADJ bilingue

bili·ous [ˈbɪlɪəs] ADJ (*Med*) biliare; (*fig: irritable*) collerico(-a); **bilious attack** attacco di bile

bill¹ [bɪl] N 1 (*account*) fattura; (*in hotel, restaurant*) conto; (*for gas, electricity*) bolletta; **could I have the bill please?** il conto, per piacere; **the gas bill** la bolletta del gas 2 (*Parliament*) progetto di legge 3 (*USA: banknote*) banconota, biglietto; **a five-dollar bill** una banconota da cinque dollari 4 (*notice*) avviso; **"post no bills"** "divieto di affissione"; **that fits the bill** (*fig*) quello fa proprio al caso mio (*or* tuo *etc*) 5 (*Theatre*) cartellone *m*, manifesto; (*smaller*) locandina; **to top the bill** essere in cima al cartellone; **on the bill** in cartellone 6 (*Comm, Fin*) cambiale *f* ♦ VT 1 (*customer*): **to bill sb for sth** mandare la fattura di qc a qn 2 (*Theatre*) mettere in cartellone

bill² [bɪl] N (*of bird*) becco ♦ VI: **to bill and coo** tubare

bill·board [ˈbɪlbɔːd] N tabellone *m* pubblicitario

bil·let [ˈbɪlɪt] N acquartieramento ♦ VT: **to billet sb (on sb)** acquartierare qn (presso qn)

bill·fold [ˈbɪlfəʊld] N (*USA*) portafoglio

bil·liards [ˈbɪljədz] NSG biliardo

bil·lion [ˈbɪljən] N miliardo; (*Brit: old*) mille miliardi

bil·low [ˈbɪləʊ] N (*of smoke*) nuvola; (*of sail*) rigonfiamento ♦ VI (*smoke*) alzarsi in volute; (*sail*) gonfiarsi

bills payable [ˈbɪlzˈpeɪəbl] NPL effetti *mpl* passivi

bills receivable [ˈbɪlzrɪˈsiːvəbl] NPL effetti *mpl* attivi

bil·ly goat [ˈbɪlɪˌgəʊt] N caprone *m*, becco

bim·bo [ˈbɪmbəʊ] N (*pej*) pollastrella, svampitella

bin [bɪn] N (*for coal, rubbish*) bidone *m*; (*for bread*) cassetta; (*Brit: dustbin*) pattumiera; (*litterbin*) cestino

bi·na·ry [ˈbaɪnərɪ] ADJ binario(-a); **binary system** (*Math*) sistema *m* binario

bind [baɪnd] (*pt, pp* **bound**) VT 1 (*tie together, make fast*) legare; (*fig*) legare, unire; (*Culin*) legare; (*Sewing: seam*) orlare; (*book*) rilegare; **bound hand and foot** legato(-a) mani e piedi 2 (*encircle*) avvolgere; (*wound, arm*) fasciare, bendare 3 (*oblige*): **to bind sb to sth/to do sth** obbligare qn a qc/a fare qc; **to be bound to essere obbligato(-a); a; the authorities are legally bound to take action** le autorità sono obbligate per legge ad intervenire ♦ N (*fam: nuisance*) scocciatura

▸ **bind together** VT + ADV (*sticks etc*) legare (insieme); (*fig*) unire

▸ **bind over** VT + ADV (*Law*) dare la condizionale a

▸ **bind up** VT + ADV (*wound*) fasciare, bendare; **to be bound up in** (*work, research etc*) essere completamente assorbito(-a) da; **to be bound up with** (*person*) dedicarsi completamente a

bind·er [ˈbaɪndəʳ] N 1 (*file*) classificatore *m* 2 (*Agr*) mietilegatrice *f*

bind·ing [ˈbaɪndɪŋ] N (*of book*) rilegatura, legatura; (*Sewing*) fettuccia, bordo; (*on skis*) attacco ♦ ADJ (*agreement, contract*) vincolante; **to be binding on sb** essere vincolante per qn

binge [bɪndʒ] (*fam*) N: **to have a binge** far baldoria; **to go on a (shopping) binge** darsi alle spese folli; **to go on a (drinking) binge** prendersi una solenne sbronza ♦ VI (*eat excessively*) mangiare in modo eccessivo; **to binge on chocolate** abbuffarsi di cioccolato

binge drinker N forte bevitore(-trice)

bin·go [ˈbɪŋgəʊ] N ≈ tombola (*giocata in stabilimenti pubblici*)

bin-liner [ˈbɪnˌlaɪnəʳ] N (*Brit*) sacchetto per l'immondizia

bin·ocu·lars [bɪˈnɒkjʊləz] NPL binocolo *sg*; **a pair of binoculars** un binocolo

bio– [baɪə...] PREF bio-

bio·chem·is·try [ˈbaɪəʊˈkemɪstrɪ] N biochimica

bio·degrad·able [ˌbaɪəʊdɪˈgreɪdəbl] ADJ biodegradabile

biodiesel [ˈbaɪəʊdiːzl] N biodiesel *m*

bio·di·ver·sity [ˌbaɪəʊdaɪˈvɜːsɪtɪ] N biodiversità

bio·fuel [ˈbaɪəʊfjʊəl] N carburante *m* biologico

bi·og·raph·er [baɪˈɒgrəfəʳ] N biografo(-a)

bio·graphi·cal [ˌbaɪəʊˈgræfɪkəl] ADJ biografico(-a)

bi·og·ra·phy [baɪˈɒgrəfɪ] N biografia

bio·logi·cal [ˌbaɪəˈlɒdʒɪkəl] ADJ biologico(-a)

biological clock N orologio biologico

bi·olo·gist [baɪˈɒlədʒɪst] N biologo(-a)

bi·ol·ogy [baɪˈɒlədʒɪ] N biologia
bio·met·ric [ˌbaɪəˈmetrɪk] ADJ biometrico(-a)
bio·phys·ics [ˌbaɪəʊˈfɪzɪks] NSG biofisica
bio·pic [ˈbaɪəʊpɪk] N film-biografia m inv
bi·op·sy [ˈbaɪɒpsɪ] N biopsia
bio·sphere [ˈbaɪəˌsfɪəʳ] N: the biosphere la biosfera
bio·tech·nol·ogy [ˌbaɪəʊtekˈnɒlədʒɪ] N biotecnologia
bio·ter·ror·ism [ˌbaɪəʊˈterərɪzm] N bioterrorismo
birch [bɜːtʃ] N (tree, wood) betulla; (for whipping) frusta (di betulla)
bird [bɜːd] N uccello; (Brit fam: woman) tipa, bambola; **have you put the bird in the oven?** hai messo il pollo (or il tacchino etc) nel forno?; **a little bird told me** (hum) me l'ha detto l'uccellino; **the early bird catches the worm** (Proverb) chi dorme non piglia pesci; **a bird in the hand is worth two in the bush** (Proverb) meglio un uovo oggi che una gallina domani; **birds of a feather flock together** (Proverb) chi si assomiglia si piglia; **to kill two birds with one stone** prendere due piccioni con una fava
bird flu N influenza aviaria
bird of prey N (uccello) rapace m
bird's-eye view [ˈbɜːdzaɪˈvjuː] N vista a volo d'uccello
bird-watcher [ˈbɜːdwɒtʃəʳ] N bird watcher m/f inv
bird-watching [ˈbɜːdˌwɒtʃɪŋ] N bird-watching m
birth [bɜːθ] N (also fig) nascita; (childbirth) parto; **it was a difficult birth** è stato un parto difficile; **at birth** alla nascita; **Italian by birth** italiano di nascita; **date of birth** data di nascita; **place of birth** luogo di nascita; **to give birth to** partorire, dare alla luce; (fig) dare inizio a
birth certificate N certificato or atto di nascita
birth control N controllo delle nascite, contraccezione f
birth·day [ˈbɜːθˌdeɪ] N compleanno ♦ ADJ (present, party, cake) del or di compleanno; **a birthday card** un biglietto d'auguri; **in my/his etc birthday suit** (fam) come mamma m'ha/l'ha etc fatto
birth·mark [ˈbɜːθˌmɑːk] N voglia (sulla pelle)
birth·place [ˈbɜːθˌpleɪs] N luogo di nascita; (town) città natale
birth rate N (indice m or tasso di) natalità
Biscay [ˈbɪskeɪ] N: the Bay of Biscay il golfo di Biscaglia
bis·cuit [ˈbɪskɪt] N (Brit) biscotto; (USA) panino al latte; **to take the biscuit** (fam) essere assolutamente incredibile
bi·sect [baɪˈsekt] VT tagliare in due (parti); (Math) bisecare
bi·sex·ual [baɪˈseksjʊəl] ADJ, N bisessuale m/f, bisex m/f inv
bish·op [ˈbɪʃəp] N vescovo; (Chess) alfiere m
bis·tro [ˈbiːstrəʊ] N bistrot m inv
bit¹ [bɪt] N 1 (piece) pezzo; (smaller) pezzetto; **a bit of** (paper, wood, cake) un pezzo di; (wine, sunshine, peace) un po' di; **a bit of cake** un pezzo di torta; **would you like another bit?** ne vuoi un altro pezzo?; **a bit of music** un po' di musica; **a bit too much** un po' troppo; **a bit bigger/smaller** un po' più grande/più piccolo(-a); **a little bit dearer** un pochino più caro(-a); **a good bit cheaper** molto più economico(-a), molto più a buon mercato; **a bit of news** (fam) una notizia; **a bit of advice** un (piccolo) consiglio; **a bit of luck** una fortuna; **a bit mad/dangerous** un po' matto(-a)/pericoloso(-a); **bit by bit** a poco a poco; **they have a bit of money** hanno un po' di soldi; **it was a bit of a shock** è stato un po' un colpo; **it's a bit of a nuisance** è un po' una scocciatura; **that's not a bit of help** questo non aiuta affatto; **to take sth to bits** smontare qc; **to come to bits** (break) andare a pezzi; (be dismantled) essere smontabile; **in bits (and pieces)** (broken) a pezzi; (dismantled) smontato(-a); **to fall to bits** cadere a pezzi; **bring all your bits and pieces** porta tutte le tue cose; **to do one's bit** fare la propria parte 2 (short time): **a bit** un momento, un attimo; **wait a bit!** aspetta un attimo! 3 (considerable sum): **a good bit, quite a bit** un bel po' 4 (USA: coin) ottavo di dollaro
bit² [bɪt] N (tool) punta; (of horse) morso
bit³ [bɪt] PT of bite
bit⁴ [bɪt] N (Comput) bit m inv
bitch [bɪtʃ] N 1 (of canines) femmina; (of dog) cagna; **a terrier bitch** un terrier femmina 2 (offensive: woman) stronza, puttana (fam!) ♦ VI (fam: complain) mugugnare
bite [baɪt] (pt bit, pp bitten) N 1 (act, wound: of dog, snake) morso; (of insect) puntura; **to take a bite at** dare un morso

a, addentare; **a dog bite** il morso di un cane; **lots of mosquito bites** molte punture di zanzara 2 (of food) boccone m; **there's not a bite to eat** non c'è niente da mettere sotto i denti; **do you fancy a bite (to eat)?** ti va di mangiare qualcosa? 3 (Fishing): **he didn't get a single bite** non ha abboccato neanche un pesce ♦ VT (gen) mordere; (subj: dog) morsicare, mordere; (: insect) pungere; **the dog bit him** il cane lo ha morso; **my dog's never bitten anyone** il mio cane non ha mai morso nessuno; **I got bitten by mosquitoes** mi hanno punto le zanzare; **to bite one's nails** mangiarsi le unghie; **once bitten twice shy** una volta scottati...; **to bite the hand that feeds you** (fig) sputare nel piatto in cui si mangia; **to bite the dust** (fam: die) lasciarci la pelle (fam) ♦ VI 1 (dog etc) mordere; (insect) pungere; (fish) abboccare 3 (fig: policy, action) farsi sentire
▸ **bite back** VT + ADV trattenersi dal dire
▸ **bite into** VI + PREP (subj: person) addentare, dare un morso a; (: acid) intaccare
▸ **bite off** VT + ADV staccare con un morso; **to bite off more than one can chew** (fig) fare il passo più lungo della gamba; **to bite sb's head off** (fig) aggredire (verbalmente) qn
▸ **bite through** VT + ADV tagliare con i denti
bit·ing [ˈbaɪtɪŋ] ADJ (cold, wind) pungente; (criticism, sarcasm) pungente, mordace; (remark) caustico(-a)
bit part N (in film, play) particina, parte f secondaria
bit·ten [ˈbɪtn] PP of bite
bit·ter [ˈbɪtəʳ] ADJ 1 (taste: gen) amaro(-a); (: of fruit) aspro(-a); **it tastes bitter** ha un sapore amaro; **a bitter pill to swallow** (fig) un boccone amaro da ingoiare 2 (icy: weather) gelido(-a); (wind) pungente; **it's bitter today** oggi si gela 3 (enemy, hatred) acerrimo(-a); (quarrel) aspro(-a); (disappointment) amaro(-a); (person) risentito(-a); **to the bitter end** fino all'ultimo, a oltranza ♦ N (Brit: beer) birra amara
bit·ter·ly [ˈbɪtəlɪ] ADV (disappoint, complain, weep) amaramente; (oppose, criticise) aspramente; (jealous) profondamente; **it's bitterly cold** fa un freddo gelido
bit·ter·ness [ˈbɪtənɪs] N (gen) amarezza; (of fruit, fig: of quarrel) asprezza
bitter·sweet [ˈbɪtəˌswiːt] ADJ (taste) agrodolce; (love affair) dolceamaro(-a)
bi·tu·men [ˈbɪtjʊmɪn] N bitume m
bivou·ac [ˈbɪvʊæk] N bivacco ♦ VI bivaccare
bi·zarre [bɪˈzɑːʳ] ADJ bizzarro(-a)
bk ABBR 1 = bank 2 = book
blab [blæb] (fam) VI (also: blab out) spifferare ♦ VI (chatter) cianciare; (to police) vuotare il sacco
black [blæk] ADJ 1 nero(-a); (in darkness) buio(-a); (fig: gloomy: prospects) poco allegro(-a); (: despair) nero(-a), cupo(-a); (: future) poco promettente; (: wicked: thought, deed) malvagio(-a); **things look pretty black** (fig) c'è poco da star allegri; **black coffee** caffè m inv nero lungo 2 (person) nero(-a) ♦ N (colour) nero; **dressed in black** vestito(-a) di or in nero; **in the black** (Fin) in attivo; **to swear that black is white** (obstinate person) negare l'evidenza; (liar) mentire spudoratamente 2 (person) nero(-a) ♦ VT (Brit: Industry: goods, firm) boicottare
▸ **black out** VT + ADV 1 (obliterate) cancellare 2 (in wartime) oscurare; (subj: power cut) far piombare nell'oscurità ♦ VI + ADV (faint) svenire
black belt N (Sport) cintura nera
black·berry [ˈblækbərɪ] N mora (di rovo); **blackberry bush** cespuglio di more
black·bird [ˈblækbɜːd] N merlo
black·board [ˈblækbɔːd] N lavagna
black box N (Aer) scatola nera
black·cur·rant [ˌblækˈkʌrənt] N ribes m inv nero; **blackcurrant jam** marmellata di ribes nero
black economy N (Brit) economia sommersa
black·en [ˈblækən] VI annerirsi; (sky) oscurarsi ♦ VT annerire; (fig: reputation) macchiare
Black Forest N: the Black Forest la Foresta Nera
black·head [ˈblækˌhed] N punto nero, comedone m
black hole N (Astron) buco nero
black ice N strato invisibile di ghiaccio (su strada)

black·jack [ˈblækˌdʒæk] N (Cards) ventuno; (at casino) blackjack m inv; (USA: truncheon) manganello
black·list [ˈblækˌlɪst] N lista nera ♦ VT mettere sulla lista nera
black·mail [ˈblækmeɪl] N ricatto ♦ VT ricattare; **to blackmail sb into doing sth** ricattare qn affinché faccia qc ♦ ADJ (letter, phone call) ricattatorio(-a); (attempt) di ricatto
black·mail·er [ˈblækˌmeɪləʳ] N ricattatore(-trice)
black market N mercato nero; (in wartime) borsa nera; **on the black market** al mercato nero; alla borsa nera
black·out [ˈblækˌaʊt] N 1 (of lights, also TV) black-out m inv; (during war) oscuramento 2 (Med) svenimento; **to have a blackout** perdere conoscenza
black pepper N pepe m nero
black pudding N sanguinaccio
Black Sea N: **the Black Sea** il mar Nero
black sheep N (fig) pecora nera
black·smith [ˈblækˌsmɪθ] N fabbro ferraio
black spot N (Aut) = **accident black spot**
blad·der [ˈblædəʳ] N (Anat) vescica (urinaria)
blade [bleɪd] N (cutting edge) lama; (of safety razor) lametta; (of propeller) pala; **blade of grass** filo d'erba
blame [bleɪm] N (responsibility) colpa, responsabilità; (censure) biasimo; **to lay the blame for sth on sb** attribuire la responsabilità di qc a qn, dare la colpa di qc a qn ♦ VT 1 (hold responsible): **to blame sb for sth** dare la colpa a qn di qc, ritenere qn responsabile di qc; **to be to blame for** essere responsabile di; **don't blame me!** non dare la colpa a me!; **he's not to blame** non è colpa sua; **blame it on the weather** dai la colpa al tempo; **you have only yourself to blame** puoi ringraziare solo te stesso 2 (reproach) criticare, biasimare; **and I don't blame him** e non gli do torto
blame·less [ˈbleɪmlɪs] ADJ irreprensibile
blanch [blɑːntʃ] VI (person) sbiancare in viso ♦ VT (Culin) scottare
bland [blænd] ADJ (smile) blando(-a); (character) insulso(-a); (food) insipido(-a); **a bland reply** una risposta evasiva; **it tastes a bit bland** è un po' insipido, ha poco sapore
blank [blæŋk] ADJ (paper, space) bianco(-a); (wall) cieco(-a); (empty: expression) vacuo(-a); (look) distratto(-a); **a blank sheet of paper** un foglio di carta bianca; **a blank CD** un CD vergine; **a look of blank amazement** uno sguardo allibito; **my mind went blank** ho avuto un vuoto ♦ N (void) vuoto; (in form) spazio in bianco; (blank cartridge) cartuccia a salve; **his mind was a blank** si sentiva la testa vuota; **fill in the blanks** riempi gli spazi in bianco; **to draw a blank** (fig) non aver nessun risultato
blank cheque, (USA) **blank check** N assegno in bianco; **to give sb a blank cheque to do sth** (fig) dare carta bianca a qn per fare qc
blan·ket [ˈblæŋkɪt] N coperta; (fig: of snow, fog) coltre f; (: of smoke) cappa
blanket cover N: **to give blanket cover** (subj: insurance policy) coprire tutti i rischi
blare [bleəʳ] N (of trumpet, car horn) strombettio; (of siren) urlo; (of radio) frastuono ♦ VT (also: **blare out**) far risuonare ♦ VI (see n) strombettare; urlare; suonare a tutto volume
blasé [ˈblɑːzeɪ] ADJ blasé inv
blas·phe·mous [ˈblæsfɪməs] ADJ blasfemo(-a)
blas·phe·my [ˈblæsfɪmɪ] N bestemmia
blast [blɑːst] N 1 (of air, steam) getto; (of wind) raffica; **(at) full blast** (also fig) a tutta forza 2 (sound: of trumpet) squillo; (: of car horn, siren) colpo; **(at) full blast** (radio) a tutto volume 3 (of explosion) spostamento d'aria; (noise) esplosione f; **a bomb blast** un'esplosione ♦ VT (strike: with explosives) far saltare; (: by lightning) bruciare; (fig: hopes, future) distruggere ♦ EXCL (Brit fam) mannaggia!; **blast him!** mannaggia a lui!
  ▸ **blast away** VI + ADV 1 (gun) sparare a raffica 2 (band) suonare a tutto volume
  ▸ **blast off** VI + ADV (Space) essere lanciato(-a)
blast·off [ˈblɑːstˌɒf] N (of rockets) lancio
bla·tant [ˈbleɪtənt] ADJ sfacciato(-a); **a blatant lie** una bugia palese
bla·tant·ly [ˈbleɪtəntlɪ] ADV sfacciatamente; **it's blatantly obvious** è lampante

blaze¹ [bleɪz] N (fire: of buildings) incendio; (glow: of fire, sun) bagliore m; (of gems, beauty) splendore m; **a blaze of colour** un'esplosione di colori; **a blaze of anger** un impeto d'ira; **in a blaze of publicity** circondato(-a) da grande pubblicità; **go to blazes!** (fam) va' al diavolo!; **like the blazes** (fam) come un matto ♦ VI (fire) ardere, fiammeggiare; (conflagration) divampare; (building) essere in fiamme; (sun) sfolgorare; (light) risplendere; **to blaze with anger** (eyes) fiammeggiare dalla rabbia; **to blaze with passion** ardere di passione
  ▸ **blaze away** VI + ADV: **to blaze away (at)** continuare a far fuoco (su)
  ▸ **blaze up** VI + ADV fare una fiammata; (fig: feelings) accendersi
blaze² [bleɪz] N (mark: on horse) stella; (: on tree) segno ♦ VT (tree) segnare; **to blaze a trail** (also fig) aprire una nuova via
blaz·er [ˈbleɪzəʳ] N blazer m inv
bleach [bliːtʃ] N decolorante m; **liquid bleach** acqua ossigenata; **household bleach** candeggina, varechina ♦ VT (material) candeggiare; (bones) sbiancare; (hair) ossigenare
bleached [bliːtʃt] ADJ decolorato(-a); **bleached hair** capelli ossigenati
bleach·ers [ˈbliːtʃəz] NPL (USA) posti mpl di gradinata
bleak [bliːk] ADJ (landscape) desolato(-a); (weather) gelido(-a); (smile) pallido(-a); (prospect, future) tetro(-a), deprimente; **a bleak area** un'area desolata; **the future looks bleak** il futuro sembra tetro; **the prospects of your getting a job here are bleak** le probabilità che tu trovi un lavoro qui sono molto scarse
bleary-eyed [ˈblɪərɪˈaɪd] ADJ: **to be bleary-eyed** avere gli occhi appannati
bleat [bliːt] N belato ♦ VI belare; (fig: fam) piagnucolare
bled [bled] PT, PP of **bleed**
bleed [bliːd] (pt, pp **bled** [bled]) VI sanguinare; **his nose is bleeding** gli sanguina il naso, gli esce il sangue dal naso; **to bleed to death** morire dissanguato(-a); **my heart bleeds for him** (iro) mi fa proprio compassione, poverino! ♦ VT 1 salassare, dissanguare 2 (brakes, radiator) spurgare
bleep [bliːp] N breve segnale m acustico, bip m inv ♦ VI suonare ♦ VT (doctor) chiamare con il cercapersone
bleep·er [ˈbliːpəʳ] N (of doctor etc) cercapersone m inv
blem·ish [ˈblemɪʃ] N imperfezione f; (on fruit) ammaccatura; (on reputation) macchia ♦ VT deturpare
blend [blend] N (gen) mescolanza, miscuglio; (of tea, whisky) miscela; (of tobacco) mistura ♦ VT (teas) mischiare; (colours) mescolare, mischiare; (Culin) amalgamare ♦ VI (harmonize): **to blend (with)** (gen) mescolarsi (a); (sounds, perfumes) confondersi (con); (styles) essere in armonia (con); (opinions, races, colours) fondersi (con)
blend·er [ˈblendəʳ] N (Culin) frullatore m
bless [bles] VT benedire; **the priest blessed the children** il prete ha benedetto i bambini; **God bless the queen!** Dio benedica la regina!; **bless you!** sei un angelo!; (after sneezing) salute!; **I'm blessed if I know!** (fam) non ne so un accidente!; **bless my soul!** santo cielo!; **to be blessed with** godere di
bless·ed [ˈblesɪd] ADJ 1 (Rel: holy) benedetto(-a); (: happy) beato(-a); **Blessed Margaret Sinclair** Beata Margaret Sinclair 2 (fam) benedetto(-a); **every blessed day** tutti i santi giorni; **where's that blessed book?** dov'è quel benedetto libro?
bless·ing [ˈblesɪŋ] N 1 (Rel) benedizione f 2 (advantage) vantaggio, fortuna; **losing my job was a blessing, really** perdere il lavoro è stata in realtà una benedizione; **to count one's blessings** ritenersi fortunato(-a); **what a blessing that ...** meno male che...; **it was a blessing in disguise** in fondo è stato un bene
blest [blest] (poet) PP of **bless**
blew [bluː] PT of **blow²**
blight [blaɪt] N (Bot) malattia che fa avvizzire le piante; (fig) piaga ♦ VT (plants etc) far avvizzire; (fig: future, hopes) rovinare, distruggere
bli·mey [ˈblaɪmɪ] EXCL (Brit fam) accidenti!
blind [blaɪnd] ADJ (person, obedience, anger) cieco(-a); **blind in one eye** cieco da un occhio, orbo; **blind as a bat** (fam) cieco come una talpa; **to go blind** diventare cieco; **he was blind to**

her faults non vedeva i suoi difetti; **to turn a blind eye to** chiudere un occhio su; **it's not a blind bit of use** (*fam*) non serve a un bel niente; **he doesn't take a blind bit of notice of ...** (*fam*) non bada minimamente a... ♦ N **1 the blind** npl i ciechi; **it's a case of the blind leading the blind** è come mettere insieme uno storpio e uno sciancato **2** (*shade*) tenda avvolgibile; **Venetian blind** veneziana ♦ ADV (*fly, land*) alla cieca; **blind drunk** (*fam*) ubriaco(-a) fradicio(-a) ♦ VT accecare; **he was blinded in the war** ha perso la vista in guerra

blind alley N vicolo cieco

blind corner N (*Brit*) svolta cieca

blind date N *appuntamento galante con qualcuno che non si conosce*

blind·ers ['blaɪndəz] NPL (*USA*) = blinkers

blind·fold ['blaɪndfəʊld] ADV con gli occhi bendati; **I could do it blindfold** potrei farlo a occhi chiusi ♦ N benda (per occhi) ♦ VT bendare (gli occhi a)

blind·ing ['blaɪndɪŋ] ADJ (*flash, light*) accecante; (*pain*) atroce

blind·ly ['blaɪndlɪ] ADV ciecamente

blind·ness ['blaɪndnɪs] N cecità; **blindness to the realities of life** rifiuto di guardare in faccia la realtà

blind spot N (*Anat*) punto cieco; (*Aut*) angolo in cui manca la visibilità; (*fig*) punto debole

bling [blɪŋ], **bling-bling** [blɪŋˈblɪŋ] (*fam!*) ADJ vistoso(-a) ♦ N stile m vistoso

blink [blɪŋk] N battito di ciglia; **to be on the blink** (*fam: car, machine*) essere scassato(-a) ♦ VT: **to blink one's eyes** sbattere le palpebre ♦ VI sbattere le palpebre; (*light*) lampeggiare

blink·ers ['blɪŋkəz] NPL (*Brit*) paraocchi mpl

blink·ing ['blɪŋkɪŋ] ADJ (*Brit fam*) dannato(-a), maledetto(-a); **this blinking ...** questo maledetto...

blip [blɪp] N (*on radar etc*) segnale m intermittente; (*on graph*) piccola variazione; (*fig*) momentanea battuta d'arresto

bliss [blɪs] N (*Rel*) beatitudine f; (*happy state*) (immensa) felicità; **ignorance is bliss** (*Proverb*) beata ignoranza; **it's bliss!** (*fam*) è meraviglioso!

bliss·ful ['blɪsfʊl] ADJ (*event, day*) stupendo(-a), meraviglioso(-a); (*smile*) beato(-a); **in blissful ignorance** nella (più) beata ignoranza

bliss·ful·ly ['blɪsfʊlɪ] ADV (*sigh, smile*) beatamente; **blissfully happy** magnificamente felice

blis·ter ['blɪstə'] N (*on skin*) vescica; (*of paint*) bolla ♦ VT (*skin*) far venire le vesciche a; (*paint*) produrre delle bolle in ♦ VI (*skin*) coprirsi di bollicine; (*paint*) formare delle bolle

blithe [blaɪð] ADJ (*thoughtless*) spensierato(-a); (*old: happy*) gioioso(-a), allegro(-a)

blithe·ly ['blaɪðlɪ] ADV (*unthinkingly*) spensieratamente; (*happily*) allegramente

blith·er·ing ['blɪðərɪŋ] ADJ (*fam*): **this blithering idiot** questo pezzo d'idiota

blitz [blɪts] N (*Mil*) blitz m inv; **to have a blitz on sth** (*fig*) prendere d'assalto qc ♦ VT bombardare

bliz·zard ['blɪzəd] N bufera di neve

bloat·ed ['bləʊtɪd] ADJ (*also fig*): **bloated (with)** gonfio(-a) (di)

blob [blɒb] N (*drop*) goccia; (*stain, spot*) macchia; (*lump: of mud*) pallina; **a blob of glue** una goccia di colla

bloc [blɒk] N (*Pol*) blocco

block [blɒk] N **1** (*of stone, ice*) blocco; (*toy*) cubo (per fare le costruzioni); (*butcher's, executioner's*) ceppo; **to knock sb's block off** (*fam*) rompere la zucca a qn **2** (*building*) palazzo; (*esp USA: group of buildings*) isolato; **he lives in our block** abita nel nostro palazzo; **block of flats** caseggiato; **to walk around the block** fare il giro dell'isolato; **3 blocks from here** a 3 isolati di distanza da qui **3** (*section: of tickets*) blocchetto; (*: of shares*) pacchetto; (*Comput*) blocco **4** (*blockage: in pipe*) ingorgo; (*Med*) blocco; **mental block** blocco mentale ♦ VT (*gen, also Comput*) bloccare; (*pipe*) ingorgare, bloccare; (*Ftbl*) stoppare; **to block sb's way** sbarrare la strada a qn; **to block sb's view** coprire la vista a qn

▸ **block in** VT + ADV **1** (*with car*) chiudere qn (con l'auto) **2** (*fill with paint*) colorare

▸ **block off** VT + ADV bloccare

▸ **block out** VT + ADV (*obscure: light*) escludere; (*obliterate: picture*) cancellare

▸ **block up** VT + ADV (*obstruct: passage*) bloccare; (*: pipe*) ingorgare, intasare; (*fill in: gap*) tappare; (*: window, entrance*) murare; **my nose is blocked up** ho il naso chiuso

block·ade [blɒˈkeɪd] N (*Mil*) blocco ♦ VT bloccare

block·age ['blɒkɪdʒ] N (*obstruction*) ingorgo; (*Med*) blocco

block and tackle N (*Tech*) paranco

block booking N prenotazione f in blocco

block·bust·er ['blɒkbʌstə'] N (*fam: film, TV series*) successo ne m

block·head ['blɒkhɛd] N (*fam*) testa di legno

block letters, block capitals NPL stampatello

block vote N (*Brit*) voto per delega

blog [blɒg] N (*Comput*) blog m inv, diario in internet

blog·ger ['blɒgə'] N (*Comput*) blogger m/f inv, redattore(-trice) di blog

blog·ging ['blɒgɪŋ] N blogging m ♦ ADJ: **blogging website** sito di blogging

blo·gos·phere ['blɒgəsfɪə'] N blogosfera f

bloke [bləʊk] N (*Brit fam*) tipo, tizio; **he's a really nice bloke** è un tipo veramente simpatico

blond [blɒnd] N (*man*) biondo ♦ ADJ biondo(-a)

blood [blʌd] N sangue m; **to give blood** donare sangue; **of royal blood** di sangue reale; **there's bad blood between them** corre cattivo sangue fra di loro; **new blood** (*fig*) nuova linfa; **it's like trying to get blood out of a stone** è come voler cavare sangue dalle pietre; **in cold blood** a sangue freddo; **blood is thicker than water** (*Proverb*) il sangue non è acqua; **it's in the blood** ce l'ho (or l'hai etc) nel sangue; **he's after my blood** (*hum*) se mi prende m'ammazza; **my blood ran cold** mi son sentito gelare il sangue

blood bank N banca del sangue

blood count N esame m emocromocitometrico

blood-curdling ['blʌdˌkɜːdlɪŋ] ADJ raccapricciante, da far gelare il sangue

blood donor N donatore(-trice) di sangue

blood group N gruppo sanguigno

blood·hound ['blʌdhaʊnd] N segugio

blood·less ['blʌdlɪs] ADJ (*pale*) smorto(-a), esangue; (*coup*) senza spargimento di sangue

blood-letting ['blʌdˌlɛtɪŋ] N (*fig*) spargimento di sangue; (*Med*) salasso

blood poisoning N setticemia

blood pressure N pressione f del sangue or sanguigna; **to have high/low blood pressure** avere la pressione alta/bassa

blood·shed ['blʌdˌʃɛd] N spargimento di sangue

blood·shot ['blʌdˌʃɒt] ADJ: **bloodshot eyes** occhi iniettati di sangue

blood·stained ['blʌdsteɪnd] ADJ insanguinato(-a), macchiato(-a) di sangue

blood·stream ['blʌdstriːm] N (circolazione f del) sangue, m

blood test N analisi fpl del sangue

blood·thirsty ['blʌdˌθɜːstɪ] ADJ sanguinario(-a), assetato(-a) di sangue

blood transfusion N trasfusione f di sangue

blood type N gruppo sanguigno

blood vessel N vaso sanguigno

bloody ['blʌdɪ] ADJ **1** (*bleeding*) sanguinante, che sanguina; (*bloodstained*) insanguinato(-a); (*cruel: battle, feud*) sanguinoso(-a); **a bloody war** una guerra sanguinosa **2** (*Brit fam*) maledetto(-a), dannato(-a); **bloody hell!** porca miseria! ♦ ADV (*Brit fam*): **that's no bloody good!** questo non serve a un cavolo!

bloom [bluːm] N (*flower*) fiore m; (*on fruit*) lanugine f; (*on complexion*) colorito roseo; **in bloom** (*flower*) sbocciato(-a); (*tree*) in fiore; **in full bloom** in piena fioritura; **in the full bloom of youth** nel fiore della giovinezza ♦ VI (*flower*) aprirsi; (*tree*) sfiorire

bloom·ing ['bluːmɪŋ] ADJ (*fam*) dannato(-a), maledetto(-a); **this blooming ...** questo dannato...

blos·som ['blɒsəm] N (*with pl sense*) fiori mpl; (*single flower*) fiore m; **apple blossom** fiori di melo ♦ VI fiorire; **to blossom into** (*fig*) diventare

blot [blɒt] N macchia; **to be a blot on the landscape** rovinare il paesaggio ♦ VT **1** (*spot with ink*) macchiare d'inchiostro;

to blot one's copy book (*fig*) farla grossa **2** (*dry: ink, writing*) asciugare ▸ **blot out** VT + ADV (*memories, words*) cancellare; (*view, sun*) nascondere, offuscare; (*nation, city*) annientare; **she blotted out all memory of the incident** ha cancellato qualsiasi ricordo dell'incidente; **clouds blotted out the sun** le nuvole nascondevano il sole

blotchy [ˈblɒtʃɪ] ADJ pieno(-a) *or* coperto(-a) di macchie

blot·ter [ˈblɒtəʳ] N tampone *m* (di carta assorbente)

blot·ting pa·per [ˈblɒtɪŋˌpeɪpəʳ] N carta assorbente, carta asciugante

blot·to [ˈblɒtəʊ] ADJ (*Brit fam*) sbronzo(-a); **to get blotto** sbronzarsi

blouse [blaʊz] N camicetta

KEYWORD
blow¹ [bləʊ] N (*gen*) colpo; (*with fist*) pugno; **a blow with a hammer** un colpo di martello; **at one blow** in un colpo (solo); **to come to blows** venire alle mani; **the news came as a great blow to her** la notizia fu un duro colpo per lei

blow² [bləʊ] (*pt* blew, *pp* blown) VT **1** (*subj: wind: ship*) spingere; (: *hair*) far svolazzare; **a gale blew the ship off course** una bufera ha fatto uscire di rotta la nave **2** (*trumpet, horn*) suonare; **to blow a whistle** fischiare; **the referee blew his whistle** l'arbitro fischiò; **to blow one's own trumpet** cantare le proprie lodi **3** (*bubbles*) fare; (*glass*) soffiare; (*kiss*) mandare; **to blow one's nose** soffiarsi il naso **4** (*fuse, safe*) far saltare; **to blow money on sth** (*fam*) buttare via dei soldi per qc; **to blow a secret** spifferare un segreto; **to blow sb's cover** scoprire il gioco di qn; **to blow one's top** (*fam*) esplodere, andare su tutte le furie; **blow the expense!** crepi l'avarizia! ♦ VI **1** (*wind, person*) soffiare; (*leaves*) svolazzare; (*flag*) sventolare; **a cold wind was blowing** soffiava un vento freddo; **to blow on one's fingers** scaldarsi le mani soffiando; **to blow on one's soup** soffiare sulla minestra; **to see which way the wind blows** (*fig*) vedere che aria tira; **his hat blew out of the window** il suo cappello è volato fuori dalla finestra; **the door blew open/shut** un colpo di vento ha spalancato/chiuso la porta **2** (*make sound: trumpet*) suonare; **they were one-all when the whistle blew** erano uno a uno quando l'arbitro ha fischiato la fine **3** (*fuse*) saltare; (*tyre or tire*) scoppiare
▸ **blow away** VI + ADV volare via ♦ VT + ADV (*papers, leaves*) far volare via; (*hat*) portare via
▸ **blow down** VI + ADV essere abbattuto(-a) dal vento ♦ VT + ADV abbattere
▸ **blow in** VI + ADV (*window*) sfasciarsi; (*enter: leaves, dust*) volar dentro; **look who's just blown in!** (*fam*) ma guarda chi è arrivato!
▸ **blow off** VI + ADV (*hat*) volar via ♦ VT + ADV (*hat*) portare via; **to blow off steam** (*fig: fam*) sfogarsi
▸ **blow out** VI + ADV (*candle*) spegnere; (*swell out: cheeks*) gonfiare; **he has blown out the candles** ha spento le candeline ♦ VI + ADV scoppiare
▸ **blow over** VT + ADV (*tree*) abbattere ♦ VI + ADV (*tree*) rovesciarsi; (*storm*) passare, calmarsi; (*fig: dispute*) calmarsi
▸ **blow up** VT + ADV (*bridge*) far saltare; (*tyre or tire, balloon*) gonfiare; (*photo*) ingrandire; (*event*) esagerare; **they blew up a plane** hanno fatto saltare un aereo; **we've blown up the balloons** abbiamo gonfiato i palloncini ♦ VI + ADV (*bomb: or fig: person*) esplodere; (*row*) scoppiare; (*storm: gather*) arrivare; **the house blew up** la casa è saltata in aria

blow-dry [ˈbləʊˌdraɪ] N (*hairstyle*) messa in piega a phon ♦ VT asciugare con il phon

blow·lamp [ˈbləʊˌlæmp] N (*Brit*) cannello per saldare/sverniciare

blown [bləʊn] PP *of* blow²

blow-out [ˈbləʊˌaʊt] N (*fam: big meal*) abbuffata; (*of tyre or tire*) scoppio; (*of fuse*) corto circuito

blow·torch [ˈbləʊˌtɔːtʃ] N (*USA*) = blowlamp

blowzy, blowsy [ˈblaʊzɪ] ADJ sciatto(-a), trasandato(-a) ♦ **blub·ber** [ˈblʌbəʳ] N (*of whales*) grasso di balena ♦ VI (*weep*) frignare

bludg·eon [ˈblʌdʒən] VT prendere a randellate; **to bludgeon sb to death** ammazzare qn a randellate; **to bludgeon sb into doing sth** (*fig*) costringere qn a fare qc

blue [bluː] ADJ **1** (*light blue*) azzurro(-a), celeste; (*darker*) blu *inv*; **bright blue** bluette *inv*; **navy blue** blu; **blue with cold** livido(-a) dal freddo; **once in a blue moon** a ogni morte di papa; **you can talk till you're blue in the face** puoi parlare fino a domani; **to be in a blue funk** (*old*) avere una fifa nera **2** (*obscene: film, book*) porno *inv*; (: *joke*) sporco(-a), sconcio(-a); **a blue movie** un film porno **3** (*fam: sad*): **to feel blue** sentirsi giù ♦ N (*colour: see adj*) azzurro, celeste *m*; blu *m inv*; **the blue** (*sky*) l'azzurro; **out of the blue** (*fig*) all'improvviso

blue baby N neonato(-a) cianotico(-a)

blue·bell [ˈbluːˌbel] N giacinto dei boschi

blue·berry [ˈbluːbərɪ] N (*USA*) mirtillo

blue·bottle [ˈbluːˌbɒtl] N moscone *m*

blue cheese N ≈ gorgonzola

blue-chip investment [ˈbluːtʃɪpɪnˈvestmənt] N investimento sicuro

blue-collar worker [ˈbluːˌkɒləˈwɜːkəʳ] N operaio(-a), tuta *f* blu, *inv*

blue jeans NPL (blue-)jeans *mpl*

blue·print [ˈbluːˌprɪnt] N cianografia; **blueprint (for)** (*fig*) formula (di)

blues [bluːz] NPL (*Mus*): **the blues** il blues; **to have the blues** (*fam: depression*) essere giù

blue·tit [ˈbluːˌtɪt] N cinciarella

bluff¹ [blʌf] ADJ (*person*) senza peli sulla lingua, brusco(-a)

bluff² [blʌf] N (*cliff*) scogliera a picco

bluff³ [blʌf] N bluff *m inv*; **to call sb's bluff** far mettere le carte in tavola a qn ♦ VT: **to bluff it out** cavarsela bluffando ♦ VI bluffare

blun·der [ˈblʌndəʳ] N (*serious mistake*) abbaglio; **to make a blunder** prendere un abbaglio ♦ VI **1** (*see n*) prendere un abbaglio **2** (*move clumsily*): **to blunder about** andare *or* muoversi a tentoni; **to blunder into sb/sth** andare a sbattere contro qn/qc

blunt [blʌnt] ADJ **1** (*not sharp: edge*) non tagliente, smussato(-a); (: *knife*) che non taglia; (: *point*) spuntato(-a); **the knife was blunt** il coltello era spuntato; **this pencil is blunt** questa matita non ha più la punta; **blunt instrument** (*Law*) corpo contundente **2** (*outspoken*) brutale; (*manners*) brusco(-a); **he was blunt with me** è stato brusco con me ♦ VT (*knife*) smussare; (*point*) spuntare; (*fig: nerves, feelings*) rendere insensibile

blunt·ly [ˈblʌntlɪ] ADV (*speak*) senza mezzi termini

blunt·ness [ˈblʌntnɪs] N (*fig: of person*) brutale franchezza

blur [blɜːʳ] N (*shape*) massa indistinta *or* confusa; **my mind was a blur** avevo la mente annebbiata ♦ VT (*writing*) rendere (quasi) illeggibile; (*outline, sight, memory, judgment*) offuscare ♦ VI (*see vt*) diventare (quasi) illeggibile; offuscarsi

blurb [blɜːb] N (*publicity material*) trafiletto pubblicitario; (*on book jacket*) note *fpl* di copertina

blurred [blɜːd] ADJ (*TV*) sfuocato(-a); (*photo*) mosso(-a)

blurt [blɜːt] VT (*also: blurt out*) spifferare

blush [blʌʃ] N rossore *m*; **with a blush** arrossendo; **without a blush** senza neppure arrossire; **to spare sb's blushes** evitare di mettere in imbarazzo qn ♦ VI: **to blush (with)** arrossire (per *or* da)

blush·er [ˈblʌʃəʳ] N **1** (*Cosmetics*) fard *m inv* **2** (*mushroom*) tignosa vinata

blus·ter [ˈblʌstəʳ] N bravate *fpl*, spacconate *fpl*; (*threats*) vuote minacce *fpl* ♦ VI (*wind*) infuriare; (*person: boast*) fare lo (la) spaccone(-a); (: *rage*) dare in escandescenze

blus·ter·ing [ˈblʌstərɪŋ] ADJ (*tone, manner*) da spaccone

blus·tery [ˈblʌstərɪ] ADJ (*wind*) a raffiche; (*day*) ventoso(-a); (*weather*) burrascoso(-a)

Blvd ABBR = Boulevard

BMX [ˌbiːemˈeks] N ABBR (= *bicycle motocross*) ciclocross *m inv*; **BMX bike** mountain bike *f inv* per cross, BMX *f inv*

bn ABBR (= *billion*) mld; **2 bn dollars** 2 mld di dollari

BO [ˌbiːˈəʊ] N ABBR **1** (= *body odour*) odori *mpl* sgradevoli (del corpo) **2** (= *box office*) botteghino *m*

boar [bɔːʳ] N (*male pig*) verro; (*wild boar*) cinghiale *m*

board [bɔːd] N **1** (*of wood*) asse *f*, tavola; (*for chess*) scacchiera; (*blackboard*) lavagna; (*on wall*) tabellone *m*; **a chopping board** un tagliere; **there were six pawns on the board**

c'erano sei pedoni sulla scacchiera; **write it on the board** scrivilo sulla lavagna; **there's a notice on the board** c'è un avviso in bacheca; **across the board** (*fig: adv*) per tutte le categorie; (: *adj*) generale; (: *adj*) generale; **to go by the board** (*fig*) andare a monte, venir messo(-a) da parte; **above board** (*fig*) regolare; **to take on board** (*fig*) recepire **2** (*provision of meals*) vitto; **half board** (*Brit*) mezza pensione *f*; **full board** (*Brit*) pensione *f* completa **3** (*Naut, Aer*): **on board** a bordo; **to go on board** salire a bordo **4** (*group of officials*) commissione *f*; **board of examiners** commissione esaminatrice *or* d'esame **5** (*institution*) ente *m* ♦ *vt* (*ship, plane*) imbarcarsi su, salire a bordo di; (*enemy ship*) andare all'abbordaggio di; (*bus, train*) salire su *or* in ♦ *vi*: **to board with sb** essere a pensione da qn
 ▸ **board out** *vt + adv* mettere a pensione presso
 ▸ **board up** *vt + adv* (*door*) chiudere con assi
board·er ['bɔːdə'] N pensionante *m/f*; (*Scol*) collegiale *m/f*, convittore(-trice)
board game N gioco da tavolo
boarding card, boarding pass N (*Aer, Naut*) carta d'imbarco
boarding house N pensione *f*
boarding party N (*to take control*) gruppo che assume il controllo di una nave come forma di protesta; (*for inspection*) squadra di ispezione (*del carico di una nave*)
boarding school N collegio, convitto
board meeting N riunione *f* di consiglio
board room N sala del consiglio
board·walk ['bɔːd,wɔːk] N **1** (*USA*) passeggiata a mare **2** passerella
boast [bəʊst] N vanteria; **it is his boast that he's never lost a match** si fa vanto di non aver mai perso un incontro ♦ *vt* (*possession, achievement*) vantare; **the country boasts many tourist attractions** il paese vanta numerosi luoghi d'interesse turistico; **the village boasted only one small store** nel paese c'era solo un negozietto ♦ *vi*: **to boast (about or of)** vantarsi (di)
boast·ful ['bəʊstful] ADJ pieno(-a) di sé, che si vanta sempre
boast·ful·ness ['bəʊstfəlnɪs] N vanagloria
boat [bəʊt] N (*gen*) barca; (*ship*) nave *f*; **to go by boat** andare in barca *or* in nave; **a rowing boat** una barca a remi; **we're all in the same boat** (*fig: fam*) siamo tutti nella stessa barca
boat·er ['bəʊtə'] N (*hat*) paglietta
boat·ing ['bəʊtɪŋ] N nautica da diporto
boat people N boat people *mpl*
boat·swain ['bəʊsn] N nostromo
bob¹ [bɒb] N (*curtsy*) riverenza, inchino ♦ *vi* (*also:* **bob up and down**) andare su e giù
 ▸ **bob up** *vi + adv* spuntare, saltare fuori
bob² [bɒb] N *pl inv* (*old, Brit: fam*) scellino
bob·bin ['bɒbɪn] N spoletta, bobina; (*of sewing machine*) rocchetto
bob·by ['bɒbɪ] N (*Brit fam*) poliziotto
bob·sleigh ['bɒb,sleɪ] N bob *m inv*
bode [bəʊd] *vi*: **to bode well** promettere bene; **to bode ill** non promettere nulla di buono
bod·ice ['bɒdɪs] N (*of dress*) corpino, corpetto
bodi·ly ['bɒdɪlɪ] ADJ (*comfort, needs*) materiale; (*functions*) corporale ♦ ADV (*carry*) in braccio; (*lift*) di peso
body ['bɒdɪ] N **1** (*of person, animal*) corpo; (*dead body*) corpo, cadavere *m*; **the human body** il corpo umano; **they've found the body** hanno trovato il cadavere; **to keep body and soul together** tirare avanti; **over my dead body!** neanche se mi ammazzi! **2** (*main part: of structure*) corpo; (: *of car*) carrozzeria; (: *of plane*) fusoliera; (: *of ship*) scafo, corpo; (: *of speech, document*) parte *f* principale **3** (*mass, collection: of facts*) massa, quantità *f inv*; (: *of laws*) raccolta; (: *of people, water*) massa; (: *of troops*) grosso; **the student body** gli studenti; **in a body** in massa **4** (*organization*) associazione *f*, organizzazione *f*, ente *m*; **a public body** un ente pubblico; **legislative body** organo legislativo; **ruling body** direttivo **5** (*of wine, hair*) corpo; **a wine with body** un vino corposo **6** (*also:* **body stocking**) body *m inv*
body blow N (*fig*) duro colpo
body building N culturismo
body·guard ['bɒdɪ,gɑːd] N (*person, group*) guardia del corpo

body language N linguaggio del corpo
body repairs NPL (*Aut*) lavori *mpl* di carrozzeria
body search N perquisizione *f* personale; **to carry out a body search on sb** effettuare una perquisizione personale su qn; **to submit to *or* undergo a body search** essere sottoposto(-a) a perquisizione personale
body·work ['bɒdɪ,wɜːk] N (*Aut*) carrozzeria
bof·fin ['bɒfɪn] N (*Brit fam*) scienziato(-a)
bog [bɒg] N palude *f*; (*Brit fam: toilet*) cesso
 ▸ **bog down** *vt + adv*: **to get bogged down (in)** impantanarsi (in)
bo·gey ['bəʊgɪ] N (*worry*) spauracchio
bog·gle ['bɒgl] *vi* (*fam*): **the mind boggles!** è incredibile!; **his eyes boggled at the sight** ha fatto tanto d'occhi davanti a quella scena
Bo·go·tá [,bəʊgə'tɑː] N Bogotà *f*
bo·gus ['bəʊgəs] ADJ (*jewels, claim*) falso(-a), fasullo(-a); (*person, attitude*) finto(-a)
Bo·he·mia [bəʊ'hiːmɪə] N Boemia
Bo·he·mian [bəʊ'hiːmɪən] ADJ (*Geog*) boemo(-a); (*artist, life*) bohémien ♦ N (*Geog*) boemo(-a); (*artist, writer*) bohémien *m inv*
boil¹ [bɔɪl] N (*Med*) foruncolo
boil² [bɔɪl] N: **to bring to the boil**, (*USA*) **to bring to a boil** portare a ebollizione; **to come to the boil**, (*USA*) **to come to a boil** raggiungere l'ebollizione; **on the boil** che bolle; **it's off the boil** ha smesso di bollire ♦ *vt* (*far*) bollire; (*potatoes, meat*) (*far*) bollire, (*far*) lessare; **boil some water** fai bollire dell'acqua; **boiled egg** uovo alla coque; **boiled ham** prosciutto cotto; **boiled potatoes** patate *fpl* bollite *or* lesse ♦ *vi* (*water etc*) bollire; **the kettle is boiling** l'acqua bolle; **to let a saucepan boil dry** lasciar evaporare tutta l'acqua da una pentola; **to boil with rage** (*fig*) bollire di rabbia
 ▸ **boil away** *vi + adv* (*liquid*) evaporare; (*fig*) sfumare
 ▸ **boil down** *vi + adv* (*fig*): **to boil down to** ridursi a
 ▸ **boil over** *vi + adv* traboccare (bollendo); (*fig: anger*) esplodere
 ▸ **boil up** *vt + adv* far bollire
boil·er ['bɔɪlə'] N (*gen*) caldaia; (*for domestic hot water*) scaldabagno, scaldaacqua *m inv*
boil·ing ['bɔɪlɪŋ] ADJ (*also fig*) bollente; **a boiling hot day** un giorno torrido; **I'm boiling (hot)** (*fam*) sto morendo di caldo; **it's boiling in here!** qui dentro si soffoca!
boiling point N punto di ebollizione
boil-in-the-bag [,bɔɪlɪnðə'bæg] ADJ (*rice etc*) da bollire nel sacchetto
bois·ter·ous ['bɔɪstərəs] ADJ (*meeting*) turbolento(-a); (*person*) chiassoso(-a); (*party*) animato(-a)
bold [bəʊld] ADJ **1** (*brave: person, attempt*) audace; (*fig: plan, move*) ardito(-a); **he was bold enough to ask her a question** fu abbastanza coraggioso da farle una domanda; **bold economic reforms** coraggiose riforme economiche **2** (*forward: child, remark*) sfacciato(-a), sfrontato(-a) **3** (*striking: line, pattern*) vistoso(-a), che salta all'occhio; (*colour*) deciso(-a)
bold·ness ['bəʊldnɪs] N (*of person, plan*) audacia; (*impudence*) sfacciataggine *f*, impudenza
bold type N (*Typ*) neretto, grassetto
Bo·livia [bə'lɪvɪə] N Bolivia
Bo·liv·ian [bə'lɪvɪən] ADJ, N boliviano(-a)
bol·lard ['bɒləd] N (*on quay*) bitta; (*Brit: to bar way*) pilastrino di chiusura al traffico; (*at junction*) colonnina luminosa
Bol·ly·wood ['bɒlɪwʌd] N cinema *m* indiano
bol·ster ['bəʊlstə'] N capezzale *m* ♦ *vt* (*also:* **bolster up**) sostenere; **to bolster sb's courage** incoraggiare qn
bolt [bəʊlt] N **1** (*on door*) chiavistello, catenaccio; (*of lock*) catenaccio; (*Tech*) bullone *m*; (*of crossbow*) dardo; (*of cloth*) pezza; **there was a heavy bolt on the door** c'era un pesante catenaccio alla porta; **nuts and bolts** dadi e bulloni; **he's shot his bolt** (*fig*) ha giocato la sua ultima carta **2** (*dash*): **to make a bolt for the door** fare un balzo *or* schizzare verso la porta; **to make a bolt for it** darsela a gambe **3** (*lightning*) fulmine *m*; **a bolt of lightning** un fulmine; **a bolt from the blue** (*fig*) un fulmine a ciel sereno ♦ ADV: **bolt upright** diritto(-a) come un fuso ♦ *vt* **1** (*door*) chiudere

con il catenaccio *or* il chiavistello, serrare; (*Tech: also:* **bolt together**) imbullonare **2** (*food: also:* **bolt down**) ingollare ♦ VI (*run away: person*) darsela a gambe; (: *horse*) imbizzarrirsi; (*rush*) scappare via

bomb [bɒm] N bomba; **it went like a bomb** (*fam: party*) è andato a meraviglia; **it goes like a bomb** (*fam: car*) va come un razzo ♦ VT (*target*) bombardare

▸ **bomb out** VT + ADV (*building*) distruggere; **they were bombed out** hanno dovuto abbandonare la casa bombardata

bom·bard [bɒm'bɑːd] VT (*Mil*): **to bombard (with)** bombardare (con); **I was bombarded with questions** sono stato bombardato di domande

bom·bard·ment [bɒm'bɑːdmənt] N bombardamento

bom·bas·tic [bɒm'bæstɪk] ADJ magniloquente, ampolloso(-a)

bomb disposal expert N artificiere *m*

bomb disposal unit N corpo degli artificieri

bomb·er ['bɒmə'] N (*aircraft*) bombardiere *m*; (*terrorist*) dinamitardo(-a), bombarolo(-a)

bomb·ing ['bɒmɪŋ] N bombardamento ♦ ADJ (*expedition*) di bombardamento

bomb scare N sospetta presenza di un ordigno esplosivo

bomb·shell ['bɒm.ʃel] N (*fig: news*) bomba

bomb site N luogo bombardato

bona fide ['bəʊnə'faɪdɪ] ADJ (*antique, excuse*) autentico(-a); (*offer*) serio(-a), onesto(-a)

bo·nan·za [bə'nænzə] N periodo di boom

bond [bɒnd] N **1** (*link*) legame *m*, vincolo; **bonds** NPL (*chains etc*) catene *fpl*; **there is a special bond between them** c'è un legame particolare tra loro **2** (*agreement*) impegno, accordo; **to enter into a bond (to do sth)** impegnarsi (a fare qc); **his word is his bond** ci si può fidare completamente della sua parola **3** (*Fin*) obbligazione *f* **4** (*Comm*): **in bond** in attesa di sdoganamento **5** (*adhesion*) aderenza **6** (*Chem*) legame *m* **7** (*also:* **bond paper**) carta fine ♦ VT (*bricks*) cementare; (*subj: glue*) far aderire, incollare ♦ VI (*people*) stabilire un legame affettivo; (*objects*) incollarsi

bond·age ['bɒndɪdʒ] N servitù, schiavitù

bond·ed ware·house ['bɒndɪd 'weəhaʊs] N magazzino doganale

bone [bəʊn] N (*gen*) osso; (*of fish*) lisca, spina; **a broken bone** un osso rotto; **I feel it in my bones** me lo sento, qualcosa me lo dice; **I have a bone to pick with you** (*fam*) devo regolare un conto con te; **she made no bones about saying what she thought** ci ha detto quello che pensava senza fare tante cerimonie ♦ VT (*meat*) disossare; (*fish*) diliscare, spinare ♦ ADJ (*buttons*) d'osso

bone china N porcellana fine

bone-dry ['bəʊn'draɪ] ADJ (*fam*) asciuttissimo(-a)

bone idle ADJ: **to be bone idle** essere un(a) fannullone(-a)

bone marrow N midollo osseo

bon·er ['bəʊnə'] N (*USA*) gaffe *f inv*; (*fam!*): **to have a boner** avere il cazzo duro (*fam!*)

bon·fire ['bɒn.faɪə'] N falò *m inv*

bonk [bɒŋk] VT, VI (*Brit: hum, fam*) scopare (*fam!*)

bonk·ers ['bɒŋkəz] ADJ (*Brit fam*): **to be bonkers** essere suonato(-a); **to go bonkers** diventare matto(-a)

Bonn [bɒn] N Bonn *f*

bon·net ['bɒnɪt] N **1** (*Brit: Aut*) cofano **2** (*woman's, baby's*) cuffia; (*esp Scot: man's*) berretto

bon·ny ['bɒnɪ] ADJ (*esp Scot*) bello(-a), carino(-a)

bo·nus ['bəʊnəs] N (*on wages*) gratifica; (*insurance etc*) dividendo; (*fig*) sovrappiù *m*; **Christmas bonus** ≈ tredicesima

bony ['bəʊnɪ] ADJ (*comp -ier, superl -iest*) (*thin: person*) angoloso(-a), ossuto(-a); (*made of bone: frame*) osseo(-a); (: *fish*) pieno(-a) di lische; (: *meat*) con parecchio osso; (*like bone*) simile a osso; **a bony face** un viso ossuto

boo [buː] EXCL bu! ♦ N; **boos** NPL fischi *mpl* ♦ VT fischiare; **he was booed off the stage** l'hanno cacciato di scena a suon di fischi

boob [buːb] N (*Brit fam: mistake*) gaffe *f inv*; (*fam: breast*) tetta

boo·by prize ['buːbɪ.praɪz] N premio per il peggior contendente

boo·by trap ['buːbɪ.træp] N trabocchetto; (*Mil*) congegno che esplode al contatto

booby-trapped ['buːbɪ.træpt] ADJ: **a booby-trapped car** una macchina carica di esplosivo

book [bʊk] N (*notebook*) quaderno; (*of matches*) bustina; (*of tickets*) blocchetto; **I read it in a book** l'ho letto in un libro; **he wrote it down in his book** l'ha scritto nel quaderno; **the books** (*Comm*) i libri contabili; **to keep** *or* **do the books** tenere la contabilità; **to be in sb's bad books** essere nel libro nero di qn; **to bring sb to book (for sth)** costringere qn a render conto (di qc); **to throw the book at sb** (*in accusing*) imputare a qn tutte le accuse possibili; (*in punishing*) condannare qn al massimo della pena; **by the book** secondo le regole; **in my book** a mio avviso, a parer mio ♦ VT **1** (*reserve: seat, room, table*) prenotare, fissare, riservare; (*ticket*) prendere, comprare **2** (*Police: driver*) fare una contravvenzione a, multare; (*Ftbl*) ammonire ♦ VI (*see vt a*) prenotare; (*ticket*) prendere il biglietto

▸ **book in** VI + ADV (*at hotel*) prendere una camera ♦ VT + ADV (*person*) prenotare (una camera) per

▸ **book up** VT + ADV riservare, prenotare; **the hotel is booked up** l'albergo è al completo; **tonight's performance is booked up** la rappresentazione di stasera è esaurita; **I'm booked up** (*fam*) sono occupatissimo

book·able ['bʊkəbl] ADJ (*seat etc*) prenotabile, riservabile; **seats are bookable** si possono prenotare i posti

book·case ['bʊk.keɪs] N libreria, scaffale *m*

book ends NPL reggilibri *mpl*

book·ing ['bʊkɪŋ] N (*Brit: in hotel*) prenotazione *f*; (: *Sport*) ammonizione *f*

booking office N (*Rail*) biglietteria, ufficio *m* prenotazioni, *inv*; (*Theatre*) botteghino

book-keeping ['bʊk.kiːpɪŋ] N contabilità

book·let ['bʊklɪt] N opuscolo, libretto

book·maker ['bʊk.meɪkə'] N bookmaker *m inv*, allibratore *m*

book·mark ['bʊkmɑːk] N (*also Comput*) segnalibro ♦ VT (*Comput*) mettere un segnalibro a

book·seller ['bʊk.selə'] N libraio

book·shelf ['bʊk.ʃelf] N mensola per libri; **bookshelves** NPL (*bookcase*) libreria

book·shop ['bʊk.ʃɒp], **book·store** (*USA*) ['bʊk.stɔː'] N libreria

book·stall ['bʊk.stɔːl] N (*in station*) edicola, chiosco (dei giornali); (*secondhand books*) bancarella (dei libri)

book token N buono *m* libro, *inv*

book value N valore *m* contabile

book·worm ['bʊk.wɜːm] N (*fig*) topo di biblioteca

boom¹ [buːm] N (*in prices, shares*) forte incremento; (*of product*) boom *m inv*, improvvisa popolarità; (*of sales*) esplosione *f*; (*period of growth*) boom (economico); **a boom in popularity** un aumento improvviso della popolarità ♦ VI (*trade*) andare a gonfie vele; (*sales*) aumentare vertiginosamente; (*industry, town*) essere in forte espansione, svilupparsi enormemente

boom² [buːm] N (*of guns, thunder*) rombo, rimbombo; (*deeper*) boato ♦ VI (*voice, radio, sea: also:* **boom out**) rimbombare; (*gun*) tuonare ♦ VT (*also:* **boom out**) urlare con voce tonante

boom·er·ang ['buːməræŋ] N boomerang *m inv* ♦ VI (*fig*) avere effetto contrario; **to boomerang on sb** ritorcersi contro qn

boom town N ≈ città *f inv* in rapidissima espansione

boon [buːn] N (*blessing*) benedizione *f*

boor·ish ['bʊərɪʃ] ADJ (*manners*) da zoticone, da bifolco

boost [buːst] N **1** (*encouragement*) spinta, sprone *m*; **to give a boost to** (*morale*) tirar su; **it gave a boost to his confidence** è stata per lui un'iniezione di fiducia **2** (*upward thrust: to person*) spinta (in su); (: *to rocket*) spinta propulsiva ♦ VT (*increase: sales, production*) incentivare; (*fig: hopes*) rinforzare; (*promote: product*) promuovere (sul mercato); (*Elec: voltage*) aumentare; (*radio signal*) amplificare; (*Space*) lanciare; **they're trying to boost the economy** stanno cercando di dare una spinta all'economia; **the win boosted the team's morale** la vittoria ha sollevato il morale della squadra

boost·er ['buːstə'] N (*TV*) amplificatore *m* di segnale; (*Elec*) amplificatore; (*booster rocket*) razzo vettore; (*Med: injection*) (iniezione *f* di) richiamo

booster seat, booster cushion N seggiolino

boot¹ [buːt] N **1** (*gen*) stivale *m*; (*ankle boot*) stivaletto; (*of soldier, skier, workman*) scarpone *m*; (*for hiking*) scarpone da montagna; **football boots** scarpe *fpl* da calcio; **to give sb the boot** (*fam*) mettere qn alla porta **2** (*Brit: Aut*) portabagagli *m inv*, bagagliaio ♦ VT **1** (*fam: kick*) dare un calcio a; **to boot sb out** buttar fuori *or* cacciar via qn (a pedate) **2** (*Comput*) inizializzare

boot² [buːt] N (*old, liter*): **to boot** (*in addition*) in (*or* per di) più, per giunta, come se non bastasse

booth [buːð] N (*at fair*) bancarella, baraccone *m*; (*Telec: voting booth*) cabina

boot·leg [ˈbuːtˌlɛg] ADJ di contrabbando; **bootleg recording** registrazione *f* pirata, *inv*

boo·ty [ˈbuːtɪ] N bottino, refurtiva

booze [buːz] (*fam*) N alcolici *mpl*; **bring your own booze** portatevi da bere ♦ VI sbevazzare, alzare il gomito

booz·er [ˈbuːzəʳ] (*fam*) N (*person*) beone *m*; (*Brit: pub*) osteria

bor·der [ˈbɔːdəʳ] N **1** (*frontier*) confine *m*; **the Borders** (*Brit*) zona al confine tra la Scozia e l'Inghilterra; **we crossed the Hungarian border** abbiamo passato il confine con l'Ungheria **2** (*edge: as decoration*) bordo, orlatura, orlo; (: *as boundary*) margine *m*, limite *m* **3** (*in garden*) aiuola (laterale) ♦ VT (*line, adjoin*) fiancheggiare, costeggiare

  ▸ **border on, border upon** VI + PREP confinare con; (*fig: come close to being*) sfiorare, rasentare

border·line [ˈbɔːdəˌlaɪn] ADJ (*candidate*) su cui è difficile decidere; **borderline case** caso limite; **he was a borderline failure** è stato bocciato per poco ♦ N (*fig*) linea di demarcazione

bore¹ [bɔːʳ] N (*person*) noioso(-a), seccatore(-trice), noia; (*event*) noia, barba; **what a bore!** che noia!; **the party/office bore** l'attaccabottoni *m/f inv* (di una festa/un ufficio) ♦ VT (*person*) annoiare

bore² [bɔːʳ] N (*also*: **bore hole**) foro di sonda; (*diameter*) diametro interno; (*of gun*) calibro; **a 12-bore shotgun** un fucile calibro 12 ♦ VT (*hole*) praticare; (*tunnel*) scavare ♦ VI: **to bore for** perforare *or* trivellare alla ricerca di

bore³ [bɔːʳ] PT *of* bear¹

bored [bɔːd] ADJ annoiato(-a); **to get bored** annoiarsi; **he's bored to tears** *or* **bored to death** *or* **bored stiff** è annoiato a morte, si annoia da morire

bore·dom [ˈbɔːdəm] N noia

bor·ing [ˈbɔːrɪŋ] ADJ (*tedious*) noioso(-a)

born [bɔːn] ADJ nato(-a); **to be born** (*also fig*) nascere; **I was born in 1955** sono nato nel 1955; **born blind** cieco(-a) dalla nascita; **a Roman born and bred** un romano di Roma, un romano doc; **the revolution was born of the workers' discontent** la rivoluzione scaturì dallo scontento degli operai; **to be born again** rinascere; **I wasn't born yesterday!** (*fam*) non sono nato ieri!; **in all my born days** (*fam*) in tutta la mia vita; **a born actor/musician** un attore/musicista nato; **a born liar** un(a) bugiardo(-a) matricolato(-a); **a born fool** un(a) perfetto(-a) cretino(-a)

born-again [ˌbɔːnəˈgɛn] ADJ: **born-again Christian** convertito(-a) alla chiesa evangelica

borne [bɔːn] PP *of* bear¹

Bor·neo [ˈbɔːnɪəʊ] N Borneo

bor·ough [ˈbʌrə] N comune *m*, circoscrizione *f* amministrativa; (*in London*) distretto

bor·row [ˈbɔrəʊ] VT: **to borrow (from)** prendere in prestito (da), farsi prestare (da); (*idea, word*) prendere (da); **to borrow sth from sb** farsi prestare qc da qn; **could I borrow your car?** puoi prestarmi la macchina?

bor·row·er [ˈbɔrəʊəʳ] N (*gen*) chi prende in prestito; (*Econ*) mutuatario(-a)

bor·row·ing [ˈbɔrəʊɪŋ] N prestito

bor·stal [ˈbɔːstl] N (*Brit*) riformatorio

Bos·nia [ˈbɒznɪə] N Bosnia

Bosnia-Herzegovina [ˌbɒznɪəhɜːtsəgəʊˈviːnə], **Bosnia-Hercegovina** [ˌbɒznɪəhɜːtsəˈɡɒvɪnə] N Bosnia-Erzegovina

Bos·nian [ˈbɒznɪən] ADJ, N bosniaco(-a)

bos·om [ˈbʊzəm] N (*of woman, also fig*) seno; **in the bosom of the family** in seno alla famiglia

bosom friend N amico(-a) del cuore

boss [bɒs] N (*employer, owner*) capo, padrone *m*, principale *m*; (*manager, of organization*) capo; (*of criminal organization*) boss *m inv* ♦ VT (*also*: **boss about** *or* **around**: *pej*) comandare a bacchetta; **stop bossing everyone about!** smettila di dare ordini a tutti!

bossy [ˈbɒsɪ] ADJ (*person*) autoritario(-a); **don't you get bossy with me!** non cominciare a darmi ordini!

bo·sun [ˈbəʊsən] N = boatswain

bo·tan·ical [bəˈtænɪkəl], **bo·tan·ic** [bəˈtænɪk] ADJ botanico(-a)

bota·nist [ˈbɒtənɪst] N botanico(-a)

bota·ny [ˈbɒtənɪ] N botanica

botch [bɒtʃ] N (*of job*) pasticcio, macello ♦ VT (*job*) raffazzonare; (*attempt*) fallire

  ▸ **botch up** VT (*job*) raffazzonare

both [bəʊθ] ADJ tutti(-e) e due, entrambi(-e) *pl*, ambedue *inv*; **both books/boys** tutti e due *or* entrambi *or* ambedue i libri/ragazzi ♦ PRON tutti(-e) e due, entrambi(-e) *pl*, ambedue *inv*; **they were both there**, **both of them were there** c'erano tutti e due; **both of us went, we both went** ci siamo andati tutt'e due; **both are to blame** la colpa è di tutti e due; **both of us agree** siamo d'accordo tutti e due; **come in both of you** entrate tutti e due ♦ ADV: **both... and** sia... che, sia... sia; **John and I both went** ci siamo andati sia John che io; **both you and I saw it** l'abbiamo visto sia tu sia io; **both this and that** sia questo che quello; **she was both laughing and crying** piangeva e rideva a un tempo *or* allo stesso tempo; **he both plays and sings** oltre a suonare canta; **they sell both meat and poultry** vendono sia carne che pollame

both·er [ˈbɒðəʳ] N (*nuisance*) seccatura, noia; (*trouble*) fastidio, disturbo; **it is a bother to have to go** è una seccatura dover andare; **(it's) no bother**, **I'll see to it** non c'è problema, ci penso io; **the children were no bother at all** i bambini non hanno dato nessun fastidio; **it wasn't any bother** (*don't mention it*) si figuri!, s'immagini!; **he had a spot of bother with the police** ha avuto delle noie con la polizia ♦ VT (*worry*) preoccupare; (*annoy*) seccare, infastidire, dar fastidio a; **to bother doing** *or* **to do sth** darsi la pena di fare qc; **what's bothering you?** cosa c'è che ti preoccupa?; **I'm sorry to bother you** scusa se ti disturbo; **I'm sorry to bother you with my problems** mi spiace importunarti con i miei problemi; **does the noise bother you?** ti dà fastidio il rumore?; **don't bother me!** lasciami in pace!; **I can't be bothered going out** *or* **to go out** proprio non mi va di uscire; **his leg bothers him** gli fa un po' male la gamba; **he didn't even bother to write** non si è nemmeno sprecato a scrivere due righe; **I'm not bothered** per me fa lo stesso ♦ VI: **to bother (about)** preoccuparsi (di *or* per); **please don't bother** non si scomodi, lasci perdere ♦ EXCL uffa!, accidenti!

Bot·swa·na [ˌbɒtsˈwɑːnə] N Botswana *m*

bot·tle [ˈbɒtl] N bottiglia; (*of perfume, shampoo*) flacone *m*; (*baby's*) biberon *m inv*, poppatoio; **bottle of wine/milk** bottiglia di vino/latte; **wine/milk bottle** bottiglia da vino/del latte ♦ VT (*wine*) imbottigliare; (*fruit*) conservare (in vasetti)

  ▸ **bottle up** VT + ADV (*emotion*) soffocare, reprimere

bottle bank N contenitore *m* per la raccolta del vetro

bottle-fed [ˈbɒtlˌfɛd] ADJ allattato(-a) artificialmente

bottle·neck [ˈbɒtlˌnɛk] N (*road*) strozzatura; (*traffic*) ingorgo

bottle-opener [ˈbɒtlˌəʊpnəʳ] N apribottiglie *m inv*

bot·tom [ˈbɒtəm] N (*gen*) fondo; (*of mountain, tree*) piedi *mpl*; (*of shoe*) suola; (*of chair*) sedile *m*; (*of ship*) opera viva; (*of person*) sedere *m*; **at the bottom of** (*hill, ladder*) ai piedi di; (*road, list*) in fondo a; **at the bottom of the page** in fondo alla pagina, a piè di pagina; **to be bottom of the class** essere l'ultimo(-a) della classe; **on the bottom of** (*shoe etc*) sotto; (*sea, lake etc*) sul fondo (di); **the boat floated bottom up** la barca galleggiava capovolta; **I fell flat on my bottom** sono caduto battendo il sedere; **at bottom** in fondo; **from the bottom of my heart** con tutto il cuore, dal profondo del cuore; **to get to the bottom of sth** (*fig*) andare al fondo di *or* in fondo a qc; **he's at the bottom of it** (*fig*) qui ci dev'essere il suo zampino; **bottoms up!** (*fam*) cin-cin!; **bikini bottom** slip *mpl* del bikini ♦ ADJ (*lowest: shelf, step*) più basso(-a), inferiore; (*corner, part*) inferiore; **the bottom shelf** il ripiano inferiore

  ▸ **bottom out** VI + ADV assestarsi al livello più basso

bot·tom·less ['bɒtəmlɪs] ADJ (*pit*) senza fondo; (*funds, supply*) inesauribile

bottom line N: the bottom line (*Fin*) il risultato finanziario; (*essential point*) l'essenziale *m*; (*result*) il risultato

botu·lism ['bɒtjʊ,lɪzəm] N botulismo

bough [baʊ] N ramo

bought [bɔːt] PT, PP *of* buy

boul·der ['bəʊldə'] N masso, macigno

boule·vard ['buːləvɑː'] N viale *m*

bounce [baʊns] N (*of ball*) rimbalzo; (*springiness: of hair, mattress*) elasticità; **he's got plenty of bounce** (*fig*) è molto esuberante ♦ VT (*ball*) far rimbalzare ♦ VI (*ball*) rimbalzare; (*child*) saltare, balzare; (*fam: cheque*) essere scoperto(-a) *or* a vuoto; **the ball bounced** la palla è rimbalzata; **the cheque he gave me bounced** (*fam*) l'assegno che mi ha dato era scoperto (*or* a vuoto); **to bounce in** entrare di slancio *or* con foga

‣ **bounce back** VI + ADV (*person*) riprendersi

bounc·er ['baʊnsə'] N (*fam*) buttafuori *m inv*

bound¹ [baʊnd] PT, PP *of* bind ♦ ADJ **1** (*prisoner*) legato(-a); **bound hand and foot** legato(-a) mani e piedi **2** (*book*) rilegato(-a) **3** (*certain*): **he's bound to say yes** vedrai che dirà di sì; **he's bound to fail** sicuramente fallirà; **there are bound to be price rises** ci sarà sicuramente un aumento dei prezzi; **it was bound to happen** doveva succedere, era da prevedersi **4** (*obliged*): **to be bound to do sth** essere obbligato(-a) *a or* tenuto(-a) a fare qc; **I'm bound to say that ...** devo dire che...

bound² [baʊnd] ADJ (*destined*): **bound for** (*person, train, ship*) diretto(-a) a, in viaggio per; (*parcel*) indirizzato(-a) a, diretto(-a) a; **where are you bound (for)?** dove sei diretto?; **California bound** diretto(-a) in California; **westbound traffic** traffico diretto verso ovest

bound³ [baʊnd] N (*jump*) salto, balzo ♦ VI (*person, animal*) saltare, balzare; **he bounded out of bed** è saltato fuori *or* è balzato giù dal letto; **his heart bounded with joy** il cuore gli balzò in petto dalla gioia

bound⁴ [baʊnd] VT: **bounded by** limitato(-a) da

bounda·ry ['baʊndərɪ] N confine *m*

bound·less ['baʊndlɪs] ADJ (*also fig*) illimitato(-a), sconfinato(-a)

boun·ti·ful ['baʊntɪfʊl] ADJ (*person*) munifico(-a); (*God*) misericordioso(-a); (*supply*) abbondante

boun·ty ['baʊntɪ] N (*generosity*) liberalità, munificenza; (*reward*) taglia

bounty hunter N cacciatore *m* di taglie

bou·quet ['bʊkeɪ] N (*of flowers, wine*) bouquet *m inv*

bour·bon ['bʊəbən], **bourbon whiskey** N (*USA*) bourbon *m inv*

bour·geois ['bʊəʒwɑː] ADJ, N borghese *m/f*

bout [baʊt] N **1** (*of illness, malaria*) attacco, accesso; **a severe bout of flu** una brutta influenza; **a drinking bout** una sbronza; **he's had several bouts of illness** è stato ammalato diverse volte; **a bout of hard work** un periodo di intenso lavoro **2** (*boxing match*) incontro

bou·tique [buːˈtiːk] N boutique *f inv*

bow¹ [bəʊ] N arco; (*Mus*) archetto; (*knot*) fiocco, nodo

bow² [baʊ] N inchino; **to take a bow** inchinarsi al pubblico *or* all'applauso del pubblico ♦ VI (*lower: head*) chinare; (*bend: back*) curvare, piegare; **bowed down by cares** schiacciato(-a) dalle preoccupazioni ♦ VI: **to bow (to)** inchinarsi (a), fare un inchino (a); (*fig: yield*) inchinarsi (di fronte a); **to bow to the inevitable** rassegnarsi all'inevitabile

‣ **bow down** VI + ADV: **to bow down (to)** prostrarsi (davanti a)

‣ **bow out** VI + ADV (*fig*) uscire di scena

bow·el ['baʊəl] N (*gen pl*) intestino, intestini *mpl*; **cancer of the bowel** cancro all'intestino; **bowels of the earth** viscere *fpl* della terra

bowl¹ [bəʊl] N **1** (*for soup*) scodella; (*for cereal, fruit*) coppetta; (*mixing bowl*) terrina; (*for salad*) insalatiera; (*for washing up*) bacinella, catino; **bowl of cornflakes** ciotola di cornflakes; **bowl of soup** piatto di minestra **2** (*hollow: of lavatory*) tazza; (: *of spoon*) incavo, cavo; (: *of pipe*) fornello **3** (*USA: stadium*) stadio

‣ **bowl over** VT + ADV rovesciare (a terra); (*fig*) lasciare strabiliato(-a)

bowl² [bəʊl] VT (*ball*) lanciare ♦ VI (*Cricket*) servire; (*Bowls*) tirare

bow-legged [,bəʊˈlegɪd] ADJ (*person*) con le gambe arcuate

bowl·er ['bəʊlə'] N **1** (*Cricket*) lanciatore(-trice); (*Bowls*) giocatore(-trice) di bocce **2** (*Brit: also*: **bowler hat**) bombetta

bowl·ing ['bəʊlɪŋ] N (*indoor*) bowling *m inv*; (*on grass*) gioco delle bocce; **to go bowling** andare a giocare a bowling

bowling alley N (pista da) bowling *m inv*

bowling green N campo da bocce (*su erba*)

bowls [bəʊlz] NSG gioco delle bocce; **he plays bowls** gioca a bocce

bow tie [,bəʊˈtaɪ] N (cravatta a) farfalla

box¹ [bɒks] N **1** scatola; (*crate, also for money*) cassetta; (*for jewels*) cofanetto; (*on page*) casella; **a box of matches** una scatola di fiammiferi; **the box** (*fam: TV*) la tele; **to watch the box** guardare la tele **2** (*Theatre*) palco; (*Law: for witness, press etc*) banco

‣ **box in** VT + ADV (*bath*) incassare; (*car*) incastrare; **to feel boxed in** sentirsi imprigionato(-a)

❏ **box** is not translated by the Italian word *box*

box² [bɒks] N: **a box on the ear** uno scappaccione ♦ VT: **to box sb's ears** prendere qn a scappaccioni ♦ VI (*Sport*) fare il pugile; (*fight*) combattere

box·er ['bɒksə'] N (*Sport*) pugile *m*, boxeur *m inv*; (*dog*) boxer *m inv*

boxer shorts ['bɒksəʃɔːts] NPL boxer; **a pair of boxer shorts** un paio di boxer

box·ing ['bɒksɪŋ] N (*Sport*) pugilato, boxe *f*

boxing gloves NPL guantoni *mpl* (da pugile *or* da boxe)

boxing ring N ring *m inv*

box number N (*for advertisements*) casella

box office N botteghino

box·room ['bɒks,rʊm] N (*Brit*) ripostiglio, stanzino

boy [bɔɪ] N **1** ragazzo; (*small*) bambino; (*son*) figlio; (*servant*) servo; **a boy of fifteen** un ragazzo di quindici anni; **a boy of seven** un bambino di sette anni; **he has two boys and a girl** ha due maschi e una femmina; **she had a boy** ha avuto un maschio; **a baby boy** un maschietto; **school for boys** scuola maschile; **when I was a boy** quand'ero piccolo; **boys will be boys** che vuoi, sono maschi; **he's out with the boys** è fuori con gli amici; **old boy** vecchio mio; **my dear boy** mio caro; **oh boy!** mamma mia!

boy band N boy band *f inv*, gruppo pop di soli ragazzi creato per far presa su un pubblico giovane

boy·cott ['bɔɪkɒt] N boicottaggio ♦ VT boicottare

boy·friend ['bɔɪˌfrend] N ragazzo; **he's not her boyfriend, they're just friends** non è il suo ragazzo, sono solo amici

boy·ish ['bɔɪʃ] ADJ (*appearance, manner*) da ragazzo

Bp ABBR = bishop

bra [brɑː] N reggiseno

brace [breɪs] N **1** (*Constr*) rinforzo, sostegno; (*dental*) apparecchio (ortodontico), macchinetta (per i denti); (*Typ*) graffa **2** (*pl inv: pair: of game birds*) coppia, paio ♦ VT (*strengthen*) rinforzare; **to brace o.s.** (*also fig*) tenersi forte

❏ **brace** is not translated by the Italian word *brace*

brace·let ['breɪslɪt] N braccialetto

braces ['breɪsɪz] NPL (*Brit*) bretelle *fpl*

brac·ing ['breɪsɪŋ] ADJ (*air*) tonificante, vivificante

brack·en ['brækən] N (*plant*) felce *f*; (*area of bracken*) felci *pl*

brack·et ['brækɪt] N **1** (*support*) sostegno; (*shelf*) mensola **2** (*Typ: usu pl*) parentesi *f inv*; **round/square brackets** parentesi tonde/quadre; **in brackets** tra parentesi **3** (*group*) categoria, gruppo; **income bracket** fascia di reddito; **age brackets** fascia d'età ♦ VT (*Typ*) mettere tra parentesi; (*fig: also*: **bracket together**) mettere insieme

brack·ish ['brækɪʃ] ADJ (*water*) salmastro(-a)

brag [bræg] VT, VI: **to brag (about/that)** vantarsi (di)

braid [breɪd] N (*on dress*) spighetta; (*Mil: on dressing gown*) cordoncino; (*trimming*) passamano; (*of hair*) treccia ♦ VT (*hair*) intrecciare

Braille [breɪl] N braille *m*

brain [breɪn] N **1** (*Anat*) cervello; (*Culin*); **brains** NPL cervella *sg*; **to blow one's brains out** farsi saltare le cervella; **he's got cars on the brain** ha il chiodo fisso delle macchine **2** (*fig: fam: intelligence*); **brains** NPL testa; **he's got brains** ha (del) cervello, è intelligente; **he's the brains of the family** è il cervellone di casa ♦ VT (*fam*) spaccare la testa a

brain·child [ˈbreɪnˌtʃaɪld] N creatura, creazione *f*

brain·dead [ˈbreɪnˌdɛd] ADJ (*Med*) che ha subito morte cerebrale; (*fam*) decerebrato(-a), deficiente

brain·less [ˈbreɪnlɪs] ADJ deficiente, stupido(-a)

brain·storm [ˈbreɪnˌstɔːm] N **1** (*Brit fig*) attacco di pazzia **2** (*USA*) = brainwave

brain·wash [ˈbreɪnˌwɒʃ] VT: **to brainwash sb (into doing sth)** fare il lavaggio del cervello a qn (per convincerlo a fare qc)

brain·wave [ˈbreɪnˌweɪv] N (*fam*) idea brillante, lampo di genio

brainy [ˈbreɪnɪ] ADJ (*comp* -ier, *superl* -iest) (*fam*) geniale

braise [breɪz] VT (*Culin*) brasare

brake [breɪk] N (*on vehicle*) freno; **to put on** *or* **apply the brakes** (*Aut*) azionare i freni; **to put the brakes on sth** (*fig*) mettere un freno a qc ♦ VI frenare

brake light N (fanalino dello) stop *m inv*

brake pedal N pedale *m* del freno

bram·ble [ˈbræmbl] N rovo; (*fruit*) mora

bran [bræn] N crusca

branch [brɑːntʃ] N **1** (*also fig*) ramo; (*in road, railway, pipe*) diramazione *f*; (*Comm: of company, bank*) filiale *f*, succursale *f* ♦ VI (*road*) diramarsi, ramificarsi

▸ **branch off** VI + ADV (*road, path*) diramarsi; (*speaker*) divagare

▸ **branch out** VI + ADV: **to branch out into** (*business*) estendere la propria attività nel ramo di; (*person*) mettersi nel ramo di; **he's branched out on his own** si è messo in proprio

branch line N (*Rail*) linea secondaria

branch manager N direttore *m* di filiale

brand [brænd] N **1** (*Comm*) marca **2** (*on cattle, prisoner*) marchio; **a famous brand name** una marca famosa; **brand loyalty** fedeltà a un marchio ♦ VT (*cattle: or fig: person*) marchiare; **his name is branded on my memory** il suo nome è impresso indelebilmente nella mia memoria; **he was branded (as) a traitor** (*fig: pej*) fu tacciato di tradimento

bran·dish [ˈbrændɪʃ] VT brandire

brand name N marca

brand-new [ˈbrændˈnjuː] ADJ nuovo(-a) di zecca, nuovo(-a) fiammante

bran·dy [ˈbrændɪ] N brandy *m inv*

brash [bræʃ] ADJ (*impudent*) sfrontato(-a), sfacciato(-a)

Bra·silia [brəˈzɪljə] N Brasilia

brass [brɑːs] N **1** ottone *m*; **the brass** (*Mus*) gli ottoni **2** (*fam*) **to have the brass (neck) to do sth** avere la faccia tosta di fare qc; **the top brass** (*Mil*) i pezzi grossi dell'esercito ♦ ADJ (*ornament etc*) d'ottone

brass band N fanfara

bras·siere [ˈbræsɪəʳ] N reggiseno

brass tacks NPL: **to get down to brass tacks** (*fam*) venire al sodo

brat [bræt] N (*fam: pej*) moccioso(-a)

bra·va·do [brəˈvɑːdəʊ] N spavalderia

brave [breɪv] ADJ coraggioso(-a); **be brave** coraggio!, sii forte! ♦ N (*Native American*) guerriero *m* pellerossa, *inv* ♦ VT (*weather, danger*) sfidare; **to brave it out** affrontare la situazione

brav·ery [ˈbreɪvərɪ] N coraggio

bra·vo [ˈbrɑːˈvəʊ] EXCL bravo!, bene!

brawl [brɔːl] N rissa ♦ VI azzuffarsi

brawn [brɔːn] N muscoli *mpl*; (*Culin*) ≈ soppressata

brawny [ˈbrɔːnɪ] ADJ muscoloso(-a)

bray [breɪ] N raglio ♦ VI ragliare

bra·zen [ˈbreɪzn] ADJ (*shameless*) sfacciato(-a) ♦ VT: **to brazen it out** continuare con la massima faccia tosta

bra·zi·er [ˈbreɪzɪəʳ] N braciere *m*

Bra·zil [brəˈzɪl] N Brasile *m*

Bra·zil·ian [brəˈzɪljən] ADJ, N brasiliano(-a)

Brazil nut N noce *f* del Brasile

breach [briːtʃ] N **1** (*violation: of law*) violazione *f*; (: *of rules*) infrazione *f*; (: *of duty*) abuso **2** (*gap: in wall*) apertura, varco; (*Mil*) breccia; (*estrangement*) rottura ♦ VT (*defences*) far breccia in

bread [brɛd] N pane *m*; (*fam: money*) grana; **brown bread** pane integrale; **sliced white bread** pancarrè *m*; **to earn one's daily bread** guadagnarsi il pane; **to know which side one's bread is buttered on** saper da che parte conviene stare

bread·bin [ˈbrɛdˌbɪn] N (*Brit*) cassetta *f* portapane, *inv*

bread·board [ˈbrɛdˌbɔːd] N tagliere *m* (per il pane); (*Comput*) pannello per esperimenti

bread·box [ˈbrɛdˌbɒks] N (*USA*) cassetta *f* portapane, *inv*

bread·crumbs [ˈbrɛdˌkrʌmz] NPL briciole *fpl*; (*Culin*) pangrattato; **fried in breadcrumbs** panato(-a) e fritto(-a)

bread·line [ˈbrɛdˌlaɪn] N: **to be on the breadline** sbarcare a malapena il lunario

breadth [brɛtθ] N (*also fig*) larghezza; **to be 2 metres in breadth** misurare 2 metri di larghezza, essere largo(-a) 2 metri

bread·winner [ˈbrɛdˌwɪnəʳ] N chi mantiene la famiglia, chi porta i soldi a casa (*fam*); **to be the breadwinner** guadagnare il pane per tutta la famiglia

---

KEYWORD

break [breɪk] (*pt* **broke**, *pp* **broken**) N

1 (*gen*) rottura; (*fracture*) fenditura; (*in bone*) frattura; (*in wall, fence*) apertura; (*gap*) breccia; (*in line, row, electric circuit*) interruzione *f*; **with a break in her voice** con voce rotta *or* incrinata dall'emozione; **a break in the clouds** una schiarita; **a break in the weather** un cambiamento di tempo; **at break of day** allo spuntare del giorno, sul far del giorno; **to make a break for it** darsela a gambe

2 (*in conversation*) pausa, interruzione *f*; (*rest: in journey*) sosta; (*tea break*) intervallo; (*Scol*) ricreazione *f*, intervallo; (*holiday*) vacanza; **the Christmas break** le vacanze di Natale; **to have** *or* **take a break** (*few minutes*) fare una pausa; (*rest, holiday*) prendere un po' di riposo; **without a break** senza una pausa

3 (*fam: chance*) possibilità *f inv*; **a lucky break** un colpo di fortuna; **give me a break!** dammi questa possibilità!; (*leave me alone*) lasciami respirare!; (*be reasonable*) ma per carità!

♦ VT

1 (*gen*) rompere; (*bone*) rompere, fratturare; (*skin*) lacerare; (*surpass: record*) battere; **I've broken a glass** ho rotto un bicchiere; **to break one's back/leg** rompersi la schiena/gamba; **he broke the world record** ha battuto il record mondiale; **to break the surface** (*submarine, diver*) affiorare (alla superficie); **to break a code** decifrare un codice; **to break sb's heart** (*fig*) spezzare il cuore a *or* di qn; **to break the ice** (*fig*) rompere il ghiaccio

2 (*law, rule*) violare; (*promise*) mancare a; (*vow*) rompere; (*appointment*) disdire, mandare all'aria; **to break the law** infrangere la legge

3 (*resistance, spirits*) fiaccare, annientare; (*health*) rovinare; (*strike*) domare, stroncare; **I can't break the habit** non riesco a perdere il vizio; **to break sb** (*financially*) mandare in rovina qn

4 (*silence, spell*) rompere; (*journey*) spezzare, interrompere; (*electrical circuit*) interrompere

5 (*soften: force*) smorzare; (: *fall, blow*) attutire

6 (*bad news*): **to break the news to sb** comunicare per primo la notizia a qn; **try to break it to her gently** cerca di dirglielo con tatto

♦ VI

1 (*gen*) rompersi; (*wave*) frangersi, infrangersi; (*fig: heart*) spezzarsi; **careful, it'll break!** stai attento che si rompe!; **to break into tiny pieces** andare in frantumi *or* in mille pezzi; **the stick broke in two** il bastone si è spezzato in due; **let's break for lunch** facciamo una sosta per pranzo; **to break with sb** (*fig*) rompere con qn; **to break free** *or* **loose** liberarsi

2 (*dawn, day*) spuntare; (*storm*) scoppiare; (*news*) saltare fuori

3 (*health, spirits*) cedere; (*weather*) cambiare; (*heatwave*) finire; (*voice: boy's*) cambiare; (: *in emotion*) rompersi

▸ **break away** VI + ADV: **to break away (from)** staccarsi (da); (*Ftbl, etc*) scattare via (da)

▸ **break down** VT + ADV 1 (*door*) buttare giù, abbattere; (*resistance*) stroncare 2 (*analyse: figures*) analizzare; (: *substance*) scomporre ♦ VI + ADV (*machine*) rompersi, guastarsi; (*Aut*) restare in panne, avere un guasto, rompersi; (*person: under pressure*) crollare; (: *from emotion*) scoppiare in lacrime; (: *mentally*) avere un esaurimento (nervoso); (*health*) cedere; (*talks*) arenarsi; **she broke down and wept** è crollata e si è messa a piangere

▸ **break even** VI (*in business*) coprire le spese; (*in gambling*) finire pari

▸ **break in** VT + ADV 1 (*door*) sfondare 2 (*train: horse*) domare; (: *new recruit*) addestrare ♦ VI 1 (*burglar*) fare irruzione; **the thief had broken in through a window** il ladro era entrato forzando una finestra 2 (*interrupt*): **to break in (on sb/sth)** interrompere (qn/qc)

▸ **break into** VI + PREP 1 (*house*) fare irruzione in; (*safe*) scassinare, forzare; (*savings*) intaccare; **thieves broke into the house** dei ladri sono entrati in casa 2 (*begin suddenly*): **to break into song/a trot** mettersi a cantare/trottare

▸ **break off** VT + ADV (*piece*) staccare, spezzare; (*talks, engagement*) rompere ♦ VI + ADV 1 (*twig*) staccarsi 2 (*speaker*) interrompersi; (*stop*): **to break off (from doing sth)** smettere (di fare qc); **to break off from work** interrompere il lavoro

▸ **break open** VT (*door*) sfondare

▸ **break out** VI + ADV 1 (*prisoners*): **to break out (of)** evadere (da) 2 (*war, fire, argument*) scoppiare; (*violence*) esplodere; **to break out in spots** coprirsi di macchie

▸ **break through** VI + ADV (*Mil*) aprirsi un varco, sfondare; **the sun broke through** il sole ha fatto capolino tra le nuvole ♦ VI + PREP (*defences, barrier*) penetrare in, sfondare; (*crowd*) aprirsi un varco in *or* tra, aprirsi un passaggio in *or* tra

▸ **break up** VT + ADV (*rocks etc*) fare a pezzi, spaccare; (*marriage*) finire; (*crowd, clouds*) disperdere; (*fight etc*) interrompere, far cessare; **police broke up the demonstration** la polizia ha disperso i dimostranti ♦ VI + ADV (*ship*) andare in *or* a pezzi, sfondarsi; (*ice*) spaccarsi, disintegrarsi; (*partnership, meeting*) sciogliersi; (*couple*) separarsi; (*marriage*) andare in pezzi, finire; (*crowd, clouds*) disperdersi; (*school*) chiudere; **Richard and Marie have broken up** Richard e Marie si sono lasciati

break·able ['breɪkəbl] ADJ fragile

break·age ['breɪkɪdʒ] N danni *mpl*; **to pay for breakages** pagare i danni

break·away ['breɪkəˌweɪ] ADJ (*group*) scissionista, dissidente

break-dancing ['breɪkˌdɑːnsɪŋ] N breakdance *f*

break·down ['breɪkdaʊn] N 1 (*of machine*) guasto, rottura; (*in system, communications*) interruzione *f*, sospensione *f* di servizio; (*Aut*) guasto, panne *f inv*; (*of talks, in relations*) rottura; (*Med*) collasso; (*mental*) esaurimento nervoso; **accidents and breakdowns** incidenti e guasti; **we had a breakdown near Leeds** siamo rimasti in panne vicino a Leeds; **the breakdown of their marriage** la fine del loro matrimonio 2 (*of figures*) resoconto analitico; (*Chem*) scomposizione *f*; **a breakdown of the costs** un'analisi dei costi

breakdown service N servizio di soccorso stradale

breakdown van N carro *m* attrezzi, *inv*

break·er ['breɪkə'] N (*wave*) frangente *m*

break·even point ['breɪkˌiːvən'pɔɪnt] N punto di rottura *or* pareggio

break·fast ['brekfəst] N (prima) colazione *f*; **to have breakfast** fare colazione ♦ VI: **to breakfast (on)** fare colazione (con)

breakfast cereal N fiocchi *mpl* d'avena (*or* di mais *etc*)

break-in ['breɪkˌɪn] N irruzione *f*

break·ing point ['breɪkɪŋˌpɔɪnt] N punto di rottura; (*fig: of person*) limite *m* di sopportazione

break·through ['breɪkθruː] N (*in research*) scoperta decisiva; (*Mil*) breccia; **they have made a breakthrough in the search for the cause of the disease** hanno fatto una scoperta decisiva nella ricerca sulle cause della malattia

break-up ['breɪkʌp] N (*of partnership, marriage*) rottura

break-up value N (*Comm*) valore *m* di realizzo

break·water ['breɪkˌwɔːtə'] N frangiflutti *m inv*

breast [brest] N (*Anat, Culin*) petto; (*of woman*) seno, mammella; **chicken breast** petto di pollo; **to make a clean breast of it** (*fig*) vuotare il sacco ♦ VT (*finishing tape*) toccare

breast-feed ['brestfiːd] (*pt, pp* **breast-fed**) VT, VI allattare (al seno)

breast pocket N taschino

breast·stroke ['brestˌstrəʊk] N (nuoto a) rana; **to swim** *or* **do the breaststroke** nuotare a rana

breath [breθ] N fiato, alito; (*act of breathing*) respiro; **she drew a deep breath** fece un respiro profondo; **bad breath** alito cattivo; **in the same breath** nello stesso istante; **out of breath** senza fiato; **under one's breath** sotto voce; **to go out for a breath of air** uscire a prendere una boccata d'aria; **to hold one's breath** trattenere il fiato *or* il respiro; **to get one's breath back** riprendere fiato; **it took my breath away** mi ha lasciato senza fiato, mi ha mozzato il respiro

breathe [briːð] VT (*air*) respirare; (*sigh*) tirare; **he breathed garlic all over me** mi ha soffiato addosso il suo alito puzzolente d'aglio; **I won't breathe a word about it** non fiaterò; **to breathe new life into sb/sth** (*fig*) ridar vita a qn/qc ♦ VI respirare; **to breathe heavily** ansimare, avere il fiato grosso; **now we can breathe again** (*fig*) adesso possiamo riprendere fiato

▸ **breathe in** VI + ADV inspirare ♦ VT + ADV respirare

▸ **breathe out** VT + ADV, VI + ADV espirare

breath·er ['briːðə'] N (*fam*) attimo di respiro

breath·ing ['briːðɪŋ] N respiro, respirazione *f*; **heavy breathing** (*on phone*) respiro ansimante (di maniaco)

breathing space N (*fig*) attimo di respiro

breath·less ['breθlɪs] ADJ (*exhausted*) senza fiato; (*with excitement*) con il fiato sospeso; (*silence*) religioso(-a); (*anticipation, anxiety*) vivissimo(-a); **his asthma makes him breathless** l'asma gli fa mancare il fiato

breath·taking ['breθˌteɪkɪŋ] ADJ (*sight*) mozzafiato *inv*

breath test N ≈ prova del palloncino

bred [bred] PT, PP *of* **breed**

-bred [bred] SUFF: **to be well/ill-bred** essere beneducato(-a)/ maleducato(-a)

breed [briːd] (*pt, pp* **bred**) N razza, varietà *f inv*; (*fig*) tipo, specie *f inv* ♦ VT allevare; (*fig: hate, suspicion*) generare, provocare; **to breed dogs** allevare cani ♦ VI (*animals*) riprodursi; **they rarely breed in captivity** in cattività si riproducono raramente

breed·er ['briːdə'] N 1 (*person*) allevatore(-trice) 2 (*Phys: also:* **breeder reactor**) reattore *m* autofertilizzante

breed·ing ['briːdɪŋ] N (*of stock*) allevamento; (*reproduction*) riproduzione *f*; (*of person: also:* **good breeding**) (buona) educazione *f*

breeze [briːz] N brezza, venticello; **land/sea breeze** brezza di terra/di mare ♦ VI: **to breeze in/out** (*jauntily*) entrare/ andarsene *etc* allegramente come se niente fosse; (*briskly*) entrare/andarsene *etc* in fretta

breezy ['briːzɪ] ADJ (*day, weather*) ventoso(-a); (*spot*) ventilato(-a), ventoso(-a); (*optimism*) superficiale; (*person's manner*) brioso(-a), gioviale

Bret·on ['bretən] ADJ bretone ♦ N (*person*) bretone *m/f*; (*language*) bretone *m*

brev·ity ['brevɪtɪ] N brevità

brew [bruː] N (*of beer*) fermentazione *f*; (*of tea, herbs*) infuso; **a strong brew** (*of beer*) una qualità forte; (*of tea*) un tè forte ♦ VT (*beer*) produrre; (*tea, coffee*) fare; (*herbs*) fare un infuso di; (*fig: scheme, mischief*) macchinare, tramare ♦ VI (*beer*) fermentare; (*tea*) farsi; (*fig: storm, crisis*) prepararsi; (: *plot*) ordirsi; **there's trouble brewing** c'è aria di burrasca; **something's brewing** qualcosa bolle in pentola

▸ **brew up** VI + ADV (*Brit*) 1 (*make tea*) preparare il tè 2 (*storm, dispute*) prepararsi; **a big storm was brewing up** si preparava un grosso temporale

brew·er ['bruːə'] N birraio

brew·ery ['bruːərɪ] N fabbrica di birra

bri·ar ['braɪə'] N (*bramble*) rovo; (*wild rose*) rosa selvatica; (*pipe*) pipa in radica

bribe [braɪb] N bustarella ♦ VT corrompere; **to bribe sb to do sth** pagare qn sottobanco perché faccia qc

brib·ery ['braɪbərɪ] N corruzione f

bric-a-brac ['brɪkəˌbræk] N no pl bric-à-brac m inv

brick [brɪk] N (single) mattone m; (material) mattoni mpl; (toy) cubo; **building bricks** (gioco delle) costruzioni fpl; **he came down on me like a ton of bricks** (fig) ancora un po' e mi mangiava; **to drop a brick** (fig: fam) fare una gaffe; **to meet** or **come up against a brick wall** (fig) trovarsi davanti un ostacolo insormontabile; **I felt I was banging my head against a brick wall** mi sembrava di parlare al muro; **you can't make bricks without straw** (Proverb) non si può far niente senza l'occorrente

  ► **brick in, brick up** VT + ADV murare

brick·layer ['brɪkˌleɪəʳ] N muratore m

brick·work ['brɪkˌwɜːk] N muratura in mattoni

brick·works ['brɪkˌwɜːks] N fabbrica di mattoni

brid·al ['braɪdl] ADJ (veil, gown) da sposa, nuziale; (feast, procession) nuziale; **bridal party** corteo nuziale

bride [braɪd] N sposa; **the bride and groom** gli sposi, gli sposini

bride·groom ['braɪdˌɡruːm] N sposo

brides·maid ['braɪdzˌmeɪd] N damigella d'onore

bridge¹ [brɪdʒ] N (gen, also Dentistry) ponte m; (Naut) ponte di comando, plancia; **bridge of the nose** setto nasale ♦ VT gettare un ponte su; **to bridge a gap** (fig: in knowledge) colmare una lacuna; (: in budget) colmare un disavanzo

bridge² [brɪdʒ] N (Cards) bridge m inv

bridg·ing loan ['brɪdʒɪŋˌləʊn] N (Brit) prefinanziamento

bri·dle ['braɪdl] N briglia ♦ VT mettere le briglie a, imbrigliare ♦ VI (with indignation) adombrarsi, adontarsi

bridle path N sentiero (per cavalli)

brief [briːf] ADJ (visit, period, moment, speech) breve; (glimpse) veloce, breve; **for a brief moment I thought ...** per un attimo ho creduto...; **I caught a brief glimpse of the queen** ho intravisto per un attimo la regina; **in brief ...** in breve..., a farla breve... ♦ N 1 (Law) dossier m inv 2 (Mil: gen) istruzioni fpl; **that's outside my brief** non è di mia competenza ♦ VT (Mil) dare istruzioni a; **to brief sb (about sth)** (person) mettere qn al corrente (di); (Law) affidare una causa a

brief·case ['briːfˌkeɪs] N cartella, ventiquattr'ore f inv

brief·ing ['briːfɪŋ] N briefing m inv, istruzioni fpl

brief·ly ['briːflɪ] ADV (speak, visit) brevemente; (glimpse) di sfuggita

brief·ness ['briːfnɪs] N brevità

briefs [briːfs] NPL (man's) slip m inv, mutande fpl; (woman's) slip m inv, mutandine fpl; **a pair of briefs** un paio di slip

Brig. ABBR = brigadier

bri·gade [brɪˈɡeɪd] N (Mil, also hum) brigata

briga·dier [ˌbrɪɡəˈdɪəʳ] N generale m di brigata

bright [braɪt] ADJ 1 (day, weather) sereno(-a); (room) luminoso(-a); (eyes, star, gem, surface) lucente, brillante; (sunshine) splendente, (light, lamp) forte; (fire, flame) vivo(-a); (colour) vivace; **bright intervals** (Met) schiarite fpl; **bright red** rosso acceso 2 (cheerful: person) vispo(-a), allegro(-a); (: expression) radioso(-a), animato(-a); (: future) brillante, radioso(-a); **bright and early** di buon'ora, di buon mattino; **to look on the bright side** vedere il lato positivo delle cose 3 (clever: person) intelligente, dotato(-a); (: idea, move) brillante, geniale; **he's not very bright** non è molto sveglio

bright·en ['braɪtn] VT (also: **brighten up**: room, situation) migliorare ♦ VI (also: **brighten up**: person) rianimarsi, rallegrarsi; (eyes, expression) illuminarsi; (weather) schiarirsi

bright·ly ['braɪtlɪ] ADV (smile) radiosamente; (behave, talk) con animazione; (shine) vivamente, intensamente

bril·liance ['brɪljəns] N (of light) intensità; (of colour) vivacità; (fig: of person) genialità

bril·liant ['brɪljənt] ADJ (sunshine) sfolgorante; (light, idea, person, success) brillante; **it's a brilliant idea!** è un'idea fantastica!; **we had a brilliant time!** ci siamo divertiti moltissimo!; **a brilliant scientist** uno scienziato geniale

brim [brɪm] N (of cup) orlo; (of hat) tesa, falda ♦ VI: **to brim (over)** with traboccare di; **eyes brimming with tears** occhi colmi di lacrime

brim·ful ['brɪmˈfʊl] ADJ: **brimful (of)** pieno(-a) fino all'orlo (di), traboccante (di); (fig: confidence, enthusiasm) pieno(-a) (di); **brimful of happiness** traboccante di felicità

brine [braɪn] N (Culin) salamoia; (liter: sea water) mare m; **tuna in brine** tonno al naturale

KEYWORD

bring [brɪŋ] (pt, pp **brought**) VT (gen) portare; (dissatisfaction, storm) provocare; (consequences) avere; **bring warm clothes** porta vestiti pesanti; **can I bring a friend?** posso portare un amico?; **I've brought you a present** ti ho portato un regalo; **to bring relief** dare sollievo; **to bring luck** portare fortuna; **to bring tears to sb's eyes** fare venire a qn le lacrime agli occhi; **to bring sth to an end** mettere fine a qc; **to bring sth on o.s.** (fig) tirarsi qc addosso; **he was brought to justice** fu consegnato alla giustizia; **I couldn't bring myself to say no** non ce l'ho fatta a dirgli di no

  ► **bring along** VT + ADV portare con sé

  ► **bring about** VT + ADV 1 (change, crisis) causare, provocare 2 (turn): **to bring a boat about** far virare di bordo un'imbarcazione

  ► **bring back** VT + ADV 1 (person, object) riportare; (souvenir) portarsi a casa; (memories) risvegliare; (old method) reintrodurre; **he's taken your drill — he'll bring it back tomorrow** ti ha preso il trapano — te lo riporterà domani; **she brought a friend back for dinner** ha portato un'amica a casa per cena; **that song brings back memories** quella canzone mi fa tornare in mente tanti ricordi

  ► **bring down** VT + ADV 1 (lower: prices, temperature) far scendere; (opponent, also Ftbl, Rugby) atterrare; (enemy plane) abbattere; (government) far cadere

  ► **bring forth** VT + ADV 1 (protests, criticism) suscitare 2 (child) mettere al mondo

  ► **bring forward** VT + ADV 1 (person) far venire avanti; (chair) spostare in avanti; (witness, proof) produrre 2 (advance time of: meeting) anticipare; **the date was brought forward** la data è stata anticipata 3 (Book-keeping) riportare

  ► **bring in** VT + ADV 1 (person) fare entrare; (object) portare dentro; (Parliament: bill) presentare; (: legislation) introdurre; (Law: verdict) emettere 2 (produce: income) rendere

  ► **bring off** VT + ADV 1 (plan, enterprise) far riuscire, realizzare; (deal) concludere; **he didn't bring it off** (fam) (il colpo) non gli è riuscito 2 (people from wreck) portare in salvo

  ► **bring on** VT + ADV 1 (illness) provocare; (crops, flowers) far spuntare 2 (Theatre: performer) fare entrare; (: object) portare in scena; (Sport: player) mandare in sostituzione, far scendere in campo

  ► **bring out** VT + ADV (meaning) mettere in luce; (colour, weaknesses) far risaltare; (qualities) valorizzare, mettere in luce; (new product) lanciare; (book) pubblicare, fare uscire

  ► **bring round** VT + ADV 1 (persuade): **to bring sb round (to the idea of sth)** persuadere qn (a fare qc) 2 (steer: conversation): **to bring round to** portare su, far cadere su 3 (unconscious person) far rinvenire, rianimare

  ► **bring to** VT (unconscious person) far rinvenire

  ► **bring together** VT + ADV (people: introduce) far incontrare; (: reconcile) riconciliare

  ► **bring up** VT + ADV (person) far salire; (rear: child) allevare; (mention: question) sollevare; (: fact, problem) far presente; (vomit) rimettere, rigurgitare; **she brought up five children on her own** ha allevato cinque figli da sola

brink [brɪŋk] N orlo; **on the brink of doing sth** sul punto di fare qc; **she was on the brink of tears** era lì lì per piangere; **on the brink of collapse** sull'orlo di un collasso

brisk [brɪsk] ADJ (person, tone) spiccio(-a), sbrigativo(-a); (abrupt) brusco(-a); (walk) svelto(-a); (wind) fresco(-a); (trade) vivace, attivo(-a); **she was brisk and efficient** era svelta ed efficiente; **business is brisk** gli affari vanno bene; **at a brisk pace** di buon passo; **to go for a brisk walk** fare una camminata di buon passo

bris·tle ['brɪsl] N (of beard, animal) pelo; (of boar, brush) setola; **pure bristle brush** spazzola di pura setola; **brush with nylon bristles** spazzola di nylon ♦ VI (also: **bristle up**) rizzarsi; **to bristle with** (fig: pins, difficulties) essere irto(-a) di; (police-men, guards) brulicare di; **he bristled with anger** fremeva di rabbia

bris·tly [ˈbrɪslɪ] ADJ (*chin*) ispido(-a); (*beard, hair*) irsuto(-a), ispido(-a)

Brit [brɪt] N ABBR (*fam: = Briton*) inglese *m/f*

Brit·ain [ˈbrɪtən] N (*also:* **Great Britain**) la Gran Bretagna

Brit·ish [ˈbrɪtɪʃ] ADJ (*economy, team*) britannico(-a), inglese; (*ambassador*) della Gran Bretagna, inglese ♦ NPL: **the British** gli inglesi

British Summer Time N ora legale (*in Gran Bretagna*)

Brit·on [ˈbrɪtən] N inglese *m/f*, britannico(-a)

Brit·ta·ny [ˈbrɪtənɪ] N Bretagna

brit·tle [ˈbrɪtl] ADJ fragile

bro. ABBR = **brother**

broach [brəʊtʃ] VT (*subject*) affrontare; (*bottle of wine*) stappare

broad [brɔːd] ADJ (*street, smile*) largo(-a); (*mind, view*) aperto(-a); (*hint*) chiaro(-a), esplicito(-a); (*accent*) marcato(-a), spiccato(-a); (*distinction*) netto(-a); **he's got broad shoulders** ha le spalle larghe; **3 metres broad** largo 3 metri; **with a broad smile** con un gran sorriso; **the broad outlines** le grandi linee; **in broad daylight** in pieno giorno; **in the broadest sense** nel senso più ampio ♦ N (*USA fam, offensive*) femmina

broad·band [ˈbrɔːdbænd] (*Comput*) N banda larga ♦ ADJ a banda larga

broad bean N fava

broad·cast [ˈbrɔːdkɑːst] (*pt, pp* **broadcast**) N (*TV, Radio*) trasmissione *f* ♦ VT (*TV*) (tele)trasmettere, mandare in onda; (*Radio*) (radio)trasmettere, mandare in onda; (*fig: news, rumour*) diffondere; **don't broadcast it!** non spargerlo ai quattro venti! ♦ VI (*station*) trasmettere; (*person*) fare una trasmissione; **to broadcast live** trasmettere in diretta

broad·cast·er [ˈbrɔːdkɑːstəʳ] N giornalista *m/f* radiotelevisivo(-a)

broad·cast·ing [ˈbrɔːdkɑːstɪŋ] N (*TV*) televisione *f*; (*Radio*) radiodiffusione *f*; (*broadcasts*) trasmissioni *fpl*

broadcasting station N stazione *f* trasmittente

broad·en [ˈbrɔːdn] VT (*scope, outlook*) allargare; **the party needs to broaden its appeal** il partito deve far presa su un maggior numero di persone; **to broaden one's mind** allargare i propri orizzonti ♦ VI (*also:* **broaden out**) allargarsi

broad·ly [ˈbrɔːdlɪ] ADV: **broadly speaking** grosso modo, in linea di massima; **smiling broadly** con un gran sorriso

broad-minded [ˌbrɔːdˈmaɪndɪd] ADJ (*person*) di mente aperta, di larghe vedute; (*attitude*) aperto(-a)

broad·sheet [ˈbrɔːdʃiːt] N (*Brit: newspaper*) quotidiano di grande formato

broc·co·li [ˈbrɒkəlɪ] N (*Bot*) broccolo; (*Culin*) broccoli *mpl*

bro·chure [ˈbrəʊʃʊəʳ] N opuscolo, dépliant *m inv*

brogue¹ [brəʊg] N (*shoe*) scarpone *m*

brogue² [brəʊg] N (*accent*) accento irlandese

broil [brɔɪl] VT (*USA: Culin*) fare alla griglia

broil·er [ˈbrɔɪləʳ] N 1 (*chicken*) galletto 2 (*pan*) griglia

broke [brəʊk] PT *of* **break** ♦ ADJ: **to be broke** (*fam*) essere al verde, essere spiantato(-a); **to go broke** andare in fallimento

bro·ken [ˈbrəʊkən] PP *of* **break** ♦ ADJ 1 (*gen*) rotto(-a); (*stick*) spezzato(-a); (*fig: marriage*) fallito(-a); (: *promise, vow*) infranto(-a), non rispettato(-a); (: *appointment*) mancato(-a); (: *health*) rovinato(-a); (: *spirit*) a pezzi; (: *heart*) infranto(-a); **a broken glass** un vetro rotto; **he comes from a broken home** i suoi sono divisi; **he's a broken old man** è un vecchio finito 2 (*uneven: surface, coastline*) irregolare; (: *ground*) accidentato(-a); (*interrupted: line*) spezzato(-a); (: *sleep*) agitato(-a); **to have a broken night** non riuscire a dormire una notte di filato; **he speaks broken English** parla un inglese stentato

broken-down [ˈbrəʊkənˈdaʊn] ADJ (*car*) in panne, rotto(-a); (*machine*) guasto(-a), fuori uso; (*house*) abbandonato(-a), in rovina

broken-hearted [ˌbrəʊkənˈhɑːtɪd] ADJ affranto(-a) dal dolore, col cuore spezzato; **to be broken-hearted** avere il cuore spezzato

bro·ker [ˈbrəʊkəʳ] N (*Comm*) mediatore(-trice); (*stock broker*) agente *m/f* di cambio

bro·ker·age [ˈbrəʊkərɪdʒ] N (*Comm*) commissione *f* di intermediazione

bron·chi·tis [brɒŋˈkaɪtɪs] N bronchite *f*

bronze [brɒnz] N bronzo ♦ ADJ (*made of bronze*) di bronzo; (*colour*) bronzeo(-a), color del bronzo *inv*; **the bronze medal** la medaglia di bronzo ♦ VI abbronzarsi ♦ VT (*skin*) abbronzare; (*metal*) bronzare

bronzed [brɒnzd] ADJ (*person*) abbronzato(-a)

brooch [brəʊtʃ] N spilla, fermaglio

brood [bruːd] N (*of chicks*) covata; (*of birds*) nidiata; (*hum: of children*) prole *f* ♦ VI (*bird*) covare; (*fig: person*) rimuginare, stare a pensare; **there's no point brooding about the past** non c'è motivo di rimuginare sul passato

▸ **brood on** VI + PREP rimuginare su, stare a pensare a

broody [ˈbruːdɪ] ADJ (*fig*) cupo(-a) e taciturno(-a)

brook [brʊk] N ruscello

broom [brʊm] N (*brush*) scopa; (*Bot*) ginestra

broom·stick [ˈbrʊmstɪk] N manico di scopa

Bros. ABBR (*Comm: = brothers*) F.lli

broth [brɒθ] N minestra (in brodo), brodo

broth·el [ˈbrɒθl] N bordello

broth·er [ˈbrʌðəʳ] N (*gen, also Rel*) fratello; (*Trade Union etc*) compagno; **do you know her brother?** conosci suo fratello?

brother·hood [ˈbrʌðəhʊd] N fratellanza, fraternità; (*group*) confraternita

brother-in-law [ˈbrʌðərɪnlɔː] N cognato

broth·er·ly [ˈbrʌðəlɪ] ADJ fraterno(-a)

brought [brɔːt] PT, PP *of* **bring**

brought forward ADJ (*Comm*) riportato(-a)

brow [braʊ] N (*forehead*) fronte *f*; (*old: eyebrow*) sopracciglio; (: *of hill*) cima; (: *on road*) dosso; **he wiped his brow** si è asciugato la fronte; **the brow of the hill** la cima della collina

brow·beat [ˈbraʊbiːt] (*pt* browbeat, *pp* browbeaten) VT intimidire; **to browbeat sb into doing sth** costringere qn a fare qc con la prepotenza

brown [braʊn] ADJ (*gen*) marrone, bruno(-a); (*hair*) castano(-a); (*bronzed: skin*) scuro(-a), abbronzato(-a); **to go brown** (*person*) abbronzarsi; (*leaves*) ingiallire ♦ N marrone *m* ♦ VT (*Culin: meat*) rosolare; (: *onion*) dorare ♦ VI (*Culin*) rosolarsi

brown bread N pane *m* integrale, pane nero

Brownie [ˈbraʊnɪ] N coccinella (*scout*), giovane esploratrice *f*

brown paper N carta da pacchi *or* da imballaggio

brown rice N riso integrale

brown sugar N zucchero greggio

browse [braʊz] VI 1 (*in bookshop*) curiosare (*leggicchiando qua e là*); (*in other shop*) guardare in giro, curiosare; (*animal*) brucare; **to browse through a book** sfogliare un libro; **I'm just browsing!** sto solo curiosando! 2 (*Comput*) navigare ♦ VT: **to browse the Web** navigare in internet ♦ N: **to have a browse (around)** dare un'occhiata (in giro)

brows·er [ˈbraʊzəʳ] N (*Comput*) browser *m inv*

bruise [bruːz] N (*on person*) livido; (*on fruit*) ammaccatura ♦ VT (*leg etc*) farsi un livido a; (*fruit*) ammaccare; (*fig: feelings*) urtare ♦ VI (*fruit*) ammaccarsi; **I bruise easily** mi vengono facilmente i lividi sulla pelle

Brum·mie [ˈbrʌmɪ] N (*fam: resident*) abitante *m/f* di Birmingham; (: *native*) originario(-a) di Birmingham

brunch [brʌntʃ] N (*fam*) ricca colazione consumata a tarda mattina che sostituisce il pranzo

bru·nette [bruːˈnɛt] N ragazza (*or* donna) bruna

brunt [brʌnt] N: **to bear the brunt of sth** (*of attack, criticism*) sostenere l'urto di qc; (*of work, cost*) sostenere il peso di qc

brush [brʌʃ] N 1 (*gen*) spazzola; (*broom*) scopa; (*hearth brush*) scopettino, scopino; (*scrubbing brush*) spazzola per pavimenti; (*paint brush*) pennello; **hair/shoe brush** spazzola per capelli/da scarpe 2 (*act of brushing*) spazzolata, colpo di spazzola 3 (*quarrel*) schermaglia; **to have a brush with sb** (*verbally*) avere uno scontro con qn; (*physically*) venire alle mani con qn; **to have a brush with the police** avere delle noie con la polizia 4 (*light touch*) lieve tocco; **he felt the brush of her hair against his face** sentiva i capelli di lei che gli sfioravano il viso 5 (*undergrowth*) boscaglia, sottobosco ♦ VT 1 (*clean: floor*) scopare; (: *clothes, hair*) spazzolare; (: *shoes*) lucidare, spazzolare; (: *teeth*) lavarsi; **to brush one's teeth** lavarsi i denti 2 (*touch lightly*) sfiorare

▶ **brush against** VI + PREP sfiorare

▶ **brush aside** VT + ADV (*fig: protest, objection*) ignorare, rifiutarsi di ascoltare; (: *idea, feeling*) ignorare

▶ **brush away** VT + ADV (*dirt: on clothes*) togliere (con la spazzola); (: *on floor*) scopar via; (*tears*) asciugarsi; (*insects*) cacciare (via)

▶ **brush down** VT + ADV dare una spazzolata a

▶ **brush off** VT + ADV (*mud*) levare con la spazzola; (*fig: suggestion*) scartare; (: *criticism, attentions*) ignorare

▶ **brush past** VI + PREP sfiorare (passando)

▶ **brush up** VT + ADV **1** (*crumbs*) raccogliere (con la spazzola) **2** (*also:* brush up on: *revise*) dare una rinfrescata *or* una ripassata a; **to brush up one's English** rispolverare il proprio inglese

brushed [brʌʃt] ADJ **1** (*Tech: steel, chrome*) sabbiato(-a) **2** (*nylon, denim*) pettinato(-a)

brush-off ['brʌʃˌɒf] N (*fam*): **to give sb the brush-off** mandare qn a quel paese

brush·wood ['brʌʃˌwʊd] N (*undergrowth*) sottobosco; (*cuttings*) rami *mpl* tagliati

brusque [bruːsk] ADJ (*person, manner*) brusco(-a); (*tone*) secco(-a)

Brus·sels ['brʌslz] N Bruxelles *f*

Brussels sprout N cavoletto di Bruxelles

bru·tal ['bruːtl] ADJ brutale

bru·tal·ity [bruːˈtælɪtɪ] N brutalità

bru·tal·ize ['bruːtəlaɪz] VT (*harden*) abbrutire; (*ill-treat*) brutalizzare

brute [bruːt] N (*animal*) bestia; (*person*) bruto; **you brute!** mostro! ♦ ADJ (*force, strength*) bruto(-a); **by brute force** a viva forza, con la forza

brut·ish ['bruːtɪʃ] ADJ da bruto

BS [biːˈɛs] N ABBR **1** (= *British Standard*) numero di standardizzazione assegnato a un certo prodotto dal BSI **2** (*USA: Univ:* = *Bachelor of Science*) laurea in Scienze **3** (*USA fam!:* = *bullshit*) stronzate *fpl* (*fam!*)

BSA [ˌbiːɛsˈeɪ] N ABBR (*USA:* = *Boy Scouts of America*)

BSE [ˌbiːɛsˈiː] N ABBR (= *bovine spongiform encephalopathy*) encefalite *f* bovina spongiforme

btu [ˌbiːtiːˈjuː] N ABBR (= *British thermal unit*) Btu *f* (= *unità termica britannica*)

bubble ['bʌbl] N **1** bolla; (*smaller*) bollicina; **soap bubble** bolla di sapone **2** (*Comm: also:* **speculative bubble**) bolla speculativa **3** (*of cartoon: also:* **speech bubble**) fumetto ♦ VI ribollire, fare bollicine; (*champagne*) spumeggiare

▶ **bubble over** VI + ADV traboccare; **to bubble over (with)** (*fig*) scoppiare (di *or* da), traboccare (di)

bubble bath N bagnoschiuma *m*

bubble gum N chewing-gum *m inv*

bubble-jet printer [ˌbʌbldʒetˈprɪntəʳ] N stampante *f* a getto d'inchiostro

bub·bly ['bʌblɪ] ADJ (*liquid*) effervescente; (*fig: personality*) spumeggiante ♦ N (*fam*) champagne *m inv*

Bu·cha·rest [ˌbuːkəˈrest] N Bucarest *f*

buck [bʌk] N **1** (*USA fam: dollar*) dollaro; **this means big bucks for sb** vuol dire un sacco di soldi per qn **2** (*Zool*) maschio **3** (*of horse*) sgroppata; **to give a buck** dare una sgroppata **4** to pass the buck (*fam*) scaricare le proprie responsabilità (*or* colpe *etc*) sugli altri ♦ VI (*horse*) sgroppare

▶ **buck up** (*fam*) VI + ADV (*cheer up*) tirarsi su; (*hurry up*) sbrigarsi, muoversi ♦ VT + ADV **1** (*make cheerful*) tirar su (il morale di) **2 to buck one's ideas up** (*fam*) darsi una mossa

buck·et ['bʌkɪt] N secchio; (*large*) secchia; **to kick the bucket** (*fam*) tirare le cuoia

Buck·ing·ham Pal·ace [ˌbʌkɪŋəmˈpælɪs] N Buckingham Palace *m* (la residenza ufficiale a Londra del sovrano britannico)

buck·le ['bʌkl] N fibbia, fermaglio ♦ VT **1** (*shoe, belt*) allacciare **2** (*wheel, girder*) distorcere, piegare; (*warp*) deformare ♦ VI (*see vt*) allacciarsi, chiudersi con una fibbia; distorcersi, piegarsi

▶ **buckle down** VI + ADV: **to buckle down to a job** mettersi a lavorare d'impegno *or* di buzzo buono, mettersi sotto

bud [bʌd] N (*of flower*) bocciolo, boccio; (*on tree, plant*)

gemma, germoglio; **to be in bud** (*flower*) essere in boccio; (*tree*) germogliare ♦ VI (*plant, tree*) germogliare, mettere le gemme; (*flower*) sbocciare

Bu·da·pest [ˌbjuːdəˈpest] N Budapest *f*

Buddha ['bʊdə] N Budda *m inv*

Bud·dhism ['bʊdɪzəm] N buddismo

Bud·dhist ['bʊdɪst] ADJ, N buddista *m/f*

bud·ding ['bʌdɪŋ] ADJ (*fig: talent*) in erba; (*flower*) in boccio ♦ N (*Bot*) gemmazione *f*

bud·dy ['bʌdɪ] N (*esp USA*) amico, compagno; **they've been buddies for years** sono amiconi da anni

budge [bʌdʒ] VT (*move*) spostare, smuovere; **I couldn't budge him an inch** (*fig*) non sono riuscito a smuoverlo di un dito ♦ VI muoversi, spostarsi; (*fig*) smuoversi; **she refused to budge from London** si è rifiutata di spostarsi da Londra; **they'll not budge on this point** non cambieranno opinione su questo punto

budg·eri·gar [ˌbʌdʒərɪgɑːʳ] N pappagallino

budget ['bʌdʒɪt] N bilancio (preventivo), budget *m inv*; **to be on a tight budget** avere un budget limitato; **I'm on a tight budget** ho i soldi contati; **she works out her budget every month** fa il preventivo delle spese ogni mese; **the defence budget** il budget per la Difesa; **budget price** prezzo ridotto ♦ ADJ (*airline, flight*) a basso costo; (*prices, travel, holiday*) economico(-a) ♦ VI fare un preventivo; (*household*) fare i propri conti; **I'm learning how to budget** sto imparando a gestire le mie finanze

▶ **budget for** VI + PREP mettere in conto *or* in preventivo, preventivare

budgie ['bʌdʒɪ] N ABBR = **budgerigar**

Bue·nos Aires ['bweɪnɒsˈaɪrɪz] N Buenos Aires *f*

buff¹ [bʌf] ADJ **1** (*colour*) color paglierino *inv* *or* camoscio *inv* **2** (*fam*) in forma, tonico(-a) ♦ VT (*also:* **buff up**) lucidare, lustrare ♦ N: **in the buff** (*fam*) nudo(-a) come un verme

buff² [bʌf] N (*fam: enthusiast*) patito(-a), appassionato(-a); **a film buff** un esperto di cinema

buf·fa·lo ['bʌfələʊ] N (*pl* buffaloes) (*wild ox*) bufalo(-a); (*esp USA: bison*) bisonte *m*

buff·er ['bʌfəʳ] N **1** (*for railway engine*) respingente *m*; (*fig*) cuscinetto **2** (*Comput*) buffer *m inv*

buff·er·ing ['bʌfərɪŋ] N (*Comput*) bufferizzazione *f*, memorizzazione *f* transitoria

buffer state N stato *m* cuscinetto, *inv*

buffer zone N zona *f* cuscinetto, *inv*

buf·fet¹ ['bʊfeɪ] N (*for refreshments*) buffet *m inv*, bar *m inv*; (*meal*) buffet, rinfresco; **a cold buffet** un buffet freddo; **a buffet lunch** un buffet

buf·fet² ['bʌfɪt] N (*blow*) schiaffo; **the buffets of fate** (*fig*) le avversità della sorte ♦ VT (*ship, car etc*) sballottare; (*house*) sferzare; (*fig: person*) travolgere

buffet car ['bʊfeɪˌkɑːʳ] N (*Brit: Rail*) ≈ servizio ristoro

buffet lunch [ˌbʊfeɪˈlʌntʃ] N pranzo in piedi

buf·foon [bəˈfuːn] N buffone(-a); **to play the buffoon** fare il (la) buffone(-a)

bug [bʌg] (*fam*) N **1** (*insect*) insetto; (*germ*) infezione *f*, virus *m inv*; (*fig: obsession*) mania, pallino; **there's a bug going round** c'è in giro un virus; **a stomach bug** una gastroenterite; **I've got the travel bug** (*fig*) mi è presa la mania dei viaggi **2** (*bugging device*) microspia, cimice *f* **3** (*Comput: in program*) errore *m* (nel programma), bug *m inv* ♦ VT **1** (*telephone*) mettere sotto controllo; (*room*) installare microspie in **2** (*fam: annoy*) scocciare; **it really bugs me** mi rompe da morire

bug·bear ['bʌgˌbɛəʳ] N spauracchio

bug·gy ['bʌgɪ] N (*also:* **baby buggy**) passeggino; (*cart: two-wheeled*) calesse *m*; (: *four-wheeled*) baghero

bu·gle ['bjuːgl] N (*Mus*) tromba

build [bɪld] (*pt, pp* built) N (*of person*) corporatura, fisico ♦ VT (*house*) costruire, fabbricare; (*ship, town, machine*) costruire; (*nest*) fare; (*fig: relationship, career, empire*) costruire; **they're going to build houses here** qui costruiranno delle case; **a new bridge is being built** è in costruzione un nuovo ponte

▶ **build on** VT + ADV aggiungere ♦ VT + PREP (*fig*) fondare su, basare su

▸ **build up** VT + ADV (*develop: business*) consolidare; (: *reputation*) fare, consolidare; (*increase: production*) allargare, incrementare; (*stocks etc*) accumulare; (*collection*) mettere insieme; (*spirits, morale*) tirar su; (*hopes*) far crescere; **he has built up a huge collection of stamps** ha messo insieme una vasta collezione di francobolli; **don't build your hopes up too soon** non sperarci troppo; **to build up one's strength** rimettersi in forze ♦ VI + ADV (*pressure*) salire; (*Fin: interest*) accumularsi; **the music built up to a crescendo** la musica aumentava in un crescendo continuo; **debts are building up** si stanno accumulando i debiti

build·er ['bɪldə'] N (*contractor*) costruttore *m*, imprenditore *m* (*edile*); (*workman*) muratore *m*; (*fig*) creatore(-trice)

build·ing ['bɪldɪŋ] N **1** (*place*) costruzione *f*, edificio; (*block*) palazzo **2** (*no pl: activity*) costruzione *f*

building contractor N costruttore *m*, imprenditore *m* (*edile*)

building industry, building trade N industria edilizia

building site N cantiere *m* di costruzione

build-up ['bɪldʌp] N (*of pressure, gas*) aumento, accumulo; (*Mil: of troops*) ammassamento; (*of traffic*) aumento di volume, intensificarsi *m*; (*fig: of tension*) aumento **2** (*publicity*) campagna pubblicitaria; **to give sb/sth a good build-up** fare buona pubblicità a qn/qc

built [bɪlt] PT, PP *of* build

built-in ['bɪlt,ɪn] ADJ (*cupboard*) a muro; (*device, feature*) incorporato(-a); **built-in wardrobe** armadio a muro

built-up ['bɪlt,ʌp] ADJ: **built-up area** abitato

bulb [bʌlb] N (*Bot: of thermometer*) bulbo; (*Elec*) lampadina; **a 100-watt bulb** una lampadina da 100 watt

bulb·ous ['bʌlbəs] ADJ a forma di bulbo, bulboso(-a)

Bul·garia [bʌl'gɛərɪə] N Bulgaria

Bul·gar·ian [bʌl'gɛərɪən] ADJ bulgaro(-a) ♦ N **1** (*person*) bulgaro(-a) **2** (*language*) bulgaro

bulge [bʌldʒ] N **1** (*in surface*) rigonfiamento; (*in plaster, metal*) bolla; (*curve: of thighs, hips*) curva **2** (*in birth rate, sales*) punta, rapido aumento; **the postwar bulge** l'esplosione demografica del dopoguerra ♦ VI (*stomach, muscles*) sporgere; (*pocket*): **to bulge (with)** essere gonfio(-a) (di); **the muscles in his neck bulged** gli sporgono i muscoli dal collo

bu·limia [bə'lɪmɪə] N bulimia

bulimic [bjuː'lɪmɪk] ADJ, N bulimico(-a)

bulk [bʌlk] N (*of thing*) volume *m*, massa; (*of person*) corporatura massiccia; **the bulk of** la maggior parte di; **the bulk of the work** il grosso del lavoro; **to buy in bulk** comprare in grande quantità

bulk buy·ing ['bʌlk'baɪɪŋ] N acquisto di merce in grande quantità

bulk carrier N grossa nave *f* da carico

bulk·head ['bʌlk,hed] N (*Naut*) paratia

bulky ['bʌlkɪ] ADJ grosso(-a), voluminoso(-a); **Mick's bulky figure** la figura massiccia di Mick

bull¹ [bʊl] N **1** toro; (*male of elephant, seal*) maschio; **like a bull in a china shop** come un elefante; **to take the bull by the horns** (*fig*) prendere il toro per le corna **2** (*Stock Exchange*) rialzista *m/f*
❑ **bull** is not translated by the Italian word *bullo*

bull² [bʊl] N (*Rel*) bolla (papale)

bull·dog ['bʊl,dɒg] N bulldog *m inv*

bull·doze ['bʊl,dəʊz] VT aprire o spianare col bulldozer; **I was bulldozed into doing it** (*fig*) mi ci hanno costretto con la prepotenza

bull·doz·er ['bʊldəʊzə'] N bulldozer *m inv*, apripista *m inv*

bul·let ['bʊlɪt] N proiettile *m*, pallottola

bul·letin ['bʊlɪtɪn] N (*statement*) comunicato (ufficiale); (*journal*) bollettino; **a bulletin was released at 3 o'clock** fu trasmesso un bollettino alle 3; **a news bulletin** un notiziario

bulletin board N (*Comput*) bulletin board *m inv*, bacheca elettronica

bullet point N punto; **bullet points** elenco *sg* puntato

bullet·proof ['bʊlɪt,pruːf] ADJ a prova di proiettile; **bulletproof vest** giubbotto *m* antiproiettile, *inv*

bull·fight ['bʊl,faɪt] N corrida

bull·fighter ['bʊl,faɪtə'] N torero

bull·fighting ['bʊl,faɪtɪŋ] N tauromachia

bul·lion ['bʊljən] N oro (*or* argento) in lingotti

bull·ock ['bʊlək] N manzo

bull·ring ['bʊl,rɪŋ] N arena (*per corride*)

bull's-eye ['bʊlz,aɪ] N (*of target*) centro (del bersaglio); **to hit the bull's-eye** (*fig*) far centro, colpire nel segno

bull·shit ['bʊl,ʃɪt](*fam!*) N stronzate *fpl* (*fam!*) ♦ VI, VT raccontare stronzate (a) (*fam!*)

bul·ly ['bʊlɪ] N bullo, prepotente *m/f*; **he's a big bully** è un grande prepotente ♦ VT (*also:* **bully around**) fare il (la) prepotente con; (*subj: children*) fare le prepotenze a; **to be bullied by** essere oggetto di prepotenze da parte di; **to bully sb into doing sth** far fare qc a qn con la prepotenza

bul·ly·ing ['bʊlɪɪŋ] N prepotenze *fpl* ♦ ADJ (*person, tone, behaviour*) prepotente

bum¹ [bʌm] N (*Brit fam: bottom*) culo

bum² [bʌm] N (*esp USA: idler*) fannullone(-a); (*tramp*) barbone(-a), vagabondo(-a) ♦ ADJ scadente; **bum advice** consiglio di merda (*fam!*) ♦ VT (*money, food*) scroccare
▸ **bum around** VI + ADV (*fam*) vagabondare

bumble·bee ['bʌmbl,biː] N (*Zool*) bombo

bumf [bʌmf] N (*fam: documents, forms*) scartoffie *fpl*

bump [bʌmp] N **1** (*blow*) botta, colpo; (*noise*) botto; (*jolt of vehicle*) botta, scossa **2** (*lump*) bernoccolo, bozzo, gonfiore *m*; (*on skin*) gonfiore; (*on road*) cunetta, bozzo; **we felt a sudden bump** abbiamo sentito una scossa improvvisa; **I've got a bump on my forehead** ho un bernoccolo sulla fronte ♦ VT (*car*) urtare, sbattere; **to bump one's head** sbattere la testa
▸ **bump along** VI procedere sobbalzando
▸ **bump into** VI + PREP **1** (*vehicle*) andare a sbattere contro **2** (*fam: meet*) imbattersi in, incontrare per caso; **I bumped into Paul yesterday** ho incontrato per caso Paul, ieri; **fancy bumping into you!** ma guarda chi si vede!
▸ **bump off** VT + ADV (*fam*) far fuori
▸ **bump up** VT + ADV (*fam: increase: prices*) far salire, far aumentare; (: *sales*) incrementare

bump·er¹ ['bʌmpə'] N (*Aut*) paraurti *m inv*

bump·er² ['bʌmpə'] ADJ: **bumper harvest** raccolto eccezionale

bumper cars NPL autoscontro

bumph [bʌmf] N = bumf

bump·tious ['bʌmpʃəs] ADJ arrogante, presuntuoso(-a)

bumpy ['bʌmpɪ] ADJ (*surface, road*) accidentato(-a), dissestato(-a), irregolare; (*journey, flight*) movimentato(-a); **we had a bumpy flight** abbiamo ballato *or* si ballava in volo

bun [bʌn] N (*Culin*) panino dolce; (*of hair*) chignon *m inv*, crocchia; **to wear one's hair in a bun** portare lo chignon

bunch [bʌntʃ] N (*of flowers, keys*) mazzo; (*posy*) mazzetto, mazzolino; (*of bananas*) casco; (*of grapes*) grappolo; (*set of people*) gruppo; **to wear one's hair in bunches** portare le codine; **the best of a bad bunch** il (*or* la etc) meno peggio
▸ **bunch together** VT + ADV (*objects*) ammucchiare ♦ VI + ADV (*people*) ammucchiarsi

bun·dle ['bʌndl] N (*of clothes, rags*) fagotto, involto; (*of sticks*) fascina; (*of papers*) mucchio; (*of newspapers*) fascio; **to be a bundle of nerves** essere tesissimo(-a), essere un fascio di nervi ♦ VT (*also:* **bundle up**) (*clothes*) fare un fagotto di, raccogliere in un mucchio; (*papers*) fare un fascio di **2** (*put hastily*) riporre in fretta; (*person*) spingere, caricare in gran fretta; **he was bundled into a car** è stato spinto in fretta su una macchina; **it's cheaper to buy software bundled with a PC** costa meno comprare il software assieme al PC
▸ **bundle off** VT + ADV (*person*) mandare via in gran fretta; **he was bundled off to Australia** l'hanno spedito in fretta e furia in Australia
▸ **bundle out** VT + ADV far uscire (senza tante cerimonie)

bung [bʌŋ] N tappo, turacciolo

bun·ga·low ['bʌŋgə,ləʊ] N bungalow *m inv*, villetta a un piano

bun·gee jump·ing ['bʌndʒɪ'dʒʌmpɪŋ] N salto nel vuoto da ponti, grattacieli ecc, con un cavo fissato alla caviglia

bun·gle ['bʌŋgl](*fam*) VT fare un pasticcio di ♦ VI fare pasticci

bunion ['bʌnjən] N callo (al piede)

bunk [bʌŋk] N (*Naut, Rail*) cuccetta

bunk beds NPL letti mpl a castello
bun·ker [ˈbʌŋkəʳ] N (coal bunker) carbonaia; (Mil, Golf) bunker m inv
bun·ny [ˈbʌnɪ] N (also: bunny rabbit) coniglietto
bunny hill N (USA: Skiing) pista per principianti
bunt·ing [ˈbʌntɪŋ] N (Naut) gran pavese m; (in street) bandierine fpl
buoy [bɔɪ] N boa, gavitello
▸ **buoy up** VT + ADV (person, boat) tenere a galla; (fig: spirits) tener su; (: hopes) alimentare
buoy·an·cy [ˈbɔɪənsɪ] N (Phys) galleggiamento; (of ship, object) galleggiabilità; (fig: of person) ottimismo
buoy·ant [ˈbɔɪənt] ADJ (ship, log) che galleggia (bene), galleggiante; (fig: person) di ottimo umore, su di corda; (: nature) ottimista; (Fin: market) sostenuto(-a); (prices, currency) stabile; **a buoyant economy** un'economia fiorente
bur·den [ˈbɜːdn] N (load) carico, peso; (fig: of years, responsibility) peso; (of taxes, payment) onere m; **the burden of proof lies with him** spetta a lui l'onere della prova; **to be a burden to sb** essere di peso a qn ♦ VT: **to burden (with)** (cares etc) opprimere (con); **burdened with debts** oberato(-a) di debiti
bu·reau [ˈbjʊərəʊ] N 1 (office) ufficio, agenzia; (government department) dipartimento, sezione f 2 (Brit: desk) secrétaire m inv; scrittoio; (USA: chest of drawers) cassettone m
bu·reau·cra·cy [bjʊəˈrɒkrəsɪ] N burocrazia
bu·reau·crat [ˈbjʊərəʊˌkræt] N burocrate m/f
bu·reau·crat·ic [ˌbjʊərəʊˈkrætɪk] ADJ burocratico(-a)
bureau de change [-dəˈʃɑ̃ʒ] (pl **bureaux de change**) N cambiavalute m inv
bu·reaux [ˈbjʊərəʊz] NPL of **bureau**
bur·geon [ˈbɜːdʒən] VI (liter) svilupparsi rapidamente
burg·er [ˈbɜːɡəʳ] N hamburger m inv
bur·glar [ˈbɜːɡləʳ] N ladro(-a), scassinatore(-trice)
burglar alarm N antifurto m inv
bur·glar·ize [ˈbɜːɡləˌraɪz] VT (USA) svaligiare
bur·gla·ry [ˈbɜːɡlərɪ] N furto (con scasso)
bur·gle [ˈbɜːɡl] VT (house, shop) svaligiare; **I've been burgled** mi hanno svaligiato la casa (or il negozio etc)
Bur·gun·dy [ˈbɜːɡəndɪ] N Borgogna
bur·ial [ˈbɛrɪəl] N sepoltura, seppellimento
burial ground N cimitero
bur·ly [ˈbɜːlɪ] ADJ ben piantato(-a), robusto(-a)
Bur·ma [ˈbɜːmə] N Birmania
Bur·mese [ˈbɜːˈmiːz] ADJ birmano(-a) ♦ N (person, cat) birmano(-a); (language) birmano
burn [bɜːn] (pt, pp **burned** or **burnt**) N (gen) bruciatura; (superficial) scottatura; (Med) ustione f ♦ VT 1 (gen) bruciare; (set fire to) incendiare; (person, skin: also of sun) bruciare, scottare; (toast, meat etc) (far) bruciare; **to burn wood/coal** (use as fuel: boiler etc) andare a legna/carbone; **I burned the cake** ho bruciato la torta; **I've burned my hand** mi sono bruciato la mano; **badly burnt** ustionato(-a); **to be burnt to death** morire tra le fiamme, morire bruciato(-a) or carbonizzato(-a); (at stake) essere bruciato(-a) vivo(-a); **I've burnt myself!** mi sono bruciato!; **to burn one's boats** or **bridges** (fig) bruciarsi i ponti alle spalle; **he's been burning the candle at both ends for too long** (fig) è da troppo tempo che abusa delle proprie energie 2 (Comput) masterizzare; **to burn a CD** masterizzare un CD ♦ VI (gen) bruciare; (fire) ardere; (skin, person) bruciarsi, scottarsi; (meat, pastry etc) bruciarsi; (light, gas) essere or rimanere acceso(-a); **to burn with anger** (fig) fremere di rabbia; **to burn with fever** scottare per la febbre; **to burn to do sth** morire dalla voglia di fare qc
▸ **burn down** VT + ADV (building) bruciare, dare alle fiamme ♦ VI + ADV (house) essere distrutto(-a) dal fuoco, bruciarsi; (candle, fire) consumarsi, abbassarsi; **the factory burned down** la fabbrica è andata distrutta in un incendio
▸ **burn off** VT + ADV (paint) togliere col fuoco
▸ **burn out** VT + ADV (subj: writer): **to burn o.s. out** esaurirsi; (: talent): **to burn itself out** esaurirsi (: enthusiasm) spegnersi ♦ VI (fuse) saltare; (candle, lamp) spegnersi; (fire) estinguersi
▸ **burn up** VI (fire) ravvivarsi, divampare ♦ VT + ADV (rubbish) bruciare

burn·er [ˈbɜːnəʳ] N (on cooker or stove) fornello; (Tech) bruciatore m, becco (a gas)
burn·ing [ˈbɜːnɪŋ] N bruciato; **I can smell burning** sento odore di bruciato ♦ ADJ (building, forest) in fiamme; (coals) acceso(-a); (flame) vivo(-a), ardente; (fig: thirst, fever, desire) bruciante, divorante; (tears) cocente; (question, topic, issue) scottante
bur·nish [ˈbɜːnɪʃ] VT brunire
burnt [bɜːnt] PT, PP of **burn**
burnt sugar N (Brit) caramello
burp [bɜːp] (fam) N rutto; (of baby) ruttino ♦ VI ruttare, fare un rutto ♦ VT (baby) far fare il ruttino a
bur·row [ˈbʌrəʊ] N (of rabbit) tana, cunicolo ♦ VT (hole) scavare; **to burrow one's way (under/through** etc) scavarsi un tunnel (sotto/attraverso etc) ♦ VI (rabbits) scavare gallerie; **he burrowed under the bedclothes** si è rintanato sotto le coperte
bur·sar [ˈbɜːsəʳ] N (Univ) economo(-a)
bur·sa·ry [ˈbɜːsərɪ] N (grant) borsa di studio
burst [bɜːst] (pt, pp **burst**) N (of shell etc) scoppio, esplosione f; (in pipe) rottura; (of shots) raffica, scarica; **a burst of applause** uno scroscio d'applausi; **a burst of laughter/activity** uno scoppio di risa/attività; **a burst of speed** uno scatto (di velocità) ♦ VT (gen) far scoppiare or esplodere; (bag) sfondare, spaccare; **the river has burst its banks** il fiume ha rotto gli argini or ha straripato ♦ VI 1 (gen) scoppiare; (tyre or tire: blow out) scoppiare; (: puncture) bucarsi; (shell, firework) scoppiare, esplodere; (bag) sfondarsi, spaccarsi; (dam) cedere; (blood vessel) rompersi; **the balloon burst** il palloncino è scoppiato; **the door burst open** la porta si è spalancata di colpo; **filled to bursting point** pieno(-a) da scoppiare; **to be bursting with** (health, energy) scoppiare di; **to be bursting with pride** sprizzare soddisfazione da tutti i pori; **to be bursting at the seams (with)** essere pieno(-a) zeppo(-a) (di), traboccare (di); **the room was bursting at the seams** la stanza rigurgitava di persone; **I was bursting to tell you** (fam) morivo dalla voglia di dirtelo 2 (go suddenly): **to burst out of the room** scappare precipitosamente dalla stanza; **the sun burst through the clouds** è sbucato il sole
▸ **burst into** VI + PREP (room) irrompere in; **to burst into flames** prendere fuoco, andare in fiamme; **to burst into tears** scoppiare a piangere
▸ **burst out** VI + ADV 1 (exclaim) esclamare 2 (start): **to burst out laughing** scoppiare a ridere; **to burst out singing** mettersi (improvvisamente) a cantare
bury [ˈbɛrɪ] VT (body, treasure) seppellire; (plunge: claws, knife): **to bury (in)** affondare (in); **he buried his face in his hands** si coprì il volto con le mani; **buried by an avalanche** travolto(-a) da una valanga; **to bury the hatchet** (fig) seppellire l'ascia di guerra; **to bury one's head in the sand** (fig) fare la politica dello) struzzo
bus [bʌs] N (pl **buses** or **busses** (USA)) autobus m inv; **to go by bus** andare in autobus; **I came by bus** sono venuto con l'autobus; **the school bus** il pulmino della scuola ♦ ADJ (driver, service, ticket) d'autobus
bus boy N (USA) aiuto cameriere m
bush [bʊʃ] N 1 cespuglio 2 (in Africa, Australia): **the bush** la boscaglia
bushed [bʊʃt] ADJ (fam: exhausted) distrutto(-a)
bush·el [ˈbʊʃl] N staio
bush·fire [ˈbʊʃˌfaɪəʳ] N grande incendio in aperta campagna
bushy [ˈbʊʃɪ] ADJ (plant, tail, beard) folto(-a); (eyebrows) irsuto(-a)
busi·ly [ˈbɪzɪlɪ] ADV con impegno, alacremente
busi·ness [ˈbɪznɪs] N 1 (commerce, trading) affari mpl; selling books is her business di mestiere vende libri; **he's in the insurance business** lavora nel campo delle assicurazioni; **he's in the wool business** è nel commercio della lana; **I'm here on business** sono qui per affari; **to be away on business** essere via per affari; **to do business with sb** fare affari con qn; **let's get down to business** (fam) bando alle chiacchiere; **business is business** gli affari sono affari; **now we're in business!** ci siamo!; **she means business** fa sul serio, non scherza 2 (firm) impresa, azienda; **to set up a business** metter su un'impresa; **it's a family business** è un'impresa familiare; **he's got his**

own business ha un'impresa in proprio **3** (*task, duty, concern, matter*) affare *m*; **to make it one's business to do sth** incaricarsi di fare qc; **that's none of your business** non sono affari tuoi, non ti riguarda; **that's my business** (è) affar mio, (sono) affari miei; **it's his business to see that ...** spetta a lui accertarsi che...; **you had no business to do that** non stava a te farlo; **mind your own business** bada ai fatti tuoi, non t'impicciare **4** (*fam: affair, matter*) storia, faccenda; **what an awful business it was!** che orrore che è stato!; **it's a nasty business** è una brutta faccenda, è un brutto affare ♦ ADJ (*deal, quarter, relationship*) d'affari; (*studies*) commerciale

business address N indirizzo sul lavoro
business card N biglietto da visita della ditta
business class N (*Aviation*) business class *f*
business·like [ˈbɪznɪsˌlaɪk] ADJ (*approach, transaction*) efficiente; (*firm, company*) serio(-a); (*person, manner*) pratico(-a), efficiente
business·man [ˈbɪznɪsmən] N (*pl* **-men**) uomo d'affari, imprenditore
business trip N viaggio d'affari
business·woman [ˈbɪznɪsˌwʊmən] N (*pl* **-women**) imprenditrice
busk·er [ˈbʌskəʳ] N (*Brit*) suonatore(-trice) ambulante
bus lane N (*Brit*) corsia preferenziale (per autobus)
bus pass N tessera dell'autobus
bus shelter N pensilina, fermata coperta
bus station N stazione *f* delle corriere, autostazione *f*
bus stop N fermata d'autobus
bust¹ [bʌst] N (*bosom*) petto, seno; (*Art*) busto
  ▸ **bust up** VT + ADV (*fam*) sfasciare
bust² [bʌst] (*fam*) ADJ (*broken*) rotto(-a), scassato(-a); **to go bust** (*bankrupt*) fallire, fare fallimento ♦ VT **1** = **burst 2** (*Police: arrest*) pizzicare, beccare; (: *raid*) fare irruzione in **3** (*break*) scassare
bus·tle [ˈbʌsl] N trambusto ♦ VI (*person: also:* **bustle about**) darsi da fare, affaccendarsi; (*place*) essere animatissimo(-a)
bus·tling [ˈbʌslɪŋ] ADJ (*person*) affaccendato(-a), indaffarato(-a); (*place, town*) animatissimo(-a)
bust-up [ˈbʌstˌʌp] N (*fam: argument*) lite *f*; **they had a bust-up** hanno rotto
busy [ˈbɪzɪ] ADJ **1** (*occupied: person*) occupato(-a); **she's busy** (*at the moment*) è occupata; **she's a busy woman** è una donna molto impegnata *or* indaffarata; **he's busy studying/cooking** sta studiando/cucinando; **he's busy at his work** sta lavorando, è molto preso dal lavoro; **let's get busy** (*fam*) diamoci da fare **2** (*active: day, time*) movimentato(-a), intenso(-a); (: *place, town*) animato(-a); **I'd had a busy day and was tired** avevo avuto una giornata intensa ed ero stanco; **Christmas is a busy time of year** a Natale ci sono sempre mille cose da fare; **the Strand is one of London's busiest streets** lo Strand è una delle vie più animate di Londra; **the roads are busy** c'è molto traffico sulle strade **3** (*esp USA: telephone, line*) occupato(-a) ♦ VT: **to busy o.s.** (**doing** sth/**with** sth) darsi da fare (a fare qc/con qc)
busy·body [ˈbɪzɪˌbɒdɪ] N ficcanaso *m/f*, impiccione(-a)
busy signal N (*USA*) segnale *m* di occupato

KEYWORD
but [bʌt] CONJ (*gen*) ma; **never a week passes but she's ill** mai una settimana che non stia male; **it's small but comfortable** (*car*) è piccola ma comoda
  ♦ ADV solo, soltanto; **she's but a child** è solo una bambina, non è che una bambina; **had I but known** se solo l'avessi saputo; **I cannot help but think that ...** non posso fare a meno di pensare che...; **you can but try** tentar non nuoce
  ♦ PREP eccetto, tranne, meno; **all but finished** quasi finito(-a); **anything but that** tutto ma non questo; **anything but finished** tutt'altro che finito(-a); **but for you** (*Brit*) se non fosse per te; **the last but one** il (la) penultimo(-a); **I live in the next street but one** abito due strade più in su (*or* giù); **no one but him** solo lui; **no one but him can do it** è l'unico che lo sappia fare; **nothing but** null'altro che; **he was nothing but trouble** non dava altro che guai
  ♦ N: **no buts about it!** non c'è ma che tenga!
bu·tane [ˈbjuːteɪn] N (*also:* **butane gas**) butano

butch [bʊtʃ] ADJ (*woman: pej*) mascolina; (*man*) macho *inv*
butch·er [ˈbʊtʃəʳ] N (*also: fig*) macellaio; **butcher's knife** coltello da macellaio; (*Culin*) coltello per carne (cruda); **butcher's (shop)** macelleria; **at the butcher's** dal macellaio
  ♦ VT macellare
but·ler [ˈbʌtləʳ] N maggiordomo
butt¹ [bʌt] N (*end*) estremità più grossa; (*of gun*) calcio; (*of cigar, cigarette*) mozzicone *m*; (*USA fam*) sedere *m*; **the butt of the rifle** il calcio del fucile; **a cigarette butt** un mozzicone di sigaretta
  ▸ **butt in** VI + ADV (*interrupt*) interrompere; (*meddle*) immischiarsi
butt² [bʌt] N (*Shooting, Archery*): **the butts** il campo *or* poligono di tiro; (*Brit fig*) bersaglio, zimbello; **she's the butt of his jokes** è il bersaglio dei suoi scherzi, è il suo zimbello
butt³ [bʌt] N (*push with head*) testata; (*of goat*) cornata
  ♦ VT dare una testata (*or* una cornata) a
but·ter [ˈbʌtəʳ] N burro; **he looks as if butter wouldn't melt in his mouth** ha una faccia d'angelo ♦ VT (*bread*) imburrare, spalmare di burro
  ▸ **butter up** VT + ADV: **to butter sb up** arruffianarsi con qn
butter·cup [ˈbʌtəˌkʌp] N ranuncolo
butter dish N burriera
butter·fingers [ˈbʌtəˌfɪŋɡəz] N (*fam*) mani *fpl* di ricotta
butter·fly [ˈbʌtəˌflaɪ] N **1** farfalla; **I've got butterflies (in my stomach)** ho il batticuore **2** (*Swimming: also:* **butterfly stroke**) (nuoto a) farfalla
but·tock [ˈbʌtək] N natica
but·ton [ˈbʌtn] N (*on garment*) bottone *m*; (*on doorbell, machine*) pulsante *m*, bottone ♦ VT (*also:* **button up**) abbottonare ♦ VI abbottonarsi
button·hole [ˈbʌtnˌhəʊl] N asola, occhiello; **to wear a buttonhole** portare un fiore all'occhiello ♦ VT (*person*) attaccar bottone a *or* con
but·tress [ˈbʌtrɪs] N contrafforte *m*, sperone *m* ♦ VT armare di contrafforti, rafforzare (con speroni); (*fig*) tener su, tenere in piedi; (*argument*) avvalorare
bux·om [ˈbʌksəm] ADJ formoso(-a)
buy [baɪ] (*pt, pp* **bought**) N: **a good/bad buy** un buon/cattivo acquisto *or* affare *m* ♦ VT comprare, acquistare; (*tickets, petrol*) fare, prendere; (*Comm: company*) acquistare; (*fig: time*) guadagnare; **to buy sb sth/sth from sb** comprare qc per qn/qc da qn; **I've bought my mother some flowers** ho comprato dei fiori per mia madre; **the victory was dearly bought** la vittoria è stata pagata a caro prezzo; **to buy sb a drink** offrire da bere a qn; **he won't buy that explanation** (*fam*) quella scusa non se la beve
  ▸ **buy back** VT + ADV riprendersi, prendersi indietro
  ▸ **buy in** VT + ADV (*Brit: goods*) far provvista di
  ▸ **buy into** VI + PREP (*Brit: Comm*) acquistare delle azioni di
  ▸ **buy off** VT + ADV (*fam: bribe*) comprare
  ▸ **buy out** VT + ADV (*business*) rilevare
  ▸ **buy up** VT + ADV (*property etc*) accaparrarsi
buy·er [ˈbaɪəʳ] N acquirente *m/f*
buyout [ˈbaɪaʊt] N (*Comm*) acquisto di una società da parte dei suoi dipendenti
buzz [bʌz] N ronzio; (*of conversation*) brusio; **the buzz of an insect** il ronzio di un insetto; **to give sb a buzz** (*fam: telephone call*) dare un colpo di telefono a qn (*fam: pleasant intoxication*) senso di ebbrezza ♦ VT (*call on intercom*) chiamare al citofono; (*with buzzer*) chiamare col cicalino; (*Aer: plane, building*) passare rasente; **Julie buzzed me** Julie mi ha dato uno squillo; **to get a buzz out of sth** (*fam*) farsi prendere da qc; **it gives me a buzz** (*fam*) mi esalta; **it has a buzz about** *or* **to it** è proprio eccitante ♦ VI (*insect, ears*) ronzare; **my head is buzzing** mi gira la testa
  ▸ **buzz off** VI + ADV (*Brit fam*) filare, levarsi di torno
buz·zard [ˈbʌzəd] N poiana
buzz·er [ˈbʌzəʳ] N cicalino; (*in factory*) sirena
buzz word N (*fam*) termine *m* in voga

KEYWORD
by [baɪ] ADV (li) vicino; **by and by** (*in past*) poco dopo; (*in future*) fra breve; **by and large** nel complesso, nell'insieme; **close by** vicinissimo, molto vicino; **to go by** passare; **hard**

by vicinissimo, molto vicino; **to lay sth by** mettere qc da parte; **to pass by** passare; **to put sth by** mettere qc da parte; **to rush by** passare correndo

♦ PREP

1 (*close to*) vicino a, accanto a, presso; **I've got it by me** ce l'ho a portata di mano *or* sottomano; **the house by the river** la casa sul fiume; **a holiday by the sea** una vacanza al mare
2 (*via, through*) per; **we came by Boston** siamo venuti via Boston
3 (*past*) davanti a; **I go by the post office every day** passo davanti alla posta ogni giorno; **she walked by me** mi è passata accanto
4 (*during*): **by day** di giorno; **by night** di notte
5 (*not later than*) per; **by then it was too late** ormai era troppo tardi; **by this time tomorrow I'll be in Spain** domani a quest'ora sarò in Spagna; **by the time I got there it was too late** quando sono arrivato era ormai troppo tardi; **by that time I knew** ormai lo sapevo; **it must be finished by 4 o'clock** dev'essere terminato entro le 4
6 (*amount*) a; **by degrees** gradualmente; **by the hour** a ore; **to increase by the hour** aumentare di ora in ora; **by the kilo** a chili; **little by little** a poco a poco; **by the metre** a metri; **one by one** uno(-a) per uno(-a)
7 (*agent, cause*) da; **killed by lightning** ucciso(-a) da un fulmine; **a painting by Picasso** un quadro di Picasso; **surrounded by enemies** circondato(-a) da nemici
8 (*method, manner, means*) per; **by bus** in autobus, con l'autobus; **by car** in macchina, con la macchina; **to pay by cheque** pagare con (un) assegno; **by force** con la forza; **made by hand** fatto(-a) a mano; **to lead sb by the hand** portare qn per mano; **by land and by sea** per terra e per mare; **by moonlight** al chiaro di luna; **(all) by oneself** tutto(-a) solo(-a); **by rail** *or* **train** con il treno, in treno; **by saving hard, he ...** risparmiando molto, lui...

9 (*according to*) per; **to play by the rules** attenersi alle regole; **it's all right by me** per me va bene
10 (*measuring difference*) di; **it missed me by inches** non mi ha preso *or* mi ha mancato per un millimetro; **it's wider by a metre** è un metro più largo
11 (*Math: measure*) per; **to divide/multiply by** dividere/moltiplicare per; **a room 3 metres by 4** una stanza di 3 metri per 4
12 (*points of compass*): **north by north-east** nord-nordest
13 (*in oaths*): **I swear by Almighty God** giuro dinanzi a Dio *or* nel nome di Dio
14 by the way *or* **by the by(e)** a proposito; **this wasn't my idea by the way** tra l'altro l'idea non era mia

bye [baɪ] EXCL (*fam: also:* **bye-bye**) ciao!, arrivederci
by-election, bye-election [ˈbaɪɪˌlekʃən] N (*Brit*) elezione *f* straordinaria
Bye·lo·rus·sia [ˌbjeləʊˈrʌʃə] N Bielorussia
Bye·lo·rus·sian [ˌbjeləʊˈrʌʃən] ADJ bielorusso(-a) ♦ N (*person*) bielorusso(-a); (*language*) bielorusso
by·gone [ˈbaɪˌɡɒn] ADJ passato(-a); **in bygone days** una volta
♦ N: **let bygones be bygones** mettiamoci una pietra sopra
by-law, bye-law [ˈbaɪˌlɔ] N ordinanza locale
by·pass [ˈbaɪˌpɑːs] N (*road*) circonvallazione *f*; (*Med*) by-pass *m inv* ♦ VT (*town*) (fare una deviazione per) evitare; (*fig: person*) scavalcare; (*difficulty*) aggirare
by-product [ˈbaɪˌprɒdʌkt] N (*Chem, etc*) sottoprodotto; (*fig*) conseguenza; **it's a by-product of petrol refining** è un sottoprodotto della raffinazione del petrolio
by·road [ˈbaɪrəʊd], **by·way** [ˈbaɪˌweɪ] N strada secondaria
by·stander [ˈbaɪˌstændəʳ] N astante *m/f*, spettatore(-trice)
byte [baɪt] N (*Comput*) byte *m inv*
by·word [ˈbaɪˌwɜːd] N: **his name is a byword for success** il suo nome è sinonimo di successo
by-your-leave [ˈbaɪjʊəˈliːv] N: **without so much as a by-your-leave** senza nemmeno chiedere il permesso

Cc

C¹, c¹ [siː] N 1 (*letter*) C, c *f inv*, *m inv*; **C for Charlie** ≈ C come Como 2 (*Mus*) do *m inv* 3 (*Scol: mark*) ≈ 6 (*sufficiente*)

C² ABBR (= *Celsius; centigrade*) C

c. ABBR 1 (= *century*) sec 2 (= *circa*) ca 3 (*USA, etc*) = **cent(s)**

CA ABBR 1 = **Central America** 2 (*USA Post* = **California**)

ca. ABBR (= *circa*) ca

C/A ABBR 1 = **capital account** 2 = **credit account** 3 = **current account**

cab [kæb] N 1 (*taxi*) taxi *m inv*; **by cab** in taxi 2 (*of train, truck, lorry*) cabina 3 (*horsedrawn*) carrozza

caba·ret [ˈkæbəreɪ] N cabaret *m inv*

cab·bage [ˈkæbɪdʒ] N cavolo

cab·by [ˈkæbɪ] N (*fam*) tassista *m/f*

cab driver N tassista *m/f*

cab·in [ˈkæbɪn] N (*hut*) capanna; (*Naut, Aer*) cabina

cabin crew N personale *m* di bordo

cabin cruiser N cabinato

cabi·net [ˈkæbɪnɪt] N 1 (*cupboard*) armadietto; (*glass-fronted*) vetrina; **bathroom cabinet** armadietto del bagno 2 (*Pol: also:* **Cabinet**) Consiglio dei Ministri

cabinet-maker [ˈkæbɪnɪtˌmeɪkəʳ] N ebanista *m*

cabinet minister N ministro (*membro del Consiglio*)

ca·ble [ˈkeɪbl] N (*rope*) cavo, fune *f*; (*Elec*) cavo; (*cablegram*) cablogramma *m* ♦ VT (*information*) trasmettere per cablogramma, cablare; (*person*) mandare un cablogramma a, telegrafare a

cable car [ˈkeɪblˌkɑːʳ] N funivia; (*on rail*) funicolare *f*

ca·ble·gram [ˈkeɪblˌɡræm] N cablogramma *m*

cable railway N funicolare *f*

cable television N televisione *f* via cavo

cache [kæʃ] N (*of arms, food*) deposito segreto

cack·le [ˈkækl] N (*of hen*) coccodè *m*; (*laugh*) risolino (stridulo); (*chatter*) chiacchierio ♦ VI (*hen*) fare coccodè; (*person: laugh*) ridacchiare

cac·tus [ˈkæktəs] N (*pl* **cactuses** *or* **cacti** [ˈkæktaɪ]) cactus *m inv*

CAD [kæd] N ABBR (= *computer-aided design*) progettazione *f* assistita dall'elaboratore

cad·die, cad·dy [ˈkædɪ] N (*in golf*) caddie *m inv*

ca·det [kəˈdɛt] N (*Mil, etc*) cadetto; **cadet officer** allievo ufficiale; **police cadet** allievo poliziotto

cadge [kædʒ] VT (*fam: money, cigarette etc*): **to cadge (from)** scroccare a; **to cadge a lift from sb** scroccare un passaggio a qn

ca·dre [ˈkædrɪ] N (*Pol: group*) gruppo scelto

Cae·sar·ean, Ce·sar·ean (*USA*) [siːˈzɛərɪən] N (*also:* **Caesarean section**) (*taglio*) cesareo

café [ˈkæfeɪ] N caffè *m inv*, bar *m inv* (*senza licenza per alcolici*)

caf·eteria [ˌkæfɪˈtɪərɪə] N self-service *m inv*; (*in factory etc*) mensa

caf·feine, caf·fein [ˈkæfiːn] N caffeina

cage [keɪdʒ] N (*gen, in mine*) gabbia ♦ VT mettere in gabbia

▸ **cage in** VT + ADV ingabbiare

cag·ey [ˈkeɪdʒɪ] ADJ (*fam*) evasivo(-a); **to give a cagey answer** dare una risposta evasiva

ca·hoots [kəˈhuːts] NPL (*fam*): **to be in cahoots (with sb)** essere in combutta (con qn)

CAI [siːˈeɪ] N ABBR (= *computer-aided instruction*) istruzione *f* assistita dall'elaboratore

Cai·ro [ˈkaɪərəʊ] N il Cairo *f*

ca·jole [kəˈdʒəʊl] VT (*coax*) convincere con le buone; (*deceitfully*) convincere con lusinghe; **to cajole sb into doing sth** convincere qn a fare qc

cake [keɪk] N 1 (*large*) torta; (*small*) pasticcino; **chocolate cake** torta al cioccolato; **a coffee and a cake** un caffè e una pasta; **piece of cake** fetta di torta; **it's a piece of cake** (*fam*) è una cosa facile *or* da nulla; **driving is a piece of cake** non ci vuole niente a guidare; **to sell like hot cakes** (*fam*) andare a ruba; **he wants to have his cake and eat it** (*fig*) vuole la botte piena e la moglie ubriaca 2 (*of wax*) tavoletta; **cake of soap** saponetta ♦ VT: **to cake (with)** incrostare (di) ♦ VI (*blood*) raggrumarsi; (*mud*) incrostarsi

cake shop N pasticceria

Cal. ABBR (*USA*: = **California**)

ca·lami·tous [kəˈlæmɪtəs] ADJ disastroso(-a)

ca·lam·ity [kəˈlæmɪtɪ] N calamità *f inv*

cal·cium [ˈkælsɪəm] N (*Chem*) calcio

cal·cu·late [ˈkælkjʊleɪt] VT (*cost, distance etc*) calcolare; (*estimate: chances, effect*) valutare; **they are calculating the likely cost** stanno calcolando quanto possa costare; **to be calculated to do sth** essere fatto(-a) *or* studiato(-a) per fare qc ♦ VI (*Math*) fare (i) conti

▸ **calculate on** VI + PREP: **to calculate on sth/on doing sth** contare su qc/di fare qc, tenere conto di qc/di fare qc; **he hadn't calculated on the arrival of the night watchman** non aveva fatto i conti con l'arrivo del guardiano notturno

cal·cu·lat·ed [ˈkælkjʊleɪtɪd] ADJ (*insult, action*) calcolato(-a), intenzionale; **a calculated risk** un rischio calcolato

cal·cu·lat·ing [ˈkælkjʊleɪtɪŋ] ADJ (*scheming*) calcolatore(-trice)

cal·cu·la·tion [ˌkælkjʊˈleɪʃən] N calcolo

cal·cu·la·tor [ˈkælkjʊleɪtəʳ] N calcolatrice *f*

cal·cu·lus [ˈkælkjʊləs] N calcolo; **differential/integral calculus** calcolo differenziale/integrale

cal·en·dar [ˈkælɪndəʳ] N calendario; **the Church calendar** il calendario ecclesiastico

calendar year N anno civile

calf¹ [kɑːf] N (*pl* **calves** [kɑːvs]) 1 (*young cow*) vitello; **seal/elephant calf** piccolo di foca/elefante 2 = **calfskin**

calf² [kɑːf] N (*pl* **calves** [kɑːvs]) (*Anat*) polpaccio

cali·brate [ˈkælɪbreɪt] VT (*gun etc*) calibrare; (*scale of measuring instrument*) tarare

cali·bre, cali·ber (*USA*) [ˈkælɪbəʳ] N (*also fig*) calibro

cali·co [ˈkælɪkəʊ] N (*tela di*) cotone *m* grezzo; (*USA*) cotonina stampata; **calico cat** gatto tartarugato

Calif. ABBR (*USA*) = **California**

Cali·for·nia [ˌkælɪˈfɔːnɪə] N California

cali·pers [ˈkælɪpəz] NPL (*USA*) = **callipers**

call [kɔːl] N 1 (*shout*) richiamo, urlo, grido; (*of bird*) canto; **to give a call** lanciare un grido; **within call** a portata di voce; **please give me a call at 7** per piacere mi chiami alle 7; **whose call is it?** (*Cards*) a chi tocca (giocare)? 2 **a 911/999 call** numero telefonico d'emergenza negli Stati Uniti/nel Regno Unito, una chiamata al 911/999 3 (*Telec: also:* **phone call**) telefonata, chiamata; **long-distance call** chiamata interurbana; **to make a call** fare una telefonare, fare una telefonata; **thanks for your call** grazie per la chiamata 4 (*summons: for flight etc*) chiamata; (*fig: lure*) richiamo; **to be on call** essere a disposizione; (*doctor*) essere reperibile; **the call of the sea** il richiamo del mare; **to answer the call of duty** fare il proprio dovere 5 (*short visit, also Med*) visita; **port of call** (*porto di*) scalo; **to pay a call on sb** fare (una) visita a qn 6 (*need*): **there is no call for alarm** non ci sono motivi di allarme 7 (*claim*): **there are many calls on my time** sono molto preso, ho molti impegni ♦ VT 1 chiamare; (*Telec*) chiamare, telefonare a; **to call 911/999** chiamare il 911/99 2 (*announce: flight*) annunciare; (*meeting, strike*) indire, proclamare; (*waken*) svegliare, chiamare; **we called the police** abbiamo chiamato la polizia 3 (*name*) chiamare; (*describe as*) considerare; **can I call you by your first name?** posso chiamarti per nome?; **to be called** chiamarsi; **what are you called?** come ti chiami?; **she's called Jane** si chiama Jane; **would you call Italian a difficult language?** diresti che l'italiano è una lingua difficile?; **I call it an insult** questo lo chiamo un insulto, lo considero un insulto; **are you calling me a liar?** mi stai dando del bugiardo?; **let's call it £50** facciamo 50 sterline; **let's call it a day** (*fam*) smettiamo, basta per oggi ♦ VI **1** (*shout: person*) chiamare; (*bird*) lanciare un richiamo; **to call to sb** gridare a qn **2** (*Telec*): **who's calling?** chi parla?; **I'll call him you called** gli dirò che hai telefonato; **London calling** (*Radio*) qui Londra **3** (*also:* **call in**, **call round**: *visit*) passare; **I'll call in at the office later** passerò più tardi in ufficio

▸ **call aside** VT + ADV chiamare da parte *or* in disparte

▸ **call at** VT + PREP (*subj: ship*) fare scalo a

▸ **call away** VT + ADV: **to be called away on business** dovere andare via per lavoro

▸ **call back** VT + ADV (*Telec*) ritelefonare a, richiamare; **can I call you back?** ti posso richiamare? ♦ VI + ADV (*Telec*) ritelefonare, richiamare; (*return*) ritornare; **I'll call back later** (*on the phone*) richiamo più tardi; (*in person*) ripasso più tardi

▸ **call down** VT + PREP: **to call down sth** (**on sb**) (*curses*) invocare qc (su qn)

▸ **call for** VI + PREP (*summon: wine, the bill*) chiedere; (*demand: courage, action*) richiedere; (*collect: person*) passare a prendere; (: *goods*) ritirare; **this job calls for strong nerves** questo lavoro richiede nervi saldi; **shall I call for you at seven thirty?** passo a prenderti alle sette e mezzo?; **this calls for a drink!** qui ci vuole un brindisi!

▸ **call forth** VT + ADV (*frm: protest, emotion*) suscitare

▸ **call in** VT + ADV **1** (*doctor, expert, police*) chiamare, far venire **2** (*Comm, etc: faulty goods*) riprendere; (: *currency*) mettere fuori corso ♦ VI + ADV = **call 3**

▸ **call off** VT + ADV **1** (*meeting, race*) disdire, revocare; (*deal*) cancellare; **the strike was called off** lo sciopero è stato revocato; **the match was called off** la partita è stata rinviata **2** (*dog*) richiamare

▸ **call on** VI + PREP **1** (*visit*) far visita a, andare a trovare, passare da **2** (*invite*): **to call on sb to do sth** invitare qn a fare qc; (*request*) chiedere a qn di fare qc; **I now call on Mr Brown to speak** ora invito il signor Brown a parlare

▸ **call out** VT + ADV (*doctor, police, troops*) chiamare; **to call workers out on strike** invitare gli operai a fare sciopero ♦ VI + ADV (*in pain*) urlare; (*to person*) chiamare; **to call out for help** invocare *or* chiamare aiuto

▸ **call round** VI + ADV passare; **to call round to see sb** passare da qn

▸ **call up** VT + ADV **1** (*Mil*) richiamare, mobilitare **2** (*Telec*) chiamare, telefonare a **3** (*fig: memories*) richiamare, evocare

▸ **call upon** VI + PREP = **to call on sb to do sth**

call·box [ˈkɔːlˌbɒks] N (*Brit*) cabina telefonica

call centre N call centre *m inv*

cal·ler [ˈkɔːləʳ] N (*visitor*) visitatore(-trice) *m/f*; (*Telec*) persona che chiama

call girl N ragazza *f* squillo, (*pegg*) *inv*

call-in [ˈkɔːlˌɪn] N (*USA*) = **phone-in**

call·ing [ˈkɔːlɪŋ] N vocazione *f*

calling card N (*USA*) biglietto da visita

cal·li·pers, cal·ipers (*USA*) [ˈkælɪpəz] NPL (*Med*) gambale *m*; (*Math*) calibro

cal·lous [ˈkæləs] ADJ (*person*) insensibile; (*remark*) crudele

cal·lous·ness [ˈkæləsnɪs] N (*of person*) insensibilità; (*of remark*) durezza

cal·low [ˈkæləʊ] ADJ immaturo(-a)

calm [kɑːm] ADJ (*gen*) calmo(-a); (*weather*) sereno(-a); **calm and collected** padrone(-a) di sé; **keep calm!** sta' calmo! ♦ N calma, pace *f*; **the calm before the storm** la quiete che precede la tempesta ♦ VT (*also:* **calm down**: *person*) calmare; **he calmed her down** l'ha calmata

▸ **calm down** VT + ADV = **calm** VT ♦ VI + ADV calmarsi; **calm down!** calmati!

calm·ly [ˈkɑːmlɪ] ADV tranquillamente, con calma

calm·ness [ˈkɑːmnɪs] N calma, tranquillità

calo·rie [ˈkælərɪ] N caloria; **low-calorie product** prodotto a basso contenuto calorico

calve [kɑːv] VI figliare

calves [kɑːvz] NPL *of* calf[1] calf[2]

CAM [kæm] N ABBR (= *computer-aided manufacturing*) fabbricazione *f* assistita dall'elaboratore

cam·ber [ˈkæmbəʳ] N (*of road*) curvatura, bombatura

Cam·bo·dia [kæmˈbəʊdɪə] N Cambogia

Cam·bo·dian [kæmˈbəʊdɪən] ADJ, N cambogiano(-a)

cam·cord·er [ˈkæmkɔːdəʳ] N camcorder *f inv*

came [keɪm] PT *of* **come**

cam·el [ˈkæməl] N cammello ♦ ADJ (*colour*) color cammello *inv*

cameo [ˈkæmɪəʊ] N cammeo ♦ ADJ (*ring, brooch*) con cammeo; (*Cine, Theatre: role, part*) breve apparizione *f* (*di un attore o un'attrice famoso(-a)*)

cam·era [ˈkæmərə] N **1** macchina fotografica; (*movie camera*) cinepresa; (*Cine, TV*) telecamera **2** (*Law*): **in camera** a porte chiuse

❏ **camera** is not translated by the Italian word *camera*

camera·man [ˈkæmərəˌmæn] N (*pl* -**men**) cameraman *m inv*

camera phone N telefonino con fotocamera integrata

Cam·eroon [ˌkæməˈruːn] N il Camerun *m*

camouflage [ˈkæməflɑːʒ] N camuffamento; (*Mil*) mimetizzazione *f* ♦ VT camuffare; (*Mil*) mimetizzare; **they were well camouflaged, and invisible from the air** erano ben mimetizzati ed invisibili dall'alto

camp[1] [kæmp] N (*gen*) accampamento, campo; (*holiday camp*) campeggio; (*Pol, etc*) campo, schieramento; **summer camp** campeggio estivo; **refugee camp** campo *m* profughi, *inv* ♦ VI campeggiare, accamparsi; **to go camping** andare in campeggio; **we went camping in Cornwall** siamo andati in campeggio in Cornovaglia

▸ **camp out** VI + ADV accamparsi, attendarsi, campeggiare

camp[2] [kæmp] ADJ (*fam: theatrical*) melodrammatico(-a); (: *fam*) ostentatamente effeminato(-a)

cam·paign [kæmˈpeɪn] N (*Mil, Pol, etc*) campagna; **advertising campaign** campagna pubblicitaria ♦ VI (*Mil, also fig*): **to campaign (for/against)** fare una campagna (per/contro); **they are campaigning for a change in the law** stanno facendo una campagna per cambiare la legge

cam·paign·er [kæmˈpeɪnəʳ] N (*Mil*): **old campaigner** veterano, vecchio combattente *m*; **campaigner for** fautore(-trice) di; **campaigner against** oppositore(-trice) di

camp·er [ˈkæmpəʳ] N (*person*) campeggiatore(-trice); (*vehicle*) camper *m inv*

camp·ing [ˈkæmpɪŋ] N campeggio; **I like camping** mi piace il campeggio

❏ **camping** is not translated by the Italian word *camping*

camp site, camping site N (zona di) campeggio

cam·pus [ˈkæmpəs] N campus *m inv*

cam·shaft [ˈkæmˌʃæft] N albero a camme; **single camshaft** monoalbero

<hr>

KEYWORD

can[1] [kæn] (*neg* **cannot**, **can't**, *cond, pt* **could**) MODAL AUX VB

1 (*be able to*) potere; **I'll tell you all I can** ti dirò tutto quello che posso; **she was as happy as could be** più felice di così non poteva essere; **he can do it if he tries hard** è capace di farlo se si sforza; **they couldn't help it** non potevano farci niente; **I can't** *or* **cannot go any further** non posso andare oltre

2 (*know how to*) essere capace di, sapere; **I can speak French** so parlare francese; **can you speak Italian?** parli italiano?; **I can swim/drive** so nuotare/guidare; **he can't swim/drive** non sa nuotare/guidare

3 (*may*) potere; **can't I come too?** non posso venire anch'io?; **could I have a word with you?** potrei parlarti un attimo?; **can I use your telephone?** posso usare il tuo telefono?

4 (*expressing disbelief, puzzlement*): **how could you lie to me!** come hai potuto dirmi una bugia!; **you can't be serious!** scherzi?; **this can't be true!** non può essere vero!; **what can he want?** cosa può mai volere?; **they can't have left already!** non è possibile che siano già partiti!

5 (*expressing possibility, suggestion etc*): **they could have forgotten** potrebbero essersene dimenticati; **he could be in the library** può darsi che sia in biblioteca, potrebbe essere in biblioteca; **I could have cried/screamed!** mi sarei messo a piangere/urlare!

6 (*not translated*): **can you hear me?** mi senti?; **I can't see you** non ti vedo

can² [kæn] N (*container: for foodstuffs*) scatola; (: *for oil, water*) latta; (: *esp USA: garbage can*) bidone *m*; **a can of peas** una scatola di piselli; **a can of beer** una lattina di birra ♦ VT (*food*) inscatolare

Cana·da [ˈkænədə] N Canada *m*

Ca·na·dian [kəˈneɪdɪən] ADJ, N canadese *m/f*

ca·nal [kəˈnæl] N canale *m*

ca·nary [kəˈnɛərɪ] N canarino

Canary Islands NPL: **the Canary Islands** le isole *fpl* Canarie

Can·ber·ra [ˈkænbərə] N Canberra

can·cel [ˈkænsəl] VT **1** (*call off: holiday, booking*) cancellare, annullare, disdire; (*meeting, event*) cancellare, sospendere; (*train*) sopprimere; (*annul: order, contract*) annullare; **they cancelled their booking at the last moment** hanno annullato la prenotazione all'ultimo momento; **I had to cancel my appointment** ho dovuto disdire l'appuntamento; **our flight was cancelled** il nostro volo è stato cancellato; **the train has been cancelled** il treno è stato soppresso **2** (*obliterate: name*) cancellare, radiare; (: *stamp*) timbrare, annullare; (: *cheque*) annullare **3** (*Math: figures*) semplificare

▸ **cancel out** VT + ADV (*Math*) semplificare; (*fig*) annullare; **they cancel each other out** (*also fig*) si annullano a vicenda ♦ VI + ADV (*Math*) semplificarsi

can·cel·la·tion [ˌkænsəˈleɪʃən] N (*see vt a, c*) cancellazione *f*, annullamento, disdetta; sospensione *f*; soppressione *f*; annullamento; semplificazione *f*

can·cer [ˈkænsəʳ] N (*Med*) cancro; **he's got cancer** ha il cancro

can·cer·ous [ˈkænsərəs] ADJ canceroso(-a)

cancer patient N malato(-a) di cancro

cancer research N ricerca sul cancro

can·did [ˈkændɪd] ADJ franco(-a), onesto(-a)

can·di·da·cy [ˈkændɪdəsɪ], **can·di·da·ture** (*Brit*) [ˈkændɪdətʃəʳ] N candidatura

can·di·date [ˈkændɪˌdeɪt] N candidato(-a)

can·died [ˈkændɪd] ADJ candito(-a); **candied peel** scorzette *fpl* di frutta candita; **candied apple** (*USA*) mela caramellata

can·dle [ˈkændl] N candela; (*in church*) cero; **he lit a candle** ha acceso una candela; **a cake with fifteen candles** una torta con quindici candeline

candle·light [ˈkændlˌlaɪt] N lume *m* di candela; **by candlelight** a lume di candela

candle·stick [ˈkændlˌstɪk], **candle·holder** [ˈkændlˌhəʊldəʳ] N bugia, portacandele *m inv*; (*large, ornate*) candeliere *m*

can·dour, can·dor (*USA*) [ˈkændəʳ] N candore *m*, franchezza, sincerità

C & W [ˈsiːənˈdʌbljuː] N ABBR = **country and western (music)**

can·dy [ˈkændɪ] N (*USA: sweet*) caramella; (: *sweets, confectionery*) dolciumi *mpl*; **do you want a candy?** vuoi una caramella?; **I don't eat candy** non mangio dolciumi ♦ VT (*fruit*) candire

candy store N (*USA*) ≈ pasticceria

cane [keɪn] N (*Bot*) canna; (*for baskets, chairs*) bambù *m*; (*wicker*) vimini *m*; (*stick: for walking*) bastone *m* (da passeggio); (: *for punishment*) bacchetta; **he leaned on a cane** si appoggiava ad un bastone; **to get the cane** (*Scol*) prenderle con la bacchetta ♦ VT (*Brit Scol: pupil*) picchiare con la bacchetta

❑ **cane** is not translated by the Italian word *cane*

can·ine [ˈkeɪnaɪn] ADJ canino(-a) ♦ N (*canine tooth*) (dente *m*) canino

can·is·ter [ˈkænɪstəʳ] N (*for tea, coffee*) barattolo (*metallico*); (*for gas*) candelotto

can·na·bis [ˈkænəbɪs] N canapa indiana

canned [kænd] PT, PP of **can²** ♦ ADJ (*food*) in scatola; (*fam: recorded: music*) registrato(-a); (*Brit fam: drunk*) sbronzo(-a); (*USA fam: worker*) licenziato(-a)

can·ni·bal [ˈkænɪbəl] N cannibale *m/f*

can·ni·bal·ism [ˈkænɪbəlɪzəm] N cannibalismo

can·non [ˈkænən] N (*pl* **cannon** *or* **cannons**) (*gun*) cannone *m* ♦ VI: **to cannon into** *or* **against** sbattere violentemente contro

cannon·ball [ˈkænənˌbɔːl] N palla di cannone

cannon fodder N carne *f* da cannone

can·not [ˈkænɒt] = **can not**

can·ny [ˈkænɪ] ADJ (*comp* **-ier**, *superl* **-iest**) furbo(-a)

ca·noe [kəˈnuː] N canoa ♦ VI andare in canoa; **on holiday we canoed and swam** in vacanza siamo andati in canoa e abbiamo nuotato

ca·noe·ing [kəˈnuːɪŋ] N (*sport*) canottaggio; **I like canoeing** mi piace il canottaggio; **we went canoeing** abbiamo fatto canottaggio

ca·noe·ist [kəˈnuːɪst] N canoista *m/f*, canottiere *m*

can·on [ˈkænən] N **1** (*clergyman*) canonico **2** (*principle*) canone *m*

can·on·ize [ˈkænəˌnaɪz] VT canonizzare

can opener N apriscatole *m inv*

can·o·py [ˈkænəpɪ] N (*above bed, throne*) baldacchino; (*Naut*) tendalino

cant¹ [kænt] N (*hypocritical talk*) discorsi *mpl* ipocriti; (*jargon*) gergo

cant² [kænt] VI (*tilt*) inclinarsi ♦ VT inclinare; (*overturn*) rovesciare

can't [kɑːnt] = **can not**

can·tan·ker·ous [kænˈtæŋkərəs] ADJ irascibile, stizzoso(-a)

can·teen [kænˈtiːn] N (*restaurant*) mensa

❑ **canteen** is not translated by the Italian word *cantina*

can·ter [ˈkæntəʳ] N piccolo galoppo; **counter canter** galoppo rovescio ♦ VI andare a piccolo galoppo

can·ti·lever [ˈkæntɪˌliːvəʳ] N trave *f* a sbalzo

can·vas [ˈkænvəs] N tela; **under canvas** (*in a tent*) in tenda; (*Naut*) a vele spiegate

can·vass [ˈkænvəs] VT (*Pol: district*) fare un giro elettorale di; (: *person*) fare propaganda elettorale a; (*Comm: district*) battere (*per raccogliere ordinazioni*); (: *citizens, opinions*) fare un sondaggio di; **they canvassed the views of local people** hanno fatto un sondaggio d'opinione tra la gente del posto ♦ VI (*Pol*) raccogliere voti; (*Comm*) battere la zona per raccogliere ordinazioni; **she canvassed for the Labour Party in the last election** ha fatto propaganda per il partito laburista alle ultime elezioni

can·vass·er [ˈkænvəsəʳ] N (*Pol*) propagandista *m/f* (elettorale); (*Comm*) piazzista *m*

can·vass·ing [ˈkænvəsɪŋ] N sollecitazione *f*

can·yon [ˈkænjən] N canyon *m inv*

cap [kæp] N **1** (*hat, also Sport*) berretto; (*for swimming*) cuffia; (*riding cap*) cap *m inv*; **cap in hand** (*fig*) umilmente; **if the cap fits wear it** chi ha orecchie per intendere intenda; **he's got his cap for England** (*Sport*) è stato scelto per la nazionale inglese **2** (*of bottle, radiator etc*) tappo; (*of pen*) cappuccio; (*Brit: contraceptive: also:* **Dutch cap**) diaframma *m*; **please put the cap back on the toothpaste** rimetti il tappo al dentifricio, per favore ♦ VT **1** (*bottle*) tappare; (*tooth*) ricoprire **2** (*surpass: story, joke*) superare, essere meglio di; **and to cap it all, he ...** e per completare l'opera, lui... **3** **he's been capped 15 times for the USA** (*Brit: Sport*) ha rappresentato gli Stati Uniti 15 volte; **this is his second cap for Scotland** è la seconda volta che veste la maglia della nazionale scozzese

ca·pa·bil·i·ty [ˌkeɪpəˈbɪlɪtɪ] N (*no pl: competence*) capacità, competenza, abilità; (*potential ability*) possibilità *f inv*

ca·pable [ˈkeɪpəbl] ADJ **1** (*competent*) capace, abile **2** (*able to*): **capable of (doing) sth** in grado di fare qc, capace di fare qc; **your son's capable of doing better at school** suo figlio potrebbe riuscire meglio a scuola; **they realized he was capable of murder** capirono che era capace di uccidere; **she's quite capable of letting someone else take the blame** sarebbe capace di dar la colpa a un altro

ca·pa·cious [kəˈpeɪʃəs] ADJ capace

ca·pac·i·ty [kəˈpæsɪtɪ] N **1** (*Elec, Phys: of container etc*) capacità; (*of lift etc*) capienza; **the tank has a 40-litre capacity** il serbatoio ha una capacità di 40 litri; **seating capacity** capienza; **filled to capacity** pieno(-a); zeppo(-a); **the auditorium was filled to capacity** la sala era al completo; **to work at full capacity** (*factory etc*) lavorare a pieno ritmo **2** (*position*) posizione *f*, funzione *f*; **in my capacity as chairman** nella mia veste di presidente, in qualità di presidente; **in an advisory capacity** a titolo consultativo; **in his official**

capacity nell'esercizio delle sue funzioni **3** (*ability*) capacità; **to have a capacity for hard work** essere un(-a) gran lavoratore(-trice); **this work is beyond my capacity** questo lavoro è al di là delle mie possibilità

cape¹ [keɪp] N (*Geog*) capo

cape² [keɪp] N (*garment*) cappa, mantello; (*of policeman, cyclist*) mantella

Cape of Good Hope N Capo di Buona Speranza

ca·per¹ ['keɪpəʳ] N (*Culin*) cappero

ca·per² ['keɪpəʳ] N (*escapade*) scherzetto, birichinata; (*leap*) saltello ♦ VI (*child*) saltellare

Cape Town N Città del Capo

capi·ta ['kæpɪtə] *see* **per capita**

capi·tal ['kæpɪtl] N **1** (*also:* **capital letter**) (lettera) maiuscola; **in capitals** in stampatello **2** (*also:* **capital city**) capitale *f*; **Cardiff is the capital of Wales** Cardiff è la capitale del Galles **3** (*Fin*) capitale *m*; **to make capital out of sth** (*fig*) sfruttare qc ♦ ADJ **1** (*letter*) maiuscolo(-a); **with a capital C** con la C maiuscola **2** (*Law*): **capital offence** delitto passibile di pena capitale **3** (*old: idea*) meraviglioso(-a), splendido(-a)

capital account N conto capitale

capital allowance N ammortamento fiscale

capital assets NPL capitale *msg* fisso

capital expenditure N spese *fpl* in capitale

capital gains tax N imposta sulla plusvalenza

capital goods N beni *mpl* d'investimento, beni capitali

capital-intensive ['kæpɪtlɪn'tensɪv] ADJ ad alta intensità di capitale

capi·tal·ism ['kæpɪtəlɪzəm] N capitalismo

capi·tal·ist ['kæpɪtəlɪst] ADJ, N capitalista *m/f*

capi·tal·ize ['kæpɪtə,laɪz] VT **1** (*Fin: provide with capital*) capitalizzare **2** (*word*) scrivere (in) maiuscolo
  ► **capitalize on** VI + PREP (*fig*) trarre vantaggio da

capital punishment N pena capitale

capital transfer tax N (*Brit*) imposta sui trasferimenti di capitali

Capi·tol ['kæpɪtəl] N: **the Capitol** il Campidoglio

ca·pitu·late [kə'pɪtjʊleɪt] VI capitolare

ca·pitu·la·tion [kə,pɪtjʊ'leɪʃən] N capitolazione *f*

ca·pri·cious [kə'prɪʃəs] ADJ capriccioso(-a)

Cap·ri·corn ['kæprɪ,kɔːn] N Capricorno; **to be Capricorn** (*Astrol*) essere del Capricorno

caps [kæps] NPL, ABBR (= *capital letters*) *see* **capital**

cap·size [kæp'saɪz] VT ribaltare, capovolgere ♦ VI ribaltarsi, capovolgersi; (*boat*) ribaltarsi, scuffiare; **the boat capsized** la barca si è capovolta

cap·stan ['kæpstən] N (*Naut*) argano

cap·sule ['kæpsjuːl] N capsula

Capt. ABBR (= *captain*) Cap.

cap·tain ['kæptɪn] N capitano, comandante *m*; **captain of industry** capitano d'industria ♦ VT (*team*) essere capitano di, capitanare; (*ship*) comandare

cap·tion ['kæpʃən] N (*heading*) intestazione *f*; (*to cartoon*) fumetto; (*for illustration, table*) didascalia

cap·ti·vate ['kæptɪ,veɪt] VT affascinare, incantare, avvincere

cap·tive ['kæptɪv] ADJ (*person*) prigioniero(-a); (*animal*) in cattività; **he had a captive audience** i presenti hanno dovuto ascoltarlo per forza ♦ N prigioniero(-a); **to hold sb captive** tenere prigioniero qn

cap·tiv·ity [kæp'tɪvɪtɪ] N prigionia; (*of animal*) cattività; **in captivity** (*animal*) in cattività

cap·tor ['kæptəʳ] N (*lawful*) chi ha catturato; (*unlawful*) rapitore(-trice); **he managed to escape from his captors** riuscì a sfuggire a quelli che l'avevano catturato

cap·ture ['kæptʃəʳ] N (*of animal, soldier, escapee*) cattura; (*of city etc*) presa; (*thing caught*) preda; (*data capture*) registrazione *f* or rilevazione *f* di dati ♦ VT (*animal*) catturare, prendere; (*escapee, soldier*) prendere, far prigioniero; (*city etc*) prendere; (*fig: attention*) attirare, cattivare; (*Art: atmosphere etc*) cogliere, rendere

car [kɑːʳ] N **1** (*Aut*) macchina, automobile *f*, auto *f inv*; **by car** in macchina; **we went by car** siamo andati in macchina **2** (*esp USA: in train*) vagone *m*; (: *in tram*) vettura; **dining car** vagone ristorante

Caracas [kə'rækəs] N Caracas *f*

ca·rafe [kə'ræf] N caraffa

carafe wine N (*in restaurant*) ≈ vino sfuso

cara·mel ['kærəməl] N caramello; (*sweet*) caramella ♦ ADJ (*custard, flavouring*) al caramello

car·at ['kærət] N carato; **18 carat gold** oro a 18 carati

cara·van ['kærə,væn] N **1** (*gipsies'*) carrozzone *m*; (*Brit: Aut*) roulotte *f inv* **2** (*in desert*) carovana ♦ VI viaggiare con la roulotte

cara·way ['kærə,weɪ] N (*Bot*) cumino (dei prati); **caraway seed** seme *m* di cumino

carb [kɑːb] N (*fam*) cibo *m* ad alto contenuto di carboidrati

car·bo·hy·drate [,kɑːbəʊ'haɪdreɪt] N (*Chem: starchy food*) carboidrato

car·bo·lic acid [kɑː'bɒlɪk'æsɪd] N acido fenico, fenolo

car bomb N autobomba *inv*

car·bon ['kɑːbən] N (*Chem*) carbonio; (*also:* **carbon paper**) carta carbone

car·bon·at·ed ['kɑːbə,neɪtɪd] ADJ (*drink*) gassato(-a)

carbon copy N (*Typing*) copia (in carta carbone); (*fig*) copia *f* carbone, *inv*; **he's a carbon copy of his father** è tutto suo padre, è la copia carbone di suo padre, è identico a suo padre

carbon credit N carbon credit *m inv*, credito sull'emissione di anidride carbonica

carbon dioxide N anidride *f* carbonica, biossido di carbonio

carbon monoxide N monossido di carbonio

carbon-neutral ADJ a zero emissioni di gas serra

carbon offset N riduzione *f* delle emissioni di gas serra

carbon paper N carta carbone

carbon ribbon N nastro carbonato

car·bu·ret·tor, carburetor (USA) [,kɑːbjʊ'retəʳ] N carburatore *m*

car·cass, car·case ['kɑːkəs] N (*of animal*) carcassa

car·cino·gen·ic [,kɑːsɪnə'dʒenɪk] ADJ (*Med*) cancerogeno(-a)

card [kɑːd] N (*greetings card, visiting card*) biglietto; (*membership card*) tessera; (*index card*) scheda; (*playing card*) carta (da gioco); (*thin cardboard*) cartoncino; **I'd like to send him a card for his birthday** vorrei spedirgli un biglietto per il suo compleanno; **here is my card** ecco il mio biglietto da visita; **to play cards** giocare a carte; **I like playing cards** mi piace giocare a carte; **it's on the cards** (*fig*) è probabile; **to lay one's cards on the table** (*also fig*) mettere le carte in tavola; **to play one's cards right** (*fig*) giocare bene le proprie carte ♦ VT (*Golf*) totalizzare; (*Ftbl*): **to be red-/yellow-carded** essere ammonito(-a) con il cartellino rosso/giallo

car·da·mom ['kɑːdəməm], **car·da·mon** ['kɑːdəmən] N cardamomo

card·board ['kɑːd,bɔːd] N cartone *m*

cardboard box N (scatola di) cartone *m*

card-carrying ['kɑːd,kærɪŋ] ADJ tesserato(-a); (*fig*) convinto(-a)

card game N gioco di carte

car·di·ac ['kɑːdɪæk] ADJ (*Med*) cardiaco(-a)

car·di·gan ['kɑːdɪgən] N cardigan *m inv*

car·di·nal ['kɑːdɪnl] ADJ, N cardinale *m*

card index N schedario

card·phone ['kɑːdfəʊn] N telefono a scheda (magnetica)

card·sharp ['kɑːdʃɑːp] N baro

care [keəʳ] N **1** (*worry*) preoccupazione *f*; **without a care in the world** senza alcuna preoccupazione; **he hasn't a care in the world** non ha preoccupazioni di sorta; **the cares of State** i problemi di Stato **2** (*carefulness*) attenzione *f*, cura; (*charge*) cura, custodia; **"with care"** "fragile", "con cura"; **to take care to do sth** fare attenzione a or badare a fare qc; **take care!** (*as warning*) (stai) attento!; (*as good wishes*) stammi bene!; **to take care of** (*details, arrangements*) occuparsi di, curarsi di; (*sick person*) curare qn; **I take care of the children on Saturdays** io mi occupo dei bambini di sabato; **I'll take care of him!** (*fam*) lo sistemo io!; **she can take care of herself** sa badare a se stessa; **take care not to drop it!** stai attento a non farlo cadere!; **care of** (*on letter*) presso; **I'll leave it/him in your care** te lo affido; **the child has been taken into care** il bambino è stato affidato ad un ente assistenziale ♦ VI (*be concerned*): **to**

care (about) interessarsi (di), preoccuparsi (di); **of course I care about him** certo che m'importa di lui; **I don't care** non m'importa, non me ne importa; **I couldn't care less** non me ne importa un bel niente; **to care deeply about** tenere molto a; **for all I care** per quello che mi interessa; **who cares?** chi se ne frega? (*fam!*), chi se ne importa? 2 (*be concerned*): **I don't care what you think** non mi interessa quello che pensi; **I couldn't care less what people say** me ne infischio di quel che dice la gente 2 (*frm: like*) volere, desiderare; **would you care to come this way?** le dispiacerebbe venire da questa parte?; **I wouldn't care to do it** non lo vorrei fare; **I shouldn't care to meet him** preferirei non incontrarlo

▸ **care for** VI + PREP 1 (*look after*) curare, aver cura di; **they'll employ a nurse to care for her** assumeranno un'infermiera che si prenderà cura di lei 2 (*be fond of: person*) voler bene a; **I still care a lot for you** ti voglio ancora tanto bene; **she no longer cares for him** non le importa più niente di lui; **I don't care for coffee** non amo particolarmente il caffè; **would you care for a drink?** gradiresti qualcosa da bere?

ca·reen [kəˈriːn] VI (*ship*) sbandare ♦ VT carenare

ca·reer [kəˈrɪəʳ] N (*occupation*) professione *f*; (*working life*) carriera; **she had a successful career in journalism** ha fatto una brillante carriera come giornalista ♦ VI (*also:* **career along**) sfrecciare, andare di gran carriera ♦ ADJ (*diplomat, soldier etc*) di carriera

careers officer N consulente *m/f* d'orientamento professionale

care·free [ˈkɛəfriː] ADJ spensierato(-a), libero(-a) da preoccupazioni; **a carefree childhood** un'infanzia spensierata

care·ful [ˈkɛəful] ADJ 1 (*taking care, cautious*) attento(-a), cauto(-a); **(be) careful!** (stai) attento!, attenzione!; **to be careful with sth** fare attenzione a qc; **he's very careful with his money** sta molto attento a quanto spende; **be careful what you say to him** stai attento a come gli parli; **he was careful not to offend her** badava a non offenderla 2 (*painstaking: work*) accurato(-a); (: *writer, worker etc*) attento(-a), diligente, zelante

care·ful·ly [ˈkɛəfəlɪ] ADV (*cautiously*) attentamente, con attenzione, cautamente; (*painstakingly*) con cura, accuratamente; **think carefully!** pensaci attentamente!; **drive carefully!** guida con prudenza!; **she carefully avoided talking about it** ha evitato accuratamente di parlarne

caregiver (*USA*) N 1 (*professional*) badante *m/f* 2 (*unpaid*) persona che si prende cura di un parente malato o anziano

care·less [ˈkɛəlɪs] ADJ (*worker, driver, driving*) distratto(-a), disattento(-a), negligente; (*work*) fatto(-a) con poco impegno; (*thoughtless: remark*) senza tatto, privo(-a) di tatto; **she's very careless** è molto sbadata; **careless mistake** errore *m* di distrazione; **careless driver** guidatore(-trice) distratto(-a)

care·less·ly [ˈkɛəlɪslɪ] ADV (*act, drive*) con disattenzione, distrattamente; (*work*) con poco impegno, negligentemente; (*speak*) senza tatto

care·less·ness [ˈkɛəlɪsnɪs] N (*see adj*) disattenzione *f*; mancanza d'impegno, negligenza; mancanza di tatto

car·er [ˈkɛərəʳ] N familiare che bada a persone anziane o disabili

ca·ress [kəˈrɛs] N carezza ♦ VT carezzare, accarezzare

care·taker [ˈkɛəˌteɪkəʳ] N custode *m/f*; (*of school*) bidello(-a)

car-ferry [ˈkɑːˌfɛrɪ] N traghetto, nave *f* traghetto, *inv*

car·go [ˈkɑːgəʊ] N carico

cargo boat N cargo

cargo plane N aereo da carico

Car·ib·be·an [ˌkærɪˈbiːən] ADJ caraibico(-a) ♦ N: **the Caribbean** i Caraibi; **we're going to the Caribbean** andremo ai Caraibi; **the Caribbean (Sea)** il Mar dei Caraibi

cari·ca·ture [ˈkærɪkəˌtjʊəʳ] N caricatura ♦ VT fare una caricatura di

car·ing [ˈkɛərɪŋ] ADJ (*parent, person*) affettuoso(-a), premuroso(-a); (*society, organization*) umanitario(-a); **the caring professions** professioni in campo medico o sociale; **ours is not a caring society** viviamo in una società ben poco altruista

car·nage [ˈkɑːnɪdʒ] N carneficina

car·nal [ˈkɑːnl] ADJ carnale

car·na·tion [kɑːˈneɪʃən] N garofano

car·ni·val [ˈkɑːnɪvəl] N (*public celebration*) carnevale *m*; (*USA: funfair*) luna park *m inv*

car·niv·o·rous [kɑːˈnɪvərəs] ADJ carnivoro(-a)

car·ol [ˈkærəl] N: (Christmas) carol canto di Natale, canto natalizio

ca·rouse [kəˈraʊz] VI far baldoria

carou·sel [ˌkærəˈsɛl] N (*USA: merry-go-round*) giostra; (: *at airport: conveyor belt*) nastro trasportatore

carp[1] [kɑːp] N (*fish*) carpa

carp[2] [kɑːp] VI (*complain*): **to carp at** avere *or* trovare da ridire su

car park N parcheggio

car·pen·ter [ˈkɑːpɪntəʳ] N carpentiere *m*

car·pen·try [ˈkɑːpɪntrɪ] N carpenteria

car·pet [ˈkɑːpɪt] N tappeto; (*fitted carpet*) moquette *f inv*; **Persian carpet** tappeto persiano ♦ VT (*floor, house*) coprire con tappeto; (*with fitted carpet*) rivestire di moquette, mettere la moquette a

carpet bombing N bombardamento a tappeto

carpet slippers NPL pantofole *fpl*

carpet sweeper N battitappeto

car rental N (*USA*) autonoleggio

car·riage [ˈkærɪdʒ] N 1 (*Brit: Rail*) carrozza, vagone *m*, vettura; (*horse-drawn*) carrozza; (*of typewriter*) carrello 2 (*of person: bearing*) portamento 3 (*Comm: of goods*) trasporto; (*cost of carriage*) (spese *fpl* di) trasporto

carriage return N (*on typewriter*) leva (*or* tasto) del ritorno a capo

carriage·way [ˈkærɪdʒˌweɪ] N (*Brit: Aut*) carreggiata

car·ri·er [ˈkærɪəʳ] N 1 (*of goods: person*) corriere *m*; (: *company*) impresa di trasporti, vettore *m*; **by carrier** per corriere 2 (*Med: of disease*) portatore(-trice); **typhoid carrier** portatore(-trice) del tifo 3 (*aircraft carrier*) portaerei *f inv*

carrier bag N (*Brit*) sacchetto, borsa (di plastica)

carrier pigeon N piccione *m* viaggiatore

car·ri·on [ˈkærɪən] N carogna

car·rot [ˈkærət] N carota

car·ry [ˈkærɪ] VT 1 (*gen*) portare; (*have on one's person: money, documents*) portare *or* avere con sé; (*transport: goods*) trasportare; (: *passengers*) portare; (*message, news*) recare, portare; (*subj: pillar*) sostenere; (*involve: responsibilities etc*) comportare; **I'll carry your bag** porto io la tua borsa; **to carry sth about with one** portarsi dietro qc; **a plane carrying 100 passengers crashed last week** la scorsa settimana è caduto un aereo che trasportava 100 passeggeri; **the wind carried the sound to him** il vento trasportò il suono verso di lui; **the offence carries a £50 fine** il reato prevede una multa di 50 sterline; **both papers carried the story** entrambi i giornali riportarono la storia; **he carries his drink well** regge bene l'alcool; **you're carrying things too far!** stai esagerando! 2 (*Comm: stock*) tenere 3 (*Math: figure*) riportare; (*Fin: interest*) avere; **this loan carries 10% interest** questo prestito ha un interesse del 10% 4 (*approve: motion, bill*) approvare, far passare; (*win: election, point*) vincere; **to carry the day** avere successo 5 **he carries himself like a soldier** ha il portamento di un militare; **she carries herself well** ha un bel portamento ♦ VI (*sound*) trasmettersi, farsi sentire, diffondersi

▸ **carry away** VT + ADV portare via; **to be carried away** (*fig*) farsi trascinare; **to get carried away by sth** (*fig*) farsi *or* lasciarsi prendere da qc

▸ **carry back** VT + ADV (*also fig: remind*) riportare

▸ **carry forward** VI + ADV (*Math, Fin*) riportare

▸ **carry off** VT + ADV (*seize, take away*) portare via; (*kidnap*) sequestrare, rapire; (*win: prize, medal*) vincere; **he carried it off very well** se l'è cavata molto bene

▸ **carry on** VT + ADV (*continue: tradition etc*) portare avanti, continuare; (: *business, trade*) mandare avanti; **to carry on a conversation** conversare, parlare ♦ VI + ADV 1 **to carry on with sth/doing sth** continuare qc/a fare qc; **she carried on talking** continuò a parlare; **carry on!** va avanti!; **am I boring you?** - **no, carry on!** ti annoio? - no, va' avanti! 2 (*fam: make a fuss*) fare storie; **how you do carry on!** quante storie fai! 3 (*fam: have an affair*): **to carry on (with)** intendersela (con), filare (con)

▸ **carry out** VT + ADV (*accomplish: plan*) realizzare; (*perform, implement: idea, threat*) mettere in pratica; (: *orders*) eseguire;

(: *experiment, search, repairs*) effettuare; (: *investigation*) svolgere; **make sure that he carries out my orders** assicurati che esegua i miei ordini
  ▸ **carry over** VT + ADV riportare
  ▸ **carry through** VT + ADV (*accomplish: task*) portare a termine, realizzare; (*sustain: person*) sostenere
carry-on [ˌkærɪˈɒn] N (*fam: fuss*) casino, confusione *f*
cart [kɑːt] N carretto; **a horse and cart** un carro trainato da un cavallo; **to put the cart before the horse** (*fig*) mettere il carro davanti ai buoi ◆ VT (*fam*) trascinare
carte blanche [ˈkɑːtˈblɑːntʃ] N: **to give sb carte blanche** dare carta bianca a qn
car·tel [kɑːˈtɛl] N (*Comm*) cartello
car·ti·lage [ˈkɑːtɪlɪdʒ] N cartilagine *f*
car·tog·ra·pher [kɑːˈtɒɡrəfə*] N cartografo(-a)
car·tog·ra·phy [kɑːˈtɒɡrəfɪ] N cartografia
car·ton [ˈkɑːtən] N (*of milk, yogurt*) cartone *m*; (*of ice cream*) vaschetta; (*of cigarettes*) stecca; (*box*) scatola di cartone
car·toon [kɑːˈtuːn] N (*in newspaper etc*) vignetta; (*Cine, TV*) cartone *m* animato; (*Art*) cartone; **strip cartoon** fumetto
car·toon·ist [ˌkɑːˈtuːnɪst] N (*in newspaper*) vignettista *m/f*; (*Cine, TV*) disegnatore(-trice) di cartoni animati
car·tridge [ˈkɑːtrɪdʒ] N (*for gun, pen*) cartuccia; (*for camera*) caricatore *m*; (*music tape*) cassetta; (*of record player*) testina
cart·wheel [ˈkɑːtˌwiːl] N: **to turn a cartwheel** (*Sport, etc*) fare la ruota
carve [kɑːv] VT (*Culin: meat*) tagliare; (*stone, wood*) scolpire, intagliare; (*name on tree*) incidere; **dad carved the roast** papà ha tagliato l'arrosto; **a carved oak chair** una sedia di quercia intagliata; **to carve out a career for o.s** farsi una carriera ◆ VI (*Culin*) tagliare la carne
  ▸ **carve up** VT + ADV (*meat*) tagliare; (*fig: country, money, profits*) suddividere
carv·ing [ˈkɑːvɪŋ] N (*Art: in wood, stone*) scultura
carving knife, carv·er [ˈkɑːvə*] N trinciante *m*
car wash N lavaggio auto; **automatic car wash** autolavaggio automatico
cas·cade [kæsˈkeɪd] N cascata ◆ VI scendere a cascata
case[1] [keɪs] N 1 (*gen, also Med, Gram*) caso; **the doctor has a lot of cases to see today** il dottore oggi deve vedere molti pazienti; **in any case** in ogni caso, comunque; **in that case** in quel *or* questo caso; **(just) in case** non si sa mai, per precauzione, per sicurezza; **take some money, just in case** prendi un po' di soldi per sicurezza; **I think she knows you're coming, but just in case, you'd better phone her** penso che sappia del tuo arrivo, ma per sicurezza faresti meglio a telefonarle; **in case it rains** caso mai dovesse piovere; **in case he changes his mind** caso mai lui cambiasse idea; **in case of emergency** in caso di emergenza; **a case in point** un esempio tipico; **it's a clear case of murder** è un chiaro caso di omicidio; **in some cases** in alcuni casi; **in most cases** nella maggior parte dei casi, in genere; **it's generally the case that people are selfish** di solito succede che la gente sia egoista; **if this** *or* **that is the case** quand'è così, se così è; **as the case may be** a seconda del caso 2 (*Law*) caso, processo, causa; (*argument*) motivo, ragione *f*; **the case for the defence/prosecution** le ragioni *or* argomentazioni della difesa/dell'accusa; **the police are investigating the case** la polizia sta indagando sul caso; **to state one's case** esporre le proprie ragioni; (*fig*) perorare la propria causa; **to have a good case** avere pretese legittime; **there's a strong case for reform** ci sono validi argomenti a favore della riforma
case[2] [keɪs] N 1 (*suitcase*) valigia; (*briefcase*) valigetta, cartella; (*packing case*) cassa; (*for camera*) custodia; (*for jewellery*) scatolina, astuccio; (*for spectacles*) custodia, astuccio; (*display case*) vetrinetta; (*of watch*) cassa; **I've packed my case** ho fatto la valigia; **a case of wine** una cassa di vini 2 (*Typ*): **lower/upper case** (carattere *m*) minuscolo/maiuscolo
case history N (*Med*) cartella clinica
case-sensitive [ˈkeɪsˌsɛnsɪtɪv] ADJ (*Comput*) sensibile alle maiuscole o minuscole
case study N casistica
cash [kæʃ] N 1 (*coins, notes*) soldi *mpl*, denaro; **in cash** in contanti; **£200 in cash** 200 sterline in contanti; **to pay (in) cash** pagare in contanti; **ready cash** (*fam*) (denaro) contante

m; **cash in hand** fondo di cassa 2 (*immediate payment*): **to pay cash down** pagare in contanti; **cash with order/on delivery** (*Comm*) pagamento all'ordinazione/alla consegna 3 (*fam: money*) quattrini *mpl*; **he's got plenty of cash** ha un sacco di quattrini; **to be short of cash** essere a corto di soldi ◆ VT (*cheque*) riscuotere, incassare
  ▸ **cash in** VT + ADV (*insurance policy*) riscuotere, riconvertire
  ▸ **cash in on** VI + ADV + PREP sfruttare
cash account N conto *m* cassa, *inv*
cash-and-carry [ˈkæʃˌəndˈkærɪ] N cash and carry *m inv*
cash-book [ˈkæʃˌbʊk] N libro *or* giornale *m* di cassa
cash box N cassetta *f* portavalori, *inv*
cash card N carta per prelievi automatici, carta *f* bancomat, *inv*
cash discount N sconto contanti
cash dispenser N sportello automatico, bancomat *m*
cash·ew [ˈkæˈʃuː] N (*also: cashew nut*) anacardio
cash flow N liquidità, cash-flow *m inv*
cash·ier [kæˈʃɪə*] N cassiere(-a)
cash·ier [kæˈʃɪə*] VT (*esp Mil: officer*) destituire
cash·mere [kæˈʃmɪə*] N cachemire *m inv*, cashmere *m inv* ◆ ADJ di cachemire; **cashmere jumper** maglione *m* di cachemire
cash payment N pagamento in contanti
cash price N prezzo per contanti
cash register N registratore *m* di cassa
cash sale N vendita per contanti
cas·ing [ˈkeɪsɪŋ] N (*Tech*) rivestimento; (*of tyre* or *tire*) copertone *m*
ca·si·no [kəˈsiːnəʊ] N casinò *m inv*
cask [kɑːsk] N barile *m*, botte *f*
cas·ket [ˈkɑːskɪt] N (*for jewels*) scrigno, cofanetto; (*USA: coffin*) bara
Cas·pian [ˈkæspɪən] N: **the Caspian Sea** il mar Caspio
cas·se·role [ˈkæsəˌrəʊl] N (*utensil*) casseruola (a due manici); (*food*): **chicken/veal casserole** pollo/vitello in casseruola; **to make a casserole** fare uno spezzatino; **casserole dish** casseruola
cas·sette [kæˈsɛt] N cassetta
cassette deck N piastra di registrazione
cassette player N riproduttore *m* a cassetta
cassette recorder N registratore *m* a cassetta
cast [kɑːst] (*pt, pp* **cast**) N 1 (*Fishing*) lancio 2 (*mould*) stampo, forma; (*Med: plaster cast*) gesso, ingessatura; **cast of mind** mentalità *f inv* 3 (*Theatre*) cast *m inv*; **after the play we met the cast** dopo la commedia abbiamo incontrato il cast 4 (*Med: squint*) strabismo; **he has a cast in his right eye** ha l'occhio destro strabico ◆ VT 1 (*also fig: throw*) gettare; (*fishing line*) lanciare; (*shadow, light*) gettare, proiettare; **to cast doubt on sth** far sorgere dubbi su qc; **to cast one's vote (for)** votare (per); **to cast one's eyes over sth** dare un'occhiata a qc 2 (*shed*) spogliarsi di; (*horseshoe*) perdere; **the snake casts its skin** il serpente ha cambiato la pelle 3 (*metal*) colare, fondere; (*plaster*) gettare; (*bronze etc statue*) fondere, gettare 4 (*Theatre, Cine: part*) affidare; (*: actor*) scritturare, ingaggiare; **to cast sb as Hamlet** scegliere qn per la parte di Amleto
  ▸ **cast about for** VI + ADV + PREP cercare di trovare
  ▸ **cast aside** VT + ADV (*reject*) mettere da parte
  ▸ **cast away** VT + ADV (*Naut*): **to be cast away** naufragare
  ▸ **cast down** VT + ADV: **to be cast down** essere giù (di corda), essere depresso(-a)
  ▸ **cast off** VT + ADV (*Knitting*) diminuire, calare ◆ VI + ADV (*Naut*) levare gli ormeggi, salpare; (*Knitting*) diminuire, calare
  ▸ **cast on** (*Knitting*) VT + ADV avviare ◆ VI + ADV avviare (le maglie)
  ▸ **cast out** VT + ADV (*liter*) abbandonare
  ▸ **cast up** VT + ADV: **to cast sth up (at sb)** rinfacciare qc (a qn)
cas·ta·nets [ˌkæstəˈnɛts] NPL castagnette *fpl*, nacchere *fpl*
cast·away [ˈkɑːstəˌweɪ] N naufrago(-a)
caste [kɑːst] N casta ◆ ADJ di casta
cas·ter sug·ar [ˈkɑːstə*ˌʃʊɡə*] N zucchero semolato

cast·ing vote [ˈkɑːstɪŋˈvəʊt] N (*Brit*) voto decisivo
cast iron N ghisa
cas·tle [ˈkɑːsl] N castello; (*fortified*) rocca; (*Chess*) torre *f*; **castles in the air** (*fig*) castelli in aria
cas·tor [ˈkɑːstəʳ] N = **caster**
castor oil N olio di ricino
cas·trate [kæsˈtreɪt] VT castrare
cas·ual [ˈkæʒjʊəl] ADJ **1** (*by chance: meeting*) fortuito(-a), casuale; (: *walk, stroll*) senza meta precisa; (: *glance*) di sfuggita; (: *remark*) fatto(-a) di sfuggita; **a casual remark** un'osservazione buttata là; **we're just casual acquaintances** ci conosciamo appena; **to have casual sex** avere avventure **2** (*unconcerned: attitude, person*) noncurante, indifferente, disinvolto(-a); **he was very casual about it** si è mostrato indifferente **3** (*informal: discussion, tone etc*) informale; (: *clothing*) sportivo(-a), casual; **casual wear** casual *m*; **I prefer casual clothes** preferisco i vestiti sportivi **4** (*irregular: work*) saltuario(-a); (: *worker*) saltuario(-a), avventizio(-a); **it's just a casual job** è solo un lavoro saltuario
♦ **casuals** NPL (*shoes*) calzature *fpl* sportive
casual labour N manodopera avventizia
casu·al·ly [ˈkæʒjʊlɪ] ADV (*see adj 1, 2, 3*) casualmente; senza meta precisa; di sfuggita; con noncuranza, con disinvoltura; in modo informale; in modo sportivo *or* informale; **to dress casually** vestirsi sportivo
casu·al·ty [ˈkæʒjʊltɪ] N (*Mil: dead*) vittima, morto, caduto; (: *wounded*) ferito; (*in accident: dead*) vittima; (: *injured*) ferito; **heavy casualties** grosse perdite *fpl*; **there are no reports of casualties** non è stato segnalato nessun ferito
❏ **casualty** is not translated by the Italian word *casualità*
cat [kæt] N gatto(-a); (*species*) felino(-a); **big cats such as lions ...** grossi felini come leoni...; **Siamese cat** gatto siamese; **that's put the cat among the pigeons!** ha suscitato un vespaio!; **that's let the cat out of the bag** questo non è più un segreto; **to fight like cat and dog** essere come cane e gatto; **when the cat's away the mice will play** quando il gatto non c'è i topi ballano
cata·combs [ˈkætəˌkuːmz] NPL catacombe *fpl*
cata·logue, cata·log (*USA*) [ˈkætəˌlɒg] N catalogo ♦ VT catalogare
cata·lyst [ˈkætəlɪst] N (*all senses*) catalizzatore *m*
cata·lyt·ic con·vert·er [ˌkætəˈlɪtɪkkənˈvɜːtəʳ] N (*Aut*) marmitta catalitica, catalizzatore *m*
cata·pult [ˈkætəˌpʌlt] N (*slingshot*) fionda; (*Mil, Aer*) catapulta ♦ VT catapultare
cata·ract [ˈkætəˌrækt] N (*Geog, Med*) cateratta
ca·tarrh [kəˈtɑːʳ] N catarro
ca·tas·tro·phe [kəˈtæstrəfɪ] N catastrofe *f*
cata·stroph·ic [ˌkætəˈstrɒfɪk] ADJ catastrofico(-a)
cat·call [ˈkætˌkɔːl] N (*at meeting etc*) fischio ♦ VI fischiare
catch [kætʃ] (*pt, pp* **caught**) N **1** (*of ball*) presa; (*fish caught*) pescato; **a brilliant catch** un'ottima presa; **he spent all day fishing without a single catch** passò tutta la giornata a pescare senza prendere niente; **he's a good catch** (*fig*) è un buon partito **2** (*fastener: on suitcase, door*) gancio, fermo **3** (*trick, snag*) tranello, inganno, trabocchetto; **what's/where's the catch?** dove sta l'inganno? **4** **with a catch in one's voice** con la voce spezzata *or* rotta ♦ VT **1** (*ball*) afferrare, prendere; (*fish*) prendere, pescare; (*thief*) prendere, acchiappare, acciuffare; (*bus, train*) prendere; (*entangle*) impigliare; **I caught my fingers in the door** mi son chiuso le dita nella porta; **I caught my coat on that nail** mi si è impigliato il cappotto in quel chiodo; **to catch sb's attention/eye** attirare l'attenzione/lo sguardo di qn; **to catch sight of** scorgere **2** (*take by surprise: person*) cogliere, sorprendere; **to catch sb doing sth** sorprendere qn a fare qc; **you won't catch me doing ...** non mi vedrai mai fare...; **caught in the act** colto(-a) sul fatto; **caught in the rain** sorpreso(-a) dalla pioggia **3** (*hear, understand: remark*) afferrare, cogliere; (*portray: atmosphere, likeness*) cogliere **4** (*disease*) prendere, contrarre; (*hit*) colpire; **to catch cold** prendere freddo; **to catch fire** prendere fuoco; **the punch caught him on the chin** è stato colpito al mento con un pugno; **to catch one's breath** (*from shock etc*) restare senza fiato; (*after effort*) riprendere fiato; **you'll**

catch it! (*fam*) vedrai! ♦ VI **1** (*get entangled*) impigliarsi, restare impigliato(-a) **2** (*fire, wood*) prendere
▸ **catch at** VI + PREP (*object*) afferrare; (*opportunity*) cogliere
▸ **catch on** VI + ADV **1** (*understand*): **to catch on (to sth)** capire (qc) **2** (*become popular*) affermarsi, far presa
▸ **catch up** VT + ADV (*snatch up*) afferrare; **to catch sb up** (*walking, working etc*) raggiungere qn; **she caught me up** mi ha raggiunto ♦ VI + ADV: **to catch up with sb** raggiungere qn; **to catch up on one's work** mettersi in pari col lavoro; **I've got to catch up on my work** devo rimettermi in pari col lavoro; **to catch up with the news** aggiornarsi
catch-22 [ˈkætʃˌtwɛntɪˈtuː] N: **it's a catch-22 situation** non c'è via d'uscita
catch·ing [ˈkætʃɪŋ] ADJ (*Med, also fig*) contagioso(-a); **don't worry, it's not catching!** non preoccuparti, non è contagioso!
catchment area N (*Brit: of school, hospital*) bacino di utenza; (*Geog*) bacino imbrifero
catch phrase N slogan *m inv*, tormentone *m*
catchy [ˈkætʃɪ] ADJ (*tune*) orecchiabile
cat·echism [ˈkætɪˌkɪzəm] N catechismo
cat·egori·cal [ˌkætɪˈgɒrɪkəl], **cat·egor·ic** [ˌkætɪˈgɒrɪk] ADJ categorico(-a)
cat·ego·rize [ˈkætɪgəˌraɪz] VT catalogare, classificare, dividere per categorie
cat·ego·ry [ˈkætɪgərɪ] N categoria
ca·ter [ˈkeɪtəʳ] VI (*provide food*) provvedere alla ristorazione ♦ VT (*esp USA: wedding, party*) provvedere ai rinfreschi per
▸ **cater for** VI + PREP (*Brit: wedding, party*) provvedere ai rinfreschi per; (: *needs*) provvedere a; (*readers, consumers*) incontrare i gusti di
▸ **cater to** VI + PREP (*Brit: whims, demands*) soddisfare
ca·ter·er [ˈkeɪtərəʳ] N chi si occupa di catering *or* ristorazione
ca·ter·ing [ˈkeɪtərɪŋ] N catering *m inv*, ristorazione *f* (collettiva)
catering trade N settore *m* (della) ristorazione
cat·er·pil·lar [ˈkætəˌpɪləʳ] N (*Zool*) bruco; (*vehicle*) cingolato
cat flap N gattaiola
ca·thedral [kəˈθiːdrəl] N cattedrale *f*, duomo
cath·ode [ˈkæθəʊd] N (*Elec*) catodo
cathode-ray tube [ˈkæθəʊdˌreɪˈtjuːb] N (*Elec*) tubo a raggi catodici
Catho·lic [ˈkæθəlɪk] (*Rel*) ADJ (*Roman Catholic*) cattolico(-a); **the Catholic Church** la Chiesa Cattolica ♦ N cattolico(-a); **I'm a Catholic** sono cattolico(-a)
catho·lic [ˈkæθəlɪk] ADJ (*wide-ranging: taste, interests*) ampio(-a), vasto(-a), eclettico(-a)
CAT scanner [ˈkætˌskænəʳ] N (*Med*) apparecchiatura per la TAC *f inv*
cat's-eye [ˈkætsˌaɪ] N (*Brit: Aut*) catarifrangente *m*
cat·sup [ˈkætsəp] N (*USA*) ketchup *m inv*
cat·tle [ˈkætl] NPL bestiame *m*
cat·ty [ˈkætɪ] ADJ (*comp* **-ier**, *superl* **-iest**) (*fam*) maligno(-a), dispettoso(-a)
cat·walk [ˈkætˌwɔːk] N passerella (*in sfilata di moda*)
Cau·ca·sian [kɔːˈkeɪzɪən] ADJ, N caucasico(-a)
Caucasus [ˈkɔːkəsəs] N Caucaso
cau·cus [ˈkɔːkəs] N (*USA Pol*) (riunione *f* del) comitato elettorale; (*Brit Pol: group*) comitato di dirigenti
caught [kɔːt] PL, PP *of* **catch**
cau·li·flow·er [ˈkɒlɪˌflaʊəʳ] N cavolfiore *m*
cause [kɔːz] N **1** (*reason*) motivo, ragione *f*; **cause and effect** causa ed effetto; **with good cause** a ragione; **to be the cause of** essere (la) causa di; **there's no cause for alarm** non c'è motivo di allarme; **there is no cause for concern** non c'è ragione di preoccuparsi; **he had no cause for complaint** non aveva motivo di lamentarsi **2** (*purpose*) causa; **in the cause of justice** per la (causa della) giustizia; **to make common cause with** far causa comune con; **it's all in a good cause** (*fam*) è tutto a fin di bene ♦ VT causare; **to cause sth to be done** far fare qc; **to cause sb to do sth** far fare qc a qn
cause·way [ˈkɔːzˌweɪ] N strada rialzata
caus·tic [ˈkɔːstɪk] ADJ (*Chem, also fig*) caustico(-a)
cau·tion [ˈkɔːʃən] N (*care*) attenzione *f*, prudenza; (*warning*)

avvertimento, ammonizione *f*; (*from police*) diffida; **a note of caution** una nota di avvertimento; **it should be handled with the utmost caution** dev'essere maneggiato con la massima cautela ♦ VT: **to caution sb** (*subj: official*) ammonire qn; (: *policeman*) diffidare qn; **to caution sb against doing sth** diffidare qn dal fare qc

cau·tious [ˈkɔːʃəs] ADJ cauto(-a), prudente

cau·tious·ly [ˈkɔːʃəslɪ] ADV cautamente, prudentemente

cau·tious·ness [ˈkɔːʃəsnɪs] N prudenza, cautela

cava·lier [ˌkævəˈlɪəʳ] N (*knight*) cavaliere *m* ♦ ADJ (*pej: offhand: person*) brusco(-a); (: *attitude*) non curante

cav·al·ry [ˈkævəlrɪ] N cavalleria

cave [keɪv] N grotta, caverna ♦ VI: **to go caving** fare speleologia
  ▸ **cave in** VI + ADV (*ceiling, roof*) sfondarsi, crollare; (*ground*) franare, cedere
  ❏ **cave** is not translated by the Italian word *cava*

cave·man [ˈkeɪvmæn] N (*pl* **-men**) cavernicolo, uomo delle caverne

cav·ern [ˈkævən] N caverna

cavi·ar, cavi·are [ˈkævɪˌɑːʳ] N caviale *m*

cav·ity [ˈkævɪtɪ] N cavità

ca·vort [kəˈvɔːt] VI saltellare, far capriole

cay·enne [ˈkeɪɛn] N: **cayenne (pepper)** pepe *m* di Caienna

CB [ˌsiːˈbiː] N ABBR (= *Citizens' Band* (*Radio*)) CB *m*; **CB radio (set)** baracchino

cc [ˌsiːˈsiː] ABBR **1** (= *cubic centimetres*) cc **2** (*on email*) Cc

CCU [ˌsiːsiːˈjuː] N ABBR (*USA*: = *coronary care unit*) unità coronarica

CD [ˌsiːˈdiː] N ABBR **1** (= *compact disc*) CD *m inv* **2** (*Mil: Brit:* = **Civil Defence (Corps)**); (: *USA:* = **Civil Defense**) ♦ ABBR (*Brit:* = *Corps Diplomatique*) CD

CD burner, CD writer N masterizzatore *m*

CDC [ˌsiːdiːˈsiː] N ABBR (*USA:* = **Center for Disease Control**)

CD player N lettore *m* CD, *inv*

Cdr. ABBR (= *commander*) Com.

CD-ROM [ˌsiːdiːˈrɒm] N ABBR (= *compact disc read-only memory*) CD-rom *m inv*

CDT [ˌsiːdiːˈtiː] ABBR (*USA – Central Daylight Time*) ora estiva nel fuso orario degli Stati Uniti centrali

CD writer N = **CD burner**

cease [siːs] VT, VI cessare, smettere

cease-fire [ˌsiːsˈfaɪəʳ] N cessate il fuoco *m inv*

cease·less [ˈsiːslɪs] ADJ incessante, continuo(-a), senza sosta

ce·dar [ˈsiːdəʳ] N cedro ♦ ADJ di cedro

cede [siːd] VT (*territory*) cedere; (*argument*) cedere su

cei·lidh [ˈkeɪlɪ] N festa con musiche e danze popolari scozzesi o irlandesi

ceil·ing [ˈsiːlɪŋ] N (*of room etc*) soffitto; (*of boat*) pagliolato; (*fig: upper limit*) tetto, limite *m* massimo

cel·ebrate [ˈselɪˌbreɪt] VT (*event, festival, birthday*) celebrare, festeggiare; (*mass*) celebrare; **I celebrated my birthday last week** ho festeggiato il mio compleanno la settimana scorsa ♦ VI far festa

cel·ebrat·ed [ˈselɪˌbreɪtɪd] ADJ celebre

cel·ebra·tion [ˌselɪˈbreɪʃən] N (*act*) celebrazione *f*; (*festivity*) celebrazione, festa

ce·leb·rity [sɪˈlɛbrɪtɪ] N celebrità *f inv*

ce·leri·ac [səˈlɛrɪˌæk] N sedano *m* rapa, *inv*

cel·ery [ˈselərɪ] N sedano; **head/stick of celery** testa/gambo di sedano

ce·les·tial [sɪˈlɛstɪəl] ADJ (*also fig*) celestiale, celeste

celi·ba·cy [ˈselɪbəsɪ] N celibato

cell [sel] N (*in prison, monastery*) cella; (*Bio*) cellula; (*Elec*) elemento (di batteria); **prisoners spend many hours in their cells** i prigionieri trascorrono molte ore in cella; **dry cell** (*Chem*) cella a secco

cel·lar [ˈselə] N cantina; **in the cellar** in cantina

cel·list [ˈtʃelɪst] N violoncellista *m/f*

cel·lo [ˈtʃeləu] N violoncello

cell·phone [ˈselfəun] N cellulare *m*

cel·lu·lar [ˈseljʊlə] ADJ (*Bio*) cellulare; **cellular blanket** coperta a tessitura rada

cel·lu·loid [ˈseljʊlɔɪd] N celluloide *f*

cel·lu·lose [ˈseljʊləus] N cellulosa

Celsius [ˈselsɪəs] ADJ Celsius *inv*; **Celsius scale of temperature** scala Celsius

Celt [kelt, selt] N celta *m/f*

Celt·ic [ˈkeltɪk, ˈseltɪk] ADJ celtico(-a) ♦ N (*language*) celtico

ce·ment [səˈment] N cemento; (*glue*) adesivo; **cement floor** pavimento di cemento ♦ VT cementare

cement mixer N betoniera

cem·etery [ˈsɛmɪtrɪ] N cimitero, camposanto

ceno·taph [ˈsenəˌtɑːf] N cenotafio

cen·sor [ˈsensəʳ] N censore *m* ♦ VT censurare, sottoporre a censura

cen·sor·ship [ˈsensəˌʃɪp] N censura

cen·sure [ˈsenʃəʳ] N biasimo, censura ♦ VT biasimare, censurare

cen·sus [ˈsensəs] N censimento

cent [sent] N (*coin: of dollar, euro*) centesimo; **I haven't a cent** non ho una lira *or* un centesimo; *see also* **per cent**

cen·te·nary [senˈtiːnərɪ] N centenario

cen·ter [ˈsentə] (*USA*) = **centre**

cen·ti·grade [ˈsentɪˌɡreɪd] ADJ centigrado(-a); **30 degrees centigrade** 30 gradi centigradi

cen·ti·li·tre, cen·ti·li·ter (*USA*) [ˈsentɪˌliːtəʳ] N centilitro

cen·ti·me·tre, cen·ti·me·ter (*USA*) [ˈsentɪˌmiːtəʳ] N centimetro

cen·ti·pede [ˈsentɪˌpiːd] N millepiedi *m inv*, centopiedi *m inv*

cen·tral [ˈsentrəl] ADJ centrale

Central African Republic N la Repubblica Centrafricana

Central America N l'America centrale

central heating N riscaldamento autonomo

cen·tral·ize [ˈsentrəˌlaɪz] VT centralizzare, accentrare

central processing unit N (*Comput*) unità *f inv* centrale di elaborazione

central reservation N (*Brit: Aut*) banchina *f* spartitraffico, *inv*

cen·tre, cen·ter (*USA*) [ˈsentəʳ] N centro; **the city centre** il centro della città; **sports centre** centro sportivo; **she is the centre of attention** è al centro dell'attenzione ♦ VT **1** centrare, mettere al centro **2** (*concentrate*): **to centre (on)** concentrare (su); **their demands centred round pay** gran parte delle loro richieste riguardavano il salario ♦ VI centrare

centre·fold, centerfold (*USA*) [ˈsentəˌfəuld] N (*of magazine*) paginone *m* centrale

centre forward [ˌsentəˈfɔːwəd] N (*Sport*) centravanti *m inv*

centre half [ˌsentəˈhɑːf] N (*Sport*) centromediano

centre·piece, centerpiece (*USA*) [ˈsentəˌpiːs] N centrotavola *m*; (*fig*) pezzo forte, punta di diamante

centre spread N (*Brit*) pubblicità *f inv* a doppia pagina

centre-stage [ˌsentəˈsteɪdʒ] N: **to take centre-stage** porsi al centro dell'attenzione

cen·trifu·gal [senˈtrɪfjuɡəl] ADJ (*Phys*) centrifugo(-a)

cen·tri·fuge [ˈsentrɪˌfjuːʒ] N centrifuga

cen·tu·ry [ˈsentʃərɪ] N secolo; (*in cricket*) cento punti; **in the twenty first century** nel ventunesimo secolo

CEO [ˌsiːiːˈəu] N ABBR = **chief executive officer**

ce·ram·ic [sɪˈræmɪk] ADJ in *or* di ceramica; (*arts*) ceramico(-a) ♦ **ceramics** NPL ceramica

ce·real [ˈsɪərɪəl] N (*crop*) cereale *m*; (*breakfast cereal*) cereali *mpl*; **I have cereal for breakfast** mangio cereali per colazione

cere·bral [ˈsɛrɪbrəl] ADJ (*frm*) cerebrale

cer·emo·nial [ˌsɛrɪˈməunɪəl] ADJ (*rite*) formale, solenne; (*dress*) da cerimonia; **on ceremonial occasions** in occasione di cerimonie ufficiali ♦ N cerimoniale *m*; (*rite*) rito

cer·emo·ny [ˈsɛrɪmənɪ] N (*event*) cerimonia; (*no pl: formality*) cerimonie *fpl*; **to stand on ceremony** attenersi all'etichetta, fare complimenti

cer·tain [ˈsɜːtən] ADJ **1** (*sure*) certo(-a), sicuro(-a); (*inevitable: death, success*) sicuro(-a); (*cure*) infallibile, garantito(-a); **he's certain to leave his job** è certo che lui lascerà il lavoro; **it is certain that ...** è certo che...; **I am certain he's not coming** sono certo che non verrà; **I am certain of it** ne sono certo; **he is certain to be there** lui ci sarà certamente; **for certain** per certo, di sicuro; **I can't say for certain that ...** non posso dire con certezza che...; **be certain to tell her** ricordati or non dimenticarti di dirglielo; **to make certain of sth** accertarsi di qc **2** (*before n: particular*) certo(-a); **a certain person** una certa persona; **a certain gentleman called** ha telefonato un certo signore

cer·tain·ly [ˈsɜːtənlɪ] ADV certamente, certo; **certainly!** (ma) certo!; **certainly not!** no di certo!; **I shall certainly be there** ci sarò sicuramente, ci sarò certamente

cer·tain·ty [ˈsɜːtəntɪ] N certezza; **faced with the certainty of disaster** di fronte al sicuro disastro; **we know for a certainty that ...** sappiamo per certo che...

cer·tifi·cate [səˈtɪfɪkɪt] N (*gen*) certificato; (*academic*) diploma *m*; **birth certificate** certificato di nascita

certified letter N (*USA*) lettera raccomandata

certified public accountant N (*USA*) ≈ commercialista *m/f*

cer·ti·fy [ˈsɜːtɪfaɪ] VT **1** certificare, attestare; **the will has been certified** il testamento è stato autenticato **2** (*Med*): **to certify sb** dichiarare malato(-a) di mente qn

cer·vi·cal [ˈsɜːvɪkəl] ADJ (*Anat*): **cervical cancer** cancro al collo dell'utero or alla cervice uterina

cer·vix [ˈsɜːvɪks] N (*pl* **cervices** [səˈvaɪsiːz]) (*Anat*) collo dell'utero, cervice *f* uterina

Ce·sar·ean [siːˈzɛərɪən] N, ADJ (*USA*) = **Caesarean**

ces·sa·tion [sɛˈseɪʃən] N (*frm*) cessazione *f*, arresto

cess·pit [ˈsɛspɪt], **cess·pool** [ˈsɛspuːl] N pozzo nero

CET [siːiːˈtiː] ABBR (= *Central European Time*) fuso orario dell'Europa Centrale

Ceylon [sɪˈlɒn] N Ceylon *f*

cf. ABBR (= *compare*) Cfr.

CFC [siːɛfˈsiː] N ABBR = **chlorofluorocarbon**; **CFCs** NPL CFC *m*

CG [siːˈdʒiː] ABBR (*USA*) = **coastguard**

cg ABBR (= *centigram*) cg

ch. ABBR (= *chapter*) cap.

Chad [tʃæd] N Ciad *m*

chafe [tʃeɪf] VT (*irritate: skin*) sfregare contro, irritare; (*rub to warm*) frizionare ♦ VI **1** (*become sore*) irritarsi **2** (*fig*): **to chafe (at)** irritarsi (per); **to chafe against** scontrarsi con

chaf·finch [ˈtʃæfɪntʃ] N fringuello

cha·grin [ˈʃæɡrɪn] N (*frm*) disappunto, dispiacere *m*

chain [tʃeɪn] N (*gen*) catena; **gold chain** catenina d'oro; **the gate was fastened with a chain** il cancello era chiuso con una catena; **a chain of events** una serie di avvenimenti ♦ VT (*also:* **chain up**) incatenare

▸ **chain up** VT + ADV (*prisoner*) incatenare; (*dog*) mettere alla catena

chain reaction N reazione *f* a catena

chain-smoke [ˈtʃeɪnsməʊk] VI fumare una sigaretta dopo l'altra

chain store N grande magazzino o supermercato che fa parte di una catena

chair [tʃɛəʳ] N sedia, seggiola; (*armchair*) poltrona; (*seat*) posto (a sedere); (*Univ*) cattedra; (*USA: electric chair*): **the chair** la sedia elettrica; **a table and four chairs** un tavolo e quattro sedie; **a sofa and two chairs** un divano e due poltrone; **dentist's chair** poltrona del dentista; **to take the chair** (*at meeting*) assumere la presidenza ♦ VT (*meeting*) presiedere

chair lift N seggiovia

chair·man [ˈtʃɛəmən] N (*pl* **-men**) presidente *m*

chair·person [ˈtʃɛəpɜːsn] N presidente(-essa)

chair·woman [ˈtʃɛəwʊmən] N (*pl* **-women**) presidentessa

cha·let [ˈʃæleɪ] N (*in mountains*) chalet *m inv*; (*in holiday camp etc*) bungalow *m inv*

chal·ice [ˈtʃælɪs] N calice *m*

chalk [tʃɔːk] N gesso; **a (piece of) chalk** un gesso; (*child's*) un gessetto; **not by a long chalk** (*fam*) proprio per niente or nulla, niente affatto ♦ VT (*message*) scrivere col gesso; (*luggage*) segnare col gesso

▸ **chalk up** VT + ADV scrivere col gesso; (*fig: success*) ottenere; (*: victory*) riportare

chalk·board [ˈtʃɔːkbɔːd] N (*USA: blackboard*) lavagna

chal·lenge [ˈtʃælɪndʒ] N sfida; (*of sentry*) intimazione *f*; **to issue a challenge** lanciare una sfida; **to take up the**

challenge accettare or raccogliere la sfida; **this task is a great challenge** questo compito è una grande sfida ♦ VT (*to contest*) sfidare; (*subj: sentry*) intimare l'alt *etc* a; (*dispute: fact, point, statement, right*) mettere in dubbio, contestare; **to challenge sb to a fight/game** sfidare qn a battersi/ad una partita; **she challenged me to a race** mi ha sfidato ad una gara; **to challenge sb to do sth** sfidare qn a fare qc; **to challenge sb to a duel** sfidare qn a duello

chal·leng·er [ˈtʃælɪndʒəʳ] N (*Sport*) sfidante *m/f*

chal·leng·ing [ˈtʃælɪndʒɪŋ] ADJ (*situation, work*) impegnativo(-a); (*remark, look*) provocatorio(-a); (*book*) stimolante; **a challenging job** un lavoro impegnativo

cham·ber [ˈtʃeɪmbəʳ] N (*of parliament*) camera; (*old: room*) stanza; **chambers** NPL (*of judge, lawyer*) studio

chamber·maid [ˈtʃeɪmbəmeɪd] N cameriera al piano

chamber music N musica da camera

chamber·pot [ˈtʃeɪmbəpɒt] N vaso da notte

cha·me·le·on [kəˈmiːlɪən] N camaleonte *m*

cham·ois [ˈʃæmwɑː] N (*Zool*) camoscio

chamois leather N (pelle *f* di) camoscio

cham·pagne [ʃæmˈpeɪn] N champagne *m inv*

cham·pers [ˈʃæmpəz] NSG, NPL (*Brit fam*) sciampagnino

cham·pi·on [ˈtʃæmpjən] N (*Sport*) campione(-essa); (*of cause*) difensore *m*; **boxing champion** campione di boxe ♦ VT difendere, lottare per

cham·pi·on·ship [ˈtʃæmpjənʃɪp] N (*contest*) campionato

chance [tʃɑːns] N **1** (*possibility*) probabilità *f inv*; **the chances are that ...** probabilmente..., è probabile che... + *sub*; **the team's chances of winning** le possibilità di vittoria della squadra; **he doesn't stand** or **he hasn't a chance of winning** non ha nessuna possibilità di vittoria; **there is little chance of his coming** è molto improbabile che venga; **no chance!** impossibile! **2** (*opportunity*) possibilità *f inv*, occasione *f*; **it's the chance of a lifetime** è un'occasione unica; **he never had a chance in life** non ha mai avuto nessuna possibilità nella vita; **to give sb a chance** dare a qn la possibilità (di fare qc); **to have an eye to the main chance** (*pej*) essere sempre pronto(-a) ad approfittare, non perdere occasioni; **I'll write when I get the chance** scriverò quando ne avrò l'opportunità **3** (*risk*) rischio; **an element of chance** una parte di fortuna; **to take a chance** rischiare; **I'm taking no chances** non voglio lasciare niente al caso, non intendo rischiare; **4** (*luck*) caso; **game of chance** gioco d'azzardo; **by chance** per caso; **do you by any chance know each other?** per caso vi conoscete?; **to leave nothing to chance** non lasciare nulla al caso ♦ VT (*happen*): **to chance to do sth** (*frm*) fare per caso qc; **I'll chance it** (*risk*) ci provo, rischio ♦ ADJ (*meeting, remark, error*) casuale, fortuito(-a); **a chance meeting** un incontro casuale

▸ **chance on, chance upon** VI + PREP (*person*) incontrare per caso, imbattersi in; (*thing*) trovare per caso

chan·cel [ˈtʃɑːnsəl] N coro

chan·cel·lor [ˈtʃɑːnsələʳ] N cancelliere *m*; (*of university*) rettore *m* (onorario)

chan·de·lier [ʃændəˈlɪəʳ] N lampadario
   ❑ **chandelier** is not translated by the Italian word **candeliere**

change [tʃeɪndʒ] N **1** cambiamento; **a change for the better/worse** un miglioramento/peggioramento, un mutamento per il meglio/peggio; **just for a change** tanto per cambiare; **he likes a change** gli piace cambiare; **change of address** cambiamento di indirizzo; **a change of clothes** un cambio (di vestiti); **to have a change of heart** cambiare idea; **to have a change of scene** cambiare aria; **there's been a change in the weather** il tempo è cambiato; **there's been a change of plan** c'è stato un cambiamento di programma **2** (*small coins*) moneta, spiccioli *mpl*; (*money returned*) resto; **small** or **loose change** spiccioli *mpl*; **can you give me change for £1?** mi può cambiare una sterlina?; **I haven't got any change** non ho spiccioli; **here's your change** ecco il resto; **keep the change** tenga il resto; **you don't get much change out of £20** non avanza molto da 20 sterline ♦ VT **1** (*by substitution*) cambiare; **to change hands** cambiare padrone, passare di mano; **a sum of money changed hands** c'è stato un movimento di denaro; **to change gear** (*Aut*) cambiare (marcia); **to change places** (*two people*) scambiarsi di posto; **I changed places with him** ho scambiato il mio posto con il suo, ci siamo scambiati di posto; **to change trains/buses (at)** cambiare treno/autobus (a); **to change the rein** (*Horse-riding*) cambiare di mano; **to change sides** (*Pol, etc*) cambiare bandiera; **let's change the subject** cambiamo argomento; **he wants to change his job** vuole cambiare lavoro **2** (*exchange: in shop*) cambiare; **to change ends** (*Tennis, Ftbl*) effettuare il cambio di campo **3** (*alter: person, idea*) cambiare; (*transform: person*) trasformare; (: *thing*) tramutare; **to change one's mind** cambiare idea; **I've changed my mind** ho cambiato idea **4** (*money*) cambiare; **I'd like to change £50** vorrei cambiare 50 sterline ♦ **VI 1** (*alter*) cambiare, mutare; **you've changed!** come sei cambiato!; **the town has changed a lot** la città è molto cambiata **2** (*change clothes*) cambiarsi; **to get changed** cambiarsi; **I've got to get changed** devo cambiarmi **3** (*Rail*) cambiare; **all change!** si cambia!

▸ **change down** VI + ADV (*Aut*) scalare (la marcia)

▸ **change into** VI + PREP **1** (*become*) trasformarsi in **2** (*different clothes*): **she changed into an old skirt** si è cambiata e ha messo una vecchia gonna ♦ VT + PREP: **to change sb/sth into** trasformare qn/qc in

▸ **change over** VI + ADV (*make complete change*): **to change over from sth to sth** passare da qc a qc; (*players etc*) scambiarsi (*di posto o di campo*)

▸ **change up** VI + ADV (*Aut*) cambiare, mettere una marcia superiore

change·able [ˈtʃeɪndʒəbl] ADJ (*person*) mutevole; (*weather*) mutevole, variabile

change machine N distributore *m* automatico di monete

change·over [ˈtʃeɪndʒˌəʊvə'] N cambiamento, passaggio

chang·ing [ˈtʃeɪndʒɪŋ] ADJ (*face, expression*) mutevole; (*colours*) cangiante

changing room N (*Brit: in shop*) camerino; (: *Sport*) spogliatoio; **three garments only allowed in the changing room** si possono portare solo tre articoli nel camerino

chan·nel [ˈtʃænl] N (*Geog, TV, also fig*) canale *m*; (*of river, sea*) alveo; **to go through the usual channels** seguire la normale procedura; **green/red channel** (*Customs*) uscita "niente da dichiarare"/"merci da dichiarare" ♦ VT (*hollow out: course*) scavare; (*direct: river*) far scorrere, convogliare; (*fig: interest, energies*): **to channel into** concentrare su, indirizzare verso, canalizzare

channel-hopping [ˈtʃænlhɒpɪŋ] N (*TV*) zapping *m*

Channel Islands NPL: **the Channel Islands** le Isole Normanne *or* del Canale (della Manica)

Channel Tunnel N: **the Channel Tunnel** il tunnel sotto la Manica

chant [tʃɑːnt] N (*of crowd*) slogan *m inv*; (*Rel, Mus*) canto, salmodia ♦ VT (*Rel, Mus*) cantare; (*subj: crowd*): **the demonstrators chanted their disapproval** i dimostranti lanciavano slogan di protesta ♦ VI (*see vt*) cantare, salmodiare; lanciare slogan

cha·os [ˈkeɪɒs] N caos *m*; **to be in chaos** essere nel caos

chaos theory N teoria del caos

cha·ot·ic [keɪˈɒtɪk] ADJ caotico(-a), confuso(-a)

chap¹ [tʃæp] N (*Brit fam: man*) tipo, tizio; **he's a nice chap** è un tipo simpatico; **he's the sort of chap everyone likes** è il tipo di persona che piace a tutti; **old chap** vecchio mio; **poor little chap** povero piccolo

chap² [tʃæp] N (*on lip*) screpolatura ♦ VT (*skin*) screpolare

chap·el [ˈtʃæpəl] N (*of church, school*) cappella; (*small church*) cappella, chiesetta

chap·er·one, chap·er·on [ˈʃæpəˌrəʊn] N accompagnatore(-trice) ♦ VT fare da accompagnatore(-trice), accompagnare

chap·lain [ˈtʃæplɪn] N cappellano

chapped [tʃæpt] ADJ (*skin*) screpolato(-a)

chap·ter [ˈtʃæptə'] N capitolo; **to quote chapter and verse** (*fig*) dare dei riferimenti precisi; **a chapter of accidents** una serie di imprevisti

char¹ [tʃɑː'] VT (*burn black*) carbonizzare

char² [tʃɑː'] (*Brit*) N (*charwoman*) donna a ore ♦ VI lavorare come donna a ore

char·ac·ter [ˈkærɪktə'] N (*gen, also Comput*) carattere *m*; (*in novel, play, film*) personaggio; (*eccentric*) originale *m*; **a man of character** un uomo di polso; **a person of good character** una persona a modo; **can you give me some idea of his character?** puoi descrivermi un po' il suo carattere?; **it's quite in/out of character for him to be rude** è/non è nella sua natura essere maleducato; **he's quite a character** è un tipo originale; **character reference** referenza; **Gothic characters** caratteri gotici

character code N (*Comput*) codice *m* di carattere

char·ac·ter·is·tic [ˌkærɪktəˈrɪstɪk] ADJ caratteristico(-a), tipico(-a); **characteristic of** tipico(-a) di; **with (his) characteristic enthusiasm** con l'entusiasmo che lo caratterizza ♦ N caratteristica

char·ac·ter·ize [ˈkærɪktəˌraɪz] VT **1** (*be characteristic of*) caratterizzare **2** (*describe*): **to characterize (as)** descrivere (come)

cha·rade [ʃəˈrɑːd] N **1** (*pretence*) farsa **2** **charades** NPL (*game*) sciarada *fsg*

char·coal [ˈtʃɑːkəʊl] N carbone *m* di legna; (*for sketching*) carboncino; **dark charcoal** color antracite scuro

charge [tʃɑːdʒ] N **1** (*cost*) tariffa, prezzo; **is there a charge?** c'è da pagare?; **is there a charge for delivery?** c'è qualcosa da pagare per la spedizione?; **free of charge** gratis, gratuito(-a); (*adv*) gratuitamente; **extra charge** supplemento; **monthly charge** tariffa mensile; **labour charges** costi *mpl* del lavoro; **I'd love to reverse the charges** vorrei fare una chiamata a carico del destinatario **2** (*Law*) accusa, imputazione *f*; **to bring a charge against sb** accusare qn, imputare qn; **to be on a charge of** essere accusato di; **he's on a charge of robbery** è accusato di furto; **he was arrested on a charge of murder** fu arrestato sotto accusa di omicidio **3** (*control, responsibility*): **the person in charge** il (la) responsabile; **to be in charge** essere responsabile; **who is in charge here?** chi è il responsabile qui?; **to be in charge of** essere responsabile di *or* per; **she was in charge of the group** era responsabile per il gruppo; **to take charge (of)** (*firm, situation*) assumere il controllo (di); (*project*) incaricarsi (di); **can you take charge here?** se ne occupa lei?; **to have charge of sb** aver cura di qn; **these children are my charges** questi bambini sono affidati a me **4** (*Mil: attack*) carica **5** (*Phys, Elec*) carica; **my phone is out of charge** il telefono scarico ♦ VT **1** (*price*) chiedere, far pagare; (*customer*) far pagare a; **what did they charge you for it?** quanto te l'hanno fatto pagare?; **to charge an expense to sb** addebitare una spesa a qn; **charge it to my account** lo metta *or* addebiti sul mio conto **2** (*Law*): **to charge sb (with)** accusare qn (di); **the police have charged him with murder** la polizia lo ha accusato di omicidio **3** (*gun, battery*) caricare; **I have to charge my phone** devo caricare il telefono **4** (*Mil: attack*) caricare ♦ VI (*Mil, etc*) caricare; (*fam: rush*) precipitarsi, lanciarsi; **to charge in/out** precipitarsi dentro/fuori; **to charge up/down the stairs** lanciarsi su/giù per le scale

charge account N (*USA*) conto

charge card N carta di credito commerciale

char·gé d'af·faires [ˈʃɑːʒeɪdæˈfeə'] N incaricato d'affari

charge hand N (*Brit*) caposquadra *m/f*

charg·er [ˈtʃɑːdʒə'] N (*Elec: also: battery charger*) caricabatterie *m inv*; (*old: warhorse*) destriero

char·i·ot [ˈtʃærɪət] N cocchio, carro

char·is·mat·ic [ˌkærɪzˈmætɪk] ADJ carismatico(-a)

char·i·table [ˈtʃærɪtəbl] ADJ (*organization, society*) filantropico(-a), di beneficenza; (*person*) caritatevole; (*deed*) buono(-a), di carità, caritatevole; (*remark, view*) indulgente, caritatevole

char·ity [ˈtʃærɪtɪ] N **1** (*virtue*) carità; **out of charity** per carità *or* misericordia; **to live on charity** vivere di elemosine; **charity begins at home** (*Proverb*) il primo prossimo è la tua famiglia **2** (*organization*) opera pia, associazione *f* benefica; **to collect for charity** raccogliere denaro per beneficenza

char·la·tan [ˈʃɑːlətən] N ciarlatano

charm [tʃɑːm] N (*of person*) fascino; (*of object*) incanto; (*also fig: magic spell*) incanto, incantesimo; (*on bracelet*) ciondolo; **it worked like a charm** (*fig*) ha funzionato perfettamente; **lucky charm** amuleto ♦ VT affascinare, incantare; **to lead a charmed life** essere nato(-a) con la camicia

charm bracelet N braccialetto con ciondoli

charm·ing [ˈtʃɑːmɪŋ] ADJ delizioso(-a), incantevole; **he's a charming boy** è una ragazzo delizioso; **Prince Charming** il Principe azzurro

chart [tʃɑːt] N (*table*) tabella, tavola; (*graph: Med*) grafico; (*Met: weather chart*) carta del tempo; (*Naut: map*) carta (nautica); **the chart shows the rise of unemployment** il grafico mostra l'aumento della disoccupazione; **the charts** la Hit Parade; **to be in the charts** (*record, pop group*) essere nella Hit Parade, essere in classifica; **his song has been in the charts for ten weeks** la sua canzone è nella Hit Parade da dieci settimane ♦ VT (*plot: course*) tracciare; (: *sales, progress*) tracciare il grafico di; (*Naut*) fare la carta nautica di

char·ter [ˈtʃɑːtə̆ʳ] N 1 (*document*) carta; (*of city, organization*) statuto 2 (*Naut, Aer, etc hire*) noleggio; **on charter** a nolo ♦ VT (*plane etc*) noleggiare

char·tered ac·count·ant [ˈtʃɑːtə̆dəˈkaʊntənt] N (*Brit*) ≈ commercialista *m/f*

charter flight N volo *m* charter, *inv*

char·woman [ˈtʃɑːˌwʊmən] N (*pl* -**women**) donna delle pulizie, donna a ore

chase [tʃeɪs] N inseguimento, caccia; **the chase** (*Hunting*) la caccia; **to give chase** dare la caccia, mettersi all'inseguimento; **a car chase** un inseguimento in macchina ♦ VT inseguire; **the policeman chased the thief** il poliziotto ha inseguito il ladro ♦ VI: **to chase after sb** correre dietro a qn

▸ **chase away, chase off** VT + ADV cacciare via

▸ **chase up** (*Brit*), **chase down** (*USA*) VT + ADV (*information*) scoprire, raccogliere; (*person*) scovare

chasm [ˈkæzəm] N voragine *f*, abisso

chas·sis [ˈʃæsɪ] N (*Aut*) telaio

chas·tened [ˈtʃeɪsnd] ADJ abbattuto(-a), provato(-a)

chas·ten·ing [ˈtʃeɪsnɪŋ] ADJ che fa riflettere

chas·tise [tʃæsˈtaɪz] VT (*frm: punish*) punire, castigare

chas·tity [ˈtʃæstɪtɪ] N castità

chat [tʃæt] N chiacchierata; **to have a chat** fare quattro chiacchiere, fare una chiacchierata ♦ VI: **to chat** (**with** *or* **to**) chiacchierare (con); **I was chatting to my neighbour** stavo chiacchierando con il mio vicino

▸ **chat up** VT + ADV (*Brit fam*) agganciare, abbordare

chat room N (*Comput*) chat line *f inv*

chat·tel [ˈtʃætl] N *see* goods

chat·ter [ˈtʃætə̆ʳ] N (*talk*) parlottio, chiacchiere *fpl*, ciarle *fpl* ♦ VI (*person*) chiacchierare, ciarlare; (*birds*) cinguettare; **her teeth were chattering** batteva i denti

chatter·box [ˈtʃætəˌbɒks] N (*fam*) chiacchierone(-a)

chat·ter·ing classes [ˈtʃætərɪŋˈklɑːsɪz] NPL: **the chattering classes** (*fam, pej*) gli intellettualoidi

chat·ty [ˈtʃætɪ] ADJ (*person*) ciarliero(-a); (*style*) familiare; **a chatty letter** una lettera scritta in tono cordiale e informale

chauf·feur [ˈʃəʊfə̆ʳ] N autista *m/f*

chau·vin·ism [ˈʃəʊvɪˌnɪzəm] N (*male chauvinism*) maschilismo; (*nationalism*) sciovinismo

chau·vin·ist [ˈʃəʊvɪnɪst] N (*male chauvinist*) maschilista *m*; (*nationalist*) sciovinista *m/f*; (**male**) **chauvinist pig** (*fam, pej*) sporco maschilista

chau·vin·is·tic [ˌʃəʊvɪˈnɪstɪk] ADJ (*jingoistic*) sciovinistico(-a); (*sexist*) maschilista

cheap [tʃiːp] ADJ (*comp* -**er**, *superl* -**est**) (*low cost: goods*) a buon mercato, a basso *or* buon prezzo, economico(-a); (*reduced*: *ticket*) a prezzo ridotto; (: *fare*) ridotto(-a); (*poor quality*) scadente, di cattiva qualità; (*vulgar, mean: joke, behaviour, trick*) volgare, grossolano(-a), dozzinale; **cheap flight** volo economico; **it was cheap at the price** sono stati soldi ben spesi; **cheaper** meno caro(-a), più economico(-a); **the bus is cheaper** l'autobus è più economico; **the cheapest seats are £5** i posti più economici vengono cinque sterline; **cheap money** (*Fin*) denaro a basso tasso di interesse; **to feel cheap** (**about**) provare vergogna *or* vergognarsi (di *or* per) ♦ ADV a buon prezzo *or* mercato ♦ N: **on the cheap** (*fam*) a risparmio

cheap day return N biglietto ridotto di andata e ritorno valido in giornata

cheap·en [ˈtʃiːpən] VT: **to cheapen o.s.** svendersi, screditarsi

cheap·ly [ˈtʃiːplɪ] ADV a buon prezzo, a buon mercato

cheat [tʃiːt] N (*deception*) imbroglio, truffa; (*person*) imbroglione(-a), truffatore(-trice) ♦ VT imbrogliare, truffare; (*rob*) soffiare, fregare; **to cheat sb out of sth** fregare qc a qn; **I was cheated out of the job** mi è stato soffiato il lavoro ♦ VI (*at games*) barare, imbrogliare; (*in exam*) copiare; **you're cheating!** stai imbrogliando!; **he's been cheating on his wife** ha tradito sua moglie

cheat·ing [ˈtʃiːtɪŋ] N truffe *fpl*, imbrogli *mpl*

Chechnya [tʃɪtʃˈnjaː] N Cecenia

check [tʃek] N 1 (*inspection*) controllo, verifica; **a thorough check** un controllo accurato; **to keep a check on sb/sth** controllare qn/qc, fare attenzione a qn/qc 2 (*control, restraint*) limitazione *f*; **to hold** *or* **keep sb/sth in check** tenere qn/qc sotto controllo; **to act as a check on sth** fare da freno a qc 3 (*Chess*): **in check** in scacco; **check!** scacco (al re)! 4 (*USA: bill*) conto; (: *receipt*) scontrino 5 (*USA*) = **cheque 6 checks** (*pattern*) quadretti *mpl*, quadri *mpl*, scacchi *mpl* ♦ VT 1 (*examine: facts, figures*) verificare; (: *passport, ticket, tyres* *or* *tires, oil*) controllare; **could you check the oil, please?** può controllare l'olio, per favore? 2 (*stop, halt*) bloccare, fermare, arrestare; (*restrain*) contenere, frenare, controllare; **to check o.s.** frenarsi, controllarsi, contenersi 3 (*USA: tick*) spuntare ♦ VI controllare; **to check with sb** chiedere a qn; **I'll check with the driver what time the bus leaves** chiederò al conducente quando parte l'autobus; (*official etc*) informarsi presso qn ♦ ADJ (*also*: **checked**: *pattern, cloth*) a scacchi, a quadretti, a quadri

▸ **check in** VI + ADV (*at airport*) fare il check-in; (*at hotel: arrive*) arrivare; (: *register*) firmare il registro ♦ VT + ADV (*luggage*) registrare, fare il check-in di

▸ **check off** VT + ADV controllare, spuntare

▸ **check on** VI + PREP (*facts, dates*) controllare, verificare; (*fam: person*) informarsi su

▸ **check out** VI + ADV (*from hotel*) lasciare la camera e saldare il conto ♦ VT + ADV 1 (*luggage*) ritirare 2 (*investigate: story*) controllare, verificare; (: *fam: person*) prendere informazioni su; **check it out** vedi di che si tratta

▸ **check up** VI + ADV controllare

▸ **check up on** VI + ADV + PREP (*story*) controllare, verificare; (*person*) controllare; **to check up (on sth)** investigare (qc)

check·book [ˈtʃekˌbʊk] N (*USA*) = **chequebook**

check·ered [ˈtʃekəd] ADJ (*USA*) = **chequered**

check·ers [ˈtʃekəz] NPL (*USA*) dama

check guarantee card N (*USA*) carta *f* assegni, *inv*

check-in [ˈtʃekˌɪn] N (*also*: **check-in desk**: *at airport*) check-in *m inv*, accettazione *f* bagagli, *inv*

check·ing ac·count [ˈtʃekɪŋəˈkaʊnt] N (*USA*) conto corrente

check·list [ˈtʃekˌlɪst] N lista di controllo

check·mate [ˈtʃekˌmeɪt] N (*in chess, also fig*) scacco matto, scaccomatto ♦ VT dare scacco matto a; (*fig*) bloccare

check·out [ˈtʃekˌaʊt] N (*in supermarket*) cassa

check·point [ˈtʃekˌpɔɪnt] N posto di blocco

check·room [ˈtʃekˌrʊm] N (*USA: for coats*) guardaroba *m inv*; (*for luggage*) deposito *m* bagagli, *inv*

check·up [ˈtʃekˌʌp] N (*Med*) check-up *m inv*, controllo medico globale; **to have a checkup** fare una visita di controllo

ched·dar [ˈtʃedə̆ʳ] N (*also*: **cheddar cheese**) *tipo di formaggio*

cheek [tʃiːk] N 1 guancia; (*fam: buttock*) natica; **to dance cheek to cheek** ballare guancia a guancia; **a kiss on the cheek** un bacio sulla guancia; **cheek by jowl** gomito a gomito 2 (*fam: impudence*) faccia tosta, sfacciataggine *f*; **what a cheek!** che faccia tosta! ♦ VT essere sfacciato(-a) con

cheek·bone [ˈtʃiːkˌbəʊn] N zigomo

cheeky [ˈtʃiːkɪ] ADJ sfacciato(-a), impudente; **don't be cheeky!** non essere sfacciato(-a)!

cheep [tʃiːp] N (*of bird*) pigolio ♦ VI pigolare

cheer [tʃɪə̆ʳ] N (*shout*) evviva *m inv*; (*applause*) applauso; **three cheers for the winner!** tre urrà per il vincitore! ♦ VT 1 (*applaud: winner etc*) applaudire 2 (*gladden*) rallegrare ♦ VI applaudire

▸ **cheer on** VT + ADV (*person*) incitare

▸ **cheer up** VI + ADV rallegrarsi, farsi animo; **cheer up!** coraggio!, su con la vita! ♦ VT + ADV rallegrare, tirar su di morale; **to cheer sb up** tirare qn su di morale; **I was trying to cheer him up** cercavo di tirarlo su di morale

cheer·ful [ˈtʃɪəfʊl] ADJ allegro(-a)
cheer·ful·ness [ˈtʃɪəfʊlnɪs] N allegria
cheerio [ˌtʃɪərɪˈəʊ] EXCL (Brit fam) ciao!
cheer·leader [ˈtʃɪəˌliːdəʳ] N cheerleader f inv
cheer·less [ˈtʃɪəlɪs] ADJ (atmosphere) triste; (room, place) desolato(-a)
cheese [tʃiːz] N formaggio; **say cheese!** (Phot) sorridi!
cheese·board [ˈtʃiːzˌbɔːd] N piatto portaformaggio
cheese·burg·er [ˈtʃiːzˌbɜːgəʳ] N cheeseburger m inv, hamburger m inv al formaggio
cheese·cake [ˈtʃiːzˌkeɪk] N torta al formaggio, a volte con frutta
chee·tah [ˈtʃiːtə] N ghepardo
chef [ʃef] N chef m inv, capocuoco
chemi·cal [ˈkemɪkəl] ADJ chimico(-a) ♦ N prodotto chimico
chemical engineering N ingegneria chimica
chem·ist [ˈkemɪst] N (Brit: pharmacist) farmacista m/f; (scientist) chimico(-a); **chemist's (shop)** (Brit) farmacia
chem·is·try [ˈkemɪstrɪ] N chimica; **chemistry lab** laboratorio di chimica
chemo [ˈkiːməʊ] N (fam) chemio f inv
chemo·thera·py [ˌkeməʊˈθerəpɪ] N chemioterapia
cheque, check (USA) [tʃek] N assegno; **a cheque for £20** un assegno di 20 sterline; **he wrote a cheque** ha fatto un assegno; **to pay by cheque** pagare per assegno or con un assegno; **can I pay by cheque?** posso pagare con un assegno?
cheque·book, check·book (USA) [ˈtʃekˌbʊk] N libretto degli assegni
cheque card N (Brit) carta f assegni, inv
chequ·ered, check·ered (USA) [ˈtʃekəd] ADJ a scacchi, a quadretti, a quadri; (fig) movimentato(-a); **a chequered career** una carriera movimentata
cher·ish [ˈtʃerɪʃ] VT (person) avere caro(-a); (hope etc) nutrire; **I cherish the memory of it** ne conservo un caro ricordo
che·root [ʃəˈruːt] N sigaro spuntato
cher·ry [ˈtʃerɪ] N. (fruit) ciliegia; (cherry tree) ciliegio ♦ ADJ (pie, jam) di ciliegie
chess [tʃes] N scacchi mpl; **he likes playing chess** gli piace giocare a scacchi
chess·board [ˈtʃesˌbɔːd] N scacchiera
chess·man [ˈtʃesˌmæn] N (pl -men) pezzo (degli scacchi)
chess·player [ˈtʃesˌpleɪəʳ] N scacchista m/f
chest [tʃest] N 1 (Anat) petto, torace m; **I've got a pain in my chest** ho un dolore al petto; **to get sth off one's chest** (fam) togliersi un peso (dallo stomaco), alleggerirsi or scaricarsi la coscienza 2 (box) cassa m, cassa, cassapanca
chest measurement N giro m torace, inv
chest·nut [ˈtʃesˌnʌt] N (fruit) castagna; (chestnut tree) castagno; **sweet chestnut** (tree) castagno comune or dolce ♦ ADJ (hair) castano(-a); (horse) sauro(-a)
chest of drawers N comò m inv, cassettone m
chew [tʃuː] VT masticare; **to chew the cud** ruminare
  ▸ **chew over** VT + ADV rimuginare su
  ▸ **chew up** VT + ADV mangiucchiare
chew·ing gum [ˈtʃuːɪŋˌgʌm] N chewing-gum m inv, gomma (americana or da masticare)
chic [ʃiːk] ADJ chic inv, elegante
chick [tʃɪk] N (baby bird) piccolo (di volatile), uccellino; (baby hen) pulcino; (fam) pollastrella
chick·en [ˈtʃɪkɪn] N pollo; (fam: coward) coniglio; **don't count your chickens before they're hatched** (Proverb) non dire quattro finché non l'hai nel sacco ♦ ADJ (stock, breast, liver) di pollo; (farmer, farming) di polli; **chicken leg** coscia di pollo
  ▸ **chicken out** VI + ADV (fam) avere fifa; **to chicken out of sth** tirarsi indietro da qc per fifa or paura
chicken feed N (fig): **he earns chicken feed** guadagna una miseria
chicken·pox [ˈtʃɪkɪnˌpɒks] N varicella
chick flick N (fam) filmetto rosa
chick·pea [ˈtʃɪkˌpiː] N cece m
chico·ry [ˈtʃɪkərɪ] N cicoria
chide [tʃaɪd] VT riprendere, rimproverare
chief [tʃiːf] N (principal: reason etc) principale; (in rank) capo inv; **his chief reason for resigning was the low pay**

la ragione principale per cui si è licenziato è lo stipendio basso; **chief steward** (Aer) commissario di bordo ♦ N capo; **chief of security** capo della sicurezza
Chief Constable N (Brit) ≈ questore m
chief executive, chief executive officer N direttore m generale
chief·ly [ˈtʃiːflɪ] ADV principalmente, per lo più
chief operating officer N direttore(-trice), operativo(-a), (operativa)
chif·fon [ˈʃɪfɒn] N chiffon m inv ♦ ADJ di chiffon
chil·blain [ˈtʃɪlˌbleɪn] N gelone m
child [tʃaɪld] N (pl children) (gen) bambino(-a); (son/daughter) figlio(-a), bambino(-a); **a child of six** un bambino di sei anni; **I like children** mi piacciono i bambini; **Susan is our eldest child** Susan è la nostra figlia maggiore; **they've got three children** hanno tre figli
child abuse N molestie fpl a minori
child abuser [ˈtʃaɪldəˈbjuːzəʳ] N molestatore(-trice) di bambini
child benefit N (Brit) ≈ assegni mpl familiari
child·birth [ˈtʃaɪldˌbɜːθ] N parto; **to die in childbirth** morire di parto
child·hood [ˈtʃaɪldhʊd] N infanzia; **from childhood** fin dall'infanzia, fin da piccolo(-a)
child·ish [ˈtʃaɪldɪʃ] ADJ (pej) infantile, puerile
child·less [ˈtʃaɪldlɪs] ADJ senza figli
child·like [ˈtʃaɪldˌlaɪk] ADJ ingenuo(-a), innocente
child prodigy N bambino(-a) prodigio inv
chil·dren [ˈtʃɪldrən] NPL of **child**
children's home N istituto per l'infanzia (abbandonata o maltrattata)
Chile [ˈtʃɪlɪ] N Cile m
Chil·ean [ˈtʃɪlɪən] ADJ, N cileno(-a)
chill [tʃɪl] ADJ (wind) freddo(-a), gelido(-a) ♦ N freddo; (Med) infreddatura, colpo di freddo; **there's a chill in the air** l'aria è fredda; **to take the chill off (a room)** riscaldare un po' (una stanza); **to catch a chill** (Med) prendere un colpo di freddo ♦ VT (food, drink) mettere in fresco; **"serve chilled"** "servire fresco"; **to chill sb's blood** (fig) far gelare il sangue a qn; **to be chilled to the bone** essere gelato(-a) fino alle ossa
  ▸ **chill out** VI (esp USA: fam) darsi una calmata
chilli, chili (USA) [ˈtʃɪlɪ] N peperoncino; **chilli con carne** piatto di carne macinata e fagioli con il peperoncino
chill·ing [ˈtʃɪlɪŋ] ADJ (story, thought) agghiacciante; (wind) gelido(-a)
chil·ly [ˈtʃɪlɪ] ADJ (weather, room) fresco(-a), freddo(-a); (fig: person, look, reception) freddo(-a), gelido(-a); (sensitive to cold) freddoloso(-a); **I feel chilly** ho or sento freddo, sono or mi sento infreddolito
chime [tʃaɪm] N rintocco ♦ VT, VI suonare
  ▸ **chime in** VI + ADV (fam: interrupt, join in) intervenire; (: echo) fare eco, far coro
chim·ney [ˈtʃɪmnɪ] N (of house) camino; (of factory) ciminiera
chimney sweep N spazzacamino
chim·pan·zee [ˌtʃɪmpænˈziː] N scimpanzé m inv
chin [tʃɪn] N mento; **(keep your) chin up!** (fam) coraggio!, testa alta!
Chi·na [ˈtʃaɪnə] N Cina; **People's Republic of China** Repubblica Popolare Cinese
chi·na [ˈtʃaɪnə] N (porcelain) porcellana; (dishes) porcellane fpl ♦ ADJ di porcellana; **a china plate** un piatto di porcellana
Chi·nese [ˈtʃaɪˈniːz] ADJ cinese ♦ N (person: pl inv) cinese m/f; (language) cinese m; **the Chinese** i cinesi
chink¹ [tʃɪŋk] N (opening) fessura; **a chink in the curtains** una fessura tra le tende; **a chink in his armour** (fig) il suo punto debole
chink² [tʃɪŋk] N (noise) tintinnio; **the chink of glasses** il tintinnio dei bicchieri ♦ VT far tintinnare ♦ VI tintinnare
chip [tʃɪp] N 1 (piece) frammento; (of glass, wood, stone) scheggia; **he's a chip off the old block** (fig) è della stessa razza del padre; **he's got a chip on his shoulder because** ... gli è rimasto sullo stomaco il fatto che... 2 (gen pl: Culin: Brit: French fry) patatina fritta; (: USA: crisp) patatina; **potato chips** (USA) patatine fpl 3 (in crockery, furniture) scheggiatura; **there's a chip in this cup** questa tazza è scheggiata

4 (*in gambling*) fiche *f inv*; **when the chips are down** (*fig*) nei momenti critici, nel momento della verità, alla resa dei conti; **to have had one's chips** (*fig: fam*) aver giocato l'ultima carta **5** (*Comput: microchip*) chip *m inv* ♦ VT (*cup, plate*) scheggiare; **chipped potatoes** (*Culin*) patatine *fpl* fritte ♦ VI scheggiarsi

▸ **chip in** VI + ADV (*fam: contribute*) contribuire; (: *interrupt*) intromettersi

▸ **chip off** VI + ADV (*paint*) scrostarsi ♦ VT + ADV (*paint*) scrostare

chip·board [ˈtʃɪpˌbɔːd] N truciolato, agglomerato

chip·munk [ˈtʃɪpˌmʌŋk] N tamia *m* striato

chip·pings [ˈtʃɪpɪŋz] NPL: **loose chippings** brecciame *msg*

chip shop N (*also:* **fish-and-chip shop**) friggitoria

chi·ropo·dist [kɪˈrɒpədɪst] N (*Brit*) callista *m/f*, podiatra *m/f*

chi·ropo·dy [kɪˈrɒpədɪ] N (*Brit*) chiropodia, podiatria, mestiere *m* di callista

chirp [tʃɜːp], **chir·rup** [ˈtʃɪrəp] N (*of birds*) cinguettio; (*of crickets*) cri cri *m* ♦ VI (*see n*) cinguettare; fare cri cri

chirpy [ˈtʃɜːpɪ] ADJ (*fam*) pimpante, frizzante

chis·el [ˈtʃɪzl] N scalpello; (*smaller*) cesello; (*for engraving*) bulino ♦ VT (*pt, pp* **chiselled** *or* **chiseled**) (*USA*) *also:* **chisel out**) scolpire; cesellare; incidere con il bulino

chit [tʃɪt] N nota *f* spese, *inv*

chit·chat [ˈtʃɪtˌtʃæt] N (*fam*) chiacchiere *fpl*

chiv·al·rous [ˈʃɪvəlrəs] ADJ cavalleresco(-a)

chiv·al·ry [ˈʃɪvəlrɪ] N cavalleria

chives [ˈtʃaɪvz] NPL erba cipollina

chlo·ride [ˈklɔːraɪd] N (*Chem*) cloruro

chlo·rin·ate [ˈklɒrɪneɪt] VT clorare

chlo·rine [ˈklɔːriːn] N cloro

chock [tʃɒk] N cuneo

chock-a-block [ˈtʃɒkəˈblɒk] ADJ: **chock-a-block (with)** pieno(-a) zeppo(-a) (di)

choco·late [ˈtʃɒklɪt] N (*substance*) cioccolato, cioccolata; (*individual sweet*) cioccolatino; (*drink*) cioccolata; **hot** *or* **drinking chocolate** cioccolata (calda); **a box of chocolates** una scatola di cioccolatini ♦ ADJ (*biscuit, cake*) al cioccolato; (*egg*) di cioccolato; (*colour*) (color) cioccolato *inv*; **chocolate cake** torta al cioccolato

choice [tʃɔɪs] N scelta; **he's not really my choice** non è proprio quello che sceglierei io; **I did it by** *or* **from choice** l'ho fatto di mia volontà *or* per mia scelta; **a wide choice** un'ampia scelta; **I had no choice** non avevo scelta; **she had no choice but to go** non aveva altra scelta che andare; **take your choice!** scegli pure!; **the treatment/weapon of choice** la cura/l'arma preferita ♦ ADJ (*fruit, wine*) di prima scelta; (*hum: example, remark*) bello(-a); **his language was really choice!** il suo tono non era esattamente garbato!

choir [ˈkwaɪəʳ] N coro

choir·boy [ˈkwaɪəˌbɔɪ] N corista *m* (*ragazzo*)

choke [tʃəʊk] N (*Aut*) (valvola dell')aria ♦ VT (*person*) soffocare; (*strangle*) strangolare; (*also:* **choke up**: *pipe*) intasare ♦ VI **1** soffocare; **help him, he's choking!** aiutatelo, sta soffocando! **2** (*fam: lose confidence*) farsi prendere dalla sfiducia

▸ **choke back** VT + ADV soffocare

chol·era [ˈkɒlərə] N colera *m*

cho·les·ter·ol [kəˈlestərɒl] N colesterolo

choose [tʃuːz] (*pt* chose, *pp* chosen) VT scegliere; **she chose a career as a soloist** ha scelto una carriera da solista; **to choose to do sth** scegliere *or* decidere di fare qc ♦ VI scegliere; **to choose between** scegliere tra; **there is nothing to choose between them** uno vale l'altro; **I don't know which to choose** non so quale scegliere; **have you already chosen?** hai già scelto?; **to choose from** scegliere da *or* tra; **there were several to choose from** vi era parecchia scelta; **as/when I choose** come/quando voglio *or* decido io

choosy [ˈtʃuːzɪ] ADJ (*comp* **-ier**, *superl* **-iest**) (*fam*): **to be choosy** fare lo (la) schizzinoso(-a) *or* difficile

chop [tʃɒp] N **1** (*blow*) colpo secco, colpo netto; **to get the chop** (*Brit fam: project*) essere bocciato(-a); (: *person: be sacked*) essere licenziato(-a) **2** (*Culin*) costoletta; **pork chop** cotoletta di maiale ♦ VT (*wood*) tagliare, spaccare; (*meat, vegetables*) tagliare (a pezzetti)

▸ **chop down** VT + ADV (*tree*) abbattere

▸ **chop off** VT + ADV tagliare (via)

▸ **chop up** VT + ADV (*wood*) spaccare; (*vegetables, meat*) tagliare (a pezzetti)

choppy [ˈtʃɒpɪ] ADJ (*sea*) mosso(-a)

chopsticks [ˈtʃɒpstɪks] NPL bastoncini *mpl* cinesi

choral [ˈkɔːrəl] ADJ corale

chord [kɔːd] N (*Mus*) accordo; (*Geom*) corda; **to touch the right chord** (*fig*) toccare il tasto giusto

chore [tʃɔːʳ] N faccenda; (*pej*) rottura; **household chores** faccende *fpl* (domestiche); **to do the chores** sbrigare *or* fare le faccende; **doing your homework is a bit of a chore** fare i compiti è un po' una scocciatura

cho·reog·ra·pher [ˌkɒrɪˈɒɡrəfəʳ] N coreografo(-a)

cho·reog·ra·phy [ˌkɒrɪˈɒɡrəfɪ] N coreografia

chor·is·ter [ˈkɒrɪstəʳ] N (*Rel*) corista *m/f*

chor·tle [ˈtʃɔːtl] VI ridacchiare, fare risolini

cho·rus [ˈkɔːrəs] N **1** (*musical work, people*) coro; **in chorus** in coro **2** (*refrain, also fig*) ritornello; **everyone joined in the chorus** tutti cantarono insieme il ritornello ♦ VT (*answer*) rispondere in coro

chose [tʃəʊz] PT *of* choose

cho·sen [ˈtʃəʊzn] PP *of* choose ♦ ADJ: **the chosen (people)** gli eletti

chow·der [ˈtʃaʊdəʳ] N (*esp USA: Culin*) zuppa di pesce

Christ [kraɪst] N Cristo

chris·ten [ˈkrɪsn] VT battezzare

chris·ten·ing [ˈkrɪsnɪŋ] N battesimo

Chris·tian [ˈkrɪstɪən] ADJ cristiano(-a); (*also:* **christian**, *fig*) caritatevole ♦ N cristiano(-a)

Chris·ti·an·ity [ˌkrɪstɪˈænɪtɪ] N cristianesimo

Christian name N nome *m* (di battesimo)

Christ·mas [ˈkrɪsməs] N Natale *m*; **at Christmas** a Natale; **Happy** *or* **Merry Christmas!** Buon Natale! ♦ ADJ (*tree, cake, present, party*) di Natale

Christmas card N biglietto di auguri natalizi

Christmas carol N canto natalizio

Christmas Day N il giorno di Natale

Christmas dec·o·ra·tions N addobbi natalizi

Christmas Eve N la vigilia di Natale

Christmas Island N Isola Christmas

Christmas pudding [ˈkrɪsməsˈpʊdɪŋ] N *dolce con frutta secca e spezie cotto a vapore e servito tradizionalmente al termine del pranzo di Natale*

Christmas tree N albero di Natale

chro·mium [ˈkrəʊmɪəm], **chrome** [krəʊm] N cromo; (*also:* **chromium plating**) cromatura

chro·mo·some [ˈkrəʊməsəʊm] N cromosoma *m*

chron·ic [ˈkrɒnɪk] ADJ (*invalid, disease*) cronico(-a); (*fig: liar, drunkard*) incallito(-a); (*fam: weather, actor etc*) allucinante; **chronic back pain** mal di schiena cronico; **a chronic problem** un grave problema

chroni·cle [ˈkrɒnɪkl] N cronaca

chrono·logi·cal [ˌkrɒnəˈlɒdʒɪkəl] ADJ cronologico(-a); **in chronological order** in ordine cronologico

chry·san·themum [krɪˈsænθəməm] N crisantemo

chub·by [ˈtʃʌbɪ] ADJ paffuto(-a), grassoccio(-a)

chuck [tʃʌk] VT (*fam*) **1** (*throw*) gettare **2** (*also:* **chuck away**) buttare, gettare; **I chucked the letter in the bin** ho gettato la lettera nella spazzatura **3** (*also:* **chuck up**, **chuck in**: *job*) piantare **4** (*boyfriend, girlfriend*) piantare

▸ **chuck out** VT + ADV (*fam: useless article*) buttare via; (: *person*) sbattere *or* buttare fuori; **you should chuck that stuff out** dovresti buttar via quella roba

chuck·le [ˈtʃʌkl] N risolino ♦ VI ridacchiare; **to chuckle at** *or* **over** ridere *or* ridacchiare per

chug [tʃʌɡ] VI **1** (*boat*) sbuffare; (*motor*) scoppiettare **2** (*also:* **chug along**: *boat*) muoversi sbuffando

chum [tʃʌm] N (*fam*) compagno(-a), amicone(-a)

chump [tʃʌmp] N (*fam*) zuccone(-a)

chunk [tʃʌŋk] N (*bel*) pezzo; (*of bread*) tocco; **cut the meat into chunks** taglia la carne a grossi pezzi

chunky [ˈtʃʌŋkɪ] ADJ (*comp* **-ier**, *superl* **-iest**) (*furniture etc*) basso(-a) e largo(-a); (*person*) ben piantato(-a); (*knitwear*) di lana grossa

Chun·nel [ˈtʃʌnəl] N (*fam*) = Channel Tunnel

church [tʃɜːtʃ] N chiesa; **to go to church** andare in chiesa; **after church** dopo la funzione; (*for Catholics*) dopo la messa; **to enter the Church** prendere gli ordini

church·yard [ˈtʃɜːtʃjɑːd] N cimitero (*annesso a una chiesa*)

churl·ish [ˈtʃɜːlɪʃ] ADJ rozzo(-a), sgarbato(-a)

churn [tʃɜːn] N (*for butter*) zangola; (*Brit: for milk*) bidone *m* per il latte ◆ VT (*butter*) fare (nella zangola); (*fig: also:* **churn up:** *water*) agitare ◆ VI (*water*) agitarsi; (*stomach*) torcersi; **his stomach was churning** aveva il voltastomaco
> **churn out** VT + ADV (*often pej*) sfornare in gran quantità

chute [ʃuːt] N 1 (*for parcels, coal, in swimming pool*) scivolo; (*also:* **rubbish chute**) canale *m* di scarico 2 (*fam*) = **parachute**

chut·ney [ˈtʃʌtnɪ] N salsa piccante (di frutta, zucchero e spezie)

CIA [ˌsiːaɪˈeɪ] N ABBR (*USA:* = *Central Intelligence Agency*) CIA *f*

ci·der [ˈsaɪdəʳ] N sidro

ci·gar [sɪˈɡɑːʳ] N sigaro

ciga·rette [ˌsɪɡəˈret] N sigaretta; **he's smoking a cigarette** sta fumando una sigaretta

cigarette case N portasigarette *m inv*

cigarette end N mozzicone *m* (di sigaretta), cicca

cigarette holder N bocchino

cigarette lighter N accendino

C-in-C ABBR = commander in chief

cinch [sɪntʃ] N (*fam*): **it's a cinch** (*easy thing*) è una cretinata *or* una sciocchezza, è presto fatto; (*sure thing*) è una cosa sicura

cin·der [ˈsɪndəʳ] N cenere *f*, brace *f*; **burned to a cinder** (*fig: food*) carbonizzato(-a)

Cinderella [ˌsɪndəˈrelə] N Cenerentola

cin·ema [ˈsɪnəmə] N cinema *m inv*

cin·na·mon [ˈsɪnəmən] N cannella

ci·pher [ˈsaɪfəʳ] N (*code*) codice *m* (cifrato); (*Math*) zero; (*fig: faceless employee etc*) persona di nessun conto, nullità *f inv*; **in cipher** in codice

circa [ˈsɜːkə] PREP circa

cir·cle [ˈsɜːkl] N (*gen*) cerchio; (*of friends etc*) circolo; (*in theatre, cinema*): **the circle** la galleria; **great/small circle** (*Geom*) cerchio massimo/minore; **to stand in a circle** mettersi in cerchio; **we stood in a circle** ci siamo messi in cerchio; **in some circles** in certi ambienti; **she moves in wealthy circles** frequenta l'alta società; **the family circle** la cerchia familiare; **to come full circle** (*fig*) ritornare al punto di partenza; **to go round in circles** (*fam*) girare sempre attorno allo stesso punto ◆ VT (*surround*) accerchiare, circondare; (*move round*) girare attorno *or* intorno a; (*draw round*) segnare con un cerchio, cerchiare ◆ VI girare in circolo

cir·cuit [ˈsɜːkɪt] N (*journey around*) giro; (*Sport, Elec*) circuito; (*of judge*) distretto giudiziario; (*Cine*) rete *f* di distribuzione

circuit board N (*Elec*) piastra; (*Comput*) tavola dei circuiti

cir·cui·tous [sɜːˈkjuːɪtəs] ADJ: **to go by a circuitous route** prendere la strada più lunga

cir·cu·lar [ˈsɜːkjʊləʳ] ADJ circolare ◆ N (*letter*) circolare *f*; (*as advertisement*) volantino pubblicitario

cir·cu·late [ˈsɜːkjʊleɪt] VI (*gen*) circolare; (*person: socially*) girare e andare un po' da tutti ◆ VT far circolare; **they are circulating a petition** stanno facendo circolare una petizione

cir·cu·lat·ing capi·tal [ˈsɜːkjʊˌleɪtɪŋˈkæpɪtl] N (*Comm*) capitale *m* d'esercizio

cir·cu·la·tion [ˌsɜːkjʊˈleɪʃən] N (*gen*) circolazione *f*; (*of news*) diffusione *f*; (*of newspaper etc*) tiratura; **she has poor circulation** (*Med*) ha una cattiva circolazione; **to withdraw sth from circulation** togliere *or* ritirare qc dalla circolazione; **the newspaper has a circulation of around 8000** il giornale ha una tiratura di circa 8000 copie; **he's back in circulation** (*fam*) è tornato in circolazione

cir·cum·cise [ˈsɜːkəmsaɪz] VT circoncidere

cir·cum·fer·ence [səˈkʌmfərəns] N circonferenza

cir·cum·flex [ˈsɜːkəmfleks] N (*also:* **circumflex accent**) accento circonflesso

cir·cum·scribe [ˈsɜːkəmskraɪb] VT (*limit*) limitare; (*Math*) circoscrivere

cir·cum·spect [ˈsɜːkəmspekt] ADJ circospetto(-a)

cir·cum·stances [ˈsɜːkəmstənsɪz] NPL 1 (*conditions*) circostanze *fpl*; **in the circumstances** date le circostanze; **under no circumstances** in nessun caso 2 (*financial state*) condizioni *fpl* finanziarie; **to be in easy/poor circumstances** trovarsi in buone/cattive condizioni finanziarie

cir·cum·stan·tial [ˌsɜːkəmˈstænʃəl] ADJ (*report, statement*) circostanziato(-a), dettagliato(-a)

cir·cum·vent [ˌsɜːkəmˈvent] VT (*frm: rule etc*) aggirare

cir·cus [ˈsɜːkəs] N (*entertainment*) circo; (*street name*): **Circus** piazza (*di forma circolare*)

cir·rho·sis [sɪˈrəʊsɪs] N (*also:* **cirrhosis of the liver**) cirrosi *f inv* (epatica)

cis·sy [ˈsɪsɪ] N (*Brit: fam*) femminuccia

cis·tern [ˈsɪstən] N serbatoio, cisterna; (*in toilet*) serbatoio d'acqua

ci·ta·tion [saɪˈteɪʃən] N citazione *f*

cite [saɪt] VT citare; **he was cited to appear in court** (*Law*) fu citato in tribunale; **to cite as an example** portare come esempio

citi·zen [ˈsɪtɪzn] N (*of state*) cittadino(-a); (*of city*) abitante *m/f*; **the citizens of this town** gli abitanti di questa città

citi·zen·ship [ˈsɪtɪznʃɪp] N cittadinanza

cit·ric acid [ˌsɪtrɪkˈæsɪd] N acido citrico

cit·rus fruit [ˈsɪtrəsˌfruːt] N agrume *m*

city [ˈsɪtɪ] N (grande) città *f inv* ◆ ADJ (*centre*) della città; (*life*) di città

city centre N (*Brit*) centro (città)

City Hall N (*USA*) ≈ Comune *m*

civ·ic [ˈsɪvɪk] ADJ civico(-a)

civic centre N (*Brit*) centro civico

civ·il [ˈsɪvl] ADJ 1 (*war, law, marriage*) civile 2 (*polite*) educato(-a), gentile

civil disobedience N resistenza passiva

civil engineer N ingegnere *m* civile

civil engineering N ingegneria civile

ci·vil·ian [sɪˈvɪlɪən] ADJ (*clothes, government*) civile, borghese; (*life*) da civile, da borghese ◆ N civile *m/f*, borghese *m/f*

civi·li·za·tion [ˌsɪvɪlaɪˈzeɪʃən] N civiltà *f inv*

civi·lized [ˈsɪvɪlaɪzd] ADJ (*country, society*) civilizzato(-a), progredito(-a); (*behaviour, manner*) civile, cortese; **in civilized countries** nei paesi civilizzati

civil law N codice *m* civile; (*study*) diritto civile

civil liberties NPL libertà *fpl* civili

civil rights NPL diritti *mpl* civili

civil servant N impiegato(-a) statale

civil service N: **the Civil Service** l'amministrazione *f* pubblica

civil war N guerra civile

civ·vies [ˈsɪvɪz] NPL (*fam*): **in civvies** in borghese

CJD [ˌsiːdʒeɪˈdiː] N (*Med:* = *Creutzfeldt-Jacob Disease*) malattia di Creutzfeldt-Jacob

cl ABBR (= *centilitre*) cl

clad [klæd] ADJ (*old, liter*) vestito(-a); **clad in** vestito(-a) di

claim [kleɪm] N 1 (*demand: to title, right*) pretesa, diritto; (: *for expenses, damages, increased pay*) richiesta; (: *insurance claim*) domanda d'indennizzo; **the poor have a claim to our sympathy** i poveri hanno diritto alla nostra comprensione; **there are many claims on my time** sono molto preso; **to lay claim to sth** avanzare pretese su qc; **to put in a claim for sth** fare una richiesta di qc; **to put in a claim for a pay rise** chiedere un aumento di stipendio; **to put in a claim for gasoline expenses** chiedere il rimborso delle spese per la benzina; **we sent in a claim to our insurance company** abbiamo mandato una richiesta di risarcimento alla nostra assicurazione 2 (*assertion*) affermazione *f*, pretesa; **the manufacturer's claims are obviously untrue** le affermazioni del fabbricante sono ovviamente false; **I make no claim to be infallible** non pretendo di essere infallibile ◆ VT 1 (*rights, territory*) pretendere, rivendicare; (*expenses, damages*) (ri)chiedere; (*lost property*) reclamare; **he's claiming compensation from the company** chiede un risarcimento da parte della società; **she's claiming unemployment benefit** riceve il sussidio di disoccupazione; **the explosion claimed five victims** l'esplosione ha fatto cinque vittime 2 (*assert*) dichiarare, sostenere; **the new system can claim many advantages over the old one** si può dire che il nuovo sistema offre molti vantaggi rispetto a quello vecchio; **to claim that/ to be ...** affermare *or* sostenere che/di essere...; **he claims he found the money** sostiene di aver trovato il denaro; **he claims to have seen her** sostiene di averla vista ♦ VI *(for insurance)* fare una domanda d'indennizzo

claim·ant [ˈkleɪmənt] N *(to social benefit)* richiedente *m/f*; *(in court)* citante *m/f*; *(to throne etc)* pretendente *m/f*

claim form N *(gen)* modulo per ricorsi; *(for expenses)* modulo di rimborso spese

clair·voy·ant [kleəˈvɔɪənt] ADJ, N chiaroveggente *(m/f)*

clam [klæm] N vongola
  ▸ **clam up** VI + ADV *(fam)* zittirsi

clam·ber [ˈklæmbəʳ] VI arrampicarsi

clam·my [ˈklæmɪ] ADJ *(comp* **-ier,** *superl* **-iest)** *(hands)* sudaticcio(-a); viscido(-a); *(weather)* appiccicoso(-a), caldo(-a) e umido(-a)

clam·our, clam·or *(USA)* [ˈklæməʳ] N *(noise)* clamore *m*; *(protest)* protesta ♦ VI: **to clamour for sth** chiedere a gran voce qc

clamp [klæmp] N morsetto, morsa ♦ VT *(hold in a vice)* stringere con un morsetto; *(immobilize: car)* applicare i ceppi bloccaruote a
  ▸ **clamp down** VI + ADV *(fig)*: **to clamp down (on)** dare un giro di vite a

clamp·down [ˈklæmp,daʊn] N stretta; **a clampdown on sth/ sb** un giro di vite a qc/qn

clan [klæn] N clan *m inv*

clan·des·tine [klænˈdestɪn] ADJ clandestino(-a)

clang [klæŋ] N suono metallico ♦ VI emettere un suono metallico; **the gate clanged shut** il cancello si chiuse con fragore

clans·man [ˈklænzmən] N membro di un clan

clap [klæp] N *(on shoulder)* pacca; *(of the hands)* battimano; *(applause)* applauso; **a clap of thunder** un tuono ♦ VT *(applaud)* applaudire; **to clap one's hands** battere le mani; **clap your hands** batti le mani; **to clap a hand over sb's mouth** chiudere la bocca (con la mano) a qn ♦ VI *(applaud)* applaudire; **everybody clapped** tutti applaudirono

clap·ping [ˈklæpɪŋ] N applausi *mpl*

clap·trap [ˈklæp,træp] N *(pej, fam)* chiacchiere *fpl*, sciocchezze *fpl*

clar·et [ˈklærət] N chiaretto (originario della regione di Bordeaux)

clari·fi·ca·tion [,klærɪfɪˈkeɪʃən] N chiarificazione *f*, chiarimento

clari·fy [ˈklærɪfaɪ] VT *(statement etc)* chiarire, chiarificare

clari·net [,klærɪˈnet] N clarinetto

clar·ity [ˈklærɪtɪ] N chiarezza

clash [klæʃ] N **1** *(noise)* fragore *m*, frastuono **2** *(Mil: of personalities, interests)* scontro, conflitto; *(of dates, programmes)* conflitto; *(of colours)* contrasto, disarmonia; **a clash with the police** uno scontro con la polizia; **a clash of wills** uno scontro di idee ♦ VT *(cymbals)* far risuonare; *(swords)* far cozzare ♦ VI: **to clash (with)** *(fig: have an argument)* scontrarsi (con); *(personalities, interests)* scontrarsi (con), essere in conflitto (con); *(colours)* stridere (con), stonare (con); *(dates, events)* coincidere (con); **red clashes with orange** il rosso stona con l'arancio; **the date of the party clashes with the meeting** la data della festa coincide con quella della riunione

clasp [klɑːsp] N fibbia, fermaglio ♦ VT afferrare; **to clasp one's hands (together)** stringere le mani; **to clasp sb in one's arms** stringere qn tra le braccia

class [klɑːs] N *(social class, also Bio, Scol, Univ)* classe *f*; *(group, category)* tipo, categoria; *(lesson)* lezione *f*; **we're in the same class** siamo in classe insieme; **I go to dancing class** vado a lezione di ballo; **to have class** *(fam)* avere classe; **to be in a class of one's own** essere impareggiabile ♦ VT: **to class sb as sth** definire qn qc

class-conscious [ˈklɑːs,kɒnʃəs] ADJ che ha coscienza di classe

class consciousness N coscienza di classe

clas·sic [ˈklæsɪk] ADJ classico(-a); **a classic example** un esempio classico ♦ N classico(-a); **this song is a classic** questa canzone è un classico; *see also* **classics**

clas·si·cal [ˈklæsɪkəl] ADJ classico(-a); **classical scholar** studioso(-a) di lettere antiche; **classical music** musica classica

clas·sics [ˈklæsɪks] NPL *(Scol, Univ)* studi *mpl* umanistici

clas·si·fi·ca·tion [,klæsɪfɪˈkeɪʃən] N classificazione *f*

clas·si·fied [ˈklæsɪfaɪd] ADJ *(information)* segreto(-a), riservato(-a); **classified advertisements** *or* **ads** *(in newspaper)* piccola pubblicità

clas·si·fy [ˈklæsɪfaɪ] VT classificare

class·less [ˈklɑːslɪs] ADJ *(society)* aclassista, senza distinzioni di classe

class·mate [ˈklɑːs,meɪt] N compagno(-a) di classe

class·room [ˈklɑːs,rʊm] N classe *f*, aula

classroom assistant N *(Brit)* assistente *m/f* (in classe) dell'insegnante

classy [ˈklɑːsɪ] ADJ *(comp* **-ier,** *superl* **-iest)** *(fam)* di classe, chic *inv*

clat·ter [ˈklætəʳ] N *(of plates)* acciottolio; *(of hooves)* scalpitio ♦ VI *(metal object etc)* sferragliare; *(hooves)* scalpitare; **the gate clattered behind her** il cancello sbattè con fragore dietro di lei; **to clatter in/out** correre rumorosamente dentro/fuori ♦ VT *(plates)* acciottolare

clause [klɔːz] N *(Gram)* proposizione *f*; *(in contract, law, will)* clausola; **main clause** proposizione *f* principale

claus·tro·pho·bia [,klɔːstrəˈfəʊbɪə] N claustrofobia

claus·tro·pho·bic [,klɔːstrəˈfəʊbɪk] ADJ *(person)* claustrofobico(-a); *(atmosphere)* claustrofobico(-a), da claustrofobia

claw [klɔː] N *(of cat, small bird)* unghia; *(of lion, eagle, bird of prey)* artiglio; *(of lobster)* chela, tenaglia ♦ VT graffiare; **to claw sth to shreds** dilaniare qc ♦ VI: **to claw at** graffiare; *(prey)* ghermire
  ▸ **claw back** VT + ADV *(tax, duty etc)* recuperare

clay [kleɪ] N *(gen)* argilla; *(for pottery)* creta, argilla

clean [kliːn] ADJ *(comp* **-er,** *superl* **-est)** *(gen)* pulito(-a); *(sheet of paper)* nuovo(-a); *(smooth, clear: outline, movement, break)* netto(-a); *(fair: fight, game)* leale, corretto(-a); **to wipe sth clean** pulire qc; **to make a clean sweep** fare piazza pulita; **the doctor gave me a clean bill of health** il medico ha garantito che godo di ottima salute; **to make a clean breast of sth** togliersi qc dalla coscienza; **a clean record** *(Police)* una fedina penale pulita; **to have a clean driving licence,** *(USA)* **to have a clean record** non aver mai preso contravvenzioni ♦ ADV: **he clean forgot** si è completamente dimenticato; **he got clean away** se l'è svignata senza lasciare tracce; **the ball went clean through the window** la palla prese in pieno la finestra; **to come clean** *(fam: admit guilt)* confessare; (: *tell unpleasant truth*) dire veramente come stanno le cose ♦ N pulita, ripulitura ♦ VT *(gen)* pulire; *(blackboard)* cancellare; *(shoes)* lucidare; **to clean one's teeth** *(Brit)* lavarsi i denti; **he never cleans the bath** non pulisce mai la vasca da bagno
  ▸ **clean off** VT + ADV *(mark)* togliere; *(chalk)* cancellare
  ▸ **clean out** VT + ADV *(also fig)* ripulire
  ▸ **clean up** VT + ADV *(room, mess)* pulire, ripulire; *(fig: city, area)* fare un po' di pulizia in; **to clean o.s. up** darsi una ripulita ♦ VI + ADV ripulire, far pulizia; *(fig: make profit)* fare una barca di soldi
  ▸ **clean up after** VT + ADV + PREP: **to clean up after sb** pulire lo sporco lasciato da qn

clean-cut [ˈkliːnˈkʌt] ADJ *(line, shape)* netto(-a), nitido(-a); *(man)* curato(-a); *(situation etc)* ben definito(-a), chiaro(-a)

clean·er [ˈkliːnəʳ] N *(person)* addetto(-a) alle pulizie; *(product)* detersivo, detergente *m*; *(also:* **dry cleaner)** tintoria, lavanderia; **he took his coat to the cleaner's** ha portato il cappotto in lavanderia *or* tintoria

clean·ing [ˈkliːnɪŋ] N pulizia; **to do the cleaning** fare le pulizie

cleaning lady N donna delle pulizie

clean·li·ness [ˈklenlɪnɪs] N pulizia

clean·ly [ˈkliːnlɪ] ADV in modo netto

cleanse [klenz] VT pulire; *(fig: soul etc)* purificare

cleans·er [ˈklenzəʳ] N *(detergent)* detersivo; *(cosmetic)* detergente *m* *(latte, gel, emulsione)*

clean-shaven [ˈkliːnˈʃeɪvn] ADJ senza barba né baffi, sbarbato(-a)

clean sweep N *(Sport)*: **to make a clean sweep of sth** far piazza pulita di qc

clean technology N tecnologie *fpl* ambientali

clean·up [ˈkliːnˌʌp] N (*of house*) pulita, ripulita; **this room could do with a good cleanup** questa stanza avrebbe bisogno di una bella ripulita

clear [klɪəʳ] ADJ (*comp* **-er**, *superl* **-est**) **1** (*water*) chiaro(-a), limpido(-a); (*glass, plastic*) trasparente; (*air, sky, weather*) sereno(-a); (*complexion*) senza brufoli o macchie; (*photograph, outline*) nitido(-a); (*conscience*) pulito(-a); **a clear plastic bottle** una bottiglia di plastica trasparente; **on a clear day** in una giornata limpida **2** (*sound*) chiaro(-a), distinto(-a); (*impression, meaning, explanation*) chiaro(-a); (*motive, consequence*) ovvio(-a); (*understanding, proof*) certo(-a), sicuro(-a); (*profit, majority*) netto(-a); **a clear case of murder** un chiaro caso di omicidio; **to make o.s. clear** spiegarsi bene; **have I made myself clear?** mi sono spiegato?, sono stato chiaro?; **to make it clear to sb that ...** far capire a qn che...; **it is clear to me that ...** per me è evidente che...; **as clear as day** chiaro come il sole; **three clear days** tre giorni interi; **to win by a clear head** (*horse*) vincere di un'incollatura **3** (*free: road, way, space*) libero(-a), sgombro(-a); **wait till the road is clear** aspetta finché la strada sarà libera; **I have a clear day tomorrow** (*Brit*) non ho impegni domani; **we had a clear view** avevamo una buona visuale; **the ship was clear of the rocks** la nave aveva superato il pericolo delle rocce; **all clear!** cessato pericolo! ♦ ADV **1** *see* **loud 2** *clear of* distante da; **to keep clear of sb/sth** tenersi lontano da qn/qc, stare alla larga da qn/qc; **to stand clear of sth** stare lontano da qc **3** (*completely*) completamente; **to get clear away** svignarsela senza lasciar tracce ♦ N: **to be in the clear** (*out of debt*) essere in attivo; (*out of suspicion*) essere a posto; (*out of danger*) essere fuori pericolo ♦ VT **1** (*place, surface, road, railway track*) liberare, sgombrare; (*site, woodland*) spianare; (*pipe*) sbloccare; (*Med: blood*) purificare; **to clear a space for sth/sb** fare posto *or* spazio per qc/qn; **they are clearing the road** stanno liberando la strada; **he cleared the path of leaves** ha sgombrato le foglie dal viale; **to clear the table** sparecchiare (la tavola); **to clear one's throat** schiarirsi la gola; **to clear the air** (*fig*) chiarire le cose; **to clear one's conscience** togliersi un peso dalla coscienza **2** (*get over: fence etc*) scavalcare; (*get past: rocks*) evitare; **to clear 2 metres** (*athlete, horse*) superare i 2 metri **3** (*declare innocent*) discolpare; **to clear sth (with sb)** (*get permission for*) ottenere il permesso (di qn) per qc; **to be cleared of ...** essere scagionato dall'accusa di...; **he was cleared of murder** fu scagionato dall'accusa di omicidio; **to clear o.s.** provare la propria innocenza; **he'll have to be cleared by the security department** dovrà superare il controllo del dipartimento di sicurezza **4** (*debt*) liquidare, saldare; (*stock*) svendere, liquidare; (*cheque*) fare la compensazione di; **to clear a profit** avere un profitto netto ♦ VI (*weather, sky*) schiarirsi, rasserenarsi; (*smoke, fog*) dissolversi, andarsene
  ▸ **clear away** VI + ADV (*mist, fog*) dissiparsi; (*clear the table*) sparecchiare ♦ VT + ADV togliere
  ▸ **clear off** VT + ADV (*debt*) saldare, liquidare ♦ VI + ADV (*fam: go away*) tagliare la corda, squagliarsela; **clear off and leave me alone!** vattene e lasciami in pace!
  ▸ **clear out** VT + ADV (*cupboard*) liberare, sgombrare; (*rubbish*) gettare via ♦ VI + ADV = **clear off** VT + ADV
  ▸ **clear up** VT + ADV **1** (*matter, mystery*) chiarire, risolvere; **I'm sure we can clear up this problem right away** sono sicuro che possiamo chiarire subito il problema **2** (*tidy: room etc*) mettere in ordine, rassettare; **who's going to clear all this up?** chi metterà tutto in ordine? ♦ VI + ADV **1** (*weather*) schiarirsi, rasserenarsi; **I think it's going to clear up** penso che schiarirà **2** (*tidy up*) fare ordine

clear·ance [ˈklɪərəns] N **1** (*of road, room, surface*) sgombero; (*of woodland*) spianamento; (*of site, slum*) demolizione *f*; (*of rubbish, litter*) rimozione *f*; **clearance of mines** rimozione delle mine **2** (*for boat, car*) spazio libero **3** (*authorization*) autorizzazione *f*, permesso; (*by customs*) sdoganamento, **clearance for take-off** (*Aer*) permesso di decollo **4** (*Ftbl*) rinvio

clearance sale N svendita, (vendita di) liquidazione *f*

clear-cut [ˈklɪəˌkʌt] ADJ ben definito(-a) *or* delineato(-a), distinto(-a)

clear·ing [ˈklɪərɪŋ] N (*in wood*) radura; (*Brit: Banking*) clearing *m*

clearing bank N (*Brit: Fin*) banca che fa uso della camera di compensazione

clearing house N (*Fin*) camera di compensazione

clear·ly [ˈklɪəlɪ] ADV chiaramente; **clearly this project will cost money** chiaramente il progetto avrà un costo; **to speak clearly** parlare chiaro

clear·way [ˈklɪəˌweɪ] N (*Brit: Aut*) strada in cui è vietata la sosta

cleav·age [ˈkliːvɪdʒ] N décolleté *m inv*

cleav·er [ˈkliːvəʳ] N mannaia; **meat cleaver** (*Culin*) marrancio

clef [klɛf] N (*Mus*) chiave *f*

cleft [klɛft] PT, PP *of* **cleave** ♦ N (*in rock*) crepa, fenditura

clem·en·cy [ˈklɛmənsɪ] N (*frm*) clemenza

clem·ent [ˈklɛmənt] (*frm*) ADJ (*person*) clemente; (*weather*) mite, clemente

clench [klɛntʃ] VT stringere; **to clench sth in one's hand** stringere in pugno qc; **she clenched her fists** strinse i pugni

cler·gy [ˈklɜːdʒɪ] N clero

clergy·man [ˈklɜːdʒɪmən] N (*pl* **-men**) ecclesiastico

cleri·cal [ˈklɛrɪkəl] ADJ **1** (*Comm: job*) d'ufficio, da impiegato(-a); **clerical worker** impiegato(-a); **clerical error** svista **2** (*Rel*) clericale

clerk [klɑːk, (*USA*) klɜːk] N (*in office, bank*) impiegato(-a); (*USA: shop assistant*) commesso(-a); (: *in hotel*) impiegato(-a) della reception; **Clerk of the Court** (*Law*) cancelliere *m*

clev·er [ˈklɛvəʳ] ADJ (*comp* **-er**, *superl* **-est**) (*gen*) intelligente; (*deft, skilful*) abile; (*ingenious: idea, person, device*) geniale; **she's very clever** è molto intelligente; **to be clever at sth** essere abile in qc; **he is very clever with his hands** è molto abile *or* bravo nei lavori manuali; **he was too clever for us** era più furbo di noi; **a clever system** un sistema ingegnoso; **what a clever idea!** che idea geniale!

clev·er·ly [ˈklɛvəlɪ] ADV abilmente

clew [kluː] N (*USA*) = **clue**

cli·ché [ˈkliːʃeɪ] N cliché *m inv*

click [klɪk] N (*of camera etc*) scatto; (*of high heels*) tacchettio; (*of soldiers' boots*) battito; (*of tongue*) schiocco ♦ VT (*heels*) battere; (*tongue*) far schioccare ♦ VI (*camera etc*) scattare; (*heels*) ticchettare; **the door clicked shut** la porta si chiuse con uno scatto; **suddenly it all clicked (into place)** (*fig: fam*) di colpo tutto è diventato chiaro, improvvisamente ho capito; **we immediately clicked** ci siamo subito piaciuti; **to click on** cliccare su

click·able [ˈklɪkəbl] (*Comput*) ADJ cliccabile

cli·ent [ˈklaɪənt] N cliente *m/f*

cli·en·tele [ˌkliːɑ̃ːnˈtɛl] N clientela

cliff [klɪf] N scogliera, rupe *f*

cliff·hanger [ˈklɪfˌhæŋəʳ] N (*TV, also fig*) episodio o situazione ecc. ricco di suspense

cli·mac·tic [klaɪˈmæktɪk] ADJ culminante

cli·mate [ˈklaɪmɪt] N clima *m*; **the climate of popular opinion** l'opinione pubblica

climate change N cambiamenti *mpl* climatici

cli·max [ˈklaɪmæks] N culmine *m*; (*of play etc*) momento più emozionante, climax *m inv*; (*sexual climax*) orgasmo; **the climax of her career** l'apice della sua carriera

climb [klaɪm] N (*gen*) ascesa, salita; (*of mountain*) scalata, arrampicata; (*Aer*) ascesa ♦ VT (*also:* **climb up**) (*tree, ladder etc*) salire su, arrampicarsi su; (*staircase*) salire; (*mountain, wall*) scalare; **to climb a rope** arrampicarsi su una corda; **they climbed a tree** sono saliti su un albero; **her ambition is to climb Mount Everest** la sua ambizione è quella di scalare l'Everest; **we had to climb three flights of stairs to get there** abbiamo dovuto salire tre rampe di scale per arrivarci ♦ VI (*road, person*) salire; (*plane*) prendere quota; (*plant*) arrampicarsi; **the pilot climbed into the cockpit** il pilota si è infilato nella cabina di pilotaggio; **to climb over a wall** scavalcare un muro
  ▸ **climb down** VI + PREP scendere da ♦ VI + ADV scendere; (*fig: abandon one's position*) tornare sui suoi (*or miei etc*) passi

climb-down [ˈklaɪmˌdaʊn] N ritirata

climb·er [ˈklaɪməʳ] N (*rock climber*) alpinista *m/f*, scalatore(-trice); (*Bot*) rampicante *m*

climb·ing [ˈklaɪmɪŋ] N (*rock climbing*) arrampicata; **to go climbing** fare arrampicata

clinch [klɪntʃ] N: **in a clinch** (*fam: embrace*) abbracciati(-e) stretti(-e) ♦ VT (*settle: deal*) concludere; (: *argument*) chiudere; **that clinches it** è fatta

clinch·er [ˈklɪntʃəʳ] N (*fam*): **the clincher** il fattore decisivo

cling [klɪŋ] VI (*pt, pp* clung) **1 to cling to** (*support, also fig*) aggrapparsi a, tenersi stretto a; **he clung to the wreckage** era aggrappato al relitto; **to cling to one another** stringersi l'uno(-a) all'altro(-a) **2 to cling (to)** (*subj: clothes*) aderire strettamente (a); (: *smell*) impregnare; **the smell clung to her clothes** l'odore aveva impregnato i suoi abiti

cling·film [ˈklɪŋˌfɪlm], **clingwrap** [ˈklɪŋˌræp] N pellicola trasparente (*per alimenti*)

clin·ic [ˈklɪnɪk] N (*hospital, dental clinic etc*) clinica; (*for guidance etc*) centro; (*session*) seduta

clinical [ˈklɪnɪkəl] ADJ clinico(-a); (*fig*) freddo(-a), distaccato(-a); **his approach was too clinical** il suo approccio era troppo distaccato; **clinical trials** sperimentazione *fsg* clinica

clink [klɪŋk] N tintinnio ♦ VT: **to clink glasses with sb** brindare *or* fare cin cin con qn ♦ VI tintinnare

clip¹ [klɪp] N (*Cine*) sequenza; **some clips from her latest film** alcune sequenze del suo ultimo film ♦ VT (*cut: gen*) tagliare; (*sheep, dog*) tosare; (*hedge*) potare, tagliare; (*ticket*) forare; (*article from newspaper*) ritagliare; **to clip sb's wings** (*fig*) tarpare le ali a qn

clip² [klɪp] N (*paperclip*) graffetta; (*Brit: bulldog clip*) fermafogli *m inv*; (*hair clip*) molletta; (*brooch*) spilla, fermaglio; (*holding hose etc*) anello d'attacco ♦ VT (*also:* **clip together:** *papers*) attaccare (con una graffetta)
  ▸ **clip on** VT + ADV (*brooch*) agganciare; (*document: with paper clip etc*) attaccare
  ▸ **clip together** VT + ADV attaccare (con una graffetta)

clip·pers [ˈklɪpəz] NPL (*for nails*) tagliaunghie *m inv*; (*for hair*) macchinetta per capelli; (*for hedge*) tosasiepi *m inv*, cesoie *fpl*

clip·ping [ˈklɪpɪŋ] N (*from newspaper*) ritaglio

clique [kliːk] N cricca

cloak [kləʊk] N cappa, mantello; **under the cloak of darkness** (*fig*) sotto il manto delle tenebre ♦ VT avvolgere

cloak·room [ˈkləʊkˌrʊm] N (*for coats*) guardaroba *m inv*; (*Brit: euph*) toilette *f inv*

clock [klɒk] N (*gen*) orologio; (*of taxi*) tassametro; **around the clock** ventiquattr'ore su ventiquattro; **to sleep round the clock** *or* **the clock round** dormire un giorno intero; **to work against the clock** lavorare in gara col tempo; **alarm clock** sveglia ♦ VT (*time*) registrare; (*of runner*) cronometrare
  ▸ **clock in, clock on** VI + ADV (*Brit*) timbrare il cartellino (all'entrata)
  ▸ **clock off, clock out** VI + ADV (*Brit*) timbrare il cartellino (all'uscita)
  ▸ **clock up** VT + ADV (*Aut*) registrare, fare; (*miles, hours etc*) fare

clock·wise [ˈklɒkˌwaɪz] ADV in senso orario

clock·work [ˈklɒkˌwɜːk] N: **to go like clockwork** (*fig*) funzionare alla perfezione ♦ ADJ (*toy, train*) a molla

clog [klɒg] N zoccolo ♦ VT (*also:* **clog up**) (*pipe, drain*) ostruire, intasare; (*machine, mechanism*) bloccare ♦ VI (*also:* **clog up**) intasarsi, bloccarsi

clois·ter [ˈklɔɪstəʳ] N chiostro

clone [kləʊn] N clone *m* ♦ VT clonare

close¹ [kləʊs] ADV vicino, dappresso; **close by, close at hand** qui *or* lì vicino; **to hold sb close** tenere stretto(-a) qn; **close together** vicino; **stay close to me** stammi vicino; **to follow close behind** seguire da vicino; **come closer** avvicinati ♦ ADJ **1** (*near*) vicino(-a); (*relative, connection, resemblance*) stretto(-a); (*friend*) intimo(-a); (*almost equal: result*) quasi pari; (: *fight, contest, election, race*) combattuto(-a); **the shops are very close** i negozi sono molto vicini; **the house is close to the shops** la casa è vicina ai negozi; **they're very close** (*in age*) sono molto vicini come età; (*emotionally*) sono molto uniti; **I'm very close to my sister** io e mia sorella siamo molto unite; **we're just inviting close relations** invitiamo solo i parenti stretti; **she's a close friend of mine** è una mia amica intima; **she was close to tears** stava per piangere; **at close quarters** da vicino; **close combat** combattimento

corpo a corpo; **that was a close shave** (*fig: fam*) l'ho (*or* l'hai *etc*) scampata per un pelo; **it was a very close contest** è stata una gara molto combattuta **2** (*exact, detailed: examination, study*) accurato(-a), attento(-a); (: *investigation, questioning*) approfondito(-a); (: *surveillance, control, watch*) stretto(-a); **to pay close attention to sb/sth** stare ben attento(-a) a qn/qc; **to keep a close watch on sb** guardare qn a vista **3** (*handwriting, texture, weave*) fitto(-a) **4** (*stuffy: atmosphere, room*) soffocante; (*weather*) afoso(-a); **it's rather close in here** c'è aria viziata; **it's close this afternoon** c'è afa questo pomeriggio

close² [kləʊz] N (*end*) fine *f*, chiusura; **to bring sth to a close** terminare qc; **to draw to a close** avvicinarsi alla fine ♦ VI (*shut: shop etc*) chiudere; (: *lid, door etc*) chiudersi; (*end*) chiudersi, concludersi, finire; **the shops close at five thirty** i negozi chiudono alle cinque e mezza; **the doors close automatically** le porte si chiudono automaticamente ♦ VT **1** (*shut: door, road, shop etc*) chiudere; **please close the door** chiudi la porta, per favore; **to close the gap between two things** (*fig*) colmare il divario tra due cose; **to close one's eyes to sth** (*fig*) ignorare qc **2** (*end: discussion, meeting*) chiudere, concludere; (: *bank account*) chiudere, estinguere; (: *bargain, deal*) concludere
  ▸ **close down** VI + ADV (*business*) chiudersi, chiudere; (*TV, Radio*) terminare le trasmissioni ♦ VT + ADV chiudere (definitivamente)
  ▸ **close in** VI + ADV (*hunters*) stringersi attorno; (*evening, night, fog*) calare; **the days are closing in** le giornate si accorciano; **to close in on sb** accerchiare qn
  ▸ **close off** VT + ADV (*area*) chiudere
  ▸ **close round** VI + PREP stringersi attorno a
  ▸ **close up** VI + ADV (*people in queue*) stringersi; (*wound*) rimarginarsi ♦ VT + ADV (*shop, house, opening*) chiudere; (*wound*) chiudere, suturare

closed [kləʊzd] ADJ chiuso(-a); **sociology is a closed book to me** per me la sociologia è un mistero

closed-circuit tele·vi·sion [ˈkləʊzdˌsɜːkɪtˈtelɪˌvɪʒən] N televisione *f* a circuito chiuso

closed shop N (*Industry*) fabbrica, ditta *or* negozio che assume solo lavoratori iscritti al sindacato

close-knit [ˌkləʊsˈnɪt] ADJ (*community, group, family*) molto unito(-a)

close·ly [ˈkləʊslɪ] ADV (*guard*) strettamente, attentamente; (*examine, study, watch, follow*) da vicino, attentamente; (*listen*) attentamente; (*resemble*) molto; (*connected*) strettamente; **a closely guarded secret** un segreto gelosamente custodito; **a closely fought race** una gara molto combattuta; **we are closely related** siamo parenti stretti

clos·et [ˈklɒzɪt] N (*USA: cupboard*) armadio; **to come out of the closet** (*fam*) uscire allo scoperto ♦ VT: **to be closeted with sb** essersi appartato(-a) con qn

close-up [ˈkləʊsʌp] N primo piano

clos·ing [ˈkləʊzɪŋ] ADJ (*stages, remarks*) conclusivo(-a), finale; **closing speech** discorso di chiusura; **closing price** (*Stock Exchange*) prezzo di chiusura

closing time N (*of pub, shop*) orario di chiusura; **when is closing time?** a che ora chiude?

closure [ˈkləʊʒəʳ] N chiusura; (*Psych*) il mettersi alle spalle un fatto negativo

clot [klɒt] N (*Med: also:* **blood clot**) coagulo, grumo; (*fam: idiot*) scemo(-a), zuccone(-a); **to have a clot on the brain/in the leg** avere un grumo (di sangue) nel cervello/in una gamba ♦ VI coagularsi

cloth [klɒθ] N (*material*) tessuto, stoffa; (*for cleaning*) panno, straccio; (*Brit: also:* **teacloth**) telo per i piatti; (*also:* **tablecloth**) tovaglia; **5 metres of cloth** cinque metri di stoffa; **wipe it with a damp cloth** puliscilo con uno straccio umido; **a man of the cloth** (*Rel*) un religioso, un ecclesiastico

clothe [kləʊð] VT vestire

clothes [kləʊðz] NPL vestiti *mpl*, abiti *mpl*; **to put one's clothes on** vestirsi; **to take one's clothes off** togliersi i vestiti, svestirsi, spogliarsi

clothes brush N spazzola per abiti

clothes line N corda del bucato

clothes peg, (*USA*) **clothes pin** N molletta (da bucato)

cloth·ing [ˈkləʊðɪŋ] N abbigliamento; **article of clothing** capo di vestiario or di abbigliamento

clot·ted cream [ˌklɒtɪdˈkriːm] N (Brit) panna rappresa (ottenuta per riscaldamento)

cloud [klaʊd] N (Met) nuvola, nube f; (of dust, smoke, gas) nube; (of insects) nugolo; **to be under a cloud** essere malvisto(-a); **he has his head in the clouds** ha la testa tra le nuvole; **to be on cloud nine** essere al settimo cielo; **every cloud has a silver lining** (Proverb) non tutto il male vien per nuocere ♦ VT (liquid) intorbidire; (mirror) appannare; (fig: judgement) confondere; (: thinking) turbare; **a clouded sky** un cielo nuvoloso; **to cloud the issue** imbrogliare la questione
  ► **cloud over** VI + ADV (also fig) rannuvolarsi, offuscarsi

cloud·burst [ˈklaʊdbɜːst] N acquazzone m

cloud-cuckoo-land [ˌklaʊdˈkʊkuːˌlænd] N mondo dei sogni

cloudy [ˈklaʊdɪ] ADJ (sky) nuvoloso(-a), coperto(-a); (liquid) torbido(-a)

clout [klaʊt] N (blow) ceffone m; (fig: power, influence) influenza; **someone with clout** qn con una certa influenza ♦ VT colpire

clove [kləʊv] PT of cleave ♦ N chiodo di garofano; **clove of garlic** spicchio d'aglio

clo·ver [ˈkləʊvə'] N trifoglio; **a four-leaved clover** un quadrifoglio; **red clover** trifoglio pratense or rosso; **white clover** trifoglio bianco; **to be in clover** (fam) nuotare nell'abbondanza

clover·leaf [ˈkləʊvəˌliːf] N (Bot) foglia di trifoglio; (Aut) raccordo (a quadrifoglio)

clown [klaʊn] N (in circus) pagliaccio, clown m inv; (fam) buffone m ♦ VI (also: **clown about** or **around**) fare il buffone or il pagliaccio

cloy·ing [ˈklɔɪɪŋ] (taste, smell) stucchevole

club [klʌb] N 1 (society) circolo, club m inv; **tennis club** circolo di tennis; **youth club** circolo giovanile; **join the club!** (fig) non sei il solo! 2 (stick) randello; (of caveman) clava; **golf club** mazza da golf 3 (nightclub) locale notturno; **we had dinner and went on to a club** abbiamo cenato e poi siamo andati in un locale notturno 4 **clubs** (Cards) fiori mpl; **he played a club** ha giocato (una carta di) fiori ♦ VT (person) bastonare; **clubbed to death with sticks** ucciso(-a) a colpi di bastone

club car N (USA: Rail) carrozza or vagone m ristorante

club class N (Aer) classe f club, inv

club·house [ˈklʌbˌhaʊs] N circolo

club soda N (USA) soda

cluck [klʌk] VI chiocciare

clue [kluː] N indicazione f; (in a crime etc) indizio; (in crosswords) definizione f; **an important clue** un indizio importante; **I'll give you a clue** ti metto sulla strada giusta; **I haven't a clue** (fam) non (ne) ho la minima idea

clued-up [kluːdˈʌp], **clued-in** ADJ (fam) (ben) informato(-a)

clump [klʌmp] N (of trees) gruppo; (flowers) macchia; (of grass) ciuffo

clum·sy [ˈklʌmzɪ] ADJ (person, action, gesture) goffo(-a), maldestro(-a); (painting, forgery) malfatto(-a); (object) mal costruito(-a); (tool) poco pratico(-a); (remark) maldestro(-a); (apology) goffo(-a)

clung [klʌŋ] PT, PP of cling

clus·ter [ˈklʌstə'] N (of houses, people, trees) gruppo; (of grapes) grappolo; (of stars) ammasso ♦ VI (people, things): **to cluster (round sb/sth)** raggrupparsi (intorno a qn/qc)

clutch [klʌtʃ] N 1 (Aut) frizione f; (pedal) (pedale m della) frizione 2 (grip, grasp) presa, stretta; **to fall into sb's clutches** cadere nelle grinfie di qn ♦ VT (catch hold of) afferrare; (hold tightly) tenere stretto(-a), stringere forte; **she clutched my arm and begged me not to go** mi ha afferrato il braccio e mi ha pregato di non andarmene ♦ VI: **to clutch at** cercare di afferrare; **to clutch at straws** (fig) crearsi delle illusioni

clut·ter [ˈklʌtə'] N confusione f, disordine m; **there's so much clutter in here** c'è un gran disordine qua dentro; **in a clutter** in disordine ♦ VT (also: **clutter up**) ingombrare; **to be cluttered up with sth** essere pieno(-a) zeppo(-a) or ingombro(-a) di qc

cm ABBR (= centimetre) cm

CO N ABBR (= commanding officer) Com. ♦ ABBR (USA Post: = Colorado)

Co. ABBR 1 (= company) C.ia 2 = county 3 and **Co.** (fam) e company; **Joe and Co.** Joe e company

c/o ABBR (= care of) c/o

coach [kəʊtʃ] N 1 (bus) corriera, pullman m inv; (for excursions) pullman m inv; (Brit: of train) carrozza, vettura; (: horse drawn) carrozza; (: stage coach) diligenza; **by coach** in corriera; **coach station** stazione f delle corriere 2 (Sport) allenatore(-trice); (tutor) chi dà ripetizioni ♦ VT (team) allenare; (student) dare ripetizioni a

coach trip N escursione f or viaggio in pullman

co·agu·late [kəʊˈægjʊleɪt] VT coagulare ♦ VI coagularsi

coal [kəʊl] N carbone m; **to carry coals to Newcastle** (fig) portare acqua al mare ♦ ADJ (fire) di carbone; (industry) del carbone; (stove) a carbone

coal·face [ˈkəʊlˌfeɪs] N fronte f di abbattimento (di filone carbonifero)

coal·field [ˈkəʊlˌfiːld] N bacino carbonifero

coa·li·tion [ˌkəʊəˈlɪʃən] N (Pol) coalizione f

coal·man [ˈkəʊlˌmæn] N (pl -men) carbonaio

coal mine N miniera di carbone

coal miner N minatore m

coal mining N estrazione f del carbone

coarse [kɔːs] ADJ (comp -er, superl -est) (texture, skin, material) ruvido(-a); (salt, sand) grosso(-a); (sandpaper) a grana grossa; (vulgar: character, laugh, remark) volgare; **the bag was made of coarse black cloth** la borsa era fatta di una stoffa nera ruvida; **the sand is very coarse on that beach** la sabbia di quella spiaggia è molto grossa

coast [kəʊst] N costa; (also: **coastline**) litorale m; **on the coast** sulla costa; **the coast is clear** (fig) la via è libera ♦ VI (Aut) andare in folle; (Cycling) andare a ruota libera

coast·al [ˈkəʊstəl] ADJ costiero(-a)

coast·er [ˈkəʊstə'] N 1 (Naut) nave f da cabotaggio 2 (for glass) sottobicchiere m

coast·guard [ˈkəʊstˌgɑːd] N (person) guardacoste m inv; (organization) guardia costiera

coast·line [ˈkəʊstˌlaɪn] N litorale m, linea costiera

coat [kəʊt] N 1 (garment) cappotto, soprabito; **a nice warm coat** un bel cappotto caldo 2 (of animal) pelo, mantello 3 (layer) mano f; (of paint) mano f; **a coat of paint** una mano di pittura 4 **coat of arms** stemma m, blasone m ♦ VT: **to coat sth with** ricoprire qc con uno strato di; (paint) dare a qc una mano di

coat hanger [ˈkəʊtˌhæŋə'] N gruccia, stampella

coat·ing [ˈkəʊtɪŋ] N (film, layer) mano, strato; (for protection) rivestimento (esterno)

co·author [ˈkəʊˌɔːθə'] N coautore(-trice)

coax [kəʊks] VT: **to coax sth out of sb** ottenere qc da qn (con le buone); **to coax sb into/out of doing sth** convincere or indurre (con moine) qn a fare/non fare qc

cob [kɒb] N see corn[1]

cob·ble [ˈkɒbl] N (also: **cobblestone**) ciottolo

cob·bled [ˈkɒbld] ADJ: **cobbled street** strada pavimentata con ciottoli

cob·bler [ˈkɒblə'] N calzolaio

cobble-stones [ˈkɒblˌstəʊnz] NPL ciottoli mpl

COBOL [ˈkəʊbɒl] N ABBR (Comput: = common business oriented language) COBOL m

co·bra [ˈkəʊbrə] N cobra m inv

cob·web [ˈkɒbˌweb] N ragnatela

co·caine [kəˈkeɪn] N cocaina

cock [kɒk] N 1 (rooster) gallo; (male bird) maschio 2 (fam!: penis) cazzo (fam!) ♦ VT (gun) armare; **to cock (up) one's ears** (also fig) drizzare le orecchie; **to cock a snook at** (make rude gesture) fare marameo a; (fig) burlarsi di

cock-a-hoop [ˌkɒkəˈhuːp] ADJ esultante, euforico(-a)

cock·er·el [ˈkɒkərəl] N galletto

cock-eyed [ˈkɒkˌaɪd] ADJ (crooked) storto(-a); (absurd) assurdo(-a), strampalato(-a)

cock·le [ˈkɒkl] N (shellfish) cardio; **it warmed the cockles of my heart** mi riempì il cuore di gioia

cock·ney [ˈkɒknɪ] N (person) cockney m/f inv, abitante dei *quartieri dell'East End di Londra; (dialect)* cockney *m;* **he's got a cockney accent** ha un accento cockney

cock·pit [ˈkɒkˌpɪt] N *(Aer)* cabina di pilotaggio, abitacolo

cock·roach [ˈkɒkˌrəʊtʃ] N scarafaggio, blatta

cock·tail [ˈkɒkˌteɪl] N *(drink)* cocktail *m inv;* **fruit cocktail** macedonia di frutta; **prawn cocktail,** *(USA)* **shrimp cocktail** cocktail *m inv* di gamberetti

cocktail cabinet N mobile *m* bar, *inv*

cocktail party N cocktail *m inv*

cock·tail shak·er [ˈkɒtˌteɪlˈʃeɪkə'] N shaker *m inv*

cocky [ˈkɒkɪ] ADJ *(comp* -ier, *superl* -iest) *(pej)* troppo sicuro(-a) di sé

co·coa [ˈkəʊkəʊ] N cacao; *(drink)* cioccolata calda

coco·nut [ˈkəʊkəˌnʌt] N *(fruit)* noce *f* di cocco; *(tree: also:* **coconut palm)** palma di cocco; *(substance)* cocco

co·coon [kəˈkuːn] N bozzolo

COD [ˌsiːəʊˈdiː] ABBR = **cash on delivery, collect on delivery** *(USA); see* **collect**

cod [kɒd] N merluzzo

code [kəʊd] N codice *m;* *(Telec)* prefisso; **in code** in codice; **it's written in code** è scritto in codice; **what's the code for London?** qual è il prefisso di Londra?; **code of behaviour** regole *fpl* di condotta ♦ VT cifrare

co·deine [ˈkəʊdiːn] N codeina

codg·er [ˈkɒdʒə'] N: **an old codger** *(Brit fam)* un nonnetto

codi·cil [ˈkɒdɪsɪl] N *(Law)* codicillo

codi·fy [ˈkəʊdɪfaɪ] VT codificare *(leggi)*

cod-liver oil [ˈkɒdˌlɪvər'ɔɪl] N olio di fegato di merluzzo

co-driver [ˈkəʊdraɪvə'] N *(in race)* copilota *m/f;* *(of truck)* secondo autista *m*

co-ed [ˈkəʊˈed] *(fam)* ADJ misto(-a)

co·edu·ca·tion·al [ˌkəʊedjʊˈkeɪʃənl] ADJ misto(-a)

co·erce [kəʊˈɜːs] VT: **to coerce sb (into doing sth)** costringere qn (a fare qc)

co·er·cion [kəʊˈɜːʃən] N forza; *(Law)* coercizione *f*

co·ex·ist·ence [ˌkəʊɪgˈzɪstəns] N coesistenza

C. of C. [ˌsiːəvˈsiː] N ABBR = **chamber of commerce**

C of E [ˌsiːəvˈiː] N ABBR = **Church of England**

cof·fee [ˈkɒfɪ] N caffè *m inv;* **cup of coffee** tazza di caffè; **black coffee** caffè nero; **white coffee,** *(USA)* **coffee with cream** caffè con latte; **two white coffees, please** due caffè con latte, per favore

coffee bar N *(Brit)* caffè *m inv*

coffee bean N grano *or* chicco di caffè *m inv*

coffee break N pausa per il caffè

coffee cake [ˈkɒfɪˌkeɪk] N *(USA)* panino dolce all'uva

coffee cup N tazzina da caffè

coffee·pot [ˈkɒfɪˌpɒt] N caffettiera

coffee shop N 1 *(bar)* caffè *m inv* 2 *(shop)* torrefazione *f*

coffee table N tavolino

cof·fin [ˈkɒfɪn] N bara

cog [kɒg] N dente *m;* **a cog in the wheel** *(fig)* una rotella in un grande ingranaggio

co·gent [ˈkəʊdʒənt] ADJ *(frm)* convincente

cog·nac [ˈkɒnjæk] N cognac *m inv*

cog·ni·tive [ˈkɒgnɪtɪv] ADJ *(frm)* cognitivo(-a)

cog·wheel [ˈkɒgˌwiːl] N ruota dentata

co·hab·it [kəʊˈhæbɪt] VI *(frm):* **to cohabit (with sb)** coabitare (con qn)

co·her·ent [kəʊˈhɪərənt] ADJ coerente

co·he·sion [kəʊˈhiːʒən] N coesione *f*

co·he·sive [kəʊˈhiːsɪv] ADJ *(fig)* unificante, coesivo(-a)

coil [kɔɪl] N 1 *(roll)* rotolo; *(single loop)* anello, giro; *(of hair)* ciocca; *(of snake)* spira; *(of smoke)* filo; **a coil of rope** un rotolo di spago 2 *(Aut, Elec)* bobina 3 **the coil** *(contraceptive)* la spirale ♦ VT avvolgere; **to coil sth up** avvolgere qc (in un rotolo) ♦ VI attorcigliarsi

coin [kɔɪn] N moneta; **a 5p coin** una moneta da 5 pence ♦ VT *(fam: money)* fare soldi a palate; *(fig: word etc)* coniare; **to coin a phrase** *(hum)* per così dire

coin·age [ˈkɔɪnɪdʒ] N 1 *(money, system)* moneta, sistema *m* monetario 2 *(coining)* coniazione *f*, invenzione *f*

coin box N *(Brit)* telefono pubblico a monete

co·in·cide [ˌkəʊɪnˈsaɪd] VI: **to coincide (with)** coincidere (con)

co·in·ci·dence [kəʊˈɪnsɪdəns] N *(chance)* coincidenza, combinazione *f*

coin-operated [ˌkɔɪnˈɒpəreɪtɪd] ADJ *(machine)* (che funziona) a monete

coke [kəʊk] N 1 *(fuel)* carbone *m* coke 2 *(fam: cocaine)* coca

Col. ABBR = **colonel**

col·an·der [ˈkʌləndə'] N colapasta *m inv*

cold [kəʊld] ADJ *(comp* -er, *superl* -est) *(also fig)* freddo(-a); **it's cold** fa freddo; **it's a cold day** fa freddo oggi; **I'm cold** ho freddo; **are you cold?** hai freddo?; **my feet are cold** ho freddo ai piedi, ho i piedi freddi; **to catch cold** prendere freddo; **to get cold** *(person)* infreddolirsi; *(food etc)* freddarsi, diventare freddo(-a); **it's getting cold** *(weather)* comincia a far freddo; **the room's getting cold** comincia a far freddo in questa stanza; **I can't stand the cold** non sopporto il freddo; **to be out cold** *(fam: unconscious)* essere privo(-a) di sensi; **to knock sb (out) cold** mettere qn fuori combattimento; **in cold blood** a sangue freddo; **it leaves me cold** *(fam)* non mi fa né caldo, né freddo; **to get cold feet** *(fig)* avere fifa; **it's cold comfort** è una magra consolazione; **to put sth into cold storage** *(food)* mettere qc in cella frigorifera; *(fig: project)* accantonare qc ♦ N 1 *(Met)* freddo; **to feel the cold** sentire il freddo; **to be left out in the cold** *(fig)* essere lasciato(-a) in disparte 2 *(Med: also:* **common cold)** raffreddore *m;* **to catch a cold** prendere un raffreddore; **to have a cold** avere il raffreddore

❏ **cold** is not translated by the Italian word *caldo*

cold-blooded [ˌkəʊldˈblʌdɪd] ADJ a sangue freddo; *(fig)* spietato(-a)

cold call N *(Comm: on phone)* vendita telefonica; *(: visit)* vendita porta a porta ♦ VT vendere per telefono; *(visit)* vendere porta a porta

cold cream N crema emolliente

cold·ly [ˈkəʊldlɪ] ADV *(fig)* freddamente

cold sore N *(Med)* febbre *f* (sulle labbra), herpes simplex *m inv*

cold sweat N: **to be in a cold sweat (about sth)** sudare freddo (per qc)

cold turkey N *(fam):* **to go cold turkey** avere la scimmia

cold war N: **the Cold War** la guerra fredda

cole·slaw [ˈkəʊlˌslɔː] N *no pl* insalata di cavolo bianco, carote e altre verdure con maionese

col·ic [ˈkɒlɪk] N colica

col·icky [ˈkɒlɪkɪ] ADJ che soffre di coliche

col·labo·rate [kəˈlæbəˌreɪt] VI: **to collaborate (with sb in** *or* **on sth)** collaborare (con qn a *or* in qc)

col·labo·ra·tion [kəˌlæbəˈreɪʃən] N collaborazione *f*

col·labo·ra·tor [kəˈlæbəˌreɪtə'] N *(on project)* collaboratore(-trice); *(pej: with enemy)* collaborazionista *m/f*

col·lage [kɒˈlɑːʒ] N *(Art)* collage *m inv*

col·la·gen [ˈkɒlədʒən] N collageno

col·lapse [kəˈlæps] N *(gen)* crollo; *(of government)* caduta; *(of plans, scheme, business)* fallimento; *(of health)* collasso ♦ VI *(see n)* crollare, cadere; fallire; avere un collasso; *(fam: with laughter)* piegarsi in due dalle risate; **the bridge collapsed during the storm** il ponte è crollato durante la tempesta; **he collapsed while playing tennis** ha avuto un collasso mentre giocava a tennis

col·laps·ible [kəˈlæpsəbl] ADJ pieghevole

col·lar [ˈkɒlə'] N *(of shirt, blouse, coat)* colletto, collo; *(for dog)* collare *m;* *(Tech)* anello, fascetta; **to grab sb by the collar** afferrare qn per il bavero ♦ VT *(fam: person, object)* beccare

collar·bone [ˈkɒləˌbəʊn] N clavicola

col·late [kɒˈleɪt] VT collazionare

col·lat·er·al [kɒˈlætərəl] N *(Fin)* garanzia

col·la·tion [kəˈleɪʃən] N 1 *(of information)* collazione *f* 2 *(frm: light meal)* pasto leggero

col·league [ˈkɒliːg] N collega *m/f*

col·lect [kəˈlekt] VT 1 *(gen)* raccogliere; *(as hobby: stamps, valuables)* fare collezione di, collezionare; **the teacher collected the exercise books** l'insegnante ha raccolto i quaderni; **he collects stamps** fa collezione di francobolli;

to collect o.s. riprendersi; **to collect one's thoughts** raccogliere le idee **2** (*Brit: call for, pick up: person*) andare *or* passare a prendere; (: *post, ticket*) ritirare; (: *pension, rent, taxes*) riscuotere; (: *donations, subscriptions*) fare una colletta di; (: *rubbish*) portare via, raccogliere; (: *dust*) accumulare; **their mother collects them from school** la mamma li va a prendere a scuola; **I'm collecting for UNICEF** faccio una colletta per l'UNICEF ♦ VI (*people*) riunirsi, adunarsi, radunarsi; (*water, dust*) accumularsi; (*rubbish etc*) ammucchiarsi, accumularsi; **to collect for charity** fare una raccolta di beneficenza; **collect on delivery** (*USA: Comm*) pagamento alla consegna ♦ ADV (*USA*): **to call collect** (*Telec*) fare una chiamata a carico del destinatario
▸ **collect up** VT + ADV raccogliere

col·lect·ed [kəˈlɛktɪd] ADJ **1** (*works, poems*) raccolto(-a); **the collected works of Shakespeare** l'opera completa di Shakespeare **2** (*frm: person: composed*) padrone(-a) di sé

col·lec·tion [kəˈlɛkʃən] N (*of information etc*) raccolta; (*of taxes*) riscossione *f*; (*of refuse*) rimozione *f*; (*of stamps*) collezione *f*, raccolta; (*of miscellaneous objects, people*) miscuglio; (*Rel*) questua; (*for charity*) colletta, raccolta; (*Post*) levata; **my CD collection** la mia collezione di CD; **a collection for charity** una colletta per beneficenza

col·lec·tive [kəˈlɛktɪv] N collettivo ♦ ADJ collettivo(-a)

collective bargaining N trattative *fpl* (sindacali) collettive

col·lec·tor [kəˈlɛktəʳ] N (*of stamps etc*) collezionista *m/f*; (*of taxes*) esattore *m*; **collector's item** *or* **piece** pezzo da collezionista

col·lege [ˈkɒlɪdʒ] N **1** (*of technology, agriculture etc*) istituto superiore; (*Brit, USA: Univ*) college *m inv*; **college of art** scuola d'arte; **college of music** conservatorio; **to go to college** (*university*) andare all'università; (*other institution*) andare a un istituto di specializzazione; **college students** studenti *mpl* universitari **2** (*body*) collegio

col·lide [kəˈlaɪd] VI: **to collide (with)** scontrarsi (con)

col·lie [ˈkɒlɪ] N (*dog*) collie *m inv*

col·liery [ˈkɒlɪərɪ] N (*Brit*) miniera di carbone

col·li·sion [kəˈlɪʒən] N scontro, collisione *f*; **to be on a collision course** (*also fig*) essere in rotta di collisione; **collision damage waiver** (*Insurance*) clausola che esclude la copertura per danni della vettura assicurata

col·lo·quial [kəˈləʊkwɪəl] ADJ (*word, phrase*) familiare; (*style*) colloquiale

col·lu·sion [kəˈluːʒən] N collusione *f*; **in collusion with** in accordo segreto con

Colo. ABBR (*USA*): = Colorado

Co·logne [kəˈləʊn] N (*Geog*) Colonia

co·logne [kəˈləʊn] N (*also: eau de cologne*) acqua di colonia

Co·lom·bia [kəˈlɒmbɪə] N Colombia

Co·lom·bian [kəˈlɒmbɪən] ADJ, N colombiano(-a)

co·lon [ˈkəʊlən] N **1** (*punctuation*) due punti *mpl* **2** (*Anat*) colon *m inv*

colo·nel [ˈkɜːnl] N colonnello

co·lo·nial [kəˈləʊnɪəl] ADJ coloniale; (*architecture*) di stile coloniale

colo·nize [ˈkɒlənaɪz] VT colonizzare

colo·ny [ˈkɒlənɪ] N colonia

col·or [ˈkʌləʳ] (*USA*) = colour

Colorado [ˌkɒləˈrɑːdəʊ] N il Colorado

Colorado beetle N dorifora

co·los·sal [kəˈlɒsl] ADJ colossale

col·our, col·or [ˈkʌləʳ] (*USA*) N **1** (*gen*) colore *m*; **what colour is it?** di che colore è?; **to change colour** cambiare colore **2** (*complexion*) colore *m*, colorito; **to get one's colour back** riprendere colore; **the colour drained from his face** impallidì **3 colours** NPL (*Mil, Naut*) colori *mpl*; (*of party, club*) emblemi *mpl*; **to see sth in its true colours** (*fig, usu pej*) vedere qc come veramente è; **to show one's true colours** (*fig, usu pej*) rivelare la propria vera personalità; **to come through (with) flying colours** (*fig*) passare (qc) a pieni voti ♦ VT (*gen*) colorare; (*tint, dye*) tingere; (*fig: affect*) influenzare; **to colour sth green** tingere *or* colorare qc di verde ♦ VI (*blush: also:* **colour up**) arrossire ♦ ADJ (*film, slide, photograph, television*) a colori; **colour TV** televisore *m* a colori
▸ **colour in** VT + ADV colorare

colour-blind, color-blind (*USA*) [ˈkʌləˌblaɪnd] ADJ daltonico(-a)

coloured, colored (*USA*) [ˈkʌləd] ADJ colorato(-a); **a straw-coloured hat** un cappello color paglia; **highly-coloured** (*tale, account*) molto colorito(-a)

col·our·ful, col·or·ful (*USA*) [ˈkʌləfʊl] ADJ (*dress*) dai colori vivaci; (*picture*) ricco(-a) di colore; (*personality*) originale, vivace; (*story*) avvincente

col·our·ing, col·or·ing (*USA*) [ˈkʌlərɪŋ] N colorazione *f*; (*substance*) colorante *m*; (*complexion*) colorito

colour scheme, color scheme (*USA*) N combinazione *f* di colori

colt [kəʊlt] N puledro

col·umn [ˈkɒləm] N (*gen*) colonna; (*in newspaper*) colonna; (*fashion column, sports column etc*) rubrica; **the editorial column** l'articolo di fondo; **the advertising columns** gli annunci economici; **columns of figures** colonne di cifre

col·umn·ist [ˈkɒləmnɪst] N giornalista *m/f* (*che cura una rubrica*), articolista *m/f*

coma [ˈkəʊmə] N (*Med*) coma *m inv*; **to go into a coma** entrare in coma

comb [kəʊm] N pettine *m*; **to run a comb through one's hair** darsi una pettinata ♦ VT **1** (*hair*) pettinare; **to comb one's hair** pettinarsi; **you haven't combed your hair** non ti sei pettinato **2** (*search: area, countryside etc*) rastrellare, setacciare, battere a tappeto

com·bat [ˈkɒmbæt] N lotta, combattimento; (*Mil*) combattimento ♦ VT (*fig*) combattere, lottare contro

com·bi·na·tion [ˌkɒmbɪˈneɪʃən] N combinazione *f*

combination lock N serratura a combinazione

com·bine [*vb* kəmˈbaɪn, *n* ˈkɒmbaɪn] VT: **to combine (with)** (*projects, proposals*) combinare (con); (*qualities*) unire a; **our combined incomes** i nostri stipendi messi insieme; **to combine business with pleasure** unire l'utile al dilettevole; **the film combines humour with suspense** il film unisce umorismo e suspense; **to combine forces with sb** unire le proprie forze con qn; **a combined effort** uno sforzo collettivo; **a combined operation** (*Mil*) operazione *f* combinata ♦ VI **1** unirsi, mettersi insieme; **to combine with** unirsi a; **to combine against sth/sb** unirsi contro qc/qn **2** (*Chem*): **to combine (with)** combinarsi (con); **combining power** valenza ♦ N lega; (*Comm, Fin*) trust *m inv*, associazione *f*; (*Agr: also:* **combine harvester**) mietitrebbia *f inv*

com·bo [ˈkɒmbəʊ] N (*Jazz*) gruppo

com·bus·tible [kəmˈbʌstɪbl] ADJ combustibile

com·bus·tion [kəmˈbʌstʃən] N combustione *f*

come [kʌm] VI (*pt* came, *pp* come) **1** (*gen*) venire; (*arrive*) venire, arrivare; (*have its place*) venire, trovarsi; **come with me** vieni con me; **Helen came with me** Helen è venuta con me; **can I come too?** posso venire anch'io?; **they came late** sono arrivati tardi; **the letter came this morning** la lettera è arrivata stamattina; **come home** vieni a casa; **come and see us soon** vieni a trovarci presto; **we have come to help you** siamo venuti ad aiutarti; **she has come from London** è venuta da Londra; **we've just come from Paris** siamo appena arrivati da Parigi; **this necklace comes from Spain** questa collana viene dalla Spagna; **they have come a long way** vengono da lontano; (*fig*) hanno fatto molta strada; **people were coming and going all day** c'era gente che andava e veniva tutto il giorno; **to come running** venire di corsa; **to come for sb/sth** venire a prendere qn/qc; **we'll come after you** ti seguiamo; **coming!** vengo!, arrivo!; **we came to a village** siamo arrivati a un paese; **to come to a decision** arrivare *or* giungere a una decisione; **the water only came to her waist** l'acqua le arrivava solo alla vita; **it came to me that** (*idea: occur*) mi è venuto in mente che; **it may come as a surprise to you ...** può sorprenderti...; **it came as a shock to her** è stato un colpo per lei; **when it comes to choosing** dovendo scegliere; **when it comes to mathematics** quanto alla matematica; **the time will come when ...** verrà il giorno in cui...; **the new ruling comes into force next year** il nuovo regolamento entrerà in vigore l'anno prossimo; **A comes before B** A viene prima di B; **he came 3rd in the race** è arrivato 3° nella gara **2** (*happen*) accadere, succedere; **come what may** qualunque cosa succeda; **no good will come of it** andrà a finire male; **nothing came of it** non ne è saltato fuori niente, non ha portato a niente; **that's what comes of being careless** ecco cosa succede a non far attenzione; **how come?** (*fam*) come mai? **3** (*be, become*) diventare; **my dreams came true** i miei sogni si sono avverati; **to come undone/loose** slacciarsi/allentarsi; **my shoelaces have come undone** i lacci (delle scarpe) si sono sciolti; **your zip has come undone** ti si è aperta la chiusura lampo *or* la cerniera; **it comes naturally to him** gli viene spontaneo; **those shoes come in two colours** quelle scarpe sono disponibili in due colori; **I have come to like her** ho finito col trovarla simpatica; **now I come to think of it** ora che ci penso **4** (*phrases*): **in (the) years to come** negli anni futuri *or* a venire; **if it comes to it** in tal caso; **if it comes to that ...** se è per questo...; **come again?** (*fam*) come?; **he had it coming to him** ha avuto quello che si meritava; **I could see it coming** me lo aspettavo; **he's as daft as they come** è sce mo come ce ne sono pochi; **to come between two people** mettersi fra due persone **5** (*fam: have an orgasm*) venire

‣ **come about** VI + ADV accadere, succedere

‣ **come across** VI + ADV **1** (*gen*) attraversare **2** (*fig*): **to come across well/badly** fare una buona/cattiva impressione; **to come across as** dare l'impressione di essere; **she came across as a very nice person** ha dato l'impressione di essere una persona molto simpatica ♦ VI + PREP (*find*) trovare (per caso); **I came across a dress that I hadn't worn for years** ho trovato per caso un vestito che non mettevo da anni

‣ **come along** VI + ADV **1 come along!** sbrigati!, avanti!, andiamo!, forza! **2** (*accompany*) venire **3** (*progress*) far progressi, procedere, migliorare; (*pupil, work*) fare progressi; **how's your arm coming along?** come va il tuo braccio?

‣ **come apart** VI + ADV (*break*) andare in pezzi; (*become detached: sleeve, jacket*) staccarsi (scucendosi); **my jacket is coming apart** la mia giacca si sta scucendo

‣ **come at** VI + PREP **1** (*attack*) avventarsi su; **he came at me with a knife** si è avventato su di me con un coltello **2** (*reach*) arrivare; **to come at the truth** arrivare alla verità

‣ **come away** VI + ADV (*leave*) venir via; (*become detached*) staccarsi; **come away from there!** levati di lì!, vieni via di là!

‣ **come back** VI + ADV **1** (*return*) tornare; **he came back an hour later** è tornato un'ora dopo; **to come back to what we were discussing ...** per tornare all'argomento di prima... **2** (*reply: fam*): **can I come back to you on that one?** possiamo riparlarne più tardi? **3** (*return to mind*): **it's all coming back to me** mi sta tornando in mente

‣ **come by** VI + PREP: **to come by sth** procurarsi qc

‣ **come down** VI + PREP scendere ♦ VI + ADV (*person*): **to come down (from/to)** scendere (da/a); (*building*) essere demolito(-a); (*prices, temperature*) diminuire, calare; **to come down in the world** ridursi male; **she came down on him like a ton of bricks** gli ha fatto una sfuriata; **to come down with a cold** prendersi un raffreddore

‣ **come down to** VI + ADV + PREP: **it all comes down to ...** è tutta questione di...

‣ **come for** VI + PREP **1** (*attack*) avventarsi su **2** (*collect*) passare a prendere; **I'll come for you at seven** passo a prenderti alle sette

‣ **come forward** VI + ADV farsi avanti, presentarsi

‣ **come from** VI + PREP venire *or* provenire da

‣ **come in** VI + ADV (*person*) entrare; (*train*) arrivare; (*tide*) salire; (*in race*) arrivare; (*in election*) salire al potere; **they came in together** entrarono insieme; **come in!** avanti!; **where do I come in?** dove entro in ballo io?; **they have no money coming in** non hanno entrate

‣ **come in for** VI + ADV + PREP (*criticism, blame*) essere oggetto di

‣ **come into** VI + PREP (*inherit*) ereditare; **where do I come into it?** (*be involved*) come vi entro io?; **money doesn't come into it** i soldi non c'entrano

‣ **come off** VI + ADV (*button etc*) staccarsi; (*stain*) andare via; **I don't think this stain will come off** non penso che la macchia andrà via **2** (*event*) avere luogo; (*plans*) attuarsi; (*attempt, experiment*) riuscire **3** (*acquit o.s.*): **to come off best/worst** avere la meglio/la peggio ♦ VI + PREP: **a button came off my jacket** mi si è staccato un bottone dalla giacca; **she came off her bike** è caduta dalla bicicletta; **come off it!** (*fam*) piantala!, ma va'!

‣ **come on** VI + ADV **1** (*progress*) = come along **3 2** (*exhortation*): **come on!** avanti!, andiamo!, forza! **3** (*protest*): **come on!** ma dai! **4** (*start*) cominciare; **I feel a cold coming on** mi sta venendo un raffreddore; **winter is coming on now** l'inverno si avvicina **5** (*lights, electricity*) accendersi **6** (*Theatre*) entrare in scena

‣ **come on to** VI + ADV + PREP (*turn to*) passare a; (*sexually*) fare delle avance di natura sessuale *or*

‣ **come out** VI + ADV (*person, object*) uscire; (*flower*) sbocciare; (*sun, stars*) apparire; (*news: esp scandal*) essere divulgato(-a); (*truth*) saltare fuori; (*book, film, magazine*) uscire, essere pubblicato(-a); (*declare one's sexual orientation*) dichiararsi **Bill has come out** Bill si è dichiarato (*qualities; show*) rivelarsi, mostrarsi; (*stain*) andare via; (*strike*) entrare in sciopero; **to come out of sth** uscire da qc; **we came out of the cinema at 10** siamo usciti dal cinema alle dieci; **her book comes out in May** il suo libro esce a maggio; **none of my photos came out** non è venuta nessuna delle mie foto; **they came out on strike** entrare in sciopero; **he came out in a rash** gli è venuto uno sfogo; **the dye has come out of your jumper** il tuo maglione è scolorito; **to come out on strike** entrare in sciopero, fare sciopero; **to come out against sth** dichiararsi decisamente contrario(-a) a qc

‣ **come over** VI + ADV venire; **they came over to England for a holiday** sono venuti in Inghilterra per una vacanza; **you'll soon come over to my way of thinking** presto sarai anche tu della mia idea; **her speech came over very well** il suo discorso ha fatto una buona impressione, il suo discorso è riuscito bene ♦ VI + PREP: **I don't know what's come over him!** non so cosa gli sia preso!; **a feeling of weariness came over her** un forte senso di stanchezza la assalì

‣ **come round** VI + ADV **1** passare, venire; **he is coming round to see us** passa da noi, viene a trovarci **2** (*occur regularly*) ricorrere, venire; **Christmas seems to come round earlier every year** ogni anno sembra che il Natale venga prima **3** (*make detour*): **to come round (by)** passare (per); **we came round by the longer route** abbiamo fatto la strada più lunga **4** (*change one's mind*) cambiare idea; **she'll soon come round to your way of thinking** presto la penserà come te **5** (*throw off bad mood*): **leave him alone, he'll soon come round** lascialo in pace *or* perdere, presto gli passerà **6** (*regain consciousness*) riprendere conoscenza, rinvenire; **he came round after about ten minutes** ha ripreso conoscenza dopo circa dieci minuti

‣ **come through** VI + ADV **1** (*survive*) sopravvivere, farcela **2** (*telephone call*): **the call came through** abbiamo ricevuto la telefonata ♦ VI + PREP (*survive: war, danger*) superare, uscire indenne da; **they came through a difficult time in their marriage** hanno superato un periodo difficile del loro matrimonio

‣ **come to** VI + PREP (*add up to: amount*): **how much does it come to?** quanto costa?, quanto viene? ♦ VI + ADV (*regain consciousness*) riprendere conoscenza, rinvenire; **she came to in a hospital bed** ha ripreso conoscenza in un letto d'ospedale

‣ **come together** VI + ADV (*assemble*) riunirsi; (*meet*) incontrarsi

‣ **come under** VI + PREP (*heading*) trovarsi sotto; (*influence*) cadere sotto, subire

‣ **come up** VI + ADV **1** salire; **he came up to us with a smile** ci si avvicinò sorridendo **2** (*matters for discussion*) essere sollevato(-a); **to come up (before)** (*accused*) comparire (davanti a); (*lawsuit*) essere ascoltato(-a) (da) ♦ VI + PREP venire su, salire; **something has come up so I'll be late home** è saltato fuori un problema, per cui tornerò a casa tardi

‣ **come up against** VI + ADV + PREP (*resistance, difficulties*) urtare contro; **she came up against complete opposition to her proposals** le sue proposte hanno incontrato la più completa opposizione

‣ **come up to** VI + ADV + PREP arrivare (fino) a; **the film didn't come up to our expectations** il film ci ha deluso

‣ **come up with** VI + ADV + PREP (*suggest: idea, plan*) suggerire, proporre; (*offer: money, suggestion*) offrire; **he came up with an idea** venne fuori con un'idea

‣ **come upon** VI + PREP (*object, person*) trovare per caso

come·back [ˈkʌmˌbæk] N 1 (*Theatre, Cine*) rentrée *f*, ritorno; **to make a comeback** (*attore, politico*) tornare sulle scene; (*abiti ecc*) tornare di moda 2 (*reaction*) reazione *f*; (*response*) risultato, risposta

co·median [kəˈmiːdɪən] N attore comico

co·medi·enne [kəˌmiːdɪˈɛn] N attrice *f* comica

come·down [ˈkʌmˌdaʊn] N *no pl* passo indietro

com·edy [ˈkɒmɪdɪ] N (*gen*) commedia brillante; (*humour*) lato comico

com·et [ˈkɒmɪt] N cometa

come·up·pance [ˌkʌmˈʌpəns] N: **she got her comeuppance** ha avuto quello che si meritava

com·fort [ˈkʌmfət] N 1 (*physical comfort*) comodità *f inv*, benessere *m*; **in the comfort of your own home** nella comodità della propria casa; **to live in comfort** vivere nell'agiatezza; **that car was a bit too close for comfort** quella macchina è passata troppo vicino per i miei gusti 2 (*solace*) consolazione *f*, conforto; **you're a great comfort to me** mi sei di gran conforto ♦ VT confortare, consolare

com·fort·able [ˈkʌmfətəbl] ADJ (*house*) confortevole; (*chair, shoes, life*) comodo(-a); (*income, majority*) più che sufficiente; (*temperature*) piacevole; **their house is small but comfortable** la loro casa è piccola ma confortevole; **to make o.s. comfortable** mettersi a proprio agio; **make yourself comfortable** si metta a suo agio; **are you comfortable, sitting there?** sta comodo, seduto lì?; **I don't feel very comfortable about it** non mi sento molto tranquillo

com·fort·ably [ˈkʌmfətəblɪ] ADV (*sit etc*) comodamente; (*live*) bene; **to be comfortably off** vivere agiatamente; **to win comfortably** vincere agevolmente

com·fort·er [ˈkʌmfətə'] N (*person*) consolatore(-trice); (*scarf*) sciarpa di lana; (*baby's dummy*) ciuccio, succhiotto; (*USA: quilt*) trapunta

comfort station N (*USA: euph*) toilette *f inv*

com·ic [ˈkɒmɪk] ADJ comico(-a) ♦ N (*person*) comico (attrice comica); (*magazine*) giornalino (a fumetti)

comic book N (*USA*) fumetti *mpl*; **he reads a lot of comic books** legge un sacco di fumetti

comic strip N fumetto

com·ing [ˈkʌmɪŋ] ADJ (*next*) prossimo(-a); (*future*) futuro(-a); **in the coming weeks/election** nelle prossime settimane/elezioni ♦ N avvento, arrivo

coming and going N, **comings and goings** NPL andirivieni *m inv*, viavai *m inv*; **there have been a lot of comings and goings** c'è stato un continuo andirivieni

com·ma [ˈkɒmə] N virgola

com·mand [kəˈmɑːnd] N (*esp Mil: order*) ordine *m*, comando; (: *control*) comando; (: *mastery*) padronanza; (*Comput*) comando; **by** *or* **at the command of** per ordine di; **under the command of** sotto il comando di; **to be in command (of)** essere al comando (di); **to have/take command of** avere/prendere il comando di; **to have at one's command** (*money, resources etc*) avere a propria disposizione; **to have a good command of English** avere una buona padronanza dell'inglese ♦ VT (*order*): **to command sb to do sth** ordinare *or* comandare a qn di fare qc; (*lead: men, ship*) essere al comando di; (*have at one's disposal: resources*) disporre di, avere a propria disposizione; (*respect*) incutere; **that picture will command a high price** quel quadro sarà venduto ad un prezzo elevato

command economy N = **planned economy**

com·man·deer [ˌkɒmənˈdɪə'] VT requisire

com·mand·er [kəˈmɑːndə'] N capo; (*Mil*) comandante *m*

commander in chief N (*Mil*) comandante *m* in capo

com·mand·ing [kəˈmɑːndɪŋ] ADJ (*appearance*) imponente; (*voice, tone*) autorevole; (*lead, position*) dominante

commanding officer N comandante *m*

com·mand·ment [kəˈmɑːndmənt] N (*Bible*) comandamento

command module N (*Space*) modulo di comando

com·man·do [kəˈmɑːndəʊ] N (*group*) commando *m inv*; (*soldier*) soldato appartenente ad un commando

com·memo·rate [kəˈmɛməreɪt] VT commemorare

com·memo·ra·tion [kəˌmɛməˈreɪʃən] N commemorazione *f*; **in commemoration of** in memoria di

com·memo·ra·tive [kəˈmɛmərətɪv] ADJ commemorativo(-a)

com·mence [kəˈmɛns] VT cominciare; **to commence doing sth** cominciare a fare qc ♦ VI cominciare

com·mence·ment [kəˈmɛnsmənt] N (*frm*) inizio

com·mend [kəˈmɛnd] VT 1 (*praise*) lodare 2 (*recommend*) raccomandare; **the proposal has little to commend it** la proposta dà poco affidamento 3 (*entrust*): **to commend (to)** affidare a

com·mend·able [kəˈmɛndəbl] ADJ lodevole

com·men·da·tion [ˌkɒmɛnˈdeɪʃən] N (*for bravery etc*) encomio, lode *f*; (*recommendation*) raccomandazione *f*

com·men·su·rate [kəˈmɛnsərɪt] ADJ: **commensurate with** proporzionato(-a) a, commisurato(-a) a

com·ment [ˈkɒmɛnt] N (*remark: written or spoken*) commento, osservazione *f*; (: *critical*) critica; **he made no comment** non fece commenti; **"no comment"** "(non ho) niente da dire"; **to cause comment** provocare critiche ♦ VI: **to comment (on)** fare commenti *or* dichiarazioni (su); **the police have not commented on these rumours** la polizia non ha fatto commenti sulle voci ♦ VT: **to comment that** osservare che

com·men·tary [ˈkɒməntərɪ] N 1 (*Radio*) radiocronaca; (*TV*) telecronaca 2 (*on text*) commento

com·men·ta·tor [ˈkɒmənteɪtə'] N (*Radio*) radiocronista *m/f*; (*TV*) telecronista *m/f*

com·merce [ˈkɒmɜːs] N commercio; **commerce between the two countries** scambi commerciali fra i due paesi

com·mer·cial [kəˈmɜːʃəl] ADJ commerciale; **the commercial world** il mondo del commercio ♦ N (*TV: also:* **commercial break**) pubblicità *f inv*, spot *m inv* (pubblicitario)

commercial bank N banca commerciale

commercial college N ≈ istituto commerciale

com·mer·cial·ism [kəˈmɜːʃəˌlɪzəm] N (*pej*) affarismo

commercial television N televisione *f* privata

commercial traveller, commercial traveler (*USA*) N viaggiatore *m or* rappresentante di commercio, commesso viaggiatore

commercial vehicle N veicolo per il trasporto di merci, veicolo commerciale

com·mis·er·ate [kəˈmɪzəreɪt] VI: **to commiserate with** esprimere il proprio rincrescimento a

com·mis·sion [kəˈmɪʃən] N 1 (*order for work: esp of artist*) incarico 2 (*for salesman*) commissione *f*, provvigione *f*; **to work/sell on commission** lavorare/vendere a provvigione; **I get 10% commission** ricevo il 10% sulle vendite; **he gets commission on top of his basic salary** oltre allo stipendio base prende una provvigione; **the bank charges one per cent commission** la banca fa pagare una commissione dell'uno per cento 3 (*committee*) commissione *f*; **commission of inquiry** (*Brit*) commissione *f* d'inchiesta; **a commission has been set up to investigate the tragedy** è stata nominata una commissione per indagare sulla tragedia 4 (*Mil*): **to get one's commission** ricevere la nomina ad ufficiale 5 **out of commission** (*machine*) fuori uso; (*Naut*) in disarmo ♦ VT 1 (*expert, consultant, artist*): **to commission sb to do sth** incaricare qn di fare qc; **to commission sth from sb** (*work of art*) commissionare qc a qn 2 (*Mil*) nominare ufficiale

com·mis·sion·aire [kəˌmɪʃəˈnɛə'] N (*Brit: at shop, cinema etc*) portiere *m* in livrea

com·mis·sion·er [kəˈmɪʃənə'] N membro di una commissione; (*Police*) questore *m*; **commissioner of police** ≈ questore *m*

com·mit [kəˈmɪt] VT 1 (*crime, act*) commettere; **to commit a crime** commettere un delitto; **to commit suicide** suicidarsi 2 **to commit o.s. (to sth/to doing sth)** impegnarsi (in qc/nel fare qc); **I don't want to commit myself** non voglio impegnarmi 3 (*consign*): **to commit sth to sb's care** affidare qc a qn; **to commit to memory** imparare a memoria; **to commit to writing** mettere per iscritto; **to commit sb for trial** rinviare qn a giudizio

com·mit·ment [kəˈmɪtmənt] N (*responsibility*) impegno; (*devotion*) dedizione *f*; **he refused to make any commitment** ha rifiutato d'impegnarsi in alcun modo

com·mit·ted [kəˈmɪtɪd] ADJ (*Christian*) convinto(-a); (*writer*) impegnato(-a)

com·mit·tee [kəˈmɪtɪ] N (*takes sg or pl vb*) comitato,

commissione f; (*Parliament*) commissione; **committee of inquiry** commissione d'inchiesta; **to be on a committee** far parte di un comitato *or* di una commissione

committee meeting N riunione f di comitato *or* di commissione

com·mod·ity [kəˈmɒdɪtɪ] N prodotto, articolo; (*food*) derrata; **basic commodities** beni *mpl* di prima necessità
❑ **commodity** is not translated by the Italian word *comodità*

commodity exchange N borsa f merci, *inv*

com·mon [ˈkɒmən] ADJ **1** comune; (*usual*) normale; **it's a common name** è un nome comune; **it's a common belief that ...** si tende a credere che...; **it's a common occurrence** succede di frequente; **it's common knowledge that ...** è risaputo *or* notorio che..., è di dominio pubblico che...; **it's common courtesy** è una questione di semplice cortesia; **in common use** di uso comune; **common or garden** ordinario(-a); **the common man** l'uomo della strada; **in common parlance** nel linguaggio corrente; **the common people** il popolo; **for the common good** nell'interesse generale, per il bene comune **2** (*pej: vulgar*) volgare, grossolano(-a) ♦ N **1** (*land*) parco comunale; **a walk on the common** una passeggiata nel parco comunale **2 in common** in comune; **we have** *or* **we've got a lot in common** abbiamo molto in comune

common cold N: **the common cold** il raffreddore

common denominator N denominatore m comune

com·mon·er [ˈkɒmənəʳ] N cittadino(-a) (non nobile)

common ground N (*fig*) punto *mpl* d'incontro *or* d'intesa, terreno comune

common land N terreno di uso pubblico

common-law N diritto consuetudinario

common-law [ˈkɒmənˌlɔː] ADJ: **common-law wife** convivente f more uxorio

com·mon·ly [ˈkɒmənlɪ] ADV (*see adj*) comunemente, usualmente; in modo volgare

Common Market N: **the Common Market** il Mercato Comune

common·place [ˈkɒmənˌpleɪs] ADJ comune; (*pej*) banale, ordinario(-a) ♦ N (*statement*) luogo comune

common room N (*Scol: staff room*) sala dei professori; (: *for students*) sala di ritrovo

Com·mons [ˈkɒmənz] NPL (*Brit Pol*): **the (House of) Commons** la Camera dei Comuni

common sense N buon senso

Common·wealth [ˈkɒmənˌwɛlθ] N: **the Commonwealth** il Commonwealth

com·mo·tion [kəˈməʊʃən] N confusione f, tumulto, trambusto; **to make** *or* **cause a commotion** causare confusione

com·mu·nal [ˈkɒmjuːnl] ADJ (*facilities*) in comune; (*for common use*) pubblico(-a); (*life*) di comunità

com·mune [n ˈkɒmjuːn, vb kəˈmjuːn] N (*group*) comune f ♦ VI: **to commune with nature** comunicare con la natura

com·mu·ni·cate [kəˈmjuːnɪˌkeɪt] VT: **to communicate sth (to sb)** (*thoughts, information*) comunicare qc (a qn); (*frm: disease*) trasmettere qc (a qn) ♦ VI (*speak etc*): **to communicate (with)** comunicare (con), mettersi in contatto (con); **communicating rooms** stanze *fpl* comunicanti

com·mu·ni·ca·tion [kəˌmjuːnɪˈkeɪʃən] N comunicazione f; **to be in communication with** (*frm*) essere in contatto con

communications network N rete f delle comunicazioni

communications satellite N satellite m per telecomunicazioni

com·mu·ni·ca·tive [kəˈmjuːnɪkətɪv] ADJ (*gen*) loquace; **communicative skills** (*Scol*) capacità f inv espressive

com·mun·ion [kəˈmjuːnɪən] N (*also Rel*) comunione f; **to take communion** ricevere la comunione

communiqué [kəˈmjuːnɪˌkeɪ] N comunicato, bollettino

com·mun·ism [ˈkɒmjʊnɪzəm] N comunismo

com·mun·ist [ˈkɒmjʊnɪst] ADJ, N comunista m/f

com·mu·nity [kəˈmjuːnɪtɪ] N (*gen*) comunità f inv; (*of goods, interests*) comunanza; **the black community** la comunità nera; **the Italian community in Glasgow** la comunità italiana a Glasgow; **the student community** gli studenti

community centre N circolo ricreativo, centro sociale

community chest N (*USA*) fondo di beneficenza

community health centre N centro socio-sanitario (di quartiere)

community service N (*Brit*) servizio civile (volontario o in sostituzione della pena per reati minori)

community spirit N (*responsibility*) spirito civico; (*solidarity*) spirito di solidarietà

com·mu·ta·tion tick·et [ˌkɒmjʊˈteɪʃənˈtɪkɪt] N (*USA*) biglietto di abbonamento

com·mute [kəˈmjuːt] VI fare il (la) pendolare; **she commutes between Oxford and London** fa la pendolare tra Oxford e Londra ♦ VT (*payment*): **to commute for** *or* **into** commutare in; (*Law: sentence*): **to commute (to)** commutare (a)

com·mut·er [kəˈmjuːtəʳ] N pendolare m/f; **the commuter belt** (*Brit*) la periferia abitata dai pendolari; **commuter aircraft** aereo interregionale

com·pact [kəmˈpækt] ADJ compatto(-a); **this house is very compact** questa casa è piccola ma funzionale

com·pact [ˈkɒmpækt] N **1** (*agreement*) patto, contratto **2** (*also: powder compact*) portacipria m inv

compact disc N compact disc m inv

compact disc player N lettore m di compact disc

com·pan·ion [kəmˈpænjən] N compagno(-a); (*lady's*) dama di compagnia; (*book*) manuale m, guida

com·pan·ion·ship [kəmˈpænjənˌʃɪp] N compagnia

com·pan·ion·way [kəmˈpænjənˌweɪ] N (*Naut*) scala

com·pa·ny [ˈkʌmpənɪ] N (*gen, also Mil, Theatre*) compagnia; (*Comm, Fin*) società f inv, compagnia; **ship's company** equipaggio; **insurance company** compagnia di assicurazione; **theatre company** compagnia teatrale; **he works for a big company** lavora per una grossa società; **Smith and Company** Smith e soci; **he's good/poor company** è di buona/cattiva compagnia; **to keep sb company** tenere *or* fare compagnia a qn; **I'll keep you company** ti farò compagnia; **to get into bad company** farsi cattive amicizie; **to keep bad company** frequentare cattive compagnie; **to part company with sb** dividersi *or* separarsi da qn; **we have company this evening** abbiamo ospiti stasera

company car N macchina (di proprietà) della ditta

company director N amministratore m, consigliere m di amministrazione

company secretary N (*Brit: Comm*) segretario(-a) generale

com·pa·rable [ˈkɒmpərəbl] ADJ simile; **comparable to** *or* **with** paragonabile a

com·para·tive [kəmˈpærətɪv] ADJ (*freedom, luxury, cost*) relativo(-a); (*adjective, adverb*) comparativo(-a); (*study, literature*) comparato(-a); **she's a comparative stranger** la conosco relativamente poco; **the comparative safety of Britain** la relativa sicurezza della Gran Bretagna ♦ N (*Gram*) comparativo

com·para·tive·ly [kəmˈpærətɪvlɪ] ADV (*see adj*) relativamente; comparativamente; **a comparatively easy exercise** un esercizio relativamente facile

com·pare [kəmˈpeəʳ] VT: **to compare sth/sb with/to** paragonare qc/qn a, mettere a confronto *or* confrontare qc/qn con; **compare the two illustrations** mettete a confronto le due illustrazioni; **people always compare him with his brother** tutti lo paragonano a suo fratello; **they compared his work to that of Joyce** hanno paragonato la sua opera a quella di Joyce; **compared with** *or* **to** a paragone di, rispetto a; **Oxford is small compared with London** Oxford è piccola rispetto a Londra; **to compare notes with sb** (*fig*) scambiare le proprie impressioni con qn ♦ VI: **to compare (with)** essere paragonabile (a), reggere il confronto (con); **how do they compare for speed?** che velocità fanno rispettivamente?; **how do the prices compare?** che differenza di prezzo c'è?; **it doesn't compare with yours** non è paragonabile al tuo ♦ N: **beyond compare** (*liter: adj*) senza confronto *or* paragone; (: *adv*) incomparabilmente

com·pari·son [kəmˈpærɪsn] N paragone m, confronto; **in comparison with, by comparison with** rispetto a, in confronto a/di; **by comparison** a confronto

com·part·ment [kəmˈpɑːtmənt] N compartimento, scomparto; (*Brit: Rail*) scompartimento; **a first class compartment** uno scompartimento di prima classe

com·pass [ˈkʌmpəs] N 1 (*Naut, etc*) bussola 2 (*Math*): **(a pair of) compasses** un compasso 3 (*fig: range*) portata; **within the compass of** entro i limiti di

com·pas·sion [kəmˈpæʃən] N compassione *f*

com·pas·sion·ate [kəmˈpæʃənɪt] ADJ (*person*) compassionevole; **on compassionate grounds** per motivi personali

compassionate leave N congedo straordinario (*per gravi motivi di famiglia*)

com·pat·ibil·ity [kəmˌpætəˈbɪlɪtɪ] N compatibilità

com·pat·ible [kəmˈpætɪbl] ADJ: **compatible (with)** compatibile (con)

com·pel [kəmˈpɛl] VT 1 (*force*): **to compel sb (to do sth)** forzare qn (a fare qc), costringere *or* obbligare qn (a fare qc) 2 (*demand: obedience*) esigere; (: *respect*) incutere

com·pel·ling [kəmˈpɛlɪŋ] ADJ (*argument, reason: powerful*) convincente; (*poem*) avvincente; (*painting*) affascinante; **he put forward a compelling argument against the death penalty** ha sollevato un argomento convincente contro la pena di morte; **it's a violent yet compelling film** è un film violento ma avvincente

com·pen·dium [kəmˈpɛndɪəm] N (*summary*) compendio, sommario

com·pen·sate [ˈkɒmpənˌseɪt] VT: **to compensate sb (for sth)** compensare qn (per qc); (*financially*) indennizzare *or* risarcire qn (per qc); **workers made redundant will be compensated** i lavoratori in esubero riceveranno un indennizzo ♦ VI: **to compensate for** compensare

com·pen·sa·tion [ˌkɒmpənˈseɪʃən] N (*see vb*) compensazione *f*; indennità, risarcimento; **in compensation (for)** come compenso (per), come indennizzo (per)

com·père [ˈkɒmpɛəʳ] N presentatore(-trice) ♦ VT (*show*) presentare

com·pete [kəmˈpiːt] VI (*Comm*): **to compete (with)** essere in concorrenza (con), fare concorrenza (a); (*vie*) essere in competizione (con); **to compete in** partecipare a; **I'm competing in the marathon** partecipo alla maratona; **to compete for sth** contendersi qc; (*take part*) concorrere in qc, concorrere per qc; **there are fifty students competing for six places** ci sono cinquanta studenti che concorrono per sei posti; **to compete with one another** farsi concorrenza

com·pe·tence [ˈkɒmpɪtəns], **com·pe·ten·cy** [ˈkɒmpɪtənsɪ] N competenza

com·pe·tent [ˈkɒmpɪtənt] ADJ competente; **this court is not competent to deal with that** questa corte non è competente in materia

com·pet·ing [kəmˈpiːtɪŋ] ADJ (*theories, ideas*) opposto(-a); (*companies*) in concorrenza; (*explanations*) in contrasto tra di loro

com·pe·ti·tion [ˌkɒmpɪˈtɪʃən] N 1 (*Comm*) concorrenza; **in competition with** in concorrenza con; **competition in the computer sector is fierce** c'è una grossa concorrenza nel settore informatico 2 (*gen, also Sport*) gara, competizione *f*, concorso; **singing competition** gara di canto; **to go in for** *or* **enter a competition** partecipare ad una gara *or* un concorso; **she won £5000 in a newspaper competition** ha vinto 5000 sterline in un concorso organizzato da un quotidiano

com·peti·tive [kəmˈpɛtɪtɪv] ADJ 1 (*sports*) agonistico(-a); (*person*) che ha spirito di competizione; (*in sport*) che ha spirito agonistico, che ha spirito di competizione; **I'm a very competitive person** sono molto competitivo(-a); **competitive examination** concorso 2 (*Comm: price*) concorrenziale, competitivo(-a); (: *goods*) a prezzo concorrenziale *or* competitivo; **to have a competitive advantage in sth** essere avvantaggiato(-a) sulla concorrenza in qc

com·peti·tor [kəmˈpɛtɪtəʳ] N concorrente *m/f*

com·pile [kəmˈpaɪl] VT compilare

com·pla·cen·cy [kəmˈpleɪsnsɪ] N autocompiacimento, eccessivo compiacimento

com·pla·cent [kəmˈpleɪsnt] ADJ compiaciuto(-a), soddisfatto(-a) di sé; **to be complacent** adagiarsi

com·plain [kəmˈpleɪn] VI: **to complain (to sb about sth)** lamentarsi (con qn di qc), lagnarsi (con qn di qc); (*make a formal complaint*) fare un reclamo (a qn per qc), reclamare (con qn per qc); **we're going to complain to the manager** presenteremo un reclamo al direttore

▸ **complain of** VI + PREP lamentarsi di; (*Med*) accusare

com·plaint [kəmˈpleɪnt] N lamentela; (*to manager of shop etc*) reclamo; (*Med: illness*) disturbo, malattia

com·ple·ment [*n* ˈkɒmplɪmənt, *vb* ˈkɒmplɪˌmɛnt] N 1 (*gen, also Gram, Math*) complemento 2 (*staff, crew*) effettivo ♦ VT (*enhance*) accompagnarsi bene a, completare

com·ple·men·tary [ˌkɒmplɪˈmɛntərɪ] ADJ complementare; **the food and wine were complementary** il cibo e il vino erano ben assortiti

com·plete [kəmˈpliːt] ADJ (*whole*) completo(-a); (*finished*) completo(-a), finito(-a); **complete with** completo(-a) di; **it's a complete disaster** è un vero disastro ♦ VT (*set, collection*) completare; (*piece of work*) finire, completare; (*fill in: form*) riempire; **and to complete my misfortunes** e per colmo di sfortuna

com·plete·ly [kəmˈpliːtlɪ] ADV completamente

com·ple·tion [kəmˈpliːʃən] N completamento; **to be nearing completion** essere in fase di completamento; **on completion of contract** alla firma del contratto

com·plex [ˈkɒmplɛks] ADJ (*all senses*) complesso(-a) ♦ N 1 (*Psych*) complesso; **he's got a complex about his weight** ha il complesso del peso, è complessato per il peso 2 (*of buildings*) complesso; **sports/housing complex** complesso sportivo/edilizio

com·plex·ion [kəmˈplɛkʃən] N (*of face*) carnagione *f*; (*fig: aspect, appearance*) aspetto; **that puts a different complexion on it** (*fig*) ciò fa apparire la cosa sotto tutta un'altra luce *or* tutto un altro aspetto

com·plex·ity [kəmˈplɛksɪtɪ] N complessità *f inv*

com·pli·ance [kəmˈplaɪəns] N 1 (*with rules, orders, wishes*): **in compliance with** in conformità con 2 (*submissiveness*) arrendevolezza, acquiescenza

com·pli·ant [kəmˈplaɪənt] ADJ (*submissive*) arrendevole, acquiescente

com·pli·cate [ˈkɒmplɪˌkeɪt] VT complicare

com·pli·cat·ed [ˈkɒmplɪˌkeɪtɪd] ADJ complicato(-a), complesso(-a)

com·pli·ca·tion [ˌkɒmplɪˈkeɪʃən] N complicazione *f*

com·pli·ment [*n* ˈkɒmplɪˌmənt, *vb* ˈkɒmplɪmənt] N 1 complimento; **to pay sb a compliment** fare un complimento a qn (per qc); **he's always paying her compliments** le fa sempre complimenti; **thanks for the compliment** grazie del complimento 2 compliments NPL (*frm: greetings*) rispetti *mpl*, ossequi *mpl*; **compliments of the season** auguri per le festività; **with our compliments** con i nostri omaggi; **with the compliments of Mr X** con gli omaggi del Signor X ♦ VT: **to compliment sb (on sth/on doing sth)** congratularsi *or* complimentarsi con qn (per qc/per aver fatto qc); **they complimented me on my Italian** si sono complimentati con me per il mio italiano

com·pli·men·tary [ˌkɒmplɪˈmɛntərɪ] ADJ (*remark etc*) lusinghiero(-a), elogiativo(-a); (*free: ticket*) (in) omaggio *inv*

complimentary ticket N biglietto d'omaggio

compliments slip N (*Comm*) cartoncino della società

com·ply [kəmˈplaɪ] VI: **to comply with** (*rules etc*) attenersi a, conformarsi a, osservare; (*wishes, request*) assecondare

com·po·nent [kəmˈpəʊnənt] ADJ, N componente (*m*)

com·pose [kəmˈpəʊz] VT 1 (*music, poetry*) comporre; (*letter*) mettere insieme; **to be composed of** essere composto(-a) di 2 (*calm: thoughts*) riordinare; **to compose o.s.** ricomporsi

com·posed [kəmˈpəʊzd] ADJ (*person*) calmo(-a), composto(-a)

com·pos·er [kəmˈpəʊzəʳ] N (*Mus*) compositore(-trice)

com·po·site [ˈkɒmpəzɪt] ADJ (*gen, also Math*) composto(-a); (*Archit*) composito(-a)

com·po·si·tion [ˌkɒmpəˈzɪʃən] N composizione *f*

com·post [ˈkɒmpɒst] N concime *m*

com·po·sure [kəmˈpəʊʒəʳ] N calma, padronanza di sé

com·pound [*n* ˈkɒmpaʊnd, *adj* kəmˈpaʊnd] N 1 (*enclosed area*) recinto 2 (*Chem*) composto; (*Ling*) parola composta, composto ♦ ADJ composto(-a); **compound substance** composto ♦ VT (*fig: problem, difficulty*) peggiorare

compound fracture N frattura esposta

compound interest N interesse *m* composto

com·pre·hend [ˌkɒmprɪˈhɛnd] VT capire, comprendere

com·pre·hen·sion [ˌkɒmprɪˈhenʃən] N (*understanding*) comprensione *f*; (*Scol*) esercizio di comprensione

com·pre·hen·sive [ˌkɒmprɪˈhensɪv] ADJ (*study*) esauriente; (*knowledge*) esteso(-a); (*description*) dettagliato(-a); (*report, review*) completo(-a), esauriente; (*measures*) di vasta portata; **a comprehensive guide to New Zealand** una guida completa della Nuova Zelanda; **comprehensive insurance policy** (*Aut*) polizza *f* casco, *inv*, polizza *f* multi-rischio, *inv*

com·press [*vb* kəmˈpres, *n* ˈkɒmpres] VT (*substance*) comprimere; (*text etc*) condensare ♦ N (*Med*) compressa

com·pres·sion [kəmˈpreʃən] N compressione *f*

com·prise [kəmˈpraɪz] VT (*also:* **be comprised of:** *be made up of*) comprendere; (*make up*) costituire

com·pro·mise [ˈkɒmprəˌmaɪz] N compromesso ♦ VI: **to compromise (with sb over sth)** venire a un compromesso (con qn su qc) ♦ VT compromettere ♦ ADJ (*decision, solution*) di compromesso

com·pul·sion [kəmˈpʌlʃən] N 1 costrizione *f*, pressione *f*; **under compulsion** sotto costrizione, dietro *or* sotto pressione; **he is under no compulsion (to do it)** nessuno lo costringe (a farlo) 2 desiderio incontrollabile; **a compulsion to tell lies** un impulso incontrollabile a mentire

com·pul·sive [kəmˈpʌlsɪv] ADJ 1 (*Psych: desire, behaviour*) incontrollabile; (: *liar*) patologico(-a); **he's a compulsive drinker/smoker/gambler** ha il vizio del bere/del fumo/del gioco 2 (*novel, film*) avvincente

com·pul·so·ry [kəmˈpʌlsərɪ] ADJ obbligatorio(-a)

compulsory purchase N espropriazione *f*

com·punc·tion [kəmˈpʌŋkʃən] N scrupolo; **to have no compunction about doing sth** non farsi scrupoli a fare qc

com·put·er [kəmˈpjuːtəʳ] N computer *m inv*, elaboratore *m* elettronico ♦ ADJ (*printout*) del computer; (*software*) per computer

computer game N computer game *m inv*, videogioco per computer

computer-generated ADJ realizzato(-a) al computer

com·put·eri·za·tion [kəmˌpjuːtəraɪˈzeɪʃən] N computerizzazione *f*

com·put·er·ize [kəmˈpjuːtəˌraɪz] VT computerizzare

computer language N linguaggio *m* macchina, *inv*

computer-literate [kəmˈpjuːtəˈlɪtərɪt] ADJ: **to be computer-literate** avere dimestichezza coi computer

computer peripheral N unità *f inv* periferica

computer program N programma *m* di computer

computer programmer N programmatore(-trice) di computer

computer programming N programmazione *f* di computer

computer science N informatica

computer scientist N informatico(-a)

com·put·ing [kəmˈpjuːtɪŋ] N informatica

com·rade [ˈkɒmrɪd] N compagno(-a)

com·rade·ship [ˈkɒmrɪdˌʃɪp] N cameratismo

con [kɒn] (*fam*) VT truffare; **to con sb into doing sth** indurre qn a fare qc con raggiri, indurre qn a fare qc raggirandolo; **I've been conned!** mi hanno fregato! ♦ N truffa

con·cave [kɒnˈkeɪv] ADJ concavo(-a)

con·ceal [kənˈsiːl] VT: **to conceal (sth from sb)** nascondere (qc a qn); (*news*) tenere nascosto(-a) (qc a qn); **concealed lighting** illuminazione *f* indiretta

con·cede [kənˈsiːd] VT (*admit: point, defeat*) ammettere; (: *argument*) riconoscere la validità di; (: *territory*) cedere; **he finally conceded that Nancy was right** alla fine ammise che Nancy aveva ragione; **to concede victory** darla vinta ♦ VI cedere

con·ceit [kənˈsiːt] N vanità *f inv*, presunzione *f*

con·ceit·ed [kənˈsiːtɪd] ADJ pieno(-a) di sé, presuntuoso(-a), vanitoso(-a)

con·ceiv·able [kənˈsiːvəbl] ADJ concepibile; **it is conceivable that ...** può anche darsi che...

con·ceiv·ably [kənˈsiːvəblɪ] ADV: **he may conceivably be right** può anche darsi che abbia ragione

con·ceive [kənˈsiːv] VT (*child, idea*) concepire ♦ VI: **to conceive of sth/of doing sth** immaginare qc/di fare qc

con·cen·trate [ˈkɒnsənˌtreɪt] VT concentrare; **to concentrate one's thoughts on sth** concentrarsi su qc ♦ VI 1 (*pay attention*): **to concentrate (on)** concentrarsi (in *or* su); **I couldn't concentrate** non riuscivo a concentrarmi; **concentrate on getting well** pensa soprattutto a guarire 2 (*group closely*) concentrarsi ♦ N (*Chem*) concentrato

con·cen·tra·tion [ˌkɒnsənˈtreɪʃən] N (*of mind, also Tech*) concentrazione *f*; (*of people, troops*) concentramento

concentration camp N campo di concentramento

con·cen·tric [kənˈsentrɪk] ADJ concentrico(-a)

con·cept [ˈkɒnsept] N concetto

con·cep·tion [kənˈsepʃən] N 1 (*idea*) concetto, concezione *f* 2 (*of child*) concepimento

con·cern [kənˈsɜːn] N 1 **what concern is it of yours?** non vedo come ti possa riguardare; **it's of no concern to me, it's no concern of mine** non mi riguarda 2 (*anxiety*) ansietà *f inv*, preoccupazione *f*; **it is a matter for concern that ...** è preoccupante che...; **they expressed concern about the situation** hanno espresso la loro preoccupazione per la situazione 3 (*firm*) impresa, azienda, ditta; **a going concern** un'azienda in attivo ♦ VT riguardare, interessare; **this shouldn't concern you** (*affect*) questo non dovrebbe cambiarti nulla; **this matter does not concern you** questa faccenda non ti riguarda; **their safety is what most concerns me** ciò che mi preoccupa maggiormente è la loro sicurezza; **"to whom it may concern"** "a tutti gli interessati"; **as far as I am concerned** per quanto mi riguarda; **as far as I'm concerned, you can come any time you like** per quanto mi riguarda, puoi venire quando vuoi; **the department concerned** (*under discussion*) l'ufficio in questione; (*relevant*) l'ufficio competente; **it was tragic for everyone concerned** è stato tragico per tutti; **to be concerned with** occuparsi di; **to be concerned in** interessarsi a; **to concern o.s. with** occuparsi di; **they are more concerned to save money than to save lives** ciò che li preoccupa maggiormente è risparmiare denaro e non salvare vite umane

con·cern·ing [kənˈsɜːnɪŋ] PREP riguardo a, circa; **for further information concerning the job, contact Mr Ross** per maggiori informazioni riguardo al lavoro, contatti il signor Ross

con·cert [ˈkɒnsət] N (*Mus*) concerto; **in concert** in concerto; (*fig*) di concerto ♦ ADJ concertistico(-a)

con·cert·ed [kənˈsɜːtɪd] ADJ (*effort, attack*) concertato(-a), collettivo(-a)

concert hall N sala da concerti

con·cer·ti·na [ˌkɒnsəˈtiːnə] N piccola fisarmonica ♦ VI accartocciarsi, piegarsi come una fisarmonica

con·cer·to [kənˈtʃɛətəʊ] N concerto

con·ces·sion [kənˈseʃən] N concessione *f*

con·ces·sion·aire [kənˌseʃəˈnɛəʳ] N (*Comm*) concessionario

con·ces·sion·ary [kənˈseʃənərɪ] ADJ (*ticket, fare*) a prezzo ridotto

con·cili·ation [kənˌsɪlɪˈeɪʃən] N conciliazione *f*

con·cilia·tory [kənˈsɪlɪətərɪ] ADJ conciliante, conciliatorio(-a), conciliativo(-a)

con·cise [kənˈsaɪs] ADJ conciso(-a)

con·clave [ˈkɒnkleɪv] N (*meeting*) riunione *f* segreta; (*Rel*) conclave *m*

con·clude [kənˈkluːd] VT (*all senses*) concludere ♦ VI: **to conclude (with)** (*events*) concludersi (con); (*speaker*) concludere

con·clud·ing [kənˈkluːdɪŋ] ADJ (*remarks etc*) conclusivo(-a), finale

con·clu·sion [kənˈkluːʒən] N (*all senses*) conclusione *f*; **in conclusion** in conclusione; **to come to the conclusion that ...** concludere che..., arrivare alla conclusione che...

con·clu·sive [kənˈkluːsɪv] ADJ conclusivo(-a)

con·coct [kənˈkɒkt] VT (*food, drink*) mettere insieme; (*lie, story, excuse*) inventare; (*scheme*) architettare

con·coc·tion [kənˈkɒkʃən] N (*food, drink*) miscuglio

con·cord [ˈkɒnkɔːd] N (*harmony*) armonia, concordia; (*treaty*) accordo

con·course [ˈkɒnkɔːs] N (*of people*) folla; (*place*) luogo di assembramento; (*in station*) atrio

con·crete [ˈkɒnkriːt] N 1 (*object, advantage*) concreto(-a) 2 (*Constr*) di calcestruzzo ♦ N (*Constr*) calcestruzzo ♦ VT (*path*) rivestire di calcestruzzo

concrete mixer N betoniera

con·cur [kən'kɜː'] VI (frm) **1** (agree): **to concur (with)** (opinions etc) coincidere (con), concordare (con); (person) essere d'accordo (con) **2** (happen at the same time) coincidere

con·cur·rent·ly [kən'kʌrəntlɪ] ADV: **concurrently (with)** simultaneamente (a)

con·cus·sion [kən'kʌʃən] N (Med) commozione f cerebrale
❏ **concussion** is not translated by the Italian word *concussione*

con·demn [kən'dɛm] VT (person) condannare; (declare unfit: building) dichiarare inagibile; (: food) dichiarare immangiabile; **to condemn sb to death** condannare qn a morte; **the government has condemned the EU's decision** il governo ha condannato la decisione dell'Unione europea

con·dem·na·tion [ˌkɒndɛm'neɪʃən] N condanna

con·den·sa·tion [ˌkɒndɛn'seɪʃən] N condensazione f

con·dense [kən'dɛns] VT condensare ♦ VI condensarsi

con·densed milk [kən'dɛnst'mɪlk] N latte m condensato

con·de·scend [ˌkɒndɪ'sɛnd] VI: **to condescend to sb** trattare qn con sussiego; **to condescend to do sth** degnarsi di fare qc, abbassarsi a fare qc

con·de·scend·ing [ˌkɒndɪ'sɛndɪŋ] ADJ sussiegoso(-a)

con·di·tion [kən'dɪʃən] N **1** condizione f; **on condition that** a condizione di, a condizione che + sub; **I'll do it, on one condition...** lo farò, ma ad una condizione...; **under** or **in the present conditions** nelle attuali condizioni or circostanze; **in good/poor condition** in buone/cattive condizioni; **to be in no condition to do sth** non essere in condizione di fare qc; **to be out of condition** (person) essere fuori forma; **physical condition** (of person) condizioni fisiche; **physical conditions** condizioni ambientali; **weather conditions** condizioni meteorologiche; **conditions of sale** condizioni di vendita **2** (disease) malattia; **to have a heart condition** soffrire di (mal di) cuore ♦ VT condizionare, regolare

con·di·tion·al [kən'dɪʃənl] ADJ condizionale; **to be conditional upon** dipendere da

con·di·tion·er [kən'dɪʃənə'] N (for hair) balsamo; (for clothes) ammorbidente m

con·do ['kɒndəʊ] N ABBR (USA fam: = condominium) condominio

con·do·lences [kən'dəʊlənsɪz] NPL condoglianze fpl

con·dom ['kɒndəm] N preservativo

con·do·min·ium [ˌkɒndə'mɪnɪəm] N (USA) condominio

con·done [kən'dəʊn] VT (forgive) perdonare, scusare; (overlook) passare sopra a; **I do not condone violence** non giustifico la violenza

con·du·cive [kən'djuːsɪv] ADJ: **to be conducive to** favorire, essere favorevole a

con·duct [n 'kɒndʌkt, vb kən'dʌkt] N condotta; **civilized conduct** comportamento civile ♦ VT (gen, also Phys) condurre; (guide) accompagnare; (Law) presentare; (Mus) dirigere; (manage) dirigere, amministrare; **to conduct o.s.** comportarsi

con·duct·ed tour [kən'dʌktɪd'tʊə'] N giro guidato, visita guidata

con·duc·tor [kən'dʌktə'] N (of orchestra) direttore m d'orchestra; (on bus) bigliettaio(-a); (USA: Rail) controllore m; (Phys: of heat, electricity) conduttore m

con·duit ['kɒndɪt] N (pipe) conduttura, condotto, tubo

cone [kəʊn] N (gen: of ice cream) cono; (Aut) birillo; (Bot) pigna; **ice-cream cone** cono di gelato
▸ **cone off** VT + ADV chiudere al traffico (un'area o un tratto stradale, delimitandolo con birilli)

con·fec·tion·er [kən'fɛkʃənə'] N pasticciere m; **confectioner's (shop)** ≈ pasticceria

con·fec·tion·ery [kən'fɛkʃənərɪ] N (sweets) dolciumi mpl

con·fed·er·ate [kən'fɛdərɪt] ADJ confederato(-a) ♦ N (pej) complice m/f; (USA: History) confederato

con·fed·era·tion [kənˌfɛdə'reɪʃən] N confederazione f

con·fer [kən'fɜː'] VT: **to confer sth on sb** conferire qc a qn ♦ VI: **to confer (with sb about sth)** consultarsi (con qn su qc)

con·fer·ence ['kɒnfərəns] N (convention, meeting) conferenza, convegno, congresso; (participants) partecipanti mpl alla conferenza or al convegno etc; **to be in conference** essere in riunione

conference room N sala f conferenze pl inv

con·fess [kən'fɛs] VT confessare, ammettere; **to confess o.s. guilty of** (sin, crime) confessare di essere colpevole di, dichiararsi colpevole di ♦ VI (make one's confession) confessarsi; (admit): **to confess (to sth/to doing sth)** confessare (qc/di aver fatto qc); **he confessed to the murder** ha confessato di aver commesso l'omicidio

con·fes·sion [kən'fɛʃən] N confessione f; **to go to confession** andare a confessarsi; **to make one's confession** confessarsi; **to hear sb's confession** ascoltare la confessione di qn

con·fes·sion·al [kən'fɛʃənl] N confessionale m

con·fes·sor [kən'fɛsə'] N confessore m

con·fet·ti [kən'fɛtɪ] N coriandoli mpl

con·fide [kən'faɪd] VT confidare ♦ VI: **to confide in sb (about sth)** confidare in qn (su qc)

con·fi·dence ['kɒnfɪdəns] N **1** (trust) fiducia; **to have (every) confidence in sb** avere (piena) fiducia in qn; **I've got a lot of confidence in him** ho molta fiducia in lui; **to have (every) confidence that** essere (assolutamente) certo(-a) che; **motion of no confidence** (Parliament) mozione f di sfiducia **2** (also: self-confidence) sicurezza di sé, fiducia in se stesso(-a); **to gain confidence** acquistare sicurezza; **she lacks confidence** non ha fiducia in se stessa **3** (secret) confidenza; **in confidence** in via confidenziale; **I'm telling you this in strict confidence** te lo dico in via strettamente confidenziale; **to take sb into one's confidence** confidarsi con qn; **to write in confidence to sb** scrivere a qn con la massima riservatezza

confidence trick N truffa

confident ['kɒnfɪdənt] ADJ sicuro(-a), fiducioso(-a); (also: self-confident) sicuro(-a) (di sé); **she seems very confident** sembra molto sicura di sé; **to be confident of doing sth/that** essere sicuro di fare qc/che; **I'm confident everything will be okay** sono sicuro(-a) che tutto andrà bene

con·fi·den·tial [ˌkɒnfɪ'dɛnʃəl] ADJ (letter, report, remark) confidenziale, riservato(-a); (secretary) particolare

con·fi·den·ti·al·ity [ˌkɒnfɪˌdɛnʃɪ'ælɪtɪ] N riservatezza, carattere m confidenziale

con·figu·ra·tion [kənˌfɪgjʊ'reɪʃən] N (Comput) configurazione f

con·fine [kən'faɪn] VT **1** (imprison, shut up) rinchiudere; **confined to barracks** consegnato(-a) (in caserma); **confined to bed** costretto(-a) a letto **2** (limit) limitare; **to confine o.s. to doing sth** limitarsi a fare qc; see also **confines**

con·fined [kən'faɪnd] ADJ (space) ristretto(-a); **a confined space** uno spazio ristretto

con·fine·ment [kən'faɪnmənt] N **1** (imprisonment) reclusione f, detenzione f; (Mil) consegna; **solitary confinement** cella di isolamento **2** (Med) parto

con·fines ['kɒnfaɪnz] NPL (bounds) confini mpl

con·firm [kən'fɜːm] VT (gen) confermare; (strengthen: belief) rafforzare; (Rel) cresimare

con·fir·ma·tion [ˌkɒnfə'meɪʃən] N conferma; (Rel) cresima; **a confirmation of their suspicions** una conferma dei loro sospetti

con·firmed [kən'fɜːmd] ADJ (smoker, habit etc) incallito(-a), inveterato(-a); (bachelor) impenitente; (admirer) fervente

con·fis·cate ['kɒnfɪsˌkeɪt] VT: **to confiscate sth (from sb)** confiscare qc (a qn)

con·fis·ca·tion [ˌkɒnfɪs'keɪʃən] N confisca

con·fla·gra·tion [ˌkɒnflə'greɪʃən] N (frm) conflagrazione f

con·flict [n 'kɒnflɪkt, vb kən'flɪkt] N conflitto ♦ VI: **to conflict (with)** essere in conflitto (con)

con·flict·ing [kən'flɪktɪŋ] ADJ (reports, evidence, opinions) contraddittorio(-a); (opinions) contrastante

con·form [kən'fɔːm] VI: **to conform (to)** conformarsi (a)

con·form·ist [kən'fɔːmɪst] ADJ conformistico(-a) ♦ N conformista m/f

con·found [kən'faʊnd] VT (confuse) confondere; (amaze) sconcertare; (defeat) sconfiggere; **confound it!** al diavolo!

con·found·ed [kən'faʊndɪd] ADJ maledetto(-a)

con·front [kən'frʌnt] VT (enemy, danger) affrontare; (defiantly) fronteggiare; **to confront sb with sth** mettere qn a

confronto con qc; **I decided to confront him** decisi di affrontarlo; **the problems which confront us** i problemi da affrontare; **the task now confronting them** il compito che ora devono affrontare
❑ **confront** is not translated by the Italian word *confrontare*

con·fron·ta·tion [ˌkɒnfrənˈteɪʃən] N scontro

con·fron·ta·tion·al [ˌkɒnfrənˈteɪʃənəl] ADJ polemico(-a), aggressivo(-a)

con·fuse [kənˈfjuːz] VT confondere

con·fused [kənˈfjuːzd] ADJ confuso(-a); **in a confused state** (*person*) in stato confusionale; (*room, papers*) in disordine; **to get confused** confondersi

con·fus·ing [kənˈfjuːzɪŋ] ADJ (*signals*) ambiguo(-a); (*plot, layout*) confuso(-a); **it's all very confusing** è tutto molto confuso

con·fu·sion [kənˈfjuːʒən] N confusione *f*

con·geal [kənˈdʒiːl] VI rapprendersi; (*blood*) coagularsi, rapprendersi
❑ **congeal** is not translated by the Italian word *congelare*

con·gen·ial [kənˈdʒiːnɪəl] ADJ (*place, work, company*) piacevole; (*person*) simpatico(-a)

con·geni·tal [kənˈdʒenɪtl] ADJ (*Med*) congenito(-a)

con·ger [ˈkɒŋgəʳ] N (*also:* **conger eel**) grongo

con·gest·ed [kənˈdʒestɪd] ADJ (*gen, also Med*) congestionato(-a); (*telephone lines*) sovraccarico(-a)

con·ges·tion [kənˈdʒestʃən] N (*with traffic, also Med*) congestione *f*; (*with people*) sovraffollamento

congestion charge N pedaggio da pagare per poter circolare in automobile nel centro di alcune città

con·glom·er·ate [kənˈglɒmərɪt] N (*Comm, Geol*) conglomerato

con·glom·era·tion [kənˌglɒməˈreɪʃən] N conglomerazione *f*

Con·go [ˈkɒŋgəʊ] N: **the Congo** (*country, river*) il Congo

con·gratu·late [kənˈgrætjʊleɪt] VT: **to congratulate sb (on sth/on doing sth)** congratularsi con qn (per qc/per aver fatto qc); **my friends congratulated me on passing my test** i miei amici si sono congratulati con me per aver passato l'esame di guida

con·gratu·la·tions [kənˌgrætjʊˈleɪʃənz] NPL: **congratulations (on)** congratulazioni *fpl* (per); **to give sb one's congratulations** fare le (proprie) congratulazioni a qn; **congratulations!** congratulazioni!, rallegramenti!; **congratulations on your new job!** congratulazioni per il tuo nuovo lavoro!

con·gre·gate [ˈkɒŋgrɪgeɪt] VI radunarsi, congregarsi, riunirsi

con·gre·ga·tion [ˌkɒŋgrɪˈgeɪʃən] N (*worshippers*) assemblea (dei fedeli); (*parishioners*) parrocchiani *mpl*, congregazione *f*

con·gress [ˈkɒŋgres] N congresso

congress·man [ˈkɒŋgresmən] N (*pl* **-men**) (*USA*) membro del Congresso

congress·woman [ˈkɒŋgresˌwʊmən] N (*pl* **-women**) (*USA*) (donna) membro del Congresso

coni·cal [ˈkɒnɪkəl] ADJ conico(-a); **conical hat** cappello a cono

co·ni·fer [ˈkɒnɪfəʳ] N conifera

co·nif·er·ous [kəˈnɪfərəs] ADJ (*forest*) di conifere; (*tree*) conifero(-a)

con·jec·ture [kənˈdʒektʃəʳ] N congettura ◆ VT, VI (*frm*) congetturare

con·joined twin [kənˈdʒɔɪndˈtwɪn] N fratello (*or* sorella) siamese

con·ju·gal [ˈkɒndʒʊgəl] ADJ (*frm*) coniugale

con·ju·gate [ˈkɒndʒʊgeɪt] VT coniugare ◆ VI coniugarsi ◆ ADJ (*Geom*) coniugato(-a)

con·ju·ga·tion [ˌkɒndʒʊˈgeɪʃən] N (*Gram*) coniugazione *f*

con·junc·tion [kənˈdʒʌŋkʃən] N (*Gram*) congiunzione *f*; **2 in conjunction with** in accordo con, insieme con *or* a

con·junc·ti·vi·tis [kənˌdʒʌŋktɪˈvaɪtɪs] N (*Med*) congiuntivite *f*

con·jure [ˈkʌndʒəʳ] VI fare giochi di prestigio; **a name to conjure with** un nome prestigioso *or* molto importante
▸ **conjure up** VT + ADV (*memories*) evocare, rievocare; (*ghost, spirit*) evocare; (*meal*) inventare, improvvisare
❑ **conjure** is not translated by the Italian word *congiurare*

con·jur·er, con·jur·or [ˈkʌndʒərəʳ] N prestigiatore(-trice), illusionista *m/f*

con·jur·ing [ˈkʌndʒərɪŋ] N giochi *mpl* di prestigio, prestidigitazione *f* ◆ ADJ: **conjuring trick** gioco di prestigio

conk·er [ˈkɒŋkəʳ] N (*Brit fam*) castagna (d'ippocastano)

conk out [ˌkɒŋkˈaʊt] VI + ADV (*fam: break down*) rompersi

con man N truffatore *m*

Conn. ABBR (*USA:* = Connecticut)

con·nect [kəˈnekt] VT **1** (*gen*) collegare, connettere; (*install: cooker, telephone*) installare, allacciare; **now connect the wires** ora collega i fili; **to connect (with)** (*Telec: caller*) mettere in comunicazione (con); **to connect (to)** (*pipes, drains*) collegare (con); **I am trying to connect you** (*Telec*) sto cercando di darle la linea; **to connect sth (up)** to the mains (*Elec*) collegare qc alla rete; **to connect to the internet** collegarsi a internet **2** (*associate*): **to connect sb/sth (with)** associare qn/qc (con), collegare qn/qc (con); **the evidence clearly connected him with the crime** le prove dimostravano chiaramente che era implicato nel delitto; **I wouldn't have connected the two facts** non avrei collegato i due fatti ◆ VI collegarsi; (*train, planes*): **to connect with** essere in coincidenza con

Con·nec·ti·cut [kəˈnetɪkət] N il Connecticut

connecting flight N volo in coincidenza

con·nec·tion, con·nex·ion [kəˈnekʃən] N **1** (*Tech, Elec, Telec*) collegamento, connessione *f*; (*train, bus, plane*) coincidenza; (*connecting point*) giuntura; **to miss/make a connection** perdere/prendere la coincidenza; **we missed our connection** abbiamo perso la coincidenza; **internet connection** collegamento a internet; **loose connection** filo staccato **2** (*relationship*) rapporto, relazione *f*, legame *m*; **connection between/with** rapporto tra/con; **what is the connection between them?** in che modo sono legati?; **there's no connection between the two events** non c'è rapporto tra i due fatti; **in connection with** con riferimento a, a proposito di; **in this connection** riguardo a questo; **she has many business connections** ha molti rapporti d'affari; **she's got the right connections** conosce le persone giuste

con·ning tow·er [ˈkɒnɪŋˌtaʊəʳ] N (*of submarine*) torretta di comando

con·nive [kəˈnaɪv] VI: **to connive at** (*pej: pretend not to notice*) chiudere un occhio su; (: *aid and abet*) essere connivente in

con·nois·seur [ˌkɒnəˈsɜːʳ] N conoscitore(-trice), intenditore(-trice)

con·no·ta·tion [ˌkɒnəˈteɪʃən] N connotazione *f*

con·nu·bial [kəˈnjuːbɪəl] ADJ (*frm*) coniugale

con·quer [ˈkɒŋkəʳ] VT (*territory, nation, castle*) conquistare; (*enemy*) vincere, battere, sconfiggere; (*habit, feelings*) vincere, superare

con·quer·or [ˈkɒŋkərəʳ] N conquistatore *m*

con·quest [ˈkɒŋkwest] N conquista

cons [kɒnz] NPL see **convenience**

con·science [ˈkɒnʃəns] N coscienza; **with a clear conscience** con la coscienza pulita *or* a posto; **to have a clear/guilty conscience** avere la coscienza pulita/sporca; **to have sth on one's conscience** avere qc sulla coscienza; **in all conscience** onestamente, in coscienza

con·sci·en·tious [ˌkɒnʃɪˈenʃəs] ADJ coscienzioso(-a)

conscientious objector N (*Mil*) obiettore *m* di coscienza

con·scious [ˈkɒnʃəs] ADJ **1** (*aware*): **conscious (of sth/of doing)** consapevole (di qc/di fare), conscio(-a) (di qc/di fare); **she was conscious of the noise** non si era consapevole; **to become conscious of sth/that** rendersi conto di qc/che **2** (*deliberate: insult, error*) intenzionale, voluto(-a); **he made a conscious decision to tell nobody** ha deciso deliberatamente di non dirlo a nessuno **3** (*Med*) cosciente; **to become conscious** riprendere coscienza; **he was still conscious when the doctor arrived** era ancora in sé quando è arrivato il dottore

con·scious·ness [ˈkɒnʃəsnɪs] N **1** (*awareness*): **consciousness (of)** consapevolezza *or* coscienza (di) **2** (*Med*) conoscenza; **to lose/regain consciousness** perdere/riprendere conoscenza *or* i sensi; **I lost consciousness** ho perso conoscenza

con·script [*n* ˈkɒnskrɪpt, *vb* kənˈskrɪpt] N coscritto ◆ VT arruolare, chiamare alle armi

con·scrip·tion [kənˈskrɪpʃən] N arruolamento (obbligatorio), coscrizione f

con·se·crate [ˈkɒnsɪˌkreɪt] VT consacrare

con·secu·tive [kənˈsekjʊtɪv] ADJ consecutivo(-a); **consecutive clause** (Gram) proposizione f consecutiva; **on three consecutive occasions** tre volte di fila, tre volte consecutive

con·sen·sus [kənˈsensəs] N consenso; **the consensus of opinion** l'opinione f unanime or comune

con·sent [kənˈsent] N consenso, benestare m; **by mutual consent** per mutuo consenso; **by common consent** di comune accordo; **age of consent** età legale per avere rapporti sessuali ♦ VI: **to consent (to sth/to do sth)** acconsentire (a qc/a fare qc)

consenting adults [kənˈsentɪŋˈædʌlts] NPL adulti mpl consenzienti

con·se·quence [ˈkɒnsɪkwəns] N 1 (result) conseguenza, risultato; **in consequence** di conseguenza 2 (importance) importanza; **of consequence** importante; **it is of no consequence** non ha nessuna importanza

con·se·quent·ly [ˈkɒnsɪkwəntlɪ] ADV di conseguenza, dunque, quindi

con·ser·va·tion [ˌkɒnsəˈveɪʃən] N conservazione f, tutela; (of nature) tutela dell'ambiente; **it's a report on the conservation of rain forests** è una relazione sulla tutela delle foreste pluviali; **people are conscious of the need for conservation** la gente è conscia di quanto sia importante la tutela dell'ambiente; **conservation project** progetto di salvaguardia ambientale; **energy conservation** risparmio energetico

con·ser·va·tion·ist [ˌkɒnsəˈveɪʃənɪst] N ambientalista m/f

con·ser·va·tive [kənˈsɜːvətɪv] ADJ (Pol: person, style) conservatore(-trice); (estimate, guess) prudente ♦ N conservatore(-trice)

con·serva·tory [kənˈsɜːvətrɪ] N (greenhouse) serra; (Mus) conservatorio

con·serve [kənˈsɜːv] VT conservare; **to conserve one's strength** risparmiare le forze ♦ N conserva di frutta

con·sid·er [kənˈsɪdəʳ] VT 1 (think about: problem, possibility) considerare, prendere in considerazione; (question, matter, subject) valutare, studiare; **to consider doing sth** considerare la possibilità di fare qc; **all things considered** tutto sommato or considerato; **it is my considered opinion that ...** sono fermamente convinto che...; **I'm considering the idea** sto prendendo in considerazione l'idea 2 (take into account) considerare, tener conto di 3 (be of the opinion) ritenere, considerare; **he considers it a waste of time** la ritiene una perdita di tempo; **his teacher considers him too lazy to pass the exams** il suo insegnante lo considera or lo ritiene troppo pigro per superare gli esami; **consider yourself lucky** puoi dirti fortunato

con·sid·er·able [kənˈsɪdərəbl] ADJ considerevole, notevole; **to a considerable extent** in gran parte, in misura notevole

con·sid·er·ably [kənˈsɪdərəblɪ] ADV notevolmente, decisamente

con·sid·er·ate [kənˈsɪdrɪt] ADJ riguardoso(-a), premuroso(-a)

con·sid·era·tion [kənˌsɪdəˈreɪʃən] N 1 (no pl: thought, reflection) considerazione f; **to be under consideration** essere in esame; **after due consideration** dopo un attento esame; **to take sth into consideration** considerare qc, prendere qc in considerazione; **taking everything into consideration** tutto considerato or sommato 2 (no pl: thoughtfulness) attenzione f, premura; **out of consideration for** per riguardo a; **to show consideration for sb's feelings** avere riguardo per qn 3 (factor) elemento; **my first consideration is my family** il mio primo pensiero è per la mia famiglia; **his age is an important consideration** la sua età è un fattore importante; **it's of no consideration** non ha nessuna importanza 4 (payment) rimunerazione f, ricompensa; **for a consideration** dietro compenso

con·sid·ered [kənˈsɪdəd] ADJ: **it is my considered opinion that ...** dopo lunga riflessione il mio parere è che...

con·sid·er·ing [kənˈsɪdərɪŋ] PREP considerando, considerato(-a) ♦ CONJ: **considering (that)** se si considera or tiene conto (che); **considering we were there for a month ...** dato che ci siamo rimasti per un mese... ♦ ADV: **he did very well, considering** è stato molto bravo, tutto sommato

con·sign [kənˈsaɪn] VT 1 **to consign sb/sth (to)** (frm: banish) relegare qn/qc (in); (commit, entrust) affidare qn/qc (a) 2 (Comm: send) consegnare, spedire

con·signee [ˌkɒnsaɪˈniː] N consegnatario(-a), destinatario(-a)

con·sign·ment [kənˈsaɪnmənt] N (of goods) partita, consegna, spedizione f

consignment note N (Comm) nota di spedizione

con·sign·or [kənˈsaɪnəʳ] N mittente m/f

con·sist [kənˈsɪst] VI: **to consist of** essere composto(-a) di, constare di, consistere di; **to consist in sth/in doing sth** consistere in qc/nel fare qc

con·sist·en·cy [kənˈsɪstənsɪ] N 1 (of person, action) coerenza 2 (density) consistenza

con·sist·ent [kənˈsɪstənt] ADJ 1 (constant: results, action) costante; (: person) costante 2 (coherent: argument) coerente, logico(-a); **to be consistent with** essere coerente con; **it is consistent with his views** è coerente con il suo modo di pensare; **consistent player** giocatore(-trice) dal rendimento costante

❏ **consistent** is not translated by the Italian word
 · **consistente**

con·so·la·tion [ˌkɒnsəˈleɪʃən] N consolazione f

con·sole [kənˈsəʊl] VT: **to console (sb for sth)** consolare (qn per qc)

con·sole [ˈkɒnsəʊl] N (control panel) console f inv, quadro di comando

con·soli·date [kənˈsɒlɪˌdeɪt] VT 1 (position, influence) consolidare 2 (combine) unire, fondere

con·som·mé [kɒnˈsɒmeɪ] N (Culin) consommé m inv, brodo ristretto

con·so·nant [ˈkɒnsənənt] N consonante f

con·sort [n ˈkɒnsɔːt, vb kənˈsɔːt] N consorte m/f; **prince consort** principe m consorte ♦ VI (often pej): **to consort with sb** frequentare qn

con·sor·tium [kənˈsɔːtɪəm] N (pl consortia [kənˈsɔːtɪə]) consorzio

con·spic·u·ous [kənˈspɪkjʊəs] ADJ (person, behaviour) che si fa notare; (clothes) vistoso(-a); (sign, notice) ben visibile; (bravery, difference) notevole, evidente; **a conspicuous lack of** una notevole mancanza di qc; **to make o.s. conspicuous** farsi notare; **I felt very conspicuous** sentivo tutti gli sguardi su di me; **to be conspicuous by one's absence** brillare per la propria assenza

con·spira·cy [kənˈspɪrəsɪ] N cospirazione f, congiura

con·spira·to·rial [kənˌspɪrəˈtɔːrɪəl] ADJ cospiratorio(-a)

con·spire [kənˈspaɪəʳ] VI 1 (people): **to conspire (with sb against sth)** congiurare or cospirare (con qn contro qn/qc) 2 (events): **to conspire to do sth** contribuire a fare qc; **everything had conspired to make him happy** tutto aveva contribuito a renderlo felice

con·sta·ble [ˈkʌnstəbl] N (Brit: also: police constable) agente m/f (di polizia)

con·stabu·lary [kənˈstæbjʊlərɪ] N polizia

con·stant [ˈkɒnstənt] ADJ (interruptions) continuo(-a), incessante; (use) continuo(-a), costante; (speed, temperature, rhythm) costante; (affection) costante, stabile; (friend, love) fedele; **meat must be kept at a constant temperature** la carne deve essere tenuta a temperatura costante ♦ N (Math, Phys) costante f

con·stant·ly [ˈkɒnstəntlɪ] ADV continuamente, costantemente

con·stel·la·tion [ˌkɒnstəˈleɪʃən] N costellazione f

con·ster·na·tion [ˌkɒnstəˈneɪʃən] N costernazione f, sgomento; **filled with consternation (at)** costernato(-a) (per)

con·sti·pat·ed [ˈkɒnstɪˌpeɪtɪd] ADJ (Med) stitico(-a)

con·sti·pa·tion [ˌkɒnstɪˈpeɪʃən] N (Med) stitichezza

con·stitu·en·cy [kənˈstɪtjʊənsɪ] N (district) collegio elettorale; (people) elettori mpl (del collegio)

constituency party N sezione f locale (del partito)

con·stitu·ent [kənˈstɪtjʊənt] N (Pol: voter) elettore(-trice); (part) ingrediente m, componente m ♦ ADJ costitutivo(-a)

con·sti·tute [ˈkɒnstɪˌtjuːt] VT costituire

con·sti·tu·tion [ˌkɒnstɪˈtjuːʃən] N costituzione f

con·sti·tu·tion·al [ˌkɒnstɪˈtjuːʃənl] ADJ costituzionale

constitutional monarchy N monarchia costituzionale

con·strain [kən'streɪn] VT costringere

con·strained [kən'streɪnd] ADJ (awkward) forzato(-a); **to feel/be constrained to do sth** sentirsi/essere costretto(-a) a fare qc

con·straint [kən'streɪnt] N no pl (compulsion) costrizione f; (restraint) limitazione f; (embarrassment) imbarazzo, soggezione f

con·strict [kən'strɪkt] VT (throat, waist, blood vessels) stringere; (movements) impedire; (freedom) limitare

con·struct [kən'strʌkt] VT costruire

con·struc·tion [kən'strʌkʃən] N (gen) costruzione f; (fig: interpretation) interpretazione f; **under construction** in costruzione

construction industry N edilizia, industria edile

con·struc·tive [kən'strʌktɪv] ADJ costruttivo(-a)

con·strue [kən'struː] VT (interpret) interpretare

❑ **construe** is not translated by the Italian word costruire

con·sul [ˈkɒnsəl] N console m; **consul general** console generale

con·su·late [ˈkɒnsjʊlɪt] N consolato

con·sult [kən'sʌlt] VT: **to consult sb (about sth)** consultare qn (su or riguardo a qc) ♦ VI: **to consult each other** consultarsi

con·sul·tan·cy [kən'sʌltənsɪ] N consulenza ♦ ADJ (fees, business) di consulenza

consultancy fee N onorario di consulenza

con·sult·ant [kən'sʌltənt] N consulente m/f; (Brit: Med) specialista m/f; **legal/management consultant** consulente legale/gestionale; **consultant to the government** consulente del governo

con·sul·ta·tion [ˌkɒnsəl'teɪʃən] N consultazione f; (Med, Law) consulto; **in consultation with** consultandosi con

con·sul·ta·tive [kən'sʌltətɪv] ADJ (document) di consulenza; **in a consultative capacity** in veste di consulente

consulting room N (Brit: Med) ambulatorio, studio medico

con·sume [kən'sjuːm] VT (gen) consumare; **to be consumed with** (envy) essere roso(-a) da; (grief) consumarsi di

con·sum·er [kən'sjuːməʳ] N consumatore(-trice); (of electricity, gas etc) utente m/f

consumer credit N credito al consumatore

consumer durables NPL beni mpl durevoli

consumer goods NPL beni mpl di consumo

con·sum·er·ism [kən'sjuːmə,rɪzəm] N (consumer protection) tutela del consumatore; (Econ) consumismo

consumer society N società consumista or dei consumi

consumer watchdog N comitato di difesa dei consumatori

con·sum·mate [adj kən'sʌmɪt, vb 'kɒnsə,meɪt] ADJ consumato(-a), abile; **with consummate ease** con estrema facilità ♦ VT (marriage) consumare

con·sump·tion [kən'sʌmpʃən] N 1 (of food, fuel) consumo; **not fit for human consumption** non commestibile; **fuel consumption** consumo di carburante 2 (old: tuberculosis) consunzione f

cont., cont'd ABBR (= continued) segue

con·tact ['kɒntækt] N (gen) contatto; (person) conoscenza, contatto; **to be in contact with sb/sth** essere in contatto con qn/qc; **I'm in contact with her** sono in contatto con lei; **to make contact with sb** mettersi in contatto con qn; **to lose contact (with sb)** perdere i contatti (con qn), perdere di vista qn; **business contacts** contatti mpl d'affari ♦ VT mettersi in contatto con, contattare

contact lens N (pl -es) lente f a contatto

con·ta·gious [kən'teɪdʒəs] ADJ contagioso(-a), infettivo(-a)

con·tain [kən'teɪn] VT contenere; (fire, disease) arginare; **to contain o.s.** contenersi

con·tain·er [kən'teɪnəʳ] N (box, jug) contenitore m, recipiente m; (Comm: for transport, shipping) container m inv ♦ ADJ (train, truck, ship) da container; (dock, depot, transport) per container

con·tain·er·ize [kən'teɪnə,raɪz] VT mettere in container

con·tami·nate [kən'tæmɪ,neɪt] VT contaminare

con·tami·na·tion [kən,tæmɪ'neɪʃən] N contaminazione f

cont'd ABBR = cont.

con·tem·plate ['kɒntɛm,pleɪt] VT (gaze at, reflect upon) contemplare; **to contemplate sth/doing sth** (consider) pensare a qc/di fare qc

con·tem·pla·tion [ˌkɒntɛm'pleɪʃən] N contemplazione f

con·tem·po·rary [kən'tɛmpərərɪ] ADJ contemporaneo(-a); (design) moderno(-a) ♦ N contemporaneo(-a)

con·tempt [kən'tɛmpt] N disprezzo, disdegno; **to hold sth/sb in contempt** disprezzare qc/qn; **contempt of court** (Law) oltraggio alla Corte; **it's beneath contempt** è oltremodo vergognoso

con·tempt·ible [kən'tɛmptəbl] ADJ vergognoso(-a), spregevole

con·temp·tu·ous [kən'tɛmptjʊəs] ADJ (person): **contemptuous (of)** sprezzante (di); (manner, gesture) sprezzante, altezzoso(-a), sdegnoso(-a)

con·tend [kən'tɛnd] VT: **to contend that** (frm) sostenere che, asserire che ♦ VI (fig): **to contend (with sb) for sth** contendersi qc (con qn); **we have many problems to contend with** dobbiamo lottare contro molti problemi; **you'll have me to contend with** dovrai vedertela con me; **he has a lot to contend with** ha un sacco di guai

con·tend·er [kən'tɛndəʳ] N contendente m/f, concorrente m/f

con·tent ['kɒntɛnt] N contenuto; **contents** NPL (of box, case) contenuto; (table of) contents (of book) indice m

con·tent [kən'tɛnt] ADJ: **content (with)** contento(-a) or soddisfatto(-a) (di); **to be content to do sth** essere contento(-a) di fare qc ♦ N contentezza; **to one's heart's content** quanto si ha voglia; **to eat and drink to one's heart content** mangiare e bere a sazietà ♦ VT fare contento(-a), soddisfare, contentare; **to content o.s. with sth/with doing sth** accontentarsi di qc/di fare qc

con·tent·ed [kən'tɛntɪd] ADJ: **contented (with)** contento(-a) (di), soddisfatto(-a) (di)

con·tent·ed·ly [kən'tɛntɪdlɪ] ADV con soddisfazione

con·ten·tion [kən'tɛnʃən] N (strife) contesa, disputa; (frm: assertion) tesi f inv; **to be in contention** essere in lizza; **bone of contention** pomo della discordia

con·ten·tious [kən'tɛnʃəs] ADJ polemico(-a)

con·tent·ment [kən'tɛntmənt] N contentezza, soddisfazione f

con·test [n 'kɒntɛst, vb kən'tɛst] N (struggle) gara, lotta; (Boxing, Wrestling) incontro; (competition) gara, concorso; **beauty contest** concorso di bellezza; **fishing contest** gara di pesca; **he won the leadership contest by a large margin** ha vinto la lotta per la leadership con un largo margine ♦ VT (dispute: argument) contestare; (: right) contestare, disputare; (Law) impugnare; (compete for) contendersi, disputare; (election, seat) essere in lizza per

❑ **contest** is not translated by the Italian word contesto

con·test·ant [kən'tɛstənt] N (in competition) concorrente m/f; (Sport) contendente m/f, avversario(-a); **contestant for a title** aspirante m/f a un titolo

con·text ['kɒntɛkst] N contesto; **in/out of context** nel/fuori dal contesto

con·ti·nent ['kɒntɪnənt] N 1 continente m 2 (Brit): **the Continent** l'Europa continentale; **on the Continent** in Europa

con·ti·nen·tal [ˌkɒntɪ'nɛntl] ADJ continentale; (Brit: European) europeo(-a), dell'Europa continentale ♦ N (Brit) abitante m/f dell'Europa continentale

continental breakfast N colazione f (senza cibi caldi)

continental quilt N (Brit) piumino

con·tin·gen·cy [kən'tɪndʒənsɪ] N contingenza, evenienza, eventualità f inv; **in certain contingencies** in certi frangenti

contingency plan N misura or piano d'emergenza

con·tin·gent [kən'tɪndʒənt] (frm) ADJ: **to be contingent upon** dipendere da ♦ N (Mil) contingente m; (group) gruppo

con·tin·ual [kən'tɪnjʊəl] ADJ continuo(-a)

con·tinu·al·ly [kən'tɪnjʊəlɪ] ADV continuamente, senza tregua, di continuo

con·tinu·ation [kən,tɪnjʊ'eɪʃən] N continuazione f; (resumption) ripresa; (of serial story) seguito

con·tinue [kən'tɪnjuː] VT (gen): **to continue (doing or to do**

sth) continuare (a fare qc); **she continued talking to her friend** ha continuato a parlare alla sua amica; *(start again)* riprendere, continuare; **we continued working after lunch** abbiamo ripreso a lavorare dopo pranzo; **to be continued** continua; **continued on page 10** segue *or* continua a pagina 10 ♦ VI *(gen)* continuare; *(resume)* riprendere, continuare; *(extend)* estendersi, proseguire; **to continue on one's way** continuare per la propria strada

con·tinu·ing edu·ca·tion [kən'tɪnjuːɪŋedjʊ'keɪʃən] N formazione *f* continua; *(USA)* corsi *mpl* di aggiornamento

con·ti·nu·ity [ˌkɒntɪ'njuːɪtɪ] N continuità; *(Cine)* (ordine *m* della) sceneggiatura

con·tinu·ous [kən'tɪnjʊəs] ADJ continuo(-a), ininterrotto(-a); **continuous performance** *(Cine)* spettacolo continuato; **continuous stationery** *(Comput)* modulo continuo

con·tinu·ous·ly [kən'tɪnjʊəslɪ] ADV *(unceasingly)* in continuazione; *(uninterruptedly)* ininterrottamente

con·tort [kən'tɔːt] VT contorcere

con·tor·tion [kən'tɔːʃən] N *(of acrobat)* contorsione *f*, contorcimento

con·tor·tion·ist [kən'tɔːʃənɪst] N contorsionista *m/f*

con·tour ['kɒntʊə'] N contorno, profilo; *(also:* **contour line**) curva di livello, isoipsa

contra·band ['kɒntrəbænd] N contrabbando ♦ ADJ di contrabbando

contra·cep·tion [ˌkɒntrə'sepʃən] N contraccezione *f*

contra·cep·tive [ˌkɒntrə'septɪv] ADJ contraccettivo(-a), anticoncezionale ♦ N contraccettivo, anticoncezionale *m*

con·tract [*n, adj* 'kɒntrækt, *vb* kən'trækt] N contratto; **contract of employment** contratto di lavoro; **to enter into a contract with sb to do sth/for sth** stipulare un contratto con qn per fare qc/per qc; **to be under contract to do sth** aver stipulato un contratto per fare qc; **to put work out to contract** dare del lavoro in appalto, appaltare un lavoro; **by contract** per contratto; **there's a contract out for him** *(fig: fam)* c'è una taglia su di lui ♦ VT *(all senses)* contrarre; **to contract with sb to do sth** stipulare un contratto con qn per fare qc ♦ VI *(muscles, lips)* contrarsi; *(metal)* restringersi; *(economy)* essere in fase di contrazione ♦ ADJ *(date)* del contratto; *(price)* secondo contratto; *(work)* a contratto, in appalto

con·trac·tion [kən'trækʃən] N contrazione *f*; *(of metal)* restringimento

con·trac·tor [kən'træktə'] N *(Constr)* appaltatore *m*, imprenditore *m*; *(Law)* contraente *m*

con·trac·tual [kən'træktʃʊəl] ADJ contrattuale

contra·dict [ˌkɒntrə'dɪkt] VT contraddire

contra·dic·tion [ˌkɒntrə'dɪkʃən] N contraddizione *f*; **to be in contradiction with** discordare con; **contradiction in terms** contraddizione (in termini)

contra·dic·tory [ˌkɒntrə'dɪktərɪ] ADJ contraddittorio(-a); **to be contradictory to** contraddire

con·tral·to [kən'træltəʊ] N contralto

con·trap·tion [kən'træpʃən] N *(fam, pej)* aggeggio

con·tra·ry ['kɒntrərɪ] ADJ **1** contrario(-a) (a), opposto(-a) (a); **contrary to nature** contro natura; **contrary to** contrariamente a; **contrary to what you may have heard, I am not resigning** contrariamente a quello che potete aver sentito, non mi dimetto; **contrary to what we thought** contrariamente a quanto pensavamo **2** [kən'treərɪ] *(self-willed)* difficile, cocciuto(-a), bisbetico(-a) ♦ N contrario; **on the contrary** al contrario; **unless you hear to the contrary** salvo contrordine

con·trast [*n* 'kɒntrɑːst, *vb* kən'trɑːst] N contrasto; **in contrast to** *or* **with** a differenza di, contrariamente a ♦ VT: **to contrast (with)** mettere a confronto (con), opporre (a) ♦ VI: **to contrast (with)** contrastare (con)

con·trast·ing [kən'trɑːstɪŋ] ADJ contrastante, di contrasto; **a contrasting colour** un colore che contrasta

contra·vene [ˌkɒntrə'viːn] VT *(frm)* contravvenire a

contra·ven·tion [ˌkɒntrə'venʃən] N: **contravention (of)** *(frm)* contravvenzione *f* (a), infrazione *f* (di)

con·trib·ute [kən'trɪbjuːt] VT *(sum of money)* offrire, donare, contribuire con; *(help)* offrire; **to contribute an article to a newspaper** contribuire a un giornale con un articolo ♦ VI:

to contribute to *(charity, collection, success)* contribuire a; *(discussion)* partecipare a; *(newspaper)* collaborare a *or* con, scrivere per; *(Admin)* pagare i contributi per; **everyone contributed to the success of the play** tutti hanno contribuito al successo della commedia; **she contributed £10 to the collection** ha contribuito alla colletta con 10 sterline; **he didn't contribute to the discussion** non ha partecipato alla discussione

con·tri·bu·tion [ˌkɒntrɪ'bjuːʃən] N *(money, goods)* contributo, offerta, donazione *f*; *(help, assistance)* contributo, contribuzione *f*; *(Brit: payment)* contributi *mpl*; *(article, story)* contributo, collaborazione; *(in discussion)* intervento

con·tri·bu·tor [kən'trɪbjʊtə'] N *(of money)* donatore(-trice); *(to journal, newspaper)* collaboratore(-trice)

con·tribu·tory [kən'trɪbjʊtərɪ] ADJ *(cause)* che contribuisce; **it was a contributory factor in ...** quello ha contribuito a...

con·trite ['kɒntraɪt] ADJ mortificato(-a); *(Rel)* contrito(-a)

con·triv·ance [kən'traɪvəns] N *(machine, device)* congegno; *(scheme)* espediente *m*, stratagemma *m*

con·trive [kən'traɪv] VT *(plan, scheme)* inventare, escogitare; **to contrive a means of doing sth** escogitare un sistema per fare qc; **to contrive to do sth** trovare un modo per fare qc

con·trol [kən'trəʊl] N **1** *(no pl: gen)* controllo; *(of traffic)* regolamentazione *f*; *(of pests)* eliminazione *f*; **the control of cancer** la lotta contro il cancro; **they have no control over their son** non hanno alcuna autorità sul figlio; **to keep sth/sb under control** tenere qc/qn sotto controllo; **to lose control of sth** perdere il controllo di qc; **to lose control of o.s.** perdere il controllo di sé; **he always seems to be in control** non perde mai il controllo della situazione; **to be in** *or* **keep control of** tenere sotto controllo; **she can't keep control of the class** non riesce a tenere la classe sotto controllo; **to take control of** assumere il controllo di; **to bring a fire under control** arginare *or* circoscrivere un incendio; **everything is under control** tutto è sotto controllo; **the car went out of control** la macchina non rispondeva più ai comandi; **to be out of control** essere scatenato(-a); **the class was quite out of control** la classe era in subbuglio; **due to circumstances beyond our control** per circostanze indipendenti dalla nostra volontà; **who is in control?** chi è il responsabile? **2** *(Tech, TV, Radio)*: **the controls** i comandi; **to take over the controls** prendere i comandi **3 wage/price controls** NPL *restrictions)* limitazione *f* dei salari/prezzi **4** *(in experiment)* gruppo di controllo ♦ VT *(check)* controllare; *(traffic)* dirigere, regolare; *(operation etc)* dirigere; *(company)* avere controllo di; *(crowd)* tenere sotto controllo; *(disease, fire)* arginare, limitare; *(emotions)* controllare, frenare, dominare; **to control o.s.** controllarsi; **please control yourself, everyone's looking at us** per favore, controllati, tutti ci guardano; **he can't control the class** non riesce a tenere la classe sotto controllo

control key N *(Comput)* tasto di controllo

controlled substance [kən'trəʊld-] N sostanza stupefacente

controlling interest N *(Comm)* maggioranza delle azioni

control panel N *(on aircraft, ship, also TV)* quadro dei comandi

control point N punto di controllo

control room N *(Naut, Mil)* sala di comando; *(Radio, TV)* sala di regia

control tower N *(Aer)* torre *f* di controllo

control unit N *(Comput)* unità *f inv* di controllo

con·tro·ver·sial [ˌkɒntrə'vɜːʃəl] ADJ *(subject, speech, decision, book)* controverso(-a), discusso(-a), che suscita polemiche; *(person)* discusso(-a), polemico(-a); **euthanasia is a controversial subject** l'eutanasia è un argomento controverso

con·tro·ver·sy [kən'trɒvəsɪ] N controversia, polemica; **it has caused a lot of controversy** ha causato molte polemiche

con·ur·ba·tion [ˌkɒnɜː'beɪʃən] N conurbazione *f*

con·va·lesce [ˌkɒnvə'les] VI fare la convalescenza, rimettersi

con·va·les·cence [ˌkɒnvə'lesns] N convalescenza

con·va·les·cent [ˌkɒnvə'lesnt] ADJ, N convalescente *m/f*; convalescent home convalescenziario

con·vec·tor [kən'vektə'] N *(also:* **convector heater, convection heater**) convettore *m*

con·vene [kən'viːn] vt (*people*) convocare; (*meeting*) indire, convocare ♦ vi riunirsi, adunarsi, convenire

con·veni·ence [kən'viːnɪəns] n 1 (*of house, plan, person*) comodità; **at your earliest convenience** (*Comm*) appena possibile; **at your convenience** a suo comodo 2 **conveniences** NPL (*amenities: of house*) comodità *fpl*; **all modern conveniences**, (*Brit*) **all mod cons** tutte le comodità moderne 3 (*frm: toilet*) gabinetto

convenience foods NPL cibi *mpl* precotti

con·veni·ent [kən'viːnɪənt] ADJ (*tool, size, place etc*) comodo(-a); (*event, time, occasion*) adatto(-a), opportuno(-a); **the house is convenient for the shops** la casa è vicina ai *or* comoda per i negozi; **it is more convenient to eat in the kitchen** è più comodo mangiare in cucina; **if it is convenient to you** se per lei va bene, se non la incomoda; **would tomorrow be convenient?** andrebbe bene domani?; **is it convenient to call tomorrow?** potrei passare domani?; **it's not a convenient time for me** non sono libero a quell'ora

con·veni·ent·ly [kən'viːnɪəntlɪ] ADV (*happen*) a proposito; (*situated*) in una posizione comoda; **very conveniently he arrived late** (*luckily*) è stata una fortuna che sia arrivato in ritardo

con·vent ['kɒnvənt] n convento (di suore)

con·ven·tion [kən'vɛnʃən] n (*custom, agreement*) convenzione *f*; (*meeting*) congresso, convegno; **the journalists' annual convention** il convegno annuale dei giornalisti; **a social convention** una convenzione sociale

con·ven·tion·al [kən'vɛnʃənl] ADJ (*person, style, weapons*) convenzionale; (*methods*) tradizionale; **conventional weapons** armi *fpl* convenzionali; **my parents are very conventional** i miei genitori sono molto tradizionalisti

convent school n scuola retta da suore

con·verge [kən'vɜːdʒ] vi: **to converge (on)** convergere (su)

con·ver·sant [kən'vɜːsənt] ADJ: **to be conversant with** (*car engines, machinery*) essere pratico(-a) di; (*facts*) essere al corrente di; (*language, subject*) avere una buona conoscenza di

con·ver·sa·tion [ˌkɒnvə'seɪʃən] n conversazione *f*; **in conversation with** a colloquio con; **to have a conversation with sb** conversare con qn, parlare con qn; **we had a long conversation** abbiamo fatto una lunga conversazione; **what was your conversation about?** di che cosa parlavate?

con·ver·sa·tion·al [ˌkɒnvə'seɪʃənl] ADJ (*style, tone*) colloquiale; (*Comput*) conversazionale

con·ver·sa·tion·al·ist [ˌkɒnvə'seɪʃnəlɪst] n conversatore (-trice)

con·verse [kən'vɜːs] vi: **to converse (with sb about sth)** (*frm*) conversare (con qn su *or* di qc)

con·verse ['kɒnvɜːs] n inverso, contrario, opposto; (*Math*) opposto ♦ ADJ opposto(-a), contrario(-a)

con·verse·ly [kən'vɜːslɪ] ADV al contrario, per contro

con·ver·sion [kən'vɜːʃən] n (*gen, also Rel*) conversione *f*; (*Brit: of house*) trasformazione *f*, rimodernamento; (*Rugby, American Football*) trasformazione

conversion table n tavola *or* tabella di conversione

con·vert [n 'kɒnvɜːt, *vb* kən'vɜːt] n convertito(-a) ♦ vt 1 (*Rel*): **to convert (to)** convertire a 2 **to convert (to, into)** (*gen*) convertire (in); (*house*) trasformare (in), convertire (in); **we've converted the loft into a bedroom** abbiamo trasformato la soffitta in una camera da letto 3 (*Rugby, American Football*) trasformare

con·vert·ible [kən'vɜːtɪbl] ADJ (*currency*) convertibile; **convertible settee** divano letto ♦ n (*car*) (auto *f inv*) decappottabile, *f*

con·vex ['kɒn'vɛks] ADJ convesso(-a)

con·vey [kən'veɪ] vt (*goods, passengers*) trasportare; (*subj: pipeline*) convogliare; (*thanks, congratulations, sound, order*) trasmettere; (*meaning, ideas*) comunicare, esprimere; **to convey to sb that** comunicare a qn che; **he did not convey the information to his parents** non ha riferito il messaggio ai suoi genitori; **words cannot convey ...** le parole non possono esprimere...; **the name conveys nothing to me** il nome non mi dice niente; **the picture conveys a feeling of tranquillity** il quadro trasmette un senso di tranquillità

con·vey·ance [kən'veɪəns] n (*of goods*) trasporto; (*vehicle*) mezzo di trasporto

con·vey·anc·ing [kən'veɪənsɪŋ] n (*Law*) redazione *f* di transazioni di proprietà

conveyor belt n (*Industry*) nastro trasportatore

con·vict [n 'kɒnvɪkt, *vb* kən'vɪkt] n carcerato(-a) ♦ vt: **to convict (of)** riconoscere colpevole (di), dichiarare colpevole (di); **convicted murderer** persona riconosciuta colpevole di omicidio; **he was convicted of the murder** è stato dichiarato colpevole di omicidio

con·vic·tion [kən'vɪkʃən] n 1 (*belief*) convinzione *f*; **it is my conviction that** sono convinto che; **to carry conviction** essere convincente; **she spoke with great conviction** ha parlato con grande convinzione 2 (*Law*) condanna; **he has three previous convictions for robbery** ha tre precedenti condanne per furto

con·vince [kən'vɪns] vt: **to convince sb (of sth/that)** convincere qn (di qc/che), persuadere qn (di qc/che)

convinced ADJ: **convinced of/that** convinto(-a), (convinta) di/che

con·vinc·ing [kən'vɪnsɪŋ] ADJ (*gen*) convincente; (*win*) netto(-a)

con·vinc·ing·ly [kən'vɪnsɪŋlɪ] ADV (*see adj*) in modo convincente; nettamente

con·viv·ial [kən'vɪvɪəl] ADJ allegro(-a), gioviale

con·vo·lut·ed ['kɒnvəluːtɪd] (*frm*) ADJ (*shape*) attorcigliato(-a), avvolto(-a); (*argument*) involuto(-a)

con·voy ['kɒnvɔɪ] n convoglio; (*escort*) scorta; **in convoy** in convoglio; **under convoy** sotto scorta

con·vulse [kən'vʌls] vt sconvolgere; **to be convulsed with pain/laughter** contorcersi dal dolore/dalle risa

con·vul·sion [kən'vʌlʃən] n (*fit, seizure*) convulsione *f*; **in convulsions** (*fam: laughter*) piegato(-a) in due (dalle risate)

COO N ABBR = **chief operating officer**

coo [kuː] vi (*dove*) tubare ♦ vt sussurrare dolcemente; **to coo over a baby** fare versetti a un bimbo

cook [kʊk] n cuoco(-a); **head cook and bottlewasher** (*fig: hum*) tuttofare *m/f* ♦ vt 1 cuocere, cucinare; (*meal*) preparare; **she's cooking lunch** sta preparando il pranzo; **shall I cook you an omelette?** ti cucino *or* ti faccio un'omelette?; **the chicken isn't cooked** il pollo non è cotto; **to cook sb's goose** (*fig: fam*) rompere le uova nel paniere a qn; **to cook one's own goose** (*fig: fam*) darsi la zappa sui piedi 2 (*fam: falsify: accounts*) falsificare, alterare; **to cook the books** falsificare i libri contabili ♦ vi (*food*) cuocere; (*person*) cucinare; **I can't cook** non so cucinare; **what's cooking?** (*fig: fam*) cosa bolle in pentola?

▸ **cook up** vt + ADV (*fam: excuse, story*) inventare

cook·book ['kʊkbʊk] n (*USA*) libro di ricette, ricettario

cook·er ['kʊkə'] n (*stove*) cucina (elettrodomestico); (*cooking apple*) mela da cuocere; **gas cooker** cucina a gas

cook·ery ['kʊkərɪ] n cucina (*attività*)

cookie ['kʊkɪ] n 1 (*USA: biscuit*) biscotto; **that's the way the cookie crumbles** purtroppo è così, così va il mondo 2 (*Comput*) cookie *m inv*

cook·ing ['kʊkɪŋ] n cucina (*attività e cibo*); **she loves your cooking** adora quello che cucini tu; **French cooking** la cucina francese ♦ ADJ (*apples, chocolate*) da cuocere; (*utensils, salt, foil*) da cucina

cook·out ['kʊkaʊt] n (*USA*) pranzo cucinato all'aperto

cool [kuːl] ADJ (*comp* **-er**, *superl* **-est**) (*gen*) fresco(-a); (*drink*) freddo(-a); (*dress*) fresco(*or* a), leggero(-a); (*calm*) calmo(-a); (*unenthusiastic, unfriendly*) freddo(-a); (*impertinent*) sfacciato(-a); **it's cool** (*weather*) fa fresco; **a cool top** una maglietta leggera; **to keep sth cool** *or* **in a cool place** tenere qc in fresco *or* al fresco; **to be cool towards sb** essere freddo(-a) con qn; **to keep cool** mantenersi fresco(-a); (*fig*) conservare la calma; **keep cool!** calma!; **play it cool!** fa' finta di niente!; **they think it's cool to do drugs** pensano che sia figo drogarsi; **to be as cool as a cucumber** (*fig*) essere imperturbabile, conservare il sangue freddo; **he's a pretty cool customer** (*fam*) ha un gran sangue freddo; (*pej*) ha una bella faccia tosta; **that was very cool of you!** (*fam*) che sangue freddo!; **we paid a cool £290,000 for that house** (*fam*) abbiamo pagato la bellezza di 290.000 sterline per quella casa ♦ n: **in the cool of the evening** nella frescura serale; **to keep sth in the cool** tenere qc al fresco; **to keep one's cool** (*fam*) conservare la calma; **keep your cool!** calma!; **to lose one's cool** (*fam*) perdere la calma *or* le staffe ♦ VT (*air*) rinfrescare, raffreddare; (*food*) raffreddare; (*engine*) far raffreddare; **cool it!** (*fam*) calmati!; **to cool one's heels** (*fam*) aspettare (a lungo) ♦ VI (*air, liquid*) raffreddarsi

▸ **cool down** VI + ADV raffreddarsi; (*fig: person, situation*) calmarsi ♦ VT + ADV far raffreddare; (*fig*) calmare

▸ **cool off** VI + ADV (*become less angry*) calmarsi; (*lose enthusiasm, become less affectionate*) diventare più freddo(-a)

cool·ant [ˈkuːlənt] N (*Tech*) (liquido) refrigerante *m*

cool box N borsa termica

cool·ing [ˈkuːlɪŋ] ADJ rinfrescante; **cooling fan** (*Aut*) ventilatore *m* di raffreddamento

cooling tower N torre *f* di raffreddamento *or* refrigerazione

cool·ly [ˈkuːlɪ] ADV (*calmly*) con padronanza di sé; (*audaciously*) come se niente fosse; (*unenthusiastically*) freddamente

cool·ness [ˈkuːlnɪs] N (*of air, weather*) frescura, fresco; (*of drink*) freschezza; (*calmness*) calma, controllo, sangue *m* freddo; (*of welcome*) freddezza; (*impudence*) sfacciataggine

coop [kuːp] N stia

▸ **coop up** VT + ADV (*fig*) rinchiudere

co-op [ˈkəʊˈɒp] N ABBR (= *cooperative (society)*) coop *f inv*

co·oper·ate [kəʊˈɒpəˌreɪt] VI: **to cooperate (with sb in** *or* **on sth/to do sth)** cooperare (con qn in qc/per fare qc), collaborare (con qn in qc/per fare qc); **will he cooperate?** sarà disposto a collaborare?

co·opera·tion [kəʊˌɒpəˈreɪʃən] N cooperazione *f*, collaborazione *f*

co·opera·tive [kəʊˈɒpərətɪv] ADJ 1 (*person*) disposto(-a) a collaborare; **you're not very cooperative!** non sei di grande aiuto! 2 (*farm etc*) cooperativo(-a) ♦ N cooperativa

co·opt [kəʊˈɒpt] VT: **to coopt sb onto/into sth** cooptare qn per qc

co·or·di·nate [*n* kəʊˈɔːdnɪt, *vb* kəʊˈɔːdɪˌneɪt] N (*Math*) coordinata; **coordinates** NPL (*clothes*) coordinati *mpl* ♦ VT coordinare

co·or·di·na·tion [kəʊˌɔːdɪˈneɪʃən] N coordinazione *f*

coot [kuːt] N (*Zool*) folaga

co-ownership [ˌkəʊˈəʊnəʃɪp] N comproprietà *f inv*

cop [kɒp] (*fam*) N 1 (*policeman*) poliziotto(-a); **to play at cops and robbers** giocare a guardie e ladri 2 **it's not much cop** (*Brit*) non è un granché ♦ VT 1 **to cop it** buscarle 2 (*something unexpected, unpleasant*) beccare, beccarsi

▸ **cop out** VI + ADV (*fam*) piantare tutto; **to cop out of sth** tirarsi indietro da qc

cope [kəʊp] VI farcela; **to cope with** (*task, child*) farcela con; (*situation, difficulties, problems: tackle*) affrontare, far fronte a; (: *solve*) risolvere; **she's got a lot of problems to cope with** ha molti problemi da affrontare; **he's coping pretty well** se la cava abbastanza bene; **it was hard, but we coped** è stato difficile ma ce l'abbiamo fatta; **leave it to me, I'll cope** lascia stare, ci penso io

Co·pen·ha·gen [ˌkəʊpnˈheɪgən] N Copenhagen *f*

copi·er [ˈkɒpɪəʳ] N (*also*: **photocopier**) (foto)copiatrice *f*

co-pilot [ˈkəʊˈpaɪlət] N secondo pilota *m/f*, copilota *m/f*

co·pi·ous [ˈkəʊpɪəs] ADJ (*tears*) copioso(-a); (*harvest*) abbondante, copioso(-a); (*notes, supply*) abbondante

cop·per [ˈkɒpəʳ] N 1 rame *m*; (*coin*) monetina; **coppers** NPL spiccioli *mpl* 2 (*Brit fam: police*) poliziotto(-a) ♦ ADJ (*wire, kettle*) di rame; (*colour*) (color) rame *inv*, ramato(-a); **copper bracelet** braccialetto di rame

cop·pice [ˈkɒpɪs], **copse** [kɒps] N bosco ceduo

copu·late [ˈkɒpjʊleɪt] VI accoppiarsi

copy [ˈkɒpɪ] N 1 (*gen*) copia; (*book etc*) esemplare *m*; (*of painting*) copia, riproduzione *f*; **rough/fair copy** brutta/ bella (copia) 2 (*material: for printing*) materiale *m*, testo; **to make good copy** (*story, scandal*) fare notizia ♦ VT (*imitate*) imitare; (*make copy of, cheat*) copiare; **he copied in the exam** all'esame ha copiato

▸ **copy out** VT + ADV ricopiare, trascrivere

copy·cat [ˈkɒpɪˌkæt] N (*pej*) copione(-a) ♦ ADJ (*crime*) di emulazione

copy·right [ˈkɒpɪˌraɪt] N diritti *mpl* d'autore, copyright *m inv*; **copyright reserved** tutti i diritti riservati

copy typist N dattilografa

copy·writer [ˈkɒpɪˌraɪtəʳ] N copywriter *m/f inv*, autore(-trice) di testi pubblicitari

cor·al [ˈkɒrəl] N corallo ♦ ADJ (*island*) corallino(-a); **coral necklace** collana di corallo

coral reef N barriera corallina

Coral Sea N: **the Coral Sea** il mar dei Coralli

cord [kɔːd] N 1 (*gen*) corda; (*for pyjamas*) cintura; (*round parcel etc*) corda, spago; (*Elec*) filo 2 (*fabric*) velluto a coste; **cords** NPL (*trousers*) calzoni *mpl* di velluto a coste

cor·dial [ˈkɔːdɪəl] ADJ cordiale ♦ N cordiale *m*

cord·less [ˈkɔːdlɪs] ADJ (*iron*) senza filo; (*telephone*) cordless *inv*

cor·don [ˈkɔːdn] N cordone *m*

▸ **cordon off** VT + ADV fare cordone intorno a

cor·du·roy [ˈkɔːdəˌrɔɪ] N velluto a coste

core [kɔːʳ] N (*of fruit*) torsolo; (*of cable*) centro; (*of Earth, nuclear reactor*) nucleo; (*Mineralogy: sample*) carota; (*of problem*) cuore *m*, nocciolo; **a hard core of resistance** uno zoccolo duro di resistenza; **rotten to the core** marcio(-a) fino al midollo; **English to the core** inglese in tutto e per tutto ♦ VT (*fruit*) togliere il torsolo a

Cor·fu [kɔːˈfuː] N Corfù *f*

co·ri·an·der [ˌkɒrɪˈændə] N coriandolo (*pianta*)

cork [kɔːk] N (*substance*) sughero; (*of bottle*) tappo (di sughero), turacciolo; **to pull the cork out of a bottle** stappare una bottiglia ♦ VT (*bottle: also*: **cork up**) tappare ♦ ADJ di sughero

cork·age [ˈkɔːkɪdʒ] N somma che il cliente di un ristorante paga per farsi stappare bottiglie (di vino) comprate altrove

corked [kɔːkt], (*USA*) **corky** [ˈkɔːkɪ] ADJ (*wine*) che sa di tappo

cork·screw [ˈkɔːkˌskruː] N cavatappi *m inv*

cor·mo·rant [ˈkɔːmərənt] N cormorano

corn¹ [kɔːn] N (*Brit: wheat*) grano, frumento; (*USA: maize*) granturco, mais *m*; **fields of corn** campi *mpl* di grano
❏ **corn** is not translated by the Italian word *corno*

corn² [kɔːn] N (*on foot*) callo

cor·nea [ˈkɔːnɪə] N (*Anat*) cornea

corned beef [ˈkɔːndˈbiːf] N carne *f* di manzo in scatola

cor·ner [ˈkɔːnəʳ] N 1 angolo; (*of table*) spigolo, angolo; **it's just around the corner** (*also fig*) è proprio dietro l'angolo (*in time*) è molto vicino; **the shop on the corner** il negozio all'angolo; **to turn the corner** (*fig*) superare una crisi; **in odd corners** nei posti più strani *or* impensati; **the four corners of the world** i quattro angoli del mondo; **out of the corner of one's eye** con la coda dell'occhio; **to drive sb into a corner** (*fig*) mettere qn con le spalle al muro; **to be in a (tight) corner** (*fig*) essere nei pasticci *or* guai; **to cut a corner** (*Aut*) tagliare una curva; **to cut corners** (*fig*) prendere una scorciatoia 2 (*Ftbl: also: corner kick*) calcio d'angolo, corner *m inv* ♦ VT 1 (*animal*) intrappolare; (*fugitive*) mettere in trappola; (*fig: person: catch to speak to*) bloccare 2 (*Comm: market*) monopolizzare; (: *goods*) accaparrare ♦ VI (*Aut*) curvare, prendere una curva ♦ ADJ (*seat, table*) d'angolo

corner flag N (*Ftbl*) bandierina d'angolo

corner kick N (*Ftbl*) calcio d'angolo, corner *m inv*

corner shop N ≈ negozio sotto casa

corner·stone [ˈkɔːnəˌstəʊn] N (*also fig*) pietra angolare

cor·net [ˈkɔːnɪt] N 1 (*Mus*) cornetta 2 (*Brit: ice cream*) cornetto, cono

corn·flakes [ˈkɔːnˌfleɪks] NPL fiocchi *mpl* di granturco, cornflakes *mpl*

corn·flour [ˈkɔːnˌflaʊəʳ] N (*Brit*) ≈ fecola di patate

cor·nice [ˈkɔːnɪs] N (*Archit*) cornicione *m*; (*interior*) cornice *f*

Cor·nish [ˈkɔːnɪʃ] ADJ della Cornovaglia

corn oil N olio di mais

corn·starch [ˈkɔːnˌstɑːtʃ] N (*USA*) = **cornflour**

cor·nu·co·pia [ˌkɔːnjʊˈkəʊpɪə] N (*frm*) grande abbondanza

Corn·wall [ˈkɔːnwəl] N Cornovaglia

corny [ˈkɔːnɪ] ADJ (*comp* **-ier**, *superl* **-iest**) (*fam: unoriginal*) banale; (: *sentimental*) sdolcinato(-a)

cor·ol·lary [kəˈrɒlərɪ] N corollario

coro·nary [ˈkɒrənərɪ] ADJ (*artery*) coronario(-a); (*disease*) coronarico(-a) ♦ N (*heart attack*) infarto

coro·na·tion [ˌkɒrəˈneɪʃən] N incoronazione f

coro·ner [ˈkɒrənəʳ] N coroner m inv (pubblico ufficiale che indaga casi di morte sospetta)

coro·net [ˈkɒrənɪt] N diadema m; (of peer) corona nobiliare

Corp. ABBR = corporation

cor·po·ral [ˈkɔːpərəl] N (Mil) caporalmaggiore m

cor·po·rate [ˈkɔːpərɪt] ADJ (joint: action, effort) congiunto(-a), unitario(-a); (ownership, responsibility) comune; (Comm) corporativo(-a), costituito(-a) (in corporazione); **corporate body** ente unico avente personalità giuridica

corporate hospitality N omaggi mpl aziendali (consistenti in biglietti per spettacoli, cene ecc)

corporate identity, corporate image N (of organization) immagine f dell'azienda

cor·po·ra·tion [ˌkɔːpəˈreɪʃən] N (Comm) società f inv; (USA) società di capitali; (of town) consiglio comunale

corporation tax N ≈ imposta sul reddito di persone giuridiche

corps [kɔːʳ] N (pl **corps** [kɔːz]) corpo; **press corps** ufficio m stampa, inv

corpse [kɔːps] N cadavere m

cor·pus·cle [ˈkɔːpʌsl] N corpuscolo; (of blood) globulo (both red and white)

cor·ral [kɒˈrɑːl] N recinto

cor·rect [kəˈrekt] ADJ (answer) corretto(-a), esatto(-a), giusto(-a); (temperature, time, amount, forecast) esatto(-a), giusto(-a); (behaviour) corretto(-a); (dress) adatto(-a); (procedure) giusto(-a), corretto(-a); **the correct answer** la risposta esatta; **that's correct** è giusto; **to be correct** avere ragione; **you're absolutely correct** ha proprio ragione ♦ VT (mistake, work, proofs) correggere; **I stand corrected** (ammetto che) ho torto

cor·rec·tion [kəˈrekʃən] N correzione f

cor·re·late [ˈkɒrɪˌleɪt] VT correlare, mettere in relazione or correlazione ♦ VI essere in correlazione; **to correlate with** essere in rapporto con

cor·re·la·tion [ˌkɒrɪˈleɪʃən] N correlazione f

cor·re·spond [ˌkɒrɪsˈpɒnd] VI 1 (be in accordance): **to correspond (with)** corrispondere a; **to correspond (to)** (be equivalent) corrispondere a, equivalere (a) 2 (by letter): **to correspond (with sb)** corrispondere (con qn), essere in corrispondenza (con qn); **they correspond** si scrivono

cor·re·spond·ence [ˌkɒrɪsˈpɒndəns] N 1 (agreement): **correspondence (between)** accordo (tra) 2 (letters) corrispondenza; (collection of letters) carteggio 3 (Math) corrispondenza

correspondence course N corso per corrispondenza

cor·re·spond·ent [ˌkɒrɪsˈpɒndənt] N corrispondente m/f; **foreign correspondent** (Press) corrispondente dall'estero

cor·re·spond·ing [ˌkɒrɪsˈpɒndɪŋ] ADJ corrispondente

cor·ri·dor [ˈkɒrɪdɔːʳ] N corridoio

cor·robo·rate [kəˈrɒbəˌreɪt] VT corroborare, confermare

cor·rode [kəˈrəud] VT corrodere ♦ VI corrodersi

cor·ro·sion [kəˈrəuʒən] N corrosione f

cor·ro·sive [kəˈrəuzɪv] ADJ corrosivo(-a)

cor·ru·gat·ed [ˈkɒrəˌgeɪtɪd] ADJ ondulato(-a), increspato(-a)

corrugated iron N lamiera di ferro ondulata

cor·rupt [kəˈrʌpt] ADJ corrotto(-a); **corrupt practices** (dishonesty, bribery) pratiche fpl illecite; **corrupt officials** funzionari mpl corrotti ♦ VT corrompere

cor·rup·tion [kəˈrʌpʃən] N corruzione f

cor·set [ˈkɔːsɪt] N (undergarment) corsetto, busto; (Med) busto (ortopedico)

Cor·si·ca [ˈkɔːsɪkə] N Corsica

Cor·si·can [ˈkɔːsɪkən] ADJ, N corso(-a)

cor·tège [kɔːˈteɪʒ] N corteo

cor·ti·sone [ˈkɔːtɪˌzəun] N cortisone m

co·rus·cat·ing [kəuˈsɪgnətərɪ] ADJ (frm) scintillante

cosh [kɒʃ] (Brit) N manganello, randello ♦ VT (fam) pestare, manganellare

co·sig·na·tory [kəuˈsɪgnətərɪ] N cofirmatario(-a)

co·si·ness [ˈkəuzɪnɪs] N (of room) comodità; (of atmosphere) intimità, calore m

cos lettuce [ˈkɒsˈletɪs] N lattuga romana

cos·met·ic [kɒzˈmetɪk] ADJ (preparation) cosmetico(-a); (surgery) estetico(-a); (fig: reforms) solo apparente ♦ N cosmetico, prodotto di bellezza

cosmetic surgery N chirurgia plastica

cos·mic [ˈkɒzmɪk] ADJ cosmico(-a)

cos·mo·naut [ˈkɒzmə,nɔːt] N cosmonauta m/f

cos·mo·poli·tan [ˌkɒzmə'pɒlɪtən] ADJ, N cosmopolita m/f

cos·mos [ˈkɒzmɒs] N cosmo

cos·set [ˈkɒsɪt] VT coccolare, vezzeggiare

cost [kɒst] N costo; (Law): **costs** spese fpl; **to be ordered to pay costs** (Law) essere condannato(-a) a pagare le spese; **cost, insurance and freight** (Comm) costo, assicurazione e nolo; **to bear the cost of** sostenere la spesa di; **at great cost** a caro prezzo; **at cost (price)** a prezzo di costo; **at any cost, at all costs** (fig) a tutti i costi, a ogni costo; **whatever the cost** (fig) costi quel che costi; **to my cost** (fig) a mie spese; **at the cost of his life/health** rimettendoci la vita/la salute ♦ 1 (pt, pp cost) costare; **how much does it cost?** quanto costa?, quanto viene?; **what will it cost to have it repaired?** quanto costerà farlo riparare?; **it cost him a lot of money** gli è costato un sacco di soldi; **it costs the earth** (fam) costa un occhio della testa; **it cost him his life/job** gli è costato la vita/il lavoro; **it cost me a great deal of time/effort** mi è costato molto tempo/molta fatica; **it costs nothing to be polite** essere educati non costa nulla; **whatever it costs** (fig) costi quel che costi; **it costs £5/too much** costa 5 sterline/troppo 2 (pt, pp costed: Comm) stabilire il prezzo di

cost accountant N analizzatore m dei costi

co-star [ˈkəustɑːʳ] N co-protagonista m/f

Cos·ta Rica [ˈkɒstəˈriːkə] N Costa Rica

cost centre N (also: costing centre) centro di costo

cost control N controllo dei costi

cost-effective [ˌkɒstɪˈfektɪv] ADJ (Comm) redditizio(-a), efficiente; (gen) conveniente, economico(-a)

cost-effectiveness [ˌkɒstɪˈfektɪvnɪs] N convenienza

cost·ing [ˈkɒstɪŋ] N (determinazione f dei) costi, mpl

cost·ly [ˈkɒstlɪ] ADJ costoso(-a), caro(-a)

cost-of-living [ˈkɒstəvˈlɪvɪŋ] ADJ: **cost-of-living allowance** indennità f inv di contingenza; **cost-of-living index** indice m del costo della vita

cost price N (Brit) prezzo all'ingrosso

cos·tume [ˈkɒstjuːm] N (gen) costume m

costume jewellery N bigiotteria

cosy, cozy (USA) [ˈkəuzɪ] ADJ (comp -ier, superl -iest) (room, atmosphere) accogliente, intimo(-a); (clothes) bello(-a) caldo(-a); **I'm very cosy here** sto proprio bene qui; **we had a cosy chat** abbiamo fatto due chiacchiere in confidenza ♦ N (tea cosy) copriteiera m inv; (egg cosy) copriuovo

cot [kɒt] N (Brit: child's) lettino; (USA: folding bed) brandina

Cots·wolds [ˈkɒts,wəuldz] NPL: **the Cotswolds** zona collinare del Gloucestershire

cot·tage [ˈkɒtɪdʒ] N villetta, cottage m inv

cottage cheese N fiocchi mpl di latte

cottage industry N industria artigianale basata sul lavoro a cottimo

cottage pie N pasticcio di carne macinata e patate

cot·ton [ˈkɒtn] N (cloth, plant) cotone m; (thread) (filo di) cotone ♦ ADJ (shirt, dress) di cotone
 ▸ **cotton on** VI + ADV (fam): **to cotton on (to sth)** afferrare (qc)

cotton candy N (USA) zucchero filato

cotton wool N (Brit) cotone m idrofilo

couch [kautʃ] N (gen) divano, sofà m inv; (in doctor's surgery) lettino; **he was sitting on the couch** era seduto sul divano ♦ VT (statement, request) esprimere

cou·chette [kuːˈʃet] N cuccetta

couch potato N (fam) pigrone(-a) teledipendente

cough [kɒf] N (single instance) colpo di tosse; (illness) tosse f; **I've got a cough** ho la tosse ♦ VI tossire
 ▸ **cough up** VT + ADV (blood, phlegm) sputare; (fig: fam: money) tirare fuori ♦ VI + ADV (fig: fam) cacciare i soldi

cough drop, cough sweet N pasticca per la tosse

cough mixture, cough syrup N sciroppo per la tosse

could [kud] PT, COND of **can**[1]

couldn't [ˈkʊdnt] PT, COND = **could not**

coun·cil [ˈkaʊnsl] N consiglio; **council of war** consiglio di guerra; **city** or **town council** consiglio comunale; **he's on the council** fa parte del consiglio comunale; **the Security Council of the United Nations** il Consiglio di Sicurezza delle Nazioni Unite; **Council of Europe** Consiglio d'Europa

council estate N (Brit) complesso di case popolari

council house N (Brit) casa popolare

council housing N (Brit) alloggi mpl popolari

coun·cil·lor [ˈkaʊnsɪlə'] N consigliere m; **local councillor** consigliere m/f comunale

council tax N (Brit) imposta comunale sugli immobili

coun·sel [ˈkaʊnsəl] N 1 (advice) consiglio, consultazione f; **to keep one's own counsel** tenere le proprie opinioni per sé 2 (pl inv: Law) avvocato(-essa); **counsel for the defence/the prosecution** avvocato difensore/di parte civile; **Queen's (or King's) Counsel** avvocato della Corona ♦ VT: **to counsel sth/sb to do sth** consigliare qc/a qn di fare qc; (caution) raccomandare qc/a qn di fare qc

coun·sel·ling, coun·sel·ing (USA) [ˈkaʊnsəlɪŋ] N terapia; **marriage counselling** terapia di coppia

coun·sel·lor, coun·se·lor (USA) [ˈkaʊnslə'] N (adviser) consulente m/f; (Psych) assistente m/f socio-psicologico(-a); (USA: lawyer) avvocato(-essa)

count[1] [kaʊnt] N 1 conteggio; (of votes at election) spoglio; **to be out for the count** (Boxing) essere fuori combattimento; (fam) essere K.O.; **to keep count of sth** tenere il conto di qc; **you made me lose count** mi hai fatto perdere il conto 2 (Law): **he was found guilty on all counts** è stato giudicato colpevole di tutti i capi di accusa ♦ VT 1 (gen) contare; (one's change etc) controllare; **don't count your chickens before they're hatched** non vendere la pelle dell'orso prima di averlo ucciso, non dir quattro se non l'hai nel sacco; **to count sheep** (fig) contare le pecore; **to count the cost of** calcolare il costo di; (fig) valutare il prezzo di; **without counting the cost** (also fig) senza badare al prezzo; **count your blessings** considera la tua fortuna 2 (include) contare; (consider): **to count sb among** annoverare qn tra; **not counting the children** senza contare i bambini; **ten counting him** dieci compreso lui; **count yourself lucky** considerati fortunato; **will you count it against me?** te la prenderai con me?; **I count it an honour (to do/that)** mi ritengo onorato (a fare/che + sub) ♦ VI 1 contare; **to count (up) to 10** contare fino a 10; **counting from today** a partire da oggi, oggi compreso 2 (be considered, be valid) valere, contare; **two children count as one adult** due bambini valgono come un adulto; **that doesn't count** quello non conta; **it will count against him** deporrà a suo sfavore; **it counts for very little** non conta molto, non ha molta importanza

▸ **count in** VT + ADV comprendere nel conto; **count me in!** (fam) ci sto anch'io!

▸ **count on, count upon** VI + PREP contare su; **you can count on me** puoi contare su di me; **to count on doing sth** contare di fare qc

▸ **count out** VT + ADV 1 (Boxing): **to be counted out** essere dichiarato(-a) K.O. 2 (money, small objects) contare 3 (fam): **count me out!** non ci sto!

▸ **count towards** VI + PREP (subj: payment) andare a incrementare

▸ **count up** VT + ADV contare; (column of figures) sommare, addizionare

count[2] [kaʊnt] N (nobleman) conte m

count·down [ˈkaʊntdaʊn] N conto alla rovescia

coun·te·nance [ˈkaʊntɪnəns] (frm) N (face) (espressione f del) volto; **to keep one's countenance** restare impassibile ♦ VT (permit): **to countenance sth/sb doing sth** ammettere qc/che qn faccia qc

count·er [ˈkaʊntə'] N 1 (of shop, canteen) banco, bancone m; (position: in post office, bank) sportello; **to buy under the counter** (fig) comperare sottobanco 2 (in game) gettone m 3 (Tech) contatore m

coun·ter [ˈkaʊntə'] ADV: **counter to** contrariamente a; **to run counter to** andare contro a ♦ VT: **to counter sth with sth/by doing sth** rispondere a qc con qc/facendo qc; **to counter an attack** rispondere ad un attacco ♦ VI: **to counter with** rispondere con; (words) ribattere con

counter·act [ˌkaʊntər'ækt] VT (counterbalance) controbilanciare, agire in opposizione a; (neutralize) neutralizzare, annullare gli effetti di; **pills to counteract high blood pressure** pillole per combattere l'alta pressione

counter·at·tack [ˈkaʊntərəˌtæk] N contrattacco ♦ VT, VI contrattaccare

counter·bal·ance [ˌkaʊntə'bæləns] N contrappeso ♦ VT controbilanciare, fare da contrappeso a

counter·clockwise [ˌkaʊntə'klɒk,waɪz] ADV (USA) in senso antiorario

counter·es·pio·nage [ˌkaʊntər'espɪ,nɑːʒ] N controspionaggio

counter·feit [ˈkaʊntəfɪt] ADJ contraffatto(-a), falsificato(-a), falso(-a); (money) falso(-a) ♦ N falso, contraffazione f; (coin) moneta falsa ♦ VT contraffare, falsificare

counter·foil [ˈkaʊntəfɔɪl] N matrice f

counter·in·tel·li·gence [ˌkaʊntərɪn'telɪdʒəns] N = **counterespionage**

counter·mand [ˈkaʊntəˌmɑːnd] VT annullare

countermeasure [ˈkaʊntəˌmeʒə'] N contromisura

counteroffensive [ˈkaʊntərəˌfensɪv] N controffensiva

counter·pane [ˈkaʊntəˌpeɪn] N copriletto m inv

counter·part [ˈkaʊntəˌpɑːt] N (of person) omologo(-a); (of document etc) copia, duplicato; **the minister and his French counterpart** il ministro e la sua controparte francese

counter·pro·duc·tive [ˌkaʊntəprə'dʌktɪv] ADJ controproducente

counter·pro·pos·al [ˈkaʊntəprə,pəʊzəl] N controproposta

counter·sign [ˈkaʊntəˌsaɪn] VT controfirmare

counter·sink [ˈkaʊntəˌsɪŋk] VT (pt **countersank**, pp **countersunk**) (hole) svasare; (screw) accecare

counterterrorism [ˈkaʊntə'terərɪzəm] N antiterrorismo

coun·tess [ˈkaʊntɪs] N contessa

count·less [ˈkaʊntlɪs] ADJ: **on countless occasions** in mille occasioni, in innumerevoli occasioni; **countless numbers of** un'infinità di

coun·tri·fied [ˈkʌntrɪˌfaɪd] ADJ rustico(-a), campagnolo(-a)

coun·try [ˈkʌntrɪ] N 1 (gen) paese m; (native land) patria; **to go to the country** (Pol) indire le elezioni; **to die for one's country** morire per la patria; **the border between the two countries** il confine tra i due paesi 2 (as opposed to town) campagna; (terrain, land) territorio; (region) regione f; **in the country** in campagna; **I live in the country** abito in campagna; **there is some lovely country further south** ci sono delle campagne bellissime più a sud; **mountainous country** territorio montagnoso; **unknown country** (also fig) terra sconosciuta ♦ ADJ (life, road) di campagna

country and western, country and western music N musica country e western, country m inv

country dancing N (Brit) danza popolare

country house N villa di campagna

country·man [ˈkʌntrɪmən] N (pl **-men**) (compatriot) compatriota m, connazionale m; (country dweller) campagnolo

country·side [ˈkʌntrɪ,saɪd] N campagna

country-wide [ˈkʌntrɪ,waɪd] ADJ (su scala) nazionale, diffuso(-a) in tutto il paese ♦ ADV in tutto il paese, su scala nazionale

coun·ty [ˈkaʊntɪ] N contea ♦ ADJ (boundary, court) di contea

county council N (Brit) consiglio di contea

county town N (Brit) capoluogo (di contea)

coup [kuː] N (Pol: also: **coup d'état**) colpo di stato, golpe m inv; (triumph) bel colpo; **getting her to take the part was a real coup** convincerla ad accettare la parte è stato veramente un bel colpo

cou·pé [ˈkuːpeɪ] N (Aut) coupé m inv

cou·ple [ˈkʌpl] N (of animals, people) coppia; **a couple of times/hours/books** (two or three) un paio di volte/ore/libri; **the couple who live next door** la coppia che vive qui accanto ♦ VT 1 (idea, name): **to couple with** associare con 2 (railway carriages): **to couple (on** or **up)** agganciare

cou·plet [ˈkʌplɪt] N distico

cou·pling [ˈkʌplɪŋ] N (Rail) agganciamento

cou·pon [ˈkuːpɒn] N (voucher) buono; (Comm) coupon m inv; (football pools coupon) schedina

cour·age [ˈkʌrɪdʒ] N coraggio; **I haven't the courage to refuse** non ho il coraggio di rifiutare; **to have the courage of one's convictions** avere il coraggio delle proprie opinioni or convinzioni; **to take one's courage in both hands** prendere il coraggio a due mani

cou·ra·geous [kəˈreɪdʒəs] ADJ coraggioso(-a)

cour·gette [ˌkʊəˈʒet] N (Brit) zucchina, zucchino

cou·ri·er [ˈkʊrɪəʳ] N (messenger) corriere m; (for tourists) accompagnatore(-trice) turistico(-a), tour leader m/f inv; **they sent it by courier** l'hanno spedito con il corriere ♦ VT: **to courier sth to sb** mandare con il corriere qc a qn

course [kɔːs] N 1 **of course** naturalmente, ovviamente, senz'altro, certo; **yes, of course!** sì, certo!; **(no) of course not!** certo che no!, no di certo!; **do you love me? - of course I do!** mi ami? - ma certo!; **of course you can** certo che puoi; **of course I won't do it** certo che non lo farò 2 (Scol, Univ) corso; **a French course** un corso di francese; **to take a course in French** seguire un corso di francese; **a course of lectures on a subject** una serie di conferenze or lezioni su un argomento; **a course of treatment** (Med) una cura 3 (part of meal) piatto, portata; **a three-course meal** un pasto di tre portate; **first course** primo piatto; **main course** portata principale 4 (route: of ship) rotta; (: of river) corso; (: of planet) orbita; **to set course for** (Naut) far rotta per; **to change course** (Naut, also fig) cambiare rotta; **to go off course** deviare dalla rotta; **to hold one's course** seguire or mantenere la rotta; **to take/follow a course of action** (fig) imboccare/seguire una politica; **we have no other course but to ...** non possiamo far altro che...; **there are two courses open to us** abbiamo due possibilità; **the best course would be to ...** la cosa migliore sarebbe...; **to let things/events take** or **run their course** lasciare che le cose/gli eventi seguano il loro corso; **as a matter of course** come una cosa scontata 5 (duration): **in the course of** (life, disease, events) nel corso di; **in the course of time** a tempo debito; **in the course of time** col passare del tempo; **in the normal** or **ordinary course of events** normalmente; **in (the) course of construction** in (via di) costruzione; **in the course of the next few days** nel corso dei prossimi giorni 6 (Sport: golf course) campo (di golf); (: race course) pista ♦ VI (water, tears) scorrere; **it sent the blood coursing through his veins** gli ha rimescolato il sangue nelle vene

court [kɔːt] N 1 (Law) corte f; (room) aula; **to take sb to court** (over sth) citare in tribunale qn (per qc); **to settle a case out of court** conciliare una causa in via amichevole; **to rule out of court** dichiarare inammissibile; **he was brought before the court on a charge of theft** fu processato sotto accusa di furto 2 (also: **tennis court**) campo da tennis 3 (royal) corte f ♦ VT corteggiare, fare la corte a; (fig: favour, popularity) cercare di conquistare; (: death, disaster) sfiorare, rasentare ♦ VI (old: Culin) corteggiarsi

cour·teous [ˈkɜːtɪəs] ADJ cortese

cour·tesan [ˌkɔːtɪˈzæn] N cortigiana

cour·tesy [ˈkɜːtɪsɪ] N (politeness) cortesia, gentilezza; (polite act) cortesia, piacere m; **by courtesy of** per gentile concessione di; **with the utmost courtesy** con la massima cortesia; **you might have had the courtesy to tell me** avresti potuto farmi la cortesia di dirmelo; **to exchange courtesies** scambiarsi convenevoli

courtesy car N vettura sostitutiva

courtesy coach N autobus m inv gratuito (di hotel, aeroporto)

courtesy light N (Aut) luce f interna

court·house [ˈkɔːthaʊs] N (USA) tribunale m, palazzo di giustizia

cour·ti·er [ˈkɔːtɪəʳ] N cortigiano(-a)

court martial [ˈkɔːtˈmɑːʃəl] N (pl court martials or courts martial) corte f marziale

court·room [ˈkɔːtˌruːm] N aula (di tribunale)

court shoe N scarpa f décolleté, inv

court·yard [ˈkɔːtˌjɑːd] N cortile m

cous·in [ˈkʌzn] N cugino(-a)

cove [kəʊv] N piccola baia, cala

cov·enant [ˈkʌvɪnənt] N accordo (scritto) ♦ VT: **to covenant to do sth** impegnarsi (per iscritto) a fare qc

cov·er [ˈkʌvəʳ] N 1 (gen) copertura; (of dish, bowl, saucepan) coperchio; (of furniture, typewriter) fodera; (for merchandise,

on vehicle) telo, telone m; (bedspread) copriletto; (often pl: blanket) coperta; (of book, magazine) copertina; **under separate cover** (Comm) a parte, in plico separato; **to read a book from cover to cover** leggere un libro dalla prima all'ultima pagina 2 (shelter) riparo; (covering fire) copertura; **to take cover** (hide) nascondersi; (Mil: shelter) ripararsi; **to break cover** uscire allo scoperto; **under cover** al coperto, al riparo; (hiding) nascosto(-a); **under cover of darkness** con il favore delle tenebre, protetto(-a) dall'oscurità 3 (Fin, Comm, Insurance: in espionage etc) copertura; **without cover** (Fin) senza copertura; **fire cover** copertura contro i rischi d'incendio 4 (frm: at table) coperto 5 (Mus: also: **cover version**) cover f inv, riedizione f di canzone di successo ♦ VT 1 (gen): **to cover (with)** coprire (con or di); **covered with confusion** (fig) tutto(-a) confuso(-a); **covered with shame** pieno(-a) di vergogna; **to cover o.s. with glory/disgrace** coprirsi di gloria/infamia; **he covered his face** si coprì il viso 2 (hide: facts, mistakes) nascondere; (: noise) coprire 3 (protect: Mil, Sport, Insurance) coprire; **he only said that to cover himself** lo disse solo per coprirsi le spalle; **I've got you covered!** ti corro jo! 4 (be sufficient for, include) coprire; **£100 will cover everything** 100 sterline saranno sufficienti; **we must cover all possibilities** dobbiamo prevedere tutte le possibilità 5 (distance) coprire, percorrere; **to cover a lot of ground** (also fig) fare molta strada 6 (Press: report on) fare un servizio su 7 (Mus) fare una cover or una riedizione di ♦ VI: **to cover for sb** (at work etc) sostituire qn

▸ **cover over** VT + ADV (ri)coprire

▸ **cover up** VT + ADV (child, object): **to cover up (with)** coprire (con or di); (fig: hide: truth, facts) nascondere; **the government tried to cover up the details of the accident** il governo ha cercato di tenere nascosti i particolari dell'incidente; **to cover up one's tracks** (also fig) cancellare le tracce ♦ VI + ADV (warmly) coprirsi; **to cover up for sb** (fig) coprire qn

cov·er·age [ˈkʌvərɪdʒ] N (Press, TV, Radio): **to give full coverage to an event** fare un ampio servizio su un avvenimento, dare grande spazio or risonanza a un avvenimento; **the visit got nationwide coverage** (Radio, TV) la visita fu trasmessa su tutta la rete nazionale

cover·alls [ˈkʌvərˌɔːlz] NPL (USA) tuta

cover charge N (in restaurant) coperto (quota)

cov·er·ing [ˈkʌvərɪŋ] N copertura; (of snow, dust etc) strato

covering letter, (USA) **cover letter** N nota esplicativa, lettera d'accompagnamento

cover note N (Insurance) polizza (di assicurazione) provvisoria

cover price N prezzo di copertina

cov·ert [ˈkʌvət] ADJ (gen) nascosto(-a); (glance) di sottecchi, furtivo(-a)

cover-up [ˈkʌvərˌʌp] N occultamento (di informazioni)

cov·et [ˈkʌvɪt] VT concupire, bramare

cow [kaʊ] N (bovine) mucca, vacca; (female elephant) elefantessa; (female seal) (foca) femmina ♦ VT (person) intimidire; **a cowed look** un'aria da cane bastonato ♦ ADJ femmina

cow·ard [ˈkaʊəd] N vigliacco(-a)

cow·ard·ice [ˈkaʊədɪs], **cow·ard·li·ness** [ˈkaʊədlɪnɪs] N vigliaccheria

cow·ard·ly [ˈkaʊədlɪ] ADJ vigliacco(-a)

cow·boy [ˈkaʊˌbɔɪ] N cowboy m inv

cow·er [ˈkaʊəʳ] VI acquattarsi (per paura)

cow·shed [ˈkaʊˌʃed] N stalla

cow·slip [ˈkaʊˌslɪp] N (Bot) primula odorosa

cox·swain [ˈkɒksən] N nocchiere m

coy [kɔɪ] ADJ (comp -er, superl -est) (affectedly shy: person) che fa il (la) vergognoso(-a); (: smile) falsamente timido(-a); (evasive) evasivo(-a); (coquettish) civettuolo(-a)

coy·ote [kɔɪˈəʊtɪ] N coyote m inv

cozy [ˈkəʊzɪ] ADJ (USA) = **cosy**

CP N ABBR (= Communist Party) P.C. m

cp. ABBR (= compare) cfr.

CPA N ABBR (USA) = **certified public accountant**

CPI N ABBR (USA: = Consumer Price Index) indice dei prezzi al consumo

Cpl. ABBR = **corporal**

cps [ˌsiːpiːˈɛs] ABBR (= *characters per second*) cps
CPU [ˌsiːpiːˈjuː] N ABBR = **central processing unit**
cr. ABBR 1 = **credit** 2 = **creditor**
crab [kræb] N granchio
crab apple N (*fruit*) mela selvatica; (*tree*) melo selvatico
crack [kræk] N 1 (*split, slit: in glass, pottery*) incrinatura, scheggiatura; (: *in wall, plaster, ground, paint*) crepa, spaccatura; (: *in skin*) screpolatura; **to open the door a crack** aprire la porta lasciandola accostata; **through the crack in the door** (*slight opening*) dalla fessura della porta; **at the crack of dawn** alle prime luci dell'alba 2 (*noise: of twigs*) scricchiolio, crepitio; (: *of whip*) schiocco; (: *of rifle, of gun*) colpo; (: *of thunder*) boato 3 (*blow*): **a crack on the head** una botta in testa 4 (*fam: attempt*): **to have a crack at sth** tentare qc; **I'll have a crack at it** ci proverò 5 (*fam: joke, insult*) battuta 6 (*Drugs*) crack m *inv* ♦ VT (*break: glass, pottery*) incrinare; (: *wood*) schiantare; (: *nut*) schiacciare; (: *egg*) rompere; (*fig: fam: safe*) scassinare; (: *bottle*) stappare, aprire; **to crack one's skull** spaccarsi la testa; **he cracked his head on the pavement** ha sbattuto la testa sul marciapiedi; **to crack sb over the head** dare un colpo in testa a qn 2 (*cause to sound: whip, finger joints*) (far) schioccare; **to crack jokes** (*fam*) dire battute, scherzare 3 (*case, mystery: solve*) risolvere; (*code*) decifrare; **I think we've cracked it!** penso che ci siamo! ♦ VI 1 (*break: pottery, glass*) incrinarsi; (*ground, wall*) creparsi; (*dry wood*) schiantarsi; (*skin*) screpolarsi; **to crack under the strain** (*person*) non reggere alla tensione 2 (*whip*) schioccare; (*dry wood*) scricchiolare; **to get cracking** (*fam*) darsi una mossa ♦ ADJ (*team, regiment*) scelto(-a); (*athlete*) di prim'ordine; **a crack shot** un tiratore infallibile
  ▸ **crack down** VI + ADV: **to crack down (on)** prendere serie misure contro, porre freno a; **the police are cracking down on motorists who drive too fast** la polizia sta prendendo serie misure contro gli automobilisti che vanno troppo veloci
  ▸ **crack up**(*fam*) VI + ADV crollare; **I must be cracking up!** (*hum*) sto dando i numeri! ♦ VT + ADV: **he's not all he's cracked up to be** non è così meraviglioso come dicono
crack·down [ˈkrækˌdaʊn] N repressione *f*
cracked [krækt] ADJ (*fam: mad*) tocco(-a), matto(-a)
crack·er [ˈkrækəʳ] N 1 (*biscuit*) cracker m *inv* 2 (*firework*) petardo; (*Christmas cracker*) specie di mortaretto natalizio con sorpresa
crack·le [ˈkrækl] VI (*twigs burning*) crepitare, scoppiettare; (*sth frying*) sfrigolare ♦ N (*see vb*) crepitio, scoppiettio; sfrigolio; (*on telephone*) disturbo
crack·ling [ˈkræklɪŋ] N 1 (*sound*) crepitio; (*on radio, telephone*) disturbo; (*of frying food*) sfrigolio 2 (*of pork*) cotenna (di maiale) arrostita
crack·pot [ˈkrækˌpɒt](*fam*) N imbecille m/f con idee assurde ♦ ADJ (*idea*) assurdo(-a)
cra·dle [ˈkreɪdl] N culla; (*of telephone*) forcella; (*Constr*) gabbia ♦ VT (*child*) tenere tra le braccia; (*object*) reggere tra le braccia
craft [krɑːft] N 1 (*handicraft*) artigianato; (*art*) arte *f*, mestiere m; (*profession*) mestiere; (*fig: skill*) abilità, maestria 2 (*cunning: pej*) furbizia, astuzia 3 (*boat: pl inv*) barca, imbarcazione *f*
crafts·man [ˈkrɑːftsmən] N (*pl* -**men**) artigiano
crafts·man·ship [ˈkrɑːftsmənˌʃɪp] N (*skill*) arte *f*, abilità, maestria; **a piece of craftsmanship** un pezzo di artigianato
crafty [ˈkrɑːftɪ] ADJ (*comp* -**ier**, *superl* -**iest**) (*person*) furbo(-a), astuto(-a); (*action*) abile
crag [kræg] N rupe *f*
cram [kræm] VT (*stuff: books, papers*): **to cram into** infilare in, stipare in, pigiare in (*people, passengers*) ammassare in; (*fill*): **to cram sth with** riempire qc di; **we crammed our stuff into the trunk** abbiamo stipato la nostra roba nel bagagliaio; **she crammed her bag with books** ha riempito la borsa di libri; **to cram in** far stare, trovare posto per; **his head is crammed with strange ideas** ha la testa piena di idee strane; **the room was crammed with furniture/people** la stanza era stipata di mobili/affollata di gente; **to cram o.s. with food** abbuffarsi, rimpinzarsi ♦ VI 1 (*people*): **to cram (into)** affollarsi (in), accalcarsi (in), stiparsi (in) 2 (*pupil: for exam*) fare una sgobbata finale

cram·ming [ˈkræmɪŋ] N (*fig: pej*) sgobbare m
cramp [kræmp] N (*Med*): **cramp (in)** crampo (a) ♦ VT (*hinder: person*) impacciare, inibire; (: *progress*) ostacolare, frenare; **you're cramping my style** mi inibisci
cramped [kræmpt] ADJ (*room etc*) angusto(-a); (*writing*) fitto(-a); (*position*) rannicchiato(-a)
cram·pon [ˈkræmpɒn] N (*Mountaineering*) rampone m
cran·berry [ˈkrænbərɪ] N mirtillo
crane [kreɪn] N (*Zool, Tech*) gru *f inv* ♦ VT, VI: **to crane forward, to crane one's neck** allungare il collo
cra·nium [ˈkreɪnɪəm] N (*pl* **cranium**) (*Anat*) cranio
crank [kræŋk] N 1 (*Tech*) manovella 2 (*person*) eccentrico(-a), persona stramba ♦ VT (*also:* **crank up**) avviare a manovella; (*musica*) alzare il volume
crank·shaft [ˈkræŋkˌʃɑːft] N (*Aut*) albero motore, albero a gomiti
cranky [ˈkræŋkɪ] ADJ (*comp* -**ier**, *superl* -**iest**) (*strange: ideas, people*) eccentrico(-a), strambo(-a); **to be cranky** (*bad-tempered*) avere i nervi, essere di malumore
cran·ny [ˈkrænɪ] N *see* **nook**
crap [kræp](*fam!*) N merda (*fam!*); (*nonsense*) cazzate *fpl* (*fam!*); **to have a crap** cacare (*fam!*)
crap·py [ˈkræpɪ] ADJ (*comp* -**ier**, *superl* -**iest**) (*fam!*) di merda (*fam!*)
crash [kræʃ] N 1 (*accident*) incidente m; **there has been a plane crash** un aereo è precipitato 2 (*noise*) fragore m, fracasso; (*of thunder*) fragore 3 (*of business*) fallimento; (*Stock Exchange*) crollo ♦ VT (*smash: car*) avere un incidente con, fracassare, sfasciare; **he crashed the car into a wall** andò a sbattere contro un muro con la macchina; **the pilot crashed the plane** il pilota ha fatto precipitare l'aereo ♦ VI 1 (*car*) avere un incidente; (*plane*) cadere, precipitare; (*collide: two vehicles*) scontrarsi; **to crash into sth** scontrarsi con qc, andare a sbattere contro qc, schiantarsi contro qc; **the plane crashed** l'aereo è precipitato; **the two cars crashed** le due macchine si sono scontrate; **the plates came crashing down** i piatti sono andati in frantumi 2 (*business*) fallire, andare in rovina; (*stock market*) crollare 3 (*computer*) impiantarsi; **it nearly finished when my computer crashed** avevo quasi finito quando il computer si è impiantato ♦ ADJ (*diet, course*) intensivo(-a), rapido(-a)
crash barrier N (*Brit: Aut*) guardrail m *inv*
crash course N corso intensivo
crash helmet N casco (di protezione)
crash landing N atterraggio forzato, atterraggio di fortuna
crass [kræs] ADJ crasso(-a)
crate [kreɪt] N cassa, cassetta
cra·ter [ˈkreɪtəʳ] N cratere m
cra·vat [krəˈvæt] N (*for men*) foulard m *inv* da collo
crave [kreɪv] VT 1 (*desire*) desiderare disperatamente 2 (*frm: pardon, permission*) implorare ♦ VI: **to crave for** = **crave 1**
crav·ing [ˈkreɪvɪŋ] N: **craving (for)** (*for food, cigarettes etc*) (gran) voglia (di); (*in pregnancy*) voglia; (*for affection, attention*) desiderio estremo
crawl [krɔːl] N 1 (*slow pace*) passo lento; **the traffic went at a crawl** il traffico procedeva a passo d'uomo 2 (*Swimming*) stile m libero, crawl m; **to do the crawl** nuotare a stile libero, nuotare a crawl ♦ VI 1 (*drag o.s.*) trascinarsi, strisciare; (*child*) andare gattoni *or* carponi; (*traffic*) avanzare lentamente, procedere a passo d'uomo; (*time*) non passare mai; **to crawl in/out** *etc* trascinarsi carponi dentro/fuori *etc*; **to be crawling with ants** brulicare di formiche 2 (*fam: suck up*): **to crawl to sb** arruffianarsi qn
cray·fish [ˈkreɪˌfɪʃ] N gambero (d'acqua dolce)
cray·on [ˈkreɪən] N (*wax*) pastello a cera; (*chalk*) gessetto; (*coloured pencil*) matita colorata
craze [kreɪz] N mania ♦ VT 1 far diventare pazzo(-a) 2 (*pottery, glaze*) incrinare ♦ VI (*pottery, glaze, windscreen*) incrinarsi
crazed [kreɪzd] ADJ (*look, person*) folle, pazzo(-a); (*pottery, glaze*) incrinato(-a)
cra·zy [ˈkreɪzɪ] ADJ (*comp* -**ier**, *superl* -**iest**) 1 (*mad*) pazzo(-a), matto(-a), folle; **to go crazy** uscire di senno, impazzire; **crazy with jealousy** pazzo(-a) di gelosia; **it was a crazy idea** era un'idea folle; **you were crazy to do it** sei stato un pazzo a

farlo **2** (*fam: keen*): **to be crazy about sb** essere pazzo(-a) di qn; **she's crazy about him** è pazza di lui; **to be crazy about sth** andare matto(-a) per qc; **Paul is crazy about football** Paul va matto per il calcio **3** (*angle, slope*) pericolante

creak [kriːk] VI (*wood, shoe etc*) scricchiolare; (*hinge etc*) cigolare; **the floorboards creaked** le assi del pavimento scricchiolavano ♦ N (*see vb*) scricchiolio; cigolio

cream [kriːm] N **1** (*Culin*) panna; **single/double cream** panna da cucina liquida/densa; **whipped cream** panna montata; **a chocolate cream** (*a sweet*) un cremino al cioccolato; **cream of tomato soup** crema di pomodoro; **strawberries and cream** fragole con panna; **the cream of society** (*fig*) la crème della società **2** (*lotion: for face, shoes etc*) crema; **sun cream** crema solare ♦ ADJ (*colour*) (color) crema *inv*, (color) panna *inv*; (*Culin: made with cream*) alla panna; **a cream silk blouse** una camicetta di seta color crema ♦ VT (*mix: also:* **cream together**) amalgamare; **creamed potatoes** puré m di patate

　▸ **cream off** VT + PREP (*best talents, part of profits*) portarsi via

cream cake N torta alla panna

cream cheese N formaggio fresco spalmabile, formaggio cremoso

cream·ery [ˈkriːmərɪ] N (*factory*) caseificio; (*shop*) latteria

creamy [ˈkriːmɪ] ADJ (*comp* **-ier**, *superl* **-iest**) (*taste, texture*) cremoso(-a); (*colour*) crema *inv*, panna *inv*

crease [kriːs] N (*fold: in trousers*) piega; (*wrinkle: in cloth*) grinza; (: *in face*) ruga, grinza ♦ VT sgualcire, spiegazzare; **his face was creased with laughter** aveva il volto contratto dalle risate ♦ VI sgualcirsi

crease-resistant [ˈkriːsrɪˌzɪstənt] ADJ ingualcibile

cre·ate [kriːˈeɪt] VT (*gen*) creare; (*impression, fuss, noise*) fare; **to create a sensation** destare or fare scalpore; **he was created a peer by the Queen** fu nominato pari dalla Regina ♦ VI (*fam*) fare un sacco di storie

crea·tion [kriːˈeɪʃən] N creazione f

crea·tive [kriːˈeɪtɪv] ADJ creativo(-a) ♦ N creativo(-a)

crea·tiv·ity [ˌkriːeɪˈtɪvɪtɪ] N creatività

crea·tor [kriːˈeɪtəʳ] N creatore(-trice)

crea·ture [ˈkriːtʃəʳ] N (*gen*) creatura; **the creatures of the deep** (*liter*) le creature degli abissi; **a creature from outer space** un extraterrestre; **the poor creature had no home** il poverino era senza casa; **a creature of habit** una persona abitudinaria

crèche [kreɪʃ] N asilo m nido, *inv*

cre·dence [ˈkriːdəns] N credenza, fede f

cre·den·tials [krɪˈdenʃəlz] NPL (*qualifications*) titoli *mpl*; (*identifying papers, of diplomat*) credenziali *fpl*; (*letters of reference*) referenze *fpl*

cred·ibil·ity [ˌkredəˈbɪlɪtɪ] N (*see adj*) credibilità; attendibilità

cred·ible [ˈkredɪbl] ADJ (*gen*) credibile; (*witness, source*) attendibile

cred·it [ˈkredɪt] N **1** (*Fin*) credito; **to give sb credit** fare credito a qn; **you have £100 to your credit** lei ha 100 sterline a suo credito; **on credit** a credito; **is his credit good?** gli si può dare credito?; **in credit** in attivo; **to be in credit** (*person*) essere creditore(-trice); (*bank account*) essere coperto(-a) **2** (*honour*) onore m; **to one's credit** a proprio onore; **it is to his credit that** ... bisogna riconoscergli che...; **he's a credit to his family** fa onore alla sua famiglia; **to give sb credit for (doing) sth** riconoscere a qn il merito di (aver fatto) qc; **I gave you credit for more sense** ti reputavo più sensato; **it does you credit** ti fa onore; **to take credit for (doing) sth** attribuirsi il merito di (aver fatto) qc **3** (*Univ, esp USA*) certificato di compimento di una parte di un corso universitario; *see also* **credits** ♦ VT **1** (*believe: also:* **give credit to**) credere, prestar fede a **2** (*attribute*) attribuire il credito a; **to credit sb with sth** attribuire qc a qn; **I credited him with more sense** credevo che avesse più cervello; **he credited them with the victory** attribuì a loro il merito della vittoria **3** (*Comm*): **to credit £50 to sb, to credit sb with £50** accreditare 50 sterline a qn ♦ VT (*limit, agency etc*) di credito; **on the credit side** (*fig*) a suo favore

cred·it·able [ˈkredɪtəbl] ADJ che fa onore, lodevole, degno(-a) di lode

credit account N (*in shop etc*) conto (di credito), conto (aperto)

credit agency, (*USA*) **credit bureau** N agenzia di analisi di credito

credit balance N saldo attivo

credit bureau N (*USA*) agenzia di analisi di credito

credit card N carta di credito

credit control N controllo dei crediti

credit crunch N improvvisa stretta di credito

credit facilities NPL agevolazioni *fpl* creditizie

credit limit N limite m di credito

credit note N (*Brit*) nota di credito

credi·tor [ˈkredɪtəʳ] N creditore(-trice)

cred·its [ˈkredɪts] NPL (*Cine, TV: opening*) titoli *mpl* di testa; (: *closing*) titoli *mpl* di coda

credit transfer N bancogiro, postagiro

credit·worthy [ˈkredɪtˌwɜːðɪ] ADJ autorizzabile al credito

cre·du·lity [krɪˈdjuːlɪtɪ] N credulità

creed [kriːd] N credo, dottrina

creek [kriːk] N (*inlet*) insenatura; (*USA*) piccolo fiume m

creel [kriːl] N cestino per il pesce; (*also:* **lobster creel**) nassa

creep [kriːp] (*pt, pp* **crept**) VI (*animal*) strisciare; (*plant*) arrampicarsi; (*person: stealthily*) avanzare furtivamente; (: *slowly*) avanzare lentamente; **to creep in/out** entrare/uscire quatto(-a) quatto(-a); **to creep up on sb** avvicinarsi quatto(-a) quatto(-a) a qn; (*fig: old age etc*) cogliere qn alla sprovvista; **a feeling of peace crept over him** lo avvolse un senso di pace; **it made my flesh creep** mi fece accapponare la pelle; **an error has crept in** ci è scappato un errore ♦ N (*fam*): **it gives me the creeps** mi fa venire la pelle d'oca; **he's a creep** è un tipo viscido

creep·er [ˈkriːpəʳ] N (*Bot*) rampicante m

creepy [ˈkriːpɪ] ADJ (*comp* **-ier**, *superl* **-iest**) (*frightening*) che fa accapponare la pelle; **it was a really creepy place** era un posto che dava proprio i brividi

creepy-crawly [ˈkriːpɪˌkrɔːlɪ] N (*fam*) bestiolina, insetto

cre·mate [krɪˈmeɪt] VT cremare

cre·ma·tion [krɪˈmeɪʃən] N cremazione f

crema·to·rium [ˌkreməˈtɔːrɪəm] N (*pl* **crematoria** [ˌkreməˈtɔːrɪə]) (forno) crematorio

creo·sote [ˈkrɪəsəʊt] N creosoto ♦ VT dare il creosoto a

crêpe [kreɪp] N **1** (*fabric*) crespo **2** (*also:* **crêpe rubber**) para **3** (*pancake*) crêpe f *inv*, crespella

crêpe paper N carta crespata

crêpe sole N (*on shoes*) suola di para

crept [krept] PT, PP *of* **creep**

cre·scen·do [krɪˈʃendəʊ] N (*Mus, also fig*) crescendo

cres·cent [ˈkresnt] ADJ (*moon*) crescente; (*shape*) a mezzaluna ♦ N (*shape*) mezzaluna; (*street*) via (*a semicerchio*)

cress [kres] N crescione m

crest [krest] N (*of bird, wave, mountain*) cresta; (*on helmet*) pennacchio; (*Heraldry*) cimiero; **to be on the crest of the wave** (*fig*) essere sulla cresta dell'onda

crest·fallen [ˈkrestˌfɔːlən] ADJ abbattuto(-a), mortificato(-a); **to look crestfallen** avere un'aria mogia

Crete [kriːt] N Creta

cre·vasse [krɪˈvæs] N crepaccio

crev·ice [ˈkrevɪs] N crepa, fessura

crew [kruː] N (*Naut, Aer*) equipaggio; (*Rowing, etc team*) squadra; (*gang*) banda, compagnia; **film crew** troupe f *inv* cinematografica ♦ VI (*Sailing*): **to crew for sb** far parte dell'equipaggio di qn

crew cut N: **to have a crew cut** avere i capelli a spazzola

crew-neck [ˈkruːˌnek] ADJ: **crew-neck sweater** maglione m a girocollo

crib [krɪb] N **1** (*small cot*) culla; (*Rel*) presepio; (*manger*) mangiatoia **2** (*plagiarism*) plagio; (*Scol: answer book*) traduttore m, bigino (*fam*) ♦ VT (*Scol*) copiare

crib·bage [ˈkrɪbɪdʒ] N *tipo di gioco di carte*

crick [krɪk] N: **crick in the neck** torcicollo; **crick in the back** dolore m alla schiena ♦ VT: **to crick one's neck** prendere il torcicollo; **to crick one's back** farsi male alla schiena

crick·et¹ [ˈkrɪkɪt] N (*sport*) cricket m; **I play cricket** gioco a cricket; **that's not cricket** (*fig*) questo non è leale

crick·et² [ˈkrɪkɪt] N (*insect*) grillo
crick·et·er [ˈkrɪkɪtəʳ] N giocatore(-trice) di cricket
crime [kraɪm] N (*in general*) criminalità; (*instance*) crimine *m*, delitto; **crime is rising** la criminalità è in aumento; **he committed a crime** ha commesso un crimine; **the scene of the crime** la scena del delitto; **it's a crime** (*fig*) è una vergogna
crime wave N ondata di criminalità
crimi·nal [ˈkrɪmɪnl] N criminale *m/f*; **a dangerous criminal** un pericoloso criminale ♦ ADJ criminale; (*fig*) vergognoso(-a); **criminal lawyer** (avvocato) penalista *m/f*; **criminal offence** reato; **to study criminal law** fare studi penalistici; **to have a criminal record** avere precedenti penali; **to take criminal proceedings against sb** istruire una causa penale contro qn
crimp [krɪmp] VT (*hair*) arricciare; (*material*) pieghettare
crim·son [ˈkrɪmzn] ADJ, N cremisi *m inv*
cringe [krɪndʒ] VI (*in terror*): **to cringe (from)** ritrarsi impaurito(-a) (da); **to cringe (before)** (*in servility*) strisciare (davanti a); **the very thought of it makes me cringe** (*fam*: *in embarrassment*) solo a pensarci mi sento sprofondare
crin·kle [ˈkrɪŋkl] VT spiegazzare, sgualcire
crip·ple [ˈkrɪpl] N (*lame*) zoppo(-a); (*disabled*) invalido(-a); (*maimed*) mutilato(-a) ♦ VT 1 rendere invalido(-a); **crippled with arthritis** invalido(-a) per l'artrite 2 (*production, exports*) paralizzare
crip·pling [ˈkrɪplɪŋ] ADJ (*disease*) che provoca invalidità; (*taxes, debts*) esorbitante
cri·sis [ˈkraɪsɪs] N (*pl* **crises** [ˈkraɪsiːz]) crisi *f inv*; **to come to a crisis** entrare in crisi; **we have a crisis on our hands** ci troviamo di fronte a una crisi
crisp [krɪsp] ADJ (*comp* **-er**, *superl* **-est**) (*bacon, biscuit, lettuce*) croccante; (*snow*) fresco(-a); (*bank note*) nuovo(-a) di zecca; (*linen*) inamidato(-a); (*air*) fresco(-a), frizzante; (*manner, tone, reply*) secco(-a), brusco(-a); (*style*) conciso(-a) e vivace
crisps [krɪsps] NPL (*Brit*) patatine *fpl*; **a bag of crisps** un sacchetto di patatine
crispy [ˈkrɪspɪ] ADJ (*comp* **-ier**, *superl* **-iest**) croccante
criss-cross [ˈkrɪskrɒs] ADJ (*lines*) incrociato(-a), intrecciato(-a); (*pattern*) a linee incrociate ♦ VT incrociare
cri·teri·on [kraɪˈtɪərɪən] N (*pl* **criteria** [kraɪˈtɪərɪə]) criterio; **I don't understand what their criteria were** non riesco a capire i criteri che hanno seguito; **only one candidate met all the criteria** un solo candidato soddisfaceva tutti i requisiti
crit·ic [ˈkrɪtɪk] N critico(-a)
criti·cal [ˈkrɪtɪkəl] ADJ (*all senses*) critico(-a); **to be critical of sb/sth** criticare qn/qc, essere critico(-a) verso qn/qc; **at a critical moment** in un momento critico; **a critical success** (*book, play*) un successo di critica
criti·cal·ly [ˈkrɪtɪkəlɪ] ADV criticamente; **to be critically ill** versare in gravi condizioni, versare in condizioni critiche, essere gravemente malato(-a); **critically important** di importanza vitale
criti·cism [ˈkrɪtɪsɪzəm] N critica
criti·cize [ˈkrɪtɪsaɪz] VT criticare
cri·tique [krɪˈtiːk] N critica, saggio critico
croak [krəʊk] N (*of raven*) gracchio; (*of frog*) gracidio, gracidare *m* ♦ VI (*raven*) gracchiare; (*frog*) gracidare; (*person*) dire con voce rauca
Cro·at [ˈkrəʊæt] N croato(-a)
Croa·tia [krəʊˈeɪʃə] N Croazia
Croa·tian [krəʊˈeɪʃən] ADJ croato(-a) ♦ N (*person*) croato(-a); (*language*) croato
cro·chet [ˈkrəʊʃeɪ] N lavoro all'uncinetto ♦ VT, VI lavorare all'uncinetto
crock [krɒk] N coccio; (*fam*: *person*) (*also*: **old crock**) rottame *m*; (: *car, bicycle*) rottame *m*, macinino
crock·ery [ˈkrɒkərɪ] N (*earthenware*) vasellame *m* (di terracotta); (*plates, cups*) stoviglie *fpl*
croco·dile [ˈkrɒkədaɪl] N coccodrillo
cro·cus [ˈkrəʊkəs] N croco
croft [krɒft] N (*Scot*) piccola fattoria
croft·er [ˈkrɒftəʳ] N (*Scot*) fattore *m* (di piccola fattoria)
crois·sant [ˈkrwæsɒŋ] N croissant *m inv*, cornetto
crone [krəʊn] N vecchiarda

cro·ny [ˈkrəʊnɪ] N (*fam*) amicone(-a)
crook [krʊk] N 1 (*fam*: *thief*) ladro(-a), truffatore(-trice); **he's a crook** è un imbroglione; **a petty crook** un piccolo delinquente 2 **the crook of one's arm** l'incavo del braccio 3 (*shepherd's*) bastone *m* (da pastore); (*bishop's*) pastorale *m* ♦ VT (*arm, finger*) piegare
crook·ed [ˈkrʊkɪd] ADJ (*stick, person*) curvo(-a), storto(-a); (*picture*) storto(-a); (*path*) tortuoso(-a); (*smile*) forzato(-a); (*dishonest*: *deal, means, person*) disonesto(-a); **a crooked line** una linea storta; **a crooked policeman** un poliziotto disonesto
crop [krɒp] N 1 (*produce*) coltivazione *f*; (*amount produced*: *of fruit, vegetables*) raccolto; (: *of cereals*) raccolto, messe *f*; (: *fig*: *of problems, applicants*) serie *f inv*; **the crops** il raccolto 2 (*of bird*) gozzo, ingluvie *f* 3 (*of whip*) manico; (*riding crop*) frustino ♦ VT (*cut*: *hair*) tagliare, rapare; (*subj*: *animals*: *grass*) brucare
  ▸ **crop up** VI + ADV (*fig*: *arise*) sorgere, presentarsi; **something must have cropped up** dev'essere capitato *or* successo qualcosa
crop·per [ˈkrɒpəʳ] N (*fam*): **to come a cropper** (*fall badly*) fare un capitombolo; (*fail completely*) fare fiasco
crop spraying [-spreɪɪŋ] N spruzzatura di antiparassitari
cro·quet [ˈkrəʊkeɪ] N croquet *m*
cro·quette [krəʊˈket] N (*Culin*) crocchetta
cross [krɒs] N 1 (*mark, symbol*) croce *f*; (*on questionnaire*) crocetta, croce; **Greek/Latin cross** croce greca/latina; **to mark with a cross** segnare con una crocetta; **we each have our cross to bear** (*fig*) ognuno ha la propria croce (da portare) 2 (*Zool, Bio*) incrocio, ibrido; **it's a cross between geography and sociology** è un misto di geografia e sociologia 3 (*bias*): **cut on the cross** tagliato(-a) in sbieco ♦ ADJ (*comp* **-er**, *superl* **-est**) (*Brit*: *angry*) arrabbiato(-a), seccato(-a); **to be/get cross with sb (about sth)** essere arrabbiato(-a)/arrabbiarsi con qn (per qc); **it makes me cross when ...** mi fa arrabbiare quando...; **he was cross about something** era arrabbiato per qualcosa ♦ VT 1 (*gen*) attraversare; (*threshold*) varcare; **this road crosses the motorway** questa strada incrocia *or* interseca l'autostrada; **it crossed my mind that ...** mi è venuto in mente che...; **we'll cross that bridge when we come to it** (*fig*) ogni cosa a tempo debito 2 (*cheque, letter t*) sbarrare; **to cross o.s.** farsi il segno della croce, segnarsi; **cross my heart!** giuro (sulla mia vita!) 3 (*arms*) incrociare; (*legs*) accavallare, incrociare; **to keep one's fingers crossed** (*fig*) fare gli scongiuri; **to cross swords with sb** (*fig*) scontrarsi con qn; **we've got a crossed line** (*Brit*: *on telephone*) c'è un'interferenza; **they've got their lines crossed** (*fig*) si sono fraintesi 4 (*thwart*: *person, plan*) contrastare, ostacolare 5 (*animals, plants*) incrociare ♦ VI 1 (*also*: **cross over**): **the boat crosses from Dieppe to Newhaven** il traghetto fa la traversata da Dieppe a Newhaven 2 (*roads*) intersecarsi; (*letters, people*) incrociarsi
  ▸ **cross off, cross out** VT + ADV cancellare (tirandoci una riga sopra)
  ▸ **cross over** VI attraversare
cross·bar [ˈkrɒsbɑːʳ] N (*of bicycle*) canna; (*of goal post*) traversa
cross·bow [ˈkrɒsbəʊ] N balestra
cross·breed [ˈkrɒsbriːd] N incrocio, ibrido
cross-Channel fer·ry [krɒsˈtʃænlˈferɪ] N traghetto che attraversa la Manica
cross-check [ˌkrɒsˈtʃek] N controprova ♦ VT fare una controprova di ♦ VI fare una controprova
cross-country [ˌkrɒsˈkʌntrɪ] ADJ (*race*) campestre, cross-country *inv*; **cross-country skiing** sci *m* di fondo; **a cross-country race** una corsa campestre ♦ ADV (*walk, travel*) attraverso i campi, cross-country, cross-country *m inv*
cross-dressing [ˌkrɒsˈdresɪŋ] N travestitismo
cross-examination [ˈkrɒsɪɡˌzæmɪˈneɪʃən] N (*Law*) interrogatorio in contraddittorio, controinterrogatorio
cross-examine [ˌkrɒsɪɡˈzæmɪn] VT (*Law*) interrogare in contraddittorio, controinterrogare
cross-eyed [ˈkrɒsaɪd] ADJ strabico(-a)
cross·fire [ˈkrɒsfaɪəʳ] N fuoco incrociato

cross·ing [ˈkrɒsɪŋ] N (*sea-passage*) traversata; (*of equator*) attraversamento; (*road junction*) incrocio, crocicchio; (*also:* **pedestrian crossing**) strisce *fpl* pedonali, passaggio pedonale; (*level crossing*) passaggio a livello; **a ten-hour crossing** una traversata di dieci ore; **cross at the crossing** attraversa sulle strisce

crossing guard (*USA*) N *dipendente comunale che aiuta i bambini ad attraversare la strada*

crossing point N valico di frontiera

cross-purposes [ˌkrɒsˈpɜːpəsɪz] NPL: **to be at cross-purposes with sb** (*disagree*) essere in contrasto con qn; (*misunderstand*) fraintendere qn; **to talk at cross-purposes** fraintendersi

cross-question [ˈkrɒsˌkwestʃən] VT (*witness*) sottoporre a controinterrogatorio; (*fig*) interrogare

cross-reference [ˌkrɒsˈrefrəns] N rinvio, rimando

cross·roads [ˈkrɒsrəʊdz] NSG incrocio, crocicchio

cross section N (*Bio, etc*) sezione *f* trasversale; (*of population*) rappresentativo *m*; (*Typ*) profilo trasversale

cross·walk [ˈkrɒswɔːk] N (*USA*) strisce *fpl* pedonali, passaggio pedonale

cross·wind [ˈkrɒswɪnd] N vento di traverso

cross·wise [ˈkrɒswaɪz] ADV (*in the form of a cross*) a forma di croce; (*across*) di traverso

cross·word [ˈkrɒswɜːd] N: **crossword (puzzle)** parole *fpl* crociate, cruciverba *m inv*

crotch [krɒtʃ] N (*also:* **crutch**: *Anat*) inforcatura; (*of garment*) cavallo

crotch·et [ˈkrɒtʃɪt] N (*Brit: Mus*) semiminima

crotch·ety [ˈkrɒtʃɪtɪ] ADJ (*fam: person*) burbero(-a), irritabile, stizzoso(-a)

crouch [kraʊtʃ] VI (*also:* **crouch down**: *person, animal*) accucciarsi, accovacciarsi, acquattarsi

croup [kruːp] N (*Med*) crup *m*

crou·ton [ˈkruːtɒn] N (*Culin*) crostino

crow [krəʊ] N 1 (*bird*) cornacchia; **hooded crow** cornacchia grigia; **as the crow flies** in linea d'aria 2 (*noise: of cock*) canto del gallo, chicchirichì *m inv*; (*: of baby, person*) gridolino ♦ VI 1 (*pt* **crowed** *or* **crew** *pp* **crowed**: *cock*: cantare, fare chicchirichì 2 (*pt, pp* **crowed**) (*child*) lanciare gridolini; (*fig*): **to crow over** *or* **about sth** vantarsi di qc; **to crow with delight** lanciare gridolini di piacere

crow·bar [ˈkrəʊbɑː] N piede *m* di porco

crowd [kraʊd] N folla; **crowds of people** un sacco di gente; **the crowd** (*common humanity*) la massa; **to follow the crowd** (*fig*) seguire la massa; **I don't like that crowd at all** non mi piace affatto quella gente; **she is part of the university crowd** appartiene alla cricca dell'università ♦ VT (*place*) affollare, gremire; **to crowd sth into** (*things*) ammassare qc in, stipare qc in ♦ VI affollarsi, ammassarsi; **to crowd in** entrare in massa; **to crowd round sb/sth** affollarsi attorno a qn/qc, accalcarsi intorno a qn/qc; **the children crowded round the model** i bambini si sono affollati attorno al modellino

crowd·ed [ˈkraʊdɪd] ADJ (*meeting, event, place etc*) affollato(-a), gremito(-a); (*town*) molto popolato(-a); (*day*) pieno(-a); (*profession*) inflazionato(-a); **crowded with** pieno(-a) di, gremito(-a) di, stipato(-a) di

crowd scene N (*Cine, Theatre*) scena di massa

crowd·source [ˈkraʊdsɔːs] VT ricorrere al crowdsourcing per

crowd·sourcing [ˈkraʊdsɔːsɪŋ] N crowdsourcing *m*

crown [kraʊn] N 1 corona; **the Crown** (*Law*) ≈ il Pubblico Ministero 2 (*top: of hat, head*) cocuzzolo; (*: of hill*) cima, vetta, cocuzzolo; (*: of road: raised centre*) centro; (*: of tooth*) corona; (*: artificial*) capsula ♦ VT 1 (*king etc, also fig*) incoronare; (*tooth*) incapsulare; **and to crown it all** ... (*fig*) e per giunta..., e come se non bastasse... 2 (*fam: hit*) dare una botta in testa a; **I'll crown you if you do that again!** se lo fai ancora ti do una botta in testa!

crown·ing [ˈkraʊnɪŋ] ADJ (*achievement, glory*) supremo(-a)

crown jewels NPL gioielli *mpl* della Corona

crown prince N principe *m* ereditario

crow's-feet [ˈkrəʊzfiːt] NPL zampe *fpl* di gallina

crow's-nest [ˈkrəʊzˌnest] N (*Naut*) coffa

cru·cial [ˈkruːʃəl] ADJ cruciale, decisivo(-a); **crucial to** essenziale per

cru·ci·fix [ˈkruːsɪfɪks] N crocifisso

cru·ci·fix·ion [ˌkruːsɪˈfɪkʃən] N crocifissione *f*

cru·ci·fy [ˈkruːsɪfaɪ] VT crocifiggere; (*fig: punish*) mettere in croce, fare a pezzi; (*: criticize: performance, actor*) stroncare; **if he catches us he'll crucify us** se ci pesca ci ammazza

crude [kruːd] ADJ (*comp* **-r**, *superl* **-st**) 1 (*pej: clumsy, unsophisticated: method, idea*) rozzo(-a); (*light, colour*) violento(-a) 2 (*simple: device, tool*) rudimentale; (*: drawing*) (appena) abbozzato(-a); **to make a crude attempt at doing sth** fare un rozzo tentativo di fare qc 3 (*vulgar*) volgare, grossolano(-a); **crude language** linguaggio volgare 4 (*unprocessed: materials*) grezzo(-a); (*: oil*) greggio(-a) ♦ N (*also:* **crude oil**) (petrolio) greggio
❑ **crude** is not translated by the Italian word *crudo*

cru·el [ˈkruːəl] ADJ (*comp* **-ler**, *superl* **-lest**): **cruel (to** *or* **towards)** crudele (con *or* nei confronti di)

cru·el·ty [ˈkruːəltɪ] N crudeltà *f inv*; **mental cruelty** crudeltà mentale

cru·et [ˈkruːɪt] N saliera e pepiera

cruise [kruːz] N crociera; **to go on a cruise** fare una crociera ♦ VI (*ship, plane*) viaggiare a velocità di crociera; (*holidaymakers*) fare una crociera; (*taxi, patrol car*) circolare; **the car cruises at 100 kph** (*Aut*) la velocità dell'auto è di 100 km/h

cruise missile N missile *m* cruise, *inv*

cruis·er [ˈkruːzə] N (*Naut*) incrociatore *m*

cruis·ing speed [ˈkruːzɪŋspiːd] N velocità *f inv* di crociera

crumb [krʌm] N (*of bread, cake etc*) briciola; (*inner part of bread*) mollica; **a crumb of comfort** (*fig*) un bricìolo di conforto; **crumbs of information** ben poche informazioni; **crumbs!** (*fam*) accidenti!

crum·ble [ˈkrʌmbl] VT sbriciolare ♦ VI (*bread*) sbriciolarsi; (*earth, land*) sbriciolarsi, franare; (*building etc*) andare in rovina; (*plaster, bricks*) sgretolarsi; (*fig: hopes, power*) crollare

crum·bly [ˈkrʌmblɪ] ADJ friabile

crum·my [ˈkrʌmɪ] ADJ (*fam: apartment*) scadente; (*: idea*) stupido(-a); **a crummy town** un postaccio

crum·pet [ˈkrʌmpɪt] N 1 (*Culin*) specie di crespella piuttosto spessa da tostare e mangiare calda con burro, marmellata ecc. 2 **a piece of crumpet** (*fam!*) un bel tocco di ragazza

crum·ple [ˈkrʌmpl] VT (*also:* **crumple up**: *paper*) accartocciare; (*clothes*) stropicciare, sgualcire, spiegazzare ♦ VI (*see vt*) accartocciarsi; stropicciarsi, sgualcirsi, spiegazzarsi; **the man crumpled to the ground** l'uomo si è accasciato al suolo

crunch [krʌntʃ] N (*of broken glass, gravel*) scricchiolio; **if** *or* **when it comes to the crunch** (*fig*) al momento cruciale ♦ VT (*with teeth*) sgranocchiare ♦ VI (*gravel*) scricchiolare

crunchy [ˈkrʌntʃɪ] ADJ (*comp* **-ier**, *superl* **-iest**) croccante

cru·sade [kruːˈseɪd] N crociata ♦ VI (*fig*): **to crusade for/ against** fare una crociata per/contro

cru·sad·er [kruːˈseɪdə] N (*History*) crociato; (*fig*): **crusader (for)** sostenitore(-trice) (di)

crush [krʌʃ] N 1 (*crowd*) ressa, calca, folla 2 (*fam: infatuation*) cotta; **to have a crush on sb** avere una cotta per qn; **she's had a crush on him for months** ha una cotta per lui da mesi 3 (*drink*): **orange/lemon crush** spremuta di arancia/limone ♦ VT (*squash, also fig*) schiacciare; (*crumple: clothes, paper*) sgualcire; (*: garlic*) tritare, schiacciare; (*: ice*) tritare; (*: grapes*) pigiare; (*: scrap metal*) pressare; (*: stones*) frantumare; **to be crushed to a pulp** essere ridotto(-a) in poltiglia; **crush two cloves of garlic** tritate due spicchi d'aglio ♦ VI (*clothes*) sgualcirsi, spiegazzarsi

crush·ing [ˈkrʌʃɪŋ] ADJ (*defeat, blow*) schiacciante; (*reply*) mordace

crust [krʌst] N crosta; (*layer*) strato; **the Earth's crust** la crosta terrestre

crus·ta·cean [krʌsˈteɪʃən] N (*Zool*) crostaceo

crusty [ˈkrʌstɪ] ADJ (*comp* **-ier**, *superl* **-iest**) (*bread*) croccante; (*fam: person*) brontolone(-a); (*: remark*) brusco(-a)

crutch [krʌtʃ] N 1 (*Med*) stampella, gruccia; (*support*) sostegno 2 = **crotch 1**

crux [krʌks] N 1 **the crux of the matter** il nocciolo della questione 2 (*Mountaineering*) passaggio chiave

cry [kraɪ] N 1 (*call, shout*) grido, urlo; (*of animal*) verso; **to**

give a cry emettere un grido; **a cry for help** un grido di aiuto; **it's a far cry from ...** (*fig*) è tutt'un'altra cosa da...; **with a cry, she rushed forward** con un grido si lanciò in avanti; **"jobs, not bombs" was their cry** "lavoro non bombe" era il loro slogan **2** (*weep*): **she had a good cry** si è fatta un bel pianto ♦ VI **1** (*also*: **cry out**: *call out, shout*) gridare, urlare; **he cried (out) with pain** urlò di dolore; **to cry for help** gridare aiuto; **to cry for mercy** invocare pietà; **"you're wrong," he cried** "hai torto", gridò **2** (*weep*) piangere; **what are you crying about?** perché piangi?; **the child was crying for his mother** il bambino piangeva perché voleva la mamma; **I laughed till I cried** risi fino alle lacrime; **I'll give him something to cry about!** (*fam*) glielo darò io un motivo per piangere!; **it's no good crying over spilt milk** (*fig*) è inutile piangere sul latte versato ♦ VT **1** gridare, urlare **2 to cry o.s. to sleep** piangere fino ad addormentarsi

▸ **cry off** VI + ADV (*fam*) ritirarsi

▸ **cry out** VI + ADV (*shout*) urlare, gridare; **this car is crying out to be resprayed** (*fam*) questa macchina ha un gran bisogno di essere riverniciata ♦ VT + ADV **1** (*call*) gridare, urlare **2 to cry one's eyes** *or* **heart out** piangere tutte le proprie lacrime

▸ **cry out against** VI + ADV + PREP protestare vigorosamente contro

cry·ing [ˈkraɪɪŋ] ADJ (*child*) in lacrime, piangente; (*fam: need*) disperato(-a), urgente; (*injustice*) palese; **it's a crying shame** è una vera vergogna ♦ N (*weeping*) pianto

crypt [krɪpt] N cripta

cryp·tic [ˈkrɪptɪk] ADJ (*mysterious*) oscuro(-a); (*puzzling*) enigmatico(-a); **cryptic crossword** cruciverba *m* a crittogramma

crys·tal [ˈkrɪstl] N (*gen*) cristallo; (*watch glass*) vetro ♦ ADJ (*glass, vase*) di cristallo; (*clear: water, lake*) cristallino(-a)

crystal-clear [ˌkrɪstlˈklɪəʳ] ADJ (*water, wine*) cristallino(-a); (*fig*) chiaro(-a) (come il sole)

crys·tal·lize [ˈkrɪstəˌlaɪz] VT (*Chem*) cristallizzare; (*fig*) concretizzare, concretare; **crystallized fruits** (*Brit*) frutta candita ♦ VI (*see vt*) cristallizzarsi; concretizzarsi, concretarsi

CT ABBR (*USA Post*: = **Connecticut**)

ct ABBR = **carat**

cu. ABBR = **cubic**

cub [kʌb] N **1** cucciolo; **lion cub** leoncino; **wolf cub** lupetto **2** (*also*: **cub scout**) lupetto

Cuba [ˈkjuːbə] N Cuba

Cu·ban [ˈkjuːbən] ADJ, N cubano(-a)

cubby·hole [ˈkʌbɪˌhəʊl] N angolo, cantuccio

cube [kjuːb] N cubo; (*of sugar*) cubetto, zolletta; **to cut into cubes** tagliare a cubetti ♦ VT (*Math*) elevare al cubo *or* alla terza potenza

cube root N radice *f* cubica

cu·bic [ˈkjuːbɪk] ADJ (*shape, volume*) cubico(-a); (*metre, foot*) cubo(-a); **cubic capacity** (*Aut*) cilindrata; **cubic function** (*Math*) funzione *f* cubica; **cubic metre** metro cubo

cu·bi·cle [ˈkjuːbɪkəl] N cabina; **shower cubicle** box *m inv* doccia; (*office*) (ufficio a) cubicolo

cuckoo [ˈkʊkuː] N cuculo, cucù *m inv* ♦ ADJ (*fam*) tocco(-a), matto(-a)

cuckoo clock N orologio a cucù

cu·cum·ber [ˈkjuːkʌmbəʳ] N cetriolo; **tomatoes and cucumbers** pomodori e cetrioli; **to be as cool as a cucumber** essere imperturbabile

cud [kʌd] N: **to chew the cud** (*cows*) ruminare; (*fig*) rimuginare

cud·dle [ˈkʌdl] N abbraccio, coccole *fpl*; **come and give me a cuddle** vieni ad abbracciarmi; **kisses and cuddles** baci e carezze ♦ VT abbracciare, coccolare ♦ VI: **to cuddle down** accoccolarsi; **to cuddle up to sb** accoccolarsi contro qn

cud·dly [ˈkʌdlɪ] ADJ (*comp* -**ier**, *superl* -**iest**) (*child, animal*) coccolone(-a); (*toy*) morbido(-a), da tenere stretto(-a); **cuddly toy** animale *m* di peluche

cudg·el [ˈkʌdʒəl] N (*weapon*) manganello, randello; **to take up the cudgels for sb/sth** (*fig*) mettersi a lottare per qn/qc ♦ VT: **to cudgel one's brains** scervellarsi, spremersi le meningi

cue [kjuː] N **1** (*Theatre: verbal, by signal*) segnale *m*, imbeccata; (*Mus: by signal*) segnale; **to give sb his cue** suggerire a qn

la battuta, dare l'imbeccata a qn; **to take one's cue from sb** (*fig*) prendere esempio da qn **2 right on cue** esattamente al momento giusto; (*Billiards*) stecca

▸ **cue in** VT + ADV (*Theatre*) chiamare in scena; (*Radio, TV*) dare il segnale a

cuff¹ [kʌf] N (*blow*) schiaffo ♦ VT dare uno schiaffo a

cuff² [kʌf] N (*of shirt, coat*) polsino; (*USA: of trousers*) risvolto; **off the cuff** (*fig*) improvvisando

cuff link N gemello

cu. ft. ABBR = **cubic feet**

cu. in. ABBR = **cubic inches**

cui·sine [kwɪˈziːn] N cucina; **French cuisine** la cucina francese

cul-de-sac [ˈkʌldəˈsæk] N vicolo cieco

culi·nary [ˈkʌlɪnərɪ] ADJ culinario(-a)

cull [kʌl] VT (*select: fruit*) scegliere; (*kill selectively: animals*) selezionare e abbattere ♦ N selezione *f*; **seal cull** abbattimento selettivo delle foche

cul·mi·nate [ˈkʌlmɪˌneɪt] VI: **to culminate in** culminare con *or* in

cul·mi·na·tion [ˌkʌlmɪˈneɪʃən] N culmine *m*; (*Astron*) culminazione *f*

cu·lottes [kjuːˈlɒts] NPL gonna *f* pantalone, *inv*

cul·pable [ˈkʌlpəbl] ADJ colpevole

cul·prit [ˈkʌlprɪt] N colpevole *m/f*

cult [kʌlt] N (*Rel, also fig*) culto; **to make a cult of sth** avere un culto per qc

cult figure N idolo

cul·ti·vate [ˈkʌltɪˌveɪt] VT (*also fig*) coltivare

cul·ti·va·tion [ˌkʌltɪˈveɪʃən] N (*Agr*) coltivazione *f*, coltura

cul·tur·al [ˈkʌltʃərəl] ADJ culturale

cul·ture [ˈkʌltʃəʳ] N **1** cultura; (*civilization*) civiltà **2** (*Bio, Agr*) coltura; **people from different cultures** persone *fpl* di culture diverse

cul·tured [ˈkʌltʃəd] ADJ (*person, mind*) colto(-a); (*voice*) da persona colta; (*manners*) raffinato(-a); (*pearl*) coltivato(-a)

cum·ber·some [ˈkʌmbəsəm] ADJ ingombrante

cum·in [ˈkʌmɪn] N (*spice*) cumino

cu·mu·la·tive [ˈkjuːmjʊlətɪv] ADJ cumulativo(-a); **cumulative frequency** (*Statistics*) frequenza cumulata

cun·ning [ˈkʌnɪŋ] ADJ (*pej: crafty*) furbo(-a), astuto(-a); (*clever: device, idea*) ingegnoso(-a); **a cunning plan** un piano ingegnoso ♦ N furbizia, astuzia

cup [kʌp] N (*for tea*) tazza; (*as prize, of brassière*) coppa; **a cup of tea/coffee** una tazza di tè/caffè; **tea cup** tazza da tè; **it's not everyone's cup of tea** (*fam*) non è una cosa che piace a tutti; **that's just not my cup of tea** (*fam*) non è proprio il mio genere ♦ VT (*hands*) riunire a (coppa); **to cup one's hands round sth** prendere qc fra le mani

cup·board [ˈkʌbəd] N armadio

cup final N (*Brit: Ftbl*) finale *f* di coppa

Cupid [ˈkjuːpɪd] N (*Myth*) Cupido; **Cupid's bow** (*lip shape*) labbro arcuato

cup·id·ity [kjuːˈpɪdɪtɪ] N cupidigia

cu·po·la [ˈkjuːpələ] N cupola

cup·pa [ˈkʌpə] N (*Brit fam*) tazza di tè

cup tie N (*Brit: Ftbl*) partita eliminatoria

cur·able [ˈkjʊərəbl] ADJ guaribile, curabile

cu·rate [ˈkjʊərɪt] N curato, cappellano

cu·ra·tor [kjʊəˈreɪtəʳ] N direttore(-trice) (di museo *etc*)

curb¹ [kɜːb] N freno ♦ VT (*fig: temper, impatience etc*) frenare, tenere a freno; (: *expenditure*) limitare

curb² [kɜːb] N (*USA*) = **kerb**

curd [kɜːd] N (*usu pl*); **curds** NPL latte *m* cagliato

curd cheese N cagliata

cur·dle [ˈkɜːdl] VT (*gen*) far cagliare; (*mayonnaise*) far impazzire ♦ VI (*usu vi*) cagliarsi, cagliare; impazzire; **it made my blood curdle** mi ha gelato il sangue nelle vene

cure [kjʊəʳ] N (*remedy*) cura; (*recovery*) guarigione *f*; **to take a cure** fare una cura ♦ VT **1** (*Med: disease, patient*) guarire; (*fig: poverty, injustice, evil*) eliminare; **to be cured of sth** essere guarito(-a) da qc; **to cure sb of a habit** far perdere un'abitudine a qn **2** (*preserve: in salt*) salare; (: *by smoking*) affumicare; (: *by drying*) seccare, essiccare; (: *animal hide*) conciare, trattare

cure-all [ˈkjʊərˌɔːl] N (*also fig*) panacea, toccasana *m inv*

cur·few [ˈkɜːfjuː] N coprifuoco

cu·rio [ˈkjʊərɪəʊ] N curiosità *f inv*, oggetto insolito

cu·ri·os·i·ty [ˌkjʊərɪˈɒsɪtɪ] N curiosità *f inv*; **curiosity killed the cat** la curiosità si paga cara

cu·ri·ous [ˈkjʊərɪəs] ADJ 1 (*inquisitive*) curioso(-a); **I'm curious about him** m'incuriosisce; **I'd be curious to know** sarei curioso di sapere 2 (*strange*) strano(-a), curioso(-a)

cu·ri·ous·ly [ˈkjʊərɪəslɪ] ADV (*see adj*) con curiosità; stranamente; **curiously enough, ...** per quanto possa sembrare strano,...

curl [kɜːl] N (*of hair*) ricciolo, riccio; (*of smoke*) anello ♦ VT (*hair*) ondulare; (*tightly*) arricciare; **she curled her lip in scorn** arricciò sprezzantemente le labbra ♦ VI (*hair*) arricciarsi; **it's enough to make your hair curl** (*fam*) è una cosa da far drizzare i capelli

> **curl up** VI + ADV (*leaves, paper*) accartocciarsi; (*cat*) acciambellarsi; (*person, dog*) accoccolarsi, rannicchiarsi; (*fam: with shame*) sprofondare (dalla vergogna); (*with laughter*) piegarsi in due (dalle risate)

curl·er [ˈkɜːlə^r] N 1 (*for hair*) bigodino 2 (*Sport*) giocatore(-trice) di curling

cur·lew [ˈkɜːluː] N chiurlo

curl·ing [ˈkɜːlɪŋ] N (*Sport*) curling *m*

curling tongs, (*USA*) **curling irons** NPL (*for hair*) arricciacapelli *m inv*

curly [ˈkɜːlɪ] ADJ (*comp* -ier, *superl* -iest) (*gen*) riccio(-a), ricciuto(-a); (*eyelashes*) ricurvo(-a); **curly hair** capelli ricci

cur·rant [ˈkʌrənt] N (*dried grape*) uva passa; (*bush, fruit*) ribes *m inv*

cur·ren·cy [ˈkʌrənsɪ] N 1 moneta; **foreign currency** valuta estera; **hard currency** moneta forte; **paper currency** banconote *fpl* 2 (*fig: of ideas*): **to gain currency** acquistare larga diffusione, acquistare credito; **to have wide currency** essere molto diffuso(-a)

cur·rent [ˈkʌrənt] ADJ (*fashion, opinion, year*) corrente; (*tendency, price, event*) attuale; (*phrase*) di uso corrente; **in current use** in uso corrente, d'uso comune; **the current financial year** l'anno finanziario corrente; **the current issue of a magazine** l'ultimo numero di una rivista; **her current boyfriend** il suo attuale ragazzo; **the current situation is quite unacceptable** la situazione attuale è del tutto inaccettabile ♦ N (*of air, water, also Elec, also fig*) corrente *f*; **direct/alternating current** (*Elec*) corrente continua/alternata; **to go against the current** (*fig*) andare controcorrente

current account N (*Brit: Bank*) conto corrente

current affairs [ˈkʌrəntˈfeəz] NPL attualità *f inv*; **she presents a current affairs programme on Monday evenings** presenta un programma d'attualità il lunedì sera

current assets [ˈkʌrəntˈæsets] NPL (*Fin*) attivo realizzabile e disponibile

current liabilities [ˈkʌrəntlaɪəˈbɪlɪtɪz] NPL (*Fin*) passività *fpl* correnti

cur·rent·ly [ˈkʌrəntlɪ] ADV attualmente, al momento

cur·ric·u·lum [kəˈrɪkjʊləm] N (*pl* **curricula** *or* **curriculums** [kəˈrɪkjʊlə]) (*Scol, Univ*) programma *m*

cur·ric·u·lum vi·tae [kəˌrɪkjʊləmˈviːtaɪ] N curriculum vitae *m inv*

cur·ry [ˈkʌrɪ] N (*dish*) pietanza al curry; (*spice*) curry *m inv*; **chicken curry** pollo al curry; **beef/vegetable curry** manzo/verdure al curry; **a spoonful of curry** un cucchiaio di curry; **to go out for a curry** andare al ristorante indiano ♦ VT cucinare al curry

cur·ry [ˈkʌrɪ] VT: **to curry favour with sb** cercare di accattivarsi (il favore di) qn

curry powder N curry *m*

curse [kɜːs] N 1 maledizione *f*; **curses!** NPL (*fam*) maledizione!; **to put a curse on sb** maledire qn; **there seems to be a curse on my family** sembra esserci una maledizione sulla mia famiglia 2 (*bane*) rovina, flagello; **the curse of it is that ...** il guaio è che... 3 (*swearword*) imprecazione *f*; (*blasphemous*) bestemmia ♦ VT maledire ♦ VI bestemmiare

cur·sor [ˈkɜːsə^r] N (*Comput*) cursore *m*

cur·sory [ˈkɜːsərɪ] ADJ (*glance*) di sfuggita, superficiale; **a cursory reading** una rapida scorsa, una lettura veloce

curt [kɜːt] ADJ brusco(-a), secco(-a); **with a curt nod** con un breve cenno del capo

❏ **curt** is not translated by the Italian word *corto*

cur·tail [kɜːˈteɪl] VT (*visit etc*) accorciare; (*wages, expenditure*) ridurre, decurtare, tagliare

cur·tain [ˈkɜːtn] N tenda; (*Theatre*) sipario; **to draw the curtains** (*together*) chiudere *or* tirare le tende; (*apart*) aprire le tende; **it'll be curtains for you!** (*fam*) per te sarà la fine!

> **curtain off** VT + ADV separare con una tenda

curtain call N (*Theatre*) chiamata alla ribalta

curt·sy, curt·sey [ˈkɜːtsɪ] N inchino, riverenza ♦ VI fare un inchino *or* una riverenza

cur·va·ture [ˈkɜːvətʃə^r] N curvatura; **curvature of the spine** (*Med*) deviazione *f* della colonna vertebrale

curve [kɜːv] N (*gen*) curva; (*of river*) ansa; **simple closed curve** (*Math*) curva semplice; **throw sb a curve** (*ball*) (*USA*) prendere qn di sorpresa ♦ VT curvare ♦ VI (*road, river*) fare una curva; (*line, surface, arch*) curvarsi

curved [kɜːvd] ADJ curvo(-a)

cush·ion [ˈkʊʃən] N cuscino; (*of billiard table*) sponda (elastica) ♦ VT (*blow, fall, shock*) attutire, fare da cuscinetto a; **to cushion sb against sth** proteggere qn da qc

cushy [ˈkʊʃɪ] ADJ (*comp* -ier, *superl* -iest) (*fam*): **a cushy job** un lavoro di tutto riposo

cus·tard [ˈkʌstəd] N (*pouring*) crema (pasticcera); (*set*) ≈ budino

custard powder N (*Brit*) preparato in polvere per crema

cus·to·dial sen·tence [kʌsˌtəʊdɪəlˈsentəns] N condanna ad una pena detentiva

cus·to·dian [kʌsˈtəʊdɪən] N (*gen*) custode *m/f*; (*of museum etc*) sovrintendente *m/f*

cus·to·dy [ˈkʌstədɪ] N (*Law: of child*) custodia; (*for offenders*) arresto; (*police custody*) detenzione *f* (preventiva); **to be in custody** essere in stato di detenzione; **to take sb into custody** mettere qn in detenzione preventiva; **in safe custody** al sicuro; **in the custody of** alla custodia di

cus·tom [ˈkʌstəm] N 1 costume *m*, usanza, consuetudine *f*; (*Law*) consuetudine; **social customs** convenzioni *fpl* sociali; **it is her custom to go for a walk each evening** è sua consuetudine fare una passeggiata ogni sera 2 (*Brit: Comm*): **to get sb's custom** ottenere qn per cliente; **the shop has lost a lot of custom** il negozio ha perso molti clienti; *see also* **customs**

cus·tom·ary [ˈkʌstəmərɪ] ADJ consueto(-a); **it is customary to wear black** è consuetudine vestire di nero

custom-built [ˈkʌstəmˌbɪlt] ADJ *see* **custom-made**

cus·tom·er [ˈkʌstəmə^r] N cliente *m/f*; **he's an awkward customer** (*fam*) è un tipo incontentabile; **ugly customer** (*fam*) brutto tipo

customer profile N profilo del cliente

cus·tom·ize [ˈkʌstəmaɪz] VT personalizzare; **customized software** software *m inv* personalizzato

cus·tom·ized [ˈkʌstəˌmaɪzd] ADJ personalizzato(-a); (*car*) fuoriserie *inv*

custom-made [ˈkʌstəmˈmeɪd] ADJ (*clothes*) fatto(-a) su misura; (*other goods: also*: **custom-built**) fatto(-a) su ordinazione

cus·toms [ˈkʌstəmz] NPL (*also*: **Customs**) dogana; **to go through (the) customs** passare la dogana

Customs and Excise N (*Brit*) Ufficio Dazi e Dogana

customs officer N doganiere *m*

cut [kʌt] (*pt, pp* **cut**) N 1 (*gen*) taglio; (*Med*) taglio, incisione *f*; (*Cards*) alzata; **the cut and thrust of politics** i vivaci contrasti della politica; **he's a cut above the others** è di gran lunga migliore degli altri 2 (*reduction: in salary, spending*) riduzione *f*, taglio; (*deletion: in film, text*) taglio; **power cut** interruzione di corrente elettrica; **to take a cut in salary** avere una riduzione dello stipendio 3 (*of clothes, hair*) taglio 4 (*of meat: piece*) taglio, pezzo, parte *f*; (*fam: share*) parte; **cold cuts** (*USA*) affettati *mpl* ♦ ADJ (*flowers*) reciso(-a); (*glass*) intagliato(-a) ♦ VT (*gen*) tagliare; (*Cards*) alzare; **to cut o.s.** tagliarsi; **to cut one's finger** tagliarsi un dito; **to cut a tooth** mettere un dente; **to cut sth in half/in two** tagliare qc a metà/in due; **he is cutting his own throat** (*fig*) si sta dando la zappa sui piedi; **to cut to pieces** (*army, also fig*) fare a pezzi, distruggere; **to cut sth to size** tagliare qc su misura; **to**

cut open aprire con un coltello (*or* con le forbici *etc*); **he cut his head open** si è spaccato la testa; **to cut sb free** liberare qn (*tagliando* qc); **it cut me to the quick** *or* **the heart** (*fig*) mi ha ferito profondamente **2** (*shape: gen, jewel*) tagliare; (*steps, channel*) scavare; (*key*) fare una copia di, riprodurre; (*glass*) lavorare; (*figure, statue*) scolpire; (*engrave*) incidere, intagliare; (*record*) incidere; **to cut one's way through** aprirsi la strada attraverso; **to cut one's coat according to one's cloth** (*fig*) non fare il passo più lungo della gamba **3** (*clip, trim: hair, nails, hedge etc*) tagliare; **to get one's hair cut** farsi tagliare i capelli **4** (*reduce: wages, prices, production etc*) ridurre; (*expenses*) ridurre, limitare, tagliare; (*speech*) abbreviare; (*text, film*) tagliare; (*interrupt*) interrompere; **to cut sb/sth short** interrompere qn/qc; **to cut 30 seconds off a record** (*Sport*) abbassare un record di 30 secondi **5** (*intersect*) intersecare, tagliare **6** (*fam: avoid: class, lecture, appointment*) saltare; **to cut sb dead** ignorare qn completamente ♦ **VI 1** (*person, knife*) tagliare; **she cut into the melon** ha affondato il coltello nel melone; **it cuts both ways** (*fig*) è un'arma a doppio taglio; **to cut and run** (*fam*) tagliare la corda; **to cut loose (from sth)** (*fig*) staccarsi (da qc) **2** (*hurry*): **to cut across country/through the lane** tagliare per la campagna/ per il sentiero; **I must cut along now** ora devo avviarmi **3** (*Cine*): **the film cut from the bedroom to the garden** la scena del film si è spostata dalla stanza da letto al giardino; **cut!** stop! **4** (*Cards*) tagliare il mazzo
► cut away VT + ADV tagliare via
► cut across VI + PREP (*fig: barriers, boundaries*) trascendere
► cut back VI + ADV (*on costs etc*) limitare *or* tagliare le spese; (*on staff*) ridurre il personale ♦ VT + ADV (*plants*) potare; (*production, expenditure, staff*) ridurre
► cut down VT + ADV **1** (*tree*) abbattere; (*enemy*) falciare **2** (*reduce: consumption, expenses*) ridurre, tagliare; **to cut sb down to size** (*fig*) sgonfiare *or* ridimensionare qn
► cut down on VI + PREP ridurre, diminuire; **I'm cutting down on coffee and cigarettes** sto riducendo il caffè e le sigarette
► cut in VI + ADV: **to cut in (on)** (*interrupt: conversation*) intromettersi (in); (*Aut*) tagliare la strada (a)
► cut off VT + ADV **1** (*gen*) tagliare; **to cut off one's nose to spite one's face** (*fam*) farsi dispetto **2** (*disconnect: telephone, gas, electricity*) tagliare; (*engine*) spegnere; **the electricity has been cut off** l'elettricità è stata tagliata; **we've been cut off** (*Telec*) è caduta la linea **3** (*isolate*) isolare; **they feel very cut off** si sentono tagliati fuori dal mondo *or* isolati; **to cut o.s. off from sth/sb** allontanarsi *or* isolarsi da qc/qn; **to cut off the enemy's retreat** tagliare la ritirata al nemico; **to cut sb off without a penny** diseredare qn
► cut out VI + ADV (*engine*) spegnersi; **the engine cut out at the traffic lights** il motore si è spento al semaforo ♦ VT + ADV **1** (*article, picture*) ritagliare; (*statue, figure*) scolpire; (*dress etc*) tagliare; **I'll cut the article out of the paper** ritaglierò l'articolo dal giornale; **to be cut out for sth/to do sth** (*fig*) essere tagliato(-a) per qc/per fare qc; **you'll have your work cut out for you** avrai un bel daffare **2** (*delete*) eliminare, togliere **3** (*stop, give up*) eliminare; **cut it out!** (*fam*) dacci un taglio!
► cut up VT + ADV **1** (*gen*) tagliare; (*chop: food*) sminuzzare **2** (*fam*): **to be cut up about sth** (*hurt*) rimanere sconvolto(-a) per qc; (*annoyed*) essere arrabbiato(-a) per qc ♦ VI + ADV: **to cut up rough** (*fam*) perdere le staffe
cut-and-dried [ˌkʌtənˈdraɪd] ADJ (*also:* **cut-and-dry**, *fig*) assodato(-a)
cut·away [ˈkʌtəˌweɪ] ADJ, N: **cutaway (drawing)** spaccato
cut·back [ˈkʌtbæk] N **1** (*in expenditure, staff, production*) taglio, riduzione *f* **2** (*Cine: flashback*) flashback *m inv*
cute [kjuːt] ADJ (*esp USA: sweet*) carino(-a), grazioso(-a); (*clever*) furbo(-a), astuto(-a)
cut glass N cristallo
cu·ti·cle [ˈkjuːtɪkl] N (*of fingernails*) cuticola, pellicina; (*Bot, Zool*) cuticola

cut·lery [ˈkʌtlərɪ] N posate *fpl*
cut·let [ˈkʌtlɪt] N cotoletta, costoletta
cut-off [ˈkʌtˌɒf] N (*also:* **cutoff point**) limite *m*
cutoff switch N interruttore *m*
cut·out [ˈkʌtˌaʊt] N (*paper, cardboard figure*) ritaglio; (*switch*) interruttore *m*
cut-price [ˈkʌtˌpraɪs], (*USA*) **cut-rate** [ˈkʌtˌreɪt] ADJ (*goods*) scontato(-a), a prezzo ridotto; (*shop*) che fa prezzi bassi
cut·throat [ˈkʌtˌθrəʊt] N assassino(-a) ♦ ADJ (*razor*) da barbiere; (*business*) spietato(-a); **cutthroat competition** concorrenza spietata
cut·ting [ˈkʌtɪŋ] N **1** (*of plant*) talea **2** (*Brit: from newspaper*) ritaglio; (*Cine*) montaggio **3** (*Brit: for road, railway*) scavo ♦ ADJ (*cold: wind etc*) pungente; (*fig: remark*) tagliente, mordace
cutting edge N **1** (*of knife*) taglio, filo **2** (*fig*): **on** *or* **at the cutting edge of sth** all'avanguardia di qc
cuttle·fish [ˈkʌtlˌfɪʃ] N seppia
cut-up [ˈkʌtˌʌp] ADJ sconvolto(-a)
CV [ˌsiːˈviː] N ABBR CV *m inv*, curriculum vitae *m inv*
cwt. ABBR *of* **hundredweight**
cya·nide [ˈsaɪəˌnaɪd] N cianuro
cyber attack N attacco *m* informatico
cy·ber·café [ˈsaɪbəˌkæfeɪ] N cibercaffè *m*
cy·ber·crime [ˈsaɪbəˌkraɪm] N delinquenza informatica
cy·ber·net·ics [ˌsaɪbəˈnetɪks] NSG cibernetica
cy·ber·se·cu·rity [saɪbəsɪˈkjʊrɪtɪ] N sicurezza *f* informatica
cy·ber·space [ˈsaɪbəspeɪs] N ciberspazio
cy·ber·ter·ror·ism [ˌsaɪbəˈterərɪzəm] N ciberterrorismo
cyc·la·men [ˈsɪkləmən] N ciclamino
cy·cle [ˈsaɪkl] N **1** (*bicycle*) bicicletta **2** (*of seasons, poems*) ciclo ♦ VI andare in bicicletta; **I cycle to school** vado a scuola in bicicletta
cycle hire N noleggio *m* biciclette *pl inv*
cycle lane N pista ciclabile
cycle path N pista ciclabile
cycle race N gara *or* corsa ciclistica
cycle rack N rastrelliere per biciclette *m inv*
cycle track N **1** percorso ciclabile **2** (*in velodrome*) pista
cy·cling [ˈsaɪklɪŋ] N ciclismo; **the roads round here are ideal for cycling** le strade qua attorno sono l'ideale per andare in bicicletta
cy·clist [ˈsaɪklɪst] N ciclista *m/f*
cy·clone [ˈsaɪkləʊn] N ciclone *m*
cyg·net [ˈsɪgnɪt] N cigno giovane
cyl·in·der [ˈsɪlɪndəʳ] N cilindro; **a 6-cylinder engine** un motore a 6 cilindri; **to fire on all four cylinders** avere tutti e quattro i cilindri in azione; (*fig*) andare a tutto gas
cylinder head N testata
cylinder head gasket N guarnizione *f* della testata del cilindro
cym·bal [ˈsɪmbəl] N piatto (*Mus*)
cyn·ic [ˈsɪnɪk] N cinico(-a)
cyni·cal [ˈsɪnɪkəl] ADJ cinico(-a)
cyni·cism [ˈsɪnɪsɪzəm] N cinismo
cy·press [ˈsaɪprɪs] N cipresso; **Lawson's cypress** cedro bianco
Cyp·ri·ot [ˈsɪprɪət] ADJ, N cipriota *m/f*
Cy·prus [ˈsaɪprəs] N Cipro; **in Cyprus** a Cipro
cyst [sɪst] N cisti *f inv*
cys·ti·tis [sɪsˈtaɪtɪs] N (*Med*) cistite *f*
czar [zɑːʳ] N zar *m inv*
Czech [tʃɛk] ADJ ceco(-a) ♦ N (*person*) ceco(-a); (*language*) ceco; **the Czechs** i cechi
Czecho·slo·vak [ˌtʃɛkəʊˈsləʊvæk], **Czecho·slo·vakian** [ˈtʃɛkəʊsləˈvækɪən] ADJ cecoslovacco(-a) ♦ N (*person*) cecoslovacco(-a); (*language*) cecoslovacco
Czecho·slo·va·kia [ˈtʃekəsləˈvækɪə] N Cecoslovacchia
Czech Republic ADJ: **the Czech Republic** la repubblica Ceca

Dd

D, d [diː] N **1** (*letter*) D, d *f inv, m inv*; **D for David**, (*USA*) **D for Dog** ≈ D come Domodossola **2** (*Mus*) re *m inv*

d [diː] ABBR (*Brit: old*) = **penny**

d. ABBR (= *died*) *see* **die**

DA [diːˈeɪ] N ABBR (*USA*) = **district attorney**

dab [dæb] N (*light stroke*) colpetto, tocco; (*of paint*) pennellata; (*small amount*) pochino, punta; (*of glue*) goccio; **a dab of paint** un colpetto di vernice ♦ VT (*touch lightly: also:* **dab at**) picchiettare lievemente; (*eyes, wound*) tamponare; (*apply: paint, cream*): **to dab sth on sth** applicare qc con colpetti leggeri su qc

dab·ble [ˈdæbl] VT: **to dabble one's hands/feet in the water** sguazzare con le mani/i piedi nell'acqua ♦ VI (*fig*): **to dabble in sth** occuparsi di qc a tempo perso, dilettarsi di qc; **to dabble in politics** dilettarsi di politica

Dac·ca [ˈdækə] N Dacca

dachs·hund [ˈdækshʊnd] N bassotto

dad [dæd], **dad·dy** [ˈdædɪ] N (*fam*) papà *m inv*, babbo; **I'll ask Dad** lo chiederò a papà

daddy-long-legs [ˌdædɪˈlɒŋlegz] N *pl inv* zanzarone *m*, tipula (*Zool*)

daf·fo·dil [ˈdæfədɪl] N trombone *m*, giunchiglia

daft [dɑːft] ADJ (*comp* **-er**, *superl* **-est**) (*fam*) sciocco(-a); **to be daft about sb** aver perso la testa per qn; **to be daft about sth** andare pazzo(-a) per qc

dag·ger [ˈdægə'] N pugnale *m*, stiletto; (*Typ*) croce *f*; **to look daggers at sb** fare gli occhiacci a qn

dahl·ia [ˈdeɪljə] N dalia

dai·ly [ˈdeɪlɪ] ADJ (*routine, task*) quotidiano(-a), giornaliero(-a); (*wage, output, consumption*) giornaliero(-a); **he takes a daily walk** fa una passeggiata ogni giorno; **the daily bread** il nostro pane quotidiano; **the daily grind** il tran-tran quotidiano ♦ ADV quotidianamente, ogni giorno, tutti i giorni; **twice daily** due volte al giorno; **the pool is open daily from nine until six** la piscina è aperta ogni giorno dalle nove alle diciotto ♦ N (*also:* **daily paper**) quotidiano

dain·ty [ˈdeɪntɪ] ADJ (*comp* **-ier**, *superl* **-iest**) (*person, figure*) minuto(-a); (*child, manners*) aggraziato(-a); (*flowers, gesture*) delicato(-a), grazioso(-a); (*dishes, food*) delicato(-a); (*dress, shoes*) grazioso(-a)

dairy [ˈdɛərɪ] N (*shop*) latteria; (*organization, on farm*) caseificio ♦ ADJ caseario(-a); (*breed, cow*) da latte; **dairy farm** caseificio; **dairy farming** industria casearia; **dairy ice cream** gelato gusto crema; **dairy produce** latticini *mpl*

dais [ˈdeɪs] N pedana, palco

dai·sy [ˈdeɪzɪ] N (*wild*) pratolina, margheritina; (*cultivated*) margherita

daisy wheel N (*on printer*) margherita

daisy-wheel printer [ˈdeɪzɪˌwiːlˈprɪntə'] N stampante *f* a margherita

Da·kar [ˈdækə'] N Dakar *f*

dale [deɪl] N (*in North of England, also liter*) valle *f*

dal·ly [ˈdælɪ] VI (*delay*) dilungarsi; **to dally about** perdere tempo; **to dally over sth** perdere tempo con qc

dal·ma·tian [dælˈmeɪʃən] N (*dog*) dalmata *m*

dam [dæm] N (*wall*) diga, sbarramento; (*reservoir*) bacino artificiale ♦ VT (*also:* **dam up**) (*river*) sbarrare con una diga; (*lake*) costruire una diga su; (*fig*) arginare, frenare

dam·age [ˈdæmɪdʒ] N **1** (*also fig*) danno, danni *mpl*; **damage to property** danni materiali; **to suffer damage** riportare *or* subire danni; **the fire did a lot of damage** l'incendio ha provocato danni ingenti; **to do damage to a relationship** pregiudicare un rapporto; **what's the damage?** (*fam: cost*) quanto ci tocca sborsare? **2 damages** NPL (*Law*) danni *mpl*; **liable for damages** tenuto(-a) al risarcimento dei danni; **to pay £5000 in damages** pagare 5000 sterline di indennizzo ♦ VT (*furniture, crops, machine*) danneggiare; (*health, eyesight*) rovinare; (*hopes, reputation*) compromettere; (*relationship*) guastare; (*cause*) compromettere, recar danno a

dam·ag·ing [ˈdæmɪdʒɪŋ] ADJ: **damaging (to)** nocivo(-a) (a)

Da·mas·cus [dəˈmɑːskəs] N Damasco *f*

dame [deɪm] N (*title, also USA: fam*) donna, madama; (*in pantomime*) personaggio comico di donna attempata recitato da un uomo

damn [dæm] VT (*Rel*) dannare; (*curse*) maledire; (*condemn: film, book*) stroncare; **damn it!** (*fam*) accidenti!; **damn him/you!** (*fam*) accidenti a lui/a te!; **well I'll be damned!** (*fam*) che mi venga un accidente!; **I'll be damned if I will!** (*fam*) (non lo faccio) manco morto! ♦ N (*fam*): **I don't give a damn** me ne infischio, non me ne importa un fico; **it's not worth a damn** non vale un fico secco ♦ ADJ (*fam: also:* **damned**) maledetto(-a); **this damn machine won't work** questa maledetta macchina non funziona; **it's a damn nuisance!** che gran seccatura! ♦ ADV (*fam: also:* **damned**): **it's damn hot** fa un caldo del diavolo; **he knew damn well** lo sapeva benissimo

dam·nable [ˈdæmnəbl] ADJ (*old: behaviour*) vergognoso(-a); (*: weather*) orribile

dam·na·tion [dæmˈneɪʃən] N (*Rel*) dannazione *f* ♦ EXCL (*old*) dannazione!, diavolo!

damn·ing [ˈdæmɪŋ] ADJ (*implications*) fortemente negativo(-a); **damning evidence** prove *fpl* schiaccianti; **damning criticism** stroncatura

damp [dæmp] ADJ (*comp* **-er**, *superl* **-est**) umido(-a); **damp with perspiration** madido(-a) di sudore ♦ N (*dampness*) umidità, umido ♦ VT = **dampen**

▸ damp down VT (*fire*) coprire

damp-course [ˈdæmpˌkɔːs] N strato *m* isolante antiumido, *inv*

damp·er [ˈdæmpə'] N (*Mus*) sordina; (*of fire*) valvola di tiraggio; **to put a damper on sth** (*fig: atmosphere*) gelare; (*: enthusiasm*) raffreddare

damp·ness [ˈdæmpnɪs] N umidità, umido

dam·son [ˈdæmzən] N (*fruit*) susina *or* prugna selvatica; (*tree*) damaschino, susino selvatico

dance [dɑːns] N (*activity*) ballo, danza; (*traditional, in ballet*) danza; (*event*) ballo, serata danzante; **the last dance was a waltz** l'ultimo ballo era un valzer; **it's a Scottish dance** è una danza scozzese; **to lead sb a dance** (*fig*) far girare qn come una trottola ♦ VT (*waltz, tango*) ballare ♦ VI ballare, danzare; (*fig: flowers, boat on waves*) danzare; **will you dance with me?** vuoi ballare (con me)?; **to go dancing** andare a ballare; **to dance about** saltellare; **to dance for joy** ballare dalla gioia *or* dalla contentezza

dance floor N pista da ballo

dance hall N dancing *m inv*, sala da ballo

danc·er [ˈdɑːnsə'] N ballerino(-a)

danc·ing [ˈdɑːnsɪŋ] N ballo

D and C N ABBR (*Med*: = *dilation and curettage*) raschiamento

dan·de·lion [ˈdændɪlaɪən] N dente *m* di leone

dan·druff [ˈdændrəf] N forfora

dan·dy [ˈdændɪ] N dandy *m inv*, elegantone *m* ♦ ADJ (*comp* **-ier**, *superl* **-iest**) (*USA fam*) fantastico(-a)

Dane [deɪn] N danese *m/f*

dan·ger [ˈdeɪndʒə'] N pericolo; **in danger** in pericolo; **out of danger** fuori pericolo; **to put sb's life in danger** mettere in pericolo la vita di qn; **to be in danger of falling** rischiare di cadere; **there was no danger that he would be caught** non c'era pericolo che lo prendessero; **there is a danger of fire** c'è pericolo di incendio; **"danger! men at work"** "attenzione! lavori in corso"; **"danger! keep out"** "pericolo! vietato l'accesso" ♦ ADJ (*zone, sign*) di pericolo

danger list N (*Med*): **on the danger list** in prognosi riservata

dan·ger·ous [ˈdeɪndʒrəs] ADJ (*gen*) pericoloso(-a); (*illness*) grave, pericoloso(-a)

dan·ger·ous·ly [ˈdeɪndʒrəslɪ] ADV (*gen*) pericolosamente; (*wounded*) gravemente; **dangerously ill** in pericolo di vita, gravemente malato(-a)

danger zone N area di pericolo

dan·gle [ˈdæŋgl] VT (*arm, leg*) (far) dondolare; (*object on string*) far oscillare; (*fig: tempting offer*): **to dangle sth in front of sb** allettare qn con qc ◆ VI pendere, penzolare; **with one's legs dangling** con le gambe penzoloni

Dan·ish [ˈdeɪnɪʃ] ADJ danese ◆ N (*language*) danese *m*

Danish pastry N *dolce di pasta sfoglia*

dank [dæŋk] ADJ (*comp* -er, *superl* -est) freddo(-a) e umido(-a)

Dan·ube [ˈdænjuːb] N: **the Danube** il Danubio

dap·per [ˈdæpəʳ] ADJ (*man*) azzimato(-a)

Dar·da·nelles [ˌdɑːdəˈnelz] NPL: **the Dardanelles** i Dardanelli

dare [dɛəʳ] VT 1 osare; **to dare (to) do sth** osare fare qc; **I don't dare tell him; how dare you!** come osa!, come osa! 2 **I dare say** immagino; **I dare say he'll turn up** immagino che spunterà 3 (*challenge*): **to dare (sb to do sth)** sfidare (qn a fare qc); **I dare you!** ti sfido a farlo! ◆ N sfida
❑ **dare** is not translated by the Italian word *dare*

dare·devil [ˈdɛəˌdevl] N scavezzacollo *m/f*

Dar-es-Salaam [ˈdɑːressəˈlɑːm] N Dar-es-Salaam *f*

dar·ing [ˈdɛərɪŋ] ADJ audace, ardito(-a) ◆ N audacia

dark [dɑːk] ADJ (*comp* -er, *superl* -est) 1 (*lacking light: room, night*) scuro(-a), buio(-a); **it is/is getting dark** è/si sta facendo buio; **the dark side of the moon** l'altra faccia della luna 2 (*in colour*) scuro(-a); (*complexion, hair, colour*) scuro(-a), bruno(-a); **dark blue/red** blu/rosso scuro *inv*; **a dark green sweater** un maglione verde scuro; **dark brown hair** capelli castano scuro; **he's tall, dark and handsome** è alto, bruno e bello; **dark chocolate** cioccolata amara 3 (*fig: sad, gloomy*) nero(-a), tetro(-a), cupo(-a); (: *sinister: secret, plan, threat*) oscuro(-a); **to keep sth dark** non far parola di qc ◆ N: **the dark** il buio, l'oscurità; **in the dark** al buio; **before dark** prima che faccia (*or* facesse) buio; **after dark** col buio, a notte fatta; **until dark** fino a sera; **to be in the dark about sth** (*fig*) essere all'oscuro di qc

dark·en [ˈdɑːkən] VT (*room*) oscurare; (*colour, photo*) scurire ◆ VI (*room, sky*) oscurarsi; (*colour*) scurirsi

dark glasses NPL occhiali *mpl* da sole

dark horse N (*fig*): **to be a dark horse** essere un'incognita

dark·ly [ˈdɑːklɪ] ADV (*sinisterly*) minacciosamente; (*gloomily*) cupamente, con aria cupa

dark·ness [ˈdɑːknɪs] N oscurità, buio; (*of hair*) colore *m* scuro; **the house was in darkness** la casa era immersa nel buio *or* nell'oscurità

dark·room [ˈdɑːkrum] N camera oscura

dar·ling [ˈdɑːlɪŋ] N tesoro; **he's a little darling** è un amore; **be a darling ...** (*fam*) sii un angelo *or* un tesoro...; **come here darling** vieni qui tesoro ◆ N (*daughter, husband*) caro(-a); (*dress, house*) adorabile, delizioso(-a)

darn [dɑːn] VT (*socks, clothes*) rammendare ◆ N rammendo

dart [dɑːt] N 1 dardo, freccia; (*Sport*) freccetta; **to play darts** giocare a freccette 2 (*Sewing*) pince *f inv*, ripresa 3 **to make a dart towards** precipitarsi verso ◆ VI (*look*) lanciare ◆ VI: **to dart in/out** *etc* entrare/uscire *etc* come una freccia; **to dart away** sfrecciare via; **to dart at sth** lanciarsi verso qc; **to dart towards** precipitarsi verso; **to dart along** passare come un razzo

dart·board [ˈdɑːt,bɔːd] N bersaglio per freccette

darts [dɑːts] NSG tiro al bersaglio con freccette; **to play darts** giocare a freccette

dash [dæʃ] N 1 (*rush*): **to make a dash (at, towards)** lanciarsi (verso), scattare (verso); **he had to make a dash for it** ha dovuto fare una corsa; **a dash to the hospital** una corsa all'ospedale; **the 100-metre dash** (*USA*) i 100 metri piani 2 (*small quantity: of liquid*) goccio, goccino; (: *of seasoning*) pizzico; (: *of colour*) tocco; **a dash of vinegar** un goccio d'aceto 3 (*punctuation mark*) lineetta, trattino; (*Morse*) linea ◆ VT 1 (*throw*) scaraventare, gettare con violenza; **to dash sth to pieces** mandare qc in frantumi; **to dash one's head**

against sth battere la testa contro qc 2 (*fig: spirits*) abbattere; (: *hopes*) infrangere; **all his hopes were dashed** tutte le sue speranze naufragarono ◆ VI 1 (*smash: object, waves*): **to dash against** infrangersi su *or* contro 2 (*rush*) precipitarsi; **everyone dashed to the window** tutti si sono precipitati alla finestra; **I must dash** (*fam*) devo scappare; **to dash away** scappare via; **to dash in/out** entrare/uscire di corsa; **to dash towards** precipitarsi verso
▸ **dash off** VT + ADV (*letter, drawing*) buttar giù

dash·board [ˈdæʃˌbɔːd] N (*Aut*) cruscotto

dash·ing [ˈdæʃɪŋ] ADJ brillante, affascinante

das·tard·ly [ˈdæstədlɪ] ADJ (*old*) vile

data [ˈdeɪtə] NSG, NPL dati *mpl*

data·base [ˈdeɪtəˌbeɪs] N database *m inv*

data capture N registrazione *f* di dati

data processing N elaborazione *f* (elettronica) dei dati

data transmission N trasmissione *f* di dati

date¹ [deɪt] N 1 data; **what's the date today?** quanti ne abbiamo oggi?; **date of birth** data di nascita; **closing date** scadenza, termine *m*; **to date** fino a oggi; **to be up to date** (*person, document, information*) essere aggiornato(-a); (*person: fashionable*) essere alla moda; (: *with one's work*) essere nei termini; (*building*) essere moderno(-a); **to bring up to date** (*correspondence, information*) aggiornare; (*method*) modernizzare; (*person*) mettere al corrente, aggiornare; **to be out of date** (*information*) non essere aggiornato(-a); (*document*) essere scaduto(-a); (*person, style*) essere fuori moda; (*technology*) superato(-a) 2 (*fam: appointment*) appuntamento; (: *boyfriend*) ragazzo; (: *girlfriend*) ragazza; **to make a date with sb** fissare un appuntamento con qn; **I have a date with Mark** ho un appuntamento con Mark; **he asked her for a date** le ha chiesto di uscire con lui ◆ VT 1 (*letter*) datare; (*ruin, manuscript*) attribuire una data a, datare; **dated the 13th** datato il 13; **thank you for your letter dated 5th July** *or* **July 5th** la ringrazio per la sua lettera in data 5 luglio; **his style of dress dates him** il suo abbigliamento tradisce la sua età 2 (*esp USA: girl, boy*) uscire con ◆ VI 1 **to date (back) from** risalire a 2 (*become old-fashioned*) passare di moda

date² [deɪt] N (*fruit*) dattero; (*also: date palm*) palma da dattero

dat·ed [ˈdeɪtɪd] ADJ (*style*) antiquato(-a), fuori moda, passato(-a) di moda; (*film*) datato(-a)

date·line [ˈdeɪtˌlaɪn] N linea del cambiamento di data

date stamp N (*on library book*) timbro datario; (*on fresh food*) scadenza; (*postmark*) timbro

daub [dɔːb] VT: **to daub (with)** imbrattare (di)

daugh·ter [ˈdɔːtəʳ] N figlia

daughter-in-law [ˈdɔːtərɪnlɔː] N nuora

daunt [dɔːnt] VT scoraggiare, intimidire; **nothing daunted ...** per nulla scoraggiato...

daunt·ing [ˈdɔːntɪŋ] ADJ (*prospect*) non allettante

daunt·less [ˈdɔːntlɪs] ADJ (*liter*) impavido(-a), intrepido(-a)

daw·dle [ˈdɔːdl] VI (*in walking*) ciondolare, bighellonare; **to dawdle over one's work** gingillarsi con il lavoro

dawn [dɔːn] N 1 alba; **at dawn** all'alba; **from dawn to dusk** dall'alba al tramonto 2 (*fig: also: dawning: of civilization*) albori *mpl*; **the dawn of a new age** l'inizio di una nuova era · ◆ VI (*day*) spuntare
▸ **dawn on, dawn upon** VI + PREP: **the truth gradually dawned on us** poco a poco cominciammo a vederci chiaro; **the idea dawned upon me that ...** mi è balenata nella mente l'idea che...; **it suddenly dawned on him that ...** improvvisamente gli è venuto in mente che...

dawn chorus N (*Brit*) coro mattutino degli uccelli

day [deɪ] N 1 (*24 hours*) giorno; **what day is it today?** che giorno è oggi?; **2 days ago** 2 giorni fa; **one day** un giorno; **(on) the day that ...** il giorno che *or* in cui...; **(on) that day** quel giorno; **the day before** il giorno avanti *or* prima; **the day before yesterday** l'altro ieri; **the day before his birthday** la vigilia del suo compleanno; **the day after** il giorno dopo; **the following day** il giorno seguente; **the day after tomorrow** dopodomani; **her mother died 3 years ago to the day** oggi sono 3 anni che è morta sua madre; **he works 8 hours a day** lavora 8 ore al giorno; **any day now** da un giorno all'altro; **every day** ogni giorno; **every other day** un giorno sì e uno no, ogni due giorni; **twice a day** due volte al giorno; **one of these days** uno di questi giorni, un giorno o l'altro; **the other day** l'altro giorno; **from one day to the next** da un giorno all'altro; **day after day** giorno dopo giorno; **day in day out** un giorno dopo l'altro, tutti i santi giorni; **for days on end** per giorni e giorni; **day by day** giorno per giorno; **to live from day to day** *or* **from one day to the next** vivere alla giornata; **he's fifty if he's a day!** (*fam*) cinquant'anni li ha di sicuro! **2** (*daylight hours*) giorno, giornata; (*working hours*) giornata; **by day** di giorno; **to travel by day** *or* **during the day** viaggiare di giorno *or* durante il giorno; **to work all day** lavorare tutto il giorno; **to work day and night** lavorare giorno e notte; **it's a fine day** è una bella giornata; **to arrive on a fine/wet day** arrivare col bel tempo/con la pioggia; **one summer's day** un giorno d'estate; **a day off** un giorno libero; **to work an 8-hour day** avere una giornata lavorativa di 8 ore; **it's all in a day's work** fa parte del mestiere; **paid by the day** pagato(-a) a giornata; **to work days** fare il turno di giorno **3** (*period of time, age*) tempo, tempi *mpl*, epoca; **in this day and age** ai nostri tempi; **these days** di questi tempi, oggigiorno; **to this day** ... ancor oggi...; **in days to come** in futuro; **in those days** a quell'epoca; **in the days when** ... all'epoca in cui...; **in Queen Victoria's day** ai tempi della regina Vittoria; **he was famous in his day** ai suoi tempi era famoso; **in his younger days** quand'era (più) giovane; **in the good old days** ai bei tempi; **the happiest days of one's life** il periodo più felice della propria vita

day·book ['deɪˌbʊk] N (*Brit*: *Book-keeping*) brogliaccio

day·break ['deɪbreɪk] N: **at daybreak** allo spuntar del giorno, all'alba

day-care centre ['deɪˌkɛəˈsɛntəʳ] N (*USA*) scuola materna

day·dream ['deɪˌdriːm] N sogno a occhi aperti ♦ VI sognare a occhi aperti

day·light ['deɪˌlaɪt] N luce *f* (del giorno); **at daylight** (*dawn*) alle prime luci, all'alba; **in the daylight, by daylight** alla luce del giorno; **it is still daylight** è ancora giorno; **daylight attack** attacco di giorno

daylight-saving time ['deɪlaɪtˈseɪvɪŋtaɪm] N (*USA*) ora legale

day release N: **to be on day release** avere un congedo settimanale per formazione professionale

day return N (*Brit*: *also*: **day return ticket**) biglietto giornaliero di andata e ritorno

day shift N turno di giorno; **to be on day shift** fare il turno di giorno

day·time ['deɪtaɪm] N giorno; **in the daytime** di giorno ♦ ADJ di giorno; **daytime TV** televisione *f* del mattino e del pomeriggio

day-to-day ['deɪtəˌdeɪ] ADJ (*routine*) quotidiano(-a); (*expenses*) giornaliero(-a); **on a day-to-day basis** a giornata

day trader N (*Fin*) day dealer *m/f inv*, operatore che compra e vende titoli nel corso della stessa giornata

day trip N gita (di un giorno)

day tripper N gitante *m/f*

daze [deɪz] N: **in a daze** stordito(-a), inebetito(-a) ♦ VT (*subj*: *drug*) inebetire; (: *blow*) stordire

dazed [deɪzd] ADJ stordito(-a), (stordita)

daz·zle ['dæzl] VT abbagliare

daz·zling ['dæzlɪŋ] ADJ (*light*) abbagliante; (*colour*) violento(-a); (*smile*) smagliante

dB, db N ABBR = decibel

DC [ˌdiːˈsiː] N ABBR (*Elec*: = *direct current*) c.c. ♦ ABBR (*USA Post*: = *District of Columbia*) distretto della Columbia; **Washington DC** Washington DC *f*

D-day ['diːˌdeɪ] N D-day *m*, giorno dello sbarco alleato in Normandia

DDS [ˌdiːdiːˈes] N ABBR (*USA*: = *Doctor of Dental Surgery*) titolare di un dottorato in odontoiatria

DDT [ˌdiːdiːˈtiː] N ABBR (= *dichlorodiphenyl trichloroethane*) DDT *m*

DE [ˌdiːˈiː] ABBR (*USA Post*: = Delaware)

dea·con ['diːkən] N diacono

dead [dɛd] ADJ **1** (*person, animal, plant*) morto(-a); (*matter*)

inanimato(-a); (*fingers, leg*): **to go dead** intorpidirsi; **to fall** *or* **drop (down) dead** morire; **he was dead** era morto; **he was shot dead** fu colpito a morte; **he's been dead for 2 years** è morto da due anni; **dead and buried** (*also fig*) morto(-a) e sepolto(-a); **dead or alive** vivo(-a) o morto(-a); **over my dead body!** (*fam*) manco morto!; **I feel absolutely dead!** (*fig*: *fam*) sono (stanco) morto!; **to be a dead duck** (*fam*) essere spacciato(-a) **2** (*volcano, cigarette*) spento(-a); (*battery*) scarico(-a); (*telephone line*) caduto(-a); (*language, town, party*) morto(-a); (*custom*) scomparso(-a), estinto(-a); **the line has gone dead** (*Telec*) è caduta la linea; **he was dead to the world** (*fig*) era proprio partito (*fig*) **3** (*complete*: *silence, calm*) assoluto(-a), totale; **to hit sth dead centre** centrare qc in pieno; **to come to a dead stop** fermarsi (del tutto); **to fall into a dead faint** cadere in svenimento ♦ ADV (*completely*): **dead certain** assolutamente certo(-a), sicurissimo(-a); **to stop dead** fermarsi di colpo; **you're dead right!** hai assolutamente ragione!; **dead ahead** sempre dritto; **it's dead ahead of us** è proprio davanti a noi; **dead on time** in perfetto orario; **to land dead on target** fare centro; **dead slow** (*Aut*) a passo d'uomo; (*Naut*) avanti piano; **to be dead set on doing sth** volere fare qc a tutti i costi; **to be dead set against sth** (*fam*) essere assolutamente contrario(-a) a qc; **dead broke** (*fam*) senza il becco di un quattrino; **dead drunk** (*fam*) ubriaco(-a) fradicio(-a); **dead tired** (*fam*) stanco(-a) morto(-a) ♦ N **1 the dead** *npl* i morti **2 at dead of night** nel cuore della notte; **in the dead of winter** nel cuore dell'inverno

dead beat ADJ (*fam*) stanco(-a) morto(-a)

dead·en ['dɛdn] VT (*noise, pain, blow, sound*) attutire; (*nerve*) rendere insensibile

dead end N (*also fig*) vicolo cieco

dead-end [dɛdˈend] ADJ: **a dead-end job** un lavoro senza sbocchi

dead heat N (*Sport*): **it was a dead heat** è stata una vittoria a pari merito; **to finish in a dead heat** finire alla pari

dead-letter office [ˌdɛdlɛtəˈɒfɪs] N ufficio della posta in giacenza

dead·line ['dɛdˌlaɪn] N termine *m* (di consegna), scadenza; **to work to a deadline** avere una scadenza da rispettare; **we'll never meet the deadline** ci sarà impossibile rispettare la scadenza

dead·lock ['dɛdˌlɒk] N punto morto, impasse *f inv*

dead loss N (*fam*): **to be a dead loss** (*person, thing*) non valere niente

dead·ly ['dɛdlɪ] ADJ (*comp* **-ier**, *superl* **-iest**) (*gen*) mortale; (*weapon, poison, aim*) micidiale; (*disease*) letale; **they are deadly enemies** sono acerrimi nemici; **the seven deadly sins** i sette peccati capitali; **he is in deadly earnest** fa (*or* parla) sul serio, non scherza; **this book is deadly** (*fam*: *very boring*) questo libro è un mattone ♦ ADV: **deadly dull** di una noia mortale; **deadly pale** pallido(-a) come un cadavere

dead·pan ['dɛdˌpæn] ADJ (*face*) impassibile; (*humour*) all'inglese ♦ ADV (*with a straight face*) senza fare una piega

Dead Sea N: **the Dead Sea** il mar Morto

deaf [dɛf] ADJ (*comp* **-er**, *superl* **-est**) sordo(-a); **deaf in one ear** sordo(-a) da un orecchio; **to be deaf to sth** (*fig*) restare sordo(-a) a qc; **to turn a deaf ear to sth** fare orecchi da mercante a qc ♦ NPL: **the deaf** i sordi

deaf·en ['dɛfn] VT assordare

deaf·en·ing ['dɛfnɪŋ] ADJ assordante, fragoroso(-a)

deaf-mute ['dɛfˌmjuːt] N sordomuto(-a)

deaf·ness ['dɛfnɪs] N sordità

deal [diːl] (*pt, pp* **dealt**) N **1** (*agreement*) accordo; (*also*: **business deal**) affare *m*; **to do** *or* **strike a deal with sb** fare un affare con qn; **he made a deal with the kidnappers** ha fatto un accordo con i rapitori; **it's a deal!** (*fam*) affare fatto!; **a new deal** (*Pol, Econ, Sociol*) un piano di riforme; **to get a good/bad deal** (*Comm*) fare/non fare un buon affare; **he got a good deal from them** l'hanno trattato bene; **a fair deal for working mothers** un trattamento equo per le madri che lavorano; **to get a rough/raw deal** venir trattato(-a) ingiustamente **2** (*Cards*) turno (*nel dare le carte*); **it's my deal** adesso tocca a me dare le carte **3** (*in expressions of quantity*): **a good** *or* **great deal** molto, parecchio; **to have a great deal to do** avere molto da fare; **there's a good deal of**

truth in what he says c'è molto di vero in quel che dice; **she spends a great deal of her time alone** passa buona parte del suo tempo da sola; **he thinks a great deal of his father** ha una grande stima di suo padre; **that's saying a good deal** non è dire poco; **it means a great deal to me** vuol dire molto per me ♦ VT **1 to deal sb a blow** assestare un colpo a qn **2** (*Cards: also:* **deal out**) distribuire, dare

▸ **deal in** VI + PREP (*Comm*) occuparsi di; (*drugs*) spacciare; **they deal in antiques** trattano oggetti d'antiquariato

▸ **deal out** VT + ADV (*cards, money*) distribuire; **to deal out justice** far giustizia

▸ **deal with** VI + PREP **1** (*handle: person, task, application*) occuparsi di; (: *problem*) affrontare; (*Comm: order*) sbrigare; **he promised to deal with it immediately** ha promesso di occuparsene immediatamente; **I'll deal with you later!** con te facciamo i conti più tardi!; **to know how to deal with sb** sapere come prendere qn; **he's not easy to deal with** è un tipo difficile **2** (*subj: book, film: be about*) trattare di; **the part of the book which deals with the subject** la parte del libro che tratta dell'argomento **3** (*Comm: company, organization, person*) trattare con

deal·er [ˈdiːləʳ] N **1** (*Comm*) commerciante m/f (di); **an antique dealer** un(a) antiquario(-a) **2** (*also:* **drug dealer**) spacciatore(-trice) **3** (*Cards*) chi fa *or* dà le carte

deal·er·ship [ˈdiːləˌʃɪp] N (*Comm*) concessione f

deal·ings [ˈdiːlɪŋz] NPL **1** (*relationship*) rapporti mpl; **to have dealings with sb** avere a che fare con qn **2** (*Comm, Stock Exchange: in goods, shares*) transazioni fpl

dealt [dɛlt] PT, PP of **deal**

dean [diːn] N (*of college, university*) preside m/f; (*Rel*) decano

dear [dɪəʳ] ADJ (*comp* **-er**, *superl* **-est**) **1** (*loved, lovable*) caro(-a); **I hold it very dear** mi è molto caro; **my dearest wish** il mio più ardente desiderio; **what a dear little boy!** che amore di bambino!; **a dear little cottage** una casetta deliziosa **2** (*in letter writing*): **Dear Daddy/Peter** Caro papà/ Peter; **Dearest Paul** Carissimo Paul; **Dear Mr/Mrs Smith** Gentile Signor/Signora Smith; **Dear Mr and Mrs Smith** Gentili Signori Smith; **Dear Sir/Madam** Egregio Signore/Gentile Signora **3** (*expensive*) caro(-a); **dear money** (*Comm*) denaro ad alto interesse ♦ EXCL: **oh dear!** oh Dio!, mamma mia!; **dear me!** Dio mio! ♦ N caro(-a); **my dear** caro(-a) mio(-a); **my dearest** amore mio; **(you) poor dear!** poverino!; **he's a dear!** (*fam*) è un tesoro! ♦ ADV caro; **to pay dear for sth** pagare caro qc

dear·ly [ˈdɪəlɪ] ADV: **to love sb/sth dearly** amare qn/qc moltissimo; **I should dearly love to go there** mi piacerebbe moltissimo andarci; **to pay dearly for sth** (*esp fig*) pagar qc caro *or* a caro prezzo

dearth [dɜːθ] N (*of food, resources, ideas, money*) penuria, mancanza

death [dɛθ] N morte f; (*Med, Admin, Law*) decesso; (*of plans, hopes*) fine f; **to be burnt to death** morire carbonizzato(-a); **to drink o.s. to death** uccidersi a forza di bere; **to sentence sb to death** condannare a morte qn; **to put sb to death** mettere a morte qn, giustiziare qn; **a fight to the death** un duello all'ultimo sangue; **to be at death's door** essere in punto di morte; **it will be the death of him** sarà la sua rovina; **you'll be the death of me** (*fam, fig*) mi farai morire; **you look like death warmed up** (*fam*) sembri un morto che cammina; **bored to death** (*fam*) annoiato(-a) a morte; **I'm sick** *or* **tired to death of it** (*fam*) ne ho fin sopra i capelli

death·bed N letto di morte; **on one's deathbed** in punto di morte ♦ ADJ (*confession*) in punto di morte

death certificate N (*Admin*) certificato di morte

death duty N (*gen pl: Brit*) tassa di successione

death·ly [ˈdɛθlɪ] ADJ (*comp* **-ier**, *superl* **-iest**) (*pallor*) mortale; (*appearance*) cadaverico(-a); (*silence*) di tomba ♦ ADV: **deathly pale** pallido(-a) come un cadavere

death penalty N pena di morte

death rate N (*tasso di*) mortalità

death row N (*USA*): **to be on death row** essere nel braccio della morte

death sentence N condanna a morte, pena di morte

death squad N squadra della morte

death·trap [ˈdɛθˌtræp] N trappola mortale

deb [dɛb] N ABBR (*Brit: fam:* = *debutante*) ragazza di buona famiglia che debutta in società

de·ba·cle [deɪˈbɑːkl] N disastro; (*defeat*) disfatta; (*collapse*) sfacelo

de·bar [dɪˈbɑːʳ] VT (*frm*): **to debar sb from sth** escludere qn da qc; **to debar sb from doing sth** vietare a qn di fare qc

de·base [dɪˈbeɪs] VT (*person, relationship, word*) degradare, svilire; (*coinage*) svilire, adulterare

de·bat·able [dɪˈbeɪtəbl] ADJ discutibile; **that's debatable** questo è discutibile; **it is debatable whether ...** è in dubbio se...

de·bate [dɪˈbeɪt] VT (*discuss*) discutere, dibattere; (*consider*): **he debated the advisability of leaving** si chiedeva se fosse saggio partire; **we debated whether to go or not** discutemmo se andare o meno ♦ VI: **to debate (with sb about sth)** discutere (con qn di qc); **to debate with o.s. (about, (up) on sth)** essere in dubbio (su qc) ♦ N dibattito, discussione f; **after much debate** dopo lunga discussione

de·bauch·ery [dɪˈbɔːtʃərɪ] N dissolutezza

de·ben·ture [dɪˈbentʃəʳ] N (*Fin*) obbligazione f

de·bili·tate [dɪˈbɪlɪteɪt] VT (*frm*) debilitare

deb·it [ˈdɛbɪt] (*Fin*) N addebito ♦ VT addebitare; **to debit sb/ sb's account with a sum, to debit a sum to sb** *or* **to sb's account** addebitare una somma a qn/sul conto di qc

debit balance N saldo passivo *or* debitore

debit card N carta di addebito

debit note N nota di addebito

debo·nair [ˌdɛbəˈneəʳ] ADJ (*young man*) gioviale e disinvolto(-a)

de·brief [ˌdiːˈbriːf] VT (*Mil*) chiamare a rapporto (a operazione ultimata)

de·brief·ing [ˌdiːˈbriːfɪŋ] N rapporto *or* resoconto (a operazione ultimata)

de·bris [ˈdɛbriː] N detriti mpl

debt [dɛt] N debito; **debts of £5000** debiti di 5000 sterline; **he's stopped paying off his debts** sta ancora pagando i debiti; **a debt of honour/gratitude** un debito d'onore/di gratitudine *or* di riconoscenza; **to be in debt (to sb)** essere indebitato(-a) (con qn), avere debiti (con qn); **I am £500 in debt** sono in debito di 500 sterline; **to be in sb's debt** (*fig*) essere in debito verso qn; **to get into debt** far debiti, indebitarsi; **to be out of debt** essere libero(-a) da debiti; **debt burden** indebitamento; **debt forgiveness** cancellazione f del debito; **debt relief** riduzione f del debito

debt collector N agente m di recupero crediti

debt·or [ˈdɛtəʳ] N debitore(-trice)

de·bug [diːˈbʌg] VT (*Comput: program*) localizzare e rimuovere errori da; (*room*) togliere i microfoni da

de·bunk [diːˈbʌŋk] VT (*theory*) demistificare; (*claim*) smentire; (*person, institution*) screditare

de·but [ˈdeɪbjuː] N debutto; **to make one's debut** debuttare, fare il proprio debutto; **to make one's stage/film debut** debuttare sulle scene/sullo schermo

debu·tante [ˈdɛbjuːtɑːnt] N debuttante f

Dec. ABBR (= *December*) dic. (= *dicembre*)

dec·ade [ˈdɛkeɪd] N decennio

deca·dence [ˈdɛkədəns] N decadenza

deca·dent [ˈdɛkədənt] ADJ decadente

de·caf·fein·at·ed [diːˈkæfɪneɪtɪd] ADJ decaffeinato(-a)

de·camp [dɪˈkæmp] VI filarsela

de·cant [dɪˈkænt] VT (*wine*) decantare

de·cant·er [dɪˈkæntəʳ] N bottiglia di cristallo (*per liquori o vini*)

de·cath·lon [dɪˈkæθlən] N decathlon m inv

de·cay [dɪˈkeɪ] VI (*teeth*) cariarsi; (*vegetation, flesh*) decomporsi; (*Phys: radioactive nucleus*) disintegrarsi; (*building, urban area*) andare in rovina; (*fig: civilization*) decadere; (: *one's faculties*) deteriorarsi ♦ N (*of teeth*) carie f; (*of vegetation, body*) decomposizione f; (*of radioactivity*) disintegrazione f; (*of building, urban area*) stato di abbandono, decadimento; (*of civilization*) rovina; (*of faculties*) deterioramento

de·cease [dɪˈsiːs] (*Law*) N decesso ♦ VI decedere

de·ceased [dɪˈsiːst] (*Law, also frm*) ADJ deceduto(-a) ♦ N: **the deceased** il (la) defunto(-a)

de·ceit [dɪˈsiːt] N (*quality*) disonestà; (*action*) inganno, truffa
de·ceit·ful [dɪˈsiːtfʊl] ADJ (*person*) falso(-a), disonesto(-a); (*words, behaviour*) menzognero(-a), ingannatore(-trice)
de·ceive [dɪˈsiːv] VT ingannare; **she deceived me into thinking that ...** mi ha ingannato facendomi credere che...; **unless my eyes deceive me** se gli occhi non m'ingannano; **don't be deceived by appearances** non ti fare ingannare dalle apparenze; **to deceive o.s.** ingannarsi, illudersi
de·cel·er·ate [diːˈsɛləreɪt] VT, VI decelerare
De·cem·ber [dɪˈsɛmbəʳ] N dicembre *m*; *see* July
de·cen·cy [ˈdiːsənsɪ] N (*moral sense*) rispetto per i valori umani; (*propriety*) decenza, decoro; **he has no sense of decency** non ha un minimo di rispetto; **to have the decency to do sth** avere la decenza di fare qc; **out of common decency** per gentilezza, se non altro
de·cent [ˈdiːsənt] ADJ 1 (*respectable: person, house*) perbene *inv*, ammodo *inv*; (*proper: clothes, behaviour, language*) decente 2 (*kind*) gentile, bravo(-a); **to do the decent thing** fare quello che è giusto; **they were very decent about it** sono stati molto corretti in merito 3 (*satisfactory: meal, house*) decente, discreto(-a)
de·cent·ly [ˈdiːsəntlɪ] ADV (*respectably*) decentemente, convenientemente; (*kindly*) gentilmente
de·cen·trali·za·tion [diːˌsɛntrəlaɪˈzeɪʃən] N (*Admin, Pol*) decentramento
de·cen·tral·ize [diːˈsɛntrəlaɪz] VT (*Admin, Pol*) decentrare
de·cep·tion [dɪˈsɛpʃən] N inganno; **to practice deception on sb** raggirare qn
de·cep·tive [dɪˈsɛptɪv] ADJ (*likely to deceive*) ingannevole; (*meant to deceive*) ingannatore(-trice)
deci·bel [ˈdɛsɪbɛl] N decibel *m inv*
de·cide [dɪˈsaɪd] VT (*question, argument*) decidere, risolvere; **to decide to do sth** decidere di fare qc, decidersi a fare qc; **to decide that** decidere che; **the goal that decided the match** il gol decisivo per la partita; **I decided to write to her** ho deciso di scriverle; **he decided not to go** ha deciso di non andare; **to decide sb to do sth** ... **; what decided him ...** ciò che l'ha fatto decidere... ♦ VI decidere, decidersi; **to decide for** *or* **in favour of sb** decidere a favore di qn; **to decide on/against sth** optare per/contro qc; **to decide on doing sth** scegliere *or* decidere di fare qc; **to decide against doing sth** decidere di non fare qc; **I can't decide** non so decidermi
de·cid·ed [dɪˈsaɪdɪd] ADJ (*tone, improvement*) deciso(-a); (*risk*) certo(-a); (*opinions, views*) chiaro(-a), preciso(-a)
de·cid·ed·ly [dɪˈsaɪdɪdlɪ] ADV (*extremely*) decisamente; (*emphatically*) in modo deciso
de·cid·ing [dɪˈsaɪdɪŋ] ADJ decisivo(-a); **the deciding factor** il fattore decisivo
de·cid·u·ous [dɪˈsɪdjuəs] ADJ deciduo(-a)
deci·mal [ˈdɛsɪməl] ADJ decimale; **the decimal system** il sistema decimale; **to 3 decimal places** al terzo decimale ♦ N (*numero*) decimale *m*
deci·mal·ize [ˈdɛsɪməlaɪz] VT (*Brit*) convertire al sistema metrico decimale
decimal point N ≈ virgola (*in numero decimale*)
deci·mate [ˈdɛsɪmeɪt] VT decimare
de·ci·pher [dɪˈsaɪfəʳ] VT decifrare
de·ci·sion [dɪˈsɪʒən] N decisione *f*; **to make a decision** prendere una decisione
de·ci·sive [dɪˈsaɪsɪv] ADJ (*victory, factor*) decisivo(-a); (*influence*) determinante; (*manner, person*) risoluto(-a), deciso(-a); (*reply*) deciso(-a), categorico(-a)
deck [dɛk] N 1 (*Naut*) (ponte *m* di) coperta; **to go up on deck** salire in coperta; **below deck** sotto coperta; **to clear the decks** (*fig*) sgombrare il campo; **to hit the deck** (*fam*) cascare a terra (*bocconi*) 2 (*of bus*): **top** *or* **upper deck** piano di sopra; **bottom** *or* **lower deck** piano di sotto 3 (*of cards*) mazzo 4 (*of record player*) piatto; **record deck** piatto (*giradischi*); **cassette deck** piastra (di registrazione) 5 piattaforma di legno (*in giardino*) ♦ VT 1 (*also:* **deck out**): **to deck (with)** decorare (con) 2 (*fam*) stendere
deck·chair [ˈdɛktʃɛəʳ] N sedia *f* sdraio, *inv*
deck hand N mozzo
dec·la·ra·tion [ˌdɛkləˈreɪʃən] N dichiarazione *f*
de·clare [dɪˈklɛəʳ] VT (*gen*) dichiarare; (*Fin, Pol: results*) annunciare; **have you anything to declare?** (*Customs*) ha qualcosa da dichiarare?, dichiara?; **to declare that** dichiarare che; **he declared that he was innocent** ha dichiarato di essere innocente, si è dichiarato innocente; **to declare war (on** *or* **against sb)** dichiarare guerra (a qn); **to declare for** pronunciarsi a favore di
de·clas·si·fy [diːˈklæsɪˌfaɪ] VT (*documents, records*) declassificare
de·cline [dɪˈklaɪn] N: **decline (in)** (*decrease*) calo (di); (*deterioration*) declino (di); **decline in living standards** abbassamento del tenore di vita; **to be on the decline** (*gen*) essere in diminuzione; (*prices*) essere in ribasso ♦ VT 1 (*frm: refuse: invitation*) declinare, rifiutare; **to decline to do sth** rifiutare *or* rifiutarsi di fare qc; **he declined the offer** ha rifiutato l'offerta 2 (*Gram*) declinare ♦ VI 1 (*power, influence*) diminuire, declinare; (*empire*) decadere; (*health*) deteriorare; **the birth rate is declining** il tasso di natalità sta calando; **in his declining years** negli ultimi anni della sua vita; (*of public figure*) negli anni del suo declino; **to decline in importance** diminuire d'importanza 2 (*Gram*) declinarsi
de·clutch [diːˈklʌtʃ] VI (*Aut*) premere la frizione
de·code [diːˈkəʊd] VT (*message*) decifrare; (*Comput, Ling*) decodificare
de·cod·er [diːˈkəʊdəʳ] N (*Comput, TV*) decodificatore *m*
de·com·pose [ˌdiːkəmˈpəʊz] VI decomporsi ♦ VT decomporre
de·com·po·si·tion [ˌdiːkɒmpəˈzɪʃən] N decomposizione *f*
de·com·pres·sion [ˌdiːkəmˈprɛʃən] N decompressione *f*
decompression chamber N camera di decompressione
de·con·gest·ant [ˌdiːkənˈdʒɛstənt] N decongestionante *m*
de·con·tami·nate [ˌdiːkənˈtæmɪˌneɪt] VT decontaminare
de·con·trol [ˌdiːkənˈtrəʊl] VT (*trade*) liberalizzare; (*prices*) togliere il controllo governativo a
dé·cor [ˈdeɪkɔːʳ] N arredamento, decorazione *f*
deco·rate [ˈdɛkəˌreɪt] VT 1 **to decorate (with)** (*adorn*) decorare (con) 2 (*paint and wallpaper: room*) pitturare e tappezzare 3 (*honour: soldier*) decorare
deco·ra·tion [ˌdɛkəˈreɪʃən] N decorazione *f*; **Christmas decorations** decorazioni natalizie; addobbi natalizi
deco·ra·tive [ˈdɛkərətɪv] ADJ decorativo(-a)
deco·ra·tor [ˈdɛkəreɪtəʳ] N decoratore(-trice)
de·co·rum [dɪˈkɔːrəm] N decoro; **out of a sense of decorum** per rispetto delle convenienze; **a breach of decorum** una sconvenienza
de·coy [ˈdiːkɔɪ] N (*bird*) (uccello da) richiamo; (*fig: bait: thing*) tranello; (: *person*) esca; **police decoy** poliziotto in borghese (*usato come esca*)
de·crease [*n* ˈdiːkriːs, *vb* diːˈkriːs] N: **decrease (in)** (*amount, numbers, population, power*) diminuzione *f* (di); (*birth rate, value, production, enthusiasm*) calo (di); (*prices*) ribasso (di); (*strength, dose*) riduzione *f* (di); **to be on the decrease** essere in diminuzione; **there has been a decrease in the number of people out of work** c'è stata una diminuzione del numero dei disoccupati ♦ VT (*see n*) diminuire; far calare; ribassare; ridurre; **after three weeks I decreased the dose** dopo tre settimane ho diminuito la dose ♦ VI (*amount, numbers etc*) diminuire; (*prices, birthrate etc*) calare; (*Knitting*) calare (le maglie); **to decrease by 10%** diminuire del 10%; **the number has decreased** il numero è diminuito
de·creas·ing [diːˈkriːsɪŋ] ADJ in diminuzione
de·cree [dɪˈkriː] N (*Law, Pol*) decreto; (*municipal*) ordinanza; (*divorce*): **decree absolute** sentenza di divorzio definitiva; **decree nisi** sentenza provvisoria di divorzio ♦ VT: **to decree (that)** decretare (che) + *sub*
de·crep·it [dɪˈkrɛpɪt] ADJ (*building*) cadente; (*person*) decrepito(-a)
de·cry [dɪˈkraɪ] VT (*frm*) condannare, deplorare
dedi·cate [ˈdɛdɪˌkeɪt] VT dedicare, consacrare; (*book etc*) dedicare; **to dedicate one's life** *or* **o.s. to sth/to doing sth** dedicare la propria esistenza a qc/a fare qc
dedi·cat·ed [ˈdɛdɪˌkeɪtɪd] ADJ coscienzioso(-a); (*Comput*) dedicato(-a); **a very dedicated teacher** un insegnante che ama molto il suo lavoro
dedi·ca·tion [ˌdɛdɪˈkeɪʃən] N (*in book*) dedica; (*devotion*) dedizione *f*

de·duce [dɪ'djuːs] VT: **to deduce sth from sth** dedurre qc da qc; **to deduce that** dedurre che

de·duct [dɪ'dʌkt] VT: **to deduct (from)** (*gen*) dedurre (da); (*from wages*) trattenere (su); (*from price*) fare una riduzione (su); (*Scol: marks*) togliere (da)

de·duc·tion [dɪ'dʌkʃən] N 1 (*inference*) deduzione *f* 2 (*subtraction*) detrazione *f*; (*from wages*) trattenuta

deed [diːd] N 1 azione *f*, atto; **brave deed** impresa; **good deed** buona azione; **in deed** di fatto 2 (*Law*) atto (notarile); **deed of covenant** atto di donazione

deem [diːm] VT (*frm*) giudicare, ritenere; **she deemed it wise to go** ha ritenuto prudente andarsene

deep [diːp] ADJ (*comp* **-er**, *superl* **-est**) 1 (*water, hole, wound*) profondo(-a); (*snow*) alto(-a); **the lake was 16 metres deep** il lago era profondo 16 metri; **how deep is the water?** quanto è profonda l'acqua?; **knee-deep in water** in acqua fino alle ginocchia; **we were ankle-deep in mud** il fango ci arrivava alle caviglie; **to be in deep water** (*fig*) navigare in cattive acque; **the deep end** (*of swimming pool*) la parte più profonda; **to be thrown in (at) the deep end** (*fig: fam*) avere il battesimo del fuoco; **to go off (at) the deep end** (*fig: fam: angry*) partire per la tangente 2 (*shelf, cupboard*) profondo(-a); (*border, hem*) lungo(-a); **these kitchen units are 30 cm deep** questi mobili da cucina hanno una profondità di 30 cm 3 (*voice, sigh*) profondo(-a); **deep breathing exercises** esercizi *mpl* respiratori; **he took a deep breath** fece un respiro profondo 4 (*feeling, sleep, writer, insight*) profondo(-a); (*colour*) intenso(-a), cupo(-a); (*relief*) immenso(-a); (*interest, concern*) vivo(-a); **to be deep in thought/in a book** essere immerso(-a) nei propri pensieri/nella lettura ♦ ADV: **deep in her heart** in fondo al cuore; **to dig deep** scavare in profondità; **deep in the forest** nel cuore della foresta; **deep into the night** fino a tarda notte; **to be deep in debt** essere nei debiti fino al collo; **buried deep in snow** coperto(-a) da uno spesso strato di neve ♦ N: **the deep** (*liter*) il mare

deep·en [diːpən] VT (*hole, knowledge, understanding*) approfondire; (*sound, friendship, love*) rendere più profondo(-a); (*colour*) scurire; (*interest*) ravvivare; (*sorrow*) aggravare ♦ VI (*gen*) diventare più profondo(-a), approfondirsi; (*colour*) diventare più intenso(-a); (*mystery*) infittirsi; (*darkness*) farsi più intenso(-a)

deep-freeze [diːp'friːz] (*pt* **deep-froze**, *pp* **deep-frozen**) VT surgelare

deep-fry [ˌdiːp'fraɪ] VT friggere in olio abbondante

deep·ly ['diːplɪ] ADV (*breathe*) profondamente; (*dig*) in profondità; (*drink*) a gran sorsi; (*interested, concerned*) vivamente; (*moving*) estremamente; (*grateful, offended*) profondamente; **to regret sth deeply** rammaricarsi profondamente di qc; **to go deeply into sth** approfondire qc; **deeply depressed** estremamente depresso

deep-rooted [ˌdiːp'ruːtɪd] ADJ (*prejudice*) profondamente radicato(-a); (*affection*) profondo(-a); (*habit*) inveterato(-a)

deep-sea [ˌdiːp'siː] ADJ (*creatures, plants*) pelagico(-a), abissale; (*fisherman, fishing*) d'alto mare; **deep-sea diver** palombaro; **deep-sea diving** immersione *f* a grande profondità

deep-seated [ˌdiːp'siːtɪd] ADJ (*beliefs*) radicato(-a)

deep-set [ˌdiːp'sɛt] ADJ: **deep-set eyes** occhi *mpl* infossati

deep vein thrombosis N (*Med*) trombosi *f inv* venosa profonda

deer [dɪə'] N *pl inv* cervo(-a); **the deer family** la famiglia dei cervidi

deer·skin ['dɪəˌskɪn] N pelle *f* di daino

deer·stalker ['dɪəˌstɔːkə'] N (*hat*) berretto da cacciatore

de·face [dɪ'feɪs] VT (*wall, monument*) deturpare; (*work of art*) sfregiare; (*statue*) mutilare; (*poster*) imbrattare

defa·ma·tion [ˌdefə'meɪʃən] N (*frm*) diffamazione *f*

de·fama·tory [dɪ'fæmətərɪ] ADJ (*frm*) diffamatorio(-a)

de·fault [dɪ'fɔːlt] N 1 **by default** per esclusione; **he got the job by default** ha ottenuto il lavoro in assenza di altri candidati; **judgement by default** (*Law*) sentenza in contumacia; **to win by default** vincere per abbandono dell'avversario; **in default of** in mancanza di 2 (*Comput: also:* **default value**) default *m inv* ♦ VI (*gen*) essere inadempiente; (*Law: not appear*) non presentarsi in giudizio, essere contumace; (*: not pay*) risultare inadempiente; **to default on a debt** non onorare un debito

de·fault·er [dɪ'fɔːltə'] N (*on debt*) inadempiente *m/f*, debitore(-trice) moroso(-a); (*Law: at trial*) contumace *m/f*

default option N (*Comput*) opzione *f* di default

de·feat [dɪ'fiːt] N (*of army, team*) sconfitta; (*more serious*) disfatta; (*of ambition, plan*) fallimento, insuccesso ♦ VT (*army, team, opponent*) sconfiggere, battere; (*plan, ambition, efforts*) frustrare; (*Pol: party*) sconfiggere; (: *bill, amendment*) respingere; **she refused to let these problems defeat her** non ha voluto che i problemi prendessero il sopravvento su di lei; **to defeat one's own ends** far fallire i propri obiettivi

de·feat·ism [dɪ'fiːtɪzəm] N disfattismo

de·feat·ist [dɪ'fiːtɪst] N, ADJ disfattista *m/f*

def·ecate ['defəkeɪt] VI (*frm*) defecare

de·fect [*n* 'diːfɛkt, *vb* dɪ'fɛkt] N (*gen*) difetto ♦ VI (*from country*) scappare; (*from political party*) defezionare; **to defect to the enemy/the West** passare al nemico/all'Ovest

de·fec·tive [dɪ'fɛktɪv] ADJ (*machine, workmanship, eyesight*) difettoso(-a); (*system, reasoning*) cattivo(-a); (*Gram*) difettivo(-a); **to be defective in sth** mancare di qc

de·fec·tor [dɪ'fɛktə'] N fuor(i)uscito(-a); (*political*) rifugiato(-a) politico(-a)

de·fence, de·fense (*USA*) [dɪ'fɛns] N difesa; **in defence of** in difesa di; **in his defence** in sua difesa; **the Ministry of Defence**, (*Brit*) **the Department of Defense** (*USA*) il Ministero della Difesa; **the case for the defence** la difesa; **witness for the defence** teste *m/f* a difesa; **the body's defences against disease** le difese naturali dell'organismo contro la malattia; **as a defence against** per ripararsi da, come difesa contro ♦ ADJ (*policy, strategy*) di difesa; **defence spending** *spese per la difesa*

de·fence·less, de·fense·less (*USA*) [dɪ'fɛnslɪs] ADJ inerme, indifeso(-a), senza difesa

de·fend [dɪ'fɛnd] VT (*gen*) difendere; (*decision, action*) giustificare; (*opinion*) sostenere; **to defend o.s. (against)** difendersi (da)

de·fend·ant [dɪ'fɛndənt] N (*Law*) imputato(-a)

de·fend·er [dɪ'fɛndə'] N (*Sport*) difensore (difenditrice); (*of title*) detentore(-trice); **Defender of the Faith** (*Brit: title of monarch*) difensore *m* della fede

de·fend·ing [dɪ'fɛndɪŋ] ADJ: **defending champion** (*Sport*) campione(-essa) in carica; **defending counsel** (*Law*) avvocato difensore

de·fense [dɪ'fɛns] N (*USA*) = **defence**

de·fen·sive [dɪ'fɛnsɪv] ADJ (*weapon*) difensivo(-a); (*person*) sulla difensiva ♦ N: **on the defensive** sulla difensiva

de·fer [dɪ'fɜː'] VT (*postpone*) rimandare, rinviare; (*Law: case*) aggiornare ♦ VI (*submit*): **to defer to sb/sth** rimettersi a qn/qc; **to defer to sb's (greater) knowledge** rimettersi alla scienza di qn

def·er·ence ['defərəns] N deferenza, riguardo; **out of** *or* **in deference to** per riguardo a

de·fi·ance [dɪ'faɪəns] N (atteggiamento di) sfida; **in defiance of** a dispetto di; **in defiance of orders/the law** sfidando gli ordini/la legge; **his courageous defiance of the government** la sua coraggiosa sfida al governo

de·fi·ant [dɪ'faɪənt] ADJ (*person*) ribelle; (*tone, attitude*) di sfida; (*reply*) insolente

de·fi·ant·ly [dɪ'faɪəntlɪ] ADV con aria (*or* tono) di sfida

de·fi·cien·cy [dɪ'fɪʃənsɪ] N 1 (*of goods*) mancanza, insufficienza; (*of vitamins, minerals, protein*) carenza 2 (*in system, plan*) carenza

deficiency disease N malattia da carenza

de·fi·cient [dɪ'fɪʃənt] ADJ deficiente, insufficiente; **to be deficient in sth** mancare di qc

defi·cit ['defɪsɪt] N (*Fin*) deficit *m inv*, disavanzo; **to be in deficit** essere in deficit

de·file¹ [dɪ'faɪl] VT (*frm: pollute*) deturpare

de·file² ['diːfaɪl] N (*liter: passage*) gola ♦ VI (*march*) sfilare

de·fine [dɪ'faɪn] VT (*all senses*) precisare, definire; **the skyscraper was clearly defined against the sky** il grattacielo si stagliava nettamente contro il cielo; **to define a block of text** (*Comput*) definire un blocco di testo

defi·nite ['defɪnɪt] ADJ 1 (*exact, clear: date, plan, intention*) preciso(-a); (: *answer, agreement*) definitivo(-a); (*positive, decided: sale, order*) sicuro(-a); (: *tone, manner*) deciso(-a); **I**

haven't got any definite plans non ho un programma preciso; **is it definite that ...?** è sicuro che...?; **maybe we'll go to Spain, but it's not definite** forse andremo in Spagna, ma non è sicuro; **it's too soon to give a definite answer** è troppo presto per dare una risposta definitiva; **he was definite about it** (*certain*) ne era sicuro; (*unequivocal*) è stato chiaro al proposito **2** (*clearly noticeable*) netto(-a); **it's a definite improvement** è un netto miglioramento **3** (*Gram*): **past definite tense** passato remoto

defi·nite·ly [ˈdefɪnɪtlɪ] ADV (*certainly*) di sicuro, certamente; (*emphatically*: *state*) categoricamente; (*appreciably*: *better, worse*) decisamente; **he's definitely the best player** è decisamente il miglior giocatore; **yes, definitely!** sicuramente!; **definitely not!** no di certo!

defi·ni·tion [ˌdefɪˈnɪʃən] N (*Ling, Phot, TV*) definizione *f*

de·fini·tive [dɪˈfɪnɪtɪv] ADJ definitivo(-a)

de·flate [diːˈfleɪt] VT **1** (*tyre* or *tire*) sgonfiare; (*fig*: *person*) fare abbassare la cresta a **2** (*Econ*) deflazionare

de·fla·tion [diːˈfleɪʃən] N (*Econ*) deflazione *f*

de·fla·tion·ary [diːˈfleɪʃənərɪ] ADJ (*Econ*) deflazionistico(-a)

de·flect [dɪˈflekt] VT (*ball, bullet, attention, criticism*) (far) deviare; (*person*): **to deflect (from)** distogliere (da)

de·fog [diːˈfɒg] VT (*USA: Aut*) sbrinare

de·fog·ger [diːˈfɒgəʳ] N (*USA: Aut*) sbrinatore *m*

de·form [dɪˈfɔːm] VT deformare

de·formed [dɪˈfɔːmd] ADJ (*person, limb, body*) deforme; (*structure*) deformato(-a)

de·form·ity [dɪˈfɔːmɪtɪ] N (*of body*) deformità *f inv*

de·fraud [dɪˈfrɔːd] VT: **to defraud (of)** defraudare (di)

de·fray [dɪˈfreɪ] VT (*frm: expenses*) sostenere

de·friend [diːˈfrend] VT (*internet*) cancellare dagli amici

de·frost [diːˈfrɒst] VT (*refrigerator*) sbrinare; (*frozen food*) scongelare

deft [deft] ADJ (*comp* -**er**, *superl* -**est**) abile, destro(-a)

de·funct [dɪˈfʌŋkt] ADJ (*company*) scomparso(-a); (*scheme*) morto(-a) e sepolto(-a)

de·fuse [diːˈfjuːz] VT (*bomb*) disinnescare; **to defuse the situation** fare in modo che la situazione non degeneri; **to defuse tensions** allentare la tensione

defy [dɪˈfaɪ] VT **1** (*person*) rifiutare di obbedire a; (*authority, death, danger*) sfidare; (*resist: efforts*) resistere a; **thousands defied the ban** migliaia di persone si sono rifiutate di obbedire al divieto; **it defies description** supera ogni descrizione **2** (*challenge*): **to defy sb (to do sth)** sfidare qn (a fare qc); **I defy you to find a single advantage in the scheme** ti sfido a trovare anche un solo vantaggio nel programma

de·gen·er·ate [*vb* dɪˈdʒenəˌreɪt, *adj, n* dɪˈdʒenərɪt] VI: **to degenerate (into)** degenerare (in) ♦ ADJ (*person*) degenere; (*morals, art*) degenerato(-a) ♦ N degenerato(-a)

deg·ra·da·tion [ˌdegrəˈdeɪʃən] N degradazione *f*

de·grade [dɪˈgreɪd] VT degradare

de·grad·ing [dɪˈgreɪdɪŋ] ADJ degradante, umiliante

de·gree [dɪˈgriː] N **1** (*gen, also Math, Geog*) grado; **10 degrees below freezing** 10 gradi sotto zero; **a temperature of thirty degrees** una temperatura di trenta gradi **2** (*amount*): **a high degree of uncertainty** un largo margine d'incertezza; **a considerable degree of risk** una grossa percentuale di rischio **3** (*step in scale*): **by degrees** a poco a poco, gradualmente; **to some degree, to a certain degree** in certa misura, fino a un certo punto **4** (*Univ*) ≈ laurea; **first degree** ≈ laurea; **honorary degree** ≈ laurea ad honorem; **to get one's degree** = prendere la laurea, laurearsi; **I'm doing a degree in languages** sono iscritto a lingue; **a (first) degree in math(s)** ≈ una laurea in matematica

de·hy·dra·ted [diːhaɪˈdreɪtɪd] ADJ (*person, vegetables*) disidratato(-a); (*milk, eggs*) in polvere

de·hy·dra·tion [ˌdiːhaɪˈdreɪʃən] N disidratazione *f*

de-ice [diːˈaɪs] VT (*car windows*) sbrinare; (*roads*) liberare dal ghiaccio

de-icer [ˈdiːˈaɪsəʳ] N (*thermal*) sbrinatore *m*; (*chemical*) scongelante *m*

deign [deɪn] VT: **to deign to do sth** degnarsi di fare qc

de·ity [ˈdiːɪtɪ] N divinità *f inv*, dio (dea); **the Deity** la Divinità, Dio

déjà vu [ˌdeɪʒɑːˈvuː] N déjà vu *m inv*; **a feeling** or **sense of déjà vu** una sensazione di déjà vu

de·ject·ed [dɪˈdʒektɪd] ADJ abbattuto(-a), avvilito(-a); **to become dejected** abbattersi

de·jec·tion [dɪˈdʒekʃən] N abbattimento, avvilimento

Del. ABBR (*USA*: = **Delaware**)

De·la·ware [ˈdeləweəʳ] il Delaware

de·lay [dɪˈleɪ] N ritardo; **a delay of twenty minutes** un ritardo di venti minuti; **without delay** immediatamente; **without further delay** senza ulteriore indugio; **delays to traffic** rallentamenti *mpl* al traffico ♦ VT (*postpone: journey*) rimandare, rinviare; (: *payment*) differire; (*hold up: person*) trattenere; (: *traffic*) far rallentare; (: *action, event*) ritardare; **we decided to delay our departure** decidemmo di rimandare la partenza; **his train must have been delayed** il suo treno avrà fatto ritardo; **our flight was delayed** il nostro volo ha subito un ritardo; **don't delay!** non perdere tempo! ♦ VI: **to delay (doing sth)** ritardare (a fare qc)

delayed-action [dɪˌleɪdˈækʃən] ADJ (*Phot: shutter*) ad azione ritardata; **delayed-action bomb** ordigno a scoppio ritardato

de·lec·table [dɪˈlektəbl] ADJ delizioso(-a)

del·egate [*n* ˈdelɪgɪt, *vb* ˈdelɪgeɪt] N: **delegate (to)** delegato(-a) al ♦ VT (*duties, responsiblities, power*) delegare; **to delegate sth to sb** delegare qc a qn; **to delegate sb to do sth** delegare qn a fare qc

del·ega·tion [ˌdelɪˈgeɪʃən] N **1** (*of work, power*) delega **2** (*group*) delegazione *f*

de·lete [dɪˈliːt] VT (*gen, also Comput*) cancellare; **to delete (from)** (*item: from list, catalogue*) togliere (da); (*mistake, line*) cancellare (da)

Del·hi [ˈdelɪ] N Delhi *f*

deli [ˈdelɪ] N ABBR (*fam: shop*: = **delicatessen**) gastronomia

de·lib·er·ate [*adj* dɪˈlɪbərɪt, *vb* dɪˈlɪbəˌreɪt] ADJ **1** (*intentional: insult, action*) intenzionale, voluto(-a); (: *mistake*) voluto(-a); (: *lie*) calcolato(-a) **2** (*cautious, thoughtful*) ponderato(-a); (*unhurried: manner, voice*) posato(-a); (*pace*) misurato(-a) ♦ VT (*think about*) considerare, riflettere su; (*discuss*) discutere ♦ VI: **to deliberate (on)** deliberare (su)

de·lib·er·ate·ly [dɪˈlɪbərɪtlɪ] ADV (*intentionally*) deliberatamente, volutamente; (*cautiously, slowly*) posatamente

de·lib·era·tion [dɪˌlɪbəˈreɪʃən] N **1** (*consideration*) riflessione *f*; (*discussion*) discussione *f*, deliberazione *f*; **after due deliberation** dopo matura riflessione **2** (*slowness*) ponderatezza, posatezza

deli·ca·cy [ˈdelɪkəsɪ] N **1** (*of person, thing*) delicatezza; (*of workmanship*) finezza **2** (*special food*) specialità *f inv*, ghiottoneria; **local delicacies** specialità locali

deli·cate [ˈdelɪkɪt] ADJ (*gen*) delicato(-a); (*workmanship, design*) fine

deli·cate·ly [ˈdelɪkɪtlɪ] ADV (*gen*) delicatamente; (*act, express*) con delicatezza

deli·ca·tes·sen [ˌdelɪkəˈtesn] N ≈ salumeria

de·li·cious [dɪˈlɪʃəs] ADJ delizioso(-a), squisito(-a)

de·light [dɪˈlaɪt] N (*feeling of joy*) piacere *m*, gioia; (*pleasurable thing*) delizia, (*gran*) piacere *m*; **the delights of good food** i piaceri della buona tavola; **to my delight** con mia grande gioia; **it is a delight to the eye** è un piacere guardarlo; **to take delight in sth** dilettarsi di qc; **to take delight in doing sth** divertirsi a fare qc; **to be the delight of** essere la gioia di ♦ VT riempire di gioia

▸ **delight in** + PREP: **to delight in sth/in doing sth** dilettarsi di qc/nel fare qc

de·light·ed [dɪˈlaɪtɪd] ADJ (*person, place, meal*) delizioso(-a); (*manner, smile*) incantevole; **thank you for a delightful evening** grazie per l'incantevole serata

de·limit [diːˈlɪmɪt] VT (*frm*) delimitare

de·lin·eate [dɪˈlɪnɪˌeɪt] VT (*frm*) delineare

de·lin·quen·cy [dɪˈlɪŋkwənsɪ] N delinquenza

de·lin·quent [dɪˈlɪŋkwənt] ADJ (*behaviour*) delinquenziale, da delinquente; **a delinquent youth** un giovane delinquente ♦ N delinquente *m/f*

de·liri·ous [dɪ'lɪrɪəs] ADJ (*Med, also fig*) delirante, in delirio; **to be delirious** delirare; (*fig*) farneticare; **delirious with joy** pazzo(-a) di gioia

de·lir·ium [dɪ'lɪrɪəm] N (*Med*) delirio; **delirium tremens** delirium *m inv* tremens, *inv*

de·liv·er [dɪ'lɪvə'] VT **1** (*goods*) consegnare; (*letter, parcel*) recapitare, consegnare; **they delivered the parcel this morning** mi hanno consegnato il pacco stamattina; **he delivered me home safely** mi ha portato a casa sano e salvo; **to deliver a message** dare un messaggio; **he delivered the goods** (*fig: fam*) ha fatto quel che doveva fare **2** (*speech, sermon, verdict*) pronunciare; (*lecture*) tenere, fare; (*ultimatum*) dare; (*blow, punch*) tirare **3** (*subj: doctor, midwife: baby*) far nascere **4** (*old: rescue*): **to deliver (from)** liberare (da)

de·liv·er·ance [dɪ'lɪvərəns] N (*old*) liberazione *f*

de·liv·ery [dɪ'lɪvərɪ] N **1** (*of goods, parcels*) consegna; (*of mail*) recapito; **allow 28 days for delivery** calcola 28 giorni per la consegna; **there is no delivery on Sundays** (*Post*) non c'è posta la domenica; **to take delivery of** prendere in consegna **2** (*of speaker*) dizione *f* **3** (*Med*) parto

delivery note N bolla di consegna

delivery van, (*USA*) **delivery truck** N furgoncino (per le consegne)

del·ta ['dɛltə] N delta *m inv*

de·lude [dɪ'luːd] VT illudere, ingannare; **to delude sb into thinking that ...** indurre qn a credere che...; **to delude o.s** illudersi, farsi (delle) illusioni

   ❏ **delude** is not translated by the Italian word *deludere*

del·uge ['dɛljuːdʒ] N diluvio; **a deluge of protests** un diluvio di proteste ♦ VT (*fig*): **to deluge (with)** subissare (di), inondare (di)

de·lu·sion [dɪ'luːʒən] N illusione *f*; (*Psych*) fissazione *f*

   ❏ **delusion** is not translated by the Italian word *delusione*

de·luxe [dɪ'lʌks] ADJ di lusso

delve [dɛlv] VI: **to delve into** (*pocket, bag*) frugare in; (*subject*) far ricerche in

Dem.(*USA Pol*) N ABBR = **Democrat** ♦ ADJ = **Democratic**

dema·gogue ['dɛməgɒg] N (*pej*) demagogo

de·mand [dɪ'mɑːnd] VT **1** (*request*): **demand (for)** (*help, money*) richiesta (di); (*better pay*) richiesta (di), rivendicazione *f* (di); **by popular demand** a richiesta generale; **on demand** su richiesta; **I have many demands on my time** sono impegnatissimo **2** (*Comm*): **demand (for)** domanda (di); **to be in demand** essere richiesto(-a) ♦ VT (*ask for*): **to demand sth (from or of sb)** pretendere qc (da qn), esigere qc (da qn); (*need*) richiedere; **to demand that** richiedere che + *sub*; **I demand an explanation** pretendo una spiegazione; **I demand to see the manager** esigo di vedere il direttore

   ❏ **demand** is not translated by the Italian word *domandare*

demand draft N (*Comm*) tratta a vista

de·mand·ing [dɪ'mɑːndɪŋ] ADJ (*person*) esigente; (*work: physically*) stancante; (: *mentally*) impegnativo(-a); **a demanding child** un bambino esigente; **it's a very demanding job** è un lavoro molto impegnativo

de·mar·ca·tion [ˌdiːmɑː'keɪʃən] N (*frm*) demarcazione *f*; **demarcation dispute** controversia settoriale *or* di categoria; **demarcation line** linea di demarcazione

de·mean [dɪ'miːn] VT svilire; **to demean o.s** abbassarsi

de·mean·our, de·mean·or (*USA*) [dɪ'miːnə'] N (*frm*) contegno

de·ment·ed [dɪ'mɛntɪd] ADJ folle, demente

de·mili·ta·rized zone [diː'mɪlɪtəˌraɪzd'zəʊn] N zona smilitarizzata

de·mise [dɪ'maɪz] N (*frm*) decesso

de·mist [diː'mɪst] VT (*Brit: Aut*) sbrinare

de·mist·er [diː'mɪstə'] N (*Brit: Aut*) sbrinatore *m*

demo ['dɛməʊ] N ABBR (*fam*) **1** (*Brit: demonstration*) manifestazione *f* **2** (*of music*) demo *f inv* **3** (*Comput: software*) demo *f inv*

de·mo·bi·lize [diː'məʊbɪlaɪz] VT smobilitare

de·moc·ra·cy [dɪ'mɒkrəsɪ] N democrazia

demo·crat ['dɛməˌkræt] N **1** democratico(-a) **2** **Democrat** (*USA Pol*) democratico(-a)

demo·crat·ic [ˌdɛmə'krætɪk] ADJ **1** democratico(-a) **2** **Democratic** (*USA Pol*) democratico(-a)

de·mog·ra·phy [dɪ'mɒgrəfɪ] N demografia

de·mol·ish [dɪ'mɒlɪʃ] VT (*gen*) demolire; (*hum: cake, food*) far fuori

demo·li·tion [ˌdɛmə'lɪʃən] N demolizione *f*; **demolition zone** area *or* zona di demolizione

de·mon ['diːmən] N (*also fig*) demonio ♦ ADJ: **a demon squash player** un mago dello squash; **a demon driver** un asso del volante

dem·on·strate ['dɛmənˌstreɪt] VT **1** (*truth, ability*) dimostrare; (*emotion*) manifestare; **you have to demonstrate that you are reliable** devi dimostrare di essere affidabile **2** (*appliance*) fare una dimostrazione di; **she demonstrated the technique** ha fatto una dimostrazione della tecnica ♦ VI (*Pol*): **to demonstrate (for/against)** manifestare (per/contro); **they demonstrated outside the court** hanno manifestato fuori dal tribunale

dem·on·stra·tion [ˌdɛmən'streɪʃən] N dimostrazione *f*; (*Pol*) manifestazione *f*; **to hold a demonstration** (*Pol*) tenere una manifestazione

de·mon·stra·tive [dɪ'mɒnstrətɪv] ADJ (*person*) espansivo(-a); (*Gram*) dimostrativo(-a)

de·mon·stra·tor ['dɛmənstreɪtə'] N (*Pol*) dimostrante *m/f*; (*Comm: sales person*) dimostratore(-trice); (: *USA: car, computer*) modello per dimostrazione

de·mor·al·ize [dɪ'mɒrəˌlaɪz] VT demoralizzare

de·mote [dɪ'məʊt] VT degradare

de·mo·tion [dɪ'məʊʃən] N degradazione *f*

de·mur [dɪ'mɜː'] VI (*frm*): **to demur (at)** sollevare obiezioni (a *or* su) ♦ N: **without demur** senza obiezioni

de·mure [dɪ'mjʊə'] ADJ pieno(-a) di contegno; (*smile*) contegnoso(-a)

de·mur·rage [dɪ'mʌrɪdʒ] N (*Comm*) controstallia

den [dɛn] N (*of wild animal*) tana, covo; (*room*) stanzetta; **a lion's den** la tana di un leone; **he's up in his den reading** è su in camera sua a leggere; **a den of iniquity** un luogo di perdizione; **a den of thieves** un covo di ladri

de·na·tion·ali·za·tion [ˈdiːˌnæʃnəlaɪ'zeɪʃən] N snazionalizzazione *f*, denazionalizzazione *f*

de·na·tion·al·ize [diːˈnæʃnəˌlaɪz] VT snazionalizzare, denazionalizzare

de·ni·al [dɪ'naɪəl] N **1** (*of accusation, guilt*) diniego, rifiuto; **the government issued an official denial** il governo ha rilasciato una smentita ufficiale; **to be in denial** non accettare la realtà **2** (*refusal: of request*) rifiuto; (: *of rights*) mancato riconoscimento

den·ier ['dɛnɪə'] N denaro (*di filati, calze*)

deni·grate ['dɛnɪˌgreɪt] VT denigrare

den·im ['dɛnɪm] N tessuto jeans; **denims** NPL (*clothes*) blue jeans *mpl* ♦ ADJ (*jacket, skirt*) di jeans; **a denim jacket** una giacca di jeans

deni·zen ['dɛnɪzn] N (*liter: inhabitant*) abitante *m/f*

Den·mark ['dɛnmɑːk] N Danimarca

de·nomi·na·tion [dɪˌnɒmɪ'neɪʃən] N (*Rel*) confessione *f*; (*of coin*) valore *m*; **bank notes in small denominations** banconote di piccolo taglio

de·nomi·na·tor [dɪ'nɒmɪˌneɪtə'] N (*Math*) denominatore *m*

de·note [dɪ'nəʊt] VT (*indicate*) denotare, indicare; (*subj: word*) significare

de·nounce [dɪ'naʊns] VT (*accuse publicly*) accusare; (*to police*) denunciare; **to denounce sb as a liar** accusare pubblicamente qn di essere un bugiardo

dense [dɛns] ADJ (*comp* -**r**, *superl* -**st**) (*fog*) denso(-a), fitto(-a); (*forest, crowd*) fitto(-a); (*fur*) folto(-a); (*fam: person: stupid*) tonto(-a), ottuso(-a); **dense smoke prevented firefighters from entering the building** un fumo denso impedìva ai pompieri di entrare; **he's so dense!** è così ottuso!

dense·ly ['dɛnslɪ] ADV: **densely populated** densamente popolato(-a); **densely wooded** coperto(-a) di fitti boschi

den·sity ['dɛnsɪtɪ] N densità *f inv*; **single-/double-density disk** (*Comput*) disco a singola/doppia densità

dent [dɛnt] N (*in metal*) ammaccatura, bozzo; (*in wood*) tacca,

intaccatura; **to make a dent in** (*fig*) intaccare; **the holiday left a dent in our savings** la vacanza ha intaccato i nostri risparmi ♦ vt (*car, hat*) ammaccare; (*fig*) intaccare
❏ **dent** is not translated by the Italian word *dente*

den·tal [ˈdɛntl] ADJ (*surgery, care*) dentistico(-a), odontoiatrico(-a); (*appointment*) dal dentista; **dental treatment** cure dentistiche; **dental orthopaedics** ortodonzia; **dental technician** odontotecnico

dental floss N filo interdentale

dental surgeon N medico dentista *m/f*, odontoiatra *m/f*

den·tist [ˈdɛntɪst] N dentista *m/f*; **dentist's chair** poltrona del dentista

den·tis·try [ˈdɛntɪstrɪ] N odontoiatria

den·tures [ˈdɛntʃəz] NPL (*false teeth*) dentiera

de·nun·cia·tion [dɪˌnʌnsɪˈeɪʃən] N denuncia; (*in public*) pubblica accusa

deny [dɪˈnaɪ] vt 1 (*possibility, truth of statement, charge*) negare; (*report*) smentire; **there's no denying it** è innegabile; **he denies having said it** nega di averlo detto 2 (*refuse*): **to deny sb sth** negare qc a qn, rifiutare qc a qn; **to deny o.s. sth** negarsi qc, privarsi di qc

de·odor·ant [diːˈəʊdərənt] N deodorante *m*

de·part [dɪˈpɑːt] vi: **to depart (from)** (*train*) partire (da); (*person*) andar via (da), allontanarsi (da); **to depart from tradition/the truth** scostarsi dalla tradizione/dalla verità

de·part·ed [dɪˈpɑːtɪd] ADJ (*bygone: glory*) trascorso(-a), passato(-a); (*dead*) scomparso(-a) ♦ N: **the dear departed** il (la) caro(-a) estinto(-a)

de·part·ment [dɪˈpɑːtmənt] N (*Admin*) sezione *f*, reparto; (*in shop*) reparto; (*in government*) ministero; (*Univ*) istituto, dipartimento; **the English Department** (*in school*) i professori di inglese; (*in university*) l'istituto di inglese; **the toy department** il reparto giocattoli; **that's not my department** (*fig*) questo non è di mia competenza; **Department of State** (*USA*) Dipartimento di Stato

de·part·men·tal [ˌdiːpɑːtˈmentl] ADJ (*meeting*) di sezione; **departmental manager** caporeparto *m/f*

department store N grande magazzino

de·par·ture [dɪˈpɑːtʃə] N (*gen*) partenza; (*fig: from custom, principle*): **departure from** deviazione *f* da, abbandono di; **after his departure** dopo la sua partenza; **a new departure** (*fig*) una svolta (decisiva); **departure board** (*Aer*) tabellone *m* (delle partenze); **departure lounge** (*Aer*) sala d'attesa

de·pend [dɪˈpend] vi 1 **to depend (up)on** (*rely*) contare su, dipendere da; (*be dependent on*) dipendere (economicamente) da, essere a carico di; **you can depend on it** sta pur certo 2 **to depend (on)** (*be influenced by*) dipendere (da); **it (all) depends on the weather** (tutto) dipende dal tempo; **it (all) depends what you mean** dipende da che cosa vuoi dire; **that depends, it depends** dipende; **depending on a** seconda di; **depending on the result ...** a seconda del risultato...

de·pend·able [dɪˈpendəbl] ADJ (*person*) fidato(-a), serio(-a); (*machine, car*) affidabile

de·pend·ant [dɪˈpendənt] N persona a carico

de·pend·ence [dɪˈpendəns] N: **dependence (on)** dipendenza (da)

de·pend·ent [dɪˈpendənt] ADJ: **to be dependent (on)** (*gen*) dipendere (da); (*child, relative*) essere a carico (di); **psychologically he's dependent on her** psicologicamente dipende da lei ♦ N = **dependant**

de·pict [dɪˈpɪkt] vt (*in picture*) rappresentare; (*in words*) descrivere, dipingere; **a picture depicting a sunset** un quadro che raffigura un tramonto; **he was depicted as a lonely old man** era descritto come un vecchio solitario

de·pila·tory [dɪˈpɪlətərɪ] N (*also*: **depilatory cream**) crema depilatoria

de·plet·ed [dɪˈpliːtɪd] ADJ diminuito(-a); **depleted uranium** uranio impoverito

de·plor·able [dɪˈplɔːrəbl] ADJ (*frm*) deplorevole, lamentevole; **this deplorable incident** questo deplorevole incidente

de·plore [dɪˈplɔː] vt (*frm*) deplorare

de·ploy [dɪˈplɔɪ] vt (*Mil: soldiers, forces*) schierare, spiegare; (*fig: resources*) impiegare, far uso di

de·popu·late [diːˈpɒpjuleɪt] vt spopolare

de·popu·la·tion [diːˌpɒpjʊˈleɪʃən] N spopolamento

de·port [dɪˈpɔːt] vt deportare

de·por·ta·tion [ˌdiːpɔːˈteɪʃən] N deportazione *f*; **deportation order** ≈ foglio di via obbligatorio

de·por·tee [ˌdiːpɔːˈtiː] N deportato(-a)

de·port·ment [dɪˈpɔːtmənt] N (*old: bearing*) portamento; (*: behaviour*) comportamento

de·pose [dɪˈpəʊz] vt (*monarch, leader*) deporre

de·pos·it [dɪˈpɒzɪt] N 1 (*in bank*) deposito; (*Comm: part payment*) acconto; (*: returnable security*) cauzione *f*; **to put down a deposit of £50** versare un acconto di 50 sterline; **you get the deposit back when you return the bike** quando riporti la bici ti ridanno la cauzione 2 (*Chem, Geol*) deposito, sedimento; (*of ore, oil*) giacimento ♦ vt 1 (*put down*) posare; (*leave: luggage*) mettere *or* lasciare in deposito, depositare 2 (*money: in bank*) depositare

deposit account N ≈ libretto di risparmio

de·posi·tor [dɪˈpɒzɪtə] N depositante *m/f*

de·posi·tory [dɪˈpɒzɪtərɪ] N 1 (*place*) deposito 2 (*person*) depositario(-a)

de·pot [ˈdepəʊ, (*USA*) ˈdiːpəʊ] N (*storehouse*) magazzino, deposito *m* merci, *inv*; (*Brit: bus garage*) deposito; (*USA: railway station*) stazione *f* ferroviaria; (*: bus station*) stazione *f* degli autobus; **an arms depot** un deposito di armi

de·praved [dɪˈpreɪvd] ADJ (*frm*) depravato(-a)

de·prav·ity [dɪˈprævɪtɪ] N (*frm*) depravazione *f*

dep·re·cate [ˈdeprɪkeɪt] vt (*frm*) deprecare

dep·re·cat·ing [ˈdeprɪkeɪtɪŋ], **dep·re·ca·tory** [ˈdeprɪkətərɪ] ADJ (*disapproving*) di biasimo, di disapprovazione; (*apologetic*): **a deprecating smile** un sorriso di scusa

de·pre·ci·ate [dɪˈpriːʃɪeɪt] vi deprezzarsi, svalutarsi ♦ vt deprezzare, svalutare

de·pre·cia·tion [dɪˌpriːʃɪˈeɪʃən] N deprezzamento, svalutazione *f*

de·press [dɪˈpres] vt 1 (*person*) deprimere; (*spirits*) buttar giù 2 (*trade*) ridurre; (*prices*) far scendere, abbassare 3 (*frm: press down: lever*) abbassare

de·pres·sant [dɪˈpresnt] N (*Med*) sedativo

de·pressed [dɪˈprest] ADJ 1 (*person*) depresso(-a); **to feel depressed** sentirsi depresso(-a); **to get depressed** deprimersi 2 (*area*) depresso(-a); (*industry*) in crisi; (*Fin: market, trade*) stagnante, in ribasso

de·press·ing [dɪˈpresɪŋ] ADJ deprimente, demoralizzante

de·pres·sion [dɪˈpreʃən] N (*gen, also Med, Econ, Met*) depressione *f*; **the economy is in a state of depression** è in atto una crisi economica; **the Depression** la Grande depressione

dep·ri·va·tion [ˌdeprɪˈveɪʃən] N (*act*) privazione *f*; (*state*) indigenza

de·prive [dɪˈpraɪv] vt: **to deprive sb of sth** privare qn di qc; **to deprive o.s. of sth** privarsi di qc

de·prived [dɪˈpraɪvd] ADJ bisognoso(-a)

dept. ABBR = **department**

depth [depθ] N (*gen: of knowledge, thought*) profondità *f inv*; (*of snow*) altezza, spessore *m*; (*of shelf*) profondità, larghezza; (*of colour, feeling*) intensità *f inv*; **at a depth of 3 metres** a 3 metri di profondità, a una profondità di 3 metri; **the depths of the sea** gli abissi del mare; **to be out of one's depth** (*swimmer*) non toccare; (*fig*) non sentirsi all'altezza della situazione; **in the depths of the forest** nel cuore della foresta; **in the depths of winter** in pieno inverno, nel cuore dell'inverno; **in the depths of despair** in preda alla disperazione; **to study sth in depth** studiare qc in profondità

depth charge N (*Mil*) bomba di profondità

depu·ta·tion [ˌdepjʊˈteɪʃən] N deputazione *f*, delegazione *f*

depu·tize [ˈdepjʊtaɪz] vi: **to deputize (for sb)** fare le veci (di qn), sostituire (qn)

depu·ty [ˈdepjʊtɪ] N (*second-in-command*) vice *m/f*; (*replacement*) sostituto(-a), supplente *m/f* ♦ ADJ: **deputy chairman** vicepresidente *m*; **deputy head** (*Scol*) vicepreside *m/f*; **deputy leader** (*Brit Pol*) sottosegretario; **deputy secretary** vicesegretario

de·rail [dɪˈreɪl] vt far deragliare; **to be derailed** deragliare

de·rail·ment [dɪˈreɪlmənt] N deragliamento

de·ranged [dɪˈreɪndʒd] ADJ (*mind*) sconvolto(-a); (*person*) squilibrato(-a)

der·by [ˈdɑːbɪ] N **1** (*sporting event*) derby *m inv* **2** (*USA: hat*) bombetta

de·regu·late [dɪˈrɛɡjʊˌleɪt] VT deregolamentare

de·regu·la·tion [dɪˌrɛɡjʊˈleɪʃən] N deregolamentazione *f*

der·elict [ˈdɛrɪlɪkt] ADJ (*ruined*) cadente, fatiscente; (*abandoned*) abbandonato(-a) ♦ N (*frm: person*) derelitto(-a)

de·ride [dɪˈraɪd] VT deridere

de·ri·sion [dɪˈrɪʒən] N derisione *f*

de·ri·sive [dɪˈraɪsɪv] ADJ (*laughter*) di scherno, di derisione; (*smile*) beffardo(-a)

de·ri·sory [dɪˈraɪsərɪ] ADJ **1** (*amount*) irrisorio(-a) **2** = **derisive**

deri·va·tion [ˌdɛrɪˈveɪʃən] N derivazione *f*

de·riva·tive [dɪˈrɪvətɪv] ADJ (*pej: literary work, style*) poco originale ♦ N (*Chem, Ling*) derivato; (*Math*) derivata

de·rive [dɪˈraɪv] VT: **to derive (from)** (*profit, comfort, pleasure*) ricavare (da), trarre (da); (*name*) derivare (da); (*origins*) trarre (da) ♦ VI: **to derive from** (*subj: word, language*) derivare da; (*: power, fortune*) provenire da

der·ma·ti·tis [ˌdɜːməˈtaɪtɪs] N dermatite *f*

der·ma·tol·ogy [ˌdɜːməˈtɒlədʒɪ] N dermatologia

de·roga·tory [dɪˈrɒɡətərɪ] ADJ (*remark*) denigratorio(-a); (*term*) spregiativo(-a)

der·rick [ˈdɛrɪk] N (*in port*) albero di carico, gru *f inv*; (*over oil well*) derrick *m inv*

de·sali·na·tion [diːˌsælɪˈneɪʃən] N desalinizzazione *f*, dissalazione *f*

de·scend [dɪˈsɛnd] VT **1** (*frm: stairs*) scendere **2 to be descended from sb** (*Genealogy*) discendere da qn ♦ VI **1** (*go down*): **to descend (from)** (di)scendere (da); (*road*) scendere (da); **we descended to the cellar** scendemmo in cantina; **in descending order of importance** in ordine decrescente d'importanza **2** (*property, customs*): **to descend from ... to** passare da...a; **to descend from generation to generation** tramandarsi di generazione in generazione

▸ **descend on, descend upon** VI + PREP (*subj: enemy, large group, angry person*) assalire, piombare su, invadere; (*liter: gloom, silence*) scendere su; **hordes of tourists descend on the village every summer** il paese è invaso ogni estate da orde di turisti; **visitors descended on us** ci sono capitati ospiti inaspettati

▸ **descend to** VI + PREP (*lower o. s. to*): **to descend to sth** abbassarsi a qc; **to descend to doing sth** abbassarsi a fare qc

de·scend·ant [dɪˈsɛndənt] N discendente *m/f*

de·scent [dɪˈsɛnt] N (*going down*) discesa; (*ancestry*): **descent (from)** discendenza (da), origine *f* (da)

de·scribe [dɪsˈkraɪb] VT descrivere; **describe him for us** descrivicelo

de·scrip·tion [dɪsˈkrɪpʃən] N **1** (*of person, scene, object*) descrizione *f*; (*of event*) racconto; (*of suspect*) connotati *mpl*, descrizione; **beyond description** oltre ogni dire **2** (*sort*) genere *m*, specie *f*; **of every description** di ogni genere e specie

de·scrip·tive [dɪsˈkrɪptɪv] ADJ descrittivo(-a)

des·ecrate [ˈdɛsɪˌkreɪt] VT profanare

des·ert [ˈdɛzət] N deserto ♦ ADJ (*climate, region*) desertico(-a)

de·sert [dɪˈzɜːt] VT abbandonare, lasciare; **his courage deserted him** il coraggio l'ha abbandonato; **her husband deserted her** suo marito l'ha abbandonata ♦ VI (*Mil*): **to desert (from)** disertare (da); **to desert (to)** passare (a)

de·sert·ed [dɪˈzɜːtɪd] ADJ (*streets*) deserto(-a); (*husband/wife*) abbandonato(-a)

de·sert·er [dɪˈzɜːtəʳ] N (*Mil*) disertore *m*

de·ser·tion [dɪˈzɜːʃən] N (*Mil*) diserzione *f*; (*of spouse*) abbandono del tetto coniugale

desert island [ˌdɛzətˈaɪlənd] N isola deserta

de·serts [dɪˈzɜːts] NPL: **to get one's just deserts** avere ciò che ci si merita

de·serve [dɪˈzɜːv] VT meritare; **he deserves to win** merita di vincere; **he got what he deserved** ha avuto quel che si meritava

de·serv·ed·ly [dɪˈzɜːvɪdlɪ] ADV meritatamente, giustamente

de·serv·ing [dɪˈzɜːvɪŋ] ADJ (*person, case, cause*) che merita aiuto; (*praiseworthy*) meritevole; **deserving of** degno(-a) di; **an idea deserving of consideration** un'idea degna di considerazione; **a crime deserving of severe punishment** un delitto che merita una severa punizione

des·ic·ca·ted [ˈdɛsɪˌkeɪtɪd] ADJ essiccato(-a); **desiccated coconut** noce *f* di cocco essiccata

de·sign [dɪˈzaɪn] N **1** (*plan, drawing: of building*) progetto, disegno; (*: of dress, car*) modello; (*: of machine*) progettazione *f*; (*style*) linea, design *m inv*; (*pattern*) disegno, fantasia, motivo; (*art of design*) design *m*; **a new design of lawnmower** un nuovo modello di tagliaerba; **the design of the plane makes it safer** il design rende più sicuro l'aereo; **a design fault** un difetto di progettazione; **dress with a floral design** vestito a fiori; **a geometric design** un disegno geometrico; **industrial design** disegno industriale **2** (*intention*) intenzione *f*; **by design** intenzionalmente, di proposito; **to have designs on sb/sth** avere delle mire su qn/qc ♦ VT **1** (*building etc*) disegnare; (*Industry*) progettare; (*perfect crime, scheme*) concepire, elaborare; **she designed the dress herself** ha disegnato lei stessa il vestito; **we will design an exercise plan specially for you** elaboreremo un programma di esercizi apposta per te **2** (*intend*): **to be designed for sb/sth** espressamente per qn/qc; **a well designed house** una casa progettata bene

des·ig·nate [*vb* ˈdɛzɪɡˌneɪt, *adj* ˈdɛzɪɡnɪt] VT: **to designate sb/sth (as)** designare qn/qc (come); **to designate sb to do sth** designare qn a fare qc ♦ ADJ (*after n*) designato(-a)

des·ig·na·tion [ˌdɛzɪɡˈneɪʃən] N (*title*) titolo, designazione *f*

de·sign·er [dɪˈzaɪnəʳ] N (*fashion designer*) stilista *m/f*, disegnatore(-trice) di moda; (*of machines etc*) disegnatore(-trice), progettista *m/f*; (*of furniture*) designer *m/f inv*; (*of theatre sets*) scenografo(-a); **designer clothes** abiti firmati; **a furniture designer** un designer di mobili

de·sir·abil·ity [dɪˌzaɪərəˈbɪlɪtɪ] N (*allure*) desiderabilità; (*value*) vantaggio

de·sir·able [dɪˈzaɪərəbl] ADJ (*woman, man*) desiderabile; (*house, job*) attraente; (*offer*) vantaggioso(-a); **it is desirable that** è opportuno che + *sub*; **desirable qualities** qualità auspicabili

de·sire [dɪˈzaɪəʳ] N desiderio, voglia; (*sexual*) desiderio; **desire (for/to do sth)** desiderio (di/di fare qc); **I have no desire to see him** non ho nessuna voglia di vederlo ♦ VT (*person*) desiderare; **to desire sth/to do sth/that** desiderare qc/di fare qc/che + *sub*; **it leaves much to be desired** lascia molto a desiderare

de·sir·ous [dɪˈzaɪərəs] ADJ (*frm*): **desirous (of)** desideroso(-a) (di)

desk [dɛsk] N (*in office*) scrivania; (*Scol: in hotel, at airport*) banco; (*Brit: in shop, restaurant*) cassa; **desk diary** agenda da tavolo; **desk job** lavoro d'ufficio; **desk lamp** lampada da tavolo

desk·top, desk-top [ˈdɛsktɒp] N (*Comput: icons*) desktop *m inv*

desk·top com·put·er [ˌdɛskˌtɒp kəmˈpjuːtəʳ] N (computer) desk top *m inv*

deso·late [ˈdɛsəlɪt] ADJ (*place*) desolato(-a), deserto(-a); (*building*) abbandonato(-a); (*outlook, future*) nero(-a); (*person: grief-stricken*) affranto(-a) (dal dolore), desolato(-a); (*: friendless*) abbandonato(-a) da tutti

deso·la·tion [ˌdɛsəˈleɪʃən] N (*bleakness, grief*) desolazione *f*; (*liter: devastation*) devastazione *f*

des·pair [dɪsˈpɛəʳ] N disperazione *f*; **in despair** disperato(-a); **to drive sb to despair** far disperare qn ♦ VI: **to despair (of)** disperare (di); **don't despair!** non disperare!

des·patch [dɪsˈpætʃ] N, VT = **dispatch**

des·per·ate [ˈdɛspərɪt] ADJ (*gen*) disperato(-a); (*criminal*) capace di tutto; (*measures*) estremo(-a); **a desperate situation** una situazione disperata; **we are getting desperate** siamo sull'orlo della disperazione; **to be desperate to do sth** volere disperatamente fare qc; **I'm desperate for money** (*fam*) ho un disperato bisogno di soldi

des·per·ate·ly [ˈdɛspərɪtlɪ] ADV (*say, look*) con disperazione; (*fight*) disperatamente; (*extremely*) terribilmente, estremamente; **he was desperately trying to persuade her** stava tentando disperatamente di convincerla; **we're desperately worried** siamo estremamente preoccupati; **desperately ill** gravemente malato(-a), tra la vita e la morte; **desperately in love** perdutamente innamorato(-a)

des·pera·tion [ˌdɛspəˈreɪʃən] N disperazione *f*; **an act of desperation** un gesto disperato; **in (sheer) desperation** per (pura) disperazione

des·pic·able [dɪsˈpɪkəbl] ADJ spregevole; (*behaviour*) vergognoso(-a); (*person*) ignobile

des·pise [dɪsˈpaɪz] VT (*person*) disprezzare, sdegnare; (*sb's attentions, offer*) disdegnare

de·spite [dɪsˈpaɪt] PREP malgrado, a dispetto di, nonostante

de·spond·ent [dɪsˈpɒndənt] ADJ (*frm*): **despondent (about)** avvilito(-a) (per), abbattuto(-a) (per); **he is despondent about his future** quanto al suo futuro è molto demoralizzato

des·pot [ˈdespɒt] N despota *m*

des·sert [dɪˈzɜːt] N dessert *m inv*, dolce *m*; **dessert plate** piatto da dessert; **dessert wine** vino da dessert

dessert·spoon [dɪˈzɜːtˌspuːn] N cucchiaio da dessert

de·sta·bi·lize [diːˈsteɪbɪˌlaɪz] VT (*regime*) destabilizzare

des·ti·na·tion [ˌdestɪˈneɪʃən] N destinazione *f*

des·tine [ˈdestɪn] VT (*frm*) destinare

des·tined [ˈdestɪnd] ADJ PRED **1** (*destined for sth/sb/to do sth (by fate)*) destinato(-a) a qc/qn/a fare qc; **we were destined to meet** eravamo destinati a incontrarci **2** (*bound for*): **destined for London** con destinazione Londra, diretto(-a) a Londra

des·ti·ny [ˈdestɪnɪ] N destino, sorte *f*

des·ti·tute [ˈdestɪˌtjuːt] ADJ (*frm*) indigente; **utterly destitute** ridotto(-a) in miseria; **destitute of** privo(-a) di
- ❏ **destitute** is not translated by the Italian word *destituito*

de·stroy [dɪsˈtrɔɪ] VT (*gen*) distruggere; (*kill: dangerous or diseased animal*) abbattere; (*: pet*) sopprimere; (*: vermin*) eliminare; (*: mood, appetite*) rovinare

de·stroy·er [dɪsˈtrɔɪəʳ] N (*Naut*) cacciatorpediniere *m*

de·struc·tion [dɪsˈtrʌkʃən] N (*gen*) distruzione *f*; (*caused by war, fire*) danni *mpl*

de·struc·tive [dɪsˈtrʌktɪv] ADJ (*person*) distruttore(-trice); (*policy*) rovinoso(-a); (*action, power, criticism*) distruttivo(-a)

des·ul·tory [ˈdesəltərɪ] (*frm*) ADJ (*conversation*) sconnesso(-a); (*reading*) disordinato(-a); (*contact*) saltuario(-a), irregolare

de·tach [dɪˈtætʃ] VT staccare, distaccare

de·tach·able [dɪˈtætʃəbl] ADJ staccabile, smontabile

de·tached [dɪˈtætʃt] ADJ **1** staccato(-a), separato(-a) **2** (*impartial: opinion*) imparziale, obiettivo(-a); (*unemotional: manner, attitude*) distaccato(-a), distante

detached house N villetta unifamiliare, villa

de·tach·ment [dɪˈtætʃmənt] N **1** (*aloofness*) distacco **2** (*Mil*) distaccamento

de·tail [ˈdiːteɪl] N **1** (*gen*) particolare *m*, dettaglio; (*part of painting*) particolare; **I can't remember the details** non ricordo i dettagli; **his attention to detail** la sua minuziosità; **in detail** nei particolari; **to go into detail(s)** entrare nei dettagli **2** (*Mil*) piccolo distaccamento ♦ VT **1** (*list: items, facts*) elencare dettagliatamente **2** (*Mil*) distaccare; **to detail sb (for)** assegnare qn (a)

de·tailed [ˈdiːteɪld] ADJ dettagliato(-a), particolareggiato(-a)

de·tain [dɪˈteɪn] VT (*delay*) trattenere; (*in custody*) detenere

de·tainee [ˌdiːteɪˈniː] N detenuto(-a)

de·tect [dɪˈtekt] VT (*signs, traces, drug, motive*) scoprire; (*feeling*) avvertire; (*Radar*) individuare; (*gas, smoke*) avvertire la presenza di

de·tec·tion [dɪˈtekʃən] N scoperta, individuazione *f*; **crime detection** indagini *fpl* criminali; **to escape detection** (*mistake*) passare inosservato(-a); (*criminal*) eludere le ricerche

de·tec·tive [dɪˈtektɪv] N investigatore(-trice); (*private detective*) investigatore(-trice) privato(-a)

detective story N romanzo poliziesco, (*romanzo*) giallo

de·tec·tor [dɪˈtektəʳ] N rivelatore *m*, detector *m inv*; **radiation detector** indicatore *m* di radiazioni

de·tente, dé·tente [deɪˈtɑːnt] N (*frm*) distensione *f*

de·ten·tion [dɪˈtenʃən] N (*of criminal, spy*) detenzione *f*; (*of schoolchild*) punizione *f* (*trattenendo l'alunno alla fine delle lezioni*); **to get a detention** essere trattenuto a scuola

de·ter [dɪˈtɜːʳ] VT: **to deter sb (from doing sth)** dissuadere qn (dal fare qc)

de·ter·gent [dɪˈtɜːdʒənt] N detersivo, detergente *m*

de·terio·rate [dɪˈtɪərɪəˌreɪt] VI deteriorarsi

de·terio·ra·tion [dɪˌtɪərɪəˈreɪʃən] N deterioramento

de·ter·mi·na·tion [dɪˌtɜːmɪˈneɪʃən] N **1** (*of person*): **determination (to do)** determinazione *f* (di fare) **2** (*of cause, position*) determinazione *f*, individuazione *f*

de·ter·mine [dɪˈtɜːmɪn] VT **1** (*decide*) determinare; (*outcome, situation*) decidere **2** (*ascertain: cause, meaning*) determinare, stabilire **3** (*resolve*): **to determine to do sth** decidere di fare qc; **to determine sb to do sth** far decidere a qn di fare qc
- ▸ **determine on** VI + PREP decidersi per

de·ter·mined [dɪˈtɜːmɪnd] ADJ (*person*) risoluto(-a), deciso(-a); **she's a very determined woman** è una donna molto determinata; **a determined effort** uno sforzo di volontà; **to be determined to do sth** essere determinato(-a) or deciso(-a) a fare qc; **she's determined to succeed** è determinata a riuscire

de·ter·rence [dɪˈterəns] N deterrenza

de·ter·rent [dɪˈterənt] N deterrente *m*; **to act as a deterrent** funzionare or fungere da deterrente

de·test [dɪˈtest] VT detestare

de·test·able [dɪˈtestəbl] ADJ detestabile

deto·nate [ˈdetəˌneɪt] VT far detonare ♦ VI detonare

deto·na·tor [ˈdetəˌneɪtəʳ] N detonatore *m*

de·tour [ˈdiːtʊəʳ] N giro più lungo, deviazione *f*; **to make a detour (through)** fare una deviazione (passando per)

detox [ˈdiːtɒks] VT disintossicare ♦ VI disintossicarsi ♦ N disintossicazione *f*

detoxification [diːˌtɒksɪfɪˈkeɪʃən] N disintossicazione *f*

detoxify [diːˈtɒksɪfaɪ] VT disintossicare ♦ VI disintossicarsi

de·tract [dɪˈtrækt] VI: **to detract from** (*value*) sminuire; (*reputation*) intaccare; (*pleasure*) attenuare

de·trac·tor [dɪˈtræktəʳ] N detrattore(-trice)

det·ri·ment [ˈdetrɪmənt] N detrimento, danno; **to the detriment of** a or con detrimento di, a danno di; **without detriment to** senza danno a

det·ri·men·tal [ˌdetrɪˈmentl] ADJ: **detrimental (to)** dannoso(-a) (a), nocivo(-a) (a); **to be detrimental to sth** pregiudicare qc

deuce [djuːs] N (*Tennis*) deuce *m inv*, quaranta pari *m inv*

de·valua·tion [ˌdiːvæljʊˈeɪʃən] N (*Fin*) svalutazione *f*

de·value [diːˈvæljuː] VT (*Fin*) svalutare

dev·as·tate [ˈdevəˌsteɪt] VT (*place*) devastare; (*opponent, opposition*) sbaragliare, annientare; (*upset greatly*) sconvolgere; **he was devastated by the news** la notizia l'aveva sconvolto

dev·as·tat·ing [ˈdevəˌsteɪtɪŋ] ADJ (*flood, storm*) devastatore(-trice); (*news, effect*) micidiale; (*beauty*) travolgente; **she received some devastating news** ha ricevuto notizie sconvolgenti; **unemployment has a devastating effect on people** la disoccupazione ha un effetto devastante sulle persone

dev·el·op [dɪˈveləp] VT **1** (*skill, ability, also Phot*) sviluppare; (*mind*) allargare **2** (*acquire: habit*) prendere (a poco a poco or gradualmente); **to develop a taste for sth** imparare a gustare qc; **she has developed an interest in politics** è sorto in lei un interesse per la politica **3** (*resources*) sviluppare, valorizzare; (*region*) valorizzare, promuovere lo sviluppo di; **to develop land** costruire su un terreno; **this land is to be developed** qui costruiranno ♦ VI **1** (*gen*) svilupparsi; (*person: mentally, emotionally*) maturare; (*baby*) crescere; (*plot, illness*) progredire; **the area has developed industrially** la zona si è sviluppata sotto il profilo industriale; **to develop into** diventare, trasformarsi in; **the argument developed into a fight** la discussione si trasformò in una lite **2** (*come into being: symptoms, feelings*) comparire, manifestarsi; (*come about: crisis, situation*) verificarsi, prodursi

de·vel·op·er [dɪˈveləpəʳ] N **1** (*also: property developer*) costruttore *m* (edile) **2** (*Phot*) sviluppatore *m*

developing country N paese *m* in via di sviluppo

de·vel·op·ment [dɪˈveləpmənt] N (*gen*) sviluppo; **to await developments** attendere ulteriori sviluppi; **the latest developments** gli ultimi sviluppi (della situazione); **development process** processo di sviluppo; **development grant** finanziamento per un programma di sviluppo

development area N (*Brit*) area di sviluppo industriale

de·vi·ant [ˈdiːvɪənt] ADJ (*behaviour*) deviante; (*development*)

anormale; (*sexually*) pervertito(-a) ♦ N deviante *m/f*; (*also:*
sexual deviant) pervertito(-a)
de·vi·ate [ˈdiːvɪˌeɪt] VI: **to deviate (from)** deviare (da), discostarsi da
de·via·tion [ˌdiːvɪˈeɪʃən] N: **deviation (from)** deviazione *f*
(da); **standard deviation** (*Math*) scarto quadratico medio
de·vice [dɪˈvaɪs] N 1 (*gadget*) congegno, dispositivo 2
(*scheme*) stratagemma *m*; **leave him to his own devices** lascia che si arrangi da solo 3 (*also:* **explosive device**) ordigno
esplosivo
dev·il [ˈdɛvl] N 1 (*evil spirit*) diavolo; **the Devil** il Diavolo, il
Demonio 2 (*fam: person*) diavolo; **poor devil** povero diavolo!; **you little devil!** monellaccio! 3 (*fam: as intensifier*): **to**
work/run like the devil lavorare/correre come un dannato; **how/what/who the devil ...?** come/che/chi diavolo...?;
there will be the devil to pay saranno guai 4 (*phrases.*): **be-**
tween the devil and the deep blue sea tra Scilla e Cariddi;
speak *or* **talk of the devil!** (*fam*) lupus in fabula!, si parla del
diavolo...; **(to) give the devil his due ...** bisogna riconoscer-
glielo..., siamo giusti...
dev·il·ish [ˈdɛvlɪʃ] ADJ (*wicked*) diabolico(-a); (*mischievous:*
child) indiavolato(-a); (: *mood*) infernale ♦ ADV (*old*) terribilmente
devil-may-care [ˈdɛvlmeɪˈkeəʳ] ADJ (*attitude*) sprezzante
devil's advocate [ˈdɛvəlzˈædvəˌkɪt] N: **to play (the) devil's**
advocate fare l'avvocato del diavolo
de·vi·ous [ˈdiːvɪəs] ADJ (*person, means, methods, mind*) sub-
dolo(-a); (*path, argument*) tortuoso(-a)
de·vise [dɪˈvaɪz] VT escogitare, concepire, ideare
de·void [dɪˈvɔɪd] ADJ: **devoid of** privo(-a) di, senza
de·vo·lu·tion [ˌdiːvəˈluːʃən] N (*Pol*) decentramento
de·volve [dɪˈvɒlv] VT (*power, responsibility*) devolvere ♦ VI: **to**
devolve (up)on ricadere su; **it devolved on me to tell him** è
stato compito mio dirglielo
de·vote [dɪˈvəut] VT: **to devote (to)** dedicare (a); **to devote**
o.s. to dedicarsi a; (*to a cause*) consacrarsi a, dedicarsi a
de·vot·ed [dɪˈvəutɪd] ADJ (*friend, admirer*) devoto(-a); (*father,*
aunt) amoroso(-a); **to be devoted to sb** essere molto attac-
cato(-a) a qn; **he's completely devoted to her** le è estremamente attaccato
devo·tee [ˌdevəuˈtiː] N 1 **devotee (of)** (*enthusiast*) appas-
sionato(-a) di 2 (*Rel*) devoto(-a)
de·vo·tion [dɪˈvəuʃən] N: **devotion (to)** (*studies etc*) devozione *f* (a), dedizione *f* (a); (*friend, family*) attaccamento (a),
fedeltà (a); **devotions** NPL (*Rel*) devozioni *fpl*
de·vour [dɪˈvauəʳ] VT (*food*) divorare; **devoured by jealousy**
divorato(-a) dalla gelosia
de·vout [dɪˈvaut] ADJ (*person*) devoto(-a), pio(-a); (*prayer,*
hope) devoto(-a), fervido(-a)
dew [djuː] N rugiada
dex·ter·i·ty [deksˈterɪtɪ] N (*of hands*) dexterity (in doing sth)
destrezza (a fare qc); (*of mind*) abilità (nel fare qc)
dex·ter·ous, dex·trous [ˈdekstrəs] ADJ (*skilful*) destro(-a),
abile; (*movement*) agile
dg [ˌdiːˈdʒiː] ABBR (= *decigram*) dg
dia·be·tes [ˌdaɪəˈbiːtiːz] N diabete *m*
dia·bet·ic [ˌdaɪəˈbetɪk] N diabetico(-a) ♦ ADJ (*gen*) diabeti-
co(-a); (*chocolate, jam*) per diabetici
dia·bol·i·cal [ˌdaɪəˈbɒlɪkəl] ADJ (*fam: dreadful*) infernale,
atroce; (: *incredible*) incredibile; (*satanic*) diabolico(-a)
di·aer·esis, di·er·esis [daɪˈerɪsɪs] N (*pl* **diaereses, diereses**
[daɪˈerɪsiːz]) dieresi *f inv*
di·ag·nose [ˈdaɪəgnəuz] VT diagnosticare; **it was diagnosed**
as bronchitis hanno diagnosticato una bronchite
di·ag·no·sis [ˌdaɪəgˈnəusɪs] N (*pl* **diagnoses** [ˌdaɪəgˈnəusiːz])
diagnosi *f inv*
di·ag·o·nal [daɪˈægənl] ADJ, N diagonale *f*
dia·gram [ˈdaɪəˌgræm] N diagramma *m*, schema *m*; (*Math*)
diagramma, grafico
dial [ˈdaɪəl] N (*of clock, instrument*) quadrante *m*; (*of radio*)
scala; (*of telephone*) disco (combinatore) ♦ VT (*Telec: num-*
ber) fare; (*more formal*) comporre; **to dial a wrong number**
sbagliare numero; **can I dial London direct?** si può chiamare Londra in teleselezione?; **to dial 999** ≈ chiamare il 113
dial. ABBR = **dialect**

dia·lect [ˈdaɪəˌlekt] N dialetto; **the local dialect** il dialetto del
luogo; **dialect word** termine *m* dialettale
dial·ling code [ˈdaɪəlɪŋˌkəud], (*USA*) **dial code** N (*Telec*)
prefisso
dial·ling tone [ˈdaɪəlɪŋˌtəun], (*USA*) **dial tone** N (*Telec*) segnale *m* di libero
dia·logue [ˈdaɪəlɒg] N dialogo
di·aly·sis [daɪˈælɪsɪs] N (*Med*) dialisi *f*
di·am·eter [daɪˈæmɪtəʳ] N diametro; **it is one metre in diam-**
eter misura un metro di diametro
dia·met·ri·cal·ly [ˌdaɪəˈmetrɪkəlɪ] ADV: **diametrically op-**
posed (to) diametralmente opposto(-a) (a)
dia·mond [ˈdaɪəmənd] N 1 (*stone*) diamante *m*, brillante *m*; (*shape*) rombo, losanga 2 (*Cards*): **diamonds**
NPL quadri *mpl*; **the Queen of diamonds** la donna di quadri
♦ ADJ (*necklace*) di diamanti *or* brillanti; **diamond ring** anello di brillanti; (*with single diamond*) anello con brillante; **dia-**
mond-shaped a forma di losanga
dia·per [ˈdaɪəpəʳ] N (*USA*) pannolino
dia·phragm [ˈdaɪəfræm] N diaframma *m*
di·ar·rhoea, di·ar·rhea (*USA*) [ˌdaɪəˈriːə] N diarrea
dia·ry [ˈdaɪərɪ] N (*daily record*) diario; (*for engagements*) agenda; **to keep a diary** tenere un diario; **her diaries are being**
published i suoi diari saranno pubblicati
dia·tribe [ˈdaɪəˌtraɪb] N (*frm*): **diatribe (against)** diatriba
(contro)
dice [daɪs] N *pl inv* dado; **throw the dice** getta i dadi; **to play**
dice giocare a dadi ♦ VT (*Culin*) tagliare a dadini ♦ VI: **to**
dice with death scherzare con la morte
dicey [ˈdaɪsɪ] ADJ (*fam*): **it's a bit dicey** è un po' un rischio
di·choto·my [dɪˈkɒtəmɪ] N (*frm*) dicotomia
dick·head [ˈdɪkˌhed] N (*fam!*) testa *m*, *f* di cazzo (*fam!*)
dic·tate [*vb* dɪkˈteɪt, *n* ˈdɪkteɪt] VT, VI (*all senses*) dettare; **he**
decided to act as circumstances dictated decise di agire
come gli dettavano le circostanze ♦ **dictates** NPL (*of heart,*
fashion) dettami *mpl*
▸ **dictate to** VI + PREP (*person*) dare ordini a, dettar legge a;
he cannot be allowed to dictate to us non dovrebbe po-
terci dare ordini; **I won't be dictated to** non ricevo ordini
dic·ta·tion [dɪkˈteɪʃən] N (*to secretary*) dettatura; (*Scol*) dettato; **at dictation speed** a velocità di dettatura
dic·ta·tor [dɪkˈteɪtəʳ] N dittatore(-trice)
dic·ta·tor·ship [dɪkˈteɪtəˌʃɪp] N dittatura
dic·tion [ˈdɪkʃən] N dizione *f*
dic·tion·ary [ˈdɪkʃənrɪ] N vocabolario, dizionario
did [dɪd] PT *of* **do**[1]
di·dac·tic [daɪˈdæktɪk] ADJ (*frm: educational*) didattico(-a); (*pej:*
person) pedante
didn't [ˈdɪdnt] = **did not**
die [daɪ] (*prp* **dying**) VI (*person, animal, plant*): **to die (of** *or*
from) morire (di); (*engine*) spegnersi, fermarsi; (*fig: friend-*
ship) finire; (: *interest, enthusiasm*) spegnersi; **he died last**
year è morto l'anno scorso; **I'm dying of boredom** muoio
di noia; **to be dying** star morendo; **to be dying for sth/to**
do sth morire dalla voglia di qc/di fare qc; **to die a natural/**
violent death morire di morte naturale/violenta; **he died a**
hero è morto da eroe; **the daylight was dying fast** si stava
facendo buio in fretta; **never say die** (*fig: fam*) non bisogna
disperare; **I nearly died** (*laughing*) per poco non morivo (dal
ridere); (*with embarrassment*) avrei voluto sprofondare; **old**
habits die hard il lupo perde il pelo ma non il vizio
▸ **die away** VI + ADV affievolirsi
▸ **die back** VI + ADV (*plant*) seccarsi
▸ **die down** VI + ADV (*fire*) spegnersi; (*flames*) abbassarsi,
languire; (*storm, wind, emotion*) calmarsi; **the wind died**
down il vento si calmò
▸ **die off** VI + ADV (*plants, animals, people*) morire uno(-a)
dopo l'altro(-a)
▸ **die out** VI + ADV estinguersi, scomparire
die·hard [ˈdaɪˌhɑːd] N conservatore(-trice) ♦ ADJ (*supporter,*
opponent) convinto(-a)
die·sel [ˈdiːzəl] N (*car*) diesel *m inv*; (*fuel*) gasolio; **our car is a**
diesel la nostra macchina è un diesel
diesel engine N motore *m* diesel, *inv*

diesel fuel, diesel oil N gasolio (per motori diesel)
diet [ˈdaɪət] N 1 (*customary food*) alimentazione *f*, regime *m* alimentare; **a healthy diet** un'alimentazione sana; **to live on a diet of** nutrirsi di 2 (*restricted food*) dieta; **to be/go on a diet** essere/mettersi a dieta; **I'm on a diet** sono in dieta ♦ VI seguire una dieta; **I've been dieting for two months** sto seguendo una dieta da due mesi ♦ ADJ (*food, drink*) dietetico(-a); **diet drinks** bibite dietetiche; **diet yoghurt** yoghurt *m inv* magro
di·eti·cian [ˌdaɪəˈtɪʃən] N dietista *m/f*
dif·fer [ˈdɪfəʳ] VI 1 (*be unlike*): **to differ from sth** differire da qc, essere diverso(-a) da qc; **this version differs from the original in several ways** questa versione differisce da quella originale in molti modi 2 (*disagree*): **to differ (with sb on or over or about sth)** dissentire (da qn su qc), discordare (da qn su qc); **we differed over the matter** ci siamo trovati in disaccordo sulla questione
dif·fer·ence [ˈdɪfrəns] N 1 **difference (in/between)** differenza (di/tra); **there's not much difference in age between us** non c'è molta differenza d'età tra noi; **the new system has made a big difference** il nuovo sistema ha apportato un grosso miglioramento; **that makes all the difference** questo cambia tutto; **it makes no difference to me** per me è lo stesso; **a car with a difference** una macchina diversa dalle altre; **I'll make up the difference later** (*of money*) ti do il resto dopo; **common difference** (*Math*) ragione *f* 2 (*quarrel*): **a difference of opinion** una divergenza di opinioni; **they could not settle their differences** non sono riusciti a mettersi d'accordo
dif·fer·ent [ˈdɪfrənt] ADJ 1 (*not alike*): **different (from or to)** diverso(-a) (da), differente (da); (*changed*) altro(-a), diverso(-a); **London is different from Rome** Londra è diversa da Roma; **that's quite a different matter** è tutt'altra cosa, è una faccenda completamente diversa; **I feel a different person** mi sento un altro 2 (*various*) diverso(-a), vario(-a); **it comes in several different colours** è disponibile in diversi or vari colori
dif·fer·en·tial [ˌdɪfəˈrenʃəl] N (*Econ*) scarto salariale; (*Math, Aut*) differenziale *m* ♦ ADJ differenziale; **differential calculus** (*Math*) calcolo differenziale; **differential erosion** erosione *f* selettiva
dif·fer·en·ti·ate [ˌdɪfəˈrenʃɪeɪt] VT: **to differentiate (from)** (*distinguish*) distinguere (fra); (*make different*) differenziare (da) ♦ VI: **to differentiate (between)** (*perceive a difference*) distinguere (tra), differenziare (tra)
dif·fer·ent·ly [ˈdɪfrəntlɪ] ADV in modo diverso or differente; **she thinks quite differently now** la pensa diversamente adesso
dif·fi·cult [ˈdɪfɪkəlt] ADJ difficile; **difficult to understand** difficile da capire; **I find it difficult to believe (that ...)** mi pare difficile da credere (che...)
dif·fi·cul·ty [ˈdɪfɪkəltɪ] N difficoltà *f inv*; **he has difficulty in walking/breathing** ha difficoltà a camminare/di respirazione; **to have difficulties with** (*police, landlord*) avere noie con; **to get o.s. into difficulty** mettersi nei guai; **to be in difficulty or difficulties** essere or trovarsi in difficoltà; **to be in (financial) difficulties** avere delle difficoltà economiche
dif·fi·dence [ˈdɪfɪdəns] N riservatezza
❏ **diffidence** is not translated by the Italian word *diffidenza*
dif·fi·dent [ˈdɪfɪdənt] ADJ (*person*) poco sicuro(-a) di sé; (*smile*) timido(-a), imbarazzato(-a); **to be diffident about doing sth** esitare a fare qc
❏ **diffident** is not translated by the Italian word *diffidente*
dif·fuse [*vb* dɪˈfjuːz, *adj* dɪˈfjuːs] VT (*light, heat, gas, information*) diffondere; (*heat, perfume*) emanare ♦ VI diffondersi ♦ ADJ (*light*) diffuso(-a); (*style, writing*) prolisso(-a); (*organization*) ramificato(-a)
dig [dɪg] (*pt, pp* dug) N 1 (*with elbow*) gomitata; **to give sb a dig in the ribs** dare una gomitata (nel fianco) a qn 2 (*fam: taunt*) frecciata, insinuazione *f*; **to have a dig at sb/sth** lanciare una frecciata a qn/qc 3 (*Archeol*) scavo, scavi *mpl* ♦ VT 1 (*ground, hole*) scavare; (*garden*) zappare, vangare; **they're digging a hole in the road** stanno scavando un buco nella

strada; **Dad's out digging the garden** il papà è fuori a zappare il giardino 2 (*poke, thrust*): **to dig sth into sth** conficcare qc in qc; **to dig one's nails into** conficcare le unghie in 3 (*old, fam*): **I don't dig that kind of scene** (*old, fam*) quell'ambiente non mi va a genio; **he really digs jazz** (*old, fam*) va pazzo per il jazz ♦ VI (*gen, or Tech*) scavare; (*Archeol*) fare degli scavi; **to dig for minerals** scavare alla ricerca di minerali; **to dig into one's pockets for sth** frugarsi le tasche cercando qc
▸ **dig in** VI + ADV 1 (*fam: eat*) attaccare a mangiare; **dig in!** dateci sotto! 2 (*also:* **dig o.s. in:** *Mil*) trincerarsi; (*fig*) insediarsi, installarsi ♦ VT + ADV (*compost*) interrare; (*knife, claw*) affondare; **to dig in one's heels** (*fig*) impuntarsi
▸ **dig out** VT + ADV (*survivors, car from snow*) tirar fuori (scavando), estrarre (scavando); (*fig*) scovare
▸ **dig up** VT + ADV (*potatoes, treasure, body*) dissotterrare; (*tree etc*) sradicare; (*weeds*) estirpare; (*fig: fam: fact, information*) scovare; **the cat's dug up my plants** il gatto ha sradicato le mie piante; **they're trying to dig up evidence against him** stanno cercando di tirar fuori delle prove contro di lui
di·gest [*vb* daɪˈdʒest, *n* ˈdaɪdʒest] VT digerire; (*information*) assimilare; **it is easily digested** (*food*) è facilmente digeribile ♦ VI digerirsi ♦ N (*summary*) compendio
di·gest·ible [dɪˈdʒestəbl] ADJ digeribile
di·ges·tion [dɪˈdʒestʃən] N digestione *f*
di·ges·tive [dɪˈdʒestɪv] ADJ digestivo(-a); **digestive system** apparato digerente; **digestive (biscuit)** *biscotto tipo frollino di farina integrale*
dig·it [ˈdɪdʒɪt] N (*Math*) cifra; (*frm: finger, thumb, toe*) dito
dig·i·tal [ˈdɪdʒɪtəl] ADJ (*clock, computer*) digitale
dig·ni·fied [ˈdɪgnɪfaɪd] ADJ dignitoso(-a), pieno(-a) di dignità
dig·ni·tary [ˈdɪgnɪtərɪ] N dignitario
dig·ni·ty [ˈdɪgnɪtɪ] N dignità; **it would be beneath his dignity to do it** non si abbasserebbe mai a farlo
di·gress [daɪˈgres] VI: **to digress (from)** divagare (da), fare digressioni (da)
di·gres·sion [daɪˈgreʃən] N digressione *f*
di·lapi·da·ted [dɪˈlæpɪdeɪtɪd] ADJ (*building*) in pessime condizioni, cadente; (*vehicle*) sgangherato(-a), scassato(-a)
di·late [daɪˈleɪt] VI (*pupils, eyes, cervix*) dilatarsi ♦ VT dilatare
di·la·tory [ˈdɪlətərɪ] ADJ (*frm: person*) lento(-a); (*action, policy*) dilatorio(-a)
di·lem·ma [daɪˈlemə] N dilemma *m*; **to be in a dilemma** essere di fronte a un dilemma
dili·gent [ˈdɪlɪdʒənt] ADJ (*person*) diligente, attento(-a); (*work, search*) accurato(-a), diligente
dill [dɪl] N aneto
dilly-dally [ˈdɪlɪˌdælɪ] VI (*fam*) gingillarsi
di·lute [daɪˈluːt] VT (*concentrated liquid*) diluire, allungare; (*wine*) annacquare; (*fig: statement, concept*) diluire; **"dilute to taste"** "aggiungere acqua a piacere" ♦ ADJ diluito(-a)
dim [dɪm] ADJ (*comp -mer, superl -mest*) (*light*) debole, fioco(-a); (*sight*) debole; (*forest*) oscuro(-a); (*room*) in penombra; (*shape, outline, memory, sound*) indistinto(-a), vago(-a); (*fam: person*) tonto(-a), ottuso(-a); **a dim light** una luce debole; **the prospects are dim** le prospettive sono scarse; **to grow dim** (*light*) affievolirsi; (*eyesight*) indebolirsi; **to take a dim view of sth** (*fam*) non vedere qc di buon occhio ♦ VT (*light*) abbassare; (*USA: headlights*) abbassare; (*sound, memory, colour*) affievolire; (*shape, outline, beauty, glory*) offuscare; (*sight, senses*) annebbiare; (*metal*) annerire ♦ VI (*light, sight, memory*) affievolirsi; (*outline*) divenire indistinto(-a)
dime [daɪm] N (*USA and Canada*) *monetina da 10 cent*; **they're a dime a dozen** (*fam*) ce n'è un sacco
di·men·sion [daɪˈmenʃən] N (*size*) dimensione *f*, proporzione *f*; (*Math, fig*) dimensione; **to add a new dimension to** (*fig*) dare una dimensione nuova a
-dimensional [daɪˈmenʃənl] ADJ SUFF: **two-dimensional** bidimensionale; **three-dimensional** tridimensionale
di·min·ish [dɪˈmɪnɪʃ] VT (*effect, enthusiasm, authority, speed*) diminuire, ridurre; (*value, person*) sminuire ♦ VI diminuire, ridursi; (*value*) scendere; **the threat of nuclear war has diminished** la paura di una guerra nucleare è diminuita

di·min·ished [dɪˈmɪnɪʃt] ADJ (*value, importance*) ridotto(-a)
di·minu·tive [dɪˈmɪnjʊtɪv] ADJ (*frm*) minuto(-a), minuscolo(-a) ♦ N (*Gram*) diminutivo
dim·ly [ˈdɪmlɪ] ADV (*hear, remember*) vagamente; (*shine*) debolmente; **she dimly recalled the circumstances** si ricordava vagamente le circostanze; **dimly lit** illuminato debolmente
dim·mer [ˈdɪmə^r] N (*also:* **dimmer switch**) dimmer *m inv*, interruttore *m* a reostato
dim·ple [ˈdɪmpl] N (*in cheek, chin etc*) fossetta
dim-witted [dɪmˈwɪtɪd] ADJ (*fam*) sciocco(-a), stupido(-a)
din [dɪn] N (*from people, in classroom*) chiasso, fracasso, baccano; (*from machine, factory, traffic*) rumore *m* infernale ♦ VT: **to din sth into sb** (*fam*) ficcare qc in testa a qn; **he tried to din it into her that ...** ha cercato di ficcarle in testa che...
dine [daɪn] VI (*frm*) cenare; **to dine (on)** pasteggiare (a *or* con); **to dine out** cenare fuori
din·er [ˈdaɪnə^r] N (*person: in restaurant*) cliente *m/f*; (*Rail*) carrozza *or* vagone *m* ristorante, *inv*; (*USA: eating place*) tavola calda
din·ghy [ˈdɪŋgɪ] N (*rubber boat*) gommone *m*; (*sailing dinghy*) dinghy *m inv*
din·gy [ˈdɪndʒɪ] ADJ (*shabby*) squallido(-a); (*dark*) scuro(-a), tetro(-a)
din·ing area [ˈdaɪnɪŋˌɛərɪə] N zona *f* pranzo, *inv*
din·ing car [ˈdaɪnɪŋˌkɑː^r] N carrozza *or* vagone *m* ristorante, *inv*
din·ing room [ˈdaɪnɪŋˌrʊm] N sala da pranzo
din·ing ta·ble [ˈdaɪnɪŋˌteɪbl] N tavola *or* tavolo da pranzo
din·ner [ˈdɪnə^r] N (*evening meal*) cena; (*lunch*) pranzo; (*banquet*) banchetto; **dinner is at seven o'clock** la cena è alle sette; **to have dinner** cenare; **we're having people to dinner this evening** abbiamo gente a cena stasera; **to go out to dinner in a restaurant/at friends** andare a cena fuori/da amici; **they have dinner at school** pranzano a scuola; **the dinner hour** l'intervallo del pranzo; **it's half past twelve — nearly dinner time!** è mezzogiorno e mezza — è quasi ora di pranzo!; **dinner's ready!** a tavola!; **school dinners** refezione *f* scolastica
dinner jacket N (*Brit*) smoking *m inv*
dinner party N cena (con amici)
dinner service N servizio da tavola
dinner time N ora di pranzo (*or* cena)
di·no·saur [ˈdaɪnəsɔː^r] N dinosauro
dint [dɪnt] N: **by dint of (doing) sth** a forza di (fare) qc
dio·cese [ˈdaɪəsɪs] N diocesi *f inv*
di·ox·ide [daɪˈɒksaɪd] N (*Chem*) biossido; **carbon dioxide** anidride *f* carbonica
dip [dɪp] N **1** (*swim*) nuotatina; **to go for a dip** andare a fare una nuotatina **2** (*hollow*) cunetta; (*slope*) pendenza, discesa **3** (*Culin*) salsetta **4** (*for sheep*) bagno ♦ VT (*into liquid*) immergere, bagnare; (*hand: into bag*) infilare; (*sheep*) immergere nel disinfestante; **he dipped his hand in the water** ha immerso la mano nell'acqua; **to dip one's pen in ink** intingere la penna nell'inchiostro; **he dipped a biscuit into his tea** ha inzuppato un biscotto nel tè ♦ VI (*slope down: road*) essere in pendenza, andare in discesa; (*move down: bird, plane*) abbassarsi; (*temperature, sun*) calare; **the boat dipped slightly under his weight** la barca si è abbassata leggermente sotto il suo peso; **the sun dipped below the horizon** il sole è sceso sotto l'orizzonte; **to dip into one's pocket/savings** (*fig*) attingere al portafoglio/ai propri risparmi; **to dip into a book** scorrere un libro; **to dip into an author** leggere brani di un autore
Dip. ABBR (*Brit*) = **diploma**
diph·theria [dɪfˈθɪərɪə] N difterite *f*
diph·thong [ˈdɪfθɒŋ] N dittongo
di·plo·ma [dɪˈpləʊmə] N diploma *m*; **to have a diploma in** avere un diploma in, essere diplomato(-a) in
di·plo·ma·cy [dɪˈpləʊməsɪ] N (*Pol, also fig*) diplomazia
dip·lo·mat [ˈdɪpləmæt] N diplomatico
dip·lo·mat·ic [ˌdɪpləˈmætɪk] ADJ (*also fig*) diplomatico(-a); **diplomatic bag**, (*USA*) **diplomatic pouch** valigia diplomatica; **diplomatic service** diplomazia; **to break off diplomatic relations** rompere le relazioni diplomatiche

diplomatic corps N corpo diplomatico
diplomatic immunity N immunità diplomatica
dip·stick [ˈdɪpˌstɪk] N (*Aut*) astina dell'olio
dip·switch [ˈdɪpˌswɪtʃ] N (*Aut*) levetta dei fari
dire [ˈdaɪə^r] ADJ (*warning*) minaccioso(-a); (*consequences*) disastroso(-a); (*event*) terribile; (*poverty*) nero(-a); **a dire warning** un terribile avvertimento; **dire necessity** dura necessità; **in dire straits** nei guai
di·rect [daɪˈrekt] ADJ (*gen*) diretto(-a); (*answer*) chiaro(-a); (*refusal*) esplicito(-a); (*manner, person*) franco(-a), diretto(-a); **direct object** (*Gram*) complemento oggetto; **the most direct route** la strada più diretta; **to be a direct descendant of** discendere in linea diretta da; **the direct opposite of** l'esatto opposto; **the direct opposite of** esattamente il contrario di; **to make a direct hit** colpire in pieno ♦ ADV (*go*) direttamente; (*fly*) senza scalo; (*dial*) in teleselezione; **you can go direct, without changing at Crewe** si può andarci direttamente senza cambiare a Crewe ♦ VT **1** (*aim: remark, gaze, attention*): **to direct at/to** dirigere a, rivolgere a; (*address: letter*): **to direct sth to** indirizzare qc a; **is that remark directed at me?** è diretta a me questa osservazione?; **can you direct me to the station?** può indicarmi la strada per la stazione? **2** (*control: traffic, business, actors*) dirigere; (*play, film, programme*) curare la regia di, dirigere **3** (*frm: instruct*): **to direct sb to do sth** dare direttive a qn di fare qc
direct cost N (*Comm*) costo diretto
direct current N (*Elec*) corrente *f* continua
direct debit N mandato di pagamento permanente
direct dialling [daɪˌrekt ˈdaɪəlɪŋ] N (*Telec*) ≈ teleselezione *f*
direct hit N (*Mil*) colpo diretto
di·rec·tion [dɪˈrekʃən] N **1** (*way*) direzione *f*; (*fig*) scopo, direzione; **in the direction of** in direzione di; **we're going in the wrong direction** stiamo andando nella direzione sbagliata; **sense of direction** senso dell'orientamento **2** (*management: of business*) direzione *f*, amministrazione *f*; (*of play, film, programme*) regia **3 directions** NPL (*instructions: to a place*) indicazioni *fpl*; (*: for use*) istruzioni *fpl*; (*advice*) chiarimenti *mpl*; **to ask for directions** chiedere la strada; **stage directions** didascalie *fpl*
di·rec·tive [dɪˈrektɪv] N direttiva, ordine *m*; **a government directive** una disposizione governativa
direct labour N manodopera diretta
di·rect·ly [dɪˈrektlɪ] ADV (*gen*) direttamente; (*at once*) subito; (*descended*) in linea diretta; (*frankly: speak*) con franchezza, senza peli sulla lingua; (*completely: opposite*) proprio; **the ball went directly to the goalkeeper** la palla è arrivata direttamente al portiere; **directly below me** proprio sotto di me; **directly after the meeting** subito dopo l'incontro ♦ CONJ (*non*) appena; **he'll come directly he's ready** verrà non appena sarà pronto
direct mail N mailing *m*
di·rect·ness [daɪˈrektnɪs] N (*of person, speech*) franchezza
di·rec·tor [dɪˈrektə^r] N (*Comm*) dirigente *m/f*, direttore(-trice) (d'azienda); (*of play, film, TV programme*) regista *m/f*; **the artistic director** il direttore artistico
di·rec·tory [dɪˈrektərɪ] N (*telephone directory*) elenco (telefonico); (*street directory*) stradario; (*trade directory*) repertorio del commercio; (*Comput*) directory *m inv*
directory enquiries, (*USA*) **directory assistance** N (*Telec*) servizio informazioni, informazioni *fpl* elenco abbonati
dirt [dɜːt] N (*on face, clothes etc*) sporco, sporcizia; (*earth*) terra; (*mud*) fango; **I started to scrub off the dirt** ho cominciato a grattare via la sporcizia; **dog dirt** bisogni *mpl* di un cane; **to treat sb like dirt** (*fam*) trattare qn come uno straccio; **to dig up dirt about sb** (*fam*) pescare nel torbido a proposito di qn; **to spread the dirt about sb** (*fam*) sparlare di qn; **have you heard the latest dirt on ...?** (*fam*) hai sentito l'ultimo scandalo riguardo a...?
dirt-cheap [ˈdɜːtˈtʃiːp] (*fam*) regalato(-a)
dirt road N strada non asfaltata
dirty [ˈdɜːtɪ] ADJ (*comp* -**ier**, *superl* -**iest**) (*gen*) sporco(-a); (*cut, wound*) infetto(-a); (*indecent: novel, story, joke*) sporco(-a), spinto(-a); **dirty socks** calzini sporchi; **to get dirty** sporcarsi; **dirty trick** brutto scherzo; **to play a dirty trick on sb**

farla sporca a qn, giocare un brutto scherzo a qn; **to give sb a dirty look** (*fam*) lanciare un'occhiataccia a qn; **to have a dirty mind** pensare solo a quello; **a dirty old man** un vecchio sporcaccione; **dirty word** parolaccia; **it's a dirty word these days** oggigiorno è un argomento tabù; **do your own dirty work!** non passare a me le tue gatte da pelare!
♦ vt sporcare, insudiciare

dis·abil·ity [ˌdɪsəˈbɪlɪtɪ] N (*injury etc*) menomazione *f*, infermità *f inv*; (*state*) invalidità *f inv*, handicap *m inv*; (*Law, fig*) incapacità *f inv*; **people with disabilities** persone con invalidità; **disability allowance** ≈ pensione *f* d'invalidità

dis·able [dɪsˈeɪbl] vt (*subj: illness, accident*) rendere invalido(-a); (*tank, gun*) mettere fuori uso; (*Law: disqualify*) rendere inabile

dis·abled [dɪsˈeɪbld] ADJ handicappato(-a), invalido(-a); (*maimed*) mutilato(-a); (*through illness, old age*) inabile; **disabled ex-serviceman** invalido di guerra ♦ **the disabled** NPL i disabili, gli invalidi

dis·ad·vant·age [ˌdɪsədˈvɑːntɪdʒ] N svantaggio; **to be to sb's disadvantage** tornare a svantaggio *or* sfavore di qn; **to be at a disadvantage** essere svantaggiato(-a)

dis·ad·van·taged [ˌdɪsədˈvɑːntɪdʒd] ADJ (*person*) svantaggiato(-a)

dis·ad·van·ta·geous [ˌdɪsædvɑːnˈteɪdʒəs] ADJ svantaggioso(-a), sfavorevole

dis·af·fect·ed [ˌdɪsəˈfektɪd] ADJ (*voters, supporters*) deluso(-a); (*young people*) ribelle

dis·af·fec·tion [ˌdɪsəˈfekʃən] N malcontento, insoddisfazione *f*

dis·agree [ˌdɪsəˈɡriː] vi **1 to disagree (with sb** *or* **about sth)** essere in disaccordo (con qn su qc), dissentire (da qn su qc); (*quarrel*) litigare; (*stories, accounts, figures: conflict*) essere discordante; **I disagree with you** non sono d'accordo con te; **we always disagree** non siamo mai d'accordo **2 to disagree with sth** (*oppose*) non essere d'accordo su qc **3 to disagree with** (*subj: climate, food*) non fare bene a; **a hot climate disagrees with me** il clima caldo non mi si confà; **onions disagree with me** non digerisco la cipolla

dis·agree·able [ˌdɪsəˈɡriːəbl] ADJ (*gen*) spiacevole; (*weather*) brutto(-a); (*person*) antipatico(-a); (*tone of voice*) sgradevole

dis·agree·ment [ˌdɪsəˈɡriːmənt] N (*with opinion*) disaccordo; (*quarrel*) dissapore *m*, litigio; (*between stories, accounts, figures*) discordanza, discordia; **to have a disagreement with sb** litigare con qn

dis·al·low [ˈdɪsəˈlaʊ] vt respingere; (*Ftbl: goal*) annullare

dis·ap·pear [ˌdɪsəˈpɪəʳ] vi scomparire, sparire; **he disappeared from sight** è scomparso alla vista; **to make sth disappear** far sparire qc

dis·ap·pear·ance [ˌdɪsəˈpɪərəns] N scomparsa, sparizione *f*; **the disappearance of the money** la scomparsa del denaro

dis·ap·point [ˌdɪsəˈpɔɪnt] vt deludere

dis·ap·point·ed [ˌdɪsəˈpɔɪntɪd] ADJ deluso(-a)

dis·ap·point·ing [ˌdɪsəˈpɔɪntɪŋ] ADJ deludente

dis·ap·point·ment [ˌdɪsəˈpɔɪntmənt] N (*cause of dejection*) delusione *f*; (*dejection*) disappunto

dis·ap·prov·al [ˌdɪsəˈpruːvəl] N disapprovazione *f*

dis·ap·prove [ˌdɪsəˈpruːv] vi: **to disapprove (of sb/sth)** disapprovare (qn/qc)

dis·ap·prov·ing [ˌdɪsəˈpruːvɪŋ] ADJ di disapprovazione

dis·arm [dɪsˈɑːm] vt disarmare ♦ vi (*Mil*) disarmarsi

dis·arma·ment [dɪsˈɑːməmənt] N disarmo; **disarmament talks** conferenza sul disarmo

dis·arm·ing [dɪsˈɑːmɪŋ] ADJ (*smile*) disarmante

dis·ar·ray [ˌdɪsəˈreɪ] N: **in disarray** (*troops*) in rotta; (*thoughts*) confuso(-a); (*clothes*) in disordine; **to throw into disarray** (*things, plans*) buttare all'aria; (*people*) portare lo scompiglio in

dis·as·ter [dɪˈzɑːstəʳ] N (*also fig*) disastro; **disaster area** zona disastrata; **disaster fund** raccolta di fondi a favore delle vittime di un disastro

dis·as·trous [dɪˈzɑːstrəs] ADJ disastroso(-a)

dis·band [dɪsˈbænd] vt (*army*) congedare, smobilitare; (*organization*) sciogliere ♦ vi sciogliersi; **the party disbanded** il partito si sciolse

dis·be·lief [ˈdɪsbəˈliːf] N incredulità; **in disbelief** incredulo(-a)

dis·be·lieve [ˈdɪsbəˈliːv] vt (*person, story*) non credere a, mettere in dubbio; **I don't disbelieve you** non è che non ti creda

disc [dɪsk] N **1** (*gen, record, also Anat*) disco; (*identity disc: of dog*) targhetta di riconoscimento; (: *of soldier*) piastrina di riconoscimento **2** (*Comput*) = **disk**

dis·card [dɪsˈkɑːd] vt (*clothes*) smettere; (*unwanted things*) sbarazzarsi di; (*idea, plan, playing card*) scartare; (*people*) abbandonare

disc brakes NPL (*Aut*) freni *mpl* a disco

dis·cern [dɪˈsɜːn] vt (*frm*) distinguere, discernere

dis·cern·ible [dɪˈsɜːnəbl] ADJ (*frm*) percepibile

dis·cern·ing [dɪˈsɜːnɪŋ] ADJ (*buyer, reader, collector*) esperto(-a), perspicace; (*eye*) da intenditore(-trice); (*taste*) raffinato(-a), sicuro(-a)

dis·charge [*n* dɪsˈtʃɑːdʒ, *vb* dɪsˈtʃɑːdʒ] N **1** (*of cargo*) operazione *f* di scarico; (*of gun*) scarica **2** (*of patient*) dimissione *f*; (*of worker*) licenziamento; (*of soldier*) congedo; (*of prisoner*) rilascio; (*of duty*) adempimento; (*of debt*) estinzione *f* **3** (*Elec*) scarica; (*of gas, chemicals*) emissione *f*; (*of water, waste*) scarico; (*Med: from wound*) secrezione *f*; (: *vaginal discharge*) perdite *fpl* (bianche) ♦ vt **1** (*ship, load*) scaricare; (*waste*) scaricare; (*shot*) far partire; (*liquid*) versare; (*Med: pus etc*) spurgare, emettere; **to discharge one's gun** fare fuoco **2** (*dismiss: employee*) licenziare; (*soldier*) congedare; (*patient*) dimettere; (*prisoner*) rilasciare; (*defendant*) prosciogliere; **discharged bankrupt** fallito cui il tribunale ha concesso la riabilitazione **3** (*settle: debt*) pagare, estinguere; (*complete: task*) assolvere, adempiere a; (*duties*) compiere ♦ vi (*wound, sore*) spurgare; (*Elec*) scaricarsi

dis·ci·ple [dɪˈsaɪpl] N (*also fig*) discepolo(-a)

dis·ci·pli·nary [ˈdɪsɪplɪnərɪ] ADJ disciplinare; **to take disciplinary action against sb** prendere un provvedimento disciplinare contro qn

dis·ci·pline [ˈdɪsɪplɪn] N disciplina; (*punishment*) punizione *f*, castigo; **to keep/maintain discipline** tenere/mantenere la disciplina ♦ vt (*punish*) punire, castigare; **to discipline o.s. to do sth** imporsi di fare qc; **to discipline o.s** darsi una regola

disc jockey N disc jockey *m inv*

dis·claim [dɪsˈkleɪm] vt (*frm*) negare, smentire; **to disclaim all knowledge of sth** negare di essere a conoscenza di qc

dis·claim·er [dɪsˈkleɪməʳ] N (*frm*) smentita; **to issue a disclaimer** pubblicare una smentita

dis·close [dɪsˈkləʊz] vt (*all senses*) rivelare, svelare

dis·clo·sure [dɪsˈkləʊʒəʳ] N rivelazione *f*

dis·co [ˈdɪskəʊ] N (*fam: place*) discoteca; (: *event*) festa (con disc jockey)

dis·col·our, dis·col·or (*USA*) [dɪsˈkʌləʳ] vt scolorire, sbiadire; (*whites*) ingiallire ♦ vi scolorirsi, sbiadire; (*whites*) ingiallire

dis·col·oura·tion, dis·col·ora·tion (*USA*) [dɪsˌkʌləˈreɪʃən] N (*see adj*) scolorimento; ingiallimento

dis·col·oured, dis·col·ored (*USA*) [dɪsˈkʌləd] ADJ scolorito(-a), sbiadito(-a); (*whites*) ingiallito(-a)

dis·com·fort [dɪsˈkʌmfət] N (*lack of comfort*) scomodità *f inv*; (*uneasiness*) disagio, imbarazzo; **his wound gave him some discomfort** la ferita gli procurava un certo disagio

dis·con·cert [ˌdɪskənˈsɜːt] vt sconcertare

dis·con·nect [ˌdɪskəˈnekt] vt (*pipe, television*) staccare; (*electricity, gas, water*) sospendere (l'erogazione di); **I've been disconnected** (*Telec: for non-payment*) mi hanno staccato il telefono; (: *in mid-conversation*) è caduta la linea, si è interrotta la comunicazione

dis·con·nec·ted [ˌdɪskəˈnektɪd] ADJ (*speech, thoughts, facts*) sconnesso(-a)

dis·con·so·late [dɪsˈkɒnsəlɪt] ADJ sconsolato(-a)

dis·con·tent [ˈdɪskənˈtent] N scontentezza, dispiacere *m*; (*Pol*) malcontento, scontento

dis·con·tent·ed [ˈdɪskənˈtentɪd] ADJ: **discontented (with/about)** scontento(-a) (di), insoddisfatto(-a) (di)

dis·con·tinue [ˈdɪskənˈtɪnjuː] vt interrompere, cessare; (*Comm*) **discontinued line** articolo fuori produzione; **to be discontinued** (*product*) uscire di produzione

dis·cord [ˈdɪskɔːd] N disaccordo, discordia; (*Mus*) dissonanza

dis·cord·ant [dɪsˈkɔːdənt] ADJ (*gen*) discordante; (*sound*) dissonante, stonato(-a)

dis·co·theque [ˈdɪskəʊtɛk] N discoteca

dis·count [*n* 'dıskaʊnt, *vb* dıs'kaʊnt] N (*reduction*) sconto, riduzione *f*; **a discount for students** una riduzione per studenti; **a twenty per cent discount** uno sconto del venti per cento; **to be at a discount** (*Comm*) essere scontato(-a); (*fig*: *little valued*) essere svalutato(-a); **to buy at a discount** comprare a prezzo scontato; **to give sb a discount on sth** fare uno sconto a qn su qc; **discount for cash** sconto cassa *inv*; **discount rate** tasso di sconto ♦ VT (*Comm*) scontare; (*fig*: *report, idea, theory*) non badare a

discount house N 1 (*Brit*: *Fin*) istituto di sconto, discount house *f inv* 2 (*USA*) = **discount store**

dis·cour·age [dıs'kʌrıdʒ] VT 1 (*dishearten*) scoraggiare; **I don't want to discourage you, but ...** non vorrei scoraggiarti, ma...; **to get discouraged** scoraggiarsi 2 (*dissuade, deter*) tentare di dissuadere; **to discourage sb from doing sth** tentare di dissuadere qn dal fare qc

dis·cour·age·ment [dıs'kʌrıdʒmənt] N (*dissuasion*) disapprovazione *f*; (*depression*) scoraggiamento; **to act as a discouragement to** scoraggiare

dis·cour·ag·ing [dıs'kʌrıdʒıŋ] ADJ scoraggiante, avvilente

dis·cour·teous [dıs'kɜːtıəs] ADJ scortese

dis·cov·er [dıs'kʌvə'] VT (*gen*) scoprire; (*after search*) scovare, trovare; (*notice*: *loss, mistake*) scoprire, accorgersi di

dis·cov·ery [dıs'kʌvərı] N scoperta

dis·cred·it [dıs'kredıt](*frm*) VT discredito; **to bring discredit on sb/sth** far cadere qn/qc in discredito ♦ VT screditare

dis·creet [dıs'kriːt] ADJ discreto(-a)

dis·creet·ly [dıs'kriːtlı] ADV discretamente, con discrezione

dis·crep·an·cy [dıs'krepənsı] N discrepanza

dis·cre·tion [dıs'kreʃən] N discrezione *f*; **at your/his** *etc* **discretion** a tua/sua *etc* discrezione; **use your own discretion** giudica tu

dis·cre·tion·ary [dıs'kreʃənərı] ADJ (*powers, payment*) discrezionale

dis·crimi·nate [dıs'krımı͵neıt] VI: **to discriminate (between)** (*gen*) distinguere (tra); **to discriminate against/in favour of** fare discriminazioni ai danni di/a favore di; **to discriminate against women** fare discriminazioni contro le donne

dis·crimi·nat·ing [dıs'krımı͵neıtıŋ] ADJ (*person*) esigente; (*judgment*) acuto(-a); (*ear*) fine

dis·crimi·na·tion [dıs͵krımı'neıʃən] N 1 (*prejudice*): **discrimination (against/in favour of)** discriminazione *f* (ai danni di/a favore di); **racial/sexual discrimination** discriminazione razziale/sessuale 2 (*good judgment*) discernimento

dis·cus ['dıskəs] N disco; **discus thrower** lanciatore(-trice) di disco

dis·cuss [dıs'kʌs] VT (*general topic*) discutere di; (*problem, plan*) discutere; (*debate*) dibattere; **we discussed the topic all evening** abbiamo discusso tutta la sera dell'argomento; **to discuss sth at length** dibattere qc a lungo

dis·cus·sion [dıs'kʌʃən] N discussione *f*; (*meeting*) colloquio, dibattito; **it's still under discussion** (*plan, policy*) non è ancora definitivo

dis·dain [dıs'deın] N disdegno ♦ VT sdegnare; **to disdain to do sth** disdegnare di fare qc

dis·ease [dı'ziːz] N malattia

dis·eased [dı'ziːzd] ADJ malato(-a)

dis·em·bark [dısım'bɑːk] VI, VT sbarcare

dis·em·bar·ka·tion [͵dısembɑː'keıʃən] N sbarco

dis·em·bod·ied ['dısım'bɒdıd] ADJ incorporeo(-a); (*voice*) etereo(-a); (*soul, spirit*) disincarnato(-a)

dis·em·bow·el [dısım'baʊəl] VT sbudellare, sventrare

dis·en·chant·ed [͵dısın'tʃɑːntıd] ADJ disincantato(-a); **disenchanted (with)** deluso(-a) (da)

dis·en·fran·chise ['dısın'fræntʃaız] VT privare del diritto di voto; (*Comm*) togliere il privilegio commerciale a

dis·en·gage [͵dısın'geıdʒ] VT (*object, hand*) liberare; (*Aut*: *clutch*) disinnestare; (*Mil*: *forces*) disimpegnare ♦ VT (*see vt*): **to disengage (from)** disinnestarsi (da); disimpegnarsi (da)

dis·en·tan·gle ['dısın'tæŋgl] VT (*string, wool*) sbrogliare; **to disentangle o.s. from** (*fig*) districarsi da, sbrogliarsi da

dis·fa·vour,   **dis·fa·vor** (*USA*) [dıs'feıvə'] N (*frm*) disapprovazione *f*; **to fall into disfavour** cadere in disgrazia; **to be in disfavour with sb** avere la disapprovazione di qn; **to look with disfavour on** disapprovare

dis·fig·ure [dıs'fıgə'] VT (*person*) sfigurare; (*landscape*) deturpare

dis·gorge [dıs'gɔːdʒ] VT (*contents*) scaricare; (*subj*: *vehicle, building*) scaricare

dis·grace [dıs'greıs] N (*state of shame*) disonore *m*, vergogna; (*shameful thing*) vergogna; (*disfavour*) disgrazia; **he's a disgrace to the school/family** è il disonore della scuola/della famiglia; **he's brought disgrace upon himself** si è ricoperto di vergogna; **he resigned in disgrace** caduto in disgrazia, si è dimesso; **to be in disgrace** essere in disgrazia; (*child, dog*) essere in castigo; **it's a disgrace!** è una vergogna! ♦ VT (*family, country*) disonorare, far cadere in disgrazia; **he disgraced himself** ha fatto una pessima figura; **he was publicly disgraced** fu svergognato pubblicamente

dis·grace·ful [dıs'greısful] ADJ vergognoso(-a), scandaloso(-a)

dis·grun·tled [dıs'grʌntld] ADJ (*person*) di malumore, di cattivo umore; (*look*) seccato(-a)

dis·guise [dıs'gaız] N travestimento; **in disguise** travestito(-a) ♦ VT (*gen*) travestire; (*voice*) contraffare; (*feelings*) mascherare; **to disguise o.s.** mascherarsi; **to disguise o.s. as** travestirsi da; **there's no disguising the fact that ...** non si può nascondere (il fatto) che...

dis·gust [dıs'gʌst] N disgusto; **much to my disgust** con mio profondo disgusto; **she left in disgust** se n'è andata disgustata ♦ VT disgustare, far schifo a

dis·gust·ed [dıs'gʌstıd] ADJ: **to be disgusted (at)** essere disgustato(-a) (di fronte a)

dis·gust·ing [dıs'gʌstıŋ] ADJ schifoso(-a), disgustoso(-a)

dish [dıʃ] N piatto; (*food*) piatto, pietanza; **a vegetarian dish** un piatto vegetariano; **put the peas in a serving dish** metti i piselli in un piatto da portata; **to wash** *or* **do the dishes** lavare *or* fare i piatti

  ▸ **dish out** VT + ADV (*food*) servire; (*advice*) dispensare; (*money*) sganciare; (*exam papers*) distribuire

  ▸ **dish up** VT + ADV (*food*) servire; (*facts, statistics*) presentare

dish·cloth ['dıʃ͵klɒθ] N strofinaccio dei piatti

dis·heart·en [dıs'hɑːtn] VT scoraggiare

di·shev·elled, di·shev·eled (*USA*) [dı'ʃevəld] ADJ (*hair*) arruffato(-a); (*clothes*) tutto(-a) in disordine

dis·hon·est [dıs'ɒnıst] ADJ (*person, action*) disonesto(-a); (*means*) sleale

dis·hon·es·ty [dıs'ɒnıstı] N (*see adj*) disonestà *f inv*; slealtà *f inv*

dis·hon·our, dis·hon·or (*USA*) [dıs'ɒnə'] N (*frm*) disonore *m*; **to bring dishonour on** gettare il disonore su, far disonore a ♦ VT (*family, woman*) disonorare; (*cheque*) non onorare

dis·hon·our·able, dis·hon·or·able (*USA*) [dıs'ɒnərəbl] ADJ disonorevole

dish·towel ['dıʃ͵taʊəl] N strofinaccio dei piatti

dish·washer ['dıʃ͵wɒʃə'] N (*machine*) lavastoviglie *f inv*; (*person*: *in restaurant*) lavapiatti *m/f inv*

dis·il·lu·sion [͵dısı'luːʒən] VT disilludere, disingannare; **to become disillusioned (with)** perdere le illusioni (su) ♦ N = **disillusionment**

dis·il·lu·sion·ment [͵dısı'luːʒənmənt] N disillusione *f*, disinganno

dis·in·cen·tive [͵dısın'sentıv] N (*frm*): **to act as a disincentive (to)** agire da freno (su); **to be a disincentive to** scoraggiare

dis·in·clined ['dısın'klaınd] ADJ: **to be disinclined to do sth** essere poco propenso(-a) a fare qc

dis·in·fect [͵dısın'fekt] VT disinfettare

dis·in·fect·ant [͵dısın'fektənt] N disinfettante *m*

dis·in·fla·tion [͵dısın'fleıʃən] N (*Econ*) disinflazione *f*

dis·in·for·ma·tion [͵dısınfə'meıʃən] N disinformazione *f*

dis·in·her·it [͵dısın'herıt] VT diseredare

dis·in·te·grate [dıs'ıntıgreıt] VI disintegrarsi; (*fig*: *society, theory*) disgregarsi

dis·in·ter·est·ed [dıs'ıntrıstıd] ADJ (*impartial*) disinteressato(-a); (*strictly incorrect*: *uninterested*) non interessato(-a), indifferente

dis·joint·ed [dıs'dʒɔıntıd] ADJ sconnesso(-a), slegato(-a)

disk [dısk] N 1 = **disc** 2 (*Comput*) disco; **the hard disk** il disco rigido

disk drive N (*Comput*) unità disco

disk·ette [dɪsˈkɛt] N (*Comput*) dischetto, floppy disk *m inv*

disk operating system N (*Comput*) sistema *m* operativo a disco

dis·like [dɪsˈlaɪk] N: dislike (of) antipatia (per), avversione *f* (per); **to take a dislike to sb/sth** prendere in antipatia qn/qc; **my likes and dislikes** ciò che mi piace e ciò che non mi piace ♦ VT (*thing, person*): **I dislike it** non mi piace; **I dislike the idea** l'idea non mi va; **I dislike her intensely** mi è fortemente antipatica, mi è antipaticissima

dis·lo·cate [ˈdɪsləʊkeɪt] VT (*Med*) slogare, lussare; (*fig: plans*) scombussolare; **he dislocated his shoulder** si è lussato una spalla

dis·lodge [dɪsˈlɒdʒ] VT (*gen*) rimuovere; (*enemy*) far sgomberare

dis·loy·al [ˈdɪsˈlɔɪəl] ADJ: **disloyal (to)** sleale (verso)

dis·mal [ˈdɪzməl] ADJ (*gloomy*) tetro(-a), cupo(-a); (*weather*) grigio(-a); **it was a dismal failure** è stato un misero fallimento

dis·man·tle [dɪsˈmæntl] VT (*machine etc*) smontare; (*service, system*) smantellare; (*fort, warship*) disarmare

dis·may [dɪsˈmeɪ] N sgomento, costernazione *f*; **in dismay** costernato(-a); **much to my dismay** con mio gran sgomento ♦ VT costernare, sgomentare

dis·miss [dɪsˈmɪs] VT **1** (*worker*) licenziare; (*official*) destituire; (*assembly*) sciogliere **2** (*gen*) congedare; (*charge, accusation*) respingere; (*problem, possibility, idea*) scartare; **she dismissed the suggestion immediately** ha scartato subito il suggerimento; **the judge dismissed the case** (*Law*) il giudice ha dichiarato il non luogo a procedere; **class dismissed!** (*Scol*) potete andare! ♦ VI (*Mil*) rompere i ranghi

dis·mis·sal [dɪsˈmɪsəl] N congedo; (*of worker*) licenziamento; (*of official*) destituzione *f*; (*of assembly*) scioglimento; **the dismissal of public opinion** l'ignorare l'opinione pubblica; **the dismissal of a case** (*Law*) il non luogo a procedere

dis·mount [dɪsˈmaʊnt] VI: **to dismount (from)** smontare (da), scendere (da) ♦ VT **1** (*gun*) smontare **2** (*rider*) disarcionare

dis·obedi·ence [ˌdɪsəˈbiːdɪəns] N disubbidienza

dis·obedi·ent [ˌdɪsəˈbiːdɪənt] ADJ disubbidiente

dis·obey [ˈdɪsəˈbeɪ] VT (*person, order*) disubbidire a; (*rule*) trasgredire; **he disobeyed instructions** ha disobbedito alle istruzioni

dis·or·der [dɪsˈɔːdəʳ] N **1** (*confusion*) confusione *f*, caos *m*; (*untidiness*) disordine *m*; **in disorder** in disordine **2** (*Pol: rioting*) disordini *mpl*, tumulto; **civil disorder** disordini *mpl* (interni) **3** (*Med*) disturbi *mpl*

dis·or·der·ly [dɪsˈɔːdəlɪ] ADJ (*room*) disordinato(-a); (*behaviour, crowd*) turbolento(-a); (*meeting*) tumultuoso(-a), burrascoso(-a)

disorderly conduct N (*Law*) comportamento atto a turbare l'ordine pubblico

dis·or·gan·ize [dɪsˈɔːgənaɪz] VT disorganizzare

dis·or·gan·ized [dɪsˈɔːgənaɪzd] ADJ (*person, life*) disorganizzato(-a); (*system, meeting*) male organizzato(-a)

disorientated [dɪsˈɔːrɪənteɪtɪd] ADJ disorientato(-a), (disorientata)

dis·own [dɪsˈəʊn] VT rinnegare, ripudiare

dis·par·ag·ing [dɪsˈpærɪdʒɪŋ] ADJ (*comment, remark*) denigratorio(-a); **to be disparaging about sb/sth** denigrare qn/qc

dis·par·ate [ˈdɪspərɪt] ADJ (*frm*) disparato(-a)

dis·par·ity [dɪsˈpærɪtɪ] N disparità *f inv*

dis·pas·sion·ate [dɪsˈpæʃənɪt] ADJ (*unbiased*) spassionato(-a), imparziale; (*unemotional*) calmo(-a)

dis·patch, des·patch [dɪsˈpætʃ] N **1** (*sending: of goods*) spedizione *f*, invio; (*: of person*) invio; **dispatch department** reparto spedizioni **2** (*Mil, Press: report*) dispaccio; **mentioned in dispatches** (*Mil*) citato(-a) all'ordine del giorno **3** (*promptness*) prontezza, rapidità ♦ VT **1** (*send: letter, goods*) spedire, inviare; (*: messenger, troops*) inviare **2** (*deal with: business*) sbrigare **3** (*old: kill*) uccidere, ammazzare; (*hum*) mandare all'altro mondo

dispatch rider N (*Mil*) corriere *m*, portaordini *m inv*

dis·pel [dɪsˈpɛl] VT (*doubts, fears*) dissipare, scacciare

dis·pen·sa·ry [dɪsˈpɛnsərɪ] N farmacia; (*clinic*) dispensario, ambulatorio

dis·pense [dɪsˈpɛns] VT (*food, money*) dispensare, distribuire; (*justice*) amministrare; (*medicine*) preparare e dare; **to dispense prescriptions** preparare e dare medicine su ricetta
▸ **dispense with** VT + PREP (*do without*) fare a meno di

dis·pens·er [dɪsˈpɛnsəʳ] N (*container*) distributore *m*

dis·pens·ing chem·ist [dɪsˈpɛnsɪŋˈkɛmɪst] N (*Brit: shop*) farmacia; (*: person*) farmacista *m/f*

dis·per·sal [dɪsˈpɜːsəl] N (*gen*) dispersione *f*; (*Bot*) disseminazione *f*

dis·perse [dɪsˈpɜːs] VT (*crowd, demonstrators, oil slick*) disperdere ♦ VI (*crowd*) disperdersi; (*mist*) dissiparsi

dis·pir·it·ed [dɪsˈpɪrɪtɪd] ADJ abbattuto(-a), scoraggiato(-a); (*sigh*) di avvilimento

dis·place [dɪsˈpleɪs] VI (*move*) spostare; (*replace*) rimpiazzare, soppiantare; (*remove from office*) destituire; (*water: Naut*) dislocare; (*: Phys*) spostare

dis·placed per·son [dɪsˈpleɪsdˈpɜːsn] N (*Pol*) profugo(-a)

dis·place·ment [dɪsˈpleɪsmənt] N (*see vb*) spostamento; rimpiazzo; destituzione *f*; dislocamento

dis·play [dɪsˈpleɪ] N **1** (*of goods for sale, paintings*) mostra, esposizione *f*; (*also: window display*) vetrina; (*of emotion*) manifestazione *f*; (*of strength, authority, force, interest*) dimostrazione *f*; (*pej: ostentation*) sfoggio, ostentazione *f*; **on display** (*gen*) in mostra; (*goods*) in vetrina; (*results, art*) esposto(-a); **a firework display** uno spettacolo di fuochi d'artificio; **display window** vetrina; **the assistant took the watch out of the display** il commesso ha preso l'orologio dalla vetrina **2** (*military display*) parata (militare) **3** (*computer display*) display *m inv* ♦ VT (*gen*) esporre; (*ostentatiously*) ostentare, far sfoggio di; (*emotion, ignorance*) mostrare, manifestare; (*notice, results*) affiggere; (*departure/arrival times*) indicare; **the watches displayed in the shop window** gli orologi esposti in vetrina; **she proudly displayed her medal** ha mostrato con orgoglio la sua medaglia

display advertising N (*Press*) pubblicità tabellare

dis·please [dɪsˈpliːz] VT dispiacere a, scontentare; **displeased with** scontento(-a) di

dis·pleas·ure [dɪsˈplɛʒəʳ] N: **displeasure (at)** dispiacere *m* (per)

dis·pos·able [dɪsˈpəʊzəbl] ADJ (*not reusable: razor, camera*) usa e getta *inv*; **disposable income** reddito netto; **disposable diaper** (*Brit*) pannolino

dis·pos·al [dɪsˈpəʊzəl] N (*of rubbish*) eliminazione *f*, smaltimento; (*of property etc: by selling*) vendita; (*: by giving away*) cessione *f*; **to put sth at sb's disposal** mettere qc a disposizione di qn; **to have at one's disposal** avere a propria disposizione

dis·pose [dɪsˈpəʊz] VT (*frm: arrange: furniture*) disporre; (*: troops*) disporre, schierare
▸ **dispose of** VI + PREP **1** (*get rid of: unwanted goods, evidence, rubbish*) sbarazzarsi di, disfarsi di; (*Comm: sell*) vendere **2** (*deal with: matter, problem*) sistemare

dis·posed [dɪsˈpəʊzd] ADJ: **to be disposed to do sth** essere disposto(-a) a fare qc; **to be well disposed towards sb/sth** essere ben disposto(-a) verso qn/qc

dis·po·si·tion [ˌdɪspəˈzɪʃən] N (*frm*) **1** (*temperament*) indole *f*, temperamento; (*tendency*) disposition to sth/to do sth tendenza a qc/a fare qc, inclinazione *f*; **he was always of a nervous disposition** è sempre stato ansioso di carattere **2** (*arrangement*) disposizione *f*

dis·pos·sess [ˌdɪspəˈzɛs] VT: **to be dispossessed (of sth)** (*property*) essere spossessato(-a) (di qc)

dis·pro·por·tion [ˌdɪsprəˈpɔːʃən] N sproporzione *f*

dis·pro·por·tion·ate [ˌdɪsprəˈpɔːʃnɪt] ADJ: **disproportionate (to)** sproporzionato(-a) (a o rispetto a)

dis·prove [dɪsˈpruːv] VT confutare

dis·pute [dɪsˈpjuːt] N (*quarrel*) disputa; (*controversy*) discussione *f*, controversia; (*legal*) lite *f*; **a dispute between neighbours** una lite tra vicini; **industrial dispute** controversia sindacale; **beyond dispute** fuori discussione; **the company is in dispute with the government** la società è in disaccordo con il governo; **to be in dispute** (*matter*) essere in discussione; (*territory*) essere oggetto di contesa ♦ VT **1**

(*question: statement, claim*) contestare; **I don't dispute the fact** non contesto questo fatto **2** (*debate: matter, question*) discutere **3** (*compete for: possession, victory*) disputarsi ♦ VI (*argue*): **to dispute (about** *or* **over)** discutere (su)

dis·quali·fi·ca·tion [dɪsˌkwɒlɪfɪˈkeɪʃən] N (*from competition*) squalifica; (*of member*) espulsione *f*; (*Brit: from driving*) ritiro della patente

dis·quali·fy [dɪsˈkwɒlɪfaɪ] VT: **to disqualify sb (from)** (*from competition*) squalificare qn (da); **to disqualify sb from doing sth** vietare a qn di fare qc; **to disqualify sb from driving** (*Brit*) ritirare la patente a qn; **it disqualified him for the job** lo ha reso non adatto al lavoro

dis·qui·et [dɪsˈkwaɪət] N (*frm*) inquietudine *f*

dis·qui·et·ing [dɪsˈkwaɪətɪŋ] ADJ (*frm*) inquietante, allarmante

dis·re·gard [dɪsrɪˈɡɑːd] N (*indifference*): **disregard (for)** (*feelings*) insensibilità, indifferenza (verso); (*danger*) sprezzo (di); (*money*) disprezzo (di); (*non-observance*): **disregard (of)** (*law, rules*) inosservanza (di) ♦ VT (*remark, feelings, fact*) ignorare, non tenere conto di; (*duty*) trascurare; (*authority*) non curarsi di

dis·re·pair [dɪsrɪˈpɛəʳ] N cattivo stato; **to fall into disrepair** (*building*) andare in rovina; (*road*) deteriorarsi

dis·repu·table [dɪsˈrɛpjʊtəbl] ADJ (*person*) poco raccomandabile; (*clothing, behaviour*) indecente; (*area*) malfamato(-a), poco raccomandabile

dis·re·pute [dɪsrɪˈpjuːt] N: **to bring into disrepute** rovinare la reputazione di; **to fall into disrepute** rovinarsi la reputazione

dis·re·spect·ful [dɪsrɪsˈpɛktfʊl] ADJ (*person*) poco rispettoso(-a); (*comment*) irriverente; **to be disrespectful to** *or* **towards** mancare di rispetto a *or* verso

dis·rupt [dɪsˈrʌpt] VT (*meeting, lesson*) disturbare, interrompere; (*public transport*) creare il caos in; (*plans*) scombussolare

dis·rup·tion [dɪsˈrʌpʃən] N (*see vb*) interruzione *f*; caos *m*; scombussolamento; **the disruption of rail services** il caos dei servizi ferroviari

dis·rup·tive [dɪsˈrʌptɪv] ADJ (*pupil*) indisciplinato(-a); (*influence*) negativo(-a), deleterio(-a); (*strike action*) paralizzante

dis·sat·is·fac·tion [ˌdɪsˌsætɪsˈfækʃən] N scontentezza; **dissatisfaction (with)** insoddisfazione *f* (per), scontento (per *or* a causa di)

dis·sat·is·fied [dɪsˈsætɪsfaɪd] ADJ: **dissatisfied (with)** insoddisfatto(-a) (di), scontento(-a) (di); **a dissatisfied customer** un cliente insoddisfatto; **we were dissatisfied with the service** non eravamo soddisfatti del servizio

dis·sect [dɪˈsɛkt] VT (*animal, body, specimen*) sezionare; (*fig*) sviscerare

dis·semi·nate [dɪˈsɛmɪˌneɪt] VT (*information*) diffondere

dis·sent [dɪˈsɛnt] N dissenso ♦ VI (*gen*): **to dissent (from)** dissentire (da)

dis·sent·er [dɪˈsɛntəʳ] N (*Rel, Pol*) dissidente *m/f*

dis·ser·ta·tion [ˌdɪsəˈteɪʃən] N (*Univ*) tesi *f inv*, dissertazione *f*

dis·ser·vice [dɪsˈsɜːvɪs] N: **to do sb a disservice** rendere un cattivo servizio a qn

dis·si·dent [ˈdɪsɪdənt] (*Pol*) N dissidente *m/f* ♦ ADJ (*speech, voice*) dissenso; (*group*) dissidente

dis·simi·lar [dɪˈsɪmɪləʳ] ADJ: **dissimilar (to)** dissimile (da), diverso(-a) (da); **two very dissimilar cases** due casi molto diversi tra loro

dis·si·pate [ˈdɪsɪˌpeɪt] VT (*frm*) dissipare

dis·si·pat·ed [ˈdɪsɪˌpeɪtɪd] ADJ (*person, life*) dissipato(-a); (*behaviour*) dissoluto(-a)

dis·so·ci·ate [dɪˈsəʊʃɪˌeɪt] VT: **to disassociate (from)** dissociare (da), separare (da); **to disassociate o.s. from** dichiarare di non avere niente a che fare con; (*from political line*) dissociarsi da

dis·so·lute [ˈdɪsəˌluːt] ADJ dissoluto(-a)

dis·solve [dɪˈzɒlv] VT (*gen*) dissolvere, sciogliere; (*partnership, business, marriage: Pol*) sciogliere ♦ VI dissolversi, sciogliersi; (*Pol*) sciogliersi; **it dissolves in water** si scioglie in acqua; **to dissolve into tears** scoppiare in lacrime; **to dissolve into thin air** svanire nel nulla

dis·suade [dɪˈsweɪd] VT: **to dissuade sb (from doing)** dissuadere qn (dal fare), distogliere qn (dall'idea di fare)

distaff side [ˈdɪstɑːfˌsaɪd] N: **on the distaff side** per parte di madre

dis·tance [ˈdɪstəns] N (*between two things*) distanza; **the distance between the houses** la distanza *or* lo spazio tra le case; **it's a good distance** dista un bel po', è parecchio lontano; **it's within walking distance** ci si arriva a piedi; **a distance of forty kilometres** una distanza di quaranta chilometri; **at a distance of 2 metres** a 2 metri di distanza; **in the distance** in lontananza; **from a distance** da lontano; **distance race** gara di fondo; **distance runner** fondista *m/f*; **distance ratio** rapporto di distanza; **at this distance in time** a distanza di tanto tempo; **to keep sb at a distance** tenere qn a distanza; **to keep one's distance** tenersi a distanza ♦ VT (*fig*) allontanare; **to distance o.s from** allontanarsi da, staccarsi da

dis·tant [ˈdɪstənt] ADJ (*gen*) lontano(-a); (*country*) distante, lontano(-a); (*likeness*) vago(-a), lontano(-a); (*fig: aloof: manner, person*) distaccato(-a); **in the distant past/future** nel lontano passato/futuro

dis·taste [dɪsˈteɪst] N: **distaste (for)** ripugnanza (per)

dis·taste·ful [dɪsˈteɪstfʊl] ADJ sgradevole, ripugnante; **the very idea is distasteful to me** la sola idea mi ripugna

Dist. Atty. ABBR (*USA*) = district attorney

dis·tem·per¹ [dɪsˈtɛmpəʳ] N (*paint*) tempera

dis·tem·per² [dɪsˈtɛmpəʳ] N (*disease*) cimurro

dis·tend [dɪsˈtɛnd] VT dilatare ♦ VI dilatarsi

dis·tend·ed [dɪsˈtɛndɪd] ADJ (*stomach*) dilatato(-a)

dis·til, dis·till (*USA*) [dɪsˈtɪl] VT distillare; **distilled water** acqua distillata

dis·till·ery [dɪsˈtɪlərɪ] N distilleria

dis·tinct [dɪsˈtɪŋkt] ADJ **1** (*different: species, type*): **distinct (from)** diverso(-a) (da), distinto(-a) (da); **the book is divided into two distinct parts** il libro si divide in due parti distinte; **as distinct from** a differenza di **2** (*clear: sound, shape*) chiaro(-a), distinto(-a); (: *unmistakable: increase, change*) palese, netto(-a); (*definite: preference, progress, feeling*) definito(-a)

dis·tinc·tion [dɪsˈtɪŋkʃən] N (*difference*) distinzione *f*, differenza; (*mark of honour*) onorificenza; **a writer of distinction** un eminente scrittore; **to make** *or* **draw a distinction between** fare (una) distinzione tra; **she got a distinction in English** (*Scol*) ha avuto il massimo dei voti in inglese; (*Univ*) ≈ ha ottenuto la lode

dis·tinc·tive [dɪsˈtɪŋktɪv] ADJ tutto(-a) particolare

dis·tinct·ly [dɪsˈtɪŋktlɪ] ADV (*see, hear*) distintamente; (*promise, remember*) chiaramente; (*prefer*) nettamente; (*better, odd*) decisamente

dis·tin·guish [dɪsˈtɪŋɡwɪʃ] VT distinguere, discernere; **he could just distinguish the form of a man** riusciva a malapena a distinguere la sagoma di un uomo; **he can't distinguish red from green** non distingue il rosso dal verde; **to distinguish o.s. (as)** distinguersi (come) ♦ VI: **to distinguish (between)** distinguere (tra)

dis·tin·guished [dɪsˈtɪŋɡwɪʃt] ADJ (*eminent: pianist, writer*) eminente, noto(-a); (: *scholar*) insigne; (: *career*) brillante; (*refined*) distinto(-a), signorile

dis·tin·guish·ing [dɪsˈtɪŋɡwɪʃɪŋ] ADJ (*marks, characteristics, features*) distintivo(-a), caratteristico(-a)

dis·tort [dɪsˈtɔːt] VT (*also fig*) distorcere; (*face, also Tech*) deformare; (*account, news*) falsare; **the media distort reality** i mass media distorcono la realtà; **a distorted impression** una falsa impressione

dis·tor·tion [dɪsˈtɔːʃən] N (*gen*) distorsione *f*; (*of truth*) alterazione *f*; (*of facts*) travisamento; (*Tech*) deformazione *f*

dis·tract [dɪsˈtrækt] VT (*person*): **to distract sb (from sth)** distrarre qn (da qc); **to distract sb's attention (from sth)** distrarre *or* sviare l'attenzione di qn (da qc)

dis·tract·ed [dɪsˈtræktɪd] ADJ (*confused*) confuso(-a); (*inattentive*) distratto(-a); **to drive sb distracted** far impazzire qn

dis·trac·tion [dɪsˈtrækʃən] N **1** (*interruption*) distrazione *f*; (*entertainment*) distrazione, diversivo; **a distraction from our concerns** una distrazione dalle nostre preoccupazioni **2** (*distress, madness*): **to drive sb to distraction** far impazzire qn

dis·traught [dɪsˈtrɔːt] ADJ stravolto(-a), sconvolto(-a)

dis·tress [dɪsˈtrɛs] N 1 (*mental anguish*) angoscia, pena; (*pain*) dolore *m*; **to be in great distress** essere sconvolto(-a) *or* affranto(-a) dal dolore; **to cause someone distress** arrecare sofferenza a qualcuno 2 (*poverty*) bisogno 3 (*danger*) pericolo; **in distress** (*Brit: ship*) in difficoltà, in pericolo ♦ VT addolorare, affliggere

dis·tress·ing [dɪsˈtrɛsɪŋ] ADJ penoso(-a), doloroso(-a)

distress signal N segnale *m* di richiesta di soccorso

dis·trib·ute [dɪsˈtrɪbjuːt] VT (*leaflets, prizes, load*) distribuire; (*tasks*) ripartire

dis·tri·bu·tion [ˌdɪstrɪˈbjuːʃən] N distribuzione *f*; **distribution costs** costi *mpl* di distribuzione

dis·tribu·tor [dɪsˈtrɪbjʊtəʳ] N 1 (*Comm*) concessionario; (*Cine*) distributore *m* 2 (*Aut, Tech*) distributore *m*; **distributor cap** calotta dello spinterogeno

dis·trict [ˈdɪstrɪkt] N (*of country*) regione *f*; (*of town*) quartiere *m*; (*administrative area*) distretto; **the shopping district** la zona dei negozi; **district manager** responsabile *m* di zona

district attorney N (*USA*) ≈ Procuratore *m* della Repubblica

district nurse N (*Brit*) infermiere(-a) (*che fa visite a domicilio*)

dis·trust [dɪsˈtrʌst] N: **distrust (of)** diffidenza (verso), sfiducia (nei confronti di) ♦ VT diffidare di, non fidarsi di

dis·trust·ful [dɪsˈtrʌstfʊl] ADJ diffidente

dis·turb [dɪsˈtɜːb] VT 1 (*bother*) disturbare, importunare; (*inconvenience*) scomodare; **sorry to disturb you** scusi se la disturbo; **"please do not disturb"** "non disturbare" 2 (*worry: person*) turbare; (*disrupt: sleep, order, meeting*) turbare, disturbare; (*ruffle: water*) turbare 3 (*disarrange: papers*) scompigliare; (*move*) spostare

dis·turb·ance [dɪsˈtɜːbəns] N 1 (*uneasiness, upset*) turbamento; (*interruption*) interruzione *f*; **sleep disturbance** disturbi del sonno 2 (*social, political*) disordini *mpl*, tumulto; (*affray*) tafferuglio

dis·turbed [dɪsˈtɜːbd] ADJ turbato(-a); **he was disturbed to hear that ...** lo ha preoccupato la notizia che...; **to be emotionally disturbed** (*Psych*) avere problemi emotivi

dis·turb·ing [dɪsˈtɜːbɪŋ] ADJ inquietante

dis·use [dɪsˈjuːs] N: **to fall into disuse** cadere in disuso

dis·used [dɪsˈjuːzd] ADJ abbandonato(-a), in disuso

ditch [dɪtʃ] N fosso; (*irrigation channel*) fosso *or* canale *m* d'irrigazione ♦ VT (*fam: get rid of: car*) abbandonare, mollare; (*: person*) piantare, mollare

dith·er [ˈdɪðəʳ] (*fam*) N: **to be in a dither** essere in agitazione ♦ VI titubare; **to dither over a decision** tentennare di fronte a una decisione

dit·to [ˈdɪtəʊ] N (*in lists*) idem come sopra; **ditto marks** virgolette *fpl*; **a coffee, please — ditto (for me)** (*fam*) per me caffè — per me idem ♦ ADV (*likewise*): **I'm really fed up — ditto!** sono proprio stufa — anch'io!

di·van [dɪˈvæn] N divano; **divan bed** divano *m* letto, *inv*

dive [daɪv] N 1 (*of swimmer, goalkeeper*) tuffo; (*of submarine*) immersione *f*; (*Aer*) picchiata 2 (*pej, fam: club etc*) bettola, buco ♦ VI 1 (*swimmer*): **to dive (into)** tuffarsi (in); (*submarine*) immergersi; (*Aer*) scendere in picchiata; (*Ftbl*) tuffarsi 2 (*fam: move quickly*): **to dive into** (*doorway, hole*) buttarsi dentro; (*car, taxi*) saltare su; **he dived into the crowd** si tuffò *or* si lanciò tra la folla; **he dived for cover** si è buttato al riparo; **he dived for the exit** si è lanciato *or* precipitato verso l'uscita

div·er [ˈdaɪvəʳ] N 1 (*swimmer*) tuffatore(-trice); (*deep-sea diver*) palombaro; **diver's buoy** segnasub *m inv* 2 (*Zool*) strolaga

di·verge [daɪˈvɜːdʒ] VI divergere

di·ver·gent [daɪˈvɜːdʒənt] ADJ divergente

di·verse [daɪˈvɜːs] ADJ svariato(-a), vario(-a)

di·ver·si·fi·ca·tion [ˌdaɪvɜːsɪfɪˈkeɪʃən] N diversificazione *f*

di·ver·si·fy [daɪˈvɜːsɪfaɪ] VT rendere vario(-a); (*Comm*) diversificare ♦ VI (*Comm*) diversificarsi

di·ver·sion [daɪˈvɜːʃən] N (*Brit: Aut*) deviazione *f*; (*of river*) diversione; (*distraction*) divertimento; (*old: pastime*) diversivo, distrazione *f*; **to create a diversion** creare un'azione diversiva

di·ver·sion·ary tac·tics [daɪˈvɜːʃnərɪˈtæktɪks] NPL tattica *fsg* diversiva

di·ver·sity [daɪˈvɜːsɪtɪ] N varietà *f inv*, diversità *f inv*

di·vert [daɪˈvɜːt] VT 1 (*traffic, river*) deviare; (*conversation, attention, person*) sviare; (*train, plane*) dirottare 2 (*old: amuse*) distrarre, divertire

di·vest [daɪˈvɛst] VT (*frm*): **to divest of** spogliare di

di·vide [dɪˈvaɪd] VT 1 (*divide (from/into*) dividere (da/in); **divide the pastry in half** dividete la pasta a metà; **to divide (between** *or* **among)** dividere (tra), ripartire (tra); **to divide 6 into 36** *or* **36 by 6** dividere 36 per 6; **40 divided by 5** 40 diviso 5 ♦ VI (*road, river*) dividersi, biforcarsi; (*Math*) essere divisibile; **we divided into two groups** ci siamo divisi in due gruppi

▸ **divide off** VI + ADV (*road*) separarsi ♦ VT + ADV (*area*) separare

▸ **divide out** VT + ADV: **to divide out (between** *or* **among)** (*sweets, proceeds*) distribuire (tra); (*tasks*) distribuire *or* ripartire (tra)

▸ **divide up** VT + ADV dividere

di·vid·ed [dɪˈvaɪdɪd] ADJ (*country, couple*) diviso(-a); **divided opinions** *fpl* discordi; **to be divided in one's mind about sth** essere indeciso(-a) su qc

divided highway N (*USA*) strada a doppia carreggiata

divided skirt N gonna *f* pantalone, *inv*

divi·dend [ˈdɪvɪdɛnd] N (*Fin*) dividendo

di·vid·ers [dɪˈvaɪdəz] NPL (*Math*) compasso a punte fisse

di·vine [dɪˈvaɪn] ADJ (*Rel, or fig: old*) divino(-a); **what divine weather!** che tempo favoloso! ♦ VT (*future*) divinare, predire; (*truth*) indovinare; (*water*) individuare (*tramite rabdomanzia*)

div·ing [ˈdaɪvɪŋ] N tuffi *mpl*

diving board N trampolino

diving suit N scafandro

di·vin·ity [dɪˈvɪnɪtɪ] N divinità *f inv*; (*as study*) teologia

di·vi·sion [dɪˈvɪʒən] N (*gen*) divisione *f*; (*Brit: Ftbl*) serie *f inv*; **the division into two states** la divisione in due stati; **the sales division** il reparto vendite; **First Division** serie A; **to call a division** (*Parliament*) procedere alla votazione, passare ai voti

di·vi·sive [dɪˈvaɪsɪv] ADJ che causa discordia

di·vorce [dɪˈvɔːs] N divorzio; **divorce proceedings** pratiche *fpl* per il divorzio ♦ VI divorziare ♦ VT divorziare da; (*fig*) separare; **she divorced him last year** ha divorziato da lui l'anno scorso

di·vorced [dɪˈvɔːst] ADJ divorziato(-a)

di·vor·cee [dɪˌvɔːˈsiː] N divorziata

div·ot [ˈdɪvɪt] N (*Golf*) zolla di terra (*sollevata accidentalmente*)

di·vulge [daɪˈvʌldʒ] VT divulgare, rivelare; (*evidence, information*) rendere pubblico(-a)

DIY [ˌdiːaɪˈwaɪ] (*Brit*) N ABBR = **do-it-yourself** N ABBR fai da te *m* ♦ ADJ ABBR di fai da te

diz·zi·ness [ˈdɪzɪnɪs] N capogiro, vertigini *fpl*; **an attack of dizziness** un capogiro

diz·zy [ˈdɪzɪ] ADJ (*height*) vertiginoso(-a); **I am** *or* **feel dizzy** ho il capogiro, mi gira la testa; **to make sb dizzy** far girare la testa a qn; **the height made me dizzy** la grande altezza mi ha dato le vertigini

DJ [diːˈdʒeɪ] N ABBR (= *disc jockey*) DJ *m/f inv*, disc jockey *m/f inv*

dj [diːˈdʒeɪ] N ABBR = **dinner jacket**

Dja·kar·ta [dʒəˈkɑːtə] N Giacarta

dl ABBR (= *decilitre*) dl

dm ABBR (= *decimetre*) dm

DMZ [diːɛmˈzɛd] N ABBR = **demilitarized zone**

DNA [diːɛnˈeɪ] N ABBR (= *deoxyribonucleic acid*) DNA *m inv*

DNA test N test *m inv* del DNA

KEYWORD

do¹ [duː] (*3rd pers sg present* **does**, *pt* **did**, *pp* **done**) AUX VB

1 **do you speak English?** parla inglese?; **do you understand?** capisci?; **I don't understand** non capisco; **do you want some?** ne vuoi?; **didn't you ask?** non (l')hai chiesto?; **didn't you know?** non lo sapevi?; **he didn't laugh** non ha riso

2 (*for emphasis*): **DO come!** dai, vieni!; **so you DO know him!** dunque è vero che lo conosci!; **but I DO like it!** sì che mi piace!; **DO shut up!** ma sta' zitto!; **DO sit down** (*polite*) si

accomodi la prego, prego si sieda; (*annoyed*) insomma siediti; **DO tell me!** su, dimmelo!; **I DO wish I could ...** magari potessi...

3 (*used to avoid repeating verb*): **neither do we** nemmeno noi; **he doesn't like it and neither do we** a lui non piace e a noi nemmeno; **so does he** anche lui; **you speak better than I do** parli meglio di me

4 (*in question tags*): **he lives here, doesn't he?** abita qui, vero?, abita qui, no?; **I don't know him, do I?** non lo conosco, vero?

5 (*in answers, replacing verb*): **do you speak English?** — **yes, I do/no, I don't** parli inglese? — sì/no; **do you agree?** — **I do** è d'accordo? — sì; **may I come in?** — **please do!** posso entrare? — certo!; **who made this mess?** — **I did** chi ha fatto questo disordine? — io!, sono stato io!; **do you really?** davvero?, ah sì?

♦ VT

1 (*gen*) fare; **I'll do all I can** farò tutto il possibile; **I've got nothing to do** non ho niente da fare; **I shall do nothing of the sort** non farò niente del genere; **that's done it!** (*fam*) sono fregato! (*or* siamo fregati! *etc*); **have you done the washing?** hai fatto il bucato?; **I'm going to do the washing up** adesso faccio i piatti; **well done!** bravo!, benissimo!; **what are you doing tonight?** che fai stasera?; **what does he do for a living?** cosa fa per vivere?; **what am I to do with you?** dimmi tu come devo fare con te!; **what can I do for you?** (*in shop*) desidera?; **what's to be done?** che fare?; **what's done cannot be undone** quello che è fatto è fatto; **it will have to be done again** è tutto da rifare

2 who does your hair? chi ti fa i capelli?; **to do one's nails** farsi le unghie; **to do Shakespeare** (*Scol*) fare Shakespeare; **to do one's teeth** (*Brit*) pulirsi i denti

3 (*only as past tense, past participle: finish*): **the job's done** il lavoro è fatto; **I haven't done telling you** (*fam*) non ho ancora finito la storia

4 (*visit: city, museum*) fare, visitare; **we did the museums** abbiamo visitato i musei

5 (*Aut*) fare; **the car was doing 100 (mph)** ≈ la macchina faceva i 160 (km/h); **we've done 200 km already** abbiamo già fatto 200 km

6 (*fam: be sufficient*) bastare; (*: be suitable*) andar bene; **that won't do him** questo non gli basta; **that'll do me nicely** per me va benissimo

7 (*play role of*) fare (la parte di); (*mimic*) imitare

8 (*fam: cheat*) imbrogliare, farla a; (*: rob*) ripulire; **to do sb out of sth** fregare qc a qn; **he did her out of a job** le ha fregato *or* soffiato il posto; **I've been done!** mi hanno fregato!

9 (*Culin*) fare; **to do the cooking** cucinare; **how do you like your steak done?** come preferisci la bistecca?; **the meat's done** la carne è pronta; **well done** ben cotto(-a)

♦ VI

1 (*act*) fare, agire; **do as I do** fai come me, fai come faccio io; **he did well to take your advice** ha fatto bene a seguire il tuo consiglio

2 (*get on, fare*) andare; **he's doing badly at school** va male a scuola; **how are you doing?** (*fam*) come va?; **how do you do?** (*in introductions*) piacere; **she did well at university** era molto brava all'università; **his business is doing well** gli affari gli vanno bene

3 (*finish: in past tenses only*): **I've done** ho fatto, ho finito; **have you done?** hai fatto?, hai finito?

4 (*suit*) andare bene; **this coat will do as a cover** questo cappotto potrà fare da coperta; **to make do (with)** arrangiarsi (con); **you'll have to make do with £10** dovrai arrangiarti con 10 sterline; **this room will do** questa stanza va bene; **will it do?** andrà bene?; **that will never do!** non se ne parla nemmeno!; **will it do if I come back at 8?** va bene se torno alle 8?

5 (*be sufficient*) bastare; **will £5 do?** bastano *or* vanno bene 5 sterline?; **that'll do** basta così; **that'll do!** (*in annoyance*) ora basta!

♦ N (*fam*)

1 (*party*) festa; (*formal gathering*) ricevimento; **it was rather a grand do** è stato un ricevimento piuttosto imponente

2 (*in phrases*): **the dos and don'ts** le regole del gioco

► **do away with** VT + PREP (*abolish*) abolire; (*kill*) far fuori

► **do by** VI + PREP: **to do well/badly by sb** comportarsi bene/male con qn; **to be hard done by** essere *or* venire trattato(-a) male

► **do for** VI + PREP (*finish off: project*) mandare all'aria; (*: person*) spacciare; **he's done for!** è spacciato!

► **do in** VT + ADV (*fam: kill*) far fuori

► **do out** VT + ADV (*room*) fare

► **do over** VT + ADV (*fam*) **1** (*USA: do again: work, essay*) rifare; (*: redecorate: house*) rimettere a posto (*pitturare, tapezzare etc*) **2** (*Brit: rob: house*) ripulire **3** (*Brit: hurt*) pestare

► **do up** VT + ADV **1** (*dress, shoes*) allacciare; (*zip*) tirar su; (*buttons*) abbottonare; **books done up in paper** libri impacchettati **2** (*renovate: house, room*) rimettere a nuovo, rifare; **to do o.s. up** farsi bello(-a)

► **do with** VT + PREP **1** (*with could: need*) avere bisogno di; **I could do with some help** mi servirebbe una mano; **I could do with a drink** un bicchierino non guasterebbe; **it could do with a wash** una lavata non gli farebbe male **2 what has that got to do with it?** che c'entra?; **it has to do with ... ** ha a che vedere *or* fare con...; **money has a lot to do with it** è una questione di soldi; **that has nothing to do with you!** non sono affari tuoi!, non ti riguarda!; **I won't have anything to do with it** non voglio aver niente a che farci **3 what have you done with my slippers?** cosa hai fatto delle mie pantofole?; **what did he do with the cat?** che ne ha fatto del gatto?; **what's he done with his hair?** che si è fatto ai capelli?

► **do without** VI + PREP fare a meno di ♦ VI + ADV fare senza

do² [dəʊ] N (*Mus*) do *m inv*

do. ABBR = ditto

DOA [ˌdiːəʊˈeɪ] ABBR (= *dead on arrival*) morto(-a) durante il trasporto

DOB ABBR = date of birth; *see* date¹

doc [dɒk] N (*fam*) dottore(-essa)

doc·ile [ˈdəʊsaɪl] ADJ docile

dock¹ [dɒk] N (*Naut*) bacino; (*wharf*) molo; (*for repairs*) darsena; **docks** dock *m inv*, porto; **dock dues** diritti *mpl* di banchina ♦ VT mettere in bacino ♦ VI entrare in bacino

dock² [dɒk] N (*in court*) banco degli imputati

dock³ [dɒk] VT **1** (*tail*) mozzare **2** (*pay*) decurtare

dock·er [ˈdɒkəʳ] N scaricatore *m* (di porto), portuale *m*

dock·et [ˈdɒkɪt] N (*on parcel etc*) etichetta, cartellino

dock·yard [ˈdɒkjɑːd] N cantiere *m* (navale)

doc·tor [ˈdɒktəʳ] N **1** (*Med*) dottore(-essa), medico; **Doctor Brown** il Dottor Brown; **doctor's office** (*USA*) studio medico, ambulatorio **2** (*Univ: Ph.D.*) dottore(-essa), **Doctor of Philosophy** (*degree*) ≈ dottorato di ricerca; (*person*) ≈ titolare *m/f* di un dottorato di ricerca ♦ VT **1** (*interfere with: food, drink*) adulterare; (*: text, document*) alterare, manipolare **2** (*treat: cold*) curare **3** (*fam: castrate: cat*) castrare

doc·tor·ate [ˈdɒktərɪt] N ≈ dottorato di ricerca

doc·trine [ˈdɒktrɪn] N dottrina

docu·dra·ma [ˈdɒkjʊˈdrɑːmə] N (*TV*) ricostruzione *f* filmata

docu·ment [*n* ˈdɒkjʊmənt, *vb* ˈdɒkjʊment] N documento; **document case** cartella, borsa portadocumenti; **document wallet** cartelletta ♦ VT documentare

docu·men·tary [ˌdɒkjʊˈmentərɪ] ADJ documentario(-a); (*evidence*) documentato(-a); **documentary letter of credit** lettera di credito contro documenti ♦ N (*Cine, TV*) documentario

docu·men·ta·tion [ˌdɒkjʊmenˈteɪʃən] N documentazione *f*

DOD [ˌdiːəʊˈdiː] N ABBR (*USA: = Department of Defense*) *see* defense

dod·der·ing [ˈdɒdərɪŋ], **dod·dery** [ˈdɒdərɪ] ADJ malfermo(-a) sulle gambe

dod·dle [ˈdɒdəl] N (*Brit fam*): **it's a doddle** è un gioco da ragazzi

Do·deca·nese [ˌdəʊdɪkəˈniːz] NPL: **the Dodecanese** il Dodecanneso; **the Dodecanese Islands** le isole del Dodecanneso

dodge [dɒdʒ] N (*fam: trick*) espediente *m*, trucco; **a tax dodge** un trucchetto per evadere le tasse ♦ VT (*blow, missile*) schivare; (*pursuer, question, difficulty*) eludere; (*tax*) evadere; (*work, duty*) sottrarsi a; **to dodge the issue** girare intorno all'argomento ♦ VI scansarsi; (*Sport*) fare una schivata; **to dodge out of the way** scansarsi; **to dodge through the**

traffic destreggiarsi nel traffico; **to dodge behind a tree** nascondersi dietro un albero

dodgy [ˈdɒdʒɪ] ADJ (*comp* **-ier**, *superl* **-iest**) (*fam: plan*) azzardato(-a), rischioso(-a); (: *deal*) sospetto(-a), poco chiaro(-a); (: *person*) losco(-a); **a dodgy character** un tipo losco; **we're in a dodgy situation** navighiamo in cattive acque

DOE [ˌdiːəʊˈiː] N ABBR (*USA*) = **Department of Energy**

doe [dəʊ] N (*deer*) femmina di daino; (*rabbit*) coniglia

does [dʌz] 3RD PERS SG PRESENT *of* **do**[1]

doesn't [ˈdʌznt] = **does not**

dog [dɒg] N (*male*) cane m; (*female*) cagna; (*male fox, wolf*) maschio; **he's a lucky dog** (*fam*) è nato con la camicia; **every dog has its day** ognuno ha il suo momento di gloria; **he's a dog in the manger** non lascia che gli altri si godano ciò che lui non può godersi; **to go to the dogs** (*person*) lasciarsi andare, ridursi male; (*nation*) andare in malora; **it's a dog's life!** che vita da cani!; **he hasn't a dog's chance** non ha la benché minima probabilità (di successo) ♦ VT (*follow closely*) pedinare; (*fig: subj: problems, injuries*) perseguitare; **dogged by ill luck** perseguitato(-a) dalla scalogna; **he dogs my footsteps** mi sta alle costole, mi sta alle calcagna ♦ ADJ (*breed, show*) canino(-a); (*fox, wolf*) maschio; **dog biscuits** biscotti mpl per cani; **dog food** cibo per cani

dog collar N (*fam: clergyman's*) collarino; (*dog's*) collare m

dog-eared [ˈdɒgˌɪəd] ADJ (*book*) con orecchie

dog·ged [ˈdɒgɪd] ADJ tenace, accanito(-a)

dog·gy, dog·gie [ˈdɒgɪ] N (*fam*) cane m, cagnolino

doggy bag N sacchetto per gli avanzi da portare a casa

dog·ma [ˈdɒgmə] N dogma m

dog·mat·ic [dɒgˈmætɪk] ADJ (*person, attitude*) dogmatico(-a); (*tone*) autoritario(-a)

do-gooder [ˈduːˈgʊdəʳ] N (*fam, pej*): **to be a do-gooder** fare il filantropo

dogs·body [ˈdɒgzˌbɒdɪ] N (*Brit fam*) tirapiedi m/f inv

doi·ly, doy·ley, doy·ly [ˈdɔɪlɪ] N centrino di carta sottopiatto

do·ing [ˈduːɪŋ] N: **this is your doing** è opera tua!, sei stato tu!; **that takes some doing** non è una cosa facile

do·ings [ˈduːɪŋz] NPL 1 (*exploits*) imprese fpl 2 (*Brit fam: thing*): **that doings over there** quel coso là

do-it-yourself [ˈduːɪtjəˈsɛlf] N fai da te m inv, bricolage m inv; **do-it-yourself magazine** rivista di bricolage; **do-it-yourself store** negozio di bricolage

dol·drums [ˈdɒldrəmz] NPL (*fig*): **to be in the doldrums** (*person*) essere giù (di corda); (*business*) attraversare un momento difficile

dole [dəʊl] N (*Brit fam*) sussidio di disoccupazione; **to be on the dole** ricevere un sussidio di disoccupazione; **to go on the dole** fare domanda per il sussidio di disoccupazione

▸ **dole out** VT + ADV distribuire

dole·ful [ˈdəʊlfʊl] ADJ (*expression*) afflitto(-a); (*song, prospect*) triste

doll [dɒl] N bambola; **doll's house** casa delle bambole

▸ **doll up** VT + ADV: **to doll o.s. up** (*fam*) farsi bello(-a); **to get (all) dolled up** mettersi in ghingheri

dol·lar [ˈdɒləʳ] N dollaro; **dollar area** area del dollaro; **dollar bill** biglietto da un dollaro

dol·lop [ˈdɒləp] N (*of jam etc*) cucchiaiata

dol·ly [ˈdɒlɪ] N (*fam*) bambola; (*cine*) carrello

dol·phin [ˈdɒlfɪn] N (*Zool*) delfino

do·main [dəʊˈmeɪn] N (*lands*) domini mpl; (*fig*) campo, sfera; (*Math*) dominio; **in the domain of art** nel campo dell'arte; **in the public domain** di dominio pubblico

dome [dəʊm] N cupola

do·mes·tic [dəˈmɛstɪk] ADJ 1 (*industry, flight*) nazionale; (*affairs, policy*) interno(-a); (*news*) dall'interno 2 (*chores, duties, animal*) domestico(-a); **domestic bliss** le gioie della famiglia; **domestic peace** pace in famiglia; **to be in domestic service** essere a servizio; **domestic servant** domestico(-a) ♦ N (*cleaner*) inserviente m/f

domestic appliance N elettrodomestico

do·mes·ti·cat·ed [dəˈmɛstɪˌkeɪtɪd] ADJ (*animal*) addomesticato(-a); (*person*) casalingo(-a)

do·mes·ti·city [ˌdəʊmesˈtɪsɪtɪ] N vita di famiglia

domi·cile [ˈdɒmɪˌsaɪl] N (*frm*) domicilio

domi·nant [ˈdɒmɪnənt] ADJ (*gen, also Mus*) dominante; (*influence*) predominante

domi·nate [ˈdɒmɪˌneɪt] VT, VI dominare

domi·na·tion [ˌdɒmɪˈneɪʃən] N dominazione f

domi·neer·ing [ˌdɒmɪˈnɪərɪŋ] ADJ dispotico(-a), autoritario(-a)

Dominican Republic N Repubblica Dominicana

do·min·ion [dəˈmɪnɪən] N (*rule*) dominio, sovranità; (*territory*) dominio, possedimenti mpl; (*Brit Pol*) dominion m inv

domi·no [ˈdɒmɪnəʊ] N tessera del domino; **dominoes** NPL (*game*) domino msg

don[1] [dɒn] N (*Brit: Univ*) docente m/f universitario(-a)

don[2] VT (*old: garment*) indossare

do·nate [dəʊˈneɪt] VT elargire; **he donated his collection to the museum** ha donato la sua collezione al museo

do·na·tion [dəʊˈneɪʃən] N elargizione f

done [dʌn] PP *of* **do**[1]

don·gle [ˈdɒŋgl] N (*Comput*) chiave f di protezione da copie illegali

don·key [ˈdɒŋkɪ] N asino(-a); **I've known him for donkey's years** (*fam*) lo conosco da secoli

do·nor [ˈdəʊnəʳ] N (*gen: Med*) donatore(-trice)

donor card N tessera di donatore di organi, ≈ tessera dell'A.I.D.O.

don't [dəʊnt] = **do not**

do·nut [ˈdəʊnʌt] N (*USA*) = **doughnut**

doo·dle [ˈduːdl] N scarabocchio ♦ VI scarabocchiare

doom [duːm] N (*ruin*) rovina; (*fate*) destino; **impending doom** disastro incombente; **it's not all doom and gloom** non è tutto nero come sembra ♦ VT (*destine*): **to doom (to)** condannare (a); **doomed to failure** destinato(-a) al fallimento

dooms·day [ˈduːmzˌdeɪ] N: **till doomsday** (*fig*) fino al giorno del giudizio

door [dɔːʳ] N (*gen*) porta; (*of vehicle*) sportello, portiera; (*of aircraft*) portello; **the first door on the right** la prima porta a destra; **at the door** alla porta; **pay at the door** pagare all'entrata; **front/back door** porta principale/di servizio; **doors down the street** 3 case più giù; **from door to door** di porta in porta

door·bell [ˈdɔːˌbel] N campanello

door·handle [ˈdɔːˌhændl] N maniglia della porta

door·knob [ˈdɔːˌnɒb] N pomello

door·man [ˈdɔːˌmæn] N (*pl* **-men**) (*in hotel*) portiere m (in livrea); (*in block of apartments*) portinaio

door·mat [ˈdɔːˌmæt] N stoino, zerbino; (*fam: downtrodden person*) pezza da piedi

door·step [ˈdɔːˌstep] N gradino della porta, soglia; **on our doorstep** (*close by*) a un passo ♦ VT: **to doorstep sb** recarsi a casa di qn per intervistarlo (*spesso contro la sua volontà*)

door-to-door [ˈdɔːtəˈdɔːʳ] ADJ (*selling*) porta a porta; (*salesperson*) a domicilio

door·way [ˈdɔːˌweɪ] N porta; **in the doorway** nel vano della porta

dope [dəʊp] N 1 (*fam: drugs*) roba (*fam*); (*Sport*) droga; **he takes dope** si droga; **dope test** (*controllo*) anti-doping m inv 2 (*fam: information*) informazioni fpl; **to give sb the dope (on sth)** fare una soffiata a qn (su qc) 3 (*fam: stupid person*) tonto(-a) ♦ VT (*horse, person, drink*) drogare

dopey [ˈdəʊpɪ] (*fam*) ADJ (*comp* **-ier**, *superl* **-iest**) (*drugged*) inebetito(-a); (*stupid*) stupidotto(-a); (*sleepy*) addormentato(-a)

dor·mant [ˈdɔːmənt] ADJ (*Bot: volcano*) quiescente; (*energy*) latente; **to lie dormant** (*fig*) rimanere latente

dor·mer [ˈdɔːməʳ] N (*also:* **dormer window**) abbaino

dor·mi·tory [ˈdɔːmɪtrɪ] N, ADJ dormitorio; (*USA: hall of residence*) casa dello studente; **the boys' dormitory** il dormitorio dei ragazzi; **dormitory town** città f inv dormitorio, inv

dor·mouse [ˈdɔːˌmaʊs] N (*pl* **dormice** [ˈdɔːˌmaɪs]) ghiro

DOS [dɒs] N ABBR (*Comput: = disk operating system*) DOS m

dos·age [ˈdəʊsɪdʒ] N (*on medicine bottle*) posologia

dose [dəʊs] N (*of medicine*) dose f; (*Brit: of fever etc*) attacco; **to get a dose of flu** prendersi l'influenza; **in small doses**

(*fig*) a piccole dosi ♦ VT: **to dose sb with sth** somministrare qc a qn

dos·si·er [ˈdɒsɪeɪ] N: **dossier (on)** dossier *m inv* (su)

DOT [ˌdiːəʊˈtiː] N ABBR (*USA*) = **Department of Transportation**

dot [dɒt] N (*gen*) punto; (*on material*) pois *m inv*; (*stain*) macchiolina; (*in punctuation*): **dots** puntini *mpl* di sospensione; **dots and dashes** punti *mpl* e linee, *fpl*; **polka dots** pois; **on the dot** (*fig*) in punto ♦ VT (*fig*): **to dot one's i's and cross one's t's** mettere i puntini sulle i; **a field dotted with flowers** un campo punteggiato di fiori

dot·com [dɒtˈkɒm] N (*Comput*) azienda che opera in internet

dot command N (*Comput*) commando punto

dote on [dəʊt ɒn] VI + PREP stravedere per

dot-matrix printer [ˌdɒtˈmeɪtrɪksˈprɪntəʳ] N stampante *f* ad aghi

dot·ted line [ˈdɒtɪdˈlaɪn] N linea punteggiata; **to sign on the dotted line** firmare (nell'apposito spazio); (*fig*) accettare; **to tear along the dotted line** strappare lungo la linea tratteggiata

dot·ty [ˈdɒtɪ] ADJ (*Brit fam: mad*) tocco(-a), strambo(-a)

dou·ble [ˈdʌbl] ADJ 1 (*gen*) doppio(-a); **a double helping** una porzione doppia; **a double whisky** un doppio whisky; **double spacing** (*Typ*) interlinea doppia 2 (*dual*) duplice; **with a double meaning** a doppio senso; **to lead a double life** avere una doppia vita; **to play a double game** fare il doppio gioco 3 (*Brit: repeated*): **double five two six (5526)** (*Telec*) cinque cinque due sei; **spelt with a double "l"** scritto con due elle *or* con doppia elle ♦ ADV (*bend*) in due; (*see*) doppio; **double the amount (of sth)** il doppio (di qc); **to cost double** costare il doppio ♦ N 1 (*amount*) doppio; (*person*) sosia *m inv*; (*Cine*) controfigura; **at the double** *or* **on the double** (*running*) a passo di corsa ♦ (*bet*) accoppiata ♦ VT 1 (*increase twofold: money, quantity etc*) raddoppiare 2 (*fold: also:* **double over**) piegare in due ♦ VI 1 (*quantity etc*) raddoppiare 2 **to double as** (*have two uses*) funzionare *or* servire anche da; (*Theatre, Cine*) fare anche la parte di

▸ **double back** VI + ADV (*person*) tornare sui propri passi

▸ **double up** VI + ADV 1 (*bend over*) piegarsi in due; **he doubled up with laughter** si sbellicava dal ridere 2 (*share bedroom*) dividere la stanza

double bass [ˌdʌblˈbeɪs] N contrabbasso

double bed N letto matrimoniale, letto a due piazze

double-breasted [ˌdʌblˈbrestɪd] ADJ (*jacket*) doppiopetto *inv*

double-check [ˌdʌblˈtʃek] VT, VI ricontrollare

double-click [ˈdʌblˈklɪk] VI (*Comput*): **to double click (on)** fare doppio click (su)

double-clutch [ˈdʌblˈklʌtʃ] VI (*USA: Aut*) = **double-declutch**

double cream N (*Brit*) panna da cucina

double-cross [ˌdʌblˈkrɒs] VT (*fam*) fare il doppio gioco con

double-decker [ˌdʌblˈdekəʳ] N (*also:* **double-decker bus**) autobus *m inv* a due piani; (*also:* **double-decker sandwich**) doppio tramezzino

double-declutch [ˌdʌblˈdiːˈklʌtʃ], (*USA*) **double-clutch** [ˈdʌblˈklʌtʃ] VI (*Aut*) fare la doppietta

double exposure N (*Phot*) sovrimpressione *f*

double glazing [ˌdʌblˈɡleɪzɪŋ] N (*Brit*) doppiovetro; **to put in double glazing** mettere i doppivetri

double-page [ˈdʌblˈpeɪdʒ] ADJ: **double-page spread** pubblicità a doppia pagina

double parking N parcheggio in doppia fila

double room N camera per due, (camera) doppia, (camera) matrimoniale *f*

dou·bles [ˈdʌblz] NPL (*Tennis*) doppio; **a game of mixed/ladies' doubles** un doppio misto/femminile

double time N tariffa doppia per lavoro straordinario

dou·ble wham·my [ˌdʌblˈwæmɪ] N (*fam*) doppia mazzata (*fig*)

double yellow lines NPL (*Brit: Aut*) linea gialla doppia continua che segnala il divieto di sosta

dou·bly [ˈdʌblɪ] ADV doppiamente; **to be doubly careful** stare doppiamente attento(-a)

doubt [daʊt] N dubbio; **to be in doubt** essere in dubbio; **without (a) doubt** senza dubbio; **beyond doubt** fuor di dubbio; **if in doubt** nell'incertezza, in caso di dubbio; **no**

doubt sicuramente; **as you no doubt know ...** come saprai sicuramente...; **no doubt he will come** è probabile che venga; **there is no doubt of that** su questo non c'è dubbio; **I have my doubts about whether he'll come** ho i miei dubbi che venga ♦ VT 1 (*truth of statement*) dubitare di; **I don't doubt her honesty** non dubito della sua onestà; **to doubt one's own eyes** non credere ai propri occhi; **I doubt it very much** ne dubito proprio; **you're a real doubting Thomas** sei proprio come San Tommaso 2 (*be uncertain*): **to doubt whether** *or* **if** *or* **that** dubitare che + *sub*; **I don't doubt that he will come** non dubito *or* non ho dubbi che verrà

doubt·ful [ˈdaʊtful] ADJ (*uncertain: person*) poco convinto(-a); (: *look*) dubbioso(-a); (: *result, success, future*) dubbio(-a), incerto(-a); (*debatable: question*) discutibile; (*questionable: taste, reputation*) dubbio(-a); **she sounds doubtful** sembra poco convinta; **to be doubtful about sth** non essere convinto(-a) di qc, avere dei dubbi su qc; **I'm doubtful about going by myself** sono incerto se andare da solo; **I'm a bit doubtful** non sono tanto sicuro; **it's doubtful whether ...** non è sicuro che... + *sub*

doubt·less [ˈdaʊtlɪs] ADV senza dubbio, indubbiamente

dough [dəʊ] N 1 impasto, pasta 2 (*fam: money*) grana

dough·nut, do·nut (*USA*) [ˈdəʊnʌt] N krapfen *m inv*, bombolone *m*; **a jam doughnut** un krapfen con la marmellata

dour [dʊəʳ] ADJ (*grim*) arcigno(-a)

douse [daʊs] VT (*with water*) infradiciare; (*flames*) spegnere

dove [dʌv] N colombo(-a); (*fig: Pol*) colomba; **collared dove** colombo(-a) dal collare

dove·tail [ˈdʌvˌteɪl] N (*also: dovetail joint*) incastro a coda di rondine ♦ VT (*fig*): **to dovetail with/into** connettere a/con ♦ VI (*fig*) combaciare, collimare

dowa·ger [ˈdaʊədʒəʳ] N vedova titolata

dowdy [ˈdaʊdɪ] ADJ (*comp* -**ier**, *superl* -**iest**) scialbo(-a)

Dow-Jones average [ˈdaʊˈdʒəʊnzˈævərɪdʒ] N (*USA*): **the Dow-Jones average** l'indice *m* Dow-Jones

down¹ [daʊn] ADV 1 (*movement*) giù; (*to the ground*) giù, a terra; (*to a dog*): **down!** a cuccia!; **get down!** scendi!; **to fall down** cadere; **to run down** correre giù; **he threw down his racket** ha gettato a terra la racchetta; **he came down from Glasgow** è venuto giù da Glasgow; **from the year 1600 down to the present day** dal 1600 fino ai giorni nostri; **from the biggest down to the smallest** dal più grande al più piccolo; **down with traitors!** abbasso i traditori! 2 (*position*) giù; **down there** là in fondo, laggiù; **down here** quaggiù; **the blinds are down** le tapparelle sono tirate giù *or* abbassate; **to kick a man when he's down** (*fig*) uccidere un uomo morto; **his office is down on the first floor** il suo ufficio è giù al primo piano; **I'll be down in a minute** scendo tra un minuto; **I've been down with flu** sono stato a letto con l'influenza; **he lives down south** abita nel sud; **his temperature is down** la febbre gli è scesa; **England is two goals down** l'Inghilterra sta perdendo per due goal; **the price of meat is down** il prezzo della carne è sceso; **write this down** scrivi; **I've got it down in my diary** ce l'ho sulla mia agenda; **you're down for the next race** sei iscritto alla prossima gara 3 (*as deposit*): **to pay £20 down** dare 20 sterline in acconto *or* di anticipo ♦ PREP (*indicating movement*) giù per; (*at a lower point on*) più giù; **he ran his finger down the list** percorse la lista col dito; **he went down the hill** discese la collina; **he's down the hill** è in fondo alla collina; **he lives down the street** abita un po' più giù; **looking down this road, you can see ...** guardando fino in fondo alla strada, vedrai...; **down the ages** nel corso della storia; **he's gone down town** (*fam*) è andato in città ♦ ADJ (*train, line*) che parte da una grande città; **I'm feeling a bit down** (*fam*) mi sento un po' giù; **to be down** (*computer*) non funzionare ♦ VT (*opponent*) atterrare; (*fam: drink*) scolarsi; **he downed a pint of beer** si è scolato una pinta di birra; **to down tools** (*fig*) incrociare le braccia (*fig*) ♦ N: **to have a down on sb** (*fam*) avercela con qn

down² [daʊn] N (*on bird, in quilts*) piumino *m inv*; (*on person, fruit*) peluria, lanugine *f*

down³ [daʊn] N (*hill*) collina, colle *m*

down-and-out [ˈdaʊnəndˈaʊt] ADJ (*destitute*) sul lastrico ♦ N (*tramp*) barbone *m*

down-at-heel [ˌdaʊnətˈhiːl] ADJ scalcagnato(-a); (*fig*) trasandato(-a)

down·beat [ˈdaʊnˌbiːt] N (*Mus*) tempo in battere ♦ ADJ (*fam: gloomy*) pessimistico(-a); (: *relaxed*) distaccato(-a)

down·cast [ˈdaʊnˌkɑːst] ADJ (*sad*) abbattuto(-a), avvilito(-a); (*eyes*) basso(-a)

down·er [ˈdaʊnə'] N (*fam: drug*) sedativo; **to be on a downer** (*depressed*) essere giù

down·fall [ˈdaʊnˌfɔːl] N rovina, caduta

down·grade [ˈdaʊnˌɡreɪd] VT (*job, hotel*) declassare; (*person*) degradare

down·hearted [ˌdaʊnˈhɑːtɪd] ADJ scoraggiato(-a), demoralizzato(-a); **don't be downhearted!** non scoraggiarti!

down·hill [ˌdaʊnˈhɪl] ADV: **to go downhill** (*road*) andare in discesa; (*car*) andare giù per la discesa; (*fig: person*) lasciarsi andare; (: *business*) andare sempre peggio, andare a rotoli; **downhill race** (*Skiing*) gara di discesa (libera); **downhill racer** discesista *m/f*; **downhill ski** sci *m inv* a valle

Downing Street [ˈdaʊnɪŋˌstrɪt] N (*Brit*): **10 Downing Street** residenza del primo ministro inglese

down·load [vb ˈdaʊnˌləʊd, n ˈdaʊnləʊd] VT (*Comput*) scaricare ♦ N (*Comput*) download *m inv*, scaricamento

down·load·able [ˌdaʊnˈləʊdəbl] ADJ scaricabile

down·market [daʊnˌmɑːkɪt] ADJ rivolto(-a) ad una fascia di mercato inferiore; (*product*) dozzinale ♦ ADV: **to go down-market** rivolgersi ad una fascia inferiore di pubblico

down payment N acconto

down·play [ˈdaʊnˌpleɪ] VT (*USA*) minimizzare

down·pour [ˈdaʊnˌpɔː'] N acquazzone *m*

down·right [ˈdaʊnˌraɪt] ADJ (*person, manner*) franco(-a); (*lie, liar*) bell'e buono(-a); (*refusal*) categorico(-a), assoluto(-a); **downright bad manners** vera e propria maleducazione ♦ ADV (*rude, disgusting*) davvero; **downright dangerous** davvero pericoloso

Downs [daʊnz] NPL (*Brit*): **the Downs** colline di gesso nel sud-est dell'Inghilterra

down·size [ˈdaʊnˌsaɪz] VT (*workforce*) ridurre

down·stairs [ˈdaʊnˈsteəz] ADJ (*on the ground floor*) al pianterreno, al pianterra; (*on the floor underneath*) al piano di sotto; **the downstairs bathroom** il bagno al piano terra ♦ ADV di sotto, giù; **to come** *or* **go downstairs** scendere (al piano di sotto); **she lives downstairs** abita al piano di sotto; **the people downstairs** le persone che abitano al piano di sotto

down·stream [ˈdaʊnˈstriːm] ADV: **downstream (from)** a valle (di)

Down syndrome [ˈdaʊnˌsɪndrəʊm] N sindrome *f* di Down

down·time [ˈdaʊnˌtaɪm] N (*Comm*) tempi *mpl* morti

down-to-earth [ˈdaʊntʊˈɜːθ] ADJ (*person*) coi piedi per terra, pratico(-a); (*advice, approach*) pratico(-a)

down·town [ˈdaʊnˈtaʊn] ADV (*USA*) in città, in centro; **he works downtown** lavora in centro ♦ ADJ: **downtown San Francisco** il centro di San Francisco ♦ N centro (città)

down·trod·den [ˈdaʊnˌtrɒdn] ADJ oppresso(-a)

down under (*fam*) N gli antipodi ♦ ADV agli antipodi

down·ward [ˈdaʊnwəd] ADJ (*curve, movement etc*) in giù, verso il basso; (*slope*) in discesa; **a downward trend** una diminuzione progressiva; **a downward trend in prices** una tendenza al ribasso dei prezzi

down·ward [ˈdaʊnwəd], **down·wards** [ˈdaʊnwədz] ADV (*go*) in giù, in discesa; (*look*) verso il basso; **face downwards** (*person*) bocconi; (*object*) a faccia in giù; **from the President downwards** dal Presidente in giù

dow·ry [ˈdaʊrɪ] N dote *f*

doz. ABBR = **dozen**

doze [dəʊz] N sonnellino, pisolino ♦ VI sonnecchiare

   ▸ **doze off** VI + ADV appisolarsi

doz·en [ˈdʌzn] N dozzina; **80p a dozen** 80 pence la dozzina; **a dozen eggs** una dozzina d'uova; **two dozen** due dozzine; **dozens of times** centinaia *or* migliaia di volte; **dozens of people** decine *fpl* di persone

Dr. ABBR **1** (= *doctor*) Dott. (Dott.ssa) **2** (*in street names*) = **Drive**

drab [dræb] ADJ (*comp* **-ber**, *superl* **-best**) (*colour*) cupo(-a); (*clothes*) triste; (*life*) grigio(-a), tetro(-a)

draft [drɑːft] N **1** (*outline*) abbozzo, bozza (copia); (*of contract, document*) minuta; **draft letter** prima stesura (di una lettera); **a draft law** un progetto di legge **2** (*Mil: detachment*) distaccamento; **the draft** (*USA Mil: conscription*) la leva **3** (*Comm: also:* **banker's** *or* **bank draft**) tratta, assegno circolare **4** (*USA*) = **draught** ♦ VT **1** (*also:* **draft out**) abbozzare; (*plan*) tracciare; (*document, report*) stendere (in versione preliminare) **2** (*Mil: for specific duty*) distaccare; (*USA Mil: conscript*) arruolare

drag [dræg] N **1** (*Aer, Naut: resistance*) resistenza (aerodinamica) **2** (*fam: boring thing, task, person*) noia, strazio; **what a drag!** che scocciatura! **3** (*on cigarette*) tirata **4** (*women's clothing worn by men*): **in drag** travestito (da donna) ♦ VT **1** (*object*) trascinare, tirare; (*person*) trascinare; **to drag one's feet over sth** (*fig*) farla lunga con qc, trascinare qc **2** (*sea bed, river*) dragare ♦ VI **1** (*anchor*) arare **2** (*go very slowly: evening, conversation etc*) trascinarsi, non finire mai

   ▸ **drag along** VT + ADV (*person*) trascinare (controvoglia); (*object*) tirare

   ▸ **drag away** VT + ADV: **to drag away (from)** tirare via (da)

   ▸ **drag down** VT + ADV trascinare giù, trascinare in basso; **to drag sb down to one's own level** (*fig*) far abbassare qn al proprio livello

   ▸ **drag in** VT + ADV (*subject, topic*) tirare in ballo

   ▸ **drag into** VT + PREP: **to drag sb/sth into** (*introduce unnecessarily*) trascinare qn/qc in

   ▸ **drag on** VI + ADV (*meeting, conversation*) trascinarsi, passare lentamente

   ▸ **drag up** VT + ADV (*mention unnecessarily*) ritirare in ballo, tirar fuori di nuovo

drag·net [ˈdræɡˌnet] N rete *f* a strascico; (*fig*) rastrellamento

drag·on [ˈdræɡən] N drago

dragon·fly [ˈdræɡənˌflaɪ] N libellula

dra·goon [drəˈɡuːn] N (*Mil: cavalryman*) dragone *m* ♦ VT: **to dragoon sb into doing sth** (*Brit*) costringere qn a fare qc

drain [dreɪn] N **1** (*outlet*) scarico, canale *m* di scolo; (*pipe*) tubatura di scarico; (*drain cover*) tombino; **to throw one's money down the drain** (*fig*) buttare i soldi dalla finestra **2 the drains** NPL (*sewage system*) le fognature; **the drains are blocked** gli scarichi sono ostruiti **3** (*fig: source of loss*): **a drain on** (*energies, resources*) un salasso per; **it has been a great drain on her** l'ha veramente spossata ♦ VT (*land, lake*) prosciugare; (*marshes*) bonificare, drenare; (*vegetables, pasta*) scolare; (*glass, bottle of wine*) svuotare; (*radiator*) (far) svuotare; (*Med: wound*) drenare; **to feel drained (of energy)** (*fig*) sentirsi svuotato(-a) (di energie), sentirsi sfinito(-a) ♦ VI (*washed dishes, vegetables*) scolare; (*liquid, stream*): **to drain (into)** defluire (in)

   ▸ **drain away** VT + ADV (*liquid*) far scolare ♦ VI + ADV (*liquid*) scolare; (*strength*) esaurirsi

   ▸ **drain off** VT + ADV (*liquid*) far scolare

drain·age [ˈdreɪnɪdʒ] N (*of land: natural*) scolo; (: *artificial*) drenaggio; (*of lake*) prosciugamento; (*system of drains*) fognature *fpl*

drain·ing board [ˈdreɪnɪŋˌbɔːd], (*USA*) **drain·board** [ˈdreɪnbɔːd] N piano del lavello

drain·pipe [ˈdreɪnˌpaɪp] N **1** tubo di scarico **2 drainpipes** (*trousers*) pantaloni *mpl* a tubo

drake [dreɪk] N maschio dell'anatra

dram [dræm] N bicchierino (di whisky *etc*)

dra·ma [ˈdrɑːmə] N (*gen*) dramma *m*, teatro; (*play*) commedia; (*event*) dramma; **a TV drama** un dramma televisivo; **drama critic** critico teatrale; **drama school** scuola d'arte drammatica; **drama student** studente(-essa) di arte drammatica; **drama is my favourite subject** la recitazione è la mia materia preferita

dra·mat·ic [drəˈmætɪk] ADJ (*change*) spettacolare; (*event, improvement, effect*) straordinario(-a); (*entrance*) teatrale; (*art*) drammatico(-a); **dramatic news** notizie sensazionali; **the dramatic arts** le arti drammatiche

dra·mati·cal·ly [drəˈmætɪkəlɪ] ADV (*improve, change*) in modo straordinario, moltissimo; (*enter, pause*) in modo teatrale

drama·tist [ˈdræmətɪst] N drammaturgo(-a)

drama·tize [ˈdræmətaɪz] VT (*events, situation*) drammatizzare; (*novel: for TV*) ridurre *or* adattare per la televisione; (: *for cinema*) ridurre *or* adattare per il grande schermo

drank [dræŋk] PT *of* **drink**

drape [dreɪp] N *see* **drapes** ♦ VT: **to drape (with)** (*altar*) drappeggiare (con); (*shoulders*) avvolgere (in); **to drape (over)** (*cloth, clothing*) avvolgere (intorno a)

drap·er [ˈdreɪpəʳ] N (*Brit: old*) negoziante *m/f* di stoffe

drapes [dreɪps] NPL (*USA*) tende *fpl*

dras·tic [ˈdræstɪk] ADJ drastico(-a); **to take drastic action** agire in modo drastico

dras·ti·cal·ly [ˈdræstɪkəlɪ] ADV drasticamente

draught, draft (*USA*) [drɑːft] N **1** (*of air*) corrente *f* (d'aria), spiffero; (*for fire*) tiraggio; (*Naut*) pescaggio **2** (*drink*): **he took a long draught of beer** ha bevuto una lunga sorsata di birra; **on draught** alla spina

draught beer N birra alla spina

draught·board [ˈdrɑːftˌbɔːd] N scacchiera

draughts [drɑːfts] N (*Brit*) (gioco della) dama

draughts·man, draftsman (*USA*) [ˈdrɑːftsmən] N (*pl -men*) (*in drawing office*) disegnatore(-trice)

draughts·man·ship, drafts·man·ship (*USA*) [ˈdrɑːftsmənʃɪp] N (*skill*) arte *f* del disegno

draw [drɔː] (*pt* drew, *pp* drawn) N **1** (*lottery*) lotteria, riffa; (*picking of tickets*) estrazione *f*, sorteggio; (*for sporting events*) sorteggio **2** (*Sport: equal score*) pareggio; **the match ended in a draw** la partita è finita con un pareggio **3** (*attraction*) attrazione *f* **4 to be quick on the draw** essere veloce con la pistola; (*fig*) avere i riflessi pronti ♦ VT **1** (*pull: bolt, curtains*) tirare; (*: caravan, trailer*) trainare, rimorchiare; (*: bow*) tendere la corda di; **he drew his finger along the table** ha passato il dito sul tavolo; **he drew his hat over his eyes** si è calato il cappello sugli occhi; **she drew him to one side** lo tirò da una parte; **she's drawn the curtains** ha tirato le tende **2** (*extract: from pocket, bag*) tirar fuori; (*: from well, tap*) attingere; (*: sword*) sguainare; (*: teeth*) estrarre; (*: cork*) cavare; (*: salary, money from bank*) ritirare; (*: cheque*) cambiare, riscuotere; (*Culin: fowl*) pulire; **to draw a bath** preparare un bagno; **to draw blood** fare uscir il sangue; (*fig*) colpire nel vivo; **to draw a card** estrarre una carta (dal mazzo); **to draw a breath** tirare un respiro; **to draw breath** (ri)prendere fiato; **to draw comfort from sth** trovare conforto in qc; **to draw a smile from sb** strappare un sorriso a qn **3** (*attract: attention, crowd, customer*) attrarre, attirare; **to feel drawn to sb** sentirsi attratto(-a) verso qn, provare attrazione per qn **4** (*sketch: picture, portrait*) fare; (*: object, person*) disegnare; (*: plan, line, circle*) tracciare; (*: map*) disegnare, fare; (*fig: situation*) fare un quadro di; (*: character*) disegnare; **to draw a picture** fare un disegno; **to draw a picture of sb** fare il ritratto a qn; **he drew a line** ha tracciato una linea; **I draw the line at (doing) that** (*fig*) mi rifiuto (di farlo) **5** (*formulate: conclusion*): **to draw (from)** trarre (da), ricavare (da); (*: comparison, distinction*): **to draw (between)** fare (tra) **6** (*Ftbl, etc*): **to draw a match** pareggiare ♦ VI **1** (*move*): **to draw (towards)** avvicinarsi (a), avanzare (verso); **he drew to one side** si è tirato da parte or in disparte; **the train drew into the station** il treno è entrato in stazione; **he drew ahead of the other runners** ha staccato gli altri corridori; **to draw level** affiancarsi; **to draw near** avvicinarsi; **to draw to an end** or **to a close** volgere alla fine, avvicinarsi alla conclusione **2** (*in cards*): **to draw for trumps** scegliere il seme or la briscola **3** (*chimney*) tirare **4** (*Sport: be equal: two teams*) pareggiare; **we drew two-all** abbiamo pareggiato due a due; **the teams drew for second place** le due squadre sono arrivate seconde a pari merito **5** (*sketch*) disegnare; **I can't draw** non so disegnare

▸ **draw aside** VI + ADV (*person*) scostarsi ♦ VT + ADV (*person*) tirare in disparte; (*object*) spostare (da un lato)

▸ **draw away** VI + ADV: **to draw away (from)** (*go away*) allontanarsi (da); (*move ahead: athlete*) portarsi in vantaggio (su) ♦ VT + ADV (*person*) allontanare, portare via; (*object*) togliere

▸ **draw back** VT + ADV (*object, hand*) tirare indietro, ritirare; (*curtains*) tirare ♦ VI + ADV (*move back*): **to draw back (from)** indietreggiare (di fronte a), tirarsi indietro (di fronte a)

▸ **draw down** VT + ADV (*gen*) abbassare; (*blame*): **to draw down (on)** tirare addosso a

▸ **draw in** VT + ADV (*breath*) tirare; (*air*) aspirare; (*pull back in: claws*) ritirare; (*attract: crowds*) richiamare

▸ **draw off** VT + ADV (*siphon off*) spillare

▸ **draw on** VI + ADV (*time*) avanzare ♦ VT + ADV (*gloves, stockings*) infilare lentamente ♦ VI + PREP (*resources*) attingere a; (*imagination, person*) far ricorso a; **he drew on his own experience to write the book** ha fatto ricorso alla propria esperienza per scrivere il libro

▸ **draw out** VI + ADV (*lengthen*) allungarsi ♦ VT + ADV **1** (*take out: handkerchief*) tirar fuori; (*money from bank*) ritirare; **to draw sb out (of his shell)** (*fig*) tirare qn fuori dal suo guscio **2** (*prolong: meeting*) tirare per le lunghe

▸ **draw up** VT + ADV **1** (*formulate: will*) redigere; (*: contract*) stendere; (*: plans*) formulare; (*: document*) compilare; **she drew up a list of priorities** compilò un elenco di priorità **2** (*chair*) avvicinare; (*troops*) schierare; **to draw o.s. up (to one's full height)** raddrizzarsi (con tutta la persona) ♦ VI + ADV (*stop*) arrestarsi, fermarsi; **to draw up (beside sth/sb)** accostarsi (a qc/qn)

draw·back [ˈdrɔːbæk] N inconveniente *m*, svantaggio

draw·bridge [ˈdrɔːbrɪdʒ] N ponte *m* levatoio

drawee [drɔːˈiː] N (*Fin*) trassato, trattario

draw·er [drɔːʳ] N **1** (*furniture*) cassetto **2** (*of cheque*) traente *m/f*

draw·ing [ˈdrɔːɪŋ] N (*picture*) disegno; **I'm no good at drawing** non so disegnare; **drawing pen** (*Art*) tiralinee *m inv*

drawing board N tavolo da disegno; **back to the drawing board!** (*fig*) ricominciamo da capo!

drawing pin N (*Brit*) puntina da disegno

drawing room N salotto

drawl [drɔːl] N cadenza strascicata ♦ VT strascicare ♦ VI strascicare le parole

drawn [drɔːn] PP *of* draw ♦ ADJ (*haggard: with tiredness*) tirato(-a); (*: with pain*) contratto(-a) (dal dolore)

draw·string [ˈdrɔːstrɪŋ] N cordone *m*, cordoncino

dread [dred] N terrore *m* ♦ VT avere il terrore di, tremare all'idea di

dread·ful [ˈdredful] ADJ (*crime, sight, suffering*) terribile, spaventoso(-a), orribile; (*weather*) tremendo(-a); **a dreadful mistake** un terribile errore; **you look dreadful** hai un aspetto orribile; **I feel dreadful!** (*ill*) mi sento uno straccio!; (*ashamed*) vorrei scomparire (dalla vergogna)!

dream [driːm] (*pt, pp* dreamed *or* dreamt) N sogno; **to have a dream about sb/sth** sognare di qn/qc; **I had a bad dream** ho fatto un brutto sogno; **sweet dreams!** sogni d'oro!; **that museum is an archaeologist's dream** quel museo è un paradiso per gli archeologi; **it worked like a dream** ha funzionato a meraviglia; **it's my dream house** è la casa dei miei sogni; **dream world** mondo immaginario ♦ VT sognare; (*imagine*) sognarsi, credersi; **I didn't dream that ...** non mi sarei mai sognato che... + *sub*; **who could have dreamt such a thing would happen?** chi avrebbe mai potuto immaginare un disastro come questo? ♦ VI sognare; (*imagine*) sognarsi; **to dream (of** *or* **about sb/sth)** sognare ((di) qn/qc); **she dreamed about her son** ha sognato di suo figlio; **there were more than I'd ever dreamed of** ce n'erano di più di quanto avessi mai immaginato; **I wouldn't dream of it!** non me lo sognerei neanche!; **I'm sorry, I was dreaming** mi scusi, stavo fantasticando

▸ **dream up** VT + ADV (*reason, excuse*) inventare; (*plan, idea*) escogitare

dream·er [ˈdriːməʳ] N sognatore(-trice)

dreamt [dremt] PT, PP *of* dream

dreamy [ˈdriːmɪ] ADJ (*comp* -ier, *superl* -iest) (*person*) distratto(-a), sognatore(-trice); (*look, voice*) sognante; (*music, quality*) di sogno

dreary [ˈdrɪərɪ] ADJ (*comp* -ier, *superl* -iest) (*landscape*) tetro(-a); (*weather*) deprimente; (*life*) squallido(-a); (*work, book, speech*) noioso(-a), monotono(-a)

dredge [dredʒ] VT (*river*) dragare

▸ **dredge up** VT + ADV tirare alla superficie; (*fig: unpleasant facts*) rivangare

dredg·er [ˈdredʒəʳ], **dredge** [dredʒ] N (*ship*) draga

dregs [dregz] NPL (*also fig*) feccia *fsg*

drench [drentʃ] VT inzuppare, infradiciare; **to get drenched** bagnarsi fino all'osso; **drenched to the skin** bagnato(-a) fradicio(-a), bagnato(-a) fino all'osso

dress [dres] N (*frock*) vestito, abito; (*no pl: clothing*) abbigliamento; **in summer dress** in abiti estivi ♦ VT **1** vestire; **to**

dress o.s., **to get dressed** vestirsi; **dressed in green** vestito(-a) di verde **2** (*Culin: salad*) condire; (: *chicken, crab*) preparare **3** (*Med: wound*) medicare, fasciare **4** (*decorate: shop window*) allestire ♦ vi vestirsi; **I got up, dressed, and went downstairs** mi alzai, mi vestii e scesi dabbasso

▸ **dress down** vi + adv **1** (*Brit: casually*) mettersi qualcosa di meno elegante (del solito) **2** (*scold*): **to dress sb down** fare una lavata di capo a qn; *see also* **dressing-down**

▸ **dress up** vi + adv (*in smart or elegant clothes*) vestirsi bene; (*in fancy dress*) vestirsi in costume, mascherarsi ♦ vt + adv (*improve appearance of: facts*) presentare sotto una veste migliore

dress circle n prima galleria

dress designer n stilista *m/f*

dress·er [ˈdresə] n **1** (*in kitchen*) credenza; (*USA: dressing table*) toilette *f inv* **2** (*Theatre*) assistente *m/f*

dress·ing [ˈdresɪŋ] n **1** (*act*) il vestirsi; (*style*) (modo di) vestire **2** (*Med: bandage*) fasciatura, benda **3** (*Culin: salad dressing*) condimento

dressing gown n (*Brit*) vestaglia, veste *f* da camera

dressing room n (*in theatre*) camerino; (*Sport*) spogliatoio

dressing table n toilette *f inv*

dress·maker [ˈdresˌmeɪkə] n sarto(-a)

dress·making [ˈdresˌmeɪkɪŋ] n sartoria; (*school subject*) taglio e cucito

dress rehearsal n prova generale

dress shirt n camicia da sera

dressy [ˈdresɪ] adj (*comp* -**ier**, *superl* -**iest**) (*fam*) elegante

drew [druː] pt of **draw**

drib·ble [ˈdrɪbl] n (*of saliva*) bava, filo di saliva; (*Ftbl*) dribbling *m* ♦ vt (*liquid*) sbrodolare ♦ vi (*baby*) sbavare; (*liquid*) sgocciolare; (*Ftbl*) dribblare, fare un dribbling; (*people*): **to dribble in/out** entrare/uscire alla spicciolata

dried [draɪd] adj (*fruit, beans, flowers, herbs*) secco(-a); (*milk, eggs*) in polvere; (*soup*) liofilizzato(-a)

dri·er [ˈdraɪə] n = **dryer**

drift [drɪft] n **1** (*direction: of current*) direzione *f*; (: *of events*) corso; (: *of conversation, opinion*) tendenza **2** (*meaning: of questions*) senso; **the drift of the speech** il senso generale del discorso; **to catch sb's drift** capire dove qn vuole arrivare **3** (*loss of direction*) deriva **4** (*mass of snow, sand*) cumulo, mucchio; **a snow drift** un'cumulo di neve ♦ vi (*in wind, current*) andare alla deriva; (*clouds*) essere sospinto(-a) dal vento; (*boat*) essere trasportato(-a) dalla corrente; (*sand, snow*) accumularsi, ammucchiarsi; (*person*) vagare; (*events*): **to drift (towards)** scivolare (verso); **to drift downstream** venir portato(-a) a valle dalla corrente; **he drifted into marriage** ha finito con lo sposarsi; **to drift into crime** scivolare nell'illegalità; **to let things drift** lasciare che le cose vadano come vogliono; (*friends*) perdersi di vista; (*lovers*) allontanarsi l'uno dall'altro

▸ **drift off** vi + adv (*fall asleep*) scivolare nel sonno

drift·er [ˈdrɪftə] n persona che ha una vita instabile

drift·wood [ˈdrɪftwʊd] n legno portato dalla corrente

drill¹ [drɪl] n (*for wood, metal, dentist's drill*) trapano; (*in mine, quarry*) perforatrice *f*; (*in oilfield*) trivella; (*pneumatic drill*) martello pneumatico ♦ vt (*wood etc*) forare, trapanare; (*tooth*) trapanare; (*oil well*) trivellare, scavare; **to drill a hole** fare un buco con il trapano ♦ vi: **to drill (for)** fare trivellazioni (alla ricerca di)

drill² [drɪl] n (*Scol: exercises*) esercizi *mpl*; (*Mil*) esercitazione *f*; **a grammar drill** un esercizio orale di grammatica ♦ vt (*soldiers*) esercitare, addestrare; (*pupils: in grammar*) fare esercitare, far fare esercizi a; **to drill sb** far esercitare qn; **to drill good manners into a child** far entrare la buona educazione in testa a un bambino ♦ vi (*Mil*) fare esercitazioni

drill·ing [ˈdrɪlɪŋ] n (*of metal, wood*) perforazione *f*; (*for oil*) trivellazione *f*; (*by dentist*) trapanazione *f*; **drilling ship** nave *f* per la trivellazione

drilling rig n (*on land*) torre *f* di perforazione; (*at sea*) piattaforma (*per trivellazioni subacquee*)

dri·ly [ˈdraɪlɪ] adv = **dryly**

drink [drɪŋk] (*pt* **drank**, *pp* **drunk**) n **1** (*liquid to drink*) bevanda, bibita; **a cold drink** una bibita fresca; **a hot drink** una bevanda calda; **there's food and drink in the kitchen** c'è da

mangiare e da bere in cucina; **would you like a drink?** vuoi qualcosa da bere?; **could I have a drink?** posso avere qualcosa da bere?; **can I have a drink of water, please?** mi dai un po' d'acqua?; **to give sb a drink** dare qualcosa da bere a qn **2** (*glass of alcohol*): **a drink** un bicchierino; **we had drinks before lunch** abbiamo preso l'aperitivo; **let's have a drink** beviamo qualcosa; **to go out for a drink** andare fuori a bere qualcosa; **I need a drink** ho bisogno di bere qualcosa di forte; **to invite sb for drinks** invitare qn a bere qualcosa **3** (*alcoholic liquor*) alcolici *mpl*; **to smell of drink** puzzare d'alcool; **his worries drove him to drink** le preoccupazioni lo hanno spinto al bere ♦ vt (*gen*) bere; (*soup*) mangiare; **she drank her tea** ha bevuto il suo tè; **would you like something to drink?** vuole qualcosa da bere?; **what would you like to drink?** cosa vuoi da bere?; **to drink sb under the table** far finire qn sotto il tavolo (completamente ubriaco(-a)) ♦ vi (*gen*) bere; **he doesn't drink** non beve (alcolici); **"don't drink and drive"** "non bevete se dovete guidare"; **he drinks like a fish** beve come una spugna; **to drink to sth/sb** bere a qc/alla salute di qn

▸ **drink in** vt + adv (*subj: person: fresh air*) aspirare; (: *story*) ascoltare avidamente; (: *sight*) ammirare, bersi con gli occhi

▸ **drink up** vt + adv bere tutto ♦ vi + adv finire di bere; **drink up!** (*to child*) su, finiscilo!; (*in pub*) finisci il bicchiere!

drink·able [ˈdrɪŋkəbl] adj (*not polluted: water*) potabile; (*palatable*) bevibile

drink·er [ˈdrɪŋkə] n bevitore(-trice); **a heavy drinker** un forte bevitore

drink·ing [ˈdrɪŋkɪŋ] n (*of alcohol*) il bere; **drinking song** ≈ canzone *f* goliardica

drinking fountain n fontanella

drinking water n acqua potabile

drip [drɪp] n **1** (*droplet*) goccia; (*of blood, dew*) stilla; (*sound: of water*) sgocciolio **2** (*fam: spineless person*) lavativo(-a) **3** (*Med*) fleboclisi *f inv*; **he's on a drip** gli stanno facendo la flebo ♦ vt (*liquid*) sbrodolare; **you're dripping paint everywhere!** stai schizzando vernice dappertutto! ♦ vi (*tap*) perdere, gocciolare; (*washing*) sgocciolare; (*wall*) trasudare; **to be dripping with sweat/blood** grondare sudore/sangue

drip-dry [ˈdrɪpˈdraɪ] adj (*shirt*) che non si stira

drip-feed [ˈdrɪpˌfiːd] vt alimentare mediante fleboclisi

drip·ping [ˈdrɪpɪŋ] n (*Culin*) grasso (dell'arrosto) ♦ adj (*tap*) che gocciola; (*washing, coat*) tutto(-a) bagnato(-a) ♦ adv: **dripping wet** (*fam*) bagnato(-a) fradicio(-a)

drive [draɪv] (*pt* **drove**, *pp* **driven**) n **1** (*outing*) giro; (*journey*) tragitto; **to go for a drive** andare a fare un giro in macchina; **it's a long drive** è un lungo viaggio; **it's 3 hours' drive from London** è a 3 ore di macchina da Londra **2** (*leading to house*) vialetto (d'accesso); **he parked his car in the drive** ha parcheggiato la macchina nel vialetto **3** (*Tennis*) diritto; (*Golf*) drive *m inv* **4** (*energy*) grinta, energia; (*motivation*) spinta, stimolo; (*Psych*) impulso; (*effort*) sforzo eccezionale; **sex drive** libido *f inv*; **to have drive** avere grinta **5** (*Comm, Pol*) campagna; **sales drive** campagna di vendita; **a national recruitment drive** una campagna di reclutamento a livello nazionale **6** (*Tech*) trasmissione *f*; (*Aut*): **front-/rear-wheel drive** trazione *f* anteriore/posteriore; **left-/right-hand drive** guida a sinistra/destra; **four-wheel drive** a quattro ruote motrici **7** (*Comput: also*: **disk drive**) disk drive *m inv*, unità *f inv* a dischi magnetici ♦ vt **1** (*cause to move: people, animals*) condurre; (*clouds, leaves*) sospingere; **the gale drove the ship off course** la tempesta ha spinto la nave fuori rotta; **to drive sb hard** (*fig*) far sgobbare qn; **to drive sb to (do) sth** spingere qn a (fare) qc; **I was driven to it** sono stato costretto a farlo; **he is driven by greed/ambition** è spinto dall'avidità/dall'ambizione; **to drive sb mad** far impazzire qn; **he drives her mad** la fa diventare matta; **to drive sb to despair** ridurre qn alla disperazione **2** (*vehicle*) guidare; (*passenger*) portare (in macchina *etc*); **he drives a taxi** fa il tassista; **he drives a Mercedes** ha una Mercedes; **I'll drive you home** ti porto a casa (in macchina) **3** (*operate: machine*) azionare; **steam-driven train** treno a vapore; **machine driven by electricity** macchina che funziona a elettricità **4** (*nail, stake*): **to drive (into)** conficcare (in), piantare (in); **to drive this point home, she pointed out that ...** per farsi capire bene, ha sottolineato che... ♦ vi (*drive a car*) guidare;

(*travel by car*) andare in macchina; **to drive away/back** partire/ritornare in macchina; **he drove from London to Edinburgh** ha guidato da Londra ad Edimburgo; **we never drive into the town centre** non andiamo mai in macchina in centro; **can you drive?** sai guidare?; **to drive at 50 km an hour** guidare *or* andare a 50 km all'ora; **to drive on the left** guidare a sinistra

▸ **drive at** VI + PREP (*fig: intend, mean*) mirare a, voler dire

▸ **drive back** VT + ADV (*person, army*) respingere, ributtare indietro

▸ **drive off** VT + ADV (*enemy*) cacciare

▸ **drive on** VI + ADV proseguire, andare (più) avanti ♦ VT + ADV (*incite, encourage*) sospingere, spingere

▸ **drive out** VT + ADV cacciare; (*fig*) fare allontanare

▸ **drive up** VI + ADV (*car*) sopraggiungere, arrivare; (*person*) arrivare (in macchina)

drive-by [ˈdraɪvˌbaɪ] N (*also:* **drive-by shooting**) sparatoria dalla macchina; **he was killed in a drive-by shooting** lo hanno ammazzato sparandogli da una macchina in corsa

drive-in [ˈdraɪvˌɪn] N (*esp USA*) drive-in *m inv* ♦ ADJ: **drive-in cinema/restaurant/bank** cinema/fastfood/banca drive-in; **drive-in window** sportello di drive-in

driv·el [ˈdrɪvl] N (*fam: nonsense*) stupidaggini *fpl*, sciocchezze *fpl*

▸ **drivel on** VI + ADV (*fam*): **to drivel on (about)** non smettere di cianciare (di)

driv·en [ˈdrɪvn] PT *of* drive

driver [ˈdraɪvəʳ] N 1 (*of car*) guidatore(-trice); (*professional: of car, truck*) autista *m/f*; (*: of bus*) conducente *m/f*, autista *m/f*; (*: of taxi*) tassista *m/f*; **to be in the driver's seat** essere seduto(-a) nel posto del conducente; (*fig*) essere al timone; **he's a good driver** guida bene; **he's a terrible driver** è un pessimo guidatore 2 (*Comput*) driver *m inv*

driver's license N (*USA*) = driving licence

drive·way [ˈdraɪvˌweɪ] N vialetto d'accesso

driv·ing [ˈdraɪvɪŋ] N (*Aut*) guida; **his driving is awful** guida veramente male ♦ ADJ 1 (*Aut*) di guida; **driving instructor** istruttore(-trice) di (scuola) guida; **driving lesson** lezione *f* di guida; **driving mirror** specchietto retrovisore; **driving school** scuola guida *inv*; **driving test** esame *m* di guida; **to pass/fail one's driving test** superare/non superare l'esame di guida 2 (*necessity*) impellente; (*force*) trainante; (*rain, sleet*) battente, sferzante

driving licence, (*USA*) **driver's license** N patente *f* (di guida)

driz·zle [ˈdrɪzl] N pioggerella, acquerugiola ♦ VI piovigginare

droll [drəʊl] ADJ (*old: humour*) ameno(-a); (*: expression*) buffo(-a), strambo(-a)

drom·edary [ˈdrɒmɪdərɪ] N dromedario

drone [drəʊn] N 1 (*male bee*) fuco, pecchione *m* 2 (*noise: of bees, aircraft*) ronzio; (*: of voices*) brusio ♦ VI (*bee, engine, aircraft*) ronzare; (*person: also:* **drone on**) continuare a parlare (in modo monotono); (*voice*) continuare a ronzare

drool [druːl] VI (*baby*) sbavare; **to drool over sb/sth** (*fig*) andare in estasi per qn/qc

droop [druːp] VI (*head*) chinarsi; (*with sleep*) cadere; (*shoulders*) piegarsi; (*flower, plant*) afflosciarsi; (*person*) abbattersi; **she was drooping with tiredness** cascava di stanchezza; **his spirits drooped** si è molto abbattuto, si è avvilito

drop [drɒp] N 1 (*gen*) goccia; (*of wine, tea*) goccio, goccino; **would you like some milk? - just a drop** vuoi del latte? - solo una goccia; **drop by drop** goccia a goccia; **a drop in the ocean** (*fig*) una goccia nel mare; **he's had a drop too much** (*fam*) ha bevuto un bicchiere di troppo; **drops** NPL (*Med*) gocce *fpl*; **lemon drops** (*sweets*) caramelle *fpl* al limone 2 (*fall: in price*) calo, ribasso; (*: in temperature*) abbassamento; (*: in salary*) riduzione *f*, taglio; **a drop of 10%** un calo del 10%; **a drop in temperature** un calo della temperatura; **at the drop of a hat** in quattro e quattr'otto 3 (*downward slope*) salto, dislivello; (*fall*) salto; **a drop of 10 metres** un salto di 10 metri 4 (*unloading by parachute: of supplies, arms*) lancio ♦ VT 1 (*let fall*) far *or* lasciar cadere; (*bomb*) lanciare, sganciare; (*liquid*) gocciolare; (*stitch*) lasciar cadere; (*lower: hemline*) allungare; (*: price, eyes, voice*) abbassare; (*set down from car: object, person*) lasciare; (*from boat: cargo, passengers*)

sbarcare; **could you drop me at the station?** puoi lasciarmi alla stazione?; **to drop anchor** gettare l'ancora 2 (*utter casually: remark, name, clue*) lasciar cadere; **to drop a word in sb's ear** dire una parolina nell'orecchio a qn; **to drop (sb) a hint about sth** far capire qc (a qn) 3 (*postcard, note*) mandare, scrivere; **to drop sb a line** mandare due righe a qn 4 (*omit: word, letter*) dimenticare; (*: aitches*) omettere, non pronunciare; (*: intentionally: person*) escludere; (*: thing*) omettere 5 (*abandon: work*) lasciare; (*: topic*) lasciar cadere; (*: idea*) abbandonare; (*: candidate*) escludere; (*: boyfriend, girlfriend*) piantare, mollare; **let's drop the subject** lasciamo perdere; **I'm going to drop chemistry** ho intenzione di non fare più chimica; **drop it!** (*fam: subject*) piantala!; (*: gun*) buttalo! 6 (*lose: money, game*) perdere ♦ VI 1 (*fall: object*) cadere, cascare; **the book dropped onto the floor** il libro è caduto sul pavimento; **I'm ready to drop** (*fam*) sto morendo; **drop dead!** (*fam*) va' al diavolo! 2 (*decrease: wind, temperature, price*) calare; (*: numbers, attendance*) diminuire; (*: voice*) abbassare; **the temperature will drop tonight** la temperatura diminuirà stanotte

▸ **drop back** VI + ADV (rallentare per) restare indietro; **he dropped back on purpose** ha rallentato apposta per restare indietro

▸ **drop behind** VI + ADV restare indietro

▸ **drop down** VI + ADV cadere, cascare

▸ **drop in** VI + ADV (*fam: visit*): **to drop in (on)** fare un salto (da), passare (da)

▸ **drop off** VI + ADV 1 (*fall asleep*) addormentarsi 2 (*decline: sales, interest*) calare, diminuire; (*: craze*) passare ♦ VT + ADV: **to drop sb off** (*from car*) far scendere qn; **to drop sth off** lasciare qc

▸ **drop out** VI + ADV (*contents*) cascar fuori; (*fig: from contest*) ritirarsi; (*: student*) smettere di studiare; **to drop out of society/university** abbandonare la società/gli studi universitari

drop·let [ˈdrɒplɪt] N gocciolina

drop·out [ˈdrɒpaʊt] N 1 (*from school, university*) chi ha abbandonato gli studi; (*from society*) chi si mette ai margini della società; **the school/college dropout rate** la percentuale di abbandono della scuola/università 2 (*Rugby*) calcio di rinvio

drop·per [ˈdrɒpəʳ] N (*Med*) contagocce *m inv*

drop·pings [ˈdrɒpɪŋz] NPL (*of bird, animal*) escrementi *mpl*, sterco *msg*

dross [drɒs] N (*Metallurgy*) scoria; (*fig: rubbish*) spazzatura

drought [draʊt] N siccità

drove [drəʊv] PT *of* drive ♦ N (*of cattle*) mandria; **droves of people** centinaia *fpl* di persone; **they came in droves** sono arrivati a frotte

drown [draʊn] VT (*people, animals*) affogare, annegare; (*land*) allagare; (*also:* **drown out:** *sound*) coprire; **you look like a drowned rat** (*fam*) sei tutto fradicio! ♦ VI (*also:* **to be drowned**) annegare, affogare

drowse [draʊz] VI sonnecchiare, essere mezzo assopito(-a)

drowsy [ˈdraʊzɪ] ADJ (*comp* **-ier,** *superl* **-iest**) (*sleepy: person, smile, look*) assonnato(-a); (*soporific: afternoon, atmosphere*) sonnolento(-a); **to feel drowsy** sentirsi insonnolito(-a)

drudge [drʌdʒ] N (*person*) uomo (donna) di fatica

drudg·ery [ˈdrʌdʒərɪ] N fatica; **housework is sheer drudgery** sbrigare le faccende domestiche è un lavoro pesante e ingrato

drug [drʌg] N (*Med*) medicina, medicinale *m*, farmaco; (*addictive substance*) droga, stupefacente *m*; **hard drugs** droghe pesanti; **soft drugs** droghe leggere; **to take drugs** drogarsi; **he's on drugs** si droga; (*Med*) è in cura ♦ ADJ di droga; **drug dealer** spacciatore(-trice) di droga; **drug runner** trafficante *m/f* di droga; **drug running, drug traffic** traffico di droga ♦ VT (*person, wine, food*) drogare; **to be in a drugged sleep** dormire sotto l'effetto di narcotici

drug abuser [-əˈbjuːzəʳ] N chi fa abuso di droghe

drug addict N tossicodipendente *m/f*, tossicomane *m/f*

drug·gist [ˈdrʌgɪst] N (*USA*) farmacista *m/f*

drug·store [ˈdrʌgˌstɔːʳ] N (*USA*) negozio di generi vari con un bar

drum [drʌm] N 1 (*Mus*) tamburo; **a drum kit** una batteria; **the drums** la batteria; **to play the drums** suonare la

batteria; **big drum** grancassa; **drum roll** rullio di tamburi **2** (*container: for oil, petrol*) bidone *m*, fusto; (*Tech: cylinder, machine part*) tamburo ♦ vt: **to drum one's fingers on the table** tamburellare con le dita sul tavolo; **to drum sth into sb** (*fig*) ficcare qc in testa a qn ♦ vi (*Mus*) battere *or* suonare il tamburo; (*tap: with fingers*) tamburellare; **the noise was drumming in my ears** il rumore mi martellava nel cervello
► **drum up** vt + adv (*enthusiasm, support*) conquistarsi

drum·mer [ˈdrʌməʳ] N (*in military band*) tamburo; (*in jazz band, pop group*) batterista *m/f*

drum·stick [ˈdrʌmˌstɪk] N **1** (*Mus*) bacchetta **2** (*chicken leg*) coscia di pollo

drunk [drʌŋk] PP *of* **drink** ♦ ADJ ubriaco(-a); (*fig*) ebbro(-a), ubriaco(-a); **to get drunk** ubriacarsi; **to arrest sb for being drunk and disorderly** arrestare qn per ubriachezza molesta ♦ N ubriaco(-a)

drunk·ard [ˈdrʌŋkəd] N beone(-a), ubriacone(-a)

drunk·en [ˈdrʌŋkən] ADJ (*intoxicated*) ubriaco(-a); (*habitually*) alcolizzato(-a); (*brawl, orgy*) di ubriachi; (*rage*) provocato(-a) dall'alcol; (*voice*) da ubriaco; **drunken hooligans** hooligans ubriachi; **drunken driving** guida in stato di ebbrezza

drunk·en·ness [ˈdrʌŋkənnɪs] N (*state*) ubriachezza, ebbrezza; (*habit, problem*) abuso di alcolici

dry [draɪ] ADJ (*comp* **-ier**, *superl* **-iest**) **1** (*gen*) secco(-a); (*clothes*) asciutto(-a), (*day*) senza pioggia; (*battery*) a secco; **it's been exceptionally dry this spring** il clima è stato insolitamente secco in primavera; **a long dry period** un lungo periodo senza pioggia; **on dry land** sulla terraferma; **as dry as a bone** completamente asciutto(-a); **to be dry** (*thirsty*) avere la gola secca; **the reservoir ran dry** il lago artificiale si è prosciugato **2** (*humour*): **a dry sense of humour** un senso dell'umorismo all'inglese; (*uninteresting: lecture, subject*) poco avvincente ♦ vt (*subj: person: hair, hands, clothes, child*) asciugare; (: *herbs, figs, flowers*) far seccare; (*subj: sun, wind*) seccare; **to dry one's hands/hair/eyes** asciugarsi le mani/i capelli/gli occhi; **to dry the dishes** asciugare i piatti; **to dry o.s** asciugarsi ♦ vi asciugarsi
► **dry off** vi + adv (*clothes etc*) asciugarsi ♦ vt + adv asciugare
► **dry out** vi + adv seccarsi; (*alcoholic*) disintossicarsi ♦ vt + adv asciugare
► **dry up** vi + adv **1** (*river, well*) seccarsi; (*moisture*) asciugarsi; (*source of supply*) esaurirsi; (*fig: imagination*) inaridirsi **2** (*dry the dishes*) asciugare (i piatti) **3** (*fall silent: speaker*) azzittirsi; **dry up!** (*fam*) chiudi il becco!

dry-clean [ˌdraɪˈkliːn] vt pulire *or* lavare a secco; "**dry-clean only**" (*on label*) "pulire a secco"

dry-cleaner's [ˌdraɪˈkliːnəz] N lavasecco *m inv*, tintoria

dry-cleaning [ˌdraɪˈkliːnɪŋ] N lavaggio a secco; **shall I pick up your dry-cleaning for you?** vado a prenderti la roba in tintoria?

dry dock N (*Naut*) bacino di carenaggio

dry·er, dri·er [ˈdraɪəʳ] N (*for hair*) föhn *m inv*, asciugacapelli *m inv*; (*at hairdresser's*) casco *m* asciugacapelli, *inv*; (*for clothes*) asciugabiancheria *m inv*; **tumble dryer** asciugabiancheria; **hair dryer** asciugacapelli

dry goods NPL (*USA: Comm*) tessuti *mpl* e mercerie, *fpl*; **dry goods store** negozio di stoffe

dry ice N ghiaccio secco

dry·ly, dri·ly [ˈdraɪlɪ] ADV (*coldly*) con fare distaccato; (*with dry humour*) con una punta d'ironia

dry·ness [ˈdraɪnɪs] N (*gen*) secchezza; (*of ground*) aridità; **she remarked with some dryness that ...** osservò con una punta d'ironia che...

dry rot N fungo del legno

dry run N (*fig*) prova

dry ski slope N pista artificiale

DST [ˌdiːˌesˈtiː] ABBR (*USA*) = **daylight-saving time**

DT's [ˌdiːˈtiːz] NPL ABBR = **delirium tremens**(*fam*): **the DT's** delirium *m inv* tremens, *inv*

dual [ˈdjʊəl] ADJ doppio(-a), duplice; **dual controls** doppi comandi *mpl*; **dual nationality** doppia nazionalità ♦ N (*Gram*) duale *m*; (*Geom*) duale *f*

dual-purpose [ˈdjʊəlˈpɜːpəs] ADJ a doppio uso

dubbed [dʌbd] ADJ (*film*) doppiato(-a)

du·bi·ous [ˈdjuːbɪəs] ADJ (*gen*) dubbio(-a); (*look, smile*) dubbioso(-a); (*character, manner*) ambiguo(-a), equivoco(-a); **to feel dubious about** or **as to what to do next** essere incerto(-a) sul da farsi; **I'm very dubious about it** ho i miei dubbi in proposito

Dub·lin [ˈdʌblɪn] N Dublino *f*

Dub·lin·er [ˈdʌblɪnəʳ] N dublinese *m/f*

duch·ess [ˈdʌtʃɪs] N duchessa

duck [dʌk] N anatra; **wild duck** anatra selvatica; **she's taken to her new school like a duck to water** si è trovata subito benissimo nella nuova scuola; **to play (at) ducks and drakes** tirare i sassi a fior d'acqua ♦ vt (*plunge in water: person, head*) spingere sotto (acqua); **to duck one's head** abbassare la testa ♦ vi (*also: **duck down***) accucciarsi; (*in fight*) fare una schivata; (*under water*) tuffarsi sott'acqua
► **duck out of** vi + prep (*fam*): **to duck out of doing sth** svignarsela per evitare di fare qc

duck·ling [ˈdʌklɪŋ] N anatroccolo

duct [dʌkt] N (*Tech, Anat*) condotto, canale *m*

dud [dʌd] (*fam*) ADJ (*shell, bomb*) inesploso(-a); (*not working: machine*) inservibile; (*false: coin, note*) falso(-a); (: *cheque*) a vuoto ♦ N: **to be a dud** (*object, tool*) non servire a un bel niente, non funzionare; (*person*) essere una nullità; (*shell*) fare cilecca

due [djuː] ADJ **1** (*owing: sum, money*) dovuto(-a); **due date** (*Comm*) data di scadenza; **the rent's due on the 30th** l'affitto scade il 30; **our thanks are due to him** gli è dovuto un grazie; **I am due 6 days' leave** mi spettano 6 giorni di ferie **2** (*proper: care, respect, attention*) dovuto(-a), giusto(-a); **with all due respect** con rispetto parlando; **after due consideration** dopo un attento esame; **in due course** a tempo debito **3** (*expected*) atteso(-a); **the train is due at 8** il treno è atteso per le 8; **she is due back tomorrow** dovrebbe essere di ritorno domani; **he's due to arrive tomorrow** lo attendiamo per domani; **it is due to be demolished** è destinato alla demolizione; **when's the baby due?** quando deve nascere il bambino? **4 due to** (*caused by*) dovuto(-a) a; (*because of*) a causa di; (*thanks to*) grazie a; **the trip was cancelled due to bad weather** il viaggio è stato annullato a causa del maltempo ♦ ADV: **due west of** direttamente a ovest di; **to go due north** andare dritto verso nord; **to face due south** guardare dritto verso sud ♦ N: **to give him his due, he did try hard** per essere onesti (nei suoi confronti), bisogna riconoscere che c'ha messa tutta; *see also* **dues**

duel [ˈdjʊəl] N duello ♦ vi battersi in duello

duet [djuːˈet] N duetto; **to sing/play a duet** cantare/suonare un duetto; **a violin/piano duet** (*performance*) un duetto al violino/al piano; (*composition*) un duetto per violino/per piano

duffel bag N sacca da viaggio di tela

duffel coat N ≈ duffel

duf·fer [ˈdʌfəʳ] N (*fam*) schiappa

dug [dʌg] PT, PP *of* **dig**

dug·out [ˈdʌɡaʊt] N **1** (*Mil*) trincea coperta; (*Sport*) panchina **2** (*canoe*) canoa ricavata da un tronco d'albero

duke [djuːk] N duca *m*

dull [dʌl] ADJ (*comp* **-er**, *superl* **-est**) **1** (*boring: book, evening*) noioso(-a); (: *person, style*) insulso(-a); **he's nice, but a bit dull** è simpatico, ma un po' noioso; **as dull as ditchwater** una vera pizza **2** (*dim: colour, eyes*) spento(-a); (*metal*) opaco(-a); (*overcast: weather, day, sky*) cupo(-a), scuro(-a), fosco(-a); (*muffled: sound, pain, thud*) sordo(-a); (*Comm: trade, business*) stagnante; (*lacking spirit: person, mood*) svogliato(-a); (*blade*) smussato(-a); **a dull day** una giornata nuvolosa **3** (*sight, hearing*) debole; (*slow-witted: person, mind*) ottuso(-a); (: *pupil*) lento(-a) ♦ vt (*mind, senses*) ottundere, annebbiare; (*blade*) smussare; (*impression, memory*) offuscare; (*pleasure, pain, grief*) attenuare, attutire; (*sound, colour*) smorzare; (*metal*) rendere opaco(-a)

duly [ˈdjuːlɪ] ADV (*properly*) come si deve, debitamente; (*as expected*) come previsto, secondo le previsioni; (*on time*) a tempo debito; **he duly arrived at 3** è arrivato alle 3 come previsto; **everybody was duly shocked** tutti sono rimasti debitamente scioccati

dumb [dʌm] ADJ (*comp* **-er**, *superl* **-est**) **1** (*Med: fam!*) muto(-a);

(*with surprise*) senza parole, ammutolito(-a); **I was so dumb!** che stupido sono stato!; **to act dumb** fare lo gnorri

dumb·bell [ˈdʌmˌbel] N (*Sport*) manubrio, peso

dumb·found·ed [ˌdʌmˈfaʊndɪd] ADJ: **to be dumbfounded** rimanere sbigottito(-a)

dum·my [ˈdʌmɪ] N 1 (*Comm: imitation*) cosa finta, riproduzione *f*; (*tailor's model*) manichino; (*ventriloquist's dummy*) pupazzo; (*Sport*) finta; (*Bridge*) morto 2 (*Brit: for baby*) tettarella, succhiotto 3 (*fam: idiot*) tonto(-a) ♦ ADJ (*not real*) finto(-a), falso(-a); **dummy weapons** armi giocattolo

dummy run N giro di prova

dump [dʌmp] N 1 (*pile of rubbish*) mucchio di immondizie *or* di rifiuti; (*place for refuse*) discarica pubblica; **to be (down) in the dumps** (*fam*) essere giù di corda 2 (*Mil*) deposito 3 (*pej, fam: town, hotel etc*) buco; (: *house*) catapecchia; **it's a real dump!** è proprio un postaccio! 4 (*Comput*) stampa della memoria, dump *m inv* ♦ VT 1 (*get rid of: rubbish etc*) buttare; (: *Comm: goods*) svendere; (: *fam: person*) piantare, scaricare 2 (*put down: load*) scaricare; (: *fam: parcel, passenger, coat*) mollare; **we dumped our bags at the hotel and went to the beach** abbiamo mollato i bagagli all'albergo e siamo andati in 3 (*Comput*) riversare

dump·ing [ˈdʌmpɪŋ] N 1 (*of rubbish*) scarico; "**no dumping**" (*of waste, rubbish*) "vietato lo scarico" 2 (*Econ*) dumping *m inv*

dump·ling [ˈdʌmplɪŋ] N (*Culin*) gnocco di pasta

dumpy [ˈdʌmpɪ] ADJ tracagnotto(-a)

dunce [dʌns] N (*Scol*) asino(-a), somaro(-a)

dune [djuːn] N duna

dung [dʌŋ] N (*of horse, cow*) sterco; (*as manure*) letame *m*, concime *m*

dun·ga·rees [ˌdʌŋɡəˈriːz] NPL (*gen*) tela grezza di cotone; (*child's*) tutina; (*adult's*) salopette *f inv*; (*of workmen*) tuta

dun·geon [ˈdʌndʒən] N segreta, prigione *f* sotterranea

dunk [dʌŋk] VT intingere, inzuppare; **to dunk one's bread in one's soup** inzuppare il pane nella minestra

duo [ˈdjuːəʊ] N (*gen, also Mus*) duo *m inv*

duo·de·nal [ˌdjuːəʊˈdiːnl] ADJ (*ulcer*) duodenale

duo·denum [ˌdjuːəʊˈdiːnəm] N duodeno

dupe [djuːp] N zimbello(-a); **to be sb's dupe** lasciarsi ingannare da qn ♦ VT ingannare, gabbare; **to dupe sb into doing sth** ingannare qn per fargli fare qc

du·plex [ˈdjuːpleks] N (*USA: also:* **duplex apartment**) appartamento su due piani

du·pli·cate [*vb* ˈdjuːplɪˌkeɪt, *n, adj* ˈdjuːplɪkɪt] VT (*document*) fare una doppia copia di; (*on machine*) riprodurre, duplicare; (*repeat: action*) ripetere, riprodurre ♦ N (*document*) duplicato; **in duplicate** in duplice copia, in doppia copia; **duplicate key** doppione *m* della chiave ♦ ADJ (*copy*) conforme, esattamente uguale; **duplicate key** doppione; **duplicate receipt pad** bollettario

du·plic·ity [djuːˈplɪsɪtɪ] N (*frm*) doppiezza, duplicità

du·rabil·ity [ˌdjʊərəˈbɪlɪtɪ] N (*of materials*) resistenza; (*of relationship*) durevolezza

du·rable [ˈdjʊərəbl] ADJ (*material, clothes*) resistente; (*Comm*) durevole; (*friendship*) duraturo(-a); **durable goods** beni durevoli

du·ra·tion [djʊəˈreɪʃən] N durata; **of 6 years' duration** della durata di 6 anni

du·ress [djʊəˈrɛs] N: **under duress** sotto costrizione, con la coercizione

dur·ing [ˈdjʊərɪŋ] PREP durante

dusk [dʌsk] N (*twilight*) crepuscolo; (*gloom*) (semi)oscurità; **at dusk** sul far della sera, al crepuscolo; **in the dusk** (*liter*) nella semioscurità

dusky [ˈdʌskɪ] ADJ (*complexion, room, light*) scuro(-a); **dusky pink** rosa antico *inv*

dust [dʌst] N (*on furniture etc*) polvere *f* ♦ VT, VI (*furniture*) spolverare; **she dusted the cake with sugar** ha spolverato il dolce di zucchero
▸ **dust off** VT + ADV rispolverare

dust·bin [ˈdʌstˌbɪn] N bidone *m* della spazzatura

dust·er [ˈdʌstə*r*] N (*cloth*) straccio per la polvere; (*for blackboard*) cancellino, cimosa

dust jacket, dust cover N (*of book*) sopraccoperta, copertina

dust·man [ˈdʌstmən] N (*pl* **-men**) (*Brit*) netturbino

dust·pan [ˈdʌstˌpæn] N paletta

dusty [ˈdʌstɪ] ADJ (*comp* **-ier**, *superl* **-iest**) polveroso(-a); **to get dusty** impolverarsi

Dutch [dʌtʃ] ADJ olandese; **Dutch elm disease** fungo parassita dell'olmo ♦ N 1 **the Dutch** (*npl: people*) gli olandesi 2 (*language*) olandese *m* ♦ ADV: **to go Dutch** *or* **dutch** (*fam*) fare alla romana

Dutch auction N asta all'olandese

Dutch·man [ˈdʌtʃmən] N (*pl* **-men**) olandese *m*

du·ti·able [ˈdjuːtɪəbl] ADJ soggetto(-a) a dazio

du·ti·ful [ˈdjuːtɪfʊl] ADJ (*child*) rispettoso(-a); (*husband*) premuroso(-a); (*employee*) coscienzioso(-a)

duty [ˈdjuːtɪ] N 1 (*moral, legal*) dovere *m*; **it was his duty to tell the police** era suo dovere dirlo alla polizia; **I carried out my duties** ho svolto i miei compiti; **to do one's duty (by sb)** fare il proprio dovere (verso qn); **to make it one's duty to do sth** assumersi l'obbligo di fare qc 2 (*often pl: task, responsibility*) mansione *f*, funzione *f*; **on duty** (*Med: in hospital*) di guardia; (*Mil*) di servizio; (*Admin, Scol*) di turno; **off duty** (*Mil*) fuori servizio; (*Mil*) in libera uscita 3 (*tax*) tassa; (*at customs*) dazio; **to pay duty on sth** pagare il dazio su qc; **import duties** tassi d'importazione

duty-free [ˌdjuːtɪˈfriː] ADJ (*goods*) esente da dogana *or* dazio; (*at airport*) duty-free *inv*

duty officer N (*Mil*) ufficiale *m* di servizio

du·vet [ˈduːveɪ] N (*Brit*) piumone *m*

DV [ˌdiːˈviː] ADV ABBR = **Deo volente**

DVD [ˌdiːviːˈdiː] N (= *digital video or versatile disk*) DVD *m inv*

DVD player N lettore *m* DVD, *inv*

DVM [ˌdiːviːˈem] N ABBR (*USA:* = *Doctor of Veterinary Medicine*)

DVT [ˌdiːviːˈtiː] N ABBR *see* **deep vein thrombosis**

dwarf [dwɔːf] ADJ, N nano(-a) ♦ VT (*subj: building, person*) fare sembrare piccolissimo(-a), far scomparire; (*achievement*) eclissare

dwell [dwel] (*pt, pp* **dwelt**) VI (*poet*) dimorare
▸ **dwell on, dwell upon** VI + PREP (*think about*) rimuginare; (*talk about*) soffermarsi su, indugiare su; (*subj: conversation*) aggirarsi su; **let's not dwell upon it** non insistiamo su questo punto

dwell·er [ˈdwelə*r*] N abitante *m*/*f*; **city dweller** cittadino(-a)

dwell·ing [ˈdwelɪŋ] N (*frm, liter*) dimora; **dwelling house** (*Law*) abitazione *f*

dwelt [dwelt] PT, PP *of* **dwell**

dwin·dle [ˈdwɪndl] VI (*numbers, supplies*) assottigliarsi, diminuire, decrescere; (*interest*) affievolirsi; **to dwindle to** ridursi a

dwin·dling [ˈdwɪndlɪŋ] ADJ (*strength, interest*) che si affievolisce; (*resources, supplies*) in diminuzione

dye [daɪ] N colore *m*; (*chemical*) colorante *m*, tintura; **hair dye** tinta per capelli, tintura per capelli; **the dye has run** si è stinto ♦ VT (*fabric*) tingere; **to dye sth red** tingere qc di *or* in rosso; **to dye one's hair blond** farsi biondo(-a); **dyed hair** capelli *mpl* tinti

dye·stuffs [ˈdaɪˌstʌfs] NPL sostanze *fpl* coloranti (per tintura)

dy·ing [ˈdaɪɪŋ] N (*death*) morte *f*; **the dying** *npl* i morenti ♦ ADJ (*person, plant*) morente; (*custom, race*) in via di estinzione; **his dying words were ...** le sue ultime parole furono...; **to my dying day** finché vivrò

dyke [daɪk] N (*barrier*) diga, argine *m*; (*channel*) canale *m* di scolo; (*causeway*) sentiero rialzato

dy·nam·ic [daɪˈnæmɪk] ADJ dinamico(-a)

dy·nam·ics [daɪˈnæmɪks] NSG dinamica

dy·na·mite [ˈdaɪnəˌmaɪt] N 1 dinamite *f* 2 (*fig: fam*): **he's dynamite!** è una bomba!; **the story is dynamite** è una storia esplosiva ♦ VT far saltare con la dinamite

dy·na·mo [ˈdaɪnəməʊ] N dinamo *f inv*

dyn·as·ty [ˈdɪnəstɪ, (*USA*) ˈdaɪnəstɪ] N dinastia

dys·en·tery [ˈdɪsɪntrɪ] N dissenteria

dys·lexia [dɪsˈleksɪə] N dislessia

dys·lex·ic [dɪsˈleksɪk] ADJ, N dislessico(-a)

dys·pep·sia [dɪsˈpepsɪə] N dispepsia

dys·tro·phy [ˈdɪstrəfɪ] N distrofia; **muscular dystrophy** distrofia muscolare

Ee

E¹, e¹ [iː] N 1 (*letter*) E, e *f inv or m inv*; **E for Edward**, (*USA*) **E for Easy** ≈ E come Empoli 2 (*Mus*): **E mi** *m*

E² ABBR (= *east*) E

e- [iː] PREF (*Comput*) e-

ea. ABBR = **each**

each [iːtʃ] ADJ ogni *inv*, ciascuno(-a); **in each hand** in ciascuna mano; **each day** ogni giorno; **each one** ognuno(a); **each one of them** ciascuno(-a) *or* ognuno(-a) di loro ♦ PRON 1 ognuno(-a), ciascuno(-a); **each of us** ciascuno(-a) *or* ognuno(-a) di noi; **a little of each please** un po' di tutto, per favore 2 **each other** l'un(a) l'altro(-a), si (*or* ci *etc*); **they love each other** si amano; **we hate each other** ci odiamo; **you know each other** vi conoscete; **we write to each other** ci scriviamo; **people must help each other** ci si deve aiutare a vicenda *or* l'un l'altro; **separated from each other** separati l'uno dall'altro; **next to each other** uno accanto all'altro; **you are jealous of each other** siete gelosi l'uno dell'altro ♦ ADV l'uno(-a), per uno(-a), ciascuno(-a); **they have ten points each** hanno dieci punti ciascuno; **we gave them an apple each** abbiamo dato una mela a ciascuno; **they cost £5 each** costano 5 sterline l'uno; **they have 2 books each** hanno 2 libri ciascuno

eager [ˈiːgəʳ] ADJ (*keen: pupil*) appassionato(-a), attento(-a); (*: search, desire*) appassionato(-a); **to be eager to do sth** (*impatient*) essere impaziente *or* ansioso(-a) di fare qc, non veder l'ora di fare qc; **he was eager to tell us about his experiences** era impaziente di raccontarci le sue esperienze; **to be eager for** (*knowledge, power*) essere avido(-a) di; (*affection*) essere desideroso(-a) di; (*happiness*) desiderare ardentemente

eagle [ˈiːgl] N aquila

ear¹ [ɪəʳ] N orecchio, orecchia; **to keep one's ears open** tenere le orecchie aperte; **to be all ears** essere tutt'orecchi; **he could not believe his ears** non credeva alle proprie orecchie; **your ears must have been burning** non ti fischiavano le orecchie?; **it goes in one ear and out the other** mi (*or* ti *etc*) entra da un orecchio ed esce dall'altro; **to be up to one's ears in debt** essere nei debiti fino al collo; **to be up to one's ears in work** avere una mole enorme di lavoro; **to have a good ear for music** avere molto orecchio; **to play sth by ear** (*tune*) suonare qc a orecchio; **I'll play it by ear** (*fig*) vedrò come si mettono le cose

ear² [ɪəʳ] N (*of wheat, barley*) spiga; (*of corn*) pannocchia

ear·ache [ˈɪəreɪk] N mal m d'orecchi; **to have earache** avere mal d'orecchi

ear·drum [ˈɪədrʌm] N timpano

ear·ful [ˈɪəfʊl] N: **to give sb an earful** fare una ramanzina a qn

earl [ɜːl] N conte *m*

ear·ly [ˈɜːlɪ] (*comp* -ier, *superl* -iest) ADV presto; (*ahead of time*) in anticipo; **I came home early** sono tornato a casa presto; **as early as possible** il più presto possibile; **early in the morning/afternoon** nelle prime ore del mattino/del pomeriggio; **early in the spring/19th century** all'inizio della primavera/dell'Ottocento; **he was 10 minutes early** è arrivato con 10 minuti di anticipo; **to book early** prenotare in anticipo; **I can't come any earlier** non posso venire prima; **I saw him earlier** l'ho visto prima; **earlier on** poco tempo prima ♦ ADJ (*man*) primitivo(-a); (*Christians, settlers*) primo(-a); (*fruit, plant*) precoce; (*death*) prematuro(-a); (*reply*) pronto(-a); **it's still early** è ancora presto; **an early general election** elezioni *fpl* generali anticipate; **at an early date** prossimamente; **an early edition of the book** una precedente edizione del libro; **you're early!** sei in anticipo!; **to be an early riser** *or* **an early bird** essere mattiniero(-a); **at an early hour** presto; **in the early morning** al mattino presto; **in the early 19th century** ai primi dell'Ottocento; **she's in her early forties** ha appena passato la quarantina;

from an early age fin dall'infanzia; **his early youth** la sua prima giovinezza; **Shakespeare's early work** le prime opere di Shakespeare; **an early Victorian table** un tavolo del primo periodo vittoriano; **to have an early night** andare a letto presto; **to make an early start** iniziare presto; **at your earliest convenience** (*Comm*) non appena possibile

early retirement N pensionamento anticipato, prepensionamento

early warning system N sistema *m* di preallarme

ear·mark [ˈɪəmɑːk] VT: **to earmark (for)** (*money*) mettere da parte (per); (*person, job*) destinare (a)

earn [ɜːn] VT (*money, salary*) guadagnare; (*Fin: interest*) maturare; (*praise, reward, rest*) meritare, meritarsi; **she earns five pounds an hour** guadagna cinque sterline all'ora; **to earn one's living** guadagnarsi da vivere

earned income [ˈɜːndˈɪnkʌm] N (*Brit: Fin*) reddito derivante da lavoro

ear·nest [ˈɜːnɪst] ADJ (*person, character, request*) serio(-a); (*wish*) sincero(-a) ♦ N 1 **in earnest** (*with determination*) con serietà, con coscienza; (*seriously*) sul serio 2 (*Law: also:* **earnest money**) caparra

earn·ings [ˈɜːnɪŋz] NPL (*of individual*) guadagni *mpl*; (*salary*) stipendio *sg*; (*of company*) proventi *mpl*; **average earnings rose two percent last year** l'anno scorso lo stipendio medio è aumentato del due percento

ear nose and throat specialist N otorinolaringoiatra *m/f*

ear·phones [ˈɪəfəʊnz] NPL (*Telec*) cuffia *sg*

ear·plug [ˈɪəplʌg] N tappo per le orecchie

ear·ring [ˈɪərɪŋ] N orecchino

ear·shot [ˈɪəʃɒt] N: **out of/within earshot** fuori portata/a portata d'orecchio; **wait till he's out of earshot before you say anything** aspetta che si allontani prima di parlare

earth [ɜːθ] N 1 (*the world*) terra; **(the) Earth** la Terra; **on earth** sulla terra; **the silliest man on earth** l'uomo più stupido del mondo; **it tasted like nothing on earth** (*fam*) aveva un sapore tremendo; **it must have cost the earth!** (*fam*) deve essere costato un occhio della testa!; **where/who/what on earth ...?** (*fam*) dove/chi/che diavolo...? 2 (*ground*) terra; (*soil*) terra, terreno; **to fall to earth** cadere a terra, cadere al suolo 3 (*of fox, badger*) tana; **to run to earth** (*animal*) inseguire fino alla tana; (*person*) scovare, stanare 4 (*Brit: Elec*) terra, massa ♦ VT (*Brit: Elec: apparatus*) mettere *or* collegare a terra

earthen·ware [ˈɜːθənwɛəʳ] N terraglie *fpl*, terracotta ♦ ADJ di terracotta

earth·ly [ˈɜːθlɪ] ADJ terreno(-a); **earthly paradise** paradiso terrestre; **there is no earthly reason to think ...** non vi è nessunissima ragione di pensare...; **it's of no earthly use** non serve assolutamente a nulla

earth·quake [ˈɜːθkweɪk] N terremoto

earth·shattering [ˈɜːθˌʃætərɪŋ] ADJ stupefacente; (*momentous*) molto importante

earth tremor N scossa sismica

earthworks [ˈɜːθwɜːks] NPL lavori *mpl* di sterro

earth·worm [ˈɜːθwɜːm] N lombrico

earthy [ˈɜːθɪ] ADJ 1 (*taste, smell*) di terra 2 (*person*) terra terra *inv*; (*humour*) grossolano(-a)

ear·wax [ˈɪəwæks] N cerume *m*

ear·wig [ˈɪəwɪg] N (*insect*) forbicina

ease [iːz] N 1 disinvoltura, scioltezza; **the camera's ease of use** la facilità d'impiego della macchina fotografica; **with ease** senza difficoltà 2 (*freedom from worry*) tranquillità, agio; **a life of ease** una vita comoda; **to feel at ease/ill at ease** sentirsi a proprio agio/a disagio; **to put sb at his** *or* **her ease** mettere qn a suo agio; **(stand) at ease!** (*Mil*) riposo! ♦ VT (*task*) facilitare; (*pain*) alleviare, calmare; (*rope, strap, pressure*) allentare; (*collar*) slacciare; **to ease the pain ...**

per calmare il dolore...; **to ease sb's mind** tranquillizzare *or* rassicurare qn; **to ease sth out/in** facilitare l'uscita/l'entrata di q c; **to ease in the clutch** (*Aut*) rilasciare la frizione dolcemente ♦ **VI** (*situation*) distendersi; **the pressure has eased** la pressione è diminuita

▸ **ease off** **VI** + ADV (*slow down*) rallentare; (*work, business*) diminuire; (*pressure, tension*) allentarsi; (*pain*) calmarsi; (*relax*) rilassarsi

▸ **ease up** **VI** + ADV (*person*) calmarsi; (*situation*) distendersi; **ease up a bit!** prenditela calma!; **the pressure had eased up** la pressione era diminuita; **we can't ease up yet** non possiamo mollare ancora

easel [ˈiːzl] N cavalletto

easi·ly [ˈiːzɪlɪ] ADV (*without effort: win, climb*) facilmente, agevolmente; **this can easily be done** questo si può fare facilmente; **he may easily change his mind** potrebbe benissimo cambiare idea; **it's easily the best** è senza dubbio il migliore, è di gran lunga il migliore; **there were easily 500 at the meeting** c'erano almeno 500 persone alla riunione

easi·ness [ˈiːzɪnɪs] N 1 facilità, semplicità 2 (*of manners*) disinvoltura

east [iːst] N est *m*, oriente *m*; **the mysterious East** l'Oriente misterioso; **the East** (*Geog*) l'Oriente; (*Pol: formerly*) i Paesi dell'Est; **in the east** ad est; **the wind is in the east** *or* **from the east** il vento viene da est; **to the east** of a est di; **in the east of** nella parte orientale di ♦ ADJ (*side, coast*) orientale; (*wind*) dell'est, di levante; **the East End** il quartiere est (di Londra); **East Africa** l'Africa orientale ♦ ADV (*travel*) a est, verso est, a oriente; **east of the border** est della frontiera

east·bound [ˈiːstˌbaʊnd] ADJ (*traffic*) diretto(-a) a est; (*carriageway*) che porta a est

East·er [ˈiːstəʳ] N Pasqua; **at Easter** a Pasqua ♦ ADJ (*holidays*) pasquale, di Pasqua; (*week*) di Pasqua

Easter egg N uovo di Pasqua

Easter Island N Isola di Pasqua

east·er·ly [ˈiːstəlɪ] ADJ (*point, aspect*) orientale; (*wind*) da est, di levante, dell'est; **in an easterly direction** in direzione est

Easter Monday N Pasquetta

east·ern [ˈiːstən] ADJ orientale, d'oriente; **France's eastern border** il confine orientale della Francia; **Eastern Europe** l'Europa orientale, l'Europa dell'est; **the Eastern bloc** (*Pol: formerly*) i Paesi *mpl* dell'Est; **Eastern Standard Time** (*USA*) ora invernale *nel* fuso orario della costa orientale degli Stati Uniti

Easter Sunday N domenica di Pasqua

East Germany N la Germania dell'Est (*la Repubblica Democratica Tedenca, esistente dal 1949 al 1990*)

east·ward [ˈiːstwəd] ADJ (*direction*) est *inv* ♦ ADV a est, verso est, verso levante

easy [ˈiːzɪ] ADJ (*comp* -ier, *superl* -iest) 1 (*not difficult*) facile; **it's easy to understand** è facile da capire; **it is easy to see that ...** è facile comprendere che...; **he's easy to get on with** ha un buon carattere; **he came in an easy first** ha vinto di larga misura; **easier said than done** si fa presto a dirlo; **easy money** facili guadagni *mpl* 2 (*carefree: life*) agiato(-a), tranquillo(-a); (: *relationship*) cordiale; (*relaxed: manners, style*) disinvolto(-a); **payment on easy terms** (*Comm*) facilitazioni *fpl* di pagamento ♦ ADV: **easy does it!** piano!; **to take it** *or* **things easy** prendersela con calma; **take it easy!** (*don't worry*) non prendertela!; (*don't rush*) calma!; **go easy with the sugar** vacci piano con lo zucchero; **go easy on him** non essere troppo duro con lui

easy chair N poltrona

easy-going [ˈiːzɪˈgəʊŋ] ADJ (*person*) accomodante; (*attitude*) tollerante; **to be easy-going** avere un buon carattere

eat [iːt] (*pt* ate, *pp* eaten) VT (*food*) mangiare; **would you like sth to eat?** vuoi mangiare qc?; **we slowly ate our sandwiches** abbiamo mangiato lentamente i nostri panini; **to eat one's fill** mangiare a sazietà; **he's eating us out of house and home** (*fam*) è un mangiapane a tradimento; **he won't eat you** (*fam*) non ti mangia mica; **what's eating you?** (*fam*) che cosa ti rode?; **to eat one's words** (*fig*) rimangiarsi quello che si è detto ♦ VI mangiare; **he eats like a horse** mangia come un lupo; **I've got him eating out of my hand** pende dalle mie labbra, fa tutto quello che voglio io

▸ **eat away** VT + ADV (*subj: sea*) erodere; (: *acid*) corrodere; (: *mice*) rosicchiare

▸ **eat away at** VI + PREP rodere

▸ **eat in** VI + ADV mangiare a casa

▸ **eat into** VI + PREP rodere; (*subj: acid*) corrodere; (*savings*) intaccare

▸ **eat out** VI + ADV mangiare fuori ♦ VT + ADV: **to eat one's heart out** mangiarsi *or* rodersi il fegato

▸ **eat up** VT + ADV (*meal*) finire di mangiare; **it eats up electricity** consuma un sacco di corrente; **this car eats up the miles** questa macchina macina i chilometri ♦ VI + ADV: **eat up!** finisci di mangiare!

eat·able [ˈiːtəbl] ADJ (*fit to eat*) mangiabile; (*safe to eat*) commestibile

eat·en [ˈiːtn] PP *of* eat

eau de Co·logne [ˈəʊdəkəˈləʊn] N acqua di colonia

eaves [iːvz] NPL gronda *sg*

eaves·drop [ˈiːvzdrɒp] VI: **to eavesdrop (on a conversation)** origliare (una conversazione)

ebb [ɛb] N (*of tide*) riflusso; **ebb and flow** flusso e riflusso; (*business*) andar male, diminuire ♦ VI rifluire; (*fig: also:* ebb away): **to ebb and flow** (*tide*) fluire e rifluire; **his strength was ebbing fast** le forze gli venivano meno rapidamente

ebb tide N marea discendente

eb·ony [ˈɛbənɪ] N ebano

e-book [ˈiːbʊk] N (*Comput*) libro elettronico, e-book *m inv*

ebul·lient [ɪˈbʌlɪənt] ADJ esuberante

e-business [ˈiːˌbɪznɪs] N (*business*) azienda che opera in internet; (*activity*) commercio elettronico, e-business *m inv*

EC [ˌiːˈsiː] N ABBR (= *European Community*) CE *f* (= *Comunità Europea*)

e-card [ˈiːkɑːd] N e-card *f inv*, cartolina virtuale

ec·cen·tric [ɪkˈsɛntrɪk] ADJ, N eccentrico(-a)

ec·cle·si·as·tic [ɪˌkliːzɪˈæstɪk] N, ADJ ecclesiastico(-a)

ec·cle·si·as·ti·cal [ɪˌkliːzɪˈæstɪkəl] ADJ ecclesiastico(-a)

ECG [ˌiːsiːˈdʒiː] N ABBR (= *electrocardiogram*) ECG *m inv*

echo [ˈɛkəʊ] N (*pl* echoes) eco *m, f* ♦ VI (*sound*) echeggiare, riecheggiare; **the room echoed with their laughter** la stanza riecheggiava delle loro risate ♦ VT fare eco a, ripetere

éclair [ɛɪkˈlɛəʳ] N ≈ bignè *m inv*

eclipse [ɪˈklɪps] N eclissi *f inv* ♦ VT eclissare

eco– [ˈiːkəʊ] PREF eco-

eco-friendly [ˈiːkəʊˈfrɛndlɪ] ADJ ecologico(-a), che rispetta l'ambiente

eco·logi·cal [ˌiːkəʊˈlɒdʒɪkəl] ADJ ecologico(-a)

ecolo·gist [ɪˈkɒlədʒɪst] N (*scientist*) ecologo(-a); (*conservationist*) ecologista *m/f*

ecol·ogy [ɪˈkɒlədʒɪ] N ecologia

e-commerce [ˈiːˌkɒmɜːs] N commercio elettronico, e-commerce *m inv*

eco·nom·ic [ˌiːkəˈnɒmɪk] ADJ 1 (*problems, development, geography*) economico(-a) 2 (*profitable: price*) vantaggioso(-a); (: *business*) redditizio(-a)

eco·nomi·cal [ˌiːkəˈnɒmɪkəl] ADJ (*method, appliance, car*) economico(-a); (*person*) parsimonioso(-a), economo(-a); **economical with the truth** non dell tutto sincero

eco·nomi·cal·ly [ˌiːkəˈnɒmɪkəlɪ] ADV 1 con economia 2 (*regarding economics*) dal punto di vista economico; **economically strong** forte dal punto di vista economico

eco·nom·ics [ˌiːkəˈnɒmɪks] NSG (*science*) economia; **he's doing economics at university** fa economia all'università ♦ NPL (*financial aspects*) aspetto *or* lato economico

econo·mist [ɪˈkɒnəmɪst] N economista *m/f*

econo·mize [ɪˈkɒnəˌmaɪz] VI: **to economize (on)** fare economia (di), risparmiare (su)

econo·my [ɪˈkɒnəmɪ] N (*all senses*) economia; **the economy is doing well** l'economia sta andando bene; **economy size** confezione economica

economy class N (*Aer*) classe *f* turistica

economy class syndrome N sindrome *f* della classe economica

economy size N confezione *f* economica

eco·sys·tem [ˈiːkəʊˌsɪstəm] N ecosistema *m*

eco-tourism [ˈiːkəʊˈtʊərɪzəm] N turismo ecologico

ec·sta·sy [ˈɛkstəsɪ] N 1 (*Rel, also fig*) estasi *f inv*; **to go into ecstasies over** andare in estasi per 2 (*drug*) ecstasy *f*

ec·stat·ic [ɛksˈtætɪk] ADJ estatico(-a), in estasi

ECU [ˈeɪkjuː] N ABBR (= *European Currency Unit*) ECU *m inv, f inv*, ecu *m inv, f inv*

Ecua·dor [ˈɛkwə,dɔː] N Ecuador *m*

ecu·meni·cal [ˌiːkjʊˈmenɪkəl] ADJ ecumenico(-a)

ec·ze·ma [ˈɛksɪmə] N eczema *m*

eddy [ˈɛdɪ] VI (*water*) far mulinelli; (*wind, air*) turbinare ♦ N (*of water*) mulinello, gorgo; (*of wind, air*) turbine *m*

edge [ɛdʒ] N (*of table, plate, cup*) orlo, bordo; (*of cube, brick*) spigolo; (*of page*) margine *m*; (*of lake*) sponda; (*of road*) ciglio; (*of forest*) limitare *m*; (*of knife, razor*) taglio, filo; (*of ski*) lamina; **the water's edge** il bagnasciuga; **on the edge of the town** ai margini della città; **the trees at the edge of the road** gli alberi lungo il ciglio della strada; **a book with gilt edges** un libro con i bordi dorati; **to be on edge** (*fig*) essere nervoso(-a), avere i nervi a fior di pelle; **it sets my teeth on edge** (*voice, accent*) mi dà sui nervi; **to be on the edge of disaster** essere sull'orlo del disastro; **to be on the edge of extinction** stare per estinguersi; **that took the edge off my appetite** mi ha calmato i morsi della fame; **to have the edge over sb/sth** essere in vantaggio su qn/qc ♦ VT **1 to edge (with)** (*garment, garden*) bordare (di) **2** (*move carefully*) spostare piano piano ♦ VI **1 to edge past** passar rasente; **to edge forward** avanzare a poco a poco; **to edge away from sb/sth** allontanarsi piano piano da qn/qc **2** (*Skiing*) spigolare

edge·ways [ˈɛdʒ,weɪz] ADV di fianco; **I couldn't get a word in edgeways** (*fam*) non sono riuscito a infilare neppure una parola

edg·ing [ˈɛdʒɪŋ] N bordo

edgy [ˈɛdʒɪ] ADJ nervoso(-a), teso(-a)

ed·ible [ˈɛdɪbl] ADJ (*fit to eat*) mangiabile; (*produce, mushrooms*) commestibile

edict [ˈiːdɪkt] N editto

edi·fice [ˈɛdɪfɪs] N costruzione *f*, edificio

edi·fy·ing [ˈɛdɪ,faɪɪŋ] ADJ edificante

Ed·in·burgh [ˈɛdɪnbərə] N Edimburgo *f*

edit [ˈɛdɪt] VT (*newspaper, magazine*) dirigere; (*book, series*) curare; (*article, speech, text*) fare la revisione di; (*tape, film: TV: programme*) montare; (: *Comput*) editare, correggere e modificare

  ▸ **edit out** VT + ADV tagliare

edi·tion [ɪˈdɪʃən] N edizione *f*

edi·tor [ˈɛdɪtə] N (*of newspaper, magazine: managing director*) direttore(-trice); (: *editorial director*) redattore(-trice) capo; (: *of section of newspaper, magazine*) redattore(-trice); (*publisher's editor: of series*) editore(-trice); (: *of text*) redattore(-trice); (: *of author's work*) curatore(-trice); (*film editor*) responsabile *m/f* del montaggio; **the political editor** il redattore della pagina politica

edi·to·rial [ˌɛdɪˈtɔːrɪəl] ADJ redazionale, editoriale; **editorial assistant** assistente *m/f* di redazione; **editorial staff** redazione *f* ♦ N (*in newspaper*) editoriale *m*, articolo di fondo

EDT [ˌiːdiːˈtiː] N ABBR (*USA*: = *Eastern Daylight Time*) ora estiva nel fuso orario di New York

edu·cate [ˈɛdjʊkeɪt] VT (*pupil*) istruire; (*the public, the mind*) educare; (*tastes*) affinare; **I was educated abroad** ho fatto i miei studi all'estero; **to be educated at a private school** frequentare una scuola privata

edu·cat·ed [ˈɛdjʊ,keɪtɪd] ADJ (*person*) istruito(-a), colto(-a)
  ❏ **educated** is not translated by the Italian word *educato*

educated guess N supposizione *f inv* ben fondata

edu·ca·tion [ˌɛdjʊˈkeɪʃən] N (*schooling*) istruzione *f*; (*teaching*) insegnamento; (*knowledge, culture*) cultura; (*studies*) studi *mpl*; (*training*) formazione *f*; (*Univ: subject etc*) pedagogia; **she wants to complete her education** vuole completare la sua istruzione; **there should be more investment in education** si dovrebbero fare più investimenti nella scuola; **Ministry of Education** Ministero della Pubblica Istruzione; **primary education**, (*USA*) **elementary education** scuola elementare *or* primaria; **secondary education** scuola secondaria; **physical education** educazione *f* fisica

edu·ca·tion·al [ˌɛdjʊˈkeɪʃənl] ADJ (*establishment, institution*) scolastico(-a); (*methods*) didattico(-a), d'insegnamento;

(*system*) pedagogico(-a); (*film, visit, role*) educativo(-a); (*experience, event*) istruttivo(-a); **educational technology** tecnologie *fpl* applicate alla didattica

Ed·ward·ian [ɛdˈwɔːdɪən] ADJ edoardiano(-a)

EEG [ˌiːiːˈdʒiː] N ABBR (= *electroencephalogram*) EEG *m inv*

eel [iːl] N anguilla

EENT N ABBR (*USA: Med*) = **eye, ear, nose and throat**

EEOC [ˌiːiːəʊˈsiː] N ABBR (*USA*) = **Equal Employment Opportunity Commission**

eerie [ˈɪərɪ] ADJ sinistro(-a), che fa accapponare la pelle

EET [ˌiːiːˈtiː] N ABBR (= *Eastern European Time*) fuso orario dell'Europa orientale

ef·fect [ɪˈfɛkt] N **1** (*result*) effetto; **to have an effect on sb/sth** avere *or* produrre un effetto su qn/qc; **to have no effect** non avere *or* produrre alcun effetto; **to no effect** invano; **to such good effect that** con risultati così buoni che; **to recover from the effects of an illness** rimettersi dai postumi di una malattia; **to put into effect** (*rule*) rendere operativo; (*plan*) attuare; **to take effect** (*drug*) fare effetto; **to come into** *or* **take effect** (*Law*) entrare in vigore; **in effect** in realtà, effettivamente, in effetti; **his letter is to the effect that ...** (*frm*) il tenore della sua lettera è che...; **or words to that effect** o qualcosa di simile **2** (*impression*) effetto, impressione *f*; **to create an effect** fare effetto; **he said it for effect** l'ha detto per far colpo; *see also* **effects** ♦ VT (*bring about*) effettuare; (*saving, transformation, reunion*) operare

ef·fec·tive [ɪˈfɛktɪv] ADJ **1** (*efficient*) efficace; **to become effective** (*Law*) entrare in vigore **2** (*striking: display, outfit*) che fa colpo **3** (*actual*) effettivo(-a); **effective date** data d'entrata in vigore

ef·fec·tive·ly [ɪˈfɛktɪvlɪ] ADV (*efficiently*) efficacemente; (*in effect*) in effetti; (*strikingly*) ad effetto; (*in reality*) di fatto
  ❏ **effectively** is not translated by the Italian word *effettivamente*

ef·fec·tive·ness [ɪˈfɛktɪvnɪs] N efficacia

ef·fects [ɪˈfɛkts] NPL **1** (*Cine, Theatre: visual*) effetti *mpl* scenici; (: *sound*) effetti *mpl* sonori **2** (*property*) effetti *mpl*

ef·femi·nate [ɪˈfɛmɪnɪt] ADJ effeminato(-a)

ef·fer·ves·cent [ˌɛfəˈvɛsnt] ADJ effervescente

ef·fi·ca·cy [ˈɛfɪkəsɪ] N (*frm*) efficacia

ef·fi·cien·cy [ɪˈfɪʃənsɪ] N (*see adj*) efficienza; efficacia; rendimento

efficiency apartment N (*USA*) miniappartamento

ef·fi·cient [ɪˈfɪʃənt] ADJ (*person*) efficiente; (*remedy, product, system*) efficace; (*machine, car*) che ha un buon rendimento

ef·fi·cient·ly [ɪˈfɪʃəntlɪ] ADV (*see adj*) efficientemente; efficacemente; **the new machine works efficiently** il nuovo macchinario ha un buon rendimento

ef·fi·gy [ˈɛfɪdʒɪ] N effigie *f*

ef·flu·ent [ˈɛfluːənt] N effluente *m*

ef·fort [ˈɛfət] N sforzo; **to make an effort to do sth** sforzarsi di fare qc; **to make every effort to do sth** fare il possibile per fare qc; **he made no effort to be polite** non si è sforzato minimamente di essere gentile; **he won a prize for effort** gli è stato dato un premio per l'impegno dimostrato; **it's not worth the effort** non vale la pena; **that's a good effort** (*fam*) non è niente male; **his latest effort** (*fam, pej*) la sua ultima fatica

ef·fort·less [ˈɛfətlɪs] ADJ (*success*) facile; (*movement*) disinvolto(-a)

ef·fron·tery [ɪˈfrʌntərɪ] N sfrontatezza, sfacciataggine *f*

ef·fu·sive [ɪˈfjuːsɪv] ADJ (*person*) espansivo(-a); (*welcome, letter*) caloroso(-a); (*thanks, apologies*) interminabile

EFL [ˌiːɛfˈɛl] N ABBR (*Scol*: = **English as a Foreign Language**)

e.g., eg [ˌiːˈdʒiː] ADV ABBR (= *exempli gratia: for example*) ad es.

egali·tar·ian [ɪˌɡælɪˈtɛərɪən] ADJ egualitario(-a)

egg [ɛɡ] N uovo; (*Bio: seed*) ovulo; **a hard-boiled egg** un uovo sodo; **scrambled eggs** uova strapazzate; **egg custard** ≈ crema pasticciera; **don't put all your eggs in one basket** (*fig*) non puntare tutto su una sola carta; **to get egg on one's face** (*fig*) fare una brutta figura

  ▸ **egg on** VT + ADV: **to egg sb on (to do sth)** incitare *or* spingere qn (a fare qc)

egg cup N portauovo *m inv*

egg·plant [ˈɛɡplɑːnt] N (*esp USA*) melanzana

egg·shell [ˈɛgˌʃɛl] N guscio d'uovo ♦ ADJ *(paint finish)* a guscio d'uovo; *(colour)* color guscio d'uovo *inv*

egg-timer [ˈɛgˈtaɪməʳ] N clessidra *(per misurare il tempo di cottura delle uova)*

egg white N albume *m*, bianco d'uovo

egg yolk N tuorlo, rosso (d'uovo)

ego [ˈiːgəʊ] N *(Psych)* ego, io; *(pride)* amor *m* proprio

ego·ism [ˈɛgəʊɪzəm] N egoismo

ego·ist [ˈɛgəʊɪst] N egoista *m/f*

ego·tism [ˈɛgəʊˌtɪzəm] N egotismo

ego·tist [ˈɛgəʊtɪst] N egotista *m/f*

ego trip N *(fam)*: to be on an ego trip gasarsi

Egypt [ˈiːdʒɪpt] N Egitto

Egyp·tian [ɪˈdʒɪpʃən] ADJ egiziano(-a), egizio(-a) ♦ N *(person)* egiziano(-a); *(ancient)* egizio(-a); *(language)* egiziano

eider·down [ˈaɪdəˌdaʊn] N *(quilt)* trapunta di piuma

eight [eɪt] ADJ otto *inv* ♦ N otto *m inv*

eight·een [ˈeɪˈtiːn] ADJ diciotto *inv* ♦ N diciotto *m inv*

eight·eenth [ˈeɪˈtiːnθ] ADJ diciottesimo(-a) ♦ N *(in series)* diciottesimo(-a); *(fraction)* diciottesimo

eighth [eɪtθ] ADJ ottavo(-a) ♦ N *(in series)* ottavo(-a); *(fraction)* ottavo

eighti·eth [ˈeɪtɪəθ] ADJ ottantesimo(-a) ♦ N *(in series)* ottantesimo(-a); *(fraction)* ottantesimo

eighty [ˈeɪtɪ] ADJ ottanta *inv* ♦ N ottanta *m inv*

Eire [ˈɛərə] N Repubblica d'Irlanda

either [ˈaɪðəʳ] ADJ 1 *(one or other)* l'uno(-a) o l'altro(-a); either day would suit me mi va bene sia un giorno che l'altro 2 *(each)* ciascuno(-a), ciascuno(-a); on either side su entrambi i lati; in either hand in ciascuna mano ♦ PRON: either (of them) (o) l'uno(-a) o l'altro(-a); I don't want either of them non voglio né l'uno né l'altro; give it to either of them dallo a uno dei due; take either of them prendi quello che vuoi; do either of you smoke? uno di voi due fuma?; which bus will you take? — either che autobus prendi? — uno qualsiasi dei due; I don't like either non mi piace né l'uno né l'altro ♦ CONJ: either ...or... o; *(after neg)* né... né; either today or tomorrow oggi o domani; either come in or stay out o entri o stai fuori; I have never been to either Paris or Rome non sono mai stato né a Parigi né a Roma; I haven't seen either one or the other non ho visto né l'uno né l'altro ♦ ADV neanche, nemmeno, neppure; he can't sing either non sa neppure cantare, non sa cantare neppure or nemmeno or neanche tui; I don't like milk, and I don't like eggs either non mi piace il latte e neanche le uova; no, I don't/haven't either no, neanch'io, no, nemmeno io

ejacu·la·tion [ɪˌdʒækjʊˈleɪʃən] N *(see vb)* eiaculazione *f*; esclamazione *f*

eject [ɪˈdʒɛkt] VT *(Tech)* sganciare, eiettare; *(flames)* emettere; *(cartridge)* espellere; *(troublemaker)* espellere, allontanare ♦ VI *(pilot)* catapultarsi; the pilot ejected il pilota si è lanciato dall'aereo

ejec·tor seat [ɪˈdʒɛktəʳˌsiːt] N *(in plane)* seggiolino eiettabile

eke [iːk] VT: to eke out *(food, supplies, money)* far bastare, far durare; *(income)* arrotondare; to eke out a living sbarcare il lunario

EKG [ˌiːkeɪˈdʒiː] N ABBR *(USA: = electrocardiogram)* ECG *m inv*

el [ɛl] N ABBR *(USA fam)* = elevated railroad

elabo·rate [adj ɪˈlæbərɪt, vb ɪˈlæbəˌreɪt] ADJ *(gen)* elaborato(-a); *(design, pattern)* complicato(-a); *(plan)* minuzioso(-a), particolareggiato(-a); *(hairstyle)* elaborato(-a); *(style of writing)* elaborato(-a), ricercato(-a); *(meal)* raffinato(-a); an elaborate system un sistema elaborato ♦ VT *(work out)* elaborare; *(describe)* illustrare ♦ VI entrare in dettagli; to elaborate on sth approfondire qc

elapse [ɪˈlæps] VI *(time)* trascorrere, passare

elas·tic [ɪˈlæstɪk] ADJ elastico(-a) ♦ N elastico

elastic band N *(Brit)* elastico

elas·tici·ty [ˌiːlæsˈtɪsɪtɪ] N elasticità

elat·ed [ɪˈleɪtɪd] ADJ esultante, euforico(-a)

ela·tion [ɪˈleɪʃən] N esultanza, euforia

el·bow [ˈɛlbəʊ] N *(Anat)* gomito; at his elbow al suo fianco, accanto ♦ VT: to elbow sb aside scostare qn a gomitate; to elbow one's way through the crowd farsi largo tra la folla a gomitate

elbow grease N *(fam)* olio di gomito

elbow·room [ˈɛlbəʊˌrʊm] N spazio; give me some elbow-room fammi spazio

el·der [ˈɛldəʳ] ADJ *(brother, sister)* maggiore, più vecchio(-a); my elder sister la mia sorella maggiore ♦ N 1 he is your elder è più anziano di te; one's elders i più anziani; you should respect your elders devi rispettare chi è più anziano di te 2 elders NPL *(of tribe)* anziani *mpl*

el·der [ˈɛldəʳ] N *(Bot)* sambuco

el·der·ly [ˈɛldəlɪ] ADJ anziano(-a) ♦ NPL: the elderly gli anziani

elder statesman N *(Pol)* uomo politico di grande esperienza e prestigio

eld·est [ˈɛldɪst] ADJ maggiore; my eldest brother il maggiore dei miei fratelli; the eldest (child) il (la) maggiore (dei bambini)

elect [ɪˈlɛkt] VT 1 *(Pol, etc)*: to elect (to) eleggere (a); he was elected chairman è stato eletto presidente 2 to elect to do *(decide)* decidere or scegliere di fare; he elected to remain ha deciso di restare ♦ ADJ futuro(-a); the president elect il presidente designato

elec·tion [ɪˈlɛkʃən] N elezione *f*; *(of Government)* elezioni *fpl*; to hold an election indire un'elezione; the election will be held next week l'elezione avrà luogo la settimana prossima

election campaign N campagna elettorale

elec·tion·eer·ing [ɪˌlɛkʃəˈnɪərɪŋ] N propaganda elettorale

elec·tor [ɪˈlɛktəʳ] N elettore(-trice)

elec·tor·al [ɪˈlɛktərəl] ADJ elettorale

electoral college N collegio elettorale

electoral roll, electoral register N *(Brit)* liste *fpl* elettorali

electoral system N sistema *m* elettorale

elec·tor·ate [ɪˈlɛktərɪt] N elettorato

elec·tric [ɪˈlɛktrɪk] ADJ elettrico(-a); the atmosphere was electric *(fig)* l'atmosfera era elettrica

elec·tri·cal [ɪˈlɛktrɪkəl] ADJ elettrico(-a)

electrical engineer N elettrotecnico

electrical failure N guasto all'impianto elettrico

electric blanket N coperta elettrica, termocoperta

electric chair N sedia elettrica

electric cooker N cucina elettrica

electric current N corrente *f* elettrica

electric fire N *(Brit)* stufa elettrica

elec·tri·cian [ɪlɛkˈtrɪʃən] N elettricista *m*

elec·tric·ity [ɪlɛkˈtrɪsɪtɪ] N elettricità; to switch on/off the electricity attaccare/staccare la corrente

electricity board N *(Brit)* ente *m* regionale per l'energia elettrica

electric light N luce *f* elettrica

electric shock N scossa (elettrica)

electric stove N *(USA)* cucina elettrica

elec·tri·fy [ɪˈlɛktrɪˌfaɪ] VT *(railway system, fence)* elettrificare; *(audience)* elettrizzare

electro– [ɪˈlɛktrəʊ] PREF elettro-

elec·tro·car·dio·gram [ɪˌlɛktrəʊˈkɑːdɪəˌgræm] N elettrocardiogramma *m*

elec·tro·con·vul·sive thera·py [ɪˌlɛktrəʊkənˈvʌlsɪvˈθɛrəpɪ], **elec·tro·shock thera·py** [ɪˈlɛtrəʊˌʃɒkˈθɛrəpɪ] N elettroshockterapia

elec·tro·cute [ɪˈlɛktrəˌkjuːt] VT folgorare *(con la corrente elettrica)*; giustiziare sulla sedia elettrica

elec·trode [ɪˈlɛktrəʊd] N elettrodo

elec·tro·en·cepha·lo·gram [ɪˌlɛktrəʊɛnˈsɛfələˌgræm] N elettroencefalogramma *m*

elec·troly·sis [ɪlɛkˈtrɒlɪsɪs] N elettrolisi *f*

elec·tro·mag·net·ic [ɪˈlɛktrəʊmægˈnɛtɪk] ADJ elettromagnetico(-a)

elec·tron [ɪˈlɛktrɒn] N elettrone *m*

elec·tron·ic [ɪlɛkˈtrɒnɪk] ADJ elettronico(-a); electronic configuration *(Chem)* configurazione *f* degli elettroni

electronic mail N posta elettronica

elec·tron·ics [ɪlɛkˈtrɒnɪks] NSG, NPL elettronica

electron microscope N microscopio elettronico

elec·tro·plat·ed [ɪˈlɛktrəʊˌpleɪtɪd] ADJ galvanizzato(-a), placcato(-a) *(mediante galvanostegia)*

elec·tro·thera·py [ɪˌlektrəʊˈθerəpɪ] N elettroterapia

el·egance [ˈelɪɡəns] N eleganza

el·egant [ˈelɪɡənt] ADJ elegante

el·ement [ˈelɪmənt] N (gen) elemento; (of surprise, luck) fattore m, componente f; (of heater, kettle) resistenza; **the elements** (weather) gli elementi; **the elements of mathematics** i fondamenti della matematica; **to be in one's element** essere nel proprio elemento or ambiente naturale

el·emen·ta·ry [ˌelɪˈmentərɪ] ADJ elementare; **elementary physics** i primi rudimenti di fisica

elementary school N ≈ scuola primaria

el·ephant [ˈelɪfənt] N elefante(-essa)

el·evate [ˈelɪˌveɪt] VT 1 (raise in rank, importance): **to elevate (to)** elevare (a) 2 (fig: mind) elevare

elevated railroad N (USA) (ferrovia) soprelevata

el·eva·tion [ˌelɪˈveɪʃən] N (gen) elevazione f; (Archit) prospetto; (of style, thought) alto livello; (altitude) altitudine f, altezza

el·eva·tor [ˈelɪˌveɪtəʳ] N (USA: lift) ascensore m; (hoist) montacarichi m inv

elev·en [ɪˈlevn] ADJ undici inv ♦ N undici m inv

elev·en·ses [ɪˈlevnzɪz] NPL (Brit fam) ≈ pausa per il caffè a metà mattina

elev·enth [ɪˈlevnθ] ADJ undicesimo(-a); **at the eleventh hour** (fig) all'ultimo minuto ♦ N (in series) undicesimo(-a); (fraction) undicesimo

elf [elf] N (pl **elves**) elfo

elic·it [ɪˈlɪsɪt] VT: **to elicit sth (from sb)** (truth, secret) strappare qc (a qn); (admission, reply) ottenere qc (da qn)

eli·gible [ˈelɪdʒəbl] ADJ (suitable): **eligible (for)** idoneo(-a) (a); (for membership, grant) che ha i requisiti richiesti (per); (public office) eleggibile a; **to be eligible for a pension** essere pensionabile; **to be eligible to vote** avere diritto di voto

elimi·nate [ɪˈlɪmɪˌneɪt] VT (gen) eliminare; (suspect, possibility) scartare

elimi·na·tion [ɪˌlɪmɪˈneɪʃən] N eliminazione f; **by process of elimination** per eliminazione

élite [eɪˈliːt] N élite f inv

élit·ist [eɪˈliːtɪst] ADJ elitario(-a)

elix·ir [ɪˈlɪksəʳ] N elisir m inv

Eliza·bethan [ɪˌlɪzəˈbiːθən] ADJ, N elisabettiano(-a)

el·lipse [ɪˈlɪps] N ellisse f

el·lip·tical [ɪˈlɪptɪkəl], **el·lip·tic** [ɪˈlɪptɪk] ADJ ellittico(-a)

elm [elm] N olmo; **English elm** olmo inglese

elo·cu·tion [ˌeləˈkjuːʃən] N dizione f, elocuzione f

elon·gat·ed [ˈiːlɒŋˌɡeɪtɪd] ADJ allungato(-a)

elope [ɪˈləʊp] VI (lovers) fuggire insieme (per sposarsi)

elope·ment [ɪˈləʊpmənt] N fuga romantica

elo·quence [ˈeləkwəns] N eloquenza

elo·quent [ˈeləkwənt] ADJ eloquente

else [els] ADV 1 (other) altro; **anybody else would have done it** chiunque altro l'avrebbe fatto; **is it anybody else's?** è di qualcun altro?; **I'd prefer anything else rather than ...** preferirei qualsiasi altra cosa piuttosto che...; **is there anything else I can do?** posso fare qualcos'altro?; **anything else, sir?** (shop assistant) desidera altro, signore?; **I'd go anywhere else but there** andrei ovunque fuorché lì; **have you tried anywhere else?** hai provato da qualche altra parte?; **everyone else** tutti gli altri; **everything else** tutto il resto; **everywhere else** in qualsiasi altro luogo; **nobody else** nessun altro (nessun'altra); **nothing else** nient'altro; **nothing else, thank you** (in shop) è tutto, grazie; **nowhere else** nessun altro posto; **I sell nowhere else** non sono andato in nessun altro posto; **somebody else** qualcun altro (qualcun'altra); **somebody else** qualcos'altro; **it's something else!** (fam) è qualcosa di speciale!; **somewhere else** da qualche altra parte, altrove; **who/what/where/how else?** chi/che/dove/come altro?; **where else?** in quale altro luogo?; **little else** poco altro; **there is little else to be done** rimane ben poco da fare 2 (otherwise): **or else** altrimenti; **keep quiet or else go away** stai zitto, altrimenti vai via; **do as I say, or else!** (fam) fai come ti dico, se no vedi!

else·where [ˈelsˈweəʳ] ADV altrove; **these flowers cannot be found elsewhere** questi fiori non si trovano da nessun'altra parte

ELT [ˌiːelˈtiː] N ABBR (Scol: = **English Language Teaching**)

elu·ci·date [ɪˈluːsɪˌdeɪt] VT delucidare

elude [ɪˈluːd] VT (arrest, pursuit, enemy, observation) sfuggire a; (question) eludere; **success has eluded him** il successo non gli ha arriso

elu·sive [ɪˈluːsɪv] ADJ (prey, enemy) inafferrabile; (thoughts, word, success etc) che sfugge; (glance) sfuggevole; **he is very elusive** è proprio inafferrabile; **it is an extremely elusive concept** è un concetto del tutto inafferrabile

elves [elvz] NPL of **elf**

ema·ci·at·ed [ɪˈmeɪsɪˌeɪtɪd] ADJ emaciato(-a)

e-mail, e-mail [ˈiːmeɪl] N ABBR = **electronic mail** (sistema) e-mail f, posta elettronica; (messaggio) e-mail, mail f inv; **email account** account m inv di posta elettronica; **email address** indirizzo di posta elettronica, indirizzo e-mail ♦ VT: **to email sb** inviare un'e-mail a qn

ema·nate [ˈeməˌneɪt] VI: **to emanate from** (frm) provenire da, emanare da

eman·ci·pate [ɪˈmænsɪˌpeɪt] VT (women, slaves) emancipare; (fig) liberare

eman·ci·pa·tion [ɪˌmænsɪˈpeɪʃən] N emancipazione f

emas·cu·late [ɪˈmæskjʊˌleɪt] VT (fig) rendere impotente

em·balm [ɪmˈbɑːm] VT imbalsamare

em·bank·ment [ɪmˈbæŋkmənt] N (of path) terrapieno; (of road, railway) massicciata; (of canal, river) argine m; (dike) diga

em·bar·go [ɪmˈbɑːɡəʊ] (pl **-es**) N (Comm, Naut) embargo; **to put an embargo on sth** mettere l'embargo su qc ♦ VT mettere l'embargo su

em·bark [ɪmˈbɑːk](Naut, Aer) VI imbarcarsi ♦ VT imbarcare
► **embark on** VI + PREP (journey) intraprendere; (business venture, explanation, discussion) imbarcarsi in

em·bar·ka·tion [ˌembɑːˈkeɪʃən] N imbarco

embarkation card N carta d'imbarco

em·bar·rass [ɪmˈbærəs] VT mettere in imbarazzo, imbarazzare; **to be embarrassed** essere imbarazzato(-a); **I was embarrassed by the question** la domanda mi ha messo in imbarazzo; **to be financially embarrassed** avere difficoltà economiche

em·bar·rass·ing [ɪmˈbærəsɪŋ] ADJ imbarazzante

em·bar·rass·ment [ɪmˈbærəsmənt] N imbarazzo; **to be an embarrassment to sb** essere fonte d'imbarazzo per qn; **financial embarrassments** difficoltà fpl economiche

em·bas·sy [ˈembəsɪ] N ambasciata; **the Italian Embassy** l'ambasciata italiana

em·bed [ɪmˈbed] VT (in wood, cement, rock) incastrare; (weapon, teeth) conficcare; (jewel) incastonare; **it is embedded in my memory** è impresso nella mia memoria

em·bel·lish [ɪmˈbelɪʃ] VT: **to embellish (with)** (decorate) abbellire (con); (fig: story, truth) infiorettare (con)

em·bers [ˈembəz] NPL braci fpl

em·bez·zle [ɪmˈbezl] VT appropriarsi indebitamente di

em·bez·zle·ment [ɪmˈbezlmənt] N appropriazione f indebita, malversazione f

em·bez·zler [ɪmˈbezləʳ] N malversatore(-trice)

em·bit·ter [ɪmˈbɪtəʳ] VT amareggiare, inasprire; **embittered by constant failure** amareggiato(-a) dai continui fallimenti

em·blem [ˈembləm] N emblema m

em·bodi·ment [ɪmˈbɒdɪmənt] N incarnazione f, personificazione f

em·body [ɪmˈbɒdɪ] VT 1 (spirit, quality) incarnare; (thought, theory, ideas): **to embody (in)** esprimere (in) 2 (include: features) comprendere, racchiudere

em·bold·en [ɪmˈbəʊldən] VT incitare, incoraggiare

em·bo·lism [ˈembəlɪzəm] N (Med) embolia

em·bossed [ɪmˈbɒst] ADJ (see vb) a sbalzo; impresso(-a) in rilievo, goffrato(-a); **embossed with ...** con in rilievo...

em·brace [ɪmˈbreɪs] VT 1 (person, religion, cause) abbracciare 2 (include) comprendere ♦ VI abbracciarsi ♦ N abbraccio

em·broi·der [ɪmˈbrɔɪdəʳ] VT ricamare; (fig: truth, facts, story) ricamare su, abbellire

em·broi·dery [ɪmˈbrɔɪdərɪ] N ricamo; **embroidery thread** filo da ricamo

em·broil [ɪmˈbrɔɪl] VT: **to embroil sb in sth** coinvolgere qn in qc; **to become embroiled (in sth)** restare invischiato(-a) (in qc)

em·bryo [ˈɛmbrɪ‚əʊ] N (*also fig*) embrione *m*; **in embryo** in embrione

em·cee [‚ɛmˈsiː] N ABBR = master of ceremonies

emend [ɪˈmɛnd] VT (*text*) correggere, emendare

em·er·ald [ˈɛmərəld] N (*stone*) smeraldo; (*colour*) verde *m* smeraldo ♦ ADJ (*necklace, bracelet etc*) di smeraldi; (*colour: also:* **emerald green**) verde smeraldo *inv*

emerge [ɪˈmɜːdʒ] VI: **to emerge (from)** spuntare (da); (*from water, fig: truth, facts, theory*) emergere (da); (: *problems, new nation*) sorgere (da); **it later emerged that ...** più tardi emerse che...

emer·gence [ɪˈmɜːdʒəns] N (*of new ideas, theory*) apparizione *f*; (*of submarine*) emersione *f*; (*of nation*) nascita
❏ **emergence** is not translated by the Italian word *emergenza*

emer·gen·cy [ɪˈmɜːdʒənsɪ] N emergenza; **this is an emergency!** questa è un'emergenza!; **in an emergency** in caso di emergenza; **to declare a state of emergency** dichiarare lo stato di emergenza ♦ ADJ (*measures, powers*) di sicurezza; (*repairs*) di fortuna; (*Med: operation*) d'urgenza; (*rations, fund*) di riserva

emergency brake (*USA*) N freno a mano

emergency exit N uscita di sicurezza

emergency landing N atterraggio di fortuna

emergency lane N (*USA: Aut*) corsia d'emergenza

emergency road service N (*USA*) servizio di soccorso stradale

emergency room N (*USA*) pronto soccorso

emergency service N servizio di pronto intervento

emergency stop N (*Aut: Brit*) frenata d'emergenza

emer·gent [ɪˈmɜːdʒənt] ADJ emergente; **emergent nation** paese *m* in via di sviluppo

emery board N limetta (di carta smerigliata) per unghie

emery paper N carta vetrata, carta smerigliata

emet·ic [ɪˈmɛtɪk] N emetico

emi·grant [ˈɛmɪgrənt] N emigrante *m/f*

emi·grate [ˈɛmɪgreɪt] VI emigrare

emi·gra·tion [‚ɛmɪˈgreɪʃən] N emigrazione *f*

émi·gré [ˈɛmɪ‚greɪ] N (*frm*) esule *m*

emi·nence [ˈɛmɪnəns] N 1 (*fame*) eminenza, reputazione *f*; **to gain** *or* **win eminence** farsi un nome *or* una reputazione 2 (*Rel*): **His Eminence** Sua Eminenza 3 (*frm: hill*) altura

emi·nent [ˈɛmɪnənt] ADJ (*person*) eminente, insigne; (*quality*) eccellente

emi·nent·ly [ˈɛmɪnəntlɪ] ADV assolutamente, perfettamente

emir·ate [ɛˈmɪərɪt] N emirato

emis·sion [ɪˈmɪʃən] N (*of fumes, gas*) esalazione *f*

emit [ɪˈmɪt] VT (*radiation*) emettere; (*fumes*) esalare

emolu·ment [ɪˈmɒljʊmənt] N (*often pl: frm*) emolumento

emo·ti·con [ɪˈməʊtɪkən] N (*Comput*) faccina, emoticon *m inv*

emo·tion [ɪˈməʊʃən] N emozione *f*; (*love, jealousy etc*) sentimento; **his voice trembled with emotion** gli tremava la voce dall'emozione; **reason and emotion** ragione e sentimento

emo·tion·al [ɪˈməʊʃənl] ADJ (*person, nature*) emotivo(-a); (*moment, experience, story, scene*) commovente; (*tone, speech*) carico(-a) d'emozione; **emotional state** condizione *f* mentale; **to be in a very emotional state** essere in uno stato di estrema confusione mentale

emo·tion·al·ly [ɪˈməʊʃnəlɪ] ADV (*behave, be involved*) sentimentalmente; (*speak*) con emozione; **to be emotionally deprived** soffrire di carenze affettive; **to be emotionally disturbed** avere turbe emotive

emo·tive [ɪˈməʊtɪv] ADJ che fa presa sui sentimenti; **emotive power** capacità di commuovere; **it's an emotive issue** è una questione che ha un grosso impatto emotivo

em·pa·thy [ˈɛmpəθɪ] N immedesimazione *f*; **to feel empathy with sb** immedesimarsi nei sentimenti di qn

em·per·or [ˈɛmpərə'] N imperatore *m*

em·pha·sis [ˈɛmfəsɪs] N (*pl* **emphases** [ˈɛmfəsiːz]) enfasi *f inv*; (*in word, phrase*) accento; **to speak with emphasis** parlare con enfasi; **with great emphasis** con grande enfasi; **to lay** *or* **place emphasis on sth** (*fig*) mettere in risalto *or* in evidenza qc, dare importanza a; **the emphasis is on sport** si dà molta importanza allo sport

em·pha·size [ˈɛmfə‚saɪz] VT (*word, fact, point, feature*) sottolineare; (*subj: garment etc*) mettere in evidenza; **he emphasized the importance of the point** ha sottolineato l'importanza della questione; **I must emphasize that ...** devo sottolineare il fatto che...

em·phat·ic [ɪmˈfætɪk] ADJ (*tone, manner, person*) energico(-a), vigoroso(-a); (*speech*) enfatico(-a); (*condemnation, denial*) categorico(-a), netto(-a); **they were emphatic that they had seen nobody** hanno detto chiaramente di non aver visto nessuno

em·phati·cal·ly [ɪmˈfætɪkəlɪ] ADV (*speak*) con enfasi; (*deny, refuse*) categoricamente

em·phy·sema [‚ɛmfɪˈsiːmə] N (*Med*) enfisema *m*

em·pire [ˈɛmpaɪə'] N impero

em·piri·cal [ɛmˈpɪrɪkəl] ADJ empirico(-a)

em·ploy [ɪmˈplɔɪ] VT (*give job to*) dare lavoro a, impiegare; (*appoint*) assumere; (*make use of: thing, method, person*) servirsi di, impiegare; (: *time*) impiegare; **the factory employs six hundred people** la fabbrica dà lavoro a seicento persone; **to be employed** lavorare; **he's employed in a bank** lavora in banca; **we employed a painter to decorate the house** ci siamo serviti di *or* abbiamo assunto un imbianchino per pitturare la casa ♦ N (*frm*): **in the employ of sb** alle dipendenze di qn

em·ployee [‚ɛmplɔɪˈiː] N dipendente *m/f*

em·ploy·er [ɪmˈplɔɪə'] N datore(-trice) di lavoro; **employer's contribution** (*to National Insurance*) contributi *mpl* (versati dal datore di lavoro)

em·ploy·ment [ɪmˈplɔɪmənt] N occupazione *f*, impiego; (*a job*) lavoro; **to take up employment** prendere servizio; **to find employment** trovare impiego *or* lavoro; **without employment** disoccupato(-a); **full employment** piena occupazione; **place of employment** (*frm*) sede dell'attività lavorativa

employment agency N agenzia di collocamento

employment exchange N (*old*) ufficio *m* di collocamento

em·pow·er [ɪmˈpaʊə'] VT (*give control over*) dare maggior potere a; **to empower sb to do sth** (*authorize*) concedere l'autorità a qn di fare qc

em·press [ˈɛmprɪs] N imperatrice *f*

emp·ti·ness [ˈɛmptɪnɪs] N vuoto

emp·ty [ˈɛmptɪ] ADJ (*comp* **-ier**, *superl* **-iest**) (*gen*) vuoto(-a); (*street, area*) deserto(-a); (*post*) vacante; (*fig: threat, promise*) vano(-a); (*words*) vacuo(-a), privo(-a) di significato; **on an empty stomach** a stomaco vuoto ♦ VT (*contents, container*) vuotare; (*liquid*) versare; **to empty (out) one's pockets** vuotarsi le tasche; **to empty a liquid from** *or* **out of sth into sth** travasare un liquido da qc in qc; **she emptied everything out of her bag onto the bed** ha rovesciato sul letto il contenuto della borsa ♦ VI (*room, container*) vuotarsi; (*liquid*) scaricarsi; (*river*): **to empty into** gettarsi in

empty-handed [‚ɛmptɪˈhændɪd] ADJ a mani vuote; **to arrive/ leave empty-handed** arrivare/andarsene a mani vuote

empty-headed [‚ɛmptɪˈhɛdɪd] ADJ sciocco(-a)

EMT N ABBR (*USA*: = emergency medical technician)

emu·late [ˈɛmjʊ‚leɪt] VT emulare

emul·sion [ɪˈmʌlʃən] N (*liquid*) emulsione *f*; (*also:* **emulsion paint**) pittura (murale)

en·able [ɪˈneɪbl] VT: **to enable sb to do sth** consentire *or* permettere a qn di fare qc

en·act [ɪnˈækt] VT 1 (*law*) emanare 2 (*play, scene*) rappresentare

enam·el [ɪˈnæməl] N smalto ♦ VT smaltare ♦ ADJ smaltato(-a)

enamel paint N vernice *f* a smalto

en·am·oured, en·am·ored (*USA*) [ɪˈnæməd] ADJ: **enamoured of** innamorato(-a) di

enc. ABBR = encl.

en·camp·ment [ɪnˈkæmpmənt] N accampamento

en·case [ɪnˈkeɪs] VT: **to encase in** (*contain*) racchiudere in; (*cover*) rivestire di

en·chant [ɪnˈtʃɑːnt] VT incantare; (*subj: magic spell*) stregare

en·chant·ing [ɪnˈtʃɑːntɪŋ] ADJ incantevole, affascinante

en·cir·cle [ɪnˈsɜːkl] VT circondare; (*Mil*) accerchiare; (*waist, shoulders*) stringere

encl., enc. ABBR (*on letter:* = enclosed, enclosure) all., alleg.

en·close [ɪnˈkləʊz] VT 1 (*land, garden*) recintare, recingere, circondare **2** (*with letter*): **to enclose (with)** allegare (a); **please find enclosed a copy of ...** si allega copia di...; **please find enclosed ... in allegato...**

en·clo·sure [ɪnˈkləʊʒəʳ] N (*act*) recinzione *f*; (*place*) recinto; (*at racecourse*) tondino; (*in letter*) allegato

en·cod·er [ɪnˈkəʊdəʳ] N (*Comput*) codificatore *m*

en·com·pass [ɪnˈkʌmpəs] VT comprendere

en·core [ɒŋˈkɔːʳ] EXCL bis ♦ N bis *m inv*; **to give an encore** concedere un bis

en·coun·ter [ɪnˈkaʊntəʳ] VT (*person*) incontrare; (*difficulty, danger, enemy*) imbattersi in ♦ N incontro

en·cour·age [ɪnˈkʌrɪdʒ] VT (*person*) incoraggiare; (*industry, growth etc*) favorire; **to encourage sb (to do sth)** incoraggiare qn (a fare qc)

en·cour·age·ment [ɪnˈkʌrɪdʒmənt] N incoraggiamento

en·cour·ag·ing [ɪnˈkʌrɪdʒɪŋ] ADJ incoraggiante

en·croach [ɪnˈkrəʊtʃ] VI: **to encroach (up)on** (*rights*) usurpare; (*land: of neighbour*) sconfinare in; (*subj: sea: land*) avanzare sopra; (*time*) abusare di

en·crust·ed [ɪnˈkrʌstɪd] ADJ: **encrusted with** (*diamonds*) tempestato(-a) di; (*rust*) incrostato(-a) di

en·crypt [ɪnˈkrɪpt] VT (*also Comput*) criptare

en·cum·bered [ɪnˈkʌmbəd] ADJ: **to be encumbered (with)** essere carico(-a) di

en·cy·clo·pedia,   en·cy·clo·paedia [ɪnˌsaɪkləʊˈpiːdɪə] N enciclopedia

end [ɛnd] N **1** (*of line, table, rope*) estremità *f inv*; (*of pointed object*) punta; (*of town*) parte *f*; **3rd from the end** il 3° a partire dalla fine; **at the end of the street** in fondo alla strada; **to place end to end** mettere un'estremità contro l'altra; **from end to end** da un'estremità all'altra; **to stand sth on end** mettere qc in piedi *or* ritto(-a); **his hair stood on end** gli si sono rizzati i capelli; **to change ends** (*Sport*) cambiare campo; **it's the end of the road** *or* **line for us** (*fig*) non abbiamo futuro; **to make ends meet** (*fig*) far quadrare il bilancio, sbarcare il lunario **2** (*conclusion*) fine *f*; **the end of the film** la fine del film; **at the end of the day** (*Brit fig*) in fin dei conti; **it's not the end of the world** (*fam*) non è poi la fine del mondo; **we'll never hear the end of it** (*fam*) non avremo più pace; **there's no end to it** (*fam*) non finisce mai; **that was the end of that!** e quella fu la fine!; **to the bitter end** fino all'ultimo sangue; **to come to a bad end** finire male; **in the end** alla fine, da ultimo; **to be at an end** essere finito(-a), arrivare alla fine; **to get to the end of** (*book, supplies, work etc*) finire; **to be at the end of** (*strength, patience*) essere al limite di; **to bring to an end** (*work, speech*) concludere; **to draw to an end** stare per finire; **to come to an end** finire; **to put an end to** (*argument, relationship, sb's tricks*) porre fine a; **for hours on end** per ore e ore; **for 5 hours on end** per 5 ore di fila; **no end of trouble** (*fam*) problemi a non finire; **it upset me no end** (*adv: fam*) mi ha turbato enormemente; **without end** a non finire **3** (*remnant: of loaf, meat*) avanzo; (: *of candle*) moccolo; **cigarette end** mozzicone *m* di sigaretta **4** (*aim*) fine *m*, scopo; **to achieve one's ends** raggiungere i propri scopi; **it's an end in itself** è fine a se stesso; **to no end** invano; **to this end, with this end in view** a questo fine; **the end justifies the means** il fine giustifica i mezzi ♦ VT finire, terminare; (*road, period of time*) terminare; **what time does the film end?** a che ora finisce il film?; **to end by saying** concludere dicendo; **to end in** (*dispute, conflict*) sfociare in; (*subj: word*) finire per *or* in ♦ VT (*gen*) porre fine a; (*speech, writing, broadcast*): **to end (with)** concludere (con); **to end one's life** mettere fine ai propri giorni; **to end it all** (*fam*) farla finita; **that was the meal to end all meals!** (*fam*) quel pranzo era imbattibile!

▸ **end up** VI + ADV (*finish*) finire, terminare; **to end up in prison** finire in prigione

en·dan·ger [ɪnˈdeɪndʒəʳ] VT mettere in pericolo; **he endangered patients' lives** ha messo in pericolo la vita dei pazienti; **to endanger one's life** mettere a repentaglio la propria vita; **an endangered species** (*of animal*) una specie in via di estinzione

en·dear [ɪnˈdɪəʳ] VT: **to endear sb to** rendere qn caro(-a) (a); **to endear o.s. to sb** accattivarsi le simpatie di qn

en·dear·ing [ɪnˈdɪərɪŋ] ADJ (*smile*) accattivante; (*characteristic, personality*) simpatico(-a)

en·dear·ment [ɪnˈdɪəmənt] N: **to whisper endearments** sussurrare tenerezze; **term of endearment** vezzeggiativo, appellativo affettuoso

en·deav·our, en·deav·or (*USA*) [ɪnˈdɛvəʳ] (*frm*) VT: **to endeavour to do sth** cercare *or* sforzarsi di fare qc ♦ N (*attempt*) sforzo, tentativo; **to make every endeavour to do sth** fare ogni sforzo per fare qc

en·dem·ic [ɛnˈdɛmɪk] ADJ endemico(-a)

end·ing [ˈɛndɪŋ] N fine *f*, conclusione *f*; (*Gram*) desinenza; **I didn't like the ending** non mi è piaciuto il finale; **a film with a happy ending** un film a lieto fine

en·dive [ˈɛndaɪv] N (*curly*) indivia (riccia); (*smooth, flat*) indivia belga

end·less [ˈɛndlɪs] ADJ (*gen*) senza fine; (*road, speech*) interminabile, senza fine; (*attempts*) innumerevole; (*arguments*) continuo(a); (*patience*) infinito(-a); (*possibilities*) illimitato(-a); (*resources*) inesauribile

en·dorse [ɪnˈdɔːs] VT (*approve: opinion, claim, plan*) approvare, appoggiare; (*Brit: driving licence*) annotare un'infrazione su; (*sign: cheque*) girare

en·dor·see [ˌɪndɔːˈsiː] N giratario(-a)

en·dorse·ment [ɪnˈdɔːsmənt] N (*approval*) approvazione *f*; (*Brit: on driving licence*) infrazione *f* annotata; (*signature*) girata, firma

en·dor·ser [ɪnˈdɔːsəʳ] N girante *m/f*

en·dow [ɪnˈdaʊ] VT **1** (*equip*): **to endow with** fornire di, dotare di; **to be endowed with** (*fig*) essere dotato(-a) di **2** (*prize*) istituire; (*hospital*) fondare; (*provide with money: institution*) devolvere denaro a; **to endow sth with sth** devolvere qc a favore di qc

en·dow·ment [ɪnˈdaʊmənt] N **1** (*gift of money*) donazione *f* **2** (*see vt 2*) istituzione *f*; fondazione *f*; donazione **3** (*frm: talent*) talento

end product N (*Industry*) prodotto finale *or* finito (*fig*) risultato

end result N risultato finale

en·dur·able [ɪnˈdjʊərəbl] ADJ sopportabile

en·dur·ance [ɪnˈdjʊərəns] N resistenza; **to come to the end of one's endurance** arrivare al limite della propria sopportazione; **past or beyond endurance** al di là di ogni sopportazione

endurance test N prova di resistenza

en·dure [ɪnˈdjʊəʳ] VT sopportare; **I can't endure being teased** non sopporto di essere preso in giro ♦ VI (*friendship, memory, peace*) durare; (*book, building*) resistere

en·dur·ing [ɪnˈdjʊərɪŋ] ADJ duraturo(-a)

end user N (*Econ*) consumatore(-trice) finale; (*Comput*) utente *m/f* finale

en·ema [ˈɛnɪmə] N (*Med*) clistere *m*

en·emy [ˈɛnəmɪ] N (*person*) nemico(-a); (*Mil*) nemico; **to make an enemy of sb** inimicarsi qn; **he is his own worst enemy** è il peggior nemico di se stesso ♦ ADJ (*territory, forces, aircraft*) nemico(-a); (*morale, strategy*) del nemico

en·er·get·ic [ˌɛnəˈdʒɛtɪk] ADJ (*person, protest etc*) energico(-a); (*day*) attivo(-a); **she's very energetic** è molto attiva; **do you feel energetic enough to go for a walk?** sei abbastanza in forze per fare una passeggiata?

en·er·gy [ˈɛnədʒɪ] N energia; **I haven't the energy** non ho la forza; **to put all one's energy into sth** dedicare tutte le proprie energie *or* forze a qc; **Department of Energy** Ministero delle risorse energetiche

energy crisis N crisi *f* energetica

energy drink N bevanda energetica

energy-saving [ˈɛnədʒɪˌseɪvɪŋ] ADJ (*policy*) di risparmio energetico; (*device*) che risparmia energia ♦ N risparmio energetico

en·er·va·ting [ˈɛnəˌveɪtɪŋ] ADJ snervante

en·force [ɪnˈfɔːs] VT (*decision, policy*) attuare; (*law, regulation*) far osservare, far rispettare; (*obedience*) imporre; (*argument*) rafforzare

en·forc·ed [ɪnˈfɔːst] ADJ imposto(-a), forzato(-a)

en·fran·chise [ɪnˈfræntʃaɪz] VT (*frm: give vote to*) concedere il diritto di voto a; (: *set free*) affrancare

en·gage [ɪnˈgeɪdʒ] VT (*occupy: attention, interest*) assorbire; (*attract: attention*) attrarre; (*Brit: hire: servant, worker*) assumere; (: *actor*) ingaggiare; (: *lawyer*) incaricare; (*reserve: room*) prenotare; (*Mil: enemy*) attaccare; **to engage to do sth** impegnarsi a fare qc; **to engage sb in conversation** attaccare conversazione con qn; **to engage gear/the clutch** (*Tech*) innestare la marcia/la frizione ♦ vi (*Tech*) innestarsi, ingranare; **to engage in** (*discussion, politics*) impegnarsi in

en·gaged [ɪnˈɡeɪdʒd] ADJ **1** (*to be married*) fidanzato(-a); **to get engaged** fidanzarsi; **she's engaged to Brian** è fidanzata con Brian **2** (*occupied*): **to be engaged in doing sth** essere impegnato(-a) a fare qc; **she is engaged in research/a survey** si occupa di ricerca/di un'inchiesta; **to be engaged on sth** occuparsi di qc **3** (*Brit: phone number, lavatory*) occupato(-a)

en·gage·ment [ɪnˈɡeɪdʒmənt] N **1** (*appointment, undertaking*) impegno; **I have a previous engagement** ho già un impegno **2** (*of worker, servant*) assunzione *f*; (*of actor, speaker*) ingaggio; (*of lawyer*) nomina **3** (*to marry*) fidanzamento; **to break off one's engagement** rompere il fidanzamento **4** (*Mil: battle*) scontro, combattimento

engagement ring N anello di fidanzamento

en·gag·ing [ɪnˈɡeɪdʒɪŋ] ADJ attraente

en·gen·der [ɪnˈdʒɛndə^r] VT produrre, causare

en·gine [ˈɛndʒɪn] N (*motor: in car, ship, plane*) motore *m*; (*Rail*) locomotiva; **facing/with your back to the engine** nel senso della/in senso contrario alla marcia; **front-to-back engine** (*Aut*) motore longitudinale

engine driver N (*Brit: of train*) macchinista *m*

en·gi·neer [ˌɛndʒɪˈnɪə^r] N (*gen*) ingegnere *m*; (*mechanic*) meccanico; (*Brit: for electrical appliances*) tecnico; (*Naut, USA: Rail*) macchinista *m*; **civil/mechanical engineer** ingegnere civile/meccanico; **the Engineers** (*Mil*) il Genio ♦ VT (*contrive*) architettare, organizzare

en·gi·neer·ing [ˌɛndʒɪˈnɪərɪŋ] N ingegneria ♦ ADJ (*works, factory, worker*) metalmeccanico(-a)

engine failure N guasto al motore

engine trouble N panne *f inv*

Eng·land [ˈɪŋɡlənd] N Inghilterra

Eng·lish [ˈɪŋɡlɪʃ] ADJ inglese; **English people** gli inglesi ♦ N **1 the English** (*npl: people*) gli inglesi **2** (*language*) inglese *m*; **do you speak English?** parli inglese?; **in plain English** in parole povere; **the King's** or **Queen's English** l'inglese corretto; **English students** chi studia l'inglese; **the English teacher** l'insegnante di inglese

English Channel N: **the English Channel** il Canale della Manica

English·man [ˈɪŋɡlɪʃmən] (*pl* -**men**) N inglese *m*

English-speaking [ˈɪŋɡlɪʃˈspiːkɪŋ] ADJ di lingua inglese

English·woman [ˈɪŋɡlɪʃˌwʊmən] (*pl* -**women**) N inglese *f*

en·grave [ɪnˈɡreɪv] VT (*Art, Typ, etc*) incidere; (*wood*) intagliare; (*fig*) imprimere

en·grav·ing [ɪnˈɡreɪvɪŋ] N (*picture*) incisione *f*

en·grossed [ɪnˈɡrəʊst] ADJ: **engrossed in** assorto(-a) in, immerso(-a) in, preso(-a) da

en·gulf, in·gulf [ɪnˈɡʌlf] VT (*also fig*) inghiottire

en·hance [ɪnˈhɑːns] VT (*beauty, attraction*) valorizzare; (*position, reputation*) migliorare; (*chances, value*) aumentare, accrescere; **this qualification will enhance your chances of employment** questa qualifica aumenterà le tue probabilità di trovare un impiego

enig·ma [ɪˈnɪɡmə] N enigma *m*

en·ig·mat·ic [ˌɛnɪɡˈmætɪk] ADJ enigmatico(-a)

en·joy [ɪnˈdʒɔɪ] VT **1** (*take delight in*): **did you enjoy the film/wine/book?** ti è piaciuto il film/vino/libro?; **I enjoy reading** mi piace leggere; **he enjoys (going for) long walks** gli piace fare lunghe passeggiate; **to enjoy life** godersi la vita; **to enjoy o.s** divertirsi; **enjoy yourself!** divertiti! **2** (*have: success, fortune*) avere; (*: income, advantage*) fruire di

en·joy·able [ɪnˈdʒɔɪəbl] ADJ piacevole

en·joy·ment [ɪnˈdʒɔɪmənt] N piacere *m*; **to find enjoyment in sth/in doing sth** provare piacere in qc/nel fare qc

en·large [ɪnˈlɑːdʒ] VT (*Phot*) ingrandire; (*house, circle of friends*) ampliare

▸ **enlarge on, enlarge upon** VI + ADV (*subject*) dilungarsi su

en·larged [ɪnˈlɑːdʒd] ADJ (*edition*) ampliato(-a); (*Med: organ, gland*) ingrossato(-a); (: *pores*) dilatato(-a)

en·large·ment [ɪnˈlɑːdʒmənt] N (*gen*) ampliamento; (*Med*) ingrossamento; (*Phot*) ingrandimento

en·light·en [ɪnˈlaɪtn] VT (*inform*): **to enlighten sb (about** or **on sth)** illuminare qn (su qc)

en·light·ened [ɪnˈlaɪtnd] ADJ illuminato(-a)

en·light·en·ing [ɪnˈlaɪtnɪŋ] ADJ istruttivo(-a)

en·light·en·ment [ɪnˈlaɪtnmənt] N (*explanations*) chiarimenti *mpl*; **the (Age of) Enlightenment** (*History*) l'Illuminismo

en·list [ɪnˈlɪst] VT **1** (*Mil: men*) arruolare **2** (*support*) assicurarsi, procurarsi; **to enlist sb's help** assicurarsi l'aiuto di qn ♦ VI (*Mil*): **to enlist (in)** arruolare (in); **enlisted man** (*USA Mil*) soldato semplice

en·liv·en [ɪnˈlaɪvn] VT (*people*) rallegrare; (*events*) ravvivare

en·mity [ˈɛnmɪtɪ] N inimicizia

en·no·ble [ɪˈnəʊbl] VT nobilitare; (*with title*) conferire un titolo nobiliare a

enor·mity [ɪˈnɔːmɪtɪ] N (*of crime, action*) atrocità *f inv*; (*of problem*) gravità

enor·mous [ɪˈnɔːməs] ADJ (*gen*) enorme; (*patience*) infinito(-a); (*strength*) prodigioso(-a); (*risk*) immenso(-a); **an enormous number of** (*people, things*) una moltitudine di

enor·mous·ly [ɪˈnɔːməslɪ] ADV enormemente

enough [ɪˈnʌf] ADJ, N (*sufficient*) abbastanza; **enough people/money/time** abbastanza gente/soldi/tempo; **more than enough money** denaro più che sufficiente; **have you had enough to eat?** hai mangiato abbastanza?; **have you got enough?** ne hai abbastanza or a sufficienza?; **we earn enough to live on** guadagniamo quel tanto che basta per vivere; **will £5 be enough?** bastano 5 sterline?; **that's enough** basta così; **that's enough, thank you** basta, grazie; **there's more than enough for everyone** ce n'è più che a sufficienza per tutti; **enough!** basta!; **enough's enough!** (*fam*) adesso basta!; **I've had enough!** (*protest*) non ne posso più!; **I've had enough of (doing) this** ne ho avuto abbastanza di (fare) questo; **I've had enough of his lies!** ne ho abbastanza delle sue bugie!; **it's enough to drive you mad** (*fam*) è sufficiente a farti diventare matto; **it was enough to prove his innocence** è stato sufficiente a dimostrare la sua innocenza ♦ ADV abbastanza; **big enough** abbastanza grande; **it's hot enough (as it is!)** fa già abbastanza caldo (così)!; **he was kind enough to lend me the money** è stato così gentile da prestarmi i soldi; **you know well enough that ...** sai molto bene che...; **he has not worked enough** non ha lavorato abbastanza; **oddly enough, ...** stranamente...; **sure enough** come volevasi dimostrare; **fair enough!** (*fam*) d'accordo!

en·quire [ɪnˈkwaɪə^r] VT, VI = **inquire**

enquiry [ɪnˈkwaɪərɪ] N (*esp Brit*) = **inquiry**

en·rage [ɪnˈreɪdʒ] VT fare arrabbiare

en·rich [ɪnˈrɪtʃ] VT arricchire

en·rol, en·roll (*USA*) [ɪnˈrəʊl] VT (*gen*) iscrivere; (*Univ*) immatricolare ♦ VI: **to enrol (in)** iscriversi a

en·rol·ment, en·roll·ment (*USA*) [ɪnˈrəʊlmənt] N (*see vb*) iscrizione *f*; immatricolazione *f*

en route [ɒnˈruːt] ADV: **en route for/from/to** in viaggio per/da/a; **it was stolen en route** è stato rubato durante il viaggio

en·sem·ble [ɑ̃ːnˈsɑ̃ːmbl] N **1** (*gen*) insieme *m* **2** (*Mus*) ensemble *m inv* **3** (*outfit*) completo

en·shrine, in·shrine [ɪnˈʃraɪn] VT custodire

en·sign N **1** [ˈɛnsən] (*flag*) insegna, bandiera **2** [ˈɛnsən] (*Mil*) portabandiera *m inv* **3** [ˈɛnsaɪn] (*USA: Naut*) guardiamarina *m inv*

en·slave [ɪnˈsleɪv] VT rendere schiavo(-a), schiavizzare

en·sue [ɪnˈsjuː] VI (*follow*) seguire; **to ensue (from)** (*result*) risultare (da)

en suite [ɑ̃ːnˈswiːt] ADJ: **en suite bedroom** stanza con bagno; **en suite facilities** servizi *mpl* ♦ ADV (*in hotel*): **with bathroom en suite** con stanza da bagno annessa

en·sure [ɪnˈʃʊə^r] VT garantire, assicurare; **to ensure that ...** assicurarsi che...

ENT [ˌiːɛnˈtiː] N ABBR (= *Ear, Nose & Throat*) ORL (= *Otorinolaringoiatria*)

en·tail [ɪnˈteɪl] VT comportare; **it entailed buying a new car** comportava l'acquisto di una nuova macchina

en·tan·gle [ɪn'tæŋgl] VT (*thread*) impigliare; **to become entangled in sth** (*fig*) rimanere impegolato(-a) in qc

en·ter ['entə'] VT **1** (*go into: house, vehicle*) entrare in; (*road*) prendere; (*navy, army*) arruolarsi in; (*profession*) intraprendere; (*college, school*) iscriversi a; (*club*) associarsi a; (*debate, discussion, contest, competition*) partecipare a; **the thought never entered my head** non mi è mai passato per la testa *or* l'anticamera del cervello; **he entered the Church** si è fatto prete **2** (*write down: name, amount, order*) registrare; (*Comput: data*) immettere, inserire, introdurre; **they entered the name into the computer** hanno immesso il nome nel computer; **to enter sb/sth for sth** (*enrol: pupil, candidate, racehorse*) iscrivere qn/qc a qc ♦ VI entrare; **enter Othello** (*Theatre*) entra Otello; **to enter for** (*competition, race*) iscriversi a
　▸ **enter into** VI + PREP **1** (*participate in*) entrare in; (*negotiations, argument, debate*) prendere parte a, partecipare a; (*explanation*) lanciarsi in; (*agreement*) concludere; **to enter into conversation with sb** intavolare una conversazione con qn **2** (*sb's plans, calculations*) rientrare in; **that doesn't enter into it** questo non c'entra **3 to enter into the spirit of things** entrare nello spirito delle cose
　▸ **enter upon** VI + PREP cominciare
en·ter·i·tis [ˌentə'raɪtɪs] N enterite *f*
en·ter·prise ['entə,praɪz] N **1** (*firm, undertaking, company*) impresa **2** (*initiative*) iniziativa
en·ter·pris·ing ['entə,praɪzɪŋ] ADJ (*person*) intraprendente; (*venture*) audace
en·ter·tain [ˌentə'teɪn] VT **1** (*audience*) divertire; (*guest*) intrattenere, ricevere; **he entertained us with his stories** ci ha divertito con le sue storie; **to entertain sb to dinner** invitare qn a cena **2** (*consider: idea, proposal, plan*) prendere in considerazione; (*hopes, doubts*) nutrire ♦ VI (*have visitors*) avere ospiti
en·ter·tain·er [ˌentə'teɪnə'] N artista *m/f* (di cabaret, radio, TV)
en·ter·tain·ing [ˌentə'teɪnɪŋ] ADJ divertente ♦ N: **to do a lot of entertaining** ricevere molti ospiti
en·ter·tain·ment [ˌentə'teɪnmənt] N **1** (*amusement*) divertimento; (*of guests*) trattenimento; **the most popular form of entertainment** la forma di intrattenimento più popolare **2** (*show*) spettacolo; **Las Vegas is the capital of entertainment** Las Vegas è la capitale del divertimento
entertainment allowance N spese *fpl* di rappresentanza
en·thral, en·thrall (*USA*) [ɪn'θrɔːl] VT affascinare, avvincere
en·thral·ling [ɪn'θrɔːlɪŋ] ADJ affascinante, avvincente
en·thuse [ɪn'θuːz] VI: **to enthuse** (**over** *or* **about**) entusiasmarsi (per)
en·thu·si·asm [ɪn'θuːzɪˌæzəm] N entusiasmo; **it failed to arouse my enthusiasm** non mi ha entusiasmato
en·thu·si·ast [ɪn'θuːzɪˌæst] N appassionato(-a); **a jazz etc enthusiast** un(a) appassionato(-a) di jazz *etc*
en·thu·si·as·tic [ɪn,θuːzɪ'æstɪk] ADJ (*response*) entusiastico(-a); (*person*) entusiasta; **to be enthusiastic about sth/sb** essere entusiasta di qc/qn; **to become enthusiastic about sth** entusiasmarsi per qc
en·tice [ɪn'taɪs] VT allettare, attirare; **to entice sb away from sb/sth** persuadere qn a lasciare qn/qc; **to entice sb into doing sth** indurre qn a fare qc; **to entice sb with food/an offer** *etc* allettare qn col cibo/con un'offerta *etc*
en·tic·ing [ɪn'taɪsɪŋ] ADJ allettante, attraente
en·tire [ɪn'taɪə'] ADJ (*whole*) intero(-a), tutto(-a); (*complete*) completo(-a), intero(-a); (*unreserved*) assoluto(-a), pieno(-a); **the entire world** il mondo intero
en·tire·ly [ɪn'taɪəlɪ] ADV completamente, interamente; (*agree*) assolutamente, pienamente; **an entirely new approach** un approccio completamente nuovo; **I agree entirely** sono pienamente d'accordo
en·tirety [ɪn'taɪərətɪ] N: **in its entirety** nel suo complesso
en·ti·tle [ɪn'taɪtl] VT **1** (*book, poem*) intitolare **2 to entitle sb to ...** dare diritto a qn di...; **this entitles him to a free ticket/to do it** questo gli dà diritto ad un biglietto gratis/a farlo; **to be entitled to sth/to do sth** avere diritto a qc/a fare qc
en·ti·tled [ɪn'taɪtld] ADJ (*book*) che si intitola, dal titolo
en·tity ['entɪtɪ] N entità *f inv*
entrails ['entreɪlz] NPL interiora *fpl*

en·trance¹ ['entrəns] N (*way in, of person*) entrata, ingresso; (*right to enter*) ammissione *f*, ingresso; **to gain entrance to** (*university etc*) essere ammesso(-a) a; **to make one's entrance** (*Theatre*) fare il proprio ingresso
en·trance² [ɪn'trɑːns] VT estasiare, incantare
entrance examination N (*to school*) esame *m* di ammissione
entrance fee N (*for club etc*) quota di ammissione, tassa d'iscrizione; (*to museum etc*) biglietto d'ingresso
en·tranc·ing [ɪn'trɑːnsɪŋ] ADJ incantevole
en·trant ['entrənt] N (*in race, competition*) concorrente *m/f*, partecipante *m/f*; (*Brit: in exam*) candidato(-a)
en·treat [ɪn'triːt] VT: **to entreat sb (to do sth)** implorare *or* supplicare qn (di fare qc)
en·treaty [ɪn'triːtɪ] N supplica; **a look of entreaty** uno sguardo supplichevole; **at his earnest entreaty** dietro sua viva supplica
en·trée ['ɒntreɪ] N (*Culin*) entrée *f inv*
en·trenched [ɪn'trentʃt] ADJ (*Mil*) trincerato(-a); (*fig*) radicato(-a)
en·tre·pre·neur [ˌɒntrəprə'nɜː'] N imprenditore(-trice)
en·tre·pre·neur·ial [ˌɒntrəprə'nɜːrɪəl] ADJ imprenditoriale
en·trust [ɪn'trʌst] VT: **to entrust sth to sb, to entrust sb with sth** affidare qc a qn
en·try ['entrɪ] N **1** (*way in*) ingresso, entrata **2** (*act*) ingresso; **"no entry"** "vietato l'ingresso", "ingresso vietato"; (*Aut*) "divieto d'accesso" **3** (*Sport, etc: total*) numero degli iscritti; (: *thing, person entered in competition*) iscrizione *f* **4** (*in reference book*) voce *f*; (*in diary, ship's log*) annotazione *f*; (*in account book, ledger, list*) registrazione *f*; **single/double entry book-keeping** partita semplice/doppia
entry form N modulo d'iscrizione
en·twine [ɪn'twaɪn] VT intrecciare
enu·mer·ate [ɪ'njuːməreɪt] VT enumerare
enun·ci·ate [ɪ'nʌnsɪeɪt] VT (*words*) articolare, pronunciare; (*sound*) articolare; (*theory, idea*) enunciare, esporre
en·vel·op [ɪn'veləp] VT: **to envelop (in)** avvolgere (in), avviluppare (in)
en·velope ['envələup] N busta; **in a sealed envelope** in busta sigillata *or* chiusa; **on the back of an envelope** sulla carta del droghiere; **to push the envelope** superare i limiti
en·vi·able ['envɪəbl] ADJ invidiabile
en·vi·ous ['envɪəs] ADJ: **envious (of sb/sth)** invidioso(-a) (di qn/qc)
en·vi·ron·ment [ɪn'vaɪərənmənt] N ambiente *m*; **Department of the Environment** (*Brit*) ≈ Ministero dell'Ambiente
en·vi·ron·men·tal [ɪn,vaɪərən'mentl] ADJ ambientale; **environmental studies** *or* **science** (*in school*) ecologia
en·vi·ron·men·tal·ist [ɪn,vaɪərən'mentəlɪst] N ambientalista *m/f*
en·vi·ron·men·tal·ly [ɪn,vaɪərən'mentəlɪ] ADV: **environmentally friendly** che rispetta l'ambiente
Environmental Protection Agency N (*USA*) ≈ Agenzia nazionale di protezione ambientale
en·vis·age [ɪn'vɪzɪdʒ], (*USA*) **en·vi·sion** [ɪn'vɪʒən] VT (*expect*) prevedere; (*imagine*) prefigurare
en·voy ['envɔɪ] N (*gen*) inviato(-a); (*diplomat*) ministro plenipotenziario
envy ['envɪ] N invidia; **her new car was the envy of all the neighbours** la sua macchina nuova era l'invidia di tutto il vicinato ♦ VT: **to envy (sb sth)** invidiare (qn per qc)
en·zyme ['enzaɪm] N enzima *m*
EPA N ABBR (*USA:* = Environmental Protection Agency)
ephem·er·al [ɪ'femərəl] ADJ effimero(-a)
epic ['epɪk] ADJ epico(-a) ♦ N poema *m* epico, epopea; (*film*) epopea
epi·cen·tre, epi·cen·ter (*USA*) ['epɪ,sentə'] N epicentro
epi·dem·ic [ˌepɪ'demɪk] ADJ epidemico(-a) ♦ N epidemia
epi·lep·sy ['epɪ,lepsɪ] N epilessia
epi·lep·tic [ˌepɪ'leptɪk] ADJ, N epilettico(-a)
epileptic fit N attacco epilettico
epi·logue ['epɪ,lɒg] N epilogo
Epipha·ny [ɪ'pɪfənɪ] N Epifania
epis·co·pal [ɪ'pɪskəpəl] ADJ episcopale

epi·sode [ˈɛpɪsəʊd] N episodio
epis·tle [ɪˈpɪsl] N epistola
epi·taph [ˈɛpɪtɑːf] N epitaffio
epi·thet [ˈɛpɪθɛt] N epiteto
epito·me [ɪˈpɪtəmɪ] N (frm): **the epitome of kindness** la personificazione della gentilezza
epito·mize [ɪˈpɪtəmaɪz] VT (frm) incarnare
epoch [ˈiːpɒk] N (period) epoca, era
epoch-making [ˈiːpɒkˌmeɪkɪŋ] ADJ che fa epoca
epony·mous [ɪˈpɒnɪməs] ADJ (liter) eponimo
eq·uable [ˈɛkwəbl] ADJ (character) tranquillo(-a); (climate) costante
equal [ˈiːkwəl] ADJ: **equal (to)** uguale (a); **divide the mixture into three equal parts** dividi l'impasto in tre parti uguali; **equal numbers of men and women** un numero uguale di uomini e donne; **an equal amount of time** lo stesso tempo; **to be equal in strength** avere la stessa forza; **all things being equal** se tutto va bene; **with equal ease/indifference** con la stessa facilità/indifferenza; **on equal terms** su un piano di parità; **to be/feel equal to** (task) essere/sentirsi all'altezza di ♦ N (person, thing) pari m/f inv, simile m/f, uguale m/f; **without equal** senza pari ♦ VT (Math) fare; (record, rival) uguagliare; **eight and twelve equals twenty** otto più dodici è uguale a venti; **this score has never been equalled** questo punteggio non è stato mai eguagliato; **there is nothing to equal it** non ha rivali
equali·ty [ɪˈkwɒlɪtɪ] N uguaglianza; (parity) parità
equal·ize [ˈiːkwəlaɪz] VT (society) livellare; (wealth, possessions) distribuire uniformemente; (salaries) equiparare; (pressure, temperature) rendere uniforme ♦ VI (Sport) pareggiare
equal·iz·er [ˈiːkwəlaɪzəʳ] N 1 (Sport) pareggio 2 (Tech) equalizzatore m
equal·ly [ˈiːkwəlɪ] ADV ugualmente; (share) in parti uguali; **they are equally clever** sono intelligenti allo stesso modo; **she is equally clever** è altrettanto intelligente; **equally, you must remember ...** allo stesso modo, ti devi ricordare...
Equal Opportunities Commission N Commissione f per le pari opportunità
equal sign, equals sign N (Math) segno d'uguale or d'uguaglianza
equa·nim·ity [ˌɛkwəˈnɪmɪtɪ] N equanimità, serenità d'animo
equate [ɪˈkweɪt] VT 1 **to equate (with)** identificare (con), considerare uguale a; (compare) paragonare (a); **I don't equate money and happiness** non identifico il denaro con la felicità 2 (Math: make equal) uguagliare; **to equate A to B** mettere in equazione A e B
equa·tion [ɪˈkweɪʒən] N (Math) equazione f; **equations of motion** (Phys) equazioni del moto
equa·tor [ɪˈkweɪtəʳ] N: **the equator** l'equatore m
Equatorial Guinea N Guinea Equatoriale
eques·trian [ɪˈkwɛstrɪən] ADJ equestre ♦ N (man) cavaliere m; (woman) amazzone f
equi·lib·rium [ˌiːkwɪˈlɪbrɪəm] N equilibrio
equi·nox [ˈiːkwɪnɒks] N equinozio
equip [ɪˈkwɪp] VT: **to equip (with)** (room etc) equipaggiare (con), attrezzare (con); (person) preparare a; **vocational courses equip you for a particular job** i corsi di formazione professionale preparano per un lavoro specifico; **equipped with** (machinery etc) dotato(-a) di; (supplies etc) fornito(-a) di; **he is well equipped for the job** ha i requisiti necessari per quel lavoro; **ill/poorly equipped** (hospital, expedition) male equipaggiato(-a)/attrezzato(-a)
equip·ment [ɪˈkwɪpmənt] N no pl attrezzatura; (Tech, Elec) apparecchiatura; **skiing equipment** attrezzatura da sci
equi·table [ˈɛkwɪtəbl] ADJ equo(-a)
equi·ties [ˈɛkwɪtɪz] NPL (Brit: shares) azioni fpl ordinarie
equi·ty [ˈɛkwɪtɪ] N equità
equity capital N capitale m azionario
equiva·lent [ɪˈkwɪvələnt] ADJ equivalente; **to be equivalent to** equivalere a ♦ N equivalente m
equivo·cal [ɪˈkwɪvəkəl] ADJ equivoco(-a); (open to suspicion) dubbio(-a)
equivo·cate [ɪˈkwɪvəkeɪt] VI esprimersi in modo equivoco
equivo·ca·tion [ɪˌkwɪvəˈkeɪʃən] N parole fpl equivoche

ER ABBR 1 (Brit: = Elizabeth Regina) 2 (USA) = **emergency room**
ERA [ˌiːɑːrˈeɪ] N ABBR (USA Pol: = Equal Rights Amendment) proposta di emendamento per le pari opportunità nella Costituzione statunitense
era [ˈɪərə] N era
eradi·cate [ɪˈrædɪkeɪt] VT sradicare
erase [ɪˈreɪz] VT cancellare
eras·er [ɪˈreɪzəʳ] N (frm, also Brit: rubber) gomma (da cancellare)
erect [ɪˈrɛkt] (frm) VT (statue, monument, temple) erigere; (apartments, factory) costruire; (barricade, mast) innalzare; (machinery, tent) montare; (theory, system) edificare; (obstacles) creare ♦ ADJ eretto(-a), dritto(-a); **with head erect** a testa alta
erec·tion [ɪˈrɛkʃən] N 1 (act: gen) erezione f; (of building) costruzione f; (of machinery) montaggio 2 (Anat) erezione f
er·go·nom·ics [ˌɜːgəˈnɒmɪks] NSG ergonomia
Eri·trea [ˌɛrɪˈtreɪə] N Eritrea
ERM [ˌiːɑːrˈɛm] N ABBR = **Exchange Rate Mechanism**
er·mine [ˈɜːmɪn] N ermellino
erode [ɪˈrəʊd] VT (Geol) erodere; (metal, fig) corrodere
erog·enous [ɪˈrɒdʒɪnəs] ADJ: **erogenous zone** zona erogena
ero·sion [ɪˈrəʊʒən] N (see vb) erosione f; corrosione f
erot·ic [ɪˈrɒtɪk] ADJ erotico(-a)
eroti·cism [ɪˈrɒtɪsɪzəm] N erotismo
err [ɜː] VI (be mistaken) sbagliare, errare; (sin) peccare; **it is better to err on the side of caution** la prudenza non è mai troppa
er·rand [ˈɛrənd] N commissione f; **to run errands** fare commissioni; **errand of mercy** atto di carità
errand boy N fattorino
er·rat·ic [ɪˈrætɪk] ADJ (person, conduct, opinions, mood) incostante, imprevedibile; (results etc) irregolare, discontinuo(-a); (driving) irregolare; (Geol) erratico(-a) ♦ N (Geol) masso erratico
er·ro·neous [ɪˈrəʊnɪəs] ADJ erroneo(-a)
er·ror [ˈɛrəʳ] N errore m; **typing/spelling error** errore di battitura/di ortografia; **in error** per errore; **to see the error of one's ways** riconoscere i propri errori
error message N (Comput) messaggio di errore
erst·while [ˈɜːstˌwaɪl] (old) ADJ di un tempo ♦ ADV un tempo, tempo addietro
eru·dite [ˈɛrʊdaɪt] ADJ erudito(-a)
erupt [ɪˈrʌpt] VI (volcano) entrare in eruzione or in attività; (spots) spuntare; (anger) esplodere; (fighting, quarrel) scoppiare; **he erupted into the room** ha fatto irruzione nella stanza
erup·tion [ɪˈrʌpʃən] N (of volcano, spots) eruzione f; (of anger, violence) esplosione f
es·ca·late [ˈɛskəleɪt] VI 1 (violence, fighting, bombing) intensificarsi; **the dispute could escalate** la controversia può inasprirsi 2 (costs) salire ♦ VT intensificare
es·ca·la·tion [ˌɛskəˈleɪʃən] N escalation f inv; (of prices) aumento
es·ca·la·tor [ˈɛskəleɪtəʳ] N scala mobile
es·ca·pade [ˌɛskəˈpeɪd] N (adventure) avventura; (misdeed) scappatella
es·cape [ɪsˈkeɪp] N (gen) fuga; (of prisoner) fuga, evasione f; (of gas) fuga, fuoriuscita; **to have a lucky escape** scamparla bella; **to make one's escape** evadere ♦ VT (capture, pursuers, punishment) sfuggire a; (death) scampare a; (danger) scampare a; (consequences) sottrarsi a; **he narrowly escaped being killed** per poco non è rimasto ucciso; **his name escapes me** il suo nome mi sfugge; **to escape notice** passare inosservato(-a); **it had escaped his notice** era sfuggito alla sua attenzione; **nothing escapes her** (attention) non le sfugge nulla ♦ VI (gen) scappare; (prisoner) evadere; (liquid, gas) fuoriuscire; (Comput) uscire; **a lion has escaped** è scappato un leone; **to escape from** (person) sfuggire a; (prison) evadere da; **to escape to** (another place) fuggire in; (freedom, safety) fuggire verso; **he escaped with a few bruises** (fig) se l'è cavata con qualche livido; **to escape unhurt** (fig) rimanere illeso(-a); **an escaped prisoner** un(a) evaso(-a)
escape artist N = **escapologist**
escape clause N (in agreement) clausola liberatoria

es·ca·pee [ɪskeɪˈpiː] N evaso(-a)
escape hatch N (*in submarine, space rocket*) portello di sicurezza
escape key N (*Comput*) tasto di escape
escape route N percorso di fuga
es·cap·ism [ɪsˈkeɪpɪzəm] N escapismo, evasione *f* (dalla realtà)
es·cap·ist [ɪsˈkeɪpɪst] ADJ d'evasione ♦ N persona che cerca di evadere dalla realtà
es·ca·po·lo·gist [ˌɛskəˈpɒlədʒɪst] N (*Brit*) *illusionista specializzato nel liberarsi da funi, catene ecc.*
es·carp·ment [ɪsˈkɑːpmənt] N scarpata
eschew [ɪsˈtʃuː] VT (*frm*) evitare
es·cort [*n* ˈɛskɔːt, *vb* ɪsˈkɔːt] N (*Mil, Naut*) scorta; (*male companion*) cavaliere *m*, accompagnatore *m*; (*female companion*) accompagnatrice *f*; **a police escort** una scorta di polizia ♦ VI accompagnare; (*Mil, Naut*) scortare
escort agency N agenzia di accompagnatrici
Es·ki·mo [ˈɛskɪˌməʊ] (*pl* **Eskimos** *or* **Eskimo**) ADJ eschimese ♦ N (*person*) eschimese *m/f*; (*language*) eschimese *m*
ESL [ˌiːɛsˈɛl] N ABBR (*Scol*: = **English as a Second Language**)
esopha·gus [ɪˈsɒfəgəs] N (*USA*) = **oesophagus**
eso·ter·ic [ˌɛsəˈtɛrɪk] ADJ esoterico(-a)
ESP [ˌiːɛsˈpiː] N ABBR = **extrasensory perception**
esp. ABBR (= *especially*) spec.
es·pe·cial·ly [ɪsˈpɛʃəlɪ] ADV (*particularly*) particolarmente; (*above all*) soprattutto, specialmente; (*expressly*) appositamente, espressamente; **it is especially difficult** è particolarmente difficile; **it's very hot there, especially in the summer** fa molto caldo lì, soprattutto d'estate; **especially when it rains** soprattutto quando piove; **why me, especially?** perché proprio io?
es·pio·nage [ˌɛspɪəˈnɑːʒ] N spionaggio
es·pla·nade [ˌɛspləˈneɪd] N lungomare *m*
es·pouse [ɪsˈpaʊz] VT (*fig: frm*) abbracciare
es·quire [ɪsˈkwaɪəʳ] N: **Colin Smith Esquire** Egregio Signor Colin Smith
es·say [ˈɛseɪ] N (*Literature*) saggio; (*Scol*) tema *m*, composizione *f*; **a history essay** un tema di storia
es·sence [ˈɛsəns] N (*gen, also Culin*) essenza; **this is the essence of the problem** questa è l'essenza del problema; **in essence** in sostanza; **speed is of the essence** la velocità è di estrema importanza
es·sen·tial [ɪˈsɛnʃəl] ADJ (*gen*) essenziale; (*basic*) fondamentale; (*important*) indispensabile; **it is essential that** è essenziale che + *sub* ♦ N (*often pl*) elemento essenziale
es·sen·tial·ly [ɪˈsɛnʃəlɪ] ADV essenzialmente, fondamentalmente
essentials NPL: **the essentials** l'essenziale *msg*
EST [ˌiːɛsˈtiː] N ABBR (*USA*: = **Eastern Standard Time**) *see* **eastern**
est. ABBR 1 (= *established*): **est. 1900** dal 1900 2 = **estimate(d)**
es·tab·lish [ɪsˈtæblɪʃ] VT (*set up: company*) costituire; (: *business*) avviare; (: *state*) creare; (: *committee*) istituire; (: *custom, precedent, relations*) stabilire; (: *power, authority, reputation*) affermare; (: *peace, order*) ristabilire; **they finally established contact** alla fine hanno stabilito un contatto; **he established his reputation as an architect** si è affermato come architetto 2 (*prove: fact, identity, sb's innocence*) dimostrare; **tests have established she is not their child** alcuni test hanno accertato che non è figlia loro
es·tab·lish·ment [ɪsˈtæblɪʃmənt] N 1 (*of company*) costituzione *f*; (*of state*) creazione *f*; (*of committee*) istituzione *f*; (*of law*) instaurazione *f*; (*of reputation*) affermazione *f* 2 (*business*) azienda; (*Admin, Mil, Naut: personnel*) effettivo; **commercial establishments** aziende; **a teaching establishment** un istituto d'istruzione; **the Establishment** la classe dirigente, l'establishment *m inv*; **the values of the Establishment** i valori tradizionali; **the cultural Establishment** l'establishment culturale
es·tate [ɪsˈteɪt] N 1 (*land*) proprietà *f inv*, tenuta; (*Brit: also:* **housing estate**) complesso edilizio; **I live on a new estate** vivo in un nuovo complesso edilizio; **country estate** tenuta in campagna 2 (*Law: on death*) patrimonio, beni *mpl*; **his estate is valued at $150,000** il suo patrimonio è valutato 150.000 dollari
❑ **estate** is not translated by the Italian word *estate*

estate agency N (*Brit*) agenzia immobiliare
estate agent N (*Brit*) agente *m/f* immobiliare
estate car N (*Brit*) auto modello familiare, station wagon *f inv*
es·teem [ɪsˈtiːm] (*frm*) N stima; **I hold him in high esteem** gode della mia più alta stima ♦ VT (*think highly of*) stimare; (*consider*) considerare; **I would esteem it an honour** sarebbe un onore per me
es·thet·ic [iːsˈθɛtɪk] ADJ (*USA*) = **aesthetic**
es·ti·mate [*n* ˈɛstɪmɪt, *vb* ˈɛstɪˌmeɪt] N (*judgment*) valutazione *f*, stima; (*Comm: for work to be done*) preventivo; **to give sb an estimate of** fare a qn un preventivo (*or* una stima) di; **at a rough estimate** ad un calcolo approssimativo ♦ VT valutare, stimare; (*Comm*) preventivare; **we estimate the cost to be £150** preventiviamo un costo di circa 150 sterline; **they estimated it would take three weeks** hanno calcolato che ci sarebbero volute tre settimane ♦ VI (*Comm*): **to estimate for** fare il preventivo per
es·ti·ma·tion [ˌɛstɪˈmeɪʃən] N 1 (*judgment*) giudizio; **in my estimation** a mio giudizio, a mio avviso 2 (*esteem*) stima, opinione *f*; **she has gone up in my estimation** ho maggiore stima di lei
Es·ton·ia, Es·tho·nia [ɛˈstəʊnɪə] N Estonia
Es·to·nian, Es·thon·ian [ɛˈstəʊnɪən] ADJ estone ♦ N (*person*) estone *m/f*; (*language*) estone *m*
es·tranged [ɪˈstreɪndʒd] ADJ separato(-a); **to become estranged** allontanarsi, disaffezionarsi
es·trange·ment [ɪsˈtreɪndʒmənt] N allontanamento
es·tro·gen [ˈiːstrədʒən] N (*USA*) = **oestrogen**
es·tu·ary [ˈɛstjʊərɪ] N estuario
ET [ˌiːˈtiː] ABBR (*USA:* = **Eastern Time**) fuso orario della costa orientale
ETA [ˌiːtiːˈeɪ] N ABBR 1 (= *estimated time of arrival*) ora di arrivo prevista 2 (*Basque separatist organization:* = **Euzkadi ta Askatsuna**) ETA *f*
e-tailer [ˈiːteɪləʳ] N venditore(-trice) in internet
e-tailing [ˈiːteɪlɪŋ] N commercio in internet
et al. [ɛtˈæl] ABBR (= *et alii: and others*) ed altri
etc ABBR (= *et cetera*) ecc., etc.
etch [ɛtʃ] VT incidere all'acquaforte
etch·ing [ˈɛtʃɪŋ] N (*process*) incisione *f* all'acquaforte; (*print made from plate*) acquaforte *f*
ETD [ˌiːtiːˈdiː] N ABBR (= *estimated time of departure*) ora di partenza prevista
eter·nal [ɪˈtɜːnl] ADJ eterno(-a); (*pej: complaints etc*) continuo(-a)
eter·nity [ɪˈtɜːnɪtɪ] N eternità
ether [ˈiːθəʳ] N etere *m*
ethe·real [ɪˈθɪərɪəl] ADJ etereo(-a)
ethi·cal [ˈɛθɪkəl] ADJ etico(-a), morale; **ethical bank/investment** banca/investimento etico
eth·ics [ˈɛθɪks] N (*sg: study*) etica; (*pl: principles, system*) morale *f*
Ethio·pia [ˌiːθɪˈəʊpɪə] N Etiopia
Ethio·pian [ˌiːθɪˈəʊpɪən] ADJ etiopico(-a), etiope ♦ N (*person*) etiope *m/f*; (*language*) etiope *m*
eth·nic [ˈɛθnɪk] ADJ etnico(-a); **an ethnic minority** una minoranza etnica
ethnic cleansing N pulizia etnica
eth·nol·ogy [ɛθˈnɒlədʒɪ] N etnologia
ethos [ˈiːθɒs] N (*of culture, group*) ethos *m*, norma di vita
e-ticket [ˈiːtɪkɪt] N biglietto acquistato in internet
eti·quette [ˈɛtɪˌkɛt] N etichetta; **court etiquette** (*royal*) cerimoniale di corte; **medical etiquette** prassi *f* medica
ety·mol·ogy [ˌɛtɪˈmɒlədʒɪ] N etimologia
EU [ˌiːˈjuː] N ABBR (= *European Union*) UE *f*
euca·lyp·tus [ˌjuːkəˈlɪptəs] N eucalipto
eulogy [ˈjuːlədʒɪ] N elogio, encomio
eu·phe·mism [ˈjuːfəˌmɪzəm] N eufemismo
euphemis·tic [ˌjuːfəˈmɪstɪk] ADJ eufemistico(-a)
eupho·ria [juːˈfɔːrɪə] N euforia
Eura·sia [jʊəˈreɪʃə] N Eurasia
Eura·sian [jʊəˈreɪʃn] ADJ eurasiatico(-a) ♦ N eurasiano(-a)
euro [ˈjʊərəʊ] N euro *m inv*
Euro- [ˈjʊərəʊ] PREF euro-

Euro·cheque [ˈjʊərəʊˌtʃɛk] N eurochèque *m inv*

Euro·crat [ˈjʊərəʊˌkræt] N eurocrate *m/f*

Euro·dol·lar [ˈjʊərəʊˌdɒləʳ] N eurodollaro

euro·land, Euroland [ˈjʊərəʊlænd] N Eurolandia

Europe [ˈjʊərəp] N Europa

Euro·pean [ˌjʊərəˈpiːən] ADJ europeo(-a); **European plan** (*USA: in hotel*) solo pernottamento (pasti esclusi) ♦ N europeo(-a)

European Court of Justice N Tribunale *m* della Comunità Europea

European Union N Unione *f* europea

Euro·pol [ˈjʊərəʊpɒl] N Europol *f*

Euro·sceptic [ˈjʊərəʊˌskɛptɪk] N euroscettico(-a)

Euro·zone [ˈjʊərəʊzəʊn] N zona euro

eutha·na·sia [ˌjuːθəˈneɪzɪə] N eutanasia

evacu·ate [ɪˈvækjʊˌeɪt] VT (*people*) sfollare; (*building, area: Med*) evacuare

evacu·ation [ɪˌvækjʊˈeɪʃən] N (*see vb*) sfollamento; evacuazione *f*

evac·uee [ɪˌvækjʊˈiː] N sfollato(-a)

evade [ɪˈveɪd] VT (*capture, pursuers*) sfuggire a; (*punishment, blow*) schivare; (*question*) eludere; (*issue, truth, sb's gaze*) evitare; (*responsibility, duties, obligation, military service*) sottrarsi a; (*tax, customs duty*) evadere

evalu·ate [ɪˈvæljʊˌeɪt] VT valutare

evan·gelist [ɪˈvændʒəlɪst] N (*writer: also:* **Evangelist**) evangelista *m*; (*preacher*) predicatore *m* evangelista

evan·gelize [ɪˈvændʒɪˌlaɪz] VT evangelizzare ♦ VI predicare il vangelo

evapo·rate [ɪˈvæpəreɪt] VT (*liquid*) far evaporare ♦ VI (*liquid*) evaporare; (*fig: hopes, fears, anger*) svanire

evapo·rat·ed milk [ɪˈvæpəˌreɪtɪdˈmɪlk] N latte *m* condensato

evapo·ra·tion [ɪˌvæpəˈreɪʃən] N evaporazione *f*

eva·sion [ɪˈveɪʒən] N evasione *f*

eva·sive [ɪˈveɪsɪv] ADJ (*answer*) evasivo(-a); (*person*) sfuggente; **to take evasive action** defilarsi

eve [iːv] N vigilia; **on the eve of** alla vigilia di; **Christmas Eve** la vigilia di Natale; **New Year's Eve** la vigilia di Capodanno, la notte di San Silvestro

even [ˈiːvən] ADV 1 perfino, anche; **even on Sundays** perfino di domenica; **not even ...** nemmeno *or* neppure *or* neanche...; **he didn't even say hello** non ha neanche salutato; **even though** anche se; **even as** proprio nel momento in cui; **even now he can't do it** non lo sa fare nemmeno ora; **without even reading it** senza neppure leggerlo; **he can't even read** non sa nemmeno leggere; **even so** ciò nonostante; **not even if/when** nemmeno *or* neppure se/ quando 2 (+ *comp adj or adv*) ancora; **even faster** ancora più veloce; **even more** ancora di più; **you'll have even more fun tomorrow** domani vi divertirete ancora di più ♦ ADJ 1 (*smooth*) liscio(-a); (*level*): **even (with)** allo stesso livello (di); **to make even** livellare; **an even surface** una superficie liscia 2 (*uniform: speed, breathing*) regolare; (*temperature*) costante; (*temper*) calmo(-a); (*tone, voice, colour*) uniforme 3 (*equal: quantities*) uguale; (: *score*) di parità, pari *inv*; **the scores are even** sono a pari punteggio; **to have an even chance (of doing sth)** avere una buona probabilità (di fare qc); **to get even with sb** vendicarsi di qn; **to break even** (*Fin*) chiudere in pareggio; **that makes us even** (*in game, also fig*) siamo pari; **they are an even match** sono allo stesso livello 4 (*number*) pari *inv*

  ▸ **even out** VT + ADV (*smooth, also fig*) appianare; (*number, score*) pareggiare ♦ VI + ADV pareggiarsi

  ▸ **even up** VT + ADV (*smooth, also fig*) appianare

even-handed [ˌiːvənˈhændɪd] ADJ imparziale, equo(-a)

eve·ning [ˈiːvnɪŋ] N sera; (*as duration, event*) serata; **in the evening** di sera, la sera; **this evening** stasera, questa sera; **tomorrow/yesterday evening** domani/ieri sera; **on Sunday evening** domenica sera; **on the evening of the 30th** la sera del 30; **all evening** tutta la sera; **we had a lovely evening** è stata una bella serata; **good evening!** buona sera! ♦ ADJ (*paper, prayers, service*) della sera; (*performance*) serale

evening class N corso serale

evening dress N (*woman's*) abito da sera; **in evening dress** (*man*) in abito scuro; (*woman*) in abito lungo

even·ly [ˈiːvənlɪ] ADV (*distribute, space, spread*) uniformemente; (*divide*) in parti uguali; (*breathe*) in modo regolare

even·song [ˈiːvənˌsɒŋ] N ≈ vespro

event [ɪˈvɛnt] N avvenimento; (*Sport: in a programme*) gara; **it was one of the most important events in his life** è stato uno degli avvenimenti più importanti della sua vita; **she took part in two events at the last Olympic Games** ha preso parte a due gare alle ultime Olimpiadi; **a sporting event** una manifestazione sportiva; **"Events"** "Spettacoli e manifestazioni"; **social events for the students** iniziative per gli studenti; **at all events, in any event** in ogni caso; **in either event** in entrambi i casi; **in the event of/that ...** in caso di/ che + *sub* ...; **in the event** in realtà, di fatto; **in that event** in quel caso; **in the normal course of events** secondo le regole, nel corso naturale delle cose; **in the course of events** nel corso degli eventi

event·ful [ɪˈvɛntfʊl] ADJ (*life*) ricco(-a) di avvenimenti; (*match, day*) movimentato(-a), denso(-a) di eventi

event·ing [ɪˈvɛntɪŋ] N (*Sport*) concorso ippico

even·tual [ɪˈvɛntʃʊəl] ADJ finale; **the eventual outcome** il risultato finale; **it resulted in the eventual loss of many lives** ha avuto come risultato finale la perdita di molte vite umane

  ❏ **eventual** is not translated by the Italian word *eventuale*

even·tu·al·ity [ɪˌvɛntʃʊˈælɪtɪ] N eventualità *f inv*, possibilità *f inv*; **to be ready for any eventuality** essere pronto(-a) a ogni evenienza

even·tu·al·ly [ɪˈvɛntʃʊəlɪ] ADV (*at last*) alla fine, finalmente; **eventually the species will become extinct** (*given time*) la specie finirà per estinguersi

  ❏ **eventually** is not translated by the Italian word *eventualmente*

ever [ˈɛvəʳ] ADV 1 (*always*) sempre; **ever ready** sempre pronto(-a); **ever since (then) they have been very careful** da allora in poi sono stati molto prudenti; **ever since I met him** da quando l'ho incontrato; **ever since I've known him** sin da quando lo conosco; **it will become ever more complex** diventerà sempre più complicato; **with ever increasing frequency** con sempre maggior frequenza; **they lived happily ever after** e vissero per sempre felici e contenti; **ever come** sempre; **for ever** per sempre; **they are for ever fighting** litigano di continuo; **yours ever** (*Brit: in letters*) sempre tuo(-a) 2 (*at any time*) mai; **hardly ever** quasi mai; **nothing ever happens** non succede mai nulla; **if you ever go there** se ti capita di andarci; **did you ever meet him?** l'hai mai incontrato?; **have you ever been there?** ci sei mai stato?; **we haven't ever tried it** non l'abbiamo mai provato; **more handsome than ever** più bello che mai; **now if ever is the time** *or* **moment to ...** ora o mai più è il momento di...; **for the first time ever** per la prima volta in assoluto; **the best ever** il (la) migliore che ci sia mai stato(-a); **the best film ever** il miglior film che ci sia mai visto; **he's a liar if ever there was one** se c'è un bugiardo al mondo quello è lui 3 (*emphasizing*): **as soon as ever you can** al più presto possibile; **why ever did you do it?** perché mai l'hai fatto?; **why not?** ma perché no?; **never ever** mai e poi mai; **ever so pretty** così bello(-a); **we're ever so grateful** siamo estremamente grati; **thank you ever so much** grazie mille; **as if I ever would!** come se mai lo dicessi!

Ev·er·est [ˈɛvərɪst] N (*also:* **Mount Everest**) l'Everest *m*, il monte *m* Everest

ever·green [ˈɛvəˌgriːn] ADJ, N sempreverde *m, f*

ever·lasting [ˌɛvəˈlɑːstɪŋ] ADJ eterno(-a); (*pej*) continuo(-a)

every [ˈɛvrɪ] ADJ (*each*) ogni *inv*; (*all*) tutti(-e) *pl*; **every pupil** ogni scolaro; **every one of them** ognuno(-a) di loro; **every one of tutti**; **every one of the components was faulty** tutti i componenti erano difettosi; **I gave you every assistance** ti ho dato tutta l'assistenza; **I have every confidence in him** ho piena fiducia in lui; **we wish you every success** ti auguriamo ogni successo; **every day** ogni giorno, tutti i giorni; **every other day** un giorno sì e uno no; **every other car** una macchina su due; **every second month** ogni due mesi; **every third day** ogni tre giorni; **every few days** ogni due o tre giorni; **every so often, every now and then, every now and again** di tanto in tanto, di quando in quando, ogni tanto; **every time that** ogni volta che; **every single time** proprio tutte le volte; **her every wish** ogni suo desiderio; **I enjoyed every minute of the party** mi sono divertito moltissimo alla festa; **every bit as clever as** tanto intelligente quanto; **in every way** sotto tutti i profili; **every man for himself** ognuno per sé

every·body [ˈɛvrɪˌbɒdɪ] PRON ognuno, ciascuno; (all) tutti(-e) pl; **everybody knows about it** lo sanno tutti; **everybody makes mistakes** tutti fanno errori; **everybody has their** or (frm) **his own view** ognuno or ciascuno la pensa come crede; **everybody else** tutti gli altri

every·day [ˈɛvrɪˌdeɪ] ADJ quotidiano(-a), di ogni giorno; (expression) di uso corrente; (use, occurrence, experience) comune; (shoes, clothes) di tutti i giorni; **in everyday life** nella vita quotidiana; **it is not an everyday event** non capita tutti i giorni

every·one [ˈɛvrɪˌwʌn] PRON = **everybody**

every·thing [ˈɛvrɪˌθɪŋ] PRON tutto, ogni cosa; **you've thought of everything!** hai pensato a tutto!; **everything is ready** è tutto pronto; **everything you say is true** tutto ciò che dici è vero; **this shop sells everything** questo negozio vende di tutto; **he did everything possible** ha fatto tutto il possibile

every·where [ˈɛvrɪˌwɛəʳ] ADV dappertutto, in ogni luogo; (wherever) ovunque; **I looked everywhere, but I couldn't find it** ho cercato dappertutto, ma non l'ho trovato; **everywhere you go you meet ...** ovunque tu vada trovi...

evict [ɪˈvɪkt] VT sfrattare

evic·tion [ɪˈvɪkʃən] N sfratto

eviction notice N avviso di sfratto

evi·dence [ˈɛvɪdəns] N INV (proof) prova; (testimony) testimonianza; (sign) indizio, traccia; **there is no evidence to support this theory** non c'è prova a sostegno di questa teoria; **to show evidence of** mostrare segni di, dare segni di; **evidence of a break-in** tracce di scasso; **to give evidence** testimoniare, deporre; **his cousin gave evidence against him** suo cugino ha deposto contro di lui; **to turn King's** or **Queen's** or (USA) **State's evidence** testimoniare contro i propri complici; **to be in evidence** essere visibile or in vista

evi·dent [ˈɛvɪdənt] ADJ evidente, chiaro(-a); **it is evident from his speech that ...** risulta chiaro or evidente dal suo discorso che...

evi·dent·ly [ˈɛvɪdəntlɪ] ADV (clearly) chiaramente; (apparently) evidentemente; **evidently he cannot come** evidentemente non può venire

evil [ˈiːvl] N male m; **the lesser of two evils** il minore tra due mali; **a necessary evil** un male necessario ♦ ADJ (person, deed) malvagio(-a), cattivo(-a); (reputation, influence) pessimo(-a); (spirit, spell, influence) malvagio(-a); (unhappy: hour, times) infausto(-a)

evince [ɪˈvɪns] VT (frm) manifestare

evoca·tive [ɪˈvɒkətɪv] ADJ: **evocative (of)** evocativo(-a) (di)

evoke [ɪˈvəʊk] VT (memories) evocare; (admiration) suscitare

evo·lu·tion [ˌiːvəˈluːʃən] N (development) sviluppo; (Bio) evoluzione f

evolve [ɪˈvɒlv] VT (system, theory, plan) elaborare, sviluppare ♦ VI (species) evolversi; (system, plan, science) svilupparsi

ewe [juː] N pecora

ex [ɛks] N (ex-husband, ex-wife) ex m/f inv; **he's one of my exes** è uno dei miei ex

ex- [ɛks] PREF (former: husband, president) ex-

ex·ac·er·bate [ɪɡˈzæsəˌbeɪt] (frm) VT (pain) aggravare; (relations, situation) esacerbare, inasprire

ex·act [ɪɡˈzækt] ADJ (number, value, meaning, time) esatto(-a); (instructions, description) preciso(-a); **it's an exact copy of the original** è una copia perfetta dell'originale; **her exact words were ...** le sue precise parole sono state...; **in exact, there were three of us** per essere precisi eravamo in tre; **the exact opposite (of)** l'esatto contrario (di) ♦ VT: **to exact sth (from)** (frm) esigere qc (da)

ex·act·ing [ɪɡˈzæktɪŋ] ADJ (task, profession, work) impegnativo(-a); (person) esigente; **exacting standards** standard molto alti

ex·acti·tude [ɪɡˈzæktɪˌtjuːd] N precisione f, esattezza

ex·act·ly [ɪɡˈzæktlɪ] ADV (describe, know, resemble) esattamente; (of time) in punto; **exactly the same** esattamente uguale;

exactly! esatto!; **that's exactly what I thought** è proprio quello che pensavo; **it's exactly 5 o'clock** sono le 5 in punto

ex·ag·ger·ate [ɪɡˈzædʒəˌreɪt] VT (overstate) esagerare; (emphasize) accentuare ♦ VI esagerare

ex·ag·gera·tion [ɪɡˌzædʒəˈreɪʃən] N esagerazione f

ex·alt [ɪɡˈzɔːlt] VT (frm) **1** (in rank) promuovere **2** (praise) esaltare, magnificare

ex·alt·ed [ɪɡˈzɔːltɪd] ADJ (frm: high: rank, position, person) elevato(-a); (: elated) esaltato(-a)

exam [ɪɡˈzæm] N (Scol: = examination) esame m; **a French exam** un esame di francese; **the exam results** i risultati degli esami; **to take an exam** fare un esame

ex·ami·na·tion [ɪɡˌzæmɪˈneɪʃən] N (Scol) esame m; (inspection: of machine, premises) ispezione f; (: of accounts, passport, at Customs) controllo; (: of witness, suspect) interrogatorio; (Med) visita; **to take** or **sit an examination** sostenere or dare un esame; **on examination** in seguito all'esame; **the matter is under examination** la questione è all'esame; **a medical examination** una visita medica

ex·am·ine [ɪɡˈzæmɪn] VT (inspect: machine, wreckage) ispezionare; (: luggage, passport) controllare; (Med) visitare, esaminare; (witness, suspect) interrogare; (test: pupil, candidate): **to examine sb in** esaminare qn in; (orally) interrogare qn in; **experts are examining the wreckage of the plane** gli esperti stanno esaminando il relitto dell'aereo; **he examined her passport** le ha controllato il passaporto; **the doctor examined him** il dottore l'ha visitato

ex·am·in·er [ɪɡˈzæmɪnəʳ] N esaminatore(-trice)

ex·am·ple [ɪɡˈzɑːmpl] N (gen) esempio; (person) esempio, modello; (copy) esemplare m; **for example** ad or per esempio; **to quote sth/sb as an example** portare qc/qn come esempio; **to set a good/bad example** dare il buon/cattivo esempio; **to make an example of sb** dare l'esempio (punendo qn); **to punish sb as an example** punire qn per dare l'esempio

ex·as·per·ate [ɪɡˈzɑːspəˌreɪt] VT esasperare; **exasperated by** or **at** or **with** esasperato(-a) da; **to become exasperated** esasperarsi

ex·as·per·at·ing [ɪɡˈzɑːspəˌreɪtɪŋ] ADJ esasperante

ex·as·pera·tion [ɪɡˌzɑːspəˈreɪʃən] N esasperazione f

ex·ca·vate [ˈɛkskəˌveɪt] VT (ground) scavare; (Archeol) effettuare gli scavi di

ex·ca·va·tion [ˌɛkskəˈveɪʃən] N scavo; (Archeol) scavi mpl

ex·ca·va·tor [ˈɛkskəˌveɪtəʳ] N (machine) escavatrice f, escavatore m

ex·ceed [ɪkˈsiːd] VT (gen: speed limit): **to exceed (by)** superare (di); (limit, bounds) oltrepassare; (powers, instructions, duty) eccedere; (time limit) superare

ex·ceed·ing·ly [ɪkˈsiːdɪŋlɪ] ADV estremamente

ex·cel [ɪkˈsɛl] VT superare; **to excel o.s.** superare se stesso ♦ VI: **to excel at** or **in** eccellere in; **to excel as** primeggiare come

ex·cel·lence [ˈɛksələns] N superiorità

Ex·cel·len·cy [ˈɛksələnsɪ] N: **His Excellency** Sua Eccellenza

ex·cel·lent [ˈɛksələnt] ADJ eccellente, ottimo(-a); **her results were excellent** i suoi risultati erano eccellenti

ex·cept [ɪkˈsɛpt] PREP (also: **except for, excepting**) eccetto, salvo, tranne; **everyone except me** tutti tranne me; **except that/ if/when** salvo che/se/quando; **there is nothing we can do except wait** non c'è nulla che possiamo fare se non aspettare; **except for** ad eccezione di ♦ VT: **to except (from)** escludere (da); **present company excepted** esclusi i presenti; **always excepting the possibility ...** sempre se si esclude la possibilità...; **not excepting ...** senza esclusione di...

ex·cep·tion [ɪkˈsɛpʃən] N eccezione f; **with the exception of** ad eccezione di, fatta eccezione per; **without exception** senza eccezioni; **to make an exception** fare un'eccezione; **the exception proves the rule** l'eccezione conferma la regola; **to take exception to** fare obiezione a, trovare da ridire su

ex·cep·tion·al [ɪkˈsɛpʃənl] ADJ eccezionale; (unusual) insolito(-a)

ex·cep·tion·al·ly [ɪkˈsɛpʃənəlɪ] ADV eccezionalmente

ex·cerpt [ˈɛksɜːpt] N (from film) spezzone m; (from TV play) estratto; (from book: Mus) brano

ex·cess [ɪkˈsɛs] N eccesso; **the excess of losses over profits** l'eccedenza delle perdite sui guadagni; **in excess of** al di sopra di; **sums in excess of £10,000** somme superiori alle 10.000 sterline; **to excess** all'eccesso; **to carry sth to excess** spingere qc all'eccesso ♦ ADJ (*profit, weight*) in eccesso; **excess fat** grasso in eccesso

excess baggage, excess luggage N bagaglio in eccedenza

excess fare N supplemento di prezzo *or* di tariffa

ex·ces·sive [ɪkˈsɛsɪv] ADJ (*drinking, spending, interest*) smodato(-a); (*charges, rates*) eccessivo(-a); (*fear*) esagerato(-a)

excess supply N eccesso di offerta

ex·change [ɪksˈtʃeɪndʒ] N 1 scambio; **in exchange (for)** in cambio (di); **what will you give me in exchange?** cosa mi darai in cambio?; **I'd like to do an exchange with an Italian student** vorrei fare uno scambio con uno studente italiano; **an exchange of gunfire** uno scontro a fuoco 2 (*Comm*): **foreign exchange** cambio 3 (*also:* **telephone exchange**) centralino ♦ VT: **to exchange sth for sth/with sb** scambiare qc con qc/con qn; (*prisoners, stamps, greetings*) scambiarsi; **to exchange blows** venire alle mani

exchange control N (*Fin*) controllo dei cambi

exchange market N mercato dei cambi

exchange rate N tasso di cambio

Ex·cheq·uer [ɪksˈtʃekəʳ] N: **the Exchequer** (*Brit*) ≈ il ministero delle Finanze

ex·cis·able [ɪkˈsaɪzəbl] ADJ soggetto(-a) a dazio

ex·cise [*n* ˈeksaɪz, *vb* ɪkˈsaɪz] N (*also:* **excise tax**) dazio ♦ VT (*frm*) asportare

excise duties [ˈeksaɪzˈdjuːtɪz] NPL dazi *mpl*

ex·cit·able [ɪkˈsaɪtəbl] ADJ eccitabile

ex·cite [ɪkˈsaɪt] VT 1 (*person*) far agitare; (*pleasantly*) riempire di gioia (*or* interesse *etc*); (*sexually*) eccitare; **to excite sb to anger** far arrabbiare qn 2 (*anger*) provocare; (*interest, enthusiasm*) suscitare

ex·cit·ed [ɪkˈsaɪtɪd] ADJ: **excited (about)** eccitato(-a) (per); **to get excited (about sth)** agitarsi (per qc); **it's nothing to get excited about** (*fig*) non è niente di particolare

ex·cite·ment [ɪkˈsaɪtmənt] N eccitazione *f*, agitazione *f*; **in the excitement of the departure/preparations** nell'eccitazione *or* agitazione della partenza/dei preparativi; **the book caused great excitement** il libro ha fatto sensazione

ex·cit·ing [ɪkˈsaɪtɪŋ] ADJ (*idea, fashion, person*) entusiasmante; (*film, book*) appassionante; **an exciting match** una partita entusiasmante; **an exciting story** una storia appassionante; **an exciting adventure** un'avventura eccitante

excl. ABBR 1 = **excluding** 2 = **exclusive (of)**

ex·claim [ɪksˈkleɪm] VI esclamare ♦ VI: **to exclaim at sth** (*indignantly*) indignarsi per qc; (*admiringly*) esprimere meraviglia davanti a qc

ex·cla·ma·tion [ˌekskləˈmeɪʃən] N esclamazione *f*

exclamation mark, (*USA*) **exclamation point** N (*Gram*) punto esclamativo

ex·clude [ɪksˈkluːd] VT (*gen*) escludere; (*possibility*) scartare; **I'm excluded from taking part** non ho il diritto di partecipare

ex·clud·ing [ɪksˈkluːdɪŋ] PREP: **excluding VAT** IVA esclusa; **excluding the cleaners** escluse le donne delle pulizie

ex·clu·sion [ɪksˈkluːʒən] N esclusione *f*; **women's exclusion from political power** l'esclusione delle donne dal potere politico; **to the exclusion of** escludendo; **exclusion from school** espulsione dalla scuola

exclusion clause N clausola di esclusione di rischi

exclusion zone N area interdetta

ex·clu·sive [ɪksˈkluːsɪv] ADJ 1 (*gen, club*) esclusivo(-a); (*district*) snob *inv*; (*interest, attention*) totale; **you will have exclusive use of the pool** avrete uso esclusivo della piscina; **exclusive agency agreement** (*Comm*) accordo di esclusiva; **exclusive rights** diritti *mpl* esclusivi; **an interview exclusive to ...** un'intervista in esclusiva a... 2 (*not including*): **exclusive of postage** spese postali escluse; **exclusive of service** servizio escluso; **exclusive of VAT** IVA esclusa

ex·clu·sive·ly [ɪksˈkluːsɪvlɪ] ADV esclusivamente

ex·com·mu·ni·cate [ˌekskəˈmjuːnɪˌkeɪt] VT scomunicare

ex·cre·ment [ˈekskrɪmənt] N (*frm*) escremento

ex·cru·ci·at·ing [ɪksˈkruːʃɪˌeɪtɪŋ] ADJ (*pain, suffering: also fam: film*) atroce; (*noise*) insopportabile

ex·cur·sion [ɪksˈkɜːʃən] N (*journey*) escursione *f*, gita; (*fig*) digressione *f*

excursion ticket N biglietto a tariffa turistica

ex·cus·able [ɪksˈkjuːzəbl] ADJ scusabile, perdonabile

ex·cuse [*n* ɪksˈkjuːs, *vb* ɪksˈkjuːz] N scusa; **there's no excuse for this** non ci sono scuse *or* scusanti per questo; **on the excuse that ...** con la scusa *or* il pretesto che...; **to make excuses for sb** trovare giustificazioni per qn ♦ VT 1 (*forgive*) scusare; **excuse me!** (*to attract attention, apologize*) scusi!; (*when you want to get past*) permesso!; **now, if you will excuse me ...** ora mi scusi ma...; **excuse me?** (*USA*) come (dice), scusi? 2 (*justify*) giustificare; **to excuse o.s. (for (doing) sth)** giustificarsi (per (aver fatto) qc) 3 (*exempt*): **to excuse sb (from sth/from doing sth)** esonerare *or* dispensare qn (da qc/dal fare qc); **to excuse o.s. (from sth/from doing sth)** farsi esonerare *or* dispensare (da qc/dal fare qc); **to ask to be excused** chiedere di essere scusato(-a)

ex·ecrable [ˈeksɪkrəbl] ADJ (*frm: gen*) pessimo(-a); (: *manners*) esecrabile

ex·ecute [ˈeksɪkjuːt] VT 1 (*put to death: prisoner*) giustiziare 2 (*carry out: plan, movement*) eseguire; (: *scheme*) attuare; (: *work of art*) realizzare; (*Law: will*) rendere esecutivo(-a)

ex·ecu·tion [ˌeksɪˈkjuːʃən] N (*see vb*) esecuzione *f*; attuazione *f*; realizzazione *f*; **in the execution of one's duty** nell'adempimento del proprio dovere

ex·ecu·tion·er [ˌeksɪˈkjuːʃnəʳ] N boia *m inv*

ex·ecu·tive [ɪgˈzekjʊtɪv] ADJ (*powers, committee*) esecutivo(-a); (*position, job, duties*) direttivo(-a); (*secretary*) di direzione; (*offices, suite*) della direzione; (*car, plane*) dirigenziale ♦ N (*Admin, Industry*) dirigente *m/f*, manager *m/f*; **the executive** (*Pol*) l'esecutivo

executive director N amministratore(-trice)

ex·ecu·tor [ɪgˈzekjʊtəʳ] N (*of will*) esecutore(-trice) testamentario(-a)

ex·em·pla·ry [ɪgˈzemplərɪ] ADJ esemplare

ex·em·pli·fy [ɪgˈzemplɪˌfaɪ] VT (*illustrate*) spiegare con esempi, esemplificare; (*be an example of*) essere un esempio di

ex·empt [ɪgˈzempt] ADJ: **exempt (from)** (*person: from tax*) esentato(-a) (da); (: *from military service etc*) esonerato(-a) (da); (*goods*) esente (da); **tax exempt** esentasse ♦ VT: **to exempt (from)** (*see adj*); esentare (da); esonerare (da)

ex·emp·tion [ɪgˈzempʃən] N (*see adj*) esenzione *f*; esonero

ex·er·cise [ˈeksəˌsaɪz] N (*gen*) esercizio; (*physical activity*) esercizio fisico; (*Mil*) esercitazione *f*; **page 10, exercise 3** pagina 10, esercizio numero 3; **in the exercise of one's duties** nell'esercizio delle proprie funzioni; **to take** *or* **do exercise** fare del movimento *or* moto, fare ginnastica ♦ VT 1 (*use: authority, right, influence*) esercitare; (: *patience, restraint, tact*) usare 2 (*mind, muscle, limb*) tenere in esercizio; (*dog*) fare passeggiare, portar fuori ♦ VI fare del movimento *or* moto

exercise bike, exercise cycle N cyclette *f inv*

exercise book N quaderno

ex·ert [ɪgˈzɜːt] VT (*force*) impiegare; (*influence, authority*) esercitare; **to exert o.s** (*physically*) fare uno sforzo; **don't exert yourself!** (*hum*) non sforzarti troppo!

ex·er·tion [ɪgˈzɜːʃən] N sforzo

ex gra·tia [ˌeksˈgreɪʃə] ADJ: **ex gratia payment** gratifica

ex·hale [eksˈheɪl] VT, VI espirare

ex·haust [ɪgˈzɔːst] N (*also:* **exhaust pipe**) tubo di scappamento ♦ VT (*gen*) esaurire; (*tire out: person*) stremare; **an exhausting journey/day** un viaggio/una giornata estenuante; **to exhaust o.s** sfiancarsi

ex·haust·ed [ɪgˈzɔːstɪd] ADJ (*tired*) esausto(-a), sfinito(-a); (*used up: supplies*) esaurito(-a)

ex·haust·ing [ɪgˈzɔːstɪŋ] ADJ estenuante, sfibrante

ex·haus·tion [ɪgˈzɔːstʃən] N esaurimento; **nervous exhaustion** sovraffaticamento mentale, surmenage *m*

ex·haus·tive [ɪgˈzɔːstɪv] ADJ (*research, inquiry, inspection*) approfondito(-a), minuzioso(-a); (*account, description*) esauriente; (*list*) completo(-a)

ex·hib·it [ɪgˈzɪbɪt] VT (*painting*) esporre; (*signs of emotion*) mostrare; (*courage*) dar prova di; (*skill, ingenuity*) dimostrare ♦ N (*painter*) esporre ♦ N (*object on show*) oggetto esposto; (*Law*) reperto

ex·hi·bi·tion [ˌeksɪˈbɪʃən] N (*act*) esposizione *f*, dimostrazione *f*; (*of rudeness*) dimostrazione; (*a public show*) mostra; **to be on exhibition** essere esposto(-a); **to make an exhibition of o.s** dare spettacolo di sé

ex·hi·bi·tion·ist [ˌɛksɪˈbɪʃənɪst] N esibizionista *m/f*

ex·hibi·tor [ɪgˈzɪbɪtə'] N espositore(-trice)

exhilarating [ɪgˈzɪləreɪtɪŋ] ADJ (*see vb*) tonificante; che rallegra

ex·hila·ra·tion [ɪgˌzɪləˈreɪʃən] N allegria

ex·hort [ɪgˈzɔːt] VT (*frm*): **to exhort sb (to sth/to do sth)** esortare qn (a qc/a fare qc)

ex·ile [ˈɛksaɪl] N (*state*) esilio; (*person*) esule *m/f*; **in(to) exile** in esilio ♦ VT esiliare

ex·ist [ɪgˈzɪst] VI **1** (*live*) vivere; **to exist on sth** vivere di qc **2** (*be in existence*) esistere; (*doubt*) sussistere; (*occur*) trovarsi

ex·ist·ence [ɪgˈzɪstəns] N esistenza; **to be in existence** esistere; **to come into existence** essere creato(-a); **the only one in existence** l'unico esistente

ex·is·ten·tial·ism [ˌɛgzɪsˈtenʃəˌlɪzəm] N esistenzialismo

ex·ist·ing [ɪgˈzɪstɪŋ] ADJ (*law, state of affairs*) attuale

exit [ˈɛksɪt] N uscita; **to make one's exit** uscire ♦ VI (*Theatre, Comput*) uscire

exit poll N exit poll *m inv*

exit ramp N (*USA: Aut*) rampa di uscita

exit visa N visto d'uscita

exo·dus [ˈɛksədəs] N (*gen, also Rel*) esodo

ex of·fi·cio [ˌɛksəˈfɪʃɪəʊ](*frm*) ADV (*act*) d'ufficio ♦ ADJ (*member*) di diritto

ex·on·er·ate [ɪgˈzɒnəˌreɪt] VT (*frm*): **to exonerate sb (from sth)** discolpare qn (da qc)

ex·or·bi·tant [ɪgˈzɔːbɪtənt] ADJ (*price*) esorbitante; (*demands*) spropositato(-a)

ex·or·cise, ex·or·cize [ˈɛksɔːsaɪz] VT esorcizzare

ex·ot·ic [ɪgˈzɒtɪk] ADJ esotico(-a)

ex·pand [ɪksˈpænd] VT (*chest, muscles, economy*) sviluppare; (*market, operations*) espandere; (*statement, notes*) ampliare; (*knowledge*) approfondire; (*horizons*) allargare; (*influence*) estendere; **we want to expand our business** vogliamo espandere l'attività ♦ VI (*see vt*) svilupparsi; espandersi; (*gas*) espandersi; (*metal, lungs*) dilatarsi; **the ceramic industry expanded at the end of the century** l'industria della ceramica si è sviluppata alla fine del secolo; **the economy is expanding** l'economia è in espansione; **to expand on** (*notes, story etc*) ampliare, approfondire; **he didn't expand on his previous remarks** non ha approfondito ciò che aveva detto prima

ex·panse [ɪksˈpæns] N distesa, estensione *f*

ex·pan·sion [ɪksˈpænʃən] N (*gen*) espansione *f*; (*of town, economy, idea*) sviluppo; (*of production*) aumento; (*of knowledge*) approfondimento; (*of influence*) estendersi *m*; (*of gas*) espansione, dilatazione *f*; (*of metal*) dilatazione

ex·pan·sion·ism [ɪksˈpænʃənɪzəm] N espansionismo

ex·pan·sion·ist [ɪksˈpænʃənɪst] ADJ espansionistico(-a)

ex·pat·ri·ate [ɛksˈpætrɪˌeɪt] N espatriato ♦ ADJ espatriato(-a) ♦ VT espatriare

ex·pect [ɪksˈpɛkt] VT **1** (*anticipate*) aspettarsi, prevedere; (*count on*) contare su; (*hope for*) sperare in; (*wait for: letter, guests, baby*) aspettare; **I didn't expect that from him** non me l'aspettavo da lui; **I didn't expect him to agree** non mi aspettavo che fosse d'accordo; **it's easier than I expected** è più facile del previsto; **as expected** come previsto; **to expect to do sth** pensare *or* contare di fare qc; **I expected as much** me l'aspettavo; **that was (only) to be expected** non potevamo che aspettarcelo; **I did not know what to expect** non sapevo che cosa aspettarmi; **we'll expect you for supper** ti aspettiamo per cena; **she's expecting a baby** sta aspettando un bambino; **I'll expect you when I see you** (*fam*) ci vediamo quando ci vediamo **2** (*suppose*) pensare, supporre; **I expect he'll be late** immagino che arriverà tardi; **I expect so** credo di sì, immagino di sì; **yes, I expect it is** sì, non ne dubito **3** (*require*): **to expect sth (from sb)** esigere qc (da qn); **to expect sb to do sth** pretendere *or* esigere che qn faccia qc; **I expect you to be punctual** esigo che tu sia puntuale; **you can't expect too much from him** non puoi pretendere troppo da lui; **what do you expect me to do about it?** cosa vuoi che ci faccia? ♦ VI: **to be expecting** (*a baby*) essere incinta *or* in stato interessante

ex·pec·tan·cy [ɪksˈpɛktənsɪ] N attesa; **life expectancy** speranza (media) di vita

ex·pec·tant [ɪksˈpɛktənt] ADJ (*person, crowd*) in attesa; (*look*) di attesa

ex·pect·ant·ly [ɪksˈpɛktəntlɪ] ADV (*look, listen*) con un'aria d'attesa; **the crowds waited expectantly** c'era un'aria di attesa tra la folla

expectant mother N gestante *f*

ex·pec·ta·tion [ˌɛkspɛkˈteɪʃən] N attesa, aspettativa; **there is little expectation of sunshine today** ci sono poche speranze che venga fuori il sole oggi; **in expectation of** in previsione di; **against** *or* **contrary to all expectation(s)** contro ogni aspettativa; **to come** *or* **live up to sb's expectations** rispondere alle aspettative di qn; **beyond (all) expectation** al di là di ogni aspettativa; **the results exceeded expectations** i risultati furono superiori alle aspettative

ex·pedi·ence [ɪksˈpiːdɪˌəns], **ex·pedi·en·cy** [ɪkˈpiːdɪənsɪ] N (*advisability*) convenienza, opportunità *f inv*; (*pej*) interesse personale; **for the sake of expedience** per una questione di convenienza

ex·pedi·ent [ɪksˈpiːdɪənt] N espediente *m* ♦ ADJ (*convenient, politic*) conveniente, opportuno(-a)

ex·pedite [ˈɛkspɪdaɪt] VT (*frm: speed up*) accelerare; (: *official matter, legal matter*) sollecitare; (: *task*) affrettare

❑ **expedite** is not translated by the Italian word *spedire*

ex·pedi·tion [ˌɛkspɪˈdɪʃən] N spedizione *f*

ex·pedi·tion·ary force [ˌɛkspɪˈdɪʃənərɪˈfɔːs] N (*Mil*) corpo di spedizione

ex·pedi·tious [ˌɛkspɪˈdɪʃəs] ADJ (*frm*) spedito(-a), sollecito(-a)

ex·pel [ɪksˈpɛl] VT espellere; **to get expelled** essere espulso(-a)

ex·pend [ɪksˈpɛnd] VT (*frm: money*) spendere; (: *time, effort, energy*) consacrare; (*use up*) consumare

ex·pend·able [ɪksˈpɛndəbl] ADJ sacrificabile

ex·pendi·ture [ɪksˈpɛndɪtʃə'] N (*of money etc*) spesa; (*of time, effort*) dispendio; **an item of expenditure** una spesa; **expenditure on health** la spesa per la sanità

ex·pense [ɪksˈpɛns] N (*cost*) spesa; **an unnecessary expense** una spesa inutile; **expenses** spese; **can you claim this on expenses?** puoi metterlo tra le spese?; **at the expense of** (*fig*) a spese di; **at the expense of his life** a prezzo della vita; **at great expense** con grande impiego di mezzi; **at their own expense** a proprie spese; **at my expense** a mie spese; (*fig*) alle mie spalle; **to go to the expense (of)** sobbarcarsi la spesa (di); **regardless of expense** senza badare a spese; **to put sb to the expense of** fare affrontare a qn la spesa di; **to meet the expense of** affrontare la spesa di

expense account N conto *m* spese, *inv*

ex·pen·sive [ɪksˈpɛnsɪv] ADJ (*dear*) caro(-a); (*costly*) costoso(-a); (*fig: victory*) a caro prezzo

ex·peri·ence [ɪksˈpɪərɪəns] N (*all senses*) esperienza; **to learn by experience** imparare per esperienza; **I know from bitter experience** ho imparato a mie spese; **he has no experience of grief/being out of work** non sa che cosa voglia dire il dolore/restare senza lavoro; **she has plenty of experience** ha moltissima esperienza; **have you any previous experience?** ha esperienza in questo campo?; **practical/teaching experience** esperienza pratica/d'insegnamento; **to have a pleasant/frightening experience** avere un'esperienza piacevole/terrificante; **it was quite an experience** (*also iro*) è stata una bella esperienza ♦ VT (*feel: emotions, sensations, pleasure*) provare; (*suffer: defeat, losses, hardship etc*) subire; **he experienced fear and pain** ha provato paura e dolore; **they're experiencing some problems** stanno avendo qualche problema; **she experiences some difficulty in walking** ha qualche difficoltà a camminare

ex·peri·enced [ɪksˈpɪərɪənst] ADJ (*teacher, lawyer*) che ha esperienza; (*driver, politician*) consumato(-a); **experienced (in)** esperto(-a) di

ex·peri·ment [*n* ɪksˈpɛrɪmənt, *vb* ɪksˈpɛrɪmɛnt] N esperimento; **to perform** *or* **carry out an experiment** fare un esperimento; **as an experiment** a titolo di esperimento ♦ VI fare un esperimento, sperimentare; **to experiment with a new vaccine** sperimentare un nuovo vaccino

ex·peri·men·tal [ɪksˌperɪˈmentl] ADJ sperimentale; **the process is still at the experimental stage** il procedimento è ancora allo stadio sperimentale

ex·pert [ˈekspɜːt] ADJ (gen) esperto(-a); (advice, help) da esperto; **expert in** or **at doing sth** esperto(-a) nel fare qc ♦ N esperto(-a); **an expert on sth/in** or **at doing sth** un(a) esperto(-a) di qc/nel fare qc

ex·per·tise [ˌekspɜːˈtiːz] N (frm) competenza

ex·pire [ɪksˈpaɪəʳ] VI (document, time limit) scadere; (die) spirare

ex·pi·ry [ɪksˈpaɪərɪ] N scadenza

expiry date N (of medicine, food item) data di scadenza

ex·plain [ɪksˈpleɪn] VT (gen) spiegare; (mystery) chiarire; **to explain o.s.** spiegarsi

▸ **explain away** VT cercare di dare una motivazione a

ex·pla·na·tion [ˌekspləˈneɪʃən] N spiegazione f; **to find an explanation for sth** trovare una spiegazione per qc; **what have you to say in explanation?** qual è la sua giustificazione?

ex·plana·tory [ɪksˈplænətərɪ] ADJ (words) di spiegazione; (notes) esplicativo(-a)

ex·ple·tive [ɪksˈpliːtɪv] N (frm: swear word) imprecazione f

ex·plic·it [ɪksˈplɪsɪt] ADJ (definite) netto(-a); (instructions, intention, denial) esplicito(-a); (details) chiaro(-a)

ex·plode [ɪksˈpləʊd] VI esplodere; **to explode with laughter** scoppiare dalle risa ♦ VT far esplodere; (fig: theory) demolire; **to explode a myth** distruggere un mito; **exploded drawing** disegno esploso

ex·ploit [vb ɪksˈplɔɪt, n ˈeksplɔɪt] VT sfruttare ♦ N impresa

ex·ploi·ta·tion [ˌeksplɔɪˈteɪʃən] N sfruttamento

ex·plo·ra·tion [ˌeksplɔːˈreɪʃən] N esplorazione f

ex·plora·tory [ɪksˈplɒrətərɪ] ADJ (talks) esplorativo(-a); (expedition) d'esplorazione; (step, discussion) preliminare; **exploratory operation** (Med) intervento esplorativo

ex·plore [ɪksˈplɔːʳ] VT (gen, also Med) esplorare; (fig: problems, subject, possibilities) esaminare; **to explore every avenue** sondare tutte le possibilità

ex·plor·er [ɪksˈplɔːrəʳ] N esploratore(-trice)

ex·plo·sion [ɪksˈpləʊʒən] N (also fig) esplosione f

ex·plo·sive [ɪksˈpləʊzɪv] ADJ (also fig) esplosivo(-a) ♦ N esplosivo

ex·po·nent [ɪksˈpəʊnənt] N **1** (person) esponente m/f **2** (Math) esponente m

ex·port [n ˈekspɔːt, vb ɪksˈpɔːt] N esportazione f; (item) merce f d'esportazione ♦ VT esportare ♦ ADJ (goods, permit, duty) d'esportazione

ex·por·ta·tion [ˌekspɔːˈteɪʃən] N esportazione f

ex·port·er [ɪksˈpɔːtəʳ] N esportatore(-trice)

export licence N licenza d'esportazione

ex·pose [ɪksˈpəʊz] VT (gen, also Phot) esporre; (uncover) scoprire; (sexual parts) esibire; (fig: reveal: plot) rivelare; (: criminal) smascherare; (: one's ignorance) mettere a nudo; **they were exposed to high levels of radiation** erano esposti ad alti livelli di radiazioni; **after the scandal was exposed, ...** dopo che emerse lo scandalo,...; **he was exposed as a liar** è risultato essere un bugiardo; **to be exposed to view** offrirsi alla vista; **to expose sb/o.s. to ridicule** esporre qn/esporsi al ridicolo; **to expose o.s.** (indecently) fare l'esibizionista

ex·posed [ɪksˈpəʊzd] ADJ (land, house, town) esposto(-a); (Elec, wire: Mil: terrain, country) scoperto(-a); (pipe, beam) a vista

ex·po·si·tion [ˌekspəˈzɪʃən] N (frm) esposizione f

ex·po·sure [ɪksˈpəʊʒəʳ] N (gen) esposizione f; (of plot) smascheramento; (Phot) esposizione; (photo) posa; (Med) assideramento; **exposure to lead** esposizione al piombo; **exposure on television** pubblicità per televisione; **to die of exposure** morire assiderato(-a); **to threaten sb with exposure** minacciare di denunciare qn

exposure meter N (Phot) esposimetro

ex·pound [ɪksˈpaʊnd] VT (theory, text) spiegare; (one's views) esporre

ex·press [ɪksˈpres] ADJ (all senses) espresso(-a); **express letter** espresso ♦ ADV: **to send sth express** spedire qc per espresso ♦ N (also: **express train**) espresso ♦ VT esprimere; **to express o.s.** esprimersi

ex·pres·sion [ɪksˈpreʃən] N (all senses) espressione f; **set expression** modo di dire

ex·pres·sion·ism [ɪksˈpreʃənɪzəm] N espressionismo

ex·pres·sive [ɪksˈpresɪv] ADJ (look, face, language) espressivo(-a); (gesture) eloquente

ex·press·ly [ɪksˈpreslɪ] ADV espressamente

ex·press·way [ɪksˈpresˌweɪ] N (esp USA) autostrada urbana

ex·pro·pri·ate [eksˈprəʊprɪˌeɪt] VT espropriare

ex·pul·sion [ɪksˈpʌlʃən] N espulsione f

ex·quis·ite [eksˈkwɪzɪt] ADJ (gen) squisito(-a); (manners, sensibility, charm) raffinato(-a); (sense of humour) sottile; (pain) acuto(-a); (joy, pleasure) vivo(-a)

ex-serviceman [ˌeksˈsɜːvɪsmən] N (Brit) ex combattente m

ext. ABBR (Telec: = extension) int. (= interno)

ex·tem·po·rize, ex·tem·po·rise [ɪksˈtempəˌraɪz] VI (frm) improvvisare

ex·tend [ɪksˈtend] VT **1** (frm: stretch out: hand, arm) tendere; (: offer: friendship, help, hospitality) offrire; (: thanks, condolences, welcome) porgere; (: invitation) estendere; (Fin: credit) accordare **2** (prolong: road, line, deadline) prolungare; (: visit) protrarre; (enlarge: building, business, vocabulary) ampliare; (: knowledge, research) approfondire; (: powers) estendere; (: frontiers) allargare; **they decided to extend their visit** hanno deciso di protrarre la visita; **perhaps the deadline could be extended** forse si potrebbe prorogare la scadenza ♦ VI (land, wall): **to extend to** or **as far as** estendersi fino a; **the caves extend for 18 km** le grotte si estendono per 18 chilometri; **to extend to/for** (term, meeting) protrarsi fino a/per; **the contract extends to/for ...** il contratto è valido fino a/per...

ex·ten·sion [ɪksˈtenʃən] N (for table, electric flex) prolunga; (of road, term) prolungamento; (of contract, deadline) proroga; (building) annesso; (telephone: in private house) derivazione f; (in office) interno; **he's been given a six month extension** gli hanno dato una proroga di sei mesi; **to have an extension built onto one's house** far ingrandire la casa; **extension 3718** interno 3718

extension cable, extension lead(Brit), **extension cord** (USA) N (Elec) prolunga

ex·ten·sive [ɪksˈtensɪv] ADJ (grounds, forest, damage) vasto(-a), esteso(-a); (knowledge, research) approfondito(-a); (inquiries, reforms, investments) su vasta scala; (use) largo(-a); (alterations) radicale; **extensive research** ricerche approfondite; **to get extensive coverage** essere trattato ampiamente; **extensive damage** danni ingenti

ex·ten·sive·ly [ɪksˈtensɪvlɪ] ADV (altered, damaged etc) radicalmente; (study, investigate) a fondo; (use, travel) molto; **he's travelled extensively** ha viaggiato molto

ex·tent [ɪksˈtent] N (of land) estensione f; (of road) lunghezza; (of knowledge, activities, power) portata; (degree: of damage, loss) proporzioni fpl; **the extent of the damage is not yet known** non è ancora nota l'entità dei danni; **to what extent** in che misura, fino a che punto; **to some extent** in una certa misura; **to a certain/large extent** in certa/larga misura; **to such an extent that** a tal punto che; **to the extent of** fino al punto di; **to some extent** fino a un certo punto

ex·tenu·at·ing [ɪksˈtenjuˌeɪtɪŋ] ADJ (frm): **extenuating circumstances** (circostanze) attenuanti fpl

ex·te·ri·or [ɪksˈtɪərɪəʳ] ADJ esterno(-a), esteriore ♦ N (of house, box) esterno; (of person) aspetto esteriore; **on the exterior** all'esterno; (fig) in apparenza

ex·ter·mi·nate [ɪksˈtɜːmɪˌneɪt] VT sterminare

ex·ter·mi·na·tion [ɪksˌtɜːmɪˈneɪʃən] N sterminio

ex·ter·nal [eksˈtɜːnl] ADJ (walls etc) esterno(-a); (appearance) esteriore; (Pol) affari mpl esteri; **for external use only** (Med) solo per uso esterno; **external examiner** esaminatore(-trice) esterno(-a); **external processes** (Geol) fenomeni mpl esogeni ♦ N: **the externals** le apparenze

ex·ter·nal·ly [eksˈtɜːnəlɪ] ADV dall'esterno, esternamente

ex·tinct [ɪksˈtɪŋkt] ADJ (volcano) spento(-a), inattivo(-a); (animal, race) estinto(-a); **dinosaurs are extinct** i dinosauri sono estinti; **to become extinct** estinguersi

ex·tinc·tion [ɪksˈtɪŋkʃən] N (of fire) estinzione f, spegnimento; (of race) estinzione f

ex·tin·guish [ɪksˈtɪŋgwɪʃ] VT (frm: fire) estinguere, spegnere; (: cigarette) spegnere; (fig) annientare

ex·tin·guish·er [ɪksˈtɪŋgwɪʃəʳ] N estintore m

ex·tol, ex·toll (USA) [ɪksˈtəʊl] VT (frm: merits, virtues) magnificare; (person) celebrare

ex·tort [ɪksˈtɔːt] VT: **to extort (from)** (money, confession) estorcere a; (promise) strappare a

ex·tor·tion [ɪksˈtɔːʃən] N estorsione f

ex·tor·tion·ate [ɪksˈtɔːʃənɪt] ADJ esorbitante

ex·tra [ˈekstrə] ADJ in più; **an extra blanket** una coperta in' più; **an extra charge** un supplemento; **wine is extra** il vino è escluso; **breakfast is extra** la colazione è a parte; **take extra care!** stai molto attento!; **for extra safety** per maggior sicurezza; **extra transport** corse fpl supplementari or straordinarie; **they won after extra time** hanno vinto dopo i tempi supplementari ♦ ADV (specially) eccezionalmente; (in addition: pay, charge) di più; **extra fine** extra sottile; **extra large** taglie fpl forti; **be extra careful!** stai attentissimo! ♦ N extra m inv; (Cine, Theatre: actor) comparsa

extra– PREF extra–

ex·tract [n ˈekstrækt, vb ɪksˈtrækt] N (from book) brano; (from film) spezzone m; (Culin, Chem) estratto ♦ VT: **to extract (from)** (take out) estrarre (da); (obtain: promise, confession, money) estorcere a, strappare a; (select: from book etc) stralciare (da)

ex·trac·tion [ɪksˈtrækʃən] N estrazione f; (descent) origine f; **of German extraction** di origine tedesca

ex·trac·tor fan [ɪkˈstræktəˌfæn] N aspiratore m

extra·cur·ricu·lar [ˈekstrəkəˈrɪkjʊləʳ] ADJ (Scol) parascolastico

extra·dite [ˈekstrədaɪt] VT: **to extradite sb (from/to)** estradare qn (da/in)

extra·di·tion [ˌekstrəˈdɪʃən] N estradizione f

extra·mari·tal [ˈekstrəˈmærɪtl] ADJ extraconiugale

extra·mu·ral [ˈekstrəˈmjʊərəl] ADJ (Univ): **extramural course** corso libero tenuto da docenti accreditati presso l'università

extra·neous [ɪksˈtreɪnɪəs] ADJ (frm): **extraneous (to)** estraneo(-a) (a)

extraor·di·nary [ɪksˈtrɔːdnrɪ] ADJ (gen) straordinario(-a); (very strange) strano(-a); **the extraordinary thing is that ...** la cosa strana è che...

extraordinary general meeting N assemblea generale straordinaria

ex·trapo·la·tion [ˌɪkstræpəʊˈleɪʃən] N estrapolazione f

extra·sen·so·ry per·cep·tion [ˈekstrəˈsensərɪ pəsepʃən] N percezione f extrasensoriale

extra time N (Ftbl) tempo supplementare

ex·trava·gance [ɪksˈtrævəgəns] N (excessive spending) sperpero; (wastefulness) spreco; (thing bought) stravaganza

ex·trava·gant [ɪksˈtrævəgənt] ADJ stravagante; (spending, claim, opinion) eccessivo(-a); (lavish: person) prodigo(-a); (: tastes) dispendioso(-a); (exaggerated: praise) esagerato(-a); (: prices) esorbitante

ex·treme [ɪksˈtriːm] ADJ estremo(-a); (sorrow, anger) profondo(-a); **the extreme left/right** (Pol) l'estrema sinistra/destra; **the extreme end of sth** l'estremità di qc; **there's no need to be so extreme** non c'è bisogno di essere così drastico ♦ N estremo; **extremes of temperature** gli estremi mpl della scala termica; **dangerous in the extreme** estremamente pericoloso(-a); **to go/be driven to extremes** arrivare/essere spinto(-a) agli estremi

ex·treme·ly [ɪksˈtriːmlɪ] ADV estremamente

ex·trem·ist [ɪksˈtriːmɪst] ADJ,N estremista m/f

ex·trem·ity [ɪksˈtremɪtɪ] N (gen) estremità f inv; (fig: of despair etc) culmine

ex·tri·cate [ˈekstrɪˌkeɪt] VT (object) liberare; **to extricate sth (from)** districare qc (da); **to extricate sb/o.s. from a difficult situation** togliere qn/togliersi d'impaccio

extro·vert [ˈekstrəʊvɜːt] N estroverso(-a)

exu·ber·ance [ɪgˈzuːbərəns] N esuberanza

exu·ber·ant [ɪgˈzuːbərənt] ADJ esuberante

ex·ude [ɪgˈzjuːd] VT,VI trasudare, stillare; (fig) emanare

ex·ult [ɪgˈzʌlt] VI (frm): **to exult in** or **over** or **at** esultare per

ex·ult·ant [ɪgˈzʌltənt] ADJ (frm: person, smile) esultante; (: shout, expression) di giubilo

ex·ul·ta·tion [ˌegzʌlˈteɪʃən] N giubilo; **in exultation** per la gioia

eye [aɪ] N occhio; (of needle) cruna; (for hook) occhiello; **I've got green eyes** ho gli occhi verdi; **he gave me a black eye** gli ha fatto un occhio nero; **eyes right/left!** (Mil) attenti a destra/sinistra!; **as far as the eye can see** a perdita d'occhio; **it happened before my very eyes** mi è successo proprio sotto gli occhi; **I saw it with my own eyes** l'ho visto con i miei occhi; **keep your eyes on the road ahead!** guarda la strada!; **I could hardly keep my eyes open** non riuscivo a tenere gli occhi aperti; **to catch sb's eye** attirare l'attenzione di qn; **to look sb (straight) in the eye** guardare qn (dritto) negli occhi; **to be in the public eye** essere in vista; **in the eyes of** agli occhi di; **under the (watchful) eye of** sotto lo sguardo (vigile) di; **to keep an eye on sb/sth** tenere d'occhio qn/qc; **to keep an eye on things** (fam) tenere d'occhio la situazione; **to keep an eye out for sth/sb, one's eyes open for sth/sb** tenere gli occhi aperti per trovare qc/qn; **to look at sth with the eye of an expert** guardare qc con l'occhio dell'esperto; **with an eye to sth** in vista di qc; **with an eye to doing sth** (Brit) con l'idea di fare qc; **with one's eyes (wide) open** (fig) perfettamente conscio(-a) di ciò che si fa; **to shut one's eyes to sth** (fig: to the truth, dangers, evidence) chiudere gli occhi di fronte a qc; (: to sb's shortcomings) chiudere un occhio su qc; **to have an eye for sth** avere occhio per qc; **there's more to this than meets the eye** non è così semplice come sembra; **I don't see eye to eye with him** non condivido il suo punto di vista; **it's five years since I last set** or **laid eyes on him** sono cinque anni che non lo vedo; **use your eyes!** (fam) guarda un po' meglio!; **to cry one's eyes out** piangere a calde lacrime; **to make eyes at sb** (fam) fare gli occhi dolci a qn; **an eye for an eye and a tooth for a tooth** occhio per occhio dente per dente ♦ VT (look at carefully) scrutare; (ogle) adocchiare; **the children eyed the parcel with interest** i bambini scrutavano il pacco con interesse

  ▸ **eye up** VT + ADV (fam) occhieggiare; **he's been eyeing me up all evening** non mi ha staccato gli occhi di dosso per tutta la sera

eye·ball [ˈaɪbɔːl] N bulbo oculare; **eyeball to eyeball** (fig) faccia a faccia

eye·bath [ˈaɪbɑːθ], (USA) **eye cup** N occhino

eye·brow [ˈaɪbraʊ] N sopracciglio; **to raise one's eyebrows** inarcare le sopracciglia

eyebrow pencil N matita per le sopracciglia

eye-catching [ˈaɪˌkætʃɪŋ] ADJ che attira l'attenzione

eye cup N = eyebath

eye·drops [ˈaɪˌdrɒps] N collirio

eye·ful [ˈaɪfʊl] N (fam): **to get an eyeful (of)** avere l'occasione di dare una bella sbirciata

eye·glass [ˈaɪglɑːs] N monocolo; **eyeglasses** NPL occhiali mpl

eye·lash [ˈaɪlæʃ] N ciglio

eye·let [ˈaɪlɪt] N occhiello

eye·lev·el [ˈaɪlevl] ADJ all'altezza degli occhi

eye·lid [ˈaɪlɪd] N palpebra

eye·liner [ˈaɪlaɪnəʳ] N eye-liner m inv

eye-opener [ˈaɪˌəʊpnəʳ] N rivelazione f

eye·shadow [ˈaɪˌʃædəʊ] N ombretto

eye·sight [ˈaɪsaɪt] N vista

eye·sore [ˈaɪsɔːʳ] N pugno in un occhio

eye·strain [ˈaɪstreɪn] N: **to get eyestrain** stancarsi gli occhi

eye-tooth [ˈaɪtuːθ] N (pl -teeth) canino superiore; **to give one's eye-teeth for sth/to do sth** (fam, fig) dare non so che cosa per qc/per fare qc

eye·wash [ˈaɪwɒʃ] N (liquid) collirio; (fam: nonsense) balle fpl

eye·witness [ˈaɪwɪtnɪs] N testimone m/f oculare

ey·rie [ˈɪərɪ] N nido d'aquila

Ff

F¹, f¹ [ɛf] N 1 (*letter*) F, f *f inv*, *m inv*; **F for Frederick**, (*USA*) **F for fox** ≈ F come Firenze 2 (*Mus*): **F** fa *m inv*

F² ABBR (= *Fahrenheit*) F

FA [ɛf'eɪ] N ABBR (*Brit*: = **Football Association**)

fa·ble ['feɪbl] N favola

fab·ric ['fæbrɪk] N 1 (*cloth*) stoffa, tessuto 2 (*Archit*) struttura; **the fabric of society** (*fig*) la struttura della società
❏ **fabric** is not translated by the Italian word *fabbrica*

fab·ri·cate ['fæbrɪkeɪt] VT fabbricare

fab·ri·ca·tion [ˌfæbrɪ'keɪʃən] N fabbricazione *f*

fabric ribbon N (*Typ*) nastro dattilografico

fabu·lous ['fæbjʊləs] ADJ (*mythical*) favoloso(-a); (*fam: wonderful*) meraviglioso(-a), fantastico(-a)

fa·çade, fa·cade [fə'sɑːd] N (*Archit*) facciata; (*fig*) facciata, apparenza

face [feɪs] N (*gen*) faccia; (*Anat*) faccia, volto, viso; (*expression*) faccia, espressione *f*; (*grimace*) smorfia; (*of dial, watch, clock*) quadrante *m*; (*surface: of the Earth*) faccia, faccia; (*of building*) facciata; (*of mountain, cliff*) parete *f*; **face down(wards)** (*person*) a faccia in giù, bocconi; (*object*) a faccia in giù; (*card*) coperto(-a); **face up(wards)** (*person, object*) a faccia in su; (*card*) scoperto(-a); **the north face of the mountain** la parete nord della montagna; **in the face of** (*difficulties etc*) di fronte a; **to laugh in sb's face** ridere in faccia a qn; **to look sb in the face** guardare qn in faccia; **to say sth to sb's face** dire qc in faccia a qn; **I told him to his face** gliel'ho detto in faccia; **you can shout till you're black or blue in the face ...** puoi urlare fino a sgolarti...; **he was red in the face** era rosso in faccia; **don't show your face here again!** non farti più vedere qui!; **it's vanished off the face of the Earth** è sparito(-a) dalla faccia della terra; **to have a good memory for faces** essere un(a) buon, (a) fisionomista; **to pull a long face** fare la faccia lunga, fare il muso; **to keep a straight face** rimanere serio(-a); **to pull a face** fare una smorfia; **to make *or* pull faces (at sb)** fare le boccacce (a qn); **his face fell** (*fig*) ha fatto una faccia!; **on the face of it** a prima vista; **they put a brave face on it** hanno fatto buon viso a cattivo gioco; **to lose/save face** perdere/salvare la faccia; **to take sth at face value** giudicare qc dalle apparenze ♦ VT 1 (*be facing, be opposite*) essere di fronte a; (*overlook: road*) dare su; (*: sea*) guardare verso; **face the wall!** girati verso il muro!; **to sit facing the engine** (*on train*) sedersi nella direzione della marcia; **the picture facing page 20** la figura a fianco di pagina 20; **they faced each other** erano uno di fronte all'altro; **the difficulties facing us** i problemi che ci aspettano 2 (*confront: attacker, danger*) affrontare, fronteggiare; **I can't face him** (*ashamed*) non ho il coraggio di guardarlo in faccia; (*reluctant*) non ho nessuna voglia di vederlo; **I can't face doing it** non ho nessuna voglia di farlo; **to face the music** (*fig*) far fronte alla tempesta; **to face the facts** affrontare la realtà; **to face the fact that ...** riconoscere *or* ammettere che...; **we are faced with serious problems** ci troviamo di fronte a gravi problemi; **let's face it!** (*fam*) diciamocelo chiaramente; **it has no basis in fact** non si basa su fatti realmente accaduti; **as a matter of fact, in point of fact** per la verità; **the fact (of the matter) is that ...** la verità è che...; **in fact** realtà, in effetti 3 (*Tech*) rivestire, ricoprire; **a wall faced with concrete** un muro rivestito di cemento ♦ VI (*person*): **to face this way** girarsi da questa parte; **it faces east/towards the east** è esposto(-a) a/guarda verso est
▸ **face down** VT + ADV (*USA fig*): **to face sb down** sfidare qn
▸ **face up to** VI + ADV + PREP (*difficulty etc*) affrontare, far fronte a; **to face up to the fact that ...** accettare che...; **he refuses to face up to his responsibilities** rifiuta di accettare le proprie responsabilità

face cloth N (*Brit*) ≈ guanto di spugna

face cream N crema per il viso

face·less ['feɪslɪs] ADJ anonimo(-a)

face lift N lifting *m inv*; (*of façade, building*) ripulita, restauro

face pack N maschera di bellezza

face powder N cipria

face-saving ['feɪsˌseɪvɪŋ] ADJ che salva la faccia

fac·et ['fæsɪt] N (*of gem*) sfaccettatura, faccetta; (*fig*) sfaccettatura, aspetto, lato

fa·cetious [fə'siːʃəs] ADJ faceto(-a); **don't be facetious** non fare lo spiritoso

face-to-face [ˌfeɪstə'feɪs] ADV, ADJ faccia a faccia, a quattr'occhi

face value N (*of coin*) valore *m* facciale *or* nominale; **to take sth at face value** (*fig*) giudicare qc dalle apparenze

fa·cia ['feɪʃə] N = **fascia**

fa·cial ['feɪʃəl] ADJ del viso, facciale ♦ N trattamento di bellezza per il viso

fac·ile ['fæsaɪl] ADJ (*gen: pej: remark, answer*) superficiale; (*: victory*) facile

fa·cili·tate [fə'sɪlɪteɪt] VT facilitare, agevolare

fa·cil·ity [fə'sɪlɪtɪ] N 1 (*easiness*) facilità; (*skill*) abilità; (*with languages*) predisposizione *f* 2 **facilities** NPL (*gen*) servizi *mpl*; (*educational, leisure*) attrezzature *fpl*; (*transport*) mezzi *mpl*; **credit facilities** facilitazioni *fpl* di credito

fac·ing ['feɪsɪŋ] N (*Constr: of wall etc*) rivestimento; (*Sewing*) passafino

fac·simi·le [fæk'sɪmɪlɪ] N facsimile *m inv*

facsimile machine N facsimile *m inv*, telecopiatrice *f*

fact [fækt] N fatto; **it's a fact that ...** è un dato di fatto che...; **to know for a fact that ...** sapere per certo che...; **the facts of life** (*sex*) i fatti riguardanti la vita sessuale; (*realities*) le realtà della vita; **facts and figures** fatti *mpl* e cifre, *fpl*; **fact and fiction** realtà e fantasia; **story founded on fact** storia basata sui fatti; **it has no basis in fact** non si basa su fatti realmente accaduti; **as a matter of fact, in point of fact** per la verità; **the fact (of the matter) is that ...** la verità è che...; **in fact** realtà, in effetti

fact-finding ['fæktˌfaɪndɪŋ] ADJ: **a fact-finding tour/mission** un viaggio/una missione d'inchiesta

fac·tion ['fækʃən] N fazione *f*

fac·tion·al ['fækʃənəl] ADJ (*fighting*) tra fazioni

fac·tor ['fæktə'] N 1 (*fact*) fattore *m*, elemento; **the human factor** il fattore umano; **safety factor** coefficiente *m* di sicurezza 2 (*Math*) fattore *m* 3 (*Comm: company*) società *f inv* di factoring; (*: agent*) factor *m inv* ♦ VI (*Comm*) esercitare il factoring

fac·to·ry ['fæktərɪ] N fabbrica, stabilimento; **a car factory** una fabbrica di automobili ♦ ADJ (*inspector, work*) di fabbrica
❏ **factory** is not translated by the Italian word *fattoria*

factory farming N (*Brit*) allevamento su scala industriale

factory floor N: **the factory floor** (*workers*) gli operai; (*area*) il reparto produzione; **on the factory floor** nel reparto produzione

factory ship N nave *f* fattoria, *inv*

fac·tual ['fæktjʊəl] ADJ (*report, description*) che si limita ai fatti; (*error*) che riguarda i fatti

fac·ul·ty ['fækəltɪ] N facoltà *f inv*; (*USA: teaching staff*) corpo insegnante; **faculty of Engineering** facoltà di ingegneria

fad [fæd] N (*fashion*) moda, mania; (*personal*) capriccio, mania, fisima

fade [feɪd] VI 1 (*flower*) appassire; (*colour, fabric*) scolorire *or* scolorirsi, sbiadire *or* sbiadirsi; **my jeans have faded** i miei jeans si sono scoloriti 2 (*also: fade away*) (*light*) affievolirsi, attenuarsi; (*eyesight, hearing, memory*) indebolirsi; (*hopes, smile*) svanire; (*sounds*) affievolirsi, attutirsi; (*person*) deperire; (*object*): **to fade from sight** scomparire alla vista; **hopes of a peaceful solution are fading** sta svanendo ogni speranza di trovare una soluzione

▸ **fade in** VT + ADV (*TV, Cine*) aprire in dissolvenza; (*Radio: sound*) aumentare gradualmente d'intensità ♦ VI + ADV (*TV, Cine*) aprirsi in dissolvenza; (*Radio*) aumentare gradualmente d'intensità

▸ **fade out** VT + ADV (*TV, Cine*) chiudere in dissolvenza; (*Radio*) diminuire gradualmente l'intensità di ♦ VI + ADV (*TV, Cine*) chiudere in dissolvenza; (*Radio*) diminuire gradualmente d'intensità

fae·ces, fe·ces (*USA*) ['fiːsiːz] NPL feci *fpl*

Fahr·en·heit ['færənhaɪt] ADJ Fahrenheit *inv*; **Fahrenheit scale** scala Fahrenheit

fail [feɪl] VI **1** (*gen*) fallire; (*in exam: candidate*) essere respinto(-a) *or* bocciato(-a); (*show, play*) essere un fiasco; **to fail in one's duty** mancare al proprio dovere; **to fail to do sth** non riuscire a fare qc; **they failed to reach the quarter-finals** non sono riusciti a raggiungere i quarti di finale; **a quarter of the students failed** un quarto degli studenti sono stati bocciati **2** (*power, light, supplies*) mancare; (*crops*) andare perduto(-a); (*sight: light*) indebolirsi; (*strength, health*) venire a mancare; (*plan*) fallire; (*engine*) fermarsi; (*brakes*) non funzionare; **the truck's brakes failed** i freni del camion non hanno funzionato; **the plan failed** il piano è fallito ♦ VT **1** (*exam, subject*) non superare, essere bocciato(-a) in; (*candidate*) respingere, bocciare, rimandare; **he failed his driving test** non ha superato l'esame di guida **2** (*subj: person, memory, nerve*) abbandonare, mancare a; **don't fail me!** non deludermi!; **his courage failed him** gli è mancato il coraggio; **words fail me!** mi mancano le parole! **3 to fail to do sth** (*neglect*) non fare qc, mancare di fare qc; (*be unable*) non riuscire a fare qc; **I fail to see why/what** etc non vedo perché/ che cosa *etc* ♦ N: **without fail** senza fallo, senz'altro; **D is a pass, E is a fail** con D si passa, con E si viene bocciati

fail·ing ['feɪlɪŋ] PREP in mancanza di; **failing that** se questo non è possibile ♦ N difetto

fail·safe ['feɪl,seɪf] ADJ (*device etc*) di sicurezza

fail·ure ['feɪljə'] N (*gen*) fallimento; (*in exam*) bocciatura; (*of crops*) perdita; (*breakdown*) guasto; (*person*) fallito(-a); (*omission*): **his failure to come/answer** il fatto che non sia venuto/abbia risposto; **to end in failure** fallire; **I feel a failure** mi sento un fallito; **failure rate** (*gen*) numero di insuccessi; (*Scol*) numero di respinti; **heart failure** insufficienza cardiaca

faint [feɪnt] ADJ (*comp* -er, *superl* -est) (*smell, breeze, trace*) leggero(-a); (*outline, mark*) indistinto(-a); (*sound, voice*) fievole, debole; (*hope*) debole; (*idea, recollection, resemblance*) vago(-a); **to feel faint** sentirsi svenire; **I haven't the faintest (idea)** (*fam*) non ne ho la più pallida idea; **faint with hunger** debole per la fame; **his voice was very faint** la sua voce era molto debole ♦ N svenimento ♦ VI: **to faint (from)** svenire (da)

faint-hearted [feɪnt'hɑːtɪd] ADJ pusillanime ♦ NPL: **the faint-hearted** tipi impressionabili

faint·ly [feɪntlɪ] ADV (*call, say, shine, smile*) debolmente; (*write, mark*) leggermente; **faintly reminiscent of** che ricorda vagamente

faint·ness ['feɪntnɪs] N (*of voice, sound etc*) debolezza

fair¹ [feə'] ADJ (*comp* -er, *superl* -est) **1** (*person, decision etc*) giusto(-a), equo(-a); (*hearing*) imparziale; (*sample*) rappresentativo(-a); (*fight, competition, match*) leale; **it's/that's not fair!** non è giusto!; **to be fair (to her)** ... per essere giusti (nei suoi confronti)...; **it's only fair that ...** è più che giusto che...; **it's fair to say that ...** bisogna riconoscere che...; **fair enough!** d'accordo!, va bene!; **by fair means** *or* **foul** con ogni mezzo; **his fair share of** la sua buona parte di **2** (*reasonable, average: work, result*) discreto(-a); **he has a fair chance** *or* **hope of success** ha buone probabilità di riuscire; **I have a fair chance of winning** ho discrete probabilità di vincere **3** (*quite large: sum*) discreto(-a), bello(-a), considerevole; (: *speed, pace*) buono(-a); **a fair amount of** un bel po' di; **that's a fair distance** è una bella distanza **4** (*light-coloured: hair, person*) biondo(-a); (: *complexion, skin*) chiaro(-a) **5** (*fine: weather*) bello(-a) ♦ ADV: **to play fair** giocare correttamente; **to act/win fair and square** agire/vincere onestamente

fair² [feə'] N (*market*) fiera, mercato; (*trade fair*) fiera campionaria; (*Brit: funfair*) luna park *m inv*, parco dei divertimenti

fair copy N bella copia

fair game N: **to be fair game** (*person*) essere bersaglio legittimo

fair·ground ['feə,graʊnd] N luna park *m inv*

fair-haired [feə'heəd] ADJ (*person*) biondo(-a)

fair·ly ['feəlɪ] ADV **1** (*justly*) in modo imparziale *or* equo, equamente; (*according to the rules*) lealmente, correttamente; **the money was divided fairly** il denaro è stato diviso equamente **2** (*quite*) abbastanza, piuttosto; **I'm fairly sure** sono abbastanza sicuro; **fairly good** discreto(-a); **my car is fairly new** la mia macchina è abbastanza nuova **3** (*fam: utterly*) completamente

fair·ness ['feənɪs] N **1** onestà, equità, giustizia; (*of decision*) imparzialità; **in all fairness** per essere giusti, a dire il vero; **in (all) fairness to him** per essere giusti nei suoi confronti **2** (*of hair, skin*) chiarezza

fair play N correttezza

fair trade N commercio equo e solidale ♦ ADJ (*product*) del commercio equo e solidale

fair·way [feə,weɪ] N: **the fairway** (*Golf*) il fairway *m inv*

fairy ['feərɪ] N **1** fata; **fairy queen** regina delle fate **2** (*offensive: gay man*) finocchio (*fam!*)

fairy godmother N fata buona

fairy tale N fiaba; (*lie*) frottola

faith [feɪθ] N **1** (*trust*) fiducia; **to have faith in sb/sth** avere fiducia in qn/qc; **to put one's faith in sb/sth** fidarsi di qn/qc; **to keep/break faith with sb** mantenere la parola/mancare di parola con qn; **to lose faith in sb/sth** perdere fiducia in qn/qc; **people have lost faith in the government** la gente ha perso fiducia nel governo; **in (all) good faith** in buona fede; **in bad faith** in malafede **2** (*Rel: belief*) fede *f*, religione *f*; **Faith, Hope and Charity** Fede, Speranza e Carità

faith·ful ['feɪθfʊl] ADJ: **faithful (to)** fedele (a) ♦ NPL: **the faithful** (*Rel*) i fedeli

faith·ful·ly ['feɪθfəlɪ] ADV fedelmente; **he promised faithfully to come** ci ha dato la sua parola che sarebbe venuto; **yours faithfully** (*Brit: in letters*) distinti saluti

faith healer N guaritore(-trice)

fake [feɪk] N (*picture*) falso; (*thing*) imitazione *f*; (*person*) impostore(-a); **his illness is a fake** fa finta di essere malato; **the painting was a fake** il quadro era un falso ♦ ADJ falso(-a), fasullo(-a); **a fake banknote** una banconota falsa; **a fake fur coat** una pelliccia sintetica ♦ VT (*accounts*) falsificare; (*illness, feelings*) fingere; (*painting*) contraffare ♦ VI fingere

fal·con ['fɔːlkən] N falco, falcone *m*

Falk·land Is·lands ['fɔːlklənd,aɪləndz], **Falk·lands** ['fɔːlkləndz] NPL: **the Falkland Islands** *or* **Falklands** le isole *fpl* Falkland, le isole Malvine

fall [fɔːl] (*pt* **fell**, *pp* **fallen**) N **1** (*gen*) caduta; (*decrease*) diminuzione *f*, calo; (*in prices*) ribasso; (*in temperature*) abbassamento; **he had a bad fall** ha fatto una brutta caduta; **a fall of earth** uno smottamento; **a fall of snow** (*Brit*) una nevicata; **a heavy/light fall of rain** una pioggia forte/leggera **2** (*USA: autumn*) autunno; **in the fall** in autunno; *see also* **falls** ♦ VI **1** (*gen*) cadere; (*building*) crollare; (*decrease: temperature, price*) abbassarsi, diminuire; **he tripped and fell** è inciampato e caduto; **she's fallen** è caduta; **prices are falling** i prezzi stanno calando; **night is falling** scende la notte; **darkness is falling** si fa buio; **to fall to** *or* **on one's knees** cadere in ginocchio; **to fall on one's feet** cadere in piedi; **to let sth fall** lasciar cadere qc; **to let fall that ...** lasciar capire che...; **to fall into bad habits** *or* **bad ways** prendere delle cattive abitudini; **to fall into conversation with sb** mettersi a parlare con qn; **his poems fall into three categories** le sue poesie si dividono in tre categorie; **to fall from grace** (*Rel*) perdere la grazia di Dio; (*fig*) cadere in disgrazia; **he fell in my estimation** ha perso ai miei occhi; **it all began to fall into place** (*fig*) ha cominciato a prendere forma; **the responsibility falls on you** la responsabilità ricade su di te; **my birthday falls on a Saturday** il mio compleanno cade di sabato; **it falls to me to say ...** (*frm*) tocca a me *or* è mio compito dire...; **to fall short of** (*sb's expectations*) non corrispondere a; (*perfection*) non raggiungere; **the dart fell short of the board** la freccetta è caduta poco prima del bersaglio; **to fall flat** (*on one's face*) cadere bocconi; (*subj: joke, party*) essere un fiasco; (: *plan*) fallire, fare cilecca; **to fall foul of** scontrarsi con **2** (*become*): **to fall asleep** addormentarsi; **to fall into**

arrears accumulare degli arretrati; **to fall due** scadere; **to fall ill** ammalarsi; **to fall in love (with sb/sth)** innamorarsi (di qn/qc); **to fall silent** farsi silenzioso(-a)

▸ **fall about** VI + ADV (*fig: fam*) torcersi dalle risa
▸ **fall apart** VI + ADV cadere a pezzi; (*fig*) crollare
▸ **fall away** VI + ADV (*slope steeply: ground*) scendere; (*crumble: plaster*) scrostarsi, sgretolarsi; (*fig: diminish*) diminuire
▸ **fall back** VI + ADV (*retreat*) indietreggiare; (*Mil*) ritirarsi
▸ **fall back on** VI + ADV + PREP (*also fig*): **to have sth to fall back on** avere qc di riserva
▸ **fall behind** VI + ADV (*in race etc*) rimanere indietro; (*fig: with payments*) essere in arretrato; (: *with work*) essere indietro
▸ **fall down** VI + ADV (*person*) cadere; (*building, hopes*) crollare; **but it falls down in one aspect** (*fig*) ma ha un punto debole; **to fall down on the job** (*fig*) non essere all'altezza del lavoro
▸ **fall for** VI + PREP 1 (*fam: person*) prendere una cotta per, innamorarsi di 2 (*fam: be deceived by*): **to fall for a trick** (*or a story etc*) cascarci; **they fell for it!** ci sono cascati!
▸ **fall in** VI + ADV 1 (*person*) cadere dentro; (*roof, walls*) crollare 2 (*Mil*) mettersi in riga, allinearsi ♦ VI + PREP: **to fall in(to)** cadere in
▸ **fall in with** VI + ADV + PREP: **to fall in with sb** (*meet*) trovare qn; **to fall in with sb's plans** (*person*) trovarsi d'accordo con i progetti di qn; (*event*) coincidere con i progetti di qn
▸ **fall off** VI + ADV (*person, leaf*) cadere; (*part*) staccarsi; (*diminish: demand, numbers, interest*) diminuire, abbassarsi; (: *quality*) scadere; **the exhaust fell off** è caduto il tubo di scarico; **unemployment has fallen off** la disoccupazione è diminuita ♦ VI + PREP cadere da
▸ **fall on, fall upon** VI + PREP (*attack*) scagliarsi su; (*responsibility*) ricadere su
▸ **fall out** VI + ADV 1 (*person, object*): **to fall out (of)** cadere (da) 2 (*Mil*) rompere le righe 3 (*fig: quarrel*): **to fall out (with sb over sth)** litigare (con qn per qc) 4 (*happen*): **it fell out that ...** è andata a finire che...
▸ **fall over** VI + ADV cadere ♦ VI + PREP: **he fell over the table** è inciampato nel tavolino ed è caduto; **he was falling over himself** *or* **over backwards to be polite** (*fam*) si faceva in quattro per essere gentile; **they were falling over each other to get it** (*fam*) si accapigliavano per averlo
▸ **fall through** VI + ADV (*plan, project*) fallire
▸ **fall upon** VI + PREP = **fall on**

fal·la·cy [ˈfæləsɪ] N errore m
fall·back [ˈfɔːlˌbæk] ADJ: **fallback position** posizione *f* di ripiego
fall·en [ˈfɔːlən] PP *of* **fall** ♦ ADJ caduto(-a); (*morally*) perduto(-a) ♦ NPL: **the fallen** (*Mil*) i caduti
fal·li·ble [ˈfæləbl] ADJ (*frm*) fallibile
fall·ing [ˈfɔːlɪŋ] ADJ: **falling market** (*Fin*) mercato in ribasso
falling-off [ˈfɔːlɪŋˈɒf] N calo
Fal·lo·pian tube [fəˌləʊpiənˈtjuːb] N (*Anat*) tuba di Fallopio
fall·out [ˈfɔːlˌaʊt] N pioggia radioattiva; (*fig: repercussions*) ripercussione *f*; **fallout shelter** rifugio antiatomico
fal·low [ˈfæləʊ] ADJ incolto(-a), a maggese; **to lie fallow** rimanere a maggese
falls [fɔːlz] NPL (*waterfall*) cascate *fpl*; **the Niagara Falls** le cascate del Niagara
false [fɔːls] ADJ (*gen*) falso(-a); **false ceiling** controsoffitto; **a false step** un passo falso; **under false pretences** con l'inganno; **with a false bottom** con doppio fondo
false alarm N falso allarme *m*
false·hood [ˈfɔːlshʊd] N (*frm: lie*) menzogna; **truth and falsehood** il vero e il falso
false·ly [ˈfɔːlslɪ] ADV (*accuse*) a torto; (*state*) falsamente
false teeth NPL (*Brit*) denti *mpl* finti, dentiera
fal·si·fy [ˈfɔːlsɪˌfaɪ] VT falsificare; (*figures*) alterare
fal·ter [ˈfɔːltəʳ] VI (*voice, speaker*) esitare; (*interest*) scemare; (*engine*) perder colpi; **his voice faltered with emotion** la sua voce era rotta dall'emozione; **his steps faltered** ha vacillato
fame [feɪm] N fama, celebrità; **his fame as a musician** la sua fama di musicista
fa·mil·iar [fəˈmɪljəʳ] ADJ 1 (*well-known: face, person, place*) conosciuto(-a), familiare; (*common: experience, complaint,*

event) comune; **her face looks familiar** la sua faccia non mi è nuova; **the name sounded familiar to me** il nome mi suonava familiare; **to be on familiar ground** (*fig*) trovarsi sul proprio terreno 2 (*well-acquainted*): **to be familiar (with sb/sth)** conoscere bene (qn/qc); **I'm familiar with his work** conosco bene i suoi lavori; **to make o.s. familiar with** familiarizzarsi con, acquistare dimestichezza con 3 (*language*) familiare; (*intimate: tone of voice*) di eccessiva confidenza; **to be on familiar terms with** essere in confidenza con; **to get too familiar with sb** (*pej*) prendersi troppa confidenza con qn
fa·mili·ar·ity [fəˌmɪlɪˈærɪtɪ] N (*knowledge*): **familiarity (with)** conoscenza (di), dimestichezza (con); (*of tone etc*) confidenza, familiarità, intimità; **familiarity breeds contempt** dar troppa confidenza fa perdere il rispetto
fa·mil·iar·ize [fəˈmɪlɪəˌraɪz] VT: **to familiarize o.s. with** familiarizzarsi con; **to familiarize sb with sth** far conoscere qc a qn
fami·ly [ˈfæmɪlɪ] N (*gen*) famiglia; **the Cooke family** la famiglia Cooke; **it runs in the family** è di famiglia ♦ ADJ (*jewels, life, business*) di famiglia, familiare
family business N impresa familiare
family doctor N (*Brit*) medico di famiglia
family life N vita familiare
family man N uomo amante della famiglia, padre *m* di famiglia
family planning N pianificazione *f* familiare
family planning clinic N consultorio familiare
family tree N albero genealogico
fam·ine [ˈfæmɪn] N carestia
fam·ished [ˈfæmɪʃt] ADJ affamato(-a); **I'm famished!** (*fam*) ho una fame da lupi!
fa·mous [ˈfeɪməs] ADJ famoso(-a), celebre; **famous last words!** (*fam, hum*) le ultime parole famose!
fa·mous·ly [ˈfeɪməslɪ] ADV (*get on*) a meraviglia
fan [fæn] N ventaglio; (*machine*) ventilatore *m*; **a silk fan** un ventaglio di seta ♦ VT (*face, person*) fare aria a, fare vento a; (*fire*) alimentare; **to fan the flames** (*fig*) soffiare sul fuoco
▸ **fan out** VI + ADV spargersi (a ventaglio)
fa·nat·ic [fəˈnætɪk] ADJ, N fanatico(-a)
fa·nati·cal [fəˈnætɪkəl] ADJ fanatico(-a)
fan belt N (*Aut*) cinghia della ventola
fan·cied [ˈfænsɪd] ADJ 1 (*imaginary*) immaginario(-a) 2 (*horse, candidate*) favorito(-a)
fan·ci·ful [ˈfænsɪfʊl] ADJ (*explanation*) fantastico(-a); (*person, idea, drawing*) fantasioso(-a); (*object*) di fantasia
fan club N fan club *m inv*
fan·cy [ˈfænsɪ] N 1 (*whim*) voglia, capriccio; **a passing fancy (for sth)** una voglia passeggera (di qc); **when the fancy takes him** quando ne ha voglia; **to take a fancy to** (*person, thing*) affezionarsi a, incapricciarsi di; (*catch or take sb's fancy*) entusiasmare qn; **it took** *or* **caught my fancy** mi è piaciuto 2 (*imagination*) fantasia, immaginazione *f*; **in the realm of fancy** nel regno della fantasia; **I have a fancy that he'll be late** (*vague idea*) ho la vaga impressione che arriverà tardi; **is it just my fancy, or did I hear a knock at the door?** mi sbaglio o hanno bussato alla porta? ♦ ADJ (*comp* **-ier**, *superl* **-iest**) 1 (*ornamental*) elaborato(-a); **a fancy design** un disegno fantasia; **nothing fancy** niente di speciale; **fancy cakes** pasticcini *mpl* 2 (*pej: price*) esorbitante; (: *idea*) stravagante ♦ VT 1 (*imagine*) immaginare, credere; **to fancy that** immaginare che; **I rather fancy he's gone out** credo proprio che sia uscito; **fancy that!** (*fam*) pensa un po'!, ma guarda!; **fancy meeting you here!** (*fam*) che combinazione incontrarti qui! 2 (*feel like, want*) avere voglia di; **do you fancy (going for) a stroll?** hai voglia *or* ti va di fare una passeggiatina?; **I don't fancy the idea** l'idea non mi attira; **he fancies himself** (*fam*) ha un'alta opinione di sé; **he fancies himself as a footballer** (*fam*) crede di essere un gran calciatore; **she fancies him** (*fam*) lui le piace (*sessualmente*) 3 (*predict success for: team, horse*) dare per vincente; **I don't fancy his chances of winning** non credo che vincerà
fancy dress N costume *m*, maschera; **fancy-dress ball** ballo in maschera; **fancy-dress party** festa mascherata
fancy goods NPL articoli *mpl* da regalo

fan·fare [ˈfænfɛə] N fanfara

fang [fæŋ] N zanna; (*of snake*) dente *m*

fan heater N (*Brit*) termoventilatore *m*

fan·light [ˈfænˌlaɪt] N lunetta (a ventaglio)

fan·ta·size [ˈfæntəˌsaɪz] VI fantasticare, sognare

fan·tas·tic [fænˈtæstɪk] ADJ (*gen*) fantastico(-a); (*idea*) assurdo(-a)

fan·ta·sy [ˈfæntəsɪ] N (*imagination*) fantasia, immaginazione *f*; (*fanciful idea, wish*) sogno, idea fantastica, chimera; **in a world of fantasy** in un mondo fantastico; **fantasies of romance** fantasie romantiche

fan·zine [ˈfænˌziːn] N fanzine *f inv*

FAQ [ˌefeɪˈkjuː] NPL ABBR = **frequently asked questions**(*Comput*) FAQ *fpl*, domande *fpl* frequenti ♦ ABBR (= *free alongside quay*) FAQ, franco lungo banchina

far [fɑː] (*comp*, farther *or* further *superl* farthest *or* furthest) ADV **1** lontano; **is it far (away)?** è lontano?; **is it far to London?** è lontana Londra?; **how far is it?** quanto è distante?; **how far is it to the river?** quanto è lontano il fiume?; **it's not far (from here)** non è lontano (da qui); **it's not far from London** non è lontano da Londra; **as far as** fino a; **as far as the eye can see** a perdita d'occhio; **to go as far as Milan** andare fino a Milano; **to come from as far away as Milan** venire addirittura da Milano; **she swam as far as the others** ha nuotato tanto lontano quanto gli altri; **as far back as I can remember** per quanto *or* per quello che posso ricordare; **as far back as 1945** già nel 1945; **as** *or* **so far as I know** per quel che ne so, per quanto ne sappia; **as** *or* **so far as I am concerned** per quanto mi riguarda; **as far as possible** nei limiti del possibile; **I would go as** *or* **so far as to say that ...** arriverei al punto di dire...; **from far and near** da ogni parte; **to come from far and wide** venire da ogni parte; **to travel far and wide** viaggiare in lungo e in largo; **far away** *or* **off** lontano, distante; **far away** *or* **off in the distance** in lontananza; **not far away** *or* **off** lontano; **far away from one's family** lontano dalla famiglia; **Christmas is not far off** Natale non è lontano, non manca molto a Natale; **far beyond** molto al di là di; **far from** (*place*) lontano da; **far from (doing sth)** invece di (fare qc); **we are far from having finished** siamo ben lungi dall'aver finito; **far from it!** al contrario!; **he is far from well** non sta affatto *or* per niente bene; **far be it from me to interfere, but ...** non ho la minima intenzione di immischiarmi, ma...; **far from easy** tutt'altro che facile; **far into the night** fino a notte inoltrata; **far out at sea** in alto mare; **our calculations weren't far out** i nostri calcoli non erano poi così sbagliati; **to go far** (*person*) andare lontano; **he'll go far** farà molta strada; **it won't go far** (*money, food*) non basterà; **how far are you going?** fin dove vai?; **how far have you got with your work?** dove sei arrivato con il tuo lavoro?; **he's gone too far this time** questa volta ha esagerato *or* oltrepassato i limiti; **he's gone too far to back out now** si è spinto troppo oltre per tirarsi indietro adesso; **the plans are too far advanced** i piani sono a uno stadio troppo avanzato; **he was far gone** (*fam: ill*) era molto malato; (: *drunk*) era ubriaco fradicio; **this far** (*in distance*) fin qui; **so far** (*in time*) finora, fino ad ora; **so far so good** fin qui tutto a posto; **so** *or* **thus far and no further** fin qui non oltre **2** (*with comp: very much*) di gran lunga; **far better** assai migliore; **it's far and away the best** *or* **it's by far the best** è di gran lunga il migliore; **this car is far faster (than)** questa macchina è molto più veloce (di); **it is far better not to go** è molto meglio non andare ♦ ADJ: **the Far North** l'estremo Nord; **the far east** *etc* of the country la zona orientale *etc* del paese; **on the far side of** dall'altra parte di; **at the far end** of in fondo a, all'altro capo di; **the far left/right** (*Pol*) l'estrema sinistra/destra

far·away [ˈfɑːrəˌweɪ] ADJ (*distant*) lontano(-a); (*voice, look*) assente

farce [fɑːs] N (*Theatre, also fig*) farsa

far·ci·cal [ˈfɑːsɪkl] ADJ farsesco(-a), ridicolo(-a); **the trial was farcical** il processo fu una farsa

fare [feə] N **1** (*cost: on trains, buses*) tariffa; (: *in taxi*) prezzo della corsa; **full fare** la tariffa intera; **"fares please!"** (*conductor on bus*) "biglietti?" **2** (*passenger in taxi*) passeggero(-a), cliente *m/f* **3** (*frm: food*) cibo, vitto; **bill of fare** (*menu*) lista delle vivande ♦ VI: **how did you fare?** com'è andata?; **I think**

they will fare badly if ... penso che le cose si metteranno male per loro se...

Far East N: **the Far East** l'Estremo Oriente *m*

fare·well [ˌfeəˈwel] N, EXCL addio; **to bid farewell (to sb)** salutare (qn), dire addio (a qn) ♦ ADJ (*party*) d'addio; (*dinner, speech*) d'addio, di commiato

far-fetched [ˌfɑːˈfetʃt] ADJ (*explanation*) stiracchiato(-a), forzato(-a); (*idea, scheme, story*) inverosimile

farm [fɑːm] N fattoria, podere *m*; **farm produce** prodotti *mpl* agricoli ♦ VT coltivare ♦ VI (*as profession*) fare l'agricoltore
> **farm out** VT + ADV (*work*): **farm out (to sb)** dare in consegna (a qn); (*children*): **to farm out (on)** affidare (a)

farm·er [ˈfɑːmə] N agricoltore *m*, contadino(-a), coltivatore(-trice); (*owner of farm*) proprietario(-a) terriero(-a)

farm·hand [ˈfɑːmˌhænd] N bracciante *m/f*

farm·house [ˈfɑːmˌhaʊs] N casa colonica, fattoria

farm·ing [ˈfɑːmɪŋ] N agricoltura; **organic farming** agricoltura biologica; **sheep farming** allevamento di pecore; **farming community** comunità *f inv* agricola; **farming methods** metodi *mpl* di coltivazione

farm la·bour·er, farm laborer (*USA*) N = **farmhand**

farm·land [ˈfɑːmˌlænd] N terreno coltivo

farm worker N = **farmhand**

farm·yard [ˈfɑːmˌjɑːd] N aia

Faroe Is·lands [ˈfeərəʊˈaɪləndz], **Faroes** [ˈfeərəʊz] NPL: **the Faroe Islands** le isole *fpl* Faeroer

far-reaching [ˈfɑːˈriːtʃɪŋ] ADJ (*effect*) di larga *or* vasta portata

far-sighted [ˌfɑːˈsaɪtɪd] ADJ **1** (*person*) previdente, lungimirante; (*plan, decision, measure*) lungimirante **2** (*USA: long-sighted*) presbite

fart [fɑːt] (*fam!*) N scoreggia, peto (*fam!*) ♦ VI scoreggiare, fare un peto (*fam!*)

far·ther [ˈfɑːðə] COMP *of* far ♦ ADV *see* further ♦ ADJ più lontano(-a); **on the farther side of the street** dall'altra parte della strada

far·thest [ˈfɑːðɪst] ADJ, ADV, SUPERL *of* far; *see* furthest

fas·cia, fa·cia [ˈfeɪʃɪə] N **1** (*Aut*) cruscotto **2** (*of mobile phone*) mascherina

fas·ci·nate [ˈfæsɪˌneɪt] VT affascinare; **it fascinates me how/why ...** sono affascinato da come/perché...

fas·ci·nat·ing [ˈfæsɪˌneɪtɪŋ] ADJ affascinante

fas·ci·na·tion [ˌfæsɪˈneɪʃən] N fascino

fas·cism [ˈfæʃɪzəm] N fascismo

fas·cist [ˈfæʃɪst] ADJ, N fascista *m/f*

fash·ion [ˈfæʃən] N **1** (*manner*) modo, maniera; **after a fashion** (*finish, manage etc*) così così; **in his usual fashion** nel solito modo; **in similar fashion** in maniera simile; **in the Greek fashion** alla greca **2** (*vogue: in clothing, speech etc*) moda; **to set a fashion for sth** lanciare la moda di qc; **to be in fashion** essere di/alla moda; **to be out of fashion** essere fuori moda, essere passato(-a) di moda; **to come into/go out of fashion** diventare/passare di moda; **the latest fashion** l'ultima moda; **the new Spring fashions** i nuovi modelli per la primavera; **it's no longer the fashion** non va più di moda; **women's/men's fashions** moda femminile/maschile ♦ VT (*gen*) fabbricare; (*in clay*) modellare ♦ ADJ (*editor, house, show*) di moda

fash·ion·able [ˈfæʃnəbl] ADJ alla moda, di moda; (*writer*) di grido; **it is fashionable to do ...** è/va di moda fare...

fashion designer N stilista *m/f*, disegnatore(-trice) di moda

fast¹ [fɑːst] (*comp* **-er**, *superl* **-est**) ADJ **1** (*speedy*) veloce, svelto(-a), rapido(-a); (*film*) ad alta sensibilità; **fast train** rapido; **a fast car** una macchina veloce; **he's a fast worker** (*fig*) non perde certo tempo; **to pull a fast one on sb** (*fam*) giocare un brutto tiro a qn **2** (*clock*): **to be fast** andare avanti; **my watch is 5 minutes fast** il mio orologio va avanti di 5 minuti **3** (*dissipated*) dissoluto(-a); (*life*) dissipato(-a), dissoluto(-a) **4** (*firm: friend*) devoto(-a), fedele; (: *colour, dye*) resistente, che non stinge ♦ ADV **1** (*quickly*) in fretta, velocemente, rapidamente; **to drive too fast** correre troppo; **as fast as I can** più in fretta possibile; **he ran off as fast as his legs would carry him** è corso via come il vento *or* più veloce che poteva; **how fast can you type?** a che velocità scrivi a macchina?; **not so fast!** piano!; **the rain was falling fast** pioveva forte *or* a dirotto **2** (*firmly: stuck, held*) saldamente, bene; **tie it fast** legalo bene; **it's stuck fast** (*door*) è saldamente bloccato; (*nail, screw*) è completamente incastrato; **fast asleep** profondamente addormentato(-a)

fast² [fɑːst] N digiuno ♦ VI digiunare

fas·ten [ˈfɑːsn] VT (*with rope, string etc*) legare; (*with nail*) inchiodare; (*secure: belt, dress, seat belt*) allacciare; (: *door, box, window*) chiudere; (*attach*) attaccare, fissare; **fasten your seat belt** allacciatevi le cinture di sicurezza; **to fasten the blame/responsibility (for sth) on sb** (*fig*) dare la colpa/addossare la responsabilità (di qc) a qn ♦ VI (*door etc*) chiudersi; (*dress*) allacciarsi, abbottonarsi
  ▸ **fasten down** VT + ADV fissare bene
  ▸ **fasten on** VT + ADV fissare
  ▸ **fasten up** VT + ADV (*clothing, coat*) allacciare, abbottonare
  ▸ **fasten on, fasten upon** VI + PREP (*idea*) cogliere al volo; (*excuse*) ricorrere a

fas·ten·er [ˈfɑːsnəʳ], **fas·ten·ing** [ˈfɑːsnɪŋ] N chiusura, fermaglio; (*zip*) chiusura *f* lampo, *inv*

fast food N fast food *m inv*

fas·tid·i·ous [fæˈstɪdɪəs] ADJ (*person: about cleanliness*) pignolo(-a); (: *in taste*) difficile, esigente
  ❑ **fastidious** is not translated by the Italian word *fastidioso*

fast lane N (*Aut*) ≈ corsia di sorpasso; **in the fast lane** nella corsia di sorpasso

fat [fæt] (*comp* -**ter**, *superl* -**test**) ADJ (*person, meat*) grasso(-a); (*face, cheeks*) paffuto(-a); (*arm, leg*) grassoccio(-a); (*book*) grosso(-a); (*wallet*) gonfio(-a); (*wage packet*) cospicuo(-a); **to get fat** ingrassare, diventare grasso(-a); **he grew fat on the proceeds/profits** (*fig*) si è arricchito con i guadagni/gli incassi; **a fat lot of good that is!** (*fam, iro*) bella roba! ♦ N grasso; (*Anat*) adipe *m*; **to fry in deep fat** friggere in molto olio; **it's very high in fat** contiene molti grassi; **to live off the fat of the land** vivere nel lusso, avere ogni ben di Dio; **the fat's in the fire** (*fig*) adesso son guai

fa·tal [ˈfeɪtl] ADJ (*injury, disease, accident*) fatale, mortale; (*mistake*) fatale; (*consequences, result*) disastroso(-a); (*influence*) nefasto(-a); (*fateful: words, decision*) fatidico(-a)

fa·tal·ism [ˈfeɪtəlɪzəm] N fatalismo

fa·tal·ity [fəˈtælɪtɪ] N (*death*) incidente *m* mortale; (*person killed*) morto(-a), vittima

fa·tal·ly [ˈfeɪtəlɪ] ADV (*wounded, injured*) mortalmente, a morte; (*damaged, flawed*) irrimediabilmente; (*exposed, incriminated*) in modo disastroso; **fatally ill** condannato(-a)

fate [feɪt] N 1 (*force*) destino, sorte *f*, fato; **the Fates** (*Myth*) le Parche; **what has fate in store for us?** cosa ci riserva il destino? 2 (*person's lot*) sorte *f*, destino; **to leave sb to his fate** abbandonare qn alla propria sorte *or* al proprio destino; **a terrible fate** un terribile destino; **to meet one's fate** (*death*) trovare la morte

fat·ed [ˈfeɪtɪd] ADJ (*governed by fate*) destinato(-a); (*person, project, friendship etc*) destinato(-a) a finire male; **it was fated that ...** era destino che...

fate·ful [ˈfeɪtful] ADJ (*momentous: day, event*) fatale; (*prophetic: words*) fatidico(-a)

fat-free [ˈfætˈfriː] ADJ senza grassi

fa·ther [ˈfɑːðəʳ] N (*gen*) padre *m*; **my father** mio padre; **Our Father** (*Rel*) Padre Nostro; **from father to son** di padre in figlio; **like father like son** tale padre tale figlio; **Old Father Time** il Tempo

Father Christmas N Babbo Natale

father·hood [ˈfɑːðəhʊd] N paternità

father-in-law [ˈfɑːðərɪnˌlɔː] N suocero

father·land [ˈfɑːðəlænd] N patria

fa·ther·ly [ˈfɑːðəlɪ] ADJ paterno(-a)

fath·om [ˈfæðəm] N (*Naut*) braccio (*Brit*=1,83m/*USA*= 1.83m) ♦ VT (*fig: also:* **fathom out**) capire; (*mystery*) penetrare, sondare; **I can't fathom why** non riesco a capire perché; **I couldn't fathom what he meant** non sono riuscito a comprendere cosa intendeva

fa·tigue [fəˈtiːɡ] N stanchezza, fatica; **to be on fatigue** (*Mil*) essere di corvé ♦ VT (*frm*) affaticare, stancare

fat·ness [ˈfætnɪs] N grassezza

fat·ten [ˈfætn] VT, VI (*also:* **fatten up**) ingrassare

fat·ten·ing [ˈfætnɪŋ] ADJ ingrassante; **to be fattening** far

ingrassare; **chocolate is fattening** la cioccolata fa ingrassare; **some foods are not fattening** alcuni cibi non fanno ingrassare

fat·ty [ˈfætɪ] ADJ (*foods*) grasso(-a); (*Anat: tissue*) grasso(-a), adiposo(-a) ♦ N (*fam*) ciccione(-a)

fatu·ous [ˈfætjʊəs] ADJ fatuo(-a)

fau·cet [ˈfɔːsɪt] N (*USA*) rubinetto

fault [fɔːlt] N 1 (*defect*) difetto; (*mistake*) errore *m*; (*Tennis*) fault *m inv*, fallo; (*Geol*) faglia; **he has his faults, but I still like him** ha i suoi difetti, ma mi piace lo stesso; **a technical fault** un guasto tecnico; **generous to a fault** eccessivamente generoso(-a); **to find fault with sb/sth** trovare da ridire su qn/qc; **to be at fault** avere torto; **your memory is at fault** non ti ricordi bene 2 (*responsibility*) colpa; **it's all your fault** è tutta colpa tua; **it wasn't my fault** non è stata colpa mia; **whose fault is it (if ...)?** di chi è la colpa (se...)? ♦ VT trovare da ridire su, criticare

fault·less [ˈfɔːltlɪs] ADJ (*person, behaviour*) irreprensibile; (*work, English*) impeccabile, perfetto(-a)

faulty [ˈfɔːltɪ] ADJ (*comp* -**ier**, *superl* -**iest**) difettoso(-a)

fau·na [ˈfɔːnə] N fauna

faux pas [fəʊˈpɑː] N INV gaffe *f inv*

fa·vour, fa·vor (*USA*) [ˈfeɪvəʳ] N 1 (*kindness*) favore *m*; **to do sb a favour** fare un favore *or* una cortesia a qn; **to ask a favour of sb** chiedere un favore a qn; **as a favour to me** per farmi un favore; **could you do me a favour?** potresti farmi un favore?; **do me a favour and close the window** fammi un favore, chiudi la finestra 2 (*approval*) favore *m*; **to be in favour (with sb)** (*person*) essere nelle grazie di qn; (*idea*) essere ben visto(-a) (da qn); **to be out of favour** (*person*) essere in disgrazia; (*idea, practice*) essere mal visto(-a); **to find favour with sb** (*subj: person*) entrare nelle buone grazie di qn; (: *suggestion*) avere l'approvazione di qn; **to gain sb's favour** *or* **gain favour with sb** guadagnarsi la stima di qn 3 (*support, advantage*) favore *m*; **to be in favour of sth** essere favorevole a qc, essere a favore di qc; **to be in favour of doing sth** essere favorevole a fare qc; **that's a point in his favour** è un punto a suo favore; **to decide in favour of sb/ sth** decidere in favore di qn/qc; **to decide in favour of doing sth** decidere di fare qc; **to show favour to sb** mostrarsi parziale verso qn, favorire qn ♦ VT (*approve: idea, scheme, approach*) essere a favore di; (*prefer: person, party, proposition*) preferire, essere favorevole a; (: *pupil*) favorire; (: *team*) essere per

fa·vour·able, fa·vor·able (*USA*) [ˈfeɪvərəbl] ADJ: **favourable (to sb/sth, for doing sth)** favorevole (a qn/qc, a fare qc)

fa·vour·ably, fa·vor·ably (*USA*) [ˈfeɪvərəblɪ] ADV favorevolmente

fa·vour·ite, fa·vor·ite (*USA*) [ˈfeɪvərɪt] ADJ favorito(-a), preferito(-a) ♦ N favorito(-a), preferito(-a); (*Horse-racing*) favorito(-a); **it's my favourite** è il mio preferito; **she's a favourite of mine** è uno dei miei preferiti, è tra i miei favoriti; **he sang some old favourites** ha cantato dei vecchi successi

fa·vour·it·ism, fa·vor·it·ism (*USA*) [ˈfeɪvərɪtɪzəm] N favoritismo

fawn¹ [fɔːn] N 1 (*Zool*) cerbiatto 2 (*colour*) marroncino ♦ ADJ (*also:* **fawn-coloured**) marroncino(-a)

fawn² [fɔːn] VI: **to fawn (up)on sb** (*subj: dog*) fare le feste a qn; (: *person, fig*) adulare servilmente qn

fax [fæks] N (*document, machine*) facsimile *m inv*, fax *m inv* ♦ VT spedire via fax, teletrasmettere; **to fax sb sth** spedire via fax qc a qn; **I'll fax you the document** ti spedirò via fax il documento

FBI [ˌɛfbiːˈaɪ] N ABBR (*USA:* = *Federal Bureau of Investigation*) FBI *f*

FD [ˌɛfˈdiː] N ABBR (*USA*) = **fire department**

FDA [ˌɛfdiːˈeɪ] N ABBR (*USA:* = *Food and Drug Administration*) *organismo federale statunitense per il controllo di alimenti e farmaci*

fear [fɪəʳ] N paura, timore *m*; **there are fears that ...** si teme che...; **grave fears have arisen for ...** si nutrono seri timori per...; **for fear of sb/of doing sth** per paura di qn/qc; **for fear that** per paura di (*or* che + *sub*); **to live in fear of sb/sth/doing sth** vivere con la paura di qn/qc/fare qc; **to go in fear of one's life/of being discovered** temere per la propria vita/di essere scoperto(-a); **fear of heights** vertigini *fpl*; **fear of enclosed spaces** claustrofobia; **have no fear!** non temere!; **in fear and trembling** tremante di paura; **to put the fear of God into sb** (*fam*) far venire una paura del diavolo a qn; **no fear!** (*fam*) neanche per sogno!; **there's no fear of that!** neanche per sogno! ♦ VT (*person, God*) temere, avere paura di; **to fear the worst** temere il peggio; **to fear that** temere di (*or* che + *sub*), avere paura di (*or* che + *sub*); **I fear I/he may be late** temo di essere in ritardo/che sia in ritardo; **I fear so/not** temo di sì/di no, ho paura di sì/di no ♦ VI: **to fear for** temere per, essere in ansia per

fear·ful [ˈfɪəfʊl] ADJ 1 (*frightened*): **to be fearful of** temere, avere paura di; **to be fearful that ...** temere *or* avere paura che ... 2 (*frightening: accident*) pauroso(-a), spaventoso(-a); (: *sight, noise*) terrificante, spaventoso(-a), terribile; **there may be fearful consequences** ci potrebbero essere terribili conseguenze

fear·ful·ly [ˈfɪəfəlɪ] ADV 1 (*timidly*) timorosamente 2 (*fam: very*) terribilmente, spaventosamente

fear·less [ˈfɪəlɪs] ADJ intrepido(-a), senza paura; **to be fearless of** non aver paura di

fear·some [ˈfɪəsəm] ADJ (*opponent*) formidabile, terribile; (*sight*) terrificante

fea·sibil·ity [ˌfiːzəˈbɪlɪtɪ] N fattibilità, attuabilità

feasibility study N studio di fattibilità, studio delle possibilità di realizzazione

fea·sible [ˈfiːzəbl] ADJ 1 (*practicable: plan, suggestion*) realizzabile, fattibile, attuabile 2 (*likely: theory, explanation*) verosimile, credibile

feast [fiːst] N (*meal*) pranzo, banchetto; (*Rel, fig*) festa; **feast day** festa, festività *f inv* ♦ VT: **to feast one's eyes on sth/sb** deliziarsi alla vista di qc/qn ♦ VI banchettare; **to feast on sth** banchettare a qc, gustare qc

feat [fiːt] N impresa, prodezza; **a feat of engineering** un trionfo dell'ingegneria; **that was quite a feat** è stata un'impresa non da poco, non è stata un'impresa da poco

feath·er [ˈfeðə⁷] N penna, piuma; **as light as a feather** leggero(-a) come una piuma; **that is a feather in his cap** è un fiore all'occhiello per lui; **you could have knocked me down with a feather** (*fam*) avresti potuto farmi cadere con un soffio ♦ VT: **to feather one's nest** (*fig*) arricchirsi ♦ ADJ (*mattress, bed, pillow*) di piuma

feather·weight [ˈfeðəˌweɪt] (*Boxing*) ADJ dei pesi piuma ♦ N peso *m* piuma, *inv*

fea·ture [ˈfiːtʃə⁷] N 1 (*gen, also Comm, Tech*) caratteristica 2 (*of face*); **features** NPL lineamenti *mpl*, fisionomia *fsg*, fattezze *fpl* 3 (*also:* **feature film**) film *m inv* (principale), lungometraggio 4 (*Press*) articolo, servizio speciale; **a regular feature in** (*newspapers*) un articolo che appare regolarmente in; **a (special) feature on sth/sb** un servizio speciale su qc/qn ♦ VT (*person*) avere come protagonista; (*event, news*) presentare, dare risalto a ♦ VI (*Cine*) apparire, essere protagonista, figurare; **it featured prominently in ...** (*gen*) ha avuto un posto di primo piano in ...

fea·ture·less [ˈfiːtʃəlɪs] ADJ privo(-a) di carattere, anonimo(-a)

Feb. ABBR (= *February*) feb. (= *febbraio*)

Feb·ru·ary [ˈfebruərɪ] N febbraio; **in February** in febbraio; *see* **July**

feces [ˈfiːsiːz] NPL (*USA*) = **faeces**

feck·less [ˈfeklɪs] ADJ irresponsabile, incosciente

Fed [fed] ABBR (*USA*) 1 = **federal** 2 = **federation**

fed [fed] PT, PP *of* **feed**

Fed. N ABBR (*USA fam*) = **Federal Reserve Board**

fed·er·al [ˈfedərəl] ADJ federale

Federal Republic of Germany N Repubblica Federale Tedesca

Federal Reserve Board N (*USA*) *organo di controllo del sistema bancario statunitense*

Federal Trade Commission N (*USA*) *organismo di tutela contro pratiche commerciali abusive*

fed·era·tion [ˌfedəˈreɪʃən] N federazione *f*

fed up ADJ (*fam*): **to be fed up (with** *or* **of)** essere stufo(-a) (di); **to be fed up doing sth** essere stufo(-a) di fare qc

fee [fiː] N pagamento; (*of doctor, lawyer*) onorario, parcella; (*entrance fee, membership fee*) quota d'iscrizione; **course** *or*

tuition fees (*Univ*) tasse *fpl* universitarie; **school fees** tasse *fpl* scolastiche; (*for examination*) tassa d'esame; **for a small fee** per una somma modesta

fee·ble [ˈfiːbl] ADJ (*comp* **-er**, *superl* **-est**) (*gen*) debole; (*joke*) pietoso(-a); (*fam: person*) rammollito(-a)

feeble-minded [ˌfiːblˈmaɪndɪd] ADJ deficiente, sciocco(-a)

feed [fiːd] (*pt, pp* **fed**) N (*baby's*) pappa; (*fodder*) mangime *m*, foraggio; (*amount, portion*) razione *f*; (*fam: meal*): **to have a good feed** fare una bella mangiata ♦ VT 1 (*gen*) nutrire; (*family, horse etc*) dare da mangiare a; **have you fed the cat?** hai dato da mangiare al gatto?; **to feed sth to sb** *or* **sth** dare qc da mangiare a qn; **he worked hard to feed his family** lavorava sodo per mantenere la famiglia 2 (*fire, machine*) alimentare; (*information*) fornire; **to feed sth into a machine** introdurre qc in una macchina; **to feed material into sth** introdurre materiale in qc; **to feed information into a computer** introdurre dati in un computer ♦ VI (*baby, animal*) mangiare; (*at breast/on bottle*) poppare; **to feed on sth** nutrirsi di qc

▸ **feed back** VT + ADV (*results*) riferire
▸ **feed in** VT + ADV (*wire, tape*) introdurre
▸ **feed on** VI + PREP nutrirsi di
▸ **feed up** VT + ADV (*person, animal*) ingrassare

feed·back [ˈfiːdˌbæk] N (*from person*) reazioni *fpl*; **to get feedback on one's work** avere un riscontro del lavoro svolto; **the feedback from customers has been positive** i clienti hanno risposto positivamente; (*from computer*) feed-back *m*

feed·er [ˈfiːdə⁷] N 1 (*baby, animal*) mangiatore(-trice); **a heavy feeder** un(-a) mangione(-a) 2 (*road, rail*) secondario(-a)

feel [fiːl] (*pt, pp* **felt**) N (*sense of touch*) tatto; (*sensation*) sensazione *f*; (*of substance*) consistenza; **to be rough to the feel** essere ruvido(-a) al tatto; **to know sth by the feel of it** riconoscere qc al tatto; **let me have a feel!** fammi toccare!; **to get the feel of sth** (*fig*) abituarsi a qc ♦ VT 1 (*touch*) tastare, sentire, toccare; **to feel sb's pulse** sentire *or* tastare il polso a qn; **to feel one's way (towards)** avanzare a tastoni (verso); **I'm still feeling my way** (*fig*) sto ancora tastando il terreno 2 (*be aware of*) sentire; (*experience: pain, pity, anger*) provare, sentire; **he doesn't feel the cold** non sente il freddo; **I didn't feel much pain** non sentivo molto dolore; **she felt a hand on her shoulder** sentì una mano sulla spalla; **I felt something move** ho sentito qualcosa che si muoveva; **we are beginning to feel the effects** cominciamo a sentire gli effetti; **I felt a great sense of relief** ho sentito un grande sollievo; **he feels the loss of his father very deeply** sta risentendo molto della morte del padre 3 (*think, believe*): **to feel (that)** credere (che), pensare (che); **I feel that you ought to do it** penso che dovresti farlo; **he felt it necessary to point out that ...** ritenne necessario far notare che...; **since you feel so strongly about it ...** visto che ci tieni tanto...; **I feel it in my bones that ...** me lo sento nelle ossa che...; **what do you feel about it?** cosa ne pensi? ♦ VI 1 (*physically, mentally*) sentirsi; **to feel cold/hungry/sleepy** avere freddo/fame/sonno; **to feel ill** sentirsi male; **I don't feel well** non mi sento bene; **I feel much better** mi sento molto meglio; **to feel lonely** sentirsi solo(-a); **I felt lonely** mi sentivo solo; **she's not feeling quite herself** non si sente molto bene; **I felt (as if I was going to) faint** mi sono sentito svenire; **to feel ashamed** avere vergogna; **I feel sure that ...** sono sicuro che...; **to feel sorry for sb** dispiacersi per qn; **I feel very cross/sorry** *etc* sono molto arrabbiato/triste *etc*; **I feel as if there is nothing we can do** ho la sensazione che non ci possiamo fare niente; **how do you feel about him/about the idea?** che ne pensi di lui/dell'idea?; **to feel like sth/doing sth** avere voglia di qc/di fare qc; **I don't feel like going out tonight** non ho voglia di uscire stasera; **do you feel like an ice cream?** hai voglia di un gelato?; **what does it feel like to do that?** che effetto ti fa fare ciò?; **I don't feel up to (doing) it** non me la sento (di farlo); **I felt (like) a fool** mi sono sentito uno stupido; **I feel for you!** (*sympathize*) come ti capisco! 2 (*objects*): **to feel hard/cold/damp (to the touch)** essere duro(-a)/freddo(-a)/umido(-a) al tatto; **it feels soft** è morbido al tatto; **the house feels damp** la casa sembra umida; **it feels like silk** sembra seta al tatto; **it feels colder out here** sembra più freddo qui fuori; **it feels like (it might) rain** sembra che voglia piovere; **it felt like being drunk** *or* **as if I was drunk** mi sentivo come se fossi ubriaco **3** (*grope*) cercare a tastoni; **to feel about** *or* **around for** cercare a tastoni; **to feel about** *or* **around for sth in the dark** cercare a tastoni qc al buio; **to feel (about** *or* **around) in one's pocket for** frugarsi in tasca per cercare

feel·er [ˈfiːlə˞] N (*of insect, snail*) antenna; (*of octopus*) tentacolo; **to put out feelers** (*fig*) tastare il terreno

feel-good [ˈfiːlɡʊd] ADJ (*film, song*) dei buoni sentimenti

feel·ing [ˈfiːlɪŋ] N **1** (*physical*) senso, sensazione *f*; **a cold feeling** una sensazione di freddo; **a burning feeling** una sensazione di bruciore; **to have no** *or* **to have lost all feeling in one's arm** aver perso completamente la sensibilità in un braccio **2** (*emotion*) sentimento, emozione *f*; (*sensitivity*) sensibilità; **bad** *or* **ill feeling** ostilità, rancore *m*; **to speak/sing with feeling** parlare/cantare con sentimento; **he shows no feeling for her** non mostra nessuna simpatia per lei; **a woman of great feeling** una donna molto sensibile; **what are your feelings about the matter?** che cosa ne pensi?; **you can imagine my feelings** puoi immaginare quello che sento/ho sentito; **to hurt sb's feelings** urtare i sentimenti di qn, ferire qn; **he was afraid of hurting my feelings** aveva paura di urtare i miei sentimenti; **feelings ran high about it** la cosa aveva provocato grande eccitazione; **no hard feelings!** senza rancore! **3** (*impression*) senso, impressione *f*; **a feeling of security/isolation** un senso di sicurezza/di isolamento; **my feeling is that ...** ho l'impressione che...; **I have a (funny) feeling that ...** ho la (strana) sensazione che...; **I got the feeling that ...** ho avuto l'impressione che...

feet [fiːt] NPL *of* **foot**

feign [feɪn] VT (*liter*) fingere, simulare

fe·lici·tous [fɪˈlɪsɪtəs] ADJ (*frm*) felice

fell¹ [fɛl] PT *of* **fall**

fell² [fɛl] VT (*with a blow: person*) atterrare; (*: tree*) abbattere

fell³ [fɛl] ADJ: **with one fell blow** con un colpo terribile; **at one fell swoop** in un colpo solo

fell⁴ [fɛl] N (*Brit: mountain*) monte *m*; (*: uplands*): **the fells** *npl* versante montuoso con scarsa vegetazione; **fell-walking** passeggiate *fpl* in montagna

fel·low [ˈfɛləʊ] N **1** (*fam: man, boy*) uomo, individuo, tipo; (*: boyfriend*) ragazzo; **poor fellow!** povero diavolo!; **my dear fellow** mio caro, caro mio **2** (*comrade*) compagno; (*equal*) pari *m inv* **3** (*of association, society etc*) membro; (*Univ*) ≈ docente *m/f* ♦ ADJ: **fellow citizen** concittadino(-a); **fellow countryman/woman** compatriota *m/f*; **one's fellow creatures** i (le) propri(e) simili; **fellow doctor** collega *m/f* (medico); **their fellow prisoners/students/workers** i loro compagni di prigione/studio/lavoro; **fellow men** simili *mpl*

fellow feeling N simpatia

fel·low·ship [ˈfɛləʊˌʃɪp] N (*companionship*) compagnia; (*club, society*) associazione *f*; (*Univ*): **a research fellowship** un posto di ricercatore(-trice) all'università

fellow traveller N compagno(-a) di viaggio; (*Pol: with communists*) compagno(-a) di strada

fel·on [ˈfɛlən] N (*Law*) criminale *m/f*

felo·ny [ˈfɛlənɪ] N (*Law*) reato, crimine *m*

felt¹ [fɛlt] PT, PP *of* **feel**

felt² [fɛlt] N feltro ♦ ADJ di feltro; **felt hat** cappello di feltro

felt-tip pen [ˈfɛltˌtɪpˈpɛn] N (*also:* **felt-tip**) pennarello

fe·male [ˈfiːmeɪl] N (*animal, plant, also Elec*) femmina *inv*; (*subject, member, worker*) di sesso femminile; (*company, vote*) di donne; (*sex, quality, character*) femminile; **two of the puppies were female** due dei cuccioli erano femmine; **female student/worker** studentessa/operaia; **male and female students** studenti e studentesse; **female MPs** le parlamentari ♦ ADJ (*animal: woman: pej*) femmina

femi·nine [ˈfɛmɪnɪn] ADJ femminile; **the feminine form** (*Gram*) il femminile ♦ N (*Gram*) femminile *m*; **in the feminine** al femminile

femi·nin·ity [ˌfɛmɪˈnɪnɪtɪ] N femminilità

femi·nism [ˈfɛmɪˌnɪzəm] N femminismo

femi·nist [ˈfɛmɪnɪst] ADJ, N femminista *m/f*

fen [fɛn] N (*often pl: Brit*) zona paludosa; *see also* **Fens**

fence [fɛns] N **1** recinto, steccato; (*Racing*) ostacolo; **to sit on the fence** (*fig*) rimanere neutrale **2** (*fam: receiver of stolen*

goods) ricettatore(-trice) ♦ VT recintare ♦ VI (*Sport*) tirare di scherma

▸ **fence in** VT + ADV **1** (*field*) recintare, recingere **2** (*fig*): **to feel fenced in** sentirsi imprigionato(-a)

▸ **fence off** VT + ADV separare con un recinto

fenc·ing [ˈfɛnsɪŋ] N **1** (*Sport*) scherma; **fencing match** incontro di scherma **2** (*material*) materiale *m* per recintare

fend [fɛnd] VI: **to fend for o.s.** arrangiarsi, badare a se stesso(-a)

▸ **fend off** VT + ADV (*attack, attacker*) respingere, difendersi da; (*blow*) parare; (*awkward question*) eludere

fend·er [ˈfɛndə˞] N (*round fire*) paracenere *m*, parafuoco; (*USA: Aut: wing*) parafango; (*USA: Rail*) paraurti *m inv*; (*Naut*) parabordo

fen·nel [ˈfɛnl] N finocchio

fer·ment [*n* ˈfɜːment, *vb* fəˈment] N (*excitement*) eccitazione *f*, agitazione *f*, fermento; **to be in a state of ferment** essere in fermento *or* in uno stato di agitazione ♦ VT far fermentare; (*fig*) fomentare ♦ VI fermentare

fer·men·ta·tion [ˌfɜːmenˈteɪʃən] N fermentazione *f*

fern [fɜːn] N felce *f*

fe·ro·cious [fəˈrəʊʃəs] ADJ feroce

fe·roc·ity [fəˈrɒsɪtɪ] N ferocia

fer·ret [ˈfɛrɪt] N furetto ♦ VI cacciare con il furetto

▸ **ferret about, ferret around** VI + ADV (*fam*) frugare

▸ **ferret out** VT + ADV (*fam: secret, truth*) scoprire; (*: person*) scovare, scoprire

fer·ry [ˈfɛrɪ] N (*also:* **ferryboat**) (*small*) traghetto; (*large: for cars etc*) nave *f inv* traghetto ♦ VT: **to ferry sth/sb across** *or* **over** traghettare qc/qn da una parte all'altra; **to ferry sb to and fro** portare qn avanti e indietro

ferry·man [ˈfɛrɪmən] N (*pl* **ferrymen**) traghettatore *m*

fer·tile [ˈfɜːtaɪl] ADJ (*gen*) fertile; (*creature, plant*) fecondo(-a); **fertile period** periodo di fecondità

fer·til·ity [fəˈtɪlɪtɪ] N (*see adj*) fertilità; fecondità

fertility drug N farmaco contro la sterilità

fer·ti·lize [ˈfɜːtɪˌlaɪz] VT (*egg*) fecondare; (*Agr: land, soil*) fertilizzare

fer·ti·liz·er [ˈfɜːtɪˌlaɪzə˞] N fertilizzante *m*

fer·vent [ˈfɜːvənt], **fer·vid** [ˈfɜːvɪd] ADJ (*believer, supporter*) fervente; (*desire*) ardente, fervido(-a); **a fervent admirer of her work** un grandissimo ammiratore del suo lavoro; **in the fervent hope that ...** sperando ardentemente che...

fer·vour, fer·vor (*USA*) [ˈfɜːvə˞] N (*frm*) fervore *m*, ardore *m*

fes·ter [ˈfɛstə˞] VI (*Med*) suppurare; (*anger, resentment*) covare

fes·ti·val [ˈfɛstɪvl] N (*Rel, etc*) festa; (*Art, Mus*) festival *m inv*; **a jazz festival** un festival di musica jazz

fes·tive [ˈfɛstɪv] ADJ di festa; **in a festive mood** di umore allegro; **a festive atmosphere** un'atmosfera di festa

fes·tiv·ity [fɛsˈtɪvɪtɪ] N **1** (*festival*) festa **2** (*celebrations*): **festivities** NPL festeggiamenti *mpl*

fes·toon [fɛsˈtuːn] VT: **to festoon with** ornare di, decorare con

fetch [fɛtʃ] VT **1** (*bring*) portare; (*go and get*) andare a prendere; (*doctor*) andare a chiamare; **fetch the bucket** vai a prendere il secchio; **fetch it!** (*to dog*) prendi! **2** (*sell for*) essere venduto(-a) per; **how much did it fetch?** a *or* per quanto lo hai venduto?; **his painting fetched five thousand pounds** il suo quadro è stato venduto per cinquemila sterline

fetch·ing [ˈfɛtʃɪŋ] ADJ attraente

fête [feɪt] N festa all'aperto (*spesso a scopo di beneficenza*) ♦ VT festeggiare

fet·id [ˈfɛtɪd], **foet·id** [ˈfiːtɪd] ADJ (*frm*) fetido(-a)

fet·ish [ˈfɛtɪʃ] N (*obsession*) fissazione *f*, mania; (*object of cult*) feticcio

fet·ter [ˈfɛtə˞] VT (*person*) incatenare; (*fig*) ostacolare

fet·ters [ˈfɛtəz] NPL catene *fpl*; (*fig*) restrizioni *fpl*

fet·tle [ˈfɛtl] N (*Brit*): **in fine fettle** in gran forma

fe·tus [ˈfiːtəs] (*USA*) N = **foetus**

feud [fjuːd] N faida, contesa, lotta; **a family feud** una faida familiare ♦ VI: **to feud (with sb)** essere in lotta (con qn)

feu·dal [ˈfjuːdl] ADJ feudale

feu·dal·ism [ˈfjuːdəˌlɪzəm] N feudalesimo

fe·ver [ˈfiːvə˞] N **1** (*high temperature*) febbre *f*; **he has a fever** ha la febbre; **a bout of fever** un accesso di febbre; **a high/**

slight fever una febbre alta/leggera **2** (*excitement*) eccita-zione *f*; **gambling fever** (*fig*) la febbre del gioco; **in a fever of excitement** in uno stato di eccitazione febbrile; **fever pitch** il colmo; **excitement has reached fever pitch** l'eccitazione ha raggiunto il colmo

fe·ver·ish [ˈfiːvərɪʃ] ADJ (*also fig*) febbrile; (*person*) febbrici-tante; **feverish preparations** preparativi *mpl* febbrili

few [fjuː] ADJ, PRON (*comp* -er, *superl* -est) **1** (*not many*) pochi(-e); **few books** pochi libri; **he has few friends** ha pochi amici; **few of them** pochi di loro; **few (people) man-aged to do it** pochi riuscirono a farlo; **few succeed** pochi ci riescono; **she is one of the few (people) who ...** è una delle poche persone che...; **the few who ...** i pochi che...; **in** *or* **over the past few days** in questi ultimi giorni, negli ulti-mi giorni; **in** *or* **over the next few days** nei prossimi giorni; **every few days/months** ogni due o tre giorni/mesi; **with few exceptions** con *or* salvo poche eccezioni; **every few weeks** a intervalli di qualche settimana; **they are few and far between** sono rari; **there are very few of us** *or* **we are very few** siamo pochi; **the last** *or* **remaining few minutes** i pochi minuti che rimangono; **as few as three of them** solo tre di loro; **too few** troppo pochi; **there were three too few** ne mancavano tre **2** (*some, several*): **a few** alcuni(-e), qual-che; **a few books** alcuni libri, qualche libro; **I invited a few old friends** ho invitato alcuni vecchi amici; **I know a few** ne conosco alcuni; **a few of them** alcuni di loro; **a few more days** qualche altro giorno; **in a few more days** fra qualche giorno; **a good few** *or* **quite a few** parecchi; **a good few** *or* **quite a few books** parecchi libri, un bel po' di libri; **quite a few people** un bel po' di gente; **a good few** *or* **quite a few (people) came** è venuta un bel po' di gente

few·er [ˈfjuːəʳ] COMP *of* **few** ♦ ADJ, PRON meno *inv*, meno nu-merosi(-e); **fewer than 10** meno di 10; **fewer than you** meno di te; **no fewer than ...** non meno di...; **there are fewer of them now** adesso ce ne sono di meno; **there were fewer people than yesterday** c'era meno gente di ieri

few·est [ˈfjuːɪst] SUPERL *of* **few** ♦ ADJ, PRON il minor numero di; **we were fewest in number** eravamo i meno numerosi

FFA [ˌɛfɛfˈeɪ] N ABBR = **Future Farmers of America**

FHA [ˌɛfeɪtʃˈeɪ] N ABBR (*USA:* = **Federal Housing Administra-tion**)

fi·an·cé [fiːˈɑ̃ŋseɪ] N fidanzato

fi·an·cée [fiːˈɑ̃ŋseɪ] N fidanzata

fi·as·co [fiˈæskəʊ] N fiasco

fib [fɪb] (*fam*) N bugia, frottola; **to tell a fib** dire una bugia ♦ VI dire bugie, raccontare storie

fi·bre, fi·ber (*USA*) [ˈfaɪbəʳ] N fibra

fibre·board, fiber·board (*USA*) [ˈfaɪbəbɔːd] N pannello di fibre

fibre·glass, fiber·glass (*USA*) [ˈfaɪbəˌɡlɑːs] N fibra di vetro ♦ ADJ di fibra di vetro

fi·bro·si·tis [ˌfaɪbrəˈsaɪtɪs] N fibrosite *f*, cellulite *f*

fick·le [ˈfɪkl] ADJ incostante, volubile

fic·tion [ˈfɪkʃən] N **1** (*Literature*) narrativa; **a work of fiction** un'opera di narrativa; **light fiction** narrativa leggera **2** (*sth made up*) finzione *f*

❑ **fiction** is not translated by the Italian word *fiction*

fic·tion·al [ˈfɪkʃənl] ADJ immaginario(-a)

fictionalize [ˈfɪkʃənəˌlaɪz] VT romanzare

fic·ti·tious [fɪkˈtɪʃəs] ADJ **1** = **fictional 2** (*false*) falso(-a), fittizio(-a)

fid·dle [ˈfɪdl] N **1** (*violin*) violino; **to play second fiddle to sb** (*fig*) avere un ruolo di secondo piano rispetto a qn **2** (*fam: cheating*) imbroglio, truffa; **it's a fiddle** è un imbroglio; **tax fiddle** frode *f* fiscale; **an insurance fiddle** una truffa assicu-rativa; **to work a fiddle** fare un imbroglio; **to be on the fiddle** imbrogliare ♦ VI (*fidget*) giocherellare, gingillarsi; **do stop fiddling!** stai fermo!; **to fiddle (about) with sth** giocherel-lare/gingillarsi con qc ♦ VT (*Brit fam: accounts, results etc*) falsificare, alterare

▸ **fiddle about, fiddle around** VT + ADV gingillarsi, giocherellare

fid·dler [ˈfɪdləʳ] N **1** (*Mus*) violinista *m/f* **2** (*fam: cheat*) im-broglione(-a)

fid·dly [ˈfɪdlɪ] ADJ (*comp* -ier, *superl* -iest) (*task*) da certosino; (*object*) complesso(-a)

fi·del·ity [fɪˈdɛlɪtɪ] N (*in relationships*) fedeltà; (*accuracy*) esat-tezza, accuratezza

fidg·et [ˈfɪdʒɪt] N (*person*) persona irrequieta; **to have the fidgets** essere irrequieto(-a) *or* agitato(-a) ♦ VI (*also:* **fidget about** *or* **around**) agitarsi; **to fidget with sth** giocherellare con qc

fidg·ety [ˈfɪdʒɪtɪ] ADJ agitato(-a), irrequieto(-a)

fi·du·ci·ary [fɪˈduːʃɪərɪ] ADJ, N (*Law*) fiduciario(-a)

field [fiːld] N (*gen, also Comput*) campo; (*Geol*) giacimento; (*sphere of activity*) campo, settore *m*; **a field of wheat** un campo di grano; **to give sth a year's trial in the field** (*fig*) sperimentare qc sul campo per un anno; **to study sth in the field** osservare *or* studiare qc sul campo; **to die in the field** (*Mil*) cadere sul campo di battaglia; **to take the field** (*Sport*) scendere in campo; **to lead the field** (*Sport, Comm*) essere in testa, essere al primo posto; **my particular field** la mia specialità, il mio campo *or* settore; **field of vision** campo vi-sivo ♦ VT (*team*) far giocare, far scendere in campo; (*Cricket: catch: ball*) prendere

field glasses NPL (*binoculars*) binocolo

field hospital N ospedale *m* da campo

field marshal N feldmaresciallo

field·work [ˈfiːldˌwɜːk] N (*Sociol, etc*) ricerche *fpl* esterne; (*Ar-cheol, Geog, Geol*) lavoro sul campo

fiend [fiːnd] N demonio; **you little fiend!** (*fam*) piccolo delin-quente!; **a football fiend** un fanatico *or* patito del calcio

fiend·ish [ˈfiːndɪʃ] ADJ (*cruelty, smile, plot*) diabolico(-a); (*fam: difficult and unpleasant*) tremendo(-a)

fierce [fɪəs] ADJ (*comp* -er, *superl* -est) (*gen*) feroce; (*opponent*) accanito(-a); (*enemy*) acerrimo(-a); (*look, fighting*) fiero(-a); (*wind, storm*) furioso(-a); (*heat*) intenso(-a); **there's fierce competition between companies** c'è una concorrenza spietata tra società; **a fierce attack** un violento attacco

fiery [ˈfaɪərɪ] ADJ (*comp* -ier, *superl* -iest) (*gen*) infocato(-a), ardente; (*red*) di fuoco; (*temperament, temper, person*) fo-coso(-a); (*liquor*) che brucia la gola

FIFA [ˈfiːfə] N ABBR (= *Fédération Internationale de Football As-sociation*) FIFA *f*

fif·teen [fɪfˈtiːn] ADJ quindici *inv*; **about fifteen people** una quindicina di persone ♦ N quindici *m inv*; (*Rugby*) squadra

fif·teenth [fɪfˈtiːnθ] ADJ quindicesimo(-a) ♦ N (*in series*) quindicesimo(-a); (*fraction*) quindicesimo

fifth [fɪfθ] ADJ quinto(-a); **the fifth floor** il quarto piano; **I was (the) fifth to arrive** sono stato il quinto ad arrivare; **he came fifth in the competition** è arrivato quinto al concorso, si è piazzato al quinto posto; **Henry the Fifth** Enrico Quinto; **the fifth of July, July the fifth** il cinque luglio; **I wrote to him on the fifth** gli ho scritto il cinque; **fifth form** (*Brit Scol*) ≈ terzo anno di scuola superiore ♦ N (*in series*) quin-to(-a); (*fraction*) quinto; (*Mus*) quinta

fif·ti·eth [ˈfɪftɪɪθ] ADJ cinquantesimo(-a) ♦ N (*in series*) cinquantesimo(-a); (*fraction*) cinquantesimo

fif·ty [ˈfɪftɪ] ADJ cinquanta *inv*; **about fifty people/cars** una cinquantina di persone/di macchine; **he'll be fifty (years old) next birthday** al prossimo compleanno avrà/com-pirà cinquant'anni; **he's about fifty** è sulla cinquantina ♦ N cinquanta *m inv*; **the fifties** (*1950s*) gli anni cinquanta; **to be in one's fifties** avere passato la cinquantina; **the tem-perature was in the fifties** la temperatura era al di sopra dei cinquanta gradi (Fahrenheit); **to do fifty** (*Aut*) andare a 50 (all'ora)

fifty-fifty [ˈfɪftɪˈfɪftɪ] ADJ, ADV: **to go fifty-fifty with sb** fare a metà con qn; **they split the prize money fifty-fifty** hanno diviso a metà i soldi del premio; **we have a fifty-fifty chance of success** abbiamo una probabilità su due di successo

fig [fɪɡ] N fico

fight [faɪt] (*pt, pp* **fought**) N (*Mil*) combattimento, lotta; (*Box-ing*) incontro; (*between 2 persons*) lotta *f*; (*brawl*) zuffa, rissa; (*fighting spirit*) combattività; (*struggle, campaign*): **fight (for/against)** lotta (a favore di/contro); **fight (over)** disputa (su); **Muhammad Ali's last fight** l'ultimo incontro di Muham-mad Ali; **there was a fight in the pub** c'è stata una rissa al pub; **to have a fight with sb** (*quarrel, struggle*) avere una lite con qn, litigare con qn; **she had a fight with her best friend** ha litigato con la sua migliore amica; **to put up a good fight** battersi *or* difendersi bene; **there was no fight left in him** aveva perduto la sua combattività; **the fight against cancer** la lotta contro il cancro ♦ ᴠᴛ (*Mil: enemy, battle*) combattere; (*fire, disease, proposals*) lottare contro, combattere; (*Law: case*) difendere; **she has fought racism all her life** ha lottato per tutta la vita contro il razzismo; **to fight a duel** battersi in duello; **to fight one's way through a crowd/across a room** farsi strada a fatica tra la folla/attraverso una stanza ♦ ᴠɪ (*person*) azzuffarsi; (*animal*) battersi; (*troops, countries*): **to fight (against)** combattere (contro); **to fight (with sb)** litigare (con qn); **to fight (for/against)** lottare (per/contro); **the fans started fighting** i tifosi hanno cominciato ad azzuffarsi; **the demonstrators fought with the police** i dimostranti si sono scontrati con la polizia; **to fight for one's life** lottare per la (propria) vita; **let us fight for peace** lottiamo per la pace; **they fight sometimes, but they're good friends** a volte litigano ma sono buoni amici

► **fight back** ᴠɪ + ᴀᴅᴠ difendersi; (*Sport: after illness*) riprendersi; **the attackers ran away when the man fought back** gli assalitori sono scappati quando l'uomo ha reagito ♦ ᴠᴛ + ᴀᴅᴠ (*tears*) trattenere; (*anger*) reprimere; (*despair, doubts*) scacciare

► **fight down** ᴠᴛ + ᴀᴅᴠ (*anger, anxiety*) vincere; (*urge*) reprimere

► **fight off** ᴠᴛ + ᴀᴅᴠ (*attack, attacker*) respingere; (*disease, sleep, urge*) lottare contro

► **fight on** ᴠɪ + ᴀᴅᴠ continuare a combattere

► **fight out** ᴠᴛ + ᴀᴅᴠ: **to fight it out** risolvere la questione a pugni

fight·er [ˈfaɪtəʳ] ɴ combattente *m/f*; (*plane*) caccia *m inv*; **he's a fighter for the cause of …** lotta per la causa di…

fighter-bomber [ˈfaɪtəˈbɒməʳ] ɴ cacciabombardiere *m*

fighter pilot ɴ pilota *m* di caccia

fight·ing [ˈfaɪtɪŋ] ɴ (*Mil*) combattimento; (*in streets*) scontri *mpl*; (*in pub etc*) risse *fpl*, zuffe *fpl*; **fighting broke out outside the pub** è scoppiata una rissa fuori dal pub ♦ ᴀᴅᴊ (*forces, strength, troops*) da combattimento; **fighting spirit** spirito combattivo; **a fighting chance** una buona probabilità

fig·ment [ˈfɪgmənt] ɴ: **it's a figment of the imagination** è frutto dell'immaginazione, è un parto della fantasia

fig·ura·tive [ˈfɪgərətɪv] ᴀᴅᴊ (*meaning*) figurato(-a); (*Art*) figurativo(-a)

fig·ure [ˈfɪgəʳ] ɴ **1** (*number*) cifra; **to be good at figures** essere bravo(-a) a fare i conti; **a mistake in the figures** un errore nei calcoli, un errore di calcolo; **can you give me the exact figures?** puoi darmi le cifre esatte?; **to reach double/three figures** raggiungere le due/tre cifre **2** (*body, outline*) figura, forma; **to lose one's figure** perdere la linea; **I have to watch my figure** devo stare attento alla linea **3** (*person*) figura, personaggio; **public figure** personaggio pubblico; **she's an important political figure** è un importante personaggio politico **4** (*drawing, Geom*) figura; (*diagram*) illustrazione *f* ♦ ᴠɪ (*appear*) figurare **2** (*esp USA: make sense*) essere logico(-a), spiegarsi; **that figures!** (*fam*) è logico! ♦ ᴠᴛ (*esp USA: think, calculate*) pensare, immaginare

► **figure on** ᴠᴛ + ᴘʀᴇᴘ (*USA*) contare su; **I figured on him arriving by 6 o'clock** contavo sul fatto che sarebbe arrivato per le 6

► **figure out** ᴠᴛ + ᴀᴅᴠ (*understand*) riuscire a capire; (*calculate: sum*) calcolare; **I just can't figure it out!** non ci arrivo!

figure·head [ˈfɪgəˌhɛd] ɴ (*Naut*) polena; (*fig*) figura rappresentativa; (*pej*) prestanome *m/f inv*; **he's little more than a figurehead** è poco più che un prestanome

figure skating ɴ pattinaggio artistico

Fiji [ˈfiːdʒiː] ɴ: **the Fiji Islands** le isole *fpl* Figi

fila·ment [ˈfɪləmənt] ɴ filamento

filch [fɪltʃ] ᴠᴛ (*fam: steal*) grattare

file¹ [faɪl] ɴ (*folder*) cartella, cartellina; (*ring binder*) raccoglitore *m*; (*dossier*) pratica, incartamento; (*in cabinet*) scheda; (*Comput*) file *m inv*; **there was stuff in that file that was private** c'erano delle cose riservate in quella pratica; **the police have a file on him** è schedato dalla polizia; **she put the photocopy into her file** ha messo la fotocopia nella sua cartella ♦ ᴠᴛ **1** (*also:* **file away**) (*notes, information, papers*)

raccogliere; (*under heading*) archiviare **2** (*Law: claim, application, complaint*) presentare; **to file a suit against sb** (*Law*) intentare causa contro qn

file² [faɪl] ɴ (*tool*) lima; (*for nails*) lima, limetta ♦ ᴠᴛ (*metal, wood*) limare; **to file one's nails** limarsi le unghie; **she was filing her nails** si stava limando le unghie

file³ [faɪl] ɴ (*row*) fila; **in single file** in fila indiana ♦ ᴠɪ: **to file in/out** entrare/uscire in fila; **to file past (sth/sb)** sfilare (davanti a qc/qn), marciare in fila (davanti a qc/qn)

file name ɴ (*Comput*) nome (del) file

file-sharing [ˈfaɪlˌʃɛərɪŋ] ɴ (*Comput*) file-sharing *mpl*, condivisione *f* di informazioni in internet

fili·bus·ter [ˈfɪlɪˌbʌstəʳ] (*esp USA Pol*) ɴ ostruzionismo ♦ ᴠɪ fare ostruzionismo

fil·ing [ˈfaɪlɪŋ] ɴ archiviazione *f*; *see also* **filings**

filing cabinet ɴ schedario, casellario

filing clerk, file clerk (*USA*) ɴ archivista *m/f*

fil·ings [ˈfaɪlɪŋz] ɴᴘʟ limatura

Fili·pi·no [ˌfɪlɪˈpiːnəʊ] ᴀᴅᴊ filippino(-a) ♦ ɴ **1** (*person*) filippino(-a) **2** (*language*) tagal *m*

fill [fɪl] ᴠᴛ (*gen*) riempire; (*tooth*) otturare; (*position*) coprire; (*subj: wind: sails*) gonfiare; (*supply: order, requirements, need*) soddisfare; **to fill with** riempire di *or* con; **she filled the glass with water** ha riempito il bicchiere d'acqua; **we've already filled that vacancy** abbiamo già assunto qualcuno per quel posto; **they asked her to fill the vacancy** le hanno offerto il posto; **the position is already filled** il posto è già preso; **filled with admiration (for)** pieno(-a) di ammirazione (per); **filled with remorse/despair** in preda al rimorso/alla disperazione; **that fills the bill** è quello che ci vuole ♦ ᴠɪ: **to fill (with)** riempirsi (di *or* con) ♦ ɴ: **to eat/drink one's fill** mangiare/bere a sazietà; **to have one's fill of sth** (*fig*) averne le tasche piene di qc

► **fill in** ᴠᴛ + ᴀᴅᴠ **1** (*hole, gap, outline*) riempire **2** (*one's name*) mettere; (*form*) riempire, compilare; (*details, report*) completare; **can you fill this form in, please?** può riempire questo modulo, per favore?; **to fill sb in on sth** (*fam*) mettere qn al corrente di qc; **I'll fill you in on what's been happening** ti metterò al corrente su quello che succede ♦ ᴠɪ + ᴀᴅᴠ: **to fill in for sb** sostituire qn

► **fill out** ᴠᴛ + ᴀᴅᴠ (*form, receipt*) riempire, compilare ♦ ᴠɪ + ᴀᴅᴠ (*person, face*) ingrassare, ingrassarsi; (*sail*) gonfiarsi

► **fill up** ᴠɪ + ᴀᴅᴠ **1** (*Aut*) fare il pieno **2** (*room etc*) riempirsi, gremirsi ♦ ᴠᴛ + ᴀᴅᴠ (*container*) riempire; **fill it** *or* **her up, please** (*fam: Aut*) mi faccia il pieno, per piacere

fil·let [ˈfɪlɪt] ɴ filetto ♦ ᴠᴛ (*meat*) disossare; (*fish*) tagliare a filetti, sfilettare; **filleted cod** filetti *mpl* di merluzzo

fillet steak ɴ (bistecca di) filetto

fill·ing [ˈfɪlɪŋ] ɴ (*for tooth*) otturazione *f*; (*Culin*) ripieno ♦ ᴀᴅᴊ (*food*) sostanzioso(-a)

filling station ɴ stazione *f* di rifornimento

fil·lip [ˈfɪlɪp] ɴ stimolo, incentivo

fil·ly [ˈfɪlɪ] ɴ puledra

film [fɪlm] ɴ **1** (*at cinema*) film *m inv*; (*Phot*) pellicola; **a 36 exposure film** un rullino da 36 pose *or* foto; **film buff** appassionato(-a) di cinema; **film camera** macchina da presa **2** (*thin layer*) strato sottile, velo; (*wrap*) pellicola ♦ ᴠᴛ (*scene*) filmare

film script ɴ copione *m*

film star ɴ divo(-a) del cinema

film·strip [ˈfɪlmˌstrɪp] ɴ filmina

film studio ɴ studio cinematografico

fil·ter [ˈfɪltəʳ] ɴ filtro ♦ ᴠᴛ filtrare ♦ ᴠɪ: **to filter to the left** (*Aut*) immettersi nella corsia di svincolo

► **filter in, filter out, filter through** ᴠɪ + ᴀᴅᴠ (*news*) trapelare; **the news started to filter out** le notizie hanno cominciato a trapelare

filter coffee ɴ caffè *m* da passare al filtro

filter tip ɴ filtro

filth [fɪlθ] ɴ sudiciume *m*, sporcizia; (*fig*) oscenità; **mess and filth** disordine e sporcizia; **it's just sheer filth** non è altro che una porcheria

filthy [ˈfɪlθɪ] ᴀᴅᴊ (*comp* **-ier**, *superl* **-iest**) sudicio(-a), sozzo(-a); (*language*) volgare, osceno(-a); **a filthy joke** una barzelletta sporca

fin [fɪn] N (of fish) pinna; (of plane, bomb) impennaggio verticale

fi·nal ['faɪnl] ADJ (last) ultimo(-a); (conclusive) finale, definitivo(-a); (victory) conclusivo(-a); (exam) finale; **a final attempt** un ultimo tentativo; **a final decision** una decisione definitiva; **final demand** (Comm) ingiunzione f (di pagamento); **the judge's decision is final** la decisione del giudice è inappellabile; **... and that's final!** ...e basta!; **I'm not going and that's final!** non ci vado e basta! ♦ N (Sport) finale f; **Federer is in the final** Federer è in finale; see also **finals**

fi·na·le [fi'nɑːlɪ] N finale m; **the grand finale** (also fig) il gran finale

fi·nal·ist ['faɪnəlɪst] N (Sport) finalista m/f

fi·nal·ity [faɪ'nælɪtɪ] N irrevocabilità; **with an air of finality** con risolutezza

fi·nal·ize ['faɪnəlaɪz] VT (preparations, arrangements, plans) mettere a punto; (agreement, decision, contract) definire; (report, text) dare una stesura definitiva a; (date) fissare

fi·nal·ly ['faɪnəlɪ] ADV (lastly) alla fine; (in conclusion) infine; (eventually) finalmente; (once and for all) definitivamente; **finally, I would like to say ...** vorrei dire, infine...; **they finally decided to leave on Saturday** alla fine hanno deciso di partire sabato; **the food finally arrived** finalmente arrivò da mangiare; **and finally...** e per concludere...

fi·nance [faɪ'næns] N 1 (money management) finanza; (funds) fondi mpl, capitale m; **Minister of Finance** Ministro delle Finanze; **small businesses have difficulty getting finance** le piccole imprese hanno difficoltà a reperire fondi 2 (resources) finances NPL finanze fpl ♦ VT finanziare ♦ ADJ (page, section, company) finanziario(-a)

fi·nan·cial [faɪ'nænʃəl] ADJ finanziario(-a); **financial management** gestione f finanziaria; **financial statement** estratto conto finanziario

financial adviser N consulente m/f finanziario(-a)

fi·nan·cial·ly [faɪ'nænʃəlɪ] ADV finanziariamente

financial year N anno finanziario, esercizio finanziario

fi·nan·ci·er [fɪ'nænsɪə'] N finanziatore(-trice)

find [faɪnd] (pt, pp found) VT 1 (gen) trovare; (sth lost) trovare, ritrovare; (learn) scoprire; **I can't find the exit** non riesco a trovare l'uscita; **I've found it** l'ho trovato; **the book is nowhere to be found** il libro non si trova da nessuna parte; **this plant is found all over Europe** questa pianta si trova in tutta Europa; **it has been found that ...** è stato or si è scoperto che...; **if you can find the time** se riesci a trovare il tempo; **no cure has been found** non è stata trovata nessuna cura; **I found it impossible to tell the difference** non riuscivo a distinguerli; **he finds it easy/difficult to do ...** non trova/trova difficoltà a or nel fare...; **to find (some) difficulty in doing sth** trovare delle difficoltà nel fare qc; **I find him very pleasant** lo trovo molto simpatico; **we found him in bed/reading** l'abbiamo trovato a letto/che stava leggendo; **I found myself at a loss** non sapevo cosa dire, non riuscivo a trovare le parole; **can you find your (own) way to the station?** sai che andare alla stazione?; **this found its way into my drawer** questo è andato a finire nel mio cassetto; **leave everything as you find it** lascia tutto come trovi; **to find fault with sb/sth** trovare da ridire sul conto di qn/su qc; **to find sb guilty** (Law) giudicare qn colpevole; **he was found innocent** (Law) fu dichiarato innocente; **to find one's feet** (fig) ambientarsi 2 (obtain) trovare; **go and find me a pencil** vai a cercarmi una matita; **there are no more to be found** non ce ne sono più; **wages all found** stipendio più vitto e alloggio ♦ VI (Law): **to find for/against sb** emettere un verdetto a favore di/contro qn ♦ N scoperta, trovata

▸ **find out** VT + ADV informarsi di; (truth, secret, answer) scoprire; **to find out that ...** scoprire che...; **to find sb out** smascherare qn ♦ VI + ADV: **to find out about** scoprire; (by investigation) informarsi su; **we found out about his death** abbiamo scoperto che era morto; **we found out all about ...** abbiamo scoperto tutto su...; **find out as much as possible about the town** informati il più possibile sulla città

find·ings ['faɪndɪŋz] NPL (of report, of inquiry) conclusioni fpl; (Law) verdetto

fine¹ [faɪn] ADJ (comp -r, superl -st) 1 (small, delicate, narrow) fine; (rain) leggero(-a); (fig: distinction) sottile; **not to put too fine a point on it** per dirlo con schiettezza; **he's got it down to a fine art** lo fa alla perfezione 2 (not coarse: metal) fino(-a); (: sense) sottile; (: taste) raffinato(-a); (: feelings) elevato(-a); **she's got very fine hair** ha i capelli molto sottili; **fine workmanship** lavorazione f raffinata 3 (good) ottimo(-a); (beautiful, imposing) bello(-a); (clothes) elegante; **if the weather is fine** se il tempo è bello; **it's a fine day today** è una bella giornata oggi; **he's a fine man** è un'ottima persona; **it'll be ready tomorrow — that's fine, thanks** sarà pronto domani — va bene, grazie; **he's fine** sta bene; **how are you? — fine, thanks!** come stai? — bene, grazie!; **I feel fine** mi sento bene; **a fine friend you are!** bell'amico sei!; **you're a fine one to talk!** senti chi parla!; **a fine thing!** bella roba!; **one fine day** un bel giorno ♦ ADV 1 (well) molto bene; **you're doing fine** te la cavi benissimo 2 (finely) finemente; **to cut it fine** (of time, money) farcela per un pelo

▸ **fine down** VT + ADV affinare

fine² [faɪn] N multa; **to get a fine for sth/doing sth** ricevere una multa per qc/per aver fatto qc ♦ VT: **to fine sb (for sth/for doing sth)** multare qn or fare una multa a qn (per qc/per aver fatto qc)

fine arts NPL: **the fine arts** (le) belle arti fpl

fine·ly ['faɪnlɪ] ADV 1 (written, sewn) con raffinatezza 2 (chop) finemente; (adjust) con precisione

fine print N: **the fine print** i caratteri minuti

fin·ery ['faɪnərɪ] N abiti mpl eleganti; **to be dressed in all one's finery** essere tutto(-a) in ghingheri

fi·nesse [fi'nɛs] N finezza; (Cards) impasse f

fine-tooth comb ['faɪntuːθˈkəʊm] N: **to go through sth with a fine-tooth comb** (fig) passare qc al setaccio

fin·ger ['fɪŋɡə'] N dito; **a ring on every finger** un anello su ogni dito; **my little finger** il mignolo; **keep your fingers crossed** fai gli scongiuri; **he didn't lift a finger to help** non ha mosso un dito per aiutare; **I can't quite put my finger on what's wrong** non riesco a vedere cosa c'è di sbagliato; **to twist sb round one's little finger** fare quello che si vuole di qn; **to have a finger in every pie** avere le mani in pasta dappertutto; **to pull one's finger out** (fig: fam) darsi una mossa ♦ VT toccare, tastare; (keyboard) far scorrere le dita su

finger·nail ['fɪŋɡəneɪl] N unghia

finger·print ['fɪŋɡəprɪnt] N impronta digitale ♦ VT (person) prendere le impronte digitali di or a

finger·stall ['fɪŋɡəstɔːl] N ditale m

finger·tip ['fɪŋɡətɪp] N punta del dito; **to have sth at one's fingertips** (fig) avere qc sulla punta delle dita; **fingertip hold** (Mountaineering) gratton m inv

fin·icky ['fɪnɪkɪ] ADJ 1 (person): **finicky (about)** pignolo(-a) (su), difficile (per) 2 (job) minuzioso(-a)

fin·ish ['fɪnɪʃ] N 1 (end, esp Sport) fine f; (Sport: line) traguardo; (Mountaineering) uscita; **from start to finish** dall'inizio alla fine; **to be in at the finish** essere presente alla fine; **a fight to the finish** un combattimento all'ultimo sangue 2 (appearance) finitura ♦ VT (gen) finire, terminare; (use up) esaurire; **to finish doing sth** finire di fare qc; **that last mile nearly finished me** (fam) quell'ultimo miglio mi ha quasi distrutto ♦ VI (session) finire, terminare; (book, game) finire, concludersi; (contract) scadere; (Mountaineering) uscire; **I've finished!** ho finito!; **have you finished eating?** hai finito di mangiare?; **the party was finishing** la festa stava per finire; **she finished by saying that ...** ha concluso dicendo che...; **to finish first/second** (Sport) arrivare primo(-a)/secondo(-a); **I've finished with the paper** ho finito col giornale; **he's finished with politics** ha chiuso con la politica; **she's finished with her boyfriend** (broken relationship) ha chiuso con il suo ragazzo

▸ **finish off** VT + ADV finire; (kill) uccidere

▸ **finish up** VI + ADV finire; **he finished up in Paris** è finito a Parigi, **it finished up as ...** ha finito col diventare... ♦ VT + ADV (food etc) finire

fin·ished ['fɪnɪʃt] ADJ 1 (product) finito(-a); (performance) perfetto(-a) 2 (fam: tired) sfinito(-a); (: done for) finito(-a)

fin·ish·ing line ['fɪnɪʃɪŋlaɪn] N (Sport) traguardo, linea d'arrivo

fin·ish·ing school ['fɪnɪʃɪŋskuːl] N scuola privata di perfezionamento (per signorine)

fin·ish·ing touches [ˌfɪnɪʃɪŋˈtʌtʃɪz] NPL ultimi ritocchi mpl;

to put the finishing touches to sth dare gli ultimi ritocchi a qc

fi·nite [ˈfaɪnaɪt] ADJ 1 (*limited*) limitato(-a); **finite resources** risorse limitate 2 (*Gram: verb*) finito(-a)

Fin·land [ˈfɪnlənd] N la Finlandia

Finn [fɪn] N finlandese *m/f*

Finn·ish [ˈfɪnɪʃ] ADJ finlandese ♦ N (*language*) finlandese *m*

fiord [fjɔːd] N = **fjord**

fir [fɜːʳ] N (*also:* **fir tree**) abete *m*

fire [ˈfaɪəʳ] N 1 (*gen*) fuoco; (*house fire etc*) incendio; **electric/gas fire** stufa elettrica/a gas; **forest fire** incendio boschivo; **to set fire to sth** *or* **set sth on fire** dar fuoco a qc, incendiare qc; **to catch fire** prendere fuoco; **to be on fire** essere in fiamme; **he made a fire to warm himself up** ha acceso un fuoco per scaldarsi; **the house was destroyed by a fire** la casa è stata distrutta da un incendio; **insured against fire** assicurato(-a) contro gli incendi; **to play with fire** (*fig*) scherzare col fuoco 2 (*Mil*) fuoco; **to open fire (on sb)** aprire il fuoco (contro *or* su qn); **to hold one's fire** cessare il fuoco; **to be/come under fire (from)** essere/finire sotto il fuoco *or* il tiro (di); **the government has come under fire from the opposition** il governo è finito sotto il tiro dell'opposizione ♦ VT 1 (*gun, shot, salute*) sparare; (*rocket etc*) lanciare; **to fire a gun at sb** fare fuoco contro qn; **to fire questions at sb** bombardare qn di domande 2 (*pottery: in kiln*) cuocere; (*fig: imagination*) accendere, infiammare 3 (*fam: dismiss*) licenziare; **you're fired!** sei licenziato!; **he was fired from his job** è stato licenziato ♦ VI 1 (*Mil, etc*): **to fire (at)** sparare (a), far fuoco (contro); **she fired at him** gli ha sparato; **fire away** *or* **ahead!** (*fig: fam*) spara! 2 (*Aut: subj: engine*) accendersi

fire alarm N allarme *m* antincendio, *inv*

fire·arm [ˈfaɪərɑːm] N arma da fuoco

fire brigade, (*USA*) **fire department** N (corpo dei) pompieri *mpl* *or* vigili *mpl* del fuoco

fire chief N (*USA*) comandante *m* dei vigili del fuoco

fire department N (*USA*) = **fire brigade**

fire door N porta *f* tagliafuoco, *inv*

fire drill, fire practice N esercitazione *f* antincendio, *inv*

fire engine N autopompa

fire escape N scala di sicurezza

fire exit N uscita di sicurezza

fire extinguisher N estintore *m*

fire·guard [ˈfaɪəˌɡɑːd] N (*Brit*) parafuoco

fire hazard N: **that's a fire hazard** può provocare un incendio

fire hydrant N idrante *m*

fire insurance N assicurazione *f* contro gli incendi

fire·man [ˈfaɪəmən] N (*pl* **-men**) vigile *m* del fuoco, pompiere *m*

fire·place [ˈfaɪəˌpleɪs] N caminetto, focolare *m*

fire·plug [ˈfaɪəˌplʌɡ] N (*USA*) = **fire hydrant**

fire practice N = **fire drill**

fire·proof [ˈfaɪəˌpruːf] ADJ (*material*) resistente al fuoco; (*dish*) resistente al calore

fire regulations NPL norme *fpl* antincendio

fire screen N = **fireguard**

fire·side [ˈfaɪəˌsaɪd] N angolo del focolare; **by the fireside** intorno al focolare

fire station N caserma dei pompieri

fire truck N (*USA*) autopompa

fire·wall [ˈfaɪəwɔːl] N (*Comput*) firewall *m inv*

fire·wood [ˈfaɪəˌwʊd] N legna da ardere

fire·works [ˈfaɪəˌwɜːks] NPL (*show*) fuochi *mpl* d'artificio; (*fig: temper*) parole *fpl* grosse; (*: virtuosity*) virtuosismi *mpl*

fir·ing [ˈfaɪərɪŋ] N (*Mil*) spari *mpl*, tiro

firing line N linea del fuoco; **to be in the firing line** (*fig: liable to be criticized*) essere sulla linea del fuoco

firing squad N plotone *m* d'esecuzione

firm¹ [fɜːm] ADJ (*comp* **-er**, *superl* **-est**) (*gen*) solido(-a); (*steady*) saldo(-a); (*belief*) fermo(-a); (*measures*) severo(-a); (*look, voice*) risoluto(-a); (*prices*) stabile; (*offer, decision*) definitivo(-a); **firm tomatoes** pomodori non troppo maturi; **a firm mattress** un materasso rigido; **a firm grip** una presa salda; **a firm refusal** un netto rifiuto; **as firm as a rock** solido(-a) come una roccia; **to be a firm believer in sth** credere fermamente in qc; **to be firm with sb** essere deciso(-a) con qn; **they are firm friends** sono molto amici; **to keep a firm hold on** tenere saldamente; **to be on firm ground** (*fig*) andare sul sicuro; **to stand firm** *or* **take a firm stand over sth** (*fig*) tener duro per quanto riguarda qc

❏ **firm** is not translated by the Italian word *firma*

firm² [fɜːm] N azienda, ditta, impresa

firm·ly [ˈfɜːmlɪ] ADV (*fixed*) saldamente, solidamente; (*speak*) con fermezza; (*believe*) fermamente

firm·ness [ˈfɜːmnɪs] N (*of voice, decision etc*) fermezza; (*of object*) solidità

first [fɜːst] ADJ primo(-a); **the first of January** il primo (di) gennaio; **the first time** la prima volta; **Charles the First** Carlo Primo; **to win first place** arrivare primo; **in the first place** per prima cosa, innanzitutto; **in the first instance** in primo luogo, prima di tutto; **first thing in the morning** la mattina presto; **I'll do it first thing tomorrow** lo farò per prima cosa domani; **first things first!** prima le cose più importanti!; **I don't know the first thing about it** (*fam*) non ne so un bel niente ♦ ADV 1 (*firstly*) prima; (*before other things*) per primo(-a); (*when listing reasons etc*) per prima cosa; **first one, then another** prima uno, poi un altro; **first of all** prima di tutto, innanzitutto; **first and foremost** prima di tutto, innanzitutto; **first and last** (*above all*) prima di tutto; **ladies first!** prima le signore!; **we arrived first** siamo arrivati per primi; **she came first in the race** è arrivata prima nella gara; **at first** sulle prime, all'inizio, dapprima; **it was difficult at first** all'inizio è stato difficile; **finish this work first** finisci questo lavoro prima; **I want to get a job, but first I have to pass my exams** voglio trovare un lavoro, ma prima devo passare gli esami; **head first** a capofitto 2 (*for the first time*) per la prima volta; **I first met him in Paris** l'ho incontrato per la prima volta a Parigi 3 (*rather*) piuttosto; **I'd die first!** piuttosto morirei! ♦ N (*person: in race*) primo(-a); **the first to arrive** il (la) primo(-a) ad arrivare; **first come, first served** chi tardi arriva, male alloggia; **from the (very) first** fin dall'inizio; **from first to last** dall'inizio alla fine; **in first (gear)** (*Aut*) in prima (marcia)

first aid N pronto soccorso

first-aid [ˈfɜːstˈeɪd] ADJ: **first-aid classes** corso di pronto soccorso; **first-aid kit** *or* **box** cassetta di pronto soccorso; **first-aid post** posto di pronto soccorso

first-class [ˈfɜːstˈklɑːs] ADJ 1 di prima classe; **first-class ticket** (*Rail, etc*) biglietto di prima classe; **first-class compartment** (*Rail*) scompartimento di prima classe; **first-class honours degree** (*Univ*) ≈ laurea con centodieci e lode 2 (*very good*) di prima qualità; **a first-class meal** un pranzo eccellente 3 **a first-class stamp** un francobollo per posta prioritaria ♦ ADV: **to travel first-class** viaggiare in prima classe; **to send a letter first-class** ≈ spedire una lettera per espresso

first-class mail N ≈ espresso

first-hand [ˈfɜːstˈhænd] ADJ diretto(-a), di prima mano ♦ ADV direttamente

First Lady N (*USA*) moglie *f* del presidente

first·ly [ˈfɜːstlɪ] ADV prima, innanzitutto, in primo luogo

first name N nome *m* (di battesimo)

first night N (*Theatre*) prima

first-rate [ˈfɜːstˈreɪt] ADJ di prim'ordine, ottimo(-a)

first-time buyer [ˈfɜːstˈtaɪmˈbaɪəʳ] N acquirente *m/f* di prima casa

First World War N: **the First World War** la prima guerra mondiale

fis·cal [ˈfɪskəl] ADJ fiscale

fish [fɪʃ] N (*pl* **fish** *or* **fishes**) pesce *m*; **I caught three fish** ho pescato tre pesci; **I don't like fish** non mi piace il pesce; **fish and chips** pesce impanato e patatine; **to be like a fish out of water** sentirsi come un pesce fuor d'acqua; **I've got other fish to fry** (*fam*) ho altro da fare ♦ VI pescare; **to go fishing** andare a pesca; **to go salmon fishing** andare a pesca di salmoni; **to fish for trout** pescare (le) trote; **to fish for compliments/for information** (*fig*) andare a caccia di complimenti/di informazioni; **to fish (around) in one's pockets for sth** frugarsi le tasche in cerca di qc ♦ VT (*river, pond*) pescare in; (*trout, salmon*) pescare

▸ **fish out** VT + ADV (*from water*) ripescare; (*from box etc*) tirare fuori

fish-and-chip shop [ˈfiʃəndˈtʃɪpˌʃɒp] N (*Brit*) *see* chip shop
fish·bone [ˈfiʃˌbəʊn] N lisca, spina
fisher·man [ˈfiʃəmən] N (*pl* -men) pescatore *m*
fish·ery [ˈfiʃərɪ] N zona di pesca
fish farm N vivaio
fish-hook [ˈfiʃˌhʊk] N amo
fish·ing [ˈfiʃɪŋ] N pesca
fishing boat N peschereccio
fishing industry N industria della pesca
fishing line N lenza
fishing net N rete *f* da pesca
fishing rod N canna da pesca
fishing tackle N attrezzatura da pesca
fish market N mercato del pesce
fish·monger [ˈfiʃˌmʌŋgəʳ] N (*Brit*) pescivendolo; **fishmonger's (shop)** pescheria
fish slice N (*Brit*) paletta forata *or* per fritti
fish sticks [ˈfiʃˌstɪks] NPL (*USA*) = **fish fingers**
fishy [ˈfiʃɪ] ADJ (*comp* -ier, *superl* -iest) 1 (*smell, taste, usu pej*) di pesce 2 (*fam: suspicious*) losco(-a), sospetto(-a)
fis·sion [ˈfiʃən] N fissione *f*; **atomic/nuclear fission** fissione atomica/nucleare
fis·sure [ˈfiʃəʳ] N fessura, fenditura
fist [fist] N pugno; **to shake one's fist (at sb)** minacciare (qn) con il pugno
fist·fight [ˈfistˌfait] N scazzottata
fit [fit] ADJ (*comp* -ter, *superl* -test) 1 (*suitable*) adatto(-a); (*proper*) appropriato(-a), conveniente; **fit for** adatto(-a) a; **to be fit for sth** andare bene per qc; **only two of the bikes were fit for the road** solo due bici erano utilizzabili; **to be fit for nothing** non essere buono(-a) a niente; **a meal fit for a king** un pranzo da re; **he's not fit for the job** non è la persona adatta per questo lavoro; **fit for habitation** abitabile; **to be fit to play** essere in condizione di giocare; **they're not fit to govern** non sono in grado di governare; **he's not fit to teach** non è adatto all'insegnamento; **he's not fit to drive** non è in condizione di guidare; **you're not fit to be seen** non sei presentabile; **it's not fit to eat** *or* **to be eaten** non è mangiabile *or* commestibile; **the water wasn't fit to drink** l'acqua non era potabile; **do as you think** *or* **see fit** fai come meglio credi 2 (*in health*) in forma; (*Sport*) in buone condizioni fisiche, in forma; **to keep fit** tenersi in forma; **to be fit for work** (*after illness*) essere in grado di riprendere il lavoro; **to be (as) fit as a fiddle** essere sano(-a) come un pesce ♦ N: **to be a good fit** (*shoes*) calzare bene; (*clothes*) andare *or* stare bene; **it's a rather tight fit** mi sta un po' stretto ♦ VT 1 (*subj: clothes*) andare/stare bene a; (: *key etc*) adattarsi a; **it fits you well** ti sta bene; **it fits me like a glove** mi sta a pennello 2 (*match: facts etc*) concordare con; (: *description*) corrispondere a; **the punishment should fit the crime** la punizione dovrebbe essere adeguata al reato 3 (*put in place*) mettere, fissare; **to fit a key in the lock** mettere una chiave nella serratura; **to have a carpet fitted** far mettere la moquette; **to fit sth into place** sistemare qc; **to fit sth on sth** mettere qc a *or* su qc 4 (*equip*) fornire, dotare, equipaggiare; **a car fitted with a radio** una macchina fornita di radio; **she has been fitted with a new hearing aid** le hanno messo un nuovo apparecchio acustico ♦ VT (*make fit*) rendere adatto(-a); (*adjust*) aggiustare; **to fit a dress (on sb)** provare un vestito (a qn); **her experience fits her for the job** la sua esperienza la rende adatta a questo lavoro ♦ VI 1 (*clothes*) andare *or* stare bene; (*part*) adattarsi; (*key, object*) andare, entrare; **does it fit?** ti va bene? 2 (*match: facts*) quadrare; (: *story*) reggere; (: *description*) calzare; **it all fits now!** tutto è chiaro adesso!
  ▸ **fit in** VI + ADV (*person*) adattarsi; **to fit in (with)** (*fact, statement*) corrispondere (a), concordare (con); **that story doesn't fit in with what he told us** la storia non corrisponde a quanto ci ha detto; **to fit in with sb's plans** adattarsi ai progetti di qn; **he left because he didn't fit in** se ne è andato perché non riusciva ad integrarsi; **she fitted in well at her new school** si è ambientata bene nella nuova scuola ♦ VT + ADV (*object*) far entrare; (*fig: appointment, visitor*) trovare il tempo per; (*plan, activity*): **to fit in (with)** conciliare (con); **the doctor can't fit you in today** il dottore non ha tempo di vederla oggi

  ▸ **fit out** VT + ADV (*Brit: ship*) allestire, equipaggiare; (: *person*) fornire, equipaggiare
  ▸ **fit up** VT + ADV 1 (*provide*): **to fit sb up with sth** fornire qc a qn 2 (*arrange: room etc*) attrezzare 3 (*fam: incriminate*) incastrare
  ❏ **fit** is not translated by the Italian word *fitto*
fit·ful [ˈfitfʊl] ADJ saltuario(-a); (*breeze, showers*) intermittente; (*wind*) a raffiche; (*sleep*) agitato(-a)
fit·ment [ˈfitmənt] N (*accessory: of machine*) accessorio
fit·ness [ˈfitnis] N 1 (*suitability: for post etc*): **fitness (for)** idoneità (a) (*of remark*) appropriatezza 2 (*health*) forma fisica
fitness instructor N instruttore(-trice) di fitness
fit·ted [ˈfitid] ADJ (*garment*) modellato(-a); **fitted carpet** moquette *f inv*; **fitted cupboards** armadi *mpl* a muro; **fitted kitchen** (*Brit*) cucina componibile; **fitted sheet** lenzuolo con gli angoli
fit·ter [ˈfitəʳ] N (*Tech*) installatore(-trice); (*of garment*) sarto(-a)
fit·ting [ˈfitiŋ] ADJ (*suitable*) adatto(-a), appropriato(-a); **it is fitting that** (*frm*) è opportuno che ♦ N (*of dress*) prova; (*of piece of equipment*) installazione *f*; *see also* **fittings**
fitting room N (*in shop*) camerino
fittings [ˈfitiŋz] NPL (*of house*) accessori *mpl*, attrezzature *fpl*; **bathroom fittings** accessori per il bagno
five [faiv] ADJ cinque *inv*; **she is five (years old)** ha cinque anni; **they live at number five/at five Green Street** vivono al numero cinque/al numero cinque di Green Street; **there are five of us** siamo in cinque; **all five of them came** sono venuti tutti e cinque; **it costs five pounds** costa cinque sterline; **five and a quarter/half** cinque e un quarto/mezzo; **it's five (o'clock)** sono le cinque ♦ N cinque *m inv*; **to divide sth into five** dividere qc in cinque parti; **they are sold in fives** sono venduti in gruppi di cinque
five-day week [ˈfaivˈdeiˈwiːk] N settimana di cinque giorni (lavorativi)
fiv·er [ˈfaivəʳ] N (*fam: Brit*) biglietto da cinque sterline; (: *USA*) biglietto da cinque dollari
fix [fiks] N 1 (*fam: predicament*) pasticcio, guaio; **to be in a fix** essere in un pasticcio, essere nei guai; **to get o.s. into a fix** cacciarsi nei guai 2 (*fam: of drug*) pera 3 **the fight was a fix** (*fam*) l'incontro è stato truccato 4 (*Aer, Naut*) posizione *f*; **to take a fix on** fare il punto su ♦ VT 1 (*gen, also Phot, fig*) fissare; (*with string etc*) legare, fissare; **she fixed the picture to the wall** ha fissato il quadro al muro; **to fix one's gaze on** fermare lo sguardo su; **to fix the blame on sb/sth** darè *or* attribuire la colpa a qn/qc; **to fix sth in one's mind** imprimersi qc nella mente 2 (*date, price*) fissare, stabilire; (*fight, race*) truccare; **let's fix a date for the party** fissiamo una data per la festa; **I'll fix everything** ci penso io, sistemo tutto io; **I'll fix him!** (*fam*) lo sistemo io!, lo metto a posto io! 3 (*repair*) riparare, aggiustare; **can you fix my bike?** puoi aggiustarmi la bici? 4 (*USA: make ready: meal, drink*) preparare; **can I fix you a drink?** cosa posso offrirti da bere?; **I'm fixing lunch** sto preparando da mangiare; **to fix one's hair** darsi una pettinata
  ▸ **fix on** VT + ADV (*badge, lid*) fissare, attaccare ♦ VI + PREP (*decide on*) fissare
  ▸ **fix up** VT + ADV 1 (*arrange: date, meeting*) fissare, stabilire; **to fix sb up with sth** procurare qc a qn; **I fixed up an appointment to see her** ho fissato un appuntamento per vederla 2 (*clean, repair*) sistemare; **I've fixed up Paul's old room** ho sistemato la vecchia camera di Paul
fixa·tion [fikˈseiʃən] N (*Psych, also fig*) fissazione *f*, ossessione *f*; **to have a fixation on sth** avere la mania di qc
fixed [fikst] ADJ (*smile*) fisso(-a), ad un'ora stabilita; **fixed price** prezzo fisso; **there's a fixed charge** c'è una quota fissa 2 **how are you fixed for money?** (*fam*) a soldi come stai?
fixed assets NPL beni *mpl* patrimoniali
fixed penalty, fixed penalty fine N multa di importo fisso
fix·ture [ˈfikstʃəʳ] N 1 (*of house etc*); **fixtures** NPL impianti *mpl* 2 (*Sport*) incontro; **their next fixture** il loro prossimo incontro
fizz [fiz] N effervescenza ♦ VI frizzare
  ▸ **fizz up** VI + ADV spumeggiare

fiz·zle ['fɪzl] VI (*sputter*) sibilare
▸ **fizzle out** VI + ADV (*fire, firework*) finire per spegnersi; (*enthusiasm, interest*) smorzarsi, svanire; (*plan*) fallire
fizzy ['fɪzɪ] ADJ (*comp* -**ier**, *superl* -**iest**) (*drink*) gassato(-a), frizzante, effervescente
fjord, fiord [fjɔːd] N fiordo
FL ABBR (*USA Post*: = Florida)
flab·ber·gast·ed ['flæbə,gɑːstɪd] ADJ sbalordito(-a)
flab·by ['flæbɪ] ADJ (*comp* -**ier**, *superl* -**iest**) flaccido(-a), floscio(-a)
flag[1] [flæg] N (*gen*) bandiera; (*for charity etc*) bandierina; **flag of convenience** bandiera di convenienza
▸ **flag down** VT + ADV (*taxi, motorist*) fare cenno (di fermarsi) a
flag[2] [flæg] VI (*strength*) indebolirsi; (*person*) stancarsi; (*enthusiasm etc*) affievolirsi; (*conversation*) languire
flag[3] [flæg] N (*also*: **flag stone**) pietra per lastricare
flag·on ['flægən] N bottiglione m
flag·pole ['flæg,pəʊl] N pennone m
fla·grant ['fleɪgrənt] ADJ flagrante
flag stop N (*USA: for bus*) fermata a richiesta, fermata facoltativa
flair [fleə'] N (*for business etc*) fiuto; (*for languages etc*) predisposizione f; **to have a flair (for)** essere portato(-a) per; **she's got a flair for business** ha fiuto per gli affari; **he's got a flair for languages** ha predisposizione per le lingue
flak [flæk] N 1 (*Mil*) fuoco d'artiglieria 2 (*fam: criticism*) critiche *fpl*
flake [fleɪk] N 1 (*of paint, rust*) scaglia; (*of skin*) squama; (*of snow, cereal*) fiocco 2 (*USA fam*) strambo(-a) ♦ VI (*also*: **flake off**) (*paint*) scrostarsi; (*skin*) squamarsi; (*stone*) sfaldarsi
▸ **flake out** VI + ADV (*fam: collapse*) svenire; (*fall asleep*) crollare
flaky ['fleɪkɪ] ADJ (*comp* -**ier**, *superl* -**iest**) (*paintwork*) scrostato(-a); (*skin*) squamoso(-a); (*person, thing: USA: fam*) strambo(-a)
flam·boy·ant [flæm'bɔɪənt] ADJ (*character, speech*) stravagante; (*dress etc*) sgargiante, vistoso(-a); (*style*) fiorito(-a), ornato(-a)
flame [fleɪm] N fiamma; **to burst into flames** divampare; (*Comput*) violento attacco via e-mail ♦ VI (*also*: **flame up**) divampare; **her cheeks flamed with embarrassment** arrossì per l'imbarazzo ♦ VT attaccare violentemente via e-mail
fla·min·go [flə'mɪŋgəʊ] N fenicottero
flam·mable ['flæməbl] ADJ infiammabile
flan [flæn] N (*Brit: Culin: sweet*) flan m inv, torta; (: *savoury*) flan m inv, tortino; **a raspberry flan** una torta di lamponi; **a cheese and onion flan** un tortino di formaggio e cipolla
Flan·ders ['flɑːndəz] NSG le Fiandre *fpl*
flange [flændʒ] N (*Tech: on wheel*) flangia
flank [flæŋk] N (*gen, also Mil*) fianco ♦ VT fiancheggiare
flan·nel ['flænl] N (*fabric*) flanella; (*Brit*) (*also*: **face flannel**) guanto di spugna ♦ ADJ di flanella
flan·nel·ette [,flænə'let] N flanella di cotone
flap [flæp] N 1 (*of pocket*) patta, battente m; (*of envelope*) linguetta; (*of table*) ribalta; (*Aer*) flap m inv 2 (*movement*): **to give sth a flap** sbattere qc; **they could have the flap of the sails** (*sound*) sentivano sbattere le vele; **to be in a flap** (*fam*) essere in agitazione; **to get into a flap** (*fam*) farsi prendere dal panico ♦ VT (*subj: bird: wings*) sbattere, battere; (*shake: sheets, newspaper*) agitare, sbattere ♦ VI 1 (*wings, sails, flag*) sbattere 2 (*fam: panic*) farsi prendere dal panico
flap·jack ['flæp,dʒæk] N (*Brit: biscuit*) biscotto di avena; (*USA: pancake*) frittella
flare [fleə'] N 1 (*blaze*) chiarore m; (*signal*) segnale m luminoso; (*Mil: for target*) razzo illuminante 2 (*in skirt*) svasatura 3 (*trousers*); **flares** NPL pantaloni *mpl* a zampa d'elefante *or* a campana ♦ VI (*match, torch*) accendersi con una fiamma
▸ **flare up** VI + ADV (*fire*) divampare; (*fig: person*) infiammarsi di rabbia, saltar su; (: *revolt, situation etc*) scoppiare
flared ['fleəd] ADJ (*skirt, trousers*) svasato(-a)
flash [flæʃ] N 1 (*of light*) sprazzo, lampo; (*USA: torch*) torcia

elettrica, lampadina tascabile; **flash of lightning** lampo; **flash of inspiration** lampo di genio; **a flash in the pan** (*fig*) un fuoco di paglia; **in a flash** in un baleno, in un lampo 2 (*also*: **news flash**) flash m inv, notizia f lampo, inv 3 (*Phot*) flash m inv ♦ VT (*light, torch*) far lampeggiare; (*look*) lanciare; (*send: message*) trasmettere; **to flash one's headlights** (*Aut*) lampeggiare; **a truck driver flashed him** un camionista gli ha lampeggiato coi fari; **to flash sth about** (*fig: fam: flaunt*) ostentare qc; **stop flashing your money about!** smettila di ostentare i tuoi soldi! ♦ VI 1 (*light, eyes*) lampeggiare; (*lightning*) guizzare, balenare; (*jewels*) brillare, scintillare; **a light was flashing** una luce stava lampeggiando 2 (*move quickly: person, vehicle*): **to flash by** *or* **past** passare come un lampo; **he flashed by** *or* **past us** sfrecciò davanti a noi
flash·back ['flæʃ,bæk] N (*Cine*) flashback m inv
flash·bulb ['flæʃ,bʌlb] N flash m inv
flash card N (*Scol*) scheda didattica
flash·cube ['flæʃ,kjuːb] N (*Phot*) cubo-flash m inv
flash·er ['flæʃə'] N 1 (*Aut*) lampeggiatore m 2 (*Brit fam: man*) esibizionista m
flash·light ['flæʃ,laɪt] N (*USA: torch*) torcia elettrica, lampadina tascabile
flash·point ['flæʃ,pɔɪnt] N punto di infiammabilità; (*fig*) livello critico
flashy ['flæʃɪ] ADJ (*comp* -**ier**, *superl* -**est**) (*pej: car, clothes*) vistoso(-a); (*person*) appariscente
flask [flɑːsk] N (*for brandy etc*) fiaschetta; (*also*: **vacuum flask**) thermos m inv; (*Chem*) pallone m, beuta; **a flask of coffee** un thermos di caffè; **a flask of brandy** una fiaschetta di brandy
flat[1] [flæt] ADJ (*comp* -**ter**, *superl* -**test**) 1 (*gen*) piatto(-a); (*smooth*) liscio(-a), piano(-a); (*tyre or tire*) sgonfio(-a), a terra; **a flat surface** una superficie piatta; **I've got a flat tyre** ho una gomma a terra; **as flat as a pancake** (*fam*) completamente piatto(-a) (*Aut: tyre or tire*) completamente sgonfio(-a) *or* a terra; **to fall flat on one's face** cadere a terra lungo(-a) disteso(-a), finire faccia a terra; **flat race** corsa piana; **flat shoes** scarpe basse 2 (*final: refusal, denial*) categorico(-a), netto(-a) 3 (*Mus: key*) bemolle inv; (: *instrument*) scordato(-a); **C flat** do m inv bemolle 4 (*dull, lifeless: taste, style*) piatto(-a); (: *joke*) che non fa ridere; (: *drink*) che ha perso l'effervescenza, sgassato(-a); (: *battery*) scarico(-a); (: *colour*) scialbo(-a); **to be feeling rather flat** sentirsi giù di corda *or* di morale 5 (*fixed*): **flat rate of pay** tariffa unica di pagamento; **at a flat rate** a una tariffa unica ♦ ADV 1 (*absolutely: refuse, tell etc*) seccamente, recisamente; **flat broke** (*fam*) al verde, in bolletta; **in ten minutes flat** in dieci minuti spaccati; (**to work**) **flat out** (*lavorare*) a più non posso 2 **to spread a map out flat on the floor** stendere una cartina sul pavimento; **to be flat out** (*lying*) essere disteso(-a) *or* sdraiato(-a); (*asleep*) dormire della grossa 3 (*Mus: sing, play*) in modo stonato ♦ N (*of hand*) palmo; (*of sword*) parte f piatta; (*Mus*) bemolle m inv; (*Aut*) gomma a terra
flat[2] [flæt] N (*Brit*) appartamento
flat-footed ['flæt'fʊtɪd] ADJ: **to be flat-footed** avere i piedi piatti
flat·ly ['flætlɪ] ADV (*refuse etc*) categoricamente, nettamente
flat·mate ['flæt,meɪt] N: **he's my flatmate** (*Brit*) divide l'appartamento con me
flat·ness ['flætnɪs] N (*gen*) piattezza; (*dullness*) piattezza, monotonia; (*of land*) assenza di rilievi
flat-pack ['flætpæk] ADJ: **flat-pack furniture** mobili *mpl* in kit ♦ N kit m inv
flat-screen ['flæt'skriːn] ADJ a schermo piatto
flat·ten ['flætn] VT (*road, field*) spianare, appiattire; (*house, city*) abbattere, radere al suolo; (*map*) spiegare, aprire; **the town was flattened in the war** la città fu rasa al suolo durante la guerra; **to flatten o.s. against sth** appiattarsi contro qc; **he flattened himself against the wall** si è appiattato contro il muro
▸ **flatten out** VI + ADV (*road, countryside*) appiattirsi ♦ VT + ADV (*path, paper*) spianare
flat·ter ['flætə'] VT (*praise*) adulare, lusingare; (*show to advantage*) donare a; **she was just flattering me** mi stava solo adulando; **clothes that flatter you** vestiti che ti donano; **this photo flatters you** in questa foto sei venuto molto bene; **to flatter o.s. that one is …** illudersi di essere…

flat·ter·er [ˈflætərə] N adulatore(-trice)
flat·ter·ing [ˈflætərɪŋ] ADJ (*person, remark*) lusinghiero(-a); (*clothes etc*) che dona, che abbellisce; **this photo of you is not very flattering** questa foto non ti fa onore
flat·tery [ˈflætərɪ] N adulazione *f*, lusinghe *fpl*
flatu·lence [ˈflætjʊləns] N flatulenza
flaunt [flɔːnt] VT (*pej*) sfoggiare, ostentare
fla·vour, fla·vor (*USA*) [ˈfleɪvə] N sapore *m*, gusto; (*of ice-cream etc*) gusto; (*flavouring*) aroma *m*; (*fig*) atmosfera; **a very strong flavour** un sapore molto forte; **which flavour ice cream would you like?** che gusto di gelato vuoi? ◆ VT: **to flavour (with)** (*Culin: cake etc*) aromatizzare (con); (*: savoury dish*) condire (con), insaporire (con); **vanilla-flavoured** al gusto di vaniglia
fla·vour·ing, fla·vor·ing (*USA*) [ˈfleɪvərɪŋ] N (*for cake etc*) aroma *m*, essenza (artificiale); (*for savoury dish*) condimento; **vanilla flavouring** aroma di vaniglia
flaw [flɔː] N (*gen*) difetto; (*crack: in china*) incrinatura
flaw·less [ˈflɔːlɪs] ADJ perfetto(-a), senza difetti
flax [flæks] N lino
flax·en [ˈflæksən] ADJ biondo(-a)
flea [fliː] N pulce *f*; **to send sb off with a flea in his ear** (*fam*) mandare qn a quel paese
flea market N mercato delle pulci
fleck [flɛk] N (*of mud, paint, colour*) macchiolina; (*of dust*) granello ◆ VT (*with blood, mud etc*) macchiettare; **brown flecked with white** marrone screziato di bianco
fled [flɛd] PT, PP *of* **flee**
fledg·ling, fledge·ling [ˈflɛdʒlɪŋ] N uccellino
flee [fliː] (*pt, pp* **fled**) VT (*town, country*) fuggire da, scappare da; (*danger, enemy*) sfuggire a ◆ VI: **to flee (from)** fuggire (da *or* davanti a); **to flee to sb/sth** correre da qn/verso qc; **to flee to safety** mettersi in salvo
fleece [fliːs] N vello ◆ VT (*fig: fam: rob*) pelare
fleecy [ˈfliːsɪ] ADJ (*comp* **-ier,** *superl* **-iest**) (*blanket*) soffice; (*cloud*) come ovatta
fleet [fliːt] N flotta; (*of cars*) parco; (*of lorries etc*) convoglio; **the British fleet** la flotta britannica; **they were followed by a fleet of cars** erano seguiti da un corteo di macchine
fleet·ing [ˈfliːtɪŋ] ADJ (*glimpse*) fuggevole; (*moment, beauty*) fugace, passeggero(-a), effimero(-a); (*visit*) volante, veloce
Flem·ish [ˈflɛmɪʃ] ADJ fiammingo(-a) ◆ N 1 (*language*) fiammingo 2 (*people*): **the Flemish** *npl* i Fiamminghi
flesh [flɛʃ] N (*gen*) carne *f*; (*of fruit*) polpa; **in the flesh** in carne ed ossa; **my own flesh and blood** la mia famiglia; **it's more than flesh and blood can stand** è più di quanto un essere umano possa sopportare; **to demand one's pound of flesh** (*fig*) esigere tutto il dovuto
flesh wound N ferita superficiale
flew [fluː] PT *of* **fly²**
flex [flɛks] N (*of lamp, telephone*) filo (flessibile) ◆ VT (*body, knees*) piegare, flettere; (*muscles*) contrarre
flexi·bil·ity [ˌflɛksɪˈbɪlɪtɪ] N flessibilità, elasticità
flex·ible [ˈflɛksɪbl] ADJ flessibile; **flexible working hours** orario di lavoro flessibile
flexi·time [ˈflɛksɪˌtaɪm] N orario flessibile
flick [flɪk] N (*gen*) colpetto; *see also* **flicks** ◆ VT dare un colpetto a; **he flicked the horse with his whip** ha dato un colpetto al cavallo con la frusta; **she flicked her hair out of her eyes** buttò i capelli di una parte ◆ VI: **the snake's tongue flicked in and out** la lingua del serpente guizzava
▸ **flick off** VT + ADV (*dust, ash*) mandar via con un colpetto; **he flicked a mosquito off his leg** ha cacciato via la zanzara dalla gamba con un colpetto
▸ **flick through** VI + PREP (*book, pages*) sfogliare, scartabellare
flick·er [ˈflɪkə] N (*of light, flame*) tremolio; (*of eyelid*) battito; (*of hope*) barlume *m*; **a flicker of light** un breve bagliore ◆ VI (*light*) tremolare; (*flame*) guizzare
flick knife N (*Brit*) coltello a serramanico
flicks [flɪks] NPL: **the flicks** (*Brit fam*) il cine
fli·er [ˈflaɪə] N aviatore(-trice)
flies [flaɪz] NPL *of* **fly²**
flight¹ [flaɪt] N 1 (*Aer: gen*) volo; (*of bullet*) traiettoria; **in**
volo; **how long does the flight take?** quanto dura il volo?; **what time is the flight to Paris?** a che ora è il volo per Parigi?; **"flight closing"** (*Aer*) "volo in chiusura"; **flights of fancy** (*fig*) voli di fantasia; **in the top flight** (*fig*) fra i migliori 2 **flight (of stairs)** rampa (di scale); **he lives two flights up** abita due piani sopra
flight² [flaɪt] N (*act of fleeing*) fuga; **to put to flight** mettere in fuga; **to take flight** darsi alla fuga; **they took flight** si sono dati alla fuga
flight attendant N (*USA*) steward *m*, hostess *f inv*
flight crew N equipaggio
flight deck N (*on aircraft carrier*) ponte *m* di volo; (*of aeroplane*) cabina di pilotaggio
flight path N (*of aircraft*) aerovia; (*of rocket, projectile*) traiettoria
flight recorder N registratore *m* di volo
flim·sy [ˈflɪmzɪ] ADJ (*comp* **-ier,** *superl* **-iest**) (*thin: dress*) leggero(-a); (*weak: construction*) poco solido(-a); (*: excuse*) debole; (*: argument*) che non sta in piedi, inconsistente; **a flimsy excuse** una debole scusa; **a flimsy nightgown** una camicia da notte leggera
flinch [flɪntʃ] VI trasalire; **without flinching** senza batter ciglio; **to flinch from sth** tirarsi indietro di fronte a qc
fling [flɪŋ] (*pt, pp* **flung**) N (*love affair*) avventura; **to have a last fling** fare un'ultima follia; **to have one's fling** godersela; **to have a fling at doing sth** cercare *or* tentare di fare qc ◆ VT (*stone etc*) lanciare, gettare, scagliare; **he flung the dictionary onto the floor** ha gettato il dizionario sul pavimento; **to fling one's arms round sb** gettare le braccia al collo di qn; **the door was flung open** la porta fu spalancata; **to fling o.s. into a chair** buttarsi su una poltrona; **to fling o.s. into a job** gettarsi a capofitto in un lavoro; **to fling on one's clothes** vestirsi in fretta e furia
▸ **fling away** VT + ADV (*waste*) gettare via, sperperare
▸ **fling off** VT + ADV togliersi in fretta e furia
▸ **fling on** VT + ADV (*clothes*) mettersi in fretta e furia
▸ **fling out** VT + ADV (*unwanted object*) buttare via; (*person*) buttar fuori
▸ **fling up** VT + ADV lanciare in aria; **to fling up one's arms** alzare le braccia al cielo; **she flung up her head** ha buttato la testa all'indietro
flint [flɪnt] N (*Geol*) selce *f*; (*for lighter*) pietrina; **a flint axe** un'ascia di selce
flip [flɪp] N colpetto ◆ VT (*switch*) dare un colpetto a; (*USA: pancake*) rivoltare (*dando un colpo alla padella*); **to flip a coin** lanciare una moneta in aria, fare a testa e croce; **he flipped the book open** ha aperto il libro con un rapido gesto della mano ◆ VI 1 (*fam: lose temper*) uscire dai gangheri 2 **to flip for sth** (*USA*) fare a testa e croce per qc ◆ ADJ (*fam: remark*) poco serio(-a)
▸ **flip through** VI + PREP (*book, records*) dare una scorsa a
flip-flops [ˈflɪpˌflɒps] NPL (*sandals*) infradito *mpl*
flip·pant [ˈflɪpənt] ADJ (*remark, tone*) poco serio(-a); (*attitude*) frivolo(-a)
flip·per [ˈflɪpə] N pinna
flip side N (*of coin*) retro
flirt [flɜːt] N (*woman*) civetta; (*man*): **he's a terrible flirt** è un gran donnaiolo ◆ VI: **to flirt (with)** flirtare (con); (*woman only*) civettare (con); **to flirt with an idea** trastullarsi con un'idea
flir·ta·tion [flɜːˈteɪʃən] N flirt *m inv*
flit [flɪt] VI (*bats, butterflies*) svolazzare; **to flit in/out** (*person*) entrare/uscire svolazzando
float [fləʊt] N galleggiante *m*; (*cork*) sughero; (*vehicle in parade*) carro; (*cash*) soldi *mpl* in cassa (*per dare il resto*) ◆ VT (*boat, logs*) far galleggiare; (*refloat*) riportare a galla; (*launch: project, plan*) lanciare; (*Fin: company*) lanciare (*emettendo azioni*); (*: currency*) far fluttuare; **to float an idea** ventilare un'idea ◆ VI (*gen*) galleggiare; (*ship*) stare a galla; (*bather*) fare il morto; (*Fin: currency*) fluttuare; **to float downstream** essere trascinato(-a) dalla corrente
▸ **float away, float off** VI + ADV (*in water*) andare alla deriva; (*in air*) volare via
float·ing [ˈfləʊtɪŋ] ADJ a galla
flock [flɒk] N (*of sheep, also Rel*) gregge *m*; (*of birds*) stormo;

(of people) stuolo, folla ♦ vi *(crowd)* affollarsi, ammassarsi; **to flock around sb** affollarsi intorno a qn

floe [fləʊ] N *(also:* **ice floe**) banchisa

flog [flɒɡ] vt frustare, flagellare; **to flog a dead horse** *(fig: fam)* perdere il proprio tempo; **to flog o.s. to death** *(fig: fam)* ammazzarsi di fatica

flood [flʌd] N inondazione *f,* alluvione *f; (of words, tears)* diluvio; **the rain has caused serious floods** la pioggia ha causato gravi inondazioni; **the river is in flood** il fiume è in piena; **the Flood** *(Rel)* il diluvio universale; **he received a flood of letters** ha ricevuto una marea di lettere ♦ vt *(town, fields, also fig)* inondare, allagare; *(Aut: carburettor)* ingolfare; **the river has flooded the village** il fiume ha allagato il paese; **to flood the market** *(Comm)* inondare il mercato ♦ vi *(river)* strapipare; **the crowd flooded into the streets** la folla si riversò nelle strade
  ► **flood in** vi + ADV entrare in grande quantità; **the light flooded in through the window** una gran luce entrava dalla finestra
  ► **flood out** vt + ADV *(house)* inondare; **they were flooded out** l'inondazione li ha costretti ad abbandonare le loro case

flood·ing [ˈflʌdɪŋ] N inondazione *f*

flood·light [ˈflʌdˌlaɪt] *(pt, pp* **floodlighted** *or* **floodlit**) N riflettore *m;* **to play a match under floodlights** giocare una partita in notturna ♦ vt illuminare a giorno

flood·lit [ˈflʌdˌlɪt] PT, PP *of* **floodlight** ♦ ADJ illuminato(-a) a giorno

flood tide N alta marea, marea crescente

flood·water [ˈflʌdˌwɔːtəʳ] N acque *fpl (di inondazione)*

floor [flɔː] N **1** *(gen)* suolo; *(of room)* pavimento; *(of sea, valley)* fondo; *(dance floor)* pista; *(fig: at meeting):* **the floor** il pubblico; **a tiled floor** un pavimento a piastrelle; **on the floor** per terra, sul pavimento; **to take the floor** *(dancer)* mettersi a ballare; **to have the floor** *(speaker)* prendere la parola **2** *(storey)* piano; **ground floor** *(Brit)* pianterreno, piano terra; **on the first floor** *(Brit)* al primo piano; *(USA)* al pianterreno; **top floor** ultimo piano ♦ vt **1** *(room):* **to floor (with)** pavimentare *(con)* **2** *(fam: knock down: opponent)* atterrare; *(: baffle)* confondere

floor·board [ˈflɔːbɔːd] N asse *f* di pavimento

floor·ing [ˈflɔːrɪŋ] N *(floor)* pavimento; *(material)* materiale *m* per pavimentazioni

floor lamp N *(USA)* lampada a stelo

floor show N spettacolo di varietà

floor·walker [ˈflɔːˌwɔːkəʳ] N *(esp USA)* caporeparto *m/f (in grande magazzino)*

flop [flɒp] N *(fam: failure)* fiasco; **the film was a flop** il film è stato un fiasco ♦ vi **1** *(person):* **to flop (into/on)** lasciarsi cadere (in/su) **2** *(fam: play)* far fiasco; *(: scheme)* fallire

flop·py [ˈflɒpɪ] ADJ *(comp* **-ier,** *superl* **-iest)** floscio(-a), molle; **floppy hat** cappello floscio

flo·ra [ˈflɔːrə] N flora

flo·ral [ˈflɔːrəl] ADJ *(arrangement)* floreale; *(fabric, dress)* a fiori; **floral tribute** omaggio floreale

Flor·ence [ˈflɒrəns] N Firenze *f*

Flor·en·tine [ˈflɒrənˌtaɪn] ADJ, N fiorentino(-a)

flor·id [ˈflɒrɪd] ADJ *(complexion)* florido(-a); *(style)* fiorito(-a)

Flo·ri·da [ˈflɒrɪdə] N la Florida

flo·rist [ˈflɒrɪst] N fioraio(-a); **at the florist's (shop)** dal fioraio

flo·ta·tion [fləʊˈteɪʃən] N *(Fin)* lancio

flounce¹ [flaʊns] vi: **to flounce in/out** entrare/uscire stizzito(-a) ♦ N balzo

flounce² [flaʊns] N *(frill)* balza

floun·der¹ [ˈflaʊndəʳ] vi *(also:* **flounder about)** *(in water, mud)* dibattersi, annaspare; *(in speech etc)* impappinarsi, esitare

floun·der² [ˈflaʊndəʳ] N *(fish)* passera di mare

flour [ˈflaʊəʳ] N farina

flour·ish [ˈflʌrɪʃ] N abbellimento; *(movement)* gran gesto; *(under signature)* svolazzo; *(Mus: fanfare)* fanfara; **to do sth with a flourish** fare qc con ostentazione ♦ vi *(gen)* fiorire; *(person)* essere in piena forma; *(writer, artist)* avere successo; *(business etc)* prosperare; **the business flourished** la ditta prosperava ♦ vt *(weapon, stick)* brandire

flour·ish·ing [ˈflʌrɪʃɪŋ] ADJ *(plant)* rigoglioso(-a); *(person)* florido(-a), in gran forma; *(business)* fiorente, prospero(-a)

flout [flaʊt] vt *(order)* contravvenire a; *(advice)* ignorare deliberatamente; *(conventions, society)* sfidare; **they persist in flouting the law** continuano a contravvenire alla legge; **he dared to flout convention** ha osato sfidare le convenzioni

flow [fləʊ] N *(of river, also Elec)* corrente *f; (of tide)* flusso; *(of blood: from wound)* uscita; *(: in veins)* circolazione *f; (of words)* fiume *m; (of insults, orders)* caterva, sfilza; **the flow of traffic** la circolazione ♦ vi *(gen)* fluire; *(tide)* salire; *(blood in veins, traffic)* circolare; *(hair)* ricadere (morbidamente), scendere; **money flowed in** *(fig)* i soldi sono arrivati in grande quantità; **the river flows into the sea** il fiume sfocia nel mare; **to keep the conversation flowing** mantenere viva la conversazione

flow chart N schema *m* di flusso

flow diagram N diagramma *m* di flusso, organigramma *m*

flow·er [ˈflaʊəʳ] N fiore *m;* **a bunch of flowers** un mazzo di fiori; **in flower** in fiore ♦ vi fiorire

flower·bed [ˈflaʊəˌbed] N aiuola

flower·pot [ˈflaʊəˌpɒt] N vaso da fiori

flow·ery [ˈflaʊərɪ] ADJ *(meadow)* fiorito(-a), in fiore; *(dress, material)* a fiori; *(style, speech)* fiorito(-a)

flown [fləʊn] PP *of* **fly²**

fl. oz. N ABBR = **fluid ounce**

flu [fluː] N *(fam)* influenza

fluc·tu·ate [ˈflʌktjʊˌeɪt] vi *(cost, rate, speed)* fluttuare, oscillare; *(person):* **he fluctuated between fear and excitement** passava da uno stato di paura a uno stato di eccitazione

fluc·tua·tion [ˌflʌktjʊˈeɪʃən] N fluttuazione *f,* oscillazione *f*

flue [fluː] N canna fumaria

flu·en·cy [ˈfluːənsɪ] N facilità, scioltezza; **his fluency in English** la sua scioltezza nel parlare l'inglese

flu·ent [ˈfluːənt] ADJ *(style)* fluido(-a), scorrevole; *(speaker)* dalla parola facile; *(speech)* facile, sciolto(-a); *(French)* corrente; **he's a fluent speaker/reader** si esprime/legge senza difficoltà; **he speaks fluent Italian, he's fluent in Italian** parla l'italiano correntemente

flu·ent·ly [ˈfluːəntlɪ] ADV *(speak a language)* correntemente; *(speak, write)* con scioltezza, con facilità

fluff [flʌf] N *(from blankets etc)* pelucchi *mpl; (of chicks, kittens)* lanugine *f* ♦ vt **1** *(also:* **fluff out)** rendere soffice *or* vaporoso(-a); *(feathers)* arruffare; **to fluff up the pillows** sprimacciare i cuscini **2** *(fam: make mistake in)* impaperarsi nel recitare

fluffy [ˈflʌfɪ] ADJ *(toy)* di peluche; *(kitten, chick)* coperto(-a) di lanugine; *(pullover)* morbido(-a) e peloso(-a); **fluffy towels** asciugamani morbidi

flu·id [ˈfluːɪd] ADJ *(substance, movement)* fluido(-a); *(plan, arrangements)* flessibile, elastico(-a) ♦ N fluido, liquido; *(in diet)* liquido

fluid ounce N *unità di misura di capacità pari a 0.028 l (Brit) o 0.030 l (USA)*

fluke [fluːk] N *(fam)* colpo di fortuna; **by a fluke** per puro caso

flum·mox [ˈflʌməks] vt *(fam)* sconcertare, rendere perplesso(-a)

flung [flʌŋ] PT, PP *of* **fling**

flunky [ˈflʌŋkɪ] N tirapiedi *m/f inv*

fluo·res·cent [ˌflʊəˈresənt] ADJ *(lighting, tube)* fluorescente

fluo·ride [ˈflʊəˌraɪd] N fluoruro

fluo·rine [ˈflʊəˌriːn] N fluoro

flur·ry [ˈflʌrɪ] N *(of snow)* turbine *m; (of wind)* folata; **a flurry of activity/excitement** un'intensa attività/un'improvvisa agitazione; **in a flurry** in uno stato di agitazione *or* eccitazione

flush [flʌʃ] N **1** *(lavatory flush)* sciacquone *m;* **he heard the flush of a toilet** ha sentito il rumore di uno sciacquone **2** *(blush)* rossore *m;* **there was a slight flush on his cheeks** c'era un leggero rossore sulle sue guance **3** *(of beauty, health, youth)* rigoglio, pieno vigore *m; (fig: exhilaration)* ebbrezza; **in the first flush of victory** nell'ebbrezza della vittoria; **in a flush of excitement** in uno stato di eccitazione **4** *(in poker)* colore *m* ♦ ADJ **1** *(level):* **flush (with)** a livello (di *or* con); **a door flush with the wall** una porta a livello con la parete **2** *(fam):* **to be flush (with money)** essere pieno(-a) di soldi

♦ vi (person, face): **to flush (with)** arrossire (di); **flushed with success** eccitato(-a) dal successo ♦ vt **1** pulire con un getto d'acqua; **to flush the lavatory** or **the toilet** tirare l'acqua **2** (also: **flush out**) (game, birds) far alzare in volo; (fig: criminal) stanare

  ▸ **flush away** vt + adv (down lavatory) buttare nel gabinetto (e tirare l'acqua)

flushed [flʌʃt] adj tutto(-a) rosso(-a)

flus·ter [ˈflʌstəʳ] n agitazione f ♦ vt (confuse, upset) mettere in agitazione, innervosire; **to get flustered** agitarsi

flus·tered [ˈflʌstəd] adj sconvolto(-a), in uno stato di confusione

flute [fluːt] n flauto

flut·ter [ˈflʌtəʳ] n agitazione f; (of eyelashes) battito; (of wings) battito, frullio; (fig) (fig) essere in uno stato di agitazione; **to have a flutter** (fam: gamble) fare una scommessa ♦ vt (wings) battere; **to flutter one's eyelashes at sb** fare gli occhi dolci a qn ♦ vi svolazzare; (bird etc) battere le ali; (flag) sventolare; (heart) palpitare

flux [flʌks] n **1 to be in a state of flux** essere in continuo mutamento **2** (Med, Phys) flusso; (Metallurgy) fondente m

fly¹ [flai] n (insect) mosca; **he wouldn't hurt a fly** non farebbe male a una mosca; **they were dropping like flies** morivano come mosche; **the fly in the ointment** (fig) la piccola pecca che sciupa tutto; **there are no flies on him** (fig) non è nato ieri, non si fa prendere per il naso

fly² [flai] (pp **flew**, pt **flown**) vt **1** (gen) volare; (passengers) andare in aereo; (flag) sventolare; **the plane flew over London** l'aereo ha sorvolato Londra; **he flew from London to Moscow** è andato in aereo da Londra a Mosca; **he's never flown** non è mai andato in aereo **2** (move quickly: time) volare, passare in fretta; **to fly past sb** (subj: car, person) sfrecciare davanti a qn; **the door flew open** la porta si è spalancata all'improvviso; **to knock** or **send sth/sb flying** far volare qc/qn; **I must fly!** devo scappare!; **to let fly at sb** scagliarsi contro qn; **to fly into a rage** infuriarsi; **to fly off the handle** perdere le staffe **3** (flee) fuggire, scappare; **to fly for one's life** salvare la pelle scappando ♦ vt (aircraft) pilotare; (passenger, cargo) trasportare (in aereo); (distances) percorrere; (flag) battere; **to fly the Atlantic** sorvolare l'Atlantico; **to fly a kite** far volare un aquilone ♦ n (on trousers: also: **flies**) patta

  ▸ **fly away** vi + adv volar via

  ▸ **fly in** vi + adv (plane) arrivare; (person) arrivare in aereo; **he flew in from Rome** è venuto da Roma in aereo ♦ vt + adv (supplies, troops) trasportare in aereo

  ▸ **fly off** vi + adv volare via

  ▸ **fly out** vi + adv (plane) partire; (person) partire in aereo

fly-drive [ˈflaidraiv] adj fly-and-drive inv

fly-fishing [ˈflaiˌfiʃiŋ] n pesca con la mosca

fly·ing [ˈflaiiŋ] adj (gen) volante; **to pass an exam with flying colours** superare un esame con risultati brillanti; **to take a flying leap** or **jump** fare un gran balzo ♦ n (action) volo; (activity) aviazione f; **he doesn't like flying** non gli piace viaggiare in aereo

flying buttress n (Archit) arco rampante

flying picket n picchetto (proveniente da fabbriche ecc non direttamente coinvolte nello sciopero)

flying saucer n disco volante

flying squad n (Police) (squadra) volante f

flying start n partenza lanciata; **to get off to a flying start** (fig) partire come un razzo, avere un inizio brillante

fly·leaf [ˈflaiˌliːf] n (pl **-leaves**) risguardo

fly·over [ˈflaiˌəuvəʳ] n (Brit: bridge) cavalcavia m inv

fly·past [ˈflaipɑːst] n parata aerea

fly·sheet [ˈflaiˌʃiːt] n (for tent) soprattetto

fly·weight [ˈflaiˌweit] (Boxing) n peso m mosca, inv ♦ adj (contest) di pesi mosca

fly·wheel [ˈflaiˌwiːl] n (Tech) volano

FM [ˌefˈem] n abbr **1** (Radio: = frequency modulation) FM **2** (Brit Mil) = **field marshal**

FO [ˌefˈəu] n abbr (Brit) = **Foreign Office**

foal [fəul] n puledro

foam [fəum] n (gen) schiuma ♦ vi (sea) spumeggiare; **to foam at the mouth** avere la schiuma alla bocca

fob [fɒb] vt: **to fob sb off (with sth)** appioppare or rifilare (qc) a qn; **to fob sb off with promises** tenere qn buono(-a) con delle promesse ♦ n (also: **watch fob**) (chain) catena per orologio; (band of cloth) nastro per orologio

  ▸ **fob off on** vt + adv + prep rifilare a

fo·cal [ˈfəukl] adj (Tech) focale

focal point n (fig) centro; (of lens, mirror) punto focale

fo·cus [ˈfəukəs] n (pl **focuses** or **foci** [ˈfəukai]) (gen) fuoco; (of attention, interest) centro; **he was the focus of attention** era al centro dell'attenzione; **to be out of focus** (Phot) essere sfocato(-a); **in focus** a fuoco ♦ vt: **to focus (on)** (camera, instrument, field glasses) mettere a fuoco (su); (attention, eyes) focalizzare (su); (light rays) far convergere (su) ♦ vi: **to focus (on)** (light, heat, rays) convergere (su); (person) fissare lo sguardo (su); **to focus on sth** (eyes, person) mettere a fuoco qc; (subject, problem) concentrarsi su qc

focus group n (Pol) gruppo di discussione, focus group m inv

fod·der [ˈfɒdəʳ] n foraggio

foe [fəu] n (liter) nemico(-a)

foe·tus, fe·tus [ˈfiːtəs] n feto

fog [fɒg] n nebbia ♦ vt (lens) far appannare; **to fog the issue** (fig) confondere le cose

fog·bound [ˈfɒgˌbaund] adj fermo(-a) a causa della nebbia

fog·gy [ˈfɒgi] adj (comp **-ier**, superl **-iest**) nebbioso(-a); **it's foggy** c'è nebbia; **a foggy day** una giornata nebbiosa; **I haven't the foggiest (idea)** (fam) non ne ho la più pallida idea

fog light, fog lamp (Brit) n (Aut) faro m antinebbia, inv

foi·ble [ˈfɔibl] n debolezza, mania

foil¹ [fɔil] n **1** lamina di metallo; (also: **tinfoil**, **kitchen foil**) carta stagnola or d'alluminio; **to act as a foil to sb/sth** (fig) far risaltare qn/qc **2** (Fencing) fioretto

foil² [fɔil] vt (thief) fermare; (attempt) far fallire, sventare

foist [fɔist] vt: **to foist sth on sb** rifilare qc a qn

fold¹ [fəuld] n (Agr) ovile m; **to come back to the fold** (fig) tornare all'ovile

fold² [fəuld] n (bend, crease, also Geol) piega ♦ vt (gen) piegare; (wings) ripiegare; **she folded the paper in two** piegò in due la carta; **to fold one's arms** incrociare le braccia ♦ vi (chair, table) piegarsi; (fam: fail: business venture) crollare; (: play) chiudere

  ▸ **fold away** vi + adv (table, bed) piegarsi, essere pieghevole ♦ vt + adv (clothes, linen) piegare, mettere a posto

  ▸ **fold back** vt + adv ripiegare

  ▸ **fold over** vt + adv ripiegare

  ▸ **fold up** vi + adv (fam: fail: business) fallire, crollare ♦ vt + adv (map, paper) piegare, ripiegare

fold·er [ˈfəuldəʳ] n (file: for papers) cartella, cartellina; (binder) raccoglitore m

fold·ing [ˈfəuldiŋ] adj (chair, doors, bed) pieghevole

fo·li·age [ˈfəulidʒ] n fogliame m

folk [fəuk] n **1** (people) gente f; **country/city folk** gente di campagna/di città; **my folks** (fam) la mia famiglia, i miei **2** (also: **folk music**) folk m inv

folk·lore [ˈfəuklɔːʳ] n folclore m

folk music n musica f folk, inv

folk singer n cantante m/f folk, inv

folk song [ˈfəukˌsɒŋ] n canto popolare, canzone f folk, inv

fol·low [ˈfɒləu] vt (gen) seguire; (football team) fare il tifo per; **the road follows the coast** la strada segue la costa; **we're being followed** qualcuno ci sta seguendo; **to follow sb's advice** seguire il consiglio di qn; **he followed suit** ha fatto altrettanto; **I don't quite follow you** non sono sicuro di capirti or seguirti; **following his resignation ...** in seguito alle sue dimissioni... ♦ vi **1** (gen) seguire; **as follows** come segue; **you go first and I'll follow** vai tu per primo, io ti seguo; **to follow in sb's footsteps** seguire le orme di qn; **what is there to follow?** che c'è dopo?; **I don't follow** non capisco **2** (result, deduction etc) risultare, conseguire; **it follows that ...** ne consegue che...; **it doesn't follow that ...** non vuol dire che...; **that doesn't follow** non necessariamente

  ▸ **follow about, follow around** vt + adv seguire dappertutto

  ▸ **follow on** vi + adv (continue): **to follow on from** seguire

▸ **follow out** vt + adv (*implement: idea, plan*) eseguire, portare a termine
▸ **follow through** vt + adv = **follow out** ♦ vi + adv (*Golf*) portare a termine l'azione; (*Tennis*) accompagnare la palla
▸ **follow up** vt + adv **1** (*investigate: case, clue*) esaminare, seguire; **the police are following up several leads** la polizia sta seguendo diverse piste **2** (*take further action on: offer, suggestion*) seguire **3** (*reinforce: success, victory*) rafforzare, sfruttare; (*letter, offer*) fare seguito a ♦ vi + adv (*Ftbl, etc*): **to follow up with another goal** segnare di nuovo

fol·low·er ['fɒləʊəʳ] n (*disciple*) seguace m/f, discepolo(-a); (*of team*) tifoso(-a)

fol·low·ing ['fɒləʊɪŋ] adj seguente, successivo(-a); **following wind** vento in poppa; **the following day** il giorno seguente, l'indomani **1** (*Pol, etc*) seguito, proseliti mpl; (*Sport*) tifosi mpl; **they have a large following** hanno un grande seguito **2 he said the following** ha detto quanto segue; **see the following** (*in document etc*) vedi quanto segue; **the following is the text of the statement** riportiamo qui di seguito il testo della dichiarazione

follow-up ['fɒləʊˌʌp] n seguito

fol·ly ['fɒlɪ] n follia, pazzia

fond [fɒnd] adj (*comp* -**er**, *superl* -**est**) (*loving: memory, look*) affettuoso(-a), tenero(-a); (*doting*) che stravede; (*foolish: hope, desire*) vano(-a); **to be fond of sb** voler bene a qn; **she's fond of swimming** le piace nuotare; **she's fond of dogs** le piacciono i cani

❏ **fond** is not translated by the Italian word *fondo*

fon·dle ['fɒndl] vt accarezzare

fond·ly ['fɒndlɪ] adv (*lovingly*) affettuosamente; (*naïvely*) ingenuamente; **he fondly believed that ...** ha avuto l'ingenuità di credere che...

fond·ness ['fɒndnɪs] n: **fondness (for sth)** predilezione f (per qc); **fondness (for sb)** affetto (per qn)

font [fɒnt] n **1** (*in church*) fonte m battesimale **2** (*Typ*) carattere m (di scrittura)

food [fuːd] n cibo; (*for plants*) fertilizzante m; **I left some food for the cat** ho lasciato un po' di cibo per il gatto; **Italian food is very popular** la cucina italiana è molto popolare; **I've no food left in the house** non c'è più niente da mangiare in casa; **to be off one's food** (*fam*) aver perso l'appetito; **food for thought** (*fig*) qualcosa su cui riflettere

food chain n catena alimentare
food mixer n frullatore m
food poisoning n intossicazione f alimentare
food processor n tritatutto m inv elettrico
food stamp n (*USA*) buono alimentare dato agli indigenti
food·stuffs ['fuːdˌstʌfs] npl generi mpl alimentari

fool [fuːl] n **1** sciocco(-a), stupido(-a), fesso(-a); (*jester*) buffone m, giullare m; **you fool!** stupido!; **don't be a fool!** non fare lo stupido!; **I was a fool not to go** sono stato stupido a non andare; **to play the fool** fare lo (la) stupido(-a); **he is nobody's fool** non è mica scemo; **to make a fool of sb** far fare a qn la figura dello scemo, prendere in giro qn; **to make a fool of o.s.** rendersi or coprirsi di ridicolo(-a); **to go on a fool's errand** fare la strada per niente **2** (*Culin*) frullato ♦ adj (*USA*) sciocco(-a) ♦ vt (*deceive*) ingannare, far fesso(-a); **you can't fool me** non mi inganni ♦ vi scherzare; **I was only fooling** stavo solo scherzando
▸ **fool about, fool around** vi + adv **1** (*waste time*) perdere tempo **2** (*act the fool*) fare lo (la) stupido(-a)

fool·hardy ['fuːlˌhɑːdɪ] adj (*rash*) avventato(-a), imprudente

fool·ish ['fuːlɪʃ] adj (*senseless*) sciocco(-a), stupido(-a), insensato(-a); (*ridiculous*) ridicolo(-a), assurdo(-a); (*unwise*) imprudente; **that was very foolish of you** è stato molto sciocco da parte tua

fool·ish·ly ['fuːlɪʃlɪ] adv stupidamente

fool·ish·ness ['fuːlɪʃnɪs] n stupidità

fool·proof ['fuːlˌpruːf] adj (*method, plan etc*) infallibile, sicurissimo(-a); (*machine*) facile da usare

fools·cap ['fuːlzˌkæp] n carta protocollo

foot [fʊt] n (*pl* **feet**) **1** (*gen*) piede m; (*of animal*) zampa; (*of page, stairs etc*) fondo; **on foot** a piedi; **she's got big feet** ha i piedi grandi; **to be on one's feet** essere in piedi; (*after illness*) essersi rimesso(-a); **to jump/rise to one's feet** balzare/

alzarsi in piedi; **it's wet under foot** è bagnato per terra **2** (*fig phrases*): **to fall on one's feet** cadere in piedi; **to find one's feet** ambientarsi; **to get cold feet** avere fifa; **to get under sb's feet** stare tra i piedi a qn; **to have one foot in the grave** avere un piede nella fossa; **to put one's foot down** (*say no*) imporsi; (*Aut*) schiacciare l'acceleratore; **to get a foot in the door** fare il primo passo; **to put one's foot in it** fare una gaffe; **to put one's feet up** (*fam*) riposarsi; **I've never set foot there** non ci ho mai messo piede; **to put one's best foot forward** (*hurry*) sbrigarsi; **to get off on the right/wrong foot** partire col piede giusto/sbagliato **3** (*measure*) piede m (= 304 mm or 12 inches); **he's 6 foot or feet tall** ≈ è alto 1 metro e 80 ♦ vt: **to foot the bill** (*fam*) pagare il conto

foot·age ['fʊtɪdʒ] n (*Cine*) sequenza; (*material*) ≈ metraggio

foot-and-mouth ['fʊtəndˈmaʊθ], **foot-and-mouth disease** n afta epizootica

foot·ball ['fʊtˌbɔːl] n (*ball*) pallone m; (*Sport: Brit*) calcio; (*: USA*) football m americano; **I like playing football** mi piace giocare a calcio; **Paul threw the football over the fence** Paul ha gettato il pallone oltre lo steccato ♦ adj (*team, supporters*) di calcio

foot·ball·er ['fʊtˌbɔːləʳ] n (*Brit*) calciatore(-trice)
football ground n campo di calcio
football match n (*Brit*) partita di calcio
football player n (*Brit*) calciatore(-trice); (*USA*) giocatore m di football americano

foot brake n freno a pedale

foot·bridge ['fʊtˌbrɪdʒ] n passerella

foot·hills ['fʊtˌhɪlz] npl contrafforti fpl, colline fpl pedemontane

foot·hold ['fʊtˌhəʊld] n punto d'appoggio; **to gain a foothold** (*fig: idea, movement*) prendere piede; (*: newcomer*) farsi accettare; **to gain a foothold in a market** (*Comm*) imporsi sul mercato

foot·ing ['fʊtɪŋ] n (*foothold*) punto d'appoggio; (*fig: basis*) posizione f; **to lose one's footing** perdere l'equilibrio, mettere un piede in fallo; **on an equal footing** (*fig*) su un piano di parità, in una situazione di parità; **to be on a friendly footing with sb** essere in rapporti d'amicizia con qn

foot·lights ['fʊtˌlaɪts] npl (*in theatre*) luci fpl della ribalta
foot·man ['fʊtmən] n (*pl* -**men**) lacchè m inv
foot·note ['fʊtˌnəʊt] n nota a piè di pagina
foot·path ['fʊtˌpɑːθ] n (*track*) sentiero
foot·print ['fʊtˌprɪnt] n orma, impronta
foot·rest ['fʊtˌrest] n poggiapiedi m inv
foot·sie ['fʊtsɪ] n (*fam*): **to play footsie with sb** fare piedino a qn

foot·sore ['fʊtˌsɔːʳ] adj: **to be footsore** avere i piedi doloranti, avere mal di piedi

foot·step ['fʊtˌstep] n passo
foot·wear ['fʊtweəʳ] n calzature fpl
FOR [ˌɛfəʊˈɑːʳ] abbr (= *free on rail*) franco vagone

KEYWORD

for [fɔːʳ] prep
1 (*indicating destination, intention*) per; **he left for Rome** è partito per Roma; **here's a letter for you** ecco una lettera per te; **is this for me?** è per me questo?; **for sale** in vendita, vendesi; **he swam for the shore** nuotò verso la riva; **it's time for lunch** è ora di pranzo; **the train for London** il treno per Londra
2 (*indicating purpose*) per; **clothes for children** vestiti per bambini; **a cupboard for toys** un armadio per i giocattoli; **fit for nothing** buono(-a) a niente; **to pray for peace** pregare per la pace; **he went down for the paper** è sceso a prendere il giornale; **what for?** perché?, per cosa?; **what's this button for?** a cosa serve questo bottone?
3 (*representing*) per; **I'll ask him for you** glielo chiederò a nome tuo; **G for George** G come George; **member for Hove** deputato che rappresenta Hove; **I took him for his brother** l'ho scambiato or preso per suo fratello
4 (*in exchange for*) per; **to pay 50 pence for a ticket** pagare 50 penny per un biglietto; **I sold it for £50** l'ho venduto per 50 sterline
5 (*with regard to*) per; **anxious for success** avido(-a) di successo; **as for him/that** quanto a lui/ciò; **it's cold for July** è

freddo per essere luglio; **for each one who voted yes, 50 voted no** per ogni voto a favore ce n'erano 50 contro; **a gift for languages** un dono per le lingue; **he's mature for his age** è maturo per la sua età

6 (*in favour of*) per, a favore di; **are you for or against us?** sei con noi o contro di noi?; **I'm all for it** sono completamente a favore; **the campaign for** la campagna a favore di *or* per; **vote for me!** votate per me!

7 (*because of*) per, a causa di; **famous for its cathedral** famoso(-a) per la sua cattedrale; **for fear of being criticised** per paura di essere criticato(-a); **to shout for joy** gridare di gioia; **for this reason** per questa ragione; **do it for my sake** fallo per me; **if it were not for you** se non fosse per te

8 (*in spite of*): **for all that** malgrado ciò; **for all his money** malgrado tutto il suo denaro

9 (*distance*) per; **there were roadworks for 5 km** c'erano lavori in corso per 5 km; **we walked for miles** abbiamo camminato per chilometri

10 (*time*): **can you do it for tomorrow?** lo puoi fare per domani?; **I haven't seen him for a week** non lo vedo da una settimana, è una settimana che non lo vedo; **I'll be away for 3 weeks** starò via (per) 3 settimane; **it has not rained for 3 weeks** non piove da 3 settimane; **he won't be back for a while** non tornerà per un po'; **he was away for 2 years** è stato via per 2 anni; **I have known her for years** la conosco da anni

11 (*with infinitive clauses*): **for this to be possible ...** perché ciò sia possibile...; **it would be best for you to go** sarebbe meglio che te ne andassi; **he brought it for us to see** l'ha portato per farcelo vedere; **it's not for me to decide** non sta a me decidere; **there is still time for you to do it** hai ancora tempo per farlo

♦ conj dal momento che, poiché

for·age [ˈfɒrɪdʒ] N piante *fpl* foraggere ♦ vi: **to forage (for)** andare in cerca (di)

forage cap N bustina

for·ay [ˈfɒreɪ] N (*esp Mil*) incursione *f*

for·bade, for·bad [fəˈbæd] pt of **forbid**

for·bear·ing [fɔːˈbɛərɪŋ] ADJ paziente, tollerante

for·bid [fəˈbɪd] (pt **forbad** or **forbade** pp **forbidden**) vt proibire, vietare; **to forbid sb sth** proibire qc a qn; **to forbid sb to do sth** proibire a qn di fare qc; **"smoking forbidden"** "vietato fumare"; **God forbid!** Dio non voglia!

forbidden [fəˈbɪdn] ADJ vietato(-a)

for·bid·ding [fəˈbɪdɪŋ] ADJ arcigno(-a), d'aspetto minaccioso

force [fɔːs] N **1** (*gen*) forza; **he's against the use of force** è contrario all'uso della forza; **to resort to force** ricorrere alla violenza; **force of gravity** forza di gravità; **a force 5 wind** un vento forza 5; **the forces of evil** (*fig*) le forze del male; **by force** con la forza; **by force of habit** per abitudine; **by sheer force of character, he ...** grazie alla sua forza di carattere, lui...; **to be in force** (*Law*) essere in vigore; **to come into force** (*Law*) entrare in vigore; **to turn out in force** manifestare in gran numero *or* in massa **2** (*body of men*) gruppo; (*Mil*) forza; **the force** (*police force*) la polizia, il corpo di polizia; **UN forces** le forze dell'ONU; **the sales force** (*Comm*) l'effettivo dei rappresentanti **3 the Forces** (*Brit Mil*) le forze armate ♦ vt **1** (*compel: person*) forzare, costringere; **to force sb to do sth** costringere qn a fare qc **2** (*impose*): **to force sth on sb** imporre qc a qn; **to force o.s. on sb** imporsi a qn, imporre la propria presenza a qn **3** (*push, squeeze*) schiacciare; **he forced the clothes into the suitcase** ha fatto entrare a forza i vestiti nella valigia; **to force one's way into** entrare con la forza in; **to force one's way through** (*crowd*) farsi strada tra; (*opening*) penetrare a forza in, passare a forza attraverso **4** (*break open: lock*) forzare; **to force an entry** entrare con la forza; **to force sb's hand** (*fig*) forzare la mano a qn **5** (*produce with effort*): **to force a smile/a reply** sorridere/rispondere; **don't force the situation** non forzare le cose **6** (*obtain by force: smile, confession*) strappare

▸ **force back** vt + ADV (*crowd, enemy*) respingere; (*urge*) reprimere; (*tears*) ingoiare

▸ **force down** vt + ADV (*food*) sforzarsi di mangiare; (*aircraft*) forzare ad atterrare

▸ **force out** vt + ADV (*person*) costringere ad uscire; (*cork*) far uscire con la forza

forced [fɔːst] ADJ (*labour, marriage*) forzato(-a)

force-feed [ˈfɔːsˌfiːd] (pt, pp **force-fed**) vt sottoporre ad alimentazione forzata

force·ful [ˈfɔːsfʊl] ADJ (*personality*) forte; (*argument*) valido(-a)

force·meat [ˈfɔːsˌmiːt] N (*Brit: Culin*) ripieno

for·ceps [ˈfɔːsɛps] NPL forcipe *msg*

for·cibly [ˈfɔːsəblɪ] ADV (*by force: take*) con la forza; (*vigorously: argue*) energicamente, vigorosamente

ford [fɔːd] N guado ♦ vt guadare, passare a guado

fore [fɔː] N (*section, part: of animal, ship, aircraft*) anteriore ♦ ADV (*Naut*): **fore and aft** da prua a poppa ♦ N: **to the fore** in primo piano; **to come to the fore** mettersi in evidenza *or* in luce

fore·arm [ˈfɔːrˌɑːm] N avambraccio

fore·bear [ˈfɔːˌbɛəʳ] N antenato(-a)

fore·bod·ing [fɔːˈbəʊdɪŋ] N (*cattivo*) presagio, presentimento; **a sense of foreboding** un brutto presentimento

fore·cast [ˈfɔːˌkɑːst] (pt, pp **forecast** or **forecasted**) N pronostico, previsione *f*; (*also: weather forecast*) previsioni *fpl* del tempo; (*Horse Racing*) accoppiata ♦ vt (*also Met*) prevedere

fore·close [fɔːˈkləʊz] vt (*Law: also:* **foreclose on**) pignorare

fore·clo·sure [fɔːˈkləʊʒəʳ] N pignoramento

fore·court [ˈfɔːˌkɔːt] N (*of garage*) spiazzo; (*of station*) piazzale *m*

fore·fathers [ˈfɔːˌfɑːðəz] NPL progenitori *mpl*, antenati *mpl*, avi *mpl*

fore·finger [ˈfɔːˌfɪŋɡəʳ] N (*dito*) indice *m*

fore·front [ˈfɔːˌfrʌnt] N: **to be in the forefront of** essere all'avanguardia di

fore·go [fɔːˈɡəʊ] vt = **forgo**

fore·going [fɔːˈɡəʊɪŋ] ADJ precedente

fore·gone [ˈfɔːˌɡɒn] pp of **forego** ♦ ADJ: **it was a foregone conclusion** era un risultato scontato

fore·ground [ˈfɔːˌɡraʊnd] N (*Art*) primo piano; **in the foreground** (*fig*) in una posizione di primo piano ♦ ADJ (*Comput*) foreground *inv*, di primo piano

fore·hand [ˈfɔːˌhænd] N (*Tennis*) diritto

fore·head [ˈfɔːˌhɛd] N fronte *f*

for·eign [ˈfɒrɪn] ADJ **1** (*language, tourist*) straniero(-a); (*policy, trade*) estero(-a); **foreign countries** paesi stranieri; **foreign investment** investimento all'estero **2** (*not natural*) estraneo(-a); **deceit is foreign to his nature** ingannare non è nel suo carattere

foreign body N (*frm*) corpo estraneo

foreign currency N valuta estera

for·eign·er [ˈfɒrɪnəʳ] N straniero(-a)

foreign exchange N cambio di valuta; (*currency*) valuta estera; **foreign exchange market** mercato dei cambi

foreign exchange rate N cambio

foreign minister N ministro degli Esteri

Foreign Office N (*Brit*) ministero degli Esteri

foreign secretary N (*Brit*) ministro degli Esteri

fore·leg [ˈfɔːˌlɛɡ] N zampa anteriore

fore·man [ˈfɔːmən] N (pl **-men**) (*of workers*) caposquadra *m*; (*Law: of jury*) portavoce *m* della giuria

fore·most [ˈfɔːˌməʊst] ADJ (*outstanding: writer, politician*) più importante, principale, più in vista ♦ ADV: **first and foremost** innanzitutto

fore·name [ˈfɔːˌneɪm] N nome *m* di battesimo

fo·ren·sic [fəˈrɛnsɪk] ADJ (*evidence, laboratory*) medico-legale; **forensic scientist** *or* **expert** esperto(-a) della (polizia) scientifica

fore·play [ˈfɔːˌpleɪ] N preliminari *mpl* (*nel rapporto sessuale*)

fore·run·ner [ˈfɔːˌrʌnəʳ] N precursore *m*; (*Skiing*) apripista *m/f inv*

fore·see [fɔːˈsiː] (pt **foresaw**, pp **foreseen**) vt prevedere; **he had foreseen the problem** aveva previsto il problema

fore·see·able [fɔːˈsiːəbl] ADJ (*opportunity*) prevedibile; **in the foreseeable future** nell'immediato futuro

fore·seen [fɔːˈsiːn] pp of **foresee**

fore·shad·ow [fɔːˈʃædəʊ] vt (*liter*) presagire, far prevedere

fore·short·en [fɔːˈʃɔːtn] vt (*figure*) rappresentare in scorcio

fore·sight [ˈfɔːˌsaɪt] N previdenza

fore·skin [ˈfɔːˌskɪn] N (*Anat*) prepuzio

for·est ['fɒrɪst] N foresta

fore·stall [fɔː'stɔːl] VT (anticipate: event, accident) prevenire; (: rival, competitor) anticipare

for·est·ry ['fɒrɪstrɪ] N selvicoltura

fore·taste ['fɔːteɪst] N assaggio

fore·tell [fɔː'tel] (pt, pp **foretold**) VT predire

fore·thought ['fɔːθɔːt] N previdenza; **to act with fore-thought** essere previdente

fore·told [fɔː'təʊld] PT, PP of **foretell**

for·ever [fɔː'evəʳ] ADV (eternally) per sempre, eternamente; (for good) per sempre; (fam: incessantly, repeatedly) sempre, di continuo; (: for ages): **it lasted forever** è durato un'eternità; **it'll take forever** ci vorrà una vita; **yours forever** tuo per sempre; **those days are gone forever** quei giorni non torneranno più

fore·warn [fɔː'wɔːn] VT avvisare in precedenza; **forewarned is forearmed** uomo avvisato è mezzo salvato

forewent [fɔː'went] PT of **forego**

fore·word ['fɔːwɜːd] N prefazione f

for·feit ['fɔːfɪt] N (penalty) ammenda; (in game) penitenza ♦ VT (esp Law: one's right, status) perdere; (one's happiness, health) giocarsi

for·gave [fə'geɪv] PT of **forgive**

forge [fɔːdʒ] N (of blacksmith) fucina ♦ VT 1 (metal, iron) fucinare, forgiare; (fig: friendship, plan, unity) forgiare, formare 2 (falsify: signature, document) contraffare, falsificare

▸ **forge ahead** VI + ADV andare avanti (con determinazione)

forg·er ['fɔːdʒəʳ] N falsario(-a), contraffattore(-trice)

forg·ery ['fɔːdʒərɪ] N (activity) falsificazione f, contraffazione f; (thing) falso; **the letter was a forgery** la lettera era un falso

for·get [fə'get] (pt **forgot**, pp **forgotten**) VT dimenticare; **I've forgotten his name** ho dimenticato il suo nome; **to forget to do sth** dimenticare di fare qc; **to forget how to do sth** dimenticare come si fa qc; **she never forgets a face** è molto fisionomista; **never to be forgotten** indimenticabile; **forget it!** (fam) lascia perdere!; **if that's what you're hoping, you can forget it!** se questo è quello che speri puoi scordartelo!; **to forget o.s.** (lose self-control) perdere la testa ♦ VI dimenticarsi, scordarsi; **I've forgotten all about it** me ne sono completamente dimenticato; **let's forget about it!** non ne parliamo più!

for·get·ful [fə'getfʊl] ADJ (absent-minded) distratto(-a), di poca memoria; **forgetful of** dimentico(-a) di; **it was very forgetful of me not to …** è stata una grande dimenticanza quella di non…

forget-me-not [fə'getmɪˌnɒt] N nontiscordardimé m inv

for·give [fə'gɪv] (pt **forgave**, pp **forgiven**) VT (person, fault) perdonare; **in the end he forgave me** alla fine mi ha perdonato; **to forgive sb for sth/for doing sth** perdonare qc a qn/a qn di aver fatto qc

for·give·ness [fə'gɪvnɪs] N (pardon) perdono; (willingness to forgive) clemenza, indulgenza

for·giv·ing [fə'gɪvɪŋ] ADJ indulgente

for·go [fɔː'gəʊ] (pt **forwent**, pp **forgone**) VT (do without) rinunciare a, fare a meno di

for·got [fə'gɒt] PT of **forget**

for·got·ten [fə'gɒtn] PP of **forget**

fork [fɔːk] N (for eating) forchetta; (for gardening) forca, forcone m; (in road) bivio, biforcazione f; **mix it with a fork** mescolalo con una forchetta; **take the left fork** al bivio volta a sinistra ♦ VI (road) biforcarsi

▸ **fork out** VT + ADV (fam: money, cash) sborsare, tirare fuori ♦ VI + ADV tirare fuori i soldi, pagare

forked [fɔːkt] ADJ (tail, tongue, branch) biforcuto(-a)

fork-lift truck ['fɔːk.lɪft'trʌk] N carrello elevatore

for·lorn [fə'lɔːn] ADJ (person) sconsolato(-a); (deserted: place, house) abbandonato(-a); (desperate: attempt) disperato(-a); **a forlorn hope** una speranza vana; **she looked forlorn** sembrava sconsolata

form [fɔːm] N 1 (gen) forma; **in the form of** a forma di, sotto forma di; **I'm against all forms of hunting** sono contrario a qualsiasi forma di caccia; **the same thing in a new form** la stessa cosa presentata in modo diverso; **a form of apology** una specie di scusa; **form and content** forma e contenuto; **to take form** prendere forma; **the correct form of address for a bishop** il corretto modo di rivolgersi a un vescovo 2 (Sport, also fig): **to be in good form** essere in forma; **in top form** in gran forma; **true to form** come sempre; **he was in great form last night** era in piena forma ieri sera 3 (document) modulo; **to fill in a form** riempire un modulo 4 (old: etiquette) forma; **it's a matter of form** è una questione di forma; **it's bad form** è maleducato 5 (bench) banco 6 (Brit Scol) classe f; **in the first form** ≈ in prima media; **he's in my form** è in classe con me ♦ VT (gen) formare; (plan) concepire; (idea, opinion) formarsi, farsi; (habit) prendere; **to form a circle/a queue** fare or formare un cerchio/una coda; **he formed it out of a lump of clay** l'ha plasmato or modellato su un blocco di creta; **to form a government/group** formare un governo/gruppo; **those who formed the group** quelli che facevano parte del gruppo; **to form part of sth** far parte di qc ♦ VI formarsi

for·mal ['fɔːmal] ADJ (gen) formale; (person) cerimonioso(-a); (official: visit, offer, acceptance) ufficiale; **a formal dinner** una cena ufficiale; **formal language** lingua formale; **formal clothes** abiti mpl da cerimonia; **there was no formal agreement** non c'era un contratto formale; **formal garden** giardino all'italiana; **formal training** preparazione f specifica

for·mal·ity [fɔː'mælɪtɪ] N formalità f inv; **it's a mere formality** è una semplice formalità

for·mal·ize ['fɔːməˌlaɪz] VT rendere ufficiale

for·mal·ly ['fɔːməlɪ] ADV (see adj) in modo formale; ufficialmente; **formally dressed** in abito da cerimonia; **to be formally invited** ricevere un invito ufficiale

for·mat ['fɔːmæt] N formato ♦ VT (Comput) formattare

for·ma·tion [fɔː'meɪʃən] N formazione f

forma·tive ['fɔːmətɪv] ADJ formativo(-a); **formative years** anni mpl formativi

for·mer ['fɔːməʳ] ADJ 1 (earlier, previous) vecchio(-a) (before n), precedente; (chairman, wife etc) ex inv (before n); **in former days** nei tempi passati, in altri tempi; **a former pupil** un ex alunno; **the former president** l'ex presidente; **the former Yugoslavia/Soviet Union** l'ex Jugoslavia/Unione Sovietica 2 (of two) primo(-a) ♦ PRON: **the former (…the latter)** il (la) primo(-a) (… l'ultimo(-a)), quello(-a)… (questo(-a)); **given the choice, I prefer the former** potendo scegliere, preferisco il primo

for·mer·ly ['fɔːməlɪ] ADV in passato, precedentemente

form feed N (on printer) alimentazione f della carta

for·mi·dable ['fɔːmɪdəbl] ADJ (task, difficulties) formidabile, terribile; (person, appearance) che incute rispetto

for·mu·la ['fɔːmjʊlə] N (pl **formulae** or **formulas** ['fɔːmjʊˌliː]) (Math, Chem, fig: plan) formula; (USA: baby's feed) latte m in polvere

for·mu·late ['fɔːmjʊˌleɪt] VT formulare

for·ni·cate ['fɔːnɪˌkeɪt] VI fornicare

for·sake [fə'seɪk] (pt **forsook**, pp **forsaken**) VT (person) abbandonare; (place) lasciare

fort [fɔːt] N (Mil) forte m

for·te ['fɔːtɪ] N forte m

forth [fɔːθ] ADV (old) 1 in avanti; **to go back and forth** andare avanti e indietro; **to set forth** mettersi in cammino; **from this day forth** d'ora in poi 2 **and so forth** e così via, e via dicendo

forth·com·ing [ˌfɔːθ'kʌmɪŋ] ADJ (event, election) prossimo(-a); (film) che sta per uscire, imminente; (book) di prossima pubblicazione; (character) aperto(-a), comunicativo(-a); **it will be discussed at the forthcoming meeting** verrà discusso nella prossima riunione; **if help is forthcoming** se c'è che è disposto ad aiutare; **he wasn't very forthcoming about it** non sembrava molto disposto a parlarne

forth·right ['fɔːθ.raɪt] ADJ (person, answer etc) franco(-a), schietto(-a)

forth·with [ˌfɔːθ'wɪθ] ADV (frm) immediatamente, subito

for·ti·eth ['fɔːtɪɪθ] ADJ quarantesimo(-a) ♦ N (in series) quarantesimo(-a); (fraction) quarantesimo

for·ti·fi·ca·tion [ˌfɔːtɪfɪ'keɪʃən] N fortificazione f

for·ti·fied wine ['fɔːtɪˌfaɪd'waɪn] N vino ad alta gradazione alcolica

for·ti·fy [ˈfɔːtɪˌfaɪ] VT (*Mil*) fortificare; (*fig: person*) rinvigorire, rafforzare; (*enrich: food*) arricchire

for·ti·tude [ˈfɔːtɪˌtjuːd] N forza d'animo

fort·night [ˈfɔːtnaɪt] N (*Brit*) quindici giorni *mpl*, quindicina di giorni, due settimane *fpl*; **to go on a fortnight's holiday** fare due settimane di vacanza; **a fortnight (from) today** oggi a quindici; **it's a fortnight since ...** sono due settimane da quando...; **for a fortnight** per quindici giorni

fort·night·ly [ˈfɔːtˌnaɪtlɪ](*Brit*) ADJ quindicinale, bimensile ♦ ADV ogni quindici giorni

for·tress [ˈfɔːtrɪs] N fortezza, rocca

for·tui·tous [fɔːˈtjuːɪtəs] ADJ fortuito(-a)

for·tu·nate [ˈfɔːtʃənɪt] ADJ (*coincidence, event, person*) fortunato(-a); **he is fortunate to have ...** ha la fortuna di avere...; **it is fortunate that** è una fortuna che + *sub*; **it's fortunate that I remembered the map** è una fortuna che mi sia ricordato della cartina

for·tu·nate·ly [ˈfɔːtʃənɪlɪ] ADV fortunatamente

for·tune [ˈfɔːtʃən] N 1 (*chance*) fortuna; **the fortunes of war** le vicende della guerra; **by good fortune** per fortuna; **to tell sb's fortune** predire l'avvenire *or* il futuro a qn 2 (*money*) fortuna; **to come into a fortune** ereditare una fortuna; **to make a fortune** farsi una fortuna *or* un patrimonio; **he made his fortune in Peru** ha fatto fortuna in Perù; **a small fortune** (*fam*) un patrimonio; **it cost a fortune** è costato una fortuna

fortune-teller [ˈfɔːtʃənˌtɛləʳ] N indovino(-a), chiromante *m/f*

for·ty [ˈfɔːtɪ] N quaranta *m inv* ♦ ADJ quaranta *inv*; **to have forty winks** (*fam*) fare *or* schiacciare un pisolino

fo·rum [ˈfɔːrəm] N (*History*) foro; (*fig*) tribuna

for·ward [ˈfɔːwəd] ADJ 1 (*in movement, position*) in avanti; (*in time*) in anticipo; (*Naut*) prodiero(-a); (*Sport*) linea d'attacco; (*Mil*) prima linea; **forward planning** pianificazione *f*; **forward thinking** (*person*) dalle idee innovatrici 2 (*precocious: child*) precoce; (*presumptuous: person, remark*) insolente, sfacciato(-a) 3 (*Comm: delivery, sales, exchange*) a termine ♦ ADV (*in place*) in avanti; (*in time*) avanti, innanzi; **to step forward** fare un passo avanti; **to push o.s. forward** farsi avanti, mettersi in evidenza; **to come forward** farsi avanti; **to move sth forward** spostare qc in avanti; **from this time forward** d'ora in poi, d'ora innanzi ♦ N (*Sport*) attaccante *m*, avanti *m inv* ♦ VT (*dispatch: parcel, goods*) spedire; (*send on: letter*) inoltrare; (*fig: sb's plans*) promuovere, appoggiare; **"please forward"** "si prega di inoltrare"

for·ward·ing ad·dress [ˈfɔːwədɪŋˈdrɛs] N: **he didn't leave a forwarding address** non ha lasciato un nuovo recapito

for·wards [ˈfɔːwədz] ADV = forward

for·went [fɔːˈwɛnt] PT *of* forgo

fos·sil [ˈfɒsl] N, ADJ fossile *m*

fos·ter [ˈfɒstəʳ] VT (*child*) avere in affidamento; (*hope, ambition*) nutrire, accarezzare; (*encourage*) incoraggiare; **she has fostered more than fifteen children** ha avuto in affidamento più di quindici bambini ♦ ADJ (*parent, mother, father*) affidatario(-a); (*child*) preso(-a) in affido; **foster brother** fratellastro, fratello adottivo; **foster sister** sorellastra, sorella adottiva

foster child N bambino(-a), (bambina) preso(-a), (presa) in affidamento

foster mother N madre *f* affidataria

fought [fɔːt] PT, PP *of* fight

foul [faul] ADJ (*putrid, disgusting: smell, breath, taste*) disgustoso(-a), rivoltante; (: *water, air*) puzzolente, fetido(-a); (*nasty: weather*) brutto(-a), orribile; (: *mood*) pessimo(-a), nero(-a); (*obscene: language*) volgare, osceno(-a); (*deed*) infame; **the weather was foul** il tempo era orribile; **it smells foul** ha un odore disgustoso; **to use foul language** parlare sboccatamente; **to fall foul of sb/the law** entrare in contrasto con qn/ con la giustizia ♦ N (*Ftbl*) fallo; (*Boxing*) colpo basso ♦ VT 1 (*pollute: air*) appestare; **the dog fouled the pavement** il cane ha sporcato il marciapiede 2 (*Sport: opponent*) commettere un fallo su 3 (*entangle: anchor, propeller*) impigliare

▸ **foul up** VT + ADV (*fam: plan, project*) rovinare

foul play N 1 (*murder*) delitto, atto criminale; (*dishonesty*) imbroglio, raggiro; **the police suspect foul play** la polizia sospetta si tratti di un delitto 2 (*Sport*) gioco scorretto

found¹ [faund] PT, PP *of* find

found² [faund] VT (*establish*) fondare; (*opinion, belief*) fondare, basare; **a statement founded on fact** una dichiarazione basata sulla realtà

foun·da·tion [faunˈdeɪʃən] N 1 (*founding, organization*) fondazione *f* 2 **foundations** NPL (*Archit*) fondamenta *fpl*; **to lay the foundations** gettare le fondamenta; (*fig*) gettare le basi 3 (*basis*) fondamento, base *f*; **the course gives students a good foundation** il corso fornisce agli studenti una buona base 4 (*justification*): **the story is without foundation** la storia è infondata

foundation stone N: **to lay the foundation stone** posare la prima pietra

found·er¹ [ˈfaundəʳ] N fondatore(-trice)

found·er² [ˈfaundəʳ] VI (*Naut, also fig*) affondare, colare a picco

found·ing [ˈfaundɪŋ] ADJ (*principle, assumption*) di base ♦ N fondazione *f*

found·ry [ˈfaundrɪ] N fonderia

fount [faunt] N 1 (*liter: source*) fonte *f*, sorgente *f* 2 (*Typ*) carattere *m* (di stampa)

foun·tain [ˈfauntɪn] N (*also fig*) fontana; **the fountains in Rome** le fontane di Roma

fountain pen N penna stilografica

four [fɔː] ADJ quattro *inv* ♦ N quattro *m inv*; **on all fours** (a) carponi

four-by-four [ˈfɔːbaɪˈfɔːʳ] N quattro per quattro *f inv*

four-letter word [ˈfɔːˌlɛtəˈwɜːd] N parolaccia

four-poster [ˈfɔːˈpəustəʳ] N (*also:* **four-poster bed**) letto a baldacchino

four·some [ˈfɔːsəm] N (*game*) partita a quattro; **we went in a foursome** siamo andati in quattro

four·teen [ˈfɔːˈtiːn] ADJ, N quattordici *m inv*

four·teenth [ˈfɔːˈtiːnθ] ADJ quattordicesimo(-a) ♦ N (*in series*) quattordicesimo(-a); (*fraction*) quattordicesimo

fourth [fɔːθ] ADJ quarto(-a); **fourth finger** anulare *m* ♦ N (*in series*) quarto(-a); (*fraction*) quarto; (*Aut: also:* **fourth gear**) quarta

four-wheel drive [ˈfɔːwiːlˈdraɪv] N (*Aut*): **a four-wheel drive** una (macchina a) quattro ruote motrici; **with four-wheel drive** con quattro ruote motrici

fowl [faul] N pollame *m*, volatile *m*

fox [fɒks] N volpe *f*; **a sly fox** (*fig*) una volpe, un furbacchione ♦ VT (*puzzle*) lasciare perplesso(-a), confondere; (*deceive*) ingannare

fox fur N (pelliccia di) volpe *f*

fox·glove [ˈfɒksˌɡlʌv] N (*Bot*) digitale *f*

fox-hunting [ˈfɒksˌhʌntɪŋ] N caccia alla volpe

foy·er [ˈfɔɪeɪ] N (*Theatre*) ridotto, foyer *m inv*

Fr. ABBR (*Rel*) = father

fr. ABBR (= *franc*) fr.

fra·cas [ˈfrækɑː] N rissa, lite *f*

frac·tion [ˈfrækʃən] N (*Math*) frazione *f*; **move it just a fraction** (*fig*) spostalo un pochino

frac·tion·al·ly [ˈfrækʃnəlɪ] ADV un tantino, minimamente

frac·tious [ˈfrækʃəs] ADJ (*person, mood*) irritabile; **to be in a fractious mood** essere irritabile *or* di cattivo umore

frac·ture [ˈfræktʃəʳ] N frattura ♦ VT fratturare; **to fracture one's arm** fratturarsi un braccio ♦ VI fratturarsi

frag·ile [ˈfrædʒaɪl] ADJ fragile; **I'm feeling rather fragile this morning** (*hum: esp after drinking*) mi sento piuttosto debole stamattina

frag·ment [N ˈfrægmənt, vb frægˈmɛnt] N frammento; **fragments of conversation** brani *mpl* di conversazione ♦ VI frammentarsi

frag·men·tary [ˈfrægməntərɪ] ADJ frammentario(-a)

fra·grance [ˈfreɪɡrəns] N (*of flowers*) fragranza, profumo; (*perfume, of toiletries*) profumo

fra·grant [ˈfreɪɡrənt] ADJ fragrante, profumato(-a)

frail [freɪl] ADJ (*comp* **-er**, *superl* **-est**) (*person, health, structure*) fragile, delicato(-a); (*fig: hope, relationship*) tenue, debole

frame [freɪm] N 1 (*of person*) corpo, ossatura; (*of ship, building, tent*) struttura, armatura; (*of bicycle*) telaio; (*of picture*) cornice *f*; (*of window, door*) telaio, intelaiatura; **a silver frame** una cornice d'argento 2 (*Cine*) immagine *f* 3 (*of spectacles*):

frames NPL montatura; **glasses with plastic frames** occhiali con la montatura di plastica ♦ VT **1** (*picture*) incorniciare **2** (*formulate: plan*) ideare; (: *question*) formulare; (: *sentence*) costruire **3 to frame sb** (*fam: incriminate*) incastrare qn

frame·work ['freɪmˌwɜːk] N (*also fig*) struttura

France [frɑːns] N la Francia

fran·chise ['fræntʃaɪz] N (*Pol*) diritto di voto; (*Comm*) concessione *f*; (*Marine Insurance*) franchigia

fran·chisee ['fræntʃaɪ'ziː] N concessionario(-a)

fran·chis·er ['fræntʃaɪzəʳ] N concedente *m*

frank¹ [fræŋk] ADJ (*comp* -er, *superl* -est) franco(-a), sincero(-a), aperto(-a)

frank² [fræŋk] VT (*letter*) affrancare

Frank·furt ['fræŋkfɜːt] N Francoforte *f*

frank·fur·ter ['fræŋkfɜːtəʳ] N würstel *m inv*

frank·ing ma·chine ['fræŋkɪŋməˌʃiːn] N affrancatrice *f*

frank·ly ['fræŋklɪ] ADV francamente, sinceramente

frank·ness ['fræŋknɪs] N franchezza

fran·tic ['fræntɪk] ADJ (*activity, pace*) frenetico(-a); (*desperate: desire*) pazzo(-a), sfrenato(-a); (*need*) disperato(-a); (*search*) affannoso(-a); (*person*) fuori di sé; **frantic with worry** fuori di sé dalla preoccupazione; **frantic with joy** pazzo(-a) di gioia; **to go frantic** perdere la testa; **I was going frantic** stavo perdendo la testa

fran·ti·cal·ly ['fræntɪkəlɪ] ADV (*gen*) freneticamente, affannosamente

fra·ter·nal [frə'tɜːnl] ADJ fraterno(-a)

fra·ter·nity [frə'tɜːnɪtɪ] N fraternità; (*club*) associazione *f*; (*spirit*) fratellanza; (*USA: Univ*) *associazione studentesca maschile*

frat·er·nize ['frætəˌnaɪz] VI: **to fraternize (with)** fraternizzare (con)

fraud [frɔːd] N (*Law*) frode *f*; (*trickery, trick*) truffa; (*person*) imbroglione(-a), impostore(-a); **he was jailed for fraud** è stato messo in prigione per truffa; **you're a fraud!** sei un impostore!

fraudu·lent ['frɔːdjʊlənt] ADJ (*behaviour*) disonesto(-a); (*claims*) fraudolento(-a)

fraught [frɔːt] ADJ (*tense*) teso(-a); **the situation is rather fraught** la situazione è un po' tesa; **fraught with** (*pain*) *or* carico(-a) di; **fraught with danger** pieno(-a) di pericoli

fray¹ [freɪ] N (*old: fight*) zuffa, baruffa; **ready for the fray** (*also fig*) pronto(-a) a battersi; **to return to the fray** ributtarsi nella mischia

fray² [freɪ] VT (*cloth, cuff, rope*) consumare, logorare; **tempers were getting frayed** (tutti) cominciavano a innervosirsi, cresceva il nervosismo; **her nerves were frayed** aveva i nervi a pezzi ♦ VI consumarsi, logorarsi

freak [friːk] N (*abnormal: person*) fenomeno da baraccone; (: *animal, plant*) mostro; (: *event*) avvenimento eccezionale; (*fam: enthusiast*) fanatico(-a); **a freak of nature** un capriccio della natura; **the result was a freak** il risultato è stato un caso eccezionale; **health freak** (*fam*) salutista *m/f*; **computer freaks** fanatici del computer♦ ADJ (*storm, conditions*) anormale; (*victory*) inatteso(-a)

▸ **freak out** VI + ADV (*fam: get angry*) uscire dai gangheri; (: *get excited*) andare su di giri; (: *on drugs*) andare fuori di testa

freak·ish ['friːkɪʃ] ADJ (*result, appearance*) strano(-a), bizzarro(-a); (*moods*) capriccioso(-a); (*weather*) anormale

freck·le ['frekl] N lentiggine *f*

free [friː] ADJ (*comp* -r, *superl* -st) **1** (*at liberty*): **free (from** *or* **of)** libero(-a) (da); **free from ties/cares** senza legami/preoccupazioni; **to be free of pain** non soffrire; **feel free** fai pure; **to break free (of)** liberarsi (da); **to set free** liberare; **free and easy** rilassato(-a); **he is not free to choose** non è libero di scegliere; **to give free rein to one's anger** *etc* dare libero sfogo alla propria rabbia *etc*; **to give sb a free hand** dare carta bianca a qn **2** (*not occupied*) libero(-a); **is this seat free?** è libero questo posto?; **are you free tomorrow?** sei libero domani?; **to have one's hands free** avere le mani libere **3 free (with)** (*generous*) prodigo(-a) (di); **to be free with one's money** spendere con facilità; **he's too free with his remarks** è sempre pronto alla critica **4** (*costing nothing*: *ticket, delivery*) gratuito(-a), gratis *inv*; **a free brochure** un

opuscolo gratuito; **a free gift** un omaggio; **free of charge** gratuito(-a); **admission free** entrata libera; **free baggage allowance** (*Aer*) franchigia bagaglio **5** (*improper: behaviour*) sfrontato(-a); (*language*) spinto(-a) ♦ ADV (*without charge*) gratuitamente, gratis; **I got in free** *or* **for free** (*fam*) sono entrato gratis ♦ VT (*gen*) liberare; (*jammed object*) districare; (*untie: person, animal*) sciogliere; **to free o.s. from** *or* **of sth** sbarazzarsi di qc

free·bie ['friːbɪ] N (*fam*): **it's a freebie** è in omaggio

free·dom ['friːdəm] N: **freedom (from)** libertà (da); **to give sb the freedom of one's house** mettere la propria casa a disposizione di qn; **the freedom of the press** la libertà di stampa; **to give sb the freedom of the city** dare a qn la cittadinanza onoraria; **freedom of speech** libertà di parola; **freedom of movement** libertà di movimento

freedom fighter N combattente *m/f* per la libertà

free enterprise N liberalismo economico

free-for-all ['friːfəˌrɔːl] N parapiglia *m* generale

free gift N regalo, omaggio

free·hold ['friːˌhəʊld] N (*Law*) proprietà assoluta

free kick N (*Ftbl*) calcio di punizione

free·lance ['friːlɑːns] ADJ: **freelance contributor** collaboratore(-trice) esterno(-a); **freelance work** collaborazione *f* esterna; **a freelance photographer** un fotografo freelance ♦ N collaboratore(-trice) esterno(-a) ♦ VI (*journalist*) essere un(a) giornalista *m/f* indipendente

free·loader ['friːˌləʊdəʳ] N (*pej*) scroccone(-a)

free·ly ['friːlɪ] ADV (*confess, speak*) liberamente, francamente; (*generously*) generosamente; **you may come and go freely** puoi andare e venire come vuoi

free-market economy ['friːˌmɑːkɪt'kɒnəmɪ] N economia di libero mercato

Free·mason ['friːˌmeɪsən] N massone *m*

free·masonry ['friːˌmeɪsənrɪ] N massoneria

free-range ['friːˌreɪnʒ] ADJ (*hen*) ruspante; (*eggs*) di gallina ruspante

free sample N campione *m* gratuito

free speech N libertà di parola

free·style ['friːstaɪl] N (*in swimming*) stile *m* libero

free trade N libero scambio

free·way ['friːˌweɪ] N (*USA*) superstrada

free·wheel ['friːˌwiːl] VI (*coast: on bicycle*) andare a ruota libera; (: *in car*) andare in folle

free·wheel·ing [ˌfriːˈwiːlɪŋ] ADJ (*fam: person*) indipendente

free will N libero arbitrio; **of one's own free will** di spontanea volontà

freeze [friːz] (*pt* froze, *pp* frozen) VT (*water*) gelare; (*food*) congelare; (*industrially*) surgelare; (*prices, assets, salaries*) bloccare, congelare ♦ VI (*Met*) gelare; (*water, lake*) ghiacciare; (*food*) congelarsi; (*keep still*) bloccarsi; **freezing fog** nebbia gelata; **the lake froze last winter** il lago è gelato lo scorso inverno; **to freeze to death** morire assiderato(-a); **he froze in his tracks** si bloccò; **freeze!** non muoverti!, fermo! ♦ N (*Met*) gelata; (*of prices, wages etc*) blocco

▸ **freeze over** VI + ADV (*lake, river*) ghiacciarsi; (*windows, windscreen*) coprirsi di ghiaccio

▸ **freeze up** VI + ADV gelarsi

freeze-dried ['friːzˌdraɪd] ADJ liofilizzato(-a)

freez·er ['friːzəʳ] N (*cabinet*) congelatore *m*; (*also:* **freezer compartment**) freezer *m inv*

freez·ing ['friːzɪŋ] N (*also:* **freezing point**) punto di congelamento; **5 degrees below freezing** 5 gradi sotto zero ♦ ADJ (*room, weather*) gelido(-a); **I'm freezing** sono congelato; **it's freezing!** si gela!

freight [freɪt] N (*goods transported*) merce *f*, merci *fpl*; (*charge*) spese *fpl* di trasporto; **freight forward** (*Comm*) spese a carico del destinatario; **freight inward** spese di trasporto sulla merce in entrata ♦ VT (*transport: goods*) trasportare ♦ ADJ (*yard*) merci *inv* ♦ ADV: **to send sth freight** spedire qc per via ordinaria

freight car N (*USA*) carro *m* merci, *inv*

freight·er ['freɪtəʳ] N (*Naut*) nave *f* mercantile *or* da carico, mercantile *m*; (*Aer*) aereo da trasporto merci

freight for·ward·er ['freɪt'fɔːwədəʳ] N spedizioniere *m*

freight train N (*USA*) treno *m* merci, *inv*

French [frɛntʃ] ADJ francese; (*lesson, teacher etc*) di francese
♦ N 1 (*language*) francese *m*; **I can speak French** parlo il
francese; **the French teacher** l'insegnante di francese 2
(*people*): **the French** *npl* i francesi
French bean N fagiolino
French bread N baguette *f inv*
French Canadian ADJ, N franco-canadese *m/f*
French doors NPL portafinestra
French dressing N (*Culin*) condimento per insalata
French fried potatoes, French fries(*esp USA*) NPL patate
fpl fritte
French Gui·ana [frɛntʃgaɪˈænə] N la Guiana francese
French loaf N filoncino
French·man [ˈfrɛntʃmən] N (*pl* -men) francese *m*
French Riviera N: **the French Riviera** la Costa Azzurra
French stick, French loaf N filoncino
French windows (*USA*) NPL portafinestra
French·woman [ˈfrɛntʃwʊmən] N (*pl* -women) francese *f*
fre·net·ic [frɪˈnɛtɪk] ADJ frenetico(-a)
fren·zy [ˈfrɛnzɪ] N frenesia
fre·quen·cy [ˈfriːkwənsɪ] N frequenza; **high/low frequency**
alta/bassa frequenza
frequency modulation N modulazione *f* di frequenza
fre·quent [*adj* ˈfriːkwənt, *vb* frɪˈkwɛnt] ADJ (*gen*) frequente;
(*visitor*) abituale ♦ VT frequentare
fre·quent·ly [ˈfriːkwəntlɪ] ADV frequentemente, spesso
fres·co [ˈfrɛskəʊ] N affresco
fresh [frɛʃ] ADJ (*comp* -er, *superl* -est) 1 (*gen: not stale*)
fresco(-a); (*new: sheet of paper, supplies, approach*) nuovo(-a);
(*: news*) recente; **is the fish fresh?** il pesce è fresco?; **to make
a fresh start** ricominciare da capo; **as fresh as a daisy**
fresco(-a) come una rosa 2 (*invigorating: breeze*) fresco(-a);
it's a bit fresh (*Met*) fa un po' freschino 3 (*not salt: water*)
dolce 4 (*fam: cheeky*) sfacciato(-a); **to get fresh with sb**
prendersi delle libertà con qn ♦ ADV (*baked, picked*) appena, da poco; **bread fresh from the oven** pane appena uscito
dal forno; **to come fresh from New York** essere arrivato(-a)
fresco(-a) da New York; **a teacher fresh from college** un insegnante appena uscito dall'università
fresh·en [ˈfrɛʃn] VI (*wind, air*) rinfrescare
  ▸ **freshen up** VI + ADV rinfrescarsi ♦ VT + ADV rinfrescare; **to
freshen o.s. up** darsi una rinfrescata
fresh·en·er [ˈfrɛʃnəʳ] N (*also:* **skin freshener**) tonico rinfrescante
fresh·er [ˈfrɛʃəʳ] N (*Brit: Univ: fam*) = **freshman**
fresh·ly [ˈfrɛʃlɪ] ADV di recente, di fresco, appena
fresh·man [ˈfrɛʃmən] N (*pl* -men) (*Univ*) matricola *f*
fresh·ness [ˈfrɛʃnɪs] N (*of food, air*) freschezza; (*of approach*)
novità; (*impertinence*) impertinenza
fresh·water [ˈfrɛʃˌwɔːtəʳ] ADJ: **freshwater fish** pesce *m* d'acqua dolce
fret [frɛt] VI (*worry*) preoccuparsi, agitarsi, affliggersi; **don't
fret** non preoccuparti
fret·ful [ˈfrɛtfʊl] ADJ (*child*) irritabile
Freud·ian [ˈfrɔɪdɪən] ADJ freudiano(-a)
FRG [ˌɛfɑːˈdʒiː] N ABBR (= *Federal Republic of Germany*) RFT *f*
(= *Repubblica Federale Tedesca*)
Fri. [a] ABBR (= *Friday*) ven. (= *venerdì*)
fri·ar [ˈfraɪəʳ] N frate *m*
fric·tion [ˈfrɪkʃən] N frizione *f*, attrito
friction feed N (*on printer*) trascinamento ad attrito
Fri·day [ˈfraɪdɪ] N venerdì *m inv*; *see* **Tuesday**
fridge [frɪdʒ] N (*Brit*) frigorifero, frigo
fridge-freezer [frɪdʒˈfriːzəʳ] N frigocongelatore *m*
fried [fraɪd] PT, PP *of* **fry**[1] ♦ ADJ (*Culin*) fritto(-a); **fried egg**
uovo fritto *or* al tegamino; **fried chicken** pollo fritto
friend [frɛnd] N amico(-a); (*at school*) compagno(-a); (*at
work*) collega *m/f*; **a friend of mine** un(a) mio(-a) amico(-a);
to make friends with sb fare amicizia con qn; **let's be
friends** facciamo pace; **we're just good friends** siamo solo
buoni amici ♦ VT (*Comput: on Facebook*): **to friend sb** aggiungere qn agli amici
friend·li·ness [ˈfrɛndlɪnɪs] N cordialità
friend·ly [ˈfrɛndlɪ] ADJ (*comp* -ier, *superl* -iest) cordiale,

amichevole; **to be friendly to sb** essere cordiale con qn; **to
be friendly with sb** essere amico di qn ♦ N (*also:* **friendly
match**) (partita) amichevole *f*
friendly fire N (*Mil*) fuoco amico
friendly society N società *f inv* di mutuo soccorso
friend·ship [ˈfrɛndʃɪp] N amicizia
fries [fraɪz] NPL (*esp USA*) patate *fpl* fritte
frieze [friːz] N (*Archit*) fregio
frig·ate [ˈfrɪgɪt] N (*Naut*) fregata
fright [fraɪt] N paura, spavento; **to get** *or* **have a fright** spaventarsi; **what a fright you gave me!** mi hai fatto paura!; **to
take fright (at)** spaventarsi (all'idea di)
fright·en [ˈfraɪtn] VT spaventare, far paura a; **horror films
frighten him** i film dell'orrore gli fanno paura; **to fright-
en sb out of their wits** far morire qn dallo spavento; **to be
frightened of sth** avere paura di qc; **he was frightened into
doing it** l'ha fatto per paura; **I was frightened to death** ero
morto di paura
  ▸ **frighten away, frighten off** VT + ADV (*birds, children*)
scacciare (facendogli paura)
fright·ened [ˈfraɪtnd] ADJ: **to be frightened (of)** avere paura
(di)
fright·en·ing [ˈfraɪtnɪŋ] ADJ pauroso(-a), spaventoso(-a)
fright·ful [ˈfraɪtfʊl] ADJ terribile, spaventoso(-a), orribile
fright·ful·ly [ˈfraɪtfʊlɪ] ADV (*fam: late, cold*) terribilmente,
spaventosamente; **I'm frightfully sorry** mi dispiace moltissimo
frig·id [ˈfrɪdʒɪd] ADJ (*atmosphere, look*) glaciale; (*Psych*) frigi-
do(-a)
fri·gid·ity [frɪˈdʒɪdɪtɪ] N (*of manners, look*) freddezza; (*sexual*)
frigidità
frill [frɪl] N (*on dress*) fronzolo, balza; **without frills** (*fig*) senza
fronzoli
frilly [ˈfrɪlɪ] ADJ (*dress*) con pizzi e merletti
fringe [frɪndʒ] N 1 (*on shawl, rug*) frangia; (*Brit: of hair*) frangia, frangetta; **I want my fringe cut** vorrei che mi tagliasse
la frangia 2 **fringes** NPL (*of forest*) margine *m*; (*of city*) periferia; **on the fringe(s) of society** ai margini della società
♦ VT (*shawl*) frangiare; **a road fringed with trees** una strada
fiancheggiata da alberi
fringe benefits NPL benefici *mpl* aggiuntivi, fringe benefits
mpl
fringe theatre N teatro d'avanguardia
frisk [frɪsk] VT (*fam: suspect*) perquisire ♦ VI (*frolic*) saltellare
allegramente
frisky [ˈfrɪskɪ] ADJ (*comp* -ier, *superl* -iest) (*person, horse*) vis-
po(-a), vivace
frit·ter [ˈfrɪtəʳ] N (*Culin*) frittella
  ▸ **fritter away** VT + ADV sprecare
fri·vol·ity [frɪˈvɒlɪtɪ] N frivolezza
frivo·lous [ˈfrɪvələs] ADJ frivolo(-a)
friz·zy [ˈfrɪzɪ] ADJ (*comp* -ier, *superl* -iest) (*hair*) crespo(-a); **to
go frizzy** incresparsi
fro [frəʊ] ADV: **to and fro** avanti e indietro; **to go to and fro**
between **fare la spola tra**
frock [frɒk] N abito, vestito; (*of monk*) tonaca
frog [frɒg] N rana; **to have a frog in one's throat** avere la voce
rauca
frog·man [ˈfrɒgmən] N (*pl* -men) sommozzatore *m*, uomo *m*
rana, *inv*
frog·march [ˈfrɒgˌmɑːtʃ] VT (*Brit*): **to frogmarch sb in/out**
portar qn dentro/fuori con la forza
frol·ic [ˈfrɒlɪk] VI (*pt, pp* **frolicked**) VI saltellare allegramente

KEYWORD

from [frɒm] PREP
  1 (*indicating starting place*) da; **where has he come from?** da
dove arriva?; **to escape from sb/sth** fuggire da qn/qc; **from
London to Glasgow** da Londra a Glasgow; **from house to
house** di casa in casa; **where is he from?** da dove viene?,
di dov'è?
  2 (*indicating time*) da; **(as) from Friday** (a partire) da venerdì;
from January da gennaio in poi; **from now on** d'ora in poi,
d'ora innanzi; **from time to time** ogni tanto, di tanto in tanto; **from one o'clock to** *or* **until** *or* **till two** dall'una alle due

3 (*indicating distance*) da; **the hotel is 1 km from the beach** l'albergo è a 1 km dalla spiaggia; **a long way from home** lontano(-a) da casa

4 (*indicating source, origin*) da; **a telephone call from Mr Smith** una telefonata dal Signor Smith; **to drink from a stream/the bottle** bere a un ruscello/dalla bottiglia; **where did you get that from?** dove l'hai trovato?; **a letter from my sister** una lettera da mia sorella; **painted from life** dipinto(-a) dal vero; **a quotation from Shakespeare** una citazione da Shakespeare; **to steal sth from sb** rubare qc a qn; **take the gun from him!** levagli la pistola!; **tell him from me** diglielo da parte mia

5 (*indicating price, number*) da; **prices range from £10 to £50** i prezzi vanno dalle 10 alle 50 sterline; **there were from 10 to 15 people there** c'erano tra le 10 e le 15 persone; **we have shirts from £18 upwards** abbiamo camicie da 18 sterline in su

6 (*indicating change*): **things went from bad to worse** le cose andarono di male in peggio; **the interest rate increased from 6% to 10%** il tasso d'interesse è aumentato dal 6% al 10%

7 (*indicating difference*): **to be different from sb** essere diverso(-a) da qn; **he can't tell red from green** non sa distinguere il rosso dal verde

8 (*because of, on the basis of*): **to act from conviction** agire per convinzione; **from experience** per esperienza; **to die from exposure** morire assiderato(-a); **weak from hunger** debole per la fame; **from what I can see** a quanto vedo; **from what I understood** da quanto ho capito; **from what he says** a quanto dice

9 (*with preposition*): **from above sth** da sopra qc, dall'alto di qc; **from among the crowd** dalla folla; **from beneath sth** da sotto qc; **from inside the house** dall'interno della casa; **from outside the house** dall'esterno della casa; **from over sth** da sopra qc, dall'alto di qc; **from underneath sth** da sotto qc

frond [frɒnd] N fronda

front [frʌnt] ADJ (*tooth*) davanti *inv*; (*garden*) sul davanti; (*wheel*) anteriore; (*row, page*) primo(-a); (*carriage*) di testa; (*view*) frontale; **the front seats of the car** i sedili davanti della macchina ♦ N **1** (*gen*) davanti *m inv*; (*of house*) facciata, davanti; (*of book*) copertina; (*of train*) testa; (*fig: appearance*) facciata; **in front** davanti; **in front of** davanti a; **Irene sits in front of me in class** Irene è seduta davanti a me in classe; (*opposite*) di fronte a; **at the front of the line** *or* **queue** in cima *or* all'inizio della fila; **at the front of the train** in testa al treno; **to be in front** (*Sport*) essere in testa; **he sat at the front of the class** era seduto nei primi banchi (della classe); **to put on a bold front** (*fig*) mostrare coraggio; **to be a front for sth** (*fam*) servire da copertura per qc **2** (*Mil, Pol, Met*) fronte *m*; **on all fronts** su tutti i fronti; **a united front** un fronte unito **3** (*also: sea front: promenade*) lungomare *m* ♦ VI: **to front onto sth** dare su qc, guardare verso qc

front·age ['frʌntɪdʒ] N facciata

front·al ['frʌntl] ADJ frontale

front bench N (*Brit Pol*): **the front bench** (*government ministers*) i ministri *pl*; (*opposition leaders*) i principali esponenti dell'opposizione

front·bench·er [frʌnt'bentʃəʳ] N *parlamentare che detiene una carica presso il governo*

front desk N (*USA: in hotel*) reception *f inv*; (: *at doctor's*) accettazione *f*

front door N porta d'ingresso

fron·tier [frʌntɪəʳ] N frontiera, confine *m*

fron·tis·piece ['frʌntɪspiːs] N frontespizio

front page N prima pagina

front-page ['frʌnt,peɪdʒ] ADJ (*news, article*) di prima pagina

front room N (*Brit*) salotto

front runner N (*fig*) favorito(-a)

front-wheel drive ['frʌnt,wiːl'draɪv] N (*Aut*) trazione *f* anteriore

frost [frɒst] N gelo; (*also: hoar frost*) brina; (*on window*) ghiaccio; **a keen frost** un gelo pungente; **there was frost on the ground** c'era brina sulla terra; **an overnight frost** gelata notturna; **4 degrees of frost** 4 gradi sotto zero ♦ VT (*esp USA: ice: cakes*) glassare

frost·bite ['frɒst,baɪt] N congelamento

frost·ed ['frɒstɪd] ADJ (*glass*) smerigliato(-a); (*esp USA: cake*) glassato(-a)

frost·ing ['frɒstɪŋ] N (*esp USA: icing*) glassa

frosty ['frɒstɪ] ADJ (*comp* -**ier**, *superl* -**iest**) (*weather, also fig*) gelido(-a); (*surface, window*) coperto(-a) di ghiaccio *or* di brina; **it was frosty last night** ha gelato durante la notte; **one frosty morning** una mattinata gelida; **they gave him a frosty reception** gli hanno riservato un'accoglienza gelida

froth [frɒθ] N schiuma, spuma ♦ VI schiumare, spumare; **the dog was frothing at the mouth** il cane aveva la schiuma alla bocca

frown [fraʊn] N: **he gave me a worried frown** mi ha guardato con aria preoccupata; **he gave me a frown of disapproval** mi ha lanciato un'occhiata di disapprovazione ♦ VI aggrottare le sopracciglia; **to frown at sth/sb** guardare qc/qn con cipiglio

‣ **frown upon, frown on** VI + PREP (*fig*) disapprovare

froze [frəʊz] PT *of* **freeze**

fro·zen ['frəʊzn] PP *of* **freeze** ♦ ADJ (*food*) congelato(-a); (*industrially deep frozen*) surgelato(-a); (*Econ: assets*) bloccato(-a); **I'm frozen stiff** sono gelato fino alle ossa

FRS [ɛfɑːr'ɛs] N ABBR **1** (*Brit:* = Fellow of the Royal Society) **2** (*USA:* = Federal Reserve System) sistema bancario degli Stati Uniti

fru·gal ['fruːgəl] ADJ (*person*) economo(-a); (*meal*) frugale

fruit [fruːt] N (*collectively*) frutta; (*Bot*) frutto; **would you like some fruit?** vuoi della frutta?; **to bear fruit** dare frutti; (*fig*) dare frutto; **the fruits of one's labour** (*fig*) i frutti del proprio lavoro

fruit fly N mosca della frutta

fruit·ful ['fruːtful] ADJ (*profitable*) fruttuoso(-a); (*soil*) fertile

frui·tion [fruː'ɪʃən] N: **to come to fruition** (*frm*) realizzarsi

fruit juice N succo di frutta

fruit·less ['fruːtlɪs] ADJ (*fig*) vano(-a), inutile

fruit salad N macedonia

frump [frʌmp] N donnetta scialba

frus·trate [frʌ'streɪt] VT (*plan, effort, hope*) rendere vano(-a); (*person*) frustrare

frus·trat·ed [frʌ'streɪtɪd] ADJ (*person*) frustrato(-a); (*effort*) reso(-a) vano(-a); **he's a frustrated artist** è un artista mancato; **I got more and more frustrated with it** ci sono impazzito

frus·trat·ing [frʌ'streɪtɪŋ] ADJ (*job*) frustrante; (*day*) disastroso(-a); **how frustrating!** che seccatura!

frus·tra·tion [frʌ'streɪʃən] N (*feeling: of hopes*) frustrazione *f*; (*of plans*) inutilità; (*setback*) scocciatura

fry¹ [fraɪ] VT, VI friggere

fry² [fraɪ] NPL (*Zool*) avannotti *mpl; see also* **small fry**

fry·ing pan ['fraɪŋ'pæn] N padella; **to jump out of the frying pan into the fire** cadere dalla padella nella brace

ft. ABBR = **foot, feet**

FTC [ɛftiː'siː] N ABBR (*USA*) = Federal Trade Commission

fuch·sia ['fjuːʃə] N (*Bot*) fucsia; (*colour*) fucsia *m* ♦ ADJ fucsia *inv*

fuck [fʌk](*fam!*) VT **1** fottere **2** **fuck you!** va' a farti fottere! (*fam!*) ♦ EXCL: **fuck!** cazzo!

‣ **fuck off** VI + ADV (*fam!*): **fuck off!** vaffanculo! (*fam!*)

fud·dled ['fʌdld] ADJ (*muddled*) confuso(-a); (*tipsy*) brillo(-a)

fuddy-duddy ['fʌdɪ,dʌdɪ] N (*pej*) parruccone *m*

fudge [fʌdʒ] N (*Culin*) specie di caramella a base di latte, burro e zucchero ♦ VT (*figures, results*) falsificare; (*question, issue*) eludere

fuel [fjʊəl] N (*gen*) combustibile *m*; (*for engine*) carburante *m*; **the plane ran out of fuel** l'aereo ha finito il carburante; **to add fuel to the flames** (*fig*) soffiare sul fuoco, gettar olio sul fuoco ♦ VT (*furnace etc*) alimentare; (*aircraft, ship*) rifornire di carburante ♦ VI (*aircraft, ship*) rifornirsi di carburante

fuel oil N olio combustibile, nafta

fuel poverty N povertà energetica

fuel pump N (*Aut*) pompa del carburante

fuel tank N (*industrial, domestic*) serbatoio del carburante, deposito *m* nafta, *inv*; (*on vehicle*) serbatoio (della benzina)

fug [fʌg] N (*Brit*) aria viziata

fu·gi·tive [ˈfjuːdʒɪtɪv] N fuggitivo(-a), profugo(-a); (*from prison*) evaso(-a) ♦ ADJ fuggitivo(-a); (*liter: fleeting*) fugace, fuggevole

ful·fil, ful·fill (*USA*) [fʊlˈfɪl] VT (*duty, function*) compiere; (*promise*) mantenere; (*ambition*) realizzare; (*wish, desire*) soddisfare, appagare; (*order*) eseguire; **to fulfil o.s.** realizzarsi; **he fulfilled his dream to visit China** ha realizzato il suo sogno di fare un viaggio in Cina

ful·filled [fʊlˈfɪld] ADJ (*person*) realizzato(-a), soddisfatto(-a)

ful·fil·ment, ful·fill·ment (*USA*) [fʊlˈfɪlmənt] N (*see vb*) compimento; mantenimento; realizzazione *f*; soddisfazione *f*, appagamento; esecuzione *f*; **sense of fulfilment** soddisfazione

full [fʊl] ADJ (*comp -er, superl -est*) **1** (*gen*) pieno(-a); (*vehicle, hotel*) completo(-a); (*timetable*) denso(-a); **the tank's full** il serbatoio è pieno; **to be full of ...** essere pieno(-a) di...; **full of people** gremito(-a) di gente; **to be full of o.s.** essere pieno(-a) di sé; **we are full up for July** siamo al completo per luglio; **he's had a full life** ha avuto una vita piena *or* intensa; **I'm full (up)** (*fam*) sono pieno *or* sazio **2** (*complete*) completo(-a); (*member*) effettivo(-a); (*price*) intero(-a); (*details*) ampio(-a); **to pay full fare** pagare la tariffa intera *or* completa; **to fall full length** cadere lungo(-a) disteso(-a); **in full bloom** in piena fioritura; **in full colour** (*illustration*) a colori; **in full dress** in abito da cerimonia; **army at full strength** esercito al gran completo; **to be in full swing** essere in pieno fervore; **in the fullest sense of the word** nel pieno senso della parola; **at full speed** a tutta velocità; **full speed ahead** (*Naut*) avanti tutta; **full price** prezzo intero; **the full particulars** tutti i particolari; **full information** tutte le informazioni; **I waited a full hour** ho aspettato un'ora intera **3** (*rounded: face*) pieno(-a); (: *figure*) pienotto(-a); (: *lips*) carnoso(-a); (: *skirt, sleeves*) largo(-a), ampio(-a) ♦ ADV: **to know full well that** sapere benissimo che; **it hit him full in the face** l'ha colpito in pieno viso ♦ N: **to write sth in full** scrivere qc per intero; **to pay in full** pagare tutto; **to the full** fino in fondo, al massimo

full·back [ˈfʊlbæk] N (*Ftbl, Rugby*) terzino

full·blooded [ˌfʊlˈblʌdɪd] ADJ (*vigorous: attack, support*) vigoroso(-a); (*virile*) virile

full·cream [ˌfʊlˈkriːm] ADJ (*Brit*): **full-cream milk** latte *m* intero

full·grown [ˌfʊlˈɡrəʊn] ADJ maturo(-a)

full·length [ˌfʊlˈlɛŋθ] ADJ (*portrait*) in piedi; (*dress*) lungo(-a); (*film*) a lungometraggio

full moon N luna piena

full·scale [ˈfʊlskeɪl] ADJ (*search, retreat*) su vasta scala; (*drawing, model*) a grandezza naturale; **a full-scale prototype** un prototipo in grandezza naturale; **a full-scale nuclear war** una guerra nucleare su vasta scala

full·sized [ˌfʊlˈsaɪzd], **full·size** [ˌfʊlˈsaɪz] ADJ (*full-grown*) adulto(-a); (*portrait, model*) a grandezza naturale

full stop N punto

full·time [ˌfʊlˈtaɪm] ADJ, ADV (*work*) a tempo pieno

ful·ly [ˈfʊlɪ] ADV **1** (*completely*) completamente, pienamente, interamente; **fully dressed** completamente vestito(-a) **2** (*at least*) almeno; **fully as big** almeno così grosso(-a)

fully·fledged [ˈfʊlɪˈflɛdʒd] ADJ (*bird*) adulto(-a); (*fig: teacher, member*) a tutti gli effetti

ful·some [ˈfʊlsəm] ADJ (*pej: praise*) esagerato(-a), eccessivo(-a); (: *manner*) insincero(-a)

fum·ble [ˈfʌmbl] VI (*also:* **fumble about**): **to fumble (about) in one's pockets** frugare *or* rovistare nelle tasche; **to fumble in the dark** andare a tastoni *or* a tentoni, brancolare; **to fumble with sth** armeggiare con qc ♦ VT: **to fumble a catch** mancare una presa; **to fumble a ball** lasciarsi sfuggire di mano una palla

fume [fjuːm] VI (*angry person*) essere furioso(-a); (*car exhaust*) fumare; **to be fuming with rage at** *or* **about sth** fumare di rabbia per qc

fu·mi·gate [ˈfjuːmɪˌɡeɪt] VT (*room*) suffumicare, fumigare

fun [fʌn] N (*enjoyment*) divertimento, spasso; **for** *or* **in fun** per scherzo, per ridere, per divertimento; **it's great fun** è molto divertente; **it's not much fun** non è molto divertente; **don't spoil our fun** non fare il guastafeste; **there'll be fun and games with that** (*fig: iro*) ci sarà da divertirsi; **to do sth for**

the fun of it fare qc tanto per ridere; **to have fun** divertirsi; **have fun!** divertiti!; **to make fun of** *or* **poke fun at sb** canzonare *or* prendere in giro qn

func·tion [ˈfʌŋkʃən] N **1** (*purpose, also Math*) funzione *f* **2** (*reception*) ricevimento; (*official ceremony*) cerimonia, funzione *f* ♦ VI (*operate*) funzionare; **the system ceased to function** il sistema ha smesso di funzionare; **to function as** fungere da

func·tion·al [ˈfʌŋkʃnəl] ADJ funzionale

function key N (*Comput*) tasto *m* funzione, *inv*

fund [fʌnd] N **1** (*reserve of money*) fondo, cassa; (*supply*) provvista, riserva; **a pension fund** un fondo pensione; **to be a fund of information** essere una miniera d'informazioni **2** (*cash*): **funds** NPL fondi *mpl*; **to raise funds for** raccogliere fondi per ♦ VT (*project*) finanziare

fun·da·men·tal [ˌfʌndəˈmɛntl] ADJ fondamentale; **his fundamental honesty** la sua innata onestà

fun·da·men·tal·ism [ˌfʌndəˈmɛntəˌlɪzəm] N fondamentalismo

fun·da·men·tal·ist [ˌfʌndəˈmɛntəlɪst] ADJ, N fondamentalista *m/f*

fun·da·men·tal·ly [ˌfʌndəˈmɛntəlɪ] ADV fondamentalmente, essenzialmente

fund·ing [ˈfʌndɪŋ] N finanziamento, fondi *mpl*

fund·raising [ˈfʌndˌreɪzɪŋ] N raccolta di fondi ♦ ADJ (*event*) per la raccolta di fondi

fu·ner·al [ˈfjuːnərəl] N funerale *m*; (*procession*) corteo funebre; (*state funeral*) funerali *mpl*; **that's your funeral!** (*fam*) è affar tuo

funeral director N impresario di pompe funebri

funeral parlour, funeral parlor (*USA*) N impresa di pompe funebri

funeral service N ufficio funebre

fu·nereal [fjuːˈnɪərɪəl] ADJ funereo(-a), lugubre

fun·fair [ˈfʌnˌfɛəʳ] N (*Brit*) luna park *m inv*

fun·gus [ˈfʌŋɡəs] N (*pl* fungi [ˈfʌŋɡaɪ]) fungo; (*mould*) muffa

fu·nicu·lar [fjuːˈnɪkjʊləʳ] N (*also:* **funicular railway**) funicolare *f* ♦ ADJ funicolare

funky [ˈfʌŋkɪ] ADJ (*comp -ier, superl -iest*) (*music*) funky *inv*; (*clothes, look etc*) alla moda; (*fam: excellent*) figo(-a)

fun·nel [ˈfʌnl] N (*for pouring*) imbuto; (*of steam engine, ship*) fumaiolo, ciminiera

fun·ni·ly [ˈfʌnɪlɪ] ADV **1** in modo divertente **2** (*oddly*) stranamente; **funnily enough** strano a dirsi, per una strana coincidenza

fun·ny [ˈfʌnɪ] ADJ (*comp -ier, superl -iest*) **1** divertente, buffo(-a); **it was so funny I couldn't stop laughing** era così divertente che non riuscivo a smettere di ridere; **that's not funny** c'è poco da ridere; **to try to be funny** fare lo spiritoso(-a) **2** (*strange*) strano(-a), bizzarro(-a); **this tastes funny** ha uno strano sapore; **a funny feeling came over me** mi sono sentito strano; **the funny thing about it is that ...** la cosa strana è che...; **there's some funny business going on here** (*fam*) qui c'è qualcosa di losco; **there's something funny about him** ha qualcosa di strano ♦ N: **the funnies** (*USA fam*) i fumetti

funny bone N (*fam*) osso cubitale

fun run N marcia non competitiva

fur [fɜːʳ] N (*of animal*) pelo, pelame *m*; (*single skin*) pelle *f*; (*as clothing*) pelliccia; (*Brit: in kettle*) incrostazione *f*, calcare *m*; **the cat's fur** il pelo del gatto

fur coat N pelliccia

fu·ri·ous [ˈfjʊərɪəs] ADJ (*person*) furioso(-a), infuriato(-a); (*argument*) violento(-a); (*effort*) grande; **at a furious speed** a velocità folle; **to be furious with sb** essere furioso(-a) con qn; **to be furious at sth/at having done sth** essere furioso(-a) per qc/per aver fatto qc

fu·ri·ous·ly [ˈfjʊərɪəslɪ] ADV furiosamente, accanitamente

furl [fɜːl] VT (*sail*) piegare

fur·long [ˈfɜːlɒŋ] N = 201,17 m

fur·lough [ˈfɜːləʊ] N (*esp USA*) licenza, permesso, congedo

fur·nace [ˈfɜːnɪs] N fornace *f*

fur·nish [ˈfɜːnɪʃ] VT **1** (*room, house*): **to furnish (with)** arredare (con), ammobiliare (con); **furnishing fabric** tessuto da arredamento; **furnished flat** *or* (*USA*) **furnished apartment**

appartamento ammobiliato 2 (*frm: supply: excuse, informa-tion*) fornire, dare; **to furnish sb with sth** dare qc a qn
fur·nish·ings [ˈfɜːnɪʃɪŋz] NPL mobili *mpl*, mobilia
fur·ni·ture [ˈfɜːnɪtʃəˈ] N mobili *mpl*, mobilia; **a piece of fur-niture** un mobile; **the furniture is new** i mobili sono nuovi; **to be part of the furniture** (*fig: fam*) confondersi con la tappezzeria
❏ **furniture** is not translated by the Italian word *fornitura*

fu·ro·re [fjʊəˈrɔːrɪ], **fu·ror** (*USA*) [fjʊəˈrɔːˈ] N (*protests*) scal-pore *m*; (*enthusiasm*) entusiasmo
❏ **furore** is not translated by the Italian word *furore*

fur·ri·er [ˈfʌrɪəˈ] N pellicciaio(-a)
fur·row [ˈfʌrəʊ] N (*Agr*) solco; (*on forehead*) solco, ruga
♦ VT (*forehead, brow*) segnare di rughe, solcare
fur·ry [ˈfʌrɪ] ADJ (*animal*) peloso(-a); (*toy*) di peluche
fur·ther [ˈfɜːðəˈ] COMP *of* **far** ♦ ADV 1 (*in time*) oltre, più avanti; (*in place*) più lontano, oltre, più avanti; **further back** più indietro; **further on** (*also fig*) più avanti; **how much further is it?** quanto manca *or* dista?; **London is further from here than Oxford** Londra è più lontana da qui rispetto a Oxford; **any further** più; **I can't walk any further** non ce la faccio più a camminare; **I got no fur-ther with him** (*fig*) non sono riuscito a cavare un ragno dal buco; **nothing is further from my thoughts** non ci penso neanche 2 (*more*) inoltre, di più; **and I further be-lieve that ...** e inoltre *or* per di più credo che...; **further to your letter of ...** (*Comm*) con riferimento alla vostra lettera del...; **further to our conversation ...** facendo seguito alla nostra conversazione...; **he heard nothing further** non c'è stato alcun seguito ♦ ADJ 1 = **farther** 2 (*additional*) ulteriore, altro(-a), supplementare; **until further notice** fino a nuovo avviso; **after further con-sideration** dopo un più attento esame; **please write to us if you need any further information** ci scriva se ha bisogno di ulteriori informazioni ♦ VT (*a cause*) appogg-iare, promuovere, favorire; **to further one's interests** fare i propri interessi
further·more [ˈfɜːðəˌmɔːˈ] ADV inoltre, per di più
further·most [ˈfɜːðəˌməʊst] ADJ più lontano(-a)
fur·thest [ˈfɜːðɪst] SUPERL *of* **far** ♦ ADV: **this is the furthest you can go** non puoi andare più lontano ♦ ADJ più lontano(-a), più distante

fur·tive [ˈfɜːtɪv] ADJ (*glance, action*) furtivo(-a); (*person*) circo-spetto(-a)
fury [ˈfjʊərɪ] N (*of storm, person*) furia, furore *m*
fuse, (*USA*) **fuze** [fjuːz] N (*Elec*) fusibile *m*, valvola; (*of bomb*) spoletta, miccia; **to blow a fuse** far saltare una valvola; **a fuse has blown** è saltata una valvola, è saltato un fusibile ♦ VT 1 (*Elec*): **to fuse the lights** far saltare le valvole 2 (*metals*) fondere ♦ VI 1 (*Elec*): **the lights have fused** sono saltate le valvole 2 (*metals*) fondersi
fuse box N scatola *or* cassetta dei fusibili
fu·selage [ˈfjuːzəlɑːʒ] N fusoliera
fuse wire N (filo) fusibile *m*
fu·sil·lade [ˌfjuːzɪˈleɪd] N scarica, raffica; (*fig*) raffica
fu·sion [ˈfjuːʒən] N fusione *f*
fuss [fʌs] N (*complaints, arguments*) storie *fpl*; (*anxious prepara-tions*) agitazione *f*; **to make a fuss about sth** fare storie per qc; **don't make such a fuss!** non fare tante storie!; **what's all the fuss about?** cosa sono tutte queste storie?; **to make a fuss of sb** (*Brit*) coprire qn di attenzioni ♦ VI agitarsi ♦ VT (*person*) infastidire, scocciare
▸ **fuss about, fuss around** VI + PREP affannarsi
▸ **fuss over** VI + PREP (*person*) circondare di premure
fuss·pot [ˈfʌsˌpɒt] N (*Brit fam*) pignolo(-a)
fussy [ˈfʌsɪ] ADJ (*comp* **-ier**, *superl* **-iest**) (*person: difficult to please*) difficile, esigente; (: *excessively punctilious*) punti-glioso(-a), pignolo(-a); (*clothes*) pieno(-a) di fronzoli; (*style*) elaborato(-a); **I'm not fussy** (*fam*) per me è lo stesso
fus·ty [ˈfʌstɪ] ADJ (*comp* **-ier**, *superl* **-iest**) (*pej: musty: smell*) che sa di stantio; (: *old-fashioned: ideas, outlook*) stantio(-a)
fu·tile [ˈfjuːtaɪl] ADJ futile, vano(-a)
fu·til·ity [fjuːˈtɪlɪtɪ] N futilità
fu·ton [ˈfuːtɒn] N futon *m inv*, materasso giapponese
fu·ture [ˈfjuːtʃəˈ] ADJ futuro(-a); **the future king** il futuro re; **the future tense** il futuro; **at some future date** in futuro ♦ N futuro, avvenire *m*; (*Gram*) futuro; **in future** in futuro; **in the near future** in un prossimo futuro; **in the immediate future** nell'immediato futuro; **there's no future in it** non c'è futuro in questo campo
fu·tur·is·tic [ˌfjuːtʃəˈrɪstɪk] ADJ futurista, futuristico(-a)
fuze [fjuːz] N, VT, VI (*USA*) = **fuse**
fuzzy [ˈfʌzɪ] ADJ (*comp* **-ier**, *superl* **-iest**) (*hair*) crespo(-a); (*blurred: photo*) sfocato(-a), indistinto(-a); (: *memory*) confu-so(-a); **a fuzzy image** un'immagine indistinta

Gg

G¹, g¹ [dʒiː] N **1** (*letter*) G, g *f inv*, *m inv*; **G for George** ≈ G come Genova **2** (*Mus*) sol *m*

G² [dʒiː] N ABBR (*USA: Cine:* = *General Audiences*) per tutti

g [dʒiː] ABBR **1** (= *gram*) g **2** = **gravity**

GA ABBR (*USA Post:* = **Georgia**)

gab [ɡæb] N (*fam*): **to have the gift of the gab** avere parlantina

gab·ble [ˈɡæbl] VT borbottare ♦ VI farfugliare

gab·er·dine [ˌɡæbəˈdiːn] N (*material*) gabardine *m*; (*coat*) (soprabito di) gabardine

ga·ble [ˈɡeɪbl] N frontone *m*

Ga·bon [ɡəˈbɒn] N Gabon *m*

gad about [ˈɡædəˈbaʊt] VI + ADV (*fam*, *old*) bighellonare, vagabondare

gadg·et [ˈɡædʒɪt] N aggeggio, arnese *m*

Gael·ic [ˈɡeɪlɪk] ADJ gaelico(-a) ♦ N (*language*) gaelico

gaffe [ɡæf] N gaffe *f inv*

gaf·fer [ˈɡæfə'] N (*Brit fam*) capo

gag [ɡæɡ] N **1** (*over mouth*) bavaglio **2** (*fam: joke*) battuta, gag *f inv* ♦ VT (*silence: prisoner etc*) imbavagliare; **he was bound and gagged** è stato legato ed imbavagliato ♦ VI (*choke*) soffocare; (*retch*) avere conati di vomito

gaga [ˈɡɑːɡɑː] ADJ (*fam*): **to go gaga** rimbambire; **to go gaga over sb/sth** andare matto(-a) per qn/qc

gage [ɡeɪdʒ] N, VT (*USA*) = **gauge**

gai·ety [ˈɡeɪtɪ] N allegria, gaiezza

gai·ly [ˈɡeɪlɪ] ADV (*sing, chatter*) allegramente, gaiamente; (*painted, decorated*) vivacemente; **gaily coloured** dai colori allegri

gain [ɡeɪn] N (*increase*) aumento; (*improvement*) miglioramento; (*advantage*) vantaggio, utile *m*; (*profit*) guadagno, profitto; **gain in weight** aumento di peso; **to do sth for gain** fare qc per lucro; **his loss is our gain** lui ci perde, noi ci guadagniamo; **the Conservatives made several gains** i Conservatori hanno guadagnato parecchi seggi ♦ VT (*obtain, acquire: respect, approval*) ottenere; (: *reputation*) farsi; (: *experience, wealth, knowledge, territory*) acquistare; (*reach: summit, shore*) raggiungere, guadagnare; (: *objective*) raggiungere; (*increase: weight*) aumentare di; **to gain 3lbs/kilos (in weight)** aumentare di 3 libbre/chili; **what do I have to gain by staying here?** che ci guadagno restando qui?; **to gain experience** fare esperienza; **I gained valuable experience by working there** ho fatto molta esperienza lavorando lì; **to gain strength** (*person*) riprendere le forze; (*theory*) avvalorarsi; **to gain possession of** impadronirsi di, impossessarsi di; **to gain ground** guadagnare terreno; **to gain speed** acquistare velocità; **to gain weight** aumentare di peso; **my watch has gained 5 minutes** il mio orologio va avanti di 5 minuti; **to gain an advantage over sb** avvantaggiarsi rispetto a qn ♦ VI (*person*) guadagnare; (*watch*) andare avanti; **to gain in/by** aumentare di/con; **to gain in weight** aumentare di peso; **to gain in popularity** acquistare popolarità

▸ **gain upon, gain on** VI + PREP accorciare le distanze da, riprendere

gain·ful [ˈɡeɪnfʊl] ADJ (*employment*) remunerativo(-a)

gain·ful·ly [ˈɡeɪnfʊlɪ] ADV: **to be gainfully employed** avere un lavoro retribuito

gain·say [ˌɡeɪnˈseɪ] (*pt, pp* gainsaid [ˌɡeɪnˈsɛd]) VT (*frm: fact, argument*) contestare, negare; (: *person*) contraddire

gait [ɡeɪt] N (*frm*) passo, andatura

gal. ABBR = **gallon**

gala [ˈɡɑːlə] N (*festive occasion*) festa; (*important*) gran galà *m inv*; **a gala evening** una serata di gala

Ga·la·pa·gos Is·lands [ɡəˈlæpəɡəsˈaɪləndz] NPL: **the Galapagos Islands** le (isole) Galapagos *fpl*

gal·axy [ˈɡæləksɪ] N galassia

gale [ɡeɪl] N (*strong wind*) bufera, vento forte; (*at sea*) burrasca; **gale force 10** vento forza 10

gall [ɡɔːl] N (*Anat*) bile *f*; (*fig: impudence*) fegato, faccia (tosta) ♦ VT seccare; **it galled him to have to ask permission** gli seccava dover chiedere il permesso

gal·lant [ˈɡælənt] ADJ (*brave*) valoroso(-a), prode; galante; **gallant soldiers** soldati valorosi; **a gallant gentleman** un signore galante

gal·lant·ry [ˈɡæləntrɪ] N (*see adj*) valore *m* militare, prodezza; galanteria

gall bladder N cistifellea

gal·leon [ˈɡælɪən] N galeone *m*

gal·lery [ˈɡælərɪ] N (*also:* **art gallery**) (*state owned*) museo; (*private*) galleria, loggia; (*for spectators*) tribuna; (*in theatre*) loggione *m*, balconata; **to play to the gallery** parlare (*per accattivarsi il pubblico*)

gal·ley [ˈɡælɪ] N (*ship*) galea; (*ship's kitchen*) cambusa

Gal·lic [ˈɡælɪk] ADJ (*of Gaul*) gallico(-a); (*French*) francese

gall·ing [ˈɡɔːlɪŋ] ADJ (*irritating*) seccante, irritante; (*humiliating*) umiliante

gal·lon [ˈɡælən] N gallone *m* (*Brit=4,55 litri; USA=3,79 litri*)

gal·lop [ˈɡæləp] N (*pace*) galoppo; (*ride*) galoppata; **at a gallop** al galoppo ♦ VI (*horse, rider*) galoppare, andare al galoppo; **to gallop away** galoppare via; (*fig*) andarsene di gran carriera

gal·lows [ˈɡæləʊz] NPL forca, patibolo

gall·stone [ˈɡɔːlˌstəʊn] N calcolo biliare

ga·lore [ɡəˈlɔː'] ADV a iosa, a profusione

gal·va·nize [ˈɡælvəˌnaɪz] VT galvanizzare; (*fig*) galvanizzare, elettrizzare; **to galvanize sb into action** spronare qn all'azione

Gam·bia [ˈɡæmbɪə] N: **the Gambia** il Gambia

gam·bit [ˈɡæmbɪt] N (*Chess*) gambetto; (*fig*) mossa; **opening gambit** prima mossa

gam·ble [ˈɡæmbl] N azzardo, rischio; **to take a gamble** rischiare; **the gamble came off** è valsa la pena rischiare; **it's a gamble** è un salto nel buio, è un rischio ♦ VT (*money*) giocare; **he gambled one hundred pounds at the casino** ha giocato cento sterline al casinò ♦ VI (*money*) giocare (d'azzardo); **to gamble on the Stock Exchange** giocare in Borsa; **to gamble on sth** puntare su qc, giocare su qc; **few firms want to gamble on new products** poche ditte vogliono puntare su prodotti nuovi

▸ **gamble away** VT + ADV (*money*) perdere al gioco, giocarsi

gam·bler [ˈɡæmblə'] N giocatore(-trice) d'azzardo

gam·bling [ˈɡæmblɪŋ] N gioco (d'azzardo)

gam·bol [ˈɡæmbəl] VI saltellare

game [ɡeɪm] N **1** (*gen*) gioco; (*match*) partita; **games** NPL (*Scol*) attività *fpl* sportive; **a game of football** una partita di calcio; **that's three games to you and two to me** siamo tre a due; **to have a game of cards/chess/tennis** fare una partita a carte/scacchi/tennis; **the children were playing a game** i bambini stavano facendo un gioco; **he plays a good game of golf** gioca bene al golf; **game of chance** gioco d'azzardo; **game, set and match** (*Tennis*) game, set e partita; **he was off his game** non era nella sua forma migliore; **to play the game** (*also fig*) rispettare le regole del gioco; **to play sb's game** fare il gioco di qn; **to beat sb at his own game** battere qn con le sue stesse armi; **the game is up** è finita, è la fine; **I wonder what his game is?** mi chiedo a che gioco stia giocando; **two can play at that game** ti (*or* lo *etc*) ripagherò con la stessa moneta **2** (*Culin, Hunting*) selvaggina; **big game** caccia grossa; **there's game on the menu** c'è selvaggina nel menù ♦ ADJ (*willing*): **to be game** starci; **to be game (for sth/to do sth)** (*ready*) essere pronto(-a) (a qc/a fare qc); **game for anything** pronto(-a) a tutto

game bird N uccello da cacciagione

game·keeper [ˈgeɪmˌkiːpəʳ] N guardacaccia *m inv*
game·ly [ˈgeɪmlɪ] ADV coraggiosamente
gam·er [ˈgeɪməʳ] N appassionato(-a) di videogiochi
game reserve N riserva di caccia
games console N console *f inv*
game·show [ˈgeɪmˌʃəʊ] N gioco a premi (*televisivo o radiofonico*)
games·man·ship [ˈgeɪmzmənˌʃɪp] N: **to be a master of gamesmanship** essere una vecchia volpe
gam·ing [ˈgeɪmɪŋ] N 1 (*frm, old*) gioco d'azzardo 2 (*Comput*) videogiochi *mpl*
gam·mon [ˈgæmən] N (*ham*) ≈ prosciutto; (*smoked*) ≈ prosciutto affumicato; (*bacon*) ≈ pancetta
gam·ut [ˈgæmət] N gamma; **to run the (whole) gamut of emotions** provare uno dopo l'altro tutti i sentimenti possibili
gang [gæŋ] N (*of thieves, youths*) banda; (*of friends*) comitiva; (*of workmen*) squadra
  ▸ **gang up** VI + ADV: **to gang up (with)** mettersi insieme (a *or* con); **to gang up on** *or* **against sb** far comunella contro qn
Gan·ges [ˈgændʒiːz] N: **the Ganges** il Gange
gang·land [ˈgæŋˌlænd] ADJ della malavita; **gangland killer** sicario
gan·gling [ˈgæŋglɪŋ] ADJ allampanato(-a)
gan·gly [ˈgæŋglɪ] ADJ = **gangling**
gang·plank [ˈgæŋˌplæŋk] N passerella
gan·grene [ˈgæŋgriːn] N cancrena
gang·ster [ˈgæŋstəʳ] N gangster *m inv*
gang·way [ˈgæŋˌweɪ] N (*Naut*) passerella; (*Brit: aisle: in theatre, cinema*) corsia; (: *in train*) corridoio; (: *in bus*) passaggio; **gangway!** largo!
gan·try [ˈgæntrɪ] N (*for crane, railway signal*) cavalletto; (*for rocket*) torre *f* di lancio
GAO [ˌdʒiːeɪˈəʊ] N ABBR (*USA*: = *General Accounting Office*) ≈ Corte *f* dei Conti
gaol *etc* [dʒeɪl] N, VT (*Brit*) = **jail**
gap [gæp] N 1 (*gen*) spazio vuoto; (*in line, traffic*) interruzione *f*; (*in trees, crowd, defences*) vuoto; (*in wall, fence*) apertura, buco; (*mountain pass*) passo, valico; (*between teeth*) spazio; (*between floorboards*) interstizio; (*fig: in knowledge*) lacuna; (: *in conversation*) pausa; (: *in time*) intervallo; **there's a gap in the hedge** c'è un buco nella siepe; **a gap of four years** un intervallo di quattro anni 2 (*difference*): **gap (between)** divario (tra); **the generation gap** il gap *m inv* generazionale; **the gap between them widened** la distanza tra di loro si fece più grande
gape [geɪp] VI 1 (*mouth, hole*) essere spalancato(-a) 2 (*person*) restare a bocca aperta; **to gape (at sb/sth)** guardare (qn/qc) a bocca aperta
gap·ing [ˈgeɪpɪŋ] ADJ (*wound*) aperto(-a); (*hole*) grosso(-a); **gaping seam** larga scucitura
gap year N (*Brit*) anno di pausa preso prima di iniziare l'università (*per lavorare o viaggiare*)
gar·age [ˈgærɑːʒ] N (*of private house*) garage *m inv*; (*for car repairs*) officina, autofficina; (*filling station*) stazione *f* di servizio
garb [gɑːb] N abiti *mpl*, vesti *fpl*
gar·bage [ˈgɑːbɪdʒ] N (*esp USA*) immondizie *fpl*, spazzatura, rifiuti *mpl*; (*fig: film, book*) porcheria, robaccia; (: *nonsense*) fesserie *fpl*; **garbage collection** raccolta della spazzatura; **that's garbage** sono fesserie
garbage can N (*USA*) bidone *m* della spazzatura
garbage collector N (*USA*) netturbino(-a)
garbage disposal unit N (*USA*) tritarifiuti *m inv*
garbage truck N (*USA*) camion *m inv* della nettezza urbana
gar·bled [ˈgɑːbld] ADJ (*speech, account*) ingarbugliato(-a), distorto(-a); (*words*) incomprensibile
gar·den [ˈgɑːdn] N giardino; **gardens** NPL (*public*) giardino *sg* (pubblico); (*of stately home*) parco *sg*, giardino; **a lovely garden** un bel giardino; **the Garden of Eden** il Paradiso Terrestre, l'Eden *m* ♦ VI fare (lavori di) giardinaggio
garden centre N vivaio
garden city N (*Brit*) città giardino *f inv*

gar·den·er [ˈgɑːdnəʳ] N giardiniere(-a); **he's a gardener** fa il giardiniere
gar·den·ing [ˈgɑːdnɪŋ] N giardinaggio
gar·gle [ˈgɑːgl] N (*act*) gargarismo; (*liquid*) collutorio ♦ VI fare gargarismi
gar·goyle [ˈgɑːgɔɪl] N gargolla, gargouille *f inv*
gar·ish [ˈgɛərɪʃ] ADJ sgargiante, vistoso(-a); (*light*) abbagliante
gar·land [ˈgɑːlənd] N ghirlanda
gar·lic [ˈgɑːlɪk] N aglio
gar·ment [ˈgɑːmənt] N (*frm*) articolo di vestiario, indumento
gar·ner [ˈgɑːnəʳ] VT (*frm*) raccogliere
gar·nish [ˈgɑːnɪʃ] N (*Culin*) decorazione *f* ♦ VT: **to garnish (with)** guarnire (con)
gar·ret [ˈgærət] N soffitta, mansarda
gar·ri·son [ˈgærɪsən] N guarnigione *f* ♦ VT (*town*) piazzare truppe in; (*subj: troops*) presidiare
gar·ru·lous [ˈgærʊləs] ADJ loquace, ciarliero(-a)
gar·ter [ˈgɑːtəʳ] N giarrettiera; (*USA: suspender*) gancio (di reggicalze)
garter belt N (*USA*) reggicalze *m inv*
gas [gæs] N 1 (*gen*) gas *m inv*; (*as anaesthetic*) etere *m*; **a gas leak** una fuga di gas 2 (*USA: also: gasoline*) benzina; **I'll stop soon and get gas** mi fermerò presto a fare benzina; **a tank of gas** un pieno di benzina ♦ VT (*person*) asfissiare (col gas); (*Mil*) uccidere col gas asfissiante, gassare; **to gas o.s.** asfissiarsi, suicidarsi col gas ♦ VI (*fam: chatter*) chiacchierare, cianciare ♦ ADJ (*industry, pipe*) del gas
gas cooker N (*Brit*) cucina a gas
gas cylinder N bombola del gas
gas·eous [ˈgæsɪəs] ADJ gassoso(-a)
gas fire N (*Brit*) stufa a gas
gas-fired [ˈgæsˌfaɪəd] ADJ (*central heating*) (alimentato(-a)) a gas
gash [gæʃ] N (*in flesh*) taglio profondo, squarcio; (*on face*) sfregio; (*in material*) spacco ♦ VT (*arm, head*) fare un brutto taglio in; (*face*) sfregiare; (*seat*) squarciare
gas·ket [ˈgæskɪt] N (*Tech*) guarnizione *f*
gas mask N maschera *f* antigas, *inv*
gas meter N contatore *m* del gas
gaso·line [ˈgæsəʊliːn] N (*USA*) benzina
gasp [gɑːsp] N ansito; **she gave a gasp of surprise** la sorpresa le mozzò il fiato; **to be at one's last gasp** star tirando l'ultimo respiro ♦ VI ansare, ansimare; (*in surprise*) restare senza fiato; **she was gasping** stava ansimando; **she gasped at the sight of it** è rimasta senza fiato quando lo ha visto; **to gasp for breath** or **air** respirare a fatica, boccheggiare
  ▸ **gasp out** VT + ADV dire affannosamente
gas pedal(*esp USA*) N pedale *m* dell'acceleratore
gas ring N fornello a gas
gas station N (*USA*) distributore *m* di benzina
gas stove N cucina a gas
gas·sy [ˈgæsɪ] ADJ (*usu pej*) troppo gassato(-a)
gas tank N (*USA: Aut*) serbatoio (della benzina)
gas tap N (*on pipe*) rubinetto del gas; (*on cooker*) manopola del gas
gas·tric [ˈgæstrɪk] ADJ gastrico(-a); **gastric flu** influenza *m inv* gastro-intestinale; **gastric band** bendaggio gastrico
gastric ulcer N ulcera gastrica
gas·tro·en·teri·tis [ˌgæstrəʊˌentəˈraɪtɪs] N gastroenterite *f*
gas·trono·my [gæsˈtrɒnəmɪ] N gastronomia
gas·works [ˈgæsˌwɜːks] NSG, NPL impianto di produzione del gas
gate [geɪt] N 1 (*in garden, field*) cancello; (*of castle, town: Skiing*) porta; (*at airport*) uscita; (*at level crossing*) barriera 2 (*Sport: attendance*) (numero di) spettatori *mpl*, presenze *fpl*; (: *entrance money*) incassi *mpl*
ga·teau [ˈgætəʊ] N (*pl gateaux* [ˈgætəʊz]) torta
gate-crash [ˈgeɪtˌkræʃ] VT (*fam: party*) intrufolarsi in, imbucarsi in; (: *enter without paying*) fare il portoghese
gate-crasher [ˈgeɪtˌkræʃəʳ] N (*fam: at party*) intruso(-a), imbucato(-a); (: *at concert etc*) portoghese *m/f*
gated community [ˈgeɪtɪd-] N gruppo di case recintate e con entrata sorvegliata

gate·house [ˈgeɪtˌhaʊs] N casetta del custode (*all'entrata di un parco*)

gate·way [ˈgeɪtˌweɪ] N porta; **the gateway to success** la chiave del successo

gath·er [ˈgæðəʳ] VT 1 (*also:* **gather together**) (*people*) radunare, riunire; (*objects*) raccogliere, radunare; (*also:* **gather up:** *papers, possessions*) raccogliere; (*also:* **gather in**) (*material*) riprendere, increspare; (*taxes*) riscuotere; **to gather the harvest** fare il raccolto; **to gather dust** raccogliere polvere; **to gather one's thoughts/strength** raccogliere i propri pensieri/le proprie forze 2 (*gain*): **to gather speed** prendere *or* acquistare velocità; **to gather strength** (*wind, waves*) aumentare d'intensità 3 (*understand*): **to gather (from/ that)** comprendere (da/che), dedurre (da/che); **I gathered that ...** ne dedussi che...; **I gather (that) you are leaving** ho saputo che parti; **as you will have gathered** come avrai indovinato; **as far as I can gather** da quel che ho potuto capire; **from what he says I gather that ...** da quel che dice mi pare di capire che... ♦ VI (*people*) (*also:* **gather together**) raccogliersi, radunarsi; (*crowd*) assembrarsi; (*dust*) accumularsi; (*clouds*) addensarsi

▸ **gather round** VI + ADV radunarsi

gath·er·ing [ˈgæðərɪŋ] N (*meeting*) raduno, riunione *f*; (*crowd*) gruppo

gauche [gəʊʃ] ADJ goffo(-a)

gaudy [ˈgɔːdɪ] ADJ (*comp* -ier, *superl* -iest) vistoso(-a), chiassoso(-a)

gauge [geɪdʒ] N (*standard measure: of bullet*) calibro; (: *of pipe, wire*) diametro; (: *of railway track*) scartamento; (*instrument*) indicatore *m* di livello; (*fig*) metro, criterio; **petrol gauge**, (*USA*) **gas gauge** indicatore *m or* spia della benzina; **oil gauge** spia dell'olio; **pressure gauge** manometro ♦ VT (*temperature, pressure*) misurare; (*fig: sb's capabilities, character*) valutare, stimare; **distance is gauged in kilometres rather than miles** la distanza viene misurata in chilometri piuttosto che in miglia; **he gauged the distance** ha calcolato la distanza; **a survey to gauge consumer reaction** un sondaggio per valutare la reazione dei consumatori; **to gauge the right moment** calcolare *or* valutare il momento giusto

gaunt [gɔːnt] ADJ emaciato(-a); (*face*) smunto(-a), scarno(-a); (*grim, desolate*) desolato(-a)

gaunt·let [ˈgɔːntlɪt] N (*of knight*) guanto d'armatura, manopola; (*of motorcyclist*) (grosso) guanto; **to run the gauntlet of an angry crowd** (*fig*) sottoporsi al fuoco di fila di una folla ostile; **to throw down the gauntlet** gettare il guanto

gauze [gɔːz] N garza

gave [geɪv] PT *of* **give**

gawky [ˈgɔːkɪ] ADJ (*comp* -ier, *superl* -iest) goffo(-a), sgraziato(-a)

gawp [gɔːp] VI = **gape** 2

gay [geɪ] ADJ (*comp* -er, *superl* -est) 1 (*orientation*) omosessuale, gay *inv* 2 (*liter: person*) allegro(-a), gaio(-a); (*colour*) vivace, vivo(-a) ♦ N (*orientation*) gay *m*

gaze [geɪz] N sguardo (insistente *or* fisso) ♦ VI: **to gaze at** guardare (con insistenza *or* fisso), fissare; **to gaze in wonderment at sb/sth** guardare rapito(-a) qn/qc; **to gaze into space** guardare nel vuoto

ga·zelle [gəˈzel] N gazzella

ga·zette [gəˈzet] N (*newspaper*) gazzetta; (*official publication*) pubblicazione *f* ufficiale

gaz·et·teer [ˌgæzɪˈtɪəʳ] N (*book*) dizionario di nomi geografici; (*section of book*) indice *m* dei nomi geografici

GB [ˌdʒiːˈbiː] ABBR (= *Great Britain*) GB

GCSE [ˌdʒiːsiːesˈiː] N ABBR (*Brit*: = *General Certificate of Secondary Education*) serie di esami sostenuti alla fine del quinto anno della scuola secondaria in Inghilterra e Galles

GDP [ˌdʒiːdiːˈpiː] N ABBR (= *gross domestic product*) PIL *m* (= *prodotto interno lordo*)

GDR [ˌdʒiːdiːˈɑːʳ] N ABBR = **German Democratic Republic**

gear [gɪəʳ] N 1 (*Aut: mechanism*) cambio; (: *speed*) marcia; **in gear** in marcia; **he left the car in gear** ha lasciato la macchina con la marcia inserita; **in first gear** in prima; **the car is in gear** la macchina ha la marcia inserita; **out of gear** in folle; **first** *or* **bottom gear** prima; **low gear** marcia bassa;

top gear, (*USA*) **high gear** marcia alta; **to put the car into gear** innestare *or* inserire la marcia; **to change gear** cambiare marcia; **she changed into second gear** ha messo *or* inserito la seconda; **to move into top gear** inserire la quinta; **production has moved into high** *or* **top gear** la produzione ha subito una forte accelerazione 2 (*equipment*) attrezzatura, equipaggiamento; (*belongings*) roba, cose *fpl*; (*clothing*) vestiti *mpl*; **camping gear** attrezzatura da campeggio; **sports gear** abbigliamento *or* attrezzatura da ginnastica; **dressed in the latest gear** (*fam*) bardato(-a) all'ultima moda 3 (*Tech*) ruota dentata ♦ VT (*fig: adapt*) adattare; **the book is geared to adult students** il libro si rivolge a studenti di età adulta

▸ **gear up** VI + ADV: **to gear up (to do)** prepararsi (a fare); **we are geared up (and ready) to do it** siamo tutti pronti a farlo

gear·box [ˈgɪəˌbɒks] N (*Aut*) scatola del cambio

gear lever, (*USA*) **gear·shift** [ˈgɪəˌʃɪft] N leva del cambio

GED [ˌdʒiːiːˈdiː] N ABBR (*USA Scol*) = **general educational development**

geese [giːs] NPL *of* **goose**

gee·zer [ˈgiːzəʳ] N (*Brit fam*) tizio

Geiger count·er [ˈgaɪgəˌkaʊntəʳ] N (contatore *m*) geiger, *m inv*

gel [dʒel] N gel *m inv*; **hair gel** gel per capelli

gela·tine [ˈdʒeləˌtiːn], **gela·tin** [ˈdʒelətɪn] N gelatina; **in gelatin(e)** in gelatina

gel·ig·nite [ˈdʒelɪgˌnaɪt] N gelatina esplosiva, gelignite *f*

gem [dʒem] N gemma, pietra preziosa; (*fig: person*) gioiello, perla

Gem·i·ni [ˈdʒemɪˌnaɪ] N Gemelli *mpl*; **to be Gemini** essere dei Gemelli; **I'm Gemini** sono dei Gemelli

Gen. ABBR (*Mil*: = *General*) Gen.

gen·der [ˈdʒendəʳ] N (*Gram*) genere *m*; (*frm: sex*) sesso; **of the same gender** dello stesso sesso

gene [dʒiːn] N (*Bio*) gene *m*

ge·neal·o·gy [ˌdʒiːnɪˈælədʒɪ] N genealogia

gen·er·al [ˈdʒenərəl] ADJ (*gen*) generale; (*not detailed: plan, view*) generale, complessivo(-a); (: *enquiry*) generico(-a); (*not specialized: trader, store*) di generi vari; **a general improvement** un miglioramento generale; **in general use** d'uso comune *or* corrente; **in general terms** in termini generici, in generale; **as a general rule** di norma, di regola; **the general idea is to ...** l'idea base sarebbe di... ♦ ADV: **in general** (*usually*) generalmente, in generale; (*as a whole*) nel complesso ♦ N (*Mil*) generale *m*

general anaesthetic N anestesia totale

general delivery N (*USA*) fermo posta *m*

general election N elezioni *fpl* politiche

gen·er·ali·za·tion [ˌdʒenərəlaɪˈzeɪʃən] N (*often pej*) generalizzazione *f*

gen·er·al·ize [ˈdʒenərəˌlaɪz] VI: **to generalize (about)** generalizzare (per quel che riguarda); **to generalize from** generalizzare sulla base di

gen·er·al·ly [ˈdʒenərəlɪ] ADV (*usually*) in genere, di solito, generalmente; (*for the most part*) nel complesso; **it's generally true that ...** in genere è vero che...; **he's generally disliked** è antipatico a tutti; **generally speaking** (parlando) in generale

general manager N direttore *m* generale

general practitioner N medico generico; (*personal doctor*) medico di famiglia

general store N emporio

general strike N sciopero generale

gen·er·ate [ˈdʒenəˌreɪt] VT generare

gen·era·tion [ˌdʒenəˈreɪʃən] N 1 (*age group*) generazione *f*; **the younger/older generation** la nuova/vecchia generazione; **the generation gap** il gap *m inv* generazionale 2 (*of electricity*) produzione *f*

gen·era·tor [ˈdʒenəˌreɪtəʳ] N generatore *m*

ge·ner·ic [dʒɪˈnerɪk] ADJ generico(-a)

gen·er·os·ity [ˌdʒenəˈrɒsɪtɪ] N generosità

gen·er·ous [ˈdʒenərəs] ADJ (*gen*) generoso(-a); (*plentiful: supply, quantity*) abbondante, generoso(-a); **to be generous with sth** essere prodigo(-a) di qc; **that's very generous of you** è molto generoso da parte tua

gen·esis [ˈdʒenɪsɪs] N genesi *f*; **Genesis** (*Bible*) la Genesi
ge·net·ic [dʒɪˈnetɪk] ADJ genetico(-a)
genetically modified [dʒɪˈnetɪklɪˈmɔdɪfaɪd] ADJ geneticamente modificato(-a), transgenico(-a); **genetically modified organism** organismo geneticamente modificato
ge·net·ic finger·print·ing [dʒɪˈnetɪkˈfɪŋgəˌprɪntɪŋ] N rilevamento delle impronte genetiche
ge·net·ics [dʒɪˈnetɪks] NSG genetica
Ge·neva [dʒɪˈniːvə] N Ginevra; **Lake Geneva** il lago di Ginevra
gen·ial [ˈdʒiːnɪəl] ADJ (*manner, person*) cordiale, affabile
❏ **genial** is not translated by the Italian word *geniale*
geni·tals [ˈdʒenɪtlz] NPL genitali *mpl*
geni·tive [ˈdʒenɪtɪv] ADJ genitivo(-a) ♦ N genitivo; **in the genitive** al genitivo
ge·ni·us [ˈdʒiːnɪəs] N genio; **to have a genius for sth/for doing sth** essere molto bravo(-a) in qc/a fare qc
Genoa [ˈdʒenəʊə] N Genova
geno·cide [ˈdʃenəʊˌsaɪd] N genocidio
Geno·ese [dʒenəʊˈiːz] ADJ, N *pl inv* genovese *m/f*
gent [dʒent] N ABBR (*Brit fam*: = *gentleman*) signore *m*
gen·teel [dʒenˈtiːl] ADJ (*affectedly polite*) affettato(-a); (*old: refined*) distinto(-a), raffinato(-a)
❏ **genteel** is not translated by the Italian word *gentile*
gen·tle [ˈdʒentl] ADJ (*comp* **-r**, *superl* **-st**) (*person, slope, voice*) dolce; (*touch*) delicato(-a); (*hint, reminder*) velato(-a); (*rebuke*) discreto(-a); (*heat, exercise*) moderato(-a); (*breeze, sound*) leggero(-a); **to be gentle with sb** trattare qn con delicatezza; **I gave him a gentle push** gli ho dato una leggera spinta
❏ **gentle** is not translated by the Italian word *gentile*
gentle·man [ˈdʒentlmən] N (*pl* **-men**) signore *m*; (*well-mannered, well-bred man*) gentiluomo, signore *m*; **gentlemen!** signori!; **(to be) a perfect gentleman** (dimostrarsi) un vero gentiluomo; **gentleman's agreement** impegno sulla parola, gentleman's agreement *m inv*
gentle·man·ly [ˈdʒentlmənlɪ] ADJ da gentiluomo
gen·tle·ness [ˈdʒentlnɪs] N (*see adj*) dolcezza; delicatezza; discretezza *f*; leggerezza
gen·tly [ˈdʒentlɪ] ADV (*say, smile*) dolcemente; (*touch*) lievemente, delicatamente; **gently does it!** piano!
gen·try [ˈdʒentrɪ] NPL piccola nobiltà
gents [dʒents] N (*fam: public toilet*) toilette *f inv* or bagno degli uomini; **"gents"** "uomini"
genu·ine [ˈdʒenjʊɪn] ADJ **1** (*person, belief*) sincero(-a) **2** (*authentic: leather, silver*) vero(-a); (: *painting, antique*) autentico(-a); **these are genuine diamonds** questi sono diamanti veri
genu·ine·ly [ˈdʒenjʊɪnlɪ] ADV (*believe, welcome*) sinceramente, veramente
ge·og·ra·pher [dʒɪˈɒɡrəfə'] N geografo(-a)
geo·graph·ic [dʒɪəˈɡræfɪk], **geo·graph·ical** [dʒɪəˈɡræfɪkəl] ADJ geografico(-a)
ge·og·ra·phy [dʒɪˈɒɡrəfɪ] N geografia
geo·logi·cal [dʒɪəʊˈlɒdʒɪkəl] ADJ geologico(-a)
ge·olo·gist [dʒɪˈɒlədʒɪst] N geologo(-a)
ge·ol·ogy [dʒɪˈɒlədʒɪ] N geologia
geo·met·rical [dʒɪəʊˈmetrɪkəl], **geo·met·ric** [dʒɪəʊˈmetrɪk] ADJ geometrico(-a)
ge·om·etry [dʒɪˈɒmɪtrɪ] N geometria
Geor·die [ˈdʒɔːdɪ] (*fam*) ADJ di Tyneside ♦ N abitante *m/f* or originario(-a) del Tyneside
Geor·gia [ˈdʒɔːdʒə] N (*in US, Europe*) Georgia
Geor·gian [ˈdʒɔːdʒən] ADJ (*History, Geog*) georgiano(-a) ♦ N (*Geog*) georgiano(-a); (*language*) georgiano
ge·ra·nium [dʒɪˈreɪnɪəm] N geranio
geri·at·ric [ˌdʒerɪˈætrɪk] ADJ geriatrico(-a)
germ [dʒɜːm] N (*Med*) microbo; (*Bio, also fig*) germe *m*
Ger·man [ˈdʒɜːmən] ADJ tedesco(-a) ♦ N **1** (*person*) tedesco(-a) **2** (*language*) tedesco; **the Germans** i tedeschi; **our German teacher** il nostro insegnante di tedesco

German Democratic Republic N (*formerly*) Repubblica Democratica Tedesca
ger·mane [dʒɜːˈmeɪn] ADJ (*frm*): **to be germane to sth** essere attinente a qc
German measles N rosolia
Ger·ma·ny [ˈdʒɜːmənɪ] N Germania; **East/West Germany** Germania dell'Est/dell'Ovest
ger·mi·na·tion [dʒɜːmɪˈneɪʃən] N germinazione *f*
germ warfare N guerra batteriologica
ger·ry·man·der·ing [ˌdʒerɪˈmændərɪŋ] N *alterazione del confine dei distretti elettorali che avvantaggia un solo partito*
ges·ta·tion [dʒesˈteɪʃən] N (*Bio*) gestazione *f*
ges·ticu·late [dʒesˈtɪkjʊˌleɪt] VI gesticolare
ges·ture [ˈdʒestʃə'] N gesto; **as a gesture of friendship** in segno d'amicizia; **she made a threatening gesture** ha fatto un gesto minaccioso; **a mere gesture** un gesto simbolico ♦ VI: **he gestured towards the door** fece un gesto verso la porta; **to gesture to sb to do sth** far segno a qn di fare qc

---

KEYWORD

get [get] (*pt* **got**, *pp* **got** *or* **gotten** (*USA*)) VT
1 (*obtain by effort: money, visa*) ottenere, procurarsi; (: *results, permission*) avere, ottenere; (*find: job, apartment*) trovare; (*buy*) comprare, prendere; (*fetch: person, doctor*) chiamare; (: *object*) prendere; (*Telec: number*) avere; (*TV, Radio: channel, station*) prendere; **to get breakfast** preparare la colazione; **can I get you a drink?** bevi qualcosa?; **to get sth for sb** prendere *or* procurare qc a qn; **I'll get it for you** vado a prendertelo io; **I've been trying to get you (on the phone) all morning** ti ho cercato tutta la mattina al telefono
2 (*receive: present, letter*) ricevere; (: *prize*) ricevere, vincere; (*acquire: reputation*) farsi; **how much did you get for it?** quanto ti hanno dato?; **he got 5 years for robbery** si è beccato 5 anni per rapina; **he gets it from his father** in questo prende da suo padre; **where did you get that idea from?** come ti sei fatta quest'idea?; **I didn't get much from the film** quel film non mi è parso un granché; **I'll get it!** (*phone*) rispondo io!; (*door*) vado io!; **this room gets very little sun** questa stanza è poco soleggiata; **he's in it for what he can get** lo fa per interesse
3 (*catch*) prendere, acchiappare; (*hit: target*) colpire; **the bullet got him in the leg** il proiettile l'ha colpito alla gamba; **to get sb by the arm/throat** afferrare qn per un braccio/alla gola; **I'll get you for that!** (*fam*) ti faccio vedere io!; **you've got me there!** (*fam*) m'hai preso in castagna!; **got you!** (*fam*) beccato!
4 (*take, move*) portare; **crying won't get you anywhere** piangere non serve a niente; **the discussion got us nowhere** la discussione non è servita a nulla; **to get sth past customs** riuscire a far passare qc alla dogana; **we'll get you there somehow** in un modo o nell'altro ti ci portiamo; **to get sth to sb** far avere qc a qn; **I'll never get this upstairs** non riuscirò mai a portarlo di sopra; **where will that get us?** (*fam*) ma a che pro?
5 (*understand*) afferrare, capire, comprendere; (*hear*) sentire; **I've got it!** ci sono arrivato!, ci sono!; **get it?** (*fam*) capito?; **I don't get it** (*fam*) non capisco, non ci arrivo; **sorry, I didn't get your name** scusi, non ho capito il suo nome
6 (*fam: annoy*) dare ai nervi a
7 (*fam: thrill*) toccare
8 (*have, possess*): **to have got** avere; **how many have you got?** quanti ne hai?
9 to get sth done (*do o.s.*) fare qc; (*have done by sb else*) far fare qc; **I wonder how he got his leg broken** mi chiedo come abbia fatto a rompersi la gamba; **to get one's hair cut** farsi tagliare i capelli; **to get one's hands dirty** sporcarsi le mani; **to get the washing/dishes done** fare il bucato/i piatti; **to get sb drunk** (far) ubriacare qn; **to get the car going** *or* **to go** mettere in moto *or* far partire la macchina; **to get sb/sth ready** preparare qn/qc; **to get sb to do sth** far fare qc a qn; **I can't get the lock to turn** non riesco a far scattare la serratura
♦ VI
1 (*go*) andare; (*reach*) arrivare; **I've got as far as page 10** sono arrivato (fino) a pagina 10; **he won't get far** non andrà lontano; **to get from** andare da; **how did you get here?** come sei

venuto?; **to get home** arrivare *or* tornare a casa; **to get nowhere** (*fig*) non approdare a nulla; **to get somewhere** avere dei risultati; **to get to** andare a; (*reach*) arrivare a

2 (*become, be*) diventare, farsi; **to get (o.s.) dirty** sporcarsi; **to get killed** venire *or* rimanere ucciso(-a); **it's getting late** si sta facendo tardi; **how did it get like that?** (*fam*) come ha fatto a ridursi così?; **to get married** sposarsi; **to get old** invecchiare; **when do I get paid?** quando mi pagate?; **to get tired** stancarsi; **to get used to sth** abituarsi a qc; **I'm not getting any younger!** il tempo passa anche per me!

3 (*begin*) mettersi a, cominciare a; **let's get going** *or* **started** muoviamoci!; **to get talking to sb** mettersi a parlare con *or* a qn; **to get to know sb** cominciare a conoscere meglio qn; **I'm getting to like him** incomincia a piacermi

4 (*must*): **why have I got to do it?** perché devo farlo?; **you've got to tell the police** devi dirlo alla polizia

5 (*be allowed to*): **I never get to go on vacation on my own** non riesco mai ad andare in vacanza da sola

▸ **get about** VI + ADV (*go out: socially, after illness*) uscire, muoversi; (*fig: news, rumour*) spargersi, diffondersi

▸ **get across** VT + ADV far capire; **to get sth across to sb** (*message, meaning*) comunicare qc a qn ♦ VI + ADV **1** (*cross road*) attraversare **2 to get across to** comunicare con

▸ **get after** VT + PREP inseguire

▸ **get ahead** VI + ADV andare avanti, farsi strada; **to get ahead of sb** sorpassare *or* superare qn

▸ **get along** VI + ADV **1** (*leave*) andarsene, scappare; **get along with you!** vattene! **2** (*progress*) procedere; (*manage*) farcela, cavarsela; **how is your son getting along at school?** come va tuo figlio a scuola? **3** (*to be on good terms*) essere in buoni rapporti; **to get along well with sb** andare d'accordo con qn

▸ **get around** VI + ADV **1** = **get about 2** = **get round** ♦ VI + PREP = **get round**

▸ **get at** VI + PREP **1** (*gain access to: object*) arrivare a (prendere); (*: place*) raggiungere, arrivare a; (*ascertain: facts, truth*) accertare, scoprire; **just let me get at him!** (*fam*) lascia che mi capiti fra le mani! **2 to get at sb** (*fam: criticize, attack*) prendersela con qn **3** (*fam: imply*) avere in mente; **what are you getting at?** dove vuoi arrivare?

▸ **get away** VI + ADV (*depart*) partire; (*go on holiday*) andar via; (*go away: work, party*) andarsene (da); (*escape*) liberarsi (da), scappare (da); **to get away from it all** andarsene lontano da tutto e da tutti; **there's no getting away from it** (*fam*) non c'è niente da fare

▸ **get away with** VI + ADV + PREP **1** (*steal*) dileguarsi con **2** (*fam: go unpunished*): **to get away with sth/with doing sth** fare qc e passarla liscia; **he'll never get away with it!** non riuscirà a passarla liscia!; **to get away with murder** essere libero(-a) di fare tutto quello che si vuole

▸ **get back** VT + ADV **1** (*recover: possessions*) recuperare; (*: sth borrowed*) farsi restituire; (*: strength*) riprendere **2** (*return: object, person*) riportare ♦ VI + ADV (ri)tornare; **get back!** indietro!; **to get back (home)** ritornare a casa, rincasare; **to get back to** (*start again*) ritornare a; (*contact again*) rimettersi in contatto con; **to get back to sleep** riaddormentarsi

▸ **get back to** VI + ADV + PREP: **to get back to sb (for sth)** rendere pan per focaccia a qn (per qc)

▸ **get behind** VI + ADV rimanere indietro

▸ **get by** VI + ADV **1** (*pass*) passare **2** (*manage*) cavarsela; (*be acceptable*) essere passabile; **I can get by in Dutch** mi arrangio in olandese; **don't worry, he'll get by** non preoccuparti, se la caverà

▸ **get down** VT + ADV **1** (*take down*) tirar giù **2** (*swallow*) mandar giù **3** (*note down*) prender nota di **4** (*fam: depress*) buttar giù; **don't let it get you down** non devi abbatterti per questo ♦ VI + ADV (*descend*): **to get down (from *or* off)** scendere (da); **quick, get down!** giù presto!

▸ **get down to** VI + ADV + PREP: **to get down to (doing) sth** mettersi a (fare) qc; **to get down to business** venire al dunque

▸ **get in** VT + ADV **1** (*bring in: harvest*) raccogliere; (*buy, obtain: coal, shopping, supplies*) fare provvista di **2** (*plant: bulbs, seeds*) piantare **3** (*summon: expert*) chiamare, far venire **4** (*insert: object*) far entrare, infilare; (*: comment, word*) infilare ♦ VI + ADV **1** (*enter*) entrare **2** (*arrive: train*) arrivare; (*reach*

home: person) rientrare **3** (*be admitted: to club*) entrare; (*be elected: party*) salire al potere; (*: MP*) essere eletto(-a); **he got in with a bad crowd** si è messo con una banda di cattivi soggetti

▸ **get in on** VI + ADV + PREP (*fam*) intrufolarsi in

▸ **get into** VI + PREP (*house, clothes*) entrare in; (*vehicle*) salire in, montare in; (*club*) entrare in, essere ammesso(-a) a; **to get into difficulties** trovarsi in difficoltà; **to get into trouble** ficcarsi nei guai; **to get into the habit of doing sth** prendere l'abitudine di fare qc; **to get into bed** mettersi a letto; **to get into a rage** andare su tutte le furie

▸ **get off** VT + ADV **1** (*remove: clothes, stain*) levare, togliere **2** (*send off*) spedire **3** (*save from punishment*) far assolvere, tirar fuori **4** (*have as holiday: day, time*) prendersi; **we got 2 days off** abbiamo avuto 2 giorni liberi ♦ VI + PREP (*bus, train, plane, bike*) scendere da; (*fam: escape: chore, lessons*) evitare, sfuggire a ♦ VI + ADV **1** (*from bus, train, plane, bike*) scendere; **to tell sb where to get off** (*fam*) dire a qn di andare a farsi benedire; **to get off to a good start** (*fig*) cominciare bene **2** (*depart: person*) andare via **3** (*escape injury, punishment*) cavarsela; **he got off with a fine** se l'è cavata con una multa **4** (*from work*) staccare

▸ **get off with** VI + ADV + PREP (*fam: start relationship with*) mettersi con

▸ **get on** VI + PREP (*vehicle*): **to get on the bus/train** salire *or* montare in autobus/in treno, salire *or* montare sull'autobus/ sul treno; **to get on a horse** montare a cavallo ♦ VI + ADV **1** (*mount*) montare, salire **2 to get on (with sth)** (*proceed*) continuare a fare (qc); **get on with it!** su, muoviti! **3** (*progress*) far progressi; (*fare: in exam, interview*): **how did you get on?** com'è andata?; **how are you getting on?** come va (la vita)?; **to be getting on** (*person*) essere avanti negli anni; **he's getting on for 70** va per i 70; **time is getting on** si sta facendo tardi **4** (*succeed*) farsi strada **5** (*be on good terms*): **to get on (with sb)** andare d'accordo (con qn)

▸ **get on to** VI + ADV + PREP (*fam: contact: on phone*) contattare, rintracciare; (*deal with*) occuparsi di

▸ **get out** VT + ADV: **to get out (of)** (*take out*) tirare fuori (da); (*money: from bank*) ritirare (da); (*stain*) levare (da), togliere (da); (*book: from library*) prendere in prestito (da); **get those children out of here!** leva quei bambini di torno! ♦ VI + ADV (*news*) venirsi a sapere, spargersi; **to get out (of)** (*go out*) uscire (da); (*leave*) andar via (da), uscire (da); (*from vehicle*) scendere (da); (*escape*) scappare (da)

▸ **get out of** VT + ADV + PREP (*extract: confession, words*) tirare fuori di bocca a; (*gain from: pleasure, benefit*) trarre da; **to get sb out of bed** far alzare qn ♦ VI + ADV + PREP **1** (*difficulty*) togliersi da; (*escape: duty, punishment*) sottrarsi a **2** (*give up*): **to get out of the habit of doing sth** perdere l'abitudine di fare qc; *see also* **get out**

▸ **get over** VT + ADV (*cross*) attraversare ♦ VI + PREP **1** (*cross*) attraversare **2** (*recover from: illness*) riprendersi da, rimettersi da; (*: disappointment*) superare; (*: surprise, shock*) riaversi da; **I can't get over it!** non riesco a crederci!; **you'll get over it!** ti passerà! **3** (*overcome: difficulty*) superare; (*: shyness*) vincere ♦ VT + ADV **1** (*transport across*) far passare **2** (*have done with*) finire una buona volta; **let's get it over (with)** facciamolo, così ci togliamo il pensiero **3** (*communicate: idea*) comunicare, passare

▸ **get round** VI + PREP (*difficulty: problem*) aggirare, superare; (*law, regulation*) eludere; (*fig: person*) rigirare ♦ VI + ADV: **to get round to doing sth** trovare il tempo di fare qc; **I'll get round to it** prima o poi lo farò

▸ **get through** VI + PREP **1** (*pass through: window*) passare per *or* da; (*: crowd*) passare attraverso, farsi strada attraverso **2** (*finish: work*) sbrigare; (*use up: food, money*) far fuori, dar fondo a; **we got through a lot of work today** abbiamo sbrigato molto lavoro oggi **3** (*pass: exam*) passare ♦ VT + PREP (*cause to succeed: student*) far passare; (*: proposal, bill*) far passare a, far approvare a ♦ VT + ADV (*succeed in sending: message, supplies*) far arrivare *or* pervenire; (*Pol: bill*) far passare *or* approvare ♦ VI + ADV **1** (*pass through*) passare; (*news, supplies: arrive*) raggiungere **2** (*pass, be accepted*) passare; **they got through to the semifinal** sono entrati in semifinale **3** (*finish*) finire, terminare **4** (*Telec*) ottenere la comunicazione *or* la linea; **to get through to sb** mettersi in

contatto con qn; (*fig: communicate with*) comunicare con qn
- **get together** vt + adv (*people*) radunare; (*objects, thoughts, ideas*) raccogliere ♦ vi + adv (*group, club*) riunirsi; **to get together about sth** vedersi per discutere qc
- **get up** vi + adv **1** (*rise: from chair, bed*) alzarsi; (*wind*) alzarsi, levarsi **2** (*climb up*) salire ♦ vt + adv **1** (*person: from chair, floor*) sollevare, tirar su; (: *wake*) far alzare, svegliare **2** (*gather: strength, speed*) prendere; **to get up enthusiasm for sth** entusiasmarsi per qc **3** (*fam: organize: celebrations*) organizzare **4** (*fam: dress up: person*): **to get o.s. up in** farsi bello(-a) con; **to get o.s. up as** travestirsi da ♦ vi + prep (*tree*) arrampicarsi su; (*ladder*) salire su per
- **get up to** vi + adv + prep **1** (*reach*) raggiungere, arrivare a; **I've got up to chapter 4** sono arrivato *or* sono al capitolo 4 **2 to get up to mischief** combinarne di tutti i colori; **what have you been getting up to?** cosa hai combinato?

get·away [ˈɡɛtəˌweɪ] N: **to make one's getaway** darsi alla fuga; **a quick getaway** una rapida fuga

getaway car N macchina per la fuga

get-together [ˈɡɛtətəˌɡɛðəʳ] N (piccola) riunione *f*; (*party*) festicciola

get-up [ˈɡɛtˌʌp] N (*fam: outfit*) tenuta

get-well card [ɡɛtˈwɛlˌkɑːd] N cartolina di auguri di pronta guarigione

gey·ser [ˈɡiːzəʳ] N (*Geog*) geyser *m inv*; (*water heater*) scaldabagno

Gha·na [ˈɡɑːnə] N Ghana *m*

Gha·na·ian [ɡɑːˈneɪən] ADJ del Ghana, ganaense ♦ N ganaense *m/f*

ghast·ly [ˈɡɑːstlɪ] ADJ (*horrible*) atroce, spaventoso(-a), orribile; (*pale*) spettrale; (*fam: very bad: experience*) pauroso(-a); **a ghastly mistake** un terribile errore; **ghastly weather** tempo orribile

gher·kin [ˈɡɜːkɪn] N cetriolino

ghet·to [ˈɡɛtəʊ] N ghetto

ghetto blaster [-ˌblɑːstəʳ] N maxistereo portatile

ghost [ɡəʊst] N fantasma *m*, spettro; **the ghost of a smile** (*fig*) una parvenza di sorriso; **he hasn't the ghost of a chance** (*fig*) non ha la minima possibilità ♦ vt (*book*) scrivere per conto di altri

ghost·ly [ˈɡəʊstlɪ] ADJ spettrale; **a ghostly apparition** uno spettro

ghost·writ·er [ˈɡəʊstˌraɪtəʳ] N ghost writer *m/f inv*, scrittore(-trice) fantasma *inv*

ghoul [ɡuːl] N vampiro che si nutre di cadaveri

ghoul·ish [ˈɡuːlɪʃ] ADJ (*tastes*) macabro(-a)

GHQ [ˌdʒiːeɪtʃˈkjuː] N ABBR (*Mil: = general headquarters*) QG (= *quartier generale*)

GI [ˌdʒiːˈaɪ] N ABBR (*USA fam: = government issue*) soldato americano

gi·ant [ˈdʒaɪənt] N gigante(-essa); (*fig*) gigante *m*, colosso ♦ ADJ (*fern, panda*) gigante; (*strides*) da gigante; **giant (size) packet** confezione *f* gigante

gib·ber [ˈdʒɪbəʳ] vi (*monkey*) squittire confusamente; (*idiot*) farfugliare; **to gibber with rage** non connettere più dalla rabbia

gib·ber·ish [ˈdʒɪbərɪʃ] N parole *fpl* senza senso

gibe [dʒaɪb] N frecciata, malignità *f inv* ♦ vi: **to gibe (at)** lanciare frecciate (a)

gib·lets [ˈdʒɪblɪts] NPL rigaglie *fpl*

Gi·bral·tar [dʒɪˈbrɔːltəʳ] N Gibilterra

gid·di·ness [ˈɡɪdmɪs] N vertigini *fpl*

gid·dy [ˈɡɪdɪ] ADJ (*comp -ier, superl -iest*) (*dizzy*): **to be giddy** aver le vertigini; (*causing dizziness: height*) vertiginoso(-a); (: *speed*) folle; **I feel giddy** mi gira la testa

gift [ɡɪft] N **1** (*present*) dono, regalo; (*Comm: also:* **free gift**) omaggio; **a lovely gift** un bel regalo; **as a free gift** in omaggio, in dono; **it's a gift!** (*fam: easy*) è uno scherzo! **2** (*talent*): **to have a gift for sth** essere portato per qc; **Dave's got a gift for painting** Dave è portato per la pittura

gift·ed [ˈɡɪftɪd] ADJ: **gifted (at)** dotato(-a) (per); **one of the most gifted artists** uno degli artisti più dotati

gift shop, (*USA*) **gift store** N negozio di souvenir

gift voucher, gift token N buono (acquisto *inv*)

gig [ɡɪɡ] N (*fam: of musician*) serata

giga·byte [ˈɡaɪɡəˌbaɪt] N gigabyte *m inv*

gi·gan·tic [dʒaɪˈɡæntɪk] ADJ gigantesco(-a)

gig·gle [ˈɡɪɡl] N risolino (sciocco); **to get the giggles** farsi prendere dalla ridarella ♦ vi ridacchiare (scioccamente), avere la ridarella

GIGO [ˈɡaɪɡəʊ] ABBR (*Comput: fam = garbage in, garbage out*) qualità di input = qualità di output

gild [ɡɪld] vt (*metal, frame*) dorare; (*fig*) indorare; **to gild the lily** (*fig*) aggiungere inutili fronzoli

gill¹ [ɡɪl] N (*of fish*) branchia; **to be green around the gills** (*fig: fam*) essere verde per la paura

gill² [dʒɪl] N (*measure*) ≈ 0,142 l

gilt [ɡɪlt] N doratura ♦ ADJ dorato(-a)

gilt-edged [ˌɡɪltˈedʒd] ADJ **1** (*Fin: stocks, securities*) della massima sicurezza **2** (*book*) dal taglio dorato

gim·let [ˈɡɪmlɪt] N (*for wood*) succhiello

gim·mick [ˈɡɪmɪk] N trovata; **sales gimmick** trovata commerciale

gin [dʒɪn] N (*liquor*) gin *m inv*; **gin and tonic** gin tonic *m inv*

gin·ger [ˈdʒɪndʒəʳ] N zenzero ♦ ADJ (*hair*) rosso(-a); **she's got ginger hair** ha i capelli rossi; **ginger snap** biscotto allo zenzero
- **ginger up** vt + adv animare

ginger ale N bibita gassata allo zenzero

ginger·bread [ˈdʒɪndʒəˌbred] N pan *m* pepato *or* di zenzero

ginger-haired [ˌdʒɪndʒəˈheəd] ADJ rossiccio(-a)

gin·ger·ly [ˈdʒɪndʒəlɪ] ADV con circospezione, cautamente

ging·ham [ˈɡɪŋəm] N (*material*) percalle *m* a righe (*or* quadretti)

gin·seng [ˈdʒɪnseŋ] N ginseng *m inv*

gip·sy [ˈdʒɪpsɪ] = **gypsy**

gi·raffe [dʒɪˈrɑːf] N giraffa

gird·er [ˈɡɜːdəʳ] N trave *f*

gir·dle [ˈɡɜːdl] N (*corset*) busto, corsetto; (*belt*) cintura

girl [ɡɜːl] N (*child*) bambina, ragazzina; (*young unmarried woman*) signorina, ragazza; (*daughter*) figlia, figliola; (*fam: girlfriend*) ragazza; **a little girl** una bambina; **a five-year-old girl** una bambina di cinque anni; **an English girl** una ragazza inglese; **they've got a girl and two boys** hanno una femmina e due maschi

girl band N girl band *f inv*, gruppo pop di sole donne creato per far presa su un pubblico giovane

girl·friend [ˈɡɜːlˌfrend] N (*of man*) ragazza; (*of woman*) amica; **Paul's girlfriend is called Lee** la ragazza di Paul si chiama Lee; **she often went out with her girlfriends** usciva spesso con le sue amiche

girl·ish [ˈɡɜːlɪʃ] ADJ da ragazza

Girl Scout N (*USA*) Giovane Esploratrice *f*

Giro [ˈdʒaɪrəʊ] N: **the National Giro** (*Brit*) ≈ la *or* il Bancoposta

giro [ˈdʒaɪrəʊ] N (*Brit fam: also:* **giro cheque**) assegno postale (*per indennità di disoccupazione o malattia*); (*also:* **bank giro**) bancogiro; (*also:* **post office giro**) postagiro

girth [ɡɜːθ] N (*for saddle*) sottopancia *m inv*; (*measure: of tree*) circonferenza; (*of person's waist*) (giro) vita

gist [dʒɪst] N (*of speech, conversation*) succo, nocciolo; **to get the gist of sth** capire il succo di qc

give [ɡɪv] N (*pt* **gave**, *pp* **given**) vt **1** (*gen*) dare; (*as gift*) regalare, dare (in dono); (*description, promise, surprise*) fare; (*particulars*) dare, fornire; (*decision*) annunciare; (*title, honour*) conferire, dare; (*assign: job*) assegnare, dare; (*dedicate: life, time*) consacrare, dedicare; **to give sb sth** *or* **sth to sb** dare qc a qn; **I gave my sister some money** ho dato dei soldi a mia sorella; **he gave me ten pounds** mi ha dato dieci sterline; **I gave him some money** gli ho dato dei soldi; **to give sb a present** fare un regalo a qn; **they gave their teacher a present** hanno fatto un regalo alla maestra; **one must give and take** bisogna fare delle concessioni; **how much did you give for it?** quanto (l')hai pagato?; **to give sb a kick/push** dare un calcio/una spinta a qn; **to give sb a cold** passare *or* attaccare il raffreddore a qn; **to give sb news of sth** dar notizie di qc a qn; **to give sb something to eat** dare (qualcosa) da mangiare a qn; **12 o'clock, give or take a few minutes** mezzogiorno, minuto più minuto meno; **give or take ten miles** dieci miglia in più o meno; **to give as good as**

one gets rendere pan per focaccia; **he gave it everything he'd got** (fig) ce l'ha messa tutta; **I'd give a lot/the world/anything to know ...** (fam) darei moltissimo/tutto l'oro del mondo/non so che cosa per sapere...; **I can give you 10 minutes** posso darti 10 minuti; **give them my regards** salutali da parte mia; **give yourself an hour to get there** calcola un'ora per arrivare; **that gave me an idea** mi ha fatto venire un'idea; **he's honest, I'll give you that** è onesto, te lo concedo **2** (produce) dare, produrre; (result, help, advice) dare; **3 times 4 gives 12** 3 per 4 fa 12; **to give the right/wrong answer** dare la risposta giusta/sbagliata **3** (perform etc: jump, smile) fare; (deliver: speech, lecture) fare, tenere; (utter: cry) lanciare; (: sigh) tirare, fare; **give us a song** cantaci qualcosa; **he gave a good performance** (musician) è stata una buona esecuzione; (actor) ha recitato bene ♦ VI **1** (give presents) dare, donare; **to give to charity** fare della beneficenza **2** (also: **give way**: collapse) (roof, ground, door) cedere; (knees) piegarsi; **something's got to give!** (fam) non si può andare avanti così! ♦ N (of material) elasticità; (of bed) morbidezza

‣ **give away** VT + ADV **1** (money, goods) dar via, donare; (bride) condurre all'altare; (distribute: prizes) distribuire; **we have six copies to give away** abbiamo sei copie da dare via **2** (reveal: secret) rivelare; (betray: person) tradire; **her accent gave her away** il suo accento l'ha tradita

‣ **give back** VT + ADV (return: sb's property): **to give back (to)** restituire (a), rendere (a), ridare (a); **I gave the book back to him** gli ho restituito il libro

‣ **give in** VT + ADV (hand in: form, essay) consegnare; **to give in one's name** dare il proprio nome ♦ VI + ADV (yield): **to give in (to sb)** cedere (a qn); (in guessing game): **I give in!** mi arrendo!

‣ **give off** VT + ADV (smell, smoke, heat) emettere, sprigionare

‣ **give onto** VI + PREP (subj: door, window) dare su

‣ **give out** VT + ADV **1** (distribute) distribuire; **he gave out leaflets in the street** distribuiva volantini per strada **2** (make known: news) annunciare ♦ VI + ADV (be exhausted: supplies) esaurirsi, venir meno; (: fuel: engine) fermarsi; (: strength) mancare; (: legs) non reggere più

‣ **give over** VT + ADV **1** (devote): **to give over to** dedicare a **2** (transfer): **to give over to** consegnare a ♦ VI + ADV (fam: stop) piantarla, smetterla; **give over!** piantala!, smettila!

‣ **give up** VT + ADV **1** (surrender: place) cedere; (hand over: ticket) consegnare; **to give o.s. up** arrendersi; **he gave himself up** si è arreso; **to give o.s. up to the police** costituirsi alla polizia **2** (renounce: friend, boyfriend, job) lasciare; (abandon: idea) rinunciare a, abbandonare; (abandon hope for: patient) dare per spacciato(-a); (: expected visitor) non aspettare più; **I gave it up as a bad job** (fam) ci ho rinunciato, ho abbandonato l'idea; **to give up drinking/smoking** smettere di bere/fumare; **he gave up smoking** ha smesso di fumare **3** (devote: one's life, time): **to give up to** dedicare (a); **to give up (for)** (sacrifice: one's life, career) donare (per), dare (per) ♦ VI + ADV (stop trying) rinunciare, arrendersi; **I give up!** (trying to guess) mi arrendo!; **I couldn't do it, so I gave up** non riuscivo a farlo, così ho lasciato perdere

‣ **give way** VI + ADV **1** see **give 2** (yield): **to give way (to)** cedere (a); **to give way to despair** lasciarsi andare alla disperazione **3** (make room for): **to give way (to)** lasciare il posto (a) **4** (Brit: Aut) dare la precedenza

give-and-take [ˌɡɪvənˈteɪk] N (fam) elasticità; **there has to be a bit of give-and-take** bisogna venirsi un po' incontro

give·away [ˈɡɪvəˌweɪ] N (fam): **her expression was a dead giveaway** le si leggeva tutto in volto; **the exam was a giveaway!** l'esame è stato uno scherzo! ♦ ADJ: **giveaway prices** prezzi mpl stracciati

giv·en [ˈɡɪvn] PP of **give** ♦ ADJ **1** (fixed: time, amount) dato(-a), determinato(-a) **2 to be given to doing sth** essere incline or propenso(-a) a fare qc ♦ CONJ: **given (that) ...** ammesso che..., supposto che...; **given the circumstances ...** date le circostanze...; **given time, it would be possible** se ci fosse tempo, sarebbe possibile

gla·cial [ˈɡleɪsɪəl] ADJ glaciale; **glacial advance** espansione f glaciale; **glacial retreat** ritiro dei ghiacciai

glaci·er [ˈɡlæsɪər] N ghiacciaio

glad [ɡlæd] ADJ (comp **-der**, superl **-dest**) (pleased) conten-

to(-a), compiaciuto(-a); (news, occasion) lieto(-a); **to be glad about sth/that** essere contento(-a) or lieto(-a) di qc/che + sub; **I am glad to hear it** mi fa molto piacere, ne sono felice; **I was glad of his help** gli sono stato grato del suo aiuto; **he was only too glad to do it** non chiedeva di meglio che farlo

glad·den [ˈɡlædn] VT rallegrare, allietare

glade [ɡleɪd] N radura

glad·ly [ˈɡlædlɪ] ADV (joyfully) lietamente; (willingly) con piacere, volentieri

glam·or·ous, glam·our·ous [ˈɡlæmərəs] ADJ (gen) favoloso(-a); (person) affascinante; (occasion) brillante, elegante

glam·our, glam·or (USA) [ˈɡlæmər] N fascino

glance [ɡlɑːns] N sguardo, occhiata; **to take** or **have a glance at** dare un'occhiata a; **we exchanged glances** ci siamo scambiati un'occhiata; **at a glance** a colpo d'occhio; **at first glance** a prima vista ♦ VI (look): **to glance at** (person) lanciare uno sguardo or un'occhiata a; (headlines) dare uno sguardo or un'occhiata a; **Peter glanced at his watch** Peter ha dato un'occhiata all'orologio; **to glance away** distogliere lo sguardo; **to glance through a report** dare una scorsa a un rapporto

‣ **glance off** VI + PREP (bullet): **to glance off sth** rimbalzare di striscio su qc

glanc·ing [ˈɡlɑːnsɪŋ] ADJ (blow) di striscio

gland [ɡlænd] N (Anat) ghiandola

glan·du·lar [ˈɡlændjʊlər] ADJ ghiandolare

glare [ɡlɛər] N **1** (of light, sun) luce f or bagliore m accecante; **the glare of publicity** (fig) il chiasso della pubblicità **2** (look) occhiata fulminante, sguardo furioso ♦ VI **1** (light) sfolgorare **2** (look): **to glare at** fulminare con lo sguardo

glar·ing [ˈɡlɛərɪŋ] ADJ (dazzling: sun, light) sfolgorante, accecante; (: colour) sgargiante; (obvious: evidence) lampante; (: mistake) palese

glas·nost [ˈɡlæsˌnɒst] N glasnost f inv

glass [ɡlɑːs] N (material, pane of glass) vetro; (glassware) cristalleria; (drinking vessel, glassful) bicchiere m; (barometer) barometro; (mirror) specchio; **a glass of milk** un bicchiere di latte; **a wine glass** un bicchiere da vino, calice m; **grown under glass** di serra, coltivato(-a) in serra; see also **glasses** ♦ ADJ (bottle, eye) di vetro; (industry) del vetro; **a glass door** una porta di vetro

glass-blowing [ˈɡlɑːsˌbləʊɪŋ] N soffiatura del vetro

glass ceiling N (fig) barriera invisibile

glasses [ˈɡlɑːsɪz] NPL (spectacles) occhiali mpl; **he wears glasses** porta gli occhiali

glass fibre N fibra di vetro

glass·house [ˈɡlɑːsˌhaʊs] N (for plants) serra

glass·ware [ˈɡlɑːsˌwɛər] N cristalleria, articoli mpl di vetro

glassy [ˈɡlɑːsɪ] ADJ (comp **-ier**, superl **-iest**) (sea, lake) come uno specchio; (eye, look) vitreo(-a)

Glas·we·gian [ɡlæzˈwiːdʒən] ADJ di Glasgow ♦ N abitante m/f or originario(-a) di Glasgow

glaze [ɡleɪz] N (on pottery) smalto; (Culin) glassa ♦ VT **1** (window, door) mettere i vetri a, fornire di vetri **2** (pottery) invetriare; (Culin) glassare ♦ VI: **his eyes glazed over** i suoi occhi si fecero vitrei

glazed [ɡleɪzd] ADJ (tiles, pottery) invetriato(-a); (fig: eye) vitreo(-a)

gla·zi·er [ˈɡleɪzɪər] N vetraio

gleam [ɡliːm] N (of light) bagliore m; (of moonlight) chiarore m; (of metal, water) luccichio m; **with a gleam in one's eye** con gli occhi scintillanti; (mischievous) con uno sguardo furbesco; **a gleam of hope** un barlume di speranza ♦ VI (light, furniture) brillare; (metal, water) luccicare; (eyes): **to gleam (with)** brillare (di); **her eyes gleamed with excitement** le brillavano gli occhi dall'eccitazione

gleam·ing [ˈɡliːmɪŋ] ADJ brillante, lucente; **the house was gleaming** la casa era uno specchio

glean [ɡliːn] VT (gather: information) racimolare

glee [ɡliː] N: **with glee** (gen) con gioia; (laugh) di gusto

glee·ful [ˈɡliːfʊl] ADJ (smile, laugh) gioioso(-a), allegro(-a); (malicious) malizioso(-a)

glen [ɡlɛn] N vallone m

glib [ɡlɪb] ADJ (person) dalla lingua sciolta; (explanation, excuse) facile, disinvolto(-a); **glib promises** promesse fatte con leggerezza; **a glib attitude** un atteggiamento facilone; **glib answers** risposte superficiali

glide [glaɪd] N (*of dancer etc*) volteggio; (*Aer*) planata; (*Skiing*) scivolata ♦ vi (*move smoothly*) scivolare silenziosamente; (*dancer*) volteggiare; (*Aer: birds*) planare; **the boat glided over the water** la barca scivolava sull'acqua; **waiters glided between the tables** i camerieri volteggiavano tra i tavoli; **to glide in** (*person*) entrare silenziosamente

glid·er [ˈglaɪdə^r] N (*Aer*) aliante *m*

glid·ing [ˈglaɪdɪŋ] N (*Aer*) volo a vela; (*with glider*) volo con l'aliante; **my hobby is gliding** il mio hobby è il volo con l'aliante

glim·mer [ˈglɪmə^r] N (*of light, also fig*) barlume *m*; (*of water*) lucchichio ♦ vi (*light*) baluginare; (*water*) luccicare

glimpse [glɪmps] N: **to catch a glimpse of** vedere di sfuggita, intravedere ♦ vt intravedere

glint [glɪnt] N (*of metal etc*) scintillio, lucchichio; **he had a glint in his eye** nei suoi occhi brillava una luce strana; **he had an angry glint in his eye** gli occhi gli scintillavano dalla rabbia ♦ vi brillare, luccicare

glis·ten [ˈglɪsn] vi (*wet surface, water*) luccicare; (*eyes*): **to glisten (with)** brillare (di)

glit·ter [ˈglɪtə^r] N (*of gold etc*) scintillio; (*on Christmas cards etc*) polvere *f* d'oro ♦ vi (*gold etc*) luccicare, scintillare; **all that glitters is not gold** non è tutt'oro quel che luccica

glitz [glɪts] N (*fam*) vistosità, chiassosità

gloat [gləʊt] vi gongolare; **to gloat over** (*money etc*) covare con gli occhi; (*victory, enemy's misfortune*) gongolare (di gioia) per, esultare per

glob·al [ˈgləʊbl] ADJ (*world-wide*) mondiale; (*comprehensive*) globale; **on a global scale** su scala mondiale; **a global view** una visione globale

glob·al·i·za·tion [ˌgləʊbəlaɪˈzeɪʃən] N globalizzazione *f*

global warming [-ˈwɔːmɪŋ] N riscaldamento dell'atmosfera terrestre

globe [gləʊb] N globo, sfera; (*spherical map*) mappamondo, globo

globe·trotter [ˈgləʊbˌtrɒtə^r] N giramondo *m/f inv*

glob·ule [ˈglɒbjuːl] N (*of water etc*) gocciolina; (*Anat*) globulo

gloom [gluːm] N 1 (*darkness*) oscurità, buio; **in the gloom** nell'oscurità, al buio; **she peered into the gloom** aguzzava gli occhi nell'oscurità 2 (*sadness*) tristezza, malinconia; **a feeling of deep gloom** un senso di profonda tristezza

gloomy [ˈgluːmɪ] ADJ (*comp* -**ier**, *superl* -**iest**) (*place, character*) cupo(-a), tetro(-a); (*person*) triste; (*atmosphere, weather, day*) deprimente; (*sky*) fosco(-a); (*outlook*) nero(-a); **a huge gloomy church** una chiesa enorme e tetra; **to feel gloomy** sentirsi giù *or* depresso(-a); **to feel gloomy about sth** essere pessimista su qc; **to take a gloomy view of things** vedere tutto nero

glo·ri·fi·ca·tion [ˌglɔːrɪfɪˈkeɪʃən] N glorificazione *f*

glo·ri·fy [ˈglɔːrɪˌfaɪ] vt (*exalt: God*) glorificare; (: *person*) onorare; (*pej: war, deeds*) magnificare, esaltare; **it was just a glorified ...** non era altro che...

glo·ri·ous [ˈglɔːrɪəs] ADJ (*deeds, victory*) glorioso(-a); (*weather, view*) stupendo(-a), magnifico(-a); (*colours*) festoso(-a)

glo·ry [ˈglɔːrɪ] N gloria; (*splendour*) splendore *m*, magnificenza; **a moment of glory** un momento di gloria; **one of the glories of the city** uno dei vanti della città; **Rome at the height of its glory** Roma all'apogeo della gloria; **there she was in all her glory** (*fam*) stava lì in tutto il suo splendore; **glory be!** (*fam*) buon Dio! ♦ vi: **to glory in sth** (*one's success etc*) gloriarsi di qc; (*another's misfortune*) gustare *or* assaporare qc

glory hole N (*fam*) ripostiglio

Glos ABBR (*Brit:* = *Gloucestershire*)

gloss [glɒs] N 1 (*explanation*) glossa, nota esplicativa 2 (*shine*) lucentezza, lustro; (*also:* **gloss paint**) vernice *f* lucida
► **gloss over** vt + ADV (*play down*) sorvolare su; (*hide*) coprire, mascherare

glos·sa·ry [ˈglɒsərɪ] N glossario

glossy [ˈglɒsɪ] ADJ (*comp* -**ier**, *superl* -**iest**) (*gen*) lucido(-a); **glossy hair** capelli lucidi

glove [glʌv] N guanto; **a pair of gloves** un paio di guanti

glove compartment N (*Aut*) vano portaoggetti

glow [gləʊ] N (*of lamp, sunset etc*) luce *f* (diffusa); (*of cigarette, fire, city*) bagliore *m*; (*of bright colour*) luminosità; (*of cheeks*) colorito acceso; (*warm feeling: of pride etc*) vampata ♦ vi (*lamp, sunset etc*) ardere; (*fire*) sfavillare; (*colour, face*) essere luminoso(-a); **to glow with health** sprizzare salute (da tutti i pori)

glow·er [ˈglaʊə^r] vi: **to glower (at sb)** guardare (qn) in cagnesco

glow·ing [ˈgləʊɪŋ] ADJ (*light etc*) caldo(-a); (*fire*) ardente; (*complexion*) luminoso(-a); (*cheeks, colour*) acceso(-a); (*person: with health*) florido(-a); (: *with pleasure*) raggiante; (*fig: report, description etc*) entusiasta

glow-worm [ˈgləʊˌwɜːm] N lucciola

glu·cose [ˈgluːkəʊs] N glucosio

glue [gluː] N colla ♦ vt: **to glue (to)** incollare (a); **to glue two things together** incollare due cose insieme; **he was glued to the spot** (*fig*) rimase di sasso

glum [glʌm] ADJ (*comp* -**mer**, *superl* -**mest**) (*person*) abbattuto(-a); (*mood*) nero(-a); (*expression*) cupo(-a); **to feel glum** sentirsi giù

glut [glʌt] N sovrabbondanza, surplus *m inv*, eccesso ♦ vt (*market*) inondare, saturare; (*with food*) saziare

glu·ti·nous [ˈgluːtɪnəs] ADJ colloso(-a), appiccicoso(-a)

glut·ton [ˈglʌtn] N goloso(-a), ghiottone(-a); **a glutton for work** uno(-a) stacanovista, un(a) patito(-a) del lavoro; **a glutton for punishment** un(a) masochista

glut·ton·ous [ˈglʌtənəs] ADJ ghiotto(-a), goloso(-a)

glut·tony [ˈglʌtənɪ] N ghiottoneria, golosità; (*sin*) gola

glyc·er·in [ˈglɪsərɪn], **glyc·er·ine** [ˌglɪsəˈriːn] N glicerina

GM [ˌdʒiːˈem] ADJ ABBR = **genetically modified**

gm (*pl* **gms**) ABBR = **gram(s)**

GMAT [ˌdʒiːemˈtiː] N ABBR (*USA:* = *Graduate Management Admissions Test*) esame di ammissione all'ultimo biennio di scuola superiore

GM crop N pianta transgenica

GM food N cibo transgenico

GM-free [ˌdʒiːemˈfriː] ADJ senza OGM

GMO [ˌdʒiːemˈəʊ] N ABBR (= *genetically modified organism*) OGM *m inv* (= *organismo geneticamente modificato*)

GMT [ˌdʒiːemˈtiː] ABBR (= *Greenwich Mean Time*) TMG (= *Tempo Medio di Greenwich*)

gnarled [nɑːld] ADJ nodoso(-a)

gnash [næʃ] vt: **to gnash one's teeth** digrignare i denti

gnat [næt] N moscerino

gnaw [nɔː] vt (*chew*) rosicchiare, rodere; (*fig: subj: remorse*) rodere; (: *hunger, pain*) tormentare ♦ vi: **to gnaw through** rosicchiare da una parte all'altra; **to gnaw at** rosicchiare; (*fig*) rodere

gnome [nəʊm] N gnomo

GNP N ABBR (= *gross national product*) PNL *m* (= *prodotto nazionale lordo*)

go [gəʊ] (*3rd pers sg present* **goes**, *pt* **went**, *pp* **gone**) vi 1 (*gen*) andare; **to go to London** andare a Londra; **to go by car/on foot** andare in macchina/a piedi; **to go at 50 km/h** andare a 50 km l'ora *or* a 50 all'ora; **to go looking for sb/sth** andare in cerca di qn/qc; **to go swimming/shopping** andare a nuotare/a fare spese *etc*; **to go for a walk/swim** andare a fare due passi/una nuotata; **to go to a party/to the dentist's** andare a una festa/dal dentista; **to go and see sb** andare a trovare qn; **to go past sth** passare davanti a qc; **the bus goes past the school** l'autobus passa davanti alla scuola; **we went home** siamo andati a casa; **I'm going to the cinema tonight** vado al cinema stasera; **halt, who goes there?** alt, chi va là?; **you go first** (*vai*) prima tu; **there he goes!** eccolo (là)!; **he went that way** è andato di là; **there you go again!** (*fam*) ci risiamo! 2 (*depart*) andar via, andarsene; (*train etc*) partire; (*disappear: person, object*) sparire; (: *time*) passare; (: *money*): **to go (on)** andarsene (in); **to go (for)** essere venduto(-a) (per); **where's Judy? - She's gone** dov'è Judy? - È andata via; **I'm going now** io vado; **my voice has gone** m'è andata via la voce; **the cake is all gone** il dolce è finito; **that cupboard will have to go** dobbiamo sbarazzarci di quell'armadio; **go!** (*Sport*) via!; **here goes!** (*fam*) Dio me la mandi buona!; **gone are the days when ...** sono finiti i tempi in cui...; **the day went slowly** la giornata non passava mai; **it's just gone 7** sono appena passate le 7; **only 2 days to go** mancano solo 2 giorni; **going, going, gone!** uno, due, tre, aggiudicato!; **it went for £100** è stato venduto per 100 sterline; **it's going cheap** (*fam*) costa poco **3** (*extend*) arrivare; **the garden goes down to the lake** il giardino arriva fino al lago; **money doesn't go far nowadays** non si fa molto coi soldi oggigiorno; **it's good as far as it goes, but …** quello che c'è va bene, ma…; **as cooks go, she's quite good** come cuoca non è male; **as hotels in Milan go, it's quite cheap** questo albergo non è molto caro, per essere a Milano **4** (*function: machine etc*) andare; **I couldn't get the car to go at all** non sono riuscito a far partire la macchina; **to keep going** (*person, also fig*) andare avanti; (*machine*) andare; **to make sth go, to get sth going** far funzionare qc; (*engine, machine*) mettere in moto qc; **let's get going** muoviamoci **5** (*progress, turn out*) andare; **the meeting went well** la riunione è andata bene; **how did it go?** com'è andata?; **how did the exam go?** com'è andato l'esame?; **how's it going?** (*fam*) come va (la vita)?; **we'll see how things go** (*fam*) vediamo come vanno *or* come si mettono le cose; **he has a lot going for him** molte cose giocano a suo favore; **how does that song go?** come fa quella canzone? **6 to go (with)** (*match*) andare (con); (*coincide, co-occur*) accompagnarsi a; **does this blouse go with that skirt?** questa camicia va con quella gonna?; **the curtains don't go with the carpet** le tende non si intonano col tappeto; **the house goes with the job** la casa è parte integrante del suo contratto di lavoro; **to go with sb** (*also fam*) andare con qn **7** (*become*) diventare, farsi; **to go blind** perdere la vista; **to go hungry** fare la fame; **to go without** sth non avere qc; **to go bad** (*food*) andare a male, guastarsi; **to go mad** impazzire; **to go to sleep** addormentarsi **8** (*fit, be contained*) andare, starci; **it won't go in the case** non sta nella valigia; **4 into 3 won't go** il 4 nel 3 non ci sta **9** (*be acceptable*) andare, essere ammesso(-a) *or* ammissibile; **anything goes** (*fam*) tutto è permesso; **that goes for me too** questo vale anche per me; **what he says goes** la sua parola è legge **10** (*break etc: material*) consumarsi, logorarsi; (: *rope*) rompersi, cedere; (: *fuse, button*) saltare; (*health, eyesight etc*) deteriorarsi **11** (*be available*): **is there any tea going?** c'è un po' di tè? **12** (*prize, inheritance*): **to go (to)** andare (a), toccare (a); **the money goes to charity** il denaro va in beneficenza; **the money will go towards our vacation** questi soldi li mettiamo da parte per la vacanza; **all his money goes on drink** tutti i suoi soldi se ne vanno in alcolici; **the qualities which go to make him a great writer** le qualità che fanno di lui un grande scrittore **13** (*make: sound, movement*) fare; (*doorbell, phone*) suonare; **go like that (with your right hand)** fai così (con la destra) **14** (*USA*): **… to go** (*food*) …da portar via, da asporto ♦ **VT AUX vb: I'm going to do it** lo farò; (*intention*) ho intenzione di farlo; **I was going to do it** stavo per farlo; (*intention*) volevo farlo; **I'm going to do it tomorrow** lo farò domani; **it's going to be difficult** sarà difficile; **it's going to rain** sta per piovere; **there's going to be trouble** saranno guai ♦ **VT** (*fam*): **to go it alone** farlo da solo(-a); **to go one better** (*action*) fare di meglio; (*story*) avere di meglio ♦ **N** (*pl goes*) **1** (*fam: energy*) dinamismo; **he's always on the go** non si ferma un minuto; **I've got two projects on the go** ho due progetti per le mani; **it's all go** non c'è un attimo di respiro **2** (*success*): **to make a go of sth** riuscire in qc; (*scheme*) mandare in porto qc; **it's no go** (*fam*) (non c'è) niente da fare **3** (*attempt*) tentativo; **to have a go (at doing sth)** provare (a fare qc); **at** *or* **in one go** in un sol colpo; **whose go is it?** a chi tocca?; **it's your go** tocca a te **4 from the word go** (*fam*) (fin) dal primo momento; **all systems (are) go** tutto a posto

▸ **go about VI + PREP 1** (*set to work on: task*) affrontare; **how does one go about getting the tickets?** come si fa a procurarsi i biglietti?; **how do I go about this?** qual è la prassi per questo? **2** (*busy o.s. with*) continuare a fare; **to go about one's business** occuparsi delle proprie faccende ♦ **VI + ADV** (*also:* **go around:** *wander about*) aggirarsi; (*circulate: flu etc*) essere(-a) in giro; (: *rumour*) correre, circolare

▸ **go after VI + PREP** (*pursue*) correr dietro a, rincorrere; (*criminal etc*) inseguire; (*job, record etc*) mirare a; (*person*) star dietro (a), fare il filo (a); **quick, go after them!** veloce, rincorrili!

▸ **go against VI + PREP** (*be unfavourable to: result, events*)

essere contro; (*be contrary to: principles, conscience, sb's wishes*) andare contro

▸ **go ahead VI + ADV** (*carry on*) andare *or* tirare avanti; **the show went ahead as planned** lo spettacolo proseguì come previsto; **to go ahead with** mettere in atto; **we'll go ahead with your suggestion** metteremo in atto il tuo suggerimento; **he went ahead with his plan** mise in atto il suo piano; **go (right) ahead!** fai pure!

▸ **go along VI + ADV** (*proceed*) andare avanti, avanzare; **check as you go along** verifica man mano che procedi; **as we went along …** andando avanti…; **to go along with** (*accompany*) andare con, accompagnare; (*agree with: idea*) sottoscrivere, appoggiare; (: *person*) essere d'accordo con

▸ **go around VI + ADV** *see* **go about, go round**

▸ **go at VI + PREP** (*fam: attack*); (*tackle: job etc*) buttarsi in; **he really went at it** si è veramente buttato

▸ **go away VI + ADV** (*depart*) andarsene; **go away!** vattene!

▸ **go back VI + ADV 1 to go back (to)** (*return, revert*) (ri)tornare (a); **we went back to the same place** siamo ritornati allo stesso posto; **there's no going back now** non si può più tornare indietro **2** (*date back*) risalire; **the controversy goes back to 1929** la controversia risale al 1929 **3** (*extend: garden, cave*) estendersi; (*go again*) andare di nuovo

▸ **go back on VI + ADV + PREP** (*word, promise*) rimangiarsi, ritirare; (*decision*) tornare su

▸ **go before VI + ADV** (*happen before*) accadere prima, succedere prima

▸ **go by VI + PREP 1** (*be guided by: watch, compass*) seguire, basarsi su, attenersi a; **to go by appearances** giudicare dalle apparenze; **going by what he says …** stando a ciò che dice… **2 to go by the name of X** farsi chiamare X ♦ **VI + ADV** (*pass by: person, car etc*) passare; (*opportunity*) scappare; (*years, time*) scorrere; **two policemen went by** sono passati due poliziotti; **as time goes by** col passare del tempo

▸ **go down VI + ADV 1** (*sun*) tramontare, calare; (*person: downstairs*) scendere, andar giù; (*sink: ship*) affondare; (: *person*) andar sotto; (*be defeated*) crollare; **he went down the stairs** ha sceso le scale; **that should go down well with him** dovrebbe incontrare la sua approvazione **2** (*be written down*) venire registrato(-a); **to go down in history/to posterity** passare alla storia/ai posteri **3** (*decrease: price, temperature etc*) scendere, calare; **the price of computers has gone down** il prezzo dei computer è sceso; **he has gone down in my estimation** è sceso nella mia stima

▸ **go down with VI + ADV + PREP** (*fam*): **to go down with flu** beccarsi l'influenza

▸ **go for VI + PREP 1** (*attack*) lanciarsi contro *or* su, avventarsi *or* contro; (*fig*) dare addosso a, attaccare; **suddenly the dog went for me** improvvisamente il cane mi ha attaccato **2** (*fam: apply to*): **that goes for me too** questo vale anche per me **3** (*fam: like, fancy*) andar matto(-a) per; **I don't go for his films** i suoi film non mi dicono un granché

▸ **go forward VI + ADV 1** (*proceed: with plan etc*): **to go forward (with)** procedere con **2** (*be put forward: suggestion*) essere avanzato(-a), venire avanzato(-a)

▸ **go in VI + ADV 1** (*enter*) entrare; **they all went in** sono entrati tutti **2 the sun went in** il sole si è oscurato *or* nascosto **3** (*fit*) entrarci, andarci

▸ **go in for VI + PREP 1** (*enter for: race, competition*) prendere parte a; (: *exam*) presentarsi a **2** (*be interested in: hobby, sport*) interessarsi di, essere appassionato(-a) di; (*take as a career*) scegliere

▸ **go into VI + PREP 1** (*investigate, examine*) indagare, esaminare a fondo; (*embark on*) lanciarsi in, imbarcarsi in; **to go into details** entrare nei particolari; **let's not go into all that now** non parliamone per ora **2** (*embark on: career*) darsi a **3** (*trance, coma*) entrare in; **to go into fits of laughter** essere preso(-a) da un convulso di risa

▸ **go off VI + ADV 1** (*leave*) partire, andarsene; **they went off after lunch** se ne sono andati dopo pranzo; **to go off (to sleep)** addormentarsi **2** (*cease to operate: lights etc*) spegnersi; **all the lights went off** si sono spente tutte le luci **3** (*explode*) esplodere, scoppiare; (*alarm clock*) suonare; **the bomb went off at ten o'clock** la bomba è scoppiata alle 10; **the gun went off by accident** è partito un colpo accidentalmente; **my alarm goes off at seven** la sveglia suona alle sette **4** (*food*) andare a male, guastarsi; **this milk has gone off** il latte è andato a male **5** (*event*) andare; **the party went off well** la festa è riuscita bene ♦ VI + PREP (*cease to like: thing*) perdere il gusto di; (: *person*) non poter più vedere; **I've gone off the idea** l'idea non mi piace più; **I've gone off chocolate** la cioccolata non mi piace più

▸ **go off with** VI + ADV + PREP (*boyfriend*) scappare con; (*book*) andarsene con

▸ **go on** VI + PREP (*be guided by: evidence etc*) basarsi su, fondarsi su; **there's nothing to go on** non abbiamo niente su cui basarci ♦ VI + ADV **1** (*continue: war, talks*) protrarsi, continuare; (: *on journey*) proseguire; **the concert went on until eleven o'clock** il concerto è durato fino alle undici; **to go on doing** continuare a fare; **he went on reading** ha continuato a leggere; **he went on to say that ...** ha aggiunto che...; **to go on about sth** (*fam*) non finirla più con qc; **go on!** forza!; **go on, tell me what the problem is!** forza, dimmi qual è il problema!; **what a way to go on!** (*pej*) bel modo di comportarsi! **2** (*lights*) accendersi; (*machine*) partire, mettersi in moto **3** (*happen*) succedere, svolgersi; **what's going on here?** che succede *or* che sta succedendo qui? **4** (*pass: time, years*) passare; **as time went on** con l'andar del tempo

▸ **go on at** VI + ADV + PREP (*nag*) assillare

▸ **go on for** VI + ADV + PREP: **it's going on for 3 years now** sono quasi 3 anni ormai; **he's going on for 60** va per la sessantina; **it's going on for 2 o'clock** sono quasi le 2

▸ **go on with** VI + ADV + PREP continuare, proseguire

▸ **go out** VI + ADV **1** (*be extinguished: fire, light*) spegnersi; **suddenly, the lights went out** improvvisamente si sono spente le luci **2** (*leave*) uscire, andar fuori; (*socially*) uscire; (*in cards*) chiudere; (*ebb: tide*) calare; **to go out shopping/for a meal** andare a far spese/a mangiare fuori; **to go out (of fashion)** passare (di moda); **to go out with sb** uscire con qn; **I went out with Steven last night** ieri sera sono uscita con Steven; **to be going out with sb** stare insieme a qn; **I've been going out with him for two months** sono due mesi che stiamo insieme; **they've been going out together for 2 years** sono due anni che stanno insieme, fanno coppia fissa da due anni

▸ **go over** VI + PREP **1** (*examine: report etc*) riguardare, controllare **2** (*rehearse, review: speech, lesson etc*) ripassare; **to go over sth in one's mind** pensare bene a qc ♦ VI + ADV **1 to go over (to)** (*cross over*) andare (a *or* in); (*fig: change habit, size etc*) passare (a) **2** (*be received*) essere accolto(-a); **his speech went over well** il suo discorso è stato accolto bene

▸ **go round** VI + ADV **1** (*revolve*) girare; (*circulate: news, rumour*) circolare; **there is a rumour going round that ...** corre voce che...; **there's a bug going round** c'è un virus in circolazione **2** (*suffice*) bastare (per tutti); **is there enough food to go round?** c'è abbastanza da mangiare per tutti? **3** (*visit*): **to go round (to sb's)** passare (da qn); **let's go round to John's place** facciamo un salto da John **4** (*make a detour*): **to go round (by)** passare (per)

▸ **go through** VI + PREP **1** (*suffer*) passare; **I know what you're going through** so cosa stai passando **2** (*examine: list, book*) leggere da capo a fondo; (*search through*) frugare in; **someone had gone through her things** qn aveva frugato tra le sue cose **3** (*use up: money*) spendere, mangiarsi; (*consume, wear out*) consumare **4** (*perform*) fare; (*formalities*) sbrigare; **let's go through that scene again** rifacciamo quella scena (da capo) **5** (*town etc*) attraversare ♦ VI + ADV (*bill, law*) essere approvato(-a); (*deal*) essere concluso(-a)

▸ **go through with** VI + ADV + PREP (*plan, crime*) mettere in atto, eseguire; **I couldn't go through with it** non sono riuscito ad andare fino in fondo

▸ **go under** VI + ADV (*sink: ship*) affondare, colare a picco; (: *person*) andare sotto; (*fig: business, firm*) fallire

▸ **go up** VI + ADV **1** (*rise: temperature, prices etc*) salire, aumentare; **to go up in price** aumentare (di prezzo); **the price has gone up** il prezzo è salito **2** (*ascend*) andare su **3** (*be built: tower block etc*) venire costruito(-a); (: *new district etc*) sorgere; (: *scaffolding etc*) venire montato(-a) **4** (*explode*) saltare in aria; **to go up in flames** andare in fiamme ♦ VI + PREP (*ascend*) salire (su per); **she went up the stairs** ha salito le scale

▸ **go without** VI + PREP fare a meno di

goad [ɡəʊd] VT: **to goad sb into doing sth** (*fig*) pungolare qn perché faccia qc; **to goad sb on** (*fig*) spronare qn, incitare qn

go-ahead [ˈɡəʊəˌhɛd] ADJ (*firm, director*) intraprendente, pieno(-a) d'iniziativa; (*policy, ideas*) avanzato(-a) ♦ N: **to give sb/sth the go-ahead** dare l'okay a qn/qc

goal [ɡəʊl] N **1** (*Sport: score*) goal *m inv*, gol *m inv*; (: *net etc*) rete *f*, porta; **to win by 4 goals to 2** vincere per 4 reti a 2; **to play in goal** giocare in porta; **he scored the first goal** ha segnato il primo gol **2** (*aim: in life*) scopo, fine *m*, obiettivo; (: *in journey*) meta; **his goal is to become the world champion** il suo obiettivo è quello di diventare campione del mondo

goal difference N differenza *f* reti, *inv*

goalie [ˈɡəʊlɪ] N (*Brit fam*) portiere *m*

goal·keeper [ˈɡəʊlˌkiːpə'] N portiere *m*

goal·post [ˈɡəʊlpəʊst] N palo (della porta)

goat [ɡəʊt] N capra; **to get sb's goat** (*fam*) far uscire qn dai gangheri; **goat's cheese** formaggio di capra

gob·ble [ˈɡɒbl] VT (*also: gobble down, gobble up*) trangugiare, ingurgitare

go-between [ˈɡəʊbɪˌtwiːn] N intermediario(-a)

Gobi De·sert [ˈɡəʊbɪˈdɛzət] N: **the Gobi Desert** il Deserto del Gobi

gob·let [ˈɡɒblɪt] N calice *m*

gob·lin [ˈɡɒblɪn] N folletto

go-cart [ˈɡəʊˌkɑːt] N go-kart *m inv*

god [ɡɒd] N **1 God** Dio; **I believe in God** credo in Dio; **God save the Queen** Dio salvi la Regina; **(my) God!** (*fam*) Dio (mio)!; **for God's sake!** per amor di Dio!; **God forbid!** per carità!; (*stronger*) Dio ce ne scampi e liberi!; **God willing** a Dio piacendo; **God (only) knows** Dio (solo) lo sa **2** (*Myth*) dio **3** (*Brit: Theatre*): **the gods** la piccionaia *sg*, il loggione *sg*

god-awful [ˈɡɒdˌɔːful] ADJ (*fam*) orrendo(-a)

god·child [ˈɡɒdˌtʃaɪld] N (*pl* **-children**) figlioccio(-a)

god·damn [ˈɡɒdˈdæm], **god·damned** [ˈɡɒdˈdæmd] (*esp USA*)(*fam*) EXCL: **goddamn!** dannazione!, maledizione! ♦ ADJ dannato(-a) ♦ ADV dannatamente

god·daughter [ˈɡɒdˌdɔːtə'] N figlioccia

god·dess [ˈɡɒdɪs] N dea

god·father [ˈɡɒdˌfɑːðə'] N padrino

god-fearing [ˈɡɒdˌfɪərɪŋ] ADJ timorato(-a) di Dio, (molto) pio(-a)

god-forsaken [ˈɡɒdfəˌseɪkən] ADJ (*fam: place*) dimenticato(-a) da Dio e dagli uomini, sperduto(-a)

god·mother [ˈɡɒdˌmʌðə'] N madrina

god·parents [ˈɡɒdˌpɛərənts] NPL: **the godparents** il padrino e la madrina

god·send [ˈɡɒdˌsɛnd] N dono del cielo; **it was a godsend to us** è stata una vera manna per noi

god·son [ˈɡɒdˌsʌn] N figlioccio

goes [ɡəʊz] 3RD PERS SG PRESENT OF **go**

go·fer [ˈɡəʊfə'] N (*fam*) galoppino(- a)

go-getter [ˈɡəʊˌɡɛtə'] N arrivista *m/f*

gog·gle [ˈɡɒɡl] VI (*look astonished*) sbarrare gli occhi, sgranare tanto d'occhi; **to goggle at** (*stare*) stare con gli occhi incollati *or* appiccicati (a *or* addosso a)

gog·gles [ˈɡɒɡlz] NPL (*of skin-diver*) maschera; (*of skier*) occhiali *mpl* da sci; (*for workman*) occhiali (di protezione)

go·ing [ˈɡəʊɪŋ] N **1** (*pace*) andatura, ritmo; **it was slow going** si andava a rilento; **that was good going** è stata una cosa veloce **2** (*state of road surface etc*) percorribilità; (*in horse-racing etc*) terreno; **let's get out while the going is good** è meglio uscire finché sia possibile ♦ ADJ **1 a going concern** un'azienda avviata **2** (*current: price*) corrente, attuale; **the going rate** la tariffa in vigore; **a going concern** un'azienda avviata

going-over [ˈɡəʊɪŋˈəʊvə'] N (*fam*) **1** (*check*) controllata; **they gave the car a thorough going-over** hanno dato una bella controllata alla macchina **2** (*search*): **to give a house a going-over** perquisire una casa **3** (*violent attack*) pestaggio; **to give sb a going-over** pestare qn

goings-on [ˈɡəʊɪŋzˈɒn] NPL (*fam*) fatti *mpl* strani, cose *fpl* strane

go-kart [ˈɡəʊˌkɑːt] N = **go-cart**

gold [gəʊld] N oro; **it's made of gold** è d'oro; **rolled gold** oro laminato ♦ ADJ (*bracelet, tooth, mine*) d'oro; (*reserves*) aureo(-a); **gold braid** gallone *m* d'oro; **a gold necklace** una collana d'oro

gold·en ['gəʊldən] ADJ (*made of gold*) d'oro, in oro; (*hair etc*) biondo oro *inv*; (*era*) d'oro; (*afternoon*) meraviglioso(-a); (*gold in colour*) dorato(-a); **golden brown** marrone *m* dorato; **her golden hair** i suoi capelli dorati; **a golden opportunity** un'occasione d'oro; **the golden mean** il giusto mezzo; **golden wedding** (*anniversary*) nozze *fpl* d'oro

golden age N età *f inv* d'oro

golden handshake N (*Brit*) gratifica di fine servizio

golden rule N regola d'oro

gold·fish ['gəʊldfɪʃ] N pesce *m* rosso

gold leaf N lamina d'oro

gold medal N (*Sport*) medaglia d'oro

gold·mine ['gəʊldˌmaɪn] N miniera d'oro

gold·plated [ˌgəʊld'pleɪtɪd] ADJ laminato(-a) *or* placcato(-a) d'oro

gold·smith ['gəʊldsmɪθ] N (*dealer*) orefice *m*; (*artisan*) orafo

gold standard N tallone *m* aureo

golf [gɒlf] N golf *m*; **to play golf** giocare a golf ♦ VI: **to go golfing** giocare a golf

golf ball N palla da golf; (*on typewriter*) pallina

golf club N (*organization*) circolo di golf; (*stick*) bastone *m or* mazza da golf

golf course N campo da golf

golf·er ['gɒlfəʳ] N giocatore(-trice) di golf

golf·ing ['gɒlfɪŋ] N il giocare a golf

gon·do·la ['gɒndələ] N gondola

gon·do·lier [ˌgɒndə'lɪəʳ] N gondoliere *m*

gone [gɒn] PP *of* **go**

gon·er ['gɒnəʳ] N (*fam*): **I thought you were a goner** pensavo che ormai fossi spacciato

gong [gɒŋ] N gong *m inv*

good [gʊd] ADJ (*comp* **better**, *superl* **best**) **1** (*gen*) buono(-a); **to lead a good life** condurre una vita virtuosa; **he's a good man** è una brava persona; (*saintly*) è un sant'uomo; **good manners** buona educazione *f*, buone maniere; **he has good judgment** sa giudicare; **be good!** fai il bravo!; **good for you!** bravo!; **she's too good for him** lui non se la merita; **it's just not good enough!** è inaccettabile!; **the job is as good as done** il lavoro è praticamente finito; **as good as new** come nuovo(-a); (**that's**) **good!** bene!, ottimo!; **that's a good one!** (*iro*) questa sì che è bella! **2** (*pleasant: holiday, day, weather*) bello(-a); (: *news*) buono(-a), bello(-a); **to feel good** sentirsi bene; **have a good journey!** buon viaggio!; **it's good to see you** mi fa piacere vederti **3** (*handsome: looks, features*) bello(-a); **you look good in that dress** quel vestito ti dona *or* ti sta bene **4** (*beneficial, advantageous, wholesome*) buono(-a); **good to eat** buono(-a) da mangiare; **he's on to a good thing** ha trovato una miniera d'oro; **it's good for you** ti fa bene; **it's a good thing you were there** meno male che c'eri **5** (*child*) bravo(-a); (*competent: teacher, doctor*) bravo(-a), buono(-a); **to be good at** essere bravo(-a) in; **he's good at English/telling jokes** è bravo in inglese/a raccontare barzellette; **she's good with children** ci sa fare coi bambini; **to be good for** andar bene per; **a ticket good for 3 months** un biglietto valido (per) 3 mesi; **he's good for £10** 10 sterline le sgancia; **are you good for another kilometre?** ce la fai a fare un chilometro? **6** (*kind*) gentile, buono(-a); **to be good to sb** essere gentile con *or* verso qn; **he's a good sort** (*fam*) è una brava persona; **would you be so good as to sign here?** avrebbe la gentilezza di firmare qui?; **that's very good of you** è molto gentile da parte sua; **good deeds** *or* **works** buone azioni *fpl*, opere *fpl* buone **7** (*considerable, not less than*) buono(-a); **a good many/few people** parecchia/un bel po' di gente; **a good deal of money** un bel po' di soldi; **a good deal of work** parecchio lavoro; **a good 3 hours** 3 ore buone; **it's a good distance from here** dista parecchio *or* un bel po' da qui **8** (*thorough*) bello(-a); **to have a good cry** farsi un bel pianto; **to take a good look (at sth)** guardare bene (qc) **9** (*in greetings*): **good morning** buongiorno; **good afternoon** buongiorno; **good evening** buonasera; **good night** buonanotte ♦ ADV **1 a good strong**

stick un bel bastone robusto; **good and strong** (*fam*) bello forte; **to hold good (for)** valere (per), reggere (in) **2** (*esp USA: fam: well*) bene ♦ N **1** (*what is morally right*) bene *m*; **to do good** fare del bene; **good and evil** il bene e il male; **he's up to no good** ne sta combinando qualcuna **2** (*advantage, benefit*) bene *m*, interesse *m*; **it's for your own good** è per il tuo bene; **for the common good** nell'interesse generale, per il bene comune; **to come to no good** andare a finire male; **what's the good of that?** a che pro?, a che serve?; **is this any good?** (*will it do?*) va bene questo?; (*what's it like?*) com'è?; **that's no good to me** non mi va bene, non fa al caso mio; **that's all to the good!** tanto meglio!, tanto di guadagnato!; **it's no good complaining** lamentarsi non serve a niente; **a (fat) lot of good that will do you** (*iro, fam*) sai quanto ne ricavi **3** (*people of virtue*): **the good** *npl* i buoni **4** (*for ever*): **for good (and all)** per sempre, definitivamente; **the theatre has closed for good** il teatro ha chiuso per sempre; *see also* **goods**

good·bye [ˌgʊd'baɪ] EXCL arrivederci ♦ N saluto, addio; **to say goodbye to** (*person*) salutare; (*fig: holiday, promotion etc*) dire addio a

good faith N buona fede

good-for-nothing ['gʊdfəˌnʌθɪŋ] ADJ, N buono(-a) a nulla

Good Friday N Venerdì *m* Santo

good-humoured [ˌgʊd'hjuːməd] ADJ (*person*) di buon umore; (*remark, joke*) bonario(-a); (*discussion*) cordiale; **to be good-humoured about doing sth** fare qc di buon grado

good-looking [ˌgʊd'lʊkɪŋ] ADJ bello(-a), piacente

good-natured [ˌgʊd'neɪtʃəd] ADJ (*person*) affabile; (*discussion*) amichevole, cordiale

good·ness ['gʊdnɪs] N (*virtue, kindness*) bontà (d'animo); (*good quality*) (buona) qualità *f* ♦ EXCL (*fam*): **(my) goodness!, goodness gracious!** santo cielo!, mamma mia!; **for goodness' sake!** per amor del cielo!

goods [gʊdz] NPL (*Comm, etc*) merci *fpl*, articoli *mpl*; **leather goods** articoli di *or* in pelle; **canned goods** scatolame *m*; **faulty goods** merce *f* difettosa; **all my worldly goods** (*frm*) tutti i miei beni *or* i miei averi; **all his goods and chattels** tutti i suoi beni ed effetti

good·will [gʊd'wɪl] N buona volontà, buona fede *f*; (*Comm*) (valore *m* d')avviamento; **as a gesture of goodwill** in segno di buona volontà; **to gain sb's goodwill** ingraziarsi qn

goody-goody [ˌgʊdɪˌgʊdɪ] N (*pej*) santarellino(-a)

goo·ey ['guːɪ] (*Brit fam*) ADJ (*comp* **-ier**, *superl* **-iest**) (*mess*) appiccicoso(-a); (*cake, dessert*) molto ricco(-a); (*fig: sentimental*) sdolcinato(-a)

goo·gle ['guːgl] VT cercare con Google

goose [guːs] N (*pl* **geese**) oca; **a flock of geese** (*on the ground*) un branco di oche; (*in the air*) uno stormo di oche; **the goose that lays the golden eggs** la gallina dalle uova d'oro; **don't be such a goose!** (*fam*) non essere così stupido!

goose·berry ['gʊzbəri] N uva spina

goose·flesh ['guːsˌfleʃ] N, **goose·pimples** ['guːsˌpɪmplz] NPL pelle *f inv* d'oca

goose step N (*Mil*) passo dell'oca

GOP [ˌdʒiːəʊ'piː] N ABBR (*USA Pol: fam:* = *Grand Old Party*) partito repubblicano

go·pher ['gəʊfəʳ] N **1** (*Zool*) geomide *m* **2** (*employee*) = **gofer**

gore[1] [gɔːʳ] N sangue *m*

gore[2] [gɔːʳ] VT (*subj: bull etc*) incornare

gorge [gɔːdʒ] N (*Geog, Anat*) gola ♦ VT: **to gorge o.s. (with** *or* **on)** rimpinzarsi (di), ingozzarsi (di)

gor·geous ['gɔːdʒəs] ADJ (*person, dress, holiday*) stupendo(-a), magnifico(-a); (*meal etc*) fantastico(-a)

go·ril·la [gə'rɪlə] N gorilla *m inv*

gorm·less ['gɔːmlɪs] ADJ (*Brit fam*) tonto(-a); (*stronger*) deficiente

gorse [gɔːs] N ginestrone *m*

gory ['gɔːri] ADJ (*comp* **-ier**, *superl* **-iest**) (*battle, death*) sanguinoso(-a); **the gory details** (*hum*) i dettagli più scabrosi, i particolari più piccanti

gosh [gɒʃ] EXCL (*fam*) cribbio!, perdinci!

go-slow [ˌgəʊ'sləʊ] N (*Brit*) ≈ sciopero bianco

gospel ['gɒspəl] N **1** (*Rel*) vangelo; **the Gospel according to**

St John il Vangelo secondo (San) Giovanni; **you can take it as gospel** (*fam*) puoi giurarci **2** (*music*) gospel *m inv*

gos·sa·mer [ˈgɒsəməʳ] N (*fabric*) garza, mussolina; (*cobweb*) filo di ragnatela

gos·sip [ˈgɒsɪp] N (*talk*) chiacchiere *fpl*; (*scandal*) pettegolezzi *mpl*; (*person*) pettegolo(-a), chiacchierone(-a); **a piece of gossip** un pettegolezzo; **it's just gossip** sono solo pettegolezzi; **tell me the gossip!** dimmi le ultime! ♦ VI (*talk*) chiacchierare; **to gossip (about)** (*talk scandal*) fare pettegolezzi (su), chiacchierare (sul conto di)

gossip column N cronaca mondana

got [gɒt] PT, PP *of* **get**

Goth·ic [ˈgɒθɪk] ADJ gotico(-a)

got·ten [ˈgɒtn] (*USA*) PP *of* **get**

gouge [gaʊdʒ] VT (*also:* **gouge out**) (*hole etc*) scavare; (*initials*) scolpire; (*sb's eyes*) cavare

gourd [gʊəd] N zucca

gour·met [ˈgʊəmeɪ] N gourmet *m inv*, buongustaio(-a)

gout [gaʊt] N (*Med*) gotta

gov·ern [ˈgʌvən] VT (*rule: country*) governare; (*subj: king*) regnare (in); (*control: business*) dirigere; (*: city*) amministrare; (*: choice, decision*) regolare; (*: person*) guidare; (*: emotions*) dominare; (*Gram*) reggere

gov·er·ness [ˈgʌvənɪs] N governante *f*, istitutrice *f*

gov·ern·ing [ˈgʌvənɪŋ] ADJ (*Pol*) al potere, al governo; **governing class** classe *f* dirigente

gov·ern·ment [ˈgʌvənmənt] N governo; **local government** amministrazione *f* locale

gov·ern·men·tal [ˌgʌvənˈmentl] ADJ governativo(-a)

government housing N (*USA*) alloggi *mpl* popolari

government stock N titoli *mpl* di stato

gov·er·nor [ˈgʌvənəʳ] N **1** (*of colony, state, bank etc*) governatore *m*; (*director: of school, hospital*) membro del consiglio di amministrazione; (*Brit: of prison*) direttore(-trice) **2** (*of engine*) controllo automatico della velocità

Govt ABBR = **government**

gown [gaʊn] N (*dress*) abito; (*Law, Univ*) toga

GP [ˌdʒiːˈpiː] N ABBR (= *general practitioner*) medico generico; **who's your GP?** chi è il suo medico di famiglia?

GPO [ˌdʒiːpiːˈəʊ] N ABBR (*USA*: = *Government Printing Office*) ≈ Istituto poligrafico dello Stato

GPS [ˌdʒiːpiːˈes] ABBR (= *Global Positioning System*): **GPS receiver** GPS *m inv*

gr. ABBR (*Comm*) = **gross**

grab [græb] N **1** (*snatch*): **to make a grab at** *or* **for sth** cercare di afferrare qc **2** (*Tech*) benna ♦ VT (*seize*) afferrare, acchiappare; (*property, power*) impossessarsi di, impadronirsi di; (*greedily*) agguantare; (*fig: chance etc*) cogliere al volo; **he grabbed my arm** mi ha afferrato il braccio; **to grab sth from sb** strappare qc di mano a qn ♦ VI: **to grab at** tentare disperatamente di afferrare; (*in falling*) cercare di aggrapparsi a

grace [greɪs] N (*Rel: elegance: of form, movement etc*) grazia; (*graciousness*) garbo, cortesia; **the Graces** (*Myth*) le (tre) Grazie; **the grace of a dancer** la grazia di una ballerina; **he had the grace to apologise** ha avuto il buon gusto di scusarsi, per lo meno si è scusato; **to do sth with good/bad grace** fare qc volentieri/malvolentieri; **his sense of humour is his saving grace** il suo senso dell'umorismo è quello che lo salva; **three days' grace** tre giorni di proroga, una dilazione *f* di tre giorni; **by the grace of God** per grazia di Dio; **to say grace** dire una preghiera (*prima del pasto*); **to be in sb's good graces** essere nelle grazie di qn; **His Grace** (*duke, archbishop*) Sua Eccellenza ♦ VT (*adorn*) adornare; (*honour: occasion, event*) onorare con la propria presenza; **he graced the meeting with his presence** ci ha fatto l'onore di presenziare alla riunione

grace·ful [ˈgreɪsfʊl] ADJ (*gen*) aggraziato(-a), pieno(-a) di grazia; (*apology*) garbato(-a)

gra·cious [ˈgreɪʃəs] ADJ (*hostess, permission*) cortese; (*smile*) benevolo(-a); (*mansion*) di raffinata eleganza; (*God*) misericordioso(-a); **gracious living** vita da gran signore ♦ EXCL: (*good*) **gracious!** madonna (mia)!

gra·da·tion [grəˈdeɪʃən] N gradazione *f*

grade [greɪd] N **1** (*on scale*) categoria, livello; (*in hierarchy,*

also Mil) grado; (*Comm*) qualità *f inv*; (*size*) misura, grandezza; **grade A fruit** frutta di prima scelta; **to make the grade** (*fig*) essere all'altezza **2** (*Scol: mark*) voto; (*: USA: class*) classe *f*, anno; **good grades** bei voti **3** (*USA: gradient*) pendenza, gradiente *m* ♦ VT **1** (*goods, eggs*) classificare; (*level of difficulty*) graduare; **graded profile** (*Geol*) profilo di equilibrio **2** (*Scol: mark*) giudicare, dare un voto a

grade crossing N (*USA: Rail*) passaggio a livello

grade school N (*USA*) scuola elementare *or* primaria

gra·di·ent [ˈgreɪdɪənt] N **1** (*of road*) pendenza, gradiente *m*; **a gradient of 1 in 7** una pendenza del 7 per cento **2** (*Math, Phys*) gradiente *m*

grad·ual [ˈgrædjʊəl] ADJ (*change*) graduale; (*slope*) dolce, lieve

gradu·al·ly [ˈgrædjʊəlɪ] ADV gradualmente, poco alla volta

gradu·ate [*n* ˈgrædjʊɪt, *vb* ˈgrædjʊ,eɪt] N (*Univ*) laureato(-a); (*USA Scol*) diplomato(-a), licenziato(-a); **he's a French graduate** *or* **a graduate in French** è laureato *or* ha la laurea in francese ♦ VT (*thermometer etc*) graduare ♦ VI (*Univ*) ≈ laurearsi; (*USA Scol*) diplomarsi; **he graduated from London University last year** si è laureato alla London University l'anno scorso

❏ **graduate** is not translated by the Italian word *graduato*

gradu·at·ed pen·sion [ˈgrædjʊ,eɪtɪdˈpenʃən] N *pensione calcolata sugli ultimi stipendi*

gradua·tion [ˌgrædjʊˈeɪʃən] N (*Univ: ceremony*) consegna delle lauree; (*USA Scol*) consegna dei diplomi; **after graduation he went abroad** dopo la laurea è andato all'estero

graf·fi·ti [grəˈfiːti] NPL graffiti *mpl*

graft [grɑːft] N **1** (*Bot, Med*) innesto; **skin graft** innesto di pelle; **kidney graft** trapianto del rene **2** (*fam: corruption*) corruzione *f*; (*: hard work*) duro lavoro ♦ VT innestare

grain [greɪn] N **1** (*no pl: cereals*) cereali *mpl*; (*USA: corn*) grano **2** (*single seed: of wheat, rice etc*) chicco, granello; (*particle: of sand, salt, sense*) grano, granello; **there's not a grain of truth in what you say** non c'è un briciolo di verità in quello che dici **3** (*of wood, marble*) venatura; (*of leather, also Phot*) grana; **it goes against the grain** (*fig*) va contro la mia (*or* la sua *etc*) natura

gram, gramme [græm] N grammo

gram·mar [ˈgræməʳ] N grammatica; **that's bad grammar** è sgrammaticato; **a grammar book** un libro di grammatica

grammar school N (*Brit*) ≈ liceo

gram·mat·i·cal [grəˈmætɪkəl] ADJ (*exercise*) di grammatica; (*structure*) grammaticale; **to be grammatical** (*sentence, language*) essere corretto(-a) grammaticalmente; **grammatical rules** regole grammaticali; **grammatical English** inglese corretto dal punto di vista grammaticale

gramme [græm] N = **gram**

gramo·phone [ˈgræmə,fəʊn] N (*Brit*) grammofono

gran [græn] N (*Brit*) nonna

grana·ry [ˈgrænərɪ] N granaio

grand [grænd] ADJ (*comp* -**er**, *superl* -**est**) (*splendid: occasion, person*) splendido(-a), magnifico(-a); (*person: important*) altolocato(-a); (*style, house*) sontuoso(-a), grandioso(-a); (*fam: very pleasant*) eccezionale, stupendo(-a); **her house is very grand** la sua casa è molto sontuosa; **we had a grand time** ce la siamo proprio spassata ♦ N (*fam*) mille dollari *mpl* (*or* sterline *fpl*)

❏ **grand** is not translated by the Italian word *grande*

grand·ad, grand·dad [ˈgrænˌdæd] N (*Brit fam*) = **grandpa**

grand·child [ˈgræn,tʃaɪld] N (*pl* -**children**) nipote *m/f*, nipotino(-a) (*di nonni*)

grand·daughter [ˈgræn,dɔːtəʳ] N nipote *f*, nipotina (*di nonni*)

gran·deur [ˈgrændjəʳ] N (*of occasion, scenery etc*) grandiosità *f inv*, maestosità *f inv*; (*of style, house*) splendore *m*; **the grandeur of the scenery** lo splendore del paesaggio; **the grandeur of the occasion** la maestosità della cerimonia

grand·father [ˈgrænd,fɑːðəʳ] N nonno

gran·di·ose [ˈgrændɪəʊz] ADJ grandioso(-a); (*pej*) pomposo(-a)

grand jury N (*USA*) giuria (*formata da 12 a 23 membri*)

grand·ma [ˈgræn,mɑː], **grand·mama** [ˈgrænmə,mɑː] N (*fam*) nonna, nonnina

grand·mother [ˈɡræn‚mʌðəʳ] N nonna
grand·pa [ˈɡræn‚pɑː], **grand·papa** [ˈɡrænpə‚pɑː] N (fam) nonno, nonnino
grand·parent [ˈɡræn‚pɛərənt] N nonno(-a)
grand piano N pianoforte m a coda
Grand Prix [ɡrɒnˈpriː] N (Aut) Gran Premio, Grand Prix m inv
grand·son [ˈɡræn‚sʌn] N nipote m, nipotino (di nonni)
grand·stand [ˈɡræn‚stænd] N (Sport) tribuna coperta
grand total N somma complessiva
gran·ite [ˈɡrænɪt] N granito
gran·ny, gran·nie [ˈɡrænɪ] N (pl grannies) (fam) nonna, nonnina
grant [ɡrɑːnt] N (Admin: of money) sovvenzione f, sussidio; (Brit: Univ) ≈ borsa di studio; a grant to restore the church una sovvenzione per il restauro della chiesa; some students get grants alcuni studenti ottengono delle borse di studio ♦ VT (allow: extension, favour) accordare; (: pension) assegnare; (: a request) accogliere; (admit): to grant (that) ammettere (che), concedere (che); granted or granting that ... ammesso che...; I grant him that glielo concedo; he grants few interviews concede poche interviste; to take sth for granted dare qc per scontato; to take sb for granted non rendersi conto di quanto qn sia importante
granu·lat·ed [ˈɡrænjʊleɪtɪd] ADJ: **granulated sugar** zucchero semolato
gran·ule [ˈɡrænjuːl] N granello
grape [ɡreɪp] N acino, chicco d'uva; **grapes** NPL uva; **a bunch of grapes** un grappolo d'uva
  ❏ **grape** is not translated by the Italian word *grappa*
grape·fruit [ˈɡreɪp‚fruːt] N pompelmo
grape·vine [ˈɡreɪp‚vaɪn] N vite f; I heard it on the grapevine (fig) l'ho sentito dire
graph [ɡrɑːf] N grafico, diagramma m
graph·ic [ˈɡræfɪk] ADJ (gen) grafico(-a); (vivid: description etc) di grande efficacia, vivido(-a); the graphic arts le arti grafiche
graphic designer N grafico(-a)
graphic equalizer N equalizzatore m grafico
graph·ics [ˈɡræfɪks] N (sg: art, process) grafica; (pl: drawings) illustrazioni fpl
graph·ite [ˈɡræfaɪt] N grafite f
graph paper N carta millimetrata
grap·ple [ˈɡræpl] VI (wrestlers etc): to grapple (with) essere alle prese (con), lottare (con); to grapple with a problem (fig) essere alle prese con un problema
grap·pling iron [ˈɡræplɪŋ‚aɪən] N (Naut) grappino
grasp [ɡrɑːsp] VT (grip) presa; to lose one's grasp on reality (fig) perdere contatto con la realtà; to have sth within one's grasp avere qc a portata di mano; it is within everybody's grasp (fig) è alla portata di tutti; it is beyond my grasp non ci arrivo; to have a good grasp of (subject) avere una buona padronanza di; he has a good grasp of the difficulties si rende perfettamente conto dei problemi ♦ VT 1 (take hold of) afferrare; (hold firmly) stringere; (fig: chance, opportunity) cogliere (al volo) 2 (understand: meaning, hint) afferrare
  ▸ **grasp at** VI + PREP (rope etc) afferrarsi a, aggrapparsi a; (fig: opportunity) non farsi sfuggire, approfittare di
grasp·ing [ˈɡrɑːspɪŋ] ADJ (fig) avido(-a)
grass [ɡrɑːs] N 1 (plant) erba; (lawn) prato; (pasture) pascolo, prato; "keep off the grass" "vietato calpestare l'erba"; not to let the grass grow under one's feet (fig) non tirarla per le lunghe; to put out to grass (also fig) mettere a riposo 2 (slang: marijuana) erba
  ▸ **grass over** VT + ADV mettere a prato
grass·hopper [ˈɡrɑːs‚hɒpəʳ] N cavalletta
grass·land [ˈɡrɑːs‚lænd] N prateria
grass roots NPL (fig) base f
grass snake N biscia d'erba
grassy [ˈɡrɑːsɪ] ADJ (comp -ier, superl -iest) erboso(-a)
grate¹ [ɡreɪt] N (in fireplace) grata, griglia
grate² [ɡreɪt] VT 1 (cheese etc) grattugiare, grattare 2 (scrape: metallic object, chalk etc) far stridere; to grate one's teeth

digrignare i denti ♦ VI (hinge) cigolare, stridere; to grate (on or against) (chalk) stridere (su); it really grates (on me) (fig) mi dà veramente ai or sui nervi
grate·ful [ˈɡreɪtfʊl] ADJ: grateful (for) grato(-a) (per), riconoscente (per); I am most grateful to you le sono enormemente grato
grate·ful·ly [ˈɡreɪtfəlɪ] ADV con gratitudine
grat·er [ˈɡreɪtəʳ] N grattugia
grati·fi·ca·tion [‚ɡrætɪfɪˈkeɪʃən] N soddisfazione f
grati·fy [ˈɡrætɪfaɪ] VT (person) far piacere a, dare soddisfazione a; (desire, whim etc) soddisfare, appagare
grati·fy·ing [ˈɡrætɪ‚faɪɪŋ] ADJ gradito(-a), soddisfacente
grat·ing [ˈɡreɪtɪŋ] N (in wall, pavement) grata
grat·ing [ˈɡreɪtɪŋ] ADJ (sound) stridulo(-a), stridente
grati·tude [ˈɡrætɪtjuːd] N gratitudine f, riconoscenza
gra·tui·tous [ɡrəˈtjuːɪtəs] ADJ gratuito(-a)
gra·tu·ity [ɡrəˈtjuːɪtɪ] N (Mil) indennità f inv di congedo; (frm: tip) mancia
  ❏ **gratuity** is not translated by the Italian word *gratuità*
grave¹ [ɡreɪv] ADJ (comp -r, superl -st) (gen) grave, serio(-a); it had grave consequences for the nation si ripercosse pesantemente su tutta la nazione
grave² [ɡreɪv] N tomba
grave·dig·ger [ˈɡreɪv‚dɪɡəʳ] N becchino, affossatore m
grav·el [ˈɡrævəl] N ghiaia ♦ ADJ (path, pit) di ghiaia
grave·ly [ˈɡreɪvlɪ] ADV gravemente, solennemente; gravely ill in pericolo di vita
grave·stone [ˈɡreɪv‚stəʊn] N pietra tombale, lapide f
grave·yard [ˈɡreɪv‚jɑːd] N cimitero
gravi·tate [ˈɡrævɪ‚teɪt] VI (fig): to gravitate (towards) gravitare (verso)
grav·ity [ˈɡrævɪtɪ] N (all senses) gravità; the law of gravity la legge di gravità
gra·vy [ˈɡreɪvɪ] N (Culin) sugo dell'arrosto, intingolo della carne
gravy boat N salsiera
gravy train N: to ride the gravy train (esp USA: fam) aver trovato la cuccagna
gray [ɡreɪ] ADJ = grey
graze¹ [ɡreɪz] VI pascolare, pascere ♦ VT (grass, field) mettere or lasciare a pascolo; (cattle, sheep) far pascolare; they graze sheep in the mountains fanno pascolare le pecore in montagna
graze² [ɡreɪz] N (injury) scorticatura, escoriazione f ♦ VT (touch lightly) sfiorare, rasentare; (scrape: skin) scorticare, escoriare; to graze one's knees sbucciarsi or escoriarsi le ginocchia; I grazed my knee mi sono sbucciato un ginocchio
graz·ing [ˈɡreɪzɪŋ] N pascolo
grease [ɡriːs] N (fat) grasso, unto; (lubricant) grasso, lubrificante m ♦ VT (baking tin) ungere; (Aut, etc) ingrassare, lubrificare; like greased lightning (fam) come una saetta; to grease the skids (USA fig) spianare la strada
grease gun N ingrassatore m
grease·paint N cerone m
grease·proof pa·per [ˈɡriːs‚pruːf‚peɪpəʳ] N (Brit) carta oleata
greasy [ˈɡriːsɪ] ADJ (comp -ier, superl -iest) (substance etc) grasso(-a); (hair) untuoso(-a), grasso(-a); (Brit: road, surface) scivoloso(-a); (hands, clothes) unto(-a); (stains) d'unto
great [ɡreɪt] ADJ (comp -er, superl -est) 1 (gen) grande; (pain, heat) forte, intenso(-a); (care etc) molto(-a); (age) venerando(-a); they're great friends sono grandi amici; he was in great pain soffriva molto; it's of no great importance non ha molta importanza; he took great care to explain clearly si è impegnato per spiegare in modo chiaro; he's a great reader è un lettore accanito; a great oak tree una grande quercia; great big (fam) enorme; a great many moltissimi; Alexander the Great Alessandro Magno or il Grande; the great thing is that ... il bello è che...; great Scott! (fam) perbacco! 2 (fam: excellent) meraviglioso(-a), magnifico(-a), favoloso(-a); it was great! è stato fantastico!; he's great at football nel calcio è una cannonata; he's great on jazz sa tutto sul jazz; we had a great time ci siamo divertiti un mondo; you look great hai un aspetto splendido

Great Barrier Reef N: the Great Barrier Reef la grande barriera corallina

Great Britain N la Gran Bretagna

great-grandchild [ˌɡreɪtˈɡrænˌtʃaɪld] N (pl **-children**) pronipote m/f (di bisnonni)

great-grandfather [ˌɡreɪtˈɡrænˌfɑːðəʳ] N bisnonno

great-grandmother [ˌɡreɪtˈɡrænˌmʌðəʳ] N bisnonna

Great Lakes NPL: the Great Lakes i Grandi Laghi

great·ly [ˈɡreɪtlɪ] ADV (gen) molto; **greatly superior** di gran lunga superiore; **it is greatly to be regretted that ...** (frm) ci rincresce infinitamente che...; **you are greatly mistaken** ti sbagli di grosso

great·ness [ˈɡreɪtnɪs] N grandezza

Gre·cian [ˈɡriːʃən] ADJ greco(-a)

Greece [ɡriːs] N Grecia

greed [ɡriːd] N: **greed (for)** (for money) avidità (di), desiderio smodato (di); (for food: also: **greediness**) golosità (per), ingordigia (di); **greed for power** sete f di potere

greedi·ly [ˈɡriːdɪlɪ] ADV (see adj) avidamente; golosamente, ghiottamente, ingordamente

greedy [ˈɡriːdɪ] ADJ (comp **-ier**, superl **-iest**): **greedy (for)** (gen) avido(-a) (di); (for food) goloso(-a) (di), ghiotto(-a) (di), ingordo(-a) (di); **greedy for power** avido di potere

Greek [ɡriːk] ADJ greco(-a) ♦ N **1** (person) greco(-a); **the Greeks** i greci **2** (language) greco; **ancient/modern Greek** greco antico/moderno; **it's (all) Greek to me** (fam) per me è arabo

green [ɡriːn] ADJ (comp **-er**, superl **-est**) (colour, or Pol) verde; (unripe) acerbo(-a), verde; (inexperienced) alle prime armi, inesperto(-a); (gullible) ingenuo(-a); **a green car** una macchina verde; **dark green** verde scuro; **to have green fingers**, (USA) **to have a green thumb** (fig) avere il pollice verde; **to turn green** (fig: with nausea) sbiancare; (: with envy) diventare verde; **I'm not as green as I look!** (fig: fam) non sono mica nato ieri!; **green salad** insalata verde ♦ N **1** (colour) verde m; (grassy area) prato, spiazzo erboso; (bowling green) campo di bocce; (of golf course) green m inv; (also: **village green**) ≈ piazza del paese; **greens** NPL (Culin) verdura sg **2** (Pol): **the Greens** i verdi

green belt N (round town) cintura di verde

green card N (Brit: Aut) carta verde; (USA: residence permit) permesso di soggiorno

green·ery [ˈɡriːnərɪ] N verde m

green·fly [ˈɡriːnˌflaɪ] N afide m

green·gage [ˈɡriːnˌɡeɪdʒ] N susina Regina Claudia

green·grocer [ˈɡriːnˌɡrəʊsəʳ] N (Brit) fruttivendolo(-a); **"greengrocer's"** "frutta e verdura"

green·house [ˈɡriːnˌhaʊs] N serra

greenhouse effect N: the greenhouse effect l'effetto serra

greenhouse gas N gas m inv responsabile dell'effetto serra

green·ish [ˈɡriːnɪʃ] ADJ verdognolo(-a), verdastro(-a)

Green·land [ˈɡriːnlənd] N Groenlandia

Green·land·er [ˈɡriːnləndəʳ] N groenlandese m/f

green light N (of traffic light) verde m; **to give sb/sth the green light** dare il via libera a qn/qc ♦ VT (fam) dare il via libera a; **to be greenlighted** ottenere il via libera

green pepper N peperone m verde

green tax N ecotassa

greet [ɡriːt] VT accogliere, salutare; **a strange sight greeted his eyes** una strana scena si presentò ai suoi occhi; **the statement was greeted with loud laughter** l'affermazione fu salutata da or con grasse risate; **he greeted me with a kiss** mi ha salutata con un bacio

greet·ing [ˈɡriːtɪŋ] N saluto; (welcome) accoglienza; **greetings** NPL saluti mpl; **Season's greetings** Buone Feste; **Christmas/birthday greetings** auguri mpl di Natale/di compleanno

greeting card, greetings card N biglietto d'auguri

gre·gari·ous [ɡrɪˈɡɛərɪəs] ADJ (animal) gregario(-a); (person) socievole

gre·nade [ɡrɪˈneɪd] N (also: **hand grenade**) granata, bomba a mano

grew [ɡruː] PT of grow

grey [ɡreɪ] ADJ (comp **-er**, superl **-est**) grigio(-a); (complexion) smorto(-a); (outlook, prospect) poco roseo(-a); **a grey suit** un completo grigio; **to go grey** diventar grigio(-a), ingrigirsi; **to go grey with fear** (person) sbiancarsi in viso dalla paura; **grey skies** cielo grigio ♦ N (colour) grigio ♦ VI (hair) diventare grigio(-a)

grey-haired [ˌɡreɪˈhɛəd] ADJ dai capelli grigi

grey·hound [ˈɡreɪˌhaʊnd] N levriero

grid [ɡrɪd] N (grating) grata, griglia; (Elec, Gas: network) rete f; (on map) reticolato; (USA: Aut) area d'incrocio; **the national grid** la rete elettrica nazionale; **a grid of streets** una rete di strade
- ❏ **grid** is not translated by the Italian word grido

grid·dle [ˈɡrɪdl] N (esp USA) piastra

grid·iron [ˈɡrɪdˌaɪən] N graticola

grid·lock [ˈɡrɪdˌlɒk] N (traffic jam) paralisi f inv del traffico

grief [ɡriːf] N (sorrow) dolore m; (cause of sorrow) dolore, pena; **to come to grief** (plan) naufragare; (person) finire male; **good grief!** (fam) mio Dio!

griev·ance [ˈɡriːvəns] N (complaint) lagnanza, rimostranza; (cause for complaint) motivo di risentimento; **their main grievance is low pay** il loro principale motivo di risentimento è la paga bassa; **a sense of grievance** un senso di ingiustizia

grieve [ɡriːv] VT addolorare; **it grieves me to see ...** mi rattrista vedere... ♦ VI addolorarsi, soffrire; **to grieve for** or **over sb** (dead person) piangere qn; **she was grieving over the death of her husband** stava piangendo la morte di suo marito; **the family is still grieving** la famiglia è ancora in lutto; **I need time to grieve** ho bisogno di tempo per piangere la sua morte

grievous bodily harm N (Law) lesione f personale grave

grill [ɡrɪl] N **1** (Brit: on cooker) griglia; (gridiron) graticola; (in restaurant: also: **grillroom**) grill-room m inv; **a mixed grill** una grigliata mista **2** (also: **grille**) (grating) griglia; (at window) grata ♦ VT **1** (Culin) cuocere ai ferri or alla griglia; **grilled meat** carne ai ferri or alla griglia **2** (fam: interrogate) fare il terzo grado a

grille [ɡrɪl] N grata; (Aut) griglia

grill·room [ˈɡrɪlˌrʊm] N grill-room m inv

grim [ɡrɪm] ADJ (comp **-mer**, superl **-mest**) (hard, unpleasant: gen) duro(-a); (: struggle) accanito(-a); (: silence) sinistro(-a); (: landscape) desolato(-a); (: humour, tale) macabro(-a); (determined: face) risoluto(-a), determinato(-a); (determination) feroce; **to hold on (to sth) like grim death** attaccarsi (a qc) con le unghie e coi denti; **to feel grim** (fam: ill) sentirsi poco bene, sentirsi giù

gri·mace [ɡrɪˈmeɪs] N smorfia ♦ VI fare smorfie

grime [ɡraɪm] N sporcizia, sudiciume m

grimy [ˈɡraɪmɪ] ADJ sudicio(-a), sporco(-a)

grin [ɡrɪn] N (smile) sorriso smagliante; (cheeky) sorrisetto ♦ VI: **to grin (at)** fare un gran sorriso (a); **Dave grinned at me** Dave mi fece un gran sorriso; **to grin and bear it** stringere i denti e andare avanti

grind [ɡraɪnd] (pt, pp ground) VT (coffee, corn) macinare; (USA: meat) tritare, macinare; (car gears) grattare; (sharpen: knife) arrotare; (polish: gem, lens) molare; **have you ground the coffee?** hai macinato il caffè?; **to grind one's teeth** digrignare i denti; **to grind sth into the earth** schiacciare qc col piede ♦ VI stridere, cigolare; **to grind to a halt** (vehicle) rallentare fino a fermarsi; (fig: talks, scheme) insabbiarsi; (: work, production) cessare del tutto ♦ N (fam: work) sgobbata; **the daily grind** (fam) il tran tran m inv quotidiano
- ▸ **grind away** VI + ADV (fam) sgobbare
- ▸ **grind down** VT + ADV (substance) levigare; (fig: oppress) schiacciare, opprimere
- ▸ **grind on** VI + ADV continuare; **the years grind on** gli anni avanzano inesorabilmente
- ▸ **grind up** VT + ADV polverizzare

grind·er [ˈɡraɪndəʳ] N (machine: for coffee, pepper) macinino; (: for sharpening) affilacoltelli m inv

grind·stone [ˈɡraɪndˌstəʊn] N: **to keep one's nose to the grindstone** darci sotto or dentro

grip [ɡrɪp] N **1** presa; **to have a firm grip on sb/sth** tenere saldamente qn/qc; **to take a grip on oneself** farsi forza; **to lose one's grip** perdere or allentare la presa; (fig) perdere la grinta; **in the grip of the recession** (fig) nel pieno della recessione; **to get to grips with sb/sth** (*also fig*) venire alle prese con qn/qc; **to come to grips with** affrontare, cercare di risolvere; **to have a good grip of a subject** avere una buona padronanza di una materia; **get a grip on yourself!** (*fam*) controllati! **2** (*of racket, oar*) impugnatura **3** (*holdall*) sacca, borsa da viaggio ♦ VT **1** (*hold*) afferrare, stringere; **to grip the road** (*tyres* or *tires*) far presa sulla strada; (*car*) tenere bene la strada **2** (*fig: enthral*) far presa su; (: *subj: fear*) prendere

gripe [graɪp] N (*fam: complaint*) lagna; **the gripes** (*stomach ache*) colica ♦ VI (*fam: complain*): **to gripe (about)** lagnarsi (di)

grip·ping [ˈgrɪpɪŋ] ADJ (*story, novel*) avvincente, appassionante

gris·ly [ˈgrɪzlɪ] ADJ (*comp* **-ier**, *superl* **-iest**) (*murder*) raccapricciante

grist [grɪst] N (*fig*): **it's (all) grist to the mill** tutto aiuta

gris·tle [ˈgrɪsl] N cartilagine *f*

grit [grɪt] N (*gravel*) ghiaia; (*fig: courage*) fegato; **I've got a piece of grit in my eye** ho un bruscolino nell'occhio; *see also* **grits** ♦ VT **1** (*road*) ricoprire di ghiaia **2 to grit one's teeth** stringere i denti

grits [grɪts] NPL (*USA*) macinato grosso (di granturco)

griz·zle [ˈgrɪzl] VI (*Brit: cry*) piagnucolare

griz·zly [ˈgrɪzlɪ] N (*also:* **grizzly bear**) orso grigio, grizzly *m inv*

groan [grəʊn] N (*of pain*) gemito ♦ VI gemere; (*tree, floorboard*) scricchiolare; **he groaned with pain** gemette dal dolore

gro·cer [ˈgrəʊsə'] N negoziante *m/f* di (generi) alimentari; **grocer's (shop)** negozio di (generi) alimentari

gro·ceries [ˈgrəʊsərɪz] NPL (generi) alimentari *mpl*; **a shop selling groceries** un negozio che vende generi alimentari; **a bag of groceries** una borsa di roba da mangiare; **to go out for some groceries** fare la spesa

gro·cery [ˈgrəʊsərɪ], **grocery store** N (*shop*) negozio di (generi) alimentari

grog [grɒg] N grog *m inv*

grog·gy [ˈgrɒgɪ] ADJ (*comp* **-ier**, *superl* **-iest**) (*dazed*) stordito(-a), intontito(-a); (*shaky*) malfermo(-a), barcollante

groin [grɔɪn] N inguine *m*

groom [gruːm] N (*in stable*) palafreniere *m*; (*also:* **bridegroom**) sposo; **the groom and his best man** lo sposo e il suo testimone ♦ VT **1** (*horse*) pulire, strigliare **2** (*prepare: person*): **to groom sb for** avviare qn alla carriera di

groove [gruːv] N **1** (*in wood, metal*) solco, scanalatura; (*of record*) solco **2** (*fam: music*) ritmo

grope [grəʊp] VI (*also:* **grope around**, **grope about**) brancolare, andare a tentoni; **to grope for sth** cercare qc a tentoni or a tastoni; **he groped for the light switch** cercò a tentoni l'interruttore della luce; (*fig: for words*) cercare (disperatamente) ♦ VT: **to grope one's way through** farsi strada a tentoni in or tra; **to grope one's way towards** andare a tentoni verso; **to grope sb** (*fam: sexually*) mettere le mani addosso a qn

gross [grəʊs] ADJ (*comp* **-er**, *superl* **-est**) **1** (*fat: body*) obeso(-a); (*vegetation*) lussureggiante; (*behaviour, language, error*) grossolano(-a); (*impertinence*) sfacciato(-a); **it was really gross!** è stato veramente disgustoso! **2** (*total: profit, income*) complessivo(-a), totale; (*Comm: weight, income*) lordo(-a); **gross interest** interesse *m* lordo; **£10,000 gross** 10.000 sterline lorde ♦ N *pl inv* (*twelve dozen*) grossa ♦ VT (*Comm*) incassare, avere un incasso lordo di

❏ **gross** is not translated by the Italian word *grosso*

gross domestic product N prodotto interno lordo

gross·ly [ˈgrəʊslɪ] ADV (*exaggerate*) enormemente; (*overestimate*) di molto; **it's grossly unfair!** è proprio ingiusto!; **we're grossly underpaid** siamo decisamente sottopagati

gross national product N prodotto nazionale lordo

gro·tesque [grəʊˈtesk] ADJ grottesco(-a)

grot·to [ˈgrɒtəʊ] N grotta

grot·ty [ˈgrɒtɪ] ADJ (*Brit fam*) squallido(-a)

grouch [graʊtʃ] (*fam*) VI brontolare ♦ N (*person*) brontolone(-a)

ground¹ [graʊnd] N **1** (*soil*) terra, suolo, terreno; **the**

ground's wet la terra è bagnata; **on the ground** per terra **2** (*terrain*) terreno; **high ground** altura; **hilly ground** zona collinosa; **to gain/lose ground** guadagnare/perdere terreno; **to be on dangerous ground** muoversi su un terreno minato **3** (*surface*) terra; (*background*) terreno, sfondo; **on the ground** per terra, a terra; **above ground** in superficie; **below ground** sottoterra; **to fall to the ground** cadere a or per terra or al suolo; (*fig*) andare in fumo; **to get off the ground** (*aircraft*) decollare; (*plans*) prendere il via; **to stand one's ground** mantenere le proprie posizioni; **he covered a lot of ground in his lecture** ha toccato molti argomenti nel corso della conferenza **4** (*Sport*) campo; (*also:* **football ground**) campo di calcio; **grounds** NPL (*gardens*) giardini *mpl* **5 grounds** NPL (*of coffee*) fondi *mpl* (di caffè) **6** (*USA: Elec: also:* **ground wire**) (presa a) terra **7** (*reason: usu pl*) ragione *f*, motivo; **on medical grounds** per motivi di salute; **we've got grounds for complaint** abbiamo motivo or ragione di lamentarci; **on the ground(s) that** per il motivo che ♦ VT **1** (*plane, pilot*) bloccare a terra; (*ship*) far incagliare **2** (*argument, hope*) basare **3** (*USA: Elec*) mettere a terra ♦ VI (*Naut*) incagliarsi, arenarsi

ground² [graʊnd] PT, PP *of* **grind** ♦ ADJ (*coffee, pepper*) macinato(-a); **ground glass** vetro smerigliato; **ground rice** farina di riso; **ground meat** carne *f* macinata

ground cloth N (*USA*) = **groundsheet**

ground control N (*Aer, Space*) base *f* di controllo

ground floor N pianterreno, pianoterra *m*; **on the ground floor** al pianterreno

ground·ing [ˈgraʊndɪŋ] N (*educational*) fondamento, basi *fpl*; **he has a good grounding in French** ha delle buone basi in francese

ground·less [ˈgraʊndlɪs] ADJ infondato(-a)

ground·nut [ˈgraʊnd,nʌt] N arachide *f*

ground rules NPL: **the ground rules** i principi fondamentali

grounds·man [ˈgraʊndzmən] (*pl* **-men**), **grounds·keep·er** (*USA*) [ˈgraʊndz,kipə'] N (*Sport*) custode *m* (di campo sportivo)

ground staff N (*Aer*) personale *m* di terra

ground·swell [ˈgraʊnd,swel] N mareggiata; (*fig*) ondata

ground-to-air [ˈgraʊndtə'ɛə'] ADJ terra-aria *inv*

ground-to-ground [ˈgraʊndtə'graʊnd] ADJ terra-terra *inv*; **ground-to-ground missile** missile *m* terra-terra

ground·work [ˈgraʊnd,wɜːk] N lavoro preparatorio, preparazione *f*

group [gruːp] N (*gen*) gruppo; (*set, clique: of people*) circolo, gruppo; (*Mus: pop group*) complesso, gruppo ♦ VT (*also:* **group together**) raggruppare ♦ VI (*also:* **group together**) raggrupparsi ♦ ADJ (*discussion, photo*) di gruppo, collettivo(-a)

groupie [ˈgruːpɪ] N (*fam*) groupie *m/f*, fanatico seguace di un gruppo o cantante rock

group therapy N (*Psych*) terapia di gruppo

grouse¹ [graʊs] N *pl inv* gallo cedrone, urogallo

grouse² [graʊs] (*fam*) N (*complaint*) mugugno ♦ VI: **to grouse (about)** brontolare (su)

grove [grəʊv] N boschetto

grov·el [ˈgrɒvl] VI (*also fig*): **to grovel to** or **before sb** strisciare di fronte a qn

grow [grəʊ] (*pt* **grew**, *pp* **grown**) VT (*Agr*) coltivare, far crescere; (*business, economy*) far crescere; **to grow a beard** farsi crescere la barba; **I'm growing a beard** mi sto facendo crescere la barba; **he grew a moustache** si è fatto crescere i baffi; **he grew vegetables in his garden** coltivava ortaggi in giardino; **lettuce was grown by the Ancient Romans** gli antichi romani coltivavano l'insalata ♦ VI **1** (*plant, person, hair, business, economy*) crescere; (*increase: in numbers*) aumentare, salire; (: *in membership*) ingrandirsi; (*develop: friendship, love*) rafforzarsi; (: *custom, idea*) affermarsi, diffondersi; **haven't you grown!** come sei cresciuto!; **to grow in stature/popularity** veder aumentare il proprio prestigio/la propria popolarità **2** (*become*) farsi, diventare; **to grow dark** farsi buio; **to grow rich/weak** arricchirsi/indebolirsi; **to grow tired of waiting** stancarsi di aspettare; **to grow to like sb** imparare ad apprezzare qn

▸ **grow apart** VI + ADV (*fig*) estraniarsi

▸ **grow away from** VI + ADV + PREP (*fig*) allontanarsi da,

staccarsi da; **we have grown away from each other** i nostri rapporti si sono gradatamente raffreddati
▸ **grow in** vi + adv (*nail*) incarnarsi
▸ **grow into** vi + prep **1** (*clothes*): **he'll grow into them** quando crescerà gli andranno bene **2** (*become*) farsi, diventare
▸ **grow on** vi + prep: **that painting is growing on me** quel quadro più lo guardo più mi piace
▸ **grow out of** vi + adv + prep **1** (*clothes*) non entrare più in; (*habit*) perdere (col tempo); **he's grown out of his jacket** non entra più nella giacca; **he'll grow out of it** gli passerà **2** (*arise from*) nascere da, essere la conseguenza di
▸ **grow up** vi + adv **1** (*become adult*) diventar grande, crescere; **I grew up in the country** sono cresciuto in campagna; **I grew up in Rome** sono cresciuto a Roma; **grow up!** (*fam*) non fare il bambino! **2** (*develop: idea, friendship*) nascere

grow·er [ˈɡrəʊəʳ] n (*Agr*) coltivatore(-trice); (*of wine*) viticoltore(-trice)

grow·ing [ˈɡrəʊɪŋ] adj (*fear, amount*) crescente; **to have a growing desire to do sth** avere un desiderio sempre più forte di fare qc

growl [ɡraʊl] n (*of animal*) ringhio; (*of thunder*) brontolio; **the dog gave a growl** il cane ringhiò ◆ vi ringhiare; (*person, thunder*) brontolare

grown [ɡrəʊn] pp of **grow** ◆ adj (*also:* **fully grown**) adulto(-a), grande; **he's a grown man** è un adulto

grown-up [ˈɡrəʊnˈʌp] adj da grande; **he's very grown-up** è molto maturo ◆ n grande *m/f*, adulto(-a)

growth [ɡrəʊθ] n **1** (*increase*) crescita, aumento; (*development*) sviluppo; **economic growth** crescita economica; **he has 5 days' growth (of beard)** ha una barba di 5 giorni; **to reach full growth** raggiungere il pieno sviluppo **2** (*Med*) tumore *m*

growth rate n (*Econ*) tasso di crescita

grub [ɡrʌb] n **1** (*larva*) bruco **2** (*fam: food*) roba da mangiare; **grub('s) up!** si mangia!, a tavola!; **get yourself some grub** prenditi qc da mangiare

grub·by [ˈɡrʌbɪ] adj (*comp* **-ier**, *superl* **-iest**) sudicio(-a), sporco(-a)

grudge [ɡrʌdʒ] n: **grudge (against)** risentimento (verso), rancore *m* (verso); **to bear a grudge against sb** portare *or* serbare rancore a qn ◆ vt: **to grudge sb sth** (*money*) dare qc a qn malvolentieri *or* a malincuore; **I don't grudge you your success** non t'invidio il tuo successo; **to grudge doing sth** fare qc malvolentieri *or* a malincuore

grudg·ing·ly [ˈɡrʌdʒɪŋlɪ] adv (*accept, support*) malvolentieri, a malincuore

gru·el·ling, gru·el·ing (USA) [ˈɡrʊəlɪŋ] adj estenuante

grue·some [ˈɡruːsəm] adj orrendo(-a), orribile, agghiacciante

gruff [ɡrʌf] adj (*comp* **-er**, *superl* **-est**) burbero(-a)

grum·ble [ˈɡrʌmbl] n (*complaint*) lamentela; (*noise*) brontolio; (*of guns*) rombo; **without a grumble** (*agree, accept*) senza lagnarsi ◆ vi (*person: complain*): **to grumble (about)** brontolare (su), lagnarsi (di); (*thunder*) rombare

grumpy [ˈɡrʌmpɪ] adj (*comp* **-ier**, *superl* **-iest**) scorbutico(-a)

grunge [ɡrʌndʒ] n (*Mus*) grunge *m*; (*style*) moda grunge

grunt [ɡrʌnt] n grugnito; **to give a grunt** emettere un grugnito ◆ vi grugnire

G-string [ˈdʒiːstrɪŋ] n (*garment*) tanga *m inv*

GU abbr (USA Post: = Guam)

guar·an·tee [ˌɡærənˈtiː] n garanzia; (*guarantor*) garante *m/f*, mallevadore *m*; **a year's guarantee** (*on appliances, watch etc*) un anno di garanzia; **it's still under guarantee** è ancora in garanzia; **there's no guarantee that it won't happen again** nessuno ti garantisce che non accadrà di nuovo ◆ vt (*gen*) garantire; **I can't guarantee that he did it** non posso garantire che lo abbia fatto; **he can't guarantee (that) he'll come** non può garantire che verrà

guar·an·tor [ˌɡærənˈtɔːʳ] n garante *m/f*, mallevadore *m*

guard [ɡɑːd] n **1** (*gen, also Mil, Sport*) guardia; (*security guard*) guardia giurata; (*esp USA: prison guard*) secondino; (*Brit: Rail*) ≈ capotreno; (*also:* **guard duty**: *watch*) (turno di) guardia, turno di vigilanza; (*fig: watchfulness*) vigilanza; **to change guard**

(*Mil*) cambiare la guardia; **to be on guard** (*Mil*) essere di guardia; **to be on one's guard** (*fig*) stare in guardia; **to keep sb under guard** tenere qn sotto vigilanza; **to catch sb off his/her guard** cogliere *or* prendere qn alla sprovvista; **to keep guard over sb/sth** (*Mil, also fig*) fare la guardia a qn/qc **2** (*safety device: on machine*) schermo protettivo; (*protection*) riparo, protezione *f*; (*also:* **fire guard**) parafuoco; (*mud guard*) parafango ◆ vt (*prisoner, treasure*) fare la guardia a, stare a guardia di; (*secret*) custodire; (*protect*): **to guard (against or from)** proteggere (da), salvaguardare (da); **they guarded the palace** facevano la guardia al palazzo ◆ adj: **guard duty** turno di guardia; **on guard duty** di guardia
▸ **guard against** vi + prep (*take care to avoid: illness*) guardarsi da; (: *suspicion, accidents*) premunirsi contro; **to guard against doing sth** guardarsi dal fare qc
❑ **guard** is not translated by the Italian word *guardare*

guard dog n cane *m* da guardia

guard·ed [ˈɡɑːdɪd] adj (*reply, tone*) guardingo(-a), cauto(-a), circospetto(-a)

guard·ian [ˈɡɑːdɪən] n custode *m/f*; (*of minor*) tutore(-trice); **parent or guardian** genitore o tutore
❑ **guardian** is not translated by the Italian word *guardiano*

Gua·te·ma·la [ˌɡwɑːtɪˈmɑːlə] n Guatemala *m*

Guern·sey [ˈɡɜːnzɪ] n (*island*) (isola di) Guernsey *f*; (*cow*) mucca di Guernsey

guer·ril·la [ɡəˈrɪlə] n guerrigliero(-a); **guerrilla group** gruppo di guerriglieri; **guerrilla tactics** tattica di guerriglia

guerrilla warfare n guerriglia

guess [ɡes] n supposizione *f*, congettura; **to take** *or* **make** *or* **have a guess** cercare di indovinare, provare a indovinare; **have a guess!** prova a indovinare!; **at a (rough) guess** a occhio e croce; **my guess is that …** suppongo che…; **it's anybody's guess** Dio solo (lo) sa; **your guess is as good as mine** ne so quanto te; **it's just a guess** è solo una supposizione ◆ vt **1** (*gen*) indovinare; **can you guess what it is?** sai cos'è?; **guess what!** (*fam*) sai l'ultima?; **I guessed as much** me lo immaginavo **2** (*esp USA: suppose*) supporre, credere; **I guess so** direi di sì, suppongo di sì; **I guess you're right** forse hai ragione ◆ vi **1** indovinare; **to guess at sth** provare a indovinare qc; **to guess correctly** azzeccarci; **she's just guessing** sta tirando a indovinare; **to keep sb guessing** tenere qn in sospeso *or* sulla corda **2** (*esp USA: suppose*) supporre, credere; **he's happy, I guess** è felice, immagino

guess·ti·mate [ˈɡestɪmɪt] n (*fam*) stima approssimativa

guess·work [ˈɡeswɜːk] n congettura; **I got the answer by guesswork** ho azzeccato la risposta; **it remains a matter of guesswork** resta un mistero

guest [ɡest] n (*in house, on TV programme*) ospite *m/f*; (*at party*) invitato(-a); (*at hotel*) cliente *m/f*; (*in boarding house*) pensionante *m/f*; **we have guests staying with us** abbiamo degli ospiti da noi; **guest of honour** ospite d'onore; **be my guest** (*fam*) fai come ti pare

guest·house [ˈɡesthaʊs] n pensione *f*

guest room n stanza *or* camera degli ospiti

guff [ɡʌf] n (*fam*) stupidaggini *fpl*, assurdità *fpl*

guf·faw [ɡʌˈfɔː] n risata fragorosa *or* sonora ◆ vi ridere fragorosamente

guid·ance [ˈɡaɪdəns] n (*counselling*) consigli *mpl*, guida; (*leadership*) guida, direzione *f*; **for your guidance** a titolo informativo; **help and guidance** aiuto e consigli; **vocational guidance** consulenza per l'avviamento professionale

guide [ɡaɪd] n **1** (*gen*) guida; (*manual*) guida, manuale *m*; (*fig: indication, model*) indicazione *f*; **let conscience be your guide** lasciati guidare dalla coscienza; **as a rough guide** approssimativamente **2 Guide** (*Brit*) Giovane Esploratrice *f*; **the Guides** le Giovani Esploratrici ◆ vt guidare; **to be guided by sb/sth** farsi *or* lasciarsi guidare da qn/qc

guide·book [ˈɡaɪdbʊk] n guida

guided missile n missile *m* teleguidato

guide dog n cane *m* per ciechi

guide·lines [ˈɡaɪdlaɪnz] npl (*fig*) direttive *fpl*

guild [ɡɪld] n (*History*) corporazione *f*, arte *f*, gilda; (*club*) associazione *f*

guild·hall [ˈɡɪldˌhɔːl] N (*Brit: town hall*) (palazzo del) municipio

guile [ɡaɪl] N astuzia

guile·less [ˈɡaɪllɪs] ADJ franco(-a), candido(-a)

guil·lo·tine [ɡɪləˈtiːn] N ghigliottina; (*for paper*) taglierina

guilt [ɡɪlt] N (*being guilty*) colpevolezza; (*feeling guilty*) colpa, senso di colpa; **feelings of guilt** sensi di colpa; **tormented by guilt** tormentato(-a) dal senso di colpa; **they were convinced of his guilt** erano convinti della sua colpevolezza

guilty [ˈɡɪltɪ] ADJ (*comp* -**ier**, *superl* -**iest**) (*gen, also Law*) colpevole; (*conscience*) sporco(-a); **guilty of sth** colpevole di qc; **to have a guilty conscience** avere la coscienza sporca; **the guilty person** *or* **party** il (la) responsabile; **to feel guilty (about)** sentirsi in colpa (per); **he felt guilty about lying to her** si sentiva in colpa per averle mentito; **to find sb guilty** riconoscere qn colpevole; **she was found guilty** fu riconosciuta colpevole; **to plead guilty/not guilty** dichiararsi colpevole/innocente

Guinea [ˈɡɪnɪ] N: **Republic of Guinea** la Repubblica di Guinea

guinea [ˈɡɪnɪ] N (*Brit: old*) ghinea, ≈ 21 shillings

guinea pig N porcellino d'India, cavia; (*fig*) cavia

guise [ɡaɪz] N maschera, parvenza; **under the guise of** mascherato da

gui·tar [ɡɪˈtɑːʳ] N chitarra

gui·tar·ist [ɡɪˈtɑːrɪst] N chitarrista *m/f*

gulch [ɡʌltʃ] N (*USA*) burrone *m*

gulf [ɡʌlf] N (*bay*) golfo; (*chasm, also fig*) abisso; **the (Persian) Gulf** il Golfo Persico; **there's a gulf between rich and poor** c'è un abisso tra ricchi e poveri

Gulf States NPL: **the Gulf States** gli stati del Golfo Persico

Gulf Stream N: **the Gulf Stream** la corrente del Golfo

gull [ɡʌl] N gabbiano

gul·let [ˈɡʌlɪt] N gargarozzo

gul·li·bil·ity [ˌɡʌlɪˈbɪlɪtɪ] N credulità, semplicioneria

gul·lible [ˈɡʌlɪbl] ADJ credulone(-a), sempliciotto(-a)

gul·ly [ˈɡʌlɪ] N (*ravine*) burrone *m*, gola; (*channel*) canale *m* di scolo

gulp [ɡʌlp] N (*of liquid*) sorso; (*of food*) boccone *m*; **a gulp of tea** un sorso di te; **in** *or* **at one gulp** in un sorso, (tutto) d'un fiato ♦ VT (*also*: **gulp down**) tranguiare, tracannare, inghiottire; **I quickly gulped my tea** ho buttato giù in fretta il mio tè ♦ VI (*while drinking*) deglutire; (*through fear*) sentirsi serrare la gola; (*from emotion*) avere un nodo alla gola

gum[1] [ɡʌm] N (*Anat*) gengiva; **gums** le gengive; **my gums are bleeding** mi sanguinano le gengive

gum[2] [ɡʌm] N (*glue*) colla; (*also*: **gum tree**) albero della gomma; (*chewing gum*) gomma americana, chewing-gum *m inv*; (*sweet*) caramella gommosa; **I'm chewing gum** sto masticando una gomma ♦ VT (*stick together*) incollare, ingommare; (*also*: **gum down**: *label*) attaccare, incollare; **gummed label** etichetta adesiva

  ▸ **gum up** VT + ADV: **to gum up the works** (*fam*) mettere il bastone tra le ruote

gum·boil [ˈɡʌmˌbɔɪl] N ascesso gengivale

gum·boots [ˈɡʌmˌbuːts] NPL (*Brit*) stivali *mpl* di gomma

gump·tion [ˈɡʌmpʃən] N (*fam: initiative*) spirito d'iniziativa; (: *common sense*) buon senso, senso pratico

gun [ɡʌn] N (*handgun*) pistola, rivoltella; (*rifle*) fucile *m*, carabina; (*shotgun*) fucile da caccia; (*cannon*) cannone *m*; **gun barrel** canna di fucile; **to draw a gun on sb** spianare la pistola contro qn; **to carry a gun** portare la pistola; **the big guns** (*Mil*) l'artiglieria pesante; (*fig: fam: people*) i pezzi grossi; **to stick to one's guns** (*fig*) tener duro; **to be going great guns** (*fam*) andare a tutto gas ♦ VT (*also*: **gun down**) abbattere a colpi di pistola *or* fucile

  ▸ **gun for** VI + PREP (*fig*) avercela a morte con

gun·boat [ˈɡʌnˌbəʊt] N cannoniera

gun dog N cane *m* da caccia

gun·fire [ˈɡʌnˌfaɪəʳ] N colpi *mpl* d'arma da fuoco, spari *mpl*

gung-ho [ˈɡʌŋˈhəʊ] ADJ (*fam*) fanatico(-a); (*eager to fight in war*) guerrafondaio(-a)

gunk [ɡʌŋk] N porcherie *fpl*

gun·man [ˈɡʌnmən] N (*pl* -**men**) bandito; (*hired*) sicario

gun·ner [ˈɡʌnəʳ] N artigliere *m*

gun·point [ˈɡʌnˌpɔɪnt] N: **at gunpoint** sotto la minaccia delle armi

gun·powder [ˈɡʌnˌpaʊdəʳ] N polvere *f* da sparo

gun·runner [ˈɡʌnˌrʌnəʳ] N trafficante *m/f* *or* contrabbandiere(-a) di armi

gun·running [ˈɡʌnˌrʌnɪŋ] N traffico *or* contrabbando d'armi

gun·shot [ˈɡʌnˌʃɒt] N (*noise*) sparo; **within gunshot** a portata di tiro

gun·smith [ˈɡʌnˌsmɪθ] N armaiolo

gur·gle [ˈɡɜːɡl] N (*all senses*) gorgoglio ♦ VI gorgogliare, ciangottare

guru [ˈɡʊruː] N (*Rel, also fig*) guru *m inv*

gush [ɡʌʃ] N (*of liquid*) getto, fiotto; (*of blood*) fiotto; (*of feeling*) ondata ♦ VI **1** (*also*: **gush out**: *water, blood*): **to gush (from)** sgorgare (da); **water gushed from the pipe** l'acqua sgorgava dal tubo **2** (*pej: enthuse*): **to gush (about** *or* **over)** abbandonarsi ad effusioni

gush·ing [ˈɡʌʃɪŋ] ADJ (*water*) zampillante; (*pej: person*) svenevole; (: *compliments*) affettato

gus·set [ˈɡʌsɪt] N (*in tights, pants*) rinforzo; (*in skirt*) gherone *m*; (*in glove*) quadrello

gust [ɡʌst] N (*of wind*) folata; (*stronger*) raffica; (*of rain*) scroscio; (*of smoke*) sbuffo; (*of laughter*) scoppio

  ❏ **gust** is not translated by the Italian word *gusto*

gus·to [ˈɡʌstəʊ] N: **with gusto** di *or* con gusto

gusty [ˈɡʌstɪ] ADJ (*comp* -**ier**, *superl* -**iest**) (*wind*) a raffiche; (*day*) tempestoso(-a)

gut [ɡʌt] N **1** (*Anat*) intestino; (*for violin, racket*) minugia, budello; **the human gut** l'intestino umano **2 guts** NPL (*fam: innards*) budella *fpl*; (: *of animals*) interiora *fpl*; (: *fig: courage*) fegato; **it takes guts** ci vuole fegato; **blood and guts** sangue e interiora; **to hate sb's guts** odiare qn a morte ♦ VT **1** (*poultry, fish*) levare le interiora a, sventrare **2** (*building*): **the blaze gutted the entire building** le fiamme hanno sventrato completamente l'edificio

gut reaction N reazione *f* istintiva

gutsy [ˈɡʌtsɪ] ADJ (*comp* -**ier**, *superl* -**iest**) (*fam: style*) che ha mordente; (: *plucky*) coraggioso(-a)

gutted [ˈɡʌtɪd] ADJ (*fam: upset*) distrutto(-a)

gut·ter [ˈɡʌtəʳ] N (*in street*) cunetta, (canaletta di) scolo; (*on roof*) grondaia; **to rise from the gutter** (*fig*) venire dai bassifondi *or* dalla strada

gut·tur·al [ˈɡʌtərəl] ADJ gutturale

guy[1] [ɡaɪ] N (*fam: man*) tizio, tipo; (*effigy*) fantoccio che si brucia la notte di Guy Fawkes; **a tough guy** un duro; **he's a nice guy** è simpatico; **who's that guy?** chi è quel tipo?; *see also* **wise guy**

guy[2] [ɡaɪ] N (*also*: **guy-rope**: *for tent*) tirante *m*, cavo

Guy·ana [ɡaɪˈænə] N Guyana

guz·zle [ˈɡʌzl] VT (*food*) ingozzare; (*drink*) tracannare; (*hum: petrol*) bere ♦ VI gozzovigliare

gym [dʒɪm] N (*gymnasium*) palestra; (*gymnastics*) ginnastica; **I go to the gym every day** vado in palestra ogni giorno; **gym classes** corso di ginnastica

gym·kha·na [dʒɪmˈkɑːnə] N gimcana

gym·na·sium [dʒɪmˈneɪzɪəm] N palestra

gym·nast [ˈdʒɪmnæst] N ginnasta *m/f*

gym·nas·tics [dʒɪmˈnæstɪks] NSG (*art*) ginnastica ♦ NPL (*exercises*) ginnastica

gym shoes NPL scarpe *fpl* da ginnastica

gy·nae·colo·gist, gy·ne·colo·gist (*USA*) [ˌɡaɪnɪˈkɒlədʒɪst] N ginecologo(-a)

gy·nae·col·ogy, gy·ne·col·ogy (*USA*) [ˌɡaɪnɪˈkɒlədʒɪ] N ginecologia

gyp·sy, gip·sy [ˈdʒɪpsɪ] N zingaro(-a) ♦ ADJ (*life*) da zingaro, zingaresco(-a); (*caravan*) degli zingari; (*music*) zigano(-a)

gy·rate [dʒaɪəˈreɪt] VI (*spin*) roteare, girare (su se stesso); (*dance*) volteggiare

gy·ro·scope [ˈdʒaɪərəskəʊp] N giroscopio

Hh

H, h [eɪtʃ] N (*letter*) H, h *f inv, m inv*; **H for Harry**, (*USA*) **H for How** = H come hotel

ha·beas cor·pus [ˌheɪbɪəs ˈkɔːpəs] N (*Law*) habeas corpus *m inv*

hab·er·dash·ery [ˌhæbəˈdæʃərɪ] N merceria; (*USA*) camiceria

hab·it [ˈhæbɪt] N 1 (*customary behaviour, individual habit*) abitudine *f*; **a bad habit** una brutta *or* cattiva abitudine; **to be in the habit of doing sth** avere l'abitudine di fare qc; **to fall into bad habits** prendere delle cattive abitudini; **to get out of/into the habit of doing sth** perdere/prendere l'abitudine di fare qc; **to get sb into the habit of doing sth** abituare qn a fare qc; **don't make a habit of it!** che non diventi un'abitudine! 2 (*dress: of monk, nun*) tonaca; (: *riding habit*) costume *m* da amazzone 3 (*fam: addiction*) assuefazione
□ **habit** is not translated by the Italian word *abito*

hab·it·able [ˈhæbɪtəbl] ADJ abitabile

habi·tat [ˈhæbɪˌtæt] N habitat *m inv*

habi·ta·tion [ˌhæbɪˈteɪʃən] N abitazione *f*; **fit for human habitation** abitabile

ha·bitu·al [həˈbɪtjʊəl] ADJ abituale, consueto(-a); (*drunkard, smoker*) incallito(-a); (*liar*) inveterato(-a); **his habitual geniality** la sua consueta genialità; **habitual criminals** delinquenti abituali; **a habitual burglar** un ladro incallito

ha·bitu·al·ly [həˈbɪtjʊəlɪ] ADV abitualmente, d'abitudine

hack¹ [hæk] N (*of sword, axe*) colpo; (*of sabre*) fendente *m* ♦ VT 1 (*cut*) tagliare; **to hack one's way through** aprirsi un varco (a colpi d'ascia *etc*) tra; **to hack sth to pieces** tagliare a pezzi qc 2 **to hack into** (*Comput: program, system*) inserirsi illegalmente in
▸ **hack down** VT + ADV (*tree etc*) abbattere (a colpi d'ascia *etc*)

hack² [hæk] N 1 (*old horse*) ronzino; (*ride*) passeggiata a cavallo 2 (*pej: writer*) scribacchino(-a); **to do hack writing** fare lo scribacchino(-a) ♦ VI: **to go hacking** (andare a) fare una passeggiata a cavallo

hack·er [ˈhækə'] N (*Comput*) hacker *m/f inv*

hack·les [ˈhæklz] NPL: **to make sb's hackles rise** (*fig*) far arrabbiare qn

hack·ney cab [ˈhæknɪˌkæb] N carrozza a nolo

hack·neyed [ˈhæknɪd] ADJ (*saying*) trito(-a); **hackneyed expression** luogo comune; **a hackneyed metaphor** una metafora trita e ritrita

hack·saw [ˈhækˌsɔː] N seghetto per metalli

had [hæd] PT, PP *of* **have**

had·dock [ˈhædək] N eglefino (*tipo di merluzzo*)

hadn't [ˈhædnt] = had not

haema·tol·ogy, hema·tol·ogy (*USA*) [ˌhiːməˈtɒlədʒɪ] N ematologia

haemo·glo·bin, hemo·glo·bin (*USA*) [ˌhiːməʊˈɡləʊbɪn] N emoglobina

haemo·philia, hemo·philia (*USA*) [ˌhiːməʊˈfɪlɪə] N emofilia

haem·or·rhage, hem·or·rhage (*USA*) [ˈhɛmərɪdʒ] N emorragia ♦ VI avere un'emorragia

haem·or·rhoids, hem·or·rhoids (*USA*) [ˈhɛmə.rɔɪdz] NPL emorroidi *fpl*

hag [hæɡ] N (*ugly*) befana; (*nasty*) megera; (*witch*) strega

hag·gard [ˈhæɡəd] ADJ (*careworn*) tirato(-a); (*gaunt*) smunto(-a)

hag·gis [ˈhæɡɪs] N (*Scot: Culin*) insaccato a base di avena e frattaglie di pecora

hag·gle [ˈhæɡl] VI: **to haggle (over)** (*bargain*) contrattare (su); (*argue*) discutere (su); **I didn't haggle over the price** non ho contrattato sul prezzo

hag·gling [ˈhæɡlɪŋ] N contrattazione *f*

Hague [heɪɡ] N: **the Hague** l'Aia

hail¹ [heɪl] N (*Met*) grandine *f*; (*fig: of bullets*) pioggia; (: *of abuse*) valanga ♦ VI grandinare; **it's hailing** grandina

hail² [heɪl] N (*greeting, call*) grido di saluto; **within hail** a portata d'orecchio ♦ EXCL (*old, liter*): **hail, Caesar!** ave, Cesare! ♦ VT (*acclaim*): **to hail (as)** acclamare (come); (*greet*) salutare; (*signal: taxi*) fermare; (*call*) chiamare; **he was hailed in the press as a hero** la stampa lo acclamò come un eroe ♦ VI: **where does that ship hail from?** qual è il porto di provenienza di quella nave?; **he hails from Scotland** viene dalla Scozia

hail·stone [ˈheɪlˌstəʊn] N chicco di grandine

hail·storm [ˈheɪlˌstɔːm] N grandinata

hair [hɛə'] N 1 (*collective: of person*) capelli *mpl*; (: *on body*) peli *mpl*; (: *of animal*) pelo; **to comb one's hair** pettinarsi; **to do one's hair** acconciarsi; **to put one's hair up** raccogliersi i capelli; **to have one's hair done** andare dal parrucchiere; **to get one's hair cut** farsi tagliare i capelli; **to remove unwanted hair** (*from legs, armpits*) depilarsi; **to make sb's hair stand on end** far rizzare i capelli (in testa) a qn; **to let one's hair down** (*fig*) lasciarsi andare 2 (*single hair: of head*) capello; (: *of body, animal*) pelo; **he's got hairs on his chest** ha il petto villoso; **to split hairs** (*fig*) spaccare il capello in quattro, cercare il pelo nell'uovo; **try a hair of the dog (that bit you)** (*fam*) prendi un bicchierino per farti passare la sbornia

hair·band [ˈhɛəˌbænd] N (*elastic*) fascia per i capelli; (*rigid*) cerchietto

hair·brush [ˈhɛəˌbrʌʃ] N spazzola per capelli

hair·cut [ˈhɛəˌkʌt] N taglio (di capelli); **a nice haircut** un bel taglio; **to have** *or* **get a haircut** farsi tagliare i capelli; **I need a haircut** devo tagliarmi i capelli

hair·do [ˈhɛəˌduː] N (*fam*) pettinatura

hair·dresser [ˈhɛəˌdrɛsə'] N parrucchiere(-a); **at the hairdresser's** dal parrucchiere

hair·dryer [ˈhɛəˌdraɪə'] N asciugacapelli *m inv*, föhn *m inv*

-haired [hɛəd] ADJ SUFF: **fair/long-haired** dai capelli biondi/lunghi

hair·grip [ˈhɛəˌɡrɪp] N molletta (per i capelli)

hair·line [ˈhɛəˌlaɪn] N attaccatura dei capelli; **to have a receding hairline** essere stempiato(-a)

hairline fracture N (*Med*) frattura capillare

hair·net [ˈhɛəˌnɛt] N retina (per capelli)

hair oil N brillantina

hair·piece [ˈhɛəˌpiːs] N toupet *m inv*

hair·pin¹ [ˈhɛəˌpɪn] N forcina; **fasten it with hairpins** fissalo con delle forcine

hairpin², hairpin bend, (*USA*) **hairpin curve** N tornante *m*

hair·raising [ˈhɛəˌreɪzɪŋ] ADJ (*story, adventure*) da far rizzare i capelli, terrificante

hair remover N crema depilatoria

hair spray N lacca per capelli

hair·style [ˈhɛəˌstaɪl] N pettinatura, acconciatura

hairy [ˈhɛərɪ] ADJ (*comp* **-ier**, *superl* **-iest**) 1 peloso(-a), irsuto(-a) 2 (*fam: frightening*) da far rizzare i capelli

Hai·ti [ˈheɪtɪ] N Haiti *f*

hake [heɪk] N nasello

hal·al [həˈlɑːl] ADJ: **halal meat** carne macellata secondo la legge mussulmana

hal·cy·on [ˈhælsɪən] ADJ sereno(-a)

hale [heɪl] ADJ: **hale and hearty** che scoppia di salute

half [hɑːf] N (*pl* **halves**) 1 (*part*) metà *f inv*, mezzo(-a); **half (of it)** la metà; **half (of)**, **half the amount of** la metà di; **half of the cake** metà torta; **one half of the apple** la *or* una metà della mela; **half an orange** mezza arancia; **half a dozen** mezza dozzina; **half a pound** mezza libbra; **half a kilo** mezzo chilo; **two and a half** due e mezzo; **half an hour**

mezz'ora; **three and a half hours** tre ore e mezza; **half of my friends** (la) metà dei miei amici; **to cut in half/into halves** tagliare a metà/in due; **I can do the job in half the time** posso fare il lavoro in metà del tempo; **half the time I don't know what he's talking about** spesso non so di che cosa stia parlando; **his** (*or* **her**) **better half** (*fam*, *hum*) la sua (dolce) metà; **she doesn't do things by halves** non fa mai le cose a metà; **to go halves** (**with sb**) fare a metà (con qn); **bigger by half** una volta e mezzo più grande; **he's too clever by half** (*fam*) è troppo furbo per i miei gusti, per favore **2** (*Sport: of match*) tempo; (: *of ground*) metà campo; (: *player*) mediano; **left/right half** mediano sinistro/destro **3** (*of beer*) mezza pinta **4** (*child's ticket*) (ridotto per) bambino ♦ ADJ (*bottle, quantity, fare, pay*) mezzo(-a), metà *inv*; **a half chicken** mezzo pollo; **half a glass, a half glass** (un) mezzo bicchiere; **half measures** mezze misure *fpl* ♦ ADV **1** (a) metà, (a) mezzo; **half empty/closed** mezzo(-a) vuoto(-a)/chiuso(-a), semivuoto(-a)/semichiuso(-a); **half asleep** mezzo(-a) addormentato(-a); **she's half French, half Italian** è mezza francese, mezza italiana; **half as big** (**as**) la metà (di); **half as big again** una volta e mezzo più grande; **I was half afraid that ...** avevo un po' paura che... + *sub*; **not half!** (*fam*) altroché!, eccome!; **it isn't half hot!** (*fam*) scotta! **2** (*time*): **half past 3** le 3 e mezza; **half past 12** le 12 e mezza

half·back [ˈhɑːfˌbæk] N (*Sport*) mediano

half-baked [ˌhɑːfˈbeɪkt] ADJ (*fig: fam: idea, scheme*) mal combinato(-a), che non sta in piedi

half board (*Brit*) N mezza pensione

half-brother [ˈhɑːfˌbrʌðəʳ] N fratellastro

half-caste [ˈhɑːfˌkɑːst] N meticcio(-a) (*offensive*)

half day N mezza giornata

half fare N tariffa a metà prezzo

half-hearted [ˌhɑːfˈhɑːtɪd] ADJ (*effort*) poco convinto(-a), svogliato(-a); **he made a half-hearted attempt** ha fatto un mezzo tentativo

half-hour [ˌhɑːfˈaʊəʳ] N mezz'ora

half-mast [ˌhɑːfˈmɑːst] N: **at half-mast** (*flag*) a mezz'asta

half·penny [ˈheɪpnɪ] N (*pl* **-pennies** *or* **-pence** [ˈheɪpəns]) (*Brit*) mezzo penny *m inv*

half-price [ˈhɑːfˈpraɪs] ADV, ADJ a metà prezzo; **I bought it half-price** l'ho comprato a metà prezzo

half-sister [ˌhɑːfˈsɪstəʳ] N sorellastra

half term N (*Brit Scol*) vacanza a *or* di metà trimestre

half-time [ˌhɑːfˈtaɪm] N (*Sport*) intervallo ♦ ADJ, ADV all'intervallo; **to work half-time** lavorare mezza giornata

half·way [ˈhɑːfˈweɪ] ADV a metà strada; **Reading is halfway between Oxford and London** Reading è a metà strada tra Oxford e Londra; **halfway up** (*or* **down**) **the stairs** a metà delle scale; **to meet sb halfway** (*fig*) arrivare a un compromesso con qn; **halfway through sth** a metà di qc; **halfway through the film** a metà del film; **we are halfway through the work** abbiamo fatto metà del lavoro ♦ ADJ (*mark*) di mezzo; **halfway line** (*Sport*) linea mediana

halfway house N (*hostel*) centro di riadattamento alla vita sociale per ex detenuti; (*fig*) via di mezzo; **to be a halfway house between** essere una via di mezzo tra

half-wit [ˈhɑːfˌwɪt] N grullo(-a), idiota *m/f*

half-yearly [ˈhɑːfˈjɪəlɪ] ADV semestralmente, ogni sei mesi ♦ ADJ semestrale

hali·but [ˈhælɪbət] N ippoglosso, halibut *m inv*

hali·to·sis [ˌhælɪˈtəʊsɪs] N alitosi *f*

hall [hɔːl] N **1** (*entrance hall*) ingresso, entrata; (*USA: passage*) corridoio; **he hung his coat in the hall** ha appeso il cappotto nell'ingresso; **her room is down the hall** la sua camera è in fondo al corridoio **2** (*large room*) salone *m*, sala; **church hall** sala dell'oratorio; **a concert hall** una sala concerti; **a sports hall** una palestra; **village hall** sala comunale a disposizione del pubblico **3** (*mansion*) palazzo, maniero, grande villa; (*Brit: Univ: also*: **hall of residence**) ≈ casa dello studente

hall·mark [ˈhɔːlˌmɑːk] N (*also fig*) marchio

hal·lo [həˈləʊ] EXCL = **hello**

Hal·low·een [ˌhæləʊˈiːn] N vigilia d'Ognissanti (31 di ottobre)

hal·lu·ci·na·tion [həˌluːsɪˈneɪʃən] N allucinazione *f*

hal·lu·ci·no·gen·ic [həˌluːsɪnəʊˈdʒenɪk] ADJ allucinogeno(-a)

hall·way [ˈhɔːlˌweɪ] N (*corridor*) corridoio; (*entrance*) ingresso

halo [ˈheɪləʊ] N (*of saint*) aureola; (*Astron*) alone *m*

halt [hɔːlt] N sosta, fermata; (*train stop*) fermata; **to come to a halt** fermarsi, arrestarsi; **to call a halt (to sth)** (*fig*) mettere *or* porre fine (a qc) ♦ VT (*vehicle, production*) fermare, arrestare; **the government failed to halt economic decline** il governo non è riuscito ad arrestare il declino economico ♦ VI fermarsi, arrestarsi; **halt!** alt!

hal·ter [ˈhɔːltəʳ] N (*for horse*) cavezza

halter·neck [ˈhɔːltəˌnek] ADJ allacciato(-a) dietro il collo

halve [hɑːv] VT (*divide*): **to halve (between)** dividere a metà *or* in due (tra); (*reduce by half*) dimezzare, ridurre della metà; **halve the apples** dividi a metà le mele; **the workforce has been halved** la manodopera è stata dimezzata

halves [hɑːvz] NPL *of* **half**

ham [hæm] N **1** (*Culin*) prosciutto; **a ham sandwich** un panino al prosciutto; **ham and eggs** uova *fpl* al prosciutto **2** (*fam: radio ham*) radioamatore(-trice); (: *ham actor*) gigione(-a)

▸ **ham up** VT + ADV: **to ham it up** (*fam*) fare l'esagerato(-a)

Ham·burg [ˈhæmbɜːg] N Amburgo *f*

ham·burg·er [ˈhæmˌbɜːgəʳ] N hamburger *m inv*

ham-fisted [ˌhæmˈfɪstɪd], **ham-handed** (*USA*) [ˌhæmˈhændɪd] ADJ maldestro(-a)

ham·let [ˈhæmlɪt] N paesetto, paesino

ham·mer [ˈhæməʳ] N (*tool*) martello; (*of gun*) percussore *m*; **to go at it hammer and tongs** (*fam: work*) darci dentro; (: *argue*) azzuffarsi ♦ VT martellare; (*fig: fam: defeat*) stracciare; (: *thrash*) picchiare; **to hammer nails into wood** piantare chiodi nel legno; **to hammer sth into shape** (*metal*) dare una forma a qc col martello; (*fig: team, plan*) mettere a punto qc; **to hammer a point home to sb** cacciare un'idea in testa a qn ♦ VI dare colpi di martello; **to hammer on** *or* **at the door** picchiare alla porta

▸ **hammer down** VT + ADV (*lid*) fissare con colpi di martello; (*nail*) piantare (a martellate)

▸ **hammer out** VT + ADV (*metal*) spianare (a martellate); (*fig: solution, agreement*) mettere a punto

ham·mock [ˈhæmək] N amaca

ham·per [ˈhæmpəʳ] N (*basket*) cesto, cestino

ham·per [ˈhæmpəʳ] VT (*hinder*) impedire, ostacolare

ham·ster [ˈhæmstəʳ] N criceto

ham·string [ˈhæmˌstrɪŋ] (*pt, pp* **hamstrung**) N (*Anat*) tendine *m* del ginocchio; (*of horse*) corda del garretto ♦ VT tagliare i tendini delle gambe a; (*fig*) tagliare le gambe a

hand [hænd] N **1** (*of person*) mano *f*; (*of clock*) lancetta; **to have in one's hand** (*knife, victory*) avere in mano *or* in pugno; (*book, money*) avere in mano; **to take sb by the hand** prendere per mano qn; **on** (**one's**) **hands and knees** carponi, a quattro zampe; **wash your hands!** lavati le mani!; **hands up!** (*during hold-up*) mani in alto!; (*to pupils*) alzate la mano!; **hands off!** (*fam*) giù le mani!; **to be clever** *or* **good with one's hands** avere le mani d'oro; **made/delivered by hand** fatto(-a)/consegnato(-a) a mano; **to live from hand to mouth** vivere alla giornata; **they gave him a big hand** (*fig*) gli hanno fatto un bell'applauso **2** (*worker: in factory*) operaio(-a), manovale *m*; (: *farm hand*) bracciante *m/f*; (: *ship hand*) marinaio; **all hands on deck!** (*Naut*) tutti in coperta!; **to be an old hand** essere vecchio(-a) del mestiere **3** (*liter: handwriting*) scrittura, mano *f*; **in one's own hand** di proprio pugno, di propria mano **4** (*Cards*) mano *f*; **a hand of bridge/poker** una mano a bridge/poker **5** (*measurement: of horse*) ≈ dieci centimetri **6** (*phrases with verb*): **to be hand in glove with sb** essere in combutta con qn; **to change hands** (*property*) cambiare (di) mano; **to force sb's hand** forzare la mano a qn; **to give** *or* **lend sb a hand** dare una mano a qn; **to keep one's hand in** tenersi in esercizio, non perdere la mano; **she can turn her hand to anything** sa fare un po' di tutto; **he asked for her hand (in marriage)** ha chiesto la sua mano; **to wait on sb hand and foot** essere a totale disposizione di qn; **to have one's hands full (with sb/sth)** essere troppo preso(-a) (con qn/qc); **to win hands down** vincere senza difficoltà; **to be making/losing money hand over fist** fare/perdere un sacco di soldi; **to have a free hand** avere carta bianca; **to have the upper hand** avere la meglio *or* il sopravvento; **to have a hand in sth** essere immischiato(-a)

in qc **7** (*phrases with prep before n*): **at hand** a portata di mano; **to be near** *or* **close at hand** essere a due passi; **at first hand** di prima mano; **hand in hand** mano nella mano; **to go hand in hand (with)** (*fig*) andare insieme (a); **to be in sb's hands** essere nelle mani di qn; **in hand** (*work*) in corso; **to have £50 in hand** avere ancora 50 sterline a disposizione; **we have the situation in hand** abbiamo la situazione sotto controllo; **we have the matter in hand** ci stiamo occupando della cosa; **to take sb in hand** controllare qn; **to play into sb's hands** fare il gioco di qn; **to fall into the hands of the enemy** cadere in mano al nemico; **on hand** (*person*) disponibile; (*object*) sottomano, a portata di mano; (*emergency services*) pronto(-a) a intervenire; **on the right/left hand** sulla destra/sinistra; **on the other hand** d'altra parte; **on the one hand ... on the other hand ...** da un lato..., dall'altro...; **to have sth left on one's hands** ritrovarsi con qc, rimanere con qc; **to take sth off sb's hands** togliere qc di torno a qn; **to condemn sb out of hand** condannare qn a priori; **to get out of hand** sfuggire di mano; **to hand** (*information*) a portata di mano ♦ VT (*pass*): **to hand sb sth, hand sth to sb** passare qc a qn; **he handed me the book** mi passò il libro; **you've got to hand it to him** (*fam*) questo glielo devi riconoscere; **it was handed to him on a plate** (*fam*) glielo hanno dato su un piatto d'argento
  ► **hand back** VT + ADV restituire
  ► **hand down** VT + ADV (*suitcase*) passare, dare (*con movimento dall'alto al basso*); (*tradition*) tramandare; (*heirloom*) lasciare in eredità; (*USA: sentence, verdict*) emettere
  ► **hand in** VT + ADV (*form*) consegnare; (*resignation*) rassegnare, dare; **Martin handed his exam paper in** Martin consegnò il compito scritto
  ► **hand on** VT + ADV trasmettere, dare, passare
  ► **hand out** VT + ADV (*leaflets*) distribuire; (*advice*) elargire; **the teacher handed out the books** l'insegnante distribuì i libri
  ► **hand over** VT + ADV consegnare; (*powers, property, business*) cedere; **she handed the keys over to me** mi ha consegnato le chiavi
  ► **hand round** VT + ADV (*information, papers*) far circolare; (*distribute: chocolates, cakes*) far girare; (*subj: hostess*) offrire
hand·bag ['hændˌbæg] N borsa, borsetta
hand baggage N bagaglio a mano
hand·ball ['hændˌbɔːl] N pallamano *f*; **we played handball** giocavamo a pallamano
hand·basin ['hændˌbeɪsn] N lavandino
hand·book ['hændˌbʊk] N (*manual*) manuale *m*, libretto di istruzioni; (*for tourists*) guida (turistica)
hand·brake ['hændˌbreɪk] N freno a mano
hand cream N crema per le mani
hand·cuff ['hændˌkʌf] VT ammanettare ♦ N: **handcuffs** NPL manette *fpl*
hand·ful ['hændfʊl] N (*quantity*) manciata, pugno; **a handful of sand** una manciata di sabbia; **a handful of people** un gruppetto di persone; **that child's a real handful** (*fam*) quel bambino è proprio un terremoto
hand-held ['hænd'held] ADJ a mano ♦ N portatile *m inv*
handi·cap ['hændɪˌkæp] N (*fig, also Sport*) handicap *m inv* ♦ VT (*disable*) handicappare, menomare; (*hamper*) ostacolare; **to be handicapped** essere handicappato
handi·craft ['hændɪˌkrɑːft] N (*art*) lavoro artigianale; **handicrafts** NPL (*products*) prodotti di artigianato
handi·work ['hændɪˌwɜːk] N (*work*) lavoro, opera; (*craft work*) lavorazione *f* a mano; **this looks like his handiwork** (*pej*) qui c'è il suo zampino
hand·ker·chief ['hæŋkətʃɪf] N fazzoletto
han·dle ['hændl] N (*gen*) manico; (*of knife*) manico, impugnatura; (*of door, drawer*) maniglia; (*of wheelbarrow*) stanga; (*of pump*) braccio; (*for winding*) manovella; (*of cup*) ansa; **he was too small to reach the door handle** era troppo piccolo per arrivare alla maniglia della porta; **a knife with a plastic handle** un coltello con il manico di plastica; **to fly off the handle** (*fig*) perdere le staffe, uscire dai gangheri ♦ VT **1** (*touch*) toccare; **"handle with care" "fragile"; the police handled him roughly** è stato malmenato dalla polizia; **to handle the ball** (*Ftbl*) fare un fallo di mano **2** (*deal with: theme*) trattare; (: *situation*) far fronte a; (: *resources*) amministrare; (*cope*

with: people) saper come prendere; (: *animals*) occuparsi di; (*Comm: goods*) trattare, occuparsi di; (*ship, car*) manovrare; (*use: gun, machine, money*) maneggiare; **I'll handle this** me ne occupo io, ci penso io; **Kathy handled the travel arrangements** Kathy si è occupata dell'organizzazione del viaggio; **she's good at handling children** sa come trattare i bambini; **it was a difficult situation, but he handled it well** era una situazione difficile, ma l'ha gestita bene; **we handle 2000 travellers a day** abbiamo un traffico di 2000 passeggeri al giorno ♦ VI (*ship, plane, car*) rispondere ai comandi
handle·bars ['hændlˌbɑːz] NPL , **handle·bar** ['hændlˌbɑːʳ] N (*on bicycle*) manubrio
han·dling ['hændlɪŋ] N **1** (*touching, fingering*) maneggio; **these goods have been damaged through too much handling** questa merce è danneggiata perché è stata maneggiata troppo **2** (*of theme, animals*) trattamento; (*of resources*) amministrazione *f*; (*of car, ship*) controllo; (*of gun*) maneggiamento; **he was criticized for his handling of the situation/the crowd** fu criticato per il suo modo di affrontare *or* trattare la situazione/la folla
handling charges NPL (*for goods*) commissione *f* per la prestazione; (*Banking*) spese *fpl* bancarie
hand·luggage ['hændˌlʌgɪdʒ] N bagaglio a mano
hand·made [ˌhænd'meɪd] ADJ (*clothes, paper*) fatto(-a) a mano; (*biscuits*) fatto(-a) in casa
hand·out ['hændˌaʊt] N (*leaflet*) volantino; (*press handout*) comunicato stampa; (*at lecture*) fotocopia; (*fam: money*) elemosina; **a state handout** una sovvenzione statale
hand-picked [ˌhænd'pɪkt] ADJ (*staff, team*) scelto(-a); (*produce*) scelto(-a), selezionato(-a)
hand·rail ['hændˌreɪl] N (*on staircase*) corrimano
hand·set ['hændset] N (*Telec*) ricevitore *m*
hands-free [ˌhænds'friː] ADJ (*telephone*) con auricolare; (*microphone*) vivavoce *inv*
hand·shake ['hændˌʃeɪk] N stretta di mano
hand·some ['hænsəm] ADJ (*comp* **-r**, *superl* **-st**) (*gen*) bello(-a); (*salary*) buono(-a); (*considerable: profit, fortune*) considerevole, grosso(-a); (*reward*) generoso(-a); **my father's very handsome** mio padre è un bell'uomo
hands-on [ˌhændz'ɒn] ADJ (*approach*) pragmatico(-a); (*training*) pratico(-a); **hands-on experience** esperienza diretta *or* pratica
hand·stand ['hændˌstænd] N: **to do a handstand** fare la verticale
hand-to-mouth [ˌhændtə'maʊθ] ADJ (*existence*) precario(-a)
hand·writing ['hændˌraɪtɪŋ] N scrittura, calligrafia
hand-written ['hændˌrɪtn] ADJ (*gen*) scritto(-a) a mano, manoscritto(-a); (*text, musical score*) manoscritto(-a)
handy ['hændɪ] ADJ (*comp* **-ier**, *superl* **-iest**) **1** (*close at hand*) a portata di mano, sottomano **2** (*convenient*) comodo(-a); (*useful: machine, gadget*) pratico(-a), utile; **this knife's very handy** questo coltello è molto pratico; **have you got a pen handy?** hai una penna a portata di mano?; **to come in handy** tornare utile; **that would come in very handy** farebbe proprio molto comodo; **the money came in very handy** il denaro è tornato molto utile **3** (*fam: skilful*) bravo(-a); **he's handy with a paintbrush** è proprio bravo come imbianchino
handy·man ['hændɪˌmæn] N (*pl* **-men**) (*paid*) tuttofare *m inv*; (*amateur*) uno bravo a fare piccole riparazioni e lavoretti; **the hotel's handyman** il tuttofare dell'albergo
hang [hæŋ] (*pt, pp* **hung**) VT **1** (*gen*) appendere; (*washing*) stendere; (*door*) montare (sui cardini); (*wallpaper*) mettere, incollare; (*coat, hat*): **to hang (on)** appendere (a); **Mike hung the painting on the wall** Mike ha appeso il quadro al muro; **the walls were hung with tapestries** i muri erano coperti di arazzi; **the Christmas tree was hung with lights** l'albero di Natale era decorato di *or* con luci colorate **2** (*pt, pp* **hanged**; *criminal*) impiccare; **in the past criminals were hanged** in passato i criminali venivano impiccati; **hang (it)!** (*fam*) accidenti!, porca miseria! **3 to hang one's head** abbassare la testa (per la vergogna) ♦ VI **1** (*rope, dangling object*): **to hang (from)** penzolare (a), pendere (da); (*garment*) cadere; (*hair*) scendere; (*criminal*) essere impiccato(-a); **there was a red bulb hanging from the ceiling** c'era una lampadina rossa che pendeva dal soffitto; **that dress hangs well** quel vestito cade bene **2 to hang over** (*smoke, fog*)

sovrastare; (*threat*) incombere su; (*hawk*) essere sospeso(-a) su ♦ N: **he couldn't get the hang of the game** (*fam*) non riusciva ad afferrare il senso del gioco; **you'll soon get the hang of this** (*fam*) ti farai presto la mano a questo
► **hang about** VI + ADV (*also:* **hang around**) (*loiter*) gironzolare, ciondolare; (*wait*) rimanere ad aspettare; **to keep sb hanging about** far aspettare qn; **they hang around all day playing computer games** non fanno niente tutto il giorno e giocano col computer ♦ VI + PREP (*the streets*) aggirarsi per
► **hang back** VI + ADV (*hesitate*): **to hang back (from doing)** essere riluttante (a fare)
► **hang down** VI + ADV ricadere ♦ VT + ADV far ricadere
► **hang on** VI + PREP 1 (*depend on: decision*) dipendere da 2 (*listen eagerly*) bersi le parole di; **she hung on his every word** pendeva dalle sue labbra ♦ VI + ADV 1 (*keep hold*): **to hang on (to)** aggrapparsi (a), attaccarsi (a); **to hang on to** (*keep*) tenere 2 (*fam: wait*) aspettare; **hang on a minute!** aspetta un momento!; (*polite: on phone*) attenda un attimo!
► **hang out** VT + ADV (*washing*) stendere (fuori); (*flags*) metter fuori ♦ VI + ADV 1 **to hang out of sth** penzolare *or* pendere fuori da qc; **his shirt was hanging out** gli usciva la camicia dai pantaloni 2 (*fam: frequent*) frequentare; **he hangs out in the local bars** bazzica nei bar locali
► **hang together** VI + ADV (*fam: people*) stare insieme; (*cohere: argument*) stare in piedi
► **hang up** VT + ADV (*coat*) appendere; (*picture*) attaccare, appendere ♦ VI + ADV (*Telec*) riattaccare, riagganciare; **to hang up on sb** metter giù il ricevitore a qn
hang·ar [ˈhæŋəʳ] N hangar *m inv*, aviorimessa
hang·dog [ˈhæŋˌdɒg] ADJ (*guilty: look, expression*) da cane bastonato
hang·er [ˈhæŋəʳ] N (*for clothes*) ometto, gruccia
hanger-on [ˌhæŋəˈrɒn] N (*pl* **hangers-on**) (*pej*) parassita *m/f*
hang·glider [ˈhæŋˌglaɪdəʳ] N deltaplano (*velivolo*)
hang·gliding [ˈhæŋˌglaɪdɪŋ] N (volo col) deltaplano
hang·ing [ˈhæŋɪŋ] N 1 (*execution*) impiccagione *f* 2 (*curtains*); **hangings** N pl tende *fpl*, tendaggi *mpl* ♦ ADJ (*bridge*) sospeso(-a); (*offence, matter*) da punire con l'impiccagione; **hanging lamp** lampadario
hang·man [ˈhæŋmən] N (*pl* -**men**) boia *m inv*
hang·over [ˈhæŋˌəʊvəʳ] N 1 (*after drinking*) postumi *mpl* della sbornia; **I woke up with a hangover** mi sono svegliato con un cerchio alla testa 2 (*sth left over*) residuato
hang-up [ˈhæŋˌʌp] N (*fam*) complesso, ossessione *f*
hank [hæŋk] N (*of wool*) matassa; (*of hair*) ciocca; (*Naut*) garroccio
hank·er [ˈhæŋkəʳ] VI: **to hanker after** *or* **for** (*fame, power*) essere assetato(-a) di, bramare; (*sympathy, possessions*) desiderare intensamente
hank·er·ing [ˈhæŋkərɪŋ] N: **to have a hankering for sth/to do sth** avere una voglia matta di qc/di fare qc
hanky [ˈhæŋkɪ] N (*fam: handkerchief*) fazzoletto
Hants ABBR (*Brit:* = Hampshire)
hap·haz·ard [ˌhæpˈhæzəd] ADJ (fatto(-a)) a caso *or* a casaccio; (*arrangement*) casuale, fortuito(-a)
hap·less [ˈhæplɪs] (*liter*) ADJ (*wretched*) disgraziato(-a); (*unfortunate*) sventurato(-a)
hap·pen [ˈhæpən] VI 1 succedere, accadere, capitare; **what's happening?** cosa succede?, cosa sta succedendo?; **what happened?** cos'è successo?; **these things will happen** sono cose che capitano *or* succedono; **don't let it happen again** che non si ripeta *or* succeda mai più; **as if nothing had happened** come se niente fosse; **what has happened to him?** (*befallen*) cosa gli è successo?; (*become of*) che fine ha fatto?; **if anything should happen to him** ... se gli dovesse accadere qualcosa... 2 (*chance*): **it happened that** ... si dava il caso che...; **do you happen to know** ... sai per caso se...; **if anyone should happen to see John** se a qualcuno capita di vedere John; **I happen to know that** ... si dà il caso che io sappia che...; **she happened to be free** per caso era libera; **as it happens** (per) combinazione; **it so happened that** ... guarda caso...
► **happen on, happen upon** VI + PREP imbattersi in
hap·pen·ing [ˈhæpnɪŋ] N (*event*) avvenimento, evento; (*in theatre*) happening *m inv*

hap·pi·ly [ˈhæpɪlɪ] ADV (*contentedly: play, work*) tranquillamente; (*cheerfully: say*) con gioia; (: *laugh*) con allegria; (*fortunately*) per fortuna, fortunatamente; **he's happily married** è felicemente sposato; **and they lived happily ever after** e vissero per sempre felici e contenti; **happily, everything went well** fortunatamente tutto è andato bene
hap·pi·ness [ˈhæpɪnɪs] N felicità, contentezza, gioia
hap·py [ˈhæpɪ] ADJ (*comp* -**ier**, *superl* -**iest**) 1 (*pleased, content*) contento(-a), felice; (*cheerful*) allegro(-a); (*at ease, unworried*) tranquillo(-a); **Janet looks happy** Janet sembra felice; **happy with** (*arrangements*) soddisfatto(-a) di; **we are not entirely happy about the plan** non siamo del tutto contenti del progetto; **we're very happy for you** ci rallegriamo per te, siamo molto felici per te; **yes, I'd be happy to** (*certo*), con piacere, (ben) volentieri; **I'm very happy with your work** sono molto soddisfatto del tuo lavoro; **I am happy to tell you that** ... sono felice *or* ho il piacere di informarti che...; **a happy ending** un lieto fine; **to be as happy as a lark** essere felice *or* contento(-a) come una pasqua; **happy birthday!** buon compleanno!; **happy Christmas/New Year!** buon Natale/anno! 2 (*well-chosen: phrase, idea*) felice, indovinato(-a); (*lucky: position*) fortunato(-a), favorevole; **by a happy chance** per fortuna
happy-go-lucky [ˈhæpɪgəʊˌlʌkɪ] ADJ spensierato(-a)
happy hour N orario in cui le consumazioni alcoliche in un bar hanno prezzi ridotti
ha·rangue [həˈræŋ] N tirata, arringa ♦ VT arringare
har·ass [ˈhærəs] VT (*attack persistently*) tormentare; (*trouble*) assillare
har·assed [ˈhærəst] ADJ (*under attack*) tormentato(-a); (*troubled*) assillato(-a); (*under pressure*) stressato(-a)
har·ass·ment [ˈhærəsmənt] N (*action*) persecuzione *f*; (*less severe*) molestia; (*feeling*) insofferenza; **sexual harassment** molestie sessuali
har·bour, har·bor (*USA*) [ˈhɑːbəʳ] N porto ♦ VT (*hold: grudge, resentment*) covare, nutrire; (*shelter: criminal, spy*) dar rifugio a, tener nascosto(-a)
harbour dues, harbor dues (*USA*) NPL diritti *mpl* portuali
harbour master, harbor master (*USA*) N capitano di porto
hard [hɑːd] (*comp* -**er**, *superl* -**est**) ADJ 1 (*substance*) duro(-a); (*mud*) indurito(-a); **this cheese is very hard** questo formaggio è davvero duro; **to grow hard** indurirsi; **hard cover** (*of book*) copertina cartonata; **a hard nut to crack** (*problem, person*) un osso duro 2 (*severe, tough: gen*) duro(-a); (: *climate, weather, winter*) rigido(-a); (: *frost*) forte; **to take a long hard look at sth** esaminare qc attentamente; **the hard fact is that** ... la verità nuda e cruda è che...; **a hard luck story** una storia pietosa; **he's as hard as nails** (*physically*) è forte come un toro *or* una quercia; (*in temperament*) è duro di cuore; **to take a hard line over sth** adottare una linea dura in merito a qc; **to be hard on sb** essere severo(-a) con qn; **to be a hard worker** essere un(a) gran (grande) lavoratore(-trice) 3 (*difficult: gen*) arduo(-a), difficile; **this exercise is too hard for me** quest'esercizio è troppo difficile per me; **I find it hard to believe that** ... stento *or* faccio fatica a credere che... + *sub*; **to be hard to please** essere esigente, essere difficile da accontentare ♦ ADV (*push*) forte; (*work*) sodo; (*think, try*) bene; (*hit*) forte, duramente; **to work hard** lavorare sodo; **to freeze hard** gelare; **it's snowing/raining hard** sta nevicando/piovendo forte; **he was breathing hard** respirava affannosamente; **to be hard hit** (*fig*) essere duramente colpito(-a); **to be hard at it** (*fam*) darci dentro; **to be hard put (to it) to do sth** essere in difficoltà a fare qc; **to try one's hardest to do sth** fare di tutto per fare qc; **to take sth hard** prendere (molto) male qc; **to be hard up for sth** essere a corto di qc; **to look hard at sth** guardare fissamente, esaminare attentamente
hard-and-fast [ˌhɑːdənˈfɑːst] ADJ ferreo(-a)
hard·back [ˈhɑːdbæk] N (*book*) libro con copertina rigida *or* in edizione rilegata ♦ ADJ (*edition*) rilegato(-a)
hard·board [ˈhɑːdbɔːd] N faesite *f*
hard-boiled [ˌhɑːdˈbɔɪld] ADJ (*egg*) sodo(-a); (*fig: tough, cynical*) duro(-a)
hard cash N (denaro) contante
hard copy N copia su carta; **on hard copy** su carta; (*Comput*) hard copy *f inv*

hard-core [ˌhɑːd'kɔːr] ADJ 1 (*pornography*) hard-core *inv* 2 (*supporters*) irriducibile ♦ N 1 (*supporters*) zoccolo duro 2 (*for roads, foundations*) massicciata

hard court N (*Tennis*) campo in terra battuta

hard disk N (*Comput*) hard disk *m inv*, disco rigido

hard drive N (*Comput*) hard drive *m inv*

hard·en [ˈhɑːdn] VT (*gen*) indurire; (*steel*) temprare; (*fig: determination*) rafforzare; **to harden one's heart** non lasciarsi commuovere ♦ VI (*substance*) indurirsi; **the glue soon hardens** la colla si indurisce presto

hard·ened [ˈhɑːdnd] ADJ (*criminal*) incallito(-a); **to be hardened to sth** essere (diventato(-a)) insensibile a qc

hard graft N: **by sheer hard graft** lavorando da matti

hard-headed [ˌhɑːd'hedɪd] ADJ pratico(-a)

hard-hearted [ˌhɑːd'hɑːtɪd] ADJ che non si lascia commuovere, dal cuore duro

hard-hitting [ˌhɑːd'hɪtɪŋ] ADJ molto duro(-a); **a hard-hitting documentary** un documentario verità *inv*

hard labour N lavori *mpl* forzati

hard·liner [ˌhɑːd'laɪnər] N sostenitore(-trice) *or* fautore(-trice) della linea dura

hard-luck story [ˌhɑːd'lʌkˌstɔːrɪ] N storia lacrimosa (*per commuovere qn*)

hard·ly [ˈhɑːdlɪ] ADV (*scarcely*) appena, a mala pena; **that can hardly be true** non può essere vero; **I hardly know him** lo conosco appena; **it's hardly the case** non è proprio il caso; **I can hardly believe it** stento a crederci; **I need hardly point out that ...** non c'è bisogno che io faccia notare che...; **this is hardly the time** non è di sicuro il momento; **hardly anyone/anything** quasi nessuno/niente; **I've got hardly any money** ho pochissimo denaro; **hardly ever** quasi mai; **hardly anywhere** quasi da nessuna parte; **hardly!** figuriamoci!, neanche per idea!

hard·ness [ˈhɑːdnɪs] N (*gen*) durezza

hard-nosed [ˌhɑːd'nəʊzd] ADJ (*fam: person*) duro(-a); (: *attitude*) da duro

hard-pressed [ˌhɑːd'prest] ADJ in difficoltà

hard sell N (*Comm*) tecnica aggressiva di vendita; **I don't like his hard sell approach** non mi piace quel suo approccio così aggressivo

hard·ship [ˈhɑːdʃɪp] N privazioni *fpl*, avversità *f inv*; (*suffering*) sofferenze *fpl*; **a life of hardship** una vita di sacrifici e privazioni; **economic hardship** difficoltà *fpl* economiche; **the worst hardship is being separated from my family** il sacrificio più grande per me è vivere separato dalla famiglia

hard shoulder N (*Brit: Aut*) corsia d'emergenza

hard·ware [ˈhɑːdˌweər] N (*for domestic use*) ferramenta *fpl*; (*Mil*) armamenti *mpl*; (*Comput*) hardware *m*

hardware shop, (*USA*) **hardware store** N (negozio di) ferramenta

hard-wearing [ˌhɑːd'weərɪŋ] ADJ (*gen*) resistente, robusto(-a); (*shoes*) robusto(-a)

hard-won [ˌhɑːd'wʌn] ADJ sudato(-a)

hard-working [ˌhɑːd'wɜːkɪŋ] ADJ che lavora sodo

har·dy [ˈhɑːdɪ] ADJ (*comp* -ier, *superl* -iest) forte, robusto(-a); (*Bot*) resistente al gelo; **hardy people** gente robusta; **hardy plants** piante resistenti al gelo

hare [heər] N lepre *f*

hare-brained, hair-brained [ˈheəˌbreɪnd] ADJ scervellato(-a)

hare·lip [ˌheə'lɪp] N labbro leporino

har·em [ˈhɑːriːm] N harem *m inv*

hark [hɑːk] VI: **hark!** (*liter*) udite!; **hark at him!** (*fam*) ma sentilo!

▸ **hark back** VI + PREP: **to hark back to** (*former days*) rievocare; (*earlier occasion*) ritornare a *or* su

harm [hɑːm] N (*gen*) male *m*; (*damage*) danno; **to do sb harm** far del male a qn; **to do harm to** (*reputation, interests*) danneggiare; **out of harm's way** al sicuro; **to keep out of harm's way** tenersi alla larga; **there's no harm in trying** tentar non nuoce; **it might do more harm than good** potrebbe fare più male che bene; **you will come to no harm** non ti succederà nulla; **he means no harm** non ha nessuna cattiva intenzione ♦ VT (*person*) far male a; (*reputation, interests, health*) danneggiare, nuocere a; (*object, crops*) danneggiare

harm·ful [ˈhɑːmfʊl] ADJ: **harmful (to)** dannoso(-a) (a), nocivo(-a) (a)

harm·less [ˈhɑːmlɪs] ADJ (*gen*) innocuo(-a), inoffensivo(-a); (*innocent: conversation, joke*) innocente

har·mon·ic [hɑːˈmɒnɪk] ADJ armonico(-a)

har·moni·ca [hɑːˈmɒnɪkə] N armonica a bocca

har·mon·ics [hɑːˈmɒnɪks] NPL (*Mus*) armonia ♦ NSG (*Phys*) armonica

har·mo·ni·ous [hɑːˈməʊnɪəs] ADJ armonioso(-a)

har·mo·nium [hɑːˈməʊnɪəm] N armonium *m inv*

har·mo·nize [ˈhɑːməˌnaɪz] VT (*Mus*) armonizzare; (*colours*) intonare, armonizzare ♦ VI (*Mus*) armonizzare; **to harmonize (with)** (*colours*) armonizzarsi con, intonarsi (a)

har·mo·ny [ˈhɑːmənɪ] N armonia

har·ness [ˈhɑːnɪs] N (*for horse*) bardatura, finimenti *mpl*; (*for baby*) briglie *fpl*; (*safety harness*) imbracatura ♦ VT (*horse*) bardare, mettere i finimenti a; (*to carriage*) attaccare a; (*resources*) sfruttare; **attempts to harness natural energy** tentativi di sfruttare le fonti energetiche naturali

harp [hɑːp] N arpa

▸ **harp on** VI + ADV (*fam*): **to harp on (about)** continuare a menarla (con)

harp·ist [ˈhɑːpɪst] N arpista *m/f*

har·poon [hɑːˈpuːn] N arpione *m* ♦ VT arpionare

harp·si·chord [ˈhɑːpsɪˌkɔːd] N clavicembalo, cembalo

har·row [ˈhærəʊ](*Agr*) N erpice *m* ♦ VT erpicare

har·row·ing [ˈhærəʊɪŋ] ADJ (*experience, story*) straziante, sconvolgente

har·ry [ˈhærɪ] VT (*pester*) assillare; (*attack persistently*) attaccare

harsh [hɑːʃ] ADJ (*comp* -er, *superl* -est) 1 (*punishment, person*) severo(-a), duro(-a); (*words*) duro(-a); (*weather*) rigido(-a); (*taste*) pungente; **a harsh climate** un clima rigido 2 (*discordant: voice*) sgradevole; (: *colour*) chiassoso(-a), squillante; (: *light*) troppo forte; (: *contrast*) brusco(-a)

harsh·ly [ˈhɑːʃlɪ] ADV (*treat, punish*) duramente; (*speak*) duramente, aspramente

harsh·ness [ˈhɑːʃnɪs] N 1 (*of punishment, person*) durezza; (*of weather*) inclemenza; (*of taste*) asprezza; (*of cloth*) ruvidezza 2 (*of voice*) sgradevolezza; (*of colour*) chiassosità; (*of light*) intensità; (*of contrast*) violenza

har·vest [ˈhɑːvɪst] N (*of crop*) raccolto; (*of grapes*) vendemmia; **a poor harvest** un raccolto scarso ♦ VT (*gen*) fare il raccolto di, raccogliere; (*grain*) mietere; (*grapes*) vendemmiare; **they're harvesting the olives** stanno raccogliendo le olive ♦ VI (*on farm*) fare il raccolto, mietere; (*in vineyard*) vendemmiare

har·vest·er [ˈhɑːvɪstər] N (*person*) mietitore(-trice); (*machine*) mietitrice *f*; (*combine harvester*) mietitrebbia

has [hæz] 3RD PERS SG PRESENT *of* have

has-been [ˈhæzˌbiːn] N (*fam: person*): **he's/she's a has-been** ha fatto il suo tempo (*thing*) anticaglia

hash [hæʃ] N 1 (*Culin*) spezzatino fatto con avanzi di carne cotta 2 (*fam*): **to make a hash of sth** fare un bel pasticcio di qc 3 (*fam: hashish*) erba

hash·ish [ˈhæʃɪʃ] N hashish, hascisc *m*

hash·tag [ˈhæʃtæg] N 1 (*on Twitter*) hashtag *m inv* 2 cancelletto

hasn't [ˈhæznt] = has not

has·sle [ˈhæsl](*fam*) N seccatura, scocciatura ♦ VT seccare, scocciare

haste [heɪst] N fretta, premura; **to make haste** sbrigarsi, affrettarsi; **more haste less speed** (*Proverb*) presto e bene raro avviene; **in haste** in fretta

has·ten [ˈheɪsn] VT (*growth*) accelerare; (*steps*) affrettare, accelerare; **to hasten sb's departure** affrettare la partenza di qn ♦ VI: **to hasten (to do sth)** affrettarsi (a fare qc); **I hasten to add that ...** mi preme aggiungere che...

has·ti·ly [ˈheɪstɪlɪ] ADV (*hurriedly*) in (gran) fretta, in fretta e furia; (*without thinking*) senza riflettere, precipitosamente; **he hastily suggested that ...** s'è affrettato a proporre che...; **he left hastily** se n'è andato in gran fretta

has·ty [ˈheɪstɪ] ADJ (*comp* -ier, *superl* -iest) (*hurried*) frettoloso(-a); (*rash*) affrettato(-a), precipitoso(-a); **a hasty escape** una fuga precipitosa; **a hasty meal** un pasto frettoloso; **hasty preparations** preparativi *mpl* affrettati

hat [hæt] N cappello; **to pass the hat round** (*fig*) fare la colletta; **I take my hat off to him** (*fig*) gli faccio tanto di cappello; **to keep sth under one's hat** (*fig*) tenere qc per sé; **keep it under your hat!** acqua in bocca!; **to talk through one's hat** (*fam*) dire delle stupidaggini; **that's old hat!** (*fam*) sono storie vecchie!

hat·box [ˈhætˌbɒks] N cappelliera

hatch¹ [hætʃ] N (*Naut: hatchway*) boccaporto; (*Brit: service hatch*) sportello passavivande; **down the hatch!** (*fam: when drinking*) salute!

hatch² [hætʃ] VT (*chick*) fare nascere; (*eggs*) fare schiudere; (*fig: scheme, plot*) elaborare, mettere a punto ♦ VI (*chick*) uscire dal *or* rompere il guscio; (*egg*) schiudersi; **the eggs will hatch soon** le uova si schiuderanno presto

hatch·back [ˈhætʃˌbæk] N (*car*) auto a tre (*or* cinque) porte

hatch·et [ˈhætʃɪt] N accetta, ascia

hatchet job N (*fam*) stroncatura

hatchet man N (*fam*) scagnozzo

hate [heɪt] N odio ♦ VT (*person: thing*) odiare; (*weaker*) detestare; **I hate having to do it** detesto doverlo fare; **I hate to trouble you, but …** mi dispiace disturbarla, ma…; **she hates to be** *or* **she hates being corrected** non sopporta le critiche *or* le osservazioni

hate·ful [ˈheɪtfʊl] ADJ odioso(-a), detestabile

ha·tred [ˈheɪtrɪd] N: hatred (of) odio (per)

hat trick N (*Brit, Sport, also fig*) tripletta

haugh·ty [ˈhɔːtɪ] ADJ (*comp* **-ier,** *superl* **-iest**) altezzoso(-a), altero(-a)

haul [hɔːl] N **1** (*distance*) tragitto, viaggio; **it's a long haul** è una lunga tirata **2** (*amount taken: from robbery*) bottino; (*: of fish*) retata, pescata ♦ VT (*drag: person, heavy object*) tirare, trascinare; **to haul sb over the coals** (*fig*) dare una strigliata a qn

▸ **haul down** VT + ADV (*gen*) tirare giù; (*flag, sail*) ammainare

▸ **haul in** VT + ADV (*subj: police, authorities: suspect*) fare una retata di; (*net, catch, drowning person*) tirare a riva

▸ **haul up** VT + ADV (*flag, sail, load*) issare; (*suspect*) portare

haul·age [ˈhɔːlɪdʒ] N (*road transport*) trasporto, autotrasporto; (*cost*) costo del trasporto; **a haulage company** una società di trasporti

haulage contractor N (*Brit: firm*) impresa di trasporti; (*: person*) autotrasportatore *m*

haul·ier [ˈhɔːljə], **haul·er** (*USA*) [ˈhɔːlə] N autotrasportatore *m*

haunch [hɔːntʃ] N (*of person, animal*) anca; (*Culin*) coscia; **a haunch of venison** una coscia di cervo; **to sit/squat on one's haunches** (*person*) accucciarsi; (*animal*) sedersi (sulle zampe posteriori)

haunt [hɔːnt] N (*of criminals*) covo; **it's one of his favourite haunts** è un dei suoi posticini favoriti ♦ VT (*subj: ghost*) abitare; (*fig: memory*) perseguitare; (*: fear*) pervadere; **these thoughts haunted her** questi pensieri la tormentavano; **a ghost haunts this house** questa casa è abitata da un fantasma; **he haunts the local bars** frequenta assiduamente i bar della zona

haunt·ed [ˈhɔːntɪd] ADJ (*castle, house*) infestato(-a) dai fantasmi *or* dagli spiriti; (*look*) ossessionato(-a), tormentato(-a)

haunt·ing [ˈhɔːntɪŋ] ADJ (*sight, music*) che non si riesce a togliere dalla mente, ossessionante

Ha·vana [həˈvænə] N L'Avana

have [hæv] (*3rd pers sg present* **has,** *pt, pp* **had**) AUX VB

1 (*gen*) avere; (*with many intransitive verbs*) essere; **to have arrived** essere arrivato(-a); **he has been kind/promoted** è stato gentile/promosso; **to have eaten** aver mangiato; **having finished** *or* **when he had finished,** he left dopo aver finito se n'è andato; **has/hasn't she told you?** te l'ha/non te l'ha detto?

2 (*in tag questions*): **you've done it, haven't you?** l'hai fatto, (non è) vero?; **he hasn't done it, has he?** non l'ha fatto, vero?

3 (*in short answers and questions*): **you've made a mistake — no I haven't/so I have** hai fatto uno sbaglio — ma no, niente affatto/eh sì, è vero; **we haven't paid — yes we have!** non abbiamo pagato — sì che abbiamo pagato!; **I've been there before, have you?** ci sono già stato, e tu?

♦ MODAL AUX VB (*be obliged*): **to have (got) to do sth** dover fare qc; **I had better leave** è meglio che io vada; **this has got to be a mistake** dev'essere un errore, deve trattarsi di un errore; **she has to do it** lo deve fare; **I have (got) to finish this work** devo finire questo lavoro; **it will have to wait till tomorrow** bisogna rimandarlo a domani; **I don't have to wear glasses** non ho bisogno di portare gli occhiali

♦ VT

1 (*possess*) avere; **he has (got) blue eyes** ha gli occhi azzurri; **I haven't got blue eyes, I don't have blue eyes** non ho gli occhi azzurri; **I have (got) an idea** ho un'idea, mi è venuta un'idea; **have you (got)** *or* **do you have a pen?** hai una penna?; **I've got somebody staying next week** ho un ospite la settimana prossima; **I have (got) no Spanish** non so una parola di spagnolo

2 (*meal, shower*) fare; (*drink*) prendere; **to have breakfast** far colazione; **she had a cigarette** fumò una sigaretta; **I'll have a coffee** prendo un caffè; **to have dinner** cenare; **I must have a drink** devo bere qualcosa; **to have lunch** pranzare; **will you have some more?** ne vuoi ancora?; **what will you have?** cosa bevi *or* prendi?

3 (*receive, obtain*) avere, ricevere; **let me have your address** dammi il tuo indirizzo; **there was no bread to be had** non avevano più or non c'era più pane; **I must have it by tomorrow** mi occorre per domani; **to have a child** avere un figlio; **you can have it for £5** te lo lascio per 5 sterline; **I have it on good authority that …** so da fonte sicura che…

4 (*hold*) avere, tenere; **he had him by the throat** lo teneva per la gola; **I have (got) him where I want him** ce l'ho in mano *or* in pugno

5 (*maintain, allow*): **rumour has it (that) …** si dice *or* corre voce che…; **I won't have it** questo non mi va affatto; **she won't have it said that …** non permette che si dica che…; **I won't have this nonsense** non tollero queste assurdità

6 (*causative*): **to have sth done** far fare qc; **to have sb do sth** far fare qc a qn; **to have one's luggage brought up** farsi portar su le valigie; **to have one's hair cut** farsi tagliare i capelli; **he had them all dancing** è riuscito a farli ballare tutti; **what would you have me do?** cosa vuoi che faccia?; **I'd have you know that …** voglio che tu sappia che…; **he had a suit made** si fece fare un abito

7 (*experience, suffer*): **to have an operation** avere *or* subire un'operazione; **she had her bag stolen** le hanno rubato la borsa

8 (+ *noun = verb identical with noun*): **let's have a look** diamo un'occhiata; **to have a swim** fare una nuotata; **let me have a try** fammi *or* lasciami provare; **to have a walk** fare una passeggiata

9 (*phrases*): **to have a pleasant evening** passare una piacevole serata; **you've been had!** (*fam*) ci sei cascato!; **let him have it!** (*fam*) dagliele!, picchialo!; **you've had it!** (*fam*) sei fritto!, sei fregato!; **thank you for having me** grazie dell'ospitalità; **you have me there!** questo proprio non lo so!; **to have a party** dare una festa; **to have a good time** divertirsi

▸ **have in** VT + ADV **1** (*visitor*) avere (in casa); (*candidate*) far passare *or* entrare; (*doctor*) chiamare **2 to have it in for sb** (*fam*) avercela con qn

▸ **have on** VT + ADV **1** (*garment*) avere addosso **2** (*Brit: be busy with*) avere da fare, avere in programma; **have you anything on tomorrow?** hai qualcosa in programma per domani? **3** (*Brit fam*): **to have sb on** prendere in giro qn ♦ VT + PREP (*money*): **I don't have any money on me** non ho soldi con me

▸ **have out** VT + ADV **1** (*tooth, tonsils*) farsi togliere *or* levare **2 to have sth out with sb** chiarire *or* mettere in chiaro qc con qn

▸ **have up** VT + ADV: **to be had up** (*fam: in court*) essere chiamato(-a) in tribunale

ha·ven [ˈheɪvn] N rifugio, riparo; **a haven of peace** un'oasi di pace

haven't [ˈhævnt] = have not

hav·er·sack [ˈhævəˌsæk] N zaino

haves [hævz] NPL: **the haves and the have-nots** gli abbienti e i non abbienti

hav·oc [ˈhævək] N distruzione *f*, devastazione *f*; **to wreak havoc on** devastare; (*fig*) scombussolare, mettere in subbuglio; **to play havoc with** (*fig*) scombussolare, mettere in subbuglio; **strikes are causing havoc** gli scioperi stanno provocando grande confusione

Ha·waii [hə'waɪɪ] N le Hawaii

Ha·wai·ian [hə'waɪjən] ADJ hawaiano(-a) ♦ N 1 (*person*) hawaiano(-a) 2 (*language*) hawaiano

hawk[1] [hɔːk] N (*also fig*) falco

hawk[2] [hɔːk] VT (*goods for sale*) vendere per strada

hawk·er ['hɔːkə'] N venditore(-trice) ambulante

hawk·ish ['hɔːkɪʃ] ADJ (*politician*) che sostiene la linea dura

haw·thorn ['hɔːθɔːn] N biancospino

hay [heɪ] N fieno; **to make hay while the sun shines** (*Proverb*) battere il ferro finché è caldo

hay fever N raffreddore *m* da fieno

hay·stack ['heɪstæk] N pagliaio

hay·wire ['heɪwaɪə'] ADJ (*fam*): **to go haywire** (*person*) dare i numeri, perdere la testa; (*machine*) impazzire; (*scheme, system*) andare a catafascio

haz·ard ['hæzəd] N (*risk*) rischio; (*more serious*) pericolo; (*chance*) azzardo; **a potential hazard** un potenziale rischio; **occupational hazard** rischio del mestiere; **natural hazard** calamità naturale; **to be a health hazard** essere dannoso(-a) alla salute ♦ VT (*one's life*) rischiare, mettere a repentaglio; (*remark*) azzardare; **to hazard a guess** tirare a indovinare; **he refused to hazard people's lives** si rifiutò di mettere a repentaglio la vita delle persone

haz·ard·ous ['hæzədəs] ADJ rischioso(-a), pericoloso(-a); **hazardous waste** rifiuti *mpl* pericolosi; **hazardous to health** rischioso per la salute

hazard pay N (*USA*) indennità di rischio

hazard warning lights NPL (*Aut*) luci *fpl* di emergenza

haze [heɪz] N (*mist*) foschia; (*of smoke*) velo

ha·zel ['heɪzl] N (*tree*) nocciolo ♦ ADJ (*eyes*) (color) nocciola *inv*

ha·zel·nut ['heɪzl,nʌt] N nocciola

hazy ['heɪzɪ] ADJ (*comp* -ier, *superl* -iest) (*day*) di foschia; (*weather*) caliginoso(-a); (*view*) indistinto(-a); (*photograph*) leggermente sfocato(-a); (*uncertain: person*) confuso(-a); (*unclear: memory, details, idea*) vago(-a); **a hazy notion** una vaga nozione; **hazy sky** cielo fosco

H-bomb ['eɪtʃ,bɒm] N bomba H

HD ABBR (= *high definition*) HD, alta definizione

HDTV [,eɪtʃdiːtiː'viː] N ABBR (= *high definition TV*) televisione *f* ad alta definizione

HE [,eɪtʃ'iː] ABBR (*Diplomacy*: = *His* (or *Her*) *Excellency*) SE (= *Sua Eccellenza*); (*Rel*: = *His Eminence*) SE (= *Sua Eminenza*)

he [hiː] PERS PRON lui, egli; **he has gone out** è uscito; **he loves dogs** lui ama i cani; **there/here he is** eccolo; **"come here," he said** "vieni qui," disse; **it is he who ...** è lui che...; **HE didn't do it** non è stato lui a farlo; **he who hesitates is lost** chi si ferma è perduto ♦ N: **it's a he** (*animal: also fam: baby*) è un maschio

head [hɛd] N 1 (*Anat*) testa, capo; **mind your head!** attenzione alla testa!; **head of hair** capigliatura; **head down** a testa bassa; **head first** a capofitto, di testa; **my head is aching** mi fa male la testa, ho mal di testa; **to fall head over heels in love with sb** innamorarsi perdutamente *or* follemente di qn; **from head to foot** dalla testa ai piedi; **his head's in the clouds** ha la testa fra le nuvole; **to keep one's head above water** (*fig*) mantenersi a galla; **the horse won by a head** il cavallo ha vinto per una testa; **on your head be it** a tuo rischio e pericolo; **I could do it standing on my head** (*fam*) potrei farlo a occhi chiusi; **they went over my head to the manager** mi hanno scavalcato e sono andati direttamente dal direttore; **wine goes to my head** il vino mi dà *or* va alla testa; **success has gone to his head** il successo gli ha dato alla testa; **to shout one's head off** (*fam*) sgolarsi 2 (*intellect, mind*) cervello, testa; **two heads are better than one** (*Proverb*) due occhi vedono meglio di uno; **it never entered my head** non mi è mai passato per la testa; **to have a head for business** essere tagliato(-a) per gli affari; **to have no head for heights** soffrire di vertigini; **to lose one's head** perdere la testa; **to keep one's head** non perdere la testa, mantenere la calma; **she always manages to keep her head in difficult**

situations riesce sempre a mantenere la calma nelle situazioni difficili; **he lost his head and started screaming** ha perso la testa e ha cominciato a gridare; **let's put our heads together** (*fam*) non te lo saprei dire così su due piedi; **to do a sum in one's head** fare un calcolo a mente; **I couldn't tell you off the top of my head** (*fam*) non te lo saprei dire così su due piedi; **to get sth into one's head** ficcarsi in testa qc; **to be off one's head** (*fam*) essere fuori di testa 3 (*leader: of family, business*) capo; (: *of school*) direttore(-trice), preside *m/f*; **head of state** (*Pol*) capo di Stato 4 (*on coin*) testa; **heads or tails?** testa o croce?; **I couldn't make head nor tail of it** per me non aveva né capo né coda 5 (*no pl: unit*): **20 head of cattle** 20 capi *mpl* di bestiame; **£10 a** *or* **per head** 10 sterline a testa 6 (*of hammer, bed, flower*) testa; (*of nail*) capocchia; (*of arrow*) punta; (*of lettuce*) cespo; (*of river*) sorgente *f*; (*of stairs, page*) cima; (*on beer*) schiuma; (*on computer*) testina; **at the head of** (*organization*) a capo di; (*train, procession*) in testa a, alla testa di; (*queue*) all'inizio di; **to sit at the head of the table** sedersi a capotavola; **to come to a head** (*abscess*) maturare; (*fig: situation*) precipitare 7 (*Naut: of ship*) prua; (*of sail*) penna ♦ VT 1 (*parade, poll*) essere in testa a; (*company, group*) essere a capo di; **she headed the list** era in cima all'elenco 2 (*Ftbl*): **to head a ball** colpire di testa una palla 3 (*chapter*) intitolare ♦ VI dirigersi; **to head for** dirigersi *or* andare verso; **to head home** andare a casa; **she was heading up the stairs** stava salendo le scale; **he is heading for trouble** sta andando incontro a dei guai ♦ ADJ (*clerk*) capo *inv*

  ► **head for** VI + PREP dirigersi verso; **they headed for the church** si sono diretti verso la chiesa

  ► **head off** VT + ADV (*threat, danger*) sventare; (*person, animal*) far cambiare direzione a

  ► **head up** VT + ADV (*USA: team, group*) essere a capo di

head·ache ['hɛdeɪk] N (*pain*) mal *m* di testa; (*fig*) grattacapo; **to have a headache** avere mal di testa; **I've got a headache** ho mal di testa; **this is a real headache for us** questo è un vero grattacapo per noi

head·band ['hɛd,bænd] N fascia per i capelli

head·board ['hɛd,bɔːd] N testiera (del letto)

head cold N raffreddore *m* di testa

head·dress ['hɛd,drɛs] N (*made of feathers*) copricapo; (*of bride*) acconciatura

head·er ['hɛdə'] N (*Brit fam: Ftbl*) colpo di testa; (: *fall*) caduta di testa; **he took a header into the water** fece un tuffo di testa nell'acqua

head-first [,hɛd'fɜːst] ADV a testa in giù, a capofitto; (*fig*) senza pensare

head·hunt ['hɛd,hʌnt] VT: **to be headhunted** avere un'offerta di lavoro da un cacciatore di teste

head·hunt·er ['hɛd,hʌntə'] N cacciatore *m* di teste

head·ing ['hɛdɪŋ] N (*title*) titolo; (*section*) sezione *f*; (*on letter*) intestazione *f*

head·land ['hɛdlənd] N punta, promontorio

head·light ['hɛd,laɪt] N, **head·lamp** ['hɛd,læmp] N (*Aut*) faro, fanale *m*

head·line ['hɛd,laɪn] N (*in newspaper*) titolo; (*TV, Radio*) headlines NPL (*main points*) sommario; **to hit the headlines** fare titolo ♦ VT: **to be headlined** (*newspaper etc*) essere titolato(-a); (*show*) avere come attrazione principale

head·long ['hɛd,lɒŋ] ADJ (*fall, dive*) a capofitto, a testa in giù; (*rush*) a tutta velocità ♦ ADV (*fall*) a capofitto, a tutta velocità; (*rush*) precipitosamente; **he fell headlong** è caduto a testa in giù; **they rushed headlong to the door** si sono precipitati verso la porta

head·master [,hɛd'mɑːstə'] N (*of primary school*) direttore *m*; (*of secondary school*) preside *m*

head·mistress [,hɛd'mɪstrɪs] N (*of primary school*) direttrice *f*; (*of secondary school*) preside *f*

head office N sede *f* centrale

head-on [,hɛd'ɒn] ADJ (*collision*) frontale; (*confrontation*) diretto(-a), faccia a faccia ♦ ADV (*collide*) frontalmente

head·phones ['hɛd,fəʊnz] NPL cuffia *fsg*

head·quarters ['hɛd,kwɔːtəz] NPL (*Mil*) quartier *msg* generale; (*of party, organization*) sede *f* centrale; (*Police*) centrale *f*

head·rest ['hɛd,rɛst] N poggiatesta *m inv*

head·room [ˈhedˌrʊm] N (*under ceiling*) spazio (per la testa); (*under bridge*) altezza libera di passaggio; (*in car*) altezza dell'abitacolo

head·scarf [ˈhedˌskɑːf], **head·square** [ˈhedˌskweəʳ] N foulard *m inv*

head·set [ˈhedˌset] N cuffia

head·stone [ˈhedˌstəʊn] N (*on grave*) lapide *f*, pietra tombale

head·strong [ˈhedˌstrɒŋ] ADJ testardo(-a), cocciuto(-a)

head·teacher N 1 (*of primary school*) direttore(-trice) 2 (*of secondary school*) preside *m/f*

head waiter N capocameriere *m*

head·way [ˈhedˌweɪ] N (*Naut*) abbrivio; **to make headway** (*fig*) fare progressi *or* passi avanti; (*Naut*) avanzare

head·wind [ˈhedˌwɪnd] N vento di prua; **to cycle against a headwind** pedalare controvento

heady [ˈhedɪ] ADJ (*comp* -**ier**, *superl* -**iest**) (*wine, scent, success*) inebriante; (*atmosphere*) euforico(-a)

heal [hiːl] VT (*wound*) guarire, cicatrizzare; (*person*) guarire; (*fig: differences*) appianare ♦ VI (*also:* **heal up**) cicatrizzarsi

health [helθ] N (*gen*) salute *f*; **Ministry of Health** Ministero della Sanità; **Health Minister** ministro della Sanità; **Department of Health** ≈ ministero della Sanità; **to be in good/bad health** essere in buona/cattiva salute; **to drink sb's health** bere alla salute di qn; **your health!** (alla tua) salute!

health care N assistenza sanitaria ♦ ADJ (*provision*) sanitario(-a); (*worker*) che lavora nella sanità

health centre N (*Brit*) poliambulatorio

health food N cibo macrobiotico

health hazard N pericolo per la salute

Health Service N: **the Health Service** (*Brit*) ≈ il Servizio Sanitario Nazionale

healthy [ˈhelθɪ] ADJ (*comp* -**ier**, *superl* -**iest**) (*person*) sano(-a), in buona salute; (*skin, diet, attitude*) sano(-a); (*air, place, climate*) salubre; (*appetite*) robusto(-a); (*exercise, food, fig: respect*) salutare; (: *interest*) vivace; (: *economy*) florido(-a); (: *bank balance*) in attivo

heap [hiːp] N (*pile*) mucchio, cumulo; (*fam: old car*) macinino; (: *lots*): **heaps (of)** un mucchio (di), un mucchio (di); **we have heaps of time** abbiamo un mucchio *or* sacco di tempo; **a heap of stones** un mucchio di sassi; **I was struck** *or* **knocked all of a heap** (*fam*) sono rimasto di stucco ♦ VT: **to heap sth onto sth** ammucchiare qc su qc; **the waitress heaped potatoes onto my plate** la cameriera mi ha dato una montagna *or* un mucchio di patate; **to heap sth with sth** colmare qc di qc; **to heap favours/praise/gifts on sb** ricolmare qn di favori/lodi/regali; **heaped spoonful** (*Culin*) cucchiaio colmo

▸ **heap up** VT + ADV accumulare, ammucchiare

hear [hɪəʳ] (*pt, pp* **heard** [hɜːd]) VT (*gen*) sentire; (*be informed of: piece of news*) apprendere, sentire; (*news on radio, TV*) ascoltare; (*lecture*) assistere a; (*Law: case*) esaminare; **I can't hear you** non ti sento; **can you hear me?** mi senti?; **I could hardly make myself heard** facevo fatica a farmi sentire; **I didn't hear anything** non ho sentito niente; **I hear you've lost your watch** ho saputo che hai perso l'orologio; **to hear him speak you'd think ...** a sentirlo parlare si direbbe che... ♦ VI (*gen*) sentire; (*get news*) aver notizie; **she can't hear very well** non sente molto bene; **to hear about** sentire parlare di; (*have news of*) avere notizie di; **I heard about him from her mother** ho avuto sue notizie tramite sua madre; **did you hear about the move?** hai saputo del trasloco?; **to hear from sb** ricevere notizie da qn; **she was never heard of again** non se ne seppe più nulla; **I've never heard of that book** non ho mai sentito parlare di quel libro; **I've never heard of such a thing** non ho mai sentito una cosa simile; **I won't hear of it** (*allow*) non ne voglio proprio sapere; **I won't hear of you paying for this** non è proprio il caso che tu paghi; **hear! hear!** (*bravo*) bravo!, bene!

▸ **hear out** VT + ADV ascoltare senza interrompere; **hear me out!** fammi finire!

hear·ing [ˈhɪərɪŋ] N 1 (*sense of hearing*) udito; **she has excellent hearing** ha un udito eccellente; **to be within/out of hearing** (*distance*) essere/non essere a portata di voce; **in my hearing** in mia presenza 2 (*Law*) udienza; **to give sb a hearing** dare udienza a qn; (*of witnesses*) audizione *f*,

escussione *f*; **the hearing was adjourned** l'udienza è stata aggiornata

hearing aid N apparecchio acustico

hear·say [ˈhɪəˌseɪ] N diceria, chiacchiere *fpl*; **by hearsay** per sentito dire

hearse [hɜːs] N carro funebre

heart [hɑːt] N 1 (*also fig*) cuore *m*; **to have a weak heart** avere il cuore debole; **he's a man after my own heart** è proprio il tipo che mi piace; **he's a good boy at heart** in fondo è un bravo ragazzo; **to have sb's interests at heart** avere a cuore gli interessi di qn; **from the (bottom of one's) heart** dal profondo del cuore, con tutto il cuore; **in her heart of hearts** nel suo intimo; **heart and soul** anima e corpo; **his heart was in his boots** (*dejected*) aveva la morte nel cuore; **to wear one's heart on one's sleeve** non fare mistero dei propri sentimenti; **my heart sank** mi sono scoraggiato; **to learn/know/recite by heart** imparare/sapere/ripetere a memoria; **to one's heart's content** quanto si ha voglia; **her heart is in the right place** è di buon cuore; **to cry one's heart out** piangere disperatamente *or* a calde lacrime; **have a heart!** (*fam*) sii buono!; **she has a heart of gold** ha un cuore d'oro; **to take sth to heart** prendersi a cuore qc; **his heart was not in it** gli mancava l'entusiasmo; **to set one's heart on sth/on doing sth** tenere molto a qc/a fare qc; **with all one's heart** con tutto il cuore; **to break sb's heart** spezzare il cuore a qn; **to be in good heart** essere su di morale; **I did not have the heart to tell her** non ho avuto cuore *or* il coraggio di dirglielo; **to have one's heart in one's mouth** avere il cuore in gola; **to lose heart** perdersi di coraggio *or* d'animo, scoraggiarsi; **to take heart** farsi coraggio *or* animo; **in the heart of the country** in mezzo alla campagna; **the heart of the matter** il nocciolo della questione 2 (*Cards*); **hearts** NPL cuori *mpl*; **the ace of hearts** l'asso di cuori ♦ ADJ cardiaco(-a); **to have a heart complaint**, **to have heart trouble** avere un disturbo cardiaco *or* una cardiopatia; **to have a heart condition** essere cardiopatico(-a)

heart·ache [ˈhɑːtˌeɪk] N pene *fpl*, dolori *mpl*

heart attack N (*Med*) infarto; **to have a heart attack** avere un infarto

heart·beat [ˈhɑːtˌbiːt] N (*single*) pulsazione *f*; (*rate*) battiti *mpl* del cuore

heart·break [ˈhɑːtˌbreɪk] N immenso dolore *m*

heart·breaking [ˈhɑːtˌbreɪkɪŋ] ADJ penoso(-a), straziante

heart·broken [ˈhɑːtˌbrəʊkən] ADJ affranto(-a); **to be heartbroken** avere il cuore spezzato *or* infranto

heart·burn [ˈhɑːtˌbɜːn] N (*Med*) bruciore *m* di stomaco

heart disease N malattia di cuore

-hearted [ˈhɑːtɪd] SUFF: **a kind-hearted person** una persona di buon cuore

heart·en·ing [ˈhɑːtnɪŋ] ADJ incoraggiante

heart failure (*Med*) N (*malfunction*) collasso cardiaco; (*arrest*) arresto cardiaco

heart·felt [ˈhɑːtˌfelt] ADJ profondo(-a), sincero(-a)

hearth [hɑːθ] N focolare *m*

hearti·ly [ˈhɑːtɪlɪ] ADV (*agree*) in pieno, completamente; (*laugh*) di cuore, di gusto; (*eat*) di buon appetito, di gusto; (*thank, welcome*) calorosamente

heart·land [ˈhɑːtˌlænd] N zona centrale; **Italy's industrial heartland** il cuore dell'industria italiana

heart·less [ˈhɑːtlɪs] ADJ spietato(-a), crudele, senza cuore, insensibile

heart·strings [ˈhɑːtˌstrɪŋz] NPL: **to tug (at) sb's heartstrings** toccare il cuore a qn, toccare qn nel profondo

heart·throb [ˈhɑːtˌθrɒb] N: **a teenage heart-throb** un idolo delle ragazzine

heart-to-heart [ˌhɑːttəˈhɑːt] ADJ, ADV a cuore aperto ♦ N (*conversation*): **to have a heart to heart** parlare a cuore aperto

heart transplant N trapianto di cuore

heart-warming [ˈhɑːtˌwɔːmɪŋ] ADJ toccante

hearty [ˈhɑːtɪ] ADJ (*comp* -**ier**, *superl* -**iest**) (*person*) gioviale; (*support*) caloroso(-a); (*dislike*) vivo(-a); (*laugh*) di cuore, di gusto; (*appetite*) robusto(-a); (*meal*) abbondante, sostanzioso(-a); (*welcome, thanks*) cordiale, caloroso(-a); **a hearty eater** una buona forchetta; **a hearty breakfast** una colazione abbondante; **heartiest congratulations!** congratulazioni vivissime!

heat [hi:t] N 1 (gen) calore m; (fig) ardore m; **the heat of the sun** il calore del sole; **I can't stand the heat** non sopporto il caldo; **at low heat** (Culin: on stove) a fuoco basso; (: in oven) a calore moderato; **take the pan off the heat** togliere la pentola dal fuoco; **in the heat of the moment** (fig) nella foga del momento; **in the heat of the battle** nella furia della battaglia; **to put the heat on sb** fare pressione a or su qn 2 (Sport: also: **qualifying heat**) batteria, prova eliminatoria 3 (Zool): **in** or **on heat** in calore ♦ VT (far) scaldare; **heat gently for five minutes** scaldare a fuoco lento per cinque minuti ♦ VI scaldarsi
  ▸ **heat up** VI + ADV (liquids) scaldarsi; (room) riscaldarsi ♦ VT + ADV riscaldare

heat·ed [ˈhi:tɪd] ADJ riscaldato(-a); (fig: discussion, argument) acceso(-a), animato(-a); **a heated swimming pool** una piscina riscaldata; **heated words** parole fpl di fuoco; **to grow heated** (discussion) accendersi

heat·er [ˈhi:tə] N calorifero, termosifone m, radiatore m; (stove) stufa; **I had the heater on and the window open** avevo il riscaldamento acceso e la finestra aperta; **an electric heater** una stufa elettrica; **a water heater** uno scaldaacqua

heath [hi:θ] N (Brit: moor) landa, brughiera; (plant) erica, brugo

hea·then [ˈhi:ðən] ADJ, N pagano(-a)

heath·er [ˈhɛðə] N erica

heat·ing [ˈhi:tɪŋ] N riscaldamento

heat-resistant [ˈhi:trɪˌzɪstənt] ADJ termoresistente

heat-seeking [ˈhi:tˌsi:kɪŋ] ADJ (missile) termoguidato(-a)

heat·stroke [ˈhi:tˌstrəʊk] N (Med) colpo di calore

heat·wave [ˈhi:tˌweɪv] N ondata di caldo

heave [hi:v] N sforzo; (of waves) movimento; (Geol) rigetto ♦ VT (pull) tirare con forza; (drag) trascinare a fatica; (lift) sollevare a fatica; (throw) scagliare; **they heaved the washing machine into the bathroom** hanno trascinato a fatica la lavatrice nel bagno; **to heave a sigh** emettere or mandare un sospiro; **to heave a sigh of relief** tirare un sospiro di sollievo; **to heave anchor** (Naut) salpare l'ancora ♦ VI 1 (sea, chest, stomach) alzarsi ed abbassarsi; **to heave at** or **to heave on** (pull) tirare con forza; **he heaved with all his might** ha tirato con tutta la sua forza 2 (feel sick) avere i conati di vomito; **her stomach heaved** le si rivoltò lo stomaco 3 (liter: pt, pp hove); **to heave in sight** or **into view** comparire all'orizzonte
  ▸ **heave to** (pt, pp hove) VI + ADV (Naut) navigare in cappa

heav·en [ˈhɛvn] N 1 (Rel) cielo, paradiso; (fig) paradiso; **to go to heaven** andare in paradiso; (good) **heaven!** santo cielo!; **thank heaven!** grazie al cielo!; **heaven forbid!** Dio ce ne guardi!; **for heaven's sake!** (protesting) santo cielo!, in nome del cielo!; **this is heaven!** (fam) che meraviglia!; **to move heaven and earth to do sth** muovere mari e monti or farsi in quattro per fare qc; **in seventh heaven** al settimo cielo; **heaven on earth** il paradiso terrestre 2 **the heavens** NPL (liter: sky) il cielo, la volta celeste; **the heavens opened** si è messo a diluviare

heav·en·ly [ˈhɛvnlɪ] ADJ (Rel) celeste, divino(-a); (fam: delightful) divino(-a); **heavenly weather** tempo stupendo; **heavenly kingdom** regno dei cieli

heavi·ly [ˈhɛvɪlɪ] ADV (move) con pesantezza; (tax) fortemente; (rain, snow, gamble) forte; (breathe) con difficoltà; (sigh, sleep) profondamente; (rely, drink, smoke, load) molto; **he drinks heavily** beve molto; **it rained heavily in the night** ha piovuto molto durante la notte; **it weighs heavily on him** questo gli pesa molto; **she sat down heavily on the sofa** si è seduta pesantemente sul divano

heavy [ˈhɛvɪ] ADJ (comp **-ier**, superl **-iest**) (gen, also fig) pesante; (sigh) profondo(-a); (sleep) profondo(-a), pesante; (blow, rain, taxation) forte; (sea) grosso(-a); (after n); (expense, casualties) ingente; (traffic) intenso(-a); (atmosphere) opprimente; (crop) abbondante; (Mil: fighting) accanito(-a); (: fire) nutrito(-a), fitto(-a); (loss) grave; (smoker) accanito(-a); **this bag's very heavy** questa borsa è molto pesante; **how heavy are you?** quanto pesi?; **a heavy cold** avere un forte raffreddore; **it's a heavy burden for her to bear** è un peso troppo grande per lei; **with a heavy heart** col cuore gonfio;

air heavy with scent aria carica di profumo; **to be a heavy drinker** essere un(a) forte bevitore(-trice); **to be a heavy sleeper** avere il sonno duro or pesante; **it's heavy going** è una gran fatica

heavy cream N (USA) panna da montare

heavy-duty [ˌhɛvɪˈdju:tɪ] ADJ molto resistente

heavy goods vehicle N (Brit) autoveicolo pesante da trasporto

heavy-handed [ˌhɛvɪˈhændɪd] ADJ (clumsy, tactless) pesante; (harsh: person) che ha la mano pesante, severo(-a)

heavy metal N (Mus) heavy metal m inv

heavy-set [ˌhɛvɪˈsɛt] ADJ (esp USA) tarchiato(-a)

heavy·weight [ˈhɛvɪˌweɪt] N (Boxing) (peso) massimo; (fig: important or influential person) autorità f inv, pezzo m grosso ♦ ADJ (issue, subject) importante

He·brew [ˈhi:bru:] ADJ (language) ebraico(-a); (person, nation) ebreo(-a) ♦ N (person) ebreo(-a); (language) ebraico

Heb·ri·des [ˈhɛbrɪˌdi:z] NPL: **the Hebrides** le Ebridi

heck [hɛk] (fam) EXCL: **oh heck!** oh cavolo! ♦ N: **a heck of a lot** of un casino di

heck·le [ˈhɛkl] VT, VI: **to heckle (sb)** interrompere continuamente (qn) (un oratore)

heck·ler [ˈhɛklə] N disturbatore(-trice)

hec·tare [ˈhɛktɑ:] N ettaro

hec·tic [ˈhɛktɪk] ADJ (busy) frenetico(-a); (eventful) movimentato(-a); **my life's pretty hectic at the moment** attualmente la mia vita è piuttosto movimentata; **a hectic schedule** un orario denso

hec·tor [ˈhɛktə] VT fare il prepotente con

he'd [hi:d] = **he would**; **he had**

hedge [hɛdʒ] N siepe f; (fig) difesa; **as a hedge against inflation** per cautelarsi contro l'inflazione ♦ VT (Agr) recintare con una siepe; **to be hedged about** or **around** or **in with** (restricted) essere limitato(-a) da, essere vincolato(-a) da; **to hedge one's bets** (fig) cercare di non compromettersi ♦ VI tergiversare, essere elusivo(-a)

hedge·hog [ˈhɛdʒˌhɒg] N riccio

hedge·row [ˈhɛdʒrəʊ] N siepe f

he·don·ism [ˈhi:dənɪzəm] N (frm) edonismo

heed [hi:d] (frm) N: **to pay (no) heed to, to take (no) heed of** (non) ascoltare, (non) tener conto di ♦ VT fare attenzione a

heed·less [ˈhi:dlɪs] ADJ (not thinking) avventato(-a); (not caring) noncurante; **to be heedless of** essere insensibile or sordo(-a) a

heel¹ [hi:l] N 1 (of foot, sock) tallone m, calcagno; (of shoe) tacco; **high heels** tacchi alti; **heel, boy!** (to dog) qui!; **to bring sb to heel** (fig) riportare qn all'ordine; **to be at sb's heels** stare alle calcagna di qn; **to take to one's heels** (liter) darsela a gambe; **to turn on one's heel** girare i tacchi 2 (fam: person) carogna ♦ VT (shoe) fare or rifare i tacchi a; (ball) colpire di tacco

heel² [hi:l] VI (also: **heel over**: ship, truck) inclinarsi (pericolosamente)

hefty [ˈhɛftɪ] (fam) ADJ (comp **-ier**, superl **-iest**) (load) pesante; (person) robusto(-a), solido(-a); (piece, profit) grosso(-a) (before n); (price) alto(-a), bello(-a) (before n); **a hefty fine** una grossa multa; **a hefty shove** una forte spinta

heif·er [ˈhɛfə] N giovenca

height [haɪt] N 1 (measurement) altezza; (of person) altezza, statura; (altitude) altezza, altitudine f; (high ground) altura; **what height are you?** quanto sei alto?; **of average/medium height** di statura media; **to be 20 metres in height** essere alto(-a) 20 metri; **height above sea level** altitudine sopra il livello del mare; **to be afraid of heights** soffrire di vertigini 2 (fig: of career, success, glory) apice m; (: of rudeness, stupidity) colmo; **at the height of** (storm, battle) nel momento culminante di; **it's the height of fashion** è l'ultimo grido della moda; **in the height of summer** nel pieno dell'estate

height·en [ˈhaɪtn] VT (raise) alzare; (increase) far aumentare; (enhance: effect) mettere in risalto, accrescere; (: experience) rendere più intenso(-a)

hei·nous [ˈheɪnəs] ADJ (frm) nefando(-a), atroce

heir [ɛə] N erede m/f

heir apparent N erede m/f legittimo(-a)

heir·ess [ˈɛərɛs] N erede f; (rich) ereditiera

heir·loom [ˈɛəluːm] N: **this picture is a family heirloom** è un quadro di famiglia

heist [haɪst] N (*USA fam: hold-up*) rapina

held [hɛld] PT, PP *of* hold

heli·cop·ter [ˈhɛlɪˌkɒptəʳ] N elicottero

heli·port [ˈhɛlɪˌpɔːt] N eliporto

he·lium [ˈhiːlɪəm] N elio

hell [hɛl] N inferno; **in hell** all'inferno; **he'll go to hell** andrà all'inferno; **all hell broke loose** è successo il *or* un finimondo; **a hell of a noise** (*fam*) un casino infernale, un fracasso del diavolo; **a hell of a lot of** (*fam*) un sacco *or* mucchio *or* casino di; **we had a hell of a time** (*fam: good*) ci siamo divertiti da pazzi; (*: bad*) è stato terribile; **to have a hell of a time doing sth** (*fam*) diventar matto(-a) a fare qc; **to make sb's life hell** (*fam*) rendere la vita un inferno a qn; **to give sb hell** (*fam: address harshly*) dirne di tutti i colori a qn; **to run like hell** (*fam*) correre come un matto(-a); **what the hell do you want?** (*fam*) che diavolo vuoi?; **just for the hell of it** (*fam*) per il gusto di farlo; **go to hell!** (*fam*) va' all'inferno!, va' al diavolo!; **to hell with it!** (*fam*) al diavolo!; **oh hell!** (*fam*) porca miseria!, accidenti!

he'll [hiːl] = he will; he shall

hell·bent [ˌhɛlˈbɛnt] ADJ: **hellbent on doing sth** deciso(-a) a fare qc a tutti i costi

hell·ish [ˈhɛlɪʃ] ADJ (*fam*) infernale, bestiale

hel·lo [həˈləʊ] EXCL (*on meeting sb*) ciao!; (*more formal*) buon giorno!; (*in surprise*) ma guarda!; (*Telec*) pronto!; (*to attract attention*) ehi!

helm [hɛlm] N (*Naut*) timone *m*; **to be at the helm** (*fig*) essere al comando

hel·met [ˈhɛlmɪt] N (*of motorcyclist, construction worker*) casco; (*of miner, soldier, policeman*) elmetto; (*of knight*) elmo

helms·man [ˈhɛlmzmən] N (*pl* -**men**) timoniere *m*

help [hɛlp] N 1 (*assistance*) aiuto; **with the help of** con l'aiuto di; **without the help of sb/sth** senza l'aiuto di qn/qc; **to be of help to sb** essere di aiuto *or* essere utile a qn; **to call for help** chiedere *or* gridare aiuto; **he gave me no help** non mi ha dato nessun aiuto; **he is beyond help** è un caso senza speranza; **there's no help for it** non c'è altro *or* nient'altro da fare; **help!** aiuto! 2 (*employee*) aiutante *m/f*; (*domestic*) domestico(-a); (*daily*) donna di servizio ♦ VT 1 (*aid, assist*) aiutare; (*scheme, project*) contribuire a; (*progress*) favorire; (*pain*) far passare, alleviare; **can you help me?** mi puoi aiutare?; **to help sb (to) do sth** aiutare qn a far qc; **I'll help you carry it** ti aiuto a portarlo; **to help sb with sth** aiutare qn con qc; **I helped him with his luggage** l'ho aiutato a portare i bagagli; **I got my sister to help me** mi sono fatta aiutare da mia sorella; **that won't help much** non servirà a gran che; **can I help you?** (*in shop*) desidera?; **to help sb on/off with his/her coat** aiutare qn a mettersi/togliersi il cappotto; **to help sb across/ up/down** aiutare qn ad attraversare/a salire/a scendere 2 (*at table*): **to help sb to soup** servire la minestra a qn; **to help o.s.** (*to food*) servirsi, prendere; **help yourself!** serviti pure!; (*to other things: steal*) prendersi, arraffare 3 **he can't help coughing** non può fare a meno di tossire; **I couldn't help thinking …** non potevo fare a meno di pensare…; **I couldn't help laughing** non ho potuto fare a meno di ridere; **it can't be helped** non ci si può fare (più) niente, non c'è niente da fare; **he won't do it if I can help it** farò il possibile per impedirglielo; **he can't help himself** non può farne a meno

▸ **help out** VI + ADV aiutare, dare una mano ♦ VT + ADV aiutare, dare una mano a

help desk N (*esp Comput*) help desk *m inv*

help·er [ˈhɛlpəʳ] N aiutante *m/f*, assistente *m/f*

help·ful [ˈhɛlpfʊl] ADJ (*person: willing*) che si rende utile; (*: useful*) di grande aiuto; (*object, advice*) utile; **the staff are always friendly and helpful** il personale è sempre amichevole e disponibile; **he gave me some helpful advice** mi ha dato dei consigli utili

help·ing [ˈhɛlpɪŋ] N porzione *f*; **you've had two helpings of dessert already** ti sei già servito due volte di dolce

helping hand N aiuto; **to give sb a helping hand** dare una mano a qn

help·less [ˈhɛlpləs] ADJ (*rage, person: powerless*) impotente; (*person: vulnerable*) indifeso(-a); (*: physically weak*) debole; **helpless with laughter** morto(-a) dalle risate

help·less·ly [ˈhɛlplɪslɪ] ADV (*struggle, try*) in vano; (*lie, remain*) senza potersi muovere; (*say*) con fare impotente; **he watched helplessly as his backpack was stolen** guardava impotente mentre gli rubavano lo zaino; **to laugh helplessly** ridere senza potersi fermare

help·line [ˈhɛlpˌlaɪn] N ≈ telefono amico; (*Comm*) servizio *m* informazioni, *inv* (a pagamento)

Hel·sin·ki [ˈhɛlsɪŋkɪ] N Helsinki *f*

helter-skelter [ˈhɛltəˈskɛltəʳ] ADV in fretta e furia, in quattro e quattr'otto ♦ N (*Brit: in funfair*) scivolo (a spirale)

hem [hɛm] N (*hemline*) orlo; **to let the hem down on a skirt** allungare una gonna ♦ VT fare l'orlo a

▸ **hem in** VT + ADV cingere, circondare; **to feel hemmed in** (*fig*) sentirsi soffocare

he-man [ˈhiːˌmæn] N (*pl* -**men**) (*fam*) vero maschio

hema·tol·ogy [ˌhiːməˈtɒlədʒɪ] (*USA*) = haematology

hemi·sphere [ˈhɛmɪsfɪəʳ] N emisfero

hem·lock [ˈhɛmˌlɒk] N cicuta

hemo·glo·bin [ˌhiːməʊˈgləʊbɪn] N (*USA*) = haemoglobin

hemo·philia [ˌhiːməʊˈfɪlɪə] N (*USA*) = haemophilia

hem·or·rhage [ˈhɛmərɪdʒ] N (*USA*) = haemorrhage

hem·or·rhoids [ˈhɛmərɔɪdz] NPL (*USA*) = haemorrhoids

hemp [hɛmp] N (*for rope*) canapa; (*drug*) canapa indiana, hashish *m inv*

hen [hɛn] N (*fowl*) gallina; (*with chicks*) chioccia; (*female bird*) femmina; **hen pheasant** fagiano femmina

hence [hɛns] ADV 1 (*frm: therefore*) per cui, quindi; **the party was divided and hence very weak** il partito era diviso e quindi molto debole 2 (*old: place*) da qui, di qui 3 (*frm: time*): **5 years hence** da qui a 5 anni

hence·forth [ˈhɛnsˈfɔːθ] ADV (*frm*) d'ora innanzi *or* in poi

hench·man [ˈhɛntʃmən] N (*pl* -**men**) (*follower*) accolito; (*pej*) scagnozzo

hen·na [ˈhɛnə] N henna

hen·pecked [ˈhɛnˌpɛkt] ADJ (*fam*): **he is henpecked** è succube della moglie

hepa·ti·tis [ˌhɛpəˈtaɪtɪs] N epatite *f*

her [hɜːʳ] PERS PRON 1 (*direct: unstressed*) la, l'+ *vowel*; (*: stressed*) lei; **I hear her** la sento; **I heard her** l'ho sentita; **I saw her** l'ho vista; **I've never seen HER** lei, non l'ho mai vista 2 (*indirect*) le; **I gave her the book** le ho dato il libro; **I spoke to her** le ho parlato; **I gave her a book** le ho dato un libro 3 (*after prep, in comparisons*) lei; **without her** senza di lei; **I was thinking of her** pensavo a lei; **she had a case with her** aveva con sé una valigia; **I'm going with her** vado con lei; **look at her!** guardala!; **if I were her** se fossi in lei; **it's her** è lei; **I'm older than her** sono più vecchio di lei ♦ POSS ADJ il (la) suo(-a); *pl* i (le) suoi (sue); **this is her house** questa è la sua casa; **her brother** suo fratello; **her address** il suo indirizzo; **her parents** i suoi genitori; **Ann and her two best friends** Ann e le sue due migliori amiche; **Sarah and her father** Sarah e suo padre; **her aunt** sua zia; **she's lost her wallet** ha perduto il portafoglio; **with her hands in her pockets** con le mani in tasca; **she took off her coat** si è tolta il cappotto

her·ald [ˈhɛrəld] N araldo; (*fig*) messaggero ♦ VT annunciare

he·ral·dic [hɛˈrældɪk] ADJ araldico(-a)

her·ald·ry [ˈhɛrəldrɪ] N araldica

herb [hɜːb] N (*Med*) erba medicinale; **herbs** NPL (*Culin*) erbe *fpl* aromatiche, odori *mpl*

her·ba·ceous [hɜːˈbeɪʃəs] ADJ erbaceo(-a)

herb·al [ˈhɜːbəl] ADJ di erbe; **herbal tea** tisana

herbi·cide [ˈhɜːbɪˌsaɪd] N erbicida *m*

herd [hɜːd] N (*of cattle, horses*) mandria; (*of wild animals, swine*) branco; (*of people: pej*): **the (common) herd** il gregge ♦ VT (*drive, gather: animals*) guidare; (*: people*) radunare

▸ **herd together** VT + ADV radunare ♦ VI + ADV stringersi uno vicino all'altro

here [hɪəʳ] ADV (*place*) qui, qua; (*at this point*) qui, a questo punto; **I live here** vivo qui; **come here!** vieni qui!; **here!** (*at roll call*) presente!; **over here** da questa parte, di qua; **here is ecco; here he is!** eccolo qui!; **here I am** eccomi qua; **here are** ecco; **here are the books** ecco i libri; **here you are!** (*giving sb sth*) ecco qui!; **here she comes** eccola (che viene); **here and there** qua e là; **here, there and everywhere**

dappertutto; **winter is here** l'inverno è arrivato; **my friend here will do it** il mio amico qui lo farà; **that's neither here nor there** non ha molta importanza; **here's to John!** alla salute di John! ♦ EXCL ehi!

here·abouts [ˈhɪərəˌbaʊts] ADV da queste parti

here·after [ˌhɪərˈɑːftəʳ] ADV (frm) d'ora in poi, da qui in avanti, in futuro ♦ N: **the hereafter** l'aldilà m

here·by [ˌhɪəˈbaɪ](frm) ADV con questo (documento or atto etc); (in letter) con la presente

he·red·i·tary [hɪˈredɪtərɪ] ADJ ereditario(-a)

he·red·ity [hɪˈredɪtɪ] N eredità

her·esy [ˈherəsɪ] N eresia

her·etic [ˈheretɪk] N eretico(-a)

he·reti·cal [hɪˈretɪkəl] ADJ eretico(-a)

here·with [ˌhɪəˈwɪθ] ADV (Comm) con la presente

her·it·age [ˈherɪtɪdʒ] N (inheritance) eredità; (of country, nation) retaggio; **our national heritage** il nostro patrimonio nazionale; **cultural heritage** il patrimonio culturale

her·meti·cal·ly [hɜːˈmetɪkəlɪ] ADV ermeticamente; **hermetically sealed** ermeticamente chiuso(-a)

her·mit [ˈhɜːmɪt] N eremita m

her·nia [ˈhɜːnɪə] N ernia f

hero [ˈhɪərəʊ] N (pl heroes) eroe m

he·ro·ic [hɪˈrəʊɪk] ADJ eroico(-a)

hero·in [ˈherəʊɪn] N eroina

heroin addict N eroinomane m/f

hero·ine [ˈherəʊɪn] N eroina

hero·ism [ˈherəʊɪzəm] N eroismo

her·on [ˈherən] N airone m

hero worship N culto degli eroi

her·ring [ˈherɪŋ] N aringa

hers [hɜːz] POSS PRON il (la) suo(-a); pl i (le) suoi (sue); **a friend of hers** un suo amico, una sua amica; **hers is red, mine is green** il suo è rosso, il mio è verde; **this is hers** questo è (il) suo; **my dog and hers** il mio cane e il suo; **my parents and hers** i miei genitori e i suoi; **my car is older than hers** la mia macchina è più vecchia della sua; **my friends and hers** le mie amiche e le sue; **whose is this? - it's hers** di chi è questo? - è suo; **is that car hers?** è sua quella macchina?

her·self [hɜːˈself] PERS PRON (reflexive) si; (emphatic) lei stessa; (after preposition) sé, se stessa; **she did it herself** l'ha fatto lei; **she's not herself today** ha qualcosa che non va oggi; **by herself** da sola; **she doesn't like travelling by herself** non le piace viaggiare da sola; **she did it (all) by herself** l'ha fatto (tutto) da sola; **she's hurt herself** si è fatta male; **she looked at herself in the mirror** si è guardata allo specchio; see also oneself

Herts ABBR (Brit: = Hertfordshire)

he's [hiːz] = he is; he has

hesi·tant [ˈhezɪtənt] ADJ esitante, indeciso(-a), titubante; **to be hesitant about doing sth** esitare a fare qc

hesi·tate [ˈhezɪteɪt] VI esitare; **to hesitate to do sth** esitare a fare qc; **to hesitate about or over sth** esitare in qc; **don't hesitate to ask (me)** non aver timore or paura di chiedere

hesi·ta·tion [ˌhezɪˈteɪʃən] N esitazione f; **I have no hesitation in saying (that)** ... non esito a dire che...

hes·sian [ˈhesɪən] N tela di canapa

hetero·geneous [ˈhetərəʊˈdʒiːnɪəs] ADJ eterogeneo(-a)

hetero·sex·ual [ˌhetərəʊˈseksjʊəl] ADJ, N eterosessuale m/f

het up [ˈhetˈʌp] ADJ (fam) agitato(-a); **to get het up** scaldarsi

hew [hjuː] (pt hewed pp hewed or hewn) VT (wood) tagliare; (stone, coal) scavare; (statue) scolpire

hex [heks] (USA) N stregoneria ♦ VT stregare

hexa·gon [ˈheksəgən] N esagono

hex·ago·nal [hekˈsægənəl] ADJ esagonale

hey [heɪ] EXCL ehi

hey·day [ˈheɪdeɪ] N età or tempi mpl d'oro; **in his heyday** quand'era in auge, ai bei tempi; **in the heyday of** ai tempi d'oro di

HF [ˌeɪtʃˈef] N ABBR (= high frequency) AF (= alta frequenza)

HI ABBR (USA Post: = Hawaii)

hi [haɪ] EXCL ciao!, salve!

hia·tus [haɪˈeɪtəs] N (frm: gap) vuoto; (Gram) iato

hi·ber·nate [ˈhaɪbəˌneɪt] VI andare in letargo, ibernare

hi·ber·na·tion [ˌhaɪbəˈneɪʃən] N letargo, ibernazione f

hic·cough, hic·cup [ˈhɪkʌp] N singhiozzo; **to have hiccoughs** avere il singhiozzo ♦ VI avere il singhiozzo, singhiozzare

hick [hɪk](USA fam) N burino(-a) ♦ ADJ (ideas) da burino(-a); (town) provinciale

hid [hɪd] PT of hide[1]

hid·den [ˈhɪdn] PP of hide[1] ♦ ADJ (gen) nascosto(-a); (meaning) recondito(-a); **there are no hidden extras** è veramente tutto compreso nel prezzo

hide[1] [haɪd] (pt hid, pp hidden) VT (gen) nascondere; (feelings, truth) dissimulare; **Paula hid the present** Paula ha nascosto il regalo; **the clouds hid the sun** le nuvole hanno nascosto or coperto il sole; **to hide sth from sb** nascondere qc a qn ♦ VI nascondersi; **he hid behind a bush** si è nascosto dietro ad un cespuglio; **he's hiding behind his illness** si trincera dietro la sua malattia; **to hide one's light under a bushel** (fig) tenere nascoste le proprie virtù

  ► **hide away** VI + ADV nascondersi, rifugiarsi ♦ VT + ADV nascondere

  ► **hide out** VI + ADV nascondersi

hide[2] [haɪd] N (skin) pelle f; (leather) cuoio

hide·away [ˈhaɪdəˌweɪ] N (hiding place) nascondiglio; (secluded spot) rifugio

hid·eous [ˈhɪdɪəs] ADJ (sight, person) orribile, orrendo(-a); (crime) atroce

hide·out [ˈhaɪdˌaʊt] N nascondiglio

hid·ing [ˈhaɪdɪŋ] N: **to be in hiding** tenersi nascosto(-a); **to go into hiding** darsi alla macchia

hid·ing [ˈhaɪdɪŋ] N botte fpl; **to give sb a good hiding** (fam) suonarle a qn; **his father will give him a good hiding** suo padre gliele suonerà

hiding place N nascondiglio

hi·er·ar·chy [ˈhaɪəˌrɑːkɪ] N (frm) gerarchia

hi·ero·glyph·ic [ˌhaɪərəˈglɪfɪk] ADJ geroglifico(-a)

hi-fi [ˈhaɪˈfaɪ] ADJ ABBR, N ABBR (= high fidelity) hi-fi m inv; **hi-fi system** impianto hi-fi

higgledy-piggledy [ˈhɪgldɪˈpɪgldɪ] ADJ buttato(-a) alla rinfusa ♦ ADV alla rinfusa

high [haɪ] ADJ (comp -er, superl -est) 1 (gen) alto(-a); **the wall's two metres high** il muro è alto due metri; **a building 60 metres high** un palazzo alto 60 metri; **how high is Ben Nevis?** quanto è alto il Ben Nevis?; **to leave sb high and dry** (fig) piantare in asso qn; **to be on one's high horse** (fig) montare or salire in cattedra; **to be or act high and mighty** darsi delle arie 2 (frequency, pressure, temperature, salary, price) alto(-a); (speed, wind) forte; (character, ideals) nobile; (value, respect, number) grande; **to pay a high price for sth** pagare (molto) caro(-a) qc; **prices are higher in Germany** i prezzi sono più alti in Germania; **there's high unemployment in Europe** c'è una forte disoccupazione in Europa; **to be high in sth** avere un alto contenuto di qc; **it's very high in fat** ha un altissimo contenuto di grassi; **his colour is very high** è molto rosso in viso; **to have a high old time** (fam) spassarsela; **it's high time you were in bed** (fam) dovresti essere già a letto da un pezzo 3 (Mus: note) alto(-a); (sound, voice) acuto(-a); **she's got a very high voice** ha una voce molto acuta 4 (fam: on drugs) fatto(-a); (: on drink) su di giri 5 (Brit: Culin: meat, game) frollato(-a); (: spoilt) andato(-a) a male ♦ ADV (fly, aim, climb) in alto; **the doves flew high in the sky** le colombe volavano alte nel cielo; **the plane flew high over the mountains** l'aereo volava alto sulle montagne; **high up** molto in alto; **high above the clouds** in alto sopra le nuvole; **higher and higher** sempre più (in) alto; **the bidding went as high as £500** le offerte sono arrivate fino a 500 sterline; **to hunt high and low** cercare per mare e per terra; **feelings were running high** c'era molta tensione ♦ N 1 **on high** (in heaven) nell'alto dei cieli; **orders from on high** (also hum) ordini dall'alto 2 **exports have reached a new high** le esportazioni hanno toccato un nuovo record 3 (Met) anticiclone m, area di alta pressione

high·ball [ˈhaɪˌbɔːl] N (USA: drink) whisky (or brandy) e soda con ghiaccio

high·boy [ˈhaɪˌbɔɪ] N (USA) cassettone m

high·brow [ˈhaɪˌbraʊ] N, ADJ intellettualoide m/f

high·chair [ˈhaɪˌtʃɛəʳ] N seggiolone m
high-class [ˌhaɪˈklɑːs] ADJ (neighbourhood) elegante; (hotel) di prim'ordine; (person) di gran classe; (food) raffinato(-a)
high court N (Law) ≈ Corte f Suprema
high·er [ˈhaɪəʳ] ADJ (form of life, study) superiore ♦ ADV più in alto, più in su
higher education N istruzione f superiore or universitaria
high·fa·lu·tin [ˌhaɪfəˈluːtɪn] ADJ (fam) pomposo(-a)
high finance N alta finanza
high-flier, high-flyer [ˌhaɪˈflaɪəʳ] N (ambitious) rampante m/f, ambizioso(-a); (gifted) giovane m/f di talento
high-flying [ˈhaɪˌflaɪɪŋ] ADJ (aircraft) da alta quota; (fig: person, aim) ambizioso(-a)
high-handed [ˌhaɪˈhændɪd] ADJ dispotico(-a), autoritario(-a)
high-heeled [ˌhaɪˈhiːld] ADJ con il tacco alto
high·jack [ˈhaɪˌdʒæk] VT, N = hijack
high jump N (Sport) salto in alto
high·lands [ˈhaɪləndz] NPL zona montuosa; **the Highlands** le Highlands scozzesi
high-level [ˈhaɪˌlɛvl] ADJ (talks, conference) ad alto livello; (Comput: language) di alto livello
high·light [ˈhaɪˌlaɪt] VT (fig) mettere in evidenza; (in painting, drawing) lumeggiare ♦ N (fig: of evening, trip) clou m inv; (Art) luce f; **highlights** NPL (in hair) colpi mpl di sole, riflessi mpl; **the highlight of the evening** il clou della serata; **the highlight of the vacation** il momento più bello della vacanza
high·light·er [ˈhaɪˌlaɪtəʳ] N (pen) evidenziatore m
high·ly [ˈhaɪlɪ] ADV estremamente, molto; **highly paid** pagato(-a) molto bene; **highly spiced dishes** piatti molto piccanti; **highly specialized** altamente specializzato(-a); **to think highly of sb** avere molta stima di qn; **to speak highly of** parlare molto bene di
highly-strung [ˌhaɪlɪˈstrʌŋ] ADJ nervoso(-a), teso(-a)
High Mass N messa cantata or solenne
high·ness [ˈhaɪnɪs] N: **Your Highness** Vostra Altezza
high-pitched [ˌhaɪˈpɪtʃt] ADJ acuto(-a)
high point N: **the high point** (of show, evening, holiday) il clou m inv
high-powered [ˌhaɪˈpaʊəd] ADJ (engine) molto potente, ad alta potenza; (fig: person) di prestigio
high-pressure [ˌhaɪˈprɛʃəʳ] ADJ ad alta pressione; (fig) aggressivo(-a)
high-rise [ˈhaɪˌraɪz] ADJ: **high-rise building** palazzone m
high school N (Brit) ≈ scuola media inferiore e superiore (dagli 11 ai 18 anni); (USA) ≈ scuola media superiore
high season N (Brit) alta stagione f
high spirits NPL buonumore msg; **to be in high spirits** essere euforico(-a)
high street N (Brit) strada principale, corso
high-tech [ˌhaɪˈtɛk] ADJ high-tech inv, ad alto contenuto tecnologico
high·way [ˈhaɪˌweɪ] N strada principale or maestra; **public highway** strada pubblica; **he knows all the highways and byways of Tuscany** conosce tutte le strade e stradine della Toscana; **a six-lane highway** una strada a sei corsie
highway·man [ˈhaɪˌweɪmən] N (pl -men) = bandito
hi·jack [ˈhaɪˌdʒæk] VT (aircraft) dirottare; (truck, car) impadronirsi di ♦ N dirottamento
hi·jack·er [ˈhaɪˌdʒækəʳ] N (of aircraft) dirottatore(-trice)
hike [haɪk] N **1** escursione f a piedi; **to go on** or **for a hike** fare un'escursione or una gita a piedi **2** (fam: in prices) aumento ♦ VI fare un'escursione or una gita a piedi; **to go hiking** fare escursioni a piedi ♦ VT (fam) aumentare
hik·er [ˈhaɪkəʳ] N escursionista m/f
hik·ing [ˈhaɪkɪŋ] N escursioni fpl a piedi
hi·lari·ous [hɪˈlɛərɪəs] ADJ spassosissimo(-a)
hi·lar·ity [hɪˈlærɪtɪ] N ilarità
hill [hɪl] N collina; (lower) colle m; (slope) pendio, costa; **hills and lakes** colline e laghi; **we pushed the car to the top of the hill** abbiamo spinto la macchina in cima al pendio; **up hill and down dale** per monti e per valli; **to be over the hill** (fig: fam) essere sul viale del tramonto; **as old as the hills** vecchio(-a) come Matusalemme

hill·bil·ly [ˈhɪlˌbɪlɪ] N (USA) montanaro del sud degli Stati Uniti; (pej) zotico(-a)
hill·ock [ˈhɪlək] N collinetta, poggio
hill·side [ˈhɪlˌsaɪd] N pendio
hill start N (Aut) partenza in salita
hill-walking [ˈhɪlwɔːkɪŋ] N: **to go hill-walking** fare passeggiate in collina
hilly [ˈhɪlɪ] ADJ (comp -ier, superl -iest) collinoso(-a), montagnoso(-a); **this road is very hilly** questa strada è un continuo saliscendi
hilt [hɪlt] N (of sword) elsa, impugnatura; **to back sb to the hilt** dare il proprio appoggio incondizionato a qn; **to mortgage sth up to the hilt** ipotecare completamente qc
him [hɪm] PERS PRON **1** (direct: unstressed) lo, l' + vowel; (: stressed) lui; **I hear him** lo sento; **I heard him** l'ho sentito; **I saw him** l'ho visto; **I've never seen HIM** lui, non l'ho mai visto **2** (indirect) gli; **I gave him the book** gli ho dato il libro; **I spoke to him** gli ho parlato **3** (after prep, in comparatives) lui; **without him** senza di lui; **I was thinking of him** pensavo a lui; **he had a case with him** aveva con sé una valigia; **I'm going with him** vado con lui; **look at him!** guardalo!; **if I were him** se fossi in lui; **it's him** è lui; **I'm older than him** sono più vecchio di lui
Hima·la·yas [ˌhɪməˈleɪəz] NPL: **the Himalayas** l'Himalaia msg
him·self [hɪmˈsɛlf] PERS PRON (reflexive) si; (emphatic) lui stesso; (after preposition) sé, se stesso; **(all) by himself** (tutto) da solo or da sé; **he doesn't like travelling by himself** non gli piace viaggiare da solo; **he's not himself today** ha qualcosa che non va oggi; **he's hurt himself** si è fatto male; **he was looking at himself in the mirror** si guardava allo specchio; **he did it himself** l'ha fatto lui; **he talked mainly about himself** parlava principalmente di sé; see also **oneself**
hind[1] [haɪnd] ADJ (leg) posteriore; **he would talk the hind leg off a donkey** (fam) parla come una macchinetta
hind[2] [haɪnd] N (Zool) cerva
hin·der [ˈhɪndəʳ] VT (prevent): **to hinder sb (from doing sth)** impedire a qn (di fare qc); (delay) ritardare; (obstruct) ostacolare, intralciare; **I want to help, not hinder you** voglio aiutarti, non intralciarti; **the loss of documents hindered the investigation** la perdita di documenti ha ritardato l'indagine
hind·quarters [ˈhaɪndˌkwɔːtəz] NPL (Zool) posteriore msg
hin·drance [ˈhɪndrəns] N intralcio, impedimento, ostacolo; **to be a hindrance to** intralciare, ostacolare
hind·sight [ˈhaɪndˌsaɪt] N senno di poi; **with the benefit of hindsight** con il senno di poi
Hin·du [ˈhɪnˈduː] ADJ, N indù m/f inv
Hin·du·ism [ˈhɪnduːˌɪzəm] N (Rel) induismo
hinge [hɪndʒ] N (of door, gate) cardine m; (of box) cerniera ♦ VI: **to hinge on** (fig) dipendere da
hint [hɪnt] N (suggestion) allusione f, accenno; (advice) consiglio; **a hint of garlic** una punta d'aglio; **hints on do-it-yourself** consigli pratici per il fai-da-te; **a gentle hint** una velata allusione; **to give sb a broad hint** far capire chiaramente a qn; **to drop a hint** lasciar capire; **to take the hint** capire l'antifona; **I told him I was a bit tired, but he didn't take the hint** gli ho detto che ero un po' stanca, ma non ha capito; **with a hint of irony/sadness** con una punta d'ironia/tristezza; **give me a hint** (clue) dammi almeno un'idea, dammi un'indicazione ♦ VT: **to hint (to sb) that** ... lasciar capire (a qn) che ...; **he hinted that I had a good chance of getting the job** ha lasciato capire che avevo buone probabilità di ottenere il lavoro
► **hint at** VI + PREP accennare a, alludere a, fare allusione a; **just what are you hinting at?** cosa vuoi insinuare?
hip[1] [hɪp] N (Anat) anca; (side) fianco; **to put one's hands on one's hips** mettersi le mani sui fianchi; **she put her hands on her hips** si è messa le mani sui fianchi
hip[2] [hɪp] N (Bot) frutto della rosa canina
hip flask N fiaschetta
hip hop N hip-hop m inv
hip·pie, hip·py [ˈhɪpɪ] N hippy m/f inv
hip·po [ˈhɪpəʊ] N ippopotamo
hip pocket N tasca posteriore dei calzoni

hip·po·pota·mus [ˌhɪpəˈpɒtəməs] N (pl **hippopotamuses** or **hippopotami** [ˌhɪpəˈpɒtəmaɪ]) ippopotamo

hippy [ˈhɪpɪ] N = **hippie**

hire [ˈhaɪəʳ] N noleggio; (cost) nolo; **car hire** noleggio auto; "**for hire**" "noleggiasi"; (taxi) "libero"; **on hire** a nolo ♦ VT (Brit: car, equipment) noleggiare; (employee) ingaggiare; **we hired a car** abbiamo noleggiato una macchina; **they hired a lawyer** hanno assunto un avvocato; **hired hand** bracciante m/f; **hired assassin** sicario prezzolato

▸ **hire out** VT + ADV noleggiare, dare a nolo or noleggio, affittare

hired car [ˌhaɪədˈkɑː], **hire car** N (Brit) macchina a nolo

hire-purchase [ˌhaɪəˈpɜːtʃɪs] N (Brit) acquisto (or vendita) a rate; **to buy sth on hire-purchase** comprare qc a rate

his [hɪz] POSS ADJ, PRON il (la) suo(-a); pl i (le) suoi (sue); **his address** il suo indirizzo; **his house** la sua casa; **his brother** suo fratello; **his aunt** sua zia; **Joe and his father** Joe e suo padre; **his parents** i suoi genitori; **his opinions** le sue opinioni; **a friend of his** un suo amico; **his is red, mine is green** il suo è rosso, il mio è verde; **this is his** questo è (il) suo; **he took off his coat** si è tolto il cappotto; **he's washing his hair** si sta lavando i capelli; **my dog and his** il mio cane e il suo; **my parents and his** i miei genitori e i suoi; **my car is older than his** la mia macchina è più vecchia della sua; **my shoes and his** le mie scarpe e le sue; **whose is this?** - **it's his** di chi è questo? - è suo; **is that car his?** è sua quella macchina?

Hispanic [hɪsˈpænɪk] ADJ ispanico(-a), (ispanica)

hiss [hɪs] N (of snake) sibilo; (of kettle, protest) fischio; (of cat) soffio; **shouts and hisses** grida e fischi ♦ VI (see n) sibilare; fischiare; soffiare; **the audience hissed** il pubblico fischiò ♦ VT (speaker) fischiare; "**get out**" **she hissed** "sparisci" sibilò

his·to·gram [ˈhɪstəˌgræm] N istogramma m

his·to·rian [hɪsˈtɔːrɪən] N storico(-a)

his·tor·ic [hɪsˈtɒrɪk] ADJ storico(-a)

his·to·ry [ˈhɪstərɪ] N storia; **a history book** un libro di storia; **to make history** fare storia; **to go down in history** passare alla storia; **there's a long history of that illness in his family** ci sono molti precedenti (della malattia) nella sua famiglia; **a history of drinking problems** un passato da alcolista; **he's history** è finito

his·tri·on·ics [ˌhɪstrɪˈɒnɪks] NPL (pej) scene fpl

hit [hɪt] (pt, pp **hit**) N 1 (blow) colpo; (Sport) tiro, colpo; **she made three hits and two misses** ha messo a segno tre colpi e ne ha mancati due; **to score a direct hit** colpire in pieno 2 (Mus, Theatre, Cine) successo; **to be a hit** essere un (gran) successo; **the song is a big hit** è una canzone di successo; **the band's latest hit** l'ultimo successo del complesso; **she's a hit with everyone** (fam) ha successo con tutti, fa colpo su tutti; **to get a hit/10,000 hits** (Comput) trovare una pagina Web/10.000 pagine Web ♦ VT 1 (strike, affect: gen) colpire; (thrash: person) picchiare; (knock against) battere; (collide with: car) urtare, sbattere contro; **he hit the ball** ha colpito la palla; **Andrew hit him** Andrew l'ha picchiato; **he was hit by a car** è stato investito da una macchina; **to hit the target** colpire il bersaglio; **to hit sb a blow** dare un colpo a qn; **to hit a man when he's down** (fig) infierire su chi non può difendersi; **to hit the mark** colpire nel segno, raggiungere lo scopo; **then it hit me** (realization: fam) solo allora me ne sono reso conto; **the news hit him hard** la notizia è stata un brutto colpo per lui 2 (reach: target, musical note) raggiungere; (: road) trovare, raggiungere; (: speed) toccare; (: difficulty, snag) incontrare, imbattersi in; (fam: arrive at: town) arrivare in; **to hit the papers** finire sui giornali; **to hit the headlines** far titolo; **to hit the front page** apparire in prima pagina; **to hit the bottle** (fam) darsi al bere; **to hit the ceiling** (fam) andare su tutte le furie; **to hit the road** or **the trail** (fam) levare le tende; **to hit the hay** or **the sack** (fam) andare a letto ♦ ADJ (song, film) di successo

▸ **hit against** VI + PREP sbattere contro; **to hit against sth** sbattere contro qc

▸ **hit back** VI + ADV restituire il colpo; **to hit back at sb** (fig) reagire contro qn ♦ VT + ADV: **to hit sb back** restituire il colpo a qn

▸ **hit off** VT + ADV: **to hit it off with sb** andare d'accordo con qn

▸ **hit on** VI + PREP: **to hit on sb** (USA fam) fare avance sessuali a qn

▸ **hit out at** VI + ADV + PREP sferrare (dei) colpi contro; (fig) attaccare

▸ **hit on, hit upon** VI + PREP (answer) imbroccare, azzeccare; (solution) trovare (per caso)

hit-and-run [ˈhɪtənˈrʌn] ADJ: **hit-and-run driver** pirata m della strada; **hit-and-run raid** (Mil) attacco m lampo, inv; **hit-and-run tactics** (Mil) tattica dell'attacco lampo

hitch [hɪtʃ] N (impediment, obstacle) intoppo, contrattempo; (difficulty) difficoltà f inv; **there's been a slight hitch** c'è stato un piccolo intoppo; **technical hitch** difficoltà tecnica; **without a hitch** senza intoppi, a gonfie vele ♦ VT 1 (fasten) attaccare; (to post) legare; **to get hitched** (fam) sposarsi 2 (fam): **to hitch a lift** fare l'autostop ♦ VI (fam) = **hitchhike**

▸ **hitch up** VT + ADV (trousers) tirarsi su; (horse, cart) attaccare

hitch·hike [ˈhɪtʃˌhaɪk] VI fare l'autostop; **we hitchhiked through Europe** abbiamo girato tutta l'Europa in autostop

hitch·hiker [ˈhɪtʃˌhaɪkəʳ] N autostoppista m/f

hitch·hiking [ˈhɪtʃˌhaɪkɪŋ] N autostop m

hi-tech [ˈhaɪˈtɛk] ADJ (Industry) tecnologicamente avanzato(-a), hi-tech inv ♦ N (Industry) tecnologia avanzata; (Archit, Design) hi-tech m inv, f inv

hith·er·to [ˈhɪðəˈtuː] ADV (frm) finora

hit list N: **to be on a hit list** essere un bersaglio

hit man N (fam) sicario, killer m inv

hit-or-miss [ˈhɪtɔːˈmɪs] ADJ (approach) disinvolto(-a); (work) così cosà; **the service in this hotel is very hit-or-miss** il servizio in questo albergo lascia a desiderare

hit parade N hit-parade f inv

HIV [ˌeɪtʃaɪˈviː] N ABBR (= human immunodeficiency virus) HIV m inv

hive [haɪv] N alveare m; (bees collectively) sciame m; **the shop was a hive of activity** (fig) c'era una grande attività nel negozio

▸ **hive off** VI + ADV: **to hive off (from)** staccarsi (da) ♦ VT + ADV staccare; (privatize) privatizzare; **waste collection will be hived off to another company** la raccolta dei rifiuti verrà trasferita ad un'altra società

hl ABBR (= hectolitre) hl

HM [ˌeɪtʃˈɛm] N ABBR (= His (or Her) Majesty) SM (= Sua Maestà)

HMO [ˌeɪtʃɛmˈəʊ] N ABBR (USA: = health maintenance organization) organo per la salvaguardia della salute pubblica

HMS [ˌeɪtʃɛmˈɛs] N ABBR (Brit: = His (or Her) Majesty's Ship)

hoard [hɔːd] N (of food) provviste fpl, scorta; (of money) gruzzolo ♦ VT (also: **hoard up**) (provisions) fare incetta di, provvista di; (money) ammonticchiare; (old newspapers) accumulare

hoard·ing [ˈhɔːdɪŋ] N (Brit: for advertisements) tabellone m or riquadro per affissioni; (wooden fence) staccionata, palizzata

hoar-frost [ˈhɔːˈfrɒst] N brina

hoarse [hɔːs] ADJ (comp -r, superl -st) rauco(-a); **they shouted themselves hoarse** si sono sgolati a forza di urlare

hoax [həʊks] N scherzo; (bomb scare) falso allarme m; **it was a hoax** è stato un falso allarme; **the warning call was a hoax** la telefonata minatoria è stata uno scherzo ♦ VT prendere in giro; **he hoaxed me into believing that ...** mi ha fatto credere che...

hob [hɒb] N piastra (con fornelli)

hob·ble [ˈhɒbl] VI zoppicare; **to hobble in/out** entrare/uscire zoppicando

hob·by [ˈhɒbɪ] N hobby m inv, passatempo (preferito)

hobby-horse [ˈhɒbɪˌhɔːs] N 1 (fig) chiodo fisso 2 (toy) giocattolo di legno raffigurante la testa di un cavallo montata su un bastone

hob·nail boots [ˈhɒbneɪlˈbuːts], **hob·nailed boots** [ˌhɒbneɪldˈbuːts] NPL scarponi mpl chiodati

hob·nob [ˈhɒbˌnɒb] VI (fam): **to hobnob (with)** essere in confidenza (con)

hobo [ˈhəʊbəʊ] N (USA) vagabondo

hock¹ [hɒk] N (of animal, also Culin) garretto

hock² [hɒk] N (Brit: wine) vino bianco del Reno

hock³ [hɒk] (fam) N: **to be in hock** (debt) essere indebitato(-a) ♦ VT (pawn) impegnare

hock·ey [ˈhɒkɪ] N hockey *m* (su prato)
hockey stick N bastone *m* da hockey
hocus-pocus [ˌhəʊkəsˈpəʊkəs] N (*trickery*) trucco; (*words: of magician*) abracadabra *m inv*; (*talk*) ciance *fpl*
hod [hɒd] N (*Tech*) cassetta per portare i mattoni
hodge·podge [ˈhɒdʒˌpɒdʒ] N = hotchpotch
hoe [həʊ] N zappa ♦ vt (*ground*) zappare; (*weeds*) sarchiare
hog [hɒg] N porco, maiale *m*; **to go the whole hog** (*fig*) fare le cose fino in fondo ♦ vt (*fam*) accapararsi; **to hog the road** guidare nel mezzo della strada
Hog·man·ay [ˈhɒgməˌneɪ] N (*in Scotland*) ≈ San Silvestro
hog·wash [ˈhɒgwɒʃ] N (*fam*) stupidaggini *fpl*, cretinate *fpl*
hoist [hɔɪst] vt issare ♦ N paranco; (*goods lift*) montacarichi *m inv*; see also **petard**
hoity-toity [ˌhɔɪtɪˈtɔɪtɪ] ADJ (*fam*) altezzoso(-a)
hold [həʊld] (*pt, pp* held) N 1 presa; **to seize** *or* **grab hold of sth/sb** afferrare qc/qn; **to catch** *or* **get (a) hold of** afferrare, attaccarsi a; **to get hold of sth** procurarsi qc; **where can I get hold of some red paint?** dove posso procurarmi della vernice rossa?; **to get (a) hold of o.s.** (*fig*) trattenersi, controllarsi; **no holds barred** (*fig*) senza esclusione di colpi; **to have a hold over sb** (*fig*) avere un forte ascendente *or* molta influenza su qn 2 (*Naut, Aer*) stiva 3 (*Mountaineering*) appiglio ♦ vt 1 (*gen*) tenere; (*contain*) contenere; (*fig: audience*) mantenere viva l'attenzione di; (: *attention, interest*) mantenere; (: *belief, opinion*) avere; **he was holding her in his arms** la teneva tra le braccia; **he held the pistol in his right hand** teneva la pistola con la mano destra; **to hold hands** tenersi per mano; **to hold a baby** tenere in braccio un bambino; **she was holding the baby** teneva in braccio il bambino; **it holds ten litres** contiene dieci litri; **the hall holds 500 people** nella sala c'è posto per 500 persone; **the chair won't hold you** la sedia non sopporterà il tuo peso; **to hold o.s. upright/ready** tenersi dritto(-a)/pronto(-a); **to hold one's head high** andare a testa alta; **to hold sb to a promise** far mantenere una promessa a qn; **to hold one's own** sapersi difendere, difendersi bene; **she holds the view that ...** è del parere che...; **to hold the line** (*Telec*) rimanere *or* restare in linea; **hold the line!** resti in linea!; **this car holds the road well** questa macchina tiene bene la strada; **what does the future hold?** cosa ci riserva il futuro? 2 (*restrain: person*) trattenere; **there's no holding him** non lo ferma più nessuno; **to hold one's breath** trattenere il respiro *or* il fiato; **I held my breath in amazement** sono rimasto a bocca aperta per lo stupore; **to hold one's tongue** (*fig*) tacere, star zitto(-a); **hold it!** (*fam*) alt!, fermati! 3 (*position, title, passport*) avere; (*shares: Fin*) possedere, avere; (*record: Sport*) detenere; (*position: Mil*) tenere, mantenere; **to hold office** (*Pol*) essere in carica 4 (*meeting, election*) tenere, indire; (*conversation*) tenere, sostenere; (*Rel: service*) celebrare 5 (*consider*): **to hold (that)** ritenere (che), sostenere (che); **to hold sb in high esteem** avere molta stima di qn; **to hold sth/sb dear** tenere molto a qc/qn; **to hold sb responsible for sth** considerare *or* ritenere qn responsabile di qc ♦ vi (*rope, nail*) tenere; (*continue*) mantenersi, durare; (*be valid*) essere valido(-a); **to hold firm** *or* **fast** resistere bene, tenere
▸ **hold against** vt + prep: **to hold sth against sb** (*fig*) volerne a qn per qc
▸ **hold back** vi + adv: **to hold back from sth** tirarsi indietro da qc; **to hold back from doing sth** trattenersi dal fare qc; **he always holds back when he meets new people** quando incontra gente nuova è sempre poco espansivo ♦ vt + adv 1 (*restrain: crowd, river*) trattenere, contenere; (: *emotions, tears*) trattenere, frenare; **to hold sb back from doing sth** impedire a qn di fare qc 2 (*information, name*) nascondere, non dare, celare; **he's holding something back** non sta dicendo tutta la verità
▸ **hold down** vt + adv 1 (*keep low, on ground*) tener giù; (*keep in place*) tener fermo(-a) 2 (*job*) conservare, mantenere
▸ **hold forth** vi + adv fare *or* tenere una concione
▸ **hold in** vt + adv (*stomach*) tirare *or* tenere in dentro; **to hold o.s. in** (*fig*) frenarsi, trattenersi
▸ **hold off** vt + adv (*enemy*) tenere a distanza; (*attack*) sventare; (*visitor*) far aspettare ♦ vi + adv (*rain*): **if the rain holds**

off se non si mette a piovere
▸ **hold on** vi + adv (*endure*) resistere; (*wait*) aspettare; **hold on, I'm coming!** aspettami, arrivo!; **hold on!** (*Telec*) resti in linea! ♦ vi + adv tenere a posto
▸ **hold on to** vt + adv + prep (*grasp*) tenersi (attaccato(-a)) a, tenersi (stretto(-a)) a; (*keep*) tenere, conservare; (*fig: retain: hope*) rimanere aggrappato(-a) a
▸ **hold out** vi + adv 1 (*supplies*) durare 2 (*stand firm*) tener duro; **to hold out for more money** (*fam*) continuare a chiedere più soldi; **to hold out (against)** resistere (a) ♦ vt + adv: **to hold out (sth to sb)** allungare (qc a qn); (*one's arms, hand*) tendere; (*fig: offer*) presentare, offrire; (: *hope*) nutrire
▸ **hold on** vt + adv + prep: **you've been holding out on me!** (*fam*) mi hai tenuto nascosto qualcosa!
▸ **hold over** vt + adv (*meeting*) rimandare, rinviare
▸ **hold together** vi + adv (*group*) restare unito(-a) ♦ vt + adv (*factions*) tenere uniti(-e)
▸ **hold up** vt + adv 1 (*raise*) sollevare, alzare; **hold up your hand** alza la mano; **to hold sth up to the light** alzare qc verso la luce 2 (*support: roof*) sostenere 3 (*delay: person*) trattenere; (: *traffic*) rallentare; (*stop*) bloccare 4 (*rob: bank*) assaltare; (: *person*) assalire ♦ vi + adv (*survive, last*) resistere; **how are your shoes holding up?** in che stato sono le tue scarpe?
hold·all [ˈhəʊldɔːl] N (*Brit*) sacca *or* borsa da viaggio, borsone *m*
hold·er [ˈhəʊldə*] N 1 (*of ticket*) possessore *m*; (*owner: of property*) proprietario(-a); (*tenant*) affittuario(-a); (*of bonds, shares*) titolare *m/f*, intestatario(-a); (*of title*) chi ha *or* possiede; (*of passport, office, post*) titolare; (*of record*) detentore(-trice) 2 (*container*) contenitore *m*; **pencil holder** portamatite *m inv*
hold·ing [ˈhəʊldɪŋ] N (*land*) podere *m*, tenuta *f*; **holdings** terre *fpl*, proprietà *fpl* terriere; **holdings** NPL (*Comm*) azioni *fpl*, titoli *mpl*
holding company N (*Comm*) holding *f inv*
hold-up [ˈhəʊldʌp] N (*robbery*) rapina a mano armata; (*stoppage, delay*) intoppo; (*Brit: of traffic*) ingorgo; **a bank clerk was injured in the hold-up** un impiegato di banca è rimasto ferito nella rapina; **no one explained the reason for the hold-up** nessuno ha spiegato i motivi dell'intoppo; **a hold-up on the motorway** un ingorgo sull'autostrada
hole [həʊl] N 1 (*in ground, road, or Golf*) buca; (*in wall, fence, clothes*) buco; (*in dam, ship*) falla; (*in defences*) breccia; (*of rabbit, fox*) tana; **to wear a hole in sth** usare qc tanto da farci un buco; **to pick holes in** (*fig: argument*) dimostrare che fa acqua; **it made a hole in my savings** ha mangiato gran parte dei miei risparmi 2 (*fig: difficulty*): **to be in a hole** essere nei guai; **she got me out of a hole** mi ha tirato fuori dai pasticci *or* dai guai 3 (*fam, pej: place*) buco ♦ vt bucare; (*Golf: ball*) mandare in buca; **the boat was holed when it hit the rocks** quando la barca ha urtato gli scogli si è aperta una falla nello scafo
▸ **hole out** vi + adv andare in buca
▸ **hole up** vi + adv nascondersi, rifugiarsi
holi·day [ˈhɒlədɪ] N (*vacation*) vacanza; (*from work*) ferie *fpl*; (*day off*) giorno di vacanza; **the school holidays** le vacanze scolastiche; **holiday with pay** ferie pagate *or* retribuite; **he took a day's holiday** ha preso un giorno di ferie; **public holiday** festa (nazionale); **next Monday is a holiday** lunedì prossimo è festa; **to be on holiday** essere in vacanza ♦ ADJ (*town*) di villeggiatura; **holiday atmosphere** aria di vacanza; **holiday spirit** spirito vacanziero
holiday home N seconda casa (*per le vacanze*)
holiday resort N luogo di villeggiatura
holiday season N stagione *f* delle vacanze
ho·li·ness [ˈhəʊlɪnɪs] N santità
hol·is·tic [həʊˈlɪstɪk] ADJ olistico(-a)
Hol·land [ˈhɒlənd] N Olanda
hol·ler [ˈhɒlə*] vt, vi (*fam*) urlare, gridare
hol·low [ˈhɒləʊ] ADJ (*comp* -er, *superl* -est) cavo(-a), vuoto(-a); (*eyes, cheeks*) infossato(-a); (*sound, voice*) cupo(-a), (*empathy*) falso(-a); (*promises*) vano(-a); **a hollow victory** una vittoria di Pirro; **to give a hollow laugh** ridere a denti stretti ♦ vt: **to beat sb hollow** (*fam*) stracciare qn ♦ N (*of back*) incavo; (*of hand*) cavo; (*in ground*) cavità *f inv*, affossamento; (*small valley*) conca; (*in landscape*) valletta, depressione *f*

▸ **hollow out** VT + ADV scavare, incavare
hol·ly ['hɒlɪ] N (*also:* holly tree) agrifoglio
hol·ly·hock ['hɒlɪˌhɒk] N malvone *m*
Hol·ly·wood ['hɒlɪˌwʊd] N Hollywood *f*
holo·caust ['hɒləˌkɔːst] N olocausto
holo·gram ['hɒləˌgræm] N ologramma *m*
hol·ster ['həʊlstəʳ] N fondina
holy ['həʊlɪ] ADJ (*comp* -ier, *superl* -iest) (*gen*) santo(-a); (*ground, bread*) consacrato(-a), benedetto(-a); (*person*) pio(-a); (*vow*) religioso(-a); **the Holy Trinity** la Santissima Trinità; **a holy terror** (*fam*) un demonio
Holy Communion N la comunione, l'eucaristia
Holy Land N: **the Holy Land** la Terra Santa
holy orders NPL ordini *mpl* (sacri)
Holy Spirit, Holy Ghost N: **the Holy Spirit, the Holy Ghost** lo Spirito Santo
hom·age ['hɒmɪdʒ] N omaggio; **to pay homage to** rendere omaggio a
home [həʊm] N 1 (*residence, house*) casa; (*country, area*) patria, paese *m* natale or natio; (*Bot, Zool*) habitat *m inv*; **to have a home of one's own** avere una casa propria; **it's near my home** è vicino a casa mia; **it's a home from home** è come essere a casa propria; **there's no place like home** non si sta mai bene come a casa propria; **she comes from a good home** viene da una buona famiglia; **he comes from a broken home** i suoi sono divisi; **to give sb/sth a home** prendersi in casa qn/qc; **he made his home in Italy** si è stabilito in Italia; **Scotland is the home of the haggis** la Scozia è la patria dell'haggis; **at home** a casa; **Celtic is playing at home on Saturday** il Celtic gioca in casa sabato; **make yourself at home** fai come se fossi a casa tua; **to make sb feel at home** mettere qn a proprio agio; **she is at home with the topic** conosce la materia benissimo; **I'm not at home to anyone** (*fig*) non ci sono per nessuno 2 (*institution*) istituto; (*for old people*) casa di riposo; **a children's home** un istituto per l'infanzia ♦ ADV 1 a casa; **to go home** andare a casa; **to come home** tornare (a casa); **to stay home** stare a or restare in casa; **to get home** arrivare a casa; **I got home at 10 o'clock** sono rientrato alle 10; **I'll be home at five o'clock** sarò a casa alle cinque; **on the way home** sulla via di casa; **can I see you home?** posso accompagnarti a casa?; **it's nothing to write home about** (*fam*) non è gran che, non è niente di speciale; **we're home and dry** (*fig*) siamo salvi 2 (*right in*) a fondo, fino in fondo; **to drive a nail home** conficcare un chiodo; **to bring sth home to sb** (*fig*) aprire gli occhi a qn su qc; **that remark hit home** ciò che ha detto ha colpito nel segno ♦ VI (*pigeons*) tornare alla base ♦ ADJ (*life*) familiare; (*cooking*) casalingo(-a); (*improvements*) alla casa; (*comforts*) di casa; (*native: village*) natale, natio(-a); (*Econ: trade, market*) nazionale, interno(-a); (*: product, industries*) nazionale; (*news*) dall'interno; (*Sport: team*) di casa; (*: match, win*) in casa
▸ **home in on** VI + ADV + PREP (*missiles*) dirigersi (automaticamente) verso
home address N indirizzo di casa or privato
home-brew [həʊmˈbruː] N birra or vino fatto(-a) in casa
home·coming ['həʊmˌkʌmɪŋ] N ritorno
Home Counties NPL: **the Home Counties** le contee intorno a Londra
home economics N economia domestica
home ground N (*fig*): **to be on home ground** essere sul proprio terreno
home-grown [ˌhəʊmˈgrəʊn] ADJ (*in locality*) nostrano(-a), di produzione locale
home help N (*Brit*) assistente a domicilio per anziani o disabili stipendiata dai servizi sociali
home·land ['həʊmˌlænd] N patria
home·less ['həʊmlɪs] ADJ senza tetto ♦ **the homeless** NPL i senzatetto
home loan N mutuo per la casa
home·ly ['həʊmlɪ] ADJ (*comp* -ier, *superl* -iest) (*food, person*) semplice, alla buona; (*atmosphere*) familiare, accogliente; (*advice*) pratico(-a); (*USA: plain: person, features*) insignificante
home-made [ˌhəʊmˈmeɪd] ADJ fatto(-a) in casa, casalingo(-a)
Home Office N (*Brit*): **the Home Office** il Ministero degli Interni

homeo·path, homoeo·path ['həʊmɪəʊpæθ] N omeopatico(-a)
homeo·path·ic, homoeo·path·ic [ˌhəʊmɪəʊ'pæθɪk] ADJ omeopatico(-a)
homeopa·thy, homoeopa·thy [ˌhəʊmɪ'ɒpəθɪ] N omeopatia
home owner N proprietario(-a) di casa
home page N (*Comput*) home page *f inv*
home rule N autogoverno, autonomia
Home Secretary N (*Brit*) ministro degli Interni
home·sick ['həʊmˌsɪk] ADJ: **to be homesick** sentire la mancanza di casa, avere nostalgia di casa
home·stead ['həʊmˌsted] N casa colonica
home town N città *f inv* natale
home·ward ['həʊmwəd] ADJ (*journey*) di ritorno ♦ ADV verso casa
home·wards ['həʊmwədz] ADV verso casa
home·work ['həʊmˌwɜːk] N (*Scol*) compiti *mpl* (per casa); **have you done your homework?** hai fatto i compiti?
homi·ci·dal [ˌhɒmɪ'saɪdl] ADJ omicida
homi·cide ['hɒmɪˌsaɪd] N omicidio
homi·ly ['hɒmɪlɪ] N (*frm*) omelia
hom·ing ['həʊmɪŋ] ADJ (*device, missile*) autoguidato(-a)
homoeopa·thy [ˌhəʊmɪ'ɒpəθɪ] = homeopathy
homo·geneous [ˌhɒmə'dʒiːnɪəs], **homo·genous** [hə'mɒdʒɪnəs] ADJ omogeneo(-a)
ho·mog·enize [hə'mɒdʒəˌnaɪz] VT omogeneizzare
homo·sex·ual ['hɒməʊˈseksjʊəl] ADJ, N omosessuale *m/f*
Hon. ABBR 1 = **honourable** 2 = **honorary**
Hon·du·ras [hɒn'djʊərəs] N Honduras *m*
hone [həʊn] VT (*sharpen*) affilare; (*fig*) affinare
hon·est ['ɒnɪst] ADJ (*person, face, actions*) onesto(-a); (*answer*) franco(-a), schietto(-a); (*means, method*) onesto(-a), lecito(-a); (*wages, profit*) decente, ragionevole; (*opinion*) sincero(-a); **an honest man** un uomo onesto; **to be quite honest with you ...** onestamente...; **to be quite honest with you ...** se devo dirti la verità...; **please be honest with me** ti prego di essere sincero con me; **tell me your honest opinion** dimmi cosa ne pensi sinceramente
hon·est·ly ['ɒnɪstlɪ] ADV onestamente; (*truly*) sinceramente, francamente; **I didn't do it, honestly!** non l'ho fatto, sul serio!; **honestly?** davvero?; **honestly!** (*exasperated*) (ma) veramente!; **did you honestly think we wouldn't notice?** pensavi davvero che non l'avremmo notato?
hon·es·ty ['ɒnɪstɪ] N 1 onestà; **in all honesty** a voler essere or per essere proprio sincero(-a), in tutta onestà 2 (*Bot*) monete *fpl* del Papa
hon·ey ['hʌnɪ] N miele *m*; (*USA fam*) tesoro, amore *m*; **a pot of honey** un vaso di miele; **hi honey, I'm here!** ciao cara(-o), sono tornato(-a)!
honey·comb ['hʌnɪˌkəʊm] N favo; (*fig*) disegno or struttura a nido d'ape ♦ VT (*fig*) sforacchiare, perforare; **honeycombed with tunnels** pieno(-a) di gallerie
honey·moon ['hʌnɪˌmuːn] N luna di miele, viaggio di nozze ♦ VI fare la luna di miele, andare in viaggio di nozze
honey·suckle ['hʌnɪˌsʌkl] N caprifoglio
Hong Kong ['hɒŋ'kɒŋ] N Hong Kong *f*
honk [hɒŋk] VI (*car*) suonare il clacson; (*goose*) schiamazzare ♦ N (*of horn*) colpo di clacson
Hono·lu·lu [ˌhɒnə'luːluː] N Honolulu *f*
hon·or·ary ['ɒnərərɪ] ADJ (*person*) onorario(-a); (*duty, title*) onorifico(-a); **an honorary degree** una laurea honoris causa or ad honorem
hon·our, hon·or (*USA*) ['ɒnəʳ] N 1 (*gen*) onore *m*; (*esteem, respect*) stima, rispetto; **in honour of** in onore di; **on my honour!** sul mio onore!; **to be on one's honour to do sth** aver dato la propria parola (d'onore) di fare qc; **to do honour to sb** or **to do sb honour** (*enhance reputation of*) fare onore a qn; **she did me the honour of attending my exhibition** mi ha fatto l'onore di presenziare alla mostra; **I would consider it an honour** sarebbe un onore per me; **to be an honour to one's profession** fare onore alla propria professione; **it's a great honour to be invited** (*frm*) è un grande onore essere

invitati; **I had the honour of meeting him** (*frm*) ho avuto l'onore d'incontrarlo; **(in) honour bound** moralmente obbligato(-a) **2 honours** NPL (*distinction, award*) onorificenze *fpl*; (*Univ*): **she got first-class honours in French** ≈ si è laureata in francese con la lode; **to be buried with full honours** essere sepolto(-a) con grandi onori; **to do the honours** (*fam*) fare gli onori di casa **3** (*title*): **Your Honour** (*judge*) Vostro Onore; (*USA: mayor*) signor sindaco ♦ VT (*dignify*): **to honour sb** (**with**) onorare qn (con); **to honour sb with a title** conferire a qn un titolo

hon·our·able, hon·or·able (*USA*) [ˈɒnərəbl] ADJ (*gen*) onorevole; (*person*) d'onore

honour-bound, honor-bound (*USA*) [ˈɒnəˌbaʊnd] ADJ: **to be honour-bound to do** dover fare per una questione di onore

hood [hʊd] N **1** (*of cloak, raincoat*) cappuccio; (*on pram: Aut*) capote *f inv*; (*USA: Aut*) cofano; (*on cooker*) cappa; **a coat with a hood** un cappotto con il cappuccio **2** (*USA fam*) malvivente *m/f*

hood·ed [ˈhʊdɪd] ADJ incappucciato(-a); (*robber*) mascherato(-a)

hood·lum [ˈhuːdləm] N teppista *m/f*

hood·wink [ˈhʊdˌwɪŋk] VT gabbare, imbrogliare, infinocchiare

hoof [huːf] N (*pl hoofs or hooves*) zoccolo

hook [hʊk] N (*gen, also Boxing*) gancio; (*Fishing*) amo; (*on dress*) gancetto; **hooks and eyes** gancetti; **he hung the painting on the hook** ha appeso il quadro al gancio; **he felt a fish pull at his hook** ha sentito che un pesce abboccava all'amo; **to take the phone off the hook** staccare il ricevitore; **to leave the phone off the hook** lasciare staccato il ricevitore; **by hook or (by) crook** in un modo o nell'altro, di riffa o di raffa; **to get sb off the hook** salvare qn; **he fell for it hook, line and sinker** (*fig*) l'ha bevuta tutta ♦ VT (*fasten*) agganciare, attaccare; (*Fishing*) prendere all'amo; **to hook one's arms/legs around sth** aggrapparsi a qc con le braccia/le gambe; **to be hooked on** (*fam*) essere fanatico(-a) di; **he's hooked on heroin** *or* **cocaine** (*fam*) è un eroinomane *or* cocainomane ♦ VI (*fasten*) agganciarsi
▸ **hook on** VI + PREP: **to hook on(to)** agganciarsi (a), attaccarsi (a) ♦ VT + PREP: **to hook on(to)** agganciare (a)
▸ **hook up** VT + ADV (*dress*) agganciare; (*Radio, TV*) allacciare, collegare

hoo·li·gan [ˈhuːlɪɡən] N teppista *m/f*, hooligan *m/f inv*

hoo·li·gan·ism [ˈhuːlɪɡənɪzəm] N teppismo

hoop [huːp] N (*gen*) cerchio; (*for skirt*) guardinfante *m*; (*croquet hoop*) archetto; **to put sb through the hoops** (*fig*) mettere qn sotto il torchio

hoot [huːt] N (*of owl*) verso; (*of horn*) colpo di clacson; (*of siren*) ululato; **a hoot of derision** una risata di scherno; **I don't give a hoot** (*fam*) non me ne importa un accidente, me ne infischio; **it was a hoot** (*fam*) è stato divertentissimo *or* uno spasso ♦ VI (*owl*) gufare; (*person: in scorn*) farsi una risata (di scherno); (*Aut: person*) strombazzare, suonare il clacson; (*ship, train, factory hooter*) fischiare; **he stopped outside the house and hooted** si è fermato davanti alla casa e ha suonato il clacson; **to hoot with laughter** farsi una gran risata; **we heard an owl hooting** abbiamo sentito il verso di una civetta

hoot·er [ˈhuːtəʳ] N (*Brit: of ship, factory*) sirena; (*Aut*) clacson *m inv*, tromba (d'automobile); (*Brit fam: nose*) nasone *m*

hooves [huːvz] NPL *of* **hoof**

hop¹ [hɒp] N (*jump*) saltello; (*dance: fam*) ballo; (*Aer*): **it's a short hop from Paris to London** è un salto da Parigi a Londra in aereo; **to catch sb on the hop** (*fam*) prendere qn alla sprovvista ♦ VI (*person, bird, animal*) saltellare; **he hopped over the wall** è balzato al di là del muro; **to hop out of bed** saltar giù *or* fuori dal letto; **hop in!** (*car*) salta dentro!, salta su!, monta su!; **hop it!** (*fam*) sparisci!, smamma!

hop² [hɒp] N (*Bot*) luppolo; *see also* **hops**

hope [həʊp] N speranza; **he is past** *or* **beyond all hope** per lui non c'è più nessuna speranza; **to live in hope** vivere sperando *or* nella speranza; **in the hope of doing sth** nella speranza di fare qc; **in the hope of sth** nella speranza di avere *or* ottenere qc; **there is no hope of that** non c'è da farci nessun conto; **with high hopes** con grandi speranze;

to raise sb's hopes far nascere delle speranze in qn; **to lose hope** perdere ogni speranza *or* tutte le speranze; **to give up hope** abbandonare ogni speranza *or* tutte le speranze; **what a hope!, some hopes!** (*fam*) figurati! ♦ VT: **to hope that/to do** sperare che/di fare ♦ VI sperare, augurarsi; **I hope he comes** spero che venga; **to hope for the best** sperare in bene *or* per il meglio; **I hope so/not** spero di sì/no; **let's hope for success** speriamo di riuscire; **to hope against hope** sperare malgrado tutto

hope·ful [ˈhəʊpfʊl] ADJ (*person*) ottimista *m/f*, pieno(-a) di speranza, fiducioso(-a); (*future, situation*) promettente; (*sign, response*) incoraggiante, buono(-a) (*before n*); **I'm hopeful that she'll manage to come** ho buone speranze che venga; **the prospects look hopeful** le prospettive sembrano incoraggianti ♦ N: **a young hopeful** un(a) giovane *m/f* di belle speranze

hope·ful·ly [ˈhəʊpfəlɪ] ADV **1** (*optimistically: speak*) con ottimismo, con speranza; **to look hopefully at sb** guardare speranzoso(-a) qn **2** (*one hopes: incorrect use*) si spera; **hopefully he will recover** speriamo che si riprenda; **hopefully he'll make it in time** si spera che arrivi in tempo

hope·less [ˈhəʊplɪs] ADJ (*impossible, useless: situation*) impossibile; (*: outlook, case*) disperato(-a), senza speranza; (*drunkard*) incorreggibile, inguaribile; (*bad: work: fam*) disastroso(-a); **I'm hopeless at it** (*fam*) sono completamente negato per questo; **it's hopeless trying to convince her** è perfettamente inutile *or* è fiato sprecato cercare di convincerla; **it is a hopeless task** è un compito impossibile; **a hopeless case** un caso disperato

hope·less·ly [ˈhəʊplɪslɪ] ADV (*live*) senza speranza; (*involved, complicated*) spaventosamente; (*late*) disperatamente, irrimediabilmente; **I'm hopelessly confused/lost** sono completamente confuso/perso; **hopelessly in love** perdutamente innamorato(-a)

hop·per [ˈhɒpəʳ] N (*chute*) tramoggia

hops [hɒps] NPL *ont mpl* di luppolo

horde [hɔːd] N orda; **hordes of screaming children** un'orda di bambini urlanti

ho·ri·zon [həˈraɪzn] N (*also fig*) orizzonte *m*; **on the horizon** all'orizzonte; **to widen one's horizons** allargare i propri orizzonti

hori·zon·tal [ˌhɒrɪˈzɒntl] ADJ orizzontale; **the shelf is horizontal to the floor** la mensola è parallela al pavimento ♦ N linea *or* piano orizzontale

hor·mone [ˈhɔːməʊn] N ormone *m*

hormone replacement therapy N terapia ormonale (*usata in menopausa*)

horn [hɔːn] N (*gen, also Mus*) corno; (*of snail*) antenna; (*Aut*) clacson *m inv*; **he sounded the horn** ha suonato il clacson; **to draw in one's horns** (*fig: back down*) cedere; (*: spend less*) ridurre le spese

horned [hɔːnd] ADJ (*animal*) cornuto(-a)

hor·net [ˈhɔːnɪt] N calabrone *m*

horny [ˈhɔːnɪ] ADJ (*comp* -**ier**, *superl* -**iest**) (*like horn*) corneo(-a); (*hands*) incallito(-a), calloso(-a); (*fam: randy*) arrapato(-a), eccitato(-a)

horo·scope [ˈhɒrəˌskəʊp] N oroscopo

hor·ren·dous [hɒˈrendəs] ADJ orrendo(-a)

hor·ri·ble [ˈhɒrɪbl] ADJ (*gen*) orribile, tremendo(-a), orrendo(-a); (*accident*) spaventoso(-a)

hor·rid [ˈhɒrɪd] ADJ (*unpleasant: person*) odioso(-a), antipatico(-a); (*: thing, weather*) orribile, orrendo(-a); (*: meal*) schifoso(-a); (*unkind*) cattivo(-a)

hor·rif·ic [hɒˈrɪfɪk] ADJ (*accident*) spaventoso(-a); (*murder*) terrificante

hor·ri·fy [ˈhɒrɪˌfaɪ] VT lasciare inorridito(-a); **I was horrified by the news** la notizia mi ha lasciato inorridito

hor·ri·fy·ing [ˈhɒrɪfaɪɪŋ] ADJ terrificante

hor·ror [ˈhɒrəʳ] N (*terror, dread*) spavento, terrore *m*; (*loathing, hatred*) orrore *m*; (*fam: pest f*; **he ran away in horror** è scappato terrorizzato; **to my horror I discovered I was locked out** ho scoperto con orrore di essere rimasto chiuso fuori

horror film N film *m inv* dell'orrore

horror-struck [ˈhɒrəˌstrʌk], **horror-stricken** [ˈhɒrəˌstrɪkən]

ADJ inorridito(-a)

hors d'oeuvres [ɔːˈdɜːvr] NPL (*course*) antipasto; (*individual items*) antipasti *mpl*

horse [hɔːs] N cavallo; **it's straight from the horse's mouth** (*fam*) è di fonte sicura; **never look a gift horse in the mouth** (*Proverb*) a caval donato non si guarda in bocca

▸ **horse about, horse around** VI + ADV (*fam*) fare lo (la) sciocco(-a)

horse·back [ˈhɔːsbæk] **on horseback** ADV a cavallo

horse·box [ˈhɔːsbɒks] N carro *or* furgone *m* per il trasporto dei cavalli

horse chestnut N (*tree*) ippocastano; (*nut*) castagna d'India

horse-drawn [ˈhɔːsdrɔːn] ADJ a cavalli, tirato(-a) da cavalli

horse·fly [ˈhɔːsflaɪ] N tafano, mosca cavallina

horse·man [ˈhɔːsmən] N (*pl* -**men**) cavaliere *m*

horse·man·ship [ˈhɔːsmənˌʃɪp] N (*riding*) equitazione *f*; (*skill*) abilità di cavaliere

horse·play [ˈhɔːspleɪ] N giochi *mpl* scatenati

horse·power [ˈhɔːspauəʳ] N cavallo (vapore)

horse·racing [ˈhɔːsreɪsɪŋ] N (*sport*) ippica; (*events*) corse *fpl* dei cavalli

horse·radish [ˈhɔːsˌrædɪʃ] N rafano

horse·shoe [ˈhɔːʃˌʃuː] N ferro di cavallo ♦ ADJ a ferro di cavallo

horse show N , **horse trials** NPL concorso ippico, gare *fpl* ippiche

horse-trading [ˈhɔːsˌtreɪdɪŋ] N mercanteggiamento

horse·whip [ˈhɔːswɪp] VT frustare

horse·woman [ˈhɔːsˌwʊmən] N amazzone *f*

horsey, horsy [ˈhɔːsɪ] ADJ (*comp* -**ier**, *superl* -**iest**) (*fam: person*) che adora i cavalli; (*appearance*) cavallino(-a), da cavallo

hor·ti·cul·ture [ˈhɔːtɪˌkʌltʃəʳ] N orticoltura

hose [həʊz] N 1 (*hosepipe*) tubo di gomma; (*also:* **garden hose**) tubo per annaffiare; (*Aut*) manicotto 2 (*pl: stockings, socks*) calza *fpl*, calzini *mpl*; (: *old*) calzamaglia

▸ **hose down** VT + ADV lavare con un getto d'acqua

ho·siery [ˈhəʊʒərɪ] N maglieria; (*in shop*) (reparto di) calze *fpl* e calzini, *mpl*

hos·pice [ˈhɒspɪs] N ospedale *specializzato nell'assistenza ai malati terminali*

hos·pi·table [hɒsˈpɪtəbl] ADJ ospitale

hos·pi·tal [ˈhɒspɪtl] N ospedale *m*; **in hospital**, (*USA*) **in the hospital** in ospedale ♦ ADJ (*staff, treatment*) ospedaliero(-a); (*bed*) di *or* dell'ospedale

hos·pi·tal·ity [ˌhɒspɪˈtælɪtɪ] N ospitalità

hos·pi·tal·ize [ˈhɒspɪtəˌlaɪz] VT ricoverare (in *or* all'ospedale)

host¹ [həʊst] N ospite *m/f*; (*TV, Radio*) presentatore(-trice); (*Bot, Zool*) ospite *m*; **we thanked our hosts** abbiamo ringraziato i nostri ospiti ♦ VT (*TV programme, games*) presentare

host² [həʊst] N (*crowd*) moltitudine *f*; **for a whole host of reasons** per tutta una serie di ragioni; **a host of problems** un mucchio di problemi

hos·tage [ˈhɒstɪdʒ] N ostaggio; **to take sb hostage** prendere qn in ostaggio

host country N paese *m* ospite, paese che ospita

hos·tel [ˈhɒstəl] N (*for students, nurses*) pensionato; (*for homeless people*) ospizio, ricovero; (*also:* **youth hostel**) ostello della gioventù

hos·tel·ling [ˈhɒstəlɪŋ] N: **to go (youth) hostelling** passare le vacanze negli ostelli della gioventù

host·ess [ˈhəʊstɛs] N ospite *f*; (*Aer*) hostess *f inv*; (*in nightclub*) entraîneuse *f inv*; **we thanked our hostess** abbiamo ringraziato la nostra ospite

hos·tile [ˈhɒstaɪl] ADJ: **hostile (to)** ostile (a)

hos·til·ity [hɒsˈtɪlɪtɪ] N ostilità *f inv*

hot [hɒt] ADJ (*comp* -**ter**, *superl* -**test**) 1 caldo(-a); **to be hot** (*person*) avere caldo; (*thing*) essere caldo(-a); (*weather*) fare caldo; **a hot bath** un bagno caldo; **I'm hot** ho caldo; **to get hot** (*person*) incominciare ad avere caldo; (*thing*) scaldarsi; (*weather*) incominciare a fare caldo; **this room is hot** fa caldo in questa stanza; **it's hot today** fa caldo oggi; **I don't like hot weather** non sopporto il caldo; **to get hot under the collar** (*fam*) scaldarsi; **to be all hot and bothered** essere

tutto accaldato(-a); (*flustered*) essere tutto agitato(-a); **to be/get into hot water** essere/cacciarsi nei guai; **you're getting hot!** (*fig: when guessing*) fuochino! 2 (*curry, spice*) piccante; (*news*) fresco(-a); (*temperament*) focoso(-a), ardente; (*conflict, contest*) accanito(-a); **the food's too hot for me** il cibo è troppo piccante per me; **hot favourite** grande favorito(-a); **I've got a hot tip for the Derby** (*fam*) ho un cavallo sicuro per il Derby; **I'll make things hot for you** (*fam*) ti renderò la vita difficile; **to be in hot pursuit of sb** stare alle calcagna di qn; **those goods are hot** (*fam: stolen*) è roba che scotta

♦ ADV: **to be hot on sb's trail** essere sulle tracce di qn; **to be hot on the heels of sb** essere alle calcagna di qn

▸ **hot up**(*fam*) VI + ADV (*situation*) farsi più teso(-a); (*party*) scaldarsi ♦ VT + ADV (*pace*) affrettare; (*car engine*) truccare

hot-air balloon [ˌhɒtˌɛəbəˈluːn] N (*Aer*) mongolfiera

hot·bed [ˈhɒtbɛd] N (*fig*) focolaio

hotch·potch [ˈhɒtʃˌpɒtʃ] N (*Brit*) pot-pourri *m*

hot dog N (*Culin*) hot dog *m inv*

ho·tel [həʊˈtɛl] N albergo, hotel *m inv*; **hotel room** camera d'albergo; **hotel workers** personale *m* alberghiero

ho·tel·ier [həʊˈtɛliəʳ] N albergatore(-trice)

hot flush, (*USA*) **hot flash** N vampata di calore

hot·foot [ˈhɒtˌfʊt] ADV di gran carriera

hot·head [ˈhɒtˌhɛd] N (*fig*) testa calda

hot·house [ˈhɒtˌhaʊs] N serra

hot line N (*Pol*) telefono rosso

hot·ly [ˈhɒtlɪ] ADV accanitamente, con accanimento, violentemente; **he was hotly pursued by the policeman** il poliziotto lo rincorreva senza dargli tregua; **a hotly contested decision** una decisione fortemente contestata

hot·plate [ˈhɒtˌpleɪt] N (*on cooker*) piastra (riscaldante); (*for keeping food warm*) scaldavivande *m inv*

hot·pot [ˈhɒtˌpɒt] N (*Brit: Culin*) stufato

hot potato N (*fam*) patata bollente; **to drop sb/sth like a hot potato** piantare in asso qn/qc

hot seat N (*fig*): **to be in the hot seat** avere un posto che scotta

hot spot N (*fig*) zona calda

hot spring N sorgente *f* termale

hot-tempered [ˌhɒtˈtɛmpəd] ADJ irascibile

hot-water bottle [ˌhɒtˈwɔːtəˌbɒtl] N borsa dell'acqua calda, boule *f inv*

hot-wire [ˈhɒtˌwaɪəʳ] VT (*fam: car*) avviare mettendo in contatto i fili dell'accensione

hound [haʊnd] N segugio; **the hounds** la muta; **to follow the hounds, to ride to hounds** fare la caccia alla volpe ♦ VT (*fig*) perseguitare

▸ **hound down** VT + ADV riuscire a stanare

▸ **hound out** VT + ADV: **to hound out of** cacciare da

hour [aʊəʳ] N ora; **a quarter of an hour** un quarto d'ora; **two and a half hours** due ore e mezza; **half an hour** mezz'ora; **they work long hours** hanno una giornata lavorativa molto lunga; **at 30 miles an hour** a 30 miglia all'ora; **hour by hour** ora per ora; **on the hour** ad ogni ora precisa; **in the early** *or* **small hours** alle ore piccole; **at all hours (of the day and night)** a tutte le ore (del giorno e della notte); **at this late hour** in questa fase avanzata; **he thought his (last) hour had come** pensò che fosse giunta la sua ora; **in the hour of danger** nel momento del pericolo; **to pay sb by the hour** pagare qn a ore; **to wait (for) hours** aspettare per (delle) ore; **hours and hours** ore e ore; **to keep regular hours** fare una vita regolare; **out of hours** fuori orario; **after hours** (*at office*) dopo le ore d'ufficio; (*at shop, pub*) dopo l'ora di chiusura

hour·ly [ˈaʊəlɪ] ADJ (*intervals*) di un'ora; (*bus service*) (ad) ogni ora; (*rate*) orario(-a); **there are hourly buses** ci sono autobus ogni ora ♦ ADV ogni ora; **to be paid hourly** essere pagato all'ora; **hourly paid workers** operai(-e) pagati a ore; **we expected him hourly** lo aspettavamo da un momento all'altro

house [*n* haʊs, *vb* haʊz] N (*pl* **houses**) 1 casa; **at** (*or* **to**) **my house** a casa mia; **to keep house** mandare avanti la casa; **to set up house** metter su casa; **house of cards** castello di carte; **to put** *or* **set one's house in order** (*fig*) sistemare i propri affari; **to get on like a house on fire** (*two people: fam*) andare d'amore e d'accordo 2 (*Pol*) camera 3 (*Theatre*) sala; **"house full"** "biglietti esauriti"; **it was a full house** lo spettacolo ha registrato il tutto esaurito; **in the front of the house** tra gli spettatori, in sala; **to bring the house down** (*fig*) scatenare un uragano di applausi; **the second house** il secondo spettacolo 4 (*Comm*) ditta, casa; **it's on the house** (*paid by company*) paga la ditta; (*free*) è offerto dalla casa 5 (*family, line*) casa, casata 6 (*music*) house music *f* ♦ VT ospitare; **this building houses 6 families** in quest'edificio abitano 6 famiglie

house arrest N arresti *mpl* domiciliari; **to put sb under house arrest** mettere qn agli arresti domiciliari

house·boat ['haʊs,bəʊt] N house boat *f inv*

house·bound ['haʊs,baʊnd] ADJ confinato(-a) in casa

house·break·ing ['haʊs,breɪkɪŋ] N furto con scasso

house-broken ['haʊs,brəʊkən] ADJ (*USA: animal*) che non sporca in casa

house·coat ['haʊs,kəʊt] N vestaglia

house·hold ['haʊs,həʊld] N casa, famiglia; **many poor households are experiencing real hardship** molte famiglie povere stanno attraversando un periodo di grosse difficoltà; **the head of the household** il capofamiglia ♦ ADJ (*accounts, expenses, equipment*) della casa, domestico(-a); **household chores** faccende domestiche

house·holder ['haʊs,həʊldə'] N padrone(-a) di casa; (*head of house*) capofamiglia *m/f*

household name, household word N nome *m* che tutti conoscono *or* conosciuto da tutti

house·hunting ['haʊs,hʌntɪŋ] N: **to go househunting** mettersi a cercar casa

house·keeper ['haʊs,kiːpə'] N governante *f*

house·keeping ['haʊs,kiːpɪŋ] N (*work*) andamento *or* governo della casa; (*also:* **housekeeping money**) soldi *mpl* per le spese di casa; (*Comput*) ausilio

house·man ['haʊsmən] N (*pl* **-men**) (*Brit: in hospital*) ≈ (medico) interno

house-owner ['haʊs,əʊnə'] N proprietario(-a) di una casa

house plant N pianta da appartamento

house-proud ['haʊs,praʊd] ADJ che ha la mania della pulizia

house-to-house [,haʊstə'haʊs] ADJ (*search*) casa per casa; (*collection*) porta a porta

house-train ['haʊs,treɪn] VT (*Brit: pet animal*) addestrare a non sporcare in casa

house-trained ['haʊs,treɪnd] ADJ (*Brit: animal*) che non sporca in casa

house-warming ['haʊs,wɔːmɪŋ] N (*also:* **house-warming party**) festa per inaugurare la casa nuova

house·wife ['haʊs,waɪf] N (*pl* **-wives**) massaia, casalinga

house wine N vino della casa

house·work ['haʊs,wɜːk] N faccende *fpl*, lavori *mpl* di casa, lavori domestici; **to do the housework** fare i lavori di casa, sbrigare le faccende

hous·ing ['haʊzɪŋ] N 1 alloggiamento 2 (*houses*) alloggi *mpl*, case *fpl* ♦ ADJ (*problem, shortage*) degli alloggi

housing association N cooperativa edilizia

housing benefit N (*Brit*) sussidio assegnato ad affittuari in difficoltà economiche

housing conditions NPL condizioni *fpl* di abitazione

housing development N zona residenziale con case popolari *e/o* private

hov·el ['hɒvəl] N tugurio

hov·er ['hɒvə'] VI (*bird*) librarsi; (*helicopter*) volare a punto fisso; **to hover on the brink of disaster** essere sull'orlo del disastro

▶ **hover about, hover around** VI + ADV stare *or* girare intorno; **to hover round sb** aggirarsi intorno a qn

hover·craft ['hɒvə,krɑːft] N hovercraft *m inv*

hover·port ['hɒvə,pɔːt] N porto per hovercraft

how [haʊ] ADV 1 (*gen*) come; **how did you do it?** come hai fatto?, come l'hai fatto?; **I know how you did it** so come hai fatto; **to know how to do sth** sapere come fare qc; **how are you?** come stai?, come va?; **how's life?** (*fam*) come va (la vita)?; **how is school?** come va la scuola?; **how was the film?** com'era il film?; **how is it that ...?** com'è che...?; **how do you say "apple" in Italian?** come si dice "apple" in italiano?; **how do you do?** molto lieto!, piacere!; **how come?** (*fam*) come mai?; **how come he's leaving?** (*fam*) come mai

se ne va?; **how about (going for) a drink?** che ne diresti di (andare a) bere qualcosa?; **and how!** (*fam*) eccome! 2 (*to what degree*) quanto(-a); **how many?** quanti?; **how much?** quanto?; **how much is it?** quanto costa?; **how long have you been here?** da quanto tempo sei qui?; **how old are you?** quanti anni hai?; **how far is it to ...?** quanto è lontano...?; **how far is it to Edinburgh?** quanto dista Edimburgo?; **how long does it take?** quanto tempo ci vuole?; **how many people?** quante persone?; **how much milk?** quanto latte?; **how often do you go?** quanto spesso ci vai?; **how lovely!** che bello!; **how kind of you!** è molto gentile da parte sua! 3 (*that*) che, di come; **she told me how she'd found the money in an old suitcase** mi ha raccontato di come aveva trovato il denaro in una vecchia valigia

how·ever [haʊ'evə'] CONJ (*still, nevertheless*) però, comunque, tuttavia ♦ ADV: **however I do it** in qualunque modo lo faccia; **however beautiful ...** per quanto bella sia...; **however cold it is** per quanto freddo faccia; **however much I try** per quanto ci possa provare; **however did you do it?** (*fam*) come diavolo hai fatto?; **however that may be** comunque sia

how·itz·er ['haʊɪtsə'] N (*Mil*) obice *m*

howl [haʊl] N (*of animal*) ululato; **a howl of pain** un urlo di dolore; **a howl of protest** un grido di protesta; **howls of laughter** scrosci *mpl* di risate ♦ VI (*person*) gridare, urlare; (*animal, wind*) ululare; (*weep*) piangere; **the dog howled all night** il cane ha ululato tutta la notte; **to howl with laughter** rotolarsi dalle risate; **he howled with pain** urlava dal dolore ♦ VT urlare

▶ **howl down** VT + ADV zittire a forza di urla

howl·er ['haʊlə'] N (*fam*) abbaglio; (*in homework*) strafalcione *m*

howl·ing ['haʊlɪŋ] ADJ (*wind, gale*) che ulula; **howling success** (*fig*) successo travolgente

hp [,eɪtʃ'piː] N ABBR (*Aut: = horsepower*) CV (*= cavallo vapore*)

HQ [,eɪtʃ'kjuː] N ABBR (*= headquarters*) QG (*= quartier generale*)

HR [,eɪtʃ'ɑː'] N ABBR 1 (*USA*) = House of Representatives 2 (*= human resources*) risorse *fpl* umane

hr (*pl* **hrs**) ABBR (*= hour*) h (*= ora*)

HRH [,eɪtʃɑːr'eɪtʃ] ABBR (*= His (or Her) Royal Highness*) SAR (*= Sua Altezza Reale*)

HRT [,eɪtʃɑː'tiː] N ABBR = hormone replacement therapy

HS ABBR (*USA*) = high school

HTML [,eɪtʃtiːem'el] N ABBR (*= hypertext markup language*) HTML *m*

hub [hʌb] N (*of wheel*) mozzo; (*fig*) centro, fulcro; **the financial hub of the country** il cuore finanziario del paese

hub·bub ['hʌbʌb] N baccano

hub·cap ['hʌb,kæp] N (*Aut*) coprimozzo

hud·dle ['hʌdl] N gruppetto, capannello; **to go into a huddle** (*fam*) fare capannello ♦ VI raggomitolarsi, rannicchiarsi

▶ **huddle down** VI + ADV accucciarsi, rannicchiarsi

▶ **huddle together** VI + ADV stringersi l'uno(-a) vicino all'altro(-a)

▶ **huddle up** VI + ADV rannicchiarsi, raggomitolarsi

hue [hjuː] N (*colour*) colore *m*, tinta

huff [hʌf] N: **in a huff** (*fam*) imbronciato(-a), stizzito(-a)

huffy ['hʌfi] ADJ (*comp* **-ier**, *superl* **-iest**) (*fam*) imbronciato(-a); **to get huffy** fare il broncio

hug [hʌg] N abbraccio, stretta; **to give sb a hug** abbracciare qn ♦ VT abbracciare, tener stretto(-a) a sé; (*subj: bear*) stringere; (*keep close to: kerb*) tenersi vicino a; **to hug the coast** tenersi sotto costa

huge [hjuːdʒ] ADJ (*comp* **-r**, *superl* **-st**) (*gen*) enorme; (*appetite, helping*) smisurato(-a); (*success*) strepitoso(-a), immenso(-a)

hulk [hʌlk] N (*abandoned ship*) nave *f* in disarmo; (*building*) costruzione *f* mastodontica; **a great hulk of a man** (*fam*) un colosso

hulk·ing ['hʌlkɪŋ] ADJ (*fam*) mastodontico(-a); **hulking (great)** grosso(-a) e goffo(-a)

hull [hʌl] N (*of ship*) scafo

hul·la·ba·loo [,hʌləbə'luː] N (*fam: noise*) fracasso

hul·lo [hʌ'ləʊ] EXCL = hello

hum [hʌm] N (*also Elec*) ronzio; (*of traffic, machines*) rumore *m*; (*of voices*) mormorio, brusio ♦ VT (*tune*) canticchiare ♦ VI (*insect*) ronzare; (*person*) canticchiare a labbra chiuse;

(*engine, machine*) rombare; (*wireless*) mandare un brusio; (*fig: fam: be busy*) animarsi; **to make things hum** (*fam*) fare procedere le cose speditamente; **to hum with activity** pullulare di attività; **to hum and haw** essere incerto(-a) sul da farsi

hu·man [ˈhjuːmən] ADJ umano(-a); **she's only human** nessuno è perfetto ♦ N essere *m* umano

hu·mane [hjuːˈmeɪn] ADJ umanitario(-a)

hu·man·ism [ˈhjuːmənɪzəm] N umanesimo

hu·mani·tar·ian [hjuːˌmænɪˈtɛərɪən] ADJ umanitario(-a)

hu·man·ity [hjuːˈmænɪtɪ] N umanità; **the humanities** gli studi letterari *or* umanistici, le lettere; **crimes against humanity** crimini contro l'umanità

hu·man·ly [ˈhjuːmənlɪ] ADV umanamente

hu·man·oid [ˈhjuːmənɔɪd] ADJ che sembra umano(-a)
♦ N umanoide *m/f*

human rights NPL diritti *mpl* dell'uomo

hum·ble [ˈhʌmbl] ADJ (*comp* -r, *superl* -st) umile; (*opinion, occupation*) modesto(-a); **of humble origins** di umili origini; **to eat humble pie** rimangiarsi tutto ♦ VT umiliare; **to humble o.s.** abbassarsi, umiliarsi

hum·bly [ˈhʌmblɪ] ADV umilmente, modestamente

hum·bug [ˈhʌmbʌg] N (*person*) impostore *m*; (*nonsense*) frottole *fpl*, falsità; (*Brit: sweet*) caramella alla menta

hum·drum [ˈhʌmdrʌm] ADJ monotono(-a), banale

hu·mid [ˈhjuːmɪd] ADJ umido(-a)

hu·midi·fi·er [hjuːˈmɪdɪˌfaɪər] N umidificatore *m*

hu·mid·ity [hjuːˈmɪdɪtɪ] N umidità

hu·mili·ate [hjuːˈmɪlɪˌeɪt] VT umiliare

hu·mili·at·ing [hjuːˈmɪlɪeɪtɪŋ] ADJ umiliante

hu·milia·tion [hjuːˌmɪlɪˈeɪʃən] N umiliazione *f*

hu·mil·ity [hjuːˈmɪlɪtɪ] N umiltà

hu·mor·ist [ˈhjuːmərɪst] N umorista *m/f*

hu·mor·ous [ˈhjuːmərəs] ADJ (*person*) spiritoso(-a); (*book, story*) divertente, umoristico(-a); (*tone*) scherzoso(-a); **a humorous magazine** un giornale umoristico

hu·mour, hu·mor (*USA*) [ˈhjuːmər] N **1** (*comic sense*) umorismo; (*of situation*) lato divertente *or* umoristico; **to have a sense of humour** avere il senso dell'umorismo **2** (*mood*) umore *m*; **to be in a good/bad humour** essere di buon/cattivo umore ♦ VT (*person*) accontentare, compiacere; (*sb's whims*) assecondare

hu·mour·less, hu·mor·less (*USA*) [ˈhjuːməlɪs] ADJ privo(-a) di umorismo

hump [hʌmp] N (*Anat*) gobba; **we're over the hump** (*fig*) il peggio è passato, il più è fatto ♦ VT **1** (*arch: back*) inarcare **2** (*fam: carry*) portare

hump·back [ˈhʌmpˌbæk] N (*also*: **humpback bridge**) ponte *m* a schiena d'asino

hu·mus [ˈhjuːməs] N humus *m*

hunch [hʌntʃ] N **1** (*fam: idea*) impressione *f*; (*premonition*) intuizione *f*; **I have a hunch that ...** ho la vaga impressione che..., ho il vago presentimento che...; **she's acting on a hunch** sta andando a naso; **to follow one's hunch** seguire il proprio fiuto **2** (*hump*) gobba ♦ VT (*also*: **hunch up**) incurvare ♦ VI star curvo(-a); **to sit hunched up** star seduto(-a) curvo(-a)

hunch·back [ˈhʌntʃˌbæk] N (*offensive*) gobbo(-a)

hunched [hʌntʃt] ADJ incurvato(-a)

hun·dred [ˈhʌndrɪd] ADJ cento *inv*; **about a hundred people** un centinaio di persone; **three hundred boys and five hundred girls** trecento ragazzi e cinquecento ragazze; **a hundred and one** centouno; **hundred and first** centunesimo(-a); **I'm a hundred per cent sure** sono sicuro(-a) al cento per cento ♦ N cento *m inv*; **to live to be a hundred** vivere fino all'età di cent'anni; (*less exactly*) diventare centenario(-a); **hundreds of people** centinaia *fpl* di persone

hun·dredth [ˈhʌndrɪdθ] ADJ centesimo(-a) ♦ N (*in series*) centesimo(-a); (*fraction*) centesimo

hundred·weight [ˈhʌndrɪdˌweɪt] N (*Brit: 112 lb*) ≈ 50.8 kg; (*USA: 100 lb*) ≈ 45.3 kg

hung [hʌŋ] PT, PP *of* hang ♦ ADJ: **a hung jury** una giuria divisa (sul verdetto)

Hun·gar·ian [hʌŋˈgɛərɪən] ADJ ungherese ♦ N **1** (*person*) ungherese *m/f* **2** (*language*) ungherese *m*

Hun·ga·ry [ˈhʌŋgərɪ] N Ungheria

hun·ger [ˈhʌŋgər] N fame *f*; (*also fig*): **hunger (for)** sete *f* (di)
▸ **hunger after, hunger for** VI + PREP desiderare ardentemente, morire dalla voglia di

hunger strike N sciopero della fame

hung over [ˌhʌŋˈəʊvər] ADJ (*fam*): **to be hungover** avere i postumi della sbornia

hun·gri·ly [ˈhʌŋgrɪlɪ] ADV (*fig*) avidamente; (*eat*) voracemente

hun·gry [ˈhʌŋgrɪ] ADJ (*comp* -ier, *superl* -iest): **to be hungry** aver fame, essere affamato(-a); **I'm not hungry** non ho fame; **to make sb hungry** far venire fame a qn; **to go hungry** (*starve*) patire la fame; (*skip a meal*) saltare il pasto; **hungry for** (*fig*) assetato(-a) di; (*lit*) affamato(-a) di

hung up ADJ (*fam*) complessato(-a)

hunk [hʌŋk] N (*of bread, cheese*) bel pezzo; **a gorgeous hunk of a man** (*fam*) un bel fusto

hunt [hʌnt] N (*gen*) caccia; (*huntsmen*) cacciatori *mpl*; (*search*): **hunt (for)** ricerca (di); **tiger hunt** caccia alla tigre ♦ VT (*animal*) andare a caccia di; (*criminal*) dare la caccia a; **they hunt foxes** vanno a caccia di volpi; **detectives have been hunting him for seven months** gli investigatori gli stanno dando la caccia da sette mesi ♦ VI (*Sport*) cacciare; (*search*) cercare; **to go hunting** andare a caccia; **to hunt for** (*animal*) cacciare; (*object, information*) cercare dappertutto; **I hunted everywhere for that book** ho cercato quel libro dappertutto; **she hunted in her bag for the keys** ha rovistato nella borsa in cerca delle chiavi
▸ **hunt down** VT + ADV (*criminal, enemy*) dar la caccia a
▸ **hunt out** VT + ADV scovare
▸ **hunt up** VT + ADV scovare

hunt·er [ˈhʌntər] N cacciatore(-trice); (*Brit: horse*) cavallo da caccia

hunt·ing [ˈhʌntɪŋ] N (*Sport*) caccia; **to go hunting** andare a caccia; **fox hunting** caccia alla volpe

hur·dle [ˈhɜːdl] N (*for fence*) graticcio; (*fig: Sport*) ostacolo; **the 100 metre hurdles** (*race*) i cento metri a ostacoli

hurl [hɜːl] VT (*throw*) scagliare, scaraventare; **to hurl o.s. at sb/sth** scagliarsi su qn/qc; **they were hurled to the ground by the blast** vennero scagliati a terra dall'esplosione; **to hurl abuse** *or* **insults at sb** scagliare *or* lanciare (degli) insulti a qn

hurl·ing [ˈhɜːlɪŋ] N (*Sport*) hurling *m*

hurly-burly [ˌhɜːlɪˈbɜːlɪ] N chiasso, baccano

hur·rah [huˈrɑː], **hur·ray** [huˈreɪ] EXCL urrà!, evviva!; **hurrah for Mr Jones!** viva Mr Jones!

hur·ri·cane [ˈhʌrɪkən] N uragano

hur·ried [ˈhʌrɪd] ADJ (*gen*) affrettato(-a); (*steps*) frettoloso(-a); (*work*) fatto(-a) in fretta; **to eat a hurried meal** buttare giù due bocconi

hur·ried·ly [ˈhʌrɪdlɪ] ADV in fretta (e furia)

hur·ry [ˈhʌrɪ] N fretta, premura; **to be in a hurry (to do)** avere una gran fretta (di fare); **to do sth in a hurry** fare qc in fretta; **done in a hurry** fatto(-a) in fretta; **are you in a hurry for this?** ti serve subito?; **what's the hurry?** che fretta c'è?; **there's no hurry** non c'è fretta *or* premura; **he won't do that again in a hurry** (*fam*) non lo rifarà tanto facilmente ♦ VT (*person*) far fretta a; (*work*) fare in fretta; **to hurry to do sth** affrettarsi a fare qc; **he won't be hurried** non gli si può far fretta; **she hurried him into the car** l'ha spinto in macchina; **he was hurried to the hospital** è stato portato d'urgenza all'ospedale; **he hurried his lunch** ha mangiato il pranzo alla svelta; **troops were hurried to the spot** le truppe furono spedite in fretta sul posto ♦ VI fare in fretta; **to hurry back/home** affrettarsi a tornare indietro/a casa; **Sharon hurried back home** Sharon si affrettò a tornare a casa; **to hurry after sb** precipitarsi dietro a qn; **to hurry in/out** entrare/uscire in fretta ♦ VT + ADV far fretta a
▸ **hurry along** VI + ADV camminare in fretta ♦ VT + ADV = hurry up
▸ **hurry away, hurry off** VI + ADV andarsene in fretta
♦ VT + ADV spedire fuori in fretta; **to be hurried off** to essere spedito(-a) in fretta a
▸ **hurry on** VI + ADV: **to hurry on to** passare in fretta a
▸ **hurry up** VI + ADV sbrigarsi, affrettarsi; **hurry up!** sbrigati!
♦ VT + ADV (*person*) far fretta a; (*work*) fare in fretta; **hurry him**

up will you! digli di fare in fretta!

hurt [hɜːt] (*pt, pp* **hurt**) ᴠᴛ **1** (*injure, also fig*) ferire; (*cause pain to, harm*) far male a; **I hurt my arm** mi sono fatto male al braccio; **you're hurting me!** mi fai male!; **to hurt o.s.** farsi male; **have you hurt yourself?** ti sei fatto male?; **where does it hurt you?** dove ti fa male?; **to get hurt** farsi male; **luckily, nobody got hurt** fortunatamente nessuno si è fatto male; (*emotionally*) essere ferito(-a); **to hurt sb's feelings** colpire la suscettibilità di qn; **his criticisms really hurt me** le sue critiche mi hanno proprio ferito **2** (*business, interests*) colpire, danneggiare ♦ ᴠɪ far male; **my arm hurts** mi fa male il braccio; **where does it hurt!** dove ti fa male?; **that hurts!** che male!, fa male! ♦ ɴ dolore *m* ♦ ᴀᴅᴊ (*foot*) ferito(-a); (*feelings, look, tone*) offeso(-a); **is he badly hurt?** è ferito gravemente?

❏ **hurt** is not translated by the Italian word *urtare*

hurt·ful [ˈhɜːtful] ᴀᴅᴊ (*upsetting: remark*) che fa male, che ferisce

hurt·le [ˈhɜːtl] ᴠɪ sfrecciare; **to hurtle past/down** passare/scendere a razzo ♦ ᴠᴛ scagliare

hus·band [ˈhʌzbənd] ɴ marito ♦ ᴠᴛ dosare; **to husband one's resources** misurare le proprie risorse

hush [hʌʃ] ɴ silenzio, calma, pace *f*; **hush!** silenzio!, zitto(-a)! ♦ ᴠᴛ quietare, calmare

▸ **hush up** ᴠᴛ + ᴀᴅᴠ (*fact*) cercare di far passare sotto silenzio; (*scandal*) mettere a tacere; (*person*) far star zitto(-a), zittire

hush-hush [ˈhʌʃˈhʌʃ] ᴀᴅᴊ (*fam*) segretissimo(-a)

husk [hʌsk] ɴ (*of wheat, rice, seed*) pula; (*of maize*) cartoccio

husky¹ [ˈhʌski] ᴀᴅᴊ (*comp* -**ier**, *superl* -**iest**) (*voice*) roco(-a); (*tough: person*) ben piantato(-a)

husky² [ˈhʌski] ɴ (*pl* -**ies**) husky *m inv*, cane *m* eschimese

hus·tings [ˈhʌstɪŋz] ɴᴘʟ (*Brit Pol*) campagna elettorale

hus·tle [ˈhʌsl] ɴ: **hustle and bustle** trambusto, via vai *m inv* ♦ ᴠᴛ (*push: person*) spingere, incalzare; **to hustle in/out** spintonare dentro/fuori; **we'll have to hustle things along** dobbiamo fare più in fretta ♦ ᴠɪ: **to hustle in/out** entrare/uscire in fretta

hut [hʌt] ɴ (*primitive dwelling*) capanna; (*in mountains*) baita, rifugio; (*Mil*) baracca; (*shed*) capanno

hutch [hʌtʃ] ɴ gabbia (per conigli)

hya·cinth [ˈhaɪəsɪnθ] ɴ giacinto

hy·brid [ˈhaɪbrɪd] ɴ ibrido ♦ ᴀᴅᴊ ibrido(-a)

hy·dran·gea [haɪˈdreɪndʒə] ɴ ortensia

hy·drant [ˈhaɪdrənt] ɴ (*also:* **fire hydrant**) idrante *m*

hy·drau·lic [haɪˈdrɔlɪk] ᴀᴅᴊ idraulico(-a); **hydraulic ramp** (*Aut*) ponte *m* (sollevatore)

hy·drau·lics [haɪˈdrɔlɪks] ɴsɢ idraulica

hydro·chlo·ric acid [ˌhaɪdrəʊˈklɒrɪkˈæsɪd] ɴ acido cloridrico or muriatico

hydro·elec·tric [ˈhaɪdrəʊɪˈlɛktrɪk] ᴀᴅᴊ idroelettrico(-a)

hydro·foil [ˈhaɪdrəˌfɔɪl] ɴ aliscafo

hydro·gen [ˈhaɪdrɪdʒən] ɴ idrogeno

hydrogen bomb ɴ bomba all'idrogeno, bomba H

hydro·pho·bia [ˌhaɪdrəˈfəʊbɪə] ɴ idrofobia

hydro·plane [ˈhaɪdrəʊˌpleɪn] ɴ idrovolante *m*

hy·ena [haɪˈiːnə] ɴ iena

hy·giene [ˈhaɪdʒiːn] ɴ igiene *f*

hy·gien·ic [haɪˈdʒiːnɪk] ᴀᴅᴊ igienico(-a)

hymn [hɪm] ɴ inno (sacro)

hype [haɪp] ɴ (*fam*) battage *m inv*

hyper·ac·tive [ˌhaɪpərˈæktɪv] ᴀᴅᴊ iperattivo(-a)

hyper·link [ˈhaɪpəlɪŋk] ɴ (*Comput*) collegamento ipertestuale

hyper·mar·ket [ˈhaɪpəˌmɑːkɪt] ɴ (*Brit*) ipermercato

hyper·ten·sion [ˌhaɪpəˈtɛnʃən] ɴ (*Med*) ipertensione *f*

hyper·text [ˈhaɪpətɛkst] ɴ ipertesto

hy·phen [ˈhaɪfən] ɴ trattino, lineetta

hyp·no·sis [hɪpˈnəʊsɪs] ɴ ipnosi *f*

hyp·not·ic [hɪpˈnɒtɪk] ᴀᴅᴊ ipnotico(-a)

hyp·no·tism [ˈhɪpnətɪzəm] ɴ ipnotismo

hyp·no·tist [ˈhɪpnətɪst] ɴ ipnotizzatore(-trice)

hyp·no·tize [ˈhɪpnəˌtaɪz] ᴠᴛ ipnotizzare; **to hypnotize sb into doing sth** far fare qc a qn sotto ipnosi

hypo·al·ler·gen·ic [ˌhaɪpəʊˌæləˈdʒɛnɪk] ᴀᴅᴊ anallergico(-a)

hypo·chon·dri·ac [ˌhaɪpəʊˈkɒndrɪæk] ɴ ipocondriaco(-a)

hy·poc·ri·sy [hɪˈpɒkrɪsɪ] ɴ ipocrisia

hypo·crite [ˈhɪpəkrɪt] ɴ ipocrita *m/f*

hypo·criti·cal [ˌhɪpəˈkrɪtɪkəl] ᴀᴅᴊ ipocrita

hypo·der·mic [ˌhaɪpəˈdɜːmɪk] ᴀᴅᴊ ipodermico(-a) ♦ ɴ (*syringe*) siringa ipodermica

hy·pot·enuse [haɪˈpɒtɪnjuːz] ɴ (*Geom*) ipotenusa

hypo·ther·mia [ˌhaɪpəʊˈθɜːmɪə] ɴ (*Med*) ipotermia

hy·poth·esis [haɪˈpɒθɪsɪs] ɴ (*pl* **hypotheses** [haɪˈpɒθɪsiːz]) ipotesi *f inv*

hypo·theti·cal [ˌhaɪpəʊˈθɛtɪkəl] ᴀᴅᴊ ipotetico(-a)

hys·ter·ec·to·my [ˌhɪstəˈrɛktəmɪ] ɴ (*Med*) isterectomia

hys·te·ria [hɪsˈtɪərɪə] ɴ (*gen*) isterismo; (*Psych*) isteria

hys·ter·i·cal [hɪsˈtɛrɪkəl] ᴀᴅᴊ isterico(-a); **to become hysterical** avere una crisi isterica; **it was hysterical!** era buffissimo!

hys·ter·ics [hɪsˈtɛrɪks] ɴᴘʟ (*tears*) crisi *f inv* isterica; (*laughter*) attacco di riso; **to be in** or **have hysterics** avere una crisi isterica; (*fam: laugh*) crepar dal ridere; **it was so funny, I was in hysterics** era così buffo, mi ha fatto morir dal ridere

Ii

I¹, i¹ [aɪ] N (*letter*) I, i *f inv*, m *inv*; **I for Isaac**, (*USA*) **I for Item** ≈ I come Imola

I² [aɪ] PERS PRON io; **I'll do it** lo faccio io; **he and I were at school together** io e lui eravamo a scuola insieme; **Ann and I** Ann ed io; **I love cats** adoro i gatti

I. ABBR (= *island, isle*) I., Is.

IA ABBR (*USA Post*: = Iowa)

ib. ABBR = ibid.

Iberian [aɪˈbɪərɪən] ADJ iberico(-a)

Iberian Peninsula N: **the Iberian Peninsula** la penisola iberica

ibid. [ˈɪbɪd] ABBR (= *ibidem: from the same source*) ibid.

ICBM [ˌaɪsiːbiːˈem] N ABBR (= *intercontinental ballistic missile*) ICBM m *inv*

ice [aɪs] N 1 ghiaccio; (*on road*) ghiaccio, strato di ghiaccio; **a sheet of ice** una lastra di ghiaccio; **to be as cold as ice** essere freddo(-a) come il ghiaccio, essere un pezzo di ghiaccio; **to break the ice** (*fig*) rompere il ghiaccio; **to keep sth on ice** (*fig: plan, project*) accantonare qc; **to skate on thin ice** (*fig*) essere sul filo del rasoio 2 (*ice cream*) gelato; **strawberry ice** gelato alla fragola; **a vanilla ice cream** un gelato alla vaniglia ♦ VT (*cake*) glassare

  ▸ **ice over, ice up** VI + ADV (*river*) gelarsi, ghiacciarsi; (*windshield, wings of plane*) incrostarsi di ghiaccio

Ice Age N: **the Ice Age** l'era glaciale

ice axe N piccozza da ghiaccio

ice·berg [ˈaɪsbəːɡ] N iceberg m *inv*; **this is only the tip of the iceberg** (*fig*) questa è solo la punta dell'iceberg

ice·box [ˈaɪsbɒks] N (*USA: refrigerator*) frigorifero; (*Brit: freezer compartment*) freezer m *inv*

ice·breaker [ˈaɪsbreɪkəʳ] N rompighiaccio m *inv*; (*fig: for group of students*) gioco o esercizio fatto per rompere il ghiaccio all'inizio di una lezione

ice bucket N secchiello del ghiaccio

ice·cap [ˈaɪskæp] N calotta glaciale; **polar icecap** calotta polare

ice-cold [ˌaɪsˈkəʊld] ADJ ghiacciato(-a), gelato(-a)

ice cream N gelato

ice-cream soda [ˌaɪskriːmˈsəʊdə] N (*USA*) (gelato) affogato al seltz

ice cube N cubetto di ghiaccio

iced [aɪst] ADJ 1 (*drink*) ghiacciato(-a); (*coffee, tea*) freddo(-a) 2 (*cake*) glassato(-a)

ice hockey N hockey m su ghiaccio

Ice·land [ˈaɪslənd] N l'Islanda f

Ice·land·er [ˈaɪsləndəʳ] N islandese m/f

Ice·land·ic [aɪsˈlændɪk] ADJ islandese ♦ N (*language*) islandese m

ice pick N piccone m per ghiaccio

ice rink N pista di pattinaggio su ghiaccio

ice-skate [ˈaɪsskeɪt] VI pattinare sul ghiaccio

ice-skating [ˈaɪsskeɪtɪŋ] N pattinaggio sul ghiaccio; **to go ice-skating** andare a pattinare sul ghiaccio

ici·cle [ˈaɪsɪkl] N ghiacciolo

ic·ing [ˈaɪsɪŋ] N 1 (*on cake*) glassa; **vanilla icing** glassa alla vaniglia 2 (*Aer*) patina di ghiaccio

icing sugar N zucchero a velo

ICJ [ˌaɪsiːˈdʒeɪ] N ABBR = International Court of Justice

icon [ˈaɪkɒn] N (*also Comput*) icona

ICU [ˌaɪsiːˈjuː] N ABBR = intensive care unit; *see* intensive care

icy [ˈaɪsɪ] ADJ (*comp* -ier, *superl* -iest) (*road, hand*) ghiacciato(-a); (*weather, temperature, stare*) gelido(-a); **it's icy cold** si gela; **an icy wind** un vento gelido; **the roads are icy** le strade sono ghiacciate

ID [ˌaɪˈdiː] N ABBR (= *identification*) identità; **have you got some ID?** ha un documento (d'identità)? ♦ ABBR (*USA Post*: = Idaho)

I'd [aɪd] = I would; I had

Ida. ABBR (*USA*: = Idaho)

I·da·ho [ˈaɪdəhəʊ] l'Idaho

ID card N = identity card

IDD [ˌaɪdiːˈdiː] N ABBR (*Brit: Telec*: = *international direct dialling*) teleselezione f internazionale

idea [aɪˈdɪə] N idea; **good idea!** buon'idea!; **that was a brilliant idea** è stata un'idea splendida; **to have an idea that ...** aver l'impressione che...; **I haven't the least** *or* **slightest** *or* **foggiest idea** non ne ho la minima *or* la più pallida idea; **it wouldn't be a bad idea to paint it** non sarebbe una cattiva idea verniciarlo; **to put ideas into sb's head** mettere delle idee in testa a qn; **it wasn't my idea** non è stata un'idea mia, non sono io che ho avuto l'idea; **if that's your idea of a joke ...** se credi di essere spiritoso...; **I've got the general idea** mi sono fatto un'idea; **that's the idea** ecco, proprio così; **what's the big idea?** (*fam*) cosa credi di fare?; **the idea is to sell it** si tratta di venderlo

ideal [aɪˈdɪəl] ADJ, N ideale m

ideal·ist [aɪˈdɪəlɪst] N idealista m/f

ideal·ly [aɪˈdɪəlɪ] ADV perfettamente; **it is ideally situated** si trova in un posto ideale; **they are an ideally matched couple** sono una coppia ideale; **ideally, I'd like to work abroad** l'ideale per me sarebbe lavorare all'estero

iden·ti·cal [aɪˈdɛntɪkəl] ADJ identico(-a)

iden·ti·fi·ca·tion [aɪˌdɛntɪfɪˈkeɪʃən] N (*recognition*) identificazione f; (*document*) documento (di riconoscimento *or* di identità); **have you got any identification?** ha un documento d'identità?; **the identification of genes** l'individuazione dei geni; **the identification of bodies** l'identificazione dei cadaveri

iden·ti·fy [aɪˈdɛntɪfaɪ] VT (*recognize, specify*) identificare, riconoscere; (*point out*) individuare; **to identify o.s. with** identificarsi con; **we managed to identify the problem** siamo riusciti ad individuare il problema; **the police have identified the body** la polizia ha identificato il corpo ♦ VI: **to identify with** identificarsi con

iden·tity [aɪˈdɛntɪtɪ] N identità f *inv*; **a case of mistaken identity** uno scambio di persona

identity card N carta d'identità

ideo·logi·cal [ˌaɪdɪəˈlɒdʒɪkəl] ADJ ideologico(-a)

ideol·ogy [ˌaɪdɪˈɒlədʒɪ] N ideologia

idio·cy [ˈɪdɪəsɪ] N idiozia

idi·om [ˈɪdɪəm] N (*phrase*) locuzione f idiomatica; (*style of expression*) stile m

idio·mat·ic [ˌɪdɪəˈmætɪk] ADJ idiomatico(-a)

idio·syn·cra·sy [ˌɪdɪəˈsɪŋkrəsɪ] N (*peculiarity, foible*) (piccola) mania; (*characteristic*) particolarità f *inv*

idi·ot [ˈɪdɪət] N deficiente m/f, stupido(-a)

idi·ot·ic [ˌɪdɪˈɒtɪk] ADJ (*person*) idiota; (*price, question*) assurdo(-a)

idle [ˈaɪdl] ADJ (*comp* -r, *superl* -st) 1 (*lazy: student*) pigro(-a), poltrone(-a); (*inactive: machine, factory, workers*) inattivo(-a); (*unemployed: worker*) disoccupato(-a); **the idle rich** i ricchi sfaccendati; **in my idle moments** nei miei momenti liberi; **an idle life** una vita d'ozio; **to stand** *or* **lie idle** (*factory, machine*) rimaner fermo(-a) *or* inattivo(-a) 2 (*fear, speculation*) infondato(-a); (*gossip, pleasures*) futile; (*question*) ozioso(-a); (*threat*) campato(-a) in aria ♦ VI (*person*) oziare; (*engine*) girare al minimo

  ▸ **idle away** VT + ADV (*time*) sprecare, buttar via

idle·ness [ˈaɪdlnɪs] N pigrizia, ozio

idler [ˈaɪdləʳ] N fannullone(-a), sfaccendato(-a)

idle time N (*esp Comm*) tempi *mpl* morti

idol [ˈaɪdl] N idolo

idol·ize [ˈaɪdəlaɪz] VT idolatrare

idyl·lic [ɪ'dɪlɪk] ADJ idilliaco(-a)

i.e. [,aɪ'iː] ABBR (= *id est: that is*) cioè

IED [aɪiː'diː] N (= *Improvised Explosive Device*) ordigno esplosivo improvvisato

if [ɪf] CONJ **1** se; **if anyone comes in** se viene *or* venisse qualcuno; **I'll go if you come with me** ci vado se vieni anche tu; **you can have it if you like** puoi prenderlo se vuoi; **I'd be pleased if you could do it** sarei molto contento se potessi farlo; **if necessary** se (è) necessario; **if I were you** se fossi in te, io al tuo posto; **if you ask me ...** secondo me... **2** (*whenever*) tutte le volte che, quando; **if we are in Scotland, we always go to see her** quando siamo in Scozia, andiamo sempre a trovarla **3** (*although*): **(even) if** anche se + *sub*; **I am determined to do it, (even) if it takes all week** sono deciso a farlo, dovessi impiegarci tutta la settimana **4** (*whether*) se; **I don't know if he is here** non so se c'è **5** (*in phrases*): **if so** se è così, allora; **are you coming? if so, I'll wait** vieni? allora ti aspetto; **if not** se no, altrimenti; **are you coming? if not, I'll go with Mark** vieni? altrimenti vado con Mark; **if only** se solo *or* soltanto; **if only she were here** se solo fosse qui; **if only I could** se soltanto potessi, magari (potessi); **I would like to see her if only for a few minutes** vorrei vederla magari *or* anche solo per pochi minuti; **if only to show him my gratitude** se non altro per esprimergli la mia gratitudine; **if only I had more money!** se solo avessi più denaro!; **as if** come se; **as if by chance** come per caso; *see* **as even** ♦ N: **there are a lot of ifs and buts** ci sono molti se e ma; **that's** *or* **it's a big if** è un grosso punto interrogativo

if·fy ['ɪfɪ] ADJ (*comp* **-ier**, *superl* **-iest**) (*fam*) incerto(-a)

ig·loo ['ɪgluː] N igloo *m inv*

ig·nite [ɪg'naɪt] VT (*fire, match*) accendere; (*wood*) incendiare ♦ VI accendersi; **the gas ignited at once** il gas si è acceso subito

ig·ni·tion [ɪg'nɪʃən] N (*Aut*) accensione *f*; (*Chem*) ignizione *f*; **to switch on/off the ignition** accendere/spegnere il motore; **the device automatically disconnects the ignition** il dispositivo esclude automaticamente l'accensione

ignition key N (*Aut*) chiave *f* dell'accensione

ig·no·ble [ɪg'nəʊbl] ADJ ignobile

ig·no·mini·ous [,ɪgnə'mɪnɪəs] ADJ vergognoso(-a), ignominioso(-a)

ig·no·ra·mus [,ɪgnə'reɪməs] N ignorante *m/f*

ig·no·rance ['ɪgnərəns] N ignoranza (di); **to keep sb in ignorance of sth** tenere qn all'oscuro di qc; **to show one's ignorance** dimostrare la propria ignoranza; **it's no use pleading ignorance of the law** la legge non ammette ignoranza

ig·no·rant ['ɪgnərənt] ADJ (*lacking education*) ignorante; **to be ignorant of** (*fact, situation, subject*) ignorare; (*events*) essere all'oscuro di

ig·nore [ɪg'nɔː'] VT (*person*) ignorare; (*problem, fact*) trascurare; (*remark*) non far caso a; (*advice, letter*) non tener in nessun conto; (*danger*) non curarsi di; (*sb's behaviour*) chiudere un occhio su

ikon ['aɪkɒn] N = **icon**

IL ABBR (*USA Post:*) **= Illinois**

ill [ɪl] ADJ (*comp* **worse**, *superl* **worst**) **1** (*sick*) ammalato(-a), malato(-a); **to fall** *or* **be taken ill** ammalarsi; **she was taken ill** si è ammalata; **to feel ill (with)** star male (per *or* a causa di); **to be in ill health** essere malaticcio(-a); **he's seriously ill** è gravemente ammalato; **she is seriously ill in hospital** è ricoverata in gravi condizioni all'ospedale **2** (*bad*) cattivo(-a); **ill fortune** *or* **ill luck** sfortuna, scalogna; **ill effects** brutte conseguenze *fpl*; **to be in an ill humour** *or* **temper** essere di cattivo umore; **it's an ill wind that blows nobody any good** (*Proverb*) non tutto il male viene per nuocere ♦ ADV male; **we can ill afford to lose him/to buy it** non possiamo certo permetterci di perderlo/di comprarlo; **to speak/think ill of sb** parlar/pensar male di qn ♦ **ills** NPL (*old, frm*) mali *mpl*, malanni *mpl*

Ill. ABBR (*USA:*) **= Illinois**

I'll [aɪl] = **I will; I shall**

ill-advised [,ɪləd'vaɪzd] ADJ (*plan, remark, decision, person*) sconsiderato(-a), avventato(-a); *see also* **advise**

ill at ease ADJ a disagio

ill-considered [,ɪlkən'sɪdəd] ADJ (*plan*) avventato(-a)

ill-disposed [,ɪldɪs'pəʊzd] ADJ: **to be ill-disposed towards sb/sth** essere maldisposto(-a) verso qn/qc *or* nei riguardi di qn/qc

il·legal [ɪ'liːgəl] ADJ illegale

il·legal·ly [ɪ'liːgəlɪ] ADV illegalmente

il·leg·ible [ɪ'ledʒəbl] ADJ illeggibile

il·legiti·mate [,ɪlɪ'dʒɪtɪmɪt] ADJ illegittimo(-a)

ill-fated [,ɪl'feɪtɪd] ADJ (*person*) sventurato(-a); (*enterprise*) sfortunato(-a)

ill-favoured, ill-favored (*USA*) [,ɪl'feɪvəd] ADJ (*ugly*) sgraziato(-a), brutto(-a); (*objectionable*) sgradevole

ill feeling N rancore *m*

ill-gotten [ɪl,gɒtn] ADJ (*frm*): **ill-gotten gains** guadagni *mpl* illeciti

ill health N problemi *mpl* di salute

il·lic·it [ɪ'lɪsɪt] ADJ illecito(-a)

ill-informed [,ɪlɪn'fɔːmd] ADJ (*person*) male informato(-a); (*comment, criticism*) che rivela ignoranza

Il·li·nois [,ɪlɪ'nɔɪ] N l'Illinois

il·lit·er·ate [ɪ'lɪtərɪt] ADJ (*person*) analfabeta, illetterato(-a); (*letter*) sgrammaticato(-a) ♦ N analfabeta *m/f*, illetterato(-a)

ill-mannered [,ɪl'mænəd] ADJ maleducato(-a), sgarbato(-a)

ill-ness ['ɪlnɪs] N malattia

il·logi·cal [ɪ'lɒdʒɪkəl] ADJ illogico(-a)

ill-suited [,ɪl'suːtɪd] ADJ (*couple*) mal assortito(-a); **he is ill-suited to the job** è inadatto a quel lavoro

ill-timed [,ɪl'taɪmd] ADJ intempestivo(-a), inopportuno(-a)

ill-treat [,ɪl'triːt] VT maltrattare

ill-treatment [,ɪl'triːtmənt] N maltrattamenti *mpl*

il·lu·mi·nate [ɪ'luːmɪneɪt] VT (*light up*) illuminare; (*fig: problem, question*) chiarire

il·lu·mi·nat·ing [ɪ'luːmɪneɪtɪŋ] ADJ (*comments, remark*) chiarificatore(-trice); (*experience, book*) istruttivo(-a)

il·lu·mi·na·tion [ɪ,luːmɪ'neɪʃən] N **1** (*lighting*) illuminazione *f* **2** (*of manuscript*) miniatura **3 illuminations** NPL (*coloured lights*) luminarie *fpl*

il·lu·sion [ɪ'luːʒən] N illusione *f*; **to be under an illusion** illudersi; **to be under the illusion that** illudersi che; **to have no illusions** non farsi illusioni

il·lu·sive [ɪ'luːsɪv], **il·lu·sory** [ɪ'luːsərɪ] ADJ illusorio(-a)

il·lus·trate ['ɪləstreɪt] VT illustrare

il·lus·tra·tion [,ɪləs'treɪʃən] N illustrazione *f*; (*example*) esemplificazione *f*; **by way of illustration** a titolo d'esempio

il·lus·tra·tor ['ɪləs,treɪtə'] N illustratore(-trice)

il·lus·tri·ous [ɪ'lʌstrɪəs] ADJ illustre

ill will N rancore *m*; **I bear you no ill will** non ti serbo rancore

ILO [,aɪel'əʊ] N ABBR (= *International Labour Organization*) OIL *f* (= *Organizzazione Internazionale del Lavoro*)

IM N (= *instant messaging*) messaggeria istantanea

I'm [aɪm] = **I am**

im·age [ɪmɪdʒ] N (*of person, group, organization*) immagine *f*; **to be the very** *or* **the spitting image of sb** essere il ritratto sputato di qn; **she's the image of her mother** è il ritratto di sua madre; **mirror image** immagine speculare

im·age·ry ['ɪmɪdʒərɪ] N (*Art, Literature*) immagini *fpl*; (*Psych*) immagini

im·agi·nable [ɪ'mædʒɪnəbl] ADJ immaginabile, che si possa immaginare

im·agi·nary [ɪ'mædʒɪnərɪ] ADJ immaginario(-a)

im·agi·na·tion [ɪ,mædʒɪ'neɪʃən] N immaginazione *f*; (*inventiveness*) immaginazione, fantasia; **it's all imagination!** sono tutte fantasie!; **it's all in your imagination** è tutto frutto della tua immaginazione; **to have a vivid imagination** avere una fervida fantasia *or* una viva immaginazione; **use your imagination!** su, un po' di fantasia!; **she has no imagination** non ha immaginazione

im·agi·na·tive [ɪ'mædʒɪnətɪv] ADJ fantasioso(-a), immaginoso(-a)

im·ag·ine [ɪ'mædʒɪn] VT **1** (*visualize*) immaginare, immaginarsi; **just imagine!** pensa un po'!; **you can imagine how I felt** puoi immaginare *or* immaginarti come mi sono sentito; **you are just imagining things** che idee!, è tutto frutto della tua immaginazione **2** (*suppose, think*) immaginare, credere;

I never imagined that he would be there non avrei mai immaginato che lui sarebbe stato lì

im·bal·ance [ɪmˈbæləns] N squilibrio

im·becile [ˈɪmbəsiːl] N ebete m/f, imbecille m/f

im·bue [ɪmˈbjuː] VT (frm): **to imbue sth with** impregnare qc di

IMF [ˌaɪɛmˈɛf] N ABBR = International Monetary Fund

imi·tate [ˈɪmɪˌteɪt] VT imitare

imi·ta·tion [ˌɪmɪˈteɪʃən] N imitazione f; **in imitation of** a imitazione di; **a painting in imitation of the famous work by Picasso** un dipinto che riproduce la famosa opera di Picasso ♦ ADJ finto(-a); **imitation leather** finta pelle

imi·ta·tor [ˈɪmɪˌteɪtəʳ] N imitatore(-trice)

im·macu·late [ɪˈmækjʊlɪt] ADJ (spotless) immacolato(-a); (flawless) impeccabile

im·ma·terial [ˌɪməˈtɪərɪəl] ADJ irrilevante, insignificante; **it is immaterial whether** poco importa se or che + sub; **it is immaterial whether we like him or not** poco importa se ci piace o no; **that's immaterial** è indifferente!; **that's quite immaterial to me** questo non ha alcuna importanza per me

im·ma·ture [ˌɪməˈtjʊəʳ] ADJ immaturo(-a)

im·ma·tu·rity [ˌɪməˈtjʊərɪtɪ] N immaturità

im·meas·ur·able [ɪˈmɛʒərəbl] ADJ incommensurabile

im·media·cy [ɪˈmiːdɪəsɪ] N immediatezza

im·medi·ate [ɪˈmiːdɪət] ADJ (decision, answer, reaction) immediato(-a); (need, problem) impellente, immediato(-a); (neighbour) della casa accanto; **in the immediate area** nelle immediate vicinanze; **in the immediate future** nell'immediato futuro; **to take immediate action** prendere immediati provvedimenti

im·medi·ate·ly [ɪˈmiːdɪətlɪ] ADV 1 (at once: reply, come, agree) immediatamente 2 (directly: affect, concern) direttamente; **immediately in front of sb/sth** proprio davanti a qn/qc ♦ CONJ (non) appena

im·mense [ɪˈmɛns] ADJ (distance) smisurato(-a); (size, difference) enorme; (enjoyment) immenso(-a)

im·mense·ly [ɪˈmɛnslɪ] ADV (differ) enormemente; (difficult, rich) estremamente; (like, enjoy) immensamente

im·men·si·ty [ɪˈmɛnsɪtɪ] N (of size, difference, problem) vastità; (of space) immensità

im·merse [ɪˈmɜːs] VT: **to immerse sth in water** immergere qc nell'acqua; **immersed in sth** (fig) immerso(-a) or assorto(-a) in qc; **to immerse o.s. in sth** (fig) buttarsi anima e corpo in qc

immersion heater N (Brit) scaldabagno elettrico

im·mi·grant [ˈɪmɪgrənt] ADJ, N (newly arrived) immigrante m/f; (already established) immigrato(-a)

im·mi·gra·tion [ˌɪmɪˈgreɪʃən] N immigrazione f

immigration authorities NPL ufficio m stranieri, inv

immigration laws NPL leggi fpl relative all'immigrazione

im·mi·nent [ˈɪmɪnənt] ADJ imminente

im·mo·bile [ɪˈməʊbaɪl] ADJ immobile

im·mo·bi·lize [ɪˈməʊbɪˌlaɪz] VT immobilizzare

im·mo·bi·liz·er [ɪˈməʊbɪlaɪzəʳ] N (Aut) immobilizer m inv, dispositivo di blocco motore

im·mo·der·ate [ɪˈmɒdərɪt] ADJ (person) smodato(-a), sregolato(-a); (opinion, reaction, demand) eccessivo(-a)

im·mod·est [ɪˈmɒdɪst] ADJ (indecent) indecente; (boastful) immodesto(-a)

im·mor·al [ɪˈmɒrəl] ADJ immorale

im·mo·ral·ity [ˌɪməˈrælɪtɪ] N immoralità

im·mor·tal [ɪˈmɔːtl] ADJ, N immortale m/f

im·mor·tal·ize [ɪˈmɔːtəˌlaɪz] VT immortalare

im·mov·able [ɪˈmuːvəbl] ADJ (object) non movibile; (person) irremovibile

im·mune [ɪˈmjuːn] ADJ: **immune (to, against)** (naturally) immune (da); (after injection) immunizzato(-a) (contro); **immune (from)** (fig) immune (a)

immune system N sistema m immunitario

im·mu·nity [ɪˈmjuːnɪtɪ] N (also fig) immunità; **diplomatic immunity** immunità diplomatica

im·mu·ni·za·tion [ˌɪmjʊnaɪˈzeɪʃən] N immunizzazione f

im·mu·nize [ˈɪmjʊˌnaɪz] VT immunizzare

imp [ɪmp] N (small devil) folletto; (child) diavoletto

im·pact [n ˈɪmpækt, vb ɪmˈpækt] N (force of collision) impatto, (forza d') urto; (fig: effect) effetto; **on impact** nell'urto, nell'impatto; **the book made a great impact on me/the public** il libro ha prodotto una forte impressione su di me/ sul pubblico ♦ VT (drive) conficcare ♦ VI (fig: influence): **to impact on** influire su

im·pair [ɪmˈpɛəʳ] VT (health) danneggiare, pregiudicare; (sight, hearing) deteriorare, menomare; (visibility) ridurre; (relations) deteriorare

im·paired [ɪmˈpɛəd] ADJ (faculties, hearing) deteriorato(-a), indebolito(-a); **visually impaired** videoleso(-a)

im·pale [ɪmˈpeɪl] VT impalare

im·part [ɪmˈpɑːt] VT (frm) 1 (make known) comunicare 2 (bestow) impartire

im·par·tial [ɪmˈpɑːʃəl] ADJ imparziale

im·par·ti·al·ity [ɪmˌpɑːʃɪˈælɪtɪ] N imparzialità

im·pass·able [ɪmˈpɑːsəbl] ADJ (road, mountain pass) intransitabile, impraticabile; (barrier) insuperabile; (river) non attraversabile

im·passe [æmˈpɑːs] N impasse f inv

im·pas·sioned [ɪmˈpæʃnd] ADJ appassionato(-a)

im·pas·sive [ɪmˈpæsɪv] ADJ impassibile

im·pa·tience [ɪmˈpeɪʃəns] N impazienza; **impatience (with sb to do sth)** impazienza (nei confronti di qn/di fare qc)

im·pa·tient [ɪmˈpeɪʃənt] ADJ (eager) impaziente; (irascible) insofferente; **to get or grow impatient (with sb/over sth)** perdere la pazienza (con qn/per qc); **to get impatient** spazientirsi; **people are getting impatient** la gente si sta spazientendo; **impatient to do sth** impaziente di fare qc; **she was impatient to get back home** era impaziente di tornare a casa

im·peach [ɪmˈpiːtʃ] VT 1 (esp USA: prosecute: public official) mettere in stato d'accusa 2 (challenge: character, motive) mettere in dubbio

im·peach·ment [ɪmˈpiːtʃmənt] N (Law) impeachment m inv

im·pec·cable [ɪmˈpɛkəbl] ADJ impeccabile

im·pecu·ni·ous [ˌɪmpɪˈkjuːnɪəs] ADJ (frm) indigente

im·pede [ɪmˈpiːd] VT ostacolare

im·pedi·ment [ɪmˈpɛdɪmənt] N 1 (obstacle) ostacolo 2 (Law) impedimento 3 (Med) difetto; **speech impediment** difetto di pronuncia

im·pel [ɪmˈpɛl] VT (force): **to impel sb (to do sth)** costringere or obbligare qn (a fare qc); (drive) spingere qn (a fare qc)

im·pend·ing [ɪmˈpɛndɪŋ] ADJ (birth, storm, retirement) imminente; (doom, disaster) incombente

im·pen·etrable [ɪmˈpɛnɪtrəbl] ADJ (jungle) impenetrabile; (fortress) inespugnabile; (fig) incomprensibile

im·pera·tive [ɪmˈpɛrətɪv] ADJ 1 (essential) essenziale; **it is imperative that he comes** è indispensabile che lui venga; **it's imperative that we act now** è vitale agire adesso 2 (authoritative: manner, voice) imperioso(-a); (Gram) imperativo(-a) ♦ N (Gram) imperativo; **in the imperative** all'imperativo

im·per·cep·tible [ˌɪmpəˈsɛptəbl] ADJ impercettibile

im·per·fect [ɪmˈpɜːfɪkt] ADJ 1 (gen) difettoso(-a); **imperfect goods** merce f difettosa; **it's an imperfect world** il mondo non è perfetto 2 (Gram) imperfetto(-a) ♦ N (Gram: also: **imperfect tense**) imperfetto; **in the imperfect** all'imperfetto

im·per·fec·tion [ˌɪmpəˈfɛkʃən] N (poor quality) imperfezione f; (flaw) difetto, imperfezione

im·perial [ɪmˈpɪərɪəl] ADJ (gen) imperiale; (imperious) imperioso(-a); (Brit: weights, measures) misurato secondo un sistema non metrico

im·peri·al·ism [ɪmˈpɪərɪəˌlɪzəm] N imperialismo

im·per·il [ɪmˈpɛrɪl] VT (frm) mettere in pericolo

im·peri·ous [ɪmˈpɪərɪəs] ADJ imperioso(-a)

im·per·son·al [ɪmˈpɜːsnl] ADJ 1 (manner, treatment) impersonale, distaccato(-a) 2 (Gram) impersonale

im·per·son·ate [ɪmˈpɜːsəˌneɪt] VT (person) fingersi; (Theatre) imitare

❏ **impersonate** is not translated by the Italian word *impersonare*

im·per·sona·tion [ɪmˌpɜːsəˈneɪʃən] N (gen, also Theatre) imitazione f; (fraudulent) usurpazione f d'identità

im·per·sona·tor [ɪmˈpɜːsəˌneɪtəʳ] N (*gen, also Theatre*) imitatore(-trice)

im·per·ti·nence [ɪmˈpɜːtɪnəns] N impertinenza

im·per·ti·nent [ɪmˈpɜːtɪnənt] ADJ: **impertinent (to)** impertinente (con *or* nei confronti di)

im·per·turb·able [ˌɪmpəˈtɜːbəbl] ADJ imperturbabile

im·per·vi·ous [ɪmˈpɜːvɪəs] ADJ: **impervious (to)** impermeabile (a); (*fig*) indifferente (a), imperturbato(-a) (di fronte a)
❑ **impervious** is not translated by the Italian word *impervio*

im·petu·ous [ɪmˈpɛtjʊəs] ADJ impetuoso(-a)

im·petus [ˈɪmpɪtəs] N (*force*) spinta, impeto; (*fig*) impulso

im·pinge [ɪmˈpɪndʒ] VI: **to impinge on** (*person, situation*) influire su; (*freedom, independence*) violare; (*rights*) ledere

imp·ish [ˈɪmpɪʃ] ADJ malizioso(-a), birichino(-a)

im·plac·able [ɪmˈplækəbl] ADJ implacabile

im·plant [*vb* ɪmˈplɑːnt, *n* ˈɪmplɑːnt] VT (*Med*) innestare; (*fig: idea, principle*) inculcare ♦ N (*Med*) innesto

im·plau·sible [ɪmˈplɔːzəbl] ADJ poco plausibile

im·ple·ment [*vb* ˈɪmplɪˌment, *n* ˈɪmplɪmənt] VT (*decision, plan, idea*) attuare; (*law*) applicare; **it'll take a few months to implement the plan** ci vorranno alcuni mesi per attuare il piano ♦ N (*for cooking*) utensile *m*; (*for garden, farm*) attrezzo

im·pli·cate [ˈɪmplɪˌkeɪt] VT: **to implicate sb in sth** implicare qn in qc

im·pli·ca·tion [ˌɪmplɪˈkeɪʃən] N **1** (*hint, suggestion*) insinuazione *f*; **the implication of your remark is that …** la tua osservazione implica che…; **by implication** implicitamente **2** (*in crime, scandal*) implicazione *f* **3 implications** NPL (*repercussions*) conseguenze *fpl*, ripercussioni *fpl*; **this event had serious implications for industry** quest'avvenimento ebbe (delle) importanti conseguenze per l'industria; **we must study all the implications** dobbiamo considerare tutte le (possibili) conseguenze

im·plic·it [ɪmˈplɪsɪt] ADJ **1** (*implied: threat*) implicito(-a); (: *agreement*) tacito(-a) **2** (*unquestioning: faith, belief*) assoluto(-a)

im·plic·it·ly [ɪmˈplɪsɪtlɪ] ADV **1** (*agree*) tacitamente; (*condone*) implicitamente **2** (*believe*) senza riserve

im·plore [ɪmˈplɔːʳ] VT: **to implore sb (to do sth)** implorare qn (di fare qc); **to implore sb's forgiveness** implorare il perdono di qn

im·ply [ɪmˈplaɪ] VT (*hint, suggest*) insinuare; (*indicate*) implicare; **it implies a lot of work** implica un sacco di lavoro; **are you implying I did it on purpose?** stai insinuando che l'ho fatto apposta?

im·po·lite [ˌɪmpəˈlaɪt] ADJ (*person, remark*) maleducato(-a)

im·pon·der·able [ɪmˈpɒndərəbl] ADJ imponderabile

im·port [*n* ˈɪmpɔːt, *vb* ɪmˈpɔːt] N **1** (*Comm: article*) articolo importato; (: *importation*) importazione *f*; **import-export** import-export *m inv* **2** (*frm: significance*) significato ♦ VT importare ♦ ADJ (*duty, licence*) d'importazione

im·por·tance [ɪmˈpɔːtəns] N importanza; **to attach great importance to sth** dare *or* attribuire molta importanza a qc; **to be of great/little importance** essere molto/poco importante

im·por·tant [ɪmˈpɔːtənt] ADJ importante; **it's not important** non ha importanza; **it is important that** è importante che + *sub*; **to try to look important** (*pej*) darsi arie d'importanza

im·por·tant·ly [ɪmˈpɔːtəntlɪ] ADV significativamente; (*pej*) con (aria d')importanza; **but, more importantly, …** ma, quel che più conta *or* importa,…

im·por·ta·tion [ˌɪmpɔːˈteɪʃən] N importazione *f*

im·port·ed [ɪmˈpɔːtɪd] ADJ importato(-a)

im·port·er [ɪmˈpɔːtəʳ] N importatore(-trice)

im·pose [ɪmˈpəʊz] VT (*conditions, fine, tax*): **to impose (sth on sb)** imporre (qc a qn)
▸ **impose on, impose upon** VI + PREP (*person*) approfittare di

im·pos·ing [ɪmˈpəʊzɪŋ] ADJ imponente

im·po·si·tion [ˌɪmpəˈzɪʃən] N (*of tax, fine, punishment*) imposizione *f*; **it's a bit of an imposition** è pretendere un po' troppo; **to be an imposition on** (*person*) abusare della gentilezza di

im·pos·sibil·ity [ɪmˌpɒsəˈbɪlɪtɪ] N: **impossibility (of sth/of doing sth)** impossibilità (di qc/di fare qc)

im·pos·sible [ɪmˈpɒsəbl] ADJ **1** (*task, enterprise, situation*) impossibile; **it is impossible for me to leave now** mi è impossibile andar via adesso; **it is impossible/not impossible for her to do that** le è impossibile/non le è impossibile farlo; **to make it impossible for sb to do sth** mettere qn nell'impossibilità di fare qc; **to do the impossible** fare l'impossibile **2** (*fam: child, person: difficult, intolerable*) impossibile, insopportabile

im·pos·tor [ɪmˈpɒstəʳ] N impostore(-a)

im·po·tence [ˈɪmpətəns] N (*frm, also Med*) impotenza

im·po·tent [ˈɪmpətənt] ADJ (*frm, also Med*) impotente

im·pound [ɪmˈpaʊnd] VT (*gen*) sequestrare, confiscare; (*stray animal*) rinchiudere

im·pov·er·ished [ɪmˈpɒvərɪʃt] ADJ impoverito(-a)

im·prac·ti·cable [ɪmˈpræktɪkəbl] ADJ inattuabile

im·prac·ti·cal [ɪmˈpræktɪkəl] ADJ (*person*) privo(-a) di senso pratico; (*plan*) poco realistico(-a), poco pratico(-a)

im·pre·cise [ˌɪmprɪˈsaɪs] ADJ impreciso(-a)

im·preg·nable [ɪmˈpregnəbl] ADJ (*fortress, defences*) inespugnabile; (*fig: person, group*) inattaccabile

im·preg·nate [ˈɪmpregˌneɪt] VT (*fertilize*) fecondare; (*saturate*): **to impregnate (with)** impregnare (di)

im·pre·sa·rio [ˌɪmprɪˈsɑːrɪəʊ] N impresario(-a)

im·press [ɪmˈpres] VT **1** (*make good impression on*) fare una buona impressione a *or* su, colpire favorevolmente; **how did she impress you?** che impressione ti ha fatto?; **he impressed me quite favourably** mi ha fatto un'impressione abbastanza buona; **he really impressed me!** mi ha veramente colpito!; **what impressed him most was …** quello che l'ha colpito di più è stato…; **a group of students trying to impress their teacher** un gruppo di studenti che cercavano di fare bella figura con l'insegnante; **I'm not impressed** non ne sono rimasto colpito **2** (*mark, stamp*) imprimere; **to impress sth on sb** (*fig*) far comprendere qc a qn

im·pres·sion [ɪmˈpreʃən] N **1** (*most senses*) impressione *f*; **to be under** *or* **have the impression that** avere l'impressione che; **he gives the impression of knowing a lot about it** dà l'impressione di saperne molto; **to make a good/bad impression on sb** fare una buona/cattiva impressione a *or* su qn; **my words made no impression on him** le mie parole non hanno avuto nessun effetto su di lui **2** (*imitation*) imitazione *f*; **to do impressions** fare delle imitazioni

im·pres·sion·able [ɪmˈpreʃnəbl] ADJ (*person*) impressionabile; **to be at an impressionable age** essere nell'età in cui si è facilmente influenzabili

im·pres·sion·ist [ɪmˈpreʃənɪst] ADJ, N (*Art*) impressionista *m/f*; (*mimic*) imitatore(-trice)

im·pres·sive [ɪmˈpresɪv] ADJ (*person, achievement*) notevole; (*occasion, event*) di notevole imponenza; (*building*) imponente; **an impressive achievement** un risultato notevole

im·print [*n* ˈɪmprɪnt, *vb* ɪmˈprɪnt] N (*Publishing*) sigla editoriale ♦ VT imprimere

im·print·ed [ɪmˈprɪntɪd] ADJ imprinted on impresso(-a) in

im·pris·on [ɪmˈprɪzn] VT incarcerare; **after being imprisoned for three weeks** dopo tre settimane di *or* in carcere

im·pris·on·ment [ɪmˈprɪznmənt] N reclusione *f*; **during his imprisonment** mentre era in carcere; **life imprisonment** l'ergastolo

im·prob·able [ɪmˈprɒbəbl] ADJ (*event*) improbabile, poco probabile; (*excuse, story*) inverosimile

im·promp·tu [ɪmˈprɒmptjuː] ADJ improvvisato(-a), estemporaneo(-a) ♦ ADV (*speak*) improvvisando, a braccio

im·prop·er [ɪmˈprɒpəʳ] ADJ (*unseemly, indecent*) sconveniente; (*wrong*) scorretto(-a); (*unsuitable*) improprio(-a), inadatto(-a); **he denies doing anything improper** nega di essersi comportato in modo scorretto

im·pro·pri·ety [ˌɪmprəˈpraɪətɪ] N (*frm: of behaviour*) scorrettezza; (: *unseemliness, indecency*) sconvenienza; (: *of expression*) improprietà *f inv*

im·prove [ɪmˈpruːv] VT (*gen*) migliorare; (*property, land*) apportare migliorie a; (*production, yield, salary*) aumentare; **to improve one's Italian** perfezionare il proprio italiano; **to improve one's chances of success** aumentare le proprie probabilità di successo; **to improve one's mind** migliorare la propria cultura; **he's improved his technique** ha migliorato la tecnica ♦ VI (*gen*) migliorare; (*person: in skill*) fare (dei) progressi; **to improve in sth** migliorare *or* fare (dei) progressi in qc; **to improve with age/use** migliorare con gli anni/con l'uso; **this wine improves with age** questo vino migliora con l'invecchiamento; **my Italian improved a lot** il mio italiano è migliorato molto

▸ **improve on, improve upon** VI + PREP (*offer*) aumentare; (*work*) ottenere dei risultati migliori rispetto a; (*method*) perfezionare; (*quality*) migliorare; **I can't improve on my offer to you** non posso farti un'offerta migliore

im·prove·ment [ɪm'pruːvmənt] N: **improvement (in)** (*gen*) miglioramento (in); (*in production, salary*) aumento (di *or* in); **it's an improvement on the old one** è meglio di quello vecchio; **there is room for improvement** si può migliorare *or* far meglio; **to make improvements to** migliorare; (*property*) apportare migliorie a; (*method*) perfezionare

im·provi·sa·tion [ˌɪmprəvaɪ'zeɪʃən] N improvvisazione *f*

im·pro·vise ['ɪmprəvaɪz] VT, VI improvvisare

im·pru·dence [ɪm'pruːdəns] N imprudenza

im·pru·dent [ɪm'pruːdənt] ADJ imprudente

im·pu·dence ['ɪmpjʊdəns] N impudenza

im·pu·dent ['ɪmpjʊdənt] ADJ impertinente, impudente

im·pugn [ɪm'pjuːn] VT (*frm*) attaccare, contestare

im·pulse ['ɪmpʌls] N impulso; **to act on impulse** agire d'impulso *or* impulsivamente

impulse buy N acquisto fatto d'impulso

im·pul·sive [ɪm'pʌlsɪv] ADJ impulsivo(-a)

im·pu·nity [ɪm'pjuːnɪtɪ] N: **with impunity** impunemente

im·pure ['ɪmpjʊə'] ADJ (*Chem: morally*) impuro(-a); (*air*) inquinato(-a)

im·pu·rity [ɪm'pjʊərɪtɪ] N impurità *f inv*

IN ABBR (*USA Post:* = **Indiana**)

<u>KEYWORD</u>

in [ɪn] PREP

1 (*place, position*) in; **in the country** in campagna; **in the garden** in giardino; **in my hand** in mano; **in here** qui dentro; **in the house** in casa; **in school** a scuola; **in the school** nella scuola; **in there** lì dentro; **in the town** in città

2 (*with place names: of town*) a; (*: of region, country*) in; **in England** in Inghilterra; **it's in France** è in Francia; **in London** a Londra; **in Sicily** in Sicilia; **it's in the United States** è negli Stati Uniti; **in Yorkshire** nello Yorkshire

3 (*time: during*) in; **in 1994** nel 1994; **at 4 o'clock in the afternoon** alle 4 del pomeriggio; **in autumn** in autunno; **in the 20th century** nel ventesimo secolo; **in those days** a quei tempi, allora; **in the daytime** di or durante il giorno, durante la giornata; **in the eighties** negli anni ottanta; **in May** in maggio, a maggio, nel mese di maggio; **in the morning** di or alla mattina, la mattina, nella mattinata; **in the mornings** di or alla mattina, la mattina; **in the past** nel or in passato; **spring** in primavera; **in (the) summer** in estate, d'estate; **in (the) winter** in inverno, d'inverno; **she has not been here in years** sono anni che non viene qui

4 (*time: in the space of*) in; (*after*) tra, fra; **it will be ready in 2 days** sarà pronto fra due giorni; **I did it in 3 hours** l'ho fatto in 3 ore; **she will return the money in a month** restituirà i soldi tra un mese

5 (*manner, means*): **a statue carved in wood** una statua intagliata nel legno; **to pay in dollars** pagare in dollari; **dressed in green/a skirt/trousers** vestito(-a) di verde/con una gonna/con i calzoni; **in English** in inglese; **in ink** a penna; **in Italian** in italiano; **the man in the hat** l'uomo con il cappello; **in alphabetical order** in ordine alfabetico; **painted in red** dipinto(-a) di rosso; **in part** in parte; **in pencil** a matita; **in person** di persona; **in large/small quantities** in grandi/piccole quantità; **in a loud/soft voice** a voce alta/bassa; **in watercolour** ad acquerello; **in a whisper** sussurrando; **in writing** per iscritto

6 (*circumstance*): **in the dark(ness)** al buio, nell'oscurità; **in (the) daylight** alla or con la luce del giorno; **to be 10 metres in height** essere alto(-a) 10 metri; **to be 10 metres in length** essere lungo(-a) 10 metri; **in the moonlight** al chiaro di luna; **a change in policy** un cambiamento di prassi; **a rise in**

prices un aumento dei prezzi; **in the rain** sotto la pioggia; **in the shade** all'ombra; **in the sun** al sole; **in all weathers** con qualsiasi tempo, qualsiasi tempo faccia; **to be 10 metres in width** essere largo(-a) 10 metri

7 (*mood, state*): **to act in anger** agire per rabbia; **in good condition** or **repair** in buono stato, in buone condizioni; **in despair** disperato(-a); **to live in luxury** vivere nel lusso; **in private** in privato; **to be in a rage** essere su tutte le furie; **in secret** in segreto; **in tears** in lacrime

8 (*ratio, number*): **in hundreds** a centinaia; **once in a hundred years** una volta ogni cento anni; **one person/car in ten** una persona/macchina su dieci; **20 pence in the pound** 20 pence per sterlina; **in twos** a due a due

9 (*people, works*) in; **this is common in children/cats** questo è comune nei or per i bambini/gatti; **she has it in her to succeed** ha in sé la capacità di riuscire; **they have a good leader in him** hanno in lui un ottimo capo; **in (the works of) Shakespeare** in Shakespeare

10 (*in profession*): **to be in the army** essere nell'esercito; **to be in publishing** lavorare nell'editoria; **to be in teaching** fare l'insegnante, insegnare

11 (*after superlative*) di; **the best pupil in the class** il migliore alunno della classe; **the biggest in Europe** il più grande d'Europa; **the smallest in Europe** il più piccolo d'Europa

12 (*with present participle*): **in saying this** dicendo questo, nel dir questo

13 in that dal momento che, visto che; **in all** in tutto

♦ ADV: **to be in** (*person*) esserci; (*train, ship, plane*) essere arrivato(-a); (*crops, harvest*) essere raccolto(-a); (*in fashion*) essere di moda; (*fam: in power*) essere al potere; **to ask sb in** invitare qn a entrare; **day in, day out** (*pej*) dalla mattina alla sera; **we're in for a snow storm** si prepara una tormenta; **he is in for trouble** lo aspettano dei guai; **he's in for it** (*fam*) è nei guai, lo aspettano guai seri; **to have it in for sb** (*fam*) avercela con qn; **is he in?** lui c'è?; **to limp in** entrare zoppicando; **my luck is in** la fortuna è dalla mia (parte); **to be in on a plan/secret** essere al corrente di un progetto/segreto; **to be in and out of work** non durare mai molto in un impiego; **to be in and out of (the) hospital/prison** essere sempre dentro e fuori dall'ospedale/di prigione

♦ N: **the ins and outs of the problem** tutti i particolari del problema

♦ ADJ (*fam*) in *inv*; **it's an in club** è un club molto 'in'; **it's an in joke** è una cosa nostra; **it's the in thing to do** (*fam*) è la cosa 'in' del momento

in. ABBR (*pl* **ins.**) = **inch**

in·abil·ity [ˌɪnə'bɪlɪtɪ] N (*physical, mental*) incapacità *f inv*; **inability to do sth** incapacità di fare qc; **his inability to control himself** la sua incapacità di controllarsi; **inability to pay** impossibilità di pagare

in·ac·ces·sible [ˌɪnæk'sesəbl] ADJ: **inaccessible (to)** inaccessibile (a)

in·ac·cu·ra·cy [ɪn'ækjʊrəsɪ] N (*see adj*) inaccuratezza; inesattezza; imprecisione *f*; (*usu pl: mistake*) errore *m*

in·ac·cu·rate [ɪn'ækjʊrɪt] ADJ (*statement, report, story*) inaccurato(-a); (*figures*) inesatto(-a); (*translation*) impreciso(-a)

in·ac·tion [ɪn'ækʃən] N inerzia, inazione *f*

in·ac·tiv·ity [ˌɪnæk'tɪvɪtɪ] N inattività

in·ad·equa·cy [ɪn'ædɪkwəsɪ] N inadeguatezza, insufficienza; (*of person*) incapacità *f inv*

in·ad·equate [ɪn'ædɪkwɪt] ADJ (*insufficient*) inadeguato(-a), insufficiente; (*person*) non all'altezza; **to feel inadequate** non sentirsi all'altezza; **he felt quite inadequate** non si sentiva assolutamente all'altezza

in·ad·mis·si·ble [ˌɪnəd'mɪsəbl] ADJ (*evidence*) inammissibile

in·ad·vert·ent [ˌɪnəd'vɜːtənt] ADJ (*unintentional*) involontario(-a); (*unthinking*) inconsapevole

in·ad·vert·ent·ly [ˌɪnəd'vɜːtəntlɪ] ADV (*unintentionally*) inavvertitamente, involontariamente; (*unawares*) inconsapevolmente

in·ad·vis·able [ˌɪnəd'vaɪzəbl] ADJ sconsigliabile

in·ane [ɪ'neɪn] ADJ (*remark*) sciocco(-a), stupido(-a)

in·ani·mate [ɪn'ænɪmɪt] ADJ inanimato(-a)

in·ap·pli·cable [ɪn'æplɪkəbl] ADJ inapplicabile

in·ap·pro·pri·ate [ˌɪnə'prəʊprɪɪt] ADJ (*action, punishment,* *treatment*) inadeguato(-a), non appropriato(-a); (*word, phrase, expression*) non appropriato(-a); (*behaviour*) sconveniente; **the scheme is inappropriate to the people's needs** il programma è inadeguato alle necessità della gente; **it would be inappropriate for us to intervene** sarebbe inopportuno da parte nostra intervenire

in·apt [ɪnˈæpt] ADJ (*remark, behaviour*) poco appropriato(-a)

in·ap·ti·tude [ɪnˈæptɪˌtjuːd], **in·apt·ness** [ɪnˈæptnɪs] N (*of remark*) improprietà

in·ar·ticu·late [ˌɪnɑːˈtɪkjʊlɪt] ADJ (*person*) che non sa esprimersi, che si esprime male; (*speech*) inarticolato(-a), confuso(-a); **he's inarticulate** si esprime male

in·as·much as [ˌɪnəzˈmʌtʃəz] CONJ (*insofar as*) in quanto, nella misura in cui; (*seeing that*) poiché

in·at·ten·tion [ˌɪnəˈtenʃən] N: **inattention (to)** mancanza di attenzione (per *or* nei confronti di), disattenzione *f* (per *or* nei confronti di)

in·at·ten·tive [ˌɪnəˈtentɪv] ADJ disattento(-a), distratto(-a)

in·audible [ɪnˈɔːdəbl] ADJ appena percettibile; **the speech was inaudible** non si riusciva a sentire il discorso

in·augu·ral [ɪˈnɔːɡjʊrəl] ADJ inaugurale

in·augu·rate [ɪˈnɔːɡjʊˌreɪt] VT (*president, official*) insediare; (*start officially: organization, festival*) inaugurare; (*frm: system, idea*) inaugurare, instaurare

in·augu·ra·tion [ɪˌnɔːɡjʊˈreɪʃən] N (*of president*) insediamento (in carica); (*opening*) inaugurazione *f*; **the inauguration of a new era** l'inizio di una nuova era

in·aus·pi·cious [ˌɪnɔːsˈpɪʃəs] ADJ poco propizio(-a)

in·between [ɪnbɪˈtwiːn] ADJ intermedio(-a)

in·born [ˈɪnˈbɔːn] ADJ (*feeling*) innato(-a); (*defect*) congenito(-a)

in·box [ˈɪnbɒks] N (*Comput*) (cartella della) posta in arrivo

in·bred [ˈɪnˈbred] ADJ (*tendency*) innato(-a); **an inbred family** (*pej*) *una famiglia con un alto indice di unioni fra consanguinei*

in·breed·ing [ˈɪnˈbriːdɪŋ] N (*Zool*) inbreeding *m inv*; (*of people*) unioni *fpl* fra consanguinei

Inc. ABBR = **incorporated**

Inca [ˈɪŋkə] ADJ (*also:* **Incan**) incaico(-a), inca *inv* ♦ N inca *m/f inv*

in·cal·cu·lable [ɪnˈkælkjʊləbl] ADJ incalcolabile

in·ca·pabil·ity [ɪnˌkeɪpəˈbɪlɪtɪ] N incapacità

in·ca·pable [ɪnˈkeɪpəbl] ADJ **incapable (of doing sth)** incapace (di fare qc); **a question incapable of solution** (*frm*) un problema irrisolvibile *or* insolubile

in·ca·paci·tate [ˌɪnkəˈpæsɪˌteɪt] VT (*person*) rendere inabile; (*Law*) inabilitare; **to incapacitate sb from doing sth** rendere qn inabile a fare qc; **a bad fall incapacitated him** una brutta caduta lo ha bloccato

in·ca·paci·tat·ed [ˌɪnkəˈpæsɪˌteɪtɪd] ADJ (*disabled*) inabile; (*Law*) inabilitato(-a); **physically incapacitated** inabile fisicamente

in·ca·pac·ity [ˌɪnkəˈpæsɪtɪ] N incapacità; (*Law*) inabilitazione *f*

in·car·cer·ate [ɪnˈkɑːsəˌreɪt] VT (*frm*) incarcerare

in·car·nate [*adj* ɪnˈkɑːnɪt, *vb* ɪnˈkɑːneɪt] ADJ (*Rel*) incarnato(-a); **the devil incarnate** il diavolo personificato *or* in persona ♦ VT incarnare

in·car·na·tion [ˌɪnkɑːˈneɪʃən] N (*Rel*) incarnazione *f*

in·cen·di·ary [ɪnˈsendɪərɪ] ADJ incendiario(-a) ♦ N (*bomb*) ordigno incendiario

in·cense [*n* ˈɪnsens, *vb* ɪnˈsens] N incenso ♦ VT (*anger*) fare infuriare

incense burner N incensiere *m*

in·cen·tive [ɪnˈsentɪv] N incentivo; **there is no incentive to work** non c'è alcun incentivo a lavorare; **it gave me an incentive** mi è servito da incentivo

incentive scheme N piano di incentivazione

in·cep·tion [ɪnˈsepʃən] N (*frm*) inizio, principio

in·ces·sant [ɪnˈsesnt] ADJ incessante

in·ces·sant·ly [ɪnˈsesntlɪ] ADV incessantemente

in·cest [ˈɪnsest] N incesto

inch [ɪntʃ] N pollice *m* (*cm 2.54; 12 per foot*); **a few inches** ≈ qualche centimetro; **the car missed me by inches** c'è mancato un pelo che la macchina mi investisse; **to lose a few inches** (*fam*) perdere un po' di ciccia; **inch by inch** a

poco a poco; **every inch of it was used** è stato utilizzato tutto fino all'ultimo millimetro *or* centimetro; **he's every inch a soldier** è un soldato dalla testa ai piedi; **within an inch of** a un pelo da; **to be within an inch of death/disaster** essere a un passo dalla morte/dalla rovina; **he didn't give** *or* **budge an inch** (*fig*) non ha ceduto di un millimetro

▸ **inch forward** VI + ADV avanzare pian piano

▸ **inch up** VI + ADV salire a poco a poco

inch tape N metro a nastro (*da sarto*)

in·ci·dence [ˈɪnsɪdəns] N (*extent, rate: of disease, crime*) incidenza; **the angle of incidence** (*Phys*) l'angolo d'incidenza

in·ci·dent [ˈɪnsɪdənt] N (*gen*) caso, avvenimento; (*diplomatic, on border*) incidente *m*; (*in book*) episodio; (*in play*) scena; **a minor incident** un piccolo incidente; **without incident** (*uneventful*) senza incidenti (di rilievo); (*without trouble*) senza problemi

in·ci·den·tal [ˌɪnsɪˈdentl] ADJ (*secondary*) secondario(-a); (*unplanned*) fortuito(-a); **incidental to** connesso(-a) con; **incidental expenses** spese *fpl* accessorie ♦ N (*minor point*) punto di secondaria importanza; **incidentals** NPL (*expenses*) spese *fpl* accessorie

in·ci·den·tal·ly [ˌɪnsɪˈdentəlɪ] ADV (*by the way*) fra parentesi, tra l'altro, per inciso

incidental music N sottofondo musicale, musica di sottofondo

incident room N (*Police*) centrale *f* operativa

in·cin·er·ate [ɪnˈsɪnəˌreɪt] VT incenerire

in·cin·era·tor [ɪnˈsɪnəˌreɪtəʳ] N inceneritore *m*

in·cipi·ent [ɪnˈsɪpɪənt] ADJ (*disease, baldness*) incipiente; (*revolt*) nascente

in·ci·sion [ɪnˈsɪʒən] N incisione *f*

in·ci·sive [ɪnˈsaɪsɪv] ADJ (*mind, remark*) acuto(-a); (*criticism*) tagliente; (*speech, style*) incisivo(-a)

in·ci·sor [ɪnˈsaɪzəʳ] N (*Anat*) incisivo

in·cite [ɪnˈsaɪt] VT: **to incite sb (to sth/to do sth)** incitare qn (a qc/a fare qc), istigare qn (a qc/a fare qc)

incl. ABBR = **including; inclusive (of)**

in·clem·ent [ɪnˈklemənt] ADJ inclemente

in·cli·na·tion [ˌɪnklɪˈneɪʃən] N 1 (*wish*) tendenza, inclinazione *f*; **he felt no inclination to join in the fun** non aveva nessuna voglia di unirsi alla gazzarra; **her inclination was to ignore him** avrebbe voluto ignorarlo; **against my inclination** controvoglia; **to follow one's inclination** seguire le proprie inclinazioni 2 (*slope*) pendio, china 3 (*bow*) cenno

in·cline [*n* ˈɪnklaɪn, *vb* ɪnˈklaɪn] N pendenza, pendio ♦ VT (*bend: head, body*) chinare, inclinare ♦ VI 1 (*slope*) declinare 2 (*tend to*): **to incline to(wards)** tendere a; **I incline to the belief/opinion that ...** sono propenso a credere che...

in·clude [ɪnˈkluːd] VT comprendere, includere; **your name is not included in the list** il tuo nome non è incluso nella lista; **he sold everything, books included** ha venduto tutto, compresi i libri; **service is/is not included** il servizio è compreso/escluso

in·clud·ing [ɪnˈkluːdɪŋ] PREP compreso(-a), incluso(-a); **including VAT** IVA compresa; **seven books including this one** sette libri compreso *or* incluso questo; **up to and including Chapter 12** fino al capitolo 12 compreso *or* incluso; **it will be two hundred pounds, including tax** sono duecento sterline, tasse comprese

in·clu·sion [ɪnˈkluːʒən] N inclusione *f*

in·clu·sive [ɪnˈkluːsɪv] ADJ (*sum, price*) tutto compreso *inv*; **the inclusive price is two hundred pounds** il prezzo tutto compreso è di duecento sterline; **inclusive of** incluso(-a); **£500, inclusive of VAT** 500 sterline, IVA compresa ♦ ADV: **from the 10th to the 15th inclusive** dal 10 al 15 incluso *or* compreso

inclusive terms NPL (*Brit*) (*prezzo m*) tutto compreso, *inv*

in·cog·ni·to [ˌɪnkɒɡˈniːtəʊ] ADV (*travel*) in incognito; **to remain incognito** mantenere l'incognito

in·co·her·ent [ˌɪnkəʊˈhɪərənt] ADJ (*person*) incoerente; **he was incoherent with rage** non connetteva per la rabbia

in·come [ˈɪnkʌm] N (*gen*) reddito; (*from receipts*) introito; **gross/net income** reddito lordo/netto; **private income** rendita; **to live within/beyond one's income** vivere secondo i propri mezzi/al di sopra dei propri mezzi; **low income families** famiglie a basso reddito

in·come support N (*Brit*) sussidio di indigenza *or* povertà

income tax N imposta sul reddito

income tax inspector N ispettore *m* delle imposte sul reddito

income tax return N dichiarazione *f* dei redditi

in·com·ing [ˈɪnˌkʌmɪŋ] ADJ (*passengers*) in arrivo; (*tide*) montante; (*government*) entrante; (*tenant*) subentrante

in·com·mu·ni·ca·do [ˌɪnkəˌmjuːnɪˈkɑːdəʊ] ADJ: **to hold sb incommunicado** tenere segregato(-a) qn

in·com·pa·rable [ɪnˈkɒmpərəbl] ADJ incomparabile

in·com·pat·ible [ˌɪnkəmˈpætɪbl] ADJ incompatibile

in·com·pe·tence [ɪnˈkɒmpɪtəns] N incompetenza

in·com·pe·tent [ɪnˈkɒmpɪtənt] ADJ (*work*) da incompetenti; (*person*): **incompetent (at)** incompetente (in fatto di)

in·com·plete [ˌɪnkəmˈpliːt] ADJ (*partial*) incompleto(-a); (*unfinished*: *work*) non finito(-a); (: *book, painting*) incompiuto(-a)

in·com·pre·hen·sible [ɪnˌkɒmprɪˈhensəbl] ADJ incomprensibile

in·con·ceiv·able [ˌɪnkənˈsiːvəbl] ADJ inconcepibile

in·con·clu·sive [ˌɪnkənˈkluːsɪv] ADJ (*debate, discussion*) inconcludente, non risolutivo(-a); (*evidence, experiment*) che lascia dubbi, inconcludente; (*argument*) poco convincente

in·con·gru·ous [ɪnˈkɒŋgrʊəs] ADJ (*appearance, behaviour*) inadeguato(-a), assurdo(-a); (*remark, act*) fuori luogo; **the top hat looked incongruous at such an occasion** il cilindro sembrava inadeguato per quell'occasione

in·con·sequen·tial [ɪnˌkɒnsɪˈkwenʃəl], **in·con·sequent** [ɪnˈkɒnsɪkwənt] ADJ (*conversation*) senza importanza; (*remark*) irrilevante

in·con·sid·er·able [ˌɪnkənˈsɪdərəbl] ADJ: **not inconsiderable** non trascurabile

in·con·sid·er·ate [ˌɪnkənˈsɪdərɪt] ADJ (*person*) privo(-a) di riguardo; (*behaviour*) poco gentile

in·con·sist·en·cy [ˌɪnkənˈsɪstənsɪ] N **1** (*of actions*) contraddizione *f*, incoerenza; (*of work*) irregolarità **2** (*of statement*) incongruenza

❏ **inconsistency** is not translated by the Italian word *inconsistenza*

in·con·sist·ent [ˌɪnkənˈsɪstənt] ADJ (*contradictory*: *action*) contraddittorio(-a), incoerente; (*uneven*: *work*) irregolare, incostante; **your work this year has been very inconsistent** il tuo rendimento quest'anno è stato incostante; **to be inconsistent with** essere in contraddizione con; **that is inconsistent with what you told me earlier** questo è in contraddizione con quanto mi avevi riferito prima; **his actions were inconsistent with his principles** le sue azioni non erano coerenti con i suoi principi

❏ **inconsistent** is not translated by the Italian word *inconsistente*

in·con·sol·able [ˌɪnkənˈsəʊləbl] ADJ inconsolabile

in·con·spicu·ous [ˌɪnkənˈspɪkjʊəs] ADJ (*place*) che non dà nell'occhio, poco in vista; (*colour*) poco appariscente; (*person, dress*) dimesso(-a); **to make o.s. inconspicuous** cercare di passare inosservato(-a); **an inconspicuous grey building** un edificio grigio che non si nota

in·con·stant [ɪnˈkɒnstənt] ADJ incostante, volubile

in·con·ti·nence [ɪnˈkɒntɪnəns] N (*Med*) incontinenza

in·con·ti·nent [ɪnˈkɒntɪnənt] ADJ (*Med*) incontinente

in·con·tro·vert·ible [ˌɪnkɒntrəˈvɜːtəbl] ADJ incontrovertibile

in·con·ven·ience [ˌɪnkənˈviːnɪəns] N (*see adj*) scomodità *f inv*; scarsa funzionalità; inopportunità; **not having a car was a great inconvenience** non aver la macchina era una gran scomodità; **to put sb to great inconvenience** creare problemi *mpl* a qn, recare disturbo a qn; **I don't want to cause any inconvenience** non vorrei dare disturbo ♦ VT disturbare, incomodare; **don't inconvenience yourself** non si disturbi *or* incomodi

❏ **inconvenience** is not translated by the Italian word *inconveniente*

in·con·ven·ient [ˌɪnkənˈviːnɪənt] ADJ (*time, appointment, location*) scomodo(-a); (*house, design*) poco funzionale; (*arrival*) inopportuno(-a); **is it an inconvenient time for you?** ti è scomodo a quest'ora?; **that time is very inconvenient for me** non è un'ora adatta per me; **if it is not inconvenient (to you)** se non è un problema; **could you let me have the key tomorrow, if it is not inconvenient** mi puoi dare la chiave domani, se non è un problema?

in·cor·po·rate [ɪnˈkɔːpəˌreɪt] VT (*include*) includere, comprendere; (*integrate*) incorporare

in·cor·po·rat·ed [ɪnˈkɔːpəˌreɪtɪd] ADJ (*USA: Comm*): **incorporated company** ≈ società *f inv* per azioni

in·cor·rect [ˌɪnkəˈrekt] ADJ (*statement, fact*) inesatto(-a); (*conclusion*) errato(-a); (*behaviour*) scorretto(-a); (*dress*) sconveniente; **that is incorrect** questo è inesatto; **the information he gave me was incorrect** le informazioni che mi ha dato erano inesatte; **you are incorrect in stating that ...** ti sbagli quando dici che...; **this backache is caused by incorrect posture** il suo mal di schiena è causato dalla postura scorretta

in·cor·ri·gible [ɪnˈkɒrɪdʒəbl] ADJ incorreggibile

in·cor·rupt·ible [ˌɪnkəˈrʌptəbl] ADJ incorruttibile

in·crease [*vb* ɪnˈkriːs, *n* ˈɪnkriːs] VI (*prices, salaries*) aumentare; (*population, demand, supply, sales*) aumentare, crescere; (*excitement, tension*) farsi più intenso(-a); (*rain, wind*) aumentare, intensificarsi; **to increase in number/size** crescere di numero/di dimensioni; **to increase in volume/weight** aumentare di volume/di peso; **to increase in value** aumentare di valore; **to increase by 100** aumentare di 100; **the number increased** il numero è aumentato; **the hole is increasing in size** il buco si sta allargando ♦ VT (*see vi*) aumentare; accrescere; intensificare; **to increase speed** aumentare la velocità; **they've increased the price** hanno aumentato il prezzo; **to increase one's efforts** moltiplicare *or* intensificare i propri sforzi ♦ N (*see vi*) aumento; crescita; intensificazione *f*; **an increase in size/volume** un aumento di dimensioni/di volume; **an increase of £5/10%** un aumento di 5 sterline/del 10%; **an increase in road accidents** un aumento degli incidenti stradali; **a salary increase** un aumento di stipendio; **to be on the increase** essere in aumento; (*prices*) essere in aumento *or* in rialzo; (*sales, trade*) essere in aumento *or* in fase di espansione

in·creas·ing [ɪnˈkriːsɪŋ] ADJ (*number*) crescente, in aumento

in·creas·ing·ly [ɪnˈkriːsɪŋlɪ] ADV sempre più

in·cred·ible [ɪnˈkredəbl] ADJ incredibile

in·cred·ibly [ɪnˈkredəblɪ] ADV incredibilmente

in·credu·lous [ɪnˈkredjʊləs] ADJ incredulo(-a)

in·cre·ment [ˈɪnkrɪmənt] N (*in salary*) aumento; (*Math*) incremento

in·crimi·nate [ɪnˈkrɪmɪˌneɪt] VT incriminare

in·crimi·nat·ing [ɪnˈkrɪmɪˌneɪtɪŋ] ADJ incriminante

in·cu·bate [ˈɪnkjʊˌbeɪt] VT (*eggs*) covare ♦ VI (*egg*) essere in incubazione; (*disease*) avere un'incubazione

in·cu·ba·tion [ˌɪnkjʊˈbeɪʃən] N incubazione *f*

incubation period N (periodo di) incubazione *f*

in·cu·ba·tor [ˈɪnkjʊˌbeɪtə*] N (*for eggs, baby*) incubatrice *f*

in·cul·cate [ˈɪnkʌlˌkeɪt] VT (*frm*): **to inculcate sth in(to) sb** inculcare qc a qn

in·cum·bent [ɪnˈkʌmbənt] (*frm*) ADJ: **it is incumbent on him to do it ...** spetta a lui farlo... ♦ N (*gen*) titolare *m/f*; (*Rel*) beneficiato

❏ **incumbent** is not translated by the Italian word *incombente*

in·cur [ɪnˈkɜː*] VT (*debt, obligation*) contrarre; (*expenses*) andare incontro a; (*loss*) subire; (*anger*) attirarsi; (*risk*) esporsi a

in·cur·able [ɪnˈkjʊərəbl] ADJ (*disease*) incurabile; (*habit*) incorreggibile; (*fig: optimist*) inguaribile

in·cur·sion [ɪnˈkɜːʃən] N incursione *f*

Ind. ABBR (*USA:* = **Indiana**)

in·debt·ed [ɪnˈdetɪd] ADJ (*fig*): **to be indebted to sb (for sth)** essere molto obbligato(-a) a qn (per *or* di qc)

in·de·cen·cy [ɪnˈdiːsnsɪ] N indecenza

in·de·cent [ɪnˈdiːsnt] ADJ (*dress, behaviour*) indecente

indecent assault N (*Brit Law*) atti *mpl* di libidine violenta

indecent exposure N esibizionismo (di organi genitali)

in·de·ci·pher·able [ˌɪndɪˈsaɪfərəbl] ADJ indecifrabile

in·de·ci·sion [ˌɪndɪˈsɪʒən] N indecisione *f*

in·de·ci·sive [ˌɪndɪˈsaɪsɪv] ADJ (*person*) indeciso(-a), esitante; (*result, discussion*) non decisivo(-a)

in·deed [ɪnˈdiːd] ADV **1** veramente, infatti, in effetti; **I feel, indeed I know, he is wrong** ho l'impressione, anzi sono certo, che si sbaglia; **there are indeed mistakes, but ...** ci sono certamente degli errori, però...; **thank you very much indeed** grazie infinite; **that is praise indeed** questa è decisamente una lode; **it's very hard indeed** è veramente molto difficile; **thank you very much indeed!** grazie infinite! **2** (*in answer to question*): **yes indeed!** certamente!; **isn't that right? — indeed it is** non è vero? — altroché; **are you coming? — indeed I am** vieni? — certo; **was I mistaken? — indeed you weren't** mi sbagliavo? — no, per niente; **know what I mean? — indeed I do** sai cosa intendo? — certamente

in·de·fati·ga·ble [ˌɪndɪˈfætɪgəbl] ADJ infaticabile, instancabile

in·de·fen·sible [ˌɪndɪˈfensəbl] ADJ (*town*) indifendibile; (*conduct*) ingiustificabile

in·de·fin·able [ˌɪndɪˈfaɪnəbl] ADJ indefinibile

in·defi·nite [ɪnˈdefɪnɪt] ADJ (*answer, plans*) vago(-a); (*time, period, number*) indeterminato(-a), indefinito(-a); (*Gram*) indefinito(-a)

in·defi·nite·ly [ɪnˈdefɪnɪtlɪ] ADV (*postpone*) a tempo indeterminato; (*wait*) indefinitamente, all'infinito

in·del·ible [ɪnˈdelɪbl] ADJ (*also fig*) indelebile

in·deli·cate [ɪnˈdelɪkɪt] ADJ (*tactless*) indelicato(-a), privo(-a) di tatto; (*not polite*) indelicato(-a)

in·dem·ni·fy [ɪnˈdemnɪˌfaɪ] VT (*compensate*): **to indemnify sb for sth** indennizzare qn per qc, risarcire qn di qc; **to indemnify sb against sth** (*safeguard*) assicurare qn contro qc

in·dem·nity [ɪnˈdemnɪtɪ] N (*see vb*) indennizzo, risarcimento; assicurazione *f*

in·dent [ɪnˈdent] VT (*Typ: text*) far rientrare dal margine ♦ VI (*Comm*): **to indent for sth** ordinare *or* commissionare qc

in·den·ta·tion [ˌɪndenˈteɪʃən] N (*dent, hollow mark*) tacca; (*in metal, car*) ammaccatura; (*Typ*) rientranza, rientro; (*notched edge*) dentellatura; (*in coastline*) frastagliatura

in·dent·ed [ɪnˈdentɪd] ADJ (*Typ*) rientrante; (*surface*) intaccato(-a), ammaccato(-a); (*coastline*) frastagliato(-a)

in·den·ture [ɪnˈdentʃəʳ] N contratto *m* formazione, *inv*

in·de·pend·ence [ˌɪndɪˈpendəns] N indipendenza; **the country gained independence in 1964** il paese ha conquistato l'indipendenza nel 1964

Independence Day N (*USA*) festa nazionale americana che si festeggia il 4 luglio

in·de·pend·ent [ˌɪndɪˈpendənt] ADJ indipendente, autonomo(-a); **of independent means** finanziariamente indipendente; **to ask for an independent opinion** chiedere un parere imparziale; **two independent studies have been carried out** sono stati condotti due studi indipendenti; **independent suspension** (*Aut*) sospensioni *fpl* indipendenti; **an independent school** una scuola privata

in·de·pend·ent·ly [ˌɪndɪˈpendəntlɪ] ADV (*move, decide*) indipendentemente, autonomamente; (*arrive*) separatamente; **independently of** indipendentemente da

in-depth [ˈɪnˌdepθ] ADJ (*investigation, study*) approfondito(-a)

in·de·scrib·able [ˌɪndɪsˈkraɪbəbl] ADJ indescrivibile

in·de·struct·ible [ˌɪndɪsˈtrʌktəbl] ADJ indistruttibile

in·de·ter·mi·nate [ˌɪndɪˈtɜːmɪnɪt] ADJ (*gen*) indeterminato(-a), indefinito(-a); (*plans, ideas*) indefinito(-a), vago(-a)

in·dex [ˈɪndeks] N **1** (*pl* **indexes**) (*in book*) indice *m*; (*in library*) catalogo; **look in the index** guarda nell'indice **2** (*pl* **indices**) (*pointer, sign*) indicazione *f*, indizio; (*Math*) indice *m*, esponente *m*; **standard index form** forma esponenziale

index card N scheda

index finger N (dito) indice *m*

index-linked [ˌɪndeksˈlɪŋkt], (*USA*) **in·dexed** [ˈɪndekst] ADJ indicizzato(-a)

In·dia [ˈɪndɪə] N India

In·dian [ˈɪndɪən] ADJ **1** (*from India*) indiano(-a) **2** (*American Indian*) indiano(-a) (d'America) ♦ N **1** (*from India*) indiano(-a) **2** (*American Indian*) indiano(-a) (d'America)

In·dia·na [ˌɪndɪˈænə] N L'Indiana

Indian ink N (inchiostro di) china

Indian Ocean N: **the Indian Ocean** l'Oceano Indiano

India paper N carta d'India, carta bibbia

India rubber N (*material*) caucciù *m*; (*eraser*) gomma da cancellare

in·di·cate [ˈɪndɪˌkeɪt] VT **1** (*point out: place*) indicare; (: *with finger*) additare; (*register: temperature, speed*) segnare, indicare **2** (*show: feelings*) denotare; (*suggest*) indicare, lasciar intendere; **this indicates a change in US policy** questo indica un cambiamento della politica statunitense ♦ VI (*Aut: Brit*) segnalare (il cambiamento di direzione), mettere la freccia; **to indicate left/right** mettere la freccia a sinistra/a destra

in·di·ca·tion [ˌɪndɪˈkeɪʃən] N indicazione *f*; **there is no indication that** non c'è niente che faccia pensare che; **this is some indication that** questo fa pensare *or* sembra indicare che; **he gave no indication he was unhappy** nulla faceva pensare che fosse infelice

in·dica·tive [ɪnˈdɪkətɪv] ADJ **1** **to be indicative of sth** essere indicativo(-a) *or* un indice di qc **2** (*Gram*) indicativo(-a) ♦ N (*Gram*) indicativo; **in the indicative** all'indicativo

in·di·ca·tor [ˈɪndɪˌkeɪtəʳ] N (*sign*) segno; (*fig*) indice *m*; (*in station, airport*) tabellone *m*; (*Brit: Aut*) indicatore *m* di direzione, freccia; (*Chem*) indicatore

in·di·ces [ˈɪndɪsiːz] NPL *of* **index 2**

in·dict [ɪnˈdaɪt] VT (*Law*): **to indict sb for** incriminare qn per

in·dict·able [ɪnˈdaɪtəbl] ADJ (*Law*): **indictable offence** reato perseguibile a norma di legge

in·dict·ment [ɪnˈdaɪtmənt] N (*Law*) atto d'accusa, imputazione *f*; **to bring an indictment against sb** formulare un'accusa *or* imputazione contro qn

in·dif·fer·ence [ɪnˈdɪfrəns] N (*see adj*) indifferenza; mediocrità

in·dif·fer·ent [ɪnˈdɪfrənt] ADJ **1** (*apathetic*): **indifferent (to)** indifferente (a); **he was indifferent to my feelings** era indifferente ai miei sentimenti **2** (*mediocre*) mediocre; **indifferent marks** voti mediocri

in·dig·enous [ɪnˈdɪdʒɪnəs] ADJ indigeno(-a)

in·di·gest·ible [ˌɪndɪˈdʒestəbl] ADJ (*food*) indigesto(-a), poco digeribile; (*fig: style*) indigesto(-a)

in·di·ges·tion [ˌɪndɪˈdʒestʃən] N cattiva digestione *f*; (*chronic*) dispepsia; **to have indigestion** non riuscire a digerire, avere qualcosa sullo stomaco

in·dig·nant [ɪnˈdɪɡnənt] ADJ indignato(-a); **to be indignant at or about sth/with sb** essere indignato(-a) per qc/contro qn; **to make sb indignant** far indignare qn

in·dig·na·tion [ˌɪndɪɡˈneɪʃən] N indignazione *f*

in·dig·nity [ɪnˈdɪɡnɪtɪ] N umiliazione *f*

in·di·go [ˈɪndɪɡəʊ] N indaco ♦ ADJ (*color*) indaco *inv*

in·di·rect [ˌɪndɪˈrekt] ADJ (*gen, also Gram*) indiretto(-a); (*road, route, answer*) non diretto(-a)

in·di·rect·ly [ˌɪndɪˈrektlɪ] ADV indirettamente

in·dis·creet [ˌɪndɪsˈkriːt] ADJ (*tactless*) indiscreto(-a); (*incautious*) imprudente

in·dis·cre·tion [ˌɪndɪsˈkreʃən] N **1** (*see adj*) indiscrezione *f*; imprudenza **2** (*action, remark*) indiscrezione

in·dis·crimi·nate [ˌɪndɪsˈkrɪmɪnɪt] ADJ (*killings*) indiscriminato(-a); (*person*) che non fa distinzioni; (*admiration*) cieco(-a)

in·dis·pen·sable [ˌɪndɪsˈpensəbl] ADJ indispensabile; **no-one is indispensable** nessuno è indispensabile

in·dis·posed [ˌɪndɪsˈpəʊzd] ADJ (*frm*) **1** (*unwell*) indisposto(-a) **2** (*unwilling*) poco incline

in·dis·po·si·tion [ˌɪndɪspəˈzɪʃən] N (*frm*) **1** (*illness*) indisposizione *f* **2** (*unwillingness*) poca inclinazione *f*

in·dis·put·able [ˌɪndɪsˈpjuːtəbl] ADJ (*evidence*) inconfutabile, incontestabile; (*fact*) indiscutibile, incontestabile; (*winner*) incontestabile

in·dis·tinct [ˌɪndɪsˈtɪŋkt] ADJ (*voice, words*) indistinto(-a); (*memory, noise*) vago(-a)

in·dis·tin·guish·able [ˌɪndɪsˈtɪŋɡwɪʃəbl] ADJ indistinguibile

in·di·vid·ual [ˌɪndɪˈvɪdjʊəl] ADJ **1** (*separate: member, case*) (ogni) singolo(-a) **2** (*own, personal: taste, style*) personale, individuale; (*for one person: portion*) individuale ♦ N individuo

in·di·vidu·al·ist [ˌɪndɪˈvɪdjʊəlɪst] N individualista *m/f*

in·di·vidu·al·ity [ˌɪndɪˌvɪdjʊˈælɪtɪ] N individualità *f inv*

in·di·vid·ual·ly [ˌɪndɪˈvɪdjʊəlɪ] ADV singolarmente, uno(-a) per uno(-a)

in·di·vis·ible [ˌɪndɪˈvɪzəbl] ADJ indivisibile
Indo·china [ˌɪndəʊˈtʃaɪnə] N l'Indocina
in·doc·tri·nate [ɪnˈdɒktrɪˌneɪt] VT indottrinare
in·doc·tri·na·tion [ɪnˌdɒktrɪˈneɪʃən] N indottrinamento
in·do·lent [ˈɪndələnt] ADJ indolente
In·do·nesia [ˌɪndəʊˈniːzɪə] N l'Indonesia
In·do·nesian [ˌɪndəʊˈniːzɪən] indonesiano(-a) ♦ N (person) indonesiano(-a); (language) indonesiano
in·door [ˈɪnˌdɔːʳ] ADJ (shoes) da casa; (plant) da appartamento; (sport: table tennis, squash) praticato(-a) al coperto; (: athletics) indoor inv; (: tennis court) al coperto; (: swimming pool) coperto(-a); (photography) di interni; (hobby) da praticare a casa; **indoor aerial** antenna interna; **indoor sports stadium** palasport m inv
in·doors [ˌɪnˈdɔːz] ADV (in building) all'interno; (at home) in casa; (under cover) al coperto; **to go indoors** rientrare, andar dentro; **they're indoors** sono dentro
in·du·bi·table [ɪnˈdjuːbɪtəbl] ADJ indubitabile
in·duce [ɪnˈdjuːs] VT (persuade) persuadere, convincere; (bring about: sleep) provocare; (: birth) indurre; **to induce sb to do sth** persuadere or convincere qn a fare qc
in·duce·ment [ɪnˈdjuːsmənt] N (incentive) incentivo
in·duct [ɪnˈdʌkt] VT (frm: install) insediare; (USA Mil) reclutare
in·duc·tion [ɪnˈdʌkʃən] N (Elec, Philosophy) induzione f; (Med: of birth) parto indotto
induction course N (Brit) corso introduttivo
in·dulge [ɪnˈdʌldʒ] VT (give into: desire, appetite) soddisfare, appagare; (: person) assecondare (i desideri di), accontentare; (spoil: child) viziare; **why not indulge yourself and have an ice-cream?** dai, concediti un gelato
  ► **indulge in** VI + PREP (activity) darsi a; (emotion) lasciarsi andare a; (chocolate, sweets) concedersi
in·dul·gence [ɪnˈdʌldʒəns] N (extravagance) piccolo lusso (che ci si concede); (habit) vizio; (leniency: Rel) indulgenza
in·dul·gent [ɪnˈdʌldʒənt] ADJ: **indulgent (to or towards sb)** indulgente (con or verso qn)
in·dus·trial [ɪnˈdʌstrɪəl] ADJ (area, town, processes) industriale; (worker) dell'industria; (accident, injury) sul lavoro; (disease) del lavoro; **industrial machinery** macchinari mpl industriali
industrial action N (strikes, working to rule) agitazione f sindacale
industrial estate, (USA) **industrial park** N zona industriale
in·dus·tri·al·ist [ɪnˈdʌstrɪəlɪst] N industriale m/f
in·dus·tri·al·ize [ɪnˈdʌstrɪəˌlaɪz] VT industrializzare
industrial park (USA) N = **industrial estate**
industrial relations NPL relazioni fpl sindacali ♦ N (field of study) relazioni fpl industriali
industrial tribunal N (Brit) organo competente a decidere le controversie di lavoro
industrial unrest N (Brit) agitazione f sindacale
in·dus·tri·ous [ɪnˈdʌstrɪəs] ADJ diligente
in·dus·try [ˈɪndəstrɪ] N **1** l'industria; **light/heavy industry** industria leggera/pesante; **the tourist industry** il turismo; **the oil industry** l'industria petrolifera **2** (frm: industriousness) operosità
in·ebri·at·ed [ɪˈniːbrɪˌeɪtɪd] ADJ (frm) ubriaco(-a)
in·ed·ible [ɪnˈedɪbl] ADJ (not to be eaten) non commestibile; (not fit to be eaten) immangiabile
in·ef·fec·tive [ˌɪnɪˈfektɪv] ADJ (remedy) inefficace; (minister, leader) poco capace
in·ef·fec·tual [ˌɪnɪˈfektʊəl] ADJ (policy) inefficace; (person) inetto(-a); **to be ineffectual** essere un(-a) incapace
in·ef·fi·cien·cy [ˌɪnɪˈfɪʃənsɪ] N inefficienza
in·ef·fi·cient [ˌɪnɪˈfɪʃənt] ADJ inefficiente
in·el·egant [ɪnˈelɪgənt] ADJ poco elegante
in·eli·gible [ɪnˈelɪdʒəbl] ADJ: **to be ineligible for sth/to do sth** non avere diritto a qc/a fare qc; **they are ineligible for unemployment benefit** non hanno diritto all'indennità di disoccupazione
in·ept [ɪˈnept] ADJ (person) inetto(-a); (remark, behaviour) inopportuno(-a); (management, handling) poco abile

in·epti·tude [ɪˈneptɪtjuːd] N (see adj) inettitudine f; inopportunità; scarsa abilità
in·equal·ity [ˌɪnɪˈkwɒlɪtɪ] N (gen) ineguaglianza, disuguaglianza; (Math) disuguaglianza
in·equi·table [ɪnˈekwɪtəbl] ADJ iniquo(-a)
in·eradi·cable [ˌɪnɪˈrædɪkəbl] ADJ (frm: feeling) tenace; (: sign, memory) incancellabile
in·ert [ɪˈnɜːt] ADJ inerte
in·er·tia [ɪˈnɜːʃə] N inerzia
inertia-reel seat belt [ɪˌnɜːʃəˌriːlˈsiːtˌbelt] N cintura di sicurezza con pretensionatore
in·es·cap·able [ˌɪnɪsˈkeɪpəbl] ADJ ineluttabile, inevitabile
in·es·sen·tial [ˌɪnɪˈsenʃl] ADJ superfluo(-a)
in·es·ti·mable [ɪnˈestɪməbl] ADJ inestimabile, incalcolabile
in·evi·table [ɪnˈevɪtəbl] ADJ inevitabile
in·evi·tably [ɪnˈevɪtəblɪ] ADV inevitabilmente
in·ex·act [ˌɪnɪɡˈzækt] ADJ inesatto(-a), impreciso(-a)
in·ex·cus·able [ˌɪnɪksˈkjuːzəbl] ADJ imperdonabile
in·ex·haust·ible [ˌɪnɪɡˈzɔːstəbl] ADJ (patience, supply) inesauribile; (person) instancabile, infaticabile
in·exo·rable [ɪnˈeksərəbl] ADJ inesorabile
in·ex·pen·sive [ˌɪnɪksˈpensɪv] ADJ a buon mercato, poco costoso(-a)
in·ex·pe·ri·ence [ˌɪnɪksˈpɪərɪəns] N inesperienza
in·ex·pe·ri·enced [ˌɪnɪksˈpɪərɪənst] ADJ inesperto(-a); **to be inexperienced in sth** essere poco pratico(-a) di qc
in·ex·pli·cable [ˌɪnɪksˈplɪkəbl] ADJ inesplicabile
in·ex·press·ible [ˌɪnɪksˈpresəbl] ADJ inesprimibile
in·ex·tri·cable [ˌɪnɪksˈtrɪkəbl] ADJ inestricabile
in·fal·libil·ity [ɪnˌfælɪˈbɪlɪtɪ] N infallibilità
in·fal·lible [ɪnˈfæləbl] ADJ infallibile
in·fa·mous [ˈɪnfəməs] ADJ (person) famigerato(-a); (crime) infame
in·fa·my [ˈɪnfəmɪ] N infamia
in·fan·cy [ˈɪnfənsɪ] N (childhood) infanzia; (Law) minore età f inv; **in its infancy** (fig: early stage) ai primi passi
in·fant [ˈɪnfənt] N bambino(-a); (Law) minorenne m/f, minore m/f
in·fan·tile [ˈɪnfənˌtaɪl] ADJ infantile
infant mortality N mortalità infantile
in·fan·try [ˈɪnfəntrɪ] N fanteria
in·fantry·man [ˈɪnfəntrɪmən] N (pl -men) fante m
infant school N (Brit) scuola elementare (per bambini dai 5 ai 7 anni)
in·fatu·at·ed [ɪnˈfætjʊˌeɪtɪd] ADJ: **infatuated (with sb)** infatuato(-a) (di qn); **to become infatuated (with sb)** infatuarsi (di qn)
in·fatu·a·tion [ɪnˌfætjʊˈeɪʃən] N infatuazione f
in·fect [ɪnˈfekt] VT (wound) infettare; (person) contagiare; (food, air) contaminare; (fig: poison) corrompere; (: influence) influenzare; **to infect sb with a disease** trasmettere una malattia a qn; **he's infected everybody with his enthusiasm** ha contagiato tutti con il suo entusiasmo
in·fec·tion [ɪnˈfekʃən] N infezione f; **an ear infection** un'infezione all'orecchio; **a throat infection** un'angina
in·fec·tious [ɪnˈfekʃəs] ADJ (disease) infettivo(-a), contagioso(-a); (person, laughter) contagioso(-a)
in·fer [ɪnˈfɜːʳ] VT: **to infer (from)** dedurre (da)
in·fer·ence [ˈɪnfərəns] N deduzione f, illazione f
in·fe·ri·or [ɪnˈfɪərɪəʳ] ADJ (in quality, rank): **inferior (to)** inferiore (a); (work, goods) scadente; **of inferior quality** di qualità inferiore; **to feel inferior** sentirsi inferiore; **their status is inferior to that of men** si trovano in una condizione di inferiorità rispetto agli uomini ♦ N inferiore m/f; (in rank) subalterno(-a)
in·fe·ri·or·ity [ɪnˌfɪərɪˈɒrɪtɪ] N inferiorità
inferiority complex N complesso di inferiorità
in·fer·nal [ɪnˈfɜːnl] ADJ (fires) dell'inferno; (spirit, powers) infernale; (fig: cruelty) diabolico(-a); (fam: noise) infernale, terribile
in·fer·no [ɪnˈfɜːnəʊ] N inferno
in·fer·tile [ɪnˈfɜːtaɪl] ADJ sterile
in·fer·til·ity [ɪnfɜːˈtɪlɪtɪ] N sterilità
in·fest·ed [ɪnˈfestɪd] ADJ: **infested (with)** infestato(-a) (di or da)

in·fi·del·ity [ˌɪnfɪˈdelɪti] N infedeltà f inv

in-fighting [ˈɪnfaɪtɪŋ] N lotte fpl interne or intestine

in·fil·trate [ˈɪnfɪlˌtreɪt] VT (troops) far penetrare; (enemy line, political organization) infiltrarsi in; **a detective infiltrated the group** un investigatore si infiltrò nel gruppo ♦ VI: **to infiltrate (into)** infiltrarsi (in)

in·fi·nite [ˈɪnfɪnɪt] ADJ infinito(-a); **we haven't got an infinite amount of time/money** non abbiamo un'illimitata quantità di tempo/denaro

in·fi·nite·ly [ˈɪnfɪnɪtli] ADV infinitamente

in·fini·tesi·mal [ˌɪnfɪnɪˈtesɪməl] ADJ infinitesimale

in·fini·tive [ɪnˈfɪnɪtɪv] ADJ (Gram) infinito(-a) ♦ N infinito; **in the infinitive** all'infinito

in·fin·ity [ɪnˈfɪnɪti] N (infiniteness) infinità; (in time, space: Math) infinito

in·firm [ɪnˈfɜːm] ADJ infermo(-a)

in·fir·ma·ry [ɪnˈfɜːmərɪ] N (hospital) ospedale m; (in school, prison, barracks) infermeria

in·fir·mity [ɪnˈfɜːmɪti] N infermità f inv

in·flamed [ɪnˈfleɪmd] ADJ (Med) infiammato(-a)

in·flam·mable [ɪnˈflæməbl] ADJ (substance, fabric) infiammabile; (fig: situation) esplosivo(-a)

in·flam·ma·tion [ˌɪnfləˈmeɪʃən] N infiammazione f

in·flam·ma·tory [ɪnˈflæmətərɪ] ADJ (speech) incendiario(-a)

in·flat·able [ɪnˈfleɪtəbl] ADJ gonfiabile

in·flate [ɪnˈfleɪt] VT (tyre or tire, balloon) gonfiare; (fig: prices, profits) gonfiare, far salire; (: idea, opinion) esagerare, gonfiare ♦ VI (tyre or tire, balloon) gonfiarsi; (fig: prices, profits) salire

in·flat·ed [ɪnˈfleɪtɪd] ADJ (price, fee) gonfiato(-a); (idea, opinion, value) esagerato(-a), gonfiato(-a); (style, language) ampolloso(-a); (tyre or tire) gonfio(-a)

in·fla·tion [ɪnˈfleɪʃən] N (Econ) inflazione f

in·fla·tion·ary [ɪnˈfleɪʃnərɪ] ADJ inflazionistico(-a)

in·flex·ible [ɪnˈfleksəbl] ADJ (object) rigido(-a); (fig: person, ideas) inflessibile, rigido(-a)

in·flict [ɪnˈflɪkt] VT: **to inflict (on)** (penalty) infliggere (a); (tax) imporre (a); (suffering, damage) procurare (a); **to inflict a blow/wound on sb** assestare un colpo a/ferire qn; **to inflict o.s. on sb** imporre la propria presenza a qn

in·flic·tion [ɪnˈflɪkʃən] N l'infliggere m

in·flight [ˈɪnˌflaɪt] ADJ a bordo; **in-flight service** servizio a bordo

in·flow [ˈɪnˌfləʊ] N afflusso

in·flu·ence [ˈɪnfluəns] N influenza; **to have an influence on sb/sth** (subj: person) avere un'influenza su qn/qc; (: event) influenzare qn/qc; (: weather) influire su qn/qc; **to have influence with sb** avere un ascendente su qn; **to be a good/bad influence on sb** avere or esercitare una buona/cattiva influenza su qn; **under the influence of drugs** sotto l'effetto della droga; **under the influence of drink** sotto l'effetto dell'alcol; (Law) in stato di ebbrezza; **he was under the influence** (fam) aveva alzato il gomito ♦ VT (person) influenzare; (action, decision) influire su, influenzare; **to be easily influenced** essere facilmente influenzabile

in·flu·en·tial [ˌɪnfluˈenʃəl] ADJ influente

in·flu·en·za [ˌɪnfluˈenzə] N (Med) influenza

in·flux [ˈɪnflʌks] N (of people, objects) afflusso; (of ideas) flusso
❑ **influx** is not translated by the Italian word *influsso*

in·fo [ˈɪnfəʊ] N (fam) informazione f

in·form [ɪnˈfɔːm] VT informare, avvertire; **to inform sb about/of sth** informare or avvertire qn di qc; **nobody informed me of the change of plan** nessuno mi ha informato del cambiamento di programma; **I am happy to inform you that** sono lieto di comunicarle che; **keep me informed** tienimi informato; **a well-informed person** una persona di cultura ♦ VI: **to inform on sb** denunciare qn

in·for·mal [ɪnˈfɔːməl] ADJ (person, manner) semplice, alla mano; (tone: of letter) non formale; (language, style) colloquiale; (dinner, party) fra amici; (visit, announcement, invitation) non ufficiale; (meeting, arrangement, discussion) informale; **"dress informal"** "non è richiesto l'abito da sera"

in·for·mal·ity [ˌɪnfɔːˈmælɪti] N (of person, manner) semplicità; (of tone) mancanza di formalità; (of language, style) tono

colloquiale; (of occasion) tono familiare; (of meeting, negotiations, announcement) carattere m non ufficiale

in·for·mal·ly [ɪnˈfɔːməli] ADV (discuss, chat) alla buona; (invite, meet) in modo non ufficiale; **the Queen visited the hospital informally** la regina ha visitato l'ospedale in forma privata; **I have been informally told that ...** mi è stato comunicato ufficiosamente che...

in·form·ant [ɪnˈfɔːmənt] N informatore(-trice)

in·for·mat·ics [ˌɪnfəˈmætɪks] NSG informatica

in·for·ma·tion [ˌɪnfəˈmeɪʃən] N: **information (about or on)** informazioni fpl (riguardo a or su); **a piece of information** un'informazione; **to give sb information about or on sb/sth** dare a qn informazioni su qn/qc; **to get information on** informarsi su; **where did you get this information?** dove hai avuto questa informazione?; **could you give me some information about ...** potrebbe darmi qualche informazione su...; **for further information contact the number below** per ulteriori informazioni contattare il numero sottostante; **for your information** (on document) a titolo d'informazione; (fam, iro) per tua norma e regola

information bureau N ufficio m informazioni, inv

information processing N (Comput) elaborazione f delle informazioni

information retrieval N (Comput) ricupero delle informazioni

information superhighway N: **the information superhighway** (Comput) l'autostrada informatica

information technology N informatica

in·forma·tive [ɪnˈfɔːmətɪv] ADJ (speech, book) istruttivo(-a)

in·formed [ɪnˈfɔːmd] ADJ (observer) (ben) informato(-a); **an informed guess** un'ipotesi f fondata

in·form·er [ɪnˈfɔːmə'] N informatore(-trice); **to turn informer** (Police) diventare un informatore(-trice)

in·fra dig [ˈɪnfrəˈdɪg] ADJ poco dignitoso(-a)

infra·red [ˌɪnfrəˈred] ADJ infrarosso(-a) ♦ N (beam) infrarosso

infra·struc·ture [ˈɪnfrəˌstrʌktʃə'] N infrastruttura

in·fre·quent [ɪnˈfriːkwənt] ADJ poco frequente, raro(-a)

in·fringe [ɪnˈfrɪndʒ] VT (law) infrangere, violare; (rights, copyright) violare; **they infringed the copyright** hanno violato il copyright ♦ VI (encroach): **to infringe on or upon** (rights) violare; (privacy) invadere

in·fringe·ment [ɪnˈfrɪndʒmənt] N (of law, rule) infrazione f, violazione f; (of rights, copyright) violazione f

in·furi·ate [ɪnˈfjʊərɪˌeɪt] VT far infuriare, rendere furioso(-a); **to become infuriated** infuriarsi, andare in bestia

in·furi·at·ing [ɪnˈfjʊərɪˌeɪtɪŋ] ADJ esasperante, estremamente irritante

in·fuse [ɪnˈfjuːz] VT 1 (with courage, enthusiasm): **to infuse sb with sth** infondere qc a qn; **to infuse courage into sb** infondere coraggio a qn 2 (Culin: herbs, tea) lasciare in infusione

in·fu·sion [ɪnˈfjuːʒən] N (tea) infuso

in·gen·ious [ɪnˈdʒiːnɪəs] ADJ ingegnoso(-a)

in·genu·ity [ˌɪndʒɪˈnjuːɪti] N ingegnosità

in·genu·ous [ɪnˈdʒenjʊəs] ADJ ingenuo(-a)

in·got [ˈɪŋgət] N lingotto

in·grained [ˈɪnˈgreɪnd] ADJ (dirt) incrostato(-a); (fig: ideas, tradition) radicato(-a); (habit, prejudice) inveterato(-a)

in·gra·ti·ate [ɪnˈgreɪʃɪˌeɪt] VT: **to ingratiate o.s. with sb** ingraziarsi qn

in·gra·ti·at·ing [ɪnˈgreɪʃɪˌeɪtɪŋ] ADJ (smile, speech) suadente, accattivante; (person) compiacente

in·grati·tude [ɪnˈgrætɪtjuːd] N ingratitudine f

in·gre·di·ent [ɪnˈgriːdɪənt] N (Culin) ingrediente m; (fig) fattore m, elemento

in·grow·ing [ˈɪnˌɡrəʊɪŋ], **in·grown** [ˈɪnˌɡrəʊn] ADJ: **ingrowing (toe)nail** unghia incarnita

in·hab·it [ɪnˈhæbɪt] VT (house) abitare (in); (town, country) vivere in

in·hab·it·able [ɪnˈhæbɪtəbl] ADJ abitabile

in·hab·it·ant [ɪnˈhæbɪtənt] N abitante m/f

in·hale [ɪnˈheɪl] VT (gas, smoke, air) respirare; (Med) inalare ♦ VI (smoker) aspirare; (Med) inspirare

in·hal·er [ɪnˈheɪlə'], **in·ha·la·tor** [ˈɪnhəˌleɪtə'] N inalatore m

in·her·ent [ɪnˈhɪərənt] ADJ: **inherent (in)** intrinseco(-a) (a); (*kindness, cruelty*) innato(-a) (a)

in·her·ent·ly [ɪnˈhɪərəntlɪ] ADV (*easy, difficult*) di per se stesso(-a), di per sé; **inherently inefficient** sostanzialmente inefficiente

in·her·it [ɪnˈhɛrɪt] VT ereditare

in·her·it·ance [ɪnˈhɛrɪtəns] N eredità *f inv*; (*fig*) retaggio

in·hib·it [ɪnˈhɪbɪt] VT inibire; **to inhibit sb from doing sth** impedire a qn di fare qc

in·hib·it·ed [ɪnˈhɪbɪtɪd] ADJ (*person*) inibito(-a)

in·hi·bi·ting [ɪnˈhɪbɪtɪŋ] ADJ inibitorio(-a)

in·hi·bi·tion [ˌɪnhɪˈbɪʃən] N inibizione *f*

in·hos·pi·table [ˌɪnhɒsˈpɪtəbl] ADJ inospitale

in-house [ˈɪnhaʊs] ADJ (*magazine, video*) per il personale, aziendale; (*training*) all'interno dell'azienda ♦ ADV (*train, produce*) all'interno dell'azienda

in·hu·man [ɪnˈhjuːmən] ADJ (*cruelty, conditions, treatment*) disumano(-a); (*appearance*) non umano(-a)

in·hu·mane [ˌɪnhjuːˈmeɪn] ADJ inumano(-a)

in·imi·table [ɪˈnɪmɪtəbl] ADJ inimitabile

in·iquity [ɪˈnɪkwɪtɪ] N iniquità *f inv*

ini·tial [ɪˈnɪʃəl] ADJ iniziale; **in the initial stages** nella fase iniziale; **in the initial stages of their relationship** agli inizi della loro storia ♦ N iniziale *f*; **to sign sth with one's initials** siglare qc con le proprie iniziali ♦ VT siglare

ini·tial·ize [ɪˈnɪʃəˌlaɪz] VT (*Comput*) inizializzare

ini·tial·ly [ɪˈnɪʃəlɪ] ADV all'inizio, inizialmente

ini·ti·ate [ɪˈnɪʃɪˌeɪt] VT **1** (*begin*) iniziare; (*talks*) iniziare, avviare; (*reform*) promuovere; **to initiate proceedings against sb** (*Law*) intentare causa a *or* contro qn **2** (*admit*): **to initiate sb (into sth)** iniziare qn (a qc)

ini·tia·tion [ɪˌnɪʃɪˈeɪʃən] N iniziazione *f*

ini·tia·tive [ɪˈnɪʃətɪv] N iniziativa; **on one's own initiative** di propria iniziativa, da sé; **to take the initiative** prendere l'iniziativa; **she's got initiative** è una che ha spirito d'iniziativa; **an important initiative** un'importante iniziativa

in·ject [ɪnˈdʒɛkt] VT (*drug*) iniettare; (*person*) fare un'iniezione a; (*fig: money*): **to inject into** immettere in; **to inject with** fare un'iniezione di; **they injected me with antibiotics** mi hanno fatto un'iniezione di antibiotici; **to inject o.s.** farsi un'iniezione; **he needs to inject himself twice a day** deve farsi un'iniezione due volte al giorno; **to inject enthusiasm into sb** dare una carica di entusiasmo a qn

in·jec·tion [ɪnˈdʒɛkʃən] N (*Med*) iniezione *f*, puntura; (*Tech, fig*) iniezione; **to give sb an injection** fare un'iniezione *or* una puntura a qn; **the doctor gave me an injection** il dottore mi ha fatto un'iniezione; **to have an injection** farsi fare un'iniezione *or* una puntura

in·ju·di·cious [ˌɪndʒuːˈdɪʃəs] ADJ (*frm*) poco saggio(-a)

in·junc·tion [ɪnˈdʒʌŋkʃən] N (*Law*) ingiunzione *f*, intimazione *f*, ordinanza

in·jure [ˈɪndʒə'] VT **1** (*physically*) ferire; **he injured his arm** si è fatto male a *or* si è ferito a un braccio; **to injure o.s.** farsi male, ferirsi **2** (*fig: reputation, trade etc*) nuocere a; (*: feelings*) offendere; (*wrong: person*) fare (un) torto a

❑ **injure** is not translated by the Italian word *ingiuriare*

in·jured [ˈɪndʒəd] ADJ (*person, leg*) ferito(-a); (*tone, feelings*) offeso(-a) ♦ NPL: **the injured** i feriti

in·ju·ri·ous [ɪnˈdʒʊərɪəs] ADJ: **injurious (to)** nocivo(-a) (a), pregiudizievole (per)

in·ju·ry [ˈɪndʒərɪ] N (*physical*) ferita, lesione *f*; (*fig: to reputation*) danno; (*: to feelings*) offesa; (*: wrong*) torto; **a serious injury** una ferita grave; **to escape without injury** rimanere illeso(-a)

❑ **injury** is not translated by the Italian word *ingiuria*

injury time N (*Sport*) (minuti *mpl* di) recupero

in·jus·tice [ɪnˈdʒʌstɪs] N ingiustizia; **you do me an injustice** sei ingiusto verso di me

ink [ɪŋk] N inchiostro; **in ink** a penna

ink-jet printer [ˈɪŋkdʒɛtˈprɪntə'] N stampante *f* a getto d'inchiostro

ink·ling [ˈɪŋklɪŋ] N (*hint*) indizio; (*suspicion, vague idea*) mezza

idea; **to give sb an inkling that** lasciar capire *or* intuire a qn che; **I had no inkling that** non avevo la minima idea che

ink pad N tampone *m or* cuscinetto per timbri

inky [ˈɪŋkɪ] ADJ (*comp* **-ier**, *superl* **-iest**) macchiato(-a) *or* sporco(-a) d'inchiostro; (*fig: darkness*) nero(-a) come l'inchiostro

in·laid [ˈɪnleɪd] ADJ (*table, box*): **inlaid (with)** intarsiato(-a) (di)

in·land [ˈɪnlænd] ADJ (*town*) dell'interno; (*mail*) nazionale, interno(-a); (*sea, waterway*) interno(-a); **inland areas** zone interne ♦ ADV (*location*) nell'entroterra; (*travel*) verso l'interno

in-laws [ˈɪnlɔːz] (*fam*) NPL (*parents-in-law*) suoceri *mpl*; (*other family members*) famiglia del marito (*or* della moglie)

in·let [ˈɪnlɛt] N **1** (*Geog*) insenatura, baia; (*of sea*) braccio di mare **2** (*Tech*) apertura di ammissione

inlet pipe N (*Tech*) tubo d'immissione

in·mate [ˈɪnmeɪt] N (*of prison*) detenuto(-a), carcerato(-a); (*of asylum*) internato(-a); (*of hospital*) ricoverato(-a)

in·most [ˈɪnməʊst] ADJ più profondo(-a), più intimo(-a); **one's inmost being** il proprio intimo; **in one's inmost heart** nel profondo del proprio cuore, nel proprio intimo

inn [ɪn] N locanda

in·nards [ˈɪnədz] NPL (*fam*) budella *fpl*

in·nate [ɪˈneɪt] ADJ innato(-a)

in·ner [ˈɪnə'] ADJ (*place*) interno(-a), interiore; (*thoughts, emotions*) intimo(-a), profondo(-a); **an inner office** un ufficio interno

inner city N centro di una zona urbana (*in degrado socio-economico*)

inner·most [ˈɪnəməʊst] ADJ = **inmost**

inner tube N camera d'aria

in·ning [ˈɪnɪŋ] N (*Baseball*) inning *m inv*

in·nings [ˈɪnɪŋz] NSG (*in cricket*) turno di battuta

in·no·cence [ˈɪnəsns] N innocenza

in·no·cent [ˈɪnəsnt] ADJ innocente; **to put on an innocent air** fare l'innocente *or* l'ingenuo(-a)

in·nocu·ous [ɪˈnɒkjʊəs] ADJ innocuo(-a)

in·no·va·tion [ˌɪnəʊˈveɪʃən] N innovazione *f*

in·no·va·tive [ˈɪnəʊˌveɪtɪv] ADJ innovativo(-a)

in·nu·en·do [ˌɪnjʊˈɛndəʊ] N (*insinuation*) insinuazione *f*; (*sexual*) allusione *f*

in·nu·mer·able [ɪˈnjuːmərəbl] ADJ innumerevole

in·ocu·late [ɪˈnɒkjʊˌleɪt] VT: **to inoculate sb with sth** inoculare qn con qc; **to inoculate sb against sth** vaccinare qn contro qc

in·ocu·la·tion [ɪˌnɒkjʊˈleɪʃən] N inoculazione *f*

in·of·fen·sive [ˌɪnəˈfɛnsɪv] ADJ inoffensivo(-a), innocuo(-a)

in·op·por·tune [ɪnˈɒpətjuːn] ADJ inopportuno(-a)

in·or·di·nate [ɪˈnɔːdɪnɪt] ADJ esagerato(-a)

in·or·di·nate·ly [ɪˈnɔːdɪmɪtlɪ] ADV: **an inordinately large sum of money** una cifra esorbitante *or* astronomica; **an inordinately large amount of food** una quantità esagerata di cibo; **an inordinately long time** un'infinità di tempo

in·or·gan·ic [ˌɪnɔːˈɡænɪk] ADJ inorganico(-a)

in·pa·tient [ˈɪnˌpeɪʃənt] N degente *m/f*, ricoverato(-a)

in·put [ˈɪnpʊt] N **1** (*outlay: of funds, labour, energy*) impiego; (*contribution: of ideas, work*) contributo; **thank you for your input** grazie per il tuo contributo; **they need more input and advice** hanno bisogno di ulteriori informazioni e consigli **2** (*Comput*) dati *mpl*, input *m inv* **3** (*Elec*) alimentazione *f*; (*in amplifiers*) ingresso ♦ VT (*Comput*) introdurre

in·quest [ˈɪnkwɛst] N (*Law*) inchiesta giudiziaria

in·quire [ɪnˈkwaɪə'] VT: **to inquire when/where/whether** domandare quando/dove/se; **to inquire sth of sb** domandare qc a qn; **"is something wrong?" he inquired** "c'è qualcosa che non va?", domandò ♦ VI: **to inquire (about sth)** informarsi (di *or* su qc), chiedere informazioni (su qc)

 ▸ **inquire after** VI + PREP (*person*) chiedere di; (*sb's health*) informarsi di

 ▸ **inquire into** VI + PREP indagare su, svolgere delle indagini su

in·quir·ing [ɪnˈkwaɪərɪŋ] ADJ (*mind*) pieno(-a) di curiosità; (*look*) interrogativo(-a), indagatore(-trice)

in·quiry [ɪnˈkwaɪərɪ] N **1** (*question*) domanda, richiesta di informazioni; "**Inquiries**" (*on sign*) "Informazioni"; **on inquiry he found that ...** essendosi informato scoprì che...; **to make inquiries (about sth)** chiedere informazioni (su qc), informarsi (di *or* su qc) **2** (*Admin, Law*) inchiesta; **committee of inquiry** commissione *f* d'inchiesta; **to hold an inquiry into sth** svolgere un'inchiesta su qc; **the police are making inquiries** la polizia sta indagando, la polizia sta svolgendo delle indagini; **there will be an inquiry into the accident** ci sarà un'inchiesta sull'incidente

inquiry desk N (*Brit*) (banco delle) informazioni *fpl*

inquiry office N (*Brit*) ufficio *m* informazioni, *inv*

in·qui·si·tion [ˌɪnkwɪˈzɪʃən] N inquisizione *f*

in·quisi·tive [ɪnˈkwɪzɪtɪv] ADJ (troppo) curioso(-a)

in·roads [ˈɪnˌrəʊdz] NPL: **to make inroads into** (*savings, supplies*) intaccare (seriamente)

ins ABBR **= inches**

in·sane [ɪnˈseɪn] ADJ (*person*) pazzo(-a), matto(-a); (*Med*) malato(-a) di mente; (*act*) folle, demenziale; **to drive sb insane** (*fig*) far impazzire *or* far diventar matto(-a) qn ♦ NPL: **the insane** i malati di mente; **an asylum for the insane** un manicomio

in·sani·tary [ɪnˈsænɪtərɪ] ADJ malsano(-a), antigienico(-a)

in·san·ity [ɪnˈsænɪtɪ] N (*Med*) infermità mentale; (*gen*) pazzia, follia

in·sa·tiable [ɪnˈseɪʃəbl] ADJ insaziabile

in·scribe [ɪnˈskraɪb] VT **1** (*engrave*) incidere; (*write*) scrivere **2** (*dedicate: book*) scrivere una dedica su; **to inscribe sth to sb** dedicare qc a qn

in·scrip·tion [ɪnˈskrɪpʃən] N (*on stone*) iscrizione *f*; (*in book*) dedica

in·scru·table [ɪnˈskruːtəbl] ADJ (*person*) imperscrutabile; (*face, eyes, gaze*) impenetrabile

in·sect [ˈɪnsekt] N insetto

insect bite N puntura *or* morsicatura di insetto

in·sec·ti·cide [ɪnˈsektɪsaɪd] N insetticida *m*

insect repellent N insettifugo

in·secure [ˌɪnsɪˈkjʊəʳ] ADJ (*structure, lock, door*) malsicuro(-a); (*Psych: person*) insicuro(-a)

in·secu·rity [ˌɪnsɪˈkjʊərɪtɪ] N (*of person*) insicurezza; (*of lock, employment, finances*) scarsa sicurezza

in·sen·sible [ɪnˈsensəbl] ADJ **1** (*unconscious*) privo(-a) di sensi *or* di conoscenza **2** (*unaware*): **insensible of** ignaro(-a) di
❏ **insensible** is not translated by the Italian word *insensibile*

in·sen·si·tive [ɪnˈsensɪtɪv] ADJ (*person*): **insensitive (to)** insensibile (a); (*action, behaviour*) privo(-a) di sensibilità

in·sen·si·tiv·ity [ɪnˌsensɪˈtɪvɪtɪ] N mancanza di sensibilità

in·sep·a·rable [ɪnˈsepərəbl] ADJ inseparabile

in·sert [*n* ˈɪnsɜːt, *vb* ɪnˈsɜːt] N inserto ♦ VT inserire; (*needle*) introdurre

in·ser·tion [ɪnˈsɜːʃən] N inserimento

in·service [ˌɪnˈsɜːvɪs] ADJ: **in-service training** corso di aggiornamento

in·shore [ˈɪnˈʃɔːʳ] ADV (*fish*) sotto costa; (*sail*) verso riva; (*blow*) dal mare ♦ ADJ (*fishing*) costiero(-a); (*wind*) dal mare

in·side [ˈɪnˈsaɪd] N **1** interno, parte *f* interiore (*of road: Brit*) sinistra; (: *USA: in Europe etc*) destra; **to overtake on the inside** (*Brit*) sorpassare a sinistra; (*USA: Europe etc*) sorpassare a destra; **to know sth from the inside** conoscere qc per esperienza diretta **2 inside out** alla rovescia; **he put his sweater on inside out** si è messo il maglione alla rovescia; **to turn sth inside out** rivoltare qc; **to know sth inside out** conoscere qc a fondo; (*place*) conoscere qc come le proprie tasche **3** (*fam: stomach*): **insides** NPL budella *fpl*, pancia ♦ ADV dentro, all'interno; **to be inside** (*fam: in prison*) essere dentro *or* al fresco ♦ PREP **1** (*of place*) dentro, all'interno di; **inside the house** in casa; **come inside!** vieni dentro! **2** (*of time*) nel giro di; **inside 10 minutes** nel giro di 10 minuti; **he is inside the record** sta battendo il record; **just inside the speed limit** sotto il limite di velocità ♦ ADJ interno(-a)

inside forward N (*Sport*) mezzala

inside lane N (*Brit*) corsia di sinistra; (*USA: Europe*) corsia di destra

inside leg measurement N (*Brit*) *lunghezza della gamba dei pantaloni partendo dal cavallo*

in·sid·er [ɪnˈsaɪdəʳ] N uno(-a) degli addetti ai lavori

insider dealing [-ˈdiːlɪŋ], **insider trading** N (*Stock Exchange*) insider trading *m inv*

in·sidi·ous [ɪnˈsɪdɪəs] ADJ insidioso(-a)

in·sight [ˈɪnsaɪt] N (*perception*) perspicacia, intuito; (*glimpse, idea*) intuizione *f*; **to gain** *or* **get an insight into sth** potersi render conto di qc; **to give sb an insight into sth** permettere a qn di capire qc

in·sig·nia [ɪnˈsɪɡnɪə] NPL insegne *fpl*

in·sig·nifi·cant [ˌɪnsɪɡˈnɪfɪkənt] ADJ insignificante

in·sin·cere [ˌɪnsɪnˈsɪəʳ] ADJ (*person,*) falso(-a), insincero(-a), ipocrita; (*smile, behaviour*) falso(-a), ipocrita

in·sin·cer·ity [ˌɪnsɪnˈserɪtɪ] N falsità, ipocrisia

in·sinu·ate [ɪnˈsɪnjʊˌeɪt] VT insinuare; **to insinuate o.s. into sb's favour** insinuarsi nelle grazie di qn

in·sinu·ation [ɪnˌsɪnjʊˈeɪʃən] N insinuazione *f*

in·sip·id [ɪnˈsɪpɪd] ADJ (*food, drink*) insipido(-a); (*fig*) insulso(-a), insipido(-a)

in·sist [ɪnˈsɪst] VI **to insist (on sth/on doing sth)** insistere (su qc/nel fare qc); **I didn't want to, but he insisted** non volevo, ma ha insistito; **she insists on leaving tomorrow** vuole assolutamente partire domani, insiste nel voler partire domani ♦ VT: **to insist that** (*order*) insistere che + *sub*; (*maintain*) sostenere *or* affermare di; **I insist that you let me pay** insisto che tu mi lasci pagare; **he insists that he is innocent** sostiene di essere innocente

in·sist·ence [ɪnˈsɪstəns] N insistenza; **at her insistence** dietro sua insistenza, perché lei ha insistito (molto)

in·sist·ent [ɪnˈsɪstənt] ADJ insistente

in·so·far as [ˌɪnsəʊˈfɑːɹəz] CONJ in quanto, nella misura in cui

in·sole [ˈɪnsəʊl] N soletta; **orthopaedic insole** plantare *m*

in·so·lence [ˈɪnsələns] N insolenza

in·so·lent [ˈɪnsələnt] ADJ insolente

in·sol·uble [ɪnˈsɒljʊbl] ADJ insolubile

in·sol·ven·cy [ɪnˈsɒlvənsɪ] N insolvenza

in·sol·vent [ɪnˈsɒlvənt] ADJ insolvente

in·som·nia [ɪnˈsɒmnɪə] N insonnia

in·som·ni·ac [ɪnˈsɒmnɪæk] N chi soffre di insonnia

in·spect [ɪnˈspekt] VT (*examine*) ispezionare; (*Brit: ticket*) controllare; (*Mil: troops*) passare in rassegna; **to inspect sth for faults** sottoporre qc a controllo *or* verifica; **the kitchens are inspected regularly** le cucine vengono ispezionate regolarmente; **my ticket was inspected twice** mi hanno controllato il biglietto due volte

in·spec·tion [ɪnˈspekʃən] N (*of goods*) controllo, ispezione *f*; (*of ticket, document*) controllo; (*Mil: of school*) ispezione; **on inspection it was found that** ad un controllo si scoprì che

in·spec·tor [ɪnˈspektəʳ] N (*police inspector*) ispettore(-trice) (di polizia); (*schools inspector*) ispettore(-trice) scolastico(-a); (*on bus, train*) controllore *m*; **inspector of taxes** ispettore *m* del fisco

in·spi·ra·tion [ˌɪnspɪˈreɪʃən] N ispirazione *f*; **to have a sudden inspiration** avere un lampo di genio; **to be an inspiration to sb** ispirare qn, essere una fonte d'ispirazione per qn; **you've been an inspiration to us all** sei stato di esempio per tutti noi

in·spire [ɪnˈspaɪəʳ] VT: **to inspire sth in sb, to inspire sb with sth** ispirare qc a qn; **to inspire sb (to do sth)** ispirare qn (a fare qc)

in·spired [ɪnˈspaɪəd] ADJ (*writer, book etc*) ispirato(-a); **in an inspired moment** in un momento d'ispirazione

in·spir·ing [ɪnˈspaɪərɪŋ] ADJ ispiratore(-trice), stimolante

inst. ABBR (*Brit: Comm: = instant: of the present month*) c.m. (*= corrente mese*)

in·stabil·ity [ˌɪnstəˈbɪlɪtɪ] N instabilità

in·stall [ɪnˈstɔːl] VT (*machine, equipment, telephone*) installare; (*mayor, official etc*) insediare

in·stal·la·tion [ˌɪnstəˈleɪʃən] N (*see vb*) installazione *f*; insediamento

in·stal·ment, in·stall·ment (*USA*) [ɪnˈstɔːlmənt] N **1** (*Comm: part payment*) rata, pagamento rateale; **to pay in instalments** pagare a rate **2** (*of serial, story*) puntata, episodio; (*of publication*) dispensa

in·stance [ˈɪnstəns] N (*example*) esempio, caso; **for instance**

per *or* ad esempio'; **in that instance** in quel caso; **in the first instance** in primo luogo; **in many instances** in molti casi

in·stant ['ɪnstənt] ADJ 1 (*reply, reaction, success*) immediato(-a); (*food*) liofilizzato(-a); **instant coffee** caffè *m* solubile; **instant potatoes** fiocchi *mpl* di patate; **it was an instant success** è stato un successo immediato 2 (*Comm: of the present month*) corrente mese *inv*; **the 10th instant** il 10 corrente mese ♦ N istante *m*, attimo; **come here this instant** vieni immediatamente *or* subito qui; **in an instant** in un attimo; **I came the instant I got the news** sono venuto non appena ho ricevuto la notizia

in·stan·ta·neous [,ɪnstən'teɪnəs] ADJ istantaneo(-a)

in·stant·ly ['ɪnstəntlɪ] ADV immediatamente, subito

instant messaging N (*Comput*) messaggistica immediata

instant replay N (*USA: TV*) replay *m inv*

in·stead [ɪn'stɛd] ADV invece; **don't take Tom, take Fred instead** non prendere Tom, prendi piuttosto Fred; **I haven't got any coffee, will cocoa do instead?** non ho caffè, va bene lo stesso il cacao?; **if you're not going, I'll go instead** se non vai tu, andrò io al posto tuo ♦ PREP: **instead of** invece di; **instead of sb** al posto di qn; **instead of doing sth** invece di fare qc; **we played tennis instead of going swimming** abbiamo giocato a tennis invece di andare a nuotare

in·step ['ɪn,stɛp] N (*of foot*) collo del piede; (*of shoe*) collo della scarpa

in·sti·gate ['ɪnstɪ,ɡeɪt] VT (*rebellion, strike, crime*) istigare a; (*new ideas*) promuovere

in·sti·ga·tion [,ɪnstɪ'ɡeɪʃən] N istigazione *f*; **at sb's instigation** per *or* in seguito al suggerimento di qn

in·stil, in·still (*USA*) [ɪn'stɪl] VT: **to instil sth into sb** instillare qc a qn

in·stinct ['ɪnstɪŋkt] N istinto; **by instinct** per istinto, istintivamente

in·stinc·tive [ɪn'stɪŋktɪv] ADJ istintivo(-a)

in·stinc·tive·ly [ɪn'stɪŋktɪvlɪ] ADV istintivamente, per istinto

in·sti·tute ['ɪnstɪtjuːt] N istituto, ente *m* ♦ VT (*start: reform*) introdurre; (: *inquiry, investigation*) avviare, aprire; (: *legal proceedings*) intentare

in·sti·tu·tion [,ɪnstɪ'tjuːʃən] N 1 (*organization*) istituzione *f*; (*charitable institution*) istituto di beneficenza; (*psychiatric institution*) istituto psichiatrico 2 (*custom, tradition*) istituzione *f*

in·sti·tu·tion·al [,ɪnstɪ'tjuːʃənl] ADJ 1 (*reforms*) istituzionale 2 (*food, furniture*) tipico(-a) degli istituti assistenziali; **institutional care** (*for children*) ricovero presso un istituto; (*for handicapped people*) assistenza medica presso un istituto; **institutional life** la vita all'interno di un istituto

in·struct [ɪn'strʌkt] VT 1 (*teach*) istruire; **to instruct sb in sth/in how to do sth** insegnare qc a qn come fare qc 2 (*order*): **to instruct sb to do sth** dare istruzioni *or* ordini a qn di fare qc; **she instructed us to wait outside** ci ha ordinato di aspettare fuori

in·struc·tion [ɪn'strʌkʃən] N 1 (*teaching*) istruzione *f* 2 instructions NPL (*orders, directions*) istruzioni *fpl*; **to give sb instructions (to do sth)** dare istruzioni a qn (di fare qc); **instructions for use** istruzioni per l'uso

instruction book N libretto di istruzioni

in·struc·tive [ɪn'strʌktɪv] ADJ istruttivo(-a)

in·struc·tor [ɪn'strʌktə'] N (*gen*) istruttore(-trice); (*Skiing*) maestro(-a); **my driving instructor** il mio istruttore di guida

in·stru·ment ['ɪnstrəmənt] N (*also Mus*) strumento; **do you play an instrument?** suoni qualche strumento?; **to fly on instruments** (*Aer*) fare il volo strumentale

in·stru·men·tal [,ɪnstrə'mɛntl] ADJ 1 **to be instrumental in sth/in doing sth** avere un ruolo importante in qc/nel fare qc 2 (*music etc*) strumentale

in·stru·men·tal·ist [,ɪnstrə'mɛntəlɪst] N strumentista *m/f*

instrument panel N (*Aer*) quadro degli strumenti di bordo

in·sub·or·di·nate [,ɪnsə'bɔːdənɪt] ADJ insubordinato(-a)

in·sub·or·di·na·tion [ˈɪnsəˌbɔːdɪ'neɪʃən] N insubordinazione *f*

in·suf·fer·able [ɪn'sʌfərəbl] ADJ intollerabile

in·suf·fi·cient [,ɪnsə'fɪʃnt] ADJ insufficiente

in·suf·fi·cient·ly [,ɪnsə'fɪʃntlɪ] ADV insufficientemente, in modo insufficiente

in·su·lar ['ɪnsjʊlə'] ADJ (*climate*) insulare; (*fig: person*) di mentalità ristretta; **insular attitude** chiusura mentale, ristrettezza di idee

in·su·late ['ɪnsjʊ,leɪt] VT (*against cold*) isolare termicamente; (*against noise*) isolare acusticamente; (*Elec: wire*) isolare; (*fig: person*): **to insulate sb (from)** tener qn lontano (da)

in·su·lat·ing tape ['ɪnsjʊ,leɪtɪŋ,teɪp] N nastro isolante

in·su·la·tion [,ɪnsjʊ'leɪʃən] N (*see vb*) isolamento termico; isolamento acustico; isolamento (elettrico); (*material*) (materiale *m*) isolante

in·su·lin ['ɪnsjʊlɪn] N insulina; **insulin injection** iniezione *f* d'insulina

in·sult [*n* 'ɪnsʌlt, *vb* ɪn'sʌlt] N insulto ♦ VT insultare, offendere

in·sult·ing [ɪn'sʌltɪŋ] ADJ offensivo(-a)

in·su·per·able [ɪn'suːpərəbl] ADJ insormontabile

in·sur·ance [ɪn'ʃʊərəns] N assicurazione *f*; **life insurance** assicurazione sulla vita; **fire insurance** assicurazione contro gli incendi; **car insurance** assicurazione della macchina; **to take out insurance (against)** fare un'assicurazione (contro), assicurarsi (contro) ♦ ADJ (*certificate, company*) di assicurazione

insurance agent N agente *m/f* d'assicurazioni

insurance broker N broker *m inv* d'assicurazioni

insurance company N società di assicurazioni

insurance policy N polizza d'assicurazione

insurance premium N premio assicurativo

in·sure [ɪn'ʃʊə'] VT (*house, car, parcel*): **to insure (against)** assicurare (contro); **to insure o.s. or one's life** assicurarsi (sulla vita); **to insure sb or sb's life** assicurare qn sulla vita; **to be insured for £50,000** essere assicurato(-a) per 50.000 sterline

in·sured [ɪn'ʃʊəd] N: **the insured** l'assicurato(-a)

in·sur·er [ɪn'ʃʊərə'] N assicuratore(-trice)

in·sur·gent [ɪn'sɜːdʒənt] ADJ ribelle ♦ N insorto(-a), rivoltoso(-a)

in·sur·mount·able [,ɪnsə'maʊntəbl] ADJ insormontabile

in·sur·rec·tion [,ɪnsə'rɛkʃən] N insurrezione *f*

in·tact [ɪn'tækt] ADJ intatto(-a)

in·take ['ɪn,teɪk] N 1 (*Tech: of air, water, gas*) immissione *f* 2 (*quantity: of pupils*) (numero di) iscrizioni *fpl*; (: *of workers*) (numero di) assunzioni *fpl*; (: *of food*) consumo; **try to limit your intake of salt** cerchi di limitare il consumo di sale; **this year's intake of students** gli studenti iscritti quest'anno

in·tan·gi·ble [ɪn'tændʒəbl] ADJ 1 (*fears, hopes*) indefinibile 2 (*Comm: asset*) immateriale

in·te·gral ['ɪntɪɡrəl] ADJ (*essential: part*) integrante; **to be an integral part of** essere parte integrante di ♦ N (*Math*) integrale *m*

in·te·grate ['ɪntɪ,ɡreɪt] VT (*gen, also Math*) integrare; (*USA: school, community*) operare l'integrazione razziale in

integrated circuit N (*Comput*) circuito integrato

in·te·gra·tion [,ɪntɪ'ɡreɪʃən] N integrazione *f*; **racial integration** integrazione razziale

in·teg·ri·ty [ɪn'tɛɡrɪtɪ] N integrità

in·tel·lect ['ɪntɪlɛkt] N intelletto

in·tel·lec·tual [,ɪntɪ'lɛktjʊəl] ADJ (*person*) intellettuale; (*interests*) culturale ♦ N intellettuale *m/f*

in·tel·li·gence [ɪn'tɛlɪdʒəns] N (*cleverness*) intelligenza; (*information*) informazioni *fpl*

intelligence quotient N quoziente *m* d'intelligenza

Intelligence Service N servizio segreto

intelligence test N test *m inv* d'intelligenza

in·tel·li·gent [ɪn'tɛlɪdʒənt] ADJ intelligente

in·tel·li·gi·ble [ɪn'tɛlɪdʒəbl] ADJ intelligibile

in·tem·per·ate [ɪn'tɛmpərɪt] (*frm*) ADJ (*remarks, response, opinion*) privo(-a) di autocontrollo; (*climate*) rigido(-a); (*habits*) smoderato(-a); (*person: lacking moderation*) intemperante; (: *drinking too much*) intemperante nel bere

in·tend [ɪn'tɛnd] VT (*mean*): **to intend to do sth** avere (l') intenzione di fare qc, intendere fare qc; (*remark, gift*): **intend sth for sb/sth** destinare qc a qn/qc; **I intend to do languages at university** ho intenzione di fare lingue all'università; **I intend him to come too** voglio che venga anche lui; **it was intended as a compliment** voleva essere un complimento; **I intended no harm** non intendevo fare del male; **did you intend that?** (*do on purpose*) l'hai fatto intenzionalmente?

in·tend·ed [ɪnˈtɛndɪd] ADJ **1** (*deliberate: insult*) intenzionale **2** (*planned: effect*) voluto(-a); (: *journey, route*) programmato(-a) ♦ N (*old, often hum*) fidanzato(-a); **he was not the intended victim** non era lui la vittima designata

in·tense [ɪnˈtɛns] ADJ (*heat, cold, expression*) intenso(-a); (*interest, enthusiasm*) vivo(-a), profondo(-a); (*person*) di forti sentimenti

in·tense·ly [ɪnˈtɛnslɪ] ADV (*difficult, hot, cold*) estremamente; (*moved*) profondamente

in·ten·si·fy [ɪnˈtɛnsɪˌfaɪ] VT intensificare ♦ VI intensificarsi

in·ten·si·ty [ɪnˈtɛnsɪtɪ] N intensità *f inv*

in·ten·sive [ɪnˈtɛnsɪv] ADJ (*study*) intenso(-a); (*course*) intensivo(-a); (*bombing*) a tappeto; **intensive farming** agricoltura intensiva

intensive care N rianimazione *f*; **to be in intensive care** essere in rianimazione; **intensive care unit** reparto *or* centro di rianimazione

in·tent [ɪnˈtɛnt] ADJ **1** (*determined*): **to be intent on doing sth** essere deciso(-a) a fare qc **2** (*absorbed*) assorto(-a); **to be intent on sth** essere intento(-a) a qc; **intent stare** sguardo attento ♦ N (*frm*) intenzione *f*, intento; **with intent to kill** con l'intento di uccidere; **to all intents and purposes** praticamente, a tutti gli effetti

in·ten·tion [ɪnˈtɛnʃən] N intenzione *f*; **I have no intention of going** non ho nessuna intenzione di andare; **I have every intention of going** ho proprio intenzione di andare; **with the best of intentions** con le migliori intenzioni del mondo

in·ten·tion·al [ɪnˈtɛnʃənl] ADJ intenzionale, deliberato(-a); **it wasn't intentional** non l'ho (*or* l'ha *etc*) fatto apposta

in·ten·tion·al·ly [ɪnˈtɛnʃnəlɪ] ADV intenzionalmente, deliberatamente

in·tent·ly [ɪnˈtɛntlɪ] ADV attentamente

in·ter [ɪnˈtɜː] VT (*frm*) seppellire

inter·act [ˌɪntərˈækt] VI interagire

inter·ac·tion [ˌɪntərˈækʃən] N interazione *f*

inter·ac·tive [ˌɪntərˈæktɪv] ADJ (*gen, also Comput*) interattivo(-a)

inter·cede [ˌɪntəˈsiːd] VI: **to intercede with sb/on behalf of sb** intercedere presso qn/a favore di qn

inter·cept [*vb* ˌɪntəˈsɛpt, *n* ˈɪntəsɛpt] VT intercettare ♦ N (*Math*) intersezione *f*

inter·cep·tion [ˌɪntəˈsɛpʃən] N intercettazione *f*

inter·change [*n* ˈɪntəˌtʃeɪndʒ, *vb* ˌɪntəˈtʃeɪndʒ] N **1** (*of views, ideas*) scambio **2** (*on motorway*) interscambio, svincolo ♦ VT (*views*) scambiarsi

inter·change·able [ˌɪntəˈtʃeɪndʒəbl] ADJ intercambiabile

inter·city [ˌɪntəˈsɪtɪ] ADJ: **intercity (train)** (treno) intercity *m inv*

inter·com [ˈɪntəˌkɒm] N (*fam*) interfono

inter·con·nect [ˌɪntəkəˈnɛkt] VI (*rooms*) essere in comunicazione

inter·con·ti·nen·tal [ˈɪntəˌkɒntɪˈnɛntl] ADJ intercontinentale

inter·course [ˈɪntəkɔːs] N **1** (*also: sexual intercourse*) rapporti *mpl* sessuali; **to have (sexual) intercourse with sb** avere rapporti sessuali con qn **2** (*frm: communication*) rapporti *mpl*, relazioni *fpl*

inter·de·pend·ent [ˌɪntədɪˈpɛndənt] ADJ interdipendente

in·ter·est [ˈɪntrɪst] N **1** (*involvement, curiosity*) interesse *m*; **she has a wide range of interests** ha moltissimi interessi; **to have** *or* **take an interest in sth** interessarsi di *or* a qc; **to have** *or* **take no interest in sth** non interessarsi di qc; **to be of interest to sb** interessare qn; **to lose interest in sth** perdere l'interesse per qc; **I have lost interest in motor racing** le corse automobilistiche non mi interessano più **2** (*profit, advantage*) interesse *m*; **in one's own interest(s)** nel proprio interesse; **to act in sb's interest(s)** agire nell'interesse di qn; **to have a vested interest in sth** essere direttamente interessato(-a) in *or* a qc; **in the public interest** nell'interesse pubblico **3** (*Comm: stake, share*) interessi *mpl*; **business interests** attività *fpl* commerciali; **British interests in the Middle East** gli interessi britannici nel Medio Oriente **4** (*Comm: on loan, shares etc*) interesse *m*; **compound/simple interest** interesse

composto/semplice; **5% interest** un interesse del 5%; **at an interest of 5%** all'interesse del 5%; **to bear interest at 5%** fruttare il 5% (di interesse); **to lend at interest** prestare denaro a interesse ♦ VT interessare; **to interest o.s. in sth** interessarsi a qc; **to interest sb in sth** (fare) interessare qn a qc

in·ter·est·ed [ˈɪntrɪstɪd] ADJ (*expression*) interessato(-a), pieno(-a) di interesse; (*person*) che s'interessa; **to be interested in sth** interessarsi di qc; **he's interested in buying a car** è interessato all'acquisto di una macchina; **I'm not interested in politics** non mi interesso di politica; **interested party** parte *f* interessata

interest-free [ˈɪntrɪstˈfriː] ADJ (*loan*) senza interesse

in·ter·est·ing [ˈɪntrɪstɪŋ] ADJ interessante

interest rate N tasso di interesse

inter·face [ˈɪntəˌfeɪs] N (*Comput*) interfaccia

inter·fere [ˌɪntəˈfɪə] VI **1 to interfere (in sth)** (*quarrel, other people's business*) interferire (in qc), intromettersi (in qc); **to interfere with sth** (*object*) manomettere qc; (*plans*) intralciare qc; (*process, activity*) interferire con qc; (*Radio, TV*) causare delle interferenze in qc; **he is always interfering** si intromette sempre in tutto; **stop interfering!** smettila di immischiarti!; **he didn't want his work to interfere with his family** non voleva che il lavoro interferisse con la famiglia **2** (*euph: sexually*): **to interfere with sb** molestare sessualmente qn

inter·fer·ence [ˌɪntəˈfɪərəns] N interferenza, intromissione *f*; (*Radio, TV, Phys*) interferenza

inter·fer·ing [ˌɪntəˈfɪərɪŋ] ADJ invadente

in·ter·im [ˈɪntərɪm] N: **in the interim** nel frattempo ♦ ADJ (*report*) provvisorio(-a); (*government*) ad interim; **interim dividend** (*Comm*) acconto di dividendo

in·te·ri·or [ɪnˈtɪərɪə] ADJ interno(-a); (*life, world, monologue*) interiore ♦ N interno; (*of country*) entroterra *m*; **Department of the Interior** Ministero degli Interni

interior decorator N (*designer*) arredatore(-trice); (*painter*) imbianchino; (*wallpaper hanger*) tappezziere

inter·jec·tion [ˌɪntəˈdʒɛkʃən] N interiezione *f*

inter·lock [ˌɪntəˈlɒk] VI ingranarsi ♦ VT ingranare

inter·lop·er [ˈɪntələʊpə] N intruso(-a)

inter·lude [ˈɪntəluːd] N parentesi *f inv*, intervallo; (*Theatre*) intermezzo; **musical interlude** interludio

inter·mar·ry [ˈɪntəˈmærɪ] VI (*races, groups*) fare matrimoni misti; (*blood relations*) sposarsi tra consanguinei

inter·medi·ary [ˌɪntəˈmiːdɪərɪ] N mediatore(-trice), intermediario(-a)

inter·medi·ate [ˌɪntəˈmiːdɪət] ADJ (*stage, position: course, level*) intermedio(-a); (*student*) che frequenta un corso intermedio

in·ter·ment [ɪnˈtɜːmənt] N (*frm*) inumazione *f*

in·ter·mi·nable [ɪnˈtɜːmɪnəbl] ADJ interminabile

inter·mis·sion [ˌɪntəˈmɪʃən] N (*pause*) interruzione *f*, pausa; (*Theatre, Cine*) intervallo

inter·mit·tent [ˌɪntəˈmɪtənt] ADJ intermittente

inter·mit·tent·ly [ˌɪntəˈmɪtəntlɪ] ADV a intermittenza

in·tern N (*USA: student*) stagista *m/f*; (: *doctor*) (medico) interno

in·ter·nal [ɪnˈtɜːnl] ADJ interno(-a); **internal injuries** lesioni *fpl* interne; **internal processes** (*Geol*) fenomeni *mpl* endogeni

in·ter·nal·ly [ɪnˈtɜːnəlɪ] ADV internamente; **to bleed internally** avere un'emorragia interna; **"not to be taken internally"** "per uso esterno"

Internal Revenue Service N (*USA: Fin*) Fisco

inter·na·tion·al [ˌɪntəˈnæʃnəl] ADJ internazionale ♦ N (*Sport: game*) incontro internazionale; (: *player*) giocatore(-trice) della squadra nazionale

International Court of Justice N Corte *f* Internazionale di Giustizia

International Date Line N linea del cambiamento di data

inter·na·tion·al·ly [ˌɪntəˈnæʃnəlɪ] ADV: **internationally famous** di fama internazionale; **internationally, the situation is even worse** a livello internazionale la situazione è anche peggiore

International Monetary Fund N Fondo monetario internazionale

international relations NPL rapporti *mpl* internazionali

inter·necine [ˌɪntəˈniːsaɪn] ADJ distruttivo(-a) per entrambe le parti

in·ternee [ˌɪntɜːˈniː] N internato(-a)

inter·net [ˈɪntənet] N: **the internet** internet *m*; **on the internet** in internet

internet service provider [-prəˈvaɪdəʳ] N (*Comput*) provider *m inv*

in·tern·ment [ɪnˈtɜːnmənt] N internamento

inter·play [ˈɪntəˌpleɪ] N interazione *f*

Inter·pol [ˈɪntəˌpɒl] N Interpol *f*

in·ter·pret [ɪnˈtɜːprɪt] VT 1 (*translate orally*): **to interpret sth (into)** tradurre qc (in) 2 (*explain, understand*) interpretare ♦ VI fare da interprete

in·ter·pre·ta·tion [ɪnˌtɜːprɪˈteɪʃən] N interpretazione *f*

in·ter·pret·er [ɪnˈtɜːprɪtəʳ] N interprete *m/f*

in·ter·pret·ing [ɪnˈtɜːprɪtɪŋ] N (*profession*) interpretariato

inter·re·lat·ed [ˌɪntərɪˈleɪtɪd] ADJ correlato(-a), in relazione (l'uno(-a) con l'altro(-a))

in·ter·ro·gate [ɪnˈterəˌgeɪt] VT interrogare

in·ter·ro·ga·tion [ɪnˌterəˈgeɪʃən] N (*of suspect, witness*) interrogatorio

in·ter·rogative [ˌɪntəˈrɒgətɪv] ADJ interrogativo(-a) ♦ N (*Gram*) interrogativo

in·ter·ro·ga·tor [ɪnˈterəˌgeɪtəʳ] N interrogatore(-trice)

in·ter·rupt [ˌɪntəˈrʌpt] VT, VI interrompere

in·ter·rup·tion [ˌɪntəˈrʌpʃən] N interruzione *f*

inter·sect [ˌɪntəˈsekt] VT (*Math*) intersecare ♦ VI (*Math*) intersecarsi; (*roads*) incrociarsi, intersecarsi

inter·sec·tion [ˌɪntəˈsekʃən] N (*crossroads*) incrocio; (*Math*) intersezione *f*

inter·sperse [ˌɪntəˈspɜːs] VT: **to intersperse sth with sth** inframmezzare qc con qc

inter·state [ˌɪntəˈsteɪt] ADJ fra stati

inter·twine [ˌɪntəˈtwaɪn] VT intrecciare ♦ VI intrecciarsi

in·ter·val [ˈɪntəvəl] N intervallo; **at intervals** di tanto in tanto, a tratti; **at regular intervals** a intervalli regolari; **sunny intervals** (*Met*) schiarite *fpl*

inter·vene [ˌɪntəˈviːn] VI (*event, circumstances*) sopraggiungere; (*time*) intercorrere; (*person*): **to intervene (in)** intervenire (in); **in the intervening years** negli anni che sono intercorsi

inter·ven·tion [ˌɪntəˈvenʃən] N intervento

inter·view [ˈɪntəˌvjuː] N (*for job, position*) colloquio; (*in paper, on radio, TV*) intervista; **to have an interview with the director** avere un colloquio con il direttore ♦ VT (*see n*) sottoporre a colloquio; intervistare; **I seized the chance to interview one of the actors** ho colto l'opportunità per intervistare uno degli attori; **to be interviewed for a job** avere un colloquio di lavoro

inter·viewee [ˌɪntəvjuːˈiː] N (*Media*) intervistato(-a); (*for job*) chi viene sottoposto ad un colloquio di lavoro

inter·view·er [ˈɪntəvjuːəʳ] N (*on radio, TV*) intervistatore(-trice)

in·tes·tate [ɪnˈtestɪt] ADJ (*Law*): **to die intestate** morire intestato(-a)

in·tes·ti·nal [ɪnˈtestɪnl] ADJ intestinale

in·tes·tine [ɪnˈtestɪn] N intestino; **large intestine** (intestino) crasso; **small intestine** (intestino) tenue *m*

in·ti·ma·cy [ˈɪntɪməsɪ] N (*friendship*) intimità; (*sexual intimacy*) rapporti *mpl* intimi

in·ti·mate [*adj* ˈɪntɪmɪt, *vb* ˈɪntɪmeɪt] ADJ intimo(-a); (*knowledge*) profondo(-a); **to be/become intimate with sb** (*friendly*) essere/diventare amico(-a) intimo(-a) di qn; (*sexually*) avere rapporti intimi con qn ♦ VT: **to intimate (that)** far *or* lasciar capire (che)
  ❏ **intimate** is not translated by the Italian word *intimare*

in·ti·mate·ly [ˈɪntɪmɪtlɪ] ADV intimamente; **to talk intimately with sb** scambiare confidenze con qn; **to be intimately involved in sth** essere direttamente coinvolto(-a) in qc

in·ti·ma·tion [ˌɪntɪˈmeɪʃən] N (*hint*) accenno
  ❏ **intimation** is not translated by the Italian word *intimazione*

in·timi·date [ɪnˈtɪmɪˌdeɪt] VT intimorire; (*witness*) minacciare,

sottoporre ad intimidazione; **he tried to intimidate me** ha cercato di intimorirmi

in·timi·da·tion [ɪnˌtɪmɪˈdeɪʃən] N intimidazione *f*

into [ˈɪntuː] PREP 1 (*of place*) in, dentro; **put it into the box** mettilo nella *or* dentro la scatola; **come into the house** vieni dentro casa; **to go into the wood** entrare nel bosco; **to walk into a wall** sbattere contro un muro; **he drove into a tree** andò a sbattere contro un albero; **to go into town/the country** andare in città/in campagna; **to get into the car** salire in macchina 2 (*change in condition*) in; **to translate sth into Italian** tradurre qc in italiano; **to burst into tears** scoppiare in lacrime; **to change pounds into dollars** cambiare delle sterline in dollari; **to cut into pieces** tagliare a pezzi; **to change into clean clothes** mettersi dei vestiti puliti; **he is really into jazz** (*fam*) è un appassionato di jazz, ha la passione del jazz 3 (*Math*): **2 into 6 goes 3 times** il 2 nel 6 sta 3 volte; **to divide 3 into 12** dividere 12 per 3

in·tol·er·able [ɪnˈtɒlərəbl] ADJ intollerabile

in·tol·er·ance [ɪnˈtɒlərəns] N intolleranza

in·tol·er·ant [ɪnˈtɒlərənt] ADJ: **intolerant (of)** intollerante (verso)

in·to·na·tion [ˌɪntəʊˈneɪʃən] N (*Linguistics*) intonazione *f*

in·toxi·cate [ɪnˈtɒksɪˌkeɪt] VT (*subj: alcohol*) ubriacare; (*subj: success*) inebriare
  ❏ **intoxicate** is not translated by the Italian word *intossicare*

in·toxi·cat·ed [ɪnˈtɒksɪˌkeɪtɪd] ADJ ubriaco(-a); **intoxicated (with)** (*fig*) inebriato(-a) (di); **to become intoxicated** ubriacarsi
  ❏ **intoxicated** is not translated by the Italian word *intossicato*

in·toxi·ca·tion [ɪnˌtɒksɪˈkeɪʃən] N (*see adj*) ubriachezza; ebbrezza

in·trac·table [ɪnˈtræktəbl] (*frm*) ADJ (*person, mood*) intrattabile; (*illness*) difficile da curare; (*problem*) insolubile

intra·net [ˈɪntrənet] N intranet *m inv*

in·tran·si·gence [ɪnˈtrænsɪdʒəns] N intransigenza

in·tran·si·gent [ɪnˈtrænsɪdʒənt] ADJ intransigente

in·tran·si·tive [ɪnˈtrænsɪtɪv] ADJ (*Gram*) intransitivo(-a)

intra-uterine device [ˌɪntrəˈjuːtəraɪndɪˈvaɪs] N dispositivo anticoncezionale intrauterino, spirale *f*

intra·venous [ˌɪntrəˈviːnəs] ADJ endovenoso(-a)

in-tray [ˈɪnˌtreɪ] N vassoio della corrispondenza in arrivo

in·trep·id [ɪnˈtrepɪd] ADJ intrepido(-a)

in·tri·ca·cy [ˈɪntrɪkəsɪ] N complessità *f inv*

in·tri·cate [ˈɪntrɪkɪt] ADJ (*plot, problem*) intricato(-a), complicato(-a); (*pattern, machinery, mechanism*) complicato(-a), complesso(-a)

in·trigue [ɪnˈtriːg] N (*plot*) intrigo; (*amorous*) tresca ♦ VT (*fascinate*) intrigare, affascinare; (*make curious*) incuriosire ♦ VI complottare, tramare

in·tri·guing [ɪnˈtriːgɪŋ] ADJ (*fascinating*) affascinante, intrigante; (*arousing curiosity*) che suscita curiosità ♦ N intrighi *mpl*

in·trin·sic [ɪnˈtrɪnsɪk] ADJ intrinseco(-a)

intro·duce [ˌɪntrəˈdjuːs] VT 1 (*bring in*: *reform, new fashion, idea*) introdurre; (: *Pol, bill*: TV, *Radio*: *programme*) presentare; **to introduce sb into a firm** far entrare qn in una ditta; **a new system is to be introduced** verrà introdotto un nuovo sistema 2 (*make acquainted*): **to introduce sb to sb** presentare qn a qn; **he introduced me to his parents** mi ha presentato ai suoi genitori; **to introduce sb to sth** (*pastime, technique*) far conoscere qc a qn, iniziare qn a qc; **may I introduce …?** permette che le presenti…?

intro·duc·tion [ˌɪntrəˈdʌkʃən] N (*see vb*) introduzione *f*; presentazione *f*; **a letter of introduction** una lettera di presentazione; **the introduction of the new system** l'introduzione del nuovo sistema

intro·duc·tory [ˌɪntrəˈdʌktərɪ] ADJ introduttivo(-a); **introductory remarks** osservazioni *fpl* preliminari; **an introductory offer** un'offerta di lancio; **an introductory course** un corso introduttivo

intro·spec·tion [ˌɪntrəʊˈspekʃən] N introspezione *f*

intro·spec·tive [ˌɪntrəʊˈspektɪv] ADJ introspettivo(-a)

in·tro·vert ['ɪntrəʊˌvɜːt] N, ADJ introverso(-a)

in·trude [ɪn'truːd] VI intromettersi; **to intrude on** or **upon** (person) importunare; (conversation) intromettersi in; **I hope I'm not intruding** spero di non disturbare

in·trud·er [ɪn'truːdəʳ] N (trespasser) intruso(-a); (burglar) ladro(-a)

in·tru·sion [ɪn'truːʒən] N intrusione f

in·tru·sive [ɪn'truːsɪv] ADJ importuno(-a)

in·tui·tion [ˌɪntjuː'ɪʃən] N (no pl: power) intuito, intuizione f; (feeling) intuito

in·tui·tive [ɪn'tjuːɪtɪv] ADJ intuitivo(-a)

in·un·date ['ɪnʌnˌdeɪt] VT: **to inundate (with)** inondare (di); (fig) sommergere (di)

in·ure [ɪn'jʊəʳ] VT: **to inure (to)** assuefare (a)

in·vade [ɪn'veɪd] VT (Mil: gen: fig) invadere; (privacy, sb's rights) violare

in·vad·er [ɪn'veɪdəʳ] N invasore m

in·va·lid¹ ['ɪnvəlɪd] N (sick person) infermo(-a); (disabled person) invalido(-a) ◆ ADJ (see n) infermo(-a); invalido(-a)
  ▸ **invalid out** VT + ADV (Mil) congedare per invalidità

in·val·id² [ɪn'vælɪd] ADJ (document, cheque) invalido(-a), non valido(-a); (excuse, argument) non valido(-a); (marriage) nullo(-a)

in·val·i·date [ɪn'vælɪˌdeɪt] VT (law, contract) invalidare; (argument, conclusion) smentire; **the will was invalidated** il testamento è stato invalidato

in·valu·able [ɪn'væljʊəbl] ADJ estremamente prezioso(-a); **your help has been invaluable** il tuo aiuto è stato estremamente prezioso

in·vari·able [ɪn'vɛərɪəbl] ADJ costante, invariabile

in·vari·ably [ɪn'vɛərɪəblɪ] ADV invariabilmente; **she is invariably late** è immancabilmente in ritardo; **they almost invariably get it wrong** sbagliano quasi sempre

in·va·sion [ɪn'veɪʒən] N invasione f; **an invasion of sb's privacy** una violazione della privacy di qn

in·vec·tive [ɪn'vektɪv] N invettiva; **a stream of invective** una sfilza d'ingiurie, una sequela di improperi

in·vei·gle [ɪn'viːgl] VT: **to inveigle sb into (doing) sth** circuire qn per fargli (farle) fare qc

in·vent [ɪn'vent] VT inventare

in·ven·tion [ɪn'venʃən] N invenzione f

in·ven·tive [ɪn'ventɪv] ADJ (genius) inventivo(-a), creativo(-a); (mind) ricco(-a) d'inventiva

in·ven·tive·ness [ɪn'ventɪvnɪs] N inventiva

in·ven·tor [ɪn'ventəʳ] N inventore(-trice)

in·ven·tory ['ɪnvəntrɪ] N inventario; **to draw up/take an inventory** fare l'inventario

inventory control N (Comm) controllo delle giacenze

in·verse ['ɪn'vɜːs] ADJ inverso(-a); **in inverse proportion (to)** inversamente proporzionale (a); **to be in inverse proportion** essere inversamente proporzionale ◆ N inverso, contrario

in·verse·ly [ɪn'vɜːslɪ] ADV all'inverso; **inversely proportionate** inversamente proporzionale

in·vert [ɪn'vɜːt] VT (object) capovolgere, rovesciare; (elements, words) invertire

in·ver·te·brate [ɪn'vɜːtɪbrɪt] N, ADJ invertebrato(-a)

in·vert·ed com·mas [ɪnˌvɜːtɪd'kɒməz] NPL (Brit) virgolette fpl; **in inverted commas** tra virgolette

in·vest [ɪn'vest] VT **1** (money, capital) investire; (fig: time, effort) impiegare **2** (endow): **to invest sb with sth** investire qn di qc ◆ VI: **to invest in** (company, property) investire in, fare (degli) investimenti in; (acquire) comprarsi

in·ves·ti·gate [ɪn'vestɪˌgeɪt] VT (crime, motive) indagare su, investigare su; (possibilities) studiare, esaminare; **the police are investigating the murder** la polizia sta indagando sull'omicidio

in·ves·ti·ga·tion [ɪnˌvestɪ'geɪʃən] N (of crime) indagine f, investigazione f giudiziaria; **police investigations** le indagini della polizia

in·ves·ti·ga·tive [ɪn'vestɪgətɪv] ADJ: **investigative journalism** giornalismo investigativo

in·ves·ti·ga·tor [ɪn'vestɪˌgeɪtəʳ] N investigatore(-trice); **a private investigator** un investigatore privato, un detective

in·ves·ti·ture [ɪn'vestɪtʃəʳ] N investitura

in·vest·ment [ɪn'vestmənt] N (Comm) investimento

investment income N reddito da investimenti

investment trust N fondo comune di investimento

in·ves·tor [ɪn'vestəʳ] N (gen) investitore(-trice); (shareholder) azionista m/f

in·vet·er·ate [ɪn'vetərɪt] ADJ (habit, gambler) inveterato(-a); (liar, smoker) incallito(-a)

in·vidi·ous [ɪn'vɪdɪəs] ADJ (comparison) ingiusto(-a); (task) poco invidiabile, antipatico(-a); (choice) imbarazzante, difficile
  ❏ **invidious** is not translated by the Italian word invidioso

in·vigi·late [ɪn'vɪdʒɪˌleɪt] VT, VI (Brit Scol) sorvegliare

in·vigi·la·tor [ɪn'vɪdʒɪˌleɪtəʳ] N (Brit) chi sorveglia agli esami

in·vig·or·at·ing [ɪn'vɪgəˌreɪtɪŋ] ADJ (exercise, walk, air, breeze) tonificante

in·vin·cible [ɪn'vɪnsəbl] ADJ invincibile

in·vio·late [ɪn'vaɪəlɪt] ADJ inviolato(-a)

in·vis·ible [ɪn'vɪzəbl] ADJ invisibile

invisible assets NPL (Brit: Econ) beni mpl immateriali

invisible ink N inchiostro simpatico

invisible mending N rammendo invisibile

in·vi·ta·tion [ˌɪnvɪ'teɪʃən] N invito; **by invitation only** esclusivamente su invito; **at sb's invitation** dietro or su invito di qn

in·vite [ɪn'vaɪt] VT (person): **to invite sb (to do)** invitare qn (a fare); (subscriptions, applications) sollecitare, richiedere (cortesemente); (opinions) chiedere; (discussion) invitare a; (ridicule) provocare, suscitare; (disbelief) incoraggiare; **to invite sb to dinner** invitare qn a cena; **to invite sb in/up** invitare qn a entrare/salire; **you're invited to a party at Claire's house** sei invitato ad una festa a casa di Claire; **to invite trouble** cercare guai
  ▸ **invite out** VT + ADV invitare fuori; **he invited us out to dinner** ci ha invitato a cena fuori
  ▸ **invite over** VT + ADV invitare (a casa)

in·vit·ing [ɪn'vaɪtɪŋ] ADJ (prospect, goods) invitante, allettante; (smile) invitante; (food, smell) invitante, appetitoso(-a)

in·voice ['ɪnvɔɪs] N fattura ◆ VT (goods) fatturare; **to invoice sb for goods** intestare a qn la fattura per le or delle merci

in·voke [ɪn'vəʊk] VT invocare

in·vol·un·tary [ɪn'vɒləntərɪ] ADJ involontario(-a)

in·volve [ɪn'vɒlv] VT **1** (associate) coinvolgere; (implicate) implicare, coinvolgere; **to be/become involved in sth** essere/rimanere coinvolto(-a) in qc; **I don't want to be involved in the argument** non voglio essere coinvolto nella discussione; **to involve o.s./sb in sth** (politics etc) impegnarsi/coinvolgere qn in qc; **we won't involve him** non lo coinvolgeremo; **don't involve me in your quarrels!** non tiratemi in mezzo alle vostre beghe!; **don't involve yourself in unnecessary expense** non metterti a fare spese inutili; **how did he come to be involved?** come ha fatto a trovarsi in mezzo?; **the factors involved** i fattori in causa or in gioco; **the persons involved** le persone in questione or coinvolte; **to feel involved** sentirsi coinvolto(-a); **to become** or **get involved with sb** (socially) legarsi a qn; (emotionally) legarsi sentimentalmente a qn; **to be involved with sb** avere una relazione con qn **2** (entail) implicare, comportare; **it involves a lot of expense/trouble** comporta un mucchio di spese/difficoltà

in·volved [ɪn'vɒlvd] ADJ (situation, discussion) complicato(-a), complesso(-a); see also **involve**

in·volve·ment [ɪn'vɒlvmənt] N **1** (being involved) impegno, partecipazione f, coinvolgimento; (emotional) legame m, relazione f; **we don't know the extent of his involvement** non sappiamo fino a che punto sia coinvolto; **their involvement in the deal** il loro coinvolgimento nell'affare; **his involvement in the activities of the group** la sua partecipazione alle attività del gruppo; **financial involvements** impegni mpl finanziari **2** (complexity) complessità

in·vul·ner·able [ɪn'vʌlnərəbl] ADJ invulnerabile

in·ward ['ɪnwəd] ADJ (peace, happiness) interiore; (thought, feeling) intimo(-a); (movement) verso l'interno ◆ ADV = **inwards**

in·ward·ly [ˈɪnwədlɪ] ADV (*feel, think*) nel proprio intimo, dentro di sé

in·wards [ˈɪnwədz] ADV verso l'interno

IOC [ˌaɪəʊˈsiː] N ABBR (= *International Olympic Committee*) CIO *m* (= *Comitato olimpico internazionale*)

iodine [ˈaɪədiːn] N iodio

ion [ˈaɪən] N ione *m*

Ionian Sea [aɪˈəʊnɪənˈsiː] N: **the Ionian Sea** il mar Ionio

iota [aɪˈəʊtə] N (*letter*) iota; (*of truth, commonsense*) briciolo

IOU [ˌaɪəʊˈjuː] N ABBR (= *I owe you*) pagherò *m inv*

Iowa [ˈaɪəʊə] l'Iowa

IPA [ˌaɪpiːˈeɪ] N ABBR (= *International Phonetic Alphabet*) AFI *m* (= *Alfabeto Fonetico Internazionale*)

IP address [aɪˈpiːəˌdres] N = **Internet Protocol address** (*Comput*) indirizzo IP

IQ [ˌaɪˈkjuː] N ABBR (= *intelligence quotient*) QI *m*

IRA [ˌaɪɑːˈreɪ] N ABBR (= *Irish Republican Army*) IRA *f*

Iran [ɪˈrɑːn] N l'Iran *m*

Ira·nian [ɪˈreɪnɪən] ADJ iraniano(-a) ♦ N (*person*) iraniano(-a); (*language*) iranico

Iraq [ɪˈrɑːk] N l'Iraq *m*

Ira·qi [ɪˈrɑːkɪ] ADJ iracheno(-a) ♦ N (*person*) iracheno(-a)

iras·cible [ɪˈræsɪbl] ADJ irascibile

irate [aɪˈreɪt] ADJ irato(-a), infuriato(-a)

Ire·land [ˈaɪələnd] N l'Irlanda; **Northern Ireland** l'Irlanda del Nord; **Republic of Ireland** la Repubblica d'Irlanda, l'Eire *f*

iris [ˈaɪərɪs] N 1 (*Anat*) iride *f* 2 (*Bot*) iris *f inv*, giaggiolo

Irish [ˈaɪərɪʃ] ADJ irlandese ♦ N 1 **the Irish** *npl* gli irlandesi 2 (*language*) irlandese *m*

Irish·man [ˈaɪərɪʃmən] N (*pl* -men) irlandese *m*

Irish Sea N: **the Irish Sea** il mar d'Irlanda

Irish·woman [ˈaɪərɪʃˌwʊmən] N (*pl* -women) irlandese *f*

irk [ɜːk] VT seccare

irk·some [ˈɜːksəm] ADJ noioso(-a), seccante

iron [ˈaɪən] N (*also fig*) ferro; (*Golf*) mazza da golf di ferro; (*for ironing clothes*) ferro (da stiro); **a will of iron** una volontà ferrea *or* di ferro; **he rules his children with a rod of iron** comanda a bacchetta i figli; **to strike while the iron is hot** (*fig*) battere finché il ferro è caldo; **to have a lot of/too many irons in the fire** (*fig*) avere molta/troppa carne al fuoco; *see also* **irons** ♦ VT (*clothes*) stirare ♦ VI: **this dress irons well** questo vestito è facile da stirare ♦ ADJ (*bridge, bar, tool etc*) di ferro; (*fig: will, determination*) ferreo(-a), di ferro; **an iron gate** un cancello di ferro; **an iron fist in a velvet glove** un pugno di ferro in un guanto di velluto

▸ **iron out** VT + ADV (*creases*) far sparire col ferro; (*fig: problems, disagreements*) appianare

Iron Curtain N (*Pol*): **the Iron Curtain** la cortina di ferro; **countries behind the Iron Curtain** gli stati d'oltrecortina

iron foundry N fonderia

iron·ic [aɪˈrɒnɪk], **ironi·cal** [aɪˈrɒnɪkəl] ADJ ironico(-a); **it's ironic that ...** è un'ironia (della sorte) che...; **an ironic remark** un commento ironico

ironi·cal·ly [aɪˈrɒnɪkəlɪ] ADV ironicamente; **ironically ...** per ironia...

iron·ing [ˈaɪənɪŋ] N (*act*) stirare *m*; (*clothes*) roba da stirare; **to do the ironing** stirare; **I hate ironing** odio stirare

ironing board N asse *f* da stiro

iron lung N (*Med*) polmone *m* d'acciaio

iron·monger [ˈaɪənˌmʌŋɡəʳ] N (*Brit*): **ironmonger's (shop)** (negozio di) ferramenta

iron ore N minerale *m* di ferro

irons [ˈaɪənz] NPL (*chains*) catene *fpl*

iron·works [ˈaɪənwɜːks] NSG stabilimento siderurgico

iro·ny [ˈaɪərənɪ] N ironia; **the irony of it is that ...** l'ironia maggiore è che...; **it's one of life's ironies** un'ironia della sorte *or* del destino

ir·ra·tion·al [ɪˈræʃənl] ADJ irrazionale; **an irrational fear** una paura irrazionale; **he had become quite irrational about it** era diventato piuttosto irragionevole al riguardo

ir·rec·on·cil·able [ɪˌrekənˈsaɪləbl] (*frm*) ADJ (*persons*) irreconciliabile; (*foes, enemies*) irriducibile; **irreconcilable with** (*opinion, proposal, view*) inconciliabile con

ir·re·deem·able [ˌɪrɪˈdiːməbl] ADJ 1 (*failing*) incorreggibile; (*selfishness*) assoluto(-a) 2 (*Comm*) irredimibile

ir·refu·table [ˌɪrɪˈfjuːtəbl] ADJ irrefutabile

ir·regu·lar [ɪˈreɡjʊləʳ] ADJ irregolare

ir·regu·lar·ity [ɪˌreɡjʊˈlærɪtɪ] N irregolarità *f inv*

ir·rel·evance [ɪˈreləvəns] N non pertinenza

ir·rel·evant [ɪˈreləvənt] ADJ non pertinente; **he either ignored the questions or gave irrelevant answers** o ignorava le domande o dava risposte non pertinenti; **that's irrelevant** non c'entra

ir·re·li·gious [ˌɪrɪˈlɪdʒəs] ADJ irreligioso(-a)

ir·repa·rable [ɪˈrepərəbl] ADJ irrimediabile, irreparabile

ir·re·place·able [ˌɪrɪˈpleɪsəbl] ADJ insostituibile

ir·re·press·ible [ˌɪrɪˈpresəbl] ADJ irrefrenabile

ir·re·proach·able [ˌɪrɪˈprəʊtʃəbl] ADJ (*conduct*) irreprensibile

ir·re·sist·ible [ˌɪrɪˈzɪstəbl] ADJ irresistibile

ir·reso·lute [ɪˈrezəluːt] ADJ (*person, character*) irresoluto(-a), indeciso(-a)

ir·re·spec·tive [ˌɪrɪˈspektɪv] **irrespective of** PREP a prescindere da; **irrespective of the weather** qualunque tempo faccia

ir·re·spon·sible [ˌɪrɪsˈpɒnsəbl] ADJ (*person, behaviour*) irresponsabile

ir·re·triev·able [ˌɪrɪˈtriːvəbl] ADJ (*object*) irrecuperabile; (*loss, damage*) irreparabile

ir·rev·er·ent [ɪˈrevərənt] ADJ irriverente

ir·revo·cable [ɪˈrevəkəbl] ADJ irrevocabile

ir·ri·gate [ˈɪrɪɡeɪt] VT irrigare

ir·ri·ga·tion [ˌɪrɪˈɡeɪʃən] N irrigazione *f*

ir·ri·table [ˈɪrɪtəbl] ADJ irritabile

ir·ri·tant [ˈɪrɪtənt] N (*annoyance*) fastidio; (*substance*) sostanza irritante

ir·ri·tate [ˈɪrɪteɪt] VT (*annoy*) irritare, seccare; (*skin*) irritare

ir·ri·tat·ing [ˈɪrɪteɪtɪŋ] ADJ (*annoying*) irritante, seccante; (*itchy*) irritante

ir·ri·ta·tion [ˌɪrɪˈteɪʃən] N (*gen, also Med*) irritazione *f*; (*fig: irritating thing*) seccatura

IRS [ˌaɪɑːˈres] N ABBR (*USA*) = **Internal Revenue Service**

is [ɪz] 3RD PERS SG PRESENT of **be**

ISBN [ˌaɪesbiːˈen] N ABBR (= *International Standard Book Number*) ISBN *m*

ISDN [ˌaɪesdiːˈen] N ABBR (= *Integrated Service Digital Network*) ISDN *m inv*

Is·lam [ˈɪzlɑːm] N Islam *m inv*

Is·lam·ic [ɪzˈlæmɪk] ADJ islamico(-a); **Islamic countries** paesi islamici

is·land [ˈaɪlənd] N isola; (*also: traffic island*) isola *f* spartitraffico, *inv*, salvagente *m*

is·land·er [ˈaɪləndəʳ] N isolano(-a)

isle [aɪl] N (*liter*) isola; **the Isle of Man** l'isola di Man; **the Isle of Wight** l'isola di Wight

isn't [ˈɪznt] = **is not**

iso·late [ˈaɪsəleɪt] VT (*gen, also Med*): **to isolate (from)** isolare (da); (*pinpoint: cause*) individuare, isolare

iso·lat·ed [ˈaɪsəleɪtɪd] ADJ isolato(-a)

iso·la·tion [ˌaɪsəˈleɪʃən] N isolamento

iso·la·tion·ism [ˌaɪsəˈleɪʃəˌnɪzəm] N isolazionismo

iso·tope [ˈaɪsətəʊp] N isotopo

ISP [ˌaɪesˈpiː] N (= *internet service provider*) provider *m inv*

Is·ra·el [ˈɪzreɪəl] N Israele *m*

Is·rae·li [ɪzˈreɪlɪ] ADJ israeliano(-a), d'Israele ♦ N israeliano(-a)

is·sue [ˈɪʃjuː] N 1 (*matter, question*) questione *f*, problema *m*; **a political issue** una questione politica; **a controversial issue** una questione controversa; **the (real/main) issue is whether ...** la questione (reale/fondamentale) è quella di sapere se...; **to confuse** *or* **obscure the issue** confondere le acque; **to avoid the issue** eludere il (vero) problema; **to face the issue** affrontare la questione; **to make an issue of sth** fare un problema di qc; **the point/matter at issue** il punto in discussione; **to take issue with sb (over sth)** prendere posizione contro qn (riguardo a qc); **I must take issue with you over your last remark** mi dispiace, ma non sono affatto d'accordo sulla tua ultima osservazione 2 (*fam: problem*) problema; **to have issues (with)** avere problemi (con) **3** (*of stamps, banknotes, shares*) emissione *f*; (*of passports, driving licences*) rilascio; (*of rations*) distribuzione *f*; **these coins are a new issue** queste monete sono di recente emissione **4** (*copy: of newspaper, magazine etc*) numero; **back issue** (numero) arretrato; **the March issue** il numero di marzo **5** (*frm: outcome*) risultato, esito **6** (*Law: offspring*) prole *sg*, discendenti *mpl*; **to die without issue** morire senza lasciare discendenti ♦ vt (*book*) pubblicare; (*stamps, cheques, banknotes, shares*) emettere; (*passports, documents*) rilasciare; (*rations, goods, equipment*) distribuire; (*tickets for performance*) mettere in vendita; (*orders*) dare, impartire; (*statement*) rilasciare, diramare; (*warrant, writ, summons*) spiccare, emettere; **the minister issued a statement yesterday** ieri il ministro ha rilasciato una dichiarazione; **to issue sth to sb** *or* **to issue sb with sth** consegnare qc a qn; **the police issued a warning to people to remain indoors** la polizia ha raccomandato alla popolazione di rimanere in casa; **staff will be issued with new uniforms** al personale verranno consegnate nuove uniformi ♦ vi: **to issue (from)** uscire (da), venir fuori (da)

Is·tan·bul [ˌɪstænˈbuːl] N Istanbul *f*

isth·mus [ˈɪsməs] N istmo

IT [ˌaɪˈtiː] N ABBR = **information technology**

<ins>KEYWORD</ins>

it [ɪt] PRON

1 (*specific: subject*) esso(-a) (*often not translated*); (*: direct object*) lo (la), l' (*before vowel*); (*: indirect object*) gli (le); **I spoke to him about it** gliene ho parlato; **she asked him about it yesterday** glielo ha chiesto ieri; **I didn't expect to meet her at it** non mi aspettavo di incontrarci lei; **what's behind it?** cosa ci sta dietro?, cosa c'è lì dietro?; **I doubt it** ne dubito; **I've come from it** vengo da lì; **there's a mistake in it** c'è un errore; **you're just in front of it** ci stai di fronte; **I'm afraid of it** ne ho paura, mi spaventa; **I'm proud of it** ne sono fiero; **it's on it** è lì sopra; **where's my book?** — **it's on the table** dov'è il mio libro? — è sul tavolo; **you won't get anything out of it** non ne ricaverai niente; **put a cover over it** mettici sopra una coperta; **he agreed to it** ha acconsentito; **did you go to it?** ci sei andato?; **there's nothing under it** non ci sta niente sotto, sotto non c'è niente; **have you seen my pen/book?** — **I can't find it anywhere** hai visto la mia penna/il mio libro? — non la/lo trovo da nessuna parte; **here's the book** — **give it back** ecco il libro — dammelo

2 (*impersonal*): **it's the 10th of October** è il 10 ottobre; **I'm against it** sono contrario; **it's cold today** oggi fa freddo; **it's easy to talk** parlare è facile; **I'm (all) for it** sono pro; **it's Friday tomorrow** domani è venerdì; **it's 2 hours on the train** sono *or* ci vogliono 2 ore di treno; **it was kind of you** è stato gentile da parte tua; **it's me** sono io; **how far is it?** — **it's 10 miles** quanto dista? — 10 miglia; **it's 6 o'clock** sono le 6; **it was Peter who phoned** è Peter che ha telefonato; **I like it here,** it's quiet qui mi piace, è tranquillo; **it's raining** sta piovendo, piove; **that's it!** (*approval, agreement*) ecco!, è proprio così!; (*disapproval*) basta!; (*finishing*) (questo) è tutto; **it's no use worrying** preoccuparsi è inutile; **what is it?** (*what do you want?*) cosa c'è?; **where is it?** dov'è?; **who is it?** chi è?

3 (*in games*): **you're it!** tocca a te!

ITA [ˌaɪtiːˈeɪ] N ABBR (*Brit:* = *initial teaching alphabet*) alfabeto fonetico semplificato per insegnare a leggere

Ital·ian [ɪˈtæljən] ADJ italiano(-a); (*lesson, teacher, dictionary*) d'italiano; (*king*) d'Italia; **our Italian teacher** il nostro insegnante di italiano ♦ N (*person*) italiano(-a); (*language*) italiano; **the Italians** gli italiani; **can you speak Italian?** parli italiano?

ital·ic [ɪˈtælɪk] ADJ (*handwriting*) corsivo(-a)

Ita·ly [ˈɪtəlɪ] N l'Italia; **in Italy** in Italia; **do you like Italy?** ti piace l'Italia?

itch [ɪtʃ] N prurito; **to have an itch to do sth** (*fig*) avere la smania di fare qc ♦ vi (*person*) avere prurito; (*part of body*) prudere; **my leg itches** mi prude la gamba; **to be itching for sth/to do sth** (*fig: fam*) aver una gran voglia di qc/di fare qc

itchy [ˈɪtʃɪ] ADJ (*comp* **-ier,** *superl* **-iest**) (*feeling*) di prurito; **my leg is itchy** ho prurito alla gamba

it'd [ˈɪtd] PRON = **it would; it had**

item [ˈaɪtəm] N (*in list, catalogue, newspaper*) articolo; (*in bill, account*) voce *f*; (*on agenda*) argomento *or* punto all'ordine del giorno; (*in programme*) numero; **items of clothing** capi *mpl* di abbigliamento; **an item of news** una notizia; **the main item of news** la notizia più importante; **a collector's item** un articolo da collezione; **the first item he bought was an alarm clock** il primo oggetto che ha comprato è stato una sveglia; **he checked the items on his bill** ha controllato le voci del conto; **the next item on the agenda is …** il prossimo punto all'ordine del giorno è …

item·ize [ˈaɪtəˌmaɪz] vt specificare (uno(-a) per uno(-a)), dettagliare

item·ized bill [ˈaɪtəˌmaɪzd'bɪl] N (*of restaurant etc*) conto dettagliato; (*Telec*) bolletta con documentazione del traffico telefonico

itin·er·ant [ɪˈtɪnərənt] ADJ (*actors*) girovago(-a); (*seller*) ambulante; (*preacher*) itinerante

itin·er·ary [aɪˈtɪnərərɪ] N itinerario

it'll [ˈɪtl] PRON = **it will; it shall**

its [ɪts] POSS ADJ il suo (la sua); *pl* i suoi (le sue); **the dog hurt its paw** il cane si è fatto male alla zampa; **this doll has lost its leg** questa bambola ha perso una gamba; **the party has concluded its annual conference** il partito ha concluso la sua conferenza annuale; **the dog is losing its hair** il cane sta perdendo il pelo

it's [ɪts] PRON = **it is; it has**

it·self [ɪtˈself] PRON **1** (*reflexive*) si; **the dog injured itself** il cane si è fatto male; **the cat is washing itself** il gatto si pulisce; **the door closed by itself** la porta si è chiusa da sé; **the heating switches itself off** il riscaldamento si spegne da solo **2** (*emphatic*): **by itself** da solo; **in itself** di per sé; **it's not a problem in itself** non è un problema di per sé; **the theatre itself** il teatro stesso; **life itself** la vita stessa; **Barra, itself a beautiful island …** Barra, di per sé un'isola bellissima…

IUD [ˌaɪjuːˈdiː] N ABBR (= *intra-uterine device*) IUD *m inv*

I've [aɪv] = **I have**

ivo·ry [ˈaɪvərɪ] N avorio ♦ ADJ (*colour*) avorio *inv*; (*object*) d'avorio

Ivory Coast N: **the Ivory Coast** la Costa d'Avorio

ivory tower N torre *f* d'avorio

ivy [ˈaɪvɪ] N (*Bot*) edera

Ivy League N le otto università più prestigiose del Nord-Est degli Stati Uniti (*Brown, Columbia, Cornell, Dartmouth College, Harvard, Princeton, University of Pennsylvania e Yale*)

J j

J, j [dʒeɪ] N (*letter*) J, j *f inv, m inv*; **J for Jack**, (*USA*) **J for Jig** ≈ J come jolly

jab [dʒæb] N (*poke*) colpo (di punta); (*Boxing*) diretto; (*fam: injection*) puntura ♦ VT: **to jab sth into** conficcare qc in; **she jabbed the needle into my arm** mi ha conficcato l'ago nel braccio; **to jab a finger at sb** puntare un dito contro qn ♦ VI: **to jab at** dare colpi a

jab·ber [ˈdʒæbə'] VI (*person*) ciarlare, chiacchierare; (*monkey*) schiamazzare; **they were jabbering away in Russian** parlavano fitto fitto in russo ♦ VT farfugliare, borbottare ♦ N (*of person*) chiacchierio, cicaleccio; (*of monkey*) schiamazzo

jack [dʒæk] N (*Tech, Aut*) cric m *inv*; (*Cards*) fante m; (*Bowls*) boccino, pallino; **the jack's in the trunk** il cric è nel cofano; **before you could say Jack Robinson** (*fam*) in men che non si dica

▸ **jack up** VT + ADV **1** (*Tech, Aut*) sollevare con il cric **2** (*fam: raise: prices, wages*) alzare

jack·al [ˈdʒækɔːl] N sciacallo

jack·ass [ˈdʒækˌæs] N (*also fig: old*) asino, somaro

jack·daw [ˈdʒækˌdɔː] N taccola

jack·et [ˈdʒækɪt] N (*garment*) giacca; (*of book*) sovraccopertina; (*of boiler*) incamiciatura; (*of potato*) buccia; **wool jacket** giacca di lana

jacket potato N *patata cotta al forno con la buccia*

jack-in-the-box [ˈdʒækɪnðəˌbɒks] N (*toy*) *scatola con pupazzo a molla*; **she popped up like a jack-in-the-box** è saltata fuori dal nulla

jack-knife [ˈdʒækˌnaɪf] N coltello a serramanico ♦ VI: **the truck jack-knifed** il rimorchio del camion si è messo di traverso

jack-of-all-trades [ˌdʒækəvˈɔːlˌtreɪdz] N uno(-a) che sa fare un po' di tutto

jack plug N (*Brit*) jack m *inv*

jack·pot [ˈdʒækˌpɒt] N primo premio (in denaro); **he won the jackpot** ha vinto il primo premio; **to hit the jackpot** (*fam*) vincere il primo premio (*fig*) fare centro

jade [dʒeɪd] N (*stone*) giada; (*colour: also:* **jade green**) verde m giada, *inv* ♦ ADJ (*statue, carving, necklace*) di giada; (*also:* **jade-green**) verde giada *inv*

jad·ed [ˈdʒeɪdɪd] ADJ (*person*) annoiato(-a), sfibrato(-a); **to have a jaded appetite** essere un po' svogliato(-a) nel mangiare

jag·ged [ˈdʒægɪd] ADJ (*edge*) dentellato(-a), irregolare; (*rock, cliffs*) frastagliato(-a)

jagu·ar [ˈdʒægjuə'] N giaguaro

jail, gaol (*Brit*) [dʒeɪl] N carcere m, prigione f; **in jail** in prigione; **to go to jail** andare in prigione; **to send sb to jail** mandare qn in prigione ♦ VT mandare in prigione; **he was jailed for 10 years** è stato condannato a 10 anni di carcere

jail·bird, gaol·bird (*Brit*) [ˈdʒeɪlˌbɜːd] N (*fam, old*) avanzo di galera

jail·break [ˈdʒeɪlˌbreɪk] N evasione f

jail·er, gaol·er (*Brit*) [ˈdʒeɪlə'] N carceriere m

ja·lopy [dʒəˈlɒpɪ] N (*fam: old car*) macinino, carretta

jam¹ [dʒæm] N (*food*) marmellata, confettura; **strawberry jam** marmellata di fragole ♦ ADJ (*tart*) alla marmellata; (*sandwich*) con la marmellata

jam² [dʒæm] VT **1** (*block: mechanism, drawer*) bloccare; (*: machine*) far inceppare; (*subj: people, cars: passage, exit*) bloccare, ingombrare, ostruire; (*Radio: station, broadcast*) disturbare con interferenze; **to jam a door open** (*or shut*) bloccare una porta; **streets jammed with people** strade molto affollate; **streets jammed with cars** strade congestionate; **demonstrators jammed the city centre** i manifestanti hanno bloccato il centro; **the telephone lines are jammed** le linee sono sovraccariche; **to jam one's brakes on** frenare

bruscamente **2** (*cram*): **to jam sth into sth** (*drawer, suitcase*) ficcare *or* infilare qc a forza dentro qc; (*room, vehicle*) far entrare qc dentro qc; **I jammed my finger in the door** mi sono schiacciato il dito nella porta ♦ VI **1** (*get stuck: mechanism, sliding part*) bloccarsi, incepparsi; (*: gun*) incepparsi **2** (*press tightly: people*): **to jam into** affollare; **twenty people jammed into the tiny office** venti persone erano ammassate nel piccolo ufficio **3** (*Mus: fam*) improvvisare ♦ N **1** (*of people*) folla, calca; (*of shoppers*) ressa; (*of cars: also:* **traffic jam**) ingorgo **2** (*fig: fam*): **to be in/get into a jam** essere/ficcarsi nei pasticci; **to get sb out of a jam** tirare qn fuori dai pasticci

Ja·mai·ca [dʒəˈmeɪkə] N la Giamaica

Ja·mai·can [dʒəˈmeɪkən] ADJ, N giamaicano(-a)

jamb [dʒæm] N stipite m

jam-packed [ˌdʒæmˈpækt] ADJ: **jam-packed (with)** pieno(-a) zeppo(-a) (di), strapieno(-a) (di)

jam session N (*Mus: fam*) jam-session *f inv*

Jan. ABBR (= *January*) gen., genn. (= gennaio)

jan·gle [ˈdʒæŋgl] VI (*bells*) scampanellare; (*bracelets, keys, chains*) tintinnare ♦ VT far risuonare ♦ N (*see vi*) scampanio; tintinnio

jani·tor [ˈdʒænɪtə'] (*esp USA, Scot*) N (*caretaker*) custode m; (*Scol*) bidello

Janu·ary [ˈdʒænjuərɪ] N gennaio; **in January** in gennaio; *see* **July**

Ja·pan [dʒəˈpæn] N il Giappone m

Japa·nese [ˌdʒæpəˈniːz] ADJ giapponese ♦ N (*person: pl inv*) giapponese m/f; (*language*) giapponese m; **the Japanese** i giapponesi

jar¹ [dʒɑː'] N (*container*) vasetto; (*of glass*) barattolo; (*of earthenware*) vaso; **jar of honey** vasetto di miele

jar² [dʒɑː'] VI (*clash: sounds*) stridere; **to jar (with)** (*colours*) stonare (con); (*opinions*) discordare (da); **to jar on sb's nerves** dare ai nervi a qn; **to jar on sb's ears** dar fastidio alle orecchie di qn ♦ VT (*also fig*) scuotere; (*elbow*) urtare ♦ N (*jolt*) scossa, scossone m; (*fig*) colpo, scossone

jar·gon [ˈdʒɑːgən] N gergo

jar·ring [ˈdʒɑːrɪŋ] ADJ (*sound, colour*) stonato(-a); **to strike a jarring note (in, at)** (*fig*) portare una nota stonata (in, a)

Jas. ABBR = James

jas·mine [ˈdʒæzmɪn] N gelsomino

jaun·dice [ˈdʒɔːndɪs] N itterizia

jaun·diced [ˈdʒɔːndɪst] ADJ (*fig: cynical*) cinico(-a); (*Med*) itterico(-a); **with a jaundiced eye** con occhio cinico; **to have** *or* **take a jaundiced view of things** vedere le cose cinicamente

jaunt [dʒɔːnt] N gita; **to go for a jaunt** fare una gita

jaun·ty [ˈdʒɔːntɪ] ADJ baldanzoso(-a); **at a jaunty angle** (*hat*) sulle ventitré

Java [ˈdʒɑːvə] N (*Geog*) Giava; (*Comput*) Java m

jave·lin [ˈdʒævlɪn] N giavellotto; **to throw the javelin** (*Sport*) lanciare il giavellotto; **javelin throwing** lancio del giavellotto

jaw [dʒɔː] N **1** (*Anat*) mascella; **my jaw dropped** sono rimasto a bocca aperta; **the jaws of death** le braccia della morte; **to snatch victory from the jaws of defeat** strappare una vittoria ormai insperata **2 jaws** NPL (*Tech: of vice, machine*) ganascia

jaw·bone [ˈdʒɔːbəʊn] N mandibola

jay [dʒeɪ] N ghiandaia

jay·walk·er [ˈdʒeɪˌwɔːkə'] N pedone m indisciplinato (*nell'attraversare la strada*)

jazz [dʒæz] N (*Mus*) jazz m; **... and all that jazz** (*fig, fam, usu pej*) ...eccetera eccetera

▸ **jazz up** VT + ADV **1** (*party, room, outfit*) vivacizzare **2**

(Mus: play) suonare a ritmo di jazz; *(: arrange)* adattare a ritmo di jazz

jazz band N banda *f* jazz, *inv*

jazzy [ˈdʒæzɪ] ADJ *(comp* -**ier**, *superl* -**iest**) *(pattern, design)* vistoso(-a), chiassoso(-a); *(rhythm)* jazzistico(-a)

JCS [ˌdʒeɪsiːˈes] N ABBR *(USA)* = **Joint Chiefs of Staff**

JD [ˌdʒeɪˈdiː] N ABBR *(USA)* **1** *(= Doctor of Laws)* ≈ dottore *m* in legge **2** *(= Justice Department)* ≈ Ministero della Giustizia

jeal·ous [ˈdʒeləs] ADJ: **jealous (of)** geloso(-a) (di); **to make sb jealous** far ingelosire qn

jeal·ous·ly [ˈdʒeləslɪ] ADV *(enviously)* con gelosia; *(possessively)* gelosamente

jeal·ousy [ˈdʒeləsɪ] N gelosia

jeans [dʒiːnz] NPL jeans *mpl*

jeep [dʒiːp] N jeep *f inv*

jeer [dʒɪəʳ] N grido di scherno ♦ VI: **to jeer (at sb)** schernire (qn)

jeer·ing [ˈdʒɪərɪŋ] ADJ *(crowd)* che lancia grida di scherno; *(remark, laughter)* di scherno ♦ N grida *fpl* di scherno

jel·ly [ˈdʒelɪ] N gelatina; **fruit jelly** gelatina di frutta

jelly·fish [ˈdʒelɪˌfɪʃ] N medusa

jeop·ard·ize [ˈdʒepədaɪz] VT mettere in pericolo, mettere a repentaglio

jeop·ardy [ˈdʒepədɪ] N: **in jeopardy** a rischio, in pericolo; **to place** *or* **put in jeopardy** mettere a repentaglio *or* in pericolo

jerk [dʒɜːk] VT *(pull)* tirare con uno strattone; **he jerked it away from me** me l'ha strappato di mano ♦ VI muoversi a scatti; **to jerk along** procedere a sbalzi; **the bus jerked to a halt** l'autobus si fermò con un sobbalzo ♦ N **1** *(movement)* sobbalzo, scossa; *(reflex)* spasmo muscolare, contrazione *f* nervosa; **he sat up with a jerk** balzò a sedere di scatto **2** *(esp USA: fam)* stronzo

jer·kin [ˈdʒɜːkɪn] N gilè *m inv*

jerky [ˈdʒɜːkɪ] ADJ *(comp* -**ier**, *superl* -**iest**) *(motion, speech)* convulso(-a), a scatti; *(ride)* pieno(-a) di scossoni

jerry-built [ˈdʒerɪˌbɪlt] ADJ costruito con materiali scadenti

jer·ry can [ˈdʒerɪˌkæn] N tanica

Jer·sey [ˈdʒɜːzɪ] N *(island)* Jersey *f*; **a Jersey (cow)** una mucca di razza Jersey

jer·sey [ˈdʒɜːzɪ] N *(garment)* maglia; *(fabric)* jersey *m*

Je·ru·sa·lem [dʒəˈruːsələm] N Gerusalemme *f*

jest [dʒest] N scherzo, facezia; **in jest** per scherzo ♦ VI scherzare

jest·er [ˈdʒestəʳ] N *(also:* **court jester)** buffone *m* (di corte)

Jesus [ˈdʒiːzəs] N Gesù *m*; **Jesus Christ** Gesù Cristo

jet [dʒet] N **1** *(plane)* jet *m inv*, aereo a reazione **2** *(of liquid, steam, gas)* getto; *(of fountain)* zampillo **3** *(nozzle: of gas burner)* becco, ugello; *(Aut)* spruzzatore *m* ♦ ADJ *(aircraft, propulsion)* a reazione; *(fuel)* per aviogetto ♦ VI *(fam: fly)* volare

jet-black [ˌdʒetˈblæk] ADJ nero(-a) come l'ebano; **jet-black hair** capelli *mpl* corvini

jet engine N motore *m* a reazione

jet lag N jet lag *m inv*; **to be suffering from jet lag** essere scombussolato(-a) per il cambiamento di fuso orario

jet·sam [ˈdʒetsəm] N oggetti gettati in mare e portati a riva dalla corrente; *see also* **flotsam**

jet-setter [ˈdʒetˌsetəʳ] N membro del jet set

Jet Ski N acquascooter *m inv*, moto *f inv* d'acqua

jet·ti·son [ˈdʒetɪsn] VT *(burden)* alleggerirsi di; *(hopes, chances)* abbandonare; *(Naut)* gettare in mare

jet·ty [ˈdʒetɪ] N *(landing pier)* imbarcadero; *(breakwater)* molo

Jew [dʒuː] N ebreo(-a); **the Jews** gli ebrei

jew·el [ˈdʒuːəl] N *(stone)* pietra preziosa; *(ornament)* gioiello; *(of watch)* rubino; *(fig)* gioiello, perla

jew·el·ler, jew·el·er *(USA)* [ˈdʒuːələʳ] N gioielliere(-a), orefice *m*; **jeweller's (shop)** gioielleria, oreficeria

jew·el·lery, jew·el·ry *(USA)* [ˈdʒuːəlrɪ] N gioielli *mpl*, gioie *fpl*; **a piece of jewellery** un gioiello; **jewellery box** (cofanetto) portagioie *m inv*

Jew·ish [ˈdʒuːɪʃ] ADJ *(mother, people)* ebreo(-a); *(festival, religion, tradition)* ebraico(-a); **he's Jewish** è ebreo; **Jewish festival** festività ebraica

jib¹ [dʒɪb] VI *(horse)* impennarsi; *(person)* impuntarsi, recalcitrare; **to jib at doing sth** essere restio(-a) a fare qc

jib² [dʒɪb] N *(Naut)* fiocco; *(of crane)* braccio

jibe [dʒaɪb] N = **gibe** ♦ VI *(USA)* combaciare, corrispondere

jif·fy [ˈdʒɪfɪ] N *(fam)*: **in a jiffy** in un baleno, in un batter d'occhio; **wait a jiffy** aspetta un attimo

jig [dʒɪg] N *(dance, tune)* giga

jig·saw [ˈdʒɪgsɔː] N **1** *(also:* **jigsaw puzzle)** puzzle *m inv* **2** *(tool)* sega da traforo

jilt [dʒɪlt] VT piantare *(fidanzato(a))*

jin·gle [ˈdʒɪŋgl] N *(of keys, coins)* tintinnio; *(of bells)* scampanellio; *(advert)* jingle *m inv*, ritornello pubblicitario ♦ VT *(see n)* far tintinnare; far scampanellare ♦ VI *(see n)* tintinnare; scampanellare

jin·go·ism [ˈdʒɪŋgəʊˌɪzəm] N sciovinismo

jinx [dʒɪŋks] N *(curse)* malocchio; *(person)* iettatore(-trice); *(thing)* cosa che porta sfortuna; **to be a jinx** portare iella; **there's a jinx on him** è iellato; **to put a jinx on sb** gettare il malocchio su qn

jit·ters [ˈdʒɪtəz] NPL *(fam)* fifa *fsg*; **to have the jitters** avere fifa; **to get the jitters** prendersi uno spavento

jit·tery [ˈdʒɪtərɪ] ADJ *(fam)* nervoso(-a), agitato(-a)

jiu·jit·su [dʒuːˈdʒɪtsuː] N = **jujitsu**

job [dʒɒb] N **1** *(work)* lavoro; *(post)* posto, impiego; **to look for a job** cercare lavoro; **to be out of a job** essere disoccupato(-a) *or* senza lavoro; **a part-time job** un lavoro part-time *or* a mezza giornata; **a full-time job** un lavoro a tempo pieno; **the government is creating new jobs** il governo sta creando nuovi posti di lavoro **2** *(piece of work)* lavoro; *(task)* compito; **on the job** sul lavoro; **to make a good/bad job of sth** fare bene/male qc; **you've done a good job!** hai fatto un ottimo lavoro!; **he's done a good job of work** ha fatto un buon lavoro; **that's not my job** non è compito mio; **to know one's job** conoscere il proprio mestiere; **he's only doing his job** sta solo facendo il suo dovere; **I had the job of telling him** è stato compito mio dirglielo; **that car is a nice little job** *(fam)* quella macchina è un gioiellino **3 to give sth up as a bad job** lasciar perdere qc perché è un'impresa impossibile; **it's a good job that ...** meno male che...; **a good job too!** meno male!; **he was caught doing a bank job** *(fam)* l'hanno preso mentre faceva un colpo alla banca

job·ber [ˈdʒɒbəʳ] N *(Brit: Stock Exchange)* jobber *m/f inv*, intermediario tra agenti di cambio

job·bing [ˈdʒɒbɪŋ] ADJ *(Brit: worker, gardener)* a cottimo

job description N mansionario, descrizione *f* delle mansioni *(relative ad un lavoro)*

job·less [ˈdʒɒblɪs] ADJ disoccupato(-a) ♦ **the jobless** NPL i disoccupati, i senza lavoro *m inv*

job lot N partita di articoli disparati

job satisfaction N soddisfazione *f* nel lavoro

job security N sicurezza del posto di lavoro

job share VI fare un lavoro ripartito ♦ N lavoro ripartito

job specification N specifica *(relativa ad un lavoro)*

Jock [dʒɒk] N *(Brit fam, pej)* termine spregiativo usato dagli inglesi per chiamare uno scozzese

jock·ey [ˈdʒɒkɪ] N fantino ♦ VI: **to jockey for position** *(fig)* manovrare per mettersi in una posizione vantaggiosa ♦ VT: **to jockey sb into doing sth** indurre qn a fare qc (con manovre)

jock·strap [ˈdʒɒkˌstræp] N sospensorio, conchiglia

jocu·lar [ˈdʒɒkjʊləʳ] ADJ *(person)* gioviale; *(remark)* scherzoso(-a)

jog [dʒɒg] VI *(Sport)* fare jogging ♦ VT *(push)* urtare, spingere; *(fig)*: **to jog sb's memory** rinfrescare la memoria a qn; **to jog sb into doing sth** *(fig)* spingere qn a fare qc ♦ N **1** *(pace)* *(also:* **jog trot)** passo lento di corsa; *(of horse)* piccolo trotto; *(run)*: **to go for a jog** andare a fare jogging **2** *(push)* spinta, colpetto

jog·ger [ˈdʒɒgəʳ] N persona che fa jogging

jog·ging [ˈdʒɒgɪŋ] N *(Sport)* jogging *m*; **to go jogging** andare a fare jogging

john [dʒɒn] N *(esp USA: fam)*: **the john** il gabinetto

join [dʒɔɪn] VT **1** *(fasten)*: **to join (together)** unire, congiungere; *(link)* collegare *(fig)* unire; **to join hands** prendersi per mano; **to join battle (with)** *(frm)* attaccare battaglia (con); **to join A and B** *or* **A to B** unire A e B *or* A a B; **to join forces**

(with) allearsi (con *or* a); (*fig*) mettersi insieme (a) **2** (*procession*) unirsi a; (*club*) divenire socio(-a) di; (*university*) entrare a; (*army, navy, religious order, firm*) entrare in; (*political party*) iscriversi a; **to join a queue** mettersi in fila; **to join one's ship** imbarcarsi; **to join one's regiment** raggiungere il proprio reggimento; **I'm going to join a ski club** ho intenzione di iscrivermi ad uno sci club **3** (*person*) unirsi a; **may I join you?, do you mind if I join you?** posso?, permette?; **will you join us?** (*come with us*) viene con noi?; (*in restaurant, bar*) vuole sedersi con noi?; **will you join us for dinner?** viene a cena con noi?; **hi Tony, come and join us!** ciao Tony, siediti qui con noi!; **will you join me for a coffee?** vieni a bere un caffè?; **will you join me in a drink?** posso offrirle qualcosa da bere?; **I'll join you later** vi raggiungo più tardi; **they joined us in protesting** si sono uniti a noi nel protestare **4** (*river*) confluire in, gettarsi in; (*road*) immettersi in ♦ VI **1 to join** (*together*) (*parts, people*) unirsi; (*lines*) incontrarsi; (*roads*) congiungersi; (*rivers*) confluire; **the parking lots are joined by a footpath** i parcheggi sono collegati da un sentiero **2** (*club member*) divenire socio(-a) ♦ N (*in wood, wallpaper*) giuntura; (*Sewing*) cucitura
  ▸ **join in** VI + PREP (*game, discussion, protest*) prendere parte a, partecipare a; **they all joined in the chorus** tutti si unirono al ritornello ♦ VI + ADV partecipare; (*in singing*): **join in!** cantate con noi!
  ▸ **join on** VT + ADV fissare, attaccare ♦ VI + ADV (*in queue*) mettersi in coda; (*part*) unirsi
  ▸ **join up** VI + ADV (*Mil*) arruolarsi ♦ VT + ADV (*wires*) unire, collegare

join·er ['dʒɔɪnə'] N falegname *m*
join·ery ['dʒɔɪnərɪ] N falegnameria
joint [dʒɔɪnt] ADJ (*action, effort, work*) comune; (*responsibility*) collettivo(-a); (*committee*) misto(-a); **joint authors** coautori(-trici); **to make a joint declaration on sth** rilasciare una dichiarazione congiunta su qc ♦ N **1** (*Anat*) articolazione *f*, giuntura; **I' ve got pains in my joints** ho dolori alle articolazioni; **out of joint** slogato(-a); **to put sb's nose out of joint** (*fig: fam*) far indispettire qn **2** (*join*) giuntura, giunto **3** (*Brit: of meat*) pezzo di carne; (*: cooked*) arrosto (*al forno*); **joint of pork** pezzo di maiale da arrosto **4** (*fam, place, esp USA*) locale *m* **5** (*fam: cannabis cigarette*) spinello ♦ VT (*chicken*) tagliare a pezzi
joint account N (*at bank*) conto comune
joint·ly ['dʒɔɪntlɪ] ADV (*held, funded*) in comune; (*agree, organize, act*) di comune accordo
joint ownership N comproprietà
joint-stock company [,dʒɔɪnt'stɒk,kʌmpənɪ] N società *f inv* per azioni
joist [dʒɔɪst] N trave *f*
joke [dʒəʊk] N (*verbal*) battuta; (*practical joke*) scherzo; (*funny story*) barzelletta; **to tell a joke** raccontare una barzelletta; **to make a joke about sth** fare una battuta su qc; **for a joke** per scherzo; **what a joke!** (*iro*) che bello scherzo!; **it's no joke** non è uno scherzo; **the joke is that ...** la cosa buffa è che...; **the joke is on you** chi ci perde, comunque, sei tu; **it's (gone) beyond a joke** lo scherzo sta diventando pesante; **to play a joke on sb** fare uno scherzo a qn; **I don't see the joke** non capisco cosa ci sia da ridere; **he can't take a joke** non sa stare allo scherzo; **don't get upset, it was only a joke** non prendertela, era solo uno scherzo ♦ VI scherzare; **I was only joking** stavo solo scherzando; **you're** *or* **you must be joking!** stai scherzando!, scherzi!
jok·er ['dʒəʊkə'] N **1** (*amusing*) burlone(-a); (*fam, pej*) buffone(-a) **2** (*Cards*) jolly *m inv*, matta
jok·ing ['dʒəʊkɪŋ] ADJ scherzoso(-a) ♦ N scherzi *mpl*
jol·lity ['dʒɒlɪtɪ] N allegria
jol·ly ['dʒɒlɪ] ADJ (*comp* -ier, *superl* -iest) (*person*) allegro(-a), gioviale; (*laugh*) allegro(-a), gioioso(-a); (*old: party*) piacevole ♦ ADV (*Brit fam*) veramente, proprio; **he's jolly lucky!** è fortunatissimo!; (*old*) benissimo! ♦ VT: **to jolly sb along** (*Brit: cheer up*) cercare di tenere qn su di morale; (*: encourage*) incoraggiare dolcemente qn
jolt [dʒəʊlt] VT (*gen*) urtare; (*fig*) scuotere; **to jolt sb into doing sth** spingere qn a fare qc ♦ VI (*vehicle*) sobbalzare; **to jolt along** avanzare a sbalzi ♦ N (*jerk*) scossa, sobbalzo; (*fig*) colpo; **it gave me a jolt** (*fig*) mi ha fatto venire un colpo

Jor·dan ['dʒɔːdn] N (*country*) la Giordania; (*river*) Giordano
Jor·da·nian [dʒɔː'deɪnɪən] ADJ, N giordano(-a)
joss stick ['dʒɒs,stɪk] N bastoncino d'incenso
jos·tle ['dʒɒsl] VT urtare, spintonare ♦ VI darsi gomitate; **to jostle against sb** urtare qn; **to jostle for a place** farsi largo a gomitate
jot [dʒɒt] N briciolo; **there's not a jot of evidence** non c'è la ben che minima prova; **not one jot** nemmeno un po'
  ▸ **jot down** VT + ADV (*ideas, notes*) buttar giù; (*address, number*) prendere
jot·ter ['dʒɒtə'] N (*Brit*) blocchetto
jour·nal ['dʒɜːnl] N (*periodical*) rivista (specializzata); (*newspaper*) giornale *m*; (*diary*) diario; (*Book-keeping*) brogliaccio; **scientific journal** rivista scientifica; **he keeps a journal** tiene un diario
jour·nal·ese [,dʒɜːnə'liːz] N (*pej*) giornalese
jour·nal·ism ['dʒɜːnə,lɪzəm] N giornalismo
jour·nal·ist ['dʒɜːnəlɪst] N giornalista *m/f*
jour·ney ['dʒɜːnɪ] N (*trip*) viaggio; (*distance, time*) tragitto; **to go on a journey** fare un viaggio; **a 5-hour journey** un viaggio *or* un tragitto di 5 ore; **my journey to school takes about half an hour** mi ci vuole una mezz'ora per andare a scuola; **to reach one's journey's end** (*liter*) giungere a destinazione; **the outward/return journey** il viaggio di andata/di ritorno; **the journey there and back** il viaggio di andata e ritorno ♦ VI viaggiare
jo·vial ['dʒəʊvɪəl] ADJ gioviale
jowl [dʒaʊl] N (*cheek*) guancia; (*jaw*) mandibola; **a man with heavy jowls** un uomo con le guance cascanti
joy [dʒɔɪ] N gioia; **to jump for joy** fare salti di gioia; **I wish you joy of it!** (*iro*) buon pro ti faccia!; **the joys of camping** (*also iro*) i piaceri del campeggio; **did you have any joy?** ci sei riuscito?; **no joy!** (*fam*) niente da fare!
joy·ful ['dʒɔɪfʊl] ADJ (*happy*) lieto(-a); (*cheerful*) gioioso(-a)
joy·ride ['dʒɔɪ,raɪd] VI: **to go joy-riding** rubare una macchina per farsi un giro ♦ N: **to go for a joy-ride** rubare una macchina per farsi un giro
joy·rider ['dʒɔɪ,raɪdə'] N chi ruba una macchina per farsi un giro
joy·stick ['dʒɔɪ,stɪk] N (*Aer*) barra di comando; (*Comput*) joystick *m inv*
JP [,dʒeɪ'piː] N ABBR = **Justice of the Peace**
Jr ABBR = **junior**
ju·bi·lant ['dʒuːbɪlənt] ADJ giubilante; **to be jubilant** essere esultante
ju·bi·la·tion [,dʒuːbɪ'leɪʃən] N (*emotion*) giubilo; **she was full of jubilation at the news of her win** esultò quando seppe di aver vinto
ju·bi·lee ['dʒuːbɪ,liː] N giubileo; **silver jubilee** venticinquesimo anniversario
judge [dʒʌdʒ] N giudice *m*; **to be a good/bad judge of sth** sapere/non sapere giudicare qc; **I'm no judge of wines** non sono un intenditore di vini; **he's no judge of character** non sa giudicare le persone ♦ VT (*Law: assess*) giudicare; (*estimate: weight, size*) calcolare, valutare; (*consider*) ritenere; **he judged the moment well** ha saputo scegliere il momento giusto; **I judged it necessary to inform him** ho ritenuto necessario informarlo; **I judged it to be right** l'ho ritenuto giusto ♦ VI (*act as judge*) fare da giudice; **judging** *or* **to judge by his expression** a giudicare dalla sua espressione; **to judge for o.s.** giudicare da sé; **as far as I can judge** a mio giudizio
judge advocate N (*Brit Mil*) magistrato militare
judg·ment, judge·ment ['dʒʌdʒmənt] N giudizio; **error of judgement** errore *m* di valutazione; **to pass judgement (on)** (*Law*) pronunciare una sentenza (nei confronti di); (*fig*) giudicare; **in my judgement** a mio giudizio; **it's against my better judgement, but ...** non ne sono affatto convinto, ma...
ju·di·cial [dʒuː'dɪʃəl] ADJ **1** (*enquiry, decision*) giudiziario(-a); **to bring judicial proceedings against sb** procedere per vie legali contro qn **2** (*mind, faculty*) critico(-a)
ju·di·ci·ary [dʒuː'dɪʃɪərɪ] N: **the judiciary** la magistratura
ju·di·cious [dʒuː'dɪʃəs] ADJ (*frm*) giudizioso(-a)
judo ['dʒuːdəʊ] N judo
jug [dʒʌg] N **1** (*container*) brocca, caraffa; (*for milk*) lattiera, bricco **2** (*fam: prison*) gattabuia

jugged hare [ˌdʒʌgd'hɛəʳ] N (*Brit*) lepre *f* in salmì

jug·ger·naut ['dʒʌgənɔːt] N (*Brit: truck*) bisonte *m* della strada

jug·gle ['dʒʌgl] VI fare giochi di destrezza ♦ VT fare giochi di destrezza con; (*fig*) manipolare

jug·gler ['dʒʌgləʳ] N giocoliere *m*

Ju·go·slav ['juːgəʊˌslɑːv] ADJ, N = Yugoslav

jugu·lar ['dʒʌgjʊləʳ] N (*also:* **jugular vein**) (vena) giugulare *f*

juice [dʒuːs] N 1 (*of fruit*) succo; (*of meat*) sugo; **orange juice** succo d'arancia 2 (*in stomach*); **juices** NPL succhi *mpl* gastrici 3 (*fam: petrol*) benzina; (: *electricity*) corrente *f*; **turn on the juice** accendi la luce

juicy ['dʒuːsɪ] ADJ (*comp* **-ier**, *superl* **-iest**) (*fruit*) succoso(-a); (*meat*) sugoso(-a); (*story*) piccante

juke·box ['dʒuːkˌbɒks] N juke-box *m inv*

Jul. ABBR (= *July*) lug., lu. (= *luglio*)

July [dʒuː'laɪ] N luglio; **the first of July** il primo luglio; **(on) the eleventh of July** l'undici luglio; **in July** in luglio; **in the month of July** nel mese di luglio; **at the beginning/end of July** all'inizio/alla fine di luglio; **in the middle of July** a metà luglio; **during July** durante (il mese di) luglio; **in July of next year** a luglio dell'anno prossimo; **each** *or* **every July** ogni anno a luglio; **July was wet this year** è piovuto molto a luglio, quest'anno

jum·ble ['dʒʌmbl] N 1 (*of objects, ideas*) miscuglio, accozzaglia; **a meaningless jumble of words** un miscuglio di parole senza senso 2 (*old clothes etc*) roba usata ♦ VT (*also:* **jumble together**, **jumble up**) mettere alla rinfusa

jum·bo ['dʒʌmbəʊ] ADJ (*fam*) maxi *inv*; **jumbo size** formato gigante ♦ N (*also:* **jumbo jet**) jumbo *m inv* (jet, *m inv*)

jump [dʒʌmp] VI (*gen: Sport*) saltare; (*in fright*) fare un salto, trasalire; (*prices*) aumentare di colpo; **to jump about** fare salti, saltellare; **to jump over sth** saltare oltre qc; **they jumped over the wall** hanno saltato oltre il muro; **to jump in/out** saltare dentro/fuori; **to jump off/on(to) sth** saltare giù da/su qc; **to jump out (of) the window** saltare giù dalla finestra; **to jump out of bed** saltare fuori dal letto; **he jumped into a taxi** è saltato su un tassì; **she jumped to her feet** si alzò di scatto, balzò in piedi; **to jump up** saltare in piedi; **to jump down** saltare giù; **to jump up and down** saltellare; **there's no need to jump down my throat!** (*fam*) non è il caso di aggredirmi così!; **you made me jump!** mi hai spaventato!; **I almost jumped out of my skin!** (*fam*) ho fatto un salto!; **jump to it!** (*fam*) presto, sbrigati!; **to jump to conclusions** arrivare a conclusioni affrettate ♦ VT (*ditch, fence*) saltare; (*horse*) far saltare; (*fig: company etc*) mollare; **to jump the rails** (*train*) deragliare; **to jump bail** (*Law*) scappare quando si è in libertà provvisoria sotto cauzione; **don't jump the gun!** (*fig: fam*) non correre troppo!; **to jump ship** lasciare la nave senza permesso; **to jump sb** (*fam*) assalire qn ♦ N 1 (*gen, or Sport*) salto; **my heart gave a jump** ho provato un tuffo al cuore; **a jump in prices** un'impennata dei prezzi; **to be one jump ahead of sb** (*fig*) essere un passo avanti a qn 2 (*Showjumping*) salto; (*fence*) ostacolo
▸ **jump at** VI + PREP (*fig*) cogliere o afferrare al volo; **he jumped at the offer** si affrettò ad accettare l'offerta

jumped-up ['dʒʌmpt'ʌp] ADJ (*Brit: pej*) presuntuoso(-a)

jump·er ['dʒʌmpəʳ] N (*Brit: sweater*) maglione *m*; (*USA: pinafore dress*) scamiciato; (*Sport*) saltatore(-trice)

jump leads, jumper cables (*USA*) NPL (*Aut*) cavi *mpl* per batteria

jump-start ['dʒʌmpˌstɑːt] N: **to give the car a jump-start** dare una spinta alla macchina per farla partire; (*with jump leads*) mettere in moto una macchina usando i cavi per la batteria ♦ VT: **to jump-start the car** far partire la macchina spingendola; **to jump-start the economy** dare una spinta all'economia

jump suit N tuta intera

jumpy ['dʒʌmpɪ] ADJ (*comp* **-ier**, *superl* **-iest**) nervoso(-a), agitato(-a)

Jun. ABBR 1 (= *June*) giu. (= *giugno*) 2 = **junior**

junc·tion ['dʒʌŋkʃən] N (*Brit: of roads*) bivio, incrocio; (: *Rail*) nodo ferroviario

junc·ture ['dʒʌŋktʃəʳ] N (*fig: critical point*) momento critico; **at this juncture** in questo frangente

June [dʒuːn] N giugno; **in June** in giugno; *see* July

jun·gle ['dʒʌŋgl] N giungla ♦ ADJ della giungla

jun·ior ['dʒuːnɪəʳ] ADJ (*on staff, in rank*) subalterno(-a); (*section: in competition*) per ragazzi; (*with name*): **Roy Smith, Junior** Roy Smith junior; **he's junior to me** ho più anzianità di lui; **junior sizes** (*Comm*) taglie *fpl* per ragazzi ♦ N (*in organization*) persona meno anziana; (*Brit: schoolchild*) ≈ allievo delle scuole elementari (*da 7 a 11 anni*); **3 years my junior** *or* **my junior by 3 years** è più giovane di me di 3 anni, ha tre anni meno di me

junior executive N dirigente *m*/*f* di livello inferiore

junior high school N (*USA*) ≈ scuola media (*da 11 a 14 anni*)

junior minister N (*Brit Pol*) ≈ sottosegretario (di Stato)

junior partner N socio meno anziano

junior school N (*Brit*) ≈ scuola elementare (*da 7 a 11 anni*)

ju·ni·per ['dʒuːnɪpəʳ] N ginepro; **juniper berry** bacca di ginepro

junk¹ [dʒʌŋk] N (*stuff*) roba; (*fam: goods of poor quality*) porcheria *fpl*; **the attic's full of junk** la soffitta è piena di cianfrusaglie ♦ VT disfarsi di

junk² [dʒʌŋk] N (*boat*) giunca

junk bond N (*Fin*) junk bond *m inv*, titolo *m* spazzatura, *inv*

junk dealer N rigattiere *m*, robivecchi *m inv*

jun·ket ['dʒʌŋkɪt] N 1 (*fam, pej*): **to go on a junket** fare bisboccia; (*trip*) farsi un viaggetto pagato (*dallo stato*) 2 (*Culin*) giuncata

junk food N cibo a scarso valore nutritivo; **to eat junk food** mangiare porcherie

junkie, junky ['dʒʌŋkɪ] N (*fam*) tossico(-a)

junk mail N posta spazzatura *f inv*

junk room N ripostiglio

junk shop N (*fam*) (bottega di) rigattiere

jun·ta ['dʒʌntə] N giunta

Ju·pi·ter ['dʒuːpɪtəʳ] N (*Myth, Astron*) Giove *m*

ju·ris·dic·tion [ˌdʒʊərɪs'dɪkʃən] N (*frm*) giurisdizione *f*; **it falls** *or* **comes within/outside our jurisdiction** è/non è di nostra competenza

jur·is·pru·dence [ˌdʒʊərɪs'pruːdəns] N giurisprudenza

ju·ror ['dʒʊərəʳ] N (*Law*) giurato(-a); (*for contest*) membro della giuria

jury ['dʒʊərɪ] N (*Law: for contest*) giuria; **to serve on a jury** far parte di una giuria

jury box N banco dei giurati

jury·man ['dʒʊərɪmən] N (*pl* **-men**) giurato

just¹ [dʒʌst] ADJ (*fair*) giusto(-a)

just² [dʒʌst] ADV 1 (*exactly*) proprio, esattamente; **just here/ there** proprio qui/là; **just behind/in front of/near** proprio dietro/davanti a/vicino a; **just when it was going well ...** proprio quando tutto andava a gonfie vele...; **just then** *or* **just at that moment** proprio in quel momento; **it's just on 10 o'clock** sono le 10 in punto *or* precise; **it costs just (on) £20** costa 20 sterline tonde tonde; **it's just what I wanted** è proprio quello che volevo; **just right** proprio giusto; **just what did he say?** cosa ha detto esattamente?; **come just as you are** vieni così come sei; **leave it just as it is** lascialo esattamente com'è; **they are just like brothers** sono proprio come fratelli; **that's just it!, that's just the point!** precisamente!, proprio così!, per l'appunto!; **that's just (like) him, always late** è proprio di lui arrivare sempre in ritardo; **just as I thought/expected** proprio come pensavo/mi aspettavo; **just as he was leaving** proprio mentre se ne stava andando; **just as you like** come vuoi; **he likes everything just so** (*fam*) gli piace che tutto sia fatto a puntino 2 (*recently, soon*) appena, or ora; **he's just done it/left** lo ha appena fatto/è appena partito; **just this minute** proprio adesso; **the book is just out** il libro è appena stato pubblicato; **we were just going** stavamo giusto andando; **just then** it's just (like) him, **I've just about finished here** qui ho quasi finito; **I was just about to phone** stavo proprio per telefonare; **I'm just coming!** arrivo subito! 3 (*only*) solo; **it's just me** sono io solo; **just the two of us** soltanto noi due; **it's just 3 o'clock** sono le 3; **just yesterday/this morning** soltanto ieri/stamattina; **just for a laugh** tanto per ridere; **it's just around the corner** è appena dietro l'angolo; **just a minute!, just one moment!** un attimo! 4 (*simply*) semplicemente, soltanto; **it's just a**

mistake non è che uno sbaglio; **just ask someone the way** basta che tu chieda la strada a qualcuno; **I just thought that ...** pensavo solo che...; **I just wanted to say that ...** volevo solo dire che...; **I just can't imagine** non riesco proprio a immaginare; **it's just that I don't like it** il fatto è che non mi piace; **it's just one of those things** (*fam*) così è la vita **5** (*slightly*) poco; **just over/under 2 kilos** un po' più/meno di 2 chili; **just before 5 o'clock** poco prima delle 5; **just after 5 o'clock** poco dopo le 5; **it's just after 10 (o'clock)** sono le 10 passate; **just after I arrived** subito dopo il mio arrivo; **it's just to the left/right** è subito a sinistra/destra; **just after Christmas** poco dopo Natale **6** (*barely*) appena; (*almost not*) per un pelo; **just in time** giusto *or* appena in tempo; **I had just enough money** avevo giusto i soldi che mi servivano; **just enough money for sth/to do sth** soldi appena sufficienti per qc/per fare qc; **he (only) just caught/missed it, he caught/missed it, but only just** l'ha preso/perso proprio per un pelo **7** (*in comparison*): **it's just as good** è altrettanto buono; **it's just as good as ...** è buono quanto...; **he speaks Italian just as well as I do** il suo italiano è buono almeno quanto il mio **8** (*with imperatives*) un po'; **just imagine!** pensa un po'!; **just look at this mess!** guarda un po' che disordine!; **just wait a minute!** aspetta un momento!; **just let me get my hands on him!** (*fam*) se lo prendo! **9** (*emphatic*) veramente, proprio; **that's just fine!** va bene così!; **so you regret buying it?** — **don't I just!** ti sei pentito di averlo comprato? — eccome! **10** (*phrases*): **I've had just about enough of this noise!** (*fam*) ne ho proprio avuto abbastanza di questo rumore!; **it's just as well you didn't go** per fortuna non ci sei andato; **it would be just as well if you didn't mention it** faresti bene a non parlarne; **not just yet** non ancora; **just now** proprio ora; **I did it just now** l'ho fatto proprio adesso; **I'm rather busy just now** in questo momento sono molto occupato; **not just now** non proprio ora; **take an umbrella just in case** prendi un'ombrello, che

non si sa mai; **just in case I don't see you** caso mai non ti vedessi; **just the same, I'd rather ...** ciononostante, preferirei...; **I'd just as soon not go** preferirei non andarci; **just my luck!** la mia solita sfortuna!

jus·tice [ˈdʒʌstɪs] N **1** (*Law*) giustizia; **to bring sb to justice** consegnare qn alla giustizia; **justice system** sistema *m* giudiziario **2** (*fairness*): **in justice to her, she ...** per essere giusti, lei...; **there's no justice in this world!** non c'è giustizia a questo mondo!; **this biography doesn't do him justice** questa biografia non gli rende giustizia; **this photo doesn't do you justice** questa foto non ti fa giustizia; **to do justice to** rendere giustizia a; **Lord Chief Justice** (*Brit*) ≈ presidente *m* della Corte d'Appello

Justice of the Peace N (*Brit*) giudice *m* di pace
jus·ti·fi·able [ˌdʒʌstɪˈfaɪəbl] ADJ giustificabile
jus·ti·fi·ably [ˌdʒʌstɪˈfaɪəblɪ] ADV legittimamente, a ragione
jus·ti·fi·ca·tion [ˌdʒʌstɪfɪˈkeɪʃən] N giustificazione *f*; **in justification of** *or* **for** a giustificazione di
jus·ti·fy [ˈdʒʌstɪˌfaɪ] VT (*behaviour, action, also Typ*) giustificare; **to be justified in doing sth** avere ragione di fare qc; **am I justified in thinking that ...?** mi sbaglio o...?
just·ly [ˈdʒʌstlɪ] ADV giustamente
just·ness [ˈdʒʌstnɪs] N (*of decision*) giustezza
jut [dʒʌt] VI (*also:* **jut out**) sporgere; **a cliff jutting out over the sea** una scogliera a strapiombo sul mare
jute [dʒuːt] N iuta
ju·venile [ˈdʒuːvəˌnaɪl] ADJ (*offender*) minorenne; (*crime*) minorile; (*books, sports*) per ragazzi; (*pej*) puerile, infantile ♦ N (*Law*) minorenne *m/f*
juvenile delinquency N delinquenza minorile
juvenile delinquent N delinquente *m/f* minorenne
jux·ta·pose [ˌdʒʌkstəˈpəʊz] VT giustapporre
jux·ta·po·si·tion [ˌdʒʌkstəpəˈzɪʃən] N giustapposizione *f*; **to be in juxtaposition** essere in giustapposizione

Kk

K¹, k¹ [keɪ] N (*letter*) K, k *f inv, m inv*; **K for King** ≈ K come kursaal

K² [keɪ] ABBR (= *kilo*) kg ♦ N ABBR **1** (*fam: one thousand*): **he's on 35k** prende 35.000 (sterline) **2** (*Comput: = kilobyte*) kB *m inv*

kaf·tan [ˈkæftæn] N caffettano

Ka·la·ha·ri [ˌkæləˈhɑːrɪ] N: **the Kalahari (Desert)** il deserto del Kalahari

kale [keɪl] N cavolo verde

ka·lei·do·scope [kəˈlaɪdəˌskəʊp] N caleidoscopio

ka·mi·ka·ze [ˌkæmɪˈkɑːzɪ] N (*also:* **kamikaze pilot**) kamikaze *m inv* ♦ ADJ da kamikaze

Kam·pa·la [kæmˈpɑːlə] N Kampala

Kam·pu·chea [ˌkæmpʊˈtʃɪə] N la Cambogia

kan·ga·roo [ˌkæŋgəˈruː] N canguro

Kans. ABBR (*USA* = Kansas)

Kansas [ˈkænzəs] il Kansas

ka·put [kəˈpʊt] ADJ (*fam*) kaputt *inv*

kara·oke [ˌkɑːrɪˈəʊkɪ] N karaoke *m inv*

ka·ra·te [kəˈrɑːtɪ] N karatè *m*

Kash·mir [kæʃˈmɪə'] N Kashmir *m*

Ka·zakh·stan [ˌkæzækˈstɑːn] N Kazakistan *m*

KC [ˌkeɪˈsiː] N ABBR (*Brit Law:* = *King's Counsel*) avvocato della Corona

ke·bab [kəˈbæb] N kebab *m inv* (*spiedino di carne e verdura*); **a lamb kebab** uno spiedino di agnello

keel [kiːl] N (*Naut*) chiglia; **on an even keel** (*Naut*) di pescaggio uniforme

▸ **keel over** VI + ADV (*person*) crollare; (*Naut*) capovolgersi

keen [kiːn] ADJ (*comp* **-er**, *superl* **-est**) **1** (*Brit: person*) entusiasta; **he doesn't seem very keen** non sembra molto entusiasta; **she's a keen student** è una studentessa attenta e interessata; **he's a keen gardener** è un appassionato di giardinaggio; **to be keen on sth** (*opera, theatre*) essere appassionato(-a) di qc; (*plan, idea*) essere entusiasta di qc; **to be keen to do** *or* **on doing sth** avere una gran voglia di fare qc; **I'm not keen on going** non mi va di andare **2** (*edge, blade*) affilato(-a), tagliente; (*wind, air*) tagliente; (*hearing*) fine; (*appetite*) robusto(-a); (*intelligence, eyesight, observation*) acuto(-a); (*desire, delight, sense*) intenso(-a), forte; (*interest*) vivo(-a); (*price, rate*) competitivo(-a); (*competition, match, struggle*) duro(-a)

keen·ly [ˈkiːnlɪ] ADV **1** (*acutely*) intensamente; (*deeply*) profondamente; (*fiercely*) duramente; **to feel sth keenly** sentire qc profondamente **2** (*enthusiastically*) con entusiasmo

keen·ness [ˈkiːnnɪs] N (*eagerness*) entusiasmo

keep [kiːp] (*pt, pp* **kept**) VT **1** (*retain, maintain*) tenere; **keep the change** tenga il resto; **you can keep it** lo puoi tenere; **he keeps himself to himself** se ne sta per conto suo; **to keep sb busy** tenere qn occupato(-a); **the noise kept him awake** il rumore lo teneva sveglio; **to keep time** (*clock*) andar bene; **to keep sth clean** tenere qc pulito(-a); **to keep a place tidy** tenere un posto in ordine; **the garden is well kept** il giardino è tenuto bene; **he has kept his looks** è ancora un bell'uomo; **to keep sb waiting** far aspettare qn; **sorry to keep you …** scusate il ritardo…; **keep him at it!** spingilo a continuare!; to keep the engine running tenere il motore acceso; **I'll keep you to your promise** ti farò mantenere la promessa; **to keep sth from sb** (*fig*) tenere qc nascosto(-a) a qn; **to keep sth to o.s.** tenere qc per sé; **keep it to yourself** *or* **under your hat** (*fam*) tienilo per te **2** (*put aside*) mettere da parte; (*store*) tenere, conservare; **keep it in a safe place** *or* **somewhere safe** tienilo in un posto sicuro; **"keep in a cool place"** "conservare in un luogo fresco" **3** (*detain, restrain*) trattenere; **to keep sb in prison** tenere qn in prigione; **I mustn't** *or* **don't let me keep you** non voglio trattenerti; **what kept you?** come mai sei in ritardo?; **to keep sb from doing sth** impedire a qn di fare qc; **to keep sth from happening** impedire che qc succeda; **to keep o.s. from doing sth** trattenersi dal fare qc; **you're keeping me from my work** mi stai impedendo di lavorare, così non riesco a lavorare; **keep him from school** non mandarlo a scuola **4** (*fulfil, observe: promise, vow*) mantenere; (: *law, rule, Lent*) osservare; (: *treaty, agreement*) rispettare; (: *Christmas, Easter*) celebrare; **to keep a secret** tenere un segreto; **to keep an appointment** rispettare un appuntamento **5** (*own, have: also Comm: stock*) avere; (*Agr: animals*) allevare **6** (*support: family*) mantenere; **to keep sb in food and clothing** nutrire e vestire qn **7** (*accounts, diary*) tenere; **to keep a record** *or* **note of sth** prendere nota di qc; **keep a note of how much you spend** segnati quanto spendi ♦ VI **1** (*continue*) continuare; (*remain*) stare, restare; **to keep (to the) left/right** tenere la sinistra/la destra; **to keep straight on** continuare dritto(-a); **to keep to** (*promise*) mantenere; (*subject, text*) attenersi a; **to keep doing sth** continuare a fare qc; **I keep forgetting my keys** continuo a dimenticare le chiavi; **to keep fit** tenersi *or* mantenersi in forma; **to keep in good health** mantenersi in buona salute; **keep trying!** prova ancora!; **keep going!** forza!; **to keep at sb** (*fam: pester*) non dare pace a qn; **to keep at sth** (*fam: continue*) continuare a fare qc; **keep at it!** (*fam*) continua, dai!; **to keep still** stare *or* rimanere fermo(-a); **to keep quiet** stare zitto(-a); **to keep together** rimanere insieme; **to keep from doing sth** trattenersi *or* frenarsi dal fare qc; **to keep to one's room/bed** rimanere in camera/a letto; **they keep to themselves** si tengono in disparte, stanno per conto loro **2** (*in health*): **how are you keeping?** come stai? **3** (*food*) mantenersi, conservarsi; (*fig: wait*): **this business can keep** quest'affare può aspettare ♦ N **1** (*livelihood*) vitto e alloggio; **to earn one's keep** guadagnarsi di che vivere **2** (*of castle*) torrione *m*, maschio; *see also* **keeps**

▸ **keep away** VT + ADV: **to keep sth/sb away from sb** tenere qc/qn lontano(-a) da qn; **they kept him away from school** non l'hanno mandato a scuola ♦ VI + ADV: **to keep away (from)** stare lontano(-a) (da)

▸ **keep back** VT + ADV **1** (*crowds, tears, money*) trattenere **2** (*conceal: information*): **to keep sth back from sb** nascondere qc a qn ♦ VI + ADV tenersi indietro; **please keep back!** indietro per favore!

▸ **keep down** VT + ADV **1** (*control: prices, spending*) contenere; (: *anger*) controllare, contenere; (: *dog*) tenere a bada; (: *rebellion*) soffocare, reprimere; (: *population*) opprimere; **you can't keep a good man down** una persona valida prima o poi emerge **2** (*food*) trattenere, ritenere **3** (*Scol*): **he was kept down a year** gli hanno fatto ripetere l'anno ♦ VI + ADV tenersi giù, stare giù

▸ **keep in** VT + ADV (*invalid, child*) tenere a casa; (*Scol*) trattenere un alunno oltre l'orario scolastico, per punizione; (*stomach*) tenere dentro; (*elbows*) tenere giù ♦ VI + ADV (*fam*): **to keep in with sb** tenersi buono(-a) qn

▸ **keep off** VT + ADV: **keep your hands off!** giù le mani!, non toccare! ♦ VT + PREP tenere lontano(-a) da; **keep your hands off that cake** non toccare quella torta ♦ VI + ADV: **PREP:** **"keep off the grass"** "non calpestare l'erba" ♦ VI + ADV: **if the rain keeps off** se non piove

▸ **keep on** VI + ADV (*continue*) continuare; **keep on along this road until …** continui per questa strada finché…; **to keep on doing sth** continuare a fare qc; **the car keeps on breaking down** la macchina continua a rompersi; **to keep on at sb about sth** (*nag*) non dare pace a qc per qc; **don't keep on so!**, **don't keep on about it!** basta! smettila! ♦ VT + ADV (*hat, employee*) tenere; (*light*) tenere acceso(-a)

▸ **keep out** VI + ADV (*not enter*) restare fuori; **"keep out"** "vietato l'ingresso"; **keep out of trouble** tenersi fuori dai guai; **you keep out of this!** non immischiarti! ♦ VT + ADV (*exclude: person, dog*) tenere fuori; **this coat keeps out**

the cold questo cappotto protegge dal freddo; **to keep sb out of trouble** tenere qn lontano dai guai
► **keep up** VT + ADV **1** (*continue: tradition, subscription*) mantenere; **I did French at school, but I haven't kept it up** non ho più studiato francese dai tempi della scuola; **keep up the good work!** bravo, continua così!; **he'll never keep it up!** non ce la farà mai! **2** (*maintain: property*) mantenere **3** (*hold up*) tenere su, sorreggere; **to keep up one's spirits** (*fig*) tenersi su di morale, non perdersi d'animo; **the noise kept me up all night** il rumore mi ha tenuto sveglio tutta la notte ♦ VI + ADV **1 to keep up with sb** (*in race*) mantenersi al passo con qn; (*fig: in comprehension*) seguire qn; (: *by correspondence*) mantenere i rapporti con qn; **Matthew walks so fast I can't keep up** Matthew cammina così veloce che non riesco a stargli dietro; **to keep up with sth** (*work, payments, price rises*) tener dietro a qc; **to keep up with the times** mantenersi al passo con i tempi; **to keep up with the Joneses** (*fig*) non essere da meno dei vicini **2** (*weather*) continuare; (*prices*) mantenersi allo stesso livello

keep·er ['kiːpəʳ] N **1** (*in park, zoo*) guardiano; (*in museum*) custode *m* **2** (*also:* **gamekeeper**) guardacaccia *m inv* **3** (*also:* **goalkeeper**) portiere *m*

keep·ing ['kiːpɪŋ] N **1 in keeping/out of keeping (with)** in armonia/disaccordo (con); **that modern building is out of keeping with the houses around** quella costruzione moderna stona con le case intorno **2** (*care*) custodia; **in the keeping of** in custodia a; **in his keeping** sotto la sua custodia; **in safe keeping** al sicuro

keeps [kiːps] N: **for keeps** (*fam*) per sempre

keep·sake ['kiːpˌseɪk] N ricordo

keg [keg] N barile *m*, fusto

Ken. ABBR (*USA*: = **Kentucky**)

ken·nel ['kenl] N **1** (*dog house*) canile *m* **2 kennels** NPL, NSG (*establishment: for boarding*) canile; (: *for breeding*) allevamento di cani; **to put a dog in kennels** portare un cane al canile

Ken·tu·cky [ken'tʌkɪ] il Kentucky

Ken·ya ['kenjə] N il Kenia *m*

Ken·yan ['kenjən] ADJ, N keniano(-a), keniota *m/f*

kept [kept] PT, PP *of* **keep** ♦ ADJ: **a kept woman/man** un(a) mantenuto(-a)

kerb [kɜːb] N (*Brit*) bordo *or* orlo del marciapiede

ker·nel ['kɜːnl] N (*of nut*) gheriglio; (*of fruit stone*) nocciolo, seme *m*

kero·sene, kero·sine ['kerəsiːn] N (*esp USA*) cherosene *m*

ketch·up ['ketʃəp] N (*also:* **tomato ketchup**) ketchup *m inv*

ket·tle ['ketl] N bollitore *m*; **that's a different** *or* **another kettle of fish** (*fig*) questo è un altro paio di maniche

kettle·drum ['ketlˌdrʌm] N timpano

key [kiː] N **1** (*also fig*) chiave *f*; (*for winding clock, toy*) chiave, chiavetta; (*can opener*) chiavetta; (*on map*) leg(g)enda; **a bunch of keys** un mazzo di chiavi; **the key to success** la chiave del successo **2** (*of piano, computer, typewriter*) tasto; (*of wind instrument*) chiave *f* **3** (*Mus*) chiave *f*; **in the key of C/F** in chiave di do/fa; **major/minor key** tonalità maggiore/minore; **to change key** cambiare tonalità; **to be in/off key** essere in/fuori tono ♦ ADJ (*vital: position, industry, man*) chiave *inv*; **yes, this is a key point** sì, è un punto chiave
► **key in** VT + ADV (*on computer: text*) digitare, battere

key·board ['kiːbɔːd] N tastiera ♦ VT (*text*) digitare, battere

key·board·er ['kiːbɔːdəʳ] N (*on typewriter*) dattilografo(-a); (*on computer*) tastierista *m/f*

keyed up ['kiːd ʌp] ADJ: **to be (all) keyed up** essere (tutto(-a)) agitato(-a)

key·hole ['kiːhəʊl] N buco della serratura

keyhole surgery N chirurgia mininvasiva

key·note ['kiːnəʊt] N (*Mus*) tonica; (*fig*) nota dominante ♦ ADJ (*speech*) programmatico(-a)

key·pad ['kiːpæd] N tastiera numerica

key ring N portachiavi *m inv*

key·stroke ['kiːstrəʊk] N (*on keyboard*) battuta

kg ABBR (= *kilogram*) kg

KGB [keɪdʒiː'biː] N ABBR: **the KGB** il KGB

kha·ki ['kɑːkɪ] N (*cloth*) tela cachi; (*colour*) cachi *m* ♦ ADJ cachi *inv*

kib·butz ['kɪ'bʊts] N (*pl* **kibbutzim**) kibbutz *m inv*

kick [kɪk] VT (*person*) dare *or* tirare calci a; (*ball*) calciare; (*subj: horse*) tirare un calcio a; **he kicked me** mi ha dato un calcio; **he kicked the ball hard** ha dato un forte calcio alla palla; **to kick sb downstairs** scaraventare qn giù per le scale; **to kick sth out of the way** spostare qc con un calcio; **I could have kicked myself** (*fig: fam*) mi sarei preso a schiaffi; **to kick the bucket** (*fig: fam*) tirare le cuoia; **to kick a habit** (*fig: fam*) liberarsi da un vizio ♦ VI (*person*) dare calci, tirare calci; (*baby, horse*) scalciare; **to kick at sth** dare *or* tirare un calcio a qc ♦ N **1** (*action*) calcio; (*of firearm*) contraccolpo, rinculo; **to take a kick at sth/sb** tirare un calcio a qc/qn; **to give sth/sb a kick** dare un calcio a qc/qn; **this cocktail's got a kick to it** (*fam*) è forte questo cocktail!; **it was a kick in the teeth for him** (*fig: fam*) per lui è stato uno schiaffo morale; **he needs a kick in the pants** (*fig: fam*) ha bisogno di un bel calcio nel sedere **2** (*fam: thrill*): **he gets a kick out of it** ci prova un gusto matto; **to do something for kicks** fare qc per divertimento
► **kick about, kick around** VT + ADV: **to kick a ball about** *or* **around** giocare a pallone ♦ VI + ADV (*fam: object*) essere in giro
► **kick against** VI + PREP lottare contro
► **kick back** VI + ADV (*gun*) rinculare ♦ VT + ADV (*ball*) rinviare, rimandare
► **kick down** VT + ADV abbattere a calci
► **kick in** VT + ADV abbattere, sfasciare; **to kick sb's teeth in** (*fam*) spaccare la faccia a qn
► **kick off** VI + ADV (*Ftbl*) dare il calcio d'inizio; (*fig: fam: meeting etc*) cominciare
► **kick out** VT + ADV: **to kick out (at)** tirare calci (a) ♦ VT + ADV (*fig: fam*): **to kick sb out (of)** cacciare qn via (da), buttare qn fuori (da)
► **kick up** VT + ADV (*fig: fam*): **to kick up a row** *or* **a din** scatenare un putiferio; **to kick up a fuss about** *or* **over sth** piantare un casino per qc

kick·off ['kɪkˌɒf] N (*Ftbl*) calcio d'inizio; (*fig*) inizio

kick-start ['kɪkˌstɑːt] (*Brit*) N (*also:* **kick-starter**) pedale *m* d'avviamento ♦ VT mettere in moto (col pedale); (*fig*): **to kick-start the economy** dare una spinta all'economia

kid [kɪd] N **1** (*fam: child*) bambino(-a); (: *teenager*) ragazzo(-a); (: *son, daughter*) figlio(-a); **one of the kids was crying** uno dei bambini stava piangendo; **they've got three kids** hanno tre figli **2** (*goat, leather*) capretto ♦ VT (*fam*): **to kid sb (on) that ...** dar da bere a qn che...; **to kid sb about sth** prendere in giro qn per qc; **don't kid yourself!** non illuderti! ♦ VI (*fam: also:* **kid on**) scherzare; **I'm only kidding** sto scherzando; **no kidding!** sul serio! ♦ ADJ **1** (*fam: brother, sister*) più giovane **2** (*gloves, leather*) di capretto

kid gloves NPL: **to treat sb with kid gloves** trattare qn coi guanti

kid·nap ['kɪdnæp] VT rapire, sequestrare

kid·nap·per ['kɪdnæpəʳ] N rapitore(-trice), sequestratore(-trice)

kid·nap·ping ['kɪdnæpɪŋ] N sequestro di persona

kid·ney ['kɪdnɪ] N (*Anat*) rene *m*; (*Culin*) rognone *m*; **he's got kidney trouble** ha disturbi ai reni ♦ ADJ (*disease, failure, transplant*) renale, del rene

kidney bean N fagiolo comune

kidney machine N rene *m* artificiale

Kili·man·ja·ro [ˌkɪlɪmənˈdʒɑːrəʊ] N (*also:* **Mount Kilimanjaro**) il Kilimangiaro

kill [kɪl] VT **1** uccidere, ammazzare; **she killed her husband** ha ucciso suo marito; **sixteen people were killed in the accident** nell'incidente sono rimaste uccise sedici persone; **he was killed in a car accident** è morto in un incidente stradale; **luckily, nobody was killed** fortunatamente non ci sono state vittime; **to be killed in action** essere ucciso(-a) in combattimento; **to kill two birds with one stone** (*fig*) prendere due piccioni con una fava; **this heat is killing me** (*fig: fam*) sto morendo di caldo; **my feet are killing me** (*fam*) i piedi mi fanno male da morire; **he killed himself** si è ucciso **2** (*fig: pain*) togliere; (: *rumour*) mettere fine a; (: *story*) rovinare, guastare; (: *paragraph, line*) sopprimere; (: *newspaper article*) impedire la pubblicazione di, far saltare; (: *feeling, hope*) distruggere; (: *flavour, smell*) soffocare; (: *sound*)

attutire, smorzare; (: *engine, motor*) fermare, spegnere; **to kill time** ammazzare il tempo ♦ N (*Hunting, Bullfighting*) uccisione *f*
▸ **kill off** VT + ADV sterminare; (*fig*) eliminare; (*rumour*) soffocare

kill·er [ˈkɪləʳ] N (*murderer*) assassino(-a); (*hired*) killer *m/f inv*; **the police are searching for the killer** la polizia sta cercando l'assassino; **flu can be a killer** si può morire per un'influenza ♦ ADJ (*disease*) mortale

killer instinct N (*fig*): **he has the killer instinct** sa essere spietato

kill·ing [ˈkɪlɪŋ] N (*murder*) uccisione *f*; (*massacre*) strage *f*; (*fam: profit*) colpaccio; **a brutal killing** un brutale assassinio; **to make a killing** fare un colpaccio ♦ ADJ (*blow*) mortale; (*fig: work*) estenuante; (*fam: funny*) divertentissimo(-a)

kill·joy [ˈkɪlˌdʒɔɪ] N guastafeste *m/f*

kiln [kɪln] N fornace *f*

kilo [ˈkiːləʊ] N chilo; **£5 a kilo** cinque sterline al chilo

kilo·byte [ˈkɪləʊbaɪt] N kilobyte *m inv*

kilo·gram, kilo·gramme [ˈkɪləʊɡræm] N chilogrammo

kilo·metre [ˈkɪləʊˌmiːtəʳ], (*USA*) **kilo·meter** [kɪˈlɒmɪtəʳ] N chilometro

kilo·watt [ˈkɪləʊwɒt] N chilowatt *m inv*

kilt [kɪlt] N kilt *m inv*

kil·ter [ˈkɪltəʳ] N (*fam*): **out of kilter** fuori fase

ki·mo·no [kɪˈməʊnəʊ] N chimono

kin [kɪn] N parenti *mpl*, familiari *mpl*; *see also* **kith, next of kin**

kind [kaɪnd] N (*species*) sorta, specie *f*, genere *m*; **all kinds of things** ogni genere di cose; **some kind of fish** qualche tipo di pesce; **it's a kind of sausage** è una specie di salsiccia; **he's not the kind of person to ...** non è il tipo da...; **what kind of an answer is that?, what kind of an answer do you call that?** che razza di risposta è questa?; **what kind of person do you take me for?** per chi mi prendi?; **I had a kind of feeling that would happen** avevo come il presentimento che sarebbe successo; **you know the kind of thing I mean** sai cosa intendo *or* voglio dire; **something of the kind** qualcosa del genere; **nothing of the kind!** niente affatto!; **it's not his kind of film** non è il tipo *or* genere di film che piace a lui, non è il suo genere di film; **they're two of a kind** (*pej*) sono della stessa pasta; **it's the only one of its kind** è l'unico nel suo genere; **I kind of thought this would happen** (*fam*) quasi me l'aspettavo; **she looked kind of worried** (*fam*) sembrava come preoccupata; **payment in kind** pagamento in natura; **to repay sb in kind** (*after good deed*) ricambiare la cortesia a qn; (*after bad deed*) ripagare qn con la stessa moneta ♦ ADJ (*comp* **-er**, *superl* **-est**) gentile, buono(-a); **to be kind to sb** essere gentile con qn; **would you be kind enough to ...?** sarebbe così gentile da...?; **would you be so kind as to ...?** le spiacerebbe...?; **thank you for being so kind** grazie mille; **it's very kind of you (to do ...)** è molto gentile da parte sua (fare...); **thank you for your kind assistance** (*frm*) la ringrazio per il gentile aiuto

kin·der·gar·ten [ˈkɪndəˌɡɑːtn] N asilo

kind-hearted [ˌkaɪndˈhɑːtɪd] ADJ buono(-a), di buon cuore

kin·dle [ˈkɪndl] VT (*wood*) appiccare il fuoco a; (*fire*) accendere; (*emotion, interest*) suscitare

kin·dling [ˈkɪndlɪŋ] N frasche *fpl*, ramoscelli *mpl*

kind·ly [ˈkaɪndlɪ] ADJ (*comp* **-ier**, *superl* **-iest**) (*person, smile, tone*) benevolo(-a), affabile; (*gesture*) gentile ♦ ADV (*speak, act*) con gentilezza; **they kindly offered to lend me some money** si sono offerti gentilmente di prestarmi del denaro; **kindly wait a moment** abbia la cortesia *or* gentilezza di aspettare un momento; **will you kindly ...** vuole... per cortesia; **kindly refrain from smoking** si prega di non fumare; **he doesn't take kindly to being kept waiting** non gli piace affatto dover aspettare; **he didn't take it kindly** non l'ha presa molto bene

kind·ness [ˈkaɪndnɪs] N (*towards sb*) gentilezza, bontà; (*act*) gentilezza; **out of the kindness of her heart** per bontà d'animo; **to do sb a kindness** fare una cortesia *or* una gentilezza a qn

kin·dred [ˈkɪndrɪd] ADJ (*tribes, peoples*) imparentato(-a); (*language*) affine; **to have a kindred feeling for sb** sentirsi molto vicino(-a) a qn ♦ N (*relations*) familiari *mpl*, parenti *mpl*

ki·net·ic [kɪˈnetɪk] ADJ cinetico(-a)

king [kɪŋ] N (*also fig: Chess, Cards*) re *m inv*; (*Draughts*) dama

king·dom [ˈkɪŋdəm] N regno, reame *m*; **the Kingdom of Heaven** il Regno dei Cieli; **till kingdom come** (*fam*) fino al giorno del giudizio

king·fisher [ˈkɪŋˌfɪʃəʳ] N martin *m inv* pescatore

king·pin [ˈkɪŋˌpɪn] N (*Tech, also fig*) perno

king-size [ˈkɪŋˌsaɪz], **king-sized** [ˈkɪŋˌsaɪzd] ADJ (*gen: object, bed*) king size *inv*, più grande del normale; (*packet*) formato gigante *inv*; (*cigarette*) king size, lungo(-a)

kink [kɪŋk] N (*in rope*) attorcigliamento; (*in hair*) riccio; (*fig: emotional, psychological, sexual*) aberrazione *f* ♦ VI attorcigliarsi

kinky [ˈkɪŋkɪ] ADJ (*comp* **-ier**, *superl* **-iest**) (*hair*) crespo(-a); (*fam: sexually*) dai gusti particolari; (: *person, idea, fashion*) stravagante, eccentrico(-a)

kin·ship [ˈkɪnʃɪp] N parentela

kins·man [ˈkɪnzmən] N (*pl* **-men**) (*old*) congiunto

kins·woman [ˈkɪnzˌwʊmən] N (*pl* **-women**) (*old*) congiunta

ki·osk [ˈkiːɒsk] N (*gen*) chiosco; (*Brit: also:* **telephone kiosk**) cabina telefonica; (*also:* **newspaper kiosk**) edicola

kip·per [ˈkɪpəʳ] N aringa affumicata

Kir·ghi·zia [ˌkɜːˈɡɪzɪə] N Kirghizistan *m*

kiss [kɪs] VT baciare; **to kiss sb goodbye** congedarsi da qn con un bacio; **to kiss sb goodnight** dare a qn il bacio della buonanotte; **to kiss sb's hand** baciare la mano a qn ♦ VI: **to kiss (each other)** baciarsi; **they kissed** si sono baciati ♦ N bacio

kit [kɪt] N **1** (*equipment: gen*) kit *m inv*, attrezzatura; (*Mil*) equipaggiamento; (*Sport: outfit*) tenuta; (: *gear*) attrezzi *mpl*; (*tools*) arnesi *mpl*; **a tool kit** un kit di attrezzi; **a sewing kit** un kit da cucito; **a first aid kit** una cassetta del pronto soccorso; **a puncture repair kit** l'attrezzatura per riparare la gomma; **a drum kit** una batteria **2** (*parts for assembly*) kit *m inv* di montaggio; **toy aircraft kit** kit per aeromodellismo

kit·bag [ˈkɪtˌbæg] N (*Mil*) sacco militare; (*Sport*) sacca sportiva

kitch·en [ˈkɪtʃɪn] N cucina; **a fitted kitchen** una cucina componibile; **the kitchen units** gli elementi della cucina ♦ ADJ (*cupboard, equipment etc*) da cucina; **a kitchen knife** un coltello da cucina

kitchen garden N orto

kitchen sink N lavello, acquaio; **to take everything but the kitchen sink** (*fam, hum*) portarsi dietro tutta la casa

kitchen unit N (*Brit*) (mobile *m*) componibile, *m* da cucina

kitchen·ware [ˈkɪtʃɪnˌweə] N (*dishes*) stoviglie *fpl*; (*equipment*) utensili *mpl* da cucina

kite [kaɪt] N (*toy*) aquilone *m*; (*bird*) nibbio

kith [kɪθ] N: **kith and kin** (*old*) amici *mpl* e parenti, *mpl*

kit·ten [ˈkɪtn] N gattino(-a)

kit·ty [ˈkɪtɪ] N **1** (*funds*) cassa comune; (*Cards*) posta **2** (*fam: cat*) micio(-a), micino(-a)

kiwi [ˈkiːwiː] N kiwi *m inv*; (*fam: New Zealander*) neozelandese *m/f*

klep·to·ma·ni·ac [ˌkleptəʊˈmeɪnɪæk] N cleptomane *m/f*

km ABBR (= *kilometre*) km

km/h ABBR (= *kilometres per hour*) km/h

knack [næk] N abilità, capacità; **to get the knack of sth** farsi la mano in qc; **to have the knack of doing sth** avere l'abilità di fare qc; **to learn the knack of doing sth** imparare la tecnica per fare qc; **there's a knack to doing this** c'è un trucco per fare questo

knack·ered [ˈnækəd] ADJ (*Brit fam*) fuso(-a)

knap·sack [ˈnæpˌsæk] N (*rucksack*) zainetto; (*shoulder bag*) tascapane *m*

knave [neɪv] N (*old*) furfante *m*; (*Cards*) fante *m*

knead [niːd] VT (*dough, clay*) impastare, lavorare; (*muscle*) massaggiare

knee [niː] N (*Anat, of garment*) ginocchio; **I've hurt my knee** mi sono fatto male al ginocchio; **on one's knees** in ginocchio; **on one's hands and knees** carponi; **to go down on one's knees (to sb)** inginocchiarsi (davanti a qn)

knee·cap [ˈniːkæp] N (*Anat*) rotula ♦ VT gambizzare

knee-deep [ˈniːˌdiːp] ADJ fino al ginocchio; **the water was knee-deep** l'acqua ci arrivava alle ginocchia

kneel [niːl] (*pt, pp* **knelt**) VI (*also:* **kneel down**) inginocchiarsi
knee·pad ['niːpæd] N ginocchiera
knell [nɛl] N (*liter: also:* **death knell**) campana a morto
knelt [nɛlt] PT, PP *of* **kneel**
knew [njuː] PT *of* **know**
knick·ers ['nɪkəz] NPL (*Brit*) slip *m inv* (*da donna*), mutandine *fpl*; **a pair of knickers** un paio di slip
knick-knack ['nɪk,næk] N ninnolo
knife [naɪf] N (*pl* **knives**) (*gen*) coltello; (*also:* **penknife**) temperino; **a sharp knife** un coltello affilato; **knife, fork and spoon** coperto ♦ VT (*stab*) accoltellare; **to knife sb to death** uccidere qn a coltellate
knife edge N: **to be on a knife edge** (*fig: person*) stare *or* camminare sul filo del rasoio; (: *hope, result*) essere appeso(-a) a un filo; **the success of the scheme was balanced on a knife edge** la riuscita del progetto era appesa ad un filo
knight [naɪt] N cavaliere *m*; (*Chess*) cavallo ♦ VT nominare cavaliere
knight·hood ['naɪthʊd] N (*Brit: title*) cavalierato; **to get a knighthood** essere nominato cavaliere
knit [nɪt] VT (*garment*) lavorare a maglia *or* a ferri; **to knit together** (*fig*) unire; **to knit one's brows** aggrottare le sopracciglia ♦ VI 1 (*make garment*) lavorare a maglia 2 (*also:* **knit together**) (*broken bones*) saldarsi; (*people*) andare d'accordo
knit·ted ['nɪtɪd] ADJ lavorato(-a) a maglia
knit·ting ['nɪtɪŋ] N (*activity*) il lavorare *m* a maglia; (*product*) lavoro a maglia; **I like knitting** mi piace lavorare a maglia
knitting machine N macchina per maglieria
knitting needle N ferro da calza
knitting pattern N modello per maglia
knit·wear ['nɪt,wɛə'] N maglieria
knives [naɪvz] NPL *of* **knife**
knob [nɒb] N pomo, pomello; (*on radio, TV*) manopola; **a knob of butter** (*Brit*) una noce *f* di burro
knob·bly ['nɒblɪ], (*USA*) **knob·by** ['nɒbɪ] ADJ (*comp* **-ier**, *superl* **-iest**) (*wood, surface*) nodoso(-a); (*knee*) ossuto(-a)
knock [nɒk] VT 1 (*strike*) colpire; **to knock a nail into sth** conficcare un chiodo in qc; **to knock sb on the head** colpire qn in *or* alla testa; **to knock one's head on/against sth** battere *or* sbattere la testa su/contro qc; **to knock sb unconscious** *or* **out** *or* **cold** tramortire qn; **to knock the bottom out of sth** (*box*) sfondare qc; (*fig: argument*) demolire qc; **he knocked the knife out of her hand** con un colpo le ha fatto cadere il coltello di mano; **to knock spots off sb/sth** (*fig: fam*) dare dei punti a qn/qc; **to knock sb sideways** *or* **for six** (*fig: fam*) lasciare qn di stucco; **to knock some sense into sb** (*fam*) far entrare un po' di buonsenso in testa a qn 2 (*fam: criticize*) criticare ♦ VI 1 (*strike*) bussare; **he knocked at** *or* **on the door** ha bussato alla porta; **his knees were knocking** gli tremavano le ginocchia 2 (*bump*): **to knock into** *or* **against sth/sb** sbattere *or* urtare contro qn/qc 3 (*engine*) battere in testa ♦ N 1 (*blow*) colpo; (*in collision*) botta; **there was a knock at the door** hanno bussato alla porta; **I heard a knock** ho sentito bussare; **his pride took a knock** il suo orgoglio ha subito un duro colpo 2 (*in engine*) battito in testa

▸ **knock about, knock around** VT + ADV (*person, object*) maltrattare ♦ VI + ADV (*fam: person*) vagabondare; (: *thing*): **it's knocking around here somewhere** è qui in giro, da qualche parte

▸ **knock back** VT + ADV (*fam*) 1 (*drink*) scolare, tracannare 2 (*cost*): **it knocked me back £100** mi è costato la bellezza di 100 sterline

▸ **knock down** VT + ADV 1 (*building*) demolire; (*person*) gettare a terra, stendere; (*pedestrian*) investire; (*tree*) abbattere; (*door*) buttare giù; **she was knocked down by a car** è stata investita da una macchina; **you could have knocked me down with a feather!** mi sono cadute le braccia 2 (*price*) abbassare; (*object at auction*) aggiudicare

▸ **knock in** VT + ADV (*nail*) conficcare

▸ **knock off** VT + ADV 1 (*strike off: vase on shelf*) far cadere; (*fig: from price, record*): **to knock off £10** *or* **knock £10 off the price** fare uno sconto di 10 sterline 2 (*fam: steal*) sgraffignare, fregare 3 (*fam: do quickly*) buttare giù 4 (*fam: stop*): **knock it off!** piantala! ♦ VI + ADV (*fam: stop work*) smontare, staccare

▸ **knock out** VT + ADV 1 (*stun*) stordire, stendere; (*Boxing*) mettere k.o. *or* fuori combattimento; **they knocked out the watchman** hanno stordito il guardiano 2 (*nails*) far uscire, levare; (*in fight: teeth*) spaccare; **to knock out one's pipe** svuotare la pipa 3 (*eliminate: in competition*) eliminare; **they were knocked out early in the tournament** sono stati eliminati all'inizio del torneo

▸ **knock over** VT + ADV (*object*) far cadere; (*pedestrian*) investire

▸ **knock together** VT + ADV 1 (*two objects*) battere uno contro l'altro 2 (*make hastily*) mettere insieme alla svelta, arrangiare alla meglio

▸ **knock up** VT + ADV 1 (*handle, lever*) tirare in alto 2 (*Brit: waken*) svegliare bussando alla porta 3 (*make hastily*) = **knock together** 4 (*USA: fam!*) rendere incinta

knock·down ['nɒk,daʊn] ADJ (*price*) stracciato(-a)
knock·er ['nɒkə'] N (*on door*) battente *m*; **knockers** NPL (*fam!*) tette *fpl*
knock·ing ['nɒkɪŋ] N colpi *mpl*
knock-kneed [,nɒk'niːd] ADJ che ha le gambe a X
knock-out ['nɒk,aʊt] N 1 (*Boxing*) knock out *m inv* 2 (*fam: person*) schianto, cannonata
knockout competition N gara ad eliminazione
knock-up ['nɒk,ʌp] N (*Tennis*) palleggio; **to have a knock-up** palleggiare
knot [nɒt] N (*in rope, wood: also Naut: speed*) nodo; (*group: of people*) capannello; **to tie a knot** fare un nodo; **to tie o.s. up in knots** (*fig*) ingarbugliarsi ♦ VT fare un nodo a, annodare; **to knot together** annodare insieme; **to tie the knot** (*fig*) sposarsi
knot·ty ['nɒtɪ] ADJ (*comp* **-ier**, *superl* **-iest**) (*wood*) nodoso(-a); (*fig: problem*) spinoso(-a)
know [nəʊ] (*pt* **knew**, *pp* **known**) VT 1 (*facts, dates*) sapere; **to know that ...** sapere che...; **to get to know sth** venire a sapere qc; **to know how to do sth** saper fare qc; **I don't know any German** non so una parola di tedesco; **he knows a lot about cars** sa molte cose sulle macchine; **he knows all the answers** sa rispondere a tutte le domande; (*pej*) sa sempre tutto; **he knows what he's talking about** parla con cognizione di causa; **to know one's (own) mind** sapere ciò che si vuole; **I know nothing about it** non ne so niente; **there's no knowing what may happen** chissà cosa succederà; **it soon became known that ...** si è presto venuto a sapere che...; **to make sth known to sb** far sapere qc a qn; **he is known to have been there** si sa che c'è stato; **it's worth knowing that/how** *etc* ... vale la pena sapere che cosa/come *etc*...; **to know sth backwards** conoscere qc a menadito; **let me know how you get on** fammi sapere come va; **you know how it is** sai com'è; **I knew it!** lo sapevo! 2 (*be acquainted with: person, place, author, subject*) conoscere; **I don't know him** non lo conosco; **I know London well** conosco bene Londra; **to know sb by sight/by name** conoscere qn di vista/di nome; **to get to know sb** (*gradually*) conoscere meglio qn; (*for the first time*) conoscere qn; **I don't know him to speak to** lo conosco di vista; **to make o.s. known to sb** presentarsi a qn; **he is known as X** è conosciuto con *or* sotto il nome di X 3 (*recognize*) riconoscere; **I knew him by his voice** l'ho riconosciuto dalla voce; **she knows a good painting when she sees one** sa riconoscere un buon dipinto; **to know the difference between ...** saper distinguere fra...; **to know right from wrong** distinguere il bene dal male ♦ VI sapere; **as far as I know ...** che io sappia..., per quanto ne so io...; **we'll let you know** te lo faremo sapere; **how should I know?** come vuoi che lo sappia?; **you never know!** non si sa mai!; **no, not that I know of** no, che io sappia; **there's no (way of) knowing** non c'è modo di saperlo; **it's not easy, you know** non è facile, sai; **yes, I know** sì, lo so; **I don't know** non lo so; **you ought to know better (than to ...)** dovresti saperlo da solo (che non è il caso di...); **you know best** nessuno può saperlo meglio di te; **(well,) what do you know!** (*fam*) chi l'avrebbe mai detto!; **to know about** *or* **of sth** essere a conoscenza di qc; **to know about** *or* **of sb** aver sentito parlare di qn; **to get to know about sth** venire a sapere qc ♦ N: **to be in the know** (*fam*) essere al corrente, essere beninformato(-a)

know-all [ˈnəʊɔːl] N (Brit: pej) sapientone(-a); he's such a know-all! è un gran sapientone!

know-how [ˈnəʊˌhaʊ] N know-how m inv

know·ing [ˈnəʊɪŋ] ADJ (look, smile) d'intesa; (shrewd) scaltro(-a)

know·ing·ly [ˈnəʊɪŋlɪ] ADV (intentionally) deliberatamente; (smile, look) con aria d'intesa

know-it-all [ˈnəʊɪtˌɔːl] N (USA) = know-all

knowl·edge [ˈnɒlɪdʒ] N 1 (information, awareness, understanding) conoscenza; **to have no knowledge of** ignorare, non sapere; **not to my knowledge** non che io sappia; **without my knowledge** a mia insaputa; **to (the best of) my knowledge** per quanto io ne sappia; **it is common knowledge that ...** è risaputo che...; **it has come to my knowledge that ...** sono venuto a sapere che... 2 (learning) conoscenza, sapere m; **to have a working knowledge of Italian** avere una conoscenza pratica dell'italiano; **to have a thorough knowledge of sth** conoscere qc a fondo

knowl·edge·able [ˈnɒlɪdʒəbl] ADJ (person) ben informato(-a); (remark) pertinente

known [nəʊn] PP of know ♦ ADJ (thief, facts) noto(-a); (expert) riconosciuto(-a), famoso(-a)

knuck·le [ˈnʌkl] N (Anat) nocca

‣ **knuckle down** VI + ADV (fam): **to knuckle down to some hard work** mettersi sotto a lavorare

‣ **knuckle under** VI + ADV (fam) cedere

knuckle·duster [ˈnʌklˌdʌstəʳ] N tirapugni m inv

KO, k.o. [ˈkeɪˈəʊ] N ABBR (pl KO's) (= knockout) KO, k.o. ♦ VT (pt, pp KO'd) (= knock out) mettere k.o.

koa·la [kəʊˈɑːlə] N (also: koala bear) koala m inv

kook [kuːk] N (USA fam) svitato(-a)

Ko·ran [kɒˈrɑːn] N: **the Koran** il Corano

Ko·rea [kəˈrɪə] N Corea; **North/South Korea** Corea del Nord/del Sud

Ko·rean [kəˈriːən] ADJ, N coreano(-a)

ko·sher [ˈkəʊʃəʳ] ADJ kasher inv

Kosovar, Kosovan [ˈkɒsəvɑːʳ, ˈkɒsəvən] ADJ kosovaro(-a)

Kosovo [ˈkɒsəvəʊ] N Kosovo

kow·tow [ˌkaʊˈtaʊ] VI (fam): **to kowtow to sb** prostrarsi davanti a qn (fig)

Krem·lin [ˈkremlɪn] N: **the Kremlin** il Cremlino

KS ABBR (USA Post: = Kansas)

Kt ABBR (Brit: = knight)

Kua·la Lum·pur [ˈkwɑːləˈlʊmpʊəʳ] N Kuala Lumpur f

ku·dos [ˈkjuːdɒs] NSG gloria, fama

Kurd [kɜːd] N curdo(-a)

Ku·wait [kʊˈweɪt] N il Kuwait m

Ku·wai·ti [kʊˈweɪtɪ] ADJ, N kuwaitiano(-a)

kW ABBR (= kilowatt) kW

KY ABBR (USA Post: = Kentucky)

L1

L¹, l¹ [ɛl] N (letter) L, l f inv, m inv; **L for Lucy,** (USA) **L for Love** ≈ L come Livorno

L² [ɛl] ABBR **1** (= large) L f inv **2** (Brit: Aut: = learner) P (= principiante); see also **L-plates** ♦ N ABBR (USA fam): **the L** (= the elevated (railroad)) la soprelevata

l ABBR (= litre) l.

L., l. ABBR **1** (lake) L **2** (left) sin.

LA [ˌɛlˈeɪ] (USA) N ABBR **1** = Los Angeles **2** (Post: = Louisiana)

la [lɑː] N (Mus) = lah

La. ABBR (USA: = Louisiana)

lab [læb] N ABBR = laboratory (fam) laboratorio

la·bel ['leɪbl] N etichetta, cartellino; (brand: of record) casa discografica, etichetta; **he records on the E.M.I. label** incide per la E.M.I. ♦ VT (goods) mettere l'etichetta su, marcare; (fig) classificare, etichettare; **a bottle labelled "poison"** una bottiglia con l'etichetta "veleno"

la·bor ['leɪbəʳ] (USA) = labour

la·bora·tory [ləˈbɒrətəri] N laboratorio ♦ ADJ di laboratorio

Labor Day N festa del lavoro (celebrata negli Stati Uniti e in Canada il primo lunedì di settembre)

la·bo·ri·ous [ləˈbɔːrɪəs] ADJ faticoso(-a), laborioso(-a)

labor union (USA) N sindacato

La·bour ['leɪbəʳ] N (Brit Pol: also: **the Labour Party**) il partito laburista, i laburisti; **she votes Labour** vota (per il partito) laburista ♦ ADJ laburista; **official Labour policy** politica ufficiale dei laburisti

la·bour, la·bor (USA) ['leɪbəʳ] N **1** (toil, task) lavoro; **hard labour** (Law) lavori forzati; **labour of love** lavoro fatto per il puro piacere di farlo **2** (workforce) manodopera **3** (Med) doglie fpl, travaglio (del parto); **to be in labour** avere le doglie ♦ VT (point) insistere su ♦ VI: **to labour at** (with effort) lavorare sodo or duro a; (with difficulty) faticare a fare; (engine, motor) essere sotto sforzo; **to labour under a delusion/misapprehension** essere vittima di un'illusione/di un malinteso ♦ ADJ di lavoro

labour camp, labor camp (USA) N campo di lavoro

labour cost, labor cost (USA) N costo del lavoro

labour dispute, labor dispute (USA) N conflitto tra lavoratori e datori di lavoro

la·boured, la·bored (USA) ['leɪbəd] ADJ (breathing) affannoso(-a); (style) pesante

la·bour·er, la·bor·er (USA) ['leɪbərəʳ] N (on building site) manovale m; (on farm) bracciante m

labour force, labor force (USA) N manodopera

labour-intensive, labor-intensive (USA) ['leɪbərɪn,tensɪv] ADJ che assorbe molta manodopera

labour market, labor market (USA) N mercato del lavoro

labour pains, labor pains (USA) NPL doglie fpl

labour relations, labor relations (USA) NPL relazioni fpl industriali

labour-saving, labor-saving (USA) ['leɪbə,seɪvɪŋ] ADJ che fa risparmiare fatica or lavoro

labour unrest, labor unrest (USA) N agitazioni fpl operaie

laby·rinth ['læbɪrɪnθ] N labirinto

lace [leɪs] N **1** (fabric) pizzo, merletto **2** (of shoe) laccio, stringa; (of corset) laccio; **a pair of laces** un paio di lacci ♦ ADJ di pizzo; **a lace collar** un colletto di pizzo ♦ VT **1** (also: **lace up**: shoes etc) allacciare **2** (drink: with spirits) correggere; (: with poison) avvelenare

lace-making ['leɪs,meɪkɪŋ] N fabbricazione f dei pizzi or dei merletti

lac·era·tion [ˌlæsəˈreɪʃən] N lacerazione f

lace-up ['leɪs,ʌp] ADJ (shoes) con i lacci or le stringhe

lack [læk] N mancanza, scarsità; **for** or **through lack of** per mancanza or scarsità di; **there is no lack of money** i soldi

---

non mancano; **he got the job, despite his lack of experience** ha ottenuto il lavoro nonostante la mancanza d'esperienza ♦ VT (also: **to be lacking**) mancare di; (fam) mancare il tempo di or per farlo; **he lacks confidence** non è sicuro di sé ♦ VI: **to be lacking in** mancare di; **he is lacking in confidence** non è sicuro di sé; **he lacks for nothing** non gli manca niente

lacka·dai·si·cal [ˌlækəˈdeɪzɪkəl] ADJ (careless) noncurante; (lacking enthusiasm) svogliato(-a)

lack·ey ['lækɪ] N (also pej) lacchè m inv

lack·lustre, lack·luster (USA) ['læk,lʌstəʳ] ADJ (performance) scialbo(-a); (eyes) spento(-a)

la·con·ic [ləˈkɒnɪk] ADJ laconico(-a)

lac·quer ['lækəʳ] N (for wood, hair) lacca ♦ VT (wood) laccare; (hair) mettere la lacca su

lacy ['leɪsɪ] ADJ (comp -ier, superl -iest) (made of lace) di pizzo; (like lace) che sembra un pizzo

lad [læd] N ragazzo, giovanotto; (Brit: in stable) mozzo or garzone m di stalla; **when I was a lad** quand'ero ragazzo or giovane; **come on, lads!** forza, or dai, ragazzi!

lad·der ['lædəʳ] N scala a pioli; (stepladder) scala a libretto; (Brit: in tights) smagliatura; **social ladder** scala sociale; **it's the first step up the ladder** è il primo passo sulla via del successo ♦ VT (Brit: tights) smagliare ♦ VI (Brit: tights) smagliarsi

lad·en ['leɪdn] ADJ: **laden (with)** carico(-a) or caricato(-a) (di); **fully laden** (truck, ship) a pieno carico

la·dle ['leɪdl] N (Culin) mestolo ♦ VT (soup) servire con il mestolo

▸ **ladle out** VT + ADV (soup) servire con il mestolo; (fig: advice) elargire, distribuire

lady ['leɪdɪ] N **1** signora; **the lady of the house** la padrona di casa; **ladies' hairdresser** parrucchière m per signora; **Ladies and Gentlemen!** signore e signori! **2 Our Lady** (Rel) la Madonna **3 Lady Jane Grey** lady Jane Grey

lady·bird ['leɪdɪ,bɜːd], (USA) **lady·bug** ['leɪdɪ,bʌg] N coccinella

lady-in-waiting ['leɪdɪn'weɪtɪŋ] N dama di corte

lady·like ['leɪdɪ,laɪk] ADJ (girl, woman) ben educata, distinta; (manners) da signora, distinta

lady·ship ['leɪdɪʃɪp] N: **Her Ladyship the Countess** la signora contessa; **Your Ladyship** signora contessa

lag¹ [læg] VI (also: **lag behind**) restare indietro; **we lag behind in space exploration** siamo ancora indietro nel campo dell'esplorazione spaziale ♦ N (also: **time-lag**) lasso or intervallo di tempo; see also **jet lag**

lag² [læg] VT (boiler, pipes) rivestire con or di materiale isolante

lag³ [læg] N (fam): **old lag** vecchia conoscenza della polizia

la·ger ['lɑːgəʳ] N birra chiara, birra bionda

lag·ging ['lægɪŋ] N (Tech) rivestimento termo-isolante

la·goon [ləˈguːn] N laguna

La·gos ['leɪgɒs] N Lagos f

laid [leɪd] PT, PP of **lay³**

laid-back ['leɪd'bæk] ADJ (fam) rilassato(-a); **his laid-back attitude** il suo atteggiamento tranquillo e rilassato

lain [leɪn] PP of **lie²**

lair [lɛəʳ] N (of animal) tana, covo; (of thieves) covo

laissez-faire [ˌleseɪˈfɛəʳ] N liberismo ♦ ADJ liberistico(-a)

la·ity ['leɪtɪ] COLLECTIVE N: **the laity** (as opposed to the clergy) i laici, il laicato; (as opposed to professionals) i non appartenenti ad una categoria professionale

lake [leɪk] N lago

Lake District N: **the Lake District** (Brit) la regione dei laghi (nel nord dell'Inghilterra)

lamb [læm] N (animal, meat) agnello; **my poor lamb!** oh, povero tesoro!; **he took it like a lamb** ha accettato docilmente; **Lamb of God** Agnello di Dio ♦ VI figliare, partorire (di pecora)

lamb chop N cotoletta d'agnello

lamb·skin ['læm‚skɪn] N (pelle f d') agnello
lambs·wool ['læmz‚wʊl] N lambswool m inv
lame [leɪm] ADJ (comp -r, superl -st) zoppo(-a); (also fig: argument, excuse) zoppicante; **to be lame** zoppicare, essere zoppo(-a); **to be lame in one foot** esser zoppo da un piede ♦ VT (person) rendere zoppo(-a); (horse) azzoppare
lame·ly ['leɪmlɪ] ADV (fig) in modo poco convincente
la·ment [lə'mɛnt] VT lamentare, piangere; **to lament sb** piangere qn ♦ VI: **to lament over sth** lamentarsi di qc; **to lament for sb** affliggersi per qn ♦ N (poet) lamento, elegia
lam·en·ta·ble ['læməntəbl] ADJ (performance) penoso(-a); (disregard, waste) deplorevole
lami·na·ted ['læmɪ‚neɪtɪd] ADJ (gen) laminato(-a); (card) plastificato(-a)
lamp [læmp] N (for table) lampada; (in street) lampione m; (Aut) faro, luce f; (Rail) lanterna; (bulb) lampadina
lamp·light ['læmp‚laɪt] N: **by lamplight** a lume della lampada
lam·poon [læm'puːn] N satira ♦ VT fare oggetto di satira, satireggiare
lamp·post ['læmp‚pəʊst] N lampione m
lamp·shade ['læmp‚ʃeɪd] N paralume m
lance [lɑːns] N lancia ♦ VT (Med) incidere
lance corporal N (Brit) caporale m
lan·cet ['lɑːnsɪt] N (Med) bisturi m inv
Lancs [læŋks] N ABBR (Brit: = Lancashire)
land [lænd] N 1 terra; (soil, ground) terreno; (estate) terreni mpl, terre fpl; **to go/travel by land** andare/viaggiare per via di terra; (dry) land terraferma; **to work on the land** lavorare la terra; **fewer people work on the land now** oggi c'è meno gente che lavora la terra; **to live off the land** vivere dei prodotti della terra; **to own land** possedere dei terreni, avere delle proprietà (terriere); **to see how the land lies** (fig) tastare il terreno 2 (nation, country) paese m; **throughout the land** in tutto il paese; **to be in the land of the living** essere nel mondo dei vivi ♦ VT 1 (cargo, goods) scaricare, (far) sbarcare; (passengers) (far) sbarcare; (aircraft) far atterrare; (catch: fish) tirare in secco; (fig: job, contract) accaparrarsi 2 (fam: place): **to land a blow on sb** assestare un colpo a qn; **it landed him in jail** gli è costato la galera; **to land sb in trouble** cacciare qn nei guai; **to land sb in debt** far indebitare qn; **I got landed with the job** è toccato a me fare il lavoro; **I got landed with him** mi è toccato restare con lui, me lo sono dovuto sorbire io ♦ VI 1 (plane, passenger) atterrare; (from boat, ship) sbarcare; **the plane landed at five o'clock** l'aereo è atterrato alle cinque 2 (after fall, jump) atterrare; (fig: fall) cadere; **to land on** (bird) posarsi su; **to land on one's feet** (to be lucky) cadere in piedi; **the hat landed in my lap** il cappello è finito sulle mie ginocchia; **the bomb landed on the building** la bomba è caduta sul palazzo; **the first man to land on the moon** il primo uomo a mettere piede sulla luna
▸ **land up** VI + ADV (fig: fam) andare a finire
landed gentry N proprietari mpl terrieri
land-fill site ['lændfɪl‚saɪt] N discarica pubblica (in cui i rifiuti vengono interrati)
land·ing ['lændɪŋ] N 1 (of aircraft) atterraggio; (of troops) sbarco 2 (in house) pianerottolo
landing card N carta di sbarco
landing craft N mezzo da sbarco
landing gear N (Aer) carrello d'atterraggio
landing stage N pontile m da sbarco
landing strip N pista d'atterraggio
land·lady ['lænd‚leɪdɪ] N (of apartment, house) padrona di casa; (of pub) proprietaria
land·locked ['lænd‚lɒkt] ADJ senza sbocco sul mare
land·lord ['lænd‚lɔːd] N (landowner) proprietario (di beni immobili); (of apartment) padrone m di casa; (of pub) proprietario
land·lub·ber ['lænd‚lʌbə'] N (fam) marinaio d'acqua dolce
land·mark ['lænd‚mɑːk] N punto di riferimento; (event) pietra miliare; **a landmark in history** una pietra miliare nella storia; **Big Ben is a London landmark** la torre del Big Ben è un punto di riferimento a Londra
land·owner ['lænd‚əʊnə'] N proprietario(-a) terriero(-a)

land·scape ['lænd‚skeɪp] N paesaggio ♦ VT abbellire con criteri architettonici
landscape architect N architetto del paesaggio
landscape painting N (Art) paesaggistica
land·slide ['lænd‚slaɪd] N (Geol) frana; (fig: Pol) valanga di voti, maggioranza schiacciante
lane [leɪn] N (in country) stradina, viottolo; (in town) stradina, viuzza; (Sport, Aut) corsia; **a country lane** una stradina di campagna; **the outside lane** la corsia esterna; **"keep in lane"** (Aut) "divieto di sorpasso"; **"get into lane"** (Aut) "immettersi in corsia"; **I'm in the wrong lane** (Aut) sono sulla corsia sbagliata; **a 3-lane motorway** un'autostrada a 3 corsie
❑ lane is not translated by the Italian word lana
lan·guage ['læŋgwɪdʒ] N (faculty, style of speech) linguaggio; (national tongue, also fig) lingua; **the Italian language** la lingua italiana; **a foreign language** una lingua straniera; **legal/scientific language** linguaggio legale/scientifico; **we don't speak the same language** (fig) non parliamo la stessa lingua; **to use bad language** dire parolacce, usare un linguaggio volgare; **watch your language!** attento a come parli!
language laboratory N laboratorio linguistico
language school N scuola di lingue
lan·guid ['læŋgwɪd] ADJ (liter: graceful, affected) languido(-a); (: indolent) fiacco(-a)
lan·guish ['læŋgwɪʃ] VI: **to languish for love/over sb/in prison** languire d'amore/per qn/in prigione
lank [læŋk] ADJ (hair) diritto(-a) e opaco(-a)
lanky ['læŋkɪ] ADJ (comp -ier, superl -iest) (person) allampanato(-a)
lano·lin, lano·line ['lænəlɪn] N lanolina
lan·tern ['læntən] N lanterna
Laos [laʊs] N Laos m
lap¹ [læp] N (Anat) grembo, ginocchia fpl; **to sit in or on sb's lap** sedersi in grembo a or sulle ginocchia di qn; **on his mother's lap** in grembo a sua madre; **to live in the lap of luxury** vivere nel lusso
▸ **lap up** VT + ADV (milk: cat) leccare; (: dog) lappare; (fig: compliments, attention) bearsi di
lap² [læp] N (Sport) giro; **to run a lap** fare un giro della pista; **I ran ten laps** ho fatto dieci giri di corsa; **we're on the last lap now** (fig) siamo quasi arrivati al traguardo
lap³ [læp] VT = lap up ♦ VI (waves) sciabordare; **to lap against** lambire
La Paz [læ'pæz] N La Paz f
lap·dog ['læp‚dɒg] N cagnolino da salotto; (fig: person) cagnolino
la·pel [lə'pɛl] N risvolto
Lap·land ['læp‚lænd] N Lapponia
Lapp [læp] ADJ lappone ♦ N (person) lappone m/f; (language) lappone m
lapse [læps] N 1 (fault) mancanza; (in behaviour) scorrettezza; **a lapse (of memory)** un vuoto (di memoria); **through a lapse of concentration** per mancanza di concentrazione; **a lapse into bad habits** un ritorno alle cattive abitudini 2 (of time) intervallo ♦ VI 1 (err) sgarrare; **to lapse in one's duty** mancare al proprio dovere 2 (fall slowly): **to lapse into bad habits** prendere cattive abitudini; **to lapse into one's old ways** ritornare a poco a poco alle vecchie abitudini; **to let one's attention lapse** distrarsi; **to lapse into silence** tacere; **to lapse into English** cominciare a parlare inglese; **she lapsed into unconsciousness** scivolò in uno stato di incoscienza 3 (law, act) cadere, andare in prescrizione; (membership, passport, ticket) scadere
lap·top ['læp‚tɒp] N (also: laptop computer) laptop m inv
lar·ceny ['lɑːsənɪ] N (Law) furto
lard [lɑːd] N strutto ♦ VT (speech, writing): **to lard with** infarcire di
lar·der ['lɑːdə'] N dispensa
large [lɑːdʒ] ADJ (comp -r, superl -st) (gen) grande; (item of clothing) di taglia grande; (garden, room) grande, ampio(-a); (person) grande e grosso(-a); (animal) grosso(-a); (sum, loss) grosso(-a), ingente; (family, population) numeroso(-a); (meal) lauto(-a); **a large house** una casa grande; **a large amount** una grossa cifra; **a large number of people**

molta gente, molte persone; **we had a large meal** abbiamo mangiato tanto; **on a large scale** su vasta scala; **as large as life** in carne e ossa; **larger than life** portato(-a) all'estremo; **to grow large(r)** ingrandirsi; **to make large(r)** ingrandire ♦ N: **at large** (*criminal, dangerous animal*) in libertà; (*generally*) in generale, nell'insieme; **the world at large** il mondo nel complesso ♦ ADV: **by and large** generalmente

large·ly [ˈlɑːdʒlɪ] ADV in gran parte, per la maggior parte
❑ **largely** is not translated by the Italian word largamente

large-scale [ˌlɑːdʒˈskeɪl] ADJ (*map, drawing*) a larga scala; (*reforms, business activities*) su vasta *or* larga scala; **a large-scale operation** un'operazione su vasta scala

lark[1] [lɑːk] N (*bird*) allodola

lark[2] [lɑːk] N (*Brit fam: joke*) scherzo, gioco; **for a lark** per scherzo; **what a lark!** che spasso!

lar·va [ˈlɑːvə] N (*pl* **larvae** [ˈlɑːviː]) larva

lar·yn·gi·tis [ˌlærɪnˈdʒaɪtɪs] N laringite *f*

lar·ynx [ˈlærɪŋks] N (*Anat*) laringe *f*

la·sa·gne [ləˈzænjə] N lasagne *fpl*

las·civ·i·ous [ləˈsɪvɪəs] ADJ lascivo(-a)

la·ser [ˈleɪzə'] N laser *m inv*

laser beam N raggio *m* laser, *inv*

laser printer N stampante *f* laser, *inv*

lash [læʃ] N 1 (*also: eye lash*) ciglio; **long lashes** ciglia *fpl* lunghe 2 (*thong*) laccio (di cuoio); (*stroke*) frustata, colpo di frusta; (*of tail*) colpo ♦ VT 1 (*beat etc*) frustare; (*subj: rain, waves: also: lash against*) picchiare (contro), sbattere (contro); **the wind lashed the sea into a fury** il vento ha trasformato il mare in una furia 2 (*esp Naut: tie*) legare

► **lash down** VT + ADV assicurare (con corde) ♦ VI + ADV (*rain*) scrosciare

► **lash out** VI + ADV 1 **to lash out (at** *or* **against sb/sth)** menare colpi (contro qn/a qc); (*fig*) attaccare violentemente (qn/qc), inveire (contro qn/qc); **he lashed out against the government** ha inveito contro il governo 2 (*fam*): **to lash out (on sth)** (*spend*) spendere un sacco di soldi (per qc)

lash·ing [ˈlæʃɪŋ] N 1 (*beating*) frustata, sferzata 2 **lashings of** (*Brit fam*) un mucchio di, una montagna di

lass [læs] N (*esp in Northern Britain*) ragazza

las·so [læˈsuː] N lazo *m inv*, laccio ♦ VT prendere al lazo *or* al laccio

last[1] [lɑːst] ADJ 1 (*most recent*) ultimo(-a); (*week, month, year*) scorso(-a), passato(-a); **last Monday** lunedì scorso; **last night** ieri sera *or* notte, la notte scorsa; **I got home at midnight last night** ieri sera sono arrivata a casa a mezzanotte; **I couldn't sleep last night** ieri notte non sono riuscito a dormire; **during (the) last week** nel corso della settimana scorsa; **during the last 2 years** negli ultimi 2 anni; **the night before last** l'altro ieri sera *or* notte; (*the*) **last time** l'ultima volta 2 (*final: in series*) ultimo(-a); **the last page** l'ultima pagina; **the last slice of cake** l'ultima fetta di torta; **last thing at night** prima di andare a letto; **that was the last thing I expected** era l'ultima cosa che mi sarei aspettato; **last but one, second last** penultimo(-a) ♦ N: **the last of the wine/bread** quello che resta del vino/del pane; **they were the last to arrive** erano gli ultimi arrivati, sono arrivati per ultimi; **the last in the series** l'ultimo della serie; **each one better than the last** uno meglio dell'altro; **we'll never hear the last of it** chissà per quanto ne sentiremo parlare; **at (long) last** finalmente; **to the last** fino all'ultimo ♦ ADV (per) ultimo; **to do/come/arrive last (of all)** fare come/venire per/arrivare ultimo(-a); **he arrived last** è arrivato ultimo; **last but not least** ... come ultimo, ma non per questo meno importante...; **when I last saw them** *or* **saw them last** l'ultima volta che li ho visti; **I've lost my bag. - When did you see it last?** ho perso la borsa. - Dove l'hai vista per l'ultima volta?

last[2] [lɑːst] VI (*rain, film, pain*) durare; (*also: last out*) (*person*) resistere; (*money, resources*) durare, bastare; **the concert lasts two hours** il concerto dura due ore; **this material will last (for) years** questa stoffa durerà degli anni; **he didn't last long in the job** non ha resistito a lungo in quell'impiego; **it's too good to last** è troppo bello per durare ♦ VT durare; **he won't last the winter** non sopravvivrà all'inverno; **it will last you a lifetime** ti durerà una vita

last-ditch [ˈlɑːstˌdɪtʃ] ADJ (*attempt*) ultimo(-a) e disperato(-a)

last·ing [ˈlɑːstɪŋ] ADJ duraturo(-a), durevole; **to his lasting shame** con sua profonda vergogna

last·ly [ˈlɑːstlɪ] ADV infine, per finire, per ultimo; **lastly I'd like to mention ...** infine vorrei accennare a...

last-minute [ˈlɑːstˌmɪnɪt] ADJ (*decision*) dell'ultimo momento; (*preparation*) fatto(-a) all'ultimo momento; **last-minute changes** cambiamenti fatti all'ultimo momento

latch [lætʃ] N (*metal bar*) chiavistello; (*lock*) serratura a scatto; **the door is on the latch** la porta non è chiusa a chiave

► **latch on to** VI + ADV + PREP 1 (*cling to: person*) attaccarsi a, appiccicarsi a 2 (*idea*) afferrare, capire

latch·key [ˈlætʃˌkiː] N chiave *f* di casa

late [leɪt] (*comp* **-r**, *superl* **-st**) ADJ 1 (*not on time*) in ritardo; **to be (10 minutes) late** essere in ritardo (di 10 minuti); **hurry up or you'll be late!** sbrigati o farai tardi!; **to be late arriving** arrivare tardi *or* in ritardo; **to make sb late** far fare tardi a qn; **to be late with one's work** essere in ritardo con il proprio lavoro; **the late arrival of the flight** il ritardo del volo; **late delivery** consegna ritardata 2 (*towards end of period*) tardivo(-a); (*far on in day etc*) tardo(-a); (*composition, concerto*) recente; **his late remarks on industry** le sue recenti osservazioni sull'industria 4 (*euph: dead*) defunto(-a); **the late Mrs Smith** la defunta signora Smith; **my late-lamented husband** il mio povero marito 5 (*former*): **our late prime minister** il nostro ex primo ministro ♦ ADV 1 (*not on time*) in ritardo, tardi; **to arrive/leave 10 minutes late** arrivare/partire con 10 minuti di ritardo; **to arrive/leave too late** arrivare/partire troppo tardi; **I'm often late for school** arrivo spesso in ritardo a scuola; **better late than never** meglio tardi che mai 2 (*towards end of period*) tardi; **to work late** lavorare fino a tardi; **I went to bed late** sono andato a letto tardi; **late at night** a tarda notte; **late into the night** fino a tarda notte, fino a notte fonda; **in the late afternoon** nel tardo pomeriggio; **in late May** verso la fine di maggio; **late in life** in età avanzata; **late in 1978** verso la fine del 1978 3 (*recently*): **as late as 1991** ancora nel 1991; **of late** negli ultimi tempi, di recente, recentemente

late·com·er [ˈleɪtˌkʌmə'] N ritardatario(-a)

late·ly [ˈleɪtlɪ] ADV ultimamente, di recente, recentemente; **till lately** fino a poco *or* non molto tempo fa; **I haven't seen him lately** ultimamente non l'ho visto

late·ness [ˈleɪtnɪs] N (*of person, vehicle*) ritardo; (*of event*) ora tarda

la·tent [ˈleɪtənt] ADJ latente

lat·er [ˈleɪtə'] ADV *comp of* **late** 1 (*not on time*) più tardi 2 (*after*) dopo, più tardi; **a few years later** pochi anni dopo *or* più tardi 3 **later on** (*in series of events*) più avanti; (*in time*) più tardi; **later on today** più tardi; **I'll do it later** lo farò più tardi; **see you later!** ci vediamo dopo! ♦ ADJ 1 (*not on time*): (*meeting, train*) successivo(-a); (*edition, version*) più recente, successivo(-a); (*date etc*) posteriore; **he was later than usual** è arrivato più tardi del solito; **Easter is later this year** Pasqua cade più tardi quest'anno; **at a later stage** *or* **date** in un secondo momento; **his later symphonies** le sue ultime sinfonie; **this version is later than that one** questa versione è posteriore a *or* più recente di quella

lat·er·al [ˈlætərəl] ADJ laterale

lat·est [ˈleɪtɪst] ADJ *superl of* **late**(*gen*) ultimo(-a), più recente; **her latest exhibition** la sua ultima mostra; **their latest album** il loro ultimo album; **the latest news** le ultime notizie ♦ N 1 (*fam: most recent*) ultima novità; **the latest in skin care** l'ultima novità nel campo della cosmesi; **have you heard the latest?** (*news*) hai sentito l'ultima? 2 **at the latest** tardi; **it'll arrive tomorrow at the latest** arriverà al più tardi domani; **by ten o'clock at the latest** alle dieci al più tardi

la·tex [ˈleɪteks] N latice *m*

lath [lɑːθ] N (*pl* **laths**) listello, assicella

lathe [leɪð] N tornio

lath·er [ˈlɑːðəʳ] N (soap) schiuma (di sapone); **in a lather of sweat** tutto(-a) sudato(-a); **the horse was in a lather** il cavallo era coperto di sudore; **in a lather** (fig) tutto affannato(-a) or scalmanato(-a) ♦ VT (one's face) insaponarsi, insaponare ♦ VI (soap) far schiuma

Lat·in [ˈlætɪn] ADJ (language, temperament) latino(-a); (textbook, scholar, lessons) di latino ♦ N (language) latino; **I do Latin** studio latino

Latin America [ˈlætɪnəˈmɛrɪkə] N America Latina

Latin American [ˈlætɪnəˈmɛrɪkən] ADJ dell'America Latina, latino-americano(-a) ♦ N latino-americano(-a)

lati·tude [ˈlætɪtjuːd] N **1** (Geog) latitudine f **2** (fig: freedom) libertà d'azione; **artistic latitude** libertà artistica

la·trine [ləˈtriːn] N latrina

lat·ter [ˈlætəʳ] N: **the latter** quest'ultimo(-a); **of the two, the latter is better** fra i due è meglio il secondo; **the former ..., the latter ...** il primo..., il secondo... ♦ ADJ **1** (later) ultimo(-a); **the latter years of his life** gli ultimi anni della sua vita **2** (of two): **the latter part of the story** la seconda or l'ultima parte della storia; **the latter part of the match** l'ultima parte della partita

lat·ter·ly [ˈlætəlɪ] ADV negli ultimi tempi

lat·tice [ˈlætɪs] N (gen) reticolato; (for plants) graticcio, traliccio; (Chem) reticolo cristallino

lattice window N finestra con vetrata a losanghe

Lat·via [ˈlætvɪə] N Lettonia

Lat·vian [ˈlætvɪən] ADJ lettone ♦ N (person) lettone m/f; (language) lettone m

laud·able [ˈlɔːdəbl] ADJ (frm) lodevole, degno(-a) di lode

lauda·tory [ˈlɔːdətərɪ] ADJ (frm) elogiativo(-a)

laugh [lɑːf] VI ridere; **to laugh over** or **about sth** ridere di or per qc; **we all laughed about it later** più tardi ci abbiamo riso sopra; **it's nothing to laugh about** non c'è niente da ridere; **to laugh to o.s.** ridere dentro di sé or fra sé e sé; **I laughed till I cried** ho riso fino alle lacrime; **to laugh in sb's face** ridere in faccia a qn ♦ VT: **to laugh sb/sth out of court** ridicolizzare qn/qc; **to laugh sb to scorn** deridere qn ♦ N risata; **to get** or **raise a laugh (from sb)** far ridere (qn); **to have a good laugh at sth** farsi una bella risata su or sopra qc; **do you want a laugh?** vuoi farti due risate?; **to do sth for a laugh** (fam) fare qc per scherzo or per ridere; **what a laugh!** che ridere!; (iro) che ridicolo!; **with a laugh** con una risata; **it was a good laugh** è stato molto divertente; **good for a laugh** divertente; **he's always good for a laugh** ci fa sempre fare due risate; **we'll see who has the last laugh** (fig) staremo a vedere chi l'avrà vinta

▸ **laugh at** VI + PREP (person, sb's behaviour, also fig) ridere di; **I laughed at his joke** la sua barzelletta mi fece ridere

▸ **laugh off** VT + ADV (pain, accusation) ridere sopra, prendere alla leggera; **to laugh one's head off** (fam) sbellicarsi dalle risate

laugh·able [ˈlɑːfəbl] ADJ ridicolo(-a)

laugh·ing [ˈlɑːfɪŋ] ADJ (face) ridente; **this is no laughing matter** non è una cosa da ridere

laughing gas N gas m esilarante

laughing stock N zimbello; **to make a laughing stock of o.s.** rendersi ridicolo(-a)

laugh·ter [ˈlɑːftəʳ] N risata; (laughing) riso; **he roared with laughter** si è fatto una fragorosa risata; **hysterical laughter** risate isteriche; **tears and laughter** lacrime e risa

launch [lɔːntʃ] VT (gen, also fig) lanciare; (ship, plan) varare; (shore lifeboat) far uscire; (ship's boat) calare (in mare); **they're about to launch the new model** stanno per lanciare il nuovo modello ♦ N **1** (of rocket, product) lancio; (of boat) varo **2** (also: motor launch) motolancia; (pleasure boat) battello

▸ **launch into** VI + ADV (speech, task) lanciarsi in

▸ **launch out** VI + ADV: **to launch out (into)** lanciarsi (in)

launch·ing [ˈlɔːntʃɪŋ] N lancio; (of ship) varo; (of shore lifeboat) uscita; (of ship's boat) calo, caletta (in mare)

launching pad, launch pad N rampa di lancio

laun·der [ˈlɔːndəʳ] VT lavare e stirare; (fig: money) riciclare

laun·drette [ˈlɔːndrɛt], (USA) **laun·dro·mat** [ˈlɔːndrəˌmæt] N lavanderia (automatica)

laun·dry [ˈlɔːndrɪ] N (establishment) lavanderia; (clothes)

bucato, biancheria; **to do the laundry** fare il bucato, lavare la biancheria

lau·reate [ˈlɔːrɪɪt] N: **Nobel laureate in Physics** insignito(-a) del Nobel per la fisica; see also **poet laureate**

lau·rel [ˈlɔrəl] N alloro, lauro; **to rest on one's laurels** riposare or dormire sugli allori

Lau·sanne [ləʊˈzæn] N Losanna

lava [ˈlɑːvə] N lava

lava·tory [ˈlævətrɪ] N (Brit: room) gabinetto, toilette f inv; (: appliance) water m inv, gabinetto

lavatory paper N (Brit) carta igienica

lav·en·der [ˈlævɪndəʳ] N lavanda

lav·ish [ˈlævɪʃ] ADJ (person) prodigo(-a); (meal) lauto(-a); (surroundings, apartment) sontuoso(-a), lussuoso(-a); (expenditure) considerevole; (excessive) eccessivo(-a); **a lavish production of Tosca** una ricca messa in scena della Tosca; **to bestow lavish praise on sb** coprire qn di elogi or lodi ♦ VT: **to lavish sth on sb/on sth** colmare qn/qc di qc; **to lavish money on sth** spendere molto denaro per qc

lav·ish·ly [ˈlævɪʃlɪ] ADV (give, spend) generosamente; (furnished) sontuosamente, lussuosamente

law [lɔː] N legge f; **law of gravity** legge di gravità; **law of constant energy** legge della conservazione dell'energia; **against the law** contro la legge; **by law** a norma di or per legge; **by British law** secondo la legge britannica; **civil/criminal law** diritto civile/penale; **to study law** studiare giurisprudenza or legge; **Faculty of Law** facoltà di giurisprudenza; **court of law** corte f di giustizia, tribunale m; **to go to law** ricorrere alle vie legali; **to have the law on one's side** avere la legge dalla propria (parte); **to be above the law** essere al di sopra della legge; **to be a law unto o.s.** non conoscere altra legge che la propria; **there's no law against it** nessuna legge lo vieta or impedisce; **to take the law into one's own hands** farsi giustizia da sé; **his word is law** la sua parola è legge

law-abiding [ˈlɔːəˌbaɪdɪŋ] ADJ rispettoso(-a) delle leggi

law and order N l'ordine m pubblico

law·breaker [ˈlɔːˌbreɪkəʳ] N persona che viola la legge

law court N (aula del) tribunale m, corte f di giustizia

law·ful [ˈlɔːfʊl] ADJ legale

law·ful·ly [ˈlɔːfəlɪ] ADV legalmente

law·giver [ˈlɔːˌgɪvəʳ], **law·maker** [ˈlɔːˌmeɪkəʳ] N legislatore m

law·less [ˈlɔːlɪs] ADJ (time, place) privo(-a) di legge; (action) illegale

Law Lords NPL (Brit Pol) ≈ Corte f Suprema

lawn [lɔːn] N prato all'inglese

lawn-mower, lawn mower [ˈlɔːnˌməʊəʳ] N tagliaerba m inv, tosaerba m inv

lawn tennis N tennis m sull'erba

law school N (USA) facoltà f inv di giurisprudenza or legge

law student N studente(-essa) di giurisprudenza or legge

law·suit [ˈlɔːsuːt] N causa, processo; **to bring a lawsuit against** intentare causa a; **to end in a lawsuit** finire in tribunale

law·yer [ˈlɔːjəʳ] N (in court) avvocato(-essa); (consultant) legale m/f; (for sales, wills) notaio; **I have put the matter in the hands of my lawyer** ho affidato la questione al mio avvocato

lax [læks] ADJ (comp -er, superl -est) (conduct) lassista; (person: careless) negligente; (: on discipline) permissivo(-a); **to be lax about punctuality** non tenere or badare alla puntualità

laxa·tive [ˈlæksətɪv] N lassativo

lax·ity [ˈlæksɪtɪ], **lax·ness** [ˈlæksnɪs] N (see adj) lassismo; negligenza; permissività

lay¹ [leɪ] ADJ (Rel) laico(-a), secolare; (brother, sister) laico(-a); (fig: non-specialist) profano(-a)

lay² [leɪ] PT of **lie²**

lay³ [leɪ] (pt, pp **laid**) VT **1** (put, set) mettere, posare; (carpet) stendere; (bricks) posare; (cable, pipe) installare, fare la posa di; (trail) lasciare; (subj: bird: egg) deporre, fare; **to lay sth over sth** stendere qc su qc; **to lay sth on sth** coprire qc con qc; **he laid a sheet of newspaper on the floor** ha posato un foglio di giornale sul pavimento; **she laid the baby in her cot** ha messo la bambina nel suo lettino; **to lay the facts/one's proposals before sb** presentare i fatti/delle proposte a qn; **to be laid low with flu** essere costretto(-a) a letto

con l'influenza; **to be laid to rest** (*euph: buried*) essere sepolto(-a); **to get laid** (*fam!*) scopare (*fam!*); **I don't know where to lay my hands on it** non saprei dove trovarlo; **to lay o.s. open to attack/criticism** esporsi agli attacchi/alle critiche; **to lay the blame (for sth) on sb** dar la colpa (di qc) a qn; **to lay claim to sth** reclamare qc, accampare diritti *mpl* su qc; **to lay odds** *or* **a bet on sth** scommettere su qc **2** (*prepare: fire*) preparare; (*: trap, snare*) tendere; (*: mine*) posare, piantare; (*: table*) apparecchiare; **I haven't laid the table yet** non ho ancora apparecchiato la tavola **3** (*settle: ghost*) placare, esorcizzare; (*: doubts, fears*) eliminare, dissipare ♦ vi (*bird*) fare le uova, deporre le uova
- **lay alongside** vi + ADV (*Naut*) affiancarsi
- **lay aside** vt + ADV mettere da parte
- **lay by** vt + ADV mettere da parte
- **lay down** vt + ADV **1** (*put down: luggage*) posare, metter giù; (*: arms*) deporre, posare; (*: wine*) mettere in cantina; **to lay down one's life for sb/sth** sacrificare la propria vita per qn/qc **2** (*dictate: conditions*) stabilire, fissare; (*: principle, rule, policy*) formulare, fissare; **to lay down the law** (*fig*) dettar legge
- **lay in** vt + ADV fare una scorta di
- **lay into** vi + PREP (*fam: attack, scold*) aggredire
- **lay off** vt + ADV (*permanently*) licenziare; (*temporarily*) ≈ mettere in cassa integrazione; **my father's been laid off** mio padre è stato licenziato ♦ vi + ADV (*fam*) smettere ♦ vi + PREP (*fam*): **lay off it!** piantala!; **lay off him!** non rompergli le scatole! (*fam!*), lascialo in pace!
- **lay on** vt + ADV (*provide: water, electricity, gas*) installare, mettere; (*: meal etc*) fornire; (*: paint*) applicare; **to lay on (for)** (*meal, entertainment*) offrire (a); (*facilities*) mettere a disposizione (di); **to lay it on thick** (*fam: flatter*) andarci pesante con i complimenti; (*: exaggerate*) metterla più dura
- **lay out** vt + ADV **1** (*plan: garden, house, town*) pianificare, progettare; (*: page, letter*) impostare; **the way the house is laid out** la disposizione della casa **2** (*put ready: clothes*) preparare; (*display: goods for sale*) sistemare, disporre, presentare; (*make ready: body for burial*) preparare, comporre **3** (*spend*) sborsare **4** (*knock out*) stendere
- **lay over** vi + ADV (*USA*) fermarsi, far tappa
- **lay up** vt + ADV **1** (*store: provisions*) far scorta *or* provvista di, accumulare; **to lay up trouble for o.s.** crearsi dei guai **2** (*put out of service: boat*) mettere in disarmo, ritirare in cantiere; (*subj: illness*) costringere a letto; **to be laid up with flu** essere costretto(-a) a letto con l'influenza

lay·about ['leɪəˌbaʊt] N (*fam*) sfaccendato(-a), fannullone(-a)
lay-by ['leɪˌbaɪ] N (*Brit: Aut*) piazzola (di sosta)
lay days NPL (*Naut*) giorni di stallia
lay·er ['leɪə] N strato
lay·ette [leɪ'et] N corredino (per neonato)
lay·man ['leɪmən] N (*pl* **-men**) (*Rel*) laico; (*fig: non-professional*) profano; **in layman's terms** detto con parole semplici
lay-off ['leɪˌɒf] N (*permanent*) licenziamento; (*temporary*) ≈ messa in cassa integrazione
lay·out ['leɪˌaʊt] N (*of town*) piano urbanistico; (*of house, garden*) disposizione *f*; (*Typing*) impostazione *f*; (*Press*) impaginazione *f*
laze [leɪz] vi (*also*: **laze around** *or* **about**) oziare
la·zi·ness ['leɪzɪnɪs] N pigrizia
lazy ['leɪzɪ] ADJ (*comp* **-ier**, *superl* **-iest**) pigro(-a)
lb ABBR (= *libra: pound*) lb.
lbw [ˌelbiː'dʌbəljuː] N ABBR (*Cricket*: = *leg before wicket*) fallo dovuto al fatto che il giocatore ha la gamba davanti alla porta
LC [ˌel'siː] N ABBR (*USA*): = **Library of Congress**
lc ABBR (*Typ*) = **lower-case**
LCD [ˌelsiː'diː] N ABBR = **liquid crystal display**
Ld ABBR (*Brit*: = *lord*) titolo
lead¹ [liːd] (*pt, pp* **led**) vt **1** (*conduct*) condurre; **to lead the way** fare strada; **to lead astray** sviare; **he is easily led** si lascia facilmente convincere *or* influenzare **2** (*be the leader of: government*) essere a capo di; (*: party*) essere alla guida *or* a capo di; (*: expedition, movement*) guidare; (*: revolution*) capeggiare; (*: team*) capitanare; (*: league, procession*) essere in testa a; (*: orchestra: Brit*) essere il primo violino di; (*USA*) dirigere; **he led the party for five years** ha guidato il partito

per cinque anni; **to lead the field** essere in testa; (*fig*) essere all'avanguardia nel campo **3** (*life, existence*) condurre **4** (*induce*) indurre, portare; **to lead sb to do sth** portare qn a fare qc; **to lead sb to believe that ...** far credere a qn che...; **it led me to the conclusion that ...** mi ha portato alla conclusione che... ♦ vi **1** (*go in front*) andare avanti; (*Cards*) essere di mano **2** (*in match, race*) essere in testa; **to lead by 3 goals** avere 3 gol di vantaggio **3** (*street, corridor*) portare; **where does this door lead?** cosa c'è oltre questa porta?; **the street that leads to the station** la strada che porta alla stazione **4** (*result in*): **to lead to** portare a; **one thing leads to another** ... una cosa tira l'altra...; **the incident led to serious trouble** l'incidente ha portato a problemi seri ♦ N **1** (*front position*) posizione *f* di testa; (*distance, time ahead*) vantaggio; **to be in the lead** (*Sport*) essere in testa; (*fig*) essere all'avanguardia; **to be in the lead by 5 points to 4** condurre *or* essere in testa per 5 a 4; **to take the lead** (*Sport*) passare in testa; (*fig*) prendere l'iniziativa; **to have a 3-second lead** avere un vantaggio di 3 secondi; **to follow sb's lead** seguire l'esempio di qn; **it's your lead** (*Cards*) sei tu di mano **2** (*Elec*) filo (elettrico) **3** (*for dog*) guinzaglio **4** (*clue*) indizio, pista **5** (*Theatre*) parte *f or* ruolo principale; **male/female lead** protagonista *m/f* maschile/femminile
- **lead away** vt + ADV condurre via, portar via
- **lead back** vt + ADV riportare, ricondurre
- **lead off** vt + ADV **1** portare; **he led us off on a visit of the museum** ci ha portato a visitare il museo **2** (*fig: begin*) dare inizio a, cominciare ♦ vi + PREP partire da; **a street leading off the main road** una traversa della strada principale
- **lead on** vt + ADV **1** (*deceive*) prendere in giro, ingannare **2** (*incite*): **to lead sb on (to do sth)** incoraggiare *or* spingere *or* trascinare qn (a fare qc)
- **lead up to** vt + ADV + PREP portare (a); (*fig*) preparare la strada per; **what's all this leading up to?** dove vuoi andare a parare?

lead² [led] N (*metal*) piombo; (*in pencil*) mina; (*for sounding*) scandaglio ♦ ADJ (*pipes*) di piombo; (*paint*) a base di piombo
lead·ed ['ledɪd] ADJ: **leaded windows** vetrate *fpl* (artistiche)
lead·en ['ledn] ADJ (*colour, sky*) plombeo(-a); (*fig: atmosphere*) teso(-a); (*: silence*) opprimente; **with a leaden heart** con la morte nel cuore
lead·er ['liːdə] N **1** (*of group, expedition*) capo; (*of party, union*) capo, leader *m/f inv*; (*Mus: of orchestra: Brit*) primo violino; (*: USA*) direttore *m* d'orchestra; (*guide*) guida; (*Mountaineering*) capocordata *m inv*; **he's a born leader** è nato per comandare **2** (*Sport: in race*) chi è in testa, leader *m/f inv*; **the leaders of the First Division** (*Ftbl*) la squadra in testa alla classifica di serie A; **they are leaders in their field** (*fig*) sono all'avanguardia nel loro campo **3** (*Brit: in newspaper*) articolo di fondo, editoriale *m*
lead·er·ship ['liːdəʃɪp] N **1** direzione *f*, leadership *f inv*; **under the leadership of ...** sotto la direzione *or* guida di...; **qualities of leadership** qualità *fpl* di un capo; **the leadership of the Conservative Party** la leadership del partito conservatore **2** (*leaders*) dirigenti *mpl*, dirigenza
lead-free ['ledfriː] ADJ (*petrol*) senza piombo, verde
lead·ing ['liːdɪŋ] ADJ (*horse, car: in race*) che è in testa, di testa; (*: in procession*) che apre la sfilata; (*chief: member etc*) principale, preminente; (*: Theatre, etc role, character*) principale, di primo piano; **one of the leading figures of this century** una delle più importanti figure di questo secolo
leading lady N (*Theatre*) prima attrice
leading light N (*person*) personaggio di primo piano
leading man N (*Theatre*) primo attore
lead pencil [ˌled'pensəl] N matita con la mina di grafite
lead poisoning ['ledˌpɔɪznɪŋ] N saturnismo
lead time [liːdˌtaɪm] N (*Comm*) tempo di consegna
lead weight [ˌled'weɪt] N piombino, piombo
leaf [liːf] N (*pl* **leaves**) **1** (*of plant*) foglia **2** (*of book*) foglio, pagina; **to turn over a new leaf** (*fig*) voltare pagina, cambiar vita; **to take a leaf out of sb's book** (*fig*) prendere esempio da qn **3** (*of table: fold-down*) ribalta; (*: extending*) asse *f* estraibile
- **leaf through** vt + PREP (*book*) sfogliare

leaf·let ['liːflɪt] N (*gen*) dépliant *m inv*; (*single sheet*) volantino

leafy ['liːfɪ] ADJ (*comp* **-ier**, *superl* **-iest**) (*suburb*) ricco(-a) di verde; (*branch*) ricco(-a) di foglie

league [liːg] N **1** (*alliance*) associazione *f*, lega; **to be in league with** essere in associazione con; (*pej*) essere in combutta con, essere in lega con; **to form a league against** far lega contro **2** (*Ftbl, Rugby*) campionato; **they are at the top of the league** sono in testa al campionato; **the Premier League** ≈ la Serie A; **they're not in the same league** (*fig: fam*) non c'è paragone

league table N (*Brit: Ftbl*) classifica del campionato; (*of schools etc*) classifica (*ordinata per livello qualitativo, pubblicata dal governo*)

leak [liːk] N (*in pipe*) perdita, fuoriuscita; (*in boat*) falla; (*in roof, wall*) infiltrazione *f*; (*of gas*) fuga, perdita, fuoriuscita; (*fig: of information*) fuga di notizie; **a leak in the radiator** una perdita del radiatore; **to have** *or* **take a leak** (*fam*) andare al bagno, andare a far pipì ♦ VI (*roof, bucket*) perdere; (*ship*) far acqua; (*shoes*) lasciar passare l'acqua; **the pipe is leaking** il tubo perde; **water was leaking into the cellar** l'acqua si stava infiltrando nella cantina ♦ VT (*liquid*) gocciolare, perdere; (*fig: information*) divulgare

▸ **leak out** VI + ADV (*liquid*) uscire (fuori); (*gas*) esalare, uscire; (*fig: news*) trapelare

leak·age ['liːkɪdʒ] N (*of water, gas etc*) perdita

leaky ['liːkɪ] ADJ (*comp* **-ier**, *superl* **-iest**) (*pipe, bucket, roof*) che perde; (*shoe*) che lascia passare l'acqua; (*boat*) che fa acqua

lean¹ [liːn] ADJ (*comp* **-er**, *superl* **-est**) magro(-a); **the lean years** i tempi di magra ♦ N (*of meat*) magro, parte *f* magra (*della carne*)

lean² [liːn] (*pt, pp* **leaned** *or* **leant**) VI **1** (*gatepost, wall, slope*) essere inclinato(-a), pendere; **to lean to(wards) the left/ right** (*Pol*) avere tendenze di sinistra/di destra **2** (*for support: person*): **to lean on, lean against** appoggiarsi a; **to be leaning against** (*ladder*) essere appoggiato(-a) a *or* contro; **the ladder was leaning against the wall** la scala era appoggiata al muro; **to lean on sb** (*also fig: for support*) appoggiarsi a qn; (*fig: put pressure on*) far pressione su qn; **she leant on his arm** si appoggiò al suo braccio; **she leant on him to contribute to the fund** lo ha spinto a contribuire alla raccolta di fondi ♦ VT (*ladder, bicycle*): **to lean sth against/on sth** appoggiare qc a *or* contro/su qc; **he leaned the ladder against the wall** ha appoggiato la scala al muro; **to lean one's head on sth** appoggiare la testa su qc

▸ **lean back** VI + ADV sporgersi indietro; (*against sth*) appoggiarsi all'indietro

▸ **lean forward** VI + ADV piegarsi in avanti

▸ **lean out** VI + ADV: **to lean out (of)** sporgersi (da); **she leaned out of the window** si è sporta dal finestrino

▸ **lean over** VI + ADV (*person*) chinarsi; (*thing*) piegarsi, inclinarsi; **don't lean out too far** non chinarti troppo; **to lean over backwards to help sb** (*fig: fam*) farsi in quattro per aiutare qn ♦ VI + PREP (*balcony, gate*) sporgersi da, affacciarsi a; (*desk*) piegarsi su, chinarsi su

lean·ing ['liːnɪŋ] N: **leaning (towards)** tendenza (a), propensione *f* (per) ♦ ADJ inclinato(-a), pendente; **the leaning Tower of Pisa** la torre (pendente) di Pisa

leant [lɛnt] PT, PP *of* **lean²**

lean-to ['liːntuː] N (*roof*) tettoia; (*building*) edificio con tetto appoggiato ad altro edificio

leap [liːp] (*pt, pp* **leaped** *or* **leapt**) VI saltare, balzare; **he leapt into/out of the train** saltò sul/giù dal treno; **to leap to one's feet** scattare in piedi; **he leapt out of his chair when his team scored** è saltato in piedi quando la sua squadra ha segnato; **to leap about** saltellare qua e là; **to leap out** saltare fuori; **to leap out at sb** saltare addosso a qn; **to leap over sth** saltare qc con un balzo; **my heart leapt** ho avuto un tuffo al cuore; **to leap at an offer** afferrare al volo una proposta ♦ VT (*fence, ditch*) saltare ♦ N salto, balzo; **a leap in the dark** (*fig*) un salto nel buio; **by leaps and bounds** a passi da gigante

▸ **leap up** VI + ADV (*person*) balzare in piedi; (*flames*) divampare

leap·frog ['liːpfrɒg] N gioco della cavallina ♦ VI: **to leapfrog over sb/sth** saltare (alla cavallina) qn/qc

leapt [lɛpt] PT, PP *of* **leap**

leap year N anno bisestile

learn [lɜːn] (*pt, pp* **learned** *or* **learnt**) VT (*study*) imparare; (*hear*) (venire a) sapere; **to learn (how) to do sth** imparare a fare qc; **I'm learning to ski** sto imparando a sciare; **to learn that ...** apprendere che..., venire a sapere che...; **we were sorry to learn that it was closing down** la notizia della chiusura ci ha fatto dispiacere; **I think he's learned his lesson** (*fig*) penso che gli sia servito di lezione ♦ VI: **to learn about sth** (*study*) studiare qc, imparare qc; (*hear*) sentire qc, apprendere qc; **I've learned from experience not to trust him** l'esperienza mi ha insegnato a non fidarmi di lui; **you learn from your mistakes** sbagliando s'impara; **you'll learn!** un giorno capirai!

▸ **learn off** VT + ADV imparare a memoria

learn·ed ['lɜːnɪd] ADJ (*person*) erudito(-a), dotto(-a); (*book*) dotto(-a)

learn·er ['lɜːnə'] N principiante *m/f*; **she's a fast learner** è una che impara subito *or* con facilità; **slow learner** (*Scol*) alunno(-a) che ha difficoltà di apprendimento; **he's a learner (driver)** (*Brit*) sta imparando a guidare, è un principiante

learn·ing ['lɜːnɪŋ] N cultura, erudizione *f*, sapere *m*

learnt [lɜːnt] PT, PP *of* **learn**

lease [liːs] N contratto di affitto (*a lungo termine con responsabilità simili a quelle di un proprietario*); **on lease** in affitto; **to give sb a new lease of life** (*fig*) ridare nuova vita a qn ♦ VT (*take*) affittare, prendere in affitto; (*give: also:* **lease out**) affittare, dare in affitto

▸ **lease back** VT + ADV effettuare un lease-back *inv*

lease-back ['liːsbæk] N lease-back *m inv*

lease·hold ['liːshəʊld] ADJ in affitto ♦ N (*property*) proprietà *f inv* in affitto; (*tenure*) diritto di godimento (della proprietà)

leash [liːʃ] N guinzaglio; **on a leash** al guinzaglio

least [liːst] superl *of* **little²** ADJ minimo(-a), più piccolo(-a); **I haven't the least idea** non ne ho la minima idea; **it takes the least time** è quello per cui ci vuole meno tempo; **go for the ones with least fat** scegli quelli con meno grassi; **she wasn't in the least bit interested** non era minimamente interessata; **that's the least of my worries** è la cosa che mi preoccupa di meno *or* che meno mi preoccupa, quella è l'ultima delle mie preoccupazioni ♦ N minimo; **it's the least I can do** è il minimo che possa fare; **to say the least** a dir poco; **the least said about the meeting, the better** meno parliamo della riunione e meglio è; **at least** almeno; **at least try** posso sempre *or* almeno provarci; **...but at least nobody was hurt** ...ma almeno nessuno si è fatto male; **at the very least** come minimo; **not in the least** per nulla *or* niente, affatto ♦ ADV meno; **the least expensive car** l'auto meno cara; **the least expensive hotel** l'albergo meno costoso; **she is least able to afford it** è quella che se lo può permettere meno di tutti; **least of all me** e men che meno io, tanto meno io; **for a number of reasons, not least ...** per una serie di motivi, non ultimo il fatto che...; **history is the subject I like the least** la storia è la materia che mi piace di meno

leath·er ['leðə'] N (*hide: soft*) pelle *f*; (*: hard*) cuoio; (*wash leather*) pelle di daino ♦ ADJ (*see n*) di *or* in pelle; di *or* in cuoio; **leather goods** (articoli di) pelletteria; **a black leather jacket** una giacca di pelle nera

leave [liːv] (*pt, pp* **left**) VT **1** (*go away from: town*) lasciare, andarsene da; (*: room*) lasciare, uscire da; (*: station*) partire da; (*: hospital*) uscire da; (*: person*) lasciare; **to leave school** (*complete studies*) finire la scuola; (*prematurely*) lasciare la scuola; **to leave home** uscire di casa; (*permanently*) andarsene di casa; **she left home when she was sixteen** se n'è andata di casa quando aveva sedici anni; **we left London at six o'clock** partiamo da Londra alle sei; **they have left this address** se ne sono andati da qui; **may I leave the room?** (*Scol: euph: to go to the lavatory*) posso uscire?; **to leave the table** alzarsi da tavola; **the car left the road** la macchina è uscita di strada; **the train is leaving in 10 minutes** il treno parte fra 10 minuti **2** (*forget*) lasciare, dimenticare; (*give: in will, as tip*) lasciare; **don't leave your wallet in the car** non lasciare il portafoglio in macchina **3** (*allow to remain*) lasciare; **to leave the window open** lasciare la finestra aperta; **let's leave it at that** per ora basta (così); **leave it to me!** ci penso io!, lascia fare a me!; **leave it with me** lascia che me ne occupi io; **I'll leave it to you to decide** decidi tu, lo lascio decidere a te; **she left him to it** lo ha lasciato alle sue occupazioni; **he leaves a wife and a child** lascia la moglie e un figlio; **to leave sb alone** lasciare qn (da) solo(-a); **leave me alone** *or* **in peace!** lasciami in pace!; **don't leave anything to chance** non lasciar niente al caso; **it leaves much to be desired** lascia molto a desiderare; **take it** *or* **leave it!** prendere o lasciare!; **3 from 10 leaves 7** 10 meno 3 fa 7 **4** (*remaining*)**: to be left (over)** rimanere, restare, avanzare; **all the money I have left (over)** tutti i soldi che mi restano *or* che mi sono avanzati; **there's some milk left over** c'è rimasto del latte; **how many are (there) left?** quanti ne restano?, quanti ce ne sono ancora?; **nothing was left for me (to do)** non ho più niente da fare; **to sell it** non mi rimaneva *or* restava altro (da fare) che venderlo ♦ VI (*plane, train*) partire; (*person*) uscire, andarsene; **the bus leaves at eight** l'autobus parte alle otto; **they left yesterday** sono partiti ieri; **she's just left** è appena andata via; **he's already left for the airport** è già uscito per andare all'aeroporto ♦ N **1** (*permission*) permesso, autorizzazione *f*; **without so much as a "by your leave"** senza nemmeno chiedere il permesso **2** (*permission to be absent*) permesso; (*of public employee*) congedo; (*Mil*) licenza; **unpaid leave** ≈ aspettativa; **on leave** in congedo; **on leave of absence** in permesso; (*public employee*) in congedo; (*Mil*) in licenza; **my brother is on leave for a week** mio fratello è in licenza per una settimana **3 to take (one's) leave of sb** accomiatarsi da qn, congedarsi da qn; **have you taken leave of your senses?** ma sei uscito di senno?, ma sei impazzito?

▸ **leave about, leave around** VT + ADV lasciare in giro
▸ **leave behind** VT + ADV (*also fig*) lasciare indietro; (*forget*) dimenticare; **I left my umbrella behind in the shop** ho dimenticato l'ombrello nel negozio; **she leaves everybody else behind** è superiore a tutti gli altri; **you'll be left behind by the rest** rimarrai indietro rispetto agli altri
▸ **leave in** VT + ADV lasciare, non togliere
▸ **leave off** VT + ADV **1** (*cover, lid, clothes*) non mettere; (*heating, light*) non accendere; (*name: from list*) non inserire **2** (*fam: stop*) **to leave off doing sth** smetterla *or* piantarla di fare qc ♦ VI + ADV (*Brit fam: stop*) smetterla
▸ **leave on** VT + ADV (*lid*) lasciare su; (*light, fire, cooker*) lasciare acceso(-a); (*coat*) non togliere
▸ **leave out** VT + ADV **1** (*omit*) tralasciare; (*in reading etc*) saltare; **he feels left out** si sente escluso *or* lasciato in disparte; **not knowing the language, I felt really left out** mi sentivo proprio escluso dato che non sapevo la lingua **2** (*not put back*) lasciare fuori
▸ **leave over** VT + ADV (*postpone*) rimandare

leaves [liːvz] NPL *of* **leaf**
leave-taking [ˈliːvˌteɪkɪŋ] N commiato, addio
Leba·nese [ˌlebəˈniːz] ADJ libanese ♦ N *pl inv* libanese *m/f*
Leba·non [ˈlebənən] N: **(the) Lebanon** (il) Libano
lech·er·ous [ˈletʃərəs] ADJ lascivo(-a)
lec·tern [ˈlektən] N leggio
lec·ture [ˈlektʃəˈ] N **1** (*Univ*) lezione *f*; (*by visitor*) conferenza; **a public lecture** una conferenza pubblica; **to deliver** *or* **give a lecture on** tenere una lezione *or* una conferenza su **2** (*reproof*) paternale *f*, predica; **to give sb a lecture** fare la predica a qn ♦ VI: **to lecture (in sth)** essere professore incaricato (di qc); **to lecture (to sb on sth)** (*Univ*) tenere una conferenza (a qn su qc); (*visiting lecturer*) tenere una conferenza (a qn su qc); **she lectures at the technical college** insegna all'istituto tecnico ♦ VT (*reprove*) rimproverare, fare una ramanzina a; **he's always lecturing us** ci rimprovera sempre
❑ **lecture** is not translated by the Italian word *lettura*

lecture hall, lecture theatre N aula magna
lec·tur·er [ˈlektʃərəˈ] N (*Brit: Univ*) professore(-essa), docente *m/f* (universitario(-a)); (*speaker*) conferenziere(-a); **assistant lecturer** (*Brit*) ≈ professore(-essa) associato(-a); **senior lecturer** (*Brit*) ≈ professore(-essa) ordinario(-a)
LED [ˌeliːˈdiː] N ABBR (*Elec: = light-emitting diode*) LED *m inv*
led [led] PT, PP *of* **lead**[1]
ledge [ledʒ] N (*on wall etc*) sporgenza; (*of window*) davanzale *m*; (*of mountain*) cengia, cornice *f*
ledg·er [ˈledʒəˈ] N libro mastro, registro
lee [liː] N lato *m* sottovento, *inv*; **in the lee of** a ridosso di, al riparo di ♦ ADJ sottovento *inv*; **to have a lee helm** (*ship*) essere poggiero(-a)

leech [liːtʃ] N sanguisuga
leek [liːk] N porro
leer [lɪəˈ] N (*lustful*) espressione *f* libidinosa; (*evil*) espressione *f* malvagia ♦ VI: **to leer at sb** (*lustfully*) guardare qn con occhi vogliosi; (*cruelly*) guardare qn con malvagità
lee·ward [ˈliːwəd] (*Naut*) ADJ sottovento *inv* ♦ ADV sottovento; **to drift leeward** scarrocciare ♦ N lato sottovento; **to leeward** sottovento
lee·way [ˈliːweɪ] N (*Naut*) deriva; (*fig*) margine *m*; **they gave him a great deal of leeway** gli hanno lasciato ampia libertà di azione
left[1] [left] PT, PP *of* **leave**
left[2] [left] ADJ sinistro(-a); **my left hand** la mia mano sinistra ♦ ADV a sinistra; **turn left at the traffic lights** volta a sinistra al semaforo ♦ N sinistra; **on my left, to my left** sulla *or* alla mia sinistra; **on the left, to the left** sulla *or* a sinistra; **the Left** (*Pol*) la sinistra; **he has always been on the Left** ha sempre avuto idee di sinistra
left-click [ˈleftklɪk] VI (*Comput*): **to left-click on** fare clic con il pulsante sinistro del mouse su
left-hand [ˈleftˌhænd] ADJ a sinistra; **left-hand page** pagina a *or* di sinistra; **left-hand side** (*parte f*) sinistra; **on the left-hand side** sulla *or* a sinistra, sul lato sinistro
left-hand drive ADJ (*Brit*) guida a sinistra
left-handed [ˈleftˈhændɪd] ADJ mancino(-a); (*fig: compliment*) ambiguo(-a); **left-handed scissors** forbici *fpl* per mancini
leftie [ˈleftɪ] N (*fam*) uno(-a) di sinistra
left·ist [ˈleftɪst] (*Pol*) ADJ di sinistra ♦ N uno(-a) di sinistra
left-luggage [ˌleftˈlʌgɪdʒ] N: **left-luggage office** deposito *m* bagagli, *inv*; **left-luggage locker** armadietto per depositare i bagagli
left-overs [ˈleftˌəʊvəz] NPL avanzi *mpl*
left wing N (*Mil, Sport*) ala sinistra; (*Pol*) sinistra
left-winger [ˌleftˈwɪŋəˈ] N (*Sport*) ala sinistra; (*Pol*) uno(-a) di sinistra
lefty [ˈleftɪ] N = **leftie**
leg [leg] N **1** (*gen*) gamba; (*of animal, bird*) zampa; (*Culin: of chicken, turkey*) coscia; (*: of lamb, pork*) coscotto; (*of furniture*) piede *m*; **she's broken her leg** si è rotta la gamba; **to be on one's last legs** (*person, animal*) stare in piedi per miracolo; (*machine, car*) funzionare per miracolo; **he hasn't got a leg to stand on** (*fig*) non ha una scusa *or* una ragione che stia in piedi; **to pull sb's leg** (*fig*) prendere in giro qn; **to stretch one's legs** sgranchirsi le gambe; **to give sb a leg up** aiutare qn a salire; (*fig*) dare una mano a qn; **I got a leg up** mi hanno dato una mano; **shake a leg!** (*Brit fam*) muoviti!, sbrigati!; **show a leg!** (*fam*) alzati!; **break a leg!** in bocca al lupo!; **to get one's leg over** (*Brit fam*) scopare **2** (*stage: of journey*) tappa; (*of relay race*) frazione *f*; (*of competition*) girone *m* ♦ VT: **to leg it** (*fam*) darsela a gambe
lega·cy [ˈlegəsɪ] N eredità *f inv*; (*fig*) retaggio; **a small legacy** una piccola eredità; **a legacy from the past** un retaggio del passato
le·gal [ˈliːgəl] ADJ **1** (*lawful*) legale; (*requirement*) di legge; **these coins are no longer legal currency** queste monete sono fuori corso **2** (*relating to the law: gen*) legale; (*: error*) giudiziario; **as a member of the legal profession** come legale; **to take legal action** *or* **proceedings against sb** intentare un'azione legale contro qn, far causa a qn; **legal department** (*of a firm*) ufficio legale, contenzioso; **legal aid** assistenza legale gratuita, patrocinio legale gratuito
legal adviser N consulente *m/f* legale
le·gal·ity [lɪˈgælɪtɪ] N legalità
le·gal·ize [ˈliːgəˌlaɪz] VT legalizzare
le·gal·ly [ˈliːgəlɪ] ADV legalmente; **to be legally binding** essere (legalmente) vincolante
legal tender N moneta in corso legale
le·ga·tion [lɪˈgeɪʃən] N legazione *f*
leg·end [ˈledʒənd] N leggenda
leg·end·ary [ˈledʒəndərɪ] ADJ leggendario(-a)
-legged [ˈlegɪd] SUFF: **two-legged** a due gambe (*or* zampe), bipede
leg·gings [ˈlegɪŋz] NPL (*women's*) pantacollant *mpl*, fuseaux *mpl*; (*men's*) gambali *mpl*

leg·gy ['lɛgɪ] ADJ (comp **-ier**, superl **-iest**) dalle gambe lunghe

leg·ibil·ity [ˌlɛdʒɪ'bɪlɪtɪ] N leggibilità

leg·ible ['lɛdʒəbl] ADJ leggibile

leg·ibly ['lɛdʒəblɪ] ADV in modo leggibile

le·gion ['liːdʒən] N legione f; (fig) schiera, stuolo ♦ ADJ (frm: very many) innumerevole

le·gion·naire [ˌliːdʒə'nɛəʳ] N (French Foreign Legion) legionario

leg·is·late ['lɛdʒɪsleɪt] VI legiferare, promulgare delle leggi

leg·is·la·tion [ˌlɛdʒɪs'leɪʃən] N legislazione f; **a piece of legislation** una legge; **legislation to protect women's rights** leggi in difesa dei diritti delle donne

leg·is·la·tive ['lɛdʒɪslətɪv] ADJ legislativo(-a)

leg·is·la·tor ['lɛdʒɪsleɪtəʳ] N legislatore m

leg·is·la·ture ['lɛdʒɪslətʃəʳ] N organi mpl legislativi, potere m legislativo

le·giti·ma·cy [lɪ'dʒɪtɪməsɪ] N (gen) legittimità; (of argument, excuse) validità

le·giti·mate [lɪ'dʒɪtɪmɪt] ADJ (lawful) legittimo(-a); (argument, cause, excuse) buono(-a), valido(-a); (complaint) legittimo(-a); (conclusion) logico(-a)

le·giti·mize [lɪ'dʒɪtɪˌmaɪz] VT (gen) convalidare, rendere legittimo(-a)

leg·less ['lɛglɪs] ADJ (Brit fam) sbronzo(-a), fatto(-a)

leg·room ['lɛgˌrʊm] N spazio per le gambe

Leics ABBR (Brit: = Leicestershire)

lei·sure ['lɛʒəʳ] N svago, tempo libero; **a life of leisure** una vita comoda; **to be a lady of leisure** (hum) fare la bella vita; **do it at your leisure** fallo con comodo ♦ ADJ: **leisure activities** attività ricreative; **in one's leisure time** durante il proprio tempo libero

leisure centre N (Brit) centro sportivo e ricreativo

lei·sure·ly ['lɛʒəlɪ] ADJ (day, stroll, trip) tranquillo(-a); **in a leisurely way** (fatto(-a)) con comodo or senza fretta

leisure suit N (USA) tuta da ginnastica

lem·on ['lɛmən] N (fruit) limone m ♦ ADJ (colour) giallo limone inv

lem·on·ade [ˌlɛmə'neɪd] N (fizzy drink) gassosa; (with lemon flavour) limonata

lemon cheese, lemon curd N crema di limone (da spalmare sul pane)

lemon juice N succo di limone

lem·on squeez·er ['lɛmənˌskwiːzəʳ] N spremilimoni m inv, spremiagrumi m inv

lemon tea N tè m inv al limone

lend [lɛnd] (pt, pp **lent**) VT (gen) prestare; (fig: impart: importance, mystery, authority) conferire; **I can lend you some money** posso prestarti del denaro; **he lent me £10** mi ha prestato dieci sterline; **to lend out** prestare, dare in prestito; **to lend a hand** dare una mano; **to lend an ear to sb/sth** prestare ascolto a qn/qc; **it does not lend itself to being filmed** non si presta ad essere filmato

lend·er ['lɛndəʳ] N chi presta, prestatore(-trice)

lending library N biblioteca (con servizio di prestito di libri)

length [lɛŋθ] N **1** (size, extent) lunghezza; (duration) durata; **it is 2 metres in length** è lungo 2 metri; **what is its length?, what length is it?** quant'è lungo?; **throughout the length and breadth of Italy** in tutta Italia; **to fall full length** cadere lungo(-a) disteso(-a); **length of time** periodo (di tempo); **for what length of time?** per quanto tempo?; **1000 words in length** di 1000 parole; **their team won the boat race by 2 lengths** (Sport) la loro squadra ha vinto la gara di canottaggio per 2 lunghezze; **at length** (at last) finalmente; (lengthily) a lungo; **to speak at length** dilungarsi, parlare a lungo; **to go to any lengths to do sth** fare qualsiasi cosa pur di or per fare qc; **she went to great lengths to make sure that …** fece di tutto per assicurarsi che… **2** (piece: of road, pipe etc) pezzo, tratto; (: material) taglio, altezza; **a dress/skirt length** un taglio per vestito/gonna

length·en ['lɛŋθən] VT (distance) allungare; (time) prolungare; **he lengthened his stride** ha allungato il passo ♦ VI allungarsi; **the days are lengthening** le giornate si stanno allungando

length·ways ['lɛŋθˌweɪz], **length·wise** ['lɛŋθˌwaɪz] ADV per la lunghezza, per lungo

lengthy ['lɛŋθɪ] ADJ (comp **-ier**, superl **-iest**) lungo(-a); (tedious) interminabile

le·ni·ence ['liːnɪəns], **le·ni·en·cy** ['liːnɪənsɪ] N (of person) clemenza, indulgenza; (of sentence, punishment) mitezza

le·ni·ent ['liːnɪənt] ADJ (person) indulgente, clemente; (sentence, punishment) mite; **to be lenient with sb** essere indulgente con qn

le·ni·ent·ly ['liːnɪəntlɪ] ADV con indulgenza

lens [lɛnz] N (Anat: of the eye) cristallino; (of spectacles) lente f; (of camera etc) obiettivo; **contact lenses** lenti a contatto

Lent [lɛnt] N Quaresima; **I'm giving it up for Lent** vi rinuncio come fioretto (quaresimale)

lent [lɛnt] PT, PP of **lend**

len·til ['lɛntl] N lenticchia

Leo ['liːəʊ] N (Astron, Astrol) Leone m; **to be Leo** essere del Leone; **I'm Leo** sono del Leone

leop·ard ['lɛpəd] N leopardo; **the leopard cannot** or **doesn't change its spots** il lupo perde il pelo ma non il vizio

leo·tard ['liːətɑːd] N body m inv (per ginnastica, danza)

lep·er ['lɛpəʳ] N lebbroso(-a)

leper colony N lebbrosario

lep·ro·sy ['lɛprəsɪ] N lebbra

les·bian ['lɛzbɪən] ADJ lesbico(-a) ♦ N lesbica

le·sion ['liːʒən] N (Med) lesione f

Le·so·tho [lə'səʊtəʊ] N Lesotho m

less [lɛs] comp of **little²** ADJ meno; now we eat less bread ora mangiamo meno pane; **she has less time to spare** ha meno tempo a disposizione; **of less importance** di minor importanza ♦ PRON meno; **a bit less, please** un po' meno, per favore; **we see less of them now** li vediamo di meno adesso; **the less you read the less you learn** meno leggi meno impari; **can't you let me have it for less?** mi potrebbe fare un piccolo sconto?; **the less said about it the better** meno se ne parla e meglio è; **less than half** meno della metà; **less than £1/a kilo/3 metres** meno di una sterlina/un chilo/3 metri; **it's less than a kilometre from here** è a meno di un chilometro da qui; **less than you think** meno di quanto tu creda; **less than you/ever** meno di te/che mai; **the holiday was less than perfect** la vacanza non è stata proprio stupenda; **it's nothing less than a disaster** è un disastro bell'e buono; **a tip of £10, no less!** (fam) nientemeno che 10 sterline di mancia! ♦ ADV meno, di meno; **to go out less (often)** uscire di meno; **less and less** sempre meno; **still less** ancora meno; **none the less …** ugualmente…, lo stesso… ♦ PREP meno; **less 5%** meno il 5%

les·see [lɛ'siː] N affittuario(-a), locatario(-a)

less·en ['lɛsn] VT (gen) diminuire, ridurre; (pain) alleviare; (cost, tension) ridurre; (shock) attutire, attenuare ♦ VI (gen) diminuire, ridursi; (shock) attenuarsi

less·er ['lɛsəʳ] ADJ (importance, degree) minore; (size) più piccolo(-a); **to a lesser extent** or **degree** in grado or misura minore; **the lesser of two evils** il minore dei due mali

les·son ['lɛsn] N lezione f; **to give lessons in** dare or impartire lezioni di; **a French lesson** una lezione di francese; **to teach sb a lesson** (fig) dare una lezione a qn; **it taught him a lesson** (fig) gli è servito di lezione

les·sor [lɛ'sɔːʳ] N locatore(-trice)

lest [lɛst] CONJ (old, frm) nel timore che + sub, per paura che + sub; **lest we forget** per non dimenticare

let [lɛt] (pt, pp **let**) VT **1** (permit) lasciare, permettere; **to let sb past** lasciar or far passare qn; **to let sb do sth** lasciar fare qc a qn, lasciare che qn faccia qc; **let him come** lascialo venire; **let me have a look** fammi vedere; **to let sb have sth** dare qc a qn; **to let sb know sth** far sapere qc a qn; **I'll let you know our decision as soon as possible** ti farò sapere cosa abbiamo deciso il prima possibile; **don't let him get away with it** (fam) non lasciare che la passi liscia; **I'll let you have it back tomorrow** te lo ridò or restituisco domani; **don't let me catch** or **see you copying again!** che non ti peschi or sorprenda mai più a copiare!; **let him alone** or **be** lascialo stare or in pace; **to let go of sb/sth** mollare or lasciar andare qn/qc; **he let me go** mi ha lasciato andare; **let me go!** lasciami andare!; **let the water boil then …** lascia bollire l'acqua e quindi… **2** (in verb forms): **let's go** or **let us go!** andiamo!; **let's go to the cinema!** andiamo al cinema!; **let's have a break!**

- **yes, let's** facciamo una pausa! - va bene; **let's see, what was I saying?** dunque, cosa stavo dicendo?; **let them wait** che aspettino (pure); **let that be a warning to you!** che questo ti serva di lezione!; **let x=1 and y=2** sia x=1 e y=2 **3** (Brit: rent out) affittare, dare in affitto; **"To Let"** "Affittasi"

▸ **let away** VT + ADV lasciare andare (via)

▸ **let down** VT + ADV **1** (lower) abbassare; (dress) allungare; (hem) allungare, lasciar giù; (Brit: tyre or tire) sgonfiare; (one's hair) sciogliersi; (on rope) calare (giù) **2** (disappoint) deludere; **I won't let you down** non ti deluderò; **that car always lets me down** quella macchina mi pianta sempre in asso

▸ **let go** VI + ADV mollare ◆ VT + ADV mollare; (allow to go) lasciare andare

▸ **let in** VT + ADV far or lasciar entrare, far or lasciar passare; **to let sb in** far or lasciar entrare qn; **they wouldn't let me in because I'm under 18** non mi hanno fatto entrare perché sono minorenne; **shoes which let the water in** scarpe che lasciano passare l'acqua; **to let sb in for a lot of trouble** procurare or dare un mucchio di fastidi a qn; **what have you let yourself in for?** in che guai or pasticci sei andato a cacciarti?; **to let sb in on a secret** rivelare or confidare un segreto a qn

▸ **let into** VT + PREP **1** (allow in) lasciar entrare in **2** (allow to share) **to let sb into** far partecipe qn di **3** (inset) inglobare

▸ **let off** VT + ADV **1** (explode) far esplodere; (fireworks) accendere, lasciar partire; (smell etc) emettere; **to let off steam** (fig: fam) sfogarsi, scaricarsi **2** (allow to go) lasciar andare or uscire; (not punish) non punire; **to let sb off lightly** non calcare la mano nel punire qn; **to let sb off with a warning** limitarsi ad ammonire qn **3** (subj: taxi driver, bus driver) far scendere

▸ **let on** VI + ADV (fam) dire, lasciar capire; **to let on to sb about sth** far capire qc a qn; **to let on (that ...)** dare a intendere (che...)

▸ **let out** VT + ADV **1** (gen) far or lasciare uscire; (secret) spifferare; (news) divulgare; **don't get up, I'll let myself out** non occorre che mi accompagni alla porta; **to let out a cry/ sigh/scream** emettere un grido/un sospiro/un urlo; **to let the air out of a tyre** sgonfiare una gomma; **that lets her out** questo la esonera **2** (dress, seam) allargare **3** (rent out) affittare, dare in affitto

▸ **let up** VI + ADV (bad weather) diminuire; (talker, worker) smettere, fermarsi ◆ VT + ADV far alzare

let-down [ˈlɛtˌdaʊn] N (disappointment) delusione f

le·thal [ˈliːθəl] ADJ: **lethal (to)** (gen) letale (per); (wound, blow) mortale (per)

le·thar·gic [lɪˈθɑːdʒɪk] ADJ (physically) fiacco(-a); (mentally) apatico(-a)

leth·ar·gy [ˈlɛθədʒɪ] N (see adj) fiacchezza; apatia

let·ter [ˈlɛtəʳ] N **1** (missive) lettera; **by letter** per lettera; **letter of introduction/application/protest** lettera di presentazione/di domanda/di protesta **2** (of alphabet) lettera; **the letter G** la (lettera) G; **small/capital letter** lettera minuscola/maiuscola; **she's got a lot of letters after her name** ha un mucchio di titoli; **the letter of the law** (fig) la lettera della legge; **to follow instructions to the letter** seguire alla lettera le istruzioni

letter bomb [ˈlɛtəˌbɒm] N lettera esplosiva

letter-box [ˈlɛtəˌbɒks] N cassetta or buca delle lettere; **she pushed the key through the letterbox** infilò la chiave nella buca delle lettere sulla porta

letter·head [ˈlɛtəˌhɛd] N intestazione f

let·ter·ing [ˈlɛtərɪŋ] N (engraving) iscrizione f; (letters) caratteri mpl; **a blue sign with white lettering** un cartello blu con i caratteri bianchi

letter-opener [ˈlɛtərˌəʊpnəʳ] N tagliacarte m inv

letter·press [ˈlɛtəˌprɛs] (Typ) N (method) rilievografia; (printed page) testo

letter quality printer N stampante f ad alta definizione

letters patent NPL brevetto di invenzione

let·tuce [ˈlɛtɪs] N lattuga

let-up [ˈlɛtˌʌp] N (fam) rallentamento; **without (a) let-up** ininterrottamente, senza smettere

leu·kae·mia, leu·ke·mia (USA) [luːˈkiːmɪə] N leucemia

lev·el [ˈlɛvl] ADJ **1** (flat: ground, surface) piano(-a), piatto(-a); (: shelf) diritto(-a), orizzontale; **I'll do my level best** (fam) farò del mio meglio, farò tutto il possibile; **a level spoonful** (Culin) un cucchiaio raso **2** (steady: voice, tone) pacato(-a); (: gaze) diretto(-a), sicuro(-a); **to keep a level head** mantenere il sangue freddo or la calma **3** (equal) alla pari; **to be level with sb** (in race, league, studies) essere allo stesso livello di; (in rank) essere allo stesso grado di qn; **to draw level with** (team) mettersi alla pari di; (runner, car) affiancarsi a ◆ N **1** livello; **above/at/ below sea level** sotto il/sul/al livello del mare; **the level of the river is rising** il livello del fiume sta salendo; **talks at ministerial level** colloqui a livello ministeriale; **to be on a level with** essere al livello di; (fig) essere allo stesso livello di; **to come down to sb's level** (fig) scendere or abbassarsi al livello di qn; **to find one's own level** trovare la giusta dimensione; **on the level** piatto(-a); (fig) onesto(-a); **he's on the level** (fig: fam) è a posto **2** (also: spirit level) livella (a bolla d'aria) **3** (Brit Scol): **A-levels** diploma di studi superiori; **O-levels** (formerly) esame che si sosteneva in Inghilterra a 16 anni, ora sostituito dal GSCE ◆ VT **1** (make level: ground, site) livellare, spianare; (raze: building) radere al suolo; (fig) livellare **2** (aim): **to level (at)** (blow) tirare (a), allungare (a); (gun) puntare (verso); **to level an accusation against** lanciare un'accusa contro

▸ **level off, level out** VI + ADV (prices, curve on graph etc) stabilizzarsi; (ground) diventare pianeggiante; (aircraft) volare in quota

▸ **level with** VI + PREP (fam): **to level with sb** esser franco(-a) con qn

level crossing N (Brit) passaggio a livello

level-headed [ˌlɛvlˈhɛdɪd] ADJ equilibrato(-a), con la testa a posto or sulle spalle

lev·el·ling, lev·el·ing (USA) [ˈlɛvəlɪŋ] ADJ (process, effect) di livellamento

level playing field N: **to compete on a level playing field** competere ad armi pari

lev·er [ˈliːvəʳ, (USA) ˈlɛvəʳ] N (also fig) leva ◆ VT: **to lever sth up/off/out** sollevare/togliere/estrarre qc (con una leva)

lev·er·age [ˈliːvərɪdʒ, ˈlɛvərɪdʒ] N: **leverage (on)** forza (su); (fig) ascendente m (su); **to exert leverage on sth/sb** far leva su qc/qn

lev·ity [ˈlɛvɪtɪ](frm) N (frivolity) frivolezza; (flippancy) leggerezza

levy [ˈlɛvɪ] N (amount) imposta, tassa; (collection) riscossione f ◆ VT (tax, contributions) imporre; (fine) elevare; (army) arruolare

lewd [luːd] ADJ (comp -er, superl -est) osceno(-a)

lexi·cog·ra·pher [ˌlɛksɪˈkɒɡrəfəʳ] N lessicografo(-a)

lexi·cog·ra·phy [ˌlɛksɪˈkɒɡrəfɪ] N lessicografia

LGBT N LGBT mpl, persone lesbiche, gay, bisessuali e transessuali

LI ABBR (USA: = Long Island)

liabil·ities [ˌlaɪəˈbɪlɪtɪz] NPL (Comm) debiti mpl; (on balance sheet) passivo msg, passività f inv

lia·bil·ity [ˌlaɪəˈbɪlɪtɪ] N (Law: responsibility) responsabilità f inv; (burden) peso; (person) peso morto; **he's becoming a liability** sta diventando un peso; **they disclaimed liability** hanno declinato ogni responsabilità; see also **liabilities**

lia·ble [ˈlaɪəbl] ADJ **1** (likely): **liable to** di propenso(-a) a fare; **she's liable to get cross** è probabile che si arrabbi; **it's liable to break** è probabile che si rompa; **we are liable to get shot at here** qui c'è il rischio che ci sparino; **he's liable to colds** è soggetto a frequenti raffreddori, prende facilmente il raffreddore; **he's liable to panic** è facile che si lasci prendere dal panico **2** (subject): **to be liable for military service** essere tenuto(-a) a svolgere il servizio militare; **to be liable to a fine** essere passibile di multa **3** (responsible): **to be liable for** essere responsabile di

li·aise [liːˈeɪz] VI: **to liaise (with)** mantenere i contatti (con)

liai·son [liːˈeɪzɒn] N (also euph) relazione f; (coordination) coordinamento; (Mil) collegamento

liar [ˈlaɪəʳ] N bugiardo(-a)

li·bel [ˈlaɪbəl] N (Law: crime) diffamazione f; (: written statement) libello ◆ VT diffamare

li·bel·lous, li·bel·ous (USA) [ˈlaɪbələs] ADJ diffamatorio(-a)

lib·er·al [ˈlɪbərəl] ADJ (*generous*) liberale, generoso(-a); (*views*) liberale; **to be liberal with** essere prodigo(-a) di

Liberal Democrat ADJ, N liberaldemocratico(-a)

lib·er·al·ity [ˌlɪbəˈrælɪtɪ] N (*generosity*) liberalità, generosità

lib·er·al·ize [ˈlɪbərəˌlaɪz] VT liberalizzare

liberal-minded [ˌlɪbərəlˈmaɪndɪd] ADJ tollerante

lib·er·ate [ˈlɪbəˌreɪt] VT liberare

lib·era·tion [ˌlɪbəˈreɪʃən] N liberazione *f*

liberation theology N teologia della liberazione

Li·beria [laɪˈbɪərɪə] N Liberia

Li·berian [laɪˈbɪərɪən] ADJ, N liberiano(-a)

lib·er·ty [ˈlɪbətɪ] N libertà *f inv*; **liberty of conscience** libertà di coscienza; **at liberty** (*not detained*) in libertà; **to be at liberty to do sth** essere libero(-a) di fare qc; **to take the liberty of doing sth** prendersi la libertà di fare qc, permettersi di fare qc; **to take liberties** prendersi delle libertà; **what a liberty!** (*fam*) come ti permetti? (*or* si permette? *etc*)

li·bi·do [lɪˈbiːdəʊ] N (*Psych*) libido *f inv*

Li·bra [ˈliːbrə] N (*Astron, Astrol*) Bilancia; **to be Libra** essere della Bilancia; **I'm Libra** sono della Bilancia

li·brar·ian [laɪˈbrɛərɪən] N bibliotecario(-a)

li·brary [ˈlaɪbrərɪ] N biblioteca

❑ **library** is not translated by the Italian word *libreria*

li·bret·to [lɪˈbrɛtəʊ] N libretto

Libya [ˈlɪbɪə] N Libia

Liby·an [ˈlɪbɪən] ADJ, N libico(-a)

lice [laɪs] NPL *of* **louse**

li·cence [ˈlaɪsəns], **license** (*USA*) N 1 (*permit*) autorizzazione *f*, permesso; (*for car*) bollo, tassa di circolazione; (*also:* **driving licence**) (*USA*) (*also:* **driver's licence**) patente *f* di guida; (*Comm*) licenza; (*for dog*) tassa; (*TV, Radio*) abbonamento; (*amount paid*) canone *m*, abbonamento; **they were married by special licence** si sono sposati con dispensa; **provisional driving licence** ≈ foglio rosa; **pilot's licence** brevetto (di pilota); **import licence** licenza di importazione; **produced under licence** prodotto(-a) su licenza; **he lost his licence for a year** gli hanno ritirato la patente per un anno 2 (*freedom*) libertà; (*excessive freedom*) licenza, eccessiva libertà

licence number N (*Brit: Aut*) numero di targa

li·cense VT 1 (*person*): **to license sb to do** autorizzare qn a fare 2 (*car: subj: owner*) pagare la tassa di circolazione; (*: subj: licensing authority*) rilasciare il bollo (di circolazione)

li·censed [ˈlaɪsənst] ADJ (*restaurant, premises*) autorizzato(-a) alla vendita di bevande alcoliche

licensed trade N commercio di bevande alcoliche con licenza speciale

li·cen·see [ˌlaɪsənˈsiː] N (*in pub*) titolare *m/f* di licenza per la vendita di bevande alcoliche

license plate N (*esp USA: Aut*) targa (automobilistica)

li·cens·ing laws [ˈlaɪsənsɪŋlɔːz] N (*Brit*) leggi *fpl* che regolamentano la vendita di alcolici

li·cen·tious [laɪˈsɛnʃəs] ADJ (*frm*) licenzioso(-a)

li·chen [ˈlaɪkən] N lichene *m*

lick [lɪk] VT 1 (*with tongue*) leccare; (*subj: flames*) lambire; **to lick one's plate clean** pulire il piatto con la lingua; **to lick one's lips** leccarsi le labbra; (*hungrily*) leccarsi i baffi; **to lick one's wounds** (*also: fig*) leccarsi le ferite; **to lick sb's boots** (*fig: fam*) leccare i piedi a qn; **to lick sth into shape** (*fig: fam*) mettere a punto qc 2 (*fam: defeat*) suonarle a, stracciare ♦ N 1 leccata; **a lick of paint** una passata di vernice; **a lick and a promise** (*fig: fam*) una pulitina sommaria 2 (*fam: speed*): **at full lick** a tutta birra

lico·rice [ˈlɪkərɪs] N = **liquorice**

lid [lɪd] N coperchio; **to take the lid off sth** (*fig*) smascherare qc; **that puts the lid on it** (*fam*) ci mancava solo questo

lido [ˈliːdəʊ] N (*esp Brit: swimming pool*) piscina (all'aperto); (*part of the beach*) lido, stabilimento balneare

lie[1] [laɪ] N bugia, menzogna; **to tell lies** raccontare *or* dir bugie; **to give the lie to** smentire ♦ VI (*prp* **lying**) mentire; **I know she's lying** so che sta mentendo; **you lied to me!** mi hai mentito!

lie[2] [laɪ] (*pt* **lay**, *pp* **lain**, *prp* **lying**) VI 1 (*also:* **lie down**) sdraiarsi, distendersi; (*be lying*) essere sdraiato(-a) *or* disteso(-a), giacere; (*dead body*) giacere; **he was lying on the sofa** era disteso sul divano; **she had lain there for hours** è rimasta distesa lì per ore; **he lay where he had fallen** giaceva a terra nel punto in cui era caduto; **to lie still** giacere immobile; **he lay in bed until 10 o'clock** è rimasto a letto fino alle 10; **to lie low** (*fig*) tenersi nell'ombra (*hide*) nascondersi 2 (*be situated*) trovarsi, essere; (*remain*) rimanere; **the book lay on the table** il libro giaceva sul tavolo; **the snow lay half a metre deep** la neve formava una coltre di mezzo metro; **the town lies in a valley** la città è situata *or* si trova in una valle; **the plain lay before us** la pianura si stendeva dinanzi a noi; **in spite of the obstacles lying in his way** nonostante gli ostacoli che aveva di fronte; **where does the difficulty/difference lie?** dove'è *or* qual è la difficoltà/differenza?; **the fault lies with you** l'errore è tuo; **the challenge lies in …** la difficoltà sta nel…; **the best remedy lies in …** il miglior rimedio consiste nel…

▸ **lie about, lie around** VI + ADV (*things*) essere in giro; (*person*) bighellonare; **it must be lying about somewhere** dev'essere in giro da qualche parte

▸ **lie back** VI + ADV stendersi; **lie back and enjoy yourself!** rilassati e divertiti!

▸ **lie behind** VI + PREP essere dietro; **what lies behind his refusal?** cosa c'è dietro il suo rifiuto?

▸ **lie down** VI + ADV stendersi, sdraiarsi; **lie down!** (*to dog*) cuccia!; **why not go and lie down for a bit?** perché non vai a distenderti per un po'?; **to take sth lying down** (*fig*) accettare supinamente qc

▸ **lie in** VI + ADV (*stay in bed*) rimanere a letto (*al mattino*)

▸ **lie up** VI + ADV (*hide*) nascondersi

Liech·ten·stein [ˈlɪktənˌstaɪn] N Liechtenstein *m*

lie detector N macchina della verità

lie-down [ˈlaɪˌdaʊn] N (*Brit fam*) riposino

lie-in [ˈlaɪˌɪn] N: **to have a lie-in** (*Brit fam*) rimanere a letto (*al mattino*)

lieu [luː] N: **in lieu of** invece di, al posto di

Lieut. ABBR (= *lieutenant*) Ten.

lieu·ten·ant [lɛfˈtɛnənt, (*USA*) luːˈtɛnənt] N (*Mil*) tenente *m*; (*Naut*) tenente *m* di vascello

lieutenant-colonel [lɛfˈtɛnəntˈkɜːnl, (*USA*) luːˈtɛnəntˈkɜːnl] N tenente *m* colonnello

life [laɪf] N (*pl* **lives**) 1 (*gen*) vita; **life on earth** vita terrestre *or* sulla terra; **bird life** gli uccelli; **a matter of life and death** una questione di vita o di morte; **to bring sb back to life** riportare in vita qn; **to come to life** rianimarsi, riprendere vita 2 (*existence*) vita; (*of battery etc*) durata; **to spend one's life doing sth** passare la vita a fare qc; **during the life of this government** durante questo governo, nel corso di questa amministrazione; **to begin life as** cominciare come; **to be sent to prison for life** essere condannato(-a) all'ergastolo; **in early life** in gioventù; **in later life** nella maturità; **all my life** tutta la vita; **a quiet/hard life** una vita tranquilla/dura; **country/city life** vita di campagna/di città; **how's life?** (*fam*) come va (la vita)?; **that's life** così è la vita; **to lose one's life** perdere la vita; **three lives were lost** tre persone sono morte *or* hanno perso la vita; **to take one's own life** (*euph: commit suicide*) togliersi la vita; **a danger to life and limb** un pericolo mortale; **to risk life and limb** rischiare l'osso del collo; **you'll be taking your life in your hands if you climb up there** (*fam*) rischi la pelle se ti arrampichi lassù; **his life won't be worth living** rimpiangerà di esser nato; **not on your life!** (*fam*) neanche morto!, fossi matto!; **to see life** vedere il mondo; **to run for one's life** correre per mettersi in salvo; **I can't for the life of me imagine …** (*fam*) non riesco assolutamente a immaginare…; **true to life** fedele alla realtà; **to paint from life** dipingere dal vero 3 (*liveliness: of place*) vita, animazione *f*; (*: of person*) vita, vivacità; **the life and soul of the party** l'anima della festa; **to put** *or* **breathe new life into** (*person*) ridare entusiasmo a; (*project, area etc*) ridare nuova vita a ♦ ADJ (*for life: membership*) a vita; (*in life: chances*) di vita

life annuity N rendita vitalizia

life assurance N (*Brit*) = **life insurance**

life belt, life buoy N salvagente *m*

life·blood [ˈlaɪfˌblʌd] N (*fig*) linfa vitale

life·boat [ˈlaɪfˌbəʊt] N (*from shore*) lancia di salvataggio; (*from ship*) scialuppa di salvataggio

life expectancy N aspettativa di vita

life·guard [ˈlaɪfˌgɑːd] N (*on beach*) bagnino(-a)

life imprisonment N ergastolo

life insurance, (*Brit*) **life assurance** N assicurazione *f* sulla vita

life jacket N giubbotto di salvataggio

life·less [ˈlaɪflɪs] ADJ (*body*) privo(-a) di vita, inanimato(-a); (*fig: person*) privo(-a) di energia; (: *style*) piatto(-a); (: *hair*) senza corpo

life·like [ˈlaɪfˌlaɪk] ADJ che sembra vero(-a), realistico(-a)

life·line [ˈlaɪfˌlaɪn] N (*on ship*) sagola di salvataggio; (*for diver*) cavo di recupero *or* di salvataggio; **it was his lifeline** (*fig*) era vitale per lui

life·long [ˈlaɪfˌlɒŋ] ADJ (*ambition etc*) di tutta la mia *or* sua *etc* vita; (*friend*) di sempre

life pre·serv·er [ˈlaɪfprɪˌzɜːvəʳ] N 1 (*USA: life belt*) salvagente *m*; (: *life jacket*) giubbotto di salvataggio 2 (*Brit: bludgeon*) sfollagente *m inv*

lif·er [ˈlaɪfəʳ] N (*fam*) ergastolano(-a)

life raft N zattera di salvataggio

life-saver [ˈlaɪfˌseɪvəʳ] N (*person*) bagnino(-a); **it/he** *etc* **was a life-saver** (*fig*) mi ha salvato la vita

life sentence N condanna all'ergastolo

life-size [ˈlaɪfˌsaɪz], **life-sized** [ˈlaɪfˌsaɪzd] ADJ in *or* a grandezza naturale

life span N (durata della) vita

life style N stile *m* di vita

life support system N (*Med*) respiratore *m* automatico

life·time [ˈlaɪfˌtaɪm] N vita; **a lifetime's work, the work of a lifetime** il lavoro di tutta una vita; **in my lifetime** nel corso della mia vita, durante la mia vita; **I don't think it will happen in my lifetime** non credo che succederà finché sono vivo; **in a lifetime** nell'arco della vita, in tutta la vita; **a trip of a lifetime** un viaggio memorabile; **the chance of a lifetime** un'occasione unica *or* che capita una sola volta nella vita; **it seemed a lifetime** sembrò (che fosse passata) un'eternità *or* una vita

lift [lɪft] VT 1 (*thing, person*) sollevare, alzare; **it's too heavy, I can't lift it** è troppo pesante, non riesco a sollevarlo; **to lift sb over sth** far passare qn sopra qc; **to lift one's head** alzare *or* sollevare la testa; **she never lifts a finger to help** non alza *or* muove mai neanche un dito per aiutare 2 (*fig: restrictions, ban*) revocare 3 (*fam: steal: idea, quotation*) riprendere *or* copiare pari pari ♦ VI sollevarsi, alzarsi; (*fog*) alzarsi ♦ N 1 (*Brit: elevator*) ascensore *m*; (*for goods*) montacarichi *m inv*; **the lift isn't working** l'ascensore non funziona 2 (*esp Brit: in car*) passaggio; **to give sb a lift** dare un passaggio a qn; **he gave me a lift to the cinema** mi ha dato un passaggio al cinema 3 (*Aer*) spinta; **it gave him a tremendous lift** (*fig*) lo ha tirato su moltissimo

▸ **lift down** VT + ADV tirar giù

▸ **lift off** VT + ADV togliere ♦ VI + ADV (*aircraft, rocket*) decollare

▸ **lift out** VT + ADV tirar fuori; (*troops, evacuees etc*) far evacuare per mezzo di elicotteri (*or* aerei)

▸ **lift up** VT + ADV sollevare, alzare

lift-off [ˈlɪftˌɒf] N decollo

liga·ment [ˈlɪgəmənt] N legamento

light¹ [laɪt] (*pt, pp* lit *or* lighted) N 1 (*gen*) luce *f*; electric light illuminazione *f or* luce elettrica; **at first light** alle prime luci dell'alba; **by the light of the moon** alla luce della luna, al chiaro di luna; **in the cold light of day** (*also fig*) alla luce del giorno; **you're (standing) in my light** mi fai ombra; **to hold sth up to** *or* **against the light** tenere qc controluce 2 (*fig*): **in the light of** alla luce di; **to bring to light** portare alla luce; **to come to light** venire in luce, emergere; **to cast** *or* **shed** *or* **throw light on** gettare *or* far luce su; **I was hoping that you could shed some light on it (for me)** speravo che tu potessi darmi dei chiarimenti su questo; **to see the light** (*Rel*) convertirsi; (*fig*) ravvedersi; **to reveal sb/sth in a new light** mostrare qn/qc sotto una nuova luce; **according to my lights** secondo quanto mi è dato di capire 3 (*single*

light) luce *f*; (*lamp*) luce, lampada; (*Aut, Aer*) fanale *m*, faro, luce; **to turn the light on/off** accendere/spegnere la luce; **he switched on the light** ha acceso la luce; **he switched off the light** ha spento la luce; **rear lights** luci di posizione posteriori; **the (traffic) lights were red** il semaforo era rosso 4 (*flame*) fiamma; **pilot light** (*on stove, water heater*) fiammella di sicurezza; **have you got a light?** (*for cigarette*) hai da accendere?; **to put a light to sth** dar fuoco a qc ♦ ADJ (*comp* -er, *superl* -est) 1 (*bright*) chiaro(-a); **to get lighter** rischiararsi, schiarirsi 2 (*colour, skin, hair, room*) chiaro(-a); **light yellow** giallo chiaro *inv*; **a light blue sweater** una maglia azzurro chiaro ♦ VT 1 (*illuminate*) illuminare, rischiarare; **to light sb's way** far luce a qn; **lit by electricity** illuminato(-a) elettricamente 2 (*cigarette, fire, candle*) accendere; **to light a bonfire** accendere un falò; **to light the fire** accendere il fuoco; **she lit the candles on the cake** ha acceso le candeline sulla torta ♦ VI (*ignite*) accendersi

▸ **light up** VI (*lamp*) accendersi; (*face, eyes*) illuminarsi 2 (*fam: smoke*) accendersi una sigaretta (*or* la pipa *etc*) ♦ VT + ADV illuminare, rischiarare

▸ **light upon** VI + PREP: **her eyes lit upon the jewels** il suo sguardo cadde sui gioielli

light² [laɪt] ADJ (*comp* -er, *superl* -est) (*gen*) leggero(-a); **a light jacket** una giacca leggera; **a light meal** un pasto leggero; **light ale** birra chiara; **some light reading** una lettura leggera; **she is a light sleeper** ha il sonno leggero; **as light as a feather** leggero(-a) come una piuma; **to be light on one's feet** avere il passo leggero; **with a light heart** a cuor leggero; **to make light work of sth** fare qc con molta facilità; **to make light of sth** (*fig*) prendere alla leggera qc, non dar peso a qc ♦ ADV (*travel*) leggero, con poco bagaglio

light bulb N lampadina

light·en [ˈlaɪtn] VT (*darkness*) rischiarare, illuminare; (*hair, colour*) schiarire ♦ VI schiararsi; (*room*) rischiararsi

light·en [ˈlaɪtn] VT (*load*) alleggerire; (*fig: make cheerful: heart, atmosphere*) sollevare

light·er [ˈlaɪtəʳ] N 1 (*also:* **cigarette lighter**) accendino, accendisigari *m inv* 2 (*boat*) chiatta

light-fingered [ˌlaɪtˈfɪŋgəd] ADJ lesto(-a) di mano

light-headed [ˌlaɪtˈhedɪd] ADJ (*by temperament*) svampito(-a); (*dizzy*) intontito(-a), stordito(-a); (*with fever*) vaneggiante; (*with excitement*) eccitato(-a); **the drink made him feel light-headed** il liquore gli ha fatto girare la testa

light-hearted [ˌlaɪtˈhɑːtɪd] ADJ (*person, laugh*) spensierato(-a), gaio(-a); (*discussion*) non impegnato(-a)

light·house [ˈlaɪtˌhaʊs] N faro

light·ing [ˈlaɪtɪŋ] N (*system*) illuminazione *f*; (*in theatre*) luci *fpl*

lighting-up time [ˌlaɪtɪŋˈʌpˌtaɪm] N (*Brit: Aut*) ora in cui bisogna accendere i fari

light·ly [ˈlaɪtlɪ] ADV leggermente; **to fry sth lightly** (*Culin*) far soffriggere qc; **to sleep lightly** avere il sonno leggero; **to get off lightly** cavarsela a buon mercato; **lightly salted** leggermente salato; **to take sth lightly** prendere qc alla leggera

light meter N (*Phot*) esposimetro

light·ness [ˈlaɪtnɪs] N 1 (*brightness*) chiarezza 2 (*in weight etc*) leggerezza

light·ning [ˈlaɪtnɪŋ] N fulmine *m*, lampo; **a lot of lightning** molti lampi; **thunder and lightning** tuoni *mpl* e fulmini; **a flash of lightning** un fulmine; **as quick as lightning, like (greased) lightning** (*fam*) (veloce) come un fulmine, in un lampo

lightning conductor, (*USA*) **lightning rod** N parafulmine *m*

lightning strike N sciopero a sorpresa *or* a gatto selvaggio

light pen N (*Comput*) penna ottica

light·ship [ˈlaɪtˌʃɪp] N battello *m* faro, *inv*

light-weight [ˈlaɪtˌweɪt] ADJ (*also fig*) leggero(-a); (*Boxing*) dei pesi leggeri; **a lightweight suit** un vestito leggero ♦ N (*Boxing*) peso leggero

light year [ˈlaɪtˌjɪəʳ] N anno *m* luce, *inv*

Li·gu·rian [lɪˈgjʊərɪən] ADJ, N ligure *m/f*

like¹ [laɪk] PREP 1 (*similar to*) come, uguale a; (*in comparisons*) come; **to be like sb/sth** essere come qn/qc; **they are very like each other** si somigliano molto; **a house like mine** una casa come la mia; **people like that** tipi del genere; **what's he like?** che tipo è?, com'è?; **what's the weather like?** che tempo fa?; **what was Turkey like?** com'era la Turchia?; **this portrait is not like him** questo ritratto non gli somiglia affatto; **it's a bit like salmon** assomiglia un po' al salmone; **to look like sb** assomigliare a qn; **you look like my brother** assomigli a mio fratello; **what does she look like?** che aspetto ha?; **he thinks like us** la pensa come noi; **that's just like him** è proprio da lui; **it's not like him to do that** non è da lui fare così, non è tipo da fare cose del genere; **I never saw anything like it** non ho mai visto una cosa simile, non ho mai visto niente di simile; **that's more like it** (*fam*) così va meglio; **it's fine like that** così va bene; **that's nothing like it** non ha niente a che vedere con quello; **something like that** qualcosa del genere; **don't talk like that** non parlare così; **do it like this** fallo così; **there's nothing like a holiday** non c'è niente di meglio di una vacanza; **it happened like this** ... è andata così...; **like father like son** tale padre tale figlio; **we ran like mad** (*fam*) abbiamo fatto una corsa pazzesca; **it rained like mad** (*fam*) ha piovuto a dirotto; **I feel like a drink** avrei voglia di bere qualcosa, berrei volentieri qualcosa; **it looks like a diamond** sembra un diamante **2** (*such as*) come; **a city like Paris** una città come Parigi ♦ ADJ simile, uguale; **in like cases** in casi simili *or* analoghi; **rabbits, mice and like creatures** conigli, topi e animali simili; **to be as like as two peas (in a pod)** essere come due gocce d'acqua ♦ ADV: **it's nothing like as hot as it was** non fa più così caldo come faceva prima; **as like as not** (molto) probabilmente ♦ CONJ (*as*) come; **like we used to (do)** come facevamo una volta ♦ N: **we shall not see his like again** non ci sarà mai più uno come lui; **did you ever see the like (of it)?** hai mai visto niente del genere?; **the like of which I never saw** come non ne avevo mai visti; **sparrows, blackbirds and the like** passeri, merli e altri uccelli simili; **the likes of him** (*fam, pej*) quelli come lui

like² [laɪk] VT **1** (*impers*) piacere; **I like swimming/that book/ chocolate** mi piace nuotare/quel libro/il cioccolato; **I like hats** mi piacciono i cappelli; **I don't like dogs** non mi piacciono i cani; **I like Mary** Mary mi è simpatica; **which do you like best?** quale preferisci?; **how did you like the trip?** ti è piaciuto il viaggio?; **well, I like that!** (*fam, hum*) questa sì che è bella! **2** (*want*) desiderare, volere; **I would like, I'd like** mi piacerebbe, vorrei; **would you like ...?** vuoi...?; **would you like to come?** vuoi venire?; **what would you like?** cosa vuoi?; **if you like** se vuoi; **would you like a coffee?** vuole un caffè?, gradirebbe un caffè?; **I'd like an orange juice, please** vorrei un'aranciata, per favore; **I'd like to wash my hands** vorrei lavarmi le mani; **he'd like to leave early** vorrebbe andarsene presto; **I would like more time** vorrei *or* mi piacerebbe avere più tempo; **I should like to know why** vorrei *or* mi piacerebbe sapere perché; **would you like me to wait outside?** vuoi *or* desideri che aspetti fuori?; **I didn't like to (do it)** non volevo (farlo); **as you like** come vuoi; **if you like** se vuoi; **whenever you like** quando vuoi ♦ **likes** NPL gusti *mpl*, preferenze *fpl*; **his likes and dislikes** i suoi gusti

like·able [ˈlaɪkəbl] ADJ simpatico(-a)

like·li·hood [ˈlaɪklɪˌhʊd] N probabilità; **in all likelihood** con ogni probabilità, molto probabilmente; **there is no likelihood of that** è da escludersi; **there is little likelihood that he'll come** è difficile che venga

like·ly [ˈlaɪklɪ] ADJ (*comp* **-ier**, *superl* **-iest**) (*outcome, winner*) probabile; (*place*) adatto(-a), buono(-a); (*story, explanation*) plausibile; **a likely explanation** una spiegazione attendibile *or* plausibile; **that's not very likely** non è molto probabile; **a likely story!** (*iro*) ma a chi la racconti?, e io dovrei crederci?; **when is the likeliest time to find you at home?** quando è più probabile trovarti a casa?; **an incident likely to cause trouble** un incidente che probabilmente causerà dei problemi; **it's not likely that he'll come, he is not likely to come** è difficile che venga; **he's likely to leave** è probabile che parta, probabilmente partirà ♦ ADV probabilmente; **most** *or* **very likely they've lost it** con molta probabilità *or* molto probabilmente l'hanno perso; **not likely!** (*fam*) neanche per sogno!

like-minded [ˈlaɪkˈmaɪndɪd] ADJ che la pensa allo stesso modo

lik·en [ˈlaɪkən] VT: **to liken sth to** paragonare qc a

like·ness [ˈlaɪknɪs] N **1** (*similarity*) somiglianza; **there is a family likeness** ci sono tratti caratteristici della famiglia; **she saw a family likeness** vedeva una somiglianza con gli altri membri della famiglia; **that's a good likeness of you** ti rassomiglia molto **2** (*form*): **in the likeness of** sotto le apparenze *or* l'aspetto di

like·wise [ˈlaɪkˌwaɪz] ADV (*similarly*) nello *or* allo stesso modo; (*also*) anche; (*moreover*) inoltre, per di più; **to do likewise** fare altrettanto, fare lo stesso

lik·ing [ˈlaɪkɪŋ] N (*for person*) simpatia; (*for thing*) predilezione *f*; **to have a liking for sb/sth** avere un debole per qn/qc; **to be to sb's liking** essere di gusto *or* gradimento di qn; **to take a liking to sb** prendere qn in simpatia; **to take a liking to sth/to doing sth** scoprire il piacere di qc/di fare qc; **is the meal to your liking?** è di tuo gradimento il pranzo?

li·lac [ˈlaɪlək] N (*flower*) lillà *m inv*; (*colour*) lilla *m inv* ♦ ADJ lilla *inv*

lilt [lɪlt] N cadenza

lilt·ing [ˈlɪltɪŋ] ADJ melodioso(-a)

lily [ˈlɪlɪ] N giglio

Lima [ˈliːmə] N Lima

limb [lɪm] N (*Anat*) arto; (*of tree*) (grosso) ramo; **a man with strong limbs** un uomo dalle membra robuste; **to be out on a limb** (*fig*) trovarsi in difficoltà; **to go out on a limb** (*fig*) esporsi; **to tear limb from limb** sbranare, fare a pezzettini ❏ **limb** is not translated by the Italian word *lembo*

limb·er up [ˌlɪmbərˈʌp] VI + ADV scaldarsi (i muscoli)

limbo [ˈlɪmbəʊ] N (*Rel, also fig*) limbo

lime¹ [laɪm] N (*Chem, Geol*) calce *f*; **slaked lime** calce spenta

lime² [laɪm] N (*Bot: linden*) tiglio

lime³ [laɪm] N (*Bot: citrus fruit*) limetta; **lime green** giallo-verdino

lime juice N succo di limetta

lime·light [ˈlaɪmˌlaɪt] N: **to be in the limelight** essere alla ribalta, essere in vista

lim·er·ick [ˈlɪmərɪk] N poesiola umoristica di 5 versi

lime·stone [ˈlaɪmˌstəʊn] N (*Geol*) calcare *m*, pietra calcarea; **limestone cliffs** scogliere *fpl* di pietra calcarea

lim·it [ˈlɪmɪt] N limite *m*; **weight/speed limit** limite di peso/ di velocità; **there's a limit to my patience** la mia pazienza ha un limite; **within limits** entro certi limiti; **there is a limit to what one can do** c'è un limite a quello che si può fare; **he's the limit!** (*fam*) lui passa tutti i limiti!; **well, that's the limit!** (*fam*) questo è il massimo *or* il colmo! ♦ VT limitare; **to limit o.s. to a few remarks** limitarsi ad alcune osservazioni; **I limit myself to 10 cigarettes a day** mi limito a (fumare) 10 sigarette al giorno

limi·ta·tion [ˌlɪmɪˈteɪʃən] N limitazione *f*, restrizione *f*; **he has/knows his limitations** ha/conosce i suoi limiti; **the limitation of nuclear weapons** la limitazione delle armi nucleari

lim·it·ed [ˈlɪmɪtɪd] ADJ limitato(-a), ristretto(-a); (*means, income*) scarso(-a); **a limited amount** una quantità limitata; **to a limited extent** entro certi limiti, fino a un certo punto; **they are limited in what they can do** hanno una possibilità di agire limitata; **limited edition** edizione a bassa tiratura

limited company, limited liability company N (*Brit*) ≈ società *f inv* a responsabilità limitata

lim·it·less [ˈlɪmɪtlɪs] ADJ illimitato(-a)

lim·ou·sine [ˈlɪməziːn] N limousine *f inv*

limp¹ [lɪmp] VI zoppicare; **to limp in/out** entrare/uscire zoppicando; **the ship limped home** la nave è tornata faticosamente in porto ♦ N: **to walk with** *or* **have a limp** zoppicare

limp² [lɪmp] ADJ (*gen*) molle; (*dress*) floscio(-a); (*person*) fiacco(-a); **she went limp** si afflosciò; **let your arm go limp** rilassa completamente il braccio; **limp cover(s)** (*on book*) rilegatura in brossura

lim·pet [ˈlɪmpɪt] N (*Zool*) patella; (*fig*) persona appiccicosa

lim·pid [ˈlɪmpɪd] ADJ (*liter*) limpido(-a)

linch·pin [ˈlɪntʃpɪn] N (*in axle*) acciarino, bietta; (*fig*) perno

Lincs [lɪŋks] ABBR (*Brit*: = Lincolnshire)

line¹ [laɪn] N **1** (*gen*) linea; (*pen stroke*) tratto; (*wrinkle*) ruga; **a straight line** una linea retta; **to draw a line under sth** sottolineare qc; (*fig*) dimenticare qc; **I want to draw a line under the experience** voglio dimenticare quell'esperienza;

to draw a line through sth tirare una riga sopra qc; **to draw the line at (doing) sth** rifiutarsi di fare qc; **to know where to draw the line** (*fig*) saper rispettare i limiti; **in line to the throne** nella linea di successione al trono; **she comes from a long line of teachers** i suoi sono insegnanti da generazioni **2** (*rope*) corda, fune *f*; (*fishing line*) lenza; (*wire*) filo; (*Elec*) linea; **clothes line** filo *or* corda del bucato **3** (*Telec*) linea; **the line went dead** è caduta la linea **4** (*row, series*) fila; (*queue*) fila, coda; **a line of people** una fila di persone; **to stand in line** mettersi in fila; **to be in line for sth** (*fig*) essere in lista per qc; **to bring sth into line with sth** mettere qc al passo con qc; **to fall into line with sb/sth** adeguarsi a qn/qc; **to step out of line** (*fig*) sgarrare; **to cut in line** (*USA*) passare avanti **5** (*direction, course*) linea, direzione *f*; **line of inquiry** pista; **in the line of fire** (*Mil*) sulla linea di tiro; **line of attack** (*Mil*) piano d'attacco; (*fig*) piano d'azione; **to follow** *or* **take the line of least resistance** seguire la via più facile; **in the line of duty** nell'esercizio delle proprie funzioni; **line of argument** filo del ragionamento; **line of research/business** settore *m* di ricerca/d'attività; **in his line of business** nel suo ramo (di affari); **line of interest** sfera di interesse; **it's not my line** (*fam: speciality*) non sono un esperto in materia; **to take a strong** *or* **firm line on sth** essere deciso(-a) per quanto riguarda qc; **to take the line that ...** essere del parere che...; **to toe** *or* **follow the party line** attenersi alla *or* seguire la linea politica del partito; **in line with** in linea con, d'accordo con; **along the same lines** dello stesso tipo *or* genere; **we are thinking along the same lines** la pensiamo più o meno allo stesso modo **6** (*of print*) riga; (*of verse*) verso; **he wrote a few lines** ha scritto qualche riga; **to learn one's lines** (*Theatre*) imparare le battute; **to read between the lines** (*fig*) leggere fra le righe; **drop me a line** scrivimi due righe **7** (*Rail: route*) linea; (*shipping company*) compagnia di navigazione; **all along the line** (*fig*) fin da principio; **to reach** *or* **come to the end of the line** (*fig: relationship*) arrivare a un punto di rottura **8** (*Comm*) linea; **a new line in cosmetics** una nuova linea di cosmetici; **our best-selling line** la linea che vendiamo di più
 ▸ **line up** VT + ADV (*people, objects*) allineare, mettere in fila; **have you got anyone lined up for the job?** hai già in mente qualcuno per quel posto?; **to have sth lined up** avere qc in programma ♦ VI + ADV (*in queue*) mettersi in fila; (*in row*) allinearsi; **line up in twos** mettetevi in fila per due

line² [laɪn] VT: **to line (with)** (*clothes*) foderare (di); (*box*) rivestire (di), foderare (di); (*subj: trees, crowd*) fiancheggiare; **crowds lined the street** c'erano molte persone ai bordi della strada; **the street was lined with trees** la strada era alberata

lin·ear [ˈlɪnɪəʳ] ADJ lineare

lined¹ [laɪnd] ADJ (*paper*) a righe, rigato(-a); (*face*) rugoso(-a)

lined² [laɪnd] ADJ (*clothes*) foderato(-a)

line feed N (*Comput*) avanzamento di una interlinea

lin·en [ˈlɪnɪn] N (*cloth*) (tela di) lino; (*sheets, tablecloth etc*) biancheria; **embroidered linen** biancheria per la casa ricamata; **to wash one's dirty linen in public** (*fig*) lavare i panni sporchi in pubblico ♦ ADJ (*garment*) di lino; (*basket, cupboard*) della biancheria; **a linen jacket** una giacca di lino

line printer N stampante *f* parallela

lin·er [ˈlaɪnəʳ] N **1** (*ship*) nave *f* di linea, transatlantico **2 dustbin liner** sacchetto per la pattumiera

lines·man [ˈlaɪnzmən] N (*pl* -**men**) (*Sport*) guardalinee *m inv*, segnalinee *m inv*; (*Telec*) guardafili *m inv*

line-up [ˈlaɪnʌp] N (*row*) fila, allineamento *m*; (*Sport*) formazione *f*; (*USA: identity parade*) confronto all'americana

lin·ger [ˈlɪŋgəʳ] VI (*person: dawdle*) indugiare; (: *wait*) attardarsi; (: *be on the point of death*) trascinarsi; (*smell, memory, tradition*) persistere; **to linger over a meal** attardarsi a tavola; **to linger on a subject** dilungarsi su un argomento; **the smell lingered for weeks** l'odore è rimasto per settimane

lin·gerie [ˈlænʒəriː] N lingerie *f inv*, biancheria intima (femminile)

lin·ger·ing [ˈlɪŋgərɪŋ] ADJ (*smell, doubt*) insistente, lungo(-a); (*look*) insistente, lungo(-a); (*death*) lento(-a)

lin·go [ˈlɪŋgəʊ] N (*fam, pej*) qualunque lingua straniera che risulti incomprensibile; (*jargon*) gergo

lin·guist [ˈlɪŋgwɪst] N (*academic*) linguista *m/f*; **I'm no**

linguist sono negato per le lingue; **to be a good linguist** essere portato per le lingue; **he's an excellent linguist** è molto portato per le lingue

lin·guis·tic [lɪŋˈgwɪstɪk] ADJ linguistico(-a)

lin·guis·tics [lɪŋˈgwɪstɪks] NSG linguistica

lin·ing [ˈlaɪnɪŋ] N (*of clothes etc*) fodera; (*Tech*) rivestimento (interno); (*of brake*) guarnizione *f*

link [lɪŋk] N (*of chain*) anello; (*fig: connection*) legame *m*, collegamento, rapporto; (*Comput*) link *m inv*, collegamento; **cultural links** rapporti culturali; **rail link** collegamento ferroviario; **the link between smoking and cancer** il collegamento tra fumo e cancro; **there's a link to another site** c'è un collegamento ad un altro sito; *see also* **links** ♦ VT (*also fig*) collegare, congiungere, unire; (*Comput*) creare un collegamento con; **to link arms with sb** prendere sottobraccio qn ♦ VI: **to link to a site** creare un collegamento con un sito
 ▸ **link up** VI + ADV (*people: meet*) ritrovarsi, riunirsi; (: *join*) unirsi, associarsi; (*spaceships etc*) agganciarsi; (*railway lines, roads*) congiungersi ♦ VT collegare, unire

links [lɪŋks] NPL (*golf links*) terreno *or* campo da golf

link-up [ˈlɪŋkʌp] N legame *m*; (*of roads*) nodo; (*of spaceships*) aggancio; (*Radio, TV*) collegamento

lino [ˈlaɪnəʊ], **li·no·leum** [lɪˈnəʊlɪəm] N linoleum *m inv*

lin·seed oil [ˈlɪnsiːdˈɔɪl] N olio di semi di lino

lint [lɪnt] N (*Med*) garza

lin·tel [ˈlɪntl] N architrave *m*

lion [ˈlaɪən] N leone *m*; (*fig: person*) celebrità *f inv*; **to get** *or* **take the lion's share** fare la parte del leone

lion cub N leoncino

li·on·ess [ˈlaɪənɪs] N leonessa

lip [lɪp] N (*Anat*) labbro; (*of jug*) beccuccio; (*of glass, of cup etc*) orlo; (*fam: insolence*) sfacciataggine *f*; **red lips** labbra rosse

lipo·suc·tion [lɪpəʊˌsʌkʃən] N liposuzione *f*

lip-read [ˈlɪpˌriːd] VI, VT leggere (sul)le labbra

lip salve N burro di cacao

lip service N: **to pay lip service to sth** essere favorevole a qc solo a parole; **he pays lip service to environmentalism but ...** si professa ambientalista ma...

lip·stick [ˈlɪpˌstɪk] N rossetto

liq·ue·fy [ˈlɪkwɪˌfaɪ] VT liquefare; **liquefied gas** gas *m* liquido ♦ VI liquefarsi

li·queur [lɪˈkjʊəʳ] N liquore *m*

liq·uid [ˈlɪkwɪd] ADJ (*gen*) liquido(-a) ♦ N liquido

liquid assets NPL (*Fin*) attività *fpl* liquide

liq·ui·date [ˈlɪkwɪdeɪt] VT liquidare

liq·ui·da·tion [ˌlɪkwɪˈdeɪʃən] N liquidazione *f*; **to go into liquidation** (*Fin*) andare in liquidazione

liq·ui·da·tor [ˈlɪkwɪˌdeɪtəʳ] N (*Fin*) liquidatore *m*

liquid crystal display N visualizzatore *m* a cristalli liquidi

li·quid·ity [lɪˈkwɪdɪtɪ] N (*Fin*) liquidità

liq·uid·ize [ˈlɪkwɪˌdaɪz] VT (*Brit: Culin*) passare al frullatore

liq·uid·iz·er [ˈlɪkwɪˌdaɪzəʳ] N (*Brit: Culin*) frullatore *m* (a brocca)

liq·uor [ˈlɪkəʳ] N (*esp USA*) bevanda alcolica, alcolico

liquo·rice [ˈlɪkərɪs] N liquirizia

liquor store N (*USA*) negozio di alcolici

Lis·bon [ˈlɪzbən] N Lisbona

lisp [lɪsp] N lisca (*fam*); **with a lisp** con la lisca (*fam*) ♦ VI parlare con la lisca (*fam*)

lis·som [ˈlɪsəm] ADJ (*liter*) leggiadro(-a)

list¹ [lɪst] N lista, elenco; (*Comm*) listino; **shopping list** lista *or* nota della spesa ♦ VT (*include in list*) mettere in lista; (*write down*) fare una lista di; (*expenses etc*) fare la nota di; (*enumerate*) elencare; (*Comput*) listare; **it is not listed** non è *or* non figura nell'elenco

list² [lɪst] VI (*ship*) inclinarsi, sbandare ♦ N (*of ship*) sbandamento

list·ed build·ing [ˈlɪstɪdˈbɪldɪŋ] N (*Brit: Archit*) edificio sotto la protezione delle Belle Arti

list·ed com·pa·ny [ˈlɪstɪdˈkʌmpənɪ] N società *f inv* le cui azioni sono quotate in Borsa

lis·ten [ˈlɪsn] VI ascoltare; **to listen to sb/sth** ascoltare qn/qc; **listen!** ascolta!, senti!; **he wouldn't listen to me** non mi ha voluto dar retta *or* ascolto; **he wouldn't listen to reason** non ha voluto sentire ragione; **listen (out) for the car** senti se arriva la macchina; **listen (out) for your name** aspetta che ti chiamino; **to listen in on a conversation** ascoltare di nascosto una conversazione

lis·ten·er ['lɪsnə'] N (*to speaker*) ascoltatore(-trice); (*to radio*) radioascoltatore(-trice); **to be a good listener** saper ascoltare

lis·teria [ˌlɪs'tɪərɪə] N listeria

list·ing ['lɪstɪŋ] N (*entry*) voce *f*; (*Comput*) lista stampata

list·less ['lɪstlɪs] ADJ (*gen*) fiacco(-a), svogliato(-a); (*uninterested*) apatico(-a)

list·less·ly ['lɪstlɪslɪ] ADV (*see adj*) fiaccamente, svogliatamente; apaticamente

list price N prezzo di listino

lit [lɪt] PT, PP *of* **light**[1]

lita·ny ['lɪtənɪ] N litania

li·ter ['liːtə'] N (*USA*) = **litre**

lit·era·cy ['lɪtərəsɪ] N il saper leggere e scrivere

literacy campaign N lotta contro l'analfabetismo

lit·er·al ['lɪtərəl] ADJ (*meaning, translation*) letterale; (*account*) testuale; (*person*) prosaico(-a) ♦ N (*Brit: Typ*) refuso

lit·er·al·ly ['lɪtərəlɪ] ADV (*gen*) letteralmente; (*interpret*) alla lettera; **it was literally impossible to work there** era letteralmente impossibile lavorare lì

lit·er·ary ['lɪtərərɪ] ADJ letterario(-a); **a literary man** un letterato

lit·er·ate ['lɪtərɪt] ADJ che sa leggere e scrivere; **highly literate** molto colto(-a), molto istruito(-a)

lit·er·a·ture ['lɪtərɪtʃə'] N (*publications, also Literature*) letteratura; (*brochures etc*) opuscoli *mpl*, materiale *m*, informativo

lithe [laɪð] ADJ (*frm*) agile, flessuoso(-a)

li·thog·ra·phy [lɪ'θɒgrəfɪ] N litografia

Lithua·nia [ˌlɪθju'eɪnɪə] N Lituania

Lithua·nian [ˌlɪθju'eɪnɪən] ADJ lituano(-a) ♦ N lituano(-a); (*language*) lituano

liti·gate ['lɪtɪgeɪt] VI essere in causa

liti·ga·tion [ˌlɪtɪ'geɪʃən] N causa (giudiziaria)

lit·mus pa·per ['lɪtməsˌpeɪpə'] N (*also fig*) cartina al tornasole

li·tre ['liːtə'] N litro

lit·ter ['lɪtə'] N **1** (*rubbish*) rifiuti *mpl*; (*papers*) cartacce *fpl* **2** (*young animals*) nidiata, figliata; (*of dogs*) cucciolata **3** (*Agr: bedding*) lettiera ♦ VT (*subj: person*) lasciare rifiuti in; (: *books, rubbish*) coprire; **littered with** coperto(-a) di; **the room was littered with books** nella stanza c'erano libri dappertutto

litter bin, litter basket N cestino dei rifiuti

litter lout, (*USA*) **litter·bug** ['lɪtəˌbʌg] N persona che butta per terra le cartacce o i rifiuti

lit·tle[1] ['lɪtl] ADJ **1** (*small: gen*) piccolo(-a); **a little chair** una seggiolina; **a little cup** una tazzina; **my little brother** il mio fratellino; **a little girl** una bambina; **little finger** mignolo; **poor little thing!** poverino! **2** (*short*) breve; **we went for a little ride/walk** siamo andati a fare un giretto/una passeggiatina; **for a little while** per un po'; **it's only a little way to the station** la stazione non è lontana; **a little holiday** una breve vacanza

lit·tle[2] ['lɪtl] (*comp* **less**, *superl* **least**) ADJ, PRON (*not much*) poco(-a); (*some*) un poco *or* un po' di; **a little milk** un po' di latte; **how much would you like? - just a little** quanto ne vuoi? - solo un po'; **it's okay, we've still got a little time** va bene, abbiamo ancora un po' di tempo; **little money** pochi soldi; **with little difficulty** senza fatica *or* difficoltà; **it makes little difference** fa poca differenza; **we've got very little time** abbiamo molto poco tempo; **little is known about his childhood** si sa poco della sua infanzia; **to see/do little** non vedere/fare molto, vedere/fare poco; **do what little we could** abbiamo fatto quel poco che abbiamo potuto; **little or nothing** poco o nulla; **that has little to do with it!** questo c'entra ben poco!; **as little as £5** soltanto 5 sterline; **to make little of sth** (*fail to understand*) capire poco di qc; (*belittle*) tenere qc in poco conto, dare poca importanza a qc; **little by little** poco a poco ♦ ADV **1 a little** un po'; **a little too big** un po' troppo grande; **a little longer** un po' più a lungo; **we were a little surprised** eravamo un po' sorpresi; **a little more milk** ancora un po' di latte; **a little more** ancora un po' **2** (*not much*): **a little-known fact** un fatto poco noto; **it's**

little better non va molto meglio; **it's changed very little** è cambiato molto poco; **as little as possible** il meno possibile; **little more than a month ago** appena più di un mese fa; **I like it as little as you do** non mi piace più di quanto piaccia a te; **little does he know that ...** quello di cui non si rende conto è che...

lit·ur·gy ['lɪtədʒɪ] N liturgia

live[1] [lɪv] VI **1** (*exist, survive*) vivere; **to live to be 100** vivere fino all'età di *or* a 100 anni; **he hasn't long to live** non gli resta molto da vivere; **as long as I live** finché vivo *or* campo; **to live through an experience** sopravvivere a un'esperienza; **he lived through two wars** ha visto due guerre; **to live like a lord** vivere da signore *or* come un re; **how can people live like that?** come si può vivere così?; **I'm living for the day when ...** vivo solo nell'attesa del giorno in cui...; **the doctors have given her three months to live** i medici le hanno dato tre mesi di vita; **you'll live!** (*iro*) vedrai che non morirai!; **to live with a memory** essere perseguitato(-a) da un ricordo; **he's not easy to live with** non è facile vivere con lui; **you live and learn** c'è sempre qualcosa da imparare; **live and let live** vivi e lascia vivere; **to live by doing ...**/**by doing ...** guadagnarsi da vivere con.../facendo...; **long live the King!** viva il re! **2** (*reside*) abitare, vivere; **where do you live?** dove abiti?; **I live in Edinburgh** abito ad Edimburgo; **to live in London** abitare *or* vivere a Londra; **I live in Grange Road** abito in Grange Road; **I live with my grandmother** vivo con mia nonna ♦ VT: **to live a happy life/a life of hardship** avere una vita felice/dura; **to live life to the full** godersi la vita; **to live a life of luxury** vivere nel lusso; **to live the part** (*Theatre, also fig*) immedesimarsi nella parte

▸ **live down** VT + ADV (*disgrace*) far dimenticare (alla gente)

▸ **live in** VI + ADV (*students, nurses*) essere interno(-a); (*servants*) avere vitto e alloggio

▸ **live off** VT + PREP (*land, food*) vivere di; (*pej: parents*) vivere alle spalle *or* a spese di

▸ **live on** VI + PREP (*food, fruit, salary*) vivere di; **to live on £50 a week** vivere con 50 sterline la settimana; **enough to live on** abbastanza per vivere ♦ VI + ADV continuare a vivere, sopravvivere

▸ **live out** VI + ADV (*Brit: students*) essere esterno(-a); (*housekeeper*) essere a mezzo servizio ♦ VT + ADV: **to live out one's days** *or* **life** trascorrere gli ultimi anni

▸ **live together** VI + ADV (*cohabit*) vivere insieme, convivere

▸ **live up** VT + ADV: **to live it up** (*fam*) fare la bella vita

▸ **live up to** VI + ADV + PREP (*principles*) tenere fede a, non venir meno a; (*reputation*) essere all'altezza di; **the film didn't live up to our expectations** il film ci ha deluso

▸ **live with** VI + PREP (*cohabit with*) vivere con; (*put up with*): **I'll learn to live with it** mi ci abituerò; **I can't live with that pink door any more** non sopporto più quella porta rosa

live[2] [laɪv] ADJ **1** (*animal*) vivo(-a); (*issue*) scottante, d'attualità; (*Radio, TV: broadcast*) in diretta; (*music, concert*) dal vivo; **a real live crocodile** un coccodrillo in carne e ossa; **I'm against tests on live animals** sono contrario agli esperimenti su animali vivi; **live yoghurt** yogurt ricco di fermenti lattici vivi **2** (*shell, ammunition: not blank*) carico(-a); (: *unexploded*) inesploso(-a); (*Elec: rail*) sotto tensione; (: *wire*) ad alta tensione; (*still burning: coal*) ardente ♦ ADV: **to be broadcast live** essere trasmesso(-a) in diretta

live-in ['lɪvɪn] ADJ (*fam: partner*) convivente; (: *servant*) che vive in casa

live·li·hood ['laɪvlɪˌhʊd] N mezzi *mpl* di sostentamento; **to earn one's livelihood** guadagnarsi da vivere; **fishermen who depend on the sea for their livelihood** pescatori che dipendono dal mare per il loro sostentamento

live·li·ness ['laɪvlɪnɪs] N vivacità, brio

live·ly ['laɪvlɪ] ADJ (*comp* **-ier**, *superl* **-iest**) (*gen*) vivace, vivo(-a); (*imagination*) fervido(-a); (*conversation, argument*) animato(-a); (*interest*) vivo(-a); (*party, scene etc*) movimentato(-a); (*pace*) sostenuto(-a); **things are getting lively** l'ambiente *or* l'atmosfera comincia a scaldarsi

liv·en up [ˌlaɪvən'ʌp] VT + ADV (*room etc*) ravvivare; (*discussion, evening*) animare ♦ VI + ADV animarsi

liv·er ['lɪvə'] N (*Anat, Culin*) fegato ♦ ADJ di fegato

liv·er·ish ['lɪvərɪʃ] ADJ: **to be liverish** *or* **feel liverish** sentirsi il fegato ingrossato, avere mal di fegato; (*fig*) scontroso(-a)

Liv·er·pud·lian [ˌlɪvəˈpʌdliən] ADJ di Liverpool ♦ N abitante *m/f or* originario(-a) di Liverpool

liv·ery [ˈlɪvəri] N livrea

lives [laɪvz] NPL *of* life

live·stock [ˈlaɪvˌstɒk] N bestiame *m*

live wire [ˈlaɪvwaɪəʳ] N (*fam*): **to be a live wire** essere pieno(-a) di vitalità

liv·id [ˈlɪvɪd] ADJ **1** (*furious*) furioso(-a), livido(-a) di rabbia, furibondo(-a) **2** (*in colour: complexion*) livido(-a); (: *sky*) plumbeo(-a); (: *bruise*) bluastro(-a); **she was absolutely livid** era assolutamente furibonda

liv·ing [ˈlɪvɪŋ] ADJ (*alive: gen*) vivo(-a); (: *person*) vivente, in vita; **within living memory** a memoria d'uomo; **the greatest living pianist** il più grande pianista vivente; **there wasn't a living soul** non c'era anima viva ♦ N vita; **what do you do for a living?** come ti guadagni da vivere?; **to earn** *or* **make a living** guadagnarsi da vivere; **the living** (*people*) i vivi

living conditions NPL condizioni *fpl* di vita

living expenses NPL spese *fpl* di mantenimento

living room N soggiorno, salotto

living standards NPL tenore *m or* livello di vita

living wage N salario sufficiente per vivere

living will N testamento biologico

liz·ard [ˈlɪzəd] N lucertola

lla·ma [ˈlɑːmə] N lama *m inv*

LMT [ˌɛlɛmˈtiː] ABBR (*USA*: = *Local Mean Time*) tempo medio locale

load [ləʊd] N **1** (*Elec, Tech: burden*) carico; (*weight*) peso; **a heavy load** un pesante carico **2** (*fig*) **that's (taken) a load off my mind** mi sono tolto un peso; **loads of, a load of** (*fam*) un sacco *or* un mucchio di; **they've got loads of money** hanno un sacco di soldi ♦ VT (*also:* **load up**): **to load (with)** (*truck, ship*) caricare (di); (*gun, camera*): **to load (with)** caricare (con); **to load (down) with debts/worries** è carico di debiti/preoccupazioni; **to load a program** (*Comput*) caricare un programma; **I can't load the program** non riesco a caricare il programma

load·ed [ˈləʊdɪd] ADJ **1 a loaded question** una domanda tendenziosa **2** (*dice*) truccato(-a); **the dice are loaded against him** (*fig*) ha tutto contro di lui **3 to be loaded** (*fam: rich*) essere pieno(-a) di soldi; **he's loaded** è pieno di soldi **4 loaded with** carico(-a) di; **a cart loaded with hay** un carro carico di fieno; **loaded with responsibilities** pieno(-a) di responsabilità

load·ing bay [ˈləʊdɪŋˌbeɪ] N piazzola di carico

loaf[1] [ləʊf] N (*pl* **loaves**) pagnotta, pane *m*; **half a loaf is better than no bread** (*Proverb*) meglio poco che niente

loaf[2] [ləʊf] VI (*also:* **loaf about, loaf around**) oziare, bighellonare

loam [ləʊm] N terriccio (fertile)

loan [ləʊn] N prestito; **to give sb the loan of sth** prestare *or* dare in prestito qc a qn; **to ask for the loan of** chiedere in prestito; **on loan** (*book, painting*) in prestito; (*employee*) distaccato(-a); **to raise a loan** (*money*) ottenere un prestito *or* un mutuo ♦ VT prestare, dare in prestito

loan capital N capitale *m* di prestito

loan-shark [ˈləʊnˌʃɑːk] N (*fam, pej*) strozzino(-a)

loath [ləʊθ] ADJ: **to be loath to do sth** essere riluttante *or* restio(-a) a fare qc

loathe [ləʊð] VT (*thing, person*) detestare, odiare; **I loathe her** la detesto; **I loathe doing it** è detesto farlo; **to loathe sb's doing sth** detestare che qn faccia qc

loath·ing [ˈləʊðɪŋ] N (*hatred*) odio; (*disgust*) ribrezzo, disgusto; **it fills me with loathing** mi riempie di disgusto, mi fa ribrezzo

loath·some [ˈləʊðsəm] ADJ (*gen*) ripugnante, disgustoso(-a); (*person*) detestabile, odioso(-a)

loaves [ləʊvz] NPL *of* loaf[1]

lob [lɒb] VT (*ball*) lanciare; **to lob sth over to sb** lanciare qc a qn

lob·by [ˈlɒbɪ] N **1** atrio, hall *f inv*; **the lobby of the museum** l'atrio del museo **2** (*Pol: pressure group*) gruppo di pressione, lobby *f inv* ♦ VT (*Pol*) far pressione su ♦ VI fare pressioni; **to lobby for a reform** fare pressioni per ottenere una riforma

lob·by·ist [ˈlɒbɪɪst] N appartenente *m/f* ad un gruppo di pressione, lobbista *m/f*

lobe [ləʊb] N (*Anat*) lobo

lob·ster [ˈlɒbstəʳ] N aragosta

lobster pot N nassa per aragoste

lo·cal [ˈləʊkəl] ADJ (*gen*) locale; (*resident, shop*) del posto; **the local paper** il giornale locale; **local doctor** medico della zona ♦ N (*fam*) **1 he's a local** è uno del posto; **the locals** la gente del posto **2** (*Brit: pub*) ≈ bar *m inv* sotto casa

local anaesthetic, local anesthetic (*USA*) N anestesia locale

local authority N autorità *f inv* locale; **local education authority** ≈ provveditorato agli studi; **local health authority** ≈ unità *f inv* sanitaria locale

local call N (*Telec*) telefonata urbana, chiamata urbana

local government N amministrazione *f* locale; **local government officer** *or* **official** funzionario dell'amministrazione locale; **local government elections** elezioni *fpl* amministrative

lo·cal·ity [ləʊˈkælɪtɪ] N (*place*) località *f inv*; (*neighbourhood*) vicinanze *fpl*

lo·cal·ize [ˈləʊkəlaɪz] VT localizzare

lo·cal·ly [ˈləʊkəlɪ] ADV (*nearby*) nei paraggi, nelle vicinanze; (*in the locality*) sul posto, in loco; **there will be showers locally** il tempo sarà localmente piovoso, ci saranno locali rovesci; **he lives locally** vive nei paraggi; **the money will be spent locally** il denaro verrà speso a livello locale

lo·cate [ləʊˈkeɪt] VT (*situate*) situare, collocare; (*find*) trovare; (*cause*) individuare, trovare; **where can he be located?** dove lo si può rintracciare?; **we're trying to locate him** stiamo cercando di trovarlo; **to be located** essere situato; **the office is located in York** l'ufficio è situato a York

lo·ca·tion [ləʊˈkeɪʃən] N **1** (*place*) posto; (*placing*) posizione *f*, ubicazione *f*; (*Geog*) localizzazione *f*; **a beautiful location** una bellissima posizione **2** (*Cine*): **on location** in esterni; **film shot on location** film girato in esterni; **to be on location in Mexico** girare gli esterni in Messico

loch [lɒx] N (*Scot*) lago

lock[1] [lɒk] N (*of hair*) ciocca; **locks** (*liter*) chioma

lock[2] [lɒk] N **1** (*on door, box*) serratura; **under lock and key** sotto chiave; **lock stock and barrel** (*fig*) in blocco; **he moved out, lock stock and barrel** se n'è andato con armi e bagagli **2** (*of canal*) chiusa **3** (*Brit: Aut: turning*) sterzo; **on full lock** a tutto sterzo ♦ VT (*door*) chiudere a chiave; (*Tech: immobilize*) bloccare; **make sure you lock your door** non dimenticare di chiudere la porta a chiave; **she locked the steering mechanism** ha messo il bloccasterzo; **to lock sb/sth in a place** chiudere qn/qc in un posto; **behind locked doors** a porte chiuse; **they were locked in each other's arms** erano abbracciati stretti; **to be locked in combat** lottare corpo a corpo ♦ VI (*door etc*) chiudersi; (*wheels*) bloccarsi, incepparsi
  ▸ **lock away** VT + ADV (*valuables*) tenere (rinchiuso-a) al sicuro; (*criminal*) mettere dentro; (*psychiatric patient*) rinchiudere
  ▸ **lock in** VT + ADV chiudere dentro (a chiave)
  ▸ **lock out** VT + ADV chiudere fuori; **the door slammed and I was locked out** la porta si è chiusa di colpo e sono rimasto chiuso fuori; **to lock workers out** (*Industry*) fare una serrata
  ▸ **lock up** VT + ADV (*object*) mettere al sicuro, chiudere (a chiave); (*criminal*) mettere dentro; (*psychiatric patient*) rinchiudere; (*funds*) vincolare, immobilizzare; **she checked that the house was properly locked up** ha controllato che tutto fosse ben chiuso ♦ VI + ADV chiudere tutto (a chiave)

lock·er [ˈlɒkəʳ] N armadietto; (*Naut*) gavone *m*; **left-luggage lockers** armadietti per deposito bagagli

locker room N spogliatoio

lock·et [ˈlɒkɪt] N medaglione *m* (*portaritratti*)

lock·out [ˈlɒkaʊt] N (*Industry*) serrata

lock·smith [ˈlɒkˌsmɪθ] N fabbro

lock-up [ˈlɒkˌʌp] N (*prison*) prigione *f*; (*cell*) guardina; (*Brit: also:* **lock-up garage**) box *m inv*

lo·co·mo·tive [ˌləʊkəˈməʊtɪv] N (*Rail*) locomotiva

lo·cum [ˈləʊkəm] N (*doctor*) medico sostituto; (*priest*) vicario

lo·cust [ˈləʊkəst] N locusta, cavalletta

lodge [lɒdʒ] N (*house*) casetta del guardiano; (*porter's lodge*) portineria, guardiola; (*Freemasonry*) loggia; **a ski lodge** uno chalet in montagna ♦ VT (*person: give lodging*) dare alloggio a; (: *find lodging*) trovare alloggio per; (*money*) depositare; (*complaint, appeal etc*) fare, presentare; (*statement*) rilasciare; **to lodge an appeal** (*Law*) ricorrere in corte d'appello; **we lodged a complaint** abbiamo presentato un reclamo ♦ VI **1** (*person*): **to lodge (with)** (*landlady*) essere a pensione (presso *or* da); (*friends*) alloggiare (con); **I'd rather lodge with a family** preferirei alloggiare presso una famiglia **2** (*bullet*) conficcarsi; **to lodge (itself) in/between** piantarsi dentro/ fra; **a bullet lodged in his leg** una pallottola gli si è conficcata nella gamba

lodg·er [ˈlɒdʒəʳ] N (*with room and meals*) pensionante *m/f*; (*room only*) persona che ha una camera in affitto; **she takes in lodgers** fa l'affittacamere

lodg·ing [ˈlɒdʒɪŋ] N (*accommodation*) alloggio; **board and lodging** vitto e alloggio; *see also* **board**

lodging house N (*Brit*) casa con camere in affitto

lodg·ings [ˈlɒdʒɪŋz] NPL (*room*) camera in affitto, camera ammobiliata; (*small apartment*) appartamentino; **to look for lodgings** cercarsi un alloggio

loft [lɒft] N soffitta, solaio; (*also:* **hayloft**) granaio, fienile *m*; (*USA*) loft *m inv*

lofty [ˈlɒftɪ] ADJ (*comp* -ier, *superl* -iest) (*frm: sentiments, aims*) nobile; (*haughty: manner*) di superiorità, altezzoso(-a); (*liter: mountain*) alto(-a); **a lofty ceiling** un soffitto alto; **lofty ambitions** grandi ambizioni *fpl*; **lofty ideals** ideali *mpl* nobili

log [lɒg] N **1** (*for fire*) ceppo; (*tree trunk*) tronco **2** = **logbook** ♦ N ABBR (= *logarithm*) log ♦ VT **1** (*Naut, Aer*) annotare *or* registrare sul giornale di bordo **2** (*Aut: also:* **log up**: *speed*) fare; (*distance*) coprire; **to log 50 mph** ≈ fare 80 km/h
   ▸ **log in, log on** VI + ADV (*Comput*) aprire una sessione (con codice di riconoscimento)
   ▸ **log off, log out** VI + ADV (*Comput*) fare il log-off

loga·rithm [ˈlɒgərɪðəm] N logaritmo; **common logarithm** logaritmo decimale *or* volgare

log·book [ˈlɒgbʊk] N (*Naut, Aer*) giornale *m or* diario di bordo; (*Aut: registration document*) libretto di circolazione; (*of events, movement of goods*) registro

log cabin N capanna di tronchi

log fire N fuoco di legna

log·ger [ˈlɒgəʳ] N boscaiolo, taglialegna *m inv*

log·ger·heads [ˈlɒgəhɛdz] NPL: **at loggerheads (with sb)** in violento contrasto (con qn), ai ferri corti (con)

log·ic [ˈlɒdʒɪk] N logica

logi·cal [ˈlɒdʒɪkəl] ADJ logico(-a)

logi·cal·ly [ˈlɒdʒɪkəlɪ] ADV logicamente; **logically, we should ...** a rigor di logica, dovremmo...

login [ˈlɒgɪn] N (*Comput*) nome *m* utente *pl inv*

lo·gis·tics [lɒˈdʒɪstɪks] NSG logistica

log·jam [ˈlɒgdʒæm] N: **to break the logjam** superare l'impasse *f inv*

logo [ˈləʊgəʊ] N logo *m inv*

loin [lɔɪn] N (*of meat*) lombata

loi·ter [ˈlɔɪtəʳ] VI (*idle*) bighellonare; (*lag behind*) attardarsi, fermarsi (ad ogni passo); **to loiter (about)** indugiare, bighellonare; **to loiter (with intent)** (*Law*) aggirarsi (con intenzioni sospette); **I loitered in the airport shops** ho gironzolato per i negozi dell'aeroporto

LOL ABBR (*fam:* = *laugh out loud*) LOL, grandi risate (*nel gergo di internet*)

loll [lɒl] VI (*head, tongue*) ciondolare; **to loll about** *or* **around** starsene pigramente sdraiato(-a), essere stravaccato(-a); **to loll against sth, loll back on sth** appoggiarsi pigramente a qc

lol·li·pop [ˈlɒlɪpɒp] N lecca lecca *m inv*

lol·ly [ˈlɒlɪ] N (*Brit fam*) **1** (*lollipop*) lecca lecca *m inv*; (*also:* **ice lolly**) ghiacciolo **2** (*money*) grana, quattrini *mpl*

Lom·bardy [ˈlɒmbədɪ] N Lombardia

Lon·don [ˈlʌndən] N Londra; **I'm from London** sono di Londra

Lon·don·er [ˈlʌndənəʳ] N londinese *m/f*

lone [ləʊn] ADJ (*frm: person*) solitario(-a), solo(-a); (: *house*) solitario(-a); **to play a lone hand** (*fig*) agire da solo

lone·li·ness [ˈləʊnlɪnɪs] N solitudine *f*

lone·ly [ˈləʊnlɪ] ADJ (*comp* -ier, *superl* -iest) (*person*) solitario(-a); (*place: isolated*) isolato(-a); (: *deserted*) deserto(-a); **to be** *or* **feel lonely** sentirsi solo(-a); **I sometimes feel lonely** qualche volta mi sento solo; **a lonely cottage** una villetta isolata

lonely hearts ADJ: **lonely hearts ad** annuncio per cuori solitari; **lonely hearts column** messaggi *mpl* personali; **lonely hearts club** club *m inv* dei cuori solitari

lone parent N (*mother*) madre single (*or* divorziata *or* vedova); (*father*) padre single (*or* divorziato *or* vedovo)

lon·er [ˈləʊnəʳ] N tipo solitario, persona solitaria, solitario(-a)

lone·some [ˈləʊnsəm] ADJ (*esp USA*) solo(-a); **to feel lonesome** sentirsi solo

long[1] [lɒŋ] ADJ (*comp* -er, *superl* -est) **1** (*in size*) lungo(-a); **she's got long hair** ha i capelli lunghi; **how long is it?** quant'è lungo?; **how long is this river?** quanto è lungo questo fiume?; **it is 6 metres long** è lungo 6 metri; **to get longer** allungarsi **2** (*in time*) lungo(-a); (*for*) **a long time** (per) molto tempo; **it takes a long time** ci vuole molto tempo; **I've been waiting a long time** aspetto da molto tempo; **how long is the film?** quanto dura il film?; **how long will it take?** quanto ci vorrà?; **how long did you stay there?** per quanto tempo sei rimasto lì?; **2 hours long** che dura 2 ore, di 2 ore; **a long walk/holiday** una lunga camminata/ vacanza; **a long job** un lavoro lungo; **to have a long memory** avere buona memoria; **it's been a long day** (*fig*) è stata una giornata lunga; **to take a long look at sth** esaminare ben bene qc; **at long last** finalmente ♦ ADV a lungo, per molto tempo; **I shan't be long** non ne avrò per molto; **he won't be long finishing** non ci metterà molto a finire; **we didn't stay (for) long** non ci siamo fermati a lungo; **I have long believed that ...** è da molto tempo che credo che...; **he had long understood that ...** aveva capito da molto tempo che...; **long before** molto tempo prima; **long before now** molto tempo prima; **long before you came** molto prima che tu arrivassi; **before long** (+ *future*) presto, fra poco; (+ *past*) poco tempo dopo; **he's long since departed** se n'è andato molto tempo fa; **how long is it since you saw them?** da quant'è che non li vedi?; **how long have you been here?** da quanto sei qui?; **how long has he been learning Italian?** da quanto studia l'italiano?; **how long ago?** quanto tempo fa?; **as long ago as 1960** nientemeno che nel 1960; **he no longer comes** non viene più; **all day long** tutto il giorno; **so long as, as long as** (*while*) finché; (*provided that*) sempre che + *sub*; **I'll come as long as it's not too expensive** verrò, sempre che non costi troppo; **so long!** (*fam, esp USA*) ciao!; **don't be long!** fai presto!; **it won't take long** è questione di poco ♦ N: **the long and the short of it is that ...** (*fig*) a farla breve...

long[2] [lɒŋ] VI: **to long for sth/sb** desiderare molto qc/qn; **to long to do sth** morire dalla voglia di fare qc; **to long for sb to do sth** desiderare tanto che qn faccia qc

long-distance [ˌlɒŋˈdɪstəns] ADJ (*Telec: call*) interurbano(-a); (*race*) di fondo; **long-distance runner** fondista *m/f*

long-haired [ˌlɒŋˈhɛəd] ADJ (*person*) dai capelli lunghi; (*animal*) dal pelo lungo

long·hand [ˈlɒŋhænd] N scrittura (normale)

long·ing [ˈlɒŋɪŋ] N desiderio; (*for food*) voglia; (*nostalgia*) nostalgia; **a longing for affection** un desiderio d'affetto ♦ ADJ (*look*) pieno(-a) di desiderio *or* di nostalgia

long·ing·ly [ˈlɒŋɪŋlɪ] ADV con desiderio (*or* nostalgia)

lon·gi·tude [ˈlɒŋgɪtjuːd] N longitudine *f*

long johns NPL (*fam*) mutandoni *mpl*

long jump N salto in lungo

long-life [ˈlɒŋlaɪf] ADJ a lunga conservazione

long-lost [ˈlɒŋlɒst] ADJ perduto(-a) da tempo; (*friend*) che non si vede da molto tempo

long-playing [ˈlɒŋpleɪɪŋ] ADJ: **long-playing record** (disco a) 33 giri *m inv*, long-playing *m inv*

long-range [ˈlɒŋreɪndʒ] ADJ (*gun, missile*) a lunga portata *or* gittata; (*aircraft*) a lungo raggio d'azione; (*weather forecast*) a lungo termine

long·shore·man [ˈlɒŋʃɔːmən] N (*pl* -men) (*USA*) portuale *m*, scaricatore *m* di porto

long-sighted [ˌlɒŋˈsaɪtɪd] ADJ presbite; (*Med*) ipermetrope; (*fig*) lungimirante

long-standing [ˈlɒŋˈstændɪŋ] ADJ di vecchia data

long-suffering [ˈlɒŋˈsʌfərɪŋ] ADJ estremamente paziente, infinitamente tollerante

long-term [ˈlɒŋˈtɜːm] ADJ (*plans, effects*) a lungo termine; **to take a long-term view of sth** proiettare qc nel futuro

long wave N (*Radio*) onde *fpl* lunghe

long-winded [ˌlɒŋˈwɪndɪd] ADJ (*speaker*) prolisso(-a); (*account, explanation*) interminabile

loo [luː] N (*Brit fam: toilet*) gabinetto, cesso

loo·fah, loo·fa [ˈluːfə] N luffa

look [lʊk] VI 1 (*see, glance*) guardare; **I'm just looking** (*in shop*) sto solo dando un'occhiata; **I'll look and see** vado a vedere; **look who's here!** (ma) guarda chi si vede!; **to look the other way** guardare dall'altra parte; (*fig*) far finta di non vedere; **to look ahead** guardare avanti; (*fig*) cominciare a pensare al futuro; **to look south** (*building etc*) dare a sud; **look before you leap** (*fig*) non buttarti alla cieca 2 (*seem, appear*) sembrare, aver l'aria; **she looks surprised** sembra sorpresa; **that cake looks nice** la torta sembra buona; **he looks about 60 (years old)** dimostra una sessantina d'anni; **it looks about 4 metres long** sarà lungo un 4 metri; **you don't look yourself** non mi sembri in forma; **you look** *or* **you're looking well** ti trovo bene; **it looks good on you** ti sta bene, ti dona; **it makes you look younger** ti ringiovanisce, ti fa sembrare più giovane; **it looks all right to me** a me pare che vada bene 3 **to look like** assomigliare a; **he looks like his brother** assomiglia a suo fratello; **what does she look like?** che aspetto ha?; **this photo doesn't look like him** in questa foto non sembra lui; **it looks like cheese to me** mi sembra formaggio; **it certainly looks like it** ne ha tutta l'aria; **the party looks like being fun** la festa promette bene; **it looks like rain** mi sa che sta per piovere; **it looks as if** *or* **as though the train will be late** mi sa tanto che il treno sarà in ritardo ♦ VT guardare; **to look sb (straight) in the eye** *or* **in the face** guardare qn (dritto) negli occhi *or* in faccia; **to look sb up and down** squadrare qn da capo a piedi; **look where you're going!** guarda dove vai!; **to look one's best** essere in gran forma; **you must look your best for this interview** dovresti cercare di presentarti a questo colloquio ben vestito e ben curato; **to look one's age** dimostrare la propria età ♦ N 1 (*glance*) occhiata; (*expression*) sguardo, aria; **with a look of despair** con un'aria *or* un'espressione disperata; **to have a look at sth** dare un'occhiata a qc; **have a look at this!** dai un'occhiata a questo!; **let me have a look** fammi vedere; **to take a good look at sb/sth** guardare (per) bene qn/qc; **to have a look for sth** cercare qc; **shall we have a look round the town?** andiamo a visitare la città?; **she gave me a dirty look** mi ha lanciato un'occhiataccia 2 (*air, appearance*) aspetto, aria; **he has a look of his mother about him** ha qualcosa di sua madre; **there's a mischievous look about that child** quel bambino ha un'aria birichina; **by the look of things it's going to rain** ha tutta l'aria di (voler) piovere; **by the look of him** a vederlo; **I don't like the look of him** ha un'aria che non mi piace; **I don't like the look of it** non mi piace per niente; **the new look for summer** (*Fashion*) il nuovo look *m inv* per l'estate; *see also* **looks**

▸ **look after** VI + PREP (*gen*) occuparsi di; (*possessions*) prendersi cura di; (*keep an eye on*) guardare, badare a; **I look after my little sister** mi occupo della mia sorellina; **to look after sth for sb** dare un'occhiata a qc per qn; **he doesn't look after himself** si trascura; **she's old enough to look after herself** è abbastanza grande per badare a se stessa

▸ **look around** VI + ADV guardarsi intorno; **to look around for sb/sth** cercare qn/qc

▸ **look at** VT + PREP (*person, object*) guardare; (*problem, situation*) considerare; **look at the picture on page three** guardate la figura a pagina tre; **it isn't much to look at but ...** (*fam*) non è bellissimo(-a) ma...; **could you look at the engine for me?** puoi dare un'occhiata al motore?; **I wouldn't even look at such a low offer** non prenderei nemmeno in considerazione un'offerta così bassa

▸ **look away** VI + ADV distogliere lo sguardo

▸ **look back** VI + ADV girarsi *or* voltarsi indietro; (*remember*) ripensare al passato; **to look back at sth/sb** voltarsi a guardare qc/qn; **he's never looked back** (*fig*) non ha fatto che migliorare; **to look back on** (*event, period*) ripensare a

▸ **look down** VI + ADV abbassare gli occhi *or* lo sguardo; (*from height*) guardare giù; **to look down at sb/sth** guardare giù verso qn/qc

▸ **look down on** VI + ADV + PREP guardare giù verso; (*fig*) guardare dall'alto in basso, disprezzare

▸ **look for** VI + PREP cercare; **to look for sb/sth** cercare qn/qc; **I'm looking for my passport** sto cercando il mio passaporto

▸ **look forward to** VI + ADV + PREP: **to look forward to doing sth** non veder l'ora di fare qc; **I'm looking forward to his visit/the film** non vedo l'ora che venga/di vedere il film; **I'm looking forward to meeting you** non vedo l'ora di incontrarti; **I'm looking forward to the holidays** non vedo l'ora che arrivino le vacanze; **I'm not looking forward to it** non ne ho nessuna voglia; **looking forward to hearing from you** (*in letter*) aspettando tue notizie

▸ **look in** VI + ADV guardar dentro

▸ **look in on** VI + ADV + PREP (*visit*) fare un salto da

▸ **look into** VI + PREP (*matter, possibility*) esaminare

▸ **look on** VI + ADV rimanere a guardare, fare da spettatore ♦ VI + PREP considerare

▸ **look onto** VI + PREP dare su, affacciarsi su; **to look onto the sea** dare sul mare; **my room looks onto the garden** la mia camera si affaccia *or* dà sul giardino

▸ **look out** VI + ADV 1 (*watch*) guardar fuori 2 **to look out (for)** stare attento(-a) (a); **look out!** attento! ♦ VT + ADV (*find*) tirar fuori

▸ **look out for** VI + PREP (*seek*) cercare; **to look out for sb/sth** (*watch out for*) guardare se arriva qn/qc

▸ **look over** VT + ADV (*essay*) dare un'occhiata a, riguardare; (*building*) ispezionare; (*person*) esaminare

▸ **look upon** VT + PREP considerare, ritenere

▸ **look round** VI + ADV (*turn*) girarsi, voltarsi; (*in shops*) dare un'occhiata; **I shouted and he looked round** ho gridato e lui si è voltato; **I'm just looking round** sto solo dando un'occhiata; **to look round for sb/sth** guardarsi intorno per cercare qn/qc ♦ VI + PREP (*museum, factory*) visitare; (*shops*) dare un'occhiata a; **to look round an exhibition** visitare una mostra

▸ **look through** VI + PREP 1 (*papers, book*) esaminare; (*briefly*) scorrere; (*revise*) rivedere 2 (*telescope*) guardare attraverso

▸ **look to** VI + PREP (*turn to*) rivolgersi a; (*look after*) badare a, stare attento(-a) a; (*rely on*) contare su

▸ **look up** VI + ADV 1 (*glance*) alzare gli occhi 2 (*improve: prospects*) migliorare; (*: business*) riprendersi; (*: sales*) aumentare; (*: shares*) essere in rialzo; (*: weather*) mettersi al bello; **things are looking up** le cose stanno migliorando ♦ VT + ADV 1 (*information, word*) cercare; **if you don't know a word, look it up in the dictionary** se non conosci qualche parola cercala sul dizionario 2 (*visit: friend*) andare a trovare

▸ **look up to** VI + ADV + PREP avere rispetto per

look-out [ˈlʊkˌaʊt] N 1 **to keep a look-out** fare la guardia; **keep a look-out for a post box** guarda se vedi una buca per le lettere; **to be on the look-out for sth** cercare qc 2 (*viewpoint*) posto di vedetta, posto d'osservazione; (*person: thief*) palo; (*: Mil*) sentinella; (*: Naut*) vedetta 3 (*prospect*) prospettiva; **it's a grim** *or* **poor look-out** è una prospettiva poco allegra; **that's his look-out!** questo è affar suo!

loom[1] [luːm] N (*weaving loom*) telaio

loom[2] [luːm] VI (*also: loom up: building, mountain*) apparire in lontananza; **the ship loomed (up) out of the mist** nella nebbia apparve la nave; (*fig*) essere imminente, incombere; **the threat of a war is looming** incombe la minaccia di una guerra; **a new crisis is looming** si profila all'orizzonte una nuova crisi

loony [ˈluːnɪ] ADJ, N (*fam*) pazzo(-a), matto(-a)

loop [luːp] N (*in string etc*) cappio; (*fastening*) asola; (*for belt*) passante *m*; (*bend: in river*) ansa; (*Comput*) loop *m inv*, sequenza ciclica di istruzioni ♦ VT: **to loop a rope round a post** passare una corda intorno a un palo; **to loop the loop** (*Aer*) fare il giro della morte

loop·hole [ˈluːpˌhəʊl] N (*fig*) scappatoia, via d'uscita; **a legal loophole** una scappatoia legale

loose [luːs] ADJ (comp -r, superl -st) **1** (not firmly attached: plaster, button) che si stacca; (: knot, shoelace, screw) allentato(-a); (: hair) sciolto(-a); (: skin) floscio(-a); (: tooth) che tentenna; (: page) staccato(-a); (: sheet of paper) volante; (: stone) sconnesso(-a); (animal) in libertà, scappato(-a); **a loose screw** una vite allentata; **to come** or **work loose** allentarsi; **to turn** or **let loose** (animal) lasciare in libertà; **to get loose** (animal) scappare; **loose chippings** (Aut) ghiaino; **loose connection** (Elec) filo che non fa contatto **2** (not tight: clothes) ampio(-a), largo(-a); **a loose shirt** una camicia larga; **loose weave** a trama or maglia larga **3** (not packed: fruit, cheese) non confezionato(-a), sfuso(-a) **4** (fig: translation) libero(-a); (: style) prolisso(-a); (: discipline) rilassato(-a); (: associations, links, thinking) vago(-a), poco rigoroso(-a); (: life, morals) dissoluto(-a); **loose living** vita dissipata ♦ N (fam): **to be on the loose** (criminal, animal) essere in libertà ♦ VT (frm: free) liberare; (: untie) sciogliere; (: slacken) allentare; (also: **loose off**: arrow) scoccare; **to loose one's gun (off) at** sparare a or contro; **to loose the dogs on** or **at sb** sguinzagliare i cani dietro a or contro qn

loose change N spiccioli mpl, moneta
loose-fitting [ˈluːsˌfɪtɪŋ] ADJ ampio(-a), largo(-a)
loose-leaf [ˈluːsˈliːf] ADJ: **loose-leaf binder** or **folder** raccoglitore m a fogli mobili
loose-limbed [ˈluːsˈlɪmd] ADJ snodato(-a), agile
loose·ly [ˈluːslɪ] ADV (hold, tie) senza stringere; (associate) vagamente; (translate) liberamente; (use word) in modo improprio
loosely-knit [ˈluːslɪˈnɪt] ADJ non rigidamente strutturato(-a)
loos·en [ˈluːsn] VT (slacken: screw, belt, knot) allentare; (: rope, grip) mollare; (: clothing) slacciare; (untie) disfare; (fig: tongue) sciogliere ♦ VI (all senses) allentarsi
  ▸ **loosen up** VI + ADV (before game) sciogliere i muscoli, scaldarsi; (fam: relax) rilassarsi
loot [luːt] N bottino ♦ VT saccheggiare, depredare ♦ VI: **to go looting** darsi al saccheggio
loot·er [ˈluːtəʳ] N saccheggiatore(-trice)
loot·ing [ˈluːtɪŋ] N saccheggio
lop [lɒp] VT (also: **lop off**) tagliar (via), recidere
lop-sided [ˈlɒpˈsaɪdɪd] ADJ (smile) di traverso; (structure) sbilenco(-a)
lord [lɔːd] N **1** signore m; **lord of the manor** signore del castello; **lord and master** signore e padrone; **to live like a lord** vivere da signore or come un re **2** (Brit): **Lord Smith** Lord Smith; **my Lord** (to bishop, noble) Eccellenza; (to judge) signor giudice **3 Our Lord** (Rel) Nostro Signore; **the Lord** il Signore; **the Lord's prayer** il Padrenostro; **good Lord!** Dio mio! ♦ VT: **to lord it over sb** (fam) darsi arie da gran signore con qn
lord·ly [ˈlɔːdlɪ] ADJ (pej: person, manner) altero(-a), altezzoso(-a); (bearing, castle) nobile, maestoso(-a)
lord·ship [ˈlɔːdʃɪp] N: **his lordship** the Count etc Sua Signoria il conte etc; **your Lordship** (Brit) Vostra Signoria
lore [lɔːʳ] N tradizioni fpl; **plant/weather lore** cognizioni fpl sulle piante/sul tempo
lor·ry [ˈlɒrɪ] N (Brit) camion m inv
lorry driver N (Brit) camionista m/f
lose [luːz] (pt, pp lost) VT **1** (gen) perdere; **I've lost my purse** ho perso il portamonete; **to get lost** (object) andare perso(-a) or perduto(-a) or smarrito(-a); (person) perdersi, smarrirsi; **I was afraid I'd get lost** avevo paura di perdermi; **get lost!** (fam) vattene!, sparisci!; **to lose one's life** perdere la vita; **many lives were lost** ci sono state molte vittime; **there were no lives lost** non ci sono stati morti, non ci sono state vittime; **he's lost his licence** (Aut) gli è stata ritirata la patente; **you've got nothing to lose** non hai niente da perdere; **to lose one's way** perdersi; **to lose interest/one's appetite** perdere interesse/l'appetito; **to lose weight** dimagrire; **to lose patience** perdere la pazienza, spazientirsi; **to lose no time (in doing sth)** non perdere tempo (a fare qc); **there's no time to lose** non c'è tempo da perdere; **he managed to lose his pursuers** è riuscito a seminare i suoi inseguitori; **you've lost me there** (fig) ho perso il filo **2** that mistake **lost us the game** quell'errore ci ha fatto perdere il gioco; **they lost the match** hanno perso la partita **3** this watch **loses 5 minutes every day** quest'orologio resta indietro di

5 minuti al giorno ♦ VI perdere; **they lost (by) 3 goals to 2** hanno perso (per) 3 a 2; **to lose to sb** perdere contro qn; **to lose (out) on sth** (deal) rimetterci in qc; (trip) perdersi; **you can't lose** in tutti i casi ci guadagni; **the clock is losing** l'orologio resta indietro
los·er [ˈluːzəʳ] N perdente m/f; **he's a born loser** è un perdente nato; **to be a good/bad loser** saper/non saper perdere
loss [lɒs] N **1** perdita; **heavy losses** (Mil) gravi perdite; **without loss of life** senza perdita di vite umane; **to cut one's losses** rimetterci il meno possibile; **it's your loss!** quello che ci rimette sei tu!; **he's a dead loss** (fam) è un disastro; **he's no great loss** (fam) nessuno lo rimpiange di certo; **to make a loss** perderci; (Comm) subire una perdita; **to sell sth at a loss** vendere qc perdendoci **2 to be at a loss** essere perplesso(-a); **to be at a loss to explain sth** non saper come fare a spiegare qc; **to be at a loss for words** essere senza parole
loss adjuster N (Insurance) liquidatore m/f
loss leader N (Comm) articolo m civetta, inv
lost [lɒst] PT, PP of **lose** ♦ ADJ (gen, also fig) perso(-a); (bewildered) smarrito(-a); **I realized I was lost** ho capito che mi ero perso; **a lost sheep** una pecorella smarrita; **some lost children** dei bambini che si erano smarriti; **lost in thought** immerso(-a) or perso(-a) nei propri pensieri; **to feel a bit lost** sentirsi smarrito(-a); **the remark/joke was lost on him** non ha capito l'osservazione/la barzelletta; **my advice was lost on her** non ha ascoltato il mio consiglio; **I feel lost without my car/him** mi sento perso senza la mia macchina/di lui; **to make up for lost time** recuperare il tempo perduto; **to give sth up for lost** dare qc per perso(-a); **lost baggage claim** ritiro bagagli smarriti; **lost at sea** perito(-a) in mare
lost property, (USA) **lost and found** N oggetti mpl smarriti; **lost property office** or **department** ufficio oggetti smarriti
lot [lɒt] N **1** (large amount) molto; **a lot of money, lots of money** (fam) un sacco di soldi; **I drink a lot of coffee** bevo molto caffè; **we saw a lot of interesting things** abbiamo visto molte cose interessanti; **a lot of people, lots of people** (fam) molta gente, molti; **he's got lots of friends** ha molti amici; **she's got lots of self-confidence** ha molta fiducia in se stessa; **do you like football? - not a lot** ti piace il calcio? - non molto; **quite a lot of noise** parecchio rumore; **such a lot of people** talmente tanta gente; **the most we could say/do** c'era ben poco da dire/da fare; **I'd give a lot to know ...** darei non so cosa per sapere...; **I read a lot** leggo molto; **he feels a lot** or (fam) **lots better** si sente molto meglio; **thanks a lot!** (also iro) grazie tante! **2** (fam): **the lot** (all, everything) tutto(-a) (quanto(-a)); **he took the lot** ha preso tutto (quanto); **that's the lot** (questo) è tutto; **the (whole) lot of them** tutti quanti **3** (destiny) sorte f, destino; **the common lot** il destino comune; **it fell to my lot to do it** è toccato a me farlo; **to throw in one's lot with sb** unirsi a qn **4** (random selection) sorte f; **to draw lots (for sth)** tirare a sorte (per qc) **5** (at auction) lotto, partita; **he's a bad lot** (fig) è un pessimo soggetto **6** (plot of land) lotto di terreno; **building lot** lotto edificabile
lo·tion [ˈləʊʃən] N lozione f
lot·tery [ˈlɒtərɪ] N lotteria; **to win the lottery** vincere alla lotteria
loud [laʊd] ADJ (comp -er, superl -est) (gen) forte; (laugh, applause, thunder) fragoroso(-a), forte; (noisy: behaviour, party, protests) rumoroso(-a); (pej: gaudy: colour, clothes) chiassoso(-a), vistoso(-a), sgargiante; **the radio's too loud** il volume della radio è troppo alto ♦ ADV (speak etc) forte; **out loud** ad alta voce; **loud and clear** chiaro e forte, molto chiaramente
loud·hailer [ˌlaʊdˈheɪləʳ] N megafono
loud·ly [ˈlaʊdlɪ] ADV (gen) forte; (laugh, applaud) fragorosamente; (protest) rumorosamente; (proclaim :out loud) ad alta voce; (: on banner etc) a lettere cubitali
loud·speaker [ˌlaʊdˈspiːkəʳ] N altoparlante m
Lou·i·si·a·na [luːˌiːzɪˈænə] la Louisiana
lounge [laʊndʒ] N soggiorno, salotto; (of hotel) salone m; (of airport) sala d'attesa; **in the lounge** nel soggiorno; **the departure lounge** la sala attesa per l'imbarco ♦ VI (also: **lounge about**) oziare, poltrire, starsene colle mani in mano
lounge bar N (Brit) bar m inv con servizio al tavolino
lounge suit N (Brit) completo da uomo

louse [laʊs] N (pl **lice**) pidocchio m; (pej, fam: person) verme m ▸ **louse up** VT + ADV (USA fam) rovinare

lousy ['laʊzɪ] ADJ (Med) pidocchioso(-a); (fam: very bad) schifoso(-a); (: headache, cough) orrendo(-a); **to feel lousy** stare da cani; **I feel lousy** sto da cani; **a lousy trick** uno sporco trucco; **the food's lousy** il cibo è pessimo

lout [laʊt] N giovinastro

lou·vre, lou·ver (USA) ['luːvəʳ] ADJ (door, window) con apertura a gelosia

lov·able ['lʌvəbl] ADJ adorabile, carino(-a)

love [lʌv] N **1 love (of, for)** amore m (di, per); (of hobby, object) passione f (per); **true love** vero amore; **it was love at first sight** è stato amore a prima vista or un colpo di fulmine; **he studies history for the love of it** studia storia per il puro piacere di farlo; **to be in love (with sb)** essere innamorato(-a) (di); **she's in love with Paul** è innamorata di Paul; **to fall in love (with sb)** innamorarsi (di qn); **to make love** fare l'amore; **to make love to sb** (old: woo) fare la corte a qn; **there is no love lost between them** non si possono soffrire; **love from Anne, love, Anne** (in letter) con affetto, Anne; **to send one's love to sb** mandare i propri saluti a qn; **give Gloria my love** salutami Gloria **2 (my) love** amore m (mio), tesoro (mio) **3** (Tennis, etc): **love all** zero a zero; **"15 love"** "15 a zero" ♦ VT (person: spouse, child) amare; (: relative, friend) voler bene a; (food, activity, place) amare, adorare; **I love you** ti amo; **everybody loves her** tutti le vogliono bene; **I love chocolate** mi piace molto la cioccolata; **he loves tennis/ Florence** gli piace (molto) il tennis/Firenze; **he loves swimming** or **to swim** gli piace (molto) nuotare; **I'd love to...** mi piacerebbe molto...; **I'd love to come** mi piacerebbe venire; **would you like to come? — I'd love to** vuoi venire? — mi piacerebbe molto

love affair N relazione f

loved ones ['lʌvd wʌnz] NPL: **my loved ones** i miei cari

love-hate relationship [ˌlʌvˌheɪtrɪˈleɪʃənʃɪp] N rapporto m amore-odio, inv

love letter N lettera d'amore

love life N vita sentimentale

love·ly ['lʌvlɪ] ADJ (comp **-ier**, superl **-iest**) (beautiful: gen) bello(-a); (delightful: meal, voice) delizioso(-a); (: evening, party) bellissimo(-a); (: holiday, weather) bello(-a); (delicious: smell, meal, food) buono(-a); **what a lovely surprise!** che bella sorpresa!; **they've got a lovely house** hanno una bella casa; **is your meal okay? — yes, it's lovely** ti piace il pranzo? — sì, è buonissimo; **she's a lovely person** è una persona deliziosa; **it's lovely and warm** fa un bel calduccio; **it's been lovely seeing you** è stato un vero piacere vederti; **have a lovely time!** divertiti!; **we had a lovely time** ci siamo divertiti molto

lov·er ['lʌvəʳ] N **1** (sexually) amante m/f; (romantically) innamorato(-a) **2 lover (of)** (enthusiast) appassionato(-a) (di); **he's a lover of good food** è un buongustaio, è un amante della buona tavola

love·sick ['lʌvˌsɪk] ADJ malato(-a) d'amore

love·song ['lʌvˌsɒŋ] N canzone f d'amore

lov·ing ['lʌvɪŋ] ADJ affettuoso(-a); (care) tenero(-a), amoroso(-a); **loving parents** genitori affettuosi

low¹ [ləʊ] ADJ (comp **-er**, superl **-est**) (gen) basso(-a); (bow) profondo(-a); (murmur) sommesso(-a); (intelligence) scarso(-a); (quality) scadente; (Bio, Zool: form of life) primitivo(-a); (pej: opinion, taste) cattivo(-a); (: character) pessimo(-a); (: behaviour) ignobile; (: café, place) malfamato(-a); **a low trick** un tiro mancino, uno scherzo ignobile; **to feel low** (depressed) sentirsi (un po') giù; **he was feeling a bit low** era un po' giù; **he's very low** (ill) è molto debole; **supplies are low** le scorte si stanno esaurendo; **we are low on flour** non c'è rimasta molta farina; **in a low voice** a bassa voce; **in low gear** (Aut) in una marcia bassa; **on low ground** in pianura; **lower down** più in basso; **lower deck/floor** ponte/ piano inferiore ♦ ADV (aim) in basso; (sing) a bassa voce; (fly) a bassa quota, basso; (bow) profondamente; **that plane is flying very low** quell'aereo vola molto basso; **to sink lower** sprofondare sempre di più; **to fall** or **sink low** (fig) cadere in basso; **to turn sth down low** (gas, radio etc) abbassare qc; **supplies are running** or **getting low** le scorte stanno per finire ♦ N **1** (Met) depressione f, zona di bassa pressione **2**

(fig: low point): **to reach a new** or **an all-time low** toccare il livello più basso or il minimo

low² [ləʊ] VI (cow) muggire

low-alcohol ['ləʊˈælkəˌhɒl] ADJ a basso contenuto alcolico

low-brow ['ləʊˌbraʊ] ADJ (pej: person) poco colto(-a); (: interests, entertainment) senza pretese intellettuali ♦ N persona poco colta or senza pretese intellettuali

low-calorie ['ləʊˈkælərɪ] ADJ a basso contenuto calorico

low-carb ['ləʊˈkɑːb] ADJ (fam) a basso contenuto di carboidrati

low-cut ['ləʊˈkʌt] ADJ (dress) scollato(-a)

low-down ['ləʊˌdaʊn] N (fam): **he gave me the low-down on it** mi ha messo al corrente dei fatti ♦ ADJ (mean) ignobile

low·er¹ ['ləʊəʳ] COMP of **low¹** ♦ VT (gen) calare; (flag, sail) ammainare; (reduce: price) abbassare, ridurre; (resistance) indebolire; **they have lowered interest rates** hanno abbassato i tassi d'interesse; **to lower sb's morale** demoralizzare qn; **to lower one's guard** (Boxing, also fig) abbassare la guardia; **to lower one's voice** abbassare la voce; **to lower o.s. to do sth** (fig) abbassarsi a fare qc

low·er² ['laʊəʳ] VI (person): **to lower (at sb)** dare un'occhiataccia (a qn); (sky) oscurarsi, essere minaccioso(-a)

lower-case ['ləʊəˈkeɪs] ADJ (Typ) minuscolo(-a)

low-fat ['ləʊˈfæt] ADJ magro(-a)

low-key [ˌləʊˈkiː] ADJ moderato(-a); (operation) condotto(-a) con discrezione; **to keep sth low-key** fare qc con discrezione

low·land ['ləʊlənd] N bassopiano, pianura; **the Lowlands of Scotland** le Lowlands scozzesi

low-level ['ləʊˌlɛvl] ADJ a basso livello; (flying) a bassa quota

low-loader [ˌləʊˈləʊdəʳ] N camion m inv a pianale basso

low·ly ['ləʊlɪ] ADJ modesto(-a), umile

low-lying ['ləʊˌlaɪɪŋ] ADJ (land) a basso livello

low-paid ['ləʊˈpeɪd] ADJ mal pagato(-a)

low-rise ['ləʊˈraɪz] ADJ (Archit) di altezza contenuta, basso(-a)

low-tech ['ləʊˈtɛk] ADJ a basso contenuto tecnologico

loy·al ['lɔɪəl] ADJ (comp **-er**, superl **-est**) leale, fedele

loy·al·ist ['lɔɪəlɪst] N, ADJ lealista m/f

loy·al·ty ['lɔɪəltɪ] N lealtà f inv, fedeltà f inv; **undying loyalty** fedeltà eterna

loyalty card N carta f fedeltà, inv

loz·enge ['lɒzɪndʒ] N (Med) pastiglia; (Geom) losanga

LP [ˌɛlˈpiː] N ABBR (= long-playing record) LP m inv, ellepi m inv

LPG [ˌɛlpiːˈdʒiː] N ABBR (= liquefied petroleum gas) GPL m inv (= gas di petrolio liquefatto)

LPN [ˌɛlpiːˈɛn] N ABBR (USA = Licensed Practical Nurse) ≈ infermiere(-a) diplomato(-a)

LSD [ˌɛlɛsˈdiː] N ABBR **1** (= lysergic acid diethylamide) LSD m **2** (Brit = pounds, shillings and pence) sistema monetario in vigore in Gran Bretagna fino al 1971

Lt. ABBR (= lieutenant) Ten.

Ltd ABBR (Comm: = limited) ≈ S.r.l.

lub·ri·cant ['luːbrɪkənt] N lubrificante m

lu·bri·cate ['luːbrɪˌkeɪt] VT lubrificare; **lubricating oil** lubrificante m

lu·cid ['luːsɪd] ADJ (person) lucido(-a); (instructions) chiaro(-a); (moments) di lucidità

lu·cid·ity [luːˈsɪdɪtɪ] N (of person) lucidità; (of instructions) chiarezza

luck [lʌk] N fortuna, sorte f; **good luck** (buona) fortuna; **bad luck** mala sorte, sfortuna; **good luck!** buona fortuna!; **bad luck!** che sfortuna!; **just my luck!** la mia solita sfortuna!; **it's good/bad luck to do ...** porta fortuna/sfortuna fare...; **no such luck!** magari!, purtroppo no!; **with any luck** con un po' di fortuna; **to be in luck** essere fortunato(-a); **to be out of luck** essere sfortunato(-a); **to be down on one's luck** essere scalognato(-a); **I had the luck to** ho avuto la fortuna di; **better luck next time!** andrà meglio la prossima volta!; **to trust to luck** affidarsi al caso; **as luck would have it** come volle il caso; **it's the luck of the draw** (fig) è una questione di fortuna

lucki·ly ['lʌkɪlɪ] ADV per fortuna, fortunatamente

luck·less ['lʌklɪs] ADJ (liter) sfortunato(-a)

lucky ['lʌkɪ] ADJ (comp **-ier**, superl **-iest**) (gen) fortunato(-a);

(*horseshoe, number*) portafortuna *inv*, che porta fortuna; he's lucky, he's got a job è fortunato, ha un lavoro; **lucky break** colpo di fortuna; **lucky charm** portafortuna *m inv*; **black cats are lucky in Britain** i gatti neri portano fortuna in Gran Bretagna; **that was lucky!** per fortuna!; **it was a lucky guess** è stata tutta fortuna; **he's lucky to be alive** è vivo per miracolo; **lucky you!, you lucky thing!** beato te!; **it was very lucky for you (that ...)** per fortuna (che...)

luc·ra·tive [ˈluːkrətɪv] ADJ lucrativo(-a), redditizio(-a)

lu·di·crous [ˈluːdɪkrəs] ADJ ridicolo(-a), assurdo(-a)

ludo [ˈluːdəʊ] N (*Brit*) ≈ gioco dell'oca

lug [lʌg] VT (*fam*) trascinare

lug·gage [ˈlʌgɪdʒ] N bagagli *mpl*, bagaglio; **my luggage was left behind** hanno dimenticato i miei bagagli

luggage rack N (*on train etc*) reticella (per i bagagli); (*Aut*) portapacchi *m inv*, portabagagli *m inv*

luggage van N (*Brit: Rail*) bagagliaio

lu·gu·bri·ous [lʊˈguːbrɪəs] ADJ (*liter*) lugubre

luke·warm [luːkˈwɔːm] ADJ **1** (*tepid: water*) tiepido(-a) **2** (*unenthusiastic: support, response*) tiepido(-a); (: *person*) poco entusiasta

lull [lʌl] N (*gen*) momento di calma; (*in business*) periodo di stasi; (*in conversation*) pausa; (*in fighting*) tregua ♦ VT (*fear*) calmare; (*person*) calmare, acquietare; (*child*) cullare; **to lull a baby to sleep** cullare un bambino finché si addormenti; **to be lulled into a false sense of security** illudersi che tutto vada bene; **to lull sb into a false sense of security** dare a qn un falso senso di sicurezza

lulla·by [ˈlʌləˌbaɪ] N ninnananna

lum·ba·go [lʌmˈbeɪgəʊ] N lombaggine *f*

lum·ber [ˈlʌmbəʳ] N (*wood, esp USA*) legname *m*; (*junk, esp Brit*) roba vecchia

lum·ber [ˈlʌmbəʳ] VI (*also:* **lumber about, lumber along**) muoversi pesantemente; **to lumber past** (*vehicle*) passare facendo fracasso

lumber·jack [ˈlʌmbəˌdʒæk] N tagliaalegna *m inv*, boscaiolo

lumber room N ripostiglio, sgabuzzino

lumber yard N (*USA*) segheria

lu·mi·nous [ˈluːmɪnəs] ADJ luminoso(-a)

lump [lʌmp] N (*gen*) pezzo; (*of earth*) zolla; (*of sugar*) zolletta; (*in sauce*) grumo; (*swelling*) gonfiore *m*; (*hard swelling*) nodulo; (*bump*) bernoccolo; (*person: fam, pej*) bestione *m*; **a lump of butter** un pezzo di burro; **he's got a lump on his forehead** ha un bernoccolo sulla fronte; **with a lump in one's throat** (*fig*) con un nodo alla gola ♦ VT (*fam: endure*): **if he doesn't like it he can lump it** dovrà mandarla giù, che gli piaccia o no
  ▸ **lump together** VT + ADV mettere insieme, riunire

lump sum N somma forfettaria; (*payment*) pagamento forfettario

lumpy [ˈlʌmpɪ] ADJ (*comp* **-ier**, *superl* **-iest**) (*sauce*) grumoso(-a); (*mattress*) bitorzoluto(-a)

lu·na·cy [ˈluːnəsɪ] N demenza; (*fig*) pazzia, follia; **it's sheer lunacy!** ma è una vera pazzia!

lu·nar [ˈluːnəʳ] ADJ lunare; **lunar landing** allunaggio; **lunar module** modulo lunare

lu·na·tic [ˈluːnətɪk] N (*idiot*) pazzo(-a); (*old: intellectually disabled person*) matto(-a); **he's an absolute lunatic** è completamente pazzo ♦ ADJ (*person*) pazzo(-a); (*idea: crazy*) pazzo(-a), pazzesco(-a); (: *stupid*) idiota; (*driving*) da pazzi
  ❏ **lunatic** is not translated by the Italian word *lunatico*

lunatic asylum N (*old, offensive*) manicomio

lunch [lʌntʃ] N pranzo, (*seconda*) colazione *f*; **a delicious lunch** un pranzo squisito; **to invite sb to** *or* **for lunch** invitare qn a pranzo; **to have lunch** pranzare; **we have lunch at 12:30** pranziamo a mezzogiorno e mezza

lunch break N intervallo del pranzo

lunch·eon [ˈlʌntʃən] N (*frm*) pranzo

luncheon meat N ≈ mortadella

luncheon voucher N buono *m* pasto, *inv*

lunch hour N = **lunch break**

lunch·time [ˈlʌntʃˌtaɪm] N ora di pranzo

lung [lʌŋ] N polmone *m*; **to shout at the top of one's lungs** gridare a squarciagola

lung cancer N cancro del polmone

lunge [lʌndʒ] N balzo (in avanti); (*Fencing*) affondo ♦ VI (*also:* **lunge forward**) fare un balzo in avanti; **to lunge at sb** balzare su qn; **to lunge out with one's fists/feet** tirare dei pugni/calci

lu·pin, lu·pine (*USA*) [ˈluːpɪn] N lupino

lurch¹ [lɜːtʃ] N sobbalzo; (*of ship, plane*) rollata; **a lurch forward** un improvviso scatto in avanti ♦ VI (*person, car*) avere un sobbalzo; (*ship, plane*) rollare; **she lurched forward** è scattata in avanti; **to lurch along** (*person*) procedere barcollando; (*car*) procedere a scatti

lurch² [lɜːtʃ] N scatto improvviso; **to leave sb in the lurch** (*fam*) piantare in asso qn

lure [ljʊəʳ] N (*decoy, bait*) richiamo, esca; (*fig: charm*) attrazione *f*, lusinga; **the lure of country life** il richiamo della vita di campagna ♦ VT attirare (con l'inganno); **to lure sb into a trap** attirare qn in una trappola; **they were lured into an ambush** sono stati attirati in un'imboscata; **to lure out** far uscire con l'inganno

lu·rid [ˈljʊərɪd] ADJ **1** (*details, description etc: gruesome*) impressionante, sconvolgente; (: *sensational*) sensazionale, scandalistico(-a) **2** (*colour*) violento(-a), sgargiante; (*sunset*) fiammeggiante
  ❏ **lurid** is not translated by the Italian word *lurido*

lurk [lɜːk] VI (*person: hide*) stare in agguato, appostarsi; (: *creep about*) girare furtivamente; (*danger*) stare in agguato; (*doubt*) persistere

lus·cious [ˈlʌʃəs] ADJ (*food*) appetitoso(-a), succulento(-a); (*taste, smell*) delizioso(-a)

lush [lʌʃ] ADJ rigoglioso(-a), lussureggiante

lust [lʌst] N (*sexual*) libidine *f*, desiderio; **lust for** (*greed*) sete *f* di
  ▸ **lust after, lust for** VI + PREP (*person*) desiderare; (*power, wealth etc*) aver sete di

lust·ful [ˈlʌstful] ADJ pieno(-a) di desiderio

lus·tre, (USA) lus·ter [ˈlʌstəʳ] N lustro, splendore *m*

lusty [ˈlʌstɪ] ADJ (*comp* **-ier**, *superl* **-iest**) (*person*) vigoroso(-a), robusto(-a); (*cry etc*) forte

lute [luːt] N liuto

Lux·em·bourg [ˈlʌksəmˌbɜːg] N (*city*) Lussemburgo *f*; (*state*) Lussemburgo *m*

luxu·ri·ant [lʌgˈzjʊərɪənt] ADJ (*growth, jungle*) lussureggiante, rigoglioso(-a); (*beard*) folto(-a); (*fig: imagination*) ricco(-a), fervido(-a)

luxu·ri·ous [lʌgˈzjʊərɪəs] ADJ (*gen*) lussuoso(-a), di lusso; (*surroundings*) di lusso; (*meal, tastes*) raffinato(-a), di lusso
  ❏ **luxurious** is not translated by the Italian word *lussurioso*

luxu·ry [ˈlʌkʃərɪ] N (*gen*) lusso; (*article*) (oggetto di) lusso; **it was luxury!** è stato un vero lusso! ♦ ADJ (*goods, apartment*) di lusso; **a luxury hotel** un albergo di lusso
  ❏ **luxury** is not translated by the Italian word *lussuria*

ly·ing [ˈlaɪŋ] ADJ (*statement, story*) falso(-a); (*person*) bugiardo(-a) ♦ N bugie *fpl*, menzogne *fpl*

lynch [lɪntʃ] VT linciare

lynx [lɪŋks] N lince *f*

Ly·ons [ˈlaɪənz] N Lione *f*

lyre [ˈlaɪəʳ] N lira

lyr·ic [ˈlɪrɪk] ADJ lirico(-a) ♦ N (*poem*) lirica; **lyrics** NPL (*words of song*) parole *fpl*

lyri·cal [ˈlɪrɪkəl] ADJ lirico(-a); (*fig*) entusiasta; **to wax** *or* **become lyrical about sth** infervorarsi a parlare di qc

lyri·cism [ˈlɪrɪˌsɪzəm] N lirismo

Mm

M¹, m¹ [ɛm] N (*letter*) M, m *f inv*, m *inv*; **M for Mary**, (*USA*) **M for Mike** ≈ M come Milano

M² [ɛm] ABBR **1** (*Brit*: = *motorway*) ≈ A *f* (= *autostrada*); **on the M6** sulla M6 **2** (= *medium*) M *f inv* (*taglia media*)

m [ɛm] ABBR **1** (= *metre*) m **2** = **mile 3** = **million**

MA [ɛmˈeɪ] N ABBR **1** (*Univ*: = *Master of Arts*) master *m inv* in materie umanistiche **2** (*USA*): = **Military Academy** ♦ ABBR (*USA Post*: = **Massachusetts**)

ma [mɑː] N (*fam*) mamma

mac [mæk] N ABBR (*Brit fam*: = *mackintosh*) impermeabile *m*

ma·ca·bre [məˈkɑːbrə] ADJ macabro(-a)

maca·ro·ni [ˌmækəˈrəʊnɪ] N maccheroni *mpl*

maca·roon [ˌmækəˈruːn] N ≈ amaretto (*biscotto*)

mace¹ [meɪs] N (*weapon, ceremonial*) mazza

mace² [meɪs] N (*spice*) macis *m, f*

Mac·edo·nia [ˌmæsɪˈdəʊnɪə] N la Macedonia

Mac·edo·nian [ˌmæsɪˈdəʊnɪən] ADJ macedone ♦ N (*person*) macedone *m/f*; (*language*) macedone *m*

machi·na·tions [ˌmækɪˈneɪʃənz] NPL macchinazioni *fpl*, intrighi *mpl*

ma·chine [məˈʃiːn] N (*gen*) apparato, macchina; (*Pol*) apparato, macchina; (*washing machine*) lavatrice *f*; **it's a complicated machine** è una macchina complicata; **I put clothes in the machine** ho messo i vestiti in lavatrice ♦ VT (*Tech*) lavorare (a macchina); (*Sewing*) cucire a macchina

machine code N (*Comput*) codice *m* (di) macchina

machine gun N mitragliatrice *f*

machine language N (*Comput*) linguaggio *m* macchina, *inv*

machine-readable [məˈʃiːnˌriːdəbl] ADJ (*Comput*) leggibile dalla macchina

ma·chin·ery [məˈʃiːnərɪ] N (*machines*) macchine *fpl*, macchinari *mpl*; (*mechanism*) meccanismo; (*fig*) macchina, apparato

machine shop N officina meccanica

machine tool N macchina utensile

machine washable ADJ lavabile in lavatrice

ma·chin·ist [məˈʃiːnɪst] N (*Tech*) macchinista *m/f*; (*Sewing*) operaio(-a) addetto(-a) alla macchina da cucire

macho [ˈmætʃəʊ] ADJ (da) macho *inv*

macke·rel [ˈmækrəl] N *pl inv* sgombro

mack·in·tosh [ˈmækɪnˌtɒʃ] N impermeabile *m*

macro– [ˈmækrəʊ] PREF macro-

macro·eco·nom·ics [ˌmækrəʊˌiːkəˈnɒmɪks] NSG macroeconomia

mad [mæd] ADJ (*comp* **-der**, *superl* **-dest**) **1** (*deranged*: *person*) pazzo(-a), matto(-a); (: *bull*) furioso(-a); (: *dog*) rabbioso(-a); (*foolish*) sciocco(-a); (*rash*: *person, idea, plan*) folle; **to go mad** impazzire, diventare matto(-a); **to drive sb mad** far diventare matto(-a) qn, far impazzire qn; **as mad as a hatter** *or* **a March hare** matto(-a) da legare; **are you mad?** sei matto?, sei impazzito?; **have you gone mad?** sei impazzito?; **you're mad!** tu sei pazzo!; **mad with grief** pazzo(-a) di dolore; **I'm in a mad rush** ho una fretta terribile; **like mad** (*adv phrase*: *fam*) come un(a) pazzo(-a) **2** (*fam*: *angry*): **mad (at** *or* **with sb)** furioso(-a) *or* furibondo(-a) (con qn); **he's hopping mad** (*fam*) è furibondo

Madagascar [ˌmædəˈɡæskə] N Madagascar *m*

mad·am [ˈmædəm] N **1** signora; **can I help you, madam?** (la signora) desidera?; **Madam Chairman** Signora Presidentessa **2** (*of brothel*) tenutaria

mad·cap [ˈmædˌkæp] ADJ (*fam*) senza senso, assurdo(-a)

mad cow disease N morbo della mucca pazza

mad·den [ˈmædn] VT (*infuriate*) far impazzire, esasperare

mad·den·ing [ˈmædnɪŋ] ADJ esasperante

made [meɪd] PT, PP of **make**

Ma·dei·ra [məˈdɪərə] N (*Geog*) Madera; (*wine*) madera *m*

made-to-measure [ˌmeɪdtəˈmeʒəʳ] ADJ (*Brit*) (fatto(-a)) su misura

made-up [ˌmeɪdˈʌp] ADJ (*story*) inventato(-a); (*face, person, eyes*) truccato(-a)

mad·house [ˈmædhaʊs] N (*also fig*) manicomio

mad·ly [ˈmædlɪ] ADV (*behave*) come un(a) pazzo(-a); (*love*) alla follia; **to be madly in love with sb** essere follemente innamorato(-a) di qn

mad·man [ˈmædmən] N (*pl* **-men**) pazzo, folle *m*

mad·ness [ˈmædnɪs] N pazzia, follia; **it's absolute madness** è pura pazzia

Ma·drid [məˈdrɪd] N Madrid *f*

Ma·fia [ˈmæfɪə] N: **the Mafia** la mafia

mag [mæg] N ABBR (*Brit fam*: = *magazine*) rivista

maga·zine [ˌmæɡəˈziːn] N **1** (*Press*) rivista **2** (*of firearm*) caricatore *m*; (*Mil*: *store*) deposito, magazzino

mag·got [ˈmæɡət] N verme *m*, baco

mag·ic [ˈmædʒɪk] ADJ (*spell*) magico(-a); (*beauty*) straordinario(-a); **a magic potion** una pozione magica; **there's no magic solution** non ci sono soluzioni miracolose; **to say the magic word** pronunciare la parola magica; **it was magic!** è stato fantastico! ♦ N magia; (*conjuring tricks*) giochi *mpl* di prestigio; **like magic** come per magia *or* per incanto

magi·cal [ˈmædʒɪkəl] ADJ magico(-a)

ma·gi·cian [məˈdʒɪʃən] N mago(-a); (*conjuror*) illusionista *m/f*

mag·is·trate [ˈmædʒɪˌstreɪt] N magistrato

mag·nani·mous [mæɡˈnænɪməs] ADJ magnanimo(-a)

mag·nate [ˈmæɡneɪt] N magnate *m*

mag·ne·sium [mæɡˈniːzɪəm] N magnesio

mag·net [ˈmæɡnɪt] N calamita, magnete *m*

mag·net·ic [mæɡˈnetɪk] ADJ magnetico(-a)

magnetic disk N (*Comput*) disco magnetico

magnetic tape N nastro magnetico

mag·net·ism [ˈmæɡnɪˌtɪzəm] N magnetismo

mag·ni·fi·ca·tion [ˌmæɡnɪfɪˈkeɪʃən] N ingrandimento

mag·nifi·cence [mæɡˈnɪfɪsəns] N magnificenza

mag·nifi·cent [mæɡˈnɪfɪsənt] ADJ magnifico(-a); **a magnificent view** una vista magnifica; **it is a magnificent achievement** è un grosso risultato

mag·ni·fy [ˈmæɡnɪˌfaɪ] VT **1** (*gen*) ingrandire; (*sound*) amplificare **2** (*exaggerate*) esagerare

mag·ni·fy·ing glass [ˈmæɡnɪfaɪɪŋˌɡlɑːs] N lente *f* d'ingrandimento

mag·ni·tude [ˈmæɡnɪtjuːd] N (*gen*) vastità *f inv*, grandezza, ampiezza; (*importance*) importanza; (*Astron*) magnitudine *f*; **an operation of this magnitude** un'operazione di questa importanza

mag·no·lia [mæɡˈnəʊlɪə] N magnolia

mag·pie [ˈmæɡpaɪ] N gazza

ma·hoga·ny [məˈhɒɡənɪ] N mogano ♦ ADJ di *or* in mogano

maid [meɪd] N **1** (*servant*) domestica; (*in hotel*) cameriera **2** (*old, liter*: *young girl*) ragazza, fanciulla

maid·en [ˈmeɪdn] N (*old, liter*) fanciulla, ragazza ♦ ADJ (*flight, voyage*) inaugurale

maiden name N nome *m* da ragazza *or* da nubile

mail [meɪl] N **1** posta; **by mail** per posta ♦ VT spedire (per posta), inviare (per posta); **he mailed me the contract** mi ha spedito il contratto per posta; **I forgot to mail the letter** ho dimenticato di imbucare la lettera

mail·box [ˈmeɪlbɒks] N (*USA*) cassetta delle lettere; (*Comput*) mailbox *m inv*, *f inv*

mail·ing list [ˈmeɪlɪŋˌlɪst] N elenco di indirizzi, indirizzario (*per l'invio di materiale pubblicitario*)

mail·man [ˈmeɪlˌmæn] N (*pl* **-men**) (*USA*) portalettere *m inv*, postino

mail-order [ˈmeɪlˌɔːdəʳ] ADJ: **mail-order firm** *or* **house** ditta di vendita per corrispondenza

mail·shot ['meɪl.ʃɒt] N campagna promozionale a mezzo posta, mailing *m inv*

mail truck N (*USA: Aut*) furgone *m* postale

mail van N (*Brit: Aut*) furgone *m* postale; (: *Rail*) vagone *m* postale

maim [meɪm] VT storpiare, mutilare

main [meɪn] ADJ (*gen*) principale; **the main body of an army** il grosso di un esercito; **the main points** i punti principali; **the main thing is to ...** l'essenziale è...; **the main thing to remember is ...** soprattutto non bisogna dimenticare che... ♦ N 1 (*pipe: for water, gas*) conduttura *or* tubatura principale; (*Elec*) linea principale; **main (sewer)** collettore *m*; *see also* **mains** 2 **in the main** nel complesso, nell'insieme

main course N (*Culin*) piatto principale, piatto forte, secondo

Maine [meɪn] il Maine

main·frame ['meɪn.freɪm] N (*also:* **mainframe computer**) mainframe *m inv*

main·land ['meɪnlənd] N continente *m*, terraferma; **the Greek mainland** la Grecia continentale

main·line ['meɪn.laɪn](*slang*) VT (*heroin*) bucarsi di ♦ VI bucarsi

main line N (*Rail*) linea principale

main·ly ['meɪnlɪ] ADV principalmente, soprattutto

main road N strada principale

mains [meɪnz] NPL: **the mains** (*supply: gas, water, electricity*) le condutture

main·stay ['meɪn.steɪ] N (*support*) sostegno, pilastro

main·stream ['meɪn.striːm] N (*fig*) corrente *f* principale

Main Street (*USA*) N via principale; (*people*) l'americano medio che vive in una piccola città

main·tain [meɪn'teɪn] VT 1 (*keep up: gen*) mantenere; (: *attack*) continuare; (: *lead in race*) mantenere, conservare; **if the improvement is maintained** se il miglioramento continua; **teachers try hard to maintain standards** gli insegnanti ce la mettono tutta per mantenere un certo livello scolastico 2 (*support: family, army*) mantenere 3 (*keep in good condition*) mantenere in buono stato 4 (*claim*): **to maintain that ...** sostenere che...; **she had always maintained her innocence** aveva sempre sostenuto la propria innocenza

main·te·nance ['meɪntɪnəns] N (*gen*) mantenimento; (*of car, building*) manutenzione *f*; (*alimony*) alimenti *mpl*

maintenance contract N contratto di manutenzione

maintenance order N (*Law*) obbligo degli alimenti

mai·son·ette [ˌmeɪzə'nɛt] N (*Brit*) appartamentino su due piani

maize [meɪz] N granturco, mais *m*

Maj. ABBR (*Mil*) = **major**

ma·jes·tic [mə'dʒɛstɪk] ADJ maestoso(-a)

maj·es·ty ['mædʒɪstɪ] N maestà *f inv*; **His Majesty** Sua Maestà

ma·jor ['meɪdʒə'] ADJ (*greater, also Math, Mus*) maggiore; (*in importance*) principale, importante; (*repairs*) grosso(-a), sostanziale; (*disaster, loss*) grave; (*interest, artist, success*) grande; **a major operation** (*Med*) un complesso intervento chirurgico; (*undertaking*) un'operazione considerevole; **major road** strada con diritto di precedenza; **drugs are a major problem** la droga è un grosso problema; **a major new film** un importante nuovo film ♦ N 1 (*Mil*) maggiore *m* 2 (*Law*) maggiorenne *m/f* 3 (*USA: Univ*) materia di specializzazione ♦ VI (*USA: Univ*): **to major (in)** specializzarsi (in)

Ma·jor·ca [mə'jɔːkə] N Maiorca

major general N (*Mil*) generale *m* di divisione

ma·jor·ity [mə'dʒɒrɪtɪ] N 1 maggioranza; **the majority of people** la maggior parte della gente; **elected by a majority of two** eletto con una maggioranza di due voti; **to be in the majority** essere in maggioranza; **the vast majority of our products** la grande maggioranza dei nostri prodotti 2 (*Law*): **the age of majority** la maggiore età ♦ ADJ (*verdict*) maggioritario(-a); (*government*) di maggioranza

majority holding N (*Fin*): **to have a majority holding** essere il (la) maggiore azionista

make [meɪk] (*pt, pp* **made**) VT 1 (*gen*) fare; (*Comm*) produrre, fabbricare; (*building*) costruire; (*points, score*) fare, segnare; **she made the material into a dress** con la stoffa ha fatto un vestito; **made of silver** (fatto(-a)) d'argento; **made in Italy** fabbricato(-a) in Italia; (*on label*) made in Italy; **it's well made** è ben fatto; **I'd like to make a phone call** vorrei fare una telefonata; **I make my bed every morning** mi faccio il letto ogni mattina; **they were made for each other** erano fatti l'uno per l'altra 2 (*cause to be or become*) fare; (+ *adj*) rendere; **to make sb happy/sad** rendere *or* far felice/triste qn; **to make sb angry** far arrabbiare qn; **to make sth into sth else** fare di qc qualcos'altro; **to make sb a judge** nominare qn giudice; **let's make it 6 o'clock** facciamo alle 6; **to make o.s. heard** farsi sentire; **make yourself comfortable** si accomodi; **you'll make yourself ill!** starai male! 3 (*cause to do*) fare; (*stronger*) costringere; **to make sb do sth** far fare qc a qn; costringere *or* obbligare qn a fare qc; **my mother makes me do my homework** mia madre mi obbliga a fare i compiti; **to make sb wait** far aspettare qn; **to make sth do, to make do with sth** accontentarsi di qc; (*because it's the only available*) arrangiarsi con qc 4 (*earn*) guadagnare; **to make money** far soldi; **he makes a lot of money** guadagna un sacco di soldi; **to make a profit of £500** ricavare un profitto di 500 sterline; **to make a loss of £500** subire una perdita di 500 sterline; **he made a profit/loss** ci ha rimesso/guadagnato; **he made £500 on the deal** l'affare gli ha fruttato 500 sterline 5 (*reach: destination*) arrivare a; (*catch: bus, train*) prendere; **we made Exeter by seven o'clock** siamo arrivati ad Exeter per le sette; **they made (it to) the finals** sono entrati in finale; **to make it** (*in time*) arrivare; (*achieve sth*) farcela; **can you make it for four o'clock?** ce la fai per le quattro?; **sorry, I can't make it to the party** mi dispiace, ma non riesco a venire alla festa; **to make it in life** riuscire nella vita; **to make good** (*succeed*) aver successo; **to make port** raggiungere il porto 6 (*cause to succeed*): **he's made for life** il suo avvenire è assicurato, è a posto per sempre; **this film made her** questo film l'ha resa celebre; **that's made my day!** questo ha trasformato la mia giornata!; **to make or break sb** essere il successo o la rovina di qn 7 (*equal, constitute*) fare; **2 and 2 make 4** 2 più 2 fa 4; **that makes 20** questo fa 20; **does that book make good reading?** è un libro interessante?; **these records make a set** questi dischi formano un set; **he made a good husband** è stato un buon marito 8 (*estimate*): **what do you make of this?** cosa pensi di questo?; **what do you make of him?** che te ne pare di lui?; **I make the total cost £1200** penso che il costo complessivo sia di milleduecento sterline ♦ VI 1 (*go*): **to make towards the door** dirigersi verso la porta; **to make after sb** inseguire qn 2 **to make as if to do sth** fare (come) per fare qc ♦ N 1 (*action*) fabbricazione *f*; (*brand*) marca; **it's our own make** è di nostra produzione 2 **to be on the make** (*fam*) essere a caccia di successo

▸ **make away** VI + ADV = **make off**

▸ **make away with** VI + ADV + PREP (*kill*) far fuori, togliere di mezzo

▸ **make for** VI + PREP 1 (*place*) essere diretto(-a) a, avviarsi verso; (*subj: ship*) far rotta verso 2 (*fig: result in*) produrre; (: *contribute to*) contribuire a

▸ **make off** VI + ADV svignarsela; **to make off with sth** svignarsela con qc

▸ **make out** VT + ADV 1 (*write out: cheque, receipt, list*) fare; (: *document*) redigere; (: *form*) riempire, compilare; **to make a cheque out to sb** intestare un assegno a qn; **to make out a case for sth** presentare delle valide ragioni in favore di qc 2 (*see, discern*) riuscire a vedere, distinguere; (*decipher*) decifrare; (*understand*) (riuscire a) capire; **I can't make out the address on the label** non riesco a decifrare l'indirizzo sull'etichetta; **how do you make that out?** che cosa te lo fa pensare?; **I can't make her out at all** non riesco proprio a capirla 3 (*claim, imply*): **to make out (that ...)** voler far credere (che...), darla ad intendere (che...); **to make sb out to be stupid** far passare qn per stupido; **they're making out it was my fault** vogliono far credere che sia colpa mia ♦ VI + ADV (*fam: get on*) cavarsela

▸ **make out with** VI + ADV + PREP (*fam*): **to make out with sb** farsi qn, sbaciucchiare

▸ **make over** VT + ADV (*assign*): **to make over (to)** passare (a), trasferire (a)

▸ **make up** VT + ADV **1** (*invent: story*) inventare; **he made up the whole story** ha inventato tutta la storia **2** (*put together, prepare: list, parcel, bed*) fare; (*food, medicine*) preparare; **she made the books up into a parcel** ha impacchettato i libri **3** (*settle: dispute*) mettere fine a; **to make it up with sb** far la pace con qn **4** (*complete: total, quantity*) completare; **I need £5 to make up the sum we require** mi occorrono 5 sterline per raggiungere la somma stabilita **5** (*compensate for: loss, deficit, lost time*) recuperare, compensare, colmare; **to make it up to sb (for sth)** compensare qn (per qc); **I'll make it up to you somehow, I promise** ti ricompenserò in qualche modo, prometto **6** (*constitute*) comporre; **to be made up of** essere composto(-a) di *or* formato(-a) da; **women make up thirteen per cent of the police force** il tredici percento del corpo di polizia è formato da donne **7** (*apply cosmetics to*) truccare ♦ VI + ADV **1** (*after quarrelling*) fare la pace, riconciliarsi; **they had a quarrel, but soon made up** hanno litigato, ma hanno subito fatto la pace **2** (*apply cosmetics*) truccarsi **3** (*catch up*): **to make up on sb** riprendere qn

▸ **make up for** VI + ADV + PREP (*lost time*) recuperare; (*trouble caused*) farsi perdonare; (*mistake*) rimediare a; (*loss, injury*) compensare; **money can't make up for the stress I've suffered** il denaro non può compensare lo stress che ho subito

▸ **make up to** VI + ADV + PREP (*fam: curry favour with*) cercare di entrare nelle simpatie di *or* di accattivarsi il favore di, lisciare

make-believe ['meɪkbɪ,liːv] N: **the land of make-believe** il mondo delle favole; **it's just make-believe** (*activity*) è solo per finta; (*story*) sono frottole, è tutta un'invenzione

makeover ['meɪkəʊvəʳ] N cambio di immagine; **to give sb a makeover** far cambiare immagine a qn

mak·er ['meɪkəʳ] N (*manufacturer*) fabbricante *m*; (*creator*) creatore(-trice); (*originator*) autore(-trice); (*Rel*): **our Maker** il Creatore; **Italy's biggest car maker** il più grosso fabbricante di automobili in Italia

make·shift ['meɪk,ʃɪft] ADJ di fortuna, improvvisato(-a)

make-up ['meɪk,ʌp] N **1** (*cosmetics*) trucco, cosmetici *mpl*; **to put on one's make-up** truccarsi; **she put on her make-up** si è truccata **2** (*nature: of object, group*) composizione *f*; (: *of football team*) formazione *f*; (: *of person*) carattere *m*

make-up bag N borsa del trucco

make-up remover N struccante *m*

mak·ing ['meɪkɪŋ] N **1** (*Comm: gen*) fabbricazione *f*; (*of dress, food*) confezione *f*; **it's still in the making** non è ancora finito; **it's history in the making** è un momento storico; **it was the making of him** ha fatto di lui un uomo **2** **he has the makings of an actor** (*qualities, potential*) ha la stoffa dell'attore; **the makings of a good film** quello che ci vuole per fare un buon film

mal·ad·just·ed [,mælə'dʒʌstɪd] ADJ (*Psych*) disadattato(-a)

mala·droit [,mælə'drɔɪt] ADJ maldestro(-a)

ma·laise [mæ'leɪz] N malessere *m*

ma·laria [mə'lɛərɪə] N malaria

Ma·la·wi [mə'lɑːwɪ] N il Malawi

Ma·lay [mə'leɪ] ADJ malese ♦ N (*person*) malese *m/f*; (*language*) malese *m*

Ma·la·ya [mə'leɪə] N la Malesia

Ma·lay·an [mə'leɪən] ADJ, N = **Malay**

Ma·lay·sia [mə'leɪzɪə] N la Malaysia

Ma·lay·sian [mə'leɪzɪən] ADJ, N malaysiano(-a)

Mal·dive Islands ['mɔːldaɪv,aɪləndz], **Mal·dives** ['mɔːldaɪvz] NPL: **the Maldive Islands, the Maldives** le (isole *fpl*) Maldive

male [meɪl] ADJ (*gen, sex*) maschile; (*animal, child*) maschio *inv*; **not all football players are male** non tutti i giocatori di calcio sono maschi; **sex: Male** sesso: Maschile; **male and female students** studenti e studentesse ♦ N (*Bio, Elec*) maschio

male chauvinist N maschilista *m*

male nurse N infermiere *m*

ma·levo·lence [mə'levələns] N malevolenza, malanimo

ma·levo·lent [mə'levələnt] ADJ malevolo(-a)

mal·func·tion [,mæl'fʌŋkʃən] N cattivo funzionamento

mal·ice ['mælɪs] N cattiveria, malevolenza; **I bear him no malice** non gli serbo nessun rancore

ma·li·cious [mə'lɪʃəs] ADJ cattivo(-a), malevolo(-a); (*Law*) doloso(-a); **malicious gossip** malignità *fpl*

ma·lign [mə'laɪn] ADJ malefico(-a), nocivo(-a) ♦ VT diffamare, calunniare, malignare su

ma·lig·nant [mə'lɪgnənt] ADJ maligno(-a), malevolo(-a); (*Med: tumour*) maligno(-a)

ma·lin·ger·er [mə'lɪŋgərəʳ] N uno(-a) che si finge malato(-a) (*per non lavorare*), scansafatiche *m/f inv*

mall [mɔːl] N (*USA: also:* **shopping mall**) centro commerciale

mal·le·able ['mælɪəbl] ADJ malleabile

mal·let ['mælɪt] N (*tool*) mazzuolo; (*in croquet*) maglio; (*in polo*) mazza

mal·nu·tri·tion [,mælnjʊ'trɪʃən] N denutrizione *f*, malnutrizione *f*

mal·prac·tice [,mæl'præktɪs] N (*by doctor*) negligenza (colposa); (*by minister, lawyer*) prevaricazione *f*

malt [mɔːlt] N malto; (*also:* **malt whisky**) whisky *m* di malto ♦ ADJ (*vinegar, whisky*) di malto

Mal·ta ['mɔːltə] N Malta

Mal·tese [,mɔːl'tiːz] ADJ maltese ♦ N INV (*person*) maltese *m/f*; (*language*) maltese *m*

mal·treat [,mæl'triːt] VT maltrattare

mal·ware ['mælwɛəʳ] N (*Comput*) malware *mpl*, software *mpl* maligni

mam·mal ['mæməl] N mammifero

mam·moth ['mæməθ] N mammut *m inv* ♦ ADJ colossale, mostruoso(-a), enorme, gigantesco(-a); **a mammoth task** un lavoro mostruoso

man [mæn] N (*pl* **men**) **1** (*gen, also Mil, Sport*) uomo; (*in office, shop*) impiegato; (*Chess*) pezzo; (*Draughts*) pedina; **an old man** un vecchio; **a blind man** un cieco; **man and wife** marito e moglie; **the man in the street** l'uomo della strada; **he's a man about town** è un uomo di mondo; **a man of the world** un uomo di mondo *or* di grande esperienza; **men say that ... si dice che...; no man** nessuno; **any man** chiunque; **that man Jones** quel Jones; **as one man** come un solo uomo; **he's not the man for the job** non è l'uomo adatto per questo lavoro; **he's a family man** è un uomo tutto casa e famiglia; **he's a Glasgow man** è di Glasgow; **the ice-cream man** il gelataio; **come on, man!** dai, forza! **2** (*humanity*): **Man** l'uomo, l'umanità *f inv* ♦ VT (*ship, fortress*) fornire di uomini; (*fleet*) armare; **the ship is manned by Americans** l'equipaggio della nave è americano; **man the guns!** uomini ai cannoni!

Man. ABBR (*Canada:* = **Manitoba**)

mana·cles ['mænəklz] NPL manette *fpl*

man·age ['mænɪdʒ] VT **1** (*direct: company, organization, hotel*) dirigere; (: *shop, restaurant*) gestire; (: *household, property, affairs*) amministrare; (: *football team, pop star*) essere il manager di; **the election was managed** (*pej*) le elezioni erano truccate; **she manages a big store** dirige un grande negozio **2** (*handle, control: tool*) maneggiare; (: *ship, vehicle*) manovrare; (: *person, child*) saper prendere *or* trattare; **I can manage him** so come trattarlo *or* prenderlo **3 to manage to do sth** riuscire a fare qc; **luckily I managed to pass the exam** fortunatamente sono riuscito a passare l'esame; **he managed not to get his feet wet** è riuscito a non bagnarsi i piedi; **£5 is the most I can manage** posso metterci 5 sterline ma non di più; **I shall manage it** ce la farò; **can you manage 8 o'clock?** alle 8 ti va bene? ♦ VI farcela; **can you manage?** ce la fai?; **how do you manage?** come riesci a farcela?; **I have to manage on £20** mi devo arrangiare con 20 sterline; **to manage without sb/sth** fare a meno di qn/qc; **we haven't got much money, but we manage** non abbiamo molto denaro, ma ci arrangiamo

man·age·able ['mænɪdʒəbl] ADJ (*car, boat, size, proportions*) maneggevole; (*person*) trattabile, arrendevole; (*task*) fattibile; **it was a manageable task** era fattibile

man·age·ment ['mænɪdʒmənt] N **1** (*act: see vb 1a*) direzione *f*; gestione *f*; amministrazione *f* **2** (*persons: of business, firm*) dirigenti *mpl*, direzione *f*; (: *of hotel, shop, theatre*) direzione *f*; **"under new management"** "nuova gestione"; **the restaurant is under new management** il ristorante ha una nuova gestione; **management and workers** dirigenti e lavoratori

management accounting N contabilità *f inv* di gestione

management buyout N acquisto di una società da parte dei suoi dirigenti

management consultant N consulente m/f aziendale

man·ag·er ['mænɪdʒə'] N (gen) direttore m; (of shop, restaurant) gestore m, gerente m; (of football team, pop star, artiste) manager m inv; (of estate) amministratore m; **sales manager** direttore m delle vendite; **I complained to the manager** mi sono lamentato con il direttore; **the England manager** il commissario tecnico dell'Inghilterra

mana·ge·rial [,mænə'dʒɪərɪəl] ADJ (class) dirigente, manageriale, dirigenziale; (ability, post) direttivo(-a), manageriale, dirigenziale

man·ag·ing di·rec·tor ['mænɪdʒɪŋ,dɪ'rɛktə'] N amministratore m delegato

Man·cu·nian [mæŋ'kjuːnɪən] ADJ di Manchester ◆ N (resident) abitante m/f di Manchester; (native) originario(-a) di Manchester

man·da·rin ['mændərɪn] N 1 (person) mandarino 2 (also: mandarin orange) mandarino

man·date ['mændeɪt] N delega, mandato

man·da·tory ['mændətərɪ] ADJ obbligatorio(-a)

man·do·lin, man·do·line ['mændəlɪn] N mandolino

mane [meɪn] N criniera

ma·neu·ver [mə'nuːvə'] (USA) = manoeuvre

man·ful ['mænfʊl] ADJ coraggioso(-a), valoroso(-a)

man·ful·ly ['mænfəlɪ] ADV coraggiosamente, valorosamente

man·ga·nese [,mæŋgə'niːz] N manganese m

mange·tout ['mãʒ'tuː] N pisello dolce, taccola

man·gle¹ ['mæŋgl] VT (mutilate: body) straziare, maciullare; (: object) stritolare

man·gle² ['mæŋgl] N strizzatoio

man·go ['mæŋgəʊ] N mango

man·grove ['mæŋgrəʊv] N mangrovia

man·gy ['meɪndʒɪ] ADJ rognoso(-a)

man·handle ['mæn,hændl] VT (treat roughly) malmenare; (move by hand: goods) spostare a mano

man·hole ['mænhəʊl] N botola stradale

man·hood ['mænhʊd] N 1 (state) età f inv virile 2 (manliness) virilità f inv 3 (men) uomini mpl

man-hour ['mæn,aʊə'] N (Industry) ora di lavoro

man·hunt ['mæn,hʌnt] N caccia all'uomo

ma·nia ['meɪnɪə] N mania; **to have a mania for (doing) sth** avere la mania di (fare) qc

ma·ni·ac ['meɪnɪæk] N maniaco(-a); **sports maniac** (fig: fam) maniaco(-a) dello sport; **a dangerous maniac** un pericoloso maniaco; **he drives like a maniac!** guida come un pazzo!

man·ic ['mænɪk] ADJ (Psych) maniaco(-a), maniacale

manic-depressive [,mænɪkdɪ'presɪv](Psych) ADJ maniaco-depressivo(-a) ◆ N persona affetta da psicosi maniaco-depressiva

mani·cure ['mænɪ,kjʊə'] N manicure f inv ◆ VT: **to manicure one's hands** (or one's nails) fare manicure; **well-manicured hands** mani ben curate

manicure set N trousse f inv della manicure

mani·fest ['mænɪ,fest] ADJ evidente, manifesto(-a), palese ◆ VT manifestare ◆ N (Aer, Naut) manifesto

mani·fes·ta·tion [,mænɪfes'teɪʃən] N manifestazione f

mani·fes·to [,mænɪ'festəʊ] N (pl **manifestoes**) manifesto

mani·fold ['mænɪ,fəʊld] ADJ molteplice ◆ N (Aut): **exhaust manifold** collettore m di scarico; **intake manifold** collettore m di aspirazione

Ma·nila [mə'nɪlə] N Manila

ma·nila, ma·nil·la [mə'nɪlə] ADJ (paper, envelope) manilla inv

ma·nipu·late [mə'nɪpjʊleɪt] VT (tool) maneggiare; (controls) azionare; (Med, fig: person) manipolare; (situation, system) manovrare; **he tried to manipulate the situation** ha cercato di pilotare la situazione a proprio vantaggio

ma·nipu·la·tion [mə,nɪpjʊ'leɪʃən] N (see vb) maneggiare m; capacità f inv di azionare; manipolazione f; capacità f inv di manovrare

man·kind [mæn'kaɪnd] N l'umanità f inv, il genere m umano

man·li·ness ['mænlɪnɪs] N virilità f inv

man·ly ['mænlɪ] ADJ (comp **-ier**, superl **-iest**) virile, coraggioso(-a)

man-made ['mæn,meɪd] ADJ artificiale, sintetico(-a)

man·na ['mænə] N manna

man·ne·quin ['mænɪkɪn] N (dummy) manichino; (fashion model) indossatrice f

man·ner ['mænə'] N 1 (mode) modo, maniera; **in this manner** in questo modo, così; **she was behaving in an odd manner** si comportava in modo strano; **in such a manner that** in modo tale che (+ indicativo (risultato reale) o + congiuntivo (risultato voluto)); **he spoke in such a manner as to offend them** ha parlato in modo tale da offenderli or che li ha offesi; **after** or **in the manner of X** alla maniera di X, nello stile di X; **in a manner of speaking** per così dire; **(as) to the manner born** come se ce l'avesse nel sangue 2 (behaviour) comportamento; (attitude) atteggiamento; **I don't like his manner** ha un modo di fare che non mi piace; **a confident manner** un modo di fare molto sicuro 3 (good) **manners** buona educazione f, buone maniere fpl; **bad manners** maleducazione f; **it's bad manners to talk with your mouth full** è da maleducati parlare con la bocca piena; **to teach sb manners** insegnare l'educazione a qn 4 (class, type): **all manner of** ogni sorta di

man·ner·ism ['mænə,rɪzəm] N 1 (habit) vezzo, tic m inv 2 (Art) manierismo

man·ner·ly ['mænəlɪ] ADJ educato(-a), civile

ma·noeu·vrable, ma·neu·ver·able (USA) [mə'nuːvrəbl] ADJ (gen) facile da manovrare; (car) maneggevole; (ship, plane) manovriero(-a)

ma·noeu·vre, ma·neu·ver (USA) [mə'nuːvə'] N manovra; **the soldiers were out on manoeuvres** i soldati stavano facendo le manovre or le esercitazioni ◆ VT (also Mil) manovrare; **I couldn't manoeuvre the settee through the door** non sono riuscito a far passare il divano attraverso la porta; **they manoeuvred the statue into position** hanno messo la statua in posizione; **he manoeuvred himself into a job** è riuscito a ottenere un posto con abili manovre; **to manoeuvre sb into doing sth** costringere abilmente qn a fare qc ◆ VI (Mil, also fig) manovrare; (Aut) far manovra

man·or ['mænə'] N (also: **manor house**) maniero

man·power ['mæn,paʊə'] N (gen, also Industry) manodopera; (Mil) effettivi mpl

man·servant ['mæn,sɜːvənt] N (pl **menservants**) servitore m, domestico

man·sion ['mænʃən] N (in town) palazzo (signorile); (in country) villa, maniero

❑ **mansion** is not translated by the Italian word mansione

man·slaughter ['mæn,slɔːtə'] N omicidio colposo

mantel·piece ['mæntl,piːs] N mensola del caminetto

man·tle ['mæntl] N (old: garment) mantello, manto; (also: **gas mantle**) reticella; (Geol) mantello; **a mantle of snow** un manto di neve

man-to-man [,mæntə'mæn] ADJ, ADV da uomo a uomo

Man·tua ['mæntjʊə] N Mantova

manu·al ['mænjʊəl] ADJ manuale ◆ N (book) manuale m

manual worker N manovale m; **manual workers** la manovalanza

manu·fac·ture [,mænjʊ'fæktʃə'] N (act) fabbricazione f, manifattura; (of clothes) confezione f; (product) manufatto ◆ VT (gen) fabbricare; (clothes) confezionare; (fig: excuse, lie) architettare, inventare

manu·fac·tured goods [,mænjʊ'fæktʃəd'gʊdz] NPL manufatti mpl

manu·fac·tur·er [,mænjʊ'fæktʃərə'] N fabbricante m

manu·fac·tur·ing in·dus·tries [,mænjʊ'fæktʃərɪŋ'ɪndəstrɪz] NPL industrie fpl manifatturiere

ma·nure [mə'njʊə'] N concime m; (organic) letame m ◆ VT concimare

manu·script ['mænjʊ,skrɪpt] N manoscritto

many ['menɪ] ADJ, PRON molti(-e), tanti(-e); **many a …** più di un(a)…, molti(-e)…; **a great many** un gran numero (di), moltissimi(-e); **so many** tanti; **he told so many lies** ha detto tante bugie; **so many books** (così) tanti libri; **many people** molta or tanta gente, molte persone; **he hasn't got many friends** non ha molti amici; **as many as** quanti; **take as many as you like** prendine quanti ne vuoi; **he has as many**

as I have ne ha tanti quanti ne ho io; **there were as many as 100 at the meeting** alla riunione c'erano ben 100 persone; **as many again** altrettanti; **twice as many** due volte tanto; **many a man** più d'uno, molti; **many a time** più volte; **a good** *or* **great many houses** moltissime case, un gran numero di case; **how many?** quanti(-e)?; **how many do you want?** quanti ne vuoi?; **how many people?** quanta gente?, quante persone?; **too many** troppi(-e); **too many difficulties** troppe difficoltà; **sixteen people?** that's **too many** sedici persone? sono troppe; **there are too many of you** siete (in) troppi; **there's one too many** ce n'è uno in più; he's had one too many ha bevuto un bicchiere di troppo; **however many there may be** per quanti ce ne siano; **many of them came** molti di loro sono venuti

Mao·ri [ˈmaʊrɪ] ADJ, N maori *m*/*f inv*

map [mæp] N (*gen*) carta (geografica); (*of town*) pianta; **a map of Egypt** una carta geografica dell'Egitto; **maps and guide books** cartine *fpl* e guide, *fpl*; **a map of the city** una pianta della città; **treasure map** mappa del tesoro; **this will put Eastdean on the map** (*fig*) questo renderà famoso *or* farà conoscere Eastdean; **off the map** (*fig*) in capo al mondo ♦ VT tracciare una carta (*or* una pianta *or* una mappa) di

▸ **map out** VT + ADV tracciare una carta (*or* una pianta *or* una mappa) di; (*fig: career, holiday, essay*) pianificare

ma·ple [ˈmeɪpl] N acero; **field maple** acero campestre

mar [mɑː] VT sciupare, guastare

Mar. ABBR (= *March*) mar. (= *marzo*)

mara·thon [ˈmærəθən] N maratona ♦ ADJ (*debate*) lunghissimo; **a marathon session** una seduta fiume

marathon runner N maratoneta *m*/*f*

ma·raud·er [məˈrɔːdə'] N predone *m*, saccheggiatore(-trice), predatore(-trice)

mar·ble [ˈmɑːbl] N 1 (*material, sculpture*) marmo; **a marble statue** una statua di marmo 2 (*toy*) bilia, biglia; **to play marbles** giocare a bilie ♦ ADJ di marmo

March [mɑːtʃ] N, in **March** in marzo; *see* **July**

march [mɑːtʃ] N (*gen*) marcia; (*demonstration*) marcia, dimostrazione *f*; **on the march** in marcia; **a day's march** una giornata di cammino ♦ VI (*gen*) marciare; **quick march!** avanti, marsc!; **the soldiers marched 50 miles** i soldati hanno marciato per cinquanta miglia; **the demonstrators were marching along the main street** i dimostranti stavano sfilando sulla via principale; **to march into a room** entrare a passo deciso in una stanza; **to march past** sfilare; **to march past sb** sfilare davanti a qn; **to march up to sb** andare risolutamente da qn ♦ VT (*Mil*) far marciare; **to march sb off to prison/to bed** spedire qn in prigione/a letto

march·er [ˈmɑːtʃə'] N dimostrante *m*/*f*

march past N (*Mil*) sfilata

mare [mɛə'] N giumenta, cavalla
❑ **mare** is not translated by the Italian word *mare*

mar·ga·rine [ˌmɑːdʒəˈriːn] N margarina

mar·gin [ˈmɑːdʒɪn] N (*gen, also fig*) margine *m*; **to win by a wide/narrow margin** vincere con largo margine/di stretta misura

mar·gin·al [ˈmɑːdʒɪnl] ADJ marginale ♦ N (*Brit Pol: also:* **marginal seat**) collegio elettorale con una stretta maggioranza a favore del partito al governo

mar·gin·al·ly [ˈmɑːdʒnəlɪ] ADV (*bigger, better*) lievemente, di poco; (*different*) un po'

mari·gold [ˈmærɪˌɡəʊld] N calendola

ma·ri·jua·na, ma·ri·hua·na [ˌmærɪˈhwɑːnə] N marijuana

ma·ri·na [məˈriːnə] N porticciolo, marina

mari·nade [ˌmærɪˈneɪd] N marinata ♦ VT = **marinate**

mari·nate, mari·nade [ˈmærɪˌneɪt] VT marinare

ma·rine [məˈriːn] ADJ (*animal, plant*) marino(-a); (*products*) del mare; (*vegetation, forces*) marittimo(-a); (*engineering*) navale ♦ N 1 **merchant** *or* **mercantile marine** marina mercantile 2 (*Mil*) fante *m* di marina; (*USA*) marine *m inv*; **tell that to the marines!** (*fam*) va' a raccontarla a un altro!

marine insurance N assicurazione *f* marittima

mari·tal [ˈmærɪtl] ADJ coniugale, maritale

mari·time [ˈmærɪˌtaɪm] ADJ (*climate, nation, museum*) marittimo(-a); (*plant, creature*) marino(-a)

maritime law N diritto marittimo

mar·jo·ram [ˈmɑːdʒərəm] N maggiorana

mark¹ [mɑːk] N 1 (*gen*) segno; (*stain*) macchia; (*of shoes, fingers: in mud*) impronta; (*of skid*) traccia; **to leave a mark on sth** lasciare un segno su qc; **to leave one's mark on sth** (*fig*) lasciare un segno in qc; **there wasn't a mark on him** *or* **on his body** non aveva nemmeno un graffio; **you've got a mark on your shirt** hai una macchia sulla camicia; **it bears the mark of genius** ha l'impronta del genio; **to make one's mark (as)** (*fig*) farsi un nome (come); **as a mark of my gratitude** come segno della mia gratitudine; **punctuation marks** segni di punteggiatura 2 (*instead of signature*) croce *f*; **to make one's mark** fare una croce 3 (*Brit Scol*) voto; **good/bad mark** buon *or* bel/brutto voto; **I get good marks for French** prendo bei voti in francese 4 (*Brit: Tech*): **Mark 1/2** prima/seconda serie *f* 5 (*Sport: target*) bersaglio; **to hit the mark** far centro; (*fig*) azzeccare in pieno; **to be wide of the mark** essere lontano(-a) dal bersaglio; (*fig*) essere lontano(-a) dal vero 6 (*Sport: starting line*) linea di partenza; **on your marks! get set! go!** ai vostri posti! pronti! (attenti!) via!; **to be quick off the mark (in doing sth)** (*fig*) non perdere tempo (per fare qc); **up to the mark** (*in health*) in forma; (*in efficiency*) all'altezza ♦ VT 1 (*make a mark on*) segnare; (*stain*) macchiare, lasciare dei segni su 2 (*indicate: score*) segnare; (: *price*) mettere; (: *place*) indicare, segnare; (: *change, improvement*) indicare; **this marks the frontier** questo segna la frontiera; **mark its position on the map** segna il posto in cui si trova sulla cartina; **the qualities which mark a good swimmer** le qualità che contraddistinguono un buon nuotatore 3 (*heed*): **mark my words** fa' attenzione a quello che ti dico 4 (*Brit Scol: correct*) correggere; (: *exam*) dare un voto a; **the teacher hasn't marked my homework yet** il professore non mi ha ancora corretto il compito; **to mark sth wrong** segnare qc come errore 5 (*Sport: player*) marcare 6 **to mark time** (*Mil, also fig*) segnare il passo ♦ VI macchiarsi

▸ **mark down** VT + ADV 1 (*reduce: prices, goods*) ribassare, ridurre; **the shirts were marked down at the beginning of the week** le camicie sono state ribassate all'inizio della settimana 2 (*note down*) prendere nota di

▸ **mark off** VT + ADV 1 (*separate*) dividere, separare 2 (*tick off*) spuntare, cancellare

▸ **mark out** VT + ADV 1 (*zone, road*) delimitare 2 (*single out: for promotion*) designare; (*characterize*) distinguere

▸ **mark up** VT + ADV 1 (*write up*) segnare 2 (*increase: goods*) aumentare il prezzo di; (: *price*) aumentare
❑ **mark** is not translated by the Italian word *marca*

mark² [mɑːk] N (*currency*) marco; **three million marks** tre milioni di marchi

marked [mɑːkt] ADJ (*accent, contrast, bias*) marcato(-a); (*improvement, increase*) sensibile, spiccato(-a), chiaro(-a); **he's a marked man** è sotto tiro

mark·ed·ly [ˈmɑːkɪdlɪ] ADV visibilmente, notevolmente, marcatamente

mark·er [ˈmɑːkə'] N (*stake*) paletto; (*pen*) pennarello; (*sign*) segno; (*in book*) segnalibro; (*Brit Scol*) persona addetta a correggere le prove d'esame; (*scorekeeper in games*) segnapunti *m inv*

mar·ket [ˈmɑːkɪt] N (*gen*) mercato; (*also:* **stock market**) mercato azionario or dei titoli; **to go to market** andare al mercato; **open market** mercato libero; **there is a good market for videos** c'è una grossa richiesta di video; **is there a market for that?** c'è uno sbocco sul mercato per quello?; **it appeals to the Italian market** è richiesto sul mercato italiano; **to be in the market for sth** avere intenzione di comprare qc; **to be on the market** essere (messo(-a)) in vendita *or* in commercio; **to come on(to) the market** essere introdotto(-a) sul mercato; **to play the market** giocare *or* speculare in borsa ♦ VT (*Comm: sell*) vendere, mettere in vendita; (: *promote*) lanciare sul mercato

mar·ket·able [ˈmɑːkɪtəbl] ADJ commercializzabile

market analysis N analisi *f inv* di mercato

market day N giorno di mercato

market demand N domanda del mercato

market economy N economia di mercato

market forces NPL forze *fpl* di mercato

mar·ket·ing [ˈmɑːkɪtɪŋ] N marketing *m inv*

market·place [ˈmɑːkɪtˌpleɪs] N (*square*) (piazza del) mercato; (*world of trade*) piazza, mercato
market price N prezzo di mercato
market research N indagini *fpl* or ricerche *fpl* di mercato
market value N valore *m* di mercato
mark·ing [ˈmɑːkɪŋ] N **1** (*on animal*) marcatura di colore; (*on road*) segnaletica orizzontale **2** (*Brit Scol*) correzione *f* (dei compiti) **3** (*Ftbl*) marcamento, marcatura
marks·man [ˈmɑːksmən] N (*pl* -**men**) tiratore *m* scelto
marks·man·ship [ˈmɑːksmənˌʃɪp] N abilità *f inv* nel tiro
mark·up [ˈmɑːkˌʌp] N (*Comm: margin*) margine *m* di vendita; (: *increase*) aumento
mar·ma·lade [ˈmɑːməˌleɪd] N marmellata d'arance
ma·roon [məˈruːn] ADJ, N (*colour*) bordeaux *m inv*
❏ **maroon** is not translated by the Italian word *marrone*
ma·roon [məˈruːn] VT (*on island*) abbandonare; (*subj: sea, traffic, snow*) bloccare; **to be marooned (in** *or* **at)** (*fig*) essere abbandonato(-a) (in)
mar·quee [mɑːˈkiː] N grande tenda, padiglione *m*
mar·quis, mar·quess [ˈmɑːkwɪs] N marchese *m*
Mar·ra·kech, Mar·ra·kesh [ˌmærəˈkeʃ] N Marrakesh *f*
mar·riage [ˈmærɪdʒ] N matrimonio; **he's my uncle by marriage** è uno zio acquisito ◆ ADJ (*vows*) di matrimonio; (*bed*) coniugale
marriage bureau N agenzia matrimoniale
marriage certificate N certificato di matrimonio
marriage guidance, (*USA*) **marriage counseling** N consulenza matrimoniale
marriage of convenience N matrimonio di convenienza
mar·ried [ˈmærɪd] ADJ (*person*) sposato(-a); (*life, love*) coniugale, matrimoniale; (*name*) da sposata
mar·row [ˈmærəʊ] N **1** (*Anat*) midollo; **bone marrow** il midollo osseo; **to be frozen to the marrow** sentirsi il gelo *or* il freddo nelle ossa **2** (*vegetable*) zucca; **baby marrow** zucchino
mar·ry [ˈmærɪ] VT (*take in marriage*) sposare, sposarsi con; (*subj: father, priest*) dare in matrimonio; **he wants to marry her** vuole sposarla ◆ VI (*also:* **to get married**) sposarsi; **my sister's getting married in June** mia sorella si sposa in giugno; **to marry again** risposarsi; **to marry into a rich family** imparentarsi con una famiglia ricca
▸ **marry up** VT + ADV (*pattern*) far combaciare
Mars [mɑːz] N (*Astron, Myth*) Marte *m*
Mar·seilles [mɑːˈseɪlz] N Marsiglia
marsh [mɑːʃ] N palude *f*
mar·shal [ˈmɑːʃəl] N (*Mil*) maresciallo; (*for demonstration, meeting*) membro del servizio d'ordine; (*USA*) (*also:* **fire marshal**) capo; (*also:* **police marshal**) capitano ◆ VT (*soldiers, procession*) schierare, adunare; (*fig: facts*) ordinare
mar·shal·ling yard [ˈmɑːʃəlɪŋˌjɑːd] N (*Brit*) scalo smistamento
marsh·mal·low [ˌmɑːʃˈmæləʊ] N (*sweet*) caramella soffice e gommosa
marshy [ˈmɑːʃɪ] ADJ (*comp* -**ier**, *superl* -**iest**) paludoso(-a)
mar·su·pial [mɑːˈsuːpiəl] ADJ, N marsupiale *m*
mar·tial [ˈmɑːʃəl] ADJ marziale
martial arts NPL arti *fpl* marziali
martial law N legge *f* marziale
Mar·tian [ˈmɑːʃən] N marziano(-a)
mar·tin [ˈmɑːtɪn] N (*bird: also:* **house martin**) balestruccio; **sand martin** topino
mar·tyr [ˈmɑːtəʳ] N martire *m/f* ◆ VT martirizzare
mar·tyr·dom [ˈmɑːtədəm] N martirio
mar·vel [ˈmɑːvəl] N (*of nature*) meraviglia; (*of science, skill*) prodigio ◆ VI: **to marvel (at)** (*awestruck*) rimanere incantato(-a) (davanti a); (*surprised*) stupirsi (di fronte a), meravigliarsi (di)
mar·vel·lous, mar·ve·lous (*USA*) [ˈmɑːvələs] ADJ meraviglioso(-a); **the weather was marvellous** il tempo era stupendo
Marx·ism [ˈmɑːksɪzəm] N marxismo
Marx·ist [ˈmɑːksɪst] ADJ, N marxista *m/f*
Ma·ry·land [ˈmɛərɪlænd] N il Maryland

mar·zi·pan [ˌmɑːzɪˈpæn] N marzapane *m*
mas·cara [mæsˈkɑːrə] N mascara *m inv*
mas·cot [ˈmæskət] N mascotte *f inv*, portafortuna *m inv*
mas·cu·line [ˈmæskjʊlɪn] ADJ (*also Gram*) maschile; (*pej: woman*) mascolino(-a) ◆ N (*Gram*) (genere *m*) maschile, *m*
mas·cu·lin·ity [ˌmæskjʊˈlɪnɪtɪ] N virilità *f inv*, mascolinità *f inv*; (*pej: of woman*) mascolinità *f inv*
MASH [mæʃ] N ABBR (*USA Mil*: = *Mobile Army Surgical Hospital*) ospedale da campo di unità mobile dell'esercito
mash [mæʃ] N **1** (*Brit fam: also:* **mashed potatoes**) purè *m* (di patate) **2** (*for animals*) pastone *m* ◆ VT (*Culin*) passare, schiacciare
mask [mɑːsk] N (*gen, Elec*) maschera ◆ VT mascherare
maso·chism [ˈmæsəʊˌkɪzəm] N masochismo
maso·chist [ˈmæsəʊkɪst] N masochista *m/f*
ma·son [ˈmeɪsn] N **1** (*builder*) muratore *m*; (*also:* **stonemason**) scalpellino **2** (*also:* **freemason**) massone *m*
ma·son·ic [məˈsɒnɪk] ADJ massonico(-a)
ma·son·ry [ˈmeɪsnrɪ] N **1** (*stonework*) muratura; (*skill*) arte *f* muratoria **2** (*also:* **freemasonry**) massoneria
mas·quer·ade [ˌmæskəˈreɪd] N (*fig: pretence*) mascherata, finzione *f*, montatura; (*masked ball*) ballo in maschera ◆ VI: **to masquerade as** farsi passare per
mass¹ [mæs] N (*Rel*) messa; **to say mass** dire (la) messa; **to go to mass** andare a *or* alla messa; **Sunday mass** messa della domenica
mass² [mæs] N (*gen*) massa, moltitudine *f*; (*Phys*) massa; **a mass of books and papers** una massa di libri e carte; **he's a mass of bruises** è coperto di lividi; **in the mass** nella gran maggioranza; **the masses** le masse; **masses (of)** (*fam*) un sacco (di), un mucchio (di) ◆ VI (*Mil*) adunarsi, concentrarsi; (*crowd*) ammassarsi; (*clouds*) addensarsi ◆ VT adunare ◆ ADJ (*culture, demonstration*) di massa; (*education*) delle masse; (*hysteria*) collettivo(-a); (*murders*) in massa; **mass grave** fossa comune
Mass. ABBR (*USA:* = *Massachusetts*)
Mas·sa·chu·setts [ˌmæsəˈtʃuːsɪts] il Massachusetts
mas·sa·cre [ˈmæsəkəʳ] N massacro ◆ VT massacrare
mas·sage [ˈmæsɑːʒ] N massaggio ◆ VT massaggiare
mas·seur [mæˈsɜːʳ] N massaggiatore *m*
mas·seuse [mæˈsɜːz] N massaggiatrice *f*
mas·sive [ˈmæsɪv] ADJ massiccio(-a), enorme
mass market N mercato di massa
mass media NPL mass media *mpl*, mezzi *mpl* di comunicazione, *f* di massa
mass meeting N (*of everyone concerned*) riunione *f* generale; (*huge*) adunata popolare
mass-produce [ˈmæsprəˌdjuːs] VT produrre in serie
mass production N produzione *f* in serie
mast [mɑːst] N (*Naut*) albero; (*flagpole*) asta; (*Radio, TV*) pilone *m* (a traliccio)
mastectomy [mæsˈtektəmɪ] N mastectomia
mas·ter [ˈmɑːstəʳ] N **1** (*of servant, dog*) padrone *m*; **the master of the house** il padrone di casa; **to be one's own master** non aver padroni; **I am (the) master now** ora comando io; **to be master of the situation** essere padrone della situazione **2** (*Naut: of ship*) capitano **3** (*musician, painter*) maestro **4** (*Brit: teacher: in primary school*) maestro; (: *in secondary school*) professore *m*; **fencing master** maestro di scherma **5** (*title for boys*): **Master Paul Moran** il signorino Paul Moran; (*on letters*) (il) signor Paul Moran ◆ VT **1** (*animal*) domare; (*person*) dominare; (*one's emotions*) controllare **2** (*theory: understand*) conoscere a fondo; (*learn: subject, skill*) imparare a fondo; **she soon mastered the technique** si è impadronita rapidamente della tecnica
master disk N (*Comput*) disco *m* master, *inv*, disco principale
mas·ter·ful [ˈmɑːstəfʊl] ADJ (*imperious*) imperioso(-a); (*authoritative*) magistrale
master key N passe-partout *m inv*
mas·ter·ly [ˈmɑːstəlɪ] ADJ magistrale, da maestro
master·mind [ˈmɑːstəˌmaɪnd] N (*genius*) mente *f* superiore; (*in crime*) cervello ◆ VT ideare e dirigere, essere il cervello di
Master of Arts/Science N (*degree*) master *m inv* in materie umanistiche/scienze; (*person*) titolare di un master in lettere/scienze

master·piece [ˈmɑːstəˌpiːs] N capolavoro

master plan N piano generale, progetto di massima

master·stroke [ˈmɑːstəˌstrəʊk] N colpo magistrale *or* da maestro

mas·tery [ˈmɑːstərɪ] N: **mastery (of)** (*subject, musical instrument*) padronanza (di); (*of the seas*) dominio (su), supremazia (su); **mastery (at)** (*skill*) virtuosità *f inv* (a *or* in), maestria (a *or* in); **mastery (over)** (*competitors*) superiorità *f inv* (su)

mas·tiff [ˈmæstɪf] N mastino

mas·tur·bate [ˈmæstəˌbeɪt] VI masturbarsi ♦ VT masturbare

mas·tur·ba·tion [ˌmæstəˈbeɪʃən] N masturbazione *f*

mat¹ [mæt] N (*on floor*) tappetino; (*of straw*) stuoia; (*also:* **doormat**) zerbino, stoino; (*on table*) tovaglietta all'americana

mat² [mæt] ADJ = **matt**

match¹ [mætʃ] N **1** (*of colours*): **to be a good match (for)** intonarsi a, andar bene con; **Paul and Jane make a good match** Paul e Jane sono una bella coppia; **it's an exact match** è identico **2** (*equal*) uguale *m/f*, pari *m/f inv*; **to be a match/no match for sb** riuscire/non riuscire a tenere testa a qn; **to meet one's match** trovare pane per i propri denti **3** (*marriage*) partito **4** (*game*) incontro; (*Ftbl, Rugby*) partita, incontro; **are you going to the match?** vai alla partita? ♦ VT **1** (*find similar to: also:* **match up**): **can you match this wool for me?** ha della lana che vada bene con questa?; **to match sb against sb** opporre qn a qn; **they are well matched** (*opponents*) son ben assortiti; (*two friends*) sono una coppia bene assortita; (*husband and wife*) sono una bella coppia; **match the pictures to the titles** fai corrispondere le immagini ai titoli **2** (*equal*) uguagliare; **the results did not match our hopes** i risultati non hanno corrisposto alle nostre speranze; **I can't match that** per me è troppo **3** (*go well with: colours*) intonarsi a; (*: clothes*) andare benissimo con; **his tie matches his socks** la sua cravatta s'intona ai calzini ♦ VI (*colours, materials*) intonarsi; **with a skirt to match, with a matching skirt** con una gonna adatta *or* intonata; **the jacket matches the trousers** la giacca si intona con i pantaloni
  ▸ **match up to** VI + ADV + PREP essere all'altezza di

match² [mætʃ] N fiammifero; **a box of matches** una scatola di fiammiferi; **to put a match to sth** dar fuoco a qc

match·box [ˈmætʃˌbɒks] N scatola di fiammiferi

match·ing [ˈmætʃɪŋ] ADJ (*colours*) intonato(-a), ben assortito(-a); **with matching shoes and bag** con scarpe e borsa intonate

match·less [ˈmætʃlɪs] ADJ senza pari

match·maker [ˈmætʃˌmeɪkəʳ] N (*arranger of marriages*) sensale *m/f* di matrimoni; (*Sport*) organizzatore(-trice) di incontri sportivi

mate¹ [meɪt] N **1** (*at work*) compagno(-a) di lavoro; (*fam: friend*) amico(-a); **he always goes on holiday with his mates** va sempre in vacanza con i suoi amici **2** (*assistant*) aiutante *m/f* **3** (*Zool*) compagno(-a), maschio (*or* femmina) **4** (*in merchant navy*) secondo ♦ VT (*Zool*) accoppiare ♦ VI (*Zool*) accoppiarsi

mate² [meɪt] N (*Chess*) scaccomatto

ma·terial [məˈtɪərɪəl] ADJ **1** (*things, needs, success*) materiale **2** (*important*) sostanziale, essenziale; (*relevant*): **material to** pertinente a; (*Law: evidence*) determinante; **a material witness** un testimone chiave ♦ N **1** (*substance*) materiale *m*, materia; (*cloth*) stoffa, tessuto; **the curtains are made of thin material** le tende sono fatte di una stoffa sottile; **she is university material** è una che dovrebbe continuare gli studi; **he is officer material** ha la stoffa dell'ufficiale **2** (*equipment*): **materials** NPL occorrente *m*; **building materials** materiali *mpl* da costruzione; **raw materials** materie prime; **have you any writing materials?** hai l'occorrente per scrivere? **3** (*for novel, report*) materiale *m*, documentazione *f*; **I'm collecting material for my project** sto raccogliendo materiale per la mia ricerca

ma·teri·al·is·tic [məˌtɪərɪəˈlɪstɪk] ADJ materialista

ma·teri·al·ize [məˈtɪərɪəˌlaɪz] VI materializzarsi; (*idea, hope*) avverarsi, realizzarsi; **so far he hasn't materialized** (*fam*) per ora non si è visto

ma·teri·al·ly [məˈtɪərɪəlɪ] ADV (*see adj*) dal punto di vista materiale; sostanzialmente

ma·ter·nal [məˈtɜːnl] ADJ materno(-a)

ma·ter·nity [məˈtɜːnɪtɪ] N maternità *f inv* ♦ ADJ di maternità

maternity benefit N sussidio di maternità

maternity home, maternity hospital N ≈ clinica ostetrica

maternity leave N congedo per maternità

matey [ˈmeɪtɪ] ADJ (*Brit fam*) amicone(-a)

math [mæθ] N ABBR (*USA:* = *mathematics*) matematica

math·emati·cal [ˌmæθəˈmætɪkəl] ADJ matematico(-a)

math·ema·ti·cian [ˌmæθəməˈtɪʃən] N matematico(-a)

math·emat·ics [ˌmæθəˈmætɪks] NSG matematica

maths [mæθs] N ABBR (*Brit fam*: = *mathematics*) matematica

mati·née [ˈmætɪˌneɪ] N matinée *f inv*

mat·ing [ˈmeɪtɪŋ] N accoppiamento ♦ ADJ dell'accoppiamento

mating call N chiamata all'accoppiamento

mating season N stagione *f* degli amori

ma·tri·ar·chal [ˌmeɪtrɪˈɑːkl] ADJ matriarcale

ma·tri·ces [ˈmeɪtrɪsiːz] NPL *of* **matrix**

ma·tricu·la·tion [məˌtrɪkjʊˈleɪʃən] N immatricolazione *f*

mat·ri·mo·nial [ˌmætrɪˈməʊnɪəl] ADJ (*vows*) di matrimonio; (*state, troubles*) coniugale, matrimoniale

mat·ri·mo·ny [ˈmætrɪmənɪ] N matrimonio

ma·trix [ˈmeɪtrɪks] N (*pl* **matrices** *or* **matrixes**) matrice *f*

ma·tron [ˈmeɪtrən] N (*Brit: in hospital*) capoinfermiera; (*: in school*) infermiera; (*older woman*) matrona

ma·tron·ly [ˈmeɪtrənlɪ] ADJ (*figure, behaviour*) da matrona; (*woman*) imponente e di una certa età

matt [mæt] ADJ opaco(-a)

mat·ted [ˈmætɪd] ADJ (*hair*) arruffato(-a); (*sweater*) infeltrito(-a)

mat·ter [ˈmætəʳ] N **1** (*substance: gen: Phys*) materia, sostanza; **colouring matter** colorante *m*; **foreign matter** sostanza estranea; **advertising matter** pubblicità *f inv*; **reading matter** (*Brit*) qualcosa da leggere **2** (*content*) contenuto **3** (*question, affair*) questione *f*, faccenda; **money matters** questioni finanziarie; **the matter in hand** l'argomento *or* la faccenda in questione; **there's the matter of my wages** ci sarebbe la questione del mio stipendio; **and to make matters worse** ... e come se non bastasse...; **that will only make matters worse** questo servirà solo a peggiorare la situazione; **it's a matter of great concern to us** è una cosa che ci preoccupa molto; **it's no laughing matter** è una cosa *or* faccenda seria; **it's a matter of life and death** è una questione di vita o di morte; **it will be a matter of a few weeks** ci vorrà qualche settimana; **it's a matter of a few pounds** si tratta di poche sterline; **in the matter of** in fatto di, per quanto riguarda; **for that matter** peraltro; **as a matter of course** di conseguenza, come cosa naturale; **as a matter of fact** per (dire) la verità, in verità; **it's a matter of opinion** è una questione di punti di vista; **that's another matter** quella è un'altra faccenda; **it's a matter of habit** è una questione di abitudine **4** (*importance*): **no matter!** non importa!; **do it, no matter how** non importa come, basta che tu lo faccia; **no matter how you do it** comunque tu lo faccia; **no matter what** qualsiasi cosa accada; **no matter what he says** qualsiasi *or* qualunque cosa dica; **no matter how big it is** per quanto grande sia; **no matter when** in qualunque momento, non importa quando; **no matter who** chiunque **5** (*difficulty, problem*): **what's the matter?** cosa c'è (che non va)?; **what's the matter with you?** cos'hai?; **there's something the matter with my arm** c'è qualcosa che non va al braccio; **as if nothing was the matter** come se niente fosse; **something's the matter with the lights** le luci hanno qualcosa che non va; **nothing's the matter** non è successo niente; **nothing's the matter with me** non ho niente **6** (*Med: pus*) pus *m* ♦ VI importare; **it doesn't matter** (*I don't mind*) non importa, non fa niente; **I can't give you the money today — it doesn't matter** non ti posso dare i soldi oggi — non importa; **what does it matter?** cosa importa?, che importanza ha?; **what does it matter to you?** ma a te che te ne importa?; **why should it matter to me?** e perché dovrebbe importarmi?; **it matters a lot to me** è molto importante per me

matter-of-fact [ˌmætərəvˈfækt] ADJ (*person, attitude*) pratico(-a), prosaico(-a); (*tone, voice*) neutro(-a), piatto(-a); (*account*) che si limita ai fatti

mat·ting [ˈmætɪŋ] N stuoia

mat·tress [ˈmætrɪs] N materasso

ma·ture [məˈtjʊəʳ] ADJ (comp -r, superl -st) (gen) maturo(-a); (cheese) stagionato(-a); **he's much more mature** è molto più maturo ♦ VI (gen) maturarsi, maturare; (Fin) maturare, scadere; (cheese) stagionarsi, stagionare

mature student N studente(-essa) universitario(-a) di età superiore ai 25 anni

ma·tur·ity [məˈtjʊərɪtɪ] N maturità f inv

maud·lin [ˈmɔːdlɪn] ADJ piagnucoloso(-a)

maul [mɔːl] VT (subj: tiger) dilaniare, sbranare; **mauled to death** sbranato(-a) vivo(-a)

Mau·ri·ta·nia [ˌmɔːrɪˈteɪnɪə] N la Mauritania

Mau·ri·tius [məˈrɪʃəs] N (l'isola di) Maurizio f

mau·so·leum [ˌmɔːsəˈlɪəm] N mausoleo

mauve [məʊv] ADJ (color) malva inv

mav·er·ick [ˈmævərɪk] N chi sta fuori del branco ♦ ADJ anticonformista

mawk·ish [ˈmɔːkɪʃ] ADJ svenevole, sdolcinato(-a), insipido(-a)

max. ABBR (= maximum) max

max·im [ˈmæksɪm] N massima

maxi·ma [ˈmæksɪmə] NPL of **maximum**

max·im·ize [ˈmæksɪˌmaɪz] VT (profits) massimizzare; (chances) aumentare al massimo; (Comput: window) ingrandire a pieno schermo

maxi·mum [ˈmæksɪməm] N (pl maxima or maximums) massimo ♦ ADJ massimo(-a)

May [meɪ] N maggio; **in May** in maggio; see **July**

may [meɪ] (pt might) MODAL AUX VB 1 (possibility): **she may come** può darsi che venga, può venire; **he might come** potrebbe venire, può anche darsi che venga; **it may rain** potrebbe piovere; **are you going to the party? — I don't know, I may ...** vai alla festa? - non so, forse...; **they may have thought you were joking** forse hanno pensato che scherzassi; **I might well go** potrei anche andare; **he might be there** può darsi che ci sia; **he may not be hungry** potrebbe non aver fame, può darsi che non abbia fame; **they may well be connected** può darsi benissimo che ci sia un legame; **that's as may be** può darsi che sia; **you may well ask!** è quello che mi chiedo anch'io! 2 (of permission): **may I smoke?** posso fumare?; **may I have a cigarette? — yes, of course** posso avere una sigaretta? — sì, prego; **may I sit here?** le dispiace se mi siedo qua?; **if I may say so** se mi è concesso dirlo; **may I?** permette?; **might I suggest that ...?** con il suo permesso suggerirei che...; **he said I might leave** mi ha detto che potevo andare 3 **I hope he may succeed** (frm) spero che ci riesca; **I hoped he might succeed this time** speravo che stavolta ci sarebbe riuscito; **we may or might as well go** tanto vale che ci andiamo; **he might have offered to help** avrebbe potuto offrirsi di aiutare; **as you might expect** come c'era da aspettarsi; **you might like to try** forse le piacerebbe provare 4 (in wishes): **may you have a happy life together** possiate vivere insieme felici; **may God bless you!** (che) Dio la benedica!

may·be [ˈmeɪbiː] ADV forse, può darsi; **maybe not** forse no, può darsi di no; **maybe tomorrow** forse or magari domani; **maybe he'll come** può darsi che venga, magari or forse verrà

May·day [ˈmeɪˌdeɪ] N (Aer, Naut) mayday m inv, S.O.S. m inv

May Day N il primo maggio (in cui si festeggia l'arrivo della primavera)

may·hem [ˈmeɪhem] N cagnara

may·on·naise [ˌmeɪəˈneɪz] N maionese f

mayor [meəʳ] N sindaco

may·pole [ˈmeɪˌpəʊl] N palo ornato di fiori attorno a cui si danza durante la festa del primo maggio

maze [meɪz] N dedalo, labirinto

MB [ˌemˈbiː] N ABBR 1 (Med: = Bachelor of Medicine) laurea in Medicina 2 (Comput: = megabyte) ♦ ABBR = **Manitoba**

MBA [ˌembiːˈeɪ] N ABBR (= Master of Business Administration) master m inv in gestione aziendale

MC [ˌemˈsiː] N ABBR 1 = **master of ceremonies** 2 (USA: = Member of Congress) membro del Congresso

MCAT [ˌemsiːeɪˈtiː] N ABBR (USA: = Medical College Admissions Test) esame di ammissione alla Facoltà di Medicina

MD [ˌemˈdiː] N ABBR 1 (= Doctor of Medicine) Dottore m in Medicina 2 (Comm: = managing director) ♦ ADJ m (= Amministratore Delegato) ♦ ABBR (USA Post: = **Maryland**)

Md. ABBR (USA: = **Maryland**)

MDT [ˌemdiːˈtiː] ABBR (USA: = Mountain Daylight Time) ora estiva nel fuso delle Montagne Rocciose

ME [ˌemˈiː] N ABBR (Med) 1 (= myalgic encephalomyelitis) sindrome f da affaticamento cronico 2 = **medical examiner** ♦ ABBR (USA Post: = **Maine**)

me [miː] PERS PRON 1 (direct: unstressed) mi, m' (+ vowel or silent 'h'); (: stressed) me; **he can hear me** mi sente; **excuse me!** mi scusi!; **it's me** sono io; **he heard me** mi ha or m'ha sentito; **he heard ME!** ha sentito ME! 2 (indirect) mi, m' (+ vowel or silent 'h'); **he gave me the money, he gave the money to me** mi ha or m'ha dato i soldi; **he gave them to me** me li ha dati; **give them to me** dammeli; **could you lend me your pen?** puoi prestarmi la penna? 3 (stressed, after prep) me; **it's for me** è per me; **without me** senza (di) me; **look at me!** guardami!; **come with me!** vieni con me!; **without me** senza di me

mead·ow [ˈmedəʊ] N prato, pascolo

mea·gre, mea·ger (USA) [ˈmiːɡəʳ] ADJ magro(-a)

meal[1] [miːl] N (flour) farina

meal[2] [miːl] N pasto; **to have a meal** mangiare; **to have a good meal** mangiar bene; **to go out for a meal** mangiare fuori; **what a lovely meal** che pranzo delizioso (or cena deliziosa); **to make a meal of sth** (fam) fare di qc un affare di stato; **before meals** prima dei pasti; **enjoy your meal!** buon appetito!

meals on wheels NSG (Brit) distribuzione di pasti caldi a domicilio a persone malate o anziane

meal·time [ˈmiːlˌtaɪm] N ora di mangiare; **at mealtimes** all'ora dei pasti

mealy-mouthed [ˌmiːlɪˈmaʊðd] ADJ evasivo(-a)

mean[1] [miːn] (pt, pp meant) VT 1 (signify) significare, voler dire; **what does that word mean?** che significa quella parola?; **what does "trap" mean?** cosa significa "trap"?; **what do you mean by that?** cosa vuoi dire con questo?; **you don't mean that, do you?** non parli sul serio, vero?; **do you really mean it?** dici sul serio?; **he said it as if he meant it** l'ha detto senza scherzare or sul serio; **I mean what I say** parlo sul serio; **it means a lot of expense for us** per noi questo vuol dire una grossa spesa; **the play didn't mean a thing to me** la commedia non mi ha detto niente; **her name means nothing to me** il suo nome non mi dice niente; **you mean a lot to me** significhi molto per me; **your friendship means a lot to me** la tua amicizia è molto importante per me; **he means nothing to me** non conta niente per me 2 (intend): **to mean to do sth** aver l'intenzione di fare qc, intendere fare qc; **to be meant for** essere destinato(-a) a; **I meant it for her** era destinato a lei; **that's not what I meant** non era quello che intendevo; **I meant it as a joke** volevo solo scherzare; **he means what he says** parla sul serio; **do you really mean it?** parli sul serio?; **what do you mean to do?** cosa intendi fare?, cosa pensi di fare?; **he didn't mean to do it** non intendeva or non era sua intenzione farlo; **I didn't mean to hurt you** non volevo farti del male; **do you mean me?** (are you speaking to me?) dici a me?; (about me) ti riferisci a me?, intendi me?; **was that remark meant for me?** quell'osservazione era diretta a me?; **Roberta is meant to do it** è Roberta che lo deve fare; **I mean to be obeyed** intendo essere ubbidito; **he means well** le sue intenzioni sono buone

mean[2] [miːn] ADJ (comp -er, superl -est) 1 (with money) avaro(-a), spilorcio(-a), gretto(-a); **mean with** avaro(-a) con; **he's too mean to buy presents** è troppo avaro per comprare regali 2 (unkind, spiteful) meschino(-a), maligno(-a); **a mean trick** uno scherzo ignobile; **that's a really mean thing to say!** che cosa meschina da dire!; **you're being mean to me** sei cattivo con me 3 (USA: vicious: animal) cattivo(-a); (: person) perfido(-a) 4 (poor: appearance, district) misero(-a)

mean[3] [miːn] N (middle term) mezzo; (Math) media; **the golden** or **happy mean** il giusto mezzo; see also **means** ♦ ADJ (average) medio(-a)

me·ander [mɪˈændə'] N meandro ◆ VI (*river*) serpeggiare; (*person*) girovagare; (*fig*) divagare

mean·ing [ˈmiːnɪŋ] N significato, senso; **a look full of meaning** uno sguardo eloquente; **do you get my meaning?** capisci cosa voglio dire?; **what's the meaning of this?** (*as reprimand*) e questo cosa significa?

mean·ing·ful [ˈmiːnɪŋfʊl] ADJ (*word, look*) significativo(-a), eloquente; (*relationship*) profondo(-a)

mean·ing·less [ˈmiːnɪŋlɪs] ADJ senza senso; **your remarks are quite meaningless** i tuoi commenti non vogliono dire niente

mean·ness [ˈmiːnnɪs] N (*see adj*) avarizia, spilorceria; meschinità *f inv*; cattiveria; perfidia

means [miːnz] N INV (*method or way of doing*) mezzo, modo; **a means of transport** un mezzo di trasporto; **to find a means to do** *or* **of doing sth** trovare il modo per fare qc; **there is no means of doing it** non c'è mezzo *or* modo di farlo; **he'll do it by any possible means** lo farà con ogni mezzo possibile; **a means to an end** un modo *or* mezzo per raggiungere i propri fini; **by means of** per mezzo di; **by this means** in questo modo, così; **by some means or other** in un modo o nell'altro; **by all means!** ma certamente!; **can I come? — by all means!** posso venire? — ma certamente!; **by no means, not by any means** per niente, niente affatto; **by all manner of means** in tutti i modi ◆ NPL *(frm: pl)* mezzi *mpl*; **private means** rendite *fpl*; **to live within/beyond one's means** vivere secondo i/al di sopra dei propri mezzi

means test N (*Admin*) accertamento dei redditi (*per concedere di prestito*)

meant [mɛnt] PT, PP *of* **mean¹**

mean·time [ˈmiːnˌtaɪm], **mean·while** [ˈmiːnˌwaɪl] ADV (*also:* **in the meantime**) nel frattempo, (e) intanto

mea·sles [ˈmiːzlz] N morbillo

mea·sly [ˈmiːzlɪ] ADJ (*comp* **-ier**, *superl* **-iest**) (*fam*) misero(-a), miserabile

meas·ur·able [ˈmɛʒərəbl] ADJ misurabile

meas·ure [ˈmɛʒəʳ] N 1 (*gen*) misura; (*also:* **tape measure**) metro; **a litre measure** dare il peso giusto (*or* la quantità giusta); **for good measure** (*fig*) in più, in aggiunta; **to be a measure of ...** essere un sintomo di...; **her happiness was beyond measure** era immensamente felice; **in some/large measure** in parte/gran parte; **some measure of success** un certo successo 2 (*step, action*) misura, provvedimento; **to take measures to do sth** prendere provvedimenti per fare qc; **to take measures against ...** prendere provvedimenti contro... ◆ VT misurare; (*take sb's measurements*) prendere le misure di *or* a; **to measure one's length** (*fig: fall*) cadere lungo(-a) disteso(-a)

▸ **measure against** VT + PREP: **to measure sb/sth against sb/sth** valutare qn/qc confrontandolo a qn/qc

▸ **measure off** VT + ADV misurare

▸ **measure out** VT + ADV dosare

▸ **measure up** VI + ADV: **to measure up (to)** dimostrarsi *or* essere all'altezza (di)

meas·ured [ˈmɛʒəd] ADJ misurato(-a)

meas·ure·ment [ˈmɛʒəmənt] N (*act*) misurazione *f*; (*measure*) misura; **to take sb's measurements** prendere le misure di *or* a qn; **chest/hip measurement** giro petto/fianchi; **are you sure the measurements are correct?** sei sicuro che le misure siano giuste?; **the measurement of blood pressure** la misurazione della pressione sanguigna

meat [miːt] N carne *f*; **cold meats** (*Brit*) affettati *mpl*; **I don't eat meat** non mangio carne; **meat and drink** da mangiare e da bere; **one man's meat is another man's poison** (*proverb*) ciò che giova a uno nuoce a un altro

meat·ball [ˈmiːtˌbɔːl] N polpetta di carne

meat pie N torta salata in pasta con ripieno di carne

meaty [ˈmiːtɪ] ADJ (*comp* **-ier**, *superl* **-iest**) (*flavour*) di carne; (*fig: book, talk*) sostanzioso(-a)

Mec·ca [ˈmɛkə] N La Mecca

me·chan·ic [mɪˈkænɪk] N meccanico; **motor mechanic** motorista *m*

me·chani·cal [mɪˈkænɪkəl] ADJ (*also fig*) meccanico(-a)

mechanical engineering N (*science*) ingegneria meccanica; (*industry*) costruzioni *fpl* meccaniche

me·chan·ics [mɪˈkænɪks] N 1 (*sg: science*) meccanica 2 (*pl: of car*) meccanismo, meccanica; (: *fig: of legal system*) meccanismo; (: *of writing, novel, plot*) meccanismo

mecha·nism [ˈmɛkəˌnɪzəm] N meccanismo

mecha·ni·za·tion [mɛkənaɪˈzeɪʃən] N (*see vb*) meccanizzazione *f*; motorizzazione *f*

med·al [ˈmɛdl] N medaglia

med·al·lion [mɪˈdæljən] N medaglione *m*

med·al·list, med·al·ist (*USA*) [ˈmɛdəlɪst] N (*Sport*): **to be a gold/silver medallist** essere medaglia d'oro/d'argento

med·dle [ˈmɛdl] VI (*interfere*): **to meddle (in)** immischiarsi (in); **to meddle with sth** (*tamper*) toccare qc; **stop meddling!** smettila di impicciarti!

med·dle·some [ˈmɛdlsəm], **med·dling** [ˈmɛdlɪŋ] ADJ (*interfering*) impiccione(-a), ficcanaso *m/f*

me·dia [ˈmiːdɪə] NPL 1 (*Press, Radio, TV*): **the media** i mass media; **all the media were there** stampa, radio e televisione erano tutte sul posto 2 (*frm: plural*) *of* **medium 2**

media circus N carrozzone *m* dell'informazione

me·di·aeval [ˌmɛdɪˈiːvəl] ADJ = **medieval**

me·dian [ˈmiːdɪən] N (*Math, Statistics*) mediana; (*USA: also:* **median strip**) banchina *f* spartitraffico, *inv*

media research N sondaggio tra gli utenti dei mass media

me·di·ate [ˈmiːdɪˌeɪt] VI fare da mediatore(-trice) ◆ VT (*settlement*) mediare

me·dia·tion [ˌmiːdɪˈeɪʃən] N mediazione *f*

me·dia·tor [ˈmiːdɪeɪtəʳ] N mediatore(-trice)

Medi·caid [ˈmɛdɪˌkeɪd] N (*USA*) *programma di assistenza medica ai poveri*

medi·cal [ˈmɛdɪkəl] ADJ (*school, ward*) di medicina; (*test, treatment*) medico(-a); **the medical profession** il corpo dei medici; **medical treatment** cure *fpl* mediche; **a medical student** uno studente di medicina ◆ N visita medica; **he had his medical last week** ha fatto una visita medica la settimana scorsa

medical certificate N certificato medico

medical examiner N (*USA*) medico legale

medical student N studente(-essa) di medicina

Medi·care [ˈmɛdɪˌkeəʳ] N (*USA*) *programma di assistenza medica agli anziani*

medi·ca·ted [ˈmɛdɪˌkeɪtɪd] ADJ medicato(-a)

medi·ca·tion [ˌmɛdɪˈkeɪʃən] N (*medicine*) medicinali *mpl*, farmaci *mpl*; **to be on medication** prendere medicinali

me·dici·nal [mɛˈdɪsɪnl] ADJ medicinale, medicamentoso(-a)

medi·cine [ˈmɛdsɪn, ˈmɛdɪsɪn] N 1 (*drug*) medicina; **to give sb a taste of his own medicine** (*fig*) rendere pan per focaccia a qn 2 (*science*) medicina

medicine cabinet, medicine chest N armadietto farmaceutico *or* dei medicinali

medicine man N stregone *m*

me·di·eval [ˌmɛdɪˈiːvəl] ADJ medievale, del medio evo; **medieval studies** medievalistica *sg*

me·dio·cre [ˌmiːdɪˈəʊkəʳ] ADJ mediocre

me·di·oc·rity [ˌmiːdɪˈɒkrɪtɪ] N mediocrità *f inv*

medi·tate [ˈmɛdɪˌteɪt] VI: **to meditate (on** *or* **about)** meditare (su) ◆ VT meditare

medi·ta·tion [ˌmɛdɪˈteɪʃən] N meditazione *f*

Medi·ter·ra·nean [ˌmɛdɪtəˈreɪnɪən] ADJ mediterraneo(-a); **the Mediterranean (Sea)** il (mar) Mediterraneo

me·dium [ˈmiːdɪəm] ADJ medio(-a); **small, medium or large?** piccola, media *or* grande?; **medium walk/trot** (*Horse-riding*) passo/trotto ordinario ◆ N 1 (*spiritualist*) medium *m/f inv* 2 (*pl* **media** *or* **mediums**): (*gen: Phys*) mezzo; **through the medium of** per mezzo della stampa; **an advertising medium** un organo di pubblicità; **the artist's medium** i mezzi espressivi dell'artista; *see also* **media 3** (*midpoint*): **a happy medium** una giusta misura *or* una via di mezzo 4 (*environment*) ambiente *m*, habitat *m inv*

medium-dry [ˈmiːdɪəmˈdraɪ] ADJ (*wine*) semisecco(-a), demisec *inv*

medium-sized [ˈmiːdɪəmˌsaɪzd] ADJ (*tin, packet*) di grandezza media; (*clothes*) di taglia media

medium wave N (*Radio*) onde *fpl* medie

med·ley [ˈmɛdlɪ] N (*mixture*) miscuglio, accozzaglia; (*Mus*) pot-pourri *m inv*, selezione *f*

meek [miːk] ADJ (*comp* -er, *superl* -est) mite, umile; **meek and mild** mite come un agnello

meet [miːt] (*pt, pp* met) VT 1 (*gen*) incontrare; (*coming in opposite direction*) incrociare; (*by arrangement*) rivedere, ritrovare; **to arrange to meet sb** dare appuntamento a qn; **I met Paul in town** ho incontrato Paul in città; **I'm going to meet my friends at the swimming pool** mi trovo con i miei amici in piscina; **she ran out to meet us** ci è corsa incontro; **to meet sb off the train** (andare a) aspettare *or* andare a prendere qn al treno; **the car will meet the train** ci sarà una macchina all'arrivo del treno; **I'll meet you at the station** verrò a prenderla (*or* a prenderti) alla stazione; **to meet sb's eye** *or* **gaze** incrociare lo sguardo di qn; **a terrible sight met him** *or* **his eyes** gli si presentò un orrendo spettacolo; **there's more to this than meets the eye** è molto più complicato di quanto possa sembrare a prima vista 2 (*for the first time*) fare la conoscenza di, essere presentato(-a) a; **meet my brother** le presento mio fratello; **come and meet my dad** vieni che ti presento mio padre; **pleased to meet you!** lieto di conoscerla!, piacere (di conoscerla)! 3 (*encounter: team, difficulty*) incontrare; (*face: enemy, danger, death*) affrontare; **to meet one's death** trovare la morte 4 (*satisfy: requirement, demand, need*) soddisfare, andare incontro a; (*: criticism, objection*) ribattere a; (*pay: bill, expenses*) far fronte a; **we agree to meet your expenses** siamo d'accordo a rimborsarle le spese ♦ VI 1 (*gen*) incontrarsi; (*by arrangement*) darsi appuntamento, trovarsi; (*committee, society*) riunirsi; **we met by chance** ci siamo incontrati per caso; **until we meet again!** arrivederci (alla prossima volta)!; **haven't we met before?** non ci conosciamo già? 2 (*join: rivers, teams, armies*) incontrarsi ♦ N (*Brit: Hunting*) raduno (*dei partecipanti alla caccia alla volpe*); (*USA: Sport*) raduno (*sportivo*)

▸ **meet up** VI + ADV incontrarsi, vedersi; **to meet up with sb** incontrare qn; **they arranged to meet up with the others at eight o'clock** hanno stabilito di incontrarsi con gli altri alle otto

▸ **meet with** VI + PREP 1 (*success, difficulties, praise*) incontrare; (*welcome*) ricevere; **they met with an accident** hanno avuto un incidente 2 (*have meeting with*) incontrarsi con

meet·ing [ˈmiːtɪŋ] N 1 (*between individuals*) incontro; (*arranged*) appuntamento; (*interview*) intervista, colloquio; **their first meeting** il loro primo incontro; **the minister had a meeting with the ambassador** il ministro ha avuto un colloquio con *or* si è incontrato con l'ambasciatore 2 (*session: of club, committee, council*) riunione *f*; (*of members, citizens, employees*) assemblea; **to call a meeting** convocare una riunione; **a business meeting** una riunione di lavoro; **Mrs Stark is in a meeting** la signora Stark è in riunione 3 (*Sport: rally*) raduno; (*Horse Racing*) riunione *f* ippica

meeting place N luogo d'incontro

mega·byte [ˈmɛgəˌbaɪt] N megabyte *m inv*

mega·lo·ma·ni·ac [ˌmɛgələʊˈmeɪnɪæk] N megalomane *m/f*

mega·phone [ˈmɛgəfəʊn] N megafono

mega·pix·el [ˈmɛgəpɪksl] N megapixel *m inv*

mega·watt [ˈmɛgəˌwɒt] N megawatt *m inv*

mel·an·choly [ˈmɛlənkəlɪ] ADJ (*person*) malinconico(-a); (*duty, subject*) triste ♦ N malinconia

mel·low [ˈmɛləʊ] ADJ (*comp* -er, *superl* -est) (*fruit*) ben maturo(-a); (*wine*) maturo(-a) e pastoso(-a); (*colour, light*) caldo(-a) e morbido(-a); (*person, character*) addolcito(-a) dall'età; (*sound*) melodioso(-a); **after a few glasses of wine he was quite mellow** dopo qualche bicchiere di vino era piuttosto brillo ♦ VI (*fruit, wine*) maturare, maturarsi; (*colour, sound*) attenuarsi, smorzarsi; (*person, character*) addolcirsi ♦ VT: **old age has mellowed him** con l'età si è addolcito

me·lo·dious [mɪˈləʊdɪəs] ADJ melodioso(-a)

melo·dra·ma [ˈmɛləʊˌdrɑːmə] N melodramma *m*

melo·dra·mat·ic [ˌmɛləʊdrəˈmætɪk] ADJ melodrammatico(-a)

melo·dy [ˈmɛlədɪ] N melodia

mel·on [ˈmɛlən] N melone *m*

melt [mɛlt] VT 1 (*gen*) sciogliere, struggere; (*metal*) fondere; **melted butter** burro fuso; **melt two ounces of butter in a saucepan** sciogliete sessanta grammi di burro in una

casseruola 2 (*fig: heart*) intenerire; (*: anger*) far svanire; (*: person*) commuovere ♦ VI 1 (*gen*) sciogliersi, struggersi; (*metals*) fondersi; **it melts in the mouth** si scioglie in bocca; **the snow is melting** la neve si sta sciogliendo 2 (*fig: anger, determination*) svanire; (*: heart*) intenerirsi; **he melted into the crowd** si confuse tra la folla

▸ **melt away** VI + ADV (*snow, ice*) sciogliersi completamente; (*fog*) dileguarsi; (*fig: anger, anxiety, opposition*) svanire; (*: savings*) andare in fumo; (*: crowd*) disperdersi; **he melted away into the crowd** svanì tra la folla

▸ **melt down** VT + ADV fondere

melt·down [ˈmɛltˌdaʊn] N melt-down *m inv*

melting point N punto di fusione

melting pot N (*fig*) crogiolo; **to be in the melting pot** essere ancora in discussione

mem·ber [ˈmɛmbə'] N (*gen*) membro; (*of club*) socio(-a), iscritto(-a); (*of political party*) iscritto(-a); **a member of NATO** un membro della NATO; **she's like a member of the family** è come una di famiglia; **"members only"** "riservato ai soci"; **member of staff** (*Scol, Univ*) insegnante *m/f*; **a member of the staff** (*gen*) un(a) dipendente *m/f*; **member of the public** privato(-a) cittadino(-a)

Member of Congress (*USA*) N membro del Congresso

Member of Parliament N (*Brit*) deputato(-a)

Member of the European Parliament N eurodeputato(-a)

Member of the House of Representatives N (*USA*) membro della Camera dei Rappresentanti

Member of the Scottish Parliament (*Brit*) N deputato(-a) del Parlamento scozzese

mem·ber·ship [ˈmɛmbəˌʃɪp] N 1 (*state*): **membership (of)** iscrizione *f* (a), adesione *f* (a); **I'm going to apply for membership** farò domanda d'iscrizione 2 (*number of members*): **the club has a membership of 950** il club ha 950 iscritti

membership card N tessera (di iscrizione)

mem·brane [ˈmɛmbreɪn] N membrana

me·men·to [məˈmɛntəʊ] N ricordo, souvenir *m inv*

memo [ˈmɛməʊ] N ABBR (= *memorandum*) promemoria *m inv*; (*to staff*) comunicazione *f* interna *or* di servizio
❑ **memo** is not translated by the Italian word **memo**

mem·oir [ˈmɛmwɑː'] N (*essay*) saggio monografico; (*biography*) nota biografica

memo pad N blocchetto per appunti

memo·rable [ˈmɛmərəbl] ADJ (*day*) memorabile; (*beauty*) notevole

memo·ran·dum [ˌmɛməˈrændəm] N (*pl* memoranda) (*gen*) promemoria *m inv*; (*Diplomacy, Comm*) memorandum *m inv*; (*within company*) comunicazione *f* interna *or* di servizio

me·mo·rial [mɪˈmɔːrɪəl] ADJ commemorativo(-a) ♦ N monumento commemorativo; **as a memorial to** in commemorazione di; **a memorial service** una funzione commemorativa; **a war memorial** un monumento ai caduti

Memorial Day N (*USA*) festa dei caduti in guerra, si celebra l'ultimo lunedì di maggio

memo·rize [ˈmɛməˌraɪz] VT imparare a memoria, memorizzare

memo·ry [ˈmɛmərɪ] N 1 (*faculty, of computer*) memoria; **to have a good/bad memory** aver buona/cattiva memoria; **I've got a terrible memory** ho una pessima memoria; **loss of memory** amnesia, perdita di memoria; **I have a bad memory for faces** non sono molto fisionomista; **he recited the poem from memory** ha recitato la poesia a memoria 2 (*recollection*) ricordo; **happy memories** bei ricordi; **I have no memory of it** non me lo ricordo affatto 3 **in memory of** in memoria *or* ricordo di; **to the memory of** alla memoria di

memory card N (*Comput*) espansione *f* di memoria

memory stick N (*Comput*) stick *m inv* di memoria

men [mɛn] NPL *of* **man**

men·ace [ˈmɛnɪs] N (*threat*) minaccia; (*fam: nuisance*) peste *f*; **he's a menace** è una peste; **a public menace** un pericolo pubblico ♦ VT minacciare

men·ac·ing [ˈmɛnɪsɪŋ] ADJ minaccioso(-a)

me·nag·erie [mɪˈnædʒərɪ] N serraglio

mend [mɛnd] VT (*repair: fence, car, clothes*) aggiustare, riparare; (*darn*) rammendare; **to mend one's ways** (*improve*) correggersi; **to mend matters** risolvere le cose ♦ VI (*broken bone*) rimettersi a posto ♦ N: **to be on the mend** star migliorando, essere in via di guarigione

mend·ing [ˈmɛndɪŋ] N (*act*) rammendo; (*items to be mended*) cose *fpl* da rammendare

me·nial [ˈmiːnɪəl] ADJ (*position*) subalterno(-a); (*work, task*) umile, servile

men·in·gi·tis [ˌmɛnɪnˈdʒaɪtɪs] N meningite *f*

meno·pause [ˈmɛnəʊpɔːz] N menopausa

men·servants [ˈmɛnˌsɜːvənts] NPL *of* **manservant**

men's room N (*esp USA*): **the men's room** la toilette degli uomini

men·stru·ate [ˈmɛnstrʊˌeɪt] VI avere le mestruazioni, mestruare

men·strua·tion [ˌmɛnstrʊˈeɪʃən] N mestruazione *f*

mens·wear [ˈmɛnzˌweər] N (*Comm: clothing*) abbigliamento maschile; (*also:* **menswear department**) (reparto) abbigliamento uomo

men·tal [ˈmɛntl] ADJ 1 (*gen*) mentale, della mente; (*ability, powers*) intellettuale; (*treatment*) psichiatrico(-a); **to make a mental note of sth** prendere mentalmente nota di qc; **mental patient** malato(-a) di mente; **mental strain** tensione *f* 2 (*fam: mad*) pazzo(-a)

mental hospital, mental institution N ospedale *m* psichiatrico

men·tal·ity [mɛnˈtælɪtɪ] N mentalità *f inv*

men·tal·ly [ˈmɛntlɪ] ADV (*calculate*) mentalmente, a mente; **to be mentally handicapped** avere una disabilità intellettiva

men·thol [ˈmɛnθɒl] N mentolo ♦ ADJ al mentolo

men·tion [ˈmɛnʃən] N menzione *f*, accenno; **it's hardly worth a mention** non è neanche il caso di parlarne ♦ VT (*gen*) accennare a; (*name, person*) fare il nome di, menzionare; **I mentioned it to him** gliel'ho accennato; **he didn't mention it to me** non me ne ha parlato; **just mention my name** basta che tu faccia il mio nome; **all those people, too numerous to mention, who ...** tutti coloro che qui sarebbe troppo lungo elencare, i quali...; **I need hardly mention that ...** inutile dire che...; **I mentioned she might come later** ho detto che poteva passare più tardi; **not to mention, without mentioning** per non parlare di, senza contare; **don't mention it!** non c'è di che!, prego!

men·tor [ˈmɛntɔː] N mentore *m*

menu [ˈmɛnjuː] N (*also Comput*) menù *m inv*; **a set menu** un menù a prezzo fisso

menu-driven [ˈmɛnjuːˌdrɪvn] ADJ (*Comput*) guidato(-a) da menù

MEP [ˌɛmiːˈpiː] N ABBR = **Member of the European Parliament**

mer·can·tile [ˈmɜːkənˌtaɪl] ADJ mercantile; (*law*) commerciale

mer·ce·nary [ˈmɜːsɪnərɪ] ADJ (*person*) mercenario(-a); (*motive*) venale ♦ N mercenario

mer·chan·dise [ˈmɜːtʃənˌdaɪz] N merce *f*, merci *fpl* ♦ VT commercializzare

mer·chan·dis·er [ˈmɜːtʃənˌdaɪzər] N merchandiser *m inv*

mer·chant [ˈmɜːtʃənt] N (*trader*) commerciante *m/f*; (*shopkeeper*) negoziante *m/f*, commerciante *m/f*; **timber/wine merchant** commerciante di legname/vino

merchant bank N (*Brit*) banca d'affari

mer·chant·man [ˈmɜːtʃəntmən] N (*pl* **-men**) (*ship*) mercantile *m*

merchant navy, (*USA*) **merchant marine** N marina mercantile

mer·ci·ful [ˈmɜːsɪfʊl] ADJ (*Rel*) misericordioso(-a); (*person*) compassionevole, pietoso(-a), clemente; **it was a merciful release** è stata una vera liberazione

mer·ci·ful·ly [ˈmɜːsɪfəlɪ] ADV (*act*) con clemenza, con misericordia; (*fortunately*) per fortuna

mer·ci·less [ˈmɜːsɪlɪs] ADJ spietato(-a)

mer·cu·rial [mɜːˈkjʊərɪəl] ADJ (*unpredictable*) volubile

mer·cu·ry [ˈmɜːkjʊrɪ] N (*Chem*) mercurio

mer·cy [ˈmɜːsɪ] N pietà *f inv*, clemenza; (*Rel*) misericordia; **to be at the mercy of sb/sth** essere alla mercé *or* in balia di qn/qc; **to have mercy on sb** avere pietà di qn; **to be left to the tender mercies of sb** essere lasciato(-a) alle buone cure di qn; **it's a mercy that** è una fortuna che + *sub*

mercy killing N eutanasia

mere [mɪər] ADJ (*formality*) semplice, puro(-a) (*before n*); (*thought*) solo(-a) (*before n*); (*chance, coincidence*) puro(-a) (*before n*); **by the merest chance** per mero caso; **it's a mere formality** è una semplice formalità; **a mere five percent** solo il cinque per cento; **the merest** il minimo; **the merest hint of criticism** il minimo accenno di critica

mere·ly [ˈmɪəlɪ] ADV soltanto, semplicemente, non... che; **I merely said that ...** ho semplicemente detto che...

merge [mɜːdʒ] VT (*Comm*) fondere, unire; (*Comput: files, text*) unire ♦ VI 1 (*colours, sounds, shapes*): **to merge (into, with)** fondersi (con), confondersi (con); **to merge (with)** (*roads*) unirsi (a); (*river*) confluire (in); **the rivers merge here** i fiumi confluiscono qui 2 (*Comm*) fondersi, unirsi; **the companies merged last year** le compagnie si sono fuse lo scorso anno

mer·ger [ˈmɜːdʒər] N (*Comm*) fusione *f*

me·rid·ian [məˈrɪdɪən] N meridiano

me·ringue [məˈræŋ] N meringa

mer·it [ˈmɛrɪt] N merito, valore *m*; **to look** *or* **inquire into the merits of sth** valutare *or* pesare i pro e i contro di qc; **to treat a case on its merits** trattare un caso con obiettività; **the idea has some merit** l'idea ha qualche valore ♦ VT meritare

meri·toc·ra·cy [ˌmɛrɪˈtɒkrəsɪ] N meritocrazia

mer·maid [ˈmɜːmeɪd] N sirena

mer·ri·ment [ˈmɛrɪmənt] N allegria, gaiezza; (*laughter*) ilarità *f inv*

mer·ry [ˈmɛrɪ] ADJ (*comp* **-ier**, *superl* **-iest**) (*cheerful*) allegro(-a), gaio(-a), festoso(-a); (*Brit fam: tipsy*) brillo(-a); **Merry Christmas!** Buon Natale!

merry-go-round [ˈmɛrɪɡəʊˌraʊnd] N giostra, carosello

mesh [mɛʃ] N 1 (*in net*) maglia; **a 6-cm mesh net** una rete con maglie di 6 cm 2 (*network, net*) rete *f*; **wire mesh** rete *f* metallica 3 (*gears*): **in mesh** ingranato(-a) ♦ VI (*gears*) ingranare

mes·mer·ize [ˈmɛzməˌraɪz] VT ipnotizzare; **she was mesmerized** (*fig*) non riusciva a distogliere lo sguardo

mess [mɛs] N 1 (*confusion of objects*) disordine *m*, confusione *f*; (*dirt*) sporcizia; (*awkward predicament*) pasticcio; **you look a mess!** guarda in che stato sei!; **to be (in) a mess** (*house, room*) essere in disordine, essere molto sporco(-a); (*fig: marriage, life*) essere un caos *or* un disastro; **I'll be in a mess if I fail the exam** sarò in un bel guaio se non passerò l'esame; **to make a mess** fare un gran disordine dappertutto, sporcare dappertutto; **the dog has made a mess** il cane ha sporcato; **to make a mess of** (*dirty*) sporcare; (*tear*) strappare; (*wreck*) sfasciare; **to make a mess of one's life/career** rovinarsi la vita/la carriera; **I made a mess of the exam** ho fatto un pasticcio all'esame; **to be/get (o.s.) in a mess** (*fig*) essere/cacciarsi in un pasticcio 2 (*Mil*) mensa

▸ **mess about, mess around** (*fam*) VI + ADV (*waste time*) perdere tempo, trastullarsi; (*play the fool*) far confusione; (*in water, mud*) pasticciare; **what are you doing? — just messing about** cosa fai? — niente di speciale ♦ VT + ADV (*person*) menare per il naso; (*plans*) scombinare

▸ **mess about with, mess around with** (*fam*) VI + ADV + PREP (*plans*) fare un pasticcio di; **to mess about with sth** armeggiare *or* trafficare con qc; **stop messing about with my computer!** smettetela di trafficare con il mio computer!; **to mess about with sb** divertirsi con qn

▸ **mess up** VT + ADV (*room*) mettere sottosopra; (*dress*) sporcare; (*hair*) scompigliare; (*fig: plan, marriage, situation*) mandare a monte, rovinare; **I messed up my chemistry exam** mi è andato male l'esame di chimica

❏ **mess** is not translated by the Italian words *massa* or *messa*

mes·sage [ˈmɛsɪdʒ] N messaggio; **to get the message** (*fig: fam*) capire l'antifona

message board N (*Comput*) bacheca elettronica

message switching [-swɪtʃɪŋ] N (*Comput*) smistamento messaggi

mes·sen·ger [ˈmɛsɪndʒər] N (*gen*) messaggero(-a); (*in office*) messo

Mes·si·ah [mɪˈsaɪə] N Messia *m*

Messrs [ˈmesəz] NPL ABBR (*on letters:* = *messieurs*) Spett.

messy [ˈmesɪ] ADJ (*comp* **-ier**, *superl* **-iest**) (*dirty:* *clothes*) sporco(-a); (: *job*) che insudicia; (*untidy*) disordinato(-a); (*confused:* *situation*) ingarbugliato(-a); **she's such a messy person!** è una persona talmente pasticciona!; **painting can be a messy activity** dipingere è un'attività con cui ci si può sporcare molto; **her writing is very messy** ha una scrittu- raccia

Met [met] N ABBR; **the Met 1** (*USA:* = the Metropolitan Op- era) **2** (*Brit:* = the Metropolitan Police)

met [met] PT, PP *of* **meet**

me·tab·o·lism [məˈtæbəˌlɪzəm] N metabolismo

met·al [ˈmetl] N metallo; **road metal** pietrisco ♦ ADJ in metal- lo ♦ VT massicciare

me·tal·lic [mɪˈtælɪk] ADJ metallico(-a)

met·al·lur·gy [meˈtæləʤɪ] N metallurgia

metal·work [ˈmetlˌwɜːk] N (*craft*) lavorazione *f* del metallo

meta·mor·pho·sis [ˌmetəˈmɔːfəsɪs] N (*pl* **metamorphoses** [ˌmetəˈmɔːfəsiːz]) metamorfosi *f inv*

meta·phor [ˈmetəfəˈ] N metafora

meta·phys·ics [ˌmetəˈfɪzɪks] NSG metafisica

mete [miːt] VI: **to mete out** (*punishment*) infliggere

me·teor [ˈmiːtɪəˈ] N meteora

me·teor·ic [ˌmiːtɪˈɒrɪk] ADJ meteorico(-a); (*fig*) fulmineo(-a)

me·teor·ite [ˈmiːtɪəˌraɪt] N meteorite *m*

me·teoro·logi·cal [ˌmiːtɪərəˈlɒʤɪkəl] ADJ meteorologico(-a)

me·teor·ol·ogy [ˌmiːtɪəˈrɒləʤɪ] N meteorologia

me·ter [ˈmiːtəˈ] N (*gen*) contatore *m*; (*parking meter*) parchime- tro; **electricity meter** contatore dell'elettricità

me·ter [ˈmiːtəˈ] N (*USA*) = **metre**

me·thane [ˈmiːθeɪn] N metano

meth·od [ˈmeθəd] N **1** (*manner, way*) metodo, sistema *m*; **my method of working** il mio metodo di lavoro; **method of payment** modo *or* modalità *fpl* di pagamento **2** (*orderliness*) metodo; **there's method in his madness** la sua follia non è priva di logica

me·thodi·cal [mɪˈθɒdɪkəl] ADJ metodico(-a)

Meth·od·ist [ˈmeθədɪst] ADJ, N metodista *m/f*

meth·yl·at·ed spir·it [ˈmeθɪˌleɪtɪdˈspɪrɪt] N , **methylated spirits** NPL (*Brit*) alcol *m inv* denaturato

me·ticu·lous [mɪˈtɪkjʊləs] ADJ meticoloso(-a)

me·tre, me·ter (*USA*) [ˈmiːtəˈ] N metro

met·ric [ˈmetrɪk] ADJ metrico(-a); **to go metric** adottare il sistema metrico decimale

met·ri·cal [ˈmetrɪkəl] ADJ (*also Poetry*) metrico(-a)

met·ri·ca·tion [ˌmetrɪˈkeɪʃən] N conversione *f* al sistema metrico decimale

metric system N sistema *m* metrico decimale

metric ton N tonnellata

metro [ˈmetrəʊ] N metro *m inv*

met·ro·nome [ˈmetrəˌnəʊm] N metronomo

me·tropo·lis [mɪˈtrɒpəlɪs] N metropoli *f inv*

met·ro·poli·tan [ˌmetrəˈpɒlɪtən] ADJ metropolitano(-a)

Metropolitan Police N (*Brit*): **the Metropolitan Police** la polizia di Londra

met·tle [ˈmetl] N: **to be on one's mettle** essere pronto(-a) a dare il meglio di se stesso(-a)

mew [mjuː] N miagolio ♦ VI miagolare

mews flat [mjuːzˈflæt] N (*Brit*) appartamentino ricavato da una *vecchia scuderia*

Mexi·can [ˈmeksɪkən] ADJ, N messicano(-a)

Mexi·co [ˈmeksɪkəʊ] N il Messico

Mexico City N Città *f inv* del Messico

mez·za·nine [ˈmezəniːn] N (*also:* **mezzanine floor**) mezza- nino

MFA [ˌemefˈeɪ] N ABBR (*USA:* = *Master of Fine Arts*) master *m inv* in Belle Arti

mfr ABBR **1** = **manufacture 2** = **manufacturer**

mg ABBR (= *milligram*) mg

Mgr ABBR **1** (= *Monseigneur, Monsignor*) mons. **2** (*Comm*) = **manager**

MHz ABBR (= *megahertz*) MHz

MI ABBR (*USA Post:* = Michigan)

MI5 [ˌemaɪˈfaɪv] N ABBR (*Brit:* = *Military Intelligence 5*) agenzia *di controspionaggio*

MI6 [ˌemaɪˈsɪks] N ABBR (*Brit:* = *Military Intelligence 6*) agenzia *di spionaggio*

MIA [ˌemaɪˈeɪ] ABBR (*USA*) *see* **missing in action**

mi·aow [miːˈaʊ] N miao ♦ VI miagolare

mic [maɪk] N ABBR (*fam*) = **mike**

mice [maɪs] NPL *of* **mouse**

Mich. ABBR (*USA:* = Michigan)

Mi·chi·gan [ˈmɪʃɪgən] il Michigan

micro– [ˈmaɪkrəʊ] PREF micro-

mi·crobe [ˈmaɪkrəʊb] N microbio, microbo

micro·bi·ol·ogy [ˌmaɪkrəʊbaɪˈɒləʤɪ] N microbiologia

micro·chip [ˈmaɪkrəʊˌtʃɪp] N (*Elec*) microcircuito integrato, microchip *m inv*

micro·com·put·er [ˌmaɪkrəʊkəmˈpjuːtəˈ] N microcomputer *m inv*

micro·cosm [ˈmaɪkrəʊˌkɒzəm] N microcosmo

micro·eco·nom·ics [ˌmaɪkrəʊˌiːkəˈnɒmɪks] NSG microecono- mia

micro·fiche [ˈmaɪkrəʊˌfiːʃ] N microfiche *f inv*

micro·film [ˈmaɪkrəʊˌfɪlm] N microfilm *m inv* ♦ VT microfil- mare

micro·light [ˈmaɪkrəʊˌlaɪt] N aereo *m* biposto, *inv*

mi·crom·eter [maɪˈkrɒmɪtəˈ] N micrometro, palmer *m inv*

micro·phone [ˈmaɪkrəˌfəʊn] N microfono

micro·pro·ces·sor [ˌmaɪkrəʊˈprəʊsesəˈ] N microprocessore *m*

micro·scooter [ˈmaɪkrəʊˌskuːtəˈ] N monopattino

micro·scope [ˈmaɪkrəskəʊp] N microscopio; **light mi- croscope** microscopio ottico; **electron microscope** mi- croscopio elettronico; **under the microscope** al microscopio

micro·scop·ic [ˌmaɪkrəˈskɒpɪk], **micro·scop·ical** [ˌmaɪkrə ˈskɒpɪkəl] ADJ microscopico(-a)

micro·wav·able, microwaveable [ˈmaɪkrəʊˌweɪvəbl] ADJ adatto(-a) al forno a microonde

micro·wave [ˈmaɪkrəʊˌweɪv] N microonda; (*also:* **microwave oven**) (forno a) microonde *m*

mid [mɪd] ADJ: **mid morning** a metà (della) mattina; **mid afternoon** metà pomeriggio; **in mid journey** a metà del viaggio; **in mid June** a metà giugno; **in mid air** a mezz'aria; **to leave sth in mid air** (*fig*) lasciare qc in sospeso; **in mid Atlantic** in mezzo all'Atlantico; **he's in his mid thirties** avrà circa trentacinque anni

mid·day [ˌmɪdˈdeɪ] N mezzogiorno; **at midday** a mezzogior- no ♦ ADJ di mezzogiorno

mid·dle [ˈmɪdl] ADJ (*of place*) di mezzo, centrale; (*in quality, size*) medio(-a); **the middle seat** il sedile di mezzo; **the mid- dle chair in the row** la sedia nel centro della fila ♦ N (*centre*) mezzo, centro; (*fam: waist*) vita, cintura; **in the middle** in mezzo; **in the middle let's put ...** e in mezzo mettiamo...; **in the middle of** in mezzo a; **the car was in the middle of the road** la macchina era in mezzo alla strada; **the potatoes were still raw in the middle** le patate erano ancora crude dentro; **she was in the middle of her exams** era sotto esa- me; **in the middle of the field** in mezzo al campo; **a village in the middle of nowhere** un paese sperduto; **in the middle of summer** in piena estate; **in the middle of the night** nel cuore della notte, a notte fonda; **I'm in the middle of read- ing it** sto proprio leggendolo ora

middle age N mezza età *f inv*

middle-aged [ˌmɪdlˈeɪʤd] ADJ di mezza età

Middle Ages NPL: **the Middle Ages** il Medioevo

middle class N: **the middle class(es)** ≈ la borghesia

Middle East N: **the Middle East** il Medio Oriente

middle·man [ˈmɪdlˌmæn] N (*pl* **-men**) (*gen*) intermediario; (*Comm*) (agente *m*) rivenditore, *m*

middle management N quadri *mpl* intermedi

middle name N secondo nome *m*

middle-of-the-road [ˌmɪdləvðəˈrəʊd] ADJ moderato(-a)

middle school N ≈ scuola media (*per ragazzi dagli 8 o 9 anni ai 12 o 13 anni in Gran Bretagna e dagli 11 anni ai 14 anni negli Stati Uniti*)

middle·weight [ˈmɪdlˌweɪt] (*Boxing*) ADJ dei pesi medi ♦ N peso medio

mid·dling [ˈmɪdlɪŋ] ADJ così così, medio(-a)

midge [mɪdʒ] N moscerino; (*biting*) pappataci *m inv*

midg·et [ˈmɪdʒɪt] N nano(-a)

midi system [ˈmɪdɪˌsɪstəm] N compatto

Mid·lands [ˈmɪdləndz] NPL: **the Midlands** le contee del centro dell'Inghilterra

mid·night [ˈmɪdˌnaɪt] N mezzanotte *f*; **at midnight** a mezzanotte ♦ ADJ (*gen*) di mezzanotte; (*attack*) a mezzanotte

mid·riff [ˈmɪdrɪf] N (*diaphragm*) diaframma *m*; (*stomach*) stomaco

midst [mɪdst] N: **in the midst of** in mezzo a; (*during*) durante; **in our midst** tra di noi, in mezzo a noi

mid·sum·mer [ˌmɪdˈsʌməʳ] N piena estate *f*

mid·way [ˌmɪdˈweɪ] ADV, ADJ: **midway (between)** a metà strada (fra); **midway between London and Worcester** a metà strada tra Londra e Worcester; **midway through the afternoon** a metà pomeriggio; **a midway point** un punto a metà strada

mid·week [ˌmɪdˈwiːk] ADV, ADJ a metà settimana

mid·wife [ˈmɪdˌwaɪf] N (*pl* **-wives**) ostetrica

mid·wife·ry [ˈmɪdˌwɪfərɪ] N ostetricia

mid·win·ter [ˌmɪdˈwɪntəʳ] N pieno inverno

miffed [mɪft] ADJ (*fam*) seccato(-a), stizzito(-a)

might¹ [maɪt] PT *of* **may**

might² [maɪt] N forza, potere *m*, forze *fpl*; **with all one's might** con tutte le proprie forze

mighty [ˈmaɪtɪ] ADJ (*comp* **-ier**, *superl* **-iest**) (*ruler, nation*) forte, potente; (*warrior*) possente; (*ocean*) vasto(-a); **a mighty bang** un forte colpo ♦ ADV (*fam*) molto; **I'm mighty proud of it** ne sono molto orgoglioso

mi·graine [ˈmiːgreɪn] N emicrania

mi·grant [ˈmaɪgrənt] ADJ (*bird, animal*) migratore(-trice); (*worker*) emigrante, emigrato(-a); (*herdsman*) nomade ♦ N (*see adj*) migratore(-trice); emigrante *m/f*; nomade *m/f*

mi·grate [maɪˈgreɪt] VI (*bird*) migrare; (*worker*) emigrare

mi·gra·tion [maɪˈgreɪʃən] N (*see vb*) migrazione *f*; emigrazione *f*

mike, mic [maɪk] N ABBR (*fam*: = *microphone*) microfono

Mi·lan [mɪˈlæn] N Milano *f*

mild [maɪld] ADJ (*comp* **-er**, *superl* **-est**) (*climate, punishment, weather*) mite; (*character, person, cheese, voice*) dolce; (*flavour, taste*) delicato(-a), non piccante; (*curry*) non piccante; (*illness, sedative, beer, cigar*) leggero(-a); (*effect*) blando(-a); **it's mild today** non fa freddo oggi; **the winters are quite mild** gli inverni sono abbastanza miti; **mild soap** sapone neutro ♦ N (*Brit*) birra leggera

mil·dew [ˈmɪldjuː] N muffa

mild·ly [ˈmaɪldlɪ] ADV (*gently*) gentilmente, dolcemente, delicatamente; (*slightly*) vagamente; **to put it mildly** (*fam*) per usare un eufemismo, a dir poco

mild·ness [ˈmaɪldnɪs] N (*of climate, punishment, weather, effect*) mitezza; (*of character, person*) mitezza, dolcezza; (*of cheese, dish*) sapore *m* delicato; (*of sedative, beer, cigar*) leggerezza; (*of illness*) non gravità *f inv*

mile [maɪl] N miglio (*1609, 33 m*); **nautical mile** miglio nautico; **to do 20 miles per gallon** ≈ fare cento chilometri con 14 litri; **miles and miles** ≈ chilometri e chilometri; **we walked for miles!** abbiamo fatto chilometri a piedi!; **they live miles away** abitano lontanissimo

mile·age [ˈmaɪlɪdʒ] N ≈ chilometraggio; **what mileage does your car do?** ≈ quanti chilometri al litro fa la tua macchina?

mileage allowance N ≈ rimborso per chilometro

mile·om·eter [maɪˈlɒmɪtəʳ] N (*Brit*) = **milometer**

mile·stone [ˈmaɪlˌstəʊn] N (*also fig*) pietra miliare

mi·lieu [ˈmiːljɜː] N ambiente *m* sociale

mili·tant [ˈmɪlɪtənt] ADJ, N militante *m/f*

mili·ta·rism [ˈmɪlɪtəˌrɪzəm] N militarismo

mili·ta·ris·tic [ˌmɪlɪtəˈrɪstɪk] ADJ militaristico(-a)

mili·tary [ˈmɪlɪtərɪ] ADJ militare ♦ NPL: **the military** i militari, l'esercito

military service N servizio militare

mili·tate [ˈmɪlɪˌteɪt] VI: **to militate against** pregiudicare, essere di ostacolo a

mi·li·tia [mɪˈlɪʃə] N milizia, milizie *fpl*

milk [mɪlk] N latte *m*; **tea with milk** tè con il latte; **it's no good crying over spilt milk** (*Proverb*) è inutile piangere sul latte versato ♦ VT (*cow*) mungere; (*fig: person*) spillare quattrini a; (: *situation*) sfruttare fino in fondo

milk float N (*Brit*) furgone *m* del lattaio

milk·ing [ˈmɪlkɪŋ] N mungitura

milk·man [ˈmɪlkmən] N (*pl* **-men**) lattaio

milk shake N frappé *m inv*, frullato

milk tooth N dente *m* di latte

milk truck N (*USA*) = **milk float**

milky [ˈmɪlkɪ] ADJ (*comp* **-ier**, *superl* **-iest**) (*substance*) lattiginoso(-a); (*colour*) latteo(-a); (*coffee*) con tanto latte

Milky Way N: **the Milky Way** la Via Lattea

mill [mɪl] N 1 (*gen*) mulino; (*Industry: for grain*) macina; (*also*: **windmill**) mulino a vento; (*small: for coffee, pepper*) macinino; **to go through the mill** (*fig*) passare un periodo duro; **to put sb through the mill** (*fig*) mettere qn sotto torchio 2 (*factory*) fabbrica, stabilimento; **a woollen mill** un lanificio ♦ VT (*coffee, pepper, flour*) macinare; (*metal*) laminare; (*coin*) zigrinare

▸ **mill about, mill around** VI + ADV (*crowd*) brulicare, formicolare

mil·len·nium [mɪˈlenɪəm] N (*pl* **millennia**) (*period*) millennio; (*anniversary*) millenario; **the millennium** periodo (futuro) di pace e felicità; **millennium bug** baco del millennio

mil·ler [ˈmɪləʳ] N mugnaio

mil·let [ˈmɪlɪt] N miglio

milli– [ˈmɪlɪ] PREF milli-

mil·li·gram, mil·li·gramme [ˈmɪlɪˌgræm] N milligrammo

mil·li·li·tre, mil·li·li·ter (*USA*) [ˈmɪlɪˌliːtəʳ] N millilitro

mil·li·metre, mil·li·meter (*USA*) [ˈmɪlɪˌmiːtəʳ] N millimetro

mil·li·ner [ˈmɪlɪnəʳ] N modista

mil·li·nery [ˈmɪlɪnərɪ] N (articoli *mpl* di) modisteria

mil·lion [ˈmɪljən] N 1 milione *m*; **a million women** un milione di donne; **two million euros** due milioni di euro; **thanks a million!** (*fam*) grazie mille!; **she's one in a million** (*fam*) come lei ce ne sono poche; **millions of** (*fam*) migliaia di, miliardi di; **you look like a million dollars** (*fam*) sei in forma smagliante

mil·lion·aire [ˌmɪljəˈneəʳ] N ≈ miliardario(-a)

mil·lionth [ˈmɪljənθ] ADJ milionesimo(-a) ♦ N (*in series*) milionesimo(-a); (*fraction*) milionesimo

mil·li·pede [ˈmɪlɪˌpiːd] N millepiedi *m inv*

mill·stone [ˈmɪlˌstəʊn] N macina, mola; **it's a millstone round his neck** è un grosso peso per lui, è una palla al piede per lui

mill·wheel [ˈmɪlˌwiːl] N ruota di mulino

mi·lom·eter, mile·om·eter [maɪˈlɒmətəʳ] N (*Brit*) ≈ contachilometri *m inv*

mime [maɪm] N (*play*) mimo; (*skill, gestures*) mimica; (*actor*) mimo(-a) ♦ VT, VI mimare

mim·ic [ˈmɪmɪk] N imitatore(-trice) ♦ VT (*subj: comedian*) imitare; (: *animal, person*) scimmiottare

mim·ic·ry [ˈmɪmɪkrɪ] N imitazioni *fpl*; (*Zool*) mimetismo

Min. ABBR (*Brit Pol*: = *Ministry*) Min.

min. ABBR 1 (= *minute or minutes*) min 2 (= *minimum*) min

mina·ret [ˌmɪnəˈret] N minareto

mince [mɪns] N (*Brit: Culin*) macinato, carne *f* macinata; **lean mince** carne macinata magra ♦ VT tritare, macinare; **he does not mince (his) words** non ha peli sulla lingua ♦ VI (*in walking*) camminare a passettini; (*in talking*) parlare con affettazione

mince·meat [ˈmɪnsˌmiːt] N composto di frutta secca tritata e spezie usato in pasticceria; **to make mincemeat of** (*fig: person*) ridurre in polpette; (: *argument*) demolire

mince pie N tortino ripieno di frutta secca

minc·er [ˈmɪnsəʳ] N (*for meat*) tritacarne *m inv*; (*all-purpose*) tritatutto *m inv*

minc·ing [ˈmɪnsɪŋ] ADJ affettato(-a), lezioso(-a)

mind [maɪnd] N 1 (*gen*) mente *f*; (*intellect*) intelletto; **a case of mind over matter** una vittoria dello spirito sulla materia; **one of Britain's finest minds** uno dei più grandi cervelli della Gran Bretagna; **I am not clear in my mind about the idea** non ho le idee chiare in proposito; **to be uneasy in**

one's mind avere dei dubbi, essere un po' preoccupato(-a); **what's on your mind?** cosa c'è ti preoccupa?; **I can't get it out of my mind** non riesco a togliermelo dalla mente; **to put** *or* **set** *or* **give one's mind to sth** concentrarsi su qc, applicarsi a qc; **that will take your mind off it** questo ti aiuterà a non pensarci (più); **it'll keep your mind off the exam** ti distrarrà dall'esame; **to bear** *or* **keep sth in mind** (*take account of*) tener presente qc; (*remember*) tenere a mente qc, non dimenticare qc; **I'll bear that in mind** lo terrò presente; **it went right out of my mind** mi è completamente passato di mente, me ne sono completamente dimenticato; **to bring** *or* **call sth to mind** riportare *or* richiamare qc alla mente 2 (*inclination, intention*) intenzione *f*, idea; **to have sb/sth in mind** avere in mente qn/qc; **to have in mind to do sth** avere intenzione *or* in mente di fare qc; **what have you got in mind?** che cos'hai in mente?; **I have a good mind to do it** avrei molta voglia di farlo; **I have half a mind to do it** ho una mezza idea di farlo; **nothing was further from my mind** non mi era nemmeno passato per l'anticamera del cervello; **it never crossed my mind** non mi ha mai sfiorato la mente; **to change one's mind** cambiare idea; **he's changed his mind** ha cambiato idea 3 (*opinion*): **to make up one's mind** decidersi, decidere; **I haven't made up my mind yet** non ho ancora deciso; **to be in two minds about sth** essere incerto(-a) *or* indeciso(-a) su qc; **to be in two minds about doing sth** non sapersi decidere se fare qc o no; **of one mind** della stessa idea; **I am still of the same mind** sono ancora dello stesso parere; **to have a mind of one's own** (*person: think for o.s.*) saper pensare con la propria testa; (: *not conform*) avere delle idee proprie; **to my mind** a mio parere, secondo me 4 (*sanity*) cervello, mente *f*, testa; **to go out of** *or* **lose one's mind** impazzire, perdere la testa; **to be out of one's mind** essere pazzo(-a), essere uscito(-a) di senno, essere fuori di sé; **are you out of your mind?** sei impazzito? ♦ **VT** 1 (*pay attention to, be careful of*) fare attenzione a, stare attento(-a) a; **never mind** (*don't worry*) non preoccuparti; (*it makes no difference*) non importa, non fa niente; **"please mind the step"** "attenti *or* attenzione al gradino"; **mind you don't fall** attento a non cadere, fa' attenzione a non cadere; **mind your language!** bada a come parli!, controlla le tue parole!; **mind you, ...** (*fam*) sì, però va detto che...; **mind your own business!** (*fam*) fatti gli affari tuoi!; **never mind him** non badargli, non fargli caso; **never mind the expense** non costa caro, pazienza!; **don't mind me!** (*iro*) per carità, non fare caso a me! 2 (*attend to, look after: shop, machine, children*) occuparsi di, badare a; **could you mind the baby this afternoon?** puoi occuparti del bambino questo pomeriggio?; **could you mind my bags for a few minutes?** può guardarmi le borse per qualche minuto? 3 (*be put out by, object to*): **I don't mind what he does** non m'importa cosa fa; **which? — I don't mind** quale? — è indifferente; **I don't mind the cold/noise** il freddo/rumore non mi dà noia *or* fastidio; **I don't mind getting up early** non mi dispiace alzarmi presto; **would you mind opening the door?** le dispiace aprire la porta?; **do you mind if I open the window?** — **I don't mind** le dispiace se apro la finestra? — faccia pure!; **I wouldn't mind a cup of tea** prenderei volentieri una tazza di tè

mind-boggling ['maɪnd,bɒglɪŋ] ADJ (*fam*) inconcepibile, incredibile

-minded ['maɪndɪd] ADJ SUFF: **fair-minded** imparziale; **an industrially-minded nation** una nazione orientata verso l'industria

mind·er ['maɪndə'] N (*Brit: child minder*) bambinaia; (: *bodyguard*) guardia del corpo

mind·ful ['maɪndfʊl] ADJ: **mindful of** conscio(-a) *or* consapevole di, attento(-a) a, memore di

mind·less ['maɪndlɪs] ADJ (*violence, crime*) insensato(-a); (*task*) che non richiede nessuna intelligenza, idiota; **mindless vandals** vandali idioti

mine¹ [maɪn] POSS PRON il (la) mio(-a); (*plural*) i (le) miei (mie); **he's a friend of mine** è un mio amico; **is this your coat? - no, mine's black** è tuo questo cappotto? - no, il mio è nero; **this is mine** questo è (il) mio; **this book is mine** questo libro è mio; **these pencils are mine** queste matite sono mie; **your marks are better than mine** i tuoi voti sono migliori dei miei; **her shoes are nicer than mine** le sue scarpe sono più belle delle mie

mine² [maɪn] N 1 (*pit*) miniera; **a coal mine** una miniera di carbone; **to work down the mines** lavorare in miniera; **a mine of information** (*fig*) una miniera di informazioni 2 (*explosive*) mina; **to lay mines** posare delle mine ♦ VT 1 (*coal, metal*) estrarre 2 (*Mil, Naut*) minare ♦ VI fare degli scavi minerari; **to mine for sth** estrarre qc

mine detector N rivelatore *m* di mine

mine·field ['maɪn,fiːld] N (*also fig*) campo minato

min·er ['maɪnə'] N minatore *m*

min·er·al ['mɪnərəl] ADJ (*substance, kingdom*) minerale; (*wealth, deposits, ore*) minerario(-a); **mineral salts** sali *mpl* minerali ♦ N minerale *m*; (*Brit: soft drink*); **minerals** NPL bevande *fpl* gasate

min·er·al·ogy [,mɪnə'rælədʒɪ] N mineralogia

mineral water N acqua minerale

mine·sweeper ['maɪn,swiːpə'] N dragamine *m inv*

min·gle ['mɪŋgl] VT: **to mingle (with)** mescolare *or* mischiare (a *or* con); **excitement mingled with fear** eccitazione mescolata a paura ♦ VI: **to mingle (with)** (*sounds*) mescolarsi *or* mischiarsi (a *or* con); **to mingle with one's guests** mescolarsi agli ospiti; **they ate and mingled** mangiarono e si mescolarono agli ospiti

min·gy ['mɪndʒɪ] ADJ (*Brit fam: person*) tirchio(-a), spilorcio(-a); (: *share, portion, amount*) misero(-a), scarso(-a)

minia·ture ['mɪnɪtʃə'] N miniatura; **in miniature** in miniatura ♦ ADJ (*gen*) in miniatura; (*poodle*) nano(-a)

mini·bar ['mɪnɪbɑː'] N minibar *m inv*, frigobar *m inv*

mini·bus ['mɪnɪˌbʌs] N minibus *m inv*, pulmino

mini·cab ['mɪnɪˌkæb] N (*Brit*) = taxi *m inv*

mini·com·put·er [,mɪnɪkəm'pjuːtə'] N minielaboratore *m*, minicomputer *m inv*

min·im ['mɪnɪm] N (*Brit: Mus*) minima

mini·ma ['mɪnɪmə] NPL *of* minimum

mini·mal ['mɪnɪməl] ADJ minimo(-a)

mini·mal·ist ['mɪnɪməlɪst] ADJ, N minimalista *m/f*

mini·mize ['mɪnɪˌmaɪz] VT minimizzare; (*Comput: window*) ridurre

mini·mum ['mɪnɪməm] N (*pl* minimums *or* minima) minimo; **he does the minimum of work** lavora il meno possibile *or* il minimo indispensabile; **to reduce to a minimum** ridurre al minimo ♦ ADJ minimo(-a); **the minimum temperature** la (temperatura) minima; **minimum wage** salario minimo garantito

minimum lending rate N (*Brit*) ≈ tasso ufficiale di sconto

min·ing ['maɪnɪŋ] N 1 estrazione *f* mineraria, industria mineraria 2 (*Mil, Naut*) posa di mine ♦ ADJ (*industry, engineer, area*) minerario(-a); (*community, family*) di minatori

minion ['mɪnjən] N (*pej*) galoppino

mini-series ['mɪnɪˌsɪəriːz] NSG miniserie *fsg*

mini·skirt ['mɪnɪˌskɜːt] N minigonna

min·is·ter ['mɪnɪstə'] N (*Brit Pol*) ministro; (*Rel*) pastore *m*; **Minister for Defence** Ministro della Difesa; **the Education Minister** il ministro della Pubblica Istruzione ♦ VI: **to minister to** (*sick person*) assistere; **to minister to sb's needs** provvedere ai bisogni di qn; **ministering angel** (*fig*) angelo del paradiso

min·is·terial [,mɪnɪs'tɪərɪəl] ADJ (*Brit Pol*) ministeriale

min·is·try ['mɪnɪstrɪ] N 1 (*Brit Pol*) ministero; **Ministry of Defence** Ministero della Difesa 2 (*Rel*): **the ministry** il ministero sacerdotale; **to go into** *or* **enter the ministry** diventare sacerdote (*or* pastore)

mink [mɪŋk] N visone *m*; **European mink** lutreola

mink coat N pelliccia di visone

Minn. ABBR (*USA:* = Minnesota)

Min·ne·so·ta [,mɪnɪ'səʊtə] N il Minnesota

min·now ['mɪnəʊ] N pesciolino d'acqua dolce

mi·nor ['maɪnə'] ADJ (*also Math, Mus*) minore; (*detail, role*) secondario(-a), di poca importanza; (*importance*) secondario(-a); (*repairs, operation, expense*) piccolo(-a); **a minor problem** un problema secondario; **a minor operation** una piccola operazione ♦ N (*Law*) minore *m/f*, minorenne *m/f* 2 (*USA: Univ*) materia complementare

Mi·nor·ca [mɪ'nɔːkə] N Minorca

mi·nor·ity [maɪ'nɒrɪtɪ] N minoranza; **to be in a minority**

essere in minoranza ♦ ADJ (*verdict*) minoritario(-a); (*government*) di minoranza

min·ster [ˈmɪnstəʳ] N (*Brit*) cattedrale *f* (*annessa a monastero*)

min·strel [ˈmɪnstrəl] N giullare *m*, menestrello

mint¹ [mɪnt] N (*Fin*) zecca; **to be worth a mint (of money)** valere un patrimonio; **the (Royal) Mint**, (*Brit*) **the (US) Mint** (*USA*) la Zecca ♦ ADJ: **in mint condition** in perfette condizioni, che sembra nuovo(-a) di zecca ♦ VT (*coins*) battere, coniare; **he's minting money** (*fig*) sta facendo soldi a palate

mint² [mɪnt] N (*plant*) menta; (*sweet*) mentina, caramella di menta; **would you like a mint?** vuoi una mentina? ♦ ADJ alla menta

minu·et [ˌmɪnjʊˈet] N minuetto

mi·nus [ˈmaɪnəs] PREP (*Math*) meno; (*fam*: *without*) senza; **sixteen minus three** sedici meno tre; **I got a B minus for my French** ho ricevuto (un voto di) B meno in francese; **minus two degrees** due gradi sotto zero; **I found my wallet, minus the money** ho ritrovato il mio portafoglio, ma senza il denaro ♦ ADJ: **minus quantity** (*Math*) quantità *f inv* negativa; **minus sign** (segno) meno *inv* ♦ N (segno) meno *inv*

mi·nus·cule [ˈmɪnəskjuːl] ADJ piccolissimo(-a), minuscolo(-a)

min·ute [mɪnɪt] N 1 (*of time*) minuto; (*of degree*) minuto, primo; **ten minutes** dieci minuti; **it is 5 minutes past 3** sono le 3 e 5 (minuti); **I'll come in a minute** vengo subito *or* tra un attimo; **wait a minute!** (aspetta) un momento!; **come here this minute!** vieni subito!; **I won't be a minute** vengo (*or* torno) subito; (*I've nearly finished*) faccio subito; **at the last minute** all'ultimo momento; **at that minute the phone rang** in quel (preciso) istante suonò il telefono; **tell me the minute he arrives** (non) appena arriva dimmelo; **up to the minute** (*fashions, news*) ultimissimo; (*equipment*) modernissimo 2 **minutes** NPL (*of meeting*) verbale *m*, verbali *mpl*; **to take the minutes of a meeting** redigere i verbali di una riunione

min·ute [maɪˈnjuːt] ADJ (*small*) minuscolo(-a); (*change, improvement*) piccolissimo(-a); (*detailed, exact*) minuzioso(-a); **in minute detail** minuziosamente; **her apartment is minute** il suo appartamento è minuscolo; **a minute amount** una quantità minima

minute book [ˈmɪnɪtˌbʊk] N libro dei verbali

minute hand [ˈmɪnɪtˌhænd] N lancetta dei minuti

mi·nute·ly [maɪˈnjuːtlɪ] ADV (*by a small amount*) di poco; (*in detail*) minuziosamente

mi·nu·tiae [mɪˈnjuːʃɪˌiː] NPL minuzie *fpl*

mira·cle [ˈmɪrəkl] N (*also fig*) miracolo; **it's a miracle that** è un miracolo che + *sub*; **by some miracle** per qualche miracolo; **to work miracles** (*also fig*) far miracoli

mi·racu·lous [mɪˈrækjʊləs] ADJ miracoloso(-a)

mi·rage [ˈmɪrɑːʒ] N miraggio

mire [maɪə] N pantano, melma

mir·ror [ˈmɪrəʳ] N specchio; (*Aut*) specchietto (retrovisore); **she got in the car and adjusted the mirror** è entrata in macchina e ha regolato lo specchietto; **hand mirror** specchio a mano; **pocket mirror** specchietto da borsetta; **to look at o.s. in the mirror** guardarsi allo specchio; **she looked at herself in the mirror** si è guardata allo specchio ♦ VT riflettere, rispecchiare

mirror image N immagine *f* speculare

mirth [mɜːθ] N ilarità *f inv*, gaiezza

mis·ad·ven·ture [ˌmɪsədˈventʃəʳ] N sfortuna, disavventura; **death by misadventure** (*Brit Law*) morte *f* accidentale

mis·an·thro·pist [mɪˈzænθrəpɪst] N misantropo(-a)

mis·ap·ply [ˌmɪsəˈplaɪ] VT impiegare male, usare erroneamente

mis·ap·pre·hen·sion [ˌmɪsˌæprɪˈhenʃən] N equivoco, malinteso; **to be (labouring) under a misapprehension** sbagliarsi

mis·ap·pro·pri·ate [ˌmɪsəˈprəʊprɪˌeɪt] VT appropriarsi indebitamente di

mis·ap·pro·pria·tion [ˌmɪsəˌprəʊprɪˈeɪʃən] N appropriazione *f* indebita

mis·be·have [ˌmɪsbɪˈheɪv] VI comportarsi male

mis·be·hav·iour, mis·be·hav·ior (*USA*) [ˌmɪsbɪˈheɪvjəʳ] N comportamento scorretto

misc. ABBR = **miscellaneous**

mis·cal·cu·late [ˌmɪsˈkælkjʊˌleɪt] VT, VI calcolare male

mis·cal·cu·la·tion [ˈmɪsˌkælkjʊˈleɪʃən] N errore *m* di calcolo

mis·car·riage [ˌmɪsˈkærɪdʒ] N 1 (*Med*) aborto spontaneo 2 **miscarriage of justice** (*fig*) errore *m* giudiziario

mis·car·ry [ˌmɪsˈkærɪ] VI 1 (*Med*) abortire 2 (*fail: plans*) andare a monte, fallire

mis·cel·la·neous [ˌmɪsəˈleɪnɪəs] ADJ (*items*) vario(-a), diverso(-a); (*collection*) misto(-a), eterogeneo(-a); **miscellaneous expenses** spese *fpl* varie; **miscellaneous items** articoli *mpl* vari

mis·cel·la·ny [mɪˈselənɪ] N misto; (*Literature*) miscellanea, raccolta; (*Radio, TV*) selezione *f*

mis·chance [ˌmɪsˈtʃɑːns] N: **by (some) mischance** per sfortuna

mis·chief [ˈmɪstʃɪf] N (*roguishness*) furberia; (*naughtiness*) birichinate *fpl*; (*maliciousness*) cattiveria, malizia; (*harm*) male *m*, danno; **he's always getting into mischief** ne combina sempre una; **to keep sb out of mischief** tenere qn occupato(-a) così che non possa combinare guai; **full of mischief** birichino(-a); **to make mischief (for sb)** rendere la vita difficile (a qn); **to make mischief between** seminare zizzania tra; **to do o.s. a mischief** (*Brit: hum*) farsi male

mis·chie·vous [ˈmɪstʃɪvəs] ADJ (*roguish*) malizioso(-a); (*child*) birichino(-a); (*harmful*) pieno(-a) di cattiveria; **mischievous rumours** (*troublemaking*) malignità *fpl*

mis·con·cep·tion [ˌmɪskənˈsepʃən] N (*false idea/opinion*) idea/convinzione *f* sbagliata; (*misunderstanding*) malinteso

mis·con·duct [ˌmɪsˈkɒndʌkt] N cattiva condotta, comportamento scorretto; (*sexual*) adulterio; **professional misconduct** reato professionale

mis·con·strue [ˌmɪskənˈstruː] VT interpretare male

mis·count [ˌmɪsˈkaʊnt] N (*gen*) calcolo errato; (*in election*) conteggio erroneo ♦ VT contare male ♦ VI sbagliare il conto

mis·deed [ˌmɪsˈdiːd] N (*old*) misfatto

mis·de·mean·our, mis·de·mean·or (*USA*) [ˌmɪsdɪˈmiːnəʳ] N infrazione *f*, trasgressione *f*, misfatto

mis·di·rect [ˌmɪsdɪˈrekt] VT (*letter*) mettere l'indirizzo sbagliato su; (*person*) dare indicazioni sbagliate a, mal indirizzare; (*operation*) organizzare male; (*Law: jury*) dare istruzioni sbagliate a

mi·ser [ˈmaɪzəʳ] N avaro(-a)

mis·er·able [ˈmɪzərəbl] ADJ 1 (*unhappy*) infelice; (*deplorable: sight, failure*) penoso(-a); **to feel miserable** sentirsi avvilito(-a) *or* giù di morale; (*physically*) sentirsi a terra; **don't look so miserable!** non fare quella faccia da funerale!; **a miserable life** una vita infelice 2 (*filthy, wretched*) miserabile; **miserable weather** brutto tempo 3 (*contemptible*) miserabile; **a miserable £2** 2 miserabili sterline; **a miserable failure** un fiasco

mis·er·ably [ˈmɪzərəblɪ] ADV (*smile, answer*) tristemente; (*fail, live, pay*) miseramente; **the attempt failed miserably** il tentativo è fallito miseramente

mi·ser·ly [ˈmaɪzəlɪ] ADJ taccagno(-a), avaro(-a)

❑ **miserly** is not translated by the Italian word *miserabile*

mis·ery [ˈmɪzərɪ] N (*unhappiness*) tristezza; (*pain*) sofferenza, tormento, dolore *m*; (*wretchedness*) miseria; (*fam: person*) lagna; **to put an animal out of its misery** uccidere un animale (per non farlo soffrire più); **to put sb out of his misery** (*fig*) mettere fine alle sofferenze di qn; **to make sb's life a misery** rovinare la vita a qn

mis·fire [ˌmɪsˈfaɪəʳ] VI (*gun, plan, joke*) far cilecca; (*engine*) perdere colpi

mis·fit [ˈmɪsˌfɪt] N (*person*) disadattato(-a), spostato(-a)

mis·for·tune [mɪsˈfɔːtʃən] N disgrazia, sventura, sfortuna

mis·giv·ing [mɪsˈgɪvɪŋ] N (*often pl*) diffidenza, apprensione *f*, dubbi *mpl*, sospetti *mpl*; **to have misgivings about sth** essere diffidente verso qc, avere dei dubbi su qc

mis·guid·ed [ˌmɪsˈgaɪdɪd] ADJ (*person*) malaccorto(-a); (*conduct*) poco assennato(-a); **a misguided belief** una convinzione sbagliata

mis·han·dle [ˌmɪsˈhændl] VT (*object*) maneggiare senza precauzioni; (*person*) non prendere per il verso giusto; (*mismanage*) condurre male; **he mishandled the whole situation** ha sbagliato tutto

mis·hap ['mɪs,hæp] N incidente m; **without mishap** senza incidenti; **a minor mishap** una piccola disavventura

mis·hear ['mɪs'hɪə'] (pt, pp **misheard**) VT, VI capire male

mish-mash ['mɪʃ,mæʃ] N (fam) minestrone m, guazzabuglio

mis·in·form [,mɪsɪn'fɔːm] VT informare male, dare informazioni erronee

mis·in·ter·pret [,mɪsɪn'tɜːprɪt] VT interpretare male

mis·in·ter·pre·ta·tion [,mɪsɪn,tɜːprɪ'teɪʃən] N interpretazione errata f; **open to misinterpretation** che dà adito ad un'interpretazione errata

mis·judge [,mɪs'dʒʌdʒ] VT (distance, amount) calcolare male; (person) giudicare male; **I may have misjudged him** posso averlo giudicato male; **the driver misjudged the bend** il guidatore ha valutato male la curva

mis·lay [,mɪs'leɪ] (pt, pp **mislaid**) VT smarrire

mis·lead [,mɪs'liːd] (pt, pp **misled**) VT trarre in inganno, sviare; **to mislead sb into thinking that ...** far credere a qn che..., indurre qn a credere che...

mis·lead·ing [,mɪs'liːdɪŋ] ADJ ingannevole, fuorviante

mis·led [mɪs'led] PT, PP of **mislead**

mis·man·age [,mɪs'mænɪdʒ] VT amministrare or gestire or condurre male

mis·man·age·ment [,mɪs'mænɪdʒmənt] N cattiva amministrazione f or gestione f

mis·no·mer [,mɪs'nəʊmə'] N: **to call her a cook is a misnomer** non si può certo definirla una cuoca

mi·sogy·nist [mɪ'sɒdʒɪnɪst] N misogino

mis·place [,mɪs'pleɪs] VT 1 (mislay) smarrire 2 **to be misplaced** (trust) essere malriposto(-a)

mis·print ['mɪs,prɪnt] N errore m di stampa, refuso

mis·pro·nounce [,mɪsprə'naʊns] VT pronunciare male

mis·quote [,mɪs'kwəʊt] VT citare erroneamente

mis·read [,mɪs'riːd] (pt, pp **misread**) VT leggere male; (misinterpret) interpretare male

mis·rep·re·sent ['mɪs,reprɪ'zent] VT (facts) travisare; (person) dare un'impressione sbagliata di

miss¹ [mɪs] N (shot) colpo mancato or a vuoto; **it was a near miss** (fig) c'è mancato poco or un pelo; **we had a near miss** per poco non ci è successo un incidente; **to give sth a miss** (fam) lasciar perdere qc ◆ VT 1 (gen: train, opportunity, film) perdere; (appointment, class) mancare a, saltare; (target) mancare; (remark: not hear) non sentire; (: not understand) non capire; (omit: meal, page) saltare; **hurry or you'll miss the bus** affrettati o perderai l'autobus; **it's too good an opportunity to miss** è un'opportunità da non perdere assolutamente; **you haven't missed much!** non hai perso molto!; **he missed the target** ha mancato il bersaglio; **you've missed a page** hai saltato una pagina; **I missed you at the station** non ti ho visto alla stazione; **sorry to have missed you** mi dispiace di non averti trovato; **to miss the boat** or **bus** (fig) perdere il treno, lasciarsi sfuggire (di mano) l'occasione; **we must have missed the sign for London** ci dev'essere sfuggito il cartello per Londra; **you can't miss our house, it's ...** non puoi sbagliarti: la nostra casa è...; **don't miss this film** non perderti questo film; **I missed what you said** mi è sfuggito quello che hai detto; **you're missing the point** non capisci 2 (escape or avoid: accident, bad weather) evitare, scampare; **the bus just missed the wall** l'autobus per un pelo non è andato a finire contro il muro; **he narrowly missed being run over** per poco non è stato investito 3 (notice loss of: money) accorgersi di non avere più; **then I missed my wallet** allora mi sono accorto che mi mancava or che non avevo più il portafoglio 4 (regret the absence of: person): **I miss you so** mi manchi tanto; **I miss him/it** sento la sua mancanza, mi manca; **I miss my family** sento la mancanza della mia famiglia; **do you miss Trieste?** senti la mancanza di or ti manca Trieste? ◆ VI (person, shot) mancare il bersaglio; **you can't miss!** non puoi fallire!

▸ **miss out on** VI + ADV + PREP (fun, party) perdersi; (chance, bargain) lasciarsi sfuggire; **I feel I've been missing out on life** sento di non aver goduto la vita come avrei potuto

miss² [mɪs] N 1 signorina 2 **Miss Smith** la signorina Smith; (on envelope) Sig.na Smith; (in letter): **Dear Miss Smith** Cara Signorina Smith; (more frm) Gentile Signorina Smith

mis·sal ['mɪsəl] N messale m

mis·shap·en [,mɪs'ʃeɪpən] ADJ deforme

mis·sile ['mɪsaɪl] N (Mil) missile m; (frm: projectile) proiettile m

missile base N base f missilistica

mis·sile launch·er ['mɪsaɪl,lɔːntʃə'] N lanciamissili m inv

mis·sing ['mɪsɪŋ] ADJ (not able to be found) smarrito(-a), perso(-a); (not there) mancante; (person, also Mil) disperso(-a); **to be missing** (thing) mancare; (persona) mancare all'appello; **to go missing** sparire; **there are several books missing** mancano diversi libri; **the missing link** l'anello mancante; **missing in action** (Mil) disperso(-a) durante un'azione militare; **missing person** disperso(-a), scomparso(-a); **reported missing** (Mil) dato(-a) per disperso

mis·sion ['mɪʃən] N (all senses) missione f; **on a mission to sb** in missione da qn; **it's her mission in life** è la sua missione nella vita

mis·sion·ary ['mɪʃənrɪ] N (Rel) missionario(-a)

Mis·sis·sip·pi [,mɪsɪ'sɪpɪ] il Mississippi

Mis·sou·ri [mɪ'zʊərɪ] il Missouri

mis·spell [,mɪs'spel] (pt, pp **misspelled** or **misspelt**) VT sbagliare l'ortografia di

mis·spent ['mɪs,spent] ADJ: **his misspent youth** la sua gioventù dissoluta

mist [mɪst] N (Met) foschia, nebbia, nebbiolina; (on glass) appannamento; (of perfume) nuvola; **through a mist of tears** attraverso un velo di lacrime; **lost in the mists of time** (fig) perduto nella notte dei tempi ◆ VI (also: **mist over**: eyes) velarsi; (also: **mist over** or **up**) (scene, landscape) annebbiarsi, offuscarsi; (mirror, window, windscreen) appannarsi

❑ **mist** is not translated by the Italian word misto

mis·take [mɪs'teɪk] (pt **mistook**, pp **mistaken**) N errore m, sbaglio; **to make a mistake** (in writing, calculating) fare uno sbaglio or un errore; **he makes a lot of mistakes when he speaks English** fa molti errori quando parla in inglese; **a spelling mistake** un errore di ortografia; **to make a mistake (about sb/sth)** sbagliarsi (sul conto di qn/su qc); **my mistake!** è colpa mia!; **you're making a big mistake** commetti un grosso or grave errore; **I made the mistake of trusting him** ho fatto l'errore di fidarmi di lui; **by mistake** per sbaglio; **he took my hat in mistake for his** ha preso il mio cappello credendo fosse il suo; **there must be some mistake** ci dev'essere un errore; **make no mistake (about it)** non aver paura, sta' tranquillo ◆ VT (meaning, remark) capir male, fraintendere; (road) sbagliare; (time) sbagliarsi su; **to mistake A for B** prendere or scambiare A per B; **he mistook me for my sister** mi ha scambiato per mia sorella

mis·tak·en [mɪs'teɪkən] PP of **mistake** ◆ ADJ (wrong: idea, conclusion) sbagliato(-a), errato(-a); (misplaced: loyalty, generosity) malriposto(-a); **in the mistaken belief that ...** credendo erroneamente che...; **to be mistaken** sbagliarsi; **if I'm not mistaken** se non sbaglio; **if you think I'm going to pay, you're mistaken** se pensi che ho intenzione di pagare ti sbagli

mistaken identity N errore m di persona

mis·tak·en·ly [mɪs'teɪkənlɪ] ADV (believe) erroneamente; (by mistake) per errore

mis·ter ['mɪstə'] N (fam) signore m; see also **Mr**

mis·tle·toe ['mɪsl,təʊ] N vischio

mis·took [mɪs'tʊk] PT of **mistake**

mis·trans·la·tion [,mɪstrænz'leɪʃən] N errore m di traduzione, traduzione f errata

mis·treat [mɪs'triːt] VT maltrattare, trattare male

mis·tress ['mɪstrɪs] N 1 (of servant) padrona; **the mistress of the house** la padrona di casa 2 (lover) amante f 3 (Brit Scol: teacher) insegnante f, professoressa

mis·trust [mɪs'trʌst] N: **mistrust (of)** diffidenza (nei confronti di); **a deep mistrust of politicians** una profonda diffidenza nei confronti dei politici ◆ VT (person, motives) diffidare di; (one's own abilities) dubitare di

mis·trust·ful [mɪs'trʌstfʊl] ADJ: **mistrustful (of)** diffidente (nei confronti di)

misty ['mɪstɪ] ADJ (comp **-ier**, superl **-iest**) (day, morning) brumoso(-a), nebbioso(-a); (mirror, window) appannato(-a); **it's misty today** c'è foschia oggi

misty-eyed [,mɪstɪ'aɪd] ADJ trasognato(-a)

mis·under·stand [ˌmɪsʌndəˈstænd] (*pt, pp* **misunderstood**) VT fraintendere, capire male; **maybe I misunderstood you** forse ho frainteso

mis·under·stand·ing [ˌmɪsʌndəˈstændɪŋ] N malinteso, equivoco; **I think there's been some misunderstanding** penso che ci sia stato un malinteso

mis·under·stood [ˌmɪsʌndəˈstʊd] PT, PP *of* **misunderstand** ♦ ADJ incompreso(-a)

mis·use [*n* ˌmɪsˈjuːs, *vb* ˌmɪsˈjuːz] N (*of power, authority*) abuso; (*of word, tool*) uso improprio; (*of resources, time, energies*) cattivo uso ♦ VT (*see n*) abusare di; usare impropriamente; fare cattivo uso di; **he misuses his position** abusa della sua posizione

MIT [ˌemaɪˈtiː] N ABBR (*USA*: = **Massachusetts Institute of Technology**)

mite [maɪt] N **1** (*small quantity*) briciolo; **the widow's mite** (*Bible*) l'obolo della vedova **2** (*Brit: small child*): **poor mite!** povera creaturina! **3** (*Zool*) acaro

mi·ter [ˈmaɪtəʳ] N (*USA*) = **mitre**

miti·gate [ˈmɪtɪˌɡeɪt] VT (*punishment*) mitigare; (*suffering*) alleviare

miti·ga·tion [ˌmɪtɪˈɡeɪʃən] N (*see vb*) mitigazione *f*; alleviamento

mi·tre, mi·ter (*USA*) [ˈmaɪtəʳ] N **1** (*Rel*) mitra **2** (*Tech: also:* **mitre joint**) giunto ad angolo retto

mitt [mɪt] N **1** (*also:* **mitten**) (*with cut-off fingers*) mezzo guanto; (*no separate fingers*) muffola, manopola **2** (*baseball glove*) guantone *m* **3** (*fam*) zampa; **keep your dirty mitts off my stuff!** giù le zampe dalla mia roba!

mix [mɪks] N mescolanza; **the school has a good social mix** gli studenti di questa scuola provengono da diverse classi sociali; **the film is a mix of science fiction and comedy** il film è un misto di fantascienza e commedia; **a cake mix** un preparato per torte ♦ VT mescolare; (*cocktail, sauce*) preparare (mescolando); **mix to a smooth paste** mescolare fino ad ottenere una pasta omogenea; **to mix sth with sth** mischiare qc a qc; **to mix business with pleasure** unire l'utile al dilettevole; **mix the flour with the sugar** mescolate la farina con lo zucchero ♦ VI mescolarsi; **he doesn't mix well** non riesce a legare; **he mixes with all sorts of people** ha a che fare con persone di ogni tipo; **they just don't mix** (*people*) non legano fra di loro; (*patterns*) non stanno bene insieme; **he doesn't mix much** non lega molto con gli altri

  ▸ **mix in** VT + ADV (*eggs*) incorporare

  ▸ **mix together** VT + ADV mescolare

  ▸ **mix up** VT + ADV **1** (*prepare: drink, medicine*) preparare **2** (*get in a muddle: documents*) confondere, mescolare; (*confuse*): **to mix sb/sth up (with)** scambiare qn/qc (per); **the travel agent mixed up the bookings** l'agente di viaggio ha confuso le prenotazioni **3 to mix sb up in sth** (*involve*) coinvolgere *or* immischiare qn in qc; **to be mixed up in sth** essere coinvolto(-a) in qc

mixed [mɪkst] ADJ (*biscuits, nuts*) assortito(-a); (*school*) misto(-a); **in mixed company** in presenza di persone di entrambi i sessi; **we had mixed weather** il tempo è stato un po' bello e un po' brutto; **I've got mixed feelings about it** ho dei sentimenti contrastanti a riguardo; **the announcement got a mixed reception** non tutti hanno accolto favorevolmente l'annuncio; **mixed metaphor** metafora che non sta in piedi; **I'm getting mixed up** sono disorientato

mixed-ability [ˌmɪkstˈbɪlɪtɪ] ADJ (*class, teaching*) alunni di capacità diverse

mixed bag N miscuglio, accozzaglia; **it's a mixed bag** (*fig: fam*) c'è un po' di tutto

mixed blessing N: **it's a mixed blessing** è una cosa buona che ha il suo risvolto negativo

mixed doubles NPL (*Sport*) doppio misto

mixed economy N economia mista

mixed marriage N matrimonio misto

mixed-up [ˌmɪkstˈʌp] ADJ (*person, ideas*) confuso(-a); (*papers*) mescolato(-a), in disordine; **I'm all mixed-up** sono disorientato

mix·er [ˈmɪksəʳ] N **1** (*for food: electric*) frullatore *m*, mixer *m inv*; (: *hand*) frullino **2** (*person*): **he's a good mixer** è molto socievole

mixer tap N (*Brit*) miscelatore *m*

mix·ture [ˈmɪkstʃəʳ] N mistura, miscuglio, mescolanza; (*Med*) sciroppo; (*blend: of tobacco*) miscela; **a mixture of spices** un miscuglio di spezie

mix-up [ˈmɪksˌʌp] N (*fam*) confusione *f*

mkt ABBR = **market**

ml ABBR (= *millilitre(s)*) ml

mm ABBR = *millimetre*) mm

MMS N ABBR (= *multimedia messaging service*) mms *m inv* (*servizio*); **MMS message** mms *m inv*

MN [ˌemˈen] N ABBR **1** (*Brit*: = **Merchant Navy**) **2** (*USA Post*: = **Minnesota**)

MO [ˌemˈəʊ] N ABBR **1** (*Brit*: = **medical officer**) **2** (*fam*: = *modus operandi*) modo d'agire ♦ ABBR (*USA Post*: = **Missouri**)

moan [məʊn] N (*gen*) gemito, lamento; (*complaint*) lamentela, lagna ♦ VI (*gen*) gemere; **to moan (about)** (*fam: complain*) lamentarsi (di)

moan·er [ˈməʊnəʳ] N (*fam*) brontolone(-a)

moan·ing [ˈməʊnɪŋ] N gemiti *mpl*, lamenti *mpl*

moat [məʊt] N fossato

mob [mɒb] N (*of people*) folla, massa; (*disorderly*) calca; (*rioting, violent*) folla inferocita; (*fam: criminal gang*) cricca, banda; **the mob** (*pej: Mafia*) la Mafia; (: *rabble*) la plebaglia ♦ VT (*person*) assalire, accalcarsi intorno a; (*place*) prendere d'assalto, accalcarsi intorno a; **to be mobbed** essere assalito(-a)

mo·bile [ˈməʊbaɪl] ADJ (*gen*) mobile ♦ N (*Art*) mobile *m inv*; (*Brit*) (*telefono*) cellulare *m*, telefonino

mobile home N grande roulotte *f inv* (*utilizzata come domicilio*)

mobile phone N telefonino

mobile shop N (*Brit*) negozio ambulante

mo·bil·ity [məʊˈbɪlɪtɪ] N mobilità *f inv*; (*of applicant*) disponibilità *f inv* a viaggiare

mo·bi·lize [ˈməʊbɪˌlaɪz] VT mobilitare ♦ VI mobilitarsi

moc·ca·sin [ˈmɒkəsɪn] N mocassino

mock [mɒk] ADJ (*gen*) finto(-a), falso(-a); (*battle*) simulato(-a); **a mock exam** una simulazione d'esame; **mock Tudor** in stile Tudor ♦ VT (*ridicule: person*) canzonare, deridere, farsi beffe di; (: *plan, efforts*) ridicolizzare, farsi beffe di; (*mimic*) scimmiottare ♦ VI: **to mock at** farsi beffe di

  ▸ **mock up** VT + ADV costruire un modello di

mock·ery [ˈmɒkərɪ] N (*derision*) scherno, derisione *f*; **it was a mockery of a trial** il processo è stato tutto una farsa; **to make a mockery of** rendere ridicolo(-a)

mock·ing [ˈmɒkɪŋ] ADJ (*gen*) beffardo(-a), derisorio(-a), di scherno

mocking·bird [ˈmɒkɪŋˌbɜːd] N mimo (*uccello*)

mock-up [ˈmɒkˌʌp] N modello dimostrativo, abbozzo

mode [məʊd] N **1** (*gen*) modo, maniera; (*of transport*) mezzo; (*Mus*) modo; (*Comput*) modalità *f inv* **2** (*fashion, also Math*) moda

mod·el [ˈmɒdl] N (*gen, also fig: Archit*) modello; (*small-scale*) modellino; (*also:* **fashion model**) indossatore(-trice), modello(-a); (*also:* **artist's model**) modello(-a); **a model of the castle** un modellino del castello; **it's the basic model** è il modello base; **4-door model** (*of car*) versione *f* 4 porte ♦ VT **1 to model sth on** modellare qc su; **to model sb on** prendere a modello per qn; **to model o.s. on sb** prendere a modello qn **2** (*make a model: in clay*) modellare, plasmare; (: *in wood*) scolpire **3** (*clothes*) indossare ♦ VI (*Art, Phot*) fare da modello(-a), posare; (*fashion*) sfilare, fare l'indossatore(-trice) *or* il (la) modello(-a) ♦ ADJ **1** (*small-scale: village, aircraft*) in miniatura **2** (*prison, school, husband*) modello *inv*

mo·dem [ˈməʊdɛm] N modem *m inv*

mod·er·ate [*adj* ˈmɒdərɪt, *vb* ˈmɒdəˌreɪt] ADJ (*gen*) moderato(-a); (*climate*) temperato(-a); (*size, income*) medio(-a); (*demands, price*) modico(-a), ragionevole; (*language, terms*) misurato(-a); (*quality, ability*) mediocre, modesto(-a); **his views are quite moderate** ha opinioni abbastanza moderate; **a moderate amount of** un po' di; **I do a moderate amount of exercise** faccio un po' di ginnastica ♦ N (*Pol*) moderato(-a) ♦ VT moderare ♦ VI (*pain, wind, anger*) calmarsi, attenuarsi, placarsi

mod·er·ate·ly [ˈmɒdərɪtlɪ] ADV (*act*) con moderazione;

(*expensive, difficult*) non troppo, moderatamente; (*pleased, happy*) abbastanza, discretamente; **moderately priced** a prezzo modico; **it was moderately successful** ha avuto un discreto successo

mod·era·tion [ˌmɒdəˈreɪʃən] N moderazione *f*, misura; **in moderation** (*eat, drink*) in quantità moderata, con moderazione; **patience and moderation** pazienza e moderazione

moderator [ˈmɒdəˌreɪtəʳ] N (*gen*) moderatore(-trice); (*Rel*) *moderatore in importanti riunioni della chiesa presbiteriana*

mod·ern [ˈmɒdən] ADJ moderno(-a); **all modern conveniences** tutti i comfort

mod·erni·za·tion [ˌmɒdənaɪˈzeɪʃən] N rimodernamento, modernizzazione *f*

mod·ern·ize [ˈmɒdəˌnaɪz] VT modernizzare

mod·est [ˈmɒdɪst] ADJ (*all senses*) modesto(-a); **to be modest about sth** non vantarsi di qc

mod·es·ty [ˈmɒdɪstɪ] N modestia; **in all modesty** in tutta modestia

modi·cum [ˈmɒdɪkəm] N: **a modicum of** un minimo di

modi·fi·ca·tion [ˌmɒdɪfɪˈkeɪʃən] N: **modification (to, in)** modifica (a); **to make modifications** fare *or* apportare delle modifiche

modi·fy [ˈmɒdɪˌfaɪ] VT (*change, also Gram*) modificare; (*moderate: demands*) moderare

mod·ish [ˈməʊdɪʃ] ADJ (*liter*) à la page *inv*

modu·lar [ˈmɒdjʊləʳ] ADJ (*furniture, unit*) modulare

modu·late [ˈmɒdjʊˌleɪt] VT modulare

modu·la·tion [ˌmɒdjʊˈleɪʃən] N modulazione *f*

mod·ule [ˈmɒdjuːl] N modulo

Moga·dishu [ˌmɒɡəˈdɪʃuː] N Mogadiscio *f*

mo·gul [ˈməʊɡəl] N 1 (*fig*) magnate *m*, pezzo grosso 2 (*Skiing*) cunetta

mo·hair [ˈməʊˌhɛəʳ] N mohair *m*

Mohammed [məʊˈhæmɪd] = **Muhammad**

moist [mɔɪst] ADJ (*comp* **-er**, *superl* **-est**) (*gen*) umido(-a); (*cake*) soffice; **eyes moist with tears** occhi umidi di lacrime; **sow the seeds in moist soil** piantate i semi nel terreno umido; **this cake is very moist** questa torta è molto soffice

mois·ten [ˈmɔɪsn] VT inumidire; **to moisten one's lips** umettarsi le labbra

mois·ture [ˈmɔɪstʃəʳ] N (*gen*) umidità *f inv*; (*on glass*) vapore *m* condensato

mois·tur·ize [ˈmɔɪstʃəˌraɪz] VT (*skin*) idratare

mois·tur·iz·er [ˈmɔɪstʃəˌraɪzəʳ] N (*prodotto*) idratante *m*

mo·lar [ˈməʊləʳ] ADJ, N molare *m*

mo·las·ses [məʊˈlæsɪz] NSG melassa

mold [məʊld] (*USA*) = **mould**¹

Mol·da·via [mɒlˈdeɪvɪə], **Mol·dova** [mɒlˈdəʊvə] N la Moldavia

Mol·da·vian [mɒlˈdeɪvɪən], **Mol·dovan** [mɒlˈdəʊvən] ADJ, N moldavo(-a)

mole¹ [məʊl] N (*Zool, also fig*) talpa
❏ **mole** is not translated by the Italian word *mole*

mole² [məʊl] N (*on skin*) neo; **I've got a mole on my back** ho un neo sulla schiena

mol·ecule [ˈmɒlɪkjuːl] N molecola

mole·hill [ˈməʊlˌhɪl] N *cumulo di terra vicino alla tana scavata da una talpa*

mo·lest [məʊˈlɛst] VT (*trouble*) importunare; (*harm: Law: sexually*) molestare

mol·lusc, mol·lusk (*USA*) [ˈmɒləsk] N mollusco

molly·coddle [ˈmɒlɪˌkɒdl] VT (*pej*) coccolare, vezzeggiare

Molotov cock·tail [ˈmɒləˌtɒfˈkɒkˌteɪl] N (*bottiglia*) Molotov *f inv*

molt [məʊlt] VI (*USA*) = **moult**

mol·ten [ˈməʊltən] ADJ (*metal*) fuso(-a); (*lava*) allo stato liquido

mom [mɒm] N (*USA fam*) = **mum**¹

mo·ment [ˈməʊmənt] N 1 momento, istante *m*; **(at) any moment** *or* **any moment now** da un momento all'altro; **at the (present) moment, at this moment in time** al momento, in questo momento; **at the last moment** all'ultimo momento; **for a** *or* **one moment** per un momento; **for the moment** per il momento, per ora; **not for a** *or* **one moment** neanche per un istante; **in a moment** (*very soon*) tra un momento;

(*quickly*) in un attimo; **one moment!, wait a moment!** (*aspetta*) un momento *or* un attimo!; **I won't be a moment** vengo (*or* torno) subito; (*I've nearly finished*) faccio subito; **it won't take a moment** è (solo) questione di un attimo; **I've just this moment heard about it** l'ho saputo in questo (preciso) istante; **the moment he arrives** (non) appena arriva; **from the moment I saw him** dal primo momento in cui l'ho visto; **the man of the moment** l'uomo del momento; **"one moment please"** (*Telec*) "attenda, prego" 2 (*Phys*) momento 3 (*frm: importance*) importanza, rilievo

mo·men·tari·ly [ˈməʊməntərɪlɪ] ADV (*for a second*) per un momento; (*USA: very soon*) da un momento all'altro

mo·men·tary [ˈməʊməntərɪ] ADJ momentaneo(-a), passeggero(-a)

mo·men·tous [məʊˈmɛntəs] ADJ (*molto*) importante, di grande importanza

mo·men·tum [məʊˈmɛntəm] N (*Phys*) momento, quantità *f inv* di moto; (*fig*) slancio, impeto, velocità *f inv* acquisita; **to gather** *or* **gain momentum** (*vehicle, person*) acquistare *or* prendere velocità, aumentare di velocità; (*fig*) prendere *or* guadagnare terreno; **to lose momentum** (*vehicle, person*) perdere velocità; (*fig*) perdere vigore

mom·my [ˈmɒmɪ] N (*USA*) = **mummy**¹

Mon. ABBR (= *Monday*) lun. (= *lunedì*)

Mona·co [ˈmɒnəˌkəʊ] N Monaco *f* (*Principato*)

mon·arch [ˈmɒnək] N monarca *m*

mon·ar·chist [ˈmɒnəkɪst] ADJ, N monarchico(-a)

mon·ar·chy [ˈmɒnəkɪ] N monarchia

mon·as·tery [ˈmɒnəstərɪ] N monastero

mo·nas·tic [məˈnæstɪk] ADJ monastico(-a)

Mon·day [ˈmʌndɪ] N lunedì *m inv*; *see* **Tuesday**

Mon·egasque [ˌmɒnəˈɡæsk] ADJ, N monegasco(-a)

mon·etar·ist [ˈmʌnɪtərɪst] ADJ monetaristico(-a) ♦ N monetarista *m/f*

mon·etary [ˈmʌnɪtərɪ] ADJ monetario(-a)

mon·ey [ˈmʌnɪ] N denaro, soldi *mpl*; **paper money** banconote *fpl*; **Italian money** moneta italiana; **I need to change some money** devo cambiare dei soldi; **there's money in it** c'è da farci i soldi; **I've got no money left** non ho più neanche una lira; **to make money** (*person*) fare (i) soldi; (*business*) rendere; **we didn't make any money on that deal** in quell'affare non ci abbiamo guadagnato niente; **to be in the money** nuotare nell'oro, essere pieno(-a) di soldi; **to get one's money's worth** spender bene i propri soldi; **to earn good money** guadagnare bene; **money doesn't grow on trees!** non me li tirano mica dietro i soldi!; **I'm not made of money** non nuoto nell'oro; **your money or your life!** o la borsa o la vita!

mon·eyed [ˈmʌnɪd] ADJ danaroso(-a), ricco(-a); **the moneyed classes** le classi più abbienti

money·lender [ˈmʌnɪˌlɛndəʳ] N chi presta soldi; (*pej*) usuraio(-a)

money·maker [ˈmʌnɪˌmeɪkəʳ] N (*Brit fam: business*) affare *m* d'oro

money·making [ˈmʌnɪˌmeɪkɪŋ] ADJ che rende (bene *or* molto), lucrativo(-a)

money market N mercato monetario

money order N vaglia *m inv* (postale)

money-spinner [ˈmʌnɪˌspɪnəʳ] N (*fam*) miniera d'oro (*fig*)

money supply N liquidità *f inv* monetaria

Mon·gol [ˈmɒŋɡəl] N (*person*) mongolo(-a); (*language*) mongolo ♦ ADJ mongolo(-a)

mon·gol [ˈmɒŋɡəl] N, ADJ (*offensive*) mongoloide *m/f*

Mon·go·lia [mɒŋˈɡəʊlɪə] N la Mongolia

Mon·go·lian [mɒŋˈɡəʊlɪən] ADJ (*people, tribe*) mongolo(-a); (*language*) mongolico(-a) ♦ N (*person*) mongolo(-a)

mon·goose [ˈmɒŋɡuːs] N mangusta

mon·grel [ˈmʌŋɡrəl] N (*dog*) (cane *m*) bastardo; **my dog's a mongrel** il mio cane è un bastardo

moni·tor [ˈmɒnɪtəʳ] N 1 (*Brit Scol*) ≈ capoclasse *m/f*; (*USA Scol*) chi sorveglia agli esami 2 (*TV, Tech: screen*) monitor *m inv*; (*Radio: person*) addetto(-a) all'ascolto delle trasmissioni dall'estero ♦ VT (*foreign station: broadcast*) ascoltare le trasmissioni di; (*machine, progress*) controllare; (*discussion*) dirigere, fare da moderatore(-trice) in *or* di

monk [mʌŋk] N frate m, monaco

mon·key [ˈmʌŋkɪ] N scimmia; (fig: child) birbante m
- **monkey about, monkey around** VI + ADV (fam) far lo (la) scemo(-a); **to monkey about with sth** armeggiare con qc

monkey business N , **monkey tricks** NPL (fam) scherzi mpl

monkey nut N (Brit) nocciolina americana, arachide f

monkey wrench N chiave f inglese a rullino

mono [ˈmɒnəʊ] ADJ mono inv; (broadcast) in mono ♦ N: **in mono** in mono

mono– [ˈmɒnəʊ] PREF mono-

mono·chrome [ˈmɒnəˌkrəʊm] ADJ (painting, print) monocromatico(-a), monocromo(-a); (television) in bianco e nero

mono·cle [ˈmɒnəkl] N monocolo

mo·noga·mous [mɒˈnɒɡəməs] ADJ monogamo(-a)

mo·noga·my [mɒˈnɒɡəmɪ] N monogamia

mono·gram [ˈmɒnəˌɡræm] N monogramma m

mono·lith [ˈmɒnəʊlɪθ] N monolito

mono·logue [ˈmɒnəlɒɡ] N monologo

mono·plane [ˈmɒnəʊpleɪn] N monoplano

mo·nopo·lize [məˈnɒpəˌlaɪz] VT monopolizzare

mo·nopo·ly [məˈnɒpəlɪ] N monopolio; **a state monopoly** un monopolio di stato

mono·rail [ˈmɒnəʊˌreɪl] N monorotaia

mono·so·dium glu·ta·mate [ˌmɒnəʊˈsəʊdɪəmˈɡluːtəˌmeɪt] N glutammato di sodio

mono·syl·lab·ic [ˌmɒnəʊsɪˈlæbɪk] ADJ (word, reply) monosillabico(-a); (person) che parla a monosillabi

mono·syl·la·ble [ˈmɒnəˌsɪləbl] N monosillabo; **to speak/ answer in monosyllables** parlare/rispondere a monosillabi

mono·tone [ˈmɒnəˌtəʊn] N: **in a monotone** con voce monotona, con tono monotono

mo·noto·nous [məˈnɒtənəs] ADJ monotono(-a)

mo·noto·ny [məˈnɒtənɪ] N monotonia

mon·ox·ide [mɒˈnɒksaɪd] N monossido

mon·soon [mɒnˈsuːn] N monsone m

mon·ster [ˈmɒnstəʳ] N mostro ♦ ADJ (enormous) gigantesco(-a)

mon·stros·ity [mɒnsˈtrɒsɪtɪ] N mostruosità f inv

mon·strous [ˈmɒnstrəs] ADJ (huge) colossale, enorme; (dreadful) mostruoso(-a); **it is monstrous that ...** è scandaloso or pazzesco che... + sub

Mont. ABBR (USA: = Montana)

Mon·ta·na [mɒnˈtænə] N il Montana

mon·tage [mɒnˈtɑːʒ] N montaggio

Mont Blanc [mɒ̃ˈblɒ̃] N il Monte Bianco

month [mʌnθ] N mese m; **last month** il mese scorso; **in the month of May** nel mese di maggio, in maggio; **300 dollars a month** 300 dollari al mese; **paid by the month** pagato(-a) mensilmente; **which day of the month is it?** quanti ne abbiamo (oggi)?; **every month** (happen) tutti i mesi; (pay) mensilmente, ogni mese

month·ly [ˈmʌnθlɪ] ADJ (gen) mensile; (ticket) valevole per un mese ♦ ADV mensilmente, ogni mese, al mese; **twice monthly** due volte al mese ♦ N (magazine) (rivista) mensile m

monu·ment [ˈmɒnjʊmənt] N monumento

monu·men·tal [ˌmɒnjʊˈmɛntl] ADJ (also fig) monumentale, colossale

monumental mason, monumental sculptor N marmista m

moo [muː] N muggito ♦ VI muggire, mugghiare

mood [muːd] N umore m; **what kind of mood are you in?** di che umore sei?; **to be in a good/bad mood** essere di buonumore/di cattivo umore; **he was in a bad mood** era di cattivo umore; **to be in a generous mood** sentirsi generoso(-a); **to be in the mood for sth/to do sth** sentirsi in vena or aver voglia di qc/di fare qc; **I'm not in the mood** non mi sento in vena; **I'm in no mood to argue** non ho voglia di discutere

moody [ˈmuːdɪ] ADJ (comp -ier, superl -iest) (variable) lunatico(-a), capriccioso(-a); (morose) imbronciato(-a), intrattabile; **he's moody and unpredictable** è lunatico e imprevedibile; **moody lyrics** parole malinconiche

moon [muːn] N luna; **full/new moon** luna piena/nuova; **there's a full moon tonight** stanotte c'è la luna piena; **by the light of the moon** al chiaro di luna; **once in a blue moon** a ogni morte di papa; **to be over the moon** (fam) essere al settimo cielo; **she's over the moon about it** è al settimo cielo
- **moon about, moon around** VI + ADV aggirarsi con aria trasognata
- **moon over** VI + PREP: **to moon over sb** sospirare per qn

moon·beam [ˈmuːnˌbiːm] N raggio di luna

moon landing N allunaggio

moon·light [ˈmuːnˌlaɪt] N chiaro di luna; **in the moonlight** al chiaro di luna ♦ VI (fam) fare del lavoro nero ♦ ADJ (walk) al chiaro di luna

moon·light·ing [ˈmuːnˌlaɪtɪŋ] N lavoro nero

moon·lit [ˈmuːnˌlɪt] ADJ illuminato(-a) dalla luna; **on a moonlit night** in una notte rischiarata dalla luna

moon·shot [ˈmuːnˌʃɒt] N lancio sulla luna

moon·struck [ˈmuːnˌstrʌk] ADJ pazzo(-a)

moony [ˈmuːnɪ] ADJ (comp -ier, superl -iest) (eyes) sognante

Moor [mʊəʳ] N moro(-a)

moor[1] [mʊəʳ] N (land) brughiera

moor[2] [mʊəʳ] VT (ship) ormeggiare ♦ VI ormeggiarsi, attraccare

moor·ings [ˈmʊərɪŋz] NPL (chains, ropes) ormeggi mpl; (place) ormeggio

Moor·ish [ˈmʊərɪʃ] ADJ moresco(-a)

moor·land [ˈmʊələnd] N brughiera

moose [muːs] N pl inv alce m

moot [muːt] ADJ: **it's a moot point** è un punto discutibile or controverso ♦ VT: **it has been mooted whether ...** è stata sollevata la questione se...

mop [mɒp] N (for floor) mocio m; (for dishes) spazzolino per i piatti; (fam: hair) cespuglio or testa di capelli ♦ VT (floor) lavare; **to mop one's brow** asciugarsi la fronte
- **mop up** VT + ADV 1 asciugare con uno straccio 2 (Mil) eliminare

mope [məʊp] VI essere depresso(-a) or avvilito(-a)
- **mope about, mope around** VI + ADV trascinarsi or aggirarsi con aria avvilita

mo·ped [ˈməʊpɛd] N (Brit) ciclomotore m

MOR [ˌɛmˌəʊˈɑːʳ] ADJ ABBR (Mus: = middle-of-the-road): **MOR music** musica melodica ♦ N ABBR (= middle-of-the-road) per il gran pubblico

mor·al [ˈmɒrəl] ADJ (gen) morale; (person) di saldi principi morali; **to lower moral standards** rilassare i costumi ♦ N 1 (lesson) morale f; **the moral of the story is ...** la morale della storia è... 2 **morals** NPL principi mpl morali, moralità f inv

mo·rale [mɒˈrɑːl] N morale m; **to raise sb's morale** risollevare il morale di qn; **morale was low** il morale era basso

mo·ral·ity [məˈrælɪtɪ] N moralità f inv

mor·al·ize [ˈmɒrəˌlaɪz] VI: **to moralize (about)** fare il (la) moralista (riguardo a), moraleggiare (riguardo a)

mor·al·ly [ˈmɒrəlɪ] ADV (act) moralmente; **morally wrong** moralmente sbagliato(-a)

moral victory N vittoria morale

mo·rass [məˈræs] N pantano, palude f; (fig) pantano

mora·to·rium [ˌmɒrəˈtɔːrɪəm] N moratoria

mor·bid [ˈmɔːbɪd] ADJ morboso(-a)
❏ **morbid** is not translated by the Italian word *morbido*

KEYWORD

more [mɔːʳ] comp of **many much** ADJ (greater in number) più inv; (in addition) altro(-a), ancora inv; **is there any more wine?** c'è ancora del vino?, c'è dell'altro vino?; **a few more weeks** ancora qualche settimana, qualche altra settimana; **many more people** molta più gente; **I have no more pennies** non ho più un penny; **do you want some more tea?** vuoi ancora un po' di tè?, vuoi dell'altro tè?; **I have more wine/money than you** ho più vino/soldi di te; **I have more wine than beer** ho più vino che birra; **there was more snow this winter than last** c'è stata più neve quest'inverno che l'inverno scorso; **more letters than we expected** più lettere di quante ne aspettavamo
♦ PRON
1 (greater amount) più inv; (further or additional amount) ancora; **4 more** ancora 4; **a few more** ancora qualcuno; **a little**

more ancora un po', un altro po'; **is there any more?** ce n'è ancora?, ce n'è dell'altro?; **you couldn't ask for more** non potresti chiedere di più; **it cost more than we had expected** è costato (di) più di quanto pensavamo; **many more** molti altri; **much more** molto di più; **there's no more** non ce n'è più; **let's say no more about it** non parliamone più; **more than** 10 più di 10; **more than ever** più che mai; **I want more** ne voglio ancora *or* di più; **and what's more ...** e per di più... 2 **(all) the more** (molto) di più; **the more you give him the more he wants** più gliene dai e più ne vuole; **the more the merrier** più gente c'è, meglio è

♦ ADV (di) più; **more and more** sempre di più; **it's more and more difficult to ...** è sempre più difficile...; **I don't want to go any more** non ci voglio più andare; **more dangerous than** più pericoloso(-a) di *or* che; **more difficult** più difficile; **more easily** più facilmente; **no more** non... più; **not any more** non... più; **once more** ancora (una volta), un'altra volta; **(all) the more so as ...** tanto più che...; **he was more surprised than angry** era più sorpreso che arrabbiato; **it will more than meet the demand** supererà ampiamente la richiesta; **more** *or* **less** più o meno

more·over [mɔːˈrəʊvəʳ] ADV per di più, inoltre

morgue [mɔːg] N obitorio

mori·bund [ˈmɒrɪˌbʌnd] ADJ moribondo(-a)

morn·ing [ˈmɔːnɪŋ] N *(part of day)* mattina, mattino; *(expressing duration)* mattinata; **this morning** stamattina, questa mattina; **yesterday morning** ieri mattina; **tomorrow morning** domani mattina, domattina; **on Monday morning** lunedì mattina; **a morning's work** il lavoro di una mattinata; **in the morning** di mattina, la mattina; *(tomorrow)* domattina; **I work in the mornings** lavoro la mattina; **at 7 o'clock in the morning** alle 7 di *or* del mattino; **on the morning of September 19th** la mattina del 19 settembre; **I'll do it first thing in the morning** lo farò domani mattina appena mi sveglio ♦ ADJ *(walk)* mattutino(-a); *(papers)* del mattino

morning-after pill [ˌmɔːnɪŋˈɑːtəˌpɪl] N pillola del giorno dopo

morning sickness N *(Med)* nausee *fpl* mattutine

Mo·roc·can [məˈrɒkən] ADJ, N marocchino(-a)

Mo·roc·co [məˈrɒkəʊ] N 1 il Marocco 2 *(also:* **Morocco leather)** marocchino

mor·on [ˈmɔːrɒn] N *(fam)* idiota *m/f*, deficiente *m/f*

mo·ron·ic [məˈrɒnɪk] ADJ cretino(-a), idiota, deficiente

mo·rose [məˈrəʊs] ADJ cupo(-a), tetro(-a), imbronciato(-a)

❑ **morose** is not translated by the Italian word *moroso*

mor·phine [ˈmɔːfiːn], **mor·phia** [ˈmɔːfɪə] N morfina

Morse [mɔːs] N *(also:* **Morse code)** alfabeto Morse

mor·sel [ˈmɔːsl] N *(of food)* boccone *m*; *(fig)* briciolo

mor·tal [ˈmɔːtl] ADJ, N mortale *m/f*

mor·tal·ity [mɔːˈtælɪtɪ] N mortalità *f inv*

mortality rate N tasso di mortalità

mor·tar [ˈmɔːtəʳ] N 1 *(cannon, bowl)* mortaio; **pestle and mortar** pestello e mortaio 2 *(cement)* malta; **bricks and mortar** mattoni e malta

mort·gage [ˈmɔːgɪdʒ] N *(in house buying)* mutuo ipotecario; *(second loan)* ipoteca; **to take out a mortgage** contrarre un mutuo *(or* un'ipoteca); **to pay off a mortgage** pagare un mutuo *(or* un'ipoteca); **I've got a mortgage** ho un mutuo ♦ VT ipotecare

mortgage company N *(USA)* società *f inv* immobiliare

mort·ga·gee [ˌmɔːgɪˈdʒiː] N creditore *m* ipotecario

mort·gag·or [ˈmɔːgɪdʒəʳ] N debitore *m* ipotecario

mor·ti·cian [mɔːˈtɪʃən] N *(USA)* impresario di pompe funebri

mor·ti·fied [ˈmɔːtɪˌfaɪd] ADJ mortificato(-a)

mortise lock N serratura incastrata

mor·tu·ary [ˈmɔːtjʊərɪ] N camera mortuaria

mo·sa·ic [məʊˈzeɪɪk] N mosaico

Mos·cow [ˈmɒskəʊ] N Mosca; **he's in Moscow** è a Mosca

Mos·lem [ˈmɒzləm] ADJ, N = **Muslim**

mosque [mɒsk] N moschea

mos·qui·to [mɒsˈkiːtəʊ] N *(pl* **mosquitoes)** zanzara; **a mosquito bite** una puntura di zanzara

mosquito net N zanzariera

moss [mɒs] N *(Bot)* muschio

mossy [ˈmɒsɪ] ADJ *(comp* **-ier,** *superl* **-iest)** muscoso(-a)

most [məʊst] *superl of* **many much** ADJ 1 più (di tutti); **the most pleasure** il piacere più grande; **who has (the) most money?** chi ha più soldi (di tutti)?; **for the most part** in gran parte, per la maggior parte; **he won the most votes** ha avuto più voti degli altri 2 *(the majority of)*: **most men** la maggior parte *or* la grande maggioranza degli uomini; **most fish** la maggior parte dei pesci; **most people** quasi tutti; **most people go out on Friday night** quasi tutti escono venerdì sera ♦ PRON: **most of it/them** quasi tutto/tutti; **most of the money/her friends/the time** la maggior parte dei soldi/dei suoi amici/del tempo; **I know most of them** conosco gran parte di loro; **do the most you can** fai più che puoi; **I did most of the work** ho fatto gran parte del lavoro; **at most** *or* **at the (very) most** al massimo; **two hours at the most** due ore al massimo; **to make the most of sth** sfruttare al massimo qc, trarre il massimo vantaggio da qc; **he made the most of his holiday** ha sfruttato al massimo la vacanza; **make the most of it!** approfittane! ♦ ADV 1 *(spend, eat, work, sleep)* di più; **I saw most** ho visto più di tutti; **the most attractive/difficult/comfortable** il (la) più attraente/difficile/confortevole; **the most expensive restaurant** il ristorante più caro; **which one did it most easily?** chi ha avuto più facilità a farlo?; **the thing she most feared** la cosa che temeva di più; **he's the one who talks most** lui è quello che parla di più 2 *(very)*: **most likely** molto probabilmente; **a most interesting book** un libro estremamente interessante; **a most unusual choice** una scelta estremamente insolita

most·ly [ˈməʊstlɪ] ADV *(chiefly)* per lo più; *(usually)* in genere; **the teachers are mostly quite nice** in genere gli insegnanti sono abbastanza gentili

mo·tel [məʊˈtɛl] N motel *m inv*

moth [mɒθ] N falena, farfalla notturna; *(also:* **clothes moth)** tarma

moth·ball [ˈmɒθˌbɔːl] N pallina di naftalina

moth-eaten [ˈmɒθˌiːtn] ADJ tarmato(-a)

moth·er [ˈmʌðəʳ] N madre *f*; **my mother** mia madre ♦ VT *(care for)* fare da madre a; *(spoil)* essere troppo chioccia con

moth·er·board [ˈmʌðəˌbɔːd] N *(Comput)* scheda *f* madre, *inv*

moth·er·hood [ˈmʌðəˌhʊd] N maternità *f inv*

mother-in-law [ˈmʌðərɪnlɔː] N *(pl* **mothers-in-law)** suocera

mother-of-pearl [ˌmʌðərəvˈpɜːl] N madreperla

Mother's Day N la festa della mamma

mother's help N bambinaia

mother-to-be [ˌmʌðətəˈbiː] N *(pl* **mothers-to-be)** futura mamma

mother tongue N lingua materna, madrelingua

moth·proof [ˈmɒθˌpruːf] ADJ antitarmico(-a)

mo·tif [məʊˈtiːf] N motivo

mo·tion [ˈməʊʃən] N 1 *(movement)* moto, movimento; **circular motion** movimento circolare; **perpetual motion** moto perpetuo; **to be in motion** *(vehicle)* essere in moto; *(machine)* essere in funzione; **to set in motion** avviare; **to go through the motions of doing sth** *(fig)* fare qc pro forma 2 *(gesture)* cenno, gesto; *(proposal: at meeting)* mozione *f* ♦ VT, VI: **to motion (to) sb to do sth** far cenno *or* segno a qn di fare qc

mo·tion·less [ˈməʊʃənlɪs] ADJ immobile

motion picture N *(USA)* film *m inv*

mo·ti·vate [ˈməʊtɪˌveɪt] VT *(act, decision)* dare origine a, motivare; *(person)* spingere, motivare

mo·ti·vat·ed [ˈməʊtɪˌveɪtɪd] ADJ motivato(-a); **he's highly motivated** è fortemente motivato

mo·ti·va·tion [ˌməʊtɪˈveɪʃən] N motivazione *f*

mo·tive [ˈməʊtɪv] N *(gen)* motivo, ragione *f*; *(for crime)* movente *m*; **the motive for the killing** il movente dell'omicidio; **from the best motives** con le migliori intenzioni; **an ulterior motive** un secondo fine ♦ ADJ motore(-trice)

mot·ley [ˈmɒtlɪ] ADJ *(many-coloured)* variopinto(-a); *(mixed)* eterogeneo(-a), molto vario(-a); **a motley crew** una banda eterogenea

mo·tor [ˈməʊtəʳ] N 1 *(engine)* motore *m*; **a boat with a motor**

una barca a motore **2** (*Brit fam: car*) macchina ♦ VI andare in automobile ♦ ADJ motore(-trice)

motor·bike [ˈməʊtəˌbaɪk] N moto *f inv*

motor·boat [ˈməʊtəˌbəʊt] N motoscafo

motor·cade [ˈməʊtəˌkeɪd] N corteo di auto

motor·car [ˈməʊtəkɑːʳ] N (*Brit: frm*) automobile *f*

motor·coach [ˈməʊtəˌkəʊtʃ] N (*Brit*) pullman *m inv*

motor·cycle [ˈməʊtəˌsaɪkl] N motocicletta

motor·cyclist [ˈməʊtəˌsaɪklɪst] N motociclista *m/f*

mo·tor·ing [ˈməʊtərɪŋ] ADJ (*accident*) d'auto, automobilistico(-a); (*offence*) di guida; **motoring holiday** vacanza in macchina; **the motoring public** gli automobilisti ♦ N (*Brit*) turismo automobilistico; **the hazards of motoring** i rischi dell'andare in macchina

mo·tor·ist [ˈməʊtərɪst] N automobilista *m/f*

mo·tor·ize [ˈməʊtəˌraɪz] VT motorizzare

motor oil N olio lubrificante

motor racing N (*Brit*) corse *fpl* automobilistiche

motor scooter N motorscooter *m inv*

motor vehicle N (*frm*) automezzo, autoveicolo

motor·way [ˈməʊtəˌweɪ] N (*Brit*) autostrada; **on the motorway** in autostrada

mot·tled [ˈmɒtld] ADJ (*leaves, bird*) variopinto(-a), variegato(-a), screziato(-a); (*marble*) variegato(-a); (*animal*) pezzato(-a), marezzato(-a); (*complexion*) a chiazze, chiazzato(-a)

mot·to [ˈmɒtəʊ] N (*pl* **mottoes**) motto

mould¹, mold¹(*USA*) [məʊld] N (*fungus*) muffa; **jam covered with mould** marmellata coperta di muffa

mould², mold²(*USA*) [məʊld] N (*Art, Culin, Tech*) stampo, forma ♦ VT (*clay, figure*) plasmare, modellare; (*fig: character*) plasmare, formare, foggiare; **parents try to mould their children** i genitori cercano di plasmare i propri figli; **mould the mixture into balls** forma delle palline con l'impasto

mould·er, mold·er (*USA*) [ˈməʊldəʳ] VI (*decay*) ammuffire; (*building*) sgretolarsi, andare in rovina

mould·ing, mold·ing (*USA*) [ˈməʊldɪŋ] N (*Archit*) modanatura

mouldy, moldy (*USA*) [ˈməʊldɪ] ADJ (*comp* **-ier**, *superl* **-iest**) ammuffito(-a); **to smell mouldy** avere odore di muffa; **to go mouldy** ammuffire

moult, molt (*USA*) [məʊlt] VI far la muta

mound [maʊnd] N rialzo, collinetta

mount¹ [maʊnt] N (*liter*) monte *m*, montagna; **Mount Everest** il monte Everest; **Mount of Olives** (*Rel*) il Monte degli Ulivi

mount² [maʊnt] N **1** (*horse*) cavalcatura **2** (*support, base*) piedistallo; (*of machine*) incastellatura di sostegno; (*of jewel, photo*) montatura; (*of slide*) telaietto ♦ VT **1** (*horse*) montare; (*platform*) salire su; (*stairs*) salire **2** (*exhibition*) organizzare; (*play*) metter su; (*attack*) sferrare, condurre; **they're mounting a publicity campaign** stanno organizzando una campagna pubblicitaria **3** (*picture, stamp*) sistemare; (*jewel*) montare **4** **to mount guard** (on *or* over) fare la guardia a; (*Mil*) montare la guardia ♦ VI **1** (*get on a horse*) montare a cavallo **2** (*quantity, price: also:* **mount up**) aumentare, salire; **tension is mounting** la tensione sta aumentando; **my savings are mounting up gradually** i miei risparmi aumentano a poco a poco

moun·tain [ˈmaʊntɪn] N (*also fig*) montagna; **in the mountains** sulle montagne, in montagna; **to take a vacation in the mountains** fare una vacanza in montagna; **to make a mountain out of a molehill** fare di una mosca un elefante; **butter mountain** (*Econ*) montagna di burro ♦ ADJ (*people*) montanaro(-a), di montagna; (*shoes*) da montagna; (*animal, plant, path*) di montagna

moun·tain·eer [ˌmaʊntɪˈnɪəʳ] N alpinista *m/f*

moun·tain·eer·ing [ˌmaʊntɪˈnɪərɪŋ] N alpinismo; **to go mountaineering** fare dell'alpinismo

moun·tain·ous [ˈmaʊntɪnəs] ADJ (*country*) montagnoso(-a), montuoso(-a); (*fig*) gigantesco(-a)

mountain range N catena montuosa *or* di montagne

mountain rescue team N ≈ squadra di soccorso alpino

moun·tain·side [ˈmaʊntɪnˌsaɪd] N fianco della montagna

mount·ed [ˈmaʊntɪd] ADJ a cavallo

mourn [mɔːn] VT piangere, lamentare; **to mourn sb** piangere

la morte di qn; **she's still mourning her father** sta ancora piangendo la morte del padre; **she mourns the loss of her idealism** rimpiange la perdita del proprio idealismo ♦ VI: **to mourn (for sb)** piangere (la morte di qn)

mourn·er [ˈmɔːnəʳ] N chi piange un defunto

mourn·ing [ˈmɔːnɪŋ] N lutto; **to be in mourning** essere in lutto; **to wear mourning** portare il lutto ♦ ADJ (*dress*) da lutto

mouse [maʊs] N (*pl* **mice**) (*gen*) topo; (*Comput*) mouse *m inv*; **house mouse** topo domestico

mouse mat, mouse pad N (*Comput*) tappetino del mouse

mouse·trap [ˈmaʊsˌtræp] N trappola per i topi

mous·sa·ka [mʊˈsɑːkə] N moussaka, *sorta di parmigiana di melanzane con ragù di carne, specialità greca*

mousse [muːs] N mousse *f inv*; **chocolate mousse** mousse al cioccolato

mous·tache [məˈstɑːʃ] N baffi *mpl*

mousy, mousey [ˈmaʊsɪ] ADJ (*comp* **-ier**, *superl* **-iest**) (*person*) timido(-a), schivo(-a); **mousy hair** capelli color castano spento

mouth [N *n* maʊθ, *vb* maʊð] N (*pl* **mouths** [maʊðz]) (*gen*) bocca; (*of cave*) imboccatura, imbocco; (*of river*) foce *f*, bocca; (*opening*) orifizio; **to keep one's mouth shut** (*fig*) tener la bocca chiusa; **shut your mouth!** ma sta' un po' zitto! ♦ VT (*insincerely*) blaterare; (*soundlessly*) esprimere col semplice movimento delle labbra

mouth·ful [ˈmaʊθfʊl] N (*of food*) boccone *m*; (*of drink*) sorsata

mouth organ N armonica (a bocca)

mouth·piece [ˈmaʊθˌpiːs] N (*Mus*) imboccatura, bocchino; (*of breathing apparatus*) boccaglio; (*of telephone*) microfono; (*fig: person*) portavoce *m/f*

mouth-to-mouth [ˈmaʊθtəˈmaʊθ],   **mouth-to-mouth resuscitation** N respirazione *f* bocca a bocca

mouth·wash [ˈmaʊθˌwɒʃ] N colluttorio

mouth·water·ing [ˈmaʊθˌwɔːtərɪŋ] ADJ che fa venire l'acquolina in bocca

mov·able [ˈmuːvəbl] ADJ mobile, movibile

move [muːv] N **1** (*movement*) movimento, mossa; **to be on the move** (*travelling*) spostarsi; (*active, busy*) essere indaffarato(-a); (*fig: developments*) essere in continuo progresso; **to get a move on** (*fam*) affrettarsi, sbrigarsi; **get a move on (with that)!** (*fam*) sbrigati (con quello)!, datti una mossa (con quello)!; **to make a move** (*start to leave, go*) andarsene; (*begin to take action*) muoversi; **he made a move towards her** fece un passo verso di lei **2** (*in game*) mossa; (*turn to play*) turno; (*fig: step, action*) passo; **it's my move** tocca a me; **a good/bad move** una mossa buona/sbagliata; **what's the next move?** e adesso cosa facciamo?; **to make the first move** (*fig*) fare il primo passo; **his first move after his victory** la prima cosa che ha fatto dopo la sua vittoria; **there was a move to oust him from the party** ci fu un tentativo di estrometterlo dal partito **3** (*change of house*) trasloco; (*to different job*) trasferimento; **our move from Oxford to Luton** il nostro trasloco da Oxford a Luton ♦ VT **1** (*change place of*) spostare; (*limbs, chesspiece*) muovere; (*transport*) trasportare; (*transfer: employee, troops*) trasferire; **move those children off the grass!** fate andare via i bambini dal prato!; **could you move your stuff please?** può spostare le sue cose per favore?; **to move house** traslocare, cambiar casa; **we asked a (removal) firm to move us** abbiamo chiesto a una ditta (di traslochi) di farci il trasloco **2** (*fig: sway*): **to move somebody from an opinion** smuovere qn da un'idea; **to move sb to do sth** indurre *or* spingere qn a fare qc; **he will not be easily moved** non cambierà facilmente idea **3** (*cause emotion in*) commuovere; **to be moved** essere commosso(-a); **to move sb to tears** commuovere qn fino alle lacrime; **to move sb to anger/pity** far arrabbiare/impietosire qn; **the book moved me deeply** il libro mi ha commossa profondamente **4** (*frm: propose*): **to move a resolution** avanzare una proposta; **to move that ...** proporre che... + *sub* ♦ VI **1** (*gen*) muoversi; (*traffic*) circolare; (*from a place*) spostarsi; **move!** muoviti!, spostati!; **let's move!** andiamo!; **don't move!** non muovetevi!; **to move towards** andare verso; **I'll not move from here** di qui non mi muovo; **the car was moving very slowly** la macchina avanzava molto lentamente; **to move freely** (*piece of machinery*) aver gioco; (*person*) circolare liberamente; (*traffic*) scorrere; **the police officer kept the traffic moving** il vigile ha fatto scorrere il traffico; **things are moving at last** finalmente qualcosa si è mosso **2** (*move house*) cambiar casa, traslocare; **the family moved to a new house** la famiglia è andata ad abitare in una nuova casa; **we're moving in July** traslochiamo in luglio; **we're moving to Scotland** ci trasferiamo in Scozia **3** (*in games*) muovere; **it's your turn to move** tocca a te **4** (*take steps*) intervenire

▸ **move about, move around** VT + ADV (*furniture*) spostare; (*person*) far spostare ♦ VI + ADV (*fidget*) agitarsi; (*walk about*) muoversi; (*travel*) spostarsi, viaggiare

▸ **move along** VT + ADV (*crowd*) far circolare; (*car*) far spostare ♦ VI + ADV spostarsi in avanti, scorrere

▸ **move away** VT + ADV (*demonstrators*) allontanare; (*employee*) trasferire; (*object*) spostare ♦ VI + ADV, VI (*move aside*) spostarsi; (*leave*) allontanarsi, andarsene; (*move house*) traslocare; **our neighbours are moving away** i nostri vicini se ne vanno

▸ **move back** VT + ADV **1** (*to former place: person*) far tornare; (*: object*) rimettere dov'era **2** (*cause to give ground: crowd*) sospingere indietro; (*: troops*) far indietreggiare ♦ VI + ADV (*return*) ritornare; **they had no intention of moving back to Britain** non avevano intenzione di ritornare in Gran Bretagna **2** (*give ground*) indietreggiare

▸ **move down** VT + ADV (*person*) far scendere; (*object*) spostare in basso; (*demote*) far retrocedere ♦ VI + ADV scendere; (*be demoted*) retrocedere

▸ **move forward** VT + ADV (*object*) spostare in avanti; (*people, troops, chesspiece*) far avanzare; (*fig: date*) anticipare ♦ VI + ADV avanzare

▸ **move in** VT + ADV (*police*) far intervenire; (*take inside*) portar dentro; **we haven't moved the furniture in yet** non ci abbiamo ancora messo i mobili ♦ VI + ADV **1** (*to a house*) traslocare, andare ad abitare; **when are the new neighbours moving in?** quando arrivano i nuovi vicini? **2** (*police*) intervenire; (*pej: try to take control*) cercare di imporsi

▸ **move off** VT + ADV (*object*) togliere ♦ VI + ADV **1** (*go away*) allontanarsi **2** (*start moving*) partire

▸ **move on** VT + ADV (*crowd*) far circolare; (*hands of clock*) spostare in avanti ♦ VI + ADV ripartire, riprendere la strada; **I felt it was time to move on** sentii che era arrivato il momento di cambiare; **the police officer asked them to move on** il poliziotto ha ordinato loro di andare via; **to move on to** (*fig: point*) passare a; **let's move on to the next question** passiamo alla prossima domanda

▸ **move out** VT + ADV (*gen*) portar fuori; (*person*) mandare fuori; (*troops*) far ritirare; **move the chair out of the corner** togli la sedia dall'angolo ♦ VI + ADV (*of house*) sgombrare, trasferirsi; (*withdraw: troops*) ritirarsi

▸ **move over** VT + ADV spostare ♦ VI + ADV spostarsi; **could you move over a bit?** puoi spostarti un po'?

▸ **move up** VT + ADV (*person*) portare su; (*object*) spostare in alto; (*promote: employee*) promuovere ♦ VI + ADV **1** (*move along*) andare avanti, avanzare **2** (*fig: shares*) salire; (*: rates*) aumentare; (*be promoted*) passare di grado

move·ment [ˈmuːvmənt] N (*gen*) movimento; (*gesture*) gesto; (*of stars, water, physical*) moto; **movement (of the bowels)** (*Med*) evacuazione *f* (intestinale); **a sudden movement** un movimento brusco; **the police questioned him about his movements** la polizia lo ha interrogato circa i suoi spostamenti; **he was asked to account for his movements** gli è stato chiesto di rendere conto dei suoi spostamenti

mov·er [ˈmuːvə'] N proponente *m/f*

movie [ˈmuːvɪ] (*esp USA*) N film *m inv*; **the movies** il cinema *m inv*; **to go to the movies** andare al cinema ♦ ADJ (*star*) del cinema; (*industry*) cinematografico(-a)

movie camera N (*USA*) cinepresa

movie·goer [ˈmuːvɪˌɡəʊə'] N (*USA*) frequentatore(-trice) di cinema

movie theater (*USA*) N cinema *m inv*

mov·ing [ˈmuːvɪŋ] ADJ **1** (*parts, staircase*) mobile; (*vehicle*) in movimento; **a moving bus** un autobus in movimento **2** (*fig: instigating*) animatore(-trice) **3** (*causing emotion*)

commovente, toccante; **a moving story** una storia commovente

mow [məʊ] (*pt mowed pp mown or mowed*) VT (*corn*) falciare; (*grass*) tagliare

▸ **mow down** VT + ADV falciare

mow·er [ˈməʊə'] N (*machine, also Agr*) falciatrice *f*; (*also: lawn mower*) tagliaerba *m inv*, tosaerba *m inv*

Mo·zam·bique [ˌməʊzəmˈbiːk] N il Mozambico

MP [ˌemˈpiː] N ABBR **1** = **Military Police 2** (*Canada:* = **Mounted Police**) **3** (*Brit:* = *Member of Parliament*) deputato(-a); (*on envelope*): **Paul Smith, MP** ≈ On. Paul Smith

MP3 [ˌempiːˈθriː] N MP3 *m inv*

mpg [ˌempiːˈdʒiː] N ABBR (= *miles per gallon*) ≈ km/l

mph [ˌempiːˈeɪtʃ] N ABBR (= *miles per hour*) ≈ km/h

Mr [ˈmɪstə'] N signore *m*; **Mr Smith** il signor Smith; (*on letter*) Sig. Smith; (*direct address*) signor Smith

Mrs [ˈmɪsɪz] N signora; **Mrs Black** la signora Black; (*on letter*) Sig.ra Black; (*direct address*) signora Black

MS [ˌemˈes] N ABBR **1** (*USA:* = *Master of Science*) master *m inv* in scienze **2** (*Med*) = **multiple sclerosis** ♦ ABBR (*USA Post:* = **Mississippi**)

Ms [mɪz] N ABBR *termine usato per evitare di distinguere tra signora e signorina*

MSG [ˌeɱesˈdʒiː] ABBR = **monosodium glutamate**

MST [ˌeɱesˈtiː] ABBR (*USA:* = *Mountain Standard Time*) *ora (invernale) nel fuso orario delle Montagne Rocciose*

MT [ˌeɱˈtiː] N ABBR = **machine translation** ♦ ABBR (*USA Post:* = **Montana**)

Mt ABBR (*Geog:* = *mount*) M.

KEYWORD

much [mʌtʃ] (*comp more, superl most*) ADJ, PRON

1 molto(-a); **how much money?** quanti soldi?; **how much is it?** quanto costa?; **it's not much** non è tanto; **there's not much to do** non c'è molto da fare; **much of this is true** molto di questo è vero; **I'm not much of a cook/singer** non sono un granché come cuoco/cantante; **that wasn't much of a party** la festa non è stata un granché; **we don't see much of each other** non ci vediamo molto spesso; **he/it isn't up to much** (*fam*) non vale granché

2 as much, as much again altrettanto(-a); **as much as you want** (*tanto*) quanto vuoi; **he drinks as much beer as I do** beve tanta birra quanto me; **it's as much as he can do to stand up** stare in piedi è il massimo che riesce a fare; **he spends as much as he earns** spende tanto quanto guadagna; **he has (just) as much money as you** ha tanti soldi quanto te; **I thought as much** c'era da aspettarselo; **three times as much tea** tre volte tanto tè

3 so much talmente tanto(-a), così (tanto(-a)); **at so much a pound** un tot *or* un tanto alla libbra; **so much for that!** pazienza!; **the problem is not so much one of money as time** non è tanto una questione di soldi quanto di tempo

4 too much troppo(-a); **that's too much!** *or* **a bit (too) much!** (*fam*) questo è (un po') troppo!

5 to make much of sb (*treat as important*) coprire qn di attenzioni; **to make much of** (*success, failure*) fare un sacco di storie per; (*item of news, scandal*) dare rilievo a; **I couldn't make much of that** (*fam*) non ci ho capito molto

♦ ADV

1 molto; **much as I would like to go I can't** per quanto abbia *or* anche se ho una gran voglia di andarci, non posso; **he was much embarrassed** era molto imbarazzato; **how much?** quanto?; **however much he tries** per quanto ci provi; **I hardly know her, much less her mother** conosco appena lei e ancora meno sua madre; **it doesn't much matter** non ha molta importanza; **I like it so much** mi piace così tanto; **so much** così (tanto); **much to my surprise** con mia grande sorpresa, con mio grande stupore; **too much** troppo; **I like it very much** mi piace moltissimo; **thank you very much** molte grazie

2 di gran lunga; **much the biggest** di gran lunga il (la) più grande; **I would much rather stay** preferirei di gran lunga restare

3 (*almost*) pressappoco, quasi; **they're much the same** sono praticamente uguali

muck [mʌk] N **1** (*dirt*) sporcizia, sudiciume *m*; (*mud*) fango;

(*manure*) letame *m*; **shoes covered with muck** scarpe coperte di fango; **muck in the engine** sporcizia nel motore; **a load of muck** un mucchio di letame **2** (*fig*) porcherie *fpl*
▸ **muck about, muck around** (*fam*) VT + ADV: **to muck sb about** complicare la vita a qn ♦ VI + ADV **1** (*lark about*) fare lo (la) stupido(-a); (*do nothing in particular*) non fare niente di speciale, gingillarsi; **stop mucking about!** finiscila di fare lo stupido! **2** (*tinker*) armeggiare; **to muck about with sth** trafficare con qc
▸ **muck in** VI + ADV (*Brit fam*) mettersi insieme
▸ **muck out** VT + ADV (*stable*) pulire
▸ **muck up** VT + ADV (*fam*) **1** (*dirty*) sporcare **2** (*spoil*) rovinare; **he's mucked up our plans** ci ha incasinato i piani

muck·rak·ing ['mʌk,reɪkɪŋ] (*fig: fam*) N scandalismo ♦ ADJ scandalistico(-a)

mucky ['mʌkɪ] ADJ (*comp* **-ier**, *superl* **-iest**) (*muddy*) fangoso(-a); (*filthy*) sudicio(-a), sporco(-a), lordo(-a)

mu·cus ['mjuːkəs] N muco

mud [mʌd] N **1** fango **2** (*fig*): **his name is mud** non è molto ben visto; **to sling mud at sb** gettar fango addosso a qn

mud·dle ['mʌdl] N (*perplexity*) confusione *f*; (*disorder*) disordine *m*; **to be in a muddle** (*room, books*) essere in disordine; (*person*) essere molto confuso(-a), non riuscire a raccapezzarsi; (*plan, arrangements*) essere per aria; **to get into a muddle** (*person: while explaining*) imbrogliarsi, fare confusione; (*things*) finire sottosopra ♦ VT (*also:* **muddle up**) **1** (*papers*) mettere sottosopra; **you've muddled up A and B** hai confuso A con B **2** (*person, story, details*) confondere; **to get muddled up** essere confuso(-a); **I'm getting muddled up** sono confuso
▸ **muddle along, muddle on** VI + ADV andare avanti a casaccio
▸ **muddle through** VI + ADV cavarsela alla meno peggio

muddle-headed ['mʌdl,hedɪd] ADJ (*person*) confusionario(-a); (*ideas*) confuso(-a)

mud·dy ['mʌdɪ] ADJ (*comp* **-ier**, *superl* **-iest**) (*road, ground, field*) fangoso(-a); (*hands*) coperto(-a) di fango; (*clothes, shoes*) infangato(-a); (*liquid*) torbido(-a); (*complexion*) smorto(-a), terreo(-a)

mud·guard ['mʌd,gɑːd] N (*Brit*) parafango

mud·pack ['mʌd,pæk] N maschera di fango

mud-slinging ['mʌd,slɪŋɪŋ] N (*fig*) infangamento

mues·li ['mjuːzlɪ] N müsli *msg*

muff¹ [mʌf] N manicotto

muff² [mʌf] VT (*shot, catch*) mancare, sbagliare; **to muff it** sbagliare tutto; **to muff one's lines** (*actor*) impappinarsi

muf·fin ['mʌfɪn] N (*Brit*) specie di pasticcino soffice da tè

muf·fle ['mʌfl] VT **1** (*wrap warmly: also:* **muffle up**) imbaccuccare **2** (*deaden: sound*) smorzare, attutire; (: *screams*) soffocare

muf·fled ['mʌfld] ADJ (*sound*) attutito(-a), smorzato(-a)

muf·fler ['mʌflə'] N (*scarf*) sciarpa (pesante); (*USA: Aut*) marmitta; (: *on motorbike*) silenziatore *m*; **a woollen muffler** una sciarpa di lana

muf·ti ['mʌftɪ] N: **in mufti** in borghese

mug [mʌg] N **1** (*cup*) tazzone *m*; (*for beer*) boccale *m*; **a mug of coffee** una tazza grande di caffè **2** (*Brit fam: fool*) salame *m*, scemo(-a); **it's a mug's game** è proprio (una cosa) da fessi **3** (*fam: face*) muso ♦ VT (*attack and rob*) aggredire, assalire; **he was mugged in the city centre** è stato aggredito in centro

mug·ger ['mʌgə'] N aggressore *m*, rapinatore(-trice)

mug·ging ['mʌgɪŋ] N aggressione *f* (a scopo di rapina)

mug·gins ['mʌgɪnz] NSG (*Brit fam*) fesso(-a), salame *m*; (*oneself*); **muggins had to do it** come sempre é toccato a me

mug·gy ['mʌgɪ] ADJ (*comp* **-ier**, *superl* **-iest**) (*weather*) afoso(-a); **it's muggy today** oggi c'è afa

mug shot N (*fam*) foto *f inv* segnaletica

Mu·ham·mad [mʊ'hɒmɪd] N Maometto

mul·berry ['mʌlbərɪ] N (*fruit*) mora (di gelso); (*tree*) gelso, moro; **black mulberry** gelso nero

mule [mjuːl] N mulo(-a); **(as) stubborn as a mule** testardo(-a) come un mulo

mull [mʌl] VT (*wine*) scaldare con aromi e zucchero
▸ **mull over** VT + ADV rimuginare

mulled wine ['mʌld,waɪn] N vin brûlé *m inv*, vino caldo

multi– ['mʌltɪ] PREF multi-

multi·ac·cess [,mʌltɪ'ækses] ADJ (*Comput*) ad accesso multiplo

multi·col·oured, multi·col·ored (*USA*) ['mʌltɪ'kʌləd] ADJ multicolore, variopinto(-a)

multi·fari·ous [,mʌltɪ'feərɪəs] ADJ molteplice, svariato(-a)

multi·lat·er·al [,mʌltɪ'lætərəl] ADJ (*Pol*) multilaterale; **multilateral trade** interscambio

multi·level ['mʌltɪ,levl] ADJ (*USA*) = **multistorey**

multi·me·dia [,mʌltɪ'miːdɪə] N (*Comput*) multimediale ♦ N multimediale *m*

multi·mil·lion·aire [,mʌltɪ,mɪljə'neə'] N multimiliardario(-a)

multi·na·tion·al [,mʌltɪ'næʃənl] N multinazionale *f* ♦ ADJ multinazionale

multi·ple ['mʌltɪpl] ADJ **1** (*with sg n*) multiplo(-a) **2** (*with pl n: many*) molteplici ♦ N **1** (*Math*) multiplo **2** (*Brit: also:* **multiple store**) grande magazzino che fa parte di una catena

multiple choice N esercizi *mpl* a scelta multipla

multiple sclerosis N sclerosi *f* a placche

multi·plex ['mʌltɪ,pleks] N (*also:* **multiplex cinema**) cinema multisale *m inv*

multi·pli·ca·tion [,mʌltɪplɪ'keɪʃən] N moltiplicazione *f*

multiplication table N tavola pitagorica; **to learn one's multiplication tables** imparare le tabelline

multi·plic·ity [,mʌltɪ'plɪsɪtɪ] N molteplicità *f inv*; **for a multiplicity of reasons** per una serie di ragioni

multi·ply [,mʌltɪ,plaɪ] VT (*Math*) moltiplicare ♦ VI **1** (*Math*) moltiplicare **2** (*increase*) moltiplicarsi

multi·racial ['mʌltɪ'reɪʃəl] ADJ multirazziale

multi·sto·rey [,mʌltɪ'stɔːrɪ], (*USA*) **multistory, multi·lev·el** ADJ (*building, parking garage*) a più piani

multi·tude ['mʌltɪ,tjuːd] N moltitudine *f*

mum¹ [mʌm] N (*Brit fam: mother*) mamma; **my mum** la mia mamma

mum² [mʌm] ADJ: **to keep mum (about sth)** non fare parola (di qc), non aprire bocca (su qc); **mum's the word!** acqua in bocca!

mum·ble ['mʌmbl] VT, VI borbottare

mum·bo jum·bo [,mʌmbəʊ'dʒʌmbəʊ] N (*pej*) sfilza di paroloni

mum·mi·fy ['mʌmɪ,faɪ] VT mummificare

mum·my¹ ['mʌmɪ] N (*Brit fam: mother*) mamma; **I want my mummy** voglio la mia mamma

mum·my² ['mʌmɪ] N (*embalmed corpse*) mummia

mumps [mʌmps] NSG orecchioni *mpl*

munch [mʌntʃ] VT, VI sgranocchiare

mun·dane [,mʌn'deɪn] ADJ (*worldly*) di questo mondo; (*pej: humdrum*) banale, terra terra *inv*

Mu·nich ['mjuːnɪk] N Monaco *f* (di Baviera)

mu·nici·pal [mjuː'nɪsɪpəl] ADJ municipale, comunale

mu·nici·pal·ity [mjuː,nɪsɪ'pælɪtɪ] N (*place*) comune *m*, municipio

mu·ni·tions [mjuː'nɪʃənz] NPL munizioni *fpl*

mu·ral ['mjʊərəl] ADJ murale ♦ N dipinto murale

mur·der ['mɜːdə'] N omicidio, assassinio; **to commit murder** commettere un omicidio; **a terrible murder** un terribile omicidio ♦ VT (*person*) assassinare; (*fig: song*) massacrare

mur·der·er ['mɜːdərə'] N assassino, omicida

mur·der·ous ['mɜːdərəs] ADJ (*intentions*) omicida; (*look*) assassino(-a); (*climate, road*) micidiale

murk [mɜːk] N oscurità *f inv*, buio

murky ['mɜːkɪ] ADJ (*comp* **-ier**, *superl* **-iest**) (*gen*) oscuro(-a), cupo(-a), tenebroso(-a), buio(-a); (*thick: darkness*) fitto(-a); (: *smoke*) denso(-a); (*fig*) torbido(-a)

mur·mur ['mɜːmə'] N (*soft speech*) mormorio; (*of traffic, voices*) brusio; (*of bees*) ronzio; (*of leaves*) fruscio; **there were murmurs of disagreement** c'era un mormorio di disapprovazione; **without a murmur** senza fiatare; **heart murmur** (*Med*) soffio al cuore ♦ VT, VI borbottare, mormorare

mus·cle ['mʌsl] N muscolo; (*fig*) energia, forza; **to have muscle** avere potere e influenza; **he never moved a muscle** rimase fermo immobile
▸ **muscle in** VI + ADV: **to muscle in (on sth)** (*fam*) intromettersi *or* immischiarsi (in qc)

mus·cu·lar [ˈmʌskjʊləʳ] ADJ muscolare; (*person, arm*) muscoloso(-a); **he's got muscular legs** ha gambe muscolose

muscular dystrophy N distrofia muscolare

muse¹ [mjuːz] N (*fig*) musa

muse² [mjuːz] VI: **to muse on** *or* **about sth** rimuginare *or* meditare su qc

mu·seum [mjuːˈzɪəm] N museo

mush [mʌʃ, mʊʃ] N (*paste*) poltiglia, pappa; (*fig*) sdolcinatezza

mush·room [ˈmʌʃrum] N (*Bot*) fungo ♦ ADJ (*soup, omelette*) ai *or* coi funghi; (*flavour*) di funghi; (*colour*) color beige rosato *inv* ♦ VI **1** (*town*) svilupparsi rapidamente; (*houses*) spuntare come funghi; **the cloud of smoke went mushrooming up** la nuvola di fumo si alzò prendendo la forma di un fungo **2 to go mushrooming** andare per funghi, andare a cercare funghi

mushy [ˈmʌʃɪ] ADJ (*comp* -ier, *superl* -iest) (*food*) spappolato(-a), come pappa; (*fig: film, novel*) sdolcinato(-a)

mu·sic [ˈmjuːzɪk] N musica; **to set to music** mettere in musica *or* musicare; **it was music to her ears** (*fig*) era musica per le sue orecchie ♦ ADJ (*teacher, lesson*) di musica

mu·si·cal [ˈmjuːzɪkəl] ADJ (*gen*) musicale; **he's very musical** (*fond of*) è amante della musica; (*skilled*) è portato per la musica; **I'm not musical** non sono portato per la musica; **she comes from a musical family** viene da una famiglia di musicisti ♦ N (*Cine, Theatre*) musical *m inv*, commedia musicale

musical chairs NSG gioco delle sedie (*in cui bisogna sedersi non appena cessa la musica*); (*fig*) scambio delle poltrone

musical instrument N strumento musicale

music box, musical box N carillon *m inv*

music centre N stereo *m inv* compatto

music hall N teatro di varietà

mu·si·cian [mjuːˈzɪʃən] N musicista *m/f*

music stand N leggio

musk [mʌsk] N muschio

mus·ket [ˈmʌskɪt] N moschetto

musk·rat [ˈmʌskˌræt] N (*animal*) topo muschiato, ondatra; (*fur*) rat musqué *m inv*

musk rose N (*Bot*) rosa muschiata

Mus·lim, Mos·lem [ˈmʊslɪm] ADJ, N musulmano(-a)

mus·lin [ˈmʌzlɪn] N mussola (di cotone) ♦ ADJ di mussola

mus·quash [ˈmʌskwɒʃ] N (*fur*) rat musqué *m inv*

mus·sel [ˈmʌsl] N cozza

must [mʌst] MODAL AUX VB **1** (*obligation*) dovere; **I must do it** devo farlo; **if you must** se proprio devi; **one must not be too hopeful** non bisogna sperare troppo; **there must be a reason** ci deve (pur) essere un motivo; **I must say** francamente; **you mustn't forget to send her an e-mail** non devi dimenticare di mandarle una mail; **you must come again next year** devi assolutamente tornare il prossimo anno; **you must be joking!** stai scherzando! **2** (*probability*): **he must be there by now** dovrebbe essere arrivato ormai; **it must be cold up there** dev'essere freddo lassù; **I must have made a mistake** devo essermi sbagliato; **there must be some problem** dev'esserci qualche problema ♦ N (*fam*): **this programme/trip is a must** è un programma/viaggio da non perdere; **for a celebration champagne is a must** per celebrare qc lo champagne è d'obbligo

mus·tache [məˈstɑːʃ] N (*USA*) = **moustache**

mus·tard [ˈmʌstəd] N senape *f*; (*also:* **grain mustard**) mostarda

mustard gas N (*Chem*) iprite *f*

mus·ter [ˈmʌstəʳ] N (*gathering*) adunata; (*roll-call*) appello; **to pass muster** (*fig*) essere (considerato(-a)) accettabile *or* passabile ♦ VT (*men, helpers*) radunare, mettere insieme; (*money, sum*) mettere insieme; (*also:* **muster up**: *strength, courage*) fare appello a; **I can't muster up any enthusiasm** non riesco ad entusiasmarmi; **he mustered his troops** ha radunato le truppe; **he mustered his courage** ha fatto appello al proprio coraggio ♦ VI radunarsi

musti·ness [ˈmʌstɪnɪs] N odor di muffa *or* di stantio

mustn't [ˈmʌsnt] = **must not**

mus·ty [ˈmʌstɪ] ADJ (*comp* -ier, *superl* -iest) (*smell*) (che sa) di stantio *or* di muffa; (*ideas*) ammuffito(-a), stantio(-a); **to smell musty** aver odore di stantio

mu·tant [ˈmjuːtənt] ADJ, N mutante *m/f*

mu·tate [mjuːˈteɪt] VI subire una mutazione

mu·ta·tion [mjuːˈteɪʃən] N mutazione *f*

mute [mjuːt] ADJ (*comp* -r, *superl* -st) muto(-a) ♦ N (*person*) muto(-a); (*Mus*) sordina

mut·ed [ˈmjuːtɪd] ADJ (*noise*) attutito(-a), smorzato(-a); (*criticism*) attenuato(-a); (*Mus*) in sordina; (*trumpet*) con sordina

mu·ti·late [ˈmjuːtɪˌleɪt] VT mutilare

mu·ti·la·tion [ˌmjuːtɪˈleɪʃən] N mutilazione *f*

mu·ti·nous [ˈmjuːtɪnəs] ADJ (*sailor, troops*) ammutinato(-a); (*attitude*) ribelle

mu·ti·ny [ˈmjuːtɪnɪ] N ammutinamento ♦ VI ammutinarsi

mut·ter [ˈmʌtəʳ] N borbottio ♦ VT borbottare, bofonchiare ♦ VI borbottare; (*thunder*) brontolare

mut·ton [ˈmʌtn] N carne *f* di montone, montone *m*; **a leg of mutton** un cosciotto di montone; **mutton dressed as lamb** (*fig*) una vecchia che vuol sembrare una giovincella

mu·tu·al [ˈmjuːtjʊəl] ADJ (*affection, suspicion*) reciproco(-a); (*interests*) mutuo(-a), reciproco(-a), comune; (*friend, cousin*) comune; **to our mutual satisfaction** in modo da soddisfare entrambi, con reciproca soddisfazione; **the feeling was mutual** il sentimento era reciproco

mu·tu·al·ly [ˈmjuːtjʊəlɪ] ADV reciprocamente; **a mutually agreed solution** una soluzione soddisfacente per entrambe le parti

muz·zle [ˈmʌzl] N (*snout*) muso; (*of gun*) bocca (da fuoco); (*for dog*) museruola ♦ VT (*dog*) mettere la museruola a; (*fig: person*) costringere a tacere

MVP [ˌɛmviːˈpiː] N = **most valuable player**(*USA: Sport*) miglior giocatore(-trice)

my [maɪ] POSS ADJ il (la) mio(-a), *pl* i (le) miei(-mie); **this is my house** questa è la mia casa; **my brother** mio fratello; **my friend** il mio amico; **my parents** i miei genitori; **my car** la mia macchina; **my opinions** le mie opinioni; **I've lost my wallet** ho perduto il portafoglio; **with my hands in my pockets** con le mani in tasca; **I want to wash my hair** voglio lavarmi i capelli; **I've hurt my foot** mi sono fatto male ad un piede

Myan·mar [ˈmaɪænmɑːˈ] N la Myanmar

my·op·ic [maɪˈɒpɪk] ADJ miope

myri·ad [ˈmɪrɪəd] N miriade *f*

my·self [maɪˈsɛlf] PERS PRON (*reflexive*) mi; (*emphatic*) io stesso(-a); (*after preposition*) me, me stesso(-a); **by myself** da solo; **I don't like travelling by myself** non mi piace viaggiare da solo; **I did it (all) by myself** l'ho fatto (tutto) da solo; **I'm not myself today** non mi sento in forma oggi; **I've hurt myself** mi sono fatto male; **I looked at myself in the mirror** mi sono guardato allo specchio; **a beginner like myself** un principiante come me; **I made it myself** l'ho fatto io; *see also* **oneself**

mys·teri·ous [mɪsˈtɪərɪəs] ADJ misterioso(-a)

mys·tery [ˈmɪstərɪ] N mistero; **it's a mystery to me where it can have gone** dove sia finito (per me) è un mistero; **a murder mystery** un romanzo giallo ♦ ADJ (*man, woman*) misterioso(-a)

mystery story N racconto del mistero

mys·tic [ˈmɪstɪk] ADJ, N mistico(-a)

mys·ti·cal [ˈmɪstɪkəl] ADJ mistico(-a)

mys·ti·fy [ˈmɪstɪˌfaɪ] VT (*bewilder*) lasciare perplesso(-a), disorientare; **I'm totally mystified!** sono totalmente confuso! ❑ **mystify** is not translated by the Italian word *mistificare*

mys·tique [mɪsˈtiːk] N fascino

myth [mɪθ] N mito; **a Greek myth** un mito greco; **that's a myth** è una credenza falsa

mythi·cal [ˈmɪθɪkəl] ADJ mitico(-a)

mytho·logi·cal [ˌmɪθəˈlɒdʒɪkəl] ADJ mitologico(-a)

my·thol·ogy [mɪˈθɒlədʒɪ] N mitologia

Nn

N¹, n¹ [ɛn] N (*letter*) N, n *f inv, m inv*; **N for Nellie**, (*USA*) **N for Nan** ≈ N come Napoli

N² ABBR (= *north*) N (= *nord*)

NA [ˌɛnˈeɪ] N ABBR **1** (*USA*: = *Narcotics Anonymous*) associazione in aiuto dei tossicodipendenti **2** (*USA*: = *National Academy*)

n/a ABBR **1** (= *not applicable*) non pertinente **2** (*Comm, etc*) = **no account**

nab [næb] VT (*fam: thief etc*) acciuffare, beccare; (: *person to speak to*) beccare, bloccare

na·dir [ˈneɪdɪəʳ] N (*Astron*) nadir *m*; (*fig*) punto più basso

nag¹ [næg] N (*pej: horse*) ronzino

nag² [næg] VT (*also:* **nag at**) assillare, tormentare; **the children nagged (at) their parents to take them to the fair** i bambini hanno tormentato i genitori per farsi portare alle giostre; **the family nagged me into buying a new car** a forza di insistere in famiglia mi hanno fatto comprare una macchina nuova ♦ VI lagnarsi, brontolare in continuazione ♦ N (*person*) brontolone(-a)

nag·ging [ˈnægɪŋ] ADJ (*person*) brontolone(-a); (*pain*) insistente, persistente; (*doubt, fear etc*) tormentoso(-a), angoscioso(-a) ♦ N brontolii *mpl*, osservazioni *fpl* continue

nail [neɪl] N **1** (*Anat*) unghia; **to bite one's nails** mangiarsi le unghie **2** (*metal*) chiodo; **he hammered a nail into the wall** ha piantato un chiodo nel muro; **to hit the nail on the head** (*fig*) cogliere *or* colpire nel segno; **to pay cash on the nail** (*Brit*) pagare subito e in contanti, pagare sull'unghia (*fam*) ♦ VT (*also fig: fam: criminal*) inchiodare; **to nail the lid on a box** inchiodare il coperchio di una cassa

▸ **nail down** VT + ADV fissare con chiodi, inchiodare; (*fig*): **to nail sb down to a date** costringere qn a una data; **to nail sb down to a promise** costringere qn a fare una promessa; **to nail sb down to a price** costringere qn ad accettare un prezzo

▸ **nail up** VT + ADV (*picture, sign*) fissare con un chiodo; (*door*) chiudere con chiodi

nail·brush [ˈneɪlbrʌʃ] N spazzolino per unghie

nail·file [ˈneɪlfaɪl] N lima *or* limetta per unghie

nail polish N smalto per unghie

nail polish remover, nail varnish remover (*Brit*) N acetone *m*, solvente *m*

nail scissors NPL forbicine *fpl* per unghie

nail varnish N (*Brit*) = **nail polish**

Nai·ro·bi [naɪˈrəʊbɪ] N Nairobi *f*

na·ive [naɪˈiːv] ADJ ingenuo(-a)

na·ive·ty [naɪˈiːvtɪ] N ingenuità *f inv*

na·ked [ˈneɪkɪd] ADJ (*person*) nudo(-a); (*hillside, trees*) spoglio(-a), nudo(-a); **the naked truth** la verità nuda e cruda; **visible to the naked eye** che si può vedere a occhio nudo; **with the naked eye** a occhio nudo

na·ked·ness [ˈneɪkɪdnɪs] N nudità *f*

name [neɪm] N nome *m*; (*of book etc*) titolo; (*reputation*) (buon) nome, fama, reputazione *f*; **what's your name?** come ti chiami?; **my name is Peter** mi chiamo Peter; **his real name** il suo vero nome; **by the name of Jones** di nome Jones; **to go by** *or* **under the name of** farsi chiamare; **she knows them all by name** li conosce tutti per nome; **I know him only by name** lo conosco solo di nome; **in the name of the law/of God** in nome della legge/di Dio; **in the name of all those present** a nome di tutti i presenti; **in name only** solo di nome; **to take sb's name and address** prendere nome e indirizzo di qn; (*Police*) prendere le generalità di qn; **to put one's name down for** (*ticket*) mettersi in lista per avere; (*school, course*) mettersi in lista per; **to call sb names** insultare qn; **he's a big name in show business** è una personalità *or* un grosso nome nel mondo dello spettacolo; **he has a name for being honest** è noto *or* famoso per la sua onestà; **to protect one's (good) name** salvaguardare il proprio buon nome; **to make a name for o.s.** farsi un nome; **the firm has a good name** l'azienda ha una buona reputazione; **to get (o.s.) a bad name** farsi una cattiva fama *or* una brutta reputazione ♦ VT **1** (*baby etc*) chiamare; (*ship*) battezzare; **a man named Jones** un uomo di nome Jones; **he was named after his father** gli è stato dato il nome del padre; **they haven't named him yet** non gli hanno ancora dato un nome **2** (*mention*) nominare, fare il nome di; (*identify*) identificare; (*accomplice*) fare il nome di, rivelare il nome di; **to name sb for a post** proporre la candidatura di qn a una carica, proporre qn per una carica; **you name it, we've got it** abbiamo tutto quello che vuoi **3** (*date, price etc*) stabilire, fissare; **have you named the day yet?** (*for wedding*) avete già fissato la data?

name-dropping [ˈneɪmˌdrɒpɪŋ] N: **there was a lot of name-dropping in his speech** il suo discorso era infarcito di nomi di gente famosa

name·less [ˈneɪmlɪs] ADJ (*unknown*) senza nome; (*anonymous*) ignoto(-a), anonimo(-a); (*indefinable: fears, crimes*) indescrivibile, indefinibile; **a certain person who shall be nameless** una persona di cui non verrà fatto il nome

name·ly [ˈneɪmlɪ] ADV vale a dire

name·plate [ˈneɪmpleɪt] N (*on door etc*) targa, targhetta

name·sake [ˈneɪmseɪk] N omonimo(-a)

nan bread [ˈnɑːnbrɛd] N tipo di pane indiano poco lievitato di forma schiacciata

nan·ny [ˈnænɪ] N (*children's*) bambinaia, tata (*fam*)

nanny goat N capra

nap¹ [næp] N (*sleep*) sonnellino, pisolino; **to have** *or* **take a nap** fare *or* farsi un sonnellino, schiacciare un pisolino; **she likes to have a nap in the afternoon** le piace fare un pisolino di pomeriggio ♦ VI: **to be caught napping** essere preso(-a) alla sprovvista

nap² [næp] N (*on cloth*) peluria; **against the nap** contropelo

na·palm [ˈneɪpɑːm] N napalm *m*

nape [neɪp] N: **nape of the neck** nuca

nap·kin [ˈnæpkɪn] N (*also:* **table napkin**) tovagliolo, salvietta

Na·ples [ˈneɪplz] N Napoli *f*

Na·po·leon·ic [nəˌpəʊlɪˈɒnɪk] ADJ napoleonico(-a)

nap·py [ˈnæpɪ] N (*Brit*) pannolino

nar·cis·sis·tic [ˌnɑːsɪˈsɪstɪk] ADJ (*frm*) narcisistico(-a)

nar·cis·sus [nɑːˈsɪsəs] N (*pl* **narcissi** [nɑːˈsɪsaɪ]) (*flower*) narciso

nar·cot·ic [nɑːˈkɒtɪk] ADJ narcotico(-a) ♦ N (*Med*) narcotico; **narcotics** (*drugs*) narcotici *mpl*, stupefacenti *mpl*

nark [nɑːk] VT (*Brit fam*) scocciare

nar·rate [nəˈreɪt] VT narrare, raccontare

nar·ra·tion [nəˈreɪʃən] N narrazione *f*

nar·ra·tive [ˈnærətɪv] ADJ narrativo(-a) ♦ N narrazione *f*; (*technique*) narrativa

nar·ra·tor [nəˈreɪtəʳ] N narratore(-trice)

nar·row [ˈnærəʊ] ADJ (*comp* **-er**, *superl* **-est**) (*gen*) stretto(-a); (*advantage, majority*) scarso(-a); (*outlook, mind*) ristretto(-a), limitato(-a); (*interpretation*) limitato(-a); (*means*) limitato(-a), modesto(-a); **to have a narrow escape** farcela per un pelo, scamparla bella; **to take a narrow view of** avere una visione limitata di ♦ VI (*also:* **narrow down**) (*road, investigations*) restringere; (*choice*) restringere, ridurre; **to narrow sth down to** ridurre qc a; **we have narrowed the field (down) to three candidates** abbiamo ristretto la scelta a tre candidati **2** (*eyes*) stringere ♦ VI (*road*) restringersi; (*majority*) ridursi; (*eyes*) stringersi; **so the question narrows down to this** la questione, quindi, si riduce a questo

narrow-gauge [ˈnærəʊˌɡeɪdʒ] ADJ (*Rail*) a scartamento ridotto

nar·row·ly [ˈnærəʊlɪ] ADV 1 (miss, escape etc): **Maria narrowly escaped drowning** per un pelo Maria non è affogata; **he narrowly missed hitting the cyclist** per poco non ha investito il ciclista 2 (interpret: rules etc) rigorosamente

narrow-minded [ˌnærəʊˈmaɪndɪd] ADJ (pej: person) di idee ristrette; (: views, outlook etc) ristretto(-a)

NAS [ɛneɪˈɛs] N ABBR (USA: = National Academy of Sciences)

NASA [ˈnæsə] N ABBR (USA: = National Aeronautics and Space Administration) N.A.S.A. f

na·sal [ˈneɪzəl] ADJ nasale

Nas·sau [ˈnæsaʊ] N Nassau f

nas·ti·ly [ˈnɑːstɪlɪ] ADV (unpleasantly) sgradevolmente; (spitefully) malignamente, con cattiveria

nas·ti·ness [ˈnɑːstɪnɪs] N (of person, remark) malignità, cattiveria

na·stur·tium [nəˈstɜːʃəm] N cappuccina, nasturzio (indiano)

nas·ty [ˈnɑːstɪ] ADJ (comp -ier, superl -iest) (smell, taste) cattivo(-a), sgradevole; (moment, experience, situation) brutto(-a), spiacevole; (accident, wound, corner, trick) brutto(-a); (person) antipatico(-a), villano(-a); (spiteful: also: remark, mind) maligno(-a), cattivo(-a)(temper, nature) brutto(-a); (weather) brutto(-a), cattivo(-a); (book, film etc) di cattivo gusto; (violent) violento(-a); **a nasty cold** un brutto raffreddore; **a nasty smell** un cattivo odore; **to smell nasty** avere un cattivo odore, non avere un buon odore; **to turn nasty** (situation) mettersi male; (weather) guastarsi; (person) incattivirsi; **he's a nasty piece of work** (fam) è un farabutto; **what a nasty mind you have!** quanto sei maligno!; **he had a nasty time of it** se l'è passata brutta; **she gave me a nasty look** mi ha dato un'occhiataccia; **it's a nasty business** è una brutta faccenda, è un brutto affare

na·tion [ˈneɪʃən] N nazione f

na·tion·al [ˈnæʃənl] ADJ nazionale; **national news** notizie fpl dall'interno; **national press** stampa (a diffusione) nazionale ♦ N cittadino(-a)

national anthem N inno nazionale

national debt N debito pubblico

national dress, national costume N costume m nazionale

National Guard N (USA): **the National Guard** la milizia nazionale (volontaria, in ogni stato)

National Health N (Brit: also: National Health Service) servizio nazionale di assistenza sanitaria; **I got it on the National Health** l'ho avuto con la mutua

National Insurance N (Brit) ≈ Previdenza Sociale

na·tion·al·ism [ˈnæʃnəˌlɪzəm] N nazionalismo

na·tion·al·ist [ˈnæʃnəlɪst] ADJ nazionalista; (sympathies) nazionalistico(-a) ♦ N nazionalista m/f

na·tion·al·ity [ˌnæʃəˈnælɪtɪ] N nazionalità f inv; (citizenship) cittadinanza, nazionalità

na·tion·al·i·za·tion [ˌnæʃnəlaɪˈzeɪʃən] N nazionalizzazione f

na·tion·al·ize [ˈnæʃnəˌlaɪz] VT nazionalizzare

na·tion·al·ly [ˈnæʃnəlɪ] ADV (consider) da un punto di vista nazionale; (broadcast) in tutto il paese; (apply etc) a livello nazionale

national park N parco nazionale

National Security Council N (USA) consiglio nazionale di sicurezza

national service N (Mil) servizio militare

National Trust N (Brit): **the National Trust** ≈ soprintendenza ai beni culturali e ambientali

nation-wide [ˈneɪʃənˌwaɪd] ADJ, ADV su scala nazionale

na·tive [ˈneɪtɪv] ADJ 1 (country, town) natale, natio(-a), nativo(-a); (dialect) nativo(-a); **he's a native Italian speaker** è di madrelingua italiana; **native language** lingua materna, madrelingua; **native land** paese m natio, patria; **my native country** il mio paese natale 2 (innate: ability) innato(-a), naturale 3 (indigenous: animal, plant) indigeno(-a), originario(-a); (: product, resources) del luogo, del paese; **native to** originario(-a) di; **Britain's native red squirrel** lo scoiattolo rosso originario della Gran Bretagna 4 (of the natives: customs, costume, rites) del luogo, del paese 5 (offensive: non-Western) indigeno(-a) ♦ N 1 (of birth, nationality) abitante m/f del luogo; **he's a native of Japan** è giapponese di nascita; **he's a native of Salzburg** è originario di Salisburgo; **he speaks Italian like a native**

parla l'italiano come un madrelingua 2 (offensive: esp in colonies) indigeno(-a)

Native American N discendente di tribù nordamericana dell'America settentrionale

Na·tiv·i·ty [nəˈtɪvɪtɪ] N (Rel): **the Nativity** la Natività

nativity play N rappresentazione f della Natività

NATO [ˈneɪtəʊ] N ABBR (= North Atlantic Treaty Organisation) N.A.T.O. f

nat·ter [ˈnætəʳ](fam) N chiacchierata; **to have a natter** fare quattro chiacchiere ♦ VI chiacchierare

natu·ral [ˈnætʃrəl] ADJ (gen) naturale; (ability) innato(-a); (manner) semplice; **death from natural causes** (Law) morte f per cause naturali; **he died a natural death** è morto di morte naturale; **a natural instinct** un istinto naturale; **in its natural state** allo stato naturale; **he never knew his natural parents** non ha mai conosciuto i suoi veri genitori; **it's natural to be tired after a long journey** è naturale essere stanchi dopo un lungo viaggio; **it seemed the natural thing to do** è sembrata la cosa più ovvia or più naturale da farsi; **it is natural that ...** è naturale che... + sub; **he's a natural painter** è un pittore nato; **C natural** (Mus) do naturale ♦ N 1 (Mus: sign) bequadro 2 **she's a natural!** ci è nata!

natural childbirth N parto naturale

natural gas N gas m metano

natural history N storia naturale

natu·ral·ist [ˈnætʃrəlɪst] N naturalista m/f

natu·rali·za·tion [ˌnætʃrəlaɪˈzeɪʃən] N (see vb) naturalizzazione f; acclimatazione f

natu·ral·ize [ˈnætʃrəˌlaɪz] VT: **to be naturalized** (person) naturalizzarsi; **to become naturalized** (animal, plant) acclimatarsi

natu·ral·ly [ˈnætʃrəlɪ] ADV 1 (gen) naturalmente; **naturally, we were very disappointed** naturalmente siamo rimasti molto delusi 2 (by nature: gifted) di natura, per natura; **he is naturally lazy** è pigro per natura; **my hair is naturally curly** i miei capelli sono ricci per natura; **a naturally optimistic person** un ottimista per natura; **it comes naturally to him to do ...** gli viene spontaneo fare... 3 (unaffectedly: behave, speak) con naturalezza, in modo naturale 4 (of course) naturalmente, certo

natu·ral·ness [ˈnætʃrəlnɪs] N naturalezza

natural resources NPL risorse fpl naturali

natural selection N selezione f naturale

natural wastage N (Industry) naturale diminuzione f di personale (per pensionamento, decesso, ecc.)

na·ture [ˈneɪtʃəʳ] N 1 natura; **a law of nature** una legge di natura; **the laws of nature** le leggi naturali or della natura; **to draw/paint from nature** disegnare/dipingere dal vero 2 (character: of person) natura, indole f; (: of thing) natura; **by nature** per natura, di natura; **it's not in his nature to say that** non è nella sua natura or nel suo carattere parlare cosi; **it's second nature to him to do that** gli viene quasi istintivo farlo 3 (kind, type) natura; **things of this nature** cose fpl di questo genere; **the ambitious nature of the project** la natura ambiziosa del progetto; **documents of a confidential nature** documenti mpl di natura riservata; **something in the nature of an apology** una specie di scusa

-natured [ˈneɪtʃəd] SUFF: **ill-natured** maldisposto(-a); **jealous-natured** geloso(-a) di natura, di temperamento geloso

nature reserve N (Brit) parco naturale

nature trail N percorso tracciato in parchi nazionali ecc. con scopi educativi

na·tur·ist [ˈneɪtʃərɪst] N naturista m/f, nudista m/f

naught [nɔːt] N 1 (Math) = **nought** 2 (old, liter: nothing) niente m, nulla m; **to come to naught** finire in nulla

naugh·ti·ness [ˈnɔːtɪnɪs] N cattiveria

naugh·ty [ˈnɔːtɪ] ADJ (comp -ier, superl -iest) 1 (child) cattivo(-a), cattivello(-a), birichino(-a); **that was a naughty thing to do** non si fanno queste cose 2 (joke, song, story, film) spinto(-a)

nau·sea [ˈnɔːzɪə] N (Med) nausea; (fig: disgust) schifo, disgusto

nau·se·ate [ˈnɔːzɪˌeɪt] VT (Med) nauseare; (fig) far schifo a, disgustare; **I was nauseated by the smell** ero nauseato dall'odore

nau·seat·ing [ˈnɔːzɪˌeɪtɪŋ] ADJ nauseante; (fig) disgustoso(-a)

nau·seous ['nɔːzɪəs] ADJ (*Med, also fig*) nauseabondo(-a); **to be nauseous** avere la nausea

nau·ti·cal ['nɔːtɪkəl] ADJ nautico(-a)

nautical mile N miglio nautico *or* marino

na·val ['neɪvəl] ADJ (*battle, strength, base, academy*) navale; (*affairs, barracks*) della marina; **naval forces** forze *fpl* navali, marina militare; **naval officer** ufficiale *m* di marina

nave [neɪv] N (*of church*) navata centrale
  ❑ nave is not translated by the Italian word *nave*

na·vel ['neɪvəl] N ombelico

navi·gable ['nævɪgəbl] ADJ (*river etc*) navigabile

navi·gate ['nævɪgeɪt] VT (*ship, plane*) pilotare, governare; (*seas, river*) navigare, percorrere navigando ♦ VI navigare; (*Aut*) fare da navigatore

navi·ga·tion [ˌnævɪ'geɪʃən] N navigazione *f*

navi·ga·tor ['nævɪgeɪtə'] N (*Naut, Aer*) navigatore *m*, ufficiale *m* di rotta; (*explorer*) navigatore *m*; (*Aut*) secondo pilota *m*, copilota *m/f*

navy ['neɪvɪ] N marina (militare *or* da guerra); **to join the navy** arruolarsi in marina; **Department of the Navy** (*USA*) Ministero della Marina; **he's in the navy** è in marina

navy-blue [ˌneɪvɪ'bluː] ADJ (*also:* **navy**) blu scuro *inv*; **a navy-blue skirt** una gonna blu scuro

Naza·reth ['næzərɪθ] N Nazareth *f*

Nazi ['nɑːtsɪ] ADJ, N nazista *m/f*

NB [ˌen'biː] N ABBR (= *nota bene*) N.B. ♦ ABBR (*Canada:* = **New Brunswick**)

NBA [ˌenbiː'eɪ] N ABBR 1 (*USA:* = *National Basket Association*) ≈ F.I.P. *f* (= *Federazione Italiana Pallacanestro*) 2 (*USA:* = **National Boxing Association**)

NC ABBR 1 (*Comm:* = *no charge*) gratis 2 (*USA Post:* = **North Carolina**)

NCO [ˌensiː'əʊ] N ABBR = **noncommissioned officer**

ND ABBR (*USA Post:* = **North Dakota**)

NE ABBR 1 (*USA Post:* = **Nebraska**) 2 (= *North East(ern*)) NE (= *nord est*)

neap [niːp] N (*also:* **neap tide**) marea di quadratura

Nea·poli·tan [nɪə'pɒlɪtən] ADJ, N napoletano(-a)

near [nɪə'] ADV vicino; **it's quite near** è abbastanza vicino; **I like to know that you are near** mi piace sapere che tu sei (qui) vicino *or* accanto; **near at hand** a portata di mano; (*event*) imminente, alle porte; **to come** *or* **draw near** (*person, event*) avvicinarsi; **come nearer** vieni più vicino, avvicinati; **to bring sth nearer (to)** portare qc più vicino (a); **he came near to being drowned** per poco non è annegato; **near to tears** sul punto di piangere; **that's near enough** va bene così; **there were 100 people there, near enough** c'erano pressappoco 100 persone; **nowhere near full** ben lontano(-a) dall'essere pieno(-a) ♦ PREP (*also:* **near to:** *of place*) vicino a, presso; (*in time*) circa, quasi; **it's very near to the school** è molto vicino alla scuola; **near here/there** qui/lì vicino; **is there a bank near here?** c'è una banca qui vicino?; **I live near Liverpool** abito vicino a Liverpool; **he was standing near the door** era in piedi vicino alla porta; **it was somewhere near midnight** era circa mezzanotte; **it's somewhere near here** dev'essere da queste parti; **the passage is near the end of the book** il brano è verso la fine del libro; **his views are very near my own** è di vedute molto simili alle mie; **nobody comes anywhere near her at cooking** nessuno può competere con lei in cucina ♦ ADJ (*comp* -**er**, *superl* -**est**) 1 (*in space, time*) vicino(-a); **where's the nearest service station?** dov'è la stazione di servizio più vicina?; **the nearest shops were three kilometres away** i negozi più vicini erano a tre chilometri di distanza; **in the near distance** a breve distanza; **the nearest way** la via *or* strada più breve; **£25,000 or nearest offer** (*Brit*) 25.000 sterline trattabili; **in the near future** in un prossimo futuro 2 (*relation*) stretto(-a), prossimo(-a) 3 **their win was a near thing** hanno vinto di misura; **that was a near thing!** per un pelo! ♦ VT (*place, event*) avvicinarsi a; **the building is nearing completion** il palazzo è quasi terminato *or* ultimato

near·by [nɪə'baɪ] ADV (qui *or* lì) vicino; **there's a supermarket nearby** c'è un supermercato qui vicino ♦ ADJ vicino(-a); **a nearby village** un paese vicino

Near East N: **the Near East** il Medio Oriente

near·ly ['nɪəlɪ] ADV 1 (*gen*) quasi; **I'm nearly fifteen** ho quasi quindici anni; **dinner's nearly ready** la cena è quasi pronta; **not nearly non... affatto; it's not nearly ready** non è affatto pronto; **that's not nearly enough** non basta per niente 2 (*with vb*): **I nearly lost it** per poco non lo perdevo; **she was nearly crying** era lì lì per piangere; **he very nearly died** ha rischiato di morire; **did you win? — very nearly!** hai vinto? — c'è mancato poco!

near miss N (*Aer*) incidente mancato; **that was a near miss** (*fig*) c'è mancato poco; **he had a near miss with that car** per un pelo non ha investito quella macchina

near·ness ['nɪənɪs] N prossimità, vicinanza

near·side ['nɪəsaɪd] N (*Aut: right-hand drive*) lato sinistro; (: *left-hand drive*) lato destro ♦ ADJ (*see n*) sinistro(-a); destro(-a)

near-sighted [ˌnɪə'saɪtɪd] ADJ miope

neat [niːt] ADJ (*comp* -**er**, *superl* -**est**) 1 (*tidy: person, handwriting*) ordinato(-a); (: *room, house, desk*) ordinato(-a), in ordine; (: *work*) accurato(-a), pulito(-a); (*well-dressed*) curato(-a) nel vestire; (*skilful: plan, solution*) indovinato(-a), azzeccato(-a); (: *USA fam: excellent*) figo(-a); **she is a neat worker** è molto accurata nel lavoro; **he has made a neat job of the bathroom** ha fatto un buon lavoro *or* un lavoro accurato nel bagno; **a neat little car** una bella macchinetta 2 (*undiluted: spirits*) liscio(-a)

neat·ly ['niːtlɪ] ADV 1 (*tidily: fold, wrap, dress*) accuratamente, con cura; (: *write*) bene, in bella calligrafia 2 (*skilfully*) abilmente; **neatly put** ben espresso(-a)

neat·ness ['niːtnɪs] N 1 (*tidiness*) ordine *m* 2 (*skilfulness*) abilità

Nebr. ABBR (*USA:* = **Nebraska**)

Ne·bras·ka [nɪ'bræskə] N il Nebraska

nebu·lous ['nɛbjʊləs] ADJ nebuloso(-a); (*fig*) nebuloso(-a), vago(-a)

nec·es·sari·ly ['nɛsɪsərɪlɪ] ADV necessariamente, per forza; (*lead to, give rise to*) inevitabilmente; **not necessarily** non necessariamente, non è detto

nec·es·sary ['nɛsɪsərɪ] ADJ (*gen*) necessario(-a); (*result, effect*) inevitabile; **a necessary evil** un male necessario; **is it necessary to make so much noise?** è proprio necessario *or* indispensabile far tanto rumore?; **it is necessary for you to go** *or* **that you go** è necessario che *or* bisogna che tu vada; **don't do more than is necessary** non fare più del necessario; **if necessary** se necessario (per); **the necessary qualifications (for)** i requisiti necessari (per); **necessary to health** necessario(-a) alla salute ♦ N (*fam: what is needed*): **to do the necessary** fare il necessario; **the necessary** (*money*) i quattrini

ne·ces·si·tate [nɪ'sɛsɪteɪt] VT rendere necessario(-a)

ne·ces·sity [nɪ'sɛsɪtɪ] N 1 necessità; **there is no necessity for you to do that** non è necessario che *or* non c'è bisogno che tu lo faccia; **the necessity of doing sth** la necessità di fare qc; **is there any necessity?** è proprio necessario?, c'è proprio bisogno?; **of necessity** di necessità, necessariamente; **from** *or* **out of necessity** per necessità *or* bisogno; **in case of necessity** in caso di necessità 2 (*necessary thing*) cosa indispensabile, necessità *f inv*; **the bare necessities** lo stretto necessario, il minimo indispensabile

neck [nɛk] N (*Anat: of bottle*) collo; (*of garment*) collo, colletto; (*Dressmaking*) scollo; **to break one's neck** rompersi il collo (*fig*) affannarsi; **to have a stiff neck** avere il torcicollo; **a V-neck sweater** un maglione con il collo a V; **the favourite won by a neck** (*Horseracing*) il favorito ha vinto per un'incollatura; **neck and neck** testa a testa; **to be up to one's neck in work** (*fam*) essere immerso(-a) nel lavoro fino al collo; **he is in it up to his neck** (*fam*) c'è dentro fino al collo; **to risk one's neck** rischiare l'osso del collo, rischiare la pelle; **to save one's neck** salvare la pelle; **to stick one's neck out** (*fam*) rischiare (forte); **in this neck of the woods** (*fam*) in questi paraggi, da queste parti; **dress with a low neck, low-necked dress** vestito scollato ♦ VI (*fam*) pomiciare, sbaciucchiarsi

neck·lace ['nɛklɪs] N collana; **pearl necklace** collana di perle

neck·line ['nɛklaɪn] N scollatura

neck·tie ['nɛktaɪ] N (*esp USA*) cravatta

nec·tar ['nɛktə'] N nettare *m*

nec·tar·ine ['nɛktərɪn] N nocepesca

née [neɪ] ADJ nata; **Mary Green née Smith** Mary Green nata Smith

need [niːd] N **1** (*necessity, obligation*) bisogno, necessità *f inv*; **if need(s) be** se necessario; **in case of need** in caso di bisogno *or* necessità; **there's no need to worry** non c'è bisogno di preoccuparsi; **there's no need for you to come too** non c'è bisogno *or* non occorre che venga anche tu; **what need is there to buy it?** che bisogno c'è di comprarlo? **2** (*want, lack*) bisogno; (*poverty*) povertà, bisogno; **to be in need of, to have need of** aver bisogno di; **it's in need of a wash** ha bisogno di una lavata; **she felt in need of a friend** sentiva il bisogno di un amico; **there's a great need for a book on this subject** c'è molto bisogno di un libro su questo argomento; **in times of need** nei momenti difficili; **to be in need** essere bisognoso(-a) **3** (*thing needed*) bisogno, necessità *f inv*; **£100 will meet my immediate needs** 100 sterline mi basteranno per le necessità più urgenti; **his needs are few** non ha grosse esigenze; **the needs of industry** le esigenze dell'industria ♦ VT aver bisogno di; **he needs money** ha bisogno di soldi, gli occorrono soldi; **I need it** ne ho bisogno, mi serve; **it's just what I need** è proprio quel che mi ci vuole; **a signature is needed** occorre *or* ci vuole una firma; **a much needed holiday** una vacanza di cui si ha proprio bisogno; **all that you need** tutto ciò che occorre; **he doesn't need me to tell him what to do** non c'è bisogno che sia io a dirgli cosa deve fare; **he needs watching** *or* **to be watched** va tenuto d'occhio; **this book needs careful reading** questo libro richiede un'attenta lettura; **the report needs no comment** il rapporto non ha bisogno di commenti; **he needs to have everything explained to him** bisogna spiegargli proprio tutto; **he doesn't need to be told all the details** non c'è bisogno di *or* non occorre dirgli tutti i particolari; **you only needed to ask** bastava che lo chiedessi; **it needed a war to alter things** c'è voluta una guerra per cambiare le cose ♦ MODAL AUX VB: **need I go?** devo (proprio) andarci?; **I need hardly tell you that ...** non c'è bisogno che io le dica *or* di dirle che...; **I need to do it** bisogna che io lo faccia, lo devo fare; **you don't need to go** non c'è bisogno che *or* non è necessario che tu vada, non devi andare per forza; **you needn't wait** non c'è bisogno che *or* non è necessario che aspetti; **you needn't have bothered to come** non occorreva che venissi; **it need not be done now** non c'è bisogno di farlo ora; **it need not follow that ...** non ne consegue necessariamente che... + *sub*

nee·dle [niːdl] N ago; (*on record player*) puntina; **knitting needle** ferro (da calza); **it's like looking for a needle in a haystack** è come cercare un ago in un pagliaio; **to give sb the needle** (*fam: annoy*) dare ai nervi a qn ♦ VT (*fam: annoy*) irritare, dare ai nervi a; (: *tease, provoke*) punzecchiare

needle·cord [niːdl kɔːd] N (*Brit*) velluto a coste sottili

need·less [niːdlɪs] ADJ inutile; **needless to say he didn't keep his promise** inutile dire che non ha mantenuto la promessa

need·less·ly [niːdlɪslɪ] ADV inutilmente

needle·work [niːdl wɜːk] N cucito; (*embroidery*) ricamo

needn't [niːdnt] = **need not**

needy [niːdɪ] ADJ (*comp* -**ier**, *superl* -**iest**) bisognoso(-a)

ne·ga·tion [nɪ geɪʃən] N negazione *f*

nega·tive [negətɪv] ADJ negativo(-a); **he's got a very negative attitude** ha un atteggiamento molto negativo ♦ N **1** (*answer*): **his answer was a firm negative** ha risposto con un fermo no *or* con. un fermo diniego; **an answer in the negative** una risposta negativa; **to answer in the negative** rispondere negativamente *or* di no **2** (*Gram*) negazione *f*; **to put a sentence into the negative** mettere una frase in forma negativa **3** (*Phot*) negativa, negativo **4** (*Elec*) polo negativo

ne·glect [nɪ glekt] VT (*friends, children, garden*) trascurare; (*opportunity*) lasciarsi sfuggire; (*obligations*) mancare a; **to neglect to do sth** trascurare *or* tralasciare di fare qc ♦ N (*lack of care*) trascuratezza; (*of child*) il trascurare; (*of duty*) negligenza; (*of rule etc*) mancata osservanza; **neglect of one's appearance** trascuratezza nel vestire; **his neglect of his friends** l'aver trascurato gli amici; **in a state of neglect** (*house, garden*) in stato di abbandono

ne·glect·ed [nɪ glektɪd] ADJ trascurato(-a)

ne·glect·ful [nɪ glektfʊl] ADJ (*gen*) negligente; (*parent*) che trascura; **to be neglectful of sb/sth** trascurare qn/qc

neg·li·gee [negli ʒeɪ] N négligé *m inv*

neg·li·gence [neglɪdʒəns] N negligenza; **through negligence** per negligenza; **criminal negligence** (*Law*) reato d'omissione

neg·li·gent [neglɪdʒənt] ADJ **1** (*careless*) negligente **2** (*offhand: gesture, manner*) noncurante, disinvolto(-a)

neg·li·gent·ly [neglɪdʒəntlɪ] ADV con negligenza

neg·li·gible [neglɪdʒəbl] ADJ trascurabile, insignificante

ne·go·tiable [nɪ gəʊʃɪəbl] ADJ **1** (*Comm, etc*) negoziabile; (*cheque*) trasferibile; **not negotiable** non trasferibile **2** (*road*) transitabile; (*river*) navigabile; (*hill*) valicabile

ne·go·ti·ate [nɪ gəʊʃɪeɪt] VT **1** (*Comm: treaty, loan, sale*) negoziare, trattare **2** (*obstacle, difficulty, hill*) superare; (*river*) passare; (*bend in road*) prendere ♦ VI trattare, condurre (le) trattative; **to negotiate with sb for sth** trattare con qn per ottenere qc

ne·go·tiat·ing ta·ble [nɪ gəʊʃɪeɪtɪŋ teɪbl] N tavolo delle trattative

ne·go·tia·tion [nɪ gəʊʃɪeɪʃən] N (*gen*) trattativa; (*Pol*) negoziato, trattativa; **to enter into negotiations with sb** entrare in trattative *or* intavolare i negoziati con qn

ne·go·tia·tor [nɪ gəʊʃɪeɪtəʳ] N negoziatore(-trice)

Ne·gro [niːgrəʊ] (*often offensive*) N (*pl* -**es**) negro(-a)

neigh [neɪ] VI nitrire ♦ N nitrito

neigh·bour, neigh·bor (*USA*) [neɪbəʳ] N vicino(-a); (*Bible, etc*) prossimo(-a)

neigh·bour·hood, neigh·bor·hood (*USA*) [neɪbəhʊd] N (*district*) quartiere *m*, vicinato; (*surrounding area*) vicinanze *fpl*; **the whole neighbourhood knows her** tutto il vicinato *or* il quartiere la conosce; **in the neighbourhood of the station** nelle vicinanze *or* nei paraggi della stazione; (*something*) **in the neighbourhood of £1,000** qualcosa come 1.000 sterline

neighbourhood watch N (*Brit: also:* **neighbourhood watch scheme**) *sistema di vigilanza reciproca in un quartiere*

neigh·bour·ing, neigh·bor·ing (*USA*) [neɪbərɪŋ] ADJ vicino(-a), confinante, limitrofo(-a)

neigh·bour·ly, neigh·bor·ly (*USA*) [neɪbəlɪ] ADJ (*action*) da buon vicino; (*feelings*) amichevole; **people here aren't very neighbourly** la gente qua non ha il senso del vicinato

nei·ther [naɪðəʳ] ADV né; **neither he nor I can go** né io né lui possiamo andare; **neither good nor bad** né buono(-a) né cattivo(-a); **he neither smokes nor drinks** non fuma né beve; **he likes neither the house nor the people** non gli piace né la casa né la gente; **neither Sarah nor Tamsin is coming to the party** alla festa non vengono né Sarah né Tamsin; **that's neither here nor there** (*fig*) questo non c'entra ♦ CONJ neanche, nemmeno, neppure; **if you aren't going, neither am I** se tu non ci vai, non ci vado neanch'io *or* nemmeno io; **I don't like it — neither do I** non mi piace — nemmeno a me; **I didn't move and neither did he** io non mi mossi e nemmeno lui; **... neither did I refuse** ...ma non ho nemmeno rifiutato ♦ ADJ: **on neither side** né da una parte né dall'altra; **neither story is true** nessuna delle due storie è vera ♦ PRON né l'uno(-a) né l'altro(-a), nessuno(-a) dei (delle) due; **neither of them has any money** né l'uno né l'altro *or* nessuno dei due ha soldi, non hanno soldi né l'uno né l'altro; **carrots or peas? — neither, thanks** vuoi carote o piselli? — nessuno dei due, grazie; **neither of them is coming** non viene nessuno dei due

neo- [niːəʊ] PREF neo-

neo·lith·ic [niːəʊ lɪθɪk] ADJ neolitico(-a)

ne·olo·gism [niː ɒlədʒɪzm] N neologismo

neon [niːɒn] N neon *m inv* ♦ ADJ al neon; **a neon light** una luce al neon

neon light N luce *f* al neon

neon sign N insegna al neon

Ne·pal [nɪ pɔːl] N il Nepal *m*

neph·ew [nevjuː] N nipote *m* (*di zii*)

nepo·tism [nepətɪzəm] N nepotismo

nerd [nɜːd] N (*fam, pej*) sfigato(-a)

nerve [nɜːv] N **1** (*Anat*) nervo; (*Bot*) nervatura; **my nerves**

are on edge ho i nervi tesi; **a fit of nerves** una crisi di nervi; **it/he gets on my nerves** mi dà ai nervi, mi fa venire i nervi **2** (*fig: courage*) coraggio; (*: calm*) sangue *m* freddo; (: *self-confidence*) fiducia in se stesso(-a); (: *fam: impudence*) sfacciataggine *f*, faccia tosta; **a man of nerve** un uomo che ha fegato; **to lose one's nerve** (*self-confidence*) perdere la fiducia in se stesso(-a); **I lost my nerve** (*courage*) mi è mancato il coraggio; **I hadn't the nerve to do it** non ho avuto il coraggio di farlo; (*cheek*) non ho avuto la faccia tosta di farlo; **he's got a nerve!** ha una bella faccia tosta! ♦ VT: **to nerve o.s. to do sth** farsi coraggio *or* animo per fare qc, armarsi di coraggio per fare qc

nerve centre N (*Anat*) centro nervoso; (*fig*) cervello, centro vitale

nerve gas N gas *m* nervino

nerve-racking [ˈnɜːvˌrækɪŋ] ADJ logorante

nerv·ous [ˈnɜːvəs] ADJ (*Anat, Med*) nervoso(-a); (*edgy*) nervoso(-a), agitato(-a), teso(-a); (*apprehensive*) ansioso(-a), apprensivo(-a); **he's full of nervous energy** è tutto nervi; **he is making me nervous** mi innervosisce; **I was nervous about speaking to her** (*apprehensive*) l'idea di parlarle mi agitava; (*excited*) ero emozionato all'idea di parlarle; **I'm nervous about flying** ho un po' paura di volare; **I bite my nails when I'm nervous** quando sono teso mi mangio le unghie; **I'm a bit nervous about the exams** sono un po' tesa per gli esami

nervous breakdown N esaurimento nervoso

nerv·ous·ly [ˈnɜːvəslɪ] ADV nervosamente; (*apprehensively*) con ansia

nerv·ous·ness [ˈnɜːvəsnɪs] N nervosismo; (*anxiousness*) ansia

nervous wreck N (*fam*): **to be a nervous wreck** avere i nervi a pezzi

nervy [ˈnɜːvɪ] ADJ (*comp* **-ier**, *superl* **-iest**) (*fam: Brit: tense*) teso(-a), nervoso(-a); (: *USA: cheeky*) sfacciato(-a)

nest [nɛst] N **1** nido **2 nest of tables** tris *m* di tavolini ♦ VI fare il nido, nidificare

nest egg N (*fig*) gruzzolo

nes·tle [ˈnɛsl] VI accoccolarsi; **to nestle up to** *or* **against sb** accoccolarsi vicino a qn, rannicchiarsi accanto a qn; **to nestle down in bed** sistemarsi ben bene nel letto; **a village nestling among hills** un paesetto annidato tra le colline

nest·ling [ˈnɛslɪŋ] N uccellino di nido, nidiaceo

Net [nɛt] N (= *the Net*) la Rete

net¹ [nɛt] N **1** (*gen, also fig*) rete *f*; (*for hair*) retina (per capelli); (*fabric*) tulle *m*; **a fishing net** una rete da pesca **2** (*Geom*) sviluppo ♦ VT (*fish, game*) prendere con la rete

net² [nɛt] ADJ (*weight, price, salary*) netto(-a); **net assets** patrimonio netto, attività *fpl* nette; **he earns £30,000 net per year** guadagna 30.000 sterline nette all'anno; **net of tax** al netto delle tasse ♦ VT (*get, obtain*) ottenere; (*make: profit*) fare; (*subj: deal, sale*) dare un utile netto di

net·ball [ˈnɛtˌbɔːl] N *sport simile alla pallacanestro*

net curtains NPL tende *fpl* di tulle

Neth·er·lands [ˈnɛðələndz] NPL: **the Netherlands** i Paesi Bassi

neti·quette [ˈnɛtɪket] N netiquette *f*, norme di comportamento per gli utenti di internet

net profit N utile *m* netto

net·surf·er [ˈnɛtsɜːfə*] N navigatore(-trice) in internet

nett [nɛt] ADJ = **net**²

net·ting [ˈnɛtɪŋ] N (*nets*) reti *fpl*; (*mesh*) rete; (*also: wire netting: for fence etc*) rete metallica, reticolato; (*fabric*) tulle *m*

net·tle [ˈnɛtl] N ortica ♦ VT esasperare; **he is easily nettled** è una persona facilmente irritabile

net·work [ˈnɛtˌwɜːk] N **1** (*Elec, TV: fig*) rete *f*; **network of roads** rete stradale; **spy network** rete spionistica *or* di spie **2** (*Comput*) rete *f*, network *m inv* ♦ VT (*TV*) trasmettere su rete nazionale

neu·ral·gia [njʊˈrældʒə] N nevralgia

neu·ro·logi·cal [ˌnjʊərəʊˈlɒdʒɪkəl] ADJ neurologico(-a)

neu·ro·sis [njʊˈrəʊsɪs] N (*pl* **neuroses** [njʊˈrəʊsiːz]) nevrosi *f inv*

neu·rot·ic [njʊˈrɒtɪk] ADJ (*person, disease*) nevrotico(-a) ♦ N nevrotico(-a)

neu·ter [ˈnjuːtə*] ADJ neutro(-a) ♦ N (*Gram*) neutro ♦ VT (*cat etc*) castrare

neu·tral [ˈnjuːtrəl] ADJ **1** (*person, country, opinion*) neutrale **2** (*Chem: colour*) neutro(-a) ♦ N (*Aut*) folle *f*; **in neutral** in folle

neu·tral·ity [njuːˈtrælɪtɪ] N neutralità

neu·tral·ize [ˈnjuːtrəˌlaɪz] VT neutralizzare

neutron bomb N bomba al neutrone

Nev. ABBR (*USA*: = Nevada)

Ne·va·da [nɪˈvɑːdə] il Nevada

nev·er [ˈnɛvə*] ADV **1** non... mai; **they never go out** non escono mai; **I have never read it** non l'ho mai letto; **have you been to Rome? — never** è mai stato a Roma? — no, mai; **never before had he been so bored** non si era mai annoiato (così) tanto; **she's never been here before** non è mai venuta qui prima; **never again!** mai più!; **I'll never go there again** non ci andrò mai più; **never in my life** mai in vita mia **2** (*emphatic negative*): **I never slept a wink all night** non ho chiuso occhio per tutta la notte; **she never so much as smiled** non ha nemmeno accennato un sorriso; **I told the boss what I thought of him — never!** *or* you never did! ho detto al capo quel che pensavo di lui — no, non mi dire! *or* non ci credo!; **well I never!** chi l'avrebbe (mai) detto!, ma guarda un po'!; **never mind** non fa niente

never-ending [ˌnɛvərˈɛndɪŋ] ADJ interminabile

never·the·less [ˌnɛvəðəˈlɛs] ADV tuttavia, ciononostante, ciononondimeno

new [njuː] ADJ (*comp* **-er**, *superl* **-est**) nuovo(-a); (*brand new*) nuovo(-a) di zecca; (*different*) nuovo(-a), altro(-a); (*bread*) fresco(-a); **he buys a new car every year** (*brand-new*) si compra una macchina nuova ogni anno; **her new boyfriend** il suo nuovo ragazzo; (*different*) si compra una nuova macchina *or* una macchina diversa ogni anno; **bring me a new glass** portami un altro bicchiere; **new potatoes** patate *fpl* novelle; **as good as new** come nuovo(-a); **that's nothing new** non è una novità; **what's new?** ci sono novità?; **are you new here?** sei nuovo di qui?; **I'm new to this job** sono nuovo del mestiere; **the idea was quite new to him** l'idea gli risultava nuova

New Age ADJ, N New Age *f inv*

new·bie [ˈnjuːbɪ] N (*Comput*) utilizzatore(-trice) inesperto(-a)

new·born [ˈnjuːbɔːn] ADJ neonato(-a); **newborn baby** neonato(-a)

new·comer [ˈnjuːkʌmə*] N nuovo(-a) venuto(-a)

new·fangled [ˈnjuːfæŋgld] ADJ (*pej*) stramoderno(-a)

New·found·land [ˈnjuːfəndlənd] N Newfoundland *m*

New Guinea N la Nuova Guinea

New Hampshire il New Hampshire

New Jersey il New Jersey

New Mexico il Nuovo Messico

new·ly [ˈnjuːlɪ] ADV (*recently*) appena, da poco, di recente; (*in a new way*) in modo nuovo; **newly made** appena fatto(-a)

newly-weds [ˈnjuːlɪˌwɛdz] NPL sposini *mpl*, sposi *mpl* novelli

new moon N luna nuova

new·ness [ˈnjuːnɪs] N novità

news [njuːz] NSG (*gen, also Press*) notizie *fpl*; (*report: on radio*) notiziario, giornale *m* radio; (: *on TV*) notiziario, telegiornale *m*; **a piece of** *or* **an item of news** una notizia; (: *in newspaper*) un articolo; **have you heard the news?** hai saputo la notizia?; **have you heard the news about Maria?** hai saputo di Maria?; **have you any news of Maria/of her?** hai notizie di Maria/sue notizie?; **it was nice to have your news** mi ha fatto piacere avere tue notizie; **that's wonderful news!** che bella notizia!; **what's your news?** (ci sono) novità?; **what's the latest news about the earthquake?** si sa qualcosa di nuovo sul terremoto?; **is there any news?** ci sono notizie?; **good/bad news** buone/cattive notizie; **I've got news for you!** non sai l'ultima!; **this is news to me** questo mi giunge nuovo; **it's in the news** (*newspapers*) è su tutti i giornali; (*radio, TV*) è in tutti i notiziari; **home/foreign news** notizie dall'interno/dall'estero; **financial news** (*Press*) pagina economica e finanziaria; (*Radio, TV*) notiziario economico

news agency N agenzia di stampa

news·agent [ˈnjuːzˌeɪdʒənt] N (*Brit*) giornalaio(-a)

news bulletin N (*Radio, TV*) notiziario

news·caster [ˈnjuːzˌkɑːstə*] N (*Radio*) annunciatore(-trice); (*TV*) presentatore(-trice)

news·dealer [ˈnjuːzˌdiːləˈ] N (USA) giornalaio(-a)
news·flash [ˈnjuːzˌflæʃ] N (notizia f) flash, m inv
news·letter [ˈnjuːzˌletəˈ] N bollettino (di ditta, associazione)
news·paper [ˈnjuːzˌpeɪpəˈ] N giornale m; **daily newspaper** quotidiano; **weekly newspaper** settimanale m
news·print [ˈnjuːzˌprɪnt] N carta da giornale
news·reader [ˈnjuːzˌriːdəˈ] N (esp Brit) = newscaster
news·reel [ˈnjuːzˌriːl] N cinegiornale m
news·room [ˈnjuːzˌrʊm] N redazione f
news·stand [ˈnjuːzˌstænd] N edicola
news·worthy [ˈnjuːzˌwɜːðɪ] ADJ che vale la pena pubblicare
newt [njuːt] N tritone m
new town N (Brit) nuovo centro urbano (creato con fondi pubblici)
New Year N anno nuovo; **Happy New Year!** Buon anno!; **to wish sb a happy New Year** augurare buon anno a qn; **to bring in the New Year** brindare all'anno nuovo; **to celebrate New Year** festeggiare l'anno nuovo ♦ ADJ (party etc) di Capodanno; (resolution) per l'anno nuovo
New Year's Day N Capodanno
New Year's Eve N la vigilia di Capodanno, la notte di San Silvestro
New York N New York f, Nuova York f; **New York State** stato di New York
New Zea·land [ˌnjuːˈziːlənd] N Nuova Zelanda ♦ ADJ neozelandese
New Zea·land·er [ˌnjuːˈziːləndəˈ] N neozelandese m/f
next [nekst] ADJ 1 (immediately adjoining: house, street, room) vicino(-a), accanto inv; (immediately following: bus stop, turning: in future) prossimo(-a); (: in past) successivo(-a), (subito) dopo; "**turn to the next page**" "vedi pagina seguente"; **the next size (up)** la misura più grande; **get off at the next stop** scendi alla prossima fermata; **he got off at the next stop** è sceso alla fermata successiva; **I arrived at 3 and Mary was next** to arrive io sono arrivato alle 3 e dopo di me è arrivata Mary; **the next room** la stanza accanto; **it's the next door but one on the right** è la seconda porta a destra; **who's next?** a chi tocca?; **you're next** tocca a lei 2 (in time: day, week etc: in future) prossimo(-a); (: in past) successivo(-a); **next time** la prossima volta; **next year** l'anno prossimo or venturo; **next month** il mese prossimo; **the next month** il mese dopo or successivo; **the week after next** fra due settimane; **(the) next time you come** quando vieni la prossima volta, la prossima volta che vieni; **this time next year** in questo periodo fra un anno; **the next day** il giorno dopo, l'indomani; **the next morning** l'indomani mattina, la mattina dopo or seguente ♦ ADV 1 (in time) dopo, poi; **first he read his e-mails and next he read the paper** prima ha letto le sue mail e dopo or poi ha letto il giornale; **what will you do next?** e adesso che farai?; **when you next see him** quando lo vedi la prossima volta, la prossima volta che lo vedi; **when next I saw him** quando l'ho visto la volta dopo or una seconda volta; **when do we meet next?** quando ci rincontriamo?; **what comes next?** che cosa viene dopo?; **what next?** e poi?; (expressing surprise etc) e che altro mai?; **the next best thing would be ...** la migliore alternativa sarebbe...; **the next to last** il (la) penultimo(-a) 2 **next to** (nearly) quasi, pressoché; **next to nothing** quasi niente; **we got it for next to nothing** non ci è costato quasi niente, l'abbiamo comprato per una sciocchezza; **there is next to no news** non si sa quasi niente ♦ PREP: **next to** (beside) di fianco a, accanto a; **his room is next to mine** la sua stanza è accanto alla mia; **next to the bank** accanto alla banca; **I don't like wearing synthetics next to the skin** non mi piacciono le fibre sintetiche a contatto della pelle ♦ N prossimo(-a); **next please!** (avanti) il prossimo!; **the next to speak is Carla** Carla è la prossima a parlare
next door ADV accanto; **next door to us** accanto a noi, nella casa accanto ♦ N la casa accanto; **from next door** della casa accanto
next of kin N parente m/f prossimo(-a)
NF [ˌenˈef] N ABBR (Brit Pol: = National Front) partito di estrema destra
NFL [ˌenefˈel] N ABBR (USA: = National Football League)
Nfld. ABBR (Canada) = Newfoundland

NGO [ˌendʒiːˈəʊ] N ABBR (= non-governmental organization)
ONG f inv (= organizzazione non governativa)
NH ABBR (USA Post: = New Hampshire)
NHL [ˌenetlˈʃɛl] N ABBR (USA: = National Hockey League) ≈ F.I.H.P f (= Federazione Italiana Hockey e Pattinaggio)
NHS [ˌenetlˈʃɛs] N ABBR (Brit: = National Health Service)
NI ABBR 1 = Northern Ireland 2 (Brit) = National Insurance
Ni·aga·ra Falls [naɪˈægrəˈfɔːlz] NPL: **the Niagara Falls** le cascate del Niagara
nib [nɪb] N (of pen) pennino
nib·ble [ˈnɪbl] VT (also: nibble at) 1 (subj: mouse) rosicchiare; (: fish) mordicchiare; (: person: biscuit, nuts) sgranocchiare; (: bread, cheese) sbocconcellare 2 (fig: offer) mostrarsi tentato(-a) da ♦ VI (person) mangiucchiare
Nica·ra·gua [ˌnɪkəˈrægjʊə] N Nicaragua m
Nica·ra·guan [ˌnɪkəˈrægjʊən] ADJ, N nicaraguense m/f
Nice [niːs] N Nizza
nice [naɪs] ADJ (comp -r, superl -st) 1 (gen: pleasant) bello(-a), piacevole, gentile; (: person) simpatico(-a), piacevole; (: taste, smell, meal) buono(-a); (attractive, pretty) carino(-a), bello(-a); **he's a nice man** è una brava persona, è un uomo simpatico; **your parents are very nice** i tuoi genitori sono molto simpatici; **he was very nice about it** è stato molto gentile; **she was always very nice to me** è sempre stata gentile con me; **be nice to him** sii gentile con lui; **it was nice of you to remember my birthday** sei stata carina a ricordarti del mio compleanno; **that's a nice dress!** che vestito carino!; **how nice you look!** come stai bene!; **did you have a nice time?** ti sei divertito?; **it's nice here** si sta bene qui; **this pasta is very nice** questa pasta è molto buona; **Pisa is a nice town** Pisa è una bella città; **nice weather** bel tempo; **it's a nice day** è una bella giornata 2 (iro) bello(-a); **that's a nice thing to say!** sono cose da dirsi, queste?; **you've got us into a nice mess!** ci hai messo in un bel pasticcio! 3 (refined, polite) gentile, garbato(-a); **he has nice manners** ha modi gentili or garbati; **that's not nice** non sta bene 4 (intensifier: fam) bello(-a) (+ aggettivo); **he gets nice long holidays** se ne vacanze sono belle lunghe; **it's nice and warm here** è bello caldo qui, c'è un bel calduccio qui; **nice and early** di buon'ora; **a nice cup of coffee** una bella tazza di caffè 5 (frm: subtle: distinction) sottile, fine
nice-looking [ˈnaɪsˌlʊkɪŋ] ADJ bello(-a)
nice·ly [ˈnaɪslɪ] ADV bene; (kindly) gentilmente; **that will do nicely** andrà benissimo; **he's getting on nicely in his new job** se la cava bene nel nuovo lavoro
ni·cety [ˈnaɪsɪtɪ] N (of judgment) accuratezza; **niceties** NPL particolari mpl, finezze fpl; **a question of some nicety** una questione piuttosto delicata; **to a nicety** alla perfezione
niche [niːʃ] N (Archit) nicchia; (Ecology) nicchia ecologica; (fig): **to find a niche for o.s.** trovare una propria collocazione
nick [nɪk] N 1 (in wood, blade) tacca; (in skin) taglietto; (in plate) scheggiatura; **in the nick of time** appena in tempo 2 (fam): **in good nick** decente, in buono stato 3 (Brit fam: prison) galera; (: police station) centrale f (di polizia); **in the nick** in galera ♦ VT 1 (see n) intaccare; tagliare; scheggiare, scalfire; **to nick o.s.** farsi un taglietto 2 (fam: steal) fregare; **somebody's nicked it** qualcuno l'ha fregato 3 (Brit fam: arrest) beccare; **to get nicked** farsi beccare
nick·el [ˈnɪkl] N (metal) nichel m; (USA: coin) (moneta da) cinque centesimi mpl di dollaro
nick·name [ˈnɪkˌneɪm] N soprannome m; (humorous, malicious) nomignolo ♦ VT: **to nickname sb sth** soprannominare qn qc
Nico·sia [ˌnɪkəˈsiːə] N Nicosia
nico·tine [ˈnɪkəˌtiːn] N nicotina
nicotine patch N cerotto antifumo (a base di nicotina)
niece [niːs] N nipote f (di zii)
nif·ty [ˈnɪftɪ] ADJ (comp -ier, superl -iest) (fam: car, jacket) chic inv; (: gadget, tool) ingegnoso(-a); **that was a nifty piece of work** è stato un bel lavoretto
Ni·ger [ˈnaɪdʒəˈ] N (country, river) il Niger m
Ni·geria [naɪˈdʒɪərɪə] N la Nigeria
Ni·gerian [naɪˈdʒɪərɪən] ADJ, N nigeriano(-a)
nig·gard·ly [ˈnɪgədlɪ] ADJ (person) tirchio(-a), spilorcio(-a); (allowance, amount) misero(-a)

nig·gle [ˈnɪgl] VT assillare ♦ VI fare il (la) pignolo(-a)

nig·gling [ˈnɪglɪŋ] ADJ (detail) insignificante; (doubt, pain) persistente; (person) pignolo(-a)

night [naɪt] N notte f; (evening) sera; **good night!** buona notte!; **at night** di notte, la notte; **in the night, during the night** durante la notte; **by night** di notte; **last night** la notte scorsa, ieri notte, stanotte; **we went to a party last night** ieri sera siamo andati ad una festa; **Tuesday night** martedì notte, la notte di martedì, la notte fra martedì e mercoledì; (evening) martedì sera, la sera di martedì; **the night before** la notte prima; (evening) la sera prima; **the night before last** l'altro ieri notte; (evening) l'altro ieri sera; **11 o'clock at night** le 11 di sera; **the last 3 nights of** (Theatre, etc) le 3 ultime serate or rappresentazioni di; **to have a night out** uscire la sera; **we had a lovely night out** abbiamo passato una bellissima serata fuori; **to spend the night** passare la notte; **I spent the night studying** ho passato la notte a studiare; **to have a good/bad night** dormire bene/male; **to have a late night** andare a letto tardi; **he's working nights** fa il turno di notte; **I want a single room for two nights** vorrei una camera singola per due notti ♦ ADJ (work, nurse, train etc) di notte; **night flight** volo notturno

night-bird [ˈnaɪtbɜːd] N uccello notturno; (fig) nottambulo(-a)

night·cap [ˈnaɪtkæp] N papalina, berretto da notte; (drink) bicchierino prima di andare a letto

night·club [ˈnaɪtklʌb] N locale m notturno, night(-club) m inv

night·dress [ˈnaɪtdres] N camicia da notte

night·fall [ˈnaɪtfɔːl] N crepuscolo; **at nightfall** al calar della notte

nightie [ˈnaɪtɪ] N (fam) camicia da notte

night·in·gale [ˈnaɪtɪŋgeɪl] N usignolo

night·life [ˈnaɪtlaɪf] N vita notturna

night·ly [ˈnaɪtlɪ] ADV ogni notte, tutte le notti; (evening) ogni sera, tutte le sere; **she appears nightly on the news** c'è ogni sera al telegiornale ♦ ADJ di ogni notte, di tutte le notti; (evening) di ogni sera, di tutte le sere; (by night) notturno(-a)

night·mare [ˈnaɪtmeəʳ] N incubo; **the whole trip was a nightmare** il viaggio è stato un vero incubo

night porter N portiere m di notte

night safe N cassa continua

night school N scuola serale

night·shade [ˈnaɪtʃeɪd] N (Bot): **deadly nightshade** belladonna

night·shirt [ˈnaɪtʃɜːt] N camicia da notte (da uomo)

night·time [ˈnaɪttaɪm] N notte f; **at night-time** di notte, la notte

night watchman N (pl -men) guardiano notturno

ni·hil·ism [ˈnaɪɪlɪzəm] N nichilismo

nil [nɪl] N nulla m; (Sport) zero; **we won one-nil** abbiamo vinto uno a zero

Nile [naɪl] N: **the Nile** il Nilo

nim·ble [ˈnɪmbl] ADJ (comp -r, superl -st) (in moving) agile; (mentally) vivace, sveglio(-a)

nine [naɪn] ADJ, N nove m inv; **nine times out of ten** (fig) nove volte su dieci; **they were dressed up to the nines** si erano messi in pompa magna; see **five**

9-11 [ˌnaɪnɪˈlevn] N 11 settembre

nine·teen [ˌnaɪnˈtiːn] ADJ, N diciannove m inv; **to talk nineteen to the dozen** (fam) parlare come una mitragliatrice

nine·teenth [ˌnaɪnˈtiːnθ] ADJ diciannovesimo(-a) ♦ N (in series) diciannovesimo(-a); (fraction) diciannovesimo

nine·ti·eth [ˈnaɪntɪɪθ] ADJ novantesimo(-a) ♦ N (in series) novantesimo(-a); (fraction) novantesimo

nine·ty [ˈnaɪntɪ] ADJ, N novanta m inv

ninth [naɪnθ] ADJ nono(-a) ♦ N (in series) nono(-a); (fraction) nono

nip¹ [nɪp] N (pinch) pizzico; (bite) morso; **there's a nip in the air** l'aria è pungente ♦ VT (pinch) pizzicare; (bite) morsicare; (prune: bud, shoot) spuntare; (subj: cold: plant) assiderare; (: face) pungere; **to nip sth in the bud** (fig) stroncare qc sul nascere ♦ VI (Brit fam): **to nip up/down** andar dentro un attimo; **to nip out/down/up** fare un salto fuori/giù/di sopra; **I nipped round to the shop** ho fatto un salto al negozio

nip² [nɪp] N (drink) goccio, bicchierino; **a nip of brandy** un goccio di brandy

nip·ple [ˈnɪpl] N (Anat) capezzolo

nip·py [ˈnɪpɪ] ADJ (comp -ier, superl -iest) fam: 1 (Brit: person, car) svelto(-a); **be nippy about it!** sbrigati!, fa' alla svelta! 2 (wind, weather) pungente; **it's nippy** l'aria è pungente

nit [nɪt] N 1 (of louse) lendine m 2 (fam: idiot) cretino(-a), scemo(-a)

nit-pick [ˈnɪtpɪk] VI (fam) cercare il pelo nell'uovo

ni·tro·gen [ˈnaɪtrədʒən] N azoto; **nitrogen cycle** ciclo dell'azoto

ni·tro·glyc·er·ine [ˌnaɪtrəʊˈglɪsəˌriːn], **ni·tro·glyc·er·in** [ˌnaɪtrəʊˈglɪsərɪn] N nitroglicerina

nitty-gritty [ˈnɪtɪˈgrɪtɪ] N (fam): **to get down to the nitty-gritty** venire al sodo

nit·wit [ˈnɪtˌwɪt] N (fam) imbecille m/f, scemo(-a)

NJ ABBR (USA Post: = New Jersey)

NL ABBR (Canada: = Newfoundland & Labrador)

NM ABBR (USA Post: = New Mexico)

KEYWORD

no [nəʊ] ADV

1 (opposite of "yes") no; **are you coming? — no** vieni? — no; **would you like some more? — no thank you** ne vuoi ancora? — no grazie

2 (emphatic): **it is no easy task** non è un'impresa facile; **it is no small matter** non è una cosa da poco; **there is no such thing** una cosa simile non esiste; **in no uncertain terms** in termini tutt'altro che ambigui

3 (in comparatives): **there were no fewer than 100 people** c'erano non meno di 100 persone; **he wants to become prime minister, no less!** vuole diventare nientemeno che primo ministro!; **I can stand it no longer** non ne posso più; **I am no taller than you** non sono più alto di te

♦ ADJ

1 (not any) nessuno(-a); **there's no denying it** non si può negarlo; **"no dogs"** "vietato l'accesso ai cani"; **"no entry"** "vietato l'accesso"; **she has no furniture** non ha mobili, non ha nessun mobile; **it is of no interest to us** non siamo interessati; **I have no money** non ho soldi; **there is no more coffee** non c'è più caffè; **who's going with you? — no one** chi ti accompagna? — nessuno; **no other man** nessun altro; **"no parking"** "divieto di sosta"; **there is no reason to believe ...** non c'è ragione di credere che...; **"no smoking"** "vietato fumare"; **it's no trouble** non c'è problema; **no two houses are alike** le case sono tutte diverse l'una dall'altra; **no two people think alike** non ci sono due persone che la pensino allo stesso modo

2 (quite other than): **he's no fool** è tutt'altro che stupido, non è affatto (uno) stupido; **he's no friend of mine** non è affatto un mio amico

♦ N (pl noes) no m inv; **I won't take no for an answer** non accetterò un rifiuto

No., no. ABBR (pl Nos.) (= number) n. (= numero)

Nobel prize [ˈnəʊbelˈpraɪz] N premio Nobel

no·bil·ity [nəʊˈbɪlɪtɪ] N nobiltà

no·ble [ˈnəʊbl] ADJ (comp -r, superl -st) nobile; (also iro) generoso(-a); **of noble birth** di nobili natali ♦ N nobile m/f

noble·man [ˈnəʊblmən] N (pl -men) nobile m, nobiluomo

no·bly [ˈnəʊblɪ] ADV (selflessly) generosamente

no·body [ˈnəʊbədɪ] PRON nessuno; **I saw nobody** non ho visto nessuno; **nobody spoke** nessuno ha parlato, non ha parlato nessuno; **there was nobody in the office** non c'era nessuno in ufficio; **nobody likes him** non è simpatico a nessuno; **nobody else** nessun altro (nessun'altra) ♦ N: **he's a nobody** è una nullità

noc·tur·nal [nɒkˈtɜːnl] ADJ notturno(-a)

nod [nɒd] N cenno del capo; **to give sb a nod** fare un cenno col capo a qn; (answering yes) accennare di sì a qn, fare di sì col capo a qn ♦ VT: **to nod one's head** fare di sì col capo; **he nodded a greeting** accennò un saluto col capo; **they nodded their agreement** accennarono di sì (col capo) ♦ VI **1** fare un cenno col capo; (say yes) far segno di sì col capo, annuire; **he nodded to me in a friendly way** mi ha salutato cordialmente con un cenno del capo; **we have a nodding acquaintance** ci conosciamo solo di vista **2** (doze) ciondolare il capo (per il sonno); (sleep) sonnecchiare

▸ **nod off** VI + ADV appisolarsi, assopirsi

no-fly zone [ˌnəʊˈflaɪˌzəʊn] N zona di interdizione aerea

noise [nɔɪz] N (*sound*) rumore *m*; (*din*) rumore, chiasso, fracasso; (*Telec, Radio, TV*) disturbo, interferenza; **to make a noise** fare un rumore; **stop making a noise!** smetta di far rumore!; **a big noise** (*fam: person*) un pezzo grosso

noise·less [ˈnɔɪzlɪs] ADJ silenzioso(-a)

noisi·ly [ˈnɔɪzɪlɪ] ADV rumorosamente

noisy [ˈnɔɪzɪ] ADJ (*comp* -ier, *superl* -iest) (*street, car*) rumoroso(-a); (*child, party*) rumoroso(-a), chiassoso(-a); **stop being noisy!** smetta di far rumore!; **the noisiest city in the world** la città più rumorosa del mondo

❑ **noisy** is not translated by the Italian word *noioso*

no·mad [ˈnəʊmæd] N nomade *m/f*

no·mad·ic [nəʊˈmædɪk] ADJ nomade

no-man's-land [ˈnəʊmænzˌlænd] N terra di nessuno

nomi·nal [ˈnɒmɪnl] ADJ (*Gram, Econ*) nominale; (*ostensible*) nominale, di nome

nomi·nate [ˈnɒmɪˌneɪt] VT: **to nominate sb** (**for sth**) (*propose*) proporre qn come candidato (a qc); (*appoint*) nominare *or* designare qn (a qc)

nomi·na·tion [ˌnɒmɪˈneɪʃən] N (*see vb*) candidatura; nomina

nomi·nee [ˌnɒmɪˈniː] N (*see vb*) candidato(-a); persona nominata

non– [nɒn] PREF non-

non-alcoholic [ˌnɒnælkəˈhɒlɪk] ADJ analcolico(-a)

non·break·able [ˈnɒnˈbreɪkəbl] ADJ infrangibile

nonce word [ˈnɒnsˌwɜːd] N parola coniata per l'occasione

non·cha·lant [ˈnɒnʃələnt] ADJ disinvolto(-a), indifferente, incurante

non·com·mis·sioned of·fic·er [ˌnɒnkəˈmɪʃəndˈɒfɪsəʳ] N sottufficiale *m*

non·com·mit·tal [ˈnɒnkəˈmɪtl] ADJ (*statement*) non impegnativo(-a), evasivo(-a); (*person*) che non si compromette, evasivo(-a)

non·con·form·ist [ˈnɒnkənˈfɔːmɪst] ADJ anticonformista ♦ N anticonformista *m/f*

non·con·tribu·tory [ˈnɒnkənˈtrɪbjʊtərɪ] ADJ: **noncontributory pension scheme** *sistema di pensionamento con i contributi interamente a carico del datore di lavoro*

non·co·op·era·tion [ˈnɒnkəʊˌɒpəˈreɪʃən] N non cooperazione *f*, non collaborazione *f*

non·de·script [ˈnɒndɪˌskrɪpt] ADJ (*person, clothes*) qualunque *inv*; (*colour*) indefinito(-a)

none [nʌn] PRON nessuno(-a), nemmeno uno(-a), neanche uno(-a); **none of them wants to go** nessuno di loro vuole andarci; **none of the machines is working** nessuna delle macchine funziona, non c'è neanche una macchina che funzioni; **I have none of the books** non ho nessuno dei libri; **I have none** non ne ho nemmeno uno; **none of this is yours** niente di questo è tuo; **none of this money** neanche un centesimo di questi soldi; **none of this wine** neanche una goccia di questo vino; **I have none left** non ne ho più; **any news? — none** ci sono novità? — niente *or* nessuna; **how many sisters have you got? — none** quante sorelle hai? — neanche una *or* nessuna; **there's none left** non ce n'è più; **none of that!** basta!; **he would have none of it** non ne ha voluto sapere; **none at all** (*nothing*) proprio niente; (*not one*) nemmeno uno; **our host was none other than the president** il nostro ospite era nientemeno che il presidente ♦ ADV: **I was none too comfortable** non ero per niente a mio agio; **it's none too warm** non fa molto caldo; **and none too soon!** ed era ora!; **I like him none the worse for it** non per questo mi piace di meno; **he is none the worse for his experience** non sembra aver risentito di quell'esperienza

non·entity [nɒnˈentɪtɪ] N persona insignificante, nullità *f inv*

non·es·sen·tial [ˈnɒnɪˈsenʃəl] ADJ non essenziale ♦ **nonessentials** NPL superfluo *sg*, cose *fpl* superflue

none·the·less [ˌnʌnðəˈles] ADV nondimeno

non·event [ˈnɒnɪˈvent] N delusione *f*; **the party turned out to be a non-event** la festa è stata deludente *or* una delusione

non·ex·ecu·tive [ˌnɒnɪgˈzekjʊtɪv] ADJ: **nonexecutive director** direttore *m* senza potere esecutivo

non·ex·ist·ent [ˌnɒnɪgˈzɪstənt] ADJ inesistente

non·fic·tion [ˈnɒnˈfɪkʃən] N *qualunque pubblicazione non di narrativa*

non·flam·mable [ˈnɒnˈflæməbl] ADJ non infiammabile

non·inter·ven·tion [ˈnɒnˌɪntəˈvenʃən] N non intervento

no-no [ˈnəʊˌnəʊ] N: **it's a no-no!** (*undesirable*) è inaccettabile!; (*forbidden*) non si può fare!

non obst. ABBR (*notwithstanding*) (= *non obstante*) nonostante

no-nonsense [ˈnəʊˈnɒnsens] ADJ che va al sodo

non·pay·ment [ˈnɒnˈpeɪmənt] N mancato pagamento

non·plussed [ˈnɒnˈplʌst] ADJ sconcertato(-a)

non-profit-making [ˈnɒnˈprɒfɪtˌmeɪkɪŋ], **non-profit** (*USA*) [ˈnɒnˈprɒfɪt] ADJ senza scopo di lucro

non·sense [ˈnɒnsəns] N sciocchezze *fpl*, assurdità *fpl*; (**what**) **nonsense!** che sciocchezze!, che assurdità!; **it is nonsense to say that …** è un'assurdità *or* non ha senso dire che…; **to talk nonsense** dire sciocchezze *or* assurdità; **that's a piece of nonsense!** è una sciocchezza!; **to make (a) nonsense of sth** rendere assurdo qc; **he stands no nonsense** con lui non si scherza

non·sen·si·cal [nɒnˈsensɪkəl] ADJ assurdo(-a), ridicolo(-a)

non·shrink [ˈnɒnˈʃrɪŋk] ADJ (*Brit*) irrestringibile

non·skid [ˈnɒnˈskɪd], **non·slip** [ˈnɒnˈslɪp] ADJ antisdrucciolo *inv*, antisdrucciolevole

non·smok·er [ˈnɒnˈsməʊkəʳ] N **1** (*person*) non fumatore(-trice); **I'm a nonsmoker** non fumo **2** (*Rail*) scompartimento per non fumatori

non·smok·ing [ˈnɒnˈsməʊkɪŋ] ADJ (*person*) che non fuma; (*area, section*) per non fumatori

non·start·er [ˌnɒnˈstɑːtəʳ] N: **it's a nonstarter** è fallito in partenza

non·stick [ˈnɒnˈstɪk] ADJ (*saucepan*) (con rivestimento) antiaderente

non·stop [ˈnɒnˈstɒp] ADJ continuo(-a), senza sosta; (*train, bus*) diretto(-a), direttissimo(-a); (*flight*) diretto(-a), senza scalo; **nonstop entertainment** spettacolo continuo ♦ ADV ininterrottamente, senza sosta; (*Rail*) diretto; **I flew non-stop to New York** ho preso un volo diretto per New York

non·tax·able [ˈnɒnˈtæksəbl] ADJ: **non-taxable income** reddito non imponibile

non-U [ˈnɒnˈjuː] ADJ ABBR (*Brit fam* = *non-upper class*) poco fine

non·vola·tile [ˈnɒnˈvɒlətaɪl] ADJ (*Comput*): **non-volatile memory** memoria permanente

non·voting [ˈnɒnˈvəʊtɪŋ] ADJ: **non-voting shares** azioni *fpl* senza diritto di voto

non-white [ˌnɒnˈwaɪt] ADJ di colore ♦ N persona di colore

noo·dles [ˈnuːdlz] NPL taglierini *mpl*, tagliatelle *fpl*; **egg noodles** pasta all'uovo

nook [nʊk] N angolino; **we searched every nook and cranny** abbiamo frugato dappertutto *or* in ogni angolo

noon [nuːn] N mezzogiorno; **at noon** a mezzogiorno

no-one [ˈnəʊˌwʌn] PRON = **nobody**

noose [nuːs] N (*loop*) nodo scorsoio, cappio; (*for animal trapping*) laccio; (*hangman's*) cappio

nor [nɔːʳ] ADV *see* **neither** ♦ CONJ = **neither**

norm [nɔːm] N norma

nor·mal [ˈnɔːməl] ADJ normale; **it was quite normal for him to object** era perfettamente normale che obiettasse; **it is perfectly normal to be left-handed** è perfettamente normale *or* naturale essere mancini ♦ N **1 to return to normal** tornare alla normalità; **above/below normal** al disopra/al disotto della normalità **2** (*Math*) normale *f*

nor·mal·ity [nɔːˈmælɪtɪ] N normalità

nor·mal·ly [ˈnɔːməlɪ] ADV normalmente

Nor·man·dy [ˈnɔːməndɪ] N Normandia

north [nɔːθ] N nord *m*, settentrione *m*; (**to the**) **north of** a nord di; **the town lies north of the border** la città si trova a nord del confine; **in the north** al nord; **in the north of** nel nord di; **the wind is from the north** il vento soffia da nord; **to veer to the north** (*wind*) girare verso nord; **a house facing north** una casa esposta a nord ♦ ADJ (*gen*) nord *inv*; (*wind*) del nord, settentrionale; (*coast*) settentrionale ♦ ADV verso nord; **to sail north** navigare verso nord; **we were travelling north** viaggiavamo verso nord

North Africa N l'Africa del Nord
North African ADJ, N nordafricano(-a)
North America N l'America del Nord
North American ADJ, N nordamericano(-a)
Northants [nɔːˈθænts] ABBR (*Brit:* = **Northamptonshire**)
north-bound [ˈnɔːθˌbaʊnd] ADJ (*traffic*) diretto(-a) a nord; (*carriageway*) nord *inv*
North Carolina il Carolina del Nord
North Dakota il Dakota del Nord
north-east [ˌnɔːθˈiːst] N nordest *m* ◆ ADJ di nordest ◆ ADV verso nordest
north-eastern [ˌnɔːθˈiːstən] ADJ di nordest
nor-ther-ly [ˈnɔːðəlɪ] ADJ (*wind*) del nord; (*direction*) verso nord; **house with a northerly aspect** casa esposta a nord; **a northerly wind** un vento settentrionale
north-ern [ˈnɔːðən] ADJ (*region*) del nord, settentrionale; (*wall*) (esposto(-a) a nord *inv*; (*coast*) settentrionale; **in northern Spain** nel nord della Spagna, nella Spagna settentrionale; **Northern Europe** l'Europa settentrionale
Northern Ireland N Irlanda del Nord
North Korea N Corea del Nord
North Pole N: **the North Pole** il Polo Nord
North Sea N: **the North Sea** il mare del Nord
North Sea oil N petrolio del mare del Nord
north-wards [ˈnɔːθwədz], **north-ward** [ˈnɔːθwəd] ADV verso nord
north-west [ˌnɔːθˈwest] N nordovest *m* ◆ ADJ di nordovest ◆ ADV verso nordovest
north-western [ˌnɔːθˈwestən] ADJ di nordovest
Nor-way [ˈnɔːˌweɪ] N Norvegia
Nor-we-gian [nɔːˈwiːdʒən] ADJ norvegese ◆ N (*person*) norvegese *m/f*; (*language*) norvegese *m*
Nos., nos. ABBR (= *numbers*) nn (= *numeri*)
nose [nəʊz] N naso; (*of animal, plane*) muso; **to speak through one's nose** parlare col naso; **to blow one's nose** soffiarsi il naso; **my nose is bleeding** perdo sangue dal naso; **nose drops** gocce *fpl* per il naso; **right under my nose** (*fig*) proprio sotto il naso; **to follow one's nose** andare a naso; **to pay through the nose (for sth)** (*fam*) pagare (qc) un occhio della testa; **to poke** *or* **stick one's nose into sth** (*fam*) ficcare *or* cacciare il naso in qc; **to turn up one's nose (at sth)** arricciare il naso (di fronte a qc); **to look down one's nose at** disprezzare; (*person*) guardare dall'alto in basso; **to have a (good) nose for** aver buon fiuto *or* buon naso per ◆ VI: **to nose (one's way)** avanzare cautamente; **the car nosed (its way) into the stream of traffic** l'auto si è infilata poco a poco nella corrente del traffico
▸ **nose about, nose around** VI + ADV curiosare
▸ **nose out** VT + ADV (*subj: dog: fig*) fiutare
nose-bleed [ˈnəʊzˌbliːd] N emorragia nasale
nose-dive [ˈnəʊzˌdaɪv] N (*Aer*) picchiata; (*fig*) calo vertiginoso ◆ VI (*see n*) scendere in picchiata; calare vertiginosamente
nos-ey [ˈnəʊzɪ] ADJ = **nosy**
nos-tal-gia [nɒsˈtældʒɪə] N nostalgia
nos-tal-gic [nɒsˈtældʒɪk] ADJ nostalgico(-a)
nos-tril [ˈnɒstrəl] N narice *f*; (*of horse*) frogia
nosy, nos-ey [ˈnəʊzɪ] ADJ (*comp* **-ier**, *superl* **-iest**) (*fam*) curioso(-a); **don't be so nosy** non fare il ficcanaso
not [nɒt] ADV non; **he is not here** non è qui, non c'è; **I haven't seen anybody** non ho visto nessuno; **it's too late, isn't it?** è troppo tardi, vero? *or* no?; **she will not** *or* **won't go** non ci andrà; **he isn't coming** non viene; **I'm not sure** non sono sicuro; **he asked me not to do it** mi ha chiesto di non farlo; **whether you go or not** che tu ci vada o no; **not that I don't like him** non che (lui) non mi piaccia; **big, not to say enormous** grosso, per non dire enorme; **why not?** perché no?; **are you coming or not?** vieni o no?; **I hope not** spero di no; **not at all** niente affatto, per niente; (*after thanks*) prego, s'immagini; **I'm not at all sure it's a good idea** non sono affatto sicuro che sia una buona idea; **you must not** *or* **mustn't do this** non deve fare questo; **not one book** neanche un libro; **not me/you** *etc* io/tu *etc* no; **not yet** non ancora; **have you finished? — not yet** hai finito? — non ancora; *see* **even much only**

no-table [ˈnəʊtəbl] ADJ (*person*) eminente; (*event*) notevole, degno(-a) di nota ◆ N notabile *m*, persona importante
no-tably [ˈnəʊtəblɪ] ADV (*noticeably*) notevolmente; (*in particular*) in particolare
no-ta-ry [ˈnəʊtərɪ] N (*also:* **notary public**) notaio
no-ta-tion [nəʊˈteɪʃən] N notazione *f*
notch [nɒtʃ] N (*in wood, blade*) tacca; (*in wheel, saw*) dente *m*; (*in belt*) buco ◆ VT (*stick, blade*) intagliare, fare tacche in
▸ **notch up** VT + ADV (*score, victory*) marcare, segnare
note [nəʊt] N **1** (*gen, also Diplomacy*) nota; **to take** *or* **make notes** prendere appunti; **remember to take notes** ricordati di prendere appunti; **I'll drop her a note** le lascerò una nota; **Italian lecture notes** appunti *mpl* di italiano; **to take** *or* **make a note of sth** prendere nota di qc, prendere atto di qc; **I must make a note to buy some more** devo tenere a mente di comprarne di più; **to compare notes** (*fig*) scambiarsi le impressioni **2** (*informal letter*) biglietto, due righe; **just a quick note to let you know ...** ti scrivo solo due righe per informarti... **3** (*Mus: of bird: fig*) nota; **to play** *or* **sing a wrong note** prendere una stecca; **to strike the right/wrong note (with)** (*fig*) intonarsi (a)/stonare (con); **with a note of anxiety in his voice** con una nota di ansia nella voce **4** (*Comm*) nota; (*also:* **banknote**) banconota, biglietto di banca; **delivery note** bolletta di consegna; **five-pound note** biglietto da cinque sterline **5** (*of person*): **of note** eminente, importante **6** (*notice*): **worthy of note** degno(-a) di nota ◆ VT (*observe*) notare, osservare; (*also:* **note down**) annotare, prendere nota di
note-book [ˈnəʊtˌbʊk] N taccuino; (*Scol*) blocco per appunti; (*for shorthand*) bloc-notes *m inv*
note-case [ˈnəʊtˌkeɪs] N (*Brit*) portafoglio
not-ed [ˈnəʊtɪd] ADJ (*Brit*): **noted (for)** celebre (per), famoso(-a) (per)
note-pad [ˈnəʊtˌpæd] N bloc-notes *m inv*, blocchetto
note-paper [ˈnəʊtˌpeɪpə] N carta da lettere
note-worthy [ˈnəʊtˌwɜːðɪ] ADJ degno(-a) di nota, importante
noth-ing [ˈnʌθɪŋ] N **1** niente *m*, nulla *m*; (*Math, Sport*) zero; **nothing happened** non è successo niente *or* nulla; **I've eaten nothing** non ho mangiato niente *or* nulla; **there is nothing to eat** non c'è niente *or* nulla da mangiare **2** (*in phrases*): **as if nothing had happened** come se niente fosse; **nothing at all** proprio niente; **nothing else** nient'altro; **nothing much/new** *etc* niente di speciale/nuovo *etc*; **nothing but** nient'altro che; **she does nothing but sleep** non fa altro che dormire; **there is nothing for it but to go** non c'è altra scelta che andare; **there is nothing in it** (*not true*) non c'è niente di vero; (*not interesting*) non è per niente interessante; (*nearly the same*) non c'è una gran differenza; **there's nothing in it for us** non ci guadagniamo niente; **there's nothing to it!** (*it's easy*) è una cosa da niente!; **to have nothing on** (*naked*) non aver niente addosso; (*not busy*) non aver niente in programma; **for nothing** (*free, unpaid*) per niente, gratis; (*in vain*) per niente, inutilmente; (*for no reason*) senza ragione; **he is nothing if not careful** è soprattutto attento; **I can do nothing about it** non posso farci nulla; **to come to nothing** finire in nulla; **to say nothing of ...** per non parlare di...; **to think nothing of doing sth** non farsi nessun problema nel fare qc; **think nothing of it!** s'immagini!, si figuri!; **I can make nothing of it** non ci capisco niente; **a mere nothing** una cosa da nulla *or* da niente; **to whisper sweet nothings to sb** sussurrare tenerezze a qn; **nothing doing!** (*fam*) niente da fare! ◆ ADV per niente, niente affatto; **it was nothing like as expensive as we thought** era molto meno caro di quanto credessimo
no-tice [ˈnəʊtɪs] N **1** (*intimation, warning*) avviso; (*period*) preavviso; **without notice** senza preavviso; **he was transferred without notice** è stato trasferito senza preavviso; **advance** *or* **previous notice** preavviso; **a week's notice** una settimana di preavviso; **at short notice** con un breve preavviso; **at a moment's notice** immediatamente, all'istante; **until further notice** fino a nuovo avviso; **to give notice** (*to tenant*) dare la disdetta a; (*to landlord*) dare il preavviso a; **to give sb notice** (*Admin: inform*) notificare a qn; (: *sack*) licenziare qn; **to give notice, to hand in one's notice** (*subj: employee*) licenziarsi; **she handed in her notice yesterday** ha dato le dimissioni ieri; **to give notice of sth** annunciare

qc; **to give sb notice of sth** avvisare qn di qc **2** (*announcement*) avviso; (*Press*) annuncio; (*sign*) cartello; (*poster*) manifesto, cartellone *m*; **to put a notice in the paper** mettere un annuncio sul giornale; **there's a notice on the board about the trip** in bacheca c'è un avviso a proposito del viaggio **3** (*Brit: review: of play etc*) critica, recensione *f* **4** (*attention*): **to bring sth to sb's notice** far notare qc a qn; **to take notice of sb/sth** notare qn/qc, fare caso a qn/qc; **to take no notice of sb/sth** non prestare attenzione a qn/qc; **he keeps waving at me — take no notice!** continua a farmi dei cenni — ignoralo!; **it has come to my notice that ...** sono venuto a sapere che...; **to escape** *or* **avoid notice** passare inosservato(-a); **it escaped my notice that ...** non ho notato che...

♦ vt accorgersi di, notare; **he pretended not to notice us** ha fatto finta di non vederci; **I notice you have a new car** vedo che ha una macchina nuova

❑ **notice** is not translated by the Italian word *notizia*

no·tice·able [ˈnəʊtɪsəbl] ADJ (*perceptible*) percettibile; (*obvious*) evidente; (*considerable*) notevole; **the scar is hardly noticeable** la cicatrice si vede appena; **there has been a noticeable increase in prices** c'è stato un notevole aumento dei prezzi

notice board N (*Brit*) bacheca

no·ti·fi·ca·tion [ˌnəʊtɪfɪˈkeɪʃən] N (*see vb*) notifica; denuncia; (*announcement*) annuncio

no·ti·fy [ˈnəʊtɪfaɪ] vt: **to notify sb of sth** informare *or* avvisare qn di qc; (*police*) denunciare qc a qn; **to notify sth to sb** notificare qc a qn; **you should notify the police that your car has been stolen** deve denunciare il furto della macchina alla polizia

no·tion [ˈnəʊʃən] N **1** idea; (*concept*) nozione *f*; **to have no notion of time** non avere la nozione del tempo; **I haven't the slightest** *or* **foggiest notion** non ho la più pallida idea; **I have no notion of what you mean** non ho la più vaga idea di cosa tu voglia dire **2 notions** NPL (*USA: haberdashery*) merceria

no·to·ri·ety [ˌnəʊtəˈraɪətɪ] N notorietà

no·to·ri·ous [nəʊˈtɔːrɪəs] ADJ (*thief, criminal, prison etc*) famigerato(-a); (*liar*) ben noto(-a); (*place, crime*) tristemente famoso(-a); **a town notorious for its fog** una città tristemente famosa per la nebbia

no·to·ri·ous·ly [nəʊˈtɔːrɪəslɪ] ADV notoriamente

Notts [nɒts] ABBR (*Brit*: = *Nottinghamshire*)

not·with·stand·ing [ˌnɒtwɪθˈstændɪŋ] PREP nonostante, malgrado ♦ CONJ: **international agreements notwithstanding ...** malgrado gli accordi internazionali...

nou·gat [ˈnuːgɑː] N torrone *m*

nought [nɔːt] N (*Math*) zero

noun [naʊn] N sostantivo, nome *m*

nour·ish [ˈnʌrɪʃ] vt nutrire

nour·ish·ing [ˈnʌrɪʃɪŋ] ADJ nutriente

nour·ish·ment [ˈnʌrɪʃmənt] N nutrimento

Nov. ABBR (= *November*) nov. (= *novembre*)

Nova Scotia [ˈnəʊvəˈskəʊʃə] N Nuova Scozia

nov·el [ˈnɒvəl] ADJ originale, nuovo(-a) (*after n*) ♦ N (*Literature*) romanzo

❑ **novel** is not translated by the Italian word *novella*

nov·el·ist [ˈnɒvəlɪst] N romanziere(-a)

nov·el·ty [ˈnɒvəltɪ] N **1** *no pl* novità **2** (*Comm*) oggettino, ninnolo

No·vem·ber [nəʊˈvɛmbəʳ] N novembre *m*; *see* July

nov·ice [ˈnɒvɪs] N principiante *m/f*; (*Rel*) novizio(-a)

NOW [naʊ] N ABBR (*USA*: = *National Organization for Women*) ≈ U.D.I. *f* (= *Unione Donne Italiane*)

now [naʊ] ADV **1** (*at present, these days*) adesso, ora; (*at that time*) allora; **right now** subito, immediatamente; **now is the time to do it** questo è il momento per farlo; **they won't be long now** ormai non tarderanno; **I saw her just now** l'ho vista proprio adesso; **that's the fashion just now** è la moda del momento; **I'm very busy just now** in questo momento sono molto occupato; **I'll read it just now** lo leggo subito; **(every) now and then** *or* **now and again** ogni tanto, di tanto in tanto; **it's now or never** ora o mai più **2** (*with prep*):

between now and Monday entro lunedì, da qui a lunedì; **I couldn't do it before now** non potevo farlo prima; **long before now** molto tempo fa; **by now** ormai; **it should be ready by now** ormai dovrebbe essere pronto; **the train should have arrived by now** il treno dovrebbe essere già arrivato; **in 3 days from now** fra 3 giorni; **from now on** d'ora in poi; **from now until then** da adesso fino a quel momento; **that's all for now** per ora basta; **until now** *or* **up to now** fino ad ora **3** (*without temporal force*): **now (then)!** dunque!, allora!; **now then, no more quarrelling** ora *or* adesso basta con i litigi; **well now** vediamo, dunque; **well now, look who it is!** ma guarda un po' chi si vede!; **be careful now!** ma sta' attento! ♦ CONJ: **now (that)** adesso che, ora che

nowa·days [ˈnaʊədeɪz] ADV al giorno d'oggi, oggi, oggigiorno, oggidì; **nowadays I haven't got time to watch television** attualmente non ho il tempo per guardare la televisione

no·where [ˈnəʊˌwɛəʳ] ADV in nessun posto *or* luogo, da nessuna parte; **I went nowhere** non sono andato in nessun posto *or* da nessuna parte; **nowhere in Italy** in nessuna parte d'Italia, da nessuna parte d'Italia; **nowhere else** in nessun altro posto; **it/he is nowhere to be found** non si riesce a trovarlo da nessuna parte; **we're getting nowhere** non stiamo concludendo nulla; **that will get you nowhere** ciò non le servirà a nulla; **he appeared from nowhere** è saltato fuori da chissà dove; **Paul is nowhere near as tall as John** Paul non è neanche lontanamente alto come John; **it's nowhere near as good** non vale neanche la metà; **nowhere near enough** ben lontano dall'essere sufficiente

no-win situation [ˌnəʊwɪnsɪtjʊˈeɪʃən] N: **to be in a no-win situation** aver perso in partenza

nox·ious [ˈnɒkʃəs] ADJ nocivo(-a)

noz·zle [ˈnɒzl] N (*of hose, vacuum cleaner, syringe*) bocchetta, boccaglio; (*of fire extinguisher*) lancia

NP [ˌɛnˈpiː] N ABBR = **notary public**

NS [ˌɛnˈɛs] ABBR (*Canada*: = *Nova Scotia*)

NSC [ˌɛnɛsˈsiː] N ABBR (*USA*) = **National Security Council**

NSF [ˌɛnɛsˈɛf] N ABBR (*USA*) = **National Science Foundation**

NSW [ˌɛnɛsˈdʌbljuː] ABBR (*Australia*: = *New South Wales*)

NT [ˌɛnˈtiː] N ABBR (= *New Testament*) N.T. (= *Nuovo Testamento*)

nth [ɛnθ] ADJ (*Math*): **to the nth power** *or* **degree** all'ennesima potenza; **for the nth time** (*fam*) per l'ennesima volta

nu·ance [ˈnjuːɑːns] N sfumatura

nu·bile [ˈnjuːbaɪl] ADJ nubile; (*attractive*) giovane e desiderabile

nu·clear [ˈnjuːklɪəʳ] ADJ nucleare; (*warfare*) atomico(-a); **nuclear power** energia nucleare

nuclear disarmament N disarmo nucleare

nuclear family N famiglia nucleare

nuclear-free zone [ˌnjuːklɪəfriːˈzəʊn] N zona denuclearizzata

nu·cleus [ˈnjuːklɪəs] N (*pl nuclei* [ˈnjuːklɪaɪ]) nucleo

nude [njuːd] ADJ nudo(-a) ♦ N (*Art*) nudo; **in the nude** nudo(-a), tutto(-a) nudo(-a)

nudge [nʌdʒ] N gomitata ♦ vt dare un colpetto col gomito a; **he nudged me out of the way** mi ha spinto via con una gomitata

nud·ist [ˈnjuːdɪst] ADJ (*colony*) nudista; (*camp, beach*) di nudisti ♦ N nudista *m/f*

nu·dity [ˈnjuːdɪtɪ] N nudità

nug·get [ˈnʌgɪt] N pepita

nui·sance [ˈnjuːsns] N (*state of affairs, thing*) fastidio, seccatura; (*person*) peste *f*; **what a nuisance!** che seccatura!; **it's a nuisance having to shave** doversi radere è una (gran) seccatura; **to make a nuisance of o.s.** rendersi insopportabile; **he's a nuisance** dà fastidio

nuke [njuːk] (*esp USA: fam*) vt attaccare con armi atomiche ♦ N bomba atomica

null [nʌl] ADJ: **null and void** (*Law*) nullo(-a)

nul·li·fy [ˈnʌlɪfaɪ] vt annullare

numb [nʌm] ADJ **1** (*fingers etc*) intorpidito(-a); **numb with cold** intirizzito(-a) (dal freddo); **my leg has gone numb** mi si è intorpidita una gamba **2** (*fig*): **numb with** (*fear, grief*) paralizzato(-a) da, impietrito(-a) da ♦ vt **1** intorpidire; **the cold numbs you as soon as you step outside** appena si esce si resta paralizzati dal freddo **2** (*fig*) rendere insensibile; **she drinks to numb her grief** beve per attenuare il dolore

num·ber ['nʌmbə'] N **1** (*Math*) numero; (*figure*) cifra, numero; **in round numbers** in cifra tonda; **even/odd number** numero pari/dispari; **the Book of Numbers** (*Bible*) i Numeri **2** (*quantity*) numero, quantità *f inv*; **a number of people** un certo numero di persone, diversa gente; **a fair number of** (*reasons, mistakes, people*) una buona quantità di; **on a number of occasions** diverse volte, in diverse occasioni; **any number of** una gran quantità di, moltissimi; **they were 15 in number** erano in 15; **times without number** tantissime volte; **one of their number** uno di loro **3** (*of house etc*) numero; **at number 15** al (numero) 15; **what's your phone number?** qual è il tuo numero di telefono?; **you've got the wrong number** ha sbagliato numero; **his number's up!** (*fam*) è venuta la sua ora!; **to look after number one** (*fam*) fare solo i propri interessi; **he's my number two** è il mio vice **4** (*issue: of magazine etc*) numero **5** (*song, act etc*) numero; (*piece of music*) pezzo ♦ VT **1** (*count, include*) contare; **to number sb among one's friends** considerare qn un amico **2** (*amount to*) ammontare a; **they numbered 10 in all** erano 10 in tutto **3** (*assign number to*) numerare; **his days are numbered** (*fig*) ha i giorni contati

num·bered ac·count [ˌnʌmbədə'kaʊnt] N (*in bank*) conto numerato

number plate N (*Brit: Aut*) targa

Number Ten N (*Brit: 10 Downing Street*) residenza del Primo Ministro del Regno Unito

numb·ness ['nʌmnɪs] N intorpidimento; (*due to cold*) intirizzimento

numb·skull ['nʌmˌskʌl] N (*fam*) imbecille *m/f*, idiota *m/f*

nu·mer·al ['njuːmərəl] N numero, cifra

nu·mer·ate ['njuːmərɪt] ADJ: **to be numerate** (*Brit*) saper far di conto

nu·meri·cal [njuːˈmɛrɪkəl] ADJ numerico(-a); **in numerical order** in ordine numerico

nu·mer·ous ['njuːmərəs] ADJ numeroso(-a)

nun [nʌn] N suora, monaca

nun·nery ['nʌnərɪ] N convento

nup·tial ['nʌpʃəl] ADJ nuziale

nurse [nɜːs] N **1** (*in hospital etc*) infermiere(-a); **student nurse** allievo(-a) infermiere(-a) **2** (*also:* **nursemaid:** *children's*) bambinaia ♦ VT **1** (*patient*) assistere, curare; (*cold*) curare; **she nursed him back to health** è guarito grazie alle sue cure; **to nurse a cold** curarsi un raffreddore **2** (*suckle:*

baby) allattare, dare il latte a **3** (*cradle*) cullare; (*fig: hope*) nutrire, cullare; (*: anger, grudge*) covare

nurse·ry ['nɜːsərɪ] N **1** (*room*) stanza dei bambini; (*institution*) asilo, nido **2** (*Agr*) vivaio

nursery rhyme N filastrocca

nursery school N scuola materna, asilo infantile

nursery slope N (*Brit: Skiing*) pista per principianti

nurs·ing ['nɜːsɪŋ] N (*care of invalids*) assistenza; (*profession*) professione *f* di infermiere (*or* di infermiera); **she's going in for nursing** ha deciso di fare l'infermiera ♦ ADJ **1** (*mother*) che allatta **2** (*of hospital*): **the nursing staff** gli infermieri, il personale infermieristico; **nursing auxiliary** infermiere(-a) non diplomato(-a)

nursing home N casa di cura, clinica

nur·ture ['nɜːtʃə'] VT (*rear*) allevare con amore; (*feed*) nutrire

nut [nʌt] N **1** (*Bot*) noce *f* (*or* nocciola *or* mandorla *etc*) (*no generic term in Italian*); **nuts** NPL frutta *sg* secca; **a bag of mixed nuts** un sacchetto di frutta secca mista **2** (*Tech*) dado; (*Mountaineering*) nut *m inv* **3** (*fam: head*) zucca; **he is off his nut** gli manca una rotella, è svitato **4** (*fam: person*) pazzo(-a), matto(-a); **he's nuts** è pazzo ♦ ADJ (*chocolate etc*) alle noci (*or* alla nocciola *or* alla mandorla *etc*); *see also* **nuts**

nut·case ['nʌtˌkeɪs] N (*fam*) matto(-a), pazzo(-a), pazzerello(-a)

nut·crackers ['nʌtˌkrækəz] NPL schiaccianoci *m inv*

nut·meg ['nʌtˌmɛg] N noce *f* moscata

nu·tri·ent ['njuːtrɪənt] N sostanza nutritiva ♦ ADJ nutriente; **nutrient cycle** (*Geol*) ciclo pedogenetico

nu·tri·tion [njuːˈtrɪʃən] N nutrizione *f*, alimentazione *f*

nu·tri·tion·ist [njuːˈtrɪʃənɪst] N nutrizionista *m/f*

nu·tri·tious [njuːˈtrɪʃəs], **nu·tri·tive** ['njuːtrɪtɪv] ADJ nutriente, nutritivo(-a)

nut·shell ['nʌtˌʃɛl] N guscio di noce (*or* nocciola *etc*) (*no generic term in Italian*); **in a nutshell** in poche parole; **to put it in a nutshell** per farla breve

nut·ty ['nʌtɪ] ADJ (*comp* **-ier,** *superl* **-iest**) **1** (*flavour, taste*) di noce (*or* nocciola *or* mandorla *etc*); (*cake*) di frutta secca; (*chocolate*) alla nocciola *etc* **2** (*fam*) pazzo(-a), matto(-a)

nuz·zle ['nʌzl] VI: **to nuzzle up to** strofinare il muso contro

NV ABBR (*USA*: = *Nevada*)

NWT [ˌɛndʌbljuːˈtiː] ABBR (*Canada*: = **Northwest Territories**)

NY [ˌɛnˈwaɪ] N ABBR (*USA Post*: = **New York**)

NYC [ˌɛnwaɪˈsiː] N ABBR (*USA Post*: = **New York City**)

ny·lon ['naɪlɒn] N nailon *m*; **nylons** NPL calze *fpl* di nailon ♦ ADJ di nailon

nymph [nɪmf] N ninfa

nym·pho·ma·ni·ac [ˌnɪmfəʊˈmeɪnɪæk] ADJ, N ninfomane *f*

Oo

O¹, o¹ [əʊ] N **1** (*letter*) O, o *f inv*, *m inv*; **O for Oliver**, (*USA*) **O for Oboe** ≈ O come Otranto **2** (*number, Telec, etc*) zero **3** (*USA Scol*: = *outstanding*) ≈ ottimo

O², o² [əʊ] EXCL (*liter*) oh!

oaf [əʊf] N zoticone(-a)

oak [əʊk] N quercia; **common oak** farnia; **English oak** rovere *m*; **red oak** quercia rossa ♦ ADJ di quercia

oar [ɔːʳ] N remo; **to put** *or* **shove one's oar in** (*fig: fam*) impicciarsi

oars·man [ˈɔːzmən] N (*pl* **-men**) rematore *m*; (*Sport*) vogatore *m*

OAS [ˌəʊeɪˈɛs] N ABBR (= *Organization of American States*) OSA *f* (= *Organizzazione degli Stati Americani*)

oasis [əʊˈeɪsɪs] N (*pl* **oases** [əʊˈeɪsiːz]) oasi *f inv*

oath [əʊθ] N **1** (*solemn promise*) giuramento; **under** *or* **on oath** sotto giuramento; **to put sb on** *or* **under oath to do sth** far giurare a qn di fare qc; **to take the oath** giurare; **to swear an oath** *or* **on one's oath** giurare solennemente **2** (*swear word*) imprecazione *f*; **a string of oaths** una sequela di imprecazioni

oat·meal [ˈəʊtmiːl] N farina d'avena ♦ ADJ (*colour*) beige *inv*

oats [ˈəʊts] NPL avena

ob·du·rate [ˈɒbdjʊrɪt](*frm*) ADJ (*unyielding*) irremovibile; (*stubborn*) caparbio(-a), pervicace; (*hard-hearted*) insensibile

OBE [ˌəʊbiːˈiː] N ABBR (*Brit*: = *Order of the British Empire*) titolo onorifico

obedi·ence [əˈbiːdɪəns] N ubbidienza; **in obedience to your orders** (*frm*) conformemente ai vostri ordini

obedi·ent [əˈbiːdɪənt] ADJ ubbidiente; **to be obedient to sb/ sth** ubbidire a qn/qc

ob·elisk [ˈɒbɪlɪsk] N obelisco

obese [əʊˈbiːs] ADJ (*frm*) obeso(-a)

obesity [əʊˈbiːsɪtɪ] N (*frm*) obesità

obey [əˈbeɪ] VT (*person*) ubbidire a; (*instructions*) seguire; (*regulations*) osservare; **to obey the rules** rispettare il regolamento; **to obey one's conscience** seguire i dettami della propria coscienza ♦ VI ubbidire

obi·tu·ary [əˈbɪtjʊərɪ] N necrologio

ob·ject [ˈɒbdʒɪkt] N **1** (*gen*) oggetto; **an object of ridicule** oggetto di scherno **2** (*aim*) scopo, intento, obiettivo; **the object of the exercise** lo scopo dell'esercizio; **with this object in view** *or* **in mind** in vista di questo scopo; **with the object of doing sth** al fine di fare; **what's the object of doing that?** a che serve farlo?; **expense is no object** non si bada a spese **3** (*Gram*) complemento; (*direct/indirect*) **object** complemento oggetto/indiretto ♦ VT [əbˈdʒekt] **to object that** obiettare che ♦ VI avere da obiettare su; **if you don't object** se non hai obiezioni; **to object to sb doing sth** disapprovare che qn faccia qc; **she objects to my behaviour** lei disapprova il mio comportamento; **a lot of people objected to the proposal** molti hanno obiettato alla proposta; **do you object to my smoking?** la disturba se fumo?; **I object!** (*frm*) mi oppongo!

ob·jec·tion [əbˈdʒekʃən] N obiezione *f*; **to make** *or* **raise an objection** sollevare un'obiezione; **there is no objection to your going** non c'è alcuna obiezione alla tua partenza; **are there any objections?** ci sono obiezioni?; **have you any objection to my smoking?** la disturba se fumo?; **if you have no objection** se non hai nulla in contrario

ob·jec·tion·able [əbˈdʒekʃnəbl] ADJ (*person*) antipatico(-a); (*conduct, method*) discutibile; (*language, attitude*) riprovevole; (*smell, colour*) sgradevole; **why are you being so objectionable?** perché sei così antipatico?; **morally objectionable** moralmente discutibile

ob·jec·tive [əbˈdʒektɪv] ADJ **1** (*impartial*) obiettivo(-a) **2** (*Gram, Philosophy*) oggettivo(-a) ♦ N (*aim*) obiettivo

ob·jec·tiv·ity [ˌɒbdʒekˈtɪvɪtɪ] N (*see adj*) obiettività; oggettività

object lesson N (*fig*): **object lesson (in)** dimostrazione *f* (di)

ob·jec·tor [əbˈdʒektəʳ] N oppositore(-trice); **a conscientious objector** un obiettore di coscienza

ob·li·ga·tion [ˌɒblɪˈgeɪʃən] N (*duty*) obbligo; (*compulsion*) impegno; **"without obligation"** "senza impegno"; **to be under an obligation to sb/to do sth** essere in dovere verso qn/ di fare qc; **I'm under no obligation to do it** non sono tenuto(-a) a farlo; **to meet one's obligations** rispettare i propri impegni; **to fail to meet one's obligations** venire meno ai propri impegni

ob·liga·tory [ɒˈblɪgətərɪ] ADJ obbligatorio(-a), d'obbligo; **to make it obligatory for sb to do sth** imporre a qn l'obbligo di fare qc

oblige [əˈblaɪdʒ] VT **1** (*compel*) obbligare, costringere; **to oblige sb to do sth** obbligare *or* costringere qn a fare qc; **to be obliged to do sth** essere obbligato(-a) *or* costretto(-a) a fare qc; **to feel obliged to do sth** sentirsi in dovere di fare qc **2** (*do a favour to*) fare una cortesia a; **anything to oblige!** (*fam*) questo e altro!; **will you oblige?** farai questa cortesia?; **to be obliged to sb for sth** essere grato(-a) a qn per qc; **much obliged!** (*old*) molto grato!, obbligato!; **I am obliged to you for your help** ti sono grato per il tuo aiuto

oblig·ing [əˈblaɪdʒɪŋ] ADJ gentile, servizievole; **it was very obliging of them** è stato molto gentile da parte loro

oblique [əˈbliːk] ADJ (*angle*) obliquo(-a); (*fig: allusion*) indiretto(-a) ♦ N (*Brit: Typ*): **oblique (stroke)** barra

oblit·erate [əˈblɪtəreɪt] VT cancellare completamente

oblivi·on [əˈblɪvɪən] N oblio; **to fall** *or* **sink into oblivion** cadere nell'oblio

oblivi·ous [əˈblɪvɪəs] ADJ: **oblivious of** *or* **to** ignaro(-a) di

ob·long [ˈɒblɒŋ] ADJ oblungo(-a) ♦ N rettangolo

ob·nox·ious [əbˈnɒkʃəs] ADJ (*person, behaviour*) detestabile, odioso(-a); (*fumes, smell*) pestifero(-a), pestilenziale

oboe [ˈəʊbəʊ] N oboe *m*

ob·scene [əbˈsiːn] ADJ osceno(-a)

ob·scen·ity [əbˈsenɪtɪ] N oscenità *f inv*

ob·scure [əbˈskjʊəʳ] ADJ (*comp* **-r**, *superl* **-st**) (*gen*) oscuro(-a); (*feeling, memory*) vago(-a) ♦ VT (*darken*) oscurare; (*hide: sun*) coprire; (*issue, idea*) confondere; **trees obscured his vision** degli alberi gli oscuravano la visione; **the mountain is obscured by fog** la montagna è nascosta dalla nebbia

ob·scu·rity [əbˈskjʊərɪtɪ] N (*also fig*) oscurità *f inv*

ob·se·qui·ous [əbˈsiːkwɪəs] ADJ (*pej*) ossequioso(-a)

ob·serv·able [əbˈzɜːvəbl] ADJ osservabile, riscontrabile; (*appreciable*) notevole

ob·serv·ance [əbˈzɜːvəns] N osservanza; **religious observances** pratiche *fpl* religiose

ob·serv·ant [əbˈzɜːvənt] ADJ (*watchful*) che ha spirito d'osservazione; **observant (of)** (*Rel, Law*) osservante (di); **you're very observant!** hai molto spirito di osservazione!

ob·ser·va·tion [ˌɒbzəˈveɪʃən] N **1** (*gen*) osservazione *f*; (*of the law*) osservanza; **the police are keeping him under observation** la polizia lo tiene sotto sorveglianza; **he is under observation in hospital** è in ospedale sotto osservazione; **powers of observation** spirito d'osservazione; **to escape observation** sfuggire alla sorveglianza **2** (*remark*) osservazione *f*, commento

observation post N (*Mil*) osservatorio (militare)

ob·ser·va·tory [əbˈzɜːvətrɪ] N osservatorio

ob·serve [əbˈzɜːv] VT osservare

ob·serv·er [əbˈzɜːvəʳ] N osservatore(-trice)

ob·sess [əbˈses] VT ossessionare; **to be obsessed by** *or* **with sb/sth** essere ossessionato(-a) da *or* con qn/qc

ob·ses·sion [əbˈseʃən] N ossessione *f*; **football is an obsession with him** è maniaco del calcio; **his obsession with her** la sua fissazione per lei; **his obsession about cleanliness**

la sua mania della pulizia; **it's getting to be an obsession with you** sta diventando una fissazione per te

ob·ses·sive [əbˈsesɪv] ADJ ossessivo(-a)

ob·so·les·cence [ˌɒbsəˈlesns] N obsolescenza; **built-in** or **planned obsolescence** (*Comm*) obsolescenza programmata

ob·so·les·cent [ˌɒbsəˈlesnt] ADJ obsolescente

ob·so·lete [ˈɒbsəliːt] ADJ obsoleto(-a), in disuso; (*word*) desueto(-a)

ob·sta·cle [ˈɒbstəkl] N ostacolo; **to be an obstacle to sb/sth** essere di ostacolo a qn/qc; **to put an obstacle in the way of sb** ostacolare qn; **that is no obstacle to our doing it** questo non ci impedisce affatto di farlo

obstacle race N (*Sport*) corsa ad ostacoli

ob·ste·tri·cian [ˌɒbstəˈtrɪʃən] N ostetrico

ob·stet·rics [ɒbˈstetrɪks] NSG ostetricia

ob·sti·na·cy [ˈɒbstɪnəsɪ] N ostinazione *f*

ob·sti·nate [ˈɒbstɪnɪt] ADJ (*gen*) ostinato(-a); (*resistance*) strenuo(-a); (*illness*) persistente; **as obstinate as a mule** testardo(-a) come un mulo

ob·strep·er·ous [əbˈstrepərəs] ADJ turbolento(-a)

ob·struct [əbˈstrʌkt] VT (*block: pipe, artery*) ostruire; (: *traffic, road: Sport*) bloccare; (*hinder*) ostacolare; **a truck was obstructing the traffic** un camion bloccava il traffico; **you're obstructing my view** mi impedisci la visuale

ob·struc·tion [əbˈstrʌkʃən] N (*sth which obstructs*) ostacolo; (*in pipe, artery*) ostruzione *f*; **an obstruction in the pipe** un'ostruzione nel tubo; **to cause an obstruction** (*in road*) bloccare la strada; **the truck was causing an obstruction** il camion stava ostruendo il traffico

ob·struc·tive [əbˈstrʌktɪv] ADJ che crea impedimenti; **stop being obstructive!** smettila di fare ostruzionismo!

ob·tain [əbˈteɪn] VT (*gen*) ottenere; **to obtain sth (for o.s.)** (*goods*) procurarsi qc; **to obtain sth for sb** procurare qc a qn ♦ VI (*frm: circumstances, custom*) esistere

ob·tain·able [əbˈteɪnəbl] ADJ **where is that obtainable?** dove si può trovare?

ob·tru·sive [əbˈtruːsɪv] ADJ (*person*) invadente, importuno(-a); (*opinions*) ostentato(-a); (*smell*) pungente; (*building*) che disturba la visuale

ob·tuse [əbˈtjuːs] ADJ (*gen, also Math*) ottuso(-a); (*remark*) stolto(-a)

ob·verse [ˈɒbvəːs] N (*frm*) opposto, inverso

ob·vi·ate [ˈɒbvɪˌeɪt] (*frm*) VT (*danger, objection*) evitare; (*necessity*) ovviare a

ob·vi·ous [ˈɒbvɪəs] ADJ (*clear, perceptible*) ovvio(-a), evidente; (*unsubtle*) scontato(-a), banale; **it's obvious that ...** è ovvio che...; **she's the obvious person for the job** è chiaramente la persona che ci vuole per quel lavoro; **the obvious thing to do is to leave** la cosa più logica da fare è andarsene; **try not to make it obvious that you're bored** cerca di non farti vedere annoiato

ob·vi·ous·ly [ˈɒbvɪəslɪ] ADV ovviamente, evidentemente; **he was obviously not drunk** si vedeva che non era ubriaco; **he was not obviously drunk** non si vedeva che era ubriaco; **she was obviously exhausted** si vedeva che era stanca; **obviously!** certo!; **obviously not!** certo che no!; **obviously I'd be sorry if we didn't go** ovviamente mi dispiacerebbe non andarci

oc·ca·sion [əˈkeɪʒən] N **1** (*point in time*) occasione *f*, circostanza; **on occasion** di tanto in tanto; **on several occasions** in varie occasioni; **on that occasion** in quell'occasione, quella volta **2** (*special occasion*) occasione *f*, avvenimento; **an important occasion** un avvenimento importante; **it was quite an occasion** è stato un avvenimento; **music written for the occasion** musica scritta per l'occasione; **on the occasion of** in occasione di; **to rise to the occasion** mostrarsi all'altezza della situazione **3** (*frm: reason*) motivo, ragione *f*; **there was no occasion for it** non ce n'era motivo; **to have occasion to do sth** avere l'occasione di fare qc; **if you ever have occasion to be in London** se ti capita di essere a Londra ♦ VT (*frm*) causare; (*remark*) dare origine a

oc·ca·sion·al [əˈkeɪʒənl] ADJ (*gen*) occasionale; (*showers*) sporadico(-a); **I like the occasional cigarette** ogni tanto mi piace fumare una sigaretta

oc·ca·sion·al·ly [əˈkeɪʒnəlɪ] ADV ogni tanto; **very occasionally** molto raramente

occasional table N tavolino (*che si usa saltuariamente*)

oc·cult [ɒˈkʌlt] ADJ occulto(-a) ♦ N: **the occult** l'occulto

oc·cu·pan·cy [ˈɒkjʊpənsɪ] N (*of house*) occupazione *f*, presa di possesso; **to take up occupancy of a house** prendere possesso di una casa

oc·cu·pant [ˈɒkjʊpənt] N (*of house*) inquilino(-a); (*of boat, car*) persona a bordo; (*of job, post*) titolare *m/f*

oc·cu·pa·tion [ˌɒkjʊˈpeɪʃən] N **1** (*job*) mestiere *m*, professione *f*; (*pastime*) occupazione *f*; **he's a joiner by occupation** è falegname di mestiere **2** (*gen, also Mil*) occupazione *f*; **army of occupation** esercito d'occupazione; **the occupation of Paris** l'occupazione di Parigi; **the house is ready for occupation** la casa è pronta per essere abitata

oc·cu·pa·tion·al [ˌɒkjʊˈpeɪʃənl] ADJ (*group, disease*) professionale; **occupational accident** infortunio sul lavoro

occupational guidance N (*Brit*) orientamento professionale

occupational pension scheme N *sistema pensionistico a disposizione di una determinata categoria di lavoratori*

occupational therapy N ergoterapia

oc·cu·pi·er [ˈɒkjʊˌpaɪəʳ] N (*of house*) inquilino(-a); (*of post*) titolare *m/f*

oc·cu·py [ˈɒkjʊˌpaɪ] VT occupare; **this job occupies all my time** questo lavoro occupa or prende tutto il mio tempo; **to be occupied with sth** essere preso(-a) da qc; **to be occupied in doing sth** essere occupato(-a) a fare qc; **she occupies herself by knitting** si tiene occupata lavorando a maglia; **to keep one's mind occupied** tenere la mente occupata; **the toilet was occupied** il bagno era occupato

oc·cur [əˈkəːʳ] VI **1** (*event*) accadere; (*difficulty, opportunity*) presentarsi; (*phenomenon*) aver luogo; (*error, word, plant*) essere presente, trovarsi; **the accident occurred yesterday** l'incidente è successo ieri; **to occur again** ripetersi **2** (*come to mind*): **to occur to sb** venire in mente a qn; **it suddenly occurred to me that ...** improvvisamente mi è venuto in mente che...; **such an idea would never have occurred to her** una tale idea non le sarebbe mai venuta in mente

❑ **occur** is not translated by the Italian word *occorrere*

oc·cur·rence [əˈkʌrəns] N evento; **an everyday occurrence** un fatto quotidiano; **this is a common occurrence** è una cosa che capita spesso; **the greatest occurrence of heart attack is in those over 65** l'infarto ha la massima incidenza nelle persone sopra i 65

❑ **occurrence** is not translated by the Italian word *occorrenza*

ocean [ˈəʊʃən] N oceano; **oceans of** (*fam*) fiumi *mpl* di

ocean bed N fondale *m* oceanico

ocean-going [ˈəʊʃənˌgəʊɪŋ] ADJ d'alto mare

Oceania [ˌəʊʃɪˈɑːnɪə] N l'Oceania

ocean liner N transatlantico

ochre, ocher (*USA*) [ˈəʊkəʳ] N ocra *f inv* ♦ ADJ (*color*) ocra *inv*

o'clock [əˈklɒk] ADV: **it is one o'clock** è l'una; **it's five o'clock** sono le cinque; **at 9 o'clock** alle 9; **at twelve o'clock** (*midday*) a mezzogiorno; (*midnight*) a mezzanotte

OCR [ˌəʊsiːˈɑːʳ] N ABBR **1** = **optical character reader 2** = **optical character recognition**

Oct. ABBR (= *October*) ott. (= *ottobre*)

oc·tag·o·nal [ɒkˈtægənl] ADJ ottagonale

oc·tane [ˈɒkteɪn] N ottano ♦ ADJ: **high-octane petrol, high-octane gas** (*USA*) benzina ad alto numero di ottani

oc·tave [ˈɒktɪv] N (*Mus*) ottava

Oc·to·ber [ɒkˈtəʊbəʳ] N ottobre *m*; **in October** in ottobre; *see* July

oc·to·gen·ar·ian [ˌɒktəʊdʒɪˈnɛərɪən] N ottuagenario(-a)

oc·to·pus [ˈɒktəpəs] N (*gen*) polpo; (*larger*) piovra

odd [ɒd] ADJ (*comp* **-er**, *superl* **-est**) **1** (*strange*) strano(-a); **how** or **that's odd!** che strano!; **he says some odd things** dice delle cose strane **2** (*number*) dispari *inv*; **an odd number** un numero dispari **3** (*extra, left over*) in più; (*unpaired: sock*) spaiato(-a); **if you have an odd minute** se hai un momento libero; **the odd man** *or* **one out** l'eccezione *f* **4** (*occasional*) occasionale; **at odd moments** in certi momenti; **he has written the odd article** ha scritto qualche articolo **5** (*and more*): **30 odd** 30 e rotti, poco più di 30; *see also* **odds**

odd·ball [ˈɒdˌbɔːl] N, ADJ (*fam*) eccentrico(-a)

odd·ity [ˈɒdɪtɪ] N **1** (*also:* **oddness**) stranezza, bizzarria **2** (*person*) originale *m/f*

odd-job man [ˈɒdˈdʒɒbˈmæn] N (*pl* **-men**) tuttofare *m inv*

odd jobs NPL lavori *mpl* occasionali

odd·ly [ˈɒdlɪ] ADV stranamente; **they are oddly similar** tra di loro c'è una strana somiglianza; **oddly enough you are right** stranamente hai ragione

odd·ments [ˈɒdmənts] NPL (*Brit: Comm*) avanzi *mpl* di magazzino

odds [ɒdz] NPL **1** (*Betting*) probabilità *fpl*; **odds of 10 to 1** una probabilità di 10 a 1; **the odds on the horse are 5 to 1** danno il cavallo 5 a 1; **short/long odds** alta/bassa probabilità; **the odds are in his favour** i pronostici sono a suo favore; **to fight against overwhelming odds** lottare contro enormi difficoltà; **to succeed against all the odds** riuscire contro ogni aspettativa; **the odds are that …** è facile *or* probabile che...; **the odds are against his coming** è poco probabile che venga **2** (*difference*): **what's the odds?** (*fam*) che differenza fa?, cosa cambia?; **it makes no odds** non fa differenza, non importa **3** (*variance, strife*): **at odds** ai ferri corti; **to be at odds with sb over sth** essere in disaccordo con qn su qc

odds-on [ɒdzˈɒn] ADJ (*fam*) probabile; **it's odds-on that … è** quasi certo che...; **odds-on favourite** (*Horse Racing*) gran favorito(-a)

ode [əʊd] N ode *f*

odi·ous [ˈəʊdɪəs] ADJ odioso(-a)

odom·eter [ɒˈdɒmɪtəʳ] N (*Aut*) odometro

odour, odor (*USA*) [ˈəʊdəʳ] N odore *m*

odour·less, odor·less (*USA*) [ˈəʊdəlɪs] ADJ inodore

oesopha·gus, esopha·gus (*USA*) [iːˈsɒfəgəs] N esofago

oes·tro·gen, es·tro·gen (*USA*) [ˈiːstrəʊdʒən] N estrogeno

of [ɒv, əv] PREP **1** (*gen*) di; **the house of my uncle** la casa di mio zio; **the love of God** l'amore di Dio; **a friend of mine** un mio amico; **that was very kind of you** è stato molto carino da parte tua; **free of charge** gratis; **the 5th of July** il 5 luglio; **loss of appetite** perdita dell'appetito; **south of Glasgow** a sud di Glasgow; **a quarter of 4** (*USA: time*) le 4 meno un quarto; **the City of New York** la città di New York; **a boy of 8** un ragazzo di 8 anni; **a man of great ability** un uomo di grande abilità; **that idiot of a minister** quell'idiota di ministro **2** (*cause*) di, per; **of necessity** necessariamente, per necessità; **to die of pneumonia** morire di polmonite **3** (*material*) di, in; **made of steel** (fatto(-a)) di or in acciaio; **it's made of wood** è di legno **4** (*concerning*) di; **what do you think of him?** cosa pensi di lui?; **what of it?** e allora? **5** (*partitive*) di; **how much of this do you need?** quanto te ne serve?; **a kilo of flour** un chilo di farina; **a handful of coins** una manciata di monete; **there were four of us** eravamo in quattro; **four of us went** quattro di noi sono andati; **there were four of them** (*people*) erano in quattro; (*things*) ce n'erano quattro

KEYWORD

off [ɒf] ADV

1 (*distance, time*): **the game was/is three days off** la gara era dopo/è fra tre giorni; **5 km off (the road)** a 5 km (dalla strada); **a place 2 miles off** un posto distante 2 miglia; **it's a long way off** è molto lontano

2 (*departure*): **I must be off** devo andare; **off we go** via, partiamo; **he's gone off to see the boss** è andato a parlare col capo; **he's off to Paris tonight** parte per Parigi stasera

3 (*removal*): **5% off** (*Comm*) sconto del 5%; **a button came off** è venuto via un bottone; **with his hat off** senza cappello; **the lid was off** non c'era il coperchio; **off with those wet clothes!** togliti quei vestiti bagnati!

4 (*not at work*): **to take a day off** prendersi una giornata di vacanza; **I'm off on Fridays** il venerdì non lavoro; **he's off sick** è in malattia

5 (*in phrases*): **off and on, on and off** di tanto in tanto; **right** *or* **straight off** subito

♦ ADJ

1 (*inoperative*): **to be off** (*machine, light, engine*) essere spento(-a); (*water, gas, tap*) essere chiuso(-a)

2 (*cancelled*) sospeso(-a); (*Brit: not available: in restaurant*) finito(-a); **the play is off** la commedia è sospesa; **the wedding is off** il matrimonio è saltato

3 (*not fresh*) andato(-a) a male; **this cheese is off** questo formaggio è andato a male; **that's a bit off, isn't it?** (*fig: fam*) non è molto carino, vero?

4 to be badly off non essere benestante; **you'd be better off staying where you are** faresti meglio a rimanere dove sei; **how are you off for cash?** come stai a soldi?; **to be well off** essere benestante; **the less well off** i meno abbienti

5 to have an off day (*fam*) avere una giornata no

♦ PREP

1 (*indicating motion, removal*) da; **there are two buttons off my coat** al mio cappotto mancano due bottoni; **to fall off a cliff** cadere da una scogliera; **he knocked £20 off the price** (*fam*) mi ha fatto uno sconto di 20 sterline; **she took the picture off the wall** tolse il quadro dalla parete; **he was off work for three weeks** è stato in malattia per tre settimane

2 (*distant from*): **his apartment is somewhere off Baker Street** il suo appartamento è dalle parti di Baker Street; **off the coast** al largo della costa; **height off the ground** altezza dal suolo; **it's just off the M1** è appena fuori della M1; **a house off the main road** una casa poco lontana della strada principale; **a street off the square** una strada che parte dalla piazza

3 I've gone off fried food non mi piacciono più i fritti; **I'm off meat** non mangio più la carne

♦ N: **from the off** (*fam*) dall'inizio

of·fal [ˈɒfəl] N frattaglie *fpl*

off·beat [ˈɒfbiːt] ADJ (*fig*) originale, anticonvenzionale

off-centre, off-center (*USA*) [ˈɒfˈsɛntəʳ] ADJ storto(-a), fuori centro

off-colour, off-color (*USA*) [ˈɒfˈkʌləʳ] ADJ **1** (*Brit: ill*) malato(-a), indisposto(-a); **to feel off-colour** sentirsi poco bene **2** (*joke, remark*) spinto(-a), osé *inv*

of·fence, of·fense (*USA*) [əˈfɛns] N **1** (*crime*) infrazione *f*, contravvenzione *f*, reato; **first offence** primo reato; **to commit an offence** commettere un reato; **it is an offence to …** è vietato dalla legge... **2** (*moral*) offesa; **to give offence (to sb)** offendere (qn); **to take offence (at sth)** offendersi (per qc)

of·fend [əˈfɛnd] VT (*person*) offendere; (*ears, eyes*) ferire; **I don't want to offend you** non voglio offenderti; **it offends my sense of justice** è un'offesa al mio senso di giustizia; **to be offended (at)** offendersi (per) ♦ VI: **to offend against** (*law, rule*) trasgredire, contravvenire a; (*God*) disubbidire a; (*common sense*) andare contro; (*good taste*) offendere

of·fend·er [əˈfɛndəʳ] N (*frm: criminal*) delinquente *m/f*; (*culprit*) reo(-a), colpevole *m/f*

of·fend·ing [əˈfɛndɪŋ] ADJ (*often hum: word, object*) incriminato(-a)

of·fense [əˈfɛns] N (*USA*) = **offence**

of·fen·sive [əˈfɛnsɪv] ADJ **1** (*causing offence, unpleasant: behaviour, remark*) offensivo(-a); (: *person*) antipatico(-a); (: *smell, sight*) sgradevole; **to be offensive to sb** offendere qn **2** (*attacking*) offensivo(-a) ♦ N (*Mil, Sport*) offensiva; **to go over to** *or* **go on** *or* **take the offensive** passare all'offensiva

of·fer [ˈɒfəʳ] N (*gen*) offerta, proposta; **offer of marriage** proposta di matrimonio; **to make an offer for sth** un'offerta per qc; **offers over £25** offerte dalle 25 sterline in su; **to be on offer** (*Comm*) essere in offerta (speciale); **"on special offer"** "in offerta speciale" ♦ VT (*gen*) offrire; (*apology*) presentare; (*comment, opinion*) dare; **to offer sth to sb** *or* **sb sth** offrire qc a qn; **can I offer you a drink?** posso offrirti qc da bere?; **to offer to do sth** offrirsi di fare qc; **he offered to help me** si è offerto di aiutarmi; **to offer resistance** opporre resistenza

of·fer·ing [ˈɒfərɪŋ] N offerta

off-grid [ˈɒfˈgrɪd] ADJ *autonomo non allacciato alla rete elettrica* (o dell'acqua, del gas, ecc.)

off·hand [ˈɒfˈhænd] ADJ (*casual*) disinvolto(-a); (*curt*) sgarbato(-a); **an offhand attitude** un atteggiamento noncurante ♦ ADV: **I can't tell you offhand** non posso dirtelo su due piedi

of·fice [ˈɒfɪs] N **1** (*place*) ufficio; (*of lawyer, doctor*) studio; **ticket office** biglietteria; **head office** sede *f* centrale **2** (*public position*) ufficio, carica; (*duty, function*) incarico, compito; **to be in** *or* **to hold office** (*person*) essere in carica; (*political party*) essere al potere; **to come into office, to take office** (*person*) assumere la carica; (*political party*) salire al potere **3 through his good offices** con il suo prezioso aiuto; **through the offices of** grazie all'aiuto di **4** (*Rel*) ufficio, funzione *f* ♦ ADJ (*staff*) d'ufficio; (*furniture*) da ufficio; (*supplies*) per ufficio

office automation N automazione *f* d'ufficio, burotica

office bearer N (*of club etc*) membro dell'amministrazione

office block, (*USA*) **office building** N complesso di uffici

office boy N fattorino

office hours NPL orario d'ufficio; (*USA: Med*) orario delle visite

office manager N capoufficio *m/f*

of·fic·er [ˈɒfɪsəʳ] N **1** (*Mil, Naut, Aer*) ufficiale *m*; **officers' mess** mensa degli ufficiali **2** (*official*) funzionario; **police officer** agente *m* di polizia; **excuse me, officer** mi scusi, agente

office work N lavoro d'ufficio

office worker N impiegato(-a)

of·fi·cial [əˈfɪʃəl] ADJ (*authorized*) ufficiale; (*formal*) ufficiale, formale; **to make official** (*position, agreement*) ufficializzare ♦ N (*civil servant*) funzionario, impiegato(-a) statale; (*of club, organization*) dirigente *m/f*

of·fi·cial·dom [əˈfɪʃəldəm] N (*pej*) burocrazia

of·fi·cial·ly [əˈfɪʃəlɪ] ADV ufficialmente

Official Receiver N: **the Official Receiver** il curatore fallimentare

of·fi·ci·ate [əˈfɪʃɪˌeɪt] VI (*Rel*) ufficiare; **to officiate as Mayor** esplicare le funzioni di sindaco; **to officiate at a marriage** celebrare un matrimonio

of·fi·cious [əˈfɪʃəs] ADJ invadente

❏ **officious** is not translated by the Italian word *ufficioso*

of·fing [ˈɒfɪŋ] N: **in the offing** (*fig*) in vista

off-key [ˌɒfˈkiː] ADJ stonato(-a) ♦ ADV fuori tono

off-licence [ˈɒfˌlaɪsns] N (*Brit*) bottiglieria

off-limits [ˌɒfˈlɪmɪts] ADJ (*USA Mil*) vietato(-a) (al personale militare), off-limits *inv*; (*not to be entered*) off-limits

off-line [ɒfˈlaɪn] (*Comput*) ADJ off-line *inv*, fuori linea; (*switched off*) spento(-a) ♦ ADV: **to go off-line** andare off-line *or* fuori linea

off-load [ˈɒfˌləʊd] VT scaricare

off-peak [ˈɒfˈpiːk] ADJ (*time*) non di punta; (*ticket, heating*) a tariffa ridotta; (*tariff*) ridotto(-a); **it's cheaper to go on vacation off-peak** costa meno andare in vacanza in bassa stagione; **train tickets are cheaper off-peak** i biglietti ferroviari sono più economici al di fuori dell'ora di punta

off-putting [ˈɒfˌpʊtɪŋ] ADJ (*Brit fam: person, manner*) antipatico(-a), scostante; (*appearance*) sgradevole; **I hope you won't find my presence off-putting** spero che la mia presenza non ti crei problemi

off-season [ˈɒfˌsiːzn] N: **the off-season** la bassa stagione ♦ ADJ di bassa stagione *f*

off·set [ˈɒfˌsɛt] (*pt, pp* offset) VT bilanciare, compensare ♦ N (*Typ*) offset *m inv*

off·shoot [ˈɒfˌʃuːt] N (*fig*) diramazione *f*; (*Bot*) germoglio

off·shore [ˈɒfˈʃɔːʳ] ADJ (*breeze*) di terra; (*island*) vicino(-a) alla costa; (*fishing*) costiero(-a); (*oil rig*) off-shore *inv*

off·side [ˈɒfˈsaɪd] ADJ **1** (*Sport*) in fuorigioco **2** (*Aut: right-hand drive*) destro(-a); (: *left-hand drive*) sinistro(-a) ♦ N (*Aut: see adj*) destra; sinistra

off·spring [ˈɒfˌsprɪŋ] N (*pl inv: of person*) rampollo; (: *with pl sense*) prole *f*; (*of animal*) piccolo(-a); (: *with pl sense*) piccoli(-e)

off·stage [ˈɒfˈsteɪdʒ] ADJ, ADV dietro le quinte

off-the-cuff [ˌɒfðəˈkʌf] ADV a braccio, improvvisando ♦ ADJ (*speech*) a braccio, improvvisato(-a); (*remark*) spontaneo(-a)

off-the-job [ˌɒfðəˈdʒɒb] ADJ (*course, training*) fuori sede *inv*

off-the-peg [ˈɒfðəˈpɛg], (*USA*) **off-the-rack** [ˈɒfðəˈræk] ADJ (*clothes*) prêt-à-porter *inv*, confezionato(-a) ♦ ADV: **to buy a dress off-the-peg** comprare un abito confezionato

off-the-record [ˌɒfðəˈrɛkəd] ADJ ufficioso(-a) ♦ ADV in via ufficiosa

off-white [ˈɒfˌwaɪt] ADJ bianco sporco *inv*

of·ten [ˈɒfn] ADV spesso; **it often rains** spesso piove; **as often as not** il più delle volte; **more often than not** quasi sempre; **every so often** (*of time*) una volta ogni tanto; (*of distance, spacing*) regolarmente, a intervalli regolari; **how often?** ogni quanto?; **how often do you see him?** ogni quanto lo vedi?; **her behaviour is often disappointing** il suo comportamento è spesso deludente; **it's not often that I ask you to help me** non è che ti chieda spesso di aiutarmi

ogle [ˈəʊgl] VT mangiarsi con gli occhi

ogre [ˈəʊgəʳ] N orco

OH ABBR (*USA Post*: = Ohio)

oh [əʊ] EXCL oh!

O·hi·o [əʊˈhaɪəʊ] N l'Ohio

OHMS [ˌəʊeɪtʃemˈes] ABBR (*Brit*: = On His (or Her) Majesty's Service*) al servizio di Sua Maestà britannica

oil [ɔɪl] N **1** (*Art, Aut, Culin*) olio; **fried in oil** fritto(-a) nell'olio **2** (*petroleum*) petrolio; (*for central heating*) nafta; **to pour oil on troubled waters** placare le acque ♦ VT (*machine*) oliare, lubrificare; **to oil the wheels** (*fig*) appianare la difficoltà ♦ ADJ (*lamp, stove*) a olio

oil·can [ˈɔɪlˌkæn] N oliatore *m*; (*for storing*) latta da olio

oil change N (*Aut*) cambio dell'olio

oil·field [ˈɔɪlˌfiːld] N giacimento petrolifero

oil filter N (*Aut*) filtro dell'olio

oil-fired [ˈɔɪlˌfaɪəd] ADJ a nafta

oil gauge N indicatore *m* del livello dell'olio

oil industry N industria petrolifera

oil level N livello dell'olio

oil painting N quadro a olio

oil refinery N raffineria di petrolio

oil rig N derrick *m inv*; (*at sea*) piattaforma per trivellazioni subacquee

oil-skins [ˈɔɪlˌskɪnz] NPL indumenti *mpl* di tela cerata

oil slick N chiazza di petrolio

oil tanker N petroliera

oil well N pozzo petrolifero

oily [ˈɔɪlɪ] ADJ (*comp* -ier, *superl* -iest) (*liquid, consistency*) oleoso(-a); (*hands*) unto(-a); (*fig: pej*) untuoso(-a)

oint·ment [ˈɔɪntmənt] N unguento

OK¹ ABBR (*USA Post*: = Oklahoma)

OK²,okay [əʊˈkeɪ] (*fam*) EXCL OK!, okay!, va bene! ♦ ADJ: **the film was OK** il film non era male; **are you OK for money?** sei a posto coi soldi?; **it's OK with** *or* **by me** per me va bene; **is it OK with you if ...?** ti va bene se...?; **is it OK?, are you OK?** tutto OK?; **did you hurt yourself? — no, I'm OK** ti sei fatto male? — no, sto bene; **is the car OK?** è a posto la macchina?; **that may have been OK last year** questo poteva forse andar bene l'anno scorso ♦ N: **to give sth one's OK** dare l'okay a qc ♦ VT (*pt, pp* OK'd *or* okayed) dare l'okay a, approvare

Okla. ABBR (*USA*: = Oklahoma)

O·kla·ho·ma [ˌəʊkləˈhəʊmə] N l'Oklahoma

old [əʊld] ADJ (*comp* -er, *superl* -est) **1** (*gen*) vecchio(-a), anziano(-a); (*ancient*) antico(-a), vecchio(-a); **an old man** un vecchio; **old people** *or* **folk(s)** i vecchi, gli anziani; **my grandfather is very old** mio nonno è molto vecchio; **to grow** *or* **get old** invecchiare; **he's old for his years** è maturo per la sua età; **the old country** la madrepatria; **as old as the hills** vecchio(-a) come Matusalemme *or* come il cucco; **the old part of Glasgow** la zona vecchia di Glasgow; **an old friend of mine** un mio vecchio amico; **here's old Peter coming!** (*fam*) ecco che arriva il vecchio Peter!; **any old thing will do** (*fam*) va bene qualsiasi cosa; **I say, old man** *or* **old boy!** (*old*) vecchio mio!; **my old man** (*fam: father*) il (mio) vecchio **2 how old are you?** quanti anni hai?; **she is 8 years old** ha 8 anni; **an 8-year-old boy** un bambino di 8 anni; **she is 2 years older than you** ha 2 anni più di te; **he's older than me** è più vecchio di me; **older brother/sister** fratello/sorella maggiore; **my older brother** mio fratello maggiore; **the older generation** i vecchi; **he's old enough to look after himself** è grande abbastanza per sbrigarsela da solo; **to be old enough to vote** avere l'età per votare; **you're old enough to know better!** alla tua età dovresti avere più senno!; **when you're older** (*to child*) quando sarai grande; **if I were 20 years older** se avessi 20 anni di più **3** (*former*) precedente; **my old school** la mia vecchia scuola; **in the old days** una volta, ai vecchi tempi; **it's not as good as our old one** non è buono come quello vecchio ♦ N **1 the old** *npl* i vecchi, gli anziani **2 of old** da tempo; **in days of old** nei tempi passati

old age N vecchiaia; **in one's old age** nella vecchiaia

old-age pension [ˌəʊldeɪdʒˈpenʃən] N pensione *f* di vecchiaia

old-age pensioner [ˌəʊldeɪdʒˈpenʃənəʳ] N (*Brit*) pensionato(-a)

old-fashioned [ˈəʊldˈfæʃnd] ADJ antiquato(-a), fuori moda; (*person*) all'antica; **my parents are rather old-fashioned** i miei sono un po' all'antica

old maid N (*pej*) vecchia zitella

old people's home N casa di riposo (per anziani)

old-style [ˈəʊldˈstaɪl] ADJ (di) vecchio stampo *inv*

old-time [ˈəʊldˌtaɪm] ADJ di una volta

old-timer [ˌəʊldˈtaɪməʳ] N veterano(-a)

old wives' tale N vecchia superstizione *f*

O-level [ˈəʊˌlɛvl] N (*Brit: formerly*) diploma di istruzione secondaria conseguito a 16 anni in Inghilterra e Galles, ora sostituito dal GCSE

ol·ive [ˈɒlɪv] N (*fruit*) oliva; (*also:* **olive tree**) olivo ♦ ADJ (*skin*) olivastro(-a); (*also:* **olive-green**) verde oliva *inv*

olive oil N olio d'oliva

Olym·pic [əʊˈlɪmpɪk] ADJ olimpico(-a)

OM [ˌəʊˈem] N ABBR (*Brit: = Order of Merit*) titolo onorifico

Oman [əʊˈmɑːn] N l'Oman *m*

OMB N ABBR (*USA: = Office of Management and Budget*) servizio di consulenza al Presidente in materia di bilancio

ome·lette, ome·let [ˈɒmlɪt] N frittata, omelette *f inv*; **ham/cheese omelette** omelette al prosciutto/al formaggio

omen [ˈəʊmən] N presagio, auspicio; **a bad omen** un cattivo presagio; **a good omen** un buon auspicio

OMG ABBR (*fam*) *nel linguaggio degli SMS, esprime sorpresa o entusiasmo*

omi·nous [ˈɒmɪnəs] ADJ (*sign*) minaccioso(-a), infausto(-a); (*event*) di malaugurio; (*look, smile, silence*) sinistro(-a); **ominous black clouds** nuvole nere minacciose; **the reappearance of tuberculosis is an ominous development** la ricomparsa della tubercolosi è un fatto preoccupante

omis·sion [əʊˈmɪʃən] N omissione *f*

omit [əʊˈmɪt] VT omettere; **to omit to do sth** tralasciare *or* trascurare di fare qc; **his name was omitted from the list** il suo nome fu omesso dalla lista

om·niv·or·ous [ɒmˈnɪvərəs] ADJ onnivoro(-a)

ON ABBR (*Canada Post: = Ontario*)

KEYWORD

on [ɒn] PREP

1 (*position*) su; (*on top of*) sopra; **on the Continent** nell'Europa continentale; **with her hat on her head** col cappello in testa; **on the left** sulla *or* a sinistra; **I haven't any money on me** non ho soldi con me; **on page 2** a pagina 2; **on the right** sulla *or* a destra; **the house is on the main road** la casa è sulla strada principale; **on the table** sul tavolo; **hanging on the wall** appeso(-a) al muro

2 (*fig*): **an attack on the government** un attacco al governo; **we did it on his authority** l'abbiamo fatto dietro sua autorizzazione; **based on fact** basato(-a) sui fatti; **he's away on business** è via per affari; **on Channel 4** su Canale 4; **he is on the committee** fa parte della commissione; **on foot** a piedi; **he's on heroin** si fa di eroina; **to be on holiday** (*Brit*) essere in vacanza; **she lives on cheese** vive di formaggio; **the march on Rome** la marcia su Roma; **have it on me** offro io; **this round's on me** questo giro lo offro io; **on the plane** sull'*or* in aereo; **he played it on the violin/piano** l'ha suonato al violino/al pianoforte; **on the radio** alla radio; **on the telephone** al telefono; **on the television** alla televisione; **on the train** sul *or* in treno; **prices are up on last year('s)** i

prezzi sono rincarati rispetto all'anno scorso; **to be on vacation** (*USA*) essere in vacanza; **we're on irregular verbs** stiamo facendo i verbi irregolari; **he's on £16,000 a year** guadagna 16.000 sterline all'anno

3 (*of time*): **on May 14th** il 14 maggio; **on my arrival** al mio arrivo; **on a day like this** in una giornata come questa; **on Friday** venerdì; **a week on Friday** venerdì a otto; **on Fridays** il *or* di venerdì; **on seeing him** nel vederlo, vedendolo

4 (*about, concerning*) su, di; **a book on physics** un libro di *or* sulla fisica; **he lectured on Keats** tenne un corso su Keats; **have you read Purnell on Churchill?** hai letto cosa scrive Purnell su Churchill?; **while we're on the subject** visto che siamo in argomento

♦ ADV

1 (*covering*): **to have one's coat on** avere indosso il cappotto; **she put her boots on** si mise gli stivali; **screw the lid on tightly** avvita il coperchio ben stretto; **with your coat! on** mettiti il cappotto!

2 (*forward*): **from that day on** da quel giorno in poi; **it's getting on for ten o'clock** sono quasi le dieci; **it was well on in the evening** era sera inoltrata; **it was well on in May** era maggio avanzato; **they talked well on into the night** continuarono a parlare fino a notte inoltrata

3 (*continuation*): **to go on, walk on, carry on** continuare, proseguire; **on and off** ogni tanto; **he rambled on and on** continuava nei suoi discorsi sconclusionati; **to read on** continuare a leggere, proseguire nella lettura; **and so on** e così via

4 (*in phrases*): **what are you on about?** cosa vai dicendo?; **my father's always on at me to get a job** (*fam*) mio padre mi sta sempre addosso perché trovi un lavoro; **the police are on to him** la polizia lo tiene d'occhio

♦ ADJ

1 (*functioning, in operation: radio, light, oven*) acceso(-a); (*: tap*) aperto(-a); (*: machine*) in moto; (*: brake*) inserito(-a); **when is this film on?** quand'è che danno questo film?; **there's a good film on at the cinema** danno un buon film al cinema; **the meeting is still on** la riunione è ancora in corso; **is the meeting still on tonight?** è confermata la riunione di stasera?; **the programme is on in a minute** il programma inizia tra un minuto; **sorry, I've got something on tonight** mi spiace, stasera sono impegnato

2 (*fam*): **you're on!** d'accordo!; **that's not on!** (*not acceptable*) non si fa così!; (*not possible*) non se ne parla neanche!

once [wʌns] ADV **1** (*on one occasion*) una volta; **I've been to Italy once before** sono già stato in Italia una volta; **I've only met him once before** prima d'ora l'ho incontrato una volta sola; **once only** solo una volta; **once or twice** un paio di volte; **once again** *or* **once more** ancora una volta; (*every*) **once in a while** (una volta) ogni tanto; **once a week** una volta alla settimana; **once and for all** una volta per tutte; **just this once** solo (per) questa volta; **for once** una volta tanto; **it never once occurred to me** non mi è mai venuto in mente; **once** (*formerly*) un tempo; **I knew him once** un tempo *or* in passato lo conoscevo; **once upon a time there was ...** c'era una volta... ♦ CONJ una volta che, quando, non appena; **once he had finished he left** una volta che *or* non appena ebbe finito andò via

on·coming [ˈɒnˌkʌmɪŋ] ADJ (*traffic*) in senso contrario

KEYWORD

one [wʌn] ADJ

1 uno(-a); **one day** un giorno; **one cold winter's day** una fredda giornata d'inverno; **one hundred and fifty** centocinquanta; **the baby is one (year old)** il bambino ha un anno; **it's one (o'clock)** è l'una; **one or two people** una o due persone, un paio di persone; **for one reason or another** per un motivo o per l'altro; **twenty-one years ago** ventun'anni fa; **that's one way of doing it** questo è uno dei modi per farlo

2 (*sole*) unico(-a), solo(-a); **his one worry** la sua unica *or* sola preoccupazione; **no one man could do it** nessuno potrebbe farlo da solo; **one and only** unico(-a); **the one and only Charlie Chaplin** l'inimitabile Charlie Chaplin; **the**

one man who il solo *or* l'unico che; **the one book which ...** l'unico libro che...

3 (*same*) stesso(-a); **they are one and the same person** sono la stessa persona; **it is one and the same thing** è la stessa cosa; **in the one car** nella stessa macchina

♦ N uno(-a); **one after the other** uno(-a) dopo l'altro(-a); **one and all** tutti; **to be at one (with sb)** andare d'accordo (con qn); **I belted him one** (*fam*) gli ho mollato un cazzotto; **to go one better than sb** fare meglio di qn; **one by one** a uno(-a) a uno(-a); **I for one am not going** per quanto mi riguarda non ci vado; **to have one for the road** bere il bicchiere della staffa; **one hundred and one** cento uno; **in ones and twos** a piccoli gruppi; **twenty-one** ventuno; **to be one up on sb** essere avvantaggiato(-a) rispetto a qn

♦ PRON

1 this one questo(-a); **any one of us** chiunque *or* uno qualsiasi di noi; **our dear ones** i nostri cari; **that's a difficult one** quello è un osso duro; **you're a fine one!** (*fam*) sei un bel tipo!; **he's a great one for chess** va matto per gli scacchi; **I'll have the grey one** prenderò quello grigio; **have you got one?** ne hai uno?; **what about this little one?** cosa ne dici di questo piccolino?; **the little ones** i bambini, i piccoli; **he is not one to protest** non è il tipo che protesta; **one or two of the books were damaged** c'erano un paio di libri rovinati; **one of them** uno(-a) di loro; **I lost one of them** ne ho perso uno; **one or two** uno(-a) o due; **that one** quello(-a); **the one on the floor** quello(-a) sul pavimento; **the one who** (*or* that *or* which) quello(-a) che; **the ones who** (*or* that *or* which) quelli(-e) che; **which one do you want?** quale vuoi?

2 one another l'un l'altro(-a); **they all kissed one another** si baciarono tutti a vicenda; **do you see one another much?** vi vedete spesso?

3 (*impersonal*): **to cut one's finger** tagliarsi un dito; **one never knows** non si sa mai; **one must eat** bisogna mangiare; **to express one's opinion** esprimere la propria opinione

one-armed bandit N slot-machine *f inv*

one-day excursion [ˌwʌndeɪksˈkɜːʃən] N (*USA*) biglietto giornaliero di andata e ritorno

one-man [ˈwʌnˈmæn] ADJ (*business*) gestito(-a) da una sola persona; (*art exhibition*) personale; (*boat*) a un posto; **one-man show** recital *m inv*

one-man band [ˈwʌnˌmænˈbænd] N (*Mus: person*) suonatore ambulante con vari strumenti; **it's a one-man band** (*fig: fam*) c'è solo una persona a mandare avanti la baracca

one-off [ˌwʌnˈɒf] N (*Brit fam*) fatto eccezionale ♦ ADJ eccezionale, più unico(-a) che raro(-a)

one-parent family [ˈwʌnˌpɛərəntˈfæmɪlɪ] N famiglia *f* monogenitore, *inv*

one-piece [ˈwʌnˌpiːs] ADJ (*bathing suit*) intero(-a), monopezzo *inv*

on·er·ous [ˈɒnərəs] (*frm*) ADJ (*task, duty*) oneroso(-a); (*responsibility*) pesante

one·self [wʌnˈsɛlf] PERS PRON (*reflexive*) si; (*after prep*) se stesso(-a), sé; (*emphatic*) se stesso; **to hurt oneself** farsi male; **to be by oneself** stare da solo(-a), stare per conto proprio; **to do sth by oneself** fare qc da solo(-a) *or* da sé; **to keep sth for oneself** tenere qc per sé; **to see for oneself** vedere con i propri occhi; **to say to oneself** dirsi; **to talk to oneself** parlare da solo *or* tra sé e sé; **one asks oneself how it could happen** ci si chiede come sia potuto succedere; **it's quicker to do it oneself** si fa più in fretta a farlo da solo

one-shot [ˌwʌnˈʃɒt] N (*USA*) = **one-off**

one-sided [ˌwʌnˈsaɪdɪd] ADJ (*decision, view*) unilaterale; (*judgment, account*) parziale; (*game, contest*) impari *inv*; **his account was one-sided** il suo resoconto non è stato obiettivo; **the match was one-sided** l'incontro era impari

one-time [ˈwʌnˌtaɪm] ADJ ex *inv*

one-to-one [ˌwʌntəˈwʌn] ADJ (*correlation*) univoco(-a); (*relationship*) tra due persone; (*interview, talk*) a quattr'occhi, faccia a faccia; (*training, therapy*) individuale; **teaching is on a one-to-one basis** l'insegnamento è organizzato in lezioni individuali ♦ ADV (*talk, discuss*) faccia a faccia, a quattr'occhi

one-upmanship [ˌwʌnˈʌpmənʃɪp] N: **the art of one-upmanship** l'arte *f* di primeggiare

one-way [ˈwʌnˌweɪ] ADJ (*traffic, street*) a senso unico; (*ticket*) di sola andata

on·going [ˈɒnˌɡəʊɪŋ] ADJ (*in progress*) in corso; (*continuing*) che si sviluppa; **the ongoing debate** il dibattito in corso; **the club's ongoing financial problems** gli attuali problemi finanziari del club

on·ion [ˈʌnjən] N cipolla

on·line [ˈɒnˌlaɪn] ADJ (*Comput*) on line *inv*, in linea; (*switched on*) acceso(-a); **online banking** servizi *mpl* bancari on-line; **online shopping** shopping *m* on-line ♦ ADV on-line

on·looker [ˈɒnˌlʊkəʳ] N astante *m/f*, spettatore(-trice)

only [ˈəʊnlɪ] ADJ solo(-a), unico(-a); **it's the only one left** è l'unico rimasto; **your only hope is to hide** la tua unica speranza sta nel nascondervi; **you are the only one who can help us** sei l'unico che possa *or* che può aiutarci; **you are not the only one** non sei l'unico; **an only child** figlio(-a) unico(-a); **the only thing I don't like about it is ...** l'unica cosa che non mi va è... ♦ ADV solo, soltanto, solamente; **we have only five** ne abbiamo solo cinque; **how much was it? — only ten pounds** quanto è costato? — solo dieci sterline; **only one choice** una sola possibilità, un'unica scelta; **only time will tell** chi vivrà vedrà; **I'm only the porter** io sono solo il portinaio; **I only touched it** l'ho soltanto toccato; **I only took one** ne ho preso soltanto uno; **we only want to stay for one night** vorremmo stare solo una notte; **only when I ...** solo quando io...; **not only A but also B** non solo A ma anche B; **I saw her only yesterday** l'ho vista appena ieri; **we can only hope** non possiamo far altro che sperare; **I'd be only too pleased to help** sarei proprio felice di essere d'aiuto; **it's only too true** è proprio vero; **only just** appena; **I only just passed the exam** ho appena passato l'esame ♦ CONJ solo che, ma (purtroppo); **I would come, only I'm very busy** verrei volentieri, solo che sono molto occupato

on·screen [ɒnˈskriːn] ADJ sullo schermo *pl inv*

on·set [ˈɒnˌsɛt] N (*of winter*) arrivo; (*of illness, old age*) inizio, principio; **the onset of winter** l'arrivo dell'inverno; **the onset of war** l'inizio della guerra

on·shore [ˈɒnˈʃɔːʳ] ADJ (*wind*) di mare; (*job*) a terra

on·slaught [ˈɒnˌslɔːt] N (*Mil, also fig*) attacco

Ont. ABBR (*Canada: = Ontario*)

on-the-job [ˈɒnðəˈdʒɒb] ADJ (*course, training*) in sede

onto [ˈɒntəʊ] PREP su, sopra; **he climbed onto the table** è salito sopra il tavolo; **to be onto sb** (*fam: suspect*) scoprire qn; **I'm onto something** (*fam*) sono su una buona pista; **to be onto a good thing** (*fam*) trovare l'America; **I'll get onto him about it** gliene parlerò io

onus [ˈəʊnəs] N *no pl* onere *m*; **the onus is on him to prove it** sta a lui dimostrarlo; **to shift the onus for sth onto sb** scaricare la responsabilità di qc su qn; **the onus of proof is on the prosecution** l'onere della prova spetta all'accusa

on·ward [ˈɒnwəd] ADJ in avanti ♦ ADV (*also:* **onwards**) in avanti; **she stumbled onward** è caduta in avanti; **from this time onward** d'ora in poi; **from the 12th century onward(s)** dal XII secolo in poi

onyx [ˈɒnɪks] N onice *f*

oops [ʊps] EXCL ops! (*esprime rincrescimento per un piccolo contrattempo*)

ooze [uːz] N melma ♦ VI (*water*) filtrare; (*gum, resin*) trasudare; (*pus*) fuoriuscire ♦ VT: **the wound oozed blood** la ferita stillava sangue; **he simply oozes confidence** (*pej*) sprizza sicurezza da tutti i pori

opa·city [əʊˈpæsɪtɪ] N opacità

opal [ˈəʊpəl] N opale *m, f*

opaque [əʊˈpeɪk] ADJ opaco(-a)

OPEC [ˈəʊpɛk] N ABBR (= *Organization of Petroleum-Exporting Countries*) OPEC *f*

open [ˈəʊpən] ADJ **1** (*gen*) aperto(-a); (*flower*) aperto(-a), sbocciato(-a); **wide open** (*door, window*) spalancato(-a); **half open, slightly open** socchiuso(-a); **open at the neck** col colletto sbottonato; **to welcome with open arms** accogliere a braccia aperte; **to cut a sack open** aprire un sacco con un taglio; **to keep open house** (*fig*) aprire la propria casa a tutti; **open to the public on Mondays** aperto(-a) al pubblico di lunedì; **the shop's open on Sunday morning** il negozio è aperto la domenica mattina **2** (*fig: letter*) aperto(-a); (: *water, channel*) navigabile; (: *cheque*) in bianco; **in the open air** all'aria aperta, all'aperto; **on the open road** su autostrada; **road open to traffic** strada aperta al traffico *or* transitabile; **open to the elements/to attack** esposto(-a) alle intemperie/all'attacco; **open country** aperta campagna; **open ground** (*among trees*) radura; (*waste ground*) terreno non edificato; **the open sea** il mare aperto; **to lay o.s. open to criticism** esporsi alle critiche; **open to persuasion** disposto(-a) a lasciarsi convincere; **it is open to doubt whether ...** è in dubbio se... **3** (*competition, scholarship*) aperto(-a) a tutti; (*meeting*) pubblico(-a); (*trial*) a porte aperte; **what choices are open to me?** che scelta ho?; **the post is still open** il posto è sempre vacante; **in open court** (*Law*) a porte aperte **4** (*person, face*) aperto(-a); (*hatred, admiration*) evidente, palese; (*enemy*) dichiarato(-a); **it's an open secret that ...** è il segreto di Pulcinella che...; **in open revolt** in aperta rivolta; **to be open with sb** essere franco(-a) con qn **5** (*undecided: question*) aperto(-a); **the race was still wide open** la gara era ancora tutta da giocare; **open verdict** dichiarazione di morte per cause non accertate; **open ticket** biglietto aperto; **to have an open mind** (**on sth**) non avere ancora deciso (su qc); **to leave the matter open** lasciare la faccenda in sospeso ♦ N **1 out in the open** (*out of doors*) fuori, all'aperto; (*in the country*) in campagna, all'aperto; **their true feelings came into the open** vennero a galla i loro veri sentimenti **2** (*Golf, Tennis*): **the Australian Open** l'open *m inv* di Australia ♦ VT (*gen*) aprire; (*legs*) divaricare; **to open sth wide** spalancare qc; **to open a road to traffic** aprire al traffico una strada; **to open a road through a forest** aprire una strada nella foresta; **to open Parliament** aprire i lavori parlamentari; **to open a bank account** aprire un conto in banca; **to open fire** (*Mil*) aprire il fuoco; **I didn't open my mouth** non ho aperto bocca; **to open one's heart to sb** confidarsi con qn; **to open one's mind to sth** aprirsi on qc ♦ VI **1** (*eyes, door, debate*) aprirsi; (*shop, bank, museum*) aprire; **what time do the shops open?** a che ora aprono i negozi?; **the shops open at 9** i negozi aprono alle 9; **the door opens automatically** la porta si apre automaticamente; **to open onto** *or* **into** dare su **2** (*begin: book, film*) cominciare; (*Cards, Chess*) aprire; **the play opens next Monday** la prima della commedia è lunedì prossimo; **the book opens with a long description** il libro comincia con una lunga descrizione

▸ **open out** VT + ADV (*unfold*) aprire, spiegare ♦ VI + ADV aprirsi, dischiudersi

▸ **open up** VT + ADV aprire; (*blocked road*) sgombrare; **to open up a country for trade** aprire il mercato di un paese ♦ VI + ADV **1** (*flower, shop*) aprirsi **2** (*start shooting*) aprire il fuoco

open-air [ˌəʊpnˈɛəʳ] ADJ all'aperto

open-and-shut [ˌəʊpnənˈʃʌt] ADJ: **open-and-shut case** caso di facile soluzione

open day N (*Brit: in school, institution*) giornata di apertura al pubblico

open-ended [ˌəʊpnˈɛndɪd] ADJ (*question*) aperto(-a); (*discussion*) senza conclusioni

open·er [ˈəʊpnəʳ] N: **bottle-opener** apribottiglie *m inv*; (*also:* **can opener** *or* **tin opener**) apriscatole *m inv*

open-heart [ˌəʊpnˌhɑːt] ADJ: **open-heart surgery** intervento *m* (chirurgico) a cuore aperto, *inv*

open·ing [ˈəʊpnɪŋ] ADJ (*gen*) d'apertura; (*ceremony, speech*) d'apertura, inaugurale **1** N (*gap*) apertura; (*in wall*) breccia; **a narrow opening** una stretta apertura **2** (*beginning*) inizio; (*also:* **official opening:** *of factory, hospital*) inaugurazione *f*; (*first performance: of film, play*) prima (rappresentazione *f*); **the opening of the book** l'inizio del libro **3** (*opportunity*) occasione *f*, possibilità *f inv*; (*post*) posto vacante; **to give one's opponent an opening** offrire il fianco all'avversario

opening hours NPL orario *msg* d'apertura

opening night N (*Theatre*) prima

open learning N sistema educativo nel quale lo studente ha maggior controllo e gestione delle modalità di apprendimento

open·ly [ˈəʊpnlɪ] ADV apertamente

open-minded [ˌəʊpnˈmaɪndɪd] ADJ aperto(-a), dalla mentalità aperta

open-necked [ˈəʊpnˌnɛkt] ADJ (*shirt, blouse*) col colletto slacciato *or* sbottonato

open·ness [ˈəʊpnnɪs] N (*frankness*) franchezza, sincerità

open-plan [ˌəʊpnˌplæn] ADJ senza pareti divisorie

open prison N (*Brit*) istituto di pena per detenuti in semilibertà

open sandwich N tartina

open shop N (*Industry*) impresa che assume anche operai non iscritti ai sindacati

op·era [ˈɒpərə] N (*work*) opera (lirica); (*genre*) opera, (*musica*) lirica

opera glasses NPL binocolo da teatro

opera house N teatro lirico *or* dell'opera, opera

opera singer N cantante *m/f* d'opera *or* lirico(-a)

op·er·ate [ˈɒpəˌreɪt] VT **1** (*machine, switchboard, brakes*) azionare, far funzionare; **a machine operated by electricity** una macchina funzionante a corrente (elettrica); **can you operate this tool?** sai usare questo strumento?; **can you operate the video?** sai far funzionare il videoregistratore? **2** (*company*) dirigere, gestire; (*service*) gestire; (*system, law*) applicare ♦ VI **1** (*function: machine, mind*) funzionare; **I don't know how the electoral system operates in Italy** non so come funziona il sistema elettorale italiano **2** (*drug, propaganda*) agire **3** (*company, firm*) operare; (*bus, airport*) essere in funzione; (*person*) agire **4** (*Med*) operare, intervenire (su); **to operate on sb** operare qn; **to be operated on** subire un'operazione *f or* un intervento (chirurgico); **she was operated on for appendicitis** fu operata di appendicite

op·er·at·ic [ˌɒpəˈrætɪk] ADJ operistico(-a), lirico(-a)

op·er·at·ing [ˈɒpəˌreɪtɪŋ] ADJ **1** (*Comm: costs*) di gestione, d'esercizio **2** (*Med*) operatorio(-a); (*nurse*) di sala operatoria

operating room N (*USA*) = **operating theatre**

operating system N (*Comput*) sistema *m* operativo

operating theatre N (*Med*) sala operatoria

op·er·a·tion [ˌɒpəˈreɪʃən] N **1** (*gen, also Mil*) operazione *f*; (*Med*) operazione *f*, intervento (chirurgico); **a minor operation** una piccola operazione; **to have an operation for appendicitis** essere operato(-a) di appendicite; **to undergo an operation** subire un'operazione *or* un intervento (chirurgico); **I've never had an operation** non sono mai stato operato; **the company's operations during the year** le operazioni dell'azienda durante l'anno **2 to be in operation** (*machine*) essere in funzione; (*plan, system*) essere in azione; (*law*) essere in vigore; **to come into operation** entrare in funzione (*or* in azione *etc*), diventare operativo(-a); **to bring** *or* **put into operation** mettere in funzione (*or* in azione); (*law*) far entrare in vigore

op·er·a·tion·al [ˌɒpəˈreɪʃənl] ADJ (*relating to operations*) operativo(-a); (*Comm*) di gestione, d'esercizio; (*ready for use or action*) in attività, in funzione; **operational research** ricerca operativa; **when the service is fully operational** quando il servizio sarà completamente operante

op·er·a·tive [ˈɒpərətɪv] ADJ **1** (*law, measure*) in vigore, operativo(-a), operante; **the operative word** la parola chiave **2** (*Med*) operatorio(-a) ♦ N (*in factory*) operaio(-a)

op·er·a·tor [ˈɒpəˌreɪtəʳ] N (*of machine*) operatore(-trice); (*Telec*) centralinista *m/f*; **tour operator** operatore(-trice) turistico(-a); **a smooth operator** (*fam*) uno(-a) che ci sa fare

op·er·et·ta [ˌɒpəˈretə] N operetta

oph·thal·mo·gist [ˌɒfθælˈmɒlədʒɪst] N oculista *m/f*

opin·ion [əˈpɪnjən] N (*belief, view*) opinione *f*, parere *m*; **public opinion** opinione pubblica; **in my opinion** secondo me, a mio avviso; **in the opinion of those who know** secondo gli esperti; **it's a matter of opinion** è discutibile *or* opinabile; **what's your opinion?** cosa ne pensi?; **what is your opinion of him?** tu che cosa pensi di lui?; **to be of the opinion that ...** essere dell'opinione che..., ritenere che...; **to ask sb's opinion** chiedere il parere di qn, consultare qn; **to give one's opinion** dare il proprio parere; **to form an opinion of sb/sth** farsi un'opinione di qn/qc; **to have a high/poor opinion of sb** avere/non avere un'alta opinione di qn, stimare molto/poco qn; **to have a high opinion of o.s.** (*pej*) avere un'alta opinione di sé, credersi chissà chi; **to seek a second opinion** (*Med*) consultare un altro medico

opin·ion·at·ed [əˈpɪnjəˌneɪtɪd] ADJ dogmatico(-a)

opinion poll N sondaggio di opinione

opium [ˈəʊpɪəm] N oppio

op·po·nent [ə'pəʊnənt] N avversario(-a); (*in debate, discussion*) oppositore(-trice); **a fierce opponent of privatization** un accanito oppositore delle privatizzazioni

op·por·tune ['ɒpə,tjuːn] ADJ opportuno(-a); **to be opportune** capitare a proposito

op·por·tun·ist [,ɒpə'tjuːnɪst] N (*frm, pej*) opportunista *m/f*

op·por·tu·nity [,ɒpə'tjuːnɪtɪ] N opportunità *f inv*, occasione *f*; **to have the opportunity to do** *or* **of doing** avere l'opportunità di fare; **I've never had the opportunity to go to Spain** non ho mai avuto l'opportunità di andare in Spagna; **to take the opportunity to do** *or* **of doing** cogliere l'occasione per fare; **at the earliest opportunity** appena possibile, alla prima occasione; **when I** (*or* **you** *etc*) **get the opportunity** quando capita l'occasione; **to miss one's opportunity** perdere l'occasione; **opportunities for promotion** possibilità *fpl* di carriera

op·pose [ə'pəʊz] VT (*gen*) opporsi a; **she opposes my leaving** è contraria alla mia partenza

op·pos·ing [ə'pəʊzɪŋ] ADJ (*tendencies, points of view*) opposto(-a); (*team*) avversario(-a); **the opposing team** la squadra avversaria

op·po·site ['ɒpəzɪt] ADV di fronte, dirimpetto; **they live directly opposite** abitano proprio di fronte ♦ PREP di fronte a; **opposite one another** l'uno(-a) di fronte all'altro(-a); **a house opposite the school** una casa di fronte alla scuola; **to play opposite sb** (*Theatre, Cine*) essere co-protagonista *m/f* insieme a qn ♦ ADJ (*house*) di fronte; (*end, direction, side*) opposto(-a); (*point of view*) opposto(-a), contrario(-a); **on the opposite side of the road** dall'altro lato della strada; **"see opposite page"** "vedere pagina a fronte" ♦ N (*reverse*) contrario, opposto; (*of word*) contrario; **quite the opposite!** al contrario!; **she said just the opposite** lei ha detto esattamente il contrario; **the opposite is true** è vero l'opposto

opposite number N omologo(-a), controparte *f*

opposite sex N: **the opposite sex** l'altro sesso

op·po·si·tion [,ɒpə'zɪʃən] N 1 (*resistance*) opposizione *f*; (*people opposing*) avversari *mpl*; **in opposition to** in contrasto con; **the plan met considerable opposition** il progetto ha incontrato una notevole opposizione; **what are the opposition like?** com'è la squadra avversaria? 2 (*Brit Pol*): **the Opposition** l'opposizione *f*; **leader of the Opposition** leader *m/f inv* dell'opposizione; **to be in opposition** essere all'opposizione

op·press [ə'pres] VT opprimere

op·pres·sion [ə'preʃən] N oppressione *f*

op·pres·sive [ə'presɪv] ADJ (*regime, system*) oppressivo(-a); (*fig: heat, thought*) opprimente

op·pro·brium [ə'prəʊbrɪəm] N (*frm*) vituperio

opt [ɒpt] VI: **to opt for** optare per; **to opt to do** scegliere di fare, optare per fare

  ► **opt out, opt out of** *vi* + *adv* + *prep* VI + ADV 1 (*of agreement, arrangement*) scegliere di non partecipare a; **I think I'll opt out of going** penso che non ci andrò; **we went to the match, but Fred opted out** noi siamo andati alla partita ma Fred non è venuto 2 (*Brit: of NHS*) scegliere di non far più parte di

op·ti·cal ['ɒptɪkəl] ADJ ottico(-a)

optical character reader N lettore *m* ottico di caratteri

optical character recognition N lettura ottica di caratteri

optical fibre N fibra ottica

op·ti·cian [ɒp'tɪʃən] N (*also:* **ophthalmic optician**) optometrista *m/f*; (*also:* **dispensing optician**) ottico

op·tics ['ɒptɪks] NSG ottica

op·ti·mism ['ɒptɪmɪzəm] N ottimismo

op·ti·mist ['ɒptɪmɪst] N ottimista *m/f*; **I'm an optimist** sono ottimista

op·ti·mis·tic [,ɒptɪ'mɪstɪk] ADJ (*attitude*) ottimistico(-a); (*person*) ottimista; **let's be optimistic** cerchiamo di essere ottimisti

op·ti·mum ['ɒptɪməm] ADJ ottimale ♦ N (*pl* **optimums** *or* **optima** ['ɒptɪmə]) optimum *m inv*, condizioni *fpl* ottimali

op·tion ['ɒpʃən] N 1 (*choice*) scelta; **I have** *or* **I've got no option** non ho scelta; **she had no option but to leave** non poteva far altro che partire; **to keep one's options open** non precludersi alcuna possibilità; **imprisonment without**

the option of bail (*Law*) carcerazione *f* senza possibilità di libertà provvisoria 2 (*Comm*) opzione *f*; **with the option to buy** con opzione di acquisto 3 (*Scol, Univ*) materia facoltativa; **I'm doing geology as my option** come materia facoltativa studio geologia

op·tion·al ['ɒpʃənl] ADJ (*course, subject, ingredient*) facoltativo(-a); **optional extra** (*Comm*) optional *m inv*

opu·lence ['ɒpjʊləns] N opulenza

opu·lent ['ɒpjʊlənt] ADJ opulento(-a)

OR ABBR (*USA Post:* = Oregon)

or [ɔːʳ] CONJ (*gen*) o; **or rather** o meglio, o piuttosto; **or else** oppure, se no, altrimenti; **do it or else!** (*fam*) fallo, altrimenti...!; **20 or so** circa 20; **hurry up or you'll miss the bus** sbrigati, altrimenti perdi l'autobus; **let me go or I'll scream!** lasciami andare o mi metto a urlare!; **would you like tea or coffee?** vuoi del tè o del caffè?; **I don't eat meat or fish** non mangio né carne né pesce; **without relatives or friends** senza (né) parenti né amici; **he can't read or write** non sa né leggere né scrivere; **he hasn't seen or heard anything** non ha (né) visto né sentito niente

ora·cle ['ɒrəkl] N oracolo

oral ['ɔːrəl] ADJ orale ♦ N (*also:* **oral exam**) (esame *m*) orale, *m*; **I've got my Italian oral soon** tra poco avrò l'orale d'italiano

or·ange ['ɒrɪndʒ] N (*fruit*) arancia; (*tree*) arancio; (*colour*) arancione *m* ♦ ADJ (*in colour*) arancione; (*juice, jelly*) d'arancia; (*marmalade*) di arance; (*cake*) all'arancia; **an orange juice** un succo d'arancia; **an orange jumper** un maglione arancione

or·ange·ade [,ɒrɪndʒ'eɪd] N aranciata

orange squash N succo d'arancia (*da diluire con acqua*)

ora·tion [ɔː'reɪʃən] N orazione *f*; **funeral oration** orazione funebre

ora·tor ['ɒrətəʳ] N oratore(-trice)

ora·to·rio [,ɒrə'tɔːrɪəʊ] N (*Mus*) oratorio

orb [ɔːb] N 1 (*frm: sphere*) orbe *m*; (*liter: celestial body*) astro 2 (*in regalia*) globo (*simbolo del potere reale e imperiale*)

or·bit ['ɔːbɪt] N orbita; **to be in/go into orbit (round)** essere/entrare in orbita (attorno a); **it's outside my orbit** (*fig*) non rientra nel mio campo ♦ VI (*satellite, astronaut*) orbitare ♦ VT (*earth, moon*) orbitare attorno a

or·bit·al ['ɔːbɪtl] N (*also:* **orbital motorway**) raccordo anulare

or·chard ['ɔːtʃəd] N frutteto; **apple orchard** meleto

or·ches·tra ['ɔːkɪstrə] N orchestra; (*USA: seating*) platea

or·ches·tral [ɔː'kestrəl] ADJ (*music, style*) orchestrale; (*concert*) sinfonico(-a)

or·ches·trate ['ɔːkɪstreɪt] VT (*Mus, also fig*) orchestrare

or·chid ['ɔːkɪd] N orchidea; **common spotted orchid** orchidea maculata

or·dain [ɔː'deɪn] VT 1 (*decree*) decretare; **it was ordained that ...** (*frm*) era destino che... 2 (*Rel*) ordinare

or·deal [ɔː'diːl] N esperienza traumatica

or·der ['ɔːdəʳ] N 1 (*sequence*) ordine *m*; **in alphabetical order** in ordine alfabetico; **in order of merit** in ordine di merito; **in order of size** in ordine di grandezza; **put these in the right order** mettili nell'ordine giusto; **to be in the wrong order** *or* **out of order** essere in ordine; **she had no order in her life** aveva una vita disordinata; **in the order of things** nell'ordine delle cose 2 (*also:* **good order**) ordine *m*; **in order** (*room*) in ordine; (*documents*) in regola; **a machine in working order** un macchinario funzionante; **to be out of order** (*machine, toilets*) essere guasto(-a); (*telephone, lift*) essere fuori servizio 3 (*peace, control*) ordine *m*; **to keep order** mantenere l'ordine; **to keep children in order** tenere i bambini sotto controllo 4 (*command*) ordine *m*, comando; (*of court: for search, arrest*) mandato; (: *for payment of fine, maintenance*) ingiunzione *f*; **by order of** per ordine di; **on the orders of** agli ordini di; **to be under orders to do sth** avere l'ordine di fare qc; **to give sb orders to do sth** dare a qn l'ordine di fare qc; **to take orders from sb** prendere ordini da qn; **to obey orders** ubbidire agli ordini; **order of the day** ordine del giorno; **violence is the order of the day** (*fig*) la violenza è all'ordine del giorno 5 (*correct procedure: at meeting, Parliament*) procedura; **order (order)!** (*in Parliament*) ordine, signori!; **order in court!** silenzio!; **to call sb to**

order richiamare qn all'ordine; **a point of order** una questione di procedura; **to be out of order** non (essere) regolamentare; **is it in order for me to go to Rome?** mi è permesso andare a Roma? **6** (*Comm*) ordinazione *f*, ordinativo; **to be on order** essere stato(-a) ordinato(-a); **to ask for a repeat order** chiedere che venga rinnovata un'ordinazione; **rush order** ordinazione urgente; **tall order** (*fig: fam*) un'impresa ardua; **made to order** fatto(-a) su misura; **to place an order for sth with sb** fare un'ordinazione di qc a qn; **the waiter took our order** il cameriere ha preso la nostra ordinazione; **to the order of** (*Banking*) all'ordine di; **payment order** (*social security*) mandato (di pagamento) **7 in order to do sth** per fare qc; **in order that** perché + *sub*; affinché + *sub*; **he does it in order to earn money** lo fa per guadagnare qualcosa; **they cancelled their vacation in order to go to the wedding** hanno cancellato la vacanza per andare al matrimonio; **in order there should be no misunderstanding** affinché non ci siano equivoci **8** *or* **in the order of** (*approximately*) nell'ordine di; **his income is of the order of £40,000 per year** il suo reddito annuale è nell'ordine delle 40.000 sterline **9** (*of society, also Bio*) ordine *m*; **the lower orders** (*pej*) i ceti inferiori; **Benedictine Order** ordine benedettino; **holy orders** ordini (sacri); **to be in/take orders** (*Rel*) aver ricevuto/prendere gli ordini ♦ VT **1** (*command*) ordinare a qn di fare qc; **the referee ordered the player off the field** l'arbitro espulse il giocatore dal campo **2** (*put in order*) ordinare, fare ordine in, mettere in ordine **3** (*meal*) ordinare; (*goods*) ordinare, commissionare; (*taxi*) chiamare; **we ordered steak and chips** abbiamo ordinato bistecca e patatine ♦ VI ordinare; **are you ready to order?** volete ordinare?

▸ **order about, order around** VT + ADV comandare, dare ordini a; **he tries to order me about** cerca di darmi ordini

order book N copiacommissione *m inv*

order form N modulo di ordinazione, modulo d'ordine

or·der·ly [ˈɔːdəlɪ] ADJ (*person*) ordinato(-a); (*mind*) metodico(-a); (*room*) in ordine, ordinato(-a); (*meeting, crowd*) disciplinato(-a) ♦ N (*Mil*) attendente *m*; (*Med*) inserviente *m*

order number N numero di commissione

or·di·nal [ˈɔːdɪnl] ADJ (*number*) ordinale ♦ N (numero) ordinale *m*

or·di·nary [ˈɔːdnrɪ] ADJ **1** (*usual*) abituale, solito(-a); **in the ordinary way** (*in the normal fashion*) nel solito modo; (*generally*) normalmente, di norma; **in ordinary use** usato(-a) normalmente; **it has 25 calories less than ordinary ice cream** ha 25 calorie in meno rispetto a un gelato normale **2** (*average*) comune, normale; (*pej*) mediocre, ordinario(-a); **an ordinary day** una giornata come tante; **he's just an ordinary guy** è uno come tanti; **the ordinary Italian** l'italiano qualunque; **the meal was very ordinary** il pranzo non era niente di speciale ♦ N: **out of the ordinary** diverso(-a) dal solito, fuori dell'ordinario

ordinary degree N *laurea*

ordinary seaman N (*Brit*) marinaio semplice

ordinary shares NPL (*Fin*) azioni *fpl* ordinarie

or·di·na·tion [ˌɔːdɪˈneɪʃən] N (*Rel*) ordinazione *f*

ord·nance [ˈɔːdnəns] (*Mil*) N (*guns*) artiglieria; (*supplies*) materiale *m* militare; **the ordnance** (*department*) il reparto di sussistenza

Ordnance Survey map N (*Brit*) ≈ carta topografica dell'Istituto Geografico Militare

ore [ɔː'] N minerale *m* grezzo; **copper ore** minerale grezzo di rame

Ore., Oreg. ABBR (*USA*: = *Oregon*)

o·reg·a·no [əˈregənəʊ] N origano

O·re·gon [ˈɒrɪɡən] l'Oregon

or·gan [ˈɔːɡən] N (*all senses*) organo

organic [ɔːˈɡænɪk] ADJ **1** (*gen, also fig*) organico(-a) **2** (*free of chemicals: vegetables, food, farming*) biologico(-a)

or·gan·ism [ˈɔːɡə,nɪzəm] N (*Bio*) organismo

or·gan·ist [ˈɔːɡənɪst] N organista *m/f*

or·gani·za·tion [ˌɔːɡənaɪˈzeɪʃən] N organizzazione *f*; **a charitable organization** un'organizzazione filantropica

organization chart N organigramma *m*

or·gan·ize [ˈɔːɡə,naɪz] VT organizzare; **to get organized** organizzarsi

or·gan·ized [ˈɔːɡə,naɪzd] ADJ organizzato(-a)

organized crime N criminalità organizzata

organized labour N manodopera organizzata (in sindacati)

or·gan·iz·er [ˈɔːɡə,naɪzə'] N organizzatore(-trice)

or·gasm [ˈɔːɡæzəm] N orgasmo

orgy [ˈɔːdʒɪ] N (*also fig*) orgia

Ori·ent [ˈɔːrɪənt] N: **the Orient** l'Oriente *m*

ori·ent [ˈɔːrɪənt], **ori·en·tate** [ˈɔːrɪənˌteɪt] VT orientare; **to orient o.s.** orientarsi

ori·en·tal [ˌɔːrɪˈentəl] ADJ orientale ♦ N (*fam!*) **Oriental** orientale *m/f*

ori·en·ta·tion [ˌɔːrɪənˈteɪʃən] N orientamento

ori·fice [ˈɒrɪfɪs] N orifizio

ori·gin [ˈɒrɪdʒɪn] N origine *f*; **country of origin** paese *m* d'origine; **to be of humble origin** *or* **have humble origins** essere di umili origini

origi·nal [əˈrɪdʒɪnl] ADJ (*gen*) originale; (*inhabitant, form, splendour*) originario(-a); **it's very original** è molto originale; **the original inhabitants** gli abitanti originari ♦ N (*manuscript, painting etc*) originale *m*; (*garment*) modello originale; (*person*) originale *m/f*; **he reads Homer in the original** legge Omero in lingua originale

origi·nal·ity [əˌrɪdʒɪˈnælɪtɪ] N originalità

origi·nal·ly [əˈrɪdʒənəlɪ] ADV (*at first*) originariamente, all'inizio; (*in an original way*) in modo originale

origi·nate [əˈrɪdʒɪˌneɪt] VT dare origine a ♦ VI: **to originate (from)** (*gen*) avere origine (da); (*suggestion, idea*) derivare (da); (*goods*) provenire (da); **to originate in** (*river*) nascere (in); (*custom*) avere origine (in); **most of these problems originate in childhood** la maggior parte di questi problemi hanno origine nell'infanzia

origi·na·tor [əˈrɪdʒɪˌneɪtə'] N ideatore(-trice)

Ork·neys [ˈɔːknɪz] NPL: **the Orkneys, the Orkney Islands** le (isole) Orcadi *fpl*

or·na·ment [*n* ˈɔːnəmənt, *vb* ˈɔːnəˌment] N (*gen*) ornamento; (*vase, figurine*) soprammobile *m*; (*trinket*) ninnolo; **a glass ornament** un soprammobile di vetro; **architectural ornaments** ornamenti architettonici; **Christmas tree ornaments** decorazioni *fpl* per l'albero di Natale ♦ VT ornare, decorare

or·na·men·tal [ˌɔːnəˈmentl] ADJ ornamentale

or·na·men·ta·tion [ˌɔːnəmenˈteɪʃən] N (*act*) ornamentazione *f*; (*ornaments*) decorazione *f*

or·nate [ɔːˈneɪt] ADJ (*decor*) ricco(-a); (*style in writing*) ornato(-a)

or·ni·tholo·gist [ˌɔːnɪˈθɒlədʒɪst] N ornitologo(-a)

or·ni·thol·ogy [ˌɔːnɪˈθɒlədʒɪ] N ornitologia

or·phan [ˈɔːfən] ADJ, N orfano(-a) ♦ VT: **to be orphaned** restare orfano(-a)

or·phan·age [ˈɔːfənɪdʒ] N orfanotrofio

ortho·dox [ˈɔːθəˌdɒks] ADJ ortodosso(-a)

ortho·paedic, ortho·pedic (*USA*) [ˌɔːθəʊˈpiːdɪk] ADJ ortopedico(-a)

OS [ˌəʊˈes] ABBR (*Brit*) **1** (*Naut*) = **ordinary seaman 2** (*clothes*) = **outsize**

O/S ABBR = **out of stock**; *see* **stock**¹

Os·car [ˈɒskə'] N (*film award*) Oscar *m inv*

os·cil·late [ˈɒsɪˌleɪt] VI oscillare

Oslo [ˈɒzləʊ] N Oslo *f*

os·ten·sible [ɒsˈtensəbl] ADJ apparente; **ostensible reason** pretesto

os·ten·sibly [ɒsˈtensəblɪ] ADV apparentemente

os·ten·ta·tion [ˌɒstenˈteɪʃən] N ostentazione *f*

os·ten·ta·tious [ˌɒstenˈteɪʃəs] ADJ (*lifestyle*) pretenzioso(-a); (*gesture, wealth*) ostentato(-a); **to be ostentatious about sth** ostentare qc

os·teo·path [ˈɒstɪəpæθ] N chiroterapista *m/f*

os·tra·cize [ˈɒstrəsaɪz] VT (*frm*) ostracizzare

os·trich [ˈɒstrɪtʃ] N struzzo

❏ *ostrich* is not translated by the Italian word *ostrica*

OT [ˌəʊˈtiː] ABBR (*Bible*: = *Old Testament*) VT *m* (= *Vecchio Testamento*)

OTB [ˌəʊtiːˈbiː] N ABBR (*USA*: = *off-track betting*) puntate effettuate fuori dagli ippodromi

oth·er [ˈʌðəʳ] ADJ altro(-a); **the other one** l'altro(-a); **this one?** — no, the other one questo? — no, l'altro; **other people** altri, altre persone *fpl*; **have you got these jeans in other colours?** avete questi jeans in altri colori?; **some other people have still to arrive** deve ancora arrivare altra gente; **the other day** l'altro giorno; **some other time** un'altra volta, un altro momento; **if there are no other questions ...** se non ci sono altre domande...; **some actor or other** un certo attore; **other people's property** la proprietà altrui ♦ PRON: **the other** l'altro(-a); **the others** gli altri (le altre); **the others are going but I'm not** gli altri ci vanno ma io no; **one after the other** uno(-a) dopo l'altro(-a); **are there any others?** ce ne sono altri?; **one or other of them will come** o uno o l'altro verrà; **somebody or other** qualcuno(-a); **no other** (*nobody else*) nessun altro (nessun'altra); (*old: nothing else*) nient'altro ♦ ADV: **other (than)** (*differently*) diversamente (da); **he could not act other than as he did** non poteva agire diversamente (da come fece); **somewhere or other** da qualche parte ♦ PREP: **other (than)** (*except*) tranne (che); **nothing other than** nient'altro che; **he's never discussed it with anyone other than David** non ne ha parlato con nessun altro a parte *or* all'infuori di David; **none other than** (*no less than*) nientemeno che; **the car was none other than Roberta's** la macchina era proprio di Roberta

other·wise [ˈʌðəˌwaɪz] ADV 1 (*in another way*) diversamente; **it cannot be otherwise** non può essere diversamente *or* altrimenti; **she was otherwise engaged** aveva già altri impegni; **except where otherwise stated** salvo indicazione contraria; **whether sold or otherwise** venduto o no 2 (*in other respects*) altrimenti, a parte ciò; **I'm tired, but otherwise I'm fine** sono stanco, ma a parte ciò sto bene; **an otherwise good piece of work** un lavoro per il resto buono ♦ CONJ (*if not*) altrimenti, se no; **note down the number, otherwise you'll forget it** scriviti il numero, altrimenti te lo dimentichi

ot·ter [ˈɒtəʳ] N lontra

ouch [aʊtʃ] EXCL ohi!, ahi!

ought [ɔːt] (*pt* ought) MODAL AUX VB 1 (*moral obligation*): **I ought to do it** dovrei farlo; **one ought not to do it** non lo si dovrebbe fare; **I ought to phone my parents** dovrei telefonare ai miei; **this ought to have been corrected** questo avrebbe dovuto essere corretto 2 (*vague desirability*): **you ought to go and see it** dovresti andare a vederlo, faresti bene ad andarlo a vedere 3 (*probability*): **that ought to be enough** quello dovrebbe bastare; **he ought to have arrived by now** dovrebbe essere arrivato, ormai; **he ought to win** dovrebbe vincere

ounce [aʊns] N oncia (= 28, 35 grammi; 16 in una libbra)

our [ˈaʊəʳ] POSS ADJ il nostro (la nostra), i nostri (le nostre) *pl*; **this is our house** questa è la nostra casa; **at our house** a casa nostra; **our brother** nostro fratello; **our dog** il nostro cane; **we took off our coats** ci siamo tolti i cappotti; **we washed our hair** ci siamo lavati i capelli

ours [ˈaʊəz] POSS PRON il (la) nostro(-a), i (le) nostri(-e) *pl*; **a friend of ours** un nostro amico; **theirs is red, ours is green** il loro è rosso, il nostro è verde; **this is ours** questo è (il) nostro

our·selves [ˌaʊəˈselvz] PERS PRON (*reflexive*) ci; (*emphatic, after preposition*) noi stessi(-e); **we did it (all) by ourselves** l'abbiamo fatto (tutto) da soli; **we really enjoyed ourselves** ci siamo divertiti moltissimo; **we built our garage ourselves** il garage l'abbiamo costruito noi; **by ourselves** da soli; **we don't like travelling by ourselves** non ci piace viaggiare da soli; *see also* oneself

oust [aʊst] VT: **to oust sb from sth** spodestare qn da qc

KEYWORD

out [aʊt] ADV
1 (*gen*) fuori; **to be out and about again**, (*Brit*) **to be out and around again** (*USA*) essere di nuovo in piedi; **the ball is out** (*Sport*) la palla è fuori; **out here** qui fuori; **they're out in the garden** sono fuori in giardino; **Mr Green is out** il signor Green non c'è *or* è uscito; **the journey out** l'andata; **to have a night out** passare una serata fuori; **speak out (loud)!** parla forte!; **out there** là fuori; **out with it!** sputa fuori!; **out!** (*Tennis*) fuori!

2 (*indicating distance*): **three days out from Plymouth** (*Naut*) a tre giorni di navigazione da Plymouth; **she's out in Kuwait** è via in Kuwait; **the boat was 10 miles out** la barca era a 10 miglia dalla costa; **it carried us out to sea** ci portò al largo

3 (*fig*): **to be out** (*person: unconscious*) essere privo(-a) di sensi; (: *on strike*) essere in sciopero; (: *out of game etc*) essere eliminato(-a); (: *out of fashion*) essere out *inv or* passato(-a) di moda; (*have appeared: sun, moon*) splendere; (: *flowers*) sbocciare; (: *news, secret*) essere rivelato(-a); (: *book*) uscire; (*extinguished: fire, light, gas*) essere spento(-a); **she is out and away the best** è di gran lunga la migliore; **it's the biggest swindle out** è la truffa più grossa che ci sia; **I was not far out** non mi sbagliavo di tanto; **he was out in his reckoning (by 5%)** si sbagliava nei suoi calcoli (del 5%); **the tide is out** c'è bassa marea; **before the week was out** prima della fine della settimana

4 **to be out for sth** cercare qc, volere qc; **he's out for all he can get** sta cercando di trarne il massimo profitto; **I'm only out for a good time** voglio solo divertirmi

5 **to be out to do sth** essere deciso(-a) a far qc, cercare di far qc; **they're out to get me** mi danno la caccia; **he's out to make money** il suo unico scopo è quello di fare soldi

♦ **out of** PREP
1 (*outside, beyond*) fuori; **to be out of danger** essere fuori pericolo; **to disappear out of sight** sparire alla vista; **to feel out of it** (*fam*) sentirsi escluso(-a); **to go out of the house** uscire di casa; **to look out of the window** guardare fuori dalla finestra; **to be out of sight** non essere visibile; **we're well out of it** (*fam*) per fortuna ne siamo fuori

2 (*cause, motive*) per; **out of curiosity** per curiosità

3 (*origin, source*) da; **to copy sth out of a book** copiare qc da un libro; **to drink sth out of a cup** bere qc da una tazza; **a box made out of wood** una scatola di *or* in legno; **it was like something out of a nightmare** era come in un incubo; **to take sth out of a drawer** prendere qc da un cassetto

4 (*from among*) su; **1 out of every 3 smokers** 1 fumatore su 3; **9 marks out of 10** 9 punti su 10

5 (*without*) senza; **to be out of sth** essere rimasto(-a) senza qc; **to be out of breath** essere senza fiato; **to be out of petrol** essere (rimasto(-a)) senza benzina; **it's out of stock** (*Comm*) non è disponibile

♦ N *see* in

♦ VT: **to out sb** rivelare pubblicamente l'omosessualità di qn

out·age [ˈaʊtɪdʒ] N (*esp USA: power failure*) black-out *m inv*, interruzione *f* (dell'erogazione) della corrente elettrica

out-and-out [ˈaʊtənˈaʊt] ADJ vero(-a) e proprio(-a)

out·back [ˈaʊtbæk] N (*in Australia*) entroterra *m*

out·bid [aʊtˈbɪd] (*pt, pp* outbid) VT offrire di più di

out·board [ˈaʊtbɔːd] ADJ, N: **outboard (motor)** (motore *m*) fuoribordo, *inv*

out·bound [ˈaʊtbaʊnd] ADJ: **outbound (for** *or* **from)** in partenza (per *or* da)

out·box [ˈaʊtbɒks] N (*Comput*) (cartella della) posta in uscita

out·break [ˈaʊtbreɪk] N (*of war*) scoppio; (*of disease*) insorgenza; (*of food poisoning*) epidemia; (*of crime*) ondata; **an outbreak of cholera** un'epidemia di colera; **at the outbreak of war** all'inizio or allo scoppio della guerra

out·build·ing [ˈaʊtbɪldɪŋ] N costruzione *f* annessa

out·burst [ˈaʊtbɜːst] N (*of anger*) scoppio; (*of applause*) scroscio

out·cast [ˈaʊtkɑːst] N reietto(-a); (*socially*) emarginato(-a)

out·class [ˌaʊtˈklɑːs] VT surclassare

out·come [ˈaʊtkʌm] N esito, risultato

out·crop [ˈaʊtkrɒp] N affioramento

out·cry [ˈaʊtkraɪ] N protesta; **to raise an outcry about sth** protestare contro qc; **the incident caused an international outcry** l'incidente sollevò una protesta internazionale

out·dat·ed [ˌaʊtˈdeɪtɪd] ADJ (*idea*) antiquato(-a), sorpassato(-a); (*custom, clothes*) fuori moda; **outdated equipment** attrezzature sorpassate

out·distance [ˌaʊtˈdɪstəns] VT distanziare

out·do [ˌaʊtˈduː] (*pt* outdid, *pp* outdone [ˌaʊtˈdʌn]) VT: **to outdo sb (in)** superare qn (in); **he was not to be outdone** non voleva essere da meno

out·door [ˈaʊtˈdɔːʳ] ADJ (activity) all'aperto; (life) all'aria aperta; (swimming pool) scoperto(-a); (clothes) pesante; **an outdoor swimming pool** una piscina scoperta; **outdoor activities** attività fpl all'aperto

out·doors [ˌaʊtˈdɔːz] ADV (go) fuori; (live, sleep) all'aria aperta ♦ NSG: **the great outdoors** l'aria aperta

out·er [ˈaʊtəʳ] ADJ esterno(-a); **the outer wall** il muro esterno; **outer suburbs** estrema periferia

outer space N spazio cosmico; **a creature from outer space** un/una extraterrestre m/f

out·fit [ˈaʊtˌfɪt] N 1 (clothes) completo; (for sports) tenuta; (for dressing up) costume m 2 (equipment) attrezzatura 3 (fam: organization) organizzazione f

out·fit·ter [ˈaʊtˌfɪtəʳ] N: **"(gent's) outfitters"** (Brit) "confezioni mpl da uomo"; **sports outfitter's** negozio di articoli sportivi

out·go·ing [ˈaʊtˌgəʊɪŋ] ADJ 1 (president, tenant) uscente; (means of transport) in partenza 2 (character) socievole, estroverso(-a); **she's very outgoing** è molto estroversa

out·go·ings [ˈaʊtˌgəʊɪŋz] NPL (Brit: expenses) spese fpl, uscite fpl

out·grow [ˌaʊtˈgrəʊ] VT (pt **outgrew** [ˌaʊtˈgruː], pp **outgrown** [ˌaʊtˈgrəʊn]) (clothes) diventare troppo grande per; (habit, attitude) perdere (col tempo)

out·house [ˈaʊthaʊs] N = **outbuilding**

out·ing [ˈaʊtɪŋ] N gita, escursione f; **to go on an outing** andare in gita

out·land·ish [aʊtˈlændɪʃ] ADJ (dress, person) bizzarro(-a)

out·last [ˌaʊtˈlɑːst] VT sopravvivere a

out·law [ˈaʊtlɔː] N fuorilegge m/f inv ♦ VT (person, practice) bandire

out·lay [ˈaʊtleɪ] N spesa

out·let [ˈaʊtlɛt] N (for water, sewage) scarico; (for air) sfogo; (of river) foce f; (Comm) mercato; (also: **retail outlet**) punto m (di) vendita, inv; (USA: Elec) presa di corrente; (fig: for emotion, talents) (valvola di) sfogo; **the washing machine outlet** lo scarico della lavatrice; **an outlet for his incredible energy** una valvola di sfogo per la sua incredibile energia; **there was only one outlet on the wall** c'era una sola presa di corrente nel muro ♦ ADJ (Tech) di scarico

out·line [ˈaʊtlaɪn] N (of object) contorno; (of face, building) profilo; (summary: general idea) abbozzo; **outlines** NPL aspetti mpl generali; **the outline of the building** il contorno dell'edificio; **give me the broad outline(s)** spiegami a grandi linee; **this is an outline of the plan** questo è un abbozzo del progetto ♦ VT (theory, plan, idea) abbozzare; (book, event, facts) descrivere a grandi linee; **to be outlined against sth** (in silhouette) stagliarsi contro qc

out·live [ˌaʊtˈlɪv] VT sopravvivere a

out·look [ˈaʊtlʊk] N (view) vista, veduta; (prospects) prospettive fpl; (opinion) visione f, concezione f; **the outlook for next Saturday is sunny** si prevede bel tempo per sabato prossimo; **it changed my outlook on life** ha cambiato la mia visione della vita; **the uncertain outlook of the motor industry** le prospettive incerte dell'industria automobilistica; **weather outlook** previsioni fpl meteorologiche

out·ly·ing [ˈaʊtˌlaɪɪŋ] ADJ (distant) fuori mano; (outside town boundary) periferico(-a)

out·ma·noeu·vre, out·ma·neu·ver (USA) [ˌaʊtməˈnuːvəʳ] VT (Mil) superare strategicamente; (fig: rival, opposition) surclassare

out·mod·ed [ˌaʊtˈməʊdɪd] ADJ = **outdated**; **an outmoded system** un sistema superato

out·num·ber [ˌaʊtˈnʌmbəʳ] VT superare numericamente

out-of-court [ˌaʊtəvˈkɔːt] ADJ (settlement) extragiudiziale ♦ ADV (settle) senza ricorrere al tribunale

out-of-date [ˌaʊtəvˈdeɪt] ADJ (passport, ticket) scaduto(-a); (theory, idea) sorpassato(-a), superato(-a); (custom) antiquato(-a); (clothes) fuori moda; **your credit card is out-of-date** la sua carta di credito è scaduta; **out-of-date medical knowledge** conoscenze fpl mediche superate; **out-of-date power stations** centrali fpl elettriche obsolete

out-of-doors [ˌaʊtəvˈdɔːz] ADV = **outdoors**

out-of-the-way [ˌaʊtəvðəˈweɪ] ADJ (remote) fuori mano; (unusual) insolito(-a)

out·pa·tient [ˈaʊtˌpeɪʃənt] N paziente m/f esterno(-a); **out-patients' department** ambulatorio (all'interno di un ospedale)

out·post [ˈaʊtpəʊst] N (Mil, also fig) avamposto

out·pour·ing [ˈaʊtˌpɔːrɪŋ] N (fig) torrente m

out·put [ˈaʊtpʊt] N (of machine, factory) produzione f; (of person) rendimento; (of computer) output m inv, dati mpl in uscita; (Elec) erogazione f; **their industrial output** la loro produzione industriale ♦ VT (Comput) emettere

out·rage [ˈaʊtreɪdʒ] N (wicked, violent deed) atrocità f inv; (emotion) sdegno; **bomb outrage** attentato dinamitardo; **who would have committed this latest outrage?** chi può aver commesso le ultime atrocità?; **it caused a public outrage** ha provocato uno scandalo; **an outrage against good taste** un oltraggio al buon gusto; **an outrage against humanity** un crimine contro l'umanità; **it's an outrage!** è una vergogna!, è uno scandalo! ♦ VT offendere; **to be outraged by sth** essere scandalizzato(-a) da qc

out·ra·geous [aʊtˈreɪdʒəs] ADJ (language, joke: offensive) scioccante; (price) esorbitante; (clothes) stravagante; (crime) atroce; **it's outrageous that ...** è scandaloso che...; **the prices they charge are outrageous** hanno prezzi esorbitanti

out·rid·er [ˈaʊtˌraɪdəʳ] N (on motorcycle) battistrada m inv

out·right [adv ˌaʊtˈraɪt, adj ˈaʊtraɪt] ADV (kill) sul colpo; (win) nettamente; (own) completamente; (buy) tutto(-a) in una volta; (refuse, reject) categoricamente; **he was killed outright** è morto sul colpo ♦ ADJ (winner, refusal) netto(-a); (liar, selfishness) bell'e buono(-a)

out·run [ˌaʊtˈrʌn] (pt **outran**, pp **outrun**) VT superare (nella corsa); (fig) superare

out·set [ˈaʊtset] N: **at the outset** all'inizio

out·shine [ˌaʊtˈʃaɪn] (pt, pp **outshone** [ˌaʊtˈʃɒn]) VT (fig) eclissare

out·side [ˌaʊtˈsaɪd] ADV fuori, all'esterno; **to be/go outside** stare/andare fuori; **seen from outside** visto(-a) dall'esterno or da fuori; **it's very cold outside** fa molto freddo fuori ♦ PREP 1 fuori di, all'esterno di; **the car outside the house** la macchina fuori della casa; **he waited outside the door** aspettò fuori della porta; **outside the city/school** fuori (della) città/scuola; **don't go outside the garden** non uscire dal giardino 2 (not included in) al di fuori di; **outside school hours** al di fuori dell'orario scolastico; **he has no interests outside his job** non ha altri interessi al di fuori del lavoro; **it's outside my experience** non ne ho una conoscenza diretta ♦ ADJ 1 (exterior) esterno(-a); **an outside seat** (in bus, plane) un posto vicino al corridoio; **outside contractor** appaltatore m esterno; **the outside walls** le mura esterne; **to get an outside opinion** chiedere un parere imparziale 2 (maximum: price) massimo(-a), massimale 3 (remote, unlikely): **an outside chance** una vaga possibilità ♦ N esterno; **the outside of the house** l'esterno della casa; **to overtake on the outside** (Aut) ≈ sorpassare sulla sinistra; **judging from the outside** (fig) a giudicare dalle apparenze; **at the (very) outside** (fig) al massimo

outside broadcast N (Radio, TV) trasmissione f in esterni

outside lane N (Aut) ≈ corsia di sorpasso

outside line N (Telec) linea esterna

out·sid·er [ˌaʊtˈsaɪdəʳ] N (stranger) estraneo(-a); (in racing, contest) outsider m/f inv; **he felt an outsider** si sentiva un estraneo; **the race was won by an outsider** la corsa è stata vinta da un outsider

out·size [ˈaʊtsaɪz] ADJ (gen) gigante; (clothes) per taglie forti; **outsize department** reparto taglie forti

out·skirts [ˈaʊtskɜːts] NPL (of town) sobborghi mpl, periferia fsg; (of wood) limitare msg, margine msg; **on the outskirts of town** in periferia

out·smart [ˌaʊtˈsmɑːt] VT superare in astuzia

out·spo·ken [ˌaʊtˈspəʊkən] ADJ franco(-a), senza peli sulla lingua (fam)

out·spread [ˌaʊtˈsprɛd] ADJ (gen) aperto(-a); (wings) spiegato(-a)

out·stand·ing [ˌaʊtˈstændɪŋ] ADJ 1 (exceptional) eccezionale; (feature) saliente 2 (not settled: bill) non pagato(-a); (: problem) irrisolto(-a); **the work is still outstanding** il lavoro non è ancora stato finito; **your account is still outstanding** deve ancora saldare il conto

out·stay [ˌaʊtˈsteɪ] VT: **to outstay sb** trattenersi più a lungo di qn; **to outstay one's welcome** abusare dell'ospitalità di qn

out·stretched [ˌaʊtˈstretʃt] ADJ (*body, legs*) disteso(-a), steso(-a); (*hand*) teso(-a); **with outstretched arms** a braccia aperte

out·strip [ˌaʊtˈstrɪp] VT (*also fig*) superare

out·tray [ˈaʊtˌtreɪ] N *vassoio per la corrispondenza e gli ordini da evadere*

out·vote [ˌaʊtˈvəʊt] VT: **it was outvoted (by ...)** fu respinto (con una maggioranza di...); **I wanted to go dancing but I was outvoted** volevo andare a ballare ma mi hanno messo in minoranza

out·ward [ˈaʊtwəd] ADJ 1 (*movement*) verso l'esterno; **on the outward journey** durante il viaggio di andata 2 (*sign, appearances*) esteriore; **with an outward show of interest** mostrando un apparente interesse

out·ward·ly [ˈaʊtwədlɪ] ADV (*on the surface*) esteriormente; (*apparently*) apparentemente; **worried but outwardly calm** preoccupato(-a) ma all'apparenza calmo(-a)

out·wards, out·ward [ˈaʊtwəd(z)] ADV verso l'esterno; **outward bound** in partenza

out·weigh [ˌaʊtˈweɪ] VT avere maggior peso di

out·wit [ˌaʊtˈwɪt] VT essere più furbo(-a) di

oval [ˈəʊvəl] ADJ, N ovale m

Oval Office N *ufficio del Presidente degli Stati Uniti*

ovar·ian [əʊˈvɛərɪən] ADJ ovarico(-a)

ova·ry [ˈəʊvərɪ] N (*Anat*) ovaia; (*Bot*) ovario

ova·tion [əʊˈveɪʃən] N ovazione *f*

oven [ˈʌvn] N forno; **in the oven** al forno; **it's like an oven in there** è un forno lì dentro

oven glove N guanto da forno

oven·proof [ˈʌvnˌpruːf] ADJ: **ovenproof dish** pirofila

oven·ready [ˈʌvnˈredɪ] ADJ pronto(-a) da infornare

oven·ware [ˈʌvnˌwɛə] N pirofile *fpl*

over [ˈəʊvə] ADV 1 (*across*): **over here** qui; **over there** laggiù, là; **over in France** in Francia; **he's over from France for a few days** è venuto dalla Francia per alcuni giorni; **over against the wall** (lì *or* là) contro il muro; **the little boy went over to his mother** il bambino andò da sua madre; **to drive over to the other side of town** andare (in macchina) dall'altra parte della città; **can you come over tonight?** puoi venire da me (*or* noi) stasera?; **over to you!** (*TV, Radio*) a te (la linea)!; **now over to our Paris correspondent** diamo ora la linea al nostro corrispondente da Parigi; **to go over to the enemy** passare al nemico 2 (*everywhere*): **the world over** in tutto il mondo; **I ache all over** mi fa male dappertutto; **I looked all over for you** ti ho cercato dappertutto; **that's him all over** è proprio di lui 3 (*indicating movement from one side to another, from upright position*): **to turn sth over (and over)** girare (e rigirare) qc; **she hit me and over I went** mi ha colpito e sono caduto 4 (*finished*) finito(-a); **the rain is over** la pioggia è cessata; **the danger was soon over** il pericolo cessò presto; **I'll be happy when the exams are over** sarò contento quando gli esami saranno finiti; **it's all over between us** tra noi è tutto finito 5 (*again*): **to tell over and over** dire mille volte; **to start (all) over again** ricominciare da capo; **several times over** diverse volte 6 (*excessively*) molto, troppo; **she's not over intelligent** (*Brit*) non è molto intelligente 7 (*remaining*) rimasto(-a); **there are three over** ne sono rimasti tre; **is there any cake left over?** è rimasta della torta? 8 (*more*): **persons of 21 and over** persone dai 21 anni in su 9 (*esp in signalling and radio*): **over and out** passo e chiudo ♦ PREP 1 (*on top of, above*) su; **to spread a sheet over sth** stendere un lenzuolo su qc; **there's a mirror over the washbasin** sopra il lavandino c'è uno specchio; **over my head** sopra la mia testa; **his speech went over my head** (*fig*) il suo discorso era troppo complicato per me; **he's over me** è un mio superiore; **to have an advantage over sb** avere un vantaggio su qn 2 (*across*): **the pub over the road** il pub di fronte; **it's over the river** è al di là del fiume; **the shop is over the road** il negozio è dall'altra parte della strada; **the bridge over the river** il ponte sul fiume; **the ball went over the wall** la palla andò al di là del muro, la palla è andata oltre il muro; **over the page** alla pagina seguente 3 (*everywhere in/on*): **all over the world** in tutto il mondo; **all over Scotland** in tutta la Scozia; **you've got mud all over your shoes** hai le scarpe tutte

infangate 4 (*more than*): **over 200** più di 200; **he must be over 60** deve aver superato i 60; **it's over twenty kilos** pesa oltre venti chili; **over and above normal requirements** oltre ai soliti requisiti; **an increase of 5% over last year's total** un aumento del 5% rispetto al totale dell'anno scorso 5 (*during*) durante, nel corso di; **over the last few years** nel corso degli ultimi anni; **over the summer/winter** durante l'estate/l'inverno; **over Christmas** durante il periodo natalizio; **let's discuss it over dinner** discutiamone a cena; **how long will he be over it?** quanto tempo ci prenderà? 6 (*means*): **I heard it over the radio** l'ho sentito alla radio 7 (*about, concerning*): **they fell out over money** litigarono per una questione di denaro

over– [ˈəʊvə] PREF: **overabundance** n sovrabbondanza; **over-protective** adj superprotettivo(-a)

over·act [ˌəʊvərˈækt] VI recitare con troppa enfasi

over·all [ˈəʊvərˌɔːl] ADJ (*improvement*) generale; (*width, length*) totale; **overall dimensions** (*Aut*) ingombro; **overall placings** (*Sport*) classifica generale; **overall improvement** miglioramento generale; **overall majority** maggioranza assoluta; **overall total** somma complessiva; **what was your overall impression?** nel complesso che impressione ti ha fatto? ♦ ADV nell'insieme, complessivamente; **overall I was disappointed** nel complesso sono rimasto deluso ♦ N (*Brit*) camice m

overall majority N maggioranza assoluta

over·anx·ious [ˌəʊvərˈæŋkʃəs] ADJ troppo ansioso(-a)

over·awe [ˌəʊvərˈɔː] VT intimidire

over·bal·ance [ˌəʊvəˈbæləns] VI sbilanciarsi ♦ VT sbilanciare

over·bear·ing [ˌəʊvəˈbɛərɪŋ] ADJ autoritario(-a), prepotente

over·board [ˈəʊvəˌbɔːd] ADV (*Naut*) fuori bordo; **to fall overboard** cadere in mare; **man overboard!** uomo in mare!; **to go overboard for sth** (*fig*) impazzire per qc

over·book [ˌəʊvəˈbʊk] VI, VT *accettare troppe prenotazioni rispetto alla disponibilità di posti*

over·came [ˌəʊvəˈkeɪm] PT *of* overcome

over·capi·tal·ize [ˌəʊvəˈkæpɪtəˌlaɪz] VT (*Fin*) sovracapitalizzare

over·cast [ˌəʊvəˈkɑːst] ADJ nuvoloso(-a), coperto(-a)

over·charge [ˌəʊvəˈtʃɑːdʒ] VT 1 **to overcharge sb for sth** far pagare troppo qc a qn; **they overcharged us for the meal** ci hanno fatto pagare troppo per il pranzo 2 (*Elec*) sovraccaricare

over·coat [ˈəʊvəˌkəʊt] N (*light*) soprabito; (*heavy*) cappotto

over·come [ˌəʊvəˈkʌm] (*pt* **overcame**, *pp* **overcome**) VT (*enemies*) sopraffare; (*obstacle, difficulty*) superare; (*rage, temptation*) vincere; (*sb's doubts*) dissolvere; **to be overcome by the heat** essere sopraffatto(-a) dall'afa; **to be overcome by remorse** essere preso(-a) dal rimorso; **overcome with grief** sopraffatto(-a) dal dolore; **I'm sure we can overcome these difficulties** sono certo che possiamo superare queste difficoltà; **they were overcome by fumes** sono stati sopraffatti dai vapori

over·con·fi·dent [ˌəʊvəˈkɒnfɪdənt] ADJ troppo sicuro(-a) (di sé), presuntuoso(-a)

over·crowd·ed [ˌəʊvəˈkraʊdɪd] ADJ sovraffollato(-a)

over·crowd·ing [ˌəʊvəˈkraʊdɪŋ] N (*in prison, housing*) sovraffollamento; (*in bus*) calca

over·do [ˌəʊvəˈduː] (*pt* **overdid** [ˌəʊvəˈdɪd], *pp* **overdone**) VT 1 (*exaggerate*) esagerare; **don't overdo these exercises** cerca di non strafare con questi esercizi (di ginnastica); **to overdo it** *or* **things** (*work too hard*) lavorare troppo; (*convalescent*) affaticarsi troppo 2 (*cook too long*) (far) cuocere troppo

over·done [ˌəʊvəˈdʌn] PP *of* overdo ♦ ADJ (*exaggerated*) esagerato(-a); (*overcooked*) troppo cotto(-a)

over·dose [ˈəʊvəˌdəʊs] N overdose *f inv* ♦ VI: **to overdose on** farsi un'overdose di

over·draft [ˈəʊvəˌdrɑːft] N (*Fin*) scoperto (di conto); **to have an overdraft at the bank** avere il conto scoperto

over·drawn [ˌəʊvəˈdrɔːn] ADJ (*account*) scoperto(-a); **to be overdrawn** avere il conto scoperto; **I'm £200 overdrawn** sono in rosso di 200 sterline

over·drive [ˈəʊvəˌdraɪv] N (*Aut*) overdrive m *inv*

over·due [ˌəʊvəˈdjuː] ADJ (*bill, rent*) arretrato(-a); (*library book*) col prestito scaduto; (*train, bus*) in ritardo; (*recognition*) tardivo(-a); (*fam: baby, period*) in ritardo; **she's a week over-due** (*pregnant woman*) è in ritardo di una settimana (*sulla data prevista del parto*); **this work is 2 days overdue** questo lavoro andava consegnato 2 giorni fa; **that change was long overdue** quel cambiamento ci voleva da tempo

over·em·pha·sis [ˌəʊvərˈemfəsɪs] N: **overemphasis on sth** importanza eccessiva data a qc

over·em·pha·size [ˌəʊvərˈemfəˌsaɪz] VT dare troppa enfasi a; **to overemphasize the importance of sth** esagerare l'importanza di qc

over·es·ti·mate [ˌəʊvərˈestɪˌmeɪt] VT (*value, amount*) sovra-stimare; (*fig: person, qualities*) sopravvalutare

over·ex·cit·ed [ˌəʊvərɪkˈsaɪtɪd] ADJ sovraeccitato(-a)

over·ex·er·tion [ˌəʊvərɪgˈzɜːʃən] N iperaffaticamento, sur-menage *m inv*

over·ex·pose [ˌəʊvərɪksˈpəʊz] VT (*Phot*) sovraesporre

over·flow [n ˈəʊvəˌfləʊ, vb ˌəʊvəˈfləʊ] N (*also:* **overflow pipe**) troppopieno; (*fig: people*): **the overflow filled the courtyard** quelli che non riuscirono ad entrare si accalcarono nel corti-le ♦ VI (*gen*) traboccare; (*river*) straripare; (*people*) riversarsi; **the theatre was overflowing with people** il teatro traboc-cava di gente

over·fly [ˌəʊvəˈflaɪ] (*pt* **overflew** [ˌəʊvəˈfluː], *pp* **overflown** [ˌəʊvəˈfləʊn]) VT sorvolare

over·gen·er·ous [ˌəʊvəˈdʒenərəs] ADJ troppo generoso(-a)

over·grown [ˈəʊvəˈgrəʊn] ADJ (*garden*): **overgrown with weeds/ivy** coperto(-a) di erbacce/edera

over·hang [*vb* ˌəʊvəˈhæŋ, *n* ˈəʊvəˌhæŋ] (*pt, pp* **overhung**) VT sporgere da ♦ VI sporgere ♦ N sporgenza

over·haul [*n* ˈəʊvəˌhɔːl, *vb* ˌəʊvəˈhɔːl] N revisione *f* ♦ VT (*ser-vice: machine*) revisionare; (*revise: system, method*) rivedere

over·head [*adv* ˌəʊvəˈhed, *adj* ˈəʊvəˌhed] ADV in alto ♦ ADJ (*railway*) sopraelevato(-a); (*cable*) aereo(-a); **overhead shot** (*Tennis*) schiacciata; **overhead valve** (*Aut*) valvola in testa

overhead projector N lavagna luminosa

over·heads [ˈəʊvəˌhedz] NPL (*Brit*) costi *mpl* di gestione

over·hear [ˌəʊvəˈhɪə'] (*pt, pp* **overheard** [ˌəʊvəˈhɜːd]) VT (*ac-cidentally*) sentire per caso; (*deliberately*) ascoltare

over·heat [ˌəʊvəˈhiːt] VI (*engine, brakes*) surriscaldarsi ♦ VT surriscaldare

over·joyed [ˌəʊvəˈdʒɔɪd] ADJ: **overjoyed (at)** pazzo(-a) di gioia (per)

over·kill [ˈəʊvəˌkɪl] N (*Mil*) potenziale *m* (nucleare) superiore al necessario; (*fig*) esagerazione *f*

over·land [ˈəʊvəˌlænd] ADV, ADJ per via di terra

over·lap [*n* ˈəʊvəˌlæp, *vb* ˌəʊvəˈlæp] N sovrapposizione *f*; (*fig*) coincidenza ♦ VI sovrapporsi; (*fig*) coincidere ♦ VT sovrap-porre

over·leaf [ˈəʊvəˈliːf] ADV a tergo

over·load [*n* ˈəʊvəˌləʊd, *vb* ˌəʊvəˈləʊd] N sovraccarico ♦ VT sovraccaricare

over·look [ˌəʊvəˈlʊk] VT 1 (*subj: building*) dare su; **the hotel overlooked the beach** l'albergo dava sulla spiaggia; **our garden is not overlooked** nel nostro giardino nessuno ci può vedere 2 (*not notice*) lasciarsi sfuggire, trascurare; (*tol-erate*) chiudere un occhio su, passare sopra a; **he had over-looked one important problem** aveva trascurato un pro-blema importante; **I'll overlook it just this once** ci passerò sopra solo per questa volta

over·lord [ˈəʊvəˌlɔːd] N capo supremo

over·man·ning [ˌəʊvəˈmænɪŋ] N esubero di manodopera

over·night [ˈəʊvəˈnaɪt] ADV (*happen*) durante la notte; (*travel*) di notte; (*fig: quickly*) da un giorno all'altro; **to stay over-night** fermarsi a dormire; **he stayed there overnight** ha passato la notte lì; **he'll be away overnight** passerà la notte fuori; **the weather remained calm overnight** il tempo è ri-masto sereno durante la notte; **we can't solve this one over-night** non possiamo risolvere questo da un giorno all'altro; **things won't change overnight** le cose non cambieranno tutto ad un tratto ♦ ADJ (*journey*) di notte; (*fig: success*) istan-taneo(-a), fulmineo(-a); **this'll mean an overnight stay at Calais** questo significa che dovremo passare la notte a Ca-lais; **an overnight success** un successo fulmineo

over·night bag N borsa da viaggio

over·pass [ˈəʊvəˌpɑːs] N (*USA*) cavalcavia *m inv*

over·pay [ˌəʊvəˈpeɪ] (*pt, pp* **overpaid**) VT strapagare; **to over-pay sb by £50** pagare 50 sterline in più a qn

over·play [ˌəʊvəˈpleɪ] VT dare troppa importanza a; **to over-play one's hand** sopravvalutare la propria posizione

over·pow·er [ˌəʊvəˈpaʊə'] VT sopraffare

over·pow·er·ing [ˌəʊvəˈpaʊərɪŋ] ADJ (*smell, heat*) asfissiante, soffocante; (*desire*) irrefrenabile, irresistibile

over·pro·duc·tion [ˌəʊvəprəˈdʌkʃən] N sovrapproduzione *f*

over·rate [ˌəʊvəˈreɪt] VT sopravvalutare

over·reach [ˌəʊvəˈriːtʃ] VT: **to overreach o.s.** volere strafare

over·react [ˌəʊvəriːˈækt] VI reagire in modo esagerato

over·ride [ˌəʊvəˈraɪd] (*pt* **overrode** [ˌəʊvəˈrəʊd], *pp* **overrid-den** [ˌəʊvəˈrɪdn]) VT (*law*) calpestare; (*person*) scavalcare; (*decision*) annullare; (*sb's wishes, orders*) non tener conto di; (*Tech: cancel*) annullare

over·rid·ing [ˌəʊvəˈraɪdɪŋ] ADJ (*factor*) preponderante; (*im-portance*) essenziale

over·rule [ˌəʊvəˈruːl] VT (*person*) prevalere su; (*request, claim*) respingere; (*decision*) annullare

over·run [ˌəʊvəˈrʌn] (*pt* **overran** [ˌəʊvəˈræn], *pp* **overrun**) VT (*Mil: country*) invadere, occupare; (*time limit*) superare; **the town is overrun with tourists** la città è invasa dai turisti ♦ VI (*meeting, event*) protrarsi

over·seas [ˈəʊvəˈsiːz] ADV (*abroad*) all'estero; **visitors from overseas** visitatori stranieri ♦ ADJ (*countries*) d'oltremare; (*foreign*) straniero(-a); (*trade, market*) estero(-a)

over·see [ˌəʊvəˈsiː] (*pt* **oversaw** [ˌəʊvəˈsɔː], *pp* **overseen** [ˌəʊvəˈsiːn]) VT sorvegliare

over·seer [ˈəʊvəˌsɪə'] N sorvegliante *m/f*; (*foreperson*) capo-squadra *m/f*

over·shad·ow [ˌəʊvəˈʃædəʊ] VT (*fig*) eclissare; **her child-hood was overshadowed by her mother's illness** la sua infanzia è stata offuscata dalla malattia della madre

over·shoot [ˌəʊvəˈʃuːt] (*pt, pp* **overshot** [ˌəʊvəˈʃɒt]) VT (*des-tination*) superare

over·sight [ˈəʊvəˌsaɪt] N (*omission*) svista; **due to an over-sight** per una svista

over·sim·pli·fy [ˌəʊvəˈsɪmplɪˌfaɪ] VT semplificare troppo

over·sleep [ˌəʊvəˈsliːp] (*pt, pp* **overslept** [ˌəʊvəˈslept]) VI non svegliarsi in tempo; **I overslept this morning** non mi sono svegliato in tempo stamattina

over·spend [ˌəʊvəˈspend] (*pt, pp* **overspent** [ˌəʊvəˈspent]) VI spendere troppo; **we have overspent by 5000 dollars** abbiamo speso 5000 dollari di troppo

over·spill [ˈəʊvəˌspɪl] N (*Brit: population*) eccedenza di popolazione; **an overspill town** ≈ una città satellite

over·staffed [ˌəʊvəˈstɑːft] ADJ: **to be overstaffed** avere trop-po personale

over·state [ˌəʊvəˈsteɪt] VT: **to overstate one's case** esagerare nel presentare le proprie ragioni

over·state·ment [ˌəʊvəˈsteɪtmənt] N esagerazione *f*

over·stay [ˌəʊvəˈsteɪ] VT: **to overstay one's welcome** tratte-nersi troppo a lungo (come ospite)

over·step [ˌəʊvəˈstep] VT: **to overstep the mark** superare ogni limite

over·stock [ˌəʊvəˈstɒk] VT sovrapprovvigionare, sovraimma-gazzinare

over·stretched [ˌəʊvəˈstretʃt] ADJ (*person*) sovraccarico(-a); (*resources, budget*) arrivato(-a) al limite

over·strike [ˌəʊvəˈstraɪk] N (*Typ*) sovrapposizione *f* (di carat-teri) ♦ VT sovrapporre

overt [əʊˈvɜːt] ADJ evidente, aperto(-a)

over·take [ˌəʊvəˈteɪk] (*pt* **overtook** [ˌəʊvəˈtʊk], *pp* **overtaken** [ˌəʊvəˈteɪkən]) VT (*catch up*) raggiungere; (*pass*) superare; **events have overtaken us** gli eventi ci hanno colto di sor-presa; **tragedy was shortly to overtake him** una disgrazia stava per travolgerlo ♦ VI sorpassare

over·tak·ing [ˌəʊvəˈteɪkɪŋ] N (*Aut*) sorpasso; "**no overtak-ing**" "divieto di sorpasso"

over·tax [ˌəʊvəˈtæks] VT (*Fin*) imporre tasse eccessive a; (*fig: strength, patience*) mettere a dura prova; **to overtax o.s.** abu-sare delle proprie forze

over·throw [*n* ˈəʊvəˌθrəʊ, *vb* ˌəʊvəˈθrəʊ] (*pt* **overthrew**

[ˌəʊvəˈθruː], *pp* **overthrown** [ˌəʊvəˈθrəʊn] N (*of government etc*) rovesciamento ♦ VT (*king, system, government*) rovesciare

over·time [ˈəʊvəˌtaɪm] N (lavoro) straordinario; **to do** *or* **work overtime** fare lo straordinario; **your imagination has been working overtime!** (*fam*) corri un po' troppo con la fantasia!

overtime ban N *rifiuto sindacale di fare gli straordinari*

over·tone [ˈəʊvəˌtəʊn] N 1 (*often pl: fig*) sfumatura 2 (*Mus*); **overtones** NPL armoniche *fpl* superiori, ipertoni *mpl*

over·took [ˌəʊvəˈtʊk] PT *of* **overtake**

over·ture [ˈəʊvəˌtjʊəʳ] N 1 (*Mus*) ouverture *f inv* 2 **to make overtures to sb** (*fig: friendly*) comportarsi amichevolmente verso qn; (*: romantic*) tentare un approccio con qn, fare delle avances a qn

over·turn [ˌəʊvəˈtɜːn] VT (*car, boat, chair*) capovolgere, ribaltare; (*government, regime*) rovesciare; (*Law: decision*) annullare, cassare; **the decision was overturned** la decisione è stata annullata ♦ VI (*car, boat*) rovesciarsi, ribaltarsi; **the car overturned** la macchina si è rovesciata

over·view [ˈəʊvəˌvjuː] N visione *f* d'insieme

over·weight [ˌəʊvəˈweɪt] ADJ: **to be overweight** (*person*) essere sovrappeso; (*luggage*) superare il peso consentito; **the parcel is a kilo overweight** il pacco pesa un chilo di troppo

over·whelm [ˌəʊvəˈwelm] VT (*opponent, team*) schiacciare; (*with questions, requests, work*) sommergere; **to be overwhelmed by grief** essere sopraffatto(-a) dal dolore; **sorrow overwhelmed him** il dolore lo sopraffece; **overwhelmed by her kindness** confuso dalla sua gentilezza; **to be overwhelmed** (*touched, impressed*) rimanere colpito(-a); **we have been overwhelmed with offers of help** siamo stati sommersi da offerte di aiuto

over·whelm·ing [ˌəʊvəˈwelmɪŋ] ADJ (*victory, majority*) schiacciante; (*defeat*) pesante; (*pressure, heat, desire, emotion*) intenso(-a); **one's overwhelming impression is of heat** l'impressione dominante è quella di caldo

over·whelm·ing·ly [ˌəʊvəˈwelmɪŋlɪ] ADV (*win*) in modo schiacciante; (*defeat*) pesantemente; (*vote*) in massa

over·work [ˌəʊvəˈwɜːk] N lavoro eccessivo; **a heart attack caused by overwork** un infarto causato dal superlavoro ♦ VI lavorare troppo, strapazzarsi ♦ VT (*staff, servants*) far lavorare troppo

over·write [ˌəʊvəˈraɪt] VT (*Comput*) sovrascrivere

over·wrought [ˌəʊvəˈrɔːt] ADJ estremamente agitato(-a)

ovu·la·tion [ˌɒvjʊˈleɪʃən] N ovulazione *f*

owe [əʊ] VT (*gen*): **to owe sb sth, to owe sth to sb** dovere qc a qn; **how much do I owe you?** quanto le devo?; **to what do I owe the honour of your visit?** (*iro*) a che devo l'onore della visita?; **you owe it to yourself to come** è per te stesso che devi venire

owing to PREP a causa di; **owing to the bad weather** a causa del maltempo

owl [aʊl] N (*small*) civetta; (*big*) gufo; **little owl** civetta notturna; **long-eared owl** gufo comune; **short-eared owl** gufo di palude

own [əʊn] ADJ proprio(-a); **this is my own recipe** è una mia ricetta; **I made it with my own hands** l'ho fatto con le mie mani; **it's all my own money** sono tutti soldi miei; **the house has its own garage** la casa ha il suo garage; **he can't trust his own judgement** non si può fidare del proprio giudizio ♦ PRON: **he has a style all his own** ha uno stile tutto

suo; **of my own** tutto(-a) per me; **I'll give you a copy of your own** ti darò una copia tutta per te; **a room of my own** una camera tutta per me; **a place of one's own** una casa tutta per sé; **can I have it for my (very) own?** posso averlo tutto per me?; **the house is her (very) own** la casa è di sua proprietà; **she has money of her own** è ricca di suo; **to come into one's own** mostrare le proprie qualità; **to be on one's own** stare per conto proprio; **on his own** da solo; **on their own** da soli; **from now on, you're on your own** (*fam*) d'ora in poi te la dovrai cavare da solo; **if I can get him on his own** se riesco a beccarlo da solo; **to do sth on one's own** (*unaided*) fare qualcosa da solo(-a); **I am so busy I have scarcely any time to call my own** sono così occupato che non ho tempo per me stesso; **without a chair to call my own** senza una sedia che possa chiamare mia; **to get one's own back** rendere pan per focaccia ♦ VT 1 (*possess*) possedere, essere proprietario(-a) di; **everything I own** tutto ciò che possiedo; **does anybody own this pen?** è di qualcuno questa penna?; **the golf course is owned by a Japanese company** il campo da golf appartiene ad una società giapponese; **he acts as if he owns the place** si comporta come se fosse il padrone; **you don't own me!** non sei il mio padrone! 2 (*old: admit*) ammettere ♦ VI (*Brit*): **to own to sth** ammettere qc; **to own to having done sth** ammettere di aver fatto qc

▸ **own up** VI + ADV: **to own up (to sth)** confessare (qc), ammettere (qc); **to own up to having done sth** ammettere di aver fatto qc

own brand N (*Comm*) marchio proprio

own·er [ˈəʊnəʳ] N proprietario(-a)

owner-occupier [ˌəʊnərˈɒkjʊˌpaɪəʳ] N proprietario(-a) della casa in cui abita

own·er·ship [ˈəʊnəʃɪp] N proprietà; **it's under new ownership** ha un nuovo proprietario; **under his ownership the business flourished** nelle sue mani la ditta prosperava; **car ownership** il possesso di una macchina

own goal N (*Sport, also fig*) autogol *m inv*, autorete *f*

ox [ɒks] N (*pl* **oxen** [ˈɒksən]) bue *m*

Ox·bridge [ˈɒksˌbrɪdʒ] (*Brit*) N *le università di Oxford e/o Cambridge* ♦ ADJ (*education, accent, attitudes*) di chi ha studiato a Oxford o Cambridge

Ox·fam [ˈɒksfæm] N ABBR (*Brit*: = *Oxford Committee for Famine Relief*) *organizzazione no-profit per aiuti al Terzo Mondo*

ox·ide [ˈɒksaɪd] N ossido

Oxon. [ˈɒksən] ABBR (*Brit* = *Oxoniensis*) (dell')Università di Oxford

ox·tail [ˈɒksˌteɪl] N: **oxtail soup** zuppa di coda di bue

oxy·acety·lene [ˌɒksɪəˈsetɪliːn] ADJ (*torch, burner*) ossiacetilenico(-a)

oxy·gen [ˈɒksɪdʒən] N ossigeno

oxygen mask N maschera a ossigeno

oxygen tent N tenda a ossigeno

oys·ter [ˈɔɪstəʳ] N ostrica; **the world is your oyster** il mondo è in tuo potere

oz. ABBR = **ounce**

ozone [ˈəʊzəʊn] N ozono

ozone-friendly [ˌəʊzəʊnˈfrendlɪ] ADJ che rispetta l'ozono, che non danneggia lo strato d'ozono

ozone layer N fascia d'ozono, strato d'ozono; **the hole in the ozone layer** il buco nell'ozono

Pp

P, p [piː] N (*letter*) P,p *f inv, m inv*; **P for Peter** ≈ P come Padova; **mind your p's and q's!** bada a come parli!

p [piː] ABBR (*Brit*) = **penny, pence**

PA [piːˈeɪ] N ABBR **1** (= *personal assistant*) assistente *m/f* personale **2** (= *public address system*): **the PA system** l'impianto di amplificazione ♦ ABBR (*USA Post:* = Pennsylvania)

pa [pɑː] N (*fam*) papà *m inv*, babbo

p.a. ABBR = **per annum**

pace [peɪs] N **1** (*step*) passo; **30 paces away** a 30 passi di distanza; **to put sb through his paces** (*fig*) mettere qn alla prova **2** (*speed*) passo, andatura; **at a good pace** (*walk*) di buon passo; (*work*) ad un buon ritmo; **at a slow pace** lentamente; **he was walking at a brisk pace** camminava a passo spedito; **the pace of life** il ritmo di vita; **to keep pace with** (*person*) andare di pari passo con; (*fig: technology*) procedere di pari passo con; (*: events*) tenersi al corrente di; **to set the pace** (*running*) fare l'andatura; (*fig*) dare il la *or* il tono ♦ VT (*room*) andare su e giù per; **to pace sth off** *or* **out** misurare a passi qc ♦ VI: **to pace up and down** camminare su e giù *or* avanti e indietro

pace·maker [ˈpeɪsˌmeɪkəʳ] N **1** (*Med*) pacemaker *m inv* **2** (*Sport*) chi fa l'andatura, battistrada *m inv*

Pa·cif·ic [pəˈsɪfɪk] N: **the Pacific (Ocean)** il Pacifico, l'Oceano Pacifico ♦ ADJ del Pacifico

paci·fi·ca·tion [ˌpæsɪfɪˈkeɪʃən] N pacificazione *f*

paci·fi·er [ˈpæsɪˌfaɪəʳ] N (*USA fam: dummy*) succhiotto, ciuccio

paci·fist [ˈpæsɪfɪst] N pacifista *m/f*

paci·fy [ˈpæsɪfaɪ] VT (*person*) calmare; (*country*) riportare la calma in, pacificare; (*creditors*) placare; (*fears*) ammansire

pack [pæk] N **1** (*packet*) pacco; (*Comm*) confezione *f*; (*of cotton, wool*) balla; (*USA: of cigarettes*) pacchetto; (*rucksack: Mil*) zaino; (*of cards*) mazzo; (*Rugby*) pacchetto; **he was carrying a heavy pack on his back** portava un grosso zaino sulle spalle; **an information pack** una serie di opuscoli informativi; **a six-pack** una confezione da sei; **a pack of cigarettes** un pacchetto di sigarette; **a pack of cards** un mazzo di carte; **a pack of lies** (*fig*) un mucchio *or* sacco di bugie **2** (*of hounds*) muta; (*of wolves*) branco; (*of thieves*) banda; (*of fools*) massa ♦ VT **1** (*objects, goods*) imballare; **packed in dozens** (*Comm*) in confezioni da dodici; **to pack one's bags** *or* **one's case** fare le valigie *or* i bagagli; (*fig*) far fagotto; **I've already packed my case** ho già fatto la valigia; **I still have a few things to pack** ho ancora qualcosa da mettere in valigia; **pack your swimming costume** metti il costume da bagno in valigia **2** (*cram full*): **to pack (with)** (*container*) riempire di; (*room, car*) stipare di; **can you pack two more into your car?** riesci a infilarcene ancora due nella tua macchina? **3** (*Comput*) comprimere, impaccare **4** (*make firm: soil etc*) comprimere, pressare ♦ VI **1** (*do one's luggage*) fare le valigie *or* i bagagli; **I'll help you pack** ti aiuto a fare i bagagli; **to send sb packing** (*fam*) dare il benservito a qn **2** (*people*): **to pack (into)** accalcarsi (in), pigiarsi (in); **thousands packed into the square** erano a migliaia stipati nella piazza; **packed like sardines** pigiati(-e) come sardine
  ► **pack away** VT + ADV riporre
  ► **pack in** (*Brit fam*) VI + ADV (*break down: watch, car*) guastarsi ♦ VT + ADV mollare, piantare; **pack it in!** piantala!
  ► **pack off** VT + ADV: **to pack sb off to school/bed** spedire qn a scuola/letto
  ► **pack up** VI + ADV (*person*) far fagotto; (*Brit fam: machine*) guastarsi ♦ VT + ADV **1** (*belongings, clothes*) mettere in una valigia; (*goods, presents*) imballare **2** = **pack in**

pack·age [ˈpækɪdʒ] N (*parcel*) pacco; (*smaller*) pacchetto; (*fig: terms of agreement*) pacchetto; **a small package** un piccolo pacco ♦ VT (*Comm: goods*) confezionare

package tour N (*Brit*) viaggio organizzato

pack·ag·ing [ˈpækɪdʒɪŋ] N confezione *f*, imballo

packed [pækt] ADJ (*crowded*) affollato(-a); **the place was packed** il posto era affollato

pack·er [ˈpækəʳ] N (*person*) imballatore(-trice); (*machine*) imballatrice *f*

pack·et [ˈpækɪt] N (*gen*) pacchetto; (*of sweets, crisps*) sacchetto; (*of needles, seeds*) bustina; **to make a packet** (*fam*) fare un mucchio *or* un sacco di soldi; **that must have cost a packet** (*fam*) dev'essere costato un sacco di soldi; **a packet of cigarettes** un pacchetto di sigarette

pack ice N banchisa, pack *m inv*

pack·ing [ˈpækɪŋ] N **1** (*of luggage*): **to do one's packing** fare le valigie *or* i bagagli **2** (*material*) (materiale *m* da) imballaggio

packing case N cassa da imballaggio

pact [pækt] N patto, trattato, accordo; **he has signed a pact** ha firmato un accordo; **a non-aggression pact** un patto di non aggressione

pad [pæd] N **1** (*to prevent friction etc*) cuscinetto; (*Ftbl*) parastinco; (*Hockey*) gambiera; (*brake pad*) pastiglia; (*for ink*) tampone *m*; **shoulder pads** spalline imbottite **2** (*writing pad*) blocco di carta da lettere; (*notepad*) bloc-notes *m inv*, blocchetto **3** (*launch pad*) rampa di lancio **4** (*of animal's foot*) cuscinetto **5** (*fam: apartment*) appartamentino ♦ VT (*cushion, shoulders etc*) imbottire ♦ VI: **to pad about/in etc** camminare/entrare etc a passi felpati
  ► **pad out** VT + ADV (*speech etc*) farcire

pad·ded [ˈpædɪd] ADJ imbottito(-a)

padded cell N cella con le pareti imbottite (*in carceri, ospedali psichiatrici*)

pad·ding [ˈpædɪŋ] N (*material*) imbottitura; (*fig: in speech, essay*) riempitivo; **it means nothing, it's just padding** non vuol dire niente, è solo un riempitivo; **protective padding** imbottitura protettiva

pad·dle [ˈpædl] N **1** (*oar*) pagaia; (*blade of wheel*) pala **2 to have a paddle** sguazzare nell'acqua bassa ♦ VT (*boat*) fare andare a colpi di pagaia ♦ VI **1** (*in boat*) pagaiare **2** (*walk in water*) sguazzare

paddle boat, paddle steamer (*Brit*) N battello a ruote

pad·dling pool [ˈpædlɪŋˌpuːl] N piscina per bambini

pad·dock [ˈpædək] N (*field*) recinto; (*of racecourse*) paddock *m inv*

pad·dy [ˈpædɪ] **paddy field** N risaia

pad·lock [ˈpædlɒk] N lucchetto ♦ VT chiudere con il lucchetto

pa·dre [ˈpɑːdrɪ] N **1** (*Mil, Naut*) cappellano **2** (*fam: clergyman*) padre *m*

Pad·ua [ˈpædʒʊə] N Padova

pae·dia·tri·cian, pe·dia·tri·cian (*USA*) [ˌpiːdɪəˈtrɪʃən] N pediatra *m/f*

pae·di·at·rics, pe·di·at·rics (*USA*) [ˌpiːdɪˈætrɪks] NSG pediatria

pae·do·phile, (*USA*) **pe·do·phile** [ˈpiːdəʊˌfaɪl] ADJ, N pedofilo(-a)

pagan [ˈpeɪɡən] ADJ, N pagano(-a)

page¹ [peɪdʒ] N (*of book etc*) pagina; **on page 2** a pagina 2; **on both sides of the page** su tutt'e due le facciate (del foglio)

page² [peɪdʒ] N (*also: pageboy*) fattorino; (*at wedding*) paggetto ♦ VT: **to page sb** (far) chiamare qn

pag·eant [ˈpædʒənt] N (*show*) spettacolo di rievocazione storica; (*procession*) corteo in costume

pag·eant·ry [ˈpædʒəntrɪ] N sfarzo, pompa

pag·er [ˈpeɪdʒəʳ] N cercapersone *m*

pagi·nate [ˈpædʒɪˌneɪt] VT (*Typ*) impaginare; (*Comput*) paginare

pagi·na·tion [ˌpædʒɪˈneɪʃən] N (*see vb*) impaginazione *f*; paginazione *f*

pa·go·da [pəˈɡəʊdə] N pagoda

paid [peɪd] PT, PP *of* **pay** ♦ ADJ (*work, official*) rimunerato(-a); **to put paid to sth** (*ruin*) metter fine a qc; **three weeks' paid vacation** tre settimane di ferie pagate

paid-up [ˈpeɪdˌʌp], (*USA*) **paid-in** [ˈpeɪdˌɪn] ADJ (*member*) che ha pagato la sua quota; (*share*) interamente pagato(-a); **paid-up capital** capitale *m* interamente versato

pail [peɪl] N secchio

pain [peɪn] N 1 dolore *m*; **to cause pain to** (*physical*) provocare dolori a; (*mental*) far soffrire; **to be in pain** soffrire; **she's in a lot of pain** soffre molto; **I have a pain in my leg** ho male *or* un dolore a una gamba; **a terrible pain** un dolore insopportabile; **he's a real pain (in the neck)** (*fam*) è un gran rompiscatole 2 **pains** NPL (*efforts*) sforzi *mpl*; **and all I got for my pains was ...** e come ringraziamento ho avuto...; **to take pains over sth** mettercela tutta in qc; **to be at (great) pains to do sth** fare di tutto per fare qc 3 (*penalty*): **on pain of death** sotto pena di morte ♦ VT (*mentally*) addolorare, affliggere

pained [peɪnd] ADJ: **a pained expression** un'aria seccata; **a pained silence** un silenzio amareggiato

pain·ful [ˈpeɪnfʊl] ADJ (*wound*) doloroso(-a); (*leg*) che fa male; (*task, sight, also fam*) penoso(-a); (*difficult*) difficile; **it is my painful duty to tell you that ...** purtroppo ho il dovere di informarla che...; **it was painful to watch** (*fam*) era penoso (a vedersi)

pain·ful·ly [ˈpeɪnfəlɪ] ADV (*walk, breathe*) a fatica; (*thin*) penosamente; **the cut throbbed painfully** la ferita pulsava e faceva male; **it was painfully clear that ...** era fin troppo chiaro che...

pain·killer [ˈpeɪnˌkɪləʳ] N analgesico, antidolorifico

pains·taking [ˈpeɪnzˌteɪkɪŋ] ADJ (*person*) coscienzioso(-a), diligente; (*work*) accurato(-a); (*accuracy*) minuzioso(-a)

paint [peɪnt] N (*Art*) colore *m*; (*for walls etc*) tinta, vernice *f*; **a tin of paint** un barattolo di tinta *or* vernice; **a box of paints** una scatola di colori ♦ VT (*house, also Art*) dipingere; (*door*) verniciare; **to paint sth blue/red** dipingere (*or* verniciare) qc di blu/rosso; **he decided to paint it green** ha deciso di verniciarlo di verde; **when did he paint the picture?** quando ha dipinto il quadro?; **to paint the town red** (*fig*) far baldoria; **he's not as black as he's painted** è meno cattivo di quanto si dica in giro ♦ VI dipingere; **to paint in oils** dipingere a olio

paint·box [ˈpeɪntˌbɒks] N scatola di colori

paint·brush [ˈpeɪntˌbrʌʃ] N pennello

paint·er [ˈpeɪntəʳ] N (*Art*) pittore(-trice); (*decorator*) imbianchino(-a); **a famous 13th century painter** un famoso pittore del XIII secolo; **the painter is coming tomorrow to redecorate the house** domani viene l'imbianchino per ridipingere la casa

paint·ing [ˈpeɪntɪŋ] N (*Art: picture*) dipinto, quadro; (: *activity*) pittura; (*decorating: of doors etc*) verniciatura; (: *of walls*) imbiancatura; **a painting by Picasso** un quadro di Picasso; **my hobby is painting** il mio hobby è la pittura

paint stripper, paint remover N prodotto sverniciante

paint·work [ˈpeɪntˌwɜːk] N (*gen*) pittura; (*of car*) vernice *f*

pair [pɛəʳ] N (*of gloves, shoes etc*) paio; (*of people*) coppia; **a pair of scissors/trousers/shoes** un paio di forbici/pantaloni/scarpe; **in pairs** a coppie; **we work in pairs** lavoriamo a coppie; **arranged in pairs** disposti(-e) a due a due; **ordered pair** (*Math*) coppia ordinata ♦ VT accoppiare, appaiare

▸ **pair off** VT + ADV trovar marito (*or* moglie) a ♦ VI + ADV: **to pair off (with sb)** fare coppia (con qn)

▸ **pair up** VI + ADV: **to pair up (with sb)** mettersi in coppia (con qn)

pa·jam·as [pəˈdʒɑːməz] NPL (*USA*) = **pyjamas**

Pa·ki·stan [ˌpɑːkɪsˈtɑːn] N Pakistan *m*

Pa·ki·stani [ˌpɑːkɪsˈtɑːnɪ] ADJ, N pakistano(-a)

PAL [pæl] N ABBR (*TV*: = *phase alternation line*) PAL *m*

pal [pæl] N (*fam*) amico(-a)

▸ **pal up** VI + ADV (*fam*) far amicizia

pal·ace [ˈpælɪs] N palazzo

pal·at·able [ˈpælətəbl] ADJ (*tasty*) gradevole (al palato); (*fig*) piacevole, gradevole

pal·ate [ˈpælɪt] N (*Anat, also fig*) palato

pa·la·tial [pəˈleɪʃəl] ADJ sontuoso(-a), sfarzoso(-a)

palaver [pəˈlɑːvəʳ] N (*fam: fuss*) storie *fpl*; (: *talk*) tiritera

pale[1] [peɪl] ADJ (*comp* **-r**, *superl* **-st**) (*gen*) pallido(-a); (*colour*) chiaro(-a), pallido(-a); **pale blue** azzurro pallido *inv*, celeste; **pale pink** rosa pallido; **pale green** verdolino; **to grow** *or* **turn pale** diventare pallido(-a), impallidire; **she still looks very pale** è ancora molto pallida ♦ VI impallidire; **to pale into insignificance (beside)** perdere d'importanza (nei confronti di)

pale[2] [peɪl] N: **to be beyond the pale** aver oltrepassato ogni limite

pale·ness [ˈpeɪlnɪs] N pallore *m*

Pal·es·tine [ˈpælɪsˌtaɪn] N Palestina

Pal·es·tin·ian [ˌpælɪsˈtɪnɪən] ADJ, N palestinese *m/f*

pal·ette [ˈpælɪt] N tavolozza

pali·sade [ˌpælɪˈseɪd] N palizzata

pall[1] [pɔːl] N (*on coffin*) drappo funebre; (*of smoke*) coltre *f*, cappa; **a pall of smoke** una cappa di fumo

pall[2] [pɔːl] VI: **to pall (on)** perdere il proprio fascino (per), diventare noioso(-a) (per)

pal·let [ˈpælɪt] N (*for goods*) pallet *m inv*

pal·lid [ˈpælɪd] ADJ pallido(-a), smorto(-a)

pal·lor [ˈpæləʳ] N pallore *m*

palm[1] [pɑːm] N (*Bot: also:* **palm tree**) palma

▸ **palm off** VT + ADV: **to palm sth off on sb** (*fam*) rifilare qc a qn

palm[2] [pɑːm] N (*Anat*) palma, palmo; **to read sb's palm** leggere la mano a qn; **to grease sb's palm** (*fig*) dare una bustarella a qn; **to have sb in the palm of one's hand** avere *or* tenere in pugno qn

palm·ist [ˈpɑːmɪst] N chiromante *m/f*

Palm Sunday N Domenica delle Palme

pal·pable [ˈpælpəbl] ADJ (*lie, mistake*) palese, evidente

pal·pi·ta·tion [ˌpælpɪˈteɪʃən] N: **to have palpitations** avere le palpitazioni

pal·try [ˈpɔːltrɪ] ADJ (*meagre*) irrisorio(-a); (*unworthy of consideration*) insignificante; **a paltry sum** una somma insignificante; **for a paltry £5** per la somma irrisoria di 5 sterline

pam·per [ˈpæmpəʳ] VT viziare, coccolare; **he's been pampered all his life** è stato viziato tutta la vita

pam·phlet [ˈpæmflɪt] N (*informative brochure*) opuscolo, dépliant *m inv*; (*political, handed out in street*) volantino, manifestino

pan [pæn] N (*Culin: also:* **saucepan**) casseruola; (*frying pan*) padella; (*milk pan*) pentolino; (*of scales*) piatto; (*of lavatory*) tazza; **roasting pan** teglia per arrosti ♦ VT 1 (*gold etc*) passare al vaglio 2 (*fam: play*) stroncare ♦ VI 1 **to pan for gold** (*lavare le sabbie aurifere per*) cercare l'oro 2 (*Cine*) fare una panoramica

▸ **pan out** VI + ADV (*develop*) andare; (*turn out well*) riuscire

pana·cea [ˌpænəˈsɪə] N panacea

pa·nache [pəˈnæʃ] N stile *m*

Pana·ma [ˌpænəˈmɑː] N Panama *f*

Panama Canal N canale *m* di Panama

Pana·ma·nian [ˌpænəˈmeɪnɪən] ADJ, N panamense *m/f*

pan·cake [ˈpænˌkeɪk] N frittella, crêpe *f inv*; **as flat as a pancake** (*fig*) piatto(-a) come una tavola

pancake roll N *crêpe ripiena di verdure alla cinese*

pan·cre·as [ˈpæŋkrɪəs] N pancreas *m inv*

pan·da [ˈpændə] N panda *m inv*

pan·dem·ic [pænˈdemɪk] N (*frm, also Med*) pandemia ♦ ADJ (*Med*) pandemico(-a)

pan·de·mo·nium [ˌpændɪˈməʊnɪəm] N pandemonio

pan·der [ˈpændəʳ] VI: **to pander to** (*person, whims*) assecondare; **the government must not pander to terrorists** il governo non deve assecondare i terroristi; **to pander to sb's tastes** piegarsi ai gusti di qn

P & H [ˌpiːəndˈeɪtʃ] N ABBR (*USA*: = *postage and handling*) affrancatura e trasporto

pane [peɪn] N vetro

pan·el [ˈpænl] N 1 (*gen*) pannello; (*of triptych*) tavola; (*of ceiling*) cassettone *m*; (*of instruments, switches*) quadro; **oak panels** pannelli *mpl* di quercia 2 (*Radio, TV: of judges*) giuria; (*of experts, researchers etc*) gruppo; (*in market research*) panel *m inv*; **the only woman on the panel** l'unica donna della giuria ♦ VT (*wall, door*) rivestire di *or* con pannelli

panel game N (*Brit*) quiz *m inv* a squadre

panelling ['pænəlɪŋ], **pan·el·ing** (*USA*) N rivestimento di *or* a pannelli

pan·el·list, pan·el·ist (*USA*) ['pænəlɪst] N partecipante *m/f* (*al quiz, alla tavola rotonda etc*)

pang [pæŋ] N: **a pang of guilt/sadness** un senso di colpa/ tristezza; **without a pang** senza rimpianti; **the pangs of hunger** i morsi della fame; **pangs of conscience** rimorsi *mpl* di coscienza; **to feel pangs of remorse** essere torturato(-a) dal rimorso

pan·han·dler ['pæn,hændlə'] N (*USA fam*) accattone(-a)

pan·ic ['pænɪk] N panico; **to get into a panic about sth** farsi prendere dal panico per qc; **to throw into a panic** (*crowd*) seminare il panico tra; (*person*) gettare in uno stato di agitazione ♦ VI lasciarsi prendere dal panico; **he panicked when he saw the blood** quando ha visto il sangue si è fatto prendere dal panico; **don't panic!** non agitarti!; **don't panic!** non agitarti!

panic buying ['pænɪk'baɪɪŋ] N accaparramento (*di generi alimentari*)

pan·icky ['pænɪkɪ] ADJ (*person*) che si lascia prendere dal panico; (*report*) allarmista; (*decision*) dettato(-a) dal panico

panic-stricken ['pænɪk,strɪkən] ADJ (*person*) preso(-a) dal panico, in preda al panico; (*look*) terrorizzato(-a)

pan·ni·er ['pænɪə'] N (*gen*) paniere *m*; (*on bicycle*) borsa; (*on animal*) bisaccia

pano·ra·ma [,pænə'rɑːmə] N panorama *m*

pano·ram·ic [,pænə'ræmɪk] ADJ panoramico(-a)

pan·sy ['pænzɪ] N (*Bot*) viola del pensiero, pensée *f inv*; (*fam: pej*) checca

pant [pænt] VI ansimare, avere il fiatone; **he was panting for a drink** moriva dalla voglia di bere; **she panted up the stairs** salì le scale ansimando

pan·tech·ni·con [pæn'teknɪkən] N (*Brit*) grosso furgone *m* per traslochi

pan·ther ['pænθə'] N pantera

panties ['pæntɪz] NPL mutandine *fpl*

pan·ti·hose ['pæntɪ,həʊz] N (*USA*) collant *m inv*

pan·to ['pæntəʊ] N (*Brit fam*) = **pantomime**

pan·to·mime ['pæntə,maɪm] N 1 (*at Christmas*) spettacolo natalizio 2 (*mime*) pantomima

pan·try ['pæntrɪ] N dispensa

pants [pænts] NPL (*Brit: underwear*) mutande *fpl*, slip *m inv*; (*USA: trousers*) pantaloni *mpl*, calzoni *mpl*; **bra and pants** reggiseno e mutande; **to catch sb with his pants down** (*fam*) beccare qn in una situazione imbarazzante

pant·suit ['pænt,suːt] N (*USA*) completo *m* pantalone, *inv*

pa·pa·cy ['peɪpəsɪ] N papato

pa·pal ['peɪpəl] ADJ papale, pontificio(-a)

pa·pa·raz·zi [,pæpə'rætsiː] NPL paparazzi *mpl*

pa·per ['peɪpə'] N 1 (*material*) carta; (*wallpaper*) carta da parati, tappezzeria; **a piece of paper** (*odd bit*) un pezzo di carta; (*sheet*) un foglio (di carta); **on paper** sulla carta; **to put sth down on paper** mettere qc per iscritto 2 (*exam questions*) prova scritta, scritto; (*lecture*) relazione *f* 3 (*newspaper*) giornale *m*; **the papers** i giornali; **it was in the papers** era su tutti i giornali; **I saw an advert in the paper** ho visto un annuncio sul giornale; **to write to the papers about sth** scrivere una lettera aperta *or* ai giornali su qc ♦ VT (*wall, room*) tappezzare ♦ ADJ (*towel, cup*) di carta; (*industry*) cartario(-a), della carta; *see also* **papers**

▸ **paper over** VI + PREP: **to paper over the cracks** (*fig*) appianare le divergenze

paper advance N (*on printer*) avanzamento della carta

paper·back ['peɪpə,bæk] N tascabile *m*, paperback *m inv*

paper bag N sacchetto di carta

paper·boy ['peɪpə,bɔɪ] N (*selling*) strillone *m*; (*delivering*) ragazzo che recapita i giornali

paper·clip ['peɪpə,klɪp] N graffetta, clip *f inv*

paper handkerchief N (*also:* **paper hankie**) fazzoletto *or* fazzolettino di carta

paper mill N cartiera

paper money N cartamoneta, moneta cartacea

paper profit N (*Fin*) utile *m* sulla carta

papers ['peɪpəz] NPL (*writings, documents*) carte *fpl*; (*identity papers*) documenti *mpl* (di riconoscimento); **old papers** scartoffie *fpl*; **Churchill's private papers** gli scritti *or* i documenti privati di Churchill

paper shop N giornalaio (*negozio*)

paper·weight ['peɪpə,weɪt] N fermacarte *m inv*

paper·work ['peɪpə,wɜːk] N parte *f* amministrativa di un lavoro; **I've got a lot of paperwork to do** ho un sacco di pratiche da sbrigare

papier-mâché [,pæpjeɪ'mæʃeɪ] N cartapesta

pap·ri·ka ['pæprɪkə] N (*spice*) paprica; (*vegetable*) peperoncino rosso

Pap test ['pæp,test], (*USA*) **Pap smear** ['pæp,smɪə'] N (*Med*) pap-test *m inv*

par [pɑː'] N 1 (*equality of value*) parità, pari *f*; (*Fin: of shares*) valore *m* nominale; **to be on a par with sb/sth** essere allo stesso livello di qn/qc; **at/above/below par** (*Fin*) alla/sopra la/sotto la pari 2 (*average*): **to feel below** *or* **under** *or* **not up to par** (*ill*) non essere *or* non sentirsi in forma; **that's par for the course** (*fig*) è normale; **to be above/below par** (*gen, also Golf*) essere al di sopra/al di sotto della norma

para·ble ['pærəbl] N parabola (*Rel*)

pa·rabo·la [pə'ræbələ] N parabola (*Math*)

para·chute ['pærə'ʃuːt] N paracadute *m inv* ♦ VT paracadutare ♦ VI (*also:* **parachute down**) paracadutarsi

parachute jump N lancio col paracadute

para·chut·ist ['pærə'ʃuːtɪst] N paracadutista *m/f*

pa·rade [pə'reɪd] N (*procession*) sfilata; (*Mil: marchpast*) parata; (*: ceremony, inspection*) rivista; **to be on parade** (*Mil: marching*) sfilare; (*: for inspection*) essere schierato(-a); **a fashion parade** (*Brit*) una sfilata di moda ♦ VT (*troops: in ceremonial order*) schierare in parata; (*: for a march*) far sfilare; (*placard etc*) portare in giro *or* in corteo; (*show off: learning, wealth, new clothes*) fare sfoggio di, sfoggiare, ostentare ♦ VI (*Mil: march*) sfilare; (*: in ceremonial order*) schierarsi in parata; (*boy scouts, demonstrators*) marciare in corteo; **to parade about** *or* **around** (*fam*) pavoneggiarsi; **the strikers paraded through the town** gli scioperanti hanno attraversato la città in corteo

parade ground N piazza d'armi

para·dise ['pærə,daɪs] N paradiso

para·dox ['pærə,dɒks] N paradosso

para·doxi·cal [,pærə'dɒksɪkəl] ADJ paradossale

para·doxi·cal·ly [,pærə'dɒksɪkəlɪ] ADV paradossalmente

par·af·fin ['pærəfɪn], (*USA*) **par·af·fin oil** ['pærəfɪn'ɔɪl] N cherosene *m*; **liquid paraffin** olio di paraffina

paraffin heater N (*Brit*) stufa al cherosene

paraffin lamp N (*Brit*) lampada a petrolio

para·gon ['pærəgən] N: **paragon of virtue** modello di virtù

❏ **paragon** is not translated by the Italian word *paragone*

para·graph ['pærəgrɑːf] N (*gen*) paragrafo; (*in newspaper*) trafiletto; **to begin a new paragraph** andare a capo

Para·guay ['pærə,gwaɪ] N Paraguay *m*

Para·guay·an [,pærə'gwaɪən] ADJ, N paraguaiano(-a)

par·al·lel ['pærəlɛl] ADJ: **parallel (with, to)** parallelo(-a) (a); **the road runs parallel to the railway** la strada corre parallela alla ferrovia ♦ N (*Geom*) parallela; (*Geog*) parallelo; (*Horse-riding*) largo; (*fig*) confronto, paragone *m*, parallelo; **to draw a parallel between** (*fig*) fare un parallelo fra ♦ VT (*fig: equal*) uguagliare; (*: be similar to*) essere analogo(-a) *or* parallelo(-a) a

pa·raly·sis [pə'ræləsɪs] N (*pl* **paralyses**) paralisi *f*

para·lyt·ic [,pærə'lɪtɪk] ADJ (*Med: person*) paralitico(-a); (*: stroke*) di paralisi

para·lyze, para·lyse ['pærə,laɪz] VT (*Med, also fig*) paralizzare; **paralyzed with fear** paralizzato(-a) dalla paura; **his leg is paralyzed** ha la gamba paralizzata

para·lyzed ['pærə,laɪzd] ADJ 1 (*Med*) paralizzato 2 (*fig: immobilized*) paralizzato; **paralyzed with fear** paralizzato dalla paura

para·medic [,pærə'mɛdɪk], **para·medi·cal** [,pærə'mɛdɪkəl] N paramedico

pa·ram·eter [pəˈræmɪtəʳ] N parametro
para·mili·tary [ˌpærəˈmɪlɪtərɪ] ADJ paramilitare
para·mount [ˈpærəˌmaʊnt] ADJ: **of paramount importance** di importanza capitale
para·noia [ˌpærəˈnɔɪə] N paranoia
para·noid [ˈpærəˌnɔɪd] ADJ (*Psych*) paranoico(-a); **paranoid (about)** (*fig*) ossessionato(-a) (da)
para·nor·mal [ˌpærəˈnɔːməl] N: **the paranormal** i fenomeni paranormali ♦ ADJ paranormale
para·pher·na·lia [ˌpærəfəˈneɪlɪə] N armamentario
para·phrase [ˈpærəˌfreɪz] N parafrasi *f inv* ♦ VT parafrasare
para·plegic [ˌpærəˈpliːdʒɪk] ADJ, N paraplegico(-a)
para·psy·chol·ogy [ˌpærəsaɪˈkɒlədʒɪ] N parapsicologia
para·site [ˈpærəˌsaɪt] N parassita *m*
para·sol [ˌpærəˈsɒl] N parasole *m inv*
para·trooper [ˈpærəˌtruːpəʳ] N (*Mil*) paracadutista *m*, parà *m inv*
par·cel [ˈpɑːsl] N (*gen*) pacchetto; (*larger*) pacco; (*of land*) appezzamento; (*fig*: *of fools, liars*) branco; (: *of lies*) mucchio
  ▸ **parcel out** VT + ADV (*inheritance*) dividere; (*land*) distribuire, spartire
  ▸ **parcel up** VT + ADV impacchettare, fare un pacco di
  ❏ **parcel** is not translated by the Italian word *parcella*
parcel bomb N (*Brit*) pacchetto esplosivo
parcel post N servizio pacchi
parch [pɑːtʃ] VT riardere
parched [pɑːtʃt] ADJ (*land, garden*) dissecato(-a), riarso(-a); (*person*) assetato(-a); **parched earth** terra arsa; **I'm parched!** (*fam*) muoio di sete!
parch·ment [ˈpɑːtʃmənt] N pergamena
par·don [ˈpɑːdn] N perdono, scusa; (*Rel*) indulgenza; (*Law*) condono della pena, grazia; **general pardon** amnistia; **a presidential pardon** una grazia del presidente ♦ VT (*forgive*) perdonare; (*Law*) graziare; **to pardon sb for sth/doing sth** perdonare qc a qn/qn per aver fatto qc ♦ EXCL (*apologizing*) mi scusi!; (*not hearing*) scusi?, come?, prego?; (**I beg your) pardon?**, (*USA*) **pardon me?** prego?
pare [pɛəʳ] VT (*nails*) tagliarsi; (*fruit*) sbucciare, pelare
  ▸ **pare down** VT + ADV (*costs*) ridurre, limitare
par·ent [ˈpɛərənt] N padre *m* (or madre *f*); **his parents** i suoi genitori
  ❏ **parent** is not translated by the Italian word *parente*
par·ent·age [ˈpɛərəntɪdʒ] N natali *mpl*; **of unknown parentage** di genitori sconosciuti
pa·ren·tal [pəˈrentl] ADJ dei genitori; (*Bio*) parentale
parent company N società *f inv* madre, *inv*
pa·ren·thesis [pəˈrenθɪsɪs] N (*pl* **parentheses** [pəˈrenθɪsiːz]) parentesi *f inv*; **in parentheses** fra parentesi
par·ent·hood [ˈpɛərənthʊd] N paternità (or maternità)
par·ent·ing [ˈpɛərəntɪŋ] N: **parenting is a full-time occupation** allevare i figli è un lavoro a tempo pieno
Par·is [ˈpærɪs] N Parigi *f*
par·ish [ˈpærɪʃ] N (*Rel*) parrocchia; (*Brit*: *civil*) ≈ comune *m* ♦ ADJ (*church*) parrocchiale; (*hall*) parrocchiale or municipale
parish council N (*Brit*) ≈ consiglio comunale
pa·rish·ion·er [pəˈrɪʃənəʳ] N parrocchiano(-a)
Pa·ris·ian [pəˈrɪzɪən] ADJ, N parigino(-a)
par·ity [ˈpærɪtɪ] N parità
park [pɑːk] N (*gen*) parco; (*public*) giardino pubblico; **why don't we go for a walk in the park?** perché non andiamo al parco a fare una passeggiata?; **a national park** un parco nazionale; **theme park** parco divertimenti; **car park** parcheggio ♦ VT (*Aut*) parcheggiare; **where can I park my car?** dove posso parcheggiare l'auto? ♦ VI (*Aut*) parcheggiare, parcheggiarsi
par·ka [ˈpɑːkə] N eskimo
park and ride N parcheggio di interscambio
park·ing [ˈpɑːkɪŋ] N (*act*) parcheggiare *m*; (*parking space*) parcheggio; **parking is difficult in the city centre** è difficile trovare parcheggio in centro; **"no parking"** "divieto di sosta" ♦ ADJ (*space*) di parcheggio

parking lights NPL luci *fpl* di posizione
parking lot N (*USA*) posteggio, parcheggio
parking meter N parchimetro
parking offence, (*USA*) **parking violation** N infrazione *f* al divieto di sosta
parking place N posto di parcheggio
parking ticket N multa per sosta vietata
parking violation N (*USA*) = **parking offence**
Parkinson's [ˈpɑːkɪnsənz] N (*also*: **Parkinson's disease**) morbo di Parkinson
park·way [ˈpɑːkˌweɪ] N (*USA*) viale *m*
par·lance [ˈpɑːləns] N: **in common/modern parlance** nel linguaggio comune/moderno
par·lia·ment [ˈpɑːləmənt] N parlamento; **to get into parliament** essere eletto(-a) al parlamento
par·lia·men·ta·ry [ˌpɑːləˈmentərɪ] ADJ parlamentare
parlour, parlor (*USA*) [ˈpɑːləʳ] N (*in house*) salotto; **ice-cream parlour** gelateria
par·lous [ˈpɑːləs] ADJ (*old, liter*) periglioso(-a)
Par·me·san [ˌpɑːmɪˈzæn] N (*also*: **Parmesan cheese**) parmigiano
pa·ro·chial [pəˈrəʊkɪəl] ADJ (*of parish*) parrocchiale; (*fig*: *pej*) provinciale, ristretto(-a)
paro·dy [ˈpærədɪ] N parodia ♦ VT parodiare
pa·role [pəˈrəʊl] N (*Law*) libertà condizionale; **on parole** in libertà condizionale; **to break (one's) parole** commettere un atto che ha per conseguenza la revoca della libertà condizionale
par·ox·ysm [ˈpærəkˌsɪzm] N (*Med*) parossismo; (*of laughter, coughing*) convulso; (*of grief, anger*) attacco
par·quet [ˈpɑːkeɪ] N (*also*: **parquet floor**) parquet *m inv*
par·rot [ˈpærət] N pappagallo
parrot-fashion [ˈpærətˌfæʃən] ADV (*learn*) a pappagallo, in modo pappagallesco
par·ry [ˈpærɪ] VT (*blow*) parare; (*fig*: *question*) eludere
par·si·mo·ni·ous [ˌpɑːsɪˈməʊnɪəs] ADJ parsimonioso(-a)
pars·ley [ˈpɑːslɪ] N prezzemolo
pars·nip [ˈpɑːsnɪp] N pastinaca
par·son [ˈpɑːsn] N (*gen*) parroco, prete *m*; (*Church of England*) pastore *m*
part [pɑːt] N **1** (*portion, fragment*) parte *f*; (*of serial*) episodio; **in part** in parte; **it was funny in parts** è stato divertente a tratti; **the first part of the play was boring** la prima parte della commedia era noiosa; **for the most part** nell'insieme, per lo più; **the greater part of it is done** il più è fatto; **for the better part of the day** per la maggior parte della giornata; **two parts of sand to one of cement** due parti di sabbia e una (parte) di cemento; **to be part and parcel of** essere parte integrante di **2** (*Tech*: *component*) pezzo *or* parte *f* (di ricambio); (*Mus*) parte; **soprano part** la parte del soprano; **2-part song** canto a 2 voci; **moving part** parte meccanica; **spare parts** pezzi di ricambio **3** (*role*, *also Theatre*) parte *f*, ruolo; **to take part in sth** prendere parte *or* partecipare a qc; **a lot of people took part in the demonstration** alla manifestazione ha partecipato molta gente; **to have no part in sth** non aver nulla a che fare con qc; **to play a part in sth/doing sth** avere un certo ruolo in qc/nel fare qc; **to look the part** essere perfetto(-a) nella parte; **she got a part in the film** ha ottenuto una parte nel film **4** (*region*) parte *f*; **in these parts** da queste parti; **a lovely part of the country** una bella regione **5** (*behalf, side*) parte *f*; **on his part** da parte sua; **to take sb's part** prendere le parti di qn, parteggiare per qn; **for my part** da parte mia, per quanto mi riguarda; **a mistake on the part of my brother** un errore da parte di mio fratello; **to take sth in good/bad part** prendere bene/male qc **6** (*USA*: *in hair*) scriminatura, riga ♦ ADV (*partly*) in parte; **a part eaten apple** una mela mezza mangiata ♦ VT (*curtains, branches*) scostare; (*lovers*) dividere, separare; (*boxers*) separare; **to part one's hair** farsi la riga *or* la scriminatura (nei capelli) ♦ VI (*boxers*) separarsi; (*curtains*) aprirsi; (*roads*) dividersi; (*rope*: *break*) spezzarsi, rompersi; (*friends, lovers*) lasciarsi; **to part (from sb)** lasciarsi (da qn); **they parted friends** si sono lasciati da buoni amici
  ▸ **part with** VI + PREP (*possessions*) separarsi da, disfarsi di; (*money*) sborsare; **I hate parting with it** mi dispiace disfarmene

par·take [pɑːˈteɪk] (*pt* **partook**, *pp* **partaken** [pɑːˈteɪkən]) vi (*frm*) **1 to partake of sth** consumare qc, prendere qc **2 to partake in an activity** partecipare *or* prender parte ad una attività

par·tial [ˈpɑːʃəl] ADJ (*gen*) parziale; **to be in partial agreement** essere parzialmente *or* in parte d'accordo; **to be partial to sth** (*like*) avere un debole per qc; **partial blindness** cecità *f inv* parziale

par·tial·ly [ˈpɑːʃəlɪ] ADV (*partly*) parzialmente, in parte

par·tici·pant [pɑːˈtɪsɪpənt] N: **participant (in)** partecipante *m*/*f* (a)

par·tici·pate [pɑːˈtɪsɪpeɪt] vi: **to participate (in)** partecipare (a), prendere parte (a)

par·tici·pa·tion [pɑːˌtɪsɪˈpeɪʃən] N: **participation (in)** partecipazione *f* (a)

par·ti·ci·ple [ˈpɑːtɪsɪpl] N participio; **past/present participle** participio passato/presente

par·ti·cle [ˈpɑːtɪkl] N (*Gram, Phys*) particella; (*of dust*) granello; (*of food*) pezzettino; (*fig: of truth, sense*) briciolo

par·ticu·lar [pəˈtɪkjʊləʳ] ADJ **1** (*specific, special*) particolare; **that particular house/train** quella casa/quel treno in particolare; **to pay particular attention to, to take particular care over** fare molta attenzione a; **to place particular emphasis on sth** dare particolare importanza a qc; **in this particular case** in questo caso particolare; **for no particular reason** senza una ragione precisa *or* particolare; **she's a particular friend of mine** è una mia carissima amica **2** (*fastidious, fussy*) pignolo(-a), difficile; (*painstaking*) meticoloso(-a); **to be very particular about** essere molto pignolo(-a) su; **he's particular about his food** è molto difficile nel mangiare; **I'm not particular** per me va bene tutto ♦ N **1** (*detail*) particolare *m* **2 in particular** in particolare, particolarmente; **nothing in particular** nulla in *or* di particolare; *see also* **particulars**

par·ticu·lar·ly [pəˈtɪkjʊləlɪ] ADV (*especially*) particolarmente; **I particularly wanted it for tomorrow** lo volevo proprio per domani; **particularly since ...** soprattutto perché...

part·ing [ˈpɑːtɪŋ] ADJ (*kiss etc*) d'addio; **his parting words** le sue ultime parole; **parting shot** (*fig*) battuta finale; **and with this parting shot he left** e detto ciò se ne andò ♦ N **1** separazione *f*; **we have reached the parting of the ways** (*fig*) a questo punto le nostre strade si dividono **2** (*Brit: in hair*) scriminatura, riga

par·ti·san [ˌpɑːtɪˈzæn] ADJ (*gen*) fazioso(-a); (*fighter*) partigiano(-a); **partisan spirit** spirito di parte ♦ N (*fighter*) partigiano(-a)

par·ti·tion [pɑːˈtɪʃən] N **1** (*wall*) parete *f* divisoria, tramezzo **2** (*of country*) suddivisione *f*, divisione *f* ♦ VT (*country etc*) suddividere, dividere

▸ **partition off** VT + ADV separare con una parete divisoria

part·ly [ˈpɑːtlɪ] ADV parzialmente, in parte

part·ner [ˈpɑːtnəʳ] N (*gen*) compagno(-a), partner *m*/*f inv*; (*Comm*) socio(-a); (*in crime*) complice *m*/*f*; (*Sport*) compagno(-a); (*at dance: male*) cavaliere *m*; (: *female*) dama ♦ VT (*Sport*) essere in coppia con; (*at dance*) accompagnare; (*in individual dance*) ballare con

part·ner·ship [ˈpɑːtnəʃɪp] N (*gen*) associazione *f*; (*Comm*) società *f inv*; **a global partnership of environmental groups** un'associazione mondiale di gruppi ambientalisti; **to take sb into partnership** prendere qn come socio(-a); **to go into partnership (with), form a partnership (with)** mettersi in società (con), associarsi (a); **the two lawyers went into partnership ten years ago** i due avvocati si sono messi in società due anni fa

part payment N acconto

par·tridge [ˈpɑːtrɪdʒ] N pernice *f*

part-time [ˈpɑːtˈtaɪm] ADV, ADJ part-time *inv*; **a part-time job** un lavoro part time; **she works part-time** lavora part time

part-timer [ˌpɑːtˈtaɪməʳ] N (*also*: **part-time worker**) impiegato(-a) *or* lavoratore(-trice) part-time *inv*

par·ty [ˈpɑːtɪ] N **1** (*Pol*) partito; **the Conservative/Labour Party** il partito conservatore/laburista **2** (*group*) gruppo; (*Mil: team*) squadra; **a party of travellers/tourists** una comitiva di viaggiatori/turisti **3** (*celebration*) festa; **to have** *or* **give** *or* **throw a party** dare una festa *or* un party; **birthday party** festa di compleanno **4** (*Law*) parte *f* (in causa); **the**

parties to a dispute le parti in causa; **to be a party to a crime** essere coinvolto(-a) in un reato; **he refused to be a party to such an agreement** si è rifiutato di entrare in un accordo del genere ♦ ADJ (*leader*) del *or* di partito; (*dress, finery*) della festa

party line N **1** (*Pol*) linea del partito **2** (*Telec*) duplex *m inv*

pass [pɑːs] N **1** (*permit*) lasciapassare *m inv*; (*for bus, train*) tesserino; (*Mil, etc*) permesso; **bus pass** abbonamento dell'autobus **2** (*Geog: in mountains*) passo, gola, valico; **the pass was blocked with snow** il valico era bloccato dalla neve **3** (*Sport*) passaggio **4** (*in exams*) sufficienza; **to get a pass in German** prendere la sufficienza in tedesco; **I got six passes** ho preso la sufficienza in sei materie **5 things have come to a pretty pass** ecco a cosa siamo arrivati **6 to make a pass at sb** (*fam*) fare delle proposte *or* delle avances a qn ♦ VT **1** (*move past*) passare, oltrepassare; (*in opposite direction*) incrociare; (*Aut: overtake*) sorpassare, superare; **they passed each other on the way** si sono incrociati per strada; **I pass his house on my way to school** passo davanti a casa sua andando a scuola **2** (*hand, give*) (far) passare; (*Sport: ball*) passare; **could you pass me the salt, please?** mi passeresti il sale, per favore?; **he passed his hand over his forehead** si passò la mano sulla fronte; **to pass a thread through a hole** far passare un filo attraverso un foro; **to pass sb sth** *or* **sth to sb** passare qc a qn **3** (*Scol: exam*) superare, passare; (: *candidate*) promuovere; **I hope I'll pass the exam** spero di passare l'esame **3** (*approve: motion, plan*) approvare, votare **5** (*spend: time*) passare, trascorrere; **we passed the weekend pleasantly** abbiamo trascorso *or* passato piacevolmente il fine settimana; **it passes the time** fa passare il tempo **6** (*express: remark*) fare; (: *opinion*) esprimere; **to pass the time of day with sb** scambiarsi i (soliti) convenevoli ♦ VI **1** (*come, go*): **to pass (through)** passare (per); (*Aut: overtake*) sorpassare; **he passed by the cinema** è passato davanti al cinema; **sales have passed the £1 million mark** le vendite hanno superato il milione di sterline; **to pass out of sight** sparire alla vista; **to pass into oblivion** cadere nell'oblio; **to pass into history** passare alla storia **2** (*be accepted: behaviour*) essere accettabile; (: *plan*) essere approvato(-a); **she could pass for twenty-five** potrebbe passare per una venticinquenne; **what passes for art these days** quel che si definisce arte oggigiorno; **is this okay?** — **oh, it'll pass** questo va bene? — sì, può andare; **I decided to let it pass** ho deciso di lasciar correre **3** (*time, day*) passare; **the time has passed quickly** il tempo è passato in fretta; **how time passes!** come passa il tempo! **4** (*pain*) passare; (*memory, opportunity*) sfuggire **5** (*in exam*) essere promosso(-a) **6** (*happen*) accadere; **all that passed between them** tutto quello che c'è stato fra loro; **should it come to pass that ...** (*frm*) dovesse accadere che... **7** (*Cards*) passare

▸ **pass along** VT + ADV far passare

▸ **pass around** VT + ADV = **pass round**

▸ **pass away** VI + ADV (*euph: die*) mancare, spegnersi

▸ **pass back** VT + ADV (*object*) passare indietro; **I will now pass you back to the studio** (*Radio, TV*) e ora ridiamo la linea allo studio

▸ **pass by** VI + ADV passare (di qui *or* lì) ♦ VT + ADV (*ignore*) ignorare, passar sopra a; **life has passed her by** non ha davvero vissuto

▸ **pass down** VT + ADV (*customs, inheritance*) tramandare, trasmettere

▸ **pass off** VI + ADV (*happen*) svolgersi, andare; (*wear off: faintness, headache*) passare ♦ VT + ADV: **to pass sb/sth off as** far passare qn/qc per

▸ **pass on** VI + ADV (*euph: die*) spegnersi, mancare; (*proceed*): **to pass on (to)** passare (a) ♦ VT + ADV (*hand on*): **to pass on (to)** (*news, information, object*) passare (a); (*cold, illness*) attaccare (a); (*benefits*) trasmettere (a); (*price rises*) riversare (su)

▸ **pass out** VI + ADV (*become unconscious*) svenire; (*Brit Mil*) uscire dall'accademia

▸ **pass over** VI + ADV (*euph: die*) spirare ♦ VT + ADV (*topic*) ignorare; (*employee, candidate*) non prendere in considerazione

▸ **pass round, pass around** VT + ADV (*bottle, photographs*) far girare; **could you pass the vegetables round?** potrebbe far passare la verdura?

▸ **pass through** VI + ADV essere di passaggio ♦ VT + ADV (*country, city*) passare per; (*hardships*) attraversare

▸ **pass up** VT + ADV (*opportunity*) lasciarsi sfuggire, perdere

pass·able [ˈpɑːsəbl] ADJ 1 (*tolerable*) passabile; (*work*) accettabile; **his French is passable** il suo francese è passabile 2 (*road*) transitabile, praticabile; (*river*) attraversabile

pas·sage [ˈpæsɪdʒ] N 1 (*way through*) passaggio; (*corridor*) corridoio 2 (*Naut: voyage*) traversata; **to grant sb safe passage** garantire a qn di passare incolume 3 (*passing*) passare m; (*of bill through parliament*) iter m inv; **with the passage of time** (*frm*) col passar del tempo 4 (*section: of book*) brano, passo; (*of music*) brano; **read the passage carefully** leggi attentamente il brano

pas·sen·ger [ˈpæsɪndʒəʳ] N (*in boat, plane, car*) passeggero(-a); (*on train*) viaggiatore(-trice), passeggero(-a) ♦ ADJ (*aircraft, liner*) di linea, passeggeri inv; (*train*) viaggiatori inv

passer-by [ˈpɑːsəˈbaɪ] N (*pl* passers-by) passante m/f

pass·ing [ˈpɑːsɪŋ] ADJ (*fleeting: fancy, thought*) passeggero(-a); (*: moment*) fuggevole; (*: glance, remark*) di sfuggita; (*car, person*) di passaggio ♦ N (*of customs: also euph: death*) scomparsa; **with the passing of the years** col passar degli anni; **to mention sth in passing** accennare a qc di sfuggita; **to mention sth in passing** accennare a qc di sfuggita

passing place N (*Aut*) piazzola (di sosta)

pas·sion [ˈpæʃən] N 1 passione f; **to have a passion for sth** aver la passione di qc, avere una passione per qc; **his passion for seafood** la sua passione per i frutti di mare; **his passion for accuracy** il suo amore per la precisione; **to get into a passion (about sth)** andare su tutte le furie (per qc) 2 (*Rel*): **the Passion** la Passione

pas·sion·ate [ˈpæʃənɪt] ADJ (*embrace, speech*) appassionato(-a); (*temperament, person*) passionale; (*believer*) convinto(-a); (*desire*) ardente

passion fruit N frutto della passione

Passion Play N rappresentazione f della Passione di Cristo

pas·sive [ˈpæsɪv] ADJ (*gen, also Gram*) passivo(-a) ♦ N passivo; **in the passive** al passivo

passive smoking N fumo passivo

pass·key [ˈpɑːsˌkiː] N passe-partout m inv

Pass·over [ˈpɑːsˌəʊvəʳ] N Pasqua ebraica

pass·port [ˈpɑːspɔːt] N passaporto; (*fig*): **passport (to)** chiave f (di)

passport control N controllo m passaporti, inv

passport office N ufficio m passaporti pl inv

pass·word [ˈpɑːsˌwɜːd] N (*also Comput*) parola f d'ordine

past [pɑːst] ADV: **to walk past, go past** passare; **to run** or **dash past** passare di corsa; **the days flew past** i giorni sono volati (via) ♦ PREP 1 (*in place: in front of*) davanti a; (*: beyond*) oltre, di là da, dopo; **I go past the school every day** passo davanti alla scuola ogni giorno; **it's just past the church** è appena oltre la chiesa 2 (*in time*) passato(-a); **it's past midnight** è mezzanotte passata; **quarter/half past four** le quattro e un quarto/e mezzo; **at twenty past four** alle quattro e venti 3 (*beyond the limits of*) al di là di, oltre; **it's past belief** è assolutamente incredibile; **I'm past caring** non me ne importa più nulla; **she's past forty** ha passato i quaranta; **to be past it** (*fam: person*) essere finito(-a); (*: object*) essere da buttar via; **I wouldn't put it past her to do it** (*fam*) non sarei affatto sorpreso se lo facesse ♦ ADJ (*gen, also Gram*) passato(-a); (*president, pupil*) ex inv; **for some time past** da qualche tempo; **for the past few days** da qualche giorno, in questi ultimi giorni; **for the past 3 days** negli ultimi 3 giorni; **in the past 5 years** negli ultimi 5 anni; **in past years** negli anni passati; **those days are past now** è passato quel tempo ♦ N passato; **in the past** in or nel passato; (*Gram*) al passato; **it's a thing of the past** è una cosa del passato

pas·ta [ˈpæstə] N (*Culin*) pasta

paste [peɪst] N 1 (*substance, consistency*) impasto; (*glue*) colla; **fish paste** pâté m inv di pesce 2 (*gems*) strass m inv ♦ ADJ (*jewellery*) di strass ♦ VT (*put glue on*) spalmare di colla, collare; (*fasten with glue*) incollare; **to paste sth to the wall** appiccicare qc al muro

pas·tel [ˈpæstəl] N (*crayon, drawing*) pastello; (*colour*) colore m pastello, inv ♦ ADJ (*colour*) pastello inv; (*drawing*) a pastello

pas·teur·ized [ˈpæstəˌraɪzd] ADJ pastorizzato(-a)

pas·tille [ˈpæstɪl] N pastiglia

pas·time [ˈpɑːsˌtaɪm] N passatempo

past master N: **to be a past master at** essere molto esperto(-a) in

pas·tor [ˈpɑːstəʳ] N (*Rel*) pastore m

pas·to·ral [ˈpɑːstərəl] ADJ (*land*) da pascolo; (*scene, poetry, also Rel*) pastorale

past participle N participio passato

pas·try [ˈpeɪstrɪ] N (*dough*) pasta (*per rustici, dolci*); (*cake*) pasta, pasticcino

pas·ture [ˈpɑːstʃəʳ] N pascolo; **to put animals out to pasture** condurre gli animali al pascolo; **to move on to new pastures** (*fig*) cambiare aria

pasty¹ [ˈpeɪstɪ] N (*pie*) sfogliatina salata ripiena di carne e patate

pasty² [ˈpeɪstɪ] ADJ (*comp* -ier, *superl* -iest) (*complexion*) smorto(-a)

pat¹ [pæt] N 1 (*with hand*) colpetto (affettuoso); (*to animal*) carezza; **to give sb/o.s. a pat on the back** (*fig*) congratularsi or compiacersi con qn/se stesso; **he deserves a pat on the back** bisogna congratularsi con lui 2 (*of butter*) panetto ♦ VT (*hair, face etc*) dare dei colpetti leggeri a; (*dog*) accarezzare; (*sb's shoulder etc*) dare un colpetto (affettuoso) su

pat² [pæt] ADJ, ADV: **the answer came** or **was too pat** la risposta è stata troppo pronta; **he has it down pat** (*USA*) lo conosce or sa a menadito

patch [pætʃ] N (*piece of cloth, material*) toppa, pezza; (*on tyre* or *tire*) toppa; (*eye patch*) benda; (*area of colour, spot*) macchia; (*piece of land*) appezzamento, pezzo; **a jacket with patches on the elbows** una giacca con le toppe sui gomiti; **a patch of blue sky** un pezzetto di cielo azzurro; **a patch of grass** uno spiazzo erboso; **a vegetable patch** un orticello; **a bald patch** una calvizie incipiente; **a bad patch** un brutto periodo; **the team is going through a bad patch** la squadra sta attraversando un brutto periodo; **it's not a patch on the other one** (*fam*) non vale neanche la metà dell'altro ♦ VT (*garment, hole*) rattoppare, mettere una pezza a

▸ **patch together** VT + ADV (*cobble together: agreement, strategy*) mettere insieme alla meglio; (*article, report*) cucire insieme alla meglio

▸ **patch up** VT + ADV (*clothes*) rattoppare; (*car, machine*) riparare alla meglio; (*quarrel*) appianare; (*marriage*) rimettere in sesto

patch·work [ˈpætʃˌwɜːk] N patchwork m inv; **a patchwork of fields** (*fig*) un mosaico di campi ♦ ADJ (*quilt*) patchwork inv

patchy [ˈpætʃɪ] ADJ (*comp* -ier, *superl* -iest) (*performance etc*) pieno(-a) di alti e bassi; (*knowledge*) incompleto(-a); (*fog*) a banchi; (*colour*) irregolare

pate [peɪt] N: **a bald pate** una testa pelata

pâté [ˈpæteɪ] N pâté m inv

pa·tent [ˈpeɪtənt] ADJ (*obvious*) evidente, palese ♦ N brevetto; **to take out a patent on sth** far brevettare qc ♦ VT brevettare

❏ **patent** is not translated by the Italian word *patente*

patent leather N vernice f (*pellame*)

pa·tent·ly [ˈpeɪtəntlɪ] ADV palesemente

patent medicine N prodotto medicinale

Patent Office N: **the Patent Office** l'ufficio brevetti

pa·ter·nal [pəˈtɜːnl] ADJ paterno(-a)

pa·ter·nity [pəˈtɜːnɪtɪ] N paternità

paternity leave N congedo di paternità

paternity suit N (*Law*) causa di paternità

path [pɑːθ] N (*pl* paths [pɑːðz]) 1 (*gen*) sentiero, viottolo; (*in garden*) vialetto; (*fig*) strada, via; **a forest path** un sentiero nella foresta; **some men blocked my path** degli uomini mi bloccavano la strada 2 (*of river*) corso; (*of sun, missile, planet*) traiettoria

pa·thet·ic [pəˈθetɪk] ADJ 1 (*pitiful*) patetico(-a), toccante 2 (*very bad*) penoso(-a), pietoso(-a); **a pathetic sight** uno spettacolo patetico; **his pathetic excuses** le sue scuse penose

patho·logi·cal [ˌpæθəˈlɒdʒɪkl] ADJ (*also fig*) patologico(-a)

pa·tholo·gist [pəˈθɒlədʒɪst] N patologo(-a)

pa·thol·ogy [pə'θɒlədʒɪ] N patologia
pa·thos ['peɪθɒs] N pathos *m inv*
path·way ['pɑːθ,weɪ] N sentiero, viottolo
pa·tience ['peɪʃəns] N 1 pazienza; to lose one's patience spazientirsi; to lose one's patience with sb/sth perdere la pazienza con qn/qc; he hasn't got much patience non ha molta pazienza; he has no patience with children non ha pazienza con i bambini 2 (*Brit*: *Cards*) solitario; to play patience fare un solitario
pa·tient ['peɪʃənt] ADJ paziente; to be patient with sb essere paziente *or* aver pazienza con qn ◆ N (*Med*) paziente *m/f*, malato(-a)
pa·tient·ly ['peɪʃəntlɪ] ADV pazientemente
pa·tio ['pætɪəʊ] N terrazza
pa·tri·ot ['peɪtrɪət] N patriota *m/f*
pat·ri·ot·ic ['pætrɪ'ɒtɪk] ADJ patriottico(-a)
pat·ri·ot·ism ['pætrɪə,tɪzəm] N patriottismo
pa·trol [pə'trəʊl] N 1 (*gen*) ronda, giro d'ispezione; (*by plane*) ricognizione *f*; (*by boat*) perlustrazione *f*; to be on patrol essere di pattuglia; essere in ricognizione; essere in perlustrazione 2 (*patrol unit*) pattuglia ◆ VT pattugliare ◆ VI essere di pattuglia; to patrol up and down andare avanti e indietro
patrol boat N guardacoste *m inv*
patrol car N autopattuglia (della polizia)
patrol·man [pə'trəʊlmən] N (*pl* -men) 1 (*USA*) agente *m* di polizia 2 (*Aut*) membro del personale del soccorso stradale
pa·tron ['peɪtrən] N (*of artist*) mecenate *m/f*; (*of charity*) benefattore(-trice); (*of society*) patrono(-essa); (*of shop, hotel*) cliente *m/f* abituale; patron of the arts mecenate *m/f*
pat·ron·age ['pætrənɪdʒ] N (*gen*) patrocinio; (*of shop etc*) frequentazione *f*; under the patronage of sotto l'alto patrocinio *or* patronato di; patronage of the arts mecenatismo
pat·ron·ize ['pætrə,naɪz] VT 1 (*fig*: *treat condescendingly*) trattare con condiscendenza; don't patronize me! non trattarmi con condiscendenza! 2 (*shop*) essere cliente abituale di; (*cinema*) frequentare
pat·ron·iz·ing ['pætrə,naɪzɪŋ] ADJ condiscendente
patron saint N patrono(-a)
pat·ter ['pætə'] N (*comedian's*) monologo; (*conjuror's*) chiacchiere *fpl*; (*sales talk*) discorsetto imbonitore
pat·ter ['pætə'] N (*of feet*) scalpiccio; (*of rain*) picchiettio ◆ VI (*person*) trotterellare; (*rain*) picchiettare
pat·tern ['pætən] N 1 (*design*) motivo, disegno; a geometric pattern un motivo geometrico 2 (*Sewing*) modello (di carta), cartamodello; (*fig*) modello; pattern of events sequenza degli avvenimenti; behaviour patterns tipi *mpl* di comportamento; the three attacks follow the same pattern le tre aggressioni seguono lo stesso schema 3 (*sample*) campione *m* ◆ VT (*model*): to pattern a dress on fare un vestito sul modello di; to pattern o.s. on sb/sth prendere a modello qn/qc
pat·terned ['pætənd] ADJ a disegni, a motivi; (*material*) fantasia *inv*
pau·city ['pɔːsɪtɪ] N (*frm*) scarsità
paunch [pɔːntʃ] N pancia
pau·per ['pɔːpə'] N indigente *m/f*; pauper's grave fossa comune
pause [pɔːz] N (*gen*) pausa; (*Mus*) pausa; (*sign*) corona; there was a pause while ... ci fu un momento di attesa mentre... ◆ VI (*gen*) fermarsi un momento; (*in speech*) fare una pausa; to pause for breath fermarsi un attimo per riprendere fiato
pave [peɪv] VT (*gen*) lastricare; (*road*) pavimentare, lastricare; the street was paved last year la strada è stata pavimentata l'anno scorso; to pave the way for (*fig*: *person*) spianare la strada a; (: *changes, reforms*) aprire la via a
pave·ment ['peɪvmənt] N (*Brit*) marciapiede *m*; (*USA*) pavimentazione *f* stradale
  ❑ **pavement** is not translated by the Italian word *pavimento*
pa·vil·ion [pə'vɪlɪən] N (*gen*) padiglione *m*; (*Sport*) tribuna annessa ad un campo da cricket in cui sono anche alloggiati gli spogliatoi
pav·ing ['peɪvɪŋ] N pavimentazione *f*

paving stone N lastra di pavimentazione
paw [pɔː] N (*of animal*: *also fam*: *hand*) zampa ◆ VT 1 (*subj*: *animal*) dare una zampata a; to paw the ground (*also fig*) scalpitare 2 (*pej*: *sexually*) palpare, mettere le zampe addosso a
pawn¹ [pɔːn] N (*Chess*) pedone *m*; (*fig*) pedina; to be sb's pawn lasciarsi manovrare da qn
pawn² [pɔːn] N: in pawn impegnato(-a) al monte di pietà; (*article pledged*) pegno; to leave *or* put sth in pawn impegnare qc ◆ VT impegnare, dare in pegno
pawn·broker ['pɔːn,brəʊkə'] N prestatore(-trice) su pegno
pawn·shop ['pɔːn,ʃɒp] N monte *m* di pietà
pay [peɪ] (*pt, pp* paid) N (*gen*) paga; to be in sb's pay essere pagato(-a) da *or* essere al servizio di qn ◆ VT 1 (*gen*) pagare; (*debt, account*) saldare, pagare; he paid him £10 gli ha dato 10 sterline; to pay for sth pagare qc; I paid £15 for that record quel disco l'ho pagato 15 sterline; how much did you pay for it? quanto l'hai pagato?; to be *or* get paid on Fridays prendere *or* riscuotere la paga il venerdì; a badly paid worker un(-a) lavoratore(-trice) mal pagato(-a); they pay me more on Sundays la domenica mi pagano di più; that's what you're paid for sei pagato per questo; to pay one's way (*to contribute one's share*) pagare la propria parte; (*to remain solvent*: *company*) coprire le spese; to put paid to (*plan, person*) rovinare; (*trip*) impedire; to pay the penalty (*fig*) pagare le conseguenze; to pay dividends (*Fin*) pagare dividendi; (*fig*) dare buoni frutti 2 (*be profitable to, also fig*) convenire a; it won't pay you to do that non ti conviene farlo 3 (*attention*) fare, prestare; (*homage*) rendere; (*respects*) porgere; I wasn't paying attention to what the teacher was saying non stavo prestando attenzione a quello che diceva l'insegnante; *see* visit ◆ VI 1 pagare; to pay in advance pagare in anticipo; don't worry, I'll pay non preoccuparti, pagherò io; can I pay by cheque? posso pagare con un assegno?; I paid by credit card ho pagato con la carta di credito 2 (*be profitable*) rendere, convenire; the business doesn't pay l'attività non rende *or* non è redditizia; it pays to be courteous ci si guadagna sempre ad essere gentile; it pays to advertise far pubblicità conviene sempre; it pays to shop around conviene confrontare i prezzi; crime doesn't pay il delitto non paga 3 (*fig*: *to suffer*) pagare; I'll make you pay for this! te la farò pagare!
  ▸ **pay back** VT + ADV 1 restituire; to pay sb back rimborsare qn; I'll pay you back tomorrow ti restituisco i soldi domani 2 (*in revenge*) farla pagare a qn; to pay sb back for doing sth farla pagare a qn per aver fatto qc
  ▸ **pay down** VT + ADV versare un acconto di
  ▸ **pay for** VI + PREP pagare
  ▸ **pay in** VT + ADV versare, depositare
  ▸ **pay off** VT + ADV 1 (*debts*) saldare; (*creditor*) pagare; (*mortgage*) estinguere; to pay sth off in instalments pagare qc a rate 2 (*discharge*) licenziare ◆ VI + ADV (*scheme, ruse*) funzionare; (*patience, decision*) dare dei frutti
  ▸ **pay out** VT + ADV 1 (*money*) sborsare, tirar fuori; (*subj*: *cashier*) pagare 2 (*rope*) far allentare
  ▸ **pay up** VT + ADV, VI + ADV saldare, pagare
pay·able ['peɪəbl] ADJ pagabile; to make a cheque payable to sb intestare un assegno a (nome di) qn
pay-as-you-go [,peɪəʒə'gəʊ] N: pay-as-you-go phone telefono con scheda prepagata
pay award N aumento salariale
pay·day ['peɪ,deɪ] N giorno di paga
payee [peɪ'iː] N beneficiario(-a)
pay envelope N (*USA*) = pay packet
pay·ing ['peɪɪŋ] ADJ (*business, scheme*) redditizio(-a)
pay·load ['peɪ,ləʊd] N carico utile
pay·ment ['peɪmənt] N (*gen*) pagamento; (*of debt, account, interest*) saldo, pagamento; (*fig*: *reward*) ricompensa; advance payment (*part sum*) anticipo, acconto; (*total sum*) pagamento anticipato; deferred payment, payment by instalments pagamento dilazionato *or* a rate; payment in full (pagamento a) saldo; payment on account acconto; payment by results = premio di produzione; in payment of (*sum owed*) come saldo di; in payment for, as payment for (*goods*) come pagamento di; (*help, efforts, kindness*) in cambio

di, come ricompensa per; **on payment of £5** dietro pagamento di 5 sterline

payout N 1 pagamento 2 *(in competition)* premio

pay packet, pay envelope *(USA)* N busta *f* paga, *inv*

pay·phone [ˈpeɪ.fəʊn], **pay station** *(USA)* N cabina telefonica

pay·roll [ˈpeɪ.rəʊl] N *(list)* lista del personale; *(money)* paga (di tutto il personale); *(employees)* personale *m*; **to be on a firm's payroll** far parte dell'organico di una ditta

pay slip *(Brit)* busta *f* paga, *inv*

pay station N *(USA)* = payphone

pay television N televisione *f* a pagamento, pay-tv *f inv*

pay·wall [ˈpeɪwɔːl] N *(Comput)* paywall *m inv*

PBS [ˌpiːbiːˈes] N ABBR *(USA: = Public Broadcasting Service)* servizio che collabora alla realizzazione di programmi per la rete televisiva nazionale

PBX [ˌpiːbiːˈeks] ABBR *(Telec: = private branch exchange)* sistema telefonico con centralino

PC [ˌpiːˈsiː] N ABBR 1 *(= personal computer)* PC *m inv* 2 *(Brit)* = police constable ♦ ABBR *(Brit)* = Privy Councillor ♦ ADJ ABBR = politically correct

pc [ˌpiːˈsiː] ABBR 1 *(= postcard)* CP *(= cartolina postale)* 2 = per cent

PD [ˌpiːˈdiː] N ABBR *(USA)* = police department

pd ABBR = paid

PDA [ˌpiːdiːˈeɪ] N ABBR = personal digital assistant *(Comput)* PDA *m inv*

PDQ ABBR *(fam)* = pretty damn quick

PDT [ˌpiːdiːˈtiː] ABBR *(USA: = Pacific Daylight Time)* ora estiva nel fuso orario del Pacifico

PE [ˌpiːˈiː] N ABBR *(= physical education)* educazione fisica ♦ ABBR *(Canada: = Prince Edward Island)*

pea [piː] N pisello; **green peas** pisellini *mpl*

peace [piːs] N *(gen)* pace *f*; **to be at peace with sb/sth** essere in pace con qn/qc; **he is at peace** *(euph: dead)* riposa in pace; **to make peace between** rappacificare; **to make one's peace with** fare la pace con; **peace of mind** tranquillità di spirito; **peace and quiet** pace e tranquillità; **to keep the peace** *(subj: police officer)* mantenere l'ordine pubblico; *(: citizen)* rispettare l'ordine pubblico; *(fig)* calmare le acque

peace·able [ˈpiːsəbl] ADJ pacifico(-a)

peace·ful [ˈpiːsfʊl] ADJ *(person, coexistence)* pacifico(-a); *(demonstration)* non violento(-a); *(period)* di pace; *(place, life, sleep)* tranquillo(-a); **a peaceful demonstration** una manifestazione pacifica; **a peaceful afternoon** un pomeriggio tranquillo

peace·keep·ing [ˈpiːsˌkiːpɪŋ] ADJ *(operation, force)* di pace; **peacekeeping force** forza di pace ♦ N mantenimento della pace; **troops responsible for peacekeeping** truppe *fpl* responsabili del mantenimento della pace

peace offering N *(fig)* dono in segno di riconciliazione

peach [piːtʃ] N 1 *(fruit)* pesca; *(tree)* pesco 2 *(fam)*: **she's a peach** è un amore ♦ ADJ *(blossom)* di pesco; *(colour)* (color) pesca *inv*

pea·cock [ˈpiːkɒk] N pavone *m*

peak [piːk] N *(of mountain)* vetta, cima; *(mountain itself)* picco; *(of roof etc)* cima; *(of cap)* visiera; *(on graph)* vertice *m*; *(fig: of power, career)* apice *m*, vertice; **to be at its peak** *(fame, career, empire)* essere all'apice; *(business)* essere nella fase culminante; *(traffic, demand)* aver raggiunto il livello massimo; **he was at the peak of fitness** era al massimo della forma fisica ♦ ADJ *(demand, production)* massimo(-a)

peak hours NPL ore *fpl* di punta

peak period N periodo di punta

peak rate N tariffa ore di punta

peaky [ˈpiːkɪ] ADJ *(comp -ier, superl -iest)* *(Brit fam)* sbattuto(-a); **I'm feeling a bit peaky** mi sento un po' giù

peal [piːl] N *(sound of bells)* scampanio; **peal of thunder** fragore *m* di tuono; **peals of laughter** scoppi *mpl* di risa ♦ VT suonare (a distesa) ♦ VI *(also: **peal out**)* *(bell)* suonare (a distesa); *(thunder)* rimbombare

pea·nut [ˈpiːˌnʌt] N arachide *f*, nocciolina americana; **a packet of peanuts** un pacchetto di nocciolina americane; **to work for peanuts** *(fam)* lavorare per una miseria

peanut butter N burro di arachidi

pear [pɛə'] N *(fruit)* pera; *(tree)* pero

pearl [pɜːl] N perla; **pearl of wisdom** *(fig)* perla di saggezza; **to cast pearls before swine** *(fig)* gettare le perle ai porci ♦ ADJ *(necklace, brooch)* di perle; *(buttons)* di madreperla

peas·ant [ˈpezənt] N contadino(-a) ♦ ADJ *(life)* dei contadini; *(societies)* contadino(-a); *(dress)* da contadino(-a)

peat [piːt] N torba

peb·ble [ˈpebl] N ciottolo

peck [pek] N *(of bird)* beccata; *(fam: kiss)* bacetto; **to take a peck at** beccare; **he gave me a peck on the cheek** mi ha dato un bacetto sulla guancia ♦ VT *(subj: bird: grain)* beccare; *(: person)* dare una beccata a; *(hole)* fare a furia di beccate ♦ VI: **to peck at** *(subj: bird)* beccare; *(: person: food)* mangiucchiare; **he pecked at his food** sbocconcellò il suo cibo

peck·ing or·der [ˈpekɪŋˌɔːdə'] N *(fig)* ordine *m* gerarchico

peck·ish [ˈpekɪʃ] ADJ *(Brit fam)*: **to feel a bit peckish** avere un languorino

pe·cu·li·ar [pɪˈkjuːlɪə'] ADJ 1 *(strange: idea, smell)* strano(-a), curioso(-a); **he's a peculiar person** è un tipo strano; **it tastes peculiar** ha un sapore strano 2 *(particular: importance, qualities)* particolare; **it has its own peculiar beauty** ha una sua bellezza particolare; **peculiar to** caratteristico(-a) di, tipico(-a) di; **it is a phrase peculiar to him** è un modo di dire tutto suo

pe·cu·li·ar·ity [pɪˌkjuːlɪˈærɪtɪ] N peculiarità *f inv*

pe·cu·ni·ary [pɪˈkjuːnɪərɪ] ADJ pecuniario(-a)

ped·al [ˈpedl] N pedale *m* ♦ VI pedalare; **to pedal up/down** pedalare su per/giù per ♦ VT: **she pedalled her bicycle up the hill** salì la collina in bicicletta

peda·lo [ˈpedələʊ] N pedalò *m inv*

pe·dan·tic [pɪˈdæntɪk] ADJ pedante, pedantesco(-a)

ped·dle [ˈpedl] VT *(goods)* andare in giro a vendere; *(drugs)* spacciare; *(gossip)* mettere in giro

ped·dler [ˈpedlə'] N *(esp USA)* = pedlar

ped·es·tal [ˈpedɪstl] N piedistallo; **to put sb on a pedestal** *(fig)* mettere qn su un piedistallo

pe·des·trian [pɪˈdestrɪən] N pedone *m*; **cyclists and pedestrians** ciclisti e pedoni ♦ ADJ 1 *(pej: style, speech)* prosaico(-a), pedestre 2 *(access)* pedonale

pedestrian crossing N *(Brit)* passaggio pedonale

pedestrian mall N *(USA)* zona pedonale

pedestrian precinct N *(Brit)* zona pedonale

pedi·gree [ˈpedɪˌgriː] N *(of person)* discendenza, stirpe *f*; *(of animal)* pedigree *m inv* ♦ ADJ di razza (pura); **a pedigree dog** un cane di razza

ped·lar [ˈpedlə'] N venditore(-trice) ambulante; *(of drugs)* spacciatore(-trice)

pee [piː] N *(fam)*: **to have a pee** fare la pipì

peek [piːk] N sbirciatina; **to take** *or* **have a peek at** dare una sbirciatina a; **I had a peek at his diary** ho dato una sbirciatina al suo diario ♦ VI sbirciare

peel [piːl] N *(gen)* buccia; *(of orange, lemon etc)* scorza, buccia; **apple peel** buccia di mela; **orange peel** scorza d'arancia ♦ VT *(fruit etc)* sbucciare; *(shrimps etc)* sgusciare; **shall I peel the potatoes?** sbuccio le patate?; **to keep one's eyes peeled** *(fam)* stare all'erta ♦ VI *(wallpaper)* staccarsi; *(paint etc)* scrostarsi; *(skin)* squamarsi; *(person)* spellarsi; **my nose is peeling** mi si sta spellando il naso

▸ **peel away** VI + ADV *(skin)* squamarsi; *(paint)* scrostarsi; *(wallpaper)* staccarsi ♦ VT + ADV *(gen)* staccare; *(paint)* scrostare; *(wrapper)* togliere

▸ **peel back** VT + ADV togliere, levare

▸ **peel off** VT + ADV 1 = peel away 2 *(clothes)* togliersi, sfilarsi ♦ VI + ADV = peel away

peel·er [ˈpiːlə'] N *(potato knife)* pelapatate *m inv*

peel·ings [ˈpiːlɪŋz] NPL bucce *fpl*

peep¹ [piːp] N *(of bird)* squittio; *(of chick)* pigolio; *(of whistle)* trillo; **we haven't heard a peep out of them** *(fam)* non hanno aperto bocca ♦ VI *(bird)* squittire; *(whistle)* trillare

peep² [piːp] N *(look)* sbirciata, sguardo furtivo; **to take** *or* **have a peep (at sth)** dare una sbirciata a qc; **he took a peep at his watch** ha dato un'occhiata all'orologio ♦ VI: **to peep at sth** sbirciare qc; **she peeped to see what he was doing** ha dato un'occhiata per vedere cosa stava facendo

▸ **peep out** VI + ADV *(Brit)* far capolino; **the sun peeped** out from behind the clouds il sole fece capolino da dietro le nuvole

peep·hole ['piːpˌhəʊl] N spioncino

peer¹ [pɪə'] N (noble) pari m inv; (equal) pari m/f inv, uguale m/f; **they get on well with their peers** vanno d'accordo con i loro pari; **children who are cleverer than their peers** bambini più intelligenti dei loro coetanei

peer² [pɪə'] VI: **to peer at sth** aguzzare gli occhi per vedere qc; **to peer into a room** guardare in una stanza

peer·age ['pɪərɪdʒ] N dignità di pari; **he was given a peerage** gli è stato conferito il titolo di pari

peer·less ['pɪəlɪs] ADJ (frm) impareggiabile, senza pari

peeved [piːvd] ADJ (fam) seccato(-a), stizzito(-a)

peev·ish ['piːvɪʃ] ADJ scontroso(-a), stizzoso(-a)

peg [pɛg] N (for tent) picchetto; (Brit: also: **clothes peg**) molletta; (for coat, hat) attaccapanni m inv; **to take sb down a peg (or two)** far abbassare la cresta a qn; **a peg on which to hang a theory** un pretesto per presentare una teoria ♦ VT (clothes) appendere con le mollette; (groundsheet, tent) fissare con i picchetti; (fig: prices, wages) fissare, stabilizzare

▸ **peg away** VI + ADV: **to peg away at sth** (fam) incaponirsi su qc

▸ **peg down** VT + ADV (tent) fissare con i picchetti

▸ **peg out** VI + ADV (fam: die) crepare, tirare le cuoia

pe·jo·ra·tive [pɪ'dʒɒrɪtɪv] ADJ spregiativo(-a), peggiorativo(-a)

Pe·kin·ese [ˌpiːkɪ'niːz] N (cane) pechinese m

Pe·king [ˌpiː'kɪŋ], **Pekin** N = **Beijing**

peli·can ['pɛlɪkən] N pellicano

pel·let ['pɛlɪt] N (of paper, bread) pallina; (for gun) pallino

pell-mell ['pɛl'mɛl] ADV disordinatamente, alla rinfusa

pel·met ['pɛlmɪt] N (wooden) cassonetto; (cloth) mantovana

pelt¹ [pɛlt] VT: **to pelt sb with sth** tirare qc addosso a qn; **to pelt sth with sth** colpire qc con qc; **the crowd pelted the car with stones** la folla ha tempestato la macchina di pietre; **they pelted him with questions** lo hanno tempestato or bombardato di domande ♦ VI **1** **the rain is pelting (down)** (fam) piove a dirotto **2** (fam: go fast): **she pelted across the road** ha attraversato sparata la strada

pelt² [pɛlt] N (of animal) pelliccia, pelle f

pelvis ['pɛlvɪs] N bacino, pelvi f inv

pen¹ [pɛn] N (for animals) recinto, chiuso; (playpen) box m inv; (USA fam: prison) gattabuia ♦ VT (also: **pen in**, **pen up**) rinchiudere

pen² [pɛn] N (gen) penna; (felt-tip pen) pennarello; **I haven't got a pen** non ho una penna; **to put pen to paper** prendere la penna in mano ♦ VT (frm) scrivere

pe·nal ['piːnl] ADJ (gen) penale; (tax, fine) oneroso(-a)

pe·nal·ize ['piːnəˌlaɪz] VT **1** (punish) punire; **bad spelling will be penalized** gli errori di ortografia verranno penalizzati **2** (Sport) penalizzare **3** (handicap) handicappare

penal servitude N lavori mpl forzati

pen·al·ty ['pɛnltɪ] N **1** (punishment) pena; (fig: disadvantage) svantaggio; (fine) ammenda; **those who break the rules do so on penalty of dismissal** coloro che infrangono il regolamento verranno puniti con il licenziamento; **the penalty for this offence is life imprisonment** la pena per questo reato è l'ergastolo; **a penalty of £1000** un'ammenda di 1000 sterline; **to pay the penalty for sth** pagare le conseguenze di qc; **I paid the penalty for her mistake** ho pagato io le conseguenze del suo errore; **the death penalty** la pena di morte **2** (Sport) penalità f inv; (Ftbl) (calcio di) rigore m

penalty area, penalty box N (Brit: Ftbl) area di rigore

penalty clause N (in contract) penale f

penalty kick N (Ftbl) calcio di rigore

penalty shoot-out [ˌpɛnəltɪ'ʃuːtˌaʊt] N (Ftbl) rigori mpl; **to beat a team in a penalty shoot-out** battere una squadra ai rigori

pen·ance ['pɛnəns] N penitenza; **to do penance for** fare la penitenza per

pence [pɛns] NPL of **penny**

pen·chant ['pɒŋʃɒŋ] N (frm) debole m, penchant m inv

pen·cil ['pɛnsl] N matita ♦ ADJ (drawing, line) a matita; **in pencil** a matita

▸ **pencil in** VT + ADV (note) scrivere a matita; (fig: date) segnarsi provvisoriamente

pencil case N astuccio per matite

pen·cil sharp·en·er ['pɛnslˌʃɑːpnə'] N temperamatite m inv

pen·dant ['pɛndənt] N pendaglio

pend·ing ['pɛndɪŋ] ADJ in sospeso ♦ PREP in attesa di; **pending the arrival of** in attesa dell'arrivo di; **pending an enquiry** in attesa di indagini

pen·du·lum ['pɛndjʊləm] N pendolo

pen·etrate ['pɛnɪˌtreɪt] VT (gen, also Mil) penetrare in; (infiltrate) infiltrarsi in; (understand: meaning, mystery) penetrare; (: truth) afferrare ♦ VI (go right through) penetrare; **the significance of what he was saying finally penetrated** il significato delle sue parole fu finalmente chiaro

pen·etrat·ing ['pɛnɪˌtreɪtɪŋ] ADJ (look, sound) penetrante; (question etc) acuto(-a); (person, mind etc) perspicace

pen·etra·tion [ˌpɛnɪ'treɪʃən] N penetrazione f

pen-friend ['pɛnˌfrɛnd] N amico(-a) di penna

pen·guin ['pɛŋgwɪn] N pinguino

peni·cil·lin [ˌpɛnɪ'sɪlɪn] N penicillina

pen·in·su·la [pɪ'nɪnsjʊlə] N penisola

pe·nis ['piːnɪs] N pene m

peni·tence ['pɛnɪtəns] N penitenza

peni·tent ['pɛnɪtənt] ADJ pentito(-a) ♦ N penitente m/f

peni·ten·tia·ry [ˌpɛnɪ'tenʃərɪ] N (esp USA: prison) penitenziario, carcere m

pen·knife ['pɛnˌnaɪf] N (pl -knives ['pɛnˌnaɪvz]) temperino

Penn., Penna. ABBR (USA: = Pennsylvania)

pen name N pseudonimo

pen·nant ['pɛnənt] N bandierina

pen·ni·less ['pɛnɪlɪs] ADJ senza un soldo or una lira

Pen·nines ['pɛnaɪnz] NPL: **the Pennines** i Pennini

Penn·syl·va·nia [ˌpɛnsɪl'veɪnɪə] N la Pennsylvania

pen·ny ['pɛnɪ] N (pl pennies or pence) (Brit) penny m inv; (USA) centesimo; **24 pence** 24 penny; **it won't cost you a penny** non ti costerà un soldo; **in for a penny, in for a pound** abbiamo fatto trenta, facciamo trentuno; **I'm not a penny the wiser** continuo a capirci quanto prima; **she hasn't a penny to her name** non ha un soldo bucato; **he turns up like a bad penny** te lo ritrovi sempre tra i piedi; **a penny for your thoughts** a che pensi?; **and then the penny dropped!** (fig) improvvisamente ci sono arrivato!

pen pal N (fam) amico(-a) di penna

pen·pusher ['pɛnˌpʊʃə'] N (pej) scribacchino(-a)

pen·sion ['pɛnʃən] N pensione f

▸ **pension off** VT + ADV mandare in pensione

pen·sion·able ['pɛnʃənəbl] ADJ pensionabile

pen·sion·er ['pɛnʃənə'] N pensionato(-a)

pension fund N fondo pensioni

pen·sive ['pɛnsɪv] ADJ pensoso(-a)

pen·ta·gon ['pɛntəgən] N pentagono

Pen·tecost ['pɛntɪˌkɒst] N (Rel) Pentecoste f

pent·house ['pɛntˌhaʊs] N attico

pent-up [ˌpɛnt'ʌp] ADJ (emotions, feelings) represso(-a)

pe·nul·ti·mate [pɪ'nʌltɪmɪt] ADJ penultimo(-a)

penu·ry ['pɛnjʊrɪ] N (frm) indigenza

❑ **penury** is not translated by the Italian word **penuria**

peo·ple ['piːpl] N **1** (pl: persons) persone fpl, gente fsg; **old people** i vecchi; **young people** i giovani; **some people** alcuni mpl, certa gente; **several people** diverse persone; **a lot of people** un sacco di gente; **six people** sei persone; **four/several people came** sono venute quattro/parecchie persone; **the people were nice** la gente era simpatica; **the room was full of people** la stanza era piena di gente; **how many people are there in your family?** quanti siete in famiglia?; **what do you people think?** e voi (altri) cosa ne pensate?; **some people are born lucky** c'è chi nasce con la camicia; **you of all people should ...** se c'è uno che dovrebbe... quello sei tu **2** (pl: in general) gente fsg; **many people think that ...** molti pensano che..., molta gente pensa che...; **people say that ...** si dice or la gente dice che... **3** (pl: inhabitants) abitanti mpl; **Italian people** gli italiani; **the people of London** i londinesi; **country people** la gente di campagna;

town people la gente di città; **the indigenous peoples of Central America** le popolazioni originarie dell'America centrale **4** (*pl: Pol: citizens*) popolo; (: *general public*) pubblico; **the people** il popolo; **people at large** il grande pubblico; **a man of the people** un uomo del popolo **5** (*pl: family*) famiglia *fsg* **6** (*sg: nation, race*) popolo, nazione *f* ♦ VT: **to people (with)** popolare (con); **to be peopled with** essere popolato(-a) di

pep [pɛp] N (*fam*) dinamismo, vitalità; **to put some pep in** vivacizzare

▸ **pep up** VT + ADV (*person*) tirar su; (*party*) animare, vivacizzare; (*food*) rendere più gustoso(-a); (*drink*) correggere

pep·per ['pɛpə'] N **1** (*spice*) pepe *m*; **white/black pepper** pepe bianco/nero; **pass the pepper, please** mi passi il pepe, per favore? **2** (*vegetable*) peperone *m*; **a green pepper** un peperone verde ♦ VT pepare; **to pepper an essay with quotations** (*fig*) infarcire un saggio di citazioni

pepper·mint ['pɛpə‚mɪnt] N **1** (*Bot*) menta peperita; (*sweet*) caramella alla menta; **would you like a peppermint?** vuoi una caramella alla menta?; **peppermint tea** il tè alla menta

pep·pero·ni [‚pɛpə'rəʊnɪ] N salsiccia piccante

pepper·pot ['pɛpə‚pɒt] N pepaiola

pep talk N (*fam*) discorso d'incoraggiamento

per [pɜː'] PREP per, a; **£7 per week/dozen** 7 sterline la *or* alla settimana/dozzina; **per day** al giorno; **per week** alla settimana; **per head** *or* **person** a testa, a *or* per persona; **per hour** all'ora, orario(-a); **30 miles per hour** 30 miglia all'ora; **per kilo** al *or* il chilo; **per pro** (*by proxy*) per procura; **as per your instructions** secondo le vostre istruzioni

per annum [‚pər'ænəm] ADV all'anno

per capita [pə'kæpɪtə] ADJ, ADV pro capite *inv*

per·ceive [pə'siːv] VT (*sound, meaning, change*) percepire; (*person, object*) notare; (*realize*) accorgersi di

per cent [pə'sɛnt] N per cento; **50 per cent** 50 per cento ♦ ADV per cento; **a 20 per cent discount** uno sconto del 20 per cento

per·cent·age [pə'sɛntɪdʒ] N percentuale *f*; **as a percentage** in percentuale; **to get a percentage on all sales** avere una percentuale sulle vendite; **on a percentage basis** a percentuale

percentage point N punto percentuale

per·cep·tible [pə'sɛptəbl] ADJ percettibile

per·cep·tion [pə'sɛpʃən] N (*gen*) percezione *f*; (*sensitiveness*) sensibilità; (*insight*) perspicacia; **one's perception of a situation** il proprio modo di vedere una situazione

per·cep·tive [pə'sɛptɪv] ADJ (*gen*) perspicace; (*analysis*) acuto(-a)

perch¹ [pɜːtʃ] N (*fish*) pesce *m* persico

perch² [pɜːtʃ] N (*of bird*) pertica, posatoio; (*in tree*) ramo; (*fig: for person etc*) posto di vedetta ♦ VT poggiare ♦ VI (*bird, person*) appollaiarsi

per·co·late ['pɜːkə‚leɪt] VT filtrare; **percolated coffee** caffè filtrato ♦ VI (*water, coffee*) passare, filtrarsi; (*fig: news*) filtrare

per·co·la·tor ['pɜːkə‚leɪtə'] N caffettiera a filtro

per·cus·sion [pə'kʌʃən] N **1** percussione *f* **2** (*Mus*) percussioni *fpl*; **I play percussion** suono le percussioni

per·emp·tory [pə'rɛmptərɪ] ADJ perentorio(-a)

per·en·nial [pə'rɛnɪəl] ADJ perenne ♦ N (*Bot*) pianta perenne

per·fect [*adj* 'pɜːfɪkt, *vb* pə'fɛkt] ADJ (*gen, also Gram*) perfetto(-a); **that's perfect!** perfetto!; **it's a perfect day for skiing** è una giornata ideale per sciare; **he's a perfect stranger to me** mi è completamente sconosciuto ♦ N (*Gram: also: perfect tense*) perfetto, passato prossimo ♦ VT perfezionare; (*skill, technique*) mettere a punto

per·fec·tion [pə'fɛkʃən] N perfezione *f*; **to perfection** a *or* alla perfezione

per·fec·tion·ist [pə'fɛkʃənɪst] N perfezionista *m/f*

per·fect·ly ['pɜːfɪktlɪ] ADV (*gen*) perfettamente, alla perfezione; **perfectly normal** perfettamente normale; **I'm perfectly happy with the situation** sono completamente soddisfatta della situazione; **you know perfectly well** sai benissimo

per·fo·rate ['pɜːfə‚reɪt] VT perforare; **perforated line** linea perforata

per·fo·rat·ed ul·cer ['pɜːfə‚reɪtɪd'ʌlsə'] N (*Med*) ulcera perforata

per·fo·ra·tion [‚pɜːfə'reɪʃən] N (*act*) perforazione *f*; (*in stamps*) dentellatura; (*hole*) foro

per·form [pə'fɔːm] VT **1** (*function, task*) svolgere, eseguire; (*duty*) adempiere a; (*miracles, experiments*) fare, compiere; (*ceremony*) celebrare; **to perform an operation** (*Med*) operare; **to perform a task** svolgere un compito; **he performed many acts of bravery** ha compiuto molti atti di coraggio **2** (*play, ballet, opera*) rappresentare; (*duet, symphony*) eseguire, suonare; (*acrobatics*) fare; **this play was first performed in 1890** questa commedia è stata rappresentata per la prima volta nel 1890 ♦ VI **1** (*theatre company*) dare una rappresentazione; (*person*) esibirsi **2** (*vehicle, machine: also fig: student*) comportarsi; **to perform brilliantly** fornire un'ottima prestazione; **if you want a car that performs really well ...** se volete una macchina che dia ottime prestazioni...

per·for·mance [pə'fɔːməns] N **1** (*see vt a*) svolgimento; adempimento; celebrazione *f*; **in the performance of his duties** nell'adempimento dei suoi doveri **2** (*presentation: of play, opera*) rappresentazione *f*; (: *of film, ballet*) spettacolo; (: *by actor, of a part*) interpretazione *f*; **the performance lasts two hours** lo spettacolo dura due ore; **he gave a splendid performance as Hamlet** la sua interpretazione di Amleto è stata magnifica; **a fine performance of the Ninth Symphony** un'ottima esecuzione della Nona sinfonia; **what a performance!** (*fam*) quante scene *or* storie! **3** (*effectiveness: of machine etc*) prestazioni *fpl*; (: *of company*) rendimento; (: *of racehorse, athlete*) performance *f inv*; **the team put up a good performance** la squadra ha giocato una bella partita; **the team's disappointing performance** la deludente prestazione della squadra

per·form·er [pə'fɔːmə'] N artista *m/f*

per·form·ing [pə'fɔːmɪŋ] ADJ (*animal*) ammaestrato(-a); **a performing seal** una foca ammaestrata

performing arts NPL: **the performing arts** le arti *fpl* dello spettacolo

per·fume [*n* 'pɜːfjuːm, *vb* pə'fjuːm] N profumo ♦ VT profumare

per·func·tory [pə'fʌŋktərɪ] ADJ (*inspection, inquiry*) superficiale, pro forma *inv*; (*nod*) meccanico(-a)

per·haps [pə'hæps, præps] ADV forse; **perhaps so/not** forse sì/no, può darsi di sì/di no; **perhaps he'll come** magari *or* forse verrà, può darsi che venga; **perhaps he's ill** forse è malato

per·il ['pɛrɪl] N pericolo; **at your peril** a tuo rischio e pericolo

peri·lous ['pɛrɪləs] ADJ pericoloso(-a)

peri·lous·ly ['pɛrɪləslɪ] ADV pericolosamente; **they came perilously close to being caught** sono stati a un pelo dall'esser presi

pe·rim·eter [pə'rɪmɪtə'] N perimetro

perimeter wall N muro di cinta

pe·ri·od ['pɪərɪəd] N **1** (*length of time*) periodo; (*stage: in career, development etc*) periodo, momento; (*USA: Ftbl*) tempo; **for a period of three weeks** per un periodo di *or* per la durata di tre settimane; **for a limited period** per un periodo limitato; **at that period (of my life)** in quel periodo (della mia vita); **the Victorian period** l'epoca *or* l'età vittoriana; **a painting of his early period** un dipinto del suo primo periodo **2** (*Scol*) ora; **each period lasts forty minutes** ogni lezione dura quaranta minuti **3** (*USA: full stop*) punto; **comma or period?** virgola o punto? **4** (*menstruation*) mestruazioni *fpl*; **I'm having my period** ho le mestruazioni ♦ ADJ (*costume*) d'epoca

pe·ri·od·ic [‚pɪərɪ'ɒdɪk] ADJ periodico(-a)

Periodic Table N la tavola periodica

pe·ri·odi·cal [‚pɪərɪ'ɒdɪkl] ADJ periodico(-a) ♦ N periodico

pe·ri·odi·cal·ly [‚pɪərɪ'ɒdɪkəlɪ] ADV periodicamente

peri·pa·tet·ic [‚pɛrɪpə'tetɪk] ADJ (*salesman*) ambulante; (*Brit: teacher*) che insegna in varie scuole

pe·riph·er·al [pə'rɪfərəl] ADJ (*gen*) periferico(-a); (*interest*) marginale ♦ N (*Comput*) unità *f inv* periferica

pe·riph·ery [pə'rɪfərɪ] N periferia

peri·scope ['pɛrɪ‚skəʊp] N periscopio

per·ish ['pɛrɪʃ] VI (*person etc*) perire, morire; **hundreds perished in the earthquake** centinaia di persone sono morte a causa del terremoto

per·ish·able [ˈperɪʃəbl] ADJ deperibile
per·ish·ables [ˈperɪʃəblz] NPL merci *fpl* deperibili
per·ish·ing [ˈperɪʃɪŋ] ADJ (*Brit fam*): **it's perishing (cold)** fa un freddo da morire
peri·to·ni·tis [ˌperɪtəˈnaɪtɪs] N peritonite *f*
per·jure [ˈpɜːdʒəʳ] VT: **to perjure o.s.** spergiurare; (*Law*) giurare il falso
per·jury [ˈpɜːdʒərɪ] N (*breach of oath*) spergiuro; (*Law*) falso giuramento; **to commit perjury** spergiurare; (*Law*) giurare il falso
perk [pɜːk] N (*fam*) vantaggio
perky [ˈpɜːkɪ] ADJ (*comp* **-ier**, *superl* **-iest**) (*cheerful*) allegro(-a); (*bright*) vivace; (*cheeky*) impertinente
perm [pɜːm] N permanente *f*; **she's got a perm** ha la permanente ♦ VT: **to perm sb's hair** fare la permanente a qn; **to have one's hair permed** farsi fare la permanente
per·ma·nence [ˈpɜːmənəns] N permanenza
per·ma·nent [ˈpɜːmənənt] ADJ (*state, building, agreement*) permanente; (*job, position*) fisso(-a); (*dye, ink*) indelebile; **a permanent ban** un divieto permanente; **I'm not permanent here** non sono fisso qui; **permanent address** residenza fissa; **permanent job** lavoro fisso
per·ma·nent·ly [ˈpɜːmənəntlɪ] ADV (*stay, leave*) definitivamente; **he is permanently drunk** è perennemente ubriaco
per·me·able [ˈpɜːmɪəbl] ADJ permeabile; **selectively permeable** semipermeabile
per·me·ate [ˈpɜːmɪeɪt] VT (*gen*) filtrare attraverso; (*Tech*) permeare; (*subj: smell*) pervadere; (: *fig: ideas etc*) diffondersi in; **permeated with** impregnato(-a) di ♦ VI filtrare; (*fig*) diffondersi
per·mis·sible [pəˈmɪsɪbl] ADJ (*action*) permesso(-a); (*behaviour*) accettabile; (*attitude*) ammissibile, permissibile; **it is not permissible to do that** non è permesso farlo
per·mis·sion [pəˈmɪʃən] N (*official*) autorizzazione *f*; **with your permission** se mi permette, con il suo permesso; **to ask permission to do sth** chiedere il permesso di fare qc; **you'll have to ask permission** dovrai chiedere il permesso; **to give sb permission to do sth** dare a qn il permesso di fare qc
per·mis·sive [pəˈmɪsɪv] ADJ (*parents, society*) permissivo(-a), tollerante
per·mit [*n* ˈpɜːmɪt, *vb* pəˈmɪt] N (*gen*) autorizzazione *f* (scritta); (*for specific activity*) permesso; (*entrance pass*) lasciapassare *m*; **fishing permit** licenza di pesca; **building/export permit** permesso *or* licenza di costruzione/di esportazione; **work permit** permesso di lavoro ♦ VT permettere; **to permit sb to do sth** permettere a qn di fare qc; **to permit sth to take place** permettere che qc avvenga ♦ VI permettere; **to permit of** (*frm*) ammettere, consentire; **weather permitting** tempo permettendo
per·mu·ta·tion [ˌpɜːmjuˈteɪʃən] N permutazione *f*
per·ni·cious [pɜːˈnɪʃəs] ADJ nocivo(-a), dannoso(-a); (*Med*) pernicioso(-a)
per·nick·ety [pəˈnɪkɪtɪ] ADJ (*fam: person*) pignolo(-a); (: *job*) da certosino
per·pen·dicu·lar [ˌpɜːpənˈdɪkjʊləʳ] ADJ (*gen, also Math*) perpendicolare; (*cliff*) a picco ♦ N perpendicolare *f*
per·pe·trate [ˈpɜːpɪtreɪt] VT perpetrare, commettere
per·pet·ual [pəˈpetjʊəl] ADJ (*gen: motion*) perpetuo(-a); (*ice, snow*) perenne; (*continuous: noise, complaining*) incessante, continuo(-a)
per·petu·ate [pəˈpetjʊeɪt] VT perpetuare
per·pe·tu·ity [ˌpɜːpɪˈtjuːɪtɪ] N: **in perpetuity** in perpetuo
per·plex [pəˈpleks] VT lasciare perplesso(-a); **I was perplexed by his behaviour** il suo comportamento mi ha lasciato perplesso
per·plex·ing [pəˈpleksɪŋ] ADJ che lascia perplesso(-a)
per·qui·site [ˈpɜːkwɪzɪt] N (*frm*) = **perk**
per·secute [ˈpɜːsɪkjuːt] VT perseguitare
per·secu·tion [ˌpɜːsɪˈkjuːʃən] N persecuzione *f*
per·sever·ance [ˌpɜːsɪˈvɪərəns] N perseveranza
per·severe [ˌpɜːsɪˈvɪəʳ] VI perseverare
Per·sia [ˈpɜːʃə] N Persia
Per·sian [ˈpɜːʃən] ADJ persiano(-a) ♦ N 1 (*person*) persiano(-a) 2 (*language*) persiano

Persian cat N (*gatto*) persiano
per·sist [pəˈsɪst] VI (*person*) persistere, ostinarsi; (*custom, rain*) persistere, durare; **to persist in sth/in doing sth** ostinarsi in qc/a fare qc, persistere in qc/nel *or* a fare qc; **why do they persist in wasting money?** perché continuano a buttar via soldi?; **if the cough persists, contact your doctor** se la tosse persiste, contattare il medico
per·sis·tence [pəˈsɪstəns] N (*tenacity*) perseveranza; (*obstinacy*) ostinazione *f*, persistenza; (*continued existence*) persistere *m*
per·sis·tent [pəˈsɪstənt] ADJ (*person, attempt, questions*) insistente, ostinato(-a); (*cough, pain, smell*) persistente; (*lateness, rain*) continuo(-a); **persistent offender** (*Law*) delinquente *m/f* abituale
per·snick·ety [pəˈsnɪkɪtɪ] ADJ (*USA*) = **pernickety**
per·son [ˈpɜːsn] N 1 (*pl* **people** *or* **persons**) (*frm*) persona; **a person to person call** (*Telec*) una chiamata con preavviso 2 (*pl* **persons**) (*Gram, Law*) persona 3 (*body, physical presence*) figura, personale *m*; (*appearance*) aspetto; **in person** di *or* in persona, personalmente; **in the person of my uncle** nella persona di mio zio; **on** *or* **about one's person** (*weapon*) su di sé; (*money*) con sé
per·son·able [ˈpɜːsnəbl] ADJ di bell'aspetto, prestante
per·son·al [ˈpɜːsnl] ADJ (*gen, Gram*) (*application*) (fatto(-a)) di persona; **personal belongings** oggetti d'uso personale; **a personal opinion** un'opinione personale; **a personal question** una domanda indiscreta; **a personal interview** un incontro privato; **for personal reasons** per motivi personali; **to make a personal appearance** apparire di persona; **to have personal knowledge of sth** conoscere qc per esperienza personale; **don't get personal!** non entriamo nel personale!; **one's personal habits** le proprie piccole manie; **"personal"** (*on letter*) "riservata", "personale"
personal allowance N (*Tax*) quota non imponibile
personal assistant N assistente *m/f* personale
personal call N (*Brit Telec: person to person*) chiamata con preavviso; (: *private*) telefonata personale
personal column N colonna degli annunci personali, colonna dei piccoli annunci
personal details NPL dati *mpl* personali
personal identification number N (*Comput, Banking*) numero di codice segreto
per·son·al·ity [ˌpɜːsəˈnælɪtɪ] N (*nature*) personalità *f inv*; (*famous person*) personalità, personaggio
per·son·al·ly [ˈpɜːsnəlɪ] ADV 1 (*for my part*) personalmente; **I feel personally responsible** mi sento personalmente responsabile; **personally I think that ...** personalmente penso che...; **personally I don't agree** personalmente non sono d'accordo; **don't take it too personally** non prenderla come un'offesa *or* una critica personale 2 (*in person*) personalmente, di persona; **to hand sth over personally** consegnare qc di persona
personal organizer N (*book*) agenda; (*electronic*) agenda elettronica
personal property N (*Law*) beni *mpl* personali
per·soni·fy [pɜːˈsɒnɪfaɪ] VT personificare
per·son·nel [ˌpɜːsəˈnel] N personale *m*
personnel department N ufficio del personale
personnel manager N direttore(-trice) del personale
per·spec·tive [pəˈspektɪv] N prospettiva; **a new perspective** una nuova prospettiva; **to see** *or* **look at sth in perspective** (*fig*) vedere qc nella giusta prospettiva; **to get sth into perspective** ridimensionare qc
per·spi·cac·ity [ˌpɜːspɪˈkæsɪtɪ] N (*frm*) perspicacia
per·spi·ra·tion [ˌpɜːspɪˈreɪʃən] N traspirazione *f*, sudore *m*; **bathed in perspiration** in un bagno di sudore, bagnato(-a) di sudore; **excessive perspiration** sudorazione eccessiva
per·spire [pəˈspaɪəʳ] VI traspirare, sudare
per·suade [pəˈsweɪd] VT persuadere; **to persuade sb of sth/that** persuadere qn di qc/che; **to persuade sb to do sth** persuadere qn a fare qc; **she persuaded me to go with her** mi ha convinto ad andare con lei; **but they persuaded me not to** ma mi hanno persuaso a non farlo; **she is easily persuaded** si lascia facilmente persuadere *or* convincere; **I am persuaded that ...** (*frm*) sono persuaso *or* convinto che... + *sub*

per·sua·sion [pə'sweɪʒən] N **1** (*persuading*) persuasione *f*; **her powers of persuasion** la sua capacità di persuasione **2** (*creed*) convinzione *f*, credo; **people of all political persuasions** gente di tutte le convinzioni politiche

per·sua·sive [pə'sweɪsɪv] ADJ (*person*) convincente; (*argument*) persuasivo(-a), convincente

pert [pɜːt] ADJ (*comp* **-er**, *superl* **-est**) (*answer*) impertinente, sfacciato(-a); (*hat*) spiritoso(-a)

per·ti·nent ['pɜːtɪnənt] ADJ pertinente

per·turb [pə'tɜːb] VT turbare, agitare; **I was perturbed to learn that ...** fui sconvolto nello scoprire che...

per·turb·ing [pə'tɜːbɪŋ] ADJ inquietante

Peru [pə'ruː] N Perù *m*

pe·rus·al [pə'ruːzəl] N lettura

Pe·ru·vian [pə'ruːvɪən] ADJ, N peruviano(-a)

per·vade [pɜː'veɪd] VT (*subj: smell, feeling, atmosphere*) pervadere; (: *influence, ideas*) insinuarsi in, diffondersi in

per·va·sive [pɜː'veɪsɪv] ADJ (*smell*) penetrante; (*influence*) dilagante; (*gloom, feelings, ideas*) diffuso(-a)

per·verse [pə'vɜːs] ADJ (*contrary: behaviour*) da bastian contrario; (*wicked*) cattivo(-a); (*desires*) perverso(-a); (*circumstances*) avverso(-a); **to be perverse** (*person*) essere un bastian contrario

per·ver·sion [pə'vɜːʃən] N (*Psych*) perversione *f*; (*of justice, truth*) travisamento, pervertimento

per·ver·sity [pə'vɜːsɪtɪ] N (*wickedness*) perversità, malvagità; (*contrariness*) spirito di contraddizione

per·vert [*vb* pə'vɜːt, *n* 'pɜːvɜːt] VT (*mind*) pervertire, corrompere; (*speech, truth etc*) travisare; **to pervert the course of justice** deviare il corso della giustizia ♦ N pervertito(-a)

pes·si·mism ['pesɪˌmɪzəm] N pessimismo

pes·si·mist ['pesɪmɪst] N pessimista *m/f*

pes·si·mis·tic [ˌpesɪ'mɪstɪk] ADJ (*attitude, forecast*) pessimistico(-a); (*person*) pessimista

pest [pest] N **1** (*Zool*) insetto (*or* animale *m*) nocivo; **garden pests** gli insetti nocivi del giardino **2** (*fig: person*) peste *f*; (: *thing*) rottura; **he's a real pest!** è un gran rompiscatole!

pest control N disinfestazione *f*

pes·ter ['pestə'] VT tormentare, molestare; **stop pestering me!** smettila di scocciarmi!

pes·ti·cide ['pestɪˌsaɪd] N pesticida *m*

pes·ti·lence ['pestɪləns] N pestilenza

pes·tle ['pesl] N pestello

pet [pet] N **1** (*animal*) animale *m* domestico; **have you got any pets?** hai qualche animale domestico?; **my dad won't let me have any pets** il mio papà non mi lascia tenere (in casa) nessun animale **2** (*favourite*) preferito(-a), favorito(-a), beniamino(-a); **the teacher's pet** il cocco dell'insegnante; **come here pet** (*fam*) vieni qua tesoro ♦ VT coccolare; (*fondle*) accarezzare ♦ VI (*sexually*) pomiciare, fare il petting ♦ ADJ **1** (*monkey*) ammaestrato(-a); (*food*) per animali domestici; **we have a pet dog** abbiamo un cane; **pet mouse** topo addomesticato **2** (*favourite: pupil, subject etc*) preferito(-a), prediletto(-a); **my pet aversion** la cosa che detesto di più

pet·al ['petl] N petalo

pe·ter ['piːtə'] VI: **to peter out** (*supply*) esaurirsi, estinguersi; (*stream*) perdersi; (*plan*) andare in fumo; (*interest, excitement*) svanire; (*conversation*) spegnersi; (*song, noise*) cessare; (*track, path*) finire

pe·tite [pə'tiːt] ADJ (*woman*) minuta e graziosa

pe·ti·tion [pə'tɪʃən] N (*list of names*) petizione *f*; (*frm: request*) richiesta, istanza ♦ VT (*person*) presentare una petizione a ♦ VI richiedere; **to petition for divorce** (*Law*) presentare un'istanza di divorzio

pet name N (*Brit*) nomignolo

pet·ri·fied ['petrɪˌfaɪd] ADJ terrorizzato(-a); **I was petrified** ero terrorizzato(-a); **to be petrified (with fear)** restare impietrito(-a) (per la paura)

pet·ri·fy ['petrɪˌfaɪ] VT (*fig*) terrorizzare ♦ VI (*turn to stone*) pietrificarsi; (*frm: stagnate*) sclerotizzarsi

pet·ro·chemi·cal [ˌpetrəʊ'kemɪkl] ADJ petrolchimico(-a) ♦ N prodotto petrolchimico

pet·ro·dol·lar ['petrəʊˌdɒlə'] N petrodollaro

pet·rol ['petrəl] (*Brit*) N benzina; **unleaded petrol** la benzina

verde; **high-octane petrol** (benzina) super *f inv*; **to run out of petrol** restare senza benzina; **they spend a lot on petrol** spendono molto per la benzina ♦ ADJ (*leak, stain*) di benzina
❑ **petrol** is not translated by the Italian word *petrolio*

petrol bomb N (bottiglia *or* bomba) molotov *f inv*

petrol can N tanica per benzina

petrol engine N motore *m* a benzina

pe·tro·leum [pɪ'trəʊlɪəm] N petrolio

petroleum jelly N vaselina

petrol pump N (*at garage, in car*) pompa della benzina

petrol station N stazione *f* di servizio *or* rifornimento, benzinaio

petrol tank N serbatoio della benzina

pet·ti·coat ['petɪˌkəʊt] N (*full-length*) sottoveste *f*; (*waist*) sottogonna *f*

pet·ti·fog·ging ['petɪˌfɒgɪŋ] ADJ (*details*) insignificante; (*objections*) cavilloso(-a)

pet·ti·ness ['petɪnɪs] N (*small-mindedness*) meschinità *f inv*

pet·ty ['petɪ] ADJ (*comp* **-ier**, *superl* **-iest**) **1** (*trivial: detail, complaint*) insignificante, di poca importanza; **petty crime** reati *mpl* minori; **petty problems** problemi *mpl* insignificanti **2** (*minor: official*) subalterno(-a) **3** (*small-minded, spiteful*) meschino(-a); **you're being petty** sei meschino(-a)

petty cash N piccola cassa

petty officer N (*Naut*) sottufficiale *m* di marina

petu·lant ['petjʊlənt] ADJ irritabile

pew [pjuː] N (*in church*) banco

pew·ter ['pjuːtə'] N peltro

PG [ˌpiː'dʒiː] N ABBR (*Cine*: = *parental guidance*) *classificazione di film la cui visione è a discrezione dei genitori date le scene poco adatte ai bambini*

PG 13 [-θɜː'tiːn] ABBR (*USA: Cine*: = *Parental Guidance 13*) vietato ai minori di 13 anni non accompagnati dai genitori

PGA [ˌpiːdʒiː'eɪ] N ABBR (= *Professional Golfers' Association*) *associazione dei giocatori di golf professionisti*

PH [ˌpiː'eɪtʃ] N ABBR (*USA Mil*) = **Purple Heart**

PHA [ˌpiːeɪtʃ'eɪ] N ABBR (*USA*: = *Public Housing Administration*) amministrazione per l'edilizia pubblica

phal·lic ['fælɪk] ADJ fallico(-a)

phan·tom ['fæntəm] ADJ fantasma *inv* ♦ N fantasma *m*

Phar·aoh ['feərəʊ] N faraone *m*

phar·ma·ceu·ti·cal [ˌfɑːmə'sjuːtɪkəl] ADJ farmaceutico(-a)

phar·ma·cist ['fɑːməsɪst] N farmacista *m/f*

phar·ma·cy ['fɑːməsɪ] N farmacia

phase [feɪz] N fase *f*, periodo; **to be out of phase** (*Tech, Elec*) essere sfasato(-a) *or* fuori fase; **it's a phase all children go through** è una fase che tutti i bambini attraversano ♦ VT (*stagger*) introdurre gradualmente; (*coordinate*) sincronizzare; **the redundancies will be phased** i licenziamenti verranno effettuati gradualmente; **phased withdrawal** ritirata progressiva
  ▸ **phase in** VT + ADV introdurre gradualmente
  ▸ **phase out** VT + ADV eliminare gradualmente

PhD N ABBR = **Doctor of Philosophy**

pheas·ant ['feznt] N fagiano

phe·nom·enal [fɪ'nɒmɪnl] ADJ fenomenale

phe·nom·enon [fɪ'nɒmɪnən] N (*pl* **phenomena** [fɪ'nɒmɪnə]) fenomeno

phew [fjuː] EXCL (*heat, tiredness*) uff!; (*relief, surprise*) uh!

phial ['faɪəl] N fiala

phi·lan·der·er [fɪ'lændərə'] N (*pej*) libertino

phil·an·throp·ic [ˌfɪlən'θrɒpɪk] ADJ filantropico(-a)

phi·lan·thro·pist [fɪ'lænθrəpɪst] N filantropo(-a)

phi·lat·elist [fɪ'lætəlɪst] N filatelista *m/f*, filatelico(-a)

phi·lat·ely [fɪ'lætəlɪ] N filatelia

Phil·ip·pines ['fɪlɪˌpiːnz] NPL: **the Philippines** le Filippine

phi·loso·pher [fɪ'lɒsəfə'] N filosofo(-a)

philo·sophi·cal [ˌfɪlə'sɒfɪkəl] ADJ (*also fig*) filosofico(-a); **he's been very philosophical about it** l'ha presa con molta filosofia

phi·loso·phy [fɪ'lɒsəfɪ] N filosofia; **her philosophy of life** la sua massima *or* filosofia

phlegm [flɛm] N flemma

phleg·mat·ic [flɛgˈmætɪk] ADJ flemmatico(-a)

pho·bia [ˈfəʊbɪə] N fobia; **to have a phobia about sth** avere la fobia di qc

phone [fəʊn] N telefono; **to be on the phone** avere il telefono; (*be calling*) essere al telefono; **she's on the phone at the moment** in questo momento è al telefono; **by phone** per telefono ♦ VT telefonare a; **I'll phone the station** alla stazione ♦ VI telefonare
▸ **phone back** VT + ADV, VI + ADV richiamare
▸ **phone up** VT + ADV: **to phone sb up** dare un colpo di telefono a qn

phone book N guida del telefono, elenco telefonico

phone box N cabina telefonica (*per strada*)

phone call N telefonata; **to make a phone call** fare una telefonata

phone·card [ˈfəʊnkɑːd] N scheda telefonica

phone-in [ˈfəʊnˌɪn] N (*Radio, TV*) trasmissione con telefonate in diretta

phone tap·ping [ˈfəʊnˌtæpɪŋ] N intercettazioni *fpl* telefoniche

pho·net·ics [fəʊˈnɛtɪks] NSG fonetica

pho·ney [ˈfəʊnɪ] (*fam*) ADJ (*comp* **-ier**, *superl* **-iest**) (*gen*) falso(-a), fasullo(-a); (*accent*) fasullo(-a) ♦ N (*person*) venditore(-trice) di fumo, ciarlatano(-a)

pho·no·graph [ˈfəʊnəˌɡrɑːf] (*old*) N fonografo; (*USA*) giradischi *m inv*

pho·ny [ˈfəʊnɪ] (*USA*) = phoney

phos·phate [ˈfɒsfeɪt] N fosfato

phos·pho·rus [ˈfɒsfərəs] N fosforo

pho·to [ˈfəʊtəʊ] N foto *f inv*; **to take a photo** fare una foto; **I took a photo of the bride and groom** ho fatto una foto agli sposi

photo– [ˈfəʊtəʊ] PREF foto-

photo album N album *m inv* fotografico (*or* di fotografie)

photo·call [ˈfəʊtəʊˌkɔːl] N convocazione di fotoreporter a scopo pubblicitario

photo·cop·i·er [ˈfəʊtəʊˌkɒpɪə'] N fotocopiatrice *f*

photo·copy [ˈfəʊtəʊˌkɒpɪ] N fotocopia ♦ VT fotocopiare

photo·elec·tric [ˌfəʊtəʊɪˈlɛktrɪk] ADJ fotoelettrico(-a)

photo·gen·ic [ˌfəʊtəʊˈdʒɛnɪk] ADJ fotogenico(-a)

photo·graph [ˈfəʊtəˌɡræf] N fotografia; **to take a photograph of sb** fare una fotografia a *or* fotografare qn; **to take a photograph of sth** fotografare qc ♦ VT fotografare

pho·tog·ra·pher [fəˈtɒɡrəfə'] N fotografo(-a); **she's a photographer** fa la fotografa; **newspaper photographer** fotoreporter *m/f inv*; **street photographer** fotografo di piazza

photo·graph·ic [ˌfəʊtəˈɡræfɪk] ADJ fotografico(-a); **to have a photographic memory** avere una memoria fotografica

pho·tog·ra·phy [fəˈtɒɡrəfɪ] N fotografia; **my hobby is photography** il mio hobby è la fotografia

photo opportunity N opportunità di scattare delle foto ad un personaggio importante

photo·syn·the·sis [ˌfəʊtəʊˈsɪnθəsɪs] N fotosintesi *f*

phrase [freɪz] N 1 (*Gram*) locuzione *f*; (*saying*) espressione *f*; **noun phrase** sintagma *m* nominale 2 (*Mus*) frase *f* ♦ VT 1 (*thought*) esprimere; (*letter*) redigere 2 (*Mus*) dividere in frasi

phrase book N vocabolarietto

physi·cal [ˈfɪzɪkəl] ADJ 1 (*of the body*) fisico(-a) 2 (*world, object*) materiale; (*of physics*) fisico(-a); **physical change** reazione *f* fisica; **physical stocktaking** (*Comm*) inventario fisico; **it's a physical impossibility** è un'impossibilità materiale

physi·cal·ly [ˈfɪzɪkəlɪ] ADV fisicamente; **it's physically impossible** è materialmente impossibile

phy·si·cian [fɪˈzɪʃən] N medico

physi·cist [ˈfɪzɪsɪst] N fisico; **nuclear physicist** fisico nucleare

phys·ics [ˈfɪzɪks] NSG fisica; **she teaches physics** insegna fisica

physio·logi·cal [ˌfɪzɪəˈlɒdʒɪkəl] ADJ fisiologico(-a)

physi·ol·ogy [ˌfɪzɪˈɒlədʒɪ] N fisiologia

physio·thera·pist [ˌfɪzɪəʊˈθerəpɪst] N fisioterapista *m/f*

physio·thera·py [ˌfɪzɪəʊˈθerəpɪ] N fisioterapia

phy·sique [fɪˈziːk] N fisico

pia·nist [ˈpɪənɪst] N pianista *m/f*

pia·no [piːˈænəʊ] N piano(forte) *m* ♦ ADJ (*lesson, teacher*) di piano(forte); (*concerto, stool*) per piano(forte)

piano accordion N fisarmonica (a tastiera)

pic·co·lo [ˈpɪkələʊ] N (*pl* **-s**) (*Mus*) ottavino

pick [pɪk] N 1 (*also:* **pickaxe**) piccone *m*; **pick and shovel** pala e piccone 2 (*choice, right to choose*) scelta; **take your pick!** scegli quello che vuoi!, prendi quello che ti pare!; **it's the pick of the bunch** è il migliore di tutti ♦ VT 1 (*choose*) scegliere; **to pick a winner** puntare sul vincente; (*fig*) fare un ottimo affare, imbroccarla giusta; **to pick one's way through** attraversare stando ben attento(-a) a dove mettere i piedi; **to pick a fight/quarrel with sb** attaccar rissa/briga con qn; **I picked the biggest piece** ho scelto il pezzo più grosso 2 (*flowers*) cogliere; (*fruit*) raccogliere; **I picked some strawberries** ho raccolto delle fragole 3 (*scab, spot*) grattarsi; **to pick one's nose** mettersi le dita nel naso; **to pick one's teeth** pulirsi i denti con uno stuzzicadenti, stuzzicarsi i denti; **to pick a lock** far scattare una serratura; **to pick a bone** spolpare un osso; **I've got a bone to pick with you!** devo fare i conti con te; **to pick holes in sth** (*fig*) trovare i punti deboli in qc; **to pick sb's pocket** alleggerire qn del portafoglio; **to pick sb's brains** farsi dare dei suggerimenti da qn ♦ VI: **to pick and choose** scegliere con cura
▸ **pick at** VI + PREP (*food, meal*) mangiare contro voglia; (*scab*) grattarsi
▸ **pick off** VT + ADV 1 (*remove: fluff*) togliere; (: *flower, leaf*) cogliere 2 (*shoot*) abbattere (uno ad *or* a dopo l'altro(-a))
▸ **pick on** VI + PREP 1 (*fam: harass*) avercela con, prendersela con; **she's always picking on me** se la prende sempre con me 2 (*single out*) beccare; **they always pick on him to do it** lo fanno sempre fare a lui
▸ **pick out** VT + ADV 1 (*choose*) scegliere; **I like them all — it's difficult to pick one out** mi piacciono tutti — è difficile sceglierne uno 2 (*place: on map*) trovare; (*person: in crowd, photo*) individuare; (: *from the line-up*) identificare; **four victims picked him out from the line-up** quattro vittime lo hanno identificato in un confronto 3 (*Mus*): **to pick out a tune on the piano** trovare gli accordi di un motivo al piano
▸ **pick over** VT + ADV (*fruit, vegetables*) selezionare, scegliere; (*rice, lentils*) mondare
▸ **pick up** VT + ADV 1 (*lift: sth dropped*) raccogliere, raccattare; (: *sth fallen*) tirar su; **could you help me pick up the toys?** mi aiuti a raccogliere i giocattoli?; **to pick o.s. up** rialzarsi; **to pick up a child** prendere in braccio un bambino; **to pick up the phone** alzare il ricevitore; **to pick up the bill** (*fig*) pagare (il conto); **to pick sb up for having made a mistake** riprendere qn per aver fatto uno sbaglio 2 (*collect: goods, person*) passare a prendere; **we'll come to the airport to pick you up** veniamo a prenderti all'aeroporto; (*subj: bus etc*) far salire, caricare; (*rescue*) raccogliere (: *from sea*) ripescare; (*arrest*) arrestare; **the car picked up speed** la macchina ha acquistato velocità *or* ha accelerato 3 (*acquire: sale bargain*) trovare; (: *information, points in exam, germ*) prendere; (*learn: habit, ideas*) prendere; (: *skill, language, tricks*) imparare; **they picked up a nasty infection** si sono presi una brutta infezione; **can you pick up some information while you're there?** puoi prendere delle informazioni mentre sei lì?; **I picked up some Spanish during my vacation** ho imparato un po' di spagnolo in vacanza 4 (*Radio, TV, Telec*) captare ♦ VI + ADV 1 (*improve: gen*) migliorare; (: *wages*) aumentare; (: *invalid, business*) riprendersi; (: *weather*) rimettersi; **things are picking up** le cose stanno migliorando 2 (*continue*) continuare, riprendere; **to pick up where one left off** riprendere dal punto in cui ci si era fermati

pick·axe, pick·ax [ˈpɪkˌæks] N piccone *m*

pick·et [ˈpɪkɪt] N 1 (*stake*) picchetto 2 (*striker, band of strikers*) picchetto; (*Mil: sentry*) sentinella; (: *group*) picchetto ♦ VT picchettare ♦ VI picchettare

picket line N cordone *m* degli scioperanti

pick·ings [ˈpɪkɪŋz] NPL (*profits*): **there are good pickings to be had here** qui si possono fare dei guadagni facili

pick·le [ˈpɪkl] N (*brine*) salamoia; (*vinegar*) aceto; **pickles** NPL (*preserved vegetables*) sottaceti *mpl*; **mixed pickles** giardiniera *fsg*; **to be in a pickle** (*fig: fam*) essere in un guaio *or* pasticcio ♦ VT mettere sott'aceto; **pickled onions** cipolline *fpl* sott'aceto

pick-me-up [ˈpɪkmiːˌʌp] N (*fam: drink*) goccetto; (: *tonic*) tonico

pick·pocket [ˈpɪkˌpɒkɪt] N borsaiolo(-a), borseggiatore(-trice)

pick-up [ˈpɪkˌʌp] N 1 (*Brit: on record player: also:* **pick-up arm**) pick-up *m inv* 2 (*also:* **pick-up truck**) camioncino

pic·nic [ˈpɪknɪk] (*pt, pp* **picnicked**) N picnic *m inv*; **to have a picnic** fare un picnic; **to go on a picnic** andare a fare un picnic; **it was no picnic** (*fig: fam*) non è stata una passeggiata ♦ VI fare un picnic

pic·nick·er [ˈpɪknɪkəʳ] N chi partecipa a un picnic

pic·to·rial [pɪkˈtɔːrɪəl] ADJ (*magazine*) illustrato(-a); (*representation*) pittoresco(-a); (*masterpiece*) di pittura; **a pictorial record of one's travels** una serie di immagini in ricordo dei propri viaggi

pic·ture [ˈpɪktʃəʳ] N 1 (*Art: painting*) quadro, pittura, dipinto; (: *drawing*) disegno; (: *portrait*) ritratto; (: *photo*) fotografia; (: *in book*) illustrazione *f*; **to paint a picture of sth** dipingere qc; **there were pictures on the walls** c'erano dei quadri alle pareti; **a picture of Queen Elizabeth I** un ritratto della regina Elisabetta I; **to draw a picture of sth** disegnare qc; **to take a picture of sb/sth** fare una foto a qn/di qc; **children's books have lots of pictures** ci sono molte illustrazioni nei libri per bambini; **my picture was in the paper** c'era la mia foto sul giornale; **he looked the picture of health** sembrava il ritratto della salute; **you're the picture of your mother** sei (proprio) il ritratto di tua madre; **the garden is a picture in June** il giardino in giugno è uno spettacolo; **his face was a picture!** avresti dovuto vedere la sua faccia!; **to be in/out of the picture** essere/non essere coinvolto(-a) 2 (*TV*) immagine *f*; **we get a good picture here** la ricezione qui è buona 3 (*Cine*) film *m inv*; **the pictures** (*esp Brit*) il cinema; **to go to the pictures** andare al cinema 4 (*mental image*) immagine *f*, idea; **the other side of the picture** il rovescio della medaglia; **he painted a black picture of the future** ha dipinto il futuro a tinte fosche; **to get the picture** afferrare l'idea; **the overall picture** il quadro generale; **to put sb in the picture** mettere qn al corrente ♦ VT (*imagine*) immaginare; (*remember*) ricordare; **I can just picture it!** me lo immagino!

picture book N libro illustrato

picture frame N cornice *f*

picture messaging N picture messaging *m*, invio di messaggini con disegni

pic·tur·esque [ˌpɪktʃəˈresk] ADJ pittoresco(-a)

picture window N finestra panoramica

pid·dling [ˈpɪdlɪŋ] ADJ (*fam*) insignificante

pidg·in Eng·lish [ˈpɪdʒɪnˈɪŋɡlɪʃ] N pidgin english *m inv*

pie [paɪ] N (*of fruit*) torta; (*of fish, meat*) pasticcio in crosta; **apple pie** torta di mele; **as easy as pie** (*fam*) (facile) come bere un bicchier d'acqua; **that's pie in the sky** sono castelli in aria

pie·bald [ˈpaɪbɔːld] ADJ (*horse*) pezzato(-a)

piece [piːs] N (*gen, also Chess*) pezzo; (*smaller*) pezzetto; (*of land*) appezzamento; (*fragment*) frammento; (*Draughts*) pedina; (*item*): **a piece of furniture/clothing/advice** un mobile/indumento/consiglio; **a piece of news/poetry** una notizia/poesia; **a piece of luck** un colpo di fortuna; **a 10p piece** (*Brit*) una moneta da 10 pence; **a six-piece band** un complesso di sei strumentisti; **a 21-piece tea set** ≈ un servizio da tè per 6 persone; **a piano piece** un pezzo *or* componimento per piano; **a small piece, please** un pezzo piccolo, per favore; **it is made all in one piece** è fatto in un pezzo solo; **in one piece** (*object*) intatto(-a); **to get back all in one piece** (*person*) tornare a casa incolume *or* sano(-a) e salvo(-a); **piece by piece** poco alla volta; **to be in pieces** (*taken apart*) essere smontato(-a); (*broken*) essere a pezzi; **to take sth to pieces** smontare qc; **to come** *or* **fall to pieces** sfasciarsi; **to smash sth to pieces** mandare in frantumi *or* in mille pezzi qc; **to go to pieces** (*fig*) crollare; **to say one's piece** dire la propria; **to give sb a piece of one's mind** dire a qn il fatto suo

▸ **piece together** VT + ADV (*also fig*) ricostruire

piece·meal [ˈpiːsmiːl] ADV poco alla volta ♦ ADJ (*approach, process*) graduale

piece rate N (*Industry*) tariffa a cottimo

piece·work [ˈpiːsˌwɜːk] N (*Industry*) (lavoro a) cottimo

pie chart N areogramma *m*, grafico a torta

Pied·mont [ˈpiːdmɒnt] N Piemonte *m*

pier [pɪəʳ] N pontile *m*; (*landing stage*) imbarcadero, pontile; (*of bridge*) pila

pierce [pɪəs] VT (*gen*) bucare, forare; (*subj: cold, wind*) penetrare; (: *shriek, light*) squarciare; (: *arrow*) trafiggere; **a bullet pierced his chest** un proiettile gli ha perforato il petto; **to have one's ears pierced** farsi fare i buchi per gli orecchini

pierc·ing [ˈpɪəsɪŋ] ADJ (*gen*) penetrante; (*cry*) lacerante, acuto(-a); (*wind, sarcasm*) pungente ♦ N (*of body part*) piercing *m inv*; **she has several piercings** ha diversi piercing

pi·ety [ˈpaɪətɪ] N pietà, devozione *f*

pif·fling [ˈpɪflɪŋ] (*fam*) ADJ insignificante

pig [pɪɡ] N 1 maiale *m*, porco; **to buy a pig in a poke** (*fig*) fare un acquisto alla cieca *or* a scatola chiusa 2 (*fam: person: nasty*) stronzo(-a); (: *greedy, dirty*) porco, maiale *m*; **to make a pig of o.s.** mangiare (e bere) come un porco

pi·geon [ˈpɪdʒən] N piccione *m*; **that's your pigeon** (*fig*) sono affari tuoi

pigeon·hole [ˈpɪdʒənˌhəʊl] N (*also fig*) casella ♦ VT (*fig*) etichettare, catalogare

pigeon-toed [ˈpɪdʒənˌtəʊd] ADJ: **to be pigeon-toed** camminare con i piedi in dentro

pig·gy bank [ˈpɪɡɪbæŋk] N salvadanaio

pig-headed [pɪɡˈhedɪd] ADJ testardo(-a), cocciuto(-a)

pig·let [ˈpɪɡlɪt] N maialino, porcellino

pig·ment [ˈpɪɡmənt] N pigmento

pig·men·ta·tion [ˌpɪɡmənˈteɪʃən] N pigmentazione *f*

pig·my [ˈpɪɡmɪ] N = **pygmy**

pig·skin [ˈpɪɡˌskɪn] N (pelle di) cinghiale *m*

pig·sty [ˈpɪɡˌstaɪ] N (*also fig*) porcile *m*

pig·tail [ˈpɪɡˌteɪl] N (*plaited*) treccina; (*loose*) codino

pike[1] [paɪk] N (*fish*) luccio; **he caught a pike** ha preso un luccio

pike[2] [paɪk] N (*spear*) picca

pilchard [ˈpɪltʃəd] N sardina

pile[1] [paɪl] N 1 (*heap: of books, records*) pila; (*less tidy*) mucchio, cumulo; **he put his things in a pile** ha ammucchiato le sue cose; **there were piles of dirty dishes in the kitchen** c'erano pile di piatti sporchi in cucina 2 (*fam: large amount*) mucchio, sacco; **piles of** un mucchio di; **I've got piles of work to do** ho un mucchio di lavoro da fare; **a pile of** una montagna di 3 (*fam: fortune*) fortuna; **my brother made a pile selling videos** mio fratello ha fatto una barca di soldi vendendo video ♦ VT (*stack*) impilare; (*heap*) ammucchiare; **a table piled high with books** un tavolo coperto da pile di libri ♦ VI (*fam*): **pile in!** salta su!; **to pile into a car** stiparsi *or* ammucchiarsi in una macchina; **to pile on/off a bus** far ressa per salire sull'autobus/scendere dall'autobus

▸ **pile on** VT + ADV: **to pile on the pressure** (*fam*) fare pressione; **to pile it on** (*fam*) esagerare, drammatizzare; **to pile work on sb** caricare qn di lavoro

▸ **pile up** VI + ADV (*also fig*) accumularsi, ammucchiarsi ♦ VT + ADV ammucchiare, accumulare

pile[2] [paɪl] N (*of carpet, cloth*) pelo

pile[3] [paɪl] N (*Constr*) palo

piles [paɪlz] NPL (*Med*) emorroidi *fpl*

pile-up [ˈpaɪlˌʌp] N (*Aut: fam*) tamponamento a catena

pil·fer [ˈpɪlfəʳ] VT rubacchiare ♦ VI fare dei furtarelli

pil·fer·ing [ˈpɪlfərɪŋ] N furtarelli *mpl*

pil·grim [ˈpɪlɡrɪm] N pellegrino(-a)

pil·grim·age [ˈpɪlɡrɪmɪdʒ] N pellegrinaggio; **to go on a pilgrimage** andare in pellegrinaggio

pill [pɪl] N pillola; **to be on the pill** (*contraceptive*) prendere la pillola; **to sweeten** *or* **sugar the pill** (*fig*) indorare la pillola

pil·lage [ˈpɪlɪdʒ] VT saccheggiare ♦ VI darsi al saccheggio

pil·lar [ˈpɪləʳ] N (*round*) colonna; (*square*) pilastro; **a pillar of smoke** una colonna di fumo; **a pillar of the church** (*fig*) uno dei pilastri della chiesa; **to be driven from pillar to post** essere sballottato(-a) a destra e a manca

pillar box N (*Brit*) buca delle lettere (a colonnina)

pil·lion [ˈpɪljən] N sellino posteriore (*di moto*); **on the pillion** sul sellino posteriore ♦ ADV: **to ride pillion** viaggiare dietro

pil·lo·ry [ˈpɪlərɪ] N berlina ♦ VT (fig) mettere alla berlina
pil·low [ˈpɪləʊ] N cuscino, guanciale m
pillow·case [ˈpɪləʊˌkeɪs], **pillow·slip** [ˈpɪləʊˌslɪp] N federa
pi·lot [ˈpaɪlət] N (Aer, Naut) pilota m/f; he's a pilot fa il pilota ♦ VT (Aer, Naut) pilotare; (fig: guide) guidare, dirigere ♦ ADJ (scheme) pilota inv
pilot boat N pilotina
pilot light N (on cooker etc) fiammella di sicurezza
pi·men·to [pɪˈmentəʊ] N peperoncino
pimp [pɪmp] N ruffiano, protettore
pim·ple [ˈpɪmpl] N foruncolo
pim·ply [ˈpɪmplɪ] ADJ (comp -ier, superl -iest) foruncoloso(-a)
PIN [pɪn] N ABBR (= personal identification number) PIN m inv
pin [pɪn] N (gen: as ornament) spillo; (safety pin) spillo di sicurezza; (Tech) perno; (in grenade) spoletta; (Med) chiodo; (Elec: of plug) spinotto; (Bowling) birillo; **fastened with a pin** fissato(-a) con uno spillo; **as neat as a (new) pin** (room) lucido(-a) come uno specchio; (person) impeccabile; **you could have heard a pin drop** non si sentiva volare una mosca ♦ VT 1 (with drawing pin) attaccare con una puntina; (sewing) attaccare con gli spilli; **they pinned a notice on the board** hanno appuntato un avviso in bacheca 2 (fig): **to pin sb against a wall** mettere qn con le spalle al muro; **to pin sb's arms to his sides** immobilizzare le braccia di qn contro i fianchi
  ▸ **pin down** VT + ADV 1 (fasten or hold down) immobilizzare 2 (fig): **to pin sb down to a date** far fissare una data a qn; **to pin sb down to their promise** costringere qn a mantenere una promessa; **to pin sb down about his beliefs** far dire a qn quello che pensa; **there's something strange here but I can't quite pin it down** c'è qualcosa di strano qua ma non riesco a capire cos'è
  ▸ **pin on** VT + PREP attaccare con uno spillo (or una puntina) a; **to pin one's hopes on sth** riporre le proprie speranze in qc; **to pin a crime on sb** (fam) addossare a qn la colpa di un delitto ♦ VT + ADV attaccare con uno spillo (or una puntina)
  ▸ **pin up** VT + ADV (notice) attaccare (al muro) con una puntina; (hair) appuntare con le forcine; (hem) appuntare con gli spilli
pina·fore [ˈpɪnəˌfɔːr] N (apron) grembiule m
pin·ball [ˈpɪnˌbɔːl] N (also: **pinball machine**) flipper m inv; **they're playing pinball** giocano a flipper
pin·cers [ˈpɪnsəz] NPL (of crab etc) pinze fpl, chele fpl; (tool) tenaglie fpl
pinch [pɪntʃ] N 1 (with fingers) pizzicotto, pizzico; **to feel the pinch** (fig) trovarsi nelle ristrettezze; **at a pinch** (fig) se è proprio necessario; **if it comes to the pinch** se le cose si mettono male 2 (small quantity) pizzico, presa; **to take sth with a pinch of salt** (fig) prendere qc con un grano di sale ♦ VT 1 (with fingers) pizzicare; **he pinched me!** mi ha pizzicato!; **my shoes are pinching me** le scarpe mi vanno strette 2 (fam: steal) fregare, grattare; (: idea) rubare; **who's pinched my pen?** chi mi ha fregato la penna? 3 (fam: arrest) pizzicare ♦ VI (shoe) essere (troppo) stretto(-a), stringere; **to pinch and scrape** fare economia (su tutto)
pinched [pɪntʃt] ADJ (face) dai lineamenti tirati; **pinched with cold** raggrinzito(-a) dal freddo; **pinched with hunger** scavato(-a) dalla fame
pin·cushion [ˈpɪnˌkʊʃn] N (cuscinetto) puntaspilli m inv
pine¹ [paɪn] N (also: **pine tree**) pino
pine² [paɪn] VI: **to pine for sb/sth** sentire tanto la mancanza di qn/qc
  ▸ **pine away** VI + ADV languire, deperire
pine·apple [ˈpaɪnˌæpl] N ananas m inv
pine cone N pigna
pine needle N ago di pino
ping [pɪŋ] N suono metallico; (of bell) tintinnio ♦ VI (see n) produrre un suono metallico; tintinnare
ping-pong [ˈpɪŋˌpɒŋ] N ping-pong m
pink [pɪŋk] N 1 (colour) rosa m inv 2 (Bot) garofano a piumino rosa 3 **to be in the pink (of health)** essere in perfetta salute ♦ ADJ 1 (colour) rosa inv; **to turn** or **go pink** (flush) arrossire 2 (Pol: fam) con tendenze di sinistra
pink·ing shears [ˈpɪŋkɪŋˌʃɪəz], **pinking scissors** NPL forbici fpl a zigzag

pin money N (Brit) denaro per spese superflue
pin·na·cle [ˈpɪnəkl] N (Archit) pinnacolo; (of rock) guglia; (top of mountain) vetta, cima; (fig) apice m, vertice m
pin·point [ˈpɪnˌpɔɪnt] VT (on map) localizzare con esattezza; (problem) mettere a fuoco, individuare con esattezza
pin·stripe [ˈpɪnˌstraɪp] ADJ: **pinstripe suit** (abito) gessato
pint [paɪnt] N (measure) pinta (Brit=0,568 litri; USA=0,4732 litri); (Brit fam: of beer) ≈ boccale m di birra; **half a pint of beer** una birra piccola; **to have a pint** bere una birra; **to go out for a pint** uscire a bere una birra
pio·neer [ˌpaɪəˈnɪər] N pioniere(-a) ♦ VT (technique, invention) essere l'ideatore(-trice) di; **he pioneered DNA tests** è stato uno dei primi a fare i test sul DNA
pi·ous [ˈpaɪəs] ADJ pio(-a); (pej) bigotto(-a); **a pious hope** una vana speranza
pip [pɪp] N (seed) seme m; (on card) seme m; (on dice) punto; (Brit Mil: fam: on uniform) stelletta; (on radar screen) segnale m; **an orange pip** un seme d'arancia
pipe [paɪp] N 1 (tube) tubo; **pipes** NPL (piping) tubatura fsg, conduttura fsg; **a plastic pipe** un tubo di plastica 2 (Mus: of organ) canna; (: wind instrument) piffero; **pipes** NPL (also: **bagpipes**) cornamusa fsg; **he plays the pipes** suona la cornamusa 3 (smoker's) pipa; **to smoke a pipe** fumare la pipa; **put that in your pipe and smoke it!** (fam) che ti piaccia o no, è così! ♦ VT 1 (water, oil etc) portare per mezzo di tubature 2 (Mus) suonare (col piffero or con la cornamusa); (speak or sing in high voice) dire (or cantare) con un tono di voce acuto; **to pipe sb aboard** (Naut) accogliere qn a bordo al suono di una banda 3 (Culin): **to pipe icing on a cake** decorare un dolce con la glassa
  ▸ **pipe down** VI + ADV (fam) fare silenzio
  ▸ **pipe up** VI + ADV (fam) farsi sentire
pipe cleaner N scovolino
piped mu·sic [ˈpaɪptˌmjuːzɪk] N musica di sottofondo
pipe dream N sogno impossibile
pipe·line [ˈpaɪpˌlaɪn] N (gen) conduttura; (also: **oil pipeline**) oleodotto; (also: **gas pipeline**) metanodotto; **to be in the pipeline** (fig) essere in arrivo; **these changes are in the pipeline** questi cambiamenti sono in arrivo
pip·er [ˈpaɪpər] N (on bagpipes) suonatore(-trice) di cornamusa
pipe tobacco N tabacco da pipa
pip·ing [ˈpaɪpɪŋ] N (tubing) tubature fpl; (Sewing) cordoncino
pi·quant [ˈpiːkənt] ADJ (sauce) piccante; (situation) intrigante; **a piquant charm** un fascino strano
pique [piːk] N dispetto, picca ♦ VT indispettire
pi·ra·cy [ˈpaɪrəsɪ] N pirateria
pi·rate [ˈpaɪrɪt] N (also fig) pirata m ♦ VT (product) contraffare; (idea) impossessarsi di; (record, video, book) riprodurre abusivamente
pirate radio N radio f inv pirata
pirou·ette [ˌpɪruˈet] N piroetta ♦ VI piroettare
Pi·sces [ˈpaɪsiːz] N Pesci mpl; **to be Pisces** essere dei Pesci
piss [pɪs] VI (fam!) pisciare (fam!)
  ▸ **piss about, piss around** VI + ADV (fam!) far cazzate (fam!)
  ▸ **piss down** VI + ADV (fam: rain) piovere a catinelle
  ▸ **piss off** (fam!) VI + ADV: **piss off!** levati dalle palle! (fam!), vaffanculo! (fam!) ♦ VT + ADV: **I'm pissed off with it** ne ho le palle piene (fam!)
pissed [pɪst] ADJ (Brit fam!: drunk) sbronzo(-a); (USA fam!) incazzato(-a); **to be pissed at sb** essere incazzato(-a) con qn
pis·tol [ˈpɪstl] N pistola
pis·ton [ˈpɪstən] N (gen) stantuffo; (Aut) pistone m
pit [pɪt] N 1 (hole in ground) buca, fossa; (on moon) cratere m; (coalmine) miniera di carbone; (quarry) cava; (to trap animals) buca; **in the pit of one's stomach** alla bocca dello stomaco; **he used to work down the pit** lavorava in miniera; **the last pit was closed twenty years ago** l'ultima miniera di carbone è stata chiusa vent'anni fa; **they dug a large pit** hanno scavato una grande buca 2 (Aut: in garage) fossa; (: Motor Racing: also: **the pits**) i box 3 (Brit: Theatre) platea; **orchestra pit** golfo mistico ♦ VT 1 (subj: chickenpox) butterare; (: rust) corrodere in più punti 2 **to pit A against B** contrapporre A a B; **to pit one's wits against sb** misurarsi contro qn

pita·pat [ˈpɪtəˈpæt] ADV: **to go pitapat** (*heart*) palpitare; (*rain*) picchiettare

pitch¹ [pɪtʃ] N (*tar*) pece *f*

pitch² [pɪtʃ] N 1 (*esp Brit: Sport*) campo; **football pitch** campo di calcio 2 (*angle, slope: of roof*) inclinazione *f* 3 (*Naut, Aer*) beccheggio 4 (*of note, voice, instrument*) intonazione *f*, altezza; (*fig: degree*) grado, punto; **I can't keep working at this pitch** non posso continuare a lavorare a questo ritmo; **at its (highest) pitch** al massimo, al colmo; **his anger reached such a pitch that ...** la sua furia raggiunse un punto tale che... 5 (*fam: also: sales pitch*) discorsetto imbonitore 6 (*Mountaineering*) tiro di corda 7 (*throw*) lancio ♦ VT 1 (*throw: ball, object*) lanciare; (: *hay*) sollevare col forcone; **he pitched the bottle into the lake** ha lanciato la bottiglia nel lago; **he was pitched off his horse** fu sbalzato da cavallo *or* disarcionato 2 (*Mus: song*) intonare; (: *note*) dare; **she can't pitch a note properly** non riesce a prendere una nota giusta; **to pitch one's aspirations too high** mirare troppo in alto; **to pitch it too strong** (*fam*) esagerare, calcare troppo la mano 3 (*set up: tent*) piantare; **we pitched our tent near the beach** abbiamo piantato la tenda vicino alla spiaggia ♦ VI 1 (*fall*) cascare, cadere; **to pitch forward** essere catapultato(-a) in avanti 2 (*Naut: Aer*) beccheggiare

  ▸ **pitch in** VI + ADV (*fam*) darci dentro *or* sotto
  ▸ **pitch into** VI + PREP (*attack*) saltare addosso a; (*start: work, food*) attaccare, buttarsi su

pitch-black [ˌpɪtʃˈblæk] ADJ (*also:* **pitch-dark**) nero(-a) come la pece; **the room was pitch-black** nella stanza c'era un buio pesto

pitched battle [ˌpɪtʃtˈbætl] N (*Mil, also fig*) battaglia campale

pitch·er [ˈpɪtʃəˈ] N (*jar*) brocca

pitch·fork [ˈpɪtʃˌfɔːk] N forcone *m* ♦ VT: **to pitchfork sb into a job** (*fig*) costringere qn ad accettare un lavoro di punto in bianco

pit·eous [ˈpɪtɪəs] ADJ pietoso(-a)

pit·fall [ˈpɪtˌfɔːl] N (*fig*) tranello, trappola

pith [pɪθ] N (*of plant*) midollo; (*of oranges, lemons*) parte *f* bianca della scorza; (*fig: core: of argument*) nocciolo, essenza, succo; (: *force*) vigore *m*

pit·head [ˈpɪtˌhɛd] N imbocco della miniera

pithy [ˈpɪθɪ] ADJ (*comp* **-ier**, *superl* **-iest**) (*fig: argument*) vigoroso(-a); (: *remarks*) arguto(-a); (: *account*) conciso(-a)

piti·able [ˈpɪtɪəbl] ADJ pietoso(-a)

piti·ful [ˈpɪtɪfʊl] ADJ 1 (*sight, story*) pietoso(-a); (*person*) che fa pietà *or* compassione 2 (*pej: attempt*) pietoso(-a); (: *cowardice*) deplorevole; (*sum*) miserabile

piti·ful·ly [ˈpɪtɪfəlɪ] ADV (*gen*) pietosamente; (*thin etc*) da far pietà; **it's pitifully obvious** è penosamente chiaro

piti·less [ˈpɪtɪlɪs] ADJ spietato(-a)

pit·tance [ˈpɪtəns] N miseria, somma miserabile; **they work for a pittance** lavorano per una miseria

pit·ted [ˈpɪtɪd] ADJ: **pitted with** (*potholes*) pieno(-a) di; (*chickenpox*) butterato(-a) da

pity [ˈpɪtɪ] N 1 compassione *f*, pietà; **to feel pity for sb** provare compassione per qn; **for pity's sake!** per amor del cielo!; (*pleading*) per pietà!; **to have** *or* **take pity on sb** aver pietà di qn 2 (*cause of regret*) peccato; **what a pity!** che peccato!; **more's the pity** purtroppo; **it is a pity that you can't come** è un peccato che tu non possa venire ♦ VT compatire, commiserare; **I don't hate him, I pity him** non lo odio, lo compatisco

pity·ing [ˈpɪtɪɪŋ] ADJ compassionevole; (*with contempt*) di commiserazione

piv·ot [ˈpɪvət] N (*Mil, Tech: fig*) perno ♦ VT imperniare ♦ VI girare su se stesso(-a)

pix·el [ˈpɪksəl] N (*Comput*) pixel *m inv*

pixie [ˈpɪksɪ] N folletto

piz·za [ˈpiːtsə] N pizza

plac·ard [ˈplækɑːd] N cartello

pla·cate [pləˈkeɪt] VT placare, calmare

placa·tory [pləˈkeɪtərɪ] ADJ (*gesture, tone, words etc*) tranquillizzante, conciliante

place [pleɪs] N 1 (*in general*) posto; (*more formally*) luogo; **it's a quiet place** è un posto tranquillo; **there are a lot of interesting places to visit** ci sono tanti posti interessanti da vedere; **to take place** (*incident*) succedere, accadere; (*meeting*) avere luogo; **elections will take place on November 25th** le elezioni avranno luogo il 25 novembre; **we came to a place where ...** siamo arrivati in un posto dove....; **from place to place** da un posto all'altro; **this is no place for you** questo non è un posto per te; **place of business** posto di lavoro; **place of worship/birth** luogo di culto/nascita; **all over the place** dappertutto; **to go places** (*travel*) andare in giro (per il mondo); **we're going places at last** (*fig: fam*) finalmente abbiamo sfondato; **it's only a small place** (*town*) è solo un paesino; (*house*) è piccolina; **his place in the country** la sua villa in campagna; **at your place** a casa tua; **come to our place** venite da noi *or* a casa nostra; **to put sth back in its place** rimettere qc al suo posto; **that remark was quite out of place** quell'osservazione era proprio fuori luogo; **I feel rather out of place here** qui mi sento un po' fuori posto; **this isn't the place to discuss politics!** questo non è il posto giusto per discutere di politica!; **to change places with sb** scambiarsi di posto con qn; **to take the place of sb/sth** sostituire qn/qc; **in place of** al posto di, invece di 2 (*in street names*) via; **market place** piazza del mercato 3 (*in book*): **to find one's place** trovare la pagina giusta; **to lose one's place** perdere il segno 4 (*seat*) posto (a sedere); (*at table*) posto (a tavola); (*in restaurant*) coperto; **to lay an extra place for sb** aggiungere un posto a tavola per qn 5 (*job, vacancy in team, school*) posto; **he found a place for his nephew in the firm** ha trovato un posto a suo nipote nella ditta; **a university place** un posto all'università 6 (*social position*) posizione *f*, rango; **friends in high places** amici altolocati *or* nelle alte sfere; **to know one's place** (*fig*) sapere stare al proprio posto; **it is not my place to do it** non sta a me farlo; **to put sb in his place** (*fig*) mettere a posto qn, mettere qn al suo posto 7 (*in series, rank etc*): **in the first/second place** in primo/secondo luogo; **she took second place in the race** si è piazzata *or* è arrivata seconda nella gara; **she took second place in the exam** ha preso il secondo miglior voto all'esame; **A won, with B in second place** A ha vinto e B è finito secondo ♦ VT 1 (*put: gen*) posare, mettere; (*on wall*) mettere; **place it on the table** mettilo *or* posalo sul tavolo; **he placed his hand on hers** ha posato la mano sulla sua; **we should place no trust in him** non dovremmo farci nessun affidamento 2 (*situate: town*) situare; (: *person*) piazzare; **we are better placed than a month ago** siamo in una situazione migliore *or* siamo messi meglio di un mese fa; **awkwardly placed** (*shop*) piazzato(-a) male; (*fig: person*) messo(-a) male; (: *in embarrassing situation*) in una posizione delicata 3 (*contract, bet*) fare; (*goods*) piazzare; **to place an order with sb (for)** fare un'ordinazione a qn (di); **to place a book with a publisher** trovare un editore per un libro; **to place sth in sb's hands** mettere qc nelle mani di qn; **we could place 200 men** possiamo procurare lavoro a 200 uomini 4 (*in exam, race etc*) classificare; **to be placed second** classificarsi *or* piazzarsi al secondo posto 5 (*recall, identify: person*) ricordarsi di; (: *face, accent*) riconoscere; **I can't place him** non riesco a ricordarmi dove l'ho visto

pla·cebo [pləˈsiːbəʊ] N placebo *m inv*

place mat N (*cork*) sottopiatto; (*linen*) tovaglietta

place·ment [ˈpleɪsmənt] N (*in group, accommodation*) collocamento; (*of trainee*) stage *m inv*; **to do a work placement** fare uno stage

place name N toponimo

pla·cen·ta [pləˈsɛntə] N placenta

plac·id [ˈplæsɪd] ADJ placido(-a), calmo(-a)

pla·cid·ity [pləˈsɪdɪtɪ] N placidità

pla·gia·rism [ˈpleɪdʒərɪzəm] N plagio

pla·gia·rist [ˈpleɪdʒərɪst] N plagiario(-a)

pla·gia·rize [ˈpleɪdʒəˌraɪz] VT plagiare

plague [pleɪg] N (*disease, also fig*) peste *f*; (*of rats, locusts*) invasione *f*; **to avoid sb/sth like the plague** evitare qn/qc come la peste ♦ VT (*fig*) tormentare; **she's plagued with money worries** è tormentata da problemi economici; **to plague sb with questions** assillare qn di domande

plaice [pleɪs] N platessa, passera di mare

plaid [plæd] N (*material*) tessuto scozzese *or* a scacchi; (*cloak*) mantellina scozzese; **a plaid shirt** una camicia a scacchi; **a plaid sports jacket** una giacca sportiva a scacchi

plain [pleɪn] ADJ (*comp* -**er**, *superl* -**est**) **1** (*clear, obvious*) chiaro(-a), palese, evidente; (*path, track*) ben segnato(-a); **it's as plain as the nose on your face** (*fam*) è chiaro come il sole; **to make sth plain to sb** far capire chiaramente qc a qn; **do I make myself plain?** mi sono spiegato?; **he's lying, that's plain** è chiaro che mente **2** (*outspoken, honest, frank*) franco(-a), aperto(-a), schietto(-a); **plain dealing** sincerità, franchezza; **in plain language** *or* **English** in parole povere; **I shall be plain with you** sarò franco con te **3** (*simple, with nothing added*) semplice; (*paper: unlined*) non rigato(-a); (*fabric: in one colour*) in tinta unita *inv*; (*without seasoning*) scondito(-a); **the plain truth** la pura verità; **he's a plain man** è un uomo semplice; **plain stitch** (*Knitting*) maglia a diritto; **a plain tie** una cravatta in tinta unita; **a plain white blouse** una camicetta bianca, semplice; **it's just plain common sense** (*fam*) è una questione di semplice buon senso; **to send sth under plain cover** spedire qc in busta riservata **4** (*not pretty*) insignificante, scialbo(-a) ♦ ADV **1** (*fam: simply, completely*) semplicemente **2** (*clearly*): **I can't put it plainer than that** non potrei esprimermi più chiaramente ♦ N **1** (*Geog*) pianura **2** (*Knitting*) (maglia a) diritto

plain chocolate N cioccolato fondente

plain·ly [ˈpleɪnlɪ] ADV (*clearly*) chiaramente; (*speak*) con franchezza, francamente; (*dress*) con semplicità, sobriamente; **he was plainly embarrassed** era chiaramente imbarazzato

plain·ness [ˈpleɪnnɪs] N (*simplicity*) semplicità; (*lack of beauty*) insignificanza

plain speak·ing [ˌpleɪnˈspiːkɪŋ] N: **there has been some plain speaking between the two leaders** i due leader si sono parlati chiaro

plain·tiff [ˈpleɪntɪf] N (*Law*) attore(-trice)

plain·tive [ˈpleɪntɪv] ADJ (*voice, song*) lamentoso(-a); (*look*) struggente; **plaintive cry** lamento

plait [plæt] N treccia ♦ VT (*raffia*) intrecciare; **to plait one's hair** farsi una treccia (*or* le trecce)

plan [plæn] N **1** (*scheme*) piano, progetto (*Pol, Econ*) piano; **plan of campaign** (*Mil, also fig*) piano di battaglia; **development plan** piano *or* progetto di sviluppo; **to draw up a plan** fare *or* elaborare un programma; **if everything goes according to plan** se tutto va secondo le previsioni *or* il previsto; **everything went according to plan** è andato tutto come previsto; **to make plans** far programmi *or* progetti; **the best plan would be to …** la cosa migliore sarebbe…; **have you got any plans for today?** che programmi hai per oggi?; **what are your plans for the holidays?** che programmi hai per le vacanze? **2** (*diagram, map: of building, town*) pianta; (: *for essay, speech*) schema *m*; **a plan of the campsite** una piantina del campeggio ♦ VT **1** (*arrange: robbery, holiday, campaign*) organizzare; (*economy, research*) pianificare; (*essay*) fare lo schema di; **we're planning a trip to France** stiamo progettando un viaggio in Francia; **plan your revision carefully** organizza bene il ripasso; **to plan one's family** pianificare le nascite **2** (*intend*) avere in progetto; **to plan to do** avere l'intenzione di fare; **how long do you plan to stay?** quanto conti di restare? **3** (*design*) progettare; **a well-planned town** una città che ha un buon piano urbanistico ♦ VI: **to plan (for)** far piani *or* progetti (per); **one has to plan months ahead** bisogna cominciare a pensarci diversi mesi prima; **to plan on sth/on doing sth** contare su qc/di fare qc
  ▸ **plan out** VT + ADV organizzare nei particolari

plane¹ [pleɪn] N aereo; **by plane** in aereo

plane² [pleɪn] ADJ (*Geom*) piano(-a) ♦ N **1** (*Art, Math*) piano **2** (*fig*) piano, livello

plane³ [pleɪn] N (*tool*) pialla ♦ VT (*also:* **plane down**) piallare; **to plane sth smooth** levigare qc con la pialla

plane⁴ [pleɪn] N (*tree*) platano; **London plane** platano di Londra

plan·et [ˈplænɪt] N pianeta *m*

plan·etar·ium [ˌplænɪˈtɛərɪəm] N planetario

plank [plæŋk] N (*of wood*) tavola, asse *f*

plank·ton [ˈplæŋktən] N plancton *m inv*

planned economy [ˌplænɪˈkɒnəmɪ] N economia pianificata

plan·ner [ˈplænə'] N (*Econ*) pianificatore(-trice); (*Industry*) progettista *m/f*; (*also:* **forward planner**) calendario; **town planner** urbanista

plan·ning [ˈplænɪŋ] N (*Pol, Econ*) pianificazione *f*; (*Industry*) progettazione *f*; **the trip needs careful planning** bisogna organizzare bene il viaggio; **family planning** pianificazione *f* familiare

plant [plɑːnt] N **1** (*Bot*) pianta; **I water my plants every week** annaffio le piante ogni settimana **2** (*no pl: machinery etc*) impianto; (*factory*) stabilimento; **a chemical plant** uno stabilimento chimico ♦ VT **1** (*trees, seeds, flowers*) piantare; **to plant a field with corn** piantare *or* coltivare un terreno a grano **2** (*position: pole*) piantare, conficcare; (*bomb*) mettere; (*kiss*) stampare; **to plant an idea in sb's mind** ficcare *or* cacciare in testa un'idea a qn; **he planted himself right in her path** le si è piantato di fronte; **to plant sth on sb** (*fam*) nascondere qc su qn (*per incriminarlo*)
  ▸ **plant out** VT + ADV (*seedlings*) trapiantare

plan·ta·tion [plænˈteɪʃən] N piantagione *f*

plant pot N vaso (per piante)

plaque [plæk] N (*on building*) placca, targa; (*on teeth*) placca batterica

plas·ma [ˈplæzmə] N plasma *m*

plasma TV N TV *f inv* al plasma

plas·ter [ˈplɑːstə'] N **1** (*Constr*) intonaco **2** (*Med*) gesso; **with his leg in plaster** con la gamba ingessata **3** (*Brit: also:* **sticking plaster**) cerotto; **have you got a plaster, by any chance?** hai un cerotto, per caso? ♦ VT **1** (*Constr*) intonacare **2** (*fam: cover*) impiastricciare; **to be plastered with** (*mud*) essere impiastricciato(-a) di; **to plaster a wall with posters** tappezzare un muro di manifesti **3** (*Med*) ingessare

plaster·board [ˈplɑːstəˌbɔːd] N lastra di cartongesso

plaster cast N (*Med*) ingessatura, gesso; (*model, statue*) modello in gesso

plas·tered [ˈplɑːstəd] ADJ (*fam: drunk*) ubriaco(-a) fradicio(-a)

plas·ter·er [ˈplɑːstərə'] N intonacatore *m*

plas·tic [ˈplæstɪk] N plastica, materia plastica; **plastics** materie *fpl* plastiche ♦ ADJ **1** (*made of plastic*) di plastica **2** (*flexible*) plastico(-a); **plastic behaviour** (*Phys*) plasticità; **the plastic arts** le arti plastiche

plastic bag N sacchetto di plastica

plastic bullet N pallottola di plastica

plastic explosive N (*esplosivo al*) plastico

plastic surgery N chirurgia plastica, chirurgia estetica

plate [pleɪt] N **1** (*flat dish, plateful*) piatto; (*for church collection*) piatto delle elemosine; **to hand sb sth on a plate** (*fig: fam*) offrire qc a qn su un piatto d'argento; **to have a lot on one's plate** (*fig: fam*) avere un sacco di cose da fare **2** **gold/silver plate** vasellame *m* d'oro/d'argento; (*electroplated*) metallo placcato in oro/in argento **3** (*Phot*) lastra; (*Tech*) placca; (*on door*) targa, targhetta; (*Aut: number plate*) targa; (*on cooker: hot plate*) piastra **4** (*dental plate*) dentiera **5** (*book illustration*) tavola (fuori testo) **6** (*Geol*) zolla **7** (*sheet of metal*) lamiera **8** (*Typ*) cliché *m inv* ♦ VT (*gen*) placcare; (*with gold*) dorare; (*with silver*) argentare

plat·eau [ˈplætəʊ] N (*pl* **plateaus** *or* **plateaux**) (*Geog*) altopiano

plate·ful [ˈpleɪtfʊl] N piatto

plate glass N vetro piano

plat·en [ˈplætən] N (*of typewriter, printer etc*) rullo

plate rack N scolapiatti *m inv*

plat·form [ˈplætˌfɔːm] N (*Brit: on bus*) piattaforma; (*at meeting, for band, stage*) palco; (*Pol: manifesto*) piattaforma, programma *m* (di base); (*Rail*) marciapiede *m*, banchina; **the soloist had just left the platform** il solista aveva appena lasciato il palco; **the train leaves from platform 7** il treno parte dal binario 7; **they were waiting on the platform** aspettavano sulla banchina

platform ticket N (*Brit*) biglietto d'ingresso ai binari

plati·num [ˈplætɪnəm] N platino

plati·tude [ˈplætɪtjuːd] N luogo comune, banalità *f inv*

pla·toon [pləˈtuːn] N (*Mil*) plotone *m*

plat·ter [ˈplætə'] N piatto da portata

plau·dits [ˈplɔːdɪts] NPL plauso *msg*

plau·sible [ˈplɔːzəbl] ADJ (*argument, story*) plausibile, credibile; (*person*) convincente; **a plausible excuse** una scusa plausibile; **he seemed plausible** sembrava convincente

play [pleɪ] N **1** (*recreation*) gioco; **the children were at play** i bambini giocavano; **to do/say sth in play** fare/dire qc per scherzo; **work and play** lavoro e svago; **a play on words** un gioco di parole **2** (*Sport*) gioco; **play began at 3 o'clock** la partita è cominciata alle 3; **there was some good play in the first half** ci sono state delle belle azioni nel primo tempo; **to be in/out of play** (*ball*) essere in/fuori gioco **3** (*Theatre*) opera teatrale; **radio/television play** commedia radiofonica/per la televisione; **a play by Shakespeare** una commedia di Shakespeare; **to put on a play** mettere in scena una commedia **4** (*Tech: movement, give*) gioco; **there's not enough play in the rope** la fune non ha abbastanza gioco **5** (*fig phrases*): **to bring** *or* **call into play** (*plan*) mettere in azione; (*emotions*) esprimere; **to give full play to one's imagination** dare libero sfogo alla propria fantasia; **to make great play of sth** giocare molto su qc; **to make a play for sb** fare il filo a qn; **to make a play for sth** darsi da fare per ottenere qc; **the play of light on the water** i giochi di luce sull'acqua ♦ VT **1** (*match, card*) giocare; (*cards, chess, tennis*) giocare a; (*opponent*) giocare contro; (*chesspiece*) muovere; **to play a game of tennis** giocare una partita a tennis; **I play hockey** gioco a hockey; **can you play pool?** sai giocare a biliardo?; **to play sb at chess** giocare contro qn a scacchi; **Italy will play Scotland next month** il mese prossimo l'Italia giocherà contro la Scozia; **they played him in goal** l'hanno fatto giocare in porta; **don't play games with me** (*fam*) non prendermi in giro; **to play a trick on sb** fare uno scherzo a qn; **my eyes must be playing tricks on me** devo avere le traveggole; **to play the field** (*sexually*) darsi da fare in campo amoroso; **to play a fish** (*Angling*) stancare un pesce **2** (*perform: role*) interpretare; (: *play*) rappresentare, dare; (*perform in: town*) esibirsi a, dare uno spettacolo (*or* una serie di spettacoli) a; **I would like to play Cleopatra** mi piacerebbe interpretare Cleopatra; **to play sth for laughs** interpretare qc in chiave comica **3** (*instrument, piece of music*) suonare; (*record*) mettere; (*radio*) ascoltare; **I play the guitar** suono la chitarra; **she's always playing that record** ascolta sempre quel disco **4** (*direct: light, hose*) puntare, dirigere ♦ VI **1** (*gen*) giocare; **to play at tennis** giocare a tennis; **to go out to play** andar fuori a giocare; **to play with a stick** giocherellare con un bastone; **he's playing with his friends** sta giocando coi gli amici; **they're playing at soldiers** stanno giocando ai soldati; **to play with fire** (*fig*) scherzare col fuoco; **to play for money** giocare a soldi; **to play for time** (*fig*) cercare di guadagnar tempo; **to play into sb's hands** (*fig*) fare il gioco di qn; **to play safe** giocare sul sicuro; **what are you playing at?** (*fam*) cosa cavolo stai facendo? **2** (*move about, form patterns*): **we watched the fountains playing** guardavamo i giochi d'acqua delle fontane; **the sun was playing on the water** il sole creava giochi di luce sull'acqua; **a smile played on his lips** un sorriso gli sfiorò le labbra **3** (*Mus*) suonare; (*radio*) essere acceso(-a); **to play on the piano** suonare il piano **4** (*Theatre, Cine*) recitare (una parte); **to play dead** (*fig*) fingere di essere morto(-a).

► **play about, play around** VI + ADV (*person*) divertirsi; **to play about** *or* **around with** (*fiddle with*) giocherellare con; (*idea*) accarezzare

► **play along** VI + ADV: **to play along with** (*fig: person*) stare al gioco di; (: *plan, idea*) fingere di assecondare ♦ VT + ADV: **to play sb along** (*fig*) illudere qn

► **play around** VI = play about

► **play back** VT + ADV riascoltare, risentire

► **play down** VT + ADV minimizzare

► **play off** VT + ADV: **to play X off against Y** mettere X e Y l'uno(-a) contro l'altro(-a) ♦ VI + ADV (*Sport*) giocare lo spareggio

► **play on** VI + ADV (*Sport*) continuare a giocare; (*Mus*) continuare a suonare ♦ VI + PREP (*sb's feelings, credulity*) giocare su; **to play on sb's nerves** dare sui nervi a qn

► **play out** VT + ADV (*enact*) mettere in atto

► **play through** VT + ADV (*piece*) suonare

► **play up** VI + ADV **1** (*Brit fam: cause trouble: child, engine*) fare i capricci; (: *leg, ulcer*) farsi sentire **2** (*fam: flatter*): **to play up to sb** adulare qn ♦ VT + ADV **1** (*fam: cause trouble to*): **to play sb up** (*subj: child*) combinarne di tutti i colori a qn; (: *leg*) fare male a qn **2** (*exaggerate*) esagerare, gonfiare

play·act ['pleɪˌækt] VI (*fig*) fare la commedia

play·boy ['pleɪˌbɔɪ] N playboy *m inv*

played out ['pleɪd'aʊt] ADJ (*exhausted: person*) spossato(-a); (: *vein in mine*) esaurito(-a); (: *argument*) superato(-a)

play·er ['pleɪə'] N (*Sport*) giocatore(-trice); (*Mus*) musicista *m/f*; (*Theatre*) attore(-trice); **players of musical instruments** suonatori di strumenti musicali; **football player** calciatore(-trice); **piano player** pianista *m/f*; **saxophone player** sassofonista *m/f*

play·ful ['pleɪfʊl] ADJ (*child, puppy*) giocherellone(-a); (*mood, smile, remark*) scherzoso(-a)

play·goer ['pleɪˌgəʊə'] N appassionato(-a) di teatro; **an actor well-loved by playgoers** un attore molto amato dal pubblico

play·ground ['pleɪˌgraʊnd] N (*in school*) cortile *m* per la ricreazione; (*in park*) parco *m* giochi, *inv*

play·group ['pleɪˌgruːp] N ≈ asilo

playing card N carta da gioco

playing field N campo sportivo

play·maker ['pleɪˌmeɪkə'] N (*Sport*) playmaker *m/f inv*

play·mate ['pleɪˌmeɪt] N compagno(-a) di gioco

play·off ['pleɪˌɒf] N (*Sport*) (partita di) spareggio, bella

play·pen ['pleɪˌpen] N box *m inv* (*per bambini*)

play·room ['pleɪˌrʊm] N stanza dei giochi

play·school ['pleɪskuːl] N ≈ asilo

play·thing ['pleɪˌθɪŋ] N (*also fig*) giocattolo

play·time ['pleɪˌtaɪm] N (*Scol*) ricreazione *f*

play·wright ['pleɪˌraɪt] N commediografo(-a), drammaturgo(-a)

plc, PLC [ˌpiːˌelˈsiː] ABBR = public limited company

plea [pliː] N **1** (*entreaty: for donations*) appello; (: *for leniency*) supplica; (*excuse*) scusa, pretesto; **a plea to humanity** un appello all'umanità; **a plea for help** una richiesta di aiuto; **to make a plea for sth** chiedere qc; **he made a plea for understanding** chiedeva comprensione; **on the plea of** con la scusa di **2** (*Law*): **to enter a plea of guilty** dichiararsi colpevole; **to put forward a plea of self-defence** invocare la legittima difesa

plea bargaining N (*Law*) patteggiamento (della pena)

plead [pliːd] (*pt, pp* **pleaded** *or* **pled**(*esp USA*)) VT **1 to plead sb's case,** (*Law*) **to plead sb's cause** (*fig*) perorare la causa di qn **2** (*as excuse: ignorance*) addurre come (*or* a) pretesto; **to plead insanity** (*Law*) invocare l'infermità mentale ♦ VI **1** (*beg*): **to plead with sb (to do sth)** supplicare *or* implorare qn (di fare qc); **to plead for sth** (*beg for*) implorare qc; (*make speech in favour of*) parlare in favore di qc; **he was pleading for mercy** chiedeva pietà **2** (*Law: lawyer*): **to plead for** perorare in favore di; **to plead guilty/not guilty** (*defendant*) dichiararsi colpevole/innocente

pleas·ant ['pleznt] ADJ (*gen*) piacevole, gradevole; (*surprise, news*) bello(-a); (*smell*) gradevole, buono(-a); (*people, smile*) simpatico(-a); (*weather*) bello(-a); **we had a pleasant time** ci siamo divertiti

pleas·ant·ly ['plezntlɪ] ADV (*smile, greet*) cordialmente; **I am pleasantly surprised** sono piacevolmente sorpreso

pleas·ant·ry ['plezntrɪ] N (*joke*) battuta di spirito, spiritosaggine *f*; (*polite remark*): **to exchange pleasantries** scambiarsi convenevoli

please [pliːz] EXCL per piacere, per favore; (*yes,*) **please** sì, grazie; **come in, please** entrate, prego; **please pass the salt, pass the salt please** per piacere *or* per favore, mi passi il sale?; **two coffees, please** due caffè, per favore; **my bill, please** il conto, per piacere; **please don't cry!** ti prego, non piangere! ♦ VI **1 if you please** (*frm: in request*) per piacere, per favore; **he wanted ten, if you please!** (*iro*) ne voleva dieci, figurati!; **he does as he pleases** fa come gli pare **2** (*cause satisfaction*) far piacere, piacere; **anxious** *or* **eager to please** desideroso(-a) di piacere; **a gift that is sure to please** un dono sicuramente gradito ♦ VT (*give pleasure to*) far piacere a; (*satisfy*) accontentare; **I did it to please you** l'ho fatto per farti piacere; **there's no pleasing him** non c'è verso di accontentarlo; **to please o.s.** far come si vuole; **please yourself!** come vuoi!, come ti pare!

pleased [pliːzd] ADJ (*happy*) felice, lieto(-a); (*satisfied*) contento(-a), soddisfatto(-a); **to be pleased (about sth)** essere contento(-a) (di qc); **pleased to meet you!** piacere!; **my mother's not going to be very pleased** mia madre non sarà molto contenta; **I am not pleased at your decision** la tua decisione non mi ha fatto piacere; **to be pleased with sb/sth** essere contento(-a) *or* soddisfatto(-a) di qn/qc; **it's beautiful: she'll be pleased with it** è bellissimo, ne sarà contenta; **to be pleased with o.s.** compiacersi, essere compiaciuto(-a) di sé; **we are pleased to inform you that ...** abbiamo il piacere di informarla che...

pleas·ing [ˈpliːzɪŋ] ADJ (*person*) simpatico(-a); (*news, sight*) piacevole, che fa piacere; **it's pleasing that ...** fa piacere che...

pleas·ur·able [ˈplɛʒərəbl] ADJ (molto) piacevole *or* gradevole

pleas·ure [ˈplɛʒər] N 1 (*satisfaction, happiness*) piacere *m*; **with pleasure** con piacere, volentieri; **it's a pleasure!, my pleasure!, the pleasure is mine!** (*frm: returning thanks*) prego!, il piacere è (tutto) mio!; **I have much pleasure in informing you that ...** sono lieto di informarla che...; **may I have the pleasure?** mi concede l'onore di questo ballo?; **Mr and Mrs Smith request the pleasure of your company** (*frm*) i Signori Smith gradirebbero averla come ospite 2 (*source of pleasure*) piacere *m*; **all the pleasures of London** tutti i divertimenti di Londra; **is this trip for business or pleasure?** è un viaggio d'affari o di piacere? 3 (*frm: will*) desiderio, volontà; **at sb's pleasure** secondo i desideri di qn; **we await your pleasure** (*Comm*) siamo a vostra disposizione; **to be detained during her Majesty's pleasure** (*Law*) essere condannato ad una pena detentiva di durata illimitata (*prevista per i reati più gravi*) ♦ ADJ (*cruise*) di piacere

pleat [pliːt] N piega ♦ VT pieghettare

plebi·scite [ˈplɛbɪsɪt] N plebiscito; **to hold a plebiscite** fare un referendum

plebs [plɛbz] NPL (*pej*) plebe *fsg*

plec·trum [ˈplɛktrəm] N plettro

pledge [plɛdʒ] N (*promise*) promessa solenne; (*security, token*) pegno; **to be under a pledge of secrecy** aver promesso di mantenere il segreto; **as a pledge of** come pegno *or* testimonianza di; **to sign** *or* **take the pledge** (*hum, fam*) promettere solennemente di non toccare alcolici ♦ VT 1 (*promise*): **to pledge sth/to do sth** promettere qc/di fare qc; **the US has pledged thirty million dollars** gli USA hanno promesso trenta milioni di dollari; **to pledge sb to secrecy** far promettere a qn di mantenere il segreto; **to pledge support for sb** impegnarsi a sostenere qn 2 (*pawn*) impegnare

ple·na·ry [ˈpliːnərɪ] ADJ plenario(-a); **in plenary session** in seduta plenaria

plen·ti·ful [ˈplɛntɪfʊl] ADJ abbondante; **to be in plentiful supply** abbondare, esserci in gran quantità

plen·ty [ˈplɛntɪ] N 1 abbondanza; **in plenty** (*in large quantities*) in abbondanza 2 **plenty of** (*lots of*) molto(-a), tanto(-a); (*enough*) abbastanza; **he has plenty of friends** ha tanti amici; **we've got plenty of time** abbiamo un sacco di tempo; **I've got plenty** ne ho abbastanza; **there's plenty to go on** (*information*) ci sono indizi più che sufficienti; **we've got plenty of time** abbiamo un sacco di tempo

pleu·ri·sy [ˈplʊərɪsɪ] N pleurite *f*

pli·able [ˈplaɪəbl], **pli·ant** [ˈplaɪənt] ADJ (*substance*) pieghevole, flessibile; (*fig: person*) malleabile

pli·ers [ˈplaɪəz] NPL (*also:* **pair of pliers**) pinze *fpl*

plight [plaɪt] N situazione *f* (critica); **their desperate plight** la loro situazione disperata; **the country's economic plight** le gravi condizioni economiche del paese

plim·soll [ˈplɪmsəl] N (*Brit*) scarpa da tennis

plinth [plɪnθ] N plinto

PLO [ˌpiːɛlˈəʊ] N ABBR (= *Palestine Liberation Organization*) OLP *f*

plod [plɒd] VI: **to plod up/down** *etc* trascinarsi su per/giù per *etc*; **to plod away at sth** (*fig*) sgobbare su qc; **we must plod on** (*fig*) dobbiamo farci forza e tirare avanti

plod·der [ˈplɒdər] N sgobbone(-a)

plod·ding [ˈplɒdɪŋ] ADJ (*gait*) pesante; (*pace of work*) lento(-a) e pesante; (*fig: person*) che sgobba

plonk[1] [plɒŋk] N (*Brit fam: wine*) vino ordinario

plonk[2] [plɒŋk] N (*sound*) tonfo ♦ ADV: **plonk in the middle** nel bel mezzo ♦ VT (*fam: also:* **plonk down**) appoggiare

pesantemente; **to plonk o.s. down** lasciarsi cadere (di peso); **he plonked himself down on the sofa** è crollato sul sofà

plot[1] [plɒt] N (*of land*) appezzamento, lotto; **a vegetable plot** un orticello; **building plot** lotto edificabile

plot[2] [plɒt] N 1 (*conspiracy*) complotto, cospirazione *f*, congiura; **a plot against the president** un complotto contro il presidente 2 (*of story, play*) intreccio, trama; **a complicated plot** una trama complicata ♦ VT 1 (*mark out: course, graph, diagram etc*) tracciare; **to plot one's position** (*Naut*) fare il punto 2 (*plan secretly*) complottare, cospirare, congiurare ♦ VI complottare, congiurare

plot·ter [ˈplɒtər] N 1 (*conspirator*) cospiratore(-trice) 2 (*Naut, Comput*) plotter *m inv*

plough, plow (*USA*) [plaʊ] N aratro ♦ VT (*field*) arare; (*furrow*) scavare; **they plough the fields in the autumn** arano i campi in autunno; **to plough one's way through a book** (*fig*) leggere con fatica un libro ♦ VI (*Agr*) arare; **the car ploughed into the wall** l'auto ha sfondato il muro

  ▸ **plough back** VT (*profits*) reinvestire

  ▸ **plough in** VT + ADV sotterrare arando

  ▸ **plough through** VI + PREP (*snow, mud*) procedere a fatica in; (*work*) procedere metodicamente in; (*speech*) leggere monotonamente

  ▸ **plough up** VT + ADV (*field*) arare

ploughing [ˈplaʊɪŋ], **plow·ing** (*USA*) N aratura

plough·man, plow·man (*USA*) [ˈplaʊmən] N (*pl* **-men**) aratore *m*

plow [plaʊ] (*USA*) = **plough**

ploy [plɔɪ] N stratagemma *m*, manovra

pls ABBR = **please**

pluck [plʌk] N (*courage*) coraggio, fegato ♦ VT (*fruit, flower*) cogliere; (*also:* **pluck out**) strappare; (*Mus: strings*) pizzicare; (: *guitar*) pizzicare le corde di; (*Culin: bird*) spennare; **to pluck one's eyebrows** depilarsi le sopracciglia; **to pluck up (one's) courage** farsi coraggio, armarsi di coraggio ♦ VI: **to pluck at sb's sleeve** tirare qn per la manica

plucky [ˈplʌkɪ] ADJ (*comp* **-ier**, *superl* **-iest**) coraggioso(-a)

plug [plʌɡ] N 1 (*of bath, basin, barrel, volcano*) tappo; (*for stopping a leak*) tampone *m* 2 (*Elec*) spina; (*Aut: also:* **spark(ing) plug**) candela; **the plug is faulty** la spina è difettosa 3 (*fam: piece of publicity*) pubblicità *f inv*, réclame *f inv*; **to give sb/sth a plug** fare pubblicità a qn/qc ♦ VT 1 (*also:* **plug up:** *hole*) tappare; (*tooth*) otturare 2 (*insert*) infilare, cacciare; **to plug a lead into a socket** inserire un filo (elettrico) in una presa di corrente 3 (*fam: publicize*) fare pubblicità a; (*: push, put forward*) fare propaganda a

  ▸ **plug away** VI + ADV (*fam*): **to plug away (at sth)** sgobbare (su qc)

  ▸ **plug in** (*Elec*) VI + ADV collegarsi; **the TV plugs in behind the table** la presa per la TV è dietro il tavolo ♦ VT + ADV (*appliance*) attaccare; **is the iron plugged in?** è attaccato il ferro da stiro?

plug·hole [ˈplʌɡhəʊl] N scarico; **it went down the plughole** è caduto nel buco del lavandino (*or* della vasca)

plug-in [ˈplʌɡɪn] ADJ 1 (*radio*) a corrente 2 (*Comput*): **plug-in memory card** scheda di memoria plug-in; **plug-in software module** applicativo plug-in

plum [plʌm] N 1 (*fruit*) prugna, susina; (*also:* **plum tree**) prugno, susino; **a real plum (of a job)** (*fig: fam*) un lavoro favoloso ♦ ADJ 1 (*tart, tree*) di prugne; (*plum-coloured*) (color) prugna *inv* 2 (*fig: fam*): **a plum role** un ruolo ambito

plum·age [ˈpluːmɪdʒ] N piume *fpl*, piumaggio

plumb [plʌm] N piombo ♦ ADV (*fam*): **plumb in the middle** esattamente nel centro; **he's plumb stupid** (*USA fam*) è proprio stupido ♦ VT scandagliare; (*sb's mind*) sondare; **to plumb the depths** scandagliare gli abissi; (*fig*) toccare il fondo

  ▸ **plumb in** VT + ADV (*washing machine*) collegare all'impianto idraulico

plumb·er [ˈplʌmər] N idraulico; **he's a plumber** fa l'idraulico

plumb·ing [ˈplʌmɪŋ] N (*craft*) lavoro *or* mestiere *m* di idraulico; (*piping*) impianto idraulico, tubature *fpl*; **the plumbing's okay** le tubature sono a posto; **brick-laying and plumbing** lavori *mpl* di muratura e di idraulica

plumb line N (*builder's*) filo a piombo; (*Naut*) scandaglio

plume [pluːm] N piuma, penna; (*on hat, helmet*) penna, pennacchio; **a plume of smoke** un pennacchio di fumo

plum·met ['plʌmɪt] VI (*bird*) calare a piombo; (*plane*) precipitare; (*temperature, price, sales*) calare bruscamente; (*spirits, morale*) calare a zero

plump [plʌmp] ADJ (*comp* **-er**, *superl* **-est**) (*person, chicken*) bene in carne; (*cheeks, face*) paffuto(-a); (*wallet, cushion*) (bello(-a)) gonfio(-a); (*arms, child, hands*) grassoccio(-a), grassottello(-a)
▸ **plump down** VT + ADV lasciar cadere di peso; **to plump sth (down) on** lasciar cadere qc di peso su ♦ VI + ADV lasciarsi cadere di peso or di schianto
▸ **plump for** VI + PREP (*fam*) decidersi per
▸ **plump up** VT + ADV (*cushion*) sprimacciare

plun·der ['plʌndə'] N (*act*) saccheggio; (*loot*) bottino ♦ VT (*gen*) saccheggiare; (*villagers*) depredare; (*objects*) far man bassa di

plunge [plʌndʒ] N (*dive*) tuffo; (*fig: into debt, of currency*) caduta; **to take the plunge** (*fig*) buttarsi, saltare il fosso, fare il gran passo ♦ VT **1** (*immerse*) immergere, tuffare; (*thrust: knife*) conficcare; (: *hand*) ficcare, tuffare; **to plunge a dagger into sb's chest** conficcare un pugnale nel petto di qn **2** (*fig*): **to plunge a room into darkness** far piombare una stanza nel buio; **we were plunged into gloom by the news** la notizia ci ha gettato nella costernazione; **to plunge sb into debt** precipitare qn nei debiti ♦ VI **1** (*dive*) tuffarsi; **she plunged into the pool** si è tuffata nella piscina **2** (*fall*) precipitare, cadere; **he plunged to his death** ha fatto una caduta mortale **3** (*share prices, currency*) calare precipitosamente; **to plunge into debt** riempirsi di debiti **4** (*fig: rush*): **he plunged into trade union activities** si buttò anima e corpo in attività sindacali; **to plunge heedlessly into danger** buttarsi allo sbaraglio

plung·er ['plʌndʒə'] N (*for clearing drain*) sturalavandini *m inv*

plung·ing ['plʌndʒɪŋ] ADJ (*neckline*) profondo(-a); (*back of dress*) profondamente scollato(-a)

plu·per·fect ['pluː'pɜːfɪkt] N (*Gram*) piuccheperfetto

plu·ral ['plʊərəl] ADJ (*Gram: form*) plurale, del plurale; (: *noun, verb*) plurale, al plurale ♦ N (*Gram*) plurale *m*; **in the plural** al plurale

plus [plʌs] PREP più; **4 plus 3 equals 7** 4 più 3 fa 7; **three children plus a dog** tre bambini e un cane ♦ ADJ (*Math, Elec*) positivo(-a); **ten/twenty plus** più di dieci/venti; **you must be 20 plus** devi avere vent'anni compiuti; **I got B plus for my essay** ho ricevuto B più nel tema; **a plus factor** (*fig*) un vantaggio ♦ N (*Math: plus sign*) più *m inv*; (*fig: advantage*) vantaggio

plus fours NPL calzoni *mpl* alla zuava

plush [plʌʃ] N felpa ♦ ADJ (*also:* **plushy**; *fam*) sontuoso(-a), lussuoso(-a)

plus-one ['plʌs'wʌn] N accompagnatore(-trice)

plu·to·nium [pluː'təʊnɪəm] N plutonio

ply[1] [plaɪ] N (*of wool*) capo; (*of wood*) strato ♦ ADJ: **three-ply wood** compensato a tre strati; **three-ply wool** lana a tre capi

ply[2] [plaɪ] VT (*knitting needle, tool etc*) maneggiare; (*sea, river, route*) viaggiare regolarmente su; **to ply one's trade** esercitare il proprio mestiere; **to ply sb with questions** continuare a far domande a qn; **to ply sb with drink** continuare a offrir da bere a qn ♦ VI: **to ply between** far la spola fra, fare servizio regolare fra; **to ply for hire** (*taxi*) andare avanti e indietro in attesa di clienti

ply·wood ['plaɪˌwʊd] N (*legno*) compensato

PM [ˌpiː'ɛm] N ABBR (*Brit fam*: = **Prime Minister**)

p.m. ['piː'ɛm] ADV ABBR (*in the afternoon*) del pomeriggio; (*in the evening*) di sera; **at 8 p.m.** alle otto di sera; **at 2 p.m.** alle quattordici

PMS [ˌpiːɛm'ɛs] N ABBR (= **premenstrual syndrome**) sindrome *f* premestruale

pneu·mat·ic [njuː'mætɪk] ADJ pneumatico(-a); **pneumatic drill** martello pneumatico

pneu·mo·nia [njuː'məʊnɪə] N polmonite *f*

PO [ˌpiː'əʊ] N ABBR (= **Post Office**) ≈ PT *fpl* ♦ ABBR (*Naut*) = **petty officer**

poach[1] [pəʊtʃ] VT (*Culin: fish*) cuocere in bianco; **poached egg** uovo affogato *or* in camicia

poach[2] [pəʊtʃ] VT (*hunt: game*) cacciare di frodo; (*fish*) pescare di frodo; (*fig: fam: steal*) soffiare, portar via ♦ VI cacciare (*or* pescare) di frodo; **to poach on sb's preserves** (*fig*) invadere il campo di qn

poached [pəʊtʃt] ADJ (*egg*) affogato(-a), (affogata)

poach·er ['pəʊtʃə'] N (*of game*) bracconiere *m*

poach·ing ['pəʊtʃɪŋ] N bracconaggio, caccia (*or* pesca) di frodo

PO Box N ABBR (= **Post Office Box**) C.P. (= *casella postale*)

pock·et ['pɒkɪt] N (*in garment etc*) tasca; **breast pocket** taschino; **with his hands in his pockets** con le mani in tasca; **to have sb in one's pocket** (*fig*) tenere in pugno qn; **to have sth in one's pocket** (*fig*) avere qc (già) in tasca; **to be in pocket** guadagnarci; **to be out of pocket** rimetterci; **to line one's pockets** arricchirsi, fare i soldi; **to put one's hand in one's pocket** (*fig*) metter mano al portafoglio; **to go through sb's pockets** frugare le tasche di qn; **to live in each other's pockets** rimanere *or* essere sempre appiccicati; **pocket of resistance/warm air** sacca di resistenza/di aria calda ♦ VT (*fig: gain, take*) intascare; **to pocket one's pride** (*fig*) metter da parte l'orgoglio ♦ ADJ (*edition, calculator*) tascabile

pocket·book ['pɒkɪtˌbʊk] N (*wallet*) portafoglio; (*notebook*) taccuino; (*USA: handbag*) borsetta; (*paperback*) tascabile *m*

pocket·knife ['pɒkɪtnaɪf] N (*pl* **-knives**) temperino

pocket money N (*of child*) paghetta; **£8 a week pocket money** una paghetta settimanale di otto sterline

pock·marked ['pɒkˌmɑːkt] ADJ (*face*) butterato(-a); (*surface*) bucherellato(-a)

pod [pɒd] N baccello, guscio ♦ VT sgusciare

pod·cast ['pɒdkɑːst] N podcast *m inv*

podgy ['pɒdʒɪ] ADJ (*comp* **-ier**, *superl* **-iest**) tracagnotto(-a)

po·dia·trist [pɒ'diːətrɪst] N (*USA*) callista *m/f*, pedicure *m/f*

po·dia·try [pɒ'diːətrɪ] N (*USA*) mestiere *m* di callista

po·dium ['pəʊdɪəm] N podio

poem ['pəʊɪm] N poesia

poet ['pəʊɪt] N poeta(-essa)

po·et·ic [pəʊ'etɪk] ADJ poetico(-a)

poet lau·reate [ˌpəʊɪt'lɔːrɪɪt] N (*Brit*) poeta di corte

po·et·ry ['pəʊɪtrɪ] N poesia; **to write poetry** scrivere (delle) poesie

poign·ant ['pɔɪnjənt] ADJ commovente, toccante

point [pɔɪnt] N **1** (*dot, punctuation mark, also Geom*) punto; (*decimal point*) virgola; **2 point 6 (2.6)** 2 virgola 6 (2,6) **2** (*on scale, compass etc*) punto; **freezing point** punto di congelamento; **from all points of the compass** da tutte le parti dei mondo; **up to a point** (*fig*) fino a un certo punto **3** (*of needle, pencil, knife*) punta; **a pencil with a sharp point** una matita appuntita; **on points** (*Ballet*) sulle punte; **at the point of a gun/sword** sotto la minaccia di un fucile/una spada; **not to put too fine a point on it** (*fig*) parlando chiaro **4** (*place*) punto; **the train stops at Carlisle and all points south** il treno ferma a Carlisle e in tutte le stazioni a sud di Carlisle; **point of contact** punto d'incontro; **point of departure** (*also fig*) punto di partenza; **a point on the horizon** un punto all'orizzonte; **at this point** (*spatially*) in questo punto; (*in time*) a questo punto; **at that point, we decided to leave** a quel punto abbiamo deciso di andarcene; **from that point on** (*in time*) da quel momento in poi; (*in space*) da quel punto in poi; **to be on the point of doing sth** essere sul punto di *or* stare (proprio) per fare qc; **when it comes to the point** quando si arriva al dunque; **when it came to the point of leaving** quando giunse il momento di partire; **abrupt to the point of rudeness** brusco al punto di essere villano **5** (*counting unit: Sport, in test: Stock Exchange*) punto; **to win on points** vincere ai punti; **they scored five points** hanno segnato cinque punti; **the index is down 3 points** l'indice è sceso di 3 punti **6** (*purpose*) scopo, motivo; (*matter*) questione *f*, argomento; (*main idea, important part: of argument, joke*) nocciolo; **there's no point in staying** è inutile *or* non ha senso restare; **I don't see** *or* **get the point** (*of joke*) mi sfugge; **I don't see the point of** *or* **in doing that** non vedo il motivo di farlo; **what's the point?** perché?; **what's the point of leaving so early?** perché partire così presto?; **the point is that ...** il fatto è che...; **that's the whole point!**

precisamente!, sta tutto lì!; **the point at issue** l'argomento in discussione *or* questione; **a 5-point plan** un piano articolato in 5 punti; **she described the process point by point** descrisse il processo punto per punto; **in point of fact** a dire il vero; **to be beside the point** non entrarci; **to get off the point** divagare; **to come** *or* **get to the point** venire al punto *or* al dunque, arrivare al punto; **to keep** *or* **stick to the point** restare in argomento; **to make a point of doing sth** non mancare di fare qc; **to make a point** fare un'osservazione; **he made some interesting points** ha fatto delle osservazioni interessanti; **to make one's point** dimostrare la propria tesi; **I take your point** so che hai ragione; **to win one's point** averla vinta; **to stretch a point** fare uno strappo (alla regola) *or* un'eccezione; **his remarks were to the point** le sue osservazioni erano pertinenti *or* a proposito; **to get sb's point** capire ciò che qn vuole dire; **yes, I get your point** sì, capisco quello che vuoi dire; **you've got a point there!** giusto!, hai ragione!; **that's a good point!** giusto!; **I missed the point of that joke** non ho afferrato quella battuta; **you've missed the whole point!** non hai capito niente!; **a point of principle** una questione di principio **7** (*characteristic*) caratteristica, qualità *f inv*; **good/bad points** lati positivi/negativi; **tact isn't one of his strong points** il tatto non è il suo forte **8** (*Brit: Rail*); **points** NPL scambio *msg* **9** (*Aut*); **points** NPL puntine *fpl* **10** (*Brit: Elec: also:* **power point**) presa (di corrente) ◆ VT **1** (*aim, direct: gun, hosepipe etc*): **to point sth (at sb/sth)** puntare qc (contro *or* su qn/qc); **to point a gun at sb** puntare una pistola contro qn; **she pointed the car at the gap in the traffic** diresse la macchina verso un varco nel traffico; **to point one's finger at sb** indicare qn con il dito, additare; **to point one's toes** stendere il piede **2** (*indicate, show*) indicare, mostrare; **to point the way** (*also fig*) indicare la strada *or* la direzione da seguire **3** (*Constr*) riempire gli interstizi *or* ◆ VI **1** indicare (con il dito), additare; **don't point!** non indicare col dito!; **to point at** *or* **to** *or* **towards sth/sb** indicare qc/qn **2** (*indicate: signpost, hand*) indicare, segnare; **everything points to him being guilty** tutti gli indizi fanno pensare che sia colpevole; **it points (to the) north** (*compass needle*) segna *or* indica il nord; **this points to the fact that ...** questo fa pensare che...

▸ **point out** VT + ADV **1** (*show*) additare, indicare; **the guide pointed out Big Ben to us** la guida ci ha indicato il Big Ben **2** (*mention*) far notare, far presente; **I'd like to point out that...** vorrei far notare che...; **she pointed out our mistakes** ci ha fatto presente i nostri errori

▸ **point up** VT + ADV sottolineare, mettere in evidenza

point-blank [ˌpɔɪntˈblæŋk] ADJ (*shot, question*) a bruciapelo; (*refusal*) categorico(-a), secco(-a); **at point-blank range** a bruciapelo ◆ ADV (*fire*) a bruciapelo; (*refuse*) categoricamente; **he was asked point-blank if he would resign** gli fu chiesto a bruciapelo se intendeva dimettersi

point duty N (*Brit: Police*) servizio di controllo del traffico; **to be on point duty** dirigere il traffico

point·ed [ˈpɔɪntɪd] ADJ **1** (*sharp: stick, chin*) appuntito(-a), aguzzo(-a); (*beard*) a punta; (*roof*) aguzzo(-a); (*arch*) a sesto acuto **2** (*obvious in intention: remark, question*) pregno(-a) di significati; **a pointed remark** un'osservazione critica; **in a pointed manner** in modo significativo

point·ed·ly [ˈpɔɪntɪdlɪ] ADV (*look*) in modo significativo; (*say*) in un tono pieno di sottintesi

point·er [ˈpɔɪntə'] N **1** (*indicator*) lancetta; (*stick*) bacchetta **2** (*dog*) pointer *m inv* **3** (*clue*) indizio; (*advice*) consiglio; **to give sb some pointers on ...** consigliare qn su...; **a useful pointer** un consiglio utile; **a pointer to the likely outcome** un indizio del probabile risultato

point·less [ˈpɔɪntlɪs] ADJ (*suffering, existence, journey*) inutile, vano(-a); (*crime*) senza senso, gratuito(-a); (*remark*) superfluo(-a); (*story, joke*) senza capo né coda; **it is pointless to refuse** è inutile rifiutarsi

poise [pɔɪz] N (*carriage of head, body*) portamento; (*balance*) equilibrio; (*composure, dignity of manner*) padronanza di sé; (*calmness*) calma ◆ VT (*balance*) mettere in equilibrio; (*hold balanced*) tenere in equilibrio

poi·son [ˈpɔɪzn] N (*also fig*) veleno; **they hate each other like poison** si odiano a morte; **what's your poison?** (*fam*) cosa bevi? ◆ VT **1** (*person, food*) avvelenare; (*air, atmosphere*)

inquinare, avvelenare **2** (*fig*): **to poison sb's mind** corrompere qn; **to poison sb's mind against sb/sth** sobillare qn contro qn/qc

poi·son·ing [ˈpɔɪznɪŋ] N (*also fig*) avvelenamento; **arsenic poisoning** avvelenamento da arsenico; **food poisoning** intossicazione *f* alimentare; **to die of poisoning** morire avvelenato(-a)

poi·son·ous [ˈpɔɪznəs] ADJ **1** (*snake, plant*) velenoso(-a); (*fumes*) venefico(-a), tossico(-a) **2** (*fig: tongue*) velenoso(-a); (: *propaganda*) venefico(-a); (: *ideas, literature*) pernicioso(-a); (: *rumours, individual*) perfido(-a); (: *fam: coffee etc*) schifoso(-a)

poke [pəʊk] N (*jab*) colpetto; (*with elbow*) gomitata; **to give the fire a poke** attizzare il fuoco ◆ VT **1** (*jab with stick, finger etc*) dare un colpetto a; **to poke sb with one's umbrella** dare un colpetto con l'ombrello a qn; **you poked me in the eye** mi hai messo *or* ficcato un dito nell'occhio; **to poke the fire** attizzare il fuoco **2** **to poke fun at sb** (*mock*) prendere in giro qn **3** (*USA fam: punch*) dare un pugno a **4** (*thrust*) cacciare, ficcare; **to poke one's head out of the window** mettere la testa fuori dalla finestra; **to poke sth in(to) sth** spingere qc dentro qc **5** (*make by poking*): **to poke a hole in sth** fare un buco in qc (*con il dito, un bastone etc*) ◆ VI: **to poke at** dare dei colpetti a

▸ **poke about, poke around** VI + ADV (*fam: in drawers, attic*) frugare, rovistare; (: *in shop*) curiosare

▸ **poke out** VI + ADV spuntar fuori, sporger fuori ◆ VT + ADV: **to poke sb's eye out** cavare un occhio a qn

pok·er[1] [ˈpəʊkə'] N (*for fire*) attizzatoio

pok·er[2] [ˈpəʊkə'] N (*Cards*) poker *m inv*; **I play poker** gioco a poker

poker-faced [ˈpəʊkəˌfeɪst] ADJ dal viso impassibile

poky, pok·ey [ˈpəʊkɪ] ADJ (*comp* **-ier,** *superl* **-iest**) (*pej*) angusto(-a)

Po·land [ˈpəʊlənd] N Polonia

po·lar [ˈpəʊlə'] ADJ (*Elec, Geog*) polare

polar bear N orso(-a) bianco(-a)

polarize [ˈpəʊləˌraɪz] (*also fig*) VT polarizzare ◆ VI polarizzarsi

Pole [pəʊl] N polacco(-a)

pole[1] [pəʊl] N (*gen*) palo; (*flagpole, for vaulting*) asta; (*of tent, fence*) paletto; (*for punting*) pertica; (*curtain pole*) bastone *m*; **telegraph pole** palo del telegrafo; **tent pole** paletto per la tenda; **ski pole** racchetta da sci; **up the pole** (*fig: fam: mad*) fuori di testa; **to send** *or* **drive sb up the pole** (*infuriate*) far uscire dai gangheri qn

pole[2] [pəʊl] N (*Elec, Geog, Astron*) polo; **the Earth's poles** i poli terrestri; **the North Pole** il polo nord; **the South Pole** il polo sud; **poles apart** (*fig*) agli antipodi

pole-axe, pole·ax [ˈpəʊlˌæks] VT (*person*) atterrare, stendere

pole·cat [ˈpəʊlˌkæt] N (*Brit*) puzzola; (*USA*) moffetta

po·lem·ic [pəˈlemɪk] N polemica

Pole Star N stella polare

pole vault N salto con l'asta

po·lice [pəˈliːs] NPL (*organization*) polizia *fsg*; (*policemen*) poliziotti *mpl*; **the railway/river police** la polizia ferroviaria/fluviale; **we called the police** abbiamo chiamato la polizia; **a large number of police were hurt** molti poliziotti sono rimasti feriti; **the police have caught him** è stato preso dalla polizia; **extra police were brought in** sono state fatte intervenire forze di polizia supplementari; **to join the police** arruolarsi nella polizia ◆ VT (*streets, city, frontier*) presidiare; (*fig: agreements, prices*) controllare; **to police a football match** presidiare lo stadio durante un incontro di calcio ◆ ADJ (*escort, protection*) di agenti di polizia

police car N macchina della polizia

police constable N (*Brit*) agente *m* di polizia

police department N (*USA*) dipartimento di polizia

police force N corpo di polizia, polizia

police·man [pəˈliːsmən] N (*pl* **-men**) poliziotto, agente *m* di polizia

police officer N (*man*) agente *m* di polizia; (*woman*) donna *f* poliziotto, *inv*

police record N: **to have a police record** avere precedenti penali

police state N stato di polizia

police station N ≈ commissariato di Pubblica Sicurezza

police·woman [pəˈliːsˌwʊmən] N (pl **-women**) donna f poliziotto, inv

poli·cy¹ [ˈpɒlɪsɪ] N (gen) politica; (of newspaper, company) linea di condotta, prassi f inv; **it is our policy to do that** fa parte della nostra prassi or politica fare questo; **to follow a policy of** seguire una politica di; **the government's policies** la politica del governo; **their economic policy** la loro politica economica; **foreign policy** politica estera; **it's a matter of policy** è una questione di principio; **it would be good/bad policy to do that** sarebbe una buona/cattiva politica fare questo ♦ ADJ (discussion, statement) sulla linea di condotta

poli·cy² [ˈpɒlɪsɪ] N (also: **insurance policy**) polizza (d'assicurazione); **to take out a policy** fare or stipulare un'assicurazione; **the terms of the policy** le condizioni della polizza

policy holder N assicurato(-a)

policy-making [ˈpɒlɪsɪˌmeɪkɪŋ] N messa a punto di programmi

po·lio [ˈpəʊlɪəʊ] N polio f; **polio victim** vittima m/f della polio

Po·lish [ˈpəʊlɪʃ] ADJ polacco(-a) ♦ N (language) polacco

pol·ish [ˈpɒlɪʃ] N 1 (for shoes, car) lucido; (for furniture, floor) cera; **shoe polish** lucido per scarpe 2 (act) lucidata; **to give sth a polish** dare una lucidata or lustrata a qc 3 (shine) lucido, lucentezza; **it has a very high polish** è molto lucido; **to put a polish on sth** far brillare qc 4 (fig: of person) raffinatezza; (: of style, performance) eleganza ♦ VT (wood, leather) lucidare; (stones, glass) levigare; (style) perfezionare, raffinare
　▸ **polish off** VT + ADV (food, drink) far fuori; (work, correspondence) sbrigare
　▸ **polish up** VT + ADV (skill, ability) perfezionare; (shoes, metal objects) lucidare, lustrare
　❑ **polish** is not translated by the Italian word pulizia

pol·ished [ˈpɒlɪʃt] ADJ (surface) lucidato(-a); (stone) levigato(-a); (fig: person, manner, performer) raffinato(-a); (: performance) impeccabile; **a polished performance** un'esecuzione impeccabile

po·lite [pəˈlaɪt] ADJ (comp **-r**, superl **-st**) educato(-a); **it's not polite to do that** non è educato or buona educazione fare questo; **to be polite to sb/about sth** essere cortese con qn/ riguardo a qc; **in polite society** nella buona società

po·lite·ly [pəˈlaɪtlɪ] ADV educatamente, cortesemente

po·lite·ness [pəˈlaɪtnɪs] N educazione f, cortesia f; **out of politeness** per educazione

poli·tic [ˈpɒlɪtɪk] ADJ (frm) prudente

po·liti·cal [pəˈlɪtɪkəl] ADJ politico(-a); **I'm not at all political** non mi interesso di politica; **political analyst** politologo(-a)

political asylum N asilo politico

po·liti·cal·ly [pəˈlɪtɪkəlɪ] ADV politicamente

politically correct ADJ politicamente corretto(-a)

poli·ti·cian [ˌpɒlɪˈtɪʃən] N politico m

poli·tics [ˈpɒlɪtɪks] N (sg: career) politica f; (: subject) scienze fpl politiche; (pl: views, policies) tendenze fpl, idee fpl politiche; **to talk politics** parlare di politica; **to go into politics** darsi alla politica; **I'm not interested in politics** non m'interesso di politica

pol·ka [ˈpɒlkə] N (dance) polca

polka dot N pois m inv

poll [pəʊl] N 1 (voting) votazione f, votazioni fpl; (election) elezioni fpl; **to take a poll (on sth)** mettere (qc) ai voti; **they got 65% of the poll** hanno ottenuto il 65% dei voti; **to go to the polls** (voters) andare alle urne; (government) indire le elezioni; **a defeat at the polls** una sconfitta alle elezioni 2 (also: **opinion poll**) sondaggio (d'opinione); **to conduct a poll** fare un sondaggio; **a recent poll revealed that ...** un recente sondaggio ha rivelato che... ♦ VT 1 (votes) ottenere 2 (in opinion poll) interrogare nel corso di un sondaggio

pol·len [ˈpɒlən] N polline m

pollen count N indice ufficiale della quantità di polline nell'aria

pol·li·na·tion [ˌpɒlɪˈneɪʃən] N impollinazione f

pol·ling [ˈpəʊlɪŋ] N 1 (Brit Pol) votazioni fpl; **polling has been heavy** c'è stata un'alta percentuale di votanti 2 (Comput) interrogazione f ciclica, polling m

polling booth N (Brit) cabina elettorale

polling day N (Brit) giorno delle elezioni

polling station N (Brit) seggio or sezione f elettorale

poll·ster [ˈpəʊlstəʳ] N chi esegue sondaggi d'opinione

poll tax N (Brit fam) imposta locale sulla persona fisica (non più in vigore)

pol·lu·tant [pəˈluːtənt] N sostanza inquinante

pol·lute [pəˈluːt] VT inquinare; (fig) inquinare, corrompere

pol·lu·tion [pəˈluːʃən] N (see vb) inquinamento; corruzione f

polo [ˈpəʊləʊ] N (sport) polo

polo neck N (collar) collo alto; (also: **polo neck sweater**) dolcevita ♦ ADJ a collo alto

poly [ˈpɒlɪ] N ABBR (Brit: = polytechnic)

poly·es·ter [ˌpɒlɪˈestəʳ] N poliestere m

po·lyga·my [pəˈlɪgəmɪ] N poligamia

poly·graph [ˈpɒlɪˌgrɑːf] N macchina della verità

Poly·nesia [ˌpɒlɪˈniːzɪə] N Polinesia

Poly·nesian [ˌpɒlɪˈniːʒən] ADJ, N polinesiano(-a)

pol·yp [ˈpɒlɪp] N (Zool, Med) polipo

poly·sty·rene [ˌpɒlɪˈstaɪriːn] N polistirolo; **polystyrene chips** palline fpl di polistirolo

poly·tech·nic [ˌpɒlɪˈteknɪk] N (Brit) istituto superiore ora inglobato nella struttura universitaria

poly·thene [ˈpɒlɪθiːn] N (Brit) polietilene m, politene m

polythene bag N sacchetto di plastica

poly·urethane [ˌpɒlɪˈjʊərɪˌθeɪn] N poliuretano

pom·egran·ate [ˈpɒmɪˌgrænɪt] N (tree) melograno; (fruit) melagrana

pom·mel [ˈpʌml] N pomo ♦ VT = **pummel**

pomp [pɒmp] N pompa, fasto; **pomp and circumstance** grande or magnifico apparato

pom·pon [ˈpɒmpɒn], **pom·pom** [ˈpɒmpɒm] N (on hat) pompon m inv

pomp·ous [ˈpɒmpəs] ADJ (pej: speech, attitude) pomposo(-a); (: person) pieno(-a) di boria

pond [pɒnd] N stagno; (in park) laghetto; **the pond** (ocean) l'Atlantico

pon·der [ˈpɒndəʳ] VT ponderare, riflettere su ♦ VI: **to ponder (on or upon)** riflettere (su), meditare (su); **they're pondering how to improve profits** stanno riflettendo su come aumentare i profitti

pon·der·ous [ˈpɒndərəs] ADJ pesante, ponderoso(-a)

pong [pɒŋ] (Brit fam) N puzzo ♦ VI puzzare

pon·tiff [ˈpɒntɪf] N pontefice m

pon·tifi·cate [pɒnˈtɪfɪˌkeɪt] VI: **to pontificate about or on** pontificare su

pon·toon [pɒnˈtuːn] N pontone m

pon·toon [pɒnˈtuːn] N (Cards) ventuno

pony [ˈpəʊnɪ] N pony m inv

pony·tail [ˈpəʊnɪˌteɪl] N (hairstyle) coda di cavallo; **she's got a ponytail** ha la coda di cavallo

poo·dle [ˈpuːdl] N barboncino

pooh-pooh [ˈpuːˈpuː] VT (fam) farsi beffe di

pool¹ [puːl] N (of water, rain, blood) pozza; (of light) cerchio; (pond) stagno; (artificial) vasca; (swimming pool) piscina; (in river) tonfano

pool² [puːl] N 1 (common fund) cassa comune; (at poker) piatto 2 (supply, source: of money, goods, workers) riserva; (: of experience, ideas) fonte f; (: of experts) équipe f inv; (: of cars) parco 3 (game) biliardo; **let's play pool** giochiamo a biliardo 4 (Comm: consortium) pool m inv; (USA: monopoly trust) trust m inv ♦ VT (money, resources) mettere insieme, mettere in un fondo comune; (efforts, knowledge) mettere insieme

poor [pʊəʳ] ADJ (comp **-er**, superl **-est**) (gen) povero(-a); (crop, light, visibility) scarso(-a); (effort, excuse) misero(-a); (memory, health, quality) cattivo(-a); (mark) mediocre; **a poor family** ly una famiglia povera; **he's a poor fencer** non sa perdere; **I'm a poor traveller** sopporto male i viaggi; **it has a poor chance of success** ha scarse possibilità di successo; **it's a poor thing when ... it** è deplorevole che... + **poor** he's poor at math(s) essere debole in matematica; **as poor as a church mouse** povero(-a) in canna; **you poor thing!** poverino!; **poor David, he's very unlucky!** povero David, è proprio sfortunato!; **you poor fool!** povero scemo! ♦ **the poor** NPL i poveri

poor·ly [ˈpuəlɪ] ADV (*badly*) male; **a poorly paid job** un lavoro mal retribuito; **a poorly furnished room** una stanza arredata squallidamente; **to be poorly off** non avere molti soldi ♦ ADJ (*ill*) indisposto(-a); **to be poorly** sentirsi poco bene; **I'm a bit poorly today** oggi mi sento poco bene

pop [pɒp] N **1** (*sound*) schiocco; **to go pop** schioccare **2** (*fam: drink*) bevanda gasata ♦ VT **1** (*balloon*) far scoppiare; (*cork*) far saltare **2** (*fam: put*) mettere; **I'll just pop my coat on** m'infilo il cappotto; **she popped her head out** (*of the window*) sporse fuori la testa; (*from under the blankets*) fece capolino; **he popped a sweet into his mouth** si è messo una caramella in bocca; **to pop the question** (*fig*) fare la proposta di matrimonio ♦ VI **1** (*balloon*) scoppiare; (*cork, buttons*) saltare; (*ears*) sbloccarsi; (*corn*) scoppiettare **2** (*fam: go quickly*): **she's just popped upstairs** è andata di sopra un attimo; **let's pop round to Joe's** facciamo un salto da Joe

▸ **pop in** VI + ADV (*fam*) fare un salto, entrare un attimo

▸ **pop off** VI + ADV (*Brit fam*) **1** (*die*) tirar le cuoia **2** (*leave*) scappare

▸ **pop out** VI + ADV (*person*) fare un salto fuori; **to pop out to the shops** fare un salto ai negozi; **his eyes nearly popped out of his head** sgranò tanto d'occhi

▸ **pop up** VI + ADV (*fam*) apparire

pop concert N concerto *m* pop, inv

pop·corn [ˈpɒpkɔːn] N popcorn *m inv*

pope [pəup] N: **the Pope** il Papa

pop·lar [ˈpɒplə˙] N pioppo; **black poplar** pioppo nero europeo

pop·lin [ˈpɒplɪn] N popeline *f*

pop·per [ˈpɒpə˙] N (*Brit*) (bottone *m*) automatico

pop·py [ˈpɒpɪ] N papavero

poppy·cock [ˈpɒpɪˌkɒk] N (*fam*) scempiaggini *fpl*

pop star N pop star *f inv*

popu·lace [ˈpɒpjuləs] N popolo, popolino

popu·lar [ˈpɒpjulə˙] ADJ **1** (*well-liked*): **to be popular (with)** (*person*) essere benvoluto(-a) *or* ben visto(-a) (da); (*decision*) essere gradito(-a) (a); (*product*) essere molto richiesto(-a) (da); **he's the most popular politician in France** è il personaggio politico più popolare in Francia; **a popular song** una canzone di successo; **a popular colour** un colore che va di moda; **this is a very popular style** questo stile è molto in voga **2** (*for the layman*) popolare; **the popular press** la stampa popolare **3** (*widespread*: *theory, fallacy*) comune; (: *support*) popolare; **by popular request** a richiesta generale

popu·lar·ity [ˌpɒpjuˈlærɪtɪ] N popolarità

popu·lar·ize [ˈpɒpjuləˌraɪz] VT **1** (*make well-liked*: *person*) rendere popolare; (*make fashionable*: *product, fashion*) diffondere **2** (*make accessible to laymen*) rendere accessibile ai più, divulgare; (*science*) volgarizzare

popu·late [ˈpɒpjuˌleɪt] VT popolare

popu·la·tion [ˌpɒpjuˈleɪʃən] N popolazione *f*

population explosion N boom *m inv* demografico

popu·lous [ˈpɒpjuləs] ADJ popoloso(-a), densamente popolato(-a)

pop-up [ˈpɒpʌp] ADJ: **pop-up book** libro per bambini con le figure a comparsa; **pop-up menu** (*Comput*) menu *m inv* a comparsa; **pop-up toaster** tostapane *m inv* a espulsione automatica ♦ N pubblicità a comparsa (sullo schermo)

porce·lain [ˈpɔːsəlɪn] N porcellana; **a piece of porcelain** una porcellana

porch [pɔːtʃ] N veranda; (*of church*) sagrato

por·cu·pine [ˈpɔːkjuˌpaɪn] N porcospino

pore[1] [pɔː˙] N (*Anat*) poro

pore[2] [pɔː˙] VI: **to pore over** (*map, problem*) studiare attentamente; (*book*) essere immerso(-a) in

pork [pɔːk] N (*carne f di*) maiale, *m*; **I don't eat pork** non mangio carne di maiale; **a pork chop** una braciola di maiale

pork chop N braciola di maiale

pork pie N pasticcio di maiale in crosta

porn [pɔːn], **porno** [ˈpɔːnəu] (*fam*) N porno *m inv* ♦ ADJ (*film*) porno *inv*

por·no·graph·ic [ˌpɔːnəˈɡræfɪk] ADJ pornografico(-a)

por·nog·ra·phy [pɔːˈnɒɡrəfɪ] N pornografia

porous [ˈpɔːrəs] ADJ poroso(-a); (*fig: border*) permeabile, facilmente oltrepassabile

por·poise [ˈpɔːpəs] N focena

por·ridge [ˈpɒrɪdʒ] N porridge *m*

port[1] [pɔːt] N (*harbour*) porto; (*town*) città *f inv* portuale; **naval/fishing port** porto militare/per pescherecci; **to come into port** entrare in porto; **any port in a storm** (*fig*) in tempo di tempesta ogni buco è porto

port[2] [pɔːt] N (*Naut, Aer: left side*) babordo; **to port** a babordo ♦ ADJ (*cabin*) di sinistra; **on the port side** a babordo

port·able [ˈpɔːtəbl] ADJ portatile; **a portable TV** una TV portatile

por·tal [ˈpɔːtl] N portale *m*

port·cul·lis [pɔːtˈkʌlɪs] N saracinesca

por·tent [ˈpɔːtɛnt] N presagio

por·ter [ˈpɔːtə˙] N (*of office etc*) portinaio(-a), portiere(-a); (*of hotel*) portiere(-a); (*Rail, Aer*) facchino, portabagagli *m inv*; (*USA: Rail*) addetto ai vagoni letto

port·fo·lio [ˌpɔːtˈfəuliəu] N (*case*) cartella; (*Fin, Pol: office*) portafoglio; (*of artist, designer etc*) portfolio *m inv*; **at the interview she showed them her portfolio** al colloquio mostrò loro la raccolta dei suoi lavori; **portfolio of shares** portafoglio *m* titoli, inv; **portfolio of investments** portafoglio di investimenti

port·hole [ˈpɔːtˌhəul] N oblò *m inv*

por·ti·co [ˈpɔːtɪkəu] N (*pl* **porticos** *or* **porticoes**) portico

por·tion [ˈpɔːʃən] N (*part, piece*) parte *f*; (*of food*) porzione *f*

▸ **portion out** VT + ADV distribuire

port·ly [ˈpɔːtlɪ] ADJ (*comp* **-ier**, *superl* **-iest**) corpulento(-a)

por·trait [ˈpɔːtrɪt] N ritratto

por·tray [pɔːˈtreɪ] VT (*painter, writer, novel*) ritrarre; (*painting*) raffigurare; (*actor*) interpretare; **journalists portray him as a despot** i giornalisti lo dipingono come un tiranno; **he portrayed the king in "Hamlet"** ha interpretato il re nell'"Amleto"

por·tray·al [pɔːˈtreɪəl] N (*see vb*) ritratto; rappresentazione *f*; interpretazione *f*

Por·tu·gal [ˈpɔːtjuɡəl] N Portogallo

Por·tu·guese [ˌpɔːtjuˈɡiːz] ADJ portoghese ♦ N (*person: pl inv*) portoghese *m/f*; (*language*) portoghese *m*; **the Portuguese** i portoghesi

Portuguese man-of-war [ˌpɔːtjuˈɡiːzˌmænəvˈwɔː˙] N (*jellyfish*) fisalia, caravella portoghese

pose [pəuz] N (*way*) posa; **to strike a pose** mettersi in posa; **it's only a pose** (*fig*) è tutta una posa ♦ VT **1** (*person*) mettere in posa **2** (*problem, difficulty*) porre, creare; (*question*) fare; **nobody dared pose the question** nessuno osò porre la domanda ♦ VI (*for artist: also fig: attitudinize*) posare; **she posed for Dalí** ha posato per Dalí; **to pose as** (*pretend to be*) atteggiarsi a, posare a, fingere di essere; **to pose as a policeman** farsi passare per un poliziotto

pos·er [ˈpəuzə˙] (*fam*) N (*problem*) domanda difficile; (*pej: person*) posatore(-trice)

po·seur [pəuˈzːː˙] N (*pej*) persona affettata

posh [pɒʃ] (*fam*) ADJ (*comp* **-er**, *superl* **-est**) (*people, neighbourhood, family*) per bene; (*car, hotel, clothes*) elegante ♦ ADV: **to talk posh** (*pej*) parlare in modo snob

▸ **posh up** (*fam*) VT + ADV (*decorate, improve*) abbellire; (*clean up*) pulire; **to posh o.s. up** agghindarsi

po·si·tion [pəˈzɪʃən] N **1** (*gen*) posizione *f*; (*of furniture etc*) disposizione *f*; (*in class, league, job*) posizione, posto; **to be in/out of position** essere/non essere al proprio posto; **in an uncomfortable position** (*also fig*) in una posizione scomoda; **in a reclining position** (*of chair*) reclinato(-a); (*of person*) semisdraiato(-a); **what position do you play?** (*Sport*) in che posizione giochi?; **he's lying in second position** si trova al secondo posto *or* in seconda posizione; **to jockey** *or* **manoeuvre for position** (*also fig*) dare l'assalto ai posti **2** (*post*) posto, impiego; **a position of trust** un posto di fiducia **3** (*fig: situation, standing*) posizione *f*; **a man in his position** un uomo nella sua posizione; **to be in a position to do sth** essere nella posizione di fare qc; **he's in no position to criticize** non sta nel proprio a lui criticare; **put yourself in my position** si metta al mio posto; **I am in an awkward position** sono in una posizione difficile **4** (*fig: point of view,* *attitude*) posizione *f*; **to take up a position on sth** prendere posizione su qc; **what's your position on this?** qual è la tua posizione riguardo a questo?; **do I make my position clear?** sono stato sufficientemente chiaro? ♦ VT (*place in position*: *chairs, lamp*) sistemare; (: *model*) mettere in posa; (: *soldiers*) disporre; **I positioned myself to get the best view** mi sono piazzato in modo da poter vedere bene

posi·tive ['pɒzɪtɪv] ADJ 1 (*gen, also Elec, Math, Phot*) positivo(-a); (*constructive*: *advice, help, criticism*) costruttivo(-a); **a positive attitude** un atteggiamento positivo; **we look forward to a positive reply** (*Comm*) in attesa di una risposta favorevole 2 (*definite*: *gen*) positivo(-a), preciso(-a); (: *improvement, increase*) deciso(-a); (: *proof*) inconfutabile; **I'm positive** ne sono sicuro; **are you sure?** — **yes, positive** sei sicuro? — sicurissimo; **to make a positive contribution to sth** dare un contributo effettivo a qc; **he's a positive nuisance** è un vero rompiscatole

posi·tive·ly ['pɒzɪtɪvlɪ] ADV (*approach*) positivamente; (*decisively*) decisamente; (*effectively*) concretamente; (*fam*: *really, absolutely*) assolutamente; **to respond positively** rispondere positivamente; **to think positively** pensare in modo costruttivo; **this is positively the last time I'll do this** è decisamente l'ultima volta che lo faccio; **it looks positively frightening** fa decisamente paura; **she was positively delighted** era assolutamente entusiasta

pos·se ['pɒsɪ] N (*USA*) gruppo armato di volontari

pos·sess [pə'zes] VT possedere; **everything they possess** tutto ciò che possiedono; **like one possessed** come un ossesso; **to be possessed by an idea** essere ossessionato(-a) da un'idea; **whatever (can have) possessed you?** cosa ti ha preso?

pos·ses·sion [pə'zeʃən] N 1 (*ownership*) possesso; **in possession of** in possesso di; **house with vacant possession** casa libera subito; **to have sth in one's possession** avere qc in proprio possesso; **to get possession of** entrare in possesso di; **to take possession of sth** impossessarsi *or* impadronirsi di qc; **to take possession of a house** prendere possesso di una casa; **to get/have possession of the ball** (*Sport*) impossessarsi/essere in possesso della palla 2 (*thing possessed*) bene *m*, avere *m*; **one's possessions** le sue cose; **have you got all your possessions?** hai tutte le tue cose?; **her most treasured possession** la cosa più cara che ha

pos·ses·sive [pə'zesɪv] ADJ (*gen, also Gram*) possessivo(-a); **to be possessive about sth/towards sb** essere possessivo(-a) nei confronti di qc/qn ♦ N (*Gram*) possessivo

pos·ses·sive·ness [pə'zesɪvnɪs] N possessività

pos·ses·sor [pə'zesə'] N possessore *m*, proprietario(-a); **to be the proud possessor of sth** essere orgoglioso(-a) di possedere qc

pos·sibil·ity [ˌpɒsə'bɪlɪtɪ] N possibilità *f inv*; **the possibility of a strike** la possibilità di uno sciopero; **it's a distinct possibility** è molto probabile; **there is no possibility of his agreeing to it** non c'è la minima possibilità *or* probabilità che accetti; **there is some possibility of success** c'è qualche probabilità di successo *or* riuscita; **he's a possibility for the part** è uno dei candidati per la parte; **to foresee all the possibilities** prevedere tutte le eventualità; **to have possibilities** (*person*) avere delle (buone) possibilità; **your idea has possibilities** la tua idea ha delle buone possibilità di successo; **this job has possibilities** questo lavoro offre molte possibilità

pos·sible ['pɒsəbl] ADJ possibile; **it is possible that he'll come** può darsi che *or* è possibile che venga; **it is possible to do it** è possibile farlo, è fattibile; **it will be possible for you to leave early** potrai uscire prima; **as soon as possible** appena possibile, al più presto possibile; **as big as possible** il più grande possibile; **as far as possible** nei limiti del possibile; **if (at all) possible** se (appena è) possibile; **the best possible result** il miglior risultato possibile; **to make sth possible for sb** rendere qc possibile a qn; **what possible excuse can you have for your behaviour?** che giustificazione puoi trovare per il tuo comportamento?; **a possible candidate** un possibile candidato ♦ N: **a list of possibles for the job** una lista dei possibili candidati al posto; **he's a possible for Saturday's match** è uno dei possibili giocatori per la partita di sabato

pos·sibly ['pɒsəblɪ] ADV 1 **he did all he possibly could** ha fatto tutto il possibile; **as often as I possibly can** quanto più spesso posso; **how can I possibly?** come posso?; **I cannot possibly do it** non posso assolutamente *or* proprio farlo; **I can't possibly come** non posso proprio venire; **could you possibly ...?** potresti...?; **if you possibly can** se le è possibile 2 (*perhaps*) forse; **are you coming to the party?** — **possibly** vieni alla festa? — forse

❑ **possibly** is not translated by the Italian word *possibilmente*

post[1] [pəʊst] N (*pole*) palo; **the ball hit the post** la palla ha colpito il palo; **starting/finishing post** (*for race*) palo di partenza/arrivo; **to be left at the post** rimanere indietro alla partenza; **to be pipped at the post** essere battuto(-a) sul filo del traguardo; (*fig*) perdere per un pelo ♦ VT 1 (*also*: **post up**: *notice, list*) affiggere 2 (*announce*) annunciare; **to post sb/sth (as) missing** (*Mil*) dare qn/qc per disperso(-a)

post[2] [pəʊst] N (*Brit*: *mail*) posta; **by post** per posta; **by return of post** a giro di posta; **to catch/miss the post** arrivare/non arrivare in tempo per la levata; **it's in the post** è stato spedito; **to take sth to the post** andare a spedire qc; **has the post come yet?** è già arrivata la posta? ♦ VT 1 (*send*) spedire per posta, mandare per posta; (*Brit*: *put in mailbox*) impostare, imbucare; **I've got some cards to post** devo imbucare delle cartoline 2 (*inform*): **to keep sb posted** tenere qn al corrente

post[3] [pəʊst] N 1 (*job*) posto; **to take up one's post** assumere la propria carica 2 (*Mil*) posto; **at one's post** al proprio posto ♦ VT 1 (*position*: *sentry*) piazzare 2 (*Brit*: *send, assign*) inviare; (: *Mil*) assegnare

post– [pəʊst] PREF post-; **post-1980** dopo il 1980

post·age ['pəʊstɪdʒ] N affrancatura; **"postage: 50p"** "spese di spedizione: 50 penny"; **postage due 40p** soprattassa (*per affrancatura insufficiente*) di 40 penny

postage stamp N francobollo

post·al ['pəʊstəl] ADJ (*service, charges*) postale; (*vote*) per posta; **postal worker** postelegrafonico(-a)

postal order N vaglia *m inv* postale

post·bag ['pəʊstbæg] N (*Brit*) sacco postale, sacco della posta

post·box ['pəʊstbɒks] (*Brit*) N (*in street*) buca delle lettere; (*in entrance hall*) cassetta per le lettere

post·card ['pəʊstkɑːd] N cartolina (postale)

post·code ['pəʊstkəʊd] N (*Brit*) codice *m* (di avviamento) postale

post·date [ˌpəʊst'deɪt] VT (*cheque*) postdatare

post·er ['pəʊstə'] N (*for advertising*) manifesto, affisso; (*for decoration*) poster *m inv*; **there are posters all over town** ci sono manifesti in tutta la città; **I've got posters on my bedrooms walls** ho dei poster sulle pareti di camera mia

poste res·tante [ˌpəʊst'restɒnt] N (*Brit*) fermo posta *m*

pos·teri·or [pɒs'tɪərɪə'] N (*hum*) deretano, didietro ♦ ADJ (*Tech*) posteriore

pos·ter·ity [pɒs'terɪtɪ] N posterità

poster paint N tempera

post-free [ˌpəʊst'friː] ADJ, ADV franco di porto

post·gradu·ate ['pəʊst'grædjʊɪt] ADJ (*studies, course*) successivo(-a) alla laurea; **a postgraduate course** un corso post-laurea ♦ N laureato che continua gli studi

post·hu·mous ['pɒstjʊməs] ADJ postumo(-a)

post·hu·mous·ly ['pɒstjʊməslɪ] ADV dopo la sua (loro *etc*) morte

post·ing ['pəʊstɪŋ] N (*Brit*) incarico; (*Comput*) messaggio lanciato in internet

post·man ['pəʊstmən] N (*pl* -men) (*Brit*) postino

post·mark ['pəʊstmɑːk] N bollo *or* timbro postale ♦ VT timbrare; **it was postmarked Rome** il timbro postale era di Roma

post·master ['pəʊstmɑːstə'] N direttore *m* di un ufficio postale

postmaster general N ≈ ministro delle Poste

post·mistress ['pəʊstmɪstrɪs] N direttrice *f* di un ufficio postale

post·mor·tem [ˌpəʊst'mɔːtəm] N (*also*: **postmortem examination**) autopsia; (*fig*) analisi *f inv* a posteriori

post·na·tal [ˌpəʊstˈneɪtl] ADJ post-parto inv
Post Office N (institution): **the Post Office** ≈ le Poste e Tele-comunicazioni
post office N (place) ufficio postale, posta
post office box N casella postale
post-paid [ˈpəʊstˈpeɪd] ADJ già affrancato(-a)
post·pone [ˌpəʊstˈpəʊn] VT: **to postpone sth for a month/until Monday** rimandare or rinviare or posticipare qc di un mese/a lunedì; **the match has been postponed until next Saturday** la partita è stata rinviata a sabato prossimo
post·pone·ment [ˌpəʊstˈpəʊnmənt] N rinvio
post·script [ˈpəʊsˌskrɪpt] N poscritto
pos·tu·late [ˈpɒstjʊˌleɪt] VT (frm) postulare
pos·ture [ˈpɒstʃəʳ] N posizione f; (carriage) portamento; (pose) posa, atteggiamento; **bad posture** postura scorretta ♦ VI (pej) mettersi in posa, posare
post·war [ˈpəʊstˈwɔːʳ] ADJ del dopoguerra; **the postwar period** il periodo postbellico or del dopoguerra
post·woman [ˈpəʊstˌwʊmən] N (Brit) postina
posy [ˈpəʊzɪ] N mazzolino (di fiori)
pot [pɒt] N 1 (for cooking) pentola, casseruola; (teapot) teiera; (coffeepot) caffettiera; (for jam) vasetto, barattolo; (piece of pottery) ceramica; (for plants) vaso; **pots and pans** pentole; **to go to pot** (fam: plans, business) andare in malora; (: person) lasciarsi andare 2 (potful): **a pot of jam** un vasetto di marmellata; **a pot of soup** una pentola di zuppa; **a pot of tea for two, please** tè per due, per piacere 3 (fam: marijuana) erba; **to smoke pot** fumare erba ♦ VT 1 (plant) mettere in un vaso, invasare; (jam) mettere nei vasetti 2 (shoot: pheasant, rabbit) ammazzare 3 (Billiards) mandare in buca or biglia
pot·ash [ˈpɒtˌæʃ] N potassa
po·tas·sium [pəˈtæsɪəm] N potassio
po·ta·to [pəˈteɪtəʊ] N (pl potatoes) patata; **baked potato** patata cotta al forno con la buccia; **mashed potatoes** purè m inv di patate
potato crisps, potato chips NPL patatine fpl
potato flour N fecola di patate
potato peeler N (knife) pelapatate m inv; (machine) pelapatate m inv
pot·bel·lied [ˈpɒtˌbelɪd] ADJ (from overeating) panciuto(-a); (from malnutrition) dal ventre gonfio
po·ten·cy [ˈpəʊtənsɪ] N (see adj) potenza; validità; (of drink) forza
po·tent [ˈpəʊtənt] ADJ (gen) potente, forte; (fig: argument, reason) validissimo(-a)
po·ten·tate [ˈpəʊtənˌteɪt] N potentato
po·ten·tial [pəʊˈtenʃəl] ADJ potenziale; **a potential problem** un potenziale problema ♦ N 1 (possibilities) potenziale m; **to realize one's full potential** realizzarsi pienamente; **sales potential** potenziale di vendita; **to show potential** promettere bene; **to have potential** essere promettente 2 (Elec, Math, Phys) potenziale m
po·ten·tial·ly [pəʊˈtenʃəlɪ] ADV potenzialmente
pot·hole [ˈpɒtˌhəʊl] N (in road) buca; (Brit: Geol) marmitta
pot·holer [ˈpɒtˌhəʊləʳ] N (Brit) speleologo(-a)
pot·hol·ing [ˈpɒtˌhəʊlɪŋ] N (Brit) esplorazione f speleologica; **to go potholing** fare della speleologia
po·tion [ˈpəʊʃən] N pozione f, filtro
pot·luck [ˌpɒtˈlʌk] N: **to take potluck** (for food) mangiare quel che passa il convento; (for other things) tentare la sorte
pot plant N pianta in vaso
pot·pour·ri [ˌpəʊˈpʊriː] N 1 (flowers) miscuglio di petali essiccati per profumare un ambiente 2 (fig: of music, writing) pot-pourri m inv
pot roast N (Culin) brasato
pot shot N: **to take a potshot at sth** sparare a casaccio contro qc
pot·ted [ˈpɒtɪd] ADJ 1 (fish, meat) conservato(-a) in vaso; (plant) in vaso 2 (fig: shortened) condensato(-a)
pot·ter¹ [ˈpɒtəʳ] N ceramista m/f
pot·ter² [ˈpɒtəʳ], (USA) **put·ter** [ˈpʌtəʳ] VI: **to potter round the shops** fare un tranquillo giretto per i negozi; **to potter round the house** sbrigare con calma le faccende di casa; **he**

likes pottering about in the garden gli piace fare qualche lavoretto in giardino
pot·tery [ˈpɒtərɪ] N (workshop) fabbrica or laboratorio di ceramiche; (craft) ceramica; (pots) ceramiche fpl; **a piece of pottery** una ceramica ♦ ADJ (dish, jug) di ceramica; **pottery classes** un corso di ceramica
pot·ty [ˈpɒtɪ] N (fam) vasino
potty-trained [ˈpɒtɪˌtreɪnd] ADJ che ha imparato a farla nel vasino
pouch [paʊtʃ] N (Anat: for tobacco) borsa; (for money) borsellino; (Zool) marsupio; **my money was in a pouch** i miei soldi erano in un borsellino; **in their mother's pouch** nel marsupio della madre
pouf, pouffe [puːf] N (seat) pouf m inv
poul·tice [ˈpəʊltɪs] N impiastro, cataplasma m
poul·try [ˈpəʊltrɪ] N pollame m
poultry farm N azienda avicola
poultry farmer N pollicoltore(-trice)
pounce [paʊns] N balzo ♦ VI (cat, tiger) balzare (sulla preda); (bird) piombare (sulla preda); **to pounce on sb/sth** (animal) balzare su qn/qc; (bird) piombare su qn/qc; (person) piombare or balzare su qn/qc; **she pounced on my offer of help** ha colto al volo la mia offerta di aiuto; **he pounced on my suggestion that …** (attack) è saltato su quando ho proposto che...
pound¹ [paʊnd] N 1 (weight = 453g, 16 ounces) libbra; **sold by the pound** venduto(-a) alla libbra; **half a pound** mezza libbra; **a pound of carrots** mezzo chilo di carote 2 (money = 100 pence) (lira) sterlina; **twenty pounds** venti sterline; **one pound sterling** una sterlina; **a pound coin** una moneta da una sterlina; **a ten-pound note** una banconota da dieci sterline
pound² [paʊnd] VT (hammer, strike: door, table, person) picchiare; (: piano) pestare i tasti di; (: typewriter) battere sui tasti di; (subj: sea, waves) sbattere contro; (: guns, bombs) martellare; (pulverize: drug, spices, nuts) pestare, polverizzare; (knead: dough) lavorare; **to pound sth to pieces** fare a pezzi qc; **to pound sth to a pulp** ridurre qc in poltiglia ♦ VI 1 (heart) battere forte; (drums) rullare; (sea) sbattere; (person): **to pound at or on** dare dei gran colpi a or su; (piano) pestare i tasti di; **to pound on the door** battere alla porta; **my heart was pounding** mi batteva forte il cuore 2 (run, walk heavily): **to pound in/out** entrare/uscire a passi pesanti
pound³ [paʊnd] N (enclosure: for dogs) canile m municipale; (for cars) deposito m auto, inv (per auto sottoposte a rimozione forzata)
pound·ing [ˈpaʊndɪŋ] N: **to take a pounding** (team) prendere una batosta; (ship) essere sbattuto(-a) violentemente dalle onde; (town: in war) venire duramente colpito(-a)
pound sterling N lira sterlina
pour [pɔːʳ] VT versare; **to pour sth off** buttar via qc, versar fuori qc; **let me pour you a drink** lascia che ti versi da bere; **shall I pour you a cup of tea?** ti verso del tè?; **she poured some water into the pan** ha versato dell'acqua nella pentola; **to pour money into a project** investire molti soldi in un progetto ♦ VI 1 **to come pouring in** (water) entrare a fiotti; (letters) arrivare a valanghe; (cars, people) affluire in gran quantità; **the sweat is pouring off you!** sei grondante di sudore! 2 **it's pouring (with rain)** sta piovendo a dirotto, sta diluviando
▸ **pour away** VT + ADV buttar via
▸ **pour in** VI + ADV (people) entrare a frotte; **tourists are pouring in** i turisti stanno arrivando in massa; **the sunshine poured into the room** la luce del sole inondava la stanza
▸ **pour out** VI + ADV (drink) versare; (dirty water) buttar via; (fig: feelings) sfogare; (: troubles) sfogarsi parlando di; (: story) raccontare tutto d'un fiato; **she poured out her complaints** si lanciò in una serie di lamentele
pour·ing [ˈpɔːrɪŋ] ADJ 1 (rain) battente; **in the pouring rain** sotto la pioggia battente; **a pouring wet day** una giornata molto piovosa 2 (custard) liquido(-a)
pout [paʊt] N broncio ♦ VI fare il broncio, mettere il muso
pov·er·ty [ˈpɒvətɪ] N miseria, povertà; **poverty of resources** mancanza di risorse; **to live in poverty** vivere in miseria

poverty line N: below the poverty line sotto la soglia di povertà

poverty-stricken ['pɒvətɪˌstrɪkən] ADJ (gen) poverissimo(-a); (hum: hard up) al verde

poverty trap N (Econ) circolo vizioso nel quale, accettando un lavoro si perderebbe parte dell'assegno di disoccupazione

POW [ˌpiːəʊˈdʌblju:] N ABBR = prisoner of war

pow·der ['paʊdəʳ] N (gen) polvere f; (face powder) cipria; (medicine) polverina; **white powder** polvere bianca ♦ VT 1 (reduce to powder) ridurre in polvere 2 (apply powder to: face) incipriarsi; **to powder one's body** mettersi il talco; **to powder one's nose** incipriarsi il naso; (euph) andare alla toilette

powder compact N portacipria m inv

powder keg N (fig: area) polveriera; (: situation) situazione f esplosiva

powder puff N piumino della cipria

powder room N toilette f inv (per signore)

pow·dery ['paʊdərɪ] ADJ (substance) come polvere; (surface) impolverato(-a), polveroso(-a); (snow) farinoso(-a)

pow·er ['paʊəʳ] N 1 (physical strength, also fig) forza; (energy) energia; (force: of engine, blow, explosion) potenza; (: of sun) intensità; (: electricity) elettricità; **to cut off the power** (Elec) togliere la corrente; **the power's off** la corrente è staccata; **the ship returned under its own power** la nave è tornata con i propri mezzi; **more power to your elbow!** (fam) dacci dentro!; **nuclear power** energia nucleare; **solar power** energia solare 2 (ability, capacity) capacità f inv, potere m; (faculty) facoltà f inv; **mental powers** capacità fpl mentali; **to do all in one's power to help sb** fare tutto quello che si può per aiutare qn; **the power of speech** la facoltà or l'uso della parola; **powers of persuasion/imagination** forza di persuasione/immaginazione 3 (Pol: authority) potere m, autorità f inv; **that is beyond my power(s)** questo è al di là dei miei poteri; **to have power over sb** avere potere su qn; **to have sb in one's power** avere qn in proprio potere; **to be in sb's power** essere in potere di qn; **to be in power** essere al potere; **the Tories were in power for 18 years** i conservatori sono stati al potere per diciotto anni; **to come to power** salire al potere; **the power behind the throne** l'eminenza grigia; **the world powers** le grandi potenze; **the powers that be** le autorità costituite; **the powers of darkness or evil** le forze del male 4 (Math) potenza; **7 to the power (of)** 3 7 al cubo or alla terza 5 (fam: a lot of): **it did me a power of good** mi ha fatto un bene enorme ♦ VT azionare; **plane powered by 4 jets** aereo azionato da 4 motori a reazione; **nuclear-powered submarine** sottomarino a propulsione atomica ♦ ADJ (saw: also Elec: cable) elettrico(-a); (supply, consumption) di energia elettrica

power·boat ['paʊəˌbəʊt] N (Brit) motobarca, imbarcazione f a motore

power cut N (Brit) interruzione f or mancanza di corrente

power failure N guasto alla linea elettrica

pow·er·ful ['paʊəfʊl] ADJ (gen) potente, forte; (person: physically) possente; (film, actor, speech) formidabile

power·house ['paʊəˌhaʊs] N (fig: person) persona molto dinamica; **a powerhouse of ideas** una miniera di idee

pow·er·less ['paʊəlɪs] ADJ impotente, senza potere; **to be powerless to do sth** essere impossibilitato a fare qc; **I felt totally powerless** mi sentivo totalmente impotente

power line N linea elettrica

power of attorney N (Law) procura

power point N (Elec) presa di corrente

power station N centrale f elettrica

power steering N (Aut: also: power-assisted steering) servosterzo

pow·wow ['paʊˌwaʊ] N (fam) riunione f

PR [ˌpiːˈɑː] N ABBR 1 (= public relations) PR 2 = proportional representation ♦ (USA Post: = Puerto Rico)

prac·ti·cabil·ity [ˌpræktɪkəˈbɪlɪtɪ] N praticabilità, attuabilità

prac·ti·cable ['præktɪkəbl] ADJ (scheme) praticabile, attuabile

prac·ti·cal ['præktɪkəl] ADJ (gen) pratico(-a); **a practical suggestion** un consiglio pratico; **for all practical purposes** in pratica, agli effetti pratici; **he's very practical** è un tipo molto pratico

prac·ti·cal·ity [ˌpræktɪˈkælɪtɪ] N (of person) senso pratico;

(of scheme, idea) aspetto pratico; **practicalities** dettagli mpl pratici

practical joke N burla

prac·ti·cal·ly ['præktɪklɪ] ADV 1 (almost) praticamente, quasi; **it's practically impossible** è praticamente impossibile 2 **practically based** (education, training) basato(-a) sulla pratica

prac·tice ['præktɪs] N 1 (habit) abitudine f, consuetudine f; **it's common practice** è d'uso; **it is not our practice to do that** generalmente non lo facciamo; **to make a practice of doing sth** avere l'abitudine di fare qc 2 (exercise) esercizio; (training) allenamento; (rehearsal) prove fpl; **target practice** pratica di tiro; **piano practice** esercizi mpl al piano; **football practice** allenamento di calcio; **to be out of practice** esser fuori esercizio (or allenamento); **I'm out of practice** sono fuori allenamento; **practice makes perfect** le cose si imparano a forza di pratica 3 (not theory) pratica; **in practice** in pratica; **in practice it's more difficult** in pratica è più difficile; **to put sth into practice** mettere qc in pratica 4 (of doctor, lawyer): **to be in practice** esercitare la professione; **he has a small practice** (doctor) ha un numero ristretto di pazienti; (lawyer) ha un numero ristretto di clienti; **his practice is in Trieste** il suo studio è a Trieste; **to set up in practice as** cominciare ad esercitare la professione di; **a medical practice** uno studio medico ♦ VT, VI (USA) = **practise**

practice match N partita di allenamento

prac·tise, prac·tice (USA) ['præktɪs] VT 1 **to practise patience/self-control** cercare di avere pazienza/di controllarsi; **to practise charity** essere caritatevole; **to practise what one preaches** mettere in pratica ciò che si predica 2 (train o.s. at: piano) esercitarsi a; (: song) esercitarsi per imparare; **to practise a shot** (Golf, Tennis) esercitarsi in un tiro; **I practise the flute every evening** mi esercito al flauto ogni sera; **I practised my Italian with her** ho fatto pratica d'italiano con lei 3 (follow, exercise: profession) esercitare; (: sport, religion) praticare; (: method) seguire, usare; (: custom) seguire ♦ VI 1 (in order to acquire skill: gen: Mus) esercitarsi; (: Sport) allenarsi; **I ought to practise more** dovrei esercitarmi di più; **the team practises on Thursdays** la squadra si allena di giovedì 2 (lawyer, doctor) esercitare

prac·tised, prac·ticed (USA) ['præktɪst] ADJ (person) esperto(-a), provetto(-a); (performance) da virtuoso(-a); (liar) matricolato(-a); **with a practised eye** con occhio esperto

prac·tising, prac·tic·ing (USA) ['præktɪsɪŋ] ADJ (lawyer) che esercita (la professione); (Jew, Catholic etc) praticante; **she's a practising Catholic** è cattolica praticante

prac·ti·tion·er [præk'tɪʃənəʳ] N (of an art) professionista m/f; (Med) medico

prag·mat·ic [præg'mætɪk] ADJ pragmatico(-a)

Prague [prɑːg] N Praga

prai·rie ['prɛərɪ] N prateria; **the prairies** le grandi praterie

praise [preɪz] N elogio, lode f; **he spoke in praise of their achievements** ha elogiato i loro risultati; **I have nothing but praise for her** non posso che lodarla; **praise be to God!** sia lodato Iddio!; **praise be!** (fam) sia ringraziato il cielo! ♦ VT lodare, elogiare; (God) render lode a; **to praise sb for sth/for doing sth** lodare or elogiare qn per qc/per aver fatto qc

praise·worthy ['preɪzˌwɜːðɪ] ADJ lodevole, degno(-a) di lode

pram [præm] N (Brit) carrozzina

prance [prɑːns] VI (horse) caracollare; (person: proudly) pavoneggiarsi; (: gaily) saltellare; **to prance in/out** entrare/uscire pavoneggiandosi (or saltellando)

prank [præŋk] N scherzetto, burla; **a childish prank** una birichinata; **to play a prank on sb** giocare un tiro a qn, fare uno scherzo a qn

prat [præt] N (Brit fam!) cretino(-a)

prat·tle ['prætl] VI chiacchierare, cianciare

prawn [prɔːn] N gambero, gamberetto

prawn cocktail N cocktail m inv di gamberetti

pray [preɪ] VI (say prayers) pregare; **to pray to God** pregare Dio; **to pray for sb/sth** pregare per qn/qc; **to pray for forgiveness** implorare il perdono; **we are praying for good weather** preghiamo che faccia bello

prayer [preə'] N preghiera; **to say one's prayers** dire *or* recitare le preghiere

prayer book N libro di preghiere

pre– [priː] PREF pre-; **pre-1970** prima del 1970

preach [priːtʃ] VT (*gen*) predicare; (*sermon*) fare ♦ VI predicare; **to preach at sb** far la predica a qn; **to preach to the converted** (*fig*) cercare di convincere chi è già convinto

preach·er ['priːtʃə'] N (*of sermon*) predicatore *m*; (*USA: minister*) pastore *m*

pre·am·ble [priːˈæmbl] N preambolo

pre·ar·ranged [ˌpriːəˈreɪndʒd] ADJ organizzato(-a) in anticipo

pre·cari·ous [prɪˈkɛərɪəs] ADJ precario(-a)

pre·cau·tion [prɪˈkɔːʃən] N precauzione *f*; **as a precaution** per precauzione; **to take precautions** prendere precauzioni; **to take the precaution of doing** prendere la precauzione di fare

pre·cau·tion·ary [prɪˈkɔːʃənərɪ] ADJ (*measure*) precauzionale

pre·cede [prɪˈsiːd] VT (*in space, time*) precedere; **he preceded me as chairman of the Society** è stato il mio predecessore nella presidenza della Società

prec·edence ['presɪdəns] N (*in rank*) precedenza; (*in importance*) priorità; **to take precedence over sb/sth** avere la precedenza su qn/qc

prec·edent ['presɪdənt] N (*also Law*) precedente *m*; **without precedent** senza precedenti; **to establish** *or* **set a precedent** creare un precedente

pre·ced·ing [prɪˈsiːdɪŋ] ADJ precedente

pre·cept [ˈpriːsept] N precetto

pre·cinct ['priːsɪŋkt] N 1 (*also:* **shopping precinct**) zona dei negozi (*chiusa al traffico automobilistico*), centro commerciale; **pedestrian precinct** zona pedonale 2 (*of cathedral*) recinto; **precincts** NPL (*environs*) dintorni *mpl* 3 (*USA: district*) circoscrizione *f*

pre·cious ['preʃəs] ADJ prezioso(-a); **a precious resource** una risorsa preziosa; **it's very precious to me** mi è molto caro; **your precious dog** (*iro*) il tuo amatissimo cane ♦ ADV (*fam*): **precious little/few** ben poco/pochi

preci·pice ['presɪpɪs] N precipizio; **on the edge of a precipice** sull'orlo del precipizio

pre·cipi·tate [*adj, n* prɪˈsɪpɪtɪt, *vb* prɪˈsɪpɪteɪt] ADJ (*hasty*) precipitoso(-a), affrettato(-a) ♦ N (*Chem*) precipitato ♦ VT 1 (*bring on: crisis*) accelerare 2 (*Chem*) precipitare; (*Met*) far condensare

pre·cipi·ta·tion [prɪˌsɪpɪˈteɪʃən] N precipitazione *f*

pre·cipi·tous [prɪˈsɪpɪtəs] ADJ (*slope, path*) a precipizio; (*decision, action*) precipitoso(-a)

pré·cis ['preɪsiː] N (*pl* **précis**) riassunto

pre·cise [prɪˈsaɪs] ADJ (*gen*) preciso(-a); (*pej: over precise*) pignolo(-a), pedante; **there were 5, to be precise** ce n'erano 5, per essere precisi; **at that precise moment** in quel preciso istante; **he's very precise in everything he does** è sempre molto preciso in quello che fa

pre·cise·ly [prɪˈsaɪslɪ] ADV con precisione; **at 4 o'clock precisely, at precisely 4 o'clock** alle 4 precise *or* in punto; **precisely!** precisamente!, proprio così!

pre·ci·sion [prɪˈsɪʒən] N precisione *f*

pre·clude [prɪˈkluːd] (*frm*) VT (*possibility*) precludere, impedire; (*misunderstanding, doubt*) non lasciar adito a; **we are precluded from doing that** siamo impossibilitati a farlo; **to preclude sb from doing** impedire a qn di fare; **his age precludes travel** l'età gli impedisce di viaggiare

pre·co·cious [prɪˈkəʊʃəs] ADJ precoce

pre·con·ceived [ˌpriːkənˈsiːvd] ADJ (*idea*) preconcetto(-a); **preconceived notions** idee preconcette

pre·con·cep·tion [ˌpriːkənˈsepʃən] N preconcetto

pre·con·di·tion [ˌpriːkənˈdɪʃən] N condizione *f* indispensabile; **to set preconditions** stabilire le condizioni necessarie

pre·cur·sor [ˌpriːˈkɜːsə'] N precursore *m*

pre·date [ˌpriːˈdeɪt] VT (*precede*) precedere; (*put earlier date on*) retrodatare

preda·tor ['predətə'] N predatore(-trice)

preda·tory ['predətərɪ] ADJ (*animal*) rapace, predatore(-trice); (*habits, army*) rapace; (*person, look*) avido(-a), cupido(-a)

pre·de·ces·sor ['priːdɪˌsesə'] N predecessore *m*

pre·des·ti·na·tion [priːˌdestɪˈneɪʃən] N predestinazione *f*

pre·de·ter·mine [ˌpriːdɪˈtɜːmɪn] VT predeterminare, determinare in anticipo

pre·dica·ment [prɪˈdɪkəmənt] N situazione *f* difficile (*or* imbarazzante); **I'm in a bit of a predicament** sono in una situazione un po' imbarazzante

predi·cate [*n, adj* ˈpredɪkɪt, *vb* ˈpredɪˌkeɪt] N (*Gram*) predicato ♦ ADJ (*Gram*) predicativo(-a) ♦ VT 1 (*frm: imply*) asserire 2 (*frm: idea*): **to be predicated on sth** dipendere da qc

pre·dict [prɪˈdɪkt] VT predire

pre·dict·able [prɪˈdɪktəbl] ADJ prevedibile

pre·dict·ably [prɪˈdɪktəblɪ] ADV (*behave, react*) in modo prevedibile; **predictably she didn't turn up** come era da prevedere, non è arrivata

pre·dic·tion [prɪˈdɪkʃən] N predizione *f*

pre·dis·pose [ˌpriːdɪsˈpəʊz] VT predisporre

pre·domi·nance [prɪˈdɒmɪnəns] N predominanza

pre·domi·nant [prɪˈdɒmɪnənt] ADJ predominante

pre·domi·nant·ly [prɪˈdɒmɪnəntlɪ] ADV prevalentemente, per lo più

pre·domi·nate [prɪˈdɒmɪˌneɪt] VI predominare

pre·eminent [ˌpriːˈemɪnənt] ADJ eccezionale, preminente

pre·empt [ˌpriːˈempt] VT acquistare per diritto di prelazione; (*fig*) anticipare

pre·emptive [ˌpriːˈemptɪv] ADJ: **pre-emptive strike** (*Mil*) azione *f* preventiva

preen [priːn] VT 1 (*feathers*) lisciare (con il becco); **the bird was preening itself** l'uccello si stava lisciando le piume; **he was preening himself in front of the mirror** (*fig: pej*) stava lisciandosi davanti allo specchio 2 **to preen o.s. on sth/on doing sth** (*liter, pej*) compiacersi di qc/di fare qc

pre·fab ['priːfæb] N (*fam*) casetta prefabbricata

pre·fab·ri·ca·ted [ˌpriːˈfæbrɪˌkeɪtɪd] ADJ prefabbricato(-a)

pref·ace ['prefɪs] N prefazione *f*; (*to speech*) introduzione *f*

pre·fect ['priːfekt] N (*Brit Scol*) allievo delle classi superiori che è incaricato della disciplina e gode di alcuni privilegi; (*Admin: in Italy, France*) prefetto

pre·fer [prɪˈfɜː'] VT 1 preferire; **which would you prefer?** quale preferisci?; **to prefer coffee to tea** preferire il caffè al tè; **I prefer chemistry to mathematics** preferisco la chimica alla matematica; **I prefer walking to going by car** preferisco camminare piuttosto che andare in macchina; **I prefer to stay home** preferisco restare a casa 2 (*Law: charges, complaint*) sporgere; (*: action*) intentare

pref·er·able ['prefərəbl] ADJ preferibile

pref·er·ably ['prefərəblɪ] ADV di preferenza, preferibilmente

pref·er·ence ['prefərəns] N preferenza; **my preference is for ..., I have a preference for ...** preferisco ...; **in preference to sth** piuttosto che qc; **to give preference to sb/sth** dare la preferenza a qn/qc

pref·er·en·tial [ˌprefəˈrenʃəl] ADJ preferenziale; **preferential treatment** trattamento di favore

pre·ferred stock [prɪˈfɜːdˈstɒk] NPL (*USA: Fin*) = **preference shares**

pre·fix ['priːfɪks] N (*Gram*) prefisso

preg·nan·cy ['pregnənsɪ] N gravidanza

pregnancy test N test *m inv* (di gravidanza)

preg·nant ['pregnənt] ADJ incinta; (*animal*) gravida; (*liter: remark, pause*) significativo(-a); **she's 3 months pregnant** è incinta di 3 mesi; **pregnant with meaning** (*liter*) pregno(-a) di significato

pre·his·tor·ic [ˌpriːhɪˈstɒrɪk] ADJ preistorico(-a)

pre·his·to·ry [ˌpriːˈhɪstərɪ] N preistoria

pre·judge [ˌpriːˈdʒʌdʒ] VT farsi a priori un giudizio di

preju·dice ['predʒʊdɪs] N 1 (*biased opinion*) pregiudizio; *collective n* pregiudizi *mpl*; **his prejudice against sb/sth** i suoi pregiudizi nei riguardi di qn/qc 2 (*Law: injury, detriment*) pregiudizio; **without prejudice to** (*frm*) senza pregiudicare ♦ VT 1 (*bias*): **to prejudice sb in favour of/against** disporre bene/male qn verso 2 (*frm: injure*) pregiudicare, ledere, compromettere

preju·diced ['predʒʊdɪst] ADJ (*person*) pieno(-a) di pregiudizi, prevenuto(-a); (*racially*) pieno(-a) di pregiudizi; (*view,* *opinion*) preconcetto(-a); **to be prejudiced against sb/sth** essere prevenuto(-a) contro qn/qc; **to be prejudiced in favour of sb/sth** essere ben disposto(-a) verso qn/qc

prel·ate [ˈprɛlɪt] N prelato

pre·limi·naries [prɪˈlɪmɪnərɪz] NPL preliminari mpl

pre·limi·nary [prɪˈlɪmɪnərɪ] ADJ preliminare ♦ PREP: **preliminary to sth/doing sth** prima di qc/fare qc

prel·ude [ˈprɛljuːd] N preludio

pre·mari·tal [ˌpriːˈmærɪtl] ADJ prematrimoniale

prema·ture [ˈprɛmətjʊəˈ] ADJ (*baby, birth, decision*) prematuro(-a); (*arrival*) (molto) anticipato(-a); **you are being a little premature** sei un po' troppo precipitoso; **premature baby** neonato prematuro

pre·medi·tat·ed [ˌpriːˈmɛdɪteɪtɪd] ADJ premeditato(-a)

pre·medi·ta·tion [priːˌmɛdɪˈteɪʃən] N premeditazione f

premenstrual syndrome N (*Med*) sindrome f premestruale

prem·ier [ˈprɛmɪəˈ] N (*Pol*) premier m inv, primo ministro; **the Australian premier** il primo ministro australiano ♦ ADJ primo(-a); **the Premier League** la prima divisione

premiere [ˈprɛmɪəˈ] N prima

prem·ise [ˈprɛmɪs] N (*hypothesis*) premessa

prem·ises [ˈprɛmɪsɪz] NPL locale msg; **on the premises** sul posto; **he was asked to leave the premises** l'hanno invitato ad abbandonare il locale; **business premises** locali commerciali; **they're moving to new premises** si trasferiscono in nuovi locali

pre·mium [ˈpriːmɪəm] N (*gen*) premio; (*additional charge*) maggiorazione f; **insurance companies charge high premiums** le compagnie assicurative fanno pagare premi elevati; **you have to pay a premium for a sea view** bisogna pagare una maggiorazione per avere la vista sul mare; **to sell at a premium** (*shares*) vendere sopra la pari; **to be at a premium** (*fig*) essere ricercatissimo(-a), scarseggiare; **in Hong Kong accommodation is at a premium** a Hong Kong le case scarseggiano

premium deal N (*Comm*) offerta speciale

premium gasoline N (*USA*) super f

premo·ni·tion [ˌprɛməˈnɪʃən] N presentimento, premonizione f

pre·oc·cu·pa·tion [priːˌɒkjʊˈpeɪʃən] N preoccupazione f; **his preoccupation with death** la sua ossessione della morte; **in his preoccupation with ...** dato che era tutto preso da...

pre·oc·cu·pied [ˌpriːˈɒkjʊpaɪd] ADJ (*absorbed*) assorto(-a); **they're preoccupied with the forthcoming wedding** sono tutti presi dall'imminente matrimonio

❏ **preoccupied** is not translated by the Italian word *preoccupato*

pre-owned [ˌpriːˈəʊnd] ADJ di seconda mano

pre·packed [ˌpriːˈpækt], **pre·pack·aged** [ˌpriːˈpækɪdʒd] ADJ preconfezionato(-a)

pre·paid [ˌpriːˈpeɪd] ADJ pagato(-a) in anticipo; (*envelope*) già affrancato(-a)

prepa·ra·tion [ˌprɛpəˈreɪʃən] N 1 (*preparing*) preparazione f; **in preparation for sth** in vista di qc; **to be in preparation** essere in (corso di) preparazione; **months of preparation** mesi di preparazione 2 **preparations** NPL (*preparatory measures*) preparativi mpl; **to make preparations** fare i preparativi; **preparations are being made for the visit of the Queen** sono in atto i preparativi per la visita della regina 3 (*Brit Scol*) compiti mpl

pre·para·tory [prɪˈpærətərɪ] ADJ (*work*) preparatorio(-a); (*measure*) preliminare; **preparatory to sth/to doing sth** prima di qc/di fare qc

preparatory school N tipo di scuola privata

pre·pare [prɪˈpɛəˈ] VT preparare; **teachers have to prepare lessons in the evening** la sera gli insegnanti devono preparare le lezioni; **prepare yourself for a shock** preparati a uno shock; **to prepare the way for sth** preparare il terreno per qc; **to prepare to do sth** prepararsi a fare qc ♦ VI: **to prepare for** (*journey, party, sb's arrival*) fare dei preparativi per; (*exam, future*) prepararsi per; **we're preparing for our skiing vacation** stiamo facendo i preparativi per le vacanze in montagna; **to prepare for war** prepararsi alla guerra

pre·pared [prɪˈpɛəd] ADJ 1 (*speech, answer*) preparato(-a)

in anticipo; (*food*) pronto(-a) 2 (*in state of readiness*) pronto(-a); **to be prepared to do sth** essere pronto(-a) a fare qc; **to be prepared for anything** essere pronto(-a) a tutto; **we were not prepared for this** questo ci ha colto alla sprovvista or non ce lo aspettavamo 3 (*willing*): **to be prepared to help sb** essere disposto(-a) or pronto(-a) ad aiutare qn; **I'm prepared to help you** sono pronto(-a) or disposto(-a) ad aiutarti

pre·pon·der·ance [prɪˈpɒndərəns] N preponderanza

prepo·si·tion [ˌprɛpəˈzɪʃən] N preposizione f

pre·pos·sess·ing [ˌpriːpəˈzɛsɪŋ] ADJ attraente

pre·pos·ter·ous [prɪˈpɒstərəs] ADJ ridicolo(-a), assurdo(-a)

prep school [prɛp-] N = **preparatory school**

pre·re·cord [ˌpriːrɪˈkɔːd] VT registrare in anticipo; **prerecorded broadcast** trasmissione f registrata

pre·requi·site [ˌpriːˈrɛkwɪzɪt] N prerequisito

pre·roga·tive [prɪˈrɒɡətɪv] N prerogativa

Pres·by·ter·ian [ˌprɛzbɪˈtɪərɪən] ADJ, N presbiteriano(-a)

pres·by·tery [ˈprɛzbɪtərɪ] N presbiterio

pre·school [ˈpriːskuːl] ADJ (*child*) in età prescolastica; (*age*) prescolastico(-a); **preschool children** bambini in età prescolare

pre·scribe [prɪˈskraɪb] VT (*gen, also Med*) prescrivere, ordinare; (*fig*) consigliare; **prescribed books** (*Scol, Univ*) testi mpl in programma

pre·scrip·tion [prɪˈskrɪpʃən] N (*Med*) ricetta (medica); **to make up a prescription, fill a prescription** (*USA*) preparare or fare una ricetta; **to make out a prescription for sb** fare una ricetta a qn; **only available on prescription** ottenibile solo dietro presentazione di ricetta medica

prescription charges NPL (*Brit*) ≈ ticket m inv

pre·scrip·tive [prɪˈskrɪptɪv] ADJ normativo(-a)

pres·ence [ˈprɛzns] N presenza; **in the presence of** in presenza di, davanti a; **to make one's presence felt** far sentire la propria presenza

pres·ent [*adj, n* ˈprɛznt, *vb* prɪˈzɛnt] ADJ 1 (*in attendance*) presente; **to be present at** (*gen*) essere presente a; (*officially*) presenziare a; **he wasn't present at the meeting** non era presente alla riunione; **those present** i presenti 2 (*of the moment*) attuale; **the present situation** la situazione attuale; **in the present circumstances** date le circostanze attuali; **at the present moment** al momento attuale; **its present value** il suo valore attuale 3 (*Gram*) presente ♦ N 1 (*present time*) presente m; (*Gram: also*: **present tense**) (tempo) presente m; **the past and the present** il passato e il presente; **at present** al momento; **for the present** per il momento, per adesso, per ora; **up to the present** fino a questo momento, finora 2 (*gift*) regalo; **to give sb a present** fare un regalo a qn; **he gave me a lovely present** mi ha fatto un bel regalo; **I got this watch as a present** questo orologio mi è stato regalato; **to make sb a present of sth** regalare qc a qn ♦ VT 1 (*hand over: gen*) presentare; (: *prize, certificate*) consegnare; (*give as gift*) offrire (in omaggio); (*proof, evidence*) fornire; (*Law: case*) esporre; **to present sb with sth, present sth to sb** fare dono di qc a qn; (*prize*) consegnare qc a qn; **the Mayor presented the winner with a medal** il sindaco ha consegnato una medaglia al vincitore; **to present arms** (*Mil*) presentare le armi; **to present o.s. for an interview** presentarsi per un colloquio 2 (*offer: difficulty, problem, opportunity*) presentare; (: *features*) offrire; **if the opportunity presents itself** se si presenterà l'opportunità 3 (*put on: play, concert, film*) dare; (*TV, Radio: act as presenter of*) presentare; **to present the news** (*TV, Radio*) leggere le notizie; **presenting Jack Nicholson as ...** con Jack Nicholson nella parte di... 4 (*frm: introduce*): **to present sb to sb** presentare qn a qn; **may I present Miss Clark?** permette che le presenti la signorina Clark?

pre·sent·able [prɪˈzɛntəbl] ADJ presentabile; **to make o.s. presentable** rendersi presentabile, mettersi in ordine

pres·en·ta·tion [ˌprɛzənˈteɪʃən] N 1 (*act of presenting*) presentazione f; (*report*) relazione f; (*Law: of case*) esposizione f; **he gave an interesting presentation** ha fatto una presentazione interessante; **on presentation of the voucher** dietro presentazione del buono; **to make a presentation of sth** (*plan, report*) presentare qc 2 (*Radio, TV, Theatre*) rappresentazione f 3 (*of prizes etc*) consegna ufficiale; (*gift*) regalo, dono; **to make the presentation** fare la consegna ufficiale; **the winners went to London for the presentation of prizes** i vincitori si sono recati a Londra per la consegna ufficiale dei premi

present-day [ˈprezntˌdeɪ] ADJ attuale, d'oggigiorno, di oggi

pre·sent·er [prɪˈzentəʳ] N (*Radio, TV*) presentatore(-trice)

pres·ent·ly [ˈprezntlɪ] ADV (*shortly*) tra poco, a momenti; (*esp USA: now*) adesso, ora; **you'll feel better presently** tra poco ti sentirai meglio; **presently a secretary came in** poco dopo è entrata una segretaria; **they're presently on tour** al momento sono in tournée

❏ **presently** is not translated by the Italian word *presentemente*

present participle N participio presente

pres·er·va·tion [ˌprezəˈveɪʃən] N conservazione *f*; (*of peace, one's dignity*) mantenimento

pre·serva·tive [prɪˈzɜːvətɪv] N (*Culin*) conservante *m*

❏ **preservative** is not translated by the Italian word *preservativo*

pre·serve [prɪˈzɜːv] VT 1 (*maintain: traditions*) conservare, mantenere; (: *dignity, peace*) mantenere; (*keep intact: buildings, memory*) conservare; **they will strive to preserve peace** lotteranno per mantenere la pace 2 (*keep from decay*) preservare, proteggere; **well preserved** ben conservato(-a); **he is well preserved** (*hum*) si conserva bene 3 (*Culin*) conservare, mettere in conserva; **to preserve fruit** fare conserve di frutta 4 (*keep from harm, save*) proteggere; **efforts to preserve the forest** sforzi per preservare la foresta ♦ N 1 (*domain*) dominio 2 (*reservation*) riserva 3 (*often pl: jam*) marmellata; (*bottled fruit*) frutta sciroppata

pre·shrunk [ˌpriːˈʃrʌŋk] ADJ (*fabric, garment*) irrestringibile

pre·side [prɪˈzaɪd] VI: **to preside (at or over)** presiedere (a)

presi·den·cy [ˈprezɪdənsɪ] N (*Pol*) presidenza; (*USA: of company*) direzione *f*

presi·dent [ˈprezɪdənt] N (*Pol*) presidente *m*; (*USA: of company*) direttore(-trice) generale

presi·den·tial [ˌprezɪˈdenʃəl] ADJ (*Pol*) presidenziale

press [pres] N 1 (*apparatus, machine: gen*) pressa; (: *for wine*) torchio 2 (*printing press*) torchio da stampa; (*place*) tipografia; **to go to press** (*newspaper*) andare in macchina; **to be in the press** (*being printed*) essere in (corso di) stampa; (*in the newspapers*) essere sui giornali; **the press** (*newspapers*) la stampa, i giornali; **to get a good/bad press** avere una buona/cattiva stampa; **a member of the press** un rappresentante della stampa ♦ VT 1 (*push: button*) premere, schiacciare; (: *doorbell*) suonare; (: *trigger*) premere; (*squeeze: grapes, olives*) pigiare; (: *flowers*) pressare; (: *hand*) stringere; **to press sb/sth to one's heart** stringersi qn/qc al petto *or* al cuore; **don't press so hard!** non premere così forte! 2 (*iron*) stirare; **she was pressing her blouse** si stava stirando la camicetta 3 (*urge, entreat*): **to press sb to do** *or* **into doing sth** fare pressione su qn affinché faccia qc; **they pressed me to stay** hanno insistito perché restassi; **to press sth on sb** (*food, gift*) insistere perché qn accetti qc; (*one's opinions*) voler imporre qc su qn; (*insist on: attack*) rendere più pressante; (: *claim, demands*) insistere su *or* in; **to press sb for an answer** insistere perché qn risponda; **to be hard pressed** essere alle strette; **to press one's opponent** incalzare l'avversario; **to press home an advantage** sfruttare al massimo un vantaggio; **to press the point** insistere sul punto; **to be pressed for time** aver poco tempo; **to be pressed for money** essere a corto di soldi; **to press sb into service** obbligare qn a lavorare; **to press sth into service** far uso di qc; **to press charges against sb** (*Law*) sporgere una denuncia contro qn ♦ VI 1 (*in physical sense*) spingere, premere; **the people pressed round him** la gente gli si è accalcata intorno; **the crowd pressed towards the exit** la folla si accalcava all'uscita; **to press ahead** *or* **forward (with sth)** (*fig*) proseguire (in qc) 2 (*urge, agitate*): **to press for sth** fare pressioni per ottenere qc; **time presses** il tempo stringe

▸ **press down** VI + ADV: **to press down (on)** premere (su) ♦ VT + ADV premere

▸ **press on** VI + ADV continuare

press agency N agenzia di stampa

press conference N conferenza *f* stampa, *inv*

press cutting, press clipping N ≈ ritaglio di giornale

press-gang [ˈpresˌgæŋ] VT: **to press-gang sb into doing sth** costringere qn a viva forza a fare qc

press·ing [ˈpresɪŋ] ADJ (*matter, problem*) urgente, pressante; (*request, invitation*) insistente, pressante; **he was very pressing** era molto insistente ♦ N stiratura

press officer N addetto(-a) stampa

press release N comunicato *m* stampa, *inv*

press stud N (bottone *m*) automatico

press-up [ˈpresˌʌp] N (*Brit*) flessione *f* sulle braccia; **to do press-ups** fare flessioni sulle braccia

pres·sure [ˈpreʃəʳ] N 1 (*Phys, Tech, Met*) pressione *f*; **at full pressure** (*Tech*) al livello massimo di pressione 2 (*compulsion, influence*) pressione *f*, pressioni *fpl*; **to be under pressure** essere sotto pressione; **he's been under a lot of pressure recently** ultimamente ha dovuto sopportare molta pressione; **to put pressure on sb** fare pressione su qn; **they are really putting the pressure on** ci (*or vi etc*) stanno assillando; **to use pressure to obtain sth** far pressione per ottenere qc; **to work under pressure** lavorare sotto pressione; **she's under a lot of pressure** è sotto un'enorme pressione; **the pressure of these events** la tensione creata da questi avvenimenti; **pressure of work prevented her from going** non è potuta andare per via del troppo lavoro ♦ VT = **pressurize**

pressure cooker N pentola a pressione

pressure gauge N manometro

pressure group N (*Pol*) gruppo di pressione

pres·sur·ize [ˈpreʃəˌraɪz] VT 1 (*Tech*) pressurizzare 2 (*fig*): **to pressurize sb to do sth** fare pressioni su qn perché faccia qc

pres·sur·ized [ˈpreʃəˌraɪzd] ADJ pressurizzato(-a)

pres·tige [presˈtiːʒ] N prestigio

pres·tig·ious [presˈtɪdʒəs] ADJ prestigioso(-a), di grande prestigio

pre·sum·ably [prɪˈzjuːməblɪ] ADV: **presumably he did it** penso *or* presumo che l'abbia fatto

pre·sume [prɪˈzjuːm] VT 1 (*suppose*): **to presume (that)** supporre (che), presumere (che); **I presume she'll come** suppongo che verrà; **I presume so** presumo di sì; **I presume he did it** suppongo che l'abbia fatto 2 (*frm: venture*): **to presume to do sth** permettersi di fare qc ♦ VI (*frm: take liberties*) prendersi troppe libertà; **to presume on sb's friendship** approfittarsi dell'amicizia di qn

pre·sump·tion [prɪˈzʌmpʃən] N 1 (*arrogance*) presunzione *f*; (*impudence*) audacia 2 (*thing presumed*) supposizione *f*; **there is a strong presumption that ...** tutto fa supporre *or* presumere che...

pre·sump·tu·ous [prɪˈzʌmptjʊəs] ADJ presuntuoso(-a)

pre·sup·pose [ˌpriːsəˈpəʊz] VT presupporre

pre-tax [ˈpriːˈtæks] ADJ al lordo d'imposta

pre·tence, pretense (*USA*) [prɪˈtens] N 1 **his pretence of innocence/sympathy** la sua finta *or* falsa innocenza/comprensione; **she is devoid of all pretence** non si nasconde dietro false apparenze; **to make a pretence of doing sth** far finta di fare qc; **he made a pretence of listening** fece finta di ascoltare; **it's all (a) pretence** è tutta una finta, è tutta scena 2 (*claim*) pretesa 3 (*pretext*) pretesto, scusa; **on** *or* **under the pretence of doing sth** con il pretesto *or* la scusa di fare qc; **under false pretences** con l'inganno

pre·tend [prɪˈtend] VT 1 (*feign*): **to pretend illness/ignorance** fingersi malato(-a)/ignorante, far finta di essere malato(-a)/ignorante; **to pretend to do sth** far finta *or* fingere di fare qc; **she's pretending she can't hear us** fa finta di non sentirci; **he was pretending to be a lawyer** si spacciava per avvocato 2 (*claim*): **to pretend to/that** pretendere di fare/che + *sub* ♦ VI (*feign*) far finta, fingere ♦ ADJ (*fam: gun, money*) finto(-a)

pre·tense [prɪˈtens] N (*USA*) = **pretence**

pre·ten·sion [prɪˈtenʃən] N (*claim*) pretesa; **to have no pretensions to sth/to being sth** non avere la pretesa di avere qc/di essere qc

pre·ten·tious [prɪˈtenʃəs] ADJ pretenzioso(-a)

pret·er·ite [ˈpretərɪt] N (*tempo*) passato, preterito

pre·text ['pri:tekst] N pretesto; **on** or **under the pretext of doing sth** col pretesto di fare qc

pret·ty ['prɪtɪ] ADJ (comp **-ier**, superl **-iest**) grazioso(-a), carino(-a); **she's very pretty** è molto carina; **he wasn't a pretty sight** non era bello a vedersi; **it'll cost you a pretty penny!** (fam) ti costerà una bella sommetta!; **pretty weather** (USA) bel tempo ♦ ADV (rather) piuttosto; (very) molto; **the weather was pretty awful** il tempo era piuttosto brutto; **pretty well** (not badly) piuttosto bene; **pretty nearly** (almost) quasi, praticamente; **pretty much** praticamente; **it's pretty much the same** (fam) è praticamente uguale

pre·vail [prɪ'veɪl] VI **1** (gain mastery): **to prevail** (against, over) prevalere (su); **in the end his view prevailed** alla fine è prevalsa la sua opinione **2** (be current: fashion, belief etc) essere diffuso(-a); **the conditions that prevail** le condizioni attuali; **the fashion which prevailed at that time** la moda che era diffusa a quel tempo **3** (persuade): **to prevail (up)on sb to do sth** convincere qn a fare qc, persuadere qn a fare qc

pre·vail·ing [prɪ'veɪlɪŋ] ADJ (conditions) attuale; (belief, customs, attitude) predominante, prevalente; (wind) dominante

preva·lent ['prevələnt] ADJ (belief, disease, fashion etc) diffuso(-a), comune, predominante; **the conditions which are prevalent in ...** le condizioni esistenti in...

pre·vari·ca·tion [prɪˌværɪ'keɪʃən] N tergiversazione f
❏ **prevarication** is not translated by the Italian word prevaricazione

pre·vent [prɪ'vent] VT (crime, accidents, fire) prevenire; **to prevent sb/sth (from doing sth)** impedire a qn/qc (di fare qc); **the police prevented the protesters from entering the building** la polizia ha impedito ai dimostranti di entrare nell'edificio; **to prevent sth happening again** fare in modo che qc non si ripeta; **to prevent sb's doing sth** (frm) impedire che qn faccia qc

pre·vent·able [prɪ'ventəbl] ADJ che può essere prevenuto(-a), evitabile

pre·ven·ta·tive [prɪ'ventətɪv] ADJ = preventive

pre·ven·tion [prɪ'venʃən] N prevenzione f; **the prevention of cruelty to animals** la protezione degli animali

pre·ven·tive [prɪ'ventɪv] ADJ preventivo(-a)

pre·view ['pri:vju:] N (of film etc) anteprima; **to give sb a preview of sth** (fig) dare a qn un'idea di qc

pre·vi·ous ['pri:vɪəs] ADJ precedente; **the previous day** il giorno prima or precedente; **previous experience** precedente esperienza; **he has no previous experience in that field** non ha esperienza in quel campo; **I have a previous engagement** ho già (preso) un impegno; **on a previous occasion** in precedenza; **in a previous life** in un'altra vita; **to have no previous convictions** (Law) non aver precedenti penali; **to have 5 previous convictions** essere già stato(-a) condannato(-a) 5 volte

pre·vi·ous·ly ['pri:vɪəslɪ] ADV (before) prima; (in the past) in precedenza; (already) già

pre·war ['pri:'wɔ:ʳ] ADJ dell'anteguerra, anteguerra inv

prey [preɪ] N (also fig) preda; **to be prey to** (fig) essere in preda a; **tourists are easy prey** i turisti sono una facile preda; **bird of prey** uccello rapace
▸ **prey on** VI + PREP (subj: animals) predare, far preda di; (: person) depredare; **to prey on sb's mind** ossessionare qn; **it was preying on his mind** gli rodeva la mente

price [praɪs] N **1** (also fig) prezzo; **to go up** or **rise in price** salire or aumentare di prezzo; **to go down** or **fall in price** scendere or calare di prezzo; **I got a good price for it** me lo hanno pagato bene; **what is the price of that painting?** quanto costa quel quadro?; **at a reduced price** a prezzo ribassato; **we pay top prices for silver** offriamo ottimi prezzi per l'argento; **every man has his price** ogni uomo ha il suo prezzo; **the price of fame** il prezzo del successo; **it's a small price to pay for it** (fig) non è che un piccolo sacrificio; **to pay a high price for sth** (also fig) pagare caro qc; **peace at any price** pace a ogni costo or costi quello che costi; **not at any price** per nessuna cosa al mondo; **he regained his freedom, but at a price** ha riconquistato la sua libertà, ma a caro prezzo **2** (value, valuation) valore m; **to put a price on sth** valutare or stimare qc; **to put a price on sb's head** mettere una taglia sulla testa di qn; **what price his promises now?** a che valgono ora le sue promesse?; **you can't put a price**

on it (fig: friendship, loyalty) è inestimabile **3** (Betting: odds) quotazione f, quota ♦ VT (fix price of) fissare il prezzo di; (put price label on) prezzare, mettere il prezzo su; (ask price of) chiedere il prezzo di; **we price the components separately** fissiamo il prezzo dei componenti separatamente; **it was priced at £20** il prezzo era di 20 sterline; **it was priced too high/low** aveva un prezzo troppo alto/basso; **to be priced out of the market** (article) essere così caro(-a) da diventare invendibile; (producer, nation) non poter sostenere la concorrenza ♦ ADV (index) dei prezzi; **prices and incomes policy** politica dei prezzi e dei salari

price control N calmiere m dei prezzi, controllo dei prezzi

price cutting N riduzione f dei prezzi

price·less ['praɪslɪs] ADJ (jewels, necklace) di valore inestimabile; (fam: amusing) impagabile, spassosissimo(-a); **friendship is priceless** l'amicizia è un bene inestimabile

price list N listino (dei) prezzi

price range N gamma di prezzi; **it's within my price range** rientra nelle mie possibilità

price tag N cartellino del prezzo

price war N guerra dei prezzi

pricey [praɪsɪ] ADJ (comp **-ier**, superl **-iest**) (Brit fam) caruccio(-a)

prick [prɪk] N **1** (act, sensation) puntura; (mark) buco; **pricks of conscience** rimorsi mpl di coscienza **2** (fam!: penis) cazzo (fam!); (: person) testa di cazzo (fam!) ♦ VT (puncture: balloon, blister) bucare; (subj: thorn, needle) pungere; (: conscience) rimordere; **to prick a hole in sth** fare un buco in qc; **to prick one's finger (with/on sth)** pungersi un dito (con/su qc); **I've pricked my finger** mi sono punto un dito
▸ **prick out, prick off** VT + ADV (seedlings) trapiantare
▸ **prick up** VT + ADV: **to prick up one's ears** (also fig) drizzare le orecchie

prick·le ['prɪkl] N **1** (on plant, animal etc) spina; **cactus prickles** spine di cactus **2** (sensation) sensazione f di prurito, pizzicore m; (of fear) brivido

prick·ly ['prɪklɪ] ADJ (comp **-ier**, superl **-iest**) **1** (plant) spinoso(-a); (animal) pieno(-a) di spine; (beard) ispido(-a); (wool) che dà prurito **2** (fig: person) permaloso(-a); (: subject) spinoso(-a)

prickly heat N (Med) sudamina

prickly pear N (plant, fruit) fico d'India

pride [praɪd] N **1** (arrogance) superbia, orgoglio; (self-respect) orgoglio, amor proprio; (satisfaction) fierezza; **his pride may be his downfall** la superbia potrebbe essere la sua rovina; **false pride** falso orgoglio; **wounded pride** orgoglio ferito; **to take (a) pride in** (appearance, punctuality) tenere molto a; (children, achievements) essere orgoglioso(-a) di; **she takes (a) pride in arriving on time** ci tiene molto ad essere sempre puntuale; **his pride was hurt** fu ferito nell'orgoglio; **her plants are her pride and joy** le sue piante sono il suo orgoglio or vanto; **to take pride of place** essere al primo posto **2** (of lions) branco ♦ VT: **to pride o.s. on sth** essere orgoglioso(-a) di qc

priest [pri:st] N prete m, sacerdote m

priest·ess ['pri:stɪs] N sacerdotessa

priest·hood ['pri:st,hud] N: **to enter the priesthood** farsi prete

prig [prɪg] N: **don't be such a prig!** non fare il(la) moralista!

prim [prɪm] ADJ (comp **-mer**, superl **-mest**) (demure: person, dress) per benino; (: house, garden) in cui nulla è fuori posto; (: manner, smile) compassato(-a); (prudish: also: **prim and proper**) per benino

pri·ma·cy ['praɪməsɪ] N (frm) suprema importanza

pri·ma fa·cie [ˌpraɪmə'feɪʃɪ] ADV a prima vista ♦ ADJ (assumption) (a prima vista) legittimo(-a); (evidence) (a prima vista) convincente; **to have a prima facie case** (Law) presentare una causa in apparenza fondata

pri·mal ['praɪməl] ADJ (origins, matter, world) originario(-a); (religion, music) primitivo(-a); (first in importance) primario(-a)

pri·mari·ly ['praɪmərɪlɪ] ADV (chiefly) principalmente, essenzialmente

pri·ma·ry ['praɪmərɪ] ADJ (chief, main: gen) principale, primario(-a); **of primary importance** di primaria or fondamentale importanza; **the primary reason for my choice was ...** la principale ragione della mia scelta è stata... ♦ N (*USA: election*) primarie *fpl*

primary colour N colore *m* primario

primary school N (*Brit*) scuola elementare

pri·mate N 1 ['praɪmeɪt](*Zool*) primate *m* 2 ['praɪmɪt](*Rel*) primate *m*

prime [praɪm] ADJ 1 (*chief, major: gen*) principale, primario(-a), fondamentale; (: *cause, reason*) primo(-a), fondamentale; **of importance** della massima importanza; **my prime concern** la mia preoccupazione principale 2 (*excellent: example*) superbo(-a); (: *meat*) di prima scelta; **of prime quality** di prima scelta; **in prime condition** (*car, athlete*) in perfette condizioni; (*fruit*) in condizioni perfette ♦ N: **in the prime of life, in one's prime** nel fiore della vita; **to be past one's prime** non essere più quello(-a) di una volta ♦ VT (*wood*) preparare; (*gun*) innescare; (*pump*) adescare; (*fig: instruct*) istruire, mettere al corrente

prime minister N primo ministro

prim·er ['praɪmə^r] N 1 (*textbook*) testo elementare 2 (*paint*) vernice *f* base, *inv*

prime time N (*Radio, TV*) fascia di massimo ascolto, prime time *m*

pri·meval [praɪˈmiːvəl] ADJ primordiale, primitivo(-a); **primeval forests** foreste originarie

primi·tive ['prɪmɪtɪv] ADJ, N primitivo(-a)

prim·rose ['prɪmˌrəʊz] N (*Bot*) primula (gialla) ♦ ADJ (*also: primrose yellow*) giallo canarino *inv*

prince [prɪns] N principe *m*; **Prince Charles** il principe Carlo

prince charming N il principe *m* azzurro

prin·cess [prɪnˈses] N principessa

prin·ci·pal ['prɪnsɪpəl] ADJ principale; **the principal violin** il primo violino ♦ N 1 (*of school, college*) preside *m/f*; (*in play*) protagonista *m/f*; (*in orchestra*) primo(-a) strumentista *m/f* 2 (*Fin*) capitale *m*

prin·ci·pal·ity [ˌprɪnsɪˈpælɪtɪ] N principato

prin·ci·pal·ly ['prɪnsɪpəlɪ] ADV principalmente

prin·ci·ple ['prɪnsɪpl] N principio; **in principle** in linea di principio; **on principle** per principio; **it's a matter of principle**, **it's the principle of the thing** è una questione di principio; **a man of principle** un uomo di saldi principi; **it's against my principles** è contrario ai miei principi

print [prɪnt] N 1 (*mark, imprint: of foot, tyre or tire, finger*) impronta; **the policeman took his prints** il poliziotto gli ha preso le impronte digitali 2 (*typeface, characters*) caratteri *mpl*; (*printed matter*) stampa; **that book is in/out of print** quel libro è disponibile/esaurito; **to see o.s. in print** vedere il proprio nome stampato; **in small/large print** stampato(-a) a caratteri piccoli/grandi 3 (*fabric*) (tessuto) stampato 4 (*Art*) stampa; (*Phot*) fotografia; **a framed print** una stampa incorniciata; **colour prints** foto *fpl* a colori ♦ VT 1 (*Typ, Textiles, Phot*) stampare; (*fig: on memory*) imprimere 2 (*publish*) pubblicare, stampare; **it was printed in Hong Kong** è stato stampato a Hong Kong 3 (*write in block letters*) scrivere in stampatello; **please print your name and address** per favore scrivere nome e indirizzo in stampatello

▸ **print out** VT + ADV (*Comput*) stampare

printed circuit board N circuito stampato

printed matter N stampe *fpl*

print·er ['prɪntə^r] N 1 (*person*) tipografo(-a); (*machine*) stampante *m*; **at the printer's** (*book*) in tipografia; **printer's error** errore *m* di stampa; **printer's ink** inchiostro tipografico

print·head ['prɪntˌhed] N (*Comput*) testina di stampa

print·ing ['prɪntɪŋ] N 1 (*process, also Phot*) stampa; **a printing error** un errore di stampa 2 (*block writing*) stampatello; (*characters*) caratteri *mpl*; (*print*) stampa 3 (*number printed*) tiratura; **the next printing** la prossima tiratura

printing press N pressa tipografica

print-out ['prɪntˌaʊt] N (*Comput*) tabulato, stampato

print wheel N margherita

pri·or[1] ['praɪə^r] ADJ precedente; **without prior notice** senza preavviso; **without prior knowledge** senza saperlo prima; **prior approval is required** occorre prima avere l'approvazione; **to have a prior claim to sth** avere un diritto di

precedenza su qc ♦ PREP: **prior to sth/to doing sth** prima di qc/di fare qc; **prior to this date** prima di questa data

pri·or[2] ['praɪə^r] N (*Rel*) priore *m*

pri·or·ity [praɪˈɒrɪtɪ] N priorità *f inv*, precedenza; **my first priority** la mia priorità; **to have *or* take priority over sth** avere la precedenza su qc; **my family takes priority over my work** la mia famiglia ha la precedenza sul lavoro; **we must get our priorities right** dobbiamo decidere quali sono le cose più importanti per noi; **to treat sth as a priority** dare la precedenza a qc; **the government's priority is to build more power plants** la priorità del governo è quella di costruire più centrali elettriche

pri·ory ['praɪərɪ] N priorato

prise, prize (*USA*) [praɪz] VT: **to prise sth open** aprire qc (forzando il coperchio); **to prise a lid up/off** aprire/togliere un coperchio facendo leva

▸ **prise out, prize out** (*USA*) VT + ADV: **to prise sth out (of sb)** (*secret*) tirar fuori qc (da qn)

prism ['prɪzəm] N (*Geom, Tech*) prisma *m*

pris·on ['prɪzn] N prigione *f*, carcere *m*; **to be in prison** essere in prigione; **to go to prison for 5 years** essere condannato(-a) a 5 anni di carcere *or* di reclusione; **to send sb to prison for 2 years** condannare qn a 2 anni di reclusione ♦ ADJ (*system*) carcerario(-a); (*conditions, food*) nelle *or* delle prigioni

prison camp N campo di prigionia

pris·on·er ['prɪznə^r] N (*under arrest*) arrestato(-a); (*convicted*) detenuto(-a); (*Mil: fig*) prigioniero(-a); **prisoners have to share cells** i detenuti devono dividere le celle; **the prisoner at the bar** l'accusato(-a), l'imputato(-a); **to take sb prisoner** far prigioniero(-a) qn

pris·sy ['prɪsɪ] ADJ (*pej*) per benino

pris·tine ['prɪstaɪn] ADJ (*unspoiled*) immacolato(-a), puro(-a); (*original*) originario(-a)

pri·va·cy ['prɪvəsɪ] N privacy *f*; **his desire for privacy** il suo desiderio di stare da solo; (*actor, popstar*) il suo desiderio di privacy; **in the privacy of one's own home** nell'intimità della propria casa; **in the strictest privacy** nella massima segretezza

pri·vate ['praɪvɪt] ADJ 1 (*not public: conversation, meeting, land*) privato(-a); (: *funeral, wedding*) in forma privata; (: *showing*) a inviti; (*confidential: letter*) personale; (: *agreement, information*) confidenziale; **"private"** (*on door*) "privato"; (*on envelope*) "riservata"; **this information must be kept private** quest'informazione deve rimanere strettamente confidenziale; **he is a very private person** è una persona molto riservata; **in (his) private life** nella vita privata; **private place** posto segreto; **private hearing** (*Law*) udienza a porte chiuse 2 (*for one person: car, house, secretary*) privato(-a), personale; (: *lessons*) privato(-a); (*personal: bank account, reasons*) personale; **a man of private means** un uomo che vive di rendita 3 (*not state-owned: company, army*) privato(-a); (: *doctor, nursing home*) non convenzionato(-a), privato(-a) ♦ N 1 (*Mil*) soldato semplice 2 **in private** = **privately**

private enterprise N l'iniziativa privata

private eye N (*USA fam*) investigatore(-trice) *or* detective *m/f inv* privato(-a)

private limited company N società *f inv* a responsabilità limitata non quotata in borsa

pri·vate·ly ['praɪvɪtlɪ] ADV 1 (*not publicly*) privatamente, in privato 2 (*secretly*) in privato; (*personally*) personalmente; (*within o.s.*) dentro di sé 3 (*unofficially*) a titolo personale

private parts NPL (*euph*) parti *fpl* intime

private property N proprietà *f inv* privata

private school N scuola privata

pri·va·tion [praɪˈveɪʃən] N 1 (*state*) privazione *f* 2 (*hardship*) privazioni *fpl*, stenti *mpl*

pri·va·tize ['praɪvɪˌtaɪz^r] VT privatizzare

priv·et ['prɪvɪt] N ligustro

privi·lege ['prɪvɪlɪdʒ] N privilegio; (*Parliament*) prerogativa; **I had the privilege of meeting her** ho avuto il privilegio *or* l'onore di incontrarla ♦ VT: **to be privileged to do sth** avere il privilegio *or* l'onore di fare qc

privi·leged ['prɪvɪlɪdʒd] ADJ privilegiato(-a); **a privileged**

few pochi privilegiati; **the privileged few** la minoranza dei privilegiati

privy [ˈprɪvɪ] ADJ: **to be privy to sth** essere a conoscenza *or* al corrente di qc ♦ N (*old: toilet*) gabinetto, ritirata

Privy Council N (*Brit*): **the Privy Council** il Consiglio della Corona

Privy Councillor N (*Brit*) Consigliere *m* della Corona

prize [praɪz] N (*gen*) premio; **to win first prize** (*in game, race, lottery*) vincere il primo premio; (*Scol*) ottenere il primo premio ♦ vт 1 (*awarded a prize*) premiato(-a); (*worthy of a prize*) eccellente; (*example*) perfetto(-a) 2 (*awarded as a prize: cup, medal*) premio (*inv* (*after n*)) ♦ vт (*honesty, friendship*) stimare, valutare; **he prizes his medals** è molto orgoglioso delle sue medaglie; **her most prized possession** il suo avere più prezioso; **a rare model, now much prized** un modello raro che oggi ha una valutazione molto alta

prize fighter N (*USA*) pugile *m* professionista

prize-giving [ˈpraɪzˌgɪvɪŋ] N premiazione *f*

prize money N soldi *mpl* del premio

prize-winner [ˈpraɪzˌwɪnəʳ] N (*in competition, lottery*) vincitore(-trice); (*Scol: in show*) premiato(-a)

prize-winning [ˈpraɪzˌwɪnɪŋ] ADJ (*gen*) vincente; (*novel, essay*) premiato(-a)

pro [prəʊ] N (*fam: Sport*) professionista *m/f*

pro- [prəʊ] PREF (*in favour of*) filo-; **pro-American** filoamericano(-a)

pro-active [ˌprəʊˈæktɪv] ADJ: **to be pro-active** avere iniziativa

prob·abil·ity [ˌprɒbəˈbɪlɪtɪ] N probabilità *f inv*; **in all probability** con ogni probabilità

prob·able [ˈprɒbəbl] ADJ probabile; **it is probable/hardly probable that ...** è probabile/poco probabile che... + *sub*

prob·ably [ˈprɒbəblɪ] ADV probabilmente

pro·bate [ˈprəʊbɪt] N (*Law*) omologazione *f* (di un testamento)

pro·ba·tion [prəˈbeɪʃən] N: **to be on probation** (*Law*) essere in libertà vigilata; (*gen: in employment*) essere in prova, fare un periodo di prova; **to put sb on probation** (*Law*) sottoporre qn a libertà vigilata

pro·ba·tion·ary [prəˈbeɪʃnərɪ] ADJ (*year, period*) di prova; (*teacher, nurse*) in prova; (*Law*) di libertà vigilata

probe [prəʊb] N 1 (*Med, Space*) sonda 2 (*inquiry*) indagine *f*, investigazione *f* ♦ vт (*hole, crack*) tastare; (*Med*) esplorare, sondare; (*Space*) esplorare; (*also: probe into*) indagare su

pro·bity [ˈprəʊbɪtɪ] N probità, rettitudine *f*

prob·lem [ˈprɒbləm] N (*also Math*) problema *m*; **to have problems with the car** avere dei problemi con la macchina; **my son is a problem** mio figlio è un problema; **the housing problem** la crisi degli alloggi; **to have a drinking problem** avere il vizio del bere; **I had no problem in finding her** non mi è stato difficile trovarla; **what's the problem?** che cosa c'è?; **no problem!** ma certamente!, non c'è problema!; **it's not my problem** è un affare che non mi riguarda; **that's no problem for/to him** per lui non è un problema ♦ ADJ (*child, family*) difficile

prob·lem·at·ic [ˌprɒblɪˈmætɪk],   **prob·lem·at·ical** [ˌprɒblɪˈmætɪkəl] ADJ problematico(-a), dubbio(-a); **it is problematic whether ...** è in dubbio se...

problem-solving N risoluzione *f* di problemi

pro·cedure [prəˈsiːdʒəʳ] N (*Admin, Law*) procedura; **the usual procedure is to ...** la procedura normale *or* prassi è di...; **cashing a cheque is a simple procedure** riscuotere un assegno è un'operazione semplice

pro·ceed [prəˈsiːd] vı 1 (*move forward*) procedere; **to proceed with sth** continuare qc; **let us proceed with caution** procediamo con cautela; **let us proceed to the next item** passiamo al prossimo punto; **things are proceeding according to plan** tutto procede *or* si svolge secondo i piani; **work was proceeding normally** il lavoro procedeva normalmente; **I am not sure how to proceed** non so bene come fare; **please proceed to gate 32** vi preghiamo di recarvi all'uscita 32 2 (*originate*): **to proceed from** (*sound*) provenire da; (*fear*) derivare da 3 **to proceed against sb** (*Law*) procedere contro qn ♦ vт: **to proceed to do sth** cominciare *or* mettersi a fare qc; **he then proceeded to tell me the whole story** quindi cominciò a raccontarmi tutta la storia

pro·ceed·ings [prəˈsiːdɪŋz] NPL 1 (*events*) avvenimenti *mpl*; (*manoeuvres*) manovre *fpl*; (*function*) cerimonia *fsg*; (*meeting*) riunione *fsg*, seduta *fsg*; (*discussions*) dibattito *msg* 2 (*esp Law: measures*) provvedimenti *mpl*, misure *fpl*; **to take proceedings (in order to do sth)** prendere i provvedimenti necessari (per fare qc); **to institute proceedings (against sb)** (*Law*) promuovere un'azione legale (contro qn) 3 (*records: of learned society*) atti *mpl*, rendiconti *mpl*

pro·ceeds [ˈprəʊsiːdz] NPL proventi *mpl*, ricavato *msg*; **the proceeds from the concert will go to charity** il ricavato del concerto sarà devoluto in beneficenza

pro·cess¹ [ˈprəʊses] N 1 processo; **the whole process** l'intera operazione; **a lengthy process** un lungo procedimento; **in the process of restoring the picture he discovered ...** stava restaurando il quadro quando ha scoperto...; **in process of construction** (in corso di) costruzione; **the process of growing up** il processo della crescita; **we are in the process of moving to ...** stiamo per trasferirci a...; **the peace process** il processo di pace 2 (*specific method*) procedimento, sistema *m*, metodo; **the Bessemer process** il metodo Bessemer 3 (*Law: action*) processo; (: *summons*) mandato di comparizione, citazione *f* in giudizio ♦ vт (*Tech*) trattare; (*Phot*) sviluppare e stampare; (*Admin: application etc*) sbrigare; (*Comput*) elaborare

pro·cess² [prəˈses] vı (*Brit: frm: go in procession*) sfilare, procedere in corteo

pro·cessed cheese [ˌprəʊsestˈtʃiːz],   (*USA*)   **process cheese** N formaggio fuso

pro·cess·ing [ˈprəʊsesɪŋ] N (*of data*) elaborazione *f*; (*of food*) trattamento; (*of film*) sviluppo e stampa; (*of application*) disbrigo

pro·ces·sion [prəˈseʃən] N (*of people, cars*) processione *f*, corteo; (*Rel*) processione; **funeral procession** corteo funebre

pro·choice [prəʊˈtʃɔɪs] ADJ per la libertà di scelta di gravidanza

pro·claim [prəˈkleɪm] vт 1 (*gen*) proclamare, dichiarare; (*peace, public holiday*) dichiarare; **to proclaim sb king/that** proclamare qn re/che 2 (*fig: reveal*) dimostrare, rivelare

proc·la·ma·tion [ˌprɒkləˈmeɪʃən] N proclama *m*, proclamazione *f*

pro·cliv·ity [prəˈklɪvɪtɪ] N (*frm*) tendenza, propensione *f*

pro·cras·ti·na·tion [prəˌkræstɪˈneɪʃən] N procrastinazione *f*

pro·crea·tion [ˌprəʊkrɪˈeɪʃən] N procreazione *f*

Procu·ra·tor Fis·cal [ˈprɒkjʊˌreɪtəˈfɪskəl] N (*in Scotland*) ≈ procuratore *m*

pro·cure [prəˈkjʊəʳ] vт 1 procurare, ottenere; **it's difficult to procure food and fuel** è difficile procurarsi cibo e carburante; **to procure sb sth, to procure sth for sb** procurare qc a qn, ottenere qc per qn; **I managed to procure a copy for myself** sono riuscito a procurarmene una copia 2 (*prostitute*) procurare

pro·cure·ment [prəˈkjʊəmənt] N (*of goods*) rifornimento, approvvigionamento

prod [prɒd] N (*push, jab*) colpetto; (*with elbow*) gomitata ♦ vт (*jab: with stick, finger*) dare un colpetto a; **he prodded the page with his finger** ha puntato il dito sulla pagina; **he has to be prodded along** (*fig*) ha bisogno di essere pungolato ♦ vı: **she prodded at the picture with a finger** ha puntato il dito sul quadro

prodi·gal [ˈprɒdɪgəl] ADJ prodigo(-a)

pro·di·gious [prəˈdɪdʒəs] ADJ prodigioso(-a), straordinario(-a)

prodi·gy [ˈprɒdɪdʒɪ] N prodigio; **child prodigy, infant prodigy** bambino(-a) prodigio *inv*

pro·duce [*n* ˈprɒdjuːs, *vb* prəˈdjuːs] N (*Agr*) prodotto; (*collective n* prodotti *mpl* ♦ vт 1 (*manufacture: gen*) produrre; (*create: book, essay*) scrivere; (: *work of art*) fare; (: *meal*) preparare; (: *ideas, profit*) dare; (*give birth to*) partorire 2 (*bring, show: gen*) tirar fuori; (: *tickets*) esibire, mostrare; (: *proof of identity*) produrre, fornire; **I can't suddenly produce £500!** da dove le tiro fuori 500 sterline? 3 (*film*) produrre; (*play*) mettere in scena 4 (*cause: gen*) causare, provocare; (: *results*) produrre; (: *interest*) suscitare; **this produced a stir** ha fatto sensazione

pro·duc·er [prəˈdjuːsəʳ] N (*Agr, Cine, TV, Theatre*) produttore(-trice)

prod·uct ['prɒdʌkt] N (*also Math*) prodotto; (*fig*) frutto

pro·duc·tion [prə'dʌkʃən] N **1** (*manufacture*) produzione *f*; **to put into production** mettere in produzione; **to take out of production** togliere dalla produzione; **the country's steel production** la produzione siderurgica del paese; **they're increasing production of luxury models** stanno aumentando la produzione di modelli di lusso **2** (*showing*) presentazione *f*; (*of documents*) produzione *f*; **on production of this ticket** dietro presentazione di questo biglietto **3** (*of film, show*) produzione *f*; (*of play*) messa in scena; (*work produced*) realizzazione *f* teatrale (*or* cinematografica); **a production of "Hamlet"** una rappresentazione di "Amleto"

production agreement N (*USA*) accordo sui tempi di produzione

production line N linea di produzione

production manager N direttore *m* di produzione, production manager *m*/*f inv*

pro·duc·tive [prə'dʌktɪv] ADJ (*gen*) produttivo(-a); (*meeting, discussion*) fruttuoso(-a); (*enterprise, business*) che rende; (*writer*) prolifico(-a); (*land, imagination*) fertile; **he had a very productive day** ha avuto una giornata molto soddisfacente

prod·uc·tiv·ity [,prɒdʌk'tɪvɪtɪ] N produttività

productivity agreement N (*Brit*) accordo sui tempi di produzione

productivity bonus N premio di produzione

Prof. ABBR (= *professor*) Prof.

pro·fane [prə'feɪn] ADJ **1** (*secular*) profano(-a) **2** (*irreverent*) irriverente; (*language*) sacrilego(-a) ♦ VT profanare

pro·fess [prə'fes] VT **1** (*faith, belief etc*) professare **2** (*claim*) dichiarare; **he professes extreme regret** si dichiara molto dispiaciuto; **he professed interest in my opinion** ha dichiarato di essere interessato alla mia opinione; **I do not profess to be an expert** non pretendo di essere un esperto

pro·fessed [prə'fest] ADJ (*Rel*) professo(-a); (*self-declared*) dichiarato(-a)

pro·fes·sion [prə'feʃən] N **1** (*gen*) professione *f*; **the professions** le professioni liberali; **by profession** di professione; **the medical profession** (*calling*) la professione medica; (*doctors collectively*) i medici **2** (*declaration*) dichiarazione *f*; **profession of faith** (*Rel*) professione *f* di fede

pro·fes·sion·al [prə'feʃənl] ADJ **1** (*capacity*) professionale; (*diplomat, soldier*) di carriera; **a professional man** un professionista; **to take professional advice** consultare un esperto; **to be a professional singer** essere un(-a) cantante *m*/*f* professionista *or* di professione; **to turn** *or* **go professional** (*Sport*) passare al professionismo **2** (*competent, skilled: worker*) esperto(-a); (: *piece of work, approach*) da professionista; (: *attitude*) professionale; **a very professional piece of work** un lavoro da professionista; **it's not up to professional standards** non è da professionista ♦ N professionista *m*/*f*

pro·fes·sion·al·ism [prə'feʃnə,lɪzəm] N professionismo

pro·fes·sion·al·ly [prə'feʃnəlɪ] ADV (*play*) come professionista; (*sing*) per professione; (*expertly*) professionalmente, in modo professionale; **she sings professionally** è una cantante professionista; **I only know him professionally** lo conosco solo per motivi di lavoro; **to be professionally qualified** essere abilitato(-a) alla professione

pro·fes·sor [prə'fesə'] N (*Univ: Brit*) docente *m*/*f*; (: *USA: teacher*) professore(-essa)

pro·fes·sor·ship [prə'fesəʃɪp] N cattedra

prof·fer ['prɒfə'] VT (*remark*) profferire; (*hand*) porgere; (*apologies*) porgere, presentare; (*advice*) fornire

pro·fi·cien·cy [prə'fɪʃənsɪ] N competenza, abilità

pro·fi·cient [prə'fɪʃənt] ADJ provetto(-a), competente

pro·file ['prəʊfaɪl] N profilo; **in profile** di profilo; **to keep a low profile** (*fig*) cercare di non farsi notare troppo, cercare di passare inosservato(-a); **to maintain a high profile** mettersi in mostra

prof·it ['prɒfɪt] N (*Comm*) profitto, utile *m*, guadagno; (*fig*) profitto, vantaggio, beneficio; **a profit of £10,000** un guadagno di 10.000 sterline; **to my profit** a mio vantaggio; **profit and loss account** conto profitti e perdite; **to make a profit out of** *or* **on sth** ricavare un utile da qc; **to sell sth at a** **profit** vendere qc con un utile ♦ VI: **to profit by** *or* **from sth** ricavare beneficio da qc

❏ **profit** is not translated by the Italian word *approfittare*

prof·it·abil·ity [,prɒfɪtə'bɪlɪtɪ] N redditività

prof·it·able ['prɒfɪtəbl] ADJ (*Comm*) remunerativo(-a), redditizio(-a); (*fig: beneficial: scheme*) vantaggioso(-a); (*meeting, visit*) fruttuoso(-a)

profit centre N centro di profitto

profi·teer·ing [,prɒfɪ'tɪərɪŋ] N (*pej*) affarismo

profit-making ['prɒfɪt,meɪkɪŋ] ADJ (*industry*) rimunerativo(-a)

profit margin N margine *m* di profitto

profit-sharing ['prɒfɪt,ʃeərɪŋ] N compartecipazione *f* agli utili

profits tax N (*Brit*) imposta sugli utili

prof·li·gate ['prɒflɪgɪt] ADJ (*dissolute: behaviour, act*) dissipato(-a); (: *person*) dissoluto(-a); **he's very profligate with his money** è uno che sperpera i suoi soldi

pro for·ma ['prəʊ'fɔːmə] ADV: **pro forma invoice** fattura pro forma

pro·found [prə'faʊnd] ADJ profondo(-a)

pro·fuse [prə'fjuːs] ADJ (*tears, bleeding*) copioso(-a); (*vegetation*) abbondante; (*thanks, praise, apologies*) infinito(-a); **she was profuse in her thanks** si è profusa in ringraziamenti

pro·fuse·ly [prə'fjuːslɪ] ADV (*sweat, bleed*) abbondantemente; (*praise*) con grande effusione; (*grow*) rigogliosamente; **he apologized profusely** si è profuso in scuse

pro·fu·sion [prə'fjuːʒən] N profusione *f*, abbondanza; **in profusion** a profusione

prog·eny ['prɒdʒɪnɪ] N (*frm*) progenie *f*, discendenti *mpl*

pro·gramme, pro·gram (*USA*) ['prəʊgræm] N (*gen, also Pol*) programma *m*; (*Radio, TV: broadcast*) programma, trasmissione *f*; (: *station*) canale *m*; **what's the programme for today?** che cosa facciamo oggi? ♦ VT (*arrange*) programmare, stabilire

pro·gram·mer ['prəʊgræmə'] N (*Comput*) programmatore(-trice); **she's a programmer** fa la programmatrice

pro·gram·ming, pro·gram·ing (*USA*) ['prəʊgræmɪŋ] N (*Comput*) programmazione *f*

programming language N (*Comput*) linguaggio di programmazione

pro·gress [*n* 'prəʊgres, *vb* prə'gres] N (*gen*) progresso, progressi *mpl*; **to make progress** (*gen*) fare progressi; (*walk forward*) avanzare; **you're making progress** stai facendo progressi!; **the pupil is making good progress** l'allievo fa dei buoni progressi; **the work is making little progress** il lavoro procede lentamente; **the progress of events** il corso degli avvenimenti; **in progress** (*meeting, work etc*) in corso; **that's progress!** questo è il progresso! ♦ VI **1** (*go forward*) avanzare, procedere **2** (*in time*) procedere; **as the match progressed** man mano che la partita procedeva **3** (*improve, make progress: person*) fare progressi; (: *investigation, studies*) progredire

pro·gres·sion [prə'greʃən] N progresso; (*Math*) progressione *f*; **arithmetic/geometric progression** progressione aritmetica/geometrica

pro·gres·sive [prə'gresɪv] ADJ **1** (*increasing: disease, taxation*) progressivo(-a); **a progressive loss of memory** una progressiva perdita della memoria **2** (*favouring progress: idea, party*) progressista

pro·gres·sive·ly [prə'gresɪvlɪ] ADV progressivamente, gradualmente

progress report N (*Med*) bollettino medico; (*Admin*) rendiconto dei lavori; (*Scol*) pagella, scheda di valutazione

pro·hib·it [prə'hɪbɪt] VT **1** (*forbid*) proibire, vietare; **to prohibit sb from doing sth** vietare *or* proibire a qn di fare qc; **"smoking prohibited"** "vietato fumare" **2** (*prevent: thing*) impedire

pro·hi·bi·tion [,prəʊɪ'bɪʃən] N proibizione *f*, divieto; **Prohibition** (*esp USA: of alcohol*) proibizionismo

pro·hibi·tive [prə'hɪbɪtɪv] ADJ (*price*) proibitivo(-a)

proj·ect [*n* 'prɒdʒekt, *vb* prə'dʒekt] N (*scheme, plan, venture*) progetto, piano; (*study*) progetto, lavoro di ricerca; (*Scol, Univ*) ricerca; **a development project** un piano di sviluppo;

a major project un importante progetto ♦ VT (*film*) proiettare; (*voice*) spiegare; (*one's personality*) mettere in luce; (*visit*) progettare ♦ VI (*jut out*) sporgere in fuori

pro·jec·tile [prə'dʒektaɪl] N proiettile *m*

pro·jec·tion [prə'dʒekʃən] N 1 (*of films, figures*) proiezione *f*; **sales projections** le proiezioni di vendita 2 (*forecast: of cost*) preventivo 3 (*overhang, protrusion*) sporgenza, prominenza

pro·jec·tion·ist [prə'dʒekʃənɪst] N (*Cine*) proiezionista *m/f*

projection room N (*Cine*) cabina di proiezione

pro·jec·tor [prə'dʒektə^r] N (*Cine*) proiettore *m*

pro·letar·ian [ˌprəʊlə'teərɪən] ADJ, N proletario(-a)

pro·letari·at [ˌprəʊlə'teərɪət] N proletariato

pro·life ['prəʊ'laɪf] ADJ per il diritto alla vita

pro·lif·er·ate [prə'lɪfəreɪt] VI (*Bio, also fig*) proliferare; (*animals*) prolificare

pro·lif·era·tion [prəˌlɪfə'reɪʃən] N (*see vb*) proliferazione *f*; prolificazione *f*

pro·lif·ic [prə'lɪfɪk] ADJ (*animal*) prolifico(-a); (*crop*) abbondante; (*writer*) fecondo(-a)

pro·logue, pro·log (USA) ['prəʊlɒg] N prologo

pro·long [prə'lɒŋ] VT prolungare

prom [prɒm] N ABBR 1 (*Brit fam*) = promenade 2 (*Brit fam*) = promenade concert ♦ N (USA) ballo studentesco

prom·enade [ˌprɒmɪ'nɑːd] N (*at seaside*) lungomare *m* ♦ VI (*stroll*) passeggiare

promenade concert N (*Brit: Mus*) concerto di musica classica (*che fa parte di una rassegna che si tiene ogni anno a Londra*)

promenade deck N (*Naut*) ponte *m* di passeggio

promi·nence ['prɒmɪnəns] N (*of ridge*) prominenza; (*conspicuousness*) imponenza; (*of role*) importanza; **to come into prominence** (*person*) venire alla ribalta

promi·nent ['prɒmɪnənt] ADJ 1 (*projecting: ridge*) prominente; (: *teeth*) sporgente; (: *cheekbones*) marcato(-a) 2 (*conspicuous*) che spicca; **put it in a prominent position** mettilo ben in vista 3 (*leading: role, feature*) di rilievo 4 (*well-known: personality*) molto in vista; **she is prominent in the field of ...** è un'autorità nel campo di...; **prominent people** gente *f* importante

promi·nent·ly ['prɒmɪnəntlɪ] ADV (*display, set*) ben in vista; **he figured prominently in the case** ha avuto una parte in primo piano nella faccenda

promis·cu·ity [ˌprɒmɪs'kjuːɪtɪ] N (*sexual*) promiscuità

pro·mis·cu·ous [prə'mɪskjʊəs] ADJ (*sexually*) promiscuo(-a)

prom·ise ['prɒmɪs] N promessa; **to make sb a promise** fare una promessa a qn; **he made me a promise** mi ha fatto una promessa; **to keep one's promise** mantenere la propria promessa; **it's a promise!** promesso!; **a young man of promise** un giovane promettente; **to show promise** promettere bene ♦ VT promettere; **to promise (sb) to do sth** promettere (a qn) di fare qc; **she promised to write** ha promesso di scrivere; **to promise sb sth, to promise sth to sb** promettere qc a qn; **to promise sb the earth** *or* **the moon** (*fig*) promettere a qn mari e monti; **to promise o.s. sth** promettere a se stesso(-a) qc ♦ VI: **I can't promise, but ...** non te (*or* ve *etc*) lo prometto, ma...; **to promise well** promettere bene

prom·is·ing ['prɒmɪsɪŋ] ADJ promettente; **it doesn't look promising** non sembra promettente; **the future is promising** il futuro promette bene; **a promising player** un giocatore promettente

prom·is·sory note ['prɒmɪsə,nəʊt] N pagherò *m inv*

prom·on·tory ['prɒməntrɪ] N promontorio

pro·mote [prə'məʊt] VT 1 (*in job*): **to be promoted** avere una promozione; **she was promoted after six months** ha avuto una promozione dopo sei mesi; **to promote sb (from sth) to sth** promuovere qn (da qc) a qc; **the team was promoted to the second division** (*Brit: Ftbl*) la squadra è stata promossa in serie B 2 (*encourage: trade, plan, concert, campaign*) promuovere; (: *product*) lanciare, reclamizzare

pro·mot·er [prə'məʊtə^r] N (*gen*) promotore(-trice); (*of sporting event*) promoter *m inv*, organizzatore(-trice), fondatore(-trice); (*of cause*) sostenitore(-trice)

pro·mo·tion [prə'məʊʃən] N (*gen*) promozione *f*; **to get (a) promotion** ottenere la promozione

prompt [prɒmpt] ADJ (*comp* -er, *superl* -est) (*action*) tempestivo(-a); (*delivery*) immediato(-a); (*payment*) pronto(-a), immediato(-a); **a prompt reply** una risposta sollecita; **to be prompt to do sth** essere sollecito(-a) nel fare qc; **he's always very prompt** (*punctual*) è sempre molto puntuale, è sempre puntualissimo ♦ ADV: **at 6 o'clock prompt** alle 6 in punto ♦ N 1 (*Theatre*) imbeccata 2 (*Comput*) prompt *m inv* ♦ VT 1 **to prompt sb to do sth** spingere qn a fare qc; **it prompts the thought that ...** questo fa pensare che... 2 (*Theatre*) suggerire a

prompt·er ['prɒmptə^r] N (*Theatre*) suggeritore(-trice)

prompt·ly ['prɒmptlɪ] ADV (*speedily*) prontamente; (*punctually*) puntualmente; **we left promptly at seven** siamo partiti puntualmente alle sette

prompt·ness ['prɒmptnɪs] N (*speed*) prontezza, sollecitudine *f*; (*punctuality*) puntualità

prone [prəʊn] ADJ 1 (*face down*) a faccia in giù, prono(-a); **he lay prone on the floor** giaceva prono sul pavimento 2 (*liable*): **prone to** incline a, propenso(-a) a, soggetto(-a) a; **to be prone to illness** essere *or* andare soggetto(-a) a malattie

prong [prɒŋ] N (*of fork*) rebbio, dente *m*; **three-pronged** (*fork*) a tre rebbi *or* denti; (*attack*) su tre fronti, triplice

pro·noun ['prəʊnaʊn] N pronome *m*

pro·nounce [prə'naʊns] VT 1 (*letter, word*) pronunciare; **how do you pronounce that word?** come si pronuncia quella parola? 2 (*declare*) dichiarare; **they pronounced him unfit to drive** lo hanno dichiarato inabile alla guida; **to pronounce o.s. for/against sth** dichiararsi in favore di/contro qc; **to pronounce sentence** (*Law*) pronunziare la sentenza ♦ VI: **to pronounce in favour of/against sth** pronunciarsi in favore di/contro qc; **to pronounce on sth** pronunciarsi su qc

pro·nounced [prə'naʊnst] ADJ (*marked*: *improvement*) netto(-a), spiccato(-a); (: *views*) preciso(-a); **he has a pronounced limp** zoppica in modo molto pronunciato

pro·nounce·ment [prə'naʊnsmənt] N dichiarazione *f*

pro·nun·cia·tion [prəˌnʌnsɪ'eɪʃən] N pronuncia

proof [pruːf] N 1 (*evidence*) prova; (*Math*) dimostrazione *f*; **proof of identity** documento d'identità; **I have proof that he did it** ho le prove che è stato lui a farlo; **as** *or* **in proof of** come prova *or* testimonianza di; **to give** *or* **show proof of** dar prova di 2 (*test, trial*): **to put sth to the proof** mettere alla prova qc 3 (*Typ*) bozza, prova di stampa; (*Phot*) provino 4 (*of alcohol*): **70% proof** ≈ 40° (alcolici) ♦ ADJ: **to be proof against** essere a prova di ♦ VT (*tent, anorak*) impermeabilizzare

proof·reader ['pruːf,riːdə^r] N correttore(-trice) di bozze

prop^1 [prɒp] N sostegno, appoggio, puntello; (*fig*) sostegno; **the army is the government's main prop** l'esercito è il principale sostegno del governo ♦ VT (*also*: **prop up**) 1 (*rest, lean: ladder*) appoggiare; **to prop sth against** appoggiare qc contro *or* a; **she propped her bike against the wall** appoggiò la bicicletta al muro 2 (*support*) sostenere, puntellare; (*fig*) tenere su, tenere in piedi

prop^2 [prɒp] N ABBR (*Theatre: fam*) (elemento del) materiale *m* di scena

propa·gan·da [ˌprɒpə'gændə] N propaganda ♦ ADJ (*campaign, leaflets*) propagandistico(-a)

propa·ga·tion [ˌprɒpə'geɪʃən] N (*see vb*) propagazione *f*; riproduzione *f*

pro·pel [prə'pel] VT spingere

pro·pel·ler [prə'pelə^r] N elica

pro·pel·ling pen·cil [prə,pelɪŋ'pensl] N (*Brit*) portamina *m inv*

pro·pen·sity [prə'pensɪtɪ] N tendenza; **propensity (for)** propensione *f* (per)

prop·er ['prɒpə^r] ADJ 1 (*suitable, appropriate: clothes, tools*) adatto(-a), appropriato(-a); (*correct, right: order, way, method*) giusto(-a); (*seemly: behaviour, person*) decente, perbene; **the proper time** il momento adatto *or* giusto; **if you had come at the proper time ...** se fossi venuto all'ora giusta...; **in the proper way** come si deve; **this is the proper way to do it** questo è il modo giusto di farlo; **to go through the proper channels** (*Admin*) seguire la regolare procedura; **you have to have the proper equipment** bisogna avere l'attrezzatura adatta; **do as you think proper** fa' come ritieni opportuno;

it isn't proper to do that non sta bene fare così; **to do the proper thing by sb** agire bene verso qn; **proper to** (*Chem, Philosophy*) proprio di 2 (*actual, authentic*) vero(-a) e proprio(-a); **physics proper** la fisica propriamente detta; **he isn't a proper doctor** non è un medico come si deve; **in the proper sense of the word** nel vero senso della parola; **in the city proper** nella città vera e propria 3 (*fam: real*: lady, *gentleman*) vero(-a), autentico(-a); (: *thorough: mess*) vero(-a), bello(-a); **it's a proper nuisance** è proprio una bella scocciatura; **we didn't have a proper lunch, just sandwiches** non abbiamo mangiato un vero pranzo, solo dei panini ♦ ADV (*Brit fam: very*) proprio; **to talk proper** (*correctly*) parlare bene

prop·er·ly ['prɒpəlɪ] ADV 1 (*correctly: speak, write*) bene, come si deve; (: *use*) in modo giusto; **you're not doing it properly** non lo stai facendo come si deve; **properly speaking** propriamente parlando 2 (*in seemly fashion*) correttamente, decentemente; **not properly dressed** vestito(-a) in maniera sconveniente; **dress properly for your interview** vestiti in modo adeguato per il colloquio 3 (*fam: really, thoroughly*) veramente

proper noun N nome *m* proprio

prop·er·ty ['prɒpətɪ] N 1 (*quality*) proprietà *f inv*, caratteristica 2 (*possessions*) beni *mpl*; (*land, building: Chem*) proprietà *f inv*; **a new property** una nuova casa; **he owns property in Spain** ha delle proprietà in Spagna; **personal property** beni *mpl* mobili; **"private property"** "proprietà privata"; **a man of property** un possidente; **is this your property?** è tuo?; **lost property** oggetti *mpl* smarriti 3 (*Theatre*) (elemento del) materiale *m* di scena

property developer N (*Brit*) costruttore *m* edile

property owner N proprietario(-a)

property tax N imposta patrimoniale

proph·ecy ['prɒfɪsɪ] N profezia

proph·esy ['prɒfɪsaɪ] VT predire, profetizzare

proph·et ['prɒfɪt] N profeta *m*

pro·phet·ic [prə'fetɪk] ADJ profetico(-a)

pro·por·tion [prə'pɔːʃən] N 1 (*ratio*) proporzione *f*, pro rata; **the proportion of boys to girls** la proporzione dei ragazzi rispetto alle ragazze; **to be in proportion** (*numbers*) essere proporzionali; **in proportion to** in relazione a; **your weight in proportion to your height** il peso in relazione alla statura; **to be in/out of proportion** (to one another) essere proporzionati/sproporzionati (tra di loro); **to be in/out of proportion to** or **with sth** essere in proporzione/sproporzione(-a) rispetto a qc; **to see sth in proportion** (*fig*) dare il giusto peso a qc; **sense of proportion** (*fig*) senso della misura 2 (*part, amount, share*) parte *f*; **they keep a proportion of the profits** si tengono una parte dei profitti 3 **proportions** NPL (*size, dimensions*) proporzioni *fpl* ♦ VT proporzionare, commisurare; **well-proportioned** ben proporzionato(-a)

pro·por·tion·al [prə'pɔːʃənl] ADJ: **proportional (to)** proporzionale (a)

proportional representation N (*Pol*) rappresentanza proporzionale

pro·por·tion·ate [prə'pɔːʃnɪt] ADJ: **proportionate (to)** proporzionato(-a) (a)

pro·po·sal [prə'pəʊzl] N (*offer*) offerta, proposta; (*of marriage*) proposta di matrimonio; (*suggestion*): **proposal (for sth/to do sth)** proposta (di qc/di fare qc); (*plan*) progetto, proposta

pro·pose [prə'pəʊz] VT 1 proporre; **to propose doing sth** proporre di fare qc; **what do you propose to do?** cosa proponi di fare?; **to propose that sth should be done** proporre che sia fatto qc; **I propose that we go by bus** propongo di andare con l'autobus; **to propose marriage to sb** fare una proposta di matrimonio a qn; **to propose sb for a job/as treasurer** proporre qn per un posto/come tesoriere; **to propose a toast to sb** proporre un brindisi a qn 2 (*have in mind*): **to propose sth/to do** or **doing sth** proporsi qc/di fare qc ♦ VI (*offer marriage*) fare una proposta di matrimonio

pro·pos·er [prə'pəʊzə'] N (*Brit: of motion*) proponente *m/f*

propo·si·tion [ˌprɒpə'zɪʃən] N 1 (*statement, also Math, Logic*) proposizione *f* 2 (*proposal*) proposta; **to make sb a proposition** proporre qc a qn; **a business proposition** una proposta d'affari 3 (*person or thing to be dealt with*): **he's a**

tough proposition è un osso duro; **that's a tough proposition** è un'impresa; **early retirement may seem an attractive proposition** il prepensionamento può sembrare una prospettiva allettante

pro·pound [prə'paʊnd] VT (*idea, scheme, theory*) proporre, presentare; (*problem, question*) porre

pro·pri·etary [prə'praɪətərɪ] ADJ (*Comm*): **proprietary article** prodotto con marchio depositato; **proprietary brand** marchio di fabbrica; **proprietary medicine** specialità farmaceutica; **proprietary name** nome depositato or registrato

pro·pri·etor [prə'praɪətə'] N proprietario(-a)

pro·pri·ety [prə'praɪətɪ] N (*seemliness*) decoro, rispetto delle convenienze sociali; (*appropriateness*) convenienza; **the proprieties** le convenzioni sociali

pro·pul·sion [prə'pʌlʃən] N: **jet propulsion** propulsione *f* a getto

pro rata ['prəʊ'rɑːtə] ADV in proporzione, pro rata

pro·sa·ic [prəʊ'zeɪɪk] ADJ (*dull*) prosaico(-a), banale

Pros. Atty. ABBR (*USA*: = prosecuting attorney)

pro·scribe [prəʊs'kraɪb] VT proscrivere

prose [prəʊz] N prosa; (*Scol: translation*) traduzione *f* dalla lingua madre or madrelingua

pros·ecute ['prɒsɪkjuːt] VT 1 (*Law*) intentare azione contro; **"trespassers will be prosecuted"** "i trasgressori saranno perseguiti a norma di legge"; **"shoplifters will be prosecuted"** "i taccheggiatori saranno perseguiti a norma di legge" 2 (*frm: carry on: inquiry*) proseguire

pros·ecut·ing at·tor·ney ['prɒsɪkjuːtɪŋə'tɜːnɪ] N (*USA*) ≈ procuratore *m*

pros·ecu·tion [ˌprɒsɪ'kjuːʃən] N (*Law: act, proceedings*) azione *f* giudiziaria; (*accusing side*) accusa; **witness for the prosecution** testimone per l'accusa; **the prosecution** ≈ il pubblico ministero

pros·ecu·tor ['prɒsɪkjuːtə'] N (*Law*): **public prosecutor** ≈ procuratore *m* della Repubblica

pros·pect [N 'prɒspekt, *vb* prə'spekt] N (*outlook*) vista; (*fig*) prospettiva; (*hope*) speranza; (*chance*) probabilità *f inv*; **future prospects** (*of person, country*) prospettive *fpl*; **it's a grim prospect** è una prospettiva poco allegra; **we are faced with the prospect of leaving** rischiamo di dovercene andare; **there's little prospect of its happening** ci sono poche probabilità che accada; **what have you got in prospect?** cos' hai in vista?; **there is every prospect of an early victory** tutto lascia prevedere una rapida vittoria; **what are his prospects?** che prospettiva ha?; **his future prospects are good** ha delle buone prospettive; **a job with no prospects** un lavoro che non offre nessuna prospettiva; **he is a good prospect for the team** è una speranza per la squadra; **to seem a good prospect** sembrare promettente ♦ VT esplorare ♦ VI: **to prospect for gold** cercare l'oro

pros·pect·ing [prəs'pektɪŋ] N (*Mining*) prospezione *f*

pros·pec·tive [prəs'pektɪv] ADJ (*buyer*) probabile; (*legislation, son-in-law*) futuro(-a); **a prospective buyer** un probabile acquirente; **the terms of the prospective deal** le condizioni della futura transazione

pro·spec·tor [prəs'pektə'] N prospettore *m*; **gold prospector** cercatore *m* d'oro

pro·spec·tus [prəs'pektəs] N prospetto

pros·per ['prɒspə'] VI (*person*) raggiungere il benessere (economico); (*business, trade*) prosperare

pros·per·ity [prɒs'perɪtɪ] N benessere *m*, prosperità

pros·per·ous ['prɒspərəs] ADJ (*industry*) prospero(-a), fiorente; (*businessman*) di successo

pros·tate ['prɒsteɪt] N (*also: prostate gland*) prostata, ghiandola prostatica

pros·ti·tute ['prɒstɪtjuːt] N prostituto(-a) ♦ VT prostituire

pros·ti·tu·tion [ˌprɒstɪ'tjuːʃən] N prostituzione *f*

pros·trate [*adj* 'prɒstreɪt, *vb* prɒ'streɪt] ADJ bocconi *inv*; (*in respect, submission*) prosternato(-a), prostrato(-a); (*exhausted*): **prostrate (with)** prostrato(-a) (da) ♦ VT: **to prostrate o.s.** (*before sb*) prostrarsi, prosternarsi; (*on the floor*) stendersi bocconi; (*fig*) abbattersi

pro·tag·o·nist [prəʊ'tægənɪst] N protagonista *m/f*

pro·tect [prə'tekt] VT (*gen*) proteggere, salvaguardare; (*from cold, heat*) riparare; (*interests, rights*) salvaguardare

pro·tec·tion [prə'tɛkʃən] N 1 protezione *f*; (*against cold, wind*) riparo; **to be under sb's protection** essere sotto la protezione di qn 2 = **protection money**
pro·tec·tion·ism [prə'tɛkʃə,nɪzəm] N protezionismo
protection racket N racket *m inv*
pro·tec·tive [prə'tɛktɪv] ADJ (*gen*) protettivo(-a); **protective custody** (*Police*) protezione *f*
pro·tec·tor [prə'tɛktə'] N protettore(-trice)
pro·té·gé, pro·té·gée ['prəʊtɪʒeɪ] N protetto(-a)
pro·tein ['prəʊtiːn] N proteina
pro tem [prəʊ'tɛm] ADV ABBR (= *pro tempore: for the time being*) pro tempore
pro·test [*n* 'prəʊtɛst, *vb* prə'tɛst] N protesta; **to do sth under protest** fare qc protestando; **he ignored their protests** ha ignorato le loro proteste; **a protest march** una manifestazione di protesta ♦ VT protestare ♦ VI: **to protest against/about** protestare contro/per; **to protest to sb** fare le proprie rimostranze a qn
Prot·es·tant ['prɒtɪstənt] ADJ, N protestante *m/f*
pro·test·er, pro·tes·tor [prə'tɛstə'] N contestatore(-trice); (*in demonstration*) dimostrante *m/f*
protest march N marcia di protesta
pro·to·col ['prəʊtə,kɒl] N protocollo
proto·type ['prəʊtəʊ,taɪp] N prototipo
pro·tract·ed [prə'træktɪd] ADJ protratto(-a), prolungato(-a)
pro·trac·tor [prə'træktə'] N (*Geom*) goniometro
pro·trude [prə'truːd] VI sporgere
pro·tu·ber·ance [prə'tjuːbərəns] N protuberanza, sporgenza
proud [praʊd] ADJ (*comp* -er, *superl* -est) 1 (*person*) orgoglioso(-a), fiero(-a); (*pej: arrogant*) superbo(-a); **to be proud to do sth** essere fiero di fare qc; **her parents are proud of her** i suoi sono orgogliosi di lei; **he was as proud as a peacock** si è gonfiato come un tacchino; **they should be proud of!** non mi pare che sia il caso di vantarsene! 2 (*splendid: ship*) superbo(-a), splendido(-a) ♦ ADV: **to do sb proud** non far mancare nulla a qn; **to do o.s. proud** non farsi mancare nulla
proud·ly ['praʊdlɪ] ADV (*see adj*) orgogliosamente, con fierezza; superbamente
prove [pruːv] (*pt* **proved** *pp* **proved** *or* **proven** ['pruːvən]) VT 1 (*verify*) provare, dimostrare; **to prove sb innocent** provare *or* dimostrare l'innocenza di qn; **he was proved right in the end** alla fine i fatti gli hanno dato ragione; **the police couldn't prove it** la polizia non è riuscita a dimostrarlo 2 (*put to the test: courage, usefulness etc*) dimostrare, mettere alla prova; **to prove o.s.** dar prova di sé 3 (*turn out*): **to prove (to be) useful** rivelarsi utile; **to prove correct** risultare vero(-a); **if it proves (to be) otherwise** dovesse rivelarsi altrimenti ♦ VI = **prove 3**
Pro·vence [prɒ'vɑ̃ːns] N Provenza
prov·erb ['prɒvɜːb] N proverbio
pro·ver·bial [prə'vɜːbɪəl] ADJ proverbiale
pro·vide [prə'vaɪd] VT 1 (*supply*) fornire; **it provides plenty of scope for development** offre molte possibilità di sviluppo; **to provide sb with sth, provide sth for sb** fornire qc a qn; **they provided us with maps** ci hanno fornito delle cartine; **to be provided with** essere dotato(-a) *or* munito(-a) di 2 (*legislation*) prevedere ♦ VI: **the Lord will provide** Dio provvederà
  ▸ **provide for** VI + PREP 1 (*financially*) provvedere a; (*in the future*) provvedere al futuro di; **he can't provide for his family any more** non è più in grado di mantenere la famiglia 2 **the treaty does not provide for that** il trattato non lo contempla; **we have provided for that** vi abbiamo provveduto
pro·vid·ed [prə'vaɪdɪd] CONJ: **provided (that)** sempre che + *sub*, a patto che + *sub*, purché + *sub*, a condizione che + *sub*; **he'll play in the next match provided he's fit** giocherà nella prossima partita sempre che sia in forma
provi·dence ['prɒvɪdəns] N provvidenza
pro·vid·ing [prə'vaɪdɪŋ] CONJ: **providing (that)** *see* **provided**
prov·ince ['prɒvɪns] N provincia; **they live in the provinces** vivono in provincia; **it's not (within) my province** (*fig*) questo non rientra nel mio campo
pro·vin·cial [prə'vɪnʃəl] ADJ (*gen*) di provincia; (*pej*) provinciale ♦ N (*usu pej*) provincialotto(-a)

pro·vi·sion [prə'vɪʒən] N 1 (*supplying: of power, water*) fornitura; (: *of food*) approvvigionamento; (: *of hospitals, housing*) costruzione *f* 2 (*supply*) provvista, riserva, rifornimento, scorta; **the provision of health care** la fornitura di prestazioni sanitarie; **provisions** (*food*) provviste, scorte; **to get** *or* **lay in provisions** fare provviste; **provisions are running short** le provviste stanno finendo; **provision of capital** (*Fin*) apporto di capitale 3 (*preparation*): **to make provision for** (*one's family, future*) pensare a; (*journey*) fare i preparativi per; **he made provision for his nephew in his will** ha pensato a suo nipote nel testamento 4 (*stipulation*) disposizione *f*, clausola; **there's no provision for this in the contract** il contratto non lo prevede; **with the provision that** a condizione che; **there's no provision for this in the contract** il contratto non lo prevede
pro·vi·sion·al [prə'vɪʒənl] ADJ provvisorio(-a)
provisional licence N (*Brit: Aut*) ≈ foglio *m* rosa, *inv*
pro·vi·sion·al·ly [prə'vɪʒnəlɪ] ADV (*accept*) provvisoriamente; (*appoint*) a titolo provvisorio
pro·vi·so [prə'vaɪzəʊ] N condizione *f*; **with the proviso that** a condizione che + *sub*, a patto che + *sub*
Pro·vo ['prəʊvəʊ] N membro dell'ala estremista dell'IRA
provo·ca·tion [,prɒvə'keɪʃən] N provocazione *f*; **she acted under provocation** ha agito così perché è stata provocata
pro·voca·tive [prə'vɒkətɪv] ADJ (*causing anger*) provocatorio(-a); (*seductive*) provocante; (*thought-provoking*) stimolante
pro·voke [prə'vəʊk] VT (*gen*) provocare, incitare; **to provoke sb to sth/to do** *or* **into doing sth** spingere qn a qc/a fare qc
pro·vok·ing [prə'vəʊkɪŋ] ADJ irritante, esasperante
prov·ost ['prɒvəst] N (*Brit: Univ*) rettore *m*; (*Scot*) sindaco
prow [praʊ] N prua
prow·ess ['praʊɪs] N (*skill*): **his prowess as a footballer** le sue capacità di calciatore
prowl [praʊl] VI (*also:* **prowl about** *or* **around**) aggirarsi ♦ N: **on the prowl** in cerca di preda
prowl·er ['praʊlə'] N: **there was a prowler in the garden** c'era un tipo sospetto che si aggirava in giardino
prox·im·ity [prɒk'sɪmɪtɪ] N vicinanza, prossimità; **in the proximity of** in prossimità di
proxy ['prɒksɪ] N (*power*) procura, delega; (*person*) mandatario(-a); **by proxy** per procura
prude [pruːd] N puritano(-a), prude *m/f*
pru·dence ['pruːdəns] N prudenza
pru·dent ['pruːdənt] ADJ prudente
prud·ish ['pruːdɪʃ] ADJ puritano(-a), che si scandalizza facilmente
prune¹ [pruːn] N (*fruit*) prugna (secca)
prune² [pruːn] VT (*tree*) potare; (*size, cost*) ridurre
pry [praɪ] VI essere troppo curioso(-a); **to pry into sb's affairs** cacciare il naso negli affari di qn; **he's always prying into other people's affairs** s'impiccia sempre degli affari altrui
PS, ps. ABBR (= *postscript*) PS
psalm [sɑːm] N salmo
pseud [sjuːd] N (*fam: poser*) intellettualoide *m/f*
pseudo– ['sjuːdəʊ] PREF pseudo–
pseudo·nym ['sjuːdə,nɪm] N pseudonimo
PST ABBR (*USA*: = *Pacific Standard Time*) ora invernale del Pacifico
psyche ['saɪkɪ] N (*Psych*) psiche *f*
psy·che·del·ic [,saɪkɪ'dɛlɪk] ADJ psichedelico(-a)
psy·chi·at·ric [,saɪkɪ'ætrɪk] ADJ (*treatment, hospital*) psichiatrico(-a); (*disease, illness*) mentale
psy·chia·trist [saɪ'kaɪətrɪst] N psichiatra *m/f*
psy·chia·try [saɪ'kaɪətrɪ] N psichiatria
psy·chic ['saɪkɪk] ADJ 1 (*supernatural*) metapsichico(-a), paranormale; (*telepathic*) che ha dei poteri telepatici; **you must be psychic!** (*fam*) devi essere un indovino!, devi avere poteri telepatici!; **psychic powers** poteri paranormali 2 (*Psych*) psichico(-a), della psiche
psy·cho ['saɪkəʊ] N (*USA fam*) folle *m/f*, psicopatico(-a)
psy·cho·ana·lyse, psy·cho·ana·lyze (*USA*) [,saɪkəʊ'ænə,laɪz] VT psicanalizzare
psy·cho·analy·sis [,saɪkəʊə'nælɪsɪs] N psicanalisi *f inv*

psy·cho·ana·lyst [ˌsaɪkəʊˈænəlɪst] N psicanalista m/f
psy·cho·logi·cal [ˌsaɪkəˈlɒdʒɪkəl] ADJ psicologico(-a)
psy·cho·lo·gist [saɪˈkɒlədʒɪst] N psicologo(-a)
psy·chol·ogy [saɪˈkɒlədʒɪ] N psicologia
psy·cho·path [ˈsaɪkəʊˌpæθ] N psicopatico(-a)
psy·cho·sis [saɪˈkəʊsɪs] N (pl **psychoses** [saɪˈkəʊsiːz']) psicosi f inv
psy·cho·so·mat·ic [ˌsaɪkəʊsəʊˈmætɪk] ADJ psicosomatico(-a)
psy·cho·thera·py [ˌsaɪkəʊˈθerəpɪ] N psicoterapia
psy·chot·ic [saɪˈkɒtɪk] ADJ, N psicotico(-a)
pt ABBR 1 = **pint** 2 = **point**
PTA [ˌpiːtiːˈeɪ] N ABBR = **parent-teacher association**
pub [pʌb] N (Brit) pub m inv
pub-crawl [ˈpʌbˌkrɔːl] N (Brit fam): **to go on a pub-crawl** fare il giro dei pub
pu·ber·ty [ˈpjuːbətɪ] N pubertà
pu·bic [ˈpjuːbɪk] ADJ pubico(-a), del pube
pub·lic [ˈpʌblɪk] ADJ (gen) pubblico(-a); (Comm: industry) statale; **in the public interest** nel pubblico interesse; **to be public knowledge** essere di pubblico dominio; **he's a public figure, he's in public life** è un personaggio della vita pubblica; **a public place** un luogo pubblico; **this place is too public to discuss it** c'è troppa gente qui per poterne discutere; **to make sth public** rendere noto or di pubblico dominio qc; **to be in the public eye** essere una persona molto in vista, essere un personaggio in vista; **her public support of** il suo aperto appoggio a; **to create more public awareness (of)** focalizzare l'attenzione del pubblico (su); **to go public** (Comm) immettere le azioni sul mercato ◆ N: **the public** il pubblico; **open to the public** aperto al pubblico; **in public** in pubblico; **the sporting/reading public** il pubblico sportivo/dei lettori
public address system N impianto di amplificazione
pub·li·can [ˈpʌblɪkən] N (Brit) gestore m (or proprietario) di un pub
pub·li·ca·tion [ˌpʌblɪˈkeɪʃən] N pubblicazione f
public company N società f inv per azioni quotata in borsa
public convenience N (Brit) gabinetti mpl pubblici
public holiday N giorno festivo, festa nazionale
public house N (Brit) pub m inv
pub·lic·ity [pʌbˈlɪsɪtɪ] N 1 pubblicità 2 (Comm: advertising, advertisements) pubblicità f inv, réclame f inv ◆ ADJ (campaign, material, budget) pubblicitario(-a); (manager) della pubblicità
pub·li·cize [ˈpʌblɪˌsaɪz] VT 1 (make public) far sapere in giro 2 (advertise) fare (della) pubblicità a, reclamizzare
public limited company N ≈ società f inv a responsabilità limitata quotata in Borsa
pub·lic·ly [ˈpʌblɪklɪ] ADV (say, do etc) pubblicamente; **a publicly owned company** una società nazionalizzata
public opinion N opinione f pubblica
public ownership N: **to be taken into public ownership** essere statalizzato(-a)
public prosecutor N (Brit) ≈ pubblico ministero; **public prosecutor's office** l'ufficio del pubblico ministero
public relations NPL relazioni fpl pubbliche
public relations officer N addetto(-a) alle pubbliche relazioni
public school N (Brit) scuola superiore privata; (USA) scuola statale
public sector N settore m pubblico
public service vehicle N (Brit) mezzo pubblico
public-spirited [ˌpʌblɪkˈspɪrɪtɪd] ADJ (attitude) che denota senso civico; (act) di civismo; (person) che ha senso civico
public transport, (USA) **public transportation** N mezzi mpl pubblici
public utility N servizio pubblico
public works NPL lavori mpl pubblici
pub·lish [ˈpʌblɪʃ] VT pubblicare; **"published weekly"** "edito settimanalmente", "pubblicato settimanalmente"
pub·lish·er [ˈpʌblɪʃəʳ] N (person) editore m; (firm) casa editrice
pub·lish·ing [ˈpʌblɪʃɪŋ] N (industry) editoria, industria editoriale; (of book) pubblicazione f

publishing company, publishing house N casa or società editrice
puce [pjuːs] ADJ color pulce inv
puck [pʌk] N (Ice Hockey) disco
puck·er [ˈpʌkəʳ] VT (also: **pucker up**) (lips) increspare; (brow) aggrottare, corrugare; (Sewing) increspare
pud·ding [ˈpʊdɪŋ] N (dessert) dolce m, dessert m inv; **what's for pudding?** cosa c'è per dessert?; (steamed pudding) dolce cotto a bagnomaria a base di uova, burro, farina e latte; **black pudding, blood pudding** (USA) sanguinaccio; **rice pudding** budino di riso
pud·dle [ˈpʌdl] N pozzanghera, pozza
pu·er·ile [ˈpjʊəraɪl] ADJ puerile, infantile
Puer·to Rico [ˈpwɜːtəʊˈriːkəʊ] N Portorico
puff [pʌf] N 1 (of breath) soffio; (of engine) sbuffare m; (of air, wind) folata, soffio; (of smoke) sbuffo; (of cigarette) tiro, boccata; **I'm out of puff** (fam) sono senza fiato 2 (powder puff) piumino della cipria 3 (Culin): **cream puff** sfogliatina alla panna ◆ VT 1 **to puff (out)** smoke etc mandar fuori (sbuffi di) fumo etc 2 (also: **puff out**: sails, cheeks) gonfiare; **his face was all puffed up** la sua faccia era tutta gonfia ◆ VI (breathe heavily) ansimare; (blow) soffiare; **he started puffing, and pedalled more slowly** cominciò ad ansimare e a pedalare più piano; **the train puffed into the station** il treno entrò sbuffando in stazione; **to puff (away) at** or **on one's pipe** tirare boccate di fumo dalla pipa
puffed [pʌft] ADJ (fam: out of breath): **I'm puffed (out)** sono senza fiato
puf·fin [ˈpʌfɪn] N pulcinella m di mare, puffino
puff pastry, (USA) **puff paste** N pasta sfoglia
puffy [ˈpʌfɪ] ADJ (comp **-ier**, superl **-iest**) gonfio(-a)
pug·na·cious [pʌɡˈneɪʃəs] ADJ bellicoso(-a), battagliero(-a)
pull [pʊl] N 1 (tug) strattone m, tirata, strappo; (of moon, magnet, the sea) attrazione f; (fig: attraction: of personality) forza di attrazione; (: of family ties) forza; **I felt a pull at my sleeve** ho sentito qualcuno che mi tirava per la manica; **to give sth a pull** dare uno strattone a qc; **he has some pull with the manager** (fam: influence) ha dell'influenza sul direttore 2 (at pipe) boccata, tirata; (at beer) sorsata; **he took a pull at the bottle** ha bevuto un sorso dalla bottiglia 3 (handle of drawer) maniglia, pomolo; (of bell) cordone m ◆ VT 1 (draw: cart) tirare, trascinare; (: curtains) tirare; (: fig: crowd) attirare; **to push and shut/open** chiudere/aprire la porta tirandola 2 (tug: handle, rope) tirare; (press: trigger) premere; **to pull sb's hair** tirare i capelli a qn; **she pulled my hair** mi ha tirato i capelli; **to pull to pieces** or **to bits** (toy) fare a pezzi; (argument) demolire; (person, play) stroncare; **to pull one's punches** (Boxing) risparmiare l'avversario; **she didn't pull any punches** (fig) non ha risparmiato nessun colpo; **to pull sb's leg** prendere in giro qn; **you're pulling my leg!** mi stai prendendo in giro!; **to pull strings (for sb)** muovere qualche pedina (per qn); **to pull one's weight** fare la propria parte, dare il proprio contributo; **to pull a face** fare una smorfia 3 (extract, draw out: gen) togliere; (: gun, knife) tirar fuori; (: weeds) strappare; (: leeks, rhubarb) raccogliere; (: beer) spillare; **to pull a gun on sb** estrarre una pistola e puntarla contro qn 4 (tear: thread) tirare; **to pull a muscle** farsi uno strappo muscolare; **to pull a tendon** farsi uno stiramento 5 (fam: carry out, do: robbery) fare; **to pull a fast one on sb** combinarla a qn ◆ VI 1 (tug) tirare; **pull!** tira!; **to pull at sb's sleeve** tirare qn per la manica; **the car is pulling to the right** lo sterzo or la macchina tira a destra; **to pull at** or **on one's pipe** tirare boccate dalla pipa 2 (move): **to pull for the shore** remare verso la riva; **the train pulled into/out of the station** il treno è entrato in/è partito dalla stazione; **he pulled alongside the kerb** ha accostato al marciapiede; **we pulled clear of the traffic** ci siamo lasciati il traffico alle spalle
▸ **pull about** VT + ADV (handle roughly: object) strapazzare; (: person) malmenare
▸ **pull along** VT + ADV trascinare; **to pull o.s. along** trascinarsi
▸ **pull apart** VT + ADV 1 (pull to pieces) smontare; (break) fare a pezzi, sfasciare; (separate) separare 2 (fig: fam: search thoroughly) frugare dappertutto in; (: criticize: novel, theory) demolire

▸ **pull away** VT + ADV strappare via ♦ VI + ADV (*move off: vehicle*) muoversi, partire; **to pull away from** (*kerb*) allontanarsi da; (*quay*) staccarsi da; (*platform*) muoversi da; (*subj: runner: competitors*) distanziare

▸ **pull back** VT + ADV (*person, lever*) tirare indietro; (*curtains*) aprire ♦ VI + ADV tirarsi indietro; (*Mil*) ritirarsi

▸ **pull down** VT + ADV **1** (*gen*) tirar giù; (*opponent*) stendere a terra **2** (*demolish: buildings*) demolire, buttar giù; **the old school was pulled down last year** la vecchia scuola fu demolita l'anno scorso

▸ **pull in** VT + ADV **1** (*rope, fishing line*) tirare su; (*Naut: sail*) cazzare; (*person: into car, room*) tirare dentro; (*stomach*) tirare in dentro **2** (*rein in: horse*) trattenere **3** (*attract: crowds*) attirare **4** (*fam: take into custody*) mettere dentro; **the police pulled him in for questioning** la polizia l'ha fermato per interrogarlo ♦ VI + ADV (*Aut: arrive*) arrivare; (*: stop*) fermarsi; **she pulled in at the side of the road** si fermò a lato della strada

▸ **pull off** VT + ADV **1** (*remove: wrapping paper*) strappare; (*: clothes, shoes, gloves*) levarsi, togliersi **2** (*fam: succeed in: plan, attack etc*) portare a termine; **he didn't pull it off** non gli è riuscito il colpo

▸ **pull on** VT + ADV (*clothes*) mettersi

▸ **pull out** VT + ADV **1** (*take out: tooth, splinter*) togliere; (*: gun, knife, person*) tirare fuori **2** (*withdraw: troops, police*) (far) ritirare ♦ VI + ADV **1** (*withdraw*) ritirarsi; **she pulled out of the tournament** si è ritirata dal torneo **2** (*leave: train, car*) uscire; **he pulled out to overtake** si è spostato per sorpassare

▸ **pull over** VT + ADV **1** (*box, table*): **pull it over here/there** tiralo in qua/in là; **pull it over to the window** tiralo vicino alla finestra **2** (*topple*) far cascare, tirar giù ♦ VI + ADV accostare; **the policeman pulled me over** il poliziotto mi ha fatto fermare la macchina

▸ **pull round** VI + ADV (*unconscious person*) rinvenire; (*sick person*) ristabilirsi

▸ **pull through** VT + ADV **1** tirare dall'altra parte **2** (*fig*) aiutare a venirne fuori ♦ VI + ADV (*fig*) cavarsela; **they think he'll pull through** pensano che se la caverà

▸ **pull together** VT + ADV (*fig*): **to pull o.s. together** ricomporsi; **pull yourself together!** datti una regolata! ♦ VI + ADV (*make common effort*) cooperare, mettersi insieme

▸ **pull up** VT + ADV **1** (*raise by pulling*) tirar su **2** (*uproot: weeds*) sradicare **3** (*stop: horse, car*) fermare **4** (*scold*) riprendere ♦ VI + ADV (*stop*) fermarsi; **a black car pulled up beside me** una macchina nera si è fermata accanto a me

pul·ley [ˈpʊlɪ] N puleggia, carrucola

pull-out [ˈpʊlˌaʊt] N inserto ♦ ADJ staccabile

pull-over [ˈpʊlˌəʊvəʳ] N pullover *m inv*

pulp [pʌlp] N **1** (*for paper*) pasta (di legno *or* stracci *etc*); **to reduce sth to pulp** spappolare qc **2** (*of fruit, vegetable*) polpa **3** (*fiction*) romanzi di qualità scadente ♦ VT (*fruit, vegetables*) spappolare; (*paper, book*) mandare al macero

pul·pit [ˈpʊlpɪt] N pulpito

pul·sate [pʌlˈseɪt] VI (*heart, blood*) pulsare; (*music*) vibrare

pulse [pʌls] N (*Anat*) polso; (*Phys*) impulso; (*fig: of drums, music*) vibrazione *f*; **to feel** *or* **take sb's pulse** sentire *or* tastare il polso a qn; **the nurse took his pulse** l'infermiera gli ha tastato il polso

pulses [ˈpʌlsɪz] NPL (*Culin*) legumi *mpl* secchi

pul·ver·ize [ˈpʌlvəˌraɪz] VT (*also fig*) polverizzare

puma [ˈpjuːmə] N puma *m inv*

pum·ice [ˈpʌmɪs] N (*also:* **pumice stone**) (pietra) pomice *f*

pum·mel [ˈpʌml] VT prendere a pugni

pump¹ [pʌmp] N pompa; **bicycle pump** pompa da bicicletta; **petrol pump** distributore *m* (di benzina) ♦ VT **1** pompare; **to pump sth dry** prosciugare qc con una pompa; **to pump air into a tyre** *or* **tire** gonfiare uno pneumatico; **to pump money into a project** immettere capitali in un progetto; **to pump sb for information** cercare di strappare delle informazioni a qn **2** (*handle*) alzare e abbassare vigorosamente; **to pump sb's hand up and down** dare una vigorosa stretta di mano a qn

▸ **pump in** VT + ADV (*water*) far passare (con una pompa); (*foam into walls*) iniettare; (*fig: money*) immettere

▸ **pump out** VT + ADV pompare fuori; **to pump out sb's stomach** fare la lavanda gastrica a qn

▸ **pump up** VT + ADV (*tyre* or *tire*) gonfiare

pump² N (*sports shoe*) scarpa da ginnastica; (*dancing shoe*) scarpetta da ballo; (*slip-on shoe*) ballerina

pump·kin [ˈpʌmpkɪn] N zucca

pun [pʌn] N gioco di parole

punch¹ [pʌntʃ] N **1** (*for making holes: in metal, leather*) punzonatrice *f*; (*: in paper*) perforatore *m*; (*: in tickets*) pinza per forare; (*for stamping metal*) punzone *m* **2** (*blow*) pugno; (*fig: vigour*) mordente *m*, forza ♦ VT **1** (*with tool: gen*) punzonare; (*: ticket*) forare; **he forgot to punch my ticket** si è dimenticato di forarmi il biglietto; **to punch a hole in sth** forare qc **2** (*with fist*): **to punch sb/sth** dare un pugno a qn/qc; **he punched me!** mi ha dato un pugno!; **to punch a ball** colpire una palla con un pugno; **to punch sb's nose** dare un pugno sul naso a qn

▸ **punch in** VI + ADV (*USA*) timbrare il cartellino (all'entrata)

▸ **punch out** VI + ADV (*USA*) timbrare il cartellino (all'uscita)

punch² [pʌntʃ] N (*drink*) punch *m inv*, ponce *m inv*

punch-drunk [ˌpʌntʃˈdrʌŋk] ADJ (*Boxing*) groggy; (*fig: stupefied*) stordito(-a)

punched card [ˌpʌntʃˈkɑːd], (*USA*) **punch card** (*esp*) N (*Comput*) scheda perforata

punch line N (*of joke*) battuta finale; (*of story*) finale *m*

punch-up [ˈpʌntʃˌʌp] N (*Brit fam*) scazzottata, rissa

punc·tu·al [ˈpʌŋktjʊəl] ADJ (*person*) puntuale; (*train*) in orario

punc·tu·al·ity [ˌpʌŋktjʊˈælɪtɪ] N puntualità

punc·tu·al·ly [ˈpʌŋktjʊəlɪ] ADV (*see adj*) puntualmente; in orario; **it will start punctually at 6** comincerà alle 6 precise *or* in punto

punc·tu·ate [ˈpʌŋktjʊˌeɪt] VT (*Gram*) mettere la punteggiatura a *or* in; **his speech was punctuated by bursts of applause** il suo discorso fu ripetutamente interrotto da scrosci di applausi

punc·tua·tion [ˌpʌŋktjʊˈeɪʃən] N (*Gram*) punteggiatura, interpunzione *f*

punctuation mark N segno d'interpunzione

punc·ture [ˈpʌŋktʃəʳ] N (*in tyre* or *tire*) foratura; (*in balloon*) foratura, buco; (*in skin*) puntura; **I have a puncture** (*Aut*) ho forato (una gomma) ♦ VT bucare, forare ♦ VI bucarsi, forarsi

pun·dit [ˈpʌndɪt] N (*iro*) esperto(-a), sapientone(-a)

pun·gent [ˈpʌndʒənt] ADJ (*smell, taste*) pungente, aspro(-a); (*smoke*) acre; (*sauce*) piccante; (*remark, satire*) caustico(-a), mordace

pun·ish [ˈpʌnɪʃ] VT **1 to punish sb for sth/for doing sth** punire qn per qc/per aver fatto qc **2** (*fig: fam: car*) mettere a dura prova; (*: horse*) sfiancare; (*: opposition*) dare una bella batosta a; (*: meal, bottle of whisky*) far fuori

pun·ish·able [ˈpʌnɪʃəbl] ADJ punibile

pun·ish·ing [ˈpʌnɪʃɪŋ] ADJ (*fig: exhausting*) sfiancante ♦ N punizione *f*

pun·ish·ment [ˈpʌnɪʃmənt] N **1** (*punishing*) punizione *f*, castigo; (*penalty*) pena; **to take one's punishment** subire il castigo; **to make the punishment fit the crime** punire secondo il reato **2** (*fig: fam*): **to take a lot of punishment** (*boxer*) incassare parecchi colpi; (*car*) essere messo(-a) a dura prova; (*furniture*) essere maltrattato(-a)

punk [pʌŋk] N **1** (*person: also:* **punk rocker**) punk *m/f inv*; (*music: also:* **punk rock**) musica punk, punk rock *m* **2** (*USA fam: hoodlum*) teppista *m*

punt¹ [pʌnt] N (*boat*) barchino; (*Ftbl*) calcio al volo; **we hired a punt** abbiamo noleggiato un barchino ♦ VT (*boat*) spingere con la pertica; (*ball*) calciare al volo ♦ VI: **to go punting** andare in barchino

punt² [pʌnt] N (*in Ireland*) sterlina irlandese; **10 Irish punts** 10 sterline irlandesi

punt·er [ˈpʌntəʳ] N (*Brit fam: gambler*) scommettitore(-trice); (*: customer*) cliente *m/f*; **to pull in the punters** attirare clienti

puny [ˈpjuːnɪ] ADJ (*comp* **-ier**, *superl* **-iest**) (*person*) gracile, striminzito(-a); (*effort*) penoso(-a)

pup [pʌp] N (*dog*) cagnolino(-a), cucciolo(-a); (*seal*) cucciolo(-a)

pu·pil¹ [ˈpjuːpl] N (*Scol*) allievo(-a), scolaro(-a)

pu·pil² [ˈpjuːpl] N (*Anat*) pupilla

pup·pet [ˈpʌpɪt] N (*glove puppet*) burattino; (*string puppet*) marionetta; (*fig*) burattino, fantoccio

puppet government N governo *m* fantoccio, *inv*

pup·py [ˈpʌpɪ] N cucciolo(-a), cagnolino(-a)

pur·chase [ˈpɜːtʃɪs] N 1 (*act*) acquisto; (*thing purchased*) acquisto, compera 2 (*grip*) presa; **to get a purchase on** trovare un appoggio su ♦ VT (*frm*) acquistare, comprare

purchase order N ordine *m* d'acquisto, ordinazione *f*

purchase price N prezzo d'acquisto

pur·chas·er [ˈpɜːtʃɪsəʳ] N acquirente *m/f*, compratore(-trice)

purchase tax N (*Brit*) imposta sugli acquisti

pur·chas·ing pow·er [ˈpɜːtʃɪsɪŋˌpaʊəʳ] N potere *m* d'acquisto

pure [pjʊəʳ] ADJ (*comp* -r, *superl* -st) puro(-a); **the pure in heart** i puri di cuore; **as pure as the driven snow** innocente come un bambino; **a pure wool jumper** un golf di pura lana; **pure mathematics** matematica pura; **pure orange juice** puro succo d'arancia; **it's laziness pure and simple** è pura pigrizia; **by pure chance** per puro caso

pure·bred [ˈpjʊəˌbred] ADJ di razza pura

pu·rée [ˈpjʊəreɪ] N purè *m inv*, purea ♦ VT schiacciare, passare

pure·ly [ˈpjʊəlɪ] ADV puramente

purge [pɜːdʒ] N (*gen, also Med*) purga; (*Pol*) epurazione *f*, purga ♦ VT 1 (*Med*) purgare; (*Pol*): **to purge (of)** epurare (da); **to purge one's sins** espiare i propri peccati; **to purge o.s. of sth** liberarsi da qc 2 (*Law: offence, crime*) espiare

pu·ri·fi·ca·tion [ˌpjʊərɪfɪˈkeɪʃən] N (*see vb*) depurazione *f*; purificazione *f*

pu·ri·fy [ˈpjʊərɪˌfaɪ] VT (*water, air*) depurare; (*person*) purificare

pur·ist [ˈpjʊərɪst] N purista *m/f*

pu·ri·tan [ˈpjʊərɪtən] ADJ, N puritano(-a)

pu·ri·tani·cal [ˌpjʊərɪˈtænɪkəl] ADJ puritano(-a)

pu·rity [ˈpjʊərɪtɪ] N purezza

purl [pɜːl] N (maglia *or* punto a) rovescio ♦ VT lavorare a rovescio

pur·loin [pɜːˈlɔɪn] VT (*frm*) sottrarre, rubare

pur·ple [ˈpɜːpl] ADJ viola *inv*; **to go purple (in the face)** diventare paonazzo(-a), farsi di porpora ♦ N (*colour*) viola *m inv*; (*Rel*): **the purple** la porpora

pur·port [*n* ˈpɜːpət, *vb* pɜːˈpɔːt] N significato, senso generale ♦ VT: **to purport to be/do** pretendere di essere/fare

pur·pose [ˈpɜːpəs] N 1 (*intention*) scopo, intenzione *f*; (*use*) uso; **she has a purpose in life** ha uno scopo nella vita; **for our purposes** per i nostri scopi; **for teaching purposes** per l'insegnamento; **for the purposes of this meeting** agli effetti di questa riunione; **for all practical purposes** a tutti gli effetti pratici, in pratica; **on purpose** di proposito, apposta; **he did it on purpose** l'ha fatto apposta; **for illustrative purposes** a titolo illustrativo; **to the purpose** a proposito, pertinente; **with the purpose of** con il proposito di; **to some purpose** con qualche risultato; **to no purpose** senza nessun risultato, inutilmente; **to good purpose** con buoni risultati; **what is the purpose of these changes?** qual è lo scopo di questi cambiamenti? 2 (*resolution, determination*): **sense of purpose** risolutezza

purpose-built [ˈpɜːpəsˌbɪlt] ADJ (*Brit*) costruito(-a) appositamente

pur·pose·ful [ˈpɜːpəsfʊl] ADJ deciso(-a), risoluto(-a)

pur·pose·ly [ˈpɜːpəslɪ] ADV di proposito, apposta

purr [pɜːʳ] N (*of cat*) le fusa *fpl* ♦ VI far le fusa

purse [pɜːs] N (*for money*) borsellino, portamonete *m inv*; (*USA: handbag*) borsetta, borsa; (*esp Sport: prize*) montepremi *m inv*; **I've got 10 pounds in my purse** ho 10 sterline nel portamonete ♦ VT: **to purse one's lips** increspare le labbra

purs·er [ˈpɜːsəʳ] N (*Naut*) commissario di bordo

purse snatch·er [ˈpɜːsˌsnætʃəʳ] N (*USA*) scippatore *m*

pur·sue [pəˈsjuː] VT 1 (*chase*) inseguire; (*pleasures*) andare in cerca di; (*subj: bad luck*) perseguitare 2 (*carry on: studies*) proseguire; (*: career*) intraprendere; (*: inquiry, matter*) portare avanti; (*: plan*) andare avanti con

pur·su·er [pəˈsjuːəʳ] N inseguitore(-trice)

pur·suit [pəˈsjuːt] N 1 (*chase*) inseguimento; (*fig: of pleasure, happiness, knowledge*) ricerca; **the pursuit of success** la ricerca del successo; **in (the) pursuit of sb** all'inseguimento di qn; **in (the) pursuit of sth** alla ricerca di qc; **with two policemen in hot pursuit** con due poliziotti alle calcagna 2 (*occupation*) attività *f inv*, occupazione *f*; (*pastime*) svago, passatempo; **scientific pursuits** ricerche *fpl* scientifiche; **outdoor pursuits** attività *fpl* all'aperto

pur·vey·or [pɜːˈveɪəʳ] N (*frm*) fornitore(-trice)

pus [pʌs] N pus *m inv*

push [pʊʃ] N 1 (*shove*) spinta, spintone *m*; **to give sb/sth a push** dare una spinta a qn/qc; **to give sb the push** (*Brit fam*) dare il benservito a qn 2 (*effort*) grande sforzo; (*Mil: offensive*) offensiva 4 (*fam*): **at a push** in caso di necessità; **if or when it comes to the push** al momento critico ♦ VT 1 (*shove, move by pushing*) spingere; (*press: button*) schiacciare, premere; **to push a door open/shut** aprire/chiudere una porta con una spinta *or* spingendola; **he pushed it into my hands** me lo ha cacciato in mano; **the accident pushed everything else out of my mind** l'incidente mi ha fatto dimenticare tutto il resto 2 (*fig: press, advance: views*) imporre; (*: claim*) far valere; (*: product*) spingere le vendite di; (*: candidate*) appoggiare; **to push home an advantage** sfruttare a fondo un vantaggio; **to push home an attack** portare a conclusione un attacco; **to push drugs** spacciare droga; **don't push your luck!** (*fam*) non sfidare la fortuna!, non tirare troppo la corda! 3 (*fig: put pressure on*): **to push sb into doing sth** costringere qn a fare qc; **to push sb to do sth** spingere qn a fare qc; **my parents are pushing me to go to university** i miei mi spingono ad andare all'università; **that's pushing it a bit** (*fam*) è un po' troppo; **to be pushed for time/money** essere a corto di tempo/soldi; **I'm hard pushed to understand how ...** mi riesce difficile capire come...; **I'm really pushed today** oggi non ho un minuto di tempo ♦ VI spingere; **to push for** (*better pay, conditions*) fare pressione per ottenere; **to push past sb** spingere qn per passare; **to push into a room** entrare in una stanza facendosi largo; **"push"** (*on door*) "spingere"; (*on bell*) "suonare"

▸ **push about, push around** VT + ADV (*fig: fam: bully*) fare il prepotente con; **he likes pushing people around** gli piace dare ordini a tutti

▸ **push ahead** VI + ADV: **to push ahead (with sth)** andare avanti (con qc)

▸ **push aside** VT + ADV spingere da parte, scostare; (*fig: suggestions*) scartare; (*: problems*) accantonare

▸ **push away** VT + ADV respingere

▸ **push back** VT + ADV (*blankets*) spingere via, buttare all'indietro; (*curtains*) aprire; (*lock of hair*) ricacciare all'indietro; (*enemy forces*) respingere

▸ **push down** VT + ADV: **to push down on** schiacciare, premere ♦ VT + ADV (*switch, knob*) abbassare, tirare giù; (*knock over: fence, person*) buttare giù

▸ **push forward** VI + ADV (*Mil*) avanzare ♦ VT + ADV spingere in avanti; **he tends to push himself forward** (*fig*) cerca sempre di mettersi in mostra

▸ **push in** VT + ADV 1 (*person*) spingere dentro; (*stick, rag: into hole*) ficcare dentro, cacciare dentro; **to push sb in(to) the water** spingere qn in acqua; **she pushed her way in** è entrata facendosi largo 2 (*break: door etc*) sfondare ♦ VI + ADV introdursi a forza

▸ **push off** VT + ADV (*gen*) buttare giù; (*lid, top*) spingere via; **he pushed me off the wall** mi ha spinto giù dal muretto ♦ VI + ADV 1 (*in boat*) prendere il largo 2 (*fam: leave*) filare, smammare; **push off!** sparisci!

▸ **push on** VI + ADV (*with journey*) continuare; (*with job*) perseverare; **I've got a lot to do, so I must push on now** ho molto da fare, quindi devo andare avanti ♦ VT + ADV (*fig: incite, urge on*) spronare, spingere

▸ **push out** VT + ADV (*car, person*) spingere fuori; (*cork*) far uscire

▸ **push over** VT + ADV 1 (*over cliff etc*) spingere giù; **to push sth over the edge** spingere qc oltre il bordo 2 (*knock over*) far cadere

▸ **push through** VT + ADV (*gen*) spingere dall'altra parte;

to push one's way through farsi largo; **I pushed my way through till I reached the front** mi sono fatto largo fino ad arrivare davanti **2** (*force acceptance of: decision*) far accettare; (: *Parliament: bill*) riuscire a far votare ♦ VI + ADV farsi strada, farsi largo; (*troops*) aprirsi un varco; **to push through a crowd** farsi largo *or* aprirsi un varco tra la folla
▸ **push to** VT + ADV (*door*) socchiudere
▸ **push up** VT + ADV **1** spingere in su **2** (*fig: raise, increase*) far salire

push-bike [ˈpʊʃˌbaɪk] N (*Brit*) bicicletta
push-button [ˈpʊʃˌbʌtn] ADJ a tastiera; **push-button warfare** guerra dei bottoni
push-chair [ˈpʊʃˌtʃɛəʳ] N (*Brit*) passeggino
push·er [ˈpʊʃəʳ] N (*fam*) **1** (*also:* **drug pusher**) spacciatore(-trice) (di droga) **2** (*ambitious person*) arrivista *m/f*
push·over [ˈpʊʃˌəʊvəʳ] N (*fam*) **1** it's a pushover è un gioco da ragazzi; **she's a pushover** si lascia convincere facilmente
push-up [ˈpʊʃˌʌp] N (*USA*) flessione *f* sulle braccia; **to do push-ups** fare flessioni sulle braccia
pushy [ˈpʊʃɪ] ADJ (*comp* **-ier**, *superl* **-iest**) (*fam, pej*) troppo intraprendente
pus·sy·cat [ˈpʊsɪˌkæt] N (*fam*) micio(-a)

put [pʊt] (*pt, pp* **put**) VT **1** (*place*) mettere; (*put down*) posare, metter giù; **where shall I put my things?** dove metto le mie cose?; **she's putting the baby to bed** sta mettendo a letto il bambino; **my brother put me on the train** mio fratello mi ha messo sul treno; **to put the ball in the net** mandare la palla in rete; **to put sth to one's ear** avvicinarsi qc all'orecchio; **she put her head on my shoulder** appoggiò la testa sulla mia spalla; **to put one's signature to sth** apporre la propria firma a qc; **to put a lot of time into sth** dedicare molto tempo a qc; **to put money into a company** investire *or* mettere dei capitali in un'azienda; **to put money on a horse** scommettere su un cavallo **2** (*thrust, direct*) cacciare; **he put his finger right in my eye** mi ha cacciato un dito nell'occhio; **I put my fist through the window** sfondai la finestra con il pugno; **to put one's pen through sth** cancellare qc con un frego; **he put his head round the door** fece capolino dalla porta; **to put the shot** (*Sport*) lanciare il peso **3** (*cause to be*): **to put sb in a good/bad mood** mettere qn di buon/cattivo umore; **to put sb in charge of sth** incaricare qn di qc; **to put sb to a lot of trouble** dare un sacco da fare a qn; **I put her to answering the phone** le ho dato l'incarico di rispondere al telefono; **he put her to work immediately** l'ha messa subito al lavoro **4** (*express*) esprimere, dire; **let me put it another way** te lo spiego in un altro modo; **how shall I put it?** come dire?; **let me put it this way** diciamo così; **as Dante puts it** come dice Dante; **to put it bluntly** per parlar chiaro; **put it to him gently** diglielo senza spaventarlo; **to put sth into French** tradurre qc in francese; **to put the words to music** mettere in musica *or* musicare le parole **5** (*expound: case, problem*) esporre, presentare; **I put it to you that ...** io sostengo che...; **to put a question to sb** rivolgere una domanda a qn **6** (*estimate*) valutare, stimare; **what would you put it at?** quanto pensi che valga?; **I'd put his age at 40** direi che ha 40 anni ♦ VI (*Naut*): **to put to sea** prendere il mare; **to put into port** entrare in porto ♦ ADV: **to stay put** (*fam*) non muoversi
▸ **put about** VT + ADV (*circulate: news, rumour*) mettere in giro ♦ VI + ADV (*Naut*) virare di bordo, invertire la rotta
▸ **put across** VT + ADV **1** (*communicate: ideas, opinion*) comunicare, far capire; (: *new product*) propagandare; **he finds it hard to put his ideas across** trova difficile riuscire a comunicare le proprie idee; **she can't put herself across** non sa far valere le sue doti **2** (*fam: play trick*): **to put one across on sb** darla a bere a qn
▸ **put aside** VT + ADV **1** (*lay down: book, game*) mettere da una parte, posare **2** (*save*) mettere da parte; (*in shop*) tenere da parte; **can you put this aside for me till tomorrow?** me lo può tenere da parte fino a domani? **3** (*fig: abandon: idea, hope, doubt*) mettere da parte, dimenticare
▸ **put away** VT + ADV **1** (*clothes, toys, dishes*) mettere via, riporre; **can you put away the dishes, please?** ti dispiace riporre i piatti? **2** = **put aside 2 3** (*fam: consume: food, drink*) far fuori **4** (*fam: lock up in prison*) mettere dentro; (: *in psy-*

chiatric hospital) rinchiudere; **I hope they put him away for a long time** spero che lo mettano dentro per un bel pezzo
▸ **put back** VT + ADV **1** (*replace*) rimettere (a posto); **put it back when you've finished with it** rimettilo a posto quando hai finito **2** (*postpone*) rimandare, rinviare; (*slow down: production*) rallentare; (*set back: watch, clock*) mettere indietro; **the meeting's been put back till two o'clock** la riunione è stata rinviata alle due; **remember to put your watch back** ricorda di mettere indietro l'orologio; **this will put us back 10 years** questo ci farà tornare indietro di 10 anni ♦ VI + ADV (*Naut*) rientrare (in porto)
▸ **put by** VT + ADV = **put aside 2**
▸ **put down** VT + ADV **1** (*set down*) mettere giù, posare; (*passenger*) far scendere; **I'll put these bags down for a minute** poso un attimo queste borse; **I couldn't put that book down** (*fig*) non riuscivo a smettere di leggere quel libro **2** (*lower: umbrella*) chiudere; (: *car roof*) abbassare **3** (*crush: revolt*) reprimere; (: *gambling, prostitution*) abolire; (: *rumour*) mettere a tacere; (*humiliate*) mortificare **4** (*pay: deposit*) versare **5** (*destroy: pet*) abbattere; **we had to have our dog put down** abbiamo dovuto far abbattere il cane **6** (*write down*) scrivere; **I've put down a few ideas** ho buttato giù alcune idee; **to put sth down in writing** mettere qc per iscritto; **put it down on my account** (*Comm*) me lo addebiti *or* metta in conto; **put me down for £15** segnami *or* mettimi in lista per 15 sterline **7** (*classify*) considerare; **I'd put him down as about forty** gli darei una quarantina d'anni; **I put him down as a troublemaker** lo considero un elemento disturbatore **8** (*attribute*): **to put sth down to sth** attribuire qc a qc ♦ VI + ADV (*Aer*) atterrare
▸ **put forward** VT + ADV **1** (*propose: gen*) proporre; (: *theory*) avanzare; (: *opinion*) esprimere **2** (*advance: date, meeting, function*) anticipare; (: *clock*) mettere avanti
▸ **put in** VT + ADV **1** (*place inside: drawer, bag*) metter dentro **2** (*insert: in book, speech*) aggiungere, inserire **3** (*interpose: remark*) fare; **she put in her piece** ha detto la sua **4** (*enter: application, complaint*) presentare; **to put in a plea of not guilty** (*Law*) dichiararsi innocente; **to put sb in for an exam** presentare qn a un esame; **to put sb in for an award** proporre qn per un premio **5** (*install: central heating*) mettere, installare **6** (*Pol: elect*) eleggere **7** (*devote, expend: time*) passare, dedicare; **to put in a few extra hours** fare qualche ora in più; **to put in a lot of work** lavorare sodo; **to put in a good day's work** fàre una bella giornata di lavoro ♦ VI + ADV (*Naut*) fare scalo
▸ **put in for** VI + ADV + PREP (*job*) far domanda per; (*promotion*) far domanda di; **he's put in a request for an assistant** ha presentato richiesta per avere un assistente
▸ **put off** VT + ADV **1** (*set down: passenger*) far scendere **2** (*postpone, delay: match, decision*) rimandare, rinviare; (: *guest*) chiedere di rimandare la visita; **to put off doing sth** rimandare qc a più tardi; **I keep putting it off** continuo a rimandarlo; **to put sb off with an excuse** liberarsi di qn con una scusa **3** (*discourage*) far passare la voglia a; **he's not easily put off** non si lascia scoraggiare facilmente; **to put sb off their food** far passare a qn la voglia di mangiare **4** (*distract*) distrarre; **stop putting me off!** smettila di distrarmi! **5** (*repel: smell*) disgustare **6** (*switch off*) spegnere; **shall I put the light off?** spengo la luce?
▸ **put on** VT + ADV **1** (*clothes, lipstick, shoes*) mettere, mettersi; **I'll put my coat on** mi metto il cappotto **2** (*assume: accent, manner*) affettare; (: *airs*) darsi; (*fam, kid, have on, esp USA*) prendere in giro; **to put on airs** darsi delle arie; **to put on an innocent expression** assumere un'aria innocente **3** (*add, increase: speed, pressure*) aumentare; **to put on weight** aumentare di peso, ingrassare; **he's put on a lot of weight** è ingrassato parecchio; **I put on four pounds** sono ingrassata di due chili **4** (*concert, exhibition*) allestire, organizzare; (*play*) mettere in scena; (*extra bus, train*) mettere in servizio; **we're putting on "Bugsy Malone"** stiamo mettendo in scena "Bugsy Malone" **5** (*switch on: light etc*) accendere; (*kettle, meal*) mettere su; **to put on the brakes** frenare; **shall I put the heating on?** accendo il riscaldamento? **6** (*inform, indicate*): **to put sb on to sb/sth** indicare qn/qc a qn; **she put us on to you** è lei che ci ha detto di rivolgerci a te; **who put the police on**

to him? chi lo ha segnalato alla polizia?; **what put you on to it?** cosa te lo ha fatto capire?

▸ **put out** VT + ADV **1** (*place outside*) mettere fuori; **to put clothes out to dry** stendere la biancheria ad asciugare; **to be put out** (*asked to leave*) essere buttato(-a) fuori; **she couldn't put him out of her head** non riusciva a non pensare a lui **2** (*stretch out: arm, foot, leg*) allungare; (: *one's hand*) porgere; (: *tongue*) tirare fuori; (*push out: leaves etc*) spuntare; **to put one's head out of the window** metter fuori *or* sporgere la testa dalla finestra; **he smiled and put out his hand** ha sorriso tendendo la mano **3** (*lay out in order*) disporre **4** (*circulate: propaganda*) fare; (: *news*) annunciare; (: *rumour*) mettere in giro; (*bring out: new book*) pubblicare; (: *regulation*) emettere **5** (*extinguish: fire, cigarette, light*) spegnere; **it took them five hours to put out the fire** ci sono volute cinque ore per spegnere l'incendio **6** (*discontent, vex*) contrariare, seccare; **to be put out** essere seccato(-a); **he's a bit put out that nobody came** è un po' seccato che non sia venuto nessuno; **to be put out by sth/sb** essere contrariato(-a) da qn/qc **7** (*inconvenience*): **to put o.s. out** (**for sb**) scomodarsi *or* disturbarsi per qn **8** (*dislocate: shoulder, knee*) lussarsi; (: *back*) farsi uno strappo a **9** (*subcontract*) subappaltare ♦ VI + ADV (*Naut*): **to put out to sea** prendere il largo; **to put out from Plymouth** partire da Plymouth

▸ **put over** VT + ADV = **put across**

▸ **put through** VT + ADV **1** (*complete: business, deal*) concludere; (*have accepted: reform, bill*) far approvare, far passare **2** (*Telec: connect: caller*) mettere in comunicazione; (*call*) passare; **can you put me through to the manager?** mi passa il direttore, per favore?; **I'm putting you through** le passo la comunicazione

▸ **put together** VT + ADV **1** mettere insieme, riunire **2** (*assemble: furniture*) montare; (: *model*) fare; (: *essay*) comporre; (: *meal*) improvvisare; (: *evidence*) raccogliere; (: *team*) mettere insieme, formare

▸ **put up** VT + ADV **1** (*raise, lift up: hand*) alzare; (: *umbrella*) aprire; (: *collar*) rialzare; (*hoist: flag, sail*) issare; **put 'em up!** (*fam: hands: in surrender*) arrenditi!; (: *in robbery*) mani in alto!; (*fists: to fight*) forza, difenditi!; **if you have any questions, put up your hand** se avete domande alzate la mano **2** (*fasten up*): **to put up (on)** attaccare (su), appendere (su); (*notice*) affiggere (su) **3** (*erect: building, barrier, fence*) costruire, erigere; (: *tent*) montare; **we put up our tent in a field** abbiamo montato la tenda in un prato **4** (*send up: space probe, missile*) lanciare, mettere in orbita **5** (*increase*) aumentare; **they've put up the price** hanno aumentato il prezzo **6** = **put forward 1 7** (*offer*): **to put sth up for sale** mettere in vendita qc; **they're going to put their house up for sale** metteranno in vendita la casa; **they put up a**

struggle hanno opposto resistenza **8** (*give accommodation to*) ospitare; **a friend will put me up for the night** un amico mi ospita per la notte **9** (*provide: money, funds*) fornire; (: *reward*) offrire **10** (*incite*): **to put sb up to doing sth** istigare qn a fare qc ♦ VI + ADV **1 to put up (at)** (*at hotel*) alloggiare (in) (*for the night*) pernottare (in) **2** (*offer o.s.*): **to put up (for)** presentarsi come candidato(-a) (per)

▸ **put upon** VI + PREP: **to be put upon** (*imposed on*) farsi mettere sotto i piedi

▸ **put up with** VI + ADV + PREP sopportare; **I'm not going to put up with it any longer** non ho intenzione di sopportarlo oltre

pu·trid [ˈpjuːtrɪd] ADJ putrido(-a); **to turn putrid** putrefarsi

putt [pʌt] N (*Golf*) putting *m* ♦ VT (*ball*) colpire leggermente

put·ter[1] [ˈpʌtəʳ] N (*Golf*) putter *m inv*

put·ter[2] [ˈpʌtəʳ] VI (*USA*) = **potter**[2]

putt·ing [ˈpʌtɪŋ] N (*game*) un tipo di golf; **putting green** green *m inv* di pratica

put·ty [ˈpʌtɪ] N (*for windows*) stucco, mastice *m* da vetrai; **to be putty in sb's hands** (*fig*) essere come la creta nelle mani di qn

put-up [ˈpʊtˌʌp] ADJ: **put-up job** (*fam*) montatura

puz·zle [ˈpʌzl] N **1** (*game*) rompicapo; (*word game*) rebus *m inv*; (*crossword*) parole *fpl* incrociate, cruciverba *m inv*; (*riddle*) indovinello; (*also: jigsaw puzzle*) puzzle *m inv* **2** (*mystery*) enigma *m*, mistero; **it's a puzzle to me how it happened** non so come sia successo, per me resta un enigma ♦ VT lasciar perplesso(-a)

▸ **puzzle out** VT + ADV (*problem*) risolvere; (*mystery, person, attitude*) capire; (*writing, instructions*) decifrare; (*answer, solution*) trovare; **I'm trying to puzzle out why** sto cercando di scoprire il perché

▸ **puzzle over, puzzle about** VT + ADV (*sb's actions*) cercare di capire; (*mystery, problem*) cercare di risolvere

puz·zled [ˈpʌzld] ADJ perplesso(-a); **to be puzzled about sth** domandarsi il perché di qc; **you look puzzled!** hai un'aria perplessa!

puz·zling [ˈpʌzlɪŋ] ADJ (*question*) poco chiaro(-a); (*attitude, set of instructions*) incomprensibile

PVC [ˌpiːviːˈsiː] N ABBR (= *polyvinyl chloride*) PVC

pyg·my [ˈpɪgmɪ] N pigmeo(-a)

py·ja·mas, (*USA*) **pa·jam·as** [pəˈdʒɑːməz] NPL pigiama *msg*; **a pair of pyjamas** un pigiama; **my pyjamas** il mio pigiama

py·lon [ˈpaɪlən] N pilone *m*

pyra·mid [ˈpɪrəmɪd] N piramide *f*

Pyr·enean [pɪrəˈniːən] ADJ pirenaico(-a), dei Pirenei

Pyr·enees [pɪrəˈniːz] NPL: **the Pyrenees** i Pirenei

py·thon [ˈpaɪθən] N pitone *m*

Qq

Q, q [kjuː] N (*letter*) Q, q *f inv*, *m inv*; **Q for Queen** ≈ Q come Quarto

Qa·tar [kæˈtɑːʳ] N il Qatar *m*

QC [ˌkjuːˈsiː] N ABBR (*Brit*: = *Queen's Counsel*) avvocato della Corona, nominato dietro raccomandazione del capo della magistratura

QED [ˌkjuːiːˈdiː] ABBR (= *quod erat demonstrandum*) qed

q.t. [kjuːˈtiː] N ABBR (*fam*: = *quiet*): **on the q.t.** di nascosto

qty ABBR = **quantity**

quack[1] [kwæk] N (*of duck*) qua qua *m inv* ♦ VI fare qua qua

quack[2] [kwæk] N (*pej*: *bogus doctor*) ciarlatano(-a); (*hum*: *doctor*) dottore(-essa)

quad [kwɒd] N ABBR = **quadrangle 2, quadruplet**

quad·ran·gle [ˈkwɒdˌræŋgl] N **1** (*Math*) quadrangolo, quadrilatero **2** (*courtyard*) cortile *m* (*di collegio, scuola*)

quad·ru·ped [ˈkwɒdrʊˌped] N quadrupede *m*

quad·ru·ple [ˈkwɒdrʊpl] ADJ quadruplo(-a), quadruplice ♦ VT quadruplicare ♦ VI quadruplicarsi; **the number has quadrupled** il numero è quadruplicato ♦ N quadruplo

quad·ru·plet [kwɒˈdruːplɪt] N uno(-a) di quattro gemelli

quag·mire [ˈkwægˌmaɪəʳ] N pantano; (*fig*) caos *m inv*

quail[1] [kweɪl] N (*bird*) quaglia

quail[2] [kweɪl] VI (*flinch*): **to quail at** *or* **before** perdersi d'animo davanti a

quaint [kweɪnt] ADJ (*comp* -**er**, *superl* -**est**) (*odd*) strano(-a), bizzarro(-a); (*picturesque*) pittoresco(-a); (*old-fashioned*) antiquato(-a) e pittoresco(-a)

quake [kweɪk] VI: **to quake (with)** tremare (di) ♦ N (*earthquake*) terremoto

Quak·er [ˈkweɪkəʳ] N quacchero(-a)

quali·fi·ca·tion [ˌkwɒlɪfɪˈkeɪʃən] N **1 qualifications** NPL (*gen*) qualifiche *fpl*, requisiti *mpl*; (*paper qualifications*) titoli *mpl* di studio; **what are your qualifications?** quali sono le sue qualifiche?; (*paper qualifications*) quali sono i suoi titoli di studio?; **what qualifications do they require?** che qualifiche richiedono?; **I've got a teaching qualification** sono abilitato *or* ho l'abilitazione all'insegnamento; **he left school without any qualifications** ha lasciato la scuola senza alcun titolo di studio; **reliability is a necessary qualification** l'affidabilità è un requisito necessario; **vocational qualifications** qualifiche professionali **2** (*reservation*) riserva, restrizione *f*; **without qualification(s)** senza condizioni *or* riserve; **I agree, with one qualification** sono d'accordo, ma con una riserva

quali·fied [ˈkwɒlɪfaɪd] ADJ **1** (*engineer, doctor, teacher*) abilitato(-a); (*nurse*) diplomato(-a); **qualified for/to do** qualificato(-a) per/per fare; **to be well qualified** avere tutti i requisiti necessari; **he's not qualified for the job** non ha i requisiti necessari per questo lavoro **2** (*support*) condizionato(-a); (*acceptance*) con riserva; **it was a qualified success** è stato un successo parziale; **the film has received qualified praise** il film non è stato accolto proprio favorevolmente

quali·fy [ˈkwɒlɪfaɪ] VT **1** (*make competent*) qualificare **2** (*modify*) modificare; (*support, approval*) porre delle condizioni a **3** (*Gram*) qualificare ♦ VI (*professionally*) abilitarsi, essere abilitato(-a); (*in competition*) qualificarsi; (*be eligible*) avere i requisiti necessari; **to qualify as an engineer** diventare un perito tecnico; (*with degree*) laurearsi in ingegneria; **to qualify for a job** avere i requisiti necessari per un lavoro; **she qualified as a teacher last year** ha ottenuto l'abilitazione all'insegnamento un anno scorso; **he hardly qualifies as a major dramatist** non si può certamente definirlo un grande drammaturgo; **our team didn't qualify for the finals** la nostra squadra non si è qualificata per le finali; **they qualify for benefit** hanno diritto al sussidio

quali·fy·ing [ˈkwɒlɪfaɪɪŋ] ADJ (*Gram*) qualificativo(-a); (*exam*) di ammissione; (*round*) eliminatorio(-a)

quali·ta·tive [ˈkwɒlɪtətɪv] ADJ qualitativo(-a)

qual·ity [ˈkwɒlɪtɪ] N qualità *f inv*; **of good quality** di buona qualità; **of poor quality** scadente ♦ ADJ di qualità; **good-quality paper** carta di buona qualità

quality control N controllo (di) qualità

qualm [kwɑːm] N (*often pl*: *fear*) apprensione *f*; (: *scruple*) scrupolo, esitazione *f*; **to have qualms about sth** avere degli scrupoli per qc; **to have no qualms about sth** non avere degli scrupoli su qc

quan·da·ry [ˈkwɒndərɪ] N: **in a quandary** in un dilemma; **to be in a quandary (about sth)** essere molto incerto(-a) (su qc)

quango [ˈkwæŋgəʊ] N ABBR (*Brit*: = *quasi-autonomous nongovernmental organization*) organizzazione autonoma di nomina governativa, dotata di fondi, che agisce in vari settori (*salute, scuola ecc*)

quan·ti·fi·able [ˈkwɒntɪfaɪəbl] ADJ quantificabile

quan·ti·fy [ˈkwɒntɪfaɪ] VT quantificare

quan·ti·ta·tive [ˈkwɒntɪtətɪv] ADJ quantitativo(-a)

quan·tity [ˈkwɒntɪtɪ] N quantità *f inv*; (*Comm*) quantità, quantitativo; **in quantity** in grande quantità

quantity surveyor N geometra *m* (*che valuta il costo del materiale e della manodopera necessari per una costruzione*)

quantum leap N (*fig*) enorme cambiamento

quar·an·tine [ˈkwɒrəntiːn] N quarantena; **in quarantine** in quarantena ♦ VT mettere in quarantena

quark [kwɑːk] N (*Phys*) quark *m inv*

quar·rel [ˈkwɒrəl] N (*argument*) litigio, lite *f*; **to have a quarrel (with sb)** litigare (con qn); **we had a quarrel** abbiamo litigato; **to pick a quarrel (with sb)** attaccar briga (con qn); **I've no quarrel with him** non ho niente contro di lui; **after their last quarrel** dopo la loro ultima lite ♦ VI **to quarrel (with sb about** *or* **over sth)** litigare (con qn per qc); **they quarrelled about** *or* **over money** hanno litigato per i soldi; **I can't quarrel with that** non ho niente da ridire su questo

quar·rel·some [ˈkwɒrəlsəm] ADJ litigioso(-a)

quar·ry[1] [ˈkwɒrɪ] N (*Hunting, also fig*) preda

quar·ry[2] [ˈkwɒrɪ] N (*mine*) cava ♦ VT cavare

quart [kwɔːt] N quarto di gallone (*Brit* = *1,136 litri*; *USA* = *0,964 litri*); **a quart** due pinte

quar·ter [ˈkwɔːtəʳ] N **1** (*fourth part*) quarto; (*of year*) trimestre *m*; **three quarters** tre quarti; **a quarter (of a pound) of tea** ≈ un etto di tè; **a quarter of a century** un quarto di secolo; **to divide sth into quarters** dividere qc in quattro (parti); **to pay by the quarter** pagare trimestralmente; **we expect fewer orders in the next quarter** ci aspettiamo meno ordini nel prossimo trimestre **2** (*USA, Canada: 25 cents*) quarto di dollaro, 25 centesimi **3** (*time*): **a quarter of an hour** un quarto d'ora; **an hour and a quarter** un'ora e un quarto; **it's a quarter to** *or* (*USA*) **of 3** sono le 3 meno un quarto, manca un quarto alle 3; **it's a quarter past** *or* (*USA*) **after 3** sono le 3 e un quarto **4** (*district*) quartiere *m* **5** (*direction*): **from all quarters** da tutte le parti *or* direzioni; **at close quarters** a distanza ravvicinata; **you won't get any help from that quarter** non otterrai nessun aiuto da quella parte **6 quarters** NPL (*accommodation*) alloggio; (*Mil*) quartiere *m*; (*temporary*) alloggiamento **7 to give sb no quarter** essere implacabile verso qn ♦ VT **1** (*divide into four*) dividere in quattro (parti) **2** (*Mil*) alloggiare

quarter·back [ˈkwɔːtəbæk] N (*American Football*) quarterback *m inv*

quarter-deck [ˈkwɔːtədek] N (*Naut*) cassero

quarter-final [ˈkwɔːtəfaɪnl] N quarti *mpl* di finale

quar·ter·ly [ˈkwɔːtəlɪ] ADJ trimestrale ♦ N periodico trimestrale ♦ ADV trimestralmente

quarter·master [ˈkwɔːtəmɑːstəʳ] N (*Mil*) furiere *m*; (*Naut*) timoniere *m*

quar·tet, quar·tette [kwɔːˈtɛt] N quartetto; **string quartet** quartetto di archi

quar·to [ˈkwɔːtəʊ] ADJ in quarto

quartz [kwɔːts] N quarzo ♦ ADJ di quarzo; (*clock, watch*) al quarzo

quash [kwɒʃ] VT 1 (*reject*) respingere; (*Law: sentence, conviction*) revocare, annullare 2 (*destroy: enemies, rebellion*) stroncare; (: *emotion*) reprimere

quasi- [ˈkwɑːzɪ] PREF semi-; (*pej*) pseudo-; **quasi-official** adj semiufficiale; **quasi-religious** adj quasi religioso(-a); **quasi-revolutionary** adj, n pseudorivoluzionario(-a)

qua·ver [ˈkweɪvəʳ] N (*when speaking*) tremolio; (*Brit: Mus: note*) croma ♦ VI (*voice*) tremare, tremolare

quay [kiː] N molo, banchina

Que. ABBR (*Canada*) = Quebec

quea·sy [ˈkwiːzɪ] ADJ (*comp* **-ier**, *superl* **-iest**) (*stomach*) nauseato(-a); **to feel queasy** avere la nausea

Que·bec [kwɪˈbɛk] N il Quebec m

queen [kwiːn] N regina; (*Cards, Chess*) regina; **Queen Elizabeth** la regina Elisabetta; **the queen of hearts** la regina di cuori

queen mother N regina madre

queer [kwɪəʳ] ADJ (*comp* **-er**, *superl* **-est**) 1 (*odd*) strano(-a), curioso(-a), singolare; **there's something queer going on here** qui c'è qualcosa che non va, qui sta succedendo qc di strano 2 (*ill*) strano(-a), non giusto(-a); **to feel queer** sentirsi poco bene 3 (*fam, offensive: orientation*) omosessuale 4 (*suspicious*) dubbio(-a), sospetto(-a)

quell [kwɛl] VT (*passion*) reprimere; (*fear*) dominare; (*rebellion*) soffocare; (*attempt*) sventare

quench [kwɛntʃ] VT (*thirst*) togliere, levare; (*flames*) spegnere; **to quench one's thirst** dissetarsi

queru·lous [ˈkwerʊləs] ADJ querulo(-a)

que·ry [ˈkwɪərɪ] N (*question*) domanda; (*question mark*) punto interrogativo; (*fig: doubt*) interrogativo, dubbio ♦ VT 1 (*ask*): **to query sb about sth** rivolgere delle domande a qn riguardo a qc 2 (*doubt*) mettere in dubbio; (*disagree with, dispute*) sollevare (dei) dubbi su, contestare; **no one queried my decision** nessuno ha messo in dubbio la mia decisione; **they queried the bill** hanno chiesto spiegazioni sul conto

quest [kwɛst] N ricerca; **in quest of** alla ricerca di, in cerca di; **my quest for a better bank continues** la mia ricerca di una banca migliore continua; **the quest to boost sales** il tentativo di aumentare le vendite

ques·tion [ˈkwɛstʃən] N 1 (*enquiry*) domanda; **to ask sb a question, put a question to sb** fare una domanda a qn; **can I ask a question?** posso fare una domanda? 2 (*matter, issue*) questione *f*, argomento; **it is an open question whether ...** resta da vedere se..., è una questione aperta se...; **the question is ...** il problema è...; **that's a difficult question** è una questione difficile; **the person/night in question** la persona/la notte in questione; **it is a question of whether ...** si tratta di sapere se...; **it's a question of doing ...** si tratta di fare...; **that is not the question** non è questo il problema; **there is no question of outside help** non c'è nessuna possibilità di aiuto esterno; **there can be no question of your resigning** che lei dia le dimissioni non è nemmeno da prendersi in considerazione; **it's out of the question** è fuori discussione; **there's some question of closing the shop** c'è chi suggerisce di chiudere il negozio 3 (*doubt*): **beyond** or **past question** fuori discussione or questione; **in question** in discussione, in dubbio; **there is no question about it** su questo non c'è (assolutamente) nessun dubbio; **to bring** or **call sth into question** mettere in dubbio qc ♦ VT 1 (*interrogate: person*) interrogare; **he was questioned by the police** è stato interrogato dalla polizia 2 (*doubt*) mettere in dubbio, dubitare di; **I question whether it is worthwhile** mi domando se ne vale or valga la pena; **nobody questions his loyalty** nessuno mette in dubbio la sua lealtà

ques·tion·able [ˈkwɛstʃənəbl] ADJ discutibile

ques·tion·er [ˈkwɛstʃənəʳ] N interrogante *m/f*

ques·tion·ing [ˈkwɛstʃənɪŋ] ADJ (*mind*) inquisitore(-trice), indagatore(-trice); (*expression*) interrogativo(-a) ♦ N interrogatorio

question mark N punto interrogativo

ques·tion·naire [ˌkwɛstʃəˈnɛəʳ] N questionario

queue [kjuː] N coda, fila; **to form a queue** mettersi in fila or in coda; **to stand in a queue** essere in fila or in coda, fare la fila or la coda; **to jump the queue** passare davanti agli altri (*in coda*) ♦ VI (*also:* **queue up**) fare la fila, fare la coda; **we had to queue for tickets** abbiamo dovuto fare la fila per i biglietti

quib·ble [ˈkwɪbl] N cavillo, sottigliezza ♦ VI cavillare, sottilizzare

quiche [kiːʃ] N quiche *f inv*

quick [kwɪk] ADJ (*comp* **-er**, *superl* **-est**) (*fast: in motion*) veloce, rapido(-a); (: *in time*) svelto(-a), veloce; (*agile: reflexes*) pronto(-a); (: *in mind*) svelto(-a); **a quick temper** un temperamento irascibile; **a quick lunch** un pranzo veloce; **it's quicker by train** è più veloce in treno; **the quickest method** il metodo più rapido; **a quick reply** una risposta pronta; **be quick about it!** fa' presto!, sbrigati!; **she's a quick learner** impara presto; **she was quick to see that ...** ha visto subito che...; **to be quick to act** agire prontamente; **to be quick to take offence** essere permaloso(-a), offendersi subito ♦ ADV in fretta, rapidamente; **come quick!** vieni subito!; **as quick as a flash** or **as lightning** veloce come un fulmine ♦ N: **to cut sb to the quick** pungere qn sul vivo

quick·en [ˈkwɪkən] VT affrettare, accelerare; (*fig: feelings*) stimolare; **to quicken one's pace** affrettare or allungare il passo ♦ VI: **the pace quickened** il ritmo divenne più veloce

quick fix N soluzione *f* tampone, *inv*

quick·lime [ˈkwɪklaɪm] N calce *f* viva

quick·ly [ˈkwɪklɪ] ADV velocemente, rapidamente; **"certainly not" she said quickly** "certo che no" disse velocemente; **we must act quickly** dobbiamo agire tempestivamente; **as quickly as possible** più velocemente possibile

quick·ness [ˈkwɪknɪs] N velocità, rapidità; (*of mind, intellect*) prontezza; (*of eye*) acutezza

quick·sand [ˈkwɪksænd] N sabbie *fpl* mobili

quick·step [ˈkwɪkstɛp] N (*dance*) quick step *m inv*

quick-tempered [ˌkwɪkˈtɛmpəd] ADJ che si arrabbia facilmente

quick-witted [ˌkwɪkˈwɪtɪd] ADJ sveglio(-a)

quid [kwɪd] N (*Brit fam: pl inv*) sterlina; **ten quid** dieci sterline

quid pro quo [ˌkwɪdprəʊˈkwəʊ] N (*reciprocal exchange*) contraccambio; **his promotion was the quid pro quo for his support** venne promosso in cambio del suo appoggio

qui·et [ˈkwaɪət] ADJ (*comp* **-er**, *superl* **-est**) 1 (*person: silent*) silenzioso(-a), tranquillo(-a); (: *reserved*) quieto(-a), taciturno(-a); (: *calm*) tranquillo(-a), calmo(-a); **quiet!** silenzio!; **be quiet!** or **keep quiet!** silenzio!, sta' zitto!; (*when moving about*) non far rumore!, fa' piano!; **you're very quiet today** sei molto silenzioso oggi; **to keep sb quiet** tener tranquillo(-a) qn; **they paid him £1000 to keep him quiet** gli hanno dato 1000 sterline perché stesse zitto 2 (*not noisy: engine*) silenzioso(-a); (: *music, voice, laugh*) sommesso(-a); (*sound*) basso(-a), leggero(-a); **the engine's very quiet** il motore è molto silenzioso 3 (*not busy: day*) calmo(-a), tranquillo(-a); (: *place*) tranquillo(-a); **a quiet little town** una cittadina tranquilla; **a quiet weekend** un fine settimana; **the shops/trains are always quiet on a Monday** i negozi/treni non sono mai affollati di lunedì; **business is quiet at this time of year** questa è la stagione morta 4 (*discreet: manner*) dolce, garbato(-a); (: *colours*) tenue, smorzato(-a); (: *humour*) garbato(-a); (: *private, intimate*) intimo(-a); **I'll have a quiet word with him** gli dirò due parole in privato; **to lead a quiet life** fare una vita tranquilla; **he managed to keep the whole thing quiet** è riuscito a tener segreta tutta la faccenda; **we had a quiet wedding** abbiamo avuto un matrimonio semplice ♦ N (*silence*) silenzio; (*calm*) pace *f*, calma, tranquillità; **on the quiet** (*fam: act*) di nascosto; (: *tell*) in confidenza ♦ VT (*USA*) = **quieten**

qui·et·en [ˈkwaɪətən] VT (*also:* **quieten down**) calmare, placare; **to quieten sb down** calmare qn ♦ VI (*also:* **quieten down**) calmarsi

qui·et·ly [ˈkwaɪətlɪ] ADV (*softly, silently*) silenziosamente, senza far rumore; (*not loudly: speak, sing*) in modo sommesso; (*calmly*) tranquillamente, con calma; **to be quietly dressed** essere vestito(-a) in modo sobrio; **to be quietly situated** (*house*) trovarsi in un posto tranquillo; **let's get married**

quietly sposiamoci con una cerimonia semplice; **he slipped off quietly to avoid being noticed** se n'è andato alla chetichella per non essere notato; **he quietly opened the door** ha aperto la porta senza far rumore; **"she's dead," he said quietly** "è morta," disse piano; **he lives quietly in the country** conduce una vita tranquilla in campagna

qui·et·ness [ˈkwaɪətnɪs] N (*silence*) silenzio; (*peacefulness*) tranquillità, calma, quiete *f*; (*softness: of voice, music*) dolcezza

quill [kwɪl] N (*feather*) penna; (*pen*) penna d'oca; (*of porcupine*) aculeo

quilt [kwɪlt] N (*traditional*) trapunta; (*continental quilt*) piumino ♦ VT trapuntare

quin [kwɪn] N ABBR = **quintuplet**

quince [kwɪns] N (*fruit*) (mela) cotogna; (*tree*) cotogno

qui·nine [kwɪˈniːn] N chinino

quin·tet, quin·tette [kwɪnˈtet] N quintetto

quin·tu·plet [kwɪnˈtjuːplɪt] N uno(-a) di cinque gemelli

quip [kwɪp] N battuta di spirito

quire [ˈkwaɪəʳ] N ventesima parte di una risma; (*Bookbinding*) segnatura di 16 pagine

quirk [kwɜːk] N (*oddity*) stranezza, bizzarria; **by some quirk of fate** per un capriccio della sorte; **one of his quirks** una delle sue stranezze

quirky [ˈkwɜːkɪ] ADJ (*comp* **-ier**, *superl* **-iest**) stravagante, capriccioso(-a)

quit [kwɪt] (*pt, pp* quit *or* quitted) VT 1 (*cease: work*) lasciare, piantare; **to quit doing sth** smettere di fare qc; **I've quit smoking** ho smesso di fumare; **I quit my job last week** ho lasciato il lavoro la settimana scorsa; **quit stalling!** (*USA fam*) non tirarla per le lunghe! 2 (*leave: place*) lasciare; **notice to quit** (*Brit*) preavviso (*dato all'inquilino*); **I've been given notice to quit** mi hanno dato lo sfratto ♦ VI (*resign*) dare le dimissioni, dimettersi; (*give up: in game*) abbandonare, mollare; (*accept defeat*) darsi per vinto(-a) ♦ ADJ: **quit of** sbarazzato(-a) di, liberato(-a) di

quite [kwaɪt] ADV 1 (*rather*) abbastanza, piuttosto; **I quite like that idea** è un'idea che non mi dispiace; **quite a few of them** non pochi di loro; **quite a few people** un bel po' di gente; **he's quite a good writer** è uno scrittore abbastanza bravo; **it's quite warm today** fa piuttosto caldo oggi; **it's quite a long way** è piuttosto lontano; **quite a lot un bel po';** **it costs quite a lot to go abroad** costa un bel po' andare all'estero; **quite a lot of money** un bel po' di denaro; **there** were **quite a few people there** c'era un bel po' di gente; **I quite liked the film, but...** il film mi è piaciuto abbastanza, ma... 2 (*completely*) proprio, perfettamente; (*entirely*) completamente, del tutto; **quite new** proprio nuovo(-a); **quite (so)!** appunto!, proprio (così)!, precisamente!; **that's quite enough** è più che abbastanza, basta così; **that's not quite right** non è proprio esatto; **I can quite believe that ...** non faccio fatica a credere che...; **not quite as many as last time** non proprio così tanti come l'ultima volta; **I quite understand** capisco perfettamente; **I'm not quite sure** non sono del tutto sicuro; **it's quite empty** è completamente vuoto

Qui·to [ˈkiːtəʊ] N Quito *f*

quits [kwɪts] ADV: **to be quits (with sb)** essere pari (con qn); **let's call it quits** adesso siamo pari

quiv·er¹ [ˈkwɪvəʳ] N (*for arrows*) faretra, turcasso

quiv·er² [ˈkwɪvəʳ] VI (*person, voice, lips*): **to quiver (with)** tremare (per *or* da)

quiz [kwɪz] N (*game*) quiz *m inv* ♦ VT (*old*): **to quiz sb about** interrogare qn su

quiz·zi·cal [ˈkwɪzɪkəl] ADJ (*glance*) interrogativo(-a) (e beffardo(-a))

quoit [kɔɪt] N anello (*per il gioco degli anelli*); **to play quoits** giocare agli anelli

quor·um [ˈkwɔːrəm] N quorum *m inv*

quo·ta [ˈkwəʊtə] N quota

quo·ta·tion [kwəʊˈteɪʃən] N 1 (*words*) citazione *f*; **a quotation from Shakespeare** una citazione da Shakespeare 2 (*estimate*) preventivo; (*of shares*) quotazione *f*; **I asked the firm to give me a quotation** ho chiesto alla ditta di farmi un preventivo

quotation marks NPL (*Typ*) virgolette *fpl*; **in quotation marks** tra virgolette

quote [kwəʊt] VT 1 (*words, author*) citare; **can you quote me an example?** puoi citarmi *or* farmi un esempio? 2 (*Comm: sum, figure, price*) indicare, fissare; (*shares*) quotare; **to quote for a job** dare un preventivo per un lavoro; **the figure quoted for the repairs** il preventivo per le riparazioni ♦ VI: **to quote from** citare; **and I quote** (*from text*) cito testualmente; (*sb's words*) riferisco *or* ripeto testualmente; **quote...unquote** (*in dictation*) aprire le virgolette... chiudere le virgolette; (*in lecture, report*) cito... fine della citazione ♦ N 1 = **quotation** 2 **quotes** NPL (*inverted commas*) virgolette *fpl*; **in quotes** tra virgolette

quo·tient [ˈkwəʊʃənt] N quoziente *m*

Rr

R, r [ɑːˈ] N (*letter*) R, r *f inv*, *m inv*; **R for Robert,** (*USA*) **R for Roger** ≈ R come Roma; **the three Rs** leggere, scrivere e far di conto

RA [ˌɑːˈeɪ] N ABBR (*Brit:* = Royal Academy, Royal Academician) ♦ ABBR = **rear admiral**

Ra·bat [rɔˈbɑːt] N Rabat *f*

rab·bi [ˈræbaɪ] N rabbino

rab·bit [ˈræbɪt] N coniglio(-a)

rabbit hole N tana di coniglio

rabbit hutch N conigliera

rab·ble [ˈræbl] N confusione *f* di gente; **the rabble** (*pej*) il popolino, la plebaglia

rab·id [ˈræbɪd] ADJ (*dog*) idrofobo(-a), rabbioso(-a); (*fig: furious*) arrabbiato(-a); (: *fanatical*) fanatico(-a)

ra·bies [ˈreɪbiz] N rabbia, idrofobia; **a dog with rabies** un cane con la rabbia

rac·coon [rɔˈkuːn] N procione *m*, orsetto lavatore

race¹ [reɪs] N (*competition, rush*) corsa; **the 100 metres race** la corsa sui 100 metri, i 100 metri (plani); **a race against time** una corsa contro il tempo; **a cycle race** una gara ciclistica; **the arms race** la corsa agli armamenti ♦ VT 1 (*horse*) far gareggiare, far correre 2 (*person*) correre contro, gareggiare contro; **I'll race you!** facciamo a gara!; **I'll race you around the block** ti sfido a una corsa intorno all'isolato 3 (*engine*) imballare ♦ VI 1 **to race (against sb)** correre (contro qn) 2 (*rush*) correre; **to race in/out** *etc* precipitarsi dentro/fuori *etc*; **he raced across the road** ha attraversato la strada di corsa; **we raced to catch the bus** abbiamo corso per prendere l'autobus 3 (*pulse*) battere precipitosamente; (*engine*) imballarsi

race² [reɪs] N razza; **students of all races** studenti di tutte le razze; **the human race** l'umanità, il genere umano ♦ ADJ (*hatred, riot*) razziale

race car N (*USA*) = **racing car**

race car driver N (*USA*) = **racing driver**

race·course [ˈreɪskɔːs] N ippodromo

race·horse [ˈreɪshɔːs] N cavallo da corsa

race relations NPL rapporti *mpl* interrazziali

race·track [ˈreɪstræk] N (*for horses, also Aut*) pista

ra·cial [ˈreɪʃəl] ADJ (*tension*) razziale; (*harmony, equality*) fra le razze

racial discrimination N discriminazione *f* razziale

ra·cial·ism [ˈreɪʃəlɪzəm] N (*Brit: old*) razzismo

ra·cial·ist [ˈreɪʃəlɪst] ADJ, N razzista *m/f*

rac·ing [ˈreɪsɪŋ] N corsa; (*horse-racing*) corse *fpl* ♦ ADJ (*cycle*) da corsa

racing car N (*Brit*) macchina da corsa

racing driver N (*Brit*) corridore *m* automobilista

rac·ism [ˈreɪsɪzəm] N razzismo

rac·ist [ˈreɪsɪst] ADJ, N razzista *m/f*

rack¹ [ræk] N 1 (*storage framework*) rastrelliera; (*for luggage*) rete *f* portabagagli, *inv*; (*for hats, coats*) appendiabiti *m inv*; (*in shops*) scaffale *m*; **magazine rack** portariviste *m inv*; **shoe rack** scarpiera 2 (*for torture*) cavalletto ♦ VT (*subj: pain, cough*) torturare, tormentare; **racked by remorse** roso(-a) dal rimorso; **to rack one's brains** scervellarsi

▸ **rack up** VT + ADV accumulare

rack² [ræk] N: **to go to rack and ruin** (*building*) andare in rovina; (*business*) andare in malora *or* a catafascio; (*country*) andare a catafascio; (*person*) lasciarsi andare completamente

rack·et¹ [ˈrækɪt] N (*for tennis*) racchetta

rack·et² [ˈrækɪt] N 1 (*din*) baccano, fracasso; **they were making a terrible racket** stavano facendo un terribile baccano 2 (*organised fraud*) traffico, racket *m inv*; (*swindle*) imbroglio, truffa; **he's on to quite a racket** (*fam*) gli sta andando bene con il suo giochetto

rack·et·eer [ˌrækɪˈtɪə] N (*esp USA*) trafficante *m/f*

ra·coon [rɔˈkuːn] N = **raccoon**

rac·quet [ˈrækɪt] N = **racket¹**

racy [ˈreɪsɪ] ADJ (*comp* **-ier,** *superl* **-iest**) (*style*) spigliato(-a), brioso(-a); (*humour, talk*) un po' spinto(-a)

ra·dar [ˈreɪdɑː] N radar *m inv* ♦ ADJ (*station, screen*) radar *inv*

radar trap N (*Aut*) multanova *m*

ra·dial [ˈreɪdɪəl] ADJ (*also:* **radial-ply**: *tyre or* tire) radiale

ra·di·ance [ˈreɪdɪəns] N (*brilliance*) splendore *m*, fulgore *m*; (*fig*) radiosità

ra·di·ant [ˈreɪdɪənt] ADJ (*Phys: heat*) radiante; (*light*) sfolgorante; (*fig*): **radiant (with)** raggiante (di); **the bride was radiant** la sposa era raggiante

ra·di·ate [ˈreɪdɪeɪt] VT (*heat*) irraggiare, irradiare; (*fig: happiness*) irraggiare; **she radiates happiness** sprizza felicità da tutti i pori ♦ VI: **to radiate from** irraggiarsi da, irradiarsi da; **the streets that radiate from the centre** le strade che si irradiano dal centro

ra·dia·tion [ˌreɪdɪˈeɪʃən] N (*nuclear*) radiazione *f*; (*of heat*) irradiamento

radiation sickness N malattia da radiazioni

ra·dia·tor [ˈreɪdɪeɪtə] N radiatore *m*

radiator cap N (*Aut*) tappo del radiatore

radiator grill N (*Aut*) mascherina, calandra

radi·cal [ˈrædɪkəl] ADJ radicale ♦ N 1 (*person*) radicale *m/f* 2 (*Math, Chem*) radicale *m*

ra·dii [ˈreɪdɪaɪ] NPL *of* **radius**

ra·dio [ˈreɪdɪəʊ] N (*Telec*) radio *f*; (*radio set*) radio *f inv*, apparecchio *m* radio, *inv*; **by radio** per radio; **on the radio** alla radio ♦ VI: **to radio to sb** comunicare via radio con qn ♦ VT (*information*) trasmettere per radio; (*one's position*) comunicare via radio; (*person*) chiamare via radio ♦ ADJ (*programme*) radiofonico(-a); (*frequency*) radio *inv*

radio– [ˈreɪdɪəʊ] PREF radio

radio·ac·tive [ˌreɪdɪəʊˈæktɪv] ADJ radioattivo(-a)

radio·ac·tiv·ity [ˌreɪdɪəʊækˈtɪvɪtɪ] N radioattività

radio announcer N annunciatore(-trice) radiofonico(-a)

radio-controlled [ˌreɪdɪəʊkənˈtrəʊld] ADJ radiocomandato(-a), radioguidato(-a)

ra·di·og·ra·pher [ˌreɪdɪˈɒɡrəfə] N radiologo(-a) (*tecnico*)

ra·di·og·ra·phy [ˌreɪdɪˈɒɡrəfɪ] N radiografia

ra·di·olo·gist [ˌreɪdɪˈɒlədʒɪst] N radiologo(-a) (*medico*)

ra·di·ol·ogy [ˌreɪdɪˈɒlədʒɪ] N radiologia

radio station N stazione *f* radio, *inv*

radio·tele·phone [ˌreɪdɪəʊˈtelɪfəʊn] N radiotelefono

radio·thera·pist [ˌreɪdɪəʊˈθerəpɪst] N radioterapista *m/f*

radio·thera·py [ˌreɪdɪəʊˈθerəpɪ] N radioterapia

rad·ish [ˈrædɪʃ] N ravanello

ra·dium [ˈreɪdɪəm] N radio

ra·dius [ˈreɪdɪəs] N (*pl* **radii** [ˈreɪdɪaɪ]) (*Math, also fig*) raggio; (*Anat*) radio; **within a radius of 50 miles** in un raggio di 50 miglia

RAF [ˌɑːreɪˈef] N ABBR (*Brit*) = **Royal Air Force**

raf·fia [ˈræfɪə] N rafia

raff·ish [ˈræfɪʃ] ADJ (*liter*) dissipato(-a)

raf·fle [ˈræfl] N lotteria, riffa ♦ VT (*object*) mettere in palio

raft [rɑːft] N zattera; **a raft of** un sacco di; **a raft of proposals** un sacco di proposte

raft·er [ˈrɑːftə] N trave *f* (del tetto), puntone *m* (*Archit*)

rag [ræɡ] N 1 (*piece of cloth*) straccio, cencio; **rags** NPL (*old clothes*) stracci *mpl*; **in rags** stracciato(-a); **dressed in rags** vestito(-a) di stracci

rag-and-bone man [ˌræɡəndˈbəʊnˌmæn] N (*pl* **-men**) straccivendolo

rag·bag [ˈræɡbæɡ] N (*fig: mixture*) guazzabuglio, accozzaglia

rag doll N bambola di pezza

rage [reɪdʒ] N **1** (*anger*) collera, furia; **to fly into a rage** andare *or* montare su tutte le furie; **to be in a rage** essere furioso(-a) *or* su tutte le furie; **he was trembling with rage** tremava dalla rabbia; **mad with rage** arrabbiatissimo(-a) **2** (*fashion, trend*) mania; **it's all the rage** fa furore ♦ VI (*person*) essere furioso(-a), andare su tutte le furie, infuriarsi; (*sea, fire, plague, wind*) infuriare

❑ **rage** is not translated by the Italian word *raggio*

rag·ged [ˈrægɪd] ADJ (*dress*) stracciato(-a); (*cuff*) logoro(-a); (*person*) lacero(-a), cencioso(-a); (*edge*) irregolare; **ragged children** bambini cenciosi; **ragged clothes** vestiti logori

rag·ing [ˈreɪdʒɪŋ] ADJ (*all senses*) furioso(-a); **in a raging temper** su tutte le furie; **I've got a raging thirst/toothache** muoio di sete/dal mal di denti

rag trade N (*fam*): **the rag trade** (il settore *m* del)l'abbigliamento

raid [reɪd] N (*Mil*) incursione *f*; (*by police*) irruzione *f*; (*by bandits*) razzia; (*by criminals*) rapina; **a police raid** un raid della polizia; **a bank raid** una rapina in banca ♦ VT (*see n*) fare un'incursione in; fare irruzione in; fare razzia in; rapinare; **the police raided a club in Soho** la polizia ha fatto irruzione in una discoteca di Soho

raid·er [ˈreɪdəʳ] N (*bandit*) bandito; (*bank raider etc*) rapinatore(-trice); (*plane*) aeroplano da incursione

rail [reɪl] N **1** (*bar*) sbarra, traversa; (*banister*) corrimano; (*on bridge, balcony*) parapetto; (*of ship*) battagliola; **he climbed the stairs, holding the rail** salì le scale tenendosi al corrimano; **he leaned over the rail** si è sporto dal parapetto; **towel rail** portasciugamani *m inv*; **bath rail** maniglia del bagno **2** (*for train*) rotaia; **to go off the rails** (*train*) deragliare, uscire dal binario; (*fig: be confused*) uscire di carreggiata; (: *err*) sviarsi; **by rail** in treno, per ferrovia; **between the rails** tra le rotaie

▸ **rail off** VT + ADV recintare una ringhiera

rail·card [ˈreɪlˌkɑːd] N (*Brit*) tessera di riduzione ferroviaria

rail·ing [ˈreɪlɪŋ] N (*also*: **railings**) ringhiera, inferriata

rail·road [ˈreɪlˌrəʊd] N (*USA*) = **railway** ♦ VT (*fig*): **to railroad sb into doing sth** costringere velocemente qn a fare qc

rail·way [ˈreɪlˌweɪ] N (*system*) ferrovia; (*track*) strada ferrata ♦ ADJ (*bridge, timetable, network*) ferroviario(-a)

railway engine N (*Brit*) locomotiva

railway line N (*Brit*) linea ferroviaria

rail·way·man [ˈreɪlˌweɪmən] N (*pl* -**men**) (*Brit*) ferroviere *m*

railway station N (*Brit*) stazione *f* ferroviaria

rain [reɪn] N pioggia; **in the rain** sotto la pioggia; **it looks like rain** per me si mette a piovere, c'è aria di pioggia; **heavy/light rain** pioggia forte/leggera; **come rain** *or* **shine** qualunque tempo faccia, col bello o col cattivo tempo; (*fig*) qualunque cosa succeda ♦ VI piovere; **it's raining** piove; **it's raining cats and dogs** piove a catinelle; **it never rains but it pours** (*Proverb*) piove sempre sul bagnato; **to rain down (on sb)** (*blows*) piovere (addosso a qn)

▸ **rain off, rain out** (*USA*) VT + ADV: **the match has been rained off** l'incontro è stato sospeso per la pioggia

rain·bow [ˈreɪnˌbəʊ] N arcobaleno

rain·coat [ˈreɪnˌkəʊt] N impermeabile *m*

rain·drop [ˈreɪnˌdrɒp] N goccia di pioggia

rain·fall [ˈreɪnˌfɔːl] N (*amount*) piovosità, precipitazioni *fpl*

rain·for·est [ˈreɪnˌfɒrɪst] N foresta pluviale *or* equatoriale

rain·proof [ˈreɪnˌpruːf] ADJ impermeabile ♦ VT impermeabilizzare

rain·storm [ˈreɪnˌstɔːm] N temporale *m*, pioggia torrenziale

rain·water [ˈreɪnˌwɔːtəʳ] N acqua piovana

rainy [ˈreɪnɪ] ADJ (*comp* -**ier**, *superl* -**iest**) (*climate*) piovoso(-a); (*season*) delle piogge; **rainy day** giorno piovoso; **to save** *or* **keep sth for a rainy day** (*fig*) mettere qc da parte per i tempi di magra

raise [reɪz] VT **1** (*lift: gen*) sollevare, alzare; (: *shipwreck*) riportare alla superficie; (: *flag*) alzare, issare; (: *dust*) sollevare; (*fig: spirits, morale*) risollevare, tirar su; (: *to power, in rank*) elevare; (*Math*): **to raise to the third power** elevare alla terza potenza; **to raise o.s. up on one's elbows** sollevarsi sui gomiti; **he raised his hat to me** si è tolto il cappello per salutarmi; **to raise one's glass to sb/sth** brindare a qn/qc; **to raise one's**

voice alzare la voce; **he didn't raise an eyebrow** non ha battuto ciglio; **he raised his hand** sollevò la mano; **to raise sb's hopes** accendere le speranze di qn; **to raise from the dead** risuscitare **2** (*erect: building, statue*) erigere **3** (*increase: salary, production*) aumentare; (: *price*) aumentare, alzare; **they want to raise standards in schools** vogliono migliorare il livello qualitativo delle scuole **4** (*crop*) coltivare; (*bring up, breed: family, livestock*) allevare **5** (*produce: question, objection*) sollevare; (: *problem*) porre; (: *doubts, suspicions*) far sorgere, far nascere; **to raise a laugh/a smile** far ridere/sorridere; **to raise hell** *or* **the roof** (*fam*) fare il diavolo a quattro; **she raised the question of unemployment** ha sollevato la questione della disoccupazione **6** (*get together: funds, army*) raccogliere; (: *taxes*) imporre; (: *money*) procurarsi; **to raise a loan** ottenere un prestito **7** (*end: siege, embargo*) togliere ♦ N (*USA*: *payrise*) aumento

rai·sin [ˈreɪzən] N uvetta

Raj [rɑːdʒ] N: **the Raj** l'impero britannico (*in India*)

rajah [ˈrɑːdʒə] N ragià *m inv*

rake[1] [reɪk] N (*tool*) rastrello ♦ VT (*sand, leaves, soil*) rastrellare; (*strafe: ship, row of men*) spazzare

▸ **rake in** VT + ADV (*fam: money*) fare; **they raked in a profit of £1000** ci hanno fatto un guadagno di 1000 sterline

▸ **rake off** VT + ADV (*fam: share of profit*) intascare

▸ **rake out** VT + ADV (*fire*) spegnere facendo cadere la brace

▸ **rake over** VT + ADV (*fig*) rivangare

▸ **rake through** VI + PREP rovistare in, frugare in

▸ **rake up** VT + ADV (*subject, memories*) rivangare, riesumare

rake[2] [reɪk] N (*old: dissolute man*) libertino

rake-off [ˈreɪkˌɒf] N (*fam: share of profit*) parte *f*, fetta

rak·ish [ˈreɪkɪʃ] ADJ **1** (*person*) libertino(-a), dissoluto(-a) **2 at a rakish angle** (*hat*) sulle ventitré

ral·ly [ˈrælɪ] N (*of troops, people, also Pol*) raduno, riunione *f*; (*Aut*) rally *m inv*; (*Tennis*) lungo scambio di colpi; **a pre-election rally** un raduno pre-elettorale; **rally driver** pilota *m/f* di rally ♦ VT (*troops, supporters*) riunire, radunare ♦ VI (*troops, supporters*) riunirsi; (*revive, recover: patient, strength, share prices*) riprendersi

▸ **rally round** VI + ADV (*fig: cause*) far fronte comune ♦ VI + PREP (*person needing help*) stringersi intorno a

ral·ly·ing point [ˈrælɪŋˌpɔɪnt] N (*Pol, Mil*) punto di raduno

RAM [ræm] N ABBR (*Comput*: = *random access memory*) RAM *f inv*

ram [ræm] N (*Zool*) montone *m*, ariete *m*; (*Astrol, Mil*) ariete ♦ VT **1 to ram (into)** (*pack tightly*) calcare (in), pigiare (in); (*push down*) ficcare (in); (*stick into*) conficcare; **they rammed their ideas down my throat** hanno cercato di imbottirmi la testa con le loro idee **2** (*collide with: ship*) speronare; (: *car*) cozzare, sbattere contro; **the car rammed the lamppost** la macchina è andata a sbattere con il muso contro il lampione

❑ **ram** is not translated by the Italian word *ramo*

Rama·dan [ˌræməˈdɑːn] N (*Rel*) ramadan *m inv*

ram·ble [ˈræmbl] N (*lunga*) passeggiata; (*hike*) escursione *f*; **to go for a ramble** fare un'escursione ♦ VI **1** (*walk*) gironzolare, vagare; (*hike*) fare escursioni **2** (*fig: in speech*) divagare, dilungarsi; **to ramble on** sproloquiare; **his mind has started to ramble** è un po' svanito

ram·bler [ˈræmbləʳ] N **1** (*hiker*) escursionista *m/f* **2** (*Bot*) rosa rampicante

ram·bling [ˈræmblɪŋ] ADJ (*plant*) rampicante; (*speech, book*) sconnesso(-a); (*house*) tutto(-a) nicchie e corridoi ♦ N escursionismo

ram·bunc·tious [ræmˈbʌŋkʃəs] ADJ (*USA*) = **rumbustious**

rami·fi·ca·tion [ˌræmɪfɪˈkeɪʃən] N ramificazione *f*

ramp [ræmp] N (*on road etc*) rampa; (*in garage*) ponte *m* idraulico; (*Aer*) scala d'imbarco; **"ramp"** (*Aut*) "fondo stradale in rifacimento"

ram·page [ræmˈpeɪdʒ] N: **to go on the rampage** scatenarsi (in modo violento) ♦ VI scatenarsi; **they went rampaging through the town** sono stati scatenati in modo violento per la città

ram·pant [ˈræmpənt] ADJ **1** (*fig: crime, disease*): **to be rampant** dilagare; **rampant corruption** corruzione *f* dilagante **2** (*Heraldry*) rampante

ram·part [ˈræmpɑːt] N terrapieno, bastione *m*

ram raid·ing [ˈræmˌreɪdɪŋ] N *il rapinare un negozio o una banca sfondandone la vetrina con un'auto-ariete*

ram·shack·le [ˈræmˌʃækl] ADJ (*house*) cadente, malandato(-a); (*car, table*) sgangherato(-a); **the present ramshackle system** l'attuale sistema sgangherato

ran [ræn] PT *of* **run**

ranch [rɑːntʃ] N ranch *m inv*

ranch·er [ˈrɑːntʃəʳ] N (*owner*) proprietario di un ranch; (*ranch hand*) cowboy *m inv*

ran·cid [ˈrænsɪd] ADJ rancido(-a); **to smell rancid** avere odore di rancido

ran·cour, ran·cor (*USA*) [ˈræŋkəʳ] N (*frm*) rancore *m*

R & B [ˌɑːrənˈbiː] N ABBR = **rhythm and blues**

R & D [ˌɑːrənˈdiː] N ABBR = **research and development**

ran·dom [ˈrændəm] ADJ (*arrangement*) casuale, fortuito(-a); (*selection, shot, killing*) a caso; **a random selection** una selezione effettuata a caso ♦ N: **at random** a caso, a casaccio

random access N (*Comput*) accesso casuale

R & R [ˌɑːrənˈɑːʳ] N ABBR (= *rest and recreation*) ricreazione *f*; (*Mil*) permesso

randy [ˈrændɪ] ADJ (*comp* **-ier**, *superl* **-iest**) (*Brit fam*) arrapato(-a)

rang [ræŋ] PT *of* **ring²**

range [reɪndʒ] N 1 (*distance attainable, scope: of gun, missile*) portata, gittata; (: *of ship, plane*) autonomia; **within (firing) range** a portata (di tiro); **out of (firing) range** fuori portata (di tiro); **at short/long range** a breve/lunga distanza; **range of vision** campo visivo 2 (*extent between limits: of temperature*) variazioni *fpl*; (: *of salaries, prices*) scala; (: *Mus: of instruments, voice*) gamma, estensione *f*; (*selection: of colours, feelings, speeds*) gamma; (: *of goods*) assortimento, gamma; (*domain, sphere*) raggio, sfera; **the range of sb's mind** le capacità mentali di qn; **a range of subjects** diverse materie; **she has a wide range of interests** ha interessi molto vari; **there's a wide range of colours** c'è una vasta gamma di colori; **price range** gamma di prezzi; **it's out of my price range** è fuori dal mio budget; **do you have anything else in this price range?** ha nient'altro più o meno a questo prezzo? 3 (*row*) serie *f inv*, fila; (*of mountains*) catena 4 (*USA: Agr*) prateria 5 (*also: shooting range*) (*in open*) poligono di tiro; (*at fair*) tiro a segno 6 (*also: kitchen range*) cucina economica ♦ VT (*arrange, place*) disporre, allineare; **ranged left/right** (*text*) allineato(-a) a destra/sinistra ♦ VI 1 (*mountains, discussion, search*) estendersi; (*numbers, opinions, results*) variare; **they were ranged along the perimeter** furono disposti lungo il perimetro; **the discussion ranged over a wide number of topics** la discussione ha toccato vari argomenti 2 (*roam*): **to range over** vagare per; **to range from ... to** andare da... a; **tickets range from four pounds to twenty pounds** i prezzi dei biglietti vanno dalle quattro alle venti sterline

rang·er [ˈreɪndʒəʳ] N (*also:* **forest ranger**) guardia forestale; (*USA: mounted policeman*) poliziotto a cavallo

Ran·goon [ræŋˈɡuːn] N Rangoon *f*

rank¹ [ræŋk] N 1 (*row*) fila; **taxi rank** posteggio di taxi 2 (*status, also Mil*) grado; **the rank of captain** il grado di capitano; **people of all ranks** gente *fsg* di tutti i ceti 3 (*Mil*): **the ranks** la truppa; **he rose from the ranks** è venuto dalla gavetta; **to close ranks** (*Mil*) serrare le righe; (*fig*) serrare i ranghi; **to break rank(s)** rompere le righe; **I've joined the ranks of the unemployed** mi sono aggiunto alla massa dei disoccupati 4 (*Math*) posizione *f* ♦ VT considerare, ritenere; **I rank him 6th** gli do il sesto posto, lo metto al sesto posto ♦ VI: **to rank 4th** essere quarto(-a), essere al quarto posto; **to rank above sb** essere superiore a qn; (*Mil*) essere superiore in grado a qn; **he ranks among the best** è uno dei migliori

rank² [ræŋk] ADJ 1 (*hypocrisy, injustice etc*) bello(-a) e buono(-a), vero(-a) e proprio(-a); (*traitor*) sporco(-a) 2 (*smell*) puzzolente, fetido(-a); (*fats*) rancido(-a) 3 (*frm: plants*) troppo rigoglioso(-a); **rank outsider** outsider *m/f inv*

ran·kle [ˈræŋkl] VI: **to rankle (with sb)** bruciare (a qn); **this rejection still rankles** questo rifiuto brucia ancora

ran·sack [ˈrænsæk] VT (*drawer, room*) frugare, rovistare; (*town*) saccheggiare; **the burglars ransacked the house** i ladri hanno rovistato in casa; **embassies and homes were ransacked** le ambasciate e le case furono saccheggiate

ran·som [ˈrænsəm] N riscatto; **to hold sb to ransom** tenere in ostaggio qn (*per denaro*); (*fig*) tenere qn in scacco ♦ VT riscattare

rant [rænt] VI (*pej*): **to rant (at sb)** inveire (contro qn)

rant·ing [ˈræntɪŋ] N (*pej*) invettiva

rap [ræp] N 1 (*noise*) colpetti *mpl*; (*at the door*) bussata; **there was a rap at the door** hanno bussato con un colpo secco alla porta; **to take the rap** (*fam*) pagare di persona 2 (*Mus*) rap *m* ♦ VT (*window*) dare dei colpetti su; (*door*) bussare a; **to rap sb's knuckles** dare un colpo secco sulle nocche di qn; (*fig*) dare una tirata d'orecchi a qn ♦ VI 1 **to rap (at)** (*see vt*): dare dei colpetti (su); bussare (a) 2 (*USA fam: talk*) chiacchierare

▸ **rap out** VT + ADV (*order*) dire bruscamente

rape¹ [reɪp] N (*also Law*) stupro, violenza carnale ♦ VT violentare, stuprare

❏ **rape** is not translated by the Italian word *rapire*

rape² [reɪp] N (*Bot*) colza

rape·seed oil [ˈreɪpˌsiːdˈɔɪl] N olio di colza

rap·id [ˈræpɪd] ADJ rapido(-a)

ra·pid·ity [rəˈpɪdɪtɪ] N rapidità

rap·id·ly [ˈræpɪdlɪ] ADV rapidamente

rap·ids [ˈræpɪdz] NPL (*in river*) rapide *fpl*

rap·ist [ˈreɪpɪst] N violentatore *m*, stupratore *m*

rap·port [ræˈpɔːʳ] N intesa

rapt [ræpt] ADJ (*person, face, expression*) rapito(-a); (*silence, attention*) profondo(-a); **to be rapt in contemplation** essere in estatica contemplazione

rap·ture [ˈræptʃəʳ] N (*liter*) estasi *f inv*; **in rapture** in estasi; **to be in raptures over sth/sb** essere estasiato(-a) di fronte a qc/qn; **to go into raptures over sth/sb** andare in estasi per qc/qn, rimanere estasiato(-a) da qc/qn

rap·tur·ous [ˈræptʃərəs] ADJ (*liter*) (*smile*) estatico(-a); (*welcome, praise, applause*) entusiastico(-a)

rare [rɛəʳ] ADJ (*comp* **-r**, *superl* **-st**) 1 raro(-a); **in a rare moment of generosity** in un raro momento di generosità; **it is rare to find that ...** capita raramente *or* di rado che... + *sub*; **a rare disease** una malattia rara 2 (*air*) rarefatto(-a) 3 (*meat*) al sangue, poco cotto(-a)

rare·bit [ˈrɛəbɪt] N: **Welsh rarebit** toast *m inv* al formaggio fuso

rar·efied [ˈrɛərɪˌfaɪd] ADJ (*atmosphere, air*) rarefatto(-a); (*fig*) raffinato(-a)

rare·ly [ˈrɛəlɪ] ADV di rado, raramente

rar·ing [ˈrɛərɪŋ] ADJ: **to be raring to go** (*fam*) non veder l'ora di cominciare

rar·ity [ˈrɛərɪtɪ] N 1 (*also: rareness*) rarità 2 (*rare thing*) rarità *f inv*

ras·cal [ˈrɑːskəl] N (*scoundrel*) mascalzone *m*; (*child*) birbante *m*

rash¹ [ræʃ] ADJ avventato(-a)

rash² [ræʃ] N (*Med: gen*) eruzione *f*, sfogo; (: *from food, allergy*) orticaria; **to come out in a rash** (*gen*) avere uno sfogo; **strawberries bring me out in a rash** le fragole mi fanno venire l'orticaria; **I've got a rash on my chest** ho un'eruzione sul petto

rash·er [ˈræʃəʳ] N: **a rasher of bacon** una fetta di pancetta

rasp [rɑːsp] N (*tool*) raspa, lima; (*sound*) stridio, suono stridulo ♦ VT (*file*) raspare, raschiare; (*speak: also:* **rasp out**) gracchiare

rasp·berry [ˈrɑːzbərɪ] N (*fruit*) lampone *m*; **to blow a raspberry** (*fam*) fare una pernacchia ♦ ADJ (*jam*) di lamponi; (*ice cream, syrup*) di lampone

raspberry bush N lampone *m* (*pianta*)

rasp·ing [ˈrɑːspɪŋ] ADJ stridulo(-a), stridente

Ras·ta·far·ian [ˌræstəˈfɛərɪən] ADJ, N rastafariano(-a)

rat [ræt] N ratto; **black rat** ratto comune; **brown rat** topo delle chiaviche; **you dirty rat!** (*fam*) brutta carogna! ♦ VI: **to rat on sb** (*fam*) fare una spiata *or* una soffiata su qn; **to rat on a deal** (*fam*) rimangiarsi la parola; **to smell a rat** subodorare qualcosa

rat·able [ˈreɪtəbl] ADJ = **rateable**

ratch·et [ˈrætʃɪt] N arpionismo

rate [reɪt] N 1 (*ratio*) tasso, percentuale *f*; (*speed*) velocità *f* *inv*; **at a rate of 60 kph** alla velocità di 60 km all'ora; **at a great rate, at a rate of knots** (*fam*) a tutta velocità; **at a slow rate** a bassa velocità; **rate of growth** tasso di crescita; **at a steady rate** a un ritmo costante; **birth/death rate** tasso *or* indice *m* di natalità/di mortalità; **failure rate** percentuale *f* dei bocciati; **rate of flow/consumption** flusso/consumo medio; **rate of reaction** (*Chem*) velocità *f inv* di reazione; **pulse rate** frequenza delle pulsazioni; **at this rate** di questo passo, con questo ritmo; **at any rate** in *or* ad ogni modo, comunque 2 (*price, charge*) tariffa; (*Comm, Fin*) tasso; **at a rate of 5% per annum** al tasso (annuo) del 5%; **postage rates** tariffe postali; **insurance rates** premi *mpl* assicurativi; **rate of exchange** tasso di cambio; **rate of pay** compenso medio; **bank rate** tasso d'interesse bancario; **a high rate of interest** un alto tasso d'interesse; **there are reduced rates for students** ci sono tariffe ridotte per gli studenti; *see also* **rates** ♦ *VT* (*evaluate, appraise*) valutare; **to rate sb/sth highly** stimare molto qn/qc; **how do you rate that film?** cosa pensi di quel film?; **I rate it as one of the best** lo considero uno fra i migliori ♦ *VI*: **it rates as one of the worst** è fra i peggiori; **to rate sb/sth among** annoverare qn/qc tra; **how does it rate among the critics?** che cosa ne hanno detto i critici?; **he was rated the best** era considerato il migliore

rateable value, ratable value N (*Brit: old*) valore *m* imponibile (*agli effetti delle imposte comunali*)

rate·payer [ˈreɪtˌpeɪəʳ] N (*Brit: old*) contribuente *m/f* (*di imposte comunali*)

rates [ˈreɪts] NPL (*Brit: old*) imposte *fpl* comunali sugli immobili

ra·ther [ˈrɑːðəʳ] ADV 1 (*preference*) piuttosto; **rather than wait, she …** piuttosto che aspettare, lei…; **I'd rather have this one than that** preferirei avere questo piuttosto che quello; **would you rather stay here?** preferisci rimanere qui?; **I'd rather you didn't come** preferirei che tu non venissi; **I'd rather not** preferirei di no; **I'd rather not come** preferirei non venire; **I would** *or* **I'd rather go** preferirei andare 2 (*to a considerable degree*) piuttosto; (*somewhat*) abbastanza; (*to some extent*) un po'; **it's rather expensive** (*quite*) è piuttosto caro; (*excessively*) è un po' troppo caro; **there's rather a lot** ce n'è parecchio; **I've got rather a lot of homework to do** ho molti compiti da fare; **I was rather disappointed** ero piuttosto deluso(-a); **a rather difficult task** un compito piuttosto difficile; **I feel rather more happy today** oggi mi sento molto più contento; **it's rather a pity** è proprio *or* davvero un peccato 3 *or* **rather** (*more accurately*) anzi, per essere (più) precisi ♦ *EXCL* eccome!

rati·fi·ca·tion [ˌrætɪfɪˈkeɪʃən] N (*frm*) ratifica

rati·fy [ˈrætɪfaɪ] VT (*frm*) ratificare

rat·ing [ˈreɪtɪŋ] N 1 (*assessment*) valutazione *f*; **it got a rating of ten out of ten** ha ottenuto una valutazione di dieci su dieci; **their popularity rating is at an all-time low** la loro popolarità ha raggiunto i minimi storici 2 (*Naut*) marinaio semplice

rat·ings [ˈreɪtɪŋz] NPL (*Radio, TV*) indice *msg* di ascolto

ra·tio [ˈreɪʃiəʊ] N rapporto, proporzione *f*; **in the ratio of 2 to 1** in rapporto di 2 a 1

ra·tion [ˈræʃən] N razione *f*; **to be on ration** (*food*) essere razionato(-a); **to be on short rations** (*person*) essere a razioni ridotte ♦ *VT* (*also:* **ration out**) razionare; **to ration sb to sth** imporre a qn un limite di qc

ra·tion·al [ˈræʃənl] ADJ (*being*) razionale; (*Med: lucid*) lucido(-a); (*faculty, action, argument*) razionale; (*solution, explanation, reasoning*) logico(-a), razionale

ra·tion·ale [ˌræʃəˈnɑːl] N fondamento logico

ra·tion·ali·za·tion [ˌræʃnəlaɪˈzeɪʃən] N razionalizzazione *f*

ra·tion·al·ize [ˈræʃnəlaɪz] VT 1 (*action, attitude*) (cercare di) spiegare razionalmente 2 (*reorganize: industry*) razionalizzare 3 (*Math*) razionalizzare

ra·tion·al·ly [ˈræʃnəlɪ] ADV (*behave, speak, think*) razionalmente

ra·tion·ing [ˈræʃnɪŋ] N razionamento

rat·pack [ˈrætˌpæk] N (*Brit fam*) stampa scandalistica

rat poison N veleno per topi

rat race N (*pej*) corsa al successo

rat·tan [ræˈtæn] N malacca

rat·tle [ˈrætl] N 1 (*of train, car*) rumore *m* di ferraglia; (*of stone*

in tin, of windows) tintinnio; (*of hail, rain, bullets*) crepitio; **a rattle of bottles/chains** un rumore di bottiglie/catene; **death rattle** rantolo 2 (*instrument: used by football fan*) raganella; (: *child's*) sonaglio ♦ *VT* 1 (*shake*) agitare; (*eybox*) far tintinnare 2 (*fam: person*) innervosire; **to get rattled** innervosirsi ♦ *VI* (*box, objects in box, machinery*) far rumore; (*bullets, hailstones*) crepitare; (*window*) vibrare; **the train rattled over the crossing** il treno passò sferragliando al passaggio a livello

▸ **rattle off** VT + ADV (*poem, speech*) snocciolare

▸ **rattle on** VI + ADV blaterare

rattle·snake [ˈrætlˌsneɪk] N crotalo, serpente *m* a sonagli

rat·ty [ˈrætɪ] ADJ (*comp* **-ier**, *superl* **-iest**) (*Brit fam*) incavolato(-a); **to get ratty** incavolarsi

rau·cous [ˈrɔːkəs] ADJ (*voice, person*) rauco(-a); (*laughter*) sguaiato(-a)

rau·cous·ly [ˈrɔːkəslɪ] ADV (*see adj*) raucamente, con voce roca; sguaiatamente

raun·chy [ˈrɔːntʃɪ] ADJ (*comp* **-ier**, *superl* **-iest**) (*fam*) sexy *inv*

rav·age [ˈrævɪdʒ] VT (*frm*) devastare

rav·ages [ˈrævɪdʒɪz] NPL (*frm*) danni *mpl*; **the ravages of time** le offese *or* ingiurie del tempo

rave [reɪv] VI (*be delirious*) delirare; (*talk wildly*) farneticare; (*rant*) infuriarsi, fare una sfuriata; (*talk enthusiastically*): **to rave (about)** andare in estasi (per), essere assolutamente entusiasta (di); **they raved about the film** erano assolutamente entusiasti del film ♦ N rave *m inv* ♦ ADJ (*scene, culture, music*) rave *inv*

ra·ven [ˈreɪvn] N corvo (imperiale)

rav·en·ous [ˈrævənəs] ADJ (*person*) affamato(-a); (*appetite, animal*) famelico(-a), vorace; **to be ravenous** avere una fame da lupi

ra·vine [rəˈviːn] N burrone *m*

rav·ing [ˈreɪvɪŋ] ADJ: **raving lunatic** pazzo(-a) furioso(-a); **you must be raving mad!** sei matto da legare!

rav·ings [ˈreɪvɪŋz] NPL vaneggiamenti *mpl*

rav·ish [ˈrævɪʃ] VT 1 (*liter: enchant, delight*) estasiare, rapire 2 (*old: rape*) violentare; (: *carry off*) rapire

rav·ish·ing [ˈrævɪʃɪŋ] ADJ (*sight, beauty*) incantevole

raw [rɔː] ADJ 1 (*food*) crudo(-a); (*spirit*) puro(-a); (*silk, leather, cotton, ore*) greggio(-a); (*sugar*) non raffinato(-a); **to get a raw deal** (*fam: bad bargain*) prendere un bidone; (: *harsh treatment*) venire trattato(-a) ingiustamente; **raw carrots** carote *fpl* crude 2 (*wind, weather*) gelido(-a) 3 (*wound: open*) aperto(-a); (: *sore*) vivo(-a); (*skin*) screpolato(-a) 4 (*person: inexperienced*) inesperto(-a); **he's still raw** è ancora un pivello *or* un novellino ♦ N: **life in the raw** la vita con's com'è

Ra·wal·pin·di [ˌrɔːlˈpɪndɪ] N Rawalpindi *f*

raw material N materia prima

ray [reɪ] N 1 raggio *m*; (*of hope*) barlume *m*, raggio; **a ray of comfort** un po' di conforto 2 (*Geom*) semiretta

ray·on [ˈreɪɒn] N raion *m*

raze [reɪz] VT (*also:* **raze to the ground**) radere al suolo

ra·zor [ˈreɪzəʳ] N rasoio; **disposable razor** rasoio usa e getta

razor blade N lametta (da barba)

razzle-dazzle [ˈræzlˈdæzl] N (*Brit fam*) brio; **to be/go on the razzle(-dazzle)** fare/andare a fare baldoria

razz·ma·tazz [ˈræzməˈtæz] N (*fam*) clamore *m*

RCAF [ˌɑːsiːˈeɪef] N ABBR = **Royal Canadian Air Force**

RCMP [ˌɑːsiːemˈpiː] N ABBR = **Royal Canadian Mounted Police**

RCN [ˌɑːsiːˈen] N ABBR = **Royal Canadian Navy**

RD [ˌɑːˈdiː] ABBR (*Post*) = **rural delivery**

Rd ABBR = **Road**

RDC [ˌɑːdiːˈsiː] N ABBR (*Brit*) = **rural district council**

reach [riːtʃ] N 1 portata; **within (easy) reach** a portata di mano, vicino(-a); **it's within easy reach by bus** ci si raggiunge facilmente in autobus; **the hotel is within easy reach of the town centre** l'albergo è vicino al centro; **out of reach** fuori portata; **keep medicine out of reach of children** non lasciare medicinali alla portata dei bambini 2 (*of river*) tratto; **the upper reaches of the Thames** l'alto corso del Tamigi 3 (*Naut*): **on a beam reach** al traverso; **on a broad reach** al gran lasco; **on a close reach** al lasco ♦ VT (*arrive at, attain*) arrivare a; (*goal, limit, person*) raggiungere; **to**

reach a conclusion arrivare ad una conclusione; **when the news reached my ears** quando mi è arrivata all'orecchio la notizia; **to reach a compromise** arrivare a *or* raggiungere un compromesso; **we reached the hotel at seven o'clock** siamo arrivati all'albergo alle sette; **eventually they reached an agreement** alla fine hanno raggiunto un accordo; **can I reach you at your hotel?** posso trovarla al suo albergo?; **to reach sb by phone** contattare qn per telefono; **we need to be able to reach him in an emergency** dobbiamo essere in grado di contattarlo in caso di emergenza ♦ VI **1** (*stretch out hand: also:* **reach down, reach over, reach across**) allungare una mano; **he reached (over) for the book** si è allungato per prendere il libro **2** (*stretch: land etc*) estendersi; (: *wire, rope*) arrivare; (: *voice, sound*) giungere

‣ **reach out** VI + ADV: **to reach out for** stendere la mano per prendere

re·act [ri:ˈækt] VI: **to react (against/to)** reagire (contro/a)

re·ac·tion [ri:ˈækʃən] N reazione *f*

re·ac·tion·ary [ri:ˈækʃənrɪ] ADJ, N reazionario(-a)

re·ac·tor [ri:ˈæktəʳ] N reattore *m*

read [ri:d] (*pt, pp* **read** [red]) VT **1** (*gen*) leggere; **to read o.s. to sleep** leggere per addormentarsi; **I read a lot** leggo molto; **to take sth as read** (*fig*) dare qc per scontato; **to take the minutes as read** (*Admin*) passare subito all'ordine del giorno; **do you read me?** (*Telec*) mi ricevete? **2** (*Univ: study*) studiare; **to read Chemistry** fare *or* studiare chimica **3** (*interpret: dream, signal*) interpretare; (: *hand*) leggere; **she can read me like a book** mi legge nel cuore, per lei sono come un libro aperto; **to read sb's thoughts** leggere nel pensiero di qn; **to read between the lines** leggere tra le righe; **to read too much into sth** attribuire troppa importanza a qc ♦ VI **1** leggere; **I read about him in the paper** ho letto qualcosa su di lui sul giornale; **I read about it in the paper** l'ho letto sul giornale; **to read to sb** leggere qualcosa a qn; **the book reads well** è un libro che si legge bene **2** (*indicate: meter, clock*) segnare; **the inscription reads "To my son"** la dedica dice "A mio figlio" ♦ N: **to have a quiet read** leggersi qualcosa in santa pace; **that book's a good read** quel libro è una buona lettura

‣ **read back** VT + ADV rileggere

‣ **read off** VT + ADV **1** (*without pause*) leggere tutto d'un fiato; **he read off the figures from the printout** (*at sight*) ha letto le cifre dal tabulato **2** (*instrument readings*) leggere

‣ **read on** VI + ADV continuare a leggere

‣ **read out** VT + ADV leggere (ad alta voce)

‣ **read over** VT + ADV rileggere attentamente

‣ **read through** VT + ADV (*quickly*) dare una scorsa a; (*thoroughly*) leggere da cima a fondo

‣ **read up, read up on** *vt + adv + prep* VT + ADV studiare bene

read·able [ˈri:dbl] ADJ (*book*) che si legge volentieri; (*writing*) leggibile; **her latest book is very readable** il suo ultimo libro si legge molto volentieri

read·er [ˈri:dəʳ] N **1** lettore(-trice); **she's a great reader** adora leggere **2** (*Brit: Univ*) ≈ (docente *m/f*) incaricato(-a) **3** (*book*) libro di lettura; (*anthology*) antologia

read·er·ship [ˈri:dəʃɪp] N (numero di) lettori *mpl*

read·ily [ˈredɪlɪ] ADV (*quickly*) prontamente; (*willingly*) volentieri; (*easily*) con facilità, facilmente; **she readily accepted** ha accettato prontamente; **the ingredients are readily available** gli ingredienti si trovano facilmente

readi·ness [ˈredɪnɪs] N prontezza; **to be in readiness for** essere pronto(-a) per; **their readiness to co-operate** la loro disponibilità a collaborare; **in readiness for the president's arrival** in preparazione all'arrivo del presidente

read·ing [ˈri:dɪŋ] N **1** (*gen*) lettura; (*of proofs*) correzione *f*; **I like reading** mi piace leggere; **reading and writing** leggere e scrivere **2** (*interpretation*) interpretazione *f*; (*of original text, manuscript*) lezione *f* **3** (*of thermometer etc*) lettura; **to take a reading** prendere *or* fare una lettura **4** (*recital: of play, poem*) reading *m inv*; **to give a poetry reading** tenere un reading di poesia

reading lamp N lampada da scrivania

reading room N sala di lettura

re·adjust [ˌri:əˈdʒʌst] VT regolare (di nuovo); **they are now readjusting their policy** ora stanno rivedendo la loro politica;

the brakes need readjusting i freni devono essere regolati ♦ VI (*person*): **to readjust (to)** riadattarsi (a); **astronauts find it difficult to readjust to life on Earth** gli astronauti fanno difficoltà a riabituarsi alla vita sulla Terra

ready [ˈredɪ] ADJ (*comp* **-ier**, *superl* **-iest**) pronto(-a); (*willing*) pronto(-a), disposto(-a); (*quick*) rapido(-a); (*available*) disponibile; **are you ready?** sei pronto?; **ready for use** pronto per l'uso; **ready for anything** pronto(-a) a tutto; **ready money** denaro contante, contanti *mpl*; **to be ready to do sth** essere pronto a fare qc; **she was always ready to help** era sempre pronta ad aiutare; **to get ready** prepararsi; **to get ready to do** prepararsi a fare; **ready to serve** (*food*) già pronto; **to get sth ready** preparare qc; **ready, steady, go!** pronti, attenti, via!; **I'm ready for him!** lo sto aspettando!; **we were ready to give up there and then** eravamo sul punto di piantare li tutto ♦ N: **at the ready** (*Mil*) pronto(-a) (a far fuoco *or* sparare); (*fig*) (tutto(-a)) pronto(-a) ♦ VT preparare

ready cash N contanti *mpl*

ready-cooked [ˌredɪˈkʊkt] ADJ già cucinato(-a) *or* cotto(-a)

ready-made [ˌredɪˈmeɪd] ADJ (*clothes*) confezionato(-a); (*excuses, solution*) bell'e pronto(-a); (*ideas*) banale; **ready-made meals** pasti *mpl* pronti; **ready-made curtains** tende *fpl* confezionate; **a ready-made topic** un argomento bell'e pronto

ready reck·on·er [ˈredɪˈrekənəʳ] N (*Brit*) prontuario di calcolo

ready-to-wear [ˌredɪtəˈwɛəʳ] ADJ prêt-à-porter *inv*

re·agent [ri:ˈeɪdʒənt] N: **chemical reagent** reagente *m* chimico

real [rɪəl] ADJ (*gen*) vero(-a); (*reason, motive*) reale, vero(-a); (*Philosophy*) reale; **in real life** nella realtà; **in real terms** (*Fin*) in termini effettivi; **real account** (*Fin: in ledger*) conto patrimoniale; **he's a real villain** è un vero mascalzone; **he wasn't a real police officer** non era un vero poliziotto; **she has no real authority** in pratica non ha alcuna autorità; **once you've tasted the real thing ...** una volta provato l'originale... ♦ ADV (*USA fam*) veramente, proprio ♦ N: **for real** (*fam*) per davvero, sul serio

real ale N tipo di birra scura prodotta secondo il metodo tradizionale

real estate N (*USA*) beni *mpl* immobili

re·al·ism [ˈrɪəlɪzəm] N (*also Art*) realismo

re·al·ist [ˈrɪəlɪst] N realista *m/f*

re·al·is·tic [rɪəˈlɪstɪk] ADJ (*thing*) realistico(-a); (*person*) realista

re·al·ity [ri:ˈælɪtɪ] N realtà *f inv*; **in reality** in realtà, in effetti

reality TV N reality TV *f inv*

re·ali·za·tion [ˌrɪəlaɪˈzeɪʃən] N (*awareness*) presa di coscienza; (*frm: of hopes, plans, assets*) realizzazione *f*; **there is a growing realization that ...** sempre più ci si rende conto che...; **at the realization that ...** quando ci rese conto che...; **the realization of their worst fears** la materializzazione delle loro peggiori paure; **the realization of their dreams** la realizzazione dei loro sogni

re·al·ize [ˈrɪəlaɪz] VT **1** (*become aware of*) rendersi conto di, accorgersi di; (*understand*) capire; **to realize sth** rendersi conto di qc; **I suddenly realized he was lying** improvvisamente mi sono reso conto che stava mentendo; **I realize that ...** mi rendo conto *or* capisco che...; **she hadn't fully realized the gravity of the situation** non si era resa completamente conto della gravità della situazione; **once they realized their mistake ...** dopo che si erano resi conto del loro errore...; **without realizing it** senza rendersene conto, senza accorgersene; **he realized how/why** ha capito come/perché **2** (*frm: hopes, ambitions, assets, project*) realizzare; (: *plan*) attuare, realizzare

re·al·ly [ˈrɪəlɪ] ADV davvero, veramente; **I don't really know** a dire la verità non lo so; **he doesn't really speak Chinese, does he?** non parla cinese sul serio, vero?; **I really ought to go home** devo proprio andare a casa; **I really don't like Tom** Tom non mi piace proprio; **a really good party** una festa bellissima; **she's really nice** è proprio simpatica; **did he hurt you? - not really** ti ha fatto male? - non è niente di grave; **I'm learning German - really?** sto studiando tedesco - davvero?

realm [relm] N (*frm*) regno; **the realm of politics** il regno della politica; **within the realms of possibility** nel possibile

real time N (*Comput*) tempo reale; **in real time** in tempo reale

Re·al·tor [ˈrɪəltɔ:ʳ] N (*USA: trademark*) agente *m/f* immobiliare

ream [riːm] N risma; **reams** NPL (*fig: fam*) pagine e pagine *fpl*

reap [riːp] VT mietere; (*fig: profit, benefit*) raccogliere; **to reap the benefit of sth** trarre beneficio da qc

reap·er [ˈriːpəʳ] N (*person*) mietitore(-trice); (*machine*) mietitrice *f*

re·appear [ˌriːəˈpɪəʳ] VI ricomparire, riapparire

re·appear·ance [ˌriːəˈpɪərəns] N ricomparsa, riapparizione *f*

re·apply [ˌriːəˈplaɪ] VI: **to reapply for** fare nuovamente domanda per

re·apprais·al [ˌriːəˈpreɪzəl] N riesame *m*

rear¹ [rɪəʳ] ADJ (*gen*) di dietro, posteriore; (*Aut: door, window, wheel*) posteriore ♦ N (*back part*) didietro, parte *f* posteriore; (*Anat: fam: buttocks*) didietro, sedere *m*; (*Mil*) retroguardia; **in** *or* **at the rear (of)** dietro (a), didietro (a); **to bring up the rear** venire per ultimo; (*Mil*) formare la retroguardia; **the rear of the building** il retro dell'edificio; **at the rear of the train** in coda al treno

rear² [rɪəʳ] VT 1 (*raise: cattle, family*) allevare 2 (*one's head*) drizzare ♦ VI (*also: rear up: esp horse*) impennarsi

rear admiral N contrammiraglio

rear-engined [ˌrɪərˈendʒɪnd] ADJ (*Aut*) con motore posteriore

rear·guard [ˈrɪəɡɑːd] N (*Mil*) retroguardia

re·arm [ˌriːˈɑːm] VT riarmare ♦ VI riarmarsi

re·arma·ment [ˌriːˈɑːməmənt] N riarmo

re·arrange [ˌriːəˈreɪndʒ] VT (*objects*) ridisporre, riordinare; (*appointment*) fissare di nuovo, spostare; **a waiter was rearranging the tables** un cameriere riordinava i tavoli; **the meeting will have to be rearranged** la data dell'incontro dovrà essere spostata

rear-view mirror [ˈrɪəˌvjuːˈmɪrəʳ] N (*Aut*) specchietto retrovisore

rear-wheel drive N trazione *fpl* posteriore

rea·son [ˈriːzn] N 1 (*motive, cause*) ragione *f*, motivo; **the reason for/why** la ragione *or* il motivo di/per cui; **the reason (why) I'm late is ...** sono in ritardo perché...; **don't ask the reason why** non chiedere il perché; **for no reason** senza ragione; **she claims with good reason that she's underpaid** si lamenta, e a ragione, di essere sottopagata; **all the more reason why you should not sell it** ragione di più per non venderlo; **we have reason to believe that ...** abbiamo motivo di ritenere che...; **by reason of** a causa di; **for security reasons** per ragioni di sicurezza 2 (*faculty, good sense*) ragione *f*; **to lose one's reason** perdere la ragione; **to listen to reason** ascoltare (la voce della) ragione; **it stands to reason** è logico; **within reason** entro limiti ragionevoli, entro certi limiti ♦ VT: **to reason that** concludere che, fare il ragionamento che ♦ VI: **to reason (with sb)** far ragionare qn

▸ **reason out** VT + ADV: **to reason sth out** risolvere qc ragionandoci su

rea·son·able [ˈriːznəbl] ADJ (*person, price*) ragionevole; (*behaviour, decision*) sensato(-a); (*standard*) accettabile; **be reasonable!** sii ragionevole!; **a perfectly reasonable thing to do** una cosa perfettamente sensata da farsi; **it is reasonable to conclude that ...** si può logicamente concludere che...; **he wrote a reasonable essay** ha fatto un tema discreto

rea·son·ably [ˈriːznəblɪ] ADV (*fairly, quite*) abbastanza; (*in a reasonable way*) ragionevolmente; **reasonably well** discretamente; **the team played reasonably well** la squadra ha giocato discretamente; **a reasonably accurate report** una relazione abbastanza accurata; **one can reasonably suppose that ...** si può logicamente supporre che...; **reasonably priced accommodation** alloggi *mpl* a prezzi ragionevoli

rea·soned [ˈriːznd] ADJ (*discussion, approach*) ragionato(-a); (*argument, opinion*) ponderato(-a)

rea·son·ing [ˈriːznɪŋ] N ragionamento

re·as·semble [ˌriːəˈsembl] VT (*machine*) rimontare, riassemblare ♦ VI (*reconvene*) tornare a riunirsi

re·as·sert [ˌriːəˈsɜːt] VT riaffermare

re·assur·ance [ˌriːəˈʃʊərəns] N rassicurazione *f*

re·assure [ˌriːəˈʃʊəʳ] VT: **to reassure sb (of)** rassicurare qn (di *or* su)

re·assur·ing [ˌriːəˈʃʊərɪŋ] ADJ rassicurante

re·awak·en·ing [ˌriːəˈweɪkənɪŋ] N risveglio

re·bate [ˈriːbeɪt] N rimborso

re·bel [ADJ, n ˈrebl, vb rɪˈbel] ADJ, N ribelle *m/f* ♦ VI: **to rebel (against sb/sth)** ribellarsi (a qn/contro qc)

re·bel·lion [rɪˈbeljən] N ribellione *f*

re·bel·lious [rɪˈbeljəs] ADJ ribelle

re·birth [ˌriːˈbɜːθ] N rinascita

re·bound [n rɪˈbaʊnd, vb rɪˈbaʊnd] N: **on the rebound** per ripicca ♦ VI (*ball*) rimbalzare

▸ **rebound on** VI + PREP ricadere su, ritorcersi contro

re·buff [rɪˈbʌf] N secco rifiuto ♦ VT rifiutare, respingere

re·build [ˌriːˈbɪld] (*pt, pp* rebuilt [ˌriːˈbɪlt]) VT ricostruire

re·buke [rɪˈbjuːk] N rimprovero ♦ VT rimproverare; **to rebuke sb for sth/for doing sth** rimproverare qn per qc/per aver fatto qc

re·but [rɪˈbʌt] VT (*frm*) confutare

re·but·tal [rɪˈbʌtl] N (*frm*) confutazione *f*

re·cal·ci·trant [rɪˈkælsɪtrənt] ADJ (*frm*) riluttante

re·call [rɪˈkɔːl] N richiamo; **beyond recall** irrimediabilmente, per sempre; **the ground has been polluted beyond recall** il terreno è stato inquinato irrimediabilmente; **those days are gone beyond recall** quei tempi sono passati per sempre; **the recall of the ambassador** il richiamo in patria dell'ambasciatore; **he has total recall of what she said** ricorda perfettamente ciò che lei ha detto ♦ VT 1 (*call back: gen: Comput*) richiamare; (: *parliament*) riconvocare; (: *past*) far rivivere; **the ambassador has been recalled** l'ambasciatore è stato richiamato 2 (*remember*) ricordare, ricordarsi di; **I don't recall where we met** non ricordo dove ci siamo conosciuti

re·cant [rɪˈkænt] (*frm*) VT (*religious belief*) abiurare; (*statement*) ritrattare ♦ VI fare abiura

re·cap [ˈriːˌkæp] (*fam*) N riepilogo ♦ VT, VI riepilogare, ricapitolare; **to recap briefly ...** per ricapitolare brevemente...

re·cap·ture [ˈriːˈkæptʃəʳ] VT (*prisoner etc*) ricatturare; (*town*) riconquistare, riprendere; (*memory, scene*) ritrovare; (*atmosphere*) ricreare

recd ABBR = **received**

re·cede [rɪˈsiːd] VI (*tide, flood*) abbassarsi; (*view*) allontanarsi; (*danger, threat*) diminuire; **the threat of an epidemic is now receding** la minaccia di un'epidemia si sta allontanando; **his hair is starting to recede** sta cominciando a stempiarsi

re·ced·ing [rɪˈsiːdɪŋ] ADJ (*forehead, chin*) sfuggente; **he's got a receding hairline** è stempiato

re·ceipt [rɪˈsiːt] N 1 (*slip of paper*) ricevuta 2 (*frm, esp Comm*) ricevimento; **to acknowledge receipt of** accusare ricevuta di; **we are in receipt of ...** abbiamo ricevuto... 3 (*money taken*); **receipts** NPL incassi *mpl*, introiti *mpl*

re·ceiv·able [rɪˈsiːvəbl] ADJ (*Comm*) esigibile; (*owed*) dovuto(-a)

re·ceive [rɪˈsiːv] VT (*gen, also Radio, TV*) ricevere; (*stolen goods*) ricettare; **"received with thanks"** (*Comm*) "per quietanza"; **to receive sb into one's home** ricevere qn in casa; **the book was not well received** il libro non ha avuto *or* ricevuto un'accoglienza favorevole

Received Pronunciation N pronuncia standard (*dell'inglese*)

re·ceiv·er [rɪˈsiːvəʳ] N 1 (*gen*) persona che riceve qualcosa; (*of letter*) destinatario(-a); (*of stolen goods*) ricettatore(-trice); (*official*) receiver (*liquidator*) curatore *m* fallimentare 2 (*Radio*) apparecchio ricevente; (*Telec*) ricevitore *m*, cornetta (*fam*); **she picked up the receiver** ha sollevato la cornetta

re·ceiv·er·ship [rɪˈsiːvəʃɪp] N curatela; **to go into receivership** andare in amministrazione controllata

re·cent [ˈriːsnt] ADJ recente; **in recent memory** in tempi recenti; **in recent years** negli ultimi anni; **in recent weeks** nelle ultime settimane; **recent events** avvenimenti *mpl* recenti

re·cent·ly [ˈriːsntlɪ] ADV di recente, recentemente, ultimamente; **as recently as 1990** soltanto nel 1990; **until recently** fino a poco tempo fa; **I haven't seen him recently** non l'ho visto di recente

re·cep·ta·cle [rɪˈseptəkl] N (*frm*) recipiente *m*

re·cep·tion [rɪˈsepʃən] N 1 (*ceremony*) ricevimento; (*welcome*) accoglienza; **to get a warm reception** avere *or* ricevere un'accoglienza calorosa; **his speech got a cool reception** il suo discorso ha ricevuto una fredda accoglienza; **the**

reception will be at a big hotel il ricevimento si terrà in un grande albergo **2** (*desk: in hotel*) reception *f inv*; (: *in hospital, at doctor's*) accettazione *f*; (: *in large building, offices*) portineria; **please leave your key at reception** si prega di lasciare le chiavi alla reception **3** (*Radio, TV*) ricezione *f* **4** (*Brit Scol*) ≈ primina

reception centre N (*Brit*) centro di raccolta

reception desk N = reception 2

re·cep·tion·ist [rɪˈsɛpʃənɪst] N (*in hotel, offices*) receptionist *m/f inv*; (*at doctor's*) addetto(-a) alla ricezione, assistente *m/f* di studio

re·cep·tive [rɪˈsɛptɪv] ADJ ricettivo(-a)

re·cess [rɪˈsɛs] N **1** (*Law, Parliament: cessation of business*) ferie *fpl*, vacanza; (*USA Law: short break*) sospensione *f*; (*Scol, esp USA*) intervallo; **a ten-minute recess** una sospensione di dieci minuti; **after the summer recess** dopo le vacanze estive **2** (*for bed*) rientranza; (*for statue*) nicchia; (*fig: of mind*) recesso; **a recess beside the fireplace** una nicchia accanto al caminetto

re·ces·sion [rɪˈsɛʃən] N (*Econ*) recessione *f*

re·charge [riːˈtʃɑːdʒ] VT (*battery*) ricaricare

re·charge·able [riːˈtʃɑːdʒəbl] ADJ (*battery*) ricaricabile

reci·pe [ˈrɛsɪpɪ] N (*also fig*) ricetta

re·cipi·ent [rɪˈsɪpɪənt] N (*of letter*) destinatario(-a); (*of cheque*) beneficiario(-a); (*of award*) assegnatario(-a)

❏ **recipient** is not translated by the Italian word *recipiente*

re·cip·ro·cal [rɪˈsɪprəkəl] ADJ reciproco(-a); **reciprocal trading** scambio commerciale

re·cip·ro·cate [rɪˈsɪprəˌkeɪt] VT, VI ricambiare, contraccambiare

re·cit·al [rɪˈsaɪtl] N (*Mus*) recital *m inv*; (*of poetry*) recita; (*account*) resoconto

re·cite [rɪˈsaɪt] VT (*poem*) recitare; (*facts, details*) elencare, enumerare ♦ VI recitare

reck·less [ˈrɛklɪs] ADJ (*driver, driving, speed*) spericolato(-a); (*disregard, pursuit*) incosciente; (*action, decision*) avventato(-a)

reck·less·ly [ˈrɛklɪslɪ] ADV (*drive*) in modo spericolato; (*gamble, bet, plunge*) avventatamente

reck·on [ˈrɛkən] VT (*calculate*) calcolare; (*believe*) pensare, credere; (*judge*) considerare, stimare; **I reckon him to be one of the best** lo considero uno dei migliori, per me è uno dei migliori; **I reckon (that) we'll be late** prevedo che saremo in ritardo; **what do you reckon?** cosa ne pensi? ♦ VI contare, calcolare; **to reckon with sb** fare i conti con qn; **he is somebody to be reckoned with** è uno da non sottovalutare; **to reckon without sb/sth** non tener conto di qn/qc; **to reckon without doing sth** non calcolare di fare qc

▸ **reckon in** VT + ADV considerare; **when everything is reckoned in ...** a conti fatti...

▸ **reckon on** VI + PREP (*bank on*) contare su; (*expect*) prevedere; **to reckon on doing sth** far conto di fare qc

▸ **reckon up** VT + ADV (*frm: cost, losses*) calcolare; **to reckon up the bill** fare il conto

reck·on·ing [ˈrɛknɪŋ] N calcoli *mpl*, conti *mpl*; **by my reckoning** secondo i miei calcoli; **to be out in one's reckoning** aver sbagliato *or* fatto male i propri conti; **the day of reckoning** (*fig*) il momento della resa dei conti

re·claim [rɪˈkleɪm] VT (*baggage, waste materials*) ricuperare; (*money*) richiedere, reclamare; (*land*) bonificare; **before leaving I reclaimed my passport** prima di partire ho chiesto indietro il passaporto; **large areas were reclaimed** ampie zone sono state bonificate

rec·la·ma·tion [ˌrɛkləˈmeɪʃən] N (*of waste materials*) ricupero; (*of land*) bonifica

re·cline [rɪˈklaɪn] VI (*person*) essere sdraiato(-a); **the seat reclines** il sedile è reclinabile *or* ribaltabile

re·clin·ing [rɪˈklaɪnɪŋ] ADJ: **reclining seat** sedile reclinabile *or* ribaltabile

re·cluse [rɪˈkluːs] N recluso(-a), eremita *m*

rec·og·ni·tion [ˌrɛkəgˈnɪʃən] N riconoscimento; **in recognition of** in *or* come segno di riconoscimento per; **to gain recognition** ottenere un riconoscimento, essere riconosciuto(-a); **to change/change sth beyond recognition**

diventare/rendere qc irriconoscibile; **transformed** *or* **changed beyond recognition** irriconoscibile; **a sign of recognition** un segno di riconoscimento

rec·og·niz·able [ˈrɛkəgˌnaɪzəbl] ADJ: **recognizable (by)** riconoscibile (a *or* da)

rec·og·nize [ˈrɛkəgˌnaɪz] VT (*all senses*) riconoscere; **to recognize (by/as)** riconoscere (a *or* da/come)

re·coil [rɪˈkɔɪl] VI **1** (*person: draw back*) tirarsi indietro; **to recoil (from) sth** indietreggiare (di fronte *or* davanti a) qc; **to recoil from doing sth** rifuggire dal fare qc **2** (*gun*) rinculare ♦ N (*of gun*) rinculo

rec·ol·lect [ˌrɛkəˈlɛkt] VT rammentare, ricordare

rec·ol·lec·tion [ˌrɛkəˈlɛkʃən] N memoria, ricordo; **to the best of my recollection** per quello che mi ricordo

rec·om·mend [ˌrɛkəˈmɛnd] VT (*course of action*) consigliare; (*product, doctor*) raccomandare, consigliare; (*person: for job*) raccomandare; **I recommend that he sees a doctor** (*frm*) gli consiglierei di vedere un medico; **what do you recommend?** che cosa ci consiglia?; **to recommend sb for sth** raccomandare qn per qc; **she has a lot to recommend her** ha molti elementi a suo favore

rec·om·men·da·tion [ˌrɛkəmɛnˈdeɪʃən] N (*of person, product*) raccomandazione *f*; (*of course of action*) consiglio; **to do sth on sb's recommendation** fare qc su *or* dietro consiglio di qn; **the committee's recommendations will be made public** le raccomandazioni della commissione verranno rese pubbliche; **on his recommendation I visited Conwy** su suo consiglio ho visitato Conwy

rec·om·pense [ˈrɛkəmpɛns] N ricompensa; (*Law: for damage*) risarcimento ♦ VT ricompensare; **to recompense sb (for sth)** (*Law*) risarcire qn (di qc)

rec·on·cil·able [ˌrɛkənˌsaɪləbl] ADJ: **reconcilable (with)** conciliabile (con)

rec·on·cile [ˈrɛkənˌsaɪl] VT (*persons*) riconciliare; (*theories, contradictions*) conciliare; **to become reconciled** (*people*) riconciliarsi; **the couple have now been reconciled** la coppia ora si è riconciliata; **to reconcile o.s. to sth** rassegnarsi a qc; **how can you reconcile your ideals with your lifestyle?** come riesci a conciliare i tuoi ideali con il tuo stile di vita?

rec·on·cilia·tion [ˌrɛkənsɪlɪˈeɪʃən] N (*of people*) riconciliazione *f*; (*of contradictions, attitudes*) conciliazione *f*

re·con·dite [rɪˈkɒndaɪt] ADJ (*frm*) recondito(-a)

re·con·di·tion [ˌriːkənˈdɪʃən] VT (*engine*) ricondizionare

re·con·nais·sance [rɪˈkɒnɪsəns] N (*Mil*) ricognizione *f*

re·con·noi·tre, re·con·noi·ter (*USA*) [ˌrɛkəˈnɔɪtəʳ](*Mil*) VT fare una ricognizione di ♦ VI fare una ricognizione

re·con·sid·er [ˌriːkənˈsɪdəʳ] VT riconsiderare

re·con·sti·tute [riːˈkɒnstɪˌtjuːt] VT ricostituire

re·con·struct [ˌriːkənˈstrʌkt] VT ricostruire

re·con·struc·tion [ˌriːkənˈstrʌkʃən] N ricostruzione *f*

re·con·vene [ˌriːkənˈviːn] VT riconvocare ♦ VI radunarsi

rec·ord [*n, adj* ˈrɛkɔːd, *vb* rɪˈkɔːd] N **1** (*report, note*) rapporto; (*file*) pratica, dossier *m inv*; (*minutes: of meeting*) verbale *m*; (*Law*) registro; (*historical report*) documento; (*Comput*) record *m inv*, registrazione *f*; **record of attendance** registro delle presenze; **public records** archivi *mpl*; **I'll check in the records** controllo in archivio; **there is no record of it** non c'è niente che lo possa comprovare; **there is no record of your booking** non c'è traccia della vostra prenotazione; **to keep a record of sth** tener nota di qc; **just for the record** tanto per mettere le cose in chiaro; **he is on record as saying that ...** ha dichiarato pubblicamente che...; **it is on record that ...** è stato registrato che...; **to place** *or* **put sth on record** mettere qc agli atti; **he told me off the record** (*fam*) me l'ha detto ufficiosamente; **to set the record straight** mettere le cose in chiaro **2** (*person's past in general*) precedenti *mpl*; (*as dossier*) resoconto; (*also:* **criminal record**) menzione *f* nel casellario giudiziale; **to have a criminal record** avere precedenti penali; **he has a clean record** ha la fedina penale pulita, non ha precedenti penali; **police records** schedario *msg* della polizia; **Italy's excellent record** i brillanti successi italiani; **the school has a poor record of exam passes** in quella scuola si registra una bassa percentuale di promozioni **3** (*Sport*) record *m inv*, primato; **to beat** *or* **break a record** battere un record *or* un primato; **to hold the record (for sth)** detenere il primato (di qc); **the world**

record il record mondiale **4** (*Mus*) disco; **one of my favourite records** uno dei miei dischi preferiti ♦ ADJ ATTR record *inv*; **in record time** a tempo di record ♦ VT **1** (*set down*) registrare, prendere nota di; (*relate*) raccontare; **to record one's vote** votare **2** (*Mus*) registrare, incidere; (*Comput*) registrare **3** (*subj: thermometer*) registrare
❑ **record** is not translated by the Italian word *ricordare*

record card [ˈrekɔːdˌkɑːd] N (*index card*) scheda
re·cord·er [rɪˈkɔːdəʳ] N **1** (*tape recorder*) registratore *m* **2** (*Mus*) flauto diritto *or* dolce; **to play the recorder** suonare il flauto dolce **3** (*Law: in England and Wales*) avvocato che *funge da giudice*
record holder [ˈrekɔːdˌhəʊldəʳ] N (*Sport*) primatista *m/f*, detentore(-trice) di (un) record
re·cord·ing [rɪˈkɔːdɪŋ] N (*of programme, song*) registrazione *f*
recording studio N sala di registrazione
record library [ˈrekɔːdˌlaɪbrərɪ] N discoteca (*raccolta*)
record player [ˈrekɔːdˌpleɪəʳ] N giradischi *m inv*
re·count¹ [rɪˈkaʊnt] VT (*narrate*) raccontare
re·count² [*n* ˈriːkaʊnt, *vb* ˌriːˈkaʊnt] N (*of votes*) nuovo conteggio ♦ VT ricontare, rifare il conteggio di
re·coup [rɪˈkuːp] VT ricuperare; **to recoup one's losses** ricuperare le perdite, rifarsi
re·course [rɪˈkɔːs] N (*frm*): **to have recourse to** ricorrere a, far ricorso a
re·cov·er [rɪˈkʌvəʳ] VT (*belongings, goods, wreck, lost time*) ricuperare; (*reclaim: money*) ottenere il rimborso di; (*Law: damages*) ottenere il risarcimento di; (*balance, appetite, health etc*) ritrovare, ricuperare; **to recover one's senses** riprendere i sensi; (*fig*) ritornare in sé ♦ VI (*all senses*) riprendersi; (*from illness*) ristabilirsi; **it took her half an hour to recover** le ci è voluta mezz'ora per riprendersi
❑ **recover** is not translated by the Italian word *ricoverare*

re·cover [ˌriːˈkʌvəʳ] VT (*chair, settee*) ricoprire
re·cov·ery [rɪˈkʌvərɪ] N **1** (*see vt*) ricupero; rimborso; risarcimento **2** (*see vi*) ripresa; **to make a recovery** (*Med*) avere *or* fare un miglioramento; (*Sport, Fin*) avere una ripresa; **to be on the way to recovery** (*Med*) essere in via di guarigione; (*Sport, Fin*) essere in ripresa
❑ **recovery** is not translated by the Italian word *ricovero*

re·cre·ate [ˌriːkrɪˈeɪt] VT ricreare
rec·rea·tion N **1** [ˌrekrɪˈeɪʃən](*leisure*) ricreazione *f*; **interests and recreations** interessi *mpl* e svaghi, *mpl* **2** [ˌriːkrɪˈeɪʃən](*restoration*) restaurazione *f*; **the recreation of the original theatre** la ricostruzione del teatro antico
rec·rea·tion·al [ˌrekrɪˈeɪʃənəl] ADJ ricreativo(-a)
recreational drug N *sostanza stupefacente usata a scopo ricreativo*
recreational vehicle N (*USA: motorhome*) camper *m inv*; (*trailer*) roulotte *f inv*
re·crimi·na·tion [rɪˌkrɪmɪˈneɪʃən] N recriminazione *f*
re·cruit [rɪˈkruːt] N (*Mil*) recluta; (*new member: of club*) nuovo(-a) iscritto(-a); (: *of staff*) nuovo(-a) assunto(-a) ♦ VT (*staff, members, soldiers*) reclutare
re·cruit·ing of·fice [rɪˈkruːtɪŋˌɒfɪs] N ufficio di reclutamento
re·cruit·ment [rɪˈkruːtmənt] N reclutamento
rec·tan·gle [ˈrekˌtæŋgl] N rettangolo
rec·tan·gu·lar [rekˈtæŋɡjʊləʳ] ADJ rettangolare
rec·ti·fy [ˈrektɪfaɪ] VT (*error*) rettificare; (*omission*) riparare a
rec·tor [ˈrektəʳ] N (*Rel*) parroco (*anglicano*); (*Univ*) rettore *m*; (*in Scottish universities*) *personalità eletta dagli studenti per rappresentarli*; (*of school*) preside *m/f*
rec·tory [ˈrektərɪ] N casa parrocchiale (*anglicana*)
rec·tum [ˈrektəm] N (*Anat*) retto
re·cu·per·ate [rɪˈkuːpəˌreɪt] VI (*Med*) ristabilirsi ♦ VT (*losses*) ricuperare
re·cur [rɪˈkɜː] VI (*pain, event, mistake*) ripetersi; (*idea, theme*) ricorrere, riapparire; (*difficulty, opportunity, symptoms*) ripresentarsi, ripetersi; **such a disaster could recur** questo disastro potrebbe riaccadere; **if the symptoms recur ...** se i sintomi si ripresentano...

re·cur·rence [rɪˈkʌrəns] N (*of pain, dream, violence*) ripetersi *m*; (*of injury, problem*) ripresentarsi *m*; (*of disease, symptoms*) ricomparsa; (*of idea, theme*) ricorrenza
re·cur·rent [rɪˈkʌrənt] ADJ ricorrente
re·cur·ring [rɪˈkɜːrɪŋ] ADJ (*Math*) periodico(-a)
recyclable [ˌriːˈsaɪkləbl] ADJ riciclabile
re·cy·cle [ˌriːˈsaɪkl] VT riciclare
re·cy·cling [ˌriːˈsaɪklɪŋ] N riciclaggio
red [red] ADJ (*comp* **-der**, *superl* **-dest**) (*all senses*) rosso(-a); **to be red in the face** (*from physical effort*) essere tutto(-a) rosso(-a), avere il viso rosso; (*embarrassed*) essere rosso(-a) (in viso); **to roll out the red carpet (for sb)** (*fig*) accogliere qn in pompa magna ♦ N (*colour*) rosso; (*Pol: pej*) rosso(-a); **in the red** (*Fin: account*) in rosso, scoperto(-a); (: *firm*) in deficit, in rosso; **to see red** (*fig*) vedere rosso
red alert N allarme rosso
red-blooded [ˌredˈblʌdɪd] ADJ (*fam*) gagliardo(-a)
red carpet treatment N trattamento d'onore
Red Cross N: **the Red Cross** la Croce Rossa
red·cur·rant [ˌredˈkʌrənt] N ribes *m inv* rosso; **redcurrant jelly** marmellata di ribes rosso
red·den [ˈredn] VT arrossare, tingere di rosso ♦ VI (*sky, leaves*) diventar rosso, tingersi di rosso; (*person*) arrossire
red·dish [ˈredɪʃ] ADJ rossiccio(-a), rossastro(-a); (*hair*) rossiccio(-a)
re·deco·rate [ˌriːˈdekəˌreɪt] VT tinteggiare (e tappezzare) di nuovo
re·deem [rɪˈdiːm] VT (*Rel: sinner*) redimere; (*buy back: pawned goods*) disimpegnare, riscattare; (*Fin: debt, mortgage*) estinguere, ammortare; (*fulfil: promise*) mantenere; (: *obligation*) adempiere a; (: *compensate for: fault*) compensare; **to redeem o.s.** farsi perdonare
re·deem·able [rɪˈdiːməbl] ADJ (*bonds, shares*) redimibile
re·deem·ing [rɪˈdiːmɪŋ] ADJ: **redeeming feature** unico aspetto positivo
re·de·fine [ˌriːdɪˈfaɪn] VT ridefinire
re·demp·tion [rɪˈdempʃən] N (*Rel*) redenzione *f*; **past** *or* **beyond redemption** irrecuperabile
re·deploy [ˌriːdɪˈplɔɪ] VT (*troops: send elsewhere*) trasferire in un altro settore; (: *reorganize*) riorganizzare lo schieramento di; (*workers*) reimpiegare; (*resources*) ridistribuire
re·deploy·ment [ˌriːdɪˈplɔɪmənt] N (*of resources*) ridistribuzione *f*
re·deve·lop [ˌriːdɪˈveləp] VT (*area*) ristrutturare
re·devel·op·ment [ˌriːdɪˈveləpmənt] N (*of area*) ristrutturazione *f*
red-haired [ˌredˈheəd] ADJ con i *or* dai capelli rossi
red-handed [ˌredˈhændɪd] ADJ: **to catch sb red-handed** prendere qn con le mani nel sacco, cogliere qn in flagrante
red·head [ˈredˌhed] N (*person with red hair*) rosso(-a)
red herring N (*fig*) falsa pista
red-hot [ˌredˈhɒt] ADJ arroventato(-a), rovente
re·di·rect [ˌriːdaɪˈrekt] VT (*letter*) rispedire (*a un nuovo indirizzo*)
re·dis·trib·ute [ˌriːdɪsˈtrɪbjuːt] VT ridistribuire
red-letter day [ˌredˈletəˌdeɪ] N giorno memorabile
red light N (*Aut*) (semaforo) rosso; **to go through a red light** passare col rosso
red-light district [ˌredˈlaɪtˌdɪstrɪkt] N quartiere *m* a luce rossa
red meat N carne *f* rossa
red·ness [ˈrednɪs] N (*of skin*) rossore *m*; (*of hair, colour*) rosso
re·do [ˌriːˈduː] VT (*pt* redid, *pp* redone) rifare
redo·lent [ˈredəʊlənt] ADJ (*liter*): **redolent of** fragrante di, profumato(-a) di; (*fig*) evocativo(-a) di
re·dou·ble [ˌriːˈdʌbl] VT raddoppiare; **to redouble one's efforts** intensificare *or* raddoppiare gli sforzi
re·draft [*n* riːˈdrɑːft, *vb* ˌriːˈdrɑːft] N nuova stesura ♦ VT stendere di nuovo, fare una nuova stesura di
re·dress [rɪˈdres](*frm*) N riparazione *f* ♦ VT riparare; **to redress the balance** ristabilire l'equilibrio
Red Sea N: **the Red Sea** il mar Rosso
red tape N lungaggini *fpl* burocratiche
re·duce [rɪˈdjuːs] VT **1** (*gen*) ridurre; (*prices, taxes*) abbassare,

ridurre, diminuire; (*speed, voltage, expenses: Med: swelling*) ridurre, diminuire; (*temperature*) far diminuire, far scendere; **to reduce sth by/to** ridurre qc di/a; "**reduce speed now**" (*Aut*) "rallentare"; **to reduce sth to ashes** ridurre qc in cenere; **to reduce sb to silence/despair/tears** ridurre qn al silenzio/alla disperazione/in lacrime; **we were reduced to begging** eravamo ridotti all'elemosina; **reduced to nothing** ridotto(-a) a zero **2** (*Mil*): **to reduce sb to the ranks** degradare qn a soldato semplice ♦ VI (*slim*) dimagrire

re·duced [rɪˈdjuːst] ADJ (*decreased*) ridotto(-a); **at a reduced price** a prezzo ribassato *or* ridotto; "**greatly reduced prices**" "grandi ribassi"; **in reduced circumstances** nelle ristrettezze

re·duc·tion [rɪˈdʌkʃən] N (*see vt a*) riduzione *f*; diminuzione *f*; **reductions in staff** riduzioni di personale; **reductions for cash** sconto per (il pagamento in) contanti; "**huge reductions!**" "grandi sconti!"

re·dun·dan·cy [rɪˈdʌndənsɪ] N (*Industry*) licenziamento (*per esubero di personale*); (*frm: profusion*) superfluità; (*Literature*) ridondanza; **compulsory redundancy** licenziamento (*per esubero*); **voluntary redundancy** forma di cassa integrazione volontaria

redundancy payment N (*Brit*) indennità *f inv* di licenziamento

re·dun·dant [rɪˈdʌndənt] ADJ (*Brit: worker*) licenziato(-a) (*per esubero di personale*); (*detail, object*) superfluo(-a); (*Literature*) ridondante; **to be made redundant** (*worker*) essere licenziato(-a) (*perché in esubero*); **these skills are now redundant** queste capacità sono ormai superflue

reed [riːd] N (*Bot*) canna; (*Mus: in mouthpiece*) ancia; (*: instrument*) strumento a fiato munito di ancia

re-educate [ˌriːˈedjʊˌkeɪt] VT rieducare

reedy [ˈriːdɪ] ADJ (*comp* -**ier**, *superl* -**iest**) (*voice, instrument*) acuto(-a)

reef [riːf] N (*Geog*) scogliera, banco di scogli; **coral reef** barriera corallina; **the ship ran onto a reef** la nave si è incagliata su una scogliera

reek [riːk] VI: **to reek of sth** puzzare di qc

reel [riːl] N **1** (*in fishing etc*) mulinello; (*cotton reel*) rocchetto, spoletta; (*Tech*) aspo; (*for tape recorder*) bobina; (*Phot: for small camera*) rotolino, rullino; (*: of cine film*) bobina, pizza **2** (*dance*) danza scozzese o irlandese molto vivace ♦ VI (*sway*) vacillare, barcollare; **my head is reeling** mi gira la testa ♦ VT (*Tech*) annaspare; (*wind up*) avvolgere
▸ **reel in** VT + ADV (*fish*) tirare su
▸ **reel off** VT + ADV snocciolare, sciorinare

re-election [ˌriːɪˈlekʃən] N rielezione *f*

re-enter [ˌriːˈentəʳ] VI rientrare; **to re-enter for an exam** ripresentarsi a un esame ♦ VT rientrare in

re-entry [ˌriːˈentrɪ] N rientro

re-export [ˌriːˈekspɔːt] VT riesportare ♦ N (*trading activity*) riesportazione *f*; (*goods*) merce *f* riesportata

ref [ref] N ABBR (*Sport: fam:* = *referee*) arbitro

ref. ABBR (*Comm*) = **reference**

re·fec·tory [rɪˈfektərɪ] N refettorio

re·fer [rɪˈfɜːʳ] VT (*gen*): **to refer sth to** (*matter, decision*) sottoporre qc a qn, deferire qc a qn; **to refer sb to sth** richiamare l'attenzione di qn su qc; **he referred me to the manager** mi ha detto di rivolgermi al direttore; **to refer sb to a specialist** mandare qn da uno specialista; "**refer to drawer**" (*on cheque*) "rivolgersi al traente" ♦ VI **1** (*relate to*) riferirsi a; **does that refer to me?** vale anche per me? **2** (*allude to: directly*) fare riferimento a; (*: indirectly*) fare allusione *or* accenno a; **he referred to a recent trip to Canada** ha fatto accenno ad un recente viaggio in Canada; **referring to your letter** (*Comm*) in riferimento alla Vostra lettera; **we will not refer to it again** non ne riparleremo più **3** (*turn attention to, see*) consultare; (*consult: person*) rivolgersi a; **please refer to section 3** vedi sezione 3

ref·er·ee [ˌrefəˈriː] N **1** (*in dispute, also Sport*) arbitro; (*Tennis*) giudice *m* di gara **2** (*Brit: for job application*) referenza; **to give sb as a referee** dare il nome di qn per referenze; **to be referee for sb** scrivere una lettera di referenze per qn ♦ VT arbitrare

ref·er·ence [ˈrefrəns] N **1** (*allusion: direct*) riferimento,

menzione *f*; (*: indirect*) allusione *f*; (*relation, connection*) rapporto; (*Comm: in letter*): **with reference to** in *or* con riferimento a; **without reference to any particular case** senza nessun riferimento specifico **2** (*from book, list*) rimando; (*on letter*) numero di riferimento; (*on map*) coordinate *fpl*; "**please quote this reference**" (*Comm*) "si prega di far riferimento al numero di protocollo"; **our reference is A32** il nostro numero di riferimento è A32 **3** (*testimonial*): **reference(s)** referenze *fpl*; **they require references** chiedono delle referenze; **may I give you as a reference?** posso dare il suo nome per referenze? ♦ ADJ (*library*) di consultazione; (*point*) di riferimento

reference book N libro *or* testo di consultazione

reference library N biblioteca per la consultazione

reference number N (*Comm*) numero di riferimento, numero di protocollo

ref·er·en·dum [ˌrefəˈrendəm] N (*pl* **referendums** *or* **referenda** [-də]) referendum *m inv*

refer·ral [rɪˈfɜːrəl] N deferimento; (*Med*): **she got a referral to a specialist** l'hanno mandata da uno specialista

re·fill [*n* ˈriːfɪl, *vb* ˌriːˈfɪl] N (*for pen etc*) ricambio ♦ VT (*gen*) riempire (di nuovo); (*pen, lighter*) ricaricare

re·fine [rɪˈfaɪn] VT (*sugar, oil, tastes, style*) raffinare; (*design, technique, machine*) perfezionare
▸ **refine on, refine upon** VI + PREP perfezionare, migliorare

re·fined [rɪˈfaɪnd] ADJ raffinato(-a)

re·fine·ment [rɪˈfaɪnmənt] N (*of person, language*) raffinatezza, finezza; (*in machine, system*) miglioramento

re·fin·ery [rɪˈfaɪnərɪ] N raffineria; **oil/sugar refinery** raffineria di petrolio/zucchero

re·fit [*n* ˈriːfɪt, *vb* ˌriːˈfɪt] N (*Naut*) raddobbo ♦ VT (*ship*) raddobbare

re·flate [ˌriːˈfleɪt] VT (*Econ*) reflazionare

re·fla·tion [ˌriːˈfleɪʃən] N (*Econ*) reflazione *f*

re·fla·tion·ary [ˌriːˈfleɪʃənərɪ] ADJ (*Econ: programme*) reflazionistico(-a)

re·flect [rɪˈflekt] VT **1** (*light, image, heat*) riflettere; (*fig*) rispecchiare; **to reflect credit on sb** fare onore a qn **2** (*think*): **to reflect that** riflettere sul fatto che ♦ VI **1** (*think, meditate*): **to reflect (on sth)** riflettere (su qc) **2** (*discredit*): **to reflect (up)on sb/sth** ripercuotersi su qn/qc

re·flec·tion [rɪˈflekʃən] N **1** (*act*) riflessione *f*; (*in mirror etc*) riflesso **2** (*thought*) riflessione *f*; **on reflection** dopo aver riflettuto, pensandoci sopra **3** (*aspersion, doubt*) dubbio; **this is no reflection on your honesty** questa non è un'insinuazione sulla tua onestà **4** (*Math*) riflessione *f*

re·flec·tor [rɪˈflektəʳ] N (*Aut: also: rear reflector*) catarifrangente *m*

re·flex [ˈriːfleks] N riflesso ♦ ADJ (*Math*) concavo(-a)

re·flex·ive [rɪˈfleksɪv] ADJ (*Gram*) riflessivo(-a); **reflexive verb** verbo riflessivo

re·form [rɪˈfɔːm] N riforma ♦ VT (*society, morals*) riformare; (*criminal*) rieducare, ricuperare socialmente; (*person's character*) correggere ♦ VI (*person*) emendarsi

re·for·mat [ˌriːˈfɔːmæt] VT (*Comput*) riformattare

Ref·or·ma·tion [ˌrefəˈmeɪʃən] N (*Rel*): **the Reformation** la Riforma

re·forma·tory [rɪˈfɔːmətərɪ] N (*USA*) riformatorio

re·formed [rɪˈfɔːmd] ADJ (*criminal*) rieducato(-a), ricuperato(-a) alla società; (*morals*) riformato(-a)

re·form·er [rɪˈfɔːməʳ] N riformatore(-trice)

re·frain [rɪˈfreɪn] VI: **to refrain from sth/from doing sth** astenersi *or* trattenersi da qc/dal fare qc; **she refrained from making any comment** si astenne dal fare qualsiasi commento

re·fresh [rɪˈfreʃ] VT (*subj: drink*) rinfrescare; (*: food, sleep, bath*) ristorare; (*: fig: memory*) rinfrescare; **this will refresh your memory** questo ti rinfrescherà la memoria

re·fresh·er course [rɪˈfreʃəˌkɔːs] N (*Brit*) corso di aggiornamento

re·fresh·ing [rɪˈfreʃɪŋ] ADJ (*drink*) rinfrescante; (*sleep*) ristoratore(-trice); (*change*) piacevole; (*idea, point of view*) originale; **it was a refreshing change** è stato un piacevole cambiamento

re·fresh·ment [rɪˈfreʃmənt] N (*eating, resting*) ristoro; **re- freshments** NPL (*food and drink*) rinfreschi *mpl*

re·frig·era·tion [rɪˌfrɪdʒəˈreɪʃən] N refrigerazione *f*

re·frig·era·tor [rɪˈfrɪdʒəˌreɪtəʳ] N frigorifero

re·fu·el [ˌriːˈfjʊəl] VI rifornirsi di carburante, fare rifornimento (di carburante) ♦ VT rifornire di carburante

ref·uge [ˈrefjuːdʒ] N (*shelter*) riparo; (*for climbers, battered wives: fig*) rifugio; **place of refuge** rifugio; **to take refuge in** (*also fig*) rifugiarsi in

refu·gee [ˌrefjʊˈdʒiː] N rifugiato(-a), profugo(-a)

refugee camp N campo *m* profughi, inv

re·fund [*n* ˈriːfʌnd, *vb* rɪˈfʌnd] N rimborso ♦ VT rimborsare; **to refund sb's expenses** rimborsare qn

re·fur·bish [ˌriːˈfɜːbɪʃ] VT (*frm*) rimettere a nuovo

re·fur·nish [ˌriːˈfɜːnɪʃ] VT ammobiliare di nuovo

re·fus·al [rɪˈfjuːzəl] N: **refusal (to do)** rifiuto (di *or* a fare); **to have first refusal on sth** avere il diritto d'opzione su qc

re·fuse¹ [rɪˈfjuːz] VT (*all senses*) rifiutare; **to refuse sb sth** rifiutare qc a qn; **to refuse to do sth** rifiutare *or* rifiutarsi di fare qc ♦ VI rifiutarsi; (*horse*) rifiutare (l'ostacolo)

ref·use² [ˈrefjuːs] N rifiuti *mpl*; **garden refuse** rifiuti del giardino

refuse collection [ˈrefjuːzkəˌlekʃən] N raccolta dei rifiuti

refuse disposal [ˈrefjuːzdɪspˌəʊzl] N smaltimento dei rifiuti

re·fuse·nik [rɪˈfjuːznɪk] N (*old*) ebreo a cui il governo sovietico impediva di lasciare il paese

re·fute [rɪˈfjuːt] VT (*frm*) confutare

re·gain [rɪˈgeɪn] VT (*gen*) riguadagnare; (*balance, consciousness*) riprendere; (*confidence*) riacquistare; (*health*) recuperare; **to regain possession of sth** rientrare in possesso di qc; **to regain one's composure** ricomporsi; **to regain control** riacquistare il controllo; **to regain consciousness** riprendere conoscenza

re·gal [ˈriːgəl] ADJ (*bearing, manners*) regale; (*person*) dal portamento regale

re·gale [rɪˈgeɪl] VT deliziare, intrattenere; **to regale sb with sth** intrattenere qn con qc

❏ **regale** is not translated by the Italian word *regalare*

re·ga·lia [rɪˈgeɪlɪə] N (*royal trappings*) insegne *fpl* reali; (*gen: insignia*) abiti *mpl* da cerimonia

re·gard [rɪˈgɑːd] N 1 (*relation*): **in** *or* **with regard to** per quanto riguarda, riguardo a; **in this regard** (*frm*) a questo riguardo *or* proposito 2 (*esteem, concern*) riguardo, stima; **out of regard for** per riguardo a; **to have a high regard for sb, hold sb in high regard** aver molta stima per qn, tenere qn in grande considerazione; **he shows little regard for their feelings** dimostra scarsa considerazione per loro 3 (*in messages*): **regards to Maria, please give my regards to Maria** salutami Maria, da' i miei saluti a Maria; (*as letter-ending*): (**kind**) **regards** cordiali saluti ♦ VT 1 (*consider*) considerare, stimare; **to regard sth as** considerare qc come; **we don't regard it as necessary** non lo riteniamo necessario 2 (*concern*) riguardare; **as regards ...** per quel che riguarda..., riguardo a...

re·gard·ing [rɪˈgɑːdɪŋ] PREP riguardo a, per quanto riguarda; **the laws regarding the export of animals** le leggi riguardanti l'esportazione di animali

re·gard·less [rɪˈgɑːdlɪs] ADJ: **regardless of** (*heedless of*) senza preoccuparsi di; (*in spite of*) a dispetto di; **regardless of rank** senza distinzioni; **regardless of race** senza distinzioni di razza ♦ ADV (*fam*): **to carry on regardless** continuare come se niente fosse; **she did it regardless** l'ha fatto lo stesso

re·gat·ta [rɪˈgætə] N regata

re·gen·cy [ˈriːdʒənsɪ] N reggenza

re·gen·er·ate [rɪˈdʒenəˌreɪt] (*frm*) VT (*Bio, also fig: society*) rigenerare; (: *feelings, enthusiasm*) far rinascere ♦ VI (*see vt*) rigenerarsi; rinascere

re·gent [ˈriːdʒənt] N reggente *m/f*

reg·gae [ˈregeɪ] N (*Mus*) reggae *m*

ré·gime [reɪˈʒiːm] N regime *m*

regi·ment [*n* ˈredʒɪmənt, *vb* ˈredʒɪˌment] N (*Mil*) reggimento ♦ VT (*fig*) irreggimentare

regi·men·tal [ˌredʒɪˈmentl] ADJ reggimentale

regi·men·ta·tion [ˌredʒɪmenˈteɪʃən] N (*pej*) irreggimentazione *f*

re·gion [ˈriːdʒən] N (*all senses*) regione *f*; **in the region of 40** (*fig*) circa 40, intorno a 40

re·gion·al [ˈriːdʒənl] ADJ regionale; **regional development** (*Brit: Admin*) sviluppo economico delle regioni; **regional development fund** fondo per lo sviluppo regionale

reg·is·ter [ˈredʒɪstəʳ] N (*gen*) registro; (*of members*) elenco; **the register of births, marriages and deaths** l'anagrafe *f*; **the hotel register** il registro dell'albergo; **to call the register** fare l'appello ♦ VT 1 (*fact, birth, death*) registrare; (*vehicle*) immatricolare; (*trademark*) depositare; (*complaint, dissatisfaction*) sporgere; **to register a protest** presentare un esposto; **he registered the birth of his son** ha denunciato all'anagrafe la nascita del figlio 2 (*Post: letter*) assicurare; (*Rail: luggage*) spedire assicurato(-a) 3 (*indicate: speed, temperature*) registrare, segnare; (: *dismay, disbelief, surprise*) dar segno di, mostrare ♦ VI 1 (*for class*) iscriversi; (*for work*) mettersi in lista; (*at hotel*) firmare il registro; **to register with a doctor** mettersi nella lista di un medico come paziente; **to register for a course** iscriversi a un corso 2 (*have impact, become clear*): **it didn't register (with me)** non me ne sono reso conto

reg·is·tered [ˈredʒɪstəd] ADJ 1 (*student, voter*) iscritto(-a); (*car*) immatricolato(-a); (*Comm: design*) depositato(-a); (*charity*) riconosciuto(-a) 2 (*Brit: letter, luggage*) assicurato(-a); **a registered letter** un'assicurata

registered company N società *f inv* iscritta all'Ufficio del Registro

registered nurse N (*USA*) infermiere(-a) diplomato(-a)

registered office N sede *f* legale

registered trademark N marchio registrato

reg·is·trar [ˌredʒɪsˈtrɑːʳ] N (*of births, deaths, marriages*) ufficiale *m* di stato civile; (*Univ*) direttore *m* amministrativo; (*Med*) medico ospedaliero superiore ad un interno; **Registrar of Companies** ≈ Ufficio del Registro

reg·is·tra·tion [ˌredʒɪsˈtreɪʃən] N (*gen*) registrazione *f*; (*of vehicle*) immatricolazione *f*; (*of voters, members*) iscrizione *f*; (*Scol*) appello; **during registration** durante l'appello; **English is the first lesson after registration** la prima lezione dopo l'appello è quella d'inglese; **L-/M- etc registration** dicitura su targhe automobilistiche che ne indica l'anno di fabbricazione; **registration of voters** iscrizione alle liste elettorali dei votanti

reg·is·try [ˈredʒɪstrɪ] N (*record office*) archivio; (*in university*) segreteria

registry office N (*Brit*) anagrafe *f*; **to get married in a registry office** ≈ sposarsi in municipio

re·gret [rɪˈgret] N 1 rimpianto, rammarico; **much to my regret, to my great regret** con mio grande dispiacere; **I have no regrets** non ho rimpianti 2 **regrets** NPL (*excuses*) scuse *fpl* ♦ VT (*news, death*) essere dispiaciuto(-a) per, essere desolato(-a) per; **to regret doing sth** rimpiangere di aver fatto qc; **try it, you won't regret it!** provalo, non te ne pentirai!; **he is very ill, I regret to say** purtroppo è molto malato; **I regret that I will be unable to attend your party** (*frm*) mi rincresce (di) non poter venire alla vostra festa; **we regret to inform you that ...** (*frm*) siamo spiacenti di informarla che...; **I regret that I/he cannot help** mi rincresce (di) non poter aiutare/che lui non possa aiutare

re·gret·ful·ly [rɪˈgretfəlɪ] ADV (*sadly*) con molto rimpianto, con rincrescimento; (*unwillingly*) a malincuore

re·gret·table [rɪˈgretəbl] ADJ (*deplorable*) increscioso(-a), deplorevole; (*unfortunate*): **her absence is regrettable** ci rincresce che sia assente

re·gret·tably [rɪˈgretəblɪ] ADV (*unfortunately*) purtroppo, sfortunatamente; **regrettably few** pochi, purtroppo

re·group [ˌriːˈgruːp] VI raggrupparsi (di nuovo) ♦ VT raggruppare (di nuovo)

Regt ABBR = **regiment**

regu·lar [ˈregjʊləʳ] ADJ 1 (*gen: shape, employment, army, verb*) regolare; **as regular as clockwork** (*person, event*) puntuale come un orologio; (*visits*) molto regolare; **at regular intervals** a intervalli regolari 2 (*habitual: visitor, client*) fisso(-a); (: *listener, reader*) fedele; (*Comm: size, price*) normale; **he's a regular customer** è un cliente abituale; **a regular portion**

of fries una porzione media di patatine fritte **3** (*permissible: action, procedure*) corretto(-a) **4** (*fam: intensive*): **it's a regular nuisance** è una solenne scocciatura ♦ N (*customer, client*) habitué *m/f inv*, cliente *m/f* abituale; (*Mil*) soldato regolare

regu·lar·ity [ˌregjʊˈlærɪtɪ] N regolarità

regu·lar·ly [ˈregjʊləlɪ] ADV regolarmente

regu·late [ˈregjʊleɪt] VT regolare

regu·la·tion [ˌregjʊˈleɪʃən] N (*rule*) regolamento, regola; (*adjustment*) regolazione *f*; **safety regulations** norme *fpl* di sicurezza; **the regulation of nurseries** la regolamentazione degli asili ♦ ADJ (*item, clothing*) di ordinanza

re·ha·bili·tate [ˌriːəˈbɪlɪteɪt] VT (*criminal, drug addict, invalid*) recuperare, reinserire

re·ha·bili·ta·tion [ˈriːəˌbɪlɪˈteɪʃən] N (*of offender, of disabled*) ricupero, reinserimento

re·hash [riːˈhæʃ] (*pej*) N rimaneggiamento ♦ VT rimaneggiare

re·hears·al [rɪˈhɜːsəl] N prova; **dress rehearsal** prova generale

re·hearse [rɪˈhɜːs] VT (*Mus, Theatre*) provare; (*one's part*) ripassare; (*what one is going to say*) ripetere

re·house [riːˈhaʊz] VT rialloggiare

reign [reɪn] N regno; **in the reign of** sotto *or* durante il regno di; **reign of terror** regno del terrore ♦ VI (*also fig*) regnare; **the reigning champion** il campione in carica; **to reign supreme** (*champion*) non avere rivali; (*justice, peace etc*) regnare sovrano(-a)

reign·ing [ˈreɪnɪŋ] ADJ (*monarch*) regnante; (*champion*) in carica

re·im·burse [ˌriːɪmˈbɜːs] VT: **to reimburse sb for sth** rimborsare qc a qn

rein [reɪn] N (*for horse*) redine *f*, briglia; **to keep a tight rein on sb** (*fig*) tenere a freno qn; **to give sb free rein** (*fig*) lasciare completa libertà a qn
‣ **rein back** VI + ADV indietreggiare
‣ **rein in** VT + ADV trattenere (tirando le briglie); (*expenditure*) limitare

re·incar·na·tion [ˌriːɪnkɑːˈneɪʃən] N reincarnazione *f*

rein·deer [ˈreɪndɪə'] N *pl inv* renna

re·inforce [ˌriːɪnˈfɔːs] VT (*army, material, structure*) rinforzare; (*fig: theory, belief*) rafforzare

re·inforced con·crete [ˌriːɪnfɔːstˈkɒnkriːt] N cemento armato

re·inforce·ment [ˌriːɪnˈfɔːsmənt] N **1** (*action*) rinforzo, rafforzamento; (*thing*) rinforzo **2** (*Mil*); **reinforcements** NPL rinforzi *mpl*

re·instate [ˌriːɪnˈsteɪt] VT (*employee, official*) reintegrare

re·instate·ment [ˌriːɪnˈsteɪtmənt] N reintegrazione *f*

re·issue [riːˈɪʃjuː] VT (*book*) fare una ristampa di, ristampare; (*record, film*) rimettere in circolazione, distribuire di nuovo

re·it·er·ate [riːˈɪtəreɪt] VT (*frm*) ripetere, reiterare

re·ject [n ˈriːdʒekt, vb rɪˈdʒekt] N (*person, thing, also Comm*) scarto ♦ VT (*offer etc*) rifiutare, respingere; (*applicant etc*) scartare, respingere; (*subj: body: food*) rifiutare; **the patient's body rejected the new organ** il paziente ha avuto una crisi di rigetto; **to feel rejected** sentirsi respinto(-a)

re·jec·tion [rɪˈdʒekʃən] N (*of offer, applicant*) rifiuto; (*of new organ*) rigetto

re·joice [rɪˈdʒɔɪs] VI (*frm*) rallegrarsi; **to rejoice in sth** godere di qc; **to rejoice (at *or* over)** provare diletto (in); **they had no cause to rejoice** non avevano motivo di rallegrarsi

re·join·der [rɪˈdʒɔɪndə'] N (*frm: retort*) replica

re·ju·venate [rɪˈdʒuːvɪneɪt] VT (*far*) ringiovanire

re·kindle [ˌriːˈkɪndl] VT (*also fig*) riaccendere

re·lapse [rɪˈlæps] N (*Med*) ricaduta; **to have a relapse** avere una ricaduta ♦ VI (*gen*): **to relapse (into)** ricadere (in); (*Med*) avere una ricaduta

re·late [rɪˈleɪt] VT **1** (*tell: story*) raccontare, riferire; **he related the whole story** ha raccontato tutta la storia **2** (*establish relation between*) collegare ♦ **to relate to** VI **1** (*connect*) riferirsi a, riguardare; **these recommendations relate to road safety** queste raccomandazioni riguardano la sicurezza sulle strade **2** (*get on with*) stabilire un rapporto con; **he can't relate to older people** non riesce a stabilire un rapporto con le persone più anziane

re·lat·ed [rɪˈleɪtɪd] ADJ **1** (*connected: subject*) connesso(-a),

collegato(-a); (: *substances, languages*) affine; **the two events were not related** non c'è alcun rapporto tra i due avvenimenti **2** (*attached by family: person*): **related to** imparentato(-a) con; **we are distantly related** siamo parenti alla lontana

re·lat·ing [rɪˈleɪtɪŋ] **relating to** PREP relativo(-a) a, che riguarda

re·la·tion [rɪˈleɪʃən] N **1** (*relationship*) rapporto, relazione *f*; (*Math*) relazione; **to bear a relation to** corrispondere a; **it has no relation to reality** non ha nessun rapporto con la realtà; **in relation to** con riferimento a; **to have good relations with sb** essere in *or* avere buoni rapporti con qn; **diplomatic/international relations** rapporti diplomatici/internazionali; **sexual relations** rapporti sessuali **2** (*family: relative*) parente *m/f*; (: *kinship*) parentela; **what relation is she to you?** che legami di parentela ha con te?; **he's a distant relation** è un lontano parente

re·la·tion·ship [rɪˈleɪʃənʃɪp] N **1** (*family ties*) legami *mpl* di parentela **2** (*connection: between two things*) rapporto, nesso; (: *with sb*) rapporti *mpl*; **to see a relationship between** vedere un nesso fra; **to have a relationship with sb** (*sexual*) avere una relazione con qn; **I'm not in a relationship at the moment** al momento non ho una relazione; **they have a good relationship** vanno molto d'accordo, hanno un bel rapporto

rela·tive [ˈrelətɪv] ADJ (*comparative, also Gram*) relativo(-a); (*connected*): **relative to** relativo(-a) a; **the relative merits of X and Y** i meriti rispettivi di X e Y ♦ N parente *m/f*

rela·tive·ly [ˈrelətɪvlɪ] ADV relativamente; (*fairly, rather*) abbastanza

re·lax [rɪˈlæks] VT (*muscles, person*) rilassare; (*restrictions*) diminuire; (*discipline*) allentare; **to relax one's hold on sth** allentare la presa di qc ♦ VI (*rest*) rilassarsi; (*amuse oneself*) svagarsi; (*slacken: sb's grip*) allentarsi; (*calm down*): **relax!** calma!; **his face relaxed into a smile** il suo viso si distese in un sorriso

re·laxa·tion [ˌriːlækˈseɪʃən] N (*rest*) relax *m*; (*of muscles*) rilassamento, rilasciamento; (*entertainment*) svago; **she plays the piano for relaxation** suona il piano per rilassarsi

re·laxed [rɪˈlækst] ADJ (*muscles*) rilassato(-a), rilasciato(-a); (*person, mood*) disteso(-a), rilassato(-a)

re·lax·ing [rɪˈlæksɪŋ] ADJ rilassante

re·lay [*n* ˈriːleɪ, *vb* rɪˈleɪ] N **1** (*of workmen, horses*) ricambio; **to work in relays** lavorare a squadre (*dandosi il cambio*) **2** (*Radio, TV*) ripetitore *m*; (*Elec*) relé *m inv*; (*Sport: also:* **relay race**) (corsa a) staffetta ♦ VT (*Radio, TV*) ripetere; (*pass on: message*) passare, trasmettere

re·lease [rɪˈliːs] N **1** (*gen*) rilascio; (*from army*) congedo; (*from suffering, obligation*) liberazione *f* **2** (*of gas*) emissione *f*; (*of film, record*) uscita, distribuzione *f*; (*of book*) pubblicazione *f*; **on general release** (*film*) in distribuzione **3** (*record, film etc*): **new release** nuovo disco (*or* film *etc*); **his latest release** il suo ultimo disco (*or* film *etc*) **4** (*also:* **release switch**) disinnesto ♦ VT **1** (*let go*) lasciare andare, mollare; (*bomb*) sganciare; (*fig: tension*) allentare; **to release one's hold of** *or* **one's grip on sth** allentare la presa di qc **2** (*set free*) rilasciare; (*Law*) rimettere in libertà; (*from wreckage*) liberare; (*from promise, vow*) sciogliere **3** (*issue: gas*) emettere; (: *book, record*) mettere in circolazione, fare uscire; (: *film*) distribuire; (: *statement*) rilasciare; (: *news*) rendere pubblico(-a) **4** (*Tech: catch, clasp, spring*) liberare; (*Phot: shutter*) far scattare; (*handbrake*) togliere; **to release the clutch** (*Aut*) staccare la frizione

rel·egate [ˈrelɪɡeɪt] VT (*demote*) relegare; (*Sport*) (far) retrocedere; **to be relegated** (*team*) essere retrocesso(-a)

re·lent [rɪˈlent] VI (*frm*) cedere
❑ **relent** is not translated by the Italian word *rallentare*

re·lent·less [rɪˈlentlɪs] ADJ implacabile

rel·evance [ˈreləvəns] N pertinenza; **relevance of sth to sth** rapporto tra qc e qc

rel·evant [ˈreləvənt] ADJ: **relevant (to)** (*remark, fact*) pertinente (a); (*information, papers, chapter*) relativo(-a) (a); (*course of action*) adeguato(-a) (a); **make sure that what you say is relevant** cerca di dire qualcosa di pertinente; **education should be relevant to real life** l'istruzione dovrebbe avere un riscontro nella vita reale; **they passed all relevant information to the police** hanno passato tutte le informazioni del caso alla polizia; **that's not relevant** questo non c'entra

❑ **relevant** is not translated by the Italian word *rilevante*

re·li·abil·ity [rɪˌlaɪəˈbɪlɪtɪ] N (*see adj*) attendibilità; affidabilità; capacità; sicurezza; (*of person*) serietà

re·li·able [rɪˈlaɪəbl] ADJ (*report, source*) attendibile; (*machine*) affidabile; (*person: trustworthy*) fidato(-a), che dà affidamento; (: *capable*) capace; (*method*) sicuro(-a); **a reliable source of information** una fonte attendibile

re·li·ably [rɪˈlaɪəblɪ] ADV: **I am reliably informed that ...** so da fonti sicure che...

re·li·ance [rɪˈlaɪəns] N: **reliance (on)** dipendenza (da)

re·li·ant [rɪˈlaɪənt] ADJ: **to be reliant on sth/sb** dipendere da qc/qn

rel·ic [ˈrelɪk] N (*Rel*) reliquia; (*fig: of the past*) retaggio

re·lief [rɪˈliːf] N 1 (*from pain, anxiety*): **relief (from)** sollievo (a); **by way of light relief** come diversivo; **that's a relief!** che sollievo! 2 (*Mil: of besieged town*) liberazione *f*; (*help, supplies*) soccorsi *mpl* 3 (*also:* **tax relief**) sgravio fiscale 4 (*Art, Geog*) rilievo; **to throw sth into relief** (*fig*) mettere qc in evidenza *or* in risalto 5 (*of guard*) cambio ♦ ADJ (*bus*) supplementare; (*driver*) che dà il cambio a un collega; (*work, organization, troops*) di soccorso

relief map N carta in rilievo

relief road N (*Brit*) circonvallazione *f*

re·lieve [rɪˈliːv] VT 1 (*pain, anxiety, boredom*) alleviare; (*person*) sollevare; (*bring help*) soccorrere; **I am relieved to hear you are better** sono sollevato dalla notizia che stai meglio; **to relieve sb of sth** (*load*) alleggerire qn di qc; (*anxiety*) sollevare qn da qc; (*duty*) esonerare qn da qc; **to relieve sb of his command** (*Mil*) esonerare qn dal comando; **to relieve one's anger** sfogare la propria rabbia; **to relieve congestion in sth** (*Med*) decongestionare qc; **to relieve o.s.** (*euph: go to lavatory*) fare i propri bisogni 2 (*take over from*) sostituire; (*replace, also Mil*) dare il cambio a; (*Mil: town*) liberare

re·lieved [rɪˈliːvd] ADJ sollevato(-a); **to be relieved that ...** essere sollevato(-a) (dal fatto) che...; **I'm relieved to hear it** mi hai tolto un peso con questa notizia

re·li·gion [rɪˈlɪdʒən] N religione *f*

re·li·gious [rɪˈlɪdʒəs] ADJ (*gen*) religioso(-a); (*conscientious*) scrupoloso(-a)

religious education N istruzione *f* religiosa

re·lin·quish [rɪˈlɪŋkwɪʃ] VT (*frm: right, control, responsibility*) rinunciare a; (: *post*) lasciare, abbandonare; **to relinquish one's hold on sth** lasciare andare qc

rel·ish [ˈrelɪʃ] N 1 relish (for) gusto (per); **to do sth with relish** fare qc con diletto 2 (*sauce*) condimento, salsa ♦ VT (*food, wine*) gustare; (*fig: like*): **I don't relish the idea** l'idea non è allettante; **I relish the challenge of difficult tasks** la sfida di un'impresa difficile mi attrae; **he didn't relish the prospect** la prospettiva non lo allettava

re·live [ˌriːˈlɪv] VT rivivere

re·load [ˌriːˈləʊd] VT ricaricare

re·lo·cate [ˌriːləʊˈkeɪt] VT (*business, person*) trasferire ♦ VI: **to relocate** trasferire la propria sede a; **rising costs forced us to relocate** l'aumento dei costi ci ha costretti a trasferire la sede

re·luc·tance [rɪˈlʌktəns] N riluttanza

re·luc·tant [rɪˈlʌktənt] ADJ (*person*) riluttante, restio(-a); (*praise, consent*) concesso(-a) a malincuore; **to be reluctant to do sth** essere restio(-a) a fare qc

re·luc·tant·ly [rɪˈlʌktəntlɪ] ADV a malincuore, di mala voglia

rely [rɪˈlaɪ] VI: **to rely on sb/sth** (*count on*) contare su qn/qc; (*be dependent on*) dipendere da qn/qc; **I'm relying on you** conto su di te; **you can rely on my discretion** puoi fidarti della mia discrezione; **you can't rely on the trains** non si può fare affidamento sui treni

re·main [rɪˈmeɪn] VI rimanere, restare; **it remains to be seen whether ...** resta da vedere se...; **it will remain in my memory** resterà sempre impresso nel mio ricordo; **the fact remains that ...** resta il fatto che...; **to remain faithful to sb** rimanere fedele a qn; **to remain silent** restare in silenzio; **to**

remain behind restare indietro; **I remain, yours faithfully** (*Brit: in letters*) distinti saluti

re·main·der [rɪˈmeɪndəʳ] N: **the remainder** (*amount, also Math*) il resto, l'avanzo; (*people*) i (le) rimanenti *pl*; **remainders** NPL (*Comm: books*) remainder *mpl*; (*other goods*) giacenze *fpl* di magazzino

re·main·ing [rɪˈmeɪnɪŋ] ADJ che rimane; **the three remaining possibilities** le tre possibilità che restano *or* che rimangono; **the remaining ingredients** il resto degli ingredienti

re·mains [rɪˈmeɪnz] NPL (*gen*) resti *mpl*; (*of food*) avanzi *mpl*; **the remains of his fortune** ciò che restava del suo patrimonio; **the remains of the picnic** i resti del picnic; **human remains** resti umani; **Roman remains** le rovine romane

re·mand [rɪˈmɑːnd] (*Law*) N: **on remand** in custodia cautelare ♦ VT rinviare a giudizio; **to remand sb in custody** ordinare la custodia cautelare di qn

re·mark [rɪˈmɑːk] N osservazione *f*, commento; **worthy of remark** (*frm*) degno(-a) di nota ♦ VT (*say, notice*) osservare, notare ♦ VI: **to remark on sth** commentare qc

re·mark·able [rɪˈmɑːkəbl] ADJ notevole

re·marry [ˌriːˈmærɪ] VI risposarsi

re·medial [rɪˈmiːdɪəl] ADJ (*Med*) correttivo(-a); (*action*) atto(-a) a porre rimedio; (*school, teaching*) speciale; (*class, tuition*) di recupero

rem·edy [ˈremədɪ] N: **remedy (for)** rimedio (contro *or* per) ♦ VT (*situation, problem, defect*) rimediare a; (*loss*) porre riparo a

re·mem·ber [rɪˈmembəʳ] VT ricordare, ricordarsi di; **I can't remember his name** non mi ricordo come si chiama; **I remember seeing it, I remember having seen it** (mi) ricordo di averlo visto; **she remembered to do it** si è ricordata di farlo; **remember to post that letter** ricordati di imbucare la lettera; **I don't remember saying that** non mi ricordo di aver detto una cosa del genere; **give me sth to remember you by** lasciami un tuo ricordo; **to remember sb in one's prayers** ricordare qn nelle proprie preghiere; **that's worth remembering** buono a sapersi

re·mem·brance [rɪˈmembrəns] N (*frm*) ricordo, memoria; **in remembrance of** in memoria di

re·mind [rɪˈmaɪnd] VT ricordare, rammentare; **to remind sb of sth/to do sth** ricordare *or* rammentare a qn qc/di fare qc; **he reminds me of Brian** mi ricorda Brian; **the scenery here reminds me of Scotland** il paesaggio mi ricorda la Scozia; **remind me to speak to Daniel** ricordami di parlare a Daniel; **that reminds me!** a proposito!

re·mind·er [rɪˈmaɪndəʳ] N 1 (*note*) promemoria *m inv*; (*Comm: letter*) (lettera di) sollecito; **to serve as a reminder of sth** servire a ricordare qc; **as a reminder that** per ricordarsi che; **the final reminder for the gas bill** l'ultimo sollecito della bolletta del gas 2 (*memento*) ricordo

remi·nisce [ˌremɪˈnɪs] VI: **to reminisce (about)** abbandonarsi ai ricordi (di)

remi·nis·cence [ˌremɪˈnɪsəns] N (*usu pl*) reminiscenza

remi·nis·cent [ˌremɪˈnɪsənt] ADJ: **to be reminiscent of** richiamare (alla mente)

re·miss [rɪˈmɪs] ADJ (*frm*) negligente; **it was remiss of me** è stata una negligenza da parte mia

re·mis·sion [rɪˈmɪʃən] N (*gen, also Rel, Med*) remissione *f*; (*Law: of debts, fee*) condono

re·mit [rɪˈmɪt] VT (*frm*) 1 (*send: amount due*) rimettere 2 (*refer: decision*) rimettere 3 (*Rel: sins*) rimettere, perdonare; (*fee, penalty*) condonare

re·mit·tance [rɪˈmɪtəns] N (*frm*) rimessa (di pagamento)

rem·nant [ˈremnənt] N (*remainder*) resto; **remnants** NPL (*of food*) avanzi *mpl*; (*of cloth*) scampoli *mpl*; **the remnants of Roman flooring** i resti della pavimentazione romana; **the remnants of the defeated army** ciò che restava dell'esercito sconfitto

re·mon·strate [ˈremənstreɪt] VI (*frm*) protestare; **to remonstrate with sb about sth** fare le proprie rimostranze a qn circa qc

re·morse [rɪˈmɔːs] N rimorso; **without remorse** senza pietà

re·morse·ful [rɪˈmɔːsfʊl] ADJ pieno(-a) di rimorsi

re·morse·less [rɪˈmɔːslɪs] ADJ (*person*) spietato(-a); (*wind, noise*) implacabile

re·mote [rɪˈməʊt] ADJ (comp -r, superl -st) **1** (place, period) remoto(-a); (ancestor) lontano(-a); (in concept: idea) lontano(-a); (person: aloof) distante; (: uninvolved) distaccato(-a); (Comput) a distanza; **a remote village** un paesino isolato; **remote from the matter in hand** non pertinente alla questione **2** (slight: possibility, resemblance) vago(-a); **not the remotest idea/hope** neanche la più vaga idea/speranza; **there is a remote possibility that ...** c'è una vaga possibilità che... + sub

remote control N (TV) telecomando

remote-controlled [rɪˌməʊtkənˈtrəʊld] ADJ telecomandato(-a)

re·mote·ly [rɪˈməʊtlɪ] ADV **1** (distantly) lontanamente, alla lontana; **remotely situated** in una posizione isolata **2** (slightly) vagamente; **there was nobody remotely resembling this description** non c'era nessuno che corrispondesse neanche vagamente alla descrizione; **I suppose it is remotely possible that ...** suppongo che ci sia una remota possibilità che...

re·mote·ness [rɪˈməʊtnɪs] N **1** (of ancestor) antichità; (of place, period, concept) lontananza; (aloofness) distacco **2** (of possibility, resemblance) vaghezza

re·mould [ˈriːˌməʊld] N (Brit: tyre or tire) pneumatico rigenerato

re·mov·able [rɪˈmuːvəbl] ADJ (detachable) staccabile

re·mov·al [rɪˈmuːvəl] N **1** (of person) allontanamento; (from post) rimozione f, destituzione f; (of problem) allontanamento; (of doubt, fear, obstacle, stain) eliminazione f; (Med) asportazione f; **the removal of a small lump in her breast** l'asportazione di un piccolo nodulo al seno **2** (move from house) trasloco

removal man N (Brit) addetto ai traslochi

removal van N (Brit) camion m inv per o dei traslochi

re·move [rɪˈmuːv] VT (gen) togliere, levare; (person) allontanare; (from post) rimuovere; (stain) togliere, eliminare; (problem) allontanare; (doubt, fear) eliminare, dissipare; (obstacle) rimuovere, eliminare; (Med) asportare; **to remove from** togliere da; **please remove your bag from my seat** le dispiace togliere la borsa dal mio sedile?; levare da; **to remove one's make-up** struccarsi; **first cousin once removed** cugino(-a) di secondo grado; **far removed from** (fig) ben lontano(-a) da ♦ VI traslocare; **to remove from London to the country** trasferirsi da Londra in campagna

re·mov·er [rɪˈmuːvə^r] N **1** (removal man) addetto ai traslochi; **removers** NPL (Brit: firm) ditta fsg o impresa fsg di traslochi **2** (of stains) smacchiatore m; (of nail varnish) solvente m; (of paint, varnish) sverniciatore m; **make-up remover** struccatore m

re·mu·ner·ate [rɪˈmjuːnəˌreɪt] VT (frm) retribuire, rimunerare

re·mu·nera·tion [rɪˌmjuːnəˈreɪʃən] N (frm) rimunerazione f

Re·nais·sance [rɪˈneɪsɑːns] N: **the Renaissance** il Rinascimento ♦ ADJ (style) (del) Rinascimento; (palace, art) rinascimentale, del Rinascimento

re·name [ˌriːˈneɪm] VT ribattezzare

rend [rɛnd] VT (pt, pp rent) (liter) lacerare

ren·der [ˈrɛndə^r] VT **1** (thanks, honour, service) rendere; (account) presentare **2** (make) rendere; **this renders it impossible for me to leave** questo rende impossibile la mia partenza **3** (interpret: sonata, role, play) interpretare; (translate: text) tradurre **4** (Culin: fat) sciogliere

ren·der·ing [ˈrɛndərɪŋ] N (translation) traduzione f; (of song, role) interpretazione f

ren·dez·vous [ˈrɒndɪˌvuː] N (meeting) appuntamento; (meeting place) punto o luogo di ritrovo ♦ VI ritrovarsi; (spaceship) effettuare un rendez-vous

ren·di·tion [rɛnˈdɪʃən] N (Mus) interpretazione f

ren·egade [ˈrɛnɪˌgeɪd] N (pej) rinnegato(-a)

re·new [rɪˈnjuː] VT (gen) rinnovare; (negotiations, discussion, strength) riprendere; **to renew one's acquaintance with sb** riprendere contatto con qn

re·new·able [rɪˈnjuːəbl] ADJ rinnovabile; **renewable resources** fonti fpl di energia rinnovabili ♦ NPL ; **renewables** NPL fonti di energia rinnovabili

re·new·al [rɪˈnjuːəl] N (see vb) rinnovo; ripresa; **urban renewal** rinnovamento urbano; **a renewal of hostilities** una ripresa delle ostilità

re·nounce [rɪˈnaʊns] VT (right, claim, title) rinunciare a; (violence, terrorism) abbandonare; **to renounce one's faith** abiurare la fede

reno·vate [ˈrɛnəʊˌveɪt] VT (house) rimettere a nuovo; (furniture, building, art work) restaurare
❑ **renovate** is not translated by the Italian word rinnovare

reno·va·tion [ˌrɛnəʊˈveɪʃən] N (see vb) rimessa a nuovo; restauro

re·nown [rɪˈnaʊn] N rinomanza, fama

re·nowned [rɪˈnaʊnd] ADJ famoso(-a), rinomato(-a)

rent [rɛnt] PT, PP of rend ♦ N (canone m di) affitto, pigione f ♦ VT **1** (take for rent: house) affittare, prendere in affitto; (: car, TV) noleggiare, prendere a noleggio **2** (also: rent out) affittare, dare in affitto; (car, TV) noleggiare, dare a noleggio

rent·al [ˈrɛntl] N (charge: on TV, telephone) abbonamento; (: on car) noleggio, noleggio

rent boy N (Brit fam) giovane prostituto

re·nun·cia·tion [rɪˌnʌnsɪˈeɪʃən] N (of right, claim, title) rinuncia; (of violence, terrorism) abbandono; (of faith) abiura

re·open [riːˈəʊpən] VT (gen) riaprire; (discussion, hostilities) riaprire, riprendere ♦ VI riaprirsi

re·open·ing [riːˈəʊpnɪŋ] N riapertura

re·or·der [riːˈɔːdə^r] N (Comm) riordino ♦ VT **1** (goods, supplies) ordinare di nuovo **2** (reorganize) riorganizzare; (rearrange) rimettere in ordine

re·or·gan·ize [riːˈɔːgənaɪz] VT riorganizzare

Rep ABBR (USA Pol) **1** = **Representative 2** = **Republican**

rep [rɛp] (fam) N ABBR **1** (Comm: = representative) rappresentante m/f **2** (Theatre: = repertory) teatro di repertorio

re·pair [rɪˈpɛə^r] N riparazione f; **under repair** in riparazione; **in good repair, in a good state of repair** in buono stato; **it is damaged beyond repair** è irrimediabilmente rovinato; **closed for repairs** chiuso(-a) per restauro ♦ VT (car, shoes etc) aggiustare, riparare; (fig: wrong) rimediare a; **to get sth repaired** far aggiustare qc; **I got the washing machine repaired** ho fatto aggiustare la lavatrice

repair kit N attrezzatura per riparazioni

repair man N (pl repair men) riparatore m

repair shop N negozio di riparazioni; (Aut) officina

rep·ar·tee [ˌrɛpɑːˈtiː] N botta e risposta m inv

re·past [rɪˈpɑːst] N (frm) pranzo

re·pat·ri·ate [riːˈpætrɪˌeɪt] VT rimpatriare

re·pay [riːˈpeɪ] VT (pt, pp repaid) (money) restituire; (debt) pagare; (lender) rimborsare, restituire i soldi a; (sb's kindness etc) ricambiare; **how can I ever repay you?** come potrò mai ricompensarti?, come potrò mai sdebitarmi?

re·pay·ment [riːˈpeɪmənt] N (of money) pagamento; (of expenses) rimborso; (compensation) ricompensa; **debt repayment** il rimborso del debito pubblico; **mortgage repayments** le rate del mutuo

re·peal [rɪˈpiːl] VT (law) abrogare; (sentence) annullare; (decree) revocare ♦ N (see vb) abrogazione f; annullamento; revoca

re·peat [rɪˈpiːt] N (gen) ripetere; (pattern) riprodurre; (promise, attack) rinnovare; **don't repeat it to anybody** non riferirlo a nessuno; **this offer cannot be repeated** questa è un'offerta irripetibile; **to repeat an order** (Comm) rinnovare un'ordinazione; **to get repeat business** fidelizzare la clientela; **in spite of repeated reminders** malgrado diversi or ripetuti solleciti ♦ VI ripetersi ♦ N ripetizione f; (Radio, TV) replica; **there are too many repeats on TV** ci sono troppe repliche in TV

re·peat·ed·ly [rɪˈpiːtɪdlɪ] ADV ripetutamente

repeat order N (Comm): **to place a repeat order (for)** rinnovare l'ordinazione (di)

repeat prescription N ricetta medica ripetibile

re·pel [rɪˈpɛl] VT (frm: force back) respingere; (disgust) ripugnare a

re·pel·lent [rɪˈpɛlənt] ADJ (disgusting) ripugnante, repellente ♦ N: **insect repellent** insettifugo; **moth repellent** antitarmico

re·pent [rɪˈpɛnt] VI (frm): **to repent (of)** pentirsi (di)

re·pent·ance [rɪˈpɛntəns] N (frm) pentimento

re·per·cus·sions [ˌriːpəˈkʌʃnz] NPL ripercussioni fpl

rep·er·toire [ˈrepətwɑːˈ] N repertorio
rep·er·tory [ˈrepətərɪ] N (*Theatre, also fig: of jokes, songs*) repertorio; **to act in repertory** far parte di una compagnia di repertorio
repertory company N compagnia di repertorio
rep·e·ti·tion [ˌrepɪˈtɪʃən] N ripetizione *f*
rep·e·ti·tious [ˌrepɪˈtɪʃəs] ADJ (*frm: speech*) pieno(-a) di ripetizioni
repetitive [rɪˈpetɪtɪv] ADJ (*work*) ripetitivo(-a), monotono(-a); (*movement*) che si ripete
re·place [rɪˈpleɪs] VT 1 (*put back*) rimettere (a posto); (*Telec: receiver*) riattaccare 2 (*get replacement for, take the place of*): **to replace (by, with)** rimpiazzare (con), sostituire (con); **computers have replaced typewriters** i computer hanno rimpiazzato le macchine da scrivere
re·place·ment [rɪˈpleɪsmənt] N (*substitute: thing*) pezzo *or* parte *f* di ricambio; (*: person*) sostituto(-a); (*: act*) sostituzione *f*; **my replacement at work** il mio sostituto al lavoro; **the replacement of faulty goods** la sostituzione di articoli difettosi
re·play [*vb* ˌriːˈpleɪ, *n* ˈriːpleɪ] (*Sport*) VT (*match*) ripetere ♦ VI ripetere l'incontro ♦ N (*of match*) partita ripetuta; (*TV: playback*) replay *m inv*; **to hold a replay** ripetere l'incontro
re·plen·ish [rɪˈplenɪʃ] VT (*frm: tank, glass*) riempire (di nuovo); (*: one's wardrobe*) rifare; **to replenish one's supplies of sth** rifornirsi di qc
re·plete [rɪˈpliːt] ADJ (*frm*): **replete (with)** sazio(-a) (di)
rep·li·ca [ˈreplɪkə] N replica, copia
re·ply [rɪˈplaɪ] N (*Post*) risposta; **in reply** in risposta; **what did you say in reply?** cos'hai risposto?; **there's no reply** (*Telec*) non risponde (nessuno) ♦ VT, VI rispondere
reply coupon N (*Post*) tagliando per la risposta
re·port [rɪˈpɔːt] N 1 (*account: written*) rapporto, relazione *f*; (*: spoken*) resoconto; (*Press, Radio, TV*) reportage *m inv*, servizio; (*Brit Scol*) pagella (scolastica); **annual report** (*Comm*) relazione annuale; **weather report** bollettino meteorologico; **to give a report on sth** fare una relazione *or* un rapporto su qc, fare un resoconto di qc; **the committee will today publish its report** la commissione pubblicherà oggi la sua relazione; **there's a report in today's paper** c'è un articolo sul giornale di oggi; **to submit a progress report on sth/sb** fare un rapporto periodico su qc/qn; **I have heard a report that ...** ho sentito (dire) che...; **he got a terrible report** ha ricevuto una bruttissima pagella 2 (*frm: bang*) detonazione *f*; (*: shot*) sparo ♦ VT (*gen, also Press, TV*) riportare; (*notify: accident, culprit*) denunciare; (*bring to notice: occurrence*) segnalare; **it is reported from Berlin that ...** ci è stato riferito da Berlino che...; **what have you to report?** che cos'ha da riferire?; **to report progress** riferire sugli sviluppi della situazione; **to report one's findings** riferire sulle proprie conclusioni; **I reported the theft to the police** ho denunciato il furto alla polizia ♦ VI 1 **to report (on)** fare un rapporto (su); (*Press, Radio, TV*) fare un reportage (su) 2 (*present oneself*): **to report (to)** presentarsi (a); **report to reception when you arrive** si presenti alla reception al suo arrivo; **to report for duty** presentarsi al lavoro; **to report sick** darsi malato(-a)
  ▸ **report back** VI + ADV 1 (*come back*) ritornare 2 (*make report*) tornare a riferire; **I'll report back as soon as I hear anything** appena ho notizie te lo faccio sapere
report card N (*USA, Scot*) pagella
re·port·ed·ly [rɪˈpɔːtɪdlɪ] ADV secondo le testimonianze; **it's reportedly the best restaurant in town** si dice che sia il miglior ristorante della città; **she is reportedly living in Spain** si dice che viva in Spagna
re·port·ed speech [rɪpɔːtɪdˈspiːtʃ] N (*Gram*) discorso indiretto
re·port·er [rɪˈpɔːtəˈ] N (*Press*) cronista *m/f*, reporter *m/f inv*; (*Radio*) radiocronista *m/f*; (*TV*) telecronista *m/f*
re·pose [rɪˈpəʊz] (*frm*) N riposo; **in repose** in riposo ♦ VI riposare
re·pos·sess [ˌriːpəˈzes] VT (*property*) rientrare in possesso di
re·pos·ses·sion or·der [ˌriːpəˈzeʃnˌɔːdəˈ] N (*for house*) ordine *m* di espropriazione
rep·re·hen·sible [ˌreprɪˈhensɪbl] ADJ (*frm*) riprovevole

re·pre·sent [ˌreprɪˈzent] VT (*all senses*) rappresentare
rep·re·sen·ta·tion [ˌreprɪzenˈteɪʃən] N 1 (*Pol*) rappresentanza; (*portrayal*) rappresentazione *f* 2 **representations** NPL (*frm: statements, protests*) rimostranze *fpl*; **to make representations to sb** fare delle rimostranze a qn
rep·re·sen·ta·tive [ˌreprɪˈzentətɪv] ADJ: **representative (of)** rappresentativo(-a) (di) ♦ N (*gen*) rappresentante *m/f*, delegato(-a); (*Comm*) rappresentante *m/f* (di commercio); (*USA Pol*): **Representative** deputato
re·press [rɪˈpres] VT reprimere
re·pres·sion [rɪˈpreʃən] N repressione *f*
re·pres·sive [rɪˈpresɪv] ADJ repressivo(-a)
re·prieve [rɪˈpriːv] N (*Law: cancellation*) commutazione *f* della pena capitale; (*: postponement*) sospensione *f* dell'esecuzione della condanna; (*delay: also gen*) proroga; **a temporary reprieve** una dilazione temporanea; **a last-minute reprieve** una sospensione all'ultimo momento dell'esecuzione della condanna ♦ VT (*Law: for good*) rinviare l'esecuzione di; (*: grant a delay*) concedere una proroga a; (*fig*) dare tregua a
rep·ri·mand [ˈreprɪmɑːnd] N rimprovero ♦ VT redarguire, rimproverare
re·print [*n* ˈriːprɪnt, *vb* ˌriːˈprɪnt] N ristampa ♦ VT ristampare
re·pris·al [rɪˈpraɪzəl] N ; **reprisals** NPL rappresaglie *fpl*; **to take reprisals** fare delle rappresaglie; **as a reprisal for** come rappresaglia per
re·proach [rɪˈprəʊtʃ] (*frm*) N rimprovero; **to look at sb with reproach** guardare qn con aria di rimprovero; **above** *or* **beyond reproach** irreprensibile ♦ VT: **to reproach sb with** *or* **for sth** rimproverare qc a qn; **to reproach sb with** *or* **for doing sth** rimproverare a qn di *or* per aver fatto qc; **don't reproach yourself for what happened** non devi sentirti in colpa per quello che è successo
re·proach·ful [rɪˈprəʊtʃfʊl] ADJ (*look*) di rimprovero
re·pro·duce [ˌriːprəˈdjuːs] VT riprodurre ♦ VI riprodursi
re·pro·duc·tion [ˌriːprəˈdʌkʃən] N (*all senses*) riproduzione *f*
re·pro·duc·tive [ˌriːprəˈdʌktɪv] ADJ riproduttore(-trice)
re·proof [rɪˈpruːf], **re·prov·al** [rɪˈpruːvəl] N (*frm*) riprovazione *f*
re·prove [rɪˈpruːv] VT (*person*): **to reprove (for)** rimproverare (di *or* per), biasimare (per)
re·prov·ing [rɪˈpruːvɪŋ] ADJ (*frm: look, frown*) di rimprovero, di disapprovazione
rep·tile [ˈreptaɪl] N rettile *m*
Repub. ABBR (*USA Pol*) = **Republican**
re·pub·lic [rɪˈpʌblɪk] N repubblica
republican [rɪˈpʌblɪkən] ADJ, N 1 repubblicano(-a) 2 **a Republican** (*USA Pol*) un(a) repubblicano(-a)
re·pu·di·ate [rɪˈpjuːdɪeɪt] (*frm*) VT (*charge, offer of friendship*) respingere; (*debt, treaty*) disconoscere, rifiutarsi di onorare; (*one's spouse*) ripudiare
re·pug·nant [rɪˈpʌɡnənt] ADJ ripugnante; **to be repugnant to sb** ripugnare a qn
re·pulse [rɪˈpʌls] VT respingere
re·pul·sion [rɪˈpʌlʃən] N ripulsione *f*, ribrezzo
re·pul·sive [rɪˈpʌlsɪv] ADJ ripugnante, ripulsivo(-a), ributtante
repu·table [ˈrepjʊtəbl] ADJ (*firm, supplier*) degno(-a) di fiducia, serio(-a); (*occupation*) rispettabile
repu·ta·tion [ˌrepjʊˈteɪʃən] N reputazione *f*; **he has a reputation for being awkward** ha la fama di essere un tipo difficile; **to live up to one's reputation** non smentirsi, non smentire la propria reputazione
re·pute [rɪˈpjuːt] N (*frm*) reputazione *f*; **of (good) repute** (*person*) che ha una buona reputazione; (*place*) che ha un buon nome; **by repute** di fama
re·put·ed [rɪˈpjuːtɪd] ADJ reputato(-a); **to be reputed to be rich/intelligent** aver fama di essere ricco(-a)/intelligente; **he is reputed to earn £500,000 a year** si dice che guadagni 500.000 sterline all'anno
re·put·ed·ly [rɪˈpjuːtɪdlɪ] ADV (*stando*) a quel che si dice, secondo quanto si dice
re·quest [rɪˈkwest] N (*formal*) richiesta, domanda; **to make a request for sth** fare richiesta di qc; **at the request of** su richiesta di; **on** *or* **by request** a *or* su richiesta; **by popular**

request a grande richiesta ♦ VT: **to request sth from** or **of sb/sb to do sth** richiedere qc a qn/a qn di fare qc; **"you are requested not to smoke"** "si prega di non fumare"

requi·em ['rekwɪɛm] N requiem m inv

re·quire [rɪ'kwaɪə'](frm) VT **1** (subj: person) aver bisogno di; (: thing, action) richiedere; **it requires careful thought** richiede un attento esame; **what qualifications are required?** che requisiti sono richiesti?, che qualifiche si richiedono?; **if required** se necessario; **when required** quando è necessario **2** (demand, order): **to require sb to do sth/sth of sb** esigere che qn faccia qc/qc da qn; **to require that sth be done** esigere che qc sia fatto; **passengers are required to show their tickets** i passeggeri devono esibire i biglietti; **required by law** prescritto(-a) dalla legge

re·quired [rɪ'kwaɪəd] ADJ (qualifications, exams) richiesto(-a); (amount) voluto(-a); **in the required time** nel tempo prescritto

re·quire·ment [rɪ'kwaɪəmənt] N (need) esigenza; (condition) requisito, condizione f (richiesta); **to meet sb's requirements** soddisfare le esigenze di qn; **she meets all the requirements for the job** risponde a tutti i requisiti (necessari per il lavoro); **entry requirements** criteri mpl d'ammissione

requi·site ['rekwɪzɪt] N occorrente m, necessario ♦ ADJ (frm) necessario(-a), richiesto(-a)

requi·si·tion [ˌrekwɪ'zɪʃən] N **1** (Mil) requisizione f **2** (request for supply) richiesta ♦ VT (see n) requisire; richiedere

re·route [ˌriː'ruːt] VT (train) deviare (il percorso di); **the train was rerouted through Blackpool** hanno fatto passare il treno per Blackpool

re·sale ['riːseɪl] N rivendita

resale price maintenance N prezzo minimo di vendita imposto

re·sat [ˌriː'sæt] PT, PP of resit

re·scind [rɪ'sɪnd] VT (law) abrogare; (contract) rescindere; (order) annullare

res·cue ['reskjuː] N (saving) salvataggio; (help) soccorso; **to come/go to sb's rescue** venire/andare in aiuto a or di qn; **a mountain rescue team** una squadra di soccorso alpino ♦ VT salvare

rescue party N squadra di salvataggio

res·cu·er ['reskjuə'] N soccorritore(-trice)

re·search [rɪ'sɜːtʃ] N ricerca, ricerche fpl; **a piece of research** un lavoro di ricerca; **to do research** fare ricerca; **she's doing some research in the library** sta facendo delle ricerche in biblioteca ♦ VI: **to research (into sth)** fare ricerca (su qc) ♦ VT documentarsi su; **a well researched book** un libro ben documentato ♦ ADJ (centre, laboratory) di ricerca

re·search·er [rɪ'sɜːtʃə'] N ricercatore(-trice)

research work N lavoro di ricerca, ricerche fpl

re·sell [ˌriː'sel] VT rivendere

re·sem·blance [rɪ'zembləns] N somiglianza; **to bear a strong resemblance to** somigliare moltissimo a

re·sem·ble [rɪ'zembl] VT (as)somigliare a

re·sent [rɪ'zent] VT risentirsi per; **to resent sb** provare risentimento nei confronti di qn; **he resents my being here** è contrariato dalla mia presenza; **I resent your remarks** le tue osservazioni mi offendono

re·sent·ful [rɪ'zentful] ADJ (person) pieno(-a) di risentimento; (tone) risentito(-a); **to be** or **feel resentful of sb** provare del risentimento per qn, essere pieno di risentimento nei confronti di qn

re·sent·ment [rɪ'zentmənt] N risentimento

res·er·va·tion [ˌrezə'veɪʃən] N **1** (booking) prenotazione f; **to make a reservation** prenotare, fare una prenotazione; **I've got a reservation for two nights** ho una prenotazione per due notti **2** (doubt) riserva; **without reservation** senza riserve; **with reservations** con le dovute riserve; **I've got reservations about it** ho delle riserve a riguardo **3** (area of land) riserva; (Brit: Aut: also: **central reservation**) spartitraffico m inv

reservation desk N (USA: in hotel) reception f inv

re·serve [rɪ'zɜːv] N **1** (most senses) riserva; (hiding one's feelings) riserbo; **keep/have in reserve** tenere/avere di riserva; **without reserve** senza riserve **2 the reserves** NPL (Mil) le

riserve ♦ VT **1** (table, seat) prenotare, riservare; (set aside) riservare; **to reserve one's strength** risparmiarsi le forze; **I'd like to reserve a table for tomorrow evening** vorrei riservare un tavolo per domani sera **2 to reserve judgment (on)** (fig) riservarsi di decidere in merito (a); **to reserve the right to do** riservarsi il diritto di fare

reserve currency N (Fin) valuta di riserva

re·served [rɪ'zɜːvd] ADJ (booked: table, seat) prenotato(-a), riservato(-a); (shy) riservato(-a)

reserve price N (Brit: at auction) prezzo minimo, prezzo m base, inv

reserve team N (Brit: Sport) seconda squadra

re·serv·ist [rɪ'zɜːvɪst] N (Mil) riservista m

res·er·voir ['rezəvwɑː'] N (artificial lake) bacino idrico; (tank etc) serbatoio

reset [ˌriː'set] VT (Comput) azzerare

re·shape [ˌriː'ʃeɪp] VT (policy) ristrutturare

re·shuf·fle [ˌriː'ʃʌfl] N: **Cabinet reshuffle** (Pol) rimpasto ministeriale or governativo

re·side [rɪ'zaɪd] VI (frm) risiedere; (fig: power, authority): **to reside in** or **with** essere nelle mani di

resi·dence ['rezɪdəns](frm) N (gen) residenza; (stay) permanenza, soggiorno; **"desirable residence for sale"** "abitazione signorile vendesi"; **to take up residence** prendere residenza; **in residence** (queen) in sede; **artist/writer in residence** artista/scrittore che insegna presso una scuola o università

residence permit N (Brit) permesso di soggiorno

resi·dent ['rezɪdənt] N abitante m/f; (of hotel) cliente m/f; **local residents** abitanti della zona ♦ ADJ (tutor, specialist) interno(-a); (population) stabile; **to be resident in a town/in London** risiedere in una città/a Londra

resi·den·tial [ˌrezɪ'denʃəl] ADJ (area) residenziale; **residential course** corso con pernottamento; **residential nurse** infermiere(-a) interno(-a)

resi·due ['rezɪdjuː] N (frm) residuo, residui mpl

re·sign [rɪ'zaɪn] VT (office, leadership) lasciare; (frm: claim) rinunciare a; **he resigned his post** ha lasciato l'impiego; **to resign one's commission** (Mil) rassegnare le dimissioni; **to resign o.s. to (doing) sth** rassegnarsi a (fare) qc ♦ VI (from) dimettersi (da), dare le dimissioni (da); **I resigned** ho dato le dimissioni

res·ig·na·tion [ˌrezɪg'neɪʃən] N **1** (from job) dimissioni fpl; **to tender one's resignation** dare le dimissioni **2** (mental state) rassegnazione f; **a feeling of resignation** un senso di rassegnazione

re·sili·ence [rɪ'zɪlɪəns] N (see adj) elasticità; capacità di ripresa

re·sili·ent [rɪ'zɪlɪənt] ADJ (substance, material) elastico(-a); (fig: person) che ha buone capacità di ripresa; **polyester is more resilient than cotton** il poliestere è più elastico del cotone

res·in ['rezɪn] N resina

re·sist [rɪ'zɪst] VT (attack) resistere a; (change) opporsi a; **he couldn't resist taking a quick look** non ha resistito alla tentazione di dare un'occhiata ♦ VI resistere

re·sist·ance [rɪ'zɪstəns] N (all senses) resistenza; **to offer resistance (to)** opporre resistenza a; **to take the line of least resistance** scegliere la strada più facile ♦ ADJ (fighter, movement) della resistenza

re·sist·ant [rɪ'zɪstənt] ADJ: **resistant (to)** resistente (a)

re·sit [vb ˌriː'sɪt, n 'riːsɪt] (pt, pp resat) VT (exam) ripresentarsi a; **I'm resitting the exam in December** mi ripresento all'esame in dicembre ♦ N: **when are the resits?** quando è la prossima sessione?; **I've got three resits** devo ripresentarmi a tre esami

reso·lute ['rezəluːt] ADJ (frm) risoluto(-a)

reso·lu·tion [ˌrezə'luːʃən] N **1** (determination) risolutezza; (resolve) fermo proposito, risoluzione f; **to make a resolution** fare un proposito; **have you made any New Year resolutions?** hai fatto dei buoni propositi per l'anno nuovo? **2** (of problem, also Chem) soluzione f **3** (on screen: also Pol: motion) risoluzione f; **a UN resolution** una risoluzione dell'ONU

re·solve [rɪ'zɒlv](frm) N (resoluteness) risolutezza; **to make a resolve to do sth** risolversi a fare qc ♦ VT **1** (sort out) risolvere; **the only way to resolve the problem** l'unico modo di risolvere il problema 2 (*decide*): **to resolve to do sth/that** decidere di fare qc/che; **the committee resolved against appointing him** il comitato ha deliberato contro la sua nomina

re·solved [rɪ'zɒlvd] ADJ risoluto(-a)

reso·nance ['rezənəns](*frm*) N (*see adj*) risonanza; sonorità

reso·nant ['rezənənt](*frm*) ADJ (*sound*) risonante; (*voice*) sonoro(-a), risonante

re·sort [rɪ'zɔːt] N 1 (*recourse*) ricorso; (*thing resorted to*) risorsa; **without resort to force** senza ricorrere *or* far ricorso alla forza; **in the last resort, as a last resort** come ultima risorsa 2 (*place*) località *f inv*; **holiday resort** località di villeggiatura; **seaside/winter sports resort** stazione *f* balneare/ di sport invernali ♦ VI: **to resort to** (*violence, treachery*) far ricorso a; **to resort to drink/stealing** *etc* mettersi *or* ridursi a bere/rubare *etc*

re·sound [rɪ'zaʊnd] VI (*frm*): **to resound (with)** risonare (di)

re·sound·ing [rɪ'zaʊndɪŋ] ADJ (*noise*) fragoroso(-a), risonante; (*victory, defeat*) clamoroso(-a); **a resounding slap** un ceffone sonoro; **a resounding victory** una vittoria clamorosa

re·source [rɪ'sɔːs] N (*asset*) risorsa; **resources** NPL (*wealth*) mezzi *mpl*; **natural resources** risorse naturali

re·source·ful [rɪ'sɔːsfʊl] ADJ (*person*) pieno(-a) di risorse, intraprendente

re·source·ful·ness [rɪ'sɔːsfʊlnɪs] N (*of person*) ingegnosità

re·spect [rɪs'pekt] N 1 (*gen*) rispetto; **respects** NPL (*regards*) ossequi *mpl*; **to have** *or* **show respect for** aver rispetto per; **I have tremendous respect for Dean** ho un grandissimo rispetto per Dean; **out of respect for** per rispetto *or* riguardo a; **with due respect (for)** con tutto il rispetto (per); **with (all) due respect I think you're mistaken** con rispetto parlando, penso che si sbagli; **to pay one's respects to sb** (*frm*) rendere omaggio a qn 2 (*point, detail*): **in some respects** sotto certi aspetti; **I like the town except in one respect** la città mi piace salvo che per una cosa 3 (*reference, regard*): **in respect of** quanto a; **with respect to** per quanto riguarda ♦ VT rispettare

re·spect·abil·ity [rɪs,pektə'bɪlɪtɪ] N rispettabilità

re·spect·able [rɪs'pektəbl] ADJ 1 (*decent*) rispettabile; **for perfectly respectable reasons** per motivi più che leciti; **in respectable society** nella società bene; **a respectable family** una famiglia rispettabile 2 (*quite big: amount, number*) considerevole; (*quite good: player, result*) niente male *inv*; **my marks were respectable** i miei voti erano discreti

re·spect·ful [rɪs'pektfʊl] ADJ rispettoso(-a)

re·spec·tive [rɪs'pektɪv] ADJ rispettivo(-a)

re·spec·tive·ly [rɪs'pektɪvlɪ] ADV rispettivamente

res·pi·ra·tion [,respɪ'reɪʃən] N respirazione *f*

res·pi·ra·tor ['respəreɪtə'] N (*Med*) respiratore *m*; (*Mil*) maschera *f* antigas, *inv*

res·pira·tory [rɪs'paɪərətərɪ] ADJ respiratorio(-a)

res·pite ['respaɪt] N (*frm*) tregua, requie; **without respite** senza tregua *or* requie; **they gave us no respite** non ci hanno dato tregua

re·splend·ent [rɪs'plendənt] ADJ (*frm*) risplendente

re·spond [rɪs'pɒnd] VI rispondere; **to respond to treatment** (*Med*) reagire (bene) alla cura; **he did not respond** non rispose; **the army responded with gunfire** l'esercito ha risposto sparando; **the government was slow to respond to the crisis** la risposta del governo alla crisi è stata lenta

re·spond·ent [rɪs'pɒndənt] N (*Law*) convenuto(-a)

re·sponse [rɪs'pɒns] N (*answer*) risposta; (*reaction*) reazione *f*; **in response to** in risposta a

re·spon·sibil·ity [rɪs,pɒnsə'bɪlɪtɪ] N responsabilità *f inv*; **to place the responsibility for sth on sb** ritenere qn responsabile di qc; **on one's own responsibility** di propria iniziativa; **to take responsibility for sth/sb** assumersi *or* prendersi la responsabilità di qc/per qn; **that's his responsibility** è compito suo

re·spon·sible [rɪs'pɒnsəbl] ADJ responsabile; (*trustworthy*) fidato(-a); **to be responsible for sth** essere responsabile di qc; **to be responsible to sb (for sth)** dover rispondere a qn (di qc); **to hold sb responsible for** ritenere qn responsabile di; **it's a responsible job** è un posto di responsabilità

re·spon·sibly [rɪ'spɒnsəblɪ] ADV responsabilmente

re·spon·sive [rɪ'spɒnsɪv] ADJ (*audience, class, pupil*) che reagisce bene; (*to affection*) affettuoso(-a); (*to needs*): **responsive to** sensibile a; **the students are responsive and full of ideas** gli studenti rispondono positivamente e sono pieni di idee

rest¹ [rest] N 1 (*repose*) riposo; (*break*) pausa; (*in walking*) sosta, tappa; **to come to rest** (*object*) fermarsi; **to have a rest** riposarsi; **to have a good night's rest** farsi una buona *or* bella dormita; **five minutes' rest** cinque minuti di riposo; **at rest** (*not moving*) fermo(-a); (*euph: dead*) in pace; **to set sb's mind at rest** tranquillizzare qn 2 (*Mus*) pausa 3 (*support*) sostegno, supporto ♦ VT 1 (*animal, dough*) (far) riposare; **God rest his soul!** pace all'anima sua!; **to rest one's eyes** *or* **gaze on** posare lo sguardo su; **he has to rest his knee** non deve affaticare il ginocchio 2 (*support: ladder, bicycle, head*): **to rest on/against** appoggiare su/contro; **I rested my bike against the window** ho appoggiato la bici alla finestra ♦ VI 1 (*repose*) riposarsi, riposare; **she's resting in her room** è in camera sua a riposare; **I feel quite rested** mi sento molto riposato; **may she rest in peace** riposi in pace; **we shall not rest until it is settled** non avremo pace finché la cosa non sarà sistemata 2 (*remain*) stare; **it rests with him to decide** sta a lui decidere; **it doesn't rest with me** non dipende da me; **rest assured that ...** stia tranquillo che...; **let the argument rest there** lascia le cose come stanno 3 **to rest on** (*perch*) posarsi su; (*be supported*) poggiare su, appoggiarsi su; (*Law: case*) basarsi su; **her head rested on my shoulder** il suo capo era appoggiato alla mia spalla; **a heavy responsibility rests on her** ha una grossa responsabilità sulle spalle ❏ **rest** is not translated by the Italian word *restare*

rest² [rest] N (*remainder*): **the rest** (*of money, substance*) il resto; (*of people, things*) gli altri (le altre) *pl*; **the rest of the money** il resto dei soldi; **the rest of them** gli altri; **the rest of them went swimming** gli altri sono andati a nuotare; **the rest of us will go later** noialtri ci andiamo più tardi; **I'll do the rest** faccio io il resto; **can you carry the rest?** porti tu quello che rimane?

re·start [,riː'stɑːt] VT (*engine*) rimettere in marcia; (*work*) ricominciare

res·tau·rant ['restərɒŋ] N ristorante *m*

restaurant car N (*Brit: Rail*) vagone *m* ristorante

rest cure N cura del riposo

rest·ful ['restfʊl] ADJ riposante

rest home N casa di riposo

res·ti·tu·tion [,restɪ'tjuːʃən] N (*act*) restituzione *f*; (*reparation*) riparazione *f*

res·tive ['restɪv] ADJ (*person*) irrequieto(-a), nervoso(-a), agitato(-a); (*horse*) restio(-a)

rest·less ['restlɪs] ADJ (*gen*) irrequieto(-a), agitato(-a); (*crowd etc*) inquieto(-a); **to get restless** spazientirsi; **I had a restless night** ho passato una notte agitata

rest·less·ly ['restlɪslɪ] ADV (*gen*) irrequietamente; (*fidget*) nervosamente

re·stock [,riː'stɒk] VT rifornire

res·to·ra·tion [,restə'reɪʃən] N 1 (*repair: of building, monument*) restauro 2 (*return: of land, property*) restituzione *f*, riconsegna; (*reintroduction: of law and order*) ripristino; (: *of confidence*) ristabilimento; (*History*): **the Restoration** la Restaurazione

re·stora·tive [rɪ'stɔːrətɪv] ADJ (*powers, effect*) corroborante ♦ N (*tonic*) ricostituente *m*; (*drink: alcoholic drink*) cordiale *m*

re·store [rɪ'stɔː'] VT 1 (*repair: building*) restaurare; **the picture has been restored** il quadro è stato restaurato 2 (*give back: gen*) restituire; (*introduce again: confidence, custom, law and order*) ripristinare; **to restore sb's confidence** far riacquistare fiducia a qn; **restored to health** ristabilito(-a); **they restored order** hanno ripristinato l'ordine

re·stor·er [rɪ'stɔːrə'] N (*Art*) restauratore(-trice)

re·strain [rɪ'streɪn] VT (*feeling*) contenere, frenare; (*dog etc*) tenere sotto controllo; **to restrain o.s.** controllarsi, trattenersi; **to restrain sb (from doing sth)** trattenere qn (dal fare qc)

re·strained [rɪ'streɪnd] ADJ (*person, style etc*) contenuto(-a), sobrio(-a); (*manner*) riservato(-a)

re·straint [rɪ'streɪnt] N 1 (*check, control*) limitazioni *fpl*, restrizioni *fpl*; **wage restraint** contenimento salariale **2** (*constraint, moderation: of manner*) ritegno, riservatezza; (*self-control*) autocontrollo; **without restraint** senza reticenze, liberamente

re·strict [rɪ'strɪkt] VT limitare, restringere

restricted area N (*Brit: Aut*) zona con limitazione di velocità

re·stric·tion [rɪ'strɪkʃən] N limitazione *f*, restrizione *f*; **to place restrictions on sth** imporre delle restrizioni su qc; **speed restriction** (*Aut*) limite *m* di velocità

re·stric·tive [rɪ'strɪktɪv] ADJ restrittivo(-a)

restrictive practices NPL (*Industry*) pratiche *fpl* restrittive di produzione

rest room N (*USA*) toilette *f inv*

re·struc·ture [ˌriː'strʌktʃəʳ] VT ristrutturare

re·sult [rɪ'zʌlt] N risultato; **as a result (of)** in *or* di conseguenza (a), in seguito (a); **as a result of the strike ...** in seguito allo sciopero...; **... and as a result, morale is low** ...e di conseguenza il morale è basso; **to get results** (*fam: person*) rendere; (: *action*) dare dei risultati; **an excellent result** un risultato eccellente ♦ VI: **to result (from)** essere una conseguenza (di), essere causato(-a) (da); **to result in** avere come conseguenza; **if the police leave, disorder will result** se la polizia se ne andrà, ci saranno dei disordini; **the inquiry resulted in several dismissals** l'inchiesta ha portato a diversi licenziamenti

re·sult·ant [rɪ'zʌltənt] ADJ (*frm*) risultante, conseguente ♦ N (*Phys, Math*) risultante *m/f*

re·sume [rɪ'zjuːm] VT (*start again*) riprendere; **to resume one's seat** rimettersi a sedere; **they've resumed work** hanno ripreso il lavoro ♦ VI (*class, meeting*) riprendere

ré·su·mé ['rezjuˌmeɪ] N **1** (*summary*) sommario; **a quick résumé** un breve riassunto **2** (*USA: CV*) curriculum vitae *m inv*

re·sump·tion [rɪ'zʌmpʃən] N ripresa

re·sur·gence [rɪ's3ːdʒəns] N (*frm*) rinascita

res·ur·rec·tion [ˌrezə'rekʃən] N risurrezione *f*

re·sus·ci·tate [rɪ'sʌsɪˌteɪt] VT (*Med*) rianimare

re·sus·ci·ta·tion [rɪˌsʌsɪ'teɪʃən] N (*frm*) rianimazione *f*

re·tail ['riːteɪl] ADJ (*price, trade*) al dettaglio, al minuto ♦ ADV al dettaglio, al minuto; **to sell retail** vendere al dettaglio ♦ VT (*Comm*) vendere al minuto *or* al dettaglio; (*gossip*) riferire ♦ VI (*Comm*): **to retail at** essere in vendita al pubblico al prezzo di

re·tail·er ['riːteɪləʳ] N **1** (*fee*) onorario (*versato in anticipo*) **2** (*servant*) servitore *m*

retail outlet N punto di vendita al minuto *or* al dettaglio

retail price N prezzo al minuto *or* al dettaglio

retail price index N indice *m* dei prezzi al consumo

re·tain [rɪ'teɪn] VT (*hold*) tenere; (*keep*) conservare, serbare; (*remember*) tenere a mente; (*sign up: lawyer*) impegnare (*pagando una parte dell'onorario in anticipo*)

re·tain·er [rɪ'teɪnəʳ] N **1** (*fee*) onorario (*versato in anticipo*) **2** (*servant*) servitore *m*

re·tali·ate [rɪ'tælɪˌeɪt] VI: **to retaliate (against sb/sth)** vendicarsi (contro qn/di qc)

re·talia·tion [rɪˌtælɪ'eɪʃən] N rappresaglie *fpl*; **by way of retaliation, in retaliation** per rappresaglia; **in retaliation for** per vendicarsi di

re·talia·tory [rɪ'tælɪətərɪ] ADJ di rappresaglia, di ritorsione

re·tard·ed [rɪ'tɑːdɪd] ADJ (*offensive: Med*) minorato(-a) mentale

retch [retʃ] VI avere (dei) conati di vomito

re·ten·tive [rɪ'tentɪv] ADJ (*memory*) ritentivo(-a)

re·think [ˌriː'θɪŋk] VT ripensare

reti·cence ['retɪsəns] N reticenza

reti·cent ['retɪsənt] ADJ reticente, riservato(-a)

reti·na ['retɪnə] N retina

reti·nue ['retɪˌnjuː] N seguito, scorta

re·tire [rɪ'taɪəʳ] VI **1** (*give up work*) andare in pensione; (*quit business*) ritirarsi **2** (*withdraw, go to bed, also Sport*) ritirarsi ♦ VT **1** (*Fin: bill of exchange*) ritirare **2** (*person*) mandare in pensione

re·tired [rɪ'taɪəd] ADJ **1** (*no longer working*) in pensione, pensionato(-a); **a retired person** un(a) pensionato(-a); **a retired**

---

teacher un insegnante in pensione **2** (*liter: quiet, secluded*) ritirato(-a), appartato(-a)

re·tire·ment [rɪ'taɪəmənt] N: **to look forward to one's· retirement** non vedere l'ora di andare in pensione; **on her retirement she hopes to ...** quando va in pensione spera di...; **since his retirement** da quando è andato in pensione; **early retirement** prepensionamento

retirement age N età del pensionamento

re·tir·ing [rɪ'taɪərɪŋ] ADJ **1** (*frm: shy*) riservato(-a) **2** (*departing: chairman*) uscente; (*age*) pensionabile

re·tort [rɪ'tɔːt] N **1** (*answer*) risposta (per le rime) **2** (*Chem*) storta ♦ VT (*answer*) ribattere ♦ VI rimbeccare, rispondere per le rime

re·trace [rɪ'treɪs] VT ripercorrere; (*recall*) ricostruire; **to retrace one's steps** (ri)tornare sui propri passi

re·tract [rɪ'trækt] VT (*statement*) ritrattare; (*draw in: claws*) ritrarre; (: *aerial*) ritirare; (: *wheels of plane*) far rientrare; **he later retracted the statement** in seguito ha ritrattato la dichiarazione; **when the wheels were retracted** quando le ruote furono fatte rientrare ♦ VI (*claws*) ritrarsi; (*aerial, wheels*) rientrare

re·tract·able [rɪ'træktəbl] ADJ (*undercarriage, nib*) retrattile

re·train [ˌriː'treɪn] VT (*worker*) riqualificare ♦ VI riqualificarsi

re·train·ing [ˌriː'treɪnɪŋ] N riqualificazione *f*

re·tread [*n* 'riːˌtred, *vb* ˌriː'tred] N gomma rigenerata; (*of book, film*) rifacimento; (*of themes*) ripetizione *f* ♦ VT (*Aut: tyre or tire*) rigenerare

re·treat [rɪ'triːt] N **1** (*place*) rifugio; (*Rel*) ritiro (spirituale); **a country retreat** una tranquilla casa in campagna, un rifugio di campagna; **to go into retreat** (*Rel*) andare in ritiro **2** (*Mil*) ritirata; **to be in retreat** essere in ritirata *or* rotta; **to beat a hasty retreat** (*fig*) battersela ♦ VT (*Mil*) ritirarsi, battere in ritirata; (*flood*) ritirarsi; (*move back*) ritrarsi; **the army retreated** l'esercito batté in ritirata

re·tri·al [ˌriː'traɪəl] N (*Law*) nuovo processo

ret·ri·bu·tion [ˌretrɪ'bjuːʃən] N castigo

re·triev·al [rɪ'triːvl] N (*Comput*) richiamo; (*see vb*) ricupero; riconquista; rimedio, richiamo

re·trieve [rɪ'triːv] VT **1** (*get back: object, money*) ricuperare; (: *honour, position*) riconquistare; (: *set to rights: error, loss, situation*) rimediare a; **we retrieved our luggage** abbiamo ritrovato i nostri bagagli; **the one person who could retrieve the situation ...** la sola persona che poteva salvare la situazione... **2** (*Comput*) richiamare; **to retrieve information** reperire informazioni

re·triev·er [rɪ'triːvəʳ] N cane *m* da riporto

retro·ac·tive [ˌretrəʊ'æktɪv] ADJ retroattivo(-a)

retro·grade ['retrəʊˌgreɪd] ADJ (*frm*): **a retrograde step** (*fig*) un passo (all')indietro

retro·spect ['retrəʊˌspekt] N: **in retrospect** ripensandoci

retro·spec·tive [ˌretrəʊ'spektɪv] ADJ (*gen*) retrospettivo(-a); (*pay rise: Law*) retroattivo(-a) ♦ N (*Art*) retrospettiva

re·turn [rɪ't3ːn] N **1** (*going, coming back*) ritorno; (*sending back*) rinvio; (*reappearance: of illness etc*) ricomparsa; **on my return** al mio ritorno; **by return of post** a stretto giro di posta; **many happy returns (of the day)!** cento di questi giorni! **2** (*of thing borrowed, lost, stolen*) restituzione *f*; (*of money*) rimborso; (*Comm: of merchandise*) reso **3** (*Fin: profit*) profitto, guadagno; **to bring in a good return** *or* **good returns** fruttare *or* dare un buon guadagno **4** (*exchange*): **in return (for)** in cambio (di); **... and I help her in return** ...e io in cambio aiuto lei **5** (*declaration*): **tax return** dichiarazione *f* dei redditi; **census/election returns** risultati *mpl* del censimento/delle elezioni **6** (*Brit: return ticket*) (biglietto di) andata e ritorno; **a return to Bangor, please** un biglietto di andata e ritorno per Bangor, per favore **7** (*Sport*) risposta; **return of serve** (*Tennis*) risposta al servizio **8** (*key*) (tasto di) invio; **hit return** premere invio ♦ VT **1** (*give back*) restituire, rendere; (*bring back*) riportare; (*put back*) rimettere; (*send back*) rinviare, mandare indietro; (*by post*) rispedire; (*Mil: gunfire*) rispondere a; (*favour, love, sb's visit*) ricambiare; **she borrows my things and doesn't return them** prende le mie cose e poi non le restituisce; **"return to sender"** "rispedire al mittente" **2** (*Law*): **to return a verdict of guilty/not guilty** pronunciare un verdetto di colpevolezza/ di innocenza **3** (*Pol: elect*) eleggere ♦ VI (*go, come back*) (ri) tornare; (*illness, symptoms etc*) ricomparire; **to return home** (ri)tornare a casa; **to return to** (*room, office*) (ri)tornare in; (*school, work*) (ri)tornare a; (*subject, argument*) (ri)tornare su; **I've just returned from holiday** sono appena tornato dalle vacanze ♦ ADJ (*Brit: ticket, fare*) di andata e ritorno; (*journey, flight*) di ritorno; **the return journey** il viaggio di ritorno

re·turn·able [rɪ'tɜːnəbl] ADJ: **returnable bottle** vuoto a rendere

re·turn·er [rɪ'tɜːnəʳ] N (*Brit*) donna che ritorna a lavoro dopo la maternità

return key N (*on computer*) tasto di invio

return ticket N (*esp Brit*) biglietto di andata e ritorno

re·tweet [riː'twiːt] N (*on Twitter*) retweet *m inv* ♦ VT ritwittare

re·union [riː'juːnjən] N riunione *f*

re·unite [ˌriːjuː'naɪt] VT riunire ♦ VI riunirsi

Rev, Revd. ABBR = **Reverend**

rev [rɛv] (*fam*) N (*Aut*) giro; **3000 revs per minute** 3000 giri al minuto; **to keep the revs up** tenere il motore su di giri ♦ VT (*engine*) mandare su di giri ♦ VI (*also: **rev up***) (*car*) andar su di giri, imballarsi; (*driver*) tenere il motore su di giri

re·valu·a·tion [ˌriːvæljʊ'eɪʃən] N rivalutazione *f*

re·vamp [ˌriː'væmp] VT (*methods, system*) modernizzare; (*company, organization*) rinnovare; (*play*) rendere di nuovo attuale

rev counter N (*Aut*) contagiri *m inv*

re·veal [rɪ'viːl] VT (*make known*) rivelare, svelare; (*uncover: hidden object*) scoprire

re·veal·ing [rɪ'viːlɪŋ] ADJ (*remarks, action*) rivelatore(-trice); (*dress*) scollato(-a)

re·veil·le [rɪ'vælɪ] N (*Mil*) sveglia

rev·el ['rɛvl] VI far baldoria; **to revel in sth/in doing sth** godere di qc/nel fare qc

rev·ela·tion [ˌrɛvə'leɪʃən] N rivelazione *f*; **(the Book of the) Revelation** (*Bible*) l'Apocalisse *f*

rev·el·ler, rev·eler (*USA*) ['rɛvləʳ] N chi fa baldoria

rev·el·ry ['rɛvlrɪ] N baldoria

re·venge [rɪ'vɛndʒ] N vendetta; (*in game etc*) rivincita; **to get one's revenge (for sth)** vendicarsi (di qc); **to take revenge on sb (for sth)** vendicarsi su qn (per qc); **this is my revenge** questa è la mia vendetta ♦ VT vendicare; **to be revenged (on sb)** prendersi la vendetta (su qn); **to revenge o.s. (on sb)** vendicarsi (su qn)

re·venge·ful [rɪ'vɛndʒfʊl] ADJ vendicativo(-a)

rev·enue ['rɛvənjuː] N entrate *fpl*, reddito

re·ver·ber·ate [rɪ'vɜːbəˌreɪt] VI (*frm: sound*) rimbombare; (*: fig*) ripercuotersi

re·ver·ber·a·tion [rɪˌvɜːbə'reɪʃən] (*frm*) N (*see vb*) rimbombo; ripercussione *f*

re·vere [rɪ'vɪəʳ] VT (*frm*) venerare

rev·er·ence ['rɛvərəns] N venerazione *f*, riverenza ♦ VT venerare

Rev·er·end ['rɛvərənd] ADJ (*in titles*) reverendo(-a)

rev·er·ent ['rɛvərənt] ADJ riverente

rev·erie ['rɛvərɪ] N fantasticheria

re·ver·sal [rɪ'vɜːsəl] N (*of roles, tendencies*) inversione *f*; (*of situation, fortunes*) capovolgimento; (*of decision*) revoca; **the reversal of industrial decline** il risollevamento delle sorti dell'industria

re·verse [rɪ'vɜːs] ADJ (*order*) inverso(-a); (*direction*) opposto(-a); (*side*) altro(-a); **in reverse order** in ordine inverso ♦ N **1** (*opposite*): **the reverse** il contrario, l'opposto; **quite the reverse** al contrario **2** (*face: of coin, paper*) rovescio **3** (*Aut*) retromarcia, marcia indietro; **to go into reverse** fare marcia indietro *or* retromarcia ♦ VT (*turn the other way round*) invertire; (*situation, position*) capovolgere, rovesciare; (*movement*) invertire la direzione di; (*garment*) rivoltare; (*Law*) cassare; **to reverse the charges** (*Brit: Telec*) fare una telefonata a carico (del destinatario); **to reverse one's car** fare marcia indietro ♦ VI (*Brit: Aut*) fare marcia indietro; **I reversed into the car behind** facendo retromarcia ho urtato la macchina di dietro

❏ **reverse** is not translated by the Italian word *riversare*

re·verse-charge call [rɪ,vɜːstʃɑːdʒ'kɔːl] N (*Brit: Telec*) telefonata a carico (del destinatario)

reverse video N (*Comput*) inversione *f* dei colori del video

re·vers·ible [rɪ'vɜːsəbl] ADJ (*garment*) double-face *inv*; (*procedure*) reversibile

re·vers·ing lights [rɪ'vɜːsɪŋ,laɪts] NPL (*Brit: Aut*) luci *fpl* di retromarcia

re·ver·sion [rɪ'vɜːʃən] N (*return to previous state*) ritorno; (*Bio*) reversione *f*

re·vert [rɪ'vɜːt] VI (*gen*): **to revert (to)** ritornare (a); **to revert to type** (*Bio*) ritornare allo stato primitivo; (*fig*) tornare alla propria natura

re·view [rɪ'vjuː] N **1** (*survey, taking stock*) revisione *f*; (*Mil: of troops*) rivista; (*critique*) critica, recensione *f*; **to come** *or* **be under review** essere preso(-a) in esame; **the play got good reviews** lo spettacolo ha ricevuto critiche favorevoli, lo spettacolo ha avuto recensioni favorevoli **2** (*journal*) rivista, periodico ♦ VT (*take stock of*) fare una revisione di; (*situation*) fare il punto di; (*Mil: troops*) passare in rivista; (*book, play, film*) fare la recensione di

re·view·er [rɪ'vjuːəʳ] N recensore *m*; **book/film reviewer** critico letterario/cinematografico

re·vile [rɪ'vaɪl] VT (*frm*) insultare

re·vise [rɪ'vaɪz] VT **1** (*look over: subject, notes*) ripassare **2** (*alter: text*) emendare; (*decision, opinion*) modificare; **to revise one's opinion** cambiare idea; **revised edition** edizione *f* riveduta e corretta ♦ VI (*for exams*) ripassare; **I haven't started revising yet** non ho ancora cominciato a ripassare

re·vi·sion [rɪ'vɪʒən] N **1** (*before exam*) ripasso; (*of text*) revisione *f* **2** (*revised version*) versione *f* riveduta e corretta

re·vi·tal·ize [riː'vaɪtə,laɪz] VT ravvivare

re·viv·al [rɪ'vaɪvəl] N (*of person, business, play*) ripresa; (*of faith, religion*) risveglio; (*of custom, usage: restoration*) ripristino; (*: reappearance*) rinascita; **a revival in car sales** una ripresa delle vendite di automobili; **a revival of 'The Seagull'** un revival de 'Il gabbiano'

re·vive [rɪ'vaɪv] VT (*person*) rianimare; (*from faint*) riprendere i sensi a; (*fig: spirits*) risollevare; (*old customs*) far tornare di moda, far rivivere; (*hopes, courage*) riaccendere; (*suspicions*) risvegliare, ridestare; (*Theatre: play*) riprendere; **the nurses tried to revive him** gli infermieri cercarono di rianimarlo ♦ VI (*person, business, trade, activity*) riprendersi, rianimarsi; (*hope, emotions*) riaccendersi, rinascere

re·voke [rɪ'vəʊk] (*frm*) VT (*law*) abrogare; (*order, decision*) revocare

re·volt [rɪ'vəʊlt] N rivolta, ribellione *f*; **to be in open revolt** essere in aperta rivolta ♦ VT (*far*) rivoltare; **to be revolted by sth** provare disgusto per qc ♦ VI **1** (*rebel*): **to revolt (against sb/sth)** ribellarsi (a qn/qc) **2** (*feel disgust*): **to revolt at** *or* **against** rivoltarsi (a *or* di fronte a)

re·volt·ing [rɪ'vəʊltɪŋ] ADJ rivoltante, ripugnante

revo·lu·tion [ˌrɛvə'luːʃən] N (*movement, change, also Pol*) rivoluzione *f*; (*of record, engine, wheel*) giro

revo·lu·tion·ary [ˌrɛvə'luːʃnərɪ] ADJ, N rivoluzionario(-a)

revo·lu·tion·ize [ˌrɛvə'luːʃəˌnaɪz] VT rivoluzionare

re·volve [rɪ'vɒlv] VT (*far*) girare ♦ VI girare; **to revolve around sth** girare *or* ruotare intorno a qc; **the Earth revolves on its own axis** la Terra ruota intorno al proprio asse; **he thinks everything revolves round him** si crede il centro dell'universo

re·volv·er [rɪ'vɒlvəʳ] N rivoltella

re·volv·ing [rɪ'vɒlvɪŋ] ADJ girevole; **revolving light** (*on police car*) lampeggiatore *m*

revolving door N porta girevole

re·vue [rɪ'vjuː] N (*Theatre*) rivista

re·vul·sion [rɪ'vʌlʃən] N ripugnanza

re·ward [rɪ'wɔːd] N ricompensa, premio; **as a reward for (doing) sth** in premio o come ricompensa per (aver fatto) qc ♦ VT: **to reward (for)** ricompensare (per), premiare (per)

re·ward·ing [rɪ'wɔːdɪŋ] ADJ (*activity*) di grande soddisfazione, gratificante; (*book*) che vale la pena di leggere; **a rewarding job** un lavoro gratificante; **financially rewarding** conveniente dal punto di vista economico

re·wind [ˌriː'waɪnd] VT **1** (*ball of wool etc*) riavvolgere, riarrotolare; (*tape, cassette*) far tornare indietro **2** (*clock, toy*) ricaricare

re·wire [ˌriː'waɪəʳ] VT (*house*) rifare l'impianto elettrico di

re·word [ˌriːˈwɜːd] VT formulare or esprimere con altre parole

re·writ·able [ˌriːˈraɪtəbl] ADJ riscrivibile

re·write [ˌriːˈraɪt] VT riscrivere

Rey·kja·vik [ˈreɪkjəˌvɪk] N Reykjavik f

RFD [ˌɑːrefˈdiː] ABBR (USA, also Post) = **rural free delivery**

Rh ABBR (= rhesus) Rh

rhap·so·dy [ˈræpsədɪ] N (Mus) rapsodia; **to go into rhapso-dies over sth** (fig) andare in estasi per qc

rhesus negative ADJ (Med) Rh-negativo(-a)

rhesus positive ADJ (Med) Rh-positivo(-a)

rheto·ric [ˈretərɪk] N retorica

rhe·tori·cal [rɪˈtɒrɪkəl] ADJ (style, question) retorico(-a)

rheu·mat·ic [ruːˈmætɪk] ADJ reumatico(-a)

rheu·ma·tism [ˈruːmə,tɪzəm] N reumatismo

rheu·ma·toid ar·thri·tis [ˈruːmətɔɪdɑːˈθraɪtɪs] N artrite f reumatoide

Rhine [raɪn] N: **the Rhine** il Reno

rhine·stone [ˈraɪn,stəʊn] N strass m inv

Rhode Island [ˌrəʊdˈaɪlənd] il Rhode Island

rhi·noc·er·os [raɪˈnɒsərəs] N rinoceronte m

rho·do·den·dron [ˌrəʊdəˈdendrən] N rododendro

Rhone [rəʊn] N: **the Rhone** il Rodano

rhu·barb [ˈruːbɑːb] N rabarbaro ♦ ADJ (jam, pie, tart) di rabarbaro

rhyme [raɪm] N rima; (verse) poesia; **in rhyme** in rima; **a little rhyme** una breve poesia; **without rhyme or reason** senza capo né coda ♦ VI: **to rhyme (with)** fare rima (con); **'Moon' rhymes with 'June'** 'Moon' fa rima con 'June'

rhythm [ˈrɪðəm] N ritmo

rhyth·mic, rhyth·mi·cal [ˈrɪðmɪk(l)] ADJ ritmico(-a)

rhyth·mi·cal·ly [ˈrɪðmɪkəlɪ] ADV ritmicamente

rhythm method N (Med): **the rhythm method** il metodo Ogino-Knaus

RI [ˌɑːˈaɪ] ABBR (USA Post: = **Rhode Island**)

rib [rɪb] N (Anat) costola; (Culin) costata; (of umbrella) stecca; (of leaf) nervatura; (Knitting) costa; **to dig or poke sb in the ribs** dare una gomitata nelle costole a qn ♦ VT (fam: tease) punzecchiare

rib·ald [ˈrɪbəld] ADJ (old: person) sguaiato(-a); (: joke) licen-zioso(-a)

ribbed [rɪbd] ADJ (knitting) a coste

rib·bon [ˈrɪbən] N (gen) nastro; (Mil) nastrino; **to tear sth to ribbons** ridurre qc a brandelli; (fig) demolire qc

rice [raɪs] N riso

rice field N risaia

rice pudding N budino di riso

rich [rɪtʃ] ADJ (comp -er, superl -est) (gen) ricco(-a); (food) con molti grassi; (colour) intenso(-a); (clothes) sontuoso(-a); **it was lovely but rather rich** era buono ma un po' troppo sos-tanzioso; **that's rich!** (fam, iro) questa sì che è bella!; **the rich** i ricchi; **to be rich in sth** essere ricco(-a) di qc; **to become or get or grow rich(er)** arricchirsi, diventar ricco(-a)

rich·ly [ˈrɪtʃlɪ] ADV (rewarded) lautamente; (endowed) abbon-dantemente; (dressed) sontuosamente; (deserved) piena-mente; **richly deserved** pienamente meritato

rick·ets [ˈrɪkɪts] NSG rachitismo

rick·ety [ˈrɪkɪtɪ] ADJ (furniture, structure) traballante

rick·shaw [ˈrɪkʃɔː] N risciò m inv

rico·chet [ˈrɪkəˌʃeɪ] N rimbalzo ♦ VI: **to ricochet (off)** rimbal-zare (contro)

rid [rɪd] (pt, pp **rid** or **ridded**) VT: **to rid sb/sth of** sbarazzare qn/qc di, liberare qn/qc da; **an attempt to rid the house of mice** un tentativo di liberare la casa dai topi; **to get rid of sb/sth, rid o.s. of sb/sth** sbarazzarsi or liberarsi di qn/qc

rid·dance [ˈrɪdəns] N: **good riddance!** (fam) che liberazione!

rid·den [ˈrɪdn] PP of **ride**

rid·dle¹ [ˈrɪdl] N (puzzle) indovinello; **to speak in riddles** par-lare per enigmi

rid·dle² [ˈrɪdl] VT (soil, coal) setacciare, vagliare; (fig): **to riddle with** (bullets) crivellare di; **riddled with holes** bucherella-to(-a); **the council was riddled with corruption** la corru-zione dilagava nel consiglio ♦ N (sieve) setaccio, vaglio

ride [raɪd] (pt **rode**, pp **ridden**) N (on horse) cavalcata; (in car, on bike) giro, corsa; (esp USA: lift) passaggio, strappo; **to go**

for a ride (on horse) andare a fare una cavalcata; (on bike) andare a fare un giro; **it was a rough ride** è stato un viaggio scomodo; **he got or was given a rough ride** (fig) passò un momentaccio; **it's a 10-minute ride on the bus** ci vogliono 10 minuti in autobus; **he gave me a ride into town** (in car) mi ha dato un passaggio in città; **it's a short bus ride to the town centre** in autobus il centro non è lontano; **to take sb for a ride** (in car, on horseback) portare qn a fare un giro; (fig: make fool of, swindle) prendere in giro qn ♦ VT: **to ride a horse** andare a cavallo, cavalcare; (: subj: jockey) montare un cavallo; **to ride a donkey/camel** cavalcare un asino/cam-mello; **to ride a bicycle** andare in bicicletta; **can you ride a bike?** sai andare in bicicletta?; **he rode his horse into town** è venuto in città a cavallo; **we rode 10 km yesterday** ieri ab-biamo fatto 10 km a cavallo (or in bicicletta); **to ride a good race** fare un'ottima gara; **to ride the bus** (USA) prendere l'autobus ♦ VI (ride a horse) andare a cavallo; (go by car/bicyc-le etc) andare in macchina/in bicicletta etc; **to ride along/ through** etc passare/attraversare etc a cavallo (or in macchi-na etc); **can you ride?** (ride a horse) sai andare a cavallo?, sai cavalcare?; **I'm learning to ride** sto imparando a cavalcare; **he rode to school on his new bike** è andato a scuola con la bici nuova; **he's riding high at the moment** in questo momento è sulla cresta dell'onda; **to ride at anchor** (ship) essere all'ancora or alla fonda; **to let things ride** lasciare che le cose seguano il loro corso

▸ **ride out** VT + ADV (Naut: storm) sostenere; (fig: difficult pe-riod) superare; **to ride out the storm** (fig) mantenersi a galla

▸ **ride up** VI + ADV (skirt, dress) salire

rid·er [ˈraɪdər] N 1 (horse rider) uomo (donna) a cavallo; (skilled man) cavallerizzo; (skilled woman) cavallerizza, amazzone f; (jockey) fantino(-a); (cyclist) ciclista m/f; (mo-torcyclist) motociclista m/f; **she's a good rider** è una buona cavallerizza 2 (addition to document) clausola addizionale

ridge [rɪdʒ] N (of mountain, hill) cresta; (of chain of mountains) crinale m; (of roof) colmo; (in ploughed field) porca; (Met): **ridge of high pressure** fascia di alta pressione; **we walked along the ridge** camminammo lungo la cresta

ridi·cule [ˈrɪdɪkjuːl] N ridicolo; **to hold sb/sth up to ridicule** mettere in ridicolo qn/qc ♦ VT ridicolizzare

ri·dicu·lous [rɪˈdɪkjʊləs] ADJ ridicolo(-a); **to make o.s. (look) ridiculous** rendersi ridicolo(-a)

rid·ing [ˈraɪdɪŋ] N (horse-riding) equitazione f; **to go riding** fare equitazione

riding school N scuola di equitazione

rife [raɪf] ADJ (frm): **to be rife** (corruption, disease) dilagare, abbondare; **speculation is rife** abbondano le congetture; **to be rife with** abbondare di; **corruption is rife** c'è molta corruzione

riff·raff [ˈrɪfˌræf] N gentaglia, canaglia

ri·fle¹ [ˈraɪfl] VT (house, till etc) ripulire, svuotare

▸ **rifle through** VI + PREP frugare

ri·fle² [ˈraɪfl] N fucile m, carabina

rifle range N (Mil) poligono di tiro; (at fair) tiro a segno

rift [rɪft] N (in family, between friends) incrinatura; (Pol: in par-ty) spaccatura; (in rock, ground) crepa, fessura; (in clouds) squarcio; **a serious rift between the President and the government** una grave incrinatura tra il Presidente e il governo

rig [rɪg] N (also: **oil rig**) impianto di trivellazione (per il petro-lio); (offshore) piattaforma petrolifera or di trivellazione ♦ VT 1 (election, competition) truccare; (prices) manipolare; (also: **rig up**: equipment, device) improvvisare, mettere su 2 (boat) armare

▸ **rig out** VT + ADV (Brit) attrezzare; (pej) abbigliare, agghin-dare; **to rig out (as/in)** vestire (da/in)

▸ **rig up** VT + ADV (also fig) improvvisare, mettere su

rig·ging [ˈrɪgɪŋ] N (Naut) attrezzatura; **standing/running rigging** manovre fpl fisse/correnti

right [raɪt] ADJ 1 (morally good) retto(-a), onesto(-a); (just) giusto(-a); **it's not right to behave like that** non sta bene fare così; **it's not right!** non è giusto!; **it is only right that ...** è più che giusto che...; **to do what is right** fare ciò che si crede giusto; **I thought it right to warn him** mi è sembrato giusto avvertirlo 2 (suitable: person, clothes, time) adatto(-a), appropriato(-a); **to choose the right moment for sth/to do**

sth scegliere il momento giusto *or* adatto per qc/per fare qc; **that's the right attitude!** così va bene!; **to say the right thing** dire la cosa giusta; **you did the right thing** hai fatto bene; **what's the right thing to do?** qual è la cosa migliore da farsi?; **to know the right people** conoscere la gente giusta **3** (*correct: answer, solution etc*) giusto(-a), esatto(-a), corretto(-a); (: *size*) giusto(-a); **right first time!** hai azzeccato al primo colpo!; **to get sth right** far giusto qc; **I got every question right** ho risposto esattamente a tutte le domande; **let's get it right this time!** cerchiamo di farlo bene stavolta!; **to get one's facts right** sapere di che cosa si parla; **get your facts right!** non parlare se non sei sicuro di quello che dici!; **(yes,) that's right** sì, esatto; **the right answer** la risposta esatta; **the right road** la strada buona; **the right time** l'ora esatta; **do you have the right time?** hai l'ora esatta?; **it isn't the right size** non è la taglia giusta; **to get on the right side of sb** (*fig*) entrare nelle grazie di qn; **to put a clock right** rimettere all'ora esatta un orologio; **to put a mistake right** (*Brit*) correggere un errore; **right you are!** *or* **right-oh!** (*fam*) va bene! **4 to be right** (*person*) aver ragione; (*answer, behaviour*) essere giusto(-a) *or* corretto(-a); **you're quite right** *or* (*fam*) **you're dead right** hai proprio *or* perfettamente ragione; **you were right to come to me** hai fatto bene a venire da me **5** (*well, in order*): **to be/feel as right as rain** essere/sentirsi completamente ristabilito(-a); **he is not quite right in the head** gli manca una rotella; **I don't feel quite right** non mi sento del tutto a posto; **all's right with the world** tutto va bene; **the stereo still isn't right** lo stereo ha ancora qualcosa che non va **6** (*not left*) destro(-a); **my right hand** la mano destra; **I'd give my right arm to know ...** darei un occhio per sapere... **7** (*Math: angle*) retto(-a) **8** (*fam: intensive*): **a right idiot** un perfetto idiota ◆ ADV **1** (*directly, exactly*): **right now** (*at this moment*) in questo momento, proprio adesso; (*immediately*) subito; **right away** subito; **I'll do it right away** lo faccio subito; **right off** subito; (*at the first attempt*) al primo colpo; **right here** proprio qui; **right against the wall** proprio contro il muro; **right ahead** sempre diritto, proprio davanti; **right behind/in front of** proprio dietro/davanti a; **right before/after** subito prima/dopo; **right after the summer** subito dopo l'estate; **right in the middle** proprio nel (bel) mezzo; (*of target*) in pieno centro; **right round sth** tutt'intorno a qc; **right at the end** proprio alla fine **2** (*completely*) completamente; **to go right back to the beginning of sth** ricominciare qc da capo; **to go right to the end of sth** andare fino in fondo a qc; **to push sth right in** spingere qc fino in fondo; **to read a book right through** leggere un libro dall'inizio alla fine **3** (*correctly*) giusto, bene; (*well*) bene; **if I remember right** se mi ricordo bene; **if everything goes right** se tutto va bene; **did I pronounce it right?** l'ho pronunciato bene? **4** (*properly, fairly*) giustamente, con giustizia; **to treat sb right** trattare qn in modo giusto; **you did right not to go** hai fatto bene a non andarci **5** (*not left*) a destra; **turn right at the traffic lights** al semaforo gira a destra; **right, left and centre** (*fig*) da tutte le parti **6 right, who's next?** bene, chi è il prossimo?; **right then, let's begin!** (va) bene allora, cominciamo! **7 all right!** va bene!, d'accordo!; (*that's enough*) va bene!; **it's all right** (*don't worry*) va (tutto) bene; **it's all right for you!** già, facile per te!; **is it all right for me to go at 4?** va bene se me ne vado alle 4?; **I'm/I feel all right now** adesso sto/mi sento bene ◆ N **1 right and wrong** il bene e il male; **to be in the right** essere nel giusto; **to know right from wrong** distinguere il bene dal male; **I want to know the rights and wrongs of it** voglio sapere chi ha ragione e chi ha torto; **two wrongs don't make a right** due errori non ammontano a una cosa giusta **2** (*claim, authority*) diritto; **film rights** diritti *mpl* di riproduzione cinematografica; **to have a right to sth** aver diritto a qc; **you have a right to your own opinions** è tuo diritto pensarla come vuoi; **the right to be/say/do sth** il diritto di essere/dire/fare qc; **what right have you got to ...?** che diritto hai di...?; **you've got no right to do that** non hai diritto di farlo; **by rights** di diritto; **to be within one's rights** avere tutti i diritti; **to own sth in one's own right** possedere qc per conto proprio **3** (*not left*) destra; (*Boxing: punch*) destro; **the Right** (*Pol*) la destra; **to the right** (*of*) sul lato destro (di); **on the right (of)** a destra (di) **4 to set** *or* **put to rights** mettere a posto ◆ VT (*correct: balance*)

ristabilire; (: *wrong, injustice*) riparare a; (: *vehicle, vessel*) raddrizzare; **to right itself** (*vehicle, vessel*) raddrizzarsi; (*situation*) risolversi da solo *or* da sé ◆ EXCL bene!

right angle N angolo retto; **at right angles (to)** ad angolo retto (con)

right-click [ˈraɪtklɪk] VI (*Comput*) fare clic con il pulsante destro del mouse

right·eous [ˈraɪtʃəs] ADJ (*person*) virtuoso(-a), retto(-a); (*indignation, anger: moralistic*) un po' troppo virtuoso(-a); (: *justified*) giustificato(-a); **righteous indignation** giusta indignazione *f*

right·eous·ness [ˈraɪtʃəsnɪs] N rettitudine *f*, virtù

right·ful [ˈraɪtfʊl] ADJ (*heir*) legittimo(-a)

right·ful·ly [ˈraɪtfəlɪ] ADV legittimamente, a buon diritto

right-hand [raɪtˈhænd] ADJ (*side*) destro(-a); **right-hand drive** (*Aut*) guida a destra

right-handed [ˌraɪtˈhændɪd] ADJ (*person*) destrimano(-a); **I'm right-handed** uso la destra

right·ly [ˈraɪtlɪ] ADV (*correctly*) correttamente; (*with reason*) a ragione, giustamente; **she rightly decided that he was lying** concluse, giustamente, che lui mentiva; **I don't rightly know** non so di preciso; **if I remember rightly** se mi ricordo bene; **rightly or wrongly** a torto o a ragione

right-minded [ˌraɪtˈmaɪndɪd], **right-thinking** [ˈraɪtˌθɪŋkɪŋ] ADJ di buon senso, sensato(-a)

right of way N (*across property*) diritto di accesso; (*Aut: precedence*) precedenza; **to have right of way** avere la precedenza

rights issue N (*Fin*) emissione *f* di azioni riservate agli azionisti, emissione *f* riservata agli azionisti

right wing N: **the right wing** (*Pol*) la destra; (*Sport, Mil: position, person*) l'ala destra

right-winger [ˌraɪtˈwɪŋəʳ] N (*Pol*) uno(-a) di destra; (*Sport*) ala destra

rig·id [ˈrɪdʒɪd] ADJ (*material*) rigido(-a); (*discipline, specifications, principle*) rigoroso(-a); (*rules*) severo(-a); (*pej: person, ideas*) inflessibile; **rigid with fear** impietrito(-a) dalla paura

ri·gid·ity [rɪˈdʒɪdɪtɪ] N (*see adj*) rigidità; rigorosità; severità; inflessibilità

rig·id·ly [ˈrɪdʒɪdlɪ] ADV (*strictly*) rigorosamente; (*inflexibly*) inflessibilmente; (*closely*) rigidamente; **to stand rigidly to attention** stare impalato(-a) sull'attenti

rig·ma·role [ˈrɪgmərəʊl] N (*pej: speech*) storia, tiritera; (: *complicated procedure*) trafila

ri·gor [ˈrɪgəʳ] N (*USA*) = **rigour**

rig·or mor·tis [ˌrɪgɔːˈmɔːtɪs] N rigor mortis *m inv*

rig·or·ous [ˈrɪgərəs] ADJ rigoroso(-a)

rig·or·ous·ly [ˈrɪgərəslɪ] ADV (*apply, test*) rigorosamente

rig·our, (*USA*) **rig·or** [ˈrɪgəʳ] N rigore *m*

rig-out [ˈrɪgaʊt] N (*Brit fam*) tenuta

rile [raɪl] VT (*fam*) irritare, seccare

rim [rɪm] N (*of cup etc*) orlo; (*of wheel*) cerchione *m*; **the rim of a cup** l'orlo di una tazza; **rims** NPL (*of spectacles*) montatura *sg*; **glasses with wire rims** occhiali con montatura metallica

rim·less [ˈrɪmlɪs] ADJ (*spectacles*) senza montatura

rimmed [ˈrɪmd] ADJ (*with colour*) bordato(-a)

rind [raɪnd] N (*of fruit*) buccia; (*of lemon*) scorza; (*of cheese*) crosta; (*of bacon*) cotenna

ring¹ [rɪŋ] N **1** (*gen*) anello; (*for napkin*) portatovagliolo; **wedding ring** fede *f*; (*of smoke*) spirale *f*; **he gave her a silver ring** le ha regalato un anello d'argento; **the rings of Saturn** gli anelli di Saturno; **to run rings round sb** (*fig*) surclassare qn **2** (*of people, objects*) cerchio; (*gang*) cricca, banda; (*of spies*) rete *f*; **they were sitting in a ring** erano seduti in circolo *or* in cerchio **3** (*arena etc: Boxing*) ring *m inv*, quadrato; (: *at circus*) pista, arena **4** (: TV *surround*) circondare, accerchiare; (*mark with ring*) fare un cerchietto intorno a

ring² [rɪŋ] (*pt* rang, *pp* rung) N **1** (*of bell*) trillo; (*of telephone*) squillo; (*tone of voice*) tono; **he answered at the first ring** ha risposto al primo squillo; **that has the ring of truth about it** questo ha l'aria d'essere vero **2** (*Brit: Telec*): **to give sb a ring** dare un colpo di telefono a qn, telefonare a qn ◆ VT **1** (*bell, doorbell*) suonare; **to ring the bell** suonare il campanello; **to ring the changes** (*fig*) variare; **the name doesn't ring a bell (with me)** (*fig*) quel nome non mi dice niente **2** (*Brit: Telec*): **to ring sb (up)** telefonare a qn, dare un colpo di telefono a qn ◆ VI **1** (*bell, telephone etc*) suonare; **the**

phone's ringing sta squillando il telefono; **to ring for sb/ sth** (suonare il campanello per) chiamare qn/chiedere qc **2** (*telephone*) telefonare; **your mother rang this morning** stamattina ha telefonato tua madre; **several friends have rung to congratulate me** mi hanno telefonato diversi amici per congratularsi **3** (*words, voice*) risuonare; (*blast*) rimbombare; (*ears*) fischiare; **their laughter rang through the room** le loro risate risuonavano nella stanza; **my ears are still ringing from the blast** mi fischiano ancora le orecchie per via dell'esplosione; **to ring true/false** (*fig*) suonare vero(-a)/falso(-a)
▸ **ring around** vi + adv = ring round
▸ **ring back** vt + adv (*Brit: Telec*) richiamare; **I'll ring back later** richiamerò più tardi
▸ **ring in** vi + adv (*Brit: Telec*) telefonare
▸ **ring off** vi + adv (*Brit: Telec*) mettere giù, riattaccare
▸ **ring out** vi + adv risuonare, riecheggiare
▸ **ring round** vi + adv fare un giro di telefonate ♦ vt + adv: **to ring round one's friends** telefonare a tutti gli amici
▸ **ring up** vt + adv = ring² 2
ring binder n classificatore *m* ad anelli
ring finger n anulare *m*
ring·ing ['rɪŋɪŋ] adj (*voice, tone*) sonoro(-a) ♦ n (*of church bells*) scampanio; (*of door bell*) scampanellata; (*of telephone*) squillo; (*in ears*) fischio, ronzio
ring·leader ['rɪŋˌliːdə'] n (*of gang*) capobanda *m/f*
ring·let ['rɪŋlɪt] n boccolo
ring road n (*Brit*) circonvallazione *f*
ring tone n suoneria
rink [rɪŋk] n (*for ice-skating*) pista di pattinaggio (su ghiaccio); (*for roller-skating*) pista di pattinaggio (a rotelle)
rinse [rɪns] n (ri)sciacquatura; (*quick*) (ri)sciacquata; (*hair-colouring*) cachet *m inv*; **to give sth a rinse** dare una sciacquata a qc ♦ vt (ri)sciacquare; **to rinse (the soap off) one's hands** sciacquarsi le mani
▸ **rinse out** vt + adv sciacquare; **to rinse out one's mouth** sciacquarsi la bocca
Rio de Ja·nei·ro [ˌriːəʊdədʒə'nɪərəʊ] n Rio de Janeiro *f*
riot ['raɪət] n disordini *mpl*; **a riot of colour(s)** un'orgia di colori; **to read sb a riot act** sopprimere i disordini; **to read sb the riot act** (*fam*) dare una lavata di capo a qn; **to run riot** (*out of control*) scatenarsi ♦ vi tumultuare, manifestare violentemente
ri·ot·er ['raɪətə'] n dimostrante *m/f* (*durante dei disordini*)
riot gear n (*Police*): **in riot gear** in assetto antisommossa
ri·ot·ous ['raɪətəs] adj (*person, mob, party*) scatenato(-a); (*living*) sfrenato(-a); (*very funny*) esilarante
ri·ot·ous·ly ['raɪətəslɪ] adv sfrenatamente; **riotously funny** esilarante
riot police n ≈ la Celere
RIP [ˌɑːraɪ'piː] abbr (= *requiescat or requiescant in pace: may he, she, or they rest in peace*) RIP
rip [rɪp] n strappo ♦ vt strappare; **to rip sth to pieces** stracciare in mille pezzi qc; **to rip open** strappare (per aprire); **I accidentally ripped the envelope** senza volere ho strappato la busta; **I've ripped my jeans** mi si sono strappati i jeans ♦ vi strapparsi; **to let rip** (*fig*) scatenarsi; **to let rip at sb** dirne di tutti di colori a qn
▸ **rip off** vt + adv **1** strappare **2** (*fam: overcharge*) pelare; (: *cheat*) fregare; **the hotel ripped us off** all'albergo ci hanno pelato
▸ **rip up** vt + adv stracciare; **he read the note and then ripped it up** ha letto il biglietto e poi l'ha strappato
rip·cord ['rɪpˌkɔːd] n (*Aer*) cavo di spiegamento
ripe [raɪp] adj (*comp* -r, *superl* -st) (*gen: fruit*) maturo(-a); (*cheese*) stagionato(-a); **to be ripe for sth** (*fig*) essere pronto(-a) per qc; **to live to a ripe old age** vivere fino a una bella età
rip·en ['raɪpən] vt maturare ♦ vi maturarsi; (*cheese*) stagionarsi
ripe·ness ['raɪpnɪs] n maturazione *f*
rip-off ['rɪpˌɒf] n (*fam*): **it's a rip-off!** è un furto!
ri·poste [rɪ'pɒst](*liter*) n replica ♦ vi replicare
rip·ple ['rɪpl] n (*of water*) ondulazione *f*; (*small wave*) increspatura; (*noise: of voices*) mormorio; (: *of laughter*) fremito;

---

ripples on the lake increspature sul lago; **a ripple of laughter** delle risate ♦ vt increspare; **the breeze rippled the water** la brezza increspava l'acqua ♦ vi incresparsi; **murmurs rippled through the audience** mormorii echeggiavano tra il pubblico
rise [raɪz] (*pt* rose, *pp* risen ['rɪzn]) n **1** (*increase: in prices, wages, inflation*): rise (in) aumento (di); **to ask for a rise** chiedere un aumento **2** (*of sun*) sorgere *m*; (*of theatre curtain*) alzarsi *m*; (*fig: ascendancy*) ascesa; **rise to power** ascesa al potere; **to get a rise out of sb** (*fam*) stuzzicare qn **3** (*upward slope*) salita, pendio; (*small hill*) altura **4** (*origin: of river*) sorgente *f*; **to give rise to** (*fig*) dar origine a **1** (*get up*) alzarsi; (*fig: building*) sorgere; **to rise to one's feet** alzarsi in piedi; **he rose to his feet** si alzò in piedi; **the House rose** (*Parliament*) la seduta della Camera è stata tolta; **to rise to the occasion** dimostrarsi all'altezza della situazione **2** (*go higher: sun*) sorgere, levarsi; (: *smoke*) alzarsi, levarsi; (: *dough, cake*) crescere (di volume), lievitare; (: *ground*) salire; (: *fig: spirits*) sollevarsi; **the plane rose to 4000 metres** l'aereo si è alzato a 4000 metri; **to rise from the ranks** (*Mil*) venir su dalla gavetta; **to rise from nothing** venir su dal niente; **he rose to be President** ascese alla carica di Presidente; **to rise to the surface** (*also fig*) venire a galla, affiorare; **to rise above sth** (*fig*) essere al di sopra di qc; **to rise to a higher sum** offrire di più, fare un'offerta più alta **3** (*increase: prices*) aumentare, rincarare; (*temperature, shares, numbers*) salire; (*wind, sea*) alzarsi; **prices rose sharply last month** i prezzi sono aumentati notevolmente il mese scorso; **his voice rose in anger** alzò la voce per la rabbia **4** (*river*) nascere; (*water*) salire
▸ **rise up** vi + adv (*rebel*) sollevarsi, insorgere
ris·en ['rɪzn] pp *of* rise
ris·ing ['raɪzɪŋ] adj **1** (*increasing: number*) sempre crescente; (: *prices*) in aumento; (: *tide*) montante; (: *anger, alarm, doubt*) crescente **2** (*getting higher: sun, moon*) nascente, che sorge; (: *ground*) in salita; (*fig: promising*) promettente ♦ n (*uprising*) sommossa
rising damp n infiltrazioni *fpl* d'umidità (*dal sottosuolo*)
rising star n (*also fig*) astro nascente
risk [rɪsk] n rischio; **fire/health/security risk** rischio d'incendio/per la salute/per la sicurezza; **to be a fire risk** essere una potenziale causa d'incendio; **there's not much risk of rain** non c'è pericolo che piova; **to take a risk** *or* **risks** correre un rischio *or* dei rischi, rischiare; **to run the risk of sth** correre il rischio di qc; **it's not worth the risk** non vale la pena di correre il rischio; **at risk** in pericolo; **to put sth at risk** mettere a repentaglio qc; **he put his job at risk** ha rischiato di giocarsi il posto; **at one's own risk** a proprio rischio e pericolo; **it's at your own risk** è a tuo rischio e pericolo; **at the risk of seeming stupid** a costo di sembrare stupido ♦ vt (*life, health, money*) rischiare, arrischiare; (*criticism, anger, defeat*) rischiare; **I'll risk it** ci proverò lo stesso; **to risk losing/being caught** rischiare di perdere/di esser preso(-a); **to risk one's neck** rischiare la pelle
risk capital n (*Fin*) capitale *m* di rischio
risky ['rɪskɪ] adj (*comp* -ier, *superl* -iest) rischioso(-a)
ris·qué ['rɪskeɪ] adj audace, spinto(-a), osé *inv*
ris·sole ['rɪsəʊl] n (*Culin*) crocchetta
rite [raɪt] n rito; (*Rel*): **the last rites** l'estrema unzione *fsg*; **rite of passage** rito di passaggio
ritu·al ['rɪtjʊəl] adj, n rituale *m*
ri·val ['raɪvl] adj (*team*) rivale; (*firm*) concorrente; (*claim, attraction*) in concorrenza; **a rival gang** una banda rivale; **a rival company** una ditta concorrente ♦ n (*see adj*) rivale *m/f*; concorrente *m/f* ♦ vt rivaleggiare con; **to rival sb/sth in** competere con qn/qc in; **the translation cannot rival the original** la traduzione non può competere con l'originale
ri·val·ry ['raɪvlrɪ] n rivalità *f inv*; (*in business*) concorrenza
riv·er ['rɪvə'] n fiume *m*; **up/down river** a monte/valle; **across the river** dall'altra parte del fiume; **the River Thames** il Tamigi ♦ adj (*port, police, basin, traffic*) fluviale
river·bank ['rɪvəˌbæŋk] n sponda (del fiume), argine *m*
river·bed ['rɪvəˌbed] n letto del fiume
river·side ['rɪvəˌsaɪd] n: **the riverside** la riva *or* la sponda (del fiume); **by the riverside** in riva al fiume; **along the riverside** lungo il fiume ♦ adj: **a riverside café** un bar sul fiume

riv·et [ˈrɪvɪt] N ribattino, rivetto ♦ VT rivettare; (fig: attention) attirare; (: audience) inchiodare; **to be riveted by sth** essere terribilmente attratto(-a) da qc

riv·et·ing [ˈrɪvɪtɪŋ] ADJ (gripping) avvincente

Rivi·era [ˌrɪvɪˈɛərə] N: **the Italian Riviera** la Riviera, la riviera ligure; **the French Riviera** la Costa Azzurra

Ri·yadh [rɪˈjɑːd] N Riad f

RN [ˌɑːrˈɛn] N ABBR 1 (Brit) = Royal Navy 2 (USA) = registered nurse

RNA [ˌɑːrɛnˈeɪ] N ABBR (Biochemistry: = ribonucleic acid) RNA

road [rəʊd] N (route, also fig) strada, via; (residential: Road) via; **main road** strada principale; **A-/B-road** ≈ strada statale/ secondaria; **country road** strada di campagna; **it takes 4 hours by road** sono 4 ore di macchina (or in camion etc); **just across the road (from)** proprio di fronte a; **to be off the road** (car: for repairs) essere in riparazione; (: laid up) essere fuori uso; **he shouldn't be allowed on the road** dovrebbero togliergli la patente; **that car shouldn't be allowed on the road** non dovrebbero lasciar circolare quella macchina; **to hold the road** (Aut) tenere la strada; **"road up"** "attenzione: lavori in corso"; **to be on the road** (pop group) essere in tournée; (salesman) viaggiare; **on the road to success** sulla via del successo; **to take to the road** (tramp) darsi al vagabondaggio; **to have one for the road** (fam) bere il bicchiere della staffa; **somewhere along the road** (fig) a un certo punto ♦ ADJ (accident, sign) stradale

road accident N incidente m stradale

road·block [ˈrəʊdblɒk] N blocco stradale

road haulage N autotrasporti mpl

road·hog [ˈrəʊdhɒg] N (fam, pej) automobilista che guida tenendosi al centro della strada così da impedire il sorpasso

road map N carta stradale, carta automobilistica; (fig) piano dettagliato; **a road map to peace** un piano di pace

road rage N aggressività al volante

road safety N sicurezza sulle strade

road·side [ˈrəʊdsaɪd] N ciglio della strada; **by the roadside** a lato della strada

road sign N cartello stradale

road·sweeper [ˈrəʊdswiːpəʳ] N (Brit: person) spazzino; (: vehicle) autospazzatrice f

road tax N (Aut) tassa di circolazione

road user N utente m/f della strada

road·way [ˈrəʊdweɪ] N carreggiata

road works NPL lavori mpl stradali; (on road sign) "lavori in corso"

road·worthy [ˈrəʊdwɜːðɪ] ADJ (vehicle) in buono stato di marcia

roam [rəʊm] VT (streets) vagabondare per, gironzolare per, vagare per; **children who roamed the streets** bambini che vagavano per le vie ♦ VI (person) vagabondare, errare, gironzolare; (thoughts) vagare; **we roamed far and wide** abbiamo vagato in lungo e in largo

roar [rɔːʳ] N (of lion) ruggito; (of bull) mugghio; (of crowd) urlo, tumulto; (of waves) fragore m; (of wind, storm) muggito; (of thunder) rimbombo; **the roar of the crowd** il tumulto della folla; **the roar of a lion** il ruggito di un leone; **with great roars of laughter** con fragorose risate ♦ VI (lion) ruggire; (bull) mugghiare; (crowd, audience) urlare, fare tumulto; (wind, storm) muggire; (thunder) rimbombare; (guns) tuonare; **to roar with laughter** ridere fragorosamente; **the truck roared past** il camion passò rombando; **the crowd roared** la folla era in tumulto; **lions roar** il leone ruggisce

roar·ing [ˈrɔːrɪŋ] ADJ (lion) ruggente; (bull) mugghiante; (crowd) urlante; (sea, thunder) fragoroso(-a); **a roaring fire** un bel fuoco, una bella fiammata; **a roaring success** un successo strepitoso; **roaring drunk** ubriaco(-a) fradicio(-a)

roast [rəʊst] N arrosto ♦ ADJ arrosto inv; **roast beef** arrosto di manzo; **roast chicken** pollo arrosto; **roast pork** arrosto di maiale ♦ VT (meat) arrostire; (coffee) tostare ♦ VI arrostire; **I'm roasting!** (fam) sto crepando dal caldo!

roast beef N arrosto di manzo

roast·ing [ˈrəʊstɪŋ] ADJ 1 (chicken) da fare arrosto; (pan) per arrosti 2 (fam): **a roasting (hot) day** una giornata torrida ♦ N (fam): **to give sb a roasting** dare una lavata di capo a qn

rob [rɒb] VT (person) derubare; (with weapon) rapinare; (till,

bank) svaligiare; **to rob sb of sth** (money) derubare qn di qc, rubare qc a qn; (fig: happiness, right) privare qn di qc; **he was robbed of his wallet** gli hanno rubato il portafoglio; **I've been robbed!** mi hanno derubato!; **to rob a bank** rapinare una banca

rob·ber [ˈrɒbəʳ] N ladro(-a); (armed) rapinatore(-trice)

rob·bery [ˈrɒbərɪ] N furto; (armed robbery) rapina (a mano armata); **robbery with violence** (Law) furto con aggressione; **a bank robbery** una rapina in banca; **it's daylight robbery!** (fam) (ma) è una rapina!

robe [rəʊb] N (garment) tunica; (also: bathrobe) accappatoio; (also: robes) abiti mpl da cerimonia; (lawyer's: Univ) toga; **scarlet robes** abiti mpl scarlatti; **a towelling robe** un accappatoio di spugna ♦ VT (frm) vestire

❏ robe is not translated by the Italian word roba

rob·in [ˈrɒbɪn] N pettirosso

ro·bot [ˈrəʊbɒt] N robot m inv, automa m

ro·bot·ics [rəʊˈbɒtɪks] NSG robotica

ro·bust [rəʊˈbʌst] ADJ robusto(-a); (material) solido(-a)

rock [rɒk] N 1 (gen) roccia; (large stone, boulder) roccia, masso; (in sea) scoglio; **the Rock of Gibraltar** la Rocca di Gibilterra; **I sat on a rock** mi sono seduto(-a) su una roccia; **the crowd started to throw rocks** la folla cominciò a lanciare sassi; **on the rocks** (drink) con ghiaccio; **their marriage is on the rocks** il loro matrimonio sta naufragando 2 **stick of rock** (Brit: sweet) bastoncino di zucchero caramellato 3 (Mus) rock m ♦ VT (gently: cradle, boat) far dondolare; (: baby) cullare; (violently: boat) sballottare; (subj: earthquake) squassare; (fig: shake, startle) sconvolgere, far tremare; **to rock the boat** (fig: fam) piantare grane; **the tremor rocked the building** la scossa ha fatto oscillare l'edificio ♦ VI (gently) dondolare; (violently) oscillare

rock and roll N rock and roll m

rock-bottom [ˈrɒkˈbɒtəm] N (fig): **to reach** or **touch rock-bottom** (person) toccare il fondo; (price) raggiungere il livello più basso; **morale was at rock-bottom** il morale era a terra; **prices have hit rock-bottom** i prezzi sono scesi tantissimo

rock climber N rocciatore(-trice), scalatore(-trice)

rock climbing N (Sport) roccia

rock·ery [ˈrɒkərɪ] N giardino roccioso

rock·et¹ [ˈrɒkɪt] N razzo; **to fire** or **send up a rocket** lanciare un razzo; **to give sb a rocket** (fig: fam) fare un cicchetto a qn ♦ VI (prices) salire alle stelle

rock·et² [ˈrɒkɪt] N 1 (Bot) ruchetta, rucola 2 (Culin) rucola

rocket launcher N lanciarazzi m inv

rock face N parete f di roccia

rock fall N caduta (di) massi

rock·ing chair [ˈrɒkɪŋtʃeəʳ] N sedia a dondolo

rock·ing horse [ˈrɒkɪŋhɔːs] N cavallo a dondolo

rocky¹ [ˈrɒkɪ] ADJ (comp -ier, superl -iest) (hill) roccioso(-a); (path) sassoso(-a)

rocky² [ˈrɒkɪ] ADJ (comp -ier, superl -iest) (shaky, unsteady) malfermo(-a), traballante; (fig: situation, marriage) instabile; **their relationship got off to a rocky start** la loro relazione ha avuto un inizio difficile

Rocky Mountains NPL: **the Rocky Mountains** le Montagne Rocciose

rod [rɒd] N (wooden, plastic) bacchetta; (metallic: Tech) asta, sbarra; (fishing rod) canna da pesca; (curtain rod) bastone m; **to rule with a rod of iron** comandare a bacchetta

rode [rəʊd] PT of ride

ro·dent [ˈrəʊdənt] N roditore m

ro·deo [ˈrəʊdɪəʊ] N rodeo

roe [rəʊ] N (of fish): **hard roe** uova fpl di pesce; **soft roe** latte m di pesce

roe deer [ˈrəʊˌdɪəʳ] N (species) capriolo; (female deer: pl inv) capriolo femmina

rogue [rəʊg] N mascalzone m; **rogues' gallery** foto fpl di pregiudicati ♦ ADJ (elephant) solitario(-a)

ro·guish [ˈrəʊgɪʃ] ADJ (look, smile) malizioso(-a); (child) birichino(-a)

role [rəʊl] N ruolo

role-model [ˈrəʊlmɒdl] N modello (di comportamento)

role play, role playing N il recitare un ruolo, role-playing *m inv*; **to do a role play** fare un gioco di ruolo

roll [rəʊl] N **1** (*of paper, wire*) rotolo; (*of hair*) chignon *m inv*; (*of banknotes*) mazzo; (*of film*) rullino; (*of cloth*) pezza, rotolo; (*of fat, flesh*) cuscinetto; **a roll of film** un rullino fotografico; **a toilet roll** un rotolo di carta igienica **2** (*also:* **bread roll**) panino; **cheese roll** panino al formaggio **3** (*list*) lista; **to have 500 pupils on the roll** avere 500 iscritti (alla scuola) **4** (*sound: of thunder*) rombo; (*of drums*) rullio, rullo **5** (*movement: of ship, plane*) rollio ♦ VT (*ball*) (far) rotolare; (*road, lawn, pitch*) cilindrare, rullare; (*cigarette*) rollare; (*also:* **roll out**: *pastry*) spianare, stendere; (*metal*) laminare; **roll the meatballs in breadcrumbs** passare le polpette nel pangrattato; **to roll one's eyes** roteare gli occhi; **to roll one's r's** arrotare la erre; **he can't roll his r's** ha la erre moscia ♦ VI **1** (*turn over*) rotolare; (*dog, horse*) rotolarsi; (*in pain*) contorcersi; **it rolled under the chair** è rotolato sotto la seggiola; **tears rolled down her cheeks** le lacrime le scendevano sulle guance; **the ball rolled into the net** la palla rotolò in rete; **they're rolling in money** *or* **they're rolling in it** (*fam*) sono ricchi sfondati **2** (*sound: thunder*) rombare; (: *drum*) rullare **3** (*ship*) rollare
  ▸ **roll about, roll around** VI + ADV (*ball, coin*) rotolare qua e là; (*person, dog*) rotolarsi; (*in pain*) contorcersi
  ▸ **roll away** VI + ADV (*ball*) rotolare (via); (*clouds, vehicle*) allontanarsi
  ▸ **roll back** VT + ADV arrotolare, togliere arrotolando
  ▸ **roll by** VI + ADV (*vehicle, years*) passare
  ▸ **roll in** VI + ADV (*money, letters*) continuare ad arrivare; (*fam: person*) arrivare
  ▸ **roll on** VI + ADV (*time*) passare; **roll on the holidays!** venite presto, vacanze!
  ▸ **roll out** VT + ADV (*pastry*) spianare; (*carpet, map*) srotolare, spiegare
  ▸ **roll over** VI + ADV (*object*) rotolare; (*person, animal*) (ri)girarsi, (ri)voltarsi
  ▸ **roll up** VI + ADV **1** (*animal*): **to roll up into a ball** appallottolarsi **2** (*arrive*) arrivare; **roll up!** venite, venite! ♦ VT + ADV (*rope, map, carpet*) arrotolare; (*sleeves*) rimboccare; **to roll o.s. up into a ball** raggomitolarsi

roll call N appello; **a roll call of** un elenco di
rolled gold [ˌrəʊld'gəʊld] N oro laminato ♦ ADJ laminato(-a) oro *inv*
roll·er [ˈrəʊləʳ] N **1** (*gen*) rullo, cilindro; (*in metallurgy*) laminatoio; (*roadroller*) rullo compressore; (*castor*) rotella; (*for hair*) bigodino **2** (*wave*) cavallone *m*
Roller·blades [ˈrəʊləˌbleɪdz] (*trademark*) pattini *mpl* in linea
roller blind N (*Brit*) avvolgibile *m*
roller coaster N montagne *fpl* russe
roller skates NPL pattini *mpl* a rotelle
roller skating N pattinaggio a rotelle
rol·lick·ing [ˈrɒlɪkɪŋ] ADJ (*person*) incredibilmente esuberante; (*party*) allegro(-a) e chiassoso(-a); **to have a rollicking time** divertirsi pazzamente
roll·ing [ˈrəʊlɪŋ] ADJ (*waves, sea*) ondeggiante; (*countryside*) ondulato(-a)
rolling mill N fabbrica di laminati
rolling pin N matterello
rolling stock N (*Rail*) materiale *m* rotabile
roll-on-roll-off [ˌrəʊlɒnrəʊl'ɒf] ADJ (*Brit: ferry*) roll-on roll-off *inv*
roly-poly [ˈrəʊlɪˈpəʊlɪ] N (*Brit: Culin*) rotolo di pasta con ripieno di marmellata
ROM [rɒm] N ABBR (*Comput: = read-only memory*) ROM *f inv*
Ro·man [ˈrəʊmən] ADJ romano(-a); **the Roman empire** l'impero romano ♦ N (*person*) Romano(-a); (*Typ*): **roman** (carattere *m*) romano; **the Romans** i romani
Roman Catholic ADJ, N cattolico(-a)
ro·mance [rəʊˈmæns] N **1** (*love affair*) storia d'amore; **a holiday romance** un amore estivo **2** (*romantic character*) fascino, romanticismo; **the romance of Paris** il fascino di Parigi **3** (*love story*) romanzo *m* rosa, *inv*; (*film*) film *m inv* d'amore; (*medieval*) romanzo (cavalleresco); (*Mus*) romanza; **she writes romances** scrive romanzi rosa
Ro·man·esque [ˌrəʊməˈnɛsk] ADJ (*Archit*) romanico(-a)

Ro·ma·nia, Ru·ma·nia [rəʊˈmeɪnɪə] N Romania
Ro·ma·nian, Ru·ma·nian [rəʊˈmeɪnɪən] ADJ romeno(-a)
  ♦ N (*person*) romeno(-a); (*language*) romeno
Roman numerals N numeri *mpl* romani
ro·man·tic [rəʊˈmæntɪk] ADJ, N romantico(-a)
ro·man·ti·cism [rəʊˈmæntɪsɪzəm] N (*Art*) romanticismo
Roma·ny [ˈrɒmənɪ] ADJ zingaresco(-a) ♦ N (*person*) zingaro(-a); (*language*) lingua degli zingari
Rome [rəʊm] N Roma *f*; **the Church of Rome** la Chiesa Romana; **when in Rome (do as the Romans do)** paese che vai usanze che trovi
romp [rɒmp] N gioco chiassoso ♦ VI (*also:* **romp about**: *children, puppies*) giocare chiassosamente; **they romped through the examination** (*fig*) ha passato l'esame a occhi chiusi; **to romp home** (*horse*) vincere senza difficoltà, stravincere
  ❑ **romp** is not translated by the Italian word
    rompere
romp·ers [ˈrɒmpəz] NPL tutina, pagliaccetto
ron·do [ˈrɒndəʊ] N (*Mus*) rondò *m inv*
roof [ruːf] N tetto; (*of tunnel, cave*) volta; **a sloping roof** un tetto spiovente; **roof of the mouth** palato; **to have a roof over one's head** avere un tetto sopra la testa; **we live under the same roof** viviamo sotto lo stesso tetto; **to go through the roof** (*fig: person*) andare su tutte le furie; (: *price*) salire alle stelle ♦ VT (*also:* **roof in, roof over**) mettere *or* fare il tetto a
roof garden N giardino pensile
roof·ing [ˈruːfɪŋ] N materiale *m* per copertura
roof rack N (*Aut*) portapacchi *m inv*, portabagagli *m inv*
rook[1] [rʊk] N (*bird*) corvo ♦ VT (*fam: swindle*) imbrogliare, truffare
rook[2] [rʊk] N (*Chess*) torre *f*
rookie [ˈrʊkɪ] N (*Mil: fam*) burba
room [rʊm] N **1** (*in house*) stanza, camera; (*in property adverts*) locale *m*, vano; (*bedroom, in hotel*) camera; (*large, public, in school*) sala; **rooms** NPL (*lodging*) alloggio *msg*; **"rooms to let"**, (*USA*) **"rooms for rent"** "si affittano camere"; **a 5-roomed house** una casa di 5 locali; **the biggest room in the house** la stanza più grande della casa; **she's in her room** è in camera sua; **a single room** una camera singola; **a double room** una camera doppia; **the music room** la sala musica; **they've always lived in rooms** hanno sempre abitato in camere ammobiliate **2** (*space*) spazio, posto; **is there room for this?** c'è spazio per questo?, ci sta anche questo?; **is there room for me?** c'è posto per me?, ci sto anch'io?; **there's no room for that box** non c'è posto per quella scatola; **to make room for sb** far posto a qn; **standing room only** solo posti in piedi; **there is no room for doubt** non c'è nessuna possibilità di dubbio; **there is room for improvement** si potrebbe migliorare
room·ing house [ˈrʊmɪŋˌhaʊs] N (*USA*) casa con camere ammobiliate
room·mate [ˈrʊmˌmeɪt] N compagno(-a) di stanza
room service N servizio in camera
room temperature N temperatura ambiente
roomy [ˈrʊmɪ] ADJ (*comp* **-ier**, *superl* **-iest**) (*apartment, cupboard etc*) spazioso(-a); (*garment*) ampio(-a)
roost [ruːst] N posatoio; **to rule the roost** dettar legge ♦ VI appollaiarsi; **now the chickens are coming home to roost!** (*fig*) ora arriva il momento della resa dei conti!
roost·er [ˈruːstəʳ] N gallo
root [ruːt] N (*gen, also Math*) radice *f*; **repeated root** (*Math*) radice *f* multipla; **to pull up by the roots** sradicare; **to take root** (*plant*) attecchire, prendere; (*idea*) far presa; **the root of the problem is that ...** il problema deriva dal fatto che...; **to put down roots in a country** mettere radici in un paese ♦ VT (*plant*) far fare le radici a, far radicare; **to be rooted to the spot** (*fig*) rimanere inchiodato(-a) sul posto ♦ VI (*Bot*) attecchire, mettere radici
  ▸ **root about, root around** VI + ADV (*fig*) frugare, rovistare
  ▸ **root for** VI + PREP (*USA fam*) fare il tifo per
  ▸ **root out** VT + ADV (*find*) scovare, pescare; (*remove*) eradicare, estirpare; **they are determined to root out corruption** sono decisi a eliminare la corruzione
  ▸ **root up** VT + ADV sradicare

root beer N (*USA*) bibita dolce a base di estratti di erbe e radici

rope [rəʊp] N fune *f*, corda; (*Naut*) cima, cavo; **to give sb more rope** (*fig*) allentare le redini a qn; **to know/learn the ropes** (*fig*) conoscere/imparare i segreti *or* i trucchi del mestiere; **a rope of pearls** una lunga collana di perle; **a rope of climbers** una cordata di alpinisti ♦ VT legare (con una fune *or* una corda); **the climbers were roped together** i rocciatori erano legati assieme

▸ **rope in** VT + ADV (*fam: fig*): **to rope sb in to help** tirar dentro qn per aiutare; **I was roped in to help with the refreshments** mi hanno tirato dentro a dare una mano con i rinfreschi

▸ **rope off** VT + ADV isolare con dei cordoni

▸ **rope up** VI + ADV (*Mountaineering*) legarsi in cordata

rope ladder N scala di corda

ropy, ropey ['rəʊpɪ] ADJ (*comp* -ier, *superl* -iest) (*fam*) scadente; **to feel rop(e)y** (*ill*) sentirsi male

ro·sary ['rəʊzərɪ] N 1 (*Rel*) rosario; **to say** *or* **recite the rosary** dire *or* recitare il rosario 2 (*rose garden*) roseto

rose[1] [rəʊz] N 1 (*flower, colour*) rosa; (*also: rose bush*) rosaio; **my life isn't all roses** (*fam*) la mia vita non è tutta rose e fiori 2 (*on shower, watering can*) bulbo (forato); (*on ceiling*) rosone *m* ♦ ADJ (*rose-coloured*) rosa *inv*

rose[2] [rəʊz] PT of **rise**

rosé ['rəʊzeɪ] N, ADJ rosé *m inv*

rose·bed ['rəʊz,bed] N rosaio, roseto

rose·bud ['rəʊz,bʌd] N bocciolo di rosa

rose·mary ['rəʊzmərɪ] N rosmarino

ro·sette [rəʊ'zet] N (*emblem, as prize*) coccarda; (*Archit*) rosone *m*

ros·ter ['rɒstə*] N = **rota**

ros·trum ['rɒstrəm] N podio, tribuna

rosy ['rəʊzɪ] ADJ (*comp* -ier, *superl* -iest) roseo(-a); **to paint a rosy picture of sth** (*fig*) dipingere qc a tinte rosa

rot [rɒt] N (*decay*) putrefazione *f*, marciume *m*; (*fam: nonsense*) fesserie *fpl*, stupidaggini *fpl*; **the rot has set in** (*fig*) le cose hanno cominciato a guastarsi; **to stop the rot** (*Brit fig*) salvare la situazione; **dry/wet rot** *funghi parassiti del legno* ♦ VT far marcire; **sugar rots your teeth** lo zucchero caria i denti ♦ VI: **to rot (away)** marcire, imputridire; **the wood had rotted** il legno era marcito

rota ['rəʊtə] N tabella dei turni; **on a rota basis** a turno; **we worked out a rota** abbiamo elaborato una tabella di turni

ro·ta·ry ['rəʊtərɪ] ADJ (*movement*) rotatorio(-a); (*blades*) rotante

ro·tate [rəʊ'teɪt] VT (*revolve*) far girare; (*change round: crops, staff*) avvicendare, fare la rotazione di; **rotate your hips** fai ruotare i fianchi; **to rotate crops** fare la rotazione delle colture ♦ VI (*wheel, Earth*) ruotare, girare; (*staff etc*) alternarsi, avvicendarsi; **the Earth rotates round the Sun** la terra ruota intorno al sole; **the presidency rotates** vi è un avvicendamento della presidenza

ro·tat·ing [rəʊ'teɪtɪŋ] ADJ (*revolving*) rotante

ro·ta·tion [rəʊ'teɪʃən] N rotazione *f*; **in rotation** a turno, in rotazione; **rotation of crops** rotazione *f* delle colture

rote [rəʊt] N: **to learn sth by rote** imparare qc a memoria; **rote learning** l'imparare *m* a memoria

ro·tor ['rəʊtə*] N rotore *m*

rot·ten ['rɒtn] ADJ 1 (*fruit, eggs*) marcio(-a); (*meat*) andato(-a) a male; (*tooth*) cariato(-a); (*wood*) marcio(-a), marcito(-a); (*fig: morally*) corrotto(-a); **rotten to the core** completamente marcio(-a) 2 (*fam: bad*) schifoso(-a), brutto(-a); (*action*) vigliacco(-a); **rotten weather** tempo da cani; **what rotten luck!** che scalogna!; **what a rotten thing to do!** che vigliaccata!, che carognata!; **I feel rotten** (*ill*) mi sento da cani; (*mean*) mi sento un verme
❏ **rotten** is not translated by the Italian word *rotto*

rot·ting ['rɒtɪŋ] ADJ in putrefazione

ro·tund [rəʊ'tʌnd] ADJ (*frm: person*) pingue; (: *object*) arrotondato(-a)

rou·ble, (USA) ru·ble ['ruːbl] N rublo

rouge [ruːʒ] N belletto

rough [rʌf] ADJ (*comp* -er, *superl* -est) 1 (*uneven: ground, road, path, edge*) accidentato(-a); (*not smooth: skin, cloth, surface,*

hands) ruvido(-a); **my hands are rough** ho le mani ruvide 2 (*voice*) rauco(-a); (*taste, wine*) aspro(-a); (*coarse, unrefined: person, manners, life*) rozzo(-a); (*harsh: person, game*) violento(-a); (*neighbourhood*) poco raccomandabile, malfamato(-a); (*sea crossing, weather*) brutto(-a); **rugby's a rough sport** il rugby è uno sport violento; **the sea is rough today** c'è mare grosso oggi, il mare è mosso oggi; **I don't want any rough stuff!** (*fam*) niente risse!; **it's a rough area** è una zona poco raccomandabile; **a rough customer** (*fam*) un duro; **to have a rough time (of it)** passare un periodaccio; **to give sb a rough time (of it)** rendere la vita dura a qn; **it's rough on him** che sfortuna per lui; **to feel rough** (*Brit fam*) sentirsi male 3 (*calculation, figures*) approssimativo(-a), approssimato(-a); (*plan*) sommario(-a); **rough work, rough draft, rough copy** brutta copia; **rough sketch** schizzo; **rough estimate** approssimazione *f*; **at a rough guess** *or* **estimate** ad occhio e croce; **I've got a rough idea** ne ho un'idea approssimativa; **he's a rough diamond** sotto quei modi un po' grezzi si nasconde un cuore d'oro ♦ ADV: **to play rough** (*Sport*) giocare pesante; (*children*) fare dei giochi violenti; **to sleep rough** (*Brit*) dormire all'addiaccio, dormire per strada; **a lot of people sleep rough in London** a Londra tanta gente dorme per strada; **to live rough** vivere per strada ♦ N 1 (*fam: person*) duro 2 **to take the rough with the smooth** prendere le cose come vengono 3 (*Golf*) erba alta, macchia ♦ VT: **to rough it** (*fam*) far vita dura

▸ **rough out** VT + ADV (*draft, plan*) fare un abbozzo di, abbozzare

▸ **rough up** VT + ADV (*fam*): **to rough sb up** malmenare qn

rough·age ['rʌfɪdʒ] N fibre *fpl*

rough-and-ready [,rʌfənd'redɪ] ADJ rudimentale

rough-and-tumble [,rʌfən'tʌmbl] N zuffa

rough·cast ['rʌf,kɑːst] N intonaco grezzo

rough·en ['rʌfn] VT (*a surface*) rendere ruvido(-a), irruvidire

rough justice N giustizia sommaria

rough·ly ['rʌflɪ] ADV 1 (*not gently: push, handle*) brutalmente; (: *speak, order*) bruscamente; **to treat sb/sth roughly** maltrattare qn/qc 2 (*not finely: make, sew*) grossolanamente; **to chop roughly** tagliare a pezzi grossi; **roughly chop the tomatoes and peppers** tagliare i pomodori e i peperoni a pezzi grossi; **to sketch sth roughly** fare uno schizzo di qc 3 (*approximately*) grosso modo, approssimativamente, pressappoco; **roughly speaking** grosso modo, ad occhio e croce; **there were roughly 50 people** c'erano pressappoco 50 persone; **it weighs roughly twenty kilos** pesa pressappoco venti chili

rough·ness ['rʌfnɪs] N (*of hands, surface*) ruvidità, ruvidezza; (*of person: abruptness*) modi *mpl* bruschi; (: *harshness*) durezza, brutalità; (*of sea*) violenza; (*of road*) cattive condizioni *fpl*; (*of terrain*) asprezza

rough·shod ['rʌf,ʃɒd] ADV: **to ride roughshod over** (*person*) mettere sotto i piedi; (*objection*) non badare minimamente a

rou·lette [ruː'let] N roulette *f inv*

round [raʊnd] ADJ rotondo(-a); (*arms, body*) grassoccio(-a); (*cheeks*) paffuto(-a); **to have round shoulders** avere le spalle tonde; **a round table** un tavolo rotondo; (*fig*) un'associazione; **a round number** una cifra tonda; **in round figures** in cifra tonda; **a round dozen** una dozzina completa ♦ ADV: **all round, right round** tutt'intorno, tutt'in giro; **there were vineyards all round** c'erano vigne tutt'intorno; **the wheels go round** le ruote girano; **all year round** (durante) tutto l'anno; **round here** da queste parti; **is there a pharmacy round here?** c'è una farmacia da queste parti?; **to ask sb round** invitare qn (a casa propria); **to go round to sb's house** andare a casa di qn; **we were round at my sister's** eravamo da mia sorella; **I'll be round at 6 o'clock** ci sarò alle 6; **to take the long way round** fare il giro più lungo ♦ PREP intorno a, attorno a; **round the table** intorno alla tavola; **we were sitting round the table** eravamo seduti intorno alla tavola; **all round the house** (*inside*) dappertutto in casa; (*outside*) tutt'intorno alla casa; **round about** circa; **it costs round about a hundred pounds** costa circa cento sterline; **round about eight o'clock** verso le otto; **she arrived round (about)** noon è arrivata verso mezzogiorno; **it's just round the corner** (*also fig*) è dietro l'angolo; **to look round a house/a town** visitare una casa/una città; **to have**

a look round dare un'occhiata in giro; **I've been round all the shops** ho fatto il giro di tutti i negozi; **to go round a museum** visitare un museo; **round the clock** ininterrottamente, 24 ore su 24; **wrap a blanket round him** avvolgilo in una coperta ♦ N **1** (*circle*) cerchio, tondo; (*Brit: slice: of bread, meat*) fetta; **a few rounds of cucumber** alcune fettine di cetriolo; **a round (of sandwiches)** due tramezzini **2** **the daily round** (*fig*) la routine quotidiana **3** (*of watchman, postman, milkman*) giro; **I've got a paper round** consegno i giornali a domicilio; **the doctor's on his rounds** il dottore sta facendo il suo giro di visite; **to go the rounds** (*illness*) diffondersi; (*story*) passare di bocca in bocca, circolare **4** (*Boxing*) round *m inv*; (*Golf*) partita; (*Showjumping*) percorso; (*in tournament, competition*) incontro; **he was knocked out in the tenth round** è andato al tappeto al decimo round; **a round of golf** una partita di golf; **another round of talks** un altro giro di consultazioni; **in the first round of the elections** nella prima tornata elettorale; **to buy a round of drinks** offrire un giro di bevute); **I think it's my round** tocca a me offrire da bere; **a round of ammunition** un colpo; **a round of applause** un applauso ♦ VT **1** (*make round: lips*) arrotondare; (: *edges*) smussare **2** (*go round: corner*) girare, voltare; (: *bend*) superare; (*Naut*) doppiare

▸ **round off** VT + ADV (*speech, series, meal, evening*) finire in bellezza; **they rounded off the meal with liqueurs** hanno terminato il pranzo con dei liquori

▸ **round on** VI + PREP (*attacker, critic*) aggredire verbalmente

▸ **round up** VT + ADV **1** (*cattle*) radunare; (*friends etc*) riunire; (*criminals*) fare una retata di **2** (*figures*) arrotondare

round·about [ˈraʊndəˌbaʊt] ADJ (*route, means*) indiretto(-a); **I heard the news in a roundabout way** ho saputo la notizia per vie traverse; **to refer in a roundabout way to sth** accennare indirettamente a qc ♦ N (*Brit: at fair*) giostra; (: *Aut*) rotatoria

round·ed [ˈraʊndɪd] ADJ (*shape*) arrotondato(-a); (*fig: sentence*) forbito(-a); (*style*) armonioso(-a)

round·ers [ˈraʊndəz] NPL (*Brit: game*) gioco simile al baseball

round·ly [ˈraʊndlɪ] ADV (*say, tell*) chiaro e tondo; (*condemn*) senza mezzi termini; **I cursed him roundly** gliene ho dette di tutti i colori

round robin N petizione *f*

round-shouldered [ˌraʊndˈʃəʊldəd] ADJ con le spalle curve

round trip N (viaggio di) andata e ritorno

round·up [ˈraʊndˌʌp] N (*of cattle, people*) raduno; (*of suspects*) retata; **a roundup of the latest news** un sommario *or* riepilogo delle ultime notizie

rouse [raʊz] VT (*person: from sleep*) svegliare; (: *from apathy*) scuotere; (*interest, suspicion, admiration*) suscitare, destare; **they roused me at six** mi hanno svegliato alle sei; **to rouse sb to action** spronare qn ad agire; **to rouse sb to fury** far infuriare qn; **to rouse o.s. from** scuotersi di dosso; **I couldn't rouse myself from my apathy** non riuscivo a scuotermi di dosso l'apatia

rous·ing [ˈraʊzɪŋ] ADJ (*cheer*) entusiasmante; (*welcome, applause*) entusiastico(-a); (*speech, song*) trascinante

rout [raʊt] N (*defeat*) disfatta, rotta ♦ VT mettere in rotta, sbaragliare

▸ **rout out** VT + ADV (*find*) scovare; (*force out*) (far) sloggiare

route [ruːt] N (*gen*) itinerario; **shipping/air routes** rotte *fpl* marittime/aeree; **bus route** percorso dell'autobus; **we're on the main bus route** abitiamo vicino alla linea dell'autobus; **the best route to London** la strada migliore per andare a Londra; **en route** per strada; **en route from ...to** viaggiando da... a; **en route for** in viaggio verso; **"all routes"** (*Aut*) "tutte le direzioni"

route map N (*Brit: for journey*) cartina di itinerario; (*for trains*) pianta di collegamenti

rou·tine [ruːˈtiːn] N (*normal procedure*) ordinaria amministrazione *f*; (*study routine, work routine*) ritmo di lavoro; (*Theatre*) numero; (*Comput*) sottoprogramma *m*; **daily routine** routine *f*; **tran tran** *m*; **my daily routine** il tran tran quotidiano ♦ ADJ (*duties, work*) abituale; (*inspection, medical examination*) periodico(-a); (*questions*) di prammatica; **a routine check** un controllo di routine; **the meeting was just routine** si è trattato di un incontro di normale amministrazione; **routine procedure** prassi *f*

rov·ing [ˈraʊvɪŋ] ADJ (*person*) vagabondo(-a); (*life*) itinerante; **to have a roving commission** avere piena libertà d'azione *or* di manovra

roving reporter N reporter *m inv* volante

row¹ [rəʊ] N (*line*) fila; (*of plants*) fila, filare *m*; (*Knitting*) ferro; (*Math*) riga; **a row of houses** una fila di case; **in a row** in fila; **in the front row** in prima fila; **for five days in a row** per cinque giorni di fila

row² [rəʊ] VT (*boat*) remare; **to row sb across a river** trasportare qn dall'altra parte di un fiume su una barca a remi ♦ VI remare; (*Sport*) vogare; **to go rowing** andare a fare una remata

row·boat [ˈrəʊˌbəʊt] N (*USA*) = **rowing boat**

row·di·ness [ˈraʊdɪnɪs] N baccano; (*fighting*) zuffa

row·dy [ˈraʊdɪ] ADJ (*comp* **-ier**, *superl* **-iest**) (*noisy*) chiassoso(-a); (*rough*) turbolento(-a) ♦ N teppista *m/f*

row·dy·ism [ˈraʊdɪɪzəm] N teppismo

row·ing [ˈrəʊɪŋ] N remare *m*; (*Sport*) canottaggio; **I like rowing** mi piace il canottaggio

rowing boat N (*Brit*) barca a remi

row·lock [ˈrɒlək] N scalmo

roy·al [ˈrɔɪəl] ADJ reale; **the royal household** la famiglia reale e il seguito; **the royal we** il pluralis maiestatis; **they gave us a royal welcome** ci hanno fatto un'accoglienza principesca ♦ N **the Royals** (*fam*) i reali, la famiglia reale

Royal Academy N (*Brit*) Accademia Reale d'Arte britannica

Royal Air Force N (*Brit*) aeronautica militare britannica

royal blue ADJ azzurro reale *inv*

roy·al·ist [ˈrɔɪəlɪst] N realista *m/f*

Royal Navy N (*Brit*) marina militare britannica

roy·al·ty [ˈrɔɪəltɪ] N **1** (*people*) reali *mpl*; **royalty and government leaders from all over the world** rappresentanti delle monarchie e dei governi di tutto il mondo **2** (*payment: also:* **royalties**) diritti *mpl* d'autore; (*from oil well, to inventor*) royalty *f inv*; **the royalties on a book** i diritti d'autore su un libro

RP [ˌɑːˈpiː] N ABBR (*Brit: = received pronunciation*) pronuncia standard

RSI [ˌɑːresˈaɪ] N ABBR (*Med: = repetitive strain injury*) lesione *f* da sforzo ripetuto

RSVP [ˌɑːresviːˈpiː] ABBR (*= répondez s'il vous plaît*) RSVP

Rt Hon. ABBR (*Brit: = Right Honourable*) ≈ On. (*= Onorevole*)

rub [rʌb] N (*with cloth*) fregata, strofinata; (*on person*) frizione *f*, massaggio; **to give sth a rub** (*furniture, mark*) strofinare qc; (*sore place*) massaggiare qc; **there's the rub!** (*liter*) qui sta il problema! ♦ VT sfregare, fregare, strofinare; **to rub one's hands together/one's nose** sfregarsi le mani/il naso; **she rubbed her eyes** si sfregò gli occhi; **to rub lotion into one's skin** frizionare sulla pelle con una lozione; **to rub sth dry** asciugare qc strofinando; **to rub a hole in sth** fare un buco in qc strofinando; **she gently rubbed the stain** ha sfregato leggermente la macchia; **there is no need to rub my nose in it!** (*fig*) non c'è bisogno che continui a ricordarmelo!; **to rub shoulders with sb** (*fig*) venire a contatto con qn ♦ VI: **to rub against sth, rub on sth** strofinarsi contro *or* su qc

▸ **rub along** VI + ADV (*fam: two people*) andare d'accordo nonostante le difficoltà

▸ **rub away** VI + ADV togliere (sfregando)

▸ **rub down** VT + ADV **1** (*body*) strofinare, frizionare; (*horse*) strigliare **2** (*door, wall*) levigare

▸ **rub in** VT + ADV (*ointment*) far penetrare (massaggiando *or* frizionando); (*cream, polish: into leather etc*) far penetrare (strofinando); **don't rub it in!** (*fam*) non rivoltare il coltello nella piaga!

▸ **rub off** VI + ADV venire (*or* andare) via; **to rub off onto sth** restare attaccato(-a) a qc; **his opinions have rubbed off on me** ho finito col pensarla come lui ♦ VT + PREP (*writing*) cancellare; (*dirt*) togliere *or* levare (strofinando)

▸ **rub out** VT + ADV cancellare

▸ **rub up** VT + ADV (*silver, vase*) lucidare; **to rub sb up the wrong way**, (*USA*) **rub sb the wrong way** (*fig*) prendere qn per il verso sbagliato, lisciare qn contropelo

rub·ber [ˈrʌbə] N (*material*) gomma, caucciù *m*; (*eraser*) gomma (da cancellare); (*fam, USA*) preservativo ♦ ADJ (*ball, dinghy, gloves*) di gomma; **rubber soles** suole *fpl* di gomma

rubber band N elastico
rubber bullet N pallottola di gomma
rubber plant N ficus *m inv*
rubber ring N (*for swimming*) ciambella
rubber stamp N timbro di gomma
rubber-stamp [ˌrʌbəˈstæmp] VT (*fig*) approvare senza discussione
rub·bery [ˈrʌbərɪ] ADJ gommoso(-a)
rub·bish [ˈrʌbɪʃ] N (*waste material*) rifiuti *mpl*; (*household rubbish*) spazzatura, immondizia; (*nonsense*) sciocchezze *fpl*, fesserie *fpl*; (*worthless stuff*) cose *fpl* senza valore, robaccia; **the rubbish is collected on Mondays** la raccolta dei rifiuti è di lunedì; **he threw the bottle in the rubbish** ha buttato la bottiglia nelle immondizie; **the film was rubbish** il film non valeva niente; **rubbish!** (*fam*) sciocchezze!, fesserie!; **don't talk rubbish!** non dire sciocchezze!; **that's a load of rubbish!** tutte sciocchezze!
rubbish bin N (*Brit*) pattumiera; (*outside house*) bidone *m* (per la spazzatura)
rubbish dump N discarica (delle immondizie)
rub·bishy [ˈrʌbɪʃɪ] ADJ (*Brit fam*) scadente, che non vale niente
rub·ble [ˈrʌbl] N detriti *mpl*; (*smaller*) pietrisco; (*of building*) macerie *fpl*; **the building was reduced to a heap of rubble** l'edificio era ridotto a un cumulo di macerie
ru·ble [ˈruːbl] N (*USA*) = **rouble**
ruby [ˈruːbɪ] N rubino ♦ ADJ (*colour*) (color) rubino *inv*; (*lips*) rosso(-a); (*made of rubies: necklace, ring*) di rubini
ruck·sack [ˈrʌkˌsæk] N zaino
ruc·tions [ˈrʌkʃənz] NPL (*fam*) putiferio *msg*, finimondo *msg*; **there will be ructions if** succederà il finimondo se
rud·der [ˈrʌdə'] N (*Naut*) timone *m*; (*Aer*) timone di direzione
rud·dy¹ [ˈrʌdɪ] ADJ (*comp* -ier, *superl* -iest) (*complexion*) rubicondo(-a); (*sky*) rossastro(-a)
rud·dy² [ˈrʌdɪ] ADJ (*comp* -ier, *superl* -iest) (*Brit fam*) dannato(-a)
rude [ruːd] ADJ (*comp* -r, *superl* -st) **1** (*impolite*) villano(-a), maleducato(-a); (*indecent*) indecente, volgare; **to be rude to sb** essere maleducato con qn; **he was very rude to me** è stato molto maleducato nei miei confronti; **it's rude to interrupt** è maleducato interrompere; **it's rude to talk with your mouth full** è cattiva educazione parlare con la bocca piena; **a rude word** una parolaccia; **a rude joke** una barzelletta sporca **2 a rude awakening** (*fig*) una doccia fredda; **to be in rude health** essere in ottima salute **3** (*liter: primitive*) rudimentale
rude·ly [ˈruːdlɪ] ADV **1** (*impolitely*) villanamente, maleducatamente; (*indecently*) indecentemente, volgarmente **2 to be rudely awoken** (*fig*) tornare bruscamente alla realtà
rude·ness [ˈruːdnɪs] N (*impoliteness*) villania, maleducazione *f*; (*indecency*) indecenza, volgarità
ru·di·men·ta·ry [ˌruːdɪˈmentərɪ] ADJ rudimentale
ru·di·ments [ˈruːdɪmənts] NPL: **the rudiments** i (primi) rudimenti *mpl*
rue [ruː] VT (*liter*) pentirsi amaramente di; **I rue the day that ...** maledico il giorno in cui...
rue·ful [ˈruːfʊl] ADJ (*liter*) mesto(-a)
ruff [rʌf] N (*Dressmaking*) gorgiera; (*Zool*) collare *m*
ruf·fian [ˈrʌfɪən] N (*old*) manigoldo
□ **ruffian** is not translated by the Italian word *ruffiano*
ruf·fle [ˈrʌfl] VT (*surface*) (far) increspare; (*hair, feathers*) arruffare, scompigliare; (*fig: person*) (far) agitare, turbare, (far) innervosire; **nothing ruffles him** non si scompone mai
rug [rʌɡ] N (*floor mat*) tappeto; (*bedside rug*) scendiletto; (*travelling rug*) coperta (da viaggio); (*in tartan*) plaid *m inv*
rug·by [ˈrʌɡbɪ] N rugby *m* ♦ ADJ (*team, player*) di rugby
rug·ged [ˈrʌɡɪd] ADJ (*terrain*) accidentato(-a); (*coastline, mountains*) frastagliato(-a); (*character*) rude; (*features*) marcato(-a), duro(-a); (*landscape*) aspro(-a); **rugged terrain** un terreno aspro; **rugged features** lineamenti *mpl* marcati
rug·ger [ˈrʌɡə'] N (*Brit fam*) = **rugby**
ruin [ruːɪn] N **1** rudere *m*; **ruins** NPL (*architectural remains*) rovine *fpl*; **the ruins of the castle** le rovine del castello; **in ruins** in rovina; **to fall into ruin** cadere in rovina **2** (*fig*) rovina ♦ VT rovinare
ru·ina·tion [ˌruːɪˈneɪʃən] N rovina
ru·in·ous [ˈruːɪnəs] ADJ (*expensive*) costoso(-a)
rule [ruːl] N **1** (*gen*) regola; (*regulation*) regola, regolamento; **the rules of the road** le norme della circolazione stradale; **rules and regulations** norme e regolamenti; **it's against the rules** è contro le regole *or* il regolamento; **as a rule** normalmente, di regola; **to make it a rule to do sth** essersi imposto(-a) la regola di fare qc; **by rule of thumb** a lume di naso **2** (*dominion*): **under British rule** sotto il dominio britannico; **majority rule** (*Pol*) governo di maggioranza **3** (*for measuring*) riga; **slide rule** regolo (calcolatore) ♦ VT **1** (*govern: also: rule over: country*) governare; **he has ruled the country since 1996** governa il paese dal 1996; **he's ruled by his wife** è sua moglie che comanda **2** (*subj: umpire, judge*): **to rule (that)** decretare (che), decidere (che) **3** (*paper, page*) rigare ♦ VI **1** (*monarch*) regnare **2** (*Law*): **to rule against/in favour of/on** pronunciarsi a sfavore di/in favore di/su
▸ **rule out** VT + ADV escludere; **murder cannot be ruled out** non si esclude che si tratti di omicidio
ruled [ruːld] ADJ (*paper*) vergato(-a), a righe
rul·er [ˈruːlə'] N **1** (*sovereign*) sovrano(-a); (*in a republic*) capo **2** (*for measuring*) righello, riga
rul·ing [ˈruːlɪŋ] ADJ (*passion, idea*) grande, dominante; (*party*) al potere; **the ruling classes** la classe dirigente ♦ N (*Law*) decisione *f*
rum¹ [rʌm] N (*drink*) rum *m inv*
rum² [rʌm] ADJ (*comp* -mer, *superl* -mest) (*Brit fam*) strambo(-a)
Ru·ma·nia [ruːˈmeɪnɪə] N = **Romania**
rum·ble [ˈrʌmbl] N (*of traffic etc*) rombo; (*thunder*) brontolio; **a rumble of thunder** il rimbombo di un tuono ♦ VI (*thunder, cannon etc*) rimbombare; (*stomach*) brontolare; (*pipe*) gorgogliare; **the train rumbled past** il treno passò sferragliando; **voices rumbled in the next room** nella stanza accanto rimbombavano delle voci; **my stomach is rumbling** il mio stomaco brontola
rum·ble [ˈrʌmbl] VT (*Brit fam*) scoprire
rum·bus·tious [rʌmˈbʌstʃəs] ADJ (*person*): **to be rumbustious** essere un terremoto
rum·mage [ˈrʌmɪdʒ] VI: **to rummage (about *or* around)** rovistare, frugare; **to rummage about in sth/for sth** rovistare *or* frugare in qc/per trovare qc
ru·mour, ru·mor (*USA*) [ˈruːmə'] N voce *f*; **rumour has it that ...** *or* **there's a rumour that ...** corre voce che... + *sub* ♦ VT: **it is rumoured that ...** si dice in giro che... + *sub*
□ **rumour** is not translated by the Italian word *rumore*
rump [rʌmp] N (*of horse*) groppa (posteriore), culatta; (*Culin*) scamone *m*
rum·ple [ˈrʌmpl] VT (*clothes*) spiegazzare, sgualcire; (*hair*) arruffare, scompigliare
rump steak N bistecca di girello
rum·pus [ˈrʌmpəs] N (*fam*) putiferio, casino; **to kick up a rumpus** scatenare un putiferio
run [rʌn] (*pt* ran, *pp* run) VI **1** correre; (*flee*) scappare; **run and see** corri a vedere; **to run in/out** *etc* entrare/uscire *etc* di corsa; **to run for the bus** fare una corsa per prendere l'autobus; **to run to help sb** accorrere in aiuto di qn, correre ad aiutare qn; **don't come running to me when you've got problems** non correre da me quando avrai dei problemi; **we shall have to run for it** ci toccherà tagliare la corda; **to run for President** candidarsi per la Presidenza; **he's running for the Presidency** si è presentato come candidato per la presidenza; **a rumour ran through the town that ...** si è sparsa la voce in città che...; **that tune keeps running through my head** continua a venirmi in mente quel motivetto; **it runs in the family** è una cosa di famiglia **2** (*bus, train*) funzionare, andare; (*travel*) fare servizio; **the train runs between Gatwick and Victoria** il treno fa servizio tra Gatwick e la stazione Victoria; **the bus runs every 20 minutes** c'è un autobus ogni 20 minuti; **to be running late** essere in ritardo **3** (*function*) funzionare, andare; **to run the engine** tenere acceso il motore; **leave the engine running** lascia

il motore acceso; **to run on petrol/on diesel/off batteries** andare a benzina/a diesel/a batterie; **things did not run smoothly for him** (*fig*) le cose non gli sono andate molto bene **4** (*extend: contract*) essere valido(-a); **it has another 5 years to run** vale per altri 5 anni; **the play ran for 2 years** lo spettacolo ha tenuto cartellone per 2 anni; **the cost ran to hundreds of pounds** alla fine la spesa è stata di centinaia di sterline; **their losses run into millions** hanno avuto una perdita di milioni **5** (*river, tears, curtains, drawer*) scorrere; (*nose*) colare; (*eyes*) lacrimare; (*tap*) perdere; (*sore, abscess*) spurgare; (*melt: butter, icing*) fondere; (*colour, ink*) sbavare; (*colour: in washing*) stingere; **the tears ran down her cheeks** le lacrime le scorrevano sulle guance; **you left the tap running** hai lasciato il rubinetto aperto; **the river runs into the sea** il fiume sfocia nel mare; **the road runs into the square** la strada sbocca nella piazza; **the milk ran all over the floor** il latte si è sparso sul pavimento; **to run high** (*river, sea*) ingrossarsi; (*feelings*) inasprirsi; **my nose is running** mi cola il naso; **his face was running with sweat** il sudore gli colava sul viso; **his blood ran cold** gli si è gelato il sangue **6** (*with adv or prep*): **to run across the road** attraversare di corsa la strada; **the road runs along the river** la strada corre lungo il fiume; **the road runs by our house** la strada passa davanti a casa nostra; **the path runs from our house to the station** il sentiero va da casa nostra fino alla stazione; **the car ran into the lamppost** la macchina è andata a sbattere contro il lampione; **he was running towards her** correva verso di lei; **he ran up to me** mi corse incontro; **she ran up the stairs** salì su per le scale di corsa ♦ *VT* **1** correre; (*race*) partecipare a; **I ran five kilometres** ho corso cinque chilometri; **to run a marathon** partecipare ad una maratona; **she ran a good race** ha fatto una buona gara; **the race is run over 4 km** la gara si svolge su un percorso di 4 km; **to let things run their course** lasciare che le cose seguano il loro corso; **to run a horse** far correre un cavallo **2** (*move*): **to run sb into town** accompagnare *or* portare qn in città; **I'll run you to the station** ti porto io alla stazione; **to run the car into a lamppost** andare a sbattere con la macchina contro un lampione; **to run errands** andare a fare commissioni **3** (*organize, manage: business, hotel*) dirigere, gestire; (*: country*) governare; (*: campaign*) organizzare; **he runs a large company** dirige una grossa società; **are they running any trains today?** ci sono treni oggi?; **they ran an extra train** hanno messo un treno straordinario; **she runs everything** è lei che manda avanti tutto; **I want to run my own life** voglio essere io a gestire la mia vita **4** (*operate: machine*) usare; **to run a program** (*Comput*) eseguire un programma; **it's a very cheap car to run** è una macchina economica **5 to be run off one's feet** doversi fare in quattro; **to run it close** *or* **fine** ridursi all'ultimo momento; **to run a (high) temperature** avere la febbre (alta); **to run a risk** correre un rischio **6** (*with adv or prep*): **to run one's eye over a letter** dare una scorsa a una lettera; **to run a fence round a field** costruire un recinto intorno a un campo; **to run a pipe through a wall** far passare un tubo attraverso un muro; **to run one's fingers through sb's hair** passare le dita fra i capelli di qn; **he ran his fingers through her hair** le passò le dita tra i capelli; **to run a comb through one's hair** darsi una pettinata; **to run water into the bath** far correre l'acqua nella vasca; **to run a bath for sb** preparare un bagno a qn ♦ *N* **1** (*act of running*) corsa; **to go for a run** andare a correre; **I go for a run every morning** vado a correre ogni mattina; **at a run** di corsa; **to break into a run** mettersi a correre; **he's on the run from the police** è ricercato dalla polizia; **a prisoner on the run** un evaso; **the criminals are still on the run** i criminali sono ancora latitanti; **to keep the enemy on the run** premere il nemico in fuga; **we've got them on the run now** adesso sono ridotti allo sbando; **he's on the run from his creditors** cerca di sfuggire ai creditori; **to make a run for it** scappare, tagliare la corda; **to give sb a run for his money** non darla vinta a qn prima del tempo; **she's had a good run** (*on death, retirement*) ha avuto il suo; **to have the run of sb's house** utilizzare la casa altrui come casa propria **2** (*outing*) giro; **to go for a run in the car** fare un giro in macchina **3** (*Rail*) percorso, tragitto; **it's a 10-minute bus run** è un tragitto di 10 minuti in autobus; **boats on the Calais run** navi che fanno il servizio per Calais **4** (*sequence*) serie

f inv; (*Cards*) scala; **a run of luck** un periodo di fortuna; **it stands out from the general run of books** è un libro fuori dal comune; **the play had a long run** lo spettacolo ha tenuto a lungo il cartellone; **in the long run** alla lunga; **in the short run** sulle prime **5** (*Comm, etc*): **there's been a run on ...** c'è stata una forte richiesta di... **6** (*for animals*) recinto **7** (*for skiing, bobsleighing*) pista **8** (*in stocking, tights*) smagliatura

▸ **run about** *VI + ADV* correre (di) qua e (di) là

▸ **run across** *VI + PREP* (*meet, find*) incontrare per caso, imbattersi in

▸ **run along** *VI + ADV* correre, andare; **run along and play** su, vai a giocare

▸ **run away** *VI + ADV* **1** scappare di corsa, fuggire; **they ran away before the police came** sono scappati prima che arrivasse la polizia; **to run away from home** scappare di casa **2** (*water*) scolare

▸ **run away with** *VI + ADV + PREP* scappare con; (*fig*): **he let his imagination run away with him** si lasciò trasportare dalla fantasia; **don't run away with the idea that ...** non credere che...

▸ **run down** *VT + ADV* **1** (*Aut*) investire, mettere sotto **2** (*reduce: production*) ridurre gradualmente; (*: factory, shop*) rallentare l'attività di **3** (*disparage*) parlar male di, denigrare **4** (*battery*) scaricare ♦ *VI + ADV* (*battery, watch*) scaricarsi

▸ **run in** *VT + ADV* **1** (*car*) rodare, fare il rodaggio di **2** (*fam: arrest*) mettere dentro

▸ **run into** *VI + PREP* (*meet: person*) incontrare per caso; (*difficulties, troubles etc*) incontrare, trovare; (*collide with*) andare a sbattere contro; **to run into debt** trovarsi nei debiti

▸ **run off** *VI + ADV* = **run away** ♦ *VT + ADV* (*copies*) fare

▸ **run off with** *VI + ADV + PREP* = **run away with**

▸ **run on** *VI + ADV* **1** (*fam: person*) parlare senza tregua; (*talk, meeting*) protrarsi (oltre il previsto) **2** (*Typ*) continuare senza andare a capo

▸ **run out** *VI + ADV* (*contract, lease*) scadere; (*food, money etc*) finire, esaurirsi; (*person*) uscire di corsa; (*liquid*) colare; **the supplies have run out** le provviste sono finite; **time is running out** ormai c'è poco tempo

▸ **run out of** *VI + ADV + PREP* non avere più; **to run out of** rimanere senza; **I ran out of petrol**, (*USA*) **I ran out of gas** sono rimasto senza benzina

▸ **run out on** *VI + ADV + PREP* (*abandon*) piantare

▸ **run over** *VI + ADV* (*overflow*) traboccare ♦ *VI + PREP* (*reread*) rileggere; (*recapitulate*) ricapitolare ♦ *VT + PREP* (*Aut*) investire, mettere sotto; **to get run over** essere investito(-a)

▸ **run through** *VI + PREP* **1** (*use up: fortune*) far fuori, dilapidare **2** (*read quickly: notes etc*) dare un'occhiata a; (*list*) scorrere **3** (*rehearse: play*) riprovare, ripetere; (*recapitulate*) ricapitolare

▸ **run up** *VT + ADV* **1** (*debt*) accumulare **2** (*dress*) mettere insieme

▸ **run up against** *VI + ADV + PREP* (*person, problem*) imbattersi in; (*difficulties*) incontrare

run·around [ˈrʌnəˌraʊnd] *N* (*fam*): **to give sb the runaround** far girare a vuoto qn

run·away [ˈrʌnəˌweɪ] *ADJ* (*slave, person*) in fuga; (*child*) scappato(-a) di casa; (*truck, train*) fuori controllo; (*horse*) imbizzarrito(-a); (*success, victory*) trascinante; **runaway inflation** inflazione *f* galoppante ♦ *N* fuggitivo(-a), fuggiasco(-a)

run·down [ˈrʌnˌdaʊn] *ADJ* (*person*) debilitato(-a); (*building*) fatiscente, in rovina ♦ *N* **1** (*Brit: of industry*) riduzione *f* graduale dell'attività di **2 to give sb a run-down on sth** (*fam*) mettere qn al corrente di qc

rung[1] [rʌŋ] *N* (*of ladder*) piolo; (*of chair*) traversa

rung[2] [rʌŋ] *PP of* **ring**[2]

run-in [ˈrʌnˌɪn] *N* (*fam*) scontro

run·ner [ˈrʌnəʳ] *N* **1** (*athlete*) corridore *m*; (*horse*) partente *m* **2** (*of sledge, aircraft*) pattino; (*of skate*) lama; (*of car seat, drawer*) guida **3** (*hall carpet*) guida, passatoia **4** (*Bot*) stolone *m*

runner bean *N* (*Brit*) fagiolino

runner-up [ˌrʌnərˈʌp] *N* secondo(-a) arrivato(-a)

run·ning [ˈrʌnɪŋ] *ADJ* (*water*) corrente; (*tap*) che cola; (*sore*) che spurga; **a running stream** un corso d'acqua; **running battle** lotta continua; **to be in good running order** (*car*) essere in buone condizioni di marcia; **for five days running** per cinque giorni consecutivi; **for the sixth time running** per la sesta volta di fila *or* di seguito ♦ N (*of business, hotel*) gestione *f*, direzione *f*; (*of campaign*) organizzazione *f*; (*of machine*) funzionamento; (*of race*) corsa; **to be in/out of the running for sth** essere/non essere più in lizza per qc; **to make the running** (*Sport: fig*) imporre il ritmo

running costs NPL (*of business*) costi *mpl* d'esercizio; (*of car*) spese *fpl* di mantenimento

running head N (*Typ*) testata, titolo corrente

running mate N (*USA Pol*) candidato(-a) alla vicepresidenza

run·ny ['rʌnɪ] ADJ (*comp* **-ier**, *superl* **-iest**) (*butter*) sciolto(-a); (*sauce*) troppo liquido(-a); (*nose*) che cola, che gocciola

run-off [rʌn,ɒf] N (*in contest, election*) ballottaggio finale; (*extra race*) spareggio

run-of-the-mill [,rʌnəvðə'mɪl] ADJ banale, solito(-a)

runt [rʌnt] N (*Zool*): **the runt of the litter** (*puppy*) il cucciolo più piccolo della figliata; (*pej: person*) omuncolo

run-through ['rʌn,θru:] N (*rehearsal*) prova generale

run-up [rʌn,ʌp] N: **the run-up to Christmas** (*Brit*) il periodo che precede natale

run·way ['rʌn,weɪ] N (*Aer*) pista

rup·ture ['rʌptʃə'] N rottura; (*Med: hernia*) ernia ♦ VT (*blood vessel etc*) far scoppiare; **to rupture o.s.** farsi venire un'ernia; **the tank ruptured** il serbatoio si è rotto

ru·ral ['ruərəl] ADJ (*gen*) rurale; (*scene*) campestre; (*life*) di campagna; **rural depopulation** deruralizzazione *f*

rural district council N (*Brit*) *fino al 1974 consiglio amministrativo di distretto rurale*

ruse [ru:z] N (*frm*) stratagemma *m*, astuzia

rush¹ [rʌʃ] N (*Bot*) giunco

rush² [rʌʃ] N **1** (*of people*) affollamento, ressa; **the Christmas rush** la ressa di Natale; **gold rush** corsa all'oro; **there was a rush to** *or* **for the door** tutti si precipitarono verso la porta; **we've had a rush of orders** abbiamo avuto una valanga di ordinazioni **2** (*hurry*) fretta, premura; **in a rush** in fretta; **to be in a rush** avere fretta; **I'm in a rush (to do)** ho fretta *or* premura (di fare); **there's no rush** non c'è fretta; **it was all done in a rush** è stato fatto tutto in gran fretta; **it got lost in the rush** nella fretta è andato perso; **what's all the rush about?** cos'è tutta questa fretta?; **is there any rush for this?** è urgente?; **we had a rush to get it ready in time** abbiamo dovuto affrettarci per prepararlo in tempo **3** (*current*): a **rush of air** una corrente d'aria; **a rush of water** un flusso d'acqua ♦ VT **1** (*person*) far fretta *or* premura a; (*work, order*) fare in fretta; **to rush sth off** spedire con urgenza qc; **I hate being rushed** non mi piace che mi si faccia premura; **we were rushed off our feet** abbiamo dovuto correre come i matti; **he was rushed (off) to (the) hospital** lo hanno portato d'urgenza all'ospedale **2** (*attack: town*) prendere d'assalto; (: *person*) precipitarsi contro; **the crowd rushed the**

barriers la folla ha dato l'assalto ai cancelli ♦ VI (*person: run*) precipitarsi; (: *be in a hurry*) essere di corsa; (*car*) andare veloce; **there's no need to rush** non c'è bisogno di affrettarsi; **don't rush at it, take it slowly** non farlo in fretta, prenditela con comodo; **to rush up/down** *etc* precipitarsi su/giù *etc*; **everyone rushed outside** tutti si precipitarono fuori; **I rushed to her side** sono corso subito da lei; **I was rushing to finish it** mi affrettavo a finirlo

▸ **rush about, rush around** VI + ADV correre su e giù

▸ **rush out** VT + ADV (*product*) immettere velocemente sul mercato; (*book*) pubblicare in tutta fretta ♦ VI + ADV precipitarsi fuori

▸ **rush over** VI + ADV: **to rush over (to sb/to do sth)** precipitarsi (da qn/a fare qc)

▸ **rush up** VI + ADV = **rush over**

▸ **rush through** VT + PREP (*meal*) mangiare in fretta; (*book*) dare una scorsa frettolosa a; (*work*) sbrigare frettolosamente; (*town*) attraversare in fretta ♦ VT + ADV (*Comm: order*) eseguire d'urgenza; (*supplies*) mandare d'urgenza

rush hour N ora di punta; **the rush hour traffic** il traffico delle ore di punta

rush job N (*urgent*) lavoro urgente; (*botched, hurried*) lavoro fatto in fretta

rush matting N stuoia

rusk [rʌsk] N fetta biscottata

Rus·sia ['rʌʃə] N Russia

Rus·sian ['rʌʃən] ADJ russo(-a) ♦ N (*person*) russo(-a); (*language*) russo; **the Russians** i russi

rust [rʌst] N ruggine *f* ♦ VI arrugginire, arrugginirsi ♦ VT (*far*) arrugginire

rustic ['rʌstɪk] ADJ (*gen*) rustico(-a); (*scene*) campestre ♦ N (*pej*) cafone(-a)

rus·tle ['rʌsl] N fruscio ♦ VT (*paper*) far frusciare ♦ VI frusciare; **the leaves rustled** le foglie frusciavano

▸ **rustle up** (*fam*) VT + ADV (*find*) ripescare; (*money*) racimolare; (*meal*) rimediare, mettere insieme

rus·tle ['rʌsl] VT (*USA: cattle*) rubare

rust·proof ['rʌst,pru:f], **rust-resistant** ['rʌstrɪ,zɪstənt] ADJ inattaccabile dalla ruggine

rust·proofing ['rʌst,pru:fɪŋ] N trattamento antiruggine

rusty ['rʌstɪ] ADJ (*comp* **-ier**, *superl* **-iest**) rugginoso(-a), arrugginito(-a); **my Greek is pretty rusty** (*fig*) il mio greco è molto arrugginito

rut¹ [rʌt] N solco; **to get into a rut** (*fig*) fossilizzarsi; **to be in a rut** (*fig*) essersi fossilizzato(-a)

rut² (*Zool*) N: **the rut** la fregola, il calore *m* ♦ VI andare in calore

ru·ta·ba·ga [,ru:tə'beɪgə] N (*USA*) rapa svedese

ruth·less ['ru:θlɪs] ADJ spietato(-a)

ruth·less·ness ['ru:θlɪsnɪs] N spietatezza

RV [,ɑ:'vi:] N ABBR (= *revised version*) *versione riveduta della Bibbia anglicana*; (*USA: = recreational vehicle*)

rye [raɪ] N segale *f*; (*USA: whisky*) whisky *m inv* di segale

Ss

S¹, s¹ [ɛs] N (letter) S, s f inv, m inv; **S for sugar** ≈ S come Savona

S² ABBR **1** (= small) S f inv **2** (= south) S **3** (Scol: = satisfactory) ≈ sufficiente

SA ABBR = South Africa, South America

Sab·bath [ˈsæbəθ], **Sab·bath Day** [ˈsæbəθˈdeɪ] N (Jewish) sabato; (Christian: old) domenica

sab·bat·i·cal [səˈbætɪkəl](Univ) N anno sabbatico; **to take a sabbatical** prendere un anno sabbatico ♦ ADJ sabbatico(-a); **sabbatical year** anno sabbatico

sabo·tage [ˈsæbə.tɑːʒ] N sabotaggio ♦ VT sabotare

sac·cha·rine, sac·cha·rin (USA) [ˈsækərɪn] N saccarina

sa·chet [ˈsæʃeɪ] N bustina

sack¹ [sæk] N **1** (bag) sacco; **sack of potatoes** sacco di patate; **coal sack** sacco per il carbone; **sack of coal** sacco di carbone **2** (fam): **to get the sack** essere licenziato(-a); **to give sb the sack** licenziare qn **3** (esp USA: fam: bed) letto ♦ VT (fam: dismiss) licenziare

sack² [sæk] N (plundering) saccheggio; **the sack of Rome** il sacco di Roma ♦ VT (plunder) saccheggiare

sack·ful [ˈsæk.fʊl] N sacco (pieno)

sack·ing [ˈsækɪŋ] N **1** (cloth) tela di sacco **2** (fam: dismissal) licenziamento

sac·ra·ment [ˈsækrəmənt] N sacramento; **the Blessed Sacrament** l'Eucaristia; **to receive the sacraments** ricevere i sacramenti

sa·cred [ˈseɪkrɪd] ADJ (holy) sacro(-a); **sacred to the memory of** dedicato(-a) alla memoria di; **a sacred promise** (fig) una promessa solenne; **is nothing sacred?** non c'è più religione!

sacred cow N (fig: person) intoccabile m/f; (: institution) caposaldo; (: idea, belief) dogma m

sac·ri·fice [ˈsækrɪ.faɪs] N sacrificio; **to make sacrifices (for sb)** fare (dei) sacrifici (per qn) ♦ VT sacrificare

sac·ri·lege [ˈsækrɪlɪdʒ] N sacrilegio

sac·ro·sanct [ˈsækrəʊ.sæŋkt] ADJ sacrosanto(-a)

sad [sæd] ADJ (comp **-der**, superl **-dest**) **1** (sorrowful, depressing) triste; **to make sb sad** rattristare qn; **how sad!** che tristezza!; **sadder but wiser** maturato(-a) dall'esperienza **2** (deplorable) deplorevole; **sad but true** è triste ma è così; **it's a sad state of affairs when ...** la situazione è proprio triste quando...

sad·den [ˈsædn] VT rattristare

sad·dle [ˈsædl] N (of horse, also Culin) sella; (of bicycle) sellino, sella; **in the saddle** in sella; **when he was in the saddle** (fig) quando aveva le redini (del potere); **saddle of lamb** sella d'agnello ♦ VT (horse: also: **saddle up**) sellare; **to saddle sb with sth** (fam: task, bill, name) appioppare qc a qn; (: responsibility) accollare qc a qn; **I got saddled with him again** me lo sono dovuto sorbire di nuovo

saddle·bag [ˈsædl.bæg] N bisaccia; (on bicycle) borsa

sad·ism [ˈseɪdɪzm] N sadismo

sad·ist [ˈseɪdɪst] N sadico(-a)

sa·dis·tic [səˈdɪstɪk] ADJ sadico(-a), sadistico(-a)

sad·ly [ˈsædlɪ] ADV (unhappily) tristemente; (regrettably) sfortunatamente; **sadly lacking in ...** completamente privo(-a) di...; **"she's gone," he said sadly** "se n'è andata" disse tristemente; **sadly, it was too late** sfortunatamente era troppo tardi

sad·ness [ˈsædnɪs] N tristezza

sado·maso·chism [.seɪdəʊˈmæsə.kɪzəm] N sadomasochismo

sa·fa·ri [səˈfɑːrɪ] N safari m inv; **to be on safari** fare un safari

safari park N zoosafari m inv

safe [seɪf] ADJ (comp **-r**, superl **-st**) **1** (not in danger: person) salvo(-a); (: money, jewels, secret) al sicuro; (out of danger: person) fuori pericolo; **safe and sound** sano e salvo(-a); as **safe as houses** sicurissimo(-a); **he didn't feel very safe up** there non si sentiva molto (al) sicuro lassù; **to be safe from** essere al sicuro da; **to feel safe** sentirsi al sicuro; **you'll be safe here** qui sarai al sicuro **2** (not dangerous: toy, beach, animal) non pericoloso(-a); (: ladder) sicuro(-a); (secure: hiding place, investment) sicuro(-a); (prudent: choice) prudente; **that dog isn't safe with children** non si dovrebbe lasciare quel cane coi bambini; **(have a) safe journey!** buon viaggio!; **in safe hands** in buone mani; **just to be on the safe side** per andare sul sicuro, per precauzione, per non correre rischi; **better safe than sorry!** meglio essere prudenti!; **it's a safe bet** è praticamente certo; **safe to drink** potabile; **is the water safe to drink?** è potabile l'acqua?; **it is safe to say that ...** si può affermare con sicurezza che...; **to play safe** giocare sul sicuro; **this car isn't safe** questa macchina non è sicura; **it might not be safe to leave your car here** potrebbe non essere prudente lasciare la macchina qui

safe bet N: **it's a safe bet** è una cosa sicura

safe-breaker [ˈseɪf.breɪkə], **safe-cracker** [ˈseɪf.krækə] (USA) N scassinatore(-trice)

safe-conduct [.seɪfˈkɒndʌkt] N salvacondotto

safe-deposit [ˈseɪfdɪ.pɒzɪt], **safety-deposit** [ˈseɪftɪdɪ.pɒzɪt] N (vault) caveau m inv; (box) cassetta di sicurezza

safe·guard [ˈseɪf.gɑːd] N salvaguardia ♦ VT salvaguardare

safe haven N zona sicura or protetta

safe-keeping [ˈseɪfˈkiːpɪŋ] N custodia; **to give sb sth for safekeeping** dare qc in custodia a qn; **I gave it to him for safekeeping** gliel'ho dato in custodia; **the key is in his safe-keeping** gli è stata affidata la custodia della chiave

safe·ly [ˈseɪflɪ] ADV (securely) al sicuro; (without danger) senza (correre) rischi, tranquillamente; (without accident): **to arrive safely** arrivare sano(-a) e salvo(-a); **I can safely say ...** posso tranquillamente asserire...

safe passage N passaggio sicuro

safe sex N sesso sicuro

safe·ty [ˈseɪftɪ] N sicurezza; **to reach safety** mettersi in salvo; **in a place of safety** al sicuro; **there's safety in numbers** l'unione fa la forza; **safety first!** la prudenza innanzitutto!; **for safety's sake** per (maggior) sicurezza ♦ ADJ (device, measure, margin) di sicurezza

safety belt N (Aut, Aer) cintura di sicurezza

safety catch N sicura

safety net N (in circus) rete f di protezione; (fig: safeguard) ancora di salvezza; **to slip through the social security safety net** (fig) scivolare attraverso le maglie dell'assistenza sociale

safety pin N spilla da balia or di sicurezza

safety valve N valvola di sicurezza

saf·fron [ˈsæfrən] N zafferano ♦ ADJ (colour) (color) zafferano inv

sag [sæg] VI (hang down: ceiling, awning, bed) incurvarsi; (: breasts) afflosciarsi; (slacken: rope) allentarsi; (fig: spirits) deprimersi; **his knees sagged** gli hanno ceduto le ginocchia; **the roof sags at one corner** il tetto è incurvato ad un'estremità; **muscles start to sag when you get to a certain age** i muscoli cominciano ad afflosciarsi ad una certa età

saga [ˈsɑːgə] N saga

sage¹ [seɪdʒ] ADJ (liter) saggio(-a) ♦ N (man) saggio

sage² [seɪdʒ] N (herb) salvia; **sage and onion stuffing** ripieno di salvia e cipolla; **chopped sage** salvia tritata

Sag·it·ta·rius [.sædʒɪˈtɛərɪəs] N (Astron, Astrol) Sagittario; **to be Sagittarius** essere del Sagittario; **I'm Sagittarius** sono del Sagittario

sago [ˈseɪgəʊ] N sagù m inv

Sa·ha·ra [səˈhɑːrə] N: **the Sahara (Desert)** il deserto del) Sahara

said [sed] PT, PP of **say** ♦ ADJ (aforementioned): **the said** il (la) suddetto(-a)

Sai·gon [saɪˈɡɒn] N Saigon *f*

sail [seɪl] N (*of boat*) vela; (*of windmill*) pala; (*trip*): **to go for a sail** fare un giro in barca a vela; **to set sail** salpare; **under sail** a vela ♦ VT 1 (*ship*) condurre, governare; **to sail a boat** condurre una barca 2 (*travel over*): **to sail the Atlantic** attraversare l'Atlantico; **to sail the seas** solcare i mari ♦ VI 1 (*travel: ship*) navigare; (: *person*) viaggiare per mare; **to sail into harbour** entrare in porto; **the ship sailed into Naples** la nave è arrivata a Napoli; **to sail round the Cape** doppiare il Capo; **to sail away/back** *etc* allontanarsi/rientrare *etc* in barca; **they sailed into Genoa** sono entrati nel porto di Genova; **to sail round the world** fare il giro del mondo in barca a vela; **to sail close to the wind** (*fig*) tirare troppo la corda 2 (*set off*) salpare; **the ship sails at 5 o'clock** la nave salpa alle 5 3 (*Sport*) fare della vela 4 (*fig: clouds*) veleggiare; (: *swan*) incedere maestosamente; **she sailed into the room** fece il suo ingresso solenne nella stanza; **the plate sailed over my head** il piatto è volato al di sopra della mia testa
► **sail through** VI + ADV (*fig*) farcela senza difficoltà ♦ VI + PREP (*fig*) fare qc senza difficoltà; (*pass: exam, driving test*) superare senza difficoltà

sail·ing [ˈseɪlɪŋ] N (*sport*) vela; (*departure*) partenza; (**pleasure**) sailing navigazione *f* da diporto; **to go sailing** fare vela; **now it's all plain sailing** il resto è liscio come l'olio

sailing boat, sail·boat [ˈseɪlˌbəʊt] N (*USA*) barca a vela

sailing ship N veliero

sail·or [ˈseɪləʳ] N marinaio

saint [seɪnt] N (*also fig*) santo(-a); **Saint John** San Giovanni; **Saint Mark's (Church)** (la chiesa di) San Marco

saint·ly [ˈseɪntlɪ] ADJ (*comp* **-ier**, *superl* **-iest**) (*expression, life*) da santo(-a); **a saintly person** una santa persona

sake [seɪk] N: **for the sake of sb/sth** per amor di qn/qc; **for my sake** per amor mio, per me; **for the sake of the children** per il bene dei bambini; **for God's/for heaven's sake!** per amor di Dio!/del cielo!; **art for art's sake** l'arte per l'arte; **for your own sake** per te (stesso), per il tuo bene; **for pity's sake** per pietà; **for old times' sake** in ricordo del passato; **for argument's sake, for the sake of argument** a titolo d'esempio

sal·ad [ˈsæləd] N insalata; **tomato salad** insalata di pomodori; **ham salad** prosciutto e insalata; **green salad** insalata verde

salad bowl N insalatiera

salad dressing N condimento per l'insalata

salad oil N olio da tavola

sa·la·mi [səˈlɑːmɪ] N salame *m*

sala·ried [ˈsælərɪd] (*person, post*) stipendiato(-a)

sala·ry [ˈsælərɪ] N stipendio

salary scale N scala salariale

sale [seɪl] N 1 (*of article*) vendita; (*also:* **auction sale**) vendita all'asta; **"for sale"** (*one article*) "vendesi"; (*two or more articles*) "vendonsi"; **for sale** in vendita; **to put a house up for sale** mettere in vendita una casa; **the house is for sale** la casa è in vendita; **to be on sale** essere in vendita; **the sale of the company** la vendita della ditta 2 (*Comm: also:* **sales**) svendita, saldi *mpl*; **to be on sale** (*USA*) essere in saldi *or* in svendita; **she bought a dress in the sale(s)** ha comprato un vestito nei saldi; **the January sales** ≈ i saldi di fine anno; **there's a sale on at Harrods** da Harrods ci sono i saldi
❏ **sale** is not translated by the Italian word *sale*

sale·room [ˈseɪlˌrʊm] N (*esp Brit*) sala di vendite all'asta

sales assistant N (*Brit*) commesso(-a)

sales clerk N (*USA*) commesso(-a)

sales conference N riunione *f* marketing e vendite

sales drive N campagna promozionale

sales force N forza di vendita

sales·man [ˈseɪlzmən] N (*pl* **-men**) (*representative*) rappresentante *m* di commercio; (*in shop*) commesso; **car salesman** rivenditore di auto

sales manager N direttore(-trice) delle vendite

sales·man·ship [ˈseɪlzmənʃɪp] N arte *f* del vendere

sales·person [ˈseɪlzˌpɜːsən] N (*in shop*) commesso(-a); (*representative*) rappresentante *m*/*f* di commercio

sales rep, sales representative N rappresentante *m*/*f* (di commercio)

sales tax N (*USA*) imposta sulle vendite

sales·woman [ˈseɪlzˌwʊmən] N (*pl* **-women**) (*in shop*) commessa; (*representative*) rappresentante *f* di commercio

sa·li·ent [ˈseɪlɪənt] ADJ (*frm*) saliente

sa·line [ˈseɪlaɪn] ADJ salino(-a)

sa·li·va [səˈlaɪvə] N saliva

sal·low [ˈsæləʊ] ADJ (*comp* **-er**, *superl* **-est**) (*complexion*) giallastro(-a)

sal·ly [ˈsælɪ] N (*witty remark*) battuta
► **sally forth, sally out** VI + ADV (*old*) uscire di gran carriera

salm·on [ˈsæmən] N salmone *m*; **salmon fishing** pesca del salmone; **salmon steak** trancio di salmone

salmon trout N trota salmonata, trota di mare

sa·lon [ˈsælɒn] N (*all senses*) salone *m*; **hair salon** il salone da parrucchiere; **beauty salon** istituto di bellezza

sa·loon [səˈluːn] N 1 (*on ship*) sala, salone *m* 2 (*Brit: car*) berlina; **a family saloon** una berlina familiare 3 (*USA: bar*) saloon *m inv*, bar *m inv*; (*Brit: also:* **saloon bar**) bar (*in pub, hotel*)

salt [sɔːlt] N sale *m*; **to rub salt into the wound** (*fig*) rigirare il coltello nella piaga; **not to be worth one's salt** non valere un granché; **he's the salt of the earth** è un bravo uomo; **an old salt** un lupo di mare ♦ VT (*flavour*) salare; (*preserve*) conservare sotto sale ♦ ADJ (*water*) salato(-a); (*beef, meat*) salato(-a), sotto sale; (*mine*) di sale; (*spoon*) per il sale
► **salt away** VT + ADV (*fam*) mettere da parte

salt·cellar [ˈsɔːltˌsɛləʳ], (*USA*) **salt shaker** N saliera

salt-free [ˌsɔːltˈfriː] ADJ senza sale

salt-water [ˌsɔːltˈwɔːtəʳ] ADJ (*fish*) di mare

salty [ˈsɔːltɪ] ADJ (*comp* **-ier**, *superl* **-iest**) (*taste*) salato(-a); (*fig: humour, remark*) piccante

sa·lu·bri·ous [səˈluːbrɪəs] (*frm*) ADJ salubre; (*fig: district*) raccomandabile

salu·tary [ˈsæljʊtərɪ] ADJ salutare

sa·lute [səˈluːt] N (*Mil: with hand*) saluto; (: *with gunfire*) salva; **to take the salute** passare in rassegna le truppe ♦ VT (*Mil, also fig*) salutare; **to salute the flag** salutare la bandiera
❏ **salute** is not translated by the Italian word *salute*

sal·vage [ˈsælvɪdʒ] N 1 (*saving: of ship etc*) salvataggio; (: *for re-use*) recupero 2 (*things saved*) oggetti *mpl* salvati *or* ricuperati; (*for re-use*) materiale *m* di ricupero 3 (*compensation*) compenso ♦ VT (*boat, cargo, goods*) ricuperare; (*fig*) salvare ♦ ADJ (*operation*) di salvataggio; (*goods*) di ricupero

salvage vessel N nave *f* di salvataggio

sal·va·tion [sælˈveɪʃən] N salvezza

Salvation Army N: **the Salvation Army** l'Esercito della Salvezza

sal·ver [ˈsælvəʳ] N vassoio (*d'argento o altro metallo*)

sal·vo [ˈsælvəʊ] N (*Mil*) salva; (*outburst: of applause*) scroscio

Sa·mari·tan [səˈmærɪtən] N 1 **the Good Samaritan** il buon Samaritano 2 **the Samaritans** (*organisation*) ≈ Telefono Amico

same [seɪm] ADJ stesso(-a), medesimo(-a); **the same book as/that** lo stesso libro di/che; **the same model** lo stesso modello; **the same table as usual** il solito tavolo; **on the same day** lo stesso giorno; **the** *or* **that same day** il *or* quel giorno stesso; **at the same time** allo stesso tempo; **it comes to the same thing** è la stessa cosa; **in the same way** allo stesso modo; **to go the same way as sb** (*fig: pej*) seguire le orme di qn; **they're exactly the same** sono esattamente uguali ♦ PRON: **the same** (*sg*) lo(-a) stesso(-a); (*pl*) gli (le) stessi(-e); **it's all the same to me** per me fa lo stesso; **just the same as usual** come al solito; **same again, please** (*in pub*) un altro, per favore; **it was wrong but I did it all** *or* **just the same** non era giusto ma l'ho fatto lo stesso; **they're one and the same** (*person*) sono la stessa persona; (*thing*) sono la stessa cosa; **it's not the same** non è lo stesso; **to do the same** fare la stessa cosa; **I'll do the same for you** farò altrettanto per te; **I would do the same again** rifarei quello che ho fatto; **to do the same as sb** fare come qn; **and the same to you!** altrettanto a te!; **I still feel the same about you** i miei sentimenti nei tuoi confronti non sono cambiati; **same here!** (*fam*) anch'io!

sam·ple [ˈsɑːmpl] N (*gen*) campione *m*; (*fig*) saggio; **to take a sample** prelevare un campione; **to take a blood sample** fare un prelievo di sangue; **free sample** campione omaggio;

a free sample of perfume un campione gratuito di profumo ♦ vt (*food, wine*) assaggiare, degustare; (*fig: experience*) provare; (*Market Research: people*) usare come campione ♦ adj (*bottle*) campione *inv*; **sample line/verse** esempio; **sample selection** campioni *mpl*; **sample copy** copia saggio; **sample survey** indagine *f* su campione

sana·to·rium [ˌsænəˈtɔːrɪəm] (*pl* sanatoria *or* sanatoriums [ˌsænəˈtɔːrɪə]) 1 casa di cura; (*for tuberculosis*) sanatorio 2 (*Brit Scol*) ≈ infermeria

sanc·ti·fy [ˈsæŋktɪˌfaɪ] vt santificare

sanc·ti·mo·ni·ous [ˌsæŋktɪˈməʊnɪəs] adj (*pej: person*) bigotto(-a), bacchettone(-a); (: *tone*) moraleggiante

sanc·tion [ˈsæŋkʃən] n (*gen*) sanzione *f*; **economic sanctions** sanzioni *fpl* economiche; **to impose economic sanctions on** *or* **against** adottare sanzioni economiche contro ♦ vt sancire, sanzionare

sanc·tity [ˈsæŋktɪtɪ] n (*of person, marriage*) santità; (*of oath, place*) sacralità

sanc·tu·ary [ˈsæŋktjʊərɪ] n (*Rel*) santuario; (*fig: Pol: refuge*) asilo; (*for wildlife, birds*) riserva; **a wildlife sanctuary** una riserva naturale; **to seek sanctuary** cercare asilo; **they sought sanctuary in the church** hanno cercato rifugio nella chiesa

sand [sænd] n sabbia; *see also* **sands** ♦ vt 1 (*road*) cospargere di sabbia 2 (*also:* **sand down:** *wood*) levigare, smerigliare

san·dal [ˈsændl] n sandalo

sand·bag [ˈsændˌbæg] n sacchetto di sabbia ♦ vt (*protect*) proteggere con sacchetti di sabbia; (*hit*) colpire (con un sacchetto di sabbia)

sand·blast [ˈsændˌblɑːst] vt sabbiare

sand·box [ˈsændˌbɒks] n (*USA*) buca della sabbia (*per i giochi dei bambini*)

sand·castle [ˈsændˌkɑːsl] n castello di sabbia

sand dune n duna

sand·er [ˈsændəʳ] n (*machine*) levigatrice *f*

sand·paper [ˈsændˌpeɪpəʳ] n carta vetrata ♦ vt cartavetrare

sand·pit [ˈsændˌpɪt] n cava di sabbia; (*Brit: for children*) buca della sabbia (*per i giochi dei bambini*); **they're playing in the sandpit** giocano nella buca della sabbia

sands [sændz] npl spiaggia *fsg*; **the sands of time** (*fig*) lo scorrere del tempo

sand·stone [ˈsændˌstəʊn] n arenaria

sand·storm [ˈsændˌstɔːm] n tempesta di sabbia

sand·wich [ˈsænwɪdʒ] n tramezzino, sandwich *m inv*; **cheese/ham sandwich** panino al formaggio/prosciutto ♦ vt (*also:* **sandwich in:** *person, appointment etc*) infilare; **to be sandwiched between** essere incastrato(-a) fra

sandwich board n cartello pubblicitario (*portato da uomo sandwich*)

sandwich course n (*Brit*) corso che alterna lo studio a periodi di pratica presso aziende o fabbriche

sandwich man n uomo *m* sandwich, *inv*

sandy [ˈsændɪ] adj (*comp* -ier, *superl* -iest) (*gen*) sabbioso(-a); (*colour*) color sabbia *inv*; (*hair*) biondo rossiccio *inv*; **a sandy beach** una spiaggia sabbiosa

sane [seɪn] adj (*comp* -r, *superl* -st) (*person*) sano(-a) di mente; (*judgment, outlook*) sensato(-a); **he seemed perfectly sane** sembrava assolutamente sano di mente; **no sane person wants conflict** nessuna persona sensata vorrebbe un conflitto

sang [sæŋ] pt *of* sing

san·guine [ˈsæŋgwɪn] adj ottimista

sani·ta·rium [ˌsænɪˈtɛərɪəm] n (*pl* sanitaria *or* sanitariums [ˌsænɪˈtɛərɪə]) (*USA*) = sanatorium

sani·tary [ˈsænɪtərɪ] adj (*clean*) igienico(-a); (*system, arrangements, fittings*) sanitario(-a)

sanitary towel, (*USA*) **sanitary napkin** n assorbente *m* (igienico)

sani·ta·tion [ˌsænɪˈteɪʃən] n (*plumbing: in house*) impianti *mpl* igienici; (: *in town*) fognature *fpl*; (*hygiene*) igiene *f*; **poor sanitation** qualità scadente delle strutture per l'igiene pubblica

sanitation department n (*USA*) ≈ assessorato alla nettezza urbana

san·ity [ˈsænɪtɪ] n (*of person*) sanità mentale; (*of judgment*) buonsenso; **sanity prevailed** il buonsenso ha avuto la meglio

sank [sæŋk] pt *of* sink[1]

San Ma·ri·no [ˌsænməˈriːnəʊ] n San Marino *f*

Santa Claus [ˌsæntəˈklɔːz] n ≈ Babbo Natale

San·tia·go [ˌsæntɪˈɑːgəʊ] n (*also:* **Santiago de Chile**) Santiago *f* (del Cile)

sap¹ [sæp] n (*of plants*) linfa

sap² [sæp] vt (*strength*) fiaccare; (*confidence*) minare

sap·ling [ˈsæplɪŋ] n alberello

sap·phire [ˈsæfaɪəʳ] n zaffiro ♦ adj (*necklace*) di zaffiri; (*colour*) blu zaffiro *inv*

sar·casm [ˈsɑːkæzəm] n sarcasmo

sar·cas·tic [sɑːˈkæstɪk] adj sarcastico(-a); **to be sarcastic** fare del sarcasmo

sar·copha·gus [sɑːˈkɒfəgəs] n (*pl* sarcophaguses *or* sarcophagi) sarcofago

sar·dine [sɑːˈdiːn] n sardina

Sar·dinia [sɑːˈdɪnɪə] n la Sardegna

Sar·din·ian [sɑːˈdɪnɪən] adj, n (*person*) sardo(-a)

sar·don·ic [sɑːˈdɒnɪk] adj sardonico(-a)

sari [ˈsɑːrɪ] n sari *m inv*

SARS [sɑːz] n abbr (= *severe acute respiratory syndrome*) SARS *f*, polmonite *f* atipica

sar·to·rial [sɑːˈtɔːrɪəl] adj (*frm*) sartoriale

SASE [ˌɛseɪesˈiː] n abbr (*USA:* = *self-addressed stamped envelope*) busta già affrancata e indirizzata a se stessi

sash [sæʃ] n (*of dress*) fusciacca; (*on uniform*) fascia

sash window n finestra a ghigliottina

Sask. abbr (*Canada:* = *Saskatchewan*)

SAT [ˌɛseɪˈtiː] n abbr (*USA:* = *Scholastic Aptitude Test*) esami attitudinali per l'iscrizione all'università

sat [sæt] pt, pp *of* sit

Sat. abbr (= *Saturday*) sab. (= *sabato*)

Satan [ˈseɪtn] n Satana *m*

sa·tan·ic [səˈtænɪk] adj satanico(-a)

satch·el [ˈsætʃəl] n cartella (*per la scuola*)

sa·ted [ˈseɪtɪd] adj (*frm*) sazio(-a)

sat·el·lite [ˈsætəˌlaɪt] n (*all senses*) satellite *m* ♦ adj satellite *inv*

satellite dish n antenna parabolica

satellite television n televisione *f* via satellite

sa·ti·ate [ˈseɪʃɪˌeɪt] vt (*frm*) saziare

sat·in [ˈsætɪn] n raso, satin *m* ♦ adj (*dress, blouse*) di raso *or* di satin; (*paper*) satinato(-a); **with a satin finish** satinato(-a)

sat·ire [ˈsætaɪəʳ] n: **satire (on)** satira (di, su)

sa·tiri·cal [səˈtɪrɪkəl] adj satirico(-a)

sati·rist [ˈsætərɪst] n (*writer etc*) scrittore(-trice) satirico(-a); (*cartoonist*) caricaturista *m/f*

sati·rize [ˈsætəˌraɪz] vt satireggiare

sat·is·fac·tion [ˌsætɪsˈfækʃən] n (*gen*) soddisfazione *f*; (*of ambitions, hopes*) realizzazione *f*; **has it been done to your satisfaction?** ne è rimasto soddisfatto?; **it gives me great satisfaction to learn that ...** mi è con immenso piacere che apprendo che...; **both sides expressed satisfaction** entrambe le parti hanno espresso soddisfazione

sat·is·fac·tory [ˌsætɪsˈfæktərɪ] adj soddisfacente; (*Scol*) sufficiente; **to bring sth to a satisfactory conclusion** concludere qc in modo soddisfacente

sat·is·fied [ˈsætɪsˌfaɪd] adj (*person, voice, customer*) soddisfatto(-a); **I'm not satisfied with that** ciò non mi basta; **I am satisfied that ...** sono convinto *or* sicuro che...

sat·is·fy [ˈsætɪsˌfaɪ] vt 1 (*make content*) soddisfare, contentare; **the offer won't satisfy everyone** l'offerta non soddisferà tutti 2 (*need, condition, creditor*) soddisfare; (*hunger*) calmare; **to satisfy the requirements** rispondere ai requisiti 3 (*convince*): **to satisfy sb (that)** convincere qn (che); **they must satisfy us that things will be different in future** devono convincerci che le cose andranno diversamente in futuro; **to satisfy o.s. of sth** accertarsi di qc; **to satisfy o.s. that** accertarsi che; **he wanted to satisfy himself that everyone was safe** voleva accertarsi che tutti fossero al sicuro

sat·is·fy·ing [ˈsætɪsˌfaɪɪŋ] adj (*gen*) soddisfacente; (*food, meal*) sostanzioso(-a)

sat·nav [ˈsætnæv] n abbr (= *satellite navigation*) navigatore *m* satellitare

sat·su·ma [ˌsætˈsuːmə] N satsuma, *tipo di mandarino*

satu·rate [ˈsætʃəˌreɪt] VT: **to saturate (with)** (*soak*) inzuppare (di); (*Chem: fig*) saturare (di); **to saturate the market** (*Comm*) saturare il mercato

saturated fat N grassi *mpl* saturi

satu·ra·tion [ˌsætʃəˈreɪʃən] N saturazione *f*

Sat·ur·day [ˈsætədɪ] N sabato; *see* **Tuesday**

sauce [sɔːs] N 1 (*containing meat, fish*) sugo; **tomato sauce** salsa di pomodoro 2 (*fam: impudence*) faccia tosta

sauce·pan [ˈsɔːspən] N pentola, casseruola

sau·cer [ˈsɔːsə] N piattino

saucy [ˈsɔːsɪ] ADJ (*comp* **-ier**, *superl* **-iest**) (*impertinent*) sfacciato(-a), impertinente; (*look*) provocante

Sau·di Ara·bia [ˌsaʊdɪəˈreɪbɪə] N Arabia Saudita

Sau·di Ara·bian [ˌsaʊdɪəˈreɪbɪən] ADJ, N (*also:* **Saudi**) saudita *m/f*

sau·na [ˈsɔːnə] N sauna

saun·ter [ˈsɔːntər] VI: **to saunter in/out** entrare/uscire con disinvoltura; **to saunter up and down** passeggiare su e giù

sau·sage [ˈsɒsɪdʒ] N (*to be cooked*) salsiccia; (*salami etc*) salame *m*

sausage roll N involtino di pasta sfoglia ripieno di salsiccia

sau·té [ˈsəʊteɪ] ADJ (*Culin: potatoes*) sauté *inv* ♦ VT (*potatoes, meat*) saltare; (*onions*) soffriggere

sav·age [ˈsævɪdʒ] ADJ 1 (*gen*) violento(-a); (*animal, murderer, attack*) feroce; **a savage attack** un feroce attacco 2 (*primitive: custom, tribe*) selvaggio(-a) ♦ N selvaggio(-a) ♦ VT (*subj: dog*) sbranare; (*fig*) fare a pezzi, attaccare violentemente

sav·age·ry [ˈsævɪdʒrɪ] N ferocia

save¹ [seɪv] VT 1 (*rescue, or Rel*): **to save (from)** salvare (da); **to save sb from falling** impedire a qn di cadere; **to save sb's life** salvare la vita a qn; **she saved his life** gli ha salvato la vita; **I couldn't do it to save my life** (*fig: fam*) sono completamente negato per quello; **to save the situation** *or* **the day** salvare la situazione; **to save one's (own) skin** (*fam*) salvare la (propria) pelle; **to save face** salvare la faccia; **to save a goal** (*Ftbl*) parare un goal; **God save the Queen!** Dio salvi la Regina! 2 (*put aside: money*) (*also:* **save up**) risparmiare, mettere da parte; (*food, newspapers*) conservare, tenere da parte; (*collect: stamps*) raccogliere; (*Comput*) memorizzare; **I've saved fifty pounds already** ho già messo da parte cinquanta sterline; **I saved you a piece of cake** ti ho tenuto da parte una fetta di dolce; **save me a seat** prendimi un posto; **to save sth till last** tenere qc per ultimo(-a); **I saved the file onto a diskette** ho memorizzato il file su un dischetto; **I'm saving up for a new bike** sto risparmiando per comprare una bici nuova 3 (*avoid using: money, effort*) risparmiare; **it saved us a lot of trouble/another journey** ci ha risparmiato una bella seccatura/un altro viaggio; **I saved money by staying in youth hostels** ho risparmiato alloggiando negli ostelli della gioventù; **it will save me an hour** mi farà risparmiare un'ora; **it saved us time** ci ha fatto risparmiare tempo; **to save time ...** per risparmiare *or* guadagnare tempo...; **save your breath** risparmia il fiato ♦ VI 1 (*also:* **save up**): **to save (for)** risparmiare (per) 2 **to save on sth** risparmiare tempo; **to save on food/transport** risparmiare *or* economizzare sul vitto/trasporto ♦ N (*Sport*) parata

save² [seɪv] PREP (*liter, old*) salvo, a eccezione di

sav·ing [ˈseɪvɪŋ] N (*of time, money*): **saving of** *or* **in** risparmio di; **to make savings** fare economia ♦ **savings** NPL (*in bank*) risparmi *mpl*; **life savings** i risparmi di tutta una vita; **to live on** *or* **off one's savings** vivere dei propri risparmi

savings account N libretto di risparmio

savings and loan association N (*USA: Fin*) società *f inv* immobiliare e finanziaria

savings bank N cassa di risparmio

sav·iour, sav·ior (*USA*) [ˈseɪvjə] N salvatore(-trice)

sa·vour, sa·vor (*USA*) [ˈseɪvə] N sapore *m*, gusto ♦ VT (*also fig*) assaporare, gustare ♦ VI: **to savour of sth** sapere di qc

sa·voury, sa·vory (*USA*) [ˈseɪvərɪ] ADJ (*not sweet*) salato(-a); (*appetizing*) saporito(-a), appetitoso(-a); **savoury flan** *or* **tart** torta salata; **is it sweet or savoury?** è dolce o salato?; **not very savoury** (*fig: district*) poco raccomandabile; (: *subject*) scabroso(-a) ♦ N (*Culin*) piatto salato, (*on toast*) crostino

sav·vy [ˈsævɪ] N (*fam*) comprendonio

saw¹ [sɔː] (*pt* **sawed** *pp* **sawed** *or* **sawn**) N (*tool*) sega ♦ VT segare; **to saw sth up** fare a pezzi qc con la sega; **to saw sth off** segare via qc ♦ VI: **to saw through** segare

saw² [sɔː] PT *of* **see**

saw·dust [ˈsɔːˌdʌst] N segatura

saw·mill [ˈsɔːˌmɪl] N segheria

sawn [sɔːn] *pp of* **saw¹**

sawn-off shotgun [ˈsɔːnɒf ˈʃɒtɡʌn], **sawed-off shotgun** [ˈsɔːdɒf ˈʃɒtɡʌn] N fucile *m* a canne mozze

saxo·phone [ˈsæksəˌfəʊn] N sassofono

say [seɪ] (*pt, pp* **said**) VT, VI 1 (*gen*) dire; (*subj: dial, gauge*) indicare; **he said (that) he'd do it** ha detto che l'avrebbe fatto; **David said he'd come** David ha detto che sarebbe venuto; **she said (that) I was to give you this** mi ha detto di darti questo; **what did he say?** cos'ha detto?; **my watch says 3 o'clock** il mio orologio fa le 3; **the rules say that ... il regolamento dice che...; **to say mass/a prayer** dire messa/una preghiera; **to say yes/no** dire di sì/di no; **to say yes/no to a proposal** accettare/rifiutare una proposta; **I wouldn't say no** (*Brit fam*) non mi dispiacerebbe; **to say goodbye/goodnight to sb** dire arrivederci/buonanotte a qn; **to say sth again** ripetere qc; **could you say that again?** potrebbe ripetere?; **say after me ...** ripetete con me...; **I've nothing more to say** non ho altro da dire; **I'll say more about it later** ne riparlerò più tardi; **let's say no more about it** non ne parliamo più; **I'd rather not say** preferisco non pronunciarmi; **I should say it's worth about £100** direi che vale sulle 100 sterline; **let's say it's worth £20** diciamo *or* ammettiamo che valga 20 sterline; **shall we say Tuesday?** facciamo martedì?; **will you take an offer of, say, £50?** accetta un'offerta di, diciamo, 50 sterline? 2 (*in phrases*): **that is to say** vale a dire, cioè; **to say nothing of** per non parlare di; **to say the least** a dir poco; **she hasn't much** *or* **has nothing to say for herself** (*by way of conversation*) non sa dire due parole; **what have you got to say for yourself?** (*by way of excuse*) qual è la tua giustificazione?; **that doesn't say much for him** non torna a suo credito; **it goes without saying (that)** va da sé (che); **there's no saying what he'll do** Dio solo sa cosa farà; **it's not for me to say** non sta a me dirlo; **what do** *or* **would you say to a walk?** che ne dici *or* diresti di una passeggiata?; **when all is said and done** in fin dei conti; **let's say that ...** mettiamo *or* diciamo che...; **it is said that** si dice che + *sub*; **they say that** dicono che + *sub*; **there is something** *or* **a lot to be said for it** ha i suoi lati positivi; **it must be said that ...** bisogna ammettere che...; **he is said to have ...** si dice che abbia...; **it is easier** *or* **sooner said than done** è più facile a dirsi che a farsi; **I say!** *or* (*USA*) **Say!** (*calling attention*) senta!, scusi!; (*in surprise, appreciation*) perbacco!; **I'll say!** (*fam*) eccome!; **I should say it is** *or* **so!, you can say THAT again!** (*fam*) altroché!; **you don't say!** (*fam, often iro*) ma va'!, ma che dici!; **you('ve) said it!** (*fam: emphatic*) l'hai detto!; **say no more!** (*fam, often hum*) non aggiungere altro! ♦ N: **to have one's say** dire la propria; **to have a say/no say in the matter** avere/non avere voce in capitolo

say·ing [ˈseɪɪŋ] N detto; **as the saying goes** come dice il proverbio

SBA [ˌɛsbiːˈeɪ] N ABBR (*USA:* = *Small Business Administration*) *organismo ausiliario per piccole imprese*

SC ABBR (*USA*) 1 = **Supreme Court** 2 (*Post:* = *South Carolina*)

scab [skæb] N 1 (*Med*) crosta 2 (*fam, pej: strikebreaker*) crumiro(-a)

scab·by [ˈskæbɪ] ADJ (*comp* **-ier**, *superl* **-iest**) crostoso(-a)

scaf·fold [ˈskæfəld] N (*Constr*) impalcatura, ponteggio; (*for execution*) patibolo

scaf·fold·ing [ˈskæfəldɪŋ] N impalcatura

scald [skɔːld] N scottatura ♦ VT (*gen*) scottare; (*Culin: milk*) sbollentare; (*sterilize*) sterilizzare

❏ **scald** is not translated by the Italian word *scaldare*

scald·ing [ˈskɔːldɪŋ] ADJ: **scalding hot** bollente

scale¹ [skeɪl] N (*of fish, reptile etc*) squama, scaglia; (*flake: of rust, chalk*) scaglia; (: *of skin*) squama ♦ VT (*fish*) squamare

scale² [skeɪl] N 1 (*on ruler, thermometer*) scala graduata; (*of model, map*) scala; **pay scale** scala salariale; **scale of charges**

tariffario; **on a scale of 1 cm to 5 km** in scala di 1 a 500.000; **on a large scale** su vasta scala; **on a small scale** su scala ridotta; **small-scale model** modello in scala ridotta; **large-scale map** carta geografica su larga scala; **to draw sth to scale** disegnare qc in scala; **he underestimated the scale of the problem** ha sottovalutato la portata del problema **2** (*Mus*) scala; *see also* **scales** ♦ VT (*wall, mountain*) scalare
▸ **scale down** VT + ADV ridurre proporzionalmente

scaled-down [ˈskeɪldˌdaʊn] ADJ su scala ridotta

scale drawing N disegno in scala

scale model N modellino in scala

scales [skeɪlz] NPL **1** (pair *or* set of) **scales** bilancia; **he tips the scales at 70 kilos** pesa 70 chili; **to turn** *or* **tip the scales in sb's/sth's favour** far pendere la bilancia dalla parte di qn/qc; **to turn** *or* **tip the scales against sb** giocare a sfavore di qn; **the scales of justice** la bilancia della giustizia **2** (*also:* **bathroom scales**) bilancia *f* pesapersone, *inv*

scal·lion [ˈskælɪən] N cipollotto; (*USA: shallot*) scalogno

scal·lop [ˈskɒləp] N **1** (*Zool*) pettine *m* **2** (*Culin*) cappa santa **3** (*Sewing*) smerlo

scalp [skælp] N cuoio capelluto; (*as trophy*) scalpo ♦ VT scotennare; (*USA: Stock Exchange*) speculare in Borsa

scal·pel [ˈskælpəl] N bisturi *m inv*

scalp·er [ˈskælpə^r] N (*USA fam: of tickets*) bagarino

scam [skæm] N (*fam*) truffa

scamp [skæmp] N (*fam: child*) peste *f*

scamp·er [ˈskæmpə^r] VI + ADV (*child*): **to scamper about** scorrazzare; **to scamper in/out** *etc* entrare/uscire *etc* di corsa; **to scamper away, scamper off** darsela a gambe

scam·pi [ˈskæmpi] NPL scampi *mpl*

scan [skæn] VT **1** (*inspect closely: horizon, sb's face, crowd*) scrutare; (: *newspaper*) leggere attentamente; **he scans the papers for European news** legge con attenzione i giornali alla ricerca di notizie dall'Europa; **she scanned the crowd for Matt** ha scrutato la folla alla ricerca di Matt **2** (*glance at quickly*) dare un'occhiata a, scorrere **3** (*machine*) leggere; (*Radar: sea bed*) scandagliare; (: *sky*) esplorare; (*image*) scannerizzare; **all luggage is scanned before loading** i bagagli vengono passati ai raggi x prima di essere caricati; **I had trouble scanning this photo** ho avuto delle difficoltà nello scannerizzare questa foto ♦ VI (*Poetry*) scandire ♦ N (*Med*) ecografia

scan·dal [ˈskændl] N **1** (*public furore, disgrace*) scandalo; **it's a scandal that** è uno scandalo *or* è scandaloso che + *sub*; **it caused a scandal** ha fatto scandalo **2** (*gossip*) chiacchiere *fpl*, pettegolezzi *mpl*; **have you heard the latest scandal about ...?** hai sentito l'ultima su...?

scan·dal·ize [ˈskændəˌlaɪz] VT scandalizzare

scan·dal·ous [ˈskændələs] ADJ scandaloso(-a)

Scan·di·na·via [ˌskændɪˈneɪvɪə] N la Scandinavia

Scan·di·na·vian [ˌskændɪˈneɪvɪən] ADJ, N scandinavo(-a)

scan·ner [ˈskænə^r] N (*Radar, Med*) scanner *m inv*; (*for bar codes*) lettore *m* di codice a barre

scant [skænt] ADJ (*comp* -er, *superl* -est) scarso(-a); **with scant courtesy** poco cortesemente; **to pay scant attention to** prestare poca attenzione a; **they have scant respect for him** hanno scarsa considerazione per lui

scanti·ly [ˈskæntɪlɪ] ADV: **scantily clad** *or* **dressed** succintamente vestito(-a)

scanty [ˈskæntɪ] ADJ (*comp* -ier, *superl* -iest) (*meal etc*) scarso(-a); (*clothing*) succinto(-a); (*swimsuit*) ridotto(-a)

scape·goat [ˈskeɪpˌgəʊt] N capro espiatorio

scar [skɑː^r] N (*Med*) cicatrice *f*; (*on face*) sfregio, cicatrice; (*fig: on landscape etc*) segno; **it left a deep scar on his mind** gli ha lasciato il segno ♦ VT (*gen*) lasciare le cicatrici su; (*face*) sfregiare; (*fig*) segnare, lasciare il segno su; **scarred by acne** butterato(-a) dall'acne; **a battle-scarred town** una città segnata dalla guerra ♦ VI (*also:* **scar over:** *heal*) cicatrizzarsi

scarce [skɛəs] ADJ (*comp* -r, *superl* -st) (*money, food, resources*) scarso(-a); (*copy, edition*) raro(-a); **to be scarce** scarseggiare; **to grow** *or* **become scarce** diventare raro(-a); **to make o.s. scarce** (*fig: fam*) squagliarsela

scarce·ly [ˈskɛəslɪ] ADV (*barely*) appena; **scarcely anybody** quasi nessuno; **scarcely ever** quasi mai; **I scarcely know what to say** non so proprio che dire; **I can scarcely believe**

it faccio fatica a crederci; **I've scarcely seen him** l'ho visto raramente; **I scarcely knew him** lo conoscevo appena; **it can scarcely be a coincidence** non può essere una coincidenza
❑ **scarcely** is not translated by the Italian word *scarsamente*

scar·city [ˈskɛəsɪtɪ], **scarce·ness** [ˈskɛəsnɪs] N (*of jobs, accommodation*) scarsezza, scarsità; (*of food*) penuria

scarcity value N: **this item has a certain scarcity value** questo oggetto ha un certo valore grazie alla sua rarità

scare [skɛə^r] N spavento, paura; **to cause a scare (amongst)** creare il panico (tra); **to give sb a scare** far prendere uno spavento a qn, mettere paura a qn; **we had a bit of a scare** abbiamo preso uno spavento; **a bomb scare** un allarme per sospetta presenza di una bomba ♦ VT spaventare, impaurire; **you scared me!** mi hai spaventato!; **to scare sb to death, scare sb stiff** (*fam*) spaventare qn a morte
▸ **scare away, scare off** VT + ADV (*dog*) mettere in fuga; (*fig: subj: price*) far scappare; **the price scared him away** il prezzo l'ha scoraggiato

scare·crow [ˈskɛəkrəʊ] N (*also fig*) spaventapasseri *m inv*

scared [skɛəd] ADJ impaurito(-a), spaventato(-a); **to be scared (of)** aver paura (di); **are you scared of him?** hai paura di lui?; **to be scared to death, be scared stiff** essere spaventato(-a) a morte, essere mezzo(-a) morto(-a) di paura; **to be scared out of one's wits** non capire più niente dalla paura

scare·monger [ˈskɛəˌmʌŋgə^r] N allarmista *m/f*

scarf [skɑːf] N (*pl* **scarfs** *or* **scarves**) **1** (*long*) sciarpa **2** (*also:* **headscarf**) foulard *m inv*

scar·let [ˈskɑːlɪt] N scarlatto ♦ ADJ scarlatto(-a); **a scarlet ribbon** un nastro scarlatto

scarlet fever N scarlattina

scarp·er [ˈskɑːpə^r] VI (*Brit fam*) darsela a gambe

scarves [skɑːvz] NPL *of* **scarf**

scary [ˈskɛərɪ] ADJ (*comp* -ier, *superl* -iest) (*fam*) che fa paura; **to be scary** fare paura; **it was really scary** faceva veramente paura; **a scary film** un film del brivido

scath·ing [ˈskeɪðɪŋ] ADJ (*remark, criticism*) aspro(-a); (*look*) sprezzante; **to be scathing about sth** essere molto critico(-a) nei confronti di qc; **a scathing attack** un duro attacco

scat·ter [ˈskætə^r] VT **1** (*gen*) spargere; (*papers*) sparpagliare **2** (*disperse: crowd, clouds*) disperdere; (: *enemy*) mettere in fuga; **her relatives are scattered about the world** la sua famiglia è sparsa per il mondo; **toys were scattered everywhere** c'erano giocattoli sparsi dappertutto ♦ VI (*crowd*) disperdersi; **the crowd scattered** la folla si disperse

scatter·brained [ˈskætəˌbreɪnd] ADJ (*fam*) sventato(-a), sbadato(-a)

scat·tered [ˈskætəd] ADJ (*books, houses*) sparso(-a), sparpagliato(-a); (*population*) sparso(-a); **scattered showers** precipitazioni *fpl* sparse; **scattered with** (*strewn*) cosparso(-a) di

scav·enge [ˈskævɪndʒ] VT (*food*) cercare; (*streets*) pulire ♦ VI (*hyenas, birds*) nutrirsi di carogne; **to scavenge (for)** (*person*) frugare tra i rifiuti (alla ricerca di)

scav·en·ger [ˈskævɪndʒə^r] N (*animal*) insetto (*or* animale *m*) necrofago; (*person*) chi fruga nei rifiuti alla ricerca di qualcosa

sce·nario [sɪˈnɑːrɪəʊ] N scenario; **try to imagine all possible scenarios** cerca di immaginare tutte le possibili situazioni

scene [siːn] N **1** (*gen, also Theatre, Cine, TV*) scena; **indoor/outdoor scenes** interni/esterni *mpl*; **the scene is set in a castle** la scena si svolge in un castello; **to set the scene** (*fig*) creare l'atmosfera; **behind the scenes** (*also fig*) dietro le quinte; **the political scene in Italy** il quadro politico in Italia; **the Punk scene** il mondo dei punk; **the music scene** il mondo della musica; **scenes of violence** scene di violenza; **to make a scene** (*fam: fuss*) fare una scenata **2** (*of crime, accident*) luogo, scena; **at the scene of the crime** sul luogo *or* sulla scena del delitto; **she needs a change of scene** ha bisogno di cambiare aria; **to appear** *or* **come on the scene** (*also fig*) entrare in scena; **it's not my scene** (*fam*) non è il mio genere **3** (*sight*) scena, spettacolo; (*view*) vista, spettacolo; **a scene of utter destruction** una scena di totale distruzione; **it was an amazing scene** è stata una scena incredibile

scen·ery [ˈsiːnərɪ] N (*landscape*) paesaggio, panorama *m*; (*Theatre*) scenario, scenari *mpl*

sce·nic [ˈsiːnɪk] ADJ (*view*) pittoresco(-a); (*road, railway*) panoramico(-a)

scent [sɛnt] N 1 (*smell, perfume*) profumo 2 (*track*) tracce *fpl*, pista; **to follow/lose the scent** seguire/perdere le tracce *or* la pista; **to pick up the scent** fiutare le tracce; **to put** *or* **throw sb off the scent** (*fig*) far perdere le tracce a qn, sviare qn ♦ VT 1 **to scent (with)** (*make sth smell nice*) profumare (di *or* con) 2 (*smell*) fiutare

scep·tic, skep·tic (*USA*) [ˈskɛptɪk] N scettico(-a)

scep·ti·cal, skep·ti·cal (*USA*) [ˈskɛptɪkəl] ADJ: **sceptical (of** *or* **about)** scettico(-a) (su *or* circa)

scep·ti·cism, skep·ti·cism (*USA*) [ˈskɛptɪˌsɪzəm] N scetticismo

scep·tre, scep·ter (*USA*) [ˈsɛptəʳ] N scettro

sched·ule [ˈʃɛdjuːl, (*USA*) ˈskɛdjuːl] N 1 (*timetable: of work, visits, events*) programma *m*, piano *m*; **the work is behind/ahead of schedule** il lavoro è in ritardo/in anticipo sul previsto; **on schedule** in orario; **we are working to a very tight schedule** il nostro programma di lavoro è molto intenso; **a busy schedule** un programma fitto d'impegni; **everything went according to schedule** tutto è andato secondo i piani *or* secondo il previsto 2 (*list: of contents, goods*) lista; (*Customs, Tax etc*) tabella ♦ VT (*date, time*) fissare, stabilire; (*visit, event*) programmare; **as scheduled** come stabilito; **scheduled flight** volo di linea; **the meeting is scheduled for 7:00** *or* **to begin at 7:00** la riunione è fissata per le 7; **this building is scheduled for demolition** questo edificio è destinato alla demolizione

scheduled flight [ˈʃɛdjuːld, (*USA*) ˈskɛdjuːld] N 1 (*date, time*) fissato(-a), (fissata) 2 (*visit, event*) programmato(-a), (programmata) 3 (*train, bus, stop*) previsto(-a) (sull'orario); **scheduled flight** volo di linea

sche·mat·ic [skɪˈmætɪk] ADJ schematico(-a)

scheme [skiːm] N 1 (*plan*) piano; (*method*) sistema *m*; **a scheme to rebuild** *or* **for rebuilding sth** un piano per la ricostruzione di qc; **a scheme of work** un piano *or* programma *m* di lavoro; **a road-widening scheme** un progetto di ampliamento della strada; **it's some crazy scheme of his** è una delle sue balzane idee; (*dishonest plan, plot*): **scheme (to do** *or* **for doing sth/for sth)** piano (per fare qc/per qc); **a scheme for making money quickly** un piano per far soldi velocemente 3 (*arrangement*) sistemazione *f*; **colour scheme** combinazione *f* di colori; **man's place in the scheme of things** (*fig*) il posto dell'uomo nell'ordine delle cose ♦ VI: **to scheme (to do)** (*intrigue*) tramare (per fare), complottare (per fare)

schem·ing [ˈskiːmɪŋ] ADJ intrigante ♦ N intrighi *mpl*, macchinazioni *fpl*

schism [ˈsɪzəm, ˈskɪzəm] N scisma *m*

schizo·phre·nia [ˌskɪtsəˈfriːnjə] N schizofrenia

schizo·phren·ic [ˌskɪtsəʊˈfrɛnɪk] ADJ, N schizofrenico(-a)

schol·ar [ˈskɒləʳ] N (*learned person*) erudito(-a), studioso(-a); **a famous Dickens scholar** un noto studioso di Dickens; **he's never been much of a scholar** non è mai stato portato per gli studi

❏ **scholar** is not translated by the Italian word *scolaro*

schol·ar·ly [ˈskɒləlɪ] ADJ dotto(-a), erudito(-a)

schol·ar·ship [ˈskɒləʃɪp] N 1 (*learning*) erudizione *f*, cultura 2 (*award, grant*) borsa di studio; **to win a scholarship** vincere una borsa di studio

school[1] [skuːl] N 1 (*gen*) scuola; **to be at/go to school** frequentare la/andare a scuola; **to leave school** terminare gli studi; **school of motoring** scuola guida, autoscuola; **the Dutch school** (*Art*) la scuola olandese; **school of thought** corrente *f* di pensiero; **of the old school** (*fig*) di vecchio stampo 2 (*Univ*) facoltà *f inv*; **medical/law school** facoltà di medicina/giurisprudenza; **art school** istituto d'arte; **she's at law school** studia legge; **School of Interpreters** Scuola Interpreti ♦ VT (*animal*) addestrare; (*reaction, voice etc*) controllare; **he schooled himself in patience** *or* **to be patient** ha imparato ad essere paziente ♦ ADJ (*year, fees etc*) scolastico(-a); **during school hours, in school time** durante l'orario scolastico

school[2] [skuːl] N (*of fish*) banco

school age N età *f inv* scolare

school·book [ˈskuːlbʊk] N libro scolastico, libro di scuola

school·boy [ˈskuːlbɔɪ] N scolaro

school·child [ˈskuːltʃaɪld] N (*pl* **-children**) scolaro(-a)

school·days [ˈskuːldeɪz] NPL tempi *mpl* della scuola

school·girl [ˈskuːlɡɜːl] N scolara

school·ing [ˈskuːlɪŋ] N istruzione *f*; **compulsory schooling** istruzione *f* obbligatoria, scuola dell'obbligo

school·master [ˈskuːlmɑːstəʳ] N (*in primary school*) maestro; (*in secondary school*) professore *m*

school·mistress [ˈskuːlmɪstrɪs] N (*in primary school*) maestra; (*in secondary school*) professoressa

school report N (*Brit*) scheda di valutazione scolastica, pagella

school·room [ˈskuːlrʊm] N aula

school·teacher [ˈskuːltiːtʃəʳ] N insegnante *m/f*

school·yard [ˈskuːljɑːd] N (*USA*) cortile *m* della scuola

schoon·er [ˈskuːnəʳ] N 1 (*Naut*) schooner *m inv*, goletta 2 (*Brit: sherry glass*) bicchiere *m* da sherry; (*USA: beer glass*) boccale *m* da birra

sci·ati·ca [saɪˈætɪkə] N (*Med*) sciatica

sci·ence [ˈsaɪəns] N scienza; (*Scol*) le materie scientifiche; **the sciences** le scienze; **the natural/social sciences** le scienze naturali/sociali ♦ ADJ (*teacher, exam*) di scienze; (*subject, equipment, laboratory*) scientifico(-a)

science fiction N fantascienza

sci·en·tif·ic [ˌsaɪənˈtɪfɪk] ADJ scientifico(-a)

sci·en·tist [ˈsaɪəntɪst] N scienziato(-a)

sci-fi [ˈsaɪˌfaɪ] N ABBR (*fam*) = **science fiction**

Scil·ly Isles [ˈsɪlˌaɪlz] NPL: **the Scilly Isles, the Scillies** le isole *fpl* Scilly

scin·til·lat·ing [ˈsɪntɪˌleɪtɪŋ] ADJ (*jewels, chandelier*) scintillante; (*wit, conversation, company*) brillante

scis·sors [ˈsɪzəz] NPL forbici *fpl*; **a pair of scissors** un paio di forbici

scle·ro·sis [sklɪˈrəʊsɪs] N (*Med*) sclerosi *f*

scoff [skɒf] VI: **to scoff (at sb/sth)** (*mock*) farsi beffe (di qn/qc); **my friends scoffed at the idea** i miei amici hanno riso dell'idea ♦ VT (*Brit fam: eat*) papparsi, spazzolare; **he scoffed the lot** si è pappato tutto, ha spazzolato tutto quello che c'era

scold [skəʊld] VT: **to scold sb (for doing sth)** sgridare qn (per aver fatto qc)

scold·ing [ˈskəʊldɪŋ] N lavata di capo, sgridata

scone [skɒn, skəʊn] N *tipo di focaccina da tè*

scoop [skuːp] N 1 (*for flour etc*) paletta; (*for ice cream*) cucchiaio dosatore; (*for water*) mestolo, ramaiolo 2 (*also:* **scoopful**) palettata; cucchiaiata; mestolata; **three scoops of ice-cream** tre palline di gelato 3 (*Press*) scoop *m inv*, colpo giornalistico; (*Comm*) affarone *m*; **a wonderful scoop** un ottimo scoop ♦ VT (*Comm: market*) accaparrarsi; (*: profit*) intascare; (*Comm, Press: competitors*) battere sul tempo; (*Press*): **to scoop an exclusive (about)** accaparrarsi l'esclusiva (su)

❏ **scoop** is not translated by the Italian word *scopo*

▸ **scoop out** VT + ADV (*flour, water etc*) svuotare (con paletta, cucchiaio etc); (*hole*) scavare

▸ **scoop up** VT + ADV (*child*) sollevare (tra le braccia); (*books*) raccogliere

scoot·er [ˈskuːtəʳ] N scooter *m inv*; (*child's*) monopattino; **he was riding a scooter** era in sella ad uno scooter

scope [skəʊp] N (*opportunity: for action*) possibilità *fpl*; (*range: of law, activity*) ambito; (*capacity: of person*) capacità *fpl*; (*: of plan, undertaking*) portata; **the scope of the plan is limited** la portata del piano à limitata; **it's beyond the scope of a child's mind** è al di sopra delle capacità di un bambino; **it's well within his scope to ...** è perfettamente in grado di...; **it is within/beyond the scope of this book** rientra/non rientra nei limiti di questo libro

❏ **scope** is not translated by the Italian word *scopo*

scorch [skɔːtʃ] N (*also:* **scorch mark**) bruciacchiatura ♦ VT (*fabric*) bruciacchiare; (*subj: sun, fire: earth, grass*) bruciare; **hot sun will scorch the leaves** il calore del sole seccherà le foglie; **the bomb scorched one side of the building** la bomba ha bruciacchiato un lato dell'edificio ♦ VI (*esp Brit: fam: car*) andare a tutta velocità

scorched earth policy [ˌskɔːtʃtˈɜːθˌpɒlɪsɪ] N tattica del fare terra bruciata

scorch·er [ˈskɔːtʃəʳ] N (fam: hot day) giornata torrida

scorch·ing [ˈskɔːtʃɪŋ] ADJ (also: **scorching hot**) rovente; (day) torrido(-a); (sun) che spacca le pietre; (sand) bollente; **it's scorching** fa un caldo pazzesco

score [skɔːʳ] N **1** (Sport, Cards) punteggio, punti mpl; **to keep (the) score** segnare i punti; **there's no score yet** (Sport) finora nessuno ha segnato (un punto); **there was no score in the match** (Sport) hanno finito zero a zero; **the score was three nil** il punteggio era tre a zero; **to know the score** (fig: fam) sapere come stanno le cose; **to have an old score to settle with sb** (fig) avere un vecchio conto da saldare con qn **2** (account) motivo, titolo; **on that score** a questo riguardo **3** (cut, mark: on wood) scalfittura; (: on leather, card) incisione f **4** (Mus: of opera) partitura, spartito; (: of film) colonna sonora **5** (twenty): **a score** venti; **a score of people** una ventina di persone; **scores of** (fig) molti(-e); **scores of times** molte volte; **scores of people** (fig) un sacco di gente ♦ VT **1** (goal, point, runs) segnare; (success) ottenere; **to score 75% in an exam** prendere 75 su 100 a or in un esame; **to score a hit** (Fencing) fare una stoccata; (Shooting) centrare il bersaglio; **to score a hit with sth** (fig) far centro con qc; **to score a hit with sb** (fig) far colpo su qn; **he scored a goal** ha segnato una rete **2** (cut: leather, wood, card) incidere **3** (music: for piano etc) comporre; (: for film) comporre la colonna sonora ♦ VI **1** (Sport: footballer) segnare; (: player) totalizzare; (: keep score) tenere il punteggio; **to score 6 out of 10** (in exam, test) prendere 6 su 10; **to score over sb** (fig) dare dei punti a qn; **who's going to score?** chi tiene il punteggio? **2** (fam!: have sex with): **to score (with sb)** portarsi a letto qn

  ► **score off** VT + ADV **1** (name, item on list) cancellare, spuntare **2** (fig: in argument): **to score points off sb** avere la meglio su qn

  ► **score out, score through** VT + ADV cancellare, cancellare (con un segno)

score·board [ˈskɔːˌbɔːd] N tabellone m segnapunti, inv

score·card [ˈskɔːˌkɑːd] N cartoncino m segnapunti, inv

score·line [ˈskɔːlaɪn] N (Sport) risultato

scor·er [ˈskɔːrəʳ] N (keeping score) segnapunti m/f inv; (player) marcatore(-trice); **the scorer of the winning goal** il marcatore del gol vincente; **I'll be the scorer** segno io i punti

scorn [skɔːn] N disprezzo, scherno; **to pour scorn on sb/sth** deridere qn/qc ♦ VT (gen) disprezzare; (attempt) ridicolizzare; (advice, offer) respingere con sdegno; **to scorn to tell a lie** (frm) rifiutarsi sdegnosamente di dire una bugia

scorn·ful [ˈskɔːnfʊl] ADJ sprezzante; **to be scornful about sth** parlare con disprezzo di qc

Scor·pio [ˈskɔːpɪəʊ] N (Astron, Astrol) Scorpione m

scor·pi·on [ˈskɔːpɪən] N scorpione m

Scot [skɒt] N scozzese m/f; **the Scots** gli scozzesi

Scotch [skɒtʃ] N (also: **Scotch whisky**) scotch m inv

scotch [skɒtʃ] VT (attempt, plan) bloccare; (revolt, uprising) stroncare; (rumour, claim) mettere a tacere

Scotch tape (USA, Trademark) scotch m

scot-free [skɒtˈfriː] ADJ: **to get off scot-free** (unpunished) farla franca; (unhurt) uscire illeso(-a)

Scot·land [ˈskɒtlənd] N la Scozia

Scots [skɒts] ADJ scozzese; **a Scots accent** un accento scozzese

Scots·man [ˈskɒtsmən] N (pl -men) scozzese m

Scots·woman [ˈskɒtsˌwʊmən] N (pl -women) scozzese f

Scot·tish [ˈskɒtɪʃ] ADJ scozzese; **the Scottish Parliament** il Parlamento scozzese

scoun·drel [ˈskaʊndrəl] N (old) canaglia, furfante m/f; (hum: child) furfantello(-a), birba

scour [ˈskaʊəʳ] VT **1** (clean: pan, floor etc) sfregare **2** (search: area, countryside) setacciare, perlustrare, battere palmo a palmo; **he scoured the photo album** ha esaminato attentamente l'album di foto; **rescue crews scoured a large area** i soccorritori hanno perlustrato una vasta zona

scour·er [ˈskaʊərəʳ] N (pad) paglietta

scourge [skɜːdʒ] N (also fig) flagello ♦ VT (beat) flagellare; (fig: bedevil) tormentare

scout [skaʊt] N (Mil) ricognitore m (persona); (boy) boy-scout m inv

  ► **scout around** VI + ADV andare alla ricerca

scowl [skaʊl] N espressione f accigliata; **with a scowl** con lo sguardo torvo ♦ VI accigliarsi; **to scowl at sb** guardare qn in malo modo, guardare qn torvo; **he scowled but said nothing** ha aggrottato le sopracciglia senza dire nulla

scrab·ble [ˈskræbl] VI (claw): **to scrabble (at)** raspare, grattare; **to scrabble about** or **around for sth** cercare a tastoni qc

scrag·gy [ˈskrægɪ] ADJ (comp -ier, superl -iest) (neck, limb) scheletrico(-a); (animal) pelle e ossa inv

scram [skræm] VI (fam) filare, filarsela

scram·ble [ˈskræmbl] VI **1** **to scramble down/along** scendere/avanzare a fatica; **to scramble out** uscire in fretta; **to scramble for** (coins, seats, job) azzuffarsi per prendere; **he scrambled up (the hill)** si è inerpicato su (per la collina); **we scrambled over the rocks** ci siamo inerpicati sulle rocce **2** (Sport): **to go scrambling** fare il motocross ♦ VT **1** (Culin: eggs) strapazzare **2** (Telec: message) disturbare con interferenze ♦ N **1** (rush) corsa; **the scramble to obtain funding** la corsa ai finanziamenti **2** (Sport: motorcycle meeting) gara di motocross

scram·bled eggs [ˌskræmbldˈegz] NPL uova fpl strapazzate

scrap[1] [skræp] N **1** (small piece) pezzo, pezzetto; (fig: of truth) briciolo; **a scrap of paper** un pezzo di carta; **a scrap of conversation** un frammento di conversazione; **there's not a scrap of proof** non c'è la benché minima prova; **it's not a scrap of use** non serve a un bel niente **2 scraps** NPL (leftovers) avanzi mpl **3** (iron, gold) scarti mpl; **to sell sth for scrap** vendere qc come rottame ♦ VT (gen) buttar via; (ship, car) demolire; (fig: plan) scartare; **in the end the plan was scrapped** alla fine il progetto venne scartato

scrap[2] [skræp] (fam) N (fight) bisticcio, zuffa; **he got into a scrap with a bigger boy** si è azzuffato con un ragazzo più grande ♦ VI: **to scrap (with sb)** bisticciare or azzuffarsi (con qn)

scrap·book [ˈskræpˌbʊk] N album m inv per ritagli (di giornali, fotografie etc)

scrap dealer, scrap merchant N rottamaio(-a), commerciante m/f in rottami

scrape [skreɪp] N **1** (act) raschiatura; (sound) stridio; (mark) graffio; (on leg, elbow) scorticatura, sbucciatura **2** (fig) pasticcio, guaio; **to get into a scrape** mettersi nei pasticci or nei guai; **to get out of a scrape** tirarsi fuori dai pasticci or dai guai ♦ VT (knee) scorticare, sbucciare; (clean: vegetables) raschiare, grattare; (: walls, woodwork) raschiare; **the truck scraped the wall** il camion ha strisciato il muro; **to scrape a living** sbarcare il lunario; **we managed to scrape enough money together** siamo riusciti a racimolare abbastanza soldi; **to scrape the bottom of the barrel** (fig) raschiare il fondo del barile ♦ VI (make sound) grattare; (rub): **to scrape (against)** strusciare (contro)

  ► **scrape along, scrape by** VI + ADV (fam: manage) cavarsela; (: live) tirare avanti

  ► **scrape off, scrape away** VT + ADV grattare via, raschiare via; **she scraped the ice off the car windows** ha grattato via il ghiaccio dai finestrini della macchina ♦ VT + PREP grattare via

  ► **scrape through** VI + ADV (succeed) farcela per un pelo, cavarsela ♦ VI + PREP (exam) passare per il rotto della cuffia; **I managed to scrape through the last exam** sono riuscito a passare l'ultimo esame per il rotto della cuffia

scrap metal N rottami mpl

scrap paper N (for scribbling on) (fogli mpl di) carta per appunti; (for recycling) carta da destinare al riciclo

scrap·py [ˈskræpɪ] ADJ (comp -ier, superl -iest) (essay etc) senza capo né coda; (knowledge, education) lacunoso(-a); (meal) arrangiato(-a)

scrap yard N deposito di rottami; (for cars) cimitero delle macchine

scratch [skrætʃ] N **1** (mark) graffio, graffiatura; **it's just a scratch** è solo un graffio; **without a scratch** (unharmed) illeso(-a), senza un graffio **2** (noise): **I heard a scratch at the door** ho sentito grattare alla porta **3 to start from scratch** (fig) cominciare or partire da zero; **his work wasn't** or **didn't come up to scratch** il suo lavoro non è stato all'altezza; **to keep sth up to scratch** mantenere qc al livello desiderato

♦ VT **1** (*gen*) graffiare; (*one's name*) incidere; **we've barely scratched the surface** (*fig: of problem, topic*) l'abbiamo appena sfiorato; **the cat scratched me** il gatto mi ha graffiato **2** (*to relieve itch*) grattare; **he scratched his head** si è grattato la testa; **you scratch my back and I'll scratch yours** (*fig*) una mano lava l'altra **3** (*cancel: meeting, game: Comput*) cancellare; (*cross off list: horse, competitor*) eliminare ♦ VI (*person, dog*) grattarsi; (*hens*) razzolare, raspare; (*pen*) raschiare; (*clothing*) pungere; **the dog scratched at the door** il cane raspava alla porta
▸ **scratch out** VT + ADV (*from list*) cancellare; **to scratch sb's eyes out** cavare gli occhi a qn
scratch card N (*card*) gratta e vinci *m inv*
scratch pad N (*USA*) bloc-notes *m inv*
scrawl [skrɔːl] N (*handwriting*) scrittura illeggibile; (*brief note*) messaggio scarabocchiato ♦ VT scarabocchiare ♦ VI scarabocchiare
scrawny ['skrɔːnɪ] ADJ (*comp* -**ier**, *superl* -**iest**) (*neck, limb*) scheletrico(-a); (*animal, person*) pelle e ossa *inv*
scream [skriːm] N (*of pain, fear*) grido, urlo; **screams of laughter** grasse risate *fpl*; **he let out a scream** cacciò un urlo; **it was a scream** (*fig: fam*) era da crepar dal ridere; **he's a scream** (*fig: fam*) è una sagoma, è uno spasso ♦ VT (*subj: person: abuse, insults*) urlare; (*subj: poster, headlines*) strombazzare ♦ VI gridare, urlare; **to scream at sb (to do sth)** gridare a qn (di fare qc); **to scream (out) with pain** gridare di *or* dal dolore; **to scream for help** gridare aiuto; **to scream with laughter** sbellicarsi dalle risa
scree [skriː] N ghiaione *m*
screech [skriːtʃ] N (*of brakes, tyres or tires*) stridio, stridore *m*; (*of owl*) strido; (*of person*) strillo; **a screech of laughter** una risata stridula ♦ VI (*person*) strillare; (*owl, brakes*) stridere
screen [skriːn] N **1** (*in room*) paravento; (*for fire*) parafuoco; (*fig: of trees*) barriera; (*: of smoke*) cortina **2** (*Cine, TV, Radar*) schermo; **stars of the big/small screen** divi(-e) del grande/piccolo schermo ♦ VT **1 to screen (from)** (*hide: from view, sight*) nascondere (da); (*protect*) schermire (da), riparare (da); **he screened his eyes (from the sun) with his hand** si schermiva gli occhi (dal sole) con la mano **2** (*TV: film, programme*) mandare in onda; (*: Cine: film*) dare al cinema; **his earlier films were only screened in France** i suoi primi film sono usciti solo in Francia **3** (*sieve: coal*) setacciare; (*fig: person: for security*) passare al vaglio; (*: for job*) selezionare; (*: for illness*) fare uno screening
screen-ing ['skriːnɪŋ] N **1** (*of film*) proiezione *f*; (*TV*) messa in onda **2** (*also:* **medical screening**) screening *m inv* **3** (*for security*) controlli *mpl* (di sicurezza)
screen memory N (*Psych*) ricordi *mpl* di copertura
screen-play ['skriːnˌpleɪ] N sceneggiatura
screen-sav-er ['skriːnˌseɪvəᵊ] N (*Comput*) screen saver *m inv*, salvaschermo
screen test N provino cinematografico
screw [skruː] N **1** vite *f*; (*Brit: old: of sweets*) cartoccio; **he's got a screw loose** (*fig: fam*) gli manca una rotella; **to put the screws on sb** (*fig: fam*) far pressione su qn **2** (*propeller*) elica **3** (*fam: prison officer*) secondino **4** (*fam!: sexual intercourse*) chiavata (*fam!*) ♦ VT **1** avvitare; **to screw sth to the wall** fissare qc al muro con viti; **I screwed the shelf to the wall** ho avvitato lo scaffale al muro; **to screw sth (up) tight** avvitare bene qc; **to screw money out of sb** (*fam*) far scucire soldi a qn; **to screw one's head round** storcere la testa; **to have one's head screwed on** avere la testa sulle spalle **2** (*fam!: have sex with*) chiavare (*fam!*); **screw you!** va' a farti fottere! ♦ VI (*fam!: have sex*) chiavare (*fam!*)
▸ **screw off** VI + ADV svitarsi ♦ VT + ADV svitare
▸ **screw together** VI + ADV avvitarsi ♦ VT + ADV (*kit*) montare con viti; (*two pieces*) avvitare
▸ **screw up** VT + ADV **1** (*paper, material*) spiegazzare; **to screw up one's eyes** strizzare gli occhi; **to screw up one's face** fare una smorfia; **to screw up one's courage** (*fig*) armarsi di coraggio **2** (*fam: ruin*) mandare all'aria; **he really screwed it up this time!** stavolta ha fatto davvero un casino!; **I've screwed everything up** ho rovinato tutto; **to screw sb up** (*fig: fam*) incasinare qn; **to be screwed up (about sth)** (*fig: fam*) essere incasinato(-a) (per qc)
screw-driver ['skruːˌdraɪvəᵊ] N cacciavite *m inv*

screwed-up [ˌskruːd'ʌp] ADJ (*fam*): **she's totally screwed-up** è nel pallone
screwy ['skruːɪ] ADJ (*comp* -**ier**, *superl* -**iest**) (*fam: mad*) strambo(-a), svitato(-a)
scrib-ble ['skrɪbl] N scarabocchio ♦ VT scribacchiare, scarabocchiare; **to scribble sth down** scarabocchiare qc ♦ VI scarabocchiare
scribe [skraɪb] N scriba *m*
script [skrɪpt] N **1** (*Cine, Theatre*) copione *m*, sceneggiatura; (*Brit: answer paper*) elaborato; (*writing system*) caratteri *mpl*, sistema di scrittura; **Arabic script** caratteri arabi **2** (*writing*) scrittura
script-ed ['skrɪptɪd] ADJ (*Radio, TV*) preparato(-a)
Scrip-ture ['skrɪptʃəᵊ] N (*also:* **Holy Scripture**) Sacre Scritture *fpl*
script-writer ['skrɪptˌraɪtəᵊ] N sceneggiatore(-trice), soggettista *m*/*f*
scroll [skrəʊl] N (*roll of parchment*) rotolo (di pergamena); (*ancient manuscript*) papiro, pergamena; (*Archit*) voluta ♦ VT (*Comput: text*) far scorrere su video; **I scrolled through the text looking for the sentence** ho scorso il testo alla ricerca della frase
scroll bar N (*Comput*) barra di scorrimento
scro-tum ['skrəʊtəm] N (*pl* **scrota** *or* **scrotums**) scroto
scrounge [skraʊndʒ] (*fam*) N: **to be on the scrounge (for sth)** scroccare (qc); **here he comes, on the scrounge again** eccolo, il solito scroccone ♦ VT (*gen*) scroccare; **to scrounge sth off** *or* **from sb** scroccare qc a qn ♦ VI: **to scrounge on** *or* **off sb** vivere alle spalle di qn
scroung-er ['skraʊndʒəᵊ] N (*fam*) scroccone(-a); (*in society*) parassita *m*
scrub[1] [skrʌb] N (*brushwood*) macchia
scrub[2] [skrʌb] N (*clean*) strofinata ♦ VT **1** (*clean*) strofinare con lo spazzolone; (*hands etc*) pulire con lo spazzolino; **to scrub sth clean** pulire qc strofinandolo(-a) **2** (*fam: cancel*) annullare; (*: holiday, plan*) cancellare
▸ **scrub down** VT + ADV (*room, wall*) pulire a fondo con lo spazzolone
▸ **scrub off** VT + ADV (*mark, stain*) togliere strofinando
▸ **scrub up** VI + ADV (*doctor etc*) lavarsi le mani
scrubbing-brush ['skrʌbɪŋˌbrʌʃ] N spazzolone *m*
scruff [skrʌf] N **1 by the scruff of the neck** per la collottola **2** (*fam: untidy person*) sciattone(-a)
scruffy ['skrʌfɪ] ADJ (*comp* -**ier**, *superl* -**iest**) (*person, clothes, appearance*) trasandato(-a), sciatto(-a); (*building*) squallido(-a); (*paintwork*) malandato(-a)
scrum [skrʌm], **scrum-mage** ['skrʌmɪdʒ] N (*Rugby*) mischia; **loose/set scrum** mischia aperta/chiusa
scru-ple ['skruːpl] N scrupolo; **to have no scruples about doing sth** non avere scrupoli a fare qc
scru-pu-lous ['skruːpjʊləs] ADJ scrupoloso(-a)
scru-pu-lous-ly ['skruːpjʊləslɪ] ADV scrupolosamente; **he tries to be scrupulously fair/honest** cerca di essere più imparziale/onesto che può
scru-ti-nize ['skruːtɪˌnaɪz] VT (*work etc*) esaminare accuratamente; (*person's face*) scrutare; (*votes*) scrutinare
scru-ti-ny ['skruːtɪnɪ] N esame *m* accurato; (*Pol: of votes*) scrutinio; **under the scrutiny of sb** sotto la sorveglianza di qn; **to come under scrutiny** essere sottoposto(-a) ad un esame accurato; **it does not stand up to scrutiny** non regge ad un esame accurato
scu-ba ['skuːbə] N autorespiratore *m*
scuba diving N immersioni *fpl* subacquee (*con autorespiratore*)
scuff [skʌf] VT (*shoes*) scorticare; (*floor*) segnare; (*feet*) strascicare
scuf-fle ['skʌfl] N tafferuglio, zuffa ♦ VI: **to scuffle (with sb)** venire alle mani *or* azzuffarsi (con qn)
scul-lery ['skʌlərɪ] N retroscucina *m inv*, *f inv*
sculp-tor ['skʌlptəᵊ] N scultore *m*
sculp-ture ['skʌlptʃəᵊ] N scultura ♦ VT, VI scolpire
scum [skʌm] N (*on liquid*) schiuma; (*fig: pej: people*) feccia; **the scum of the earth** la feccia della società; **to remove the scum (from sth)** schiumare (qc)

scup·per ['skʌpə'] vт (*Naut*) autoaffondare; (*Brit fig: plan*) far naufragare

scur·ril·ous ['skʌrɪləs] ADJ (*remark*) scurrile; (*attack*) di bassa lega

scur·ry ['skʌrɪ] vɪ: **to scurry along/away** *etc* procedere/andarsene *etc* a tutta velocità; **to scurry about** aggirarsi frettolosamente

scur·vy ['skɜːvɪ] N scorbuto

scut·tle ['skʌtl] vт (*ship*) autoaffondare ♦ N **1** (*Naut*) portellino **2** (*also:* **coal scuttle**) secchio del carbone

scut·tle ['skʌtl] vɪ: **to scuttle away** *or* **off** filare via; **to scuttle in** entrare precipitosamente

scythe [saɪð] N falce *f* ♦ vт falciare

SD ABBR (*USA Post:* = **South Dakota**)

SDLP [ˌɛsdiːɛl'piː] N ABBR (*Brit Pol*) = **Social Democratic and Labour Party**

sea [siː] N mare *m*; **by** *or* **beside the sea** (*holiday*) al mare; (*village*) sul mare; **on the sea** (*boat*) sul mare, in mare; (*village, town*) sul mare; **to go by sea** andare per mare; **to go to sea** (*person*) diventare marinaio; **to put to sea** (*sailor*) uscire in mare; (*boat*) salpare; **to spend 3 years at sea** passare 3 anni in mare; (*out*) **at sea** al largo; **to look out to sea** guardare il mare; **heavy** *or* **rough sea(s)** mare grosso *or* agitato; **a delay caused by rough seas** un ritardo causato dalle cattive condizioni del mare; **to be all at sea** (*about* *or* **with sth**) (*fig*) non capirci niente (di qc); **a sea of faces** (*fig*) una marea di gente ♦ ADJ (*salt*) marino(-a); (*fish, air*) di mare; (*route, transport, port*) marittimo(-a); (*battle, power*) navale

sea bed N fondale *m* marino

sea bird N uccello marino

sea·board ['siːbɔːd] N litorale *m*

sea breeze N brezza marina

sea·farer ['siːfɛərə'] N navigatore *m*, navigante *m*

sea·faring ['siːfɛərɪŋ] ADJ (*community*) marinaro(-a); (*life*) da marinaio

sea·food ['siːfuːd] N frutti *mpl* di mare

sea front N lungomare *m*

sea·going ['siːgəʊɪŋ] ADJ (*nation*) marinaro(-a); (*ship*) d'alto mare

sea·gull ['siːgʌl] N gabbiano

seal¹ [siːl] N (*Zool*) foca

seal² [siːl] N (*gen*) sigillo; (*on parcel*) piombino; (*of door, lid*) chiusura ermetica; **to set one's seal to sth, to give the** *or* **one's seal of approval to sth** dare il proprio beneplacito a qc; **to set the seal on** (*bargain*) concludere; (*friendship*) suggellare ♦ vт **1** (*put seal on: document*) sigillare; (*close: envelope*) chiudere, incollare; (*: jar, tin*) chiudere ermeticamente; (*Culin: meat*) rosolare; **to seal an envelope** chiudere una busta; **my lips are sealed** (*fig*) sarò una tomba **2** (*decide: sb's fate*) segnare; (*: bargain*) concludere
  ► **seal off** vт + ADV (*close up: building, room*) sigillare; (*forbid entry to: area*) bloccare l'accesso a
  ► **seal up** vт + ADV (*parcel*) sigillare; (*jar, door*) chiudere ermeticamente

sea level N livello del mare

seal·ing wax ['siːlɪŋˌwæks] N ceralacca

sea lion N leone *m* marino, otaria

seal·skin ['siːlˌskɪn] N pelle *f* di foca

seam [siːm] N **1** (*Sewing*) cucitura; (*Welding*) saldatura; **to come apart at the seams** scucirsi; **trouser seams** le cuciture dei pantaloni; **my dress is bursting at the seams** scoppio dentro questo vestito; **the hall was bursting at the seams** (*fig*) l'aula era piena zeppa **2** (*Geol: of coal*) filone *m*, vena

sea·man ['siːmən] N (*pl* **-men**) marinaio

sea·man·ship ['siːmənʃɪp] N tecnica di navigazione

seam·less ['siːmlɪs] ADJ senza cucitura

seamy ['siːmɪ] ADJ (*comp* **-ier**, *superl* **-iest**) (*fam: district*) malfamato(-a); **the seamy side of life** gli aspetti più squallidi della vita

se·ance, sé·ance ['seɪɑ̃ːns] N seduta spiritica

sea·plane ['siːpleɪn] N idrovolante *m*

sea·port ['siːpɔːt] N porto di mare *or* marittimo

search [sɜːtʃ] N **1** (*for sth lost*) ricerca; **in search of** alla ricerca di; **to make a search for sb/sth** fare delle ricerche per trovare qn/qc; **the search was abandoned** la ricerca fu abbandonata **2** (*of person, building etc*) perquisizione *f*; **to carry out a search of sth** (*subj: police, customs official*) eseguire una perquisizione di qc; (*: thief*) frugare in qc **3** (*Comput*) ricerca; **"search and replace"** "ricerca e sostituzione" ♦ vт **1 to search (for)** (*subj: police etc*) perquisire (alla ricerca di); (*: thief*) frugare (alla ricerca di); (*: area, woods etc*) perlustrare *or* setacciare (alla ricerca di); **the police searched him for drugs** la polizia l'ha perquisito alla ricerca di droga; **they searched the woods for the puppy** hanno perlustrato i boschi alla ricerca del cucciolo; **search me!** (*fig: fam*) e che ne so io? **2** (*scan: records, documents, photograph*) esaminare minuziosamente; (*: notice-board, newspaper*) leggere attentamente; (*: Comput*) ricercare; (*: one's conscience*) interrogare; (*: one's memory*) frugare in ♦ vɪ **1** (*gen*) cercare; **to search after** *or* **for sb/sth** cercare qn/qc; **they're searching for the missing climbers** stanno cercando gli alpinisti dispersi; **to search through** *or* **in sth for sth** frugare *or* rovistare qc alla ricerca di qc **2** (*Comput*): **to search for** ricercare
  ► **search out** vт + ADV scovare; **the library eventually searched out the book I wanted** la biblioteca alla fine ha rintracciato il libro che cercavo

search engine N (*Comput*) motore *m* di ricerca

search·er ['sɜːtʃə'] N chi cerca

search·ing ['sɜːtʃɪŋ] ADJ (*look*) indagatore(-trice); (*examination*) minuzioso(-a); (*question*) pressante

search·light ['sɜːtʃˌlaɪt] N riflettore *m*

search party N squadra di soccorso

search warrant N mandato di perquisizione

sear·ing ['sɪərɪŋ] ADJ (*heat*) rovente; (*pain*) acuto(-a)

sea·shore ['siːʃɔː'] N riva del mare; **by the seashore** in riva al mare; **on the seashore** sulla riva del mare

sea·sick ['siːsɪk] ADJ: **to be seasick** avere *or* soffrire il mal di mare

sea·side ['siːsaɪd] N: **at the seaside** al mare; **to go to the seaside** andare al mare ♦ ADJ (*town*) di mare; (*holiday*) al mare

seaside resort N centro *or* stazione *f* balneare

sea·son ['siːzn] N (*gen*) stagione *f*; **to be in/out of season** essere di/fuori stagione; **the Christmas season** il periodo natalizio; **"Season's Greetings"** "Buone Feste"; **the busy season** (*for shops*) il periodo di punta; (*for hotels etc*) l'alta stagione; **during the holiday season** nel periodo delle vacanze; **football/fishing season** stagione calcistica/della pesca; **the open season** (*Hunting*) la stagione della caccia; **it's against the law to hunt during the closed season** è proibito dalla legge andare a caccia quando la stagione è chiusa; **in season** (*Zool*) in calore ♦ vт **1** (*wood*) stagionare **2** (*Culin*) condire; **season with salt and pepper** condite con sale e pepe

sea·son·al ['siːzənl] ADJ stagionale; **after seasonal adjustment** (*Econ*) dopo la destagionalizzazione

sea·soned ['siːznd] ADJ (*wood*) stagionato(-a); (*fig: worker, troops*) con esperienza; (*: actor*) consumato(-a); **a seasoned campaigner** un(a) veterano(-a); **a seasoned traveller** un (un') esperto(-a) viaggiatore(-trice)

sea·son·ing ['siːznɪŋ] N condimento

season ticket N (*Theatre, Rail, etc*) abbonamento

seat [siːt] N **1** (*chair*) sedia; (*in theatre etc*) posto; (*in bus, train, car etc*) posto, sedile *m*; (*on cycle*) sella, sellino; **are there any seats left?** ci sono posti?; **to take one's seat** prendere posto; **do take a seat** prego, si accomodi; **to take a back seat** (*fig*) restare in secondo piano **2** (*Pol*) seggio; **to keep/lose one's seat** essere/non essere rieletto(-a); **to win four seats from the nationalists** strappare quattro seggi ai nazionalisti; **to take one's seat in the (House of) Commons** iniziare la propria carriera di parlamentare **3** (*of chair*) sedile *m*; (*buttocks*) didietro; (*of trousers*) fondo **4** (*centre: of government, of infection*) sede *f*; (*: of learning*) centro **5** (*Horse-riding*) assetto ♦ vт **1** (*person etc*) far sedere; **to be seated** essere seduto(-a); **please be seated** accomodatevi per favore; **please remain seated** rimanete ai vostri posti per cortesia **2** (*subj: hall, cinema etc*) essere fornito(-a) di posti a sedere per; **the theatre seats 500** il teatro può accogliere 500 persone

seat belt N (*Aut, Aer*) cintura di sicurezza

seat·ing ['siːtɪŋ] N posti *mpl* a sedere

seating arrangements NPL sistemazione *fsg or* disposizione *fsg* dei posti

seating capacity N posti *mpl* a sedere

sea water N acqua di mare

sea·weed [ˈsiːˌwiːd] N alghe *fpl*; **a strand of seaweed** un'alga

sea·worthy [ˈsiːˌwɜːðɪ] ADJ idoneo(-a) alla navigazione

SEC [ˌɛsiːˈsiː] N ABBR (*USA:* = *Securities and Exchange Commission*) commissione di controllo sulle operazioni in Borsa

sec. ABBR = **second²**

seca·teurs [ˌsɛkəˈtɜːz] NPL cesoie *fpl*

se·cede [sɪˈsiːd] VI (*frm*): **to secede (from)** staccarsi (da)

se·clud·ed [sɪˈkluːdɪd] ADJ (*house*) appartato(-a), isolato(-a); (*life*) ritirato(-a)

se·clu·sion [sɪˈkluːʒən] N isolamento; **to live in seclusion** fare vita ritirata

sec·ond¹ [ˈsɛkənd] ADJ secondo(-a); **he's a second Beethoven** è un nuovo Beethoven; **give him a second chance** dagli un'altra opportunità; **second floor** (*Brit*) secondo piano; (*USA*) primo piano; **in second gear** (*Aut*) in seconda; **to travel second class** viaggiare in seconda classe; **to ask for a second opinion** (*Med*) chiedere un altro consulto; **second person** (*Gram*) seconda persona; **Charles the Second** Carlo II; **every second day/week** ogni due giorni/settimane; **to be second to none** non essere inferiore a nessuno; **to have second thoughts (about doing sth)** avere dei ripensamenti (quanto a fare qc); **we had second thoughts about it** ci abbiamo ripensato; **on second thoughts …** ripensandoci meglio… ♦ ADV 1 (*in race, competition etc*) al secondo posto; **to come second** arrivare secondo(-a), piazzarsi al secondo posto; **it's the second largest fish I've ever caught** ho preso soltanto un pesce più grosso di questo, finora 2 (*secondly*) in secondo luogo, secondo ♦ N 1 (*Boxing: in duel*) secondo 2 **in second** (*Aut*) in seconda 3 **he came a good second** (*in race*) è arrivato secondo con un buon tempo; **he came a poor second** è arrivato secondo ma con notevole scarto 4 (*Brit: Univ*) ≈ laurea con punteggio discreto 5 (*Comm: imperfect goods*) **seconds** NPL merce *fsg* di seconda scelta 6 (*fam: second helping*); **seconds** NPL bis *m inv* ♦ VT 1 (*motion, statement*) appoggiare; **I'll second that** (*fig*) l'appoggio, sono a favore 2 [sɪˈkɒnd] (*Brit: employee*) distaccare

sec·ond² [ˈsɛkənd] N (*in time, also Geog, Math*) (minuto) secondo; **at that very second** (proprio) in quell'istante; **just a second!** un attimo!; **it won't take a second** ci vuole un attimo

sec·ond·ary [ˈsɛkəndərɪ] ADJ secondario(-a); **secondary sector** (*Industry*) settore *m* secondario; **presentation is of secondary importance** la presentazione ha un'importanza secondaria

secondary school N scuola secondaria

second-best [ˌsɛkəndˈbɛst] N ripiego; **as a second-best** in mancanza di meglio ♦ ADV: **to come off second-best** avere la peggio

second-class [ˌsɛkəndˈklɑːs] ADJ 1 (*mail*) ordinario(-a); (*ticket, carriage*) di seconda classe 2 (*pej: goods, quality*) scadente ♦ ADV: **to send sth second-class** spedire qc per posta ordinaria; **to travel second-class** viaggiare in seconda classe

second cousin N cugino(-a) di secondo grado

sec·ond·er [ˈsɛkəndəʳ] N sostenitore(-trice)

second-guess [ˌsɛkəndˈɡɛs] (*fam*) VT (*sb's reaction*) cercare di anticipare

second hand N lancetta dei secondi

second-hand [ˌsɛkəndˈhænd] ADJ di seconda mano, usato(-a); **second-hand bookshop** negozio di libri usati ♦ ADV: **to buy sth second-hand** comprare qc di seconda mano; **second-hand news** notizie *fpl* di seconda mano; **to hear sth second-hand** venire a sapere qc da terze persone

second-in-command [ˌsɛkəndɪnkəˈmɑːnd] N (*Mil*) comandante *m* in seconda; (*Admin*) aggiunto

sec·ond·ly [ˈsɛkəndlɪ] ADV secondo, in secondo luogo, secondariamente; **firstly …, secondly …** in primo luogo…, in secondo luogo…

second-rate [ˌsɛkəndˈreɪt] ADJ di second'ordine, scadente

Second World War N: **the Second World War** la seconda guerra mondiale

se·cre·cy [ˈsiːkrəsɪ] N segretezza; **there's no secrecy about …** non si fa mistero di…; **in secrecy** in segreto, in tutta segretezza

se·cret [ˈsiːkrɪt] ADJ segreto(-a); **to keep sth secret (from sb)** tenere qc nascosto (a qn); **keep it secret** che rimanga un segreto; **a secret mission** una missione segreta ♦ N segreto; **in secret** in segreto; **to keep a secret** mantenere un segreto; **can you keep a secret?** sai tenere un segreto?; **to let sb into a secret** mettere qn a parte di un segreto, confidare un segreto a qn; **to make no secret of sth** non far mistero di qc; **to do sth in secret** fare qc in segreto *or* segretamente

secret agent N agente *m* segreto

sec·re·tar·ial [ˌsɛkrəˈtɛərɪəl] ADJ (*work*) di segreteria; (*college, course*) di segretariato; **secretarial work** lavoro di segreteria(-e); **secretarial training** corso di addestramento per segretari(-e)

sec·re·tari·at [ˌsɛkrəˈtɛərɪət] N segretariato

sec·re·tary [ˈsɛkrətrɪ] N segretario(-a)

secretary-general [ˌsɛkrətrɪˈdʒɛnərəl] N segretario generale

se·crete [sɪˈkriːt] VT 1 (*Med, Anat, Bio*) secernere 2 (*frm: hide*) nascondere

se·cre·tion [sɪˈkriːʃən] N secrezione *f*

se·cre·tive [ˈsiːkrətɪv] ADJ riservato(-a); **to be secretive about sth** essere riservato(-a) a proposito di qc

se·cret·ly [ˈsiːkrɪtlɪ] ADV in segreto, segretamente

secret police N: **the secret police** la polizia segreta

secret service N servizi *mpl* segreti; **the Secret Service** (*USA*) servizi segreti incaricati di salvaguardare l'incolumità del presidente

sect [sɛkt] N setta

sec·tar·ian [sɛkˈtɛərɪən] ADJ settario(-a)

sec·tion [ˈsɛkʃən] N 1 (*part: gen*) sezione *f*, parte *f*; (: *of community, population*) settore *m*, fascia; (: *of town, esp USA*) quartiere *m*; (: *of document, law etc*) articolo; (: *of pipeline, road etc*) tratto; (: *of machine, furniture*) pezzo; **the business section** (*Press*) la pagina economica 2 (*department*) sezione *f* 3 (*cut*) sezione *f*; **vertical section** sezione verticale, spaccato ♦ VT (*cut*) sezionare, dividere in sezioni

sec·tor [ˈsɛktəʳ] N (*gen*) settore *m*; (*Geom*) settore *m* circolare

secu·lar [ˈsɛkjʊləʳ] ADJ (*authority, school*) laico(-a); (*writings, music*) profano(-a); (*clergy*) secolare

se·cure [sɪˈkjʊəʳ] ADJ (*comp -r, superl -st*) 1 (*firm: knot*) saldo(-a), sicuro(-a); (: *nail*) ben piantato(-a); (: *rope*) ben fissato(-a); (: *door*) ben chiuso(-a); (: *ladder, chair*) stabile; (: *hold*) saldo(-a); **to make sth secure** fissare bene qc; **make sure the load is secure** assicurati che il carico sia ben fissato 2 (*safe: place, container*) sicuro(-a); (*certain: career, success*) assicurato(-a); (*victory*) certo(-a); **secure from** *or* **against sth** al sicuro da qc; **a secure job** un lavoro sicuro 3 (*free from anxiety*) sicuro(-a), tranquillo(-a); **to rest secure in the knowledge that …** stare tranquillo(-a) sapendo che…; **to feel secure** sentirsi sicuro(-a) ♦ VT 1 (*fix: rope*) assicurare; (: *door, window*) chiudere bene; (*tie up: person, animal*) legare; **secure the bike to the back of the car** fissa la bici dietro la macchina 2 (*make safe*): **to secure (from** *or* **against)** proteggere (da) 3 (*frm: obtain: job, staff etc*) assicurarsi; **to secure sth for sb** procurare qc per *or* a qn; **his experience helped secure him the job** ha avuto il lavoro anche grazie alla sua esperienza 4 (*Fin: loan*) garantire

se·cured credi·tor [sɪˌkjʊədˈkrɛdɪtəʳ] N (*Fin*) creditore *m* privilegiato

se·cu·rity [sɪˈkjʊərɪtɪ] N 1 (*safety, stability*) sicurezza; **job security** sicurezza dell'impiego; **security of tenure** garanzia di titolo *or* di godimento; (*in job*) garanzia del posto di lavoro; **they have security of tenure** non possono essere sfrattati fino al termine del contratto 2 (*against theft etc*) misure *fpl* di sicurezza; **to increase/tighten security** aumentare/intensificare la sorveglianza 3 (*Fin: on loan*) garanzia; **to lend money on security** prestare denaro su *or* dietro garanzia 4 (*Stock Exchange*); **securities** NPL titoli *mpl*

Security Council N: **the Security Council** il Consiglio di Sicurezza

security forces NPL forze *fpl* dell'ordine

security guard N guardia giurata
security risk N *persona che costituisce una minaccia per la sicurezza dello stato*
secy. ABBR = **secretary**
se·dan [sɪˈdæn] N (*USA: Aut*) berlina
se·date [sɪˈdeɪt] ADJ posato(-a), pacato(-a) ♦ VT (*Med*) somministrare sedativi a
se·da·tion [sɪˈdeɪʃən] N (*Med*): **to be under sedation** essere sotto l'effetto di sedativi
seda·tive [ˈsedətɪv] ADJ calmante, sedativo(-a) ♦ N sedativo, calmante *m*
sed·en·tary [ˈsedntrɪ] ADJ sedentario(-a)
sedi·ment [ˈsedɪmənt] N (*in liquids, boiler*) deposito, fondo; (*Geol*) sedimento
se·di·tion [səˈdɪʃən] N sedizione *f*
se·duce [sɪˈdjuːs] VT sedurre
se·duc·tion [sɪˈdʌkʃən] N seduzione *f*
se·duc·tive [sɪˈdʌktɪv] ADJ (*gen*) seducente; (*dress*) sexy *inv*; (*offer*) allettante
see [siː] (*pt* **saw**, *pp* **seen**) VT, VI **1** (*gen*) vedere; **I can't see him** non lo vedo; **I saw him writing the letter** l'ho visto scrivere *or* mentre scriveva la lettera; **I saw him write the letter** l'ho visto scrivere la lettera; **have you seen that film?** hai visto quel film?; **there was nobody to be seen** non c'era anima viva; **I can't see anything** non vedo niente; **I can't see to read** non ci vedo abbastanza per leggere; **let me see** (*show me*) fammi vedere; (*let me think*) vediamo (un po'); **can you see your way to helping us?** (*fig*) puoi trovare il modo di aiutarci?; **to go and see sb** andare a trovare qn; **see you soon/later/tomorrow!** a presto/più tardi/domani!; **see you!** ci vediamo!; **now see here!** (*in anger*) ma insomma!; **so I see** sì, vedo; **see for yourself!** guarda qua!; **as you can see** come vedi; **I must be seeing things** (*fam*) devo avere le allucinazioni *or* le traveggole; **I see in the paper that ...** vedo che sul giornale è scritto che...; **I see nothing wrong in it** non ci trovo niente di male; **I don't know what she sees in him** non so che cosa ci trova in lui; **(go and) see who it is** vai a vedere chi è, vedi chi è; **this car has seen better days** questa macchina ha conosciuto tempi migliori; **I never thought I'd see the day when ...** non avrei mai creduto che un giorno... **2** (*understand, perceive*) vedere, capire; (*joke*) afferrare; **to see the funny side of sth** vedere il lato comico di qc; **I see!** capisco!; **I don't** *or* **can't see how/why** *etc* ... non vedo come/perché *ecc*...; **as far as I can see** da quanto posso vedere; **the way I see it** a parer mio, a mio giudizio **3** (*accompany*) accompagnare; **to see sb to the door/home** accompagnare qn alla porta/a casa; **I'll see you to your car** ti accompagno alla macchina **4** (*ensure, check*) vedere, assicurarsi; **to see if** vedere se + *indic*; **to see that** vedere *or* badare che + *sub*; **see that he has all he needs** vedi che non gli manchi nulla; **I'll see that he gets it** farò in modo che lo riceva **5** (*imagine*) vedere; **I can just see him as a teacher** lo vedo benissimo nei panni dell'insegnante; **I can't see myself as ...** non mi vedo come...; **I can't see him winning** non credo che lui vincerà
  ▸ **see about** VI + PREP **1** (*deal with*) occuparsi di **2** (*consider*): **I'll see about it** ci penserò, vedrò; **we'll see about it** si vedrà; **we'll see about that!** (*iro*) vedremo!
  ▸ **see in** VT + ADV: **to see the New Year in** festeggiare l'Anno Nuovo
  ▸ **see off** VT + ADV salutare alla partenza
  ▸ **see out** VT + ADV (*person*) accompagnare alla porta; **I'll see myself out** (*fam*) non c'è bisogno che mi accompagni; **I'm afraid she won't see the week out** (*survive*) temo che non passerà la settimana
  ▸ **see over, see round** VI + PREP (*visit*) visitare
  ▸ **see through** VI + PREP (*promises, behaviour*) non lasciarsi ingannare da; **I finally saw through him** finalmente ho capito che tipo è ♦ VT + ADV (*project, deal*) portare a termine; **we'll see him through** lo aiuteremo noi ♦ VT + PREP: **£100 will see him through the week** 100 sterline gli basteranno ad arrivare alla fine della settimana
  ▸ **see to** VI + PREP (*deal with*) occuparsi di; (*work-load*) sbrigare; (*mend*) mettere a posto; **please see to it that you lock all doors** si assicuri di aver chiuso tutte le porte; **the shower isn't working—can you see to it please?** la doccia non funziona—se ne può occupare, per favore?

seed [siːd] N **1** (*Bot*) seme *m*; (*for sowing*) semi *mpl*, semente *f*; **sunflower seeds** semi di girasole; **to go** *or* **run to seed** (*plant*) fare seme; **to go to seed** (*fig: person*) ridursi male **2** (*fig: origin*): **the seeds of** il seme di, il germe di; **the seeds of discontent** il seme del malcontento **3** (*Tennis: player*) testa di serie ♦ VT **1** (*lawn etc*) seminare **2** (*remove the seed: raisins, grapes*) togliere i semi a **3** (*Tennis*): **he was seeded fifth** è stato classificato quinta testa di serie ♦ VI fare seme ♦ ADJ (*potato, corn*) da semina
seed·less [ˈsiːdlɪs] ADJ senza semi
seed·ling [ˈsiːdlɪŋ] N semenzale *m*
seedy [ˈsiːdɪ] ADJ (*comp* **-ier**, *superl* **-iest**) (*fam: sordid, shabby*) squallido(-a)
see·ing [ˈsiːɪŋ] CONJ: **seeing (that)** visto che
seek [siːk] (*pt, pp* **sought**) VT (*gen*): **to seek (sth/to do sth)** cercare (qc/di fare qc); **people seeking work** le persone che cercano lavoro; **they are seeking a solution to the problem** cercano di trovare una soluzione al problema; **he sought to calm them down** ha cercato di tranquillizzarli; **to seek shelter (from)** cercar riparo (da); **to seek one's fortune** cercar fortuna; **to seek advice/help from sb** chiedere consiglio/aiuto a qn ♦ VI: **to seek after, seek for** cercare
  ▸ **seek out** VT + ADV (*person*) andare a cercare
seem [siːm] VI sembrare, parere; **she seems capable** sembra (essere) in gamba; **he seemed to be in difficulty** sembrava (trovarsi) in difficoltà; **she seems to know you** sembra *or* pare che lei ti conosca; **she seems not to want to leave** non dà segno di voler andar via; **I seemed to be sinking** mi sembrava di affondare; **I seem to have heard that before** questa mi pare di averla già sentita; **I can't seem to do it** a quanto pare non ci riesco; **how did he seem to you?** come ti è sembrato?; **it seems (that)** sembra *or* pare che + *sub*; **it seems she's getting married** pare che si sposi; **so it seems** così pare *or* sembra; **it seems not** pare di no; **it seems you're right** pare che tu abbia ragione; **it seems ages since ...** mi sembra una vita da quando...; **what seems to be the trouble?** che cosa c'è che non va?; **there seems to be a mistake** ci dev'essere un errore, sembra *or* pare che ci sia un errore; **that seems like a good idea** mi sembra una buona idea; **she died yesterday, it seems** pare che sia morta ieri; **I did what seemed best** ho fatto quello che sembrava più opportuno
seem·ing·ly [ˈsiːmɪŋlɪ] ADV (*evidently*) a quanto pare; (*from appearances*) in apparenza, apparentemente
seen [siːn] PP *of* **see**
seep [siːp] VI: **to seep (through/from/into)** filtrare (attraverso/da/in *or* dentro)
  ▸ **seep away** VI + ADV scolare a poco a poco
  ▸ **seep in** VI + ADV infiltrarsi
  ▸ **seep out** VI + ADV trapelare
seer [sɪəʳ] N (*old, liter*) veggente *m/f*
seer·sucker [ˈsɪəˌsʌkəʳ] N crespo di cotone a strisce
see·saw [ˈsiːsɔː] N altalena (a bilico) ♦ VI (*fig*) oscillare
seethe [siːð] VI (*liquid*) ribollire, gorgogliare; (*street*): **to seethe (with)** brulicare (di); (*person*): **to seethe** *or* **be seething with anger** schiumare *or* fremere di rabbia
see-through [ˈsiːθruː] ADJ trasparente
seg·ment [*n* ˈsegmənt, *vb* ˈsegˈment] N (*section*) parte *f*; (*of orange*) spicchio; (*Geom*) segmento circolare; **line segment** (*Geom*) segmento ♦ VT segmentare
seg·re·gate [ˈsegrɪgeɪt] VT: **to segregate (from)** separare (da), segregare (da)
seg·re·ga·tion [ˌsegrɪˈgeɪʃən] N segregazione *f*
Seine [seɪn] N: **the Seine** la Senna
seis·mic [ˈsaɪzmɪk] ADJ sismico(-a)
seize [siːz] VT (*clutch, grasp*) afferrare; (*Mil, Law: person, territory, power*) prendere; (*: articles*) sequestrare; (*: opportunity*) cogliere; **to seize hold of sth/sb** afferrare qc/qn; **he seized my hand** mi ha afferrato la mano; **to seize an opportunity** cogliere un'opportunità; **troops have seized the airport** le truppe si sono impadronite dell'aeroporto; **to seize power** impadronirsi del potere; **he was seized with a fit of coughing** gli è venuto un accesso di tosse; **she was seized with fear/rage** è stata presa dalla paura/rabbia; **I was seized by the desire to laugh** mi è venuta una gran voglia di ridere

‣ **seize on, seize upon** VI + PREP (*chance, mistake*) non lasciarsi sfuggire; (*idea*) sfruttare prontamente
‣ **seize up** VI + ADV (*muscle, back*) bloccarsi; (*Tech: machine*) grippare; **my back seized up** mi si è bloccata la schiena
sei·zure [ˈsiːʒəʳ] N **1** (*of goods*) sequestro, confisca; (*of land, city, ship*) presa **2** (*Med*) attacco; **he had a seizure** ha avuto un attacco
sel·dom [ˈsɛldəm] ADV di rado, raramente
se·lect [sɪˈlɛkt] VT (*team, candidate*) scegliere, selezionare; (*book, gift etc*) scegliere; **selected works** opere *fpl* scelte ♦ ADJ (*hotel, restaurant*) chic *inv*; (*club*) esclusivo(-a); (*group*) ristretto(-a); (*audience*) scelto(-a); **a select few** pochi eletti *mpl*
se·lec·tion [sɪˈlɛkʃən] N (*gen*) scelta; (*of goods etc*) scelta, selezione *f*; **selections from** (*Mus, Literature*) brani scelti da
selection committee N comitato di selezione
se·lec·tive [sɪˈlɛktɪv] ADJ (*gen*) selettivo(-a)
se·lec·tor [sɪˈlɛktəʳ] N (*person*) selezionatore(-trice); (*Tech*) selettore *m*
self [sɛlf] N (*pl* **selves**): **the self** l'io *m inv*; **my better self** la parte migliore di me stesso; **my inner self** il mio io; **his true self** il suo vero io; **he's quite his old self again** è tornato quello di una volta; **you're looking more like your usual self** sembri essere tornata quella di sempre
self-addressed envelope [ˌsɛlfəˈdrɛstˈɛnvələʊp] N busta col proprio nome e indirizzo
self-adhesive [ˌsɛlfədˈhiːsɪv] ADJ autoadesivo(-a)
self-assertive [ˌsɛlfəˈsɜːtɪv] ADJ che si fa valere
self-assurance [ˌsɛlfəˈʃʊərəns] N sicurezza di sé
self-assured [ˌsɛlfəˈʃʊəd] ADJ sicuro(-a) di sé
self-centred, self-centered (*USA*) [ˌsɛlfˈsɛntəd] ADJ egocentrico(-a)
self-cleaning [ˌsɛlfˈkliːnɪŋ] ADJ (*oven*) autopulente
self-confessed [ˌsɛlfkənˈfɛst] ADJ (*alcoholic, cheat*) dichiarato(-a); **he's a self-confessed thief/liar** ha ammesso di essere un ladro/bugiardo
self-confidence [ˌsɛlfˈkɒnfɪdəns] N fiducia in se stesso(-a)
self-confident [ˌsɛlfˈkɒnfɪdənt] ADJ sicuro(-a) di sé
self-conscious [ˌsɛlfˈkɒnʃəs] ADJ a disagio, impacciato(-a); **she was self-conscious about her height** era complessata per la statura
self-contained [ˌsɛlfkənˈteɪnd] ADJ (*Brit: flat*) indipendente
self-control [ˌsɛlfkənˈtrəʊl], **self-restraint** [ˌsɛlfrɪˈstreɪnt] N self-control *m inv*, autocontrollo, padronanza di sé
self-defeating [ˌsɛlfdɪˈfiːtɪŋ] ADJ controproducente
self-defence, self-defense (*USA*) [ˌsɛlfdɪˈfɛns] N autodifesa; **to act in self-defence** (*Law*) agire per legittima difesa; **she killed him in self-defence** l'ha ucciso per legittima difesa; **self-defence classes** corso di difesa personale
self-discipline [ˌsɛlfˈdɪsɪplɪn] N autodisciplina
self-drive [ˌsɛlfˈdraɪv] ADJ: **self-drive car** vettura da noleggio senza autista
self-employed [ˌsɛlfɪmˈplɔɪd] ADJ (*worker*) autonomo(-a), che lavora in proprio; **to be self-employed** lavorare in proprio ♦ NPL: **the self-employed** i lavoratori autonomi
self-esteem [ˌsɛlfɪsˈtiːm] N stima di sé
self-evident [ˌsɛlfˈɛvɪdənt] ADJ evidente, lampante
self-explanatory [ˌsɛlfɪksˈplænətərɪ] ADJ ovvio(-a), che non ha bisogno di spiegazioni
self-governing [ˌsɛlfˈgʌvənɪŋ] ADJ autonomo(-a)
self-harm [sɛlfˈhɑːm] N autolesionismo ♦ VI farsi del male intenzionalmente
self-help [ˌsɛlfˈhɛlp] N autoaiuto; **a self-help group** un gruppo di autoaiuto
self-importance [ˌsɛlfɪmˈpɔːtəns] N presunzione *f*, boria
self-indulgent [ˌsɛlfɪnˈdʌldʒənt] ADJ indulgente verso le proprie passioni
self-inflicted [ˌsɛlfɪnˈflɪktɪd] ADJ: **self-inflicted wound** autolesione *f*; **your problems are self-inflicted** ti sei creato da solo i tuoi problemi
self-interest [ˌsɛlfˈɪntrɪst] N interesse *m* personale
self·ish [ˈsɛlfɪʃ] ADJ egoista
self·ish·ly [ˈsɛlfɪʃlɪ] ADV egoisticamente
self·ish·ness [ˈsɛlfɪʃnɪs] N egoismo

self·less [ˈsɛlflɪs] ADJ altruista, altruistico(-a)
self·less·ly [ˈsɛlflɪslɪ] ADV altruisticamente
self·less·ness [ˈsɛlflɪsnɪs] N altruismo
self-made man N self-made man *m inv*, uomo che si è fatto da sé
self-pity [ˌsɛlfˈpɪtɪ] N autocommiserazione *f*
self-portrait [ˌsɛlfˈpɔːtrɪt] N autoritratto
self-possessed [ˌsɛlfpəˈzɛst] ADJ padrone(-a) di sé, composto(-a)
self-preservation [ˌsɛlfˌprɛzəˈveɪʃən] N istinto di conservazione
self-raising [ˌsɛlfˈreɪzɪŋ], (*USA*) **self-rising** [ˌsɛlfˈraɪzɪŋ] ADJ: **self-raising flour** miscela di farina e lievito
self-reliant [ˌsɛlfrɪˈlaɪənt] ADJ indipendente
self-respect [ˌsɛlfrɪsˈpɛkt] N dignità, amor proprio *m*
self-respecting [ˌsɛlfrɪsˈpɛktɪŋ] ADJ dignitoso(-a)
self-righteous [ˌsɛlfˈraɪtʃəs] ADJ (*pej*) presuntuoso(-a)
self-rising [ˌsɛlfˈraɪzɪŋ] ADJ (*USA*) = **self-raising**
self-sacrifice [ˌsɛlfˈsækrɪfaɪs] N abnegazione *f*
self-same [ˈsɛlfˌseɪm] ADJ stesso(-a)
self-satisfied [ˌsɛlfˈsætɪsfaɪd] ADJ soddisfatto(-a) di sé
self-sealing [ˌsɛlfˈsiːlɪŋ] ADJ autosigillante
self-service [ˌsɛlfˈsɜːvɪs] ADJ self-service *inv*
self-styled [ˌsɛlfˈstaɪld] ADJ sedicente
self-sufficient [ˌsɛlfsəˈfɪʃənt] ADJ autosufficiente
self-supporting [ˌsɛlfsəˈpɔːtɪŋ] ADJ economicamente indipendente
self-taught [ˌsɛlfˈtɔːt] ADJ autodidatta
self-test [ˌsɛlfˈtɛst] N (*Comput*) test *m inv* autodiagnostico
sell [sɛl] (*pt, pp* **sold**) VT vendere; **to sell sth for £150** vendere qc per 150 sterline; **to sell sth at £10 per dozen** vendere qc a 10 sterline la dozzina; **to sell sth to sb** vendere qc a qn; **I was sold this in London** questo me l'hanno venduto a Londra; **to sell sb an idea** (*fig*) far accettare un'idea a qn; **to sell sb down the river** (*fig*) vendere qn; **to sell sb a pup** (*fig: old*) imbrogliare qn; **to be sold on sb/sth** (*fam*) essere entusiasta di qn/qc; **he doesn't sell himself very well** non si sa vendere bene; **they're selling the house** stanno vendendo la casa; **he sold his car to his sister** ha venduto la macchina alla sorella ♦ VI essere in vendita; **they sell at** or **for 15p each** sono in vendita a 15p l'uno
‣ **sell off** VT + ADV (*stocks and shares, goods*) svendere, liquidare
‣ **sell out** VI + ADV: **to sell out to sb/sth** (*Comm*) vendere (tutto) (a qn/qc); **to sell out to the enemy** (*fig*) passare al nemico ♦ VT + ADV esaurire; **the tickets are all sold out** i biglietti sono *or* we've **sold out of bread** il pane è tutto finito (*in negozio*)
‣ **sell up** VI + ADV (*esp Brit*) vendere (tutto) ♦ VT + ADV vendere
sell-by date [ˈsɛlbaɪˌdeɪt] N data di scadenza
sell·er [ˈsɛləʳ] N **1** venditore(-trice); **seller's market** mercato favorevole ai venditori; **hot-dog seller** un venditore di hot-dog **2** (*product*): **this item's a good seller** questo articolo (si) vende molto
selling price N prezzo di vendita
sell·out [ˈsɛlˌaʊt] N **1** (*Theatre*): **to be a sellout** registrare il tutto esaurito; **it was a sellout** ha fatto registrare il tutto esaurito **2** (*betrayal: to enemy*) tradimento
selves [sɛlvz] NPL of **self**
se·man·tic [sɪˈmæntɪk] ADJ semantico(-a)
se·man·tics [sɪˈmæntɪks] NSG semantica
sema·phore [ˈsɛməˌfɔːʳ] N **1** (*system*) segnalazioni *fpl* con bandierine **2** (*Rail: signal post*) semaforo ferroviario
sem·blance [ˈsɛmbləns] N parvenza, apparenza
se·men [ˈsiːmən] N seme *m*, sperma *m*
se·mes·ter [sɪˈmɛstəʳ] N (*USA*) semestre *m*
semi- [ˈsɛmɪ] PREF semi-
semi·breve [ˈsɛmɪˌbriːv] N (*Brit: Mus*) semibreve *f*
semi·cir·cle [ˈsɛmɪˌsɜːkl] N semicerchio
semi·cir·cu·lar [ˌsɛmɪˈsɜːkjʊləʳ] ADJ semicircolare
semi·co·lon [ˌsɛmɪˈkəʊlən] N punto e virgola
semi·con·duc·tor [ˌsɛmɪkənˈdʌktəʳ] N semiconduttore *m*
semi·con·scious [ˌsɛmɪˈkɒnʃəs] ADJ parzialmente cosciente

semi·de·tached [ˌsɛmɪdɪ'tætʃt] ADJ: **semidetached house** casetta a schiera

semi·fi·nal [ˌsɛmɪ'faɪnl] N semifinale *f*

semi·nar ['sɛmɪnɑːʳ] N (*Univ*) seminario

semi·nary ['sɛmɪnərɪ] N (*Rel*) seminario

semi·precious ['sɛmɪˌprɛʃəs] ADJ semiprezioso(-a)

semi·qua·ver ['sɛmɪˌkweɪvəʳ] N (*Brit: Mus*) semicroma

semi·skilled [ˌsɛmɪ'skɪld] ADJ (*worker*) parzialmente qualificato(-a); (*work*) che richiede una specializzazione parziale

semi·skimmed [ˌsɛmɪ'skɪmd] ADJ parzialmente scremato(-a)

semi·tone ['sɛmɪˌtəʊn] N (*Mus*) semitono

semo·li·na [ˌsɛmə'liːnə] N semolino

Sen., sen. ABBR 1 = **senator** 2 = **senior**

sen·ate ['sɛnɪt] N (*Pol*) senato; (*Univ*) senato accademico

sena·tor ['sɛnɪtəʳ] N (*Pol*) senatore(-trice)

send [sɛnd] (*pt, pp* **sent**) VT 1 (*gen*) mandare; (*letter, telegram*) mandare, spedire; (*arrow, rocket, ball*) lanciare; **to send by post, (USA) send by mail** spedire per posta; **to send by telex/fax** mandare via telex/fax; **have you sent the letter?** hai spedito la lettera?; **she sent me a birthday card** mi ha mandato un biglietto d'auguri; **she sent out a hundred invitations** ha inviato cento inviti; **to send word that ...** mandare a dire che...; **she sends (you) her love** ti saluta affettuosamente; **to send sb for sth** mandare qn a prendere qc; **to send sb to do sth** mandare qn a fare qc; **to send sb home** mandare qn a casa; (*from abroad*) rimpatriare qn; **to send sb to prison/bed/school** mandare qn in prigione/a letto/a scuola; **to send sb to sleep** (*bore*) far addormentare qn; **send sb into fits of laughter** far scoppiare dal ridere qn; **the explosion sent a cloud of dust into the air** l'esplosione ha sollevato una nuvola di polvere; **to send a shiver down sb's spine** far venire i brividi a qn; **to send sb flying** mandare qn a gambe all'aria; **to send sth flying** far volare via qc 2 (*cause to become*): **to send sb mad** far impazzire qn; **that really sends me** (*fam, old*) mi manda in visibilio

▸ **send away** VT + ADV (*person*) mandare; (*get rid of*) mandare via

▸ **send away for, send off for** VI + ADV + PREP richiedere per posta, farsi spedire; **I'll send away for a brochure** mi farò spedire un depliant

▸ **send back** VT + ADV rimandare

▸ **send down** VT + ADV (*person, prices*) far scendere; (*Brit: student*) cacciare, mandar via; (*fam: imprison*) mandare in galera

▸ **send for** VI + PREP 1 (*doctor, police*) (mandare a) chiamare, far venire; (*by post*) ordinare per posta

▸ **send in** VT + ADV (*person*) far entrare; (*troops*) inviare; (*report, application, resignation*) presentare

▸ **send off** VT + ADV (*person*) mandare; (*letter, goods*) spedire; (*Ftbl: player*) espellere; **we sent off your order yesterday** ieri abbiamo spedito il suo ordinativo; **he was sent off** l'hanno espulso; **to send sb off to do sth** mandare qn a fare qc

▸ **send off for** VI + ADV + PREP = **send away for**

▸ **send on** VT + ADV (*Brit: letter*) inoltrare; (*luggage etc: in advance*) spedire in anticipo; (*: afterwards*) mandare, spedire

▸ **send out** VT + ADV 1 (*person*) far uscire; (*invitation*) mandare, spedire; **to send out for sth** mandar fuori a prendere qc, farsi portare qc; **let's send out for a pizza** facciamoci portare una pizza ♦ VT + ADV 1 (*person*) mandar fuori; (*troops*) inviare 2 (*post: invitations*) mandare, spedire 3 (*emit: light, heat*) mandare, emanare; (*: signals*) emettere

▸ **send round** VT + ADV (*letter, document etc*) far circolare; **to send sb round (to sb)** mandare qn (da qn); **I'll send it round later** te lo farò pervenire più tardi

▸ **send up** VT + ADV 1 (*person, luggage*) mandar su; (*balloon, rocket, flare*) lanciare; (*smoke, dust*) sollevare; (*prices*) far salire 2 (*Brit fam: make fun of: person, book*) fare la parodia di

send·er ['sɛndəʳ] N mittente *m/f*

send·off ['sɛndˌɒf] N: **to give sb a sendoff** festeggiare la partenza di qn

Sen·egal [ˌsɛnɪ'gɔːl] N il Senegal

Sen·ega·lese [ˌsɛnɪgə'liːz] ADJ, N *pl inv* senegalese *m/f*

se·nile ['siːnaɪl] ADJ senile; **I'm not senile yet!** non sono ancora rimbambito!

se·nil·ity [sɪ'nɪlɪtɪ] N senilità

sen·ior ['siːnɪəʳ] ADJ 1 (*in age*) maggiore, più anziano(-a); **she is 10 years senior to me** ha 10 anni più di me; **P. Jones senior** P. Jones senior *or* padre; **senior year** (*USA: Univ, Scol*) ultimo anno di studi; **senior pupils** gli studenti delle classi superiori 2 (*of higher rank: employee, officer*) di grado superiore; (*: partner*) più anziano(-a); **senior management** i dirigenti di grado superiore; **he holds a senior position in the company** occupa una posizione di responsabilità nell'azienda; **he is senior to me in the firm** ha più anzianità di me nella ditta ♦ N 1 (*in age*) persona più anziana; **he is my senior by 2 years** ha 2 anni più di me 2 (*USA: Univ*) studente(-essa) dell'ultimo anno

senior citizen N (*euph: old person*) anziano(-a); (*: pensioner*) pensionato(-a)

senior high school N (*USA*) ≈ liceo

sen·ior·ity [ˌsiːnɪ'ɒrɪtɪ] N (*in age, years of service*) anzianità; (*in rank*) superiorità

sen·sa·tion [sɛn'seɪʃən] N 1 (*physical feeling, impression*) sensazione *f*; **a strange sensation** una strana sensazione; **he is completely without sensation in that leg** ha perso completamente la sensibilità della gamba 2 (*excitement*) sensazione *f*, scalpore *m*; **to be** *or* **cause a sensation** fare sensazione, destare scalpore

sen·sa·tion·al [sɛn'seɪʃənl] ADJ (*gen: also fam: marvellous*) sensazionale; (*newspaper*) sensazionalistico(-a); (*novel etc*) a sensazione; (*account, description*) a forti tinte

sense [sɛns] N 1 (*faculty*) senso; **a keen sense of smell/hearing** un olfatto/udito fine; **to come to one's senses** (*regain consciousness*) riprendere i sensi; **the five senses** i cinque sensi; **sixth sense** sesto senso; **sense of direction** senso di orientamento; **to lose all sense of time** perdere la nozione del tempo; **sense of humour** (senso dell') umorismo 2 (*feeling*) senso, sensazione *f*; **sense of duty/guilt** senso del dovere/di colpa; **a sense of well-being** una sensazione di benessere 3 (*also: common sense*) buonsenso; **he should have had more sense than to do it** avrebbe dovuto avere il buonsenso di non farlo; **have a bit of sense!** un po' di buonsenso, via!; **there is no sense in (doing) that** non ha senso (farlo); **to make sb see sense** far ragionare qn, far intendere ragione a qn 4 (*sanity*): **senses** NPL ragione *fsg*, senno *msg*; **to come to one's senses** (*become reasonable*) tornare in sé; **to bring sb to his senses** riportare qn alla ragione, far rinsavire qn; **to take leave of one's senses** perdere il lume *or* l'uso della ragione 5 (*meaning*) senso, significato; **it makes sense** ha senso; **it doesn't make sense** non ha senso; **I can't make (any) sense of this** non ci capisco niente; **in one** *or* **a sense** in un certo senso; **in every sense (of the word)** in tutti i sensi (del termine) 6 (*Math*) verso ♦ VT (*presence, interest*) avvertire, intuire; (*danger*) sentire, percepire; **to sense that all is not well** sentire che c'è qualcosa che non va

sense·less ['sɛnslɪs] ADJ 1 (*stupid: action*) insensato(-a); (*: idea*) assurdo(-a); **acts of senseless violence** atti di violenza insensata 2 (*unconscious*) privo(-a) di sensi *or* di conoscenza; **she fell senseless to the ground** cadde a terra priva di sensi

sen·sibil·ities [ˌsɛnsɪ'bɪlɪtɪz] NPL (*frm*) suscettibilità *fsg*

sen·sible ['sɛnsəbl] ADJ 1 (*having good sense: person*) assennato(-a) 2 (*act, decision, choice*) sensato(-a), ragionevole; (*clothing, shoes*) pratico(-a); **be sensible!** sii ragionevole!; **it would be more sensible (to do)** avrebbe più senso (fare) 3 (*frm: noticeable*) notevole, rilevante

sen·si·tive ['sɛnsɪtɪv] ADJ (*person, tooth, instrument, film*): **sensitive (to)** sensibile (a); (*delicate: skin, question*) delicato(-a); (*easily offended*) suscettibile; **he is very sensitive about it** è meglio non toccare quel tasto con lui

sen·si·tiv·ity [ˌsɛnsɪ'tɪvɪtɪ] N (*see adj*) sensibilità; delicatezza; suscettibilità

sen·sual ['sɛnsjʊəl] ADJ (*gen*) sensuale; (*pleasures*) dei sensi

sen·su·ous ['sɛnsjʊəs] ADJ sensuoso(-a)

sent [sɛnt] PT, PP of **send**

sen·tence ['sɛntəns] N 1 (*gen*) frase *f*; (*Gram*) proposizione *f*; (*complex sentence*) periodo; **he wrote a sentence** ha scritto una frase 2 (*Law: verdict*) sentenza; (*: punishment*) condanna; **to pass sentence on sb** condannare qn; (*fig*) giudicare qn; **sentence of death** condanna a morte; **under sentence of death**

condannato(-a) a morte; **the judge gave him a 6-month sentence** il giudice lo ha condannato a 6 mesi di prigione; **he served a long sentence** ha scontato una lunga condanna; **he got a life sentence** ha avuto l'ergastolo ♦ VT: **to sentence sb to death/to 5 years (in prison)/to life imprisonment** condannare qn a morte/a 5 anni (di prigione)/all'ergastolo

sen·ti·ment [ˈsɛntɪmənt] N 1 (*feeling*) sentimento; (*opinion*) opinione *f*; **the sentiments expressed by the previous speaker** le opinioni espresse dall'oratore precedente; **nationalist sentiments** sentimenti nazionalisti 2 (*sentimentality*) sentimentalismo

sen·ti·men·tal [ˌsɛntɪˈmɛntl] ADJ (*emotional*) sentimentale; (*pej: film, love story*) troppo sentimentale; **I have a sentimental attachment to this pen** sono attaccato a questa penna per motivi sentimentali

sen·ti·men·tal·ity [ˌsɛntɪmɛnˈtælɪtɪ] N (*pej*) sentimentalismo

sen·try [ˈsɛntrɪ] N sentinella

sentry duty N: **to be on sentry duty** essere di sentinella

Seoul [səʊl] N Seul *f*

Sep. ABBR (= *September*) Sett.

sepa·rable [ˈsɛpərəbl] ADJ separabile

sepa·rate [*adj* ˈsɛprɪt, *vb* ˈsɛpəˌreɪt] ADJ (*gen*) separato(-a); (*organization, career*) indipendente; (*occasion, issue*) diverso(-a); **they went their separate ways** (*also fig*) sono andati ognuno per la propria strada; **we sat at separate tables** ci siamo seduti a tavoli diversi; **it was discussed at a separate meeting** è stato discusso in un'altra riunione; **they have separate rooms** hanno camere separate; **on separate occasions** in diverse occasioni; **I wrote it on a separate sheet** l'ho scritto su un altro foglio di carta; **separate from** separato(-a) da; **under separate cover** (*Comm*) in plico a parte ♦ VT (*gen*) separare, dividere; (*divide up*): **to separate into** dividere in; **to separate sth from sth** separare qc da qc; **he is separated from his wife, but not divorced** è separato dalla moglie ma non divorziato; **the police tried to separate the two groups** la polizia ha cercato di separare i due gruppi ♦ VI (*mixture, milk*) separarsi; (*married couple, boxers*) separarsi, dividersi; (*unmarried couple, friends*) lasciarsi; **they separated seven years ago** si sono separati sette anni fa; *see also* **separates**

sepa·rate·ly [ˈsɛprɪtlɪ] ADV separatamente

sepa·rates [ˈsɛprɪts] NPL (*clothes*) coordinati *mpl*

sepa·ra·tion [ˌsɛpəˈreɪʃən] N separazione *f*

Sept. ABBR (= *September*) sett., set. (= *settembre*)

Sep·tem·ber [sɛpˈtɛmbə^r] N settembre *m*; *see* **July**

sep·tic [ˈsɛptɪk] ADJ settico(-a); (*wound*) infetto(-a); **to go septic** infettarsi; **a septic finger** un dito infettato

sep·ti·cae·mia, sep·ti·cemia (*USA*) [ˌsɛptɪˈsiːmɪə] N setticemia

septic tank N fossa settica

se·quel [ˈsiːkwəl] N (*of film, book*): **sequel (to)** seguito (di); (*of event*) conseguenza (di), strascico (di)

se·quence [ˈsiːkwəns] N 1 (*order*) successione *f*, ordine *m*; **in sequence** in ordine, di seguito; **sequence of tenses** (*Gram*) concordanza dei tempi 2 (*series*) serie *f inv*; (*Mus, Cards: film sequence*) sequenza; **the sequence of events that led to the murder** la serie di avvenimenti che ha portato all'omicidio

se·quen·tial [sɪˈkwɛnʃəl] ADJ sequenziale; **sequential access** (*Comput*) accesso sequenziale

se·quin [ˈsiːkwɪn] N paillette *f inv*, lustrino

Serb [sɜːb] ADJ, N = **Serbian**

Ser·bia [ˈsɜːbɪə] N Serbia

Ser·bian [ˈsɜːbɪən] ADJ serbo(-a) ♦ N (*person*) serbo(-a); (*language*) serbo

Serbo-Croat [ˈsɜːbəʊˈkrəʊæt] N (*language*) serbocroato

ser·enade [ˌsɛrəˈneɪd] N serenata ♦ VT fare la serenata a

se·rene [sɪˈriːn] ADJ (*person, sky*) sereno(-a); (*sea*) calmo(-a)

se·ren·ity [sɪˈrɛnɪtɪ] N serenità

ser·geant [ˈsɑːdʒənt] N (*Mil*) sergente *m*; (*Police*) ≈ brigadiere *m*

sergeant major N (*Mil*) sergente *m* maggiore

se·rial [ˈsɪərɪəl] N (*in magazine*) romanzo a puntate; (*TV*) teleromanzo a puntate, serial *m inv* televisivo; (*Radio*) commedia radiofonica a puntate ♦ ADJ (*Comput*) seriale

se·rial·ize [ˈsɪərɪəˌlaɪz] VT (*Press*) pubblicare a puntate; (*TV, Radio*) trasmettere a puntate

serial killer N serial-killer *m/f inv*

serial number N (*of goods, machinery, banknotes etc*) numero di serie

se·ries [ˈsɪərɪz] N *pl inv* (*gen, also Radio, TV*) serie *f inv*; (*set of books*) collana

se·ri·ous [ˈsɪərɪəs] ADJ 1 (*earnest*) serio(-a); **to give serious thought to sth** considerare seriamente qc; **he's a serious student of jazz** s'interessa seriamente di jazz; **he's getting serious about him** si sta innamorando sul serio di lui; **are you serious (about it)?** parli sul serio?; **you can't be serious!** stai scherzando!; **you're looking very serious** hai un'aria molto seria 2 (*causing concern*) serio(-a), grave; **the patient's condition is serious** il paziente versa in gravi condizioni; **a serious illness** una grave malattia

se·ri·ous·ly [ˈsɪərɪəslɪ] ADV 1 (*in earnest*) seriamente; **to take sth/sb seriously** prendere qc/qn sul serio; **seriously though ...** scherzi a parte..., sul serio...; **we'll have to think about it seriously** dovremo pensarci seriamente 2 (*wounded*) gravemente; (*worried*) seriamente; **seriously injured** gravemente ferito(-a) 3 (*fam: extremely*): **he's seriously rich** ha un casino di soldi

se·ri·ous·ness [ˈsɪərɪəsnɪs] N (*gen*) serietà, gravità; (*of error*) gravità; **in all seriousness** in tutta sincerità; **the seriousness of the situation** la gravità della situazione

ser·mon [ˈsɜːmən] N (*in church*) sermone *m*; (*pej: lecture*) predica

ser·rat·ed [sɛˈreɪtɪd] ADJ seghettato(-a)

❑ **serrated** is not translated by the Italian word *serrato*

se·rum [ˈsɪərəm] N siero

serv·ant [ˈsɜːvənt] N (*domestic*) domestico(-a); (*fig: of the public, one's country*) servitore *m*

serve [sɜːv] VT 1 (*work for: employer*) servire; (: *God, one's country*) servire, essere al servizio di 2 (*be used for or useful as*): **to serve (as)** servire (da); **that serves to explain ...** così si spiega...; **it serves a variety of purposes** ha svariati usi; **it serves my purpose** fa al caso mio, serve al mio scopo; **it serves its purpose** serve allo scopo; **it serves no useful purpose** non serve a niente; **it serves you right** (*fam*) ben ti sta; **his knowledge served him well** la sua preparazione gli è tornata utile 3 (*in shop, restaurant*) servire; (*food, meal, also Tennis*) servire; **to serve sb (with) sth** servire qc a qn; **are you being served?** la stanno servendo?; **dinner is served** la cena è servita; **this dish should be served hot** è un piatto che va servito caldo; **the power station serves the entire region** la centrale elettrica alimenta l'intera regione; **the railway line serves five cities** la ferrovia serve cinque città 4 (*complete*): **to serve an apprenticeship** fare tirocinio; **to serve a prison sentence** scontare una condanna; **to serve time** (*fam*) essere in prigione; **he has served time (in prison)** è stato in prigione; **he has served his time** (*prisoner*) ha scontato la sua condanna; (*apprentice*) ha finito il periodo di prova 5 (*Law: summons, writ*): **to serve sth on sb** notificare qc a qn; **to serve a summons on sb** (*Law*) spiccare un mandato di comparizione contro qn ♦ VI 1 (*servant, soldier*) prestare servizio; (*shop assistant, waiter*) servire; (*Tennis*) servire, battere; **to serve on a committee/jury** far parte di un comitato/una giuria; **she served for 2 years as chairperson** è stata in carica come presidente per 2 anni 2 (*be useful*): **to serve as/for/to do** servire da/per/per fare ♦ N (*Tennis*) servizio, battuta

▸ **serve out, serve up** VT + ADV (*food*) servire; (*meal*) servire in tavola

serv·er [ˈsɜːvə^r] N 1 (*Comput*) server *m inv* 2 (*Rel*) chierichetto; (*Tennis*) chi ha il servizio, battitore(-trice) 3 (*piece of cutlery*) posata di servizio; (*tray*) vassoio, piatto da portata

ser·vice [ˈsɜːvɪs] N 1 (*gen, also Mil*) servizio; **to see service** (*Mil*) prestare servizio; **military service** servizio militare; **at your service** al suo (or vostro) servizio; **to be of service (to sb)** essere utile (a qn); **to do sb a service** fare un (gran) favore a qn; **this old chair has seen a lot of service** questa vecchia sedia ne ha viste tante; **in service** (*domestic*) a servizio; **On Her** (*or* **His**) **Majesty's Service** al servizio di Sua Maestà (Britannica); **in the service of one's country** al servizio della patria; **service is included** il servizio è compreso 2 (*department, system*) servizio; **medical/**

social services servizi sanitari/sociali; **the postal service** il servizio postale; **the essential services** i servizi primari; **goods and services** (*Econ*) beni *mpl* e servizi; **the train service to London** il servizio di treni per Londra; **the number 13 bus service** la linea del 13 **3 the Services** (*Mil*) le Forze Armate **4** (*Rel*) funzione *f*; **funeral service** rito funebre; **to hold a service** celebrare una funzione **5** (*maintenance work*) revisione *f* (periodica); **to put the car in for a service** portare la macchina in officina per una revisione **6** (*set of crockery*) servizio; **a tea/coffee/dinner service** un servizio da tè/da caffè/da tavola **7** (*on motorway*); **services** NPL stazione *fsg* di servizio **8** (*Tennis, etc*) servizio, battuta ♦ VT (*car, washing machine*) revisionare; (*group, organization*) dare assistenza a; (*Fin: debt*) pagare gli interessi su

ser·vice·able [ˈsɜːvɪsəbl] ADJ (*practical: clothes, shoes*) pratico(-a); (*usable, functioning*) usabile

service area N (*on motorway*) area di servizio

service charge N (*in restaurant*) servizio; **there's no service charge** il servizio è compreso

service industries NPL settore *msg* terziario

ser·vice·man [ˈsɜːvɪsmən] N (*pl* **-men**) militare *m*

service provider N provider *m inv*

service station N (*Aut*) stazione *f* di servizio

ser·vi·ette [ˌsɜːvɪˈet] N (*Brit*) tovagliolo, salvietta

ser·vile [ˈsɜːvaɪl] ADJ (*pej*) servile

ses·sion [ˈseʃən] N **1** (*sitting*) seduta, sessione *f*; (*meeting*) riunione *f*; **to be in session** (*parliament, court*) essere in seduta; **the court is now in session** l'udienza è aperta; **I had a long session with her** (*talk*) ho avuto un lungo colloquio con lei; (*work*) ho avuto una lunga riunione di lavoro con lei **2** (*esp USA, Scot: Scol, Univ: year*) anno scolastico (*or* accademico); (*: term*) trimestre *m or* quadrimestre *m*; **the new parliamentary session begins in October** l'attività parlamentare riprenderà a ottobre

session musician N musicista *m/f* di studio

set [set] (*pt, pp* **set**) N **1** (*gen*) serie *f inv*; (*of kitchen tools, saucepans*) batteria; (*of books*) raccolta, collezione *f*; (*of dishes*) servizio; **a set of false teeth** una dentiera; **he still has a full set of teeth** ha ancora una dentatura completa; **a set of dining-room furniture** una camera da pranzo; **a chess/checkers set** un gioco di scacchi/dama; **a painting/writing set** l'occorrente *m* per dipingere/per scrivere; **these articles are sold in sets** questi articoli si vendono in serie complete **2** (*Tennis*) set *m inv* **3** (*Math*) insieme *m*; **closed set** insieme chiuso; **empty set** insieme vuoto **4** (*Elec*) apparecchio; **television set** televisore *m* **5** (*Cine*) set *m inv*; (*Theatre*) scena **6** (*Hairdressing*) messa in piega **7** (*group, often pej*) cerchia; **the smart set** il bel mondo ♦ ADJ **1** (*unchanging: gen*) fisso(-a); (*smile*) artificiale; (*purpose*) definito(-a), preciso(-a); (*lunch*) a prezzo fisso; (*speech, talk*) preparato(-a); (*date, time*) preciso(-a), stabilito(-a); (*Scol: subjects*) obbligatorio(-a); (*: books*) in programma (per l'esame); **set in one's ways** abitudinario(-a); **set in one's opinions** rigido(-a) nelle proprie convinzioni; **a set phrase** una frase fatta; **at a set time** a un'ora stabilita **2** (*determined*) deciso(-a); (*ready*) pronto(-a); **he is (dead) set on doing it** è deciso a farlo; **he is (dead) set on a new car** si è ficcato in testa di comprare una nuova macchina; **to be (dead) set against (doing)** essere assolutamente contrario(-a) a (fare) qc; **to be all set to do sth** essere pronto(-a) a fare qc; **the scene was set for ...** (*fig*) tutto era pronto per... ♦ VT **1** (*place, put*) mettere; **a novel set in Rome** un romanzo ambientato a Roma; **to set the value of a ring at £500** valutare un anello 500 sterline; **to set sb free** liberare qn, mettere qn in libertà; **to set fire to sth** dare *or* appiccare fuoco a qc; **to set a dog on sb** aizzare un cane contro qn **2** (*arrange, adjust: clock, mechanism*) regolare; (*: alarm clock*) mettere, puntare; (*: trap*) mettere, tendere; (*: hair*) fissare, mettere in piega; (*: broken arm, leg: in plaster*) ingessare; (*: with splint*) mettere una stecca a; (*: type*) comporre; **to set a poem to music** mettere in musica una poesia; **I set the alarm for seven o'clock** ho messo la sveglia alle sette **3** (*fix, establish: date, limit*) fissare, stabilire; (*: record*) stabilire; (*: fashion*) lanciare; (*: dye, colour*) fissare; **to set course for** (*Naut*) far rotta per; **the world record was set last year** il record mondiale è stato stabilito l'anno scorso **4** (*gem*) montare **5** (*assign: task, homework*) dare,

assegnare; **to set sb a problem** porre un problema a qn; **to set sb an exam in Italian** far fare un esame d'italiano a qn; **to set an exam in Italian** preparare il testo *or* le domande di un esame d'italiano; **we'll set you a task** ti daremo un compito **6** (*start, cause to start*): **to set sth going** mettere in moto qc; **it set me thinking** mi ha fatto pensare; **to set sb to work** mettere qn al lavoro; **to set to work** mettersi al lavoro ♦ VI **1** (*sun, moon*) tramontare; **the sun was setting** il sole stava tramontando **2** (*broken bone, limb*) saldarsi; (*jelly, jam*) rapprendersi; (*concrete, glue*) indurirsi, fare presa; (*fig: face*) irrigidirsi

▸ **set about** VI + PREP **1** (*task*): **to set about doing sth** intraprendere qc, mettersi a fare qc; **I don't know how to set about it** non so da che parte cominciare **2** (*attack*) assalire

▸ **set against** VT + PREP **1** (*make hostile to*): **to set sb against sb/sth** mettere qn contro qn; **2** (*balance against*): **to set sth against sth** contrapporre qc a qc

▸ **set apart** VT + ADV (*object*) mettere da parte; (*fig: person*) distinguere

▸ **set aside** VT + ADV **1** (*book, work*) mettere via; (*money, time*) mettere da parte; (*differences, quarrels, principles*) accantonare; (*land*) mettere a riposo **2** (*reject: objection*) respingere; (*: will, judgement*) invalidare, annullare

▸ **set back** VT + ADV **1** (*clock*) mettere indietro; (*progress*) ritardare; **to set back the clock** (*by one hour*) mettere l'orologio indietro (di un'ora); **the strike has set us back 6 months** lo sciopero ci ha fatto perdere 6 mesi **2 a house set back from the road** una casa a una certa distanza dalla strada **3** (*fam: cost*): **it set me back £900** mi è costato la bellezza di 900 sterline

▸ **set down** VT + ADV **1** (*put down: object*) posare; (*: passenger*) lasciare, far scendere **2** (*record*) prendere nota di; **to set sth down in writing** *or* **on paper** mettere qc per iscritto *or* sulla carta

▸ **set forth** VT + ADV (*frm: facts, reasons, arguments*) esporre ♦ VI + ADV (*liter: set off*) mettersi in viaggio

▸ **set in** VI + ADV (*infection*) svilupparsi; (*complications*) intervenire; **the rain has set in for the day** ormai pioverà tutto il giorno; **before the rot sets in** prima che la situazione degeneri

▸ **set off** VI + ADV (*leave*) mettersi in cammino, partire; **to set off on a journey** (*to*) mettersi in viaggio (per); **we set off after breakfast** siamo partiti dopo colazione ♦ VT + ADV **1** (*bomb*) far scoppiare *or* esplodere; (*mechanism, burglar alarm*) azionare; (*process, chain of events*) mettere in moto, scatenare **2** (*enhance*) mettere in risalto, far risaltare

▸ **set out** VI + ADV: **to set out (for)** avviarsi (verso, a); (*city*) partire (per); **we set out for London at nine o'clock** siamo partiti per Londra alle nove; **to set out (from)** partire (da); **to set out in search of sb/sth** mettersi alla ricerca di qn/qc; **to set out to do sth** proporsi di fare qc ♦ VT + ADV (*goods etc: also fig: reasons, ideas*) esporre, presentare; (*chess pieces*) schierare, disporre

▸ **set to** VI + ADV: **to set to (and do sth)** mettersi all'opera (e fare qc)

▸ **set up** VI + ADV: **to set up (in business)** as a baker/lawyer aprire una panetteria/uno studio legale; **when did you set up in business?** quand'è che ti sei messo in proprio? ♦ VT + ADV **1** (*place in position: chairs, stalls, road blocks*) disporre; (*tent*) rizzare, piantare; (*monument*) innalzare **2** (*start: firm, business etc*) avviare; (*: school, organization*) fondare; (*: fund*) costituire; (*: inquiry*) aprire; (*: infection*) provocare; (*: record*) stabilire; **to set up house** trovarsi una casa; **to set up camp** accamparsi; **to set up shop** mettersi in proprio; **to set sb up in business** avviare qn agli affari; **to set o.s. up as sth** (*fig*) pretendere di essere qc; **to set sb up with sb** facilitare un incontro romantico fra due persone

▸ **set upon** VI + PREP (*attack*) assalire

set·back [ˈsetbæk] N (*hitch*) contrattempo, inconveniente *m*; (*more serious*) momento di crisi; (*in health*) ricaduta; **a setback for the peace process** un intoppo al processo di pace; **he suffered a setback in his career** la sua carriera ha avuto un momento di crisi

set menu N menù *m inv* fisso *or* turistico

set square N squadra da disegno

set·tee [seˈtiː] N divano

set·ting [ˈsetɪŋ] N 1 (of novel) ambiente m, ambientazione f; (scenery) sfondo; (of jewels) montatura; **a house in a beautiful setting** una casa in una posizione meravigliosa 2 (Mus) adattamento (musicale) 3 (of controls) posizione f; **the heating was on the highest setting** il termosifone era fissato sulla regolazione più alta 4 (of sun) tramonto

setting lotion N fissatore m (per messa in piega)

set·tle¹ [ˈsetl] N cassapanca con schienale alto

set·tle² [ˈsetl] VT 1 (place carefully) sistemare; **to settle o.s., get settled** sistemarsi 2 (decide, finalize: details, date) definire, concordare; (pay: bill, account) regolare, saldare; (solve: problem) risolvere; (: difficulty) appianare; (: dispute, argument) comporre; **to settle a case** or **claim out of court** definire una causa in via amichevole; **that should settle the problem** questo dovrebbe risolvere il problema; **I'll settle the bill tomorrow** salderò il conto domani; **that's settled then** allora è deciso; **that settles it!** (I've decided) ecco, ho deciso!; (indignant) questo è il colmo! 3 (calm down: nerves) distendere; (: doubts) dissipare; **to settle one's stomach** calmare il mal di stomaco 4 (colonize: land) colonizzare 5 (Law): **to settle sth on sb** intestare qc a qn ♦ VI 1 (bird, insect) posarsi; (sediment, dust, snow) depositarsi; (building) assestarsi; (conditions, situation) stabilizzarsi; (weather) mettersi al bello; (emotions) calmarsi; (nerves) distendersi; **to settle to sth** applicarsi a qc; **I couldn't settle to anything** non riuscivo a concentrarmi 2 (go to live: in town, country) stabilirsi; (: in new house) sistemarsi, installarsi; (: as colonist) insediarsi; **to feel settled** (in a place) sentirsi a casa 3 **to settle with sb for the price of sth** concordare il prezzo di qc con qn; **can I settle with you later?** posso darti i soldi più tardi?; **to settle out of court** (Law) giungere a un accordo in via amichevole; **to settle on sth** (choose) decidere or optare per qc

▸ **settle down** VI + ADV (person: in house, armchair etc) sistemarsi; (: become calmer) calmarsi; (: after wild youth) mettere la testa a posto; (situation) sistemarsi, tornare alla normalità; **to settle down to work** mettersi a lavorare; **has he settled down in his new job?** si è adattato bene al nuovo lavoro?; **things will settle down eventually** le cose si sistemeranno alla fine; **I want to settle down and start a family** voglio sistemarmi e metter su famiglia; **to get married and settle down** mettere su casa (e famiglia)

▸ **settle for** VI + PREP: **to settle for sth** accontentarsi di qc; **he settled for £100** ha accettato 100 sterline

▸ **settle in** VI + ADV (in new house) sistemarsi, installarsi; (in new job, neighbourhood) ambientarsi

▸ **settle up** VI + ADV: **to settle up (with sb)** saldare or regolare i conti (con qn)

set·tle·ment [ˈsetlmənt] N 1 (of bill, debt) pagamento, saldo; (of question) soluzione f; (of dispute) composizione f; **in settlement of our account** (Comm) a saldo del nostro conto 2 (agreement) accordo; **a peace settlement** un accordo di pace 3 (village) insediamento, comunità f inv; (colony) colonia

set·tler [ˈsetləʳ] N colonizzatore(-trice)

set·up [ˈsetˌʌp] N 1 portamento 2 situazione 3 (fam) inganno

setup costs [-ˌkɒsts] NPL (Comm) costi mpl d'avviamento

setup file N (Comput) file m inv di configurazione

sev·en [ˈsevn] ADJ, N sette m inv

sev·en·teen [ˌsevnˈtiːn] ADJ, N diciassette m inv

sev·en·teenth [ˌsevnˈtiːnθ] ADJ diciassettesimo(-a) ♦ N (in series) diciassettesimo(-a); (fraction) diciassettesimo

sev·enth [ˈsevnθ] ADJ settimo(-a) ♦ N (in series) settimo(-a); (fraction) settimo

sev·en·ti·eth [ˈsevntɪɪθ] ADJ settantesimo(-a) ♦ N (in series) settantesimo(-a); (fraction) settantesimo

sev·en·ty [ˈsevntɪ] ADJ, N settanta m inv

sev·er [ˈsevəʳ] VT (rope) tagliare, recidere; (limb) staccare, mozzare; (fig: relations) troncare, rompere; (: communications) interrompere; **he severed an artery** ha reciso un'arteria; **she severed all ties with her family** ha troncato tutti i legami con la famiglia

sev·er·al [ˈsevrəl] ADJ parecchi(-ie) pl, diversi(-e) pl; **several times** diverse volte ♦ PRON parecchi(-ie) pl, alcuni(-e) pl; **several of us** parecchi di noi, alcuni di noi

sev·er·ance [ˈsevərəns] N (frm: of relations) rottura

severance pay N (Industry) indennità di licenziamento

se·vere [sɪˈvɪəʳ] ADJ (comp **-r**, superl **-st**) (problem, case, flooding, injuries) grave; (climate, winter, restrictions) rigido(-a); (frost, cold) intenso(-a); (punishment, person) severo(-a); (examination) rigoroso(-a); (damage) ingente; (blow, criticism) duro(-a); (pain, headache, pressure) forte; (symptoms) acuto(-a); **to be severe (with sb)** essere severo(-a) (con qn); **a severe cold** un forte raffreddore; **severe handicaps** gravi handicap; **a severe shortage of staff** una forte carenza di personale; **a severe punishment** una punizione severa; **a severe blow** un duro colpo

se·vere·ly [sɪˈvɪəlɪ] ADV (damage, affect, injure) gravemente; (criticise, speak, strain) duramente; (punish, reprimand) severamente; (test) rigorosamente; (curtail, restrict, reduce) severamente; **to leave severely alone** (object) non toccare mai; (person) ignorare completamente; (politics etc) non interessarsi assolutamente a

se·ver·ity [sɪˈverɪtɪ] N (gen) gravità; (of punishment) severità; (of criticism) durezza; (of climate, weather) rigore m; (of damage) ingenza; (of pain) intensità; (of symptoms) acutezza

sew [səʊ] (pt **sewed** pp **sewn** or **sewed**) VT, VI cucire; **to sew a button on sth** attaccare un bottone a qc; **she was sewing** cuciva; **it was sewn by hand** era cucito a mano

▸ **sew up** VT + ADV (tear) rammendare; (wound) ricucire; (hem) cucire; (seam) fare; **it's all sewn up** (fig: fam) è tutto a posto

sew·age [ˈsjuːɪdʒ] N acque fpl di scolo, liquami mpl

sewage works N stabilimento per la depurazione dei liquami

sew·er [ˈsjʊəʳ] N fogna

sew·ing [ˈsəʊɪŋ] N (skill, activity) (il) cucire m; (piece of work) cucito; **I like sewing** mi piace cucire

sewing machine N macchina da cucire

sewn [səʊn] PP of **sew**

sex [seks] N (gender) sesso; (sexual intercourse) rapporti mpl sessuali; **to have sex with sb** avere rapporti sessuali con qn; **the opposite sex** l'altro sesso ♦ ADJ (discrimination) sessuale

sex act N atto sessuale

sex appeal N sex appeal m inv

sex education N educazione f sessuale

sex·ism [ˈseksɪzəm] N sessismo

sex·ist [ˈseksɪst] N, ADJ sessista m/f

sex life N vita sessuale

sex object N oggetto sessuale; **to be treated as a sex object** (woman) essere trattata da donna oggetto; (man) essere trattato da uomo oggetto

sex·tet [seksˈtet] N sestetto

sex·ual [ˈseksjʊəl] ADJ sessuale; **sexual discrimination** discriminazione f sessuale; **sexual assault** violenza carnale

sexu·al·ity [ˌseksjʊˈælɪtɪ] N sessualità

sexy [ˈseksɪ] ADJ (comp **-ier**, superl **-iest**) sexy inv, provocante; (fam: subject etc) stuzzicante

Sey·chelles [seɪˈʃelz] NPL: **the Seychelles** le Seychelles

SF [ˈesˈef] N ABBR = science fiction

SG [ˌesˈdʒiː] N ABBR (Brit: = Solicitor General) assistente del Procuratore Generale

Sgt. ABBR = sergeant

shab·bi·ness [ˈʃæbɪnɪs] N (of dress, person) trasandatezza; (of building) squallore m; (of treatment) meschinità

shab·by [ˈʃæbɪ] ADJ (comp **-ier**, superl **-iest**) (building) malandato(-a), squallido(-a); (clothes) sciatto(-a); (person: also: shabby-looking) trasandato(-a); (behaviour) meschino(-a); **a shabby trick** un tiro mancino

shack [ʃæk] N capanno; (in slum) baracca ♦ VI: **to shack up with sb** (fam) convivere (con qn)

shackles [ˈʃæklz] NPL ceppi mpl, ferri mpl; (fig: constraints) impacci mpl

shade [ʃeɪd] N 1 ombra; **in the shade** all'ombra; **to put in the shade** (fig) mettere in ombra, oscurare 2 (also: lampshade) paralume m 3 (also: eyeshade) visiera 4 (USA: window shade) tapparella 5 **shades** NPL (USA: sunglasses) occhiali mpl da sole 6 (of colour) tonalità f inv, sfumatura; (fig: of meaning, opinion) sfumatura; **several shades darker/lighter** di tonalità parecchio più scura/chiara; **this lipstick comes in several shades** questo rossetto è disponibile in diverse gradazioni di colore; **a beautiful shade of blue** una bella tonalità d'azzurro **7** (*small quantity*): **just a shade more** un tantino di più; **a shade bigger** un tantino più grande ♦ VT (*from sun, light*) riparare; **to shade one's eyes from the sun** ripararsi gli occhi dal sole

▸ **shade in** VT + ADV (*drawing*) ombreggiare

shad·ow [ˈʃædəʊ] N ombra; **in shadow** in ombra, all'ombra; **in the shadow (of)** all'ombra (di); **without** *or* **beyond a shadow of a doubt** senz'ombra di dubbio; **to cast a shadow over** proiettare *or* fare ombra su; (*fig*) gettare un'ombra su, offuscare; **he's only a shadow of his former self** è diventato l'ombra di se stesso; **to have shadows under one's eyes** avere le occhiaie ♦ VT (*follow*) pedinare ♦ ADJ ATTR: **the Shadow Foreign Secretary** il ministro degli Esteri del governo ombra

Shadow Cabinet N (*Pol: Brit*) governo *m* ombra, *inv*

shad·owy [ˈʃædəʊɪ] ADJ (*form, figure*) indistinto(-a), vago(-a); (*place*) pieno(-a) di ombre

shady [ˈʃeɪdɪ] ADJ (*comp* **-ier**, *superl* **-iest**) (*place*) ombreggiato(-a); (*tree*) ombroso(-a); (*fig: person, deal*) losco(-a), equivoco(-a); **a wide, shady street** una larga strada ombrosa; **shady dealings** affari loschi

shaft [ʃɑːft] N **1** (*of arrow, spear*) asta; (*of tool*) manico; (*of cart etc*) stanga; (*Aut, Tech*) albero; **shaft of light/sunlight** raggio di luce/sole **2** (*of mine, lift etc*) pozzo; **ventilator shaft** condotto di ventilazione

shag·gy [ˈʃægɪ] ADJ (*comp* **-ier**, *superl* **-iest**) (*mane, hair*) ispido(-a), arruffato(-a); (*dog*) a pelo lungo e arruffato

shake [ʃeɪk] (*pt* **shook**, *pp* **shaken**) N scossa, scrollata; **with a shake of her head ...** scuotendo *or* scrollando la testa *or* il capo...; **to give a rug a good shake** dare una bella sbattuta ad un tappeto; **he's no great shakes at swimming** (*fam*) nel nuoto non è che brilli; **in two shakes** (*fam*) in quattro e quatt'otto; **to have the shakes** avere la tremarella; **he gets the shakes when ...** gli viene la tremarella quando ... ♦ VT **1** (*person, object*) scuotere; (*building, windows*) far tremare; (*bottle, dice*) agitare; (*cocktail*) shakerare; **to shake one's fist at sb** minacciare qn col pugno; **to shake hands** stringersi la mano, darsi una stretta di mano; **they shook hands** si strinsero la mano; **to shake hands with sb** stringere la mano a qn; **to shake one's head** (*in refusal, dismay*) scuotere la testa *or* il capo; **Donald shook his head** Donald scosse il capo **2** (*harm: confidence, belief, opinion*) scuotere; (: *reputation*) minare; (*amaze, disturb*) scuotere, sconvolgere; **nothing will shake our resolve** niente ci smuoverà; **he needs to be shaken out of his apathy** bisogna scuoterlo dalla sua apatia; **I was feeling a bit shaken** ero un po' scosso(-a) ♦ VI (*person, building, voice etc*) tremare; **to shake with fear/cold** tremare di paura/freddo; **he was shaking with cold** tremava di freddo; **to shake with laughter** essere scosso(-a) dalle risate; **the walls shook at the sound** il fragore ha fatto tremare i muri

▸ **shake down** VT + ADV: **to shake down apples from a tree** scuotere un albero per far cadere le mele ♦ VI + ADV (*fam: sleep*) dormire

▸ **shake off** VT + ADV (*raindrops, snow*) scrollarsi di dosso; (*dust*) scuotersi di dosso; (*fig: cold, cough*) sbarazzarsi di; (: *habit*) togliersi; (: *pursuer*) seminare

▸ **shake out** VT + ADV (*sail*) sciogliere; (*blanket etc*) scuotere; (*bag*) svuotare scuotendo

▸ **shake up** VT + ADV **1** (*bottle*) agitare; (*pillow*) sprimacciare **2** (*upset: person*) sconvolgere, scuotere **3** (*rouse, stir: person, company etc*) scuotere, dare una scossa salutare a

shake-up [ˈʃeɪkˌʌp] N (*fig*) cambiamento

shaki·ly [ˈʃeɪkɪlɪ] ADV (*reply*) con voce tremante; (*walk*) con passo malfermo; (*write*) con mano tremante

shaky [ˈʃeɪkɪ] ADJ (*comp* **-ier**, *superl* **-iest**) (*table, building*) traballante; (*trembling: voice*) tremante; (: *hands*) tremante; (: *handwriting*) tremolante; (*fig: health*) vacillante, malfermo(-a); (: *memory*) labile; (: *knowledge*) incerto(-a); (: *start*) incerto(-a); **I feel a bit shaky** mi gira un po' la testa; **my Spanish is rather shaky** il mio spagnolo lascia un po' a desiderare; **the team got off to a shaky start** la partita ha avuto un avvio incerto per la squadra; **he answered in a shaky voice** ha risposto con voce tremante

shale [ʃeɪl] N scisto

shall [ʃæl] AUX VB **1** (*used to form 1st person in future tense and questions*): **I shall go tomorrow** ci andrò domani, ci vado domani; **I shall know more next week, I hope** ne saprò qc di più la prossima settimana, spero; **shall I open the door or will you?** devo aprire io la porta o lo fai tu?; **shall I shut the window?** chiudo la finestra?; **let's go out, shall we?** usciamo, vuoi? **2** (*in commands, promises: emphatic*): **you shall pay for this!** questa la pagherai!; **it shall be done** sarà fatto; **but I wanted to see him — and so you shall** ma volevo vederlo! — lo vedrai

shal·lot [ʃəˈlɒt] N scalogno

shal·low [ˈʃæləʊ] ADJ (*comp* **-er**, *superl* **-est**) (*water etc*) basso(-a), poco profondo(-a); (*dish*) piano(-a); (*breathing*) leggero(-a); (*fig: person*) superficiale, leggero(-a); (: *conversation*) futile, frivolo(-a) ♦ **shallows** NPL secche *fpl*

sham [ʃæm] ADJ (*piety*) falso(-a); (*politeness*) finto(-a); (*elections*) fasullo(-a); (*battle, illness*) simulato(-a); **a sham marriage** un falso matrimonio; **sham promises** promesse vuote e false ♦ N **1** (*imposture*) messinscena, finta **2** (*person*) ciarlatano(-a), impostore *m* ♦ VT fingere, simulare; **to sham illness** fingersi malato(-a) ♦ VI fingere, far finta; **he's just shamming** fa solo finta

sham·bles [ˈʃæmblz] NSG (*scene of confusion*) macello, baraonda; **the area was (in) a shambles after the earthquake** dopo il terremoto la zona era nella distruzione più totale; **the economy is (in) a complete shambles** l'economia è nel caos più totale; **the place was (in) a shambles** c'era un macello; **the game was a shambles** la partita è stata un disastro; **it's a complete shambles** è un disastro totale

sham·bol·ic [ʃæmˈbɒlɪk] ADJ (*Brit fam*) incasinato(-a)

shame [ʃeɪm] N **1** (*feeling*) vergogna, pudore *m*; (*humiliation*) vergogna; **shame on you!** vergognati!, vergogna!; **to put sb/ sth to shame** (*fig*) far sfigurare qn/qc; **I'd die of shame!** morirei di vergogna! **2** (*pity*): **it's a shame (that/to do)** è un peccato (che + *sub* /fare); **what a shame!** che peccato! ♦ VT (*make ashamed*) far vergognare; (*bring disgrace on*) disonorare; **to shame sb into doing sth** far vergognare qn a tal punto da fargli fare qc

shame·faced [ˈʃeɪmˌfeɪst] ADJ (*ashamed*) tutto(-a) vergognoso(-a); (*confused*) confuso(-a), timido(-a)

shame·ful [ˈʃeɪmfʊl] ADJ vergognoso(-a)

shame·less [ˈʃeɪmlɪs] ADJ (*unashamed, brazen*) svergognato(-a), sfrontato(-a); (*immodest*) spudorato(-a)

sham·poo [ʃæmˈpuː] N (*for hair*) shampoo *m inv*; (*for carpet*) detersivo liquido; **shampoo and set** shampoo e messa in piega ♦ VT (*hair*) lavare (con shampoo); (*carpet*) lavare (con detersivo liquido); **to shampoo one's hair** farsi lo shampoo

sham·rock [ˈʃæmˌrɒk] N trifoglio

shan·dy [ˈʃændɪ] N (*Brit*) birra con gazzosa

shan't [ʃɑːnt] = **shall not**

shanty·town [ˈʃæntɪˌtaʊn] N bidonville *f inv*, baraccopoli *f inv*

SHAPE [ʃeɪp] N ABBR (= *Supreme Headquarters Allied Powers Europe*) quartier *m* generale delle forze NATO in Europa

shape [ʃeɪp] N forma; **what shape is it?** di che forma è?, che forma ha?; **in the shape of a heart** a forma di cuore; **it is rectangular in shape** è di forma rettangolare; **his ears are a funny shape** le sue orecchie hanno una forma buffa; **a strange shape** una strana forma; **in all shapes and sizes** d'ogni forma e dimensione, di tutti i tipi; **I can't bear gardening in any shape or form** detesto il giardinaggio di qualunque specie; **to take shape** prendere forma; **to take the shape of** prendere la forma di; **the news reached him in the shape of a telegram** ha ricevuto la notizia sotto forma di telegramma; **the shape of things to come** il volto del futuro; **to lose its shape** (*sweater etc*) sformarsi; **to be in good/poor shape** (*person*) essere in (ottima) forma/giù di forma; (*object*) essere in buone/cattive condizioni; **to knock** *or* **hammer sth into shape** dar forma a qc a colpi di martello; **to knock** *or* **lick into shape** (*fig: business etc*) rimettere in sesto; (: *plan, team*) mettere a punto; (: *athlete*) rimettere in forma; **to get o.s. into shape** rimettersi in forma; **a shape loomed up out of the fog** una forma indistinta emerse dalla nebbia ♦ VT (*clay, stone*) dar forma a; (*fig: ideas, character*) formare; (: *course of events*) determinare, condizionare ♦ VI (*fig: also: shape up*): **things are shaping (up) well** le cose si mettono bene; **he's shaping (up) nicely** sta facendo dei progressi

-shaped [ʃeɪpt] SUFF: **heart-shaped** a forma di cuore; **diamond-shaped** a forma di losanga

shape·less [ˈʃeɪplɪs] ADJ informe, senza forma

shape·ly [ˈʃeɪplɪ] ADJ (comp **-ier**, superl **-iest**) ben fatto(-a)

share [ʃɛəʳ] N 1 parte f; **to have a share in the profits** partecipare agli utili; **to have a share in sth** aver parte in qc; **he has a 50% share in a new business venture** è socio al 50% in una nuova impresa commerciale; **he had a share in it** (fig) c'è entrato anche lui; **to take a share in sth** partecipare a qc; **fair shares for all** parti giuste or uguali per tutti; **she's had more than her (fair) share of suffering** ha avuto la sua buona dose di sofferenze; **I want a fair share** ne voglio una parte equa; **the minister came in for his share of criticism** il ministro ha avuto la sua parte di critiche; **he refused to pay his share of the bill** ha rifiutato di pagare la sua quota del conto; **to do one's (fair) share** fare la propria parte 2 (Fin) azione f, titolo; **he has 500 shares in an oil company** possiede 500 azioni di una compagnia di petrolio; **they've got shares in British Gas** hanno delle azioni della British Gas; **ordinary/preference shares** azioni ordinarie/privilegiate ♦ VT 1 (also: **share out**) spartirsi; **to share (out) among** or **between** dividere tra; **they shared the sweets out among the children** hanno distribuito le caramelle ai bambini; **the thieves shared (out) the money** i ladri si sono spartiti i soldi 2 (use jointly): **to share (with)** dividere (con); **I share the room with Helen** divido la stanza con Helen; **shall we share the last bottle of wine?** ci beviamo insieme l'ultima bottiglia di vino?; **shared line** (Telec) duplex m inv 3 (fig: have in common) condividere, avere in comune; **she shares his love of gardening** hanno in comune la passione del giardinaggio ♦ VI: **children must learn to share** i bambini devono imparare a dividere ciò che hanno; **share and share alike** un po' per uno non fa male a nessuno; **to share in** (gen) partecipare a; (blame) prendersi la propria parte di
❏ share is not translated by the Italian word share

share capital N (Fin) capitale m azionario
share certificate N (Fin) certificato azionario
share·holder [ˈʃɛəˌhəʊldəʳ] N azionista m/f
share index N (Fin) indice m azionario

shark [ʃɑːk] N (fish) squalo, pescecane m; (fam: swindler) pirata m; (: a successful and rich one) pescecane m

sharp [ʃɑːp] ADJ (comp **-er**, superl **-est**) 1 (edge, razor, knife) tagliente, affilato(-a); (point) acuminato(-a); (pencil) appuntito(-a); (needle, stone) aguzzo(-a); (angle) acuto(-a); (curve, bend) stretto(-a), a gomito; (features) spigoloso(-a); (nose, chin) affilato(-a), aguzzo(-a); **be careful, that knife's sharp!** stai attento, quel coltello è affilato!; **a sharp bend** una curva a gomito 2 (abrupt: change, halt) brusco(-a); (: descent) ripido(-a); (: rise, fall) improvviso(-a) e marcato(-a); **a sharp rise in prices** un brusco e notevole aumento dei prezzi 3 (well-defined: outline) nitido(-a), netto(-a); (: contrast) spiccato(-a), marcato(-a); (: TV: picture) chiaro(-a) 4 (harsh: smell, taste) acuto(-a), aspro(-a); (: pain, cry) acuto(-a); (: blow) violento(-a); (: tone, voice) secco(-a), aspro(-a); (: wind, frost) penetrante, pungente; (: rebuke) aspro(-a); (: retort, tongue) tagliente, duro(-a); (: words) pungente; **to be sharp with sb** rimproverare aspramente qn 5 (acute: eyesight, hearing, sense of smell) acuto(-a), fine; (: mind, intelligence) acuto(-a); (: person) sveglio(-a), svelto(-a); **she's very sharp** è molto sveglia 6 (Mus): **C sharp** do diesis ♦ N 1 (Mus) in diesis 2 **at 5 o'clock sharp** alle 5 in punto; **turn sharp left** gira tutto a sinistra; **look sharp!** sbrigati!, spicciati! ♦ N (Mus) diesis m inv

sharp·en [ˈʃɑːpən] VT 1 (tool, blade etc) affilare; (pencil) temperare 2 (outline) mettere in risalto, far spiccare; (contrast, difference) sottolineare, evidenziare; (TV picture) mettere a fuoco; (conflict) intensificare; (desire, pain) acuire; (appetite) aguzzare, stuzzicare; **to sharpen one's wits** aguzzare l'ingegno

sharp·en·er [ˈʃɑːpnəʳ] N (for pencils) temperamatite m inv; (for knives) affilacoltelli m inv

sharp-eyed [ʃɑːpˈaɪd], **sharp-sighted** [ʃɑːpˈsaɪtɪd] ADJ dalla vista acuta

sharp·ish [ˈʃɑːpɪʃ] ADV (Brit fam: quickly) subito

sharp·ly [ˈʃɑːplɪ] ADV 1 (abruptly: turn, rise, stop) bruscamente 2 (clearly: stand out, contrast) nettamente 3 (harshly: criticize, retort) duramente, aspramente

sharp-tempered [ʃɑːpˈtɛmpəd] ADJ irascibile

shat·ter [ˈʃætəʳ] VT (glass, window) frantumare, mandare in frantumi; (door) fracassare; (health) rovinare; (career) compromettere definitivamente; (nerves) mandare in pezzi; (self-confidence, hope) distruggere; **the bullet shattered his skull** la pallottola gli ha frantumato il cranio; **his death shattered all their hopes** la sua morte ha mandato in fumo tutte le loro speranze ♦ VI frantumarsi, andare in frantumi; **it shattered into a thousand pieces** è andato in mille pezzi; **the windscreen shattered** il parabrezza è andato in pezzi

shat·tered [ˈʃætəd] ADJ (grief-stricken) sconvolto(-a); (fam: exhausted) a pezzi, distrutto(-a); **I'm absolutely shattered!** sono proprio distrutto!; **I was shattered to hear this news** la notizia mi ha sconvolto

shatter·proof [ˈʃætəpruːf] ADJ infrangibile

shave [ʃeɪv] N: **to have a shave** farsi la barba; **I need a shave** devo farmi la barba; **to have a close shave** (fig) cavarsela per un pelo; **that was a close shave!** ce la siamo cavata per un pelo! ♦ VT (person, legs, head) radere, rasare; (wood) piallare; (fig: graze) sfiorare, rasentare; **to shave off one's beard** tagliarsi la barba; **to shave one's legs** depilarsi le gambe ♦ VI (person) farsi la barba, radersi, sbarbarsi; **he's shaving** si sta facendo la barba

shav·en [ˈʃeɪvn] ADJ (head) rasato(-a), rapato(-a) (a zero)
shav·er [ˈʃeɪvəʳ] N (also: **electric shaver**) rasoio elettrico
shav·ing [ˈʃeɪvɪŋ] N (gen pl: of wood etc) truciolo
shaving brush N pennello da barba
shaving cream N crema da barba
shaving foam N = shaving cream
shaving soap N sapone m da barba
shawl [ʃɔːl] N scialle m

she [ʃiː] PERS PRON 1 (used of people, animals) lei; **she has gone out** è uscita; **she was fifteen then** allora lei aveva quindici anni; **she's very tall** è molto alta; **there she is** eccola; **SHE didn't do it** non è stata lei a farlo 2 (used of countries, cars, ships): **she does 0 to 60 in 10 seconds** ha un'accelerazione da 0 a 60 in 10 secondi ♦ N: **it's a she** (animal: also fam: baby) è una femmina

sheaf [ʃiːf] N (pl **sheaves**) (Agr) covone m; (of papers) fascio

shear [ʃɪəʳ] (pt **sheared** pp **sheared** or **shorn**) VT (sheep) tosare
▸ **shear off** VI + ADV (break off) spezzarsi

shears [ʃɪəz] NPL (for gardening) cesoie fpl; (for dressmaking) forbici fpl; (for sheep) forbici fpl da tosatore

sheath [ʃiːθ] N (gen) guaina; (for sword) guaina, fodero; (contraceptive) preservativo

sheathe [ʃiːð] VT ricoprire; (sword) rinfoderare
sheath knife N coltello con fodero
sheaves [ʃiːvz] NPL of **sheaf**

shed¹ [ʃɛd] (pt, pp **shed**) VT 1 (get rid of: gen) perdere; (: clothes) togliersi; (: employees) disfarsi di, licenziare; **a truck shed its load on the motorway** un camion ha perso il carico sull'autostrada; **to shed leaves** perdere foglie 2 (tears) versare; (blood) spargere 3 (send out: light, warmth) diffondere; **to shed light on** (problem, mystery) far luce su

shed² [ʃɛd] N (in garden) capanno; (for bicycles) rimessa f; (Industry, Rail) capannone m; (for cattle) stalla

she'd [ʃiːd] = she had; she would

sheen [ʃiːn] N lucentezza

sheep [ʃiːp] N pl inv pecora; **to make sheep's eyes at sb** (fig) fare gli occhi dolci a qn

sheep·dog [ˈʃiːpdɒg] N cane m (da) pastore
sheep farmer N allevatore m di pecore
sheep·ish [ˈʃiːpɪʃ] ADJ (look, smile) imbarazzato(-a), mortificato(-a)
sheep·skin [ˈʃiːpskɪn] N pelle f di pecora or di montone ♦ ADJ (gloves) di montone

sheepskin jacket N (giacca di) montone m

sheer¹ [ʃɪəʳ] ADJ (comp **-er**, superl **-est**) 1 (utter: madness, greed) puro(-a); (: waste of time) totale; (: necessity) assoluto(-a); **that's sheer robbery!** è un furto bello e buono!; **it's sheer greed** è pura avidità; **the sheer impossibility of …**

l'assoluta impossibilità di...; **by sheer chance, by a sheer accident** per puro caso *or* pura combinazione **2** (*transparent*) trasparente **3** (*precipitous*) a picco; **a sheer drop** uno strapiombo ♦ ADV a picco, a perpendicolo

sheer² [ʃɪəʳ] VI (*also:* **to sheer off**: *gen: Naut*) deviare

sheet¹ [ʃiːt] N (*on bed*) lenzuolo; (*also:* **dust sheet**) telo; (*of paper, plastic*) foglio; (*of metal, glass, ice*) lastra; (*of water*) distesa; (*of flame*) muro; **cotton sheets** lenzuola di cotone; **a sheet of paper** un foglio di carta
▸ **sheet down** VI + ADV (*rain*) piovere a dirotto

sheet² [ʃiːt] N (*Naut*) scotta

sheet feed N (*on printer*) alimentazione *f* di fogli

sheet lightning N lampeggio diffuso

sheet metal N lamiera

sheet music N spartito (*non rilegato*)

sheik, sheikh [ʃeɪk] N sceicco

shelf [ʃɛlf] N (*pl* **shelves**) **1** (*in cupboard, oven*) ripiano; (*fixed to wall*) mensola **2** (*in rock face, underwater*) piattaforma

shelf life N (*Comm*) durata di conservazione

shell [ʃɛl] N **1** (*of egg, nut, tortoise*) guscio; (*of oyster, mussel*) conchiglia; (*of lobster*) corazza, guscio; (*Phys*) guscio elettronico; **to come out of one's shell** (*fig*) uscire dal (proprio) guscio; **an egg shell** un guscio d'uovo **2** (*of building*) struttura, scheletro; (*of ship*) ossatura **3** (*Mil*) granata; **an unexploded shell** una granata inesplosa ♦ VT **1** (*nuts*) sgusciare; (*peas, beans*) sgranare **2** (*Mil*) bombardare
▸ **shell out** (*fam*) VI + ADV: **to shell out (for)** sganciare soldi (per) ♦ VT + ADV: **to shell out (for)** (*money*) sganciare (per)

she'll [ʃiːl] = **she will; she shall**

shell·fish [ˈʃɛlˌfɪʃ] N *pl inv* (*crab etc*) crostaceo; (*mollusc*) mollusco; (*Culin*) frutti *mpl* di mare

shell·suit [ˈʃɛlˌsuːt] N tuta di acetato

shel·ter [ˈʃɛltəʳ] N **1** (*protection*) riparo; **under the shelter of** al riparo di; **to seek shelter (from)** cercare riparo (da *or* contro), ripararsi (da); **to take shelter (from)** mettersi al riparo (da) **2** (*construction: on mountain etc*) rifugio; **bus shelter** pensilina; **air-raid shelter** rifugio antiaereo ♦ VT **1** (*protect*): **to shelter (from)** riparare (da); (*from blame etc*) proteggere (da) **2** (*give lodging to: homeless, criminal etc*) dare rifugio *or* asilo a ♦ VI ripararsi, mettersi al riparo; **to shelter from the rain** ripararsi dalla pioggia; **to shelter under a tree** ripararsi sotto un albero

shel·tered [ˈʃɛltəd] ADJ (*place*) riparato(-a); (*childhood*) sereno(-a), senza problemi; (*environment*) protetto(-a); **she has led a very sheltered life** è vissuta nella bambagia

shelve [ʃɛlv] VT (*fig: postpone*) accantonare

shelves [ʃɛlvz] NPL *of* **shelf**

shelv·ing [ˈʃɛlvɪŋ] N scaffalature *fpl*

shep·herd [ˈʃɛpəd] N pastore *m*; **the Good Shepherd** (*Rel*) il buon Pastore; **a shepherd with his dog** un pastore con il suo cane ♦ VT: **to shepherd sb in/out** accompagnare qn dentro/fuori; **she shepherded the children across the road** ha aiutato i bambini ad attraversare la strada

shep·herd·ess [ˈʃɛpədɪs] N pastorella

shepherd's pie N (*Culin*) timballo di carne macinata e purè di patate

sher·bet [ˈʃəːbət] N (*Brit: powder*) polvere effervescente al gusto di frutta; (*USA: water ice*) sorbetto

sher·iff [ˈʃɛrɪf] N sceriffo

sher·ry [ˈʃɛrɪ] N sherry *m inv*

she's [ʃiːz] = **she is; she has**

Shet·land [ˈʃɛtlənd] N: **the Shetlands, the Shetland Islands** le (isole) Shetland

Shetland pony N pony *m inv* delle Shetland

shield [ʃiːld] N (*armour*) scudo; (*on machine etc*) schermo (di protezione) ♦ VT: **to shield sb from sth** riparare qn da qc; **to shield sb with one's body** fare scudo a qn con il proprio corpo

shift [ʃɪft] N **1** (*change: in wind, opinion etc*) cambiamento; (*movement: of load*) spostamento; (*Comm: in demand*) variazione *f* (della domanda); **a shift in government policy** un cambiamento nella politica del governo **2** (*period of work, group of workers*) turno; **to work in shifts** fare i turni (di lavoro); **the night shift** il turno di notte; **to work on night/day shift** fare il turno di notte/di giorno **3** (*old: expedient*)

espediente *m*; **to make shift with/without sth** arrangiarsi con/senza qc **4** (*USA: Aut: also:* **gear shift**) cambio ♦ VT (*gen*) spostare; (*sth stuck*) smuovere; (*dirt, stain*) togliere; (*employee*) trasferire; (*change: position etc*) cambiare; **to shift scenery** (*Theatre*) cambiare le scene; **to shift the blame on to sb** scaricare la colpa su qn; **I couldn't shift the wardrobe on my own** non riuscivo a spostare l'armadio da solo ♦ VI **1** (*gen*) spostarsi; (*opinions*) mutare; (*change one's mind*) cambiare idea; **the wind has shifted to the south** il vento ha girato verso sud; **he shifted over to the door** si è avvicinato alla porta; **shift off the sofa!** togliti dal divano!; **shift up** *or* **over** *or* **along!** spostati!; **that car's certainly shifting** (*fam*) quella macchina va molto forte; **to shift into second gear** (*Aut*) innestare la seconda (marcia) **2** **to shift for o.s.** arrangiarsi da sé, cavarsela da solo(-a)

shift key N (*on typewriter*) tasto delle maiuscole

shift·less [ˈʃɪftlɪs] ADJ: **a shiftless person** un(a) inetto(-a)

shift work N: **to do shift work** fare i turni

shifty [ˈʃɪftɪ] ADJ (*comp* **-ier**, *superl* **-iest**) (*person*) losco(-a), equivoco(-a); (*behaviour*) losco(-a), equivoco(-a); (*eyes*) sfuggente; **he looked shifty** aveva un'aria losca

Shi·ite [ˈʃiːaɪt] ADJ, N sciita *m/f*

shil·ling [ˈʃɪlɪŋ] N (*Brit*) scellino

shilly·shally [ˈʃɪlɪˌʃælɪ] VI (*fam*) tentennare, esitare; **don't shillyshally!, stop shillyshallying!** deciditi una buona volta!

shim·mer [ˈʃɪməʳ] VI (*gen*) luccicare, scintillare; (*heat haze*) tremolare

shim·mer·ing [ˈʃɪmərɪŋ] ADJ (*gen*) luccicante, scintillante; (*haze*) tremolante; (*satin etc*) cangiante

shin [ʃɪn] N stinco ♦ VI: **to shin up a tree** arrampicarsi in cima a un albero

shin·dig [ˈʃɪnˌdɪɡ] N (*fam*) festa indiavolata

shine [ʃaɪn] VI (*pt, pp* **shone**) (ri)splendere, brillare; **the sun was shining** splendeva il sole; **the light was shining in his eyes** aveva la luce negli occhi; **the light was shining under the door** si vedeva la luce sotto la porta; **the metal shone in the sun** il metallo risplendeva al sole; **her face shone with happiness** il suo viso splendeva di felicità; **her eyes shone with joy** i suoi occhi brillavano di gioia; **to shine at mathematics** (*fig*) brillare in matematica ♦ VT (*pt, pp* **shone** *or* **shined**) **1** **shine the light** *or* **your torch over here** fai luce (con la pila) in questa direzione **2** (*pt, pp* **shined**: *polish*: **lucidare, lustrare ♦ N** (*of sun, metal*) lucentezza, splendore *m*; **to give sth a shine** dare una lucidata a qc; **those shoes have got a good shine** quelle scarpe luccicano; **to take the shine off sth** far perdere il lucido a qc; (*fig*) offuscare qc; **to take a shine to sb** (*fig*) prendere qn in simpatia; **come rain or shine** ... qualunque tempo faccia..., col bello o col cattivo tempo...

shin·gle [ˈʃɪŋɡl] N **1** (*on beach*) ciottoli *mpl* **2** (*on roof*) scandola **3** (*USA: signboard*) insegna

shin·gles [ˈʃɪŋɡlz] NSG (*Med*) fuoco di Sant'Antonio

shin·ing [ˈʃaɪnɪŋ] ADJ (*surface, hair*) lucente; (*light*) brillante; (*eyes*) splendente; **a shining example** (*fig*) un fulgido esempio

shiny [ˈʃaɪnɪ] ADJ (*comp* **-ier**, *superl* **-iest**) lucido(-a)

ship [ʃɪp] N nave *f*; **Her** (*or* **His**) **Majesty's Ship Ark Royal** l'Ark Royal *f*; **on board ship** a bordo; **ship's company** equipaggio; **ship's papers** carte *fpl* di bordo; **ship's stores** riserve *fpl* di bordo ♦ VT **1** (*take on board: goods, water*) imbarcare; (: *oars*) tirare in barca **2** (*transport: usu by ship*) spedire (*via mare*); **a new engine has to be shipped out to them** hanno dovuto spedire loro un motore nuovo

ship·builder [ˈʃɪpˌbɪldəʳ] N costruttore *m* navale

ship·building [ˈʃɪpˌbɪldɪŋ] N costruzione *f* navale

ship chan·dler [ˈʃɪpˌtʃændləʳ] N (*person*) fornitore *m* marittimo; (*company*) società *f inv* di forniture navali

ship·ment [ˈʃɪpmənt] N (*act*) spedizione *f*; (*quantity*) carico

ship·owner [ˈʃɪpˌəʊnəʳ] N armatore *m*

ship·per [ˈʃɪpəʳ] N spedizioniere *m* (marittimo)

ship·ping [ˈʃɪpɪŋ] N (*ships*) imbarcazioni *fpl*; (*traffic*) navigazione *f*; **a danger to shipping** un pericolo per la navigazione; **shipping is extra** i costi di trasporto sono a parte

shipping agent N agente *m* marittimo

shipping company, shipping line N compagnia di navigazione

shipping lane N rotta (di navigazione)

ship·shape [ˈʃɪpˌʃeɪp] ADJ in perfetto ordine

ship·wreck [ˈʃɪpˌrek] N (*ship*) relitto; (*event*) naufragio ♦ VT: **to be shipwrecked** naufragare, fare naufragio

ship·yard [ˈʃɪpˌjɑːd] N cantiere *m* navale

shire [ˈʃaɪəʳ] N (*Brit*) contea

shirk [ʃɜːk] VT (*duty*) sottrarsi a, sfuggire a; (*issue*) ignorare; (*work*) scansare; **to shirk doing sth** evitare di fare qc ♦ VI fare lo(-a) scansafatiche

shirt [ʃɜːt] N (*man's*) camicia; (*woman's*) camicetta, camicia; **in one's shirt sleeves** in maniche di camicia; **to put one's shirt on sth** (*fig: Betting*) giocarsi anche la camicia su qc; **keep your shirt on!** (*fig: fam*) non ti scaldare!

shit [ʃɪt](*fam!*) EXCL merda (*fam!*) ♦ N (*excrement*) merda (*fam!*); (*rubbish*) porcheria; (*worthless person*) pezzo di merda (*fam!*) ♦ VI cacare

shiv·er [ˈʃɪvəʳ] N brivido; **it sends shivers down my spine, it gives me the shivers** mi fa venire i brividi ♦ VI: **to shiver (with)** (*cold, fear*) rabbrividire (da), tremare (da)

shoal [ʃəʊl] N (*of fish*) banco

shock [ʃɒk] N **1** (*Elec: of earthquake*) scossa; (*of explosion*) scossone *m*; (*of collision*) urto; **an electric shock** una scossa elettrica; **to get a shock** (*Elec*) prendere la scossa; **I got a shock when I touched the switch** quando ho toccato l'interruttore ho preso la scossa **2** (*emotional*) shock *m inv*, colpo; **the shock was too much for him** non ha sopportato il colpo *or* lo shock; **the news came as a shock** la notizia è stata uno shock; **it came as a shock to hear that ... è** stato uno shock venire a sapere che...; **it may come as a shock to you, but ...** per quanto possa sorprenderti...; **to give sb a shock** far venire un colpo a qn **3** (*Med*) shock *m inv*; **to be suffering from shock** essere in stato di shock ♦ VT (*affect emotionally, scandalize*) scioccare; **he is easily shocked** si scandalizza facilmente; **they were shocked by what happened** erano scioccati per ciò che era successo; **after twenty years in the police nothing shocks him** dopo vent'anni di lavoro in polizia non lo scandalizza più niente; **to shock sb out of one's complacency** far perdere a qn un po' della sua boria ♦ VI far scandalo, destare scalpore

shock absorber [-əbˈsɔːbəʳ] N (*Aut*) ammortizzatore *m*

shock·er [ˈʃɒkəʳ] N (*fam*): **it was a real shocker** è stata una vera bomba

shock·ing [ˈʃɒkɪŋ] ADJ (*appalling: news*) scioccante; (: *sight, crime*) agghiacciante; (*causing scandal: behaviour, film*) scandaloso(-a); (: *price*) sbalorditivo(-a); (: *waste*) vergognoso(-a); (*very bad: weather, handwriting*) orribile; (: *results*) disastroso(-a); **it's shocking!** è scandaloso!; **a shocking waste** uno spreco vergognoso; **the weather was shocking** il tempo era orribile

shock·proof [ˈʃɒkˌpruːf] ADJ antiurto *inv*

shock therapy, shock treatment N (*Med*) trattamento con elettroshock

shock wave N (*of explosion, earthquake*) onda d'urto; (*fig*); **shock waves** NPL impatto *msg*

shod [ʃɒd] PT, PP *of* shoe

shod·dy [ˈʃɒdɪ] ADJ (*comp* -**ier**, *superl* -**iest**) scadente

shoe [ʃuː] (*pt, pp* shod) N **1** scarpa, calzatura; **I wouldn't like to be in his shoes** non vorrei essere nei suoi panni **2** (*horseshoe*) ferro di cavallo **3** (*also*: **brake shoe**) ganascia (del freno) ♦ VT (*horse*) ferrare

shoe·brush [ˈʃuːˌbrʌʃ] N spazzola per le scarpe

shoe·horn [ˈʃuːˌhɔːn] N calzante *m*, calzascarpe *m inv*

shoe·lace [ˈʃuːˌleɪs] N laccio (di scarpa), stringa

shoe·maker [ˈʃuːˌmeɪkəʳ] N calzolaio

shoe polish N lucido *or* per scarpe

shoe shop [ˈʃuːˌʃɒp] N negozio di scarpe *or* di calzature

shoe·string [ˈʃuːˌstrɪŋ] N (*USA*) stringa (di scarpa); **on a shoestring** (*fig: do sth*) con quattro soldi; (: *live*) contando il centesimo

shoe·tree [ˈʃuːˌtriː] N forma per scarpe

shone [ʃɒn] PT, PP *of* shine

shoo [ʃuː] EXCL sciò!, via! ♦ VT (*also*: **shoo away, shoo off**) cacciare (via)

shook [ʃʊk] PT *of* shake

shoot [ʃuːt] (*pt, pp* shot) VT **1** (*hit*) colpire, sparare a; (*hunt*) cacciare, andare a caccia di; (*execute*) fucilare; (*kill*) uccidere; **he was shot in the arm** gli hanno sparato al braccio; **he was shot by a sniper** è stato colpito da un cecchino; **he was shot at dawn** è stato fucilato all'alba; **he shot himself with a revolver** si è sparato con un revolver; **to shoot sb dead** colpire a morte qn; **to shoot o.s. in the foot** (*fig*) darsi la zappa sui piedi; **you'll get shot if you do that!** (*fig: fam*) puoi rimetterci le penne! **2** (*fire: bullet*) sparare; (: *arrow*) scoccare; (: *missile*) lanciare; **to shoot one's way out** farsi largo a colpi di pistola; **to shoot an arrow at sb** tirare una freccia contro qn; **to shoot dice** tirare i dadi **3** (*direct: look, smile*) lanciare; **to shoot a look at sb** lanciare uno sguardo a qn; **to shoot a question at sb** sparare una domanda a qn **4** (*Cine: film, scene*) girare; (: *person, object*) riprendere; **the film was shot in Prague** il film è stato girato a Praga **5** (*pass quickly: rapids*) scendere ♦ VI **1 to shoot (at sb/sth)** (*with gun*) sparare a qn/qc); (*with bow*) tirare (su *or* contro qn/qc); **don't shoot!** non sparare!; **to shoot on sight** sparare a vista; **to shoot back** rispondere al fuoco; **to shoot wide** tirare a vuoto **2** (*rush*): **to shoot in/out** entrare/uscire come una freccia; **to shoot across** precipitarsi verso; **to shoot past sb** sfrecciare vicino a qn; **a car shot past me** una macchina mi è sfrecciata accanto; **the pain shot up his leg** sentì una fitta lancinante alla gamba; **the bullet shot past his head** il colpo gli ha sfiorato la testa ♦ N **1** (*Bot*) germoglio **2** (*shooting party*) partita di caccia; (*competition*) gara di tiro; (*preserve*) riserva di caccia **3** (*fig: fam*): **the whole shoot** tutto, ogni cosa

▸ **shoot down** VT + ADV (*aeroplane*) abbattere; (*person*) uccidere; (*fig: person*) distruggere; (: *argument*) demolire

▸ **shoot out** VT + ADV: **he shot out his arm and saved me** ha allungato prontamente il braccio e mi ha salvato; **to shoot it out** regolare una faccenda a colpi di pistola ♦ VI + ADV (*water*) sprizzare; (*flames*) divampare

▸ **shoot up** VI + ADV **1** (*flames, rocket*) alzarsi; (*water*) scaturire con forza; (*price*) salire alle stelle **2 he's shooting up** sta crescendo a vista d'occhio; **he has shot up** è cresciuto molto ♦ VT + ADV (*fam: heroin*) bucarsi

shoot·ing [ˈʃuːtɪŋ] N **1** (*shots*) spari *mpl*, colpi *mpl* d'arma da fuoco; (*continuous shooting*) sparatoria; **they heard shooting** hanno sentito degli spari **2** (*act: murder*) uccisione *f* (a colpi d'arma da fuoco); (: *wounding*) ferimento **3** (*Cine*) riprese *fpl* **4** (*Hunting*) caccia; **shooting and fishing** la caccia e la pesca ♦ ADJ (*pain*) lancinante

shooting range N poligono di tiro

shooting star N stella cadente

shop [ʃɒp] N **1** (*Comm*) negozio; **at the baker's shop** in panetteria; **a sports shop** un negozio di articoli sportivi; **to shut up shop** chiudere; (*fig*) chiudere bottega; **to talk shop** (*fig*) parlare di lavoro; **all over the shop** (*fig: fam*) dappertutto **2** (*Industry: workshop*) officina; **repair shop** officina di riparazione ♦ VI (*gen*) fare acquisti, fare compere; (*for food*) fare la spesa; **to go shopping** andare a fare lo shopping, andare a fare compere *or* spese; **they shop in expensive stores** vanno a fare compere in negozi costosi; **I was shopping for a dress** cercavo un vestito ♦ VT (*fam: betray*) tradire

▸ **shop around** VI + ADV (*compare prices*) confrontare i prezzi; (*fig: weigh up alternatives*) confrontare diverse possibilità

shopa·holic [ˌʃɒpəˈhɒlɪk] N (*fam*) maniaco(-a) dello shopping

shop assistant N (*Brit*) commesso(-a)

shop floor N (*Industry*): **the workers on the shop floor** gli operai; **he works on the shop floor** è un operaio

shop·keeper [ˈʃɒpˌkiːpəʳ] N negoziante *m/f*, bottegaio(-a)

shop·lift [ˈʃɒpˌlɪft] VI taccheggiare

shop·lifter [ˈʃɒpˌlɪftəʳ] N taccheggiatore(-trice)

shop·lifting [ˈʃɒpˌlɪftɪŋ] N taccheggio

shop·per [ˈʃɒpəʳ] N **1** (*person*) acquirente *m/f* **2** (*bag*) borsa per la spesa

shop·ping [ˈʃɒpɪŋ] N (*goods*) acquisti *mpl*, compere *fpl*; (*food*) spesa; **I love shopping** adoro lo shopping; **can you get the shopping from the car?** puoi prendere la spesa dalla macchina?

shopping bag N borsa per la spesa

shopping cart N (*USA*: *Comput*: *shopping trolley*) carrello
shopping centre N centro commerciale
shopping mall N centro commerciale
shop steward N (*Brit*: *Industry*) rappresentante *m/f* sindacale
shop window N vetrina
shore¹ [ʃɔː] VT: **to shore up** (*tunnel, wall*) puntellare; (*fig*) consolidare (*prices*) mantenere
shore² [ʃɔː] N (*of sea*) riva; (*of lake*) sponda, riva; (*beach*) spiaggia; (*coast*) costa; **on shore** a terra; **to go on shore** sbarcare; **the ship hugged the shore** la nave navigava sotto costa; **boats on the shore** barche sulla riva
shore leave N (*Naut*) franchigia
shorn [ʃɔːn] PP *of* **shear** ♦ ADJ **1** (*grass*) tosato(-a); (*head*) rasato(-a) **2** (*fig*): **shorn of** (*power, glory*) privato(-a) di
short [ʃɔːt] ADJ (*comp -er, superl -est*) **1** (*in length, distance*) corto(-a); (*in time*) breve; (*person*) basso(-a); **a short skirt** una gonna corta; **short hair** capelli corti; **a short break** una breve pausa; **it was a great holiday, but too short** è stata una bella vacanza, ma troppo breve; **she's quite short** è piuttosto bassa; **the days are getting shorter** le giornate si stanno accorciando; **to be short in the leg** (*person*) avere le gambe corte; (*trousers*) essere corti di gamba; **to win by a short head** (*Racing*) vincere di mezza testa *or* incollatura; **a short time ago** poco tempo fa; **time is getting short** il tempo stringe; **that was short and sweet** è stato sbrigativo; **to make short work of sb** (*fig*) sistemare qn; **to make short work of sth** (*job*) sbrigare qc; (*cake, drink*) far fuori qc **2** (*insufficient*): **I'm £30 short** mi mancano 30 sterline; **to give short weight** *or* **short measure to sb** imbrogliare qn sul peso *or* sulla misura; **to be in short supply** scarseggiare; **to be short of** (*money*) essere a corto di qc; **I'm short of time** ho poco tempo; **short of breath** senza fiato, con il fiatone; **it's little short of madness** è pazzia bella e buona; **three miles short of home** a tre miglia da casa; **at short notice** con poco preavviso **3** (*concise*) breve; **short and to the point** breve e conciso; **"Pat" is short for "Patricia"** "Pat" è il diminutivo di "Patricia"; **in short**, a farla breve; **in short, the answer is no** per farla breve, la risposta è no **4** (*reply, manner*) secco(-a), brusco(-a); **to have a short temper** essere irascibile; **to be short with sb** essere brusco(-a) con qn ♦ ADV **1** (*suddenly, abruptly*): **to stop short** fermarsi di colpo; **I'd stop short of stealing** non arriverei mai a rubare; **he wouldn't stop short of murder** arriverebbe al punto di uccidere; **to pull up short** frenare bruscamente **2** (*insufficiently*): **to run short of sth** rimanere senza qc; **we never went short (of anything)** as children da bambini non ci è mai mancato nulla; **to come** *or* **fall short of** (*expectations*) venire meno a; (*needs*) non soddisfare; **to sell sb short** (*fig*: *belittle*) sminuire qn, buttar giù qn; **to be taken** *or* **caught short** (*fam*) avere un bisognino urgente **3** (*except*): **short of selling the house, what can we do?** non vedo cos'altro potremmo fare, a parte vendere la casa; **I'll do anything short of…** farò tutto tranne che…; **nothing short of a miracle can save him** solo un miracolo potrebbe salvarlo ♦ N **1** (*Elec*) = **short circuit 2** (*fam*: *drink*) superalcolico **3** (*also*: **short film**) cortometraggio; *see also* **shorts** ♦ VT, VI (*Elec*) = **short-circuit**
short·age [ʃɔːtɪdʒ] N carenza, scarsità *f inv*; **the housing shortage** la crisi degli alloggi
short·bread [ʃɔːt,brɛd] N frollino, biscotto di pasta frolla
short-change [ʃɔːtʃeɪndʒ] VT: **to short-change sb** imbrogliare qn sul resto; (*fig*) fregare qn
short-circuit [ʃɔːtsɜːkɪt] VT (*Elec*) mettere in cortocircuito ♦ VI (*Elec*) fare cortocircuito
short·coming [ʃɔːtkʌmɪŋ] N difetto
short cut N scorciatoia
short·en [ʃɔːtn] VT (*gen*) accorciare; **the article needs to be shortened** l'articolo deve essere accorciato ♦ VI accorciarsi
short·en·ing [ʃɔːtnɪŋ] N (*Culin*) grasso (*usato in pasticceria*)
short·fall [ʃɔːt,fɔːl] N (*Fin*) deficit *m inv*; **there is a shortfall of £20,000** mancano 20.000 sterline
short·hand [ʃɔːt,hænd] N stenografia; **to take sth down in shorthand** stenografare qc
shorthand notebook N bloc-notes *m inv* per stenografia
shorthand typist N stenodattilografo(-a)

short list N graduatoria finale; (*Brit*: *for job*) rosa dei candidati
short-lived [ʃɔːt,lɪvd] ADJ (*fig*) di breve durata, effimero(-a)
short·ly [ʃɔːtlɪ] ADV **1** (*soon*) tra poco, tra breve; **shortly before/after** poco prima/dopo **2** (*curtly*) seccamente, bruscamente
short·ness [ʃɔːtnɪs] N (*of person*) bassa statura; (*of reply, manner*) bruschezza; **shortness of temper** irascibilità; **the shortness of her skirt** la sua gonna corta; **shortness of breath** affanno
short pastry, short crust pastry N (*Brit*) pasta frolla
shorts [ʃɔːts] NPL shorts *mpl*, calzoncini *mpl*
short-sighted [ʃɔːtˈsaɪtɪd] ADJ (*also fig*: *policy, decision*) miope
short-sleeved [ʃɔːtsliːvd] ADJ a maniche corte
short-staffed [ʃɔːtˈstɑːft] ADJ a corto di personale
short story N racconto, novella
short-tempered [ʃɔːtˈtɛmpəd] ADJ (*in general*) irascibile; (*in a bad mood*) di cattivo umore
short-term [ʃɔːt,tɜːm] ADJ a breve scadenza; (*solution*) di *or* a breve durata
short time N: **to work short time, be on short time** (*Industry*) essere *or* lavorare a orario ridotto
short wave N (*Radio*) onde *fpl* corte
shot [ʃɒt] N **1** (*from gun, also sound*) sparo, colpo d'arma da fuoco; (*shotgun pellets*) pallottole *fpl*; **to fire a shot at sb/sth** sparare un colpo a qn/qc; **a warning shot** un colpo di avvertimento; **good shot!** bel colpo!; **a witness said he heard a shot** un testimone ha detto di aver sentito uno sparo; **he was off like a shot** (*fig*) è partito come un razzo; **it was a shot in the dark** (*fig*) è stata un'ipotesi azzardata **2** (*person*) tiratore(-trice); **he's a good/bad shot** è un buon/pessimo tiratore; **a big shot** (*fam*) un pezzo grosso *or* da novanta, un alto papavero **3** (*Ftbl, Golf, Tennis, etc*) tiro; (*throw*) lancio; **to put the shot** lanciare il peso; **a shot at goal** un tiro in porta; **good shot!** bel tiro!, bel lancio!; **he had only one shot at goal** ha avuto solo una possibilità di segnare **4** (*attempt*) prova; (*turn to play*) turno; **to have a shot at sth/doing sth** provare a fare qc; **I'll have a shot at it** ci proverò **5** (*injection*) puntura, iniezione *f*; (*of alcohol*) bicchierino; **they gave him shots** gli hanno fatto delle iniezioni; **the economy needs a shot in the arm** (*fig*) l'economia ha bisogno di una sferzata **6** (*Phot*) foto *f inv*; (*Cine*) inquadratura; **a shot of Edinburgh castle** una foto del castello di Edimburgo ♦ PT, PP *of* **shoot**; **to get shot of sb/sth** (*fam*) sbarazzarsi di qn/qc ♦ ADJ: **shot silk** seta cangiante; **shot with blue** screziato(-a) di blu
shot·gun [ʃɒt,gʌn] N fucile *m* da caccia
should [ʃʊd] MODAL AUX VB **1** (*duty, advisability, desirability*): **all school buses should have seat belts** tutti gli autobus scolastici dovrebbero essere forniti di cinture di sicurezza; **I should go now** dovrei andare ora; **I should have been a doctor** avrei dovuto fare il medico; **I should have told you before** avrei dovuto dirtelo prima; **you shouldn't do that** non dovresti farlo; **I should go if I were you** se fossi in te andrei; **I shouldn't if I were you** se fossi in te non lo farei; **how should I know?** e che ne so io?, e come faccio a saperlo?; **I should be so lucky!** sarebbe bello! **2** (*probability*): **he should pass his exams** dovrebbe superare gli esami; **they should have arrived by now** a quest'ora dovrebbero essere già arrivati; **he should be there now** dovrebbe essere arrivato ora; **that shouldn't be too hard** non dovrebbe essere troppo difficile; **this should be good** dovrebbe essere bello **3** (*conditional uses*): **if they invited me I should go** *or* **I'd go** se mi invitassero ci andrei; **I should like to** mi piacerebbe; **I should have liked to** mi sarebbe piaciuto; **I should think so!** mi pare!, direi!; **should he phone …** (*frm*) se telefonasse…, se dovesse telefonare…; **who should I see but Maria!** e chi dovevo vedere se non Maria! **4** (*remote form of shall in indirect speech*): **I told you I should be late** ti ho detto che avrei fatto tardi
shoul·der [ʃəʊldə] N (*gen*) spalla; **to carry sth over one's shoulder** portare qc a spalla; **to cry on sb's shoulder** piangere sulla spalla di qn; **to look over one's shoulder** guardarsi alle spalle; **to look over sb's shoulder** guardare da dietro le spalle di qn; (*fig*) stare addosso a qn; **shoulder to shoulder** spalla a spalla; **to have broad shoulders** (*also fig*) avere le spalle larghe; **to put one's shoulder to the wheel** (*fig*)

mettersi all'opera; **to rub shoulders with sb** (*fig*) frequentare qn; **to give sb the cold shoulder** (*fig*) trattare qn con freddezza; **he stands head and shoulders above everybody else** è di gran lunga superiore a tutti gli altri ♦ VT (*fig: responsibilities etc*) accollarsi, addossarsi; **to shoulder sb aside** spingere qn da parte a spallate; **to shoulder one's way through the crowd** farsi largo a spallate tra la folla

shoulder bag N borsa a tracolla

shoulder blade N scapola

shoulder strap N bretella, spallina

shouldn't [ˈʃʊdnt] = should not

shout [ʃaʊt] N (*gen*) urlo, grido; **a shout of laughter** una risata fragorosa; **to give sb a shout** dare una voce a qn ♦ VT (*order, name*) gridare, urlare ♦ VI gridare, urlare; **to shout to sb to do sth** gridare a qn di fare qc; **to shout with pain** urlare per il *or* di dolore; **to shout for help** gridare aiuto; **to shout with laughter** scoppiare a ridere; **don't shout!** non urlare!; "Go away!" **he shouted** "Vattene!" urlò

▸ **shout at** VI + PREP gridare a, urlare a; **to shout at sb** (*angrily*) sgridare qn

▸ **shout down** VT + ADV: **they shouted him down** gridavano così forte che non si sentiva ciò che diceva

▸ **shout out** VI + ADV emettere un grido ♦ VT + ADV gridare

shout·ing [ˈʃaʊtɪŋ] N grida *fpl*, urla *fpl*; **it's all over bar the shouting** (*fig*) il più è fatto

shouting match N (*fam*) vivace scambio di opinioni

shove [ʃʌv] N spintone *m*; **to give sb/sth a shove** dare uno spintone a qn/qc ♦ VT (*gen*) spingere; (*thrust*) cacciare, ficcare; **he shoved me out of the way** mi ha spinto da parte in malo modo; **he shoved a cloth into my hand** mi ha ficcato in mano uno straccio; **to shove in/out** *etc* spingere dentro/fuori *etc*; **he shoved his fist/stick into my face** mi ha minacciato con il pugno/bastone ♦ VI spingere; **he shoved (his way) through the crowd** si è fatto largo tra la folla a spintoni; **to shove past sb** passare davanti a qn con uno spintone

▸ **shove off** VI + ADV 1 (*fam*) sloggiare, smammare 2 (*Naut*) prendere il largo

▸ **shove over, shove up** VI + ADV (*fam*) farsi più in là

shov·el [ˈʃʌvl] N pala ♦ VT (*coal, snow*) spalare; (*sth spilt*) raccogliere con una paletta; **he was shovelling food into his mouth** (*fig*) mangiava a quattro ganasce

show [ʃəʊ] (*pt* showed, *pp* shown) N 1 (*of feeling, emotion*) manifestazione *f*; (*of strength, goodwill*) dimostrazione *f*, prova; (*ostentation*) mostra; **a show of strength** una dimostrazione di forza; **to ask for a show of hands** chiedere una votazione per alzata di mano 2 (*exhibition: Art*) mostra, esposizione *f*; (: *Comm, Tech*) salone *m*, fiera; (: *Agr*) fiera; **a fashion show** una sfilata di moda; **to be on show** essere esposto(-a); **the garden is a splendid show** il giardino offre uno spettacolo stupendo 3 (*Theatre, Cine, etc*) spettacolo; (*variety show*) varietà *m inv*; **to go to a show** andare a vedere uno spettacolo; **we're seeing a show this evening** stasera andiamo a vedere uno spettacolo; **on with the show!** (*fig*) andiamo avanti!; (*old, fam*) bene, bravo(-a)!; **the last show** (*Theatre*) l'ultima rappresentazione; (*Cine*) l'ultimo spettacolo; **he's now got his own show** ora ha un suo programma; **she stole the show** tutti gli occhi erano puntati su di lei; **to put up a good show** (*fam*) difendersi bene; **to put up a poor show** (*fam*) essere una delusione; **it's a poor show when/if ...** (*fam*) siamo proprio ridotti male se... 4 (*outward appearance, pretence*) apparenza; **it's just for show** è solo per far scena; **to make a show of doing sth** far finta di fare qc; **to make a show of anger** far finta di essere arrabbiato(-a); **to make a show of resistance** accennare a una qualche resistenza 5 (*fam: organization*) baracca; **who's running the show here?** chi è il padrone qui?; **this is my show** qui comando io ♦ VT 1 (*gen*) mostrare; (*film, slides*) proiettare; (*goods for sale, pictures*) esporre; (*animals*) presentare ad una mostra; **to show sb sth** mostrare qc a qn; **he showed me his new car** mi ha mostrato la sua macchina nuova; **have you shown the article to your boss?** hai mostrato l'articolo al tuo capo?; **to show a film at Cannes** presentare un film a Cannes; **what's showing at the Odeon?** cosa danno all'Odeon?; **white shoes soon show the dirt** le scarpe bianche si sporcano in fretta; **don't show your face here again!** non farti mai più vedere da queste parti!;

to show one's hand *or* **one's cards** scoprire le carte; (*fig*) mettere le carte in tavola; **I have nothing to show for it** non ho niente a dimostrazione dei miei sforzi; **I'll show him!** (*fam*) gli faccio vedere io! 2 (*indicate*) indicare, segnare; **as shown in the illustration** come da illustrazione; **the motorways are shown in black** le autostrade sono segnate in nero; **to show a profit/loss** (*Comm*) registrare un utile/una perdita 3 (*reveal: interest, surprise*) (di)mostrare, dar prova di; **she showed great courage** ha dimostrato un gran coraggio; **her action showed intelligence** la sua azione ha dato prova di intelligenza; **her face showed her happiness/fear** le si leggeva la felicità/paura in viso; **the choice of dishes shows excellent taste** la scelta dei piatti rivela un ottimo gusto; **this shows him to be a coward** questo dimostra la sua vigliaccheria; **it just goes to show that ...** il che sta a dimostrare che... 4 (*direct, conduct: person*) accompagnare; **to show sb the way** indicare la strada a qn; **to show sb into a room** far entrare qn in una stanza; **to show sb to his seat/to the door** accompagnare qn al suo posto/alla porta; **to show sb the door** (*fig*) mettere qn alla porta; **to show sb round** *or* **over a house** far visitare *or* vedere la casa a qn; **to show sb in/out/up** far entrare/uscire/salire qn ♦ VI (*stain, emotion, underskirt*) vedersi, essere visibile; **it shows** si vede; **I've never been riding before - it shows** non sono mai andato a cavallo prima d'ora - si vede; **it doesn't show** non si vede; **don't worry, it won't show** sta' tranquillo, non si vedrà

▸ **show off** VI + ADV (*pej*) darsi delle arie, mettersi in mostra; **he's showing off again** ecco che ricomincia a darsi delle arie ♦ VT + ADV (*pej*) mettere in mostra; (*ability, one's figure*) mostrare; (*knowledge*) ostentare; (*subj: colour, dress: qualities, features*) mettere in risalto, valorizzare

▸ **show through** VI + ADV vedersi ♦ VI + PREP vedersi attraverso

▸ **show up** VI + ADV 1 (*be visible: gen*) risaltare, (: *mistake*) saltare all'occhio 2 (*fam: arrive*) farsi vivo(-a), farsi vedere; **he showed up late as usual** si è presentato in ritardo, come al solito ♦ VT + ADV 1 (*reveal: thief, fraud*) smascherare; (: *deception*) mettere a nudo; **he was shown up as an impostor** è stato smascherato per l'impostore che era; **the bright lighting showed up her scars** la forte luce metteva in evidenza le sue cicatrici 2 (*embarrass*) far fare una figuraccia a

show business [ˈʃəʊˌbɪznɪs], **show biz** [ˈʃəʊˌbɪz] (*fam*) N mondo dello spettacolo

show·case [ˈʃəʊˌkeɪs] N (*cabinet*) vetrina, bacheca; (*fig*) vetrina; **the tournament will be a showcase of European football** il torneo sarà la vetrina del calcio europeo

show·down [ˈʃəʊˌdaʊn] N regolamento di conti

show·er [ˈʃaʊəʳ] N 1 (*of rain*) rovescio; **a shower of hail** una grandinata; **a snow shower** una nevicata 2 (*fig: of arrows, stones*) pioggia; (: *of blows*) gragnuola, scarica; (: *of bullets*) scarica; (: *of kisses, presents*) valanga 3 (*shower bath*) doccia; **to have** *or* **take a shower** fare una doccia 4 (*USA: party*) festa di fidanzamento (*in cui si fanno regali alla persona festeggiata*) ♦ VT (*fig*): **to shower sb with** (*gifts, abuse*) coprire qn di; (*blows*) riempire qn di; (*missiles*) bersagliare qn con una pioggia di; **he was showered with invitations** è stato inondato di inviti ♦ VI (*take a shower*) fare la doccia

shower cap N cuffia da doccia

shower gel N gel *m inv* doccia, *inv*

shower·proof [ˈʃaʊəˌpruːf] ADJ impermeabile

show·ery [ˈʃaʊərɪ] ADJ (*weather*) con piogge intermittenti

show·ground [ˈʃəʊˌɡraʊnd] N area di esposizione

show·ing [ˈʃəʊɪŋ] N (*of film*) proiezione *f*; (*cinema session*) spettacolo; **to make a poor showing in the opinion polls** avere un magro risultato al sondaggio d'opinione

show·jumping [ˈʃəʊˌdʒʌmpɪŋ] N concorso ippico (*di salto ad ostacoli*)

show·man [ˈʃəʊmən] N (*pl* -men) (*at fair, circus*) impresario; **he's a great showman** (*fig*) fa sempre un po' l'attore

show·man·ship [ˈʃəʊmənˌʃɪp] N (*fig*) abilità *or* capacità di intrattenere il pubblico

shown [ʃəʊn] PP *of* show

show-off [ˈʃəʊˌɒf] N (*fam*) esibizionista *m/f*

show·piece [ˈʃəʊˌpiːs] N (*of exhibition*) pezzo forte; **that hospital is a showpiece** quello è un ospedale modello

show·room [ˈʃəʊˌrʊm] N (Comm) show-room m inv, salone m d'esposizione; (Art) sala d'esposizione

show trial N processo a scopo dimostrativo (spesso ideologico)

showy [ˈʃəʊɪ] ADJ (comp -ier, superl -iest) vistoso(-a), appariscente

shrank [ʃræŋk] PT of shrink

shrap·nel [ˈʃræpnl] N shrapnel m inv

shred [ʃred] N (gen pl: of cloth) brandello; (of paper) strisciolina; (fig: of truth, evidence) briciolo; **not a shred of truth** neanche un briciolo di verità; **you haven't got a shred of evidence** non ne hai la benché minima prova; **in shreds** a brandelli; **to tear to shreds** fare a brandelli; (fig: argument) demolire; **to tear sb to shreds** fare a pezzi qn ♦ VT (paper) stracciare, strappare; (mechanically) trinciare; (food: with grater) grattugiare; (: with knife) tagliuzzare, sminuzzare; **shred the apples and carrots** sminuzzate le mele e le carote; **the documents were shredded** i documenti furono distrutti

shred·der [ˈʃredəʳ] N (for documents, papers) distruttore m di documenti

shrew [ʃruː] N (Zool) toporagno; (fig: pej: woman) strega

shrewd [ʃruːd] ADJ (comp -er, superl -est) (person, assessment) acuto(-a), accorto(-a); (lawyer, businessman) scaltro(-a); (plan, look) astuto(-a); (guess) perspicace; **a shrewd businessman** uno scaltro uomo d'affari; **a shrewd investment** un investimento accorto; **I have a shrewd idea that ...** mi sa tanto che...

shrewd·ness [ˈʃruːdnɪs] N (see adj) acume m; accortezza; astuzia; perspicacia

shriek [ʃriːk] N strillo; **a shriek of pain** un grido di dolore; **shrieks of laughter** risate fpl stridule ♦ VI strillare; **to shriek at sb** strillare a qn; **to shriek with laughter** sbellicarsi dalle risa ♦ VT strillare

shrift [ʃrɪft] N (fig): **to give sb short shrift** trattare qn in modo sbrigativo; **to get short shrift from sb** essere trattato(-a) in modo sbrigativo da qn

shrill [ʃrɪl] ADJ (comp -er, superl -est) (bell, sound) acuto(-a), penetrante; (laugh, voice) stridulo(-a); (demand, protest) insistente

shrimp [ʃrɪmp] N (Zool) gamberetto; (fig: child) scricciolo

shrine [ʃraɪn] N (tomb) sepolcro; (place) santuario; (reliquary) reliquiario, teca

shrink [ʃrɪŋk] (pt shrank, pp shrunk) VT (wool) far restringere ♦ VI 1 (clothes) restringersi, ritirarsi; (metal) contrarsi; (gums) ritirarsi; (piece of meat) ridursi; (area, person) rimpicciolirsi; **to shrink in the wash** restringersi con il lavaggio; **my sweater shrank in the wash** il mio maglione si è ristretto durante il lavaggio; **all my sweaters have shrunk** mi si sono ristretti tutti i maglioni 2 (also: shrink away, shrink back) ritrarsi, tirarsi indietro; **to shrink from doing sth** rifuggire dal fare qc; **he didn't shrink from telling her the truth** non ha esitato a dirle la verità ♦ N (fam, pej) strizzacervelli m/f inv

shrink·age [ˈʃrɪŋkɪdʒ] N (of clothes) restringimento; (Comm: in shops) perdite fpl (dovute a danno o taccheggio)

shrink-wrap [ˌʃrɪŋkˈræp] VT cellofanare

shriv·el [ˈʃrɪvl], **shrivel up** VT (plant etc) far rinsecchire; (skin) far raggrinzire, far avvizzire ♦ VI (see vt) rinsecchirsi; raggrinzirsi, avvizzire

shroud [ʃraʊd] N (round corpse) sudario; (fig: of secrecy) alone m ♦ VT (fig): **shrouded in** (mist, darkness) circondato(-a) da; **shrouded in mystery** avvolto(-a) nel mistero

Shrove Tuesday [ʃrəʊvˈtjuːzdɪ] N martedì m inv grasso

shrub [ʃrʌb] N arbusto

shrub·bery [ˈʃrʌbərɪ] N arbusti mpl

shrug [ʃrʌg] N alzata di spalle; **a shrug of indifference** un gesto d'indifferenza; **to give a shrug of contempt** alzare le spalle con disprezzo; **...he said with a shrug** ...disse alzando le spalle ♦ VT, VI: **to shrug (one's shoulders)** alzare le spalle, fare spallucce

▸ **shrug off** VT + ADV (danger) prendere sottogamba; (insult) ignorare, passare sopra a; (troubles) minimizzare; (cold, illness) sbarazzarsi di

shrunk [ʃrʌŋk] PP of shrink

shrunk·en [ˈʃrʌŋkən] ADJ (body) rinsecchito(-a)

shud·der [ˈʃʌdəʳ] VI (person): **to shudder (with)** rabbrividire (per or da); (machinery) vibrare; **the car shuddered to a halt** dopo vari sussulti la macchina si fermò; **I shudder to think!** rabbrividisco al solo pensiero! ♦ N (of person) brivido; (of machinery) vibrazione f; **to give a shudder** (person) rabbrividire; (car) sussultare

shuf·fle [ˈʃʌfl] N 1 passo strascicato 2 (Cards) mescolata, scozzata; **to give the cards a shuffle** dare una mescolata alle carte ♦ VT 1 (feet) strascicare 2 (mix up: cards) mescolare, scozzare; (: papers) mettere sottosopra ♦ VI (walk) strascicare i piedi; **she shuffled along the corridor** strascicava i piedi lungo il corridoio; **to shuffle in/out** etc entrare/uscire etc con passo strascicato

shun [ʃʌn] VT (person, work, publicity) evitare, sfuggire; (obligation) sottrarsi a

shunt [ʃʌnt] VT (Rail: direct) smistare; (: divert) deviare; (: fig: from one place to another) spostare ♦ VI: **to shunt to and fro** fare la spola

shunting yard N fascio di smistamento

shush [ʃʊʃ] EXCL zitto(-a)! ♦ VT (fam) zittire

shut [ʃʌt] (pt, pp shut) VT (gen) chiudere; **to shut the door in sb's face** sbattere la porta in faccia a qn; **to shut one's finger in the door** chiudersi un dito nella porta; **to shut sb in a room** rinchiudere qn in una stanza; **shut your mouth** or **face!** (fam!) chiudi il becco! ♦ VI (door, window) chiudersi; (shop, bank etc) chiudere; **what time do the shops shut?** a che ora chiudono i negozi? ♦ ADJ chiuso(-a); **to keep one's mouth shut** tenere la bocca chiusa

▸ **shut away** VT + ADV (person, animal) rinchiudere, chiudere; (valuables) mettere al sicuro

▸ **shut down** VI + ADV (factory, shop) chiudere i battenti; **the cinema shut down last year** il cinema ha chiuso i battenti l'anno scorso ♦ VT + ADV (factory, shop) chiudere; (machine) fermare; (nuclear reactor) ridurre al minimo

▸ **shut in** VT + ADV rinchiudere

▸ **shut off** VT + ADV 1 (stop: power) staccare; (: water) chiudere; (: engine) spegnere 2 (isolate): **to shut off (from)** tagliar fuori (da), isolare (da)

▸ **shut out** VT + ADV (person, noise, cold) non far entrare; (block: view) impedire, bloccare; (: memory) scacciare; **to be shut out of the house** rimanere chiuso(-a) fuori casa

▸ **shut up** VI + ADV (fam: be quiet) star zitto(-a); **shut up!** stai zitto! ♦ VT + ADV 1 (factory, business, house) chiudere 2 (person, animal) rinchiudere, chiudere; (valuables) mettere al sicuro 3 (fam: silence) far stare zitto(-a)

shut·down [ˈʃʌtdaʊn] N chiusura

shut·ter [ˈʃʌtəʳ] N (on window) imposta; (for shop) battente m; (Phot) otturatore m; **shutter speed** tempo di apertura

shut·tle [ˈʃʌtl] N 1 (of loom) spola, navetta; (of sewing machine) spoletta 2 (fig: plane etc) navetta ♦ VI (subj: vehicle, person) fare la spola ♦ VT (to and fro: passengers) portare avanti e indietro; **I was/the papers were shuttled from one department to another** sono stato sballottato/la pratica è stata mandata da un ufficio all'altro

shuttle·cock [ˈʃʌtlkɒk] N (Badminton) volano

shuttle diplomacy N la gestione dei rapporti diplomatici caratterizzata dai frequenti viaggi e incontri dei rappresentanti del governo

shy [ʃaɪ] ADJ (comp -er, superl -est) timido(-a); (unsociable) schivo(-a); **to be shy of doing sth** esitare a fare qc; **don't be shy of asking for ...** non esitare a chiedere...; **to fight shy of sth** tenersi alla larga da qc; **to fight shy of doing sth** cercare in tutti i modi di non fare qc ♦ VI (horse): **to shy (at)** fare uno scarto (davanti a); **the horse shied at the noise** il cavallo ha fatto uno scarto quando ha sentito il rumore; **to shy away from sth** evitare qc; **to shy away from doing sth** (fig) rifuggire dal fare qc ♦ VT (old: throw) scagliare

shy·ness [ˈʃaɪnɪs] N timidezza

Siam [saɪˈæm] N il Siam

Sia·mese [ˌsaɪəˈmiːz] ADJ siamese ♦ N (person: pl inv) siamese m/f; (fam: cat) siamese m/f; (language) siamese m

Si·beria [saɪˈbɪərɪə] N la Siberia

sib·ling [ˈsɪblɪŋ] N (frm) fratello (sorella); **sibling rivalry** rivalità tra fratelli

Si·cil·ian [sɪˈsɪlɪən] ADJ, N siciliano(-a)

Sici·ly [ˈsɪsɪlɪ] N la Sicilia

sick [sɪk] ADJ (*comp* **-er**, *superl* **-est**) **1** (*ill*) malato(-a), ammalato(-a); **a sick person** un(a) malato(-a); **to fall** *or* **take sick** ammalarsi; **to be (off) sick** (*from work*) essere assente (per malattia); **to go sick** mettersi in malattia; **to be sick** (*vomiting*) vomitare, rimettere; **I was sick twice last night** ho vomitato due volte, ieri notte; **to feel sick** avere la nausea; **I feel sick** ho la nausea; **she looks after her sick mother** si occupa della madre malata **2** (*fig: mind, imagination*) malato(-a); (: *humour*) macabro(-a); (: *joke*) di gusto macabro; **to be sick of sth** averne abbastanza di qc; **I'm sick of your lies** ne ho abbastanza delle tue bugie; **to be sick (and tired) of sb/sth** averne fin sopra i capelli di qn/qc; **to be sick to death of sb/sth** essere stufo(-a) marcio(-a) di qn/qc; **sick at heart** desolato(-a); **to be sick of the sight of sb/sth** non poterne più di qn/qc; **you make me sick!** mi fai schifo!; **that's really sick!** è veramente di cattivo gusto! ♦ N **1** (*fam: vomit*) vomito **2** **the sick** NPL i malati

▸ **sick up** VT + ADV (*fam*) vomitare, rimettere

sick·bag [ˈsɪk,bæg] N sacchetto (*da usarsi in caso di malessere*)

sick·bay [ˈsɪk,beɪ] N infermeria

sick building syndrome N malattia causata dalla continua esposizione a ventilazione con sistemi di aria condizionata

sick·en [ˈsɪkn] VT nauseare, stomacare; (*fig*) disgustare ♦ VI sentirsi male, ammalarsi; **to sicken of sth** stufarsi di qc; **to be sickening for sth** (*cold, flu etc*) covare qc

sick·en·ing [ˈsɪknɪŋ] ADJ (*smell, sight*) nauseante; (*fig: crime, waste, behaviour*) disgustoso(-a), rivoltante; (: *crash*) pauroso(-a); (: *fam: annoying*) esasperante

sick·le [ˈsɪkl] N falcetto; **hammer and sickle** falce e martello

sick leave N: **on sick leave** in congedo per motivi di salute *or* per malattia

sickle-cell anaemia [ˌsɪklsɛləˈniːmɪə] N anemia falciforme

sick·ly [ˈsɪklɪ] ADJ (*comp* **-ier**, *superl* **-iest**) (*person*) malaticcio(-a); (*plant, animal*) malato(-a); (*smile*) stentato(-a); (*complexion*) giallastro(-a); (*taste, smell*) stomachevole; (*cake*) stucchevole; **sickly sweet** nauseante

sick·ness [ˈsɪknɪs] N malattia; **there's a lot of sickness about** c'è molta gente malata; **wave of sickness** ondata di malessere

sickness benefit N indennità di malattia

sick pay N salario erogato al dipendente in caso di malattia

sick·room [ˈsɪk,ruːm] N stanza di malato

side [saɪd] N **1** (*of person, animal*) fianco; **side of beef** quarto di bue; **at** *or* **by sb's side** al fianco di qn, accanto a qn; **side by side** (*people*) fianco a fianco; (*objects*) uno(-a) accanto all'altro(-a); **she was lying on her side** era sdraiata su un fianco **2** (*edge: of box, square etc*) lato; (: *of buildings*) fianco, lato; (: *of boat, vehicle*) fiancata, fianco; (: *of ship*) murata, fianco; (: *of lake*) riva; (: *of road*) bordo, ciglio; **at the side of the road** sul bordo della strada; **by the side of the lake** sulla riva del lago **3** (*face, surface: gen*) faccia; (: *of paper*) facciata; (: *of slice of bread*) lato; (: *fig: aspect*) aspetto, lato; **the right/wrong side** il dritto/rovescio; **the other side of the coin** (*fig*) il rovescio della medaglia; **to hear both sides of the question** sentire tutt'e due le campane **4** (*part*) parte *f*; **from all sides, from every side** da ogni parte; **from side to side** da una parte all'altra; **to move to one side** scostarsi, farsi *or* tirarsi da (una) parte; **he was driving on the wrong side of the road** guidava sul lato sbagliato della strada; **to take sb on one side** prendere qn da parte *or* in disparte; **to put sth to** *or* **on one side (for sb)** mettere qc da parte (per qn); **on the mother's side** per parte di madre; **to be on the wrong/right side of 30** aver/non aver superato la trentina; **to get on the wrong/right side of sb** prendere qn per il verso sbagliato/giusto; **on this side of town** da questa parte della città; **it's a bit on the large side** è un po' abbondante; **to make a bit (of money) on the side** (*fam*) farsi un po' di soldi extra **5** (*Sport: team*) squadra; (*Pol: faction*) parte *f*; **the other side** la parte opposta; **God is on our side** Dio è con noi; **to be on sb's side** essere dalla parte di *or* con qn; **I'm on your side** sto dalla tua parte; **to be on the side of moderation** essere per la moderazione; **to have age/the law** *etc* **on one's side** avere l'età/la legge *etc* dalla propria (parte); **to pick** *or* **choose sides** formare le squadre; **to take sides** prendere posizione; **to take sides with sb** schierarsi con qn; **to let the side**

down (*Sport, also fig*) deludere le aspettative di qn; **Arsenal was the stronger side** l'Arsenal era la squadra più forte ♦ VI: **to side with sb** prendere le parti di qn, parteggiare per qn ♦ ADJ (*door, entrance*) laterale; **a side entrance** un ingresso laterale; **a side issue** una questione secondaria

▸ **side against** VT + PREP schierarsi contro

side·board [ˈsaɪd,bɔːd] N credenza

side·boards [ˈsaɪd,bɔːdz], (USA) **side·burns** [ˈsaɪd,bɜːnz] NPL basette *fpl*

side·car [ˈsaɪd,kɑː'] N sidecar *m inv*

side dish N contorno

side drum N (*Mus*) piccolo tamburo

side effect N effetto collaterale

side·kick [ˈsaɪd,kɪk] N (*fam, esp USA: assistant*) braccio destro *m inv*; (: *friend*) amico(-a)

side·light [ˈsaɪd,laɪt] N (*Aut*) luce *f* di posizione

side·line [ˈsaɪd,laɪn] N **1** (*Ftbl, etc*) linea laterale; **to watch from the sidelines** (*fig*) guardare dall'esterno; **to be on the sidelines of** (*fig*) non prendere parte alle decisioni di **2** (*Comm*) attività *f inv* collaterale; **a profitable sideline** un'attività secondaria redditizia; **to be on the sidelines** (*fig*) essere lasciato(-a) fuori; **to watch from the sidelines** (*fig*) essere uno(-a) spettatore(-trice) passivo(-a) ♦ VT (*fig*) escludere

side·long [ˈsaɪd,lɒŋ] ADJ: **to give a sidelong glance at sth** guardare qc con la coda dell'occhio

side order N contorno (*pietanza*)

side plate N piattino

side road N strada secondaria

side·saddle [ˈsaɪd,sædl] ADV: **to ride sidesaddle** cavalcare all'amazzone

side·show [ˈsaɪd,ʃəʊ] N (*at fair*) attrazione *f*

side·step [ˈsaɪd,stɛp] VT (*question, problem*) eludere, scansare ♦ VI (*Boxing*) schivare

side street N traversa

side·track [ˈsaɪd,træk] VT (*person*) sviare, mettere fuori strada; **I got sidetracked** mi hanno distratto

side·walk [ˈsaɪd,wɔːk] N (*USA: pavement*) marciapiede *m*

side·ways [ˈsaɪd,weɪz] ADJ laterale; **to give a sideways glance at sth** guardare qc con la coda dell'occhio ♦ ADV (*move*) di lato, di fianco; (*look*) con la coda dell'occhio; **sideways on** di profilo; **I took a step sideways** ho fatto un passo di lato

sid·ing [ˈsaɪdɪŋ] N (*Rail*) binario di raccordo

si·dle [ˈsaɪdl] VI: **to sidle up to sb** avvicinarsi furtivamente a qn; **to sidle out/past** *etc* uscire/passare *etc* furtivamente

SIDS [sɪdz] N ABBR (*Med: = sudden infant death syndrome*) morte *f* improvvisa del lattante

siege [siːdʒ] N assedio; **in a state of siege** in stato d'assedio; **to lay siege to** porre l'assedio a

❏ **siege** is not translated by the Italian word *seggio*

siege economy N economia da stato d'assedio

Si·er·ra Le·o·ne [sɪˈɛərəlɪˈəʊnɪ] N Sierra Leone *f*

sieve [sɪv] N (*for flour*) setaccio; (*for coal, soil*) crivello; **to have a memory like a sieve** (*fam*) avere una memoria che fa acqua, essere smemorato(-a) ♦ VT (*soil, flour etc*) setacciare, passare al setaccio; (*coal etc*) passare al crivello

sift [sɪft] VT (*flour, sand etc*) setacciare; (*coal etc*) passare al crivello; (*fig: evidence*) vagliare; **to sift out** (*truth etc*) separare; **sift the flour and spices** setacciate la farina e le spezie; **after sifting the evidence …** dopo aver vagliato le prove… ♦ VI (*fig*): **to sift through** esaminare minuziosamente; (*statement, evidence*) vagliare accuratamente

sigh [saɪ] N (*of person*) sospiro; (*of wind*) sussurro; **Daphne heaved a sigh of relief** Daphne tirò un sospiro di sollievo ♦ VI: **to sigh (with)** sospirare (di); **to sigh over** (*sth lost*) piangere su

sight [saɪt] N **1** (*faculty, act of seeing*) vista; **to have good/poor (eye)sight** avere la vista buona/cattiva; **at first sight** a prima vista; **to know sb by sight** conoscere di vista qn; **I know her by sight** la conosco di vista; **payable at sight** (*Comm*) pagabile a vista; **to be within sight of** (*sea*) essere in vista di; (*victory*) essere vicino(-a) a; **in sight** visibile; **the bus was still in sight** l'autobus si vedeva ancora; **the end is in sight** si intravvede la fine; **a solution is in sight** è in vista una soluzione; **to come into sight** (*thing*) profilarsi all'orizzonte; **Janice came into sight** abbiamo scorto Janice; **to catch sight of sth/sb** scorgere qc/qn; **keep out of my sight!** sparisci!; **keep out of sight!** non farti vedere!; **don't let it out of your sight** non perderlo di vista; **when it's out of sight** quando non si vede più, quando non è più visibile; **out of sight out of mind** (*Proverb*) lontano dagli occhi lontano dal cuore; **to lose sight of sb/sth** perdere di vista qn/qc; **to hate the sight of sb/sth** non sopportare la vista di qn/qc; **my sight is failing** la vista mi sta calando **2** (*spectacle*) spettacolo; **the sights** le attrazioni turistiche; **to see the sights of Rome** vedere *or* visitare i monumenti di Roma; **it's not a pretty sight** non è uno spettacolo edificante; **you're a sight for sore eyes!** al solo vederti mi si allarga il cuore!; **you look a sight!** (*fam*) come sei conciato!; **it's a sight to be seen** è uno spettacolo da non perdere; **it was an amazing sight** era uno spettacolo incredibile **3** (*on gun: often pl*) mirino; **in one's sights** sotto mira; **to set one's sights on sth/on doing sth** (*fig*) mirare a qc/a fare qc; **to set one's sights too high** (*fig*) mirare troppo in alto **4** (*fam: a great deal*) molto; **a sight more** molto di più; **it isn't finished by a long sight** è ben lungi dall'essere finito; **a sight too clever** fin troppo furbo(-a) ♦ VT (*rare animal, land*) avvistare; (*person*) scorgere

sight·ed [ˈsaɪtɪd] ADJ che ha il dono della vista; **partially sighted** parzialmente cieco(-a); **sighted people** i vedenti

sight·see·ing [ˈsaɪtˌsiːŋ] N turismo; **to go sightseeing, to do some sightseeing** (*gen*) fare un giro turistico; (*in town*) visitare la città

sight·seer [ˈsaɪtˌsiːəʳ] N turista *m/f*

sign [saɪn] N **1** (*with hand etc*) segno, gesto; **to communicate by signs** comunicare a gesti; **to make a sign to sb (to do sth)** far segno a qn (di fare qc); **to make the sign of the Cross** far(si) il segno della croce **2** (*indication*) segno, indizio; **as a sign of** in segno di; **it's a sign of the times** è sintomo dei tempi che corrono; **it's a good/bad sign** è buon/brutto segno; **all the signs are that ...** tutto fa prevedere che...; **at the first** *or* **slightest sign of** al primo *or* al minimo segno di; **to show signs/no sign of doing sth** accennare/non accennare a fare qc; **there was no sign of him anywhere** non c'era traccia di lui da nessuna parte; **there was no sign of life in the village** nel paesino non c'era segno di vita; **there's no sign of improvement** non c'è alcun segno di miglioramento **3** (*also:* **road sign**) segnale *m* **4** (*also:* **shop sign**) insegna; (*notice*) cartello, avviso; **there was a big sign saying "private"** c'era un grande cartello con la scritta "privato" **5** (*written symbol*) segno; **plus/minus sign** segno del più/meno **6** (*also:* **star sign**) segno zodiacale; **what sign are you?** di che segno sei? ♦ VT **1** (*letter, contract*) firmare; **to sign one's name** firmare, apporre la propria firma; **she signs herself B. Smith** si firma B. Smith **2** (*Ftbl: player*) ingaggiare ♦ VI **1** (*with signature*) firmare; (*Ftbl*) firmare un contratto; **sign here, please** firmi qui, per favore **2** (*signal*): **to sign to sb to do sth** far segno a qn di fare qc **3** (*deaf people*) usare il linguaggio dei segni

▸ **sign away** VT + ADV (*rights etc*) cedere (*con una firma*)

▸ **sign for** VI + PREP (*letter, goods*) firmare per l'accettazione di; (*football club, record company*) firmare un contratto con

▸ **sign in** VI + ADV (*in hotel*) firmare il registro (*all'arrivo*)

▸ **sign off** VI + ADV (*TV, Radio*) chiudere le trasmissioni

▸ **sign on** VI + ADV (*as unemployed*) iscriversi all'ufficio di collocamento; (*Mil, etc enlist*) arruolarsi; (*as worker*) prendere servizio; (*enrol*): **to sign on for a course** iscriversi a un corso ♦ VT + ADV (*employees*) assumere; (*Mil: enlisted man*) arruolare

▸ **sign out** VI + ADV (*in hotel*) firmare il registro (*alla partenza*) ♦ VT + ADV (*book*) firmare il registro per il prestito di un libro

▸ **sign over** VT + ADV (*rights etc*): **to sign sth over to sb** cedere qc con scrittura legale a qn

▸ **sign up** VI + ADV (*Mil: enlist*) arruolarsi; (*enrol: for course*) iscriversi ♦ VT + ADV (*employee*) assumere; (*Mil*) arruolare

sig·nal [ˈsɪɡnl] N: **signal (for)** segnale *m* (di); **at a prearranged signal** ad un segnale convenuto; **distress signal** segnale di soccorso; **traffic signals** semafori *mpl*; **railway signals** segnali *mpl* ferroviari; **the engaged signal** (*Telec*) il segnale di occupato; **the signal is very weak** (*TV*) la ricezione è molto debole ♦ ADJ (*frm: success, importance*) notevole ♦ VT **1**

(*message*) comunicare per mezzo di segnali; **to signal a left/right turn** (*Aut*) segnalare una svolta a sinistra/destra; **to signal sb on/through** far segno a qn di avanzare/passare **2** (*signify*) indicare ♦ VI (*gen*) segnalare; (*for help*) fare segnalazioni; **to signal to sb (to do sth)** far segno a qn (di fare qc)

signal box N (*Rail*) cabina di manovra

signal·man [ˈsɪɡnlmən] N (*pl* **-men**) (*Rail*) deviatore *m*

sig·na·tory [ˈsɪɡnətərɪ] N firmatario(-a)

signature [ˈsɪɡnətʃəʳ] N **1** (*of person*) firma; **to put one's signature to sth** firmare qc, apporre la propria firma a qc; **a petition containing one thousand signatures** una petizione con mille firme **2** (*Mus*): **key signature** segnatura in chiave; **time signature** indicazione *f* del tempo ♦ ADJ tipico(-a)

signature tune N (*Brit*) sigla musicale

signet ring N anello con sigillo

sig·nifi·cance [sɪɡˈnɪfɪkəns] N (*of remark*) significato; (*of event, speech*) importanza; **that is of no significance** ciò non ha importanza

sig·nifi·cant [sɪɡˈnɪfɪkənt] ADJ (*discovery, change, event*) importante; (*increase, improvement, amount*) notevole; (*evidence*) significativo(-a); (*look, smile*) eloquente; **it is significant that ...** è significativo che...; **a significant development** uno sviluppo importante; **a significant improvement** un miglioramento notevole

sig·nifi·cant·ly [sɪɡˈnɪfɪkəntlɪ] ADV (*smile*) in modo eloquente; (*improve, increase*) considerevolmente; **and, significantly, ...** e, fatto significativo, ...

sig·ni·fy [ˈsɪɡnɪfaɪ] VT (*mean*) significare; (*indicate*) indicare; (*make known*) manifestare, esprimere ♦ VI avere importanza

sign language N linguaggio dei segni

sign·post [ˈsaɪnpəʊst] N indicazione *f* *or* cartello stradale ♦ VT (*fig*) indicare, segnalare

Sikh [siːk] ADJ, N sikh *m/f inv*

si·lage [ˈsaɪlɪdʒ] N insilato

si·lence [ˈsaɪləns] N silenzio; **silence!** silenzio!; **in** (*dead or complete*) **silence** in (totale *or* perfetto) silenzio; **there was silence on** *or* **about the subject** non si è parlato dell'argomento; **to pass over sth in silence** passare qc sotto silenzio ♦ VT (*person, critics*) ridurre al silenzio, far tacere; (*conscience*) mettere a tacere

si·lenc·er [ˈsaɪlənsəʳ] N (*Aut*) marmitta; (*on motorbike, gun*) silenziatore *m*

si·lent [ˈsaɪlənt] ADJ (*person*) silenzioso(-a); (*film, prayer etc*) muto(-a); **silent "h"** "h" muta; **to fall silent** tacere; **to keep** *or* **remain silent** tacere, stare zitto(-a)

si·lent·ly [ˈsaɪləntlɪ] ADV (*noiselessly*) silenziosamente; (*without speaking*) in silenzio

silent partner N (*USA*) = **sleeping partner**

sil·hou·ette [ˌsɪluˈet] N (*gen*) sagoma; (*drawing*) silhouette *f inv* ♦ VT: **to be silhouetted against** stagliarsi contro

sili·con [ˈsɪlɪkən] N silicio

silicon chip N chip *m inv* al silicone

sili·cone [ˈsɪlɪkəʊn] N silicone *m*

silk [sɪlk] N seta ♦ ADJ (*blouse, stockings*) di seta; (*industry*) della seta; **a silk scarf** un foulard di seta

silky [ˈsɪlkɪ] ADJ (*comp* **-ier**, *superl* **-iest**) (*hair, dress*) di seta; (*skin*) vellutato(-a); (*voice*) suadente, carezzevole

sill [sɪl] N **1** (*also:* **windowsill**) davanzale *m* **2** (*Aut*) predellino **3** (*Geol: of corrie*) soglia

sil·ly [ˈsɪlɪ] ADJ (*comp* **-ier**, *superl* **-iest**) (*stupid*) sciocco(-a), stupido(-a); (*ridiculous*) ridicolo(-a); **don't be silly** non fare lo(-a) sciocco(-a), non essere stupido(-a); **to do something silly** fare una sciocchezza

silo [ˈsaɪləʊ] N silo

silt [sɪlt] N limo

▸ **silt up** VI + ADV insabbiarsi ♦ VT + ADV ostruire

sil·ver [ˈsɪlvəʳ] N **1** (*metal*) argento **2** (*silverware, cutlery*) argenteria; **to polish the silver** lucidare l'argenteria **3** (*money*) monete *fpl* da 5, 10, 20 o 50 pence; **£5 in silver** cinque sterline in moneta ♦ ADJ (*ring, coin*) d'argento; **a silver medal** una medaglia d'argento

silver foil, silver paper N carta argentata, (carta) stagnola

silver-plated [ˌsɪlvəˈpleɪtɪd] ADJ placcato(-a) in argento, argentato(-a)

silver·smith [ˈsɪlvəˌsmɪθ] N argentiere *m*

silver·ware [ˈsɪlvəwɛəʳ] N argenteria; **jewellery and silver-ware** i gioielli e l'argenteria

sil·very [ˈsɪlvərɪ] ADJ (colour) argenteo(-a); (hair) argenta-to(-a); (sound) argentino(-a)

SIM card [ˈsɪmkɑːd] N = Subscriber Identity Module card(Telec) SIM card f inv

simi·lar [ˈsɪmɪləʳ] ADJ: **similar (to)** simile (a), dello stesso tipo (di); **similar in size** (objects) della stessa misura; (people) della stessa altezza; **...and similar products** ... e simili

simi·lar·ity [ˌsɪmɪˈlærɪtɪ] N (ras)somiglianza, similarità f inv

simi·lar·ly [ˈsɪmɪləlɪ] ADV (in a similar way) allo stesso modo; (as is similar) così pure; **and similarly, ...** e allo stesso modo,...; **similarly, the second plan too has defects** e analogamente anche il secondo piano ha dei difetti; **they were similarly dressed** erano vestiti allo stesso modo

simi·le [ˈsɪmɪlɪ] N similitudine f, paragone m

sim·mer [ˈsɪməʳ] VT cuocere a fuoco lento; **simmer the soup for ten minutes** cuocete la minestra a fuoco lento per dieci minuti ♦ VI (water) sobbollire; (food) cuocere a fuoco lento; (fig: revolt) covare; **to simmer with rage** ribollire dalla rabbia; **rebellion continued to simmer** la ribellione continuava a covare

▸ **simmer down** VI + ADV (fig: fam) calmarsi

sim·per [ˈsɪmpəʳ] N sorriso affettato ♦ VI fare lo(-a) smorfioso(-a)

sim·per·ing [ˈsɪmpərɪŋ] ADJ lezioso(-a), smorfioso(-a)

sim·ple [ˈsɪmpl] ADJ (comp -r, superl -est) (gen) semplice; (foolish) sempliciotto(-a), sprovveduto(-a); **to make simple(r)** semplificare; **it's as simple as ABC** è come bere un bicchier d'acqua; **to make it simple for you** ... per semplificarti le cose...; **the simple truth** la pura verità; **the answer is simple** la risposta è semplice; **in simple terms, in simple English** in parole povere; **for the simple reason that** ... per il semplice motivo che...; **the simple past** (Gram) il passato semplice; **simple equation** (Math) equazione f di primo grado; **a simple Simon** un(a) sempliciotto(-a); **he's a bit simple** (fam, euph: mentally impaired) è poco sveglio

simple interest N (Fin) interesse m semplice

simple-minded [ˌsɪmplˈmaɪndɪd] ADJ semplicione(-a)

sim·ple·ton [ˈsɪmpltən] N (old) semplicione(-a), sempliciotto(-a)

sim·plic·ity [sɪmˈplɪsɪtɪ] N semplicità

sim·pli·fi·ca·tion [ˌsɪmplɪfɪˈkeɪʃən] N semplificazione f

sim·pli·fy [ˈsɪmplɪfaɪ] VT semplificare

sim·ply [ˈsɪmplɪ] ADV (gen) semplicemente; **I simply said that** ... ho semplicemente detto che...; **you simply MUST come!** devi assolutamente venire!; **a simply furnished room** una stanza arredata con semplicità

simu·late [ˈsɪmjʊleɪt] VT simulare

simu·la·tion [ˌsɪmjʊˈleɪʃən] N simulazione f

sim·ul·ta·neous [ˌsɪməlˈteɪnɪəs] ADJ simultaneo(-a)

sim·ul·ta·neous·ly [ˌsɪməlˈteɪnɪəslɪ] ADV simultaneamente, contemporaneamente; **simultaneously with** contemporaneamente a

sin [sɪn] N peccato; **sins of omission** peccati di omissione; **mortal sin** peccato mortale; **it would be a sin to do that** (Rel) sarebbe peccato farlo; (fig) sarebbe peccato farlo ♦ VI peccare

Si·nai [ˈsaɪnaɪ] N il Sinai

since [sɪns] ADV da allora; **ever since** da allora (in poi); **(not) long since** da (non) molto (tempo); **I haven't seen him since** non lo vedo da allora ♦ PREP da; **since Monday** da lunedì; **since Christmas** da Natale; **(ever) since then/that** ... da allora...; **since leaving** da quando sono (or è etc) partito(-a); **how long is it since his last visit?** da quanto tempo non viene?; **I've been here since the beginning of June** sono qua dall'inizio di giugno; **we've been waiting for him since three o'clock** siamo qui ad aspettarlo dalle tre ♦ CONJ **1** (time) da quando; **(ever) since I arrived** (fin) da quando sono arrivato; **I haven't seen her since she left** non l'ho più vista da quando è partita; **how long is it since you last saw him?** da quando non lo vedi?, quant'è che non lo vedi? **2** (because) siccome, dato che; **since you're tired, let's stay at home** dato che sei stanco restiamo a casa

sin·cere [sɪnˈsɪəʳ] ADJ sincero(-a)

sin·cere·ly [sɪnˈsɪəlɪ] ADV sinceramente; **Yours sincerely** (at end of letter) Distinti saluti

sin·cer·ity [sɪnˈsɛrɪtɪ] N sincerità

sine [saɪn] N (Math) seno

sin·ew [ˈsɪnjuː] N (tendon) tendine m; **sinews** NPL (muscles) muscoli mpl; (fig: strength) forza

sin·ful [ˈsɪnfʊl] ADJ (Rel) peccaminoso(-a); (waste, act) vergognoso(-a)

sing [sɪŋ] (pt **sang**, pp **sung**) VT cantare; **to sing the tenor part** cantare come tenore; **to sing sb's praises** (fig) cantare le lodi di qn; **to sing a child to sleep** cantare la ninna nanna a un bambino ♦ VI (person, bird) cantare; (ears, kettle, bullet) fischiare; **to sing like a lark** cantare come un usignolo; **she sang in the school choir** cantava nel coro della scuola; **he has sung in the choir for two years** canta nel coro da due anni

▸ **sing out** VI + ADV (fam: call) chiamare

Sin·ga·pore [ˌsɪŋgəˈpɔː] N Singapore f

singe [sɪndʒ] VT bruciacchiare

sing·er [ˈsɪŋəʳ] N cantante m/f

Sin·gha·lese [ˌsɪŋəˈliːz] ADJ, N = Sinhalese

sing·ing [ˈsɪŋɪŋ] N (of person, bird) canto; (of kettle, bullet, in ears) fischio ♦ ADJ (lessons, teacher) di canto

sin·gle [ˈsɪŋgl] ADJ **1** (only one) solo(-a), unico(-a) (before n); **a single tree in a garden** un solo albero in un giardino; **only on one single occasion** in una sola occasione; **I haven't a single moment to spare** non ho neanche un attimo di tempo; **not a single one was left** non ne è rimasto nemmeno uno; **she didn't see a single person or soul** non ha visto anima viva; **she hadn't said a single word** non aveva detto una sola parola; **every single day** tutti i santi giorni **2** (not double) unico(-a); (flower) semplice; (ticket) di (sola) andata; **down to single figures** (inflation) inferiore a dieci; **single spacing** (Typ) interlinea uno **3** (not married: man) celibe, single inv; (: woman) nubile, single inv ♦ N **1** (Rail, etc) biglietto di (sola) andata; **a single to Oxford, please** un biglietto di sola andata per Oxford, per favore **2** (record): **a single** un 45 giri; **a CD single** un CD singolo; see also **singles**

▸ **single out** VT + ADV (choose) scegliere; (distinguish) distinguere, isolare; **his boss singled him out for special mention** il suo capo lo ha scelto per una menzione d'onore

single bed N letto a una piazza

single-breasted [ˌsɪŋglˈbrɛstɪd] ADJ (jacket) a un petto

single file N: **in single file** in fila indiana

single-handed [ˌsɪŋglˈhændɪd] ADJ (voyage) solitario(-a); (achievement) fatto(-a) da solo(-a) ♦ ADV da solo(-a), senza aiuto

single-minded [ˌsɪŋglˈmaɪndɪd] ADJ (person) deciso(-a), tenace, risoluto(-a); (ambition, attempt) ostinato(-a); **to be single-minded about sth** concentrare tutte le proprie forze in qc

single parent N genitore single

single room N camera singola

singles [ˈsɪŋglz] NPL **1** (Tennis) singolo msg; **the women's singles** il singolare femminile **2** (USA: single people) single m/fpl

singles bar N (esp USA) bar per single, dove è possibile fare amicizia

single-sex school [ˌsɪŋglsɛksˈskuːl] ADJ (for boys) scuola maschile; (for girls) scuola femminile

sin·glet [ˈsɪŋglɪt] N (esp Brit) canottiera

sin·gly [ˈsɪŋglɪ] ADV singolarmente, uno(-a) a uno(-a)

sing·song [ˈsɪŋsɔŋ] ADJ (tone) cantilenante ♦ N (Brit fam) di canto

sin·gu·lar [ˈsɪŋgjʊləʳ] ADJ **1** (Gram) singolare **2** (frm: extraordinary) strano(-a), singolare ♦ N (Gram) singolare m; **in the singular** al singolare; **in the feminine singular** al femminile singolare

sin·gu·lar·ly [ˈsɪŋgjʊləlɪ] ADV (frm) singolarmente

Sin·ha·lese [ˌsɪnhəˈliːz] ADJ, N singalese m/f

sin·is·ter [ˈsɪnɪstəʳ] ADJ sinistro(-a)

sink¹ [sɪŋk] (pt **sank**, pp **sunk**) VT **1** (ship, object) (far) affondare; (fig: project) far naufragare; (: person) distruggere; **the ship was sunk in the war** la nave venne affondata durante la guerra; **to be sunk** (fam) essere nei guai; **I'm sunk without**

it se non ce l'ho sono perso; **to be sunk in thought** essere immerso(-a) nei propri pensieri; **to be sunk in despair** essere assolutamente disperato(-a); **let's sink our differences** accantoniamo le divergenze 2 (*mineshaft, well*) scavare; (*foundations*) gettare; (*stake*) piantare, conficcare; (*pipe etc*) interrare; **to sink the ball** (*Golf*) fare buca; **to sink money into an enterprise** investire denaro in un'impresa; **lets sink a few beers** (*Brit fam*) facciamoci un paio di birre ♦ VI (*in water*) affondare; (*level of water, sun*) calare; (*ground*) cedere; (*value, voice*) abbassarsi; (*sales*) diminuire; **the ship sank** la nave è affondata; **to sink to the bottom** (*ship*) colare a picco; **to sink to one's knees** cadere in ginocchio; **he sank into a chair/the mud** sprofondò in una poltrona/nel fango; **the water sank slowly into the ground** l'acqua è penetrata lentamente nel terreno; **she's sinking fast** (*dying*) deperisce rapidamente; **he has sunk in my estimation** è scaduto ai miei occhi; **he was left to sink or swim** (*fig*) fu lasciato a cavarsela da solo; **to sink like a stone** andar giù come un sasso; **to sink out of sight** scomparire alla vista; **the shares have** *or* **the share price has sunk to 3 dollars** le azioni sono crollate a 3 dollari; **my heart** *or* **spirits sank** mi sentii venir meno

‣ **sink back** VI + ADV (*in chair*) accomodarsi bene; (*under water*) affondare di nuovo

‣ **sink down** VI + ADV: **to sink down onto a chair** lasciarsi cadere su una poltrona; **to sink down on one's knees** cadere in ginocchio; **to sink down out of sight** scomparire

‣ **sink in** VI + ADV (*person, car*) sprofondare; (*liquid: into ground, carpet*) penetrare; (*remark, explanation*) essere capito(-a); **it hasn't sunk in yet** (*fig*) non mi rendo (*or* si rende *etc*) ancora conto; **it took a long time to sink in** ci ho (*or* ha *etc*) messo molto a capirlo

sink² [sɪŋk] N (*in kitchen*) acquaio, lavello; (*in bathroom*) lavandino

sink·ing [ˈsɪŋkɪŋ] N (*shipwreck*) naufragio ♦ ADJ: **a** *or* **that sinking feeling** una stretta allo stomaco; **I have a sinking feeling that things have gone wrong** ho il brutto presentimento che le cose siano andate male; **with sinking heart** con la morte nel cuore

sinking fund N (*Comm*) fondo d'ammortamento

sink unit N blocco *m* lavello, *inv*

sin·ner [ˈsɪnə²] N peccatore(-trice)

Sinn Féin [ˌʃɪnˈfeɪn] N Sinn Féin *m inv*, braccio politico dei cattolici repubblicani (*nell'Irlanda del Nord*)

sinu·ous [ˈsɪnjʊəs] ADJ (*course, route*) sinuoso(-a), tortuoso(-a); (*dance, movement*) flessuoso(-a)

si·nus [ˈsaɪnəs] N (*Anat*) seno, cavità *f inv*

sip [sɪp] N sorso ♦ VT sorseggiare, centellinare

si·phon [ˈsaɪfən] N sifone *m* ♦ VT (*also:* **siphon off:** *liquid*) travasare (con un sifone); (*fig: funds, traffic*) deviare; **he siphoned the petrol out of the tank** ha travasato la benzina dal serbatoio; **they siphoned the money into their accounts** hanno dirottato il denaro nei loro conti correnti

sir [sɜː²] N (*frm*) signore *m*; **yes, sir** sì, signore; (*Mil*) sissignore; **Dear Sir** (*in letter*) Egregio signor (+ *surname*); **Dear Sirs** Spettabile ditta; **Sir Winston Churchill** Sir Winston Churchill

si·ren [ˈsaɪərən] N (*all senses*) sirena

sir·loin [ˈsɜːlɔɪn] N (*of beef*) controfiletto

sirloin steak N bistecca di controfiletto

si·roc·co [sɪˈrɒkəʊ] N scirocco

si·sal [ˈsaɪsəl] N sisal *f inv*

sis·sy [ˈsɪsɪ] N (*fam, pej*) femminuccia

sis·ter [ˈsɪstə²] N 1 (*relation*) sorella; **this is my sister** questa è mia sorella 2 (*Med*) (infermiera *f*) caposala, *inv*; **she's a sister at the infirmary** è infermiera caposala all'ospedale 3 (*Rel*) suora; **Sister Mary** Suor Maria

sister-in-law [ˈsɪstərɪnlɔː] N (*pl* **sisters-in-law**) cognata

sit [sɪt] (*pt, pp* **sat**) VI 1 (*also:* **sit down**) sedersi, sedere; **sit!** (*to dog*) seduto!; **sit beside me** siediti accanto a me; **he just sits at home all day** sta a casa tutto il giorno senza far nulla; **he was sitting in front of the TV** era seduto davanti alla TV; **we sat in the front row** eravamo seduti in prima fila; **this unit sits on top of that one** questo pezzo poggia su quello; **to sit still/straight** stare seduto(-a) fermo(-a)/dritto(-a); **to**

sit tight (*wait patiently*) starsene seduto(-a); **to be sitting pretty** (*fig: fam*) passarsela bene; **to sit on a committee** far parte di una commissione; **to sit for** (*a constituency*) rappresentare; **to sit in Parliament** sedere in Parlamento; **to sit for a painter/portrait** posare per un pittore/ritratto; **to sit for an examination** (*esp Brit*) dare *or* sostenere un esame; **to sit through** (*a film, play*) resistere fino alla fine di; **to sit over one's work** *or* **books** stare con la testa sui libri 2 (*assembly, committee*) riunirsi, essere in seduta; **the committee is sitting now** il comitato è in riunione; **Parliament sits from November till June** i lavori parlamentari iniziano a novembre e terminano a giugno 3 (*bird, insect*) posarsi; (*on eggs*) covare 4 (*dress etc*) cadere; **that jacket sits well** quella giacca cade bene ♦ VT 1 (*guest, child etc*) far sedere 2 (*exam*) dare, sostenere; **to sit an exam** sostenere un esame

‣ **sit about, sit around** VI + ADV star seduto(-a) senza far nulla

‣ **sit back** VI + ADV (*in seat*) appoggiarsi allo schienale; (*doing nothing*) stare con le mani in mano

‣ **sit by** VI + ADV: **to sit by while sb does sth** starsene a guardare mentre qn fa qc

‣ **sit down** VI + ADV sedersi; **he sat down at his desk** si sedette alla scrivania; **please sit down** prego, si accomodi; **to be sitting down** essere seduto(-a) ♦ VT + ADV far sedere, far accomodare

‣ **sit in** VI + ADV 1 **to sit in on a discussion** assistere ad una discussione; **to sit in for sb** (*as substitute*) fare le veci di qn, sostituire qn 2 (*demonstrate*): **to sit in a building** occupare un edificio

‣ **sit on** VI + PREP (*fig: fam*) 1 (*keep secret: news, information*) tenere segreto(-a); (*delay taking action on: document, application*) tenere nel cassetto 2 (*person: silence*) far tacere

‣ **sit out** VT + ADV (*dance etc*) non partecipare a, saltare; (*lecture, play*) restare fino alla fine di

‣ **sit up** VI + ADV 1 (*upright*) stare seduto(-a) diritto(-a); (*in bed*) tirarsi (su) a sedere; **to make sb sit up (and take notice)** (*fig*) far drizzare le orecchie a qn 2 (*stay up late*) restare alzato(-a); **to sit up with** (*invalid*) passare la notte al capezzale di; **to sit up for sb** aspettare qn alzato(-a) ♦ VT + ADV (*baby, doll*) mettere a sedere, mettere seduto(-a)

sit·com [ˈsɪtˌkɒm] N (*fam: Radio, TV*) situation comedy *f inv*

sit-down [ˈsɪtˌdaʊn] ADJ: **a sit-down strike** sciopero bianco (*con occupazione del posto di lavoro*); **a sit-down meal** un pranzo (a tavola) ♦ N (*fam*): **to have a sit-down** sedersi un momento

site [saɪt] N 1 (*of town, building*) ubicazione *f*; (*Archeol*) località *f inv*; **the site of the accident** il luogo dell'incidente; **the site of the battle** il teatro della battaglia; **an archaeological site** una zona archeologica 2 (*Constr: also:* **building site**) cantiere *m* 3 (*also:* **camp site**) campeggio 4 (*Comput*) sito; **to visit a site** visitare un sito ♦ VT collocare, situare; **a badly sited building** un edificio in una brutta posizione

sit-in [ˈsɪtˌɪn] N (*demonstration*) sit-in *m inv*; **to hold a sit-in** fare un sit-in

sit·ing [ˈsaɪtɪŋ] N ubicazione *f*

sit·ter [ˈsɪtə²] N (*Art*) modello(-a); (*also:* **babysitter**) baby-sitter *m/f inv*

sit·ting [ˈsɪtɪŋ] N (*of assembly, Parliament*) seduta; (*in canteen*) turno; (*for portrait*) seduta (di posa); **there are three sittings at lunchtime** ci sono tre turni per il pranzo; **an emergency sitting of the council** una seduta d'emergenza del consiglio ♦ ADJ: **in a sitting position** seduto(-a)

sitting member N (*Pol*) deputato in carica

sitting room N salotto, soggiorno

sitting tenant N (*Brit*) affittuario(-a), inquilino(-a)

situ·ate [ˈsɪtjʊeɪt] VT collocare, situare

situ·ated [ˈsɪtjʊeɪtɪd] ADJ situato(-a); **well situated** (*house*) in una bella posizione; **how are you situated for money?** (*fig*) come stai a soldi?

situa·tion [ˌsɪtjʊˈeɪʃən] N (*position*) posizione *f*; (*fig*) situazione *f*; (*frm, old: job*) lavoro, impiego; **"situations vacant/wanted"** (*Brit*) "offerte *fpl*/domande, *fpl* di impiego"; **to save the situation** salvare la situazione; **a difficult situation** una situazione difficile

situation comedy N (*TV, Radio, Theatre*) situation comedy *f inv*

six [sɪks] ADJ sei *inv* ♦ N sei *m inv*; **to be (all) at sixes and sevens** (*fig: person, things*) essere sottosopra; **it's six of one and half a dozen of the other** (*fig*) se non è zuppa è pan bagnato, siamo lì

six-pack ['sɪks,pæk] N confezione *f* da sei (*di birra*); (*muscles*) potenti addominali *mpl*

six·teen [,sɪks'tiːn] ADJ sedici *inv* ♦ N sedici *m inv*

six·teenth [,sɪks'tiːnθ] ADJ sedicesimo(-a) ♦ N (*in series*) sedicesimo(-a); (*fraction*) sedicesimo

sixth [sɪksθ] ADJ sesto(-a) ♦ N (*in series*) sesto(-a); (*fraction*) sesto; **the upper/lower sixth** (*Brit Scol*) ≈ l'ultimo/il penultimo anno di scuola superiore

sixth form N ≈ ultimo biennio delle superiori

sixth-form college ['sɪksθ,fɔːm'kɒlɪdʒ] N (*Brit*) *istituto che offre corsi di preparazione all'esame di maturità*

six·ti·eth ['sɪkstɪθ] ADJ sessantesimo(-a) ♦ N (*in series*) sessantesimo(-a); (*fraction*) sessantesimo

six·ty ['sɪkstɪ] ADJ sessanta *inv* ♦ N sessanta *m inv*

size [saɪz] N (*gen*) dimensioni *fpl*; (*fig: of problem, operation etc*) proporzioni *fpl*; (*of garments*) taglia, misura; (*of shoes*) numero, misura; (*of hat*) misura; **I take size 5** (*USA* 8) **shoes** ≈ porto il 38 di scarpe; **I take size 14** (*USA* 12) **in a dress** ≈ porto la 44 di vestiti; **what size** (*of*) **collar?** che misura di collo?; **what size are you?**, **what size do you take?** che taglia porti?; **he's about your size** sarà più o meno come te; **to be the size of** essere grande come; **Leeds is about the size of Florence** Leeds è grande più o meno come Firenze; **it's the size of a brick/nut** sarà grande come un mattone/una noce; **I'd like the small/large size** (*of soap powder etc*) vorrei la confezione piccola/grande; (*of clothes*) vorrei la misura piccola/grande; **plates of various sizes** piatti di varie dimensioni; **to try sth for size** misurare qc per vedere se è della taglia giusta; **to cut sth to size** tagliare qc nella misura desiderata *or* voluta; **to cut sb down to size** (*fig: fam*) ridimensionare qn; **that's about the size of it** (*fig*) le cose stanno più o meno così

► **size up** VT + ADV (*person, problem*) valutare, farsi un'idea di

size·able ['saɪzəbl] ADJ (*house, diamond*) abbastanza grande; (*sum, problem*) considerevole, notevole; **a sizeable sum** una somma considerevole; **a sizeable property** una casa abbastanza grande

siz·zle ['sɪzl] VI sfrigolare

SK ABBR (*Canada Post*: = Saskatchewan)

skate¹ [skeɪt] N (*pl inv: fish*) razza

skate² [skeɪt] N pattino; **to get one's skates on** (*fig: hurry up*) affrettarsi, sbrigarsi ♦ VI pattinare; **to go skating** andare a pattinare; **to skate across/down** etc attraversare/scendere etc pattinando; **it went skating across the room** (*fig*) è scivolato lungo la stanza

► **skate over**, **skate around** VI + PREP (*problem, issue*) prendere alla leggera, prendere sottogamba

skate·board ['skeɪt,bɔːd] N skateboard *m inv*

skate·board·ing ['skeɪt,bɔːdɪŋ] N: **to go skateboarding** andare sullo skateboard

skat·er ['skeɪtəʳ] N pattinatore(-trice)

skat·ing ['skeɪtɪŋ] N pattinaggio; **figure skating** pattinaggio artistico

skating rink N pista di pattinaggio

skel·eton ['skelɪtn] N (*of person*) scheletro; (*of building*) struttura, ossatura; (*of novel, report*) schema *m*; **a walking skeleton** (*fig*) uno scheletro ambulante; **the skeleton at the feast** (*fig*) il (la) guastafeste; **skeleton in the cupboard** *or* **closet** (*fig*) scheletro nell'armadio ♦ ADJ (*staff, service*) ridotto(-a)

skeleton key N passe-partout *m inv*

skeleton staff N personale *m* ridotto

skep·tic ['skeptɪk] (*USA*) = **sceptic**

sketch [sketʃ] N 1 (*drawing*) schizzo, abbozzo; (*fig: rough draft: of ideas, plan*) abbozzo, schema *m*; (: *description*) schizzo 2 (*Theatre, etc*) sketch *m inv* ♦ VT (*draw*) schizzare, abbozzare; (*fig: ideas, plan*) abbozzare; **to sketch a map for sb** fare una piantina per qn

► **sketch in** VT + ADV (*details*) inserire, aggiungere

► **sketch out** VT + ADV (*plan, situation*) descrivere a grandi linee

sketch·book ['sketʃ,bʊk], **sketch·pad** ['sketʃ,pæd] N album *m inv* or blocco per schizzi

sketchy ['sketʃɪ] ADJ (*comp* **-ier**, *superl* **-iest**) (*drawing, plan*) approssimato(-a); (*plans, knowledge*) vago(-a)

skew [skjuː] ADJ storto(-a); **skew distribution** (*Math*) distribuzione *f* asimmetrica; **skew lines** (*Math*) rette *fpl* sghembe ♦ VT: **to be skewed** essere inclinato(-a) *or* storto(-a) ♦ N (*Brit*): **on the skew** storto(-a), di traverso

skew·er ['skjʊəʳ] N (*for roasts*) spiedo; (*for kebabs*) spiedino ♦ VT infilzare in uno spiedo

ski [skiː] N sci *m inv* ♦ VI sciare; **to ski down a slope** fare una discesa con gli sci; **to go skiing** andare a sciare

ski boot N scarpone *m* da sci

skid [skɪd] N (*Aut*) slittamento; (*sideways slip*) sbandamento; **to go into a skid** slittare; sbandare; **to get out of a skid**, **to correct a skid** riprendere controllo del veicolo; **on the skids** (*fig*) in difficoltà ♦ VI (*Aut*) slittare; (*slip sideways*) sbandare; (*person, object*) scivolare; **to skid into sth** (*car*) slittare e sbattere contro qc; (*person, object*) scivolare contro qc

skid mark N (*Aut*) segno della frenata

ski·er ['skiːəʳ] N sciatore(-trice)

ski·ing ['skiːɪŋ] N sci *m* (*sport*) ♦ ADJ (*holiday etc*) sciistico(-a); **to go on a skiing holiday** fare una vacanza sulla neve

ski instructor N maestro(-a) di sci

ski jump N 1 trampolino 2 (*also: **ski jumping***) salto con gli sci

skil·ful, **skill·ful** (*USA*) ['skɪlfʊl] ADJ abile

skil·ful·ly, **skill·ful·ly** (*USA*) ['skɪlfəlɪ] ADV abilmente

ski lift N impianto di risalita

skill [skɪl] N 1 (*gen*) capacità *f inv*, abilità *f inv*; (*talent*) talento; **her skill in dealing with people** la sua abilità nel trattare con le persone; **his skill as a mechanic** la sua abilità come meccanico; **a writer of great skill** uno scrittore di grande talento; **it requires a lot of skill** richiede molta abilità; **to make use of sb's skills** sfruttare le capacità di qn 2 (*technique*) tecnica; **there's a certain skill to doing it** ci vuole una certa tecnica or arte nel farlo

skilled [skɪld] ADJ 1 (*gen*) abile, esperto(-a) 2 (*job, work*) specializzato(-a); (*worker*) specializzato(-a), qualificato(-a); **a skilled worker** un operaio specializzato

skil·let ['skɪlɪt] N (*USA*) padella

skill·ful ['skɪlfʊl] N (*USA*) = **skilful**

skill·fully ['skɪlfəlɪ] ADJ (*USA*) = **skilfully**

skim [skɪm] VT 1 (*soup*) schiumare; (*milk*) scremare; **to skim the fat off the soup** schiumare il brodo; **skim off the fat** schiuma via il grasso; **to skim the cream off the milk** scremare il latte 2 (*stone*) far rimbalzare; (*subj: bird, plane*): **to skim the water/ground** sfiorare *or* rasentare l'acqua/il suolo ♦ VI: **to skim across** *or* **along** sfiorare; **the boat skimmed over the waves** la barca sfiorava le onde; **the stone skimmed across the ice** il sasso rimbalzò sul ghiaccio; **to skim through a book** (*fig*) scorrere *or* dare una scorsa a un libro

skimmed milk [,skɪmd'mɪlk] N latte *m* scremato

skimp [skɪmp] VI: **to skimp on** (*material etc*) risparmiare; (*work*) raffazzonare; (*refreshments*) lesinare

skimpy ['skɪmpɪ] ADJ (*comp* **-ier**, *superl* **-iest**) (*skirt etc*) striminzito(-a), succinto(-a); (*hem*) piccolo(-a); (*allowance*) misero(-a); (*meal*) frugale

skin [skɪn] N 1 (*gen*) pelle *f*; (*of fruit, vegetable*) buccia; (*of boat, aircraft*) rivestimento; (*for duplicating*) matrice *f* per duplicatori; (*crust: on paint, milk pudding: thin*) pellicola; (: *thick*) crosta; **next to the skin** a contatto con la pelle; **to have a thick/thin skin** (*fig*) non essere/essere suscettibile; **by the skin of one's teeth** (*fig*) per un pelo; **wet** *or* **soaked to the skin** bagnato(-a) fino al midollo; **to be (all) skin and bone** (*fig*) essere pelle e ossa; **to get under sb's skin** (*fig*) dare sui nervi a qn; **I've got you under my skin** (*fig*) ti ho nella pelle; **it's no skin off my nose** (*fig: fam: does not concern me*) non sono affari miei; (: *does not hurt me*) non mi costa niente 2 (*fam*) = **skinhead** ♦ VT (*animal*) spellare, scuoiare, scorticare; (*fruit etc*) sbucciare, pelare; **to skin one's knee/elbow** sbucciarsi *or* scorticarsi un ginocchio/gomito; **I'll skin him alive!** (*fig*) lo scortico vivo!; **keep your eyes skinned for a garage** tieni gli occhi aperti per un distributore

skin cancer N cancro alla pelle
skin-deep [ˌskɪnˈdiːp] ADJ (*also fig*) superficiale
skin diver N sub *m/f*
skin diving N nuoto subacqueo
skin·flint [ˈskɪnˌflɪnt] N taccagno(-a), spilorcio(-a)
skin graft N innesto epidermico
skin·head [ˈskɪnˌhed] N testa rasata, skinhead *m/f*
skin·ny [ˈskɪnɪ] ADJ (*comp* **-ier**, *superl* **-iest**) (*usu pej: person*) magro(-a), gracile, mingherlino(-a); (*jumper*) striminzito(-a); (*milk*) magro(-a), scremato(-a) ♦ N: **the skinny** (*USA fam*) le ultime (notizie)
skin test N prova di reazione cutanea
skin·tight [ˈskɪnˌtaɪt] ADJ aderente come una seconda pelle
skip¹ [skɪp] N saltello, balzo ♦ VI saltellare, salterellare; (*with rope*) saltare con la corda; **to skip in/out** *etc* entrare/uscire *etc* saltellando; **to skip off** (*fig*) tagliare la corda; **to skip over sth** (*fig*) sorvolare su qc; **to skip from one subject to another** saltare da un argomento a un altro ♦ VT (*fig: meal, lesson, page*) saltare; (*: school*) marinare, bigiare; **let's skip it!** (*fam*) sorvoliamo!; **you should never skip breakfast** non si dovrebbe mai saltare la colazione; **to skip school** marinare la scuola
skip² [skɪp] N benna
ski pants NPL pantaloni *mpl* da sci
ski pass N ski-pass *m inv*
ski pole N = **ski stick**
skip·per [ˈskɪpəʳ] N (*Sport, Naut*) capitano; (*in boat race*) skipper *m inv* ♦ VT (*boat*) essere al comando di; (*sports team*) capitanare
skipping rope N (*Brit*) corda per saltare
ski resort N località *f inv or* stazione *f* sciistica
skir·mish [ˈskɜːmɪʃ] N scaramuccia
skirt [skɜːt] N gonna ♦ VT 1 (*road, path*) fiancheggiare, costeggiare 2 (*person: also:* **skirt around**) (*town, table*) girare intorno a; (*obstacle, difficulty*) aggirare; (*argument, subject*) schivare
skirt·ing [ˈskɜːtɪŋ], **skirt·ing board** N (*Brit*) zoccolo, battiscopa *m inv*
ski run, ski slope N pista da sci
ski stick N racchetta da sci
ski suit N tuta da sci
skit [skɪt] N (*Theatre*) sketch *m inv* satirico
ski tow N sciovia, ski-lift *m inv*
skit·tle [ˈskɪtl] N birillo; **skittles** NPL (*game*) (gioco dei) birilli *mpl*; **to play skittles** giocare a birilli
skulk [skʌlk] VI (*also:* **skulk about**) aggirarsi furtivamente; **to skulk into/out** entrare/uscire furtivamente
skull [skʌl] N (*of live person*) cranio; (*of dead person*) teschio; (*fam: head*) testa, testona; **skull and crossbones** (*danger warning*) teschio; (*flag*) bandiera dei pirati
skull·cap [ˈskʌlˌkæp] N (*worn by Jews*) zucchetto; (*worn by Pope*) papalina
skunk [skʌŋk] N (*Zool*) moffetta, puzzola; **you skunk!** (*fam*) farabutto!, carogna!
sky [skaɪ] N cielo; **to sleep under the open sky** dormire sotto le stelle *or* all'aperto; **to praise sb to the skies** portare alle stelle *qn*; **the sky's the limit** (*fig: fam*) non ci sono limiti
sky-blue [ˌskaɪˈbluː] N azzurro ♦ ADJ azzurro(-a)
sky-diving [ˈskaɪˌdaɪvɪŋ] N paracadutismo in caduta libera
sky-high [ˌskaɪˈhaɪ] ADV (*throw*) molto in alto; **to blow sth sky-high** far saltare in aria *qc*; **to blow a theory sky-high** confutare una teoria; **prices have gone sky-high** i prezzi sono saliti alle stelle ♦ ADJ (*fam*) esorbitante
sky·lark [ˈskaɪˌlɑːk] N (*bird*) allodola ♦ VI (*fig: fam*) fare il matto(-a)
sky·light [ˈskaɪˌlaɪt] N lucernario
sky·line [ˈskaɪˌlaɪn] N (*horizon*) orizzonte *m*; (*of city*) profilo
sky marshal N agente *m/f* armato a bordo (*di aereo*)
sky·scraper [ˈskaɪˌskreɪpəʳ] N grattacielo
slab [slæb] N (*of stone, metal*) lastra; (*of wood*) tavola; (*of chocolate*) tavoletta; (*of meat, cheese*) pezzo; (*fam: in mortuary*) tavolo anatomico; **a concrete slab** una lastra di cemento
slack [slæk] ADJ (*comp* **-er**, *superl* **-est**) 1 (*not tight: rope, knot*) lento(-a), allentato(-a); (*: grip*) debole 2 (*lax: work*

trascurato(-a); (*: student, worker*) negligente; (*lazy*) pigro(-a), fiacco(-a); **to be slack about one's work** essere negligente nel proprio lavoro; **to grow slack** lasciarsi andare 3 (*Comm: market*) stagnante; (*: demand*) scarso(-a); (*: period*) morto(-a); **business is slack** si fanno pochi affari; **the slack season** la bassa stagione ♦ N 1 (*part of rope etc*): **to take up the slack in a rope** tendere una corda 2 (*coal dust*) polvere *f* di carbone; *see also* **slacks** ♦ VI (*fam*) fare il (la) lavativo(-a) ♦ VT (*Naut: sail*) lascare
  ▸ **slack off** VI + ADV (*fam: activity etc*) ridursi, calare
slack·en [ˈslækən], **slacken off** VT (*rope, grip, reins, nut*) allentare; (*pressure*) diminuire; **to slacken speed** ridurre la velocità; **to slacken one's pace** rallentare il passo ♦ VI (*gen*) allentarsi; (*pressure, speed, activity*) diminuire, rallentare; (*gale*) placarsi; (*trade*) calare, ridursi
slacks [slæks] NPL pantaloni *mpl* casual, *inv*
slag [slæg] N (*waste: from coal mine, smelting*) scorie *fpl* ♦ VT (*Brit fam*): **to slag sb/sth off** sputtanare *qn/qc*
slag heap N cumulo di scorie
slain [sleɪn] PP *of* **slay** ♦ NPL (*liter*): **the slain** i caduti
slake [sleɪk] VT (*liter: one's thirst*) spegnere
sla·lom [ˈslɑːləm] (*Sport*) N slalom *m inv*; **special slalom** slalom speciale ♦ VI fare lo slalom
slam [slæm] N 1 (*of door*) colpo 2 (*Bridge*) slam *m inv*; **grand slam** (*Cards, Sport*) grande slam ♦ VT 1 (*door, lid*) sbattere; **to slam sth shut** chiudere *qc* sbattendolo(-a); **to slam down the phone** buttare giù la cornetta; **to slam sth (down) on the table** sbattere *qc* sul tavolo; **to slam on the brakes** frenare di colpo; **to slam the door (in sb's face)** sbattere la porta (in faccia a *qn*); **she slammed the door** ha sbattuto la porta 2 (*criticize*) stroncare ♦ VI (*door, lid*) sbattere
slam·mer [ˈslæməʳ] N (*fam*): **the slammer** la gattabuia
slan·der [ˈslɑːndəʳ] N calunnia; (*Law*) diffamazione *f* ♦ VT calunniare; (*Law*) diffamare
slan·der·ous [ˈslɑːndərəs] ADJ calunnioso(-a); (*Law*) diffamatorio(-a)
slang [slæŋ] N (*gen*) slang *m inv*, gergo; **school/army slang** gergo studentesco/militare; **to talk slang** parlare in gergo ♦ ADJ (*word*) gergale ♦ VT (*fam: insult, criticize*) dirne di tutti i colori a
slant [slɑːnt] N pendenza, inclinazione *f*; (*Geom*) apotema *m*; (*fig: point of view*) punto di vista, angolazione *f*; **to be on a slant** essere inclinato(-a); **the house is on a slant** la casa è in pendenza; **a different slant** un punto di vista diverso; **to give a new slant on sth** presentare *qc* sotto una nuova angolazione; **to get a new slant on sth** vedere *qc* da un'altra angolazione ♦ VT (*roof etc*) inclinare; **to slant a report** (*fig*) dare una versione distorta *or* tendenziosa dei fatti ♦ VI essere inclinato(-a), pendere
slant·ed [ˈslɑːntɪd] ADJ (*programme, report*) tendenzioso(-a)
slant·ing [ˈslɑːntɪŋ] ADJ (*handwriting*) inclinato(-a); (*roof*) spiovente; (*line*) obliquo(-a); (*rain*) che cade di traverso
slap [slæp] N schiaffo, ceffone *m*; **a slap in the face** uno schiaffo; (*fig*) uno schiaffo morale; **a slap on the wrist** (*fig*) una tirata d'orecchi; **a slap on the back** una pacca sulla spalla ♦ ADV (*fam*): **to run slap into** (*tree, lamppost*) colpire in pieno; (*person*) imbattersi in; **it fell slap in the middle** cadde proprio nel mezzo ♦ VT 1 schiaffeggiare; **to slap a child's bottom** sculacciare un bambino; **to slap sb on the back** dare una pacca sulla spalla a *qn*; **to slap sb down** (*fig: child*) zittire; (*: opposition*) stroncare 2 **he slapped the book on the table** ha sbattuto il libro sul tavolo; **slap a coat of paint on it** dagli una mano di vernice ♦ VI: **to slap against** andare a sbattere contro; **the waves slapped against the pier** le onde si infrangevano sul molo
slap·dash [ˈslæpˌdæʃ], **slap-happy** [ˈslæpˌhæpɪ] ADJ (*person*) negligente; (*work*) raffazzonato(-a); **a slapdash piece of work** un lavoro raffazzonato; **a slapdash person** una persona negligente
slap·stick [ˈslæpˌstɪk] N (*also:* **slapstick comedy**) farsa grossolana
slash [slæʃ] N 1 (*slit*) taglio; (*in dress, skirt*) spacco; (*stroke: of sword, whip*) colpo 2 (*Typ: also:* **slash mark**) barra ♦ VT (*with knife: gen*) tagliare, squarciare; (*: face, painting*) sfregiare; (*with whip, stick*) sferzare; (*fig: prices*) ridurre fortemente; **to slash one's wrists** tagliarsi le vene; **I found my tyres (or**

tires) **slashed** ho trovato le gomme tagliate; **they're slashing prices** stanno riducendo drasticamente i prezzi

slat [slæt] N (*of wood*) stecca; (*of plastic*) lamina

slate [sleɪt] N **1** (*rock*) ardesia; (*tile*) tegola (d'ardesia); (*writing tablet*) lavagnetta; **to wipe the slate clean** (*fig*) metterci una pietra sopra; **to put sth on sb's slate** mettere qc sul conto di qn; **a missing slate** una tegola d'ardesia mancante **2** (*USA Pol*) lista di candidati ♦ VT **1** (*roof*) coprire con tegole **2** (*fam: criticize*) criticare, stroncare ♦ ADJ di ardesia; **a slate roof** un tetto d'ardesia

slaugh·ter ['slɔːtə'] N (*of animals*) macellazione *f*; (*of people*) strage *f*, massacro, carneficina ♦ VT (*animals*) macellare; (*people*) trucidare, massacrare; (*fig*) distruggere, massacrare

slaughter·house ['slɔːtə,haʊs] N macello, mattatoio

Slav [slɑːv] ADJ, N slavo(-a)

slave [sleɪv] N schiavo(-a); **to be a slave to sth** (*fig*) essere schiavo(-a) di qc; **to be a slave of habit** essere schiavo(-a) delle abitudini ♦ VI: **to slave (away) at sth/at doing sth** sgobbare per qc/per fare qc

slave-driver ['sleɪv,draɪvə'] N sorvegliante *m* di schiavi; (*fig*) schiavista *m/f*

slave labour N lavoro fatto dagli schiavi

slav·er¹ ['slævə'] VI (*dribble*) sbavare

slav·er² ['sleɪvə'] N (*person*) schiavista *m/f*

slav·ery ['sleɪvərɪ] N (*condition*) schiavitù *f*; (*system*) schiavismo; **to reduce to slavery** schiavizzare

Slavic ['slævɪk] ADJ slavo(-a), (slava)

slav·ish ['sleɪvɪʃ] ADJ (*pej: devotion*) servile; (: *imitation*) pedissequo(-a)

slav·ish·ly ['sleɪvɪʃlɪ] ADV (*see adj*) servilmente; pedissequamente

Sla·von·ic [slə'vɒnɪk], (*USA*) **Slav·ic** ['slɑːvɪk] ADJ, N slavo(-a)

slay [sleɪ] (*pt* **slew**, *pp* **slain**) VT (*liter: kill*) uccidere

slea·zy ['sliːzɪ] ADJ (*comp* **-ier**, *superl* **-iest**) squallido(-a), infimo(-a)

sledge [sledʒ] N (*also:* **sled**) slitta ♦ VI: **to go sledging** andare in slitta; **to sledge down a hill** scendere in slitta giù per una collina

sledge·hammer ['sledʒ,hæmə'] N mazza

sleek [sliːk] ADJ (*comp* **-er**, *superl* **-est**) (*shiny: hair, coat*) liscio(-a) e lucente; (*cat*) dal pelo lucido; (*person: in appearance*) azzimato(-a); (: *in manner*) untuoso(-a); (*car, boat*) elegante ♦ VT: **to sleek one's hair down/back** lisciarsi i capelli

sleep [sliːp] (*pt, pp* **slept**) N sonno; **deep** *or* **sound sleep** sonno profondo; **a couple of hours' sleep** un paio di ore di sonno; **to have a good night's sleep** farsi una bella dormita; **to drop off** *or* **go to sleep** addormentarsi; **to get to sleep** (*limb*) intorpidirsi; **to put to sleep** (*patient*) anestetizzare; (*animal: euph: kill*) abbattere; **to talk in one's sleep** parlare nel sonno; **to walk in one's sleep** camminare nel sonno; (*as a habit*) essere sonnambulo(-a); **to send sb to sleep** (*bore*) far addormentare qn; **I won't lose any sleep over it** (*fig*) non starò a perderci il sonno ♦ VT: **we can sleep four** abbiamo quattro posti letto, possiamo alloggiare quattro persone; **the villa sleeps ten** la villa può alloggiare dieci persone ♦ VI dormire; **I couldn't sleep last night** ieri notte non riuscivo a dormire; **the baby slept during the journey** il bambino ha dormito lungo il tragitto; **to sleep like a log** *or* **top** dormire della grossa *or* come un ghiro; **he was sleeping soundly** *or* **deeply** era profondamente addormentato; **to sleep lightly** avere il sonno leggero; **let's sleep on it** (*fig*) la notte porta consiglio, dormiamoci sopra; **sleep tight!** sogni d'oro!; **I slept through the storm/alarm clock** non ho sentito il temporale/la sveglia; **he slept at his mother's** ha dormito dalla mamma; **to sleep with sb** (*euph: have sex*) andare a letto con qn

▶ **sleep around** VI + ADV (*fam*) andare a letto con tutti

▶ **sleep in** VI + ADV (*lie late*) alzarsi tardi; (*oversleep*) dormire fino a tardi

▶ **sleep off** VT + ADV: **to sleep sth off** smaltire qc dormendo

▶ **sleep out** VI + ADV dormire all'aperto

sleep·er ['sliːpə'] N **1** (*person*) dormiente *m/f*; **to be a heavy/ light sleeper** avere il sonno pesante/leggero **2** (*Brit: Rail: track*) traversina; (: *berth*) cuccetta; (: *coach*) vagone *m* letto, *inv* **3** (*earring*) campanella

sleepi·ly ['sliːpɪlɪ] ADV con aria assonnata

sleep·ing ['sliːpɪŋ] ADJ addormentato(-a); **the Sleeping Beauty** la Bella Addormentata nel bosco; **let sleeping dogs lie** (*Proverb*) non svegliare il can che dorme

sleeping bag N sacco a pelo

sleeping car N (*Rail*) vagone *m* letto, *inv*

sleeping partner N (*Brit: Comm*) socio inattivo

sleeping pill N sonnifero

sleeping sickness N malattia del sonno

sleep·less ['sliːplɪs] ADJ (*person*) insonne; (*night*) in bianco, insonne

sleep·less·ness ['sliːplɪsnɪs] N insonnia

sleep·over ['sliːp,əʊvə'] N *notte che un ragazzino o una ragazzina passa da amici*

sleep·walk ['sliːp,wɔːk] VI camminare nel sonno; (*as a habit*) essere sonnambulo(-a); **she sleepwalks** soffre di sonnambulismo, è sonnambula

sleep·walk·er ['sliːp,wɔːkə'] N sonnambulo(-a)

sleepy ['sliːpɪ] ADJ (*comp* **-ier**, *superl* **-iest**) (*person, voice, look*) assonnato(-a), sonnolento(-a); (*village*) addormentato(-a); **to be** *or* **feel sleepy** avere sonno

sleet [sliːt] N nevischio ♦ VI: **it was sleeting** nevischiava

sleeve [sliːv] N (*of garment*) manica; (*of record*) copertina; **to roll up one's sleeves** rimboccarsi le maniche; **to have sth up one's sleeve** (*fig*) avere in serbo qc

sleeve·less ['sliːvlɪs] ADJ (*garment*) senza maniche

sleigh [sleɪ] N slitta

sleight [slaɪt] N: **sleight of hand** (*trick*) gioco di destrezza; (*fig*) trucchetto

slen·der ['slendə'] ADJ (*person*) snello(-a), slanciato(-a); (*waist, neck, hand*) sottile; (*fig: resources, majority*) scarso(-a), esiguo(-a); (: *hope, chance*) piccolo(-a), scarso(-a)

slept [slept] PT, PP *of* **sleep**

sleuth [sluːθ] N (*hum*) segugio

slew [sluː] PT *of* **slay** ♦ VI (*Brit: also:* **slew round**) girare, virare

slice [slaɪs] N **1** (*of meat etc*) fetta; (*of lemon, cucumber*) fettina; **a slice of the profits** (*fig*) una fetta dei profitti; **a slice of life** (*fig*) uno scorcio di vita **2** (*tool*) paletta ♦ VT (*meat etc*) affettare, tagliare a fette; (*rope etc*) tagliare di netto; (*Sport: ball*) tagliare; **to slice sth thickly/thinly** affettare qc grosso/ sottile; **sliced loaf** *or* **bread** pane *m* a cassetta

▶ **slice off** VT + ADV tagliare (via)

▶ **slice through** VI + PREP tagliare di netto; (*fig: the air, waves*) fendere

▶ **slice up** VT + ADV affettare

slick [slɪk] ADJ (*comp* **-er**, *superl* **-est**) (*adroitly executed: show, performance*) brillante; (*pej: answer, excuse*) troppo pronto(-a); (: *person: glib*) dalla parlantina sciolta; (: *cunning*) scaltro(-a); (: *insincere*) untuoso(-a); **a slick character** un(a) dritto(-a) ♦ N (*also:* **oil slick**) chiazza di petrolio ♦ VT (*also:* **slick down**: *hair: with comb*) lisciare; (: *with haircream*) impomatare

slid [slɪd] PT, PP *of* **slide**

slide [slaɪd] (*pt, pp* **slid**) N **1** (*action: on ice, mud etc*) scivolone *m*; (*fig: in temperature, profits*) caduta; **the slide in share prices** la caduta del prezzo delle azioni **2** (*in playground, swimming pool*) scivolo; **some swings and a slide** alcune altalene ed uno scivolo **3** (*landslide*) frana **4** (*Brit: also:* **hair slide**) fermacapelli *m inv* **5** (*also: microscope slide*) vetrino; (*Phot*) diapositiva; **he showed us his slides** ci ha mostrato le sue diapositive ♦ VI scivolare; **these drawers slide in and out easily** questi cassetti scorrono bene; **to slide down the banisters** scivolare giù per il corrimano; **to let things slide** (*fig*) trascurare tutto ♦ VT (*box, case*) far scivolare; (*bolt*) far scorrere; **he slid the gun from its holster** ha tirato la pistola fuori dalla custodia

slide projector N (*Phot*) proiettore *m* per diapositive

slide rule N (*Math*) regolo calcolatore

slide show N (*Phot*) proiezione *f* di diapositive

slid·ing ['slaɪdɪŋ] ADJ (*part, seat*) mobile; (*door*) scorrevole; **sliding roof** (*Aut*) capotte *f inv*

sliding scale N (*Admin, etc*) scala mobile

slight [slaɪt] ADJ (*comp* **-er**, *superl* **-est**) **1** (*person: slim*) minuto(-a); (: *frail*) gracile, delicato(-a) **2** (*trivial: cold*) leggero(-a); (: *error*) piccolo(-a), insignificante; **a slight pain in**

the arm un leggero dolore al braccio **3** (*small*) piccolo(-a), leggero(-a); **a slight improvement** un leggero miglioramento; **a slight problem** un piccolo problema; **there's not the slightest possibility** non c'è la minima possibilità; **there's not the slightest danger** non c'è il benché minimo pericolo; **not in the slightest** per nulla, niente affatto ♦ N offesa, affronto ♦ VT (*person*) snobbare, ignorare

slight·ly [ˈslaɪtlɪ] ADV **1** (*better, nervous*) leggermente; **they are slightly more expensive** sono leggermente più costosi; **I know her slightly** la conosco appena **2 slightly built** esile

slim [slɪm] ADJ (*comp* -**mer**, *superl* -**mest**) **1** (*figure, person*) magro(-a), snello(-a); (*ankle, wrist, book*) sottile **2** (*fig: resources*) scarso(-a), magro(-a); (: *evidence*) insufficiente; (*excuse*) magro(-a); (: *hope*) poco(-a); **a slim chance** una scarsa possibilità; **his chances are pretty slim** le sue possibilità sono molto scarse ♦ VI dimagrire, fare *or* seguire una dieta dimagrante

slime [slaɪm] N (*mud*) melma; (*sticky substance*) sostanza viscida; (*of snail*) bava

slim·ming [ˈslɪmɪŋ] ADJ (*diet, pills*) dimagrante; (*food*) ipocalorico(-a)

slimy [ˈslaɪmɪ] ADJ (*comp* -**ier**, *superl* -**iest**) (*also fig: person*) viscido(-a); (*covered with mud*) melmoso(-a)

sling [slɪŋ] (*pt, pp* **slung**) N (*weapon*) fionda; (*catapult*) catapulta; (*Med*) fascia a tracolla; (*Mountaineering*) anello di fettuccia; **to have one's arm in a sling** avere un braccio al collo ♦ VT (*fam: throw*) scagliare, buttare; (*hang: hammock*) appendere; **he slung his bag onto the back seat** ha buttato la borsa sul sedile posteriore; **to sling over** *or* **across one's shoulder** (*rifle, load*) mettere in spalla; (*coat, shawl*) buttarsi sulle spalle

▸ **sling out** VT + ADV (*fam: object*) buttare via; (: *person*) buttare fuori

slink [slɪŋk] (*pt, pp* **slunk**) VI: **to slink away, slink off** svignarsela

slinky [ˈslɪŋkɪ] ADJ (*comp* -**ier**, *superl* -**iest**) (*fam: dress*) aderente, attillato(-a); (: *movement*) sinuoso(-a)

slip [slɪp] N **1** (*downward slide*) scivolata; (*trip*) scivolone *m* **2** (*also: landslip*) smottamento **3** (*mistake*) errore *m*, sbaglio; (*moral*) sbaglio; **a slip of the tongue** un lapsus linguae; **a slip of the pen** un lapsus calami; **a Freudian slip** un lapsus freudiano; **there must be no slips** non ci devono essere sbagli **4** (*petticoat*) sottoveste *f*; **a white slip** una sottoveste bianca **5** (*also: pillowslip*) federa **6** (*small receipt, bill*) scontrino; **a slip of paper** un foglietto; **pay slip** busta paga; **a slip of a girl** (*fig*) una ragazzina minuta **7** (*fam*): **to give sb the slip** seminare qn ♦ VI **1** (*slide*) scivolare; **I slipped** sono scivolato; **he slipped on the ice** è scivolato sul ghiaccio; **my foot slipped** mi è scivolato un piede; **it slipped from** *or* **out of her hand** mi sfuggì di mano; **to slip into bad habits** prendere delle cattive abitudini; **he let (it) slip that ...** si è lasciato sfuggire che...; **to let a chance slip through one's fingers** lasciarsi scappare un'occasione; **you're slipping!** (*fig: fam*) perdi colpi! **2** (*move quickly*): **to slip into/out of** sgattaiolare dentro/fuori da; **to slip into a dress** infilarsi un vestito; **the months/years have slipped by** i mesi/gli anni sono passati ♦ VT **1** (*slide*) far scivolare; **to slip a coin into a slot** infilare una moneta in una fessura; **to slip sb a tenner** allungare dieci sterline a qn; **to slip an arm round sb's waist** mettere il braccio attorno alla vita di qn; **to slip on/off a jumper** infilarsi/sfilarsi un maglione **2** (*escape*) sfuggire a; **the dog slipped its collar** il cane si liberò dal collare; **it slipped my memory** *or* **attention** *or* **mind** mi è sfuggito

▸ **slip away, slip off** VI + ADV svignarsela

▸ **slip in** VT + ADV (*object*) far scivolare in (*or* dentro); (*reference, remark*) aggiungere en passant

▸ **slip out** VI + ADV (*thief*) svignarsela; (*guest*) andarsene alla chetichella; (*secret, word*) sfuggire; **to slip out to the shops** fare una scappatina per la spesa; **it slipped out that ...** è saltato fuori che...

▸ **slip up** VI + ADV (*fam*) sbagliarsi

slip-on [ˈslɪp.ɒn] ADJ (*gen*) comodo(-a) da mettere; (*shoes*) senza allacciatura

slipped disc [ˌslɪptˈdɪsk] N (*Med*) ernia del disco

slip·per [ˈslɪpəʳ] N pantofola

slip·pery [ˈslɪpərɪ] ADJ sdrucciolevole, scivoloso(-a); (*fig: pej:*

person) viscido(-a); **it's slippery underfoot** il pavimento è scivoloso; **he's as slippery as they come** *or* **as an eel** è un tipo viscido

slip road N (*Brit: to motorway*) rampa di accesso

slip·shod [ˈslɪp.ʃɒd] ADJ sciatto(-a), trascurato(-a)

slip-up N (*fam: mistake*) sbaglio; **there's been a slip-up somewhere** è stato fatto uno sbaglio da qualche parte

slip·way [ˈslɪp.weɪ] N (*Naut*) scalo

slit [slɪt] (*pt, pp* **slit**) N (*opening*) fessura; (*cut*) taglio; (*tear*) strappo; (*in skirt*) spacco; **a skirt with a slit at the back** una gonna con lo spacco dietro; **she was watching through a slit in the curtains** osservava attraverso una fessura tra le tende ♦ VT tagliare; **to slit open** (*letter*) aprire; (*sack*) aprire con un taglio; **to slit sb's throat** tagliare la gola a qn

slith·er [ˈslɪðəʳ] VI (*person*) scivolare; (*snake*) strisciare; **he was slithering about on the ice** avanzava slittando sul ghiaccio

sliv·er [ˈslɪvəʳ] N (*of glass, wood*) scheggia; (*of cheese, sausage*) fettina

slob [slɒb] N (*fam*) sciattone(-a)

slog [slɒg] N faticata; **it's a hard slog to the top** è una faticaccia arrivare in cima ♦ VI **1** (*work*) faticare, sgobbare; **to slog away at sth** sgobbare su qc **2** (*walk etc*): **to slog along** avanzare a fatica; **we slogged on for 8 kilometres** ci trascinammo per 8 chilometri ♦ VT (*ball, opponent*) colpire con forza

slo·gan [ˈsləʊgən] N slogan *m inv*

slop [slɒp] VI (*also:* **slop over**) traboccare, versarsi; **the water was slopping about in the bucket** l'acqua quasi traboccava dal secchio ♦ VT versare, rovesciare

slope [sləʊp] N **1** (*gen: of hill*) pendio; (*side of hill*) versante *m*; (*of roof*) pendenza; (*of floor*) inclinazione *f*; **a steep slope** un pendio ripido; **on the slopes of Mount Etna** sulle falde *or* pendici dell'Etna; **the car got stuck on a slope** la macchina si è bloccata su una salita **2** (*also:* **ski slope**) pista (da sci) ♦ VI (*path, roof, handwriting*) essere inclinato(-a); **to slope up** essere in salita; **the garden slopes down to the stream** il giardino digrada verso il ruscello

▸ **slope off** VI + ADV (*fam*) filarsela, tagliare la corda

slop·ing [ˈsləʊpɪŋ] ADJ inclinato(-a)

slop·py [ˈslɒpɪ] (*fam*) ADJ (*comp* -**ier**, *superl* -**iest**) **1** (*work*) trascurato(-a); (*appearance, dress*) trasandato(-a), sciatto(-a) **2** (*book, film, letter*) sdolcinato(-a) **3** (*food*) brodoso(-a)

slosh [slɒʃ] (*fam*) VT **1** (*liquid*) spargere; **to slosh some water over sth** gettare dell'acqua su qc **2** (*hit: person*) colpire ♦ VI: **to slosh about in the puddles** sguazzare nelle pozzanghere

sloshed [slɒʃt] ADJ (*fam: drunk*) sbronzo(-a); **to get sloshed** prendere una sbronza

slot [slɒt] N (*in machine etc*) fessura; (*groove*) scanalatura; (*fig: in timetable: Radio, TV*) spazio; **put the money in the slot** inserite il denaro nella fessura ♦ VT (*object*) infilare; (*fig: activity, speech*) inserire ♦ VI: **to slot (into)** inserirsi (in)

sloth [sləʊθ] N **1** (*frm: vice*) indolenza **2** (*Zool*) bradipo

slot machine N (*for cigarettes, food*) distributore *m* automatico; (*for amusement*) slot-machine *f inv*

slot meter N contatore *m* a monete

slouch [slaʊtʃ] VI (*when walking*) camminare dinoccolato(-a); **don't slouch!** raddrizza la schiena!, non stare con la schiena curva!; **to slouch in/out** trascinarsi dentro/fuori; **she was slouched in the chair** era stravaccata nella poltrona ♦ N: **to be no slouch at sth** (*fam*) cavarsela benino in qc

▸ **slouch about, slouch around** VI + ADV (*laze*) oziare

Slo·vak [ˈsləʊvæk] ADJ slovacco(-a) ♦ N (*person*) slovacco(-a); (*language*) slovacco

Slo·vakia [sləʊˈvækɪə] N Slovacchia

Slo·vak·ian [sləʊˈvækɪən] ADJ, N = **Slovak**

Slo·vene [sləʊˈviːn] ADJ sloveno(-a) ♦ N (*person*) sloveno(-a); (*language*) sloveno

Slo·venia [sləʊˈviːnɪə] N Slovenia

Slo·venian [sləʊˈviːnɪən] ADJ, N = **Slovene**

slov·en·ly [ˈslʌvnlɪ] ADJ (*person*) sciatto(-a), trasandato(-a); (*work*) trascurato(-a), poco accurato(-a)

slow [sləʊ] (*comp* -**er**, *superl* -**est**) ADJ **1** (*gen*) lento(-a); **a slow truck** un camion lento; **at a slow speed** a bassa velocità; **she's a slow worker** lavora lentamente; **this car is slower than my old one** questa macchina è meno veloce di quella che avevo; **to be slow to act/decide** essere lento(-a) ad agire/a decidere; **to be slow to anger** (*liter*) non arrabbiarsi facilmente **2** (*of clock*): **to be slow** essere *or* andare indietro; **the clock's slow** l'orologio è indietro; **my watch is 20 minutes slow** il mio orologio è indietro di 20 minuti **3** (*person: stupid*) lento(-a), tardo(-a); **slow to understand/notice** tardo(-a) a capire/notare; **he's a bit slow at mathematics** fa un po' di fatica in matematica **4** (*boring, dull: film, play*) lento(-a); (*: party*) poco movimentato(-a); **life here is slow** qui la vita scorre lenta; **the game is very slow** il gioco è molto lento; **business is slow** (*Comm*) gli affari procedono a rilento **5** (*slowing down movement: pitch, track, surface*) pesante; **bake for two hours in a slow oven** cuocere per due ore nel forno a bassa temperatura; **to go slow** (*driver*) andare piano; (*in industrial dispute*) attuare uno sciopero bianco; (*be cautious*) andare con i piedi di piombo; **go slower!** vai più piano!; **"(go) slow"** "rallentare" ♦ vt (*also:* **slow down**, **slow up**) (*progress, machine*) rallentare; (*person*) far rallentare; (*pace of novel etc*) rendere più lento(-a); **the interruptions have slowed us down** le interruzioni ci hanno fatto perdere tempo; **that car slows up the traffic** quella macchina fa rallentare il traffico ♦ vi (*also:* **slow down**, **slow up**) rallentare; **production has slowed to almost nothing** la produzione si è ridotta a livelli minimi

slow-acting ['sləʊˌæktɪŋ] ADJ che agisce lentamente, ad azione lenta

slow·ly ['sləʊlɪ] ADV lentamente; **to drive slowly** andare piano; **slowly but surely** a poco a poco ma in modo certo; **work is proceeding slowly but surely** il lavoro procede piano ma bene; **to go more slowly** rallentare

slow motion N: **in slow motion** al rallentatore

slow·ness ['sləʊnɪs] N lentezza

sludge [slʌdʒ] N (*mud, sediment*) melma; (*sewage*) deposito di fognatura

slug [slʌg] N (*Zool*) lumaca; (*esp USA: fam: bullet*) pallottola; (*fam: blow*) colpo; (*: large mouthful*) sorsata; **a slug of whisky** (*fam*) un bicchierino di whisky ♦ vt (*fam: hit*) colpire

slug·gish ['slʌgɪʃ] ADJ (*indolent*) pigro(-a), fiacco(-a); (*slow-moving: river, engine, car*) lento(-a); (*: business, market, sales*) stagnante, fiacco(-a); **the car is very sluggish** la macchina manca di ripresa

sluice [sluːs] N (*also:* **sluicegate**) chiusa; (*also:* **sluiceway**) canale *m* di chiusa ♦ vt: **to sluice down** *or* **out** lavare con abbondante acqua

slum [slʌm] N (*house*) catapecchia, tugurio

slum·ber ['slʌmbəʳ] N (*often pl: liter*) sonno ♦ vi dormire (tranquillamente)

slump [slʌmp] N (*gen*) caduta, crollo; (*in production, sales*) calo, crollo; (*economic*) crisi *f inv*, depressione *f*; **the slump in the price of copper** il crollo del prezzo del rame; **a slump in property prices** un crollo dei prezzi delle case; **the slump of the early 1980s** la crisi dei primi anni '80 ♦ vi **1** (*price etc*) cadere, crollare; (*production, sales*) calare, diminuire; (*fig: morale etc*) abbassarsi; **profits have slumped** i profitti sono crollati **2 to slump into a chair** lasciarsi cadere su una sedia; **he was slumped over the wheel** era accasciato sul volante

slung [slʌŋ] PT, PP *of* **sling**

slunk [slʌŋk] PT, PP *of* **slink**

slur [slɜːʳ] N **1** (*stigma*) macchia; (*insult*) diffamazione *f*; **racial slurs** insulti razzisti; **a slur on sb's reputation** una calunnia su qn; **to cast a slur on sb** calunniare qn; **without wishing to cast a slur on his character, I think ...** senza per questo volerlo denigrare, penso che... **2** (*Mus*) legatura ♦ vt (*word etc*) farfugliare, pronunciare in modo inarticolato; (*Mus*) legare; **his speech was slurred** biascicava (*perché ubriaco*)

slurp [slɜːp] vt, vi (*fam*) bere rumorosamente ♦ N rumore fatto bevendo

slurred [slɜːd] ADJ (*speech*) confuso(-a)

slush [slʌʃ] N (*melting snow*) neve *f* sciolta, fanghiglia; (*fam: literature etc*) letteratura *etc* sdolcinata

slush fund N fondi *mpl* neri

slushy ['slʌʃɪ] ADJ (*comp* **-ier**, *superl* **-iest**) (*snow*) sciolto(-a), fangoso(-a); (*fam: Brit: poetry*) sdolcinato(-a)

slut [slʌt] N (*offensive*) (*immoral*) donnaccia, sgualdrina; (*dirty, untidy*) sciattona

sly [slaɪ] ADJ (*comp* **-ier**, *superl* **-iest**) (*wily*) astuto(-a), scaltro(-a); (*secretive*) furtivo(-a); (*mischievous: trick*) birbone(-a); (*smile*) sornione(-a), malizioso(-a); **she's sly!** è scaltra! ♦ N: **on the sly** di nascosto, di soppiatto

smack¹ [smæk] N (*slap: on buttocks*) pacca; (*: on face*) schiaffo, ceffone *m*; (*sound*) colpo secco; (*: of lips, whip*) schiocco; **it was a smack in the eye for them** è stato uno smacco *or* uno schiaffo morale per loro; **to give a child a smack** sculacciare un bambino; **to have a smack at doing sth** (*fig*) provare a fare qc ♦ vt (*child*) sculacciare; (*face*) schiaffeggiare; **she smacked the child's bottom** sculacciò il bambino; **to smack one's lips** schioccare le labbra ♦ vt: **it fell smack in the middle** (*fam*) cadde giusto nel mezzo; **she ran smack into the door** andò a sbattere dritto contro la porta

smack² [smæk] vi: **to smack of** (*fig: intrigue etc*) puzzare di

smack·er ['smækəʳ] N (*fam: kiss*) bacio; (*: Brit: old: pound note*) sterlina; (*: USA: dollar bill*) dollaro

small [smɔːl] ADJ (*comp* **-er**, *superl* **-est**) (*gen: in size, number*) piccolo(-a); (*: in height*) basso(-a); (*stock, supply, population*) scarso(-a); (*waist*) sottile; (*meal*) leggero(-a); (*letter*) minuscolo(-a); (*minor, unimportant*) piccolo(-a), insignificante; (*: increase, improvement*) piccolo(-a), leggero(-a); **a small car** una macchina piccola; **when we were small** quando eravamo piccoli; **there was only a small audience** c'era poco pubblico; **this house makes the other one look small** questa casa fa sembrare piccola l'altra; **the smallest possible number of books** il minor numero di libri possibile; **the smallest details** i minimi dettagli; **to have a small appetite** avere poco *or* scarso appetito; **in a small voice** con un filo di voce; **to feel small** (*fig*) sentirsi umiliato(-a) *or* sminuito(-a); **to get** *or* **grow smaller** (*stain, town*) rimpicciolire; (*debt, organization, numbers*) ridursi; **to make smaller** (*amount, income*) ridurre; (*garden, object, garment*) rimpicciolire; **to have small hope of success** avere scarse speranze di successo; **to have small cause** *or* **reason to do sth** non avere molti motivi per fare qc; **to start in a small way** cominciare da poco; **a small shopkeeper** un(a) piccolo(-a) negoziante ♦ N **1 the small of the back** le reni **2 smalls** NPL (*fam: underwear*) biancheria intima

small ad N (*in newspaper*) annuncio economico

small arms NPL armi *fpl* leggere

small business N piccola impresa

small change N spiccioli *mpl*

small·holder ['smɔːlˌhəʊldəʳ] N (*Brit*) piccolo proprietario

small·holding ['smɔːlˌhəʊldɪŋ] N (*Brit*) piccola tenuta

small·ish ['smɔːlɪʃ] ADJ piccolino(-a)

small-minded [smɔːl'maɪndɪd] ADJ meschino(-a)

small·pox ['smɔːlpɒks] N (*Med*) vaiolo

small print N caratteri *mpl* piccoli; (*in contract etc*) parte *f* scritta in piccolo

small-scale ['smɔːlskeɪl] ADJ (*map, model*) in scala ridotta; (*business, farming*) modesto(-a)

small talk N conversazione *f* mondana, chiacchiere *fpl*

small-time ['smɔːltaɪm] ADJ (*fam*) da poco; **a small-time criminal** un delinquente di mezza tacca; **a small-time thief** un ladro di polli

small-town ['smɔːltaʊn] ADJ (*pej*) provinciale

smarmy ['smɑːmɪ] ADJ (*comp* **-ier**, *superl* **-iest**) (*Brit fam*) untuoso(-a), servile

smart [smɑːt] ADJ (*comp* **-er**, *superl* **-est**) **1** (*elegant*) elegante, chic *inv*; (*fashionable*) di moda; **the smart set** il bel mondo; **to look smart** essere elegante; **that's a smart car** è una bella macchina **2** (*clever*) intelligente, brillante; (*quick-witted*) sveglio(-a), furbo(-a); **he thinks he's smarter than Sarah** pensa di essere più intelligente di Sarah; **that was pretty smart of you!** che furbo!; **smart work by the police led to ...** una brillante operazione della polizia ha portato a... **3** (*quick: pace, action*) svelto(-a), rapido(-a); **look smart about it!** sbrigati!, spicciati! ♦ vi **1** (*cut, graze etc*) bruciare; **my eyes are smarting** mi bruciano gli occhi **2** (*fig*): **she's still smarting from his remarks** le bruciano ancora le sue osservazioni; **to smart under an insult/a reproof** soffrire per un insulto/un rimprovero ♦ N (*pain*) dolore *m* acuto

smart·card ['smɑːtkɑːd] N (*Comput*) smart card *f inv*, carta intelligente

smart·en [ˈsmɑːtn] vt (*also:* **smarten up**) (*room, house etc*) abbellire, ravvivare; (*child*) far bello(-a); (*o.s.*) farsi bello(-a); **I'll go and smarten up** andrò a farmi bella; **a plan to smarten up the station** un progetto per abbellire la stazione ♦ vi (*also:* **smarten up**) abbellirsi, farsi bello(-a)

smash [smæʃ] n **1** (*sound*) fracasso **2** (*also:* **smash-up:** *collision*) scontro; (*Tennis, etc*) schiacciata, smash *m inv*; (*powerful blow*) pugno; (*Fin*) crollo; **he died in a car smash** è morto in un incidente automobilistico; **the smash of plates** il rumore di piatti rotti ♦ vt (*break*) rompere, fracassare; (*shatter*) infrangere, frantumare; (*beat: enemy, opponent*) schiacciare, annientare; (: *record*) polverizzare; (*wreck, also fig*) distruggere; (*Tennis, etc*) schiacciare; **they smashed the windows** hanno rotto le finestre; **he smashed it against the wall** lo scagliò contro la parete; **we will smash this crime ring** distruggeremo quest'organizzazione criminale; **he smashed his way out of the building** uscì dall'edificio spaccando tutto quello che trovava davanti ♦ vi (*break*) rompersi, andare in frantumi; **the glass smashed** il bicchiere si è rotto; **the car smashed into the wall** la macchina si schiantò contro il muro
 ‣ **smash down** vt + adv (*door*) abbattere
 ‣ **smash in** vt + adv (*door, window*) abbattere; **to smash one's way in** entrare con la forza; **to smash sb's face in** (*fam*) spaccare la faccia a qn
 ‣ **smash up** vt + adv (*car*) sfasciare; (*room*) distruggere

smash-hit [ˌsmæʃˈhɪt] n successone *m*

smash·ing [ˈsmæʃɪŋ] adj (*fam*) formidabile; **we had a smashing time** ci siamo divertiti come pazzi; **I think he's smashing** io lo trovo formidabile

smat·ter·ing [ˈsmætərɪŋ] n: **to have a smattering of** avere un'infarinatura di

smear [smɪə'] n (*smudge*) traccia; (*dirty mark, also fig*) macchia; (*insult*) calunnia; (*Med*) striscio; **a smear of grease** una macchia di grasso; **a smear against him** una calunnia nei suoi confronti ♦ vt **1** (*butter etc*) spalmare; **to smear cream on one's hands, smear one's hands with cream** spalmarsi le mani di crema; **she smeared sun cream on his back** gli ha spalmato la crema solare sulla schiena **2** (*make dirty*) sporcare; (*smudge: ink, paint*) sbavare; **the page was smeared** c'erano delle sbavature sulla pagina; **his hands were smeared with oil/ink** aveva le mani sporche di olio/inchiostro **3** (*fig: libel*) calunniare, diffamare; **an attempt to smear the organization** un tentativo di infangare il nome dell'organizzazione ♦ vi (*paint, ink etc*) sbavare

smear campaign n campagna diffamatoria

smear test n (*Brit: Med*) Pap-test *m inv*, striscio (*fam*)

smell [smel] (*pt, pp* **smelled** *or* **smelt**) n **1** (*sense of smell*) olfatto, odorato; (*of animal: fig*) fiuto; **to have a keen sense of smell** (*person*) avere l'olfatto sviluppato; (*animal*) avere un fiuto finissimo **2** (*odour*) odore *m*; (*pleasant*) profumo; (*stench*) puzza; **it has a nice smell** ha un buon odore; **there's a strong smell of gas here** qui c'è una forte puzza di gas ♦ vt (*gas, cooking*) sentire odore di; (*flower*) annusare; **to smell something burning** sentire odore di bruciato; **to smell danger** (*fig*) fiutare un pericolo; **I smell a rat** (*fig*) qui gatta ci cova; **I can smell gas** sento odore di gas; **I took a rose and smelled it** ho preso una rosa e l'ho annusata ♦ vi (*pleasantly*) sapere, odorare; (*unpleasantly*) puzzare; **to smell of sth** avere odore di qc; **it smells of petrol** ha odore di benzina; **my fingers smell of garlic** ho le dita che puzzano di aglio; **it smells like chicken** odora di pollo; **it smells good** ha un buon odore; **it smells damp in here** c'è odore di umidità qui dentro; **that dog smells!** quel cane puzza!; **his breath smells** gli puzza l'alito
 ‣ **smell out** vt + adv **1** (*animal, prey, also fig*) fiutare **2** **your feet are smelling the room out!** i tuoi piedi appestano la stanza!

smelly [ˈsmelɪ] adj (*comp* -ier, *superl* -iest) (*fam*) puzzolente; **it's smelly in here** qui c'è puzza

smelt¹ [smelt] pt, pp *of* **smell**

smelt² [smelt] vt (*ore*) fondere

smile [smaɪl] n sorriso; **with a smile on one's lips** col sorriso sulle labbra; **to be all smiles** essere raggiante; **to give sb a smile** sorridere a qn ♦ vi sorridere; **to smile at sb/sth** sorridere a qn/qc; **to keep smiling** continuare a sorridere; (*fig*)

conservare l'allegria; **fortune smiled on him** la fortuna gli arrise ♦ vt: **he smiled his appreciation** sorrise in segno di apprezzamento

smil·ing [ˈsmaɪlɪŋ] adj sorridente

smirk [smɜːk] n (*self-satisfied*) sorriso compiaciuto; (*knowing*) sorrisetto furbo; (*affected*) sorriso affettato ♦ vi (*see n*) sorridere compiaciuto(-a); fare un sorriso furbo; sorridere in modo affettato

smith [smɪθ] n fabbro

smithy [ˈsmɪðɪ] n fucina

smit·ten [ˈsmɪtn] pp *of* **smite** ♦ adj pred: **to be smitten with** (*remorse, desire, fear*) essere preso(-a) da; (*idea*) entusiasmarsi per; **to be smitten (with sb)** avere una cotta (per qn); **to be smitten with flu** essere colpito(-a) dall'influenza

smock [smɒk] n (*loose shirt*) camiciotto; (*blouse*) blusa; (*to protect clothing*) grembiule *m*

smog [smɒg] n smog *m inv*

smoke [sməʊk] n **1** fumo; **there's no smoke without fire** non c'è fumo senza arrosto; **to go up in smoke** (*house*) andare distrutto(-a) dalle fiamme; (*fig*) andare in fumo **2** **to have a smoke** (*cigarette, pipe*) fare una fumatina ♦ vt **1** (*tobacco*) fumare **2** (*bacon, fish, cheese*) affumicare ♦ vi (*gen*) fumare; (*chimney*) fare fumo; **do you smoke?** fumi?; **you should stop smoking** dovresti smettere di fumare
 ‣ **smoke out** vt + adv (*insects etc*) snidare col fumo

smoke alarm, smoke detector n rivelatore *m* di fumo

smoked [sməʊkt] adj (*bacon, fish, etc*) affumicato(-a); **smoked glass** vetro fumé

smoke·less fuel [ˌsməʊklɪsˈfjuːəl] n combustibile *m* che non dà fumo

smoke·less zone [ˌsməʊklɪsˈzəʊn] n (*Brit*) zona in cui sono vietati gli scarichi di fumo

smok·er [ˈsməʊkə'] n (*person*) fumatore(-trice), tabagista *m/f*; (*railway carriage*) carrozza (per) fumatori; **smoker's cough** tosse *f* da fumo

smoke screen n (*Mil, also fig*) cortina fumogena

smoke shop n (*USA*) tabaccheria

smok·ing [ˈsməʊkɪŋ] adj fumante ♦ n fumo; **"no smoking"** "vietato fumare"; **he's given up smoking** ha smesso di fumare; **smoking can damage your health** il fumo può danneggiare la salute; **smoking is bad for you** il fumo fa male
 ❏ **smoking** is not translated by the Italian word *smoking*

smoking car, smoking compartment n carrozza (per) fumatori

smoky [ˈsməʊkɪ] adj (*comp* -ier, *superl* -iest) (*chimney, fire*) fumoso(-a), che fa fumo; (*room, atmosphere*) fumoso(-a), pieno(-a) di fumo; (*flavour*) affumicato(-a); **a smoky room** una stanza fumosa; **to have a smoky flavour** sapere di affumicato

smol·der [ˈsməʊldə'] vi (*USA*) = **smoulder**

smoochy [ˈsmuːtʃɪ] adj (*comp* -ier, *superl* -iest) (*fam*) romantico(-a)

smooth [smuːð] adj (*comp* -er, *superl* -est) **1** (*surface, skin*) liscio(-a); (*chin: hairless*) imberbe; (*sea*) liscio(-a), calmo(-a); **as smooth as silk** liscio(-a) come la seta; **it keeps your skin soft and smooth** mantiene la pelle morbida e liscia **2** (*in consistency: paste etc*) omogeneo(-a) **3** (*movement, breathing, pulse*) regolare; (*landing, take-off, flight*) senza problemi; (*crossing, trip, life*) tranquillo(-a) **4** (*not harsh: cigarette*) leggero(-a); (: *drink*) dal gusto morbido, amabile; (: *voice, sound*) carezzevole **5** (*pej: person*) mellifluo(-a); **he's a smooth operator** (*fam*) ci sa fare; **he's a smooth talker** ha la parola facile; **he's too smooth for my liking** è troppo mellifluo per i miei gusti ♦ vt **1** (*also:* **smooth down:** *hair etc*) lisciare; **to smooth the way** *or* **path for sb** (*fig*) spianare la strada a qn **2** (*stone, wood*) levigare; **to smooth away wrinkles** far sparire le rughe **3** **to smooth cream into one's face** massaggiarsi la crema sul viso
 ‣ **smooth out** vt + adv (*fabric, creases*) lisciare, spianare; (*fig: difficulties*) appianare
 ‣ **smooth over** vt + adv: **to smooth things over** (*fig*) sistemare le cose

smooth·ly [ˈsmuːðlɪ] adv (*easily*) liscio; (*gently*) dolcemente; (*move*) senza scosse; (*talk*) in modo mellifluo; **the engine is**

running smoothly il motore non dà problemi; **everything went smoothly** tutto andò liscio

smoth·er [ˈsmʌðəʳ] VT 1 (*stifle*) soffocare 2 (*cover*) ricoprire; **to smother sb with kisses** ricoprire qn di baci; **fruit smothered in cream** frutta ricoperta di panna

smoul·der, smol·der (*USA*) [ˈsməʊldəʳ] VI (*fire*) covare sotto la cenere; (*fig: passion etc*) covare

SMS [ˌɛsɛmˈɛs] ABBR (*Telec: = short message service*) SMS (*servizio*)

SMS message N SMS *m inv*, messaggino

smudge [smʌdʒ] N sbavatura, macchia ♦ VT sporcare, imbrattare ♦ VI sbavare

smug [smʌɡ] ADJ (*comp* **-ger**, *superl* **-gest**) compiaciuto(-a)

smug·gle [ˈsmʌɡl] VT (*tobacco, drugs*) contrabbandare; **to smuggle in/out** (*goods etc*) far entrare/uscire di contrabbando *or* clandestinamente; (*fig: person, letter etc*) far entrare/uscire di nascosto; **to smuggle sth past** *or* **through Customs** passare la dogana con qc senza dichiararlo

smug·gler [ˈsmʌɡləʳ] N contrabbandiere(-a)

smug·gling [ˈsmʌɡlɪŋ] N contrabbando

smut [smʌt] N (*grain of soot*) granello di fuliggine; (*mark*) segno nero; (*in conversation etc*) sconcezze *fpl*

smut·ty [ˈsmʌtɪ] ADJ (*comp* **-ier**, *superl* **-iest**) (*crude*) osceno(-a), sconcio(-a); (*dirty*) sporco(-a), sudicio(-a)

snack [snæk] N spuntino; **to have a snack** fare uno spuntino

snack bar N snack-bar *m inv*, tavola calda (*or* fredda)

snag [snæɡ] N (*pulled thread*) filo tirato; (*difficulty*) intralcio, intoppo; **the snag is that ...** il guaio è che...; **the snag is that it costs £2000** il guaio è che costa 2000 sterline; **what's the snag?** qual è il problema?; **to run into** *or* **hit a snag** incontrare una difficoltà, trovare un intoppo ♦ VT (*jumper*) tirare un filo a; (*tights*) smagliare

snail [sneɪl] N chiocciola; **at a snail's pace** a passo di lumaca

snake [sneɪk] N serpente *m*, serpe *f*; **snake in the grass** (*fig*) traditore(-trice)

snap [snæp] N 1 (*sound, action: of sth breaking, closing*) colpo secco; (*: of fingers*) schiocco; **a cold snap** (*fam*) un'improvvisa ondata di freddo; **the dog made a snap at the biscuit** il cane ha cercato di afferrare il biscotto; **with a snap of one's fingers** schioccando le dita 2 (*Cards*) rubamazzo 3 (*fam: photo*) foto *f inv* ♦ ADJ (*sudden: strike*) selvaggio(-a); (*: answer, judgement*) immediato(-a); (*: decision*) repentino(-a) ♦ VT 1 (*break*) spezzare di netto 2 (*fingers*) schioccare; **to snap one's fingers at sb/sth** (*fig*) infischiarsi di qn/qc; **to snap a box shut** chiudere una scatola di colpo 3 "be quiet!", she snapped "sta' zitto!", sbottò 4 (*Phot*) fotografare, scattare una foto a ♦ VI 1 (*break: elastic*) spezzarsi 2 (*whip*) schioccare; **it snapped shut** si chiuse di scatto; **to snap back into place** scattare di nuovo a posto; **everything snapped into place** (*fig*) tutto fu chiaro 3 **to snap at sb** (*dog*) cercare di mordere qn; (*person*) rivolgersi a qn con tono brusco

  ▸ **snap off** VT + ADV rompere con un colpo secco; **to snap sb's head off** (*fig*) aggredire qn

  ▸ **snap out** VI + ADV: **snap out of it!** (*fam*) non lasciarti andare! ♦ VT + ADV (*order etc*) dare bruscamente

  ▸ **snap up** VT + ADV afferrare; **to snap up a bargain** (*fig*) accaparrarsi un affare, non lasciarsi sfuggire un affare

snap fastener N bottone *m* a pressione

snap·py [ˈsnæpɪ] ADJ (*comp* **-ier**, *superl* **-iest**) (*fam: slogan, answer*) d'effetto; (*: way of speaking*) sbrigativo(-a); (*: smart*) elegante; **he's a snappy dresser** è un elegantone; **make it snappy!** (*fam*) sbrigati!

snap·shot [ˈsnæpˌʃɒt] N (*Phot*) istantanea

snare [snɛəʳ] N trappola ♦ VT prendere in trappola, intrappolare

snarl¹ [snɑːl] N ringhio ♦ VI: **to snarl (at sb)** ringhiare (a qn)

snarl² [snɑːl] VI (*in wool etc*) garbuglio ♦ VT: **to get snarled up** (*wool, plans*) ingarbugliarsi; (*traffic*) intasarsi

snatch [snætʃ] N 1 (*act of snatching*): **to make a snatch at sth** cercare di afferrare qc 2 (*fam: theft*) furto, rapina; (*: kidnapping*) rapimento 3 (*snippet*) pezzo; **snatches of conversation** frammenti *mpl* di conversazione; **to sleep in snatches** dormire a intervalli ♦ VT (*grab: object*) strappare con violenza; (*: opportunity*) cogliere; (*: few days, short break*) prendersi; (*steal: also fig: kiss, victory*) rubare; (*kidnap*) rapire; **my bag**

was snatched mi hanno scippato; **to snatch a sandwich** buttar giù in fretta un panino; **to snatch some sleep** riuscire a dormire un po'; **to snatch sth from sb** strappare qc a qn; **he snatched the keys from my hand** mi ha strappato di mano le chiavi; **to snatch a knife out of sb's hand** strappare di mano un coltello a qn ♦ VI: **don't snatch!** non strappare le cose di mano!; **to snatch at** (*object*) cercare di afferrare; (*opportunity*) cogliere al volo

  ▸ **snatch away** VT + ADV: **to snatch sth away from sb** strappare qc a qn

  ▸ **snatch up** VT + ADV raccogliere in fretta, afferrare

snaz·zy [ˈsnæzɪ] ADJ (*comp* **-ier**, *superl* **-iest**) (*fam: clothes*) sciccoso(-a)

sneak [sniːk] VT: **to sneak sth out of a place** portare fuori qc di nascosto da un luogo; **to sneak a look at sth** dare una sbirciatina a qc; **to sneak a quick cigarette** fumarsi una sigaretta di nascosto ♦ VI 1 **to sneak in/out** entrare/uscire di nascosto *or* di soppiatto; **to sneak away** *or* **off** allontanarsi di nascosto *or* di soppiatto, squagliarsela; **to sneak off with sth** portare via di soppiatto qc 2 **to sneak on sb** (*fam*) fare la spia a qn ♦ N (*fam: telltale*) spione(-a)

sneak·ers [ˈsniːkəz] NPL (*USA*) scarpe *fpl* da ginnastica

sneak·ing [ˈsniːkɪŋ] ADJ (*dislike, preference*) segreto(-a); **I have a sneaking admiration for him** mio malgrado l'ammiro; **to have a sneaking feeling/suspicion that ...** avere la vaga impressione/il vago sospetto che...

sneaky [ˈsniːkɪ] ADJ (*comp* **-ier**, *superl* **-iest**) (*fam*) vile

sneer [snɪəʳ] N (*expression*) sogghigno, ghigno; (*remark*) commento sarcastico ♦ VI sogghignare; **to sneer at sb/sth** farsi beffe di qn/qc; **you may sneer, but ...** puoi ridere, ma...

sneeze [sniːz] N starnuto ♦ VI starnutire; **an offer not to be sneezed at** (*fig: fam*) un'offerta su cui non si può sputare

snide [snaɪd] ADJ (*fam*) maligno(-a)

sniff [snɪf] N (*sound*) annusata, fiutata; **to have a sniff of sth** annusare qc; **one sniff of this is enough to kill you** un'annusata a questo e muori di sicuro; **he gave a sniff of contempt** ha arricciato il naso con disprezzo ♦ VT (*gen*) annusare, fiutare; (*glue, drug*) sniffare; (*inhalant*) fare inalazioni di; **the dog sniffed my hand** il cane mi ha annusato la mano; **to sniff glue** sniffare colla ♦ VI (*person*) tirare su col naso; (*in contempt*) arricciare il naso; **stop sniffing!** smettila di tirare su col naso!

  ▸ **sniff at** VI + PREP annusare; **it's not to be sniffed at** non è da disprezzare

  ▸ **sniff out** VT + ADV fiutare; (*fig*) fiutare, subodorare

sniff·er dog [ˈsnɪfəˌdɒɡ] N cane *inv* poliziotto, *m* (*antidroga o antiterrorismo*)

snig·ger [ˈsnɪɡəʳ] (*pej*) N risolino ♦ VI ridacchiare, ridere sotto i baffi; **to snigger at** ridere sotto i baffi per

snip [snɪp] N (*cut*) taglio; (*small piece*) ritaglio; (*Brit fam: bargain*) affare *m*, occasione *f*; **with a snip of the scissors** con un colpo di forbici ♦ VT tagliare; **to snip sth off** tagliare via qc

snip·er [ˈsnaɪpəʳ] N franco tiratore *m*, cecchino

snip·pet [ˈsnɪpɪt] N (*of cloth, paper*) ritaglio; (*of information, conversation etc*) frammento

sniv·el·ling, sniv·el·ing (*USA*) [ˈsnɪvlɪŋ] ADJ piagnucoloso(-a)

snob [snɒb] N snob *m/f inv*; **he's an intellectual snob** è uno snob in fatto di cultura

snob·bery [ˈsnɒbərɪ] N snobismo

snob·bish [ˈsnɒbɪʃ] ADJ snob *inv*

snog [snɒɡ] (*Brit fam*) N pomiciata ♦ VI sbaciucchiarsi, pomiciare

snook·er [ˈsnuːkəʳ] N ≈ (gioco del) biliardo ♦ VT: **to be properly snookered** (*fig: fam*) essere in un bel casino

snoop [snuːp] (*fam, pej*) N (*act*): **to have a snoop round** curiosare ♦ VI (*also*: **snoop about**, **snoop around**) curiosare; **to snoop into sb's affairs** ficcare il naso negli affari di qn; **to snoop on sb** spiare qn

snoop·er [ˈsnuːpəʳ] N ficcanaso *m/f*

snooty [ˈsnuːtɪ] ADJ (*comp* **-ier**, *superl* **-iest**) (*fam, pej*) snob *inv*, borioso(-a), altezzoso(-a)

snooze [snuːz] N sonnellino, pisolino; **to have a snooze** fare un sonnellino, schiacciare un pisolino ♦ VI sonnecchiare

snore [snɔː'] N: **to give a loud snore** russare sonoramente ♦ VI russare

snor·ing [ˈsnɔːrɪŋ] N il russare *m*

snor·kel [ˈsnɔːkl] N *(of submarine)* presa d'aria; *(of swimmer)* respiratore *m* subacqueo, boccaglio ♦ VI: **to go snorkelling** nuotare con il boccaglio

snort [snɔːt] N sbuffata, sbuffo ♦ VI *(horse, person)* sbuffare; **to snort with laughter** soffocare dalle risate ♦ VT *(fam: drugs)* sniffare

snot·ty [ˈsnɒtɪ] ADJ *(comp* **-ier**, *superl* **-iest**) *(fam)* moccioso(-a); *(fig: snooty)* borioso(-a), altezzoso(-a)

snout [snaʊt] N *(of animal)* muso; *(of pig)* grugno

snow [snəʊ] N **1** neve *f*; *(also:* **snowfall**) nevicata; *(fam: co-caine)* neve **2** *(on TV screen)* effetto neve ♦ VT: **to be snowed in** *or* **up** essere isolato(-a) a causa della neve; **to be snowed under with work** essere sommerso(-a) di lavoro ♦ VI nevicare; **it's snowing** nevica

snow·ball [ˈsnəʊˌbɔːl] N palla di neve ♦ VI *(fig: scheme, appeal)* crescere a vista d'occhio

snow·board [ˈsnəʊˌbɔːd] N *(board)* snowboard *m*

snow·bound [ˈsnəʊˌbaʊnd] ADJ *(village)* isolato(-a) dalla neve; *(person, road)* bloccato(-a) dalla neve; *(countryside)* coperto(-a) di neve

snow·capped [ˈsnəʊˌkæpt] ADJ *(mountain)* incappucciato(-a) di neve; *(peak)* coperto(-a) di neve

snow·drift [ˈsnəʊˌdrɪft] N cumulo di neve *(ammucchiato dal vento)*

snow·drop [ˈsnəʊˌdrɒp] N bucaneve *m inv*

snow·fall [ˈsnəʊˌfɔːl] N *(fall of snow)* nevicata; *(amount that falls)* nevosità *f inv*

snow·flake [ˈsnəʊˌfleɪk] N fiocco di neve

snow·man [ˈsnəʊˌmæn] N *(pl* **-men**) pupazzo di neve; **the abominable snowman** l'abominevole uomo delle nevi

snow·plough, snow·plow *(USA)* [ˈsnəʊˌplaʊ] N spazzaneve *m inv*

snow·shoe [ˈsnəʊˌʃuː] N racchetta da neve

snow·storm [ˈsnəʊˌstɔːm] N tormenta, tempesta di neve

snowy [ˈsnəʊɪ] ADJ *(comp* **-ier**, *superl* **-iest**) *(climate, region, day etc)* nevoso(-a); *(hills, roof)* innevato(-a); *(white as snow)* candido(-a), niveo(-a); **it's been very snowy recently** ha nevicato parecchio, ultimamente

SNP [ˌesenˈpiː] N ABBR *(Brit Pol = Scottish National Party)* partito nazionalista scozzese

snub [snʌb] N affronto, offesa ♦ VT *(person)* snobbare

snub-nosed [ˌsnʌbˈnəʊzd] ADJ con il naso a patata *or* patatina

snuff [snʌf] N tabacco da fiuto; **to take snuff** fiutare tabacco ♦ VT *(also:* **snuff out:** *candle)* spegnere; **to snuff it** *(Brit fam)* tirare le cuoia

snuff movie N *(fam)* film porno dove una persona viene uccisa realmente

snug [snʌg] ADJ *(comp* **-ger**, *superl* **-gest**) *(cosy: room, house)* accogliente, comodo(-a); *(safe: harbour)* sicuro(-a); *(fitting closely)* attillato(-a); **a snug little house** una casetta accogliente; **warm and snug by the fire** accoccolato(-a) vicino al fuoco; **to be snug in bed** essere al calduccio nel letto; **it's a snug fit** è attillato(-a)

snug·gle [ˈsnʌgl] VI: **to snuggle down in bed** rannicchiarsi nel letto; **to snuggle up to sb** stringersi a qn

snug·ly [ˈsnʌglɪ] ADV comodamente; **it fits snugly** *(object in pocket etc)* ci sta giusto(-a) giusto(-a); *(garment)* sta ben attillato(-a)

KEYWORD

so [səʊ] ADV

1 *(in comparisons: before adjective and adverb)* così; **so quickly** *(soon)* così presto; *(fast)* così in fretta; **it is so big that ...** è così grosso che...; **it was so much more difficult than I expected** era molto più difficile di quanto pensassi; **she's not so clever as him** lei non è così intelligente come lui; **he's not so foolish as I thought** non è così scemo come pensavo; **I wish you weren't so clumsy** magari non fossi così maldestro

2 *(very)* così; **so much** tanto; *(+ noun)* tanto(-a); **so many** tanti(-e); **I love you so much** ti voglio tanto bene; **I'm so worried** sono così preoccupato; **I'm so glad to see you**

again sono così felice di rivederti; **I've got so much to do** ho così tanto da fare; **I've got so much to do that ...** ho così tanto da fare che...; **thank you so much** grazie infinite *or* mille

3 *(thus, in this way, likewise)* così, in questo modo; **the article is so written as to ...** l'articolo è scritto in modo da...; **if so** è così, quand'è così; **he likes things just so** vuole che tutto sia fatto a puntino; **I didn't do it — you DID so!** non l'ho fatto io — l'hai fatto tu eccome!; **so do I, so am I** *etc* anch'io; **he's wrong and so are you** lui si sbaglia e tu pure; **and so forth, and so on** e così via; **so it is!, so it does!** davvero!; **it so happens that ...** sì dà il caso che... + *sub*; **while she was so doing** mentre lo stava facendo; **you should do it so** dovresti farlo così; **I hope so** lo spero; **I think so** penso di sì; **I'm afraid so** temo di sì; **so he says** così dice; **so to speak** per così dire; **don't worry so** non preoccuparti così tanto; **I told you so** te l'avevo detto io; **so saying he walked away** così dicendo se ne andò; **do so** fallo

4 *(phrases)*: **I haven't so much as a penny** non ho neanche una lira; **at so much per week** a un tot alla settimana; **ten or so** circa una decina; **just so!, quite so!** esattamente!; **even so** comunque; **so long!** *(fam)* ciao!, ci vediamo!; **so far** finora, fin qui; *(in past)* fino ad allora

♦ CONJ

1 *(expressing purpose)*: **so as to do sth** in modo *or* così da fare qc; **we hurried so as not to be late** ci affrettammo per non fare tardi; **so (that)** perché + *sub*; **I brought it so that you could see it** l'ho portato perché tu lo vedessi; **so as to prevent cheating** così da evitare imbrogli

2 *(expressing result)*: **it was raining and so we could not go out** pioveva e così non potemmo uscire; **as her French improved so did her confidence** man mano che il suo francese migliorava acquistava più sicurezza; **so you see ...** così vedi...

3 *(in questions, exclamations)*: **so you're Spanish?** e così sei spagnolo?; **so that's the reason!** allora è questo il motivo!, ecco perché!; **so there you are!** ah eccoti qua!; **so there!** *(fam)* ecco!; **so (what)?** *(fam)* e allora?, e con questo *or* ciò?

soak [səʊk] VT **1** *(bread etc)* inzuppare; *(clothes)* mettere a mollo; **soak it in cold water** mettilo in ammollo nell'acqua fredda; **to get soaked (to the skin)** bagnarsi *or* infradiciarsi *(fino alle ossa)*; **to be soaked through** essere (bagnato(-a)) fradicio(-a) **2** *(fam)*: **to soak the rich** mungere i ricchi ♦ VI *(clothes)* inzupparsi; **to leave to soak** *(garment)* lasciare in ammollo; *(dishes)* lasciare a bagno ♦ N **1** *(in water)*: **to have a long soak in the bath** restare a lungo a mollo nella vasca **2** *(fam: drunkard)* spugna

▸ **soak in** VI + ADV penetrare; **it took a long time to soak in** *(fig)* ci è voluto tanto prima che mi *(or* gli *etc)* entrasse in testa

▸ **soak up** VT + ADV *(liquid, knowledge)* assorbire; **to soak up water** assorbire acqua; **to soak up the sunshine** *(fam)* crogiolarsi al sole

soaking [ˈsəʊkɪŋ] ADJ *(also:* **soaking wet**) bagnato(-a) fradicio(-a); **your shoes are soaking** hai le scarpe zuppe

so-and-so [ˈsəʊənˌsəʊ] N *(somebody)* un(a) tale; **Mr/Mrs so-and-so** *(fam)* signor/signora tal dei tali; **he's a so-and-so!** *(fam)* che tipo odioso che è!

soap [səʊp] N sapone *m*; *(also:* **cake of soap**) saponetta; *(TV: fam)* telenovela, soap opera *f inv* ♦ VT insaponare

soap·box [ˈsəʊpˌbɒks] N palco improvvisato *(per orazioni pubbliche)*

soap·flakes [ˈsəʊpˌfleɪks] NPL sapone *msg* in scaglie

soap opera N telenovela, soap opera *f inv*

soap powder N detersivo in polvere

soap·suds [ˈsəʊpˌsʌdz] NPL saponata *fsg*

soapy [ˈsəʊpɪ] ADJ *(comp* **-ier**, *superl* **-iest**) *(covered in soap: person)* insaponato(-a); *(: water)* saponato(-a); *(like soap)* saponoso(-a); **to taste soapy** sapere di sapone

soar [sɔː'] VI **1** *(rise: bird)* librarsi; *(: plane, ball)* volare **2** *(fig: tower etc)* elevarsi, ergersi; *(: price, morale, spirits)* salire alle stelle; *(: ambitions, hopes)* aumentare notevolmente; **the price has soared** il prezzo è lievitato; **the temperature soared** la temperatura è salita moltissimo

sob [sɒb] N singhiozzo ♦ VI singhiozzare ♦ VT: **to sob one's heart out** piangere disperatamente

s.o.b. [ˌesəʊˈbiː] N ABBR (*USA fam!* = *son of a bitch*) figlio di puttana (*fam!*)

so·ber [ˈsəʊbəʳ] ADJ 1 (*not drunk*) sobrio(-a); **to be far from sober** non essere affatto sobrio(-a); **to be as sober as a judge, be stone-cold sober** essere perfettamente sobrio(-a) 2 (*rational, sedate, dull: life, person, colour*) sobrio(-a); (: *opinion, statement, estimate*) ponderato(-a); (: *occasion*) solenne; **the sober truth** la verità pura e semplice; **in a sober mood** serio(-a) ♦ VT (*also:* **sober up**) far passare la sbornia a; (*fig*) calmare ♦ VI (*also:* **sober up**) smaltire la sbornia; (*fig*) calmarsi

so·bri·e·ty [səʊˈbraɪətɪ] N 1 (*not being drunk*) sobrietà 2 (*seriousness, sedateness*) sobrietà, pacatezza

sob story N (*fam, pej*) storia lacrimosa

Soc. ABBR (= *society*) Soc.

so-called [ˌsəʊˈkɔːld] ADJ cosiddetto(-a)

soc·cer [ˈsɒkəʳ] N calcio ♦ ADJ (*club, season, match*) calcistico(-a), di calcio; **a game of soccer** una partita di calcio

soccer pitch N campo di calcio

soccer player N calciatore m

so·cia·ble [ˈsəʊʃəbl] ADJ (*person*) socievole, cordiale; (*evening, gathering*) amichevole, tra amici; **I don't feel very sociable** non ho molta voglia di vedere gente; **I'll have one drink, just to be sociable** berrò qualcosa, tanto per gradire

so·cial [ˈsəʊʃəl] ADJ (*all senses*) sociale; **man is a social animal** l'uomo è un animale sociale *or* socievole ♦ N festicciola

social climber N arrampicatore(-trice) sociale, arrivista m/f

social club N circolo

social democrat N socialdemocratico(-a)

social insurance N (*USA*) assicurazione f sociale

so·cial·ism [ˈsəʊʃəlɪzəm] N socialismo

so·cial·ist [ˈsəʊʃəlɪst] ADJ, N socialista m/f

so·cial·ite [ˈsəʊʃəlaɪt] N persona mondana

so·cial·ize [ˈsəʊʃəlaɪz] VI (*be with people*) frequentare gente; (*make friends*) fare amicizia; (*chat*) chiacchierare; **the party will be an opportunity to socialize and relax** la festa è un'occasione per socializzare e rilassarsi; **to socialize with** socializzare con, frequentare ♦ VT (*Pol, Psych*) socializzare

social life N: **to have a good social life** avere un'intensa vita sociale

so·cial·ly [ˈsəʊʃəlɪ] ADV (*gen*) socialmente, in società; **I know him socially** lo incontro in occasioni mondane

social network N social network m inv, rete f sociale

social networking N il comunicare tramite social network

social science N scienze fpl sociali

social security N previdenza sociale; **to be on social security** (*fam*) ricevere sussidi dalla previdenza sociale

social services NPL servizi mpl sociali

social welfare N sicurezza sociale

social work N assistenza sociale

social worker N assistente m/f sociale

so·ci·e·ty [səˈsaɪətɪ] N 1 (*social community*) società f inv; **to live in society** vivere in società; **he was a danger to society** era un pericolo pubblico; **we live in a multi-cultural society** viviamo in una società multiculturale 2 (*club, organization*) società f inv, associazione f; **film society** cineclub m inv; **learned society** circolo culturale; **literary society** associazione letteraria 3 (*also:* **high society**) alta società; **polite society** società bene 4 (*frm: company*) compagnia; **in the society of** in compagnia di; **I enjoyed his society** ho gradito la sua compagnia ♦ ADJ (*party, column*) mondano(-a)

so·cio·eco·nom·ic [ˌsəʊsɪəʊˌiːkəˈnɒmɪk] ADJ socioeconomico(-a)

so·cio·logi·cal [ˌsəʊsɪəˈlɒdʒɪkəl] ADJ sociologico(-a)

so·ci·olo·gist [ˌsəʊsɪˈɒlədʒɪst] N sociologo(-a)

so·ci·ol·ogy [ˌsəʊsɪˈɒlədʒɪ] N sociologia

sock¹ [sɒk] N (*short*) calzino; (*long*) calzettone m; (*of horse*) balzana; **to pull one's socks up** (*fig*) darsi una regolata; **put a sock in it!** (*Brit fam*) chiudi il becco!

sock² [sɒk] (*fam*) N (*blow*) colpo, pugno; **to give sb a sock on the jaw** dare un pugno sul muso a qn ♦ VT colpire, picchiare; **come on, sock him one!** dai, suonagliele!

sock·et [ˈsɒkɪt] N (*of eye*) orbita; (*of joint*) cavità f inv; (*Elec: for plug*) presa (di corrente); (: *for light bulb*) portalampada m inv

sod¹ [sɒd] N (*liter: of earth*) zolla erbosa

sod² [sɒd] N (*Brit fam!*) stronzo(-a) (*fam!*)

► **sod off** VI + ADV (*Brit fam!*): **sod off!** levati dalle palle! (*fam!*)

soda [ˈsəʊdə] N 1 (*Chem*) soda 2 (*drink*) seltz m inv; **whisky and soda** whisky e soda 3 (*USA: also:* **soda pop**) gassosa

sod·den [ˈsɒdn] ADJ zuppo(-a)

so·dium [ˈsəʊdɪəm] N sodio

sodium chloride N cloruro di sodio

sofa [ˈsəʊfə] N sofà m inv, divano

sofa bed N divano m letto pl inv

So·fia [ˈsəʊfɪə] N Sofia (*città*)

soft [sɒft] ADJ (*comp* -er, *superl* -est) 1 (*not hard, rough etc: gen*) morbido(-a); (: *snow, ground*) soffice; (: *metal, stone*) tenero(-a); (: *cheese*) a pasta molle; (: *pej: muscles*) flaccido(-a); **soft cheeses** formaggi a pasta molle; **a nice soft towel** un asciugamano bello morbido; **the mattress is too soft** il materasso è troppo soffice 2 (*gentle, not harsh: breeze, rain, pressure*) leggero(-a); (: *colour*) delicato(-a); (: *light*) tenue; (: *look, smile, answer*) dolce; (: *heart*) tenero(-a); (: *life, option*) facile; (: *job*) non pesante; (: *teacher, parent*) indulgente; **you're too soft with him** sei troppo indulgente con lui; **to have a soft spot for sb** avere un debole per qn; **to be soft on sb** essere cotto(-a) di qn; **he has a soft time of it** lui se la passa bene; **soft skills** capacità fpl relazionali 3 (*not loud: sound, laugh, voice*) sommesso(-a); (: *steps, whisper*) leggero(-a); **the music is too soft** il volume della musica è troppo basso 4 (*fam: person: no stamina*) smidollato(-a); (*stupid*) **to be soft (in the head)** essere un po' tocco(-a) 5 (*Ling: consonant*) dolce

soft-boiled [ˈsɒftˌbɔɪld] ADJ (*egg*) alla coque

soft drink N bibita analcolica

soft drugs NPL droghe fpl leggere

sof·ten [ˈsɒfn] VT (*gen*) ammorbidire; (*light*) attenuare; (*sound, impression*) attutire; (*colour, anger*) smorzare; (*resistance*) fiaccare; (*person: weaken*) addolcire; **he became softened by luxurious living** vivendo nel lusso si è rammollito; **they have recently softened their position** recentemente hanno ammorbidito la loro posizione; **to soften the blow** (*fig*) attutire il colpo; **to soften the impact of** ridurre l'impatto di ♦ VI (*see vt*) ammorbidirsi; attenuarsi; attutirsi; smorzarsi; fiaccarsi; (*person, character*) addolcirsi; **her heart softened** si intenerì; **fry until the onion has softened** soffriggere finché la cipolla si ammorbidisce; **his voice softened** la sua voce si è addolcita

► **soften up** VT + ADV (*fam*): **to soften sb up** ammorbidire qn

sof·ten·er [ˈsɒfnəʳ] N ammorbidente m

soft fruit N (*Brit*) ≈ frutti mpl di bosco

soft furnishings NPL (*Brit*) tessuti mpl d'arredo

soft-hearted [ˌsɒftˈhɑːtɪd] ADJ dal cuore tenero

soft·ly [ˈsɒftlɪ] ADV (*gen*) dolcemente; (*walk*) silenziosamente; (*gently: knock*) lievemente; **he laughed softly** rise piano; **softly lit** debolmente illuminato

soft·ness [ˈsɒftnɪs] N (*of skin, bed, snow, leather*) morbidezza; (*of voice, manner, glance*) dolcezza; (*indulgence*) indulgenza

soft option N soluzione (più) facile

soft sell N persuasione f (indiretta) all'acquisto

soft target N obiettivo civile (*e quindi facile da colpire*)

soft touch N (*fam*): **to be a soft touch** lasciarsi mungere facilmente

soft toy N pupazzo di peluche

soft·ware [ˈsɒftˌweəʳ] N (*Comput*) software m inv

software package N (*Comput*) pacchetto di software

soft water N acqua non calcarea, acqua dolce

sog·gy [ˈsɒgɪ] ADJ (*comp* -ier, *superl* -iest) fradicio(-a), inzuppato(-a); (*bread, cake*) molle, pesante

soil [sɔɪl] N (*earth*) terreno, terra, suolo; **chalky/poor soil** terreno calcareo/povero; **cover it with soil** coprilo di terra; **on British soil** sul suolo britannico; **the soil** (*fig: farmland*) la terra ♦ VT (*dirty*) sporcare; (*fig: reputation, honour etc*) infangare, macchiare

soiled [sɔɪld] ADJ sporco(-a), sudicio(-a)

so·journ [ˈsɒdʒɜːn] (*liter*) N soggiorno ♦ VI soggiornare

sol·ace [ˈsɒlɪs] N consolazione f

so·lar [ˈsəʊləʳ] ADJ solare

so·lar·ium [səʊˈlɛərɪəm] N (pl **solariums** or **solaria** [səʊˈlɛərɪə]) solarium m inv

solar panel N pannello solare

so·lar plex·us [ˌsəʊləˈpleksəs] N (Anat) plesso solare

solar power N energia solare

solar system N sistema m solare

sold [səʊld] PT, PP of **sell**

sol·der [ˈsəʊldəʳ] N lega per saldatura ♦ VT saldare; **soldering iron** saldatore m (attrezzo)

sol·dier [ˈsəʊldʒəʳ] N soldato, militare m; **toy soldier** soldatino; **an old soldier** (also fig) un veterano ♦ VI fare il soldato
  ▸ **soldier on** VI + ADV perseverare

sold out ADJ (Comm) esaurito

sole[1] [səʊl] N (of foot) pianta del piede; (of shoe) suola ♦ VT risolare
  ❏ sole is not translated by the Italian word sole

sole[2] [səʊl] N (pl **sole** or **soles**) (fish) sogliola

sole[3] [səʊl] ADJ 1 (only) unico(-a), solo(-a); **the sole reason** la sola or l'unica ragione; **she was the sole woman in the group** era l'unica donna del gruppo 2 (exclusive) esclusivo(-a); **sole agent** agente m or rappresentante m esclusivo; **sole rights** diritti in esclusiva

sole·ly [ˈsəʊllɪ] ADV solamente, unicamente; **I will hold you solely responsible** ti considererò il solo responsabile

sol·emn [ˈsɒləm] ADJ solenne

sole trader N titolare m/f unico(-a) di azienda

so·lic·it [səˈlɪsɪt] VT (frm: request) richiedere, sollecitare ♦ VI (prostitute) adescare

so·lici·tor [səˈlɪsɪtəʳ] N (Brit: in court) ≈ avvocato(-essa); (: for wills etc) ≈ notaio; (USA) rappresentante m legale (di una città o un ministero)

sol·id [ˈsɒlɪd] ADJ (gen) solido(-a); (not hollow) pieno(-a); (gold, wood) massiccio(-a); (crowd, row) compatto(-a); (line) ininterrotto(-a); (vote) unanime; (meal) sostanzioso(-a); **to become solid** solidificarsi; **cut out of solid rock** scolpito(-a) nella roccia viva; **a solid wall** un muro solido; **solid gold** oro massiccio; **as solid as a rock** solido come una roccia; **to be frozen solid** essere completamente ghiacciato(-a); **we waited two solid hours** abbiamo aspettato due ore filate; **a man of solid build** un uomo di corporatura massiccia; **the street was packed solid with people** la strada era affollatissima; **a solid mass of colour** una massa uniforme di colore; **he's a good solid worker** è un lavoratore serio; **a solid argument** un argomento fondato or valido; **solid common sense** buon senso pratico; **the town is solid for Labour** nella città c'è una gran maggioranza laburista ♦ N solido

soli·dar·ity [ˌsɒlɪˈdærɪtɪ] N solidarietà

solid fuel N combustibile m solido

so·lidi·fy [səˈlɪdɪfaɪ] VT solidificare ♦ VI solidificarsi

so·lid·ity [səˈlɪdɪtɪ] N solidità

solid-state [ˈsɒlɪdˌsteɪt] ADJ (Elec) a stato solido; **solid-state physics** fisica dei solidi

so·lilo·quy [səˈlɪləkwɪ] N soliloquio

soli·taire [ˌsɒlɪˈtɛəʳ] N (game, gem) solitario

soli·tary [ˈsɒlɪtərɪ] ADJ (alone, secluded) solitario(-a); (sole: example, case) solo(-a), unico(-a); **a solitary figure** una figura solitaria; **not a solitary one** neanche uno(-a)

solitary confinement N: **to be in solitary confinement** essere in cella d'isolamento

soli·tude [ˈsɒlɪtjuːd] N solitudine f

solo [ˈsəʊləʊ] N (pl **solos**) (Mus) assolo; **a tenor solo** un assolo di tenore; **a guitar solo** un assolo di chitarra ♦ ADJ: **solo flight** volo in solitario; **passage for solo violin** brano per violino solista ♦ ADV (Mus): **to play** (or **sing**) **solo** fare un assolo; **to fly solo** volare in solitario

so·lo·ist [ˈsəʊləʊɪst] N solista m/f

Solomon Islands NPL: **the Solomon Islands** le isole Salomone

sol·stice [ˈsɒlstɪs] N solstizio

sol·uble [ˈsɒljʊbl] ADJ solubile

so·lu·tion [səˈluːʃən] N soluzione f

solve [sɒlv] VT risolvere

sol·ven·cy [ˈsɒlvənsɪ] N (Fin) solvibilità

sol·vent [ˈsɒlvənt] ADJ (Fin) solvibile; (Chem) solvente; **to be solvent** avere una discreta posizione economica ♦ N (Chem) solvente m

solvent abuse N abuso di colle e solventi (a scopo stupefacente)

So·ma·li [səʊˈmɑːlɪ] ADJ, N somalo(-a)

So·ma·lia [səʊˈmɑːlɪə] N la Somalia

Somaliland [səʊˈmɑːlɪˌlænd] N paesi mpl del Corno d'Africa

sombre, som·ber (USA) [ˈsɒmbəʳ] ADJ (mood, person) triste, tetro(-a); (colour) scuro(-a); **a sombre prospect** una triste prospettiva

---

KEYWORD

some [sʌm] ADJ
1 (a certain amount or number of): **some tea/water/biscuits/girls** del tè/dell'acqua/dei biscotti/delle ragazze; **I have some books** ho qualche libro or alcuni libri; **some children came** sono venuti dei bambini; **all I have left is some chocolate** mi è rimasto solo un po' di cioccolato; **have some more crisps** prendi ancora delle patatine; **there's some milk in the fridge** c'è un po' del latte in frigo; **there were some people outside** c'era della gente fuori; **he asked me some questions about the accident** mi ha fatto qualche domanda or alcune domande or delle domande sull'incidente; **have some tea/ice-cream** prendi un po' di tè/gelato; **if you have some time to spare** se hai un po' di tempo a disposizione

2 (certain: in contrast) certo(-a), alcuni(-e) pl; **some people hate fish** certa gente odia il pesce; **some people say that ...** certa gente dice or alcuni dicono che...; **in some ways** per certi versi, in un certo senso

3 (vague, indeterminate) un(a) certo(-a), qualche; **some day** un giorno; **some day next week** un giorno della prossima settimana; **in some form or other** in una qualche forma; **some man was asking for you** un tale chiedeva di te; **at some place in Sweden** da qualche parte in Svezia; **some politician or other** un qualche uomo politico; **some other time!** sarà per un'altra volta!

4 (considerable amount of): **it took some courage to do that** ci è voluto un bel coraggio per farlo; **some days ago** parecchi giorni fa; **some distance away** abbastanza lontano; **at some length** a lungo; **after some time** dopo un po'

5 (emphatic: a few, a little): **that's SOME consolation!** questo è già qualcosa!; **there's still SOME petrol in the tank** c'è ancora un po' di benzina nel serbatoio

6 (fam: intensive): **that's some fish!** questo sì che è un pesce!; **it was some party** è stata una grande festa; **you're some help!** (iro) sei proprio un bell'aiuto!

♦ PRON
1 (a certain number) alcuni(-e) pl, certi(-e) pl; **some of them are crazy** alcuni di loro sono pazzi; **I've got some** (books etc) ne ho alcuni; (milk, money) ne ho un po'; **some (of them) have been sold** alcuni sono stati venduti; **would you like some?** ne vorresti qualcuno?; **do take some** prendine qualcuno; **some went this way and some that** alcuni andarono di qua e altri di là

2 (a certain amount) un po'; **could I have some of that cheese?** potrei avere un po' di quel formaggio?; **have some more** prendine ancora un po'; **have some!** prendine un po'!; **I've read some of the book** ho letto parte del libro; **some of what he said was true** parte di ciò che ha detto era vero; **some of it was left** ne è rimasto un po'

♦ ADV: **some 20 people** circa 20 persone

some·body [ˈsʌmbədɪ] PRON qualcuno; **there's somebody coming** sta arrivando qualcuno; **somebody knocked at the door** hanno bussato alla porta; **somebody else** qualcun altro; **somebody Italian** un italiano; **somebody told me so** me l'ha detto qualcuno; **somebody or other** qualcuno ♦ N: **to be somebody** essere qualcuno; **she thinks she's somebody** si crede importante

some·day [ˈsʌmˌdeɪ] ADV uno di questi giorni, un giorno o l'altro

some·how [ˈsʌmˌhaʊ] ADV 1 (in some way) in qualche modo, in un modo o nell'altro; **it must be done somehow or other** bene o male va fatto; **we managed it somehow** non so come, ma ce l'abbiamo fatta; **we'll manage somehow** in un modo o nell'altro ce la faremo; **I'll do it somehow** lo farò, in un modo o nell'altro **2** (*for some reason*) per un motivo o per l'altro; **it seems odd somehow** non so perché, ma mi sembra strano; **somehow I've never succeeded** chissà perché non ce l'ho mai fatta; **somehow I don't think he believed me** qualcosa mi dice che non mi ha creduto

some·one [ˈsʌmˌwʌn] PRON = **somebody**

some·place [ˈsʌmˌpleɪs] ADV (*USA*) = **somewhere**

som·er·sault [ˈsʌməˌsɔːlt] N (*by person*) capriola; (*in air*) salto mortale; (*by car etc*) ribaltamento, cappottamento ♦ VI (*see n*) (*also*: **turn a somersault**) fare una capriola; fare un salto mortale; cappottare, ribaltarsi

some·thing [ˈsʌmˌθɪŋ] PRON qualche cosa, qualcosa; **something nice** (*pretty*) qualcosa di carino; (*to eat*) qualcosa di buono; (*to do*) qualcosa di bello; **something interesting** qualcosa di interessante; **something special** qualcosa di speciale; **something to do** qualcosa da fare; **something else** altro, qualcos'altro; **something has happened** è successo qualcosa; **something of the kind** qualcosa del genere; **she said something or other about it** mi ha detto qualcosa a tale proposito; **he's a lecturer in something or other** è professore di non so che; **he's a doctor or something** è dottore o qualcosa del genere; **wear something warm** mettiti qualcosa di pesante; **there's something the matter** c'è qualcosa che non va; **to have something to live for** avere uno scopo nella vita; **there's something in what you say** c'è del vero in quello che dici; **will you have something to drink?** vuoi qualcosa da bere?; **he's called John something** si chiama John vattelappesca; **here's something for your trouble** eccoti qualcosa per il disturbo; **I hope to see something of you** spero di vederti qualche volta; **I think you may have something there** penso che tu abbia ragione; (*good idea*) mi sembra una buona idea, la tua; **there's something about him that ...** c'è qualcosa in lui che...; **she has a certain something** ha un certo non so che; **that's really something!** mica male!; **it would be really something!** non sarebbe mica male! ♦ ADV **1 something over/under 200** un po' più/meno di 200; **something like 200** circa 200; **... or something like that** ...o giù di lì; **it cost a hundred pounds, or something like that** è costato cento sterline o giù di lì; **he's something like me** mi assomiglia un po'; **now that's something like a rose!** (*approving comment*) questa sì che è una rosa! **2 it's something of a problem** è un bel problema; **he is something of a liar** è un bel pezzo di bugiardo; **he's something of a musician** è un musicista abbastanza bravo **3** (*fam*): **the weather was something shocking** faceva un tempo da cani

some·time [ˈsʌmˌtaɪm] ADV un giorno, uno di questi giorni; **sometime last month** un giorno, il mese scorso; **sometime before tomorrow** prima di domani; **sometime next year** (nel corso del)l'anno prossimo; **sometime soon** presto, uno di questi giorni; **I'll finish it sometime** lo finirò uno di questi giorni; **I want to go to Spain sometime** voglio andare in Spagna un giorno o l'altro; **you must come and see us sometime** vieni a trovarci uno di questi giorni; **sometime or (an)other it will have to be done** bisognerà farlo prima o poi ♦ ADV (*frm*: *former*) ex

some·times [ˈsʌmˌtaɪmz] ADV qualche volta, a volte; **sometimes I think Carol hates me** a volte ho l'impressione che Carol mi detesti

some·what [ˈsʌmˌwɒt] ADV piuttosto, alquanto

some·where [ˈsʌmˌwɛəʳ] ADV **1** (*in space*) da qualche parte, in qualche posto; **somewhere else** da qualche altra parte; **I lost it somewhere** l'ho perso da qualche parte; **I've left my keys somewhere** ho lasciato le chiavi da qualche parte; **somewhere in Wales** da qualche parte nel Galles; **somewhere or other in Scotland** da qualche parte in Scozia; **now we're getting somewhere!** ora stiamo facendo dei passi in avanti **2** (*approximately*) circa, all'incirca, più o meno; **he paid somewhere around £12** l'ha pagato circa 12 sterline; **he's somewhere in his fifties** è sulla cinquantina

son [sʌn] N figlio; **come here son** (*fam*) vieni qui figliolo; **the Son of God/of Man** (*Rel*) il Figlio di Dio/dell'uomo

so·nar [ˈsəʊnɑːʳ] N sonar *m inv*

so·na·ta [səˈnɑːtə] N sonata

song [sɒŋ] N (*ballad etc*) canzone *f*; (*of birds*) canto; **give us a song!** cantaci una canzone!; **to burst into song** mettersi a cantare; **to make a great song and dance about sth** (*fig*) fare un sacco di storie per qc; **I got it for a song** (*fig*) l'ho avuto per quattro soldi

song book N canzoniere *m*

song·writer [ˈsɒŋˌraɪtəʳ] N compositore(-trice) di canzoni

son·ic [ˈsɒnɪk] ADJ sonico(-a); **sonic depth finder** ecoscandaglio

son-in-law [ˈsʌnɪnˌlɔː] N (*pl* **sons-in-law**) genero

son·net [ˈsɒnɪt] N sonetto

son·ny [ˈsʌnɪ] N (*fam*) figlio mio, ragazzo mio

soon [suːn] ADV **1** (*before long*) presto, fra poco; **come back soon!** torna presto!; **soon afterwards** poco dopo; **it will soon be summer** presto or fra poco sarà estate; **you would soon get lost** ti perderesti subito; **see you soon!** a presto!; **very/quite soon** molto/abbastanza presto; **he soon changed his mind** ha cambiato presto idea **2** (*early*) presto; **how soon can you be ready?** fra quanto tempo sarai pronto?; **Friday is too soon** venerdì è troppo presto; **it's too soon to tell** è troppo presto per dirlo; **all too soon** fin troppo presto; **we were none too soon** siamo arrivati appena in tempo; **an hour too soon** con un'ora di anticipo **3** (*with as*): **as soon as possible** prima possibile, il più presto possibile; **I'll do it as soon as I can** lo farò appena posso; **as soon as it was finished** appena finito **4** (*expressing preference*): **I would as soon not go** preferirei non andarci; **I would as soon as he didn't know** preferirei che non lo sapesse

soon·er [ˈsuːnəʳ] ADV **1** (*of time*) prima; **can't you come a bit sooner?** non puoi venire un po' prima?; **sooner or later** prima o poi; **the sooner the better** prima è meglio è; **when are you leaving? — the sooner the better** quando parti? — prima parto meglio è; **no sooner had he taken ... than ...** eravamo appena partiti, quando...; **no sooner said than done** detto fatto **2** (*of preference*): **I'd** *or* **I would sooner not do it** preferirei non farlo; **I would sooner do something useful** preferirei fare qualcosa di utile; **I'd sooner die!** (*fam*) piuttosto morirei!

soot [sʊt] N fuliggine *f*

soothe [suːð] VT (*gen*) calmare; (*pain, anxieties*) alleviare

sooth·ing [ˈsuːðɪŋ] ADJ (*ointment etc*) calmante; (*tone, words etc*) rassicurante; (*bath*) rilassante

SOP [ˌɛsəʊˈpiː] N ABBR (= **standard operating procedure**)

sop [sɒp] N **1** (*concession*): **that's only a sop** è soltanto un contentino; **as a sop to his pride** per lusingare il suo amor proprio **2 sops** NPL (*food*) pappette *fpl*
  ▸ **sop up** VT + ADV (*fam*) assorbire, bere

so·phis·ti·cat·ed [səˈfɪstɪˌkeɪtɪd] ADJ (*method, machine*) sofisticato(-a); (*person*) raffinato(-a), sofisticato(-a); (*clothes, room*) raffinato(-a); (*discussion*) sottile; (*mind, film*) complicato(-a); **a sophisticated machine** una macchina sofisticata; **sophisticated tastes** gusti raffinati

so·phis·ti·ca·tion [səˌfɪstɪˈkeɪʃən] N (*of method, machine*) complessità; (*of person, clothes etc*) raffinatezza; (*of argument etc*) sottigliezza

sopho·more [ˈsɒfəˌmɔːʳ] N (*USA*) studente del secondo anno di scuola superiore o dell'università

sopo·rif·ic [ˌsɒpəˈrɪfɪk] ADJ soporifero(-a)

sop·ping [ˈsɒpɪŋ] ADJ (*also*: **sopping wet**) bagnato(-a) fradicio(-a)

sop·py [ˈsɒpɪ] ADJ (*comp* **-ier**, *superl* **-iest**) (*Brit fam*: *sentimental*) sdolcinato(-a); (: *silly*) sciocco(-a)

so·pra·no [səˈprɑːnəʊ] N (*pl* **sopranos**) (*Mus*: *singer*) soprano *m/f*; (: *voice*) soprano *m* ♦ ADJ di soprano

sor·bet [ˈsɔːbɪt] N sorbetto

sor·cer·er [ˈsɔːsərəʳ] N stregone *m*

sor·did [ˈsɔːdɪd] ADJ (*place, room etc*) sordido(-a); (*deal, motive etc*) meschino(-a), sordido(-a)

sore [sɔːʳ] ADJ (*comp* **-r**, *superl* **-st**) **1** (*painful*) dolorante; **I feel sore all over** sono tutto indolenzito; **sore throat** mal *m* di gola; **it's sore** mi fa male; **my eyes are sore, I have sore eyes** mi fanno male gli occhi **2** (*fig*): **it's a sore point** è un punto delicato; **to touch on a sore point** mettere il dito sulla piaga; **to feel sore about sth** (*esp USA*: *fam*) essere molto seccato(-a) per qc; **don't get sore!** (*esp USA*: *fam*) non te la prendere! ♦ N (*Med*) piaga

sore·ly [ˈsɔːlɪ] ADV (*tempted*) fortemente; (*regretted*) amaramente; **it is sorely needed** ce n'è un estremo bisogno; **she is sorely missed by her family** la sua famiglia sente molto la sua mancanza; **he has been sorely tried** (*frm*) è stato duramente provato

sor·rel [ˈsɒrəl] N 1 (*Bot*) acetosa 2 (*horse*) sauro; (*colour*) giallo bruno *inv* ♦ ADJ (*colour*) giallo bruno *inv*

sor·row [ˈsɒrəʊ] N dolore *m*; **her sorrow at the death of her son** il suo dolore per la morte del figlio; **more in sorrow than in anger** più con dolore che con rabbia ♦ VI: **to sorrow over sth** (*liter*) addolorarsi per qc

sor·row·ful [ˈsɒrəʊfəl] ADJ addolorato(-a), triste

sor·ry [ˈsɒrɪ] ADJ (*comp* **-ier**, *superl* **-iest**) 1 (*in apologizing*): **sorry!** scusa! (*or* scusi! *or* scusate!); **awfully sorry!, so sorry!, very sorry!** (*more polite*) scusa (*or* scusi *or* scusate) tanto!; **to be sorry** essere spiacente *or* desolato(-a); **to say sorry (to sb for sth)** chiedere scusa (a qn per qc); **to be sorry about sth** essere dispiaciuto(-a) *or* spiacente di qc; **I'm sorry I'm late** scusa il ritardo; **I'm sorry about what happened last night** scusami per quello che è successo ieri sera; **I'm sorry, but you're wrong** scusa ma hai torto; **to be sorry to have to do sth** essere spiacente di dover fare qc 2 (*Brit: what did you say?*): **sorry?** come, scusa? 3 (*regretful, sad*) triste, addolorato(-a), desolato(-a); **I'm very sorry** mi dispiace tanto; **I'm sorry to hear that …** mi dispiace (sapere) che…; **I'm sorry to tell you that …** mi dispiace dirti che…; **it was a failure, I'm sorry to say** purtroppo è stato un fiasco; **I can't say I'm sorry** non posso dire che mi dispiaccia; **you'll be sorry for this!** te ne pentirai! 4 (*pitying*): **to be** *or* **feel sorry for sb** dispiacersi per qn; **to be** *or* **feel sorry for o.s.** compiangersi, piangersi addosso 5 (*condition, tale*) pietoso(-a); (*sight, failure*) triste; (*excuse*) misero(-a); **in a sorry state** in uno stato pietoso

sort [sɔːt] N 1 (*gen*) specie *f inv*, genere *m*, tipo; (*make: of coffee, car etc*) tipo; **what sort do you want?** che tipo vuole?; **I know his sort** conosco il suo tipo; **books of all sorts** libri di ogni genere; **he's a painter of sorts** è, per così dire, un pittore; **of the worst sort** della peggior specie; **something of the sort** qualcosa del genere; **it's tea of a sort** è una specie di tè; **I'll do nothing of the sort!** nemmeno per sogno!; **behaviour of that sort** comportamento del genere; **it takes all sorts (to make a world)** il mondo è bello perché è vario 2 **sort of**, **what sort of car?** che tipo di macchina?; **what sort of bike have you got?** che tipo di bici hai?; **what sort of man is he?** che tipo di uomo è?; **it's my sort of film** è il tipo di film che piace a me; **he's not the sort of man to say that** non è il tipo da dire cose del genere; **all sorts of dogs** cani di ogni tipo; **he's some sort of painter** è una specie di pittore; **it's a sort of dance** è una specie di danza; **and all that sort of thing** e così via; **what sort of an answer is that?** che razza di risposta è questa?; **that's the sort of person I am** io sono fatto così; **you know the sort of thing I mean** sai cosa voglio dire; **it's sort of awkward** (*fam*) è piuttosto difficile; **it's sort of yellow** (*fam*) è giallastro; **aren't you pleased?** — **sort of** (*fam*) non sei contento? — insomma; **I sort of thought that would happen** (*fam*) quasi mi lo sentivo che sarebbe successo 3 (*person*): **he's a good sort** è una brava persona; **he's not my sort** non è il mio tipo; **he's an odd sort** è un tipo strano 4 **to be out of sorts** (*in a bad temper*) avere la luna (storta *or* di traverso), non essere in vena; (*unwell*) non essere in forma ♦ VT 1 (*classify: documents, stamps*) classificare; (*put in order: papers, clothes*) mettere in ordine; (*: letters*) smistare; (*separate*) separare, dividere; **the students are sorted into three groups** gli studenti sono suddivisi in tre gruppi 2 (*Comput*) ordinare

  ▸ **sort out** VT + ADV 1 = **sort** VT 2 (*straighten out: room*) riordinare, sistemare; (*: papers, one's ideas*) riordinare; (*solve: problem etc*) risolvere; **have you managed to sort out what's happening?** sei riuscito a sapere cosa succede?; **things will sort themselves out** le cose si sistemeranno da sole; **we've got it sorted out now** la faccenda è risolta 3 **I'll sort him out!** (*fam*) lo sistemo io!

sor·tie [ˈsɔːtɪ] N (*Aer, Mil*) sortita

sort·ing of·fice [ˈsɔːtɪŋˌɒfɪs] N (*Post*) ufficio di smistamento

SOS [ˌɛsəʊˈɛs] N S.O.S. *m inv*

so-so [ˈsəʊsəʊ] ADJ, ADV (*fam*) così così; **how are you feeling?** —**so-so** come ti senti? — così così

souf·flé [ˈsuːfleɪ] N soufflé *m inv*; **cheese soufflé** soufflé di formaggio

sought [sɔːt] PT, PP *of* **seek**

sought-after [ˈsɔːtˌɑːftə] ADJ richiesto(-a)

soul [səʊl] N 1 anima; **with all one's soul** con tutta l'anima; **All Souls' Day** il giorno dei morti; **God rest his soul** pace all'anima sua; **he's the soul of discretion** è la discrezione in persona 2 (*person*) anima; **I didn't see a soul** non ho visto anima viva; **the poor soul had nowhere to sleep** il poveraccio non aveva dove dormire 3 (*also:* **soul music**) soul *m*

soul-destroying [ˈsəʊldɪˈstrɔɪɪŋ] ADJ (*fig: boring*) alienante; (*: depressing*) demoralizzante

soul·ful [ˈsəʊlfʊl] ADJ (*gen*) pieno(-a) di sentimento; (*eyes, expression*) espressivo(-a)

soul·less [ˈsəʊllɪs] ADJ (*task, factory*) alienante; (*person*) senza cuore, crudele

soul mate N anima gemella

soul-searching [ˈsəʊlˌsɜːtʃɪŋ] N: **after much soul-searching** dopo un profondo esame di coscienza

sound¹ [saʊnd] N (*gen*) suono; (*of sea, breaking glass etc*) rumore *m*; (*volume of TV*) audio; **don't make a sound!** non fare rumore!; **the sound of footsteps** il rumore di passi; **can I turn the sound down?** posso abbassare l'audio?; **the speed of sound** la velocità del suono; **to the sound of the national anthem** al suono dell'inno nazionale; **not a sound was to be heard** non si sentiva volare una mosca; **a language with many consonant sounds** una lingua piena di consonanti; **I don't like the sound of it** (*fig: of film etc*) non mi dice niente; (*: of news*) è preoccupante ♦ VT 1 (*alarm, bell, horn*) suonare; **to sound the retreat** (*Mil*) suonare la ritirata; **to sound a note of warning** (*fig*) dare un segnale d'allarme 2 **sound your "r"s more** pronuncia la r più chiaramente 3 (*Med*): **to sound sb's chest** auscultare il torace di qn ♦ VI 1 (*trumpet, bell, alarm*) suonare; (*voice, siren*) risuonare; **a cannon sounded a long way off** si sentì un colpo di cannone in lontananza 2 **it sounds hollow** dal rumore sembra vuoto; **he sounds Italian to me** da come parla mi sembra italiano; **it sounds like French** (*similar*) somiglia al francese; **it sounds better like that** suona meglio così; **that sounds like them arriving now** mi sembra di sentirli arrivare; **you sound like your mother** mi sembra di sentire parlare tua madre; **he sounded angry** (*a giudicare*) dalla voce sembrava arrabbiato 3 (*seem*): **that sounds interesting** mi sembra interessante; **that sounds very odd** sembra molto strano; **how does it sound to you?** che te ne pare?; **that sounds like a good idea** sembra una buona idea; **it sounds as if she's doing well at school** sembra che stia andando bene a scuola; **it sounds as if she won't be coming** ho l'impressione che non verrà

  ▸ **sound off** VI + ADV (*fam*): **to sound off (about)** (*give one's opinions*) fare dei grandi discorsi (su); (*boast*) vantarsi (di); (*grumble*) brontolare (per)

  ▸ **sound out** VT + ADV sondare

sound² [saʊnd] ADJ (*comp* **-er**, *superl* **-est**) 1 (*in good condition, healthy*) sano(-a); (*structure, organization, investment*) solido(-a); **to be of sound mind** essere sano(-a) di mente; **as sound as a bell** (*person*) sano(-a) come un pesce; (*thing*) in perfette condizioni; **a sound structure** una struttura solida 2 (*valid: argument, policy*) valido(-a); (*: move*) sensato(-a); (*dependable: person*) affidabile; **Julian gave me some sound advice** Julian mi ha dato un buon consiglio; **a sound conservative** un conservatore convinto; **he's sound on government policy** conosce molto bene la politica del governo 3 (*thorough*): **to give sb a sound beating** picchiare qn di santa ragione 4 (*sleep: deep, untroubled*) profondo(-a); **he's a sound sleeper** è uno che dorme sodo ♦ ADV: **to be sound asleep** dormire sodo, dormire profondamente

sound³ [saʊnd] VT (*Naut*) scandagliare, sondare; **to sound sb out about sth** sondare le opinioni di qn su qc

sound⁴ [saʊnd] N (*Geog*) stretto

sound barrier N: **the sound barrier** la barriera *or* il muro del suono

sound·bite [ˈsaʊndˌbaɪt] N frase *f* incisiva (*trasmessa per radio o per TV*)

sound effects NPL effetti *mpl* sonori

sound engineer N tecnico del suono

sound·ing [ˈsaʊndɪŋ] N (*Naut*) scandagliamento

sounding board N (*Mus*) tavola armonica; (*fig*) banco di prova

sound·ly [ˈsaʊndlɪ] ADV (*build*) solidamente; (*argue*) giudiziosamente; (*invest*) saggiamente; **to beat sb soundly** (*thrash*) picchiare qn di santa ragione; (*defeat*) battere duramente qn; **to sleep soundly** dormire profondamente

sound·proof [ˈsaʊndˌpruːf] ADJ insonorizzato(-a) ♦ VT insonorizzare

sound system N impianto m audio, *inv*

sound·track [ˈsaʊndˌtræk] N (*music*) colonna sonora; (*speech, noises*) sonoro

soup [suːp] N minestra; (*thick*) zuppa; (*clear*) brodo; **vegetable soup** minestra di verdura; **to be in the soup** (*fam*) essere *or* trovarsi nei pasticci

soup course N minestra

soup kitchen N mensa dei poveri

soup plate N piatto fondo

soup spoon N cucchiaio da minestra

sour [ˈsaʊə^r] ADJ (*comp* **-er**, *superl* **-est**) (*gen*) aspro(-a), agro(-a); (*milk: fig: person, remark*) acido(-a); (*smell*) acre; **whisky sour** *cocktail di whisky al limone*; **to go** *or* **turn sour** (*milk, wine*) inacidirsi; (*fig: relationship, plans*) guastarsi; **it was sour grapes on his part** (*fig*) ha fatto come la volpe con l'uva, è stata solo invidia da parte sua; **to be in a sour mood** (*fig*) essere di umore nero

source [sɔːs] N (*of river*) sorgente *f*; (*fig: of problem, epidemic*) fonte *f*, origine *f*; **oranges are a source of vitamin C** le arance sono ricche di vitamina C; **I have it from a reliable source that ...** ho saputo da fonte sicura che...; **renewable sources of energy** fonti di energia rinnovabile; **the source of the Severn** la sorgente del fiume Severn ♦ VT comperare; **they source their organic products from outside the UK** comperano i loro prodotti biologici da paesi al di fuori del Regno Unito

south [saʊθ] N sud *m*, meridione *m*, mezzogiorno; **(to the) south of** a sud di; **it's south of London** è a sud di Londra; **in the south of** nel sud di; **the wind is from the south** il vento soffia da sud *or* da mezzogiorno; **to veer to the south** (*wind*) girare verso sud; **the South of France** il sud della Francia, la Francia del sud *or* meridionale ♦ ADJ (*gen*) sud *inv*; (*coast*) meridionale; (*wind*) del sud; **the south coast** la costa meridionale; **South Wales** il Galles del sud *or* meridionale ♦ ADV verso sud; **south of the border** a sud del confine; **to sail due south** andare direttamente verso sud; **to travel south** viaggiare verso sud; **we were travelling south** viaggiavamo verso sud; **this house faces south** questa casa è esposta a sud *or* a mezzogiorno

South Africa N il Sudafrica

South African ADJ, N sudafricano(-a)

South America N il Sudamerica, l'America del sud

South American ADJ, N sudamericano(-a)

south·bound [ˈsaʊθˌbaʊnd] ADJ (*gen*) diretto(-a) a sud; (*carriageway*) sud *inv*

South Carolina la Carolina del Sud

South Dakota il Dakota del Sud

South-East Asia N l'Asia sudorientale

south·east [ˌsaʊθˈiːst] N sud-est *m* ♦ ADJ (*wind*) di sud-est; (*counties etc*) sudorientale ♦ ADV verso sud-est

south·east·ern [ˌsaʊθˈiːstən] ADJ di sudest, sudorientale

south·er·ly [ˈsʌðəlɪ] ADJ (*wind*) del sud; (*direction*) verso sud; **house with a southerly aspect** casa esposta a sud

south·ern [ˈsʌðən] ADJ (*region*) del sud, meridionale; (*coast*) meridionale; (*wall*) esposto(-a) a sud; **Southern Europe** l'Europa del sud *or* meridionale; **in southern Spain** nella Spagna del sud *or* meridionale, nel sud della Spagna; **the southern part of the island** la zona meridionale dell'isola

South Korea N Corea *f* del Sud

South Pole N: **the South Pole** il polo sud

South Sea Islands NPL: **the South Sea Islands** le isole dei Mari del Sud

South Seas NPL: **the South Seas** i Mari del Sud

South Vietnam N Vietnam *m* del Sud

south·ward [ˈsaʊθwəd], **south·wards** [ˈsaʊθwədz] ADV verso sud ♦ ADJ a sud

south·west [ˌsaʊθˈwest] N sud-ovest *m* ♦ ADJ di sud-ovest ♦ ADV verso sud-ovest

south·west·ern [ˌsaʊθˈwestən] ADJ di sud-ovest

sou·venir [ˌsuːvəˈnɪə^r] N souvenir *m inv*, ricordo; **a souvenir shop** un negozio di souvenir

sov·er·eign [ˈsɒvrɪn] ADJ (*gen*) sovrano(-a); **with sovereign contempt** (*fig*) con sommo disprezzo; **a sovereign remedy** (*old*) un rimedio infallibile ♦ N (*monarch*) sovrano(-a); (*coin*) sovrana

sov·er·eign·ty [ˈsɒvrəntɪ] N sovranità

so·vi·et [ˈsəʊvɪət] N Soviet *m inv* ♦ ADJ sovietico(-a); **Soviet Russia** Russia Sovietica

Soviet Union N: **the Soviet Union** l'Unione *f* Sovietica

sow[1] [səʊ] (*pt* **sowed**, *pp* **sown**) VT seminare; **to sow (the seeds of) doubt in sb's mind** far sorgere dei dubbi a qn; **to sow (the seeds of) discord** seminare zizzania

sow[2] [saʊ] N scrofa

soya [ˈsɔɪə], (*USA*) **soy** [sɔɪ] N soia

soz·zled [ˈsɒzld] ADJ (*Brit fam*) sbronzo(-a); **to get sozzled** sbronzarsi

spa [spɑː] N (*resort*) stazione *f* termale, terme *fpl*; (*USA: also:* **health spa**) centro di cure estetiche

space [speɪs] N (*all senses*) spazio; **to stare into space** guardare nel vuoto; **to clear a space for sth** fare posto per qc; **to take up a lot of space** occupare molto spazio, ingombrare; **to buy space in a newspaper** comprare spazio pubblicitario su un giornale; **blank space** spazio in bianco; **answer in the space provided** scrivere le risposte negli appositi spazi; **in a confined space** in un luogo chiuso; **there isn't enough space** non c'è abbastanza spazio; **I couldn't find a space for my car** non sono riuscito a trovare un posto per la macchina; **in a short space of time** in un breve lasso di tempo; **(with)in the space of an hour/three generations** nell'arco di un'ora/di tre generazioni; **for the space of a fortnight** per un periodo di due settimane; **after a space of two hours** dopo un intervallo di due ore ♦ VT (*also:* **space out**) (*gen*) distanziare; (*payments*) scaglionare, dilazionare; (*type*) spaziare ♦ ADJ (*research, capsule, probe etc*) spaziale

space-bar [ˈspeɪsˌbɑː^r] N (*on typewriter, computer*) barra spaziatrice

space·craft [ˈspeɪsˌkrɑːft] N *pl inv* veicolo spaziale

space·man [ˈspeɪsmən] N (*pl* **-men**) astronauta *m*, cosmonauta *m*

space·ship [ˈspeɪsˌʃɪp] N astronave *f*, navicella spaziale

space shuttle N shuttle *m inv*

space·suit [ˈspeɪsˌsuːt] N tuta spaziale

space·woman [ˈspeɪsˌwʊmən] N (*pl* **-women**) astronauta *f*, cosmonauta *f*

spac·ing [ˈspeɪsɪŋ] N (*Typing, etc*) spaziatura; **single/double spacing** spaziatura uno/due, spaziatura singola/doppia

spa·cious [ˈspeɪʃəs] ADJ spazioso(-a)

spade [speɪd] N **1** (*tool*) vanga; (*child's*) paletta; **to call a spade a spade** (*fig*) dire pane al pane (e vino al vino) **2** (*Cards*); **spades** NPL picche *fpl*; **the three of spades** il tre di picche; **the ace of spades** l'asso di picche; **to play spades** giocare picche; **to play a spade** giocare una carta di picche

spade·work [ˈspeɪdˌwɜːk] N (*fig*) il grosso dei preparativi

spa·ghet·ti [spəˈgetɪ] N spaghetti *mpl*

Spain [speɪn] N la Spagna

spam [spæm] N (*Comput*) N spamming *m* ♦ VT: **to spam sb** inviare a qn messaggi pubblicitari non richiesti via e-mail

span[1] [spæn] N (*of hand*) spanna; (*of bridge, arch, roof*) luce *f*, campata; (*of time*) periodo; **attention span** capacità di concentrazione; **a short attention span** una limitata capacità di concentrazione; **life span** durata; **the batteries have a life span of six hours** le batterie hanno una durata di sei ore; **time span** intervallo di tempo; **a span of ten years** un periodo di dieci anni ♦ VT (*subj: bridge etc*) attraversare; **to span 3 decades** abbracciare un periodo di 30 anni; **his career spanned sixteen years** la sua carriera abbracciava un periodo di sedici anni; **her interests spanned every aspect of nature** i suoi interessi abbracciavano in ogni aspetto della natura; **the bridge spanning the Avon** il ponte che attraversa il fiume Avon; **his memory spanned 50 years** i suoi ricordi risalivano a 50 anni fa

span² [spæn] PT *of* **spin**

Span·iard [ˈspænjəd] N spagnolo(-a)

span·iel [ˈspænjəl] N spaniel *m inv*

Span·ish [ˈspænɪʃ] ADJ (*gen*) spagnolo(-a); (*teacher, lesson, book*) di spagnolo; **Spanish America** America latina ♦ N 1 (*language*) spagnolo 2 **the Spanish** NPL (*people*) gli Spagnoli

spank [spæŋk] VT sculacciare

spanner [ˈspænə^r] N (*Brit*) chiave *f* inglese; **adjustable spanner** chiave *f* a rullino; **to throw a spanner in the works** (*fig*) mettere il bastone tra le ruote

spar¹ [spɑː^r] N (*Naut*) asta, palo

spar² [spɑː^r] VI: **to spar with sb** (*Boxing*) allenarsi (con qn); (*argue*) discutere (con qn)

spare [spɛə^r] ADJ 1 (*surplus*) in più, d'avanzo; (*reserve*) di riserva, di scorta; **spare batteries** pile di scorta; **the spare wheel** la ruota di scorta; **I've lost my key — have you got a spare?** ho perso la chiave — ne hai un'altra?; **I haven't enough spare cash to go on holiday** non mi avanzano soldi per andare in vacanza; **any spare change, please?** ha qualche spicciolo, per favore?; **is there any spare string?** c'è rimasto un po' di spago?; **there are two going spare** (*Brit*) ce ne sono due in più; **to go spare** (*fam*) andare su tutte le furie 2 (*person: lean*) asciutto(-a) ♦ N (*part*) pezzo di ricambio ♦ VT 1 (*be grudging with*): **she spared no effort or pains in helping me** ha fatto tutto il possibile per aiutarmi; **to spare no expense** non badare a spese 2 (*do without*) fare a meno di; **can you spare this for a moment?** puoi prestarmelo per un attimo?; **if you can spare it** se puoi farne a meno; **can you spare the time?** hai tempo?; **I can't spare the time** non ho tempo da perdere?; **there is none to spare** ce n'è appena a sufficienza; **I've a few minutes to spare** ho un attimino di tempo; **I got to the station with 3 minutes to spare** sono arrivato alla stazione con 3 minuti di anticipo; **I had £1 to spare** mi avanzava 1 sterlina; **they've got no money to spare** non hanno poi tanti soldi; **there is no time to spare** non c'è tempo da perdere 3 (*refrain from hurting, using*) risparmiare; **to spare sb's feelings** avere riguardo per i sentimenti di qn; **she doesn't spare herself** non si risparmia 4 (*save from need or trouble*): **to spare sb the trouble of doing sth** risparmiare a qn la fatica di fare qc; **spare me the details** risparmiami i particolari

spare part N pezzo di ricambio

spare room N stanza degli ospiti

spare time N tempo libero

spare tyre, (*USA*) **spare tire** N (*Aut*) gomma di scorta; (*fig*) maniglie *fpl* dell'amore

spare wheel N (*Aut*) ruota di scorta

spar·ing [ˈspɛərɪŋ] ADJ (*amount, use*) moderato(-a); **to be sparing of praise** essere avaro(-a) di lodi; **to be sparing with** essere parsimonioso(-a) con

spar·ing·ly [ˈspɛərɪŋlɪ] ADV (*eat, live*) frugalmente; (*use, drink*) con moderazione, moderatamente

spark [spɑːk] N (*from fire*) scintilla; (*fig*): **there wasn't a spark of life in the battery** la batteria non dava segni di vita; **he didn't show a spark of interest** non ha mostrato il benché minimo interesse; **bright spark** (*iro*) genio ♦ VT (*also*: **spark off**) (*debate, quarrel, revolt*) provocare; (*interest*) suscitare

spar·kle [ˈspɑːkl] N (*gen*) scintillio, sfavillio; (*fig: of person, conversation*) brio ♦ VI (*flash, shine*) scintillare, sfavillare, luccicare; (*eyes*) brillare, luccicare; (*person, conversation*) brillare; (*wine*) frizzare, spumeggiare

spar·kler [ˈspɑːklə^r] N 1 bengala *m inv*, fuoco d'artificio 2 (*fam: diamond*) brillante *m*

spar·kling [ˈspɑːklɪŋ] ADJ (*gen*) scintillante, sfavillante; (*person, conversation*) brillante; (*wine*) frizzante

spark plug, sparking plug [ˈspɑːkɪŋˌplʌɡ] N (*Aut*) candela

spar·ring part·ner [ˈspɑːrɪŋˈpɑːtnə^r] N sparring partner *m inv*; (*fig*) interlocutore abituale in discussioni, dibattiti, tavole rotonde ecc

spar·row [ˈspærəʊ] N passero

sparse [spɑːs] ADJ (*comp* **-r**, *superl* **-st**) (*vegetation, hair*) rado(-a); (*population*) scarso(-a)

Spar·tan, spar·tan [ˈspɑːtən] ADJ (*also fig*) spartano(-a)

---

spasm [ˈspæzəm] N (*Med*) spasmo; (*of coughing*) attacco, accesso; (*fig*) accesso; **a spasm of pain** uno spasmo di dolore

spas·mod·ic [spæzˈmɒdɪk] ADJ (*Med*) spasmodico(-a); (*fig: growth*) irregolare

spas·tic [ˈspæstɪk] ADJ, N (*offensive*) spastico(-a)

spat¹ [spæt] PT, PP *of* **spit²**

spat² [spæt] N (*USA*) battibecco

spate [speɪt] N (*of letters, orders*) valanga; (*of words, abuse*) torrente *m*; (*of accidents*) gran numero; **to be in spate** (*river*) essere in piena; **a spate of attacks** una lunga serie di attacchi

spa·tial [ˈspeɪʃəl] ADJ spaziale

spat·ter [ˈspætə^r] VT: **to spatter (with)** schizzare (di); **spattered with mud** inzaccherato(-a)

spatu·la [ˈspætjʊlə] N spatola

spawn [spɔːn] N (*of fish, frogs*) uova *fpl* ♦ VI deporre le uova ♦ VT (*pej*) produrre

speak [spiːk] (*pt* **spoke**, *pp* **spoken**) VT (*words, lines*) dire; (*language*) parlare; **she speaks Italian** parla italiano; **do you speak English?** parli inglese?; **to speak the truth** dire la verità; **to speak one's mind** dire quello che si pensa ♦ VI 1 (*gen*) parlare; **to speak to sb** parlare a qn; (*converse with*) parlare con qn; **have you spoken to him?** gli hai parlato?; **I spoke to her yesterday** le ho parlato ieri; **I'll speak to him about it** (*problem, idea*) gliene parlerò; (*his lateness etc*) glielo farò presente; **to speak about** (*or* **on** *or* **of**) **sth** parlare di qc; **to speak in a whisper** bisbigliare; **they haven't spoken to each other since they quarrelled** da quando hanno litigato non si rivolgono la parola; **to speak at a conference/in a debate** intervenire *or* prendere la parola ad una conferenza/in un dibattito; **he's very well spoken of** tutti ne parlano bene; **I don't know him to speak to** lo conosco solo di vista; **so to speak** per così dire; **it's nothing to speak of** non è niente di speciale; **he has no money to speak of** non si può proprio dire che sia ricco; **speaking of holidays** a proposito di vacanze; **roughly speaking** grosso modo; **speaking for myself** per quel che mi riguarda; **speaking as a student myself, I ...** in qualità di studente, io...; **generally speaking** generalmente parlando 2 (*Telec*): **speaking!** sono io!; **this is Peter speaking** sono Peter; **could I speak to Alison? — speaking!** posso parlare con Alison? — sono io!; **who's speaking?** altoparlante?

▸ **speak for** VI + PREP: **to speak for sb** parlare a nome di qn; **speak for yourself!** (*fam*) parla per te!; **let her speak for herself** lascia che dica la sua opinione; **it speaks for itself** parla da sé; **that picture is already spoken for** (*in shop*) quel quadro è già stato venduto

▸ **speak up** VI + ADV 1 (*raise voice*) parlare a voce alta; **speak up!** parli più forte! 2 (*fig: also*: **speak out**) parlare apertamente; **he finally decided to speak out** alla fine si è deciso a parlare; **to speak out against sth** dichiararsi pubblicamente contrario(-a) a qc; **to speak up for sb** parlare a favore di qn

speak·er [ˈspiːkə^r] N 1 (*gen*) chi parla; (*in discussion*) interlocutore(-trice); (*in public*) oratore(-trice); **he's a good/poor speaker** è un buon/pessimo oratore 2 (*of language*): **are you a Welsh speaker?** parla gallese?; **they're both English native speakers** sono tutti e due madrelingua inglesi 3 (*also*: **loudspeaker**) altoparlante *m*

speak·ing [ˈspiːkɪŋ] ADJ parlante; **Italian-speaking people** persone che parlano italiano; **I am not on speaking terms with her** la conosco solo di vista; **they are not on speaking terms** (*after quarrel*) non si rivolgono la parola ♦ N (*skill*) arte *f* del parlare

spear [spɪə^r] N lancia

spear·head [ˈspɪəˌhɛd] N punta di lancia; (*Mil*) reparto d'assalto; (*fig*) avanguardie *mpl* ♦ VT (*attack etc*) condurre

spear·mint [ˈspɪəmɪnt] N (*Bot, etc*) menta verde

spec [spɛk] N (*Brit fam*): **to buy sth on spec** comprare qc sperando di fare un affare; **I went to the theatre on spec** sono andato al teatro nella speranza di trovare un biglietto

spe·cial [ˈspɛʃəl] ADJ 1 (*specific*) particolare, speciale; **have you any special date in mind?** hai in mente una data particolare?; **I've no-one special in mind** non penso a nessuno in particolare 2 (*exceptional: price, favour, legislation*) speciale; (: *powers*) straordinario(-a); (*particular: care, situation, attention*) particolare; **take special care!** siate particolarmente prudenti!; **to make a special effort** fare del proprio meglio; **this is a special day for me** è una giornata speciale per me; **you're extra special** (*fam*) sei veramente speciale; **to expect special treatment** aspettarsi un trattamento speciale; **nothing special** niente di speciale; **what's so special about her?** che cosa ha di tanto speciale? ♦ N (*train*) treno straordinario; (*newspaper*) edizione *f* straordinaria; **the chef's special** la specialità dello chef

special agent N agente *m* segreto

special correspondent N (*Press*) inviato speciale

special delivery N (*Post*): **by special delivery** per espresso

special effects NPL (*Cine*) effetti *mpl* speciali

spe·cial·ist [ˈspeʃəlɪst] N specialista *m/f*; **a heart specialist** (*Med*) un cardiologo ♦ ADJ (*teacher*) specializzato(-a); (*dictionary*) specialistico(-a); (*knowlege, work*) da specialista

spe·ci·al·ity [ˌspeʃɪˈælɪtɪ], (*USA*) **spe·cial·ty** [ˈspeʃəltɪ] N specialità *f inv*; **to make a speciality of sth** specializzarsi in qc

spe·cial·ize [ˈspeʃəˌlaɪz] VI: **to specialize (in)** specializzarsi (in)

spe·cial·ly [ˈspeʃəlɪ] ADV (*specifically*) specialmente; (*on purpose*) apposta; (*particularly*) particolarmente; **it can be very cold here, specially in January** qui può fare molto freddo, specialmente in gennaio; **not specially** non particolarmente; **do you like opera? — not specially** ti piace l'opera? — non particolarmente; **it's specially designed for teenagers** è concepito apposta per i giovani

special needs N: **with special needs** con difficoltà d'apprendimento; **special needs students** studenti con difficoltà d'apprendimento; **special needs education** insegnamento di sostegno; **to teach special needs** insegnare a ragazzi con difficoltà di apprendimento

special offer N (*Comm*) offerta speciale

spe·cial·ty [ˈspeʃəltɪ] N (*USA*) = speciality

spe·cies [ˈspiːʃiːz] N *pl inv* specie *f inv*

spe·cif·ic [spəˈsɪfɪk] ADJ 1 (*example, order etc*) preciso(-a); (*meaning*) specifico(-a); **certain specific issues** certi problemi specifici; **could you be more specific?** puoi essere più preciso?; **he was very specific about that** è stato molto chiaro in proposito; **to be specific to** avere un legame specifico con 2 (*Bio, Phys, Chem, Med*) specifico(-a)

spe·cifi·cal·ly [spəˈsɪfɪkəlɪ] ADV (*explicitly: state, warn*) chiaramente, esplicitamente; (*especially: design, intend*) appositamente; **it's specifically designed for teenagers** è appositamente concepito per i giovani; **in Britain, or more specifically in England ...** in Gran Bretagna, o più specificamente in Inghilterra...; **I specifically said that...** avevo chiaramente detto che...

speci·fi·ca·tion [ˌspesɪfɪˈkeɪən] N 1 (*gen*) specificazione *f* 2 **specifications** (*of car, machine*) dati *mpl* caratteristici; (*for building*) dettagli *mpl*; **the parts do not meet our specification** i pezzi non sono conformi alle nostre specifiche

speci·fy [ˈspesɪˌfaɪ] VT specificare, precisare; **unless otherwise specified** salvo indicazioni contrarie; **he hasn't specified what action he will take** non ha precisato quale iniziativa intende adottare

speci·men [ˈspesɪmən] N (*sample: gen*) campione *m*; (: *of rock, species*) esemplare *m*; **a rare specimen** un esemplare raro; **a specimen of urine** un campione di urina; **he's an odd specimen** (*fig*) è un tipo strano

specimen signature N firma depositata

speck [spek] N (*of dust, dirt*) granello; (*of ink, paint etc*) macchiolina, puntino; **it was just a speck on the horizon** era solo un puntino all'orizzonte

speck·led [ˈspekld] ADJ maculato(-a)

specs [speks] NPL (*fam*) occhiali *mpl*

spec·ta·cle [ˈspektəkl] N spettacolo; **to make a spectacle of o.s.** (*fig*) coprirsi di ridicolo; **a bizarre spectacle** uno spettacolo bizzarro; *see also* spectacles

spectacle case N (*Brit*) custodia degli occhiali

spec·ta·cles [ˈspektəklz] NPL (*Brit*) occhiali *mpl*

spec·tacu·lar [spekˈtækjʊləʳ] ADJ (*gen*) spettacolare; (*view*) favoloso(-a) ♦ N (*Cine, TV*) kolossal *m*, film *m inv* etc spettacolare

spec·ta·tor [spekˈteɪtəʳ] N spettatore(-trice)

spectator sport N sport *m inv* come spettacolo, *inv*; **football is Britain's most popular spectator sport** in Gran Bretagna il calcio è lo sport più seguito dal pubblico

spec·tra [ˈspektrə] NPL *of* spectrum

spec·tre, spec·ter (*USA*) [ˈspektəʳ] N spettro

spec·trum [ˈspektrəm] N (*pl* spectra) (*Phys*) spettro; (*fig*) gamma; **a wide spectrum of problems** un'ampia gamma di problemi; **the colours of the spectrum** i colori dell'arcobaleno

specu·late [ˈspekjʊˌleɪt] VI (*Fin*) speculare; (*wonder*): **to speculate on the stock exchange** speculare in borsa; **to speculate (about** or **on sth/whether)** chiedersi (qc/se); **I can only speculate** posso solo fare congetture ♦ VT: **to speculate that ...** ipotizzare che...; **they speculate that he had a heart attack** ipotizzano che abbia avuto un infarto

specu·la·tion [ˌspekjʊˈleɪʃən] N (*guessing*) congetture *fpl*; (*Fin*) speculazione *f*

specu·la·tive [ˈspekjʊlətɪv] ADJ (*Philosophy, Fin*) speculativo(-a); (*expression*) indagatore(-trice)

specu·la·tor [ˈspekjʊˌleɪtəʳ] N (*Fin*) speculatore(-trice)

sped [sped] PT, PP *of* speed

speech [spiːtʃ] N 1 (*faculty*) parola; (*manner of speaking*) parlata, modo di parlare; **to lose the power of speech** perdere l'uso della parola; **freedom of speech** libertà di parola; **the development of speech in children** lo sviluppo del linguaggio nei bambini 2 (*language*) linguaggio; **children's speech** il linguaggio dei bambini 3 (*formal talk*) discorso, intervento; **to make a speech** fare un discorso; **he made a speech at the conference** ha fatto un discorso alla conferenza 4 (*Brit: Gram*): **direct/indirect speech** discorso diretto/indiretto

speech impediment N difetto di pronuncia

speech·less [ˈspiːtʃlɪs] ADJ senza parole, ammutolito(-a); **to be speechless** rimanere senza parole

speech therapy N logoterapia

speed [spiːd] N 1 (*rate of movement*) velocità; (*rapidity, haste*) rapidità; (*promptness*) prontezza; **at speed** (*Brit*) velocemente; **at full speed, at top speed** a tutta velocità; **at a speed of 70 km/h** a una velocità di 70 km all'ora; **the speed of light/sound** la velocità della luce/del suono; **what speed were you doing?** (*Aut*) a che velocità andavi?; **to pick up** or **gather speed** (*car*) acquistare velocità; (*project, work*) procedere più speditamente; **the speed of his reactions** la sua prontezza di riflessi; **shorthand/typing speeds** numero di parole al minuto in stenografia/dattilografia 2 (*Aut, Tech: gear*) marcia; **a five-speed gearbox** un cambio a cinque marce; **a ten-speed bike** una bicicletta a dieci marce 3 (*Phot: of film*) sensibilità; (*: of shutter*) tempo di apertura ♦ VI 1 (*pt, pp sped*); **to speed along** (*car, work*) procedere velocemente; **to speed away** or **off** (*car, person*) sfrecciare via; **the years sped by** gli anni sono volati 2 (*pt, pp speeded*): (*Aut: exceed speed limit*) andare a velocità eccessiva

▸ **speed up** (*pt, pp speeded up*) VI + ADV (*gen*) andare più veloce; (*Aut*) accelerare; (*walker/worker/train etc*) camminare/lavorare/viaggiare più veloce; (*engine, machine*) girare più veloce; (*production*) accelerare ♦ VT + ADV accelerare

speed·boat [ˈspiːdˌbəʊt] N motoscafo

speed dating [-ˈdeɪtɪŋ] N *sistema di appuntamenti grazie al quale si possono incontrare in pochissimo tempo diverse persone e scegliere eventualmente chi frequentare*

speedi·ly [ˈspiːdɪlɪ] ADV (*see adj*) velocemente, rapidamente; prontamente

speed·ing [ˈspiːdɪŋ] N (*Aut*) eccesso di velocità; **he was fined for speeding** ha preso la multa per eccesso di velocità

speed limit N limite *m* di velocità; **to exceed the speed limit** superare il limite di velocità

speed·om·eter [sprˈdɒmɪtəʳ] N tachimetro

speed trap N (*Aut*) *tratto di strada sul quale la polizia controlla la velocità dei veicoli*

speed·way [ˈspiːdˌweɪ] N: **speedway racing** corsa motociclistica su pista

speedy [ˈspiːdɪ] ADJ (*comp* -ier, *superl* -iest) (*gen*) veloce, rapido(-a); (*reply*) pronto(-a)

spe·leolo·gist [ˌspiːlɪˈɒlədʒɪst] N speleologo(-a)

spell¹ [spel] (*pt, pp* spelled or spelt) VT: **how do you spell**

your name? come si scrive il tuo nome?; **can you spell it for me?** me lo puoi dettare lettera per lettera?; **c-a-t spells "cat"** c-a-t formano la parola "cat"; **I can't spell** faccio errori di ortografia; **it spells disaster for us** (*fig*) significa la nostra rovina
▸ **spell out** VT + ADV (*fig*): **to spell sth out for sb** spiegare qc a qn per filo e per segno

spell² [spɛl] N (*also:* **magic spell**) incantesimo; (*words*) formula magica; **an evil spell** una stregoneria; **to cast** *or* **put a spell on sb** fare un incantesimo a qn; (*fig*) stregare qn; **to be under sb's spell** essere stregato(-a) da qn; **to fall under sb's spell** (*fig*) subire il fascino di qn; **to break the spell** (*also fig*) rompere l'incantesimo

spell³ [spɛl] N (*period of time*) periodo; **cold spell** periodo di freddo; **a spell of dry weather** un periodo di tempo secco; **to do a spell of duty** fare un turno; **they're going through a bad spell** stanno attraversando un brutto periodo

spell·bound [ˈspɛlbaʊnd] ADJ incantato(-a), affascinato(-a); **to hold sb spellbound** affascinare qn

spell·check·er [ˈspɛlˌtʃɛkəʳ] N (*Comput*) correttore *m* ortografico

spell·ing [ˈspɛlɪŋ] N ortografia; **my spelling is terrible** faccio molti errori di ortografia

spelt [spɛlt] PT, PP *of* **spell¹**

spend [spɛnd] (*pt, pp* **spent**) VT 1 (*money*) spendere; **to spend money on sb/sth** spendere soldi per qn/qc; **they spend an enormous amount of money on advertising** spendono grosse cifre per la pubblicità; **without spending a penny** senza spendere una lira 2 (*pass*) passare, trascorrere; **he spent a month in France** ha trascorso un mese in Francia; **he spends his time sleeping** passa il tempo dormendo 3 (*devote*): **to spend time/money/effort on sth** dedicare tempo/soldi/energie a qc; **I spent 2 hours writing that letter** ho passato 2 ore a scrivere quella lettera; **he spends a lot of time on his hobbies** dedica un sacco di tempo ai suoi hobby

spend·ing [ˈspɛndɪŋ] N spesa; **government spending** spesa pubblica

spending money N denaro per le piccole spese

spending power N potere *m* d'acquisto

spend·thrift [ˈspɛndˌθrɪft] ADJ spendereccio(-a) ♦ N spendaccione(-a)

spent [spɛnt] PT, PP *of* **spend** ♦ ADJ (*cartridge, bullets, match*) usato(-a); (*supplies*) esaurito(-a); **he's a spent force** è un uomo finito

sperm [spɜːm] N (*Bio*) sperma *m*

sperm bank N banca dello sperma

sperm whale N capodoglio

spew [spjuː] VT (*also:* **spew out**: *smoke, pollution*) emettere, vomitare ♦ VI 1 (*subj: smoke, pollution*) fuoriuscire 2 (*also:* **to spew up**: *fam: vomit*) rigettare

sphere [sfɪəʳ] N (*gen*) sfera; **his sphere of interest** la sua sfera d'interessi; **his sphere of activity** il suo campo di attività; **within a limited sphere** in un ambito molto ristretto; **sphere of influence** sfera d'influenza; **that's outside my sphere** non rientra nelle mie competenze

spheri·cal [ˈsfɛrɪkəl] ADJ sferico(-a)

sphinx [sfɪŋks] N (*also fig*) sfinge *f*

spice [spaɪs] N (*Culin*) droga, spezia; (*fig*) sapore *m*; **mixed spice(s)** spezie miste; **variety is the spice of life** la varietà dà sapore alla vita ♦ VT (*Culin*) condire (con spezie), aromatizzare; **a highly spiced account** un racconto molto gustoso

spick-and-span [ˌspɪkənˈspæn] ADJ pulito(-a) come uno specchio

spicy [ˈspaɪsɪ] ADJ (*comp* **-ier**, *superl* **-iest**) (*Culin, also fig*) piccante

spi·der [ˈspaɪdəʳ] N ragno; (*tool*) chiave *f* a croce; **spider's web** ragnatela

spiel [ʃpiːl] N (*fam*) tiritera

spike [spaɪk] N 1 (*point*) punta; (*on shoe*) chiodo; **rocky spike** (*Mountaineering*) spuntone *m* 2 **spikes** NPL (*Sport*) scarpe *fpl* chiodate 3 (*Elec*) punta (di corrente) 4 (*in price, volume etc*) aumento improvviso ♦ VT (*story, interview*) rifiutare di pubblicare; (*fig*): **to spike sb's guns** rompere le uova nel paniere a qn; **a spiked drink** (*fam*) una bevanda corretta ♦ VI (*price, volume etc*) aumentare improvvisamente

spike heel N (*USA*) tacco a spillo

spiky [ˈspaɪkɪ] ADJ (*comp* **-ier**, *superl* **-iest**) (*bush, branch*) spinoso(-a); (*animal*) ricoperto(-a) di aculei; (*fig: person*) spigoloso(-a)

spill [spɪl] (*pt, pp* **spilled** *or* **spilt** [spɪlt]) VT (*gen*) rovesciare, versare; (*blood*) spargere; **he spilled coffee on his pants** s'è rovesciato il caffè sui pantaloni; **to spill the beans** (*fam*) spiattellare tutto, vuotare il sacco ♦ VI rovesciarsi, versarsi
▸ **spill out** VI + ADV uscire fuori; (*fall out*) cadere fuori; **the audience spilt out of the cinema** gli spettatori si riversarono fuori dal cinema ♦ VT + ADV (*contents etc*) rovesciare; (*fig: story*) rivelare
▸ **spill over** VI + ADV: **to spill over (into)** (*liquid*) versarsi (in); (*crowd*) riversarsi (in)

spill·age [ˈspɪlɪdʒ] N (*event*) fuoriuscita; (*substance*) sostanza fuoriuscita

spin [spɪn] (*pt* **spun** *or* **span** *pp* **spun**) N 1 (*revolution*) giro; **to give a wheel a spin** far girare una ruota; **to give a long/short spin** (*in washing machine*) fare una centrifuga completa/ridotta; **to be in a flat spin** (*fam*) essere in preda al panico; **to go into a flat spin** lasciarsi prendere dal panico 2 (*on ball*) effetto; **to put a spin on a ball** imprimere l'effetto a una palla 3 (*Aer*): **to go into a spin** discendere in avvitamento; (*Aut*) fare un giretto 4 (*ride*): **to go for a spin** fare un giretto 5 (*Pol*) reinterpretazione *f*; **to put a new/different spin on sth** presentare qc da un'angolatura nuova/diversa ♦ VT 1 (*turn: wheel*) far girare; (*ball*) mettere nella centrifuga; (*ball*) imprimere l'effetto a; **to spin a coin** (*Brit*) lanciare in aria una moneta; **he spun the wheel sharply** ha girato il volante bruscamente 2 (*cotton, wool*) filare; (*subj: spider*) tessere; **to spin a yarn** (*fig*) imbastire una storia; **she spins the wool from her own sheep** fila la lana delle sue pecore ♦ VI 1 filare 2 (*revolve: person*) girarsi; (: *ball*) ruotare; (: *wheel*) girare; **to spin round and round** girare su se stesso(-a); **the car spun out of control** la macchina ha sbandato e ha girato su se stessa; **to send sb spinning** mandare qn a gambe all'aria; **it makes my head spin** mi fa girare la testa
▸ **spin out** VT + ADV (*fam: visit, holiday*) prolungare; (: *speech, food*) far durare

spi·na bi·fi·da [ˌspaɪnəˈbɪfɪdə] N spina bifida

spin·ach [ˈspɪnɪdʒ] N spinaci *mpl*; **the spinach is delicious** gli spinaci sono ottimi

spi·nal [ˈspaɪnl] ADJ spinale; **spinal injury** lesione *f* alla spina dorsale

spinal column N colonna vertebrale, spina dorsale

spinal cord N midollo spinale

spin·dly [ˈspɪndlɪ] ADJ (*comp* **-ier**, *superl* **-iest**) (*legs, arms, plant*) stecchito(-a)

spin doctor N (*Pol*) pierre addetto alla difesa di provvedimenti impopolari con interviste, interventi in TV ecc

spin-dry [ˌspɪnˈdraɪ] VT strizzare con la centrifuga

spin-dryer [ˌspɪnˈdraɪəʳ] N (*Brit*) centrifuga

spine [spaɪn] N (*Anat*) spina dorsale; (*Zool*) aculeo; (*Bot*) spina; (*of book*) dorso; (*of mountain range*) cresta

spine-chilling [ˈspaɪntʃɪlɪŋ] ADJ agghiacciante

spine·less [ˈspaɪnlɪs] ADJ (*fig*) smidollato(-a); (*animal*) invertebrato(-a)

spin·ner [ˈspɪnəʳ] N (*of thread, yarn*) tessitore(-trice); (*Fishing*) cucchiaino; (*fam: spin-dryer*) centrifuga

spin·ning [ˈspɪnɪŋ] N filatura; **spinning and weaving** la filatura e la tessitura

spinning top N trottola

spinning wheel N filatoio

spin-off [ˈspɪnˌɒf] N (*Tech, Industry*) applicazione *f* secondaria; (*product*) prodotto secondario; **this TV series is a spin-off from the famous film** questa serie televisiva è ispirata al famoso film

spin·ster [ˈspɪnstəʳ] N (*old*) zitella

spi·ral [ˈspaɪərəl] ADJ a spirale ♦ N spirale *f*; **the inflationary spiral** la spirale dell'inflazione ♦ VI (*prices*) salire vertiginosamente; **to spiral up/down** (*also Aer*) salire/scendere a spirale

spiral staircase N scala a chiocciola

spire [ˈspaɪəʳ] N guglia

spir·it [ˈspɪrɪt] N 1 (*soul*) spirito; **the human spirit** lo spirito umano; **I'll be with you in spirit** ti sarò vicino col pensiero; **one of the greatest spirits of the age** uno dei più grandi personaggi dell'epoca; **one of the leading spirits in the party** uno dei principali animatori del partito 2 (*ghost, supernatural being*) spirito; **Holy Spirit** Spirito Santo 3 (*courage*) coraggio; (*energy*) energia; (*vitality*) brio, vitalità; **everyone who knew her admired her spirit** tutti quelli che la conoscevano ammiravano il suo coraggio 4 (*attitude etc*) spirito; **community spirit, public spirit** senso civico; **in a spirit of optimism** con un atteggiamento ottimista; **to enter into the spirit of sth** entrare nello spirito di qc; **that's the spirit!** (*fam*) bravo!, così va bene!; **the spirit of the law** lo spirito della legge; **to take sth in the right/wrong spirit** prendere qc bene/male 5 (*state of mind*) NPL (*state of mind*): **high spirits** buon umore *m*; **to be in low spirits** essere giù di morale; **we kept our spirits up by singing** ci siamo tenuti su di morale cantando; **my spirits rose somewhat** mi sono tirato un po' su 6 **spirits** NPL (*alcohol*) liquori *mpl*; **raw spirits** alcol *m* puro 7 (*Chem*) spirito, alcol *m inv*

▸ **spirit away, spirit off** VT + ADV far sparire misteriosamente

spir·it·ed [ˈspɪrɪtɪd] ADJ (*horse*) focoso(-a); (*conversation*) animato(-a); (*person, attack etc*) energico(-a); (*description*) vivace, vigoroso(-a); **he gave a spirited performance** (*Mus, Theatre*) ha dato una brillante interpretazione

❑ **spirited** is not translated by the Italian word *spiritato*

spirit level N livella a bolla d'aria

spir·itu·al [ˈspɪrɪtjʊəl] ADJ spirituale ♦ N (*Mus*) spiritual *m inv*

spir·itu·al·ism [ˈspɪrɪtjʊə‚lɪzəm] N (*occult*) spiritismo

spit¹ [spɪt] N (*Culin: for roasting*) spiedo; (*of land*) lingua di terra; **on the spit** allo spiedo

spit² [spɪt] N (*pt, pp* **spat**) N (*spittle*) sputo; (*saliva*) saliva; **a bit of spit and polish** (*fam*) una bella lucidata ♦ VT sputare ♦ VI: **to spit (at)** sputare (addosso a); (*cat*) soffiare (contro); **they spat at me** mi hanno sputato addosso; **to spit on the ground** sputare per terra; **it is spitting with rain** sta piovigginando

▸ **spit out** VT + ADV (*sparks*) sprigionare; (*fat*) schizzare; **spit it out!** (*fam: say it*) sputa il rospo!; **it tasted horrible and I spat it out** aveva un saporaccio e l'ho sputato

spite [spaɪt] N 1 (*ill will*) dispetto; **out of spite** per dispetto; **to do sth out of (or from) spite** fare qc per dispetto 2 **in spite of** (*despite*) nonostante, malgrado; **in spite of the fact that** malgrado *or* nonostante (il fatto che) + *sub*; **she laughed in spite of herself** ha riso suo malgrado ♦ VT far dispetto a; **he just did it to spite me** l'ha fatto solo per farmi dispetto

spite·ful [ˈspaɪtfʊl] ADJ (*person, behaviour*) dispettoso(-a); (*tongue, remark*) maligno(-a), velenoso(-a)

spit-roast [ˈspɪtˌrəʊst] VT cuocere allo spiedo

spit·ting [ˈspɪtɪŋ] N: **"spitting prohibited"** "vietato sputare" ♦ ADJ: **to be the spitting image of sb** essere il ritratto sputato di qn

spit·tle [ˈspɪtl] N (*ejected*) sputo; (*dribbled*) saliva; (*of animal*) bava

spiv [spɪv] N (*Brit fam*) imbroglione *m*

splash [splæʃ] N (*sound*) tonfo; (*series of splashes*) sciabordio; (*mark*) spruzzo, macchia; (*fig: of colour, light*) chiazza; **I heard a splash** ho sentito un tonfo; **a splash of colour** un tocco di colore; **to make a splash** (*fig*) far furore ♦ VT schizzare; **to splash up with water** schizzare qn d'acqua; **to splash sth over sb** schizzare qc addosso a qn; **to splash one's face with water** spruzzarsi acqua sul viso; **he splashed water on his face** si spruzzò acqua sul viso; **to splash paint on the floor** schizzare il pavimento di vernice; **the story was splashed across the front page** (*fam*) la notizia è stata sbattuta in prima pagina; **don't splash me!** non schizzarmi! ♦ VI (*liquid, mud etc*) schizzare; (*person, animal in water: also:* **splash about**) sguazzare; **to splash across a stream** guadare un ruscello; **to splash into the water** (*stone*) cadere nell'acqua con un tonfo

▸ **splash down** VI + ADV ammarare

▸ **splash out** VI + ADV (*fam*) fare spese folli

▸ **splash up** VI + ADV schizzare; **the waves splashed up against the rocks** le onde s'infrangevano sugli scogli

splash-down [ˈsplæʃˌdaʊn] N ammaraggio

splay [spleɪ] VI: **splayed fingers** dita allargate

spleen [spliːn] N (*Anat*) milza; **to vent one's spleen** (*fig*) sfogarsi

splen·did [ˈsplendɪd] ADJ (*ceremony, clothes*) splendido(-a), magnifico(-a); (*idea, example*) eccellente, ottimo(-a); **that's splendid!** magnifico!, fantastico!

splen·dour, splen·dor (*USA*) [ˈsplendər] N splendore *m*, magnificenza

splice [splaɪs] VT (*rope, film*) giuntare; (*wood*) calettare

splint [splɪnt] N (*Med*) stecca; **to put sb's arm in splints** steccare il braccio di qn

splin·ter [ˈsplɪntər] N scheggia ♦ VI (*wood, glass*) scheggiarsi; (*fig: party*) staccarsi, scindersi ♦ VT (*wood, glass*) scheggiare; (*fig: party*) scindere

splinter group N gruppo scissionista

split [splɪt] (*pt, pp* **split**) N 1 (*in ground, wall, rock*) fessura, crepa; (*in wood*) spacco; (*in garment, fabric*) strappo 2 (*fig: division, quarrel*) scissione *f*, spaccatura; **there are fears of a split in the party** si teme una scissione nel partito 3 **to do the splits** fare la spaccata 4 (*cake etc*): **jam split** tortina farcita di marmellata; **banana split** banana-split *f inv* ♦ VT 1 (*cleave*) spaccare; (*tear*) strappare; **he split the wood with an axe** spaccava la legna con l'ascia; **to split the atom** scindere l'atomo; **to split sth open** aprire qc spaccandolo(-a); **he split his head open** si è spaccato la testa; **to split sth down the middle** (*also fig*) spaccare qc a metà; **to split hairs** (*fig*) spaccare il capello in quattro; **to split one's sides laughing** (*fig*) ridere a crepapelle 2 (*divide, also fig*) dividere, spartire; **to split sth into three parts** dividere qc in tre; **to split the profit five ways** dividere il guadagno in cinque parti; **they decided to split the profits** hanno deciso di dividere i guadagni; **to split the difference** (*agree price*) incontrarsi a metà strada; (*fig*) accettare una soluzione di compromesso ♦ VI 1 (*wood, stone*) spaccarsi; (*cloth*) strapparsi; (*fig: party, church*) spaccarsi, dividersi; **to split open** spaccarsi; **my head is splitting** mi scoppia la testa; **the ship hit a rock and split in two** la nave ha urtato contro una roccia e s'è spaccata in due 2 (*fam: tell tales*): **don't you split on me to the police!** non provarti a denunciarmi alla polizia!

▸ **split off** VI + ADV (*also fig*) staccarsi, separarsi ♦ VT + ADV (*also fig*) staccare, separare

▸ **split up** VI + ADV (*stone etc*) spaccarsi; (*ship on rocks*) schiantarsi; (*crowd*) disperdersi; (*into groups*) dividersi; (*meeting*) sciogliersi; (*partners*) separarsi; (*couple*) separarsi, rompere; (*friends*) rompere ♦ VT + ADV (*stone etc*) spaccare; (*movement, money, work*) dividere; (*crowd*) disperdere; (*partners*) separare

split-level [ˈsplɪtˌlevl] ADJ (*house*) a piani sfalsati

split peas NPL piselli *mpl* secchi spaccati

split personality N sdoppiamento della personalità

split second N frazione *f* di secondo

split·ting [ˈsplɪtɪŋ] ADJ: **a splitting headache** un terribile mal di testa

splut·ter [ˈsplʌtər] VI (*person: spit*) sputacchiare; (: *stutter*) farfugliare; (*fire*) crepitare; (*fat*) schizzare; (*engine*) scoppiettare

spoil [spɔɪl] (*pt, pp* **spoiled** *or* **spoilt**) VT 1 (*ruin, detract from*) rovinare, sciupare; (*ballot paper*) annullare, invalidare; **don't spoil our fun** non fare il guastafeste; **to spoil one's appetite** guastarsi l'appetito; **don't let it spoil your vacation!** non lasciare che ti rovini la vacanza! 2 (*child*) viziare; **grandparents like to spoil their grandchildren** ai nonni piace viziare i nipotini ♦ VI 1 (*food*) rovinarsi, andare a male; (*while cooking*) rovinarsi 2 **to be spoiling for a fight** morire dalla voglia di litigare

spoils [spɔɪlz] NPL: **the spoils** il bottino *msg*

spoil-sport [ˈspɔɪlˌspɔːt] N (*fam*) guastafeste *m/f inv*

spoilt [spɔɪlt] PT, PP *of* **spoil** ♦ ADJ (*child*) viziato(-a); (*meal*) rovinato(-a); (*ballot paper*) nullo(-a)

spoke¹ [spəʊk] N raggio; **to put a spoke in sb's wheel** mettere i bastoni fra le ruote a qn

spoke² [spəʊk] PT *of* **speak**

spo·ken [ˈspəʊkən] PP *of* **speak**

spokes·man [ˈspəʊksmən] N (pl -men) portavoce m inv
spokes·person [ˈspəʊksˌpɜːsən] N portavoce m/f inv
spokes·woman [ˈspəʊksˌwʊmən] N (pl -women) portavoce f inv
sponge [spʌndʒ] N spugna; (Culin: also: sponge cake) pan m di Spagna; to throw in the sponge (fig) gettare la spugna; a wet sponge una spugna bagnata ♦ VT (wash) lavare con una spugna; to sponge a stain off pulire una macchia con una spugna ♦ VI (fam: scrounge) scroccare; to sponge off or on sb vivere alle spalle di qn
  ► **sponge down** VT + ADV lavare con una spugna
sponge bag N (Brit) nécessaire m inv
sponge cake N (Culin) = sponge N
spong·er [ˈspʌndʒəʳ] N (fam) scroccone(-a); (pej) parassita m inv
spon·gy [ˈspʌndʒɪ] ADJ (comp -ier, superl -iest) spugnoso(-a)
spon·sor [ˈspɒnsəʳ] N (of enterprise, bill, for fund raising) promotore(-trice); (for loan) garante m/f; (of member) socio(-a) garante; (Radio, TV, Sport, etc) sponsor m inv; (godparent) padrino (madrina) ♦ VT (enterprise etc) promuovere, patrocinare; (borrower, member of club) garantire; (Pol: Parliamentary bill) presentare; (Radio, TV, Sport, etc) sponsorizzare; (as godparents) tenere a battesimo; the tournament was sponsored by local firms il torneo è stato sponsorizzato da imprese locali; I sponsored him at 50p a mile (in fund-raising race) mi sono impegnato a donare 50 penny per ogni miglio
spon·sor·ship [ˈspɒnsəˌʃɪp] N (financial backing) promozione f; (of arts, events) sponsorizzazione f; (of candidate) sostegno
spon·ta·neity [ˌspɒntəˈneɪɪti] N spontaneità
spon·ta·neous [spɒnˈteɪnɪəs] ADJ spontaneo(-a)
spoof [spuːf] N (fam) parodia
spooky [ˈspuːkɪ] ADJ (comp -ier, superl -iest) (fam) sinistro(-a); the house has a spooky atmosphere la casa ha un'atmosfera sinistra
spool [spuːl] N (Phot: on sewing machine, on fishing line) bobina; (spool of thread) rocchetto di filo
spoon [spuːn] N cucchiaio; to be born with a silver spoon in one's mouth essere nato(-a) con la camicia ♦ VT: to spoon out (sauce, cream) servire con il cucchiaio; to spoon sth into a plate versare qc in un piatto con il cucchiaio
spoon-feed [ˈspuːnˌfiːd] (pt, pp spoon-fed [ˈspuːnˌfɛd]) VT imboccare; (fig) scodellare la pappa a
spoon·ful [ˈspuːnfʊl] N cucchiaiata
spo·rad·ic [spəˈrædɪk] ADJ (attempts, gunfire) sporadico(-a); (work) discontinuo(-a)
sport [spɔːt] N 1 sport m inv; indoor/outdoor sports sport al chiuso/all'aria aperta; to be good at sport riuscire bene nello sport; I'm not interested in sport lo sport non mi interessa; sports NPL (meeting) gare fpl 2 (amusement) divertimento 3 (fam: person) persona di spirito; be a sport! sii buono! ♦ VT sfoggiare
sport·ing [ˈspɔːtɪŋ] ADJ (event, behaviour, attitude) sportivo(-a); there's a sporting chance that c'è una buona probabilità che + sub; to give sb a sporting chance dare a qn una possibilità (di vincere)
sports car N automobile f sportiva
sports drink N sport drink m inv
sports ground N campo sportivo
sports jacket, (USA) **sport jacket** N giacca sportiva
sports·man [ˈspɔːtsmən] N (pl -men) sportivo
sports·man·ship [ˈspɔːtsmənˌʃɪp] N spirito sportivo
sports page N pagina sportiva
sports utility vehicle, **sport utility vehicle** N (esp USA) fuoristrada m inv
sports·wear [ˈspɔːtsˌwɛəʳ] N abbigliamento sportivo
sports·woman [ˈspɔːtsˌwʊmən] N (pl -women) sportiva
sporty [ˈspɔːti] ADJ (comp -ier, superl -iest) (fam) sportivo(-a)
spot [spɒt] N 1 (dot) puntino; (on dress) pois m inv, pallino; (stain, also fig) macchia; a material with blue spots una stoffa a pallini o pois blu; there's a spot on your shirt hai una macchia sulla camicia; to knock spots off sb (fig: fam) dare dei punti a qn; to have spots before one's eyes vedere dei puntini 2 (pimple) foruncolo; to break or come out in spots coprirsi di foruncoli; he's covered in spots è pieno di

brufoli 3 (place) posto; a pleasant spot un bel posto; it's a lovely spot for a picnic è un posto ideale per un picnic; to have a tender spot on the arm avere un punto dolorante nel braccio; the reporter was on the spot il reporter era sul posto; the firemen were on the spot in 3 minutes i pompieri sono arrivati sul posto in 3 minuti; an on-the-spot broadcast una trasmissione in diretta; to do sth on the spot fare qc immediatamente or lì per lì; to be in a (tight) spot (fig) essere nei guai or nei pasticci; to put sb in a spot or on the spot (fig) mettere in difficoltà qn; that's my weak spot (fig) è il mio punto debole 4 (Brit fam: small amount): a spot of un po'di (of milk, wine etc) un goccio di; just a spot, thanks solo un goccio, grazie; we had a spot of rain yesterday c'è stata qualche goccia di pioggia ieri; would you like a spot of lunch? vuoi mangiare un boccone?; to have a spot of bother avere noie 5 (Radio, Theatre, TV: in show) numero; (Radio, TV: advertisement) spot m inv (pubblicitario) 6 (fam: also: spotlight) faretto ♦ VT 1 (speckle) macchiare (di) 2 (notice, see: mistake, person in a crowd) notare; (: car, person in the distance) scorgere; (recognize: winner) indovinare; (: talent, sb's ability) scoprire; (bargain) riconoscere; I spotted a mistake ho notato un errore
spot check N controllo casuale
spot·less [ˈspɒtlɪs] ADJ pulitissimo(-a), immacolato(-a); (fig: reputation) senza macchia; (: character) retto(-a)
spot·light [ˈspɒtˌlaɪt] N (lamp) spot m inv, faro; (beam) fascio luminoso; (Aut) faro, riflettore m; in the spotlight sotto la luce dei riflettori; (fig) al centro dell'attenzione; to turn the spotlight on sb/sth (fig) mettere in risalto qn/qc, richiamare l'attenzione su qn/qc
spot-on [ˈspɒtˈɒn] ADJ (Brit) esatto(-a)
spot price N (Comm) prezzo per contanti
spot·ted [ˈspɒtɪd] ADJ (material) a pois, a pallini; (animal) maculato(-a); spotted with punteggiato(-a) di; a spotted tie una cravatta a pallini
spot·ty [ˈspɒtɪ] ADJ (comp -ier, superl -iest) (fam) foruncoloso(-a)
spouse [spaʊs] N (frm) sposo(-a)
spout [spaʊt] N (of teapot) becco, beccuccio; (of guttering) scarico; (for tap) cannella; (column of water) getto, zampillo ♦ VT (water) gettare; (lava) eruttare; (smoke) emettere; (fam, pej: poetry) declamare ♦ VI (liquid) zampillare
sprain [spreɪn] N slogatura, storta, distorsione f; (of muscle) strappo muscolare ♦ VT (muscle) stirarsi; to sprain one's wrist/ankle slogarsi un polso o una caviglia; she's sprained her ankle s'è slogata una caviglia
sprang [spræŋ] PT of spring
sprawl [sprɔːl] VI (person: sit, lie) stravaccarsi; (: fall) cadere scompostamente; (town) estendersi in modo incontrollato; (plant) crescere disordinatamente; her handwriting sprawled all over the page la sua scrittura copriva tutta la pagina; he sprawled on the sofa, smoking si stravaccò sul divano fumando; to send sb sprawling mandare qn a gambe all'aria ♦ N: urban sprawl sviluppo urbanistico incontrollato, espansione urbana tentacolare; a sprawl of buildings lay below them un gruppo di edifici si estendeva disordinatamente dinanzi ai loro occhi
spray [spreɪ] N 1 (from hosepipe) getto; (from wet road) schizzi mpl; (of sea, fountain) spruzzi mpl; (from atomizer, aerosol) spruzzo 2 (aerosol, atomizer) spray m inv, bomboletta; (of perfume) vaporizzatore m; (for paint, garden) spruzzatore m, nebulizzatore m; (Med) spray ♦ VT (gen) spruzzare; (crops) irrorare; to spray sth/sb with water spruzzare qc/qn d'acqua; to spray sth/sb with bullets sparare una scarica di proiettili contro qc/qn; she sprayed perfume on my hand mi ha spruzzato del profumo sulla mano ♦ ADJ (deodorant) spray inv; (gun, paint) a spruzzo
spray² [spreɪ] N (of greenery) ramoscello; (of flowers) mazzolino; (brooch) spilla a forma di ramoscello
spread [spred] (pt, pp spread) N 1 (of fire, infection) propagazione f; (of idea, knowledge) diffusione f; (of crime) il dilagare; the spread of nuclear weapons la proliferazione delle armi nucleari; the spread of modern technology la diffusione della tecnologia moderna 2 (extent: of bridge) ampiezza; (: of wings, arch) apertura 3 (range: of prices, figures, marks) gamma; (: on graph, scale) distribuzione f; middle-age spread

pancetta **4** (*fam: feast*) banchetto **5** (*also:* **bedspread**) copriletto **6** (*for bread*)**: anchovy spread** ≈ pasta d'acciughe; **cheese spread** formaggio da spalmare; **chocolate spread** cioccolata da spalmare **7** (*Press, Typ: two pages*) doppia pagina; (: *across columns*) articolo a più colonne ♦ VT **1** (*open or lay out: also:* **spread out**) (*wings, sails etc*) spiegare; (*cloth*) stendere; (*fingers*) distendere; (*arms*) allargare, spalancare; **to spread a map out on the table** spiegare una cartina sul tavolo; **he spread the map out on the table** ha spiegato la cartina sul tavolo; **to spread one's wings** (*fig*) spiccare il volo; **she spread the towel on the sand** ha steso l'asciugamano sulla sabbia **2** (*butter, cream etc*) spalmare; **spread the whipped cream on the top of the cake** spalma la panna montata sopra la torta; **to spread cream on one's face** spalmarsi la crema sul viso **3** (*distribute: gen*) disporre; (*: fertilizer*)**: to spread sth on sth** cospargere qc di qc (*goods, objects*) disporre; (*cards, toys*) spargere; (*soldiers*) scaglionare; (*payments*) rateizzare, scaglionare; (*resources*) distribuire; **repayments will be spread over 18 months** i pagamenti saranno scaglionati lungo un periodo di 18 mesi **4** (*disseminate: germs, disease*) propagare, diffondere; (: *knowledge, panic etc*) diffondere; (: *news*) spargere, diffondere ♦ VI (*news, rumour etc*) diffondersi, propagarsi, spargersi; (*pain, fire, flood etc*) estendersi; (*milk etc*) spargersi; (*disease, weeds*) propagarsi; **to spread into sth** estendersi fino a qc; **margarine spreads better than butter** la margarina si spalma meglio del burro; **the news spread rapidly** la notizia si diffuse rapidamente

▸ **spread out** VI + ADV (*view, valley*) stendersi; (*soldiers, police*) disporsi; **the soldiers spread out across the field** i soldati si sparpagliarono nel campo ♦ VT + ADV = **spread 1, spread 3**

spread-eagled [ˌspredˈiːgld] ADJ**: to be** *or* **lie spread-eagled** essere disteso(-a) a gambe e braccia aperte

spread·sheet [ˈspredˌʃiːt] N (*Comput*) foglio elettronico

spree [spriː] N (*fam*)**: to go on a spending spree** fare spese folli; **to go on a spree** darsi alla pazza gioia, fare baldoria

sprig [sprɪg] N ramoscello

spright·ly [ˈspraɪtlɪ] ADJ (*comp* **-ier,** *superl* **-iest**) vivace; **a sprightly old man** un vecchietto arzillo

spring [sprɪŋ] (*pt* **sprang,** *pp* **sprung**) N **1** (*season*) primavera; **in spring, in the spring** in primavera; **spring is in the air** c'è aria di primavera **2** (*coiled metal, also Tech*) molla **3** **springs** NPL (*Aut*) sospensioni *fpl*, balestre *fpl* **4** (*of water*) sorgente *f*; **hot spring** sorgente termale **5** (*leap*) salto, balzo; **in one spring** in un salto **6** (*bounciness*) elasticità; **to walk with a spring in one's step** camminare con passo elastico ♦ VT (*trap, lock etc*) far scattare; **to spring a leak** (*pipe etc*) cominciare a perdere; **the boat has sprung a leak** s'è aperta una falla nella barca; **he sprang a question on me** (*fig*) mi ha fatto una domanda a bruciapelo; **to spring a surprise on sb** fare una sorpresa a qn; **he sprang the news on me** mi ha sorpreso con quella notizia; **he sprang it on me** mi ha preso alla sprovvista ♦ VI (*leap*) saltare, balzare; **suddenly the cat sprang** il gatto improvvisamente spiccò un balzo; **to spring aside/forward** balzare da una parte/in avanti; **to spring back** saltare *or* scattare all'indietro; **the door sprang open** la porta si aprì di scatto; **where on earth did you spring from?** (*fam*) da dove spunti?; **to spring into the air** fare un balzo in aria; **to spring into action** entrare rapidamente in azione; **to spring to one's feet** scattare in piedi; **he sprang to his feet** è balzato in piedi; **to spring to mind** venire in mente; **nothing springs to mind** non mi viene in mente niente **2** (*originate: gen*) sorgere; (: *tears*) sgorgare ♦ ADJ **1** (*of season*) di primavera, primaverile **2** (*with springs: mattress*) a molle

▸ **spring up** VI + ADV (*person*) saltar su; (*plant, weeds, building*) spuntare; (*problem, obstacle*) presentarsi; (*wind, storm*) alzarsi, levarsi; (*doubt, friendship, rumour*) nascere

spring·board [ˈsprɪŋbɔːd] N trampolino

spring-clean [ˌsprɪŋˈkliːn] VI fare le pulizie di primavera

spring onion N (*Brit*) cipollina

spring roll N involtino primavera, *involtino fritto farcito di verdure o carne, specialità cinese*

spring·time [ˈsprɪŋtaɪm] N primavera

springy [ˈsprɪŋɪ] ADJ (*comp* **-ier,** *superl* **-iest**) (*gen*) elastico(-a); (*carpet, turf*) morbido(-a); (*mattress*) molleggiato(-a)

sprin·kle [ˈsprɪŋkl] VT**: to sprinkle with** (*gen*) cospargere di; (*water*) spruzzare di; **they are sprinkled about here and there** sono sparsi un po' dovunque; **to sprinkle water** *etc* **on** spruzzàre dell'acqua *etc* su; **to sprinkle sugar** *etc* **on,** **sprinkle with sugar** *etc* spolverizzare di zucchero *etc*; **sprinkled with mistakes** infarcito(-a) di errori

sprin·kler [ˈsprɪŋklə'] N (*for lawn etc*) irrigatore *m*; (*for fire-fighting*) sprinkler *m inv*

sprin·kling [ˈsprɪŋklɪŋ] N (*of water, snow*) spruzzatina; (*of salt, sugar*) pizzico; **there was a sprinkling of young people** c'era qualche giovane

sprint [sprɪnt] N (*in race*) sprint *m inv*, scatto; (*dash*) corsa; **in a sprint finish** con uno sprint finale; **the women's 100 metres sprint** i cento metri piani femminili; **the 200-metres sprint** i 200 metri piani ♦ VI (*in race*) scattare, sprintare; (*dash: for bus etc*) fare una corsa; **she sprinted for the bus** ha fatto una corsa per prendere l'autobus

sprint·er [ˈsprɪntə'] N (*Sport*) velocista *m/f*

sprite [spraɪt] N elfo, folletto

spritz·er [ˈsprɪtsə'] N spritz *m inv*

sprock·et [ˈsprɒkɪt] N (*on printer, bicycle*) dente *m*, rocchetto

sprout [spraʊt] N (*from bulb, seeds*) germoglio; *see also* **sprouts** ♦ VT (*leaves, shoots*) mettere, produrre; **to sprout a moustache** farsi crescere i baffi ♦ VI germogliare; **skyscrapers are sprouting up everywhere** i grattacieli spuntano dappertutto

sprouts [spraʊts] NPL (*also:* **Brussels sprouts**) cavoletti *mpl* di Bruxelles

spruce¹ [spruːs] N (*Bot*) abete *m*; **Norway spruce** abete norvegese *or* rosso

spruce² [spruːs] ADJ (*outfit*) elegante; (*lawn*) curato(-a); (*person*) azzimato(-a)

▸ **spruce up** VT + ADV (*tidy*) mettere in ordine; (*smarten up: room etc*) abbellire; **to spruce o.s. up** farsi bello(-a); **all spruced up** tutto(-a) azzimato(-a) *or* agghindato(-a)

sprung [sprʌŋ] PP *of* **spring** ♦ ADJ (*seat, mattress*) a molle; **interior-sprung mattress** materasso a molle

spry [spraɪ] ADJ (*comp* **-er,** *superl* **-est**) vivace, sveglio(-a), arzillo(-a)

spun [spʌn] PT, PP *of* **spin**

spur [spɜː'] N (*also Geog*) sperone *m*; (*fig*) sprone *m*; **to be a spur to** essere d'incentivo a; **on the spur of the moment** su due piedi, d'impulso ♦ VT (*also:* **spur on:** *horse: fig*) spronare; **to spur sb on to do sth** spronare qn a fare qc

spu·ri·ous [ˈspjʊərɪəs] ADJ (*gen*) falso(-a); (*affection, interest*) falso(-a), simulato(-a)

spurn [spɜːn] VT respingere, sdegnare

spurt [spɜːt] N (*of water, steam etc*) getto; (*of speed, energy, anger*) scatto; **to put on a spurt** (*runner*) fare uno scatto; (*fig: in work etc*) affrettarsi, sbrigarsi; **a spurt of water** un getto d'acqua; **a spurt of anger** uno scatto di rabbia ♦ VI (*gush: also:* **spurt out**) sgorgare

sput·ter [ˈspʌtə'] VI = **splutter**

spy [spaɪ] N spia; **police spy** informatore(-trice) (della polizia) ♦ VT (*catch sight of*) scorgere ♦ VI spiare; **to spy on sb** spiare qn ♦ ADJ (*film, story*) di spionaggio

▸ **spy out** VT + ADV**: to spy out the land** (*fig*) tastare il terreno

spy·ing [ˈspaɪɪŋ] N spionaggio

Sq. ABBR = **Square** (*in address*) p.zza

sq. ABBR (*Math*) *of* **square**

squab·ble [ˈskwɒbl] N battibecco ♦ VI**: to squabble (over** *or* **about)** bisticciarsi (per); **stop squabbling!** smettetela di bisticciare!

squad [skwɒd] N (*Mil*) drappello, plotone *m*; (*of police, workmen etc*) squadra; **flying squad** (*Police*) (squadra) volante *f*, (squadra) mobile *f*; **a squad of soldiers** un drappello di soldati; **vice squad** buoncostume *f*; **the England World Cup squad was named today** (*Ftbl*) oggi è stata annunciata la formazione inglese convocata per i mondiali

squad car N (*Brit Police*) automobile *f* della polizia

squad·die [ˈskwɒdɪ] N (*Brit Mil: fam*) burba

squad·ron [ˈskwɒdrən] N (*Mil*) squadrone *m*; (*Aer, Naut*) squadriglia

squal·id [ˈskwɒlɪd] ADJ squallido(-a), sordido(-a)

squall [skwɔ:l] N (*Met*) bufera, burrasca ♦ VI (*baby*) strillare, urlare

squal·or [ˈskwɒlə'] N squallore *m*

squan·der [ˈskwɒndə'] VT (*money*) sperperare, dissipare, scialacquare; (*time, opportunity*) sprecare, perdere

square [skwɛə'] N 1 (*gen*) quadrato; (*instrument*) squadra; (*check on material*) quadro; **a square and a triangle** un quadrato e un triangolo; **with red and blue squares** a quadri rossi e blu; **to cut into squares** tagliare in (pezzi) quadrati; **we're back to square one** (*fig*) siamo al punto di partenza 2 (*in town*) piazza; (*USA: block of houses*) isolato; **the town square** la piazza principale 3 (*Math*) quadrato; **16 is the square of 4** 16 è il quadrato di 4 4 (*fam: old-fashioned person*) matusa *m inv*; **he's a real square** è proprio un matusa ♦ ADJ 1 (*in shape*) quadrato(-a); **a square table** un tavolo quadrato; **he's a square peg in a round hole in that job** non è tagliato per quel lavoro 2 (*Math*) quadrato(-a); **1 square metre** 1 metro quadrato; **two square metres** due metri quadrati; **it is less than a centimetre square** misura meno di un centimetro per lato; **2 metres square** di 2 metri per 2 3 **a square meal** un pasto sostanzioso 4 (*fair, honest*) onesto(-a), retto(-a); **to give sb a square deal** trattare qn onestamente; **I'll be square with you** sarò franco con te 5 (*even: accounts, figures*) in ordine; **to get one's accounts square** mettere in ordine i propri conti; **to get square with sb** (*also fig*) regolare i conti con qn; **now we're all square** (*fig*) adesso siamo pari 6 (*fam: old-fashioned: person*) all'antica; (*: idea*) sorpassato(-a); (*: style*) fuori moda ♦ ADV: **square in the middle** esattamente *or* proprio nel centro; **to look sb square in the eye** guardare qn diritto negli occhi ♦ VT 1 (*make square: stone, timber*) squadrare; (*: shape*) rendere quadrato(-a); **to square one's shoulders** raddrizzare le spalle 2 (*settle etc: accounts, books*) far quadrare; (*: debts*) saldare, regolare; **can you square it with your conscience?** riesci a conciliarlo con la tua coscienza?; **I'll square it with him** (*fam*) sistemo io le cose con lui 3 (*Math*) elevare al quadrato; **2 squared is 4** 2 al quadrato fa 4 ♦ VI (*agree*) accordarsi; **to square with** quadrare con

▸ **square off** VT + ADV (*wood, edges*) squadrare

▸ **square up** VI + ADV 1 (*Brit: settle*) saldare; **to square up with sb** regolare i conti con qn 2 **to square up (to)** (*opponent*) affrontare; (*fig: difficulties*) far fronte a

square bracket N (*Typ*) parentesi *f inv* quadra

square·ly [ˈskwɛəlɪ] ADV 1 (*directly*) direttamente; **to place sth squarely in the middle of the table** mettere qc proprio in mezzo al tavolo; **to face sth squarely** affrontare qc con coraggio 2 (*honestly, fairly*) onestamente; **to deal squarely with sb** trattare qn onestamente

square root N radice *f* quadrata

squash¹ [skwɒʃ] N 1 (*Brit: drink*): **orange/lemon squash** ≈ sciroppo di arancia/limone 2 (*crowd*) ressa, calca ♦ VT 1 (*squeeze*) schiacciare; **you're squashing me** mi stai schiacciando; **can you squash two more in?** (*passengers*) puoi farne entrare altri due?; **to be squashed together** essere schiacciati(-e) l'uno(-a) contro l'altro(-a) 2 (*fig: argument*) soffocare; (*: opposition*) mettere a tacere; (*: person*) umiliare, schiacciare ♦ VI: **to squash in** riuscire a entrare; **to squash up to make room for sb** stringersi per fare posto a qn

squash² [skwɒʃ] N (*vegetable*) zucca

squash³ [skwɒʃ] N (*Sport*) squash *m*

squat [skwɒt] ADJ (*comp* **-ter**, *superl* **-test**) (*person*) tarchiato(-a), tozzo(-a); (*building, shape etc*) tozzo(-a) ♦ VI 1 (*also:* **squat down**) accovacciarsi, acquattarsi; **he squatted to examine the footprints** si accovacciò per esaminare le impronte 2 (*on property*) occupare abusivamente; **to squat in a house** occupare abusivamente una casa ♦ N (*fam: house*) casa occupata

squat·ter [ˈskwɒtə'] N occupante *m/f* abusivo(-a)

squawk [skwɔ:k] N strido rauco ♦ VI (*parrot, baby, person*) strillare; (*fam: complain*) lamentarsi

squeak [skwi:k] N (*of hinge, wheel etc*) cigolio; (*of shoes*) scricchiolio; (*of mouse etc*) squittio; **a squeak of surprise** un gridolino di sorpresa; **I don't want to hear a squeak out of you!** non voglio sentire una parola! ♦ VI (*see n*) cigolare; scricchiolare; squittire; emettere un gridolino; **the door squeaked as it opened** la porta scricchiolò aprendosi; **she**

squeaked with delight ha lanciato un gridolino di gioia

squeaky [ˈskwi:kɪ] ADJ (*comp* **-ier**, *superl* **-iest**) (*hinge, wheel*) cigolante; (*shoes*) scricchiolante; **squeaky clean** (*hair*) splendente; (*fig: very clean: office, home*) tirato(-a) a specchio; (*: person: irreproachable*) dall'immagine cristallina

squeal [skwi:l] N (*gen*) strillo; (*of tyres or tires, brakes*) stridore *m*; **a squeal of laughter** una risatina ♦ VI (*see n*) strillare; stridere; (*fam: inform*): **to squeal (on sb)** fare una soffiata (a qn)

squeam·ish [ˈskwi:mɪʃ] ADJ (*easily nauseated*) facilmente impressionabile; **I was too squeamish to look** mi faceva troppa impressione guardare

squeeze [skwi:z] N (*pressure*) pressione *f*; (*of hand*) stretta; (*crush, crowd*) ressa, calca; **credit squeeze** (*Fin*) stretta creditizia; **to give sb's hand a squeeze** dare una breve stretta di mano a qn; **it was a tight squeeze to get through** c'era appena il posto per passare; **we're in a tight squeeze** (*fig: fam*) ci troviamo in difficoltà; **a squeeze of lemon** una spruzzata di limone; **give me a squeeze of toothpaste** dammi un po' di dentifricio; **to put the squeeze on sb** far pressione su qn ♦ VT (*gen*) premere; (*sponge*) strizzare; (*lemon etc*) spremere; (*hand, arm*) stringere; **to squeeze the juice out of a lemon** spremere un limone; **squeeze two large lemons** spremete due limoni grossi; **to squeeze toothpaste out of a tube** spremere il dentifricio da un tubetto; **to squeeze clothes into a case** pigiare i vestiti in una valigia; **to squeeze information out of sb** strappare delle informazioni a qn; **she squeezed my hand reassuringly** mi ha stretto la mano con fare rassicurante; **can you squeeze two more in?** riesci a farcene entrare altri due?; **I can squeeze you in at two o'clock** le posso dare un appuntamento alle due ♦ VI: **to squeeze past/under sth** passare vicino/sotto a qc con difficoltà; **to squeeze in** infilarsi; **to squeeze through a hole** passare a forza attraverso un buco; **to squeeze through the crowd** riuscire ad aprirsi un varco tra la folla; **the thieves squeezed through a tiny window** i ladri si sono introdotti attraverso una finestrella

▸ **squeeze out** VT + ADV spremere

squelch [skweltʃ] VI: **to squelch in/out** *etc* entrare/uscire sguazzando; **he squelched through the mud** faceva cic ciac nel fango

squib [skwɪb] N petardo

squid [skwɪd] N calamaro

squint [skwɪnt] N (*Med*) strabismo; (*sidelong look*) occhiata, sbirciata; **to have a squint** (*Med*) essere strabico(-a); **let's have a squint** (*fam*) diamo un'occhiata ♦ VI (*Med*) essere strabico(-a); **to squint at sth** guardare qc di traverso; (*quickly*) sbirciare qc; **he squinted in the sunlight** la luce del sole gli faceva strizzare gli occhi

squire [ˈskwaɪə'] N (*old: landowner*) possidente *m*

squirm [skwɜ:m] VI contorcersi; **to squirm with embarrassment** sentirsi morire dall'imbarazzo

squir·rel [ˈskwɪrəl] N scoiattolo; **red squirrel** scoiattolo eurasiatico; **grey squirrel** scoiattolo grigio

squirt [skwɜ:t] N (*of water*) schizzo; (*of detergent, perfume*) spruzzo ♦ VT spruzzare ♦ VI schizzare

Sr ABBR = **senior, sister 3**

Sri Lan·ka [ˌsriˈlæŋkə] N lo Sri Lanka

SS ABBR = **steamship**

SSA [ˌɛsɛsˈeɪ] N ABBR (*USA:* = *Social Security Administration*) ≈ Previdenza Sociale

ST [ˌɛsˈti:] ABBR (*USA*) = **standard time**

St ABBR = **Saint**

stab [stæb] N 1 (*with knife*) coltellata; (*with dagger*) pugnalata; (*of pain*) fitta; **a stab in the back** (*also fig*) una pugnalata alla schiena; **he felt a stab of remorse** gli rimordeva la coscienza 2 (*fam: try*): **to have a stab at (doing) sth** provare a fare qc ♦ VT (*with dagger*) pugnalare; (*with knife*) accoltellare; **to stab sb to death** uccidere qn a coltellate; **to stab sb in the back** (*also fig*) pugnalare qn alla schiena; **he was stabbed through the heart** fu pugnalato al cuore

stab·bing [ˈstæbɪŋ] N: **there's been a stabbing** c'è stato un accoltellamento ♦ ADJ (*pain, ache*) lancinante

sta·bil·ity [stəˈbɪlɪtɪ] N (*structural, political, economic*) stabilità; (*mental, emotional*) equilibrio; (*of family, relationship*) solidità

sta·bi·li·za·tion [ˌsteɪbəlaɪˈzeɪʃən] N stabilizzazione f

sta·bi·lize [ˈsteɪbəlaɪz] VT stabilizzare; **stabilizing jacket** (*Skin diving*) giubbetto equilibratore ♦ VI stabilizzarsi

sta·bi·li·zer [ˈsteɪbəlaɪzəʳ] N (*Aer, Naut*) stabilizzatore m

sta·ble¹ [ˈsteɪbl] ADJ (*comp* -r, *superl* -st) (*government, economy*) stabile; (*relationship*) solido(-a), stabile; (*person: emotionally, mentally*) equilibrato(-a); **a stable relationship** una relazione stabile; **the patient is stable** (*Med*) le condizioni del paziente sono stazionarie

sta·ble² [ˈsteɪbl] N (*building*) stalla; (*establishment*) scuderia; **riding stables** maneggio ♦ VT (*keep in stable*) tenere in una stalla

stac·ca·to [stəˈkɑːtəʊ](*Mus*) ADV in staccato ♦ ADJ stacca-to(-a); (*sound*) scandito(-a)

stack [stæk] N 1 (*pile*) pila, catasta; (*Brit fam*) mucchio, sac-co; **there was a stack of books on the table** sul tavolo c'era una pila di libri; **stacks of** un sacco di; **they've got stacks of money** hanno un sacco di soldi; **there's stacks of time to finish it** abbiamo un sacco di tempo per finirlo 2 (*also: chimney stack*) comignolo; (*of factory*) ciminiera 3 (*Geog*) faraglione m ♦ VT (*books, boxes*) impilare, accatastare; (*chairs*) mettere l'uno(-a) sopra l'altro(-a); (*aircraft*) tenere a quote assegnate (*in attesa dell'atterraggio*); **the cards are stacked against us** (*fig*) tutto è contro di noi

sta·dium [ˈsteɪdɪəm] N stadio

staff [stɑːf] N 1 (*personnel: gen*) personale m; (*: servants*) per-sonale di servizio; (*: Mil*) Stato Maggiore; **the administra-tive staff** il personale amministrativo; **the teaching staff** il corpo insegnante; **to be on the staff** far parte del personale *or* dell'organico; **a staff of 15** un personale *or* organico di 15 persone; **to join the staff** entrare a far parte del perso-nale; **"staff only"** "passaggio di servizio" 2 (*old: stick*) ba-stone m; (*Rel*) bastone pastorale; (*of flag*) asta 3 (*Mus: also: stave*) pentagramma m, rigo ♦ VT fornire di personale; **to be staffed by Asians/women** avere un personale asiatico/cos-tituito da donne; **to be well staffed** essere ben fornito(-a) di personale

staff room N sala dei professori

Staffs ABBR (*Brit:* = Staffordshire)

stag [stæg] N (*Zool*) cervo; (*Brit: Stock Exchange*) rialzista m/f su nuove emissioni

stage [steɪdʒ] N 1 (*period, section: of process, development*) fase f, stadio; (*: of journey*) tappa; (*: of rocket*) stadio; **in stages** (*travel, work etc*) a tappe; **in** *or* **by easy stages** a piccole tappe; **in the early/final stages** negli stadi iniziali/finali; **at this stage in the negotiations** in questa fase dei negoziati; **the final stage of their world tour** la tappa conclusiva della loro tournée mondiale; **to go through a difficult stage** at-traversare un periodo difficile 2 (*platform*) palco; (*in theatre*) palcoscenico; **the stage** (*profession*) il teatro; **to go on the stage** entrare in scena; (*become an actor*) fare del teatro; **she went on stage and did her act** è salita sul palco e ha fat-to il suo show ♦ VT (*play*) mettere in scena, rappresentare; (*arrange: welcome, demonstration*) organizzare; (*fake: accident*) simulare; **to stage a scene** allestire una scena; (*fig*) fare una sceneggiata; **to stage a quick recovery** riprendersi subito; **to stage a comeback** fare ritorno

❏ **stage** is not translated by the Italian word *stage*

stage·coach [ˈsteɪdʒˌkəʊtʃ] N diligenza

stage door N ingresso degli artisti

stage fright N panico prima di andare in scena; **to get stage fright** essere assalito(-a) dal panico prima di andare in scena

stage·hand [ˈsteɪdʒˌhænd] N (*Theatre*) macchinista m

stage-manage [ˈsteɪdʒˌmænɪdʒ] VT (*event, confrontation*) montare, inscenare; (*pej*) orchestrare

stage manager N direttore(-trice) di scena

stag·ger [ˈstægəʳ] VT 1 (*amaze: person*) sbalordire; **it stag-gered me** mi ha sbalordito 2 (*holidays, payments, hours*) scaglionare; (*objects*) disporre a intervalli ♦ VI barcollare; **to stagger along/in/out** avanzare/entrare/uscire barcollando; **he staggered to the door** andò verso la porta barcollando

stag·ger·ing [ˈstægərɪŋ] ADJ (*amazing*) sbalorditivo(-a), in-credibile

stag·ing post [ˈsteɪdʒɪŋˌpəʊst] N tappa obbligata

stag·nant [ˈstægnənt] ADJ stagnante

stag·nate [stægˈneɪt] VI (*water*) stagnare; (*fig: economy*) ri-stagnare; (*: person*) vegetare; (*: mind*) intorpidirsi

stag·na·tion [stægˈneɪʃən] N (*of water, economy*) ristagno, stagnazione f; (*of mind*) intorpidimento

stag night, stag party N festa di addio al celibato

staid [steɪd] ADJ (*comp* -er, *superl* -est) compassato(-a)

stain [steɪn] N 1 (*also fig*) macchia; **grease stain** macchia di grasso; **a large stain** una grande macchia 2 (*dye*) colorante m ♦ VT 1 (*also fig*) macchiare; **to stain with** macchiare di 2 (*wood*) tingere; (*glass*) colorare ♦ VI macchiarsi

stained glass [ˌsteɪndˈglɑːs] N vetro colorato

stained-glass window [ˌsteɪndglɑːsˈwɪndəʊ] N vetrata co-lorata

stain·less [ˈsteɪnlɪs] ADJ (*steel*) inossidabile

stain remover N smacchiatore m

stair [stɛəʳ] N (*single step*) scalino, gradino; (*whole flight: usu pl*) scala; **he fell down the stairs** è caduto (giù) per le scale; **on the stairs** per le *or* sulle scale; **he left the bag on the bot-tom stair** ha lasciato la borsa sull'ultimo gradino

stair·case [ˈstɛəˌkeɪs], **stair·way** [ˈstɛəˌweɪ] N scala

stair·well [ˈstɛəˌwel] N tromba delle scale

stake [steɪk] N 1 (*share*) interesse m; (*bet*) puntata, scommes-sa; **to be at stake** essere in gioco; **to raise the stakes** alzare la posta in gioco; **to have a stake in sth** avere un interesse in qc 2 (*for fence, tree*) palo; (*for plant*) bastoncino; **a wood-en stake** un palo di legno 3 (*for execution*): **to be burnt at the stake** essere bruciato(-a) sul rogo ♦ VT 1 (*bet*): **to stake (on)** scommettere (su); **I'd stake my reputation on it** ci giocherei la reputazione 2 (*also: stake out: area*) delimitare con paletti; (*plant: stake up: plant*) legare a un bastoncino; **to stake a claim (to sth)** rivendicare (qc)

stake·out [ˈsteɪkaʊt] N (*esp USA Police*) sorveglianza

stal·ac·tite [ˈstæləkˌtaɪt] N stalattite f

stal·ag·mite [ˈstæləgˌmaɪt] N stalagmite f

stale [steɪl] ADJ (*comp* -r, *superl* -st) (*food: gen*) stantio(-a); (*: bread*) stantio(-a), raffermo(-a); (*: beer*) svaporato(-a); (*air*) viziato(-a); (*news, joke*) vecchio(-a) come il cucco, trito(-a); (*Law: claim*) caduto(-a) in prescrizione, prescritto(-a); **stale bread** pane raffermo; **stale air** aria viziata; **I'm getting stale** non ho più entusiasmo

stale·mate [ˈsteɪlˌmeɪt] N (*Chess*) stallo; (*fig*) punto morto; **to reach stalemate** (*fig*) arrivare a un punto morto; **the nego-tiations have reached a stalemate** i negoziati sono arrivati ad un punto morto

stalk¹ [stɔːk] VT (*animal, person*) inseguire ♦ VI: **to stalk in/out** *etc* entrare/uscire *etc* impettito(-a); **she stalked out of the room angrily** uscì furiosa dalla stanza

stalk² [stɔːk] N (*Bot*) gambo, stelo; (*of cabbage*) torsolo; (*of fruit*) picciolo

stall [stɔːl] N 1 (*Agr: stable*) stalla, box m inv; (*Brit: in market*) bancarella, banco; (*at exhibition, fair*) stand m inv; **a news-paper/flower stall** chiosco del giornalaio/del fioraio; **to set out your stall** (*Brit*) dire chiaramente le proprie intenzioni 2 (*Theatre*): **the stalls** la platea 3 (*Aer*) stallo ♦ VT (*plane*) far andare in stallo; **he stalled the car** gli si è spento il motore ♦ VI 1 (*car, engine*) bloccarsi; (*plane*) andare in stallo 2 (*fig: delay*): **to stall for time** prendere tempo, temporeggiare; **stop stalling!** smettila di menare il can per l'aia!

stall·holder [ˈstɔːlˌhəʊldəʳ] N (*Brit*) bancarellista m/f

stal·lion [ˈstæljən] N stallone m

stal·wart [ˈstɔːlwət] ADJ (*person: in spirit*) prode, coraggio-so(-a); (*party member*) fidato(-a); (*supporter, opponent*) riso-luto(-a), deciso(-a); **a party stalwart** un fedelissimo del partito ♦ N prode m, persona coraggiosa

sta·men [ˈsteɪmen] N stame m

stami·na [ˈstæmɪnə] N resistenza; **he's got stamina** ha molta resistenza

stam·mer [ˈstæməʳ] N balbuzie f; **he's got a stammer** è bal-buziente ♦ VI, VT balbettare

stamp [stæmp] N 1 (*also: postage stamp*) francobollo; (*also: trading stamp*) bollino premio, ≈ marchetta; **I collect stamps** faccio collezione di francobolli 2 (*rubber stamp*) timbro; (*mark*) bollo; **an official stamp** un timbro ufficiale; **it bears the stamp of genius** porta l'impronta del genio 3 **with an angry stamp of her foot** battendo il piede per terra con rabbia ♦ VT **1 to stamp one's feet** battere i piedi; (*in anger*) pestare i piedi; **the audience stamped their feet** il pubblico batteva i piedi; **to stamp the ground** (*person*) pestare i piedi per terra; (*horse*) scalpitare **2** (*letter*) affrancare **3** (*mark with rubber stamp*) timbrare, bollare; (*emboss*) imprimere su; **they stamped my passport at the border** mi hanno timbrato il passaporto al confine; **he looked at her ticket, and stamped it** le ha guardato il biglietto e l'ha timbrato ♦ VI (*single movement*) battere il piede per terra; **to stamp in/out** entrare/uscire infuriato(-a); **ouch, you stamped on my foot!** ahi, mi hai pestato un piede!

▸ **stamp out** VT + ADV (*fire*) estinguere; (*crime*) eliminare; (*opposition*) soffocare

❏ **stamp** is not translated by the Italian word *stampo*

stamp album N (*new*) album *m inv* per francobolli; (*containing stamps*) album *m inv* di francobolli

stamp collecting [-kǝˈlektɪŋ] N filatelia

stamp duty N (*Brit*) bollo

stam·pede [stæmˈpiːd] N (*of cattle*) fuga precipitosa; (*of people*) fuggi fuggi *m inv*; **a stampede for the exit** un fuggi fuggi verso l'uscita; **there was a sudden stampede for the door** ci fu un fuggi fuggi verso la porta ♦ VT (*cattle*) far scappare; **to stampede sb into doing sth** (*pej*) spingere qn a fare qc senza dargli il tempo di riflettere ♦ VI (*cattle*) fuggire precipitosamente; (*fig*) precipitarsi

stamp machine N distributore *m* automatico di francobolli

stance [stæns] N **1** (*way of standing*) posizione *f* **2** (*attitude*) presa di posizione *f*

❏ **stance** is not translated by the Italian word *stanza*

stand [stænd] (*pt,pp* **stood**) N **1** (*booth*) chiosco; (*market stall*) banco, bancarella; (*at exhibition, fair*) stand *m inv*; (*raised area*) (*also:* **bandstand**) palco; (*Sport*) tribuna; (*USA Law: also:* **witness stand**) banco; **a music stand** un leggìo; **our stand in the trade fair** il nostro stand alla fiera; **he kicked the ball into the stand** con un calcio ha tirato la palla in tribuna **2** (*position, also fig*) posizione *f*; (*resistance*) resistenza; **to take (up) one's stand at the door** prendere il proprio posto vicino alla porta; **to take a stand on an issue** prendere posizione su un problema; **to make a stand against sth** (*Mil, also fig*) opporre resistenza contro qc **3** (*also:* **taxi stand**) posteggio di taxi ♦ VT **1** (*place*) mettere, porre; **to stand sth against a wall** appoggiare qc a un muro; **to stand sth on end** mettere qc in piedi **2** (*withstand, bear: weight*) reggere a, resistere, sopportare; **it won't stand serious examination** non reggerà ad un esame accurato; **the troops stood heavy bombardment** le truppe hanno sopportato pesanti bombardamenti; **the company will have to stand the loss** la ditta dovrà sostenere la perdita; **to stand the cost of sth** sobbarcarsi le spese di **3** (*tolerate*) sopportare; **I can't stand him** non lo sopporto; **I can't stand this noise** non sopporto questo chiasso; **I can't stand the sight of him** non lo posso vedere; **I can't stand it any longer!** non ce la faccio più!; **I can't stand waiting for people** non sopporto aspettare la gente **4** (*fam: treat*): **to stand sb a drink/meal** offrire da bere/un pranzo a qn **5** (*phrases*): **to stand guard** *or* **watch** (*Mil*) essere di guardia *or* sentinella; **to stand guard over** (*Mil, also fig*) fare la guardia a ♦ VI **1** (*be upright*) stare in piedi; (*stay standing*) restare in piedi; (*get up*) alzarsi; **I had to stand** non dovuto restare in piedi; **he could hardly stand** si reggeva a malapena; **the woman standing over there** la donna in piedi laggiù; **he was standing by the door** stava in piedi vicino alla porta; **don't just stand there - help me!** non stare lì impalato - aiutami!; **the house is still standing** la casa è ancora in piedi; **they stood talking for hours** restarono a parlare per delle ore; **they kept us standing about** *or* **around for ages** ci hanno fatto aspettare in piedi per ore; **to stand on sb's foot** pestare il piede a qn; **to stand in sb's way** intralciare il passaggio a qn; **I won't stand in your way** (*fig*) non ti sarò d'ostacolo; **nothing stands in our way** la via è libera; **that was all that stood between him and ...** era tutto ciò che si frapponeva fra lui e ...; **nothing stands between us** non c'è niente che ci separi; **to be left standing** (*building*) essere rimasto(-a) in piedi; (*fig: competitor*) essere bruciato(-a) in partenza; **it made my hair stand on end** mi ha fatto rizzare i capelli; **to stand still** stare fermo(-a) (in piedi); **to stand fast** tener duro; **to stand on one's own two feet** (*fig*) cavarsela

da solo(-a); **to stand on one's head/hands** fare la verticale in appoggio/la verticale; **he could do the job standing on his head** potrebbe fare quel lavoro a occhi chiusi; **to stand on the brakes** (*Aut*) frenare di colpo; **to stand on one's dignity** stare sulle sue **2 he stands over 6 feet** è alto più di 2m; **the tower stands 50m high** la torre è alta 50m **3** (*be situated: building, tree*) trovarsi, stare; **the car stands outside all year round** la macchina sta fuori tutto l'anno; **the house stands on top of a hill** la casa è situata in cima ad una collina **4** (*Culin*): **to leave to stand** (*tea*) lasciare in infusione; (*batter*) (lasciar) riposare; **my objection still stands** la mia obiezione è ancora valida; **to let sth stand as it is** lasciare qc così com'è; **the theory stands or falls on this** è questo il presupposto su cui si basa la teoria; **it stands to reason that ...** è logico che... **5** (*fig: be placed*) stare; **to stand accused of** essere accusato(-a) di; **how do things stand?** come stanno le cose?; **as things stand** stando così le cose; **the peace process as it stands violates human rights** il processo di pace così com'è viola i diritti umani; **to stand at** (*thermometer, clock*) indicare, segnare; (*offer, price, sales*) ammontare a; (*score*) essere **6** (*Pol*): **to stand as a candidate** candidarsi; **to stand in an election** candidarsi ad un'elezione; **to stand for Parliament** candidarsi al Parlamento **7** (*Naut*): **to stand out to sea** stare al largo

▸ **stand aside** VI + ADV farsi da parte, scostarsi

▸ **stand back** VI + ADV tirarsi indietro; (*building: be placed further back*): **to stand back from** essere arretrato(-a) rispetto a

▸ **stand by** VI + ADV (*be onlooker*) stare là (a non far niente); (*be ready*) tenersi pronto(-a); **stand by for further news** tenetevi pronti a ricevere altre notizie ♦ VI + PREP (*person*) rimanere vicino(-a) a; (*promise*) mantenere; (*opinion*) sostenere

▸ **stand down** VI + ADV (*withdraw*) ritirarsi; (*Mil*) smontare di guardia; (*Law*) lasciare il banco dei testimoni; **to stand down in favour of** (*fig*) farsi da parte a favore di

▸ **stand for** VI + PREP **1** (*represent: principle, honesty*) rappresentare; (*: subj: initials*) indicare, stare per; **"BT" stands for "British Telecom"** "BT" è l'abbreviazione di "British Telecom" **2** (*tolerate*) tollerare, sopportare; **I won't stand for that** non tollero una cosa del genere; **I won't stand for it any more!** non ho intenzione di tollerarlo oltre! **3** (*Pol*) = **stand 6**

▸ **stand in** VI + ADV: **to stand in for sb** sostituire qn

▸ **stand out** VI + ADV **1** (*be noticeable: veins, eyes*) sporgere; (*: colours*) risaltare, spiccare; (*: person*) distinguersi; (*: mountains*) stagliarsi; **it stands out a mile!** si vede lontano un miglio! **2** (*be firm, hold out*) resistere, tener duro; **to stand out against sth** opporsi fermamente a qc; **to stand out for sth** rivendicare qc, insistere su qc

▸ **stand over** VI + ADV (*items for discussion*) rimanere in sospeso ♦ VT + PREP (*person*) stare addosso a

▸ **stand to** VI + ADV (*Mil*) tenersi pronto(-a)

▸ **stand up** VI + ADV (*rise*) alzarsi in piedi; (*be standing*) stare in piedi; (*fig: argument*) reggersi ♦ VT + ADV (*fam: girlfriend, boyfriend*): **she stood me up** non è venuta all'appuntamento

▸ **stand up for** VI + ADV + PREP difendere; **to stand up for sb/sth** difendere qn/qc; **stand up for your rights!** difendi i tuoi diritti!; **to stand up for o.s.** difendersi

▸ **stand up to** VI + ADV + PREP tenere testa, resistere a; **to stand up to sb** tenere testa a qn, affrontare qn con coraggio; **it stands up to hard wear** è resistente (all'uso)

stand-alone [ˈstændzˈləʊn] ADJ (*business, organization*) indipendente; (*Comput*) a sé stante, non in rete

stand·ard [ˈstændǝd] N **1** (*norm*) standard *m inv*; (*intellectual standard*) livello culturale; **the gold standard** (*Fin*) il tallone aureo; **to be** *or* **come up to standard** rispondere ai requisiti; **to set a high standard** dare il buon esempio; **at first-year university standard** a livello del primo anno d'università; **of (a) high/low standard** di alto/basso livello; **the standard is very high** il livello qualitativo è molto alto; **below** *or* **not up to standard** (*work*) mediocre **2** (*moral: usu pl*) scala di valori; **moral standards** valori *mpl* morali; **to accept sb's standards** accettare la scala di valori di qn; **to apply a double standard** avere due pesi e due misure **3** (*flag*) insegna;

(*Mil*) stendardo ♦ ADJ (*size, quality*) standard *inv*; (*reference book*) classico(-a); **standard English** inglese standard

stand·ardi·za·tion [ˌstændədaɪˈzeɪʃən] N standardizzazione *f*

stand·ard·ize [ˈstændəˌdaɪz] VT standardizzare

standard lamp N (*Brit*) lampada a stelo

standard time N ora ufficiale

stand-by [ˈstændˌbaɪ] N 1 (*person*) riserva; **have you got a stand-by, should that fail?** ha qualcosa che lo rimpiazzi nel caso che lo funzioni?; **to be on stand-by** (*gen*) tenersi pronto(-a); (*doctor*) essere di guardia 2 (*also:* **stand-by ticket**) biglietto *m* stand-by, *inv*

stand-by generator N generatore *m* d'emergenza

stand-by passenger N (*Aer*) passeggero(-a) in lista d'attesa

stand-by ticket N (*Aer*) biglietto *m* stand-by, *inv*

stand-in [ˈstændˌɪn] N sostituto(-a); (*Cine*) controfigura

stand·ing [ˈstændɪŋ] ADJ 1 (*passenger*) in piedi; (*upright: corn*) non mietuto(-a); **he was given a standing ovation** tutti si alzarono per applaudirlo; **standing start** partenza da fermo; **standing waves** (*Phys*) onde *fpl* stazionarie 2 (*permanent: rule*) fisso(-a); (*army*) regolare; (: *grievance*) continuo(-a); **it's a standing joke** è diventato proverbiale ♦ N 1 (*social position*) rango, condizione *f*, posizione *f*; (*repute*) reputazione *f*; **financial standing** standing *m*; **a man of some standing** un uomo di una certa importanza; **wealth and social standing** ricchezza e posizione sociale; **the Prime Minister's standing in the country** la reputazione del primo ministro nel paese 2 (*duration*): **of 6 months' standing** che dura da 6 mesi; **of long standing** di lunga data

standing committee N commissione *f* permanente

standing order N 1 (*Brit: at bank*) ordine *m* permanente (di pagamento) 2 **standing orders** NPL (*Mil, Parliament*) regolamento

standing room N posto in piedi

stand-off [ˈstændˌɒf] N (*stalemate*) situazione *f* di stallo

stand·offish [ˌstændˈɒfɪʃ] ADJ (*fam, pej*) scostante, freddo(-a)

stand·pat [ˈstændˈpæt] ADJ (*USA*) irremovibile

stand·pipe [ˈstændˌpaɪp] N fontanella

stand·point [ˈstændˌpɔɪnt] N punto di vista

stand·still [ˈstændˌstɪl] N: **to bring a car to a standstill** fermare una macchina; **to be at a standstill** (*vehicle*) essere fermo(-a); (*industry etc*) ristagnare, essere paralizzato(-a), il traffico è fermo; **traffic is at a standstill, to come to a standstill** (*vehicle*) fermarsi; (*industry etc*) rimanere paralizzato(-a); (*production*) arrestarsi; (*talks, negotiations*) giungere a un punto morto; **the train came to a standstill** il treno si è fermato; **the talks came to a standstill** i colloqui erano ad un punto morto

stank [stæŋk] PT *of* stink

stan·za [ˈstænzə] N stanza (*Poetry*)

sta·ple¹ [ˈsteɪpl] N (*for papers*) punto metallico ♦ VT (*also:* **staple together**) cucire con punti metallici

sta·ple² [ˈsteɪpl] ADJ (*diet, food, products*) base *inv*; (*crop, industry*) principale; **rice is their staple food** il loro alimento principale è il riso ♦ N (*chief product*) prodotto principale; (*of diet*) alimento principale

sta·pler [ˈsteɪpləʳ], **sta·pling ma·chine** [ˈsteɪplɪŋməˈʃiːn] N cucitrice *f*

star [stɑːʳ] N 1 (*gen*) stella; (*Mil*) stelletta; (*Typ, etc*) asterisco; **the moon and stars** la luna e le stelle; **four-star hotel** albergo a quattro stelle; **born under a lucky star** nato(-a) sotto una buona stella; **the stars** (*horoscope*) le stelle; **you can thank your lucky stars that** puoi ringraziare la tua buona stella che + *sub*; **to see stars** (*fig*) vedere le stelle 2 (*celebrity*) divo(-a); (*actress only*) stella; **a TV star** una star della TV ♦ VT (*Cine, etc*) essere interpretato(-a) da; **a film starring Meryl Streep** un film con Meryl Streep; **the film stars Sharon Stone** il film ha come protagonista Sharon Stone ♦ VI (*Cine, etc*): **to star in a film** essere il (*or* la) protagonista di un film; **he starred as Othello** ha interpretato il ruolo di Otello

star attraction N (*in show*) numero principale; (*in museum*) l'attrazione *f* principale

star·board [ˈstɑːbəd] N tribordo; **on the starboard side** a dritta, a tribordo

starch [stɑːtʃ] N amido ♦ VT inamidare

starched [stɑːtʃt] ADJ (*collar*) inamidato(-a)

starchy [ˈstɑːtʃɪ] ADJ (*comp* **-ier**, *superl* **-iest**) (*food*) ricco(-a) di amido

star·dom [ˈstɑːdəm] N celebrità

stare [stɛəʳ] N sguardo fisso; **a vacant stare** uno sguardo assente ♦ VT: **it's staring you in the face** (*obvious*) salta agli occhi; (*very near*) ce l'hai sotto il naso ♦ VI: **to stare at sb/sth** fissare qn/qc; **to stare into space** fissare il vuoto; **to stare at sb in surprise** fissare qn con aria sorpresa; **it's rude to stare** non sta bene fissare la gente

  ► **stare out** VT + ADV (*fissare fino a*) fare abbassare gli occhi

  ❑ **stare** is not translated by the Italian word *stare*

star·fish [ˈstɑːfɪʃ] N stella di mare

stark [stɑːk] ADJ (*comp* **-er**, *superl* **-est**) (*outline*) aspro(-a); (*landscape*) desolato(-a); (*simplicity, colour*) austero(-a); (*contrast*) forte; (*reality, poverty, truth*) crudo(-a) ♦ ADV: **stark staring** *or* **raving mad** matto(-a) da legare; **stark naked** nudo(-a) come un verme

stark·ers [ˈstɑːkəz] ADJ (*Brit fam*) nudo(-a) come un verme

star·let [ˈstɑːlɪt] N (*Cine*) stellina

star·light [ˈstɑːˌlaɪt] N: **in the starlight** alla luce delle stelle

star·ling [ˈstɑːlɪŋ] N storno

star·lit [ˈstɑːˌlɪt] ADJ stellato(-a)

starry [ˈstɑːrɪ] ADJ (*comp* **-ier**, *superl* **-iest**) stellato(-a); **starry cast** cast *m inv* di prim'ordine

starry-eyed [ˌstɑːrɪˈaɪd] ADJ (*idealistic, gullible*) ingenuo(-a); (*from wonder*) meravigliato(-a); (*from love*) perdutamente innamorato(-a)

Stars and Stripes NPL: **the Stars and Stripes** la bandiera a stelle e strisce

star sign N segno zodiacale

star-studded [ˈstɑːˌstʌdɪd] ADJ: **a star-studded cast** un cast di attori famosi

start [stɑːt] N 1 (*beginning*) inizio; (*in race*) partenza; (*starting line*) linea di partenza; (*Mountaineering*) attacco; **at the start** all'inizio; **the start of the school year** l'inizio dell'anno scolastico; **from the start** dall'inizio; **for a start** tanto per cominciare; **for a start you need to check all the names** per cominciare devi controllare tutti i nomi; **to get off to a good** *or* **flying start** cominciare bene; **to make a start** cominciare; **shall we make a start on the washing-up?** cominciamo a lavare i piatti?; **to make an early start** partire di buon'ora; **to make a fresh** (*or* **new**) **start in life** ricominciare daccapo *or* da zero; **it's not much, but it's a start** non è molto ma è pur sempre un inizio 2 (*advantage*) vantaggio; **the thieves had 3 hours' start** i ladri avevano 3 ore di vantaggio; **to give sb a 5-minute start** dare un vantaggio di 5 minuti a qn 3 (*sudden movement*) sussulto, sobbalzo; **to give a start** trasalire; **to give sb a start** far trasalire qn; **to wake with a start** svegliarsi di soprassalto ♦ VT 1 (*begin: gen*) cominciare, iniziare; (: *bottle*) aprire; (: *habit*) prendere; **to start doing sth** *or* **to do sth** iniziare a fare qc; **to start negotiations** avviare i negoziati; **he started life as a labourer** ha cominciato come operaio 2 (*cause to begin or happen: conversation, discussion*) iniziare; (: *quarrel*) cominciare, provocare; (: *rumour*) mettere in giro; (: *series of events, policy*) dare l'avvio a; (: *reform*) avviare; (: *fashion*) lanciare; (*found: business, newspaper*) fondare, creare; (*car, engine*) mettere in moto, avviare; **to start a fire** provocare un incendio; **to start a race** dare il via a una gara; **you started it!** hai cominciato tu!; **don't start anything!** non cominciare!; **don't start him on that!** non toccare quest'argomento in sua presenza!; **we'd like to start a family** ci piacerebbe avere un bambino subito; **he wants to start his own business** vuole avviare un'attività in proprio; **she started a campaign against drugs** ha lanciato una campagna contro la droga; **he couldn't start the car** non riusciva a far partire la macchina ♦ VI 1 (*begin: gen*) cominciare, iniziare; (: *rumour*) nascere; (: *on journey*) partire, mettersi in viaggio; (: *car, engine*) mettersi in moto, partire; **starting from Tuesday** a partire da martedì; **to start on a task** cominciare un lavoro; **to start at the beginning** cominciare dall'inizio; **it started (off) well/badly** è cominciato bene/male; **she started (off) down the street** s'incamminò giù per la strada; **what time does it start?** a che ora inizia?; **what shall we start (off) with?** con che cosa cominciamo?; **she started (off) as a nanny** ha cominciato

come bambinaia; **to start (off) with ...** (*firstly*) per prima cosa...; (*at the beginning*) all'inizio...; **he started (off) by saying (that) ...** cominciò col dire che...; **the car wouldn't start** la macchina non partiva; **we started off first thing in the morning** ci siamo messi in viaggio di buon mattino **2** (*in fright*): **to start (at)** trasalire (a), sobbalzare (a); **his eyes were starting out of his head** aveva gli occhi fuori dalle orbite
▸ **start off** VI + ADV (*leave*) partire ♦ VT + ADV causare, far nascere; **to start sb off** (*on complaints, story etc*) far cominciare qn; (*give initial help*) aiutare qn a cominciare; **that was enough to start him off** è bastato questo a dargli il via
▸ **start out** VI + ADV (*begin journey*) partire; (*fig*): **to start out as** cominciare come; **to start out to do sth** cominciare con l'intenzione di fare qc
▸ **start over** VI + ADV (*USA*) ricominciare
▸ **start up** VI + ADV (*engine*) mettersi in moto; (*driver*) mettere in moto; (*music*) cominciare ♦ VT + ADV (*car, engine*) mettere in moto, avviare
start·er [ˈstɑːtə'] N **1** (*Brit: Culin*): **as a starter** come or per antipasto; **for starters** (*fig*) per cominciare **2** (*Aut, etc motor*) motorino d'avviamento; (*on machine*) pulsante *m* d'accensione **3** (*Sport: judge*) starter *m inv*; (: *competitor*) concorrente *m/f*; **he was a late starter** (*child*) ha cominciato tardi a leggere e a scrivere
starting handle N (*Brit*) manovella d'avviamento
starting point N punto di partenza
starting price N (*Horse Racing*) ultima quotazione
star·tle [ˈstɑːtl] VT far trasalire, spaventare
star·tling [ˈstɑːtlɪŋ] ADJ (*surprising*) sorprendente, sbalorditivo(-a); (*alarming*) impressionante
star turn N (*Theatre, also fig: person*) vedette *f inv*; (*act*) attrazione *f* principale
star·va·tion [stɑːˈveɪʃən] N inedia, fame *f*; **to die of starvation** morire d'inedia; **they died of starvation** sono morti d'inedia; **poverty and starvation breed terrorism** il terrorismo nasce da povertà e fame; **it might be fuel starvation** (*Tech*) potrebbe essere un problema di alimentazione del carburante
starve [stɑːv] VT far patire la fame a, affamare; **to starve sb to death** far morire qn di fame; **to starve o.s.** lasciarsi morire di fame; **to starve sb into submission** prendere qn per fame; **to be starved of affection** soffrire per mancanza di affetto ♦ VI (*lack food*) soffrire la fame; **to starve (to death)** morire di fame; **people are starving** la gente muore di fame; **I'm starving!** (*fam*) sto morendo di fame!
stash [stæʃ] VT (*fam*): **to stash sth away** nascondere qc
state [steɪt] N **1** (*condition*) stato, condizione *f*; **state of emergency** stato di emergenza; **state of mind** stato d'animo; **state of war** stato di guerra; **to be in a bad/good state** essere in cattivo/buono stato; **he's not in a (fit) state to do it** non è in condizioni di farlo; **he was in no state to drive** non era in condizioni di guidare; **to be in a state of shock** essere sotto shock; **he arrived home in a shocking state** è arrivato a casa ridotto proprio male **2** (*anxiety*) agitazione *f*; **to be in a real state** essere tutto agitato(-a); **now don't get into a state** non ti agitare **3** (*pomp*): **in state** in pompa; **to lie in state** essere esposto(-a) solennemente **4** (*Pol*): **the State** lo Stato; **it's an independent state** è uno stato indipendente ♦ VT (*gen*) dichiarare, affermare; (*time, place*) decidere, fissare; (*conditions*) indicare; (*case, problem, theory, facts*) esporre; **as stated above** come indicato sopra; **state your name and address** fornisca nome e indirizzo; **cheques must state the amount clearly** gli assegni debbono indicare chiaramente la somma; **he stated his intention to resign** ha dichiarato di essere intenzionato a dimettersi ♦ ADJ (*business*) di stato; (*control*) statale; (*security*) dello stato; **the State line** (*USA*) il confine (tra due stati); **to pay a state visit to a country** andare in visita ufficiale in un paese
state control N controllo statale
stat·ed [ˈsteɪtɪd] ADJ stabilito(-a), fissato(-a); **within stated limits** entro i limiti stabiliti; **within the stated period** entro il periodo di tempo stabilito
State Department N (*USA*): **the State Department** il Dipartimento di Stato, ≈ Ministero degli Esteri
state education N (*Brit*) istruzione *f* pubblica or statale

state·less [ˈsteɪtlɪs] ADJ apolide; **a stateless person** un(a) apolide
state·ly [ˈsteɪtlɪ] ADJ (*comp -ier, superl -iest*) maestoso(-a)
stately home N (*Brit*) residenza nobiliare (*d'interesse storico e artistico*)
state·ment [ˈsteɪtmənt] N (*gen*) dichiarazione *f*; (*of views, facts*) esposizione *f*; (*Law*) deposizione *f*; (*Fin*) rendiconto; **statement of account, bank statement** estratto conto; **official statement** comunicato ufficiale; **to make a statement** rilasciare una dichiarazione; (*Law*) fare una deposizione; **he made a statement to the police** ha fatto una dichiarazione alla polizia; **I found this statement vague and unclear** ho trovato vaga e poco chiara l'affermazione
state-owned [ˈsteɪtˈəʊnd] ADJ statale, pubblico(-a)
States [steɪts] NPL: **the States** (*USA*) gli Stati *mpl* Uniti
state school N (*Brit*) scuola statale
states·man [ˈsteɪtsmən] N (*pl -men*) statista *m*
states·man·ship [ˈsteɪtsmənʃɪp] N abilità *f inv* politica
stat·ic [ˈstætɪk] ADJ statico(-a); **static electricity** elettricità statica ♦ N **1** (*Radio, TV*) scariche *fpl* **2 statics** NSG (*Phys*) statica
sta·tion [ˈsteɪʃən] N **1** (*gen, also Rail*) stazione *f*; (*also:* **fire station**) caserma (dei pompieri); (*also:* **police station**) commissariato (di Pubblica Sicurezza), questura, caserma (dei Carabinieri); (*esp Mil: post*) base *f*; **action stations** posti *mpl* di combattimento **2** (*Radio*) stazione *f* **3** (*social position*) condizione *f* sociale, rango; **to have ideas above one's station** montarsi la testa ♦ VT (*Mil: troops, sentry*) stanziare; (*fig*) piazzare; **to be stationed in** (*Mil*) essere di stanza in; **to station o.s. by the door** piazzarsi sulla porta ♦ ADJ (*Rail: staff, bookstall*) della stazione
sta·tion·ary [ˈsteɪʃənərɪ] ADJ (*gen*) fermo(-a), immobile; (*vehicle*) in sosta; (*temperature, condition*) stazionario(-a); (*not movable*) fisso(-a); **to remain stationary** rimanere fermo(-a); **stationary point** (*Math*) punto di stazionarietà
sta·tion·er [ˈsteɪʃənə'] N cartolaio(-a); **stationer's shop** cartoleria
sta·tion·ery [ˈsteɪʃənərɪ] N articoli *mpl* di cancelleria; (*writing paper*) carta da lettere
station master N (*Rail*) capostazione *m*
station wagon N (*USA: Aut*) station-wagon *f*, familiare *f*
sta·tis·tic [stəˈtɪstɪk] N statistica; *see also* **statistics**
sta·tis·ti·cal [stəˈtɪstɪkəl] ADJ statistico(-a)
sta·tis·tics [stəˈtɪstɪks] NSG (*science*) statistica ♦ NPL (*numbers*) statistiche *fpl*; **statistics show that ...** la statistica dimostra che...; **official statistics** statistiche ufficiali
statue [ˈstætjuː] N statua
statu·esque [ˌstætjʊˈesk] ADJ statuario(-a)
statu·ette [ˌstætjʊˈet] N statuetta
stat·ure [ˈstætʃə'] N **1** (*build*) statura; **to be of short stature** essere basso(-a) or di statura bassa **2** (*fig*) importanza; **a woman of considerable intellectual stature** una donna di grande levatura
sta·tus [ˈsteɪtəs] N (*of person: legal, marital*) stato; (: *economic, official etc*) posizione *f*; (*of agreement etc*) validità; (*prestige*) prestigio; **social status** status *m inv*; **the status of children in society** la posizione dei bambini nella società; **men and women of wealth and status** uomini e donne benestanti e di una certa condizione sociale
status quo [-ˈkwəʊ] N: **the status quo** lo statu quo
status symbol N status symbol *m inv*
stat·ute [ˈstætjuːt] N (*law*) legge *f*, statuto
statute book N codice *m*
statu·tory [ˈstætjʊtərɪ] ADJ (*right, wage, control etc*) stabilito(-a) dalla legge; (*offence*) legalmente punibile; **statutory meeting** (*Comm*) assemblea ordinaria
staunch¹ [stɔːntʃ] ADJ (*comp -er, superl -est*) (*supporter, friend*) fedele, leale; (*believer, Christian*) convinto(-a)
staunch² [stɔːntʃ] VT (*flow*) arrestare; (*blood*) tamponare
stave [steɪv] N (*Mus*) = **staff 3**
▸ **stave in** VT + ADV (*pt, pp stove in*) sfondare
▸ **stave off** VT + ADV (*pt, pp staved off*) (*crisis, threat, illness*) evitare; (*attack*) respingere; (*temporarily*) allontanare
stay [steɪ] N **1** (*period of time*) soggiorno, permanenza; (*in hospital*) degenza; **a stay of ten days, a ten-day stay** un

soggiorno di dieci giorni; **my stay in Italy** il mio soggiorno in Italia **2** (*Law*): **stay of execution** sospensione *f* dell'esecuzione di una sentenza ♦ VI **1** (*remain in a place or situation*) rimanere, restare; (*spend some time*) fermarsi, soggiornare; (*reside, visit: in hotel*) alloggiare, stare; (: *with friends*) stare; **you stay right there** stai fermo dove sei; **stay here!** resta qui!; **to stay to dinner** rimanere a cena; **how long can you stay?** quanto ti fermi?; **to stay with friends** stare con degli amici; **she's staying with friends** sta presso amici; **where are you staying?** dove alloggi?; **to stay the night** passare la notte; **to stay overnight with friends** passare la notte a casa di amici; **camcorders are here to stay** le videocamere non sono un fenomeno temporaneo **2** (*continue, remain: with adj*) rimanere; **if it stays fine** se il tempo si mantiene bello; **to stay put** non muoversi ♦ VT **1** (*last out*): **to stay the course** (*also fig*) resistere fino alla fine **2** (*punishment*) sospendere; (*spread of disease, flow*) fermare; **to stay sb's hand** fermare la mano a qn

▸ **stay away** VI + ADV: **to stay away from** (*person*) stare lontano da; (*school, party etc*) non andare a; **to stay away for** (*period of time*) stare via per

▸ **stay behind** VI + ADV (*after school, work etc*) fermarsi, trattenersi; (*not to go*) non andare

▸ **stay down** VI + ADV (*downstairs*) rimanere giù, rimanere di sotto; (*crouching, lying*) rimanere a terra; (*under water*) rimanere sott'acqua

▸ **stay in** VI + ADV (*person*) rimanere a casa, non uscire; (*screw*) tenere

▸ **stay on** VI + ADV rimanere, restare; **he stayed on as manager** è rimasto in carica come direttore

▸ **stay out** VI + ADV (*overnight, outside*) rimanere fuori, restare fuori; (*strikers*) continuare lo sciopero; **to stay out late** stare fuori fino a tardi; **to stay out of trouble** tenersi fuori dai pasticci; **you stay out of this!** non ti immischiare!

▸ **stay over** VI + ADV fermarsi

▸ **stay up** VI + ADV (*trousers, tent*) tenersi su; (*person: wait up*) rimanere alzato(-a) *or* in piedi; **we stayed up till midnight** siamo rimasti alzati fino a mezzanotte; **to stay up late** fare tardi

stay·ing pow·er [ˈsteɪɪŋˌpaʊəʳ] N capacità di resistenza

STD [ˌɛstiːˈdiː] N ABBR (= *sexually transmitted disease*) malattia venerea

stead [stɛd] N: **to stand sb in good stead** essere utile a qn; **in sb's stead** (*Brit*) al posto di qn

stead·fast [ˈstɛdfəst] ADJ costante, risoluto(-a)

steadi·ly [ˈstɛdɪlɪ] ADV (*walk*) con passo sicuro; (*speak*) con tono risoluto; (*improve, decrease*) gradualmente; (*rain*) di continuo; **it is getting steadily worse** continua a peggiorare; **to gaze steadily at sb** guardare qn senza distogliere lo sguardo; **to work steadily** lavorare senza interruzione *or* costantemente; **to increase steadily** essere in costante crescita; **keep breathing steadily** continua a respirare normalmente

steady [ˈstɛdɪ] ADJ (*comp* -**ier**, *superl* -**iest**) (*not wobbling: gen*) fermo(-a), stabile; (: *voice, gaze*) sicuro(-a); (: *nerves*) saldo(-a); (*not fluctuating: prices, sales*) stabile; (*regular: temperature, demand, improvement, progress*) costante; (*reliable: person, character*) serio(-a); (*boyfriend, girlfriend*) fisso(-a); **a steady job** un lavoro *or* impiego fisso; **a steady income** un reddito regolare; **a steady hand** una mano ferma; **you need a steady hand for this job** ci vuole mano ferma per fare questo lavoro; **we were going at a steady 70 km/h** andavamo a una velocità costante di 70 km l'ora ♦ ADV: **steady!** calma!, piano!; **they are going steady** (*old, fam*) fanno coppia fissa, stanno insieme ♦ VT stabilizzare; (*wobbling object*) tenere fermo(-a); (*nervous person*) calmare; **to steady o.s.** reggersi, tenersi in equilibrio; **I smoke to steady my nerves** fumo per calmarmi; **to have a steadying influence on sb** rendere più calmo(-a) qn

steak [steɪk] N (*beef*) carne *f* di manzo; (*piece of beef, pork etc*) bistecca; **a cod steak** un trancio di merluzzo; **steak and kidney pie** pasticcio di carne e rognoni di manzo in pasta sfoglia

steak·house [ˈsteɪkˌhaʊs] N ristorante specializzato in bistecche

steal [stiːl] (*pt* stole, *pp* stolen) VT (*also fig*) rubare; **to steal money/an idea from sb** rubare denaro/un'idea a qn; **to steal a glance at sb** dare un'occhiata furtiva a qn; **to steal a march on sb** battere qn sul tempo; **thieves broke in and**

stole the video sono entrati i ladri e hanno rubato il videoregistratore; **my car was stolen last week** mi hanno rubato la macchina la settimana scorsa ♦ VI **1** (*thieve*) rubare **2** (*move quietly*): **to steal in/out** *etc* entrare/uscire *etc* furtivamente; **to steal up on sb** avvicinarsi furtivamente a qn

▸ **steal away, steal off** VI + ADV svignarsela, andarsene alla chetichella

stealth [stɛlθ] N: **by stealth** furtivamente, di nascosto

stealthy [ˈstɛlθɪ] ADJ (*comp* -**ier**, *superl* -**iest**) furtivo(-a)

steam [stiːm] N vapore *m*; **to get up steam** (*train, ship*) aumentare la pressione; (*worker, project*) mettersi in moto; **to let off steam** (*fig*) sfogarsi; **under one's own steam** (*fig*) da solo, con i propri mezzi; **to run out of steam** (*fig: person*) non farcela più; (: *project, movement*) perdere vigore; **full steam ahead!** (*Naut*) avanti tutta!; **to go full steam ahead** (*fig*) andare a tutto vapore ♦ VT (*Culin*) cuocere a vapore; **to steam open an envelope** aprire una busta con il vapore ♦ VI **1** (*give off steam: liquid, food etc*) fumare; **a steaming saucepan** una pentola fumante **2** **the ship steamed into harbour** la nave entrò nel porto; **to steam along** filare; **to steam away** (*ship*) partire; (*fig: person, car*) partire a tutto gas

▸ **steam up** VI + ADV (*window*) appannarsi; **to get steamed up about sth** (*fig*) andare in bestia per qc

steam engine N (*Rail*) locomotiva a vapore

steam·er [ˈstiːməʳ] N (*steamship*) nave *f* a vapore, piroscafo; (*Culin*) pentola per cottura a vapore

steam iron N ferro a vapore

steam·roller [ˈstiːmˌrəʊləʳ] N rullo compressore

steam·ship [ˈstiːmˌʃɪp] N piroscafo, nave *f* a vapore

steamy [ˈstiːmɪ] ADJ (*comp* -**ier**, *superl* -**iest**) (*room*) pieno(-a) di vapore; (*window*) appannato(-a); (*atmosphere, heat*) umido(-a); (*fam: book, film, play*) erotico(-a)

steed [stiːd] N (*liter*) corsiero, destriero

steel [stiːl] N acciaio; **nerves of steel** nervi *mpl* di acciaio ♦ VT: **to steel one's heart against** corazzarsi contro; **to steel o.s. for sth/to do sth** armarsi di coraggio per affrontare qc/per fare qc ♦ ADJ (*knife, tool*) d'acciaio

steel band N banda di strumenti metallici a percussione (*tipica delle Antille*)

steel industry N industria dell'acciaio

steel mill N acciaieria

steel·works [ˈstiːlˌwɜːks] N *pl inv* acciaieria

steely [ˈstiːlɪ] ADJ (*comp* -**ier**, *superl* -**iest**) (*determination*) inflessibile; (*gaze*) duro(-a); (*eyes*) freddo(-a) come l'acciaio; **steely grey** color piombo *inv*

steep¹ [stiːp] ADJ (*comp* -**er**, *superl* -**est**) (*gen*) ripido(-a); (*cliff*) scosceso(-a); (*increase, drop*) drastico(-a); (*fig: fam: price*) alto(-a); (: *demands*) eccessivo(-a); (: *story*) inverosimile; **it's a bit steep!** (*fig: fam*) è un po' troppo!

steep² [stiːp] VT (*washing*): **to steep (in)** mettere a bagno (in); (*Culin*) lasciare in infusione; **a town steeped in history** (*fig*) una città impregnata di storia; **steeped in prejudice** pieno(-a) di pregiudizi

stee·ple [ˈstiːpl] N campanile *m*

steeple·chase [ˈstiːpltˌʃeɪs] N corsa ad ostacoli, steeplechase *m inv*

steeple·jack [ˈstiːplˌdʒæk] N chi ripara campanili e ciminiere

steer [stɪəʳ] VT **1** (*car*) guidare; (*fig: conversation, person*) dirigere, condurre; (*ship, boat*) dirigere; **my father let me steer the car** mio padre mi ha lasciato guidare la macchina; **he steered us into the nearest seats** ci ha guidati fino ai posti più vicini **2** (*handle controls of: ship*) governare; (: *boat*) portare ♦ VI (*in car*) sterzare; (*on ship*) dirigere; **to steer towards** *or* **for sth** dirigersi verso qc; **to steer clear of sb/sth** (*fig*) tenersi alla larga da qn/qc

steer·ing [ˈstɪərɪŋ] N (*Aut*) sterzo; **power steering** servosterzo

steering column N (*Aut*) piantone *m* dello sterzo

steering committee N (*USA*) comitato direttivo

steering wheel N (*Aut*) volante *m*, sterzo

stem [stɛm] N (*of plant*) gambo, stelo; (*of fruit, leaf*) gambo, picciolo; (*of glass*) stelo; (*of word*) radice *f* ♦ VT (*check, stop*) frenare, arrestare; (*river*) arginare, contenere; (*disease*) contenere; **to stem the tide of events** arrestare il corso degli eventi

▸ **stem from** VI + ADV derivare da

❑ **stem** is not translated by the Italian word *stemma*

stem cell N (*Bio*) cellula staminale
stench [stentʃ] N puzzo, fetore *m*
sten·cil [ˈstɛnsl] N (*for lettering etc*) stampino; (*in typing*) matrice *f* ♦ VT stampinare
ste·nog·ra·pher [stɛˈnɒɡrəfəʳ] N (*USA*) stenografo(-a)
ste·nog·ra·phy [stɛˈnɒɡrəfɪ] N (*USA*) stenografia
step [stɛp] N 1 (*movement*) passo; (*fig: move*) mossa, passo; **to take a step back/forward** fare un passo indietro/avanti; **he took a step forward** fece un passo in avanti; **it's a great step forward** (*fig*) è un gran passo avanti; **a step in the right direction** (*fig*) un passo nella direzione giusta; **step by step** un passo dietro l'altro; (*fig*) poco a poco; **to be in/out of step with** (*also fig*) stare/non stare al passo con; **to keep in step (with)** (*also fig*) mantenersi al passo (con); **to watch one's step** guardare dove si mettono i piedi; (*fig*) fare attenzione 2 (*measure*) misura; **to take steps to solve a problem** prendere le misure necessarie per risolvere un problema 3 (*stair*) gradino, scalino; (*of ladder*) piolo; (*of vehicle*) predellino; (*fig: in scale*) gradino; **steps** NPL (*stairs*) scala *fsg*; (*outside building*) scalinata *fsg*; **folding steps, pair of steps** scala a libretto; **a step up in his career** (*fig*) un passo avanti nella carriera; **she tripped over the step** ha inciampato sul gradino ♦ VI fare un passo, andare; **to step aside** farsi da parte, scansarsi; **to step inside** entrare; **she stepped out of the car** uscì dalla macchina; **to step back** tirarsi indietro; **step this way, please!** da questa parte, per favore!; **to step over sth** scavalcare qc; **to step off the pavement** scendere dal marciapiede; **to step on sth** calpestare qc; **step on it!** (*fam*) muoviti!; **to step out of line** (*fig*) sgarrare
  ▸ **step down** VI + ADV scendere; (*fig: resign*): **to step down (in favour of sb)** dimettersi *or* dare le dimissioni (a favore di qn)
  ▸ **step forward** VI + ADV fare un passo avanti; (*fig: volunteer*) farsi avanti; **I tried to step forward** ho cercato di fare un passo in avanti
  ▸ **step in** VI + ADV entrare, fare il proprio ingresso; (*fig*) intromettersi
  ▸ **step up** VT + ADV (*production*) aumentare; (*efforts, campaign*) intensificare; **to step up work on sth** accelerare i lavori per qc
step aerobics NPL step *msg*
step·brother [ˈstɛp,brʌðəʳ] N fratellastro
step·child [ˈstɛp,tʃaɪld] N (*pl -children*) figliastro(-a)
step·daughter [ˈstɛp,dɔːtəʳ] N figliastra
step·father [ˈstɛp,fɑːðəʳ] N patrigno
step·ladder [ˈstɛp,lædəʳ] N scala a libretto
step·mother [ˈstɛp,mʌðəʳ] N matrigna
step·ping stone [ˈstɛpɪŋ,stəʊn] N pietra di un guado; (*fig*): **stepping stone (to)** trampolino di lancio (verso)
step·sister [ˈstɛp,sɪstəʳ] N sorellastra
step·son [ˈstɛp,sʌn] N figliastro
ste·reo [ˈstɛrɪəʊ] N (*hi-fi equipment*) stereo *m inv*; (*sound*) stereofonia; **in stereo** in stereofonia ♦ ADJ stereofonico(-a), stereo *inv*
ste·reo·type [ˈstɛrɪə,taɪp] N stereotipo
ster·ile [ˈstɛraɪl] ADJ sterile
ste·ril·ity [stɛˈrɪlɪtɪ] N sterilità
steri·li·za·tion [,stɛrɪlaɪˈzeɪʃən] N sterilizzazione *f*
steri·lize [ˈstɛrɪlaɪz] VT sterilizzare
ster·ling [ˈstɜːlɪŋ] N (*Fin*) sterlina ♦ ADJ 1 (*silver*) al titolo di 925/1000, di buona lega; (*Econ*): **pound sterling** lira sterlina 2 (*fig*): **of sterling qualities** di gran pregio; **he is of sterling character** è una persona fidata
sterling area N (*Fin*) area della sterlina
stern¹ [stɜːn] ADJ (*comp -er, superl -est*) (*discipline*) rigido(-a); (*person, warning*) severo(-a); **I thought he was made of sterner stuff** pensavo fosse più forte
stern² [stɜːn] N (*Naut*) poppa
ster·num [ˈstɜːnəm] N (*Anat*) sterno
ster·oid [ˈstɛrɔɪd] N steroide *m*
stetho·scope [ˈstɛθəˌskəʊp] N stetoscopio
ste·vedore [ˈstiːvɪˌdɔːʳ] N scaricatore *m* di porto
stew [stjuː] N 1 (*Culin*) stufato 2 (*fig*): **to be in a stew (about sth)** essere agitato(-a) (per qc); **to get into a stew (about sth)** mettersi in agitazione (per qc) ♦ VT (*meat*) stufare,

cuocere in umido; **stewed fruit** frutta cotta ♦ VI (*tea*) diventare troppo forte; **to let sb stew in his own juice** (*fig*) lasciar cuocere qn nel suo brodo
stew·ard [ˈstjuːəd] N (*Aer, Naut, Rail*) steward *m inv*; (*on estate*) fattore *m*; (*in club*) dispensiere *m*; (*butler*) maggiordomo; (*shop steward*) rappresentante *m*/*f* sindacale
stew·ard·ess [ˈstjuːədɛs] N (*Aer, Naut*) hostess *f inv*
stew·ard·ship [ˈstjuːəd,ʃɪp] N (*frm: supervision, care*) amministrazione *f*
stew·ing steak [ˈstjuːɪŋ,steɪk], (*USA*) **stew meat** N carne *f* di manzo per stufato
stg ABBR = **sterling**
STI [,ɛstiːˈaɪ] N ABBR (= *sexually transmitted infection*) malattia venerea
stick [stɪk] (*pt, pp* **stuck**) N (*gen*) bastone *m*; (*twig*) ramoscello; (*support for plants*) asticella, bastoncino; (*of celery, rhubarb*) gambo; (*of shaving soap*) stick *m inv*; (*of dynamite*) candelotto; **dried sticks** rametti secchi; **he walks with a stick** cammina con il bastone; **a stick of celery** un gambo di sedano; **to wave the big stick** (*fig*) fare il (la) prepotente; **to get hold of the wrong end of the stick** (*fig*) fraintendere; **a few sticks of furniture** pochi mobili *mpl* sgangherati; **to live in the sticks** (*fam*) abitare a casa del diavolo; **to give sb stick** (*fig*) fare un cicchetto a qn ♦ VT 1 (*with glue etc*) incollare; **to stick two things together** incollare due cose; **he was sticking stamps into his album** attaccava i francobolli nell'album; **she stuck the envelope down** incollò la busta 2 (*thrust, poke: hand etc*) ficcare; (*sth pointed: pin, needle*) conficcare, piantare; **he stuck his hand in his pocket** ficcò una mano in tasca; **to stick a knife into sb** accoltellare qn 3 (*fam: place, put*) mettere; **stick it in your case** mettilo *or* ficcalo nella borsa; **he picked up the papers and stuck them in his briefcase** ha raccolto i documenti e li ha ficcati nella valigetta 4 (*fam: tolerate*) sopportare; **I can't stick it any longer** non ne posso più 5 **to be stuck** (*door, window*) essere bloccato(-a); (*knife, screw*) essere incastrato(-a); **it's stuck in my throat** mi si è conficcato in gola; **to be stuck with sb/sth** doversi sorbire qn/qc, dover sopportare qn/qc; **I'm stuck at home all day** sono bloccato a casa tutto il giorno ♦ VI (*glue, sticky object etc*) attaccarsi, appiccicarsi; (*food, sauce*) attaccarsi; (*get jammed: door, lift*) bloccarsi; (*: lock*) incepparsi; (*: in mud etc*) impantanarsi; (*: sth pointed*) conficcarsi; **it stuck to the wall** è rimasto attaccato al muro; **the rice stuck to the pan** il riso s'è attaccato; **the nickname seems to have stuck** (*fam*) sembra che il soprannome gli (*or le etc*) sia rimasto; **to stick to sb's wheel** (*Cycling*) incollarsi alla ruota di qn; **it stuck in my mind** mi è rimasto in mente; **just stick at it and I'm sure you'll manage it** non mollare e sono sicuro che riuscirai a farlo
  ▸ **stick around** VI + ADV (*fam*) restare, rimanere, fermarsi
  ▸ **stick by** VI + PREP (*stand by*) stare vicino(-a); **we'll all stick by you** (*support you*) siamo tutti con te; **she stuck by him through it all** è sempre rimasta al suo fianco
  ▸ **stick in** VT + ADV (*knife*) affondare; (*pin, needle etc*) appuntare; (*photo in album etc*) incollare, attaccare; **to get stuck in** (*fam*) impegnarsi seriamente; **I stuck in a few quotations from Shakespeare** ho inserito qua e là delle citazioni di Shakespeare
  ▸ **stick on** VT + ADV (*stamp, label*) incollare
  ▸ **stick out** VI + ADV 1 (*protrude*) sporgere; (*be noticeable*) spiccare; **his teeth stick out** ha i denti sporgenti; **his ears stick out** ha le orecchie a sventola; **to stick out like a sore thumb** essere un pugno nell'occhio; **it sticks out because of the colour** spicca a causa del colore; **it was sticking out of the back of the car** sporgeva dal retro della macchina 2 **to stick out for sth** battersi per qc ♦ VT + ADV (*tongue*) tirar fuori; (*arm*) allungare; (*head*) sporgere; **to stick it out** (*fam*) tener duro; **the little girl stuck out her tongue** la bambina tirò fuori la lingua
  ▸ **stick to** VI + PREP (*one's word, promise*) mantenere; (*principles*) tener fede a; (*text*) rimanere fedele a; (*facts*) attenersi a; **decide what you're going to do, then stick to it** decidi il da farsi e poi fallo
  ▸ **stick together** VI + ADV (*people*) restare uniti; (*things*) attaccarsi

▸ **stick up** VI + ADV (*protrude*) rimanere diritto(-a); **to stick up out of the water** uscire dall'acqua ♦ VT + ADV **1** (*fam: raise: hand*) alzare; (: *rob*) rapinare; **stick 'em up!** mani in alto! **2** (*notice*) affiggere

▸ **stick up for** VI + ADV + PREP difendere; **to stick up for sb/ sth** (*fam*) battersi per qn/qc

▸ **stick with** VI + PREP (*carry on with*) attenersi a; **I'll stick with the job for another few months** continuerò a fare questo lavoro per qualche altro mese

stick·er [ˈstɪkəʳ] N (*label*) etichetta; (*on car etc*) adesivo

stick·ing plas·ter [ˈstɪkɪŋˌplɑːstəʳ] N cerotto adesivo

stick·ing point [ˈstɪkɪŋˌpɔɪnt] N (*fig*) punto di stallo, impasse *f inv*

stick insect N insetto stecco

stickle·back [ˈstɪklˌbæk] N spinarello

stick·ler [ˈstɪkləʳ] N: **to be a stickler for** essere esigente in fatto di, essere pignolo(-a) su

stick·on [ˈstɪkˌɒn] ADJ (*label*) adesivo(-a)

stick shift N (*USA: Aut*) cambio manuale

stick-up [ˈstɪkˌʌp] N (*fam*) rapina a mano armata

sticky [ˈstɪkɪ] ADJ (*comp* -**ier**, *superl* -**iest**) appiccicoso(-a), vischioso(-a); (*label*) adesivo(-a); (*fam: situation*) difficile, imbarazzante; **a sticky label** un'etichetta adesiva; **my hands are sticky** ho le mani appiccicose; **a sticky situation** una situazione difficile; **he was a bit sticky about lending me the money** ha fatto un sacco di storie per prestarmi i soldi; **to come to a sticky end** (*fam*) fare una brutta fine; **sticky tape** nastro adesivo

stiff [stɪf] ADJ (*comp* -**er**, *superl* -**est**) **1** (*gen*) rigido(-a); (*starched: shirt*) inamidato(-a); (*brush*) duro(-a); (*dough*) compatto(-a), denso(-a); (*arm, joint*) rigido(-a), indolenzito(-a); (*muscle*) legato(-a); **stiff material** stoffa rigida; **to have a stiff neck/back** avere il torcicollo/mal di schiena; **to be** or **feel stiff** essere or sentirsi indolenzito(-a); **the door's stiff** la porta si apre (or si chiude) con difficoltà; **as stiff as a ramrod** or **a poker** dritto(-a) come un palo; **to keep a stiff upper lip** (*Brit fig*) restare impassibile **2** (*fig: climb, examination, test*) arduo(-a), difficile; (: *competition, breeze, drink*) forte; (: *resistance*) tenace; (: *punishment*) severo(-a); (: *price, fine*) salato(-a); (: *manner, smile, reception*) freddo(-a); **that's a bit stiff!** (*fam*) è un po' troppo!; **it was a stiff price to pay** (*fig*) l'hanno pagata cara; **bored stiff** annoiato(-a) a morte; **frozen stiff** congelato(-a); **scared stiff** morto(-a) di paura

stiff·en [ˈstɪfn] VT (*legs etc*) irrigidire; (*with starch*) inamidare; (*fig: resistance etc*) rafforzare ♦ VI (*person, manner*) irrigidirsi; (*determination*) rafforzarsi; (*morale*) risollevarsi

stiff·ness [ˈstɪfnɪs] N (*gen*) rigidità; (*of punishment*) durezza; (*of climb*) difficoltà; (*of back etc*) indolenzimento; (*of manner*) freddezza; (*of resolution*) fermezza

sti·fle [ˈstaɪfl] VT (*yawn, sob, anger*) soffocare; (*desire, smile*) reprimere; (*revolt, opposition*) stroncare ♦ VI soffocare

sti·fling [ˈstaɪflɪŋ] ADJ (*heat*) soffocante; **it's stifling in here** qui non si respira

stig·ma [ˈstɪɡmə] N stigma *m*; **the stigma attached to illegitimacy** il marchio dell'essere figli illegittimi

stig·ma·ta [ˈstɪɡmɑːtə] NPL (*Rel*) stigmate *fpl*

stile [staɪl] N scaletta (*per scavalcare una siepe*)

sti·let·to [stɪˈletəʊ] N (*knife*) stiletto; (*shoe*) scarpa con tacco a spillo

still¹ [stɪl] ADV **1** (*up to now*) ancora; **she's still in bed** è ancora a letto; **it's past midnight and he still hasn't arrived** è mezzanotte passata e non è ancora arrivato; **I still haven't finished!** non ho ancora finito!; **she still doesn't believe me** ancora non mi crede **2** (*with comp: even*) ancora; **still better, better still** meglio ancora **3** (*nevertheless*) tuttavia, nonostante ciò; **still, it was worth it** però, ne valeva la pena; **she's still your sister** è pur sempre tua sorella; **still, it's the thought that counts** in fondo è il pensiero che conta

still² [stɪl] ADJ (*comp* -**er**, *superl* -**est**) (*motionless*) fermo(-a), immobile; (*quiet*) tranquillo(-a), silenzioso(-a); (*orange juice*) non gassato(-a); **still mineral water** acqua minerale naturale; **still waters run deep** (*Proverb*) le acque chete rovinano i ponti ♦ N **1 in the still of the night** nel silenzio della notte **2** (*Cine*) fotogramma *m* ♦ ADV: **to stand still, sit still** stare fermo(-a); **to hold still** tenersi fermo(-a); **keep still!** stai fermo!

still³ [stɪl] N (*Chem*) alambicco, distillatore

still-born [ˈstɪlˌbɔːn] ADJ nato(-a) morto(-a)

still life N (*Art*) natura morta

stilt [stɪlt] N trampolo; (*pile*) palo; **to walk on stilts** camminare sui trampoli

stilt·ed [ˈstɪltɪd] ADJ (*style*) artificioso(-a); (*way of speaking*) formale; (*translation*) poco naturale

stimu·lant [ˈstɪmjʊlənt] N stimolante *m*

stimu·late [ˈstɪmjʊleɪt] VT stimolare; **to stimulate sb to do sth** stimolare qn a fare qc

stimu·lat·ing [ˈstɪmjʊleɪtɪŋ] ADJ stimolante

stimu·la·tion [ˌstɪmjʊˈleɪʃən] N stimolazione *f*

stimu·lus [ˈstɪmjʊləs] N (*pl* **stimuli** [ˈstɪmjʊlaɪ]) stimolo; **it gave trade a new stimulus** ha dato un nuovo impulso al commercio; **under the stimulus of** stimolato(-a) da

sting [stɪŋ] (*pt, pp* **stung**) N (*Zool*) pungiglione *m*; (*Bot*) pelo urticante; (*pain, mark*) puntura; (*of iodine, antiseptic*) bruciore *m*; **a bee sting** una puntura d'ape; **to take the sting out of sth** (*fig*) rendere qc meno pungente; **but there was a sting in the tail** (*fig*) ma c'era una spiacevole sorpresa ♦ VT **1** (*subj: insect, nettle*) pungere; (: *jellyfish*) pizzicare; (: *iodine*) bruciare; (: *cold wind*) tagliare; (*fig: remark, criticism*) pungere sul vivo; **he was stung into action** fu spronato all'azione; **she was stung by remorse** fu presa dal rimorso; **I got stung by a wasp** mi ha punto una vespa **2** (*fam*): **they stung me for £40** mi hanno scucito 40 sterline ♦ VI (*iodine etc*) bruciare; (*remark, criticism*) ferire; **my eyes are stinging** mi bruciano gli occhi

stin·gy [ˈstɪndʒɪ] ADJ (*comp* -**ier**, *superl* -**iest**) (*pej: person*) avaro(-a), tirchio(-a), spilorcio(-a), taccagno(-a); (: *gift etc*) misero(-a); **to be stingy with** (: *one's praise, money*) essere avaro(-a) di; (: *food*) razionare

stink [stɪŋk] (*pt* **stank**, *pp* **stunk**) N puzza, fetore *m*; **to raise** or **kick up a stink** (*fig: fam*) scatenare un putiferio, piantare un casino ♦ VI: **to stink (of)** puzzare (di); **the room stank of cigarettes** la stanza puzzava di fumo; **it stinks in here** che puzza c'è qui; **it stinks to high heaven** puzza tremendamente; **the whole thing stinks** (*fig: fam*) tutta la faccenda puzza ♦ VT (*also*: **stink out**: *room*) appestare

stink·er [ˈstɪŋkəʳ] N (*fam: person*) carogna, fetente *m/f*; **this problem is a stinker** questo problema è una bella rogna

stink·ing [ˈstɪŋkɪŋ] ADJ: **a stinking cold** un raffreddore tremendo; **what stinking weather!** che tempo da cani! ♦ ADV: **stinking rich** ricco(-a) sfondato(-a)

stint [stɪnt] N: **to do one's stint (at sth)** fare la propria parte (di qc); **I do a stint in the pool every day** faccio una nuotata in piscina ogni giorno; **to do a stint at the wheel** (*Aut*) fare il proprio turno al volante ♦ VT: **he did not stint his praises** non è stato avaro di complimenti; **don't stint yourself!** (*iro*) non farti mancare niente!

sti·pend [ˈstaɪpend] N congrua

sti·pen·di·ary [staɪˈpendɪərɪ] ADJ: **stipendiary magistrate** magistrato stipendiato

stipu·late [ˈstɪpjʊleɪt] VT: **to stipulate (that)** stabilire (che)
❑ **stipulate** is not translated by the Italian word *stipulare*

stipu·la·tion [ˌstɪpjʊˈleɪʃən] N stipulazione *f*; **on the stipulation that** a condizione che + *sub*

stir [stɜːʳ] N **1 to give sth a stir** mescolare qc **2** (*fig*) agitazione *f*, scalpore *m*; **to cause a stir** fare scalpore ♦ VT **1** (*liquid etc*) mescolare; (*fire*) attizzare; **stir the mixture well** mescolare bene l'impasto **2** (*move*) muovere, agitare; **she didn't stir a finger** non ha mosso un dito; **the breeze stirred the leaves** la brezza muoveva le foglie **3** (*fig: emotions, interest*) risvegliare; (: *person*) commuovere **2** (: *imagination, curiosity*) eccitare, stimolare; **to stir sb to do sth** incitare qn a fare qc; **come on, stir yourself!** forza, muoviti! ♦ VI (*move*) muoversi; **he never stirred from the spot** non si è mosso

▸ **stir in** VT + PREP aggiungere mescolando

▸ **stir up** VT + ADV (*memories*) risvegliare; (*hatred, revolt*) fomentare; (*trouble*) provocare; **he's always trying to stir things up** cerca sempre di creare problemi

stir-fry [ˈstɜːfraɪ] VT saltare in padella ♦ N pietanza al salto

stir·ring [ˈstɜːrɪŋ] ADJ (*exciting*) entusiasmante; (*moving*) commovente

stir·rup ['stɪrəp] N staffa

stitch [stɪtʃ] N (*Sewing*) punto; (*Med*) punto (di sutura); (*Knitting*) maglia, punto; (*pain in side*) fitta (al fianco); **to put a few stitches in sth** mettere due punti a qc; **a stitch in time saves nine** (*Proverb*) un punto in tempo ne salva cento; **to put stitches in a wound** cucire una ferita; **I had five stitches** mi hanno messo cinque punti; **she hadn't a stitch on** era completamente nuda; **we were in stitches** (*fam*) ridevamo a crepapelle ♦ VT (*Sewing*) cucire; (*Med*) suturare, cucire; **to stitch up a hem/wound** cucire un orlo/una ferita
▸ **stitch down** VT + ADV cucire
▸ **stitch on** VT + ADV (*button etc*) attaccare; (*button that's come off*) riattaccare

stoat [stəʊt] N ermellino

stock¹ [stɒk] N 1 (*supply, store*) provvista, scorta; (*in bank: of money*) riserva; (*Comm*) stock *m inv*; **out of stock** esaurito(-a); **I'm sorry, they're both out of stock** mi dispiace, sono esauriti tutt'e due; **in stock** disponibile; **is it in stock?** è disponibile?; **to have sth in stock** avere qc in magazzino, avere disponibilità di qc; **this is the last one in stock** sì, abbiamo la sua taglia; **to take stock** (*Comm*) fare l'inventario; **to take stock (of the situation)** fare il punto della situazione; **to lay in a stock of** fare una scorta di; **a small stock of medicines** una piccola scorta di medicine 2 (*Agr: also: livestock*) bestiame *m* 3 (*Culin*) brodo; **chicken stock** brodo di pollo 4 (*Rail: also: rolling stock*) materiale *m* rotabile 5 (*Fin: company's capital*) capitale *m* azionario; (: *investor's shares*) titoli *mpl*, azioni *fpl*; **stocks and shares** valori *mpl* di borsa; **government stock** titoli di Stato 6 (*descent, origin*) stirpe *f* 7 **to be on the stocks** (*ship*) essere in cantiere; (*fig: piece of work*) essere in lavorazione; **the stocks** NPL (*History: for punishment*) la gogna ♦ VT (*Comm: goods*) tenere, avere, vendere; (*supply: shop, library, freezer, cupboard*) rifornire; (: *lake, river*) ripopolare; (: *farm*) fornire di bestiame; (: *shelves*) riempire; **a well-stocked shop/library** un negozio/una biblioteca ben fornito(-a); **do you stock camping stoves?** vendete fornellini da campeggio? ♦ ADJ (*Comm: size*) standard *inv*; (*fig: response, arguments, excuse*) solito(-a), consueto(-a); (: *greeting*) usuale
▸ **stock up** VI + ADV: **to stock up (on)** rifornirsi (di), fare provvista (di); **I must stock up on candles** devo fare provvista di candele

stock² [stɒk] N (*Bot*) violacciocca

stock·ade [stɒˈkeɪd] N palizzata

stock·broker ['stɒkˌbrəʊkəʳ] N agente *m* di cambio

stock control N gestione *f* magazzino

stock cube N (*Brit: Culin*) dado (da brodo)

stock exchange N (*Fin*) borsa valori

stock·holder ['stɒkˌhəʊldəʳ] N (*Fin*) azionista *m/f*

Stock·holm ['stɒkhəʊm] N Stoccolma

stock·ing ['stɒkɪŋ] N calza ♦ ADJ: **in one's stocking(ed) feet** senza scarpe

stock-in-trade [ˌstɒkɪnˈtreɪd] N (*goods*) merce *f* a magazzino; (*tools etc*) strumenti *mpl* di lavoro; (*fig*) ferri *mpl* del mestiere; **it's his stock-in-trade** è la sua specialità

stock·ist ['stɒkɪst] N (*Brit*) fornitore *m*

stock market N (*Brit: Fin*) mercato azionario

stock phrase N frase *f* fatta, cliché *m inv*

stock·pile ['stɒkpaɪl] N riserva, scorta ♦ VT accumulare riserve di

stock·room ['stɒkrʊm] N magazzino

stock·taking ['stɒkteɪkɪŋ] N (*Brit: Comm*) inventario

stocky ['stɒkɪ] ADJ (*comp* **-ier**, *superl* **-iest**) tarchiato(-a), tozzo(-a)

stodgy ['stɒdʒɪ] ADJ (*comp* **-ier**, *superl* **-iest**) (*food, book*) pesante, indigesto(-a); (*person*) pesante

sto·ic ['stəʊɪk] N stoico(-a)

stoi·cal ['stəʊɪkəl] ADJ stoico(-a)

stoke [stəʊk] VT (*also: stoke up*) (*fire*) attizzare; (*furnace*) alimentare

stok·er ['stəʊkəʳ] N fuochista *m*

stole¹ [stəʊl] N stola

stole² [stəʊl] PT *of* **steal**

stol·en ['stəʊlən] PP *of* **steal**

stol·id ['stɒlɪd] ADJ flemmatico(-a)

stom·ach ['stʌmək] N (*gen*) stomaco; (*abdomen*) ventre *m*; **it turns my stomach** mi rivolta lo stomaco; **they have no stomach for a fight** (*fig*) non hanno il fegato di battersi; **lie down on your stomach** stenditi sulla pancia ♦ VT (*fig: fam*) sopportare, digerire

stomach ache N mal *m* di stomaco; **to have (a) stomach ache** avere mal di stomaco

stomach pump N lavanda gastrica

stomach ulcer N ulcera gastrica

stomp [stɒmp] VI: **to stomp in/out** *etc* entrare/uscire *etc* con passo pesante

stone [stəʊn] N 1 (*material*) pietra; (*single pebble, rock*) sasso, ciottolo; (*also: gemstone*) pietra preziosa, gemma; (*of fruit*) nocciolo; (*Med*) calcolo; (*also: gravestone*) lastra tombale, lapide *f*; **to turn to stone** (*vt*) pietrificare; (*vi*) rimanere pietrificato(-a); **within a stone's throw of the station** a due passi dalla stazione, ad un tiro di schioppo dalla stazione; **to leave no stone unturned** non lasciare nulla d'intentato; **a peach stone** un nocciolo di pesca 2 (*Brit: weight: pl gen inv*) ≈ 6,348 kg ♦ ADJ (*wall*) di pietra; **a stone wall** un muro di pietra ♦ VT 1 (*person*) scagliare pietre contro; **to stone sb to death** lapidare qn 2 (*fruit*) snocciolare

Stone Age N: **the Stone Age** l'età della pietra

stone-cold ['stəʊn'kəʊld] ADJ ghiacciato(-a) ♦ ADV: **stone-cold sober** perfettamente sobrio(-a)

stoned [stəʊnd] ADJ (*fam: drunk, on drugs*) fatto(-a)

stone-deaf [ˌstəʊn'def] ADJ sordo(-a) come una campana

stone·mason ['stəʊnˌmeɪsn] N scalpellino

stone·wall [ˌstəʊn'wɔːl] VI (*fig*) fare ostruzionismo ♦ VT ostacolare

stone·work ['stəʊnwɜːk] N lavoro in muratura

stony ['stəʊnɪ] ADJ (*comp* **-ier**, *superl* **-iest**) (*ground*) sassoso(-a); (*beach*) pieno(-a) di ciottoli; (*fig: glance, silence*) freddo(-a); **a stony heart** un cuore di pietra

stood [stʊd] PT, PP *of* **stand**

stooge [stuːdʒ] N (*fam: minion*) tirapiedi *m/f*; (*Theatre*) spalla

stool [stuːl] N (*seat*) sgabello; **to fall between two stools** (*fig*) fare come l'asino di Buridano

stoop [stuːp] N: **to have a stoop** avere la schiena curva; **to walk with a stoop** camminare curvo(-a) ♦ VI 1 (*bend: also: stoop down*) chinarsi, curvarsi, abbassarsi; (*have a stoop*) essere curvo(-a); **he stooped down to pick up the letter** si è chinato per raccogliere la lettera 2 (*fig*): **to stoop to sth/doing sth** abbassarsi a qc/a fare qc; **I wouldn't stoop so low!** non mi abbasserei a tanto!

stop [stɒp] N 1 (*halt*) arresto; (*break, pause*) pausa; (*overnight*) sosta; **a 20 minute stop for coffee** una pausa di 20 minuti per il caffè; **without a stop** senza fermarsi; **to come to a stop** (*traffic, production*) arrestarsi; (*work*) fermarsi; **to bring to a stop** (*traffic, production*) paralizzare; (*work*) fermare; **to make a stop** (*bus*) fare una fermata; (*train*) fermarsi; (*plane, ship*) fare scalo; **to put a stop to sth** mettere fine a qc 2 (*stopping place: for bus etc*) fermata; **a bus stop** una fermata d'autobus 3 (*Typ: also: full stop*) punto; (*in telegrams*) stop *m inv* 4 (*Mus: on organ*) registro; (: *on trombone etc*) chiave *f*; **to pull out all the stops** (*fig*) mettercela tutta ♦ VT 1 (*arrest movement of: runaway, engine, car*) fermare, bloccare; (: *blow, punch*) parare 2 (*put an end to: gen*) mettere fine a; (: *noise*) far cessare; (: *pain*) far passare; (: *production: permanently*) arrestare; (: *temporarily*) interrompere, sospendere; **she drew the curtains to stop the light coming in** tirò le tende per impedire che entrasse la luce; **rain stopped play** la partita è stata sospesa a causa del maltempo 3 (*prevent*) impedire; **to stop sb (from) doing sth** impedire a qn di fare qc; **to stop sth (from) happening** impedire che qc succeda; **can't you stop him?** non puoi fermarlo?; **to stop o.s. (from doing sth)** trattenersi (dal fare qc); **I managed to stop myself in time** sono riuscito a fermarmi in tempo 4 (*cease*) smettere; **to stop doing sth** smettere di fare qc; **I'm trying to stop smoking** sto cercando di smettere di fumare; **stop it!** smettila!; **I just can't stop it** (*help it*) proprio non riesco a smetterla 5 (*suspend: payments, wages*) sospendere; (: *subscription*) cancellare; (: *leave*) revocare; (: *cheque*) bloccare; **to stop £30 pound from sb's wages** trattenere trenta sterline dallo stipendio di qn 6 (*also: stop up: block: hole*) bloccare, otturare; (*leak, flow of blood*) arrestare, fermare; **to**

stop one's ears tapparsi *or* turarsi le orecchie ♦ vɪ 1 (*stop moving, pause: gen*) fermarsi; (*cease: gen*) cessare; (*machine, production*) arrestarsi; (*play, concert, speaker*) finire; **stop!** fermo!; **stop, thief!** al ladro!; **without stopping** senza fermarsi; **to stop to do sth** fermarsi per fare qc; **he stopped to look at the view** si è fermato per guardare il panorama; **to stop in one's tracks, stop dead** fermarsi di colpo; **to stop at nothing (to do sth)** non fermarsi davanti a niente (pur di fare qc); **to know where to stop** (*fig*) avere il senso della misura; **the bus doesn't stop there** l'autobus non si ferma lì 2 (*fam: stay*): **to stop (at/with)** fermarsi (a/da); **I'm not stopping** non mi fermo

‣ **stop away** vɪ + ADV (*fam*) stare via
‣ **stop by** vɪ + ADV (*fam*) passare, fare un salto
‣ **stop in** vɪ + ADV rimanere a casa
‣ **stop off** vɪ + ADV fermarsi, sostare brevemente
‣ **stop over** vɪ + ADV: **to stop over (in)** fermarsi (a), fare una sosta (a); (*Aer*) fare scalo (a)
‣ **stop up** vᴛ + ADV = **stop 6a** ♦ vɪ + ADV (*fam*) stare alzato(-a)

stop·cock ['stɒp,kɒk] N rubinetto di arresto
stop·gap ['stɒpɡæp] N (*person*) supplente, sostituto(-a) temporaneo(-a); (*measure*) palliativo; **a temporary stopgap** un ripiego temporaneo ♦ ADJ (*measures, solution*) tampone *inv*, sostitutivo(-a); **a stopgap solution** una soluzione tampone
stop·light ['stɒp,laɪt] N (*traffic light*) (semaforo) rosso
stop·over ['stɒp,əʊvə'] N sosta; (*Aer*) scalo intermedio; **during a stopover in London** durante una breve sosta a Londra
stop·page ['stɒpɪdʒ] N (*in pipe etc*) ostruzione *f*; (*of work*) interruzione *f*; (*strike*) interruzione *f* del lavoro; (*from wages*) detrazione *f*, trattenuta
stop·per ['stɒpə'] N tappo
stop press N ultimissime *fpl*
stop·watch ['stɒp,wɒtʃ] N cronometro
stor·age ['stɔːrɪdʒ] N (*of goods, fuel*) immagazzinamento; (*of heat, electricity*) accumulazione *f*; (*of documents*) conservazione *f*; (*Comput*) memoria; **to put sth into storage** immagazzinare qc; **the cupboards provide ample storage** gli armadi offrono ampio spazio per tenere la roba; **the storage of information on computers** l'immagazzinamento di informazioni nei computer
storage heater N (*Brit*) radiatore *m* elettrico che accumula calore
store [stɔː'] N 1 (*stock*) provvista, scorta, riserva; (*fig: of knowledge etc*) bagaglio; **stores** NPL (*food*) provviste *fpl*, scorte *fpl*, rifornimenti *mpl*; **to lay in a store of sth** fare provvista di qc; **in store** di riserva, come provvista; **we had no idea what lay in store for us** non avevamo idea di cosa ci aspettasse; **who knows what is in store for us** chissà cosa ci riserva il futuro; **to set great/little store by sth** dare molta/poca importanza a qc; **my secret store of biscuits** la mia scorta segreta di biscotti 2 (*also:* **storehouse, storeroom:** *depot*) deposito; **to put one's furniture in(to) store** mettere i mobili in un deposito 3 (*USA: shop*) negozio; (*Brit: also:* **department store**) grande magazzino; **a furniture store** un negozio di mobili ♦ vᴛ 1 (*also:* **store up**) (*food, fuel, goods*) fare provvista di; (*heat, electricity*) accumulare; (*documents*) conservare 2 (*also:* **store away**) (*food, fuel*) mettere da parte; (*grain, goods*) immagazzinare; (*information: in memory*) immagazzinare; (*in filing system*) schedare

‣ **store up** vᴛ + ADV conservare

store·house ['stɔːhaʊs] N magazzino, deposito
store·keeper ['stɔːkiːpə'] N (*USA: shopkeeper*) negoziante *m/f*
store·room ['stɔːrʊm] N deposito; (*for food*) dispensa
sto·rey, sto·ry (*USA*) ['stɔːrɪ] N piano; **a 9-stor(e)y building** un edificio a 9 piani
stork [stɔːk] N cicogna
storm [stɔːm] N 1 (*Met*) tempesta; (*at sea*) burrasca, tempesta; (*thunderstorm*) temporale *m*; (*fig: of applause*) scroscio; (: *of abuse*) torrente *m*; (: *of protests*) uragano; (: *of weeping, tears*) mare *m*; (*uproar*) scompiglio; **it caused a storm** (*fig*) ha creato scompiglio; **a storm in a teacup** (*fig*) una tempesta in un bicchier d'acqua 2 (*Mil*): **to take a town by storm**

prendere d'assalto una città; **the play took Paris by storm** (*fig*) la commedia ha trionfato a Parigi ♦ vᴛ (*Mil*) prendere d'assalto; **to storm a building** irrompere in un edificio ♦ vɪ (*wind, rain*) infuriare; (*person*): **to storm in/out** entrare/uscire come una furia; **she stormed up the stairs** si è precipitata di sopra furiosa ♦ ADJ (*signal, warning*) di burrasca
storm cloud N nube *f* temporalesca; **there are storm clouds on the horizon** (*fig*) c'è aria di burrasca
storm door N controporta
stormy ['stɔːmɪ] ADJ (*comp* -ier, *superl* -iest) (*also fig*) burrascoso(-a), tempestoso(-a)
sto·ry ['stɔːrɪ] N 1 (*account, lie*) storia; (*of book, film*) trama; (*tale: Literature*) racconto; **short story** (*Literature*) novella; **that's not the whole story** non è tutto; **it's the same old story** è sempre la solita storia; **to cut a long story short** per farla breve; **but that's another story** ma questa è un'altra storia; **that's the story of my life!** (*fam*) per me va sempre a finire così!; **to tell stories** (*fam: lies*) raccontare storie 2 (*Press*) articolo; **he covered the story of the earthquake** ha fatto il servizio sul terremoto
sto·ry ['stɔːrɪ] N (*USA*) = **storey**
story·book ['stɔːrɪ,bʊk] N libro di racconti
story·teller ['stɔːrɪ,telə'] N 1 narratore(-trice); **he's a good storyteller** è uno che sa raccontare bene le storie 2 (*fam: liar*) bugiardo(-a)
stout [staʊt] ADJ (*comp* -er, *superl* -est) (*sturdy: stick, shoes etc*) robusto(-a), solido(-a); (*fat: person*) corpulento(-a), robusto(-a); (*determined: supporter, resistance*) tenace; (: *refusal*) deciso(-a); (*brave*) coraggioso(-a); **with stout hearts** coraggiosamente, valorosamente; **a short, stout man** un uomo basso e robusto; **a stout fellow** (*old: fig*) un tipo in gamba ♦ N (*beer*) birra scura
stove [staʊv] N 1 (*for heating*) stufa 2 (*for cooking*) cucina; (*small*) fornelletto; **gas/electric stove** cucina a gas/elettrica; **camping stove** fornello da campeggio
stow [staʊ] vᴛ (*Naut: cargo*) stivare

‣ **stow away** vᴛ + ADV mettere via ♦ vɪ + ADV imbarcarsi clandestinamente

stow·away ['staʊə,weɪ] N passeggero(-a) clandestino(-a)
strad·dle ['strædl] vᴛ (*subj: person: stream*) stare a gambe divaricate su; (: *chair*) stare a cavalcioni di; (: *horse*) stare in groppa a; (*subj: bridge: stream*) essere sospeso(-a) sopra; (*subj: town: border*) essere a cavallo di
strafe [strɑːf] vᴛ mitragliare
strag·gle ['stræɡl] vɪ (*lag behind*) rimanere indietro; (*spread untidily*) estendersi disordinatamente; **to straggle in/out** entrare/uscire uno ad uno; **they straggled back to the classroom** rientrarono in classe alla spicciolata
strag·gler ['stræɡlə'] N chi rimane indietro
strag·gling ['stræɡlɪŋ], **strag·gly** ['stræɡlɪ] ADJ (*village*) sparso(-a); (*hair*) scarmigliato(-a); (*line*) irregolare; (*plant*) che cresce in modo disordinato
straight [streɪt] ADJ (*comp* -er, *superl* -est) 1 (*gen*) diritto(-a), dritto(-a); (*hair*) liscio(-a); (*Geom*) retto(-a); (*posture*) eretto(-a); **a straight road** una strada dritta; **the picture isn't straight** il quadro non è dritto; **to be (all) straight** (*tidy*) essere a posto, essere sistemato(-a); (*clarified*) essere chiaro(-a); **let's get this straight** mettiamo le cose in chiaro; **to put straight** (*picture*) raddrizzare; (*hat, tie*) aggiustare; (*house, room, accounts*) mettere in ordine; **to put things or matters straight** chiarire le cose; **he soon put me straight** mi ha corretto immediatamente; **I couldn't keep a straight face, I couldn't keep my face straight** non riuscivo a stare serio 2 (*continuous, direct*) diritto(-a); **ten straight wins** dieci vittorie di fila 3 (*honest, frank: person*) onesto(-a); (: *answer*) franco(-a); (: *denial*) netto(-a); **straight speaking, straight talking** franchezza; **I'll be straight with you** sarò franco con te 4 (*plain, uncomplicated*) semplice; (*drink*) liscio(-a); (*Theatre: part, play*) serio(-a); (*person: conventional*) normale; (: *heterosexual*) etero *inv* ♦ ADV 1 (*in a straight line: gen*) dritto; **to go straight up/down** andare dritto su/giù; **it's straight across the road from us** è proprio di fronte a noi; **straight ahead** avanti dritto; **straight on** sempre dritto; **to go straight on** andare dritto; **to go straight** (*fig*) rigare dritto 2 (*directly, without diversion*) direttamente, diritto; **I went straight home** sono andato direttamente a casa; **to**

come straight to the point venire al sodo **3** (*immediately*) subito, immediatamente; **straight away, straight off** subito; **I'll come straight back** torno subito **4** (*frankly*) chiaramente, francamente; **straight out** chiaro e tondo ♦ N (*on racecourse*) dirittura d'arrivo; (*Rail*) rettilineo; **to cut sth on the straight** tagliare qc in drittofilo; **to keep to the straight and narrow** (*fig*) seguire la retta via

straight·en [ˈstreɪtn] VT (*sth bent: also:* **straighten out**) raddrizzare; (*hair*) stirare; (*tablecloth, tie*) aggiustare; (*tidy: also:* **straighten up**) mettere in ordine; (*fig: problem: also:* **straighten out**) spianare, risolvere; **to straighten things out** mettere le cose a posto; **to straighten one's shoulders** raddrizzarsi; **straighten your shoulders!** stai su dritto! ♦ VI (*person: also:* **straighten (o.s.) up**) raddrizzarsi

straight-faced [ˌstreɪtˈfeɪst] ADJ serio(-a) ♦ ADV con espressione seria

straight·forward [ˌstreɪtˈfɔːwəd] ADJ (*honest, frank*) franco(-a), diretto(-a); (*simple*) semplice; **the question seemed straightforward enough** la questione sembrava abbastanza semplice

strain¹ [streɪn] N **1** (*Tech: on rope*) tensione *f*; (: *on beam*) sollecitazione *f*; (*on person: physical*) sforzo; (: *mental*) tensione *f*; (: *tiredness*) fatica; **to take the strain off sth** ridurre la tensione di (*or* la sollecitazione su) qc; **the bridge is showing signs of strain** il ponte mostra segni di deformazione; **the rope broke under the strain** la corda si è spezzata a causa della tensione; **she's under a lot of strain** è molto tesa, è sotto pressione; **it was a strain** è stata dura; **I can't stand the strain** non resisto, non ce la faccio più; **the strains of modern life** il logorio della vita moderna; **to put a great strain on** (*marriage, friendship*) pesare molto su **2** (*Med: sprain*) strappo **3 to the strains of** (*Mus*) sulle note di; **he continued in that strain** (*fig*) e continuò su questo tono ♦ VT **1** (*stretch*) tendere, tirare **2** (*put strain on*) sottoporre a sforzo; (*fig: relationship, marriage*) mettere a dura prova; (*resources etc*) gravare su; (*meaning*) forzare; (*Med: back, muscle, ligament*) farsi uno stiramento a; (: *eyes, heart*) affaticare; **don't strain yourself!** (*also iro*) non affaticarti troppo!; **to strain one's back** farsi male alla schiena; **to strain a muscle** farsi uno strappo muscolare; **to strain the truth** deformare la verità; **to strain every nerve to do sth** fare ogni sforzo per fare qc; **to strain one's voice** sforzare la voce; **to strain one's ears** aguzzare le orecchie; **to strain (one's eyes) to see sth** aguzzare la vista per vedere qc **3** (*soup*) passare; (*tea*) filtrare; (*vegetables, pasta*) scolare ♦ VI: **to strain at sth** (*push/pull*) spingere/tirare qc con tutte le forze; **to strain against** (*ropes, bars*) far forza contro

‣ **strain off** VT + ADV (*liquid*) togliere

strain² [streɪn] N (*breed*) razza; (*lineage*) stirpe *f*; (*of virus*) tipo; (*streak, trace*) tendenza

strained [streɪnd] ADJ (*muscle*) stirato(-a); (*arm, ankle*) slogato(-a); (*heart, eyes*) affaticato(-a); (*laugh, smile etc*) forzato(-a); (*relations*) teso(-a); (*liquid*) filtrato(-a); (*solid food*) passato(-a); **a strained muscle** uno strappo muscolare

strain·er [ˈstreɪnəʳ] N (*Culin*) passino, colino

strait [streɪt] N (*Geog*) stretto; **the Straits of Dover** lo stretto di Dover; **to be in dire straits** (*fig*) essere nei guai

strait·jacket [ˈstreɪtˌdʒækɪt] N camicia di forza

strait-laced [ˌstreɪtˈleɪst] ADJ puritano(-a)

strand [strænd] N (*of thread, pearls*) filo; (*of hair*) ciocca

strand·ed [ˈstrændɪd] ADJ: **to be (left) stranded** (*ship, fish*) essere arenato(-a); (*person: without transport*) essere lasciato(-a) a piedi, rimanere bloccato(-a); (: *without money etc*) trovarsi nei guai; **to leave sb stranded** lasciare qn nei guai

strange [streɪndʒ] ADJ (*comp* -**r**, *superl* -**st**) **1** (*odd*) strano(-a), bizzarro(-a); **it is strange that ...** è strano che...; **strange as it may seem** per quanto possa sembrare strano...; **I felt rather strange** mi sono sentito strano **2** (*unknown, unfamiliar*) sconosciuto(-a); **you'll feel rather strange at first** all'inizio ti sentirai un po' spaesato; **to wake up in a strange bed** svegliarsi in un letto che non è il proprio; **the work is strange to him** non è pratico di questo lavoro

strange·ly [ˈstreɪndʒlɪ] ADV stranamente; **strangely (enough), I've never met him** stranamente, non l'ho mai incontrato

stran·ger [ˈstreɪndʒəʳ] N (*unknown person*) sconosciuto(-a); (*from another place*) forestiero(-a), estraneo(-a); **don't speak to strangers** non parlare con gli sconosciuti; **I'm a stranger here** non sono del posto; **he's a complete stranger to me** non lo conosco affatto, per me è un perfetto sconosciuto; **I'm no stranger to Rome** conosco Roma

❑ **stranger** is not translated by the Italian word *straniero*

stran·gle [ˈstræŋgl] VT strangolare, strozzare

strangle·hold [ˈstræŋglhəʊld] N (*Wrestling*) presa di gola; **to have a stranglehold on sb/sth** (*fig*) tenere qn/qc in pugno

stran·gu·la·tion [ˌstræŋgjʊˈleɪʃən] N strangolamento

strap [stræp] N (*of watch, shoes*) cinturino; (*for suitcase*) cinghia; (*in bus etc*) maniglia a pendaglio; (*also:* **shoulder strap**) (*of bra*) bretella, spallina; (*of bag*) tracolla; **the strap of her bag** la tracolla della borsa; **I need a new strap for my watch** ho bisogno di un cinturino nuovo per l'orologio; **a top with thin straps** un top con le spalline strette; **to give sb the strap** punire qn con la cinghia ♦ VT **1** (*fasten*): **to strap down, strap in, strap on, strap up** legare; **to strap sb in** (*in car, plane*) allacciare la cintura di sicurezza a qn **2** (*Med: also:* **strap up**) fasciare

straphanging [ˈstræphæŋɪŋ] N viaggiare *m* in piedi (*su mezzi pubblici reggendosi a un sostegno*)

strap·less [ˈstræplɪs] ADJ (*bra, dress*) senza spalline

strapped [stræpt] ADJ: **strapped for cash** a corto di soldi; **financially strapped** messo(-a) male finanziariamente

strap·ping [ˈstræpɪŋ] ADJ (*person*) robusto(-a), ben piantato(-a)

Stras·bourg [ˈstræzbɜːg] N Strasburgo *f*

stra·ta [ˈstrɑːtə] NPL *of* stratum

strata·gem [ˈstrætɪdʒəm] N stratagemma *m*

stra·tegic [strəˈtiːdʒɪk] ADJ (*also fig*) strategico(-a)

strat·egist [ˈstrætɪdʒɪst] N stratega *m*

strat·egy [ˈstrætɪdʒɪ] N (*also fig*) strategia

strato·sphere [ˈstrætəʊˌsfɪəʳ] N stratosfera

stra·tum [ˈstrɑːtəm] N (*pl* **strata**) (*also fig*) strato

straw [strɔː] N paglia; (*drinking straw*) cannuccia; **he sucked the juice through a straw** ha bevuto il succo di frutta con la cannuccia; **that's the last straw!** questa è la goccia che fa traboccare il vaso!

straw·berry [ˈstrɔːbərɪ] N fragola; **wild strawberry** fragolina di bosco ♦ ADJ (*jam, tart*) di fragole; (*ice cream*) alla fragola

stray [streɪ] ADJ (*dog, cat*) randagio(-a); (*person, cow, sheep*) smarrito(-a); **a stray cat** un gatto randagio; **he was killed by a stray bullet** è stato ucciso da un proiettile vagante; **a few stray cars** qualche rara macchina ♦ N (*animal*) randagio *m* ♦ VI (*animal: get lost*) smarrirsi, perdersi; (*wander: person*) allontanarsi, staccarsi dal gruppo; (: *speaker*) divagare; (: *thoughts*) vagare; **some cows strayed into the garden** delle mucche hanno sconfinato nel giardino; **to stray into enemy territory** ritrovarsi in territorio nemico

streak [striːk] N (*line*) striscia, riga; (*of mineral*) filone *m*, vena; **he had streaks of grey in his hair** aveva delle ciocche di capelli grigi; **to have streaks in one's hair** avere le mèches; **like a streak of lightning** come un fulmine; **to have a streak of madness** avere una vena di pazzia; **he had a cruel streak (in him)** c'era un che di crudele in lui; **lucky streak** periodo di fortuna; **a winning/losing streak** un periodo fortunato/sfortunato ♦ VT rigare, screziare, striare; **streaked with** (*tears*) rigato(-a) di; (*subj: sky*) striato(-a) di; (: *clothes*) macchiato(-a) di ♦ VI (*move quickly*): **to streak away/across/past** allontanarsi/attraversare/passare come un fulmine; (*run naked*) fare lo streaking

streak·er [ˈstriːkəʳ] N streaker *m/f*

streaky [ˈstriːkɪ] ADJ (*colour, window, sky*) striato(-a); (*rock*) venato(-a), screziato(-a)

stream [striːm] N (*brook*) ruscello; (*current*) corrente *f*; (*flow: of liquid, people, words*) fiume *m*; (: *of cars*) colonna; (: *of air*) soffio; (: *of light*) fascio; **against the stream** controcorrente; **a mountain stream** un ruscello di montagna; **a stream of visitors** una marea di visitatori; **an unbroken stream of cars** un fiume ininterrotto di macchine; **divided into three streams** (*Scol*) diviso in tre gruppi di diverso livello; **the B stream** (*Scol*) il gruppo di secondo livello; **to come on**

stream (*oilwell, production line*) entrare in attività ♦ vt **1** (*water etc*) scendere a fiumi; **his nose streamed blood** grondava sangue dal naso **2** (*Scol*) dividere in gruppi di diverso livello (*di rendimento e abilità*) ♦ vi (*liquid*) scorrere; (*cars, people*) riversarsi; **her eyes were streaming** (*because of smoke*) le lacrimavano gli occhi; **her cheeks were streaming with tears** le lacrime le rigavano il volto; **cars kept streaming past me** fiumi di macchine continuavano a passarmi davanti; **to stream in/out** *etc* entrare/uscire *etc* a fiotti

stream·er [ˈstriːməʳ] n (*of paper, at parties etc*) stella filante

stream feed n (*on photocopier etc*) alimentazione *f* continua

stream·line [ˈstriːmˌlaɪn] vt dare una linea aerodinamica a; (*fig*) razionalizzare, snellire

stream·lined [ˈstriːmˌlaɪnd] adj (*see vb*) aerodinamico(-a); razionalizzato(-a), snellito(-a)

street [striːt] n strada, via; **the back streets** le strade secondarie; **a narrow street** una strada stretta; **to be on the streets** (*homeless*) essere senza tetto; (*as prostitute*) battere il marciapiede; **it's right up my street** (*fig: job*) è proprio quello che fa per me, è il mio forte; **to be streets ahead of sb** (*fam*) essere di gran lunga superiore a qn

street·car [ˈstriːtˌkɑːʳ] n (*USA*) tram *m inv*

street cred [-kred] n (*fam*) credibilità presso i giovani

street lamp n lampione *m*

street lighting n illuminazione *f* stradale

street map, street plan n pianta (della città), stradario

street market n mercato rionale

street plan n pianta (di una città)

street·wise [ˈstriːtˌwaɪz] adj (*fam*) scafato(-a); **to be streetwise** sapersela cavare

strength [streŋθ] n **1** (*gen, also fig*) forza; (*of wall, nail, wood etc*) solidità; (*of rope*) resistenza; (*of chemical solution*) concentrazione *f*; (*of wine*) gradazione *f* alcolica; **you'll soon get your strength back** presto ti rimetterai in forze; **his strength failed him** gli sono mancate le forze; **strength of character/mind** forza di carattere/d'animo; **strength of purpose** risolutezza; **on the strength of** sulla base di, in virtù di; **to go from strength to strength** andare di bene in meglio **2** (*Mil, etc*) effettivo; **below/at full strength** con gli effettivi ridotti/al completo; **to come in strength** (*fig*) venire in gran numero

strength·en [ˈstreŋθən] vt (*person, muscles*) irrobustire; (*wall, building*) rinforzare; (*economy, currency*) consolidare; (*desire, determination*) rafforzare; **they are trying to strengthen their position** stanno cercando di rafforzare la loro posizione ♦ vi (*economy, currency*) consolidarsi; (*wind*) aumentare di intensità; (*desire, determination*) rafforzarsi

strenu·ous [ˈstrenjʊəs] adj (*denial, attempt*) energico(-a), vigoroso(-a); (*game, match, day*) faticoso(-a); (*opposition, efforts, resistance*) accanito(-a); **strenuous exercise** esercizi *mpl* pesanti; **you mustn't do anything too strenuous** devi evitare di fare troppi sforzi

stress [stres] n **1** (*Tech*) sforzo; (*force, pressure*) pressione *f*; (*psychological etc: strain*) tensione *f*, stress *m*; **to be under stress** essere stressato(-a); (*fig*) essere sotto pressione; **in times of stress** in momenti di grande tensione; **a stress-related illness** una malattia legata allo stress; **the stresses and strains of modern life** il logorio or lo stress della vita moderna **2** (*emphasis*) enfasi *f*; (*Ling, Poetry*) accento; **the stress is on the first syllable** l'accento cade sulla prima sillaba; **to lay great stress on sth** dare grande importanza a qc ♦ vt (*emphasize*) sottolineare, mettere in rilievo; **I would like to stress that...** vorrei sottolineare che...

stressed [strest] adj (*syllable*) accentato(-a)

stress·ful [ˈstresfʊl] adj (*job*) difficile, stressante

stretch [stretʃ] n **1** (*distance*) tratto; (*expanse*) distesa; (*of time*) periodo; **a stretch of road** un pezzo di strada; **a stretch of time** un periodo; **for a long stretch it runs between ...** per un lungo or bel tratto passa fra...; **for three days at a stretch** per tre giorni di seguito *or* di fila; **he's done a five-year stretch** (*fam: in prison*) è stato dentro cinque anni **2** (*elasticity*) elasticità; **to have a stretch** (*person*) stiracchiarsi; **we'll begin with a few stretches** cominceremo con qualche esercizio di stretching; **to be at full stretch** lavorare a tutta forza; **by no stretch of the imagination** in nessun modo ♦ vt **1** (*pull out: elastic*) tendere, tirare; (*make larger: pullover,*

shoes) allargare; (*spread on ground etc*) stendere; **to stretch (between)** (*rope etc*) tendere (fra); **they stretched a rope between two trees** hanno teso una corda tra due alberi; **to stretch one's legs** sgranchirsi le gambe; **to stretch o.s.** (*after sleep etc*) stiracchiarsi **2** (*money, resources, meal*) far bastare **3** (*meaning*) forzare; (*truth*) esagerare; **to stretch a point** fare uno strappo alla regola **4** (*athlete, student etc*) far sforzare al massimo; **to be fully stretched** essere impegnato(-a) a fondo; **to stretch o.s.** mettercela tutta, impegnarsi a fondo ♦ vi **1** (*reach, extend: area of land*): **to stretch to** *or* **as far as** estendersi fino a; (*: meeting*): **to stretch (into)** prolungarsi (fino a); **to stretch (to)** andare (fino a); (*be enough: money, food*) bastare (per) **2** (*stretch one's limbs*) stirarsi, stiracchiarsi; **the dog woke up and stretched** il cane s'è svegliato e s'è stiracchiato; **I stretched across for the book** mi sono allungato per prendere il libro **3** (*be elastic*) essere elastico(-a); (*become larger: clothes, shoes*) allargarsi; **my sweater stretched when I washed it** il maglione s'è allargato durante il lavaggio ♦ adj (*fabric, trousers*) elasticizzato(-a)

▸ **stretch out** vi + adv (*person*) allungarsi; (*lie down*) stendersi; (*countryside etc*) estendersi, stendersi; **there wasn't enough room to stretch out** non c'era abbastanza spazio per distendersi; **to stretch out for sth** allungare la mano per prendere qc; **a life of unrelieved monotony stretched out before him** lo aspettava una vita di terribile monotonia ♦ vt + adv (*arm, leg*) allungare, tendere; (*net, blanket*) distendere, stendere; (*rope*) stendere; **she stretched out an arm and grabbed me** ha allungato un braccio per afferrarmi

stretch·er [ˈstretʃəʳ] n (*Med*) barella

stretcher-bearer [ˈstretʃˌbeərəʳ] n barelliere *m*

stretch marks npl smagliature *fpl*

strewn [struːn] adj: **strewn with** cosparso(-a) di

strick·en [ˈstrɪkən] pp (*old*) of **strike** ♦ adj (*distressed, upset*) colpito(-a); (*wounded*) ferito(-a); (*damaged: ship etc*) in avaria; (*: city*) colpito(-a); **grief stricken** affranto(-a); **she was stricken with remorse** fu presa dal rimorso; **he was stricken with cancer** fu colpito dal cancro

strict [strɪkt] adj (*comp* -er, *superl* -est) **1** (*stern, severe: person, principles, stance*) severo(-a), rigido(-a); (*: order, rule*) rigoroso(-a); (*: supervision*) stretto(-a); (*: discipline, diet*) rigido(-a) **2** (*precise: meaning, accuracy*) preciso(-a); (*absolute: secrecy, truth*) assoluto(-a); (*: time limit*) tassativo(-a); **in the strict sense of the word** nel senso stretto della parola; **in strict confidence** in assoluta confidenza

strict·ly [ˈstrɪktlɪ] adv (*see adj*) severamente; rigorosamente; strettamente; rigidamente; precisamente; assolutamente; tassativamente; **she was strictly brought up** ha ricevuto un'educazione rigida; **strictly confidential** strettamente confidenziale; **it is strictly forbidden** è severamente proibito; **strictly speaking** a rigor di termini; **strictly between ourselves** ... detto fra noi...; **strictly controlled** rigorosamente controllato; **that's not strictly true** questa non è proprio la verità

stride [straɪd] (*pt* strode, *pp* stridden [ˈstrɪdn]) n passo, falcata; **to get into one's stride** (*fig*) trovare il ritmo giusto; **to take sth in one's stride** (*fig: changes etc*) prendere con tranquillità; (*: exam*) sostenere senza grossi problemi; **to make great strides** (*fig*) fare passi da gigante; **a few strides** alcuni lunghi passi ♦ vi: **to stride in/out** *etc* entrare/uscire a grandi passi; **to stride along** camminare a grandi passi; **to stride up and down** camminare avanti e indietro

stri·dent [ˈstraɪdənt] adj (*sound*) stridente, stridulo(-a); (*voice*) stridulo(-a); (*protest*) energico(-a)

strife [straɪf] n conflitto; **industrial strife** lotte *fpl* sindacali

strike [straɪk] (*pt, pp* struck) n **1** (*by workers*) sciopero; **to be on strike** essere in sciopero; **to go on** *or* **come out on strike** entrare in sciopero; **to call a strike** organizzare uno sciopero **2** (*Mil: also*: air strike) attacco; **a military strike** un attacco militare **3** (*discovery: of oil, gold*) scoperta; **to make a strike** scoprire un giacimento **4** (*Baseball, Bowling*) strike *m inv* ♦ vt **1** (*hit: gen*) colpire; **to strike a blow at sb** sferrare un colpo a qn; **who struck the first blow?** chi ha colpito per primo?; **to strike a blow for freedom** spezzare una lancia in favore della libertà; **to strike a man when he's down** (*fig*) uccidere un uomo morto; **the president was struck by two bullets** il presidente è stato colpito da due pallottole; **the**

clock struck nine o'clock l'orologio ha suonato le nove; **to be struck by lightning** essere colpito(-a) da un fulmine; **panic struck** preso(-a) dal panico; **to strike sth out of sb's hand** far cadere qc di mano a qn; **he struck the ball hard** ha colpito forte la palla **2** (*collide with*) urtare, sbattere contro; (*rocks etc*) sbattere contro, cozzare contro; **she struck her head against the wall** ha battuto la testa contro il muro; **a ghastly sight struck our eyes** una scena orribile si presentò ai nostri occhi; **disaster struck us** siamo stati colpiti da una sciagura **3** (*produce, make: coin, medal*) coniare; (: *agreement, deal*) concludere; (: *a light, match*) accendere; (: *sparks*) far sprizzare; **to strike an attitude** assumere un atteggiamento; **to strike a balance** (*fig*) trovare il giusto mezzo; **to be struck dumb** ammutolire; **to strike terror into sb's heart** terrorizzare qn **4** (*occur to*) colpire; **the thought** *or* **it strikes me that ...** mi viene in mente che...; **it strikes me as being most unlikely** mi sembra molto improbabile; **how does it strike you?** che te ne pare?, che ne pensi?; **I'm not much struck with him** non mi ha fatto una buona impressione **5** (*find: gold, oil*) trovare; **he struck it rich** (*fig*) ha fatto fortuna, ha trovato l'America **6** (*pp, also*) **stricken**: *remove, cross out*: **to strike (from)** cancellare (da) ♦ VI **1** (*workers*) scioperare; **to strike for higher wages** scioperare per rivendicazioni salariali; **they decided to strike** hanno deciso di fare sciopero **2** (*clock*) rintoccare, suonare **3** (*attack*: *Mil, etc*) attaccare, sferrare un attacco; (: *tiger*) aggredire la preda; (: *snake*) mordere; (: *disease, disaster*) colpire, abbattersi; **now is the time to strike** questo è il momento di agire; **it strikes at our very existence** minaccia di distruggerci; **to strike at** (*person, evil*) colpire; **to strike at the root of a problem** intervenire alla radice di un problema; **they fear the killer may strike again** temono che il killer possa colpire di nuovo **4 to strike on an idea** avere un'idea ♦ ADJ (*pay, committee*) di sciopero

▸ **strike back** VI + ADV (*Mil*) fare rappresaglie; (*fig*) reagire

▸ **strike down** VT + ADV (*subj: illness etc: incapacitate*) colpire; (: *kill*) uccidere; **he was struck down in his prime** è morto nel fiore degli anni

▸ **strike off** VT + ADV (*from list*) cancellare; (*doctor*) radiare ♦ VI + PREP (*name off list*) depennare ♦ VI + ADV: **he struck off across the fields** ha tagliato per i campi

▸ **strike out** VT + ADV (*cross out*) depennare ♦ VI + ADV **1** (*hit out*): **to strike out (at)** tirare colpi (a), dare botte (a) **2** (*set out*): **to strike out (for)** dirigersi (verso); **to strike out across country** tagliare per la campagna; **to strike out on one's own** (*fig: in business*) mettersi in proprio

▸ **strike up** VT + ADV **1** (*friendship*) fare; **to strike up a conversation** attaccare discorso **2** (*tune*) attaccare ♦ VI + ADV (*band*) attaccare

strike·breaker [ˈstraɪkˌbreɪkəʳ] N crumiro(-a)

strik·er [ˈstraɪkəʳ] N (*in industry*) scioperante *m/f*; (*Sport*) attaccante *m/f*; **the strikers wanted more money** gli scioperanti volevano più soldi; **the Arsenal striker** l'attaccante dell'Arsenal

strik·ing [ˈstraɪkɪŋ] ADJ (*arresting: picture, dress, colour*) che colpisce; (: *person*) che fa colpo; (*obvious: contrast, resemblance*) evidente, lampante; (*shocking: change, sight*) impressionante; **to be within striking distance of sth** (*Mil*) essere a portata di tiro da qc; (*fig*) essere a un tiro di schioppo da qc

string [strɪŋ] (*pt, pp* **strung**) N **1** (*cord*) spago; (*of puppet*) filo; (*plait: of onions*) treccia; (*row: of beads*) filo; (: *of vehicles, people*) fila; (: *of excuses*) sfilza, serie *f inv*; (*Comput, Ling*) stringa, sequenza; **a piece of string** un pezzo di spago; **a string of victories** una serie di vittorie; **to pull strings for sb** raccomandare qn; **to get a job by pulling strings** ottenere un lavoro a forza di raccomandazioni; **with no strings attached** (*fig*) senza legami, senza obblighi **2** (*on musical instrument, racket*) corda; **the strings** (*Mus*) gli archi; **to have more than one string to one's bow** (*fig*) avere molte frecce al proprio arco ♦ VT **1** (*pearls*) infilare; (*lights, decorations*) appendere; (*rope*): **to string across/between** tendere attraverso/tra **2** (*violin, bow*) incordare; (*tennis racket*) mettere le corde a; **he can't even string two sentences together** non sa mettere insieme due parole

▸ **string along** VT + ADV (*fam*) menare per il naso

▸ **string out** VT + ADV: **to be strung out behind sb/along sth** formare una fila dietro a qn/lungo qc

▸ **string up** VT + ADV (*object*) appendere a una corda; (*fam: hang*) appendere (per il collo); **to be strung up about sth** (*fig*) essere teso(-a) per qc

string bean N fagiolino

stringed in·str·ument [ˌstrɪŋdˈɪnstrəmənt] N (*Mus*) strumento a corda

strin·gent [ˈstrɪndʒənt] ADJ (*measures, economies, tests*) rigoroso(-a); **stringent rules** regolamento *msg* stretto

string quartet N quartetto d'archi

strip [strɪp] N **1** (*gen*) striscia; (*of metal*) nastro; (*Aer*) pista; **comic strip** fumetto; **a strip of material** una striscia di stoffa; **to tear a strip off sb** (*fig: fam*) dare una lavata di capo a qn **2** (*Sport: clothes*) divisa; **wearing the Celtic strip** con la divisa del Celtic ♦ VT **1** (*person, plants, bushes*) spogliare; (*bed*) disfare; (*house*) vuotare, svuotare; (*wallpaper*) staccare; (*paint*) togliere; (*furniture, woodwork*) sverniciare; **to strip from** staccare (*or* togliere) da; **to strip sb/sth of sth** spogliare qn/qc di qc; **he was stripped of his rank** (*Mil*) è stato degradato **2** (*Tech: also: strip down: engine*) smontare ♦ VI (*undress*) spogliarsi, svestirsi; (*do striptease*) fare lo spogliarello; **to strip to the waist** spogliarsi fino alla cintola

▸ **strip off** VI + ADV spogliarsi

strip cartoon N fumetto

stripe [straɪp] N **1** riga, striscia; **white with green stripes** bianco(-a) a strisce verdi **2** (*Mil*) gallone *m*

striped [straɪpt] ADJ a strisce, a righe; **a striped skirt** una gonna a righe

strip light N (*Brit*) tubo al neon

strip·per [ˈstrɪpəʳ] N (*also: paint stripper*) sverniciatore *m*; (*striptease*) spogliarellista *m/f*

strip-search [ˈstrɪpˈsɜːtʃ] VT: **to strip-search sb** perquisire qn facendolo(-a) spogliare ♦ N perquisizione *f* (*facendo spogliare il perquisito*)

strip·tease [ˈstrɪpˌtiːz] N spogliarello

strive [straɪv] (*pt* **strove**, *pp* **striven** [ˈstrɪvn]) VI sforzarsi; **strive as he might** per quanto si sforzasse; **to strive after** *or* **for sth** lottare per ottenere qc; **to strive to do sth** sforzarsi di fare qc, fare ogni sforzo per fare qc; **she strove to read the name on the pillar** si sforzò di leggere il nome sul pilastro

strobe [strəʊb], **strobe light** N luce *f* stroboscopica

strode [strəʊd] PT *of* **stride**

stroke [strəʊk] N **1** (*blow*) colpo; **at a stroke, at one stroke** d'un solo colpo **2** (*caress*) carezza **3** (*Med*) ictus *m inv* **4** (*of pen*) tratto; (*of brush*) pennellata **5** (*Cricket, Golf*) colpo; (*Rowing*) vogata, remata; (*Swimming: single movement*) bracciata; (: *style*) nuoto; **butterfly stroke** nuoto a farfalla; **he hasn't done a stroke (of work)** non ha fatto un bel niente; **a stroke of genius** un lampo di genio; **a stroke of luck** un colpo di fortuna; **to put sb off his stroke** (*Sport*) far perdere il ritmo a qn; (*fig*) far perdere la concentrazione a qn **6** (*of bell, clock*) rintocco; **on the stroke of 12** allo scoccare delle 12 **7** (*of piston*) corsa; **two-stroke engine** motore *m* a due tempi ♦ VT (*cat, sb's hair*) accarezzare

stroll [strəʊl] N passeggiata, giretto; **to go for a stroll, have** *or* **take a stroll** andare a fare un giretto *or* due passi ♦ VI andare a spasso; **to stroll around** *or* **through** gironzolare per; **to stroll in/out** etc entrare/uscire etc tranquillamente

stroll·er [ˈstrəʊləʳ] N (*USA: pushchair*) passeggino

strong [strɒŋ] ADJ (*comp* **-er**, *superl* **-est**) (*gen*) forte; (*sturdy: table, shoes, fabric*) solido(-a), resistente; (*candidate*) che ha buone possibilità; (*protest, letter, measures*) energico(-a); (*concentrated, intense: bleach, acid*) concentrato(-a); (*marked, pronounced: characteristic*) marcato(-a); (: *accent*) marcato(-a), forte; **as strong as a horse** *or* **an ox** (*powerful*) forte come un toro; (*healthy*) sano(-a) come un pesce; **he's never been very strong** è sempre stato di salute cagionevole; **she's stronger than me** lei è più forte di me; **there's a strong possibility that ...** ci sono buone possibilità che...; **there are strong indications that ...** tutto sembra indicare che...; **to have a strong stomach** avere uno stomaco di ferro; **I have strong feelings on the matter** ho molto a cuore quel problema; **to be a strong believer in** credere fermamente in; **strong language** (*swearing*) linguaggio volgare; (*frank and critical*) linguaggio incisivo; **he's not very strong on grammar** non è molto forte in grammatica; **geography**

was never my strong point la geografia non è mai stata il mio forte; **they are 20 strong** sono in 20 ♦ ADV: **to be going strong** (*company, business*) andare a gonfie vele; (*song, singer*) andare forte, avere successo; (*old person*) essere attivo(-a)

strong-arm [ˈstrɒŋˌɑːm] ADJ (*pej: methods*) brutale; **strong-arm tactics** le maniere forti

strong·box [ˈstrɒŋˌbɒks] N cassaforte *f*

strong·hold [ˈstrɒŋˌhəʊld] N fortezza; **the last stronghold of ...** (*fig*) l'ultima roccaforte di...

strong·ly [ˈstrɒŋlɪ] ADV (*made, built*) solidamente; (*tempted, influenced*) fortemente; (*remind*) moltissimo; (*protest, support, argue*) energicamente; (*believe*) fermamente; (*feel*) profondamente, intensamente; **to feel strongly about sth** avere molto a cuore qc; **I don't feel strongly about it** per me fa lo stesso; **she strongly resembles her mother** somiglia molto a sua madre; **to smell strongly of sth** avere un forte odore di qc; **it smells strongly of garlic** ha un forte odore di aglio; **a strongly-worded letter** una lettera dura; **we recommend strongly that ...** raccomandiamo vivamente di...; **strongly built** robusto(-a)

strong·man [ˈstrɒŋˌmæn] N (*pl* **-men**) (*circus performer*) maciste

strong·room [ˈstrɒŋˌruːm] N camera blindata

strop·py [ˈstrɒpɪ] ADJ (*comp* **-ier**, *superl* **-iest**) (*Brit fam*) indisponente, scontroso(-a); **to get stroppy** mettersi a fare il (la) difficile

strove [strəʊv] PT *of* **strive**

struck [strʌk] PT, PP *of* **strike**

struc·tur·al [ˈstrʌktʃərəl] ADJ strutturale; **structural formula** (*Chem*) formula di struttura

struc·tur·al·ly [ˈstrʌktʃərəlɪ] ADV strutturalmente

struc·ture [ˈstrʌktʃəʳ] N (*gen: also Chem: of building*) struttura; (*building itself*) costruzione *f*, fabbricato; **the structure of the organization** la struttura dell'organizzazione; **a four-storey structure** una costruzione di quattro piani ♦ VT (*essay, argument*) strutturare

strug·gle [ˈstrʌgl] N (*fight*) lotta; (*effort*) sforzo; **he lost his glasses in the struggle** ha perso gli occhiali nella zuffa; **a violent struggle** una lotta violenta; **a power struggle** una lotta per il potere; **the struggle for survival** la lotta per la sopravvivenza; **without a struggle** (*surrender*) senza opporre resistenza; (*without difficulty*) senza problemi; **to have a struggle to do sth** avere dei problemi a fare qc; **it was a struggle** è stata dura ♦ VI (*physically*) lottare; **to struggle with sth/sb** lottare con qc/qn; **to struggle to one's feet** alzarsi con sforzo; **to struggle through the crowd** avanzare a fatica tra la folla ♦ VT: **to struggle to do sth** lottare per fare qc; **he struggled to get custody of his daughter** ha lottato per ottenere la custodia della figlia; **they struggle to pay their bills** riescono a stento a pagare le bollette; **to struggle to make ends meet** (*fig*) faticare a sbarcare il lunario

▸ **struggle on** VI + ADV (*fighting*) continuare a lottare; (*walking*) avanzare a fatica; (*living*) tirare avanti

▸ **struggle through** VI + ADV (*fig*): **they managed to struggle through** sono riusciti a farcela

strum [strʌm] VT (*guitar*) strimpellare

strung [strʌŋ] PT, PP *of* **string**

strut¹ [strʌt] VI: **to strut about** *or* **around** pavoneggiarsi; **he strutted past** mi passò davanti impettito; **to strut into a room** entrare impettito(-a) in una stanza

strut² [strʌt] N (*beam*) supporto, sostegno

strych·nine [ˈstrɪknɪn] N stricnina

stub [stʌb] N (*of cigarette, pencil*) mozzicone *m*; (*of candle*) moccolo; (*of cheque, receipt, ticket*) matrice *f*, talloncino ♦ VT: **to stub one's toe (on sth)** urtare *or* sbattere il dito del piede (contro qc)

▸ **stub out** VT + ADV: **to stub out a cigarette** spegnere una sigaretta

stub·ble [ˈstʌbl] N (*in field*) stoppia; (*on chin*) barba di due giorni; **to have stubble** avere la barba di due giorni

stub·born [ˈstʌbən] ADJ (*gen*) ostinato(-a); (*person*) cocciuto(-a), testardo(-a)

stub·by [ˈstʌbɪ] ADJ tozzo(-a)

stuc·co [ˈstʌkəʊ] N stucco

stuck [stʌk] PT, PP *of* **stick** ♦ ADJ **1** (*jammed*) bloccato(-a); **to**

get stuck bloccarsi, rimanere bloccato(-a); **we got stuck in a traffic jam** siamo rimasti bloccati nel traffico **2** (*stumped*): **I'm stuck** (*fam: with crossword, puzzle*) non riesco ad andare avanti; **to be stuck for an answer** non sapere cosa rispondere; **he's never stuck for an answer** ha sempre la risposta pronta

stuck-up [ˌstʌkˈʌp] ADJ (*fam*) presuntuoso(-a), arrogante

stud¹ [stʌd] N (*in road*) chiodo; (*of football boots*) tacchetto; (*decorative*) borchia; (*earring*) orecchino (*a perno*); (*also:* **collar stud, shirt stud**) bottoncino ♦ VT: **studded with** (*fig*) ornato(-a) di, tempestato(-a) di; **studded tyre** *or* **tire** pneumatico chiodato

stud² [stʌd] N (*stud farm*) scuderia di allevamento; (*also:* **stud horse**) stallone *m*

stu·dent [ˈstjuːdənt] N (*Scol, Univ*) studente(-essa); (*of human nature etc*) studioso(-a); **a law/medical student** uno(-a) studente(-essa) di legge/di medicina ♦ ADJ (*life, unrest*) studentesco(-a); (*attitudes, opinions*) degli studenti; (*canteen*) universitario(-a)

student driver N (*USA*) conducente *m/f* principiante

students' union N (*Brit: association*) associazione *f* universitaria; (*: building*) sede *f* dell'associazione universitaria

stud·ied [ˈstʌdɪd] ADJ (*calm, simplicity*) studiato(-a), calcolato(-a); (*insult*) premeditato(-a), intenzionale; (*pose, style*) affettato(-a)

stu·dio [ˈstjuːdɪəʊ] N (*TV, Radio, Cine: of artist*) studio; (*also:* **recording studio**) sala di registrazione; **a TV studio** uno studio televisivo

studio flat, (*USA*) **studio apartment** N monolocale *m*

stu·di·ous [ˈstjuːdɪəs] ADJ (*person*) studioso(-a); (*attention to detail*) accurato(-a)

stu·di·ous·ly [ˈstjuːdɪəslɪ] ADV (*see adj*) studiosamente; accuratamente; (*deliberately*) studiatamente, deliberatamente

study [ˈstʌdɪ] N (*activity, room*) studio; **to make a study of sth** fare uno studio su qc; **his face was a study!** (*fig*) ha fatto una faccia!; **it repays closer study** vale la pena di studiarlo a fondo ♦ VT (*subj*) studiare; (*examine: evidence, painting*) esaminare, studiare ♦ VI studiare; **she's studying to be a doctor** studia medicina; **to study under sb** (*Univ*) essere uno degli studenti di qn; (*subj: artist, composer*) essere allievo(-a) di qn; **to study for an exam** prepararsi a un esame

stuff [stʌf] N **1** (*substance*) roba; **there is some good stuff in that book** ci sono delle buone cose in quel libro; **it's dangerous stuff** è roba pericolosa; **do you call this stuff beer?** questa robaccia la chiami birra?; **I can't read his stuff** non riesco a leggere quello che scrive; **he's the stuff that heroes are made of** ha la stoffa dell'eroe **2** (*possessions, equipment*) cose *fpl*, roba; **have you got all your stuff?** hai tutta la tua roba? **3** (*fam: nonsense*): **all that stuff about her leaving** tutte quelle storie sulla sua partenza; **stuff and nonsense!** sciocchezze! **4** (*fam*): **to do one's stuff** fare la propria parte; **go on, do your stuff!** forza, fai quello che devi fare!; **he certainly knows his stuff** sa il fatto suo ♦ VT (*fill*) riempire; (*Culin*) farcire; (*animal: for exhibition*) impagliare; **to stuff (with)** (*container*) riempire (di); (*cushion, toy*) imbottire (di); **to stuff into** (*stow: contents*) ficcare (in); **he stuffed it into his pocket** se lo ficcò in tasca; **my nose is stuffed up** ho il naso chiuso; **get stuffed!** (*offensive*) va' a farti fottere!; **stuffed shirt** (*fam*) pallone *m* gonfiato; **to stuff o.s. (with food)** rimpinzarsi, strafogarsi

stuff·ing [ˈstʌfɪŋ] N (*in cushion etc*) imbottitura; (*Culin*) farcia, ripieno; **to knock the stuffing out of sb** (*subj: boxer, blow*) mettere al tappeto; **a stuffing for peppers** il ripieno per i peperoni

stuffy [ˈstʌfɪ] ADJ (*comp* **-ier**, *superl* **-iest**) **1** (*room*) mal ventilato(-a), senz'aria; **it's terribly stuffy in here** qui non si respira; **it smells stuffy** c'è odore di chiuso **2** (*ideas*) antiquato(-a), arretrato(-a); (*person*) all'antica

stum·ble [ˈstʌmbl] VI inciampare; (*in speech*) incespicare; **to stumble against sth** inciampare contro qc; **to stumble in/out** entrare/uscire barcollando; **to stumble on** *or* **across sth** (*fig: secret*) scoprire per caso; (*: photo etc*) trovare per caso

stum·bling block [ˈstʌmblɪŋˌblɒk] N ostacolo, scoglio

stump [stʌmp] N (*of limb*) moncone *m*; (*of pencil, tail*) mozzicone *m*; (*of tree*) troncone *m*; (*of tooth*) pezzo; (*Cricket*) paletto (*della porta*) ♦ VT (*perplex*) sconcertare, lasciare

perplesso(-a); **to be stumped for an answer** essere incapace di rispondere ♦ vi: **to stump in/out** *etc* entrare/uscire *etc* con passo pesante
▸ **stump up** vt + adv (*fam*) sganciare, sborsare ♦ vi + adv (*fam*) sborsare i soldi, sganciare i soldi

stun [stʌn] vt (*subj: blow*) stordire, tramortire; (*fig: amaze*) sbalordire, stupefare; **the news stunned everybody** la notizia sbalordì tutti; **I was stunned by the news** sono rimasto sbalordito dalla notizia; **he was stunned by the blow** il colpo lo aveva stordito

stung [stʌŋ] pt, pp *of* **sting**

stunk [stʌŋk] pp *of* **stink**

stunned [stʌnd] adj (*by blow*) stordito(-a); (*fig*) sbalordito(-a); **in stunned silence** ammutolito(-a)

stun·ning [ˈstʌnɪŋ] adj (*news etc*) sbalorditivo(-a), stupefacente; (*dress, etc*) fantastico(-a), splendido(-a)

stunt¹ [stʌnt] n (*Aer: for film etc*) acrobazia; (*Comm*) trovata pubblicitaria; **it's just a stunt to get your money** è tutto un trucco per farti tirar fuori i soldi; **he performed his own stunts** ha girato personalmente le scene pericolose

stunt² [stʌnt] vt (*tree, person*) arrestare la crescita *or* lo sviluppo di; (*growth*) arrestare

stunt·ed [ˈstʌntɪd] adj (*tree*) striminzito(-a); (*person*) rachitico(-a)

stunt·man [ˈstʌntˌmæn] n (*pl* -men) stuntman *m inv*, cascatore *m*

stu·pefac·tion [ˌstjuːpɪˈfækʃən] n stupefazione *f*, stupore *m*

stu·pefy [ˈstjuːpɪˌfaɪ] vt (*subj: tiredness, alcohol*) stordire, istupidire; (*fig: astound*) stupire, sbalordire

stu·pen·dous [stjuːˈpɛndəs] adj (*fam: film, holiday etc*) stupendo(-a), fantastico(-a); (: *price*) altissimo(-a); (: *mistake*) enorme

stu·pid [ˈstjuːpɪd] adj (*gen*) stupido(-a); (*person*) stupido(-a), sciocco(-a); (*from sleep, drink*) intontito(-a), istupidito(-a); **that was stupid of you, that was a stupid thing to do** hai fatto una stupidaggine; **he drank himself stupid last night** era ubriaco fradicio ieri sera

stu·pid·ity [stjuːˈpɪdɪtɪ] n stupidità *f inv*

stu·pid·ly [ˈstjuːpɪdlɪ] adv (*smile, say*) stupidamente; **I stupidly forgot to lock the door** mi sono stupidamente dimenticato di chiudere la porta a chiave

stu·por [ˈstjuːpəʳ] n (*from heat, alcohol*) intontimento, stordimento
❏ **stupor** is not translated by the Italian word *stupore*

stur·dy [ˈstɜːdɪ] adj (*comp* -ier, *superl* -iest) (*person, tree*) robusto(-a), forte; (*boat, material*) resistente, solido(-a); (*fig: supporter*) accanito(-a); (: *refusal*) risoluto(-a)

stur·geon [ˈstɜːdʒən] n storione *m*

stut·ter [ˈstʌtəʳ] n balbuzie *f*; **he's got a stutter** è balbuziente ♦ vi, vt balbettare

Stutt·gart [ˈstʊtɡɑːt] n Stoccarda

sty [staɪ] n (*for pigs*) porcile *m*

stye [staɪ] n (*Med*) orzaiolo

style [staɪl] n **1** (*gen*) stile *m*; **in the Renaissance style** in stile rinascimentale; **that's the style!** così va bene!; **that's not his style** non è nel suo stile **2** (*of dress etc*) modello, linea; (*also: hair style*) pettinatura; (*more elaborate*) acconciatura; **in the latest style** all'ultima moda; **something in this style** qualcosa di questo tipo **3** (*elegance: of person, car, film*) classe *f*, stile *m*; **to dress with style** vestire con un certo stile; **she has style** ha classe *or* stile; **to live in style** avere un elevato tenore di vita; **to do things in style** fare le cose in grande stile **4** (*Bot*) stilo

sty·li [ˈstaɪlaɪ] npl *of* **stylus**

styl·ish [ˈstaɪlɪʃ] adj (*person*) di classe; (*car, district, furniture*) elegante; (*film*) raffinato(-a)

styl·ist [ˈstaɪlɪst] n: **hair stylist** parrucchiere(-a); (*in advertising*) pubblicitario(-a)

styl·ized [ˈstaɪlaɪzd] adj stilizzato(-a)

sty·lus [ˈstaɪləs] n (*pl* styli) (*of record player*) puntina; (*pen*) stilo

Styro·foam [ˈstaɪrəˌfəʊm] n (*USA, Trademark*) polistirene

suave [swɑːv] adj (*person, manners*) mellifluo(-a); (*question, suggestion*) insinuante
❏ **suave** is not translated by the Italian word *soave*

sub [sʌb] n abbr **1** = **submarine 2** = **subscription**

sub- [sʌb] pref sub-, sotto-

sub·com·mit·tee [ˈsʌbkəˌmɪtɪ] n sottocommissione *f*

sub·con·scious [ˌsʌbˈkɒnʃəs] adj subcosciente ♦ n: **the subconscious** il subcosciente, il subconscio

sub·con·ti·nent [ˌsʌbˈkɒntɪnənt] n: **the (Indian) subcontinent** il subcontinente (indiano)

sub·con·tract [n ˌsʌbˈkɒntrækt, vb ˌsʌbkənˈtrækt] n subappalto ♦ vt subappaltare

sub·con·trac·tor [ˌsʌbkənˈtræktəʳ] n subappaltatore(-trice)

sub·di·vide [ˌsʌbdɪˈvaɪd] vt suddividere

sub·di·vi·sion [ˈsʌbdɪˌvɪʒən] n suddivisione *f*

sub·due [səbˈdjuː] vt (*enemy*) sottomettere; (*children*) far star buono(-a); (*high spirits*) smorzare; (*passions etc*) controllare

sub·dued [səbˈdjuːd] adj (*person: downcast*) giù di morale; (*emotions*) contenuto(-a); (*voice, tone*) sommesso(-a); (*colours*) tenue; (*lighting*) soffuso(-a); **he's rather subdued these days** ultimamente non è allegro come al solito

sub·edi·tor [ˌsʌbˈedɪtəʳ] n redattore(-trice) aggiunto(-a)

sub·ject [n, adj ˈsʌbdʒɪkt, vb səbˈdʒɛkt] n **1** (*topic: gen*) argomento, soggetto; (*Scol*) materia; **the subject of my project is the internet** l'argomento della mia ricerca è internet; **what's your favourite subject?** quale materia preferisci?; **let's keep to the subject** non divaghiamo; **let's drop the subject** lasciamo perdere; **(while we're) on the subject of money** ... a proposito di soldi...; **to change the subject** cambiare discorso **2** (*Gram*) soggetto **3** (*Pol: of country*) cittadino(-a); (: *of sovereign*) suddito(-a) ♦ adj **1 subject to** (*liable to: law, tax, disease, delays*) soggetto(-a) a; **subject to doing that** (*conditional upon*) a condizione di fare *or* che si faccia ciò; **subject to confirmation in writing** a condizione di ricevere conferma per iscritto; **these prices are subject to change without notice** questi prezzi sono suscettibili di modifiche senza preavviso; **subject to contract** (*Comm*) fino a stipulazione del contratto **2** (*people, nation*) assoggettato(-a), sottomesso(-a) ♦ vt: **to subject sb to sth** sottoporre qn a qc; **to subject o.s. to ridicule/criticism** esporsi al ridicolo/alle critiche; **she was subjected to severe criticism** è stata duramente criticata

sub·jec·tion [səbˈdʒɛkʃən] n (*state*): **subjection (to)** sottomissione *f* (a), soggezione *f* (a); **to hold a people in subjection** tenere un popolo in servitù

sub·jec·tive [səbˈdʒɛktɪv] adj soggettivo(-a)

subject matter n argomento

sub ju·di·ce [ˌsʌbˈjuːdɪsɪ] adj (*Law*) sub iudice

sub·ju·gate [ˈsʌbdʒʊˌɡeɪt] vt sottomettere, soggiogare

sub·junc·tive [səbˈdʒʌŋktɪv] (*Gram*) adj congiuntivo(-a) ♦ n congiuntivo; **in the subjunctive** al congiuntivo

sub·let [ˌsʌbˈlɛt] vt, vi (*pt, pp* sublet) subaffittare

sub·lime [səˈblaɪm] adj (*beauty, emotion, achievement*) sublime; (*indifference, contempt*) supremo(-a) ♦ n sublime *m*; **from the sublime to the ridiculous** dal sublime al grottesco ♦ vt (*Chem*) sublimare

sub·limi·nal [ˌsʌbˈlɪmɪnl] adj subliminale

sub·machine gun [ˌsʌbməˈʃiːnˌɡʌn] n mitra *m inv*

sub·ma·rine [ˌsʌbməˈriːn] n sottomarino, sommergibile *m* ♦ adj (*frm*) sottomarino(-a)

sub·merge [səbˈmɜːdʒ] vt (*flood*) sommergere; (*plunge*): **to submerge (in)** immergere (in); **the river burst its banks, submerging the village** il fiume ha rotto gli argini e ha sommerso il paese ♦ vi (*submarine*) immergersi

sub·mer·sion [səbˈmɜːʃən] n (*see vt*) sommersione *f*; immersione *f*

sub·mis·sion [səbˈmɪʃən] n sottomissione *f*; (*to committee etc*) richiesta, domanda

sub·mis·sive [səbˈmɪsɪv] adj sottomesso(-a), remissivo(-a)

sub·mit [səbˈmɪt] vt (*proposal, claim*) presentare; **I submit that ...** propongo che...; **they have submitted a claim for a pay rise** hanno presentato una richiesta di aumento ♦ vi (*give in*): **to submit to** (*pressure, threats*) cedere a; (*sb's will*) sottomettersi a; **we won't submit to their demands** non ci piegheremo alle loro richieste

sub·nor·mal [ˌsʌbˈnɔːməl] adj subnormale

sub·or·di·nate [adj, n səˈbɔːdnɪt, vb səˈbɔːdɪˌneɪt] adj (*rank, officer*) subalterno(-a); **subordinate clause** (*Gram*) proposizione *f* subordinata ♦ N subalterno(-a), subordinato(-a) ♦ VT: **to subordinate (to)** subordinare (a); **subordinating conjunction** (*Gram*) congiunzione *f* subordinativa

sub·poe·na [səb'piːnə](*Law*) N citazione *f*, mandato di comparizione ♦ VT citare in giudizio

sub·scribe [səb'skraɪb] VI: **to subscribe to** (*magazine etc*) abbonarsi a; (*fund*) sottoscrivere; (*opinion*) condividere, approvare; **to subscribe for** (*shares*) sottoscrivere; **thousands subscribed to the fund** migliaia di persone hanno contribuito alla raccolta di fondi; **to subscribe to a magazine** abbonarsi ad una rivista; **I don't subscribe to this view** non condivido questa opinione ♦ VT (*money*) devolvere

sub·scrib·er [səb'skraɪbə'] N (*to magazine, telephone*): subscriber (*to*) abbonato(-a) (a)

sub·script ['sʌb,skrɪpt] N (*Typ*) deponente *m*

sub·scrip·tion [səb'skrɪpʃən] N (*to magazine etc*) abbonamento; (*membership fee*) quota d'iscrizione; (*for shares*) sottoscrizione *f*; **to take out a subscription to** abbonarsi a

sub·se·quent ['sʌbsɪkwənt] ADJ (*later*) successivo(-a); (*further*) ulteriore; **subsequent to** in seguito a; **subsequent events** avvenimenti successivi; **subsequent modifications** ulteriori modifiche

sub·se·quent·ly ['sʌbsɪkwəntlɪ] ADV successivamente, in seguito

sub·ser·vi·ent ['sʌb'sɜːvɪənt] ADJ: **subservient (to)** sottomesso(-a) (a)

sub·side [səb'saɪd] VI (*flood*) calare, decrescere; (*road, land*) cedere, avvallarsi; (*wind, anger*) calmarsi, placarsi; **the violence is beginning to subside** la violenza sta cominciando a diminuire; **they are waiting for the water to subside** stanno aspettando che il livello dell'acqua cali; **at last the wind subsided** finalmente il vento si è calmato

sub·sid·ence [səb'saɪdəns] N (*of land etc*) cedimento, avvallamento; (*of waters etc*) abbassamento

sub·sidi·ari·ty [səb,sɪdɪ'ærɪtɪ] N (*Pol*) principio del decentramento del potere

sub·sidi·ary [səb'sɪdɪərɪ] ADJ (*company*) consociato(-a); (*role etc*) secondario(-a); (*Brit: Univ: subject*) complementare; **subsidiary cone** (*Geol*) cono vulcanico secondario ♦ N (*Comm*) filiale *f*; (*Univ*) materia complementare

sub·si·dize ['sʌbsɪ,daɪz] VT sovvenzionare

sub·si·dy ['sʌbsɪdɪ] N sovvenzione *f*, sussidio

sub·sist [səb'sɪst] VI: **to subsist on sth** vivere di qc

sub·sist·ence [səb'sɪstəns] N sopravvivenza; **means of subsistence** mezzi *mpl* di sussistenza

subsistence allowance N indennità *f inv* di trasferta

subsistence level N livello minimo di vita

sub·stance ['sʌbstəns] N (*gen*) sostanza; **to lack substance** (*argument*) essere debole; (*accusation*) essere privo(-a) di fondamento; (*film, book*) essere scarso(-a) di contenuto; **a man of substance** un uomo benestante; **in substance** sostanzialmente, fondamentalmente

substance abuse N abuso di sostanze tossiche

sub·stand·ard [,sʌb'stændəd] ADJ (*goods*) scadente; (*housing*) di qualità scadente

sub·stan·tial [səb'stænʃəl] ADJ 1 (*considerable: amount, progress*) notevole, considerevole; (: *majority, proportion*) largo(-a), grande; (: *difference*) sostanziale; (*solid: building, table*) solido(-a); (: *meal*) sostanzioso(-a); (*wealthy: landowner, businessman*) ricco(-a); **a substantial sum** una somma notevole; **a substantial lunch** un pranzo sostanzioso; **a substantial structure** una struttura solida 2 (*frm: real*) reale

sub·stan·tial·ly [səb'stænʃəlɪ] ADV 1 (*considerably*) notevolmente; **substantially bigger** molto più grande; **substantially different** notevolmente diverso(-a) 2 (*in essence*) sostanzialmente; **substantially correct** sostanzialmente corretto(-a) 3 (*solidly: built*) solidamente

sub·stan·ti·ate [səb'stænʃɪˌeɪt] VT comprovare

sub·sti·tute ['sʌbstɪˌtjuːt] N (*person*) sostituto(-a); (*teacher*) supplente *m/f*; (*Sport*) riserva; (*thing*) surrogato; **coffee substitute** surrogato di caffè; **he's looking for a substitute** sta cercando un sostituto; **a substitute came on in the 71st minute** è entrata una riserva al 71° minuto; **there's**

no substitute for butter non c'è niente di meglio del burro ♦ VT: **to substitute sb/sth (for)** sostituire qn/qc (con *or* a); **they want to substitute gas for coal** vogliono sostituire il carbone con il gas ♦ VI: **to substitute for sb** sostituire qn

sub·sti·tu·tion [,sʌbstɪ'tjuːʃən] N (*gen*) sostituzione *f*; (*in school*) supplenza

sub·ter·fuge ['sʌbtəˌfjuːdʒ] N sotterfugio

sub·ter·ra·nean [,sʌbtə'reɪnɪən] ADJ sotterraneo(-a)

sub·ti·tle ['sʌb,taɪtl] N (*Cine*) sottotitolo

sub·tle ['sʌtl] ADJ (*gen*) sottile; (*flavour, perfume*) delicato(-a)

sub·tle·ty ['sʌtltɪ] N (*see adj*) sottigliezza; delicatezza

sub·tly ['sʌtlɪ] ADV (*see adj*) sottilmente; delicatamente

sub·to·tal [,sʌb'təʊtl] N totale *m* parziale

sub·tract [səb'trækt] VT sottrarre

sub·trac·tion [səb'trækʃən] N sottrazione *f*

sub·urb ['sʌbɜːb] N sobborgo; **a London suburb** un sobborgo di Londra; **in the suburbs** in periferia; **to live in the suburbs** vivere in periferia

sub·ur·ban [sə'bɜːbən] ADJ suburbano(-a), periferico(-a); **a suburban street** una via periferica; **a suburban shopping centre** un centro commerciale fuori città

sub·ur·bia [sə'bɜːbɪə] N periferia, sobborghi *mpl*

sub·ver·sion [səb'vɜːʃən] N sovversione *f*

sub·ver·sive [səb'vɜːsɪv] ADJ, N sovversivo(-a)

sub·way ['sʌb,weɪ] N (*Brit: underpass*) sottopassaggio; (*USA: underground*) metropolitana

sub·zero [,sʌb'zɪərəʊ] ADJ: **subzero temperatures** temperature *fpl* sotto zero

suc·ceed [sək'siːd] VI (*be successful: gen*) riuscire, avere successo; **the plan did not succeed** il piano è fallito; **to succeed in life/business** avere successo nella vita/negli affari; **to succeed in doing sth** riuscire a fare qc; **they succeeded in persuading her** sono riusciti a persuaderla 2 (*follow*): **to succeed (to)** succedere (a) ♦ VT (*monarch*) succedere a; **to succeed sb in a post** succedere a qn in un posto

suc·ceed·ing [sək'siːdɪŋ] ADJ (*following: in past*) successivo(-a), seguente; (: *in future*) futuro(-a); **succeeding generations** generazioni *fpl* future; **in succeeding months** nei mesi successivi; **each succeeding year brought ...** ogni anno che passava recava...; **each succeeding year will bring further wealth** con ogni anno che passa aumenterà la ricchezza

suc·cess [sək'ses] N (*gen*) successo, riuscita; **she was a great success** ha avuto un grande successo; **without success** senza successo *or* risultato; **to make a success of sth** riuscire bene in qc; **to meet with success** avere successo

suc·cess·ful [sək'sesful] ADJ (*person: in attempt*) che ha successo; (: *in life*) affermato(-a), di successo; (*attempt, plan, venture*) riuscito(-a), coronato(-a) da successo; (*play, film*) di successo; (*business*) prospero(-a); **to be successful in doing sth** riuscire a fare qc; **a successful lawyer** un avvocato affermato

suc·cess·ful·ly [sək'sesfəlɪ] ADV con successo

suc·ces·sion [sək'seʃən] N 1 (*series*) serie *f inv*; **in succession** di seguito; **in quick succession** in rapida successione; **a succession of jobs** una serie di lavori 2 (*to post etc*) successione *f*

suc·ces·sive [sək'sesɪv] ADJ (*days, months*) consecutivo(-a); (*generations*) successivo(-a); **on three successive days** per tre giorni consecutivi *or* di seguito; **each successive failure** ogni nuovo insuccesso; **he was the winner for a second successive year** ha vinto per il secondo anno consecutivo

suc·ces·sor [sək'sesə'] N (*in office*) successore *m*; (*heir*) erede *m/f*

suc·cinct [sək'sɪŋkt] ADJ succinto(-a), breve

suc·cu·lent ['sʌkjələnt] ADJ (*tasty*) succulento(-a) ♦ N (*Bot*) succulents piante *fpl* grasse

suc·cumb [sə'kʌm] VI: **to succumb to** (*temptation, illness*) soccombere a; (*entreaties, charms*) cedere a

such [sʌtʃ] PREDETERMINER, DETERMINER 1 (*of this/that sort*) tale, del genere; **such a book** un tale libro, un libro del genere; **such books** tali libri, libri del genere; **such a thing** una cosa del genere; **I wouldn't dream of doing such a thing** non mi sognerei di fare una cosa del genere; **did you ever hear of such a thing?** hai mai sentito una cosa del genere?; **it was such a waste of time** era una tale perdita di tempo;

there's no such thing non esiste; **there's no such thing as a unicorn** gli unicorni non esistono; **there's no such place in Italy** non c'è un posto del genere in Italia; **such was his answer** questa è stata la sua risposta; **such is life** così è la vita; **I said no such thing** non ho detto niente del genere; **in such cases** in casi del genere; **we had such a case last year** si è avuto un caso del genere l'anno scorso; **some such idea** un'idea del genere; **it was such as to/that** era tale da/che; **this is my car such as it is** questa è la mia macchina, se così si può chiamare **2** (*so much, so great*) tale, tanto(-a); **he's not such a fool as you think** non è così scemo come pensi; **I had such a fright** ho preso un tale spavento; **such courage** tanto coraggio; **I was in such a hurry** avevo una tale fretta; **I was in such a hurry that ...** avevo così tanta fretta che...; **such a lot of** talmente, così tanto(-a); **such a lot of work** così tanto lavoro; **making such a noise that** facendo un rumore tale che; **a noise such as to** un rumore tale da **3** (*so very*) talmente, così; **such good food** cibo così buono; **such good books** libri così buoni; **it's such a long time since we saw each other** è da tanto tempo che non ci vediamo; **such a long time ago** tanto tempo fa; **such a long trip** un viaggio così lungo; **such nice people** gente così simpatica **4 such as** (*introducing examples*) come; **such a man as you, a man such as you** un uomo come te; **such writers as** Updike, **writers such as** Updike come Updike; **books such as these** libri come questi; **hot countries such as India** paesi caldi, come l'India; **such as?** per esempio?; **have you got such a thing as a torch?** hai una pila per caso? ♦ PRON **1** (*this, that, those*): **such as wish to go** chi desidera andare; **but such is not the case** ma non è questo il caso; **and such** (*like*) e così via; **I haven't many, but I'll give you such as I have** non ne ho molti, ma ti darò tutti quelli che ho **2 as such** (*in that capacity*) come tale, in quanto tale; (*in itself*) di per sé; **and as such he was promoted** e come tale fu promosso; **there's no garden as such** non c'è un vero e proprio giardino; **he's not an expert as such, but ...** non è un vero e proprio esperto, però...; **doctors as such are ...** i medici in quanto tali sono...; **the work as such is poorly paid** il lavoro di per sé non è pagato bene

such-and-such [ˈsʌtʃ ən ˌsʌtʃ] ADJ tale; **they live in such-and-such street** abitano nella tale strada; **such-and-such a place** il tale posto ♦ N: **Mr such-and-such** il signor tal dei tali

such·like [ˈsʌtʃlaɪk] (*fam*) ADJ simile, di tal genere; **sheep and suchlike animals** pecore *fpl* e animali, *mpl* del genere ♦ PRON: **and suchlike** e così via

suck [sʌk] VT (*gen*) succhiare; (*subj: baby*) poppare, succhiare; (: *pump, machine*) aspirare; **to suck one's thumb** succhiarsi il pollice; **to suck sth through a straw** bere qc con la cannuccia; **to suck an orange dry** succhiare tutto il succo di un'arancia; **to suck dry** (*fig: person: of money*) ripulire; (: *of energy*) esaurire ♦ VI (*baby*) succhiare, poppare; **to suck at sth** succhiare qc
▸ **suck down** VT + ADV (*subj: current, mud*) inghiottire, risucchiare
▸ **suck in** VT + ADV (*subj: machine: dust, air etc*) aspirare; **to suck one's cheeks in** succhiarsi le guance
▸ **suck out** VT + ADV succhiare, far uscire succhiando
▸ **suck up** VT + ADV (*dust, liquid etc*) aspirare ♦ VI + ADV (*fam*): **to suck up to sb** leccare i piedi a qn

suck·er [ˈsʌkəʳ] N (*fam: person*) babbeo(-a), citrullo(-a), gonzo(-a); (*Zool, Tech*) ventosa; (*Bot*) pollone *m*; (*USA: lollipop*) lecca lecca *m inv*; **he's a sucker for flattery** (*fam*) non sa resistere ai complimenti

suck·le [ˈsʌkl] VT allattare

su·crose [ˈsuːkrəʊz] N saccarosio

suc·tion [ˈsʌkʃən] N (*Tech*) aspirazione *f*

suction pump N pompa aspirante

Su·dan [suːˈdɑːn] N il Sudan

Su·da·nese [ˌsuːdəˈniːz] ADJ, A *pl inv* sudanese *m/f*

sud·den [ˈsʌdn] ADJ improvviso(-a); **this is so sudden!** non me l'aspettavo!; **all of a sudden** all'improvviso, improvvisamente; **a sudden change** un cambiamento improvviso

sudden-death [ˌsʌdnˈdeθ], **sudden-death playoff** N **1** (*in football*) rigori *mpl* a oltranza; (*in American football*) tempo supplementare (*in cui vince la prima squadra che segna*) **2**

(*Golf*): **sudden-death hole** buca supplementare *per decidere la vittoria*

sud·den·ly [ˈsʌdnlɪ] ADV improvvisamente, all'improvviso

sudoku [səˈdəʊkuː] N sudoku *m inv*

suds [sʌdz] NPL (*lather*) schiuma *fsg*; (*soapy water*) saponata *fsg*

sue [suː] VT: **to sue sb for libel/damages** *etc* citare qn per diffamazione/danni *etc*; **they're going to sue me** hanno intenzione di citarmi in giudizio ♦ VI: **to sue (for)** intentare causa (per); **to sue for divorce** intentare causa di divorzio

suede [sweɪd] N pelle *f* scamosciata; **a suede jacket** una giacca di pelle scamosciata ♦ ADJ scamosciato(-a)

suet [ˈsuːɪt] N grasso di rognone

Suez [ˈsuːɪz] N Suez *f*

suf·fer [ˈsʌfəʳ] VT **1** (*hardship, hunger*) soffrire, patire; (*pain*) provare; (*undergo: loss, setback*) subire; **to suffer pangs of hunger** provare i morsi della fame; **we have suffered a serious blow** abbiamo subito un grosso colpo **2** (*tolerate: opposition, rudeness*) sopportare, tollerare; **she doesn't suffer fools gladly** non sopporta proprio gli stupidi ♦ VI (*physically*) soffrire; (*be adversely affected: town*) subire danni; (: *regiment*) subire perdite; **to suffer from** (*rheumatism, headaches, deafness*) soffrire di; (*malnutrition, the cold*) soffrire; (*a cold, influenza, bad memory*) avere; **I suffer from hay fever** soffro di raffreddore da fieno; **she was suffering from shock** era sotto shock; **to suffer from the effects of alcohol/a fall** risentire degli effetti dell'alcol/di una caduta; **the house is suffering from neglect** la casa è in stato di abbandono; **your health will suffer** la tua salute ne risentirà; **to suffer for one's sins** scontare i propri peccati; **you'll suffer for it!** la pagherai!

suf·fer·ance [ˈsʌfərəns] N: **he was only there on sufferance** lì era più che altro sopportato

suf·fer·er [ˈsʌfərəʳ] N (*Med*): **sufferer (from)** malato(-a) (di); **diabetes sufferers** i diabetici

suf·fer·ing [ˈsʌfərɪŋ] N (*pain, grief*) sofferenza; (*hardship, deprivation*) privazione *f*

suf·fice [səˈfaɪs] (*frm*) VI bastare, essere sufficiente ♦ VT: **suffice it to say ...** basti dire che...

suf·fi·cient [səˈfɪʃənt] ADJ: **sufficient (for)** sufficiente (per); **that's sufficient** basta così; **do you have sufficient money?** hai abbastanza soldi?; **a kilo will be sufficient** un chilo sarà sufficiente

suf·fi·cient·ly [səˈfɪʃəntlɪ] ADV sufficientemente, abbastanza; **sufficiently large** (*quantity*) sufficiente; (*number*) abbastanza grande

suf·fix [ˈsʌfɪks] N suffisso

suf·fo·cate [ˈsʌfəˌkeɪt] VT, VI soffocare, asfissiare

suf·fo·ca·tion [ˌsʌfəˈkeɪʃən] N soffocazione *f*, soffocamento; (*Med*) asfissia; **to die from suffocation** morire per asfissia

suf·frage [ˈsʌfrɪdʒ] N suffragio

suf·fuse [səˈfjuːz] VT (*frm*): **to suffuse (with)** (*colour*) tingere (di); **her face was suffused with joy** la gioia si dipingeva sul suo volto; **the room was suffused with light** nella stanza c'era una luce soffusa

sug·ar [ˈʃʊgəʳ] N zucchero ♦ VT (*tea etc*) zuccherare; **to sugar the pill** (*fig*) indorare la pillola

sugar basin, sugar bowl N zuccheriera

sugar beet N barbabietola da zucchero

sugar cane N canna da zucchero

sugar-coated [ˈʃʊgəˌkəʊtɪd] ADJ ricoperto(-a) di zucchero

sugar lump N zolletta di zucchero

sugar refinery N raffineria di zucchero

sug·ary [ˈʃʊgərɪ] ADJ (*food etc*) zuccherato(-a), zuccherino(-a); (*fig: sentimental*) sdolcinato(-a), stucchevole

sug·gest [səˈdʒest] VT (*gen*) suggerire, proporre; (*evoke*) indicare, far pensare a; **to suggest doing sth** proporre *or* suggerire di fare qc; **it was you who suggested coming** sei stato tu a voler venire; **she suggested going out for a pizza** ha proposto di andare a mangiare la pizza; **he suggested (that) they should come too** ha proposto *or* suggerito che venissero anche loro; **I suggested they set off early** ho consigliato loro di partire presto; **this suggests that ...** questo fa pensare *or* indica che...; **what are you trying to suggest?** cosa stai cercando di insinuare?; **nothing suggests itself**

non mi viene in mente niente; **what do you suggest I do?** cosa mi suggerisci di fare?

sug·ges·tion [sə'dʒestʃən] N 1 suggerimento, proposta; **an interesting suggestion** una proposta interessante; **to make suggestions** avanzare delle proposte; **if I may make** *or* **offer a suggestion** se mi è concesso avanzare una proposta; **my suggestion is that ...** propongo *or* suggerisco che...; **at sb's suggestion** su *or* dietro suggerimento di qn; **there's no suggestion of** non c'è niente che indichi *or* che faccia pensare a 2 (*trace*): **a suggestion of** un'idea di

sug·ges·tive [sə'dʒestɪv] ADJ 1 (*remark*) spinto(-a); (*look*) indecente 2 (*evocative*): **to be suggestive of** far pensare a, evocare, richiamare; **a style suggestive of Conrad** uno stile che richiama Conrad

sui·cid·al [ˌsuːɪ'saɪdl] ADJ suicida; (*fig*) fatale, disastroso(-a); **I was feeling suicidal** volevo suicidarmi

sui·cide ['suːɪsaɪd] N 1 (*also fig*) suicidio; **to attempt suicide** tentare il suicidio; **to commit suicide** suicidarsi; **a case of attempted suicide** un caso di tentato suicidio 2 (*person*) suicida m/f

suicide attempt, suicide bid N tentato suicidio

suicide bomber N attentatore(-trice) suicida

suicide bombing N attentato suicida

suit [suːt] N 1 (*for man*) abito; (*for woman*) tailleur m inv; (*for bathing*) costume m; (*astronaut's*) tuta; **a suit of armour** un'armatura 2 (*lawsuit*) causa; **to bring a suit against sb** intentare causa a qn 3 (*Cards*) colore m, seme m; **to follow suit** (*fig*) fare altrettanto ♦ VT 1 (*adapt*): **to suit (to)** adattare (a); **to suit one's language to one's audience** usare un linguaggio adatto a chi ascolta; **to suit the action to the word** mettere in pratica le proprie parole; **to be suited to sth** (*suitable for*) essere adatto(-a) a qc; **they are well suited (to each other)** stanno bene insieme 2 (*be acceptable: time, day*) andare bene a; (: *food, climate*) fare per; (: *clothes, colour*) stare bene a; **what time would suit you?** a che ora ti andrebbe bene?; **that dress really suits you** quel vestito ti sta benissimo; **that suits me (down to the ground)** per me va benissimo; **it doesn't suit me to leave now** non mi va di partire ora; **the post suited her perfectly** il lavoro faceva proprio per lei 3 (*please*) contentare; **suit yourself whether you do it** *or* **not** se vuoi farlo fallo, se no lascia perdere; **suit yourself!** fa' come ti pare!

suit·able ['suːtəbl] ADJ (*gen*) adatto(-a); **a suitable time** un'ora conveniente; **I haven't anything suitable to wear** non ho niente di adatto da mettermi; **the most suitable man for the job** l'uomo più adatto a questo lavoro; **we found somebody suitable** abbiamo trovato la persona adatta; **the film is not suitable for children** non è un film adatto ai bambini; **would tomorrow be suitable?** andrebbe bene domani?

suit·ably ['suːtəblɪ] ADV (*dress*) in modo adatto; (*thank*) adeguatamente; **he was suitably impressed** ha giustamente ricevuto un'impressione favorevole; **to reply suitably** dare una risposta adeguata

suit·case ['suːtkeɪs] N valigia

suite [swiːt] N (*of rooms*) appartamento; (*in hotel*) suite f inv; (*Mus*) suite f inv; (*furniture*): **dining room suite** arredo *or* mobilia per la sala da pranzo; **a bathroom suite** i sanitari e gli arredi per il bagno; **a bedroom suite** una camera da letto; **a three-piece suite** un divano e due poltrone; **a suite at the Paris Hilton** una suite all'Hilton di Parigi

suit·or ['suːtə'] N corteggiatore m, spasimante m

sul·fate ['sʌlfeɪt] N (*USA*) = sulphate

sul·fur ['sʌlfə'] (*USA*) = sulphur

sulk [sʌlk] VI tenere il broncio *or* il muso ♦ N: **to have the sulks** tenere il broncio *or* il muso

sulky ['sʌlkɪ] ADJ (*comp* -**ier**, *superl* -**iest**) imbronciato(-a)

sul·len ['sʌlən] ADJ indisponente; (*sky*) cupo(-a); **to have a sullen face** avere il viso imbronciato

sul·phate ['sʌlfeɪt] N solfato; **copper sulphate** solfato di rame

sul·phur ['sʌlfə'] N zolfo

sulphur dioxide N anidride f solforosa, biossido di zolfo

sul·phu·ric [sʌl'fjʊərɪk] ADJ: **sulphuric acid** acido solforico

sul·tan ['sʌltən] N sultano

sul·tana [sʌl'tɑːnə] N (*fruit*) uva sultanina f inv

sul·try ['sʌltrɪ] ADJ (*weather*) afoso(-a), opprimente; (*character*) ardente, sensuale

sum [sʌm] N (*piece of arithmetic*) somma, addizione f; (*amount of money*) somma; **a sum of money** una somma di denaro; **we do sums** facciamo le addizioni; **the sum of 6 and 4 is 10** 6 più 4 fa 10; **that is the sum (total) of his achievements** questo è tutto quello che ha fatto

▸ **sum up** VT + ADV (*review*) riassumere, ricapitolare; (*evaluate rapidly*) valutare, giudicare; **to sum up an argument** riassumere una discussione; **she quickly summed him up** capì subito che tipo era; **he summed up the situation quickly** valutò subito la situazione ♦ VI + ADV riassumere; **to sum up ...** per riassumere..., riassumendo...

Su·ma·tra [suˈmɑːtrə] N Sumatra

sum·ma·rize ['sʌməraɪz] VT riassumere, riepilogare

sum·mary ['sʌmərɪ] N riassunto ♦ ADJ (*dismissal, treatment, justice*) sommario(-a); (*perusal*) sbrigativo(-a)

sum·mer ['sʌmə'] N estate f; **in (the) summer** d'estate; **in the summer of 1995** nell'estate del 1995; **last/next summer** l'estate scorsa/prossima ♦ ADJ (*gen*) estivo(-a), d'estate; **summer clothes** abiti estivi; **the summer holidays** le vacanze estive

summer camp N (*USA*) colonia estiva

summer·house ['sʌməhaʊs] N (*in garden*) padiglione m

summer·time ['sʌmətaɪm] N (*season*) stagione f estiva, estate f

summer time N (*Brit: daylight saving time*) ora legale

sum·mery ['sʌmərɪ] ADJ estivo(-a)

summing-up [ˌsʌmɪŋˈʌp] N (*Law*) ricapitolazione f del processo (*fatta dal giudice alla giuria*)

sum·mit ['sʌmɪt] N 1 cima, vetta, sommità f inv; (*fig*) culmine m; (*Pol*) vertice m, summit m inv; **the NATO summit in Rome** il vertice della NATO a Roma; **after six hours we reached the summit** dopo sei ore abbiamo raggiunto la cima

summit conference N incontro al vertice

sum·mon ['sʌmən] VT (*meeting*) convocare; (*aid, doctor, servant etc*) chiamare; (*Law*): **to summon a witness** citare un testimone

▸ **summon up** VT + ADV (*courage, interest*) trovare; **to summon up all one's courage** farsi coraggio, armarsi di coraggio; **to summon up all one's strength** fare appello a tutte le proprie forze; **I couldn't summon up the courage to tell him** non ho trovato il coraggio di dirglielo; **I summoned up my courage** ho raccolto il coraggio

sum·mons ['sʌmənz] N (*pl* -**es**) (*Law*) citazione f, mandato di comparizione; **to serve a summons on sb** notificare una citazione a qn ♦ VT citare (in giudizio)

sumo ['suːməʊ], **sumo wrestling** N sumo m inv

sump [sʌmp] N (*Aut*) coppa dell'olio, carter m inv

sump·tu·ous ['sʌmptjʊəs] ADJ sontuoso(-a)

sun [sʌn] N sole m; **to get up with the sun** alzarsi allo spuntar del sole; **the sun is in my eyes** ho il sole negli occhi; **in the sun** al sole; **you've caught the sun!** come sei abbronzato!; **a place in the sun** (*also fig*) un posto al sole; **have everything under the sun** hanno tutto ciò che possono desiderare; **there's nothing new under the sun** non c'è niente di nuovo sotto il sole ♦ VT: **to sun o.s.** godersi il sole

Sun. ABBR (= *Sunday*) dom. (= domenica)

sun·bathe ['sʌnbeɪð] VI prendere il sole

sun·beam ['sʌnbiːm] N raggio di sole

sun·bed ['sʌnbed] N lettino solare

sun·block ['sʌnblɒk] N crema a schermo totale

sun·burn ['sʌnbɜːn] N (*painful*) scottatura; (*tan*) abbronzatura

sun·burnt, sun·burned ['sʌnbɜːnt] ADJ (*tanned*) abbronzato(-a); (*painfully*) scottato(-a); **sunburnt shoulders** spalle scottate dal sole; **to get sunburnt** scottarsi

sun cream N crema solare

sun·dae ['sʌndeɪ] N coppa di gelato guarnita

Sun·day ['sʌndeɪ] N domenica; **he'll never do it in a month of Sundays** non ci riuscirà mai e poi mai; *see* **Tuesday**

Sunday paper N giornale m della domenica

Sunday school N ≈ scuola di catechismo

sun·dial [ˈsʌnˌdaɪəl] N meridiana
sun·down [ˈsʌnˌdaʊn] N (*esp USA*) tramonto
sun·dry [ˈsʌndrɪ] ADJ vari(e), diversi(e); **all and sundry** tutti quanti ♦ **sundries** NPL (*items*) varie *fpl*; (*Comm*) articoli *mpl* vari
sun·flower [ˈsʌnˌflaʊəʳ] N girasole *m*
sung [sʌŋ] PP *of* **sing**
sun·glasses [ˈsʌnˌɡlɑːsɪz] NPL occhiali *mpl* da sole
sunk [sʌŋk] PP *of* **sink**[1]
sunk·en [ˈsʌŋkən] ADJʳ (*ship*) affondato(-a); (*eyes, cheeks*) infossato(-a); (*bath*) incassato(-a)
sun·lamp [ˈsʌnˌlæmp] N lampada a raggi UVA
sun·light [ˈsʌnˌlaɪt] N (luce *f* del) sole, *m*; **in the sunlight** alla luce del sole
sun·lit [ˈsʌnˌlɪt] ADJ illuminato(-a) dal sole
sun·ny [ˈsʌnɪ] ADJ (*comp* **-ier**, *superl* **-iest**) **1** (*place, room etc*) assolato(-a), soleggiato(-a); (*day*) di sole; **it is sunny** c'è il sole; **the outlook is sunny** (*Met*) si prevede il sole **2** (*fig: person, disposition*) allegro(-a); (: *smile*) radioso(-a)
sun·rise [ˈsʌnˌraɪz] N: **at sunrise** allo spuntar del sole; **before sunrise** prima dell'alba
sun·roof [ˈsʌnˌruːf] N (*on building*) tetto a terrazzo; (*Aut*) tettuccio apribile
sun·screen [ˈsʌnˌskriːn] N (*protective ingredient*) filtro solare; (*cream, lotion*) crema (*or* lozione *f*) solare protettiva
sun·set [ˈsʌnˌsɛt] N tramonto
sun·shade [ˈsʌnˌʃeɪd] N (*portable*) parasole *m inv*; (*for eyes*) visiera; (*in car*) aletta parasole; (*awning*) tenda da sole
sun·shine [ˈsʌnˌʃaɪn] N (luce *f* del) sole, *m*; **in the sunshine** al sole; **hours of sunshine** (*Met*) ore *fpl* di sole; **six hours of sunshine** sei ore di sole
sun·spot [ˈsʌnˌspɒt] N (*Astron*) macchia solare
sun·stroke [ˈsʌnˌstrəʊk] N colpo di sole, insolazione *f*; **to get sunstroke** prendere un'insolazione
sun·tan [ˈsʌnˌtæn] N abbronzatura, tintarella
suntan lotion N lozione *f* abbronzante
sun·tanned [ˈsʌnˌtænd] ADJ abbronzato(-a)
suntan oil N olio solare
sun·trap [ˈsʌnˌtræp] N angolo molto assolato
su·per [ˈsuːpəʳ] ADJ (*fam*) fantastico(-a), splendido(-a); **we had a super time** ci siamo divertiti da morire
super·an·nua·tion [ˌsuːpərˌænjʊˈeɪʃən] N (*pension*) pensione *f*; (*contribution*) contributi *mpl* pensionistici
su·perb [suːˈpɜːb] ADJ (*quality*) superbo(-a); (*control, confidence*) magnifico(-a)
Super Bowl N (*American football*) super bowl *m inv*
super·cili·ous [ˌsuːpəˈsɪlɪəs] ADJ (*frm*) altezzoso(-a), sprezzante
super·fi·cial [ˌsuːpəˈfɪʃəl] ADJ superficiale
super·fi·cial·ly [ˌsuːpəˈfɪʃəlɪ] ADV superficialmente
super·flu·ous [suːˈpɜːflʊəs] ADJ superfluo(-a); **he felt rather superfluous** si sentì di troppo
super·glue [ˈsuːpəˌɡluː] N colla a presa rapida
super·high·way [ˈsuːpəˌhaɪweɪ] N (*USA*) autostrada; **the information superhighway** l'autostrada telematica
super·hu·man [ˌsuːpəˈhjuːmən] ADJ sovrumano(-a)
super·im·pose [ˌsuːpərɪmˈpəʊz] VT: **to superimpose (on)** sovrapporre (a)
super·in·tend [ˌsuːpərɪnˈtɛnd] VT (*work, shop, department*) dirigere, soprintendere; (*exam*) sorvegliare, vigilare; (*production*) controllare; (*counting of votes*) presiedere a
super·in·ten·dent [ˌsuːpərɪnˈtɛndənt] N soprintendente *m/f*, direttore(-trice); (*Police*) ≈ commissario (capo) di Pubblica Sicurezza
su·peri·or [sʊˈpɪərɪəʳ] ADJ (*gen*): **superior to** superiore a; (*Comm: goods, quality*) di prim'ordine, superiore; (*smug: person*) che fa il (la) superiore; (: *smile, air*) di superiorità; (: *remark*) altezzoso(-a); **superior number** (*Typ*) esponente *m*; **superior technology** tecnologia di prim'ordine; **of superior quality** di qualità superiore; **he felt rather superior** si sentì superiore ♦ N (*in rank*) superiore *m/f*; **Mother Superior** (*Rel*) (madre *f*) superiora
su·peri·or·ity [sʊˌpɪərɪˈɒrɪtɪ] N superiorità

super·la·tive [suːˈpɜːlətɪv] ADJ (*superb: quality, achievement*) eccellente; (: *indifference*) sommo(-a); (*Gram*) superlativo ♦ N (*Gram*) superlativo; **to talk in superlatives** fare largo uso di superlativi nel parlare
super·man [ˈsuːpəˌmæn] N (*pl* **-men**) superuomo
super·mar·ket [ˈsuːpəˌmɑːkɪt] N supermercato
super·model [ˈsuːpəˌmɒdəl] N top model *m/f inv*
super·natu·ral [ˌsuːpəˈnætʃərəl] ADJ, N soprannaturale *m*
super·nova [ˌsuːpəˈnəʊvə] N supernova
super·pow·er [ˈsuːpəˌpaʊəʳ] N (*Pol*) superpotenza
super·script [ˈsuːpəˌskrɪpt] N esponente *m*
super·sede [ˌsuːpəˈsiːd] VT sostituire, soppiantare; **a superseded method** un metodo sorpassato
super·son·ic [ˌsuːpəˈsɒnɪk] ADJ supersonico(-a)
super·star [ˈsuːpəstɑːʳ] N superstar *f inv*
super·sti·tion [ˌsuːpəˈstɪʃən] N superstizione *f*
super·sti·tious [ˌsuːpəˈstɪʃəs] ADJ superstizioso(-a)
super·store [ˈsuːpəstɔːʳ] N (*Brit*) ipermercato
super·tank·er [ˈsuːpəˌtæŋkəʳ] N superpetroliera
super·tax [ˈsuːpəˌtæks] N soprattassa
super·vise [ˈsuːpəˌvaɪz] VT (*person*) sorvegliare, vigilare; (*work, organization, research*) soprintendere a
super·vi·sion [ˌsuːpəˈvɪʒən] N (*of activity, process*) supervisione *f*; (*of person*) sorveglianza; **under medical supervision** sotto controllo medico; **they work under supervision** lavorano sotto sorveglianza
super·vi·sor [ˈsuːpəˌvaɪzəʳ] N sorvegliante *m/f*, soprintendente *m/f*, supervisore *m*; (*Univ*) relatore(-trice); (*in shop*) capocommesso(-a); **a supervisor in the factory** un sorvegliante della fabbrica; **he's a supervisor in a big store** è capocommesso in un grande magazzino
super·vi·sory [ˈsuːpəˌvaɪzərɪ] ADJ di sorveglianza, di vigilanza
su·pine [ˈsuːpaɪn] ADJ supino(-a)
sup·per [ˈsʌpəʳ] N (*evening meal*) cena; (*late-night snack*) spuntino; **to have supper** cenare
sup·plant [səˈplɑːnt] VT soppiantare
sup·ple [ˈsʌpl] ADJ (*comp* **-r**, *superl* **-st**) elastico(-a), flessibile; (*person*) agile; **supple leather** morbido cuoio
sup·plement [*n* ˈsʌplɪmənt, *vb* ˌsʌplɪˈmɛnt] N (*also Press*) supplemento ♦ VT (*diet etc*) integrare; (*income*) arrotondare; (*information*) completare
sup·plemen·ta·ry [ˌsʌplɪˈmɛntərɪ] ADJ supplementare
supplier [səˈplaɪəʳ] N (*Comm*) fornitore(-trice)
sup·ply[1] [səˈplaɪ] N (*delivery*) fornitura; (*stock*) provvista; (*Tech*) alimentazione *f*; **the electricity/water/gas supply** l'erogazione *f* di corrente/d'acqua/di gas; **to cut off the water supply** tagliare l'acqua; **a supply of paper** una provvista di carta; **the supply of fuel to the engine** l'afflusso di carburante al motore; **supply and demand** (*Econ*) domanda e offerta; **to be in short supply** scarseggiare, essere scarso(-a); **supplies** NPL (*food*) viveri *mpl*; (*Mil*) approvvigionamenti *mpl*, rifornimenti *mpl*; (*food only*) sussistenza; **medical supplies** materiale *msg* sanitario; **office supplies** forniture *fpl* per ufficio ♦ VT (*goods, materials, information etc*) fornire; (*fill: need, want*) soddisfare; **to supply sth (with sth)** (*system, machine*) alimentare qc (con qc); **to supply sb (with sth)** (*with goods*) fornire a qn qc; rifornire qn di qc; (*Mil*) approvvigionare qn (di qc); **she supplied us with the necessary evidence** ci ha fornito le prove necessarie; **the centre supplied us with all the equipment** il centro ci ha fornito tutta l'attrezzatura; **most towns are supplied with electricity** quasi tutte le città sono dotate di elettricità; **who will supply their needs?** chi farà fronte ai loro bisogni? ♦ ADJ (*ship, train*) di rifornimento
sup·ply[2] [ˈsʌplɪ] ADV (*bend*) agilmente
supply teacher N (*Brit*) supplente *m/f*
sup·port [səˈpɔːt] N (*gen*) sostegno, appoggio; (*object*) sostegno, supporto; **she was a great support to me** mi è stata di grande conforto; **moral support** aiuto morale; **he has no visible means of support** non è ben chiaro come si mantenga; **to speak in support of a candidate** parlare a favore di un candidato; **to lean on sb for support** (*also fig*) appoggiarsi a qn; **they stopped work in support (of)** hanno interrotto l'attività lavorativa per solidarietà (con); **our support comes from the workers** sono gli operai ad appoggiarci;

there's a great deal of support for his views le sue opinioni sono ampiamente condivise ♦ vт (*gen*) sostenere, sorreggere; (*fig: person: emotionally*) sostenere; (: *financially*) mantenere; (: *proposal, project*) appoggiare; (: *Sport: team*) tifare per; (: *corroborate: evidence*) confermare, convalidare; **to support o.s.** (*financially*) mantenersi; **my friends have always supported me** i miei amici mi hanno sempre appoggiato; **what team do you support?** per quale squadra tifi?; **she had to support five children on her own** ha dovuto mantenere cinque figli da sola; **the pillars that support the ceiling** i pilastri che sostengono il soffitto; **all that is necessary to support life** tutto ciò che rende possibile l'esistenza di una forma di vita

sup·port·er [sə'pɔːtə'] N (*of proposal, project*) sostenitore(-trice); (*of political party*) sostenitore(-trice), fautore(-trice); (*Sport*) tifoso(-a); **a Liverpool supporter** un tifoso del Liverpool; **a supporter of the Labour Party** un simpatizzante del partito Laburista; **a major supporter of the tax reform plan** un importante sostenitore del piano di riforma fiscale

sup·port·ing [sə'pɔːtɪŋ] ADJ 1 (*Theatre, Cine: role, actor, actress*) non protagonista 2 (*wall*) sostegno

sup·port·ive [sə'pɔːtɪv] ADJ 1 (*person*): **to be very supportive (towards sb)** dare il proprio appoggio (a qn); (*emotionally*) essere di grande conforto (per qn); **I have a supportive family** la mia famiglia mi appoggia 2 (*gesture, effort*) di aiuto

sup·pose [sə'pəuz] vт 1 (*assume, believe*): **I suppose she'll come** suppongo che verrà; **I don't suppose she'll come** non credo che venga; **I suppose so/not** credo di sì/di no; **I don't suppose so** non credo; **I suppose he's late** suppongo che sia in ritardo; **you're going to accept, I suppose?** accetti, immagino?; **I don't suppose you could lend me £10?** non potresti per caso prestarmi dieci sterline?; **he's supposed to be an expert** dicono che sia un esperto, passa per un esperto; **it's supposed to be ...** sembra che sia il miglior albergo della città 2 (*assume as hypothesis*) supporre + *sub*, mettere + *sub*; **let us suppose that ...** supponiamo che..., mettiamo che...; **supposing you won the lottery ...** mettiamo che tu vinca alla lotteria...; **but just suppose he's right** ma supponi *or* metti che abbia ragione; **even supposing (that) it were true** anche nel caso (che) fosse vero; **always supposing (that) he comes** ammesso e non concesso che venga; **suppose she doesn't come?** e se non venisse? 3 (*in passive: ought*): **to be supposed to do sth** essere tenuto(-a) a fare qc; **he's supposed to ...** dovrebbe...; **he's supposed to leave on Sunday** dovrebbe partire domenica; **you're not supposed to smoke in the restroom** non è consentito fumare nel bagno; **you're not supposed to do that** non bisogna farlo 4 (*in imperative: I suggest*): **suppose you do it now?** e se lo facessi adesso?; **suppose we change the subject?** e se parlassimo d'altro? 5 (*presuppose*) presupporre

sup·pos·ed·ly [sə'pəuzɪdlɪ] ADV (*presumably*) presumibilmente; (*seemingly*) apparentemente

sup·pos·ing [sə'pəuzɪŋ] CONJ se, ammesso che + *sub*

sup·po·si·tion [ˌsʌpə'zɪʃən] N (*frm*) supposizione *f*, ipotesi *f inv*; **on the supposition that** partendo dal presupposto che + *sub*

sup·pos·i·tory [sə'pɒzɪtərɪ] N supposito

sup·press [sə'prɛs] vт (*emotion, revolt*) reprimere, soffocare; (*scandal*) mettere a tacere, soffocare; (*yawn, smile*) trattenere; (*publication*) sopprimere; (*news, the truth*) tacere; (*evidence*) occultare

sup·pres·sion [sə'prɛʃən] N (*of emotions etc*) repressione *f*; (*of scandal*) soffocamento; (*of truth*) il tacere; (*of evidence*) occultamento; (*of publication*) soppressione *f*

sup·pres·sor [sə'prɛsə'] N (*Elec*) soppressore *m*

su·prem·a·cy [su'prɛməsɪ] N supremazia

su·preme [su'priːm] ADJ (*in authority*) supremo(-a); (*very great*) sommo(-a), massimo(-a); **with supreme indifference** con somma indifferenza; **the supreme sacrifice** il sacrificio supremo; **to reign supreme** (*fig*) dominare

Supreme Court N (*USA*): **the Supreme Court** la corte suprema

su·pre·mo [su'priːməu] N (*Brit fam*) grande capo

Supt ABBR (*Police*) = **superintendent**

sur·charge [ˈsɜːtʃɑːdʒ] N (*gen*) supplemento, sovrapprezzo; (*tax*) soprattassa ♦ vт far pagare un sovrapprezzo (*or* una soprattassa)

sure [ʃuə'] ADJ (*comp* -r, *superl* -st) (*gen*) sicuro(-a); (*definite, convinced*) sicuro(-a), certo(-a); **are you sure?** sei sicuro?; **it's sure to rain** pioverà di sicuro; **I'm sure it's going to rain** sono sicuro che pioverà; **I'm not sure how/why/when** non so bene come/perché/quando + *sub*; **be sure to tell me if you see him** mi raccomando, dimmi se lo vedi; **to be sure of sth** essere sicuro(-a) di qc; **to be sure of o.s.** essere sicuro(-a) di sé; **to be sure of one's facts** essere sicuro(-a) dei fatti; **you can be sure of a good time there** puoi essere sicuro che ti divertirai; **to make sure you do it right** bada di farlo bene; **I'll find out for sure** vedrò di accertarmene; **I think I locked up, but I'll just make sure** credo di aver chiuso a chiave, ma voglio assicurarmene; **to make sure that** assicurarsi che; **I'm going to make sure the door's locked** voglio assicurarmi che la porta sia chiusa a chiave; **just to make sure** per sicurezza; **do you know for sure?** ne sei proprio sicuro?; **she'll leave, for sure** senza dubbio partirà; **I'm sure I don't know, I don't know, I'm sure** che vuoi che ne sappia io?; **he's a sure thing for president** ha la presidenza assicurata ♦ ADV: **is that O.K.? — sure!** va bene? — certo! *or* sicuro!; **that sure is pretty, that's sure pretty** (*USA*) è veramente *or* davvero carino; **sure enough!** (*of course*) sicuro!, senz'altro!; **sure enough** (*predictably*) infatti; **as sure as fate** ovviamente; **as sure as I'm standing here** è com'è vero Dio

sure-fire [ˈʃuəfaɪə'] ADJ (*fam: winner, success*) sicuro(-a)

sure-footed [ˌʃuə'futɪd] ADJ dal passo sicuro

sure·ly [ˈʃuəlɪ] ADV (*certainly*) certamente, sicuramente; **surely we've met before?** ma non ci siamo già incontrati?; **surely you don't mean that!** non parlerai sul serio!; **surely you don't believe that?** non ci crederai davvero?; **surely not!** ma non è possibile!

sure·ty [ˈʃuərətɪ] N cauzione *f*; **to go** *or* **stand surety for sb** farsi garante per qn

surf [sɜːf] N (*waves*) cavalloni *mpl*; (*foam*) spuma; **to surf the internet** navigare in internet

sur·face [ˈsɜːfɪs] N (*gen*) superficie *f*; (*of road*) piano stradale; **on the surface it seems that ...** (*fig*) superficialmente sembra che...; **we've only scratched the surface** (*fig: of argument, work*) abbiamo appena iniziato ♦ vт (*road*) asfaltare ♦ vɪ (*submarine etc*) risalire in superficie; (*fig: person: after absence*) farsi vivo(-a); (: *from bed*) emergere; **he surfaces in London occasionally** ogni tanto si fa vedere a Londra ♦ ADJ (*Mil, Naut*) di superficie

surface area N superficie *f*

surface mail N posta ordinaria

surface-to-surface [ˌsɜːfɪstə'sɜːfɪs] ADJ (*Mil*) superficie-superficie *inv*

surf·board [ˈsɜːfbɔːd] N surf *m inv*

sur·feit [ˈsɜːfɪt] N (*frm*) sovrabbondanza; **a surfeit of** un surplus di

surf·er [ˈsɜːfə'] N surfista *m/f*

surf·ing [ˈsɜːfɪŋ], **surf·riding** [ˈsɜːfˌraɪdɪŋ] N surfing *m inv*, surf *m inv*; **to go surfing** fare surf

surge [sɜːdʒ] N (*of sea, sympathy*) ondata; (*of people*) marea; (*Elec*) sovratensione *f* transitoria; **a surge of anger** un impeto di rabbia; **a surge in inflation** un improvviso aumento dell'inflazione; **a surge of optimism** un'ondata di ottimismo ♦ vɪ (*water, people*) riversarsi; (*waves*) sollevarsi; (*Elec: power*) aumentare improvvisamente; **to surge into/over sth** riversarsi in/su qc; **to surge forward** buttarsi avanti; **to surge round sb/sth** accalcarsi intorno a qn/qc; **the blood surged to her cheeks** il sangue le affluì al viso

sur·geon [ˈsɜːdʒən] N chirurgo

Surgeon General N (*USA*): **the Surgeon General** ≈ il ministro della Sanità

sur·gery [ˈsɜːdʒərɪ] N (*art*) chirurgia; (*operation*) intervento chirurgico; (*Brit: Med: consulting room*) ambulatorio; (: *session*) visita ambulatoriale; (*Brit: of MP*) incontri *mpl* con gli elettori; **to undergo surgery** subire un intervento chirurgico

surgery hours NPL (*Brit*) orario *msg* di ambulatorio

sur·gi·cal [ˈsɜːdʒɪkəl] ADJ chirurgico(-a); **surgical cotton** cotone *m* idrofilo; **surgical dressing** medicazione *f*

surgical spirit N (*Brit*) alcol denaturato

sur·ly [ˈsɜːlɪ] ADJ (*comp* **-ier**, *superl* **-iest**) burbero(-a), scontroso(-a)

sur·mise [*n* ˈsɜːmaɪz, sɜːˈmaɪz, *vb* sɜːˈmaɪz] N congettura ♦ VT supporre, congetturare; **I surmised as much** me lo immaginavo

sur·mount [sɜːˈmaʊnt] VT (*difficulty*) sormontare

sur·name [ˈsɜːneɪm] N cognome *m*

sur·pass [sɜːˈpɑːs] VT (*expectations, person*) superare; **it surpassed all his hopes** è andata meglio di quanto sperasse

sur·plus [ˈsɜːpləs] N (*Fin, Comm*) surplus *m inv*; **to have a surplus of sth** avere qc in eccedenza; **labour surplus** eccedenza di manodopera; **trade surplus** surplus commerciale ♦ ADJ eccedente, d'avanzo; (*Fin, Comm*) di sovrappiù, in eccedenza; **surplus stock** merce *f* in sovrappiù; **it is surplus to our requirements** eccede i nostri bisogni

sur·prise [səˈpraɪz] N (*gen*) sorpresa; (*astonishment*) stupore *m*, sorpresa; **it came as quite a surprise to me** fu una grande sorpresa per me; **a look of surprise** uno sguardo di sorpresa; **much to my surprise, to my great surprise** con mia grande sorpresa; **to take by surprise** (*person*) cogliere di sorpresa; (*Mil: town, fort*) attaccare di sorpresa; **to give sb a surprise** fare una sorpresa a qn ♦ VT (*astonish*) sorprendere, stupire; (*catch unawares*) sorprendere, cogliere di sorpresa; **he surprised me into accepting** ho accettato perché colto alla sprovvista ♦ ADJ (*present, visit*) inaspettato(-a); (*attack*) di sorpresa

surprised ADJ: **to be surprised at** essere sorpreso(-a) di; **he was surprised to learn that ...** fu sorpreso di sapere che...; **I'm surprised at you!** mi meraviglio di te!; **I wouldn't be surprised if he accepts** non mi sorprenderebbe se accettasse; **don't be surprised if he comes** non ti meravigliare se viene

sur·pris·ing [səˈpraɪzɪŋ] ADJ sorprendente

sur·pris·ing·ly [səˈpraɪzɪŋlɪ] ADV (*good, bad*) sorprendentemente; (*somewhat*) **surprisingly, he agreed** cosa (alquanto) sorprendente, ha accettato; **not surprisingly he refused** come c'era da aspettarsi ha rifiutato

sur·re·al·ism [səˈrɪəˌlɪzəm] N surrealismo

sur·re·al·ist [səˈrɪəlɪst] ADJ, N surrealista *m/f*

sur·ren·der [səˈrɛndəʳ] N resa, capitolazione *f*; **no surrender!** non ci arrendiamo! ♦ VT (*gen, also Mil*): **to surrender (to)** consegnare (a); (*lease*) cedere; (*claim, right*) rinunciare a; (*hope*) abbandonare; (*insurance policy*) riscattare ♦ VI: **to surrender (to)** arrendersi (a)

surrender value N (*Insurance*) valore *m* di riscatto

sur·rep·ti·tious [ˌsʌrəpˈtɪʃəs] ADJ furtivo(-a)

sur·ro·gate [ˈsʌrəgɪt] N (*Brit: substitute*) surrogato ♦ ADJ surrogato(-a); **a surrogate son** un figlio sostitutivo

surrogate mother N madre *f* biologica

sur·round [səˈraʊnd] VT circondare; (*Mil*) accerchiare; **a town surrounded by hills** una città circondata da colline ♦ N bordo

sur·round·ing [səˈraʊndɪŋ] ADJ circostante; **the surrounding hills** le colline circostanti

sur·round·ings [səˈraʊndɪŋz] NPL (*of place*) dintorni *mpl*; (*environment*) ambiente *msg*; **in the surroundings** nei dintorni; **in beautiful surroundings** (*house, hotel*) in una bella posizione

sur·tax [ˈsɜːtæks] N sopratassa

sur·veil·lance [sɜːˈveɪləns] N sorveglianza; **under surveillance** sotto sorveglianza

sur·vey [*n* ˈsɜːveɪ, *vb* sɜːˈveɪ] N 1 (*comprehensive view: of situation, developments*) quadro generale 2 (*inquiry, study*) indagine *f*, studio; **a survey of public opinion** un sondaggio d'opinione; **to carry out a survey of** fare un'indagine di; **they did a survey of a thousand students** è stata fatta un'indagine su un campione di mille studenti 3 (*Surveying: of building*) perizia; (: *of land*) rilevamento; (: *of country*) rilevamento topografico ♦ VT 1 (*look at*) guardare; (*prospects, trends*) passare in rassegna; **they have surveyed a number of companies** hanno passato in rassegna diverse aziende 2 (*examine*) studiare, esaminare; **the book surveys events up**

to 2014 il libro esamina gli eventi fino al 2014; **he surveyed the room** ha esaminato la stanza 3 (*Surveying: building*) fare una perizia di; (: *land*) fare il rilevamento di; (: *country*) fare il rilevamento topografico di; **they have surveyed the area** hanno fatto un rilevamento della zona

sur·vey·ing [sɜːˈveɪɪŋ] N (*of land*) agrimensura

sur·vey·or [sɜːˈveɪəʳ] N (*of buildings*) perito; (*of land*) agrimensore *m*

sur·viv·al [səˈvaɪvəl] N (*act*) sopravvivenza; (*relic*) retaggio; **the survival of the fittest** (*Bio*) la selezione naturale; **in the business world it's a case of the survival of the fittest** nel mondo degli affari vige la legge della giungla

survival course N corso di sopravvivenza

survival kit N equipaggiamento di prima necessità

sur·vive [səˈvaɪv] VI (*gen*) sopravvivere; (*fig: in job etc*) durare; **you'll survive!** stai tranquillo che non morirai! ♦ VT sopravvivere a

▸ **survive on** VI + PREP sopravvivere con; **my salary's only just enough to survive on** col mio stipendio riesco a malapena a sopravvivere

sur·vi·vor [səˈvaɪvəʳ] N superstite *m/f*, sopravvissuto(-a); **there were no survivors** non ci sono stati superstiti

sus·cep·ti·ble [səˈsɛptəbl] ADJ 1 **to be susceptible to** (*infection, illness*) essere predisposto(-a) a, soggetto(-a) a; (*persuasion, flattery*) essere sensibile a; **young people are susceptible to adverts** la pubblicità fa facile presa sui giovani 2 (*impressionable*) (facilmente) impressionabile 3 **susceptible of change** (*frm*) suscettibile di cambiamenti

sus·pect [*adj, n* ˈsʌspɛkt, *vb* səˈspɛkt] ADJ sospetto(-a) ♦ N persona sospetta ♦ VT **to suspect (of)** sospettare (di); (*think likely*): **to suspect that** sospettare che + *sub*, supporre che + *sub*; **to suspect sb of a crime** sospettare qn di un delitto; **I suspect his motives** non mi convince; **I suspect that he is the author** immagino che sia lui l'autore; **he suspects nothing** non sospetta niente

sus·pect·ed [səˈspɛktɪd] ADJ presunto(-a); **to have a suspected fracture** avere una sospetta frattura

sus·pend [səˈspɛnd] VT (*gen*) sospendere; **it was suspended from the ceiling/between two posts** era appeso al soffitto/sospeso tra due pali; **he was suspended for cheating** è stato sospeso perché aveva imbrogliato

sus·pend·ed   **ani·ma·tion** [səˌspɛndɪdˌænɪˈmeɪʃən] N interruzione *f* delle funzioni vitali

sus·pend·ed sen·tence [səˌspɛndˈsɛntəns] N (*Law*) (condanna) condizionale *f*

suspender belt N (*Brit*) reggicalze *m inv*

sus·pend·ers [səˈspɛndəz] NPL (*Brit*) giarrettiere *fpl*; (*USA: braces*) bretelle *fpl*

sus·pense [səˈspɛns] N incertezza, apprensione *f*; (*in film, book*) suspense *f*; **we waited in suspense** attendevamo ansiosamente; **the suspense is killing me!** muoio dalla curiosità!; **the suspense was terrible** l'attesa era terribile; **a film with lots of suspense** un film ricco di suspense; **to keep sb in suspense** tenere qn in sospeso

sus·pen·sion [səˈspɛnʃən] N (*gen, also Aut*) sospensione *f*; (*of driving licence*) ritiro temporaneo

suspension bridge N ponte *m* sospeso

sus·pi·cion [səˈspɪʃən] N 1 (*suspicious belief*) sospetto; (*lack of trust*) diffidenza; **I had no suspicion that ...** non avevo il benché minimo sospetto che... + *sub*; **my suspicion is that ...** ho il sospetto che... + *sub*; **arrested on suspicion of murder** arrestato(-a) per sospetto omicidio; **to be under suspicion** essere sospettato(-a); **above suspicion** al di sopra di ogni sospetto; **I had my suspicions about him** non mi ha mai convinto troppo 2 (*hint: of danger, scandal*) segno; (: *of garlic*) punta

sus·pi·cious [səˈspɪʃəs] ADJ (*causing suspicion*) sospetto(-a); (*feeling suspicion*): **suspicious (of)** sospettoso(-a) (di), diffidente (di); **to be suspicious of** *or* **about sb/sth** nutrire dei sospetti nei riguardi di qn/qc; **that made him suspicious** questo lo ha insospettito; **a suspicious character** un(a) tipo(-a) sospetto(-a); **suspicious behaviour** un comportamento sospetto; **he was suspicious at first** all'inizio era sospettoso

suss [sʌs] VT (*Brit fam*): **I've sussed it/him out** ho capito come stanno le cose/che tipo è

sus·tain [səsˈteɪn] VT 1 (*weight*) sostenere, sopportare; (*body, life*) mantenere; (*Mus: note*) tenere; (*effort, role, pretence*) sostenere; "objection sustained" (*USA Law*) "obiezione accolta" 2 (*receive: damage, loss etc*) subire, soffrire

sus·tain·able [səsˈteɪnəbl] ADJ che può essere mantenuto(-a); (*Econ: rate, growth*) stabile; (*source, resource, energy*) rinnovabile; (*forest, timber*) che si può tagliare senza danneggiare l'ambiente; **sustainable development** sviluppo sostenibile

sus·tained [səsˈteɪnd] ADJ (*effort etc*) prolungato(-a)

sus·te·nance [ˈsʌstɪnəns] N (*food*) nutrimento; (*livelihood*) mezzi *mpl* di sussistenza *or* di sostentamento; **there's not much sustenance in it** non è molto nutriente

su·ture [ˈsuːtʃə'] N (*Med*) sutura

SUV [ˌɛsjuːˈviː] N ABBR = **sports utility vehicle**

SW ABBR 1 (= *southwest(ern)*) SO (= *sud ovest*) 2 (*Radio: = short wave*) OC *fpl* (= *onde corte*)

swab [swɒb] N (*Med: for cleaning wound, for specimen*) tampone *m* ♦ VT (*Naut: also: swab down*) redazzare

swag·ger [ˈswægə'] N andatura spavalda ♦ VI pavoneggiarsi; **to swagger in** entrare pavoneggiandosi

swal·low [ˈswɒləʊ] N (*act*) deglutizione *f*; (*of food*) boccone *m*; (*of drink*) sorso ♦ VT (*food, drink*) inghiottire, mandar giù, ingoiare; (*fig: suppress: anger, resentment*) inghiottire; (: *believe: story*) bere; **to swallow one's pride** mettere il proprio orgoglio sotto i piedi; **that's hard to swallow** è difficile crederci; **they swallowed it whole!** (*story*) se la sono bevuta in pieno! ♦ VI inghiottire; (*fig*): **he swallowed hard and said …** con l'emozione che gli serrava la gola ha detto…

▸ **swallow up** VT + ADV (*fig*) inghiottire; **they were soon swallowed up in the darkness** furono presto inghiottiti dalle tenebre; **I wished the ground would open and swallow me up** avrei voluto sprofondare

swal·low [ˈswɒləʊ] N rondine *f*

swam [swæm] PT *of* **swim**

swamp [swɒmp] N palude *f*, pantano ♦ VT (*flood*) inondare, allagare; (*boat etc*) sommergere; **to swamp (with)** (*fig*) sommergere (di)

swampy [ˈswɒmpɪ] ADJ paludoso(-a)

swan [swɒn] N cigno ♦ VI (*fam*): **to swan around** fare la bella vita; **he swanned off to New York** se n'è andato bellamente a New York

swank [swæŋk] (*fam*) N 1 (*vanity, boastfulness*) ostentazione *f*; **he does it for swank** lo fa per mettersi in mostra 2 (*person*) spaccone(-a) ♦ VI (*fam: show off*) mettersi in mostra; (: *talk boastfully*) fare lo(-a) spaccone(-a)

swan song N (*fig*) canto del cigno

swap [swɒp] N (*exchange*) scambio ♦ VT (*cars, stamps etc*) scambiare; **to swap sth for sth else** scambiare qc con qualcos'altro; **he swapped the vouchers for tickets** ha scambiato i voucher con i biglietti; **to swap places with sb** cambiare di posto con qn ♦ VI fare uno scambio; **do you want to swap?** vuoi fare scambio?

▸ **swap over, swap round** VT + ADV: **to swap sth over** *or* **round** cambiare di posto qc; **you can swap them over** li puoi cambiare di posto

swarm [swɔːm] N (*of bees, flying insects*) sciame *m*; (*of crawling insects*) schiera, esercito; (*fig: of tourists etc*) sciame *m*, frotta, stuolo; **swarm of ants** formicaio; **a swarm of people** una marea di gente; **in swarms** (*fig*) a frotte ♦ VI (*bees*) sciamare; **to swarm about** (*crawling insects, people*) brulicare; **to swarm in/out** *etc* entrare/uscire *etc* a frotte; **to swarm with** (*people, insects*) brulicare di

swarm [swɔːm] VI: **to swarm up a tree/rope** arrampicarsi su un albero/su per una corda

swarthy [ˈswɔːðɪ] ADJ (*comp* **-ier**, *superl* **-iest**) (*person*) di carnagione scura; (*skin*) scuro(-a)

swash·buck·ling [ˈswɒʃˌbʌklɪŋ] ADJ (*role, hero*) spericolato(-a); (*film, novel*) di cappa e spada

swas·ti·ka [ˈswɒstɪkə] N svastica, croce *f* uncinata

SWAT [swɒt] N ABBR (*USA: = Special Weapons and Tactics*) corpo speciale di polizia; **a SWAT team** ≈ un reparto di teste di cuoio

swat [swɒt] VT (*fly*) schiacciare ♦ N (*Brit: also:* **fly swat**) acchiappamosche *m inv*

swathe [sweɪð], **swath** [swɔːθ] N (*pl* **swathes** *or* **swaths** [swɔːðz]) (*of grass etc*) falciata

swathe [sweɪð] VT: **to swathe in** (*bandages, blankets*) avvolgere in

swat·ter [ˈswɒtə'] N (*also:* **fly swatter**) acchiappamosche *m inv*

sway [sweɪ] N 1 (*movement: gen*) ondeggiamento; (*of boat*) dondolio, rollio 2 (*rule, power*): **sway (over)** influenza (su); **to hold sway over sb** dominare qn ♦ VI (*tree, hanging object*) ondeggiare; (*bridge, building, train*) oscillare; (*person*) barcollare; **the train swayed from side to side** il treno oscilla violentemente ♦ VT 1 (*move*) far oscillare; **to sway one's hips** ancheggiare 2 (*influence*) influenzare; **these factors finally swayed me** questi fattori hanno finito per influenzarmi; **to be swayed by** essere influenzato(-a) da

Swa·zi·land [ˈswɑːzɪˌlænd] N lo Swaziland

swear [swɛə'] (*pt* **swore**, *pp* **sworn**) VT (*gen*) giurare; **to swear an oath** prestare giuramento; **I swear it!** lo giuro!; **I swear (that) I did not steal it** giuro che non l'ho rubato, giuro di non averlo rubato; **to swear to do sth** promettere di fare qc; **I could have sworn that was Louise** avrei giurato che' fosse Louise; **to swear sb to secrecy** far giurare a qn di mantenere il segreto ♦ VI 1 (*solemnly: witness etc*) giurare; **to swear on the Bible** giurare sulla Bibbia; **to swear to the truth of sth** giurare che qc è vero; **I can't swear to it** non posso giurarlo; **I swear I didn't know** giuro che non lo sapevo; **he swore he wouldn't do it again** ha giurato che non l'avrebbe rifatto 2 (*use swearwords*): **to swear (at sb)** bestemmiare *or* imprecare (contro qn), dire parolacce (a qn); **he swore under his breath** ha imprecato sottovoce; **to swear like a trooper** bestemmiare come uno scaricatore di porto

▸ **swear by** VT + PREP (*fam*): **my mother swears by hot baths for backache** mia madre dice che non c'è rimedio migliore di un bagno caldo contro il mal di schiena

▸ **swear in** VT + ADV (*jury, witness, president*) prestare giuramento

swear·word [ˈswɛəˌwɜːd] N parolaccia; (*curse*) bestemmia

sweat [swɛt] N sudore *m*; **by the sweat of one's brow** con il sudore della fronte; **to get in** *or* **into a sweat about sth** (*fam*) farsi prendere dal panico per qc; **in a sweat** in un bagno di sudore; **to be in a cold sweat** (*also fig*) avere i sudori freddi; **it was a real sweat!** è stata una faticaccia!; **no sweat!** (*fam*) non ci sono problemi! ♦ VI (*person*) sudare; (*walls*) trasudare; (*fam: work hard*): **to sweat (over sth)** sudare (su qc); **to sweat like a pig** essere in un bagno di sudore, sudare sette camicie ♦ VT: **to sweat blood** (*fig: work hard*) sudare sangue; (: *be anxious*) sudare freddo; **to sweat it out** (*fig: fam*) armarsi di pazienza

sweat·band [ˈswɛtˌbænd] N (*Sport*) fascia (elastica) (*per assorbire il sudore: da polso o da fronte*)

sweat·er [ˈswɛtə'] N maglione *m*

sweat·shirt [ˈswɛtˌʃɜːt] N felpa

sweat·shop [ˈswɛtˌʃɒp] N *azienda o fabbrica in cui i dipendenti sono sfruttati*

sweaty [ˈswɛtɪ] ADJ (*comp* **-ier**, *superl* **-iest**) (*gen*) sudato(-a), sudaticcio(-a); (*smell*) di sudore

Swede [swiːd] N svedese *m/f*

swede [swiːd] N (*Brit: vegetable*) rapa svedese

Swe·den [ˈswiːdn] N la Svezia

Swe·dish [ˈswiːdɪʃ] ADJ svedese ♦ N (*language*) svedese *m*

sweep [swiːp] (*pt, pp* **swept**) N 1 (*of room*) scopata, spazzata; (*of chimney*) pulita 2 (*also:* **chimney sweep**) spazzacamino 3 (*range*) portata; (*movement: of arm*) ampio gesto; (: *of scythe, sword*) sciabolata; (: *of beam, searchlight*) fascio luminoso; (*curve: of road, hills etc*) curva; (*expanse: of countryside*) distesa; **a wide sweep of country** una vasta distesa di campi ♦ VT (*stairs, floor*) scopare, spazzare; (*chimney*) pulire; (*dust, snow*) spazzare; **she swept the floor** ha spazzato il pavimento; **to sweep (out) a room** scopare una stanza; **to sweep a problem under the carpet** (*fig*) accantonare un problema 2 (*move over: subj: waves, wind*) spazzare; (: *searchlight*) perlustrare; (: *disease*) dilagare in; (: *fashion, craze*) invadere; **to sweep the sea for mines** dragare il mare; **to sweep the horizon** (*with eyes, binoculars*) scrutare l'orizzonte; **to sweep the board** (*fig*) fare tabula rasa 3 (*remove with sweeping movement*) spazzar via; **to be swept overboard** essere spazzato(-a) fuori bordo; **the crowd swept him along** fu trascinato dalla folla ♦ VI 1 (*with broom*) scopare, spazzare

2 (*move*): **to sweep in/out/along** entrare/uscire/procedere maestosamente; **to sweep past sb** sfrecciare davanti a qn; **the hurricane swept through the city** l'uragano infuriava sulla città; **panic swept through the crowd** la folla fu assalita dal panico; **he swept past in a sports car** è passato sfrecciando alla guida di un'auto sportiva; **the mountains sweep down to the coast** le montagne digradano maestose fino al mare

▸ **sweep aside** VT + ADV spingere di lato; (*fig: objections*) scartare

▸ **sweep away** VT + ADV (*dust, rubbish*) spazzar via; (*subj: crowd, current*) trascinare via

▸ **sweep up** VI + ADV spazzare ♦ VT + ADV (*leaves, rubbish*) raccogliere; (*pick up: books etc*) acchiappare

sweep·er ['swiːpəʳ] N **1** (*worker*) spazzino(-a) **2** (*machine*) spazzatrice *f* **3** (*Brit: Ftbl*) libero

sweep·ing ['swiːpɪŋ] ADJ (*gesture*) ampio(-a); (*statement etc*) generico(-a); (*changes, reforms*) radicale, ampio(-a)

sweep·stake ['swiːpsteɪk] N lotteria (*spesso abbinata alle corse dei cavalli*)

sweet [swiːt] ADJ (*comp* -**er**, *superl* -**est**) **1** (*taste*) dolce; **this coffee is too sweet** questo caffè è troppo dolce; **I love sweet things** adoro i dolci; **a sweet wine** un vino dolce **2** (*fresh, pleasant: smell, perfume, sound*) dolce; (: *breath*) fresco(-a); (*fig: success*) piacevole; (: *revenge*) dolce; **the sweet smell of success** il profumo del successo; **it was sweet to his ear** era musica per le sue orecchie **3** (*charming: person*) carino(-a), dolce; (: *smile, character*) dolce; (: *appearance, village, kitten*) grazioso(-a), carino(-a); **that's very sweet of you** è molto carino da parte tua; **he carried on in his own sweet way** (*iro*) ha continuato (a fare) come gli pareva ♦ ADV **to smell/ taste sweet** avere un odore/sapore dolce ♦ N (*Brit: toffee etc*) caramella; (: *dessert*) dolce *m*; **a bag of sweets** un sacchetto di caramelle; **are you going to have a sweet?** prendi il dolce?

sweet·breads ['swiːtbredz] NPL animelle *fpl*

sweet corn N granturco dolce

sweet·en ['swiːtn] VT (*tea etc*) zuccherare; (*air*) profumare; (*fig: temper*) addolcire; (: *task*) rendere più piacevole; (*also: sweeten up*): (*person*) ingraziarsi; (: *child*) tenere buono(-a)

sweet·en·er ['swiːtnəʳ] N (*Culin*) dolcificante *m*; (*fam: bribe*) zuccherino, contentino

sweet·heart ['swiːthaːt] N innamorato(-a); **yes, sweetheart** sì, tesoro

sweet·ly ['swiːtlɪ] ADV (*gen*) dolcemente, con dolcezza; **the engine is running sweetly** il motore non dà problemi

sweet·ness ['swiːtnɪs] N (*gen*) dolcezza; (*of taste*) sapore *m* dolce; (*of breath*) freschezza; **now all is sweetness and light** adesso tutti sono felici e contenti

sweet pea N pisello odoroso

sweet potato N patata americana *or* dolce

sweet shop N (*Brit*) negozio di dolciumi

sweet tooth N: **to have a sweet tooth** avere un debole per i dolci, essere goloso(-a) di dolci

swell [swel] (*pt* **swelled**, *pp* **swollen**) N (*of sea*) mare *m* lungo ♦ ADJ (*USA: fine, good*) eccezionale, favoloso(-a); **that's just swell** perfetto ♦ VI (*ankle, eye etc: also:* **swell up**) gonfiarsi; (*sails*) prendere il vento; (*in size, number*) aumentare; (*sound, music*) diventare più forte; (*river etc*) ingrossarsi; **to swell with pride** gonfiarsi d'orgoglio; **the cheers swelled to a roar** gli applausi si tramutarono in un boato; **the numbers have swelled** i numeri sono aumentati; **my ankles swelled** mi si sono gonfiate le caviglie ♦ VT (*numbers, sales etc*) far aumentare; (*sails*) gonfiare; (*river*) ingrossare

swell·ing ['swelɪŋ] N (*Med*) gonfiore *m*, tumefazione *f*

swel·ter·ing ['sweltərɪŋ] ADJ soffocante, afoso(-a); **I'm sweltering** sto soffocando; **it was sweltering** faceva un caldo soffocante

swept [swept] PT, PP *of* sweep

swerve [swɜːv] N inversione *f*; (*in car*) sterzata ♦ VI deviare bruscamente; (*in car*) sterzare; (*in ship*) virare; (*boxer*) scartare; **nothing will make him swerve from his aims** niente lo distoglierà dai suoi propositi; **I swerved to avoid the cyclist** ho sterzato per evitare il ciclista

swift [swɪft] ADJ (*comp* -**er**, *superl* -**est**) (*movement*) rapido(-a),

repentino(-a); (*runner*) veloce; (*reply, reaction*) pronto(-a) ♦ N (*bird*) rondone *m*

swift·ly ['swɪftlɪ] ADV (*see adj*) rapidamente, repentinamente; velocemente; prontamente

swift·ness ['swɪftnɪs] N (*see adj*) rapidità, repentinità; velocità; prontezza

swig [swɪg] (*fam*) N (*drink*) sorsata; **he took a swig at his bottle** ha bevuto un lungo sorso dalla bottiglia ♦ VT tracannare

swill [swɪl] N (*also pej*) broda ♦ VT **1** (*clean: also:* **swill out**) risciacquare **2** (*fam: drink: beer etc*) tracannare

swim [swɪm] (*pt* **swam**, *pp* **swum**) N **1** nuotata; **it's a long swim back to the shore** è una bella nuotata fino alla spiaggia; **to go for a swim** andare a fare una nuotata; **let's go for a swim** andiamo a fare una nuotata; **to have a swim** fare una nuotata **2** (*fam*): **to be in the swim** essere al corrente ♦ VI (*river etc*) attraversare a nuoto; (*distance*) nuotare per; **to swim the crawl** nuotare a crawl; **to swim a length** fare una vasca; **she can't swim** non sa nuotare ♦ VI (*gen*) nuotare; (*as sport*) nuotare **2** (*fam*): **can you swim?** sai nuotare?; **I swam for an hour** ho nuotato per un'ora; **I've never swum in the sea** non ho mai nuotato nel mare; **to go swimming** andare a nuotare; **to swim across a river** attraversare un fiume a nuoto; **she swam across the river** ha attraversato il fiume a nuoto; **my head is swimming** (*fig*) mi gira la testa; **the meat was swimming in gravy** la carne galleggiava nel sugo; **eyes swimming with tears** occhi inondati di lacrime

swim·mer ['swɪmə'] N nuotatore(-trice)

swim·ming ['swɪmɪŋ] N nuoto; **swimming and cycling** il nuoto ed il ciclismo; **do you like swimming?** ti piace nuotare?

swimming baths NPL (*Brit*) piscina pubblica

swimming cap N cuffia

swimming costume N (*Brit*) costume *m* da bagno

swim·ming·ly ['swɪmɪŋlɪ] ADV (*smoothly*): **everything went swimmingly** tutto è andato liscio come l'olio

swimming pool N piscina

swimming trunks NPL calzoncini *mpl* da bagno

swim·suit ['swɪmsuːt] N costume *m* da bagno (*da donna*)

swin·dle ['swɪndl] N truffa ♦ VT imbrogliare, truffare; **to swindle sb out of sth** estorcere qc a qn con l'inganno

swin·dler ['swɪndlə'] N imbroglione(-a), truffatore(-trice)

swine [swaɪn] N **1** (*fig: fam!: person*) porco (*fam!*); **you swine!** brutto porco! **2** (*pl inv: old: pig*) maiale *m*

swing [swɪŋ] (*pt, pp* **swung**) N **1** (*of pendulum, needle*) oscillazione *f*; (*distance*) arco; **to take a swing at sb** mollare un pugno a qn **2** (*seat for swinging*) altalena; **a slide and some swings** uno scivolo e alcune altalene; **to have a swing** andare sull'altalena; **it's swings and roundabouts** (*fig*) che ci vuoi fare, le cose a volte vanno bene, a volte vanno male **3** (*Pol: in attitudes, opinions, support*): **there was a swing towards/away from Labour** c'è stato un aumento/ una diminuzione di voti per i Laburisti; **a sudden swing in public opinion** un improvviso cambiamento dell'opinione pubblica; **a swing to the left** una svolta a sinistra **4** (*Boxing, Golf*) swing *m inv* **5** (*rhythm*) ritmo; **to get into the swing of things** entrare nel pieno delle cose; **to be in full swing** essere in pieno corso; **the party went with a swing** la festa è stata una bomba **6** (*also:* **swing music**) swing *m* **7 a mood swing** un cambiamento d'umore ♦ VT **1** (*pendulum*) far oscillare; (*person on swing, in hammock*) dondolare, spingere; (*arms, legs*) dondolare, ciondolare; **to swing the door open** spalancare la porta **2** (*wield: axe, sword*) brandire, roteare; **he swung the case up onto his shoulder** si è messo la valigia sulla spalla; **he swung himself over the wall** si è lanciato al di là del muro; **she swung the car round** girò di colpo la macchina **3** (*influence: opinion, decision*) influenzare; **she managed to swing it so that we could all go** (*fam*) è riuscita a fare in modo che ci potessimo andare tutti; **what swung it for me was ...** ciò che mi ha fatto decidere è stato... ♦ VI dondolare, oscillare; (*on swing, hammock*) dondolarsi; (*arms, legs*) dondolare; **to swing to and fro** dondolare avanti e indietro; **a large key swung from his belt** dalla cintura gli dondolava una grossa chiave; **the door swung open** la porta si spalancò; **the door swung shut** la porta si chiuse sbattendo; **he'll swing for it** (*fam*) lo impiccheranno; **the road swings south** la strada prende la direzione sud; **he swung**

round si voltò bruscamente; **the car swung into the square** la macchina svoltò bruscamente nella piazza; **to swing to the right** (*fig*: *Pol*) svoltare a destra; **to swing into action** entrare in azione

swing bridge N ponte *m* girevole

swing door N porta a vento

swinge·ing [ˈswɪndʒɪŋ] ADJ (*cuts*) drastico(-a); (*attack, blow*) violento(-a); (*defeat, majority*) schiacciante; (*taxation*) forte; (*price increase*) enorme

swing·ing [ˈswɪŋɪŋ] ADJ (*step*) cadenzato(-a), ritmico(-a); (*rhythm, music*) trascinante; **swinging door** (*USA*) porta a vento

swipe [swaɪp] N: **to take a swipe at sb** dare uno schiaffo a qn ♦ VT **1** (*hit*: *ball, person*) colpire; **he swiped the ball** ha colpito con forza la palla **2** (*fam*: *steal*) fregare, sgraffignare; **sb's swiped my stapler** qn mi ha fregato la cucitrice **3** (*Comput*: *card*) far passare nell'apposita macchinetta; **you get in by swiping a card** per entrare devi passare una scheda nell'apposita macchinetta ♦ VI: **to swipe at sb/sth** tentare di colpire qn/qc

swipe card N scheda magnetica

swirl [swɜːl] N (*movement*) turbinio, turbine *m*, mulinello; (*of cream etc*) ricciolo ♦ VI turbinare, far mulinello

swish [swɪʃ] N (*sound*: *of whip*) schiocco; (: *of skirts, grass*) fruscio ♦ ADJ (*fam*: *smart*) all'ultimo grido, alla moda ♦ VT (*whip*) schioccare; (*skirt*) far frusciare; (*tail*) agitare ♦ VI (*whip*) schioccare; (*skirts, grass*) frusciare

Swiss [swɪs] ADJ svizzero(-a) ♦ N *pl inv* svizzero(-a); **the Swiss** gli svizzeri

Swiss French ADJ svizzero(-a) francese

Swiss German ADJ svizzero(-a) tedesco(-a)

switch [swɪtʃ] N **1** (*Elec, etc*) interruttore *m* **2** (*Rail*: *points*) scambio **3** (*change*) cambiamento, mutamento; (*exchange*) scambio; **a rapid switch of plan** un improvviso cambiamento di programma; **a policy switch** un cambiamento di politica **4** (*stick*) bacchetta; **riding switch** frustino ♦ VT **1** (*change*: *plans, jobs*) cambiare; (: *allegiance*): **we switched partners** abbiamo cambiato partner; **to switch (to)** spostare (a) (*conversation*) spostare (su) **2** (*exchange*) scambiarsi; (*transpose*) (*also*: **switch round, switch over**) scambiare; (*two objects*) invertire; **I switched hats with him, we switched hats** ci siamo scambiati i cappelli **3** (*TV, Radio*: *programme*) cambiare; **to switch the TV to another channel** cambiare canale; **to switch the radio to another programme** cambiare stazione; **to switch the heater to high** regolare la stufa al massimo **4** (*Rail*) deviare ♦ VI (*also*: **switch over**) passare; **he switched to another topic** è passato a un altro argomento; **he has switched to Labour** è passato al partito laburista

‣ **switch back** VI + ADV (*gen*) ritornare; (*TV, Radio*): **to switch back to the other programme** rimettere l'altro programma, ritornare all'altro programma; **he switched back to being calm** è tornato alla calma ♦ VT + ADV: **can you switch the heater back to "low"?** puoi rimettere la stufa al minimo?; **to switch the light back on/off** riaccendere/ rispegnere la luce

‣ **switch off** VT + ADV (*Elec, TV, Aut*) spegnere ♦ VI + ADV (*Elec, TV*) spegnersi da solo(-a); (*fig*: *fam*: *not listen*) smettere di ascoltare

‣ **switch on** VT + ADV (*Elec, TV, etc*) accendere; (*water supply*) aprire; (*machine*: *Aut*) mettere in moto, avviare; (*ignition*) inserire; **to switch on the charm** diventare tutto(-a) gentile ♦ VI + ADV (*heater, oven*) accendersi da solo(-a)

switch·back [ˈswɪtʃˌbæk] N (*Brit*: *roller coaster*) montagne *fpl* russe

switch·blade [ˈswɪtʃˌbleɪd] N (*also*: **switchblade knife**) coltello a scatto

switch·board [ˈswɪtʃˌbɔːd] N centralino

switchboard operator N centralinista *m/f*

Swit·zer·land [ˈswɪtsələnd] N la Svizzera

swiv·el [ˈswɪvl] N perno ♦ VI (*also*: **swivel round**) girarsi

swol·len [ˈswəʊlən] PP *of* swell ♦ ADJ (*ankle, finger, stomach*) gonfio(-a); (*river*) in piena; **my ankle is swollen** ho una caviglia gonfia; **her eyes were swollen with tears** aveva gli occhi gonfi di pianto; **you'll give him a swollen head** (*fig*) gli farai montare la testa

swoon [swuːn] (*old*) N svenimento ♦ VI svenire; **to swoon over sb** (*fig*) morire dietro a qn

swoop [swuːp] N (*of bird etc*) picchiata; (*by police*): **swoop (on)** incursione *f* (in); **in one fell swoop** in un colpo solo ♦ VI (*bird*: *also*: **swoop down**) scendere in picchiata; (*police*): **to swoop (on)** fare un'incursione (in); **the plane swooped low over the village** l'aereo è sceso in picchiata sul villaggio

swop [swɒp] N, VT = **swap**

sword [sɔːd] N spada

sword·fish [ˈsɔːdˌfɪʃ] N pesce *m* spada, *inv*

swore [swɔː] PT *of* swear

sworn [swɔːn] PP *of* **swear** ♦ ADJ (*enemy*) giurato(-a); (*friend*) per la pelle; (*ally*) fedele; (*testimony*) giurato(-a), fatto(-a) sotto giuramento

swum [swʌm] PP *of* swim

swung [swʌŋ] PT, PP *of* swing

syca·more [ˈsɪkəmɔː] N sicomoro

syco·phant [ˈsɪkəfənt] N adulatore(-trice)

syco·phan·tic [ˌsɪkəˈfæntɪk] ADJ (*frm*) ossequioso(-a), adulatore(-trice)

Syd·ney [ˈsɪdnɪ] N Sydney *f*

syl·la·ble [ˈsɪləbl] N sillaba

syl·la·bus [ˈsɪləbəs] N (*Scol, Univ*) programma *m*; **on the syllabus** in programma d'esame

sym·bol [ˈsɪmbl] N simbolo

sym·bol·ic [sɪmˈbɒlɪk], **sym·bol·i·cal** [sɪmˈbɒlɪkəl] ADJ simbolico(-a); **to be symbolic of sth** simboleggiare qc

sym·bol·ism [ˈsɪmbəˌlɪzəm] N simbolismo

sym·bol·ize [ˈsɪmbəˌlaɪz] VT simboleggiare

sym·met·ri·cal [sɪˈmɛtrɪkəl] ADJ simmetrico(-a)

sym·me·try [ˈsɪmɪtrɪ] N simmetria; **line symmetry** simmetria rispetto a una retta; **rotational symmetry** simmetria rotazionale

sym·pa·thet·ic [ˌsɪmpəˈθɛtɪk] ADJ (*showing pity*) compassionevole; (*kind, understanding*) comprensivo(-a); **they were sympathetic but could not help** sono stati molto comprensivi ma non hanno potuto aiutare; **I told my teacher and she was sympathetic** l'ho detto all'insegnante e lei è stata comprensiva; **to be sympathetic to a cause** (*well-disposed*) simpatizzare per una causa; **to be sympathetic towards** (*person*) essere comprensivo(-a) nei confronti di
❏ **sympathetic** is not translated by the Italian word *simpatico*

sym·pa·theti·cal·ly [ˌsɪmpəˈθɛtɪkəlɪ] ADV (*see adj*) in modo compassionevole; con comprensione

sym·pa·thize [ˈsɪmpəˌθaɪz] VI: **to sympathize (with sb)** (*feel pity*) partecipare al dolore (di qn); (*understand*) capire (qn); **I sympathize with you in your grief** ti sono molto vicino nel dolore; **I sympathize with what you say, but ...** capisco quello che vuoi dire, ma...
❏ **sympathize** is not translated by the Italian word *simpatizzare*

sym·pa·thiz·er [ˈsɪmpəˌθaɪzə] N (*fig, esp Pol*): **sympathizer (with)** simpatizzante *m/f* (di)

sym·pa·thy [ˈsɪmpəθɪ] N **1** (*pity, compassion*) compassione *f*; **you have my deepest sympathy** *or* **sympathies** hai tutta la mia comprensione; **you won't get any sympathy from me!** non venire a piangere da me!; **with our deepest sympathy** con le nostre più sincere condoglianze; **a letter of sympathy** una lettera di cordoglio **2** (*understanding*) comprensione *f*; (*fellow-feeling, agreement*) solidarietà; **I am in sympathy with your suggestions** mi trovo d'accordo con i tuoi suggerimenti; **to strike in sympathy with sb** scioperare per solidarietà con qn
❏ **sympathy** is not translated by the Italian word *simpatia*

sym·phon·ic [sɪmˈfɒnɪk] ADJ sinfonico(-a)

sym·pho·ny [ˈsɪmfənɪ] N sinfonia

symphony orchestra N orchestra sinfonica

sym·po·sium [sɪmˈpəʊzɪəm] N (*pl symposia*) simposio

symp·tom [ˈsɪmptəm] N sintomo

symp·to·mat·ic [ˌsɪmptəˈmætɪk] ADJ: **symptomatic (of)** sintomatico(-a) (di)

syna·gogue [ˈsɪnəˌɡɒɡ] N sinagoga

sync [sɪŋk] N (*Tech*): **in/out of sync** in/fuori sincronia; **everything is out of sync** (*fig*) è tutto sballato(-a)

syn·chro·mesh [ˌsɪŋkrəʊˈmɛʃ] N cambio sincronizzato

syn·chro·nize [ˈsɪŋkrəˌnaɪz] VT sincronizzare ♦ VI: **to synchronize with** essere in sincronia con

syn·chro·nized swim·ming [ˈsɪŋkrəˌnaɪzdˈswɪmɪŋ] N nuoto sincronizzato

syn·di·cate [*n* ˈsɪndɪkɪt, *vb* ˈsɪndɪˌkeɪt] N (*Comm, etc*) sindacato; (*Press*) agenzia di stampa ♦ VT (*Press*) vendere tramite agenzia di stampa

syn·drome [ˈsɪndrəʊm] N sindrome *f*

syno·nym [ˈsɪnənɪm] N sinonimo

syn·ony·mous [sɪˈnɒnɪməs] ADJ: **synonymous (with)** sinonimo(-a) (di)

syn·op·sis [sɪˈnɒpsɪs] N (*pl* **synopses** [sɪˈnɒpsiːz]) (*of plot*) trama

syn·tax [ˈsɪntæks] N sintassi *f inv*

syn·the·sis [ˈsɪnθəsɪs] N (*pl* **syntheses** [ˈsɪnθəsiːz]) sintesi *f inv*

syn·the·siz·er [ˈsɪnθəˌsaɪzəʳ] N (*Mus*) sintetizzatore *m*

syn·thet·ic [sɪnˈθɛtɪk] ADJ (*fabric etc*) sintetico(-a) ♦ N prodotto sintetico; (*Textiles*) fibra sintetica

syphi·lis [ˈsɪfɪlɪs] N sifilide *f*

sy·phon [ˈsaɪfən] N, VB = **siphon**

Syria [ˈsɪrɪə] N la Siria

Syr·ian [ˈsɪrɪən] ADJ, N siriano(-a)

sy·ringe [sɪˈrɪndʒ] N siringa ♦ VT (*Med*) siringare

syr·up [ˈsɪrəp] N sciroppo; **golden syrup** (*Brit*) melassa raffinata

syr·upy [ˈsɪrəpɪ] ADJ (*also fig*) sciropposo(-a)

sys·tem [ˈsɪstəm] N (*method*) sistema *m*; (*network*) rete *f*; (*Anat*) apparato; **it was quite a shock to his system** è stato uno shock per il suo organismo; **to get sth out of one's system** (*fig*) sfogarsi

sys·tem·at·ic [ˌsɪstəˈmætɪk] ADJ sistematico(-a)

system disk N (*Comput*) disco di sistema

systems analyst N (*Comput*) sistemista

Tt

T, t [tiː] N (*letter*) T, t *m inv, f inv*; **T for Tommy** ≈ T come Taranto; **it fits you to a T** (*fam*) ti sta a pennello; **that's him to a T** (*fam*) è proprio lui

ta [tɑː] EXCL (*Brit fam*) grazie!

tab [tæb] N ABBR = **tabulator** ♦ N (*label*) etichetta; (*flap on garment*) linguetta; (*USA fam: bill*) conto; **to keep tabs on sb/sth** (*fig: fam*) tenere d'occhio qn/qc; **to pick up the tab** (*USA fam*) pagare il conto; **we can put it on your tab** (*USA*) possiamo metterlo sul suo conto

tab·by ['tæbɪ] N (*also:* **tabby cat**) (gatto(-a)) soriano(-a), gatto(-a) tigrato(-a)

tab·er·nac·le ['tæbə,nækl] N tabernacolo

ta·ble ['teɪbl] N 1 tavolo; (*for meals*) tavola; (*also:* **coffee table**) tavolino; **card table** tavolino da gioco; **to lay** *or* **set the table** apparecchiare *or* preparare la tavola; **to clear the table** sparecchiare; **at table** a tavola; **the entire table was in fits of laughter** l'intera tavolata moriva dalle risate; **to drink sb under the table** battere qn nel bere; **to turn the tables on sb** (*fig*) rovesciare la situazione a danno di qn 2 (*Math, Chem: illustration*) tavola; (*chart*) tabella; **table of contents** indice *m*; **league table** (*Ftbl, Rugby*) classifica ♦ VT (*bill, motion: Brit: propose*) presentare; (: *USA: postpone*) rinviare

table·cloth ['teɪbl,klɒθ] N tovaglia

table d'hôte [,tɑːblˈdəʊt] N pasto a prezzo fisso ♦ ADJ (*meal*) a prezzo fisso

table lamp N lampada da tavolo

table·mat ['teɪbl,mæt] N tovaglietta

table salt N sale *m* fino o da tavola

table·spoon ['teɪbl,spuːn] N cucchiaio da portata *or* da tavola; (*also:* **tablespoonful:** *as measurement*) cucchiaiata; **a tablespoonful of sugar** un cucchiaio di zucchero

tab·let ['tæblɪt] N (*inscribed stone*) lapide *f*, targa; (*Med*) compressa; (*for sucking*) pastiglia; (*for writing*) blocco; (*elec*) tablet; **tablet of soap** (*Brit*) saponetta

table tennis N tennis *m* da tavolo *m*

table wine N vino da tavola

tab·loid ['tæblɔɪd] N (*newspaper*) tabloid *m inv*

ta·boo [təˈbuː] ADJ, N tabù *m inv*

tabu·late ['tæbjʊˌleɪt] VT (*data, figures*) disporre in tabelle, tabulare

tabu·la·tor ['tæbjʊˌleɪtəʳ] N tabulatore *m*

tacho·graph ['tækəˌɡrɑːf] N tachigrafo

ta·chom·eter [tæˈkɒmɪtəʳ] N tachimetro

tac·it ['tæsɪt] ADJ tacito(-a)

taci·turn ['tæsɪˌtɜːn] ADJ taciturno(-a)

tack [tæk] N 1 (*nail*) bulletta; (*for upholstery*) borchia; (*USA fam: also:* **thumbtack**) puntina da disegno; **a hammer and some tacks** un martello e dei chiodi; **to get down to brass tacks** venire al sodo 2 (*Naut: course*) bordo; **to be on the port/starboard tack** avere le mura a sinistra/dritta; **to change tack** virare di bordo; (*fig*) cambiare linea di condotta; **to be on the right/wrong tack** (*fig*) essere sulla buona strada/sulla strada sbagliata; **to try a different tack** (*fig*) prendere le cose per un altro verso 3 (*stitch*) punto d'imbastitura 4 (*for horse*) selleria, equipaggiamento ♦ VT 1 (*nail*) imbullettare 2 (*Sewing*) imbastire; (*fig: add*): **to tack sth on to (the end of) sth** (*of letter, book*) aggiungere qc alla fine di qc; **I'll tack on a couple of paragraphs** aggiungerò un paio di paragrafi ♦ VI (*Naut: change direction*) virare di bordo (in prua); (*go zigzag*) bordeggiare

tack·le ['tækl] N 1 (*lifting gear*) paranco 2 (*equipment: esp for sport*) attrezzatura, equipaggiamento; **fishing tackle** attrezzatura da pesca 3 (*Ftbl*) contrasto; (*Rugby*) placcaggio ♦ VT (*Ftbl*) contrastare; (*Rugby*) placcare; (*thief, intruder*) agguantare; (*fig: person, problem, job*) affrontare; **I'll tackle him about it at once** affronterò subito la cosa con lui

tacky ['tækɪ] ADJ (*comp* **-ier,** *superl* **-iest**) (*sticky*) appiccicoso(-a), appiccicaticcio(-a); (*of paint, glue*) ancora bagnato(-a), non ancora asciutto(-a); (*fam: shabby*) scadente; (: *tasteless*) di cattivo gusto; **the paint was still tacky** la vernice era ancora appiccicaticcia; **a pair of tacky red sunglasses** un paio di occhialacci da sole rossi; **a tacky film** un filmaccio

tact [tækt] N tatto

tact·ful ['tæktfʊl] ADJ (*person*) pieno(-a) di tatto; (*remark, reply*) discreto(-a); **to be tactful** avere tatto

tact·ful·ly ['tæktfəlɪ] ADV con tatto, con discrezione

tac·ti·cal ['tæktɪkəl] ADJ tattico(-a)

tactical voting N voto tattico

tac·ti·cian [tækˈtɪʃən] N (*Mil, also fig*) stratega *m/f*

tac·tics ['tæktɪks] N, NPL tattica; **strong-arm tactics** le maniere forti

tact·less ['tæktlɪs] ADJ (*person*) privo(-a) di tatto, che manca di tatto; (*remark*) indelicato(-a)

tact·less·ly ['tæktlɪslɪ] ADV senza tatto

tad·pole ['tædˌpəʊl] N girino

taf·fy ['tæfɪ] N (*USA*) caramella *f* mou, *inv*

tag [tæg] N 1 (*label*) etichetta; (*metal point*) puntale *m*; **price/name tag** etichetta del prezzo/con il nome 2 (*game*) chiapparello

▸ **tag along** VI + ADV andare (*or* venire); **do you mind if I tag along?** ti dispiace se vengo anch'io?; **to tag along behind sb** andare (*or* venire) dietro a qn

▸ **tag on** VT + ADV: **to tag sth on (to the end of sth)** aggiungere qc (alla fine di qc)

Ta·hi·ti [tɑːˈhiːtɪ] N Tahiti *f*

tail [teɪl] N (*gen*) coda; (*of shirt*) estremità inferiore; **to put a tail on sb** (*fig: fam*) far pedinare qn; **he was right on my tail** mi stava alle calcagna; **to turn tail** voltare la schiena; **he went off with his tail between his legs** (*fig*) se n'è andato con la coda fra le gambe ♦ VT (*fam: follow: suspect*) pedinare, seguire

▸ **tail away, tail off** VI + ADV (*in size, quality*) diminuire gradatamente

tail·back ['teɪlˌbæk] N (*Brit: Aut*) coda

tail coat N frac *m inv*, marsina

tail end N (*of party, meeting*) fine *f*; (*of train, procession*) coda; **to be at the tail end of the procession/queue** essere in coda alla processione/in fondo alla coda

tail·gate ['teɪlˌɡeɪt] N (*Aut*) portellone *m* posteriore

tail light N (*Aut*) fanalino di coda; (*Rail*) luce *f* di coda

tai·lor ['teɪləʳ] N sarto; **tailor's dummy** manichino (da sarto); **tailor's (shop)** sartoria (da uomo) ♦ VT (*suit*) confezionare; (*fig*): **to tailor sth (to)** adattare qc (alle esigenze di)

tail·or·ing ['teɪlərɪŋ] N (*cut*) taglio

tailor-made [,teɪləˈmeɪd] ADJ (*also fig*) fatto(-a) su misura; (*fig*): **it's tailor-made for you** è fatto apposta per te

tail·wind ['teɪlˌwɪnd] N vento in coda

taint [teɪnt] N (*fig*) macchia; **the taint of madness** il marchio della pazzia ♦ VT (*meat, food*) far avariare; (*fig: reputation*) infangare

taint·ed ['teɪntɪd] ADJ (*food*) avariato(-a), guasto(-a), andato(-a) a male; (*water, air*) contaminato(-a); (*fig: system*) inquinato(-a); (: *reputation*) infangato(-a)

Tai·wan [taɪˈwɑːn] N la Repubblica di Taiwan

Taiwanese [taɪwəˈniːz] ADJ, N taiwanese

Ta·jiki·stan [tɑːˌdʒɪkɪˈstɑːn] N il Tagikistan

take [teɪk] (*pt* **took,** *pp* **taken**) VT 1 (*gen*) prendere; (*remove, steal*) portar via; **let me take your coat** posso prenderti il cappotto?; **to take sb's hand** prendere qn per mano; **to take sb's arm** appoggiarsi al braccio di qn; **he must be taken alive** dev'essere preso vivo; **to take the train** prendere il treno; **take the first on the left** prenda la prima a sinistra; **he hasn't taken any food for four days** non mangia nulla da quattro giorni; **to take notes** prendere appunti; **take 6 from 9** (*Math*) 9 meno 6; **he took £5 off the price** ha fatto uno sconto di 5 sterline; **to take a trick** (*Cards*) fare una presa; **"to be taken three times a day"** (*Med*) "da prendersi tre volte al dì"; **to take cold/fright** prendere freddo/paura; **to be taken ill** avere un malore; **I take size 8** porto la 36 **2** (*bring, carry*) portare; (*accompany*) accompagnare; **I took the children with me** ho portato i bambini con me; **don't forget to take your camera** non scordarti di portare la macchina fotografica; **he goes to London every week, but he never takes me** va a Londra tutte le settimane ma non mi porta mai con sé; **to take for a walk** (*child, dog*) portare a fare una passeggiata **3** (*require: effort, courage*) volerci, occorrere; (*Gram*) prendere, reggere; **it takes about an hour** ci vuole circa un'ora; **it took me two hours to do it**, **I took two hours to do it** mi ci sono volute due ore per farlo; **it won't take long** non ci vorrà molto tempo; **she's got what it takes to do the job** ha i requisiti necessari per quel lavoro; **it takes a lot of time/courage** occorre *or* ci vuole molto tempo/coraggio; **it takes a lot of money to do that** ci vogliono un sacco di soldi per farlo; **that will take some explaining** non sarà facile da spiegare **4** (*accept, receive*) accettare; (*obtain, win: prize*) vincere, ottenere; (: *1st place*) conquistare; (: *Comm: money*) incassare; **he didn't take my advice** non mi ha ascoltato; **how did he take the news?** come ha preso la notizia?; **please take a seat** prego, si sieda; **is this seat taken?** è occupato (questo posto)?; **do you take credit cards?** accettate carte di credito?; **it's worth taking a chance** vale la pena di correre il rischio; **it's £50, take it or leave it** sono 50 sterline, prendere o lasciare; **can you take it from here?** (*handing over task*) puoi andare avanti tu? **5** (*have room or capacity for: passengers*) contenere; (*support: subj: bridge*) avere una portata di; (: *chair*) tenere; **the hall will take 200 people** nel salone c'è posto per 200 persone; **the bus takes 60 passengers** l'autobus porta 60 persone; **it will take at least five litres** contiene almeno cinque litri **6** (*conduct: meeting*) condurre; (: *church service*) officiare; (*teach, study: course*) fare; (*exam, test*) fare, sostenere; **the professor is taking the French course himself** sarà il professore stesso a tenere il corso di francese; **I only took Russian for one year** ho fatto russo solo per un anno; **have you taken your driving test yet?** hai già fatto l'esame di guida?; **I took the driving test** ho fatto *or* sostenuto l'esame di guida **7** (*understand, assume*) pensare; (*consider: case, example*) prendere; **how old do you take him to be?** quanti anni pensi che abbia?; **I took him for a doctor** l'ho preso per un dottore; **I take it that ...** suppongo che...; **may I take it that ...?** allora posso star certo che...?; **take it from me!** credimi!; **take D.H. Lawrence, for example** prendete D.H. Lawrence, per esempio **8** (*put up with, tolerate: climate, alcohol*) sopportare; **she can't take the heat** non sopporta il caldo; **I can't take any more!** non ce la faccio più!; **I won't take no for an answer** non accetterò una risposta negativa *or* un rifiuto; **he can't take being criticized** non sopporta di essere criticato **9** (*negotiate: bend*) prendere; (: *fence*) saltare **10** (*attracted*): **to be taken with sb/sth** essere tutto(-a) preso(-a) da qn/qc; **I'm quite taken with the idea** l'idea non mi dispiace per niente **11** (*as function verb: see other element*): **to take a photograph** fare una fotografia; **to take a bath/shower** fare un bagno/una doccia; **take your time!** calma!; **it took me by surprise** mi ha colto di sorpresa ♦ VI (*dye, fire*) prendere; (*injection*) fare effetto; (*plant, cutting*) attecchire ♦ N (*Cine*) ripresa

▸ **take after** VI + PREP assomigliare a; **she takes after her mother** assomiglia a sua madre

▸ **take against** VI + PREP prendere in antipatia

▸ **take along** VT + ADV portare

▸ **take apart** VT + ADV (*clock, machine*) smontare; (*fig: fam: criticize*) demolire

▸ **take aside** VT + ADV prendere in disparte

▸ **take away** VI + ADV: **to take away from sth** danneggiare qc; **his bad temper took away from the pleasure of our party** ci ha guastato un po' la festa con il suo cattivo umore ♦ VT + ADV **1** (*subtract*): **to take away (from)** sottrarre (da); **you need to take this amount away from the total** devi

sottrarre questa cifra dal totale; **sixteen take away three** sedici meno tre **2** (*remove: person, thing, privilege*) togliere; (*carry away, lead away*) portar via; **they took away all his belongings** gli hanno portato via tutte le sue cose; **pizzas to take away** pizze *fpl* da asporto

▸ **take back** VT + ADV **1** (*get back, reclaim*) riprendere; (*retract: statement, promise*) ritirare; **I take it all back!** ritiro tutto quello che ho detto! **2** (*return: book, goods, person*) riportare; **I took it back to the shop** l'ho riportato al negozio; **can you take him back home?** puoi riaccompagnarlo a casa?; **it takes me back to my childhood** (*fig*) mi ha fatto tornare alla mia infanzia

▸ **take down** VT + ADV **1** (*curtains, picture, vase from shelf*) tirare giù; **she took down a book from the top shelf** ha tirato giù un libro dall'ultimo scaffale **2** (*dismantle: scaffolding*) smontare; (: *building*) demolire; **he took down the bookcase** ha smontato la libreria **3** (*write down: notes, address*) prendere; (: *letter*) scrivere; **the policeman took down the details** il poliziotto ha preso nota dei particolari

▸ **take in** VT + ADV **1** (*bring in: object, harvest*) portare dentro; (: *person*) far entrare; (: *lodger*) prendere, ospitare; (: *orphan*) accogliere; (: *stray dog*) raccogliere **2** (*receive: money*) incassare; (: *laundry, sewing*) prendere a domicilio **3** (*Sewing*) stringere **4** (*include, cover*) coprire; (*prices*) includere, comprendere; **we took in Florence on the way** abbiamo visitato anche Firenze durante il viaggio **5** (*grasp, understand: meaning, complex subject*) capire; (: *situation*) rendersi conto di; (: *impressions, sights*) assimilare; (: *visually: surroundings, people, area*) prendere nota con uno sguardo; **I didn't really take it in** non avevo capito bene; **he took the situation in at a glance** ha afferrato subito la situazione **3** (*deceive, cheat*) imbrogliare, abbindolare; **they were taken in by his story** si sono lasciati abbindolare dalla sua storia; **to be taken in by appearances** farsi ingannare dalle apparenze

▸ **take off** VI + ADV (*plane, passengers*) decollare; (*high jumper*) spiccare un salto; **the plane took off twenty minutes late** l'aereo ha decollato con venti minuti di ritardo ♦ VT + ADV **1** (*remove: clothes*) togliere *o* togliersi; (: *price tag, lid, item from menu*) togliere; (: *leg, limb*) amputare; (: *cancel: train*) sopprimere; **take your coat off** levati il cappotto **2** (*deduct: from bill, price*) she took 50p off ha fatto 50 penny di sconto **3** (*lead away: person, object*) portare; **she was taken off to the hospital** è stata portata all'ospedale; **to take o.s. off** andarsene **4** (*imitate*) imitare ♦ VT + PREP **1** (*remove: clothes, price tag, lid*) togliere da; (: *item from menu*) cancellare da; (*cancel: train*) togliere da; **to take sb off sth** (*remove from duty, job*) allontanare qn da qc **2** (*deduct: from bill, price*): **he took 5% off the price for me** mi ha fatto uno sconto del 5% sul prezzo

▸ **take on** VI + ADV **1** (*old, fam: become upset*) prendersela **2** (*song, fashion*) fare presa ♦ VT + ADV **1** (*work*) accettare, intraprendere; (*responsibility*) prendersi, addossarsi; (*bet, challenger*) affrontare **2** (*worker: also fig: qualities, form*) assumere; (*cargo, passengers*) caricare; **her face took on a wistful expression** sul suo volto si era dipinta un'espressione malinconica

▸ **take out** VT + ADV **1** (*bring, carry out*) portare fuori; **to take sb out to ...** portare qn a...; **he took her out to the theatre** l'ha portata a teatro; **can I take you out to lunch?** posso invitarti a pranzo fuori?; **he took the dog out for a walk** ha portato il cane a passeggio **2** (*extract: appendix, tooth*) togliere; (*remove: stain*) rimuovere, togliere; (*pull out: from pocket, drawer*): **to take sth out of sth** tirare fuori qc da qc, estrarre qc da qc; **he took a plate out of the cupboard** ha preso un piatto dalla credenza; **he opened his wallet and took out some money** ha aperto il portafoglio e ha tirato fuori dei soldi **3** (*insurance, patent, licence*) prendere, ottenere, procurarsi **4** **to take sb out of himself** distrarre qn; **redecorating a house takes it out of you** è spossante ridipingere una casa; **don't take it out on me!** non prendertela con me!

▸ **take over** VI + ADV (*dictator, political party*) prendere il potere; **to take over from sb** prendere le consegne da qn, subentrare a qn; **I'll take over now** ti do il cambio ♦ VT + ADV (*debts, business*) rilevare; (*company*) assumere il controllo di; **to take over from sb** subentrare a qn; **to take over sb's job** subentrare a qn nel lavoro; **they took over the**

company last year hanno assunto il controllo della società l'anno scorso; **the tourists have taken over Florence** (*fig*) i turisti hanno preso d'assalto Firenze
- **take to** VI + PREP **1** (*develop liking for: person*) prendere in simpatia; (: *games, surroundings, activity*) prendere gusto a; **I just can't take to my friend's husband** il marito della mia amica non riesce proprio a piacermi; **she didn't take kindly to the idea** l'idea non le è piaciuta per niente **2** (*form habit of*): **to take to sth** darsi a qc; **to take to doing sth** prendere *or* cominciare a fare qc **3** (*escape to*) fuggire verso; **to take to one's bed** mettersi a letto
- **take up** VI + ADV: **to take up with sb** fare amicizia con qn ♦ VT + ADV **1** (*raise, lift*) raccogliere; (*subj: bus*) prendere; (*carpet, floorboards*) sollevare; (*road*) spaccare; (*dress, hem*) accorciare **2** (*lead, carry upstairs*) portare su **3** (*continue*) riprendere **4** (*occupy: time, attention*) assorbire; (: *space*) occupare; **it will take up the whole of our Sunday** ci porterà via tutta la domenica; **he's very taken up with his work** è molto preso dal suo lavoro **5** (*absorb: liquids*) assorbire **6** (*raise question of: matter, point*) affrontare **7** (*start: job, duties*) cominciare; (: *hobby, sport*): **to take up painting/golf/photography** cominciare a dipingere/giocare a golf/fare fotografie; **to take up a career as** intraprendere la carriera di **8** (*accept: offer, challenge*) accettare; **I'll take you up on your offer** accetto la tua offerta **9** (*adopt: cause, case, person*) appoggiare
- **take upon** VT + PREP: **to take sth upon o.s.** prendersi la responsabilità di qc; **to take it upon o.s. to do sth** prendersi la responsabilità di fare qc

take·away ['teɪkə,wɔɪ] (*Brit*) N (*shop*) ≈ rosticceria; (*meal*) piatto pronto (*da asporto*) ♦ ADJ (*food*) da asporto, da portar via
take-home pay ['teɪkhəʊm,peɪ] N stipendio netto
tak·en ['teɪkn] PP *of* take
take·off ['teɪk,ɒf] N **1** (*Aer*) decollo; (*Horse-riding*) battuta **2** (*fam: imitation*) imitazione *f*
take-out ['teɪk,aʊt] ADJ (*USA*) = takeaway
take·over ['teɪk,əʊvə'] N (*Comm*) assorbimento
takeover bid N offerta di assorbimento
tak·ings ['teɪkɪŋz] NPL (*Fin*) introiti *mpl*, entrate *fpl*; (*at show*) incasso
talc [tælk], **tal·cum pow·der** ['tælkəm,paʊdə'] N talco
tale [teɪl] N (*gen*) storia; (*story*) racconto; (*legend*) leggenda; (*pej*) fandonia; **to tell tales** (*inform*) fare la spia; (*lies*) dire bugie; **he told us the tale of his escape** ci ha raccontato la storia della sua fuga
tal·ent ['tælənt] N **1** (*skill*) talento; **he's got a lot of talent** ha molto talento; **to have a talent for** essere portato(-a) per; **he has a talent for languages** è portato per le lingue, ha facilità nell'apprendere le lingue; **there isn't much musical talent in this town** non ci sono molti grandi talenti musicali in questa città; **there's not much talent about tonight** (*Brit fam: attractive people*) non c'è nessuno di decente in giro stasera **2** (*Bible*) talento
tal·ent·ed ['tæləntɪd] ADJ di talento; **she's a talented pianist** è una pianista di talento
talent scout N talent scout *m/f inv*
tal·is·man ['tælɪzmən] N talismano
talk [tɔːk] N **1** (*conversation*) conversazione *f*; (*chat*) chiacchierata; (*speech*) discorso; (*interview*) discussione *f*; **talks** NPL (*Pol*) colloqui *mpl*; **to have a talk about** parlare di; **I had a talk with my mother about it** ne ho parlato con mia mamma; **I must have a talk with you** devo parlarti **2** (*lecture*) conferenza; **to give a talk** tenere una conferenza, fare un intervento; **she gave a talk on ancient Egypt** ha fatto un intervento sull'antico Egitto; **he will give us a talk on ...** ci parlerà di...; **to give a talk on the radio** parlare alla radio **3** (*gossip*) dicerie *fpl*, chiacchiere *fpl*; **the talk was all about the wedding** non si faceva che parlare del matrimonio; **there has been a lot of talk about him** si è molto parlato di lui; **she's the talk of the town** è sulla bocca di tutti; **it's just talk** sono solo chiacchiere ♦ VI (*gen*) parlare; (*discuss*) discutere; (*chatter*) chiacchierare; **to talk about** parlare di; (*converse*) discorrere *or* conversare di; **what did you talk about?** di che cosa avete parlato?; **to talk to/with sb about or of sth** parlare a/con qn di qc; **to talk to o.s.** parlare da

solo; **try to keep him talking** cerca di farlo parlare; **to get o.s. talked about** far parlare di sé; **it's all right for you to talk!** parli bene tu!; **look who's talking!** senti chi parla!, parli proprio tu!; **now you're talking!** questo sì che è parlare!; **he talks too much** (*talkative*) parla troppo; (*indiscreet*) non sa tenere la bocca chiusa; **they are talking of going to Sicily** pensano di andare in Sicilia; **who were you talking to?** con chi stavi parlando?; **he knows what he's talking about** lui sì che se ne intende; **talking of films, have you seen ...?** a proposito di film, hai visto...? ♦ VT (*a language, slang*) parlare; **they were talking Arabic** parlavano arabo; **to talk business** parlare di affari; **to talk shop** parlare del lavoro *or* degli affari; **to talk nonsense** dire stupidaggini; **to talk sb into doing sth** persuadere *or* convincere qn a fare qc; **to talk sb out of doing sth** dissuadere qn dal fare qc
- **talk back** VI + ADV: **to talk back (to sb)** rispondere impertinentemente (a qn)
- **talk down** VI + ADV: **to talk down to sb** parlare a qn con condiscendenza ♦ VT + ADV: **to talk a plane (or pilot) down** guidare l'atterraggio dalla torre di controllo
- **talk out** VT + ADV: **to talk things out** mettere le cose in chiaro discutendone
- **talk over** VT + ADV discutere; **to talk sth over with sb** discutere qc con qn; **I'll have to talk it over with my wife** devo parlarne con mia moglie
- **talk round** VT + ADV: **to talk sb round** convincere qn ♦ VI + PREP (*subject, problem*) girare intorno a

talka·tive ['tɔːkətɪv] ADJ loquace, ciarliero(-a)
talking point N argomento di conversazione
talking-to ['tɔːkɪŋ,tuː] N (*fam*): **to give sb a good talking-to** fare una bella paternale a qn
talk show N (*USA: TV, Radio*) talk show *m inv*
tall [tɔːl] ADJ (*comp -er, superl -est*) alto(-a); **to be two metres tall** essere alto due metri; **how tall are you?** quanto sei alto?; **I'm 6 feet tall** ≈ sono alto 1 metro 80; **that's a tall order!** è una bella pretesa!
tall·boy ['tɔːl,bɔɪ] N (*Brit*) cassettone *m* alto
tall·ness ['tɔːlnɪs] N altezza
tall story N (*Brit*) storia incredibile
tal·ly ['tælɪ] N (*count*) conto, conteggio; (*running total*) totale *m*; (*score*) punteggio; **to keep a tally of sth** tener il conto di qc ♦ VI: **to tally (with)** corrispondere (a)
tal·on ['tælən] N artiglio
❑ **talon** is not translated by the Italian word *tallone*
tam·bou·rine [,tæmbə'riːn] N tamburello
tame [teɪm] ADJ (*comp -r, superl -st*) (*animal*) addomesticato(-a); (*fig: person*) docile; (: *story, style*) scialbo(-a), insipido(-a); (: *book, performance*) banale; **tame monkeys** scimmie *fpl* addomesticate; **a tame report** una relazione scialba ♦ VT (*wild creature*) addomesticare; (*lion, tiger, passion*) domare
Tam·il ['tæmɪl] ADJ tamil *inv* ♦ N (*person*) tamil *m/f*; (*language*) tamil *m*
tam·per ['tæmpə'] VI: **to tamper with** manomettere; **someone had tampered with the brakes** qualcuno aveva manomesso i freni
tam·pon ['tæmpən] N tampone *m*
tan [tæn] N (*also: suntan*) abbronzatura; (*colour*) color *m* marrone chiaro; **to get a tan** abbronzarsi ♦ ADJ marrone chiaro *inv* ♦ VI abbronzarsi ♦ VT (*person, skin*) abbronzare; (*leather*) conciare; **to tan sb's hide** (*fam*) darle a qn
tan·dem ['tændəm] N (*bicycle*) tandem *m inv* ♦ ADV: **in tandem** in tandem
tan·doori [tæn'dʊərɪ] ADJ: **tandoori chicken** (*Culin*) pollo speziato, cucinato in forno d'argilla, tipico della cucina indiana
tang [tæŋ] N (*taste*) sapore *m* forte; (*smell*) odore *m* penetrante
tan·gent ['tændʒənt] N (*Geom*) tangente *f*; **to go off at a tangent** (*fig*) partire per la tangente
tan·ge·rine [,tændʒə'riːn] N specie di mandarino
tan·gible ['tændʒəbl] ADJ (*proof, results*) tangibile; (*difference*) sostanziale; **tangible assets** patrimonio reale
Tan·gier [tæn'dʒɪə'] N Tangeri *f*
tan·gle ['tæŋɡl] N (*of wool, wire*) groviglio; (*in hair*) nodo; (*fig: muddle*) confusione *f*; **a tangle of wires** un groviglio di fili; **to get into a tangle** (*gen*) aggrovigliarsi; (*hair*) arruffarsi;

(*person*) combinare un pasticcio; **we got into a tangle** ci siamo messi in un pasticcio ♦ VT (*also:* **tangle up**) aggroviglia-re; (*hair*) arruffare ♦ VI aggrovigliarsi; (*hair*) ingarbugliarsi; **to tangle with sb** (*fig: fam*) azzuffarsi con qn

tan·go [ˈtæŋɡəʊ] N tango

tank [tæŋk] N **1** (*container: for gas, petrol*) serbatoio; (*: for rainwater*) cisterna; (*: for processing*) vasca; **fish tank** acquario; **fuel tank** serbatoio del carburante **2** (*Mil*) carro armato; **the army sent in its tanks** l'esercito ha inviato i carri armati

tank·ard [ˈtæŋkəd] N boccale *m* (con coperchio)

tank·er [ˈtæŋkəʳ] N (*ship: for oil*) petroliera; (*: for water*) nave *f* cisterna, inv; (*aircraft*) aereocisterna; (*truck*) autocisterna, autobotte *f*

tanned [tænd] ADJ abbronzato(-a)

tan·nin [ˈtænɪn] N tannino

tan·ning [ˈtænɪŋ] N **1** (*by sun*) abbronzatura; (*of leather*) conciatura **2** (*fam: beating*) botte *fpl*

tan·ta·liz·ing [ˈtæntəˌlaɪzɪŋ] ADJ (*food*) stuzzicante; (*idea, offer*) allettante

tan·ta·mount [ˈtæntəˌmaʊnt] ADJ: **to be tantamount to** equivalere a; **tantamount to** equivalente a

tan·trum [ˈtæntrəm] N accesso di collera; **to have** *or* **throw a tantrum** fare le bizze *or* i capricci

Tan·za·nia [ˌtænzəˈnɪə] N la Tanzania

Tan·za·nian [ˌtænzəˈnɪən] ADJ, N tanzaniano(-a)

tap¹ [tæp] N (*Brit: on sink*) rubinetto; **on tap** (*beer*) alla spina; (*fig: resources*) a disposizione; **the hot tap** il rubinetto dell'acqua calda ♦ VT (*barrel*) spillare; (*telephone*) mettere sotto controllo; (*telephone conversation*) intercettare; (*resources*) sfruttare, utilizzare

❑ **tap** is not translated by the Italian word *tappa*

tap² [tæp] N (*gentle blow*) colpetto; **there was a tap on the door** hanno bussato leggermente alla porta ♦ VT (*pat, knock*) picchiare leggermente su, dare un colpetto a; **I tapped him on the shoulder** gli ho dato un colpetto sulla spalla; **to tap one's foot** (*impatiently*) battere il piede; (*in time to music*) segnare il tempo con il piede; **to tap out a message in Morse** trasmettere un messaggio in Morse ♦ VI (*knock*) bussare; (*rain*) picchiettare

tap dancing N tip tap *m*

tape [teɪp] N (*gen: also Sport: for recording*) nastro; (*also:* **magnetic tape**) nastro (magnetico); (*Sewing*) fettuccia; **on tape** (*song*) su nastro; **adhesive tape** nastro adesivo; **to break the tape** (*Sport*) tagliare la linea del traguardo ♦ VT (*record*) registrare (su nastro); **did you tape the film last night?** hai registrato il film di ieri sera?; (*also:* **tape up**) legare con un nastro; **I've got him taped** (*Brit fam*) ho capito il tipo

tape deck N piastra di registrazione

tape measure N metro a nastro

ta·per [ˈteɪpəʳ] N (*waxed spill*) cerino; (*thin candle*) candelina ♦ VI (*also:* **taper off**) assottigliarsi; (*trousers*) restringersi

tape-record [ˈteɪprɪˌkɔːd] VT registrare (su nastro)

tape recorder N registratore *m* (a nastro)

tape recording N registrazione *f*

ta·pered [ˈteɪpəd] ADJ (*trouser leg, stick*) affusolato(-a)

tap·es·try [ˈtæpɪstrɪ] N (*object*) arazzo, tappezzeria; (*art*) mezzo punto

tape·worm [ˈteɪpˌwɜːm] N tenia, verme *m* solitario

tapio·ca [ˌtæpɪˈəʊkə] N tapioca

tap·pet [ˈtæpɪt] N punteria

tar [tɑːʳ] N catrame *m*; **low-/middle-tar cigarettes** sigarette a basso/medio contenuto di catrame ♦ VT (*road*) incatramare; **he's tarred with the same brush** *or* **besaglio** (*fig*) è della stessa razza

ta·ran·tu·la [təˈræntjʊlə] N tarantola

tar·dy [ˈtɑːdɪ] ADJ (*comp* **-ier**, *superl* **-iest**) (*slow*) lento(-a); (*later than expected*) tardivo(-a), tardo(-a); (*USA: late: person*) in ritardo

tar·get [ˈtɑːɡɪt] N (*gen: objective*) obiettivo; (*Mil, Archery*) bersaglio; (*fig*) bersaglio; **he achieved his target** ha raggiunto il suo obiettivo; **the bullet hit the target** il proiettile ha colpito il bersaglio; **she has been the target of criticism** è stata fatta oggetto *or* bersaglio di critiche; **the targets for production in 2020** gli obiettivi della produzione per il 2020; **to be on target** (*project*) essere nei tempi (di

lavorazione) ♦ VT puntare su; **the company targets well-off childless couples** l'azienda punta sulle coppie benestanti senza figli

target practice N (esercitazioni *fpl*) tiro al bersaglio

tar·iff [ˈtærɪf] N (*price list*) tariffa; (*tax*) tariffa doganale, dazio

tar·mac [ˈtɑːmæk] N (*Brit: on road*) macadam *m* al catrame; (*runway*): **the tarmac** la pista ♦ VT (*Brit*) macadamizzare con il catrame

tar·nish [ˈtɑːnɪʃ] VT ossidare, annerire; (*fig: reputation*) infangare, macchiare; **the affair tarnished his reputation** la storia ha macchiato la sua reputazione ♦ VI ossidarsi, annerirsi; **it never rusts or tarnishes** non si arrugginisce né si annerisce

ta·rot [ˈtærəʊ] N tarocco

tar·pau·lin [tɑːˈpɔːlɪn] N (*waterproof cover*) (tela) incerata

tar·ra·gon [ˈtærəgən] N dragoncello

tart¹ [tɑːt] ADJ (*fruit, flavour*) aspro(-a), agro(-a); (*fig: remark*) caustico(-a)

▸ **tart up** VT + ADV (*Brit fam*) agghindare

tart² [tɑːt] N **1** (*Brit: Culin: large*) crostata; (*: individual*) crostatina **2** (*fam, offensive: woman*) puttana (*fam!*)

tar·tan [ˈtɑːtən] N tartan *m inv*, tessuto scozzese ♦ ADJ di tessuto scozzese; **a tartan scarf** una sciarpa scozzese

tar·tar [ˈtɑːtəʳ] N (*on teeth*) tartaro; **cream of tartar** cremor tartaro

tartar sauce N salsa tartara

task [tɑːsk] N compito; **a difficult task** un compito difficile; **to take sb to task (for sth)** richiamare qn all'ordine (per qc), rimproverare qn (per qc)

task force N (*Mil, Police*) unità *f inv* operativa, task force *f inv*

task·master [ˈtɑːskˌmɑːstəʳ] N: **he's a hard taskmaster** è un vero tiranno

Tas·ma·nia [tæzˈmeɪnɪə] N la Tasmania

tas·sel [ˈtæsəl] N nappa, fiocco

taste [teɪst] N (*gen*) gusto; (*flavour*) sapore *m*, gusto; (*fig: glimpse, idea*) idea; **the soup had an odd taste** la minestra aveva un sapore un po' strano; **to have a taste of sth** assaggiare qc; **may I have a taste?** posso assaggiare?; **have a taste of everything!** assaggia un po' di tutto!; **to have a taste for sth** avere un'inclinazione per qc; **he acquired a taste for sports cars** gli è preso il gusto delle macchine sportive; **it's not to my taste** non è di mio gusto; **to be in bad** *or* **poor taste** essere di cattivo gusto; **a joke in bad taste** uno scherzo di cattivo gusto; **"sweeten to taste"** (*Culin*) "zuccherare a piacere" ♦ VT **1** gustare; (*sample*) assaggiare; **would you like to taste it?** vuoi assaggiare?; **just taste this** assaggiane un pochino **2** (*notice flavour of*) sentire il sapore di; **you can taste the garlic (in it)** (ci) si sente il sapore dell'aglio **3** (*fig: experience*) assaporare; **once he had tasted power** una volta assaporato il gusto del potere ♦ VI: **to taste of** (*fish, garlic*) sapere di, avere sapore di; **it tastes of fish** sa di pesce; **it tastes good/bad** ha un buon/cattivo sapore; **what does it taste like?** che sapore *or* gusto ha?; **rabbit tastes quite like chicken** il coniglio ha un sapore molto simile a quello del pollo

❑ **taste** is not translated by the Italian word *tasto*

taste bud N papilla gustativa

taste·ful [ˈteɪstfʊl] ADJ di (buon) gusto

taste·ful·ly [ˈteɪstfəlɪ] ADV con gusto

taste·less [ˈteɪstlɪs] ADJ (*food*) insipido(-a); (*decor, joke, remark*) di cattivo gusto

tasty [ˈteɪstɪ] ADJ (*comp* **-ier**, *superl* **-iest**) (*food*) saporito(-a), gustoso(-a); (*dish, meal*) succulento(-a)

tat·tered [ˈtætəd] ADJ sbrindellato(-a)

tat·ters [ˈtætəz] NPL stracci *mpl*; **in tatters** a brandelli, sbrindellato(-a)

tat·too¹ [təˈtuː] N (*on skin*) tatuaggio ♦ VT tatuare

tat·too² [təˈtuː] N (*Mil: signal*) ritirata; (*: show*) parata militare

tat·ty [ˈtætɪ] ADJ (*comp* **-ier**, *superl* **-iest**) (*Brit fam: shabby*) malandato(-a), malridotto(-a); (*: paint*) scrostato(-a)

taught [tɔːt] PT, PP of **teach**

taunt [tɔːnt] N scherno ♦ VT: **to taunt sb (with)** schernire qn (per)

Tau·rus [ˈtɔːrəs] N (*Astron, Astrol*) Toro; **to be Taurus** essere del Toro; **I'm Taurus** sono del Toro

taut [tɔːt] ADJ (*comp* -er, *superl* -est) (*also fig*) teso(-a)
tav·ern ['tævən] N (*old*) taverna
taw·dry ['tɔːdrɪ] ADJ (*comp* -ier, *superl* -iest) pacchiano(-a)
taw·ny ['tɔːnɪ] ADJ (*comp* -ier, *superl* -iest) fulvo(-a)
tax [tæks] N (*on income*) imposta, tasse *fpl* (*fam*); (*on goods, services*) tassa; **before/after tax** al lordo/netto delle imposte (*or* delle tasse); **free of tax** esente da imposte; esentasse *inv*; **a third of my wages goes in tax** un terzo del mio stipendio se ne va in tasse; **how much tax do you pay?** quanto paghi di tasse?; **to put a tax on sth** mettere una tassa su qc; **the tax on cigarettes** la tassa sulle sigarette ♦ VT 1 (*Fin: people, salary, goods*) tassare; **tobacco and petrol are heavily taxed** le tasse sul tabacco e sulla benzina sono altissime 2 (*fig: resources*) gravare su; **to tax sb's patience** mettere alla prova la pazienza di qn 3 (*fig: accuse*): **to tax sb with sth/with doing sth** accusare qn di qc/di aver fatto qc ♦ ADJ fiscale, delle tasse; **for tax purposes** per motivi fiscali
tax·able ['tæksəbl] ADJ imponibile
tax allowance N detrazione *f* d'imposta
taxa·tion [tæk'seɪʃən] N (*act*) tassazione *f*; (*taxes*) imposte *fpl*, tasse *fpl*; **this will mean higher taxation** questo significa tasse più alte; **system of taxation** sistema *m* fiscale
tax avoidance N elusione *f* fiscale
tax collector N esattore *m* delle imposte
tax evasion N evasione *f* fiscale
tax exemption N esenzione *f* fiscale
tax exile N *chi ripara all'estero per evadere le imposte*
tax-free [tæks'friː] ADJ esente da imposte, esentasse *inv* ♦ ADV senza pagare tasse
tax haven N paradiso fiscale
taxi ['tæksɪ] N taxi *m inv* ♦ VI (*Aer*) rullare
taxi·der·mist ['tæksɪˌdɜːmɪst] N tassidermista *m/f*
taxi driver N tassista *m/f*
tax inspector N ispettore *m* delle tasse
taxi rank, (*USA*) **taxi stand** N posteggio dei taxi
tax·payer ['tæksˌpeɪəʳ] N contribuente *m/f*
tax rebate N rimborso fiscale
tax relief N sgravio fiscale
tax return N dichiarazione *f* dei redditi
tax shelter N *espediente legale per pagare meno tasse*
tax year N anno fiscale
TB [ˌtiː'biː] N ABBR (= *tuberculosis*) TBC *f*
TD [ˌtiː'diː] N ABBR (*USA*) 1 (= *Treasury Department*) *see* treasury 2 (*American Football*) = touchdown
tea [tiː] N 1 (*beverage*) tè *m inv*; **I made a pot of tea** ho fatto un po' di tè; **would you like some tea?** vuoi del tè?; **a cup of tea** una tazza di tè; **tea with lemon** tè al limone; **it's just my cup of tea!** (*fig*) è proprio quello che fa per me! 2 (*Brit: main evening meal*) cena; (*also:* **afternoon tea**) tè *m inv*; **we're having sausages and beans for tea** per cena abbiamo salsicce e fagioli; **we're invited to tea at the Browns'** siamo stati invitati per il tè dai Brown ♦ ADJ di tè, del tè
tea bag N bustina di tè
tea break N (*Brit*) pausa sul lavoro (*per bere un tè, un caffè*)
tea·cake ['tiːkeɪk] N (*Brit*) panino dolce all'uvetta
teach [tiːtʃ] (*pt, pp* taught) VT insegnare; **I teach English** insegno inglese; **to teach sb sth, teach sth to sb** insegnare qc a qn; **to teach sb (how) to do sth** insegnare a qn come si fa qc; **I taught him (how) to write** gli ho insegnato a scrivere; **my sister taught me (how) to swim** mia sorella mi ha insegnato a nuotare; **it taught him a lesson** (*fig*) gli è servito da lezione; **that'll teach you!** così impari! ♦ VI insegnare; **his wife teaches in our school** sua moglie insegna nella nostra scuola
teach·er ['tiːtʃəʳ] N (*gen*) insegnante *m/f*; (*in secondary school*) professore(-essa); (*in primary school*) maestro(-a); **French teacher** insegnante di francese
teacher training college N (*for primary schools*) ≈ istituto magistrale; (*for secondary schools*) scuola universitaria per l'abilitazione all'insegnamento
teach·ing ['tiːtʃɪŋ] N (*gen*) insegnamento; **to go into teaching** fare l'insegnante; **she went into teaching 10 years ago** ha incominciato a insegnare 10 anni fa; **the teaching profession** l'insegnamento

teaching aids NPL sussidi *mpl* didattici
teaching hospital N clinica universitaria
teaching staff N (*Brit*) corpo insegnante *or* docente, insegnanti *mpl*
tea cloth N (*for dishes*) strofinaccio; (*Brit: for trolley, tray*) tovaglietta da tè
tea cosy N copriteiera *m inv*
tea·cup ['tiːˌkʌp] N tazza da tè
teak [tiːk] N teak *m*
tea leaves NPL foglie *fpl* di tè
team [tiːm] N (*of people*) équipe *f inv*; (*Sport*) squadra; (*of animals*) tiro; **home team** squadra di casa
  ▸ **team up** VI + ADV: **to team up (with)** mettersi insieme (a)
team games NPL giochi *mpl* di squadra
team·work ['tiːmˌwɜːk] N lavoro d'équipe; (*Sport*) lavoro di squadra
tea party N (*ricevimento*) tè *m inv*
tea·pot ['tiːpɒt] N teiera
tear[1] [tɛəʳ] (*pt* tore, *pp* torn) N (*rip, hole*) strappo; **your shirt has a tear in it** hai uno strappo nella camicia, hai la camicia strappata; **there was a small tear in the sleeve** c'era un piccolo strappo sulla manica ♦ VT (*gen*) strappare; **torn by remorse** tormentato(-a) dal rimorso; **torn by war** (*fig*) devastato(-a) dalla guerra; **torn by his emotions** combattuto(-a); **he was torn between going and staying** era combattuto tra andare e restare; **to tear to pieces** *or* **to bits** *or* **to shreds** (*also fig*) fare a pezzi *or* a brandelli; **to tear a muscle** strapparsi un muscolo; **to tear a hole in** (*shirt*) fare un buco in; (*argument*) dimostrare che fa acqua; **to tear a letter** *or* **an envelope open** aprire una busta strappandola; **be careful or you'll tear the page** stai attento o strapperai la pagina; **he tore his jacket** gli si è strappata la giacca; **I've torn my jeans** mi si sono strappati i jeans ♦ VI (*be ripped*) strapparsi; (*subj: person, animal*): **to tear at sth** strappare qc; **it won't tear, it's very strong** non si strappa, è molto resistente
  ▸ **tear along** VI + ADV (*rush*) correre all'impazzata ♦ VI + PREP correre per
  ▸ **tear apart** VT + ADV (*also fig*) distruggere
  ▸ **tear away** VT + ADV: **to tear o.s. away (from sth)** (*fig*) staccarsi (da qc)
  ▸ **tear down** VT + ADV (*flag, poster*) tirare giù; (*building*) demolire
  ▸ **tear into** VI + PREP (*fam*): **to tear into sb** criticare ferocemente qn
  ▸ **tear loose** VT + ADV 1 **to tear o.s. loose** liberarsi (con uno strattone) 2 **to tear sth loose** strappare via qc ♦ VI + ADV liberarsi (con uno strattone)
  ▸ **tear off** VT + ADV (*wrapping*) strappare; (*perforated section*) staccare; (*roof*) portare via ♦ VT + PREP (*piece of material*) strappare da
  ▸ **tear out** VT + ADV (*sheet of paper, cheque*) staccare; **to tear one's hair out** strapparsi i capelli ♦ VI + ADV correre fuori
  ▸ **tear up** VT + ADV 1 (*also fig*) strappare; (*agreement*) annullare 2 (*plant, stake*) sradicare; (*sheet of paper*) strappare; **he tore the letter up** ha strappato la lettera
tear[2] [tɪəʳ] N lacrima; **a few tears** qualche lacrima; **to be close to tears** stare per piangere; **to burst into tears** scoppiare in lacrime; **to bring tears to sb's eyes** far venire le lacrime agli occhi a qn
tear·away ['tɛərəˌweɪ] N (*Brit fam*) ragazzaccio
tear·drop ['tɪəˌdrɒp] N lacrima
tear·ful ['tɪəful] ADJ (*face*) coperto(-a) di lacrime; (*voice*) piangente; (*person*) in lacrime; **she looked a bit tearful** sembrava che stesse per piangere
tear gas ['tɪəˌgæs] N gas *m* lacrimogeno
tea·room ['tiːˌrum] N sala da tè
tease [tiːz] N (*person*) burlone(-a) ♦ VT (*playfully*) stuzzicare; (*make fun of*) prendere in giro, canzonare; (*cruelly*) tormentare; **he's teasing you** ti sta prendendo in giro; **I was only teasing** ti stavo solo prendendo in giro
  ▸ **tease out** VT + ADV 1 (*tangle, knots*) sbrogliare; **to tease the tangles** *or* **knots out of one's hair** sbrogliarsi i capelli 2 **to tease information out of sb** cavare delle informazioni a qn
tea service, tea set N servizio da tè

tea·shop ['tiː.ʃɒp] N (*Brit*) sala da tè

tea·spoon ['tiː.spuːn] N (*also:* **teaspoonful:** *as measurement*) cucchiaino da tè; **a teaspoonful of sugar** un cucchiaino di zucchero

tea strainer N colino per il tè

teat [tiːt] N (*of bottle*) tettarella; (*of animal*) capezzolo

tea·time ['tiː.taɪm] N ora del tè; **at teatime** all'ora del tè; **teatime!** a tavola!

tea towel N (*Brit*) strofinaccio (per i piatti)

tea urn N bollitore m per il tè

tech [tek] N ABBR **1** (*Brit fam*) = **technical college 2** (*fam*) = **technology**

tech·ni·cal ['teknɪkəl] ADJ (*process, word*) tecnico(-a); **this book is too technical for me** questo libro è troppo tecnico *or* specifico per me; **technical expert** tecnico specializzato; **technical offence** (*Law*) infrazione *f*

technical college N (*Brit*) ≈ istituto tecnico

tech·ni·cal·ity [ˌteknɪˈkælɪtɪ] N (*quality*) tecnicità *f inv*; (*detail*) dettaglio tecnico; **on a legal technicality** grazie a un cavillo legale; **I don't understand all the technicalities** non riesco a capire tutti i dettagli tecnici

tech·ni·cal·ly ['teknɪkəlɪ] ADV (*gen*) dal punto di vista tecnico; (*in theory*) tecnicamente, in teoria

tech·ni·cian [tekˈnɪʃən] N tecnico(-a)

tech·nique [tekˈniːk] N tecnica

tech·no ['teknəʊ] N (*Mus*) techno *f inv*

tech·no·crat ['teknəʊkræt] N tecnocrate *m/f*

tech·no·logi·cal [ˌteknəˈlɒdʒɪkəl] ADJ tecnologico(-a)

tech·nolo·gist [tekˈnɒlədʒɪst] N tecnologo(-a)

tech·nol·ogy [tekˈnɒlədʒɪ] N tecnologia

ted·dy bear ['tedɪˌbeəʳ] N (*also:* **teddy**) orsacchiotto

te·di·ous ['tiːdɪəs] ADJ noioso(-a), tedioso(-a)

tee [tiː] N (*Golf*) tee *m inv*

▸ **tee off** VI + ADV (*Golf*) cominciare la partita

teem [tiːm] VI **1** brulicare, abbondare; **to teem with** brulicare di; **the area was teeming with tourists** la zona brulicava di turisti **2 it's teeming (with rain)** piove a dirotto

teen [tiːn] ADJ = **teenage** ♦ N (*USA*) = **teenager**

teen·age ['tiːneɪdʒ] ADJ (*problems*) da adolescente; (*rebelliousness*) adolescenziale; (*fashions*) per teenager, per giovani; **teenage boy/girl** adolescente *m/f*; **she has two teenage daughters** ha due figlie adolescenti; **a teenage magazine** una rivista per ragazzi

teen·ager ['tiːneɪdʒəʳ] N adolescente *m/f*, teenager *m/f inv*

teens [tiːnz] NPL: **he is still in his teens** è ancora un adolescente

tee-shirt ['tiːʃɜːt] N = **T-shirt**

tee·ter ['tiːtəʳ] VI barcollare, vacillare; **to teeter on the edge or brink of** vacillare sull'orlo di

teeth [tiːθ] NPL *of* **tooth**

teethe [tiːð] VI mettere i denti

teething ring N dentaruolo

teething troubles NPL (*fig*) difficoltà *fpl* iniziali

tee·to·tal ['tiːˈtəʊtl] ADJ astemio(-a)

tee·to·tal·ler, tee·to·tal·er (*USA*) ['tiːˈtəʊtləʳ] N (*person*) astemio(-a)

TEFL ['tefl] N ABBR = **Teaching of English as a Foreign Language**

Tef·lon ['teflɒn] (*Trademark*) Teflon *m*

Te·he·ran [teəˈrɑːn] N Teheran *f*

tel. ABBR (= *telephone*) tel.

Tel Aviv ['telə'viːv] N Tel Aviv *f*

tele·cast ['telɪˌkɑːst] N trasmissione *f* televisiva ♦ VT, VI teletrasmettere

tele·com·mu·ni·ca·tions ['telɪkəˌmjuːnɪˈkeɪʃənz] NPL telecomunicazioni *fpl*

tele·con·fer·en·cing ['telɪˌkɒnfərənsɪŋ] N teleconferenze *fpl*; **teleconferencing facilities** dispositivi *mpl* per teleconferenza

tele·gram ['telɪˌgræm] N telegramma *m*

tele·graph ['telɪˌgrɑːf] N (*apparatus*) telegrafo; (*message*) telegramma *m*; **by telegraph** via telegrafo ♦ VT trasmettere per telegrafo, telegrafare

tele·graph·ic [ˌtelɪˈgræfɪk] ADJ telegrafico(-a)

telegraph pole, telegraph post N (*Brit*) palo del telegrafo

telegraph wire N filo del telegrafo

tele·path·ic [ˌtelɪˈpæθɪk] ADJ telepatico(-a)

te·lepa·thy [tɪˈlepəθɪ] N telepatia

tele·phone ['telɪˌfəʊn] N telefono; **by telephone** telefonicamente; **to have a telephone** avere il telefono; **to be on the telephone** (*Brit: subscriber*) avere il telefono; (*be speaking*) essere al telefono ♦ VI telefonare ♦ VT (*person*) telefonare a; (*message*) telefonare

telephone box, telephone booth (*USA*) N cabina telefonica

telephone call N telefonata

telephone directory, telephone book N guida del telefono, elenco telefonico

telephone exchange N centralino (telefonico)

telephone number N numero di telefono

telephone operator N centralinista *m/f*

tele·phone tap·ping ['telɪfəʊnˌtæpɪŋ] N intercettazione *f* telefonica

te·lepho·nist [tɪˈlefənɪst] N (*Brit*) telefonista *m/f*

tele·photo lens [ˌtelɪfəʊtəʊˈlenz] N teleobiettivo

tele·print·er ['telɪˌprɪntəʳ] N telescrivente *f*

Tele·Promp·Ter ['telɪˌprɒmptəʳ] (*USA, Trademark*) gobbo

tele·sales ['telɪˌseɪlz] N vendita per telefono

tele·scope ['telɪˌskəʊp] N telescopio ♦ VI chiudersi a telescopio; (*fig: vehicles*) accartocciarsi

tele·scop·ic [ˌtelɪsˈkɒpɪk] ADJ telescopico(-a); (*umbrella*) pieghevole

tele·thon ['telɪˌθɒn] N Telethon *m inv, maratona televisiva*

tele·vise ['telɪˌvaɪz] VT trasmettere per televisione, teletrasmettere

tele·vi·sion ['telɪˌvɪʒən] N (*broadcasts, broadcasting industry*) televisione *f*; (*also:* **television set**) televisore *m*, televisione; **to watch television** guardare la televisione; **on television** alla televisione ♦ ADJ televisivo(-a)

television licence N (*Brit*) abbonamento alla televisione

television programme, television program (*USA*) N programma *m* televisivo

television set N televisore *m*, televisione *f*

tele·work·ing ['telɪˌwɜːkɪŋ] N telelavoro

tel·ex ['teleks] N telex *m inv* ♦ VI mandare un telex ♦ VT (*message*) trasmettere per telex

tell [tel] (*pt, pp* **told**) VT **1** (*gen*) dire; (*story, adventure: relate*) raccontare; (*secret*) svelare; **to tell sb sth** dire qc a qn; **did you tell your mother?** l'hai detto a tua madre?; **I told him I was going on holiday** gli ho detto che andavo in vacanza; **to tell sb about sth** dire a qn di qc, raccontare qc a qn; **who told you?** chi te l'ha detto?; **I have been told that ...** mi è stato detto che...; **I am glad to tell you that ...** (*frm*) ho il piacere di comunicarle che...; **I cannot tell you how pleased I am** non so come esprimere la mia felicità; **so much happened that I can't begin to tell you** sono successe tante cose che non saprei da dove incominciare a raccontarti; **(I'll) tell you what ...** so io che cosa fare...; **I told you so!, didn't I tell you so?** te l'avevo (pur) detto!; **I was furious, I can tell you** ti dirò che ero furioso; **let me tell you** credimi; **you're telling me!** (*fam*) a me lo dici!, lo vieni a dire a me!; **don't tell me you can't do it!** non starmi a raccontare che non sei capace!; **tell me another!** (*fam*) raccontala giusta!; **to tell a story** raccontare una storia; **to tell lies** dire bugie; **to tell the time** leggere l'ora; **can you tell me the time?** puoi dirmi l'ora?; **to tell the future/sb's fortune** predire il futuro/il futuro a qn **2** (*order, instruct*): **to tell sb to do sth** dire a qn di fare qc; **he told me to wait a moment** mi ha detto di aspettare un attimo; **do as you are told!** fai come ti si dice!; **he won't be told** non dà ascolto **3** (*indicate: subj: sign, dial*): **to tell sb sth** indicare qc a qn; **there was a sign telling us which way to go** c'era un cartello che ci indicava la strada **4** (*know, be sure of*) sapere; **how can you tell what he'll do?** come fai a prevedere cosa farà?; **there's no telling what may happen** non si può prevedere cosa succederà; **you can tell he's unhappy** si vede che è infelice **5** (*distinguish*): **to tell sth from** distinguere qc da; **to tell right from wrong** distinguere il bene dal male; **I couldn't tell them apart** non riuscivo a distinguerli; **I can't tell the difference between**

them non riesco a distinguerli uno dall'altro **6 400 all told** 400 in tutto ♦ vi **1** (*talk*) parlare; (*fam: sneak, tell secrets*) fare la spia; **to tell (of)** parlare (di); **more than words can tell** più di quanto non riescano ad esprimere le parole; **that would be telling!** non te lo dico! **2** (*know, be certain*) sapere; **I can't tell** non saprei dire; **who can tell?** chi lo può dire?; **there is no telling** non si sa; **you never can tell** non si può mai dire **3** (*have effect*) farsi sentire, avere effetto; **to tell against sb** ritorcersi contro qn; **the strain is beginning to tell** la fatica incomincia a farsi sentire; **their lack of fitness began to tell** incominciavano a risentire della mancanza di forma

▸ **tell off** vt + adv (*fam*): **to tell sb off** (for sth/for doing sth) sgridare qn (per qc/per aver fatto qc)

▸ **tell on** vi + prep (*fam: inform against*) denunciare

tell·er ['tɛlə'] N **1** (*of story*) narratore(-trice) **2** (*person: in bank*) cassiere(-a); (*: at election*) scrutatore(-trice)

tell·ing ['tɛlɪŋ] ADJ (*effective: blow*) efficace; (*significant: figures, remark, detail*) rivelatore(-trice)

tell·tale ['tɛl,teɪl] ADJ (*sign*) rivelatore(-trice) ♦ N (*fam, pej: person*) spione(-a), pettegolo(-a)

tel·ly ['tɛlɪ] N ABBR (*Brit fam: = television*) tele *f inv*; **on the telly** alla tele

te·mer·ity [tɪ'mɛrɪtɪ] N (*frm*) audacia, temerarietà *f inv*

temp [tɛmp] (*Brit fam*) N ABBR (= *temporary*) lavoratore(-trice) interinale ♦ vi avere un lavoro interinale

tem·per ['tɛmpə'] N (*nature*) temperamento, carattere *m*, indole *f*; (*mood*) umore *m*; (*fit of anger*) collera; **he's got a terrible temper** ha un pessimo carattere; **to be in a temper** essere in collera; **to be in a good/bad temper** essere di buon/cattivo umore; **to keep one's temper** restare calmo(-a); **to lose one's temper** perdere le staffe, andare in collera, arrabbiarsi; **I lost my temper** mi sono arrabbiato; **in a fit of temper** in un accesso d'ira; **to fly into a temper** andare su tutte le furie; **mind your temper!, temper, temper!** cerca di controllarti!, calma, calma! ♦ vt (*moderate*) moderare; (*soften: metal*) temprare

tem·pera·ment ['tɛmpərəmənt] N (*nature*) temperamento, carattere *m*, indole *f*; (*moodiness*) umore *m* variabile

tem·pera·men·tal [,tɛmpərə'mɛntl] ADJ **1** (*moody: person*) capriccioso(-a); (: *fig: machine*) che fa i capricci; **the oven is temperamental** il forno fa i capricci **2** (*caused by one's nature*) innato(-a)

tem·per·ance ['tɛmpərəns] N (*frm: self-control*) moderazione *f*; (*in drinking*) temperanza nel bere; (*teetotalism*) astinenza dal bere

tem·per·ate ['tɛmpərət] ADJ (*climate, zone*) temperato(-a); (*frm: language, response*) moderato(-a)

tem·pera·ture ['tɛmprɪtʃə'] N temperatura; **the temperature was about 40 degrees** la temperatura era di circa 40 gradi; **to have** *or* **run a temperature** avere la febbre

tem·pered ['tɛmpəd] ADJ (*steel*) temprato(-a)

tem·pest ['tɛmpɪst] N (*liter*) tempesta

tem·pes·tu·ous [tɛm'pɛstjʊəs] ADJ (*relationship, meeting*) burrascoso(-a)

tem·pi ['tɛmpiː] NPL *of* **tempo**

template, templet (*USA*) ['tɛmplɪt] N sagoma

tem·ple ['tɛmpl] N **1** (*Rel*) tempio **2** (*Anat*) tempia

tem·po ['tɛmpəʊ] N (*pl* **tempi** ['tɛmpiː]) (*Mus*) tempo; (*fig: of life*) ritmo; **the busy tempo of city life** il ritmo veloce della vita di città

tem·po·ral ['tɛmpərəl] ADJ temporale

tem·po·rari·ly ['tɛmpərərɪlɪ] ADV temporaneamente

tem·po·rary ['tɛmpərərɪ] ADJ (*gen*) provvisorio(-a); (*powers, relief, improvement, job*) temporaneo(-a); (*worker*) avventizio(-a); **a temporary illness** una malattia passeggera; **temporary secretary** segretario(-a) temporaneo(-a) *or* straordinario(-a); **temporary teacher** supplente *m/f*

tem·po·rize ['tɛmpə,raɪz] vi (*delay deliberately*) temporeggiare; (*compromise*) adeguarsi, adattarsi (alle circostanze)

tempt [tɛmpt] vt (*person*) tentare; **to be tempted to do sth** essere tentato(-a) di fare qc; **I'm very tempted!** sono molto tentato(-a)!; **can I tempt you with another cake?** posso tentarti con un altro dolce?; **to tempt Providence** *or* **fate** sfidare il destino; **to tempt sb to do sth/into doing sth** indurre qn a fare qc

temp·ta·tion [tɛmp'teɪʃən] N tentazione *f*; **there is always a temptation to ...** si ha sempre la tentazione di ...; **I couldn't resist the temptation** non sono riuscito a resistere alla tentazione

tempt·ing ['tɛmptɪŋ] ADJ (*offer*) allettante; (*food*) appetitoso(-a)

ten [tɛn] ADJ dieci *inv* ♦ N dieci *m inv*; **she's ten** ha dieci anni; **tens of thousands** decine di migliaia; **ten to one he'll be late** (*fam*) dieci a uno che arriva tardi; **they're ten a penny** (*fam*) ce ne sono a bizzeffe

ten·able ['tɛnəbl] ADJ sostenibile

te·na·cious [tɪ'neɪʃəs] ADJ tenace

te·nac·ity [tɪ'næsɪtɪ] N tenacia

ten·an·cy ['tɛnənsɪ] N (*use of rented property*) locazione *f*, conduzione *f*; **to have a 5 year tenancy** avere un contratto d'affitto di 5 anni; **during his tenancy** durante il periodo in cui abitava lì

ten·ant ['tɛnənt] N inquilino(-a)

tend¹ [tɛnd] vi tendere; **to tend to do sth** tendere a fare qc; **that tends to be the case with young people** questa è la tendenza tra i giovani; **to tend to** *or* **towards sth** (*colour*) tendere a; (*characteristic*) propendere per qc

tend² [tɛnd] vt (*sick person*) prendersi cura di; (*cattle, machine*) badare a, occuparsi di

ten·den·cy ['tɛndənsɪ] N tendenza; **to have a tendency to do sth** avere la tendenza a fare qc

ten·der¹ ['tɛndə'] ADJ **1** tenero(-a); **to bid sb a tender farewell** salutare qn con tenerezza **2** (*sore: part of body*) sensibile, dolente; (*fig: subject*) delicato(-a); **my tummy felt tender** avevo la pancia dolorante; **tender to the touch** sensibile al tatto

ten·der² ['tɛndə'] N **1** (*Comm*) offerta; **to make a tender (for), put in a tender (for)** fare un'offerta (per); **to put work out to tender** (*Brit*) dare lavoro in appalto **2** (*Fin*): **to be legal tender** essere in corso legale ♦ vt presentare, offrire; **to tender one's resignation** (*frm*) rassegnare le proprie dimissioni ♦ vi (*Comm*): **to tender (for)** fare un'offerta (per), concorrere a un appalto (per)

ten·der·ize ['tɛndə,raɪz] vt (*Culin*) far intenerire

ten·der·ly ['tɛndəlɪ] ADV (*affectionately*) teneramente

ten·der·ness ['tɛndənɪs] N (*see adj*) tenerezza; sensibilità *f inv*

ten·don ['tɛndən] N tendine *m*

❑ **tendon** is not translated by the Italian word *tendone*

ten·ement ['tɛnɪmənt] N casamento

Ten·erife [,tɛnə'riːf] N Tenerife *f*

ten·et ['tɛnət] N principio

Tenn. ABBR (*USA*: = **Tennessee**)

Ten·nes·see [,tɛnɪ'siː] N il Tennessee

ten·ner ['tɛnə'] N (*Brit fam*) (banconota da) dieci sterline *fpl*

ten·nis ['tɛnɪs] N tennis *m* ♦ ADJ da tennis

tennis ball N palla *or* pallina da tennis

tennis court N campo da tennis

tennis elbow N (*Med*) gomito del tennista

tennis match N partita di tennis

tennis player N tennista *m/f*

tennis racket N racchetta da tennis

tennis shoes NPL scarpe *fpl* da tennis

ten·or ['tɛnə'] ADJ (*voice*) tenorile; (*part*) del tenore; (*instrument*) tenore *inv* ♦ N (*Mus, also frm: of speech, discussion*) tenore *m*

ten·pin bowl·ing [,tɛnpɪn'bəʊlɪŋ] N (*Brit*) bowling *m*

tense¹ [tɛns] N (*Gram*) tempo; **in the present tense** al presente

tense² [tɛns] ADJ (*comp* **-r**, *superl* **-st**) teso(-a); **tense with fear** teso(-a) dalla paura ♦ vt (*tighten: muscles*) tendere

tense·ness ['tɛnsnɪs] N tensione *f*

ten·sion ['tɛnʃən] N tensione *f*

tent [tɛnt] N tenda; **to pitch a tent** piantare una tenda

ten·ta·cle ['tɛntəkl] N tentacolo

ten·ta·tive ['tɛntətɪv] ADJ (*hesitant: person*) esitante, incerto(-a); (*provisional: conclusion, arrangement*) provvisorio(-a); **a tentative suggestion** un suggerimento incerto; **tentative plans** progetti *mpl* provvisori

tenter·hooks [ˈtɛntəˌhʊks] NPL: **to be on tenterhooks** essere sulle spine; **to keep sb on tenterhooks** tenere qn sulle spine

tenth [tɛnθ] ADJ decimo(-a); **the tenth floor** il decimo piano; **the tenth of August** il dieci agosto ◆ N (in series) decimo(-a); (fraction) decimo m

tent peg N picchetto (da tenda)

tent pole N palo da tenda, montante m

tenu·ous [ˈtɛnjʊəs] ADJ (thread) tenue; (argument) debole

ten·ure [ˈtɛnjʊəʳ] N (of land) possesso; (of office) incarico; **to have tenure** (guaranteed employment) essere di ruolo; **during his tenure as foreign minister** durante il suo incarico di primo ministro

tep·id [ˈtɛpɪd] ADJ (also fig) tiepido(-a)

Ter. ABBR = **Terrace**

term [tɜːm] N **1** (limit) termine m; (period) periodo; **in the short term** a breve scadenza; **in the long term** a lungo andare; **a short-term solution** una soluzione a breve termine; **during his term of office** durante il suo incarico; **a 12 month term** un periodo di 12 mesi; **term of imprisonment** periodo di detenzione or prigionia; **to serve a 3-year term of imprisonment** scontare 3 anni di carcere **2** (Scol) trimestre m; (Law) sessione f; **the autumn/spring/summer term** il primo/secondo/terzo trimestre; **it's nearly the end of term** è quasi la fine del trimestre **3** (word, expression) termine m, vocabolo; **to tell sb in no uncertain terms** dire qc chiaro e tondo a qn, dire qc a qn senza mezzi termini; **in terms of ...** in termini di... **4 terms** NPL (conditions) condizioni fpl; (Comm) prezzi mpl, tariffe fpl; **terms of employment** condizioni di impiego; **terms of reference** termini mpl (stabiliti); **"easy terms"** (Comm) "facilitazioni di pagamento"; **reduced terms for pensioners** agevolazioni fpl per i pensionati; **on one's own terms** a modo proprio; **to come to terms with** (person) arrivare a un accordo con; (problem) affrontare, accettare; **not on any terms** a nessuna condizione **5 terms** NPL (relations): **to be on good terms with** avere buoni rapporti con, essere in buoni rapporti con; **not to be on speaking terms with sb** non rivolgere la parola a qc ◆ VT (name) definire

ter·mi·nal [ˈtɜːmɪnəl] ADJ (patient) incurabile, terminale; (disease) letale; (stages) finale, terminale, conclusivo(-a) ◆ N **1** (Elec, Comput) terminale m **2** (of bus) capolinea m; (of train) stazione f terminale; (Aer: depot: for oil, containers) terminal m inv; **a computer terminal** un terminale; **an air terminal** un terminal

ter·mi·nate [ˈtɜːmɪˌneɪt] VT terminare, mettere fine a; (contract) rescindere ◆ VI (contract) terminare, concludersi; (train, bus) finire; **to terminate in** finire in or con

ter·mi·na·tion [ˌtɜːmɪˈneɪʃən] N fine f; (of contract) rescissione f; **termination of pregnancy** (Brit: Med) interruzione f di gravidanza

ter·mi·nol·ogy [ˌtɜːmɪˈnɒlədʒɪ] N terminologia

ter·mi·nus [ˈtɜːmɪnəs] N (pl termini [ˈtɜːmɪnaɪ]) (of bus) capolinea m; (of train) stazione f terminale; (building: Rail) stazione f di testa

ter·mite [ˈtɜːmaɪt] N termite f

term paper N (USA: Univ) saggio scritto da consegnare a fine trimestre

Terr., Ter. ABBR = **Terrace**

ter·race [ˈtɛrəs] N **1** (patio, porch) terrazza; **we were sitting on the terrace** eravamo seduti in terrazza **2** (Brit: row of houses) fila di case a schiera; **our house is in a terrace** abitiamo in una casa a schiera **3 the terraces** NPL (Brit: Sport) le gradinate

ter·raced [ˈtɛrɪst] ADJ (layered: hillside, garden) terrazzato(-a), a terrazze; (in a row: house, cottage) a schiera; **a terraced house** una casa a schiera

ter·rain [təˈreɪn] N terreno

ter·res·trial [tɪˈrɛstrɪəl] ADJ terrestre

ter·ri·ble [ˈtɛrəbl] ADJ (gen) terribile, tremendo(-a); (play, film) orrendo(-a); (performance, report) pessimo(-a); (weather) bruttissimo(-a); **a terrible nightmare** un incubo terribile; **to be terrible at sth** essere un disastro in qc; **to feel terrible** sentirsi malissimo

ter·ri·bly [ˈtɛrəblɪ] ADV (very) tremendamente, terribilmente; (very badly: play, sing) malissimo; **I'm terribly sorry** mi

spiace terribilmente; **he suffered terribly** ha sofferto moltissimo

ter·ri·er [ˈtɛrɪəʳ] N terrier m inv

ter·rif·ic [təˈrɪfɪk] ADJ (fam: very good: performance, book, news) fantastico(-a), stupendo(-a), formidabile, eccezionale; (extreme: heat, speed, noise, anxiety) spaventoso(-a); (: amount, scare) enorme, impressionante; **that's terrific!** fantastico!; **you look terrific!** stai benissimo!; **a terrific amount** un'enorme quantità

❑ **terrific** is not translated by the Italian word *terrificante*

terri·fied [ˈtɛrɪfaɪd] ADJ atterrito(-a)

ter·ri·fy [ˈtɛrɪfaɪ] VT terrorizzare; **to be terrified** essere atterrito(-a); **to be terrified of** avere il terrore folle di; **to be terrified of** avere il terrore folle di

ter·ri·fy·ing [ˈtɛrɪˌfaɪɪŋ] ADJ terrificante

ter·ri·to·rial [ˌtɛrɪˈtɔːrɪəl] ADJ territoriale ◆ N: **Territorial** (Brit: soldier) soldato della milizia territoriale

territorial waters NPL acque fpl territoriali

ter·ri·tory [ˈtɛrɪtərɪ] N territorio

ter·ror [ˈtɛrəʳ] N (fear) terrore m; (fam: child) peste f; **to live in terror of sth** vivere nel terrore di qc; **you little terror!** piccola peste!

terror attack N attentato terroristico

ter·ror·ism [ˈtɛrəˌrɪzəm] N terrorismo

ter·ror·ist [ˈtɛrərɪst] ADJ, N terrorista m/f; **a group of terrorists** un gruppo di terroristi; **a terrorist attack** un attentato terroristico

ter·ror·ize [ˈtɛrəˌraɪz] VT terrorizzare

terse [tɜːs] ADJ (comp -r, superl -st) (style) conciso(-a); (reply) laconico(-a)

ter·tiary [ˈtɜːʃərɪ] ADJ (gen) terziario(-a); **tertiary education** (Brit) educazione f superiore post-scolastica; **tertiary sector** (Industry) settore m terziario

TESL [ˈtɛsl] N ABBR = **Teaching of English as a Second Language**

test [tɛst] N (trial, check) prova f; (of goods in factory) controllo, collaudo; (of machinery) collaudo; (Med) analisi f inv, esame m; (Chem) analisi; (exam: of intelligence) test m inv; (: Scol: written) compito in classe; (: oral) interrogazione f; (: Med: also: driving test) esame m di guida; **to do tests on sth** fare delle prove su qc; **they're going to do some more tests** devono fare altre analisi; **to have a blood test** fare le analisi del sangue; **we've got an English test tomorrow** abbiamo un compito in classe di inglese domani; **to put sth to the test** mettere qc alla prova; **it has stood the test of time** ha resistito alla prova del tempo; **nuclear tests** test mpl inv nucleari; **tests on animals** sperimentazione f sugli animali ◆ VT (gen) provare, controllare; (try, ascertain the worth of) mettere alla prova; (machine) collaudare; (Chem) analizzare; (blood, urine) fare le analisi di; (new drug) sperimentare; (Psych) fare un test psicologico a; **to test sb's eyes** etc **tested** farsi controllare la vista etc; **to test sb's patience** mettere alla prova la pazienza di qn; **to test sb in mathematics** esaminare or interrogare qn in matematica; **to test sb for sth** fare delle analisi a qn per qc; **to be tested for drugs** essere sottoposto(-a) all'antidoping; **to test sb for sth** analizzare qc alla ricerca di qc; **to test sth out** testare qc; **the drug was tested on rats** la medicina è stata sperimentata sui ratti; **test the water with your wrist** prova l'acqua con il polso; **he tested us on the new vocabulary** ci ha interrogato sui nuovi vocaboli ◆ VI: **to test (for)** fare ricerche (per trovare); **to test positive for** risultare positivo(-a) al test di; **testing, testing ...** (Telec) prova, prova... ◆ ADJ di collaudo

tes·ta·ment [ˈtɛstəmənt] N testamento; **the Old/New Testament** (Rel) il Vecchio/Nuovo Testamento

test ban N (also: nuclear test ban) divieto dei test nucleari

test case N (Law, also fig) caso che costituisce un precedente

tes·tes [ˈtɛstiːz] NPL of **testis**

test flight N (Aer) volo di prova or collaudo

tes·ti·cle [ˈtɛstɪkl] N testicolo

tes·ti·fy [ˈtɛstɪˌfaɪ] VI (Law) testimoniare, deporre; **to testify in favour** (Brit) or **favor** (USA) **of/against sb** testimoniare a favore di/contro qn; **they won't testify against him** non testimonieranno contro di lui; **to testify to sth** (Law) testimoniare qc; (*prove*) comprovare *or* dimostrare qc; (*be sign of*) essere una prova di qc; **the excavations testify to a high level of civilization** gli scavi testimoniano un alto grado di civilizzazione

tes·ti·mo·nial [ˌtɛstɪˈməʊnɪəl] N **1** (*Brit: reference*) referenze *fpl*, benservito **2** (*gift*) tributo di riconoscimento, testimonianza di stima

tes·ti·mo·ny [ˈtɛstɪmənɪ] N (*Law*) testimonianza, deposizione *f*; **false testimony** falsa testimonianza

test·ing [ˈtɛstɪŋ] ADJ (*difficult: time*) duro(-a)

test match N (*Cricket, Rugby*) partita internazionale

tes·tos·ter·one [teˈstɒstəˌrəʊn] N testosterone *m*

test paper N (*Chem*) carta reattiva; (*Scol*) prova (scritta)

test pilot N pilota *m* collaudatore

test tube N (*Chem*) provetta

test-tube baby [ˌtɛsttjuːbˈbeɪbɪ] N bambino(-a) in provetta

tes·ty [ˈtɛstɪ] ADJ (*comp* **-ier**, *superl* **-iest**) (*impatient: person*) irritabile; (*: remark*) stizzoso(-a)

teta·nus [ˈtetənəs] N tetano; **tetanus injection** antitetanica

tetchy [ˈtetʃɪ] ADJ (*comp* **-ier**, *superl* **-iest**) irritabile, irascibile

teth·er [ˈteðəʳ] N laccio; **to be at the end of one's tether** (*fig*) non poterne più ♦ VT (*animal*) legare; **to be at the end of one's tether** non poterne più

Tex. ABBR (*USA*: = **Texas**)

Tex·as [ˈteksəs] il Texas

text [tekst] N **1** (*Telec*) sms *m inv*, messaggino **2** testo ♦ VT mandare un sms *or* messaggino a; **I'll text you** ti manderò un sms

text·book [ˈtekstˌbʊk] N libro di testo

tex·tile [ˈtekstaɪl] ADJ tessile; **textile industry** industria tessile ♦ N tessuto; **textiles** NPL (*industry*) industria tessile; (*materials*) tessuti *mpl*

text·ing [ˈtekstɪŋ], **text messaging** [-ˈmesɪdʒɪŋ] N invio di sms

text message N (*Telec*) sms *m inv*, messaggino

tex·tu·al [ˈtekstjʊəl] ADJ (*error, differences*) di testo; (*criticism*) testuale, basato(-a) sul testo

tex·ture [ˈtekstʃəʳ] N (*gen*) consistenza; (*of soil*) struttura; **I don't like the texture of this cheese** non mi piace la consistenza di questo formaggio; **the material has a rough texture** la stoffa è ruvida al tatto

TGIF [ˌtiːdʒiːaɪˈef] EXCL, ABBR (*fam*: = **thank God it's Friday**) finalmente è venerdì

Thai [taɪ] ADJ tailandese ♦ N (*person*) tailandese *m/f*; (*language*) tailandese *m*

Thai·land [ˈtaɪlænd] N la Tailandia

tha·lido·mide [θəˈlɪdəʊˌmaɪd] N talidomide *m*

Thames [temz] N: **the Thames** il Tamigi

than [ðæn, (*weak form*) ðən] CONJ che; (*with numerals, pronouns, proper names*) di; **you have more than me/Mary/ten** ne hai più di me/Mary/dieci; **she's taller than me** è più alta di me; **I've got more CDs than books** ho più CD che libri; **more than ever** più che mai; **she is older than you think** è più vecchia di quanto tu (non) creda; **it was a better play than we expected** la commedia è stata migliore di quanto (non) pensassimo; **they have more money than we have** hanno più soldi di noi; **it is better to phone than to write** è meglio telefonare che scrivere; **more/less than 90** più/meno di 90; **more than once** più di una volta; **more often than not** il più delle volte; **no sooner did he leave than the phone rang** non appena uscì il telefono suonò; **you know her better than I do** la conosci meglio di me *or* di quanto non la conosca io

thank [θæŋk] VT: **to thank sb (for sth/for doing sth)** ringraziare qn (per qc/per aver fatto qc); **don't forget to write and thank them** mi raccomando, scrivi per ringraziarli; **thank you (very much)** grazie (mille), tante grazie; **no thank you** no grazie; **to have only o.s. to thank for sth** doversi ringraziare se stesso per qc; **I have John to thank for getting me the job** devo ringraziare John per avermi trovato il lavoro; **I know who to thank!** (*iro*) so io chi devo ringraziare!; **thank heavens/God!** grazie al cielo/a Dio!; *see also* **thanks**

thank·ful [ˈθæŋkfʊl] ADJ: **thankful (to sb for sth)** grato(-a) *or* riconoscente (a qn per qc); **she was thankful for his support** gli era grata per il suo appoggio; **let us be thankful that**

it's over ringraziamo il cielo che è tutto finito; **I'm thankful I've got a job** ringrazio il cielo di avere un lavoro; **thankful for/that ...** (*relieved*) sollevato(-a) da/dal fatto che...

thank·ful·ly [ˈθæŋkfəlɪ] ADV (*gratefully*) con riconoscenza; (*with relief*) con sollievo; **thankfully there were few victims** grazie al cielo ci sono state poche vittime

thank·less [ˈθæŋklɪs] ADJ (*unrewarding: task*) ingrato(-a); **a thankless task** un compito ingrato

thanks [θæŋks] NPL ringraziamenti *mpl*, grazie *m inv*; **thanks to** grazie a; **that's all the thanks I get!** bel ringraziamento!; **thanks to you ...** (*also iro*) grazie a te...; **it's all thanks to** (*also iro*) è tutto merito di; **it's small or no thanks to you that ...** non è certo per merito tuo se...; **thanks be to God** rendiamo grazie a Dio ♦ EXCL grazie!; **(very) many thanks** grazie mille

thanks·giving [ˈθæŋksˌgɪvɪŋ] N ringraziamento

Thanksgiving Day N (*USA: also:* **Thanksgiving**) giorno del ringraziamento (negli Stati Uniti, il quarto giovedì di novembre)

KEYWORD

that [ðæt, (*weak form*) ðət] DEM ADJ (*pl* **those**) quel (quell', quello) *m*, quella (quell') *f*; (*as opposed to "this"*) quello(-a) là; **that book** quel libro; **what about that cheque?** e quel famoso assegno?; **that wretched dog!** quel cagnaccio!; **that man** quell'uomo; **I only met her that once** l'ho incontrata solo quella volta; **that one over there** quello là; **it's not this picture but that one I like** non mi piace questo quadro ma quello là; **that man** quell'uomo; **that woman** quella donna

♦ DEM PRON (*pl* **those**) ciò; (*as opposed to 'this'*) quello(-a); **after that** dopo; **and after that he left** dopodiché uscì; **at that, she ...** al che lei...; **and they were late at that** e per di più erano in ritardo; **if it comes to that** se è per quello; **that's my house** quella è la mia casa; **I prefer this to that** preferisco questo a quello; **£5? — it must have cost more than that** 5 sterline? — dev'essere costato di più; **that is (to say), ...** cioè..., vale a dire...; **that's Joe** quello è Joe; **do it like that** fallo così; **how do you like that?** (*iro*) niente male, ti pare?; **that's odd!** che strano!; **that's that!** punto e basta!; **you can't go and that's that!** non puoi andare e basta!; **that's true** è proprio vero; **what is that?** che cos'è quello?; **that's what he said** questo è ciò che ha detto; **who is that?** chi è quello?; **with that, she ...** con ciò lei...; **is that you?** sei tu?

♦ DEM ADV così; **he was that angry** (*fam*) tanto era arrabbiato; **cheer up, it isn't that bad** coraggio, non va poi così male; **that high** così alto(-a), alto(-a) così; **it's about that high** è alto circa così; **I didn't know he was that ill** non sapevo che fosse così malato; **that many** così tanti(-e); **that much** così tanto(-a); **this one isn't that much more difficult** questo non è poi tanto più difficile

♦ REL PRON **1** che, il (la) quale; (*indirect*) cui; **all (that) I have** tutto ciò che ho; **the box (that) I put it in** la scatola in cui l'ho messo; **the house (that) we're speaking of** la casa di cui stiamo parlando; **the man (that) I saw** l'uomo che ho visto; **the man (that) I gave it to** l'uomo (a) cui l'ho dato; **not that I know of** non che io sappia; **the people (that) I spoke to** le persone con cui *or* con le quali ho parlato **2** (*of time: when*) in cui; **on the day that he came** il giorno in cui *or* quando venne; **the evening/winter that** la sera/l'inverno in cui

♦ CONJ che; **I believe that he exists** credo che esista; **not that I want to, of course** non che lo voglia, naturalmente; **oh that I could ...** oh se potessi...; **he said that ...** disse che...; **that he should behave like this is incredible** è incredibile che si sia comportato così; **so that, in order that** affinché + *sub*, perché + *sub*

thatched [θætʃt] ADJ (*roof*) di paglia (*or* frasche); **a thatched cottage** un cottage con il tetto di paglia (*or* frasche)

Thatch·er·ism [ˈθætʃəˌrɪzəm] N thatcherismo

thaw [θɔː] N disgelo; (*fig: easing up*) distensione *f* ♦ VT (*also:* **thaw out:** *food*) (fare) scongelare; **I forgot to thaw the chicken** ho dimenticato di scongelare il pollo ♦ VI (*weather*) sgelare; (*ice*) sciogliersi; (*also:* **thaw out:** *frozen food, cold toes*) scongelarsi; (*fig: person*) aprirsi; (*: relations*) distendersi; **the ice began to thaw** il ghiaccio ha cominciato a sciogliersi; **it's thawing** sta sgelando

KEYWORD

the [ðiː, (*weak form*) ðə] DEF ART

1 il (lo, l') *m*, la (l') *f*, i (gli) *mpl*, le *fpl*; **in this age of the computer ...** in quest'era di computer...; **she was the elder** era la maggiore delle due; **did you see the photographs?** hai visto le fotografie?; **to play the piano** suonare il piano; **if it is within the realms of the possible** se è umanamente possibile; **the rich and the poor** i ricchi e i poveri; **do you know the Smiths?** conosci gli Smith?; **could you pass me the sugar?** mi passi lo zucchero?; **it's on the table** è sulla tavola; **I haven't the time** non ho il tempo; **it was the year of the student riots** quello era l'anno delle manifestazioni studentesche

2 (*distributive*): **0.8 euros to the dollar** 0,8 euro per un dollaro; **eggs are usually sold by the dozen** di solito le uova si vendono alla dozzina; **this car does 30 miles to the gallon** ≈ questa macchina fa 11 chilometri con un litro; **paid by the hour** pagato(-a) a ore

3 (*emphatic*): **he's THE man for the job** è proprio l'uomo adatto al lavoro

4 (*in titles*): **Richard the Second** Riccardo secondo; **Ivan the Terrible** Ivan il terribile

♦ ADV: **the more he works the more he earns** più lavora più guadagna; **(all) the more so because ...** soprattutto perché...; **the sooner the better** prima è, meglio è

theatre, theater (*USA*) ['θɪətə'] N teatro; **to go to the theatre** andare a teatro; **operating theatre** sala operatoria; **lecture theatre** auditorium *m inv*; **theatre of war** teatro di guerra

theatre·goer, theater·goer (*USA*) ['θɪətə,gəʊə'] N habitué *m/f inv* del teatro, frequentatore(-trice) abituale di teatri

the·at·ri·cal [θɪ'ætrɪkəl] ADJ (*also fig*) teatrale

theft [θeft] N furto

their [ðɛə'] POSS ADJ il (la) loro, i (le) loro *pl*; **their money** il loro denaro; **their parents** i loro genitori; **their house** la loro casa; **their girlfriends** le loro ragazze; **they took off their coats** si sono tolti il cappotto; **they washed their hair** si sono lavati i capelli; **someone has left their bag here** qualcuno ha lasciato qui la borsa

theirs [ðɛəz] POSS PRON il (la) loro, i (le) loro *pl*; **this car is theirs** questa macchina è loro; **is this car theirs?** è loro questa macchina?; **it's not our car, it's theirs** non è la nostra auto, è la loro; **a friend of theirs** un loro amico; **our garden is smaller than theirs** il nostro giardino è più piccolo del loro

them [ðem, (*weak form*) ðəm] PERS PRON PL **1** (*direct: unstressed*) li (le); (: *stressed: people*) loro; (: *things*) essi(-e); **I watched them** li ho guardati *or* le ho guardate; **he knows them** non le conosce loro; **if I were them** se io fossi in loro; **it's them!** eccoli!; **I'm looking for the tickets, have you seen them?** sto cercando i biglietti, li hai visti?; **where are the sweets, have you eaten them?** dove sono le caramelle? le hai mangiate?

2 (*indirect: people*) loro (*after verb*), gli (*fam*); (: *things*) essi(-e); **they gave them the money** ha dato loro i soldi, gli ha dato i soldi (*fam*) **3** (*after prep: people*) loro; (: *things*) essi(-e); **I'm thinking of them** penso a loro; **as for them** quanto a loro (*or* a questi); **it's for them** è per loro; **both of them** tutt'e due; **several of them** parecchi (di loro *or* di essi); **give me a few of them** dammene un po' *or* qualcuno; **I don't like either of them** non mi piace nessuno dei due; **none of them would do it** nessuno (di loro) lo voleva fare; **that was very good of them** è stato molto gentile da parte loro; **Sally came with them** Sally è venuta con loro

theme [θiːm] N (*of speech, argument*) tema *m*, argomento; (*Mus*) tema

theme park N parco a tema

theme song N (*of musical, film*) motivo conduttore; (*USA: signature tune*) sigla musicale

them·selves [ðəm'selvz] PERS PRON PL (*reflexive*) si; (*emphatic*) loro stessi(-e); (*after prep*) se stessi(-e); **did they hurt themselves?** si sono fatti(-e) male?; **between themselves** tra (di) loro; **beginners like themselves** dei principianti come loro; **by themselves** da soli; **they did it (all) by themselves** hanno fatto tutto da soli; *see also* **oneself**

then [ðen] ADV **1** (*at that time*) allora; **it was then that ...** fu allora che...; **there was no electricity then** allora non c'era

l'elettricità; **before/since then** prima di/da allora; **until then** fino ad allora; **now and then** ogni tanto; **from then on** da allora in poi; **by then** allora; **then and there** all'istante **2** (*afterwards, next*) poi, dopo; **what happened then?** e poi cos'è successo?; **and then what?** e poi?, e allora?; **I get dressed, then I have breakfast** mi vesto e poi faccio colazione **3** (*in that case*) allora, dunque; **what do you want me to do then?** allora cosa vuoi che faccia?; **my pen's run out. - use a pencil then!** è finita la penna. - allora usa una matita!; **well then** dunque; **and** *or* **but then again** no, non e resto; **I like it, but then I'm biased** mi piace, ma del resto non sono del tutto imparziale; **it would be awkward at work, and then there's the family** sarebbe difficile al lavoro, e poi c'è la famiglia ♦ ADJ: **the then president** l'allora presidente *or* il presidente di allora

theo·lo·gian [θɪə'ləʊdʒɪən] N teologo(-a)

theo·logi·cal [θɪə'lɒdʒɪkəl] ADJ teologico(-a)

the·ol·ogy [θɪ'ɒlədʒɪ] N teologia

theo·rem ['θɪərəm] N (*Math*) teorema *m*

theo·ret·ical [θɪə'retɪkəl], **theoretic** [θɪə'retɪk] ADJ (*Science*) teoretico(-a); (*possibility*) teorico(-a)

theo·rize [θɪə,raɪz] VI: **to theorize (about)** teorizzare (su)

theo·ry ['θɪərɪ] N (*statement, hypothesis*) teoria; **in theory** in teoria

thera·peu·tic [,θerə'pjuːtɪk] ADJ terapeutico(-a)

thera·pist ['θerəpɪst] N terapista *m/f*

thera·py ['θerəpɪ] N terapia

KEYWORD

there [ðɛə'] ADV

1 (*at that place*) lì *or* là; **he's not all there** (*fam*) gli manca un venerdì; **back there** là dietro; **down there** laggiù; **to go there and back** andarci e ritornare; **in there** là dentro; **we left there** ce ne andammo; **on there** lassù; **over there** là; **put it there** mettilo lì *or* là; **we will be there at 8** saremo lì alle 8; **we will be there for sure** ci saremo di sicuro; **through there** di là; **he went there** ci è andato

2 (*to draw attention to sb/sth*): **there he is!** eccolo (là)!; **mind out there!** attenzione!; **that man there** quell'uomo là; **there's the bus** ecco l'autobus; **there we differ** su questo non siamo d'accordo; **you there!** ehilà!; **there you are!** eccoti!; (*I told you so*) visto?; **there you are wrong** in questo hai torto; **there you go again** eccoti di nuovo

3 there is, there are ci sono; **there has been ...** c'è stato...; **there is no wine left** non c'è più vino; **there might be time** forse c'è tempo; **there might be room** forse c'è posto; **there was laughter at this** al che ci fu uno scoppio di risa; **there were 10 of them** erano in 10; **there will be 8 people for dinner tonight** ci saranno 8 persone a cena stasera

♦ EXCL: **there, there, don't cry** su, su, non piangere

there·abouts ['ðɛərə,baʊts] ADV (*place*) nei pressi, nei dintorni, da quelle parti; (*amount*) giù di lì, all'incirca; **ten pounds or thereabouts** dieci sterline o giù di lì

there·after [,ðɛər'ɑːftə'] ADV (*past*) da allora in poi; (*future*) in seguito

there·by [,ðɛə'baɪ] ADV con ciò

there·fore ['ðɛəfɔː'] ADV perciò, quindi; **it isn't therefore any better** per questo non è meglio

there's [ðɛəz] **1** = **there is 2** = **there has**

there·upon [,ðɛərə'pɒn] ADV (*at that point*) a quel punto; (*frm: on that subject*) in merito

ther·mal ['θɜːməl] ADJ (*currents, spring*) termale; (*underwear*) termico(-a); (*paper*) termosensibile; **thermal baths** bagni *mpl* termali; **thermal underwear** biancheria termica

ther·mo·dy·nam·ics [,θɜːməʊdaɪ'næmɪks] NSG termodinamica

ther·mom·eter [θə'mɒmɪtə'] N termometro

ther·mo·nu·clear [,θɜːməʊ'njuːklɪə'] ADJ termonucleare

ther·mos ['θɜːməs] N (*also:* **thermos flask** *or* **bottle**) thermos *m inv*

ther·mo·stat ['θɜːməˌstæt] N termostato

the·sau·rus [θɪ'sɔːrəs] N dizionario dei sinonimi

these [ðiːz] *pl of* **this** DEM ADJ questi(-e); (*as opposed to* "*those*") questi(-e) (qui); **these shoes** queste scarpe; **I want these!** voglio questi!; **these ones (over here)** questi qui; **these ones are very interesting** questi qui sono molto

interessanti; **how are you getting on these days?** come ti
va di questi tempi? ♦ DEM PRON questi(-e)

the·sis [ˈθiːsɪs] N (pl **theses** [ˈθiːsiːz]) tesi f inv

they [ðeɪ] PERS PRON PL 1 (gen) essi(-e); (people only) loro; **who
are they?** chi sono loro?; **they have gone** sono partiti (or
partite); **they were watching TV** stavano guardando la TV;
they're horrible sono bruttissimi; **there they are** eccoli (or
eccole) là; **THEY know nothing about it** LORO non ne sanno nulla 2 (people in general) si; **they say that ...** (it is said
that) si dice che...

they'd [ðeɪd] = they would; they had

they'll [ðeɪl] = they will; they shall

they're [ðeə'] = they are

they've [ðeɪv] = they have

thick [θɪk] ADJ (comp **-er**, superl **-est**) 1 (gen) grosso(-a); (wall,
layer, line) spesso(-a); (hair) folto(-a); (soup, paint, smoke)
denso(-a); (fog, vegetation) fitto(-a); (strong: accent) marcato(-a); **it's 20 cm thick** ha uno spessore
di 20 cm; **the furniture was thick with dust** sui mobili c'era
la polvere di mesi; **the air was thick with exhaust fumes**
l'aria era satura di gas di scarico; **the leaves were thick on
the ground** sul terreno c'era una spessa coltre di foglie; **a
thick accent** un forte accento; **they're thick as thieves** (fig:
fam) sono amici per la pelle 2 (fam: stupid) ottuso(-a), len-
to(-a); **he's a bit thick** è un po' tonto; **he's as thick as two
short planks** (Brit) è proprio duro di comprendonio ♦ ADV:
to spread sth thick spalmare uno spesso strato di qc; **to
cut sth thick** tagliare qc a fette grosse; **thick and fast** senza
tregua; **to lay it on (a bit) thick** (fig: fam: exaggerate) calcare
un po' la mano ♦ N: **in the thick of** (activity, situation, event)
nel mezzo di; **in the thick of battle** nel mezzo della battaglia; **he likes to be in the thick of things** gli piace buttarsi
nella mischia; **through thick and thin** nella buona e nella
cattiva sorte

thick·en [ˈθɪkən] VT (gen) ispessire; (sauce) rendere più den-
so(-a) ♦ VI (gen) ispessirsi; (grow denser: forest, jungle) infittirsi; **the plot thickens** (fig) il mistero s'infittisce, la trama
si complica

thick·et [ˈθɪkɪt] N boscaglia

thick·ly [ˈθɪklɪ] ADV (spread) a strati spessi; (cut) a fette grosse;
(populated) densamente; **the snow fell thickly** la neve cade-
va fitta fitta; **a thickly wooded slope** un pendio molto boscoso

thick·ness [ˈθɪknɪs] N (gen) spessore m; (of fog) densità f inv;
(of hair) foltezza

thick·set [ˌθɪkˈsɛt] ADJ (person) tarchiato(-a), tozzo(-a)

thick-skinned [ˌθɪkˈskɪnd] ADJ (fig: insensitive) insensibile,
coriaceo(-a)

thief [θiːf] N (pl **thieves** [θiːvz]) ladro(-a); **stop thief!** al ladro!

thiev·ing [ˈθiːvɪŋ] ADJ ladro(-a); **you thieving scoundrel!**
brutto ladruncolo! ♦ N furti mpl

thigh [θaɪ] N coscia

thigh·bone [ˈθaɪbəʊn] N femore m

thim·ble [ˈθɪmbl] N ditale m

thin [θɪn] ADJ (comp **-ner**, superl **-nest**) (gen) sottile; (paper,
glass) fine; (blanket, parcel, coat, fog) leggero(-a); (soup, paint,
honey) poco denso(-a); (vegetation, hair, crowd) rado(-a);
(population) scarso(-a); (person) esile, magro(-a); (crop, excuse, argument) magro(-a); **a thin slice** una fettina sottile; **a
thin soup** una minestra liquida; **at 20,000 metres the air
is thin** a 20.000 metri l'aria è molto rarefatta; **the crowd
seemed suddenly thinner** improvvisamente la folla sembrò essersi diradata; **she's very thin** è molto magra; **he's as
thin as a rake** è magro come un chiodo; **to vanish into thin
air** volatilizzarsi; **doctors are thin on the ground at the
moment** i dottori scarseggiano in questo periodo ♦ ADV:
to spread sth thin spalmare uno strato sottile di qc; **to cut
sth thin** tagliare qc a fette sottili ♦ VT (also: **thin down**:
sauce, paint) diluire; (also: **thin out**: trees, plants, hair) sfoltire
♦ VI (fog) diradarsi; (also: **thin out**: crowd) disperdersi; **his
hair is thinning** sta perdendo i capelli

thing [θɪŋ] N 1. cosa; (object) oggetto; (contraption) aggeggio;
a thing of beauty una bella cosa, un bell'oggetto; **things of
value** oggetti di valore; **what's that thing?** cos'è quell'affare?; **what's that thing called?** come si chiama quel coso?;
the main thing is to keep calm la cosa più importante è

mantenere la calma; **the first thing to do is (to) check the
facts** la prima cosa da fare è controllare i fatti; **the best
thing would be to ...** la cosa migliore sarebbe di...; **for one
thing** in primo luogo, tanto per cominciare; **what with one
thing and another** tra una cosa e l'altra; **if it's not one thing
it's the other** se non è una è l'altra; **it's neither one thing
nor the other** non è né carne né pesce; **first thing (in the
morning)** come or per prima cosa (di mattina); **last thing
(at night)** come or per ultima cosa (di sera); **it's a good
thing that he left** è stato un bene che se ne sia andato; **it
was a close** or **near thing** ce l'ha fatta per un pelo; **to be
just the thing for** essere proprio quello che ci vuole per; **it's
the (very) thing** è proprio quello che ci vuole; **the thing is
...** il fatto è che...; **it's just one of those things** sono cose
che capitano; **what a thing to say!** cosa dici mai!; **how are
things (with you)?** come (ti) va?; **things are going badly**
le cose vanno male; **not a thing to say/to wear** niente da
dire/da mettersi; **I haven't done a thing about it yet** non
ho ancora fatto niente; **he knows a thing or two** la sa lunga; **you did the right thing** (fam) hai fatto la cosa migliore;
to make a (big) thing out of sth (fam) fare una tragedia di
qc 2 **things** NPL (belongings, clothes, equipment) roba sg, cose
fpl; **take your wet things off** togliti quella roba bagnata di
dosso; **the tea things** le cose per il tè; **where shall I put my
things?** dove metto le mie cose?; **take your things and go!**
prendi la tua roba e vattene! 3 **to do one's own thing** (fam)
fare quello che si vuole; **she's got a thing about mice** è ter-
rorizzata dai topi; **the latest thing in hats** l'ultimo grido
in fatto di cappelli 4 (creature): **poor thing** poveretto(-a);
you poor thing! poverino(-a)!; **what a sweet little thing!**
che carino!

think [θɪŋk] (pt, pp **thought**) VI (gen): **to think of** or **about
sth** pensare a qc; (more carefully) riflettere su qc; **to think
of** or **about doing sth** pensare di fare qc; **to act without
thinking** agire senza riflettere or pensare; **think before
you reply** rifletti or pensa prima di rispondere; **think carefully** pensaci bene; **think again!** rifletti!, pensaci su!; **just
think!** ma pensa un po'!; **let me think** fammi pensare; **let's
think** pensiamoci un attimo; **to think twice before doing
sth** pensare due volte prima di fare qc; **to think straight**
concentrarsi; **to think aloud** pensare ad alta voce; **to think
for o.s.** pensare con la propria testa; see also **think about,
think of** ♦ VT 1 (use one's brain, have ideas) pensare; (imagine) pensare, immaginare; **I can't think what he can want**
non riesco ad immaginare che cosa possa volere; **did you
think to bring a corkscrew?** hai pensato di portare un cavatappi?; **I thought I might go swimming** ho pensato che
potrei andare a nuotare; **think what you've done** pensa a
ciò che hai fatto; **think what we could do** pensa che cosa
potremmo fare; **to think evil thoughts** avere cattivi pensieri 2 (believe, consider): **to think (that ...)** pensare (che...),
credere (che...); **we all thought him a fool** pensavamo tutti
che fosse un cretino; **I don't think it likely** penso che sia improbabile; **who'd have thought it possible?** chi l'avrebbe
mai pensato?; **I don't think it can be done** non penso che si
possa fare; **I think (that) you're wrong** penso che tu abbia
torto; **I thought as much** lo sapevo io; **I think/don't think
so** penso or credo di sì/no; **I should think so too!** lo credo
bene!; **what do you think?** che cosa ne pensi?; **who do you
think you are?** ma chi credi di essere?; **what do you think I
should do?** cosa pensi che dovrei fare?; **what do you think
you're doing?** ma cosa stai facendo? ♦ N: **to have a think
about sth** riflettere su qc; **I'd like to have a think about it**
vorrei pensarci su; **you've got another think coming!** (fam)
ti sbagli!, hai capito male!

▸ **think about** VI + PREP (remember) pensare a; (consider)
pensare di; **I'll think about it** ci penserò; **what are you
thinking about?** a cosa stai pensando?; **have you thought
about it?** ci hai pensato?; **what were you thinking about!**
che cosa ti è saltato in mente!

▸ **think back** VI + ADV: **to think back (to)** ripensare (a),
riandare con la mente (a)

▸ **think of** VI + PREP 1 (remember: names) ricordare; **you
can't think of everything** non ci si può ricordare di tutto,
non si può pensare a tutto; **I'll be thinking of you** ti penserò
2 (consider, reckon) pensare di; **to think of doing sth** pensare
di fare qc; **I thought of going to Spain** pensavo di andare

in Spagna; **he never thinks of other people's feelings** non si cura mai dei sentimenti degli altri; **think of the expense** pensa a quanto costa; **what do you think of him?** che cosa pensi di lui?; **what do you think of it?** che cosa ne pensi?; **I told him what I thought of him** gli ho detto ciò che pensavo di lui; **I wouldn't think of such a thing!** non mi sognerei mai di fare una cosa simile!; **to think highly of sb** stimare qn; **to think well of** avere una buona opinione di; **I didn't think much of it** non mi è piaciuto molto, non mi ha convinto **3** (*devise: plan*) escogitare; (: *solution*) trovare; **what will he think of next?** una ne fa e cento ne pensa!

▸ **think out** VT + ADV (*plan*) elaborare; (*solution*) trovare; **this needs thinking out** bisogna pensarci su

▸ **think over** VT + ADV: **to think sth over** riflettere su qc; **I'd like to think things over** vorrei pensarci su

▸ **think through** VT + ADV: **to think sth through** riflettere a fondo su qc

▸ **think up** VT + ADV (*idea, solution*) escogitare, ideare

think·ing ['θɪŋkɪŋ] ADJ: **to any thinking person** a ogni persona ragionevole; **to put on one's thinking cap** (*fam*) mettersi a pensare, mettersi a ragionare ♦ N pensiero; **to my (way of) thinking** a mio parere; **I've done some thinking about it** ci ho pensato un po' sopra

think tank N gruppo di esperti

thin·ly ['θɪnlɪ] ADV (*spread*) in uno strato sottile; (*cut*) a fette sottili; (*scantily: dressed*) scarsamente; (*disguised*) malamente

thin·ness ['θɪnnɪs] N (*gen*) sottigliezza f; (*of person*) magrezza; (*of hair*) radezza; (*of soup*) eccessiva liquidità; (*of excuse*) debolezza

third [θɜːd] ADJ terzo(-a); **the third time** la terza volta; **the third of March** il tre marzo; **third time lucky!** questa è la volta buona! ♦ N **1** (*in series*) terzo(-a); (*fraction*) terzo, terza parte f; **I came third** sono arrivato terzo; **a third of the population** un terzo della popolazione **2** (*Brit Scol: degree*) laurea col minimo dei voti

third-degree burns [ˌθɜːdɪˈɡriːˈbɜːnz] NPL ustioni fpl di terzo grado

third·ly ['θɜːdlɪ] ADV in terzo luogo, terzo

third party insurance N (*Brit*) assicurazione f contro terzi

third-rate [ˌθɜːdˈreɪt] ADJ (di qualità) scadente, di terz'ordine

Third World N: **the Third World** il Terzo Mondo

thirst [θɜːst] N sete f; **thirst for knowledge** sete di conoscenza ♦ VI: **to thirst for** (*fig*) essere assetato(-a) di

thirsty ['θɜːstɪ] ADJ (*comp* -**ier**, *superl* -**iest**) (*person*) assetato(-a), che ha sete; (*hum: work*) che fa venire sete; **to be thirsty** aver sete

thir·teen [ˌθɜːˈtiːn] ADJ, N tredici m inv; **I'm thirteen** ho tredici anni

thir·teenth [ˌθɜːˈtiːnθ] ADJ tredicesimo(-a); **the thirteenth floor** il tredicesimo piano; **the thirteenth of March** il tredici marzo ♦ N (*in series*) tredicesimo(-a); (*fraction*) tredicesimo

thir·ti·eth ['θɜːtɪɪθ] ADJ trentesimo(-a) ♦ N (*in series*) trentesimo(-a); (*fraction*) trentesimo

thir·ty ['θɜːtɪ] ADJ, N trenta m inv

KEYWORD

this [ðɪs] DEM ADJ (*pl* **these**) questo(-a); (*as opposed to "that"*) questo(-a) (qui); **this book** questo libro; **this man** quest'uomo; **this one here** questo qui; **it's not that picture but this one I like** non è quel quadro che mi piace, ma questo qui; **this time** questa volta; **this time next week** a quest'ora la settimana prossima; **this time last year** l'anno scorso in questo periodo; **this way** (*in this direction*) da questa parte; (*in this fashion*) così; **this woman** questa donna

♦ DEM PRON (*pl* **these**) questo(-a); (*as opposed to 'that'*) questo(-a) (qui); **what's all this I hear about you leaving?** mi hanno detto che te ne vai, è vero?; **this is April** è aprile; **this is Friday** è venerdì; **do it like this** fallo così; **it was like this** è successo or è andata così; **this is Mr Brown** (*in introductions, in photo*) questo è il signor Brown; (*on telephone*) sono il signor Brown; **they were talking of this and that** stavano parlando del più e del meno; **I prefer this to that** preferisco questo a quello; **what is this?** che cos'è questo?; **this is what he said** questo è ciò che ha detto; **this is where I live** io abito qui; **who is this?** chi è questo?; **and with this he left** e con ciò se ne andò; **what with this and that I was**

busy all week tra una cosa e l'altra non ho avuto un momento libero questa settimana; **where did you find this?** dove l'hai trovato?

♦ DEM ADV: **this far** fino qui; **this high** alto(-a) così, così alto(-a); **it's about this high** è alto circa così

this·tle ['θɪsl] N cardo

thong [θɒŋ] N (*underwear*) perizoma m; (*USA: shoe*) infradito m inv, f inv, laccio or cinghia di cuoio

thorn [θɔːn] N spina; **you're a thorn in my side** or **flesh** (*fig*) sei la mia spina nel fianco or la mia croce

thorny ['θɔːnɪ] ADJ (*comp* -**ier**, *superl* -**iest**) irto(-a) di spine; (*fig: tricky*) spinoso(-a), scabroso(-a)

thor·ough ['θʌrə] ADJ (*work, worker*) preciso(-a), accurato(-a); (*search*) minuzioso(-a); (*examination, knowledge, research*) approfondito(-a); (*cleaning*) a fondo; (*complete: attr only: idiot, scoundrel*) vero(-a); **a thorough check** un controllo minuzioso; **she's very thorough** è molto meticolosa; **she has a thorough knowledge of the subject** ha una profonda conoscenza in materia; **he's a thorough rascal** è una canaglia matricolata, è un vero mascalzone

thor·ough·bred ['θʌrəbrɛd] ADJ, N (*horse*) purosangue m/f inv

thor·ough·fare ['θʌrəfɛəʳ] N strada transitabile; **"no thoroughfare"** (*Brit*) "divieto di transito"

thor·ough·go·ing ['θʌrəɡəʊɪŋ] ADJ (*examination, search*) accurato(-a), minuzioso(-a); (*analysis*) approfondito(-a); (*reform*) totale; **he's a thoroughgoing idiot** è un perfetto idiota

thor·ough·ly ['θʌrəlɪ] ADV **1** (*with vb: agree*) completamente; (: *understand*) perfettamente; (: *search, clean*) accuratamente, minuziosamente, a fondo; **she thoroughly agreed** fu completamente d'accordo; **I checked the car thoroughly** ho controllato la macchina meticolosamente; **mix the ingredients thoroughly** mescolare bene gli ingredienti; **I thoroughly enjoyed myself** mi sono divertito moltissimo **2** (*with adj: very*) assolutamente; **thoroughly clean** completamente pulito(-a); **a thoroughly unpleasant person** una persona assolutamente antipatica

thor·ough·ness ['θʌrənɪs] N precisione f

those [ðəʊz] *pl of* **that** DEM ADJ quei (quegli) mpl, quelle fpl; (*as opposed to "these"*) quelli(-e) (là); **those days** quei giorni; **those pages** quelle pagine; **those students** quegli studenti; **those ones** quelli lì; **pass me those books — those ones?** passami quei libri — quelli lì? ♦ DEM PRON quelli(-e); (*as opposed to 'these'*) quelli(-e) (là); **those of you who were here yesterday** quelli di voi che erano qua ieri; **those of us who fought in the war** noi che abbiamo combattuto la guerra; **I want those!** voglio quelli!

though [ðəʊ] CONJ benché + *sub*, sebbene + *sub*; **though it's raining ...** anche se piove...; **though it was raining** benché piovesse; **he's a nice person, though he's not very clever** è simpatico, anche se non è molto sveglio; **even though** anche se; **strange though it may appear** per quanto strano possa sembrare ♦ ADV tuttavia, comunque; **it's not so easy, though** tuttavia non è così facile

thought [θɔːt] PT, PP *of* **think** ♦ N (*reflection, mental activity*) pensiero; (*idea*) idea; (*opinion*) opinione f; (*intention*) intenzione f; **to be lost** or **deep in thought** essere assorto(-a) or perso(-a) nei propri pensieri; **after much thought** dopo molti ripensamenti; **I've just had a thought** mi è appena venuta un'idea; **that's a thought!** che bell'idea!; **I shudder at the very thought of it** rabbrividisco solo al pensiero; **to collect one's thoughts** raccogliere le proprie idee; **my thoughts were elsewhere** avevo la testa altrove; **with no thought for o.s.** senza pensare a se stesso; **to give sth some thought** prendere qc in considerazione, riflettere su qc; **it's the thought that counts** è il pensiero che conta; **it was a nice thought, thank you** è stato un pensiero carino, grazie

thought·ful ['θɔːtfʊl] ADJ **1** (*pensive*) pensieroso(-a), pensoso(-a); (*serious: book*) ragionato(-a); (: *remark*) ponderato(-a) **2** (*considerate*) gentile, premuroso(-a); **she had a thoughtful expression on her face** aveva un'espressione pensierosa; **a thoughtful and caring man** un uomo premuroso ed attento; **how thoughtful of you!** che pensiero gentile!

thought·ful·ly ['θɔːtfəlɪ] ADV **1** (*pensively*) con aria pensierosa; **he looked at me thoughtfully** mi ha guardato pensieroso **2** (*considerately*) gentilmente

thought·less [ˈθɔːtlɪs] ADJ (*person, remark, words*) sconsiderato(-a); (*behaviour*) scortese; **it was thoughtless of her to mention it** è stato poco delicato da parte sua parlarne; **thoughtless of the consequences** senza pensare alle conseguenze

thought·less·ly [ˈθɔːtlɪslɪ] ADV (*see adj*) sconsideratamente; scortesemente

thought-provoking [ˈθɔːtprəˌvəʊkɪŋ] ADJ che dà da pensare, stimolante

thou·sand [ˈθaʊzənd] ADJ mille ♦ N mille *m inv*; **one/two/ five thousand** mille/duemila/cinquemila; **a thousand pounds** mille sterline; **a thousand and one/two** mille e uno/due; **about a thousand** circa un migliaio; **three thousand boys and five thousand girls** tremila ragazzi e cinquemila ragazze; **in their thousands, by the thousand** a migliaia; **thousands of** migliaia *fpl* di

thou·sandth [ˈθaʊzəndθ] ADJ millesimo(-a) ♦ N (*in classification*) millesimo(-a); (*fraction*) millesimo

thrash [θræʃ] VT (*gen*) percuotere, picchiare; (*with whip*) frustare; (*with stick*) bastonare; (*Sport: fam: defeat*) dare una batosta a, battere; **his father thrashed him** suo padre lo ha picchiato; **Liverpool will thrash them** il Liverpool li batterà ♦ VI (*also*: **thrash about, thrash around**) agitarsi, dibattersi

▸ **thrash out** VT + ADV (*problem, difficulty: discuss*) sviscerare; (: *solve*) risolvere; (: *plan*) mettere a punto con difficoltà; **a meeting to thrash out the problem** un incontro per sviscerare il problema

thrash·ing [ˈθræʃɪŋ] N: **to give sb a thrashing** (*beat*) picchiare qn di santa ragione; (*Sport: fam: defeat*) dare una batosta a qn

thread [θrɛd] N 1 filo; **cotton/nylon thread** filo di cotone/di nailon; **to hang by a thread** (*fig*) essere appeso a un filo; **to lose the thread (of what one is saying)** perdere il filo (del discorso); **to pick up the thread again** (*fig*) riprendere il filo 2 (*of screw*) filettatura, filetto ♦ VT (*needle, beads*) infilare; **to thread one's way through a crowd** infilarsi *or* farsi largo tra una folla; **to thread one's way between** infilarsi tra

thread·bare [ˈθrɛdbɛəʳ] ADJ (*coat, blanket*) logoro(-a), consumato(-a), liso(-a); (*fig: argument*) trito(-a)

threat [θrɛt] N minaccia; **to be a threat to sb/sth** costituire una minaccia per qn/qc; **to be under threat of** (*closure, extinction*) rischiare; (*exposure*) essere minacciato(-a) di

threat·en [ˈθrɛtn] VT minacciare; **to threaten sb with sth** minacciare qn di qc; **to threaten to do sth** minacciare di fare qc ♦ VI (*storm*) minacciare

threat·en·ing [ˈθrɛtnɪŋ] ADJ minaccioso(-a)

three [θriː] ADJ tre *inv*; **she's three** ha tre anni ♦ N tre *m inv*; **the best of three** (*Sport*) partita, rivincita e bella

three-dimensional [ˌθriːdaɪˈmɛnʃənl] ADJ tridimensionale

three-piece suit [ˌθriːpiːsˈsuːt] N completo (con gilè), tre pezzi *m inv*

three-piece suite [ˌθriːpiːsˈswiːt] N salotto comprendente un divano e due poltrone

three-ply [ˌθriːˈplaɪ] ADJ (*wood*) a tre strati; (*wool*) a tre capi, a tre fili

three-quarters [ˌθriːˈkwɔːtəz] NPL tre quarti *mpl*; **three-quarters full** pieno per tre quarti

three-wheeler [ˌθriːˈwiːləʳ] N (*car*) veicolo a tre ruote; (*tricycle*) triciclo

thresh [θrɛʃ] VT (*corn*) trebbiare

thresh·ing ma·chine [ˈθrɛʃɪŋməˌʃiːn] N trebbiatrice *f*, trebbia

thresh·old [ˈθrɛʃhəʊld] N (*also fig*) soglia; **to be on the threshold of** (*fig*) essere sulla soglia di

threshold agreement N (*Econ*) ≈ scala mobile

threw [θruː] PT *of* **throw**

thrift [θrɪft], **thrifti·ness** [ˈθrɪftɪnɪs] N parsimonia; **thrift is not one of his strong points** la parsimonia non è una delle sue qualità; **a life of hard work and thrift** una vita di duro lavoro e risparmio

thrifty [ˈθrɪftɪ] ADJ (*comp* **-ier**, *superl* **-iest**) parsimonioso(-a)

thrill [θrɪl] N (*of fear*) brivido; (*of pleasure, joy*) fremito; **it gave me a great thrill** è stata un'esperienza emozionante; **it was a great thrill to see my team win** che emozione vedere vincere la mia squadra! ♦ VT (*with fear*) far rabbrividire;

(*with pleasure*) entusiasmare; (*audience*) elettrizzare; **I was thrilled to get your letter** la tua lettera mi ha fatto veramente piacere ♦ VI tremare; **to thrill at** *or* **to sth** fremere (di gioia) a qc

thrilled ADJ: **I was thrilled to get your letter** la tua lettera mi ha fatto veramente piacere

thrill·er [ˈθrɪləʳ] N thriller *m inv*

thrill·ing [ˈθrɪlɪŋ] ADJ (*book, play*) pieno(-a) di suspense; (*news, discovery*) entusiasmante; **a thrilling match** una partita entusiasmante

thrive [θraɪv] VI (*be healthy: person, animal*) crescere *or* svilupparsi bene; (: *plant*) crescere rigoglioso(-a); (: *fig: business*) prosperare; **he thrives on it** gli fa bene, ne gode; **lavender thrives in poor soil** la lavanda cresce rigogliosa nei terreni poveri; **she thrives on hard work** il lavoro le fa bene; **business is thriving** il commercio prospera

thriv·ing [ˈθraɪvɪŋ] ADJ (*industry, community*) fiorente

throat [θrəʊt] N gola; **to clear one's throat** schiarirsi la gola; **to have a sore throat** avere (il) mal di gola; **to stick in sb's throat** (*fig*) restare in gola a qn

throb [θrɒb] N (*of heart*) palpito, battito; (*of pain*) fitta; (*of music*) battito; (*of engine*) vibrazione *f*; (*of drum*) rullio ♦ VI (*heart*) palpitare, battere forte; (*wound*) pulsare; (*engine*) vibrare; **my head is throbbing** mi martellano le tempie; **my arm is throbbing** ho delle fitte al braccio; **throbbing with life** (*fig: town*) pullulante di vita; **a throbbing pain** un dolore lancinante

throes [θrəʊz] NPL: **in the throes of** alle prese con; **in the throes of death** in agonia; **in the throes of war** dilaniato(-a) dalla guerra

throm·bo·sis [θrɒmˈbəʊsɪs] N trombosi *f inv*; **coronary thrombosis** trombosi coronarica

throne [θrəʊn] N trono; **to ascend to the throne** salire al trono; **the heir to the throne** l'erede *m/f* al trono

throng [θrɒŋ] N moltitudine *f* ♦ VT affollare ♦ VI affollarsi

throt·tle [ˈθrɒtl] N (*on motorcycle*) (manopola del) gas; (*valve*) valvola a farfalla; (*on motorboats*) (manetta del) gas; **to open the throttle** dare gas; **to go at full throttle** andare a tutto gas ♦ VT (*strangle*) strangolare, strozzare ♦ VI: **to throttle back** *or* **down** rallentare il motore

through [θruː] PREP 1 (*place*) attraverso; **to look through a telescope** guardare attraverso un telescopio; **to look through the window** (*look out*) guardare dalla finestra; (*look in*) guardare dentro; **to walk through the woods** camminare per *or* attraversare i boschi; **through the crowd** attraverso la folla; **he shot her through the head** le ha sparato in testa; **to go through** (*house, garden, wood*) attraversare; **to go through one's pockets** frugarsi le tasche; **to go through sb's papers** scartabellare le carte di qn 2 (*time, process*) per, durante; **all** *or* **right through the night** per tutta la notte; **he won't live through the night** non supererà la notte; (*from*) **Monday through Friday** (*USA*) da lunedì a venerdì; **to go through a bad/good period** attraversare un brutto momento/periodo felice; **I am halfway through the book** sono a metà libro 3 (*owing to*) a causa di; (*by means of*) per, per mezzo di; (*thanks to*) grazie a; **through lack of resources** per mancanza di mezzi; **through the post** per posta; **he got the job through them** ha avuto quel posto grazie a loro; **it was through you that we were late** è colpa tua se siamo arrivati tardi; **I heard it through my sister** l'ho saputo da mia sorella; **I know him through my brother** lo conosco tramite mio fratello ♦ ADV 1 (*place*): **to let sb through** lasciar passare qn; **the soldiers didn't let us through** i soldati non ci hanno lasciato passare; **please go through into the dining room** prego, entrate in sala da pranzo; **to go through Birmingham** passare per Birmingham; **does this train go through to London?** va direttamente a Londra questo treno?; **the nail went right through** il chiodo è passato da parte a parte; **I am wet through** sono bagnato fino al midollo; **my coat is wet through** ho il cappotto inzuppato; **he is through to the finals** ce l'ha fatta a entrare in finale; **the wood has rotted through** il legno è completamente marcio 2 (*Brit: Telec*) **to get through** ottenere la comunicazione; **to put sb through** passare la linea a qn; **to put sb through to sb** passare qn a qn; **you're through!** è in linea! 3 (*time, process*): **the party lasted right through until morning** la festa è andata avanti fino al mattino; **I read the book right through** ho letto il libro da cima a fondo **4 through and through** fino in fondo ♦ ADJ **1** (*attr: traffic*) di passaggio; (*ticket, train, passage*) diretto(-a); **a through train** un treno diretto; **"no through road"** (*sign: Brit*) "strada senza uscita"; **"no through traffic"** (*sign: USA*) "divieto d'accesso" **2** (*finished*): **to be through** avere finito; **we'll be through at 7** avremo finito per le sette; **I'm not through with you yet** con te non ho ancora finito; **you're through!** sei finito!

through·out [θruːˈaʊt] PREP **1** (*place*) in tutto(-a), dappertutto in; **throughout Italy** in tutta l'Italia **2** (*time, process*) per *or* durante tutto(-a); **throughout the year** per tutto l'anno; **throughout last summer** per tutta l'estate scorsa ♦ ADV **1** (*everywhere*) dappertutto; **the house is carpeted throughout** c'è la moquette dappertutto in casa **2** (*the whole time*) dal principio alla fine, sempre

through·put [ˈθruːˌpʊt] N (*of goods, materials*) materiale *m* in lavorazione; (*Comput*) volume *m* di dati immessi

throve [θrəʊv] PT *of* **thrive**

throw [θrəʊ] (*pt* **threw**, *pp* **thrown**) N (*gen*) tiro; (*Sport*) lancio; (*in judo, wrestling*) atterramento ♦ VT (*gen, or fig*) lanciare, tirare, gettare; (*ball, javelin, hammer*) lanciare; (*dice*) gettare; (*horse/rider*) disarcionare, gettare a terra; (*judo opponent*) atterrare, mettere al tappeto; (*pottery*) tornire, formare al tornio; (*fig: fam: disconcert*) sconcertare, disorientare; **to throw a ball 200 metres** lanciare una palla a duecento metri; **he threw the ball to me** mi ha lanciato la palla; **to throw a coat round one's shoulders** buttarsi un cappotto sulle spalle; **that really threw him** l'ha veramente sconcertato; **to throw a switch** (*Elec*) azionare una leva; **he was thrown from his horse** fu disarcionato; **to throw a party** dare una festa; **to throw open** (*doors, windows*) spalancare; (*house, gardens*) aprire al pubblico; (*competition, race*) aprire a tutti; **to throw o.s. off a cliff/into a river** gettarsi da una scogliera/in un fiume; **to throw o.s. at sb** (*rush at*) gettarsi *or* scagliarsi su qn; (*fig*) buttarsi su qn; **to throw o.s. into one's work** buttarsi a capofitto nel lavoro; **to throw o.s. at sb's feet** gettarsi ai piedi di qn; **to throw o.s. on sb's mercy** rimettersi alla pietà di qn

▸ **throw about, throw around** VT + ADV (*litter*) spargere; **to throw money about** *or* **around** sperperare il denaro; **to throw one's weight about** *or* **around** far pesare la propria presenza

▸ **throw away** VT + ADV (*rubbish, old things*) gettare *or* buttare via; (*chance, money, time*) sprecare, gettare *or* buttare via; **he threw it away** lo ha buttato via

▸ **throw back** VT + ADV **1** (*return: ball*) rinviare **2** (*head, hair*) buttare all'indietro; (*shoulders*) raddrizzare

▸ **throw down** VT + ADV (*object*) gettare giù; (*weapons*) deporre; **to throw o.s. down** gettarsi a terra; **to throw down the gauntlet** (*fig*) gettare il guanto

▸ **throw in** VT + ADV (*Sport: ball*) rimettere in gioco; (*add, include*) aggiungere; (*say casually: remark*) buttar lì

▸ **throw on** VT + ADV (*clothes*) buttarsi addosso; (*coal*) aggiungere

▸ **throw off** VT + ADV (*get rid of*) sbarazzarsi di, liberarsi di; (*escape: pursuers, dogs*) sbarazzarsi di, seminare ♦ VT + PREP: **to throw sb off the trail** mettere qn fuori pista

▸ **throw out** VT + ADV **1** (*rubbish, person*) buttar fuori; (*fig: proposal*) respingere **2** (*offer: idea, suggestion*) lanciare **3** (*calculation, prediction*) far sballare

▸ **throw over** VT + ADV (*person*) piantare

▸ **throw together** VT + ADV (*clothes*) raccattare; (*meal*) raffazzonare; (*essay*) buttar giù; (*people*) fare incontrare

▸ **throw up** VI + ADV (*fam: vomit*) vomitare ♦ VT + ADV (*ball*) lanciare in aria; **she threw up her hands in despair** ha alzato le braccia al cielo per la disperazione

throw·away [ˈθrəʊəˌweɪ] ADJ (*disposable: product*) da buttar via, usa e getta; (*casual: remark*) buttato(-a) lì

throw·back [ˈθrəʊˌbæk] N: **it's a throwback to** (*fig*) ciò risale a

throw-in [ˈθrəʊˌɪn] N (*Ftbl*) rimessa in gioco

thrown [θrəʊn] PP *of* **throw**

thru [θruː] PREP, ADV (*USA*) = **through**

thrush¹ [θrʌʃ] N (*bird*) tordo

thrush² [θrʌʃ] N (*Med: esp in children*) mughetto; (: *Brit: in women*) candida

---

thrust [θrʌst] (*pt, pp* **thrust**) N (*push*) spintone *m*; (*Aer, Space*) spinta; (*Mil: offensive*) attacco, offensiva; **forward thrust** spinta propulsiva; **it provides the thrust that makes the craft move** dà la spinta necessaria a far muovere l'apparecchio ♦ VT (*push*) spingere con forza; (*push in: finger, stick, dagger*) conficcare; **they thrust him into a van** lo hanno spinto con forza su un furgone; **he thrust a book into my hands** mi ha cacciato un libro tra le mani; **she thrust her head out of the window** ha sporto la testa dalla finestra; **to thrust o.s. upon sb** (*fig*) imporre la propria presenza a qn; **they thrust the job on me** (*fig*) mi hanno costretto ad accettare il lavoro; **I thrust my way through the crowd** mi sono fatto largo tra la folla; **to thrust sb/sth aside** spingere qn/qc da una parte; **to thrust an idea aside** scartare un'idea

thrust·ing [ˈθrʌstɪŋ] ADJ (*troppo*) intraprendente

thud [θʌd] N tonfo ♦ VI: **to thud to the ground** cadere a terra con un tonfo; **to thud against the wall** colpire il muro con un tonfo

thug [θʌɡ] N teppista *m/f*, delinquente *m/f*

thumb [θʌm] N (*Anat*) pollice *m*; **to be under sb's thumb** (*fig*) essere succube di qn; **to be all thumbs** (*fig: fam*) essere maldestro(-a); **to give sb/sth the thumbs up** (*fam: sign*) far segno di essere d'accordo con qn/qc; (: *approve*) dare l'okay a qn/qc; **to give sth the thumbs down** (*fam*) disapprovare *or* bocciare qc ♦ VT (*book*) sfogliare; **to thumb a lift** *or* **a ride** (*fam*) fare l'autostop; **to thumb one's nose at sb** fare marameo a qn; **to thumb one's nose at sb/sth** (*fig: fam*) beffarsi di qn/qc ♦ VI: **to thumb through a book/magazine** sfogliare un libro/una rivista

thumb index N indice *m* a rubrica

thumb·nail [ˈθʌmneɪl] N unghia del pollice

thumbnail sketch N descrizione *f* breve

thumb·tack [ˈθʌmˌtæk] N (*USA*) puntina da disegno

thump [θʌmp] N (*blow*) forte colpo; (*noise of fall*) tonfo; **it came down with a thump** è caduto con un tonfo ♦ VT (*hit hard: person*) picchiare; (: *door*) picchiare su; (: *table*) battere su ♦ VI (*person: on door, table*) picchiare, battere; (: *move heavily*) camminare pesantemente; (*pound: heart*) battere forte

▸ **thump out** VT + ADV (*tune*) suonare pestando sui tasti

thun·der [ˈθʌndəʳ] N (*Met*) tuono; (*of hooves, traffic*) fragore *m*; **with a face like thunder** nero(-a) *or* scuro(-a) in volto ♦ VI (*Met: voice, fig*) tuonare; **the guns thundered in the distance** i cannoni tuonavano in lontananza; **to thunder by** *or* **past** (*train*) passare rombando *or* con un rombo; **he thundered at him to stop** gli urlò di fermarsi

thunder·bolt [ˈθʌndəˌbəʊlt] N fulmine *m*

thunder·clap [ˈθʌndəˌklæp] N rombo di tuono

thun·der·ous [ˈθʌndərəs] ADJ (*applause*) fragoroso(-a)

thunder·storm [ˈθʌndəˌstɔːm] N temporale *m*

thunder·struck [ˈθʌndəˌstrʌk] ADJ (*fig*) sbigottito(-a)

thun·dery [ˈθʌndərɪ] ADJ (*weather*) minaccioso(-a), da temporale, temporalesco(-a)

Thurs., Thur. ABBR (= *Thursday*) gio(v). (= *giovedì*)

Thurs·day [ˈθɜːzdɪ] N giovedì *m inv*; *see* **Tuesday**

thus [ðʌs] ADV (*frm: in this way*) così; (*as a result*) perciò; **they are thus better paid than other workers** sono quindi meglio pagati di altri impiegati; **it was not always thus** non è stato sempre così; **thus far** fino ad ora

thwart [θwɔːt] VT ostacolare, contrastare

thyme [taɪm] N timo

thy·roid [ˈθaɪrɔɪd] N (*also: thyroid gland*) tiroide *f*

ti·ara [tɪˈɑːrə] N diadema *m*; (*of pope*) tiara

Ti·ber [ˈtaɪbəʳ] N: **the Tiber** il Tevere

Ti·bet [tɪˈbɛt] N il Tibet

Ti·bet·an [tɪˈbɛtən] ADJ tibetano(-a) ♦ N (*person*) tibetano(-a); (*language*) tibetano

tibia [ˈtɪbɪə] N tibia

tic [tɪk] N (*Med*) tic *m inv*

tick¹ [tɪk] N **1** (*sound: of clock*) tic tac *m inv*; **the loud tick of the alarm clock** il forte ticchettio della sveglia **2** (*Brit fam: moment*) secondo, attimo; **in a tick** in un attimo **3** (*Brit: mark*) segno, spunta; **to put a tick against sth** fare un segno a fianco di qc; **put a tick in the appropriate box** fare un segno sulla casella corrispondente ♦ VT spuntare, fare un segno su; **to tick the right answer** fare un segno sulla risposta

giusta; *see also* **tick off** ♦ VI *(clock)* ticchettare, fare tic tac; **I can't understand what makes him tick** *(fig)* non riesco a capire come ragioni
- **tick away, tick by** VI + ADV *(hours, minutes)* scorrere
- **tick off** VT + ADV **1** *(Brit: from a list)* barrare; (: *fam: scold*) sgridare; **he ticked the names off the list** ha barrato i nomi dalla lista; **she ticked me off for being late** mi ha sgridato per il ritardo **2** *(USA fam: annoy)* seccare, infastidire

tick² [tɪk] N *(Zool)* zecca

ticker tape N nastro di telescrivente; *(USA: in parades)* stelle *fpl* filanti

tick·et ['tɪkɪt] N *(gen)* biglietto; *(for library)* tessera; *(Comm: label on goods)* cartellino, etichetta; (: *from cash register*) scontrino; (: *USA Pol*) lista dei candidati; **to get a (parking) ticket** *(Aut)* prendere una multa (per sosta vietata); **return ticket,** *(USA)* **round-trip ticket** biglietto di andata e ritorno; **open/closed ticket** *(Aer)* biglietto aperto/chiuso; **admission is by ticket only** si ammettono solo le persone munite di biglietto; **the man inspecting the tickets** l'uomo che controlla i biglietti; **that's the ticket!** *(fig: fam)* è quel che ci voleva! ♦ VT *(label: goods)* etichettare ♦ ADJ di biglietti

ticket agency N *(Theatre)* agenzia di vendita di biglietti

ticket barrier N *(Brit: Rail)* cancelletto d'ingresso

ticket collector N bigliettaio

ticket holder N persona munita di biglietto

ticket inspector N controllore *m*

ticket machine N distributore *m* di biglietti

ticket office N biglietteria

tick·le ['tɪkl] VT *(person)* fare il solletico a; *(fig: palate)* stuzzicare; (: *amuse*) divertire, far ridere; **it tickled his fancy** stuzzicava la sua fantasia; **to be tickled pink** *(fam)* andare in brodo di giuggiole ♦ VI: **it tickles** mi *(or* gli *etc)* fa il solletico ♦ N solletico; **to give sb a tickle** fare il solletico a qn

tick·lish ['tɪklɪʃ], **tick·ly** ['tɪklɪ] ADJ *(fam: easily tickled: person)* che soffre il solletico; *(which tickles: blanket)* che provoca prurito; (: *cough*) che provoca una sensazione di irritazione in gola; *(fig: touchy: person)* permaloso(-a); (: *delicate: situation, problem)* delicato(-a); **to be ticklish** soffrire il solletico

tid·al [taɪdl] ADJ *(flow)* di marea; *(river, estuary)* soggetto(-a) alla marea; **tidal range** escursione *f* di marea

tidal wave N onda di marea; *(fig: of protest, enthusiasm)* ondata

tid·bit ['tɪd,bɪt] N *(USA)* = **titbit**

tiddly·winks ['tɪdlɪ,wɪŋks] NSG gioco della pulce

tide [taɪd] N marea; *(fig: of emotion)* ondata; (: *of events)* corso; **the tide of public opinion** l'orientamento dell'opinione pubblica; **high/low tide** alta/bassa marea; **the tide has turned** la marea è cambiata; *(fig)* c'è stato un cambiamento (di tendenze); **to go with the tide** *(fig)* seguire la corrente; **to swim against the tide** *(fig)* andare controcorrente ♦ VT: **to tide sb over** *or* **through (until)** aiutare qn a tirare avanti (fino a); **can you lend me £10 to tide me over until Friday?** mi puoi prestare 10 sterline per tirare avanti fino a venerdì?

ti·di·ly ['taɪdɪlɪ] ADV in modo ordinato; **to arrange tidily** sistemare; **to dress tidily** vestirsi per benino

ti·di·ness ['taɪdɪnɪs] N ordine *m*

tidy ['taɪdɪ] ADJ *(comp* -ier, *superl* -iest) *(gen)* ordinato(-a), in ordine; *(hair, dress)* in ordine, curato(-a), a posto; *(room)* lindo(-a); *(work)* accurato(-a); *(drawing)* pulito(-a); *(person: in appearance)* curato(-a); (: *in character)* ordinato(-a); (: *mind)* organizzato(-a); **a tidy sum** *(fam)* una bella sommetta ♦ VT *(also:* **tidy up)** *(room, toys)* mettere in ordine, riordinare; *(one's hair)* ravviarsi; **go and tidy your room** vai a mettere in ordine la tua camera
- **tidy away** VT + ADV mettere via
- **tidy out** VT + ADV mettere in ordine
- **tidy up** VI + ADV fare ordine ♦ VT + ADV = **tidy** VT **to tidy o.s. up** rassettarsi

tie [taɪ] N **1** *(Brit: also:* **necktie)** cravatta; *(cord, ribbon, string)* legaccio; *(fig: bond)* legame *m*; **a red tie** una cravatta rossa; **black/white tie** *(on invitation)* smoking/abito di rigore; **the children are a tie** i bambini legano; **ties of friendship** legami d'amicizia; **family ties** legami familiari **2** *(Sport: draw)* pareggio; (: *match in series)* incontro; (: *Pol)* parità *f inv* di voti; **the match ended in a tie** l'incontro è finito con un pareggio, la partita è finita in pareggio; **cup tie** *(Brit:*

Sport: match) incontro di coppa **3** *(USA: Rail)* traversina ♦ VT *(gen, or fig)* legare; *(ribbon)* annodare; *(also:* **tie up:** *shoe)* allacciare, allacciarsi; **to tie sth in a bow** annodare qc; **to tie a knot (in sth)** fare un nodo (a qc); **to get tied in knots** *(also fig: fam)* ingarbugliarsi; **to tie a necktie** fare il nodo a una cravatta; **my job ties me to London** il mio lavoro mi tiene a Londra; **his hands are tied** *(fig)* ha le mani legate ♦ VI **1** *(dress, shoes)* allacciarsi **2** *(Sport: draw)* pareggiare; **they tied three-all** hanno pareggiato tre a tre
- **tie back** VT + ADV *(curtains)* fissare; **to tie back one's hair** farsi la coda (di cavallo)
- **tie down** VT + ADV assicurare, fissare con una corda; *(fig):* **to tie sb down to sth** costringere qn ad accettare qc; **to tie sb down to a promise/a price/a time** costringere qn a mantenere una promessa/ad accettare un prezzo/a venire a una certa ora; **to be tied down to sth** *(promise, date)* essere vincolato(-a) da qc; **to be tied down** *(restricted)* essere legato(-a) mani e piedi
- **tie in** VI + ADV: **to tie in (with)** *(correspond)* corrispondere (a); *(be connected)* avere legami (con) ♦ VT + ADV: **to tie in (with)** *(meeting, visit)* far coincidere (con); *(findings)* far combaciare (con)
- **tie on** VT + ADV *(Brit: label)* attaccare
- **tie together** VT + ADV legare (insieme); **he tied the handles of the bag together** ha legato assieme i manici della borsa
- **tie up** VI + ADV *(Naut)* ormeggiare ♦ VT + ADV *(person, parcel)* legare; *(boat)* ormeggiare; *(fig: capital)* impegnare; (: *business deal)* concludere; *(connect)* ricollegare; **to be tied up (with sb/sth)** *(busy)* essere occupato(-a) *or* impegnato(-a) (con qn/a fare qc); **the traffic was tied up by the accident** il traffico è rimasto bloccato per l'incidente

tie-breaker ['taɪ,breɪkər], **tie-break** ['taɪ,breɪk] N *(Tennis)* tie-break *m inv*; *(in quiz)* spareggio

tie-on ['taɪ,ɒn] ADJ *(Brit: label)* volante

tie-pin ['taɪ,pɪn] N *(Brit)* fermacravatta *m inv*

tier [tɪər] N *(in theatre)* fila; *(in stadium)* gradinata; *(layer)* strato; *(of cake)* piano; **to arrange in tiers** disporre in file (or in strati); **tiers of seats** file di sedili; **a three-tier wedding cake** una torta nuziale a tre piani

Tier·ra del Fue·go [tɪ,erədel'fweɪgəʊ] N Terra del Fuoco

tie tack N *(USA)* fermacravatta *m inv*

tiff [tɪf] N battibecco; **a lover's tiff** un battibecco tra innamorati

ti·ger ['taɪgər] N tigre *f*

tight [taɪt] ADJ **1** *(gen: clothes, budget, bend)* stretto(-a); *(rope)* teso(-a), tirato(-a); *(usu pred: firmly fixed, hard to move)* duro(-a); *(strict: control, discipline)* severo(-a), fermo(-a); *(Brit fam: mean)* tirchio(-a); **this dress is a bit tight** *or* is a **tight fit** questo vestito è un po' stretto; **tight jeans** jeans attillati; **to be in a tight spot** *(fig: fam)* essere in una situazione difficile; **space is a bit tight** siamo un po' stretti; **money is a bit tight** siamo un po' a corto di denaro; **to keep a tight hold of sth** tenere qc stretto; **to keep a tight hold on the reins** *(fig)* tenere le redini in pugno; **under tight control** sotto stretto controllo **2** *(fam: drunk)* sbronzo(-a); **to get tight** sbronzarsi ♦ ADV *(hold)* stretto(-a); *(close)* ermeticamente; *(grasp)* saldamente; *(squeeze)* fortemente; **to be packed tight** *(suitcase)* essere pieno(-a) zeppo(-a); *(people)* essere pigiati; **screw it up tight!** avvitalo stretto!; **pull the door tight!** chiudi bene la porta!; **to hold sb tight** tenere stretto(-a) qn; **everybody hold tight!** tenetevi stretti!; **the room was packed tight with people** la stanza era piena zeppa di persone; **to sleep tight** *(soundly)* dormire sodo

tight·en ['taɪtn] VT *(also:* **tighten up)** *(gen)* stringere; *(rope)* tendere; *(regulation)* rendere più severo(-a); *(control)* intensificare; **he tightened the rope** ha teso la corda; **to tighten one's grip** stringere la presa; **to tighten security** aumentare la sicurezza; **to tighten one's belt** *(fig)* tirare la cinghia ♦ VI *(also:* **tighten up)** stringersi; *(rope)* tendersi; *(grasp)* farsi più stretto(-a)
- **tighten up** VI + ADV **1** = **tighten 1** **2 to tighten up on sth** rendere qc più severo(-a) ♦ VT + ADV = **tighten** VT

tight-fisted [,taɪt'fɪstɪd] ADJ *(fam)* avaro(-a), tirchio(-a)

tight-lipped [,taɪt'lɪpt] ADJ: **to be tight-lipped** *(silent)* essere reticente; *(angry)* tenere le labbra serrate

tight·ly ['taɪtlɪ] ADV (*grasp*) bene, saldamente; **to hold sth tightly** tenere stretto qc; **she held his hand tightly** gli tenne stretta la mano; **tightly closed** ben chiuso(-a)

tight·rope ['taɪt,rəʊp] N corda (da acrobata)

tightrope walker N funambolo(-a)

tights [taɪts] NPL (*Brit*) collant *m inv*

ti·gress ['taɪgrɪs] N tigre *f* (femmina)

tile [taɪl] N (*on roof*) tegola; (*on floor, wall*) mattonella, piastrella; **roofs with red tiles** tetti con le tegole rosse; **black and white tiles** piastrelle bianche e nere ♦ VT (*roof*) rivestire di tegole; (*floor, bathroom*) piastrellare

tiled [taɪld] ADJ (*floor, wall, bathroom*) a mattonelle, a piastrelle; (*roof*) rivestito(-a) di tegole; **a tiled roof** un tetto di tegole; **tiled walls** pareti *fpl* piastrellate

till¹ [tɪl] PREP (*fam*): **I waited till ten o'clock** ho aspettato fino alle dieci; **not... till** non... prima di; **it won't be ready till next week** non sarà pronto prima della settimana prossima; **till now** finora; **till then** fino ad allora

till² [tɪl] N (*for money*) cassa, registratore *m* di cassa; **pay at the till** pagare alla cassa

till³ [tɪl] VT (*land*) coltivare

till·er ['tɪlə'] N (*Naut*) barra del timone

tilt [tɪlt] N 1 (*slope*) pendio; **to wear one's hat at a tilt** portare il cappello sulle ventitré 2 (*fam*): **(at) full tilt** a tutta velocità ♦ VT inclinare, far pendere; **tilt it this way/the other way** inclinalo da questa/quella parte; **he tilted the mirror** ha inclinato lo specchio; **he tilted his chair back** ha inclinato la sedia indietro ♦ VI inclinarsi, pendere; **to tilt to one side** inclinarsi da una parte; **the boat tilted dangerously** la barca si è inclinata pericolosamente; **he tilted back in his chair** si è inclinato indietro con la sedia

tim·ber ['tɪmbə'] N (*material*) legname *m*; (*trees*) alberi *mpl* da legname; **timber!** cadé! ♦ ADJ (*roof, cabin*) di legno

time [taɪm] N 1 (*gen*) tempo; **time and space** il tempo e lo spazio; **how time flies** come vola il tempo!; **only time will tell** si saprà solo col tempo; **time is on our side** il tempo è dalla nostra; **all in good time** senza fretta; **to have (the) time (to do sth)** avere il tempo (di fare qc); **I'm sorry, I haven't got time** scusa, non ho tempo; **to find the time for reading** trovare il tempo per leggere; **I've no time for them** (*too busy*) non ho tempo da perdere con loro; (*contemptuous*) non li posso soffrire; **I've no time for it** (*fig*) non ho tempo da perdere con cose del genere; **he lost no time in doing it** l'ha fatto subito senza perdere tempo; **it takes time to ...** ci vuole tempo per...; **to take one's time** prenderla con calma; **time is money** (*Proverb*) il tempo è denaro; **he'll do it in his own (good) time** (*without being hurried*) lo farà quando ha (un minuto di) tempo; **he'll do it in his own time** (*out of working hours*) lo farà nel suo tempo libero; **my time is my own** dispongo del mio tempo 2 (*period of time*) tempo; **a long time** molto tempo; **a long time ago** molto tempo fa; **a short time** poco tempo; **in a short time they were all gone** nel giro di poco tempo se ne erano andati tutti; **a short time after** poco tempo dopo; **for a time** per un po' di tempo; **have you been here all this time?** sei stato qui tutto questo tempo?; **for the time being** per il momento; **in no time** in un attimo; **it will be ready in no time** sarà pronto prestissimo; **in a week's time** fra una settimana 3 (*moment*) momento; (*period*) periodo; **any time** in qualsiasi momento; **come any time you like** vieni quando vuoi; **any time now** da un momento all'altro; **at that time** allora, a quel tempo; **at the present time** al momento, adesso; **at this time of the year** in questo periodo dell'anno; **(by) this time next year** in questo periodo l'anno prossimo; **by the time he arrived** quando è arrivato; **at the same time** (*simultaneously*) contemporaneamente; **but at the same time, I have to admit ...** tuttavia devo ammettere...; **at the same time as** nello stesso momento in cui; **at times** a volte; **at all times** in ogni momento, sempre; **from time to time** di tanto in tanto; **the time has come to leave** è arrivato il momento *or* l'ora di partire; **this is no time for jokes** non è il momento di scherzare; **this is neither the time nor the place to discuss it** non è né il luogo né il momento adatto per discuterne 4 (*by clock*) ora; **what time do you make it?** che ora fai?; **have you got the (right) time?** hai l'ora (esatta)?; **what's the time?** che ora è?, che ore sono?; **it was two**

o'clock, Italian time erano le due, ora italiana; **what time do you get up?** a che ora ti alzi?; **in time** (*soon enough*) in tempo; (*after some time*) col tempo; **just in time** appena in tempo; **to arrive (just) in time for dinner** arrivare (appena) in tempo per cena; **on time** (*person*) puntuale; (*train*) in orario; **he never arrives on time** non è mai puntuale; **it's time for the news** (*on radio*) c'è il giornale radio; (*on television*) c'è il telegiornale; **time's up!** è (l')ora!; **to be 30 minutes behind/ahead of time** avere 30 minuti di ritardo/anticipo; **about time too!** era anche ora!; **it was about time you had a haircut** era proprio ora che ti tagliassi i capelli 5 (*era: often pl*) era; (*period*) periodo, epoca; **in modern times** nell'era moderna; **in Elizabethan times** nel periodo elisabettiano; **in my time** ai miei tempi; **it was before my time** non ero ancora nata; **times were hard** erano tempi duri; **in times to come** nel tempo a venire; **to be ahead of one's time** precorrere i tempi; **to be behind the times** essere rimasto(-a) indietro 6 (*experience*): **to have a good time** divertirsi; **did you have a good time?** vi siete divertiti?; **to have a bad** *or* **rough time (of it)** passarsela male; **they had a hard time of it** è stata dura per loro 7 (*occasion*) volta; **three times** tre volte; **this/next time** questa/la prossima volta; **how many times?** quante volte?; **the last time I did it** l'ultima volta che l'ho fatto; **time after time, time and again** mille volte; **many's the time ...** più di una volta...; **I remember the time when ...** ricordo ancora quando...; **for weeks at a time** per settimane; **2 at a time** 2 alla volta; **to carry 3 boxes at a time** portare 3 scatole per volta 8 (*Mus, Mil*) tempo; **to play/march in time** suonare/marciare a tempo; **to keep time** andare a tempo; **to be out of time** essere *or* andare fuori tempo 9 (*Math*): **4 times 3 is 12** 4 per *or* volte 3 fa 12; **3 times as fast (as)**, **3 times faster (than)** 3 volte più veloce (di) ♦ VT 1 (*schedule*) programmare; (*measure duration of*) calcolare la durata di; (*choose time of: joke, request*): **to time sth well/badly** scegliere il momento più/meno opportuno per qc, fare qc al momento giusto/sbagliato; **the footballer timed his shot perfectly** il giocatore ha calcolato il tiro alla perfezione; **the bomb was timed to explode 5 minutes later** la bomba era stata regolata in modo da esplodere 5 minuti più tardi 2 (*with stopwatch*) cronometrare; **to time an egg** controllare il tempo per la cottura di un uovo; **to time o.s.** prendere i propri tempi

time and motion study N analisi *f inv* dei tempi e delle fasi di produzione

time bomb N bomba a orologeria

time·card ['taɪm,kɑːd] N cartellino (di presenza)

time clock N (*Industry*) orologio marcatempo

time-consuming ['taɪmkən,sjuːmɪŋ] ADJ che richiede molto tempo

time difference N differenza di fuso orario

time frame N tempi *mpl*

time-honoured, **time-honored** (*USA*) ['taɪm,ɒnəd] ADJ consacrato(-a) dal tempo

time·keeper ['taɪm,kiːpə'] N (*Sport*) cronometrista *m/f*; **he's a good timekeeper** è sempre puntuale; **my old watch is a good timekeeper** il mio vecchio orologio non perde un secondo

time lag N (*between events*) intervallo (di tempo); (*in travel*) differenza di fuso orario

time·less ['taɪmlɪs] ADJ (*frm: unchanging*) senza tempo; (: *unending*) eterno(-a), infinito(-a)

time limit N limite *m* di tempo; **to set a time limit** fissare un limite di tempo

time·ly ['taɪmlɪ] ADJ tempestivo(-a); (*opportune*) opportuno(-a)

time off N tempo libero

tim·er ['taɪmə'] N (*in kitchen*) contaminuti *m inv*; (*hourglass*) clessidra; (*Tech*) timer *m inv*, temporizzatore *m inv*

time-saving ['taɪm,seɪvɪŋ] ADJ che fa risparmiare tempo

time scale N tempi *mpl* d'esecuzione

time-share ['taɪm,ʃɛə'] ADJ (*holiday home*) in multiproprietà ♦ N (*property*) casa in multiproprietà; (*system*) multiproprietà *f inv*

time sheet N foglio di presenza

time signal N segnale *m* orario

time switch N interruttore *m* a tempo

time·table [ˈtaɪmˌteɪbl] N (*for trains*) orario; (*programme of events*) programma *m*; **the train timetable** l'orario del treno

time zone N fuso orario

tim·id [ˈtɪmɪd] ADJ (*shy*) timido(-a); (*easily scared*) timoroso(-a), pauroso(-a)

ti·mid·ity [tɪˈmɪdɪtɪ] N timidezza

tim·ing [ˈtaɪmɪŋ] N (*of tennis player, cricketer*) coordinazione *f*; (*of musician*) tempismo; (*of comedian*) tempestività *f inv*; (*of demonstration, elections*) momento; (*of engine*) messa in fase; (*of race, industrial process*) cronometraggio; **that was good/bad timing** hai (*or* ha *etc*) scelto il momento opportuno/sbagliato; **that was perfect timing!** che tempismo!; **the timing of the announcement was carefully calculated** il momento in cui dare l'annuncio fu scelto con attenzione

timing device N (*on bomb*) timer *m inv*

tim·pa·ni [ˈtɪmpənɪ] NPL (*Mus*) timpani *mpl*

tin [tɪn] N 1 (*metal*) stagno; (*also*: **tin plate**) latta 2 (*Brit*: *can*) barattolo *or* scatola (di latta); (: *for baking*) teglia; **a tin of paint** un barattolo di vernice; **a tin of beans** una scatola di fagioli; **a biscuit tin** una scatola per biscotti ♦ VT (*Brit*) inscatolare

tin·foil [ˈtɪnˌfɔɪl] N (*carta*) stagnola

tinge [tɪndʒ] N (*of colour, also fig*) punta, sfumatura; **her hair had a tinge of red in it** i suoi capelli avevano dei riflessi rossi ♦ VT: **to be tinged with** avere una punta *or* sfumatura di

tin·gle [ˈtɪŋgl] N (*of skin*) formicolio; (*thrill*) fremito ♦ VI (*cheeks, skin: from cold*) pungere, pizzicare; (: *from bad circulation*) formicolare; **my fingers are tingling** ho le dita informicolate; **my tongue is tingling** mi pizzica la lingua; **a tingling sensation** un formicolio; **to tingle with excitement** fremere dall'eccitazione

tink·er [ˈtɪŋkəʳ] N stagnino ambulante
 ▸ **tinker with** VI + PREP armeggiare intorno a
 ▸ **tinker about with** VI + ADV + PREP (*play*) trastullarsi con; (*repair*) armeggiare intorno a, cercare di riparare; **he's always tinkering with his car** è sempre lì ad armeggiare intorno alla macchina

tin·kle [ˈtɪŋkl] N 1 (*of bell*) tintinnio; (*Brit fam*): **give me a tinkle** dammi un colpetto di telefono 2 (*fam*: *act of urinating*) fusg *fsg* ♦ VI (*bell*) tintinnare

tin mine N miniera di stagno

tinned [tɪnd] ADJ (*Brit*: *food*) in scatola; **tinned peaches** pesche in scatola

tin·ni·tus [tɪˈnaɪtəs] N (*Med*) ronzio auricolare

tin·ny [ˈtɪnɪ] ADJ (*comp* **-ier**, *superl* **-iest**) (*metallic: sound*) metallico(-a); (*pej: car, machine*) che sembra di latta

tin-opener [ˈtɪnˌəʊpnəʳ] N (*Brit*) apriscatole *m inv*

tin·sel [ˈtɪnsəl] N decorazioni *fpl* natalizie (*argentate*)

tint [tɪnt] N (*gen*) sfumatura; (*colour*) tinta; (*for hair*) shampoo *m inv* colorante; **a delicate purple tint** una leggera sfumatura di viola ♦ VT (*hair*) fare uno shampoo colorante a

tint·ed [ˈtɪntɪd] ADJ (*hair*) tinto(-a); (*spectacles, glass*) colorato(-a); **tinted windows** (*Aut*) cristalli *mpl* fumé, *inv*

tiny [ˈtaɪnɪ] ADJ (*comp* **-ier**, *superl* **-iest**) minuscolo(-a)

tip¹ [tɪp] N (*end*) punta; (*peak*) cima, vetta; (*of stick, umbrella: protective*) puntale *m*; **it's on the tip of my tongue** (*fig*) ce l'ho sulla punta della lingua; **it was just the tip of the iceberg** (*fig*) era solo la punta dell'iceberg
 ▸ **tip off** VT + ADV (*inform*) fare una soffiata a
 ▸ **tip up** VI + ADV ribaltarsi ♦ VT + ADV inclinare

tip² [tɪp] N 1 (*gratuity*) mancia 2 (*hint*) suggerimento; (*advice*) consiglio; (*for horse race*) cavallo; **I'll give you a tip** ti darò un consiglio; **he didn't leave a tip** non ha lasciato la mancia; **a useful tip** un buon consiglio ♦ VT 1 (*porter, waiter*) dare la mancia a; **I tipped him £1** gli ho dato una mancia di 1 sterlina, gli ho dato 1 sterlina di mancia 2 (*predict: winner*) pronosticare; (: *horse*) dare vincente; **he is being tipped for the job** secondo i pronostici dovrebbe avere il posto

tip³ [tɪp] VT (*tilt*) inclinare; (*empty: also*: **tip out**) svuotare, scaricare; (*overturn: also*: **tip over**) rovesciare, capovolgere; **to tip sb off his seat** far cadere qn dalla sedia; **to tip away the dishwater** svuotare l'acqua dei piatti; **to tip back a chair** inclinare una sedia all'indietro; **he tipped out the contents of the box** ha rovesciato il contenuto della scatola; **she tipped the leftovers in the bin** ha vuotato gli avanzi

nella pattumiera; **to tip over a glass of wine** rovesciare un bicchiere di vino; **to tip the balance** far pendere la bilancia da una parte ♦ VI (*incline*) pendere, essere inclinato(-a); (*also*: **tip over**) rovesciarsi

tip-off [ˈtɪpˌɒf] N (*information*) soffiata

tipped [tɪpt] ADJ (*Brit: cigarette*) col filtro; **steel-tipped** con la punta d'acciaio

tip·ple [ˈtɪpl] (*fam*) N drink *m inv* preferito; **to have a tipple** bere un bicchierino ♦ VI sbevazzare

tip·ster [ˈtɪpstəʳ] N (*Racing*) chi vende informazioni sulle corse e altre manifestazioni oggetto di scommesse

tip·sy [ˈtɪpsɪ] ADJ (*comp* **-ier**, *superl* **-iest**) brillo(-a)

tip·toe [ˈtɪpˌtəʊ] N: **to walk on tiptoe** camminare in punta dei piedi ♦ VI camminare in punta dei piedi

tip·top [ˌtɪpˈtɒp] ADJ: **in tiptop condition** in ottime condizioni

ti·rade [taɪˈreɪd] N filippica

tire¹ [ˈtaɪəʳ] VT (*exhaust*) stancare ♦ VI stancarsi; **he tires easily** si stanca facilmente; **to tire of sb/sth** stancarsi di sb/sth
 ▸ **tire out** VT + ADV sfinire, spossare; **the walk tired me out** la passeggiata mi ha sfinito

tire² [ˈtaɪəʳ] (*USA*) = **tyre**

tired [ˈtaɪəd] ADJ 1 stanco(-a); **to be/feel/look tired** essere/sentirsi/sembrare stanco(-a); **to be tired of sb/sth** essere stanco(-a) *or* stufo(-a) di qn/qc; **I'm tired of waiting** sono stufa di aspettare; **to get** *or* **grow tired of doing sth** stancarsi di fare qc 2 (*fig: cliché*) trito(-a) e ritrito(-a); (*fig: shabby*) consunto(-a)

tired·ness [ˈtaɪədnɪs] N stanchezza

tire·less [ˈtaɪəlɪs] ADJ instancabile

tire pressure N (*USA*) = **tyre pressure**

tire·some [ˈtaɪəsəm] ADJ (*job, person*) noioso(-a); (*situation*) seccante; **how tiresome!** che seccatura!

tir·ing [ˈtaɪərɪŋ] ADJ faticoso(-a)

tis·sue [ˈtɪʃuː] N 1 (*thin paper*) velina; (*paper handkerchief*) fazzolettino di carta; **she blew her nose on a tissue** si è soffiata il naso con un fazzolettino di carta 2 (*Anat*) tessuto; **muscle tissue** tessuto muscolare 3 (*fig*): **to weave a tissue of lies** ordire tutta una serie di menzogne

tissue paper N carta velina

tit¹ [tɪt] N (*bird: also*: **titmouse**) cincia

tit² [tɪt] N (*fam: breast*) tetta

tit³ [tɪt] N: **to give tit for tat** rendere pan per focaccia

ti·ta·nium [tɪˈteɪnɪəm] N titanio

tit·bit [ˈtɪtˌbɪt], (*USA*) **tid·bit** [ˈtɪdˌbɪt] N (*of food*) bocconcino, leccornia; (*fig: of news, information, gossip*) notizia ghiotta

tit·il·late [ˈtɪtɪˌleɪt] VT (*sexually*) titillare

titi·vate [ˈtɪtɪˌveɪt] VT agghindare

ti·tle [ˈtaɪtl] N 1 (*gen*) titolo; **author and title** autore e titolo; **to hold a title** detenere un titolo 2 (*Law: right*): **title (to)** diritto (a)

title deed N (*Law*) atto di proprietà

title page N frontespizio

title role N (*Theatre, Cine*) ruolo *or* parte *f* principale

tit·ter [ˈtɪtəʳ] N risatina nervosa ♦ VI ridere nervosamente, ridacchiare

tittle-tattle [ˈtɪtlˌtætl] (*fam*) N pettegolezzi *mpl*, chiacchiere *fpl* ♦ VI pettegolare

titu·lar [ˈtɪtjʊləʳ] ADJ (*in name only*) nominale

tiz·zy [ˈtɪzɪ] N (*fam*): **to be in/get into a tizzy (about sth)** essere/mettersi in agitazione (per qc)

T-junction [ˈtiːˌdʒʌŋkʃən] N (*Brit*) incrocio a T

TM [ˌtiːˈem] N ABBR 1 (= *transcendental meditation*) MT *f* 2 (*Comm*) = **trademark**

TN ABBR (*USA Post*: = **Tennessee**)

TNT [ˌtiːenˈtiː] N ABBR (= *trinitrotoluene*) TNT *m*

KEYWORD

to [tuː, *weak form* tə] PREP

1 (*direction*) a; (: *towards*) verso; (: *to a country*) in; (: *to sb's house, office, shop*) da; **have you ever been to India?** sei mai stata in India?; **to go to the doctor's** andare dal dottore; **to go to France** andare in Francia; **to the left** a sinistra; **a letter to his wife** una lettera a sua moglie; **to go to Paris** andare a Parigi; **to go to Peter's** andare da Peter; **to go to**

Portugal andare in Portogallo; **to the right** a destra; **the road to Copenhagen** la strada per Copenaghen; **to go to school** andare a scuola; **to go to the station** andare alla stazione

2 (*next to, with position*) a; **with one's back to the wall** con le spalle al muro; **the door is to the left (of)** la porta è a sinistra (di); **at right angles to sth** ad angolo retto con qc

3 (*as far as*) fino a; **to count to 10** contare fino a dieci; **to some extent** fino a un certo punto, in parte; **from here to London** da qui (fino) a Londra; **from 40 to 50 people** da 40 a 50 persone; **to be wet to the skin** essere bagnato(-a) fino al midollo

4 (*with expressions of time*) a; **it's twenty-five to 3** mancano venticinque minuti alle 3, sono le 2 e trentacinque

5 (*expressing indirect object*) a; **it belongs to him** gli appartiene, è suo; **to drink to sb** bere a qn *or* alla salute di qn; **to give sth to sb** dare qc a qn; **give it to me** dammelo; **the key to the front door** la chiave della porta d'ingresso; **to be kind to sb** essere gentile con qn; **a monument to the fallen** un monumento ai caduti; **the man I sold it to, the man to whom I sold it** (*frm*) l'uomo (a) cui l'ho venduto; **a solution to the problem** una soluzione al problema

6 (*in relation to*) (in confronto) a; **A is to B as C is to D** A sta a B come C sta a D; **30 miles to the gallon** ≈ 11 chilometri con un litro; **5 apples to the kilo** 5 mele in un chilo; **10 inhabitants to the square kilometre** 10 abitanti per chilometro quadrato; **that's nothing to what is to come** non è nulla in confronto a ciò che ancora deve venire; **superior to the others** superiore agli altri; **three goals to two** tre reti a due

7 (*about*): **that's all there is to it** questo è tutto, è tutto qui; **what do you say to this?** che cosa ne pensi?

8 (*according to*) secondo; **to the best of my recollection** per quanto mi ricordi io; **we danced to the music of ...** abbiamo ballato con la musica di...; **to my way of thinking** secondo il mio modo di pensare, a mio parere

9 (*purpose, result*): **to come to sb's aid** venire in aiuto a qn; **to sentence sb to death** condannare qn a morte; **to my great surprise** con mia grande sorpresa

♦ PARTICLE (*with verb*)

1 (*simple infinitive*): **to go/eat** andare/mangiare

2 (*following another verb*): **to start to cry** incominciare *or* mettersi a piangere; **to try to do** cercare di fare; **to want to do** voler fare

3 (*purpose, result*) per; **he did it to help you** l'ha fatto per aiutarti; **he came to see you** è venuto per vederti

4 (*with ellipsis of verb*): **you ought to** dovresti (farlo); **I don't want to** non voglio (farlo)

5 (*equivalent to relative clause*) da; **I have things to do** ho (delle cose) da fare; **he's not the sort to do that** non è il tipo da fare una cosa del genere; **now is the time to do it** è ora di farlo; **he has a lot to lose** rischia grosso; **he has nothing to lose** non ha nulla da perdere

6 (*after adjective etc*): **the first to go** il (la) primo(-a) ad andarsene; **hard to believe** difficile da credere; **too old to ...** troppo vecchio(-a) per...; **ready to go** pronto(-a) a partire; **too young to ...** troppo giovane per...

♦ ADV

1 to go to and fro andare e tornare; **to pull/push the door to** (*closed*) accostare la porta

2 to come to (*recover consciousness*) riprendere conoscenza

toad [təʊd] N rospo

toad·stool [ˈtəʊdˌstuːl] N fungo velenoso

toady [ˈtəʊdɪ] (*pej*) N leccapiedi *m/f inv* ♦ VI: **to toady to sb** leccare i piedi a qn

toast [təʊst] N **1** (*bread*) pane *m* tostato; **a piece** *or* **slice of toast** una fetta di pane tostato *or* abbrustolito **2** (*drink, speech*) brindisi *m inv*; **to propose/drink a toast to sb** proporre (di fare)/fare un brindisi a qn; **the toast of the town/nation** (*fig*) il vanto della città/nazione ♦ VT **1** (*bread*) tostare, abbrustolire **2** (*drink to*) brindare a

❑ **toast** is not translated by the Italian word *toast*

toast·er [ˈtəʊstəʳ] N tostapane *m inv*

toast·master [ˈtəʊstˌmɑːstəʳ] N direttore *m* dei brindisi

toast rack [ˈtəʊstˌræk] N portatoast *m inv*

to·bac·co [təˈbækəʊ] N tabacco; **pipe tobacco** tabacco da pipa

to·bac·co·nist [təˈbækənɪst] N (*Brit*) tabaccaio(-a); **tobacconist's (shop)** tabaccheria

To·ba·go [təˈbeɪɡəʊ] N *see* **Trinidad and Tobago**

to·bog·gan [təˈbɒɡən] N toboga *m inv*, slittino; (*child's*) slitta, slittino ♦ VI andare in slittino

to·day [təˈdeɪ] ADV oggi; (*these days*) al giorno d'oggi, oggigiorno; **a week from today, a week today, today week** (*Brit*) oggi a otto; **a fortnight today** (*Brit*), **two weeks from today** (*USA*) quindici giorni a oggi; **what day is it today?** che giorno è oggi?; **what date is it today?** quanti ne abbiamo oggi?; **today is the 4th of March** (oggi) è il 4 (di) marzo ♦ N (*also fig*) oggi *m inv*; **writers of today** gli scrittori d'oggi; **today's paper** il giornale di oggi

tod·dler [ˈtɒdləʳ] N (*small child*) bambino(-a) che impara a camminare

tod·dy [ˈtɒdɪ] N: **hot toddy** grog *m inv*

to-do [təˈduː] N (*fam: fuss*): **to cause a to-do** fare delle storie

toe [təʊ] N (*Anat*) dito del piede; (*of shoe*) punta; **big toe** alluce *m*; **little toe** mignolino; **to keep sb on his toes** (*fig*) tenere qn sull'attenti ♦ VT: **to toe the line** (*fig: conform*) conformarsi alle regole, stare in riga

TOEFL N ABBR = Test(ing) of English as a Foreign Language

toe·hold [ˈtəʊˌhəʊld] N punto d'appoggio

toe·nail [ˈtəʊˌneɪl] N unghia del piede

tof·fee [ˈtɒfɪ] N caramella *f* mou, *inv*

toffee apple N (*Brit*) mela caramellata

tofu [ˈtəʊˌfuː] N tofu *m*, *caglio di latte di soia non fermentato*

toga [ˈtəʊɡə] N toga

to·geth·er [təˈɡeðəʳ] ADV **1** (*gen*) insieme; **together with** insieme a; **all together** tutti insieme; **they were both in it together** (*pej*) vi erano implicati entrambi; **we're in this together** siamo nella stessa barca; **to bring the two sides together** far mettere d'accordo le due parti; **to gather together** radunarsi; **to put a meal together** mettere insieme un pranzo *or* una cena; **are they still together?** stanno ancora insieme? **2** (*simultaneously*) insieme, contemporaneamente, allo stesso tempo; (*continuously*) di seguito

to·geth·er·ness [təˈɡeðənɪs] N (*closeness*) intimità *f inv*; **family togetherness** intimità familiare

toggle switch N deviatore *m* a comando manuale; (*Comput*) tasto bistabile

Togo [ˈtəʊɡəʊ] N il Togo

togs [tɒɡz] NPL (*fam: clothes*) vestiti *mpl*

toil [tɔɪl] N duro lavoro, fatica ♦ VI lavorare sodo, faticare; **workers toiled for hours and hours** gli operai sgobbavano per ore ed ore; **to toil away at sth** lavorare duramente su qc; **to toil up a hill** arrancare su per una collina

toi·let [ˈtɔɪlɪt] N **1** (*Brit: lavatory*) gabinetto; **to go to the toilet** andare al gabinetto *or* al bagno; **where's the toilet?** dov'è la toilette? **2** (*old: dressing, washing*) toilette *f* ♦ ADJ (*soap*) da toilette

toilet bag N (*Brit*) nécessaire *m inv* da toilette

toilet bowl N vaso *or* tazza del gabinetto

toilet paper N carta igienica

toi·let·ries [ˈtɔɪlɪtrɪz] NPL articoli *mpl* da toilette

toilet roll N (*Brit*) rotolo di carta igienica

toilet water N acqua di colonia

to-ing and fro-ing [ˌtuːɪŋənˈfrəʊɪŋ] N (*pl* **to-ings and fro-ings**) (*Brit*) andirivieni *m inv*

to·ken [ˈtəʊkən] N **1** (*Brit: voucher*) buono; **record token** buono *m* disco, *inv*; **gift token** buono *m* omaggio, *inv* **2** (*metal disc*) gettone *m* **3** (*sign, symbol*) segno; **by the same token** (*fig*) per lo stesso motivo; **as a token of our respect** come segno di rispetto ♦ ADJ (*fee, strike*) simbolico(-a); (*resistance, gesture*) formale; **a token gesture** un gesto simbolico

to·ken·ism [ˈtəʊkəˌnɪzəm] N concessione *f* pro forma, *inv*

To·kyo [ˈtəʊkjəʊ] N Tokyo *f*

told [təʊld] PT, PP *of* **tell**

tol·er·able [ˈtɒlərəbl] ADJ **1** (*bearable*) sopportabile, tollerabile **2** (*fairly good*) passabile, discreto(-a); **the pain was tolerable** il dolore era sopportabile; **he got tolerable marks in English** ha ricevuto voti decenti in inglese

tol·er·ably [ˈtɒlərəblɪ] ADV (*good, comfortable*) abbastanza

tol·er·ance [ˈtɒlərəns] N (*of pain, hardship*) sopportazione *f*; (*of behaviour: Med, Tech*) tolleranza

tol·er·ant [ˈtɒlərənt] ADJ: **tolerant (of)** tollerante (nei confronti di)

tol·er·ate [ˈtɒləˌreɪt] VT (*gen, also Med, Tech*) tollerare, sopportare

tol·era·tion [ˌtɒləˈreɪʃən] N tolleranza

toll¹ [təʊl] N 1 (*on road*) pedaggio 2 (*losses, casualties*): **the death toll on the roads** il numero di vittime sulle strade; **the severe winter has taken its toll on the crops** l'inverno rigido ha colpito duramente il raccolto ♦ ADJ (*road, bridge*) a pedaggio

toll² [təʊl] VT, VI (*bell*) suonare lentamente e solennemente ♦ N (*of bell*) rintocco

toll·bridge [ˈtəʊlˌbrɪdʒ] N ponte *m* a pedaggio

toll call N (*USA: Telec*) (telefonata) interurbana

toll-free [ˌtəʊlˈfriː] (*USA*) ADJ senza addebito, gratuito(-a); **toll-free number** ≈ numero verde ♦ ADV gratuitamente

to·ma·to [təˈmɑːtəʊ, (*USA*) təˈmeɪtəʊ] N (*pl* **tomatoes**) pomodoro ♦ ADJ (*juice, sauce*) di pomodoro

tomb [tuːm] N tomba

tom·bo·la [ˈtɒmˈbəʊlə] N (*Brit*) tombola

tom·boy [ˈtɒmˌbɔɪ] N: **she's a tomboy** è un maschiaccio

tomb·stone [ˈtuːmˌstəʊn] N pietra tombale

tom·cat [ˈtɒmˌkæt] N gatto maschio

to·mor·row [təˈmɒrəʊ] ADV (*also fig*) domani; **tomorrow morning** domani mattina; **a week from tomorrow, a week tomorrow** (*Brit*) domani a otto ♦ N domani *m inv*; **tomorrow is Sunday** domani è domenica; **the day after tomorrow** dopodomani; **tomorrow's paper** il giornale di domani; **tomorrow is another day** (*fig*) domani è un altro giorno

ton [tʌn] N (*weight*) tonnellata (*Brit* = 1016 *kg*; *USA* = 907 *kg*); (*metric ton*) tonnellata; (*Naut*) (*also:* **register ton**) tonnellata di stazza (*2.83 cu. m*; *100 cu. ft*); (*also:* **displacement ton**) tonnellata inglese; **this suitcase weighs a ton** (*fam*) questa valigia pesa una tonnellata; **tons of sth** (*fam*) un mucchio *or* sacco di qc

to·nal [ˈtəʊnl] ADJ tonale

tone [təʊn] N (*gen*) tono; (*of colour*) tonalità *f inv*; (*of musical instrument*) timbro; (*Telec*) segnale *m* acustico; **his tone of voice** il tono della sua voce; **leave a message after the tone** lasciate un messaggio dopo il segnale acustico; **dialling** (*Brit*) *or* **dial** (*USA*) **tone** (*Telec*) segnale *m* di libero; **to praise sb in ringing tones** (*fig*) portare qn alle stelle; **they were speaking in low tones** parlavano a voce bassa; **two tones of red** due tonalità di rosso; **to raise/lower the tone of sth** migliorare/abbassare il tono di qc ♦ VI (*also:* **tone in**: *colours*) intonarsi; **the curtains tone with the carpet** le tende si intonano con la moquette

▸ **tone down** VT + ADV (*moderate: colour, sound*) attenuare; (*fig: language, criticism*) moderare

▸ **tone up** VT + ADV (*muscles*) tonificare; **exercise tones the muscles** la ginnastica tonifica i muscoli

tone-deaf [ˌtəʊnˈdɛf] ADJ stonato(-a), completamente privo(-a) di orecchio (musicale)

ton·er [ˈtəʊnəʳ] N (*for photocopier*) colorante *m* organico, toner *m inv*

Tonga Is·lands [ˈtɒŋgəˌaɪləndz] NPL , **Tonga** N le (isole *fpl*) Tonga

tongs [tɒŋz] NPL (*for coal*) molle *fpl*, tenaglie *fpl*; (*for sugar, in laboratory*) pinza

tongue [tʌŋ] N 1 (*gen*) lingua; (*of shoe*) linguetta; (*of bell*) battaglio; **have you lost your tongue?** hai perso la lingua?; **hold your tongue!** chiudi quella bocca!; **to put out one's tongue (at sb)** mostrare la lingua (a qn); **to say sth tongue in cheek** (*fig*) dire qc ironicamente; **I can't get my tongue round it** (*fig*) non riesco a pronunciarlo 2 (*frm, liter: language*) lingua

tongue-tied [ˈtʌŋˌtaɪd] ADJ (*fig*) muto(-a); **he was tongue-tied with embarrassment** l'imbarazzo lo ha fatto ammutolire

tongue-twister [ˈtʌŋˌtwɪstəʳ] N scioglilingua *m inv*

ton·ic [ˈtɒnɪk] N 1 (*Med*) ricostituente *m*; (*also:* **skin tonic**) tonico; **fresh air is the best tonic when you have a**

headache l'aria fresca è il miglior rimedio per il mal di testa 2 (*also:* **tonic water**) acqua tonica; **a bottle of tonic** una bottiglia di acqua tonica 3 (*Mus*) nota tonica ♦ ADJ (*all senses*) tonico(-a); **tonic solfa** (*Mus*) solfeggio

to·night [təˈnaɪt] ADV, N (*this evening*) questa sera, stasera; (*this night*) questa notte, stanotte; **are you going out tonight?** esci stasera?; **I'll see you tonight** ci vediamo stasera; **I'll sleep well tonight** stanotte dormirò bene; **tonight's TV programmes** (*Brit*) *or* **programs** (*USA*) i programmi della serata

ton·nage [ˈtʌnɪdʒ] N (*Naut*) tonnellaggio, stazza

tonne [tʌn] N (*Brit: metric ton*) tonnellata

ton·sil [ˈtɒnsl] N tonsilla; **to have one's tonsils out** farsi operare di tonsille

ton·sil·li·tis [ˌtɒnsɪˈlaɪtɪs] N tonsillite *f*; **to have tonsillitis** avere la tonsillite

too [tuː] ADV 1 (*excessively*) troppo; **it's too sweet** è troppo dolce; **it's too sweet for me to drink** non lo bevo, è troppo dolce per me; **it's too heavy for me** è troppo pesante per me; **it's too heavy for me to lift** non riesco a sollevarlo, è troppo pesante per me; **the water's too hot** l'acqua è troppo calda; **it's too good to be true** è troppo bello per essere vero; **I'm not too sure about that** non ne sono troppo sicuro; **too much** troppo(-a); **too many** troppi(-e); **too bad!** (*unsympathetic*) tanto peggio!; (*expressing regret*) che peccato! 2 (*also*) anche; (*moreover*) per di più; **I went too** ci sono andato anch'io; **my sister came too** è venuta anche mia sorella; **I speak French and Japanese too** parlo il francese e (anche) il giapponese; **he's famous, intelligent and rich too** è famoso, intelligente e per di più anche ricco

took [tʊk] PT *of* **take**

tool [tuːl] N 1 (*gen, also Tech*) attrezzo, utensile *m*, arnese *m*; (*set of*) **tools** (*set m inv* di) attrezzi; **the tools of one's trade** i ferri del mestiere 2 (*fig: person*) strumento; **he was a mere tool in their hands** non era che uno strumento *or* un fantoccio nelle loro mani ♦ VT lavorare con un attrezzo

tool box N cassetta degli attrezzi

tool kit N kit *m inv* di attrezzi

toot [tuːt] N colpo di clacson ♦ VT: **to toot one's horn** suonare il clacson ♦ VI suonare; (*with car horn*) suonare il clacson

tooth [tuːθ] N (*pl* **teeth**) (*Anat, Tech*) dente *m*; **to clean one's teeth** lavarsi i denti; **to have a tooth out, to have a tooth pulled** (*USA*) farsi togliere un dente; **to have a sweet tooth** essere ghiotto(-a) di dolci; **long in the tooth** (*fam: old*) vecchiotto(-a); **to be fed up to the (back) teeth with sb/sth** (*fam*) averne fin sopra i capelli di qn/qc; **to get one's teeth into** (*fig: work*) impegnarsi a fondo in; (: *subject*) immergersi in; **armed to the teeth** armato(-a) fino ai denti; **to fight tooth and nail** combattere con le unghie e con i denti; **it sets my teeth on edge** mi fa venire i brividi; **by the skin of one's teeth** per il rotto della cuffia

tooth·ache [ˈtuːθˌeɪk] N mal di denti; **to have (a) toothache** avere il mal di denti

tooth·brush [ˈtuːθˌbrʌʃ] N spazzolino da denti

tooth fairy N: **the tooth fairy** *fatina che porta soldini in regalo a un bimbo quando perde un dente da latte* ≈ topolino

tooth·paste [ˈtuːθˌpeɪst] N dentifricio

tooth·pick [ˈtuːθˌpɪk] N stuzzicadenti *m inv*

top¹ [tɒp] N 1 (*highest point: of mountain, page, ladder*) cima; (: *of list, table, queue*) testa; (: *of carpet*) apice *m*; **at the top of the hill** sulla cima della collina; **at the top of the stairs/page/street** in cima alle scale/alla pagina/alla strada; **at the top of the table** a capotavola; **to be top of the charts** essere in testa alla hit-parade; **Liverpool is at the top of the league** (*Sport*) il Liverpool è in testa alla classifica; **from top to bottom** (*fig*) da cima a fondo; **from top to toe** dalla testa ai piedi; **from the top of the hill** dalla cima della collina; **on top** sopra; **on top of** in cima a, sopra; (*Brit: in addition to*) oltre a; **on top of the cupboard** sopra l'armadio; **to fall on top of sb** cadere addosso a qn; **he's going thin on top** (*fam*) sta incominciando a perdere i capelli; **to reach the top** (*fig: of career*) raggiungere l'apice; **the men at the top** (*fig*) quelli che sono al potere 2 (*surface*) superficie *f*; (*of box, cupboard, table*) sopra *m inv*, parte *f* superiore; (*roof: of car*) tetto; (*upper part: of bus*) piano superiore; **the top of the table needs wiping** bisogna pulire la superficie *or* il piano della tavola; **oil comes to the top** l'olio sale alla superficie; **seats on top!** (*Brit: in double-decker bus*) ci sono posti di sopra!; **the top of the milk** (*Brit*) la panna 3 (*Dressmaking: blouse*) camicia; (: *T-shirt*) maglietta; (: *of pyjamas*) giacca; **a cotton top** una maglia di cotone; **a bikini top** il pezzo di sopra di un bikini 4 (*lid: of bottle*) tappo; (: *of box, jar*) coperchio; (: *of pen*) tappo, cappuccio 5 (*also:* **top gear**): **to change into top** mettere la quarta (*or* quinta) 6 (*in phrases*): **on top of (all) that** per di più, inoltre; **there's a surcharge on top of that** in più c'è un sovrapprezzo; **it's just one thing on top of another** è una cosa dietro a un'altra; **to be/feel on top of the world** (*fam*) essere/sentirsi al settimo cielo; **to be/get on top of things** (*fig*) dominare/cominciare a dominare la situazione; **to come out on top** (*fig*) uscire vincitore(-trice); **I can't tell you off the top of my head** a mente non te lo posso dire; **at the top of one's voice** (*fig*) a squarciagola; **over the top** (*Brit fam: behaviour*) eccessivo(-a); **to go over the top** (*Brit fam*) esagerare; **to be tops** essere il migliore ♦ ADJ 1 (*highest: floor, step*) ultimo(-a); (: *shelf, drawer*) (ultimo(-a)) in alto; (: *price*) più alto(-a); (: *in rank*) primo(-a); **at top speed** a tutta velocità; **top gear** la marcia più alta, quarta (*or* quinta); **the top leaders in the party** i dirigenti del partito; **a top job** un posto di prestigio; **top dog** (*fig: fam*) il grande capo 2 (*best*) migliore; **to get top marks** (*Brit*) avere i voti migliori; **he always gets top marks in Italian** ha sempre degli ottimi voti in italiano; **to come top of the class** avere i voti più alti di tutta la classe, risultare il (la) migliore della classe; **he came top in maths** *or* (*USA*) **math** ha avuto i voti migliori in matematica; **the top twenty** (*Mus*) i venti migliori dischi (della settimana); **to be on top form** (*fam*) sentirsi veramente in forma; **a top surgeon** un grande chirurgo 3 (*last: layer*) ultimo(-a); **the top coat** (*of paint*) l'ultima mano (di pittura); **she is in the top class at school** sta facendo l'ultimo anno di scuola 4 (*most important*) principale, più importante; **top model** top model *f inv* ♦ ADV: **tops** al massimo; **it's worth £200 tops** vale al massimo 200 sterline ♦ VT 1 sormontare; **a church topped by a steeple** una chiesa sovrastata da un campanile; **to top a cake with cream** coprire una torta di panna 2 (*be first in*) essere in testa a; **to top the bill** (*Theatre*) avere il primo posto sul cartellone 3 (*exceed*) superare; **and to top it all ...** (*fig*) e come se non bastasse...; **profits topped £50,000 last year** i profitti hanno superato le 50.000 sterline l'anno scorso 4 (*vegetables, fruit*) tagliare le punte a; **to top and tail fruit** tagliare le punte e i gambi alla frutta

▸ **top off** VT + ADV (*finish*): **to top off with** concludere con; **we topped off the dinner with a toast to the happy couple** abbiamo concluso il pranzo con un brindisi in onore della coppia felice

▸ **top up** VT + ADV riempire; **to top sb's glass up** riempire il bicchiere a qn, dare ancora da bere a qn; **to top up a battery** fare un rabbocco alla batteria

top² [tɒp] N (*toy*) trottola; **to sleep like a top** dormire come un ghiro

to·paz ['təʊpæz] N topazio

top-class [ˌtɒpˈklɑːs] ADJ di prim'ordine

top-coat ['tɒpˌkəʊt] N (*old: overcoat*) soprabito

top-flight [ˌtɒpˈflaɪt] ADJ di primaria importanza

top floor N ultimo piano

top hat N cilindro

top-heavy [ˌtɒpˈhɛvɪ] ADJ (*structure*) con la parte superiore troppo pesante; **this company is top-heavy** (*fig*) ci sono troppi dirigenti in questa società

top·ic ['tɒpɪk] N (*of conversation*) argomento; (*of essay*) soggetto; **the essay can be on any topic** per il tema si può scegliere un argomento qualunque

topi·cal ['tɒpɪkəl] ADJ d'attualità; **a highly topical question** un argomento di grande attualità

top·less ['tɒplɪs] ADJ (*bather*) a seno scoperto; **topless swimsuit** topless *m inv* ♦ ADV (*sunbathe*) in topless; **to go topless** mettersi in topless

top-level [ˌtɒpˈlɛvl] ADJ (*talks*) ad alto livello

top·most ['tɒpˌməʊst] ADJ il (la) più alto(-a)

top-notch [ˌtɒpˈnɒtʃ] ADJ (*fam: player, performer*) di razza; (: *school, car*) eccellente

to·pog·ra·phy [təˈpɒɡrəfɪ] N topografia

top·ping ['tɒpɪŋ] N (*Culin*) guarnizione *f*

top·ple ['tɒpl] VT (*fig: overthrow*) far cadere, rovesciare; **strong winds toppled trees and electricity lines** forti venti hanno fatto cadere gli alberi e le linee elettriche ♦ VI cadere, rovesciarsi; **he toppled backwards** cadde all'indietro

▸ **topple over** VI + ADV cadere ♦ VI + PREP cadere da; **he toppled over a cliff** è caduto da una scogliera

top-ranking [ˌtɒpˈræŋkɪŋ] ADJ di massimo grado

top-secret [ˌtɒpˈsiːkrɪt] ADJ segretissimo(-a)

top-security [ˌtɒpsɪˈkjʊərɪtɪ] ADJ (*Brit*) di massima sicurezza

topsy-turvy [ˌtɒpsɪˈtɜːvɪ] ADJ, ADV sottosopra *inv*

top-up ['tɒpˌʌp] N (*Brit fam: refill*): **would you like a top-up?** vuoi che ti riempia la tazza (*or* il bicchiere *etc*)?

top-up loan N (*Brit*) prestito integrativo

torch [tɔːtʃ] N (*Brit: electric*) torcia elettrica, lampadina tascabile; (*flaming*) torcia, fiaccola; **to carry a torch for sb** (*fig*) essere innamorato(-a) cotto(-a) di qn

tore [tɔːʳ] PT *of* **tear¹**

tor·ment [*n* ˈtɔːmɛnt, *vb* tɔːˈmɛnt] N tormento, tortura; **to be in torment** (*also fig*) soffrire le pene dell'inferno ♦ VT (*hurt*) tormentare; (*fig: annoy*) molestare, infastidire; **she was tormented by doubts** era tormentata *or* assillata dai dubbi

torn [tɔːn] PP *of* **tear¹**

tor·na·do [tɔːˈneɪdəʊ] N (*pl* **tornadoes**) tornado

tor·pe·do [tɔːˈpiːdəʊ] N (*pl* **torpedoes**) siluro ♦ VT silurare

torpedo boat N motosilurante *f*

tor·por ['tɔːpəʳ] N (*frm*) torpore *m*

tor·rent ['tɒrənt] N (*also fig*) torrente *m*; **we got caught in a torrent of rain** una pioggia torrenziale ci ha sorpresi; **the rain came down in torrents** pioveva a dirotto; **a torrent of abuse** una sfilza di improperi

tor·ren·tial [tɒˈrɛnʃəl] ADJ torrenziale

tor·rid ['tɒrɪd] ADJ (*liter*) torrido(-a); (*fig*) denso(-a) di passione

tor·so ['tɔːsəʊ] N (*Anat*) torso; (*Sculpture*) busto

tor·toise ['tɔːtəs] N tartaruga

tortoise-shell ['tɔːtəsˌʃɛl] N guscio di tartaruga ♦ ADJ di tartaruga

tor·tu·ous ['tɔːtjʊəs] ADJ tortuoso(-a)

tor·ture ['tɔːtʃəʳ] N tortura; **it was sheer torture!** (*fig*) è stata una vera tortura! ♦ VT torturare; (*fig*) tormentare

tor·tur·er ['tɔːtʃərəʳ] N torturatore(-trice)

Tory ['tɔːrɪ] ADJ tory *inv*, conservatore(-trice) ♦ N tory *m/f inv*, conservatore(-trice); **the Tories** i conservatori

toss [tɒs] N 1 (*movement: of head*) scrollata; **to take a toss** (*from horse*) fare una caduta 2 (*of coin*) lancio; **to win/lose the toss** vincere/perdere a testa e croce; (*Sport*) vincere/perdere il sorteggio; **it's pointless to argue the toss** (*Brit fam*) è inutile stare a discutere; **I don't give a toss** (*Brit fam!*) non me ne frega un cazzo (*fam!*) ♦ VT 1 (*repeatedly*) muovere bruscamente, scuotere; **the boat was tossed by the waves** l'imbarcazione era sballottata dalle onde 2 (*throw: ball*) lanciare, gettare; (: *head*) scuotere; (*subj: horse: head*) tirare su; (: *mane*) agitare; (: *rider*) disarcionare; (*subj: bull*) lanciare in aria; **to toss sth to sb** lanciare qc a qn; **she tossed me a can of beer** mi ha lanciato una lattina di birra; **to toss salad** mescolare l'insalata; **toss the salad in the dressing** mescola l'insalata con il condimento; **to toss a pancake** far saltare una crêpe; **to toss one's hair back** gettare indietro i capelli; **to toss a coin** lanciare in aria una moneta, fare a testa o croce; **I'll toss you for it** ce lo giochiamo a testa e croce ♦ VI 1 (*also:* **toss about, toss around**) agitarsi; (*boat*) rollare e beccheggiare; **to toss (in one's sleep), toss and turn** (*in bed*) agitarsi nel sonno, girarsi e rigirarsi 2 (*also:* **toss up**) tirare a sorte, fare a testa e croce; **we tossed (up) for the last piece of cake** abbiamo fatto a testa e croce per l'ultima fetta di torta

▸ **toss off** VT + ADV 1 (*drink*) buttare giù; (*book, letter*) sfornare 2 (*Brit fam!: masturbate*) fare una sega a (*fam!*) ♦ VI + ADV (*Brit fam!: masturbate*) farsi una sega (*fam!*)

tot [tɒt] N 1 (*child*) bimbetto(-a), bimbo(-a); **a tiny tot** un bimbo piccolo 2 (*Brit: drink*) bicchierino; **a tot of rum** un bicchierino di rum

▸ **tot up** VT + ADV (*Brit figures*) sommare

to·tal ['təʊtl] ADJ (*complete, utter*) totale, completo(-a); (*sum*) globale; **the total losses amount to ...** il totale delle perdite ammonta a...; **a total failure** un vero fiasco, un assoluto disastro; **he was in total ignorance of the fact that ...** non sapeva assolutamente che... ♦ N totale *m*; **grand total** somma globale; **in total** in tutto ♦ VT (*also:* **total up**) (*add*) sommare; (*amount to*) ammontare a

to·tali·tar·ian [ˌtəʊtælɪˈtɛərɪən] ADJ totalitario(-a)

to·tal·ity [təʊˈtælɪtɪ] N totalità *f inv*

to·tal·ly [ˈtəʊtəlɪ] ADV completamente

tote bag N sporta

to·tem pole N totem *m inv*

tot·ter [ˈtɒtəʳ] VI (*person*) camminare barcollando, barcollare; (*object, government*) vacillare; **to totter in/out** *etc* entrare/uscire *etc* barcollando

touch [tʌtʃ] N **1** (*sense*) tatto; (*act of touching*) contatto; **rough to the touch** ruvido(-a) al tatto; **by touch** al tatto; **at the slightest touch** al minimo contatto; **the touch of her hand** il tocco della sua mano; **a pianist with a delicate touch** un pianista dal tocco raffinato; **the personal touch** una nota personale, un tocco personale; **at the touch of a button** premendo un bottone; **it has a touch of genius** è quasi geniale; **to lose one's touch** (*fig*) perdere la mano (*with people*) perdere il proprio fascino; **to put the finishing touches to sth** dare gli ultimi ritocchi a qc **2** (*small amount:* *of milk*) goccio; (*: of colour, paint*) tocco; (*: of frost*) leggero strato; **a touch of irony** una punta *or* pizzico d'ironia; **to have a touch of flu** avere una leggera influenza **3** (*contact*) contatto; **to be in touch with sb** essere in contatto con qn; **to get in touch with sb** mettersi in contatto con qn; **I'll be in touch** mi farò sentire; **you can get in touch with me here** mi puoi rintracciare qui; **to keep in touch with sb** mantenere i rapporti con qn, tenersi in contatto con qn; **I'll keep in touch with Ann** mi terrò in contatto con Ann; **I haven't kept in touch with Hilary** non sono rimasta in contatto con Hilary; **keep in touch!** fatti vivo!; **to lose touch** (*friends*) perdersi di vista; **to lose touch with sb** perdere di vista qn; **to be out of touch with events** essere tagliato(-a) fuori **4** (*Brit: Ftbl, Rugby*): **the ball is in touch** la palla è fuori gioco ♦ VT **1** (*gen*) toccare; (*brush lightly, fig: topic, problem*) sfiorare; **he touched his arm** gli ha toccato il braccio; **his hair touches his shoulders** i capelli gli sfiorano le spalle; **touch wood!** tocchiamo ferro!; **to touch sb for £5** (*fam*) chiedere 5 sterline in prestito a qn **2** (*neg phrases*): **don't touch that!** non toccare!; **I never touch gin** non tocco mai il gin; **you haven't touched your cheese** non hai neppure toccato il formaggio; **if you admit nothing, they can't touch you** (*fig*) se non confessi non ti possono toccare **3** (*move*) commuovere; (*affect*) riguardare; **I am touched by your offer** la tua offerta mi commuove; **she was touched by his gift** fu commossa dal suo regalo; **the story touched me deeply** la storia mi ha commosso profondamente; **it touches all our lives** riguarda tutti noi, ci tocca tutti **4** (*compare*) uguagliare; **nobody can touch them for quality** per quanto riguarda la qualità non li batte nessuno; **no artist in the country can touch him** non c'è artista nel paese che lo possa uguagliare ♦ VI (*hands*) toccarsi; (*property, gardens*) confinare; **our hands touched** le nostre mani si sono sfiorate; **"do not touch"** "non toccare"

▸ **touch down** VT + ADV (*Rugby: score*): **to touch the ball down** segnare una meta ♦ VI + ADV **1** (*on land*) atterrare; (*on sea*) ammarare; (*on moon*) allunare **2** (*Rugby: score*) segnare una meta

▸ **touch off** VT + ADV (*argument, riot*) provocare

▸ **touch on** VI + PREP (*topic, subject*) sfiorare, accennare a

▸ **touch up** VT + ADV **1** (*improve*) ritoccare **2** (*fam: sexually*) mettere le mani addosso a

touch-and-go [ˌtʌtʃənˈgəʊ] ADJ incerto(-a); **it's touch-and-go whether ...** è incerto se...; **it was touch-and-go whether we'd go bankrupt** eravamo sull'orlo del fallimento; **it was touch-and-go with the sick man** il malato era tra la vita e la morte

touch·down [ˈtʌtʃdaʊn] N (*on land*) atterraggio; (*on sea*) ammaraggio; (*on moon*) allunaggio; (*Rugby*) meta

touched [tʌtʃt] ADJ (*moved*) commosso(-a); (*fam: crazy*) tocco(-a), toccato(-a); **I was really touched** ero veramente commosso(-a)

touch·ing [ˈtʌtʃɪŋ] ADJ commovente

touch·line [ˈtʌtʃlaɪn] N (*Ftbl*) linea laterale; (*Rugby*) linea di touche

touch-screen [ˈtʌtʃskriːn] N (*Comput*) touch-screen *m inv*, schermo sensibile

touch-sensitive [ˌtʌtʃˈsɛnsɪtɪv] ADJ sensibile al tatto

touch-type [ˈtʌtʃtaɪp] VI dattilografare (*senza guardare i tasti*)

touchy [ˈtʌtʃɪ] ADJ (*comp* **-ier**, *superl* **-iest**) (*person*) permaloso(-a), suscettibile; (*subject*) delicato(-a); **he's touchy about his weight** è molto suscettibile quando si parla del suo peso

tough [tʌf] ADJ (*comp* **-er**, *superl* **-est**) **1** (*substance, fabric*) resistente, duro(-a); (*conditions, regulations*) duro(-a); (*meat*) duro(-a), tiglioso(-a); (*journey*) faticoso(-a), duro(-a); (*task, problem, situation*) difficile; (*fig: resistance*) tenace; (*: fight*) accanito(-a); **tough leather gloves** guanti *mpl* di pelle resistente; **the meat is tough** la carne è dura; **as tough as old boots** duro(-a) come una suola di scarpa; **it was tough, but I managed okay** è stata dura ma ce l'ho fatta; **tough opposition** opposizione tenace **2** (*person: hardy, resilient*) robusto(-a), resistente; (*: mentally strong*) resistente, tenace; (*: hard: in character*) inflessibile; (*: rough*) violento(-a), brutale; **they got tough with the workers** hanno adottato una politica inflessibile con i lavoratori; **he's a tough man to deal with** è un tipo difficile; **a tough guy** un duro; **he thinks he's a tough guy** crede di essere un duro; **he's a tough customer** (*fam*) è un osso duro **3** (*fam: unfortunate*): **but it was tough on the others** ma è stata una sfortuna per gli altri; **tough luck!** tanto peggio!; **if you can't get here on time, that's your tough luck!** (*unsympathetic*) se non ce la fai ad arrivare in orario, peggio per te! ♦ N (*fam: gangster, lout*) delinquente *m/f*

tough·en [ˈtʌfn] VT (*also:* **toughen up**) (*substance*) rinforzare, rendere più resistente; (*metal*) indurire; (*person*) rendere più forte

tough·ness [ˈtʌfnɪs] N (*see adj*) **1** resistenza; durezza; difficoltà *f inv*; accanimento **2** resistenza; tenacia; inflessibilità *f inv*; violenza

tou·pee [ˈtuːpeɪ] N toupet *m inv*, parrucchino

tour [tʊəʳ] N (*gen*) giro; (*of building, exhibition, town*) visita; (*by performers, team*) tournée *f inv*; **package tour** viaggio organizzato; **a guided tour** una visita guidata; **a tour of the city** un giro della città; **a round-the-world tour** un giro del mondo; **to go on a tour of** (*region, country*) fare il giro di; (*museum, castle*) visitare; **to go on a walking/cycling tour of Tuscany** fare il giro della Toscana a piedi/in bicicletta; **on tour** (*Theatre*) in tournée; **to go on tour** andare in tournée, fare una tournée; **tour of inspection** giro d'ispezione ♦ VT (*subj: tourists*) fare un giro di, fare un viaggio in; (*: performers, team*) fare una tournée in; **the Prime Minister is touring the country** il primo ministro sta visitando il paese ♦ VI (*also:* **to go touring**) andare a fare un viaggio

tour·ing [ˈtʊərɪŋ] N viaggi *mpl* turistici

tour·ism [ˈtʊərɪzəm] N turismo

tour·ist [ˈtʊərɪst] N turista *m/f*; **there were lots of tourists** c'erano molti turisti ♦ ADJ (*attraction, season*) turistico(-a); **the tourist trade** il turismo ♦ ADV (*travel*) in classe turistica

tourist class N (*Aer*) classe *f* turistica

tourist office N ufficio del turismo

tour·na·ment [ˈtʊənəmənt] N torneo; **tennis tournament** torneo di tennis

tour·ni·quet [ˈtʊənɪkeɪ] N (*Med*) laccio emostatico, pinza emostatica

tour operator N (*Brit*) operatore *m* turistico

tou·sled [ˈtaʊzld] ADJ (*hair*) arruffato(-a); (*bedclothes*) sottosopra *inv*

tout [taʊt] N (*for hotels*) procacciatore *m* di clienti; (*Brit: also:* **ticket tout**) bagarino; (*Racing*) portaquote *m inv* ♦ VI: **to tout for business** raccogliere ordinazioni; (*for hotels*) procacciare clienti ♦ VT: **to tout sth (around)** (*Brit*) cercare di (ri)vendere qc; **he is being touted as the greatest living singer** lo stanno facendo passare per il miglior cantante vivente

tow [təʊ] N rimorchio; **to give sb a tow** (*Aut*) rimorchiare qn; **to be on tow** essere a rimorchio; **"on tow", "in tow"** (*USA*) "veicolo rimorchiato"; **he arrived with a friend in tow** (*fig: fam*) si è portato dietro un amico; **she had a child in tow** aveva un bimbo con sé ♦ VT (*boat, car, caravan*) rimorchiare; **he towed my car to the nearest garage** mi ha rimorchiato la macchina fino all'officina più vicina; **to tow a car away** portar via una macchina con il carro attrezzi

to·wards [tə'wɔːdz], **to·ward** [tə'wɔːd] PREP (*gen*) verso; (*of attitude*) nei confronti di, verso; (*of purpose*) per; **he came towards me** è venuto verso di me; **we walked towards the sea** ci siamo incamminati verso il mare; **the government is moving towards disaster** il governo si avvia al disastro; **towards noon/the end of the year** verso mezzogiorno/la fine dell'anno; **your attitude towards him** il tuo atteggiamento nei suoi confronti *or* verso di lui; **to feel friendly towards sb** provare un sentimento d'amicizia per qn; **to save towards sth** risparmiare per comprare qc; **half my salary goes towards paying the rent** metà del mio stipendio se ne va per l'affitto *or* in affitto; **he gave them £100,000 towards a house** ha dato loro centomila sterline per la casa

tow·el ['taʊəl] N (*also:* hand towel) asciugamano; (*also:* bath towel) telo da bagno; (*also:* tea towel, dishtowel) strofinaccio; **to throw in the towel** (*fig*) gettare la spugna ♦ VT: **to towel o.s. dry** asciugarsi con un asciugamano

tow·el·ling ['taʊəlɪŋ] N (*fabric*) (tessuto di) spugna

towel rail, towel rack N portasciugamani

tow·er ['taʊəʳ] N (*of castle, church*) torre *f*; **the towers of the castle** le torri del castello; **he was a tower of strength to me** mi ha dato un grande appoggio ♦ VI (*building, mountain*) innalzarsi; **to tower above** *or* **over sb/sth** sovrastare qn/qc

tower block N (*Brit*) palazzone *m*

tow·er·ing ['taʊərɪŋ] ADJ (*building, figure*) imponente, altissimo(-a); **in a towering rage** (*fig*) in preda a un violento accesso d'ira

tow·line ['təʊ‚laɪn] N (cavo da) rimorchio

town [taʊn] N città *f inv*; **to live in a town** vivere in città; **to be out of town** essere fuori città; **in (the) town** in città; **to go (in) to town** andare in città *or* in centro; **to go out on the town** (*fam*) uscire a far baldoria; **to go to town on sth** (*fig: fam*) fare qc in grande ♦ ADJ (*centre*) della città; (*life*) di città; (*house*) in città

town centre N (*Brit*) centro (città)

town clerk N segretario comunale

town council N (*Brit*) consiglio comunale

town cri·er [‚taʊn'kraɪəʳ] N (*Brit*) banditore(-trice)

town hall N ≈ municipio

townie ['taʊnɪ] N (*Brit fam*) persona di città

town plan N pianta della città

town planner N (*Brit*) urbanista *m/f*

town planning N (*Brit: action*) pianificazione *f* urbana; (*: study*) urbanistica

town·ship ['taʊnʃɪp] N township *f inv*

towns·people ['taʊnz‚piːpl] NPL cittadinanza, cittadini *mpl*

tow·path ['təʊ‚pɑːθ] N alzaia

tow·rope ['təʊ‚rəʊp] N (cavo da) rimorchio

tow truck N (*USA*) carro *m* attrezzi, *inv*

tox·ic ['tɒksɪk] ADJ tossico(-a)

toxic asset N (*Econ*) titolo tossico

toxic bank N (*Econ*) banca cattiva (*che investe in titoli tossici*)

tox·in ['tɒksɪn] N tossina

toy [tɔɪ] N giocattolo ♦ ADJ (*railway, house*) in miniatura; (*gun*) giocattolo *inv*

▸ **toy with** VI + PREP **1** (*play with: object*) giocherellare con; (*: food*) trastullarsi con; (*affections*) giocare con **2** (*consider: idea*) accarezzare

toy·shop ['tɔɪ‚ʃɒp] N negozio di giocattoli

trace [treɪs] N (*sign*) traccia; **there was no trace of the robbers** non c'era traccia dei ladri; **there was no trace of it** non ne restava traccia; **to vanish without trace** sparire senza lasciar traccia; **I've lost all trace of them** ho completamente perso le loro tracce; **the postmortem revealed traces of poison in the blood** l'autopsia ha rivelato tracce di veleno nel sangue ♦ VT **1** (*draw*) tracciare; (*with tracing paper*) ricalcare **2** (*follow*) seguire (le tracce di); (*find, locate*) rintracciare; **the police are trying to trace witnesses** la polizia sta cercando di rintracciare i testimoni; **I cannot trace**

any reference to the matter non riesco a rintracciare alcun riferimento alla faccenda

▸ **trace back** VT + ADV: **they traced the weapon back to here** hanno stabilito che l'arma proviene da qui; **to trace one's roots** trovare le proprie radici; **to trace back one's family to** risalire alle origini della propria famiglia fino a

trace element N oligoelemento

tra·chea [trə'kɪə] N (*Anat*) trachea

trac·ing pa·per ['treɪsɪŋ‚peɪpəʳ] N carta da ricalco

track [træk] N **1** (*mark: of person, animal*) orma, traccia, impronta; (*: of vehicle*) solco; (*: of ship*) scia; **to be on sb's track** essere sulle tracce di qn; **they followed the tracks for miles** hanno seguito le tracce per miglia; **to follow in sb's tracks** (*also fig*) seguire le orme di qn; **to keep track of** (*fig: person*) seguire le tracce di; (*: keep in touch with*) restare in contatto con; (*event*) essere al corrente di; **to lose track of** (*fig: person*) perdere le tracce di; (*: lose contact with*) perdere di vista; (*event*) non essere al corrente di; **to lose track of an argument** perdere il filo del discorso; **to make tracks (for)** (*fig: fam*) avviarsi (a *or* verso) **2** (*path*) sentiero; (*of comet, rocket*) traiettoria; (*of suspect, animal*) pista, tracce *fpl*; **a mountain track** un sentiero di montagna; **to be on the right track** (*fig*) essere sulla buona strada; **to be on the wrong track** (*fig*) essere fuori strada; **to throw sb off the track** (*fig*) mettere qn fuori strada **3** (*Sport*) pista; **two laps of the track** due giri di pista **4** (*Rail*) binario, rotaie *fpl*; **a woman fell onto the tracks** una donna è caduta sui binari; **on the right/wrong side of the tracks** (*USA fam*) nei quartieri alti/poveri della città **5** (*Mus: on tape*) pista; **a 4-track tape** un nastro a 4 piste; **the first track on the record/tape** il primo pezzo del disco/nastro; **this is my favourite track** questo è il mio pezzo preferito **6** (*Comput*) pista ♦ VT (*person, animal*) seguire le tracce di

▸ **track down** VT + ADV (*locate: person*) snidare; (*: prey*) scovare; (*: sth lost*) rintracciare; **the police never tracked down the killer** la polizia non ha mai trovato l'assassino

track·er dog ['trækə‚dɒg] N (*Brit*) cane *m* poliziotto, *inv*

track events NPL (*Sport*) gare *fpl* di atletica (*su pista*)

track·ing sta·tion ['trækɪŋ‚steɪʃən] N (*Space*) osservatorio spaziale

track meet N (*USA*) meeting *m inv* di atletica

track record N: **to have a good track record** (*fig*) avere un buon curriculum

track·suit ['træk‚suːt] N tuta sportiva *or* da ginnastica

tract¹ [trækt] N **1** (*area*) distesa **2** (*Anat*): **respiratory tract** apparato respiratorio

tract² [trækt] N (*pamphlet*) trattatello, libretto, opuscolo

trac·tion ['trækʃən] N trazione *f*

trac·tor ['træktəʳ] N trattore *m*

trade [treɪd] N **1** (*commerce*) commercio; (*business*) affari *mpl*; **to do trade with sb** fare affari con qn, essere in rapporti commerciali con qn; **foreign trade** commercio estero; **free trade** il libero scambio; **to do a brisk** *or* **roaring trade** fare affari d'oro **2** (*industry*) industria, settore *m*; **he's in the cotton/building trade** è nell'industria cotoniera/edilizia; **the tourist trade** l'industria del turismo; **the arms trade** il commercio di armi; **the book trade** l'editoria **3** (*profession*) mestiere *m*; **to learn a trade** imparare un mestiere; **he's a butcher by trade** di mestiere fa il macellaio; **tailoring is a useful trade** quello del sarto è un mestiere utile; **to sell to the trade** vendere all'ingrosso ♦ VT (*fig: swap sth for sth*) barattare; **he traded his tennis racquet for a football** ha barattato la sua racchetta da tennis con un pallone; **I'd like to trade some cards** vorrei scambiare alcune figurine ♦ VI: **to trade with sb** fare affari con qn, intrattenere rapporti commerciali con qn; **they have traded with France for centuries** commerciano con la Francia da secoli ♦ ADJ (*association, route*) commerciale

▸ **trade in** VT + ADV (*old car*) cedere in permuta, dare dentro ♦ VI + PREP commerciare in

▸ **trade on** VI + PREP (*pej*) approfittare di, sfruttare

trade barrier N barriera commerciale

trade deficit N bilancio commerciale in deficit

trade discount N sconto sul listino (*fatto al commerciante*)

trade fair N fiera campionaria

trade-in [ˈtreɪdˌɪn] N **1 to take as a trade-in** accettare in permuta **2** (*car*) *macchina ceduta a parziale pagamento di una nuova*
trade-in price N prezzo di permuta
trade·mark [ˈtreɪdˌmɑːk] N (*Comm*) marchio di fabbrica; (*fig*) marchio; **registered trademark** marchio registrato
trade mission N missione *f* commerciale
trade name N (*of product*) nome *m* depositato, marca; (*of a company*) ragione *f* sociale
trade-off [ˈtreɪdˌɒf] N (*exchange*) scambio; (*balancing*) compromesso
trad·er [ˈtreɪdə'] N commerciante *m/f*
trade secret N segreto commerciale
trades·man [ˈtreɪdzmən] N (*pl* -**men**) fornitore *m*; (*shopkeeper*) negoziante *m*; **tradesman's entrance** ingresso per i fornitori *or* di servizio
trade union, trades union(*Brit*) N sindacato ♦ ADJ (*official*) sindacale; **trade-union dues** quota di associazione al sindacato
trade unionist, trades unionist N (*Brit*) sindacalista *m/f*
trade wind N aliseo
trad·ing [ˈtreɪdɪŋ] ADJ (*port, centre*) commerciale; (*nation*) che vive di commercio ♦ N commercio
trading estate N (*Brit*) zona industriale
trading stamp N bollino premio
tra·di·tion [trəˈdɪʃən] N tradizione *f*; **traditions** NPL tradizioni, usanze *fpl*
tra·di·tion·al [trəˈdɪʃənl] ADJ tradizionale
traf·fic [ˈtræfɪk] (*pt, pp* **trafficked**) N traffico; **rail traffic** traffico ferroviario; **heavy traffic** traffico pesante; **the traffic is heavy during the rush hour** il traffico è molto intenso nelle ore di punta; **closed to heavy traffic** (*Aut*) divieto di transito per gli automezzi pesanti; **drug traffic** traffico di droga ♦ VI: **to traffic in** (*pej: liquor, drugs*) trafficare in ♦ ADJ (*Aut: regulations*) stradale
traffic calming [-ˈkɑːmɪŋ] N *misure per rallentare il traffico cittadino*
traffic circle N (*USA*) isola rotatoria
traffic island N salvagente *m*, isola *f* spartitraffico, *inv*
traffic jam N ingorgo (del traffico); **a 5-mile traffic jam** una coda di 5 miglia
traf·fick·er [ˈtræfɪkə'] N trafficante *m/f*
traffic lights NPL semaforo
traffic offence N (*Brit*) infrazione *f* al codice stradale
traffic sign N cartello stradale
traffic violation N (*USA*) = traffic offence
traffic warden N (*Brit*) ≈ vigile(-essa) (urbano(-a))
trag·edy [ˈtrædʒɪdɪ] N (*gen, also Theatre*) tragedia; **it is a tragedy that …** è una vera disgrazia che…
trag·ic [ˈtrædʒɪk] ADJ tragico(-a); **tragic actor** attore *m* tragico
trail [treɪl] N **1** (*of dust, smoke*) scia; **the hurricane left a trail of destruction** l'uragano non ha lasciato altro che distruzione dietro di sé **2** (*track*) orma; (*tracks*) pista, tracce *fpl*; **a trail of clues** una serie di indizi; **to be on sb's trail** essere sulle orme di qn, essere sulle tracce di qn **3** (*path*) sentiero; (*Skiing*) pista da fondo; **a forest trail** un sentiero nella foresta ♦ VT **1** (*drag*) trascinare, strascicare; **she trailed her fingers through the water** trascinava le dita nell'acqua; **don't trail your coat in the mud** non trascinare il cappotto nel fango; **don't trail mud into the house** non portare fango in casa **2** (*track: animal*) seguire le orme di; (*: person*) pedinare, seguire ♦ VI **1** (*object*) strisciare; (*plant*) arrampicarsi; (*dress*) strusciare; **to trail a plant over a wall** far attecchire una pianta al muro; **to trail by 2 goals** (*Sport*) essere in svantaggio di 2 goal; **Liverpool was trailing 3 to 1 at half time** il Liverpool era in svantaggio per 3 a 1 dopo il primo tempo **2** (*wearily: also:* **trail along**) trascinarsi
  ▸ **trail away, trail off** VI + ADV (*sound*) affievolirsi; (*interest, voice*) spegnersi a poco a poco
  ▸ **trail behind** VI + ADV essere al traino; **to trail behind sb** trascinarsi dietro a qn
  ▸ **trail off** VI + ADV = **trail away**
trail·er [ˈtreɪlə'] N **1** (*Aut*) rimorchio; (*for horses*) van *m inv*; (*USA: caravan*) roulotte *f inv*; **a car and trailer** un'auto con rimorchio; **they live in a trailer** vivono in una roulotte **2** (*Cine*) trailer *m inv*

trailer truck N (*USA*) autoarticolato
train [treɪn] N **1** (*Rail*) treno; **to go by train** andare in *or* col treno; **he went by train** ci è andato in treno; **to travel by train** viaggiare in treno; **in** *or* **on the train** in treno, sul treno; **to take the 3:00 train** prendere il treno delle 3; **to change trains** cambiare treno **2** (*line: of animals, vehicles*) fila; (*entourage*) seguito; (*of admirers*) codazzo **3** (*Brit: series*): **train of events** serie *f inv* di eventi; **my train of thought** il filo dei miei pensieri **4** (*of dress*) strascico, coda ♦ VT **1** (*instruct*) istruire; (*apprentice, doctor*) formare; (*Mil*) addestrare; (*sportsman*) allenare; (*mind, memory*) far esercitare; (*animal*) addestrare, ammaestrare; **to train sb to do sth** preparare qn a fare qc **2 to train on** (*direct: gun*) puntare qc contro; (*: camera, telescope*) puntare (a *or* verso) ♦ VI **1** (*learn a skill*) fare pratica, fare tirocinio; **to train as** *or* **to be a lawyer** fare pratica come avvocato; **to train as a teacher** fare tirocinio come insegnante; **where did you train?** dove hai fatto pratica *or* tirocinio? **2** (*Sport*): **to train (for)** allenarsi (per); **to train for a race** allenarsi per una gara
train attendant N (*USA*) addetto(-a) ai vagoni letto
trained [treɪnd] ADJ (*accountant, nurse*) diplomato(-a), qualificato(-a); (*teacher*) abilitato(-a) all'insegnamento; (*Sport: athlete, horse*) allenato(-a); (*animal*) addestrato(-a), ammaestrato(-a); **well-trained** (*child, dog*) ben educato(-a); **I've got him well-trained** (*hum*) l'ho addomesticato per bene; **highly trained workers** operai *mpl* altamente qualificati
trainee [treɪˈniː] N (*gen: in trade*) apprendista *m/f*; (*for profession*) tirocinante *m/f*; **she's a management trainee** sta facendo tirocinio come dirigente ♦ ADJ: **to be a trainee teacher** fare il tirocinio come insegnante; **he's a trainee chef** sta facendo tirocinio come chef; **a trainee plumber** un apprendista idraulico
train·er [ˈtreɪnə'] N **1** (*Sport*) allenatore(-trice); (*of circus animals*) domatore(-trice); (*of dogs*) addestratore(-trice) **2** (*Brit: shoe*) scarpa da ginnastica; **a language trainer** un/un'insegnante di lingua
train·ing [ˈtreɪnɪŋ] N (*in job*) pratica, tirocinio; (*for job*) formazione *f*; (*Mil*) addestramento; (*Sport*) allenamento; **to be in training** (*for race, event*) essere in allenamento; (*fit*) essere in forma; **to be out of training** essere fuori allenamento *or* forma; **he strained a muscle in training** si è fatto uno strappo durante l'allenamento ♦ ADJ (*scheme, centre: for job*) di formazione professionale; (*Sport*) di allenamento
training college N istituto professionale
training course N corso di formazione professionale
training shoe N (*Brit*) scarpa da ginnastica
train wreck N (*fig*) persona distrutta; (*pej*) rottame *m*; **he's a complete train wreck** è completamente distrutto, è un rottame
traipse [treɪps] VI (*fam*): **to traipse around** trascinarsi in giro; **to traipse around the shops** trascinarsi in giro per negozi ♦ N: **a long traipse** una camminata sfiancante
trait [treɪt] N caratteristica, tratto
trai·tor [ˈtreɪtə'] N traditore(-trice); **to turn traitor** passare al nemico
tra·jec·tory [trəˈdʒɛktərɪ] N traiettoria
tram [træm], **tram·car** [ˈtræmˌkɑː'] N (*Brit*) tram *m inv*
tram·line [ˈtræmˌlaɪn] N linea tranviaria
tramp [træmp] N **1** (*sound of feet*) rumore *m* pesante (di passi) **2** (*long walk*) camminata; **to go for a tramp in the hills** andare a fare una camminata sui colli **3** (*person*) vagabondo(-a); **she's a tramp** (*fam, pej*) è una sgualdrina ♦ VT (*walk through: town, streets*) percorrere a piedi; **to tramp the streets looking for sth** battere le strade in cerca di qc ♦ VI camminare con passo pesante; **the soldiers tramped past** i soldati sono passati marciando pesantemente; **he tramped up to the door** si è avvicinato con passi pesanti alla porta
tram·ple [ˈtræmpl] VT: **to trample (underfoot)** (*crush*) calpestare; **to trample sth into the ground** calpestare qc
  ▸ **trample on** VI + PREP calpestare; **to trample on sb's feelings** (*fig*) calpestare i sentimenti di qn
tram·po·line [ˈtræmpəlɪn] N trampolino
trance [trɑːns] N trance *f inv*; (*Med*) catalessi *f inv*; **to go into a trance** cadere in trance

tran·quil [ˈtræŋkwɪl] ADJ tranquillo(-a)
tran·quil·lity, tran·quil·ity (USA) [træŋˈkwɪlɪtɪ] N tranquillità f inv
tran·quil·liz·er, tran·quil·iz·er (USA) [ˈtræŋkwɪˌlaɪzəʳ] N (Med) tranquillante m
trans·act [trænˈzækt] VT (business) trattare
trans·ac·tion [trænˈzækʃən] N (business) trattativa; (in bank) operazione f, transazione f; **transactions** NPL (minutes) atti mpl; **a commercial transaction** una transazione commerciale; **cash transaction** operazione in contanti
trans·at·lan·tic [ˌtrænzətˈlæntɪk] ADJ transatlantico(-a)
trans·cend [trænˈsend] VT (frm: go beyond) trascendere, superare
tran·scen·den·tal [ˌtrænsenˈdentl] ADJ (frm) trascendentale
tran·scribe [trænˈskraɪb] VT trascrivere
tran·script [ˈtrænskrɪpt] N trascrizione f
tran·scrip·tion [trænˈskrɪpʃən] N trascrizione f
tran·sept [ˈtrænsept] N (Archit) transetto
trans·fer [n ˈtrænsfɜːʳ, vb trænsˈfɜːʳ] N 1 (gen) trasferimento; (Pol: of power) passaggio; (Law) cessione f; (Ftbl) cessione (or acquisto); **bank transfer** bonifico bancario; **they will be offered transfers to other locations** verrà loro proposto il trasferimento in altri posti; **the transfer of power** il passaggio di potere 2 (picture, design: stick-on) decalcomania, autoadesivo ♦ VT 1 (move): **to transfer (from/to)** trasferire (da/a): (Sport): **to be transferred (from/to)** essere ceduto(-a) (da/a); **to transfer one's affections/ambitions to sb** trasferire i propri sentimenti/le proprie ambizioni su qn; **to transfer money from one account to another** trasferire il denaro da un conto su un altro; **to transfer sth to sb's name** mettere qc a nome di qn; **to make a transferred charge call** (Brit) fare una chiamata a carico del destinatario 2 (picture, design) decalcare ♦ VI (gen) trasferirsi, passare; **she transferred from History to Classics** (Univ) è passata da Storia a Lettere Antiche
trans·fer·able [trænsˈfɜːrəbl] ADJ trasferibile; **not transferable** non cedibile, personale
trans·fix [trænsˈfɪks] VT trafiggere; (fig): **transfixed with fear** paralizzato(-a) dalla paura
trans·form [trænsˈfɔːm] VT trasformare
trans·for·ma·tion [ˌtrænsfəˈmeɪʃən] N trasformazione f
trans·form·er [trænsˈfɔːməʳ] N (Elec) trasformatore m
trans·fu·sion [trænsˈfjuːʒən] N trasfusione f; **to give sb a blood transfusion** praticare una trasfusione di sangue a qn
trans·gen·der [trænsˈdʒendəʳ] ADJ transgender
trans·gress [trænsˈgres] (frm) VI (sin) peccare ♦ VT (violate: moral law) infrangere, trasgredire
tran·ship [trænˈʃɪp] VT = transship
tran·si·ent [ˈtrænzɪənt] ADJ transitorio(-a), fugace
tran·sis·tor [trænˈzɪstəʳ] N (Elec) transistor m inv
trans·it [ˈtrænzɪt] N transito; **in transit** in transito; **their luggage was lost in transit** il loro bagaglio è stato smarrito durante il trasferimento
transit camp N campo (di raccolta) profughi
tran·si·tion [trænˈzɪʃən] N transizione f, passaggio; **transition period** or **period of transition** periodo di transizione; **the transition to democracy** il passaggio alla democrazia
tran·si·tion·al [trænˈzɪʃənl] ADJ (period, government) di transizione; (measures) transitorio(-a)
tran·si·tive [ˈtrænzɪtɪv] ADJ (Gram) transitivo(-a)
transit lounge N (Aer) sala di transito
tran·si·tory [ˈtrænzɪtərɪ] ADJ transitorio(-a)
trans·late [trænzˈleɪt] VT: **to translate (from/into)** tradurre (da/in); **it is translated as** si traduce con ♦ VI tradurre; **it won't translate** è intraducibile
trans·la·tion [trænzˈleɪʃən] N (of text) traduzione f; (Scol: as opposed to prose) versione f; (Geom) traslazione f
trans·la·tor [trænzˈleɪtəʳ] N traduttore(-trice)
trans·lu·cent [trænzˈluːsnt] ADJ traslucido(-a)
trans·mis·sion [trænzˈmɪʃən] N (Aut, TV, Radio) trasmissione f
trans·mit [trænzˈmɪt] VT (illness, programme, message) trasmettere

trans·mit·ter [trænzˈmɪtəʳ] N (TV, Radio, Telec) trasmettitore m
trans·par·en·cy [trænsˈpærənsɪ] N trasparenza; (Phot) diapositiva
trans·par·ent [trænsˈpærənt] ADJ trasparente; **a transparent lie** (fig) una menzogna palese
tran·spire [trænsˈpaɪəʳ] VI 1 (Bot, Physiology) traspirare 2 (frm: become known): **it finally transpired that ...** alla fine si è venuto a sapere che... 3 (incorrect use: happen) succedere; **what transpired at the meeting?** cos'è successo all'incontro?
trans·plant [vb trænsˈplɑːnt, n ˈtrænsˌplɑːnt] VT (also Med) trapiantare ♦ N (Med) trapianto; **to have a heart transplant** subire un trapianto cardiaco
trans·port [n ˈtrænspɔːt, vb, adj trænsˈpɔːt] N 1 (gen) trasporto; (vehicle) mezzo di trasporto; **public transport** mezzi mpl or trasporti mpl pubblici; **rail transport** il trasporto ferroviario; **have you got your own transport?** hai un tuo mezzo di trasporto?; **I haven't got any transport** non ho un mezzo 2 (fig: of delight, rage) trasporto; **to go into transports of joy** esultare dalla gioia ♦ VT 1 trasportare; (History: convicts) deportare 2 (fig): **transported with delight** deliziato(-a); **transported with joy** estasiato(-a) ♦ ADJ (system, costs) di trasporto
trans·por·ta·tion [ˌtrænspɔːˈteɪʃən] N 1 trasporto; (vehicle) mezzo di trasporto 2 (History: of convicts) deportazione f; **Department of Transportation** (USA) Ministero dei Trasporti
transport café N (Brit) trattoria per camionisti
trans·pose [trænsˈpəʊz] VT 1 (frm: words) trasporre 2 (Mus) trasporare
trans·sexu·al [trænzˈseksjʊəl] N, ADJ transessuale m/f inv
trans·verse [ˈtrænzvɜːs] ADJ trasversale
trans·ves·tite [trænzˈvestaɪt] N travestito(-a)
trap [træp] N 1 (snare, trick) trappola; **to set** or **lay a trap (for sb)** tendere una trappola (a qn); **he was caught in his own trap** si è fregato con le sue stesse mani 2 (fam: mouth) boccaccia; **shut your trap!** (fam) chiudi quella boccaccia! 3 (carriage) calesse m ♦ VT 1 prendere in trappola, intrappolare; **they trapped rabbits** catturavano conigli usando delle trappole; **to trap sb into saying sth** far raccontare qc a qn con un trucco 2 (immobilize) bloccare; (in wreckage) intrappolare, bloccare; **to be trapped** rimanere intrappolato; **six people were trapped in the burning building** sei persone sono rimaste intrappolate nell'edificio in fiamme; **to trap one's finger in the door** chiudersi il dito nella porta; **to trap the ball** (Ftbl) stoppare la palla
trap door N botola
tra·peze [trəˈpiːz] N (circus) trapezio
trap·per [ˈtræpəʳ] N cacciatore m di animali da pelliccia
trap·pings [ˈtræpɪŋz] NPL (of public office) bardatura, ornamenti mpl; (fig: of success) segni mpl esteriori; **the trappings of power** le manifestazioni esteriori del potere
trash [træʃ] N (USA: rubbish) rifiuti mpl, spazzatura; (pej: goods) ciarpame m; (fig: nonsense) sciocchezze fpl, stupidaggini fpl; **I'll take out the trash** porto fuori la spazzatura; **the book is trash** il libro è una schifezza; **they're just trash** (fam, pej: people) sono dei pezzenti
trash·can [ˈtræʃˌkæn] N (USA) secchio della spazzatura
trashy [ˈtræʃɪ] ADJ (comp -ier, superl -iest) (fam: book, film) scadente
trau·ma [ˈtrɔːmə] N trauma m
trau·mat·ic [trɔːˈmætɪk] ADJ (Med) traumatico(-a); (Psych, fig) traumatizzante, traumatico(-a)
trav·el [ˈtrævl] N il viaggiare, viaggi mpl; **travel is easier now** viaggiare è più facile al giorno d'oggi; **air travel is cheap these days** viaggiare in aereo non costa molto di questi tempi; **when are you off on your travels?** quando parti per uno dei tuoi viaggi?; **if you meet him on your travels** (fig) se lo incontri in uno dei tuoi giri ♦ VI 1 viaggiare; (make a journey) fare un viaggio; **to travel a country** percorrere un paese; **we shall be travelling in France** faremo un viaggio in Francia; **to travel round the world** fare un viaggio intorno al mondo, girare il mondo; **to travel by car** viaggiare in macchina; **I prefer to travel by train** preferisco viaggiare in treno; **they have travelled a lot** hanno viaggiato molto;

they have travelled a long way sono venuti da lontano; **we travelled over 800 kilometres** abbiamo fatto più di ottocento chilometri; **to travel light** viaggiare con poco bagaglio; **this wine doesn't travel well** questo vino non resiste agli spostamenti **2** (*go at a speed*) viaggiare, andare; **it travels at 50 km/h** fa 50 km/h; **light travels at a speed of ...** la velocità della luce è di...; **news travels fast** le notizie si diffondono molto velocemente, le notizie volano **3** (*Tech: move*) spostarsi; **it travels along this wire** si sposta lungo questo filo **4** (*Comm*) fare il (la) rappresentante (di commercio); **he travels in furs** fa il rappresentante di pellicce ♦ VT (*road, distance*) percorrere, fare; **this is a much travelled road** questa è una strada di grande traffico

travel agency N agenzia (di) viaggi

travel agent N agente *m* di viaggio

travel brochure N dépliant *m inv* di viaggi

travel insurance N assicurazione *f* di viaggio

trav·el·ler, trav·el·er (*USA*) ['trævlə'] N (*gen*) viaggiatore(-trice); (*Comm*) commesso viaggiatore; (*Brit: gypsy*) zingaro(-a); **my fellow travellers** i miei compagni di viaggio

traveller's cheque, traveler's check (*USA*) N traveller's cheque *m inv*

trav·el·ling, trav·el·ing (*USA*) ['trævlɪŋ] ADJ (*circus, exhibition*) itinerante; (*expenses, allowance*) di viaggio; (*bag, rug, clock*) da viaggio ♦ N viaggi *mpl*; **I love travelling** adoro viaggiare

travelling salesman, traveling salesman (*USA*) N commesso viaggiatore

trav·el·ogue ['trævəlɒg] N (*book*) diario di viaggio; (*film*) documentario di viaggio; (*talk*) conferenza su un viaggio

travel-sick ['trævl,sɪk] ADJ: **to get travel-sick** soffrire di mal d'auto

travel sickness N (*in car*) mal *m* d'auto; (*in plane*) mal d'aria; (*in boat*) mal di mare

trav·erse ['trævɜːs] (*frm*) N (*line*) linea trasversale; (*crossbeam*) traversa; (*Mountaineering*) traversata ♦ VT traversare, attraversare; (*Mountaineering*) traversare ♦ VI (*Mountaineering*) fare una traversata

trav·es·ty ['trævɪstɪ] N parodia; **his trial was a travesty of justice** il suo processo è stato una farsa

trawl·er ['trɔːlə'] N peschereccio (per la pesca a strascico)

tray [treɪ] N (*for carrying*) vassoio; (*filing tray*) vassoio per la corrispondenza

treach·er·ous ['tretʃərəs] ADJ (*disloyal: person, act*) sleale; (*smile*) traditore(-trice); (*answer*) infido(-a); (*fig: surface, ground, tide*) pericoloso(-a); **a treacherous friend** un amico sleale; **treacherous intentions** intenzioni *fpl* disoneste; **road conditions today are treacherous** oggi il fondo stradale è pericoloso; **the treacherous waters of the Waikato River** le acque infide del fiume Waikato

treach·ery ['tretʃərɪ] N slealtà *f inv*; **an act of treachery** un tradimento

trea·cle ['triːkl] N (*Brit*) melassa

tread [tred] (*pt* **trod**, *pp* **trodden**) N **1** (*footsteps*) passo; (*sound*) rumore *m* di passi; **to walk with (a) heavy tread** avere un'andatura pesante **2** (*of stair*) pedata; (*of tyre*) battistrada *m inv* ♦ VT (*ground*) calpestare; (*path*) percorrere; (*grapes*) pigiare; **to tread water** tenersi a galla verticalmente (*muovendo solo le gambe*); **don't tread mud into the carpet** non infangare il tappeto; **to tread a dangerous path** (*fig*) battere un sentiero pericoloso ♦ VI (*walk*) camminare; **to tread on sth** calpestare qc; **he trod on a piece of glass** ha calpestato un pezzo di vetro; **to tread on sb's toes** (*also fig*) pestare i piedi a qn; **he trod on her foot** le ha pestato un piede; **we must tread very carefully** *or* **warily** dobbiamo muoverci con molta cautela

  ▸ **tread on** VI + PREP calpestare

trea·dle ['tredl] N pedale *m*

treas. ABBR = **treasurer**

trea·son ['triːzn] N tradimento

treas·ure ['treʒə'] N (*no pl: gold, jewels*) tesori *mpl*; (*valuable object, fig: person*) tesoro; **our cleaner is a real treasure** la nostra donna delle pulizie è una vera rarità ♦ VT (*value: friendship*) apprezzare molto, tenere in gran conto; (*keep: valuables*) custodire gelosamente; (*: memory*) fare tesoro di

treasure hunt N caccia al tesoro

treas·ur·er ['treʒərə'] N tesoriere(-a)

treas·ury ['treʒərɪ] N **1** tesoreria; **the Treasury**, (*Brit*) **the Treasury Department** (*USA*) ≈ il Ministero del Tesoro **2** (*fig*) pozzo

treasury bill N ≈ buono del tesoro

treat [triːt] N (*pleasure*) piacere *m*; (*present*) sorpresa, sorpresina; **it was a treat** mi (*or ci etc*) ha fatto veramente piacere; **as a birthday treat they took me to the theatre** come regalo di compleanno mi hanno portato a teatro; **to give sb a treat** fare una sorpresa a qn; **to have a treat in store** avere una sorpresa in serbo; **this is my treat** offro io; **to work a treat** funzionare a meraviglia ♦ VT **1** (*gen, also Tech*) trattare; **to treat sb like a child** trattare qn come se fosse un bambino; **the hostages were well treated** gli ostaggi sono stati trattati bene **2** (*consider*) considerare; **to treat sth as a joke** considerare qc uno scherzo; **we treat all applications in the order in which we receive them** prendiamo in considerazione le domande nell'ordine in cui ci arrivano **3** (*give, buy for sb*): **to treat sb to sth** offrire qc a qn; **I'll treat you** offro io; **he treated himself to a new jacket** si è concesso il lusso di una giacca nuova **4** (*patient, illness*) curare; **he was treated with antibiotics/for bronchitis** è stato sottoposto a un trattamento di antibiotici/per la bronchite; **she was treated for a minor head wound** le hanno curato una ferita superficiale al capo

trea·tise ['triːtɪz] N trattato

treat·ment ['triːtmənt] N **1** trattamento; **to give sb preferential treatment** fare un trattamento di favore a qn; **we don't want any special treatment** non vogliamo un trattamento di favore; **he got good/bad treatment** è stato trattato bene/male; **our treatment of foreigners** il modo in cui trattiamo gli stranieri **2** (*Med: of illness*) cura; (*: of wound*) medicazione *f*; **to give sb medical treatment for sth** curare qc a qn; **to have treatment for sth** farsi curare qc; **an effective treatment for eczema** una cura efficace per l'eczema

trea·ty ['triːtɪ] N trattato, patto; **to sell a house by private treaty** (*agreement*) vendere una casa con un accordo privato

tre·ble ['trebl] ADV (*3 times*) tre volte ♦ ADJ **1** triplo(-a), triplice; **he now earns treble what he did** guadagna il triplo rispetto a prima **2** (*Mus: voice, part*) da soprano; (*: note, instrument*) alto(-a) ♦ N **1** (*Mus*) soprano *m/f*; (*also: boy treble*) voce *f* bianca **2** (*Horse-riding*) doppia gabbia ♦ VT triplicare *e* triplicarsi

treble clef N chiave *f* di violino

tree [triː] N **1** (*Bot*) albero; (*fig*): **to be at the top of the tree** essere all'apice **2** (*also: shoetree*) tendiscarpe *m inv*

tree-lined ['triːlaɪnd] ADJ fiancheggiato(-a) da alberi

tree·top ['triːtɒp] N cima di un albero

tree trunk N tronco di un albero

trek [trek] N (*hike*) spedizione *f*; (*fam: tiring walk*) camminata sfiancante; **a trek through the desert** una spedizione nel deserto ♦ VI (*hike*) fare una camminata lunga e faticosa; (*as holiday*) fare dell'escursionismo; (*fam*) trascinarsi; **they trekked through jungles** hanno fatto trekking nella giungla; **I trekked from shop to shop** mi sono trascinata da un negozio all'altro

trel·lis ['trelɪs] N graticcio; (*arched*) pergola

trem·ble ['trembl] N (*of fear*) tremito; (*of passion, excitement*) fremito; **to be all of a tremble** (*fam*) tremare dalla testa ai piedi, tremare come una foglia ♦ VI tremare; (*machine*) vibrare; **to tremble with** tremare per; **to tremble at the thought of sth** tremare al pensiero di qc

trem·bling ['tremblɪŋ] ADJ tremante ♦ N tremore *m*, tremito

tre·men·dous [trə'mendəs] ADJ (*enormous: difference, pleasure*) enorme; (*dreadful: storm, blow*) tremendo(-a); (*: speed*) spaventoso(-a), folle; (*terrific: success*) strepitoso(-a); (*fam: excellent*) fantastico(-a), formidabile, meraviglioso(-a); **he was a tremendous person** era una persona fantastica

tre·men·dous·ly [trə'mendəslɪ] ADV incredibilmente; **he enjoyed it tremendously** gli è piaciuto da morire

trem·or ['tremə'] N (*of fear, shock*) tremito, tremore *m*; (*of excitement*) fremito; (*also: earth tremor*) scossa di terremoto, scossa sismica; **it sent tremors down my spine** mi ha fatto venire i brividi

trench [trentʃ] N (*gen*) fosso; (*Mil*) trincea

trench coat N trench *m inv*
trench warfare N guerra di trincea
trend [trend] N (*tendency*) tendenza; (*of events*) andamento, corso; (*of prices, coastline*) andamento; (*fashion*) moda; **the latest trend** l'ultima moda; **to set a trend** lanciare una moda; **to set the trend** essere all'avanguardia; **trend towards sth/away from sth** tendenza a qc/ad allontanarsi da qc; **there is a trend towards doing sth/away from doing sth** si tende a fare qc/a non fare qc; **there's a trend towards part-time employment** il lavoro part-time è sempre più diffuso
trendy [ˈtrendɪ] ADJ (*comp* **-ier**, *superl* **-iest**) (*Brit fam: person, idea*) à la page; (: *clothes, night club*) trendy
trepi·da·tion [ˌtrepɪˈdeɪʃən] N (*frm*) trepidazione *f*
tres·pass [ˈtrespəs] VI: **to trespass (on)** (*on land*) entrare abusivamente (in); (*fig: on time, hospitality*) abusare (di); **"no trespassing"** "proprietà privata", "vietato l'accesso" ♦ N (*on land*) transito abusivo
tres·pass·er [ˈtrespəsə^r] N (*Bible, Law*) trasgressore *m*; **"trespassers will be prosecuted"** "vietato l'accesso - i trasgressori saranno puniti secondo i termini di legge"
tres·tle [ˈtresl] N cavalletto
trestle table N tavola su cavalletti
tri·al [ˈtraɪəl] N 1 (*gen*) giudizio; (*proceedings*) processo; **trial by jury** processo penale con giuria; **to be on trial (for a crime)** essere sotto processo (per un reato); **to bring sb to trial (for a crime)** portare qn in giudizio (per un reato); **to go on trial, to stand trial** essere processato(-a); **to be sent for trial** essere rinviato(-a) a giudizio; **the witnesses at the trial** i testimoni del processo 2 (*test: gen*) prova; (: *of drugs*) sperimentazione *f*; (: *of machine*) collaudo; **trials** NPL (*Athletics*) prove *fpl* di qualificazione; (*Ftbl*) prova di selezione; **horse trials** concorso ippico; **a trial of strength** una prova di forza; **by trial and error** per tentativi; **to be on trial** (*drug*) essere in via di sperimentazione; (*machine*) essere al collaudo; **to give sb a trial** (*for job*) far fare una prova a qn 3 (*hardship*) prova, difficoltà *f inv*; (*worry*) cruccio; **it was a great trial** è stata una dura prova; **that child is a great trial to them** quel bambino è una continua preoccupazione per loro; **the trials and tribulations of life** le tribolazioni della vita ♦ ADJ (*flight, order, period*) di prova; **trial offer** offerta di lancio; **trial period** periodo di prova; **on a trial basis** in prova
trial balance N (*Comm*) bilancio di verifica
trial run N periodo di prova
tri·an·gle [ˈtraɪˌæŋgl] N (*Math, Mus*) triangolo
tri·an·gu·lar [traɪˈæŋgjʊlə^r] ADJ triangolare
tri·ath·lon [traɪˈæθlɒn] N triathlon *m inv*
tribe [traɪb] N tribù *f inv*
tribes·man [ˈtraɪbzmən] N (*pl* **-men**) membro della tribù
tribu·la·tion [ˌtrɪbjʊˈleɪʃən] N (*frm*) tribolazione *f*
tri·bu·nal [traɪˈbjuːnl] N tribunale *m*; **tribunal of inquiry** commissione *f* d'inchiesta
tribu·tary [ˈtrɪbjʊtərɪ] N (*river*) affluente *m*, tributario
trib·ute [ˈtrɪbjuːt] N tributo, omaggio; **to pay tribute to sb/sth** rendere omaggio a qn/qc; **floral tribute** omaggio floreale
trice [traɪs] N: **in a trice** (*Brit fam*) in un batter d'occhio, in un attimo
trick [trɪk] N 1 (*joke, hoax*) scherzo, tiro; (*ruse, catch, special knack*) trucco; (*clever act*) stratagemma *m*; **to play a trick on sb** giocare un tiro a qn; **dirty** *or* **mean trick** scherzo di cattivo gusto; **there must be a trick in it** ci deve essere sotto qualche cosa; **he's up to his old tricks again** è tornato ai suoi vecchi trucchetti; **there's a trick to opening this door** c'è un trucco per aprire questa porta; **it's not easy, there's a trick to it** non è facile, c'è un trucco per farlo; **it's a trick of the light** è un effetto ottico; **he knows all the tricks of the trade** conosce tutti i trucchi del mestiere 2 (*habit*) mania; **he has a trick of turning up when least expected** ha il dono di spuntare quando uno meno se l'aspetta 3 (*Cards*) presa; (*also*: **conjuring trick**) gioco di prestigio; **that should do the trick** (*fam*) vedrai che funziona; **he doesn't miss a trick** (*fig*) non gliene scappa mai una ♦ VT (*deceive*) ingannare, imbrogliare; (*swindle*) imbrogliare; **I've been tricked!** mi hanno imbrogliato!; **to trick sb into doing sth** convincere qn a fare qc con l'inganno; **to trick sb out of sth** fregare qc a qn
trick·ery [ˈtrɪkərɪ] N inganno
trick·le [ˈtrɪkl] N (*of liquid*) rivolo; (*in drops*) gocciolio; (*fig*): **we've had only a trickle of customers** abbiamo avuto solo pochi clienti; **there was a steady trickle of orders** gli ordini erano pochi ma regolari; **a trickle of water** un rivolo d'acqua ♦ VI (*liquid*) gocciolare; (*ball*) rotolare lentamente; **tears trickled down his/her cheeks** le lacrime le scorrevano sulle guance; **to trickle in** (*orders, money*) arrivare a poco a poco; **to trickle in/out** (*people*) entrare/uscire alla spicciolata
trick question N domanda *f* trabocchetto, *inv*
trick·ster [ˈtrɪkstə^r] N imbroglione(-a)
tricky [ˈtrɪkɪ] ADJ (*comp* **-ier**, *superl* **-iest**) (*situation, problem*) difficile; (*job, task*) delicato(-a); (*person: sly*) astuto(-a)
tri·cy·cle [ˈtraɪsɪkl] N triciclo
tri·fle [ˈtraɪfl] N 1 (*unimportant thing*) cosa di poco valore, sciocchezza; **he worries about trifles** si preoccupa per niente; **he spends a lot on trifles** spende molto per delle sciocchezze; **it's a trifle difficult** è piuttosto difficile; **that seems a trifle ambitious** sembra un po' ambizioso; **a trifle long** un po' lungo(-a) 2 (*Brit: Culin*) ≈ zuppa inglese; **trifle or ice cream?** zuppa inglese o gelato?
  ▸ **trifle with** VI + PREP prendere alla leggera; **he's not a person to be trifled with** non è una persona da prendere alla leggera; **to trifle with sb's affections** giocare con i sentimenti di qn
tri·fling [ˈtraɪflɪŋ] ADJ insignificante
trig·ger [ˈtrɪgə^r] N (*of gun, machine*) grilletto; **to pull the trigger** premere il grilletto ♦ VT (*also*: **trigger off**: *event*) provocare, scatenare; **the incident which triggered the First World War** l'incidente che ha scatenato la prima guerra mondiale; **to trigger an alarm** far scattare l'allarme
trigo·nom·etry [ˌtrɪgəˈnɒmɪtrɪ] N trigonometria
tril·by [ˈtrɪlbɪ] N (*Brit: also:* **trilby hat**) cappello di feltro
trill [trɪl] N (*of bird, also Mus*) trillo
tril·ogy [ˈtrɪlədʒɪ] N trilogia
trim [trɪm] ADJ (*comp* **-mer**, *superl* **-mest**) curato(-a), ordinato(-a); (*house, garden*) ben tenuto(-a); (*figure*) snello(-a) ♦ N 1 **in good trim** (*car*) in buone condizioni; (*person*) in forma; **to keep in (good) trim** mantenersi in forma 2 (*haircut*) spuntata, regolata; **to have a trim** farsi spuntare i capelli 3 (*embellishment*) finiture *fpl*; (*decoration*) applicazioni *fpl*; (*on car*) guarnizioni *fpl*; **white with a black trim** bianco con una guarnizione nera; **car with grey interior trim** macchina con gli interni grigi ♦ VT 1 (*cut: hedge, beard, edges*) regolare tagliando; (: *hair*) spuntare 2 **to trim (with)** (*decorate: Christmas tree*) decorare (con); **to trim sth with sth** (*edge*) mettere un bordo di qc a qc 3 (*Naut*: *sail*) orientare
  ▸ **trim off** VT + ADV tagliare via ♦ VT + PREP: **to trim sth off sth** tagliare via qc da qc
trim·ming [ˈtrɪmɪŋ] N (*edging*) bordura; **trimmings** NPL (*embellishments*) decorazioni *fpl*; (*extras*) accessori *mpl*; (*Culin*) guarnizione *f*; (*cuttings*) ritagli *mpl*; **turkey with all the trimmings** tacchino con contorno e tutto il resto
Trini·dad and To·ba·go [ˌtrɪnɪdædəndtəˈbeɪgəʊ] N Trinidad e Tobago *f*
Trini·ty [ˈtrɪnɪtɪ] N: **the Trinity** la Trinità
trin·ket [ˈtrɪŋkɪt] N (*piece of jewellery*) ciondolo; (*ornament*) ninnolo, gingillo
trio [ˈtriːəʊ] N trio
trip [trɪp] N 1 viaggio; (*outing*) gita; (*excursion*) escursione *f*; (*away*) **on a trip** in viaggio; **to take a trip** *or* **to go on a trip** fare un viaggio; **how does 3 trips to Milan a week** va a Milano 3 volte alla settimana; **I've made 2 trips to the shops already** sono già andata 2 volte a far la spesa; **have a good trip!** buon viaggio!; **a day trip** una gita di un giorno 2 (*Drugs: slang*) trip *m inv*, viaggio 3 (*stumble*) passo falso ♦ VI 1 (*stumble*) inciampare; **I tripped and fell** sono inciampato(-a) e caduto(-a) 2 **to trip along** *or* **go tripping along** (*skip*) andare saltellando; (*move lightly*) camminare con passo leggero ♦ VT = **trip up**
  ▸ **trip over** VT + ADV inciampare ♦ VI + PREP inciampare in
  ▸ **trip up** VI + ADV inciampare; (*fig: make a mistake*) fare un passo falso ♦ VT + ADV far inciampare, fare lo sgambetto a

tri·par·tite [ˌtraɪˈpɑːtaɪt] ADJ (*agreement*) tripartito(-a); (*talks*) a tre

tripe [traɪp] N (*Culin*) trippa; (*fam, pej: rubbish*) sciocchezze *fpl*, fesserie *fpl*

tri·ple [ˈtrɪpl] ADJ triplo(-a). ♦ ADV: **triple the distance/the speed** tre volte più lontano/più veloce ♦ VT triplicare ♦ VI triplicarsi

triple jump N salto triplo

tri·plets [ˈtrɪplɪts] NPL: **to have triplets** avere tre gemelli; **she's just had triplets** ha appena avuto tre gemelli *or* un parto trigemino

trip·li·cate [ˈtrɪplɪkɪt] N: **in triplicate** in triplice copia

tri·pod [ˈtraɪpɒd] N treppiede *m*

Tripo·li [ˈtrɪpəlɪ] N Tripoli *f*

trip·per [ˈtrɪpəʳ] N (*Brit*) gitante *m/f*

trip·wire [ˈtrɪpˌwaɪəʳ] N filo in tensione che fa scattare una trappola, un allarme ecc

trite [traɪt] ADJ (*remark*) banale; (*story, idea*) trito(-a) e ritrito(-a)

tri·umph [ˈtraɪʌmf] N (*success*) successo; (*sense of triumph*) trionfo; (*victory*): **triumph (over)** trionfo (su), vittoria (su); **in triumph** in trionfo ♦ VI: **to triumph (over)** trionfare (su)

tri·um·phal [traɪˈʌmfəl] ADJ trionfale

tri·um·phant [traɪˈʌmfənt] ADJ (*jubilant*) trionfante; (*homecoming*) trionfale; (*victorious*) vittorioso(-a)

trivia [ˈtrɪvɪə] NPL banalità *fpl*

triv·ial [ˈtrɪvɪəl] ADJ (*matter*) futile; (*excuse, comment*) banale; (*amount*) irrisorio(-a); (*mistake*) di poco conto
  ❏ **trivial** is not translated by the Italian word *triviale*

trivi·al·ity [ˌtrɪvɪˈælɪtɪ] N frivolezza; (*trivial detail*) futilità *f inv*
  ❏ **triviality** is not translated by the Italian word *trivialità*

trivi·al·ize [ˈtrɪvɪəˌlaɪz] VT sminuire

trod [trɒd] PT *of* tread

trod·den [ˈtrɒdn] PP *of* tread

troll [trəʊl, trɒl] N troll *m inv* ♦ VI (*fam*) vagare

trol·ley [ˈtrɒlɪ] N (*Am*) tram *m inv*; (*Brit: in station, supermarket: also:* **tea trolley**) carrello; (: *in hospital*) lettiga

trolley bus N filobus *m inv*

trol·lop [ˈtrɒləp] N (*old, offensive*) sgualdrina

trom·bone [trɒmˈbəʊn] N trombone *m*

troop [truːp] N (*gen: of scouts*) gruppo; (*Mil*) squadrone *m*; **troops** NPL (*Mil*) truppe *fpl* ♦ VI (*walk*): **to troop in/past/off** *etc* entrare/passare/andarsene *etc* in gruppo

troop carrier N 1 (*plane*) aereo per il trasporto (di) truppe 2 (*Naut*) = **troopship**

troop·er [ˈtruːpəʳ] N (*Mil*) soldato di cavalleria; (*USA: policeman*) ≈ poliziotto, *agente della polizia di uno stato*; **to swear like a trooper** bestemmiare come un turco

troop·ship [ˈtruːpˌʃɪp] N nave *f* per il trasporto (di) truppe

tro·phy [ˈtrəʊfɪ] N trofeo

trop·ic [ˈtrɒpɪk] N tropico; **the tropics** i tropici; **Tropic of Cancer/Capricorn** tropico del Cancro/Capricorno

tropi·cal [ˈtrɒpɪkəl] ADJ tropicale; **tropical rain forest** foresta pluviale equatoriale

trot [trɒt] N 1 (*pace*) trotto; **sitting/rising trot** (*Horse-riding*) trotto seduto/sollevato; **to break into a trot** (*horse, rider*) partire al trotto; (*person*) mettersi a camminare di buon passo; **to go for a trot** (*on horse*) andare a fare una trottata 2 (*Brit fam*): **on the trot** di fila, uno(-a) dopo l'altro(-a); **three weeks on the trot** tre settimane di fila; **to be on the trot** (*fam*) essere sempre in movimento 3 **the trots** (*fam: diarrhoea*) la cacarella ♦ VI (*horse, rider*) andare al trotto, trottare; (*person*): **to trot in/past** *etc* entrare/passare *etc* di corsa
  ▸ **trot out** VT + ADV (*excuse, reason*) tirar fuori; (*names, facts*) recitare di fila

trou·ble [ˈtrʌbl] N 1 (*problems*) problemi *mpl*, difficoltà *fpl*; (*as result of doing wrong*) guai *mpl*, pasticci *mpl*; (*with sth mechanical*) noie *fpl*; (*unrest, fighting*) agitazione *f*, disordine *m*; **troubles** NPL disordini, conflitti *mpl*; **to have trouble doing sth** avere delle difficoltà a fare qc; **to be in trouble** (*having problems*) avere qualche problema *or* difficoltà; (*for doing wrong*) essere nei guai; **to get into trouble** cacciarsi nei guai; **to get sb into trouble** mettere *or* cacciare qn nei guai; **to help sb out of trouble** aiutare qn a tirarsi fuori dai

guai; **what's the trouble?** cosa c'è che non va?; **the trouble is …** c'è che…, il guaio è che…; **the trouble is, it's too expensive** il problema è che costa troppo; **don't go looking for trouble** non andare in cerca di guai; **the police are trying to prevent trouble** la polizia sta cercando di prevenire eventuali disordini; **engine trouble** noie al motore; **stomach trouble** disturbi *mpl* gastrici; **heart/back trouble** disturbi al cuore/di schiena 2 (*bother, effort*) sforzo; (*worry*) preoccupazione *f*; **it's no trouble** (*offering help*) non è un problema; **it's no trouble!** (*accepting thanks*) di niente!; **it's not worth the trouble** non vale la pena; **to go to (all) the trouble of doing sth, take the trouble to do sth** darsi la pena di fare qc; **to take a lot of trouble over sth** mettere molto impegno in qc ♦ VT 1 (*worry*) preoccupare; **my eyes have been troubling me** ho avuto dei disturbi agli occhi 2 (*bother, be nuisance to*) disturbare; **I'm sorry to trouble you** mi dispiace disturbarla; **please don't trouble yourself** non si disturbi 3 (+ *infin*: *make the effort*): **to trouble to do sth** darsi la pena di fare qc

trou·bled [ˈtrʌbld] ADJ (*person, expression*) preoccupato(-a), inquieto(-a); (*period*) travagliato(-a); (*epoch, life*) agitato(-a), difficile

trouble-free [ˌtrʌblˈfriː] ADJ (*life, car, trip*) senza problemi; (*area, factory*) tranquillo(-a); (*demonstration*) pacifico(-a)

trouble-maker [ˈtrʌblˌmeɪkəʳ] N elemento disturbatore, agitatore(-trice)

trouble-shooter [ˈtrʌblˌʃuːtəʳ] N (*Tech*) esperto(-a) (*chiamato in casi di emergenza*); (*Pol*) mediatore(-trice); (*in conflict*) conciliatore *m*

trou·ble·some [ˈtrʌblsəm] ADJ (*person*) molesto(-a), importuno(-a); (*headache*) fastidioso(-a); (*dispute, problem*) difficile, seccante; **a troublesome child** un bambino molesto

trouble spot N zona calda

trou·bling [ˈtrʌblɪŋ] ADJ (*thought*) preoccupante; **these are troubling times** questi sono tempi difficili

trough [trɒf] N 1 (*also:* **feeding trough**) mangiatoia, trogolo; (*also:* **drinking trough**) abbeveratoio; (*channel*) canale *m* 2 (*between waves*) cavo; (*on graph*) punto più basso; (*Met*): **trough of low pressure** area di bassa pressione, depressione *f*

trounce [traʊns] VT (*beat*) picchiare; (*defeat*) battere

troupe [truːp] N (*Theatre*) compagnia, troupe *f inv*

trouser press N (*Brit*) stiracalzoni *m inv*

trou·sers [ˈtraʊzəz] NPL (*Brit*) pantaloni *mpl*, calzoni *mpl*; **short trousers** calzoncini *mpl*

trouser suit N (*Brit*) completo *m* pantalone, *inv*, tailleur *m inv* pantalone, *inv*

trous·seau [ˈtruːsəʊ] N corredo da sposa

trout [traʊt] N *pl inv* trota ♦ ADJ: **trout fishing** pesca della trota

trow·el [ˈtraʊəl] N (*for garden*) paletta da giardiniere; (*builder's*) cazzuola

tru·ant [ˈtruːənt] N (*Scol*): **to play truant** marinare la scuola

truce [truːs] N tregua; **to call a truce** dichiarare una tregua
  ❏ **truce** is not translated by the Italian word *truce*

truck [trʌk] N 1 (*Brit: Rail: wagon*) carro *m* merci, *inv* (*aperto*) 2 (*esp USA: lorry*) camion *m inv*, autocarro 3 (*for luggage*) carrello *m* portabagagli, *inv*

truck driver, (*USA*) **truck·er** [ˈtrʌkəʳ] N camionista *m/f*

truck·ing [ˈtrʌkɪŋ] N (*USA*) autotrasporto, trasporto su gomma

trucking company N (*USA*) impresa di trasporti

trucu·lent [ˈtrʌkjʊlənt] ADJ aggressivo(-a), brutale

trudge [trʌdʒ] VI: **to trudge up/down/along** *etc* trascinarsi pesantemente su/giù/lungo *etc*; **to trudge round the town** girare la città in lungo e in largo

true [truː] ADJ (*comp* **-r,** *superl* **-st**) 1 (*not fiction: story*) vero(-a); (*accurate, correct: statement, description*) preciso(-a), esatto(-a), accurato(-a); (: *portrait, likeness*) fedele; **that can't be true!** non può essere vero!; **to come true** avverarsi; **I hope my dream will come true** spero che il mio sogno si avveri; **the same holds true of or for …** lo stesso vale per…; **too true!** fin troppo vero!; **true, but … sì, ma… 2 (*real, genuine: emotion, interest*) sincero(-a), vero(-a); **true love** vero amore; **to behave like a true Englishman** comportarsi da vero inglese; **in the truest sense of the word** nel vero senso della parola **3** (*wall, beam*) a piombo; (*wheel*) centrato(-a) **4** (*faithful: friend*) fedele; **to be true to sb/sth** essere fedele a qn/qc; **to be true to one's word** tenere fede alla parola data; **true to life** verosimile; **to run true to type** essere fedele alla propria immagine ♦ N: **to be out of true** (*wall, beam*) non essere a piombo; (*wheel*) non essere centrato(-a)

truf·fle [ˈtrʌfl] N tartufo

tru·ly [ˈtruːlɪ] ADV (*genuinely: believe, love*) veramente, sinceramente; (*faithfully: serve, love, reflect*) fedelmente; (*emphatic: very*) veramente, davvero; **I truly never minded looking after Tom** sinceramente non mi è mai dispiaciuto occuparmi di Tom; **it was a truly remarkable victory** è stata veramente una vittoria straordinaria; **well and truly** per bene; **yours truly** (*in letter-writing*) distinti saluti

trump [trʌmp] N (*Cards*) atout *m inv*; **hearts are trumps** l'atout è di cuori; **to turn** or **come up trumps** (*fig*) fare miracoli ♦ VT (*Cards*) tagliare, prendere con l'atout

trump card N atout *m inv*; (*fig*) asso nella manica

trumped-up [ˌtrʌmptˈʌp] ADJ (*charge*) inventato(-a), falso(-a)

trum·pet [ˈtrʌmpɪt] N tromba; **a trumpet player** (*Jazz*) un(-a) trombettista ♦ VI (*elephant*) barrire

trun·cat·ed [trʌŋˈkeɪtɪd] ADJ (*Geom*) tronco(-a)

trun·cheon [ˈtrʌntʃən] N manganello, sfollagente *m inv*

trun·dle [ˈtrʌndl] VT (*push, pull*): **to trundle along** far rotolare (a fatica) ♦ VI (*cart*) avanzare lentamente

trunk [trʌŋk] N (*of tree, person*) tronco; (*also:* **tree trunk**) tronco d'albero; (*of elephant*) proboscide *f*; (*piece of luggage*) baule *m*; (*USA: Aut: boot of car*) bagagliaio; **put it in the trunk** mettilo nel portabagagli; *see also* **trunks**

trunk call N (*Brit: old: Telec*) (telefonata) interurbana

trunk road N (*Brit*) strada principale

trunks [trʌŋks] NPL: (**swimming** or **bathing**) **trunks** calzoncini *mpl* da bagno

truss [trʌs] VT (*also:* **truss up**) legare stretto; (*Culin*) legare ♦ N (*Med*) cinto erniario

trust [trʌst] N **1 trust (in)** fiducia (in); **to put one's trust in sb** riporre la propria fiducia in qn; **to put one's trust in sth** riporre le proprie speranze in qc; **to be in a position of trust** ricoprire un incarico di fiducia; **you'll have to take it on trust** devi credermi sulla parola; **he betrayed my trust** ha tradito la mia fiducia **2** (*charge*): **to leave sth in sb's trust** affidare qc a qn or alle cure di qn **3** (*Law, Fin*) amministrazione *f* fiduciaria; **in trust** in amministrazione fiduciaria; **charitable trust** fondazione *f* benefica **4** (*Comm:* *also:* **trust company**) trust *m inv* ♦ VT **1** (*have faith, confidence in*) avere fiducia in, fidarsi di; (*rely on*) fare affidamento su, contare su; **don't trust me?** non ti fidi di me?; **trust me!** fidati di me!; **to trust sth to sb/trust sb with sth** (*entrust*) affidare qc a qn; **I wouldn't trust him an inch** non mi fiderei proprio di lui; **trust you!** (*fam*) ci avrei scommesso! **2** (*hope*): **to trust (that ...)** sperare (che...) ♦ VI (*have faith*): **to trust in** credere in; **to trust to luck/fate** (*rely*) affidarsi alla fortuna/al destino

trust·ed [ˈtrʌstɪd] ADJ (*friend, adviser*) fidato(-a)

trus·tee [trʌsˈtiː] N (*Law*) amministratore(-trice) fiduciario(-a); (*of school, institution*) amministratore(-trice)

trust·ful [ˈtrʌstfʊl], **trust·ing** [ˈtrʌstɪŋ] ADJ fiducioso(-a)

trust fund N fondo fiduciario

trust·worthy [ˈtrʌstˌwɜːðɪ] ADJ (*person*) fidato(-a), degno(-a) di fiducia; (*source of news*) attendibile

trusty [ˈtrʌstɪ] ADJ (*comp* -**ier**, *superl* -**iest**) (*hum*) fidato(-a)

truth [truːθ] N verità *f inv*; **to tell the truth** dire la verità; **to tell (you) the truth, truth to tell** a dire il vero or la verità; **the truth of the matter is that ...** la verità è che...; **the truth hurts** la verità fa male; **there is some truth in what he says** c'è del vero in ciò che dice; **there isn't a word of truth in it** non c'è nulla di vero; **truth will out** la verità viene sempre a galla

truth·ful [ˈtruːθfʊl] ADJ (*account*) veritiero(-a), esatto(-a); (*person*) sincero(-a)

truth·ful·ly [ˈtruːθfʊlɪ] ADV sinceramente

truth·ful·ness [ˈtruːθfʊlnɪs] N (*of account*) veridicità *f inv*; (*of person*) sincerità *f inv*

try [traɪ] N **1** (*attempt*) tentativo, prova; **to give sth a try**

provare qc; **why don't you give the exam a try?** perché non provi a fare l'esame?; **to have a try (at doing sth)** provare (a fare qc); **it's worth a try** vale la pena di tentare; **his third try** il suo terzo tentativo **2** (*Rugby*) meta ♦ VT **1** (*usu* + *infin*): **to try to do sth** (*attempt*) provare a fare qc; (*seek*) cercare di fare qc; **to try one's (very) best** or **one's (very) hardest** mettercela tutta **2** (*sample, experiment with: method, car, food*) provare; **would you like to try some?** vuoi assaggiare?; **why not try him for the job?** perché non gli fai fare una prova?; **try pressing that switch** prova a schiacciare quell'interruttore **3** (*test: strength, vehicle, machine*) verificare, collaudare; (*tax, strain: patience, person*) mettere alla prova; (*eyes*) affaticare; **to try one's hand at sth** (*fig*) cimentarsi in qc **4** (*Law*): **to try sb (for sth)** processare qn (per qc) ♦ VI (*attempt*) provare; **I tried, but failed** ho tentato, ma non ci sono riuscito; **you must try harder** devi tentare ancora; **to try again** ritentare; **try again!** provaci ancora!

▸ **try for** VT + ADV mirare a

▸ **try on** VT + ADV **1** (*clothes, shoes*) provare **2** (*Brit fam*): **to try it on (with sb)** cercare di farla (a qn)

▸ **try out** VT + ADV (*test: sth new, different*) provare; (*employee*) far fare una prova a; **to try sth out on sb** far provare qc a qn

try·ing [ˈtraɪɪŋ] ADJ (*tiring: situation, time*) difficile, duro(-a); (: *day, experience*) logorante, pesante; (*tiresome: person*) noioso(-a), seccante; (: *child*) insopportabile; **to have a trying time** passare un periodo difficile

tsar [zɑː] N zar *m inv*

T-shirt [ˈtiːʃɜːt] N maglietta

T-square [ˈtiːskwɛəʳ] N riga a T

tsu·na·mi [tsʊˈnɑːmi] N tsunami *m inv*

tub [tʌb] N (*for washing clothes*) tinozza, mastello; (*for flowers*) vasca; (*for ice cream*) vaschetta; (*individual*) coppetta; (*fam: also:* **bathtub**) vasca da bagno; **a tub of margarine** una vaschetta di margarina; **a hot tub** un bagno caldo

tuba [ˈtjuːbə] N tuba

tub·by [ˈtʌbɪ] ADJ (*comp* -**ier**, *superl* -**iest**) (*fam*) grassoccio(-a)

tube [tjuːb] N **1** (*pipe*) tubo; (*of toothpaste, paint*) tubetto; (*Anat*) tuba; (*for tyre* or *tire*) camera d'aria; **a cardboard tube** un tubo di cartone **2** (*Brit: London Underground*) metrò *m inv*, metropolitana **3 the tube** (*USA fam: television*) la tele ♦ ADJ (*Brit*) del metrò; **tube station** stazione *f* del metrò

tube·less [ˈtjuːblɪs] ADJ (*tyre*) senza camera d'aria

tu·ber [ˈtjuːbəʳ] N (*Bot*) tubero

tu·ber·cu·lo·sis [tjʊ,bɜːkjʊˈləʊsɪs] N tubercolosi *f*

tub·ing [ˈtjuːbɪŋ] N tubi *mpl*, tubazione *f*; **a piece of tubing** un tubo

tubu·lar [ˈtjuːbjʊləʳ] ADJ tubolare

tuck [tʌk] N (*Sewing*) pince *f inv*, piega ♦ VT (*put*) infilare, mettere, cacciare; **she tucked a blanket round him** lo ha avvolto in una coperta; **I tucked a note under her pillow** le ho infilato un biglietto sotto il cuscino ♦ VI: **to tuck into a meal** (*Brit fam*) lanciarsi sul pasto

▸ **tuck away** VT + ADV (*put away*) riporre in un luogo sicuro; (*hide*) nascondere; **she has her money safely tucked away** ha messo i soldi in un posto sicuro

▸ **tuck in** VI + ADV (*Brit fam: eat*) mangiare con grande appetito, abbuffarsi; **they all tucked into the huge breakfast** tutti hanno mangiato di gusto un'abbondante colazione; **tuck in!** abbuffati! ♦ VT + ADV (*blankets*) rimboccare; (*shirt*) mettere dentro; **she tucked the blouse into her skirt** si è messa la camicia dentro la gonna; **to tuck sb in** rimboccare le coperte a qn; **I'll come and tuck you in** vengo a rimboccarti le coperte

▸ **tuck up** VT + ADV (*skirt, sleeves*) tirare su; **to tuck sb up** rimboccare le coperte a qn; **he tucked him up** gli ha rimboccato le coperte; **to be tucked up in bed** essere a letto con le coperte ben rimboccate

Tue., Tues. ABBR (= *Tuesday*) mar. (= *martedì*)

Tues·day [ˈtjuːzdɪ] N martedì *m inv*; **(the date) today is Tuesday 23 March** oggi è martedì 23 marzo; **on Tuesday** martedì; **I saw her on Tuesday** l'ho vista martedì; **on Tuesdays** di or il martedì; **I go swimming on Tuesdays** vado in piscina il martedì; **every Tuesday** tutti i martedì; **every other Tuesday** ogni due martedì; **last/next Tuesday** martedì scorso/prossimo; **Tuesday next** martedì prossimo; **the following**

Tuesday (*in past*) il martedì successivo; (*in future*) il martedì dopo; **the Tuesday before last** martedì di due settimane fa; **the Tuesday after next** non questo martedì ma il prossimo; **a week/fortnight** (*Brit*) **on Tuesday, Tuesday week/fortnight** (*Brit*) martedì fra una settimana/quindici giorni; **Tuesday morning/lunchtime/afternoon/evening** martedì mattina/all'ora di pranzo/pomeriggio/sera; **Tuesday night** martedì sera; (*overnight*) martedì notte; **the Tuesday film** (*TV*) il film del martedì; **Tuesday's newspaper** il giornale di martedì; **Shrove Tuesday** martedì grasso

tuft [tʌft] N (*of hair*) ciuffo, ciocca; (*of grass*) ciuffo

tug [tʌg] N 1 (*pull*) strattone m; **to give sth a (good) tug** dare uno strattone a qc 2 (*ship*) (*also:* **tugboat**) rimorchiatore m ♦ VT (*pull*) tirare con forza ♦ VI: **to tug (at)** dare uno strattone (a)

tug-of-love [ˌtʌgəv'lʌv] N (*Brit fam*) contesa per la custodia dei figli; **tug-of-love children** bambini coinvolti nella contesa per la custodia

tug-of-war [ˌtʌgəv'wɔːʳ] N (*Sport*) tiro alla fune; (*fig*) braccio di ferro

tui·tion [tjʊ'ɪʃən] N (*Brit: lessons*) lezioni *fpl*; (*USA: fees*) tasse *fpl* scolastiche (*or* universitarie); **private tuition** lezioni private

tu·lip ['tjuːlɪp] N tulipano

tum·ble ['tʌmbl] N (*fall*) ruzzolone m, capitombolo; **to have a tumble, take a tumble** fare un ruzzolone *or* capitombolo ♦ VI 1 (*fall*) ruzzolare, capitombolare, fare un capitombolo; (*somersault*) fare capriole; **to tumble downstairs** ruzzolare giù dalle scale; **he tumbled down the steps** ha fatto un capitombolo giù dalle scale 2 (*rush*): **to tumble into/out of bed** buttarsi a/cadere giù dal letto; **the children tumbled out of the room/the car** i bambini si sono precipitati fuori dalla stanza/dalla macchina 3 (*suddenly understand*): **to tumble to sth** (*Brit fam*) realizzare qc ♦ VT far cadere
▸ **tumble over** VI + ADV ruzzolare

tumble-down ['tʌmbl̩ˌdaʊn] ADJ cadente, diroccato(-a)

tumble dryer N (*Brit*) asciugatrice f

tum·bler ['tʌmbləʳ] N (*glass*) bicchiere m (senza stelo)

tum·my ['tʌmɪ] N (*fam*) pancia

tumour, tu·mor (*USA*) ['tjuːməʳ] N tumore m

tu·mult ['tjuːmʌlt] N tumulto

tu·mul·tu·ous [tjuː'mʌltjʊəs] ADJ tumultuoso(-a)

tuna ['tjuːnə] N *pl inv* (*also:* **tuna fish**) tonno

tune [tjuːn] N 1 (*melody*) melodia, aria; **a familiar tune** una melodia familiare; **he gave us a tune** ci ha suonato qualcosa; **to change one's tune** (*fig*) cambiare tono; **to the tune of** (*fig: amount*) per la modesta somma di 2 **in tune** (*instrument*) accordato(-a); (*person*) intonato(-a); **out of tune** (*instrument*) scordato(-a); (*person*) stonato(-a); **to sing in tune** cantare senza stonare; **to sing out of tune** stonare; **to play in tune** essere accordato(-a); **in tune with** (*fig*) in accordo con ♦ VT (*Mus*) accordare; (*Aut: engine*) mettere a punto; (*Radio, TV*) regolare ♦ VI (*Mus: also:* **tune up**) accordare lo strumento
▸ **tune in** VI + ADV (*Radio, TV*): **to tune in (to)** sintonizzarsi (su)

tune·ful ['tjuːnfʊl] ADJ melodioso(-a)

tun·er ['tjuːnəʳ] N 1 (*Radio: control*) sintonizzatore m, tuner m *inv* 2 (*also:* **piano tuner**) accordatore(-trice) di pianoforte

tuner amplifier N amplificatore m di sintonia

tung·sten ['tʌŋstən] N tungsteno

tu·nic ['tjuːnɪk] N tunica

tun·ing ['tjuːnɪŋ] N (*Mus*) accordatura; (*Aut*) messa a punto; (*Radio, TV*) sintonizzazione f

tuning fork N diapason m *inv*

Tu·nis ['tjuːnɪs] N Tunisi f

Tu·ni·sia [tjuː'nɪzɪə] N la Tunisia

Tu·ni·sian [tjuː'nɪzɪən] ADJ, N tunisino(-a)

tun·nel ['tʌnl] N (*gen*) galleria, tunnel m *inv*; (*Min*) galleria; **the Mont Blanc tunnel** il traforo del Monte Bianco ♦ VI: **to tunnel one's way out** aprirsi un passaggio scavando; **to tunnel a passage** scavare un passaggio ♦ VI scavare una galleria

tunnel vision N (*Med*) riduzione f del campo visivo; (*fig*) visuale f ristretta

tun·ny ['tʌnɪ] N (*Brit*) = **tuna**

tur·ban ['tɜːbən] N turbante m

tur·bid ['tɜːbɪd] ADJ (*liquid: also fig: situation*) torbido(-a); (*smoke, fog*) denso(-a)

tur·bine ['tɜːbaɪn] N turbina

turbo ['tɜːbəʊ] N turbo m *inv*

tur·bo·jet [ˌtɜːbəʊ'dʒet] N turbogetto, turboreattore m

tur·bo·prop [ˌtɜːbəʊ'prɒp] N turboelica m *inv*

tur·bot ['tɜːbət] N *pl inv* rombo gigante

tur·bu·lence ['tɜːbjʊləns] N turbolenza

tur·bu·lent ['tɜːbjʊlənt] ADJ turbolento(-a); (*sea*) agitato(-a)

tu·reen [tə'riːn] N zuppiera

turf [tɜːf] N (*pl* **turfs** *or* **turves**) (*grass*) tappeto erboso; (*one piece*) zolla erbosa; **the turf** (*horse racing*) l'ippica, le corse ippiche; (*racetrack*) l'ippodromo ♦ VT (*also:* **turf over**) ricoprire di zolle erbose
▸ **turf out** VT + ADV (*Brit fam*) buttar fuori

turf accountant N (*Brit*) allibratore m

tur·gid ['tɜːdʒɪd] ADJ (*liter: prose, speech*) ampolloso(-a), pomposo(-a)

Tu·rin [tjʊə'rɪn] N Torino f

Turk [tɜːk] N turco(-a); **the Turks** i turchi

Tur·key ['tɜːkɪ] N la Turchia

tur·key ['tɜːkɪ] N tacchino

Turk·ish ['tɜːkɪʃ] ADJ turco(-a) ♦ N (*language*) turco

Turkish bath N bagno turco

Turkish delight N gelatine ricoperte di zucchero a velo

tur·mer·ic ['tɜːmərɪk] N curcuma

tur·moil ['tɜːmɔɪl] N confusione f, tumulto; **to be in a turmoil** essere in uno stato di confusione

turn [tɜːn] N 1 (*rotation*) giro; **to give sth a turn** girare qc; **done to a turn** (*Culin*) cotto a puntino 2 (*change of direction: in road*) curva; **"no left turn"** "divieto di svolta a sinistra"; **to do a left turn** (*Aut*) girare a sinistra; **take the next left turn** prendi la prossima a sinistra; **a road full of twists and turns** una strada a zigzag *or* tutta a curve; **a sharp turn** una curva secca; **to take a turn in the park** fare un giro nel parco; **at the turn of the year/century** alla fine dell'anno/del secolo; **at every turn** (*fig*) a ogni piè sospinto; **things took a new turn** (*fig*) le cose hanno preso una nuova piega; **to take a turn for the better** (*situation, events*) volgere al meglio; (*patient, health*) migliorare; **to take a turn for the worse** (*situation, events*) volgere al peggio; (*patient, health*) peggiorare; **an odd turn of mind** una strana disposizione mentale; **a turn of phrase** modo di esprimersi 3 (*Med*) attacco, crisi f *inv*; **he had a bad turn last night** la scorsa notte ha avuto una crisi *or* un peggioramento; **the news gave me quite a turn** (*fam*) la notizia mi ha fatto prendere un bello spavento 4 (*in series*) turno; **by turns** a turno; **in turn** a sua volta; **hot and cold by turns** ora caldo ora freddo; **and he, in turn, said ...** e lui, a sua volta, ha detto...; **they spoke in turn** hanno parlato a turno; **to take turns at (doing) sth, take it in turn(s) to do sth** fare qc a turno; **to take/wait/miss one's turn** fare/aspettare/saltare il proprio turno; **it's my turn** è il mio turno, tocca a me; **whose turn is it?** a chi tocca?; **your turn will come** verrà anche il tuo momento; **to take turn and turn about** fare i turni; **to take turns at the wheel** fare i turni al volante; **to take a turn at the wheel** fare un turno al volante; **to speak out of turn** (*fig*) parlare a sproposito 5 (*performance*) numero; **to do a comedy turn** fare un numero comico 6 (*action*): **to do sb a good turn** rendere un servizio a qn; **to do sb a bad turn** fare un brutto tiro a qn; **his good turn for the day** la sua buona azione quotidiana; **one good turn deserves another** una mano lava l'altra ♦ VT 1 (*wheel, handle*) girare; (*mechanically*) far girare; **turn the key in the lock** gira la chiave nella toppa 2 (*also:* **turn over:** *page, mattress, steak*) girare, voltare, rivoltare; **to turn one's ankle** storcersi una caviglia; **it turns my stomach** mi fa rivoltare lo stomaco 3 (*direct: car, object*) voltare; (: *attention*) rivolgere; (: *gun, telescope*) puntare; **the fire fighter turned the hose on the building** il pompiere ha puntato l'idrante verso l'edificio; **to turn a gun on sb** puntare la pistola contro qn; **to turn one's back on sb** (*also fig*) voltare le spalle a qn; **to turn one's back on the past** tagliare i ponti col passato; **as soon as his back is turned** non appena volta le spalle; **power/success turned his head** il potere/il successo gli ha dato alla testa; **without**

turning a hair senza battere ciglio; **to turn the other cheek** (*fig*) porgere l'altra guancia; **he turned his hand to cookery** si è dato alla cucina; **to turn the tables on sb** (*fig*) capovolgere la situazione a danno di qn; **they turned him against us** ce l'hanno messo contro 4 (*go past, round*) girare, voltare; **the car turned the corner** la macchina ha voltato l'angolo; **to have turned the corner** (*fig*) aver superato la fase critica; **he's turned 50** ha passato i 50; **it's turned four o'clock** sono le quattro passate 5 (*change*): **to turn sb/sth into sth** trasformare qn/qc in qc; **to turn iron into gold** trasformare il ferro in oro; **to turn a book into a film** fare un film da un libro; **it turned him into a bitter man** lo ha reso un uomo pieno d'amarezza; **the shock turned her hair white** le sono venuti i capelli bianchi dallo shock; **the heat has turned the milk** il caldo ha fatto andare a male il latte 6 (*shape: wood, metal*) tornire; **to turn wood on a lathe** lavorare il legno con il tornio; **a well-turned phrase** un'espressione molto elegante; **a well-turned ankle** una caviglia ben tornita ♦ VI 1 (*rotate*) girare; (*change direction: person*) girarsi, voltarsi; (: *vehicle*) girare, svoltare; (: *ship*) virare; (: *wind, tide, weather*) cambiare; (*reverse direction*) girare indietro; **my head is turning** (*fig*) mi gira la testa; **everything turns on his decision** (*fig*) tutto dipende dalla sua decisione; **to turn and go back** girare *or* girarsi e tornare indietro; **to turn left/right** (*Aut*) girare a sinistra/destra; **turn right at the lights** al semaforo gira a destra; **the car turned into a lane** la macchina ha svoltato in una stradina; **to wait for the weather to turn** aspettare che il tempo cambi; **he turned to me and smiled** si è girato verso di me e mi ha sorriso; **to turn to sb for help** rivolgersi a qn per un aiuto; **she has no-one to turn to** non ha nessuno cui potersi rivolgere; **he turned to politics** si è messo in politica, si è dato alla politica; **he turned to drink** si è dato al bere; **I don't know which way to turn** (*fig*) non so dove sbattere la testa; **the conversation turned to religion** la conversazione passò alla religione 2 (*become*) diventare; (*change*): **to turn into sth** trasformarsi in qc, cambiare in qc; **the vacation turned into a nightmare** la vacanza si è trasformata in un incubo; **the milk has turned** il latte è andato a male; **to turn red** arrossire; **to turn nasty** diventare cattivo(-a); **when he's drunk he turns nasty** quando è ubriaco diventa cattivo; **he turned into a cynic** è diventato un cinico; **they turned communist** sono diventati comunisti; **a singer turned songwriter** un cantante divenuto autore

▸ **turn about, turn around** VI + ADV girarsi indietro

▸ **turn against** VI + PREP: **to turn against sb** mettersi contro qn

▸ **turn aside** VI + ADV girarsi *or* voltarsi dall'altra parte

▸ **turn away** VI + ADV girarsi *or* voltarsi dall'altra parte; **he turned away from the awful sight** ha distolto lo sguardo da quel tremendo spettacolo ♦ VT + ADV 1 (*move: eyes*) distogliere; (: *head*) girare dall'altra parte; (: *gun*) spostare 2 (*reject: person*) mandar via; (: *business*) rifiutare

▸ **turn back** VI + ADV 1 (*on journey*) ritornare, tornare indietro; **we turned back** siamo tornati indietro 2 (*in book*) ritornare ♦ VT + ADV 1 (*fold: bedclothes*) ripiegare 2 (*send back*) far tornare indietro; **to turn back the clock 20 years** ritornare indietro di 20 anni

▸ **turn down** VT + ADV 1 (*fold: bedclothes, collar, page*) ripiegare 2 (*reduce: gas, heat, volume*) abbassare; **should I turn the heating down?** abbasso il riscaldamento? 3 (*refuse: offer*) rifiutare; (*candidate*) scartare; **he turned down the offer** ha rifiutato l'offerta

▸ **turn in** VI + ADV 1 **to turn in (to)** girare (in); **she turned in at the house** ha girato per entrare nella casa 2 (*fam: go to bed*) andare a letto ♦ VT + ADV 1 (*hand over*) consegnare; **to turn sb in** consegnare qn alla polizia 2 (*fold*) voltare in dentro

▸ **turn off** VI + ADV 1 (*from road*) girare, voltare 2 (*appliance, machine*) spegnersi ♦ VT + ADV 1 (*light, radio, machine*) spegnere; (*tap*) chiudere; **I'll turn off the radio** spegnerò la radio; **you haven't turned off the tap** non hai chiuso il rubinetto 2 (*fam: also sexually*) fare schifo a

▸ **turn on** VI + ADV (*appliance*) accendersi ♦ VT + ADV 1 (*light, radio, electricity*) accendere; (*tap*) aprire; (*engine*) avviare; **shall I turn on the light?** accendo la luce?; **she turned**

on the tap ha aperto il rubinetto 2 (*fam: person: also sexually*) eccitare

▸ **turn out** VI + ADV 1 (*appear, attend: troops, doctor*) presentarsi; **to turn out for a meeting** presentarsi a un'assemblea 2 (*prove to be*) rivelarsi; **it turned out to be true/a mistake** è risultato essere vero/un errore; **things will turn out all right** andrà tutto bene; **how did the cake turn out?** come è venuta la torta?; **it turned out that ...** si è scoperto che...; **it turned out that she was right** è risultato che aveva ragione lei ♦ VT + ADV 1 (*light, appliance, gas*) chiudere, spegnere 2 (*produce: goods*) produrre; (: *novel, good pupils*) creare; **to be well turned out** (*fig*) essere ben vestito(-a) 3 (*empty: pockets*) vuotare; (*tip out: cake*) capovolgere 4 (*clean out: room*) dare una bella pulita a 5 (*expel: tenant, employee*) mandar via 6 (*guard, police*) far uscire

▸ **turn over** VI + ADV 1 (*person*) girarsi; (*car*) capovolgersi; (*engine*) girare; **my stomach turned over** mi si è rivoltato lo stomaco; **she turned over onto her back** si è girata sulla schiena 2 (*in reading*) girare *or* voltare la pagina; (*in letter*): **please turn over** segue ♦ VT + ADV 1 (*page, mattress, card*) girare; (*patient*) far girare; **to turn sth over in one's mind** riflettere a lungo *or* rimurginare su qualcosa 2 (*hand over: object, person*) consegnare

▸ **turn round** VI + ADV 1 (*person*) girarsi; (*vehicle*) girare 2 (*rotate*) girare; **to turn round and round** girare su se stesso(-a) ♦ VT + ADV girare

▸ **turn up** VI + ADV 1 (*lost object*) saltar fuori; (*person*) arrivare, presentarsi; **something will turn up** salterà fuori qualcosa; **the painting turned up in an old house in Devon** il dipinto è saltato fuori in una vecchia casa nel Devon; **we waited but she didn't turn up** abbiamo aspettato ma non si è fatta vedere 2 (*point towards*) essere rivolto(-a) all'insù; **his nose turns up** ha il naso all'insù ♦ VT + ADV 1 (*collar, sleeve, hem*) alzare, tirare su; **to turn up one's nose at sth** (*fig*) arricciare il naso davanti a qc 2 (*heat, gas, radio*) alzare; **can you turn up the volume?** puoi alzare il volume? 3 (*find*) scoprire

turn·about ['tɜːnəbaʊt], **turn·around** ['tɜːnəraʊnd] N (*fig*) voltafaccia *m inv*, dietrofront *m inv*

turn·coat ['tɜːnkəʊt] N voltagabbana *m/f inv*

turned-up [ˌtɜːnd'ʌp] ADJ (*nose*) all'insù

turn·ing ['tɜːnɪŋ] N (*side road*) strada laterale; (*fork*) biforcazione *f*; (*bend*) curva; **the first turning on the right** la prima a destra; **we took the wrong turning** abbiamo sbagliato strada

turning circle, (*USA*) **turning radius** N diametro di sterzata

turning point N (*fig*) svolta decisiva; (*Math*) punto di ondulazione

tur·nip ['tɜːnɪp] N rapa

turn·out ['tɜːnaʊt] N 1 (*attendance*) presenza, affluenza; **there was a poor turnout** la partecipazione è stata molto scarsa 2 (*clean*) ripulita

turn·over ['tɜːnəʊvə] N 1 (*Comm: amount of money*) giro d'affari; (: *of goods*) smercio; **an annual turnover of ten million pounds** un giro d'affari annuo di dieci milioni di sterline; **these goods have a rapid turnover** di questi prodotti c'è grande smercio; **there is an extremely high turnover in staff** c'è un ricambio molto rapido di personale 2 (*Culin*): **apple turnover** ≈ sfogliatella alle mele

turn·pike ['tɜːnpaɪk] N (*USA: Aut*) autostrada (a pagamento)

turn·stile ['tɜːnstaɪl] N cancelletto girevole, tornella

turn·table ['tɜːnteɪbl] N (*of record player*) piatto; (*for trains*) piattaforma girevole

turn-up ['tɜːnʌp] N 1 (*Brit: of trousers*) risvolto 2 **that was a turn-up for the books** (*Brit fam*) è stato un colpo di scena

tur·pen·tine ['tɜːpəntaɪn] N trementina; **turpentine substitute** acquaragia

tur·quoise ['tɜːkwɔɪz] N (*stone, colour*) turchese *m* ♦ ADJ (*ring, earrings*) di turchesi; (*colour*) (color) turchese *inv*

tur·ret ['tʌrɪt] N torretta

tur·tle ['tɜːtl] N 1 testuggine *f*, tartaruga acquatica; **to turn turtle** (*boat*) scuffiare ♦ ADJ (*soup*) di tartaruga

turtle·neck ['tɜːtlˌnek] N (*also:* **turtleneck sweater**) maglione *m* con il collo alto

Tus·can ['tʌskən] ADJ toscano(-a) ♦ N (*person*) toscano(-a); (*dialect*) toscano

Tus·ca·ny ['tʌskənɪ] N la Toscana

tusk [tʌsk] N zanna

tus·sle ['tʌsl] N baruffa, mischia; **to have a tussle with** fare baruffa con; **a tussle with the goalie** uno scontro con il portiere; **a legal tussle** una battaglia legale ♦ VI: **to tussle (with sb for sth)** far baruffa (con qn per qc)

tu·tor ['tjuːtəʳ] N (*private teacher*) insegnante *m/f* privato(-a); (*living with family*) precettore *m*; (*Brit: Univ*) docente *m/f* (*responsabile di un gruppo*) ♦ VT: **to tutor sb in Italian** dare lezioni private d'italiano a qn

tu·to·rial [tjuːˈtɔːrɪəl] N (*Univ*) seminario, esercitazione *f* (*di un gruppo limitato*)

tux·edo [tʌkˈsiːdəʊ] N (*USA*) smoking *m inv*

TV [ˌtiːˈviː] N ABBR (= *television*) TV *f inv*, tivù *f inv*

.TV dinner N *pasto veloce da mangiare davanti alla TV*

twad·dle ['twɒdl] N (*fam*) scemenze *fpl*

twang [twæŋ] N (*of wire, bow*) suono acuto; (*of instrument*) suono vibrante; (*of voice*) accento nasale; **to speak with a twang** parlare con voce nasale ♦ VT (*guitar*) pizzicare le corde di ♦ VI vibrare

tweak [twiːk] N: **to give sb's nose/ear a tweak** dare un pizzicotto sul naso/una tirata d'orecchie a qn ♦ VT (*nose*) pizzicare; (*ear, hair*) tirare

tweed [twiːd] N (*cloth*) tweed *m*; **tweeds** NPL (*suit*) abito di tweed

tweet [twiːt] VI cinguettare ♦ VT (*Comput: on Twitter*) postare un tweet

twee·zers ['twiːzəz] NPL pinzette *fpl*

twelfth [twelfθ] ADJ dodicesimo(-a); **the twelfth floor** il dodicesimo piano; **the twelfth of August** il dodici agosto ♦ N (*in series*) dodicesimo(-a); (*fraction*) dodicesimo

Twelfth Night N la notte dell'Epifania

twelve [twelv] ADJ, N dodici *m inv*; **at twelve** alle dodici, a mezzogiorno; (*midnight*) a mezzanotte; **she's twelve** ha dodici anni

twen·ti·eth ['twentɪɪθ] ADJ ventesimo(-a); **the twentieth floor** il ventesimo piano; **the twentieth of May** il venti maggio ♦ N (*in series*) ventesimo(-a); (*fraction*) ventesimo

twen·ty ['twentɪ] ADJ venti *inv* ♦ N venti *m inv*; **he's twenty** ha vent'anni

twerp [twɜːp] N (*fam*) idiota *m/f*

twice [twaɪs] ADV due volte; **I tried twice** ho provato due volte; **twice as much, twice as many** il doppio, due volte tanto; **I have twice as many cigarettes as you** ho il doppio delle sigarette che hai tu; **there's twice as much wine here as beer** qui c'è vino in quantità due volte superiori alla birra; **twice a week** due volte alla settimana; **she is twice your age** ha il doppio dei tuoi anni; **twice as big** due volte più grande

twid·dle ['twɪdl] VT, VI: **to twiddle (with) sth** giocherellare con qc; **he was twiddling with the controls** stava giocherellando con i comandi; **to twiddle one's thumbs** (*fig*) girarsi i pollici

twig¹ [twɪg] N ramoscello

twig² [twɪg] VT, VI (*fam*) capire

twi·light ['twaɪlaɪt] N (*evening, also fig*) crepuscolo; (*morning*) alba; **at twilight** al crepuscolo, all'alba; **in the twilight** nella penombra

twill [twɪl] N (*fabric*) twill *m*, spigato

twin [twɪn] ADJ gemello(-a); **my twin brother** mio fratello gemello; **twin lead** (*Elec*) piattina ♦ N gemello(-a) ♦ VT: **to twin one town with another** fare il gemellaggio di una città con un'altra

twin-bedded [ˌtwɪnˈbedɪd] ADJ (*room*) a due letti

twin beds NPL letti *mpl* gemelli

twin-carburettor [ˌtwɪnkɑːbjʊˈretəʳ] ADJ a doppio carburatore

twine [twaɪn] N cordicella, spago ♦ VT intrecciare ♦ VI (*plant*) attorcigliarsi

twin-engined [ˌtwɪnˈendʒɪnd] ADJ a due motori; **twin-engined aircraft** bimotore *m*

twinge [twɪndʒ] N (*of pain*) fitta; **a twinge in my back** una fitta alla schiena; **a twinge of regret/sadness/conscience** una punta di rimpianto/tristezza/rimorso; **I've been having twinges of conscience** ho i rimorsi di coscienza

twin·kle ['twɪŋkl] N scintillio; **he had a twinkle in his eye** gli brillavano gli occhi ♦ VI scintillare; (*eyes*) brillare

twin room N (*also:* **twin-bedded room**) stanza a due letti

twin town N città *f inv* gemellata

twirl [twɜːl] N (*of body*) piroetta; (*in writing*) ghirigoro ♦ VT (*also:* **twirl round**) far roteare; (*knob*) far girare; (*moustache*) arricciare ♦ VI (*also:* **twirl round**) volteggiare, roteare

twist [twɪst] N **1** (*in wire, flex*) piega; (*of tobacco*) treccia; (*of paper*) cartoccio; (*of lemon*) fettina **2** (*twisting action*) torsione *f*; **to give sth a twist** far girare qc; **to give one's ankle/wrist a twist, twist one's ankle/wrist** (*Med*) slogarsi la caviglia/il polso; **with a quick twist of the wrist** con un rapido movimento del polso **3** (*bend*) svolta, piega; (*fig: in story*) sviluppo imprevisto; **a road full of twists and turns** una strada a zigzag or tutta a curve; **the plot has an unexpected twist** la trama ha uno sviluppo inatteso; **to go round the twist** (*Brit fam*) ammattire, impazzire **4** (*dance*) il twist; **to do the twist** ballare il twist ♦ VT (*wrench out of shape*) far piegare, deformare; (*fig: sense, words*) travisare, distorcere; (*turn*) girare; (*unscrew*) svitare; (*weave: also:* **twist together**) intrecciare; (*roll around*) arrotolare; **you're twisting my words** stai travisando le mie parole; **she twisted her head sideways** ha girato la testa di lato; **to twist (round)** (*coil*) attorcigliare (intorno a); **his face was twisted with pain** il suo volto era contratto dal dolore; **to twist one's ankle/neck/wrist** (*Med*) slogarsi la caviglia/il collo/il polso; **to twist sb's arm** (*fig*) forzare qn ♦ VI **1** (*rope*) attorcigliarsi; (*road*) snodarsi; **the road twisted and turned** la strada procedeva a zigzag **2** (*dance*) ballare il twist

▸ **twist off** VT + ADV svitare

▸ **twist round** VI + ADV (*person*) girarsi, voltarsi; (*thing*) arrotolarsi; (*road*) serpeggiare ♦ VT + ADV (*words*) travisare ♦ VT + PREP: **to twist sth round sth** mettere qc intorno a qc, avvolgere qc in qc; **to twist sb round one's little finger** (*fam*) rigirare qn

twist·ed ['twɪstɪd] ADJ (*wire, rope*) attorcigliato(-a); (*ankle, wrist*) slogato(-a); (*fig: logic, mind*) contorto(-a); **the twisted metal of the car** le lamiere contorte della macchina

twit [twɪt] N (*fam*) cretino(-a)

twitch [twɪtʃ] N (*slight pull*) tiratina; (*nervous*) tic *m inv*; **to give sth a twitch** dare una tiratina a qc ♦ VI (*hands, face, muscles*) contrarsi; (*person: in particular situation*) agitarsi; (: *habitually*) avere un tic; (*tail, ears*) drizzarsi; (*nose*) muoversi ♦ VT (*rope, sleeve*) tirare; **the dog twitched its ears** il cane drizzò le orecchie; **the rabbit twitched its nose** il coniglio arricciò il naso

two [tuː] ADJ due *inv* ♦ N due *m inv*; **she's two** ha due anni; **to break sth in two** spezzare qc in due; **two by two, in twos** a due a due; **to arrive in twos and threes** arrivare alla spicciolata; **to put two and two together** (*fig*) fare uno più uno, trarre le conclusioni; **that makes two of us** e così siamo in due

two-bit ['tuːˌbɪt] ADJ (*esp USA: fam, pej*) da quattro soldi

two-door [ˌtuːˈdɔːʳ] ADJ (*car*) a due porte

two-faced [ˌtuːˈfeɪst] ADJ (*fig: pej: person*) doppio(-a), falso(-a)

two·fold ['tuːfəʊld] ADV: **to increase twofold** aumentare del doppio ♦ ADJ (*increase*) doppio(-a); (*reply*) in due punti; **the purpose of the visit is twofold** lo scopo della nostra visita è duplice

two-piece ['tuːpiːs] ADJ a due pezzi ♦ N (*also:* **two-piece suit**) due pezzi *m inv*; (*also:* **two-piece swimsuit**) (costume *m* da bagno a) due pezzi, *m inv*

two-seater [ˌtuːˈsiːtəʳ] N (*car*) macchina a due posti; (*plane*) biposto

two·some ['tuːsəm] N (*people*) coppia; **to go out in a twosome** uscire in coppia

two-stroke ['tuːstrəʊk] N (*engine*) due tempi *m inv* ♦ ADJ a due tempi

two-tone ['tuːtəʊn] ADJ (*colour*) bicolore

two-way ['tuːweɪ] ADJ (*street*) a doppio senso; (*traffic*) a doppio senso di circolazione; **two-way radio** radio *f inv* ricetrasmittente

TX ABBR (*USA Post:* = **Texas**)

ty·coon [taɪˈkuːn] N: **(business) tycoon** magnate *m*

type [taɪp] N 1 (*gen, also Bio*) tipo; (*sort*) genere *m*, tipo; (*model*) modello; (*make: of tea, machine*) marca; **what type do you want?** che tipo vuole?; **what type of camera have you got?** che tipo di macchina fotografica hai?; **what type of person is he?** che tipo è?; **he's not my type** non è il mio tipo; **it's my type of film** è il mio genere di film; **he's a pleasant type** è un tipo piacevole 2 (*Typ: one letter*) carattere *m* (tipografico); (*: letters collectively*) caratteri (tipografici), tipi *mpl*; **in bold/italic type** in grassetto/corsivo ♦ VT 1 (*also:* **type out, type up:** *letter*) battere (a macchina), dattilografare 2 (*disease*) classificare ♦ VI dattilografare, battere a macchina

type-cast [ˈtaɪpˌkɑːst] ADJ (*actor*) a ruolo fisso

type·face [ˈtaɪpˌfeɪs] N carattere *m* (tipografico)

type·script [ˈtaɪpˌskrɪpt] N dattiloscritto

type·set [ˈtaɪpˌsɛt] VT comporre

type·set·ter [ˈtaɪpˌsɛtə'] N compositore *m*

type·writ·er [ˈtaɪpˌraɪtə'] N macchina da scrivere

type·writ·ten [ˈtaɪpˌrɪtn] ADJ dattiloscritto(-a), battuto(-a) a macchina

ty·phoid [ˈtaɪfɔɪd] N febbre *f* tifoidea

ty·phoon [taɪˈfuːn] N tifone *m*

ty·phus [ˈtaɪfəs] N tifo

typi·cal [ˈtɪpɪkəl] ADJ tipico(-a); **a typical case/example** un

caso/esempio tipico; **(isn't that just) typical!** tipico!; **that's typical of her!** questo è tipico di lei!

typi·cal·ly [ˈtɪpɪkəlɪ] ADV tipicamente; **typically, he arrived home late** come al solito è arrivato a casa tardi

typi·fy [ˈtɪpɪfaɪ] VT (*thing*) essere tipico(-a) di, caratterizzare; (*person*) impersonare

typ·ing [ˈtaɪpɪŋ] N (*skill*) dattilografia; **have you finished that typing?** hai finito quelle cose che dovevi battere a macchina? ♦ ADJ (*lesson*) di dattilografia; (*paper*) per macchina da scrivere

typing pool N ufficio *m* dattilografia, *inv*

typ·ist [ˈtaɪpɪst] N dattilografo(-a)

typo [ˈtaɪpəʊ] N ABBR (*fam:* = *typographical error*) refuso

ty·pog·ra·phy [taɪˈpɒɡrəfɪ] N tipografia

tyr·an·ny [ˈtɪrənɪ] N tirannia

ty·rant [ˈtaɪərənt] N tiranno

tyre, tire (*USA*) [ˈtaɪə'] N (*Aut*) gomma, pneumatico

tyre pressure, (*USA*) **tire pressure** N pressione *f* (dei pneumatici)

Ty·rol [tɪˈrəʊl] N: **the Tyrol** il Tirolo

Ty·ro·lean [ˌtɪrəʊˈliːən], **Tyro·lese** [ˌtɪrəˈliːz] ADJ, N tirolese *m*/*f*

Tyrrhenian Sea [tɪˌriːnɪənˈsiː] N: **the Tyrrhenian Sea** il mar Tirreno

Uu

U¹, u¹ [juː] N (*letter*) U, u *f inv*, *m inv*; **U for Uncle** ≈ U come Udine

U² [juː] N ABBR (*Brit: Cine*: = *universal*) per tutti

UAW [ˌjuːeɪˈdʌbljuː] N ABBR (*USA*: = *United Automobile Workers*) sindacato dei lavoratori del settore automobilistico

U-bend [ˈjuːˌbend] N (*in pipe*) gomito

ubiqui·tous [juːˈbɪkwɪtəs] ADJ (*frm*) onnipresente

ud·der [ˈʌdəʳ] N mammella (*di animale*)

UEFA [juːˈeɪfə] N ABBR (= *Union of European Football Associations*) UEFA *f*

UFO [ˈjuːefˈəʊ] N ABBR (= *unidentified flying object*) ufo *m inv*

Ugan·da [juːˈɡændə] N Uganda

Ugan·dan [juːˈɡændən] ADJ, N ugandese *m/f*

ugh [ɜːh] EXCL puah!

ug·li·ness [ˈʌɡlɪnɪs] N bruttezza

ugly [ˈʌɡlɪ] ADJ (*comp* -**ier**, *superl* -**iest**) **1** (*not pretty*) brutto(-a); **as ugly as sin** brutto(-a) come la fame **2** (*nasty: situation, incident*) brutto(-a); (: *rumour*) inquietante; (: *mood, look*) minaccioso(-a); (: *crime, sight*) ripugnante; (: *vice*) osceno(-a)

UHF [ˌjuːeɪtʃˈef] N ABBR (= *ultra-high frequency*) UHF *f*

UK [ˌjuːˈkeɪ] N ABBR (= *United Kingdom*): **the UK** il Regno Unito

Ukraine [juːˈkreɪn] N Ucraina

Ukrainian [juːˈkreɪnɪən] ADJ ucraino(-a) ♦ N ucraino(-a); (*language*) ucraino

ul·cer [ˈʌlsəʳ] N (*gen*) ulcera, ulcerazione *f*; (*stomach*) ulcer ulcera gastrica, ulcera allo stomaco; **mouth ulcer** afta

Ul·ster [ˈʌlstəʳ] N Ulster *m*

ul·te·ri·or [ʌlˈtɪərɪəʳ] ADJ recondito(-a); **ulterior motive** secondo fine *m*
   ❑ **ulterior** is not translated by the Italian word *ulteriore*

ul·ti·ma·ta [ˌʌltɪˈmeɪtə] (*frm*) NPL *of* **ultimatum**

ul·ti·mate [ˈʌltɪmɪt] ADJ **1** (*final: result, outcome*) finale; (: *conclusion*) definitivo(-a); (: *destination*) ultimo(-a) **2** (*greatest: insult*) massimo(-a); (: *authority*) supremo(-a), massimo(-a); **the ultimate deterrent** (*Mil*) il mezzo di dissuasione risolutivo; **the ultimate challenge** la sfida suprema **3** (*principle, cause*) fondamentale ♦ N: **the ultimate in luxury** il non plus ultra del lusso

ul·ti·mate·ly [ˈʌltɪmɪtlɪ] ADV (*in the end, eventually*) in fin dei conti, in definitiva; (*in the last analysis*) in ultima analisi; (*at last*) alla fine; **ultimately, it's your decision** in fin dei conti, la decisione è tua; **to be ultimately responsible for sth** dover rispondere per primi di qc
   ❑ **ultimately** is not translated by the Italian word *ultimamente*

ul·ti·ma·tum [ˌʌltɪˈmeɪtəm] N (*pl* **ultimatums** *or* **ultimata** [ˌʌltɪˈmeɪtə]) (*Mil, also fig*) ultimatum *m inv*; **to issue an ultimatum to** dare l'ultimatum a

ultra·son·ic [ˌʌltrəˈsɒnɪk] ADJ ultrasonico(-a)

ultra·sound [ˌʌltrəˈsaʊnd] N (*Med*) ecografia

ultra·vio·let [ˌʌltrəˈvaɪəlɪt] ADJ ultravioletto(-a)

um·bili·cal [ʌmbɪˈlaɪkəl] ADJ ombelicale

um·brage [ˈʌmbrɪdʒ] N: **to take umbrage (at sth)** adombrarsi (a *or* per qc), risentirsi (di *or* per qc)

um·brel·la [ʌmˈbrelə] N ombrello; **under the umbrella of** (*fig*) sotto l'egida di; **an umbrella organization** un'organizzazione a cui fanno capo diverse altre

um·laut [ˈʊmlaʊt] N (*Ling*) umlaut *m inv*

um·pire [ˈʌmpaɪəʳ] N arbitro ♦ VI arbitrare ♦ VT arbitrare

ump·teen [ˈʌmptiːn] ADJ (*fam*) non so quanti(-e), innumerevole; **umpteen times** centomila volte *fpl*, non so quante volte

UN [ˌjuːˈen] N ABBR (= *United Nations*): **the UN** le Nazioni Unite, l'ONU *f*

un·abashed [ˌʌnəˈbæʃt] ADJ imperterrito(-a)

un·abat·ed [ˌʌnəˈbeɪtɪd] ADJ (*energy, enthusiasm*) costante, inesauribile; **to be** *or* **continue unabated** (*storm, wind*) non accennare a diminuire; (*fighting*) senza tregua

un·able [ʌnˈeɪbl] ADJ: **to be unable to do sth** (*not to know how to*) non saper fare qc, non essere capace di fare qc; (*not to have it in one's power to*) non poter fare qc, essere nell'impossibilità di fare qc; **unfortunately, he was unable to come** purtroppo non è potuto venire

un·abridged [ˌʌnəˈbrɪdʒd] ADJ integrale

un·ac·cep·table [ˌʌnəkˈsɛptəbl] ADJ (*proposal, behaviour*) inaccettabile; (*price*) impossibile; **it's unacceptable that** è inammissibile che + *sub*

un·ac·com·pa·nied [ˌʌnəˈkʌmpənɪd] ADJ (*child, person*) non accompagnato(-a); (*luggage*) incustodito(-a); (*singing, song*) senza accompagnamento; (*violin*) solo(-a)

un·ac·count·ably [ˌʌnəˈkaʊntəblɪ] ADV (*inexplicably*) inesplicabilmente, inspiegabilmente

un·ac·count·ed [ˌʌnəˈkaʊntɪd] ADJ: **unaccounted for** mancante; **two passengers are unaccounted for** due passeggeri mancano all'appello

un·ac·cus·tomed [ˌʌnəˈkʌstəmd] ADJ **1** (*unused to*): **to be unaccustomed to sth/to doing** non essere abituato(-a) a qc/a fare **2** (*unwonted*) insolito(-a); **with unaccustomed zeal** con insolito zelo

un·ac·quaint·ed [ˌʌnəˈkweɪntɪd] ADJ: **to be unacquainted with** (*facts*) ignorare, non essere al corrente di; (*poverty*) non aver mai conosciuto

un·adul·ter·at·ed [ˌʌnəˈdʌltəˌreɪtɪd] ADJ (*water, nonsense*) puro(-a); (*wine*) non sofisticato(-a)

un·af·fect·ed [ˌʌnəˈfɛktɪd] ADJ **1** (*sincere*) naturale, spontaneo(-a); (*manner, voice*) non affettato(-a); (*gratitude*) sincero(-a) **2** (*unchanged*): **to be unaffected by** non essere toccato(-a) da; **she was wholly unaffected by the news** la notizia non le ha fatto né caldo né freddo

un·afraid [ˌʌnəˈfreɪd] ADJ: **to be unafraid** non aver paura

un·aid·ed [ʌnˈeɪdɪd] ADV senza aiuto ♦ ADJ: **by his own unaided efforts** con le sue sole forze, senza l'aiuto di nessuno

una·nim·ity [ˌjuːnəˈnɪmɪtɪ] N unanimità

unani·mous [juːˈnænɪməs] ADJ unanime

unani·mous·ly [juːˈnænɪməslɪ] ADV all'unanimità

un·an·swered [ʌnˈɑːnsəd] ADJ (*question, letter*) senza risposta; (*criticism*) non contestato(-a)

un·ap·pe·tiz·ing [ʌnˈæpɪtaɪzɪŋ] ADJ poco appetitoso(-a)

un·ap·pre·cia·tive [ˌʌnəˈpriːʃɪətɪv] ADJ che non sa apprezzare; **an unappreciative audience** un pubblico indifferente

un·armed [ʌnˈɑːmd] ADJ (*person*) disarmato(-a)

un·ashamed [ˌʌnəˈʃeɪmd] ADJ (*brazen*) sfrontato(-a), sfacciato(-a)

un·as·sist·ed [ˌʌnəˈsɪstɪd] ADJ, ADV senza nessun aiuto

un·as·sum·ing [ˌʌnəˈsjuːmɪŋ] ADJ modesto(-a), senza pretese

un·at·tached [ˌʌnəˈtætʃt] ADJ (*part*) staccato(-a); (*not married*) libero(-a), senza legami; (*independent*) indipendente, sciolto(-a)

un·at·tend·ed [ˌʌnəˈtɛndɪd] ADJ (*not looked after: luggage*) incustodito(-a); (: *patient, baby*) solo(-a), senza sorveglianza; **please do not leave your luggage unattended** si prega di non lasciare il bagaglio incustodito

un·at·trac·tive [ˌʌnəˈtræktɪv] ADJ (*person*) poco attraente; (*offer*) poco allettante; (*place*) privo(-a) di attrattiva

un·author·ized [ʌnˈɔːθəˌraɪzd] ADJ non autorizzato(-a)

un·avail·able [ˌʌnəˈveɪləbl] ADJ (*article, room, book*) non disponibile; (*person*) impegnato(-a)

un·avoid·able [ˌʌnəˈvɔɪdəbl] ADJ inevitabile

un·avoid·ably [ˌʌnəˈvɔɪdəblɪ] ADV (*detained*) per cause di forza maggiore

un·aware [ʌnəˈwɛəʳ] ADJ: **to be unaware of sth/that …** non rendersi conto di *or* ignorare qc/che…; **she was unaware of the regulations** non era a conoscenza del regolamento

un·awares [ʌnəˈwɛəz] ADV: **to catch** *or* **take sb unawares** prendere qn alla sprovvista

un·bal·anced [ʌnˈbælənst] ADJ non equilibrato(-a); *(mentally)* squilibrato(-a)

un·bear·able [ʌnˈbɛərəbl] ADJ insopportabile

un·beat·able [ʌnˈbiːtəbl] ADJ imbattibile

un·beat·en [ʌnˈbiːtn] ADJ *(team, army)* imbattuto(-a); *(record)* insuperato(-a)

un·be·com·ing [ʌnbɪˈkʌmɪŋ] ADJ *(liter: unseemly: conduct, behaviour)* sconveniente; *(: unflattering: garment)* che non dona

un·be·known [ʌnbɪˈnəʊn], **un·be·knownst** [ʌnbɪˈnəʊnst] ADV *(old)*: **unbeknown to** all'insaputa di; **unbeknown to me** a mia insaputa

un·be·lief [ʌnbɪˈliːf] N incredulità

un·be·liev·able [ʌnbɪˈliːvəbl] ADJ incredibile; **it's unbelievable that** è incredibile che + *sub*

un·be·liev·ing·ly [ʌnbɪˈliːvɪŋlɪ] ADV con aria incredula; **he looked at me unbelievingly** mi ha guardato incredulo

un·bend [ʌnˈbend] *(pt, pp* **unbent** [ʌnˈbent]*)* VT *(pipe, wire)* raddrizzare ♦ VI *(fig: person)* distendersi, rilassarsi

un·bend·ing [ʌnˈbendɪŋ] ADJ *(fig)* inflessibile, rigido(-a)

un·bi·ased, unbiassed [ʌnˈbaɪəst] ADJ obiettivo(-a), imparziale

un·blem·ished [ʌnˈblemɪʃt] ADJ senza macchia

un·block [ʌnˈblɒk] VT *(pipe)* sbloccare

un·born [ʌnˈbɔːn] ADJ non ancora nato(-a)

un·bound·ed [ʌnˈbaʊndɪd] ADJ sconfinato(-a), senza limite

un·break·able [ʌnˈbreɪkəbl] ADJ infrangibile

un·bri·dled [ʌnˈbraɪdld] ADJ *(lust, ambition)* sfrenato(-a)

un·bro·ken [ʌnˈbrəʊkən] ADJ 1 *(intact)* intatto(-a), intero(-a); **his spirit remained unbroken** ha conservato un animo indomito 2 *(continuous: sleep, silence)* ininterrotto(-a); *(line of descent)* diretto(-a) 3 *(record)* insuperato(-a) 4 *(horse)* non domato(-a)

un·buck·le [ʌnˈbʌkl] VT slacciare

un·bur·den [ʌnˈbɜːdn] VT: **to unburden o.s. to sb** sfogarsi con qn

un·but·ton [ʌnˈbʌtn] VT sbottonare

uncalled-for [ʌnˈkɔːldfɔːʳ] ADJ *(remark)* fuori luogo *inv*; *(action)* ingiustificato(-a)

un·can·ny [ʌnˈkænɪ] ADJ *(comp* **-ier,** *superl* **-iest)** *(knack, resemblance)* sconcertante; *(sound, silence)* strano(-a), inquietante; **that's uncanny!** è strano!; **an uncanny resemblance** una rassomiglianza stupefacente

un·ceas·ing [ʌnˈsiːsɪŋ] ADJ incessante

un·cer·emo·ni·ous [ʌnsɛrɪˈməʊnɪəs] ADJ *(abrupt, rude)* brusco(-a); **in unceremonious haste** in modo sbrigativo

un·cer·tain [ʌnˈsɜːtn] ADJ *(person, future, result)* incerto(-a); *(aims)* vago(-a); *(temper)* instabile; **the future is uncertain** l'avvenire è incerto; **I'm uncertain about what to do** sono incerto sul da farsi; **it is uncertain whether** non è sicuro se; **he is uncertain whether** non sa bene se; **in no uncertain terms** chiaro e tondo, senza mezzi termini

un·cer·tain·ty [ʌnˈsɜːtntɪ] N *(of situation)* incertezza; *(confusion)* dubbi *mpl*; **the uncertainties of this life** le incognite della vita

un·chal·lenged [ʌnˈtʃælɪndʒd] ADJ *(gen, also Law)* incontestato(-a); **to go unchallenged** non venire contestato(-a), non trovare opposizione; **to let a remark go unchallenged** lasciar passare un'osservazione senza replicare

un·changed [ʌnˈtʃeɪndʒd] ADJ *(plans, situation)* immutato(-a), invariato(-a); **he's completely unchanged** non è cambiato minimamente

un·chari·table [ʌnˈtʃærɪtəbl] ADJ *(attitude)* poco generoso(-a), duro(-a); *(remark)* cattivo(-a)

un·chart·ed [ʌnˈtʃɑːtɪd] ADJ inesplorato(-a)

un·checked [ʌnˈtʃɛkt] ADJ 1 *(unrestrained: anger)* incontrollato(-a); **to go unchecked** *(abuse, violence)* rimanere incontrollato(-a); *(virus, inflation)* dilagare; **to advance unchecked** *(army)* avanzare senza incontrare opposizione 2 *(not verified: facts)* non controllato(-a), non verificato(-a); *(typescript)* non corretto(-a)

un·civi·lized [ʌnˈsɪvɪˌlaɪzd] ADJ *(tribe, people)* selvaggio(-a); *(behaviour, conditions)* incivile, barbaro(-a)

un·cle [ˈʌŋkl] N zio

un·clear [ʌnˈklɪəʳ] ADJ non chiaro(-a); **I'm still unclear about what I'm supposed to do** non ho ancora ben capito cosa dovrei fare

un·coil [ʌnˈkɔɪl] VT srotolare ♦ VI srotolarsi

un·com·fort·able [ʌnˈkʌmfətəbl] ADJ 1 *(person, chair)* scomodo(-a); *(afternoon)* poco piacevole; *(situation)* sgradevole; **an uncomfortable position** una posizione scomoda; **to have an uncomfortable time** passare un brutto quarto d'ora; **to make life uncomfortable for sb** rendere la vita difficile a qn 2 *(uneasy, embarrassed)* a disagio, non a proprio agio; **to make sb feel uncomfortable** mettere qn a disagio; **the way he talks makes me feel uncomfortable** il modo in cui parla mi mette a disagio; **I had an uncomfortable feeling that …** ho avuto la sgradevole sensazione che…

un·com·fort·ably [ʌnˈkʌmfətəblɪ] ADV 1 *(sit)* scomodamente; *(dressed)* in modo poco pratico; *(hot)* eccessivamente 2 *(uneasily: say)* con voce inquieta; *(: think)* con inquietudine; **uncomfortably close** a una vicinanza preoccupante

un·com·mit·ted [ʌnkəˈmɪtɪd] ADJ *(attitude, country)* neutrale; **to be uncommitted** *(person)* non essere impegnato(-a); **to remain uncommitted to** *(policy, party)* non dare la propria adesione a

un·com·mon [ʌnˈkɒmən] ADJ 1 *(unusual)* insolito(-a); *(rare)* non comune, raro(-a); **an uncommon name** un nome insolito; **it's not uncommon that** non è raro che + *sub* 2 *(outstanding)* fuori dal comune

un·com·mu·ni·ca·tive [ʌnkəˈmjuːnɪkətɪv] ADJ poco comunicativo(-a)

un·com·pli·cat·ed [ʌnˈkɒmplɪˌkeɪtɪd] ADJ semplice, poco complicato(-a)

un·com·pro·mis·ing [ʌnˈkɒmprəˌmaɪzɪŋ] ADJ *(honesty, dedication)* assoluto(-a); *(attitude)* intransigente

un·con·cerned [ʌnkənˈsɜːnd] ADJ *(unworried)* tranquillo(-a); **she seemed unconcerned** sembrava tranquilla; **to be unconcerned about** non darsi pensiero di, non preoccuparsi di *or* per; **to be unconcerned by** essere indifferente a

un·con·di·tion·al [ʌnkənˈdɪʃənl] ADJ *(surrender, refusal)* incondizionato(-a); *(freedom)* assoluto(-a)

un·con·gen·ial [ʌnkənˈdʒiːnɪəl] ADJ *(person)* poco simpatico(-a); *(surroundings, work)* poco piacevole

un·con·nect·ed [ʌnkəˈnɛktɪd] ADJ 1 *(unrelated)* senza connessione, senza rapporto; **to be unconnected with** essere estraneo(-a) a 2 *(incoherent)* sconnesso(-a)

un·con·scious [ʌnˈkɒnʃəs] ADJ 1 *(Med)* privo(-a) di sensi, svenuto(-a); **to fall unconscious** svenire, cadere (a terra) privo(-a) di sensi; **to knock sb unconscious** far perdere i sensi a qn con un colpo 2 *(unaware)*: **unconscious (of)** inconsapevole (di), ignaro(-a) (di) 3 *(unintentional: action, desire)* inconscio(-a) ♦ N *(Psych)*: **the unconscious** l'inconscio

un·con·scious·ly [ʌnˈkɒnʃəslɪ] ADV inconsciamente, senza rendersi conto

un·con·sti·tu·tion·al [ʌnkɒnstɪˈtjuːʃənl] ADJ *(frm)* anticostituzionale

un·con·test·ed [ʌnkənˈtɛstɪd] ADJ *(champion)* incontestato(-a); *(Pol: seat, election)* non disputato(-a)

un·con·trol·lable [ʌnkənˈtrəʊləbl] ADJ *(desire, epidemic)* incontrollabile; *(child)* indisciplinato(-a); *(laughter)* irrefrenabile; *(temper, reaction)* incontrollato(-a)

un·con·trolled [ʌnkənˈtrəʊld] ADJ *(laughter, weeping)* irrefrenabile; *(child, dog)* scatenato(-a); *(inflation, price rises)* incontenibile

un·con·ven·tion·al [ʌnkənˈvɛnʃənl] ADJ poco convenzionale

un·con·vinced [ʌnkənˈvɪnst] ADJ: **to be** *or* **remain unconvinced** non essere convinto(-a)

un·con·vinc·ing [ʌnkənˈvɪnsɪŋ] ADJ non convincente, poco persuasivo(-a)

un·cork [ʌnˈkɔːk] VT stappare

un·cor·robo·rat·ed [ʌnkəˈrɒbəˌreɪtɪd] ADJ *(evidence, confession)* non convalidato(-a)

un·couth [ʌnˈkuːθ] ADJ *(old)* maleducato(-a), rozzo(-a), villano(-a)

un·cov·er [ʌnˈkʌvəˈ] VT **1** (*find out*) scoprire; (*scandal*) portare alla luce **2** (*remove coverings of*) scoprire; (*drain*) scoperchiare

unc·tu·ous [ˈʌŋktjʊəs] ADJ (*liter*) untuoso(-a)

un·dam·aged [ʌnˈdæmɪdʒd] ADJ (*goods*) in buono stato; (*fig: reputation*) intatto(-a)

un·daunt·ed [ʌnˈdɔːntɪd] ADJ: **undaunted by** per nulla intimidito(-a) da; **to carry on undaunted** continuare imperterrito(-a)

un·de·cid·ed [ˌʌndɪˈsaɪdɪd] ADJ (*person*) indeciso(-a), incerto(-a); (*matter*) irrisolto(-a); **we are still undecided whether to go** siamo ancora indecisi se andare o meno

un·de·liv·ered [ˌʌndɪˈlɪvəd] ADJ non recapitato(-a); **if undelivered return to sender** in caso di mancato recapito rispedire al mittente

un·de·ni·able [ˌʌndɪˈnaɪəbl] ADJ innegabile, indiscutibile, fuori discussione

un·der [ˈʌndəˈ] PREP **1** (*beneath*) sotto; **under the table** sotto il tavolo; **from under the bed** da sotto il letto; **it's under there** sta lì sotto; **under water** sott'acqua; **the tunnel goes under the Channel** il tunnel passa sotto il Canale della Manica **2** (*less than*) meno di; (*in rank, scale*) al di sotto di; **in under 2 hours** in meno di 2 ore; **people under 50 (years old)** gente al di sotto dei 50 (anni); **under 20 people** meno di 20 persone **3** (*fig: sb's leadership, sign of zodiac, letter in catalogue*) sotto; **under anaesthetic** sotto anestesia; **under discussion/repair/construction** in discussione/riparazione/costruzione; **to study under sb** studiare con qn *or* sotto la guida di qn; **under the circumstances** date le circostanze; **under the Romans** sotto i Romani; **under a false name** sotto falso nome; **he has 30 workers under him** ha 30 operai sotto di sé **4** (*according to*) secondo; **under the new law** secondo quanto previsto dalla nuova legge; **under British law they have done nothing wrong** in base alla legge britannica non hanno fatto nulla di male ♦ ADV **1** (*beneath: position*) sotto; (: *direction*) sotto, di sotto; **to be under** (*under anaesthetic*) essere sotto anestesia **2** (*less*) al di sotto, meno; **girls of 11 and under** ragazze dai 11 anni in giù

under– [ˈʌndəˈ] PREF **1** (*in rank*) sotto-, aiuto; (*in age*): **the under-15s** i ragazzi al di sotto dei 15 anni; **undergardener** aiuto giardiniere *m* **2** (*insufficiently*) sotto-; **underprepared** poco preparato(-a); **undercooked** poco cotto(-a)

under·age [ˌʌndərˈeɪdʒ] ADJ minorenne; **he's underage** è minorenne

under·arm [ˈʌndərˌɑːm] ADV (*throw*) da sotto in su ♦ ADJ (*temperature*) ascellare; (*deodorant*) per le ascelle; (*bowling*) da sotto in su; **underarm hair** i peli delle ascelle; **underarm serve** (*Tennis*) servizio dal basso verso l'alto

under·capi·tal·ized [ˌʌndəˈkæpɪtəˌlaɪzd] ADJ (*Fin*) carente di capitali

under·carriage [ˈʌndəˌkærɪdʒ] N (*Brit: Aer*) carrello (d'atterraggio)

under·charge [ˌʌndəˈtʃɑːdʒ] VT far pagare di meno a

under·class [ˈʌndəˌklɑːs] N sottoproletariato

under·clothes [ˈʌndəˌkləʊðz] NPL biancheria *fsg* intima

under·cover [ˌʌndəˈkʌvəˈ] ADJ (*agent*) segreto(-a); (*meeting*) clandestino(-a); **an undercover agent** un agente segreto; **she was working undercover** agiva in incognito

under·cur·rent [ˈʌndəˌkʌrənt] N corrente *f* sottomarina; (*fig*) vena nascosta

under·cut [ˌʌndəˈkʌt] (*pt, pp* undercut) VT (*Comm*) vendere a minor prezzo di; **they were able to undercut their competitors** riuscivano a vendere a prezzi inferiori rispetto ai concorrenti; **they plan to undercut fares on some routes** introdurranno tariffe concorrenziali su alcune rotte

under·de·vel·oped [ˌʌndədɪˈveləpt] ADJ (*country*) sottosviluppato(-a); (*baby, muscles, photo*) non ben sviluppato(-a)

under·dog [ˈʌndəˌdɒg] N: **the underdog** (*in fight, contest*) il (la) più debole; (*in society*) l'oppresso(-a); (*in family, organization*) l'ultima ruota del carro; **Inter were the underdogs on this occasion** in quest'occasione l'Inter era la squadra sfavorita

under·done [ˌʌndəˈdʌn] ADJ (*Culin: food*) poco cotto(-a); (: *steak*) al sangue

under·employment [ˌʌndərɪmˈplɔɪmənt] N sottoccupazione *f*

under·es·ti·mate [ˌʌndərˈestɪˌmeɪt] VT sottovalutare

under·ex·posed [ˌʌndərɪksˈpəʊzd] ADJ (*Phot*) sottoesposto(-a)

under·fed [ˌʌndəˈfed] ADJ malnutrito(-a)

under·foot [ˌʌndəˈfʊt] ADV sotto i piedi, per terra; **to trample underfoot** (*also fig*) calpestare; **the children are always getting underfoot** i bambini sono sempre tra i piedi

under·funded [ˌʌndəˈfʌndɪd] ADJ insufficientemente sovvenzionato(-a)

under·go [ˌʌndəˈgəʊ] (*pt* underwent, *pp* undergone [ˌʌndəˈgɒn]) VT sottoporsi a, subire; **to undergo changes** essere sottoposto(-a) a modifiche; **to undergo training** seguire un corso di formazione; **the car is undergoing repairs** la macchina è in riparazione

under·gradu·ate [ˌʌndəˈgrædjʊɪt] N (*also:* undergrad) studente(-essa) universitario(-a); **a group of undergraduates** un gruppo di studenti universitari ♦ ADJ (*opinion, attitudes*) degli studenti; **undergraduate courses** corsi *mpl* di laurea

under·ground [*adj* ˈʌndəˌgraʊnd, *adv* ˌʌndəˈgraʊnd] ADJ (*passage, cave, railway*) sotterraneo(-a); (*fig: political movement, press*) clandestino(-a); (: *Art, Cine*) underground *inv*; **an underground parking garage** un parcheggio sotterraneo ♦ ADV sottoterra; (*fig*) clandestinamente; **moles live underground** le talpe vivono sottoterra; **to go underground** (*fig*) entrare in clandestinità ♦ N **1** (*Brit: Rail*): **the Underground** la metropolitana; **to go by underground** *or* **on the underground** andare in *or* con la metropolitana **2** (*Mil, Pol*): **the underground** il movimento clandestino, la resistenza; (*Art*) la controcultura, l'underground *m*

under·growth [ˈʌndəˌgrəʊθ] N sottobosco

under·hand [ˌʌndəˈhænd], **under·hand·ed** [ˌʌndəˈhændɪd] ADJ (*method*) equivoco(-a), poco pulito(-a); (*trick*) subdolo(-a), mancino(-a)

under·in·sured [ˌʌndərɪnˈʃʊəd] ADJ sottoassicurato(-a)

under·lie [ˌʌndəˈlaɪ] (*pt* underlay [ˌʌndəˈleɪ], *pp* underlain [ˌʌndəˈleɪn]) VT essere alla base di; **these objectives underlie his economic policy** questi obiettivi sono alla base della sua politica economica; **an underlying nervousness** un nervosismo di fondo; **the underlying cause** il motivo di fondo

under·line [ˌʌndəˈlaɪn] VT (*also fig*) sottolineare

under·ling [ˈʌndəlɪŋ] N (*pej*) galoppino, tirapiedi *m inv*

under·men·tioned [ˌʌndəˈmenʃənd] ADJ (riportato(-a)) qui sotto *or* qui di seguito

under·mine [ˌʌndəˈmaɪn] VT (*fig*) minare; (*authority*) pregiudicare

under·neath [ˌʌndəˈniːθ] PREP sotto, al di sotto di; **underneath the carpet** sotto la moquette ♦ ADV sotto, di sotto; **I got out of the car and looked underneath** sono sceso dalla macchina e ho guardato sotto ♦ N: **the underneath** la parte di sotto

under·nour·ished [ˌʌndəˈnʌrɪʃt] ADJ denutrito(-a)

under·paid [ˌʌndəˈpeɪd] PT, PP *of* underpay ♦ ADJ mal pagato(-a), sottopagato(-a)

under·pants [ˈʌndəˌpænts] NPL (*Brit*) mutande *fpl* da uomo; (*USA*) mutande *fpl* da donna

under·pass [ˈʌndəˌpɑːs] N (*for cars*) sottopassaggio; (*for pedestrians*) sottopassaggio pedonale

under·pin [ˌʌndəˈpɪn] VT (*Archit*) puntellare; (*fig: argument, case*) corroborare

under·play [ˌʌndəˈpleɪ] VT minimizzare; **to underplay a role** (*Theatre*) recitare una parte con misura

under·popu·lat·ed [ˌʌndəˈpɒpjʊˌleɪtd] ADJ scarsamente popolato(-a), sottopopolato(-a)

under·price [ˌʌndəˈpraɪs] VT vendere sottoprezzo

under·privi·leged [ˌʌndəˈprɪvɪlɪdʒd] ADJ svantaggiato(-a); **the underprivileged** i diseredati *mpl*

under·rate [ˌʌndəˈreɪt] VT sottovalutare

under·score [ˌʌndəˈskɔːˈ] VT sottolineare

under·seal [ˌʌndəˈsiːl] VT (*Aut*) trattare con antiruggine

under·sec·re·tary [ˌʌndəˈsekrətrɪ] N sottosegretario

under·sell [ˌʌndəˈsel] (*pt, pp* undersold) VT (*competitors*) vendere a prezzi più bassi di; (*fig*) non valorizzare a sufficienza

under·shirt [ˈʌndəˌʃɜːt] N (*USA*) maglietta, canottiera

under·shorts [ˈʌndəˌʃɔːts] NPL (*USA*) mutande *fpl* da uomo

under·side [ˈʌndəˌsaid] N parte *f* di sotto

under·signed [ˈʌndəˌsaind] ADJ, N sottoscritto(-a); **I the undersigned** io sottoscritto

under·skirt [ˈʌndəˌskɜːt] N sottogonna

under·staffed [ˌʌndəˈstɑːft] ADJ a corto di personale

under·stand [ˌʌndəˈstænd] (*pt, pp* **understood**) VT 1 (*gen*) capire; **to make o.s. understood** farsi capire; **do you understand?** capisci?; **I can't understand a word of it** non ci capisco un'acca; **I don't understand the question** non ho capito la domanda; **I don't understand why ...** non capisco perché...; **she understands children** capisce i bambini; **we understand one another** ci capiamo (tra di noi); **he doesn't understand how I feel** non capisce quello che provo; **I can understand his wanting to go** posso ben capire il suo desiderio di andarsene; **is that understood?** è chiaro?; **I wish it to be understood that ...** vorrei che fosse chiaro che...; **understood!** (*agreed*) intesi! 2 (*believe*) credere; **we understood we were to be paid** a quanto avevamo capito dovevamo essere pagati; **I understand you have been absent** mi risulta che lei è stato assente; **I understand you've heard about David** credo che tu abbia saputo di David; **it's understood that ...** resta inteso che...; **he let it be understood that he was leaving** ha dato a intendere che stava per partire; **she is understood to be ill** pare che stia poco bene ♦ VI capire; **I quite understand** capisco benissimo, s'immagini; **she was, I understand, a Catholic** era, se non sbaglio, cattolica

under·stand·able [ˌʌndəˈstændəbl] ADJ comprensibile

under·stand·ing [ˌʌndəˈstændɪŋ] ADJ (*person*) comprensivo(-a); (*smile*) indulgente ♦ N 1 (*intelligence*) comprensione *f*; **his understanding of the situation is that ...** il modo in cui vede la situazione è che...; **it was my understanding that** quello che ho capito io era che + *sub*; **it is our understanding that they wanted to participate** crediamo che lei volessero partecipare; **a basic understanding of computing** una conoscenza di base dell'informatica 2 (*sympathy*) simpatia, comprensione *f*; **thank you for your patience and understanding** grazie della sua pazienza e comprensione 3 (*agreement*) accordo, intesa; **to come to an understanding with sb** giungere ad un accordo con qn; **there was an understanding between us** tra noi c'era un accordo; **on the understanding that he pays** a patto che *or* a condizione che paghi tu

under·state [ˌʌndəˈsteit] VT minimizzare, sminuire

under·state·ment [ˌʌndəˈsteitmənt] N understatement *m inv*; **that's an understatement!** a dir poco!

under·stood [ˌʌndəˈstʊd] PT, PP *of* **understand** ♦ ADJ inteso(-a); (*implied*) sottinteso(-a)

under·study [ˈʌndəˌstʌdɪ] N (*Theatre*) doppio ♦ VT sostituire

under·take [ˌʌndəˈteik] (*pt* **undertook**, *pp* **undertaken** [ˌʌndəˈteikən]) VT (*task*) intraprendere; (*responsibility*) assumersi; **to undertake a task** assumersi un compito; **to undertake to do sth** impegnarsi a fare qc

under·tak·er [ˈʌndəˌteikəʳ] N impresario di pompe funebri

under·tak·ing [ˈʌndəˌteikɪŋ] N 1 (*task*) impresa; **a massive undertaking** una grossa impresa; **it is quite an undertaking!** è una bella impresa! 2 (*promise*) promessa, assicurazione *f*; **to give an undertaking that ...** dare la propria parola che...

under·tone [ˈʌndəˌtəʊn] N 1 (*low voice*) tono sommesso; **in an undertone** a mezza voce, sottovoce, a voce bassa 2 **undertones** NPL (*comic, religious*) sfumature *fpl*

under·value [ˌʌndəˈvæljuː] VT (*person, contribution*) svalutare, sottovalutare; (*Comm, Fin*) deprezzare, svalutare

under·wa·ter [ˈʌndəˈwɔːtəʳ] ADJ (*swimming, photography*) subacqueo(-a); (*exploration*) sottomarino(-a); **underwater photography** fotografia subacquea ♦ ADV sott'acqua; **this sequence was filmed underwater** questa scena è stata girata sott'acqua

under·way [ˈʌndəˈwei] ADJ **to be underway** essere in corso

under·wear [ˈʌndəˌwɛəʳ] N biancheria intima

under·weight [ˈʌndəˈweit] ADJ (*person*) sottopeso *inv*; (*thing*) al di sotto del giusto peso

under·went [ˌʌndəˈwɛnt] PT *of* **undergo**

under·world [ˈʌndəˌwɜːld] N: **the underworld** (*criminal*) la malavita; (*hell*) gli inferi *mpl*

under·write [ˈʌndəˌrait] (*pt* **underwrote** [ˈʌndəˌrəʊt], *pp* **underwritten** [ˈʌndəˌritn]) VT (*Fin*) sottoscrivere; (*Insurance*) assicurare

under·writ·er [ˈʌndəˌraitəʳ] N (*Insurance*) assicuratore (-trice); (*Fin*) sottoscrittore(-trice)

un·de·serv·ing [ˌʌndɪˈzɜːvɪŋ] ADJ: **to be undeserving of** non meritare, non essere degno(-a) di

un·de·sir·able [ˌʌndɪˈzaiərəbl] ADJ (*effects*) indesiderato(-a); (*behaviour, habits, friendship*) discutibile; **it is undesirable for students to ...** gli studenti non devono... ♦ N persona indesiderabile

un·de·vel·oped [ˌʌndɪˈvɛləpt] ADJ (*land, resources*) non sfruttato(-a)

un·dies [ˈʌndɪz] NPL (*fam*) biancheria *fsg* intima (*da donna*)

un·di·lut·ed [ˌʌndaiˈluːtɪd] ADJ (*concentrated*) non diluito(-a); (*fig: bliss, love*) totale, assoluto(-a)

un·dip·lo·matic [ˌʌndɪpləˈmætɪk] ADJ poco diplomatico(-a)

un·dis·charged [ˌʌndɪsˈtʃɑːdʒd] ADJ (*debt*) non pagato(-a); (*bankrupt*) non riabilitato(-a)

un·dis·ci·plined [ʌnˈdɪsɪplɪnd] ADJ indisciplinato(-a)

un·dis·guised [ˌʌndɪsˈgaizd] ADJ (*dislike, amusement*) palese

un·dis·put·ed [ˌʌndɪsˈpjuːtɪd] ADJ incontrastato(-a), indiscusso(-a)

un·dis·tin·guished [ˌʌndɪsˈtɪŋgwɪʃt] ADJ (*pej: person*) qualunque, mediocre; (*: career, design, performance*) mediocre; **an undistinguished poet** un poetucolo; **an undistinguished wine** un vino qualsiasi

un·dis·turbed [ˌʌndɪsˈtɜːbd] ADJ 1 (*sleep*) tranquillo(-a); **to work undisturbed** lavorare in pace; **to leave sth undisturbed** lasciare qc così com'è 2 (*unworried*): **undisturbed (by)** indifferente (a); **the Prime Minister is undisturbed by rising inflation** l'aumento dell'inflazione non turba minimamente il primo ministro

un·di·vid·ed [ˌʌndɪˈvaidɪd] ADJ: **I want your undivided attention** esigo (da voi) la massima attenzione

undo [ʌnˈduː] (*pt* **undid**, *pp* **undone**) VT 1 (*unfasten: button*) sbottonare; (*: shoelaces*) slacciare; (*: knot*) sciogliere; (*: parcel*) aprire; (*: knitting*) disfare; **she undid her coat** si è sbottonata il cappotto; **I can't undo the knot** non riesco a sciogliere il nodo 2 (*reverse: action, wrong*) riparare (a); (*spoil*) rovinare

un·do·ing [ʌnˈduːɪŋ] N rovina

un·done [ʌnˈdʌn] PP *of* **undo** ♦ ADJ (*unfastened: button*) sbottonato(-a); **to come undone** slacciarsi; **to leave undone** (*shirt*) lasciare aperto(-a) *or* sbottonato(-a); (*job*) non fare, lasciare da fare

un·doubt·ed [ʌnˈdautid] ADJ indubbio(-a)

un·doubt·ed·ly [ʌnˈdautidlɪ] ADV indubbiamente, senza dubbio

un·dress [ʌnˈdrɛs] VT spogliare ♦ VI (*also:* **get undressed**) spogliarsi, svestirsi

un·drink·able [ʌnˈdrɪŋkəbl] ADJ (*unpalatable*) imbevibile; (*polluted*) non potabile

un·due [ʌnˈdjuː] ADJ eccessivo(-a)

un·du·lat·ing [ˈʌndjʊˌleitɪŋ] ADJ (*surface*) ondulato(-a); (*countryside*) collinoso(-a); (*sea*) ondeggiante

un·du·ly [ʌnˈdjuːlɪ] ADV troppo, eccessivamente

un·dy·ing [ʌnˈdaiɪŋ] ADJ (*liter: fame, glory*) imperituro(-a); (*: love*) eterno(-a)

un·earned [ʌnˈɜːnd] ADJ (*praise, respect*) immeritato(-a)

un·earth [ʌnˈɜːθ] VT dissotterrare; (*fig: secret*) scoprire; (*: object*) scovare; (*: evidence*) portare alla luce; **they've unearthed some important documents** hanno scoperto alcuni documenti importanti

un·earth·ly [ʌnˈɜːθlɪ] ADJ (*eerie: brightness*) innaturale; (*: noise, sound*) spettrale; **unearthly hour** (*fam*) ora impossibile

un·easy [ʌnˈiːzɪ] ADJ (*person: worried*) inquieto(-a), preoccupato(-a), agitato(-a); (*: ill at ease*) a disagio; (*calm, peace*) precario(-a); (*night, sleep*) agitato(-a); (*silence*) imbarazzato(-a); **to feel uneasy about doing sth** non sentirsela di fare qc; **to feel uneasy about sth** essere preoccupato per qc; **to become uneasy about sb/sth** cominciare a preoccuparsi per qn/qc; **to have an uneasy conscience** non avere la coscienza a posto; **to have an uneasy feeling that ...** avere la spiacevole sensazione che...; **he looked uneasy** sembrava a disagio

un·eco·nom·ic [ˌʌniːkəˈnɒmɪk] ADJ (*wasteful: method, process*) antieconomico(-a); (*unprofitable*) poco redditizio(-a)

un·edu·cat·ed [ʌnˈedjʊˌkeɪtɪd] ADJ (*person*) senza istruzione, incolto(-a); (*speech*) popolare

un·em·ployed [ˌʌnɪmˈplɔɪd] ADJ disoccupato(-a), senza lavoro ♦ NPL: **the unemployed** i disoccupati

un·em·ploy·ment [ˌʌnɪmˈplɔɪmənt] N disoccupazione *f*

unemployment benefit, (*USA*) **unemployment compensation** N sussidio di disoccupazione

un·end·ing [ʌnˈendɪŋ] ADJ interminabile, senza fine

un·en·vi·able [ʌnˈenvɪəbl] ADJ poco invidiabile

un·equal [ʌnˈiːkwəl] ADJ (*length, objects*) disuguale; (*amounts*) diverso(-a); (*division of labour*) ineguale; **to be unequal to a task** (*frm*) non essere all'altezza di un compito

un·equalled, **un·equaled** (*USA*) [ʌnˈiːkwəld] ADJ senza pari, insuperato(-a)

un·equivo·cal [ˌʌnɪˈkwɪvəkəl] ADJ (*answer*) inequivocabile; (*person*) esplicito(-a), chiaro(-a)

un·err·ing [ʌnˈɜːrɪŋ] ADJ (*aim, taste, instinct*) infallibile

UNESCO [juːˈneskəʊ] N ABBR (= *United Nations Educational, Scientific, and Cultural Organization*) UNESCO *f*

un·ethi·cal [ʌnˈeθɪkəl] ADJ (*methods*) moralmente inaccettabile; (*doctor's behaviour*) contrario(-a) all'etica professionale

un·even [ʌnˈiːvən] ADJ (*heartbeat, work, quality, performance*) irregolare; (*thickness*) ineguale; (*ground*) disuguale, accidentato(-a); **uneven distribution** distribuzione *f* poco uniforme; **an uneven surface** una superficie irregolare; **their performance has been uneven this season** il loro rendimento è stato discontinuo questa stagione

un·event·ful [ˌʌnɪˈventfʊl] ADJ senza sorprese, tranquillo(-a)

un·ex·cep·tion·al [ˌʌnɪkˈsepʃənl] ADJ che non ha niente d'eccezionale

un·ex·cit·ing [ˌʌnɪkˈsaɪtɪŋ] ADJ (*news*) poco emozionante; (*film, evening*) poco interessante; (*person*) scialbo(-a)

un·ex·pec·ted [ˌʌnɪksˈpektɪd] ADJ inatteso(-a), imprevisto(-a)

un·ex·pect·ed·ly [ˌʌnɪksˈpektɪdlɪ] ADV (*happen*) inaspettatamente; (*die*) improvvisamente, inaspettatamente; (*arrive*) senza preavviso

un·ex·plained [ˌʌnɪksˈpleɪnd] ADJ inspiegato(-a)

un·ex·plod·ed [ˌʌnɪksˈpləʊdɪd] ADJ inesploso(-a)

un·fail·ing [ʌnˈfeɪlɪŋ] ADJ (*frm: remedy*) sicuro(-a), infallibile; (: *humour, supply, energy*) inesauribile; (: *zeal, courage*) senza riserve

un·fair [ʌnˈfeə'] ADJ (*comp* -**er**, *superl* -**est**) (*person, decision, criticism*) ingiusto(-a); (*means, tactics*) sleale; (*competition*) scorretto(-a); **this is unfair!** è ingiusto!; **it's unfair that ...** non è giusto che... + *sub*; **to be unfair to sb** essere ingiusto(-a) verso qn; **unfair competition** concorrenza sleale

unfair dismissal N (*Industry*) licenziamento ingiustificato, licenziamento senza giusta causa

un·fair·ly [ʌnˈfeəlɪ] ADV (*treat, criticize*) ingiustamente; (*play*) scorrettamente

un·faith·ful [ʌnˈfeɪθfʊl] ADJ: **unfaithful (to sb)** infedele (a qn)

un·fa·mil·iar [ˌʌnfəˈmɪljə'] ADJ (*subject*) sconosciuto(-a); (*experience*) insolito(-a); (*surroundings*) estraneo(-a); **to be unfamiliar with sth** non essere pratico(-a) di qc, non avere familiarità con qc, avere scarsa familiarità con qc; **I heard an unfamiliar voice** ho sentito una voce sconosciuta

un·fash·ion·able [ʌnˈfæʃnəbl] ADJ (*clothes*) fuori moda; (*district*) non alla moda; **these pants are unfashionable** questi pantaloni sono fuori moda *or* non vanno più

un·fas·ten [ʌnˈfɑːsn] VT (*buttons, seatbelt*) slacciare; (*scarf, rope*) sciogliere; (*gate*) aprire; **don't unfasten your seat belt** non slacciarti la cintura di sicurezza

un·fath·om·able [ʌnˈfæðəməbl] ADJ (*depths, mystery*) insondabile, imperscrutabile; (*person*) impenetrabile

un·fa·vour·able, **un·fa·vor·able** (*USA*) [ʌnˈfeɪvərəbl] ADJ (*circumstances, climate*) sfavorevole; (*report, impression*) negativo(-a)

un·fa·vour·ably, **un·fa·vor·ably** (*USA*) [ʌnˈfeɪvərəblɪ] ADV (*judge, see*) in senso sfavorevole; (*speak, review*)

sfavorevolmente; **to look unfavourably upon** vedere di malocchio

un·feel·ing [ʌnˈfiːlɪŋ] ADJ insensibile, duro(-a)

un·fin·ished [ʌnˈfɪnɪʃt] ADJ (*task*) non finito(-a); (*letter*) da finire; (*business*) in sospeso; (*symphony*) incompiuto(-a); **I have some unfinished business to attend to** ho un affare in sospeso da regolare

un·fit [ʌnˈfɪt] ADJ (*unsuitable*): **unfit for** inadatto(-a) a; (*Sport: injured*) non in grado di giocare (*or* correre); (*out of training*) non in forma; **unfit for habitation** inabitabile; **to be unfit to do sth** non essere in grado di fare qc; **unfit for military service** inabile (al servizio militare); **to be unfit for work** non essere adatto(-a) al lavoro; **to be unfit to travel** non essere in grado di viaggiare; **to be unfit to hold office** non essere adatto all'incarico

un·flag·ging [ʌnˈflæɡɪŋ] ADJ instancabile

un·flap·pable [ʌnˈflæpəbl] ADJ calmo(-a), composto(-a)

un·flat·ter·ing [ʌnˈflætərɪŋ] ADJ (*dress, hairstyle*) che non dona; (*portrait, light*) poco lusinghiero(-a)

un·flinch·ing [ʌnˈflɪntʃɪŋ] ADJ risoluto(-a), che non indietreggia

un·fold [ʌnˈfəʊld] VT (*newspaper, map, wings*) spiegare, aprire; (*arms*) distendere; (*fig: plan, idea*) esporre; (: *secret*) svelare; **she unfolded the map** ha aperto la cartina ♦ VI (*flower*) schiudersi; (*fig: view*) spiegarsi; (: *story*) svolgersi

un·fore·see·able [ˌʌnfɔːˈsiːəbl] ADJ imprevedibile

un·fore·seen [ˌʌnfɔːˈsiːn] ADJ imprevisto(-a)

un·for·get·table [ˌʌnfəˈɡetəbl] ADJ indimenticabile

un·for·giv·able [ˌʌnfəˈɡɪvəbl] ADJ imperdonabile

un·for·mat·ted [ʌnˈfɔːmætɪd] ADJ (*disk, text*) non formattato(-a)

un·for·tu·nate [ʌnˈfɔːtʃnɪt] ADJ (*deserving of pity*) povero(-a); (*unlucky*) sfortunato(-a); (*unsuitable, regrettable: event, remark*) infelice; (*habit*) deplorevole; **it is most unfortunate that he left** ci rincresce molto che se ne sia andato ♦ N sfortunato(-a), sventurato(-a)

un·for·tu·nate·ly [ʌnˈfɔːtʃnɪtlɪ] ADV purtroppo, sfortunatamente; **an unfortunately worded speech** un discorso infelice

un·found·ed [ʌnˈfaʊndɪd] ADJ infondato(-a), senza fondamento

un·friend·ly [ʌnˈfrendlɪ] ADJ (*comp* -**ier**, *superl* -**iest**) (*person*): **unfriendly (to)** scostante (con), antipatico(-a) (con); (*attitude, reception*) ostile, poco amichevole; (*remark*) scortese; **the waiters are a bit unfriendly** i camerieri sono un po' antipatici

un·ful·filled [ˌʌnfʊlˈfɪld] ADJ **1** (*ambition*) non realizzato(-a); (*prophecy*) che non si è avverato(-a); (*desire*) insoddisfatto(-a); (*promise*) non mantenuto(-a); (*terms of contract*) non rispettato(-a) **2** (*person*) frustrato(-a)

un·furl [ʌnˈfɜːl] VT (*flag, banner*) spiegare

un·fur·nished [ʌnˈfɜːnɪʃt] ADJ non ammobiliato(-a)

un·gain·ly [ʌnˈɡeɪnlɪ] ADJ sgraziato(-a), goffo(-a)

un·god·ly [ʌnˈɡɒdlɪ] ADJ (*person, language, action*) empio(-a); (*fam*): **at an ungodly hour** a un'ora allucinante, a un'ora impossibile

un·grate·ful [ʌnˈɡreɪtfʊl] ADJ ingrato(-a)

un·guard·ed [ʌnˈɡɑːdɪd] ADJ **1** (*Mil*) indifeso(-a), sguarnito(-a) **2** (*fig: careless*) imprudente; **in an unguarded moment** in un momento di distrazione

un·hap·pi·ly [ʌnˈhæpɪlɪ] ADV (*miserably*) tristemente, con aria infelice; (*unfortunately*) purtroppo, sfortunatamente

un·hap·pi·ness [ʌnˈhæpɪnɪs] N infelicità

un·hap·py [ʌnˈhæpɪ] ADJ (*comp* -**ier**, *superl* -**iest**) **1** (*sad*) infelice; **to look unhappy** avere l'aria triste; **he was very unhappy as a child** da bambino era molto infelice; **an unhappy state of affairs** una situazione spiacevole **2** (*not pleased*) scontento(-a); (*uneasy, worried*) preoccupato(-a), inquieto(-a); **unhappy with** (*arrangements*) insoddisfatto(-a) di; **to be unhappy about sth/doing sth** non essere contento(-a) di qc/di fare qc **3** (*unfortunate: remark, choice*) infelice; (: *coincidence*) sfortunato(-a)

un·harmed [ʌnˈhɑːmd] ADJ (*person*) illeso(-a), sano(-a) e salvo(-a), incolume; (*thing*) intatto(-a)

UNHCR [juːˈeɪtʃsiːˈɑː'] N ABBR (= *United Nations High*

Commission for Refugees) ACNUR m (= Alto Commissariato delle Nazioni Unite per Rifugiati)

un·heal·thy [ʌnˈhɛlθɪ] ADJ (comp -ier, superl -iest) (person) cagionevole, poco sano(-a); (climate, place, complexion) malsano(-a); (curiosity, interest) morboso(-a); **an unhealthy girl** una ragazza cagionevole; **an unhealthy diet** una dieta poco sana; **an unhealthy climate** un clima insalubre

unheard-of [ʌnˈhɜːdɒv] ADJ (unprecedented) inaudito(-a), senza precedenti; (outrageous) dell'altro mondo

un·help·ful [ʌnˈhɛlpfʊl] ADJ (person) poco disponibile, di scarso aiuto; (remark, advice) di scarso aiuto

un·hesi·tat·ing [ʌnˈhɛzɪˌteɪtɪŋ] ADJ (reply, offer) pronto(-a), immediato(-a); (loyalty, faith) che non vacilla; **she was un-hesitating in her support** non ha esitato a darmi (or dargli etc) il suo appoggio

un·ho·ly [ʌnˈhəʊlɪ] ADJ profano(-a); **at an unholy hour** (fam) ad un'ora indecente; **an unholy alliance** una coalizione f paradossale

un·hook [ʌnˈhʊk] VT (remove: picture) staccare; (: trailer) sganciare; (undo: gate) aprire; (: dress) slacciare

un·hurt [ʌnˈhɜːt] ADJ incolume, illeso(-a)

un·hy·gien·ic [ˌʌnhaɪˈdʒiːnɪk] ADJ (conditions) non igienico(-a); (surroundings) insalubre

uni·corn [ˈjuːnɪkɔːn] N unicorno

uni·den·ti·fied [ˌʌnaɪˈdɛntɪˌfaɪd] ADJ non identificato(-a)

uni·form [ˈjuːnɪˌfɔːm] N (Mil: school) uniforme f, divisa; **in full uniform** in alta uniforme; **in uniform** in divisa; **out of uniform** in borghese; **school uniform** la divisa scolastica ♦ ADJ (colour, acceleration) uniforme

uni·form·ity [juːnɪˈfɔːmɪtɪ] N uniformità

uni·fy [ˈjuːnɪˌfaɪ] VT (country) unire; (different parts, systems) unificare

uni·lat·er·al [juːnɪˈlætərəl] ADJ unilaterale

un·im·agi·nable [ˌʌnɪˈmædʒɪnəbl] ADJ inimmaginabile, inconcepibile

un·im·agi·na·tive [ˌʌnɪˈmædʒɪnətɪv] ADJ privo(-a) di fantasia

un·im·paired [ˌʌnɪmˈpɛəd] ADJ (health, mental powers) buono(-a) come prima; (quality) non danneggiato(-a)

un·im·por·tant [ˌʌnɪmˈpɔːtənt] ADJ (matter) senza importanza, di scarsa importanza; (detail) trascurabile

un·im·pressed [ˌʌnɪmˈprɛst] ADJ (unmoved) niente affatto colpito(-a), indifferente; (unconvinced) niente affatto convinto(-a)

un·in·hab·it·ed [ˌʌnɪnˈhæbɪtɪd] ADJ (house) disabitato(-a); (island) deserto(-a)

un·in·hib·it·ed [ˌʌnɪnˈhɪbɪtɪd] ADJ (person, behaviour) disinibito(-a), senza inibizioni; (emotion, laughter) sfrenato(-a)

un·in·jured [ʌnˈɪndʒəd] ADJ (person) incolume; (reputation) salvo(-a)

un·in·spir·ing [ˌʌnɪnˈspaɪərɪŋ] ADJ banale

un·in·stall [ˌʌnɪnˈstɔːl] VT (Comput) disinstallare

un·in·tel·li·gent [ˌʌnɪnˈtɛlɪdʒənt] ADJ poco intelligente

un·in·ten·tion·al [ˌʌnɪnˈtɛnʃənl] ADJ involontario(-a)

un·in·ten·tion·al·ly [ˌʌnɪnˈtɛnʃnəlɪ] ADV senza volerlo, involontariamente

un·in·vit·ed [ˌʌnɪnˈvaɪtɪd] ADJ (guest) non invitato(-a); (criticism, attention) non richiesto(-a); **to arrive uninvited (at sb's house)** piovere in casa (a qn); **to help o.s. to sth uninvited** servirsi di qc senza chiedere il permesso

un·in·vit·ing [ˌʌnɪnˈvaɪtɪŋ] ADJ (place, food) poco invitante; (offer) poco allettante

un·ion [ˈjuːnjən] N 1 (also: trade union) sindacato; **do you belong to a union?** sei iscritto a un sindacato? 2 (gen, also Pol) unione f; **the union with England** l'unione con l'Inghilterra 3 (club, society) associazione f, circolo ♦ ADJ (leader, movement) sindacale

un·ion·ize [ˈjuːnjəˌnaɪz] VT sindacalizzare, organizzare in sindacato

Union Jack N bandiera nazionale britannica

Union of Soviet Socialist Republics N Unione f delle Repubbliche Socialiste Sovietiche

union shop N stabilimento in cui tutti gli operai sono tenuti ad aderire ad un sindacato

unique [juːˈniːk] ADJ unico(-a); **to be unique to** essere esclusivo di

uni·sex [ˈjuːnɪˌsɛks] ADJ unisex inv

uni·son [ˈjuːnɪzn] N: **in unison** (Mus, also fig) all'unisono

unit [ˈjuːnɪt] N 1 (gen, also Elec, Math, Mil) unità f inv; **mon-etary/linguistic unit** unità monetaria/linguistica; **unit of length** unità di lunghezza; **unit of measurement** unità di misura 2 (division, section) reparto; (of furniture) elemento (componibile); (team, squad) squadra; **a kitchen unit** un elemento componibile della cucina; **production unit** reparto m produzione, inv; **the basic social unit** il nucleo sociale di base; **research unit** (personnel) équipe f inv; (building) sede f di ricerca

unit cost N (Industry) costo unitario

unite [juːˈnaɪt] VT (join: parts, pieces) unire; (unify: parts of country) unificare; **they united their efforts** hanno unito i loro sforzi ♦ VI (join) unirsi; (companies) fondersi; **to unite with sb/in doing** or **to do sth** unirsi a qn/per fare qc; **the two parties united** i due partiti si sono uniti

unit·ed [juːˈnaɪtɪd] ADJ (family, people) unito(-a); (effort) unitario(-a); (efforts) comune, congiunto(-a)

United Arab Emirates NPL: **the United Arab Emirates** gli Emirati Arabi Uniti

United Kingdom N: **the United Kingdom** il Regno Unito

United Nations N: **the United Nations** le Nazioni Unite, l'Organizzazione f delle Nazioni Unite

United States N: **the United States (of America)** gli Stati Uniti (d'America)

unit price N (Industry) prezzo unitario

unit trust N (Brit: Fin) fondo d'investimento

unity [ˈjuːnɪtɪ] N (in party, country) unità; (of members, individuals) unione f; **in unity** in armonia, in pieno accordo

Univ. ABBR = **university**

uni·ver·sal [juːnɪˈvɜːsəl] ADJ (phenomenon, disapproval) generale; (language, values) universale; **a universal favourite** un(-a) gran favorito(-a)

uni·verse [ˈjuːnɪˌvɜːs] N: **the universe** l'universo

uni·ver·sity [juːnɪˈvɜːsɪtɪ] N università f inv; **Oxford Universi-ty** l'Università di Oxford; **to be at/go to university** essere/andare all'università ♦ ADJ (student, professor, education) universitario(-a)

university degree N (diploma m di) laurea

un·just [ʌnˈdʒʌst] ADJ ingiusto(-a); **to be unjust to sb** essere ingiusto(-a) con or verso qn

un·jus·ti·fi·able [ʌnˈdʒʌstɪˌfaɪəbl] ADJ ingiustificabile

un·jus·ti·fied [ʌnˈdʒʌstɪˌfaɪd] ADJ (remark) ingiustificato(-a), immotivato(-a); (suspicion) infondato(-a); (Typ: text) non giustificato(-a)

un·kempt [ʌnˈkɛmpt] ADJ (hair) scarmigliato(-a), spettinato(-a); (appearance) trasandato(-a)

un·kind [ʌnˈkaɪnd] ADJ (comp -er, superl -est) (person, remark) poco gentile, scortese; (stronger) villano(-a); (fate, blow) crudele; **without wishing to be unkind...** senza voler essere scortese...; **it's unkind of him to want my career to fail now** è crudele da parte sua volere che la mia carriera si interrompa adesso

un·kind·ly [ʌnˈkaɪndlɪ] ADV (speak) in modo sgarbato; (treat) male; **don't take it unkindly if...** non te la prendere se...

un·known [ʌnˈnəʊn] ADJ sconosciuto(-a), ignoto(-a); **the murderer is as yet unknown** ancora non si sa chi sia l'assassino; **unknown quantity** (Math, also fig) incognita; **his intentions are unknown to me** non conosco le sue intenzioni; **a substance unknown to scientists** una sostanza ignota agli scienziati ♦ ADV: **unknown to me** a mia insaputa; **unknown to them he was nearby** era nelle vicinanze, a loro insaputa ♦ N 1 (person) sconosciuto(-a) 2 (Math) incognita; **the unknown** l'ignoto

un·lad·en [ʌnˈleɪdn] ADJ (ship, weight) a vuoto

un·law·ful [ʌnˈlɔːfʊl] ADJ illecito(-a), illegale

un·lead·ed [ʌnˈlɛdɪd] N (also: **unleaded petrol** or **gasoline**) benzina senza piombo

un·leash [ʌnˈliːʃ] VT (dog) sguinzagliare; (fig) scatenare

un·leav·ened [ʌnˈlɛvnd] ADJ (bread) azzimo(-a), non lievitato(-a)

un·less [ʌnˈlɛs] CONJ a meno che non + sub, se non + indic, a meno di + infin; **we won't get there on time unless we leave earlier** se non partiamo prima non arriveremo in tempo; **unless otherwise stated** salvo indicazione contraria; **unless I am mistaken** se non mi sbaglio

un·li·censed [ˌʌnˈlaɪsənst] ADJ (*vehicle*) senza bollo; (*Brit: hotel, restaurant*) senza licenza per la vendita di alcolici

un·like [ˌʌnˈlaɪk] ADJ diverso(-a), dissimile; **to be unlike sth** essere diverso(-a) da qc; **that photo is quite unlike her** quella foto non le somiglia affatto; **it's quite unlike him to do that** non è da lui fare una cosa simile ♦ PREP a differenza di, contrariamente a; **I, unlike others ...** diversamente dagli *or* a differenza degli altri, io...

un·like·li·hood [ʌnˈlaɪklɪhʊd], **un·like·li·ness** [ʌnˈlaɪklɪnɪs] N improbabilità

un·like·ly [ʌnˈlaɪklɪ] ADJ (*comp* -**ier**, *superl* -**iest**) (*happening*) improbabile; (*explanation*) inverosimile; **in the unlikely event that it does happen ...** dovesse succedere, cosa assai improbabile...; **it is unlikely that he will come, he is unlikely to come** è poco probabile che venga

un·lim·it·ed [ʌnˈlɪmɪtɪd] ADJ (*time, power*) illimitato(-a); (*wealth*) smisurato(-a)

un·list·ed [ʌnˈlɪstɪd] ADJ (*item*) non elencato(-a); (*Stock Exchange: share*) non quotato(-a); (*USA: Telec*): **unlisted number** numero fuori elenco

un·lit [ʌnˈlɪt] ADJ (*lamp*) spento(-a); (*room*) senza luce; (*road*) non illuminato(-a)

un·load [ʌnˈləʊd] VT 1 scaricare 2 (*fam: get rid of*): **to unload onto sb** (*problem, children*) scaricare su qn ♦ VI scaricare

un·lock [ʌnˈlɒk] VT aprire; **he unlocked the door of the car** ha aperto la portiera dell'auto; **she left the door unlocked** non ha chiuso la porta a chiave

un·lucky [ʌnˈlʌkɪ] ADJ (*comp* -**ier**, *superl* -**iest**) (*person, day*) sfortunato(-a); (*decision*) infausto(-a), infelice; (*number, object*) che porta sfortuna *or* male, di malaugurio; **to be unlucky** (*person*) essere sfortunato(-a), non avere fortuna; (*number, thing*) portare sfortuna; **it's unlucky to walk under a ladder** porta sfortuna *or* male passare sotto una scala

un·man·age·able [ʌnˈmænɪdʒəbl] ADJ (*unwieldy: tool, vehicle*) poco maneggevole; (: *parcel, size*) ingombrante; (*uncontrollable: teenage child*) difficile; (: *hair*) ribelle; (: *situation*) difficile da gestire

un·manned [ʌnˈmænd] ADJ (*spacecraft*) senza equipaggio

un·man·ner·ly [ʌnˈmænəlɪ] ADJ maleducato(-a), scortese

un·marked [ʌnˈmɑːkt] ADJ (*unstained*) pulito(-a), senza macchie; (*unblemished: face, body*) senza rughe; (*without marking: linen*) senza cifre; (: *banknote*) non segnato(-a); (*uncorrected: essay*) non corretto(-a); **unmarked police car** auto *f* civetta, *inv*

un·mar·ried [ʌnˈmærɪd] ADJ (*man*) celibe, non sposato; (*woman*) nubile, non sposata; **unmarried couple** coppia non sposata

unmarried mother N ragazza *f* madre, *inv*

un·mask [ʌnˈmɑːsk] VT (*fig*) smascherare

un·matched [ʌnˈmætʃt] ADJ senza pari, impareggiabile

un·men·tion·able [ʌnˈmenʃənəbl] ADJ (*topic*) tabù *inv*; (*vice, disease*) innominabile; (*word*) irripetibile

un·mer·ci·ful [ʌnˈmɜːsɪfʊl] ADJ spietato(-a)

un·mis·tak·able, **un·mis·take·able** [ˌʌnmɪsˈteɪkəbl] ADJ (*person, sound*) inconfondibile; (*displeasure, meaning*) indubbio(-a), lampante; **his style was unmistakable** il suo stile era inconfondibile; **the similarities between the sisters are unmistakable** la somiglianza tra le due sorelle è indubbia

un·miti·gat·ed [ʌnˈmɪtɪˌɡeɪtɪd] ADJ (*disaster, nonsense*) totale, completo(-a); (*criminal, scoundrel*) incallito(-a)

un·named [ʌnˈneɪmd] ADJ (*fear, object*) senza nome; (*donor, author*) anonimo(-a)

un·natu·ral [ʌnˈnætʃrəl] ADJ (*gen*) innaturale; (*affected*) affettato(-a); (*abnormal*) non normale; **her back ached from lying in this unnatural position** le faceva male la schiena per la posizione innaturale in cui era sdraiata; **it's unnatural for him to behave like that** non è da lui comportarsi così

un·nec·es·sary [ʌnˈnesɪsərɪ] ADJ (*superfluous*) non necessario(-a), superfluo(-a); (*useless*) inutile; **it was unnecessary to be rude!** non c'era bisogno di essere sgarbato!; **it's unnecessary for you to attend** non è necessario che tu intervenga

un·nerve [ʌnˈnɜːv] VT (*subj: accident*) sgomentare; (: *hostile attitude*) bloccare; (: *experience*) far sentire disagio

un·no·ticed [ʌnˈnəʊtɪst] ADJ: **to go** *or* **pass unnoticed** passare inosservato(-a)

un·ob·serv·ant [ˌʌnəbˈzɜːvənt] ADJ: **to be unobservant** non avere spirito di osservazione

un·ob·tain·able [ˌʌnəbˈteɪnəbl] ADJ (*food, materials*) introvabile; **this number is unobtainable** (*Telec*) è impossibile ottenere questo numero

un·ob·tru·sive [ˌʌnəbˈtruːsɪv] ADJ discreto(-a)

un·oc·cu·pied [ʌnˈɒkjʊˌpaɪd] ADJ (*house*) vuoto(-a); (*seat, table*: *also Mil*: *zone*) libero(-a), non occupato(-a); (*person: not busy*) libero(-a), senza impegni

un·of·fi·cial [ˌʌnəˈfɪʃəl] ADJ (*visit*) privato(-a), non ufficiale; (*unconfirmed: report, news*) ufficioso(-a); **in an unofficial capacity** in veste ufficiosa; **unofficial strike** sciopero non autorizzato; **unofficial figures** cifre ufficiose

un·opened [ʌnˈəʊpənd] ADJ (*letter*) chiuso(-a); (*present*) ancora incartato(-a); (*bottle, tin*) non aperto(-a)

un·op·posed [ˌʌnəˈpəʊzd] ADJ (*enter, be elected*) senza incontrare opposizione; **the motion was unopposed by the committee** il comitato non si è opposto alla mozione

un·ortho·dox [ʌnˈɔːθəˌdɒks] ADJ poco ortodosso(-a)

un·pack [ʌnˈpæk] VT (*suitcases*) disfare; (*belongings*) sballare; **I unpacked my suitcase** ho disfatto la valigia; **I haven't unpacked my clothes yet** non ho ancora tolto i vestiti dalla valigia ♦ VI disfare le valige *or* i bagagli; **I went to my room to unpack** sono andato in camera mia a disfare le valige

un·paid [ʌnˈpeɪd] ADJ (*bill, debt*) da pagare; (*holiday*) non pagato(-a); (*work*) non retribuito(-a)

un·pal·at·able [ʌnˈpælətəbl] ADJ (*food*) immangiabile; (*drink*) imbevibile; (*fig: truth*) sgradevole

un·par·al·leled [ʌnˈpærəˌleld] ADJ senza pari, impareggiabile

un·pat·ri·ot·ic [ˌʌnpætrɪˈɒtɪk] ADJ (*person*) poco patriottico(-a); (*speech, attitude*) antipatriottico(-a)

un·planned [ʌnˈplænd] ADJ (*visit*) imprevisto(-a); (*baby, pregnancy*) non previsto(-a)

un·pleas·ant [ʌnˈplɛznt] ADJ (*smell, task*) sgradevole, spiacevole; (*person, remark*) antipatico(-a); (*day, experience*) brutto(-a); **to be unpleasant to sb** essere villano(-a) con qn; **an unpleasant situation** una situazione spiacevole; **an unpleasant smell** un odore sgradevole

un·plug [ʌnˈplʌɡ] VT staccare (la spina di); **she unplugs the TV before going to bed** stacca la presa della TV prima di andare a letto

un·pol·lut·ed [ˌʌnpəˈluːtɪd] ADJ non inquinato(-a)

un·popu·lar [ʌnˈpɒpjʊləʳ] ADJ (*gen*) impopolare; **to be unpopular with sb** (*person, law*) non riscuotere l'approvazione di qn; **to make o.s. unpopular (with)** rendersi antipatico(-a) (a); (*subj: politician*) alienarsi le simpatie (di); **I'm unpopular with the boss at the moment** non sono nelle grazie del capo in questo momento; **he's unpopular with the rest of the class** è mal visto dal resto della classe

un·prec·edent·ed [ʌnˈprɛsɪdəntɪd] ADJ senza precedenti

un·pre·dict·able [ˌʌnprɪˈdɪktəbl] ADJ imprevedibile

un·preju·diced [ʌnˈprɛdʒʊdɪst] ADJ (*not biased*) obiettivo(-a), imparziale; (*having no prejudices*) senza pregiudizi

un·pre·pared [ˌʌnprɪˈpeəd] ADJ (*person*) impreparato(-a); (*speech*) improvvisato(-a); **it caught me unprepared** mi ha trovato impreparato; **he was unprepared for her reaction** la sua reazione lo colse alla sprovvista

un·pre·pos·sess·ing [ˌʌnpriːpəˈzɛsɪŋ] ADJ poco attraente

un·pre·ten·tious [ˌʌnprɪˈtɛnʃəs] ADJ senza pretese

un·prin·ci·pled [ʌnˈprɪnsɪpld] ADJ senza scrupoli

un·pro·duc·tive [ˌʌnprəˈdʌktɪv] ADJ improduttivo(-a); (*discussion*) sterile

un·pro·fes·sion·al [ˌʌnprəˈfɛʃənl] ADJ: **unprofessional conduct** scorrettezza professionale

un·prof·it·able [ʌnˈprɒfɪtəbl] ADJ (*financially*) non redditizio(-a); (*job, deal*) poco lucrativo(-a); (*fig*) infruttuoso(-a), poco produttivo(-a); **an unprofitable afternoon** un pomeriggio poco produttivo

un·pro·tect·ed [ˌʌnprəˈtɛktɪd] ADJ (*town*) indifeso(-a); (*house*) esposto(-a), non riparato(-a); (*sex*) non protetto(-a)

un·pro·voked [ˌʌnprəˈvəʊkt] ADJ (*attack*) non provocato(-a); (*unpleasant remark*) ingiustificato(-a)

un·pun·ished [ʌnˈpʌnɪʃt] ADJ: **to go unpunished** restare impunito(-a)

un·quali·fied [ʌnˈkwɒlɪˌfaɪd] ADJ **1** (*worker*) non qualificato(-a); (*in professions*) non diplomato(-a), non abilitato(-a); (*applicant*) senza i requisiti necessari; **unqualified members of staff at the hospital** personale *m* non qualificato all'ospedale; **she was unqualified for the job** non era qualificata per il lavoro **2** (*absolute: assent, denial*) incondizionato(-a); (: *admiration*) senza riserve; (: *success, disaster*) completo(-a), assoluto(-a); **an unqualified success** un successo completo

un·ques·tion·ably [ʌnˈkwestʃənəblɪ] ADV indiscutibilmente

un·ques·tion·ing [ʌnˈkwestʃənɪŋ] ADJ (*obedience, acceptance*) cieco(-a)

un·rav·el [ʌnˈrævəl] VT (*knitting*) disfare; (*wool*) dipanare, districare; (*threads*) sfilare, sbrogliare; (*fig: mystery*) risolvere; (: *plot*) venire a capo di ♦ VI (*knitting*) disfarsi; (*threads*) sbrogliarsi

un·real [ʌnˈrɪəl] ADJ irreale; **an unreal situation** una situazione irreale; **unreal expectations** aspettative *fpl* esagerate; **it was unreal!** era incredibile!

un·re·al·is·tic [ˌʌnrɪəˈlɪstɪk] ADJ (*idea*) illusorio(-a); (*estimate*) non realistico(-a); **you're being unrealistic if you think ...** ti fai delle illusioni se credi...

un·rea·son·able [ʌnˈriːznəbl] ADJ (*person, idea, behaviour*) irragionevole; (*price, time*) irragionevole, assurdo(-a); **it is unreasonable to expect that** è un po' troppo aspettarsi che + *sub*; **he makes unreasonable demands on me** pretende troppo da me; **he was most unreasonable about it** non ha voluto sentire ragioni; **her attitude was completely unreasonable** il suo atteggiamento era del tutto irragionevole

un·rec·og·niz·able [ʌnˈrekəgˌnaɪzəbl] ADJ irriconoscibile

un·rec·og·nized [ʌnˈrekəgˌnaɪzd] ADJ (*talent, genius*) misconosciuto(-a); (*Pol: regime*) non riconosciuto(-a) ufficialmente; **he walked along the street unrecognized by passers-by** ha camminato per la strada senza che nessuno lo riconoscesse

un·re·cord·ed [ˌʌnrɪˈkɔːdɪd] ADJ non documentato(-a), non registrato(-a)

un·re·fined [ˌʌnrɪˈfaɪnd] ADJ (*petroleum*) greggio(-a); (*sugar*) non raffinato(-a); (*person, manners: coarse*) rozzo(-a)

un·re·hearsed [ˌʌnrɪˈhɜːst] ADJ (*Theatre*) improvvisato(-a); (*spontaneous*) imprevisto(-a)

un·re·lat·ed [ˌʌnrɪˈleɪtɪd] ADJ: **unrelated (to)** (*unconnected*) senza nesso *or* rapporto (con); (*by family*) non imparentato(-a) (con), senza legami di parentela (con)

un·re·lent·ing [ˌʌnrɪˈlentɪŋ] ADJ (*rain, heat*) incessante; (*activity*) senza tregua; (*attack*) che non dà tregua; (*hatred*) irriducibile, implacabile; (*person*) spietato(-a)

un·re·li·able [ˌʌnrɪˈlaɪəbl] ADJ (*person*) su cui non si può contare *or* fare affidamento; (*firm*) poco serio(-a); (*car, machine*) che non dà affidamento; **it's a nice car, but a bit unreliable** è una bella macchina, ma è un po' inaffidabile

un·re·lieved [ˌʌnrɪˈliːvd] ADJ (*pain, gloom*) costante; (*anguish, depression*) totale; (*boredom*) mortale; (*monotony*) ininterrotto(-a); (*colour*) uniforme

un·re·mit·ting [ˌʌnrɪˈmɪtɪŋ](*frm*) ADJ (*activity*) senza sosta, incessante; (*efforts, demands*) costante; (*hatred*) irriducibile, implacabile

un·re·peat·able [ˌʌnrɪˈpiːtəbl] ADJ irripetibile

un·re·pent·ant [ˌʌnrɪˈpentənt] ADJ (*sinner*) impenitente; (*believer, supporter*) irriducibile; **to be unrepentant about sth** non mostrare un'ombra di rimorso per qc

un·rep·re·senta·tive [ˌʌnreprɪˈzentətɪv] ADJ (*untypical*) atipico(-a), poco rappresentativo(-a)

un·re·served [ˌʌnrɪˈzɜːvd] ADJ **1** (*seat*) non prenotato(-a), non riservato(-a) **2** (*approval, admiration*) senza riserve

un·re·spon·sive [ˌʌnrɪsˈpɒnsɪv] ADJ che non reagisce; **unresponsive to** insensibile a

un·rest [ʌnˈrest] N (*disturbances*) agitazioni *fpl*

un·re·strict·ed [ˌʌnrɪˈstrɪktɪd] ADJ senza una regolamentazione; (*power, time*) illimitato(-a); (*access, parking*) libero(-a)

un·re·ward·ed [ˌʌnrɪˈwɔːdɪd] ADJ non ricompensato(-a); **to go unrewarded** rimanere senza ricompensa

un·ripe [ʌnˈraɪp] ADJ non maturo(-a)

un·ri·valled, un·ri·valed (*USA*) [ʌnˈraɪvəld] ADJ senza pari; **to be unrivalled** non avere *or* non temere rivali

un·roll [ʌnˈrəʊl] VT srotolare ♦ VI srotolarsi

un·ruf·fled [ʌnˈrʌfld] ADJ (*person*) imperturbato(-a); (*hair*) a posto; (*water*) senza un'increspatura

un·ru·ly [ʌnˈruːlɪ] ADJ (*comp* -ier, *superl* -iest) (*behaviour*) indisciplinato(-a); (*child, mob*) turbolento(-a); (*hair*) ribelle

un·safe [ʌnˈseɪf] ADJ (*machine, car, wiring*) pericoloso(-a); (*method*) poco sicuro(-a), rischioso(-a); **unsafe to drink** non potabile; **unsafe to eat** non commestibile; **to feel unsafe** non sentirsi sicuro(-a); **it's unsafe to go out alone at night** è pericoloso uscire da soli la sera

un·said [ʌnˈsed] ADJ non detto(-a), taciuto(-a); **consider it unsaid** come non detto; **to leave sth unsaid** passare qc sotto silenzio; **it would have been better left unsaid** sarebbe stato meglio non dirlo; **much was left unsaid** molte cose sono rimaste non dette

un·sale·able, un·sal·able (*USA*) [ʌnˈseɪləbl] ADJ invendibile

un·sat·is·fac·tory [ˌʌnsætɪsˈfæktərɪ] ADJ (*result*) poco soddisfacente; (*profits*) al di sotto delle aspettative; (*piece of work, hotel room*) che lascia a desiderare; (*on school report*) insufficiente

un·sa·voury, un·sa·vory (*USA*) [ʌnˈseɪvərɪ] ADJ (*character, business, activity*) equivoco(-a), losco(-a); (*place, district, reputation*) poco raccomandabile; (*appearance*) sgradevole

un·scathed [ʌnˈskeɪðd] ADJ senza un graffio, incolume; (*fig*) indenne

un·sci·en·tif·ic [ˌʌnsaɪənˈtɪfɪk] ADJ poco scientifico(-a)

un·screw [ʌnˈskruː] VT svitare ♦ VI svitarsi

un·scru·pu·lous [ʌnˈskruːpjʊləs] ADJ (*person*) senza scrupoli, privo(-a) di scrupoli; (*means*) disonesto(-a)

un·seat [ʌnˈsiːt] VT (*rider*) disarcionare; (*fig: official*) spodestare; (: *Members of Parliament*) far perdere il seggio a

un·secured [ˌʌnsɪˈkjʊəd] ADJ: **unsecured creditor** creditore *m* non privilegiato

un·seed·ed [ʌnˈsiːdɪd] ADJ (*Sport*) che non è una testa di serie

un·seem·ly [ʌnˈsiːmlɪ] ADJ (*pej*) sconveniente, indecoroso(-a)

un·seen [ʌnˈsiːn] ADJ (*person*) inosservato(-a); (*danger*) nascosto(-a); (*Scol: translation*) all'impronta ♦ N (*Scol*) traduzione *f* all'impronta

un·self·ish [ʌnˈselfɪʃ] ADJ (*person*) altruista; (*act*) disinteressato(-a)

un·set·tled [ʌnˈsetld] ADJ (*weather, market, situation*) instabile, variabile; (*person: restless*) irrequieto(-a); (: *itinerant*) nomade; (*frm: question, issue*) non risolto(-a); **to feel unsettled** sentirsi turbato(-a) *or* scombussolato(-a); **the staff were unsettled and demoralized** il personale era turbato e demoralizzato; **unsettled weather** tempo instabile; **an unsettled dispute** una controversia irrisolta

un·set·tling [ʌnˈsetlɪŋ] ADJ inquietante; **the news had an unsettling effect on me** la notizia mi ha scombussolato

un·shak·able, un·shake·able [ʌnˈʃeɪkəbl] ADJ irremovibile

un·shav·en [ʌnˈʃeɪvn] ADJ non rasato(-a)

un·sight·ly [ʌnˈsaɪtlɪ] ADJ (*unattractive*) sgradevole a vedersi; (*ugly*) brutto(-a)

un·skilled [ʌnˈskɪld] ADJ (*worker, manpower*) non specializzato(-a); **an unskilled worker** un operaio non specializzato

un·so·ciable [ʌnˈsəʊʃəbl] ADJ (*pej: person*) poco socievole; **he's very unsociable** è un orso

un·so·cial [ʌnˈsəʊʃəl] ADJ: **unsocial hours** orario *msg* sconveniente

un·sold [ʌnˈsəʊld] ADJ invenduto(-a)

un·so·lic·it·ed [ˌʌnsəˈlɪsɪtɪd] ADJ non richiesto(-a)

un·so·phis·ti·cat·ed [ˌʌnsəˈfɪstɪˌkeɪtɪd] ADJ (*person, dress, habits*) semplice; (*machine*) primitivo(-a), rudimentale

un·sound [ʌnˈsaʊnd] ADJ (*health*) debole, cagionevole; (*in construction: floor, foundations*) malsicuro(-a); (*argument*) che non regge; (*opinion*) poco fondato(-a); (*policy, advice*) poco sensato(-a); (*judgment, investment*) poco sicuro(-a); (*business*) poco solido(-a); **of unsound mind** (*Law*) non in pieno possesso delle proprie facoltà mentali

un·speak·able [ʌnˈspiːkəbl] ADJ (*behaviour, crime*) abominevole; (*pain, joy*) indicibile, indescrivibile

un·spoiled [ʌnˈspɔɪld], **un·spoilt** [ʌnˈspɔɪlt] ADJ (*countryside, beauty*) non deturpato(-a); (*child*) non viziato(-a); (*person*) genuino(-a)

un·spo·ken [ʌnˈspəʊkən] ADJ (*words*) non detto(-a); (*thoughts*) non espresso(-a); (*agreement, approval*) tacito(-a)

un·sta·ble [ʌnˈsteɪbl] ADJ (*structure, situation, also Chem, Phys*) instabile; (*person*) squilibrato(-a)

un·steady [ʌnˈstedɪ] ADJ (*ladder, foothold*) instabile, malsicuro(-a); (*hand, voice*) tremante; (*economy*) vacillante; **to be unsteady on one's feet** non reggersi bene sulle gambe

un·stint·ing [ʌnˈstɪntɪŋ] ADJ (*support*) incondizionato(-a); (*generosity*) illimitato(-a); (*praise*) senza riserve

un·stuck [ʌnˈstʌk] ADJ: **to come unstuck** (*label*) staccarsi, scollarsi; (*fam: plan*) andare a monte, fallire; (: *person*) fare fiasco

un·sub·scribe [ˌʌnsəbˈskraɪb] VI (*Comput*) disdire l'abbonamento

un·sub·stan·ti·at·ed [ˌʌnsəbˈstænʃɪˌeɪtɪd] ADJ (*rumour, accusation*) infondato(-a)

un·suc·cess·ful [ˌʌnsəkˈsesfʊl] ADJ (*gen*) che non ha successo; (*writer*) fallito(-a); (*businessman*) di scarso successo; **to be unsuccessful** (*play, book, actor*) non avere successo; (*idea*) non avere fortuna; (*attempt, marriage, negotiation*) non riuscire, fallire; (*application*) avere esito negativo; **to be unsuccessful in an exam** non superare un esame; **to be unsuccessful in an attempt to do sth** fallire nel tentativo di fare qc; **an unsuccessful artist** un artista fallito

un·suc·cess·ful·ly [ˌʌnsəkˈsesfəlɪ] ADV senza successo

un·suit·able [ʌnˈsuːtəbl] ADJ: **unsuitable (for)** (*clothes, colour*) non adatto(-a), inadatto(-a); (*moment*) inopportuno(-a) (a *or* per); **this film is unsuitable for children** non è un film adatto ai bambini; **unsuitable for children under 15** sconsigliabile ai minori di 15 anni; **he's unsuitable for the post** non è la persona adatta per quell'impiego; **the post is unsuitable for him** quel posto non fa per lui

un·suit·ed [ʌnˈsuːtɪd] ADJ: **to be unsuited for** *or* **to** non essere fatto(-a) per

un·sung [ʌnˈsʌŋ] ADJ: **an unsung hero** un eroe misconosciuto

un·sup·port·ed [ˌʌnsəˈpɔːtɪd] ADJ (*claim*) senza fondamento; (*theory*) non dimostrato(-a); (*mother*) senza aiuti finanziari

un·sure [ʌnˈʃʊəʳ] ADJ: **unsure of, unsure about** incerto(-a) su; **they are unsure about what to do** sono incerti(-e) su cosa fare; **to be unsure of o.s.** essere un(a) insicuro(-a)

un·sus·pect·ing [ˌʌnsəsˈpektɪŋ] ADJ (*gen*) che non sospetta nulla; (*public*) ignaro(-a)

un·sweet·ened [ʌnˈswiːtnd] ADJ (*tea*) senza zucchero; (*fruit juice*) non zuccherato(-a)

un·swerv·ing [ʌnˈswɜːvɪŋ] ADJ (*loyalty, devotion*) ferreo(-a), incrollabile

un·sym·pa·thet·ic [ˌʌnsɪmpəˈθetɪk] ADJ (*attitude*) poco incoraggiante; (*person: not understanding*) poco comprensivo(-a); (: *disagreeable*) antipatico(-a); (: *response*) gelido(-a); **to be unsympathetic to a cause** non appoggiare una causa; **I explained, but he was unsympathetic** ho spiegato le mie ragioni, ma è stato poco comprensivo

un·tan·gle [ʌnˈtæŋgl] VT (*knots, wool*) sbrogliare

un·tapped [ʌnˈtæpt] ADJ (*resources*) non sfruttato(-a)

un·taxed [ʌnˈtækst] ADJ (*goods*) esente da imposte; (*income*) non imponibile

un·think·able [ʌnˈθɪŋkəbl] ADJ impensabile, inconcepibile

un·think·ing·ly [ʌnˈθɪŋkɪŋlɪ] ADV senza pensare

un·ti·dy [ʌnˈtaɪdɪ] ADJ (*comp* **-ier**, *superl* **-iest**) (*person, room, writing*) disordinato(-a)

un·tie [ʌnˈtaɪ] VT (*parcel*): **they are unsure about what to do** sono incerti su cosa fare, disfare; (*knot, shoelaces*) sciogliere; (*hands, person, dog*) slegare; **he couldn't untie the knots** non riusciva a sciogliere i nodi

un·til [ʌnˈtɪl] PREP fino a; (*after negative*) prima di; **until now** finora; **it's never been a problem until now** non è mai stato un problema, finora; **until then** fino ad allora; **until then I'd never been to Italy** fino ad allora non ero mai stato(-a) in Italia; **until such time as I decide otherwise** fino a quando non cambio idea; **from morning until night** dalla mattina alla sera; **until his arrival** fino al suo arrivo; **I waited until**

ten o'clock ho aspettato fino alle dieci; **I didn't know anything about it until 10 minutes ago** non ne sapevo niente fino a 10 minuti fa; **it won't be ready until next week** non sarà pronto prima della settimana prossima ♦ CONJ finché (non), fino a quando; **I won't see her until I return** non la vedrò fino al mio ritorno; **wait until I get back** aspetta finché torno; **he did nothing until I told him** non ha mosso un dito finché non gliel'ho detto

un·time·ly [ʌnˈtaɪmlɪ] ADJ (*death, end*) prematuro(-a); (*remark*) fuori luogo, inopportuno(-a); **to come to an untimely end** (*person*) morire prematuramente; (*project*) naufragare anzitempo

un·told [ʌnˈtəʊld] ADJ (*loss, wealth*) incalcolabile; (*misery*) indicibile, indescrivibile; (*story, secret*) mai rivelato(-a); **untold damage** danni *mpl* incalcolabili

un·touched [ʌnˈtʌtʃt] ADJ **1** (*unchanged*) così com'era; (*unaffected*) non toccato(-a); **she left her breakfast untouched** non ha nemmeno toccato la colazione; **untouched by human hand** manipolato(-a) a distanza **2** (*safe: person*) incolume; **the thieves left our cases untouched** i ladri non hanno toccato le nostre valigie **3** (*unmoved*): **untouched by her pleas** insensibile alle sue preghiere

un·to·ward [ˌʌntəˈwɔːd] ADJ (*frm*) increscioso(-a)

un·trained [ʌnˈtreɪnd] ADJ (*worker, teacher*) privo(-a) di formazione professionale; (*troops*) privo(-a) di addestramento; **to the untrained eye/ear** ad un occhio inesperto/orecchio non esercitato

un·tram·melled, un·tram·meled (*USA*) [ʌnˈtræməld] ADJ (*liter*) senza vincoli

un·trans·lat·able [ˌʌntrænzˈleɪtəbl] ADJ intraducibile

un·true [ʌnˈtruː] ADJ (*statement*) falso(-a), non vero(-a)

un·trust·wor·thy [ʌnˈtrʌstˌwɜːðɪ] ADJ (*person*) di cui non ci si può fidare; (*source*) inattendibile, non degno(-a) di fede

un·us·able [ʌnˈjuːzəbl] ADJ inservibile, inutilizzabile

un·used [ʌnˈjuːzd] ADJ (*new*) mai usato(-a), nuovo(-a); (*not made use of*) non usato(-a), non utilizzato(-a)

un·used [ʌnˈjuːst] ADJ: **to be unused to sth/to doing sth** non essere abituato(-a) a qc/a fare qc; **the company is unused to competition** l'azienda non è abituata ad avere concorrenti

un·usual [ʌnˈjuːʒʊəl] ADJ (*uncommon*) insolito(-a); (*exceptional: event, talent*) non comune, raro(-a); **an unusual shape** una forma insolita; **it's unusual to get snow at this time of year** è raro che nevichi in questo periodo dell'anno; **it's unusual for him to be late** è strano che arrivi in ritardo; **that's unusual for her** che strano, non è da lei; **isn't it unusual!** che originale!

un·usu·al·ly [ʌnˈjuːʒʊəlɪ] ADV (*unaccustomedly*) insolitamente; (*exceptionally: tall, gifted*) eccezionalmente; **most unusually, she was late** fatto molto strano, era in ritardo

un·veil [ʌnˈveɪl] VT (*plan*) svelare; (*monument*) scoprire, inaugurare

un·want·ed [ʌnˈwɒntɪd] ADJ (*person, effect*) non desiderato(-a); (*clothes*) smesso(-a); **to feel unwanted** sentirsi respinto(-a)

un·war·rant·ed [ʌnˈwɒrəntɪd] ADJ ingiustificato(-a)

un·wary [ʌnˈweərɪ] ADJ incauto(-a)

un·wa·ver·ing [ʌnˈweɪvərɪŋ] ADJ (*support, faith*) incrollabile, fermo(-a)

un·wel·come [ʌnˈwelkəm] ADJ (*guest, news*) non gradito(-a); (*development*) sgradito(-a); **to feel unwelcome** sentire che la propria presenza non è gradita

un·well [ʌnˈwel] ADJ indisposto(-a); **to feel unwell** non sentirsi bene; **he's unwell** è indisposto

un·wieldy [ʌnˈwiːldɪ] ADJ poco maneggevole

un·will·ing [ʌnˈwɪlɪŋ] ADJ riluttante; **to be unwilling to do sth** non essere disposto(-a) a fare qc, non voler fare qc; **he was unwilling to help me** non era disposto ad aiutarmi; **he was unwilling to admit he was wrong** non voleva ammettere di aver torto

un·will·ing·ly [ʌnˈwɪlɪŋlɪ] ADV controvoglia, malvolentieri, di malavoglia

un·wind [ʌnˈwaɪnd] (*pt, pp* **unwound**) VT srotolare, svolgere; **he unwound the rope** ha srotolato la fune ♦ VI srotolarsi; (*fam: relax*) distendersi, rilassarsi; **I need time to unwind** ho bisogno di tempo per rilassarmi

un·wise [ʌnˈwaɪz] ADJ (*decision, act*) avventato(-a); **it was unwise of you to do that** è stato imprudente da parte tua farlo

un·wit·ting [ʌnˈwɪtɪŋ] ADJ (*cause*) involontario(-a); (*victim*) inconsapevole; (*insult*) non intenzionale, non voluto(-a)

un·wit·ting·ly [ʌnˈwɪtɪŋlɪ] ADV senza volerlo; **quite unwittingly** in tutta innocenza

un·work·able [ʌnˈwɜːkəbl] ADJ (*plan*) inattuabile

un·wor·thy [ʌnˈwɜːðɪ] ADJ (*undeserving*) non degno(-a); (*ignoble*) indegno(-a); **to be unworthy of sth/to do sth** non essere degno(-a) di qc/di fare qc

un·wrap [ʌnˈræp] VT (*present*) aprire, scartare; (*parcel*) disfare; **after lunch we unwrapped the presents** dopo pranzo abbiamo aperto i regali

un·writ·ten [ʌnˈrɪtn] ADJ (*agreement*) tacito(-a); **it is an unwritten law that ...** la norma vuole che...

un·zip [ʌnˈzɪp] VT aprire (la chiusura lampo di); (*Comput*) dezippare, decomprimere

---

KEYWORD

up [ʌp] ADV

1 (*upwards, higher*) su, in alto; **up above** su in alto, al di sopra; **he's been up and down all evening** non è stato fermo un momento, stasera; **to walk up and down** camminare su e giù; **to jump up and down** saltellare; **she's still a bit up and down** (*sick person*) ancora non si è ripresa del tutto; **my office is five floors up** il mio ufficio è al quinto piano; **to stop halfway up** fermarsi a metà salita; **a bit higher up** un po' più su *or* in alto; **up in the sky/mountains** su nel cielo/ in montagna; **they've got the road up** la strada è interrotta; **"this side up"** "alto"; **the sun is up** il sole è sorto il sole; **up there** lassù; **to throw sth up in the air** gettare qc in aria; **he goes up to Oxford next year** va a Oxford l'anno prossimo; **up with Leeds United!** viva il Leeds United!, forza Leeds United!

2 (*installed, built*): **to be up** (*building*) essere terminato(-a); (*tent*) essere piantato(-a); (*shutters*) essere sollevato(-a); (*wallpaper*) essere su; (*picture*) essere appeso(-a); (*notice*) essere esposto(-a)

3 (*out of bed*): **to be up** essersi alzato(-a); **to be up and about again** essere di nuovo in piedi; **to be up early** alzarsi presto; **to be up late** (*at night*) fare tardi

4 (*in price, value*): **to be up** essere andato(-a) su (di); (*standard, level*): **to be up** essere salito(-a); **we are 3 goals up** abbiamo un vantaggio di 3 gol, vinciamo per 3 gol; **prices are up on last year** i prezzi sono più alti dell'anno scorso

5 (*finished*): **it's all up with her** (*fam*) per lei è finita; **the lease is up** il contratto d'affitto è scaduto; **his leave is up** il suo congedo è scaduto; **time's up** il tempo è scaduto; **when the year was up** finito l'anno

6 (*upwards*): **from £20 up** dalle 20 sterline in su

7 (*in or towards the north*) su; **he's up for the day** è qui per la giornata; **she's up from Birmingham** è arrivata da Birmingham; **up in Scotland** su in Scozia; **up North** su al Nord; **to live/go up North** vivere/andare su al Nord

8 (*Brit: knowledgeable*): **I'm not very well up on what's going on** non sono molto al corrente di ciò che sta succedendo; **he's well up in** *or* **on politics** è informatissimo sulla politica

9 (*fam: wrong*): **there's something up with him/with the TV** (lui)/la TV ha qualcosa che non va; **what's up?** cosa c'è che non va?; **what's up with him?** che ha?, che gli prende?

10 up to (*as far as*) fino a; **up to here** fin qui, fino a qui; **up to now** finora; **up to £ 100** fino a 100 sterline

11 what is he up to? (*fam, pej: doing*) cosa sta combinando?; **he's up to no good, he's up to something** sta architettando qualcosa

12 up to (*equal to*) all'altezza di; **he is not up to it** non ne è capace; **I don't feel up to it** non me la sento; **the book isn't up to much** (*fam*) il libro non vale un granché

13 it's up to you to decide (*depends on*) sta *or* tocca a te decidere; **I'd go, but it's up to you** io ci andrei, ma dipende da te

14 to be up against opposition (*faced with*) trovarsi di fronte a una forte opposizione; **you don't know what you're up against** non sai a cosa vai incontro; **he's really up against it** sta in un bell'impiccio

♦ PREP: **to go up** (*stairs*) salire su per; (*hill*) salire su per; (*river*)

risalire; **to travel up and down the country** viaggiare su e giù per il paese; **further up the page** più su nella stessa pagina; **halfway up the stairs** a metà scala; **it's up that road** è su per quella strada; **he went off up the road** se n'è andato su per la strada; **he pointed up the street** ha indicato in fondo alla strada; **to be up a tree** essere su un albero

♦ N: **ups and downs** (*in life, career*) alti e bassi *mpl*; **the road is full of ups and downs** la strada è molto accidentata; **he's on the up and up** le cose gli vanno di bene in meglio

♦ ADJ (*train, line*) per la città

♦ VI (*fam*): **she upped and left** ha preso e se n'è andata; **he upped and punched him** gli ha mollato un pugno

♦ VT (*fam: price*) alzare

up-and-coming [ʌpəndˈkʌmɪŋ] ADJ promettente

up·beat [ˈʌpˌbiːt] N (*Mus*) tempo in levare; (*positive trend*) tendenza al rialzo ♦ ADJ (*fam*) ottimistico(-a)

up·braid [ʌpˈbreɪd] VT rimproverare

up·bring·ing [ˈʌpˌbrɪŋɪŋ] N educazione *f*

upcoming [ˌʌpˈkʌmɪŋ] ADJ imminente, prossimo(-a)

up·date [ʌpˈdeɪt] VT aggiornare

up·end [ʌpˈend] VT (*box*) mettere in piedi; (*fig: system*) rovesciare

up·front [ˌʌpˈfrʌnt] (*fam*) ADJ franco(-a), aperto(-a); **up-front payment** pagamento immediato ♦ ADV (*pay*) in anticipo

up·grade [ˈʌpˌgreɪd] VT (*employee*) promuovere, avanzare di grado; (*job*) rivalutare; (*Comput*) far l'upgrade di; (*goods*) migliorare la qualità di; **universities cannot afford to upgrade laboratory facilities** le università non possono permettersi di modernizzare i laboratori; **I expect most Windows users will upgrade to Windows Longhorn** credo che gran parte degli utenti di Windows passeranno a Windows Longhorn; **travellers may want to upgrade from economy to business class** i viaggiatori potrebbero voler passare dalla classe economica alla classe business

up·heav·al [ʌpˈhiːvl] N (*disturbance*) scompiglio; (*Pol*) sconvolgimento; (*Geol*) sollevamento; **political upheaval** sconvolgimento politico

up·hill [ʌpˈhɪl] ADV: **to go uphill** andare in salita, salire ♦ ADJ in salita, in su; (*fig: task, battle*) arduo(-a); **it was an uphill struggle** è stata dura; **uphill ski** sci *m inv* a monte; **it's uphill all the way** è tutta salita; (*fig*) è una continua lotta

up·hold [ʌpˈhəʊld] (*pt, pp* **upheld**) VT (*frm: law, principle*) difendere; (*: decision, verdict*) confermare

up·hol·stery [ʌpˈhəʊlstərɪ] N tappezzeria

up·keep [ˈʌpˌkiːp] N manutenzione *f*

up·load [ˈʌpləʊd] VT (*Comput*) inviare, trasferire (*dal proprio computer ad un altro*)

up·market [ˌʌpˈmɑːkɪt] ADJ (*product*) che si rivolge ad una fascia di mercato superiore; (*restaurant*) elegante

upon [əˈpɒn] PREP = **on 1**

up·per [ˈʌpəʳ] ADJ **1** (*jaw, lip*) superiore; (*storey*) superiore, di sopra; **on the upper floor** al piano superiore; **the upper reaches of the Po** l'alto Po **2** (*in importance, rank*) superiore, più alto(-a), più elevato(-a); **the upper school** gli ultimi anni di scuola superiore; **the upper income bracket** la fascia di reddito più alto; **the upper middle class** l'alta borghesia ♦ N (*of shoe*) tomaia; **to be on one's uppers** (*fig: fam*) non avere il becco d'un quattrino

upper case N maiuscolo

upper-class [ˌʌpəˈklɑːs] ADJ (*district*) signorile; (*people*) dell'alta borghesia; (*accent*) aristocratico(-a); (*attitude*) snob *inv*; **a wealthy upper-class family** una famiglia benestante dell'alta borghesia; **an upper-class accent** un accento aristocratico

upper-cut [ˈʌpəˌkʌt] N (*Boxing*) uppercut *m inv*, montante *m*

upper hand N: **to have the upper hand** prendere il sopravvento

Upper House N: **the Upper House** (*in Britain*) la Camera Alta, la Camera dei Lords; (*in US etc*) il Senato

upper·most [ˈʌpəˌməʊst] ADJ (*thought*) dominante; (*echelon*) più alto(-a), più elevato(-a); **it was uppermost in my mind** è stata la mia prima preoccupazione

Upper Volta N: **the Upper Volta** l'Alto Volta *m*

up·right [ˈʌpˌraɪt] ADJ **1** (*posture*) ritto(-a), eretto(-a); (*post*) verticale **2** (*fig*) retto(-a), onesto(-a) ♦ ADV dritto(-a); **to**

stand upright (*person*) stare dritto(-a); (*object*) essere in posizione verticale ♦ N 1 (*post*) supporto verticale; (*of door, window*) montante *m* 2 (*piano*) pianoforte *m* verticale *or* a mezza coda

up·ris·ing [ˈʌpˌraɪzɪŋ] N rivolta, insurrezione *f*

up·roar [ˈʌpˌrɔː] N trambusto, clamore *m*; **the whole place was in uproar** c'era un gran baccano

up·roari·ous [ʌpˈrɔːrɪəs] ADJ (*group, meeting*) chiassoso(-a); (*laughter*) fragoroso(-a); (*welcome*) entusiastico(-a); (*very funny: joke, mistake*) esilarante

up·root [ʌpˈruːt] VT sradicare

up·set [*vb, adj* ʌpˈsɛt, *n* ˈʌpˌsɛt] (*pt, pp* **upset**) VT 1 (*container, contents*) rovesciare; (*boat*) capovolgere, rovesciare; (*fig: plan, schedule*) scombussolare 2 (*emotionally: disturb*) turbare; (: *stronger*) sconvolgere; (: *offend*) offendere; (: *annoy*) contrariare, seccare; **to upset sb** turbare qn; **you'll only upset her if you mention it** riuscirai solo a turbarla menzionandolo; **don't upset yourself** non te la prendere 3 (*make ill: person*) far star male; (: *stomach*) scombussolare ♦ ADJ 1 (*emotionally: disturbed*) turbato(-a); (: *stronger*) sconvolto(-a); (: *offended*) offeso(-a); (: *annoyed*) contrariato(-a), seccato(-a); **to get upset** (*distressed*) lasciarsi turbare *or* sconvolgere; (*offended*) offendersi; (*annoyed*) seccarsi; **don't get upset** non te la prendere; **she's still a bit upset** è ancora un po' turbata 2 **I have an upset stomach** ho lo stomaco in disordine *or* scombussolato ♦ N 1 (*disturbance: in plans etc*) contrattempo, contrarietà *f inv*; (*emotional*) dispiacere *m*; **emotional upsets** disturbi emotivi 2 **to have a stomach upset** (*Brit*) avere disturbi di stomaco, avere lo stomaco scombussolato

upset price N (*USA, Scot*) prezzo di riserva

up·set·ting [ʌpˈsɛtɪŋ] ADJ (*distressing*) sconvolgente; (*disturbing*) scioccante

up·shot [ˈʌpˌʃɒt] N (*result*) risultato; **the upshot of it all was that …** la conclusione è stata che…; **the upshot is that we have unhappy employees** il risultato è che abbiamo dipendenti insoddisfatti

up·side down [ˌʌpsaɪdˈdaʊn] ADV (*person*) a testa in giù; (*object*) alla rovescia, sottosopra; **the painting was hung upside down** il quadro era appeso alla rovescia; **to turn upside down** capovolgere; (*mattress*) rivoltare; (*fig*) mettere sottosopra *or* a soqquadro ♦ ADJ (*person*) a testa in giù; (*object*) capovolto(-a); **the room was upside down** (*in disorder*) la stanza era tutta sottosopra *or* a soqquadro

up·stage [ˌʌpˈsteɪdʒ] VT: **to upstage sb** rubare la scena a qn

up·stairs [*adv, n* ˌʌpˈstɛəz, *adj* ˈʌpstɛəz] ADV al di sopra; **to go upstairs** andare di sopra; **the people upstairs** quelli di sopra; **where's your coat?** - **it's upstairs** dov'è il tuo cappotto? - è di sopra; **he went upstairs to bed** è andato di sopra a coricarsi ♦ N: **the upstairs** il piano di sopra ♦ ADJ (*room*) al piano di sopra

up·start [ˈʌpˌstɑːt] N (*pej: in society*) parvenu *m inv*; (*in organization, hierarchy*) ultimo(-a) arrivato(-a) che si dà arie d'importanza

up·stream [ˌʌpˈstriːm] ADV (*be*) a monte; (*swim*) controcorrente; **to swim upstream** nuotare controcorrente; **to sail upstream** risalire la corrente

up·surge [ˈʌpˌsɜːdʒ] N (*of enthusiasm*) ondata; (*of prices, inflation*) impennata, improvviso aumento

up·take [ˈʌpˌteɪk] N (*fam*): **slow on the uptake** duro(-a) di comprendonio; **to be quick on the uptake** capire le cose al volo; (*number of people*) numero degli utilizzatori; (*of food, water etc*) consumo

up·tight [ʌpˈtaɪt] ADJ (*fam*) teso(-a), nervoso(-a)

up-to-date [ˌʌptəˈdeɪt] ADJ (*figures, edition*) aggiornato(-a); (*person*) ben informato(-a), aggiornato(-a); (*ideas*) attuale, al passo coi tempi; (*clothes*) alla moda; **to bring sb up-to-date** (**on sth**) aggiornare qn (su qc)

up·town [ʌpˈtaʊn] (*USA*) ADV (*walk, drive*) verso i quartieri residenziali; (*live*) in un quartiere residenziale ♦ ADJ dei quartieri residenziali

up·turn [ˈʌpˌtɜːn] N (*fig: improvement*) ripresa; (*in value of currency*) rialzo; (*in luck*) svolta favorevole

up·turned [ʌpˈtɜːnd] ADJ (*box*) capovolto(-a), rovesciato(-a); (*nose*) all'insù

up·ward [ˈʌpwəd] ADJ (*movement*) verso l'alto, in su; (*curve*)

ascendente; **upward tendency** (*Fin*) tendenza al rialzo ♦ ADV (*also:* **upwards**) 1 in su, verso l'alto; **to lie face upward** giacere supino(-a) 2 (*with numbers*): **from the age of 13 upwards** dai 13 anni in su; **upwards of 500** 500 e più

upwardly-mobile [ˌʒwədliˈməʊbaɪl] N: **to be upwardly-mobile** salire nella scala sociale

Ural Mountains [ˈjʊərəlˈmaʊntɪnz] NPL: **the Ural Mountains** (*also:* **the Urals**) gli Urali, i Monti Urali

ura·nium [jʊəˈreɪnɪəm] N uranio

Ura·nus [jʊəˈreɪnəs] N (*Myth, Astron*) Urano

ur·ban [ˈɜːbən] ADJ urbano(-a); **urban sprawl** sviluppo urbanistico incontrollato, espansione *f* urbana tentacolare

ur·bane [ɜːˈbeɪn] ADJ urbano(-a), civile

ur·bani·za·tion [ˌɜːbənaɪˈzeɪʃən] N urbanizzazione *f*

ur·chin [ˈɜːtʃɪn] N monello(-a)

Urdu [ˈʊəduː] N urdu *m*

urge [ɜːdʒ] N impulso, stimolo, voglia; **to feel an urge to do sth** sentire l'impulso di fare qc ♦ VT 1 (*try to persuade*) esortare; **to urge sb to do sth** esortare qn a fare qc; **they urged him to take action** lo hanno esortato ad agire; **he urged me to visit the Uffizi** mi ha raccomandato vivamente di visitare gli Uffizi; **he needed no urging** non si è fatto pregare 2 (*frm: advocate: measure*) fare pressioni per; (: *caution, acceptance*) raccomandare vivamente; **to urge that** insistere che + *sub*; **to urge sth on** *or* **upon sb** sottolineare a qn l'importanza di qc

▸ **urge on** VT + ADV (*also fig*) incitare, spronare

ur·gen·cy [ˈɜːdʒənsɪ] N (*of case, need*) urgenza; (*of tone of voice, pleas*) insistenza; **it is a matter of urgency** è una questione della massima urgenza

ur·gent [ˈɜːdʒənt] ADJ 1 (*message, need*) urgente 2 (*earnest, persistent: plea*) pressante; (: *tone*) insistente, incalzante

ur·gent·ly [ˈɜːdʒəntlɪ] ADV (*see adj*) d'urgenza, urgentemente; in modo pressante, con insistenza

uri·nal [jʊˈraɪnl] N (*building*) vespasiano; (*vessel*) orinale *m*

uri·nate [ˈjʊərɪˌneɪt] VI orinare

urine [ˈjʊərɪn] N orina

URL [juːaːˈrɛl] N ABBR (*Comput:* = *Uniform Resource Locator*) URL *m inv*, indirizzo internet

urn [ɜːn] N 1 (*vase*) urna 2 (*also:* **tea urn**, **coffee urn**) capace contenitore provvisto di cannella per tè, caffè (*specialmente nelle mense*)

Uru·guay [ˈjʊərəˌgwaɪ] N l'Uruguay *m*

Uru·guay·an [ˌjʊərəˈgwaɪən] ADJ, N uruguaiano(-a)

US [juːˈes] N ABBR (= *United States*): **the US** gli USA, gli Stati Uniti

us [ʌs] PERS PRON PL 1 (*direct, indirect*) ci; (*stressed, after prep, in comparatives*) noi; **they saw us** ci hanno visto; **they're older than us** sono più vecchi di noi; **why don't you come with us?** perché non vieni con noi?; **we had some suitcases with us** avevamo con noi delle valigie; **let's go** andiamo; **us Scots** noialtri Scozzesi 2 (*fam: me*): **give us a kiss** dammi un bacino

USA [juːesˈeɪ] N ABBR 1 (*Geog:* = *United States of America*) USA *mpl* 2 (*Mil:* = *United States Army*)

us·able [ˈjuːzəbl] ADJ utilizzabile, usabile

USAF [juːeseɪˈef] N ABBR = **United States Air Force**

us·age [ˈjuːzɪdʒ] N 1 (*Ling: use, way of using*) uso; **to be in common usage** essere nell'uso comune 2 (*custom*) usanza, uso 3 (*treatment, handling, use*) uso; (*of energy*) utilizzo *m*; **it's had some rough usage** è stato un po' bistrattato

USB stick N pennetta USB

USCG N ABBR = **United States Coast Guard**

USDA N ABBR = **United States Department of Agriculture**

use [*n* juːs, *vb* juːz] N 1 (*gen*) uso, utilizzazione *f*, impiego; **a new use for old tyres** un nuovo modo di utilizzare vecchi copertoni; **directions for use** istruzioni *fpl* per l'uso; **for the use of the blind** ad uso dei non vedenti; **for use in case of emergency** da usarsi in caso di emergenza; **ready for use** pronto(-a) per l'uso; **to make use of sth** far uso di qc, utilizzare qc; **in use** in uso; **out of use** fuori uso; **is your old radio still in use?** funziona ancora la tua vecchia radio?; **to be in daily use** venire adoperato(-a) quotidianamente; **to be no longer in use** non essere più usato(-a); **it's gone** *or* **fallen out of use** non lo si usa più; **for one's own use** per uso personale; **fit for use** che si può ancora usare; **to make good use of sth, put sth to good use** far buon uso di qc; **to find a use for sth** trovare il modo di utilizzare qc; **we have no further use for this** questo non ci serve più **2** (*usefulness*): **to be of use** essere utile, servire; **it's (of) no use** non serve, è inutile; **it's no use!** niente da fare!; **it's no use discussing it further** non serve a niente continuare a discuterne; **what's the use of all this?** a che serve tutto ciò?; **she's no use as a teacher** non vale niente come insegnante **3** (*ability or right to use*): **to lose the use of one's legs** perdere l'uso delle gambe; **I've got the use of the car this evening** stasera posso prendere la macchina ♦ vt **1** (*gen*) usare; **to use force** usare la forza; **"to be used only in emergencies"** "da usare solo in caso d'emergenza"; **to use sth as a hammer** usare qc come martello; **what's this used for?** a che serve?; **I could use a drink** (*fam*) non mi dispiacerebbe bere qualcosa; **this room could use some paint** (*fam*) una passata di vernice non farebbe male a questa stanza; **use your head** *or* **brains!** usa la testa *or* il cervello!; **use your eyes!** apri gli occhi! **use up** vt + adv (*strength*) usare; (*left-overs*) utilizzare; (*supplies*) dare fondo a; (*petrol, paper, money*) finire; **we've used up all the paint** abbiamo finito la vernice **2** (*make use of, exploit: influence*) servirsi di, adoperare; (: *opportunity*) sfruttare, approfittare di; **to use drugs** fare uso di droghe **3** (*use up, consume*) consumare; (*finish*) finire; (*supplies*) usare, utilizzare **4** (*old, liter: treat*) trattare ♦ aux vb: **I used to go there every day** ci andavo ogni giorno, ero solito(-a) andarci ogni giorno; **I used to live in London** ho abitato a Londra; **she used to do it** era solita farlo, lo faceva (una volta); **I didn't use to like math(s) when I was at school** la matematica non mi piaceva quando andavo a scuola; **things are not what they used to be** non è più come una volta

► **use up** vt + adv (*strength*) usare; (*left-overs*) utilizzare; (*supplies*) dare fondo a; (*petrol, paper, money*) finire; **we've used up all the paint** abbiamo finito la vernice

used¹ [juːzd] adj (*secondhand: clothing*) usato(-a); (: *car*) di seconda mano, d'occasione, usato(-a); (*dirty: glass, napkin*) (già) usato(-a)

used² [juːst] adj: **to be used to sth** essere abituato(-a) a qc; **don't worry, I'm used to it** non preoccuparti, ci sono abituato(-a); **to be used to doing sth** essere abituato(-a) a *or* avere l'abitudine di fare qc; **he wasn't used to driving on the right** non era abituato(-a) a guidare sulla destra; **to get used to** abituarsi a, fare l'abitudine a

use-ful [juːsfʊl] adj **1** (*gen*) utile; **he's a useful man to know** è una conoscenza utile; **that's a useful thing to know** buono a sapersi; **it is very useful to be able to drive** saper guidare è molto utile; **to make o.s. useful** rendersi utile; **to come in useful** fare comodo, tornare utile **2** (*fam: capable: player*) bravino(-a); **he is useful with a gun** sa maneggiare il fucile

use-ful-ness [juːsfʊlnɪs] n utilità

use-less [juːslɪs] adj **1** (*no good: remedy*) inefficace; (: *device*) inutile; (*unusable: object*) inservibile; **he's useless as a forward** come centravanti non vale niente; **I'm useless at tennis!** a tennis sono un impedito!; **you are useless!** sei un inetto! **2** (*pointless*) inutile; **it's useless arguing with him** non serve a niente *or* è inutile discutere con lui

user [juːzə'] n (*of public service, dictionary*) utente *m/f*; (*of petrol, gas*) consumatore(-trice); **car users** automobilisti *mpl*; **library users** lettori *mpl*; **drug users** drogati *mpl*

user-friendly [juːzə'frendlɪ] adj (*machine, also Comput*) di facile uso

user-name [juːzə,neɪm] n (*Comput*) nome *m* utente, *inv*

ush-er [ʌʃə'] n (*Law*) usciere *m*; (*in theatre, cinema*) maschera; (*at wedding*) valletto che accompagna gli ospiti ai

loro posti ♦ vt: **to usher sb in** far entrare qn; **it ushered in a new era** (*fig*) ha inaugurato una nuova era

USM [juːɛsˈɛm] n abbr = **United States Mint; United States Mail**

USN [juːɛsˈɛn] n abbr = **United States Navy**

USPO [juːɛspiːˈəʊ] n abbr = **United States Post Office**

USS [juːɛsˈɛs] abbr = **United States Ship** (*or* **Steamer**)

USSR [juːɛsɛsˈɑː'] n abbr (= *Union of Soviet Socialist Republics*) URSS *f*

usu. abbr = **usually**

usu-al [juːʒʊəl] adj (*gen*) solito(-a); **as usual** come al solito, come d'abitudine; **more than usual** più del solito; **at the usual time** alla solita ora; **earlier than usual** prima del solito; **as is usual on these occasions** come vuole la tradizione; **as is usual with this type of housing** come sempre in questo genere di alloggi; **he's not his usual self** di solito non è così; **he'll soon be his usual self again** tornerà presto ad essere quello di sempre; **"business as usual"** "l'ufficio (*or* il negozio etc*) è aperto al pubblico"; **it's not usual for her to be late** non è sua abitudine arrivare in ritardo ♦ n: **the usual, please!** (*fam: drink*) il solito, per favore!

usu-al-ly [juːʒʊəlɪ] adv di solito; **to be more than usually careful** fare ancora più attenzione del solito

usu-rer [juːʒərə'] n (*old*) usuraio(-a)

usurp [juːˈzɜːp] vt usurpare

UT abbr (*USA Post*: = *Utah*)

U-tah [juːtɑː] lo Utah

uten-sil [juːˈtɛnsl] n utensile *m*

uter-us [juːtərəs] n utero

utili-tar-ian [juːtɪlɪˈtɛərɪən] adj **1** (*Philosophy*) utilitarista, utilitaristico(-a) **2** (*furniture*) funzionale

util-ity [juːˈtɪlɪtɪ] n (*usefulness*) utilità; (*also*: **public utility**) servizio pubblico; **privatized utilities** servizi pubblici privatizzati; **of great utility** di grande utilità

utility room n locale adibito alla stiratura dei panni ecc

uti-li-za-tion [juːtɪlaɪˈzeɪʃən] n utilizzazione *f*

uti-lize [juːtɪlaɪz] vt (*frm: facilities, resources*) utilizzare; (: *talent, opportunity*) sfruttare

ut-most [ʌtməʊst] adj **1** (*greatest: simplicity, caution*) massimo(-a); (: *danger*) estremo(-a); **with the utmost speed** a tutta velocità; **of the utmost importance** della massima importanza; **it is of the utmost importance that** è estremamente importante che + *sub* **2** (*furthest: limits*) estremo(-a) ♦ n: **to do one's utmost (to do sth)** fare tutto il possibile (per fare qc); **to the utmost of one's ability** al limite delle proprie capacità

ut-ter¹ [ʌtə'] adj (*disaster, silence*) totale, assoluto(-a); (*madness*) puro(-a); (*fool*) perfetto(-a); **that's utter nonsense** sono tutte sciocchezze

ut-ter² [ʌtə'] vt (*groan, sigh*) emettere; (*cry, insult*) lanciare; (*word*) pronunciare, proferire; **she never uttered a word** non ha fiatato

ut-ter-ance [ʌtərəns] n (*remark, statement*) parole *fpl*; (*expression*) espressione *f*

ut-ter-ly [ʌtəlɪ] adv completamente, del tutto

U-turn [juːtɜːn] n inversione *f* a U; (*fig*) voltafaccia *m inv*, cambiamento di rotta, dietro-front *m inv*; **I braked and did a U-turn** ho frenato e fatto un'inversione a U; **a humiliating U-turn** un umiliante voltafaccia

Uzbekistan [ʊzbɛkɪˈstɑːn] n l'Uzbekistan *m*

Vv

V¹, v¹ [viː] N (letter) V, v f inv, m inv; **V for Victor** ≈ V come Venezia
V² ABBR (= volt) V
v. ABBR (= verse) v. **2** (= vide) v. (= vedi) **3** = versus
VA [ˌviːˈeɪ] ABBR (USA Post: = **Virginia**)
va·can·cy [ˈveɪkənsɪ] N **1** (job) posto (vacante); **have you any vacancies?** avete bisogno di personale?; **there were no vacancies** non c'erano posti vacanti; **they have vacancies for programmers** cercano programmatori **2** (in boarding house etc) stanza libera; **"no vacancies"** "completo" **3** (emptiness) vuoto
❑ **vacancy** is not translated by the Italian word *vacanza*
va·cant [ˈveɪkənt] ADJ **1** (seat, room) libero(-a); (property, house) vuoto(-a), libero(-a); (post) vacante; **vacant lot** terreno non occupato; (for sale) terreno in vendita **2** (look, expression) vuoto(-a), vacuo(-a), assente
va·cate [vəˈkeɪt] VT (house, seat, room) lasciare libero(-a); (post) lasciare, dare le dimissioni da
va·ca·tion [vəˈkeɪʃən] N (esp USA) vacanza, ferie fpl; (Univ) vacanze fpl; **on vacation** in vacanza, in ferie; **to take a vacation** prendere una vacanza, prendere le ferie ♦ VI (USA) andare in vacanza; **he vacations in Jamaica** va in vacanza in Giamaica
vacationer, (USA) **vacationist** N vacanziere(-a), (vacanziera)
vac·ci·nate [ˈvæksɪˌneɪt] VT vaccinare
vac·ci·na·tion [ˌvæksɪˈneɪʃən] N vaccinazione f
vac·cine [ˈvæksiːn] N vaccino; **polio vaccine** vaccino antipolio
vacuum [ˈvækjəm] N (also fig) vuoto; **in a vacuum** (fig) in assoluto isolamento; **their departure has left a vacuum** la loro partenza ha lasciato un vuoto ♦ VT passare l'aspirapolvere in; **to vacuum the lounge** passare l'aspirapolvere nel salotto ♦ VI passare l'aspirapolvere; **I've already vacuumed** ho già passato l'aspirapolvere
vacuum cleaner N aspirapolvere m inv
vacuum flask, (USA) **vacuum bottle** N termos m inv
vacuum-packed [ˈvækjəmˌpækt] ADJ confezionato(-a) sottovuoto inv
vaga·bond [ˈvægəˌbɒnd] N vagabondo(-a), barbone(-a)
va·gary [ˈveɪgərɪ] N (usu pl) capriccio
va·gi·na [vəˈdʒaɪnə] N vagina
va·gran·cy [ˈveɪgrənsɪ] N vagabondaggio
va·grant [ˈveɪgrənt] N vagabondo(-a), barbone(-a)
vague [veɪg] ADJ (comp -r, superl -st) (gen) vago(-a); (directions, description) impreciso(-a), confuso(-a); (indistinct: memory) sfocato(-a); (: person: absent-minded) distratto(-a); **I have a vague idea that ...** ho la vaga impressione che...; **I haven't the vaguest idea** non ho la minima or più pallida idea; **the vague outline of a ship** la sagoma indistinta or confusa di una nave; **a vague look** uno sguardo assente or vuoto
vague·ly [ˈveɪglɪ] ADV vagamente
vain [veɪn] ADJ (comp -er, superl -est) **1** (attempt, hope) vano(-a), inutile; **in vain** invano, inutilmente; **all our efforts were in vain** tutti i nostri sforzi sono stati inutili **2** (person) vanitoso(-a); **he's terribly vain** è terribilmente vanitoso
val·ance [ˈvæləns] N volant m inv, balza
val·edic·tory [ˌvælɪˈdɪktərɪ] ADJ (frm) di commiato
val·en·tine [ˈvælənˌtaɪn] N (card) biglietto di auguri per San Valentino; (: person: sweetheart) innamorato(-a)
Valentine's Day [ˈvæləntaɪnzdeɪ] N San Valentino
val·et [ˈvæleɪ] N cameriere m personale
valet parking N servizio di parcheggio (offerto da albergo ecc ai clienti)
valet service N (for car) servizio completo di lavaggio; (for clothes) servizio di lavanderia

val·iant [ˈvælɪənt] ADJ (liter) coraggioso(-a), valoroso(-a); **a valiant knight** un prode cavaliere
val·id [ˈvælɪd] ADJ (ticket, document, excuse) valido(-a); (claim, objection) giustificato(-a)
vali·date [ˈvælɪˌdeɪt] VT (contract, document) convalidare; (argument, claim) comprovare
va·lid·ity [vəˈlɪdɪtɪ] N (of document) validità; (of argument) fondatezza, validità
va·lise [vəˈliːz] N (old) borsa da viaggio
val·ley [ˈvælɪ] N valle f
val·our [ˈvælər], **val·or** (USA) N (liter) valore m (coraggio)
valu·able [ˈvæljʊəbl] ADJ (contribution, time) prezioso(-a); (painting, object) di valore, costoso(-a); **valuable help** un aiuto prezioso; **a valuable painting** un quadro di valore
valua·tion [ˌvæljʊˈeɪʃən] N (of monetary worth) valutazione f; (of quality) valutazione, stima; **what is your valuation of him?** che opinione ti sei fatto di lui?
value [ˈvæljuː] N **1** (worth) valore m; (usefulness) utilità; **to lose (in) value** (currency) svalutarsi; (property) perdere (di) valore; **to gain (in) value** (currency) guadagnare; (property) aumentare di valore; **of no value** di nessun valore, senza valore; **to be of great value to sb** avere molta importanza per qn; **it has been of no value to him** non gli è servito a nulla; **you get good value (for money) in that shop** si compra bene in quel negozio; **this dress is good value (for money)** questo abito ha un buon prezzo **2** **values** NPL (principles) valori mpl ♦ VT (financially) valutare, stimare; (friendship, independence etc) tenere a, apprezzare; **we're going to get the house valued** abbiamo intenzione di far valutare la casa; **it is valued at £80** è valutato 80 sterline; **it's not something I value very much** non è una cosa cui do molto valore
value add·ed tax [ˌvæljʊædɪdˈtæks] N (Brit) imposta sul valore aggiunto
val·ued [ˈvæljuːd] ADJ (appreciated) stimato(-a), apprezzato(-a), tenuto(-a) in grande considerazione
valu·er [ˈvæljʊər] N stimatore(-trice)
valve [vælv] N (all senses) valvola
vam·pire [ˈvæmpaɪər] N vampiro
van [væn] N (Aut: small) furgoncino; (: for furniture) furgone m; (Rail) vagone m
van·dal [ˈvændəl] N vandalo
van·dal·ism [ˈvændəˌlɪzəm] N vandalismo
van·dal·ize [ˈvændəˌlaɪz] VT (damage) danneggiare, rovinare; (destroy) distruggere
van·guard [ˈvænˌgɑːd] N avanguardia; **to be in the vanguard of progress** essere all'avanguardia del progresso; **to be in the vanguard of a movement** essere le avanguardie fpl di un movimento
va·nil·la [vəˈnɪlə] N vaniglia ♦ ADJ (ice cream) alla vaniglia; (essence) di vaniglia
van·ish [ˈvænɪʃ] VI svanire; **to vanish into thin air** svanire nel nulla, volatilizzarsi
van·ity [ˈvænɪtɪ] N vanità f inv
vanity case N beauty case m inv
van·tage [ˈvɑːntɪdʒ] N (also: advantage: Tennis) vantaggio
va·por·ize [ˈveɪpəˌraɪz] VT vaporizzare ♦ VI vaporizzarsi
va·pour, va·por (USA) [ˈveɪpər] N vapore m
vari·able [ˈvɛərɪəbl] ADJ (output, performance) non costante; (weather, wind) variabile; (mood) mutevole ♦ N (Math) variabile f
vari·ance [ˈvɛərɪəns] N **1** **to be at variance (with sb over sth)** essere in disaccordo (con qn per qc); **to be at variance (with sth)** (facts, statements) essere in contraddizione (con qc) **2** (Math) varianza
vari·ant [ˈvɛərɪənt] N variante f ♦ ADJ diverso(-a)

vari·ation [ˌvɛərɪ'eɪʃən] N (*of amount, quality, also Mus*) variazione *f*; (*in opinion*) cambiamento

vari·cose veins [ˌværɪkəʊs'veɪnz] NPL varici *fpl*, vene *fpl* varicose

var·ied ['vɛərɪd] ADJ (*types, sizes, qualities*) vario(-a), diverso(-a); (*life*) movimentato(-a); (*diet*) diversificato(-a)

va·ri·ety [və'raɪətɪ] N (*type*) varietà *f inv*, tipo; (*range, diversity*) molteplicità, varietà; **in a wide** *or* **large variety of colours** in una vasta gamma di colori; **for a variety of reasons** per una serie di motivi; **for variety** per variare

variety show N spettacolo di varietà

vari·ous ['vɛərɪəs] ADJ (*several*) diverso(-a), vario(-a); (*different*) diverso(-a), differente; **at various times** (*different*) in momenti diversi *or* differenti; **various times** (*several*) in verse *or* varie volte; **we visited various villages in the area** abbiamo visitato vari paesini della zona; **we went our various ways home** ognuno è tornato a casa per la sua strada

var·nish ['vɑːnɪʃ] N (*for wood*) vernice *f* trasparente; (*for nails*) smalto; **a tin of varnish** un barattolo di vernice ♦ VT (*wood*) verniciare; (*nails*) smaltare; **to varnish one's nails** smaltarsi le unghie, mettersi lo smalto sulle unghie

vary ['vɛərɪ] VT variare ♦ VI 1 (*change*): **to vary (with** *or* **according to)** variare (con *or* a seconda da) 2 (*deviate*): **to vary (from)** discostarsi (da); **the temperature varies** la temperatura è variabile; **these items vary in price** questi articoli si differenziano per il prezzo

vary·ing ['vɛərɪŋ] ADJ variabile, che varia; **with varying degrees of success** con più o meno successo

vase [vɑːz, (*USA*) veɪz] N vaso

vas·ec·to·my [væ'sɛktəmɪ] N vasectomia

Vas·eline ['væsɪˌliːn] (*Trademark*) vaselina

vast [vɑːst] ADJ (*comp* **-er**, *superl* **-est**) (*territory, expanse*) vasto(-a); (*sum, amount*) ingente; (*difference, improvement*) enorme; **at vast expense** con enorme dispendio di capitale

vast·ly ['vɑːstlɪ] ADV (*grateful, rich*) enormemente; **vastly superior to** di gran lunga superiore a; **he's vastly mistaken if ...** sbaglia di grosso se...; **a vastly overrated player** un giocatore incredibilmente sopravvalutato

vast·ness ['vɑːstnɪs] N (*of territory*) vastità, immensità; **the vastness of his wealth** la vastità delle sue ricchezze

VAT ['viːeɪtiː, væt] N ABBR (*Brit*: = *value added tax*) IVA *f*

vat [væt] N (*for wine, dye*) tino

Vati·can ['vætɪkən] N: **the Vatican** il Vaticano

vat·man ['vætmən] N (*Brit fam*): **the vatman** (*inspector*) l'ispettore *m* dell'IVA; (*Inland Revenue*) il fisco

vault¹ [vɔːlt] N (*Archit*) volta; (*of bank*) caveau *m inv*; (*tomb*) cripta, tomba; **family vault** cappella di famiglia, tomba di famiglia

vault² [vɔːlt] VT, VI: **to vault (over) sth** saltare qc con un balzo

vaunt·ed ['vɔːntɪd] ADJ: **much vaunted** tanto celebrato(-a)

VC [ˌviː'siː] N ABBR 1 (*Brit*: = *Victoria Cross*) medaglia al valore 2 = **vice-chairman**

VCR [ˌviːsiː'ɑː'] N ABBR = **video cassette recorder**

VD [ˌviː'diː] N ABBR = **venereal disease**

veal [viːl] N (*carne f* di) vitello

veer [vɪə'] VI (*ship, car*) virare; (*wind*) girare; **wind veering westerly at times** vento con tendenza a provenire da occidente; **the plane veered off the runway** l'aereo ha sterzato uscendo di pista; **the country has veered to the left** il paese ha fatto una svolta a sinistra; **the conversation veered round to politics** la conversazione si è spostata sulla politica

veg [vɛdʒ] N ABBR (*Brit fam*) = **vegetable(s)**

ve·gan ['viːgən] N vegetaliano(-a), vegano(-a)

veg·eta·ble ['vɛdʒɪtəbl] N 1 verdura; **vegetables** NPL (*in restaurant*) ≈ contorno *msg* (di verdure); **would you like some vegetables?** desidera un contorno di verdure?; (*at home*) vuoi un po' di verdura? 2 (*generic term: plant*) vegetale *m* ♦ ADJ (*oil, wax*) vegetale; (*soup*) di verdura; **vegetable soup** minestra di verdura

vegetable garden N orto

veg·etar·ian [ˌvɛdʒɪ'tɛərɪən] ADJ, N vegetariano(-a)

veg·etate ['vɛdʒɪˌteɪt] VI vegetare

veg·eta·tion [ˌvɛdʒɪ'teɪʃən] N vegetazione *f*

veg·eta·tive [ˌvɛdʒɪtətɪv] ADJ (*also Bot*) vegetativo(-a)

veg·gie·burg·er, veg·e·burg·er ['vɛdʒɪˌbɜːgə'] N hamburger *m inv* vegetariano

ve·he·mence ['viːɪməns] N veemenza

ve·he·ment ['viːɪmənt] ADJ (*speech, passions*) veemente, violento(-a); (*attack*) vigoroso(-a); (*dislike, hatred*) profondo(-a); **there was vehement opposition** ci fu una dura opposizione

ve·hi·cle ['viːɪkl] N veicolo; (*fig*) mezzo

ve·hicu·lar [vɪ'hɪkjʊlə'] ADJ (*frm*): **"no vehicular traffic"** "chiuso al traffico di veicoli"

veil [veɪl] N velo; **a black veil** un velo nero; **to take the veil** (*Rel*) prendere il velo; **under a veil of secrecy** protetto(-a) da una cortina di segretezza ♦ VT velare, coprire con un velo; **the town was veiled in mist** la città era avvolta dalla nebbia

veiled [veɪld] ADJ (*also fig*) velato(-a)

vein [veɪn] N (*in body, stone, also fig*) vena; (*Bot: on leaf*) nervatura; **in melancholy vein** in un tenore *m* malinconico; **in a different vein** in un tenore *m* diverso; **to reply in similar vein** rispondere a tono

Vel·cro ['vɛlkrəʊ] (*Trademark*) velcro

vel·lum ['vɛləm] N (*writing paper*) pergamena

ve·loc·ity [vɪ'lɒsɪtɪ] N velocità *f inv*

ve·lour, velours [və'lʊə'] N velours *m inv*

vel·vet ['vɛlvɪt] N velluto ♦ ADJ (*skirt, curtain*) di velluto

vend·ing ma·chine ['vɛndɪŋməˌʃiːn] N distributore *m* automatico

ven·dor ['vɛndɔː'] N venditore(-trice); **street vendor** venditore ambulante

ve·neer [və'nɪə'] N impiallacciatura; (*fig*) parvenza, vernice *f*

ven·er·able ['vɛnərəbl] ADJ venerabile; (*older person, appearance*) venerando(-a)

venereal disease N malattia venerea

Ve·netian [vɪ'niːʃən] ADJ, N veneziano(-a)

Venetian blind N veneziana

Ven·ezue·la [ˌvɛnɪ'zweɪlə] N Venezuela *m*

Ven·ezue·lan [ˌvɛnɪ'zweɪlən] ADJ, N venezuelano(-a)

venge·ance ['vɛndʒəns] N vendetta; **to take vengeance on sb** vendicarsi di qn; **to seek vengeance on** cercare di vendicarsi di; **with a vengeance** (*fig*) a più non posso, sul serio; **it started to rain again with a vengeance** ricominciò a piovere sul serio

venge·ful ['vɛndʒfʊl] ADJ (*liter*) vendicativo(-a)

Ven·ice ['vɛnɪs] N Venezia

veni·son ['vɛnɪsən] N carne *f* di cervo

ven·om ['vɛnəm] N (*also fig*) veleno

ven·om·ous ['vɛnəməs] ADJ (*also fig*) velenoso(-a)

vent [vɛnt] N (*Tech: airhole*) presa d'aria; (*of jacket*) spacco; **to give vent to one's anger** sfogare la propria rabbia; **to give vent to one's feelings** dare sfogo ai propri sentimenti ♦ VT: **to vent one's anger (on sb/sth)** scaricare *or* sfogare la propria rabbia (su qn/qc)

❑ **vent** is not translated by the Italian word *vento*

ven·ti·late ['vɛntɪˌleɪt] VT ventilare, arieggiare

ven·ti·la·tion [ˌvɛntɪ'leɪʃən] N aerazione *f*, ventilazione *f*

ventilation shaft N condotto di aerazione

ven·ti·la·tor ['vɛntɪˌleɪtə'] N ventilatore *m*

ven·trilo·quist [vɛn'trɪləkwɪst] N ventriloquo(-a)

ven·ture ['vɛntʃə'] N impresa; **a business venture** un'iniziativa commerciale; **a new venture in publishing** una nuova iniziativa editoriale; **this new venture** questa nuova impresa; **joint venture** joint venture *f inv* ♦ VT (*money, reputation, life*) rischiare; (*opinion, guess*) azzardare; **to venture to do sth** azzardarsi a fare qc; **if I may venture an opinion** posso azzardare *or* arrischiare un parere; **nothing ventured, nothing gained** chi non risica non rosica ♦ VI: **to venture on sth** avventurarsi in qc; **to venture out (of doors)** arrischiarsi ad uscire (di casa), azzardarsi ad uscire (di casa)

venture capital N (*Fin*) capitale *m* a rischio

venue ['vɛnjuː] N luogo (designato) (*per concerto, incontro sportivo, convegno*)

Venus ['viːnəs] N (*Astron, Myth*) Venere *f*

ve·rac·ity [və'ræsɪtɪ] N (*frm*) veridicità

ve·ran·da, ve·ran·dah [və'rændə] N veranda

verb [vɜːb] N verbo

ver·bal [ˈvɜːbəl] ADJ verbale
ver·bal·ly [ˈvɜːbəlɪ] ADV a voce, verbalmente
ver·ba·tim [vɜːˈbeɪtɪm] ADV, ADJ parola per parola
ver·bose [vɜːˈbəʊs] ADJ verboso(-a), prolisso(-a)
ver·dict [ˈvɜːdɪkt] N (Law) verdetto, sentenza; (opinion) giudizio, parere m; **verdict of guilty/not guilty** verdetto di colpevolezza/non colpevolezza; **his verdict on the wine was unfavourable** ha dato un giudizio sfavorevole sul vino
verge [vɜːdʒ] N (of road) bordo, margine m; (fig) orlo; **"soft verges"** (Brit) "banchina cedevole"; **to be on the verge of** (disaster) essere sull'orlo di; (a discovery) essere alle soglie di; **a company on the verge of bankruptcy** una società sull'orlo del fallimento; **to be on the verge of doing sth** essere sul punto di fare qc
  ▸ **verge on** VI + PREP rasentare
ver·ger [ˈvɜːdʒəʳ] N (Rel) sagrestano
veri·fi·ca·tion [ˌvɛrɪfɪˈkeɪʃən] N verifica, accertamento
veri·fy [ˈvɛrɪfaɪ] VT (check) verificare, controllare; (confirm the truth of) confermare
veri·table [ˈvɛrɪtəbl] ADJ vero(-a)
ver·min [ˈvɜːmɪn] NPL animali mpl nocivi; (fig: pej) parassiti mpl
Ver·mont [vɛːˈmɒnt] il Vermont
ver·mouth [ˈvɜːməθ] N vermut m inv
ver·nacu·lar [vəˈnækjʊləʳ] N vernacolo ♦ ADJ vernacolare
ver·sa·tile [ˈvɜːsəˌtaɪl] ADJ (person) versatile; (machine, tool) multiusi inv
verse [vɜːs] N **1** (of poem) verso; (stanza) strofa; (of Bible) versetto; **the last verse** l'ultimo verso **2** (no pl: poetry) poesia, versi mpl; **in verse** in versi
versed [vɜːst] ADJ: **to be well versed in sth** essere molto versato(-a) in qc
ver·sion [ˈvɜːʃən] N versione f
ver·sus [ˈvɜːsəs] PREP (Law, Sport: gen) contro
ver·te·bra [ˈvɜːtɪbrə] N (pl **vertebrae** [ˈvɜːtɪbriː]) vertebra
ver·te·brate [ˈvɜːtɪbrɪt] ADJ, N vertebrato(-a) ♦ N vertebrato
ver·ti·cal [ˈvɜːtɪkəl] ADJ (gen) verticale, perpendicolare; (cliff) a picco; **vertical takeoff** (Aer) decollo verticale ♦ N verticale f
ver·ti·cal·ly [ˈvɜːtɪkəlɪ] ADV verticalmente
ver·ti·go [ˈvɜːtɪgəʊ] N vertigine f; **to suffer from vertigo** soffrire di vertigini; **I get vertigo** mi vengono le vertigini
verve [vɜːv] N (of person) verve f, brio; (of painting, writing) vivacità
very [ˈvɛrɪ] ADV **1** (extremely) molto, tanto; **very happy** molto felice, felicissimo(-a); **it's very cold** fa molto freddo; **very well** molto bene; **very little** molto poco; **very much** molto, tanto; (stronger) moltissimo, tantissimo; **very much younger** molto più giovane; **are you tired?** — **(yes,) very** sei stanco? — (sì,) tanto; **he's so very poor** è poverissimo **2** (absolutely): **the very first** il (la) primissimo(-a), proprio il (la) primo(-a); **the very last** l'ultimissimo(-a), proprio l'ultimo(-a); **the very latest design** l'ultimissimo modello; **they are the very best of friends** sono grandissimi amici; **to wish sb the very best of luck** augurare a qn ogni fortuna; **at the very most** al massimo; **at the very least** come minimo, almeno; **at the very latest** al più tardi; **he won't come until 9 o'clock, at the very earliest** non arriverà prima delle 9, al più presto; **the very same hat** lo stesso identico cappello; **it's my very own** è proprio mio ♦ ADJ **1** (precise) stesso(-a); **that very day** quello stesso giorno; **his very words** le sue stesse parole; **her very words were ...** le sue parole testuali furono...; **he's the very man we want** è proprio l'uomo che cercavamo; **the very book which** proprio il libro che; **the very thing!** proprio quel che ci vuole!; **at that very moment** proprio in quel momento; **the very next day** proprio il giorno dopo **2** (mere) solo(-a); **the very thought (of it) alarms me** il solo pensiero mi spaventa, sono spaventato solo al pensiero; **the very idea!** neanche per sogno! **3** (extreme): **at the very bottom/top** proprio in fondo/in cima; **at the very end** proprio alla fine; **to the very end** fino alla fine; **in the very depths of the jungle** nel cuore della giungla
ves·pers [ˈvɛspəz] NPL (Rel) vespro
ves·sel [ˈvɛsl] N (ship) vascello, nave f; (container) recipiente m; (Anat) vaso; **fishing vessel** nave da pesca; **blood vessel** vaso sanguigno

vest¹ [vɛst] N (Brit: with sleeves) maglia intima; (: sleeveless) canottiera; (USA: waistcoat) panciotto, gilè m inv; **thermal vest** canottiera termica; **bullet-proof vest** giubbotto m antiproiettile, inv
  ❏ **vest** is not translated by the Italian word veste

vest² [vɛst] VT (frm): **to vest sb with sth** investire qn di qc; **to vest powers/authority in sb** conferire poteri/autorità a qn
vest·ed in·te·rest [ˌvɛstɪdˈɪntrɪst] N: **to have a vested interest in doing sth** avere un interesse personale nel fare qc; **vested interests** NPL (Comm) diritti mpl acquisiti
ves·ti·bule [ˈvɛstɪbjuːl] N atrio, vestibolo
ves·tige [ˈvɛstɪdʒ] N vestigio; **the last vestiges of** le ultime vestigia di
vest·ment [ˈvɛstmənt] N (Rel) paramento liturgico
ves·try [ˈvɛstrɪ] N sagrestia
Ve·su·vi·us [vɪˈsuːvɪəs] N Vesuvio
vet¹ [vɛt] N (esp Brit) veterinario ♦ VT (text) rivedere; (person, application) esaminare minuziosamente; **to vet sb for a job** informarsi su qn prima di offrirgli un posto
vet² [vɛt] N ABBR (esp USA) = veteran
vet·er·an [ˈvɛtərən] N (also: **war veteran**) reduce m
vet·er·an [ˈvɛtərən] ADJ: veteran soldier veterano; **a veteran teacher** un(-a) veterano(-a) dell'insegnamento; **she's a veteran campaigner for ...** lotta da sempre per... ♦ N (also: **war veteran**) reduce m
veteran car N (Brit) auto f inv d'epoca (anteriore al 1919)
vet·eri·nar·ian [ˌvɛtərɪˈnɛərɪən] N (USA) = **veterinary surgeon**
vet·eri·nary [ˈvɛtərɪnərɪ] ADJ veterinario(-a)
veterinary surgeon N (Brit) veterinario
veto [ˈviːtəʊ] N (pl **vetoes**) veto; **to use** or **exercise one's veto** esercitare il proprio diritto di veto; **to put a veto on** (op) porre il veto a ♦ VT (op)porre il veto a
vet·ting [ˈvɛtɪŋ] N (Brit): **positive vetting** indagine per accertare l'idoneità di un aspirante ad una carica ufficiale
vex [vɛks] VT irritare, contrariare
vexed [vɛkst] ADJ **1** irritato(-a); **to be/get vexed (with sb about sth)** essere irritato(-a)/irritarsi (con qn per qc) **2** (question) controverso(-a), dibattuto(-a)
VG [ˌviːˈdʒiː] ABBR (Brit Scol: = very good) ottimo
VHF [ˌviːeɪtʃˈef] N ABBR (= very high frequency) VHF f
VI ABBR (USA Post: = Virgin Islands)
via [ˈvaɪə] PREP (by way of: place) via; (: person) attraverso, tramite; (by means of) tramite, attraverso, per mezzo di; **we went to Rome via London** siamo andati a Roma passando per Londra; **they can send their work via email** possono mandare il loro lavoro tramite posta elettronica; **via satellite** via satellite
vi·abil·ity [ˌvaɪəˈbɪlɪtɪ] N attuabilità
vi·able [ˈvaɪəbl] ADJ (proposal) attuabile, fattibile; (foetus) in grado di sopravvivere; **a viable alternative** un'alternativa possibile; **the foetus was not viable** il feto non era in grado di sopravvivere
via·duct [ˈvaɪədʌkt] N viadotto
vial [ˈvaɪəl] N fiala
vibes [vaɪbz] NPL ABBR (fam) **1** (vibrations) atmosfera; **I got good vibes** l'impressione è stata buona **2** (Mus) = **vibraphone**
vi·brant [ˈvaɪbrənt] ADJ (sound) vibrante; (colour) vivace, vivo(-a); **to be vibrant with life** sprizzare vita da tutti i pori
vi·bra·phone [ˈvaɪbrəˌfəʊn] N vibrafono
vi·brate [vaɪˈbreɪt] VI: **to vibrate (with)** (quiver) vibrare (per); (resound) risuonare (di); (footsteps) risuonare di
vi·bra·tion [vaɪˈbreɪʃən] N vibrazione f
vi·bra·tor [vaɪˈbreɪtəʳ] N (for massage) vibromassaggiatore m (elettrico); (sex toy) vibratore m
vic·ar [ˈvɪkəʳ] N (Church of England) pastore m; (Roman Catholic) vicario
vic·ar·age [ˈvɪkərɪdʒ] N canonica (anglicana)
vi·cari·ous [vɪˈkɛərɪəs] ADJ: **to get vicarious pleasure out of sth** trarre piacere indirettamente da qc
vice¹ [vaɪs] N vizio; **vices and virtues** vizi e virtù
vice² [vaɪs] N (tool) morsa; **held in a vice** stretto(-a) in una morsa
vice- [vaɪs] PREF vice-

vice-chairman [ˌvaɪsˈtʃeəmən] N (pl -men) vicepresidente m

vice-chancellor [ˌvaɪsˈtʃɑːnsələʳ] N (Brit: Univ) rettore m (eletto, non onorario)

vice-president [ˌvaɪsˈprezɪdənt] N vicepresidente m

vice-roy [ˈvaɪsrɔɪ] N viceré m inv

vice squad N (squadra del) buon costume f

vice ver·sa [ˌvaɪsɪˈvɜːsə] ADV viceversa

vi·cin·ity [vɪˈsɪnɪtɪ] N vicinanze fpl

vi·cious [ˈvɪʃəs] ADJ (attack) brutale; (blow, kick) dato(-a) con cattiveria, violento(-a); (animal) cattivo(-a); (remark, criticism) crudele; (glare) malevolo(-a), d'odio; (tongue) velenoso(-a); **a vicious habit** un vizio

vi·cious·ness [ˈvɪʃəsnɪs] N (of behaviour) brutalità, ferocia; (of remark, criticism) cattiveria, malignità

vi·cis·si·tudes [vɪˈsɪsɪtjuːdz] NPL (frm) vicissitudini fpl

vic·tim [ˈvɪktɪm] N vittima; **to be the victim of** essere la vittima di; **he was the victim of a mugging** è stato vittima di un'aggressione; **to fall victim to** (fig: desire, sb's charms) essere vittima di

vic·timi·za·tion [ˌvɪktɪmaɪˈzeɪʃən] N persecuzione f; **to be the subject of victimization by sb** essere oggetto di persecuzione da parte di qn

vic·tim·ize [ˈvɪktɪˌmaɪz] VT perseguitare

vic·tor [ˈvɪktəʳ] N (in sport, battle) vincitore(-trice)

Vic·to·rian [vɪkˈtɔːrɪən] ADJ, N vittoriano(-a)

vic·to·ri·ous [vɪkˈtɔːrɪəs] ADJ (gen) vittorioso(-a); (shout) di vittoria, trionfante

vic·to·ry [ˈvɪktərɪ] N vittoria; **to win a victory over sb** riportare una vittoria su qn

video [ˈvɪdɪəʊ] N (fam) video m inv; **it's out on video** è uscito su videocassetta; **she lent me a video** mi ha prestato una videocassetta ♦ VT registrare; **I'll video the programme** registrerò il programma

video camera N videocamera

video cassette N videocassetta

video cassette recorder, video recorder N videoregistratore m

video·disk [ˈvɪdɪəʊˌdɪsk] N videodisco

video game N videogioco

video·phone [ˈvɪdɪəʊˌfəʊn] N videotelefono

video recorder N videoregistratore m

video recording N videoregistrazione f

video shop N videonoleggio

video tape N videocassetta

video wall N maxischermo (composto da più pannelli)

vie [vaɪ] VI: **to vie (with sb) for sth** competere (con qn) per qc; **to vie with one another for sth** contendersi qc; **nationalist politicians vying for power** politici nazionalisti che si contendono il potere

Vi·en·na [vɪˈenə] N Vienna

Vi·et·nam, Viet Nam [ˌvjetˈnæm] N Vietnam m

Vi·et·nam·ese [ˌvjetnəˈmiːz] ADJ vietnamita inv ♦ N (person) vietnamita m/f; (language) vietnamita m

view [vjuː] N 1 (sight, panorama) veduta; **there's an amazing view** c'è una vista fantastica; **a splendid view of the river** una splendida veduta del fiume; **50 views of Venice** 50 vedute di Venezia; **you'll get a better view from here** da qui vedrai meglio; **back/front view of the house** la casa vista da dietro/davanti; **to be in or within view (of sth)** essere in vista (di qc); **the house is within view of the sea** la casa ha la vista sul mare; **to come into or within view** arrivare in vista; **the city suddenly came into view** la città apparve all'improvviso; **in full view of sb** sotto gli occhi di qn; **hidden from view** nascosto(-a) alla vista; **on view** (house) in visione; (exhibit) in esposizione; **an overall view of the situation** (survey) una visione globale della situazione 2 (opinion) punto di vista, opinione f; **in my view** a mio parere, a mio avviso; **to take or hold the view that ...** essere dell'opinione che...; **to take a dim or poor view of sth** accogliere male qc; **they have similar views on this matter** hanno punti di vista simili sull'argomento 3 (consideration): **in view of the fact that ...** visto che..., considerato che...; **in view of this, ...** visto ciò... 4 (intention): **to have in view** avere in mente; **to keep sth in view** non perdere qc di vista; **with this in view** a questo scopo; **with a view to doing sth** con l'intenzione di fare qc ♦ VT (house) vedere; (television) guardare; (situation) considerare; **how do you view this development?** come consideri questo sviluppo?

view·er [ˈvjuːəʳ] N 1 (TV) telespettatore(-trice) 2 (for slides) visore m

view·finder [ˈvjuːˌfaɪndəʳ] N (Phot) mirino

view·point [ˈvjuːˌpɔɪnt] N (on hill) posizione f; (fig) punto di vista

vig·il [ˈvɪdʒɪl] N veglia; **to keep vigil** vegliare; **a prayer vigil** una veglia di preghiera

vigi·lance [ˈvɪdʒɪləns] N vigilanza

vigi·lant [ˈvɪdʒɪlənt] ADJ vigile

vigi·lan·te [ˌvɪdʒɪˈlæntɪ] N vigilante m/f (privato cittadino)

vig·or·ous [ˈvɪgərəs] ADJ (handshake, speech, protest) vigoroso(-a), energico(-a); (character) vitale; (plant) forte

vig·our, vig·or (USA) [ˈvɪgəʳ] N vigore m

vile [vaɪl] ADJ (horrible) orrendo(-a); (very bad: temper) pessimo(-a); (: smell) disgustoso(-a); **a vile habit** un vizio detestabile

vili·fy [ˈvɪlɪˌfaɪ] VT (frm) diffamare

vil·la [ˈvɪlə] N villa

vil·lage [ˈvɪlɪdʒ] N paese m, villaggio ♦ ADJ (of a village, villages) di paese; (local) del paese; **a village inn** una locanda di paese; **the village inn** la locanda del paese; **the village idiot** lo scemo del villaggio

vil·lag·er [ˈvɪlɪdʒəʳ] N abitante m/f di paese, paesano(-a)

vil·lain [ˈvɪlən] N mascalzone m; (hum: rascal) briccone(-a); (scoundrel) canaglia; (in novel, film) cattivo; (fam: criminal) delinquente m
   ❑ **villain** is not translated by the Italian word villano

VIN N ABBR (USA: = vehicle identification number)

vinai·grette [ˌvɪneɪˈgret] N vinaigrette f inv

vin·di·cate [ˈvɪndɪˌkeɪt] VT (assertion, claim) provare la fondatezza di, confermare; **he was finally vindicated** fu alla fine provato che aveva ragione
   ❑ **vindicate** is not translated by the Italian word vendicare

vin·di·ca·tion [ˌvɪndɪˈkeɪʃən] N giustificazione f; **in vindication of** a conferma di

vin·dic·tive [vɪnˈdɪktɪv] ADJ vendicativo(-a); **to feel vindictive towards sb** volersi vendicare di qn

vine [vaɪn] N (grapevine) vite f; (climbing plant) rampicante m
   ❑ **vine** is not translated by the Italian word vino

vin·egar [ˈvɪnɪgəʳ] N aceto

vine·grower [ˈvaɪnˌgrəʊəʳ] N viticoltore m

vine·growing [ˈvaɪnˌgrəʊɪŋ] ADJ viticolo(-a) ♦ N viticoltura

vine·yard [ˈvɪnjəd] N vigna, vigneto

vin·tage [ˈvɪntɪdʒ] N (harvest) vendemmia; (season) periodo della vendemmia; (year) annata; **what vintage is this wine?** di che annata è questo vino?; **the 1980 vintage** il vino del 1980; **a good vintage** una buona annata

vintage car N auto f inv d'epoca

vintage wine N vino d'annata

vi·nyl [ˈvaɪnɪl] N vinile m; (record) disco di vinile

vio·la¹ [vɪˈəʊlə] N (Mus) viola

vio·la² [vɪˈəʊlə] N (Bot) viola

vio·late [ˈvaɪəˌleɪt] VT violare

vio·la·tion [ˌvaɪəˈleɪʃən] N violazione f; **in violation of sth** in contravvenzione f inv a qc

vio·lence [ˈvaɪələns] N violenza; (Pol) incidenti mpl violenti; **outbreaks of violence** episodi di violenza; **acts of violence** atti di violenza; **robbery with violence** rapina a mano armata; **sex and violence** violenza e sesso; **to do violence to sth** (fig) fare violenza a qc

vio·lent [ˈvaɪələnt] ADJ (gen) violento(-a); **to die a violent death** morire di morte violenta; **a violent temper** un temperamento violento; **to be in a violent temper** essere furioso(-a); **a violent dislike of sb/sth** una violenta avversione per qn/qc; **by violent means** con l'uso della forza

vio·lent·ly [ˈvaɪələntlɪ] ADV (attack, react) in modo violento, violentemente; (severely: sick, angry) terribilmente; **to fall violently in love with sb** innamorarsi follemente di qn

vio·let [ˈvaɪəlɪt] N (Bot) violetta; (colour) violetto ♦ ADJ violetto(-a)

vio·lin [ˌvaɪəˈlɪn] N violino ♦ ADJ (*case, concerto*) per violino
vio·lin·ist [ˌvaɪəˈlɪnɪst] N violinista *m/f*
VIP [ˌviːaɪˈpiː] N ABBR (= *very important person*) VIP *m/f inv*
vi·per [ˈvaɪpəʳ] N (*Zool, also fig*) vipera
vi·ral [ˈvaɪərəl] ADJ virale; (*advertising, marketing*) fatto(-a) da utenti internet tramite la diffusione di videoclip
vir·gin [ˈvɜːdʒɪn] N vergine *f*; **she/he is a virgin** lei/lui è vergine; **the Virgin** (*Mary*) la Beata Vergine ♦ ADJ (*fig: forest, soil*) vergine; **virgin snow** neve fresca
Vir·gin·ia [vəˈdʒɪnjə] N il Virginia
Vir·gin Is·lands le Isole Vergini
vir·gin·ity [vɜːˈdʒɪnɪtɪ] N verginità
Vir·go [ˈvɜːgəʊ] N (*Astron, Astrol*) Vergine *f*; **to be Virgo** essere della Vergine; **I'm Virgo** sono della Vergine
vir·ile [ˈvɪraɪl] ADJ virile
vi·ril·ity [vɪˈrɪlɪtɪ] N virilità
vir·tual [ˈvɜːtjʊəl] ADJ effettivo(-a), vero(-a); (*Comput, Phys*) virtuale; **the virtual leader** il capo all'atto pratico; **the strike led to the virtual closure of the dock** lo sciopero ha praticamente portato alla chiusura del porto; **it was a virtual defeat** di fatto è stata una sconfitta; **it's a virtual impossibility** è praticamente impossibile; **it's a virtual certainty** è praticamente una certezza
vir·tu·al·ly [ˈvɜːtjʊəlɪ] ADV (*in effect*) di fatto; (*to all intents and purposes*) praticamente; **she virtually runs the business** di fatto è lei che gestisce l'azienda; **it is virtually impossible to do anything** è praticamente impossibile fare qualcosa
❏ **virtually** is not translated by the Italian word *virtualmente*
virtual reality N (*Comput*) realtà *f* virtuale
vir·tue [ˈvɜːtjuː] N (*goodness*) virtù *f inv*; (*advantage*) pregio, vantaggio; **it has the virtue of simplicity** *or* **of being simple** ha il pregio di essere semplice; **its other great virtue is its quality** l'altro pregio è la qualità; **I see no virtue in doing that** non vedo nessun vantaggio nel farlo; **to make a virtue of necessity** fare di necessità virtù; **by virtue of** in virtù di, grazie a; **vices and virtues** vizi e virtù
vir·tu·os·ity [ˌvɜːtjʊˈɒsɪtɪ] N virtuosismo
vir·tu·o·so [ˌvɜːtjʊˈəʊzəʊ] N virtuoso(-a)
vir·tu·ous [ˈvɜːtjʊəs] ADJ virtuoso(-a)
viru·lent [ˈvɪrʊlənt] ADJ (*frm*) virulento(-a)
vi·rus [ˈvaɪərəs] N virus *m inv*
visa [ˈviːzə] N visto
vis-à-vis [ˌviːzɑːˈviː] PREP rispetto a, in confronto a, nei riguardi di
vis·count [ˈvaɪkaʊnt] N visconte *m*
vis·cous [ˈvɪskəs] ADJ viscoso(-a)
vise [vaɪs] N (*USA*) = **vice²**
vis·ibil·ity [ˌvɪzɪˈbɪlɪtɪ] N visibilità
vis·ible [ˈvɪzəbl] ADJ **1** visibile; **visible to the naked eye** che si può vedere ad occhio nudo, visibile ad occhio nudo; **to become visible** apparire **2** (*obvious*) evidente; **visible exports/imports** esportazioni *fpl* /importazioni, *fpl* visibili; **a visible effort** uno sforzo palese
vis·ibly [ˈvɪzəblɪ] ADV visibilmente
vi·sion [ˈvɪʒən] N **1** (*eyesight*) vista, capacità visiva; **loss of vision** la perdita della vista **2** (*imagination, foresight, apparition*) visione *f*; **a man of vision** un uomo lungimirante *or* che vede lontano; **my vision of the future** la mia visione del futuro; **his vision of society** la sua visione della società; **to see visions** avere le visioni; **to have a vision of** immaginare; **I had visions of having to walk home** già mi vedevo dover andare a casa a piedi
vi·sion·ary [ˈvɪʒənərɪ] N visionario(-a) ♦ ADJ lungimirante; (*dreamlike*) irreale
vis·it [ˈvɪzɪt] N visita; (*stay*) soggiorno; **to go on a visit to** (*person*) andare in visita da; (*place*) andare in visita a; **to pay a visit to** (*person*) fare una visita a; (*place*) andare a visitare; **on a private/official visit** in visita privata/ufficiale ♦ VT **1** (*person*) andare a trovare; (*frm*) andare in visita da; (*place: go and see*) visitare; (: *inspect*) ispezionare; **I visited my grandmother last week** sono andato(-a) a trovare mia nonna la settimana scorsa; **we'd like to visit the castle** ci piacerebbe visitare il castello **2** (*stay with: person*) essere ospite di
▸ **visit with** VI + PREP (*USA*) chiacchierare con

vis·it·ing [ˈvɪzɪtɪŋ] ADJ (*speaker, professor, team*) ospite
visiting card N biglietto da visita
visiting hours NPL orario *msg* delle visite
visi·tor [ˈvɪzɪtəʳ] N (*guest*) ospite *m/f*; (*tourist*) turista *m/f*; (*in hospital, at zoo, exhibition*) visitatore(-trice); **important visitors** visitatori importanti; **visitors to the town** i visitatori della città; **to have a visitor** avere una visita; **you've got a visitor** (*in hospital, at home*) c'è una visita per te
visitor centre, (*USA*) **visitor center** N centro informazioni *per visitatori* di museo, zoo, parco ecc
visitors' book N (*in hotel*) registro dei clienti; (*in museum*) registro dei visitatori
vi·sor [ˈvaɪzəʳ] N (*on helmet*) visiera; (*Aut*) aletta parasole
vis·ta [ˈvɪstə] N (*view*) vista; (*fig*) prospettiva
vis·ual [ˈvɪzjʊəl] ADJ visivo(-a)
visual aid N sussidio visivo
visual arts NPL: **the visual arts** le arti figurative
visual display unit N (*Comput*) videoterminale *m*
visu·al·ize [ˈvɪzjʊəlaɪz] VT (*imagine*) immaginare, immaginarsi; (*foresee*) prevedere; **to visualize sb doing sth** immaginare qn che fa qc
visu·al·ly [ˈvɪzjʊəlɪ] ADV: **visually handicapped** (*blind*) non vedente; (*visually impaired*) videoleso(-a); **visually the film was good** sul piano dell'immagine il film era buono; **visually appealing** piacevole a vedersi
vi·tal [ˈvaɪtl] ADJ **1** (*gen*) vitale; (*error*) fatale; **of vital importance (to sb/sth)** di vitale importanza (per qn/qc); **it is vital that** è essenziale che; **it's vital to sterilize the equipment** è essenziale sterilizzare l'attrezzatura; **vital information** informazioni *fpl* d'importanza vitale **2** (*lively*) pieno(-a) di vitalità
vi·tal·ity [vaɪˈtælɪtɪ] N vitalità; **his performance lacked vitality** la sua esecuzione mancava di brio
vi·tal·ly [ˈvaɪtlɪ] ADV: **vitally important** di vitale importanza; **vitally urgent** estremamente urgente
vital statistics NPL (*of population*) statistica *fsg* demografica
vita·min [ˈvɪtəmɪn] N vitamina; **with added vitamins** vitaminizzato(-a)
vit·i·ate [ˈvɪʃɪeɪt] VT (*frm: all senses*) viziare
vit·re·ous [ˈvɪtrɪəs] ADJ (*china, enamel*) vetrificato(-a); (*rock*) vetroso(-a)
vit·ri·ol·ic [ˌvɪtrɪˈɒlɪk] ADJ (*fig*) al vetriolo
viva [ˈvaɪvə] N (*also:* **viva voce**) (*esame m*) orale, *m*
vi·va·cious [vɪˈveɪʃəs] ADJ vivace, pieno(-a) di brio
vi·vac·ity [vɪˈvæsɪtɪ] N vivacità
viv·id [ˈvɪvɪd] ADJ (*colour*) vivo(-a), vivido(-a); (*dream, recollection, expression on face*) chiaro(-a); (*description, memory*) vivido(-a); **to have a vivid imagination** avere una fervida immaginazione
viv·id·ly [ˈvɪvɪdlɪ] ADV (*describe*) in modo vivido; (*remember*) chiaramente; **so vividly described** descritto(-a) così vividamente; **I remember it vividly** lo ricordo chiaramente
vivi·sec·tion [ˌvɪvɪˈsekʃən] N vivisezione *f*
vix·en [ˈvɪksn] N volpe *f* femmina; (*pej: woman*) vipera
viz ABBR (= *videlicet: namely*) cioè
VLF [ˌviːelˈef] N ABBR (= *very low frequency*) VLF (= *bassissima frequenza*)
V-neck [ˈviːnek] N maglione *m* con scollo a V
VOA [ˌviːəʊˈeɪ] N ABBR (= *Voice of America*) voce *f* dell'America (*alla radio*)
vo·cabu·lary [vəʊˈkæbjʊlərɪ] N (*gen*) vocabolario; (*in textbook*) vocabolario, dizionario; **we have to learn all the new vocabulary** dobbiamo imparare tutti i vocaboli nuovi
vo·cal [ˈvəʊkəl] ADJ **1** (*gen*) vocale **2** (*fig: vociferous*) pronto(-a) a esprimere la propria opinione
vocal chords NPL corde *fpl* vocali
vo·cal·ist [ˈvəʊkəlɪst] N cantante *m/f* (*in un gruppo*)
vo·ca·tion [vəʊˈkeɪʃən] N vocazione *f*; **to have a vocation for teaching** avere la vocazione dell'insegnamento
vo·ca·tion·al [vəʊˈkeɪʃənl] ADJ (*training*) professionale
vo·cif·er·ous [vəʊˈsɪfərəs] ADJ rumoroso(-a)
vod·ka [ˈvɒdkə] N vodka *f inv*
vogue [vəʊg] N (*fashion*) moda; (*popularity*) voga; **to be in vogue, be the vogue** essere di moda, essere in voga

voice [vɔɪs] N (gen, also Gram) voce f; **to lose one's voice** perdere la voce; **she is in fine voice again** ha riacquistato la sua bella voce; **in a loud/soft voice** a voce alta/bassa; **at the top of one's voice** a tutta voce, con quanta voce si ha in gola or in corpo; **with one voice** all'unisono; **to have a voice in the matter** aver voce in capitolo; **to give voice to** esprimere; **I heard voices** sentivo delle voci ♦ VT (feelings, opinions) esprimere

voice-mail [ˈvɔɪsˌmeɪl] N = **v-mail**

voice-over [ˈvɔɪsˌəʊvəʳ] N (TV, Cine) voce f fuori campo, inv

void [vɔɪd] ADJ (frm: Law) nullo(-a); (empty) vuoto(-a); **void of** privo(-a) di; **to make** or **render a contract void** invalidare un contratto ♦ N vuoto; **to fill the void** colmare il vuoto

voile [vɔɪl] N voile m

vol. ABBR (= volume) vol.

vola·tile [ˈvɒləˌtaɪl] ADJ (Chem) volatile; (fig: situation) esplosivo(-a); (: character) volubile

vol·can·ic [vɒlˈkænɪk] ADJ vulcanico(-a)

vol·ca·no [vɒlˈkeɪnəʊ] N (pl **volcanoes**) vulcano

vo·li·tion [vəˈlɪʃən] N: **of one's own volition** di propria volontà

vol·ley [ˈvɒlɪ] N (of shots, stones, insults) raffica, scarica; (of gunfire) salva; (Tennis) volée f inv, volata

volley·ball [ˈvɒlɪˌbɔːl] N pallavolo f

volt [vəʊlt] N volt m inv

volt·age [ˈvəʊltɪdʒ] N tensione f, voltaggio; **high/low voltage** alta/bassa tensione

vol·uble [ˈvɒljʊbl] ADJ loquace
❑ **voluble** is not translated by the Italian word *volubile*

vol·ume [ˈvɒljuːm] N 1 (book) volume m; **volume one/two** volume primo/secondo 2 (size: sound) volume m; (of tank) capacità f inv; **he turned down the volume** ha abbassato il volume; **the volume of sales** il volume delle vendite 3 **to speak volumes** (express a great deal) dire tutto; **his expression spoke volumes** la sua espressione lasciava capire tutto; **it speaks volumes for his charm** la dice lunga sul suo fascino

volume control N (Radio, TV) regolatore m or manopola del volume

volume discount N (Comm) vantaggio sul volume di vendita

vo·lu·mi·nous [vəˈluːmɪnəs] ADJ voluminoso(-a); (writer) prolifico(-a); (notes) abbondante

vol·un·tari·ly [ˈvɒləntərɪlɪ] ADV spontaneamente, volontariamente

vol·un·tary [ˈvɒləntərɪ] ADJ (statement, confession) spontaneo(-a); (attendance) facoltativo(-a); (unpaid: contribution, work, worker) volontario(-a); **attendance is voluntary** la frequenza è facoltativa; **to do voluntary work** fare volontariato; **voluntary contributions** contributi mpl volontari

voluntary liquidation N (Comm) liquidazione f volontaria

vol·un·teer [ˌvɒlənˈtɪəʳ] N (Mil: gen) volontario(-a) ♦ VT (one's help, services, suggestion) offrire spontaneamente; (information) fornire; **no-one volunteered an answer** nessuno si è offerto di rispondere; **he rarely volunteers his opinion** è raro che esprima la propria opinione spontaneamente

♦ VI (for a task) offrirsi come volontario(-a), offrirsi spontaneamente; (Mil) arruolarsi volontario(-a); **to volunteer to do sth** offrirsi spontaneamente di fare qc, offrirsi volontario(-a) per fare qc ♦ ADJ (forces, helpers) volontario(-a); (corps) di volontari

vo·lup·tu·ous [vəˈlʌptjʊəs] ADJ (pleasure, sensation) voluttuoso(-a); (lips, figure) sensuale

vom·it [ˈvɒmɪt] N vomito ♦ VT, VI vomitare

vo·ra·cious [vəˈreɪʃəs] (liter) ADJ (appetite) smisurato(-a); (reader) avido(-a)

vote [vəʊt] N voto; (ballot, election) votazione f; **vote for/against** voto a favore/contrario; **to put sth to the vote, take a vote on sth** mettere qc ai voti; **to have the vote** avere diritto di voto; **as the 1997 vote showed** com'è risultato dalle votazioni del 1997; **the Labour vote has decreased** il partito laburista ha perso voti; **they won by two votes** hanno vinto per due voti; **now let's take a vote** passiamo ora alla votazione ♦ VT (gen) votare; (sum of money) votare a favore di; **the bill was voted through parliament** la proposta di legge è stata approvata dal parlamento; **he was voted secretary** è stato eletto segretario; **to vote a proposal down** respingere una proposta ♦ VI: **to vote (for sb/sth)** votare (per qn/qc); **to vote on sth** mettere qc ai voti; **to vote Labour/Conservative** votare laburista/conservatore; **to vote to do sth** scegliere di fare qc; **to vote against/in favour of sth** votare a favore di/contro qc; **I vote we turn back** (fam) io propongo di tornare indietro
▸ **vote down** VT + ADV bocciare ai voti
▸ **vote in** VT + ADV eleggere
▸ **vote out** VT + ADV: **to vote sb out** votare a sfavore della rielezione di qn

vot·er [ˈvəʊtəʳ] N elettore(-trice)

vot·ing [ˈvəʊtɪŋ] N votazione f, voto

voting right N (of shareholder) diritto di voto

vouch [vaʊtʃ] VI: **to vouch for sth** garantire qc; **to vouch for sb** garantire per qn

vouch·er [ˈvaʊtʃəʳ] N buono, tagliando, coupon m inv; **travel voucher** voucher m inv; **a gift voucher** un buono acquisto

vow [vaʊ] N voto; **to make** or **make a vow to do sth** fare voto di fare qc; **to take one's vows** (Rel) prendere i voti ♦ VT (obedience, allegiance) giurare; **to vow to do sth/that** giurare di fare qc/che

vow·el [ˈvaʊəl] N vocale f

voy·age [ˈvɔɪdʒ] N viaggio per mare; **the voyage out/back** il viaggio di andata/di ritorno

vo·yeur [vwaːˈjɜːʳ] N guardone(-a), voyeur m inv

VP [ˌviːˈpiː] N ABBR (= vice-president) VP

vs ABBR = **versus**

VT ABBR (USA Post: = Vermont)

vul·gar [ˈvʌlgəʳ] ADJ (gen, also pej) volgare

vul·gar·ity [vʌlˈgærɪtɪ] N volgarità

vul·ner·abil·ity [ˌvʌlnərəˈbɪlɪtɪ] N vulnerabilità

vul·ner·able [ˈvʌlnərəbl] ADJ (person) vulnerabile; (position) esposto(-a)

vul·ture [ˈvʌltʃəʳ] N avvoltoio

Ww

W¹, w¹ [ˈdʌbljuː] N (*letter*) W, w *f inv*, *m inv*; **W for William** ≈ W come Washington

W² ABBR **1** (= *West*) O **2** (*Elec*: = *watt*) W

WA ABBR (*USA Post*: = **Washington**)

wad [wɒd] N (*of cloth*) tampone *m*; (*of chewing gum, putty*) pallina; (*of cotton wool*) batuffolo; (*of papers, banknotes*) fascio; **a wad of banknotes** una mazzetta di banconote

wad·ding [ˈwɒdɪŋ] N imbottitura

wad·dle [ˈwɒdl] VI camminare come una papera; **to waddle in/out** *etc* entrare/uscire *etc* camminando come una papera

wade [weɪd] VI: **to wade through** (*water, mud*) camminare in; (*long grass, corn*) farsi strada attraverso; (*fig: book*) leggere con fatica; **to wade ashore** raggiungere a piedi la riva; **to wade into sb** (*fig*) scagliarsi su qn; **he waded in and helped us** (*fig*) si rimboccò le maniche e ci aiutò ♦ VT (*river*) guadare

wa·fer [ˈweɪfəʳ] N (*Culin, Elec*) wafer *m inv*; (*with ice cream*) cialda; (*Rel*) ostia

wafer-thin [ˌweɪfəˈθɪn] ADJ sottilissimo(-a)

waf·fle [ˈwɒfl] N (*Culin*) cialda; (*fam: talk*) chiacchiere *fpl*, ciance *fpl* ♦ VI (*fam: also:* **waffle on**) cianciare, chiacchierare; (*in exam, essay*) chiacchierare molto e dire poco

waffle iron N stampo per cialde

waft [wɑːft] VT (*sound, scent*) portare ♦ VI diffondersi

wag [wæg] N: **with a wag of its tail** dimenando la coda ♦ VT: **the dog wagged its tail** il cane scodinzolò; **he wagged his head** scosse la testa; **to wag one's finger at sb** fare un cenno di rimprovero a qn scuotendo il dito ♦ VI (*tail*) dimenarsi; **that'll set the tongues wagging** (*fig*) farà scatenare le malelingue; **his tongue never stops wagging** (*fig*) non sta mai zitto

wage [weɪdʒ] N (*often pl*) paga; **a day's wages** un giorno di paga; **she gets a good wage** è pagata bene; **minimum wage** minimo salariale; **a low wage** una paga bassa; **he collected his wages** ha ritirato la paga ♦ VT (*campaign*) intraprendere; **to wage war** fare la guerra ♦ ADJ (*demand, negotiations*) salariale

wage claim N rivendicazione *f* salariale

wage differential N differenziali *mpl* salariali

wage earn·er [ˈweɪdʒˌɜːnəʳ] N salariato(-a); **the family wage earner** il sostegno economico della famiglia

wage freeze N blocco dei salari

wage packet N (*Brit*) busta *f* paga, *inv*

wa·ger [ˈweɪdʒəʳ] N: **wager (on)** scommessa (su) ♦ VT (*sum of money*): **to wager (on)** puntare (su), scommettere (su); **to wager that ...** scommettere che...

wag·gle [ˈwægl] N: **with a waggle of one's hips** ancheggiando; **with a waggle of its tail** scodinzolando ♦ VT (*tail*) dimenare, agitare; **to waggle one's hips** ancheggiare ♦ VI dimenarsi, agitarsi

wag·on, wag·gon [ˈwægən] N (*horse-drawn*) carro; (*truck*) camion *m inv*; (*Rail*) vagone *m* merci, *inv*; (*trolley*) carrello; **a horse and wagon** un carro trainato da un cavallo; **he's on the wagon again!** (*fam*) ha nuovamente smesso di bere!

wail [weɪl] N (*of suffering*) gemito; (*of baby*) vagito; (*of siren*) urlo; (*of wind*) ululato; **a wail of protest** un urlo di protesta ♦ VI (*see n*) gemere; vagire; urlare; ululare

waist [weɪst] N (*Anat: of dress*) vita; (*fig: narrow part: of violin*) strozzatura; **he put his arm round her waist** le ha messo un braccio attorno alla vita; **stripped to the waist** nudo(-a) fino alla cintura, a torso nudo; **to be up to one's waist in mud** essere nel fango fino alla vita

waist·coat [ˈweɪsˌkəʊt] N panciotto, gilè *m inv*

waist·line [ˈweɪstˌlaɪn] N vita; **to watch one's waistline** badare alla linea

wait [weɪt] N: **wait (for)** attesa (di); **to have a long wait** aspettare a lungo; **a 2-hour wait** un'attesa di 2 ore; **to lie in wait (for sb)** tendere un agguato (a qn) ♦ VT **1** (*turn, chance*) aspettare, attendere **2** (*USA: delay: dinner etc*) ritardare ♦ VI **1** to wait (for sb/sth) aspettare (qn/qc); **how long have you been waiting?** da quanto tempo aspetti?; **I'll wait for you** ti aspetto; **wait for me!** aspettami!; **to wait for sb to do sth** aspettare che qn faccia qc; **wait a moment!** (aspetta) un momento!; **wait and see!** aspetta e vedrai!; **we'll have to wait and see** dobbiamo vedere come vanno le cose; **just you wait!** ti faccio vedere io!; **wait till you're older** aspetta di essere cresciuto(-a); **to keep sb waiting** far aspettare qn; **they kept us waiting for hours** ci hanno fatto aspettare per ore; **"repairs while you wait"** "riparazioni lampo"; **I can't wait for the holidays** non vedo l'ora che arrivino le vacanze; **I can't wait to see his face** non vedo l'ora di vedere che faccia farà; **I can hardly wait!** non vedo l'ora!; **that was worth waiting for** valeva la pena aspettare tanto **2** (*as servant*): **to wait at table** servire a tavola

▸ **wait about, wait around** VI + ADV restare ad aspettare

▸ **wait behind** VI + ADV trattenersi

▸ **wait in** VI + ADV restare a casa ad aspettare

▸ **wait on** VI + PREP servire; **to wait on sb hand and foot** servire qn in tutto e per tutto

▸ **wait up** VI + ADV restare alzato(-a) (ad aspettare); **don't wait up for me** non rimanere alzato ad aspettarmi

▸ **wait upon** VI + PREP (*old: visit*) presentare i propri rispetti a

wait·er [ˈweɪtəʳ] N cameriere *m*

wait·ing [ˈweɪtɪŋ] N attesa; (*Brit: Aut*): **"no waiting"** "divieto di sosta"

waiting list N lista d'attesa

waiting room N sala d'attesa *or* d'aspetto

wait·ress [ˈweɪtrɪs] N cameriera

waive [weɪv] VT (*claim*) rinunciare a; (*rule, age limit*) non tener conto di

waiv·er [ˈweɪvəʳ] N rinuncia

wake¹ [weɪk] N (*of ship*) scia; **in the wake of** sulla scia di; **to follow in sb's wake** (*fig*) camminare dietro a qn; **it left a trail of destruction in its wake** ha lasciato dietro di sé una scia di distruzione

wake² [weɪk] N (*over corpse*) veglia funebre

wake³ [weɪk] (*pt*, **woke** *or* **waked** *pp* **woken** *or* **waked**) VI (*also:* **wake up**) svegliarsi, destarsi; **wake up!** (*also fig*) svegliati!; **there's enough noise to wake the dead!** c'è un baccano del diavolo!; **to wake up to sth** (*fig*) rendersi conto di qc ♦ VT (*also:* **wake up**) svegliare; (*memories, desires*) risvegliare; **to wake sb (up)** (*fig*) aprire gli occhi a qn su qc; **to wake one's ideas up** (*fam*) darsi una mossa

wak·en [ˈweɪkən] VT, VI = **wake³**

Wales [weɪlz] N Galles *m*; **the Prince of Wales** il Principe di Galles

walk [wɔːk] N **1** (*stroll, ramble*) passeggiata; (*path, place to walk*) percorso, sentiero; **to take sb/one's dog for a walk** portare qn/il cane a spasso; **to go for a walk** (*short*) fare quattro passi *or* un giretto; (*long*) fare una passeggiata; **we went for a walk** abbiamo fatto una passeggiata; **it's only a 10-minute walk from here** ci vogliono solo 10 minuti a piedi da qui; **there's a nice walk by the river** c'è una bella passeggiata lungo il fiume; **from all walks of life** (*fig*) con ogni tipo di esperienza **2** (*gait*) passo, andatura, camminata; **at a walk** (*of person, horse*) al passo; **he has an odd sort of walk** ha una camminata tutta particolare ♦ VT **1** (*distance*) percorrere a piedi; **we walked 40 kilometres yesterday** ieri abbiamo percorso 40 chilometri a piedi; **to walk the streets** vagare per le strade; (*prostitute*) battere il marciapiede; **you can walk it in a few minutes** puoi arrivarci a piedi in pochi minuti; **he walked it** (*fig*) è stato uno scherzo per lui **2** (*cause to walk: invalid*) aiutare a camminare; (*lead: dog*) portare a spasso *or* fuori; (*: horse*) portare; **I'll walk you home**

ti accompagno a casa; **to walk sb into the ground** *or* **off their feet** far stancare qn a furia di camminare ♦ vi (*gen*) camminare; (*for pleasure, exercise*) passeggiare; (*not drive or ride*) andare a piedi; **are you walking or going by bus?** ci vai a piedi o in autobus?; **they walked in silence for a while** hanno camminato in silenzio per un po'; **to walk in one's sleep** camminare nel sonno; (*habitually*) essere sonnambulo(-a); **can your little boy walk yet?** tuo figlio sa già camminare?; **walk a little with me** accompagnami per un pezzo; **to walk up and down (the room)** camminare su e giù (per la stanza); **we had to walk** siamo dovuti andare a piedi; **to walk home** andare a casa a piedi; **we were out walking in the hills** stavamo passeggiando in collina; **to walk into sth** (*bump into*) andare a sbattere contro qc; (*fig: fall into: trap*) cadere in qc

▸ **walk about, walk around** vi + adv camminare; **I've been walking about all afternoon** sono stato in giro tutto il pomeriggio ♦ vi + prep: **to walk about the room** camminare per la stanza; **to walk about the town** gironzolare per la città

▸ **walk across** vi + prep attraversare

▸ **walk away** vi + adv allontanarsi (a piedi), andare via; (*fig: unhurt*) uscire illeso(-a); **to walk away with sth** (*fig: win easily*) vincere facilmente qc

▸ **walk away from** vi + adv + prep **1** (*pej: job, marriage, relationship*) mollare, piantare **2 to walk away from an accident** uscire incolume da un incidente

▸ **walk in** vi + adv entrare

▸ **walk off** vi + adv = **walk away** ♦ vt + adv (*lunch*) smaltire; (*headache*) far passare camminando

▸ **walk off with** vi + adv + prep (*fam*): **to walk off with sth** (*steal*) andarsene con qc; (*win: prize, bargain*) assicurarsi qc con facilità

▸ **walk on** vi + adv (*go on walking*) continuare a camminare; (*Theatre*) fare la comparsa

▸ **walk out** vi + adv (*go out*) uscire; (*as protest*) uscire in segno di protesta; (*strike*) scendere in sciopero; **to walk out of a meeting** abbandonare una riunione in segno di protesta; **he walked out of the meeting in protest** ha abbandonato la riunione in segno di protesta; **to walk out on sb** abbandonare qn; **he walked out on his wife and family** ha abbandonato la moglie e la famiglia

▸ **walk over** vi + prep (*defeat*) schiacciare; **to walk all over sb** (*dominate*) mettere i piedi in testa a qn

▸ **walk up** vi + adv (*approach*): **to walk up (to)** avvicinarsi (a); **walk up, walk up!** (*at fair*) avanti!

walk·about [ˈwɔːkəˌbaʊt] N: **to go (on a) walkabout** avere incontri informali col pubblico durante una visita ufficiale

walk·er [ˈwɔːkəʳ] N (*person*) camminatore(-trice); (*for babies*) girello; **he's a good walker** gli piace camminare; **he's a slow walker** ha il passo lento

walkie-talkie [ˌwɔːkɪˈtɔːkɪ] N walkie-talkie *m inv*

walk·ing [ˈwɔːkɪŋ] N camminare *m*; **to do a lot of walking** camminare molto; **I did some walking in the Alps last summer** ho fatto escursionismo sulle Alpi l'estate scorsa ♦ adj: **it's within walking distance** ci si arriva a piedi; **he's a walking encyclopaedia** è un'enciclopedia ambulante; **the walking wounded** i feriti in grado di camminare; **walking boots** pedule *fpl*; **walking tour** (*of a city*) giro a piedi; **a walking tour of the hills** una lunga gita a piedi sulle colline

walking holiday N vacanza fatta di lunghe camminate

walking shoes NPL scarpe *fpl* da passeggio

walking stick N bastone *m* da passeggio

walk-on [ˈwɔːkˌɒn] ADJ (*Theatre: part*) da comparsa

walk·out [ˈwɔːkˌaʊt] N (*from conference*) abbandono; (*strike*) sciopero selvaggio *or* a sorpresa; **to stage a walkout** (*from conference*) ritirarsi in segno di protesta; (*from work*) scendere in sciopero

walk·over [ˈwɔːkˌəʊvəʳ] N (*Sport*) vittoria facile; **the exam was a walkover** l'esame è stato una vera passeggiata

walk·way [ˈwɔːkˌweɪ] N passaggio pedonale

wall [wɔːl] N (*internal, of tunnel, cave*) muro, parete *f*; (*outside*) muro; (*Anat*) parete; (*of tyre*) fianco; (*fig: of smoke*) cortina; **the Berlin Wall** il muro di Berlino; **the Great Wall of China** la Grande Muraglia Cinese; **the city walls** le mura

della città; **it drives me up the wall** (*fam*) mi fa uscire dai gangheri; **to go to the wall** (*fig: firm*) andare a rotoli *or* in rovina; **walls have ears** (*fam*) anche i muri hanno orecchi ♦ adj (*clock*) a muro

▸ **wall in** vt + adv (*garden etc*) circondare con un muro

▸ **wall off** vt + adv (*area of land*) recingere con un muro

▸ **wall up** vt + adv (*entrance etc*) murare

wall cupboard N pensile *m*

walled [wɔːld] ADJ (*city*) fortificato(-a); (*house, garden*) cinto(-a) da mura

wal·let [ˈwɒlɪt] N portafoglio

wall·flower [ˈwɔːlˌflaʊəʳ] N violaciocca (gialla); (*fig*): **to be a wallflower** fare (da) tappezzeria

wall hanging N tappezzeria

wal·lop [ˈwɒləp] (*fam*) N (*blow*) cazzotto; (*sound*): **with a wallop** con un tonfo ♦ vt (*fam: person*) suonarle a; **to wallop the table** battere il pugno sul tavolo

wal·low [ˈwɒləʊ] vi: **to wallow (in)** (*in water, mud*) rotolarsi (in); (*in bath*) sguazzare (in); **to wallow in one's grief** crogiolarsi nel proprio dolore; **to wallow in luxury** nuotare nell'oro

wall·paper [ˈwɔːlˌpeɪpəʳ] N carta da parati, tappezzeria; (*Comput*) sfondo

wall-to-wall [ˌwɔːltəˈwɔːl] ADJ: **wall-to-wall carpeting** moquette *f*

wal·nut [ˈwɔːlˌnʌt] N (*nut*) noce *f*; (*tree, wood*) noce *m* ♦ adj (*furniture*) di noce; (*cake*) di noci

wal·rus [ˈwɔːlrəs] N tricheco

waltz [wɔːlts] N valzer *m inv* ♦ vi ballare il valzer; **to waltz in/out** *etc* (*confidently*) entrare/uscire *etc* con fare sicuro; (*cheekily*) entrare/uscire *etc* con fare spavaldo

wan [wɒn] ADJ (*gen*) pallido(-a); (*look, person*) triste

wand [wɒnd] N (*also: magic wand*) bacchetta magica; (*of usher*) mazza

wan·der [ˈwɒndəʳ] N: **to go for a wander around the shops/ the town** fare un giro per i negozi/in città ♦ vi (*person*) gironzolare, girare senza meta; (*river, road*) serpeggiare; (*stray: from path*) allontanarsi; (: *thoughts, eyes*) vagare; **to wander around** gironzolare; **I just wandered around for a while** ho gironzolato per un po'; **to wander back/out** *etc* tornare indietro/uscire *etc* con calma; **don't go wandering off** non allontanarti; **to wander from** *or* **off the point** divagare; **to let one's mind** *or* **attention wander** distrarsi ♦ vt (*streets, hills*) girovagare per; **to wander the world** girare il mondo

wan·der·er [ˈwɒndərəʳ] N giramondo *m/f inv*

wan·der·ing [ˈwɒndərɪŋ] ADJ (*tribe*) nomade; (*minstrel, actor*) girovago(-a); (*path, river*) tortuoso(-a); (*mind*) distratto(-a) ♦ **wanderings** NPL peregrinazioni *fpl*, vagabondaggi *mpl*

wane [weɪn] vi (*moon*) calare; (*fig*) declinare, scemare ♦ N: **to be on the wane** = **wane**

wan·gle [ˈwæŋgl] (*fam*) N astuzia ♦ vt (*job, ticket*) rimediare *or* procurare (con l'astuzia); (*days off*) ottenere (con l'astuzia); **he wangled his way in** è riuscito ad entrare con un sotterfugio

wank·er [ˈwæŋkəʳ] N (*fam!*) testa di cazzo (*fam!*), coglione (*fam!*)

want [wɒnt] N **1** (*lack*): **want (of)** mancanza (di); **for want of** per mancanza di; **for want of anything better to do** non avendo nulla di meglio da fare; **it wasn't for want of trying** non si può dire che non ci abbia (*or* abbiamo *etc*) provato **2** (*poverty*) miseria, povertà; **to be in want** essere in miseria **3** (*need*) bisogno; **to be in want of sth** avere bisogno di qc; **it fills a long-felt want** soddisfa un bisogno che si sentiva da tempo **4** (*requirements*): **wants** NPL esigenze *fpl*; **my wants are few** ho poche esigenze ♦ vt **1** (*wish, desire*) volere, desiderare; **to want to do sth** voler fare qc; **what do you want to do tomorrow?** che cosa vuoi fare domani?; **to want sb to do sth** volere che qn faccia qc; **I want you to tell me** voglio che tu mi dica; **I want it done now** voglio che sia fatto subito; **what do you want with me?** cosa vuoi da me?; **you've got him where you want him** (*fig*) l'hai in pugno; **you don't want much!** (*iro*) ti accontenti di poco!; **do you want some cake?** vuoi un po' di torta?; **she wants £5000 for the car** vuole *or* chiede 5000 sterline per la macchina; **I don't want you interfering!** non voglio che tu ti intrometta!; **I know when I'm not wanted** so quando non mi si vuole; **you're wanted on the phone** ti vogliono al telefono; **I don't want to** non ne ho voglia; **"cook wanted"** "cercasi cuoco"; **he is wanted for murder** è ricercato per omicidio; **to want sb** (*sexually*) desiderare qn **2** (*need, require: subj: person*) avere bisogno di; (*task*) richiedere; (*ought*) dovere; **you want to see a doctor** dovresti andare dal dottore; **that's the last thing I want!** (*fam*) è l'ultima cosa che vorrei!; **it's just what we wanted!** (*fam*) è proprio quello che ci voleva!; **you want a screwdriver to do that** ti ci vuole un cacciavite per farlo; **it only wanted the parents to come in ...** bastava solo che i genitori entrassero...; **you want your head seeing to** tu hai bisogno di uno psicanalista; **the window wants cleaning** la finestra ha bisogno di una pulita ♦ VI (*lack*): **to want (for)** mancare (di); **she doesn't want for friends** gli amici non le mancano; **they want for nothing** a loro non manca nulla

▸ **want out** VI + ADV (*fam*) volerne uscire

want ads NPL (*USA*) annunci *mpl* economici

want·ing [ˈwɒntɪŋ] ADJ: **to be wanting (in)** mancare (di); **humour is completely wanting in his work** la sua opera manca totalmente di senso dell'umorismo; **he is wanting in confidence** non è abbastanza sicuro di sé; **he was tried and found wanting** lo hanno messo alla prova e non è risultato all'altezza

wan·ton [ˈwɒntən] ADJ (*wilful*) gratuito(-a), ingiustificato(-a); (*shameless*) scostumato(-a)

war [wɔːʳ] N guerra; (*fig*): **war (on or against)** lotta (contro); **to be at/go to war (with)** essere/entrare in guerra (con); **to make war (on)** fare guerra (a); **a war of words** una guerra verbale; **to have been in the wars** (*fig: hum*) essere malridotto(-a); **the war against organized crime** la lotta contro la criminalità organizzata ♦ VI: **to war (with)** guerreggiare (con), far guerra (a) ♦ ADJ (*wound, crime, bride*) di guerra

war·ble [ˈwɔːbl] N (*of bird*) trillo ♦ VI (*bird*) trillare; (*person*) gorgheggiare

war cry N grido di guerra

ward [wɔːd] N **1** (*in hospital*) corsia, reparto **2** (*Law*) pupillo(-a); **ward of court** minore *m*/*f* sotto tutela (giudiziaria) **3** (*Pol*) collegio (elettorale)

▸ **ward off** VT + ADV (*blow, attack*) parare, schivare; (*attacker*) respingere; (*danger, depression*) scongiurare

war·den [ˈwɔːdn] N (*of institution*) direttore(-trice); (*of park, game reserve*) guardiano(-a)

war·der [ˈwɔːdəʳ] N guardia carceraria

ward·robe [ˈwɔːdrəʊb] N (*cupboard*) guardaroba *m inv*, armadio; (*clothes*) guardaroba; (*Theatre*) costumi *mpl*

ware·house [ˈwɛəhaʊs] N deposito, magazzino

wares [wɛəz] NPL merci *fpl*

war·fare [ˈwɔːfɛəʳ] N (*fighting*) guerra, lotta; (*technique*) arte *f* bellica

war game N war game *m inv*

war·head [ˈwɔːhɛd] N (*Mil*) testata

wari·ly [ˈwɛərɪlɪ] ADV cautamente, con prudenza

war·like [ˈwɔːlaɪk] ADJ bellicoso(-a)

warm [wɔːm] ADJ (*comp* -**er**, *superl* -**est**) **1** (*gen*) caldo(-a); **I'm warm, I feel warm** ho caldo; **I'm too warm** ho troppo caldo; **it's warm today** oggi fa caldo; **it's warm in here** fa caldo qui; **it's warm work** è un lavoro che ti fa sudare; **warm water** acqua calda; **come and get warm** vieni a scaldarti; **keep yourself warm!** non prendere freddo!; **it keeps me warm** mi tiene caldo; **to keep sth warm** tenere qc in caldo; **am I getting warm?** (*fig: in game*) fuocherello? **2** (*fig: colour*) caldo(-a); (*: thanks, congratulations, apologies*) sentito(-a); (*: welcome, applause*) caloroso(-a); (*: person, greeting*) cordiale; (*: heart*) d'oro; (*: supporter*) convinto(-a); **with my warmest thanks** con i miei più sentiti ringraziamenti; **a warm welcome** una calorosa accoglienza ♦ VT (*gen*) scaldare; **to warm o.s.** scaldarsi; **to warm o.s. by the fire** scaldarsi vicino al fuoco; **she warmed her hands by the fire** si è scaldata le mani vicino al fuoco; **it warmed my heart** mi ha fatto tanto piacere ♦ VI (*food, water*) scaldarsi; **he warmed to his subject** si appassionò all'argomento; **I or my heart warmed to him** mi è entrato in simpatia

▸ **warm up** VI + ADV (*person*) scaldarsi, scaldarsi i muscoli; (*fig: party*) animarsi; **spend the first five minutes warming**

up innanzitutto, fai cinque minuti di riscaldamento ♦ VT + ADV (*food*) scaldare, riscaldare; (*engine*) scaldare; (*fig: party, audience*) animare; **I'll warm up some lasagne for you** ti riscaldo delle lasagne

warm-blooded [ˌwɔːmˈblʌdɪd] ADJ (*animal*) a sangue caldo

war memorial N monumento ai caduti

warm-hearted [ˌwɔːmˈhɑːtɪd] ADJ cordiale, affettuoso(-a)

warm·ly [ˈwɔːmlɪ] ADV (*recommend*) caldamente; (*welcome, thank, applaud*) calorosamente; **to dress warmly** portare indumenti pesanti

war·monger [ˈwɔːmʌŋgəʳ] N guerrafondaio

war·monger·ing [ˈwɔːmʌŋgərɪŋ] N bellicismo

warmth [wɔːmθ] N calore *m*; (*fig*) calore, calorosità

warm-up [ˈwɔːmʌp] N riscaldamento

warn [wɔːn] VT: **to warn (of or about)** avvertire (di), avvisare (di); **to warn sb not to do sth or against doing sth** avvertire qn di non fare qc; **you have been warned!** sei avvisato!; **well, I warned you!** be', ti avevo avvertito!; **to warn sb off or against sth** mettere qn in guardia contro qc

warn·ing [ˈwɔːnɪŋ] N (*gen*) avvertimento, ammonimento; (*by police, judge*) diffida; (*advance notice*): **warning (of)** preavviso (di); **to give sb a warning that** avvertire qn che; **to give sb due/a few days' warning** avvertire qn a tempo debito/con qualche giorno di anticipo; **without (any) warning** senza preavviso; **let this be a warning to you!** che ti serva da ammonimento!; **gale warning** (*Met*) avviso di burrasca

warning light N spia luminosa

warning triangle N (*Aut*) triangolo

warp [wɔːp] N (*in weaving*) ordito; (*of wood*) curvatura, deformazione *f* ♦ VT (*wood*) deformare, curvare; (*fig: mind, personality, judgment*) influenzare negativamente ♦ VI (*wood*) deformarsi, curvarsi

war·path [ˈwɔːpɑːθ] N: **to be on the warpath** (*fig*) essere sul sentiero di guerra

warped [wɔːpt] ADJ (*wood*) curvo(-a); (*fig: character, sense of humour etc*) contorto(-a)

war·rant [ˈwɒrənt] N **1** (*Law: to arrest*) mandato di cattura; (*: to search*) mandato di perquisizione; (*: for travel etc*) buono; **there is a warrant out for his arrest** è stato emesso un mandato di cattura nei suoi confronti **2** (*justification*) giustificazione *f* ♦ VT **1** (*justify, merit*) giustificare; **nothing warrants such an assumption** nulla giustifica questa ipotesi **2** (*guarantee*) garantire; **I'll warrant you he'll be back soon** ti assicuro or garantisco che sarà di ritorno presto

warrant officer N (*Mil*) sottufficiale *m*

war·ran·ty [ˈwɒrəntɪ] N (*Comm*) garanzia; **under warranty** in garanzia

war·ren [ˈwɒrən] N (*also:* **rabbit warren**) tana; (*fig*) alveare *m*; **a warren of little streets** un dedalo di stradine

war·ring [ˈwɔːrɪŋ] ADJ (*interests etc*) opposto(-a), in lotta; (*nations*) in guerra

war·ri·or [ˈwɒrɪəʳ] N guerriero(-a)

War·saw [ˈwɔːsɔː] N Varsavia

war·ship [ˈwɔːʃɪp] N nave *f* da guerra

wart [wɔːt] N (*Med*) porro, verruca

war·time [ˈwɔːtaɪm] N: **in wartime** in tempo di guerra ♦ ADJ (*regulations, rationing etc*) di guerra

wary [ˈwɛərɪ] ADJ (*comp* -**ier**, *superl* -**iest**) (*gen*) prudente; (*manner*) cauto(-a); **to be wary (of)** essere diffidente (di), diffidare (di); **to keep a wary eye on sth** tenere d'occhio qc; **to be wary about or of doing sth** andare cauto(-a) nel fare qc, esitare a fare qc

was [wɒz] 1ST PERS SG PTPL, 3RD PERS SG PT *of* **be**

wash [wɒʃ] N **1** (*act of washing*) lavata; **to have a wash** darsi una lavata, lavarsi; **to give sth a wash** dare una lavata a qc, lavare qc; **it needs a wash** ha bisogno di essere lavato; **to be in the wash** essere a lavare; **your jeans are in the wash** i tuoi jeans sono a lavare; **it ran in the wash** si è stinto nel lavaggio; **it'll all come out in the wash** (*fig: work out*) tutto si sistemerà **2** (*of ship*) scia **3** (*Art*) lavatura ♦ VT **1** (*gen*) lavare; **to wash o.s.** lavarsi; **to wash one's hands/hair** lavarsi le mani/i capelli; **he washed his hands** si è lavato le mani; **have you washed your hair?** ti sei lavata i capelli?; **to wash one's hands of sth** (*fig*) lavarsene le mani (di qc); **I'll wash the dishes** lavo io i piatti **2** (*lap: sea, waves*) bagnare, lambire; **an island washed by a blue sea** un'isola bagnata da un mare azzurro **3** (*sweep, carry: sea*) portare, trascinare; **he was washed overboard** fu trascinato in mare dalle onde ♦ vi **1** (*have a wash*) lavarsi; (*do the washing*) fare il bucato; **synthetic fabrics usually wash well** di solito i tessuti sintetici si lavano facilmente; **I'll wash if you'll wipe** (*dishes*) io lavo i piatti se tu li asciughi; **that excuse won't wash!** (*fam*) quella scusa non regge! **2** (*sea*): **to wash against sth** frangersi contro qc; **to wash over sth** infrangersi su qc

▸ **wash away** vt + adv (*mark*) togliere lavando; (*subj: river etc*) trascinare via; (*fig: sins etc*) cancellare

▸ **wash down** vt + adv (*walls, car*) lavare; (*pill, food*) mandar giù (*con acqua etc*)

▸ **wash off** vi + adv andare via con il lavaggio ♦ vt + adv (*dirt*) togliere (lavando)

▸ **wash out** vt + adv (*stain*) togliere (lavando); (*bottle, paintbrush*) sciacquare

▸ **wash through** vt + adv dare una lavata a

▸ **wash up** vi + adv (*Brit: do dishes*) lavare i piatti; (*USA: have a wash*) darsi una lavata, lavarsi ♦ vt + adv **1** (*Brit: dishes*) lavare, rigovernare **2** (*subj: sea etc*) portare, trascinare **3 to be all washed up** (*fig: fam*) essere finito(-a)

Wash. abbr (*USA*: = **Washington**)

wash·able [ˈwɒʃəbl] adj lavabile

wash·basin [ˈwɒʃˌbeɪsn], **wash·bowl** [ˈwɒʃbəʊl] n lavabo, lavandino

wash·cloth [ˈwɒʃˌklɒθ] n (*USA*) pezzuola (per lavarsi)

wash·er [ˈwɒʃəʳ] n **1** (*Tech*) rondella; **a rubber washer** una guarnizione di gomma **2** (*washing machine*) lavatrice *f*; **your shirt's in the washer** la tua camicia è in lavatrice

wash·ing [ˈwɒʃɪŋ] n **1** (*act*) lavaggio; (*of clothes*) bucato; **to do the washing** fare il bucato **2** (*clothes themselves*) bucato; **dirty washing** biancheria da lavare

washing line n (*Brit*) corda del bucato

washing machine n lavatrice *f*

washing powder n (*Brit*) detersivo in polvere per bucato

Wash·ing·ton [ˈwɒʃɪŋtən] n Washington *f*

washing-up [ˌwɒʃɪŋˈʌp] n (*dishes*) piatti *mpl* sporchi; **to do the washing-up** lavare i piatti, rigovernare

washing-up liquid n (*Brit*) detersivo liquido per i piatti

wash-out [ˈwɒʃˌaʊt] n (*fam: plan, party, person*) disastro

wash·room [ˈwɒʃˌrʊm] n bagno, gabinetto

wasn't [ˈwɒznt] = **was not**

WASP, Wasp n abbr (*USA*: = *White Anglo-Saxon Protestant*) WASP *m* (= *bianco/a protestante anglosassone*)

wasp [wɒsp] n vespa; **wasp's nest** nido di vespe

wasp·ish [ˈwɒspɪʃ] adj (*character*) litigioso(-a); (*comment*) pungente

wast·age [ˈweɪstɪdʒ] n (*gen*) spreco; (*of time: Comm: through pilfering*) perdita; (*in manufacturing*) scarti *mpl*; (*amount wasted*) scarto; **natural wastage** normale diminuzione *f* del personale

waste [weɪst] adj (*material*) di scarto; (*food*) avanzato(-a); (*land, ground: in city*) abbandonato(-a), desolato(-a); (: *in country*) incolto(-a); **to lay waste** devastare ♦ n **1** (*gen*) spreco; (*of time*) perdita; **it's such a waste!** è un tale spreco!; **it's a waste of money** è uno spreco di denaro; **it's a waste of effort** è fatica sprecata; **it's a waste of breath** è fiato sprecato; **it's a waste of time** doing that è tempo sprecato; **to go to waste** andare sprecato(-a) **2** (*waste material: industrial, chemical etc*) scorie *fpl*; (*rubbish*) spazzatura, immondizia, rifiuti *mpl*; **nuclear waste** scorie *mpl* radioattive **3** (*land: often pl*) distesa desolata; **desert waste** landa desertica ♦ vt (*gen*) sprecare; (*time, opportunity*) perdere, sprecare; **to waste time** perdere tempo; **there's no time to waste** non c'è tempo da perdere; **you didn't waste much time finding a replacement** (*iro*) non hai perso tempo a rimpiazzarmi!; **I don't like wasting money** non mi piace sprecare i soldi; **he's wasted in that job** è sprecato in quel lavoro; **sarcasm is wasted on him** non afferra il sarcasmo; **to waste one's breath** sprecare (il) fiato; **waste not, want not** (*Proverb*) chi risparmia guadagna

▸ **waste away** vi + adv deperire, consumarsi

waste·basket [ˈweɪstˌbɑːskɪt] n (*USA*) = **wastepaper basket**

waste disposal n smaltimento dei rifiuti

waste·ful [ˈweɪstfʊl] adj (*person*) sprecone(-a); (*process*) dispendioso(-a); **to be wasteful with** or **of sth** sprecare qc

waste ground n (*Brit*) terreno incolto or abbandonato

waste·land [ˈweɪstˌlænd] n terra desolata

wastepaper basket n cestino per la cartaccia

waste pipe n tubo di scarico

waste products n (*Industry*) materiali *mpl* di scarto; (*from body*) materiali *mpl* di rifiuto

wast·er [ˈweɪstəʳ] n (*good-for-nothing*) perdigiorno *m/f*; (*spendthrift*) sprecone(-a)

watch¹ [wɒtʃ] n (*also: wrist watch*) orologio (da polso); **it's 10 o'clock by my watch** il mio orologio fa le 10; **he was wearing an expensive watch** portava un orologio costoso

watch² [wɒtʃ] n **1** (*act of watching*) sorveglianza; **to be on the watch for** (*danger, person*) stare in guardia contro; (*vehicle*) stare all'erta per l'arrivo di; (*bargain*) essere a caccia di; **to keep watch over** (*prisoner*) sorvegliare; (*patient*) vigilare; **to keep a close watch on sb/sth** sorvegliare da vicino qn/qc; **to keep watch for sb/sth** stare all'erta per qn/qc **2** (*period of duty*) guardia; (*Naut*) quarto; (*sentry*) sentinella; **officer of the watch** (*Naut*) ufficiale *m* di quarto; **to be on watch** (*Naut*) essere di guardia; **I had the first watch** feci il primo turno di guardia ♦ vt **1** (*guard: gen*) tener d'occhio **2** (*observe: gen*) guardare; (*subj: police*) tenere d'occhio, sorvegliare; (*monitor: case*) seguire; **to watch sb do(ing) sth** osservare qn mentre fa qc; **you can't do that! — just you watch (me)!** non puoi farlo! — e come no, sta' a vedere!; **to watch one's chance** aspettare il momento propizio; **to watch the time** controllare l'ora; **a new actor to be watched** un nuovo attore molto promettente or da seguire; **I was watching TV** stavo guardando la TV; **the police were watching the house** la polizia sorvegliava la casa **3** (*be careful with*) stare attento(-a) a; **to watch one's language** moderare i termini, badare a come si parla; **watch it!** attento!; **watch how you drive/what you're doing** fai attenzione a come guidi/quel che fai; **watch your head** attento alla testa; **we shall have to watch our spending** dovremo limitare le spese; **to watch the clock** (*fig*) tenere d'occhio l'orologio; **to watch sb's interests** badare agli interessi di qn ♦ vi (*observe*) guardare; (*keep guard*) fare or montare la guardia; (*pay attention*) stare attento(-a); (*at bedside*) vegliare; **to watch for sb/sth** aspettare qn/qc; **the doctors are watching for any deterioration in his condition** i medici lo tengono sotto osservazione nell'eventualità che le sue condizioni peggiorino

▸ **watch out** vi + adv fare attenzione *f*, stare attento(-a); **to watch out for** (*keep watch*) fare attenzione a; (*be on the alert*) stare attento(-a) a; **watch out!** (*also threatening*) attento!, occhio!

▸ **watch over** vi + prep sorvegliare

watch·band [ˈwɒtʃˌbænd] n (*USA*) cinturino dell'orologio

watch·dog [ˈwɒtʃˌdɒg] n cane *m* da guardia; (*fig*) sorvegliante *m/f* ♦ adj di controllo; **a government watchdog committee** un comitato statale di controllo

watch·ful [ˈwɒtʃfʊl] adj: **to be watchful for sth** stare attento a qc; **to keep a watchful eye on sb** guardare con occhio vigile qn; **under the watchful eye of** sotto lo sguardo vigile di

watch·maker [ˈwɒtʃˌmeɪkəʳ] n orologiaio(-a)

watch·man [ˈwɒtʃmən] n (*pl* **-men**) guardiano; **night watchman** guardiano notturno

watch·word [ˈwɒtʃˌwɜːd] n parola d'ordine

wa·ter [ˈwɔːtəʳ] n (*gen*) acqua; **fresh/salt water** acqua dolce/salata; **"hot and cold water in all rooms"** "acqua corrente calda e fredda in tutte le camere"; **a glass of water** un bicchiere d'acqua; **I'd like a drink of water** vorrei un bicchier d'acqua; **the High Street is under water** la strada principale è inondata; **to turn on the water** aprire il rubinetto dell'acqua; **to spend money like water** spendere e spandere, avere le mani bucate; **a lot of water has flowed under the bridge since then** (*fig*) da allora è passata molta acqua sotto i ponti; **that theory won't hold water** (*fig*) quella teoria fa acqua; **to pour cold water on sth** (*fig*) mostrarsi poco entusiasta di qc; **it's like water off a duck's back** (*fig*) è come parlare al muro; **the waters of the Tiber** le acque del Tevere; **British waters** acque *fpl* (territoriali) britanniche; **to take the waters** fare la cura delle acque (termali); **the waters** (*in pregnancy*) le acque; **to pass water** orinare; **water on the brain** (*Med*)

idrocefalia; **water on the knee** (*Med*) sinovite *f* ♦ VT (*garden, plant*) annaffiare; (*horses, cattle*) abbeverare; (*wine*) annacquare; **she's watering the geraniums** sta annaffiando i gerani ♦ VI (*eyes*) lacrimare; **to make sb's mouth water** far venire l'acquolina in bocca a qn; **my mouth is watering** ho l'acquolina in bocca ♦ ADJ (*pressure, supply*) dell'acqua; (*purifier, power*) idrico(-a)
  ► **water down** VT + ADV (*milk, wine*) diluire; (*fig: claim*) moderare, attenuare; (: *report, article*) edulcorare
water closet N (*Brit: frm*) water closet *m inv*
water-colour, water-color (*USA*) [ˈwɔːtəˌkʌləʳ] N (*picture*) acquerello; (*paints*); **watercolours** NPL acquerelli *mpl*
water-cooled [ˈwɔːtəˌkuːld] ADJ raffreddato(-a) ad acqua
water-cress [ˈwɔːtəˌkrɛs] N crescione *m*
water-fall [ˈwɔːtəˌfɔːl] N cascata
water-front [ˈwɔːtəˌfrʌnt] N (*seafront*) lungomare *m*; (*at docks*) banchina, fronte *m* del porto
water heater N scaldabagno, scaldaacqua *m inv*
water hole N pozza d'acqua
water ice N (*Brit: Culin*) sorbetto
watering can N annaffiatoio
water level N livello dell'acqua; (*of flood*) livello delle acque
water lily N ninfea
water-line [ˈwɔːtəˌlaɪn] N (*Naut*) linea di galleggiamento
water-logged [ˈwɔːtəˌlɒgd] ADJ (*ground etc*) impregnato(-a) *or* imbevuto(-a) d'acqua; (*fields, football pitch*) allagato(-a); (*shoes*) inzuppato(-a)
water-mark [ˈwɔːtəˌmɑːk] N (*in paper*) filigrana; (*left by tide*) segno della marea
water-melon [ˈwɔːtəˌmɛlən] N anguria, cocomero
water polo N pallanuoto *f*
water-proof [ˈwɔːtəˌpruːf] ADJ impermeabile ♦ N impermeabile *m* ♦ VT impermeabilizzare
water-repellent [ˈwɔːtərɪˌpɛlənt] ADJ idrorepellente
water-shed [ˈwɔːtəˌʃɛd] N (*Geog, also fig*) spartiacque *m inv*; (*Brit: TV*) inizio della seconda serata (*ora dopo la quale i ragazzi in genere non guardano più la televisione*)
water-skiing [ˈwɔːtəˌskiːɪŋ] N sci *m* d'acqua *or* acquatico
water softener N addolcitore *m* d'acqua; (*substance*) anti-calcare *m*
water tank N serbatoio *or* cisterna d'acqua
water-tight [ˈwɔːtəˌtaɪt] ADJ (*compartment, seal*) stagno(-a); (*fig: excuse, argument*) inattaccabile; **the roof is not water-tight** il tetto non è a tenuta stagna
water vapour N vapore *m* acqueo
water-way [ˈwɔːtəˌweɪ] N corso d'acqua navigabile
water-works [ˈwɔːtəˌwɜːks] N (*place*) impianto idrico ♦ NPL (*fig: fam*): **to turn on the waterworks** piangere come una fontana; **to have trouble with one's waterworks** avere dei problemi alla vescica
wa-tery [ˈwɔːtərɪ] ADJ (*tea, soup*) acquoso(-a); (*coffee*) lungo(-a); (*pale: sun, colour*) slavato(-a), pallido(-a); (*eyes*) umido(-a); **to go to a watery grave** perire tra i flutti
watt [wɒt] N watt *m inv*
watt-age [ˈwɒtɪdʒ] N potenza in watt
wat-tle [ˈwɒtl] N 1 (*woven sticks*) graticcio 2 (*on turkey*) barbiglio
wave [weɪv] N 1 (*gen, also Phys, Radio*) onda; (*in hair, on surface*) ondulazione *f*; (*fig: of enthusiasm, strikes etc*) ondata; **in waves** a ondate; **short/medium/long wave** (*Radio*) onde *fpl* corte/medie/lunghe; **the new wave** (*Cine*) la nouvelle vague; (*Mus*) la new wave; **he was knocked over by a big wave** è stato travolto da una grossa onda 2 (*greeting*) cenno di saluto; (*signal*) gesto, cenno; **to give sb a wave** salutare qn con la mano; **with a wave of his hand** con un cenno della mano; **a friendly wave** un cenno amichevole ♦ VT 1 (*brandish: flag, banner, handkerchief*) sventolare; (: *stick, umbrella*) agitare; (*beckon, motion*) far segno a; **he waved the ticket under my nose** mi sventolò il biglietto sotto il naso; **to wave sb goodbye** salutare qn con la mano; **she waved a greeting to the crowd** salutò la folla con un cenno della mano; **he waved us over to the best table** ci indicò con la mano il tavolo migliore 2 (*hair*) ondulare ♦ VI 1 (*person*) gesticolare; **to wave to** *or* **at sb** fare un cenno a qn; **he waved at me** mi ha fatto un cenno con la

mano 2 (*flag, branches etc*) ondeggiare, sventolare 3 (*hair*) essere mosso(-a) *or* ondulato(-a)
  ► **wave about, wave around** VT + ADV (*object*) agitare; **to wave one's arms about** (*in talking*) gesticolare
  ► **wave aside, wave away** VT + ADV (*person*): **to wave sb aside** fare cenno a qn di spostarsi; (*fig: suggestion, objection*) respingere, rifiutare
  ► **wave down** VT + ADV: **to wave sb/a car down** far segno a qn/a un'auto di fermarsi
  ► **wave off** VT + ADV: **to wave sb off** salutare qn
  ► **wave on** VT + ADV (*subj: policeman*) fare segno di avanzare a
wave-band [ˈweɪvˌbænd] N (*Radio*) gamma di lunghezza d'onda
wave-length [ˈweɪvˌlɛŋθ] N (*Phys, Radio*) lunghezza d'onda; **we're not on the same wavelength** (*fig*) non siamo sulla stessa lunghezza d'onda
wa-ver [ˈweɪvəʳ] VI (*flame, needle etc*) oscillare; (*voice*) tremare; (*fig: hesitate*): **to waver** (*between*) tentennare, titubare; **she's beginning to waver** comincia a vacillare
wavy [ˈweɪvɪ] ADJ (*comp* -ier, *superl* -iest) (*hair, surface*) ondulato(-a); (*line*) ondeggiante, sinuoso(-a); **a wavy line** una linea ondulata; **wavy hair** i capelli mossi
wax[1] [wæks] N cera; (*for skis*) sciolina; (*in ear*) cerume *m* ♦ ADJ di cera ♦ VT (*furniture, car*) dare la cera a; (*skis*) sciolinare
wax[2] [wæks] VI (*moon*) crescere; **to wax enthusiastic** diventare entusiasta; **to wax eloquent about sth** diventare infervorato(-a) nel parlare di qc
wax-works [ˈwæksˌwɜːks] NSG, NPL museo delle cere
way [weɪ] N 1 (*road, lane*) strada; (*path, access*) passaggio; (*in street names*) via; **private/public way** strada privata/pubblica; **the way across the fields** il sentiero attraverso i campi; **the Appian Way** la via Appia; **across** *or* **over the way** di fronte 2 (*route*) strada; **the Way of the Cross** (*Rel*) la via crucis; **to ask one's way to the station** chiedere la strada per la stazione; **can you tell me the way to the station?** mi sa indicare la strada per la stazione?; **the way back** la via del ritorno; **we came a back way** siamo arrivati per strade secondarie; **she went by way of Birmingham** è andata passando per Birmingham; **to go the wrong way** andare dalla parte sbagliata; **to lose one's way** perdere la strada, perdersi; **the way in** l'entrata, l'ingresso; **the way out** l'uscita; **to find one's way into a building** riuscire a entrare in un edificio; **don't bother, I'll find my own way out** non si scomodi, troverò l'uscita; **to find a way out of a problem** trovare una via d'uscita a un problema; **to take the easy way out** scegliere la soluzione più facile; **on the way** (*en route*) per strada; (*expected*) in arrivo; **on the way to work** andando a lavorare; **you pass it on your way home** ci passi davanti andando a casa; **he lost it on the way to school** lo ha perso andando a scuola; **he's on his way to becoming an alcoholic** è sulla strada dell'alcolismo; **to be on one's way** essere in cammino *or* sulla strada; **economic recovery is on the way** siamo sulla strada della ripresa economica; **I'm on my way** sto arrivando; **he's on his way** sta arrivando; **it's time we were on our way** è ora di andare; **all the way** (*here/home*) per tutta la strada (*venendo qui/andando a casa*); **I'm with you all the way** (*fig: fam*) sono assolutamente d'accordo con te; **to make one's (own) way home** andare a casa (da solo(-a)); **I know my way about town** sono pratico della città; **I don't know the way** non so la strada; **to lead the way** fare strada; (*fig*) essere all'avanguardia; **I don't want to take you out of your way** non voglio farti deviare; **the village is rather out of the way** il villaggio è abbastanza fuori mano; **to go out of one's way to help sb** farsi in quattro per aiutare qn; **to go one's own way** (*fig*) fare di testa propria; **to make one's way in the world** farsi strada nel mondo; **he worked his way up in the company** si è fatto strada nella ditta; **the company isn't paying its way** la ditta non rende più 3 (*space sb wants to go through*) strada; **to be** *or* **get in the** *or* **sb's way** essere d'intralcio *or* d'impiccio a qn; **am I in your way?** (*of sb watching sth*) ti tolgo la visuale?; **to stand in sb's way** intralciare il passaggio a qn; (*fig*) essere d'ostacolo a qn; **"give way"** (*Brit: Aut*) "dare la precedenza"; **to stand in the way of progress** ostacolare il progresso; **to get out of the** *or* **sb's way** lasciare

passare qn; **get out of the way!** togliti di mezzo!; **to keep out of sb's way** evitare qn, stare alla larga da qn; **to keep sth out of the way** togliere di torno qc; **as soon as I've got this essay out of the way** appena mi sono liberato di questo tema; **keep those matches out of his way** tieni lontano da lui quei fiammiferi; **to push/elbow one's way through the crowd** farsi strada a spinte/gomitate tra la folla; **he lied his way out of it** se l'è cavata mentendo; **he crawled/limped his way to the gate** andò a carponi/zoppicando verso il cancello; **to make way (for sb/sth)** far strada (a qn/qc); (*fig*) lasciare il posto *or* fare largo (a qn/qc); **to leave the way open for further talks** lasciare aperta la possibilità di ulteriori colloqui **4** (*direction*) direzione *f*, parte *f*; **which way? — this way** da che parte? — da questa (parte), in quale direzione? — per di qua; **come this way** vieni da questa parte; **this way for ...** da questa parte per...; **which way did he go?** da che parte è andato?; **which way do we go from here?** da che parte dobbiamo andare da qui?; (*fig*) cosa facciamo adesso?; **are you going my way?** fai la strada che faccio io?; **the supermarket is this way** il supermercato è da questa parte; **everything is going my way** (*fig*) mi sta andando tutto liscio; **this way and that** di qua e di là; **down our way** dalle nostre parti; **she didn't know which way to look** non sapeva da che parte guardare; **put it the right way up** (*Brit*) mettilo in piedi dalla parte giusta; **to be the wrong way round** essere al contrario; **to look the other way** (*fig*) guardare dall'altra parte; **to be in a fair way to doing sth** essere sulla strada giusta per fare qc; **to split sth three ways** dividere qc in tre **5** (*indicating distance, motion, progress*): **to come a long way** (*also fig*) fare molta strada; **it's a long way** è lontano; **it's a long way away** è molto lontano da qui; **a little way along the road** un po' più avanti lungo la strada; **she'll go a long way** (*fig*) farà molta strada; **we've come a long way since those days** abbiamo fatto molta strada da allora; **it should go a long way towards convincing him** dovrebbe contribuire molto a convincerlo; **to be under way** (*work, project*) essere in corso; **to get under way** avviarsi; **the job is now well under way** il lavoro ora è ben avviato **6** (*means*) mezzo, modo; (*manner*) modo; **a way of life** uno stile di vita; **the British way of life** lo stile di vita britannico; **there are ways and means** il modo per farlo si trova; **we'll find a way of doing it** troveremo un modo per farlo; **the only way of doing it** l'unico modo per farlo; **there are no two ways about it** non ci sono dubbi; **he has his own way of doing it** ha un modo tutto suo per farlo; **she looked at me in a strange way** mi ha guardato in modo strano; **I'll do it (in) my own way** lo farò a modo mio; **they've had it all their own way too long** hanno fatto per troppo tempo a modo loro; **to get one's own way** aver la vinta; **I will help in every way possible** aiuterò in tutti i modi possibili; **he helped in a small way** ha aiutato un pochino; **in no way, not in any way** per nulla; **no way!** (*fam*) neanche per sogno!; **there's no way I'll do it** non lo farò per nessun motivo al mondo; **do it this way** fallo in questo modo *or* così; **in this way** così, in questo modo; **it was this way ...** è stato così...; **(in) one way or another** in un modo o nell'altro; **in a way** in un certo senso; **in some ways** in un certo senso, sotto certi aspetti; **in many ways** per molti versi; **to my way of thinking** a mio modo di vedere; **either way I can't help you** non ti posso aiutare in nessun caso; **to go on in the same old way** continuare nel modo di sempre; **the way things are** come stanno le cose; **in the ordinary way (of things)** normalmente **7** (*habit*) abitudine *f*; (*manner*) modo di fare; **the ways of the Spaniards** i costumi degli Spagnoli; **foreign ways** abitudini *fpl* forestiere; **it's not my way** non è mia abitudine fare così; **he has a way with people** ci sa fare con la gente; **he has a way with him** ci sa fare; **to get into/out of the way of doing sth** prendere/perdere l'abitudine di fare qc **8** (*state*): **things are in a bad way** le cose si mettono male; **he's in a bad way** è ridotto male; **to be in the family way** (*fam*) aspettare un bambino **9** (*with "by"*): **by the way** a proposito; **but that's just by the way** ma questo è tra parentesi; **by way of a warning** come avvertimento; **she's by way of being an artist** è una specie di artista ♦ ADV (*fam*): **it happened way back** è successo molto tempo fa; **way back in 1900** nel lontano 1900; **it's way out in Nevada** è nel lontano Nevada; **he was way out in his estimate** la sua valutazione era decisamente errata

way·bill ['weɪ‚bɪl] N (*Comm*) bolla di accompagnamento
way·lay [weɪ'leɪ] (*pt, pp* **waylaid**) VT (*old*) intercettare; **I got waylaid** (*fig*) ho avuto un contrattempo
way·side ['weɪ‚saɪd] N bordo della strada; **along the wayside, by the wayside** sul ciglio della strada; **to fall by the wayside** (*fig*) perdersi lungo la strada ♦ ADJ (*flowers, café*) sul bordo della strada
way station N (*USA: Rail*) stazione *f* secondaria; (*fig*) tappa
way·ward ['weɪwəd] ADJ (*self-willed*) ribelle, capriccioso(-a)
WC [‚dʌblju:'si:] N ABBR (*Brit: = water closet*) WC *m inv*
we [wi:] PERS PRON PL noi; **we understand** abbiamo capito; (*stressed*) noi sì che abbiamo capito; **here we are** eccoci; **we Italians** noi *or* noialtri italiani; **as we say in Florence ...** come si dice a Firenze...; **we all make mistakes** tutti possiamo sbagliare; **we aren't so lucky** noi non siamo così fortunati; **we'll arrive tomorrow** arriveremo domani
weak [wi:k] ADJ (*comp* **-er**, *superl* **-est**) (*gen*) debole; (*tea, coffee*) leggero(-a); (*health*) precario(-a); (*excuse, effort*) inefficace; **to grow weak(er) = weaken**; **a weak chin** un mento sfuggente; **to have weak eyes** *or* **eyesight** avere la vista debole; **to have a weak heart** soffrire di cuore; **her French is weak, she is weak at French** è scarsa in francese; **weak in the head** (*fam*) tocco(-a), toccato(-a); **to go weak at the knees** (*with excitement, hunger etc*) avere le gambe che fanno giacomo giacomo; **the weak link in the chain** l'anello debole della catena; **weak verb** verbo debole
weak·en ['wi:kən] VT (*gen*) indebolire; (*grip*) allentare; (*influence*) diminuire; (*solution, mixture*) diluire; **this fact weakens your case** questo fatto sminuisce il tuo argomento; **the recession weakened many firms** la recessione ha indebolito molte aziende ♦ VI (*gen*) indebolirsi; (*grip*) allentarsi; (*influence*) diminuire; (*give way*) cedere; **we must not weaken now** non dobbiamo cedere proprio ora; **her resolve did not weaken** la sua determinazione non si è indebolita
weak-kneed [‚wi:k'ni:d] ADJ (*fig*) debole, codardo(-a)
weak·ling ['wi:klɪŋ] N (*physically*) mingherlino(-a); (*morally*) smidollato(-a)
weak·ly ['wi:klɪ] ADJ deboluccio(-a), gracile ♦ ADV debolmente
weak·ness ['wi:knɪs] N debolezza; **chocolate is one of my weaknesses** il cioccolato è una delle mie passioni; **to have a weakness for sth** avere un debole per qc
wealth [welθ] N (*money, resources*) ricchezza, ricchezze *fpl*; (*fig: abundance*): **wealth and fame** ricchezza e fama; **wealth (of)** dovizia *or* abbondanza (di)
wealth tax N imposta sul patrimonio
wealthy ['welθɪ] ADJ (*comp* **-ier**, *superl* **-iest**) ricco(-a)
wean [wi:n] VT (*baby*) svezzare; **to wean sb (away) from alcohol** far perdere a qn il vizio del bere
weap·on ['wepən] N arma; **weapons of mass destruction** armi di distruzione di massa
wear [weəʳ] (*pt* **wore**, *pp* **worn**) N **1** (*use*) uso; **shoes for everyday wear** scarpe da mettere tutti i giorni; **there's still a lot of wear in these** (*shoes, carpets, tyres*) sono ancora in buono stato; **I've had a lot of wear out of this jacket** porto questa giacca da anni; **to stand up to a lot of wear** durare a lungo **2** (*deterioration through use*) logoramento, logorio; **wear and tear** usura; **fair wear and tear** (*Comm*) normale usura; **the wear on the engine** l'usura del motore **3** (*clothing*) abbigliamento; **children's wear** confezioni *fpl* per bambini; **sports/baby wear** abbigliamento sportivo/per neonati; **summer wear** abiti *mpl* estivi; **evening wear** abiti *mpl* da sera ♦ VT **1** (*spectacles, necklace, beard*) portare; (*clothes*) portare, indossare; (*look, smile*) avere; **to wear make-up** truccarsi; **she wasn't wearing any make-up** non era truccata; **she wore her blue dress** portava il vestito blu; **she was wearing a black coat** portava un cappotto nero; **she wore black trousers and a T-shirt** portava pantaloni neri e una maglietta; **this is the first time I've worn these shoes** è la prima volta che metto queste scarpe; **I have nothing to wear to the dinner** non ho niente da mettermi per la cena; **to wear one's hair long** portare i capelli lunghi; **he wore a big smile** sfoderò un gran sorriso **2** (*damage through use*) consumare, logorare; **I always manage to wear my sweaters at the elbow** i miei maglioni sono sempre consumati nei gomiti; **they have worn a path across the lawn** hanno

formato un sentiero nel prato a forza di camminarci sopra; **to wear a hole in sth** bucare qc a furia di usarlo(-a); **the rocks had been worn smooth** le rocce erano state levigate dal tempo **3** (*fam: believe, tolerate*) bere; **he won't wear that** questa non la beve ♦ VI **1** (*last*) durare; **she has worn well** porta bene i suoi anni; **that theory has worn well** quella teoria è ancora valida **2** (*become worn: shoes, inscription etc*) consumarsi; (: *rocks*) levigarsi; **the stone steps are beginning to wear** gli scalini di pietra cominciano a consumarsi; **the edges have worn smooth** gli spigoli si sono smussati; **that excuse is wearing a bit thin** quella scusa non regge più

▸ **wear away** VT + ADV (*rock, pattern etc*) consumare ♦ VI + ADV consumarsi

▸ **wear down** VT + ADV (*heel, tyre tread etc*) consumare; (*fig: opposition etc*) fiaccare; (: *strength*) esaurire; **to wear down sb's patience** far perdere la pazienza a qn ♦ VI + ADV (*heels, tyre tread*) consumarsi

▸ **wear off** VI + ADV (*plating, paint etc*) consumarsi; (*pain, excitement etc*) diminuire; (*anaesthetic*) perdere efficacia; **after a while the novelty wore off** dopo un po' non era più una novità; **the feeling soon wore off** presto la sensazione svanì

▸ **wear on** VI + ADV avanzare, passare; **as the evening wore on** nel corso della serata

▸ **wear out** VT + ADV consumare, logorare; (*fig: exhaust*) stancare; (: *patience*) far perdere; **he wore out his shoes wandering round the city** ha consumato le scarpe gironzolando per la città; **don't wear yourself out!** non stancarti troppo!; **to be worn out** essere consumato(-a); (*fig: person*) essere estenuato(-a) *or* distrutto(-a) ♦ VI + ADV (*shoes, carpet etc*) consumarsi; **his strength wore out** era spossato; **her patience wore out** ha perso la pazienza

▸ **wear through** VT + ADV consumare ♦ VI + ADV consumarsi

wear·able [ˈwɛərəbl] ADJ indossabile

wea·ri·ly [ˈwɪərɪlɪ] ADV stancamente

wea·ri·ness [ˈwɪərɪnɪs] N stanchezza

wea·ri·some [ˈwɪərɪsəm] ADJ (*tiring*) estenuante; (*boring*) noioso(-a)

wea·ry [ˈwɪərɪ] ADJ (*comp* **-ier,** *superl* **-iest**) (*tired*) stanco(-a), affaticato(-a); (*dispirited*) stanco(-a), abbattuto(-a); (*tiring: wait, day*) estenuante; **to be weary of sb/sth** essere stanco(-a) di qn/qc; **five weary miles** cinque lunghe miglia ♦ VT stancare ♦ VI: **to weary of sb/sth** stancarsi di qn/qc

wea·sel [ˈwiːzl] N (*Zool*) donnola

weath·er [ˈwɛðəʳ] N tempo; **in this weather** con questo tempo; **what's the weather like?** che tempo fa?; **it gets left outside in all weathers** rimane fuori con qualsiasi tempo; **to be under the weather** (*fig: ill*) sentirsi poco bene; **to make heavy weather of sth** far sembrare qc più difficile di quello che sia ♦ VT **1** (*wood*) stagionare **2** **to weather the storm** (*ship*) resistere alla tempesta; (*fig*) superare le difficoltà ♦ VI (*rocks*) logorarsi; (*wood*) stagionare ♦ ADJ (*bureau, ship, chart, station*) meteorologico(-a)

weather-beaten [ˈwɛðəˌbiːtn] ADJ (*rocks, building*) logorato(-a) dalle intemperie; (*person, skin*) segnato(-a) dal tempo

weather forecast N previsioni *fpl* del tempo

weather·man [ˈwɛðəˌmæn] N (*pl* **-men**) meteorologo

weather·proof [ˈwɛðəˌpruːf] ADJ (*garment*) impermeabile

weather report N bollettino meteorologico

weather·vane [ˈwɛðəˌveɪn] N = **weathercock**

weave [wiːv] (*pt, pp* **wove,** *pp* **woven**) N trama ♦ VT (*threads, basket*) intrecciare; (*fabric*) tessere; **I wove this rug myself** ho tessuto io stesso questo tappeto; **he wove these details into the story** ha intrecciato nella storia questi dettagli; **he wove a story round these experiences** ha intessuto una storia attorno a queste esperienze ♦ VI (*pt, pp* **weaved**) tessere; (*fig: move in and out*) zigzagare; **to weave in and out of the traffic** zigzagare nel traffico

weav·er [ˈwiːvəʳ] N tessitore(-trice)

weav·ing [ˈwiːvɪŋ] N tessitura

web [wɛb] N (*of spider*) ragnatela, tela; (*between toes*) membrana interdigitale; (*fig*) insieme *m*; **it was a web of lies** era un castello di menzogne

web address N indirizzo internet

webbed [wɛbd] ADJ: **webbed foot** piede *m* palmato

web·bing [ˈwɛbɪŋ] N (*on chair*) cinghie *fpl*

web·cam [ˈwɛbˌkæm] N (*Comput*) webcam *f inv*

web page N (*Comput*) pagina *f* web, *inv*

web·site [ˈwɛbsaɪt] N (*Comput*) sito internet

wed [wɛd] VT sposare; **to be wedded to one's job/an idea** essere consacrato(-a) al proprio lavoro/a un'idea ♦ VI sposarsi ♦ N: **the newly-weds** gli sposi novelli

Wed. ABBR (= *Wednesday*) mer(c). (= *mercoledì*)

we'd [wiːd] = **we had; we would**

wed·ded [ˈwɛdɪd] ADJ (*wife, husband*) legittimo(-a); (*bliss, life*) coniugale

wed·ding [ˈwɛdɪŋ] N matrimonio, nozze *fpl*; **silver/golden** *etc* **wedding** nozze *fpl* d'argento/d'oro *etc*; **to have a church wedding** sposarsi in chiesa ♦ ADJ (*cake, dress, reception*) nuziale

wedding anniversary N anniversario di matrimonio

wedding day N giorno delle nozze *or* del matrimonio

wedding dress N abito da sposa

wedding present N regalo di nozze

wedding ring N fede *f*, vera

wedge [wɛdʒ] N (*under door*) zeppa; (*for splitting sth*) cuneo; (*piece: of cheese, cake*) fetta; **it's the thin end of the wedge** (*fig*) è l'inizio della fine; **to drive a wedge between two people** intaccare il rapporto tra due persone ♦ VT mettere una zeppa sotto *or* in; **to wedge a door open** tenere aperta una porta con un fermo; **the car was wedged between two trucks** la macchina era incastrata tra due camion

wedge-heeled shoes [ˌwɛdʒhiːldˈʃuːz] NPL scarpe *fpl* con la zeppa

wed·lock [ˈwɛdlɒk] N (*old*) vincolo matrimoniale

Wednes·day [ˈwɛnzdɪ] N mercoledì *m inv; see* **Tuesday**

wee [wiː] ADJ (*comp* **-er,** *superl* **-est**) (*Scot: fam*) piccolo(-a); **a wee bit** un pochino

weed [wiːd] N (*plant*) erbaccia; (*weak person*) tipo(-a) allampanato(-a); **the garden's full of weeds** il giardino è pieno di erbacce ♦ VT (*flower bed*) diserbare ♦ VI strappare le erbacce

▸ **weed out** VT + ADV (*fig*) eliminare

weed-killer [ˈwiːdˌkɪləʳ] N diserbante *m*, erbicida *m*

weedy [ˈwiːdɪ] ADJ (*comp* **-ier,** *superl* **-iest**) (*fam: person*) allampanato(-a)

week [wiːk] N settimana; **once/twice a week** una volta/due volte alla settimana; **this week** questa settimana; **next/last week** la settimana prossima/scorsa; **in the middle of the week** a metà settimana; **in a week's time** tra una settimana; **a week today** oggi a otto, una settimana a oggi; **2 weeks ago** 2 settimane fa; **in 2 weeks' time** fra 2 settimane, fra 15 giorni; **Tuesday week, a week on Tuesday** martedì a otto; **to take 3 weeks' holiday** prendere 3 settimane di ferie; **the week ending January 3rd** ≈ la prima settimana di gennaio; **a 35-hour week** una settimana lavorativa di 35 ore; **week in, week out** settimana dopo settimana; **week after week** settimana dopo settimana; **every other week** una settimana sì e una no, a settimane alterne; **to knock sb into the middle of next week** (*fam*) darle di santa ragione a qn

week·day [ˈwiːkdeɪ] N giorno feriale; (*Comm*) giornata lavorativa; **on weekdays** durante la settimana, nei giorni feriali

week·end [ˌwiːkˈɛnd] N week-end *m inv,* fine settimana *m inv, f inv*; **a long weekend** un fine settimana lungo (*che include il venerdì o il lunedì*); **at the weekend** durante il fine settimana; **at weekends** al weekend *or* fine settimana; **last weekend** l'altro fine settimana; **to go away for the weekend** andare via per il weekend *or* il fine settimana ♦ ADJ (*cottage*) per il fine settimana; (*visit*) di fine settimana

weekend case N borsa da viaggio

week·ly [ˈwiːklɪ] ADJ settimanale ♦ ADV settimanalmente, ogni settimana; **£45 weekly** 45 sterline alla settimana ♦ N (*magazine*) settimanale *m*

weep [wiːp] (*pt, pp* **wept**) VT (*tears*) versare, piangere ♦ VI piangere; (*Med: wound etc*) essudare; **to weep for sb** piangere per qn; **to weep bitterly** piangere amaramente; **I could have wept!** mi sarei messo a piangere!; **she wept for hours** pianse per ore ♦ N: **to have a good weep** farsi un bel pianto

weeping willow N salice *m* piangente

weepy [ˈwiːpɪ] ADJ piagnucoloso(-a) ♦ N (*fam: film*) film *m* strappalacrime, *inv*

weft [wɛft] N (*Textiles*) trama
weigh [weɪ] VT 1 (*also fig*) pesare; **how much do you weigh?** quanto pesi?; **to weigh o.s.** pesarsi; **it weighs a ton** (*also fig*) pesa una tonnellata; **to weigh sth in one's hand** soppesare qc; **to weigh sth in one's mind** soppesare mentalmente qc; **to weigh the pros and cons** valutare i pro e i contro 2 **to weigh anchor** (*Naut*) salpare, levare l'ancora ♦ VI (*fig: be a worry*): **to weigh on sb** pesare su qn; **to weigh against sb** giocare a sfavore di qn; **to weigh with sb** avere importanza *or* contare per qn; **it weighs on her mind** la preoccupa; **that didn't weigh with him** quello per lui non aveva importanza
  ▸ **weigh down** VT + ADV (*branches*) piegare; (*person: with worry*) opprimere; **to be weighed down by sth** curvarsi sotto il peso di qc; **to be weighed down with sorrows** essere oppresso(-a) dai dispiaceri
  ▸ **weigh in** VI + ADV (*Sport*) pesarsi (prima di una gara); **he weighed in at 60 kilos** al controllo del peso era 60 chili
  ▸ **weigh out** VT + ADV (*goods*) pesare
  ▸ **weigh up** VT + ADV (*alternatives, situation*) pesare, valutare
weigh·bridge [ˈweɪˌbrɪdʒ] N bascula
weighing machine N bilancia *f* pesapersone, *inv*
weight [weɪt] N 1 (*gen, also fig*) peso; **the weight of the load** il peso del carico; **sold by weight** venduto(-a) a peso; **it** (*or* **he** *etc*) **is worth its** (*or* **his** *etc*) **weight in gold** vale tanto oro quanto pesa; **to put on/lose weight** ingrassare/dimagrire; **to carry weight** (*fig*) avere peso; **these are arguments of some weight** questi sono argomenti di un certo peso; **that's a weight off my mind** mi sono tolto un peso; **they won by sheer weight of numbers** hanno vinto solo per superiorità numerica; **to chuck** *or* **throw one's weight about** (*fam*) fare il (la) prepotente; **he doesn't pull his weight** non lavora quanto dovrebbe 2 (*for scales etc*) peso; **weights and measures** pesi e misure ♦ VT (*also:* **weight down**) mettere dei pesi su
weight·ing [ˈweɪtɪŋ] N indennità *f inv* speciale (*per carovita etc*)
weight·less·ness [ˈweɪtlɪsnɪs] N assenza di peso
weight·lifter [ˈweɪtˌlɪftəʳ] N pesista *m/f*
weight·lifting [ˈweɪtˌlɪftɪŋ] N sollevamento pesi, pesistica
weight training N: **to do weight training** allenarsi con i pesi, fare pesi
weighty [ˈweɪtɪ] ADJ (*comp* **-ier**, *superl* **-iest**) (*fig: problems, duties, considerations*) importante
weir [wɪəʳ] N sbarramento
weird [wɪəd] ADJ (*comp* **-er**, *superl* **-est**) strano(-a), bizzarro(-a)
weir·do [ˈwɪədəʊ] N (*fam*) tipo(-a) allucinante
wel·come [ˈwɛlkəm] ADJ (*gen*) gradito(-a); **welcome!** benvenuto(-a)!; **welcome to Britain!** benvenuti in Gran Bretagna!; **to be welcome** (*person*) essere il (la) benvenuto(-a); **welcome back!** bentornato(-a)!; **you will always be welcome here** qui sarai sempre il benvenuto; **to make sb welcome** accogliere bene qn; **you're welcome** (*after thanks*) prego; **thank you! — you're welcome!** grazie! — di niente!; **you're welcome to try** prova pure; **you're welcome to (borrow) it** prendilo pure; **it's a welcome change** è un piacevole cambiamento ♦ N accoglienza, benvenuto; **a cold/warm welcome** un'accoglienza fredda/calorosa; **a welcome speech** un discorso di benvenuto; **to bid sb welcome** dare il benvenuto a qn; **the crowd gave him an enthusiastic welcome** la folla lo accolse con entusiasmo; **what sort of a welcome will this product get?** che accoglienza avrà questo prodotto? ♦ VT accogliere, ricevere; (*also:* **bid welcome**) dare il benvenuto a; (*fig: change, suggestion, development*) rallegrarsi di; (: *criticism*) accettare di buon grado; **everyone was there to welcome me** erano tutti lì ad accogliermi; **I'd welcome your help** gradirei il tuo aiuto; **we welcome this step** siamo lieti di questa iniziativa; **he didn't welcome the suggestion** non ha gradito il suggerimento
wel·com·ing [ˈwɛlkəmɪŋ] ADJ accogliente
weld [wɛld] VT saldare ♦ N saldatura
weld·er [ˈwɛldəʳ] N (*person*) saldatore *m*
weld·ing [ˈwɛldɪŋ] N saldatura
wel·fare [ˈwɛlfɛəʳ] N 1 (*gen*) bene *m*; (*comfort*) benessere *m*; **the nation's welfare** il bene della nazione; **spiritual welfare** benessere spirituale; **to look after sb's welfare** preoccuparsi

di qn; **child welfare** protezione *f* dell'infanzia; **they're concerned for your welfare** si preoccupano del tuo benessere 2 (*social aid etc*) assistenza sociale; **to be on welfare** vivere con il sussidio statale; **they were living off welfare** vivevano del sussidio statale ♦ ADJ (*aid, organization*) di assistenza sociale
welfare state N: **the welfare state** lo stato sociale
welfare work N assistenza sociale
well¹ [wɛl] N (*for water etc*) pozzo; (*of stairs*) tromba; (*of lift*) gabbia ♦ VI (*tears, emotions*) sgorgare
  ▸ **well up** VI + ADV (*tears, emotions*) sgorgare
well² [wɛl] (*comp* **better**, *superl* **best**) ADV 1 (*gen*) bene; **very well** benissimo; **she plays the flute very well** suona molto bene il flauto; **you did that really well** l'hai fatto proprio bene; **he did as well as he could** ha fatto come meglio poteva; **to do well (in sth)** andare bene (in qc); **she's doing really well at school** va molto bene a scuola; **to be doing well** stare bene; **the patient is doing well** il paziente si sta rimettendo; **you did well to come** hai fatto bene a venire; **he did well to come tenth** andò bene per essere decimo con lui un buon risultato; **well done!** ben fatto!, bravo(-a)!; **to think well of sb** avere una buona opinione di qn; **to be well in with sb** essere in buoni rapporti con qn; **to do well by sb** trattare bene qn; **it was well worth it** ne valeva certo la pena; **you're well out of it** è un bene che tu ne sia uscito; **well and truly** completamente; **well over a thousand** molto *or* ben più di mille; **all** *or* **only too well** anche troppo bene; **and well I know it!** è proprio vero!; **he's well away** (*fam: drunk*) è completamente andato 2 (*probably, reasonably*): **we might just as well have ...** tanto valeva...; **one might well ask why ...** ci si potrebbe ben chiedere perché...; **you might well ask!** buona domanda!; **you might as well tell me** potresti anche dirmelo; **I might** *or* **may as well come** quasi quasi vengo; **I couldn't very well leave** non potevo andarmene così 3 **as well** (*in addition*) anche; **she sings, as well as playing the piano** oltre a suonare il piano, canta; **X as well as Y** sia X che Y; **we worked hard, but we had some fun as well** abbiamo lavorato sodo, ma ci siamo anche divertiti; **we went to Verona as well as Venice** siamo stati a Verona e anche a Venezia ♦ ADJ 1 (*healthy*): **to be well** stare bene; **I'm not very well at the moment** non sto molto bene in questo periodo; **get well soon!** guarisci presto!; **I don't feel well** non mi sento bene 2 (*acceptable, satisfactory*) buono; **all is not well** non va tutto bene; **that's all very well, but ...** va benissimo, ma..., d'accordo, ma...; **well and good** bene; **it would be as well to ask** sarebbe bene chiedere; **it's just as well we asked** abbiamo fatto bene a chiedere ♦ EXCL (*gen*) bene; (*resignation, hesitation*) be'; **well, as I was saying ...** dunque, come stavo dicendo...; **well, well, well!** ma guarda un po'!; **very well then** va bene, molto bene; **very well, if that's the way you want it** (*unenthusiastic*) va bene, se questo è quello che vuoi; **well I never!** ma no!, ma non mi dire!; **well there you are then!** ecco, hai visto!; **it's enormous! Well, quite big anyway** è gigantesco! Be', diciamo molto grande; **well? What's wrong?** allora? Cosa c'è che non va? ♦ N: **to wish sb well** augurare ogni bene a qn; (*in exam, new job*) augurare a qn di riuscire
we'll [wiːl] = **we will**; **we shall**
well-behaved [ˌwɛlbɪˈheɪvd] ADJ (*child*) che si comporta bene, beneducato(-a)
well-being [ˌwɛlˈbiːɪŋ] N benessere *m*
well-bred [ˌwɛlˈbrɛd] ADJ educato(-a), beneducato(-a)
well-built [ˌwɛlˈbɪlt] ADJ (*person*) ben fatto(-a); (*house*) ben costruito(-a)
well-chosen [ˌwɛlˈtʃəʊzn] ADJ (*remarks, words*) ben scelto(-a), appropriato(-a)
well-developed [ˌwɛldɪˈvɛləpt] ADJ ben sviluppato(-a)
well-disposed [ˌwɛldɪˈspəʊzd] ADJ: **well-disposed to(wards)** bendisposto(-a) verso
well-dressed [ˌwɛlˈdrɛst] ADJ ben vestito(-a), vestito(-a) bene
well-earned [ˌwɛlˈɜːnd] ADJ (*rest*) meritato(-a)
well-groomed [ˌwɛlˈgruːmd] ADJ (*person*) curato(-a) (nel vestire); (*horse*) ben strigliato(-a); (*dog*) ben tenuto(-a)
well-heeled [ˌwɛlˈhiːld] ADJ (*fam: wealthy*) agiato(-a), facoltoso(-a)
wel·lies [ˈwɛlɪz] NPL (*fam*) = **wellingtons**

well-informed [ˌwelɪnˈfɔːmd] ADJ (*knowledgeable*) informato(-a); (*having knowledge of*) ben informato(-a)

Wel·ling·ton [ˈwelɪŋtən] N (*city*) Wellington *f*

wel·ling·tons [ˈwelɪŋtənz] NPL (*also:* **wellington boots**) stivali *mpl* di gomma

well-kept [ˌwelˈkept] ADJ (*house, grounds*) ben tenuto(-a); (*secret*) ben custodito(-a); (*hair, hands*) ben curato(-a)

well-known [ˌwelˈnəʊn] ADJ noto(-a), famoso(-a); **a well-known film star** un famoso divo del cinema

well-mannered [ˌwelˈmænəd] ADJ (*person*) beneducato(-a); (*remark*) cortese

well-meaning [ˌwelˈmiːnɪŋ] ADJ (*person*) spinto(-a) da buone intenzioni

well-nigh [ˌwelˈnaɪ] ADV: **well-nigh impossible** quasi impossibile

well-off [ˌwelˈɒf] ADJ (*rich*) benestante, danaroso(-a); **you're well-off without him** puoi fare tranquillamente a meno di lui; **you don't know when you're well-off** non sai quanto sei fortunato ♦ NPL: **the well-off** i benestanti

well-paid [welˈpeɪd] ADJ ben pagato(-a)

well-read [ˌwelˈred] ADJ colto(-a)

well-spoken [ˌwelˈspəʊkən] ADJ che parla bene

well-stocked [ˌwelˈstɒkt] ADJ (*shop, larder*) ben fornito(-a); (*river*) pescoso(-a)

well-timed [ˌwelˈtaɪmd] ADJ opportuno(-a), tempestivo(-a)

well-to-do [ˌweltəˈduː] ADJ abbiente, benestante

well-wisher [ˈwelˌwɪʃəʳ] N ammiratore(-trice); **letters from well-wishers** lettere *fpl* di incoraggiamento

Welsh [welʃ] ADJ gallese; **Welsh Assembly** (*Pol*) organo legislativo autonomo gallese ♦ N **1 the Welsh** *npl* i gallesi **2** (*language*) gallese *m*

Welsh·man [ˈwelʃmən] N (*pl* -men) gallese *m*

Welsh rabbit, Welsh rarebit N crostino al formaggio

Welsh·woman [ˈwelʃˌwʊmən] N (*pl* -women) gallese *f*

wel·ter [ˈweltəʳ] N massa, mucchio

went [went] PT *of* **go**

wept [wept] PT, PP *of* **weep**

were [wɜːʳ] 2ND PERS SG PT, 2ND PERS PL PAST *of* **be**

we're [wɪəʳ] = **we are**

weren't [wɜːnt] = **were not**

were·wolf [ˈwɪəˌwʊlf] N (*pl* -wolves) licantropo, lupo mannaro (*fam*)

west [west] N ovest *m*, ponente *m*, occidente *m*; **the wind is in** *or* **from the west** il vento viene da ovest *or* da ponente *or* da occidente; **(to the) west of** a ovest di; **Stroud is west of Oxford** Stroud è a ovest di Oxford; **in the west** a ovest; **in the west of** nella parte occidentale di; **the West** (*Pol*) l'Occidente *m* ♦ ADJ (*gen*) ovest *inv*; (*part, coast*) occidentale; (*wind*) di ponente; **the west coast** la costa occidentale ♦ ADV verso ovest; **to sail west** navigare verso ovest; **a house facing west** una casa esposta a ovest; **we were travelling west** andavamo verso ovest

west·bound [ˈwestˌbaʊnd] ADJ (*traffic*) diretto(-a) a ovest; (*carriageway*) ovest *inv*

West Country N: **the West Country** il sud-ovest dell'Inghilterra

west·er·ly [ˈwestəlɪ] ADJ (*wind*) di ponente; **westerly wind** vento di ponente; **in a westerly direction** verso ovest

west·ern [ˈwestən] ADJ (*also Pol*) occidentale, dell'ovest; **in Western France/Europe** nella Francia/nell'Europa occidentale; **the western coast of Scotland** la costa occidentale della Scozia ♦ N (*film*) western *m inv*; (*novel*) romanzo *m* western, *inv*

west·ern·er [ˈwestənəʳ] N occidentale *m/f*

west·ern·ized [ˈwestənaɪzd] ADJ occidentalizzato(-a)

West German ADJ, N tedesco(-a) occidentale

West Germany N Germania Ovest (*la Repubblica Federale Tedesca, del esistente dal 1949 al 1990*)

West Indian ADJ delle Indie Occidentali; **the West Indian team** la squadra caraibica; **the West Indian community** la comunità caraibica ♦ N abitante *m/f* (*or* originario(-a)) delle Indie Occidentali

West Indies NPL: **the West Indies** le Indie Occidentali

West·min·ster [ˈwestˌmɪnstəʳ] N il parlamento (britannico)

West Vir·gin·ia la Virginia Occidentale

west·ward [ˈwestwəd] ADJ (*direction*) ovest *inv* ♦ ADV (*also:* **westwards**) a ovest, verso ovest

wet [wet] ADJ (*comp* -ter, *superl* -test) **1** bagnato(-a); (*damp*) umido(-a); (*soaked*) fradicio(-a); (*paint, varnish, ink*) fresco(-a); **in wet clothes** coi vestiti bagnati; **to get wet** bagnarsi; **to be wet through** *or* **wet to the skin** essere fradicio(-a) fino alle ossa; **dripping wet** gocciolante; **he's still wet behind the ears** (*fig*) ha ancora il latte alla bocca **2** (*rainy*) piovoso(-a); **a wet day** una giornata piovosa; **wet weather** tempo piovoso; **it was wet all week** è piovuto tutta la settimana **3** (*fam, pej: person*) smidollato(-a) ♦ N **1** (*moisture*) umidità; (*rain*) pioggia; **it got left out in the wet** l'hanno lasciato fuori sotto la pioggia **2** (*fam, pej: person*) smidollato(-a) ♦ VT bagnare; **to wet the bed** bagnare il letto; **to wet one's pants** *or* **o.s.** farsela addosso

wet blanket N (*fig*) guastafeste *m/f inv*; **what a wet blanket you are!** (*fam*) che pesante che sei!

wet·ness [ˈwetnɪs] N umidità

wet suit N muta (*da subacqueo*)

we've [wiːv] = **we have**

whack [wæk] N **1** (*blow*) (forte) colpo **2** (*fam: attempt*): **to have a whack at sth/at doing sth** provare qc/a fare qc, tentare qc/di fare qc **3** (*fam: share*) parte *f*, fetta **4** (*fam*): **to take a whack at sb** sputtanare pubblicamente qn **5** (*of money*) parte *f*; **to pay full whack for sth** pagare in pieno qc **6 out of whack** sballato(-a) ♦ VT (*person*) dare un ceffone a; (*ball*) colpire con forza; (*fam: defeat*) dare una batosta a

whacked [wækt] ADJ (*fam: exhausted*) sfinito(-a), stremato(-a)

whale [weɪl] N (*Zool*) balena; **we had a whale of a time** (*fam*) ci siamo divertiti da matti

whal·er [ˈweɪləʳ] N (*person*) baleniere *m*; (*ship*) baleniera

whal·ing [ˈweɪlɪŋ] N caccia alla balena

wharf [wɔːf] N (*pl* **wharfs** *or* **wharves** [wɔːvz]) banchina

---

KEYWORD

what [wɒt] ADJ che, quale; **to what extent?** fino a che punto?; **buy what food you like** compra il cibo che vuoi; **what a fool I was!** che sciocco sono stato!; **what good would that do?** a che può servire?; **what little I had** il poco che avevo; **what a mess!** che disordine!; **what a nuisance!** che seccatura!; **for what reason?** per quale motivo?; **what time is it?** che ore sono?; **in what way did it strike you as odd?** in che cosa esattamente ti è sembrato strano?

♦ PRON

1 (*interrogative*) che cosa, cosa, che; **what were you talking about?** di cosa stavate parlando?; **what is his address?** qual è il suo indirizzo?; **he asked me what she had said** mi ha chiesto che cosa avesse detto lei; **what is it** (*or* **he** *etc*) **called?** come si chiama?; **what will it cost?** quanto sarà? *or* costerà?; **what are you doing?** che *or* (che) cosa fai?; **what are you doing that for?** perché lo fai?; **what is that tool for?** a che *or* a cosa serve quello strumento?; **what's happening?** che *or* (che) cosa succede?; **it's WHAT?** come?, cosa?; **I don't know what to do** non so cosa fare; **what's the weather like?** che tempo fa?; **what's in there?** cosa c'è lì dentro?; **what is it now?** che c'è ora?; **tell me what you're thinking about** dimmi a cosa stai pensando; **tell us what you're laughing at** dicci perché stai ridendo; **what is the Italian for "book"?** come si dice "book" in italiano?; **what do you want now?** che cosa vuoi adesso?; **I wonder what he'll do now** mi chiedo cosa farà adesso

2 (*relative*) ciò che, quello che; **I saw what you did** ho visto quello che hai fatto; **is that what happened?** è andata così?; **it's just what I wanted** è proprio ciò che volevo; **I know what — let's go to the cinema** sai cosa facciamo? — andiamo al cinema; **say what you like** di' quello che vuoi; **she's not what she was** non è più quella di una volta; **I tell you what, why not come back later?** sai cosa ti dico? perché non torniamo più tardi?; **what I want is a cup of tea** ciò che voglio adesso è una tazza di tè; **I saw what was on the table** ho visto quello che c'era sul tavolo; **he knows what's what** (*fam*) sa come stanno le cose; **I'll show her what's what!** le farò vedere io!

3 what about me? e io?; **what about doing ...?** cosa ne diresti di fare...?; **what about a drink?** beviamo qualcosa?;

what about going to the cinema? e se andassimo al cinema?; ... and what have you (fam) ...e roba del genere; you know John — yes, what about him? conosci John — sì, perché?; what about it? (what do you think) cosa ne pensi?; what about that money you owe me? e quei soldi che mi devi?; and what's more e per di più; ...and what not (fam) ... e così via; so what e allora?; what with one thing and another tra una cosa e l'altra

♦ EXCL (disbelieving) cosa?!, come?!; what, no coffee! come, non c'è caffè?!

what·ev·er [wɒt'ɛvə'] PRON 1 (anything that) (tutto) ciò che, (tutto) quello che (no matter what) qualsiasi or qualunque cosa + sub; do whatever you want fa' quello or ciò che vuoi; do whatever is necessary fai qualunque cosa sia necessaria, fai tutto quello che è necessario; whatever happens qualsiasi or qualunque cosa succeda; whatever it costs costi quel che costi; or whatever they're called o come caspita si chiamano 2 (emphatic): whatever do you mean? cosa vorresti dire?; whatever did you do that for? perché mai l'hai fatto? ♦ ADJ, ADV (any): whatever book you choose qualsiasi or qualunque libro tu scelga; (all): give me whatever money you've got dammi i soldi che hai; nothing whatever proprio niente; it's no use whatever non serve proprio a nulla; for whatever reason per qualunque ragione; no reason whatever or whatsoever nessuna ragione al mondo; there was no reason whatever for the attack non c'era nessuna ragione al mondo per attaccare

what·so·ev·er [ˌwɒtsəʊ'ɛvə'] = whatever

wheat [wiːt] N grano, frumento

wheat·germ [ˈwiːtdʒɜːm] N germe m di grano

wheat·meal [ˈwiːtmiːl] N tipo di farina integrale di frumento

whee·dle [ˈwiːdl] VT: to wheedle sb into doing sth convincere qn a fare qc con lusinghe; to wheedle sth out of sb (favour etc) ottenere qc da qn con lusinghe; (secret, name) farsi dire qc da qn con lusinghe

wheel [wiːl] N (gen) ruota; (also: steering wheel) volante m; (Naut) timone m; (also: potter's wheel) tornio da vasaio; (also: spinning wheel) filatoio; at the wheel (Aut) al volante; (Naut) al timone; the front wheel la ruota anteriore; this car is a four-wheel drive questa è una macchina a quattro ruote motrici; to take the wheel prendere il volante; (Naut) prendere il timone; the wheel of fortune la ruota della fortuna; the wheels of government gli ingranaggi dello stato; there are wheels within wheels (fig) è più complesso di quello che sembra; to put one's shoulder to the wheel (fig) darci dentro; the wheel has come or turned full circle (fig) la fortuna è girata ♦ VT (push: bicycle, pram etc) spingere; we wheeled it over to the window l'abbiamo spinto verso la finestra ♦ VI (birds) roteare; to wheel left (Mil) fare una conversione a sinistra; to wheel round (person) girarsi sui tacchi, voltarsi; to wheel and deal (fam) trafficare

wheel·bar·row [ˈwiːlbærəʊ] N carriola

wheel·base [ˈwiːlbeɪs] N (Aut) interasse m, passo

wheel·chair [ˈwiːltʃeə'] N sedia a rotelle

wheel clamp N (Brit) ceppo bloccaruota

wheeler-dealer [ˈwiːləˌdiːlə'] N trafficone(-a)

wheelie bin [ˈwiːliˌbɪn] N cassonetto (con le ruote)

wheel·ing [ˈwiːlɪŋ] N: wheeling and dealing traffici mpl

wheeze [wiːz] VI ansimare ♦ N respiro affannoso

wheezy [ˈwiːzi] ADJ (comp -ier, superl -iest) (person) chi respira con affanno; (breath) sibilante

---

KEYWORD

when [wɛn] ADV quando; when did it happen? quando è successo?; I know when it happened lo so io quando è successo; say when! (pouring drinks) dimmi (quando) basta; since when do you like Indian food? da quando (in qua) ti piace la cucina indiana?

♦ CONJ

1 (at, during or after the time that) quando; when I came in quando sono entrato; be careful when you cross the road or when crossing the road stai attento quando attraversi la strada; even when anche quando; when it's finished, it will measure ... quando sarà finito misurerà...; when you've read it quando l'hai or l'avrai letto; why walk when you can take a bus? perché camminare se puoi andare in autobus?

2 (the time that): she told me about when she was in Milan mi parlò di quando era a Milano; that was when I needed you era allora che avevo bisogno di te; that's when the train arrives il treno arriva a quell'ora

3 (relative: in, on or at which) in cui; on the day when il giorno in cui; one day when it was raining un giorno che pioveva; at the very moment when ... proprio quando...; during the time when she lived abroad nel periodo in cui viveva all'estero; in the winter when ... nell'inverno in cui...

4 (whereas, although) mentre, sebbene; you call the policy rigid, when in fact it is very flexible la definisci rigida, mentre in realtà è una politica molto flessibile

when·ever [wɛn'ɛvə'] CONJ 1 (rel: at whatever time) quando, in qualsiasi momento + sub; (every time that) quando, ogni volta che; come whenever you like vieni quando vuoi; leave whenever it suits you parti quando ti fa comodo or in qualsiasi momento ti faccia comodo; I go whenever I can ci vado quando posso; whenever you see one of those, stop fermati quando ne vedi uno 2 (in questions): whenever did I say that? quando mai l'ho detto? ♦ ADV: tomorrow or whenever domani o in un altro momento; ...last month, or whenever it was ...lo scorso mese, o non ricordo quando; last week or whenever la settimana scorsa o non so più quando

where [wɛə'] ADV dove; where are you from? da dove sei?; where am I? dove sono?; where do you live? dove abiti?; where are you going (to)? dove stai andando?; where have you come from? da dove sei venuto?; did he tell you where he was going? ti ha detto dove andava?; where should we be if ...? dove saremmo se...? ♦ CONJ 1 (gen) dove; there's a cinema where the butcher's used to be dove una volta c'era la macelleria ora c'è un cinema; where possible quando è possibile, se possibile; from where I'm standing it looks fine da dove sono, mi sembra vada bene; so that's where they've got to! ecco dove erano finiti!; this is where we found it è qui che l'abbiamo trovato; that's where we got to in the last lesson è qui che siamo arrivati nell'ultima lezione; that's just where you're wrong! è proprio lì che ti sbagli!; sometimes a teacher will be listened to, where a parent might not qualche volta si è più disposti ad ascoltare un insegnante che un genitore 2 (rel: in, on, at which) dove, in (or da, su etc) cui; the town where we come from la città da cui veniamo; the house where I was born la casa in cui sono nato; the hill where the heather grows la collina dove or su cui cresce l'erica

where·abouts [ˈwɛərəˌbaʊts] ADV dove; whereabouts did you say you lived? da che parte hai detto che abiti? ♦ NPL: to know sb's whereabouts sapere dove si trova qn; his current whereabouts are unknown non si sa dove si trovi attualmente

where·as [wɛər'æz] CONJ (while on the other hand) mentre; (Law) considerato che

where·by [wɛə'baɪ] ADV (frm) per cui

where·upon [ˌwɛərə'pɒn] ADV (frm) al che, dopo di che

wher·ever [wɛər'ɛvə'] CONJ dovunque + sub; wherever you go I'll go too dovunque tu vada andrò anch'io; some people have a good time wherever they are alcune persone si divertono dovunque siano; wherever they went they were cheered venivano acclamati dovunque andassero; Udine, wherever that is un posto che non so dove sia ma che si chiama Udine; sit wherever you like sediti dove vuoi ♦ ADV 1 in Naples, Florence, or wherever a Napoli, Firenze o in qualche altro posto 2 (in questions) dove; wherever did he put it? dove (mai) l'ha messo?

where·with·al [ˈwɛəwɪðˌɔːl] N: the wherewithal (to do sth) i mezzi mpl (per fare qc)

whet [wɛt] VT (tool) affilare; (appetite, curiosity) stuzzicare

wheth·er [ˈwɛðə'] CONJ (if) se; (no matter whether) che + sub; whether you want to or not che tu voglia o no; whether it's sunny or not che ci sia il sole o no; I am not certain whether he'll come (or not) non so con certezza se verrà (o no), non sono sicuro che venga; whether they come or not che vengano o meno; I don't know whether you know ... non so se lo sai...; I doubt whether that's true dubito che sia vero; I don't know whether to accept or not non so se accettare o no; it's doubtful whether è poco probabile che

whey [weɪ] N siero

which [wɪtʃ] ADJ
1 (*interrogative*) quale; **which book do you want?** quale libro vuoi?; **she didn't say which books she wanted** non ha detto quali libri voleva; **which books are yours?** quali sono i tuoi libri?; **tell me which one you want** dimmi quale vuoi; **which one of you?** chi di voi?; **which one/ones do you want?** quale/quali vuoi?; **which way did she go?** da che parte è andata?
2 in which case nel qual caso; **he lived in Italy for a year, during which time ...** ha vissuto in Italia per un anno, periodo in cui...; **by which time** e a quel punto
♦ PRON
1 (*interrogative: the one or ones that*) quale; **I know which I'd rather have** io lo so quale preferirei; **I don't mind which** non mi importa quale; **which of these are yours?** quali di questi sono tuoi?; **which of your sisters?** quale delle tue sorelle?; **which of you?** chi di voi?; **which do you want?** quale vuoi?; **I can't tell which is which** non riesco a distinguere l'uno dall'altro
2 (*relative: that*) che; (*indirect*) cui, il (la) quale; **the book about which** il libro del quale *or* di cui; **after which** dopo di che; **the apple (which) you ate** la mela che hai mangiato; **the apple which is on the table** la mela che è sul tavolo; **the hotel at which we stayed** l'albergo in cui abbiamo soggiornato; **from which one can deduce ...** dal che si può dedurre...; **he said he was there, which is true** ha detto che c'era, il che è vero; **the meeting (which) we attended** la riunione a cui abbiamo partecipato; **the chair on which I** sedia sulla quale *or* su cui; **you're late, which reminds me ...** sei in ritardo, il che mi fa venire in mente...; **it rained a lot, which upset her** ha piovuto tanto e ciò l'ha irritata
which·ever [wɪtʃ'evə[r]] ADJ (*that one which*) quello(-a) che; (*no matter which*) qualsiasi + *sub*, qualunque + *sub*; **take whichever one you prefer** prendi quello che preferisci; **take whichever book you prefer** prendi il libro che preferisci; **whichever book you take** qualsiasi libro tu prenda; **you can choose whichever system you want** puoi scegliere il sistema che vuoi; **whichever system you have there are difficulties** qualsiasi sistema tu abbia ci sono delle difficoltà; **whichever way you ...** in qualunque modo tu...; **whichever way you look at it** da qualunque punto di vista lo si consideri ♦ PRON (*the one which*) quello(-a) che; (*no matter which one*) qualsiasi + *sub*, qualunque + *sub*; **whichever of the methods you choose** qualsiasi *or* qualunque metodo tu scelga; **choose whichever you like** scegli quello che ti piace
whiff [wɪf] N (*of gas, sth unpleasant*) zaffata; (*of sea air, perfume*) odore *m*; **to catch a whiff of sth** sentire l'odore di qc; **a few whiffs of this could knock you out** se annusi un po' di questo svieni
while [waɪl] N **1 a while** un po' (di tempo); **for a little while** per un po'; **for a long while** per un bel po', a lungo; **after a while** dopo un po', per un certo periodo; **I lived in London for a while** ho abitato a Londra per un po'; **in a while** tra poco; **once in a while** ogni tanto, una volta ogni tanto; **it will be a good while before he gets here** gli ci vorrà un bel po' (di tempo) per arrivare qui; **a little while ago** poco fa; **he was here a while ago** era qui poco fa; **in between whiles** nel frattempo; **quite a while** distanza di tempo; **I haven't seen him for quite a while** è da diverso tempo che non lo vedo; **all the while** tutto il tempo; **we'll make it worth your while** faremo in modo che non ti penta; **it might be worth your while to ...** forse ti converrebbe... ♦ CONJ **1** (*during the time that*) mentre; (*as long as*) mentre; **while this was happening** mentre avveniva questo; **she fell asleep while reading** si addormentò mentre stava leggendo; **it won't happen while I'm here** non accadrà finché sono qui io; **you hold the torch while I look inside** tieni la pila mentre io guardo dentro **2** (*although*) benché + *sub*, sebbene + *sub*, anche se; **while I agree with what you have said** benché sia d'accordo *or* anche se sono d'accordo con ciò che hai detto; **while this may seem expensive, it's worth it** anche se può sembrare costoso, vale la spesa **3** (*whereas*) mentre; **I enjoy sport, while he prefers reading** a me piace lo sport, mentre lui preferisce la lettura; **Isobel is**

very dynamic, while Kay is more laid-back** Isobel è molto attiva mentre Kay è più tranquilla
▸ **while away** VT + ADV (*time, hours*) far passare
whilst [waɪlst] CONJ = **while 1**
whim [wɪm] N capriccio; **a passing whim** una passione momentanea; **as the whim takes me** come mi gira
whim·per [ˈwɪmpə[r]] N (*of person*) gemito; (*whine*) piagnucolio; (*of dog*) mugolio ♦ VI (*see n*) gemere; piagnucolare; mugolare
whim·si·cal [ˈwɪmzɪkəl] ADJ (*person*) particolare; (*look*) curioso(-a); (*idea, story*) fantasioso(-a); **a whimsical smile** uno strano sorrisetto
whine [waɪn] N (*of dog*) guaito; (*of child*) piagnucolio; (*of engine*) sibilo; (*of bullet*) fischio ♦ VI (*dog*) guaire; (*child*) piagnucolare; (*engine*) sibilare; (*bullet*) fischiare; (*fig: fam: complain*) piagnucolare, lamentarsi; **don't come whining to me about it** non venire a piangere da me
whip [wɪp] N **1** frusta; (*also: riding whip*) frustino **2** (*Parliament: person*) capogruppo; **three-line whip** ordine *m* tassativo di votare **3** (*Culin*) mousse *f inv* ♦ VT **1** frustare, fustigare; (*Culin: cream etc*) montare; **whip the cream** montare la panna; **whip the egg whites** sbattere gli albumi **2** (*fam: move quickly*): **he whipped the book off the table** tolse rapidamente il libro dal tavolo; **he whipped a gun out of his pocket** estrasse fulmineamente una pistola dalla tasca; **the car whipped round the corner** la macchina svoltò l'angolo a gran velocità ♦ VI: **to whip along/away** *etc* fare una corsa; **she whipped round when she heard me** si voltò di scatto quando mi sentì
▸ **whip up** VT + ADV (*cream*) montare, sbattere; (*fam: meal*) improvvisare; (: *stir up: support, feeling*) suscitare
whip·lash [ˈwɪplæʃ] N (*blow from whip*) frustata; (*Med: also: whiplash injury*) colpo di frusta
whipped cream [ˌwɪptˈkriːm] N panna montata
whipping boy N (*fig*) capro espiatorio
whip-round [ˈwɪpˌraʊnd] N (*Brit fam*) colletta; **to have a whip-round for sb** fare una colletta per qn
whirl [wɜːl] N (*spin*) vortice *m*, turbinio; (*of dust, water etc*) turbine *m*; (*of cream*) ricciolo; **my head is in a whirl** mi gira la testa; **the social whirl** il vortice della vita mondana; **let's give it a whirl** (*fam*) facciamo un tentativo ♦ VT (*also: whirl round: dance partner*) far roteare, far volteggiare; **the wind whirled the leaves** il vento ha sollevato le foglie in un vortice; **he whirled us round the town** ci ha fatto visitare la città a tutta velocità *or* in un baleno; **he whirled us off to the theatre** ci trascinò con sé al teatro ♦ VI (*also: whirl round*) (*wheel, merry-go-round*) girare; (*dancers*) volteggiare; (*leaves, dust*) sollevarsi in un vortice; **the countryside whirled past us** la campagna sfrecciava accanto a noi; **the dancers whirled past us** i danzatori passarono accanto a noi volteggiando; **my head was whirling** mi girava la testa
whirl·pool [ˈwɜːlˌpuːl] N mulinello, vortice *m*
whirl·wind [ˈwɜːlˌwɪnd] N tromba d'aria, turbine *m* ♦ ADJ (*romance etc*) travolgente
whirr, whir [wɜːr] N (*of insect wings, machine*) ronzio ♦ VI ronzare
whisk [wɪsk] N (*Culin*) (*also: hand whisk*) frusta, frullino a mano; (*also: electric whisk*) frullino elettrico; **with a whisk of its tail** con un colpo di coda ♦ VT **1** (*Culin*) frullare, sbattere; (*egg whites*) montare a neve; **whisk the yolks with the sugar** sbattere i tuorli e lo zucchero **2 whisk the eggs into the mixture** incorporare le uova all'impasto mescolando energicamente; **he was whisked away in a police car** è stato trascinato via in una macchina della polizia; **the horse whisked the flies away with its tail** il cavallo scacciava le mosche con la coda; **the waiter whisked the dishes away** il cameriere tolse in fretta i piatti; **they whisked him off to a meeting** lo trascinarono di gran fretta a una riunione
whisk·ers [ˈwɪskəz] NPL (*also: side whiskers*) basette *fpl*; (*beard*) barba; (*moustache, of animal*) baffi *mpl*
whis·ky, whis·key (*USA*) [ˈwɪskɪ] N whisky *m inv*; **a whisky and soda** un whisky e soda
whis·per [ˈwɪspə[r]] N **1** (*gen*) sussurro, bisbiglio; (*of leaves*) fruscio, stormire *m*; **to speak in a whisper** bisbigliare **2** (*rumour*) voce *f* ♦ VT bisbigliare, sussurrare; **to whisper sth to sb** bisbigliare qc a qn ♦ VI (*gen*) bisbigliare; (*leaves*) frusciare, stormire; **to whisper to sb** bisbigliare a qn

whis·per·ing [ˈwɪspərɪŋ] N bisbiglio; (*of leaves*) fruscio; **there's been a lot of whispering about her** sono corse parecchie voci sul suo conto

whist [wɪst] N whist *m*

whis·tle [ˈwɪsl] N (*sound*) fischio; (*instrument*) fischietto; **the referee blew his whistle** l'arbitro fischiò; **the police searched him, but he was as clean as a whistle** la polizia lo ha perquisito ma lui era pulito; **the handle broke off as clean as a whistle** il manico si è staccato di netto; **to blow the whistle on** (*inform on*) fare una soffiata su ♦ VT: **to whistle a tune** fischiettare un motivetto ♦ VI (*gen*) fischiare; (*in low tone*) fischiettare; **he whistled for a taxi** fischiò per fermare un taxi; **the referee whistled for a foul** l'arbitro fischiò un fallo; **the bullet whistled past my ear** la pallottola mi fischiò vicino all'orecchio; **he's whistling in the dark** (*fig*) lo fa (*or* dice) per darsi coraggio; **he can whistle for it!** (*fig: fam*) se lo può sognare!
- **whistle up** VT + ADV (*taxi, dog*) fare un fischio a

whistle-stop [ˈwɪslstɒp] ADJ: **whistle-stop tour** (*Pol*) visita *f* lampo, *inv* (*in una città nel corso di una campagna elettorale*)

Whit [wɪt] (*fam*) N Pentecoste *f* ♦ ADJ (*holiday, weekend*) di Pentecoste

white [waɪt] ADJ (*comp* **-er**, *superl* **-est**) (*gen*) bianco(-a), candido(-a); **to turn** *or* **go white** (*person*) sbiancare; (*hair*) diventare bianco(-a); **a white man** un bianco; **white people** i bianchi; **a white Christmas** un Natale con la neve; **to be as white as a sheet** essere bianco(-a) come un cencio; **as white as snow** niveo(-a), bianco *or* candido come la neve; **white with fear** pallido(-a) dalla paura; **it washes the clothes whiter than white** lava più bianco del bianco; **he's got white hair** ha i capelli bianchi ♦ N (*colour, of eyes*) bianco; (*of egg*) bianco, albume *m*; **the whites** (*washing*) i capi bianchi; **tennis whites** completo *msg* da tennis; **dressed in white** vestito(-a) di bianco; **her dress was a dazzling white** il suo abito era di un bianco abbagliante 2 (*person*) bianco(-a)

white·bait [ˈwaɪtbeɪt] N bianchetti *mpl*

white-collar worker N impiegato(-a), colletto bianco

white elephant N (*fam*) cattedrale *f* nel deserto

white goods NPL (*appliances*) elettrodomestici *mpl*; (*linen*) biancheria *fsg* per la casa

white-hot [ˈwaɪtˈhɒt] ADJ (*metal*) incandescente

White House N (*USA*): **the White House** la Casa Bianca, la residenza ufficiale del presidente degli Stati Uniti

white lie N bugia pietosa, bugia innocua

white·ness [ˈwaɪtnɪs] N (*gen*) bianco; (*of skin*) candore *m*; (*pallor*) biancore *m*

white noise N (*Radio, TV*) sibilo (per interferenza)

white paper N (*Pol*) ≈ libro bianco

white·wash [ˈwaɪtwɒʃ] N (bianco di) calce *f* ♦ VT (*wall*) imbiancare (con la calce); (*fig: person, sb's faults*) coprire; (*: motives*) dissimulare; (*: event, episode*) sminuire

whit·ing [ˈwaɪtɪŋ] N INV (*fish*) merlango

Whit Monday N lunedì *m inv* di Pentecoste

Whit·sun [ˈwɪtsən] N (*also:* **Whitsuntide**) Pentecoste *f*; (*week*) settimana di Pentecoste

whit·tle [ˈwɪtl] VT (*wood*) intagliare
- **whittle away** VT + ADV (*fig*) ridurre
- **whittle down** VT + ADV (*fig*) ridurre, tagliare

whiz, whizz [wɪz] VI (*motorbike, sledge etc*) sfrecciare; (*bullet*) sibilare; **to whiz through the air** sfrecciare; **cars were whizzing past** le macchine passavano sfrecciando

whiz kid N (*fam*) mago(-a)

WHO [ˌdʌbljuːeɪtʃˈəʊ] N ABBR (= *World Health Organization*) OMS *f* (= *Organizzazione Mondiale della Sanità*)

KEYWORD

who [huː] PRON

1 (*si può anche usare al posto di "whom" nella lingua parlata: interrogative*) chi; **who should it be but Graham!** chi poteva essere se non Graham!; **who's the boy?** chi è?; **he's the author del libro?**; **who are you looking for?** chi stai cercando?; **who is it?** chi è?; **I know who it was** io so chi è stato; **who's there?** chi è?; **who does she think she is?** (*fam*) chi si crede di essere?; **you'll soon find out who's who** presto ti conoscerai

2 (*relative*) che; **my cousin who lives in New York** mio cugino che vive a New York; **those who can swim** quelli che sanno nuotare, chi sa nuotare

who·dun·it, whodunnit [huːˈdʌnɪt] N (*fam*) (romanzo) giallo

who·ever [huːˈevər] PRON 1 (*the person that, anyone that*) chiunque + *sub*, chi; (*no matter who*) chiunque + *sub*; **whoever said that was an idiot** chiunque l'abbia detto *or* chi l'ha detto è un idiota; **whoever finds it** chiunque lo trovi; **ask whoever you like** chiedi a chiunque; **invite whoever you like** invita chi vuoi; **it won't be easy, whoever does it** non sarà facile, chiunque lo faccia; **whoever she marries** chiunque lei sposi 2 (*in questions*) chi (mai); **whoever told you that?** chi (mai) te l'ha detto?

whole [həʊl] ADJ 1 (*entire*: + *sg n*) intero(-a), tutto(-a); (: + *pl n*) intero(-a); **with my whole heart** con tutto il mio cuore; **a whole lot of things** una gran quantità di cose, moltissime cose; **a whole lot of people** moltissima gente; **a whole lot better** molto meglio; **the whole lot** tutto; **the whole lot (of them)** tutti(-e); **3 whole days** 3 giorni interi; **the whole day** tutto il giorno, il giorno intero; **the whole afternoon** tutto il pomeriggio; **I read the whole book** ho letto tutto il libro *or* il libro per intero; **the whole world** tutto il mondo, il mondo intero; **the whole class** la classe intera; **a whole box of chocolates** un'intera scatola di cioccolatini; **whole villages were destroyed** interi paesi furono distrutti; **is that the whole truth?** è tutta la verità?; **but the whole purpose** *or* **point was to ...** ma lo scopo era proprio di... 2 (*intact, unbroken*) intero(-a); (*series, set*) completo(-a); **to swallow sth whole** mandar giù qc intero(-a); **he swallowed it whole** l'ha bevuta tutta; **to our surprise he came back whole** con nostra sorpresa tornò sano e salvo ♦ N 1 (*all*): **the whole of the film** tutto il film, il film intero; **the whole of the sum** la somma intera, l'intera somma; **the whole of the time** tutto il tempo; **the whole of August** tutto agosto; **the whole of Italy** tutta l'Italia, l'Italia intera; **the whole of Wales was affected** tutto il Galles è stato colpito; **the whole of the town** la città intera, tutta la città; **as a whole** nell'insieme, nel suo insieme; **on the whole** nel complesso 2 (*entire unit*) tutto; **they make a whole** formano un tutto; **two halves make a whole** due metà fanno un intero

whole·food [ˈhəʊlfuːd] N: **wholefoods** alimenti *mpl* integrali ♦ ADJ: **wholefood diet** dieta a base di prodotti integrali

whole·hearted [ˌhəʊlˈhɑːtɪd] ADJ (*approval, agreement*) incondizionato(-a), totale; (*thanks, congratulations*) sentito(-a), sincero(-a); **to be wholehearted in sth** fare qc di tutto cuore

whole·heart·ed·ly [ˌhəʊlˈhɑːtɪdlɪ] ADV (*approve, agree*) incondizionatamente; (*thank, congratulate*) sentitamente, di tutto cuore; (*do, work, play*) con impegno, mettendoci l'anima

whole·meal [ˈhəʊlmiːl] ADJ (*Brit: flour, bread*) integrale; **wholemeal bread** pane *m* integrale

whole note N (*USA: Mus*) semibreve *f*

whole·sale [ˈhəʊlseɪl] ADJ (*prices, trade*) all'ingrosso; (*fig: slaughter, destruction*) in massa, totale; (*acceptance*) in blocco; (*modification*) su vasta scala; **wholesale prices** prezzi *mpl* all'ingrosso; **wholesale destruction** distruzione *f* su vasta scala; **his work came in for wholesale criticism** il suo lavoro è stato criticato in blocco ♦ ADV (*see adj*) all'ingrosso; in massa; in blocco; su vasta scala ♦ N commercio *or* vendita all'ingrosso

whole·sal·er [ˈhəʊlseɪləʳ] N grossista *m/f*

whole·some [ˈhəʊlsəm] ADJ (*gen*) sano(-a); (*climate*) salubre

whole·wheat [ˈhəʊlwiːt] ADJ (*USA*) = **wholemeal**

whol·ly [ˈhəʊlɪ] ADV completamente, del tutto

KEYWORD

whom [huːm] PRON

1 (*spesso sostituito da "who" nella lingua parlata: interrogative*) chi; **from whom did you receive it?** da chi l'hai ricevuto?; **whom did you see?** chi hai visto?

2 (*relative: direct object*) che, prep + il (la) quale; (: *indirect*) cui; **the man whom I saw** l'uomo che ho visto; **three policemen, none of whom wore a helmet** tre poliziotti, nessuno dei quali portava il casco; **those to whom I spoke** le persone con le quali ho parlato; **the lady with whom I was talking** la signora con cui stavo parlando

whoop·ing cough [ˈhuːpɪŋˌkɒf] N pertosse *f*, tosse *f* asinina (*or* canina *or* cavallina)

whoops [wuːps] EXCL (*also:* whoops-a-daisy!: *avoiding fall etc*) ops!

whoosh [wuʃ] N: **it came out with a whoosh** (*sauce, water*) è uscito(-a) di getto; (*air*) è uscito(-a) con un sibilo

whop·per [ˈwɒpəʳ] N (*fam: large thing*) cosa enorme; (: *lie*) balla

whop·ping [ˈwɒpɪŋ] ADJ enorme

whore [hɔːʳ] N (*pej*) puttana

KEYWORD

whose [huːz] POSS PRON di chi; **whose is this?** di chi è questo?; **I know whose it is** io lo so di chi è

♦ POSS ADJ

1 (*interrogative*) di chi; **whose daughter are you?** di chi sei figlia?; **whose fault was it?** di chi era la colpa?; **whose hat is this?** di chi è questo cappello?; **whose pencil have you taken?** di chi è la matita che hai preso?

2 (*relative*) il (la) cui; **the girl whose sister you were speaking to** la ragazza alla cui sorella stavi parlando; **the man whose wife I was talking to** l'uomo alla cui moglie stavo parlando; **the man whose son you rescued** l'uomo di cui hai salvato il figlio; **the woman whose car was stolen** la donna a cui macchina è stata rubata

Who's Who N chi è *m inv*

why [waɪ] ADV, CONJ perché; **why is he always late?** perché è sempre in ritardo?; **I wonder why he said that** mi chiedo perché l'abbia detto; **why not do it now?** perché non farlo adesso?; **why did you do it?** perché l'hai fatto?; **the reason why** il motivo per cui; **there's no reason why** non c'è motivo per cui + *sub*; **why (ever) not?** perché no?; **so that's why he did it!** ecco perché l'ha fatto! ♦ EXCL (*surprise*) guarda guarda!, ma guarda un po'!; (*remonstrating*) ma via!; (*explaining*) ebbene!; **why, it's you!** guarda guarda, *or* ah sei tu!; **why, it's obvious!** ma via, è ovvio! ♦ N: **the whys and (the) wherefores** le ragioni *or* i motivi; **the why and the how** il perché e il percome

why·ev·er [waɪˈevəʳ] ADV perché mai

WI ABBR 1 (*Geog*) = **West Indies** 2 (*USA Post*: = **Wisconsin**)

wick [wɪk] N stoppino, lucignolo

wick·ed [ˈwɪkɪd] ADJ (*person, remark, smile*) cattivo(-a), malvagio(-a); (*mischievous*) malizioso(-a); (*satire*) sferzante; (*system, policy*) iniquo(-a); (*fam: price, weather etc*) allucinante; **she has a wicked temper** ha un caratteraccio; **that was a wicked thing to do** è stata una cattiveria; **a wicked sense of humour** un senso dell'umorismo un po' malizioso

wick·er [ˈwɪkəʳ] N vimini *mpl* ♦ ADJ di vimini

wick·et [ˈwɪkɪt] (*Cricket*) N porta

wicket keeper N (*Cricket*) ≈ portiere *m*

wide [waɪd] ADJ (*comp* **-er**, *superl* **-est**) (*gen*) largo(-a); (*publicity, margin*) ampio(-a); (*ocean, desert, region*) vasto(-a); (*fig: considerable: variety, choice*) grande, ampio(-a), vasto(-a); **it is 3 metres wide** è largo 3 metri; **his wide knowledge of the subject** la sua vasta conoscenza dell'argomento; **in the whole wide world** nel mondo intero, in tutto il mondo; **a wide road** una strada larga; **a wide choice of hotels** un'ampia scelta di alberghi; **the wide screen** il grande schermo ♦ ADV (*aim, fall*) lontano dal bersaglio; **set wide apart** (*houses, eyes*) ben distanziati(-e); (*legs*) divaricato(-a); **to be wide open** (*door*) essere spalancato(-a); **to open wide** spalancare; **to shoot wide** tirare a vuoto *or* fuori bersaglio; **the ball went wide** la palla ha mancato il bersaglio; **to be wide open to criticism/attack** essere esposto(-a) alle critiche/agli attacchi

wide-angle lens [ˌwaɪdæŋglˈlenz] N grandangolare *m*

wide-awake [ˌwaɪdəˈweɪk] ADJ completamente sveglio(-a); (*fig*) sveglio(-a)

wide-eyed [ˌwaɪdˈaɪd] ADJ con gli occhi spalancati

wide·ly [ˈwaɪdlɪ] ADV (*distributed, scattered*) ampiamente, largamente; (*read etc*) molto; (*travel*) in lungo e in largo; (*differing*) molto, profondamente; (*popularly, by many people*) generalmente; **widely used** di largo uso; **to be widely read** (*author*) essere molto letto(-a); (*reader*) essere molto colto(-a); **it is widely believed that** è una credenza diffusa che; **to be widely spaced** (*houses, trees*) essere molto

distanziati(-e); **it's widely available** è facilmente reperibile

wid·en [ˈwaɪdn] VT (*also fig*) ampliare, allargare; **they're widening the road** stanno allargando la strada ♦ VI (*also:* **widen out**) ampliarsi

wide·ness [ˈwaɪdnɪs] N (*see adj*) larghezza; vastità; ampiezza

wide open ADJ (*door*) spalancato(-a); (*defences*) vulnerabile; (*outcome*) aperto(-a); **the door was wide open** la porta era spalancata

wide-ranging [ˌwaɪdˈreɪndʒɪŋ] ADJ (*survey, report*) vasto(-a); (*interests*) svariato(-a)

wide-screen [ˈwaɪdskriːn] ADJ (*television*) a schermo panoramico

wide·spread [ˈwaɪdˌspred] ADJ (*disease, belief*) molto diffuso(-a); **there is widespread fear that ...** c'è una paura diffusa che...

widget [ˈwɪdʒɪt] N (*Comput*) widget *m inv*

wid·ow [ˈwɪdəʊ] N vedova; **to be left a widow** restare vedova; **she is a golf widow** (*hum*) è una vedova del gioco del golf; **widow's peak** attaccatura dei capelli a forma di V (sulla fronte) ♦ VT: **to be widowed** restare vedovo(-a)

wid·owed [ˈwɪdəʊd] ADJ (*che è rimasto(-a)*) vedovo(-a); **his widowed mother** sua madre (rimasta) vedova

wid·ow·er [ˈwɪdəʊəʳ] N vedovo

width [wɪdθ] N (*see adj*) larghezza; ampiezza; (*of fabric*) altezza; **it's 7 metres in width** è largo 7 metri

width·ways [ˈwɪdθˌweɪz], **width·wise** [ˈwɪdθˌwaɪz] ADV trasversalmente

wield [wiːld] VT (*sword, axe*) maneggiare; (*brandish*) brandire; (*power, influence*) esercitare

wife [waɪf] N (*pl* **wives**) moglie *f*; **the wife** (*fam*) la padrona; **it's just an old wives' tale** è solo una superstizione

Wi-Fi [ˈwaɪfaɪ] N WiFi *m*

wig [wɪg] N parrucca

wig·ging [ˈwɪgɪŋ] N (*Brit fam, old*) lavata di capo

wig·gle [ˈwɪgl] N: **with a wiggle of one's hips** ancheggiando ♦ VT (*fingers, loose tooth*) muovere; **to wiggle one's hips** ancheggiare ♦ VI (*person*) dimenarsi, agitarsi; (*worm*) agitarsi, muoversi; (*tooth, loose screw*) tentennare

wig·gly [ˈwɪgli] ADJ (*line*) ondulato(-a), sinuoso(-a), (*tooth*) tentennante

wiki [ˈwɪki] N (*internet*) wiki *m inv*

wild [waɪld] ADJ (*comp* **-er**, *superl* **-est**) 1 (*not domesticated: animal, plant*) selvatico(-a); (*horse*) brado(-a); (*countryside*) selvaggio(-a); **a wild animal** un animale selvatico; **in its wild state** allo stato selvatico; **to grow wild** (*plant*) crescere incolto(-a); **wild horses wouldn't make me tell you** (*fig*) non riuscirai a cavarmelo neanche con la forza; **to sow one's wild oats** (*fig*) correre la cavallina 2 (*rough: wind, weather*) violento(-a); (*sea, night*) tempestoso(-a) 3 (*unrestrained, disorderly: child*) turbolento(-a); (*appearance, look*) selvaggio(-a); (*eyes*) sbarrato(-a); (*hair*) incolto(-a); **to lead a wild life** fare una vita sregolata; **to run wild** (*children*) scatenarsi 4 (*fam: angry*) fuori di sé; **to go wild** infuriarsi; **wild with indignation** fuori di sé dall'indignazione; **it makes me wild** mi manda su tutte le furie 5 (*fam: enthusiastic*): **to be wild about** andare pazzo(-a) per; **to be wild with joy** essere fuori di sé dalla gioia; **to go wild (with)** non stare più in sé (da); **the audience went wild** la folla andò in delirio 6 (*rash, extravagant: idea*) folle; (: *laughter*) sguaiato(-a); (*erratic: shot, guess*) azzardato(-a); **it's a wild exaggeration** è una grossa esagerazione; **you've let your imagination run wild** hai lavorato troppo di fantasia ♦ N: **the wild** la natura; **to live out in the wilds** (*hum*) vivere a casa del diavolo

wild card N (*Comput*) carattere jolly *m inv*; (*fig*) incognita *f*; (*Sport*) permesso di partecipazione a una gara accordato a un giocatore che non si è qualificato

wild·cat [ˈwaɪldˌkæt] N gatto(-a) selvatico(-a)

wildcat strike N sciopero (a gatto) selvaggio

wil·der·ness [ˈwɪldənɪs] N (*gen*) deserto; (*neglected garden*) giungla; **the garden was a wilderness** il giardino era una giungla

wild·fire [ˈwaɪldˌfaɪəʳ] N: **to spread like wildfire** diffondersi a macchia d'olio

wild-goose chase [ˌwaɪldˈguːsˌtʃeɪs] N (*fig*): **to be on a wild-goose chase** seguire una pista falsa

wild·life ['waɪld‚laɪf] N natura, flora e fauna ♦ ADJ (*sanctuary, reserve*) naturale

wild·ly ['waɪldlɪ] ADV (*gen*) violentemente; (*behave*) in modo sfrenato; (*talk*) fervorosamente; (*rush around*) come un(a) pazzo(-a); (*exaggerate*) largamente; (*applaud, cheer*) freneticamente; **to guess wildly** tirare a indovinare; **wildly happy/ enthusiastic** terribilmente felice/entusiasta; **her heart was beating wildly** il cuore le batteva forte

wiles [waɪlz] NPL astuzie *fpl*

wil·ful, will·ful (*USA*) ['wɪlfʊl] ADJ (*deliberate: act*) intenzionale, premeditato(-a); (*self-willed*) testardo(-a), ostinato(-a)

wil·ful·ly, will·ful·ly (*USA*) ['wɪlfəlɪ] ADV (*see adj*) intenzionalmente, premeditatamente; testardamente

---

KEYWORD

will¹ [wɪl] (*pt* **would**) MODAL AUX VB

1 (*forming future tense*): **will you be there?** ci sarai?; **he will come** verrà; **will you do it?** — yes, I will/no, I won't lo farai? — sì (lo farò)/no (non lo farò); **I will finish it tomorrow** lo finirò domani; **I will have finished it by tomorrow** lo finirò entro domani; **you won't lose it, will you?** non lo perderai, vero?

2 (*in conjectures*): **he will** *or* **he'll be there by now** dovrebbe essere arrivato ormai; **that will be the postman** sarà il postino

3 (*in commands, requests, offers*): **will you be quiet!** vuoi fare silenzio?; **will you come?** vieni?; **won't you come with us?** non vuoi venire con noi?; **will you have a cup of tea?** vorresti una tazza di tè?; **will you help me?** mi puoi aiutare?; **I will not** *or* **won't put up with it!** non intendo tollerarlo!; **will you sit down** (*politely*) prego, si accomodi; (*angrily*) vuoi metterti seduto!

4 (*expressing habits, persistence, capability*): **the car will do 100 mph** la macchina fa 100 miglia all'ora; **accidents will happen** gli incidenti possono capitare; **he will often sit there for hours** spesso rimane seduto lì per ore; **the car won't start** la macchina non parte; **he WILL fidget!** e continua a muoversi!

♦ VI (*wish*) volere; (*just*) **as you will!** come vuoi!; **say what you will** di' quello che vuoi

will² [wɪl] N **1** volontà; **to have a will of one's own** avere una volontà indipendente; **to do sth of one's own free will** fare qc di propria volontà; **the will to win/live** la voglia di vincere/vivere; **against sb's will** contro la volontà *or* il volere di qn; **at will** a volontà; **to work with a will** lavorare di buona lena; **where there's a will there's a way** volere è potere; **a strong will** una forte volontà **2** (*testament*) testamento; **the last will and testament of** le ultime volontà di; **to make a will** fare testamento; **he made a will** ha fatto testamento

♦ VT **1** (*urge on by willpower*): **to will sb to do sth** pregare (tra sé) perché qn faccia qc; **he willed himself to stay awake** si costrinse a restare sveglio; **he willed himself to go on** andò avanti con un grande sforzo di volontà **2** (*leave in one's will*): **to will sth to sb** lasciare qc a qn in eredità

will·ing ['wɪlɪŋ] ADJ **1** (*obedience, help*) spontaneo(-a); (*helper, worker*) volenteroso(-a); **a willing pupil** un alunno volenteroso; **he's very willing** è pieno di buona volontà; **there were plenty of willing hands** erano tutti disposti a dare una mano **2 to be willing (to do sth)** essere disposto(-a) (a fare qc); **he wasn't very willing to help me** non aveva una gran voglia di aiutarmi; **God willing** se Dio vuole ♦ N: **to show willing** mostrarsi disponibile

will·ing·ly ['wɪlɪŋlɪ] ADV volentieri

will·ing·ness ['wɪlɪŋnɪs] N disponibilità, buona volontà

will-o'-the-wisp [‚wɪləðə'wɪsp] N (*also fig*) fuoco fatuo

wil·low ['wɪləʊ] N (*also:* **willow tree**) salice *m*; **white willow** salice bianco

will·power ['wɪl‚paʊə'] N forza di volontà

willy-nilly [‚wɪlɪ'nɪlɪ] ADV volente o nolente

wilt [wɪlt] VI (*flower*) appassire; (*fig: person*) crollare; (: *effort, enthusiasm*) diminuire

Wilts [wɪlts] ABBR (*Brit:* = **Wiltshire**)

wily ['waɪlɪ] ADJ (*comp* **-ier**, *superl* **-iest**) astuto(-a), furbo(-a); **he's a wily old devil** *or* **bird** *or* **fox** (*fam*) è una vecchia volpe, è un furbo matricolato *or* di tre cotte

wimp [wɪmp] N (*fam*) pappamolle *m/f*

win [wɪn] (*pt, pp* **won**) N (*in sports etc*) vittoria; **their fifth win in a row** la quinta vittoria consecutiva ♦ VT (*battle, race, cup, prize*) vincere; (*victory*) conquistare, aggiudicarsi; (*sympathy, popularity, support, friendship*) conquistare, ottenere; (*person*) accattivarsi, conquistare; (*contract*) aggiudicarsi; **I won £20 from him** gli ho vinto 20 sterline; **to win sb's favour/heart** conquistare il favore/cuore di qn; **she won it at tennis** l'ha vinto a tennis; **it won him first prize** gli ha valso il primo premio; **did you win?** hai vinto?; **he won a gold medal** ha vinto una medaglia d'oro; **to win the lottery** vincere alla lotteria; **he won the support of the poor** si è conquistato il sostegno dei poveri; **to win a victory** aggiudicarsi una vittoria; **to win the day** (*Mil, also fig*) avere il sopravvento ♦ VI vincere; **O.K., you win** (*fam*) va bene, ti do ragione

- **win back** VT + ADV riconquistare
- **win over, win round** VT + ADV convincere; **we won him over to our point of view** l'abbiamo convinto ad accettare il nostro punto di vista
- **win out, win through** VI + ADV uscire vittorioso(-a)

wince [wɪns] N: **to give a wince** rabbrividire; (*grimace*) smorfia ♦ VI rabbrividire; (*grimace*) fare una smorfia (*di dolore*); **he winced at the thought** rabbrividì al pensiero

winch [wɪntʃ] N argano, verricello ♦ VT: **to winch up/down** sollevare/abbassare con un argano

wind¹ [wɪnd] N **1** vento; **high** *or* **strong wind** vento forte; **the wind is in the west** il vento viene da ponente; **into** *or* **against the wind** controvento; **to go like the wind** filare come il vento; **to run before the wind** (*Naut*) andare con il vento in poppa; **there's something in the wind** (*fig*) c'è qualcosa nell'aria; **to get wind of sth** venire a sapere qc; **to get** *or* **have the wind up** (*fam*) agitarsi; **to take the wind out of sb's sails** smontare qn, spegnere l'entusiasmo di qn; **to sail close to the wind** (*fig*) spingere le cose troppo in là; (*act almost illegally*) rasentare l'illegalità; (*risk causing offence*) rischiare di offendere; **to throw caution to the winds** gettare la prudenza alle ortiche **2** (*flatulence*) flatulenza; **to break wind** far aria; **to bring up wind** (*baby*) far il ruttino **3** (*breath*) respiro, fiato; **to get one's wind back** *or* **one's second wind** riprendere fiato; **to be short of wind** essere senza fiato **4** (*Mus*): **the wind(s)** i fiati *mpl* ♦ VT: **to wind sb** (*with punch etc*) mozzare il fiato a qn; **to wind a baby** far fare il ruttino a un bambino

wind² [waɪnd] (*pt, pp* **wound**) VT **1** (*roll, coil*) avvolgere, arrotolare; **he wound the rope round a tree** ha avvolto la fune attorno a un albero; **to wind sth into a ball** aggomitolare qc **2** (*clock, watch, toy*) caricare ♦ VI (*also:* **wind its way**: *river, path*) serpeggiare; (*procession*) snodarsi

- **wind back** VT + ADV (*tape*) riavvolgere
- **wind down** VT + ADV (*car window*) abbassare; (*fig: production, business*) diminuire ♦ VI + ADV rilassarsi, distendersi
- **wind forward** VT + ADV (*tape*) mandare avanti
- **wind in** VT + ADV (*fishing line*) riavvolgere
- **wind on** VT + ADV (*film, tape*) far avanzare
- **wind up** VT + ADV **1** (*car window*) alzare; (*clock, toy*) caricare; **to wind sb up** (*fig: fam: annoy*) far venire i nervi a *or* innervosire qn; (: *kid, trick*) prendere in giro qn **2** (*close: meeting, debate*) concludere, chiudere; (: *company*) chiudere; **the company will be wound up** la società verrà chiusa ♦ VI + ADV (*meeting, debate*) concludersi; (*fam: end up*) finire; **we wound up in Rome** siamo finiti a Roma; **he'll wind up in jail** finirà in prigione

wind·break, wind·breaker (*USA*) ['wɪnd‚breɪk, 'wɪnd‚breɪkə'] N frangivento

wind·cheater ['wɪnd‚tʃiːtə'] N giacca a vento

wind·er ['waɪndə'] N (*Brit: on watch*) corona di carica; (*Aut: also:* **window winder**) manovella *f* alzacristalli, *inv*

wind·fall ['wɪnd‚fɔːl] N (*apple etc*) frutto fatto cadere dal vento; (*fig*) colpo di fortuna

wind farm N centrale *f* eolica

wind·ing ['waɪndɪŋ] ADJ (*road, path*) serpeggiante, tortuoso(-a); (*staircase*) a chiocciola

wind instrument N (*Mus*) strumento a fiato

wind·mill ['wɪnd‚mɪl] N mulino a vento

win·dow ['wɪndəʊ] N (*gen, also Comput*) finestra; (*of car, train*) finestrino; (*also:* **window pane**) vetro; (*also:* **stained glass**

window) vetrata; (*also*: **shop window**) vetrina; (*of booking office etc*) sportello; (*in envelope*) finestrella; **to break a window** rompere un vetro; **a broken window** un vetro rotto; **to clean the windows** pulire i vetri; **to look out of the window** guardare fuori della finestra; "**do not lean out of the window**" "vietato sporgersi dal finestrino"; **the kitchen window** la finestra della cucina

window box N cassetta per i fiori (*da tenere sul davanzale*)

window cleaner N lavavetri *m/f*

window dressing N (*Comm*) vetrinistica; (*fig*) fumo negli occhi

window envelope N busta a finestra

window frame N telaio di finestra

window ledge N davanzale *m*

window pane N vetro

window seat N (*in house*) panchetta fissa vicino alla finestra; (*in train etc*) posto vicino al finestrino

window-shopping ['wɪndəʊ'ʃɒpɪŋ] N: **to go window-shopping** andare a vedere le vetrine

window·sill ['wɪndəʊ'sɪl] N davanzale *m*

wind·pipe ['wɪnd'paɪp] N (*Anat*) trachea

wind power N energia eolica

wind·screen ['wɪndskriːn], (*USA*) **wind·shield** ['wɪndʃiːld] N parabrezza *m inv*

windscreen washer N lavacristallo

windscreen wiper N tergicristallo

wind·surfing ['wɪnd,sɜːfɪŋ] N windsurf *m inv* (*l'attività*); **to go windsurfing** fare del windsurf

wind·swept ['wɪnd,swept] ADJ (*landscape*) ventoso(-a); (*square*) spazzato(-a) dal vento; (*person*) scompigliato(-a) per il vento

wind tunnel ['wɪnd,tʌnəl] N galleria aerodinamica *or* del vento

windy ['wɪndɪ] ADJ (*comp* **-ier**, *superl* **-iest**) **1** ventoso(-a); **it's windy** c'è vento; **a windy day** una giornata ventosa **2** (*fam*, *old*: *afraid*, *nervous*): **windy (about)** teso(-a) (per), nervoso(-a) (per)

wine [waɪn] N vino; **a glass of wine** un bicchiere di vino; **white/red wine** vino bianco/rosso ♦ VT: **to wine and dine sb** offrire un ottimo pranzo a qn ♦ ADJ (*bottle*) da vino; (*vinegar*) di vino

wine bar N enoteca (*per degustazione*)

wine cellar N cantina

wine·glass ['waɪn,glɑːs] N bicchiere *m* da vino

wine list N lista *or* carta dei vini

wine merchant N commerciante *m* di vini

wine tast·ing ['waɪn,teɪstɪŋ] N degustazione *f* di vini

wine waiter N sommelier *m inv*

wing [wɪŋ] N **1** (*gen*, *also Sport*, *Archit*, *Pol*) ala; (*Brit*: *Aut*) fiancata; **to take sb under one's wing** prendere qn sotto le proprie ali; **the left wing of the Conservative Party** la sinistra del Partito Conservatore **2 the wings** NPL (*Theatre*) le quinte

wing·er ['wɪŋə'] N (*Sport*) ala

wing mirror N (*Brit*) specchietto laterale esterno

wing nut N galletto

wing·span ['wɪŋ,spæn], **wing·spread** ['wɪŋ,spred] N apertura alare, apertura d'ali

wink [wɪŋk] N (*blink*) strizzata d'occhi; (*meaningful*) occhiolino, strizzatina d'occhi; **to give sb a wink** ammiccare *or* fare l'occhiolino a qn; **in a wink** in un batter d'occhio; **I didn't sleep a wink** non ho chiuso occhio ♦ VI (*meaningfully*): **to wink (at sb)** fare l'occhiolino (a qn), ammiccare (a qn); (*blink*) strizzare gli occhi; (*light*, *star etc*) baluginare

win·kle ['wɪŋkl] N litorina ♦ VT: **to winkle a secret out of sb** carpire un segreto a qn

win·ner ['wɪnə'] N (*gen*) vincitore(-trice); **to pick a winner** (*horse*) scegliere il cavallo vincente; (*gen*) fare un affare; **it's a winner!** (*fam*) è un successone!; (*likely to be a success*) è un successo garantito!

win·ning ['wɪnɪŋ] ADJ **1** (*gen*) vincente; (*hit*, *shot*, *goal*) decisivo(-a); **the winning team** la squadra vincitrice; **the winning goal** il gol della vittoria **2** (*charming*) affascinante; **a winning smile** un sorriso accattivante; *see also* **winnings**

winning post N traguardo

win·nings ['wɪnɪŋz] NPL vincita *fsg*

win·some ['wɪnsəm] ADJ accattivante

win·ter ['wɪntə'] N inverno; **in winter** d'inverno, in inverno; **the winter of 2014** l'inverno del 2014; **it's winter** è inverno; **last winter** lo scorso inverno ♦ ADJ (*clothes*, *weather*, *day*) invernale, d'inverno

winter sports NPL sport *mpl* invernali

winter·time ['wɪntə,taɪm] N inverno, stagione *f* invernale

win·try, **win·tery** ['wɪntrɪ] ADJ invernale; (*fig*: *look*) freddo(-a)

wipe [waɪp] N pulita, passata; **to give sth a wipe** dare una pulita *or* una passata a qc ♦ VT (*gen*) pulire; (*blackboard*, *tape*: *Comput*) cancellare; **to wipe one's eyes** asciugarsi gli occhi; **to wipe one's nose** soffiarsi il naso; **to wipe one's feet** *or* **shoes** pulirsi i piedi; **to wipe one's bottom** pulirsi il sedere; **to wipe the dishes** asciugare i piatti; **to wipe sth dry** asciugare qc; **to wipe the floor with sb** (*fig*: *fam*) schiacciare qn
  ▸ **wipe away** VT + ADV (*marks*) togliere; (*tears*) asciugare
  ▸ **wipe down** VT + ADV pulire
  ▸ **wipe off** VT + ADV cancellare; (*stains*) togliere (strofinando)
  ▸ **wipe out** VT + ADV **1** (*erase*: *writing*, *memory*) cancellare; (: *debt*) liquidare **2** (*destroy*: *town*, *race*, *enemy*) annientare
  ▸ **wipe up** VI + ADV (*dry dishes*) asciugare i piatti ♦ VT + ADV asciugare

wire ['waɪə'] N **1** filo di ferro; (*Elec*) filo (elettrico); **copper wire** filo di rame; **the telephone wire** il filo del telefono; **to get one's wires crossed** (*fam*) fraintendere **2** (*telegram*) telegramma *m*; **to the wire** fino all'ultimo momento ♦ VT **1** (*Elec*: *house*) fare l'impianto elettrico di; (: *circuit*) installare; (*also*: **wire up**: *two pieces of equipment*) collegare, allacciare; **to wire a room for sound** installare un impianto di sonorizzazione in una stanza **2** (*Telec*) telegrafare **3 to wire sth to sth** (*tie*) attaccare qc a qc con un filo

wire brush N spazzola metallica

wire cutters NPL tronchese *msg*, *fsg*

wireless ['waɪəlɪs](*old*) N (*Brit*) radio *f*; (*also*: **wireless set**) (apparecchio *m*) radio, *f inv*; **on the wireless** per radio; **by wireless** via radio ♦ ADJ (*station*, *programme*) radiofonico(-a); (*technology*) wireless *inv*, senza fili

wireless technology N tecnologia wireless

wire netting N rete *f* metallica

wire service N (*USA*) = **news agency**

wire-tapping ['waɪə,tæpɪŋ] N intercettazione *f* telefonica

wir·ing ['waɪərɪŋ] N (*Elec*) impianto elettrico

wiry ['waɪərɪ] ADJ (*comp* **-ier**, *superl* **-iest**) (*person*) asciutto(-a) e muscoloso(-a); (*hair*) ispido(-a)

Wis., Wisc. ABBR (*USA*: = **Wisconsin**)

Wis·con·sin ['wɪs'kɒnsɪn] il Wisconsin

wis·dom ['wɪzdəm] N (*of person*) saggezza; (*of remark*, *action*) opportunità; **words of great wisdom** parole di grande saggezza

wisdom tooth N dente *m* del giudizio

wise[1] [waɪz] ADJ (*comp* **-r**, *superl* **-st**) (*gen*: *person*) saggio(-a); (*learned*) sapiente; (*prudent*: *advice*, *remark*) prudente; **a wise man** un saggio; **the Three Wise Men** i Re Magi; **to be wise after the event** giudicare con il senno di poi; **it was wise of you not to do that** sei stato saggio a non farlo; **I'm none the wiser** ne so quanto prima; **it would be wiser to stay at home** sarebbe più sensato rimanere a casa; **to get wise to sb/sth** (*fam*) aprire gli occhi su qn/qc; **to put sb wise to sb/sth** (*fam*) mettere qn al corrente di qn/qc
  ▸ **wise up** VI + ADV (*esp USA*: *fam*): **to wise up to** aprire gli occhi su; **wise up!** svegliati!

wise[2] [waɪz] N (*old*): **in no wise** affatto, in nessun modo; **in this wise** in tal guisa ♦ ADV ENDING: **workwise** per quel che riguarda il lavoro; **how are we foodwise?** come stiamo a cibo?

wise·crack ['waɪz,kræk] N (*fam*) battuta, spiritosaggine *f*

wish [wɪʃ] N **1** (*desire*) desiderio; (*specific desire*) richiesta; **I had no wish to upset you** non avevo nessuna intenzione di farti star male; **to go against sb's wishes** andare contro il volere di qn; **I'll grant you three wishes** ti concedo di esprimere tre desideri; **you shall have your wish** realizzerai il tuo desiderio; **to make a wish** esprimere un desiderio; **make a wish** esprimi un desiderio **2 best wishes** (*in greetings*) tanti auguri; (*in letter*) cordiali saluti; **give her my best wishes** le porga i miei più cordiali saluti; **with best wishes**

con i migliori auguri; "with best wishes, Kathy" "cari saluti, Kathy" ♦ VT **1** (*want*) volere, desiderare; **to wish sb to do sth** volere che qn faccia qc; **to wish to do sth** voler fare qc; **I wish to make a complaint** voglio fare reclamo; **I wish he'd shut up** (*fam*) magari chiudesse il becco; **I wish I'd gone too** vorrei esserci andato anch'io; **I wish you were here!** come vorrei che tu fossi qui!; **I wish I could!** mi piacerebbe!, magari! **2** (*foist*): **to wish sb on sb** appioppare *or* affibbiare qn a qn; **to wish sth on sb** rifilare qc a qn **3** (*bid, express*) augurare; **to wish sb goodbye** dire arrivederci a qn; **to wish sb good luck/a happy Christmas/a happy birthday** augurare a qn buona fortuna/buon Natale/buon compleanno; **to wish sb well** augurare ogni bene a qn; **to wish sb ill** voler del male a qn ♦ VI: **to wish for sth** desiderare qc; **she has everything she could wish for** ha tutto ciò che desidera; **what more could you wish for?** cosa vuoi di più?

wish·bone [ˈwɪʃˌbəʊn] N (*of turkey, chicken etc*) forcella

wish·ful [ˈwɪʃfʊl] ADJ: **it's just wishful thinking** è solo un'illusione

wishy-washy [ˈwɪʃɪˌwɒʃɪ] ADJ (*fam: colour*) slavato(-a); (: *person, argument, ideas*) insulso(-a)

wisp [wɪsp] N (*of straw, smoke*) filo; (*of hair*) ciuffetto

wist·ful [ˈwɪstfʊl] ADJ (*look, smile*) pieno(-a) di rammarico; (*nostalgic*) nostalgico(-a)

wit [wɪt] N **1** (*understanding: gen pl*) intelligenza; **native wit** buon senso; **to be at one's wits' end** avere esaurito tutte le risorse, non sapere più che fare; **I'm at my wits' end!** non so più cos'altro fare!; **to have** *or* **keep one's wits about one** avere presenza di spirito; **use your wits!** usa il cervello!; **to live by one's wits** vivere di espedienti; **to collect one's wits** rimettersi in sesto; **to be frightened** *or* **scared out of one's wits** essere spaventato(-a) a morte **2** (*humour, wittiness*) spirito, arguzia; **he was known for his intelligence and wit** era conosciuto per la sua intelligenza e il suo spirito **3** (*person*) persona arguta, bello spirito **4** (*namely*): **to wit** cioè

witch [wɪtʃ] N strega

witch·craft [ˈwɪtʃˌkrɑːft] N stregoneria

witch doctor N stregone *m*

witch-hunt [ˈwɪtʃˌhʌnt] N caccia alle streghe

with [wɪð, wɪθ] PREP

1 (*gen*) con; **she mixed the sugar with the eggs** mischiò lo zucchero con le uova; **she stayed with friends** è stata a casa di amici; **to stay overnight with friends** passare la notte da amici; **I was with him** ero con lui; **he had no money with him** non aveva denaro con sé; **to be with it** (*fam: up-to-date*) essere à la page; **to rise with the sun** alzarsi all'alba; **she just wasn't with us** (*fig*) era completamente assente; **I'm with you** (*fig: I understand*) ti seguo

2 (*descriptive*) con; **the fellow with the big beard** il tipo con la *or* dalla barba folta; **the man with the grey hat** l'uomo dal *or* con il cappello grigio; **a room with a view** una camera con vista (sul mare *etc*)

3 (*manner, means, cause*) con; **red with anger** rosso(-a) dalla *or* per la rabbia; **to cut wood with an axe** tagliare la legna con l'ascia; **to shake with fear** tremare di paura; **she's come down with the flu** ha preso l'influenza; **in bed with measles** a letto con il morbillo; **white with snow** bianco(-a) a causa della neve; **covered with snow** coperto(-a) di neve; **to walk with a stick** camminare con l'aiuto di un bastone; **with tears in her eyes** con le lacrime agli occhi; **with that, he left** con ciò se ne andò; **with time** col tempo

4 (*concerning: in the case of*): **he's good with children** ci sa fare con i bambini; **how are things with you?** (*fam*) come te la passi?; **the trouble with Harry is that ...** il guaio con Harry è che...

5 (*in proportion*) a seconda di; **it varies with the time of year** varia a seconda della stagione

6 (*in spite of*) nonostante; **with all his faults I still like him** nonostante i suoi difetti mi piace ancora

with·draw [wɪθˈdrɔː] (*pt* **withdrew**, *pp* **withdrawn**) VT: **to withdraw (from)** (*gen*) ritirare (da); (*money from bank*) prelevare (da); **they withdrew all their savings** hanno prelevato tutti i loro risparmi; **he withdraw his remarks** ha ritirato quanto aveva detto ♦ VI: **to withdraw from** (*gen*) ritirarsi

da; (*move away*) allontanarsi da; **to withdraw in sb's favour** ritirarsi a favore di qn; **to withdraw to a new position** (*Mil*) arretrare su una nuova posizione; **to withdraw into o.s.** chiudersi in se stesso(-a); **the troops withdrew** le truppe si sono ritirate

with·draw·al [wɪθˈdrɔːəl] N (*gen*) ritiro; (*of money*) prelievo; (*of army*) ritiro; (*Med*) sindrome *f* da astinenza; **the withdrawal of their savings** il prelievo dei loro risparmi; **the withdrawal of the troops** la ritirata delle truppe

withdrawal symptoms NPL crisi *fsg* di astinenza

with·drawn [wɪθˈdrɔːn] PP *of* **withdraw** ♦ ADJ chiuso(-a) in se stesso(-a)

with·drew [wɪθˈdruː] PT *of* **withdraw**

with·er [ˈwɪðəʳ] VT far appassire ♦ VI (*plant*) appassire; (*limb*) atrofizzarsi; (*fig: love, passion*) spegnersi; (: *beauty*) sfiorire

with·ered [ˈwɪðəd] ADJ (*plant*) appassito(-a), vizzo(-a); (*skin*) avvizzito(-a); (*limb*) atrofizzato(-a)

with·hold [wɪðˈhəʊld] (*pt, pp* **withheld**) VT (*money from pay etc*) trattenere; (*truth, news*) nascondere; (*refuse: consent*) non concedere, negare; **to withhold from** (*permission*) rifiutare a; (*information*) nascondere a; **I'm withholding my rent until the roof is repaired** non pagherò l'affitto finché il tetto non sarà stato riparato

with·in [wɪðˈɪn] PREP **1** (*inside*) dentro; **a voice within me said ...** una vocina dentro di me disse...; **within herself** dentro di sé; **to be within the law** restare nei limiti della legalità; **to live within one's income** vivere secondo i propri mezzi; **within sight of** in vista di; **within easy reach** a portata di mano, vicino(-a); **the shops are within easy reach** i negozi sono vicini; **communication within the organization** la comunicazione all'interno dell'organizzazione **2** (*less than*): **we were within 100 metres of the summit** eravamo a meno di 100 metri dalla vetta; **within a mile of** entro un miglio da; **within ten kilometres** a meno di dieci chilometri; **within a year of her death** meno di un anno prima della (*or* dopo la) sua morte; **correct to within a millimetre** preciso(-a) al millimetro; **within an hour** entro un'ora; **within an hour from now** da qui a un'ora; **within the week** entro questa settimana; **he returned within the week** è tornato prima della fine della settimana ♦ ADV: **"car for sale - apply within"** "auto in vendita - rivolgersi all'interno"

with·out [wɪðˈaʊt] PREP senza; **without speaking** senza parlare; **he did it without telling me** l'ha fatto senza dirmelo; **he came without a coat/any money** è venuto senza cappotto/soldi; **without a coat or hat** senza cappotto né cappello; **the bus left without me** l'autobus è partito senza di me; **he is without friends** non ha amici; **without anybody knowing** senza che nessuno lo sappia; **to go** *or* **do without sth** fare a meno di qc

with·stand [wɪθˈstænd] (*pt, pp* **withstood** [wɪθˈstud]) VT resistere a

wit·ness [ˈwɪtnɪs] N **1** (*person*) testimone *m/f*; **witness for the prosecution/defence** testimone a carico/discarico; **to call sb as a witness** chiamare qn a testimoniare; **there were no witnesses** non c'erano testimoni **2** (*evidence*) testimonianza; **to bear witness to sth** (*subj: person*) testimoniare qc; (: *thing, result*) provare qc ♦ VT **1** (*event, crime*) essere testimone di; (*change, improvement*) constatare **2** (*attest by signature: document*) autenticare ♦ VI (*testify*) testimoniare; **to witness to sth/having seen sth** testimoniare qc/di aver visto qc

witness box, (*USA*) **witness stand** N banco dei testimoni

wit·ti·cism [ˈwɪtɪˌsɪzəm] N arguzia

wit·ty [ˈwɪtɪ] ADJ (*comp* **-ier**, *superl* **-iest**) arguto(-a), spiritoso(-a)

wives [waɪvz] NPL *of* **wife**

wiz·ard [ˈwɪzəd] N mago, stregone *m*; (*fig*) mago; **he's a financial wizard** è un mago della finanza; **he's a wizard at mathematics** è un genio matematico

wiz·ened [ˈwɪznd] ADJ raggrinzito(-a)

wk ABBR = **week**

WMD [ˌdʌbljuːɛmˈdiː] N ABBR = **weapon of mass destruction**

WO [ˌdʌbljuːˈəʊ] N ABBR = **warrant officer**

wob·ble [ˈwɒbl] N: **to have a wobble** (*chair*) traballare; **she had a wobble in her voice** le tremava la voce ♦ VI (*table, chair, wheel, cyclist*) traballare; (*dancer, acrobat*) vacillare; (*compass needle*) oscillare; (*hand, voice*) tremare

wob·bly [ˈwɒblɪ] ADJ (comp -ier, superl -iest) (hand, voice) tremante; (table, chair) traballante; (object about to fall) che oscilla pericolosamente; (wheel) che ha troppo gioco; **to feel wobbly** (person) sentirsi debole

woe [wəʊ] N (liter: hum) dolore m; **woe is me!** me tapino(-a)!; **woe betide him who …** guai a chi…; **a tale of woe** una triste storia

woe·ful [ˈwəʊfʊl] ADJ (sad) triste; (deplorable) deplorevole, vergognoso(-a)

wok [wɒk] N wok m inv, padella concava usata nella cucina cinese

woke [wəʊk] PT of **wake³**

wok·en [ˈwəʊkən] PP of **wake³**

wolf [wʊlf] N (pl **wolves** [wʊlvz]) 1 lupo; (fig): **a wolf in sheep's clothing** un lupo in veste di agnello; **to keep the wolf from the door** sbarcare il lunario; **to cry wolf** gridare al lupo 2 (fig: fam: womanizer) mandrillo, drago ♦ VT (also: **wolf down**) divorare

wom·an [ˈwʊmən] N (pl **women**) donna; **a man and two women** un uomo e due donne; **young woman** giovane donna; **woman of the world** donna di mondo; **the little woman** (hum: wife) la mogliettina; **the woman in his life** la donna della sua vita

wom·an·ize [ˈwʊmənaɪz] VI correre dietro alle donne

wom·an·ly [ˈwʊmənlɪ] ADJ femminile

womb [wuːm] N (Anat) grembo

wom·en [ˈwɪmɪn] NPL of **woman**

women's movement N: **the women's movement** il movimento per la liberazione della donna

won [wʌn] PT, PP of **win**

won·der [ˈwʌndə'] N 1 (feeling) meraviglia, stupore m; **in wonder** con stupore; **lost in wonder** stupefatto(-a) 2 (object or cause of wonder) miracolo, portento; **the wonders of science** i miracoli della scienza; **the Seven Wonders of the World** le sette meraviglie del mondo; **it's no or little or small wonder that he left** c'è poco or non c'è da meravigliarsi che sia partito; **the wonder of it was that …** la cosa incredibile or sorprendente era che…; **to do or work wonders** fare miracoli; **no wonder!** non mi meraviglio!; **no wonder he got upset** non mi stupisce che si sia arrabbiato ♦ VT chiedersi, domandarsi; **I wonder whether or if …** mi chiedo se…; **I wonder why she said that** mi chiedo perché l'abbia detto; **I was wondering if you could give me a lift** mi chiedevo se potessi darmi un passaggio; **I wonder where/how/when** mi chiedo dove/come/quando ♦ VI 1 (ask o. s., speculate): **to wonder about** pensare di; **I was wondering about going out for dinner** pensavo di andare fuori a cena, magari; **does she know about it? — I wonder** lo sa? — è quello che mi chiedo anch'io 2 (be surprised) stupirsi, meravigliarsi; **we all wonder you're still alive** ci meravigliamo tutti che tu sia ancora vivo; **to wonder at sth** stupirsi di qc

won·der·ful [ˈwʌndəfʊl] ADJ meraviglioso(-a), stupendo(-a)

won·der·ful·ly [ˈwʌndəfʊlɪ] ADV (with adjective) meravigliosamente; (with verb) a meraviglia

won·ky [ˈwɒŋkɪ] ADJ (comp -ier, superl -iest) (Brit fam: chair, table) traballante; **to go wonky** (TV picture, machine) fare i capricci

wont [wəʊnt] N: **as is his/her wont** com'è solito(-a) fare

won't [wəʊnt] PT, PT = **will not**

woo [wuː] VT corteggiare; (fig: voters, audience) cercare di conquistare

wood [wʊd] N 1 (material) legno; (timber) legname m; **touch wood!**, (USA) **knock on wood!** tocca ferro!; **aged in the wood** invecchiato(-a) in botti di legno; **it's made of wood** è di legno 2 (forest) bosco; **woods** NPL boschi mpl; **we're not out of the wood yet** (fig) non ne siamo ancora usciti completamente; **he can't see the wood for the trees** (fig) si perde nei dettagli; **we went for a walk in the wood** siamo andati a passeggiare nel bosco 3 (Golf) mazza di legno; (Bowls) boccia ♦ VT 1 (made of wood) di legno 2 (living etc in a wood) di bosco, silvestre

wood·carving [ˈwʊdˌkɑːvɪŋ] N scultura in legno

wood·ed [ˈwʊdɪd] ADJ coperto(-a) di boschi, boscoso(-a); **thickly/sparsely wooded** a bosco fitto/rado

wood·en [ˈwʊdn] ADJ 1 (made of wood) di legno; **a wooden chair** una sedia di legno 2 (fig: movements, manner) impacciato(-a), rigido(-a); (: face, stare) inespressivo(-a); (: personality) goffo(-a); **to give a wooden performance** (actor) recitare in maniera impacciata

wood·land [ˈwʊdlənd] N zona boscosa ♦ ADJ di bosco, silvestre

wood·pecker [ˈwʊdˌpekə'] N picchio

wood pigeon N colombaccio

wood·wind [ˈwʊdˌwɪnd] NPL (Mus): **the woodwind** i legni mpl

wood·work [ˈwʊdˌwɜːk] N 1 (craft, subject) falegnameria 2 (wooden parts of room) parti fpl in legno

wood·worm [ˈwʊdˌwɜːm] N tarlo; **to have woodworm** essere tarlato(-a)

woof [wʊf] N (of dog) bau bau m ♦ VI abbaiare; **woof, woof!** bau bau!

wool [wʊl] N lana; **all wool, pure wool** pura lana; **pure new wool** pura lana vergine; **knitting wool** lana per lavorare a maglia; **a ball of wool** un gomitolo di lana; **to pull the wool over sb's eyes** (fam) gettare fumo negli occhi a qn ♦ ADJ (dress) di lana; (shop) di lane, di filati; (trade, industry) della lana

wool·len, wool·en (USA) [ˈwʊlən] ADJ (cloth, dress) di lana; (industry) della lana ♦ **woollens** NPL indumenti mpl di lana

wool·ly, wooly (USA) [ˈwʊlɪ] ADJ (comp -ier, superl -iest) (jumper etc) di lana; (fig: clouds) come batuffoli; (: ideas) confuso(-a), vago(-a); (: essay, book) sul vago ♦ N (fam) indumento di lana

woozy [ˈwuːzɪ] ADJ (comp -ier, superl -iest) (fam) stordito(-a), intontito(-a)

word [wɜːd] N 1 (gen) parola; **what's the word for "pen" in Italian?** come si dice "pen" in italiano?; **what does this word mean?** cosa vuol dire questa parola?; **the word "ginseng" is Chinese** la parola "ginseng" è cinese; **words** NPL (of song) parole fpl, testo; **in the words of Dante** come disse Dante; **word for word** parola per parola, testualmente; **words per minute** parole al minuto; **to put sth into words** esprimere qc a parole; **silly isn't the word for it!** sciocco non è la parola esatta!; **words fail me** non ho parole; **in a word** in una parola; **in other words** in altre parole, in altri termini; **not in so many words** non esplicitamente; **those were her very words** quelle furono le sue testuali parole; **the last word in** l'ultima novità in fatto di; **to have the last word** avere l'ultima parola; **to give sb a word of warning** dare a qn un piccolo avvertimento; **I can't get a word out of him** non riesco a cavargli una parola di bocca; **by word of mouth** con il passaparola; **to take the words out of sb's mouth** rubare le parole di bocca a qn; **don't put words into my mouth!** non mettermi parole in bocca!; **to have a word with sb** fare un discorsetto a qn; **could I have a word with you?** posso parlarti un attimo?; **to put in a (good) word for sb** mettere una buona parola per qn; **without a word** senza una parola; **don't say or breathe a word about it** non farne parola; **to have words with sb** (quarrel with) venire a parole con qn 2 (news) notizia, notizie fpl; **is there any word from Peter yet?** non ci sono ancora notizie da parte di Peter?; **word came from headquarters that …** il quartiere generale ci ha fatto sapere che…; **to bring/send word of sth to sb** portare/dare la notizia di qc a qn; **to leave word (with sb, for sb) that …** lasciare detto (a qn) che…; **word of command** ordine m; **to give the word to do sth** dare l'ordine di fare qc 3 (promise) parola; **word of honour** parola d'onore; **he is a man of his word** è un uomo di parola; **to be as good as one's word, keep one's word** essere di parola, tenere fede alla parola data; **to break one's word** mancare di parola; **to give sb one's word (that …)** dare a qn la propria parola (che…); **I've only got your word for it** devo fidarmi di quello che dici tu; **to take sb at his word** prendere qn in parola; **I'll take your word for it** ti credo sulla parola 4 (gospel): **the Word** il Verbo, la parola di Dio; **to preach the Word** predicare la buona novella ♦ VT (document, protest) formulare

word·ing [ˈwɜːdɪŋ] N (of contract, document) formulazione f; **to change the wording** formulare diversamente

word-perfect [ˌwɜːdˈpɜːfɪkt] ADJ (speech etc) imparato(-a) a memoria; **to be word-perfect** (actor) sapere a memoria la parte

word processing N word processing *m inv*

word processor N (*machine*) word processor *m inv*

word wrap N (*Comput*) ritorno a margine automatico

wordy ['wɜːdɪ] ADJ (*comp* -**ier**, *superl* -**iest**) verboso(-a), prolisso(-a)

wore [wɔːʳ] PT *of* **wear**

work [wɜːk] N **1** (*gen*) lavoro; **it's hard work** è un lavoro duro; **to be at work (on sth)** lavorare (a qc); **men at work** lavori in corso; **it's all in a day's work** è una cosa di ordinaria amministrazione; **to get on with one's work** continuare il proprio lavoro; **the forces at work** gli elementi che influiscono; **work on the new school has begun** sono cominciati i lavori per la nuova scuola; **a good piece of work** un buon lavoro; **to set sb to work doing sth** mettere qn a fare qc; **to set to work (on), start work (on)** mettersi al lavoro (a); **I'm trying to get some work done** sto cercando di lavorare; **to make short** *or* **quick work of** (*sth*) sbrigare in fretta; (*fig: fam: sb*) sistemare subito **2** (*employment, job*) lavoro; **to go to work** andare al lavoro; **he's at work today** oggi è al lavoro; **to look for work** cercare lavoro; **she's looking for work** sta cercando lavoro; **to be out of work** essere disoccupato(-a); **to be in work** avere un lavoro; **to put** *or* **throw sb out of work** licenziare qn; **to be off work** essere in congedo; **he's off work this week** questa settimana non lavora; **he hasn't done a day's work in his life** non ha mai lavorato in vita sua; **they have little work experience** hanno poca esperienza lavorativa **3** (*product: of writer, musician, scholar*) opera; **his life's work** il lavoro di tutta la sua vita; **he sells a lot of his work** vende molti dei suoi lavori; **good works** opere *fpl* buone; **work of art/reference** opera d'arte/di consultazione; **the works of Dickens** le opere di Dickens; **he's a nasty piece of work** (*fig*) è un tipaccio; *see also* **works** ♦ VT **1** (*students, employees*) far lavorare; **to work sb hard** far lavorare molto qn; **to work o.s. to death** ammazzarsi di lavoro **2** (*operate*) azionare; **can you work the photocopier?** sai usare la fotocopiatrice?; **I can't work the video** non riesco a far funzionare il videoregistratore; **it is worked by electricity** va a corrente **3** (*miracle*) fare; (*change*) operare; **to work wonders** fare miracoli; **they worked it so that she could come** (*fam*) hanno fatto in modo che potesse venire; **to work sth into a speech** far scivolare qc in un discorso; **to work one's passage on a ship** pagarsi il viaggio su una nave lavorando (*a bordo della stessa*); **to work one's way through college** lavorare per pagarsi gli studi; **to work one's way along sth** avanzare lentamente lungo qc; **to work one's hands free** riuscire a liberarsi le mani; **to work sth loose** far smollare qc; **to work one's way through a book** leggersi pazientemente un libro; **he worked his way up from the factory floor** ha cominciato come umile operaio; **to work one's way up to the top of a company** farsi strada fino al vertice di una società; **to work o.s. into a rage** andare in bestia **4** (*shape: metal, dough, clay, wood*) lavorare; (*exploit: mine*) sfruttare; (: *land*) coltivare; (*Sewing: design*) ricamare; **worked by hand** lavorato(-a) a mano ♦ VI **1** lavorare; **to work towards/for sth** lavorare in vista di/per qc; **to work hard** lavorare sodo; **they are working hard** lavorano sodo; **to work at** *or* **on sth** (*essay, project*) lavorare su qc; **she works in a shop** lavora in un negozio; **she's working at her desk** sta lavorando alla scrivania; **to work to rule** (*Industry*) fare uno sciopero bianco; **to work like a Trojan** lavorare come un(a) pazzo(-a) **2** (*machine, plan, brain*) funzionare; (*drug, medicine*) fare effetto; **to get sth working** far funzionare qc; **it works off the mains** funziona a corrente; **the heating isn't working** il riscaldamento non funziona; **my plan worked perfectly** il mio piano ha funzionato a meraviglia; **it worked** (*fig*) funziona nei due sensi **3** (*mouth, face, jaws*) contrarsi; **her mouth worked in her sleep** le si muoveva la bocca nel sonno **4** (*move gradually*) muoversi pian piano; **to work loose** (*screw*) allentarsi; **he worked slowly along the cliff** avanzava lentamente lungo la scogliera; **to work round to a question** formulare una domanda dopo averci girato intorno

▸ **work in** VI + ADV (*arrangement*) inserirsi ♦ VT + ADV (*reference*) inserire, infilare

▸ **work off** VT + ADV (*fat*) eliminare; (*annoyance, tension*) sfogare; (*debt*) pagare lavorando

▸ **work on** VI + PREP **1** (*task, novel*) lavorare a; **he's working**

on the car sta facendo dei lavori alla macchina; **the police are working on the case** la polizia sta facendo indagini sul caso **2** (*principle, assumption*) basarsi su; **we've no clues to work on** non abbiamo indizi su cui basarci; **we're working on the principle that ...** partiamo dal presupposto che... + *sub* **3** (*persuade, influence*): **to work on sb** lavorarsi qn

▸ **work out** VI + ADV **1** (*problem*) risolversi **2** (*amount to*): **the cost worked out at £50** il costo ammontava a 50 sterline; **it works out at £100** fa 100 sterline **3** (*succeed: plan, marriage*) riuscire, funzionare; **I hope it all works out for you** spero che ti vada tutto bene; **things aren't working out as planned** le cose non stanno andando come previsto **4** (*Sport*) allenarsi; **I work out twice a week** faccio ginnastica due volte alla settimana ♦ VT + ADV **1** (*problem, calculation*) risolvere; **I can't work out the percentage** non riesco a calcolare la percentuale; **things will work themselves out** tutto si sistemerà; **I just couldn't work it out** non riuscivo proprio a capire **2** (*devise: plan, route*) escogitare **3** (*understand: behaviour*) capire **4** (*exhaust: resources*) esaurire

▸ **work over** VT + ADV (*fam*) pestare

▸ **work up** VT + ADV **1** (*develop: trade*) sviluppare; **to work up an appetite** farsi venire appetito; **to work up enthusiasm for sth** entusiasmarsi per qc **2 to work sb up into a temper/fury** far arrabbiare/infuriare qn

▸ **work up to** VI + ADV + PREP (*point, climax*) preparare il terreno a

work·able ['wɜːkəbl] ADJ (*plan*) fattibile; (*solution*) realizzabile; (*land*) coltivabile; (*mine*) sfruttabile

worka·hol·ic [ˌwɜːkə'hɒlɪk] N stacanovista *m/f*, maniaco(-a) del lavoro

work·bench ['wɜːk,bentʃ] N banco da lavoro

worked up [ˌwɜːkt'ʌp] ADJ: **to get worked up** andare su tutte le furie; **don't get all worked up!** non agitarti tanto!

work·er ['wɜːkəʳ] N (*gen, also Agr*) lavoratore(-trice); (*esp Industry*) operaio(-a); **a good worker** un bravo lavoratore; **he's a poor worker** non lavora bene; **a factory worker** un operaio; **office worker** impiegato(-a); **management and workers** il padronato e i lavoratori

work experience [ˌwɜːkɪksˈpɪərɪəns] N **1** (*previous jobs*) esperienze *fpl* lavorative **2** (*student training placement*) tirocinio

work force N forza *f* lavoro, *inv*

work-in [ˌwɜːk,ɪn] N (*Brit*) forma di protesta in cui gli operai occupano e continuano a lavorare in una fabbrica o azienda minacciata di chiusura

work·ing ['wɜːkɪŋ] ADJ (*day*) feriale; (*week*) lavorativo(-a); (*tools, conditions, lunch*) di lavoro; (*clothes*) da lavoro; (*mother*) che lavora; (*partner*) attivo(-a); **an 8-hour working day** una giornata lavorativa di 8 ore; **working knowledge** conoscenza pratica; **in working order** funzionante

working capital N (*Comm*) capitale *m* d'esercizio

working class N classe *f* operaia *or* lavoratrice

working man N lavoratore *m*, operaio

working party N (*Brit*) commissione *f* d'inchiesta

working week N settimana lavorativa

work-in-progress [ˌwɜːkɪn'prəʊɡrɛs] (*Comm*) N (*value*) valore *m* del manufatto in lavorazione

work·load ['wɜːk,ləʊd] N carico di lavoro

work·man ['wɜːkmən] N (*pl* -**men**) operaio

work·man·ship ['wɜːkmənʃɪp] N (*of worker*) abilità professionale; (*of thing*) fattura

work·mate ['wɜːk,meɪt] N collega *m/f* di lavoro

work·out ['wɜːk,aʊt] N (*Sport*) allenamento

work permit N permesso di lavoro

workplace N posto di lavoro

works [wɜːks] N (*Brit*) **1** NPL (*of machine, clock*) meccanismo; (*Admin*) opere *fpl*; (*Mil*) opere, fortificazioni *fpl*; **road works** lavori stradali; **to give sb the works** (*fam: treat harshly*) dare una strigliata a qn **2** *pl inv: factory etc*) fabbrica, stabilimento; **works outing** gita aziendale

works council N consiglio aziendale

work sheet N scheda; (*Comput*) foglio col programma di lavoro

work·shop ['wɜːkʃɒp] N officina; (*fig*): **a music workshop** un seminario di musica; **a drama workshop** un laboratorio teatrale

work station N stazione *f* di lavoro

work study N studio di organizzazione del lavoro

work surface N piano di lavoro

work·top [ˈwɜːktɒp] N piano di lavoro

work-to-rule [ˌwɜːktəˈruːl] N (*Brit*) sciopero bianco

world [wɜːld] N **1** (*gen*) mondo; **in the world** al mondo; **all over the world** in tutto il mondo; **to be on top of the world** essere al settimo cielo; **it's a small world!** com'è piccolo il mondo!; **alone in the world** solo(-a) al mondo; **it's not the end of the world!** (*fam*) non è la fine del mondo!; **to live in a world of one's own** vivere in un mondo tutto proprio; **the business world** il mondo degli affari; **the world we live in** il mondo in cui viviamo; **to come** *or* **go down, go up** *or* **rise in the world** scendere/salire nella scala sociale; **to come into the world** venire al mondo; **the next world** l'aldilà *m inv*; **to have the best of both worlds** avere un doppio vantaggio; **it's out of this world!** (*fam*) è la fine del mondo!; **he's not long for this world** non gli rimane molto da vivere **2** (*phrases*): **I wouldn't do it for the world** *or* **for anything in the world** non lo farei per niente al mondo; **what in the world is he doing?** che caspita sta facendo?; **to think the world of sb** pensare un gran bene di qn; **there's a world of difference between ...** c'è un abisso tra...; **to do sb a world of good** fare un gran bene a qn; **the world and his wife** un miliardo di persone; **they're worlds apart** non hanno niente in comune; **the world's worst cook** la cuoca peggiore che possa esistere ♦ ADJ (*tour, power*) mondiale; (*record*) del mondo, mondiale

world champion N campione(-essa) mondiale

World Cup N (*Ftbl*): **the World Cup** il campionato mondiale *or* i mondiali *mpl* di calcio

world-famous [ˌwɜːldˈfeɪməs] ADJ di fama mondiale

world·ly [ˈwɜːldlɪ] ADJ (*comp* **-ier**, *superl* **-iest**) (*matters, person*) mondano(-a); (*attitude, pleasures*) materiale

world music N musica etnica, world music *f inv*

World Series N (*USA*: *Baseball*): **the World Series** torneo di spareggio al termine del campionato di baseball

world·wide [ˈwɜːldˈwaɪd] ADJ mondiale, universale; **his books have sold 200 million copies worldwide** i suoi libri hanno venduto 200 milioni di copie nel mondo

World Wide Web N: **the World Wide Web** (*Comput*) il Web

worm [wɜːm] N (*Zool*: *also person*: *pej*) verme *m*; **to have worms** (*Med*) avere i vermi; **the worm will turn** (*Proverb*) anche la pazienza ha un limite; **a can of worms** (*fam*) un vespaio; **you worm!** (*fam*) verme!; (*Comput*) baco ♦ VT **1 to worm one's way through a crowd** insinuarsi tra la folla; **to worm one's way into a group** infiltrarsi in un gruppo; **to worm one's way into sb's confidence** riuscire a conquistare la fiducia di qn **2 to worm a secret out of sb** carpire un segreto a qn

worn [wɔːn] PP *of* **wear** ♦ ADJ (*carpet, tyre* or *tire*) consumato(-a), logoro(-a); (*person*) stanco(-a), sfinito(-a); **the carpet is a bit worn** la moquette è un po' consumata

worn-out [ˌwɔːnˈaʊt] ADJ (*thing*) consunto(-a), logoro(-a); (*person*) sfinito(-a); **worn-out shoes** scarpe logore; **I'm worn out!** sono sfinito!

wor·ried [ˈwʌrɪd] ADJ preoccupato(-a); **to be worried about sth** essere preoccupato per qc; **I was worried about my job** ero preoccupato per il mio lavoro; **to be worried sick** (*fam*) essere preoccupatissimo(-a); **to be worried to death about sth/sb** (*fam*) essere molto ansioso(-a) per qc/qn; **to look worried** avere l'aria preoccupata

wor·rier [ˈwʌrɪəˈ] N ansioso(-a)

wor·ri·some [ˈwʌrɪsəm] ADJ **1** (*causing worry*) preoccupante **2** (*worried*) ansioso(-a)

wor·ry [ˈwʌrɪ] N preoccupazione *f*; **what's your worry?** cosa ti preoccupa?; **to cause sb a lot of worry** creare un sacco di preoccupazioni a qn; **that's the least of my worries** questa è l'ultima cosa di cui mi preoccupo ♦ VT **1** (*cause concern*) preoccupare; **to worry o.s. sick** (**about** *or* **over sth**) preoccuparsi da morire (per qc); **don't worry yourself** *or* **your head about it** non fartene un pensiero **2** (*bother*) disturbare, importunare **3** (*subj: dog: bone*) azzannare; (: *sheep*) inseguire e attaccare ♦ VI: **to worry about** *or* **over sth/sb** preoccuparsi di qc/per qn; **don't worry!** non preoccuparti!

▸ **worry at** VI + PREP **1** (*gnaw*) rosicchiare **2** (*try to deal with*): **to worry at sth** scervellarsi su qc

---

wor·ry·ing [ˈwʌrɪɪŋ] ADJ (*problem*) preoccupante; **it's a worrying time for her** è un brutto momento per lei; **she's not the worrying kind** non è il tipo che si preoccupa

worse [wɜːs] ADJ *comp of* **bad** peggiore; **worse than** peggio *or* peggiore di; **the situation is worse than we expected** la situazione è peggiore di quanto ci aspettassimo; **it was even worse than mine** era anche peggiore del mio; **it's worse than ever** è peggio che mai; **it could have been worse!** poteva andare peggio!; **he was the worse for drink** (*fam*) aveva un po' bevuto; **he is none the worse for it** non ha avuto brutte conseguenze; **to get worse, grow worse** peggiorare; **it gets worse and worse** va peggiorando (sempre di più); **in March the weather will get worse** in marzo il tempo peggiorerà; **so much the worse for you!** tanto peggio per te!; **I've got to work this weekend, worse luck** devo lavorare questo fine settimana, sfortunatamente ♦ ADV *comp of* **badly** peggio; **I'm feeling worse** mi sento peggio; **she's behaving worse than ever** si comporta peggio che mai; **I don't think any the worse of you** non per questo ti stimo meno; **I won't think any the worse of you (for having done)** non ti stimerò di meno (per aver fatto) ♦ N peggio; **a change for the worse** un cambiamento in peggio, un peggioramento; **worse followed** a questo seguì il peggio; **there is worse to come** il peggio deve ancora venire

wors·en [ˈwɜːsn] VT (*health, situation*) peggiorare; (*chances*) diminuire ♦ VI peggiorare

worse off ADJ più povero(-a); (*fig*): **you'll be worse off this way** così sarà peggio per te; **he is now worse off than before** ora è in condizioni economiche peggiori di prima

wor·ship [ˈwɜːʃɪp] N **1** (*adoration*) adorazione *f*, culto; (*also*: **organized worship**) culto; **place of worship** (*Rel*) luogo di culto **2** (*Brit: in titles*): **Your Worship** (*to judge*) Vostro Onore; (*to mayor*) signor sindaco ♦ VT adorare, venerare; **she worships her children** (*fig*) adora i suoi bambini; **he worships the ground she treads on** bacia la terra su cui lei cammina ♦ VI (*Rel*) assistere alle funzioni

wor·ship·per [ˈwɜːʃɪpəˈ] N adoratore(-trice); (*in church*) fedele *m/f*, devoto(-a)

worst [wɜːst] ADJ *superl of* **bad** il (la) peggiore; **it was the worst possible time** era il momento peggiore *or* meno opportuno; **the worst film of the three** il peggiore fra i tre film; **the worst pupil in the school** il peggior alunno della scuola; **my worst enemy** il mio peggior nemico; **one of his worst efforts** una delle sue prove peggiori ♦ ADV *superl of* **badly** peggio; **he sings worst of all** canta peggio di tutti; **to come off worst** (*in fight, argument*) avere la peggio ♦ N peggio *m, f*; (*of crisis, storm*) culmine *m*; **at (the) worst** alla peggio, per male che vada; **the worst of it is that ...** il peggio è che...; **the worst is yet to come** il peggio deve ancora venire; **if the worst comes to the worst** nel peggiore dei casi; **to get the worst of an argument** avere la peggio in una discussione; **he brings out the worst in me** risveglia in me gli istinti peggiori; **we're over** *or* **past the worst of it now** il peggio è passato, ora; **do your worst!** sono pronto al peggio!

worst-case [ˈwɜːstˈkeɪs] ADJ: **the worst-case scenario** la peggiore delle ipotesi

wor·sted [ˈwʊstɪd] N (*cloth*) pettinato; **wool worsted** lana pettinata

worth [wɜːθ] ADJ: **to be worth** valere; **how much is it worth?** quanto vale?; **it's worth £5** vale 5 sterline; **it's worth a great deal/a lot of money** vale molto/un sacco di soldi; **it's worth a great deal to me** (*sentimentally*) ha un gran valore per me; **he is worth his weight in gold** vale tanto oro quanto pesa; **I'll tell you this for what it's worth** ti dico questo, per quello che può valere; **what's it worth to you?** che valore ha per te?; **to run for all one is worth** correre a gambe levate; **it hardly seemed worth mentioning** non mi sembrava abbastanza importante da parlarne; **it's well worth the effort/expense** vale lo sforzo/la spesa; **it's not worth the paper it's written on** non vale nemmeno la carta su cui è scritto; **it's worth it** ne vale la pena; **is it worth it?** ne vale la pena?; **it's not worth it, it's not worth the trouble** non ne vale la pena; **it's more than my life is worth** non oserei mai; **is it worth doing?** vale la pena di farlo? ♦ N valore *m*; **50 pence worth of apples** 50 pence di mele; **he had no chance to show his true worth** non ebbe occasione di mostrare quanto valeva

worth·less [ˈwɜːθlɪs] ADJ (*effort, action, attempt*) inutile; (*assurance, guarantee, object*) senza valore, di nessun valore; **a worthless individual** un individuo spregevole

worth·while [ˌwɜːθˈwaɪl] ADJ (*gen*) che vale la pena; (*book, film*) che merita; (*life, work, activity*) utile; (*contribution*) valido(-a); (*cause*) lodevole; **a worthwhile trip** un viaggio che vale la pena di fare; **a worthwhile book** un libro che vale la pena leggere; **to be worthwhile** valere la pena; **it might be worthwhile to take out insurance** potrebbe valere la pena stipulare un'assicurazione

wor·thy [ˈwɜːðɪ] ADJ (*comp* **-ier**, *superl* **-iest**) (*gen*) degno(-a); (*cause, aim, motive*) lodevole; **a worthy cause** una degna causa; **worthy of** degno di; **worthy of note** *or* **mention** degno di nota ♦ N (*hum*) personalità *f inv*

KEYWORD

would [wʊd] MODAL AUX VB *cond of* **will**[1]

1 (*conditional tense*): **she would come** verrebbe; **if you asked him he would do it** se tu glielo chiedessi lo farebbe; **he would have come** sarebbe venuto; **if you had asked him he would have done it** se tu gliel'avessi chiesto l'avrebbe fatto; **you'd think she had enough to worry about** si direbbe che abbia già abbastanza preoccupazioni

2 (*in indirect speech*): **I said I would do it** ho detto che l'avrei fatto

3 (*emphatic*): **you WOULD be the one to forget!** è proprio da te dimenticartelo!; **it WOULD have to snow today!** doveva proprio nevicare oggi!; **you WOULD say that, wouldn't you!** e ti pareva! sapevo che avresti detto così!

4 (*insistence*): **she wouldn't behave** ha continuato a comportarsi male; **I told her not to but she would do it** le avevo detto di non farlo ma lei l'ha voluto fare a tutti i costi

5 (*conjecture*): **what would this be?** questo cosa sarebbe?; **it would have been about midnight** sarà stato verso mezzanotte; **it would seem so** sembrerebbe proprio di sì

6 (*wish*): **what would you have me do?** cosa desideri che faccia?; **would (that) it were not so!** (*old, liter*) magari non fosse così!

7 (*in offers, invitations, requests*): **would you ask him to come in?** lo faccia entrare per cortesia; **would you care for some tea?** gradiresti del tè?; **would you close the door, please** chiuda la porta per favore; **would you like a biscuit?** gradisce un biscotto?

8 (*habit*): **he would go there on Mondays** ci andava il lunedì; **he would paint it each year** era solito dipingerlo ogni anno

would-be [ˈwʊdˌbiː] ADJ: **a would-be poet/politician** un aspirante poeta/politico

wouldn't [ˈwʊdnt] = **would not**

wound[1] [wuːnd] N ferita; **leg/bullet wound** ferita alla gamba/di proiettile ♦ VT (*also fig*) ferire

wound[2] [waʊnd] PT, PP *of* **wind**[2]

wove [wəʊv] PT *of* **weave**

wo·ven [ˈwəʊvən] PP *of* **weave**

WP ABBR = **word processing, word processor**

wpm ABBR = **words per minute**

wran·gle [ˈræŋgl] N litigio, alterco ♦ VI: **to wrangle (about** *or* **over)** litigare (su)

wrap [ræp] N (*shawl*) scialle *m*; (*housecoat*) vestaglia; (*rug*) coperta; (*cape*) mantellina; **still under wraps** (*fig: plan, scheme*) ancora segreto(-a) ♦ VT (*also:* **wrap up**) avvolgere, incartare; **the scheme is wrapped in secrecy** il piano è avvolto nel mistero

▸ **wrap up** VT + ADV **1** (*gen*) avvolgere; (*parcel*) incartare; (*child*) coprire bene; **she's wrapping her Christmas presents** sta incartando i regali di Natale **2** (*fam: finalize*) concludere; **I think that (just) about wraps it up** direi che questo è tutto ciò che c'è da dire **3 to be wrapped up in sb/sth** essere completamente preso(-a) da qn/qc; **she's wrapped up in herself** non pensa che a se stessa ♦ VI + ADV **1** (*dress warmly*) coprirsi (bene) **2** (*fam: be quiet*): **wrap up!** chiudi il becco!

wrap·per [ˈræpəʳ] N (*on chocolate*) carta; (*postal*) fascetta; (*of book*) foderina, copertina

wrap·ping [ˈræpɪŋ] N (*for chocolate, parcel*) carta

wrapping paper N (*brown*) carta da pacchi; (*for gift*) carta da regali

wrath [rɒθ] N (*liter*) ira, collera

wreak [riːk] VT (*destruction, havoc*) portare, causare; **to wreak vengeance on** vendicarsi su

wreath [riːθ] N (*pl* **wreaths** [riːðz]) (*of flowers*) ghirlanda; (*at funeral*) corona; (*of smoke*) anello; (*mist*) corona

wreck [rek] N (*of ship, scheme etc*) naufragio; (*ship itself*) relitto; (*fig: old car etc*) rottame *m*; (: *building*) rudere *m*; **that car is a wreck!** quella macchina è un rottame!; **to be a complete wreck** essere distrutto(-a); **I'm a wreck, I feel a wreck** sono distrutto ♦ VT (*gen*) distruggere, rovinare; (*ship*) far naufragare; (*train*) far deragliare; (*house*) demolire; (*health*) rovinare; **to be wrecked** (*Naut*) fare naufragio; **the explosion wrecked the whole house** l'esplosione ha completamente distrutto la casa; **the trip was wrecked by bad weather** il brutto tempo ha rovinato la gita

wreck·age [ˈrekɪdʒ] N (*of ship*) relitto; (*of car etc*) rottami *mpl*; (*of building*) macerie *fpl*; **the wreckage of the coach** i rottami della corriera; **the wreckage of the building** le macerie dell'edificio

wreck·er [ˈrekəʳ] N (*Naut: salvager*) addetto al ricupero di relitti; (*USA: breaker, salvager*) demolitore *m*; (: *breakdown van*) carro *m* attrezzi, *inv*

wren [ren] N scricciolo

wrench [rentʃ] N **1** (*tug*) strattone *m*; **to give sth a wrench** dare uno strattone a qc **2** (*tool*) chiave *f*; **a screwdriver and a wrench** un cacciavite e una chiave **3** (*fig*) strazio; **it'll be a wrench to leave after all these years** sarà uno strazio partire dopo tutti questi anni ♦ VT **1 to wrench sth (away) from** *or* **off sb** strappare qc a qn; **they wrenched the suitcase from his hand** gli hanno strappato di mano la valigia; **he wrenched it out of my hands** me lo ha strappato di mano; **she wrenched herself free** si liberò con uno strattone; **to wrench a door open** aprire bruscamente una porta **2** (*Med*) slogare, storcere

wrest [rest] VT: **to wrest sth from sb** strappare qc a qn

wres·tle [ˈresl] N: **to have a wrestle with sb** fare la lotta con qn ♦ VI **1** lottare, fare la lotta; (*Sport*) praticare la lotta libera **2** (*fig*): **to wrestle with** (*one's conscience, device, machine*) lottare con; (*temptation, sins*) lottare contro; **they are currently wrestling with the problem of vandalism** attualmente stanno lottando contro il problema del vandalismo ♦ VT: **to wrestle sb to the ground** mettere qn a terra; **the policeman wrestled him to the ground** i poliziotti lo hanno messo a terra

wres·tler [ˈresləʳ] N (*Sport*) lottatore(-trice)

wres·tling [ˈreslɪŋ] N (*Sport*) lotta libera; (*also:* **all-in wrestling**: *Brit*) catch *m*

wrestling match N incontro di lotta libera

wretch [retʃ] N disgraziato(-a), sciagurato(-a); **little wretch!** (*often hum*) birbante!

wretch·ed [ˈretʃɪd] ADJ **1** (*house, conditions*) misero(-a), disgraziato(-a); (*life*) gramo(-a); (*pittance*) misero(-a); (*unhappy, depressed*) infelice, triste; **I feel wretched** (*fam: ill*) sto malissimo; **the outlook for these wretched people is grim** le prospettive per questi disgraziati sono ben tristi **2** (*fam: very bad: weather, behaviour*) pessimo(-a), atroce; (*holiday*) orrendo(-a), orribile; (*results*) pessimo(-a); (*child*) pestifero(-a); **I feel wretched about it** (*fam: conscience-stricken*) mi sento un verme; **what wretched luck!** (*fam*) che scalogna!; **where's that wretched dog?** (*fam*) dov'è quel maledetto cane?; **I've got to do the wretched thing again** (*fam*) devo rifare 'sta maledetta cosa

wrig·gle [ˈrɪgl] VT (*toes, fingers*) muovere; **to wriggle one's way through** (*tunnel*) attraversare strisciando; (*undergrowth*) strisciare in ♦ VI (*also:* **wriggle about** *or* **around**) agitarsi, dimenarsi; (*fish: on hook*) contorcersi; **to wriggle along/down** avanzare/scendere strisciando; **to wriggle free** liberarsi contorcendosi; **to wriggle through a hole** contorcersi per passare attraverso un buco; **he managed to wriggle out of it** (*fig*) se l'è cavata con un espediente ♦ N contorsione *f*

wring [rɪŋ] (*pt, pp* **wrung**) VT **1** (*also:* **wring out:** *wet clothes*) strizzare **2** (*twist*) torcere; **I'll wring your neck!** (*fam*) ti torco il collo!; **she wrung my hand** mi strinse forte la mano; **to wring one's hands** (*fig: in distress*) torcersi le mani; **to wring sb's heart** (*fig*) stringere il cuore a qn **3** (*also:* **wring out:** *confession, truth, money*) estorcere

wring·er [ˈrɪŋəʳ] N strizzatoio (manuale)
wring·ing [ˈrɪŋɪŋ] ADJ (also: **wringing wet**) bagnato(-a) fradicio(-a)
wrin·kle [ˈrɪŋkl] N (on face, skin) ruga; (in stockings, paper etc) grinza ♦ VT (fabric) stropicciare; (nose) arricciare; (flat surface, skin) corrugare, raggrinzire ♦ VI (see vt) stropicciarsi; arricciarsi; corrugarsi, raggrinzirsi
wrin·kled [ˈrɪŋkld], **wrin·kly** [ˈrɪŋklɪ] ADJ (fabric, paper) stropicciato(-a); (nose) arricciato(-a); (surface) corrugato(-a), increspato(-a); (skin) rugoso(-a), pieno(-a) di rughe; **his suit was wrinkled** il suo vestito era stropicciato
wrist [rɪst] N polso
wrist·band [ˈrɪstˌbænd] N (of shirt) polsino; (of watch) cinturino
wrist·watch [ˈrɪstˌwɒtʃ] N orologio da polso
writ [rɪt] N (Law) mandato; **to issue a writ against sb, serve a writ on sb** notificare un mandato di comparizione a qn
write [raɪt] (pt **wrote**, pp **written**) VT scrivere; (list) compilare; (certificate) redigere; **she wrote that she'd arrive soon** scrisse che sarebbe arrivata presto; **to write sb a letter** scrivere una lettera a qn; **he wrote me a letter last week** mi ha scritto una lettera la settimana scorsa; **I was writing a letter** stavo scrivendo una lettera; **have you written the letter?** hai scritto la lettera?; **he's just written another novel** ha appena scritto un altro romanzo; **how is his name written?** come si scrive il suo nome?; **she wrote three pages** ha scritto tre pagine; **his guilt was written all over his face** gli si leggeva in faccia che era colpevole ♦ VI scrivere; **to write to sb** scrivere a qn; **it's nothing to write home about** (fam) non è niente di speciale; **I'll write for the catalogue** scriverò per farmi mandare il catalogo; **to write for a paper** scrivere per un giornale
  ▸ **write away** VI + ADV: **to write away for** (information) richiedere per posta; (goods) ordinare per posta
  ▸ **write back** VI + ADV rispondere (con una lettera)
  ▸ **write down** VT + ADV (make a note of) segnare, annotare; (put in writing) mettere per iscritto; **I wrote down the address** ho annotato l'indirizzo; **can you write it down for me, please?** me lo può scrivere, per favore?
  ▸ **write in** VT + ADV inserire ♦ VI + ADV scrivere; **to write in for sth** scrivere per richiedere qc
  ▸ **write into** VT + PREP includere in, scrivere in
  ▸ **write off** VI + ADV = **write away** ♦ VT + ADV (debt) estinguere; (scheme) porre un termine a; (smash up: car) distruggere; **to write off a debt** estinguere un debito; **to write off a car** rottamare una macchina; **he was written off as useless** (fig) fu deciso che era un incompetente punto e basta
  ▸ **write out** VT + ADV (gen) scrivere; (list, form) compilare; (cheque) fare; (copy: essay) ricopiare
  ▸ **write up** VT + ADV (notes, diary) aggiornare; (write report on: developments etc) mettere per iscritto; **she wrote the play up in the Glasgow Herald** ha scritto una recensione della commedia sul Glasgow Herald
write-off [ˈraɪtˌɒf] N (Comm) perdita; (fig: car etc) rottame m; **the car is a write-off** la macchina è ridotta a un rottame
write-protect [ˌraɪtprəˈtɛkt] VT (Comput) proteggere contro scrittura
writ·er [ˈraɪtəʳ] N (of letter, report) autore(-trice); (as profession) scrittore(-trice); **to be a good/poor writer** scrivere/non scrivere bene; **he's a thriller writer** è un autore di gialli; **he's a writer of novels** è un romanziere; **writer's cramp** crampo dello scrivano
write-up [ˈraɪtˌʌp] N (review) recensione f
writhe [raɪð] VI contorcersi; **to writhe with embarrassment** morire di vergogna
writ·ing [ˈraɪtɪŋ] N (art) scrivere m; (sth written) scritto; (handwriting) scrittura; **writings** NPL (author's works) opera fsg; **in writing** per iscritto; **to put sth in writing** mettere qc per iscritto; **in my own writing** scritto di mio pugno; **I can't read your writing** non riesco a leggere la tua scrittura; **Aubrey's biographical writings** gli scritti biografici di Aubrey; **writing is my profession** faccio lo scrittore di professione; **writing is just a hobby with me** scrivere è solo un hobby

per me; **the writing on the wall** (fig) il presagio della rovina; **there's writing on the wall** c'è una scritta sul muro
writing case N nécessaire m inv per la corrispondenza
writing desk N scrivania
writing paper N carta da lettere
writ·ten [ˈrɪtn] PP of **write** ♦ ADJ scritto(-a)
wrong [rɒŋ] ADJ 1 (morally) sbagliato(-a), riprovevole; (unfair) ingiusto(-a), sbagliato(-a); (wicked) cattivo(-a); **it's wrong to steal, stealing is wrong** non si deve rubare; **lying is wrong** non si dicono le bugie; **you were wrong to do that** hai sbagliato a fare così; **what's wrong with a drink now and again?** che c'è di male nel bere un bicchierino ogni tanto? 2 (incorrect) sbagliato(-a), errato(-a); **to be wrong** (answer) essere sbagliato(-a); (in doing, saying) avere torto, sbagliarsi; **I was wrong in thinking that …** avevo torto a pensare che…; **you are wrong about that** ti sbagli; **the information they gave us was wrong** le informazioni che ci hanno dato erano sbagliate; **the wrong answer** la risposta sbagliata; **you've got the wrong number** ha sbagliato numero 3 (improper, not sought, not wanted) sbagliato(-a), inadatto(-a); **to say/do the wrong thing** dire/fare qc che non va 4 (amiss): **is anything or something wrong?** c'è qualcosa che non va?; **what's wrong (with you)?** che cos'hai?, cosa c'è che non va?; **what's wrong with her?** cos'ha?; **there's nothing wrong** va tutto bene; **sth must be wrong** dev'esserci qc che non va; **there is something wrong with my lights** le luci non funzionano bene; **what's wrong with your arm?** cos'hai al braccio?; **what's wrong with the car?** cos'ha la macchina che non va?; **to be wrong in the head** (fam) essere un po' tocco(-a) ♦ ADV (spell, pronounce) in modo sbagliato, erroneamente; **to do sth wrong** sbagliare; **you've done it wrong** hai sbagliato; **you're doing it all wrong** stai sbagliando tutto; **you did wrong to do it** hai fatto male sbagliando; **to get sth wrong** sbagliare qc; **don't get me wrong** (fam) non fraintendermi; **to go wrong** (on route) sbagliare strada; (in calculation) sbagliarsi, commettere un errore; (morally) prendere una cattiva strada; (plan etc) andare male, fallire; **the robbery went wrong and they got caught** la rapina è andata male e li hanno presi; **something went wrong with the brakes** è successo qualcosa ai freni; **you can't go wrong** non puoi sbagliarti; **you won't go far wrong if you follow his advice** non rischi più di tanto a seguire il suo consiglio ♦ N 1 (evil) male m; **to do wrong** far (del) male; **he can do no wrong in her eyes** ai suoi occhi lui è perfetto 2 (unjust act) torto; **to do sb a wrong** fare un torto a qn; **to be in the wrong** avere torto; **to put sb in the wrong** mettere qn dalla parte del torto; **to right a wrong** riparare a un torto; **to suffer a wrong** subire un torto ♦ VT fare (un) torto a
wrong-doer [ˈrɒŋˌduːəʳ] N malfattore(-trice)
wrong-foot [ˈrɒŋˌfʊt] VT (Ftbl, also fig) prendere in contropiede
wrong·ful [ˈrɒŋfʊl] ADJ (unjust: accusation) ingiusto(-a); (unlawful: arrest, imprisonment) illegale, illecito(-a); **wrongful dismissal** licenziamento ingiustificato
wrong·ly [ˈrɒŋlɪ] ADV (answer, do, count) erroneamente; (treat) ingiustamente; (accuse, dismiss) a torto
wrong number N: **you have the wrong number** (Telec) ha sbagliato numero
wrong side N (of cloth) rovescio
wrote [rəʊt] PT of **write**
wrought [rɔːt] PT, PP (old, liter) of **wreak**; **great changes have been wrought** sono avvenuti dei grandi cambiamenti ♦ ADJ (silver) lavorato(-a); (iron) battuto(-a)
wrung [rʌŋ] PT, PP of **wring**
wry [raɪ] ADJ beffardo(-a); **to make a wry face** fare una smorfia
wt. ABBR = **weight**
WV ABBR (USA Post: = West Virginia)
WWW N ABBR (Comput: = World Wide Web) WWW m
WY ABBR (USA Post: = Wyoming)
Wy·o·ming [waɪˈəʊmɪŋ] il Wyoming
WYSIWYG ABBR (Comput: = what you see is what you get) quello che vedi sullo schermo è quello che ottieni in stampa

Xx

X, x [ɛks] N (*letter, also Math*) X, x *f inv, m inv*; **X for Xmas** ≈ X come Xeres; **if you have x dollars a year** se hai x dollari all'anno; **x marks the spot** il punto è segnato con una croce

Xer·ox [ˈzɪərɒks] (*Trademark*) fotocopiatrice *f*

XL [ˌɛksˈɛl] ABBR (= *extra large*) XL *f inv*

Xmas [ˈɛksməs, ˈkrɪsməs] N ABBR = **Christmas**

X-rated [ˌɛksˈreɪtɪd] ADJ (*USA: film*) ≈ vietato ai minori di 18 anni

X-ray [ˈɛksˌreɪ] N (*ray*) raggio X; (*photograph*) radiografia; **x-rays** raggi X; **to have an X-ray** farsi fare una radiografia ♦ VT radiografare; **they X-rayed my arm** mi hanno fatto una radiografia al braccio ♦ ADJ (*examination*) radiografico(-a)

xy·lo·phone [ˈzaɪləˌfəʊn] N xilofono

Yy

Y, y [waɪ] N (*letter*) Y, y *f inv, m inv*; **Y for Yellow**, (*USA*) **Y for Yoke** ≈ Y come Yacht

yacht [jɒt] N yacht *m inv*, panfilo da diporto

yacht·ing [ˈjɒtɪŋ] N yachting *m*, navigazione *f* da diporto

yachts·man [ˈjɒtsmən] N (*pl* -**men**) yachtsman *m inv*

yam [jæm] N (*plant, tuber*) igname *m*; (*sweet potato*) patata dolce

Yank [jæŋk], **Yan·kee** [ˈjæŋkɪ] (*fam, often pej*) N yankee *m/f inv* ♦ ADJ yankee *inv*

yank [jæŋk] N strattone *m* ♦ VT tirare, dare uno strattone a; **to yank a nail out** strappare via un chiodo; **she yanked open the drawer** aprì il cassetto con uno strattone

yap [jæp] (*of dog*) N guaito ♦ VI (*dog*) guaire

yard¹ [jɑːd] N 1 (*measure*) iarda (*91, 44 cm*), yard *f inv*; **to sell sth by the yard** ≈ vendere qc al metro; **yards of** (*fig*) chilometri di 2 (*Naut*) pennone *m*

yard² [jɑːd] N (*courtyard, farmyard*) cortile *m*; (*USA: garden*) giardino; (*worksite*) cantiere *m*; (*for storage*) deposito; **builder's yard** deposito di materiale da costruzione; **back yard** (*Brit*) cortile sul retro; (*USA*) giardino sul retro

yard sale (*USA*) N vendita di oggetti usati nel cortile di una casa privata

yard·stick [ˈjɑːdstɪk] N (*fig*) metro, criterio

yarn [jɑːn] N 1 (*wool, thread*) filato *m* 2 (*tale*) storia, racconto; **to spin sb a yarn** raccontare a qn una grossa balla

yawn [jɔːn] N sbadiglio; **to give a yawn** fare uno sbadiglio ♦ VI sbadigliare; (*fig: hole, chasm*) aprirsi; **"yes", she yawned** "sì", disse con uno sbadiglio ♦ VT: **to yawn one's head off** non riuscire a smettere di sbadigliare

yawn·ing [ˈjɔːnɪŋ] ADJ (*fig: gap, abyss*) spalancato(-a)

yd. ABBR = **yard(s)**

yeah [jɛə] ADV (*fam*) sì

year [jɪəʳ] N 1 (*gen*) anno; **this year** quest'anno; **every year** tutti gli anni, ogni anno; **all (the) year round** (per) tutto l'anno; **year in, year out** anno dopo anno; **year by year**, **from year to year** col passar degli anni; **years and years ago** tanti anni fa; **from one year to the next** da un anno all'altro; **three times a year** tre volte all'anno; **in the year 1869** nell'anno 1869; **last year** l'anno scorso; **next year** (*looking to future*) l'anno prossimo *or* venturo; **the next year** (*in past time*) l'anno seguente *or* successivo; **he got 10 years** (*in prison*) si è beccato 10 anni; **it takes years** ci vogliono anni; **I met him a year last January** a gennaio fa un anno che l'ho conosciuto; **a year tomorrow** domani tra un anno; **I haven't seen her for years** non la vedo da anni, sono anni che non la vedo; **over the years** con gli anni; **to be 15 years old** avere quindici anni; **an eight-year-old child** un bambino di otto anni; **she's three years old** ha tre anni; **she's in her fiftieth year** compierà cinquant'anni; **it's taken years off her** l'ha ringiovanita; **a** *or* **per year** all'anno 2 (*Scol, Univ*) anno; **he's in the second year** è al secondo anno; **he was in my year at university** frequentavamo lo stesso anno di università 3 (*of wine*) annata 4 (*age*): **old/young for one's years** vecchio/giovane per i suoi anni *or* per la sua età; **from her earliest years** fin dall'infanzia, fin dalla più tenera età; **he's getting on in years** ha i suoi anni ormai

year·book [ˈjɪəˌbʊk] N annuario

year·ly [ˈjɪəlɪ] ADJ annuale; **twice-yearly** semestrale ♦ ADV annualmente; **three times yearly** tre volte all'anno

yearn [jɜːn] VI: **to yearn for sb/sth** desiderare ardentemente qn/qc; **to yearn to do sth** struggersi dal desiderio di fare qc

yearn·ing [ˈjɜːnɪŋ] ADJ (*desire*) intenso(-a); (*look, tone*) desideroso(-a), bramoso(-a) ♦ N: **yearning (for)** desiderio struggente (di)

yeast [jiːst] N lievito; **dried yeast** lievito disidratato (*or* in polvere)

yell [jɛl] N urlo; **to give a yell, let out a yell** lanciare un urlo; **a yell of laughter** una fragorosa risata ♦ VI urlare ♦ VT (*order, name*) urlare

yel·low [ˈjɛləʊ] ADJ (*comp* -**er**, *superl* -**est**) 1 (*colour*) giallo(-a); **to go** *or* **turn yellow** (*person*) diventare giallo(-a); (*leaf, paper*) ingiallire 2 (*fam, pej: cowardly*) fifone(-a) ♦ N (*colour*) giallo; (*of an egg*) rosso ♦ VI ingiallire

yellow fever N febbre *f* gialla

yel·low·ish [ˈjɛləʊɪʃ] ADJ giallastro(-a), giallognolo(-a)

Yellow Sea N: **the Yellow Sea** il mar Giallo

yelp [jɛlp] N (*of dog*) guaito; (*of person*) strillo ♦ VI (*see n*) guaire, strillare

Yem·en [ˈjɛmən] N Yemen *m*

yen¹ [jɛn] N (*currency*) yen *m inv*

yen² [jɛn] N (*fam*): **to have a yen to do sth** avere una gran voglia di fare qc

yeo·man [ˈjəʊmən] N (*pl* -**men**) (*Brit: old*) piccolo proprietario terriero

yes [jɛs] ADV sì; **to say yes (to)** dire di sì (a); **do you like it?** — **yes I do** ti piace? — sì; **don't you want any?** — **yes (I do)!** non ne vuoi? — ma sì!; **yes yes, but what if she doesn't do it?** sì, va bene, ma se non lo fa? ♦ N sì *m inv*

yes·ter·day [ˈjɛstəˌdeɪ] ADV ieri; **yesterday morning/evening** ieri mattina/sera; **the day before yesterday** l'altro ieri; **a week yesterday** (*past*) una settimana fa, ieri; **late yesterday** ieri in serata; **all (day) yesterday** ieri è piovuto tutto il giorno; **the great politicians of yesterday** i grandi politici del passato ♦ N ieri *m inv*

yet [jɛt] ADV **1** (*already, up to now, so far*) già; (*now, by now*) ancora; **I wonder if he's come yet** mi chiedo se non sia già arrivato; **not yet** non ancora; **he hasn't come yet** non è ancora arrivato; **it is not finished yet** non è ancora finito; **have you told your parents yet?** lo hai già detto ai tuoi genitori?; **I needn't go (just) yet** non è ancora il momento di andare; **don't go (just) yet** non andare già via; **this is his best film yet** finora questo è il suo film migliore; **as yet** per ora, finora; **there's no news as yet** per ora non ci sono notizie **2** (*still*) ancora; **he may come yet, he may yet come** può ancora arrivare; **that question is yet to be decided** quella questione è ancora da decidere; **a settlement might yet be possible** è ancora possibile trovare un accordo; **I'll do it yet!** prima o poi ce la farò! **3** (*in addition, even*): **yet again** di nuovo; **yet another/more** ancora un altro/più; **yet once more** ancora una volta; **a few days yet** ancora qualche giorno **4** (*frm*): **nor yet** tanto meno; **I do not like him, nor yet his sister** lui non mi piace, e tanto meno sua sorella ♦ CONJ ma, tuttavia; **and yet** eppure, tuttavia; **it was funny, yet sad at the same time** era buffo e triste nel contempo; **and yet I enjoyed it** e tuttavia mi è piaciuto

yew [juː] N (*also*: **yew tree**) tasso

YHA [ˌwaɪeɪtʃˈeɪ] N ABBR (*Brit:* = *Youth Hostels Association*) associazione degli ostelli della gioventù

Yid·dish [ˈjɪdɪʃ] ADJ, N yiddish *m inv*

yield [jiːld] N (*of land, mine*) resa; (*of investment*) rendita; (*of crops*) raccolto; **a yield of 5%** un profitto del 5% ♦ VT **1** (*produce: harvest, dividend*) fruttare; (*: results*) fornire, produrre; (*: information, opportunity*) fornire **2** (*surrender*) cedere ♦ VI (*surrender*): **to yield (to)** cedere (a), arrendersi (a); (*break, collapse*) cedere; (*USA: Aut*) dare la precedenza; **to yield to temptation** cedere alla tentazione
  ▸ **yield up** VT + ADV (*liter: secret*) svelare, rivelare

YMCA [ˌwaɪɛmsiːˈeɪ] N ABBR (= *Young Men's Christian Association*) YMCA *f*

yob [ˈjɒb], **yob·bo** [ˈjɒbəʊ] N (*Brit fam*) teppista *m/f*

yo·del [ˈjəʊdl] VI fare lo jodel ♦ N jodel *m inv*

yoga [ˈjəʊgə] N yoga *m inv*

yo·ghurt, yo·ghourt, yo·gurt [ˈjɒgət] N yogurt *m inv*

yoke [jəʊk] N **1** (*of oxen, also fig*) giogo; **under the yoke of** (*fig*) sotto il giogo di **2** (*on dress*) sprone *m* ♦ VT (*also:* **yoke together:** *oxen*) aggiogare

yolk [jəʊk] N tuorlo, rosso (d'uovo)

yon·der [ˈjɒndəʳ] ADV (*old*): **(over) yonder** laggiù, là

yonks [jɒŋks] ADV (*Brit fam*): **I haven't seen her for yonks** è un secolo che non la vedo

Yorks [jɔːks] ABBR (*Brit:* = *Yorkshire*)

KEYWORD

you [juː] PERS PRON
1 (*subject: singular*) tu; (*: plural*) voi; (*: singular: polite form*) lei; (*: plural: very formal*) loro; **you and I will go** tu ed io andiamo; **you angel!** sei un angelo!; **you are very kind** è molto gentile da parte tua (*or* sua *etc*); **here you are!** eccoti!; **that dress just isn't you** quel vestito proprio non ti si addice; **you Italians** voi *or* voialtri italiani; **if I was** *or* **were you** se fossi in te (*or* lei *etc*)
2 (*see* 1) (*object: direct*) ti; la; vi; loro (*after verb*); (*indirect*) ti; le; vi; loro (*after verb*); **I'll phone you later** ti chiamo più tardi/la chiamerò più tardi/vi chiamerò più tardi/li chiamerò più tardi; **I'll see you tomorrow** ci vediamo domani; **I gave it to you** te l'ho dato; gliel'ho dato; ve l'ho dato; l'ho dato loro
3 (*see* 1) (*stressed, after preposition, in comparisons*) te; lei; voi; loro; **it's for you** è per te (*or* lei *etc*); **she's younger than you** è più giovane di te (*or* lei *etc*); **I told YOU to do it** ho detto a TE (*or* LEI *etc*) di farlo
4 (*impersonal: one*) si; **you can't do that!** non si fanno queste cose!; **fresh air does you good** l'aria fresca fa bene; **you know who/what** sappiamo chi/cosa; **you never can tell** non si sa mai; **you never know** non si sa mai

you'd [juːd] = you would; you had

you'll [juːl] = you will; you shall

young [jʌŋ] ADJ (*comp* **-er**, *superl* **-est**) (*gen*) giovane; (*vegetables*) novello(-a); (*offender*) minorenne; **a young man** un giovanotto; **a young lady** una signorina; **young people**

i giovani; **young children** bambini piccoli; **they have a young family** hanno dei bambini piccoli; **in my young days** quand'ero giovane; **you're too young** sei troppo giovane; **she's not so young as she was** non è più tanto giovane; **younger** più giovane; **he's younger than me** è più giovane di me; **my younger brother** il mio fratello minore; **the younger son** il figlio minore; **he is two years younger than her** ha due anni meno di lei; **if I were 15 years younger** se avessi 15 anni di meno; **my youngest brother** il mio fratello minore; **the youngest** (*masculine*) il più giovane; **the youngest, he's the youngest** è il più giovane; **the youngest** (*feminine*) la più giovane; **she's the youngest in the class** è la più giovane della classe; **she is the youngest competitor** è la concorrente più giovane; **you're only young once** si è giovani una volta sola; **she's young at heart** è giovane di spirito; **he looks young for his age** sembra più giovane di quanto sia in realtà; **the night is young** la notte è appena cominciata; **to grow** *or* **get younger** ringiovanire; **the younger generation** la nuova generazione ♦ NPL (*of animals*) piccoli *mpl*, prole *fsg*; **the young** (*young people*) i giovani

young·ish [ˈjʌŋɪʃ] ADJ abbastanza giovane

young·ster [ˈjʌŋstəʳ] N (*child*) bambino(-a); (*young person*) giovane *m/f*

your [jɔːʳ] POSS ADJ **1** *sg* il (la) tuo(-a); *pl* i (le) tuoi (tue); (*sg: polite form*) il (la) suo(-a); *pl* i (le) suoi (sue); *pl* il (la) vostro(-a); *pl* i (le) vostri(-e); (*sg: polite: very formal*) il (la) loro; (*: pl*) i (le) loro; **your house** la tua (*or* sua *etc*) casa; **your brother** tuo (*or* suo *etc*) fratello; **your address** il tuo indirizzo; **your pen** la tua penna; **your parents** i tuoi genitori; **your father** tuo padre; **your mother** tua madre; **children, give these letters to your parents** ragazzi, date queste lettere ai vostri genitori; **your ticket, madam** il suo biglietto, signora; **wash your hands** lavati le mani; **remember to take your umbrella, sir** non dimenticti di prendere l'ombrello **2** (*impersonal: one's*): **it's bad for your health** danneggia la salute; **your average Italian** l'italiano medio

you're [jɔːʳ] = you are

yours [jɔːz] POSS PRON *sg* il (la) tuo(-a); *pl* i (le) tuoi (tue); *pl* il (la) vostro(-a); *pl* i (le) vostri(-e); (*sg: polite form*) il (la) suo(-a); (*: pl*) i (le) suoi (sue); (*: pl: very formal*) il (la) loro; *pl* i (le) loro; **yours is red, mine is green** il tuo è rosso, il mio è verde; **this is yours** questo è il tuo (*or* suo *etc*); **a friend of yours** un tuo (*or* suo *etc*) amico; **my garden is smaller than yours** il mio giardino è più piccolo del tuo; **that bag's not mine, it's yours** questa borsa non è la mia, è la tua; **is this bag yours?** è tua questa borsa?; **our parents and yours** i nostri genitori e i vostri; **is that car yours, sir?** è sua quella macchina, signore?; **yours faithfully/sincerely** (*in letters*) distinti/cordiali saluti; **what's yours?** (*fam: drink*) tu che prendi?

your·self [jɔːˈself] PERS PRON (*pl* **yourselves** [jɔːˈselvz]) **1** (*reflexive: sg*) ti; (*: pl*) vi; (*: sg: polite*) si; (*: pl: very formal*) si; **have you hurt yourself?** ti sei (*or* è) fatto male?; **have you hurt yourselves?** vi siete (*or* si sono) fatti male?; **did you enjoy yourself, sir?** si è divertito, signore? **2** (*emphatic: sg*) tu stesso(-a); (*: pl: very formal*) loro stessi(-e); **you yourself told me** me l'hai detto proprio tu, tu stesso me l'hai detto; **a beginner like yourself** un principiante come te; **an important person like yourself** una persona importante come lei **3** (*after prep*) te, stesso(-a); (*: polite*) lei, lei stesso(-a); (*: pl*) voi, voi stessi(-e); (*: very formal*) loro, loro stessi(-e); **(all) by yourself** (*tutto*) da solo; **do you like travelling by yourself?** ti piace viaggiare da solo? **4** (*impersonal: reflexive*) si; (*: emphatic*) se stessi; (*: after prep*) se, stessi; *see also* **oneself**

youth [juːθ] N **1** giovinezza, gioventù *f*; **in early youth** nella prima giovinezza; **in my youth** da giovane, quando ero giovane **2** (*pl* **youths** [juːðz]) (*boy*) ragazzo, giovane *m* **3** (*pl: young people*) giovani *mpl*; **the youth of today** i giovani di oggi

youth club N circolo giovanile

youth·ful [ˈjuːθfʊl] ADJ (*air, figure, manner*) giovanile; (*mistakes*) di gioventù

youth·ful·ness [ˈjuːθfʊlnɪs] N giovinezza; **youthfulness of appearance** aspetto giovanile

youth hostel N ostello della gioventù
youth movement N movimento giovanile
you've [juːv] = you have
yowl [jaʊl] N (*of dog, person*) latrato; (*of cat*) miagolio ♦ VI (*see n*) latrare; miagolare
yr ABBR = year
YT [ˌwaɪˈtiː] ABBR (*Canada*: = Yukon Territory)
Yu·go·slav [ˌjuːgəʊˈslɑːv] ADJ, N jugoslavo(-a)
Yu·go·sla·via [ˌjuːgəʊˈslɑːvɪə] N Jugoslavia; the former

Yugoslavia l'ex Jugoslavia; **in the former Yugoslavia** nell'ex Jugoslavia
Yu·go·sla·vian [ˌjuːgəʊˈslɑːvɪən] ADJ, N jugoslavo(-a)
yule log N (*cake*) tronchetto di Natale; (*piece of wood*) ceppo nel caminetto a Natale
yup·pie [ˈjʌpɪ] N yuppie *m/f inv*
YWCA [ˌwaɪdʌbljuːsiːˈeɪ] N ABBR (= *Young Women's Christian Association*) organizzazione che mette a disposizione ostelli per donne

Zz

Z, z [zɛd, (*USA*) ziː] N (*letter*) Z, z *f inv, m inv*; **Z for Zebra** ≈ Z come Zara
Za·ire [zɑːˈiːəʳ] N lo Zaire *m*
Zam·bia [ˈzæmbɪə] N lo Zambia *m*
Zam·bian [ˈzæmbɪən] ADJ, N zambiano(-a)
zany [ˈzeɪnɪ] ADJ (*comp* -ier, *superl* -iest) (*fam*) pazzoide, un po' pazzo(-a)
zap [zæp] VT (*fam*: *destroy*) far fuori; (*Comput*) cancellare; (*TV*) fare zapping; **I zapped the file** ho cancellato il file; **a plan to zap their missiles** un piano per distruggere i loro missili
zeal [ziːl] N (*fervour*) zelo; (*enthusiasm*) entusiasmo; **zeal for** ansia di
zeal·ot [ˈzɛlət] N zelota *m/f*
zeal·ous [ˈzɛləs] ADJ (*supporter, believer, worker*) zelante
zeb·ra [ˈziːbrə] N zebra
zebra crossing N (*Brit*) strisce *fpl* (pedonali), zebre *fpl*
zen·ith [ˈzɛnɪθ] N (*liter*: *of civilization*) culmine *m*; (*of career*) apice *m*; (*Astron*) zenit *m inv*
zero [ˈzɪərəʊ] N zero; **5° below zero** 5° sotto zero ♦ ADJ (*altitude, gravity*) zero *inv*; (*fam*: *interest, hope*) nullo(-a)
  ▸ **zero in on** VI + ADV + PREP (*target*) essere puntato(-a) su; (*problem, subject*) concentrarsi su
zero hour N ora zero
zero option N (*Pol*) opzione *f* zero
zero-rated [ˌzɪərəʊˈreɪtɪd] ADJ (*Brit*: *Comm*) ad aliquota zero
zest [zɛst] N **1** (*enthusiasm*): **zest (for)** gusto (per), entusiasmo (per); (*fig*: *spice*) sapore *m*; **zest for living** *or* **life** gioia di vivere **2** (*Culin*: *of orange, lemon*) buccia
zig·zag [ˈzɪgzæg] N zigzag *m inv* ♦ VI zigzagare; **to zigzag across/down/up** attraversare/scendere/salire a zigzag ♦ ADJ a zigzag
Zim·ba·bwe [zɪmˈbɑːbwɪ] N lo Zimbabwe
Zim·ba·bwean [zɪmˈbɑːbwɪən] ADJ dello Zimbabwe
zinc [zɪŋk] N zinco ♦ ADJ di zinco
Zi·on·ism [ˈzaɪəˌnɪzəm] N sionismo

Zi·on·ist [ˈzaɪənɪst] ADJ sionistico(-a) ♦ N sionista *m/f*
zip [zɪp] N **1** (*Brit*: *also*: **zip fastener**) cerniera (lampo), zip *m inv*; **the zip's stuck** la cerniera lampo è inceppata **2** (*fam*: *energy*) energia, forza; **put a bit of zip into it** mettici un po' di entusiasmo ♦ VT: **to zip up** chiudere la cerniera di; **zipped pockets** (*with zips*) tasche con cerniera; (*zipped up*) tasche con la cerniera chiusa; **he zipped the bag open/closed** ha aperto/chiuso la cerniera della borsa; (*Comput*) zippare ♦ VI: **to zip past** sfrecciare davanti; **a sports car zipped past me** una macchina sportiva mi è sfrecciata davanti; **to zip along to the shops** fare una corsa per comprare qc
zip code N (*USA Post*: codice *m* di avviamento postale
zip·per [ˈzɪpəʳ] N (*USA*) = zip 1
zit [zɪt] N brufolo
zith·er [ˈzɪðəʳ] N cetra
zo·di·ac [ˈzəʊdɪæk] N zodiaco
zom·bie [ˈzɒmbɪ] N zombie *m/f inv*; **like a zombie** come uno zombie, come un morto che cammina
zone [zəʊn] N zona; **danger zone** zona pericolosa; **war zone** zona di guerra ♦ VT zonizzare
zoo [zuː] N zoo *m inv*, giardino zoologico
zo·o·logi·cal [ˌzəʊəˈlɒdʒɪkəl] ADJ zoologico(-a)
zo·olo·gist [zəʊˈɒlədʒɪst] N zoologo(-a)
zo·ol·ogy [zəʊˈɒlədʒɪ] N zoologia
zoom [zuːm] N (*sound*) rombo ♦ VI (*go fast*): **to zoom off** sfrecciare via; **the police car zoomed by very close to him** la macchina della polizia gli è sfrecciata accanto
  ▸ **zoom in** VI + ADV (*Phot, Cine*): **to zoom in (on sb/sth)** zumare (su qn/qc)
  ▸ **zoom out** VI + ADV allargare l'immagine
zoom lens N zoom *m inv*
zuc·chi·ni [zuːˈkiːnɪ] N *pl inv* (*USA*) zucchina; **potatoes and zucchini** patate e zucchine
Zulu [ˈzuːluː] ADJ, N zulù *m/f inv*
Zü·rich [ˈzjʊərɪk] N Zurigo *f*

I numeri — L'ora

Numbers — Time

I NUMERI		NUMBERS
uno(a)	1	one
due	2	two
tre	3	three
quattro	4	four
cinque	5	five
sei	6	six
sette	7	seven
otto	8	eight
nove	9	nine
dieci	10	ten
undici	11	eleven
dodici	12	twelve
tredici	13	thirteen
quattordici	14	fourteen
quindici	15	fifteen
sedici	16	sixteen
diciassette	17	seventeen
diciotto	18	eighteen
diciannove	19	nineteen
venti	20	twenty
ventuno	21	twenty-one
ventidue	22	twenty-two
ventitré	23	twenty-three
ventotto	28	twenty-eight
trenta	30	thirty
quaranta	40	forty
cinquanta	50	fifty
sessanta	60	sixty
settanta	70	seventy
ottanta	80	eighty
novanta	90	ninety
cento	100	a hundred, one hundred
centouno	101	a hundred and one
duecento	200	two hundred
mille	1000	a thousand, one thousand
milleduecentodue	1202	one thousand two hundred and two
cinquemila	5000	five thousand
un milione	1,000,000	a million, one million

I NUMERI

NUMBERS

primo(a), 1°	first, 1st
secondo(a), 2°	second, 2nd
terzo(a), 3°	third, 3rd
quarto(a), 4	fourth, 4th
quinto(a), 5	fifth, 5th
sesto(a), 6	sixth, 6th
settimo(a)	seventh
ottavo(a)	eighth
nono(a)	ninth
decimo(a)	tenth
ndicesimo(a)	eleventh
'icesimo(a)	twelfth
~esimo(a)	thirteenth
'dicesimo(a)	fourteenth
simo(a)	fifteenth
(a)	sixteenth
no(a)	seventeenth
\	eighteenth
'a)	nineteenth
	twentieth
	twenty-first
~imo(a)	twenty-second
ventitreesimo(a)	twenty-third
ventottesimo(a)	twenty-eighth
trentesimo(a)	thirtieth
centesimo(a)	hundredth
centunesimo(a)	hundred-and-first
millesimo(a)	thousandth
milionesimo(a)	millionth

L'ORA

che ora è?, che ore sono?
è ..., sono...
mezzanotte
l'una (del mattino)
l'una e cinque
l'una e dieci
l'una e un quarto, l'una e quindici
l'una e venticinque
l'una e mezzo *o* mezza, l'una e trenta
l'una e trentacinque
le due meno venti, l'una e quaranta
le due meno un quarto, l'una e
    quarantacinque
le due meno dieci, l'una e cinquanta
mezzogiorno
le tre (del pomeriggio), le quindici
le sette (di sera), le diciannove

a che ora?
a mezzanotte
alle sette
fra venti minuti
venti minuti fa

THE TIME

what time is it?
it's...
midnight
one o'clock (in the morning), one (am)
five past one
ten past one
a quarter past one, one fifteen
twenty-five past one, one twenty-five
half past one, one thirty
twenty-five to two, one thirty-five
twenty to two, one forty
a quarter to two, one forty-five

ten to two, one fifty
twelve o'clock, midday, noon
three o'clock (in the afternoon), three (pm)
seven o'clock (in the evening), seven (pm)

at what time?
at midnight
at seven o'clock
in twenty minutes
twenty minutes ago

LA DATA

oggi
domani
dopodomani
ieri
l'altro ieri
il giorno prima
il giorno dopo
la mattina
la sera
stamattina
stasera
questo pomeriggio

THE DATE

today
tomorrow
the day after tomorrow
yesterday
the day before yesterday
the day before, the previous day
the next *or* following day
morning
evening
this morning
this evening
this afternoon

LA DATA

ieri mattina	yesterday morning
ierisera	yesterday evening
domani mattina	tomorrow morning
domani sera	tomorrow evening
nella notte tra sabato e domenica	during Saturday night, during the night of Saturday to Sunday
viene sabato	he's coming on Saturday
il sabato	on Saturdays
tutti i sabati	every Saturday
sabato scorso, lo scorso sabato	last Saturday
il prossimo sabato	next Saturday
fra due sabati	a week on Saturday
fra tre sabati	a fortnight *or* two weeks on Saturday
da lunedì a sabato	from Monday to Saturday
tutti i lunedì	every Monday
una volta alla settimana	once a week
una volta al mese	once a month
due volte alla settimana	twice a week
una settimana fa	a week ago
quindici giorni fa	a fortnight *or* two weeks ago
l'anno scorso *or* passato	last year
fra due giorni	in two days
fra una settimana	in a week
fra quindici giorni	in a fortnight *or* two weeks
il mese prossimo	next month
l'anno prossimo	next year

che giorno è oggi?, quanti ne abbiamo oggi?	what day is it?
il primo/24 ottobre 2013	the 1st/24th of October 2013, October 1st/24th 2013
nel 2013	in 2013
il millenovecentonovantacinque	nineteen ninety-five
44 a.C.	44 BC
14 d.C.	14 AD
nel diciannovesimo secolo, nel XIX secolo, nell'Ottocento	in the nineteenth century
negli anni trenta	in the thirties
c'era una volta...	once upon a time...